# GRANGER'S
## INDEX TO POETRY

# GRANGER'S
# INDEX TO POETRY

Seventh Edition, Indexing Anthologies
Published from 1970 through 1981

*GRANGER, EDITH*

**EDITED BY**
**WILLIAM JAMES SMITH**
*and*
**WILLIAM F. BERNHARDT**

## COLUMBIA UNIVERSITY PRESS

### NEW YORK 1982

Granger's Index to Poetry

**Library of Congress Cataloging in Publication Data**

Granger, Edith.
    Granger's Index to poetry.

    1. Poetry—Indexes.  2. English poetry—
Indexes.  I. Smith, William James, 1918-
II. Bernhardt, William F.  III. Title.
IV. Title: Index to poetry.
PN1022.G7  1982      016.80881      81-18155
ISBN 0-231-05002-X         AACR2

*In Memoriam*
*William James Smith*
*1918–1981*

# PREFACE

The planning for this Seventh Edition of GRANGER'S INDEX TO POETRY, as well as the selection of anthologies for inclusion, was largely completed by William James Smith prior to his illness and subsequent death in the early part of 1981. Bill had been the guiding force behind the Sixth Edition, published in 1973, and the supplementary volume covering the years 1970–1977. His knowledge of literature, his affable personality and engaging sense of humor, are sorely missed; those of us who have completed the work on this edition hope that we have adhered to the standards he set in the past.

GRANGER'S INDEX TO POETRY has been a standard reference work since its first appearance under the editorship of Edith Granger in 1904. In 1945 Columbia University Press took over the editing and publication of the work from A. C. McClurg & Co. in Chicago. The format was changed somewhat—all prose works were omitted, titles and first lines were combined into a single alphabetical listing, and the SUBJECT INDEX was greatly expanded—but the purpose of the book remained unchanged: to assist the reader in identifying and locating poems or selections from poems appearing in the most generally accessible anthologies. Each entry in the TITLE AND FIRST LINE INDEX is followed by alphabetical symbols for the anthologies in which the work appears. A KEY TO SYMBOLS will be found at the front of the book. No new symbol duplicates any used previously.

The Seventh Edition of GRANGER'S departs from previous editions in one notable way. While earlier editions incorporated a large number of older anthologies carried over from former editions, the Seventh Edition marks a fresh beginning with the year 1970 by incorporating the 1970–77 supplementary volume and adding anthologies published from 1977 to 1981. The Seventh Edition indexes a total of 248 volumes of anthologized poetry, including the 120 volumes indexed in GRANGER'S INDEX TO POETRY, 1970–1977, and 128 newer volumes. This edition includes a larger number of new anthologies than have been indexed in any previous edition of GRANGER'S.

The change in the Seventh Edition was introduced after a survey of librarians showed that many retained earlier editions of GRANGER'S on library shelves. Rather than repeat so much material from past editions, it was felt that a greater number of new anthologies could be indexed, thus giving librarians more up-to-date information on the contents of recent anthologies. Inasmuch as many older anthologies remain on library shelves, however, librarians are strongly urged to continue the common practice by retaining their copies of the Sixth Edition, at least, as the most comprehensive survey of poetry anthologies up to 1970.

It should be pointed out that the inclusive dates on the title page are not stringent. Four volumes in the current edition have copyright dates earlier than 1970, but none of them were previously indexed in GRANGER'S.

# PREFACE

The SUBJECT INDEX has been expanded for this edition to include poems under more than five thousand categories. Some subjects, such as Love, are so broad that no effort has been made to include individual poems; instead, readers are referred in the SUBJECT INDEX to anthologies devoted entirely to the subject. Librarians are reminded that the TITLE AND FIRST LINE INDEX may serve as a supplement to the SUBJECT INDEX in certain instances, although deducing a subject from the title alone is sometimes deceptive.

Continued from the 1970–77 volume, and revised, is the designation of works recommended for priority acquisition by libraries. Since many libraries cannot acquire all or most of the anthologies indexed, they may be helped by the designation in the KEY TO SYMBOLS of two asterisks for the five works recommended for primary acquisition and by the designation of one asterisk for the thirty-five works recommended for further acquisition. This feature is not presented as an infallible guide but as an aid to libraries with limited funds and no specialized requirements.

Assisting the Press in making the recommendations was a panel of experts consisting of Wayne Gossage, formerly Library Director of the Bank Street College of Education and currently library consultant with Gossage Regan Associates; Lillian Morrison, Coordinator, Young Adult Services, New York Public Library; and William Jay Smith, poet, critic, and anthologist. In addition to evaluating the new anthologies indexed, the panel revised the recommendations previously made in the 1970–77 volume.

An accompanying page lists the names of those persons whose endeavors contributed to the making of this new edition—the selection, marking, and checking of the anthologies, as well as the typing, filing, and editing of the many thousands of cards that constitute the manuscript for GRANGER's. Special thanks are due John Cafaro, who brought an intimate knowledge of the procedures followed on the 1970–77 volume to the detailed precision requisite for a work of this nature. The production process was greatly facilitated by the expertise of Gerard Mayers, head of the Production Department for the Press.

*November 1981*

WILLIAM F. BERNHARDT

# CONTENTS

PREFACE . . . . . . . . . . . . . . . . . . . . . . . . . . . . . . VII

EXPLANATORY NOTES . . . . . . . . . . . . . . . . . . . . . X

ABBREVIATIONS . . . . . . . . . . . . . . . . . . . . . . . . . XI

KEY TO SYMBOLS . . . . . . . . . . . . . . . . . . . . . . . XIII

TITLE AND FIRST LINE INDEX . . . . . . . . . . . . . . . . . 1

AUTHOR INDEX . . . . . . . . . . . . . . . . . . . . . . . . 953

SUBJECT INDEX . . . . . . . . . . . . . . . . . . . . . . . 1169

# EXPLANATORY NOTES

The TITLE AND FIRST LINE INDEX is the principal index and must be used in connection with both the AUTHOR INDEX and the SUBJECT INDEX.

In the TITLE AND FIRST LINE INDEX initial capitals in the important words of the titles distinguish titles from first lines. Symbols are listed after both titles and first lines. However, more complete information as to translators, acts and scenes, abridgments, and variant titles is given in the title entries.

When the title and first line of a poem are the same, only the title entry has been indexed. When they are so nearly the same as to be adjacent, again only the title has been indexed, with the first line added in quotation marks and in parentheses to the title entry.

In the arrangement of the title entries, indention is important. Single indention indicates a selection from the work named above; double indention with parentheses indicates a variant title.

Because the Mother Goose rhymes are so much better known by first line than by the artificial and varying titles given to them in various collections, only their first lines have been included in the TITLE AND FIRST LINE INDEX.

In such titles as "Ode," "Poem," "Song," "Sonnet," too frequent to be distinctive, the first line is added to the title given in the anthology (for example, Ode: "How sleep the brave who sink to rest"). The title is then alphabeted by first line under "Ode," "Poem," etc.

Titles and first lines beginning with "O" and "Oh" have been filed, as in previous editions, as if all were spelled "O," and are alphabeted according to the words that follow.

"Mac," "Mc," and "M'" are filed as if all were spelled "Mac."

Arabic and Chinese names in the AUTHOR INDEX are filed uninverted as if written in one word. Old-style Japanese names are handled in the same way as Chinese names (that is, as if written in one word), while modern Japanese names are usually inverted in the Western manner for filing purposes.

A KEY TO SYMBOLS is provided, with publishers, dates and editions added after titles of anthologies. Two asterisks (**) preceding a title are a recommendation for priority purchase by small libraries. One asterisk (*) indicates secondary recommendations. See PREFACE for a fuller explanation of this feature.

# ABBREVIATIONS

| | | | | |
|---|---|---|---|---|
| *abr.* | abridged | | *mod.* | modernized *or* modern |
| *ad.* | adapted | | *N.T.* | New Testament |
| *add.* | additional | | *O.T.* | Old Testament |
| *arr.* | arranged | | *orig.* | original |
| *at.* | attributed | | Pt. | part |
| Bk. | book | | *rev.* | revised |
| *br.* | brief | | sc. | scene |
| *c.* | copyright | | Sec. | section |
| *ch.* | chapter | | *sel.* | selection |
| *comp.* | compiled *or* compiler | | *sels.* | selections |
| *comps.* | compilers | | *sl.* | slightly |
| *cond.* | condensed | | *st.* | stanza |
| *diff.* | different | | *sts.* | stanzas |
| *fr.* | from | | *tr.* | translator, translation, *or* translated |
| *frag.* | fragment | | | |
| *incl.* | included *or* including | | *trs.* | translators *or* translations |
| *introd.* | introduction *or* introductory | | *var.* | various |
| *ll.* | lines | | *wr.* | wrong *or* wrongly |
| *misc.* | miscellaneous | | | |

# KEY TO SYMBOLS

*Anthologies starred with two asterisks (\*\*) are recommended for priority acquisition by small libraries, one star (\*) for further acquisition. See* PREFACE *for fuller explanation.*

811.08 AAN     Ardis Anthology of New American Poetry, The. *David Rigsbee and Ellendea Proffer, eds.* (1977) Ardis

821.08 AAS     Anchor Anthology of Sixteenth-Century Verse, The. *Richard S. Sylvester, ed.* (1974) Doubleday Anchor Books

AATT     Adam Among the Television Trees: An Anthology of Verse by Contemporary Christian Poets. *Virginia R. Mollenkott, ed.* (1971) Word Books

AcAn     Actualist Anthology, The. *Morty Sklar and Darrell Gray, eds.* (1977) The Spirit That Moves Us Press

783.952 AH     American Hymns: Old and New. *Albert Christ-Janer, Charles W. Hughes, and Carleton Sprague Smith, eds.* (1980) Columbia University Press (2 vols.; Vol. I, with music; Vol. II, notes on the hymns and biographies of the authors and composers)

AIW     As I Walked Out One Evening: A Book of Ballads. *Helen Plotz, comp.* (1976) Greenwillow Books (William Morrow & Company)

AKE     All Kinds of Everything. *Louis Dudek, ed.* (1973) Clarke, Irwin & Company

784.4 AmFP     \*American Folk Poetry: An Anthology. *Duncan Emrich, ed.* (1974) Little, Brown & Company

AmNP 811.08     \*American Negro Poetry. *Arna Bontemps, ed.* (rev. ed., 1974) Hill and Wang

AmPA 811.08     American Poetry Anthology, The. *Daniel Halpern, ed.* (1975) Avon Books

R811.08 AMV-80     Anthology of Magazine Verse and Yearbook of American Poetry. 1980 Edition. *Alan F. Pater, ed.* (1980) Monitor Book Company, Inc.

AMV-81     Anthology of Magazine Verse and Yearbook of American Poetry. 1981 Edition. *Alan F. Pater, ed.* (1981) Monitor Book Company, Inc.

AmVN     American Verse of the Nineteenth Century. *Richard Gray, ed.* (1973) Rowman & Littlefield (Published in Great Britain by J. M. Dent & Sons)

xiii

AnMo    Ancients and Moderns: An Anthology of Poetry. *Stewart A. Baker, ed.* (1971) Harper & Row

*81/.08*    ANTL    America Is Not All Traffic Lights: Poems of the Midwest. *Alice Fleming, comp.* (1976) Little, Brown & Company

APAS    Anthology of Poems on Affairs of State: Augustan Satirical Verse, 1660–1714. *George deF. Lord, ed.* (1975) Yale University Press

ATNZ    Anthology of Twentieth-Century New Zealand Poetry, An. *Vincent O'Sullivan, ed.* (1970) Oxford University Press

BBGO    Being Born and Growing Older: Poems and Images. *Bruce Vance, ed.* (1971) Van Nostrand Reinhold

BBL    Batsford Book of Light Verse for Children, The. *Gavin Ewart, ed.* (1978) B. T. Batsford

*811*    BCr    Bear Crossings: An Anthology of North American Poets. *Anne Newman and Julie Suk, eds.* (1978) The New South Company

BiP    Beginnings in Poetry. *William J. Martz, ed.* (2d ed., 1973) Scott, Foresman and Company

*(R)821.08*    BIrV    *Book of Irish Verse, The: An Anthology of Irish Poetry from the Sixth Century to the Present. *John Montague, ed.* (1974) Macmillan Publishing Company (Also published as The Faber Book of Irish Verse)

*M 784.8*    BLSH    Best Loved Songs and Hymns: Popular, Patriotic and Folk Songs, Church Hymns and Gospel Songs, Spirituals and Carols. (With music.) *James Morehead and Albert Morehead, eds.* (1965) Funk and Wagnalls

*M 784.8*    BLSo    **Best Loved Songs of the American People. (With music.) *Denes Agay, ed.* (1975) Doubleday & Company

*R784.756*    BluL    *Blues Line, The: A Collection of Blues Lyrics. *Eric Sackheim, comp.* (1969, paperback 1975) Schirmer Books

*J)821.08*    BoAnP    Book of Animal Poems, A. *William Cole, ed.* (1973) The Viking Press

*821.08*    BoLoP    *Book of Love Poetry, A. *Jon Stallworthy, ed.* (1974) Oxford University Press

*821.08*    BoReV    *Book of Religious Verse, A. *Helen Gardner, ed.* (1972) Oxford University Press (Also published as The Faber Book of Religious Verse)

*R 808.81*    BoWoP    *Book of Women Poets from Antiquity to Now, A. *Aliki Barnstone and Willis Barnstone, eds.* (1980) Schocken Books

BPAW    Best Loved Poems of the American West. *John J. Gregg and Barbara T. Gregg, eds.* (1980) Doubleday & Company

*811.08*    BPo    Black Poets, The: A New Anthology. *Dudley Randall, ed.* (1971) Bantam Books

BrS *811.08*    Brother Songs: A Male Anthology of Poetry. *Jim Perlman, ed.* (1979) Holy Cow! Press

**BTTM** Breathes There the Man: Heroic Ballads & Poems of the English Speaking Peoples. *Frank S. Meyer, ed.* (1973) Open Court Publishing Company

**BuTh** Burning Thorn, The: An Anthology of Poetry. *Griselda Greaves, ed.* (1971) Macmillan Publishing Company (First published in Great Britain by Hamish Hamilton Children's Books)

**CAAP** Contemporary American and Australian Poetry. *Thomas Shapcott, ed.* (1976) University of Queensland Press

**CABA** College Anthology of British and American Poetry, The. *A. Kent Hieatt and William Park, eds.* (2d ed., 1972) Allyn and Bacon

**CaPo** Cavalier Poets: Selected Poems. *Thomas Clayton, ed.* (1978) Oxford University Press

**CAPP** Contemporary American Poetry. *A. Poulin, Jr., ed.* (1971) Houghton Mifflin Company

**CaYB** Catch Your Breath: A Book of Shivery Poems. *Lilian Moore and Lawrence Webster, comps.* (1973) Garrard Publishing Company

**CC** Callooh! Callay! Holiday Poems for Young Readers. *Myra Cohn Livingston, ed.* (1978) Atheneum

**CDW** *Carriers of the Dream Wheel: Contemporary Native American Poetry. *Duane Niatum, ed.* (1975) Harper & Row

**CIP** Contemporary Irish Poetry: An Anthology. *Anthony Bradley, ed.* (1980) University of California Press

**CMoP** Chief Modern Poets of Britain and America. *Gerald DeWitt Sanders, John Herbert Nelson, and M. L. Rosenthal, eds.* (5th ed., 1970) Macmillan Publishing Company

**CNA** Celebrations: A New Anthology of Black American Poetry. *Arnold Adoff, ed.* (1977) Follett Publishing Company

**CNW** Contemporary Northwest Writing: A Collection of Poetry and Fiction. *Roy Carlson, ed.* (1979) Oregon State University Press

**ConAP** Contemporary American Poetry. *Donald Hall, ed.* (2d ed., 1972) Penguin Books

**CoPAm** Contemporary Poetry in America. *Miller Williams, ed.* (1973) Random House

**CPA** California Bicentennial Poets Anthology. *A. D. Winans, ed.,* (1976) Second Coming Press

**CSP** Contemporary Southern Poetry: An Anthology. *Guy Owen and Mary C. Williams, eds.* (1979) Louisiana State University Press

**CTBA** Crazy to Be Alive in Such a Strange World: Poems about People. *Nancy Larrick, comp.* (1977) M. Evans and Company

**CTV** Child's Treasury of Verse, A. *Eleanor Doan, comp.* (1977) Zondervan Publishing House

**DL** *Death in Literature. *Robert F. Weir, ed.* (1980) Columbia University Press

# KEY TO SYMBOLS

DNGG — Do Not Go Gentle: Poetry and Prose from Behind the Walls. *Michael Hogan, ed.* (1977) Blue Moon Press

DuDa — Dusk to Dawn: Poems of Night. *Helen Hill, Agnes Perkins, and Alethea Helbig, comps.* (1981) Thomas Y. Crowell Company

DuDr — Ducks and Dragons: Poems for Children. *Gene Kemp, ed.* (1980) Faber and Faber

EAP — Early American Poetry. *Jane Donahue Eberwein, ed.* (1978) University of Wisconsin Press

EAS — English and American Surrealist Poetry. *Edward B. Germain, ed.* (1978) Penguin Books

EBEV — Everyman's Book of English Verse. *John Wain, ed.* (1981) J. M. Dent & Sons

EC — Editor's Choice: Literature and Graphics from the U.S. Small Press, 1965–1977. *Morty Sklar and Jim Mulac, eds.* (1980) The Spirit That Moves Us Press

ECBV — Every Child's Book of Verse. *Sarah Chokla Gross, comp.* (1968) Franklin Watts, Inc.

EcS — Echoes of the Sea. *Elinor Parker, ed.* (1977) Charles Scribner's Sons

EPC — English Poetry, 1700–1780: Contemporaries of Swift and Johnson. *David W. Lindsay, ed.* (1974) Rowman & Littlefield (Published in England by J. M. Dent & Sons)

Epi — Episodes in Five Poetic Traditions: The Sonnet; The Pastoral Elegy; The Ballad; The Ode; Masks and Voices. *R. G. Barnes, ed.* (1972) Chandler Publishing Company

ESaP — English Satiric Poetry: Dryden to Byron. *James Kinsley and James T. Boulton, eds.* (1970) University of South Carolina Press (First published in Great Britain by Edward Arnold Publishers, 1966)

ESo — Elizabethan Sonnets. *Maurice Evans, ed.* (1977) Rowman & Littlefield (Published in Great Britain by J. M. Dent & Sons)

ExPo — Exploring Poetry. *M. L. Rosenthal and A. J. M. Smith, eds.* (2d ed., 1973) The Macmillan Company

FaBoBa — *Faber Book of Ballads, The. *Matthew Hodgart, ed.* (1965) Faber and Faber

FaBoCo — *Faber Book of Comic Verse, The. *Michael Roberts and Janet Adam Smith, eds.* (rev. ed., 1974) Faber and Faber

FaBoEE — Faber Book of Epigrams and Epitaphs, The. *Geoffrey Grigson, ed.* (1977) Faber and Faber

Faber Book of Irish Verse, The. (1974) Faber and Faber (This book is the same as The Book of Irish Verse; see above)

Faber Book of Love Poems, The. (1975) Faber and Faber (This book is the same as The Gambit Book of Love Poems; see below)

FaBoNo — *Faber Book of Nonsense Verse, The. *Geoffrey Grigson, ed.* (1979) Faber and Faber

Faber Book of Popular Verse, The. (1971) Faber and Faber (This book is the same as The Gambit Book of Popular Verse; see below)

Faber Book of Religious Verse, The. (1972) Faber and Faber (This book is the same as A Book of Religious Verse; see above)

FaBoTw    Faber Book of Twentieth-Century Verse, The. *John Heath-Stubbs and David Wright, eds.* (3d ed., 1975) Faber and Faber

FAF    Flowering After Frost: The Anthology of Contemporary New England Poetry. *Michael McMahon, ed.* (1975) Branden Press

FaPo    Familiar Poems, Annotated. *Isaac Asimov. ed.* (1977) Doubleday & Company

FaPoR    Faber Popular Reciter, The. *Kingsley Amis, ed.* (1978) Faber and Faber

FB    Forerunners, The: Black Poets in America. *Woodie King, Jr., ed.* (1975) Howard University Press

FF    *Fine Frenzy: Enduring Themes in Poetry. *Robert Baylor and Brenda Stokes, eds.* (2d ed., 1978) McGraw-Hill Book Company

FiCh    15 Chicago Poets. *Richard Friedman, Peter Kostakis, and Darlene Pearlstein, eds.* (1976) The Yellow Press

FiCP    Fifty Contemporary Poets: The Creative Process. *Alberta T. Turner, ed.* (1977) David McKay Company

FoP    Face of Poetry, The. *LaVerne Harrell Clark and Mary MacArthur, eds.* (1979) Heidelberg Graphics

FPA    First Paperback Poets Anthology, The. *Roger McDonald, ed.* (1974) University of Queensland Press

FPB    First Poetry Book, A. *John Foster, comp.* (1979) Oxford University Press

FSFS    Four Seasons Five Senses. *Elinor Parker, comp.* (1974) Charles Scribner's Sons

FSN    Favorite Songs of the Nineties: Complete Original Sheet Music for 89 Songs. *Robert A. Fremont, ed.* (1973) Dover Publications

FSW    *Folksinger's Wordbook. *Irwin Silber and Fred Silber, eds.* (1973) Oak Publications

GAS    Golden Apples of the Sun, The: Twentieth Century Australian Poetry. *Chris Wallace-Crabbe, ed.* (1980) Melbourne University Press

GBL    Gambit Book of Love Poems, The. *Geoffrey Grigson, ed.* (1975) Gambit (Originally published in Great Britain by Faber and Faber as The Faber Book of Love Poems)

GBP    *Gambit Book of Popular Verse, The. *Geoffrey Grigson, ed.* (1971) Gambit (Also published as The Faber Book of Popular Verse; see above)

# KEY TO SYMBOLS

GDP *821.008* Good Dog Poems. *William Cole, comp.* (1981) Charles Scribner's Sons

GOA *811.08* *Gift Outright, The: America to Her Poets. *Helen Plotz, ed.* (1977) Greenwillow Books (William Morrow & Company)

GP *811.08* *Geography of Poets, A: An Anthology of the New Poetry. *Edward Field, ed.* (1979) Bantam Books

GrRo *808.1* Grandfather Rock: The New Poetry and the Old. *David Morse, ed.* (1972) Delacorte Press

GSB *J784.624* Great Song Book, The. *Timothy John, ed.* (1978) Doubleday & Company

HAP *Harper Anthology of Poetry, The. *John Frederick Nims, ed.* (1981) Harper & Row

HeHu *821.08* Here & Human: An Anthology of Contemporary Verse. *F. E. S. Finn, comp.* (1976) John Murray (U.S. distributor: Transatlantic Arts, Inc.)

HeIP Heath Introduction to Poetry, The. *Joseph de Roche, ed.* (1975) D. C. Heath and Company

HeS *811.08* Heartland II: Poets of the Midwest. *Lucien Stryk, ed.* (1975) Northern Illinois University Press

HoPM *808.1* *How Does a Poem Mean? *John Ciardi and Miller Williams, eds.* (2d ed., 1975) Houghton Mifflin Company

IHMS *811.08* I Hear My Sisters Saying: Poems by Twentieth-Century Women. *Carol Konek and Dorothy Walters, eds.* (1976) Thomas Y. Crowell Company

ILP Introduction to Literature: Poems. *Lynn Altenbernd and Leslie L. Lewis, eds.* (3d ed., 1975) Macmillan Publishing Company

ILWL In Love with Love: 100 of the Greatest Mystical Poems. *Anne Fremantle and Christopher Fremantle, eds.* (1978) Paulist Press

InPK Introduction to Poetry, An. *X. J. Kennedy, ed.* (3d ed., 1974) Little, Brown & Company

InPS *821.08* Introduction to Poetry, An. *Louis Simpson, ed.* (2d ed., 1972) St. Martins Press

InW *861* Inventing a Word: An Anthology of Twentieth-Century Puerto Rican Poetry. *Julio Marzán, ed.* (1980) Columbia University Press (in association with The Center for Inter-American Relations)

IP Introduction to the Poem. *Robert W. Boynton and Maynard Mack, eds.* (rev. 2d ed., 1973) Hayden Book Company

IPM Irish Poets, 1924–1974. *David Marcus, ed.* (1975) Pan Books

IPWM Introducing Poems. *Linda W. Wagner and C. David Mead, eds.* (1976) Harper & Row

IWK *J811.008* In the Witch's Kitchen: Poems for Halloween. *John E. Brewton, Lorraine A. Blackburn, and George M. Blackburn III, comps.* (1980) Thomas Y. Crowell Company

JB — Jump Bad: A New Chicago Anthology. *Gwendolyn Brooks, ed.* (1971) Broadside Press

LAuP — Late Augustan Poetry. *Patricia Meyer Spacks, ed.* (1973) Prentice-Hall

LCL — Listen, Children, Listen: An Anthology of Poems for the Very Young. *Myra Cohn Livingston, ed.* (1972) Harcourt Brace Jovanovich

LFH — Liberating Form, The: A Handbook-Anthology of English and American Poetry. *Bert C. Bach, William A. Sessions, and William Walling, eds.* (1972) Dodd, Mead & Company

LiSp — Literature of Sports, A. *Tom Dodge, ed.* (1980) D. C. Heath and Company

LoAs — Love's Aspects: The World's Great Love Poems. *Jean Garrigue, comp.* (1975) Doubleday & Company

LP — Living Poets. *Michael Morpurgo and Clifford Simmons, comps.* (1974) John Murray

MAT — Messages: A Thematic Anthology of Poetry. *X. J. Kennedy, ed.* (1973) Little, Brown & Company

MAuV — Map of Australian Verse, A. *James McAuley, ed.* (1975) Oxford University Press

MBPR — Major British Poets of the Romantic Period. *William Heath, ed.* (1973) Macmillan Publishing Company

MetP — Metaphysical Poets, The. *Margaret Willy, ed.* (1971) University of South Carolina Press (First published in Great Britain by Edward Arnold Publishers)

MG — Mother Goose Nursery Rhymes. *Arthur Rackham, ed. and illus.* (1913, current edition 1975) The Viking Press

MiP — Mindscapes: Poems for the Real World. *Richard Peck, ed.* (1971) Delacorte Press

MIS — Made in Scotland: An Anthology of Fourteen Scottish Poets. *Robert Garioch, ed.* (1974) Carcanet Press

MIT — Mark in Time: Portraits and Poetry/San Francisco. *Nick Harvey, ed.* (1971) Glide Publications

MMD — Mountain Moving Day: Poems by Women. *Elaine Gill, ed.* (1973) The Crossing Press

MN — Mice Are Rather Nice: Poems about Mice. *Vardine Moore, comp.* (1981) Atheneum

Moon — Moonstruck: An Anthology of Lunar Poetry. *Robert Phillips, ed.* (1974) The Vanguard Press

MPA — Modern Poetry of Western America. *Clinton F. Larson and William Stafford, eds.* (1975) Brigham Young University Press

# KEY TO SYMBOLS

MPo     Modern Poetry: A Selection. *John Rowe Townsend, comp.* (1971) J. B. Lippincott Company

MS     Modern Scottish Poetry: An Anthology of the Scottish Renaissance, 1925–1975. *Maurice Lindsay, ed.* (1976) Carcanet Press (U.S. distributor: Dufour Editions, Inc.)

NAWM 1-2     Norton Anthology of World Masterpieces, The (Volumes One and Two). *Maynard Mack, general ed.* (4th Continental ed., 1980) W. W. Norton & Company

NCSH     *New Coasts and Strange Harbors: Discovering Poems. *Helen Hill and Agnes Perkins, comps.* (1974) Thomas Y. Crowell Company

NeAC     New American and Canadian Poetry. *John Gill, ed.* (1971) Beacon Press

NIL     Norton Introduction to Literature, The: Poetry. *J. Paul Hunter, ed.* (1973) W. W. Norton & Company

NMM     *No More Masks! An Anthology of Poems by Women. *Florence Howe and Ellen Bass, eds.* (1973) Doubleday Anchor Books

NNaP     New Naked Poetry, The: Recent American Poetry in Open Forms. *Stephen Berg and Robert Mezey, eds.* (1976) Bobbs-Merrill

NoAM     *Norton Anthology of Modern Poetry, The. *Richard Ellmann and Robert O'Clair, eds.* (1973) W. W. Norton & Company

NOBA     **New Oxford Book of American Verse, The. *Richard Ellmann, ed.* (1976) Oxford University Press

NOBE     **New Oxford Book of English Verse, 1250–1950, The. *Helen Gardner, ed.* (1972) Oxford University Press

NOBL     *New Oxford Book of English Light Verse, The. *Kingsley Amis, ed.* (1978) Oxford University Press

NowV     Now Voices, The: The Poetry of the Present. *Angelo Carli and Theodore Kilman, eds.* (1971) Charles Scribner's Sons

NPW     New Poets: Women. An Anthology. *Terry Wetherby, ed.* (1976) Les Femmes Publishing

NU     News of the Universe: Poems of Twofold Consciousness. *Robert Bly, comp.* (1980) Sierra Club Books

NVAP     New Voices in American Poetry: An Anthology. *David Allen Evans, ed.* (1973) Winthrop Publishers

NW     Next World, The: Poems by 32 Third World Americans. *Joseph Bruchac, ed.* (1978) The Crossing Press

NYP     New York: Poems. *Howard Moss, ed.* (1980) Avon Books

OAEL 1-2     Oxford Anthology of English Literature, The (Volumes One and Two). *Frank Kermode and John Hollander, general eds.* (1973) Oxford University Press (also published as six paperback vols.: Medieval English Literature, *J. B. Trapp, ed.;* The Literature of Renaissance England, *John Hollander and Frank Kermode, eds.;* The Restoration and the Eighteenth Century, *Martin Price, ed.;*

Romantic Poetry and Prose, *Harold Bloom and Lionel Trilling, eds.;* Victorian Prose and Poetry, *Lionel Trilling and Harold Bloom, eds.;* Modern British Literature, *Frank Kermode and John Hollander, eds.*)

OBAL    **Oxford Book of American Light Verse, The. *William Harmon, ed.* (1979) Oxford University Press

OBP    100 British Poets. *Selden Rodman, ed.* (1974) (Mentor Books) The New American Library

OBSV    Oxford Book of Satirical Verse, The. *Geoffrey Grigson, comp.,* (1980) Oxford University Press

OBVE    Oxford Book of Verse in English Translation, The. *Charles Tomlinson, ed.* (1980) Oxford University Press

OBW    Oxford Book of Welsh Verse in English, The. *Gwyn Jones, comp.* (1977) Oxford University Press

OFD    O Frabjous Day! Poetry for Holidays and Special Occasions. *Myra Cohn Livingston, ed.* (1977) Atheneum

OLR    One Little Room, an Everywhere: Poems of Love. *Myra Cohn Livingston, ed.* (1975) Atheneum

OSF    Oh, Such Foolishness! *William Cole, comp.* (1978) J. B. Lippincott Company

OSP    Other Side of a Poem, The. *Barbara Abercrombie, ed.* (1977) Harper & Row

OxBChV    Oxford Book of Children's Verse, The. *Iona and Peter Opie, eds.* (1973) Oxford University Press

OxBM    Oxford Book of Medieval English Verse, The. *Celia and Kenneth Sisam, eds.* (1970) Oxford University Press

OxBTC    *Oxford Book of Twentieth-Century English Verse, The. *Philip Larkin, ed.* (1973) Oxford University Press

PAIC    Poetry and Its Conventions: An Anthology Examining Poetic Forms and Themes. *John T. Shawcross and Frederick R. Lapides, eds.* (1972) The Free Press

PB    Poetry of Birds, The. *Samuel Carr, ed.* (1976) Taplinger Publishing Company

PBMP    Premier Book of Major Poets, The: An Anthology. *Anita Dore, ed.* (1970) Fawcett Publications

PBWP    *Penguin Book of Women Poets, The. *Carol Cosman, Joan Keefe, and Kathleen Weaver, eds.* (1978) Penguin Books

PCat    Poetry of Cats, The. *Samuel Carr, ed.* (1974) The Viking Press

PCho    Poet's Choice, The. *George E. Murphy, Jr., ed.* (1980) Tendril

PChr    Poems of Christmas. *Myra Cohn Livingston, ed.* (1980) Atheneum

PCOP    Poems for Children and Other People. *George Hornby, ed.* (rev. ed., 1980) Crown Publishers, Inc.

# KEY TO SYMBOLS

PeBB   Penguin Book of Ballads, The. *Geoffrey Grigson, ed.* (1975) Penguin Books

PeD   Pegasus Descending: A Book of the Best Bad Verse. *James Camp, X. J. Kennedy, and Keith Waldrop, eds.* (1971) The Macmillan Company

PES   Poets and the English Scene. *Elinor Parker, comp.* (1975) Charles Scribner's Sons

PF   Poetry of Flowers, The. *Samuel Carr, ed.* (1977) Taplinger Publishing Company

PFD   Poems of Faith and Doubt: The Victorian Age. *R. L. Brett, ed.* (1970) University of South Carolina Press (First published in Great Britain, 1965, by Edward Arnold Publishers)

PFIr   Poems from Ireland. *William Cole, comp.* (1972) Thomas Y. Crowell Company

PH   Poetry of Horses, The. *William Cole, comp.* (1979) Charles Scribner's Sons

PHC   Poetry Hawaii: A Contemporary Anthology. *Frank Stewart and John Unterecker, eds.* (1979) The University Press of Hawaii

PiAm   Poet in America, The: 1650 to the Present. *Albert Gelpi, ed.* (1973) D. C. Heath and Company

PIM   Poems of Inspiration from the Masters. *James R. Mills, comp.* (1979) Fleming H. Revell Company

PMW   Poems from the Medical World. *Howard Sergeant, ed.* (1980) MTP Press Limited

PoA   *Poetry Anthology, The: 1912–1977. *Daryl Hine and Joseph Parisi, eds.* (1978) Houghton Mifflin Company

PoBA   **Poetry of Black America, The: Anthology of the 20th Century. *Arnold Adoff, ed.* (1973) Harper & Row

PoIA   Poetry: An Introduction and Anthology. *Edward Proffitt, ed.* (1981) Houghton Mifflin Company

POL   Poems One Line and Longer. *William Cole, ed.* (1973) Grossman Publishers

PoPle   Poetry for Pleasure: A Choice of Poetry and Verse on a Variety of Themes. *Ian Parsons, ed.* (1977) W. W. Norton & Company

PoRo   Pop/Rock Songs of the Earth. *Jerry L. Walker, ed.* (1972) Scholastic Book Services (division of Scholastic Magazines, Inc.)

PoTa   Poet's Tales, The: A New Book of Story Poems. *William Cole, ed.* (1971) World Publishing

PoUp   Poet Upstairs, The: A Washington Anthology. *Octave Stevenson, ed.* (1979) Washington Writers' Publishing House

PoW   Poets West: Contemporary Poems from the Eleven Western States. *Lawrence P. Spingarn, ed.* (1975) Perivale Press

PPM 808.1    Poetry for Peace of Mind. *Alison Wyrley Birch, ed.* (1978) Doubleday & Company

PPoD    Poetry: Points of Departure. *Henry Taylor, ed.* (1974) Winthrop Publishers

PPoe    Pleasures of Poetry, The. *Donald Hall, ed.* (1971) Harper & Row

PPP    Poetry: Past and Present. *Frank Brady and Martin Price, eds.* (1974) Harcourt Brace Jovanovich

Prf 808.1    Preferences: 51 American Poets Choose Poems from Their Own Work and from the Past. *Richard Howard, ed.* (1974) The Viking Press

PSN    Poems Since 1900: An Anthology of British and American Verse in the Twentieth Century. *Colin Falck and Ian Hamilton, eds.* (1975) Macdonald and Jane's (U.S. distributor: Beekman Publishers)

PSoN M 784.8    *Popular Songs of Nineteenth-Century America: Complete Original Sheet Music for 64 Songs. *Richard Jackson, ed.* (1976) Dover Publications (Published in Great Britain by Constable and Company)

Psy 811.08    Psyche: The Feminine Poetic Consciousness. An Anthology of Modern American Women Poets. *Barbara Segnitz and Carol Rainey, eds.* (1973) A Dell Laurel Edition

QQQ    Of Quarks, Quasars, and Other Quirks: Quizzical Poems for the Supersonic Age. *Sara Brewton, John E. Brewton, and John Brewton Blackburn, eds.* (1977) Thomas Y. Crowell Company

RAE    Round about Eight: Poems for Today. *Geoffrey Palmer and Noel Lloyd, eds.* (1972) Frederick Warne & Company

RDB    Richard Dyer-Bennet Folk Song Book, The: 50 Traditional Songs and Ballads with Guitar Accompaniments and Piano Arrangements. *Richard Dyer-Bennet, ed.* (1971) Simon and Schuster

RFM    Room for Me and a Mountain Lion: Poetry of Open Space. *Nancy Larrick, comp.* (1974) M. Evans and Co. (U.S. distributor: J. B. Lippincott Company)

RhR    Rhyming in the Rigging: Poems of the Sea. *Lahaina Harry, ed.* (1978) Ox Bow Press

RiTi 811.08    Rising Tides: 20th Century American Women Poets. *Laura Chester and Sharon Barba, eds.* (1973) (Washington Square Press) Pocket Books

RRA    Roses Race Around Her Name, The: Poems from Fathers to Daughters. *Jonathan Cott, ed.* (1974) Stonehill Publishing Company

SA    Settling America: The Ethnic Expression of 14 Contemporary Poets. *David Kherdian, ed.* (1974) Macmillan Publishing Company

# KEY TO SYMBOLS

SBG    Salt and Bitter and Good: Three Centuries of English and American Women Poets. *Cora Kaplan, ed.* (1975) Paddington Press

SCP 1-2    Signet Classic Poets of the 17th Century (Volumes One and Two). *John Broadbent, ed.* (1974) (A Signet Classic) New American Library

SES    Speak Easy, Speak Free. *Antar S. K. Mberi and Cosmo Pieterse, eds.* (1977) International Publishers

SFF    Since Feeling Is First. *James Mecklenburger and Gary Simmons, eds.* (1971) Scott, Foresman and Company

SLP    Scottish Love Poems: A Personal Anthology. *Antonia Fraser, ed.* (1976) Penguin Books (First published by Canongate Publishing, 1975)

SO    Straight On Till Morning: Poems of the Imaginary World. *Helen Hill, Agnes Perkins, and Alethea Helbig, comps.* (1977) Thomas Y. Crowell Company

SoS    *Sounds and Silences: Poetry for Now. *Richard Peck, ed.* (1970) (Laurel-Leaf Library) Dell

SoSe    *Sound and Sense: An Introduction to Poetry. *Laurence Perrine, ed.* (4th ed., 1973; 5th ed., 1977) Harcourt Brace Jovanovich

SPo    Sports Poems. *R. R. Knudson and P. K. Ebert, eds.* (1971) (Laurel-Leaf Library) Dell

SpRo    *Speak Roughly to Your Little Boy: A Collection of Parodies and Burlesques, Together with the Original Poems, Chosen and Annotated for Young People. *Myra Cohn Livingston, ed.* (1971) Harcourt Brace Jovanovich

SPT    Social Poetry of the 1930s: A Selection. *Jack Salzman and Leo Zanderer, eds.* (1978) Burt Franklin & Company

SS    Sounds and Silences: Poems for Performing. *Robert W. Boynton and Maynard Mack, eds.* (1975) Hayden Book Companny

STS    Seven Traditional, Seven Modern Poets. *Hulon Willis, ed.* (1971) Chandler Publishing Company

TAP    *Treasury of American Poetry, The. *Nancy Sullivan, ed.* (1978) Doubleday & Company

TAT    Traveling America with Today's Poets. *David Kherdian, ed.* (1977) Macmillan Publishing Company

TC    Third Coast, The: Contemporary Michigan Poetry. *Conrad Hilberry, Herbert Scott, and James Tipton, eds.* (1976) Wayne State University Press

TCP    Twentieth Century Poetry. *Carol Marshall, ed.* (1971) Houghton Mifflin Company

TDH    They've Discovered a Head in the Box for the Bread and Other Laughable Limericks. *John E. Brewton and Lorraine A. Blackburn, comps.* (1978) Thomas Y. Crowell Company

TH     Take Hold! An Anthology of Pulitzer Prize Winning Poems. *Lee Bennett Hopkins, comp.* (1974) Thomas Nelson, Inc.

TPo     Touch of a Poet, The. *Paul C. Holmes and Harry E. Souza, eds.* (1976) Harper & Row

TSWA 808.1     To See the World Afresh. *Lilian Moore and Judith Thurman, comps.* (1974) Atheneum

TT     Twice Ten: An Introduction to Poetry. *Chad Walsh and Eva T. Walsh, eds.* (1976) John Wiley and Sons

TV 811.08     Tangled Vines: A Collection of Mother and Daughter Poems. *Lyn Lifshin, ed.* (1978) Beacon Press

TVo     Timeless Voices: A Poetry Anthology Celebrating the Fulfillment of Age. *Virginia Larrain, comp.* (1978) Celestial Arts

TVS 831.07     Tudor Verse Satire. *K. W. Gransden, ed.* (1970) The Athlone Press of the University of London (American distributor: Humanities Press)

TwMBP     Twenty-three Modern British Poets. *John Matthias, ed.* (1971) The Swallow Press

UnPo     *Understanding Poetry. *Cleanth Brooks and Robert Penn Warren, eds.* (4th ed., 1976) Holt, Rinehart and Winston

UsP     Uses of Poetry, The. *Agnes Stein, comp.* (1975) Holt, Rinehart and Winston

VGW 811.08     *Voice That Is Great Within Us, The: American Poetry of the Twentieth Century. *Hayden Carruth, ed.* (1970) Bantam Books

VLP     Victorian Literature: Poetry. *Donald J. Gray and G. B. Tennyson, eds.* (1976) Macmillan Publishing Company

VoA     Visions of America by the Poets of Our Time. *David Kherdian, ed.* (1973) Macmillan Publishing Company

VoPo     Voices of Poetry. *Allen Kirschner, ed.* (1970) (Laurel-Leaf Library) Dell

VoR 811.08     Voices of the Rainbow: Contemporary Poetry by American Indians. *Kenneth Rosen, ed.* (1975) The Viking Press

VPC     Victorian Poetry: "The City of Dreadful Night" and Other Poems. *N. P. Messenger and J. R. Watson, eds.* (1974) Rowman & Littlefield (Published in Great Britain by J. M. Dent & Sons)

VW     Voices from Wah'Kon-Tah: Contemporary Poetry of Native Americans. *Robert K. Dodge and Joseph B. McCullough, eds.* (2d ed., 1976) International Publishers Company

VWA 808.81     *Voices Within the Ark: The Modern Jewish Poets. *Howard Schwartz and Anthony Rudolf, eds.* (1980) Avon Books

WasP     Washington and the Poet. *Francis Coleman Rosenberger, ed.* (1977) University Press of Virginia

WBN     We Become New: Poems by Contemporary American Women. *Lucille Iverson and Kathryn Ruby, eds.* (1975) Bantam Books

# KEY TO SYMBOLS

WeW      Western Wind: An Introduction to Poetry. *John Frederick Nims, ed.* (1974) Random House

WIF      Words in Flight: An Introduction to Poetry. *Richard Abcarian, ed.* (1972) Wadsworth Publishing Company

WPE 808.1   Women Poets in English, The: An Anthology. *Ann Stanford, ed.* (1972) (A Herder and Herder Book) McGraw-Hill Book Company

WPW      Women Poets of the West: An Anthology, 1850–1950. *A. Thomas Trusky, ed.* (2d rev. ed., 1979) Ahsahta Press

WTO      *World Treasury of Oral Poetry, A. *Ruth Finnegan, ed.* (1978) Indiana University Press

# TITLE AND FIRST LINE INDEX

"A" (1–12), *sels.*   Louis Zukofsky.
  "Giant sparkler,/ Lights of the river," 4.   VGW
  "River that must turn full after I stop dying," 11.   VGW
A, a, a, a,/ Yet I love whereso I go.   A Bachelor's Life.
  *Unknown.*   OxBM
A, a, a, Domine Deus.   David Jones.   FaBoTw (1975 ed.)
A, a noble failure, turns his critical wits on B.   Names.   D. J.
  Enright.   FaBoCo
A. A violent order is disorder; and.   Connoisseur of Chaos.
  Wallace Stevens.   CABA (1972 ed.)
A, an Apple, sweet and gay.   A B C Objects.   *Unknown.*   ECBV
A-Apple Pie.   Walter de la Mare.   MN
A Apple-pie.   Mother Goose.   MG
A B C, An.   *Unknown.*   GBP
A B C Objects.   *Unknown.*   ECBV
A B C of Love, The.   O. B. Hardison, Jr.   PoUp
A B C's.   Cinda Kornblum.   AcAn
A B C s.   Charles Olson.   NIL
A. B. S. News.   Ruth Lechlitner.   WasP
A! Dere God, what may this be.   On the Death of Edward III.
  *Unknown.*   OxBM
A dis[h], a dis[h], a green grass.   Green Grass.   *Unknown.*
  GBP; PoPle
A. E. F.   Carl Sandburg.   CMoP (1970 ed.)
"A 11."   Louis Zukofsky.   *Fr.* "A."   VGW
A = bh over 2.   Homework for Annabelle.   Phyllis McGinley.
  BBGO
A = pi r squared.   Even Though.   John Stone.   AMV-81
A for action; the bull's head.   Vowels.   Peter West.   AKE
"A 4."   Louis Zukofsky.   *Fr.* "A."   VGW
A. "I was a Have."   B. "I was a 'Have-not.' "   Equality of
  Experience.   Kipling.   *Fr.* Epitaphs of the War.   FaBoTw
  (1975 ed.)
A Is for Abracadabra.   Eleanor Farjeon.   ECBV
A is for Angels.   Alphabet of Christmas Cheer.   Elizabeth
  Weston.   ECBV
A is for axes, you very well know.   The Lumberman's Alphabet.
  *Unknown.*   AmFP
A is the aftermost part of the ship.   The Sailors' Alphabet.
  *Unknown.*   AmFP
A is the autograph bore.   The Autograph Bore.   Oliver Herford.
  TDH
A la Bourbon.   Richard Lovelace.   CaPo
A la Claire Fontaine (By Yonder Flowing Fountain).   *Tr. fr. French*
  *by* Arthur Kevess.   FSW
A la Promenade.   Paul Verlaine, *tr. fr. French by* Arthur Symons
  OBVE
A. M.—P.M.   Theodore H. Hirschfield.   AMV-81
À Madame, Madame B, Beauté Sexagenaire.   Charles Sackville.
  APAS
A peels an apple, while B kneels to God.   A Primer of the Daily
  Round.   Howard Nemerov.   WeW
A Quoi Bon Dire.   Charlotte Mew.   OxBTC
A Terre.   Wilfred Owen.   OxBTC
A' things created have their uses.   Strictures on the Economy of
  Nature.   George Outram.   FaBoCo
A tumbled down, and hurt his Arm, against a bit of wood.
  Alphabet.   Edward Lear.   FaBoNo

A.U.C. 334: about this date.   Advice to Young Ladies.   A. D.
  Hope.   SoSe
A, U, Hinny Burd.   *Unknown.*   GBP
A was an apple-pie.   Mother Goose.   ECBV
A was an archer, and shot at a frog,/ B was a blindman.
  *Unknown.*   OxBChV
A was an archer, and [*or* who] shot at a frog,/ B was a butcher.
  *Unknown.*   ECBV; MG
A Was Once an Apple Pie.   Edward Lear.   ECBV
  (Alphabet, An.).   OxBChV
A was the archer who shot at a frog/ B was Bo-peep.   A Nursery
  Rhyme Alphabet.   *Unknown.*   ECBV
A-a-ahh/ Because the world is round.   Because.   John Lennon
  *and* Paul McCartney.   UsP
Aah . . . You Ikenne Women.   Mark Wangberg.   TC
Aardvark.   Julia Fields.   CNA; OFD
Aaron.   George Herbert.   OAEL-1
Aaron Burr's Wooing.   Edmund Clarence Stedman.   BTTM
Aaron Nicholas, Almost Ten.   Janet Campbell Hale.   VoR
Aaron Stark.   E. A. Robinson.   AmVN; STS
Aa's a broken-hairted keelman, and aa's ower heid in love.
  Cushie Butterfield.   George Ridley.   VLP
Abalone Song, The.   George Sterling.   BPAW
Abandoned Copper Refinery.   Dan Gillespie.   TAT
Abandoned Farmhouse.   Ted Kooser.   GP
Abandoned. My brother and I tiptoed.   The Slaughterhouse Boys.
  William Meissner.   AMV-81
Abasshyd.   Pittendrigh MacGillivray.   MS
Abbey Church at Bath, The.   Henry Harington.   FaBoEE
Abbey Mason, The, *sel.*   Thomas Hardy.
  "When longer yet dank death had wormed."   PeD
Abbey Tomb.   Patricia Beer.   HeHu
Abdelazer, *sel.*   Aphra Behn.
  Song: "Love in fantastic triumph sate."   NOBE; WPE
  (Love Arm'd.)   SBG
Abdul, the Bulbul Amir.   *Unknown.*   FSW
Abel.   Else Lasker-Schüler, *tr. fr. German by* Joachim
  Neugroschel.   VWA
Abel was pure and woolly.   Brothers.   Dan Pagis, *tr. by* Shirley
  Kaufman.   VWA
Abelard at Cluny.   Grover Rees III.   AMV-80
Abelard was: God is.   Sic et Non.   Sir Herbert Read.   FaBoTw
  (1975 ed.)
Abel's Blood.   Henry Vaughan.   OBW
Abel's Bride.   Denise Levertov.   VGW; WBN
Aberdarcy: The Chaucer Road.   Kingsley Amis.   *Fr.* The Evans
  Country.   NOBL
Aberdarcy: The Main Square.   Kingsley Amis.   *Fr.* The Evans
  Country.   NOBL; OxBTC
Aberdare, Llanwynno through.   Glyn Cynon Wood.   *Unknown,*
  *tr. fr. Welsh by* Gwyn Williams.   OBW
Aberdeen, Mississippi Blues.   *Unknown.*   BluL
Abide, Good Men.   *Unknown.*   OxBM
Abide in Me, O Lord, and I in Thee, *with music.*   Harriet Beecher
  Stowe.   AH
Abide Not in the Realm of Dreams, *with music.*   William Henry
  Burleigh.   AH

Abide with Me. Henry Francis Lyte. BLSH, *with music;* FaPoR; ILwL; VLP

Abigail's Lamentation for the Loss of Mr. Harley. William Walsh. APAS

Abilene. *Unknown.* FSW

Abiquiu—Thursday in Holy Week. Peggy Pond Church. WPW

Abishag. Jakov Fichman, *tr. fr. Hebrew by* Robert Friend. VWA

Abishag Writes a Letter Home. Itzik Manger, *tr. fr. Yiddish by* Ruth Whitman. VWA

Ablow the Mune. Donald Campbell. MIS

Abnegation. Adrienne Rich. WPE

Abner Silver's "Pu-leeze! Mr. Hemingway!" Ring Lardner. OBAL

Aboard at a Ship's Helm. Walt Whitman. NOBA; RhR

Abominable Snowman, The. Ogden Nash. RAE

Aboriginal Simile, An. Mary Gilmore. GAS

Aboriginal Sin. William R. Mitchell. AATT

Abortion. Ai. BoWoP

Abortion. Mei Berssenbrugge. SA

Abortion, The. Lucille Iverson. WBN

Abortion, An. Frank O'Hara. CoPAm; TAP

Abortion, The. Anne Sexton. CAPP; IHMS; MAT; NMM; VGW

Abortions will not let you forget. The Mother. Gwendolyn Brooks. BPo; CAPP; GP; ILP (1975 ed.); NMM; TT

Abou Ben Adhem. Leigh Hunt. ECBV; FaPoR; NOBE; PCOP; PIM

About a fly. The Story. Charles Simic. NNaP

About a Year after He Got Married He Would Sit Alone in an Abandoned Shack in a Cotton Field Enjoying Himself. James Whitehead. CSP; GP

About an Excavation. Charles Reznikoff. VGW; WeW

About Children. Phyllis McGinley. OBAL

About Infinity: A Self-Portrait. Norman Dubie. FoP

About Long Days. Anthony Ostroff. MPA

About Marriage. Denise Levertov. NMM

About mirrors in hotel rooms: one can say. Results of a Scientific Survey. Bruce Cutler. AMV–80

About mountains it is useless to argue. Alpine. R. S. Thomas. LiSp; POL; RFM

About My Poems. Donald Justice. PoA

About My Students. John Fandel. PoIA

About one month before my thirty-third. Thinking of You. Dick Lourie. NeAC

About Scotland, & C. Ruthven Todd. MS

About suffering, about adoration, the old masters. The Old and the New Masters. Randall Jarrell. ExPo (1973 ed.); InPK

About suffering they were never wrong. Musée des Beaux Arts. W. H. Auden. AnMo; BiP; CABA (1972 ed.); CMoP (1970 ed.); ExPo (1973 ed.); FF; HAP; HeIP; ILP (1975 ed.); InPK; InPS; IP; MPo; NIL; NoAM; NOBE; OBP; PBMP; PPoD; PPP; PSN; TCP; TT; VoPo; WEW; WIF

About suffering you were wrong, Wystan. A Letter to Auden. Robert Phillips. AMV–81

About That. Marvin Bell. HeS

About That of Which One Cannot Speak, One Must Be Silent. Rudolph von Abele. PoUp

About the cool water. Sappho, *tr. fr. Greek by* Kenneth Rexroth. OBVE

About the Heavenly Life. Luis de Leon, *tr. fr. Spanish.* ILwL

About the Phoenix. James Merrill. NoAM

About the Shark, phlegmatical one. The Maldive Shark. Herman Melville. EcS; ILP (1975 ed.); NOBA; PiAm; TAP

About the skull of the beloved, filled. Presentation Piece. Marilyn Hacker. AmPA

About the sweet bag of a bee. The Bag of a Bee. Robert Herrick. SCP–1

About the Teeth of Sharks. John Ciardi. CaYB

About the time that taverns shut. The Ballad of Minepit Shaw. Kipling. PoPle; PoTa

About those wagon wheels. Wagon Wheels. S.E. LaMoure. AMV–81

About those who have recognized the range of choice. It Is Difficult Now to Speak of Poetry. George Oppen. NNaP

About to Die. *Gond Oral Tradition, tr. by* V. Elwin *and* S. Hivale. WTO

About twenty years ago. Wild Oats. Philip Larkin. InPS

About women no one can know. There are some. Mary Magdalene. Saunders Lewis, *tr. by* Gwyn Thomas. OBW

About Yes and No. Steve Toth. AcAn

Above a surface of stars. Metropolitan Night. Jorge Guillén, *tr. by* Barbara Howes. NYP

Above, above. Behold. *Tr. fr. Hawaiian by* M. K. Pukui. WTO

Above all gifts we most should prize. Walter Savage Landor. FaBoEE

Above It All. Philip Levine. NOBA

Above Lancaut, in a sequestered dell. Tintern Abbey. Edward Davies. *Fr. Chepstow: A Poem.* OBW

Above me is the misty English sky. In the Lake Country. Kay Wissinger. AMV–80

Above me the abbey, grey arches on the cliff. Caedmon. Norman Nicholson. FaBoTw (1975 ed.)

Above my daughter in the tree. White Spider. Marita Garin. AMV–80

Above my desk/the Rabbi of Auschwitz. On a Drawing by Flavio. Philip Levine. VWA

Above my desk, whirring and [*or* but] self-important. Angel [*or* Another Angel]. James Merrill. ConAP; NoAM; PoA

Above my face is a map. The Cloud-Mobile. May Swenson. SO

Above Pate Valley. Gary Snyder. ConAP; ILP (1975 ed.)

Above Penmaenmawr. Tony Connor. MPo

Above the Bright Blue Sky, *sel.* Albert Midlane. "There's a Friend for little children." OxBChV

Above the clouds the sun is warm. Flight 382. Doris Longman. AMV–81

Above the clumps where feather trees. At the Beginnings of the Andes. Barbara Ras. AMV–81

Above the fresh ruffles of the surf. Voyages, I. Hart Crane. CABA (1972 ed.); CMoP (1970 ed.); NoAM; NOBA; PSN; TAP; VGW

Above the hidden rocks all night. The Lighthouse. John Seller Anson AMV

Above the marsh, a hollow monument. The Hangar at Sunnydale: 1937. Janet Lewis. WPW

Above the Moving River. David Kherdian. VoA

Above the pines the moon was slowly drifting. Dickens in Camp. Bret Harte. BPAW

Above the rocking heads of the mothers. Nelly Sachs, *tr. fr. German by* Ruth *and* Matthew Mead. PBWP

Above the sounds that echo eerily. The Unreturning Native. Basil Dowling. ATNZ

Above the voiceful windings of a river. At the Grave of Henry Vaughan. Siegfried Sassoon. CMoP (1970 ed.); PoPle

Above the Wall. Susannah P. Malarkey. AMV–80

Above us the solid sky is waiting. Sunning during Session Break at Camp Lake Hubert for Girls, Brainerd, Minnesota. Mary Walker. PoUp

Abraham. Stephen Mitchell. VWA

Abraham. Delmore Schwartz. VWA

Abraham. Eisig Silberschlag. VWA

Abraham and Hagar/ a marriage torn asunder. The Story of Abraham and Hagar. Edna Aphek, *tr. by* Yishai Tobin. VWA

Abraham and Isaac. Else Lasker-Schüler, *tr. fr. German.* BoWop, *tr. by* Rosemarie Waldrop; VWA, *tr. by* Joachim Neugroschel

Abraham and Sarah. Itzik Manger, *tr. fr. Yiddish by* Stephen Garrin. VWA

Abraham built a town of sod. Abraham and Isaac. Else Lasker-Schüler, *tr. by* Rosemarie Waldrop. BoWoP

Abraham in Egypt. Howard Schwartz. VWA

Abraham in the land of Eden. Abraham and Isaac. Else Lasker-Schüler, *tr. by* Joachim Neugroschel. VWA

Abraham Lincoln. Rosemary *and* Stephen Vincent Benét. CC

Abraham Lincoln Walks at Midnight. Vachel Lindsay. CMoP (1970 ed.); GOA; IPWM; NoAM; NOBA; OFD; TAP; VGW

Abraham Sutskever. Seymour Mayne. VWA

Abraham's children played with shells. Hagar and Ishmael. Else Lasker-Schüler, *tr. by* Rosemarie Waldrop. BoWoP

Abraham's Knife. George Garrett. CSP

Abraham's little sons played with seashells. Hagar and Ishmael. Else Lasker-Schüler, *tr. by* Joachim Neugroschel. VWA

Abram Bailey he'd three sons. Sir Lionel. *Unknown.* AmFP

Abridged Bestiary, An. Maxine Chernoff. FiCh

Abroad Thoughts. Edward Blishen. NOBL

Abruptly All the Palm Trees. William Jay Smith. PoA

Absalom. Zerubavel Gilead, *tr. fr. Hebrew by* Dorothea Krook. VWA

Absalom and Achitophel, Pt. I. Dryden. OAEL-1
*Sels.*
  Achitophel: The Earl of Shaftesbury. NOBE
  "Of these the false Achitophel was first." HAP; InPS
  "In pious times, ere priestcraft did begin." HAP
  "In the first rank of these did Zimri stand." HAP
  "Some by their friends, more by themselves thought wise." OBSV
  "Some of their chiefs were princes of the land." EBEV
  "What shall we think! Can people give away." ILP (1975 ed.)
  "With all these loads of injuries opprest." EBEV
  Zimri: the Duke of Buckingham. NOBE; OBSV

Absalom and Achitophel, Pt. II, *sels.* Nahum Tate *and* John Dryden.
  "Let him rail on, let his invective Muse." Dryden. OBP
  "Next these, a troop of busy spirits press." Dryden. PPP
  Portrait of "Og." Dryden. NIL
  "To make quick way I'll leap o'er heavy blocks." Dryden. OBSV

Absence. Jeannette Barnes. AMV-80

Absence. Kathy Mangan. AMV-81

Absence of Noise Presence of Sound. Olga Broumas. PCho

Absences. James Tate. CAAP

Absent, The. Edwin Muir. NoAM

Absent from thee, I languish still. Song [*or* Return]. Earl of Rochester. BoLoP; GBL; NOBE

Absent Lover, An. *Unknown.* OxBM

Absent-minded, in his shack. An Odd Old Man in Hackensack. *Unknown.* TDH

Absent-minded Professor. Howard Nemerov. NowV

Absent One, The. Mary Queen of Scots, *tr. fr. French by* Antonia Fraser. SLP

Absent, this morning. Aube Provençale. Marilyn Hacker. AmPA

Absinthe-Drinker, The. Arthur Symons. FaBoTw (1975 ed.)

Absolute, An/ patience. The Breathing. Denise Levertov. IPWM; RFM; TCP

Absolute and Abitofhell. Ronald Arbuthnott Knox. FaBoCo

Absolute, freezing, eternity. Blue Tit. John Sjoberg. AcAn

Absolute zero: the locust sings. Summer. Conrad Aiken. NoAM

Absolutely Ordinary Rainbow, An. Les A. Murray. GAS

Abstinence. Kenneth Rosen. AmPA

Abstinence sows sand all over. Blake. EBEV; FaBoEE; FF; GBL

Abstract Love Poem. John Logan. UsP

Abstracted, sour, as he reaches across a dish. Scylla and Charybdis. Thomas Kinsella. OxBTC

Abt Vogler. Robert Browning. BoReV; OAEL-2; TT; VLP

Abu. Dudley Randall. BPo; TC

Abysm past thinking on, chill. In Space-Time Aware. Abbie Huston Evans. GP

Abysmal corners will dis (be) located. Vitality. Maria Amalia Fonte Boa, *tr. by* Willis Barnstone *and* Nelson Cerqueira. BoWoP

Abyss, The. Baudelaire, *tr. fr. French by* Jackson Matthews. GrRo

Ac that most needen aren oure neighebores, and we nime good heede. Our Needy Neighbours. William Langland. *Fr.* The Vision of Piers Plowman. OxBM

Academic. James Reeves. MPo

Academic. Theodore Roethke. FaBoEE; OBAL

Academic Affair. Brenda S. Stockwell. AMV-80

Accept, my God, the praises which I bring. The Offering: Part One. Mary Lee, Lady Chudleigh. WPE

Accept, thou shrine of my dead saint. The Exequy [*or* Exequy on His Wife]. Henry King. BoLoP; CABA (1972 ed.); GBL; HAP; ILP (1975 ed.); MetP; NOBE; OBP; PAIC; PPoe; SCP-2

Acceptance. Robert Frost. CMoP (1970 ed.); UsP

Acceptance. Margaret Reynolds. MIS

Acceptance Speech. Marvin Bell. AmPA

Accepting. Vassar Miller. FiCP

Accepting Surprise. William Stafford. EC

Accessions to Autumn. John Williams. MPA

Accident, The. Len Gasparini. NeAC

Accident. Sydney Lea. NYP

Accident, An. Gael Turnbull. PMW

Accident. *Unknown.* OSF

Accident at Three Mile Island. Jim Barnes. AMV-81

Accident Has Occurred, The. Margaret Atwood. IPWM; NMM

Accomplice, The. Ron Slate. AMV

Accomplices, The. Conrad Aiken. LoAs; NOBA

Accomplishments. Cynthia MacDonald. GP

According to Brueghel. Landscape with the Fall of Icarus. William Carlos Williams. Pictures from Brueghel, II. BBGO; NIL; PPP; TT; WIF

According to some learn'd opinions. Irish Antiquities. Thomas Moore. FaBoEE

"According to the Mighty Working." Thomas Hardy. CMoP (1970 ed.)

According to the silence, winter has arrived. Shepherd. William Stafford. PoA

According to the word of the Eternal Being. L'Imprévisibilité. Zinaida Hippius, *tr. by* Temira Pachmuss. PBWP

Accra 8/75. Thulani Nkabinde. NW

Accumulation of reefs, The. The Distances. Jim Carroll. PoA

Accursed power which stands on Privilege, The. On a General Election. Hilaire Belloc. FaBoCo; FaBoEE; NOBE; NOBL; OBSV; OxBTC

Accursed the man, whom fate ordains, in spite. The Author. Charles Churchill. EsaP; FaBoCo

Accusation. Utahania, *tr. fr. Eskimo.* WTO

Ache of Marriage, The. Denise Levertov. FF; NIL; NoAM; NOBA; PiAm; RiTi; TAP

Achilles. Phillip Corwin. AMV–80

Achilles spoke thus:/ "Atrides, and all." The Funeral Games for Patroclus: The Boastful Boxer. Homer, *tr. by* Ennis Rees. *Fr.* The Iliad, XXIII. LiSp

Achilles Tendon. Coleman Barks. *Fr.* Body Poems. NVAP

Aching all over I believe I've got the pneumonia this time. Pneumonia Blues. *Unknown.* BluL

Achitophel: The Earl of Shaftesbury. Dryden. *Fr.* Absalom and Achitophel, Pt. I. NOBE

Achromatic Bear, The. Robert Bloom. AATT

Acis and Galatea, *sel.* John Gay.
Song: "O ruddier than the cherry." NOBE

Acon. Hilda Doolittle ("H. D."). VGW

Aconite, The. Thomas Noel. PF

Acorn, The. Arthur J. Bull. HeHu

Acorns. Paul Mills. MIS

Acquainted with the Night. Robert Frost. CMoP (1970 ed.); HAP; IP; IPWM; NoAM; NOBA; PoIA; PPP; PSN; SoSe (1977 ed.); STS; TAP; VGW; WeW

Acquiescence of Pure Love, The. William Cowper, *after the French of* Madame Guyon. ILwL

Acre of Grass, An. W. B. Yeats. CMoP (1970 ed.); NoAM; OBP

Acres of Clams. *Unknown.* FSW

Acrobat. Edward Watkins. AMV–80

Acrobat from Xanadu disdained all nets, The. Dan Georgakas. FF

Acrobats. Robert Graves. PSN

Acrophobe and Lapidary. James Bonk. HeS

Across a sky suddenly mid-February blue. Cranes. J. R. S. Davies. POL

Across eternity, across her snows. Dogs and Wolves. Sorley Maclean, *tr. by* Iain Crichton Smith. SLP

Across Grandmother Ingersoll's face. To the Children at the Family Album. William Stafford. PoW

Across the ages they come thundering. Say This of Horses. Minnie Hite Moody. PCOP

Across the alley from the alamo. Variation. Peter Wild. GP

Across the Bay. Donald Davie. PSN

Across the bison-dotted plain. The Last Trail. Stanton A. Coblentz. BPAW

Across the crests of the naked hills. Laramie Trail. Joseph Mills Hanson. BPAW

Across the dim frozen fields of night. Night Train. Robert Francis. DuDa

Across the dinner table from me. The General's Wife. Elton Glaser. NVAP

Across the gap made by our English hinds. August. William Morris. *Fr.* The Earthly Paradise. VPC

Across the hills to Grandma's house. You Take the Pilgrims, Just Give Me the Progress. Loyd Rosenfield. QQQ

Across the lake the lights. Late November, Madison. David Hilton. AcAn

Across the lonely beach we flit. *See* Across the narrow beach we flit.

Across the millstream below the bridge. The Blue Swallows. Howard Nemerov. AnMo; BiP

Across the narrow [*or* lonely] beach we flit. The Sandpiper. Celia Thaxter. CTV; EcS; OxBChV; PCOP

Across the night. From Creature to Ghost. Pauline Hanson. TAP

Across the open countryside. The Unsettled Motorcyclist's Vision of His Death. Thom Gunn. PoA

Across the plain the wind whines through the sage. The Snowstorm. Pearl Riggs Crouch. BPAW

Across the road. Flock. Lance Henson. VoR

Across the round field under the dark male tower. The Lovers. Alex Comfort. PoA

Across the sea will come Adze-head. Adze-Head. *Unknown, tr. by* James Carney. BIrV

Across the sky the daylight crept. Coventry Patmore. *Fr.* The Angel in the House, II, x. GBL

Across the square. A Day in Salamanca. Radcliffe Squires. MPA

Across the street. It Makes No Difference. Donald Finkel. UsP

Across the street, apples fill the gutter. When It Rains. H. A. Maxson. AMV–80

Across the street, my aunt has lost. Emergency at 8. Geof Hewitt. NeAC

Across the swiffling waves they went. The Cruise of the "P.C." *Unknown.* RhR

Across the tracks in Cheyenne, behind the biggest billboard. A Long Way Outside Yellowstone. Thomas McGrath. VGW

Across the Universe. John Lennon *and* Paul McCartney. PoRo

Across the Western Ocean. *Unknown.* FSW

Across the Wide Missouri (Shenandoah). *Unknown. See* Shenandoah.

Across to the Peloponnese. James Welch. CDW; MPA

Across upon this undulated board of verdure chequered bright. The Five Unmistakable Marks. David Jones. In Parenthesis, VII. NoAM

Acrostic. "Lewis Carroll." NIL

Acrostic for Anna Geen. Eliza R. Snow. WPW

Acrostic of My Sister's Name. Keats. MBPR

Acrostic on Wharton, An. *Unknown.* OBSV

Act, An. Kenneth Rosen. AmPA

Act, The. William Carlos Williams. VGW

Act of Faith. Arturo Trías, *tr. fr.* Spanish by Julio Marzán. InW

Act of Love, The. Robert Creeley. GP; HAP

Act of Love. Vernon Scannell. SFF

Act I/ Orlando hails. The Five-Minute Orlando Macbeth. George MacBeth. NOBL

Actaeon. Arthur Hugh Clough. VLP

Actaeon. Rayner Heppenstall. FaBoTw (1975 ed.)

Acton Beauchamp, Herefordshire. *Unknown.* GBP

Acts of God. Ben Maddow. SPT

Acts passed beyond the boundary of mere wishing. Stephen Spender. OxBTC

Actual Vision of Morning's Extrusion. Alan Dugan. PPP

Ad Henricum Wottonem. Thomas Bastard. FaBoEE

Ad Johannuelem Leporem, Lepidissimum, Carmen Heroicum. *Unknown.* FaBoNo

Ad Limina. Joseph Campbell. BIrV

Ad Vilmum Axiologum. Samuel Taylor Coleridge. MBPR

Adam and Eve. C. H. Sisson. FaBoTw (1975 ed.)

Adam and Eve. *Unknown.* PoPle
("While Adam slept, from him his Eve arose.") FaBoEE

Adam and Eve at the Garden Gate. Marsha Pomerantz. VWA

Adam and Eve in Paradise. Milton. *Fr.* Paradise Lost, IV. SCP-1

Adam Driven from Eden. *Unknown.* OxBM

Adam, Eve and the Big Apple. Edward Watkins. AMV–81

Adam in Love. Stephen Mitchell. VWA

Adam in the Garden. Elmer F. Suderman. AATT

Adam in the Garden Pinning Leaves. *Unknown.* FSW

Adam is clay, the dumb. Paradise. Chana Bloch. VWA

Adam Lay I-bowndyn [*or* Y-bounden]. *Unknown.* HAP; ILP (1975 ed.); InPS; LoAs; NOBE; OAEL-1; OxBM; PPoe (O Felix Culpa!) BoReV

Adam scrivein, if ever it thee bifalle. To Adam, His Scribe. Chaucer. OAEL-1; OxBM

Adam Smith. E. C. Bentley. *Fr.* Clerihews. FaBoCo

Adam Speaks ("Oh, why did God,/Creator wise"). Milton. *Fr.* Paradise Lost, X. NU

Adam, who thought himself immortal still. The Discovery. Monk Gibbon. PFIr

Adam's Apple. Coleman Barks. *Fr.* Body Poems. NVAP

Adam's Complaint. Denise Levertov. BoWoP; NNaP

Adam's Curse. W. B. Yeats. BIrV; CMoP (1970 ed.); ExPo (1973 ed.); LoAs; NoAM; OAEL-2; PFIr; PoIA; SoSe (1977 ed.); TT; VLP; WIF

Adam's Death. Gabriel Levin. VWA

Adam's Dream. Howard Schwartz. VWA

Adam's Footprint. Vassar Miller. NIL

Adam's Song to Heaven. Edgar Bowers. ConAP

Adam's Task. John Hollander. PPP

Adbaston. C. B. Ash. PES

Addenda. Ted Berrigan. FiCh

Adder's Epigrams. Colin Ellis. FaBoEE

Addict. Jack Montgomery. QQQ

Addict, The. Anne Sexton. CTBA

Addiction to the exceptional event. Barbarossa. Hubert Witheford. ATNZ

Addio a la Mamma. Noe Jitrik, *tr. fr. Spanish by* Yishai Tobin. VWA

Addition to Kipling's "The Dead King (Edward VII), 1910." Max Beerbohm. FaBoEE

Addition to the Family, An. Edwin Morgan. MPo; MS

Address to a Child during a Boisterous Winter Evening. Dorothy Wordsworth. OxBChV

Address to Certain Gold Fishes. Hartley Coleridge. VLP

Address to the Deil. Burns. LAuP; OAEL-1

Address to the New Tay Bridge, An. William McGonagall. PeD; PPoD, *abr.*

Address to the Refugees. John Malcolm Brinnin. GOA

Address to the Scholars of New England. John Crowe Ransom. GOA

Address to the Unco Guid, or the Rigidly Righteous. Burns. ILP (1975 ed.); NOBE

Addressed to Haydon ("Great spirits now on earth are sojourning"). Keats. MBPR

Addressed to Haydon ("Highmindedness, a jealousy for good"). Keats. MBPR

Addressing His Deaf Wife, Kansas, 1916. William Olsen. AMV-81

Adelita ("Adelita's the name of the lady"). *Unknown, tr. fr. Spanish.* FSW

Adequacy. Elizabeth Barrett Browning. SBG

Adeste Fideles. *Unknown. See* O Come, All Ye Faithful.

Adieu, dear object of my love's excess. Orinda to Lucasia Parting, October 1661, at London. Katherine Philips. SCP-2

Adieu, Farewell Earth's Bliss. Thomas Nashe. *Fr.* Summer's Last Will and Testament. EBEV; HAP; HeIP; PPoe; WeW
(In a Time of Pestilence.) HoPM (1975 ed.)
(In Plague Time.) FaPoR
(In Time of Pestilence.) NOBE; PoPle; UsP
(Litany in Time of Plague, A.) CABA (1972 ed.); DL; NIL; OAEL-1; PPoD; PPP
(Song: "Adieu, farewell earths blisse.") OBP

Adieu, Romauld! But thou canst not forget me. Ella Wheeler Wilcox. *Fr.* The Farewell of Clarimonde. PeD

Adieu, sweet Angus, Maeve and Fand. The Passing of the Shee. J. M. Synge. BIrV; FaBoEE

Adieu to the pleasure of murder and whoring. Sir Thomas Armstrong's Last Farewell to the World. *Unknown.* APAS

Adjuration. Charles Enoch Wheeler. AmNP (1974 ed.)

Adlestrop. Edward Thomas. DuDr; HAP; NOBE; OxBTC; PES

Admetus, from my marrow's core I do. Edna St. Vincent Millay. SBG

Administrator, An. Geoffrey Grigson. FaBoEE

Administration of Things, The, *sels.* Matthew Mead.
"No days but these." TwMBP
"Riot, tumult, anticipated disturbances." TwMBP
"Sword or stealth, strength or ancient blood." TwMBP

Admire Cranmer! ("Admire the old man, admire him, admire him"). Stevie Smith. NoAM

Admiral Death. Sir Henry Newbolt. VLP

Admirals All. Sir Henry Newbolt. FaPoR

Admonition to the Muse. Geoffrey Taylor. FaBoEE

Admonitions. Lucille Clifton. BPo; InPS; NMM

Adobe House, An. Witter Bynner. BPAW

Adobe walls of the house, The. Woman. Ai. GP

Adolescence—II. Rita Dove. AmPA

Adolescent night, breath of the town, The. Midsummer. Robert Fitzgerald. PoA

Adolescent's Song. Howard Moss. LoAs

Adolph Hitler Meditates on the Jewish Problem. Oscar Hahn, *tr. fr. Spanish by* James Hoggard. AMV-81

Adonais: An Elegy on the Death of John Keats. Shelley. CABA (1972 ed.); EBEV; HoPM (1975 ed.); ILP (1975 ed.); LFH, *abr.;* MBPR; OAEL-2
Mourn Not for Adonais, *sel.* BoReV; NOBE

Adonis, Dying. Praxilla, *tr. fr. Greek by* John Dillon. PBWP
("Most beautiful of things I leave is sunlight," *tr. by* Willis Barnstone. BoWoP

Adorable paratroopess alights, The. Michael Silverton. POL

Adoremus. Christopher Smart. *Fr.* A Song to David. OBP

A-down the road and gun in hand. Whiskey Bill,—a Fragment. *Unknown.* BPAW

Adrian and Bardus. John Gower. *Fr.* Confessio Amantis, V. OxBM

Adrian Henri's Talking after Christmas Blues. Adrian Henri. BuTh; MPo
(Talking after Christmas Blues.) LP

Adriani Morientis ad Animam Suam. Emperor Hadrian. *See* Hadrian's Address to His Soul When Dying.

Adult Epigram. Wallace Stevens. NIL

Adulterers and customers of whores. Womanisers. John Press. BoLoP

Adultery. James Dickey. CAPP; CSP; PPoD; TAP; WeW

Adultery. Alan Dugan. CAPP

Adultery at the Plaza. John Thompson. WeW

Adulthood. Nikki Giovanni. NMM

Adultness is thrust upon us. Bury Our Faces. Bob Millard. AMV-80

Adults Only. William Stafford. FF

Advancement of Learning, An. Seamus Heaney. NCSH

Advantages. Eve Shelnutt. TC

Advent, *sel.* Brian Coffey.
"Awakening like return to Earth from Moon." CIP

Advent. Clinton F. Larson. MPA

Advent. Christina Rossetti. VLP

Advent. *Unknown.* BoReV
(Christ's Coming.) OxBM

Advent Images, The. Paul Ramsey. CSP

Advent 1966. Denise Levertov. ILP (1975 ed.); InPS; NNaP; PiAm; Prf

Adventure ("There's a place I've dreamed about far away"). Harry Behn. CTV

Adventures of Huckleberry Finn, The, *sel.* "Mark Twain."
Emmeline Grangerford's "Ode to Stephen Dowling Bots,
Dec'd." OBAL
(Ode to Stephen Dowling Bots, Dec'd.) NIL

Adventures of Isabel. Ogden Nash. ECBV; OBAL; PPM
"Isabel met an enormous bear," *sel.* OSP

Adventures of Master F. I., The, *sel.* George Gascoigne.
"And if I did, what then?" EBEV; GBL; HAP
(Farewell, A.) NOBE

Adversary, The. Phyllis McGinley. FaBoEE

Advice. Yehuda Amichai, *tr. fr. Hebrew by* Ruth Nevo. VWA

Advice. E. di Pasquale. AMV-81

Advice. Horace Gregory. SPT

Advice. Langston Hughes. ILP (1975 ed.)

Advice, The. Sir Walter Ralegh. AAS

Advice. Ruth Stone. NMM

Advice, The. *Unknown.* APAS

Advice for good love; Don't love. Advice. Yehuda Amichai, *tr.
by* Ruth Nevo. VWA

Advice from Euterpe. Carter Revard. VoR

Advice of an Efficiency Expert, The. Augustus Young. CIP

Advice to a Neighbour Girl. Yü Hsüan-chi, *tr. fr. Chinese by*
Kenneth Rexroth *and* Ling Chung. PBWP
(For a Neighbor Girl, *tr. by* Geoffrey Waters.) BoWoP

Advice to a Painter. *Unknown.* APAS

Advice to a Prizefighter. Lucilius, *tr. fr. Greek by* Tom Dodge.
LiSp

Advice to a Prophet. Richard Wilbur. CAPP; ExPo (1973 ed.);
ILP (1975 ed.); MAT; NIL; PiAm; PPoD; PP

Advice to a Raven in Russia. Joel Barlow. NOBA

Advice to Children and Their Parents. *Unknown.* DuDr

Advice to My Best Brother, Colonel Francis Lovelace. Richard
Lovelace. CaPo

Advice to the Lovelorn. Linda Parker. HeS; TC

Advice to the Old Beaux. Sir Charles Sedley. ILP (1975 ed.);
SCP-2

Advice to the Painter. Matthew Prior. APAS

Advice to Young Ladies. A. D. Hope. SoSe

Advising Anna Doolittle the White Antelope Allusion Will Escape
Her Readers. Tom Trusky. PoW

Adze-Head. *Unknown, tr. fr. Irish by* James Carney. BIrV

Ae boat anerlie nou. Largo. Sydney Goodsir Smith. MS

Ae Fond Kiss. Burns. CABA (1972 ed.); OAEL-1; OBP; PPP;
SLP
(Song: "Ae fond kiss, and then we sever.") BoLoP

Ae nicht o thae twa year. The Widdreme. Sorley Maclean. MS

Ae weet forenicht i the yow-trummle. The Watergaw. "Hugh
MacDiarmid." MS

Aedh Hears the Cry of the Sedge. W. B. Yeats. *See* He Hears
the Cry of the Sedge.

Aedh Tells of the Rose in His Heart. W. B. Yeats. *See* Lover
Tells of the Rose in His Heart.

Aedh Thinks of Those Who Have Spoken Evil of His Beloved.
W. B. Yeats. NoAM; VLP
(He Thinks of Those Who Have Spoken Evil of His Beloved.)
PFIr

Aedh Wishes for the Cloths of Heaven. W. B. Yeats. DuDr;
NoAM
(He Wishes for the Cloths of Heaven.) CMoP (1970 ed.);
OLR

Aella, *sel.* Thomas Chatterton.
Minstrel's Song, The. HAP; OBP
("O! Synge untoe mie roundelaie.") NOBE
(Song from Aella.) LoAs

Aelred of Rievaulx. Liam Lynch. IPM

Aeneas at Washington. Allen Tate. NoAM; NOBA; PiAm;
WasP

Aeneid, The, *abr.* Virgil, *tr. fr. Latin by* Allen Mandelbaum.
NAWM-1
*Sels.*
"Affrayit, I glistnyt of sleip, and stert on feit," *fr.* II, *tr. into
Middle English by* Gavin Douglas. OBVE
"Amyd the wod his modir met thame tway," *fr.* I, *tr. into Middle
English by* Gavin Douglas. OBVE
"And oft the owle with rufull song complaind," *fr.* IV, *tr. by*
Earl of Surrey. OBVE
"And Turnus than, quhar he at erth dyd ly," *fr.* XII, *tr. into
Middle English by* Gavin Douglas. OBVE
"Arms, and the man I sing, who forc'd by fate," *fr.* I, *tr. by*
Dryden. OBVE
"As, sum tyme, dois the curser stert and ryn," *fr.* XI, *tr. into
Middle English by* Gavin Douglas. OBVE
"As this convine and ordinance was mayd," *fr.* VIII, *tr. into
Middle English by* Gavin Douglas. OBVE
"As when a fragment, from a mountain torn," *fr.* XII, *tr. by*
Dryden. OBVE
"Attentively he heard us, while we spoke," *fr.* XI, *tr. by* Dryden.
OBVE
"Batellis and the man I will descrive, The," *fr.* I, *tr. into Middle
English by* Gavin Douglas. OBVE
"Bot now the haisty, egir, and wild Dido," *fr.* IV, *tr into Middle
English by* Gavin Douglas. OBVE
"Dear Sister, my resentment had not been," *fr.* IV, *tr. by* Sir
John Denham. OBVE
"Eneas wonderit the greitnes of Cartaige," *fr.* I, *tr. into Middle
English by* Gavin Douglas. OBVE
"Exulting in his strength, he seems to dare," *fr.* XI, *tr. by*
Dryden. OBVE
Funeral Games for Anchises, The: Entellus, *fr.* V, *tr. by* Rolfe
Humphries. LiSp
"Greeks' chieftains, all irked with the war, The," *fr.* II, *tr. by*
Earl of Surrey. OAEL-1
"Heaven, the earth, and all the liquid mayne, The," *fr.* VI, *tr. by*
Sir Walter Ralegh. OBVE
"It was then night: the sound and quiet sleep," *fr.* IV, *tr. by* Earl
of Surrey. OAEL-1
"Loe! formest of a rout that followed him," *fr.* II, *tr. by* Earl of
Surrey. OBVE
"Loud report through Lybian cities goes, The," *fr.* IV, *tr. by*
Dryden. OBVE
"Now manhood and garbroyls I chaunt," *fr.* I, *tr. by* Richard
Stanyhurst. BIrV; OBVE
"Onto the hallowit steid bryng in, thai cry," *fr.* II, *tr. into Middle
English by* Gavin Douglas. OBVE
"Prince, with wonder, sees the stately tow'rs, The," *fr.* I, *tr. by*
Dryden. OBVE
"Quhen thou are careit to that cuntree," *fr.* III, *tr. into Middle
English by* Gavin Douglas. OBVE
"There Charon stands, who rules the dreary coast," *fr.* VI, *tr. by*
Dryden. OBVE
"Thir riveris and thir watteris kepit war," *fr.* VI, *tr. into Middle
English by* Gavin Douglas. OBVE
"Thus fell the King, who yet surviv'd the state," *fr.* II, *tr. by* Sir
John Denham. OBVE
"To my prowd foe thus, sister, humblie saye," *fr.* II, *tr. by* Earl
of Surrey. OBVE
"Wee leave Creete Country; and our sayls unwrapped
uphoysing," *fr.* III, *tr. by* Richard Stanyhurst. OBVE

Aeroplane, The. Derek Stuart. FPB

Aesop's Fable of the Frogs. La Fontaine, *tr. fr. French by* John
Hookham Frere. OBVE

Aesthete, The. W. S. Gilbert. *See* Bunthorne's Song: The
Aesthete.

Aesthete Weasel, The. Christian Morgenstern, *tr. fr. German by*
Geoffrey Grigson. FaBoNo

Aesthetic. Norman Rosten. PoA

Aesthetic Point of View, The. W. H. Auden. OBAL

Aesthetics of the Moon. Jack Anderson. Moon

Aestivation [an Unpublished Poem by My Late Latin Tutor].
  Oliver Wendell Holmes. *Fr.* The Autocrat of the Breakfast
  Table, *ch.* 11.  NOBL; OBAL
  (Intramural Aestivation, or Summer in Town, by a Teacher of
  Latin.) FaBoNo
Affable Irregular, An.  The Road at My Door.  W. B. Yeats.
  Meditations in Time of Civil War, V.  BIrV; NOBE
Affair of the Heart.  Peter Porter.  CAAP
Affections, instincts, principles, and powers.  Written in Butler's
  Sermons.  Matthew Arnold.  VLP
Affinities.  Adrien Stoutenburg.  TSWA
Affirmation.  Helen Armstead Johnson.  AmNP (1974 ed.)
Affirmed, Pent by power that holds it fast.  Like a Bulwark.
  Marianne Moore.  PiAm
Affliction.  Sir John Davies.  *Fr.* Nosce Teipsum.  NOBE
Affliction ("Broken in pieces all asunder").  George Herbert.
  SCP-1
Affliction ("When first thou didst entice to thee my heart").
  George Herbert.  BoReV; CABA (1972 ed.); MetP; NOBE;
  SCP-1
Affliction of Margaret, The.  Wordsworth.  MBPR
Affrayit, I glistnyt of sleip, and stert on feit.  Virgil, *tr. by* Gavin
  Douglas.  *Fr.* The Aeneid, II.  OBVE
Afoot and light-hearted I take to the open road.  Song of the
  Open Road.  Walt Whitman.  NOBA; PPM; RFM
Afraid and trackless between storm and storm.  The Hare in the
  Snow.  Gloria Rawlinson.  ATNZ
Afraid of the sun, I hide behind my sleeve.  For a Neighbor Girl.
  Yü Hsüan-chi, *tr. by* Geoffrey Waters.  BoWoP
Afraid of the sunlight.  Advice to a Neighbour Girl.  Yü Hsüan-
  chi, *tr. by* Kenneth Rexroth *and* Ling Chung.  PBWP
Afresh'd with paint the shop had glare.  New Storefront.  Russell
  Atkins.  FB
Africa.  Lucille Clifton.  CNA
Africa.  David Diop, *tr. fr.* French *by* Gerald Moore *and* Ulli
  Beier.  NIL
Africa.  Change Is Not Always Progress.  Don L. Lee.  TAP
Africa my Africa.  Africa.  David Diop, *tr. by* Gerald Moore *and*
  Ulli Beier.  NIL
African Affair, The.  Bruce McM. Wright.  AmNP (1974 ed.);
  PoBA
African China.  Melvin B. Tolson.  PoBA
African Day.  Gloria de Sant'Ana, *tr. fr.* Portuguese *by* Allan
  Francovich *and* Kathleen Weaver.  PBWP
African Dream.  Bob Kaufman.  AmNP (1974 ed.); PoBA
African Elegy, An.  Robert Duncan.  NoAM
African Poems, *sel.*  Don L. Lee.
  "We're an Africanpeople."  CNA
African Things.  Victor Hernández Cruz.  InW; SA
African Woman is dead, An.  Poem about Birth.  Anne
  Sadowski.  SES
Africa's Plea.  Roland Tombekai Dempster.  TPo
Africland.  Oliver La Grone.  FB
Afro-American Fragment.  Langston Hughes.  PBMP
After.  Philip Levine.  VWA
After.  Kendrick Smithyman.  ATNZ
After a Birthday.  Michael Dransfield.  FPA
After a black day, I play Haydn.  Allegro.  Tomas Tranströmer,
  *tr. by* Robert Bly.  EAS
After a dream in which your love's fullness.  The Sapphire.
  W. S. Merwin.  PoA
After a drifting day, visiting the bridge near Louisberg.  Summer,
  1960, Minnesota.  Robert Bly.  InPS
After a hundred years.  Emily Dickinson.  UsP
After a Journey.  Thomas Hardy.  CMoP (1970 ed.); EBEV;
  ExPo (1973 ed.); GBL; OxBTC
After a Journey.  Ken Smith.  TwMBP

After a long evening waiting for John Wayne.  George Mattingly.
  *Fr.* The Lives of the Poets.  AcAn
After a long walk I come down to the shore.  The Fallen Tree.
  Robert Bly.  PCho
After a long winter, giving/ each other nothing.  Chiyo, *tr. fr.*
  *Japanese by* David Ray.  BoWoP
After a Passage in Baudelaire.  Robert Duncan.  CMoP (1970
  ed.); ExPo (1973 ed.); PoA
After a while, in the larger cities, we.  Normal as Two Ships in
  the Night.  Walta Borawski.  AMV-81
After a while it dawns on us.  Historical Museum, Manitoulin
  Island.  Lisel Mueller.  PoA
After Advertising Ended.  Ed Ochester.  AAN
After all, Charlie, we shall see them go.  Longshore Intellectual.
  Sean Lucy.  CIP
After All These Years.  May Sarton.  AMV-81
After All You Are Quiet.  Margaret Atwood.  Psy
After an age when thunderbolts and hail.  Sonnet XVI.  Louise
  Labé, *tr. by* Willis Barnstone.  BoWoP
After an All-Night Cackle with Sloth and Co. I Enter Mansion
  and Greet the Dawn.  Gary Gildner.  GP
After an Eclipse of the Sun.  Eugene Heimler, *tr. fr. Hungarian*
  *by* Peter Sherwood *and* Keith Bosley.  VWA
After an evening of drinking.  Ryōkan.  William Heyen.  AMV-
  81
After an hundred and thirty years' nap.  On the Erection of
  Shakespeare's Statue in Westminster Abbey.  Pope.  FaBoEE
After Apple-picking.  Robert Frost.  CMoP (1970 ed.); Epi;
  NoAM; NOBA; NU; PPP; PSN; STS; TAP; TT; UnPo (1976
  ed.)
After Bad Dreams.  George Garrett.  CoPAm
After Boris slays the tsarevitch Dmitri.  Iowa.  Harry Stessel.
  AAN
After breakfast and you'd left for school.  Divorce.  Bink Noll.
  MAT
After breakfast in the Philippines.  Ode to Tropical Skiing.  John
  Forbes.  GAS
After bringing forth eighteen.  For a Shetland Pony Brood Mare
  Who Died in Her Barren Year.  Maxine W. Kumin.  PH
After casting the first act, checking sections.  God and Man.
  Samuel Hazo.  TPo
After centuries of dissecting.  Lesbian Poem.  Robin Morgan.
  IHMS
After Dark.  Adrienne Rich.  VGW
After dark vapours have oppress'd our plains.  Keats.  ILP (1975
  ed.); MBPR
After Death.  Patricia Beer.  HeHu
After Death.  Christina Rossetti.  GBL; ILP (1975 ed.)
After death nothing is, and nothing death.  Seneca, *tr. by* Earl of
  Rochester.  *Fr.* Troades, II.  EBEV; OBVE
After Derry, 30 January 1972.  Seamus Deane.  IPM
After Dilettante Concetti.  Henry Duff Traill.  FaBoCo
After dreaming some hours of the land of Cockaigne.  Thomas
  Moore.  *Fr.* The Fudge Family in Paris.  BIrV
After Drinking Water.  Daniela Gioseffi.  WBN
After each quake.  Crack in the Wall Holds Flowers.  Adam
  David Miller.  PoBA
After eight thousand years among the stars.  Space-Wanderer's
  Homecoming.  Peter Viereck.  AMV-80
After Emerson.  *Unknown.*  NOBL
After Ever Happily.  Ian Serraillier.  ECBV; SO
After experience taught me that all the ordinary.  W. D.
  Snodgrass.  CAPP; PPoD; PPP; TAP
After Five Years.  Augustus Young.  BIrV
After Frost.  Brian Patten.  EBEV
After Galen.  Oliver St. John Gogarty.  FaBoEE
After Goliath.  Kingsley Amis.  NOBL; OxBTC

After Grave Deliberation. Elizabeth Flynn. AMV–80

After great pain, a formal feeling comes. Emily Dickinson. BoWoP; CABA (1972 ed.); HAP; InPS; IP; NIL; NOBA; PiAm; PoIA; PPM; PPoe; Psy; SBG; TAP; TT; UnPo (1976 ed.); UsP; WeW

After Greece. James Merrill. ConAP; NOBA

After Grief. Stanley Plumly. AmPA

After having slain very many beasts. Sonnet XIX. Louise Labé, *tr. by* Willis Barnstone. BoWoP

After having written verses in tight corsets. To Make It Real. Peter Porter. UsP

After He Said. Stephen Dunn. BrS

After he stripped off my clothes. Vallana, *tr. fr. Sanskrit by* Willis Barnstone. BoWoP

After her pills the girl slept and counted. Tally. Josephine Miles. NoAM

After her twelfth birthday. Woman's Liberation. Sister Maura. AMV–81

After His Death. Susan Hartman. AAN

After his death we wade together. He Fishes with His Father's Ghost. Lewis Nordan. AMV–81

After Horace. Alfred Denis Godley. NOBL

After hot loveless nights, when cold winds stream. The Sisters. Roy Campbell. BoLoP; FaBoTw (1975 ed.)

After hundreds of years of common sense. Holiday. Alan Dugan. CoPAm

After I am dead/ Say this at my funeral. After My Death. Hayim Nachman Bialik, *tr. by* A. C. Jacobs. VWA

After I ate my dinner then I ate. Confession of a Glutton. Don Marquis. GDP

After I came down from the mountain, my Lord. Moses' Account. Milan Fuest, *tr. by* Andrè Ungar. VWA

After I come home from the meeting with friends. Josephine Miles. CoPAm

After I got religion and steadied down. Butch Weldy. Edgar Lee Masters. *Fr.* Spoon River Anthology. PSN

After I Had Worked All Day. Charles Reznikoff. *Fr.* Five Groups of Verse. SA; VGW

After I Have Voted. Laura Jensen. AmPA

After I watched your face, behind its mask. A Commitment. Jon Anderson. BrS

After ice-ages comes heaven and hell. Sequitor: A Love Poem. Cinda Kornblum. AcAn

After Illness. Vi Gale. GP

After its lid. Pumpkin. Valerie Worth. CC; IWK

After jump, drop and somersault. Parachutist. Samuel Hazo. SPo

After kicking on the swing. Li Ch'ing-chao, *tr. fr. Chinese by* Kenneth Rexroth *and* Ling Chung. BoWoP

After Long Busyness. Robert Bly. PoA

After Long Silence. W. B. Yeats. BoLoP; CMoP (1970 ed.); HeIP; HoPM (1975 ed.); NIL; OAEL-2; PPP; PSN; UnPo (1976 ed.); WIF

After long stormes and tempests sad assay. Amoretti, LXIII. Spenser. OAEL-1

After Looking into a Genealogy. Peggy Pond Church. WPW

After Lorca. Robert Creeley. ConAP; InPS; POL; UsP

After Lorca. Ted Hughes. PoA

After Lord Tennyson. G. K. Chesterton. NOBL

After Love. Vicente Aleixandre, *tr. fr. Spanish by* Lewis Hyde. AMV

After Love. Maxine W. Kumin. NMM; RiTi; TAP; WBN

After many long months on the market. Sold. R. R. Cuscaden. ANTL

After many winters the moss. Tale. W. S. Merwin. TH

After Margrave died, nothing. History of a Literary Movement. Howard Nemerov. PSN

After Mass. "Michael Field." WPE

After massaging you in Rose Oil. Touching. Katie Savage. PoUp

After Midnight. Louis Simpson. NoAM

After midnight I heard a scream. By Night. Robert Francis. POL; VGW

After midnight the bright moon. Frost Warning. Ron McFarland. AMV–81

After midnight the charm. Party. Donald Justice. GP

After Midsummer. E. J. Scovell. OxBTC

After miles of the same oasis up ahead. Truckdriver. Gary Sange. NVAP

After My Death. Hayim Nachman Bialik, *tr. fr.* Hebrew by A. C. Jacobs. VWA

After night's thunder far away had rolled. Haymaking. Edward Thomas. PES

After only a month or so—weary and. Melancholy Summer. Kris Hemensley. *Fr.* A Mile from Poetry. CAAP

After our fierce loving. The Profile on the Pillow. Dudley Randall. BPo; PoBA; TAP

After Paeschendale,/ After Katyn. Matthew Mead. *Fr.* Identities. TwMBP

After Picking Rosehips. Harley Elliott. NeAC

After Plotinus. William Stafford. PoA

After porridge, flapjacks, and stirrup-cups. The Ranch. Lawrence P. Spingarn. PoW

After Publication of Under the Volcano. Malcolm Lowry. FaBoTw (1975 ed.)

After Rabbi Akiba, Buxtorf, Herder. Commentaries on the Song of Songs. Judith Herzberg, *tr. by* Shirley Kaufman. VWA

After Rain. Edward Thomas. NCSH

After rain has cooled the rough skin. Barriers 2. Gerald Barrax. CSP

After rain I/ walk and looking. Room Conditioner. A. R. Ammons. PCho

After rain, through afterglow, the unfolding fan. Train Ride. John Wheelwright. VGW

After Reading Nelly Sachs. Linda Pastan. VWA

After Reading St. John the Divine. Gene Derwood. WPE

After Reading Sylvia Plath. Alta. IHMS

After Reading Takahashi. Jim Harrison. HeS

After Reading *The First Circle*. Martha Shelley. WBN

After Robert Browning. G. K. Chesterton. NOBL

After scanning its face again and again. John Muir on Mt. Ritter. Gary Snyder. *Fr.* Myths and Texts: Burning. Epi; NOBA; TCP

After Selecting the Wedding Invitations. Diane Levenberg. NPW

After Sex. Greg Kuzma. GP

After sharp words from the fine mind. The Flowering Bars. Charles Donnelly. CIP

After she finished her first abortion. Margaret, Seen through a Picture Window. Judy Grahn. *Fr.* The Common Woman, VI. GP

After Snow. Walter Clark. NCSH

After so many victories, one. Epitaph for Goliath. David R. Slavitt. CoPAm

After so many years of desperate quiet. Not Steel Alone. Norman Macleod. SPT

After some years Bohemian came to this. Epigram. J. V. Cunningham. VGW

After squid and cool white wine there is. Early Morning of Another World. Tom McKeown. AMV–80

After such knowledge of knowing. The Syllabus. Manfred Jurgensen. FPA

After Swimming in the Pacific. Cathy Colman. NPW

After Swinburne. G. K. Chesterton. NOBL

After Tennyson. Edward Lear. FaBoNo

After that war, when death had gone away. Joan Miró. Ruthven Todd. EAS

After the agony in the guest/ bedroom. Margaret Atwood. NeAC

After the Anonymous Swedish. Jim Harrison. VGW

After the Ball Is Over, *with music.* Charles Kassell Harris. BLSo; FSN; FSW

"After the ball is over," chorus. BLSH

After the ball was over/ The lady took out her glass eye. *Unknown.* OSF

After the bars and the gates and the degradation. What Is Left? Assata Shakur. AMV

After the Bombing of Barcelona. Norman Macleod. SPT

After the Broken Arm. Ron Padgett. ConAP; EAS; UsP

After the Burial. James Russell Lowell. UnPo (1976 ed.)

After the burial-parties leave. The Hyaenas. Kipling. OBSV

After the celebrated carved misericords. Cromwell. Robert Francis. GP

After the class I taught my father French. Ballet. Brenda Hillman. AMV-81

After the cloud embankments. Reconnaissance. Arna Bontemps. AmNP (1974 ed.); BPo

After the Club-Dance. Thomas Hardy. At Casterbridge Fair, III. VLP

After the cracked screams. Wife. Jenné Andrews. HeS

After the Cries of the Birds. Lawrence Ferlinghetti. CAPP

After the Dark Months. Ronald Mann. PMW

After the darkness has come. Disturbances. Anthony Thwaite. MPo

After the Death of an Elder Klallam. Duane Niatum. CDW

After the Death of Her Daughter in Childbirth. Izumi Shikibu, *tr. fr. Japanese by* Edwin A. Cranston. PBWP

After the Deformed Woman Is Made Correct. Robert Lietz. AMV-80

After the Deluge. House of the Living. Claude Vigée, *tr. by* Henry Braun. VWA

After the Dentist. May Swenson. GP

After the doctor checked to see. First Practice. Gary Gildner. AmPA; InPK; LiSp; PPoD

After the dreadful Flood was past. The Tower of Babel. Nathaniel Crouch. OxBChV

After the Engraving. David Bromige. MIT

After the entertainments of the night. The Apparition. Chris Wallace-Crabbe. MAuV

After the event the rockslide. Clarity. A. R. Ammons. TAP

After the explosion or cataclysm, that big. The Eternal City. A. R. Ammons. TT

After the Fact. Grace Cavalieri. AATT

After the Fair. Thomas Hardy. At Casterbridge Fair, VII. CMoP (1970 ed.); HAP; VLP

After the fall of the tree. After. Philip Levine. VWA

After the family dinner, language. Stroke. Susan Irene Rea. EC

After the feast, my Shapcott, see. Oberon's Palace. Robert Herrick. CaPo

After the fiercest pangs of hot desire. Richard Duke. BoLoP

After the fifth day. Food Strike. Michael Hogan. GP

After the final no there comes a yes. The Well Dressed Man with a Beard. Wallace Stevens. BiP

After the First Communion. Sunday Afternoon. Denise Levertov. ConAP; IHMS; SoS

After the First Frost. Lew Blockcolski. VoR

After the first glass of vodka. As Planned. Frank O'Hara. UsP

After the first powerful plain manifesto. The Express. Stephen Spender. CMoP (1970 ed.); ILP (1975 ed.); MPo; NoAM; NowV; WIF

After the first shallows have dropped away. Daily the Ocean between Us. Patricia Goedicke. TAP

After the first sudden rain. Rains on the Island. Gabriel Preil, *tr. by* Robert Friend. VWA

After the Funeral. Dylan Thomas. CMoP (1970 ed.); InPK; OAEL-2; OBW

After the Funeral of Assam Hamady. Sam Hamod. SA

After the glass shower. Weather Report. Elaine H. Jennings. NPW

After the Industrial Revolution, All Things Happen at Once. Robert Bly. ConAP

After the "invitation" by the preacher she collapsed in the. Jim Harrison. *Fr.* Ghazals. NoAM

After the kill, there is the feast. Small Poem about the Hounds and the Hares. Lisel Mueller. GP

After the Killing. Dudley Randall. CNA

After the Last Breath. Thomas Hardy. VLP

After the Last Bulletins. Richard Wilbur. ConAP; NIL

After the Last Dynasty. Stanley Kunitz. TAP

After the last long agate beach. Before the Dark Is Down. Mary Shumway. NVAP

After the latest mass murders. The Land of the Old Fields. Van K. Brock. CSP

After the leaves have fallen, we return. The Plain Sense of Things. Wallace Stevens. InPS

After the lilting. Voice Over. Anthony Glavin. IPM

After the Locust. Rene Gascou. PoW

After the many courses, hot bowls of rice. Photographs of China. Donald Hall. TC

After the movie, we drive down Ridge road towards home. Lilacs. Bill Pruitt. EC

After the murder. The Last Quatrain of the Ballad of Emmett Till. Gwendolyn Brooks. CAPP; CNA; PoBA; WPE

After the Navy and war. Wood Butcher. Norman Hindley. AMV-81

After the Night Hunt. James Dickey. PoA

After the Persian. Louise Bogan. PoA

After the planes unloaded, we fell down. The Dead in Europe. Robert Lowell. CMoP (1970 ed.); STS

After the Pleasure Party. Herman Melville. AmVN

After the Quarrel. Barbara Gibson. FF

After the Rain. Stanley Crouch. CNA

After the Rain. Yannis Ritsos, *tr. fr. Greek by* Nikos Stangos. TSWA

After the rare arch-poet Jonson died. Upon Mr. Ben Jonson: Epigram. Robert Herrick. CaPo; SCP-1

After the Rent. Ed Cox. PoUp

After the Revolution. Marilyn Hacker. AmPA

After the Riot. William Pillin. SPT

After the School-Feast. Charles Tennyson Turner. VPC

After the Seance. David Clewell. AMV-81

After the Second Operation. Patricia Goedicke. AAN; TAP

After the Seizer there were ten chiefs, and there was much warfare south and east. *Tr. fr. Delaware Indian by* Danile G. Brinton. *Fr.* Walam Olum; or, Red Score. OBVE

After the shot the driven feathers rock. Rainbow. Robert Huff. CoPAm

After the Spanish Chroniclers. William Bronk. GP

After the spring floods, after. River Road. Mary Shumway. NVAP

After the Storm. Joseph Kalar. SPT

After the Storm. Rosalie Moore. MIT; RiTi

After the Stormy Night. Rolly Kent. FoP

After the Successful Psychotherapy. Michael Ventura. EC

After the Surprising Conversions. Robert Lowell. CABA (1972 ed.); ConAP; HAP; ILP (1975 ed.); NoAM; PAIC; PPP; STS

After the Swimmer. Robert Wallace. LiSp

"After the terrible rain, the Annunciation." Anne Boleyn's Song. Edith Sitwell. UsP

After the thorns I came to the first page. The Sleeping Beauty; Variation of the Prince. Randall Jarrell. PoA

After the tiff there was stiff silence, till. The Lovers. W. R. Rodgers. BIrV

After the tornado, a dead moccasin. Heaved from the Earth. Besmilr Brigham. CSP; Psy

After the Unexpected Answer (Magritte). Paul Hoover. FiCh

After the usual rounds at night. A Sense of Property. Anthony Thwaite. MPo

After the Visit. Thomas Hardy. NOBE

After the War. Hayim Naggid, tr. fr. Hebrew by Shlomo Vinner and Howard Schwartz. VWA

After the whey-faced anonymity. South Country. Kenneth Slessor. GAS; MAuV

After the Winter. Claude McKay. PoBA

After the words of magnificence and doom. Country Burial. Janet Lewis. WPW

After these long still days of frost and fire. The Wind. Arthur J. Bull. HeHu

After these thirty years, Mother. Mother and I. Martha Yoak. NPW

After these words the Weather-Geat prince. Beowulf's Fight with Grendel's Mother. Unknown. tr. by Michael Alexander. Fr. Beowulf. WTO

After these years of lectures heard. To a Friend on Her Examination for the Doctorate in English. J. V. Cunningham. VGW

After they all leave. Surely You Remember. Dahlia Ravikovitch, tr. by Chana Bloch. VWA

After they passed I climbed. A Story. William Stafford. NNaP; PoTa; RFM

After this much time, it's still impossible. Spit. Charles Kenneth Williams. FoP; VWA

After those first days. Death of a Bird. Jon Silkin. BoAnP

After thy labour, take thine ease. The Mount of the Muses. Robert Herrick. CaPo

After Tonight. Gary Soto. GP

After Trinity. John Meade Falkner. OxBTC

After Twenty Years. Fadwa Tuquan, tr. fr. Arabic. PBWP

After two sittings, now our Lady State. The Last Instructions to a Painter. Andrew Marvell. APAS; OBSV

After Vacation. Katherine Hanley. AMV-81

After W.B. Yeats. G. K. Chesterton. NOBL

After waking I look down across our bodies. God. Eugene Ruggles. MIT

After Walt Whitman. G. K. Chesterton. NOBL

After watching all night from a petrified. Ah, Wilderness. Peter Cooley. NVAP

After we had burned on the water a while. Voice from Danang. Thomas Dillon Redshaw. MAT

After we had torn out. For a Marriage. Erica Jong. CTBA

After we'd turned in they gathered round. Cow-Ponies. Maurice Lesemann. BPAW

After weeks of watching the roof leak. Gary Snyder. Fr. Hitch Haiku. InPK

After what had/ to be said. Drunk. Carroll Arnett. VoR

After Winter. Sterling A. Brown. PoBA

After Work. Gary Snyder. CoPAm; HoPM (1975 ed.); NNaP

After X-Ray. Linda Pastan. POL

After years smuggling poems. A Poem in Translation. Tess Gallagher. AAN

After Yesterday. A. R. Ammons. TSWA

After you dived from the barnacled rocks. Poem for Susan. Barbara Greenberg. RiTi

After you have enriched your soul. Jonathan Swift Somers. Edgar Lee Masters. Fr. Spoon River Anthology. OBAL

After you have gone. Renaming the Evening. Eric Pankey. AMV-81

After you left me forever. Semele Recycled. Carolyn Kizer. WBN

After Your Death. David James. AMV-80

After your death. Poem. William Knott. EAS

Afterglow goldens the. The Mountain Afterglow. James Laughlin. IPWM; VGW

Afterimage. James Beall. PoUp

Afterlives. Derek Mahon. CIP

Aftermath. Longfellow. NOBA; PiAm; TAP

Aftermath. Sylvia Plath. SBG

Afternoon. David Sten Herrstrom. AATT

Afternoon. Desmond O'Grady. IPM; PFIr

Afternoon. George Scarbrough. CSP

Afternoon,/ with just enough of a breeze for him to ride it. Robert Sund. BoAnP

Afternoon: Amagansett Beach. John Hall Wheelock. EcS

Afternoon, and the houses are quiet. Afternoon. Desmond O'Grady. IPM; PFIr

Afternoon at Cannes. Paul Davis. AMV-81

Afternoon at the Beach, An. Edgar Bowers. PiAm

Afternoon at the Movies. Jim Mulac. AcAn

Afternoon cooking in the fall sun. Song. Robert Hass. AmPA

Afternoon deepening now, a dark animal growing. Hermit. David Baker. AMV-80

Afternoon Nap, The. Joan White. PoW

Afternoon of a Faun, The: Eclogue. Stéphane Mallarmé, tr. fr. French by Roger Fry. NAWM-2

Afternoon of a Girl. R. H. Deutsch. PoW

Afternoon on a Hill. Edna St. Vincent Millay. PPM; PSN

Afternoon 3. Saburoh Kuroda. EAS

Afternoon with a Baby, An. Susan Snively. AAN

Afternoons. Philip Larkin. PSN

Afternoon's Angel. Seymour Mayne. VWA

Afternoons with Baedeker, sels. Osbert Lancaster.
Eirenn. NOBL
English. FaBoCo; NOBL
French. FaBoCo; NOBL
Italian. FaBoCo
Manhattan. NOBL

After-Thought. Wordsworth. The River Duddon, XXXIV. MBPR
(Valediction to the River Duddon.) NOBE

Afterwake, The. Adrienne Rich. NOBA; Prf

Afterward. Mark Van Doren. TH

Afterward, long/ after we have taken. For Tom (1945–1975). Sheryl Dare. PHC

Afterwards. Thomas Hardy. CMoP (1970 ed.); EBEV; InPS; NOBE; OAEL-2; OBP; PoPle; SoSe; TPo

Afterwards, sel. Gertrude Stein.
"I like to have a home life in the house." OSP

Afterwards, afterwards the wind between two mountains. Prelude. David Rosenmann-Taub, tr. by Charles Guenther. VWA

Afterwards, the compromise. After Love. Maxine W. Kumin. NMM; RiTi; TAP; WBN

Afterwards, They Shall Dance. Bob Kaufman. VGW

Afterword: A Film. Michael S. Harper. NW

Afterword, An: For Gwen Brooks. Don L. Lee. JB

Afterword: Song of Song. James Broughton. GP

Afton Water. Burns. BiP; HeIP; ILP (1975 ed.); LAuP; NIL (Flow Gently, Sweet Afton.) BLSH, *with music;* FSW (Sweet Afton.) CABA (1972 ed.)

Aga Khan, The. Steve Orlen. PCho

Again. Glyn Jones. OBW

Again,/ smoke starts to rise from chimneys. The Cycle. Stephen Dunn. HeS

Again and again I go away from you. J. Michael Yates. *Fr.* The Great Bear Lake Meditations. HoPM (1975 ed.)

Again and then again . . . the year is born. New Year's Day. Robert Lowell. CABA (1972 ed.); ConAP; PPoe

Again as Evening's Shadow Falls, *with music.* Samuel Longfellow. AH

Again at Christmas did we weave. Tennyson. In Memoriam A. H. H., LXXVIII. PChr

Again, Christmas, bright colored lights. The Spirit. Doug Turner. AMV-81

Again, Father,/ I've tried to escape. Moby Christ. Gerald Barrax. CSP

Again for Hephaistos, the Last Time. Richard Howard. GP

Again, his friend's death made the man sit still. John Berryman. NOBA

Again I am summoned to the eternal field. First Love. Edwin Rolfe. SPT

Again I keep watch. Speak. Bea Opengart. AMV-80

Again I see my bliss at hand. Meeting. Matthew Arnold. Switzerland, I. VLP

Again, Kapowsin. Richard Hugo. CNW

Again last night I dreamed the dream called Laundry. The Mad Scene. James Merrill. CoPAm; NoAM; NOBA; PoA; TAP

Again let me do a lot of extraordinary talking. The Song of the Militant Romance. Percy Wyndham Lewis. FaBoTw (1975 ed.); OxBTC

Again observing how my hands. Étude for Voice and Hand. Gabriel Levin. VWA

Again the ancient, meaningless. Gary Snyder. Myths and Texts: Logging, V. CAPP

Again the call of the winter birds. Poem for Carroll, Descendant of Chiefs. Lance Henson. VoR

Again the day. If the Stars Should Fall. Samuel Allen. PoBA

Again the light of. Epitaph: Snake River. Lance Henson. VoR

Again the time and blood consuming sun crosses its corner. The Dawn Horse. William Harmon. CSP

Again the wood, and long with-drawing vale. To Spring. Charlotte Smith. WPE

Against a falling snow. A Fear. Robert Francis. GP

Against a sharp spring sky. Sky Patterns. Jeannette Maino. AMV-80

Against a yellow accordian. The Man Upstairs. David Hilton. AcAn

Against Absence. Sir John Suckling. CaPo

Against an Old Lecher. Sir John Harington. FaBoEE

Against Blame of Woman. Gerald, Earl of Desmond, *tr. fr. Late Middle Irish by* the Earl of Longford. BIrV

Against Botticelli. Robert Hass. AmPA

Against Broccoli. Roy Blount, Jr. OBAL

Against Constancy. Earl of Rochester. GBL

Against Dark's Harm. Anne Halley. NMM

Against deep seas blue-black like mussel-shells. Escape. Charles Spear. ATNZ

Against Friars. *Unknown.* OxBM

Against Fruition. Sir John Suckling. CaPo

Against Gaudy-Bragging-Undoughty Daccus. John Davies of Hereford. FaBoEE

Against Gravity. Edith E. Cutting. AMV-80

Against Idleness and Mischief. Isaac Watts. *See* How Doth the Little Busy Bee.

Against Love. Katherine Philips. BoWoP; SBG; WPE

Against Minoan sunlight. Wishes for Her. Denis Devlin. CIP

Against Parting. Natan Zach, *tr. fr. Hebrew by* Jon Silkin. VWA

Against Proud Poor Phryna. John Davies of Hereford. FaBoEE

Against Quarrelling and Fighting. Isaac Watts. OxBChV

Against Romanticism. Kingsley Amis. NoAM

Against Still Life. Margaret Atwood. NMM

Against the burly air I strode. Genesis. Geoffrey Hill. HAP; OAEL-2

Against the day of sorrow. Trifle. Georgia Douglas Johnson. AmNP (1974 ed.)

Against the Evidence. David Ignatow. NNaP

Against the Fear of Death. Lucretius, *tr. fr. Latin by* Rolfe Humphries. *Fr.* De Rerum Natura, III. DL, *abr.;* NAWM-1

   *Abr. version, tr. by* Dryden. OAEL-1; OBVE

Against the Friars. *Unknown.* OxBM

Against the Magpie. *Unknown.* GBP

Against the pleated pillars of Old Main. About My Students. John Fandel. PoIA

Against the rubber tongues of cows and the hoeing hands of men. Thistles. Ted Hughes. MPo; NoAM; OxBTC; PSN

Against the stone breakwater. The Storm. Theodore Roethke. NCSH

Against the Sun. George MacBeth. TwMBP

Against Them Who Lay Unchastity to the Sex of Women. William Habington. MetP

Against Winter. Elaine Feinstein. VWA

Against Witches. *Unknown.* GBP

Against Women, *sel. Unknown, tr. fr. Welsh by* Gwyn Williams. "Woman is by aptitude." OBW

Agamemnon. Aeschylus, *tr. fr. Greek by* Louis MacNeice. NAWM-1

Agatha. Nadine Major. POL

Agatha Christie to. Said. George Starbuck. OBAL

Age? H. R. Hays. POL

Age. Walter Savage Landor. FaBoEE; InPK

Age. Philip Larkin. CMoP (1970 ed.)

Age, The/ requires this task. A Different Image. Dudley Randall. BPo; CNA; FF; NoAM; TAP

Age and bare bone/ Are e'er allied in action. Cyril Tourneur. *Fr.* The Revenger's Tragedy, III, iv. OBP

Age, and the deaths, and the ghosts. He Resigns. John Berryman. PSN; WeW

Age demanded an image, The. Hugh Selwyn Mauberley, II. Ezra Pound. HAP; LFH; PiAm; VGW

Age in her embraces passed, An. The Mistress. Earl of Rochester. EBEV; NOBE

Age is when to a man. Samuel Beckett. *Fr.* Words and Music. BIrV

Age of Bronze, The, *sel.* Byron. "Alas, the country! how shall tongue or pen." OBSV

Age of Bronze awoke now in brutality, The. John Heath-Stubbs. *Fr.* Artorius. EBEV

Age of the Butcher, The. Stuart Friebert. AMV-80

Age saw two quiet children. Carpe Diem. Robert Frost. PAIC

Aged Aged Man, The. "Lewis Carroll." *See* White Knight's Song.

Aged in the villages, The. War. Miguel Hernandez, *tr. by* Edwin Honig. IPWM

Aged Lover Discourses in the Flat Style, The. J. V. Cunningham. NoAM; PPoD

Aged Lover Renounceth Love, The. Thomas, Lord Vaux. OAEL-1

Aged man, that mows these fields. A Dialogue betwixt Time and a Pilgrim. Aurelian Townsend. NOBE; OAEL-1; SCP-2

Aged Pilot Man, The. "Mark Twain." OBAL

Aged Wino's Counsel to a Young Man on the Brink of Marriage, The. X. J. Kennedy. FF

Aged Woman to Her Sons, The. Babette Deutsch. AMV-81

Ageing Hunter, The. Avane, *tr. fr. Eskimo.* WTO

Ageing Schoolmaster, An. Vernon Scannell. LP

Agent of Love. A. K. Redwing. VoR

Agents, The. Robert Conquest. EAS

Aghadoe. John Todhunter. PFIr

Agincourt. Michael Drayton. *See* Ballad of Agincourt, The.

Agincourt Carol, The. *Unknown.* OAEL-1; OxBM ("Deo gracis, Anglia.") EBEV

Aging. Randall Jarrell. PoA

Aging. Erica Jong. Psy; WBN

Aging. Diane Wakoski. AMV-81

Aging Athlete, The. Neil Weiss. LiSp

Aging pilgrim on a, An. Kenneth Rexroth. *Fr.* On Flower Wreath Hill. GP

Agitation of the air, An. End of Summer. Stanley Kunitz. VGW

Agitprop. Marge Piercy. MMD

Aglaura, *sels.* Sir John Suckling.
   Song: "No, no, fair heretic, it needs must be," *fr.* IV, i. CABA (1972 ed.); CaPo
   "Why So Pale and Wan, Fond Lover?" *fr.* IV, ii. BiP; BuTh; HAP; HoPM (1975 ed.); NOBE; UnPo (1976 ed.) (Encouragement to a Lover.) PBMP
   (Song: "Why so pale and wan, fond lover?") BoLoP; CABA (1972 ed.); CaPo; HeIP; ILP (1975 ed.); InPS

Agnes. Kathleen Fraser. WBN

Agnosco Veteris Vestigia Flammae. J. V. Cunningham. VGW

Agonies confirm His hour. Bahá'u'lláh in the Garden of Ridwan. Robert Hayden. PoBA

Agonies of change. Death Takes Only a Minute. Agnes Pratt. VW

Agony, The. George Herbert. SCP-1

Agony, An. As Now. Amiri Baraka. BPo; ExPo (1973 ed.); ILP (1975 ed.); IPWM; LFH; PiAm; PPP

Agony Column. A. D. Hope. SoSe

Agreed,/ Yesterday was terrible. Mark This. Sallie Chesham. AATT

Agreed that all these birds. All These Birds. Richard Wilbur. NIL; NOBA; Prf

Ah. Greg Kuzma. NVAP

Ah, ah. Lemuel Johnson. *Fr.* Hand on the Navel. AAN

Ah, Are You Digging on My Grave? Thomas Hardy. BoAnP; DL; ILP (1975 ed.); InPS

Ah Ben!/ Say how or when. An Ode for Him. Robert Herrick. CaPo

Ah blessed plant! ah lucky creeper! Entwined. *Malay Oral Tradition, tr. by* R. J. Wilkinson *and* R. O. Winstedt. WTO

Ah, broken is the golden bowl! the spirit flown forever! Lenore. Poe. WIF

Ah, but a good wife! Late Abed. Archibald MacLeish. NCSH

Ah! cease to shroud the radiance of those cheeks. Dark Aspect and Prospect. *Unknown.* PeD

Ah child, no Persian-perfect art! Horace, *tr. by* Gerard Manley Hopkins. *Fr.* Odes. InPK; OBVE

Ah, Christ, I love you rings to the wild sky. Sonnets at Christmas, II. Allen Tate. HAP; LFH; VGW

Ah, cruel maid, because I see. The Cruel Maid. Robert Herrick. CaPo

Ah! dear one, we were young so long. Alas, So Long! Dante Gabriel Rossetti. VPC

Ah dearest Love, for how long. Mechtild of Magdeburg, *tr. fr. German. Fr.* The Flowering Light of the Godhead. ILwL

Ah dextrous Chirurgeons, mitigate your plan. On Having Piles. Sir Walter Scott. FaBoEE

Ah, did you once see Shelley plain. Memorabilia. Robert Browning. CABA (1972 ed.); ILP (1975 ed.); OAEL-2; STS

Ah, fair Zenocrate, divine Zenocrate! Christopher Marlowe. *Fr.* Tamburlaine the Great, Pt. I, Act V, sc. ii. EBEV

Ah false Amyntas, can that hour. Song. Aphra Behn. *Fr.* The Dutch Lover. WPE

Ah, Faustus,/ Now hast thou but one bare hour [*or* hower] to live. Christopher Marlowe. *Fr.* Doctor Faustus, V, ii. HeIP; ILwL; LFH; OBP; PAIC

Ah Feels It in Mah Bones. Richard Wright. SPT

Ah! gentle, fleeting, wav'ring sprite. Hadrian's Address to His Soul When Dying. Emperor Hadrian, *tr. by* Byron. OBVE

Ah! Grandmother weaves! Grandmother Sleeps. Liz Sohappy Bahe. CDW

Ah hate to see de evenin' sun go down. *See* I hate to see de ev'nin' sun go down.

Ah, How Sweet It Is to Love! Dryden. *Fr.* Tyrannic Love, IV, i. HoPM (1975 ed.)

Ah, I remember well—and how can I. First Flame. Samuel Daniel. *Fr.* Hymen's Triumph. VoPo

Ah in the thunder air. Trees in the Garden. D. H. Lawrence. CMoP (1970 ed.)

Ah—it's the skeleton of a lady's sunshade. The Sunshade. Thomas Hardy. OxBTC

Ah, Lenin, you were richt. But I'm a poet. Second Hymn to Lenin. "Hugh MacDiarmid." OAEL-2; TwMBP

Ah! light lovely lady with delicate lips aglow. *Unknown, tr. fr. Irish by* Robin Flower. BIrV

Ah, little road, all whirry in the breeze. The Road. Helene Johnson. AmNP (1974 ed.)

Ah, look. The Divers. Peter Quennell. EcS

Ah! look an' zee how widely free. Air an' Light. William Barnes. VLP

Ah, look at all the lonely people! Eleanor Rigby. John Lennon *and* Paul McCartney. ExPo (1973 ed.); InPK; InPS; OBP; PPoe; WIF; WTO

Ah! Lovely Appearance of Death! *with music.* Charles Wesley. AH

Ah, Lucasta, why so bright. To Lucasta. Richard Lovelace. CaPo

Ah me! conceived in sin and born with sorrow. Childhood. Anne Bradstreet. *Fr.* The Four Ages of Man. SBG

Ah me! full sorely is my heart forlorn. The School-Mistress. William Shenstone. EPC; LAuP

Ah me, the aspidistra grows dusty behind the window pane. In North Great George's Street. "Seamas O'Sullivan." BIrV

Ah me! while up the long, long vale of time. The Destruction of the Pequods. Timothy Dwight. Greenfield Hill, Pt. IV. EAP

Ah my Anthea! must my heart still break? To Anthea. Robert Herrick. CaPo

Ah my daughter, my grandchild! All You Others, Eat. Djurberaui, *tr. fr. Aborigine by* C. H. Berndt. WTO

Ah my dear angry Lord. Bitter-sweet. George Herbert. BoReV; IPWM; NOBE; PoIA

Ah my Jill loves her nakedness. Marvelous. Allan Kaplan. POL

Ah, my Perilla! dost thou grieve to see. To Perilla. Robert Herrick. CaPo; ILP (1975 ed.)

Ah, necromancy sweet! Emily Dickinson. NOBA

Ah! no, not these! Parentage. Alice Meynell. SBG

Ah, nobody knows. Frost. Stella Benson. OxBTC

Ah not as plains that spread into us slowly. Booty. Eileen Duggan. ATNZ

Ah, not this marble, dead and cold. Washington's Monument, February 1885. Walt Whitman. OFD

Ah nuts! It's boring reading French newspapers. Les Luths. Frank O'Hara. NoAM; NOBA

Ah, Poor Bird. *Unknown.* FSW

Ah Posthumus! our years hence fly. His Age, Dedicated to His Peculiar Friend, Master John Wickes, under the Name of Posthumus. Robert Herrick. CaPo

Ah, Raleigh, when thy breath thou didst resign. Britannia and Raleigh. John Ayloffe. APAS

Ah, Spain, already your tragic landscapes. The Spanish War. "Hugh MacDiarmid." CMoP (1970 ed.)

Ah! Sun-Flower. Blake. *Fr.* Songs of Experience. CABA (1972 ed.); EBEV; ExPo (1973 ed.); HAP; LAuP; MBPR; NIL; OAEL-2; PF; PoIA; PoPle; PPP; STS; TT; UnPo (1976 ed.); WeW

Ah sweet content, where is thy mylde abode? Parthenophil and Parthenope, LXVI. Barnabe Barnes. AAS; ESo

Ah, Teneriffe! Emily Dickinson. InPS

Ah, that Roman, making proverbs after love. Proverbial Man. Martin Galvin. PoUp

Ah, the blowful is whining there, its maggots are eating the flesh. The Blowflies Buzz. Djalparmiwi, *tr. fr. Aborigine by* C. H. Berndt. WTO

Ah! there's a house that I do know. Slow to Come, Quick a-Gone. William Barnes. VLP

Ah these are the poor. Street. George Oppen. GP

Ah, these with life so done with now, might deem. October. William Morris. *Fr.* The Earthly Paradise. VLP

Ah, through the open door. Spring Morning. D. H. Lawrence. CMoP (1970 ed.)

Ah to be alone and uninhibited! American against Solitude. Alan Dugan. CAPP

Ah, wake up mama: wake up and don't sleep so sound. Sweet Patuni. *Unknown.* BluL

Ah well, the night. The Far North. Terry Savoie. AMV-80

Ah, what avails the sceptred race! Rose Aylmer. Walter Savage Landor. BoLoP; CABA (1972 ed.); GBL; HAP; HeIP; HoPM (1975 ed.); ILP (1975 ed.); NIL; NOBE; OAEL-2; UnPo (1976 ed.)

Ah, what can ail thee, wretched wight [*or* knight-at-arms]. *See* O what can ail thee, knight-at-arms.

Ah, what is love? It is a pretty thing. The Shepherd's Wife's Song. Robert Greene. *Fr.* Green's Mourning. HAP

Ah! what pleasant visions haunt me. The Secret of the Sea. Longfellow. RhR

Ah! what time wilt thou come? when shall that cry. The Dawning. Henry Vaughan. BoReV

Ah, when I was a little boy, mama, 'bout 16 inches high. Stepfather Blues. *Unknown.* BluL

Ah! who can e'er forget so fair a being? Keats. MBPR

Ah, Wilderness. Peter Cooley. NVAP

Ah, with the Grape my fading Life provide. Omar Khayyam. *Fr.* The Rubáiyát of Omar Khayyám. EBEV

Ah, Yes! I wrote the "Purple Cow." Sequel to the Purple Cow. Gelett Burgess. FaBoCo; FaBoNo; OBAL

Ah yes, when love allows. Hadewijch, *tr. fr. Dutch by* Frans van Rosevelt. PBWP

Ah, you beast of love. Hayden Carruth. VGW

Ah, you should see Cynddylan on a tractor. Cynddylan on a Tractor. R. S. Thomas. LP; MPo

A-Ha! Dorothy Aldis. IWK

Aha! Spring's a/ long way off. For John and Lucy. Joel Oppenheimer. BCr

Ahab's gaily clad fisherfriends. Evil Is No Black Thing. Sarah Webster Fabio. PoBA

Ahasuerus. Joseph Roth, *tr. fr. German by* Erna Baber Rosenfeld. VWA

Aiberdeen. Donald Campbell. *Fr.* Sonnets frae Siberia. MIS

Aiken Drum. *Unknown.* FaBoNo

Ailing fish moves in tired circles, An. Repose. Alfred Lichtenstein, *tr. by* Mary Zilzer. VWA

Aim get your sights and its sound. Canto 7: First Thesis. Tom Weatherly. PoBA

Aim Was Song, The. Robert Frost. SoSe

Aimee McPherson. *Unknown.* FSW

Ain't been on Market Street for nothing. Ballad of the Hoppy-Toad. Margaret Walker. FB; HoPM (1975 ed.)

Ain't Gonna Grieve My Lord No More. *Unknown.* FSW

Ain't Gonna Let Nobody Turn Me Round. *Unknown.* FSW

Ain't gonna work on the railroad. Roll in My Sweet Baby's Arms. *Unknown.* FSW

Ain't got no money. Things About Comin' My Way. *Unknown.* FSW

Ain't It a Sad Thing? R. Dean Taylor. PoRo

Ain't It a Shame. *Unknown.* FSW

Ain't it hard to stumble. I'm a Stranger Here. *Unknown.* FSW

Ain't No Grave Can Hold My Body Down. *Unknown.* AmFP

Ain't No More Cane on This Brazos. *Unknown.* FSW

Ain't No Tellin'. *Unknown.* BluL

Ain't no use to sit and cry. Sail Away Ladies. *Unknown.* FSW

Ainu Men, The. Gary Lawless. FAF

Air. Pamela Alexander. AAN

Air. James Rado *and* Gerome Ragni. PoRo

Air. Tomaz Salamun, *tr. fr. Slovene by* Aleksandar Nejgebauer. VWA

Air: "Cat bird singing." Robert Creeley. Prf

Air: "Love of a woman, The." Robert Creeley. VGW

Air: "Naturally it is night." W. S. Merwin. CAPP

Air an' Light. William Barnes. VLP

Air and Angels. John Donne. LoAs; MetP; OAEL-1; Prf; SCP-1

Air as the fuel of owls. Iowa. Michael Dennis Browne. ANTL

Air bites shrewdly, The; it is very cold. Shakespeare. *Fr.* Hamlet, I, iv. ExPo (1973 ed.)

Air, cold, The. Plowing at Full Moon. Leo Dangel. AMV-80

Air Force Blue, The, *with music.* Scott *and* Textor. BLSH

Air heaves at matter. Night Wind in Fall. W. R. Moses. NCSH

Air Is. John Michael Brennan. MAT

Air is, The/ Sucked clear of dross. January. H. R. Hays. EAS

Air is full of flying stars, The. Snow-Stars. Frances Frost. CTV

Air is green, The. NYC. Art Lange. FiCh

Air is interesting, The. Tom Clark. *Fr.* Sunglasses. OSP

Air is one great dripping cloud, The. Tennis Pro. Lawrence Jay Dessner. AMV-81

Air is thick with nerves and smoke, The. University Examinations in Egypt. D. J. Enright. NowV; OxBTC

Air of departures, An. Silences. Smoke. Jane Cooper. UsP

Air Vision, The. Jakov van Hoddis, *tr. fr. German by* Charles Guenther. VWA

Air War. Linda Pastan. PoUp

Air was soft, the ground still cold, The. April 5, 1974. Richard Wilbur. GP

Aire and Angells. John Donne. *See* Air and Angels.

Airedale, erect beside the chauffeur of a Rolls-Royce, An. Fashions in Dogs. E. B. White. GDP

Airey-Force Valley. Wordsworth. VLP

Airline Breakfast, An. William Matthews. AMV-80

Airplane taxis down the field, The. Taking Off. *Unknown.* CTV

Airstrip in Essex, 1960, An. Donald Hall. InPS

Airwaves. Warren Woessner. TAT

Airy, fairy Lilian. Lilian. Tennyson. PeD

Ajanta. Muriel Rukeyser. NNaP

Ajax and Ulysses. James Shirley. *See* Contention of Ajax and Ulysses, The.

Ajax the swift swerv'd never from the side. Homer, *tr. by* William Cowper. *Fr.* The Iliad, XIII. OBVE

Akedah, The. Matti Megged, *tr. fr. Hebrew by* Howard Schwartz. VWA

Akedah, The. Aliza Shenhar, *tr. fr. Hebrew by* Linda Zisquit. VWA

Akiba. Muriel Rukeyser. VWA

Akond of Swat, The. Edward Lear. FaBoCo; FaBoNo

Akriel's Consolation. William Pillin. AMV-80

Al Aaraaf, *sels.* Poe.
  Song: "Young flowers were whispering in melody." NOBA
  Sonnet—to Science, *prologue.* AmVN; InPK; PAIC; PBMP; PiAm; PPoD; TAP; WIF
  (Sonnet: To Science.) ILP (1975 ed.)
  (To Science.) LFH

Al Capone in Alaska. Ishmael Reed. MIT

Al the merier is that place. The Sun of Grace. *Unknown.* OxBM

Alabama. Margo Bohanon. SES

Alabama. Julia Fields. PoBA

Alabama. Judy Dothard Simmons. CNA

Alabama Bound. *Unknown.* BluL; FSW

Alabama Bus. *Unknown.* BluL

Alabama Centennial. Naomi Long Madgett. BPo

Alabaster legs of the lonely woman, The. The Merry Window. Francis Scarfe. EAS

Aladdin. James Russell Lowell. PCOP

Aladdin's Lamp. Charles Cantrell. AAN

Alajire, we ask you to be patient. *Yoruba Oral Tradition, tr. by* Ulli Beier. WTO

Alan walks with his head upside down. Karen L. Kent. NPW

Alarm and time clock still intrude too early. And on This Shore. M. Carl Holman. AmNP (1974 ed.); PoBA

Alarm Clock, The. Mari Evans. Psy

Alarm Clock, The. Paul Hoover. FiCh

Alarm clocks tick in a thousand furnished rooms, The. North Infinity Street. Conrad Aiken. ILP (1975 ed.)

Alarmed Skipper, The. James Thomas Fields. RhR

Alarmed to life, she encounters the cold floor. The Girl Next Door. Brendan Kennelly. IPM

Alas, Alack! Walter de la Mare. CaYB; OxBChV

Alas, alas the pull alas the bell alas the coach in china. Cooking. Gertrude Stein. *Fr.* Tender Buttons. RiTi

Alas, alas, well evil [*or* Allas, allas, wel ivel] I sped! Undo! *Unknown.* BoReV; OxBM

Alas! Carolina! J. Gordon Coogler. OBAL

Alas, dear Mother, fairest queen and best. A Dialogue between Old England and New. Anne Bradstreet. EAP

Alas, eheu, one question that sorely vexes. Ezra Pound. *Fr.* L'Homme Moyen Sensuel. OBSV

Alas! for all the pretty women who marry dull men. Meditation at Kew. Anna Wickham. BuTh; FaBoTw (1975 ed.)

Alas for Him Whose Sickness Is Love. Iseabal Ni Mheic Cailein, *tr. fr. Gaelic.* SLP

Alas for the sad standards. The Living Values. Stephen Spender. NIL

Alas! for the South. J. Gordon Coogler. OBAL

Alas have I not pain enough my friend. Astrophel and Stella, XIV. Sir Philip Sidney. Epi; OAEL-1

Alas, how pleasant are their dayes. The Unfortunate Lover. Andrew Marvell. TT

Alas! I am seized by the shark, great shark! Love Is a Shark. *Tr. fr. Hawaiian by* N. B. Emerson. WTO

Alas, I shall not shuffle in the sand. Samarkand. Arthur J. Bull. HeHu

Alas, madam, for stealing of a kiss. Sir Thomas Wyatt. BoLoP; LoAs

Alas! Mowler, the children's pride. Death of the Cat. Ian Serraillier. SO

Alas, my brothers. Hilda Doolittle ("H. D."). *Fr.* Helen in Egypt. NOBA

Alas, my love, you [*or* ye] do me wrong. Greensleeves [*or* Lady Greensleeves]. *Unknown.* BLSo; FSW; GBL; RDB

Alas! Poor Queen. Marion Angus. MS

Alas, so all things now do hold their peace. A Complaint by Night of the Lover Not Beloved. Earl of Surrey, *after* Petrarch. AAS; EBEV; LoAs; OAEL-1; OBVE; PAIC

Alas, So Long! Dante Gabriel Rossetti. VPC

Alas, that I should be. To My Infant Daughter. Yvor Winters. VGW

Alas, that I should die. Song of a Woman Abandoned by the Tribe. *Unknown, tr. by* Mary Austin. BPAW; WPE; WPW

Alas! that love whose view is muffled still. Shakespeare. *Fr.* Romeo and Juliet, I, i. LFH

Alas, the country! how shall tongue or pen. Byron. *Fr.* The Age of Bronze. OBSV

Alas, 'tis true I have gone here and there. Sonnets, CX. Shakespeare. EBEV

Alas! 'Tis Very Sad to Hear. Walter Savage Landor. WeW

Alas! what boots it that my noble steed. On a Distant Prospect of an Absconding Bookmaker. G. Rostrevor Hamilton. FaBoCo

Alas, what is the world? a sea of glass. Meditation 10. Philip Pain. NOBA; PiAm

Alas, what pleasure, now the pleasant spring. A Canzone Pastoral in Honor of Her Majesty. Edmund Bolton. PAIC

Alaskan Mountain Poem #1. Leslie Silko. VoR

Alastor; or, The Spirit of Solitude. Shelley. MBPR; OAEL-2

Alba. Samuel Beckett. BIrV

Alba: "As cool as the pale wet leaves." Ezra Pound. GBL; HAP; PiAm; WeW

Alba: "When the nightingale to his mate." Ezra Pound, *after the Provençal of* Arnaut Daniel. OBVE; PoIA; VGW; WeW

Alba for Mélusine. Ramon Guthrie. LoAs

Alba: March. Marilyn Hacker. GP

Albatross. Judy Collins. GrRo

Albatross. Lele-io-Hoku, *tr. fr. Hawaiian by* S. H. Elbert *and* N. Mahoe. WTO

Albert Ayler: Eulogy for a Decomposed Saxophone Player. Stanley Crouch. PoBA

Alberta. *Unknown.* FSW

Albino Bear. Douglas Lawder. BCr

Albion Battleship Calamity, The. William McGonagall. PeD

Albion's most lovely daughter sat on the banks of the. Mrs. Albion You've Got a Lovely Daughter. Adrian Henri. OxBTC

Album, The. C. Day Lewis. BuTh; OxBTC

Album. Carol Papenhausen. AMV-81

Album Leaf. Stéphane Mallarmé, *tr. fr. French by* Keith Bosley. OBVE

Albuquerque Indian militants. Ignacio, Colorado, for You That Time. Joy Harjo. SA

Alceste in the Wilderness. Anthony Hecht. ConAP; PoA

Alcestis. Maura Stanton. PCho

Alcestis on the Poetry Circuit. Erica Jong. AmPA; RiTi

Alchemical Cupboard, The. Asa Benveniste. VWA

Alchemist, The. Richard Church. OxBTC

Alchemist, The, *sels.* Ben Jonson.
  "I will have all my beds blown up, not stuft," *fr.* II, i. EBEV
  "Where's master?/ At's prayers, sir, he," *fr.* II, ii. LFH

Alchemist, The. Ezra Pound. CMoP (1970 ed.)

Alchemist in the City, The. Gerard Manley Hopkins. IPWM

Alchemy. Diane Levenberg. NPW

Alchemy of Day, The. Anne Hébert, *tr. fr. French by* A. Poulin, Jr. BoWoP

Alcide Pavageau. Miller Williams. TAT

Alciphron and Leucippe. Walter Savage Landor. VLP

Alcyna met them at the outer gate. Ariosto, *tr. by* Sir John Harington. *Fr.* Orlando Furioso, VII. OBVE

Aldport (Mystery Tour). Kingsley Amis. *Fr.* The Evans Country. NOBL

Aleph. Stuart Z. Perkoff. VWA

Aleph Bet, The. Fay Lipshitz. VWA

Aleph the cow with wide horns. The Letters of the Book. Rose Drachler. VWA

Alex, perhaps a colour of which neither of us had dreamt. Letter to Alex Comfort. Dannie Abse. FaBoTw (1975 ed.)

Alexander. Frederick Morgan. AMV-81

Alexander and Campaspe, *sels.* John Lyly.
  Cards and Kisses, *fr.* III, v. HoPM (1975 ed.); NOBE; PBMP
  (Cupid and My Campaspe.) CABA (1972 ed.); HeIP
  ("Cupid and my Campaspe played.") GBL; ILP (1975 ed.)
  Serving-Men's Song, A, *fr.* I, iii. NOBE
  Trico's Song: "What bird so sings, yet so does wail?" *fr.* V, i. OBP
  (Welcome to Spring.) NOBE

Alexander and the Gymnosophists. *Unknown.* OxBM

Alexander cut the knot. Alexander. Frederick Morgan. AMV-81

Alexander to His Horse. Eleanor Farjeon. PH

Alexander's Feast: or, The Power of Music. Dryden. FaPo; FaPoR; ILP (1975 ed.); NOBE; OAEL-1

Alexandrite Ring, The. Margaret Ryan. AMV-81

Alfa is nice. Her Roman eye. Safety at Forty; or, An Abecedarian Takes a Walk. L. E. Sissman. Prf

Alfonso closed his speech, and begged her pardon. Byron. *Fr.* Don Juan, I. PoIA

Alfonso was his name: his sad cantini. Skin Diving in the Virgins. John Malcolm Brinnin. TAP

Alfred, a Masque, *sel.* James Thomson *and* David Mallet.
  Rule, Britannia, *fr.* II, v. Thomson. BLSH; BTTM; FaPoR; VoPo

Alfred Corning Clark. Robert Lowell. NoAM

Alfred de Musset. Byways in Biography. Maurice Hare. BBL

Algernon Sidney's Farewell. *Unknown.* APAS

Algy Met a Bear. *Unknown.* CTV; PoPle
  (Algy.) CaYB

Ali. Lloyd M. Corbin, Jr. CNA; PoBA

Ali Ben Shufti. Anthony Thwaite. HeHu; OxBTC

Alibi. Zoe A. Tilghman. BPAW

Alicante. Jacques Prévert, *tr. fr. French by* Lawrence Ferlinghetti. BoLoP

Alice Corbin Is Gone. Carl Sandburg. PoA

"Alice, dear, what ails you." A Frosty Night. Robert Graves. LP; OxBTC

Alice Fell; or, Poverty. Wordsworth. MBPR; SpRo

Alice grown lazy, mammoth but not fat. Last Days of Alice. Allen Tate. NoAM; NOBA; PiAm; UnPo (1976 ed.)

Alice is tall and upright as a pine. Resolution in Four Sonnets, of a Poetical Question Put to Me by a Friend, Concerning Four Rural Sisters. Charles Cotton. BoLoP; Prf

Alice, Where Art Thou? Wellington Guernsey. VLP

Alice's Adventures in Wonderland, *sels.* "Lewis Carroll."
  Alice's Recitation, *fr. ch.* 10. FaBoNo; SpRo
  " 'Tis the voice of the Lobster; I heard him declare."
    FaBoCo; NOBL
    (Lobster, The, *sl. diff.*) OxBChV
  Duchess's Lullaby, The, *fr. ch.* 6. FaBoNo; SpRo
    ("Speak roughly to your little boy.") FaBoCo
  Evidence Read at the Trial of the Knave of Hearts, *fr. ch.* 12.
    FaBoNo; PBMP
    (Silence in Court.) FaBoCo
    ("They told me you had been to her.") SS
  Father William, *fr. ch.* 5. BiP; FaBoNo; HoPM (1975 ed.); SpRo; SS; TVo
    (You Are Old, Father William.) OxBChV; UnPo (1976 ed.)
    (" 'You are old, Father William,' the young man said.")
    FaBoCo; NOBL
  How Doth the Little Crocodile, *fr. ch.* 2. CTV; ECBV; FaBoCo; FaBoEE; FaBoNo; LCL; NOBL; PCOP; SpRo
    (Crocodile, The.) HoPM (1975 ed.)
  Lobster Quadrille, The, *from ch.* 10. OxBChV; PoPle
    (Mock Turtle's Song, The.) FaBoNo; VLP, *2 versions*
  Mad Hatter's Song, The, *fr. ch.* 7. FaBoNo; SpRo
    ("Twinkle, twinkle, little bat!") CTV; NOBL
  Mouse's Tale, The, *fr. ch.* 3. FaBoNo
    (Mouse's Tail, The.) MN
  Turtle Soup, *fr. ch.* 10. FaBoNo; SpRo

Alice's Recitation. "Lewis Carroll." *Fr.* Alice's Adventures in Wonderland, *ch.* 10. FaBoNo; SpRo
  " 'Tis the voice of the Lobster; I heard him declare," *sel.*
    FaBoCo; NOBL
    (Lobster, The, *sl. diff.*) OxBChV

Alien. Donald Jeffrey Hayes. AmNP (1974 ed.)

Alienation (To My Son). Lucille F. Travis. AATT

Alison. *Unknown. See* Alysoun.

Alive at the End of the Journey. James Tipton. TC

Alive in a brown stucco house. The Quilt. Karen Swenson. WBN

Alive, this man was Manes, a common slave. Anyte, *tr. fr. Greek by* Willis Barnstone. BoWoP

Alive Together. Lisel Mueller. IHMS

Alkinoos, king and admiration of men. New Coasts and Poseidon's Son. Homer, *tr. by* Robert Fitzgerald. *Fr.* The Odyssey. WTO

All/ fall it stuck. Horse. Randy Blasing. PH

All afternoon we lie, stretched out. Talking Across Kansas. Paula Kwon. AMV-80

All, All of a Piece. Dryden. *Fr.* The Secular Masque. HAP; InPS

All alone. Boy from Tennessee. Gail Killens. PPM

All alone from his dark sanctum. Mahabalipuram. Louis MacNeice. NoAM

All along the backwater. Ducks' Ditty. Kenneth Grahame. *Fr.* The Wind in the Willows. OxBChV; PoPle

All along the rail. In Texas Grass. Quincy Troupe. PoBA

All along the valley, stream that flashest white. In the Valley of Cauteretz. Tennyson. BoLoP; NOBE; VLP

All-American Guard, An. *Unknown.* TDH

All Around Man. *Unknown.* BluL

All around me, the city was falling asleep. The Quick and the Dead. Ilarie Voronca, *tr. by* Edouard Roditi. VWA

All around the cobbler's bench. Pop! Goes the Weasel. *Unknown.* BLSo; FSW

All at once, behold! Wordsworth. *Fr.* The Excursion, II. PES

All beauties vulgar eyes on earth do see. The Idea. Made of Alnwick, in His Expedition to Scotland with the Army, 1639. Lord Herbert of Cherbury. SCP-2

All beauty, resonance, integrity. Le Livre Est sur la Table. John Ashbery. EAS

All beginnings start right here. The Move Continuing. Al Young PoBA

All Being Well. W. W. Gibson. OxBTC

All Bibles or sacred codes. The Voice of the Devil. Blake. *Fr.* The Marriage of Heaven and Hell. NU

All Christian men in my behalf. On Sir John Calf. *Unknown.* FaBoEE

"All clear, all clear, all clear!" after the storm in the morning. October Morning. Mary Ursula Bethell. ATNZ

All craftsmen share a knowledge. They have held. Craftsmen. V. Sackville-West. OxBTC

All day a strong wind blew. A Strong Wind. Austin Clarke. PFIr

All day a wounded mountain followed me. Seven Preludes to Silence. Richard Shelton. MPA

All day across the sagebrush flat. The Sheep-Herder. Charles Badger Clark, Jr. BPAW

All day and every day the sea shone, steeped in its blueness. When I Was Young. Alun Llywelyn-Williams, *tr. by* Gwyn Williams. OBW

All day and night, save winter, every weather. Aspens. Edward Thomas. InPS

All day beside the shattered tank he'd lain. Reconciliation. C. Day Lewis. NoAM

All-day Bird, the artist, The. Claritas. Denise Levertov. PiAm; VGW

All day, day after day, they're bringing them home. Homecoming. Bruce Dawe. GAS

All day he had felt her stirring. The Mermaid. Lisel Mueller. RiTi

All day he stood at Weeping Cross. Karl. Charles Spear. ATNZ

All day I am before the altar. Samuel. Charles Reznikoff. *Fr.* Five Groups of Verses. SA

All day I hear the mourning doves. Looking Glass. Martha Webb. PHC

All Day I Hear the Noise of Waters. James Joyce. Chamber Music, XXXV. NoAM; SoSe; UnPo (1976 ed.)

All day I heard the water talk. Loch Brandy. Andrew Young. MS

All day I swing my level scythe. Scything. Basil Dowling. ATNZ

All Day It Has Rained. Alun Lewis. NOBE; OBW; OxBTC

All day long. Rain. "Seumas O'Sullivan." PFIr

All day long I have been working. Madonna of the Evening Flowers. Amy Lowell. RiTi

All day long, prismatic dazzle. Midnight. Mary Ursula Bethell. ATNZ

All day long she dials. Befriending the Weather. Helena Minton. FAF

All day long the clouds formed in the peaks. First Winter Storm. William Everson. NU

All day my sheep have mingled with yours. Shepherdess. Norman Cameron. Three Love Poems, III. GBL; SLP

All Day Satori. Brian Lynch. IPM

All day subdued, polite. Negro Servant. Langston Hughes. VGW

All day swaying in the tower. Out from Lobster Cove. J. D. Reed. NeAC

All day the bees have come to the garden. Falling Asleep in a Garden. David Wagoner. AMV-81

All day the black rain has fallen. Louis Johnson. *Fr.* Four Poems from the Strontium Age. ATNZ

All day the driftwood. Driftwood Dybbuk. Barbara F. Lefcowitz. VWA

All day the geese fly south. Starting Over. Shirley Kaufman. VWA

All day the mirrors kindle their brilliance. The Mirrors. Sophia de Mello Breyner Andresen, *tr. by* Allan Francovich. PBWP

All day the opposite house. The Opposite House. Robert Lowell. CMoP (1970 ed.); NYP

All day the unnatural barking of dogs. The Dog. Valentin Iremonger. BIrV

All day they/ bring the face. Ceremony. Lyn Lifshin. FAF

All day to the loose tile behind the parapet. The Wasps' Nest. George MacBeth. OxBTC

All day we walked the streets. The Fifties. Ira Sadoff. AmPA

All day where Megaphone. Merry-go-round. Gloria Rawlinson. ATNZ

All dripping in tangles green. The Tuft of Kelp. Herman Melville. FaBoEE; SoSe

All dull, my Lord, my spirits flat, and dead. Edward Taylor. Preparatory Meditations, Second Series, VII. EAP

All endeavor to be beautiful. Primer of Plato. Jean Garrigue. NOBA

All evidence. In Winter. Paul Blackburn. NYP

All fathers in Western civilization must have. The Father of My Country. Diane Wakoski. NoAM; TAP

All flesh is grass, and so are feathers too. Epitaphs on Two Piping-Bullfinches of Lady Ossory's. Horace Walpole. FaBoEE

All flesh waxeth old as a garment. Bible, Apocrypha. *Fr.* Ecclesiasticus. OBVE

All folks, who pretend to religion and grace. The Place of the Damn'd. Swift. FaBoEE; OBSV

All for the Cause. William Morris. VLP

All Friends Together: A Survey of Present-Day Australian Poetry. R. A. Simpson. GAS

All gentle folks who owe a grudge. The Gadfly. Keats. MBPR

All Goats. Elizabeth J. Coatsworth. BoAnP

All God's Children Got Shoes. *Unknown.* BLSH, *with music;* FSW

All God's spades wear dark shades. Its Curtains. Ted Joans. PoBA

All grave old men, and souldiers they had bene, but for age. Homer, *tr. by* George Chapman. *Fr.* The Iliad, III. OBVE

All Greece hates. Helen. Hilda Doolittle ("H. D."). BoWoP; NIL; NOBA; SBG; TAP

All hail, once pleasing, once inspired shade! Lines Written in Windsor Forest. Pope. EBEV

All Hail the Power of Jesus' Name. Edward Perronet. *See* Coronation.

All hail to the town of Limerick. Hail to the Town of Limerick. Langford Reed. TDH

All Hallows. Louise Glück. AmPA; NU

All-Hallows Children. Eve Shelnutt. TC

All has stilled, Magician Sleep having cast his spell. Those Last, Late Hours of Christmas Eve. Lou Ann Welte. PChr

All he owns is. Squirrel near Library. Genevieve Taggard. WPE

All his friends had gotten a hole. First Holes Are Fresh. Vivian Shipley. AMV-81

All his hopes were hands, his ventures hands. The Hands. Tony Harrison. FaBoTw (1975 ed.)

All his life, my father looked for money. The Game. Stuart Silverman. CoPAm

All human race would fain be wits. On Poetry: A Rhapsody. Swift. HAP; OBSV

All human [*or* humane] things are subject to decay. MacFlecknoe. Dryden. CABA (1972 ed.); ESaP; HAP; LFH; NIL; NOBE; OAEL-1; OBP; OBSV; PoIA; PPP; SCP-1

All hushed and still within the house. Emily Brontë. VLP

All I ask of a woman is that she. D. H. Lawrence. POL

All I can give you is broken-face gargoyles. Broken-Face Gargoyles. Carl Sandburg. ILP (1975 ed.)

All I can say is—I saw it! Natural Magic. Robert Browning. VLP

All I know is a door into the dark. The Forge. Seamus Heaney. PFIr; SoSe

All i know is his name. Cross Oceans into My Heart. Ntozake Shange. NW

All I need. What I Want. Wing Tek Lum. PHC

All I need is a regular. Gun, White Castle. Peter Klappert. AAN

All I want in this creation['s]. Black-eyed Susie. *Unknown.* AmFP; FSW

All I wanted/ was your/ love. To Mother and Steve. Mari Evans. BPo; PoBA; Psy

All Ignorance Toboggans into Know. E. E. Cummings. ILP (1975 ed.); NOBA

All in a literary parleur. Bootie Black and the Seven Giants. Mike Cook. JB

All in a row, a bendy bow. Country Rhyme. *Unknown.* ECBV

All in bunches the furred leaves. Tithes. Luci Shaw. AATT

All in Due Time. J. V. Cunningham. NIL

All in Green Went My Love Riding. E. E. Cummings. CMoP (1970 ed.); HeIP; InPK; NoAM; STS (Song: "All in green went my love riding.") PAIC

All in the Downs. John Gay. *See* Sweet William's Farewell to Black-eyed Susan.

All in the golden weather, forth let us ride to-day. The King's Highway. John S. McGroarty. BPAW

All-In Wrestlers. James Kirkup. SPo

All Intents. Larry Eigner. VGW

All Ireland's now one vessel's company. Fearghal Og MacWard, *tr. by* the Earl of Longford. *Fr.* The Flight of the Earls, 1607. BIrV

All is best, though we oft doubt. Milton. *Fr.* Samson Agonistes. NOBE

All Is God's. Jakov de Haan, *tr. fr. Dutch by* David Soetendorp. VWA

All Is Well. Arthur Hugh Clough. ILP (1975 ed.)

All Is Well with the Child. Marya Zaturenska. LoAs

All joy to mortals, joy and mirth. Song. Aphra Behn. *Fr.* Emperor of the Moon. WPE

All Kinds of Shivers. Lilian Moore. CaYB

All kings, and all their favourites. The Anniversary. John Donne. BoLoP; HAP; HoPM (1975 ed.); MetP; NOBE; OAEL-1; PoPle; TT; WeW

All-knowing God, 'Tis Thine to Know, *with music. Unknown.* AH

All La Glory. Robbie Robertson. RRA

All Last Night. Lascelles Abercrombie. FaBoTw (1975 ed.)

All Legendary Obstacles. John Montague. BIrV; CIP

All look and likeness caught from earth. Phantom. Samuel Taylor Coleridge. MBPR; OAEL-2

All men are locked in their cells. Fall Down. Calvin C. Hernton. CNA; PoBA

All Men Are . . . Socrates Is. Napoleon St. Cyr. FAF

All men are worms. But this no man. In silk. On Courtworm. Ben Jonson. SCP-1

All men,—the preacher saith,—whate'er or whence. Frederick Goddard Tuckerman. *Fr.* Sonnets. AmVN

All men wait for battle and when it comes. An Apple Tree and a Pig. Emyr Humphreys. OBW

All Morning. Terry Stokes. AmPA

All morning I watched. David Martinson. *Fr.* Nineteen Sections from a Twenty Acre Poem. TAT

All morning the mist. Steady Rain. Lynn Merrill. AMV-80

All must be used. Barracks Apt. 14. Theodore Weiss. TAP

All my favourite characters have been. Mythology. Lawrence Durrell. OxBTC

All my future plans, dear. The Blue Room. Lorenz Hart. OBAL

All my life/ they have told me. To You. Frank Horne. *Fr.* Letters Found near a Suicide. BPo

All my life I lived in a coconut. Locked In. Ingemar Gustafson, *tr. by* May Swenson. PoTa

All my neckties. Sooner or Later. John Digby. EAS

All my past life is mine no more. Love and Life. Earl of Rochester. BoLoP; FF; GBL; HAP; NOBE

All My Pretty Ones. Anne Sexton. NoAM; PoIA

All my shortcomings, in this year of grace. Dear Uncle Stranger. Conrad Aiken. NoAM; NOBA

All My Trials. *Unknown.* FSW

All my nature owns with one accord. Nature's Hymn to the Deity. John Clare. VLP

All Nature seems at work. Slugs leave their lair. Work without Hope. Samuel Taylor Coleridge. AnMo; BiP; ILP (1975 ed.); IPWM; MBPR; NOBE

All night/ you banged. To Poem. Lyn Lifshin. NeAC; Psy

All Night by the Rose. *Unknown.* HeIP ("All night by the rose, rose.") GBL

All night fell hammers, shock on shock. A London Fete. Coventry Patmore. HAP; VPC

All night from the roof of the chieftain. Or Ever God Created Adam. *Malay Oral Tradition, tr. by* R. J. Wilkinson. WTO

All night had shout of men and cry. Easter Night. Alice Meynell. BoReV

All night I clatter upon my creed. The Wife Who Would a Wanton Be. *Unknown.* FaBoCo

All night I could not sleep. *Tr. fr. Chinese by* Arthur Waley. *Fr.* Tzu Yeh Songs. BoWoP

All night I had been sweeping up broken glass. Waterlilies. Marjorie Sinclair. PHC

All night I thought on those wise men who took. Twelfth Night. John Peale Bishop. NIL

All night I walked among your spirits, Richard. A Mourning Letter from Paris. Conrad Kent Rivers. BPo

All Night Long. Nina Cassian, *tr. fr. Rumanian by* Herbert Kuhner. VWA

All Night Long. *Unknown.* FSW

All Night Long Fooling Me. *Unknown.* AmFP

All night long they race above my bed. Mares of Night. Virginia Long. AMV-81

All night the blind entrance of the children. Barren Poem. Michael Ryan. AmPA

All night the Shabbos candles. Labor. Lucille Day. VWA

All night the sound had. The Rain. Robert Creeley. CAPP; ConAP; UsP; VGW

All night the surf bangs the coast. Green Frogs. David Rigsbee. AMV-81

All night the wind swept over the house. Winter Morning. William Jay Smith. NCSH

All night they whine upon their ropes and boom. Nocturne of the Wharves. Arna Bontemps. BPo

All night waiting, in an empty house. The Streets of Air. Malcolm Cowley. *Fr.* Blue Juniata. PoA

All-Night Waitress, The. Maura Stanton. AmPA

All night we were softly tangled in the sky's/ vineyard. Fresh Fruit for Breakfast. Roderick Jellema. PoUp

All night you wallowed through my sleep. For Theodore Roethke. Robert Lowell. STS

All of a row. Mother Goose. MG

All of Cornwall held its breath. Report on a Memorial Service: A Letter to Mark Van Doren. William Claire. PoUp

All of our fathers are old but lately. The Great Depression. Patricia Goedicke. GP

All of the mattresses worn through, he lies. The Nude Poet. Charles Edward Eaton. CSP

All on a Summer's Day. *Unknown.* PoPle

All on one summer's evening when the fever were a-dawning. The Grey Cock. *Unknown.* FaBoBa

All One. Millen Brand. GP

All other joys of life he strove to warm. Modern Love, IV. George Meredith. PAIC

All Other Love Is Like the Moon. *Unknown.* OxBM

All our best ye have branded. 1867. Joseph Mary Plunkett. PFIr

All our roads go nowhere. On Inhabiting an Orange. Josephine Miles. NoAM; PoA

All our stones like as much sun as possible. Forecast. Josephine Miles. NoAM

All Out and Down. *Unknown.* BluL

All out for Illinois Central. Calling Trains. *Unknown.* AmFP

All out-of-doors looked darkly in at him. An Old Man's Winter Night. Robert Frost. AnMo; HAP; NoAM; PiAm; TT; VGW

All over the blue. Vantage. Brewster Ghiselin. MPA; PPoD

All over the district, on leather couches. Walking through the Upper East Side. Erica Jong. NYP

"All over the world," the traveller said. The Two Travellers. C. J. Boland. PFIr

All Owners of Meat Are Hospitable. Rochelle Owens. WBN

All people that on earth do dwell. Old Hundredth. William Kethe. BLSo;FaPoR; FSW

All Praise to Thee, *with music.* F. Bland Tucker. AH

All Praise to Thee, My God, This Night. Thomas Ken. BLSH, *with music*
(Evening Hymn, An.) OxBChV

All praise your face, your verses none abuse. Horace Walpole. FaBoEE

All profits disappear: the gain. The Reckoning. Theodore Roethke. PoA

All Quiet. David Ignatow. ConAP

All Quiet along the Potomac To-Night, *with music.* Ethel Lynn Beers. PSoN

All Revelation. Robert Frost. CABA (1972 ed.); PiAm

All right, gentlemen who cry blue murder as always. Draft of a Reparations Agreement. Dan Pagis, *tr. by* Stephen Mitchell. VWA

All right, I may have lied to you, and about you. Love, 20 Cents the First Quarter Mile. Kenneth Fearing. HAP; WeW

All right, I'll die, my spirit is strong. Fear. Vittoria Aganoor Pompili, *tr. by* Brenda Webster. PBWP

All right now, listen to me right good. Unloading Rails. *Unknown.* AmFP

All right. Try this. Northern Pike. James Wright. CAAP

All round about the door of your house. Regret and Refusal. *Tr. fr. Tewa Indian by* H. J. Spinden. WTO

All Saints' Day, *sel.* Margherita Guidacci, *tr. fr. Italian by* Ruth Feldman *and* Brian Swann.
"All Saints' Day; November sky." PBWP

All Saints' Day, Nov. 1. Christopher Wordsworth. VLP

All saints revile her, and all sober men. The White Goddess. Robert Graves. OAEL-2; OBP

All Shams. *Unknown.* APAS

All she took from her hand. The Return. Bruce Bennett Brown. TAT

All silence says music will follow. Onion Bucket. Lorenzo Thomas. PoBA

All Songs. B. Sanford Page. AMV-81

All Souls'. Gwen Harwood. GAS

All Souls' Night. Frances Cornford. OxBTC

All Splendor on Earth. Karin Kiwus, *tr. fr. German by* Almut McAuley. BoWoP

All such proclivities are tabulated. The Quiet Glades of Eden. Robert Graves. BoLoP

All summer I heard them. The Snakes of September. Stanley Kunitz. AMV-81

All summer you have been. Poem for a Neighbor. Pat Therese Francis. AMV-81

All Sunday I sat as lady. For Paige. Summer Brenner. RiTi

All that blazing day, swift-breasted swallows. Thunderstorm in South Dakota. Kay Boyle. WPE

All that blesses the step of the antelope. "Else a Great Prince in Prison Lies." Denise Levertov. PPP; VGW

All That Glitters. Allan Kornblum. AcAn

All That I Am, *with music.* Verna Arvey. AH

All that I know. My Star. Robert Browning. HeIP; SoSe

All that I ran from. The Mood. Quandra Prettyman. PoBA

All that I try to save him from. Sleep-Learning. Ruth Fainlight. NMM

All That Is Left. Michael Hartnett. IPM

All That Is Perfect in Woman. William Carlos Williams. BiP

All that lives of legendry. Unicorn. Nicholas Stuart Gray. ECBV

All that matters is to be at one with the living God. Pax. D. H. Lawrence. BoReV

All that remains now is her skeleton. From the Ice Age. Barbara Bloom. AMV-81

All that remains of Astronaut. Astronaut. Sean O'Meara. IPM

All that running water outside. The Marshes. Jane Mayhall. TAP

All That Time. May Swenson. FF; RiTi; UsP

All that time wasted. Out of the Desert. Diane Levenberg. NPW

All that we see, about, abroad. On the Universality and Other Attributes of the God of Nature. Philip Freneau. EAP

All That You Have Given Me, Africa. Anoma Kanié, *tr. fr. French by* Kathleen Weaver. PBWP

All That's Past. Walter de la Mare. NOBE; OAEL-2; OxBTC

All the awnings at home had to be pulled down. Cleaning Day. Jose Kozer, *tr. by* David Unger. VWA

All the bells were ringing. Christina Rossetti. LCL

All the bright lights of heaven. The God of Judgment. Swinburne. PIM

All the cages are empty. The Two Selves. Margaret Avison. NoAM

All the cautionary tales of strange girls. Mythics. Helen Chasin. IHMS

All the convicts have their roaches lit. Starry Sky. Charles Simic. POL

All the days of my life. Lifelong. Rachel Boimwall, *tr. by* Howard Schwartz. VWA

All the Dead Birds. Melvin Walker LaFollette. SFF

All the Dead Dears. Sylvia Plath. AnMo; CAPP; CoPAm; IHMS

All the Death-Room Needs. Michael Hartnett. CIP

All the flowers of the spring. Vanitas Vanitatum. John Webster. *Fr.* The Devil's Law Case. ILP (1975 ed.); NOBE; OBP

All the fruit is ripe, plunged in fire, cooked. Friedrich Hölderlin, *tr. fr. German by* Robert Bly. NU

All the golden air is full of balm and bloom. Hawthorn Dyke. Swinburne. VLP

All the heavy. Abstract Love Poem. John Logan. UsP

All the here and all the there. Our Two Worthies. John Crowe Ransom. OBAL

All the hills and vales along. Charles Hamilton Sorley. EBEV

All the hot night. Haiku. Masaoka Shiki, *tr. by* Kenneth Rexroth. PAIC

All the houses on drastic street. Mr. Clean. John William Corrington. PPoD

All the inventions that the world contains. Inventions. Samuel Butler. NIL

All the invisible hands. The Circle and the Question. Josephine Saunders. FoP

All the male poets write of orpheus. Euridice. Alta. MMD

All the Many is One. The Wild Geese. John Masefield. NoAM

All the mothers in the world. War. Miguel Hernández, *tr. by* James Wright. EC; Epi

All the new flowers flat. Cold Snap. Kathy Mangan. AMV-80

All the night in woe. The Little Girl Found. Blake. *Fr.* Songs of Experience. MBPR; RRA

All the night sleep came not upon my eyelids. Sapphics. Swinburne. LoAs; PAIC

All the Past We Leave Behind, *with music.* Walt Whitman. AH

All the perversions of the soul. A Small Farm. Michael Hartnett. CIP

All the Pretty Little Horses. *Unknown.* AmFP; FSW

All the ships are sailing away without me. The Statue of Liberty. Edward Field. TAT

All the Sioux were defeated. Report to Crazy Horse. William Stafford. MPA

All the sisters of mercy. Canto Llano. Anita Endrezze Probst. CDW

All the soft moon bends over. The Natural Mother. Jay MacPherson. CABA (1972 ed.)

All the soldiers marching along. Remembering Day. Mary Wright Saunders. CTV

All the soul indrawn. Stéphane Mallarmé, *tr. fr. French by* Roger Fry. NAWM-2

All the Spirit Powers Went to Their Dancing Place. Gary Snyder. UnPo (1976 ed.)

All the things that have harmed me. The Healing from the Beautyway Chant. *Tr. fr. Navajo Indian.* TVo

All the things. The objects. Cold Term. Amiri Baraka. BPo; CNA

All the Things You Are, *with music.* Oscar Hammerstein II. BLSo

All the trees were made. Mother. Barry Dempster. AMV-80

All the way from Florence in the train. Walking in Nice. Patricia Traxler. AMV-81

All the Way Home. Primus St. John. MPA

All the Way My Saviour Leads Me. Fanny Crosby. BLSH, *with music;* FSW

All the while, believe me, I prayed. Sappho, *tr. fr. Greek by* Willis Barnstone. BoWoP

All the windows are shaped like keyholes. At the Porno Factory. Jack Thomas. PoW

All the women/ all their kisses. A Love Poem for All the Women I Have Known. Charles Bukowski. PCho

All the words you could say. Red Eyes Lick the Night. T. L. Kryss. EC

All the World Moved. June Jordan. PoBA

All the world's a school. Schoolmaster. George Rostrevor Hamilton. FaBoEE

All the World's a Stage. Sir Walter Ralegh. *See* What Is Our Life? A Play of Passion.

All the world's a stage. Shakespeare. *Fr.* As You Like It, II, vii. FaPoR; FF; NIL; PoIA; SFF

All their lives in a box! What generations. The Silkworms. Douglas Stewart. GAS; MAuV

All there was of men was the smoke above their houses. Sacheverell Sitwell. *Fr.* Upon an Image from Dante. PES

All These Birds. Richard Wilbur. NIL; NOBA; Prf

All these illegitimate babies. Valuable. Stevie Smith. OxBTC

All these men were there inside. Fable of the Mermaid and the Drunks. Pablo Neruda, *tr. by* Alastair Reid. LP

All things are possible. Lake Walk at New Year's. Leigh Perez-Diotima. AMV-81

All things at first was God, who dwelt alone. Joseph Beaumont. *Fr.* Psyche or Love's Mystery Displaying the Intercourse betwixt Christ and the Soul, Canto VI. SCP-2

"All things become thee, being thine," I think sometimes. Woman. Randall Jarrell. NoAM; NOBA

All Things Being Equal. J. Lee Humphrey. AMV-81

All Things Bright and Beautiful. Cecil Frances Alexander. CTV; FaPoR; OxBChV (Maker of Heaven and Earth.) VLP

All Things Can Tempt Me. W. B. Yeats. CMoP (1970 ed.); PFIr

All things come alike to all. Bible, *O.T. Fr.* Ecclesiastes. NAWM-1

All things come to him who waits. At the Gates. Danny Laurino. DNGG

All things come to pass. My Name Is Afrika. Keorapetse Kgositsile. PoBA

All Things Confine. Hadewijch, *tr. fr. Dutch by* Frans van Rosevelt. PBWP

All Things Decay and Die. Robert Herrick. CaPo

All things find a place. At Night. Michael Small. DNGG

All Things Have Savour. *Unknown.* FaBoCo

All things shall perish from under the sky. Music Alone Shall Live. *Unknown.* FSW

All things uncomely and broken, all things worn out and old. The Lover [*or* Aedh] Tells of the Rose in His Heart. W. B. Yeats. CMoP (1970 ed.); ILP (1975 ed.); PFIr; VLP

All things within this fading world hath end. Before the Birth of One of Her Children. Anne Bradstreet. BoWoP; EAP; MAT; NOBA; PiAm; SBG; WPE

All this indigo, nonviolent light will triumph. Sunday Evenings. John Hollander. NYP

All this time we have been drinking. Light Showers of Light. Kathryn Lindskoog. AMV-80

All this was, was. Verses on Accepting the World. Joseph Brodsky, *tr. by* Dimitry Pospielovsky *and* Keith Bosley. VWA

All those heads those ears those eyes. Song of the Old Woman. *Tr. fr. Eskimo by* Paul Emile Victor, *ad. by* Armand Schwerner. BoWoP

All those summers, waiting. Waiting for You to Come By. Simon J. Ortiz. CDW

All those treasures that lie in the little bolted box. Slow Movement. William Carlos Williams. PoA

All those who seek Thee tempt Thee. The Book of Pilgrimage. Rainer Maria Rilke, *tr. by* Jessie Lemont. ILwL

All thoughts, all passions, all delights. Love. Samuel Taylor Coleridge. MBPR

All Three of Us. Carol Cox. MMD

All through October. Indian Summer: Vermont. Anne Stevenson. NCSH

All through the march, besides bag and blanket. Crazed Man in Concentration Camp. Agnes Gergely, *tr. by* Edwin Morgan. BoWoP

All through the Night. Harold Boulton; *also at. to* David Owen. BLSH, *with music;* FSW; GSB, *with music*

All through the night the happy sheep. The Happy Sheep. Wilfrid Thorley. CTV

All through the Rains. Gary Snyder. ConAP; VoA

All through the windless night the clipper rolled. John Masefield. Dauber, VI. CMoP (1970 ed.)

All through the years.   I Am the Soil.   Gladstone Yearwood.
SES

All thru last/ year they sang.   The Group.   Victor Hernández
Cruz.   SA

All Thumbs.   David Giber.   AMV-81

All Too Late.   *Unknown.*   OAEL-1; OxBM
("Whenne mine eyes misteth.")   EBEV

All Too Little on Pictures.   Charles Black.   AMV-80

All trembling in my arms Aminta lay.   The Dream.   Aphra Behn.
*Fr.* A Voyage to the Isle of Love.   PBWP

All Tropic Places Smell of Mold.   Karl Shapiro.   VGW

All truths are half-truths.   The Golden Pyramids of the Sun.
Alden Nowlan.   AKE

All under the leaves, the leaves of life.   The Seven Virgins.
*Unknown.*   GBP; PeBB

All Up and Down the Lines.   Robert Cooperman.   AMV-80

All veiled in black, with faces hid from sight.   Mourning Women.
Mathilde Blind.   SBG

All was as it is, before the beginning began, before.   Jacob.
Delmore Schwartz.   VWA

All was in flight.   The Wind Was There.   Bravig Imbs.   EAS

All Watched Over by Machines of Loving Grace.   Richard
Brautigan.   MAT

All We Wanted.   Paul David Ashley.   DNGG

All were to little for the merchauntes hande.   George Gascoigne.
AAS

All wheels; a man breathed fire.   The Celebration.   James
Dickey.   VGW

All Which Isn't Singing Is Mere Talking.   E. E. Cummings.
VGW

All who are not just classmates.   Rachel at Thirteen.   Yvonne.
WBN

All who want to roam in Kansas.   In Kansas.   *Unknown.*   FSW

All will die.   Forecast.   Sam Cornish.   NVAP

All winter long I lose my poise.   The Horrors.   Ogden Nash.
SFF

All winter long you listened for the boom.   The Stoic: For Laura
von Courten.   Edgar Bowers.   PiAm

All winter through I bow my head.   The Scarecrow.   Walter de la
Mare.   OxBTC

All winter your brute shoulders strained against collars, padding.
Names of Horses.   Donald Hall.   HAP; PH

All women are beautiful as they rise.   Poem for Easter.   Robert
Kelly.   VGW

All worlds have halfsight, seeing either with.   E. E. Cummings.
PiAm

All ye poets of the age.   Namby-Pamby.   Henry Carey.   OBSV

All ye that pass by this holy place.   An Epitaph.   *Unknown.*
ILP (1975 ed.)

All ye young men, I pray draw near.   The Gardener.   *Unknown.*
GBP

All year/ They have kept a careful record.   The New Year for
Trees.   Howard Schwartz.   VWA

All year round the whin.   Whinlands.   Seamus Heaney.   HeHu;
PF

All year the flax-dam festered in the heart.   Death of a Naturalist.
Seamus Heaney.   HAP; NCSH

All you ask is.   Jonathan Williams.   *Fr.* Strung Out with Elgar on
a Hill.   GP

All you can about animals as persons.   What You Should Know
to Be Poet.   Gary Snyder.   NNaP

All You Others, Eat.   Djurberaui, *tr. fr. Aborigine by* C. H.
Berndt.   WTO

All you Southerners now draw near.   The Battle of Shiloh.
*Unknown.*   AIW

All you that are single and wild in your ways.   Old Maids.
*Unknown.*   AmFP

All you violated ones with gentle hearts.   For Malcolm X.
Margaret Walker.   BPo; CNA; PoBA

All you young men an' maidens come an' listen to my song.   A
New Song on the Taxes.   *Unknown.*   WTO

Allace depairting, grund of wo.   Fairweill.   *Unknown.*   SLP

Allas, allas, wel ivel I sped!   *See* Alas, alas, well evil I sped!

Allas! what shul we freres do.   The Friars' Retort.   *Unknown.*
OxBM

Alle bakbiteres hi wendeth to helle.   Going to Hell.   *Unknown.*
OxBM

Allegiance, An.   Chris Wallace-Crabbe.   GAS

Allegiance is assigned.   Choice.   J. V. Cunningham.   PiAm;
VGW

Allegiance to Aphrodite.   Nicholas Flocos.   SA

Allegory, An.   David Ignatow.   VGW

Allegory in Black.   Carl Clark.   JB

Allegro: "After a black day, I play Haydn."   Tomas Tranströmer,
*tr. fr. Swedish by* Robert Bly.   EAS

Alleluia! Christ Is Risen Today, *with music.*   John Henry Hopkins,
Jr..   AH

Allen Ginsberg Blesses a Bride and Groom: A Wedding Night
Poem.   Robert Peters.   GP

Allen said, I am searching for the true cadence.   Helicon.   John
Hollander.   NoAM

Allen-a-Dale.   Sir Walter Scott.   *Fr.* Rokeby, III.   PoTa

Allergic to their stings, you see my words as bees.   Woman
Talking Man into Child.   Elizabeth Albrecht.   PoUp

Alley Blues.   *Unknown.*   BluL

Alley of granite arkite pillars, The.   Stones: Avesbury.   Daisy
Aldan.   PoA

Alley-Walker.   Joan Smith.   AMV-80

Alligator, The.   Beatrice Ravenel.   WPE

Alligator, beetle, porcupine, whale.   An Animal Alphabet.
*Unknown.*   ECBV

Alligator Bites.   Janet Campbell Hale.   NW

Alligator Bride, The.   Donald Hall.   ConAP; EAS

Alligator on the Escalator.   Eve Merriam.   SO

Allison Gross.   *Unknown.*   PeBB

Allotments: April.   Bernard Spencer.   PSN

All's over, then: does truth sound bitter.   The Lost Mistress.
Robert Browning.   BoLoP; NOBE; PoPle

All's Well That Ends Well, *sel.*   Shakespeare.
"For I the ballad will repeat," *fr.* I, iii.   BiP

Allusion to Horace, An.   Earl of Rochester.   APAS

Alma; or, The Progress of the Mind.   Matthew Prior.   EPC

Almighty Father, as of watery matter.   1st Week 6th Day.
Joshua Sylvester.   *Fr.* Du Bartas His Divine Weeks and
Works.   SCP-2

Almighty God in Being Was, *with music.*   Silas Ballou.   AH

Almighty God, Thy Constant Care, *with music.*   Henry S.
Washburn.   AH

Almighty has dealt bitterly with me, The.   The Great Sad One.
Uri Zvi Greenberg, *tr. by* Robert Mezey *and* Ben Zion Gold.
VWA

Almighty Lord, with One Accord, *with music.*   Melancthon W.
Stryker.   AH

Almighty Sovereign of the Skies! *with music.*   Nathan Strong.
AH

Almighty Spake, and Gabriel Sped, Th', *with music.*   George
Richards.   AH

Almost Any Evening.   Phyllis McGinley.   *Fr.* Speaking of
Television.   TH

Almost at the equator.   Once Only.   Gary Snyder.   CoPAm

Almost before the princess had grown cold.   The True Story of
Snow White.   Bruce Bennett.   AAN

Almost Human.   C. Day Lewis.   NoAM

Almost Ninety. Ruth Whitman. TVo

Almost Persuaded, *with music.* Philip Paul Bliss. AH; BLSH

Almost sexless: the white skin. Girl in a Black Bikini. Allan Brown. AMV-80

Almost singing, she stares past the crowd and flies. Old Woman Awaiting the Greyhound Bus. Duane Niatum. CDW

Almost twenty years. Drinking Cold Water. Peter Everwine. NNaP

Almswomen. Edmund Blunden. OxBTC

Aloft in heavenly mansions, doubleyou one. The Playboy of the Demi-World: 1938. William Plomer. OxBTC

Aloft, lightly on fingertips. Burial. Robert Francis. NCSH

Aloha Oe, *with music.* Queen Lydia Liliuokalani. BLSH

Alone. "Anna Akhmatova," *tr. fr. Russian by* Stephen Berg. BoWoP

Alone. Chu Shu-chen, *tr. fr. Chinese by* Kenneth Rexroth. BoWoP

Alone. Itzik Manger, *tr. fr. Yiddish by* Ruth Whitman. VWA

Alone. Poe. PiAm; VoPo

Alone. Siegfried Sassoon. PPM

Alone. E. J. Scovell. GBL

Alone, alone/ you are the eyes of midnight. The Mute City. Lazer Eichenrand, *tr. by* Gabriel Preil *and* Howard Schwartz. VWA

Alone am I, and alone I wish to be. Christine de Pisan, *tr. fr. French by* Julie Allen. BoWoP

Alone and Godless, stopped by the sudden edge. Patrick MacDonogh. *Fr.* Escape to Love. BIrV

Alone, at night, with all the world. Evil Nigger Waits for Lightnin'. Amiri Baraka. NoAM; NOBA

Alone at the end of green allées, alone. The Statues in the Public Gardens. Howard Nemerov. ConAP

Alone/ December/ Night. Victor Hernández Cruz. PBMP

Alone for the evening. Bringing Flowers. Roberta Spear. AmPA

Alone hunting. Deserted Farms Poem. Bruce Severy. VW

Alone I tiptoe through the stars. Star Journey. Naomi Long Madgett. BPo

Alone in greenwood must I roam. Hollin, Green Hollin. *Unknown.* GBP

Alone in her bed. The Two Sleepers. Robin Skelton. MPA

Alone in ourselves. At midnight. And We Are Strangers to Each Other. Ruth Lisa Schechter. RiTi

Alone in the darkling apartment the boy. Messias. Karl Shapiro. MPA

Alone in the Grange. Gregory Harrison. FPB

Alone in the House. George Bogin. AMV-80

Alone in this desert under the cold moon. If I Forget Thee. Emanuel Litvinoff. VWA

Alone Is the Hunter. Harold Littlebird. VoR

Alone on the jagged rock. November Day at McClure's. Robert Bly. NU

Alone on the lawn. The Dancing Cabman. J. B. Morton. NOBL

Alone we are born. High Country Weather. James K. Baxter. ATNZ

Alone with the Dawn. Matthew Sweeney. AMV-80

Along Ancona's hills the shimmering heat. Poppies on the Wheat. Helen Hunt Jackson. BPAW

Along came the [*or* come that] F.F.V., the swiftest on the line. George Allen [*or* Engine 143]. *Unknown.* AmFP; FSW

Along History. Muriel Rukeyser. NNaP

Along the avenue of cypresses. Giorno Dei Morti. D. H. Lawrence. NOBE

Along the Banks, *with music.* Joel Barlow. AH

Along the blushing borders bright with dew. Spring Flowers. James Thomson. *Fr.* The Seasons: Spring. NOBE; PF

Along the dark bank of the river. After the Night Hunt. James Dickey. PoA

Along the Field as We Came By. A. E. Housman. HAP; WeW

Along the path that skirts the wood. The Three Musicians. Aubrey Beardsley. VLP

Along the path where your light feet passed. Anath. Haim Guri, *tr. by* Naomi Nir *and* Howard Schwartz. VWA

Along the rim of sea and sky. The Helicopter. Ian Serraillier. RAE

Along the River. D. J. Enright. HeHu

Along the river edge. Breathe on the Glass. Raymond Stineford. AMV-81

Along the sea-edge, like a gnome. The Sandpiper. Witter Bynner. EcS

Along the shore the tall, thin grass. In Memory of Colonel Charles Young. Countee Cullen. PoBA

Along the sprawled body of the derailed. Outside Fargo, North Dakota. James Wright. NNaP; VoA

Along the streaming ground, the wet leaves. After the Storm. Rosalie Moore. MIT; RiTi

Along the Yellow Sand. Hilda Doolittle ("H. D."). LFH

Aloof. Christina Rossetti. *Fr.* The Thread of Life. UsP ("Irresponsive silence of the land, The.") NOBE

Aloof, as if a thing of mood and whim. The Schreckhorn. Thomas Hardy. OAEL-2; OBP

Aloof upon the day's immeasured dome. The Black Vulture. George Sterling. BPAW; PB

Alouette, *with music. Unknown.* BLSH

Alpaca pictures of the previous past. Confounded Nonsense. Tom Hood. FaBoNo

Alphabet ("A tumbled down, and hurt his Arm, against a bit of wood"). Edward Lear. FaBoNo

Alphabet, An ("A was once an Apple pie"). Edward Lear. *See* A Was Once an Apple Pie.

Alphabet, The. Karl Shapiro. MPA; NoAM; PoA; VWA

Alphabet Calendar of Amergin, The. *Unknown, tr. fr. Irish by* Robert Graves. BIrV (Song of Amergin.) Moon

Alphabet Came to Me, The. Jerome Rothenberg. VWA

Alphabet Murders, The, *sel.* John Tranter. "Karl Marx is a comic novelist, almost," XI. GAS

Alphabet of Christmas Cheer. Elizabeth Weston. ECBV

Alphabet of Questions, An. Charles Edward Carryl. OSF

Alphaomegadeltasigmakappazetasssssss (sing-song fashion). Greek Crazeology. Carolyn M. Rodgers. SA

Alphonso of Castile. Emerson. NOBA

Alpine. R. S. Thomas. LiSp; POL; RFM

Already autumn begins here in the mossy rocks. Thinking of "The Autumn Fields." Robert Bly. NNaP

Already blushes on thy cheek. Nemesis. Emerson. NOBA

Already I am no longer looked at with lechery or love. A Sunset of the City. Gwendolyn Brooks. PBWP

Already it's late summer. Sun-bathers go. The Divine Insect. John Hall Wheelock. PPoD

Already she seems bone thin. A Poem about Breasts. James Wright. CAAP; TAP

Already, through the splendour ere the morn. Virgil's Farewell to Dante. Dante, *tr. by* Laurence Binyon. *Fr.* Divina Commedia: Purgatorio XXVII. FaBoTw (1975 ed.)

Already we are both fans of the green and golden dragon. A Natural History of Dragons and Unicorns My Daughter and I Have Known. William Pitt Root. AMV-81

Already your name is worn on the rock. Beach Cliff Graffiti. Madeline DeFrees. CNW

Also Ulysses once—that other war. Kilroy. Peter Viereck. FF; NIL

Alston Chapel. James E. Warren, Jr. AATT

Altar, The. George Herbert. AnMo; HoPM (1975 ed.); ILP (1975 ed.); InPS; NIL; OAEL-1; SCP-1

Altar Prayers. *Tr. fr. Hawaiian by* N. B. Emerson. WTO

Altarpiece Finished, The. John Hollander. NoAM

Altars and Sacrifice. Jay Wright. FB

Altars in the Street, The. Denise Levertov. CAPP

Altarwise by Owl-Light, *sels.* Dylan Thomas.
   "Altarwise by owl-light in the half-way house," I. CMoP (1970 ed.); Epi; NoAM
   "And from the windy West came two-gunned Gabriel," V. Epi; NoAM
   "Death is all metaphors, shape in one history," II. CMoP (1970 ed.); NoAM
   "First there was the lamb on knocking knees," III. CMoP (1970 ed.); Epi
   "From the oracular archives and the parchment," IX. CMoP (1970 ed.); NoAM
   "Let the tale's sailor from a Christian voyage," X. CMoP (1970 ed.); Epi; NoAM; OAEL-2
   "This was the crucifixion on the mountain," VIII. CMoP (1970 ed.); Epi; NoAM
   "What is the metre of the dictionary?" IV. CMoP (1970 ed.)

Alter Ego. Leon Slade. FPA

Alter! When the hills do. Emily Dickinson. LoAs

Altered Circumstances. Francis Coleman Rosenberger. PoUp

Altered look about the hills, An. Emily Dickinson. PPP

Alternatives. Peter Cooley. AmPA

Although crowds gathered once if she but showed her face. Fallen Majesty. W. B. Yeats. PoA

Although, great Queen, thou now in silence lie. In Honour of That High and Mighty Princess Queen Elizabeth of Happy Memory. Anne Bradstreet. SBG

Although he has no form. Mukta Bai, *tr. fr. Marathi by* Willis Barnstone. BoWoP

Although he never stirs from home. Haiku. José Juan Tablada, *tr. by* Samuel Beckett. PBMP

Although I be the basest of mankind. St. Simeon Stylites. Tennyson. OAEL-2

Although I can see him still. The Fisherman. W. B. Yeats. BiP; CMoP (1970 ed.); HAP; LiSp; NoAM; PSN

Although I cry and though my eyes still shed. Sonnet XIV. Louise Labé, *tr. by* Willis Barnstone. BoWoP

Although I do not hope to turn again. Ash-Wednesday, VI. T. S. Eliot. BoReV

Although I feel its shape could knit my bones. The Shirt. Jon Silkin. NoAM

Although I leave Braglu, I am close to it. I Djanggawul, am paddling. Djanggawul Song-Cycle. *Aborigine Oral Tradition, tr. by* R. M. Berndt. WTO

Although I mean it, and project the meaning. The Ice-Cream Wars. John Ashbery. PoA

Although I shelter from the rain. The Lamentation of the Old Pensioner. W. B. Yeats. HAP; InPK; PFIr; WeW

Although I was her pupil,/ even I reproach Myrtis. Korinna, *tr. fr. Greek by* Willis Barnstone. BoWoP. *See also* I blame Myrtis.

Although it is a cold evening. At the Fishhouses. Elizabeth Bishop. HAP; ILP (1975 ed.)

Although it is night, I sit in the bathroom, waiting. Adolescence—II. Rita Dove. AmPA

Although it's cold no clothes I wear. *Unknown.* GBP

Although my claws weaken. Sweetness. *Unknown, tr. by* John Montague. BIrV

Although my house floats on a lawn. Blues for John Coltrane, Dead at 41. William Matthews. NVAP

Although only a fool would mock. Queen Mother to New Queen. Robert Graves. OBSV

Although she feeds me bread of bitterness. America. Claude McKay. ILP (1975 ed.); IPWM; NIL; NoAM; PoBA; TAP

Although some are afraid that to speak of a spade as a spade is a social mistake. Rigoletto. Newman Levy. OBAL

Although the aepyornis. He "Digesteth Harde Yron." Marianne Moore. CMoP (1970 ed.); NoAM

Although the house is gone, how well I know. Old House Place. Velma Sanders. AMV-80

Although the relatives in the summer house. A Poem for Bhain. John Berryman. CoPAm

Although the snow still lingers. Last Snow. Andrew Young. OxBTC

Although the summer sunlight gild. W. B. Yeats. *Fr.* Vacillation. BoReV

Although thou now put'st me in doubt. Parting with ———. Jane Barker. SCP-2

Although thy blood be frozen, and thy scalp. To a Covetous Churl. Edward May. FaBoEE

Although thy hand and faith, and good works too. Change. John Donne. Elegies, III. EBEV

Although you see the world diff'rent from me. Child of Mine. Gerry Goffin *and* Carole King. PoRo

Altitudes. Richard Wilbur. CMoP (1970 ed.)

Always. Pablo Neruda, *tr. fr. Spanish by* Donald D. Walsh. OLR

Always before, we sped in the same direction. The Queen. Kenneth Pitchford. NYP

Always Begin Where You Are. Thomas Hornsby Ferril. VGW

Always brilliant/ and all the world is queer. The Generator. Rae Desmond Jones. CAAP

Always expecting the winter. In Dream: The Privacy of Sequence. Ray A. Young Bear. CDW

Always fastidious, it removed its dying. Death of a Cat. Brian Jones. LP

Always Finish. *Unknown.* CTV

Always for the first time. André Breton, *tr. fr. French by* Wallace Fowlie. LoAs

Always for thirty years now. Fish Peddler and Cobbler. Kenneth Rexroth. NNaP

Always, from My First Boyhood. John Peale Bishop. VGW

Always happy, always bright. The Commission Man. Robert V. Carr. BPAW

Always he shadowboxed himself on Sunday evenings. Shadowbox: In a Milltown. Norman Macleod. SPT

Always, I am leaving you. Sarah's Song. Jane Flanders. PoUp

Always I have been a cottonwood. The Gathering. Dwayne Thorpe. AMV-81

Always I lay upon the brink of love. Judas. Vassar Miller. CoPAm

Always—I tell you this they learned. House Fear. Robert Frost. *Fr.* The Hill Wife. PPM

Always in December the child who was my elder brother. Christmas Poem. Brian Lynch. IPM

Always in that valley in Wales I hear the noise. Waterfalls. Vernon Watkins. NoAM

Always, in these islands, meeting and parting. Charles Brasch. The Islands, II. ATNZ

Always in training. Yet helping with his work. St. Bartholomew Remembers Jesus Christ as an Athlete. Alan Wearne. GAS

Always in transit. Tenantry. George Scarbrough. CSP; TAT

Always I've loved the transient things that die. Unseen Flight. Markos Georgeou. AMV-80

Always Learning. D. J. Enright. HeHu

Always loving or blithe. Poem. Charles Senior. MIS

Always on Monday, God's [name is] in the morning papers. The Day after Sunday. Phyllis McGinley. OBSV; UnPo (1976 ed.)

Always puzzled, the man I keep seeing. Looking for Something? Edward Lowbury. PMW

Always She Moves from Me. Shirley Kaufman. WPE

Always, the damage is irreparable. Cape Cod Murders, 1968. Mira Fish. FAF

Always the same, when on a fated night. The Onset. Robert Frost. CMoP (1970 ed.); PBMP; PPP; TT

Always the setting forth was the same. Odysseus. W. S. Merwin. NOBA

Always there is this crossing. Liberation. Mary Swanson Stroh. NPW

Always there's some boy. Coda. Fred Johnson. CNA

Always this pressing for shape. Old Mill, Newton St. Cyres. Ken Smith. TwMBP

Always to want to. The Tortoise. Cid Corman. InPK; VGW

Always too eager for future, we. Next, Please. Philip Larkin. HeIP; ILP (1975 ed.)

Always when I write I wear a mask. The Mask. Valery Larbaud, tr. by William Jay Smith. LoAs

Always you begin the same. Nantucket's Widows. Richard Foerster. AMV-81

Always your body like a foreign country. Location. Knute Skinner. MAT

Alysoun ("Bytuene Mersh [or Betwene March] and Averil"). Unknown. HAP; HeIP; OxBM
(Alison: "Betwene March and Averil.") OAEL-1
(Alison: "In March and April, thereabout.") HAP

Am I a stone and not a sheep. Good Friday. Christina Rossetti. OFD

Am I crazy. Street Iconoclasts. Pancho Aguila. NW

Am I despised because you say. To a Gentlewoman Objecting to Him His Grey Hairs. Robert Herrick. CaPo; SCP-1

Am I failing? For no longer can I cast. Modern Love, XXIX. George Meredith. CABA (1972 ed.); GBL

Am I Not Your Son? Rudolph von Abele. PoUp

Am I really old, as people say? Kim Jung-ku. TVo

Am I thy gold? Or purse, Lord, for thy wealth. Edward Taylor. Fr. Preparatory Meditations, First Series, VI. EAP; ILP (1975 ed.); TAP; VoPo

Am I to become profligate? The Galleries. Peter Kostakis. FiCh

Am I to become profligate as if I were a blonde? Meditations in an Emergency. Frank O'Hara. TAP

Am I too dangerous, that no man can let. D. B. Wyndham Lewis. Fr. If So the Man You Are. OBSV

Am I your only love—in the whole world—now? Tell Me Again. Nigâr Hanim, tr. by Tâlat S. Halman. PBWP

Am Steinplatz. D. J. Enright. HeHu

Amalek. Friedrich Torberg, tr. fr. German by Erna Baber Rosenfeld. VWA

Amana Colonies, The. Ken Smith. TwMBP

Amanda Barker. Edgar Lee Masters. Fr. Spoon River Anthology. NoAM

Amanda Dreams She Has Died and Gone to the Elysian Fields. Maxine W. Kumin. GP

Amanda Is Shod. Maxine W. Kumin. PH

Amarantha sweet and fair. To Amarantha, That She Would Dishevel Her Hair. Richard Lovelace. CaPo; HoPM (1975 ed.); SCP-2

Amateur and muddled, as their sex goes. The Professionals. Geoffrey Grigson. PoA

Amateur Flute, The. Unknown. SpRo

Amateurs, we gathered mushrooms. Fall. Robert Hass. AmPA

Amazing Grace. John Newton. BLSH, with music; BLSo, with music; FSW

Amazing monster! that, for aught I know. A Fish Replies. Leigh Hunt. Fr. The Fish, the Man, and the Spirit. NOBL

Amazing Sight! The Saviour Stands, with music. Henry Alline. AH

Amazing thing happened to me, An. A Sonnet. Daniil Kharms, tr. by George Gibian. FaBoNo

Ambassador Puser the ambassador. Memorial Rain. Archibald MacLeish. CMoP (1970 ed.); NoAM

Ambassadors, The. Paul Lawson. GP; PPoD

Amber Bead, The. Robert Herrick. CaPo

Amber husk. Sea Poppies. Hilda Doolittle ("H. D."). PiAm

Ambiguous Dog, The. Arthur Guiterman. GDP

Ambiguous Lines. Unknown. See I Saw a Peacock with a Fiery Tail.

Ambition. Robert Herrick. CaPo

Ambitious gay boy of Khartoum, An. Limerick. Unknown. NIL

Ambitious Mouse, The. John Farrar. MN

Ambitious sir, take heed! Honour. Joseph Beaumont. SCP-2

Amboyna; or, The Cruelties of the Dutch to the English Merchants, sel. Dryden.
"As needy gallants in the scriv'ners' hands," Prologue. OBSV

Ambulance Call. Lorrie Goldensohn. AMV-81

Ambulances. Philip Larkin. FaBoTw (1975 ed.); UsP

Ambulando. Charles Brasch. ATNZ

Amelia mixed the mustard. A. E. Housman. FaBoNo

Amelia Street. Frank Ormsby. CIP; IPM

Amen. Alvaro Mutis, tr. fr. Spanish by James Normington. AMV-81

Amen. Jaime Sabines, tr. fr. Spanish by Steve Kowit. AMV-81

Amen. Richard W. Thomas. PoBA

Amend Me. Unknown. OxBM

Amendis to the Telyouris and Sowtaris for the Turnament Maid on Thame, The. William Dunbar. OBSV

Amends to Nature. Arthur Symons. FSFS

America. Robert Creeley. MAT

America. Henry Dumas. PoBA

America. Allen Ginsberg. CABA (1972 ed.); CAPP; Epi; ExPo (1973 ed.); NoAM; PiAm; PPoe; PPP

America. Claude McKay. ILP (1975 ed.); IPWM; NIL; NoAM; PoBA; TAP

America. Wendy Rose. CDW

America. Samuel Francis Smith. BLSH, with music; BLSo, with music; BTTM; CTV; PSoN, with music

America. Walt Whitman. GOA

America a Prophecy. Blake. MBPR; OAEL-2

America, America! Delmore Schwartz. NYP

America Bleeds. Angelo Lewis. PoBA

America existed in/ its ribboned. Reprise of One of A.G.'s Best Poems! Amiri Baraka. PCho

America for Me. Henry van Dyke. SoSe

America Is Darken'd. R. H. W. Dillard. CoPAm

America, it is to thee. From America. James M. Whitfield. BPo

America I've given you all and now I'm nothing. America. Allen Ginsberg. CABA (1972 ed.); CAPP; Epi; ExPo (1973 ed.); NoAM; PiAm; PPoe; PPP

America the Beautiful. Katherine Lee Bates. BLSH, with music; BTTM; CTV; FSW; GOA; TAP

America: The Elephant. James Tipton. TC

America will never forgive you. H. Rap Brown. Henry Blakely. CNA

America, you ode for reality! America. Robert Creeley. MAT

American against Solitude. Alan Dugan. CAPP

American Age, The.  Richard Packer.  FPA

American Citizen, *sel.*  Kay Boyle.
  Invitation in It, The.  RiTi

American City.  Joyce Carol Oates.  IPWM

American Commencement.  Aram Boyajian.  NeAC

American Dreams.  Louis Simpson.  GP

American Eagle, The.  D. H. Lawrence.  OAEL-2

American Express called me last week.  A Reason of Numbers.
  Josephine Jacobsen.  IPWM

American Farm, 1934.  Genevieve Taggard.  VGW; WPW

American Flag, The.  Joseph Rodman Drake.  BTTM

American frigate, a frigate of fame, An.  Paul Jones's Victory.
  *Unknown.*  AmFP

American Gothic, An.  Dick Allen.  FAF

American Gothic.  Samuel Allen.  *See* To Satch.

American Heartbreak.  Langston Hughes.  BPo; CABA (1972
  ed.)

American Heritage.  Robert Sward.  OBAL

American hero must triumph over, The.  Eisenhower's Visit to
  Franco, 1959.  James Wright.  CAPP; PSN

American History.  Michael S. Harper.  BPo

American Indian, The.  *Unknown.*  FaBoCo

American Letter: For Gerald Murphy.  Archibald MacLeish.
  ILP (1975 ed.)

American Lights Seen from Off Abroad.  John Berryman.  OBAL

American Literature.  James Russell Lowell.  *Fr.* A Fable for
  Critics.  AmVN
  ("There are truths you Americans need to be told.")  OBSV

American muse, whose strong and diverse heart.  John Brown's
  Body: Invocation.  Stephen Vincent Benét.  BTTM

American Names.  Stephen Vincent Benét.  GOA; OBAL

American Plan.  John Malcolm Brinnin.  GOA

American Poetry.  Louis Simpson.  CoPAm; NoAM; NOBA;
  TAP; TH

American Poets.  Marvin Bell.  NVAP

American poets have seen their country.  The Pterodactyl and
  Powhatan's Daughter.  Donald Macrae.  MS

American poets stick together.  Now Everyone Is Writing Poems
  about Indians.  James Tipton.  HeS; TC

American Primitive.  William Jay Smith.  CoPAm; FF; InPK;
  SFF; TPo; UsP; WIF

American Rhapsody (4).  Kenneth Fearing.  MiP; PAIC; TPo

American Saturday Afternoon.  Ron Ikan.  NVAP

American Soldier, The.  Philip Freneau.  TAP

American Traveller, The.  "Orpheus C. Kerr."  FaBoCo; OBAL

American workingclass is a big-boned charmaid, The.  The Man
  from Moscow  H. H. Lewis.  SPT

Americana XIII: "Captain Patterson, the folks back home."  Carl
  Rakosi.  InPS

Americana XVII: Reminder of William Carlos Williams, A.  Carl
  Rakosi.  InPS

Americana XV: Simplicity.  Carl Rakosi.  InPS
  (Simplicity.)  GP

Americana IX: "Your correspondent must be kidding when he
  says."  Carl Rakosi.  InPS

American's a hustler, for he says so, The.  A Ballad of
  Abbreviations.  G. K. Chesterton.  NOBL

Americans pass by.  Baja—Outside Mexicali.  Michael McClure.
  GP

America's Wounded Knee.  Phillip William George.  NW; VoR

Amerikkka.  Another Commercial.  Lonnie L. Landrum.
  DNGG

Amethysts and sapphires stud the sarcophagus.  The Tomb of
  Time.  Albert Howard Carter.  AATT

Amid my Bale I bath in blisse.  A Straunge Passion of a Lover.
  George Gascoigne.  AAS

Amid the deafening traffic of the town.  To a Passer-by.
  Baudelaire, *tr.* by C. F. McIntyre.  NAWM-2

Amid the smoke of cities did you pass.  To Joanna.
  Wordsworth.  MBPR

Amidst a wood of oaks with canvas leaves.  Description of a
  Ninety Gun Ship.  William Falconer.  PeD

Amidst fruitless activity and fat idleness.  Haifa.  Dovid Knut, *tr.*
  *by* Daniel Weissbort.  VWA

Amidst the nymphs, the glory of the flood.  On Mrs. E.
  Montague's Blushing in the Cross-bath.  Thomas Flatman.
  SCP-2

Aminta, *sel.*  Tasso, *tr. fr. Italian.*
  Pastoral, A: "Oh happy golden age," *tr.* by Samuel Daniel.
  OAEL-1
  ("O lovely age of gold!," *tr.* by Leigh Hunt.)  OBVE

Amish, The.  John Updike.  OBAL; SS

Amo, Amas.  John O'Keefe.  GBL

Amoeba Named Sam, An.  *Unknown.*  QQQ

Among/ of/ green.  The Locust Tree in Flower.  William Carlos
  Williams.  PiAm

Among all lovely things my love had been.  The Glow-Worm.
  Wordsworth.  GBL; MBPR

Among bent twigs.  Thoughts from the Wall.  Damon Bordenave.
  PoW

Among boy-crawling bamboo.  Of Bombs and Boys.  Richard
  Corbin.  SoS

Among Commuters.  Jon Swan.  NYP

Among Friends.  Greg Kuzma.  AMV-80

Among Hawks.  Lance Henson.  VoR

Among Household Objects.  Gregory Jerozal.  PoUp

Among Iron Fragments.  Tuvia Ruebner, *tr. fr. Hebrew by* Robert
  Friend.  VWA

Among Mirrors in the Locker Room.  Karen Sagstatter.  PoUp

Among Mountains.  Reuben Tam.  PHC

Among Old Houses.  Ruth Dallas.  ATNZ

Among other things, he smiles at lit lightbulbs.  Seeing and
  Doing.  John Dean.  AMV-81

Among our country's outlaws.  Jesse James.  Rosemary *and*
  Stephen Vincent Benét.  BPAW

Among our flocks of hard days.  My Mother.  Hayim Naggid, *tr.*
  *by* Rose Drachler.  VWA

Among our hills and valleys, I have known.  The Old Man's
  Counsel.  Bryant.  EAP

Among Pelagian travellers.  On the Circuit.  W. H. Auden.
  NOBL; OxBTC

Among rocks, I am the loose one.  Night Song.  Lisel Mueller.
  AMV-80

Among School Children.  W. B. Yeats.  AnMo; CABA (1972
  ed.); CMoP (1970 ed.); Epi; HAP; ILP (1975 ed.); NIL;
  NoAM; NOBE; OAEL-2; OxBTC; PPoe; PPP; SoSe; STS;
  WeW

Among Sharks.  Al Lee.  AmPA

Among snake-patterned swords Weland tasted sorrow.  Deor.
  *Unknown, tr. by* John Wain.  EBEV

Among Strangers.  William Stafford.  NNaP

Among stray quartz pebbles turned up.  The Pheasant Hunter and
  the Arrowhead.  Julian Gitzen.  AMV-80

Among the first and farthest! Elk and deer.  John Day,
  Frontiersman.  Yvor Winters.  MPA

Among the high-branching, leafless boughs.  The View from an
  Attic Window.  Howard Nemerov.  ConAP

Among the iodoform, in twilight-sleep.  The Leg.  Karl Shapiro.
  HAP; MPA; UnPo (1976 ed.)

Among the Multitude ("Among the men and women the
  multitude").  Walt Whitman.  LoAs

Among the orchard weeds, from every search.  Hen's Nest.  John
  Clare.  AKE

Among the Pine Trees. Moshe Dor, *tr. fr. Hebrew by* Elaine Feinstein. VWA

Among the rain. The Great Figure. William Carlos Williams. NoAM

Among the Roman love-poets, possession. Note on Propertius 1.5. Fleur Adcock. ATNZ; BoLoP

Among the Shades. Thomas Campion, *after the Latin of* Propertius. NOBE
(Vobiscum Est Iope.) BoLoP
("When thou must home to shades of underground.") AAS; CABA (1972 ed.); EBEV; GBL; HAP; ILP (1975 ed.); LoAs; OBVE; PoPle

Among the smoke and fog of a December afternoon. Portrait of a Lady. T. S. Eliot. PSN

Among the springs which flow from Ida's head. *Unknown, formerly at. to* Homer; *tr. by* Congreve. *Fr.* The Hymn to Venus. OBVE

Among the taller wood with ivy hung. The Vixen. John Clare. BoAnP

Among the topless dancers. The Roses of Queens. Claire Nicholas White. NYP

Among them marble where the man may lie. A Thurn. John Berryman. NOBA

Among these mountains, do you know. For Allan, Who Wanted to See How I Wrote a Poem. Robert Frost. CC; PChr

Among these tempests great and manifold. His Hope or Sheet-Anchor. Robert Herrick. CaPo

Among Those Killed in the Dawn Raid Was a Man Aged a Hundred. Dylan Thomas. LFH; STS

Among thy fancies, tell me this. The Kiss: A Dialogue. Robert Herrick. PAIC

Among trees/ my father was a spruce. Family Photograph. Gerald Vizenor. VoR

Among twenty snowy mountains. Thirteen Ways of Looking at a Blackbird. Wallace Stevens. CABA (1972 ed.); CMoP (1970 ed.); InPK; IPWM; NoAM; NOBA; PoIA; TAP; TSWA; VoPo

Amor Vincit Omnia. Edgar Bowers. PiAm

Amores, *sels.* Ovid, *tr. fr. Latin.*
Corinnae Concubitus, I, 5, *tr. by* Christopher Marlowe. GBL
(Elegy: "In summer's heat and mid-time of the day.") BoLoP
("In summer's heat, and mid-time of the day.") EBEV; OBVE
(Ovid's Fifth Elegy.) OBP
"Cypassis, that a thousand ways trimm'st hair," II, 8, *tr. by* Christopher Marlowe. EBEV
"Does anyone these days respect the artist," III, 8, *tr. by* Guy Lee. NAWM-1
"Either she was foule, or her attire was bad," III, 6, *tr. by* Christopher Marlowe. OBVE
"Graecinus (well I wot) thou told'st me once," II, 10, *tr. by* Christopher Marlowe. EBEV
("Graecinus, I blame you. Yours that memorable remark," *tr. by* Guy Lee.) NAWM-1
"I ask but right: let her that caught me late," I, 3, *tr. by* Christopher Marlowe. EBEV
"I Ovid poet of my wantonnesse," II, 1, *tr. by* Christopher Marlowe. OBVE
("Another collection of verse by the man from Sulmona," *tr. by* Guy Lee.) NAWM-1
"Now ore the sea from her old love comes she," I, 13, *tr. by* Christopher Marlowe. OBVE
"Offered a sexless heaven I'd say 'No thank you'," II, 9b, *tr. by* Guy Lee. NAWM-1
"Seeing thou art faire, I barre not thy false playing," III, 13, *tr. by* Christopher Marlowe. OBVE
"So that's my role—the professional defendant?" II, 7, *tr. by* Guy Lee. NAWM-1
"Yes, Atticus, take it from me," I, 9, *tr. by* Guy Lee. NAWM-1

"Your husband? Going to the same dinner as us?" I, 4, *tr. by* Guy Lee. NAWM-1
(To His Mistress, *tr. by* Dryden.) BoLoP
"Your loveliness, I don't deny, needs lovers," III, 14, *tr. by* Guy Lee. NAWM-1

Amoretti. Spenser. AAS; ESo
*Sels.*
I. "Happy ye leaves! when as those lily hands." EBEV; LoAs; NIL; OAEL-1; PAIC
II. "Unquiet thought, whom at the first I bred." PAIC
III. "The sovereign beauty which I do admire." PAIC
VIII. "More than most fair, full of the living fire." CABA (1972 ed.)
XIV. "Return again, my forces late dismayed." SoSe
XV. "Ye tradefull merchants, that with weary toyle." HeIP; ILP (1975 ed.); NIL; OAEL-1
XVI. "One day as I unwarily did gaze." OAEL-1
XVIII. "The rolling wheel that runneth often round." Epi
XIX. "The Merry Cuckow, messenger of Spring," ILP (1975 ed.)
XXII. "This holy season fit to fast and pray." ILP (1975 ed.)
XXIII. "Penelope, for her Ulysses' sake." NIL
XXVI. "Sweet is the Rose, but growes upon a brere." ILP (1975 ed.)
XXVIII. "The laurel leaf which you this day do wear." CABA (1972 ed.)
XXX. "My love is like to ice, and I to fire." FF
XXXIV. "Lyke as a ship that through the Ocean wyde." ILP (1975 ed.)
XLI. "Is it her nature or is it her will." ILP (1975 ed.)
XLIV. "When those renoumed noble peers of Greece." CABA (1972 ed.)
LIV. "Of this worlds theatre in which we stay." ILP (1975 ed.); NIL; OAEL-1
LXII. "Weary year his race now having run, The." FSFS
LXIII. "After long stormes and tempests sad assay." OAEL-1
LXIV. "Com[m]ing to kisse her lyps, (such grace I found). EBEV; OAEL-1
LXVII. "Like [*or* Lyke] as a huntsman after weary chace." Epi; GBL; HeIP; ILP (1975 ed.); NIL
LXVIII. "Most glorious Lord of life, that on this day." CABA (1972 ed.); Epi; ExPo (1973 ed.); HAP
(Easter.) BoReV; NOBE
LXX. "Fresh spring the herald of loves mighty king." CABA (1972 ed.); FF; HAP; ILP (1975 ed.)
LXXV. "One day I wrote her name upon the strand." BoLoP; CABA (1972 ed.); EBEV; GBL; HeIP; ILP (1975 ed.); IPWM; LFH; LoAs; NIL; OAEL-1; PBMP; WeW
LXXVII. "Was it a dream, or did I see it plain?" NIL
LXXVIII. "Lackying my loue I go from place to place." LoAs
LXXXII. "Joy of my life, full oft for loving you." HeIP
LXXXIX. "Like as the culver on the bared bough." FF; GBL

Amoris Exsul, *sel.* Arthur Symons. Arques, XI. VLP

Amorous Neptune. Christopher Marlowe. *Fr.* Hero and Leander. NOBE

Amorous Señor, The. Ogden Nash. TDH

Amorous Worms' Meat, The. Petrarch, *tr. fr. Italian by* Anna Maria Armi. Sonnets to Laura: To Laura in Death, XXXVI. LoAs

Amours de Voyage. Arthur Hugh Clough.
*Sels.*
"Dear Eustatio, I write that you may write me an answer," Canto I. VPC
"*Dulce* it is, and *decorum*, no doubt, for the country to fall, Canto II, ii. OBP
"Is it illusion? or does there a spirit from perfecter ages," Canto II, *introd.*-iv. EBEV
"Now supposing the French or the Neapolitan soldier," Canto II, iv. OBP
"Tell me, my friend, do you think that the grain would sprout in the furrow," Canto III, ii. OBP

"There are two different kinds, I believe, of human attraction," Canto II, xi. OBP

"There was a time, methought it was but lately departed," *fr.* Canto V, 5. OBP

"What do the people say, and what does the government do?" Canto II. OBSV, i-iv only; VPC

"When God makes a great Man he intends all others to crush him," *fr.* Canto II. OBSV

Amphibious bedlam of mothers, The. What's Living? Linda Hogan. AMV-81

Amphibious Crocodile. John Crowe Ransom. OBAL

Amphitryon, *sel.* Dryden.
Mercury's Song to Phaedra, *fr.* IV, i. OBP

Amputation numbs with its cold logic. The Amputee. Charles Cantrell. AAN

Amputee, The. Charles Cantrell. AAN

Amputee Soldier, The. Philip Dacey. NVAP

Amsterdam. Jean Garrigue. TAP

Amsterdam Street Scene, 1972. Raphael Rudnik. AMV-81

Amused contempt, is it, that scintillates. Juan de Pareja: Painted by Velazquez. Richard A. Long. AmNP (1974 ed.)

Amusing Our Daughters. Carolyn Kizer. CNW; VGW

Amyd the wod his modir met thame tway. Virgil, *tr. into Middle English by* Gavin Douglas. Fr. The Aeneid, I. OBVE

Amyntas led me to a grove. The Willing Mistress. Aphra Behn. *Fr.* The Dutch Lover. SBG

An' oh! the jay our rest did yield. Day's Work a-Done. William Barnes. VPC

Anabasis. Rodney Nelson. AMV-81

Anabasis, *sel.* "St.-John Perse," *tr. fr. French by* T. S. Eliot. "Such is the way of the world," IV. OBVE

Anacreontic ("Born I was to be old"). Robert Herrick. CaPo

Anacreontic ("I must/ Not trust"). Robert Herrick. CaPo

Anacreontic to Flip. Royall Tyler. OBAL

Anacreontic Verse. Robert Herrick. BBL

Anacreontics: Drinking. Abraham Cowley. *See* Drinking.

Anadarko John. Carroll Arnett. VoR

Anaesthesia. Jean Valentine. TAP

Anagram, The. John Donne. Elegies, II. PAIC

Anahorish. Seamus Heaney. HeHu

Analogue of Unity in Multeity. Richard Eberhart. NoAM

Analogy. Brian Higgins. FaBoTw (1975 ed.)

Analysands. Dudley Randall. BPo; CABA (1972 ed.)

Analysis of Baseball. May Swenson. SPo

Ana(Mary-Army)gram. George Herbert. CABA (1972 ed.); OAEL-1

Anarchist. Anthony Cronin. CIP

Anarchist. Norman Dugdale. BoAnP

Anarchist's Letter, An. Harald Wyndham. POL

Anath. Haim Guri, *tr. fr. Hebrew by* Naomi Nir *and* Howard Schwartz. VWA

Anathema of Cats. John Skelton. *Fr.* Phyllyp Sparowe. PCat

Anathemata, The, *sels.* David Jones.
Angle-Land, III. NoAM; TwMBP
"Did he meet Lud at the Fleet Gate? did count the top." EBEV
Redriff. TwMBP
"Ship's master:/ before him, in the waist and before it. FaBoTw (1975 ed.)

Anatomy. Gilbert Sorrentino. POL

Anatomy of Happiness, The. Ogden Nash. PAIC; TAP

Anatomy of Melancholy, The, *sel.* Robert Burton.
Author's Abstract of Melancholy, The. SCP-2
"Methinks I hear, methinks I see."
" 'Tis my sole plague to be alone."
"When I go musing all alone."

Anatomy of Monotony. Wallace Stevens. BiP

Anatomy of the World, An, *sel.* John Donne.
First Anniversary, The.
New Philosophy, The. ExPo (1973 ed.)
"She, of whom the ancients seemed to prophesy." SCP-1
"Some months she hath been dead (but, being dead)." SCP-1

Ancestor. Thomas Kinsella. BIrV

Ancestors, The. Anita Barrows. VWA

Ancestors, The. John Peale Bishop. PoA

Ancestors, The. Barbara Drake. TC

Ancestors. Ryah Tumarkin Goodman. AAN

Ancestors. Dudley Randall. BPo; CNA

Ancestors. Harold Schimmel. VWA

Ancestral Houses. W. B. Yeats. Meditations in Time of Civil War, I. OAEL-2

Ancestry. Louis Daniel Brodsky. AMV-81

Anchises, Paris, and Adonis too. Spoken by Venus on Seeing Her Statue Done by Praxiteles. *Tr. fr. Greek.* FaBoEE

Anchorage, The. Pat Wilson. ATNZ

Anchorage in Time (I). Stanley Burnshaw. SPT

Anchorage in Time (II). Stanley Burnshaw. SPT

Anchors Aweigh, *with music.* Alfred H. Miles. BLSH

Ancient chestnut's blossoms threw, An. Alciphron and Leucippe. Walter Savage Landor. VLP

Ancient Couple on Lu Mountain, The. Mark Van Doren. VGW

Ancient Custom, An. Anatoly Steiger, *tr. fr. Russian by* John Glad. VWA

Ancient Days, The. Jonathan Williams. CSP

Ancient Law, The. Andrè Spire, *tr. fr. French by* Stanley Burnshaw. VWA

Ancient Lights. Austin Clarke. BIrV; CMoP (1970 ed.)

Ancient long-horned bovine, An. The Last Longhorn. R. W. Hall. BPAW

Ancient Monuments. John Ormond. OBW

Ancient Murderess Night. Anna Margolin, *tr. fr. Yiddish by* Ruth Whitman. VWA

Ancient Music. Ezra Pound. FaBoCo; FF; HeIP; ILP (1975 ed.); OBAL; PBMP; PoIA; SpRo

Ancient of Days, *with music.* William Croswell Doane. AH; BLSH

Ancient of Days. Anthony Rudolf. VWA

Ancient of Days bless the innocent. Clams. Stanley Moss. GP

Ancient person, for whom I. A Song of a Young Lady to Her Ancient Lover. Earl of Rochester. BoLoP; EBEV; GBL

Ancient Pistol, peacock Payne. Tennyson. FaBoEE

Ancient Prayer, An. Thomas H. B. Webb. CTV

Ancient Proverb, An. Blake. *Fr.* Several Questions Answered. MBPR

Ancient reservoir, The. The Reservoir. Edward Field. GP

Ancient store of olden time. Jarashow. Morty Sklar. AcAn

Ancient to Ancients, An. Thomas Hardy. CMoP (1970 ed.); OxBTC

Ancient tutor, awaiting failure, The. The Clarity of Apples. Terry M. Perlin. AMV-80

Ancient Wisdom, Rather Cosmic. Ezra Pound. NOBA

Ancient Yuba Miner of the Days of '49, Ye. Samuel C. Upham. AIW

Ancientness surrounds me. Death. Patty L. Harjo. VoR

And a sweet goodnight to you and you. Lights, Flowers. Judith Johnson Sherwin. WBN

And a woman who held a babe against. Kahlil Gibran. *Fr.* The Prophet. PPM

And after this quick bash in the dark. Portrait of a Young Girl Raped at a Suburban Party. Brian Patten. OxBTC

And again I see the long pouring headland. The Return. Alistair Campbell. ATNZ

And aged Tiriel stood and said: "Where does the thunder sleep?" Blake. *Fr.* Tiriel. Epi

And All Call Him Uncle. Antar S. K. Mberi. SES

And always through my window pane. Girl's Song. Marya Zaturenska. OLR

And among the divine paranoids old Ezra. Ezra Pound. Phyllis Webb. MMD

And an evening will come when I will leave. Plain Song. Benjamin Fondane, *tr. by* Matei Calinescu *and* Willis Barnstone. VWA

And answer made King Arthur, breathing hard. Tennyson. *Fr.* The Passing of Arthur. EBEV

And are always suddenly there, the knock on the glass. Two Memories of a Rented House in a Southern State. Dave Smith. CSP

And as for me, though that I konne but lyte. Chaucer. *Fr.* The Legend of Good Women. HeIP

And as in winter time when Jove his cold-sharpe javelines throwes. Homer, *tr by* George Chapman. *Fr.* The Iliad, XII. OBVE

And as many time as the ocean curls. The Undertow: Hatteras Island. Gary Stein. PoUp

And as soon as it was morning the chief priests. Bible, *N.T. Fr.* St. Mark. DL

And as we came down the staircase. Valse Oubliée. John Heath-Stubbs. OxBTC

And as when with the West-wind's flawes the sea thrusts up her waves. Homer, *tr. by* George Chapman. *Fr.* The Iliad, IV. OBVE

And at the last I cast my mine eye aside. Lady of the Arbour. *Fr.* The Flower and the Leaf. WPE

And because we lived in a democracy. Naming the State Bird. Keith Gunderson. HeS

And before hell mouth; dry plain. Ezra Pound. *Fr.* Cantos, XVI. ExPo (1973 ed.)

And believing she was a maid. The Faithless Wife. Federico García Lorca, *tr. by* A. L. Lloyd. BoLoP

And birds came crying. James Cunningham. *Fr.* The Narrator's Trance. JB

And borne with theirs, my proudest thoughts do seem. Frederick Goddard Tuckerman. *Fr.* Sonnets. AmVN

And call ye this to utter what is just. Psalm LVIII: Si Vere Utique. Countess of Pembroke, *paraphrased fr.* Bible, *O.T.* BoWoP; WPE

And can it be, that I should gain. Free Grace. Charles Wesley. BoReV

And can the physician make sick men well? Lily, Germander, and Sops-in-Wine. *Unknown. Fr.* Robin Goodfellow, Pt. II. ECBV

And Canst Thou, Sinner, Slight, *with music.* Abby Bradley Hyde. AH

And change with hurried hand has swept these scenes. Sonnet. Frederick Goddard Tuckerman. *Fr.* Sonnets. HAP; NOBA; PiAm; TAP

And, constantly, I seek/ A poetry of facts. "Hugh MacDiarmid." *Fr.* The Kind of Poetry I Want. InPS

And Death Shall Have No Dominion. Dylan Thomas. CMoP (1970 ed.); ExPo (1973 ed.); ILP (1975 ed.); MPo; NoAM; PPoe; TT

And Did the Animals? Mark Van Doren. VGW

And Did Those Feet in Ancient Time. Blake. *Fr.* Milton. CABA (1972 ed.); HAP; HeIP; InPS; IP; MAT; MBPR; NIL; OAEL-2; OBP; STS
(Jerusalem.) FaPoR; NOBE; PIM
(New Jerusalem, A.) FSW; VoPo
(Preface.) ILP (1975 ed.); PPoe

And did you not hear of a jolly young waterman. The Jolly Young Waterman. Charles Dibdin. PoPle

And did young Stephen sicken. Emmeline Grangerford's "Ode to Stephen Dowling Bots, Dec'd." "Mark Twain." *Fr.* The Adventures of Huckleberry Finn. NIL; OBAL

And does the heart grow old? You know. To My Wife. J. V. Cunningham. PiAm

And don't bother telling me anything. César Vallejo, *tr. fr. Spanish by* Robert Bly. EAS

And Doves Were Nowhere to Be Found. Jesús Papoleto Mélendez. NW

And each one to the advantage of her breasts. The Girl with 18 Nightgowns. Gregory Orr. POL

And ever against eating cares. Milton. *Fr.* L'Allegro. SCP-1

And every sky was blue and rain. Ralph Hodgson. UsP

And every yeare a worlde my will did deeme. George Gascoigne. AAS

And ev'ry man 'neath his vine and fig tree. Vine and Fig Tree. Shalom Altman. FSW

And first, the lamp-posts whose burning match-heads. Jewish Main Street. Irving Layton. VWA

And for what, except for you, do I feel love? Wallace Stevens. *Fr.* Notes toward a Supreme Fiction. NOBA

And Forgive Us Our Trespasses. Aphra Behn. EBEV

And from the Citie Tegea there came the Paragone. Ovid, *tr. by* Arthur Golding. *Fr.* Metamorphoses, X. OBVE

And from the windy West came two-gunned Gabriel. Altarwise by Owl-Light, V. Dylan Thomas. Epi; NoAM

And God created the great whales, and each. Milton. *Fr.* Paradise Lost, VII. RhR

And God said, "Let the waters generate." Creation: The Fifth Day, Fishes and Birds. Milton. *Fr.* Paradise Lost, VII. EcS; SCP-1

And God saw that the wickedness of man was great. Bible, *O.T. Fr.* Genesis. NAWM-1

And God stepped out on space. The Creation. James Weldon Johnson. MiP; PBMP; PoBA

And Gwydion said to Math, when it was Spring. The Wife of Llew. Francis Ledwidge. PFIr

And Hannah prayed, and said. Hannah's Thanksgiving. Bible, *O.T. Fr.* First Samuel. BoWoP

And hast thou left old Jemmy in the lurch? A Satire upon the French King. Thomas Brown. APAS

And Have the Bright Immensities, *with music.* Howard Chandler Robbins. AH

And have we lost another friend? John Close. *Fr.* In Respectful Memory of Mr. Yarker. FaBoCo

And he continued more firmly, although with stronger emotion. Arthur Hugh Clough. *Fr.* The Bothie of Tober-na-Vuolich. VLP

And he is risen? Well, be it so. A Drizzling Easter Morning. Thomas Hardy. CMoP (1970 ed.)

And he passed around midnight. Nathaniel Tarn. *Fr.* A Nowhere for Vallejo. TwMBP

And he said, So soule doth magnifie the Lord. Bible, *N.T. Fr.* St. Mark. OBVE

And He Shall Judge among Nations. Bible, *O.T. Fr.* Isaiah. PBMP

And heaven did curse—they found him laid. Charlotte Brontë. *Fr.* Mementos. PeD

And here face down beneath the sun. You, Andrew Marvell. Archibald MacLeish. CMoP (1970 ed.); HAP; HeIP; HoPM (1975 ed.); NoAM; NOBA; PiAm; PoIA; PPP; SoSe; VoPo; WeW

And here I wish my soul died with my breath. Ovid, *tr. by* Henry Vaughan. *Fr.* Tristium, III, 3a. OBVE

And here the precious dust is laid [*or* layd]. Maria Wentworth. Thomas Carew. CaPo; MetP; SCP-2

And here upon this final bed. Eschatology. Wade Hall. AATT

And here we are in the middle of a wind tunnel. In the Middle of a Wind Tunnel. Dave Morice. AcAn

And how beguile you? Death has no repose. James Elroy Flecker. *Fr.* The Golden Legend of Samarkand OxBTC

And How It Goes. Anselm Hollo. TwMBP

And how will I forget. Eyes. Clarisse Nicoïdski, *tr. by* Stephen Levy. VWA

And I a beginner. Answer to Yo/Question. Sonia Sanchez. BPo; RiTi

And I Am Old to Know. Pauline Hanson. TAP

And I can't buy. Addenda. Ted Berrigan. FiCh

And I come out of it. Scenario VI. Amiri Baraka. Epi

And I had forgotten about the stars. Letter from Des Moines. Thomas Swiss. AMV-81

And I have come upon this place. L'An Trentiesme de Mon Eage [*or Age*]. Archibald MacLeish. NoAM; NOBA; PAIC

And I Have Loved Thee, Ocean! Byron. *Fr.* Childe Harold's Pilgrimage, IV. SPo

And I hear the pad of feet to the union hall. Thomas McGrath. Letter to an Imaginary Friend, Part One, II, 2. NNaP

"And I perhaps am secret: Heav'n is high." Eve Contemplates Sharing Her Sin. Milton. *Fr.* Paradise Lost, IX. OBP

And I say nothing—no, not a word. My Sister Jane. Ted Hughes. SO

And I wanted to be inside you. Firebird. Alta. MMD

And I went down by that freight depot. Lost Lover Blues. *Unknown.* BluL

And if death were only the eyelid. The Never Again. Charles Dobzynski, *tr. by* Anita Barrows. VWA

And if I did, what then? A Farewell. George Gascoigne. *Fr.* The Adventures of Master F. I. EBEV; GBL; HAP; NOBE

And, if I give thee honour due. Milton. *Fr.* L'Allegro. PoPle

And if I loved you Wednesday. Thursday. Edna St. Vincent Millay. PoA

And if Moishe Leib the poet should tell. Memento Mori. Moishe Leib Halpern, *tr. by* Ruth Whitman. VWA

And if my memory live when I am dead. Wedded Memories. Philip Bourke Marston. VLP

And if sun comes. Truth. Gwendolyn Brooks. *Fr.* The Womanhood. TH

And if tonight my soul may find her peace. Shadows. D. H. Lawrence. BoReV; ILP (1975 ed.); OxBTC

And if ye stand in doubt. Colin Clout. John Skelton. OAEL-1; TVS

And if you would ask me "Where do you find your songs." Hanukah. Jakov de Haan, *tr. by* David Soetendorp. VWA

And I'm going way down. The Gone Dead Train. *Unknown.* BluL

And in conclusion I'll say. Goodbye. Bella Akhmadulina, *tr. by* Barbara Einzig. BoWoP

And in That Drowning Instant. A. M. Klein. VWA

And in the cold, bleak winter time. W. G. Vincent. *Fr.* Moonlight. ANTL

And in the frosty season, when the sun. The Skaters. Wordsworth. *Fr.* The Prelude. FSFS; LiSp; SPo

And in the Hanging Gardens. Conrad Aiken. PoTa

And is it by immutable decree. *Unknown. Fr.* Zepheria. ESo

And is it night? Are they thine eyes that shine? *Unknown.* GBL

And is the water come? Sure't cannot be. Upon Sir John Lawrence's Bringing Water over the Hills. Sir John Suckling. CaPo

And is there care in heaven? and is there love? Care in Heaven. Spenser. *Fr.* The Faerie Queene, II, 8. BoReV; OAEL-1

And is there then no earthly place. Thomas Moore. *Fr.* Rhymes on the Road. OBSV

And is this—Yarrow?—This the stream. Yarrow Visited. Wordsworth. MBPR

And it all died down. From My Lai the Thunder Went West. Richard Ryan. CIP

And it all goes twirling around. For Leon. Lorraine Sutton. NW

And it came to pass in those days, that there went out a decree from Caesar Augustus. Bible, *N.T. Fr.* St. Luke, II. NAWM-1

And it's forty miles to Nicut Hill. Prince Robert. *Unknown.* AmFP

And it's never mind, never mind, baby. Poor Man Blues. *Unknown.* BluL

And Jesus Don't Have Much Use for His Old Suitcase Anymore. Tom Kryss. NeAC

And Joshua looks down on my face. Joshua's Face. Amir Gilboa, *tr. by* Shirley Kaufman. VWA

And just because he's human. United Front. Bertolt Brecht *and* Hans Eisler. FSW

And learn O voyager to walk. Seafarer. Archibald MacLeish. NoAM

And let me the canakin, clink, clink. Shakespeare. *Fr.* Othello, II, iii. AIW

And, like a dying lady lean and pale. The Waning Moon. Shelley. Moon; PoPle

And Los and Enitharmon builded Jerusalem weeping. Vala, Night the Ninth Being the Last Judgment. Blake. *Fr.* The Four Zoas. MBPR; OAEL-2

And love hung still as crystal over the bed. Louis MacNeice. *Fr.* Trilogy for X. CIP; GBL

And Marie said, My soule doth magnifie the Lord. Bible, *N.T. Fr.* St. Luke. OBVE

And merry Bacchus practiced dancing too. Sir John Davies. *Fr.* Orchestra; or, A Poem on Dancing. NIL

And Mrs. Stephanopoulos said oh yes I am happy. Armaments Race. Evangeline Paterson. AMV-81

And my poor fool is hang'd! No, no, no life! Shakespeare. *Fr.* King Lear, V, iii. LFH

And new Philosophy calls all in doubt. The New Philosophy. John Donne. *Fr.* An Anatomy of the World: The First Anniversary. ExPo (1973 ed.)

And next morning, at the medical center. One More Time. Patricia Goedicke. AMV-80

And no sound/and no word spoken. Three Love Poems for My Wife. George Bruce. SLP

And nothing can we call our own but death. Shakespeare. *Fr.* King Richard II. DL

And now,/ wherever I walk. The Beach. Robert Peters. GP

And now another autumn morning finds me. An Ageing Schoolmaster. Vernon Scannell. LP

And now Eurynome had bath'd the king. Homer, *tr. by* George Chapman. *Fr.* The Odyssey, XXIII. OBVE

And now his well-known bow the master bore. Homer, *tr. by* Pope. *Fr.* The Odyssey, XXI. OBVE

And now in Ellesmereland there sits. Ellesmereland II. Earle Birney. CABA (1972 ed.)

And now, kind friends, what I have wrote. Julia Moore. FaBoCo

And now man-slaughtering Pallas tooke in hand. Homer, *tr. by* George Chapman. *Fr.* The Odyssey, XXII. OBVE

And now methinks I could e'en chide myself. Cyril Tourneur. *Fr.* The Revenger's Tragedy. SCP-2

And now my pampered beast. Epitaph for My Cat. Jean Garrigue. TAP

And now one prayer. The Short Lay of Sigurd. *Unknown, tr. by* William Morris *and* Eiriks Magnusson. *Fr.* The Elder Edda. OBVE

And Now Out of Sight. Lonnie L. Landrum. DNGG

And now, outside, the walls. Night Watch. Adrienne Rich. TT

And now she cleans her teeth into the lake. Camping Out. William Empson. CMoP (1970 ed.); OxBTC

And now she lets him whisper in her ear. The Seduction of Hero. Christopher Marlowe. *Fr.* Hero and Leander, Second Sestiad. NIL

And now the book is closed. Anne Waldman *and* Ted Berrigan. *Fr.* Memorial Day: A Collaboration. EAS

And now the dark comes on, all full of chitter noise. The Sound of Night. Maxine W. Kumin. WPE

And now the green household is dark. In the Tree House at Night. James Dickey. BrS

And now the heart/ overflows its beats. Beginning. Marcos Rodríguez Frese, *tr. by* Julio Marzán. InW

And now the morn arose; when o'er the plain. The Gathering. Timothy Dwight. *Fr.* The Triumph of Infidelity. EAP

And now the purple dusk of twilight time. Star Dust. Mitchell Parish. BLSo

And now the Queene of women had intent. Homer, *tr. by* George Chapman. *Fr.* The Odyssey, XXI. OBVE

And now the riverbank. For the last time. Marina Tsvetayeva, *tr. by* Paul Schmidt. *Fr.* The Daughter of Jairus, VII. BoWoP

And now the riverbank. I cling. Marina Tsvetayeva, *tr. by* Paul Schmidt. *Fr.* The Daughter of Jairus, III. BoWoP

And now the sun that through the horizon peeps. Christopher Marlowe. *Fr.* Hero and Leander, Second Sestiad. OAEL-1

And now the trembling light. Shoreham: Twilight Time. Samuel Palmer. OAEL-2

And now there came both mist and snow. Icebergs. Samuel Taylor Coleridge. *Fr.* The Rime of the Ancient Mariner. EcS

"And now to God the Father," he ends. In Church. Thomas Hardy. PoTa

And now to the abyss I pass. Andrew Marvell. *Fr.* Upon Appleton House. OAEL-1

And now 'twas done. The Death of Crazy Horse. John G. Neihardt. BPAW

And now, unveiled, the toilet stands displayed. The Toilet [*or* Belinda's Morning]. Pope. *Fr.* The Rape of the Lock. ExPo (1973 ed.); NOBE

And now was Paris come/ From his high towres. Homer, *tr. by* George Chapman. *Fr.* The Iliad, VI. OBVE

And now we know/ why coaches rage. On the Death of the Evansville University Basketball Team in a Plane Crash December 31, 1977. Robert W. Hamblin. AMV-80

And now we walked along the solid mire. Dante, *tr. by* Robert Lowell. Divina Commedia: Inferno, XV. OBVE

And now where're he strayes. Richard Crashaw. *Fr.* Saint Mary Magdalene. FaBoCo

And now you're ready who while she was here. J. V. Cunningham, *after the Greek of* Skythinos. OBVE

And of Columbus. Horace Gregory. GOA; OFD

And of trees and the river. Muscle and Bone of Song. Hone Tuwhare. ATNZ

And oft the owle with rufull song complaind. Virgil, *tr. by* Earl of Surrey. *Fr.* The Aeneid, IV. OBVE

And on My Return. Haim Guri, *tr. fr. Hebrew by* Mark Elliott Shapiro. VWA

And on that day, upon the heavenly scarp. Upon the Heavenly Scarp. A. M. Klein. PoA

And on this day, which poets unto thee. Ovid, *tr. by* Henry Vaughan. *Fr.* Tristium, V, 3. OBVE

And on This Shore. M. Carl Holman. AmNP (1974 ed.); PoBA

And one, and one, and one. Three Problems. Katharine Edgar Cobey. PoUp

And one morning while in the woods. Between the World and Me. Richard Wright. AmNP (1974 ed.); MiP; NoAM; PoBA; SPT; WIF

And One Other Thing. A. Wilber Stevens. MPA

And other wonders. Geological Faults. Barbara Unger. AMV-81

And Our Gifts to the Seasons. Thomas Clark. SLP

And Paradise does come. Joy. Gavin Bantock. OxBTC

And Pergamos,/ city of the Phrygians. Euripides, *tr. by* Hilda Doolittle ("H. D."). *Fr.* Iphigeneia in Aulis. OBVE

And prytily he wolde pant. John Skelton. *Fr.* Phyllyp Sparowe. ECBV

And Ronda with the old windows of the posadas. Yes. James Joyce. *Fr.* Ulysses. FF

And Ruth said, Intreat me not to leave thee. Bible, *O.T. Fr.* Ruth. FF

And Sam he looked again, and Sam he saw. *Unknown. Fr.* The Coming of K——. VLP

And Samson grew old in days. Samson. Amir Gilboa, *tr. by* Stephen Mitchell. VWA

And seeing the multitudes, he went up into a mountain. Bible, *N.T. Fr.* St. Matthew. BiP; NAWM-1

And semblably, though I go not upright. John Lydgate. *Fr.* The Fall of Princes: Epilogue. OxBM

And several strengths from drowsiness campaigned. The Sermon on the Warpland. Gwendolyn Brooks. BPo; NOBA; PoBA

And shall it never be again, never? Not on nights filled. To See Him Again. Gabriela Mistral, *tr. by* Doris Dana. OLR

And she, being old, fed from a mashed plate. Old Woman. Iain Crichton Smith. FaBoTw (1975 ed.); MS; OxBTC; PSN

And she—her beauty never made her cold. Frederick Goddard Tuckerman. *Fr.* Sonnets. AmVN

And she shall remain nameless. The Loves and Lays of William J. Higginson. William J. Higginson. AAN

And She Was Bad. Marvin Wyche, Jr. AmNP (1974 ed.)

And shores and strands and naked piers. Henry James at Newport. Weldon Kees. PoA

And should I thank you, my dear skin. Gratitude. Annette Lynch. FF

And silence. The End of Man Is His Beauty. Amiri Baraka. AmNP (1974 ed.)

And silence/ And not another word. Monument to Pushkin. Joseph Brodsky, *tr. by* Dimitry Pospielovsky *and* Keith Bosley. VWA

And so an easier life our Cyclops drew. Theocritus, *tr. by* Elizabeth Barrett Browning. *Fr.* Idylls, XI. OBVE

And so deciding everything has been done. Dear Oedipus. Ann Darr. WBN

And so for nights. The Night-blooming Cereus. Robert Hayden. FB; NU

And so I cross into another world. New Heaven and Earth. D. H. Lawrence. CMoP (1970 ed.)

And so I speak/ in place of that primordial cry. Monique Laederach, *tr. fr. French by* Charles Guenther. *Fr.* Penelope. BoWoP

And so it must be. Gaining, with Departure. Neil Baldwin. AAN

And so must I lose her whose mind. Prothalamium. Donagh MacDonagh. BIrV

And so, one day when the tide was away out. The Farewell. Pat Wilson. ATNZ

And so one sees all living matter perish. Sonnet. Louise Labé, *tr. by* Frederic Prokosch. LoAS

And so the day drops by; the horizon draws. Frederick Goddard Tuckerman. *Fr.* Sonnets. AmVN

And so the scene degenerates. At the Theatre. John Williams. CoPAm

And so we too came where the rest have come. The Question. F. T. Prince. BoLoP

And some are sulky, while some will plunge. Horses. Kipling. BoAnP; PH; POL

"And something that . . . that is theirs—no longer ours." The Dispossessed. John Berryman. VGW

And spoke: coopers, craftsmen, shepherds. Great God Paused among Men. Daniel Berrigan. MAT

And still they come and go: and this is all I know. Picture-Show. Siegfried Sassoon. CMoP (1970 ed.)

And summer mornings the mute child, rebellious. Eleven. Archibald MacLeish. HAP; NCSH; WeW

And suppose the darlings get to Mantua. Purgatory. Maxine W. Kumin. CoPAm

And that question which I have not asked. The Last. Ezra Zussman, tr. by D. Shnayorson. VWA

And the Americans put Pound in a cage. The Cage. John Berryman. PoA

And the child, mine. Expectation. Aliza Shenhar, tr. by Linda Zisquit. VWA

And the Cock Begins to Crow, with music. Richard K. Avery. AH

And the Communists have nothing to offer but fat cheeks and eye-glasses and lying policemen. Kral Majales. Allen Ginsberg. GP; PiAm

And the Days Are Not Full Enough. Ezra Pound. AKE

And "the earth under our feet." At Kenneth Burke's Place. William Carlos Williams. NOBA

And the first among them. Stony Brook Tavern. Ken Belford. NeAC

And the first grey of morning fill'd the east. Sohrab and Rustum. Matthew Arnold. VLP

And the gud King held forth the way. Bruce Meets Three Men with a Wether. John Barbour. Fr. The Bruce. OxBM

And the lemon is tall. The sun is tall, and descends. Lemon. Mario Satz, tr. by Willis Barnstone. VWA

And the Lord God planted a garden eastward in Eden. Bible, O.T. Fr. Genesis. OAEL-1

And the new sun broke on fields of grain. My Life Like Any Other. Philip Levine. AMV-81

And the next I remembered I'm on a table. The Loser. Charles Bukowski. MiP

And the Old Women Gathered. Mari Evans. PoBA

And the ones that got tough. The Inheritors. William Peskett. IPM

And the quiet cat. Jack Kerouac. Fr. Some Western Haikus. VoA

And the Same Words. David Ignatow. NNaP

And the Seventh Dream Is the Dream of Isis. David Gascoyne. EAS

And the Silver Turns into Night. Nathan Yonathan, tr. fr. Hebrew by Richard Flantz. VWA

And the snake was/ talking to Eve. An Old Story. Rena Lee. VWA

And the stones in the Prague cemetery were so bored. The Drunken Stones of Prague. David Scheinert, tr. by Edouard Roditi. VWA

And the storm-fiends wild rave. Shelley. Fr. St. Irvyne. PeD

And the stranger at last stood before the monument of lava and anger. The Stone and the Blade of Grass in the Warsaw Ghetto. David Scheinert, tr. by Edouard Roditi. VWA

And the sun wields mercy. The Sun Wields Mercy. Charles Bukowski. MAT

And the terrible. The Vision of Felicity. William Everson. PiAm

And the time is one/ of leavings. Long Beach, 1975. Merrill Leffler. PoUp

And the traveller hopes: let me be far from any. Journey to Iceland. W. H. Auden. PoA

And the trunk: "So sweet those words to me that I." Pier delle Vigne. Dante, tr. by John Ciardi. Fr. Divina Commedia: Inferno, XIII. HoPM (1975 ed.)

And the two reservist guys went. Look, don't shoot. The Poem on Our Mother, Our Mother Rachel. Avot Yeshurun, tr. by Harold Schimmel. VWA

And the undecided question. The Lust for Murder. Gerda Penfold. GP

And the voices dropped. T. C. (Terry Callier; True Christian). Walter Bradford. FiCh; HeS

And the way goes on in the worn earth. Prologue. Archibald MacLeish. Fr. Conquistador. NoAM

And the whole earth was of one language, and of one speech. Bible, O.T. Fr. Genesis. NAWM-1

And then? Colors and names of colors. No Way of Knowing. John Ashbery. CAAP

And then fate strikes us. First our joys decay. Wilfrid Scawen Blunt. The Love Sonnets of Proteus, LXXV. VLP

And then he would lift this finest. Out-of-the-Body Travel. Stanley Plumly. AmPA

And then I pressed the shell. The Shell. James Stephens. CMoP (1970 ed.); EcS

And Then No More. Friedrich Rückert, tr. fr. German by James Clarence Mangan. BIrV

And then the blue world daring onward. The Handball Players at Brighton Beach. Irving Feldman. NYP

And then the drug takes hold. Sleeping Pill. Diana O Hehir. AMV-81

And then the knife. Song of the Hanged. Eléni Vakaló, tr. by James Damaskos. PBWP

And then they are there all of the people depressed. Traces. David Lehman. UsP

And then went down to the ship. Ezra Pound. Cantos, I. CMoP (1970 ed.); ExPo (1973 ed.); NoAM; OBVE; PAIC; VGW

And Then What. Dave Kelly. POL

And then without his knowing, sweet sleep descended down. The Marriage in Eden. William Williams, tr. by Saunders Lewis and Gwyn Jones. Fr. A View of Christ's Kingdom. OBW

And there are times truly. An Underdeveloped Country. D. J. Enright. NOBL

And there came two angels to Sodom at even. Bible, O.T. Fr. Genesis. HoPM (1975 ed.).

"And there goes the bell for the third month." The Fight of the Year. Roger McGough. DuDr

And there he was—/ the rhinoceros! Rhinoceros. William Hart-Smith. BoAnP

And there I was. Not a dictionary. Northwest Airlines. Fred Chappell. HoPM (1975 ed.)

And there is nothing at all—neither fear. Natalya Gorbanyevskaya, tr. fr. Russian by Daniel Weissbort. BoWoP

And there it was once, on the banks. The Lake above Santos. Keith Wilson. GP

And there shall come forth a rod out of the stemme of Jesse. Bible, O.T. Fr. Isaiah. OBVE

"And There Was a Great Calm." Thomas Hardy. CMoP (1970 ed.); OAEL-2

And there were gypsies. Gypsies. Cynthia Nibblelink. TC

And there were in the same country shepherds. Bible, N.T. Fr. St. Luke. PChr

And therewith kest I doun myn eye ageyne. James I, King of Scotland. Fr. The Kingis Quair. SLP

And they both lived happily ever after. After Ever Happily. Ian Serraillier. ECBV; SO

And they went down into the king-city. Nathaniel Tarn. Fr. A Nowhere for Vallejo. TwMBP

And They Were Richt. Robert Garioch. MS

And they were there in the City of Fire, enflamed. JuJu. Askia Muhammad Touré. PoBA

And this is how you live: a woman, children. A Primary Ground. Adrienne Rich. NNaP; WBN

And This Is Love. Paula Reingold. IHMS

And This Is My Father. Marcus J. Grapes. AMV-80

And this is the way they ring. Ringing the Bells. Anne Sexton. BiP; CAPP; FF; ILP (1975 ed.); TAP; VGW

And this reft house is that, the which he built. On a Ruined House in a Romantic Country [or The House That Jack Built]. Samuel Taylor Coleridge. *Fr.* Sonnets Attempted in the Manner of Contemporary Writers. AKE; Epi

And thou, Dalhousie, the Great God of War. *Unknown.* FaBoCo

And thou wert sad—yet I was not with thee. Lines on Hearing That Lady Byron Was Ill. Byron. EBEV; MBPR

And three baby barn swallows. After an All-Night Cackle with Sloth and Co. I Enter and Greet the Dawn. Gary Gildner. GP

And through the Caribbean Sea. Margaret Danner. BPo

And thus continuing with outrageous fier. Barnabe Barnes. Parthenophil and Parthenophe, XXXVI. ESo

And thus declared that Arab lady. Solomon and the Witch. W. B. Yeats. NoAM

And Thus in Nineveh. Ezra Pound. VGW

And to Her-Without-Bounds I send. Tribal Memories. Robert Duncan. Passages, I. NOBA; PiAm

And to Private Ball it came as if a rigid beam. David Jones. *Fr.* In Parenthesis. OBW; TwMBP

And to what end aim a dry root. Lemuel Johnson. *Fr.* Hand on the Navel. AAN

And Tomorrow Wend Our Ways. *Malay Oral Tradition, tr. by* R. J. Wilkinson *and* R. O. Winstedt. WTO

And Truly It Is a Most Glorious Thing, *with music.* William Bradford. AH

And Turnus than, quhar he at erth dyd ly. Virgil, *tr. by* Gavin Douglas. *Fr.* The Aeneid, XII. OBVE

And Two Good Things. D. J. Enright. HeHu

And Was Not Improved. Lerone Bennett, Jr. CNA; PoBA

And We Are Strangers to Each Other. Ruth Lisa Schechter. RiTi

And we came caught in the dance. Lemuel Johnson. *Fr.* Hand on the Navel. AAN

And We Conquered. Rob Penny. PoBA

And we went there. The River Kleeg. Greg Kuzma. BrS

And we were speaking easily and all the light stayed low. In Judgment of the Leaf. Kenneth Patchen. VGW

And we will lace the. God Send Easter. Lucille Clifton. CNA

And What About the Children. Audre Lorde. PoBA

And what are we to do with the horses. Answer. Leah Goldberg, *tr. by* Robert Friend. VWA

And what are you that, wanting you. The Philosopher. Edna St. Vincent Millay. CMoP (1970 ed.)

And what did we see, high up there. Ravenna. David Ray. HeS

And what I have learned. Duncan Spoke of a Process. Amiri Baraka. CAPP

And what if the little girl playing with her doll. The Turning. Lawrence Russ. TC

And what is left for the others. What Is Left? István Vas, *tr. by* Emery George. VWA

And what is life? A Primer for Schoolchildren. Richard Weber. CIP

And what is love? It is a doll dress'd up. Modern Love. Keats. LoAs; MBPR

And what is love? Misunderstanding, pain. Epigram. J. V. Cunningham. CoPAm; HAP; HoPM (1975 ed.); PoA

And what is so rare as a day in June? James Russell Lowell. *Fr.* The Vision of Sir Launfal. CTV; FSFS

And What of Me? Liz Sohappy Bahe. CDW

And what price the statue of a victorian man. Lemuel Johnson. *Fr.* Hand on the Navel. AAN

And what shall I bring back from such a voyage. Voyage. Stanislaw Wygodski, *tr. by* Isaac Komem. VWA

And what shall I do back in Frankfurt? Lemuel Johnson. *Fr.* Hand on the Navel. AAN

And What Shall You Say? Joseph Seamon Cotter, Jr. PoBA

And what was the big room he walked in? Before a Fall. Geoffrey Grigson. EAS

And when/ the cold white ness. Query. Ebon Dooley. PoBA

And When I Die. Laura Nyro. WIF

And when I say eyes right I want to hear. Weapons Training. Bruce Dawe. CAAP

And when that ballad lady went. A Road in Kentucky. Robert Hayden. NCSH

And When the Green Man Comes. John Haines. ConAP; NCSH

And When the Revolution Came. Carolyn M. Rodgers. GP

And when they came together in one place. Homer, *tr. by* Tennyson. *Fr.* The Iliad, IV. OBVE

And when we die at last. Heaven and Hell. *Unknown, tr. by* Edward Field. DL; IPWM

And when you called. The Cry. Grace Cavalieri. AATT

And when you have after all this. Lemuel Johnson. *Fr.* Hand on the Navel. AAN

And when you have forgotten the bright bedclothes. When You Have Forgotten Sunday: The Love Story. Gwendolyn Brooks. BPo; FF; TT

And when you try to sleep. For Bill. Geof Hewitt. NeAC

And when you walk the world lifts up its head. To a Very Beautiful Lady. Ruthven Todd. SLP

And where? it was at some moment. Home. John Blight. CAAP

And While We Are Waiting. Carolyn M. Rodgers. JB

& white folks freakin. 1,000,001 Starlings. Karoniaktatie. NW

And Who Are You? June Jordan. RiTi

And who desires, at large to know my name. George Gascoigne. *Fr.* The Steel Glass. TVS

And who has seen the moon, who has not seen. Moonrise. D. H. Lawrence. Moon; PoA

And who shall separate the dust. Common Dust. Georgia Douglas Johnson. AmNP (1974 ed.); PoBA

And Why Are All the Voices I Hear Divided into Colors? Alta. MMD

And why does Gratt [or Fatt] teach English? Why, because. Professor Gratt [or Dr. Fatt, Instructor]. Donald Hall. OBAL; TPO

And why take ye thought for raiment? Bible, *N.T. Fr.* St. Matthew. PF

And will they always be so tender, her. Swift Love, Sweet Motor. Hildegarde Flanner. WPE; WPW

And wilt thou leave [or wylt thow leve] me thus? An Appeal. Sir Thomas Wyatt. AAS; NOBE

And with the Sorrows of This Joyousness. Kenneth Patchen. ECBV

And would you gather turds. A History of Love. William Carlos Williams. VGW

And wylt thow leve me thus? *See* And wilt thou leave me thus?

And, yeah, brothers. I Sing of Shine. Etheridge Knight. BPo; GP

And Yet. Kadya Molodovsky, *tr. fr. Yiddish by* Seymour Levitan. VWA

And yet a kiss (like blubber)'d blur and slip. Love and Death. John Frederick Nims. CoPAm; HoPM (1975 ed.); WeW

And yet hath prayer, the heav'n-breathing foliage of faith.  Ethick.
  Robert Bridges.  *Fr.* The Testament of Beauty.  OxBTC
And yet the southern whale does some time come.  The Whales.
  Marguerite Young.  WPE
And yet this great wink of eternity.  Voyages, II.  Hart Crane.
  ExPo (1973 ed.); HAP; ILP (1975 ed.); NU; PAIC; PiAm;
  PPoe; PPP; UnPo (1976 ed.); VGW
And yet this is a poem.  Poem for My Students.  Robert L.
  McRoberts.  HeS
And you are dead.  The earth has not yet covered you.  Isaac
  Leybush Peretz  Moishe Leib Halpern, *tr. by* Kathryn
  Hellerstein.  VWA
And You Are There.  Tom Clark.  LiSp
And You as Well Must Die, Beloved Dust.  Edna St. Vincent
  Millay.  TAP
And you came back.  Samar Attar.  *Fr.* The Return of the Dead.
  PBWP
And You, Helen.  Edward Thomas.  BoLoP; OBW
And you'll say a nation totters.  G. D. H. Cole.  *Fr.* Civil Riot.
  OxBTC
Andante of Snakes, The.  Arthur Symons.  VLP
Anderson, Indiana.  James L. White.  HeS
Andonis, My Daughter.  Thomas Peacock.  VoR
Andraitx—Pomegranate Flowers.  D. H. Lawrence.  NoAM
Andrea del Sarto.  Robert Browning.  CABA (1972 ed.); ILP
  (1975 ed.); OAEL-2; SoSe (1977 ed.); TT; VLP
Andrée Rexroth.  Kenneth Rexroth.  VGW
Andrew Gear of Sunderland.  *Unknown.*  FaBoCo
Andrew Jackson's Speech.  Robert Bly.  ConAP
Andrew M'Crie.  Robert Fuller Murray.  FaBoCo
Andrew Talks to Gulls.  George Roberts.  BrS
Andrew's Bedtime Story.  Ian Serraillier.  DuDa
Andromache Afterwards.  Linda Gregg.  AAN
Andromache's Lamentation.  Homer, *tr. fr. Greek by* Congreve.
  *Fr.* The Iliad, XXIV.  OBVE
Andromache's Wedding.  Sappho, *tr. fr. Greek by* Willis
  Barnstone.  BoWoP
Andromeda.  Gerard Manley Hopkins.  EBEV; VLP
Andromeda/ forgot.  Sappho, *tr. fr. Greek by* Willis Barnstone.
  BoWoP
Andromeda, by Perseus saved and wed.  Aspecta Medusa.  Dante
  Gabriel Rossetti.  VLP
Andy-Diana DNA Letter.  Andrew Weiman.  HAP
Ane Ballat of Our Lady, *sel.*  William Dunbar.
  "Empryce of prys, imperatrice."  EBEV
Ane Metaphoricall Invention of a Tragedie Called Phoenix, *sel.*
  James I, King of England.
  "For I complaine not of sic common cace."  SLP
Ane mornin when aw went te wark.  The Row between the Cages.
  Thomas Armstrong.  VLP
Ane Satyre of the Thrie Estaitis, *sel.*  Sir David Lyndsay.
  "My patent pardouns ye may see."  OBSV
Anear the centre of that northern crest.  The City's Queen.
  James Thomson ("B.V.").  The City of Dreadful Night,
  XXI.  NOBE; PFD; VLP
Anecdote for Fathers.  Wordsworth.  MBPR
Anecdote of the Jar.  Wallace Stevens.  CMoP (1970 ed.); ExPo
  (1973 ed.); HoPM (1975 ed.); ILP (1975 ed.); InPK; NIL;
  NoAM; NOBA; PoA; PPP; TAP; TT; UnPo (1976 ed.)
Anemic pictures!  Legend.  Jules Laforgue, *tr. by* Louis Simpson.
  Prf
Anemones.  Marion Angus.  MS; SLP
Angel, The.  Blake.  *Fr.* Songs of Experience.  LAuP; MBPR
Angel.  James Merrill.  ConAP; PoA
  (Another Angel.)  NoAM
Angel ("Softly and gently, dearly-ransomed soul").  Cardinal
  Newman.  *Fr.* The Dream of Gerontius.  PFD

Angel.  Gary Soto.  AMV–80
Angel and the girl are met, The.  The Annunciation.  Edwin
  Muir.  BoReV; CMoP (1970 ed.)
Angel came to me, An.  O Simplicitas.  Madeleine L'Engle.  *Fr.*
  Three Songs of Mary.  PChr
Angel came to me and said, An.  A Memorable Fancy.  Blake.
  *Fr.* The Marriage of Heaven and Hell.  NU
Angel came to me and stood by my bedside, An.  Nightmare,
  with Angels.  Stephen Vincent Benét.  MAT
Angel Collector, The.  Henry Shore.  PMW
Angel Eye of Memory.  John Malcolm Brinnin.  PoA
Angel in the House, The, *sels.*  Coventry Patmore.
  "Across the sky the daylight crept," *fr.* II, x.  GBL
  Attainment, The, *fr.* I, iii.  FaBoEE
  Cathedral Close, The, *fr.* I, i.  VPC
  Constancy Rewarded, *fr.* II, xi.  VLP
  County Ball, The, *fr.* II, iii.  VPC
  Dean, The, *fr.* I, vi.  VLP
  Demonstration, A, *fr.* II, xi.  VLP
  Impossibility, The, *fr.* I, i.  VLP
  Kiss, The, *fr.* II, viii.  BoLoP; PoPle; SoSe
  Kites, The, *fr.* II, i.  VLP
  Love at Large, *fr.* I, ii.  VPC
  Love's Reality, *fr.* I, i.  VLP
  Married Lover, The, *fr.* II, xii.  VLP
  Perspective, *fr.* II, i.  FaBoEE; GBL
  Platonic Love, *fr.* II, xi.  VLP
  Poet's Confidence, The, *fr.* I, i.  VLP
  Revelation, The, *fr.* I, viii.  GBL; HAP
  Spirit's Epochs, The, *fr.* I, viii.  EBEV; GBL
  Tribute, The, *fr.* I, iv.  EBEV
  " 'Twas when the spousal time of May," *fr.* II, vii.  GBL
  Wedding, The, *fr.* II, xi.  VLP
  "Whirl'd off at last, for speech I sought," *fr.* II, xi.  GBL
Angel Michael, The.  Anath Bental, *tr. fr. Hebrew by* Howard
  Schwartz.  VWA
Angel of Death, The.  *Unknown.*  *See* There's a Man Goin'
  'Round Takin' Names.
Angel of Peace, Thou Hast Wandered Too Long, *with music.*
  Oliver Wendell Holmes.  AH
Angel, robed in spotless white, An.  Dawn.  Paul Laurence
  Dunbar.  AmNP (1974 ed.)
"Angel!" said the Heavenly Father, "I have called my servant
  Jackson."  Ascent of T. J. Jackson: A Soldier's Tale.
  "A. N."  BTTM
Angel said to me, The: "Why are you laughing?"  Sarah.
  Delmore Schwartz.  VWA
Angel Surrounded by Paysans.  Wallace Stevens.  PPP; TT
Angel That Presided o'er My Birth, The.  Blake.  InPK
Angel told Mary, An.  A Christmas Carol.  Harry Behn.  PChr
Angela Honey (she wrote) I would it were not so.  From Lois in
  London.  Angela McCabe.  AmPA
Angelical whites of your eyes, The.  Susan.  Robin Magowan.
  EAS
Angels.  Dannie Abse.  PoA
Angels.  Richard Burns.  VWA
Angels, The.  Marguerite Young.  WPE
Angels and ministers of grace defend us!  Shakespeare.  *Fr.*
  Hamlet, I, iv.  EBEV
Angels are stooping, The.  A Cradle Song.  W. B. Yeats.  LCL
Angels by one sin fell; so, man; how then.  Edward Benlowes.
  *Fr.* Theophila; or, Love's Sacrifice, Canto II.  SCP–2
Angels guide him now, The.  In Memory of a Child.  Vachel
  Lindsay.  PIM
Angels have no memory.  God's Language.  Ruth Fainlight.
  VWA
Angels have talked with him, and showed him thrones.  The
  Mystic.  Tennyson.  VLP

Angels in the House. Jerred Metz. VWA

Angels in Winter. Nancy Willard. FiCP

Angels' Song, The. Edmund Hamilton Sears. *See* It Came upon the Midnight Clear.

Angels Sung a Carol, The, *with music.* Edward Taylor. AH

Angels walking under the palm trees. A Little Carol of the Virgin. Lope de Vega, *tr. by* Denise Levertov. PChr

Angels We Have Heard on High. R. T. Smith. AAN

Angels We Have Heard on High. *Unknown.* FSW

Angel's Weather. Bruce Beaver. GAS

Anger now be your song, immortal one. The Iliad. Homer, *tr. by* Robert Fitzgerald. NAWM-1

Anger rises with metal filings, The. A Man All Grown Up Is Supposed To. Terry Stokes. AmPA

Anger that breaks a man down into boys, The. César Vallejo, *tr. fr. Spanish by* Robert Bly. EAS

Angina Pectoris. W. R. Moses. NCSH

Angle-Land. David Jones. The Anathemata, III. NoAM; TwMBP

Angle of Geese. N. Scott Momaday. CDW; VW

Angle of Repose. Robert A. Brooks. PoUp

Angle of Vision. Martha Bosworth. AMV-80

Angle of Vision. Robert Rendall. OxBTC

Angler's Song, The ("As inward love breeds outward talk"). Izaak Walton. LiSp

Angleworms. Marie Louise Allen. CTV

Anglican curate in want, An. Ronald Knox. FaBoNo

Anglicized Utopia W. S. Gilbert. OBSV

Anglo-American Chainpoem. *Unknown.* EAS

Anglo-Saxon Race, The: A Rhyme for Englishmen. Martin Farquhar Tupper. PeD

Anglosaxon Street. Earle Birney. CABA (1972 ed.); HeIP

Angola Question Mark. Langston Hughes. BPo

Angora, The. Jim Gerard. AMV-80

Angrier than my now occasional. A Preface to the Memoirs. James Merrill. NOBA

Angry domed silo mouths. The Death Penalty. Ross Laursen. CPA

Angry Man, The. Phyllis McGinley. SoS

Angry nettle and the mild, The. The Plum Gatherer. Edna St. Vincent Millay. NoAM

Angry Old Men. Basil Payne. PFIr

Angry Poet, The. Frank O'Connor, *tr. fr. Irish.* CIP

Angry Sermon for Any Day in the Week, An. F. Eugene Warren. AATT

Anguish is always there, lurking at night. The Kingdom of Kali. May Sarton. *Fr.* The Invocation to Kali. RiTi

Anguish of a naked body is more terrible, The. A Prayer to the Lord Ramakrishna. James Wright. NNaP

Animae Superstiti. Charles Spear. ATNZ

Animal, The. Allan Block. FAF

Animal Alphabet, An. *Unknown.* ECBV

Animal Crackers. Christopher Morley. CTV

Animal Days. Lee Harwood. TwMBP

Animal Fair, The. *Unknown.* PoPle

Animal I wanted, The. Kenneth Patchen. VGW

Animal moment, when he sorted out her tail, The. John Berryman. LoAs

Animal Poems. Gwendolyn MacEwen. MMD

Animal Runs, It Passes, It Dies. *Unknown, tr. fr. Gabon Pygmy by* C. M. Bowra. WeW

Animal That Drank Up Sound, The. William Stafford. VGW

Animal, Vegetable and Mineral. Louise Bogan. SBG

Animalcule, a Tale, The. Richard Savage. PeD

Animals. Robinson Jeffers. NU

Animals, The. Edwin Muir. CMoP (1970 ed.); EBEV; HeIP; PoIA

Animals. Walt Whitman. *See* I Think I Could Turn and Live with Animals.

Animals Are Passing from Our Lives. Philip Levine. NoAM; NOBA; TAP

Animals' Arrival, The. Elizabeth Jennings. PBWP

Animals' Christmas, The. Philip Dacey. GP; HeS; NVAP

Animals, hanging around in forms, The. On Visiting Central Park Zoo. Alan Dugan. NYP

Animals in the Ark, The. *Unknown.* GBP

Animals live in darkness, The. World of Darkness. Robert Chatain. PoA

Animals own a fur world. Adults Only. William Stafford. FF

Animals That Stand in Dreams, *sel.* Harley Elliott. Panda, The. NeAC

Animation and Ego. Jody Swilky. AMV-80

Animula. T. S. Eliot. STS

Animula vagula blandula. Limerick. Conrad Aiken. FaBoNo; OBAL

Anishinabe children sing songs of sleep. For the Children. Thomas Peacock. VoR

Anishinabe Grandmothers. Gerald Vizenor. VoR

Anita, la Maldita. Teresa A. McCarthy. NPW

Ank'hor Vat. Denis Devlin. BIrV; CIP

Anklet Song. *Tr. fr. Hawaiian by* N. B. Emerson. WTO

Ann. Kaye Starbird. ECBV

Ann, Ann!/Come! quick as you can! Alas, Alack! Walter de la Mare. CaYB; OxBChV

Ann was astounded when. Claremont. Robert Peters. GP

Ann wears dresses with ruffles. Ann. Kaye Starbird. ECBV

Anna. Joe Johnson. CNA

Anna Elise. *Unknown.* ECBV

Annabel Lee, *parody.* Stanley Huntley. SpRo

Annabel Lee. Poe. AmVN; DL; HeIP; NOBA; PiAm; RhR; SpRo; TAP

"It was many and many a year ago," *sel.* PCOP

Anne and the Field-Mouse. Ian Serraillier. MN; RAE

Anne and the Peacock. Noel Welch. FF

Anne Boleyn's Song. Edith Sitwell. UsP

Anne Rutledge. Edgar Lee Masters. *Fr.* Spoon River Anthology. CMoP (1970 ed.); FaPo; HAP; NoAM; NOBA; OFD

Anne Sexton. Hans Juergensen. AMV-81

Annie appears, arrayed. Hats. R. H. W. Dillard. CoPAm; GP

Annie Laurie. William Douglas, *and* Lady John Scott. BLSH, *with music;* FSW; PoPle

Annihilation. Conrad Aiken. GBL

Annihilation of Nothing, The. Thom Gunn. NoAM

Anniversarie, The. John Donne. *See* Anniversary, The.

Anniversary, The. Ai. CAAP; GP

Anniversary. Philip Dacey. AAN; HeS

Anniversary [*or* Anniversarie], The. John Donne. BoLoP; HAP; HoPM (1975 ed.); MetP; NOBE; OAEL-1; PoPle; TT; WeW

Anniversary, An. Thomas Hardy. OxBTC

Aniversary. Daniel Weissbort. VWA

Anniversary on the Hymeneals of My Noble Kinsman, Thomas Stanley, Esquire, An. Richard Lovelace. CaPo

Anniversary Poem for the Cheyennes Who Fell at Sand Creek. Lance Henson. VoR

Anno Domini. E. M. Walker. POL

Annot and John, *orig. and mod. English prose. Unknown.* OxBM

Annotations of Auschwitz, *sel.* Peter Porter.
  "London is full of chickens, on electric spits." OxBTC

Announced by all the trumpets of the sky. The Snow-Storm. Emerson. AmVN: FSFS; ILP (1975 ed.); IPWM; NOBA; PiAm; PPoD; Prf; TAP; UnPo (1976 ed.); VoPo

Announcement, The. George Ellenbogen. AMV-80

Annoying Miss Tillie McLush. Miss Tillie McLush. Joseph S. Newman. TDH

Annunciation. John Donne. SCP-1

Annunciation. Sister Maura.. TAT

Annunciation, The. Edwin Muir. BoReV; CMoP (1970 ed.)

Annunciation. Rainer Maria Rilke, *tr. fr. German by* James Blair Leishman. OBVE

Annunciation, The ("Gabriel, from Hevene-King"). *Unknown.* OxBM

Annunciation over the Shepherds, *sel.* Rainer Maria Rilke, tr. fr. German by M. D. Herter Norton.
"Look up, you men. Men there at the fire." PChr

Annus Mirabilis, *sels.* Dryden.
Fire of London.
"At length the crackling noise and dreadful blaze." SCP-1
London after the Great Fire, 1666. NOBE
"Swell'd with our late successes on the foe." EBEV
War. SCP-1

Annus Mirabilis. Philip Larkin. NOBL

Anomie. Patricia Ramsey. AATT

Anon out of the north-est the noys bigynes. Jonah Is Cast into the Sea. *Unknown. Fr.* Patience. OxBM

Anon with gaping fearlessness they quaff. My Boots. Henry David Thoreau. PeD

Anonymous. Anne Hazlewood Brady. WBN

Anonymous as cherubs. Two Voices in a Meadow. Richard Wilbur. PBMP; SoS; UnPo (1976 ed.)

Anonymous Drawing. Donald Justice. HeIP

Another ("As loving hind that, hartless, wants her deer"). Anne Bradstreet. *See* Letter to Her Husband, Absent upon Public Employment.

Another [Epitaph on the Lady Mary Villiers] ("Purest soul that e'er was sent, The"). Thomas Carew. CaPo

Another [Epitaph on the Lady Mary Villiers] ("This little vault, this narrow room"). Thomas Carew. *See* Epitaph on the Lady Mary Villiers ("This little vault . . .").

Another [on the Snail.] Richard Lovelace. CaPo

Another ("Yes, every poet is a fool"). Matthew Prior. *See* Epigram: "Yes, every poet is a fool."

Another Academy. Charles Bukowski. TAT

Another Angel. James Merrill. *See* Angel.

Another armored animal—scale. The Pangolin. Marianne Moore. HAP; NoAM; NOBA; PBWP

Another Attempt at the Trick. Cynthia Macdonald. WBN

Another collection of verse by the man from Sulmona. Ovid, *tr. by* Guy Lee. Amores, II, 1. NAWM-1

Another Color. Frank Stewart. AMV-81

Another Commercial. Lonnie L. Landrum. DNGG

Another cove of shale. On the Marginal Way. Richard Wilbur. CAPP; NOBA

Another Cross. Stephen Gardner. AMV-80

Another dawn, leaden. Words. Philip Levine. VWA

Another Death. D. E. Borrell. FF

Another Epitaph on an Army of Mercenaries. "Hugh MacDiarmid." NoAM

Another Face. Ray A. Young Bear. CDW

Another Fan. Stéphane Mallarmé. *See* Fan for His Daughter, A.

Another Given: The Last Day of the Year. William Dickey. AMV-80

Another Grace for a Child. Robert Herrick. *See* Grace for a Child.

Another hill town. Hotel Paradiso e Commerciale. John Malcolm Brinnin. NoAM

Another Life. Philip Levine. CPA

Another Life, *sel.* Derek Walcott.
Runner at Sauteurs, The. OBP

Another Load. William Harrold. HeS

Another Love Poem. Jimmy Santiago Baca. DNGG

Another Man Done Gone. *Unknown.* FSW

Another Meeting. Lawrence A. Lucus. AMV-80

Another night of lunacy! Etude. Richard O'Connell. BCr

Another Night on the Porch Swing. Cathleen Quirk. NMM

Another on Her. Robert Herrick. SpRo

Another One for the Devil. David C. Childers. AMV-80

Another Poem for Me. Etheridge Knight. NNaP

Another Poem of the Tearing Down of the Metropolitan Opera House. A. Wilber Stevens. MPA

Another Poem on Absalom Nathan Yonathan, *tr. fr. Hebrew by* Fichard Flantz. VWA

Another season centers on this place. The Gourd Dancer. N. Scott Momaday. CDW

Another September. Thomas Kinsella. BIrV; CIP; IPM

Another shout from the wharves. Hilda Doolittle ("H. D."). *Fr.* Helen in Egypt. NOBA

Another sin I had forgot. *Unknown.* PeD

Another Song ("The winter of my infancy being over-past"). Ann Collins. SCP-2

Another Song ("Merry the green, the green hill shall be merry"). Donald Justice. ConAP; VGW

Another Song of the Same Woman, to Some Partridges, Sent to Her Alive. Florencia del Pinar, *tr. fr. Spanish by* Julie Allen. BoWoP

Another Stone Poem. Philip Dacey. AMV-81

Another summer is gone. Accessions to Autumn. John Williams. MPA

Another summer! Our Independence. Fourth of July in Maine. Robert Lowell. CAPP

Another Sunday Morning. Carter Revard. VoR

Another time I'll let him pick his own. Eve's Version. James Harrison. AMV-81

Another True Maid. Matthew Prior. FaBoEE

Another uncle/ was a pathological liar. Family 8. Lyn Lifshin. NeAC

Another View of the Beast. R. P. Dickey. FoP

Another woman: a change of tears. Theodore Roethke. POL

Another Year Come. W. S. Merwin. OFD

Another year it may betide. *Unknown.* HAP

Answer. Leah Goldberg, *tr. fr. Hebrew by* Robert Friend. VWA

Answer, The. George Herbert. Epi

Answer, The. Robinson Jeffers. CMoP (1970 ed.)

Answer, An. John Sjoberg. AcAn

Answer, The. Sara Teasdale. PoA

Answer. *Unknown. See* Reply, A.

Answer of Mr. Waller's Painter to His Many New Advisers, The. *Unknown.* APAS

Answer [*or* Answers] to a Child's Question. Samuel Taylor Coleridge. ECBV; OxBChV; PCOP; PoPle

Answer to a Man's Question, An, "What Can I Do about Women's Liberation?" Susan Griffin. MMD

Answer to a Sonnet Ending Thus. Keats. MBPR

Answer to Allegory, An. Basil Payne. IPM

Answer to an Invitation to Cambridge, An. Abraham Cowley. PAIC

Answer to Another Persuading a Lady to Marriage, An. Katherine Philips. HAP

Answer to Chloe Jealous. Matthew Prior. NOBE

Answer to Marlowe. Sir Walter Ralegh.    *See* Nymph's Reply to the Shepherd, The.

Answer to the Parson, An. Blake. FaBoEE

Answer to Voznesensky and Evtushenko. Frank O'Hara. NNaP

Answer to Yo/ Question. Sonia Sanchez. BPo; RiTi

Answerers. William Stafford. PCho

Answering. Robert Duncan. PiAm

Answering Li Ying Who Showed Me His Poems about Summer Fishing. Yü Hsüan-chi, *tr. fr. Chinese by* Geoffrey Waters. BoWoP

Answers. Elizabeth Jennings. OxBTC

Answers for Ethelbert. Ahmos Zu-Bolton II. PoUp

Answers to a Child's Question. Samuel Taylor Coleridge.    *See* Answer to a Child's Question.

Answers to the Snails. Arthur Solway. AMV-81

Ant, The. Richard Lovelace. CaPo

Ant, The. Ogden Nash. OBAL

Ant on the tablecloth, An. Departmental. Robert Frost. HeIP; HoPM (1975 ed.); InPK; NOBA; NOBL; OBAL; SoSe (1977 ed.); STS; WIF

Ant-seething city, city full of dreams. The Seven Old Men. Baudelaire, *tr. by* Roy Campbell. OBVE

Ante-Bellum Sermon, An. Paul Laurence Dunbar. BPo

Anteroom: Geneva. Denis Devlin. CIP

Anthea bade me tie her shoe. The Shoe-tying. Robert Herrick. CaPo

Anthem for Doomed Youth. Wilfred Owen. BiP; BuTh; CMoP (1970 ed.); EBEV; HAP; HeIP; HoPM (1975 ed.); NoAM; NOBE; OAEL-2; OxBTC; PPoD; PPP; PSN; SoSe; WeW; WIF, 3 *versions*

Anthology of Nouns. Parker Tyler. PoA

Anthology Poem. Petra von Morstein, *tr. fr. German by* Rosemarie Waldrop. BoWoP

Anthropology in Fort Morgan, Colorado. Sam Hamod. TAT

Anthropophagites See a Sign on NC Highway 177 That Looks like Heaven, The. Jonathan Williams. OBAL

Antichrist, or the Reunion of Christendom: An Ode. G. K. Chesterton. FaBoCo; NOBE; NOBL; OBSV

Anticipation of Sharks. Diane Wakoski. MAT

Antietam Creek: In the North They Named the Battles after Bodies of Water. Anne Becker. PoUp

Antigone. Sophocles, *tr. fr. Greek by* T. H. Banks. NAWM-1

Antigone I. Herbert Martin. PoBA

Antigone VI. Herbert Martin. PoBA

Anti-Nostalgia. Henryk Grynberg, *tr. fr. Polish by* Isaac Komem. VWA

Antipathy. Rowland Watkyns, *after the Latin of* Martial. FaBoEE

Antiphonal Hymn in Praise of Inanna. Enheduanna, *tr. fr. Sumerian*; *ad. by* Aliki *and* Willis Barnstone. BoWoP

Antiplatonick, The. John Cleveland. MetP; SCP-2

Antiquary, The. Joseph Campbell. OxBTC

Antiquary. John Donne. EBEV; FF; InPK; NIL

Antique Indian should be Henry James, The. American Plan. John Malcolm Brinnin. GOA

Antique lights, The. Ybor City. Duane Locke. CSP

Antique people are down in the dungeons, The. Goodbye and Hello. Tim Buckley. WIF

Antiques. Walter de la Mare. PoA

Antiquitez de Rome, *sels.* Joachim du Bellay, *tr. fr. French by* Spenser.
  "Thou stranger, which for Rome in Rome here seekest." OBVE
  "Who list the Romane greatnes forth to figure." OBVE

Antiquity of Freedom, The. Bryant. EAP

Anti-Semanticist, The. Everett Hoagland. BPo

Antisong. Phyllis Webb. MMD

Antiworlds. Andrei Voznesensky, *tr. fr. Russian by* Richard Wilbur. NIL

Antlered forests, The. Ank'hor Vat. Denis Devlin. BIrV; CIP

Anton Leeuwenhoek was Dutch. The Microscope. Maxine W. Kumin. PoTa; QQQ

Antonio. Laura E. Richards. CTV; TDH

Antonio's Revenge, *sel.* John Marston.
  "Being laid upon her bed she grasped my hand." SCP-2

Antony and Cleopatra, *sels.* Shakespeare.
  "Barge she sat in, like a burnish'd throne, The," *fr.* II, ii. BiP; PPoe
  Cleopatra's Lament, *fr.* V, ii. UnPo (1976 ed.)
  "Eros, thou yet behold'st me?" *fr.* IV, xiv. EBEV
  "I, that with my sword," *fr.* IV, xiv. IP
  "Miserable change now at my end, The," *fr.* IV, xiii. EBEV; PoPle

Antony to Cleopatra. William Haines Lytle. FaPo

Antrim. Robinson Jeffers. BIrV; NOBA; VGW

Ants. Katharyn Machan Aal. AMV-80

Ants, The. John Clare. BoAnP

Ants. Lewis Hyde. AMV-80

Ants and Others. Adrien Stoutenburg. BoAnP

Ants on inert cricket crawling. Haiku. José Juan Tablada, *tr. by* Samuel Beckett. PBMP

Antwerp and Bruges. Dante Gabriel Rossetti. VLP

Anxiety about Dying. Alicia Ostriker. AMV-80

Anxious Thought. Thomas Hoccleve. *Fr. De Regimine Principum.* OxBM

Any April. Cathy Beard. AMV-81

"Any cracked eggs today?" Cracked Eggs. Herbert Scott. TC

Any Complaints? Vernon Scannell. OxBTC

Any Golf Championship. Grantland Rice. SPo

Any Day Now. David McCord. QQQ

Any hound a porcupine nudges. The Porcupine. Ogden Nash. ECBV

Any Man's Advice to His Son. Kenneth Fearing. CMoP (1970 ed.); TPo

Any Night. Philip Levine. AMV-80

Any of the several names. Eulogy for Populations. Ron Welburn. PoBA

Any Part of Piggy. Noel Coward. BBL

Any time,/ any time at all. Martha Webb. PHC

Any way you hold them, they hurt. Pine Cones. Dave Smith. AMV-80

Any Wife to Any Husband. Robert Browning. VLP

Anybody Could Write This Poem. All You Have to Say Is Yes. Alta. MMD

Anyone Lived in a Pretty How Town. E. E. Cummings. AnMo; BiP; CABA (1972 ed.); CMoP (1970 ed.); HAP; ILP (1975 ed.); InPK; IP; IPWM; NOBA; NowV; PAIC; PoA; PPM; STS; TAP; VGW; WeW

Anyone who has ever lived. Why I Can't Write My Autobiography. Rodger Kamenetz. VWA

Anything Goes. Cole Porter. OBAL

Anything that promises good. First Hymn. John Gill. NeAC

Anything this recognizable. Downy Hair in the Shape of a Flame. Coleman Barks. *Fr. Body Poems.* NVAP

Anywhere I look/ the water has dominion. Dingman's Marsh. John Moore. NCSH

Anzac Ceremony. Kendrick Smithyman. ATNZ

Aodh Ruadh O'Domhnaill. Thomas MacGreevy. CIP

Aoibhinn, A Leabhrain, Do Thriall. *Unknown, tr. fr. Irish by* Flann O'Brien. BIrV

Ap Huw's Testament. R. S. Thomas. BuTh

Apache Kid. Ned White. BPAW

Apache word for love stings, The. In the Night Desert. William Stafford. MPA

Apart from Branches. Josephine Miles. MPA

Apart from my sisters, estranged. Cinderella. Olga Broumas. PoIA

Apart from Oneself. Alejandra Pizarnik, *tr. fr. Spanish by* Yishai Tobin. VWA

Apartheid. Margo Bohanon. SES

Apartment House. Gerald Raftery. SFF

Apartment Hunter, The. Philip Schultz. NYP

Apartments on First Avenue. Cynthia Macdonald. NYP

Apeneck Sweeney spreads his knees. Sweeney among the Nightingales. T. S. Eliot. CABA (1972 ed.); CMoP (1970 ed.); HAP; HeIP; InPK; NIL; NoAM; NOBA; NOBE; PAIC; PPP; TT

Apes yawn and adore their fleas in the sun, The. The Jaguar. Ted Hughes. ILP (1975 ed.)

Aphorisms. "Novalis," *tr. fr. German by* Charles E. Passage. NU

Aphrodite!/ Aphrodite of the blue sleep. Blue Sleep. Winifred Bryher. PoA

Apocalypse. D. J. Enright. OBSV

Apocalypse. Jean Lipkin. VWA

Apocalypse and Resurrection. John Bayliss. EAS

Apocalypse in Black and White. Robert Pack. CoPAm

Apocalypse in Springtime. Lex Banning. GAS

Apocrypha. Stanley Moss. VWA

Apolitical Intellectuals. Otto Rene Castillo, *tr. fr. Spanish by* Margaret Randall. EC

Apollo and Daphne. Yvor Winters. PiAm

Apollo 8. John Berryman. Moon

Apollo kept my father's sheep. A Daughter of Admetus. T. Sturge Moore. FaBoTw (1975 ed.)

Apollo of the Physiologists. Robert Graves. NIL

Apollo 113. Diderik Finne. AMV-80

Apologia. Swinburne. VLP

Apologia pro Vita Sua. A. R. Ammons. NOBA

Apologia pro Vita Sua. Samuel Taylor Coleridge. MBPR

Apologia pro Vita Sua. Pope. *Fr.* Epistle to Dr. Arbuthnot. NOBE

Apologia pro Vita Sua. Sedulius Scottus, *tr. fr. Medieval Latin by* Helen Waddell. BIrV

Apologue. Tony Connor. BoLoP

Apology. Anthony Cronin. CIP; IPM

Apology. J. V. Cunningham. PiAm

Apology, The. Emerson. AmVN

Apology, An. William Morris. *Fr.* The Earthly Paradise. OAEL–2; PAIC; VPC
(Prologue: "Of Heaven or Hell I have no power to sing.") VLP

Apology, An. Diane Wakoski. TAP

Apology. Wordsworth. *Fr.* Sonnets upon the Punishment of Death. VLP

Apology Addressed to the Critical Reviewers, The. Charles Churchill. LAuP

Apology for a Lost Classicism, An. John Ciardi. AMV–81

Apology for Apostasy? Etheridge Knight. NeAC

Apology for Bad Dreams. Robinson Jeffers. ILP (1975 ed.); NOBA

Apology for Liberals. Joy Davidman. SPT

Apology for the Fall. E. R. Cole. AATT

Apology for Understatement. John Wain. LoAs; OxBTC

Apology. Hands shaping air. Lynn Strongin. *Fr.* First Aspen. RiTi

Apology to My Lady. Edward Falco. AMV–80

Apostasy of One and But One Lady, The. Richard Lovelace. CaPo

Apostrophe to Man. Edna St. Vincent Millay. PBMP; SBG

Apostrophe to Vincentine, The. Wallace Stevens. LoAs

Apotheosis of Olde Towne, *sel.* Hugh Fox.
"Dress goods,/ Silk." TC

Apparent, The. Linda Gregg. AAN

Apparent Failure. Robert Browning. NOBE

Apparently with no surprise. Emily Dickinson. CABA (1972 ed.); ILP (1975 ed.); IP; PPP; SoSe; WIF

Apparition, The. Eiléan Ní Chuilleanáin. IPM

Apparition, The. John Donne. CABA (1972 ed.); ExPo (1973 ed.); GBL; HeIP; NOBE; OAEL–1; PAIC; SCP–1

Apparition, The. Michael Heffernan. HeS

Apparition, The. Theodore Roethke. AIW; LoAs

Apparition, The. Chris Wallace-Crabbe. MAuV

Apparition of His Mistress Calling Him to Elysium, The. Robert Herrick. CaPo

Apparition of these faces in the crowd, The. In a Station of the Metro. Ezra Pound. BBGO; CABA (1972 ed.); ExPo (1973 ed.); HAP; HeIP; ILP (1975 ed.); InPK; LFH; NIL; NoAM; NOBA; PiAm; PPoD; TAP; TPo; UnPo (1976 ed.); VGW; WeW; WIF

Apparitions, The. W. B. Yeats. CMoP (1970 ed.)

Appeal, The. Samuel Daniel. OLR

Appeal, An. Sir Thomas Wyatt. NOBE
("And wylt thow leve me thus?") AAS

Appeal to Cats in the Business of Love, An. Thomas Flatman. GBL; HAP; PCat; SCP–2

Appeal to the Moongod Nanna-Suen to Throw Out Lugalanne. Enheduanna, *tr. fr. Sumerian; ad. by* Aliki *and* Willis Barnstone. BoWoP

Appearance, An. Sylvia Plath. CAPP

Appearance and Reality. John Hollander. OBAL

Appeasement of Demeter, The. George Meredith. VLP

Appetite, The. Yom Kippur: Fasting. Ruth Whitman. OFD

Applauding youths laughed with young prostitutes. The Harlem Dancer. Claude McKay. BPo; FF; ILP (1975 ed.); IPWM; NoAM; TAP

Applause flutters onto the open air. A Snapshot for Miss Bricka. Robert Wallace. LiSp

Apple. Dave Morice. AcAn

Apple, The. *At.* to Plato, *tr. fr. Greek.* WeW

Apple a Day, An. Lee Blair. TDH

Apple Blight. Paul Zimmer. VGW

Apple Dumplings and a King, The. "Peter Pindar". OBSV

Apple Gathering, An. Christina Rossetti. OLR

Apple Hell. Mark Van Doren. PoA

Apple-Logia. Marian Frances Brand. AATT

Apple on its bough is her desire, The. Garden Abstract. Hart Crane. PSN

Apple Scoop. Emilie Glen. OSP; TVo

Apple Tree and a Pig, An. Emyr Humphreys. OBW

Apple you jerked from its stem, The. Girl on the Run. David Kresh. PoUp

Apples. Margaret Gibson. AAN

Apples. Shirley Kaufman. NMM; RiTi

Apples Be Ripe. *Unknown.* GBP

Apples, bright on the leafless bough. Apple Hell. Mark Van Doren. PoA

Apples for the little ones. Clyde Watson. *Fr.* Father Fox's Pennyrhymes. CC

Apples of Sodom and Gomorrah, The. Barbara A. Holland. WBN

Apples to Keep. Frances Frost. ECBV

Applicant, The. Sylvia Plath. MAT; NMM; NOBA; Psy; SBG; TPo; UsP

Apply for the position (I've forgotten now for what) I had to marry. In Order To. Kenneth Patchen. IP; PPoD

Appoggiatura. Donald Jeffrey Hayes. AmNP (1974 ed.); PoBA

Apposite blood red the blobs. Remembrance Day. Vernon Scannell. HeHu

Appointment, The. Maxine W. Kumin. NMM

Appointment, The. L. A. G. Strong. OxBTC

Appology, The. Countess of Winchilsea. SBG

Appreciate/ the wide pavements. Good Morning. Layle Silbert. NPW

Appreciation. Harry Graham. PoPle

Apprehension this spring . . . the leaves, the leaves. Homage and Lament for Ezra Pound in Captivity. Robert Duncan. NOBA

Apprentice Angel, An. "Hugh MacDiarmid". MS

Apprentice in the shop across from me, The. A Short Winter Tale. Natan Zach, *tr. by* Peter Everwine *and* Shula Starkman. VWA

Apprentice Painter, The. Jack Myers. AmPA

Approach of the Storm, The. *Tr. fr. Chippewa by* Frances Densmore. OBVE

Approach to the bar, The. Pole Vaulter. David Allan Evans. NVAP

Approach to Thebes, The. Stanley Kunitz. PoA

Approaches, The. W. S. Merwin. NOBA; Prf

Approaching Absolute Zero. Joyce Peseroff. PCho

Approaching the Canvas. Kathleen Spivack. PCho

Approaching the Castle. Richard Hugo. SoSe (1977 ed.)

Approaching the laboratory gates. The Liberator. Lucien Stryk. GP

Approaching the Walt/ Whitman Bridge. On the Industrial Highway. Daniel Hoffman. PCho

Approaching Washington. Charles G. Bell. WasP

Approaching Washington Heights. James Reiss. NYP

Approve the traveler who never went. The Travelers. James Reeves. POL

Après le Bain. William Carlos Williams. OBAL

Apricot Tree. Magda Isanos, *tr. fr. Rumanian by* Willis Barnstone *and* Matei Calinescu. BoWoP

April. John Linthicum. AMV–80

April. Ezra Pound. CMoP (1970 ed.)

April. Samuel Thompson. BIrV

April. Jean Valentine. TAP

April. Yvor Winters. RFM

April, and young women glorify their flesh. The Love Day. Douglas Dunn. MS

April Birthday. Ted Hughes. DuDr

April 1885. Robert Bridges. OxBTC

April 5, 1974. Richard Wilbur. GP

April Fool's Day. *Unknown.* CTV

April, in another fortnight, metropolitan April. Piano Practice. Derek Walcott. NYP

April Inventory. W. D. Snodgrass. BiP; CABA (1972 ed.); CAPP; HAP; NoAM; NowV; PPoe; SFF; TAP; WIF

April Is in My Mistress' Face. *Unknown.* GBL; HeIP

April is the cruellest month, breeding. The Waste Land. T. S. Eliot. CABA (1972 ed.); CMoP (1970 ed.); HAP; NoAM; NOBA; NOBE; OAEL–2; OxBTC; PiAm; PPoe; TAP; UnPo (1976 ed.)

April Landscape. A. L. Rowse. PES

April 1962. Paul Goodman. VGW

April Rain. Robert Loveman. CTV; PCoP

April Rain Song. Langston Hughes. LCL

April Rise. Laurie Lee. LP; MPo

April 68. Sam Cornish. CNA

April this year, not otherwise. Song of a Second April. Edna St. Vincent Millay. CMoP (1970 ed.); PPM

April 29, 1975. David Hilton. AcAn

April what an ice-cold promise. Hudson Ferry. James Schuyler. NYP

April winter. 13:IV:72. David Kherdian. BCr

Aprill. Spenser. *Fr.* The Shepheardes Calender. ILP (1975 ed.)

April's blossoms launch. Two Weeks after an April Frost. Steven Helmling. AMV–80

Aprilly. Bert Leston Taylor. OBAL

Apron, The. Stuart Friebert. FiCP

Apron of Flowers, The. Robert Herrick. CaPo

Apron Strings. Marge Piercy. TAP

Aprons of Silence. Carl Sandburg. NoAM; NOBA

Aquarium, San Francisco, The. V. Sackville-West. SBG

Ar ne couthe ich sorwe none. A Prisoner's Prayer. *Unknown.* OxBM

Arabesque. Fred Johnson. PoBA

Arabia. John Meade Falkner. OxBTC

Arabic Script. Anthony Thwaite. HeHu

Aran Islands. Irving Layton. NeAC

Arbor Vitae. Coventry Patmore. *Fr.* The Unknown Eros. VLP

Arbor Vitae. Siegfried Sassoon. PoPle

Arc Inside and Out, The. A. R. Ammons. NoAM

Arcades, *sel.* Milton.
    Song: "Nymphs and shepherds dance no more." LoAs

Arcadia, *sels.* Sir Philip Sidney.
    "My true love hath my heart, and I have his." BoLoP; GBL; ILP (1975 ed.); LoAs; PoPle
    (Bargain, The.) NOBE
    Sestina: "Farewell, Oh sun, Arcadia's clearest light." NIL; PAIC
    Since Nature's Works Be Good. ILP (1975 ed.)
    When Two Suns Do Appear. Moon
    "Ye goat-herd gods that love the grassy mountains." HAP; NOBE; OAEL–1

Arcady Revisited. Robert Funge. AMV–80

Archaeologists. Real Faucher. AMV–80

Archaeology. Richard Church. PES

Archaic Torso of Apollo. Rainer Maria Rilke, *tr. fr. German by* Robert Bly. NU

Archbishop Tait. *Unknown.* FaBoNo

Archery. Walter de la Mare. FaBoNo

Arches and Shadows. Annie Dillard. CTBA

Archetypes. Neal Bowers. AMV–81

Archne. Richard Foerster. AMV–80

Archy and Mehitabel, *sels.* Don Marquis.
    Archy Confesses. SS
    Cheerio My Deario. FaBoCo
    Freddy the Rat Perishes. MiP
    Old Trouper, The. FaBoCo

Archy at the Zoo. Don Marquis. OBAL

Arctic honey blabbed over the report causing darkness, The. Leaving the Atocha Station. John Ashbery. CAPP

Arctic Vixen. Michael Baldwin. FPB

"Arcturus" is his other name. Emily Dickinson. NOBA; WIF

Arcuconspicilla oves looks for perditas. She Lost Her Sheep. J. Moyr Smith. FaBoNo

Ardently down the backs of cousins. Hair. Maxine Silverman. VWA

Ardour and Memory. Dante Gabriel Rossetti. The House of Life, LXIV. OAEL–2

Are all such off'rings, as are crusht, and bruis'd. Francis Quarles. FaBoEE

Are all these stones. Close-Up. A. R. Ammons. PoA

Are at the end of our street. They. Donald Finkel. CoPAm; GP

Are not Abracadabra or anything slippery and remote. The Magic Words. Ronald Koertge. AMV–81

Are the desolate, dark weeks. These. William Carlos Williams. NoAM; NOBA; PBMP; TCP; UsP

Are the living so much use. At the Cenotaph. "Hugh MacDiarmid." OBP

Are the Sick in Their Beds as They Should Be? Joan McIntosh. AMV–80

Are Then Regalities All Gilded Masks? Keats. *Fr.* Endymion, III. Moon

Are there birds twittering under the earth. Under the Earth. Abraham Sutskever, *tr. by* Ruth Whitman. VWA

Are there not twelve whole hours in every day. The Day of Denial. Jones Very. NOBA

Are there two things, of all which men possess. To Asra. Samuel Taylor Coleridge. MBPR

Are these the astronauts who carried. A Farewell to the Moon. Ed Ochester. Moon

Are these the pope's grand tools? On the Murder of Sir Edmund Berry Godfrey. *Unknown.* APAS

Are these the strings that poets say. The Cat and the Lute. Thomas Master. PCat

Are they clinging to their crosses. Antichrist, or the Reunion of Christendom: An Ode. G. K. Chesterton. FaBoCo; NOBE; NOBL; OBSV

Are they shadows that we see? Shadows. Samuel Daniel. *Fr.* Tethys' Festival. ExPo (1973 ed.); NOBE

Are we quite cut off from Thee? The Trial. Gershom Scholem, *tr. by* Jonathan Griffin. VWA

"Are Ye Right There, Michael?" (A Lay of the Wild West Clare.) Percy French. WTO

Are you alive? The Pool. Hilda Doolittle. ("H. D."). CMoP (1970 ed.); ExPo (1973 ed.)

Are you asking where I'm going with these sad faces. Poem with the Final Tune. Julia de Burgos, *tr. by* Julio Marzán. InW

"Are you awake, Gemelli." Star-Talk. Robert Graves. FSFS; OxBTC

Are You Born?—I. Muriel Rukeyser. LoAs

Are You Glad? *Mongol Oral Tradition, tr. by* C. R. Bawden. WTO

Are you going to Scarborough Fair? Scarborough Fair. *Unknown.* BLSo; FSW

Are you going to Whittingham Fair? Whittingham Fair. *Unknown.* AIW; GBP

Are You Just Back for a Visit or Are You Going to Stay? Francis Coleman Rosenberger. AMV–81

Are You looking for us? We are here. The 151st Psalm. Karl Shapiro. VWA

Are you ready? soul said again. Two Trinities. Kenneth Mackenzie. GAS

"Are you really a poet?" Some 5-Day Drunk Poems. Simon J. Ortiz. NW

"Are you sad to think how often." Middle-aged Conversation. A. S. J. Tessimond. POL

Are You the New Person Drawn toward Me? Walt Whitman. LoAs; NoAM; PPP

Are You There, Mrs. Goose? John V. Hicks. AMV–80

Are you what your faire lookes expresse? Thomas Campion. AAS

Are you writing in a radiant place now, Delmore. Ode to Delmore Schwartz. Paul Carroll. FiCh

Arena, The. Hubert Witheford. ATNZ

"Aren't you fearful you'll trip and fall?" Ice-Creepers (for Cid Ricketts Sumner). Eve Merriam. TVo

Aren't You Glad. Charlotte Zolotow. CTV

Ares at last has quit the field. Under Which Lyre, a Reactionary Tract for the Times. W. H. Auden. NOBL

*Arethusa,* The. Prince Hoare. FaPoR

Arethusa. Shelley. MBPR

Argent Solipsism. Howard Blake. PoA

Argentine gaucho named Bruno, An. Limerick. *Unknown.* NOBL

Argoed. T. Gwynn Jones, *tr. fr. Welsh by* Anthony Conran. OBW

Argument. Langston Hughes. ILP (1975 ed.)

Argument, An. Thomas Moore. BoLoP

Argument, The. Jane P. Moreland. AMV–80

Argument against Metaphor. Gad Hollander. VWA

Argument begins the week we marry, The. The Argument. Jane P. Moreland. AMV–80

Argument of His Book, The. Robert Herrick. CaPo; EBEV; HAP; HeIP; ILP (1975 ed.); OAEL–1; OBP; PoPle ("I sing of brooks, of blossoms, birds and bowers.") NIL

Argument of the refrigerator wakes me, The. The Refrigerator. Howard Moss. GP

Argus and Ulysses ("Argus was a puppy"). Eleanor Farjeon. ECBV

Arid Husband, The. E. L. T. Mesens. EAS

Ariel. Sylvia Plath. AnMo; CABA (1972 ed.); CMoP (1970 ed.); ExPo (1973 ed.); HeIP; InPK; NoAM; NOBA; PBWP; PiAm; Psy

Ariel, one true. Thoughts about My Daughter before Sleep. Sandra Hochman. TV

Ariel to Miranda:—Take. With a Guitar, to Jane. Shelley. MBPR; OAEL–2

Ariel was glad he had written his poems. The Planet on the Table. Wallace Stevens. HAP

Ariel's Song: "Come unto these yellow sands." Shakespeare. *Fr.* The Tempest, I, ii. NOBE ("Come unto these yellow sands.") HeIP; PoPle; SpRo

Ariel's Song: "Full fathom five thy father lies." Shakespeare. *See* Full Fathom Five Thy Father Lies.

Ariel's Song: "Where the bee sucks, there suck I." Shakespeare. *Fr.* The Tempest, V, i. NOBE; SoSe ("Where the bee sucks, there suck I.") CABA (1972 ed.); HeIP; ILP (1975 ed.); LCL; PCOP; PoIA

Arioso, *sel.* J. Charles Green. "I call on the sun to strip/ us naked." DNGG

Ariosto. Osip Mandelstam, *tr. fr. Russian by* W. S. Merwin *and* Clarence Brown. OBVE

Arise and See the Glorious Sun, *with music.* Francis Hopkinson. AH

Arise, My Soul! With Rapture Rise! *with music.* Samuel J. Smith. AH

Arise, O Glorious Zion, *with music.* William G. Mills. AH

Arise, Ye Saints of Latter Days, *with music. Unknown.* AH

Arise, ye sons of France, to glory! La Marseillaise. Claude Joseph Rouget de Lisle, *tr. fr. French.* FSW

Arise, you pris'ners of starvation. The Internationale. Eugene Potter *and* Pierre Degeyter. FSW

Arise! you who refuse to be bond-slaves. Chee Lai! (Arise!) *Unknown, tr. fr. Chinese.* FSW

Arisen from what childhood. The Phoenix of Mozart. Claude Vigée, *tr. by* Anthony Rudolf. VWA

Aristophanes' Symposium. Rita Mae Brown. IHMS

Aristotle was a little man with. Humanities Lectures. William Stafford. NNaP

Arithmetic on the Frontier. Kipling. VLP

Arizona. *Unknown.* AmFP

Arizona Highways. James Welch. CDW

Arizona Nature Myth. James Michie. NOBL

Arizona Poems, *sels.* John Gould Fletcher.
  Mexican Quarter, II. BPAW
  Rain in the Desert, VI. BPAW; NCSH
Arizona Ruins. Lyn Lifshin. RiTi
Arjuna said:/ How shall I in battle against Bhisma. *Unknown.*
  *Fr.* The Bhagavad-Gita. DL
Ark, The, *sel.* Jay MacPherson.
  "I wait, with those that rest." PoA
Ark noisy with children, The. Noah. Chana Bloch. VWA
Arkansas. Jackman Young. TAT
Arkansas Traveler, The. *Unknown.* FSW
Arkansas Traveller, The, *with music.* Mose Case. PSoN
Arlo Will. Edgar Lee Masters. *Fr.* Spoon River Anthology.
  PBMP
Armada, The. Macaulay. FaPoR
Armada, 1588, The. John Wilson. OxBChV
Armadillo, The. Elizabeth Bishop. NoAM; NOBA; PiAm;
  TAP; VGW
Armageddon, Armageddon, *sel.* Paul Muldoon.
  "When Oisin came back to Ireland." CIP
Armagh. W. R. Rodgers. NoAM; PFIr
Armaments Race. Evangeline Paterson. AMV-81
Armed we go. we are the dancers. A Tryptych for Jan Bockelson.
  John Oliver Simon. NeAC
Armful, The. Robert Frost. CMoP (1970 ed.)
Armistice. Elizabeth Daryush. AMV-81
Armistice. Paul Dehn. OxBTC
Armistice Day. Patricia Beer. HeHu
Armless, The. Don Welch. AMV-81
Arms. Patricia Beer. HeHu
Arms and the Boy. Wilfred Owen. CABA (1972 ed.); CMoP
  (1970 ed.); HAP; ILP (1975 ed.); IP; LFH; OAEL-2; OBP;
  PBMP; PoIA; WeW
Arms, and the man I sing, who forc'd by fate. Virgil, *tr. by*
  Dryden. *Fr.* The Aeneid, I. OBVE
Arms seem clumsy at first, The. The Fever Toy. Charles Wright.
  AmPA
Armstrong Spring Creek. Lloyd Davis. AMV-81
Army Buddy Used to Say, An. John L. Sellers. DNGG
Army Corps on the March, An. Walt Whitman. InPS; PiAm;
  PPoe
Army Goes Rolling Along, The, *with music.* Edmund L. Gruber
  *and* H. W. Arberg. BLSH
Army of the Lord. I'm a Soldier in the Army of the Lord.
  *Unknown.* AmFP
Army returned home wet with sunlight, The. One Night Away
  from Day. John Digby. EAS
Arnold, warm with God. The Last Warmth of Arnold. Gregory
  Corso. NoAM; SA
Around, above my bed, the pitch-dark fly. Truth. Howard
  Nemerov. CoPAm; HoPM (1975 ed.); ILP (1975 ed.)
Around, around,/ All directions go around. The Direction. May
  Miller. PPoD
Around, around the sun we go. Mother Goose's Garland.
  Archibald MacLeish. OBAL
Around his open grave from near and far. Harry Edward Mills.
  *Fr.* Convicted. PeD
Around islands of jade and malachite. The Wave Symphony.
  Arthur Davison Ficke. *Fr.* Four Japanese Paintings. PoA
Around me roar and crash the pagan isms. The Pagan Isms.
  Claude McKay. BPo
Around me the images of thirty years. The Municipal Gallery
  Revisited. W. B. Yeats. OxBTC
Around Thanksgiving. Rolfe Humphries. OFD
Around the bend we streaked it with the leaders swingin' wide.
  The Oro Stage. Henry Herbert Knibbs. BPAW

Around the Block. Keith Waldrop. AMV-80
Around the Corner. *Unknown.* FSW
Around the fire one wintry night. The Beggar Man. Lucy Aikin.
  OxBChV
Around the fireplace, pointing at the fire. On Falling Asleep by
  Firelight. William Meredith. NoAM
Around the quays, kicked off in twos. Fishing Boats in
  Martigues. Roy Campbell. FaBoEE
Around the Year. Sara Coleridge. *See* Months, The.
Around them my cleanliness stinks. At Every Gas Station There
  Are Mechanics. Stephen Dunn. NVAP
Around us speeches of birds. I tremble. Lines to a Tree. Judah
  Leib Teller, *tr. by* Gabriel Preil *and* Howard Schwartz. VWA
A-Roving ("In Amsterdam there lived a maid"). *Unknown.*
  FSW; GSB, *with music*
Arraign'd before his worldly gods. The Execution of Cornelius
  Vane. Sir Herbert Read. NoAM
Arraignment of a Lover, The. George Gascoigne. AAS
Arraignment of Paris, The, *sel.* George Peele.
  Oenone and Paris. NOBE
Arrangements with Earth for Three Dead Friends. James Wright.
  NIL
Arrest of Oscar Wilde at the Cadogan Hotel, The. John
  Betjeman. AIW; CMoP (1970 ed.); EBEV; ILP (1975 ed.);
  NoAM; OxBTC
Arrival. John Wain. EBEV
Arrival at the Waldorf. Wallace Stevens. NYP
Arrival in Hell. Ricarda Huch, *tr. fr. German by* Susan C. Strong.
  PBWP
Arrival, New York Harbor. Robert Peters. GOA
Arrival of My Mother, The. Keith Wilson. GP
Arrival of the Bee Box, The. Sylvia Plath. PSN; TCP
Arrivals. Stewart Conn. SLP
Arrivals at a Watering-Place. Winthrop Mackworth Praed.
  NOBL
Arrive. The Ladies from the Ladies' Betterment League. The
  Lovers of the Poor. Gwendolyn Brooks. BiP; CAPP;
  NoAM; NOBA
Arrived upon the downs of asphodel. Classic Encounter.
  "Christopher Caudwell." "OxBTC
Arriving. Daniel Halpern. HoPM (1975 ed.)
Arriving. Gabriel Preil, *tr. fr. Hebrew by* Robert Friend. VWA
Arriving back in San Francisco. Letter to the Chronicle. Bob
  Kaufman. UsP
Arrow and the Song, The. Longfellow. CTV; PCOP
Arrow of Desire, The. *Gond Oral Tradition, tr. by* V. Elwin *and* S.
  Hivale. WTO
Arrowheads. Leona Gom. AMV-81
Arrows of the narrow moon flock down direct, The. Communion
  of Saints: The Poor Bastard under The Bridge. Marie
  Ponsot. VGW
Arrowy Dreams. Witter Bynner. GOA
Arroyo. Tom Weatherly. PoBA
Ars. Marina Tsvetayeva, *tr. fr. Russian by* Willis Barnstone *and*
  Edward Brown. BoWoP
Ars Longa Which is crueller. The Peacock Room. Robert
  Hayden. FB; WasP
Ars Poetica. Horace. *See* Art of Poetry, The.
Ars Poetica. X. J. Kennedy. NIL
Ars Poetica. Archibald MacLeish. BiP; CMoP (1970 ed.); HAP;
  HeIP; HoPM (1975 ed.); ILP (1975 ed.); InPK; IPWM; NIL;
  NOBA; PAIC; PiAm; PoA; PoIA; SFF; SoSe; TAP; TH;
  WIF
Ars Poetica. Arturo Trías, *tr. fr. Spanish by* Julio Marzán. InW
Ars Poetica. Adam Wazyk, *tr. fr. Polish by* Isaac Komem. VWA
Ars Poetica: Some Recent Criticism. James Wright. CAAP

Ars Victrix. Austin Dobson, *after the French of* Théophile Gautier. VLP

Arsenal at Springfield, The. Longfellow. ILP (1975 ed.)

Arsonist of flesh, An. A Small Tribute. William Harrold. HeS

Art. Ambrose Bierce. InPK

Art. Hjalmar Flax, *tr. fr. Spanish by* Julio Marzán. InW

Art. Denise Levertov. CAPP

Art. Herman Melville. NOBA; PPM

Art and Civilization. Robert Conquest. NoAM

Art and Reality. James Simmons. CIP

Art as meagre as a quilt, An. The Spare Quilt. John Peale Bishop. GOA

Art Gallery. John Dickson. AMV-81

Art in America. Theodore Weiss. AMV-80

Art Lesson, The. Robert Morgan. HeHu

Art Market: Leopoldville. Michael Jackson. ATNZ

Art of Biography, The. E. C. Bentley. *Fr.* Clerihews. NOBL

Art of Enforced Deprivation, The. Alta. GP; MMD

Art of Happiness, The. Edward Young. *Fr.* Night Thoughts, VIII. POL

Art of losing isn't hard to master, The. One Art. Elizabeth Bishop. HAP

Art of Love, The. Richard Grossman. AMV-81

Art of Love, The, *sels.* Kenneth Koch.
"Life is full of horrors and hormones." GP
"To win the love of women one should first discover." NNaP

Art of Picasso, The. Salvador Dali, *tr. fr. Spanish by* David Gascoyne. EAS

Art of Poetry, The. Darrell Gray. AcAn

Art of Poetry, The, *sels.* Horace, *tr. fr. Latin.*
"As woods whose change appeares," *tr. by* Ben Jonson. OBVE
"Should some ill painter, in a wild design," *tr. by* John Oldham. OBVE

Art of Poetry, The. Dennis Trudell. NowV

Art of Rowing, The. John Elsberg. PoUp

Art of Sinking in Poetry, The, *sel.* Pope.
"Who knocks at the door?" AnMo

Art of the Sonnet, *sel.* Gil Orlovitz.
"Night comes. Day runs for its life into my eyes." PoA

Art on the Swing-Shift, Truck Assembly. Eric Johnson. PoW

Art thou a Statist in the van. A Poet's Epitaph. Wordsworth. MBPR

Art thou afraid the adorer's prayer. Walter Savage Landor. GBL

Art thou gone in haste? Love Pursued. *Unknown. Fr.* The Thracian Wonder. GBL

Art thou pale for weariness. To the Moon. Shelley. MBPR; Moon; PBMP; PPP

Art thou poor, yet hast thou golden slumbers? Thomas Dekker. *Fr.* The Pleasant Comedy of Patient Grissell, I, i. HAP; InPS; UnPo (1976 ed.)

Artemis, Artemis: there is fading. The Night-Walker. Horace Gregory. Moon

Artery, The. Les A. Murray. *Fr.* Walking to the Cattle-Place. CAAP

Artery of the Sea. Napoleon St. Cyr. FAF

Arthritic farmer and a calf watch Dr. Graves, The. These Obituaries of Rattlesnakes Being Eaten by the Hogs. Roger Weingarten. AmPA

Arthur McBride. *Unknown.* GBP; PeBB

Arthur Mitchell. Marianne Moore. PiAm

Arthur O'Bower has broken his bands. *Unknown.* GBP

Arthur Ridgewood, M.D. Frank Marshall Davis. BPo

Artillery. George Herbert. InPS

Artisan didn't collect his gear and say, The. The Makers. Richard Kell. CIP; PFIr

Artist, An. Robinson Jeffers. VGW

Artist, The. William Carlos Williams. InPS; TPo

Artist is the creator of beautiful things, The. Preface to the Picture of Dorian Gray. Oscar Wilde. WIF

Artist must leave these woods now, The. The Departure. Reed Whittemore. TAP

Artist Underground, The. Ann Stanford. MPA

Artistry. Robert T. Kasold. DNGG

Artorius, *sels.* John Heath-Stubbs.
"Age of Bronze awoke now in brutality, The." EBEV
"It was the virgin Zennora, who dwelt." EBEV

Arts and Sciences, *sels.* Samuel Butler.
"Nature/ leaks like a tub and not a boat." SCP-2
"Rules/ Were made for novices and fools." SCP-2

Art's Variety. David McFadden. NeAC

Arundel Tomb, An. Philip Larkin. HeIP; MPo; PPP

As a/ child crawls. Home/Grown. Ralph Storey. SES

As a bathtub lined with white porcelain. The Bathtub. Ezra Pound. NIL

As a beauty I'm not a great star. The Face. Anthony Euwer. OBAL

As a Black Child I was a dreamer. Four Sheets to the Wind and a One-Way Ticket to France, 1933. Conrad Kent Rivers. AmNP (1974 ed.); CABA (1972 ed.). *See also* As a child/ I bought a red scarf.

As a boy. Now I Am a Man. Russell Marano. AMV-80

As a boy I collected stamps. On Seeing a Stamp from the Democratic Republic of Vietnam. Leslie Woolf Hedley. NowV

As a boy with a richness of needs I wandered. Clifford Dyment. OxBTC

As a boy you outdrove the masters. To an Aging Charioteer. Leontius Scholasticus, *tr. by* Tom Dodge. LiSp

As a child/ I bought a red scarf. Four Sheets to the Wind and a One-Way Ticket to France. Conrad Kent Rivers. BPo; PoBA

As a child/ I thought nests. Nests. Bruce Weber. PoUp

As a child I was. Woman. Elouise Loftin. PoBA

As a child of cedar, hemlock, and the sea. No One Remembers Abandoning the Village of White Fir. Duane Niatum. CDW

As a child running loose. Learning To Speak. Peter Everwine. NNaP

As a Child Seeing a Cardinal. John Gill. NeAC

As a child, they could not keep me from wells. Personal Helicon. Seamus Heaney. HeHu; IPM

As a critic the poet Buchanan. On Robert Buchanan, Who Attacked Him under the Pseudonym of "Thomas Maitland." Dante Gabriel Rossetti. FaBoEE

As a dare-gale skylark scanted in a dull cage. The Caged Skylark. Gerard Manley Hopkins. AnMo; CMoP (1970 ed.); ILP (1975 ed.); SoSe

As a decrepit father takes delight. Sonnets, XXXVII. Shakespeare. STS

As a fond mother, when the day is o'er. Nature. Longfellow. AmVN; TAP

As a friend to the children commend me the Yak. The Yak. Hilaire Belloc. NOBL; OxBChV

As a gray hawk's eyes. Hawk's Eyes. Yvor Winters. PoA

As a Great Prince. Edwin Honig. NoAM

As a Jew in New Mexico. A View of the Organ Mountains North of Las Cruces, New Mexico. Gene Frumkin. FoP

As a kid I believed in democracy: I. John Berryman. PPoD

As a little fat man of Bombay. *Unknown.* OxBChV

As a naked man I go. Waste Places. James Stephens. PPM

As a pale phantom with a lamp. Moonlight. Longfellow. Moon

As a Plane Tree by the Water.  Robert Lowell.  CMoP (1970 ed).; NoAM; NOBA

As a Possible Lover.  Amiri Baraka.  AmNP (1974 ed.)

As a principle underlying the apple, the road.  Apple.  Dave Morice.  AcAn

As a rare painter draws, for pleasure, here.  1st Week 5th Day. Joshua Sylvester.  *Fr.* Du Bartas His Divine Weeks and Works.  SCP-2

As a sloop with a sweep of immaculate wing on her delicate spine.  Buick.  Karl Shapiro.  BiP; CMoP (1970 ed.); HoPM (1975 ed.)

As a white candle.  The Old Woman.  Joseph Campbell.  OxBTC; WIF

As Adam Early in the Morning.  Walt Whitman.  AmVN

As an egg, when broken, never.  Thomas Holley Chivers.  *Fr.* To Allegra Florence in Heaven.  PeD

As an intruder I trudged with careful innocence.  Old Mansion. John Crowe Ransom.  NOBA

As an old traveller, I am indebted to paper-bound thrillers. Calling Spring VII-MMMC.  Ogden Nash.  FaBoCo

As an unperfect actor on the stage.  Sonnets, XXIII. Shakespeare.  BiP; OBP

As are the sandes (faire Licia) on the shore.  Giles Fletcher the Elder.  Licia, XVII.  ESo

As Aubry worked by candles.  Artistry.  Robert T. Kasold. DNGG

As aw was gannin to Durham.  Durham Old Women.  *Unknown.* GBP

As Bad as a Mile.  Philip Larkin.  InPK

As beautiful Kitty one morning was tripping.  Kitty of Coleraine. *Unknown.*  PoTa

As bird to nest, when, moodily.  Sarasvati.  James Stephens. NoAM

As Birds Are Fitted to the Boughs.  Louis Simpson.  BoLoP; OLR; WIF

As bold Mirmillo the grey dawn descries.  Sir Samuel Garth.  *Fr.* The Dispensary.  PMW

As by the streams of Babylon.  Psalm CXXXVII.  Bible, *O.T.*, *paraphrased by* Thomas Campion.  OAEL-1

As Camels Who Have Become Thirsty.  Ilmi Bowndheri, *tr. fr. Somali by* M. F. Abdillahi *and* B. W. Andrzejewski.  WTO

As careful mothers do to sleeping lay.  On the Deputy of Ireland's Child.  Sir John Davies.  FaBoEE

As clever Tom Clinch, while the Rabble was bawling.  Clever Tom Clinch Going to Be Hanged.  Swift.  FaBoBa; ILP (1975 ed.); NIL

As commanded, I looked for my origin.  The Search.  Michael Hamburger.  VWA

As Concerning Man.  Alexander Radcliffe.  OBSV

As cool as the pale wet leaves.  Alba.  Ezra Pound.  GBL; HAP; PiAm; WeW

As darkness/ is my shelter.  The Voice of the Power of This World.  Gregory Hall.  NU

As day did darken on the dewless grass.  The Wind at the Door. William Barnes.  GBL

As difference blends into identity.  Josephine Miles.  NoAM

As doctors give physic by way of prevention.  For My Own Monument [*or* For His Own Epitaph].  Matthew Prior. FaBoEE; ILP (1975 ed.)

As Down a Lone Valley, *with music.*  Timothy Dwight.  AH

As down the road she wambled slow.  Bessie Bobtail.  James Stephens.  PFIr

As down the torrent of an angry flood.  The Story of the Pot and the Kettle.  Charles Montagu.  APAS

As down through Cupid's garden for pleasure I did walk.  The 'Prentice Boy.  *Unknown.*  AmFP

As down through Moore's field one evening I went.  The Silk Weaver's Daughter.  *Unknown.*  AmFP

As down thru Sally's garden one evening as I chanced to stray. Sally's Garden.  *Unknown.*  AmFP

As, even today, the airman, feeling the plane sweat.  Icarus. Valentin Iremonger.  BIrV; CIP

As fair as morn, as fresh as May.  *Unknown.*  GBL

As far as statues go, so far there's not.  From Trollope's Journal. Elizabeth Bishop.  GOA

As far from Africa as home.  The Cheetah.  Harold Witt.  PoW

As fast as thou shalt wane, so fast thou grow'st.  Sonnets, XI. Shakespeare.  STS

As Flows the Rapid River, *with music.*  Samuel Francis Smith. AH

As fly the shadows o'er the grass.  The Irish Wolf-Hound.  Denis Florence McCarthy.  GDP

As for me/I have seen Llywelyn.  A Day Which Endures Not. Arthur Glyn Prys-Jones.  OBW

As for me, my Nanna ignores me.  Condemning the Moongod Nanna.  Enheduanna, *tr. fr. Sumerian.*  BoWoP

As Freedom Is a Breakfastfood.  E. E. Cummings.  CMoP (1970 ed.); MAT; NOBA; TAP; VGW

As from an [*or* their] ancestral oak.  Similes for Two Political Characters of 1819.  Shelley.  InPS; MBPR

As from the darkening gloom a silver dove.  Sonnet on the Death of a Friend.  Keats.  MBPR; PIM

As from the Dorset shore I travell'd home.  The White Horse of Westbury.  Charles Tennyson Turner.  EBEV; VLP

As gay for you to take your father's ax.  To a Young Wretch. Robert Frost.  OFD

As Gentle Dews Distill, *with music.*  George Rogers.  AH

As grit swirls in the wind the word spreads.  The Center of Attention.  Daniel Hoffman.  UnPo (1976 ed.)

As growth of form or momentary glance.  Transfigured Life. Dante Gabriel Rossetti.  The House of Life, LX.  VLP

As he climbs down our hill, my kestrel rises.  Esyllt.  Glyn Jones. OBW

As he comes from one of those small houses.  The Fisherman. George Bruce.  MS

As He Lay Dying.  Randolph Stow.  BoAnP

As he learned the land.  The Farmer.  Terry Stokes.  POL

As he left the ship he saw this, only this.  The Descent of the Vulture.  Marya Zaturenska.  WPE

As he moves the mine-detector.  Hunting Civil War Relics at Nimblewill Creek.  James Dickey.  ConAP; GOA

As he said vanity, so vain say I.  The Vanity of All Worldly Things.  Anne Bradstreet.  EAP

As he that loves oft looks on the dear form.  On the "Vita Nuova" of Dante.  Dante Gabriel Rossetti.  VLP

As he trudged along to school.  The Story of Johnny Head-in-Air. Heinrich Hoffmann.  OxBChV

As Hermes once took to his feathers light.  On a Dream.  Keats. LoAs

As Hoosier.  Biographical Sketch.  Charles S. Bouslog.  PHC

As I am,/ I should be able to.  Missing Beat.  Carolyn M. Rodgers.  JB

As I am a Rhymer.  On My Joyful Departure.  Samuel Taylor Coleridge.  FaBoCo

As I Am My Father's.  Rose Drachler.  VWA

As I came down from Cundiyo.  Cundiyo.  Alice Corbin.  WPW

As I came down Talbingo Hill.  Bullocky Bill.  *Unknown.* MAuV

As I came down the Cano' gate.  Merry May the Keel Row. *Unknown.*  GBP

As I came home through Drury's woods.  Cold Fear.  Elizabeth Madox Roberts.  WPE

As I came in by Tiviot side. The Generous Gentleman. Allan Ramsay. SLP

As I came in by Turra market. Barnyards of Delgaty. *Unknown.* FSW

As I came out of the New York Public Library. Nuns in the Wind. Muriel Rukeyser. NNaP

As I came over the humpbacked hill. The Green Fiddler. Rachel Field. PoTa

As I came through Sandgate. The Keel Row. *Unknown.* PoPle

As I came to the edge of the woods. Come In. Robert Frost. ILP (1975 ed.); NOBA; PoIA

As I descended black, impassive rivers. The Drunken Boat. Arthur Rimbaud, *tr. by* Stepan Stepanchev. NAWM-2

As I did the washing one day. The Shirt of a Lad. *Unknown, tr. fr. Welsh.* OBW

As I dreamed my stature (mad dream!). Jerome Rothenberg. *Fr.* The Counter-Dances of Darkness. FoP

As I drive to the junction of lane and highway. At Castle Boterel. Thomas Hardy. EBEV; NOBE

As I Ebb'd with the Ocean of Life. Walt Whitman. NOBA; TAP

As I gaed doon by the twa mill dams i' the mornin'. The Water-Hen. Violet Jacob. MS

As I Gird on for Fighting. A. E. Housman. CMoP (1970 ed.); TT

As I grow more and more each day. My Aim. Alexander Seymour. CTV

As I Grow Older and Fatten on Myself. Joseph Carson. AMV-80

As I in hoary winter's night stood shivering in the snow. The Burning Babe. Robert Southwell. BoReV; CABA (1972 ed.); HAP; HeIP; ILP (1975 ed.); InPS; NIL; NOBE; OAEL-1; OBP; PPoe; Prf

As I lay asleep in Italy. The Mask of Anarchy. Shelley. MBPR; OBSV

As I lay in a winter's night. The Debate of the Body and the Soul. *Unknown.* PAIC

As I Lay with My Head in Your Lap Camerado. Walt Whitman. BuTh

As I lie alone. *Unknown.* SFF

As I lie here in the sun. Jonah. Randall Jarrell. CoPAm

As I look in the mirror. An Israeli Soldier's Nightmare. Alison B. Carb. AMV-80

As I look out from the desk window. Laura St. Martin. FF

As I looked out of my window. Run Little Dogies. *Unknown.* BPAW

As I looked out one May morning. The Princess and the Gypsies. Frances Cornford. PoTa

As I mark a set of essays. Assignment: Descriptive Essay. Gary Willis. AMV-81

As I one evening sat before my cell. Artillery. George Herbert. InPS

As I pass her house, Martha bends over. Woman in the Window. Dennis M. Gaughan. PoUp

As I pass through my incarnations in every age and race. The Gods of the Copybook Headings. Kipling. FaPoR; OBP; OBSV; OxBTC

As I ran to catch a bus, my heart fell out. An Accident. Gael Turnbull. PMW

As I reach to close each book. Against the Evidence. David Ignatow. NNaP

As I ride, as I ride. Through the Metidja to Abd-el-Kadr. Robert Browning. PeD

As I rode out by Tom Sherman's bar-room. The Dying Cowboy. *Unknown.* FaBoBa; NIL

As I roved out impatiently. In the Ringwood. Thomas Kinsella. CMoP (1970 ed.); IPM

As I roved out on a May morning. Johnny's the Lad I Love. *Unknown.* AIW

As I roved out one summer's morning, speculating most curiously. Colleen Rue. *Unknown.* BIrV

As I sail home to Galveston. A Sailor's Song. Hazel Harper Harris. RhR

As I sat at the cafe, I said to myself. How Pleasant It Is to Have Money. Arthur Hugh Clough. *Fr.* Dipsychus. NOBE; OAEL-2; VPC

As I sat at the cafe, I said to myself. Spectator ab Extra [*Expanded version of* Dipsychus *sel.*]. Arthur Hugh Clough. FaBoCo

As I sat down one evening. The Frozen Logger. *Unknown.* FSW; OBAL

As I sat down one ev'nin' in a timber-town café. The Frozen Logger. *At. to* James Stevens. BPAW

As I sat down to breakfast in state. The Country Clergyman's Trip to Cambridge. Macaulay. OBSV

As I sat in a lonesome grove. The Little Dove. *Unknown.* AmFP

As I sat on a sunny bank. Sunny Bank. *Unknown.* GBP

As I sd to my/ friend. I Know a Man. Robert Creeley. CAPP; ConAP; CoPAm; Epi; InPK; InPS; MAT; NOBA; PPoD; PPP; TCP

As I sit looking out of a window of the building. The Instruction Manual. John Ashbery. HAP; NoAM; NOBA

As I Step over a Puddle at the End of Winter, I Think of an Ancient Chinese Governor. James Wright. CAPP; NIL; TCP; VOA

As I strole the city, oft I. Swift. *Fr.* The Legion Club. BIrV

As I strolled out one evening just as the sun went down. The Farmer and the Shanty Boy. *Unknown.* AmFP

As I strolled out one evening upon a night's career. The Fireship. *Unknown.* FSW

As I talk with learned people. A Spade Is Just a Spade. Walter Everette Hawkins. PoBA

As I view the leaf, my theme is not the shades of meaning. My Own House. David Ignatow. AMV-80; PCho

As I walked by a forest side. Stag-Hunt. *Unknown.* OxBM

As I walk'd by my self. *Unknown.* FaBoEE

As I walked down by the river. A Ballad for Katharine of Aragon. Charles Causley. FaBoTw (1975 ed.)

As I walked down on Broadway. Can't You Dance the Polka? *Unknown.* FSW

As I Walked Out. *Unknown. See* Git Along Little Dogies.

As I walked out in Dublin City. The Spanish Lady in Dublin City. *Unknown.* RDB

As I Walked Out in the Streets of Laredo. *Unknown. See* Cowboy's Lament, The

As I walked out of a London Bridge. Geordie. *Unknown.* FSW

As I Walked Out One Evening. W. H. Auden. AIW; FF; HeIP; InPK; IP; NOBE; PBMP; PoIA; UnPo (1976 ed.); WIF (Song: "As I walked out one evening.") OAEL-2

As I walked out one evening, all in the month of May. The Banks of Claudy. *Unknown.* AmFP

As I walked out one evening down by the Strawberry Lane. Captain Wedderburn's Courtship. *Unknown.* AmFP

As I walked out one May morning. The Lover Proved False. *Unknown.* AmFP

As I walked out one May morning. The Royal Fisherman. *Unknown.* GBP; PeBB

As I Walked Out One Morning. *Unknown.* AmFP

As I walked out one morning early. *See* As I went out one morning early, to breathe the sweet and pleasant air.

As I walked out one morning for pleasure. *See* As I was a-walking one morning for pleasure.

As I walked out one morning in May.   Archie O Cawfield.
*Unknown.*   AmFP

As I walked out one morning, just as day was dawning.   As I
Walked Out One Morning.   *Unknown.*   AmFP

As I walked out one summer's day to view the fields and the
lizards springing.   The Husband with No Courage in Him.
*Unknown.*   FSW

As I walked out over London Bridge.   Georgie.   *Unknown.*   GSB

As I walked out that sultry night.   Full Moon.   Robert Graves.
NOBE

As I walked over London Bridge.   Georgie.   *Unknown.*   AIW

As I walked with my friend.   Columbus.   Louis Simpson.   MPo

As I wandered on the beach.   The Great Blue Heron.   Carolyn
Kizer.   WPE

As I wandered through the eight hundred and eight streets of the
city.   Streets.   Amy Lowell.   RiTi; SBG

As I was a-goin' over Gilgary Mountain.   Whiskey in the Jar.
*Unknown.*   FSW

As I was a-gwine down the road.   *See* As I was goin' . . .

As I was a-hoeing, a-hoeing my land.   The Six Badgers.   Robert
Graves.   RAE

As I was a-roving one morning in spring.   The Mantle So Green.
*Unknown.*   AmFP

As I was a-walking/ One morning in spring.   The Pretty
Ploughboy.   *Unknown.*   AIW; GBP

As I was a-walking by Saint James Hospital.   Young Man Cut
Down in His Prime. (St. James Hospital).   *Unknown.*   FSW

As I was a-walking [*or* walked out] one morning for pleasure.   Git
Along Little Dogies [*or* Whoopee-Ti-Yi-Yo].   *Unknown.*
BLSH; BPAW; FSW

As I was a-walking to Nottingham Fair.   Nottingham Fair.
*Unknown.*   AmFP

As I was fishing off Pondy Point.   Jim Desterland.   Hyam
Plutzik.   VGW

As I was goin' [*or* a-gwine] down the road.   Turkey in the Straw.
*Unknown.*   BLSo; GBP

As I was going by Charing Cross.   King Charles the First.
*Unknown.*   GBP

As I was going down the lane.   Ballad of No Proper Man.
Daniel Hoffman.   MAT

As I Was Going Out One Day.   *Unknown.*   CaYB

As I was going over Mulberry Mountain.   Mulberry Mountain.
*Unknown.*   AmFP

As I was going through Windy Gap.   Windy Gap.   David
Campbell.   GAS

As I was going to Derby.   The Derby Ram.   *Unknown.*
FaBoNo; GBP

As I was going to St. Ives.   Mother Goose.   MG

As I was going to work that morning.   Armistice Day.   Patricia
Beer.   HeHu

As I was going up the hill.   Jack the Piper.   *Unknown.*   GBP

As I was going up the stair.   The Little Man Who Wasn't There
[*or* A Case].   Hughes Mearns.   CTV; FaBoCo

As I Was Laying on the Green.   *Unknown.*   InPK

As I was musing by myself alone.   Mirth and Melancholy.
Margaret Cavendish, Duchess of Newcastle.   WPE

As I was walkin' an' a-ramblin' one day.   The Wild Rippling
Water.   *Unknown.*   FaBoBa

As I was sitting by the fire, talking to old Reilly's daughter.
Reilly's Daughter.   *Unknown.*   FSW

As I was sitting with a jug and spoon.   The Jug of Punch.
Francis McPeake.   FSW

As I was travelling toward the city of satisfactions.   The City of
Satisfactions.   Daniel Hoffman.   Prf

As I was wa'king all alone.   *See* As I was walking all alone.

As I was walking/ I came upon.   Kore.   Robert Creeley.
ConAP; InPK; InPS

As I was walking all alane.   The Twa Corbies.   *Unknown.*   AIW;
CABA (1972 ed.); Epi; ExPo (1973 ed.); FaBoBa; HAP; ILP
(1975 ed.); InPK; LFH; PAIC; PBMP; PoPle; PoTa; PPP;
SoSe; UnPo (1976 ed.)

As I was walking [*or* wa'king] all alone [*or* alane].   The Wee Wee
Man.   *Unknown.*   AIW; EBEV; GBP; OAEL-1; PeBB

As I was walking all alone.   The Little Wee Man.   Ian Serraillier.
FPB

As I was walking among the fires of hell.   A Memorable Fancy.
Blake.   *Fr.* The Marriage of Heaven and Hell.   NU

As I was walking down by the seashore.   The Lover's Lament for
Her Sailor.   *Unknown.*   AmFP

As I was walking down the street.   Buffalo Gals.   *Unknown.*
BLSo; FSW

As I was walking in the fields last Tuesday.   The Slender Lad.
*Unknown, tr. by* Kenneth Jackson.   OBW

As I was walking on iambic feet.   Terrible Dactyl, Son of Rodan.
Edward Proffitt.   PoIA

As I was washing under a span.   The Lover's Shirt.   *Unknown, tr.
by* Gwyn Williams.   BuTh

As I watch the moon.   Native African Revolutionaries.   Paul
Jones.   AMV-80

As I watch you leave again.   Souvenirs.   Melvin Dixon.   NW

As I went a-walking one fine summer's morning.   The Shoofly.
Felix O'Hare.   AmFP

As I went by St. James's, I heard a bird sing.   An Excellent New
Ballad Called the Prince of Darkness.   *Unknown.*   APAS

As I Went Down to David's Town, *with music.*   George Craig
Stewart.   AH

As I went down to Dymchurch Wall.   In Romney Marsh.   John
Davidson.   OxBTC; PES; PoPle

As I went down to the huckleberry picnic.   The Kicking Mule.
*Unknown.*   AmFP

As I went down to the mowin' field.   Fod.   *Unknown.*   AmFP

As I went eastward, while the zun did zet.   Lowshot Light.
William Barnes.   VLP

As I went out a crow.   The Last Word of a Bluebird.   Robert
Frost.   LCL; PCOP; RAE; SO

As I went out a-walking to breathe the pleasant air.   Rolly
Trudum.   *Unknown.*   AmFP

As I went out in Dublin City.   Wheel of Fortune.   *Unknown.*
FSW

As I went out one May morning.   Bird in a Cage.   *Unknown.*
GBP

As I went [*or* walked] out one morning early, to breathe the sweet
and pleasant air.   John Riley   *Unknown.*   FSW; GSB

As I went out one morning to take the pleasant air.   Lolly-Too-
Dum.   *Unknown.*   FSW

As I went out, so I came in.   *Unknown.*   GBP

As I went out to walk.   Elizabeth Riddell.   *Fr.* Country Tunes.
GAS

As I went out walking for pleasure one day.   The Little Mohea.
*Unknown.*   AmFP

As I went out walking upon a fine day.   Little Mohee.   *Unknown.*
FSW

As I went owre the Hill o' Hoos.   *Unknown.*   GBP

As I went up the humber jumber.   *Unknown.*   FaBoNo

As I went up to Craigbilly Fair.   Craigbilly Fair.   *Unknown.*
GBP

As I were a-walking upon a fine day.   Because I Were Shy.
*Unknown.*   PoTa

As I wipe the dust off my face.   The Unexpected.   Ai.   CAAP

As I work at the pump, the wind heavy.   Mother.   Seamus
Heaney.   IPM

As if a cast of grain leapt back to the hand.   An Event.   Richard
Wilbur.   CoPAm

As If a Phantom Caress'd Me.   Walt Whitman.   GBL

As if engraved upon the dawn. Storm's End. Leonora Speyer. TH

As if he had been poured. The Grauballe Man. Seamus Heaney. CIP

As if I carried a charm. Her Going. Shirley Kaufman. RiTi

As if I didn't have enough. Small Aircraft. Bella Akhmadulina, *tr. by* Daniel Halpern. BoWoP

As if I needed some means to maintain. The Dodo. Edward Kessler. PPoD

As if it were a scene made-up by the mind. Often I Am Permitted to Return to a Meadow. Robert Duncan. CmoP (1970 ed.); HeIP; NOBA; NU; PiAm

As if somebody ordered it. Tashkent Breaks into Bloom. Anna Akhmatova, *tr. by* Richard McKane. BoWoP

As if stone Caesar shook. Fragment. Hugh McCrae. GAS

As if to symptoms we may credit give. Michael Drayton. *Fr.* To Master George Sandys, Treasurer for the English Colony in Virginia. SCP-2

As If Trooth. Robert Bloom. AATT

As If You Had Never Been. Richard Eberhart. UsP

As imperceptibly as grief. Emily Dickinson. CMoP (1970 ed.); FSFS; NOBA; PBWP

As in a pot the milk turns sour. The Shattering of Love. *Gond Oral Tradition, tr. by* V. Elwin *and* S. Hivale. WTO

As in the cool-air'd road I come by. My Love's Guardian Angel. William Barnes. GBL

As in the house I sate. Poverty. Thomas Traherne. Prf

As in the Land of Darkness. Robert Miklitsch. AMV-80

As in the lonely night. The Setting of the Moon. Giacomo Leopardi, *tr. by* John Heath-Stubbs. Moon

As in Their Time. Louis MacNeice. POL

As incense smoke thins, a stupendous. God's Measurements. Laurence Lieberman. PCho

As into the Garden. A. E. Housman. PoTa

As inward love breeds outward talk. The Angler's Song. Izaak Walton. LiSp

As it befell on a bright holiday. The Bitter Withy. *Unknown.* GBP; PeBB

As it fell one holy-day. Little Musgrave and Lady Barnard. *Unknown.* FaBoBa; PeBB

As it fell out on a Holy Day. The Bitter Withy. *Unknown.* FaBoBa

As it fell out one May morning. The Holy Well. *Unknown.* GBP; PeBB

As it fell out upon a day. Dives and Lazarus. *Unknown.* FaBoBa

As It Fell upon a Day. Thomas Hood. BBL

As it fell upon a day. Philomel. Richard Barnfield. *Fr.* The Passionate Pilgrim. GBL; NOBE

As it fell upon a day. A Vision of Truth. J. C. Squire. NOBL

As it is cold in the room and early morning. As the Snow Falls, Another Breathes in an Adjoining Room. Elizabeth Wray. PoUp

As It Looked Then. E. A. Robinson. CMoP (1970 ed.); NoAM

As It Should Be. Tom Meschery. SPo

As Jack, the jolly plowboy, was plowing of his land. The Jolly Plowboy. *Unknown.* AmFP

As Jack walked out of London city. Jack the Jolly Tar. *Unknown.* AmFP

As Joseph was a-walking. The Cherry Tree Carol. *Unknown.* PChr

As Julia once a-slumbering lay. The Captived Bee; or, The Little Filcher. Robert Herrick. CaPo; SCP-1

As kingfishers catch fire, dragonflies draw flame. Gerard Manley Hopkins. CMoP (1970 ed.); EBEV; VLP

As Lambs into the Pen. Dorothy Wellesley. FaBoTw (1975 ed.)

As landscapes richen after rain, the eye. Foliage of Vision. James Merrill. VGW

As late I lay in slumber's shadowy vale. Burke. Samuel Taylor Coleridge. *Fr.* Sonnets on Eminent Characters. MBPR

As late I rambled in the happy fields. To a Friend Who Sent Me Some Roses [*or* The Musk Rose]. Keats. MBPR; PF

As long as I continue weeping. Sonnet. Louise Labé, *tr. by* Joan Keefe *and* Richard Terdiman. PBWP

As long as I live. Me. Walter de la Mare. CTV

As Long as the Heart Beats. Christine Zawadiwsky. AMV-81

As long as they were standing, they were all that passion dares. The Cubistic Lovers. Charles Edward Eaton. AMV-81

As long as we look forward, all seems free. The Western Approach. Howard Nemerov. TAP

As love and I, late harbour'd in one inn. Michael Drayton. GBL

As loving hind that (hartless) wants her deer. A Letter to Her Husband, Absent upon Public Employment. Anne Bradstreet. SBG; SCP-2; WPE

As magicians' swords pierce wicker baskets. Prison Dorm. Robert T. Kasold. DNGG

As May was opening the rosebuds. Birth of the Foal. Ferenc Juhász, *tr. by* David Wevill. BoAnP; PH

As men oft laugh at little babes when they. Michael Drayton. *Fr.* To My Noble Friend Master William Browne: of the Evil Time. SCP-2

As much as he could learn has done no good. Lesson of the Master. William Dickey. CoPAm

As much for the seatide ages of my sons. The Alchemical Cupboard. Asa Benveniste. VWA

As my eyes search the prairie. Spring Song. *Tr. fr. Chippewa by* Frances Densmore. OBVE

As my father before my I dream. Dream of Southern Roads. William Claire. PoUp

As my new life begins, I start smiling at the people around me. Farewell to Kurdistan. Rosemary Tonks. OxBTC

As "Name of individual, partnership, or corporation to whom paid." Royalties. D. J. Enright. NOBL

As Nature H——'s clay was blending. On a Certain Effeminate Peer. John Winstanley. FaBoEE

As Near to Eden. Robert Francis. PoIA

As needy gallants in the scriv'ners' hands. Dryden. Amboyna; or, The Cruelties of the Dutch to the English Merchants, prologue. OBSV

As night creates the sun, silence. The Roads. Stephen Stepanchev. SA

As on a dark guitar. Ballad of Love and Blood. Angel Miguel Queremel, *tr. by* Rolfe Humphries. LoAs

As on a window late I cast mine eye. Love-Joy. George Herbert. OAEL-1

As on the cross, the Saviour hung. Deep Spring. *Unknown.* AmFP

As on the highway's quiet edge. The Coast: Norfolk. Frances Cornford. OxBTC

As once, if not with light regard. Ode on the Poetical Character. William Collins. LAuP; OAEL-1

As one grows older and Caesar, Hitler. The Walk Home. Reed Whittemore. ConAP

As One Non-Combatant to Another. George Orwell. OxBTC

As One Put into the Packet-Boat. John Ashbery. HAP

As piles of sand disintegrate when sucked. Nothing to Lose. Joseph Kalar. SPT

As pilot well expert in perilous wave. Spenser. *Fr.* The Faerie Queene, II, 7. OAEL-1

As Planned. Frank O'Hara. UsP

As Pluto ruled the underworld. Neptune. Eleanor Farjeon. EcS

As pools beneath stone arches take. Invocation. John Drinkwater. PoA

As praiseworthy/ the power of breathing. Lorine Niedecker. VGW

As Ralph and Nick i'th'field were plowing. The Plowman. *Unknown.* APAS

As red as a starling's his peepers. The Opium-Den. *Malay Oral Tradition, tr. by* R. J. Wilkinson *and* R. O. Winstedt. WTO

As regions may be known by their moths. Protective Colors. William Logan. AMV-81

As Rocks Rooted. Howard G. Hanson. AMV-80

As round their dying father's bed. The Father and His Children. *Unknown.* OxBChV

As Sand. Natan Zach, *tr. fr. Hebrew by* Jon Silkin. VWA

As sea-foam blown of the winds, as blossom of brine that is drifted. "Home, Sweet Home," with Variations. H. C. Bunner. OBAL

As seventh sign, the antique heavens show. Feast of the Ram's Horn. Harvey Shapiro. VGW

As Shadows Cast by Cloud and Sun, *with music.* Bryant. AH

As she jumped up to open the door. Motionless Swaying. Yannis Ritsos, *tr. by* Nikos Stangos. TSWA

As she shook her little fist. The Death of the Novel. David Young. AmPa

As ships, becalmed at eve, that lay. Qua Cursum Ventus. Arthur Hugh Clough. VLP; VPC

As shows the air when with a rainbow graced. Upon Julia's Ribband. Robert Herrick. CaPo

As silent as a mirror is believed. Legend. Hart Crane. CABA (1972 ed.); NoAM

As simple an act. Way Out West. Amiri Baraka. ExPo (1973 ed.); PoBA

As Sisyphus against the infernal steep. Byron. *Fr.* English Bards and Scotch Reviewers. OBSV

As sleep comes I imagine I'm a carpenter. Nocturnes I. Dan Gerber. TC

As slowly and sadly I strayed by the river. Lost Jimmie Whalen. *Unknown.* AmFP

As snow in summer, and as rain in harvest. Bible, *O.T.* Proverbs, XXVI. BiP

As soft as silk, as white as milk. *Unknown.* GBP; PoPle

As some brave admiral, in former war. The Disabled Debauchee. Earl of Rochester. BoLoP; CABA (1972 ed.); HAP; NIL; NOBL; OBSV; PPP; WeW

As some day it may happen that a victim must be found. They'll None of 'Em Be Missed. W. S. Gilbert. *Fr.* The Mikado. VLP

As some fond virgin, whom her mother's care. Epistle to Miss Blount, on Her Leaving the Town after the Coronation. Pope. BoLoP; EBEV; NOBE; PPP; SoSe

As some women love jewels. Ode to a Lebanese Crock of Olives. Diane Wakoski. GP

As soon as/ I speak, I. The Pattern. Robert Creeley. PPoD

As soon as he came home, straightway Pygmalion did repair. Pygmalion's Statue Comes to Life. Ovid, *tr. by* Arthur Golding. OAEL-1

As soon as I could I have called you together. The Queen's Speech. Arthur Mainwaring APAS

As soon as I lie down in my soft bed. Sonnet IX. Louise Labé, *tr. by* Willis Barnstone. BoWoP

As soon as I'm in bed at night. Mrs. Brown. Rose Fyleman. OxBChV

As Spring the Winter Doth Succeed. Anne Bradstreet. *See* Meditation: "As spring the winter doth succeed."

As summer ends and leaves fall like dust. A Cantor's Dream before the High Holy Days. Martin Robbins. VWA

As, sum tyme, dois the curser stert and ryn. Virgil, *tr. by* Gavin Douglas. *Fr.* The Aeneid, XI. OBVE

As Sun, as Sea. James Sullivan. AMV-81

As sunbeams pierce the glass and, streaming in. The Virgin Mary. Robert Herrick. SCP-1

As sunbeams stream through liberal space. Woodnotes, II. Emerson. NOBA

"As surely as I hold your hand in mine." Brown Boy to Brown Girl. Countee Cullen. PoBA

As that Arabian bird (whom all admire). William Browne. *Fr.* Britannia's Pastorals, I, Song 4. OAEL-1

As the black storm upon the mountain top. Wordsworth. *Fr.* The Prelude, VII. HAP

As [*or* when] the blackbird in the spring. Aura Lea [*or* Lee]. W. W. Fosdick. BLSo

As the body denies the means to look. Epigram. Pernette du Guillet, *tr. by* Joan Keefe *and* Richard Terdiman. PBWP

As the bull-dozer bites into the tree-ringed hill fort. Hymn to the New Omagh Road. John Montague. TwMBP

As the candle light and fire light. Cottage. "Seumas O'Sullivan." PFIr

As the car stooped, seemed to pause. Vincent Buckley. *Fr.* Golden Builders. CAAP; GAS

As the cat/ climbed over. Poem. William Carlos Williams. CABA (1972 ed.); InPK; InPS; PiAm

As the chameleon, who is known. The Chameleon. Matthew Prior. OBSV

As the child rests upon my arm. Double Mirror. Ann Stanford. MPA

As the clouds that are so light. The Clouds That Are So Light. Edward Thomas. FaBoTW (1975 ed.)

As the corn becomes higher. Cricket March. Carl Sandburg. UsP

As the dust from the wet dream of a nation. Written in Unbridled Repugnance near Sioux Falls, Alabama—April 30, 1974. A. K. Redwing. VoR

As the fireman said. Riding the Elevator into the Sky. Anne Sexton. NYP

As the first congress. First and Last. Bruce Severy. VW

As the gook woman howls. In the Mourning Time. Robert Hayden. BPo

As the leaves say. Free Will. Walter Clark. NCSH

As the liberty lads o'er the sea. Song for the Luddites. Byron. MBPR

As the night ended. My Son, My Son. Seymour Cain. AMV-81

As the player's breath warms the fipple the tone clears. Basil Bunting. *Fr.* Briggflatts. OBP

As the poets have mournfully sung. The Aesthetic Point of View. W. H. Auden. OBAL

As the poor end of each dead day drew near. He Liked the Dead. Malcolm Lowry. OxBTC

As the Queen and Prince Albert, so buxom and all pert. Old England Forever and Do It No More. *Unknown.* GBP

As the rains of spring. Izumi Shikibu, *tr. fr. Japanese by* Edwin A. Cranston. PBWP

As the Snow Falls, Another Breathes in an Adjoining Room. Elizabeth Wray. PoUp

As the snow falls I brush it away. A Snowfall. Richard Eberhart. FiCP

As the Spring Rains Fall. Buson, *tr. fr. Japanese by* Harold G. Henderson. NIL

As the stars hide in the light before daybreak. Avoiding News by the River. W. S. Merwin. CoPAm

As the stores close, a winter light. February Evening in New York. Denise Levertov. InPS; NoAM

As the story goes,/ the Jews bought for themselves. The Jews in Hell. Isaac Goldemberg, *tr. by* David Unger. VWA

As the story goes, Noah took animals of every variety. An Abridged Bestiary. Maxine Chernoff. FiCh

As the sun declined the snow at our feet. Prose Poem. Humphrey Jennings. EAS

As the sunlight in the sky. For the Cultural Campaign. Chimedin Jigmed, *tr. by* C. R. Bawden. WTO

As the swamp cooler breathes. A Sale of Smoke. Roberta Spear. AmPA

As the Team's Head-Brass. Edward Thomas. ExPo (1973 ed.); OxBTC; PoPle

As the wise men of old brought gifts. The Gift. William Carlos Williams. IPWM; TCP

As the Word came to prophets of old. Prophets for a New Day. Margaret Walker. BPo

As the World Turns. Larry Mollin. NeAC

As these two double verses, perfect linguists, create. In Eundem Macaronicon. John Donne. PAIC

As they argued, the bishop had yelled, arrogant. Franz Jagesttater's Epistemology. Mark Halperin. PCho

As thick as a plank, as unbending as Fate. Toffee-Slab. Brian Lee. FPB

As things be/ come. Word Poem. Nikki Giovanni. PoBA

As this convine and ordinance was mayd. Virgil, *tr. by* Gavin Douglas. *Fr.* The Aeneid, VIII. OBVE

As Thomas was cudgeled one day by his wife. Epigram. Swift. FaBoEE; SoSe

As those who are not athletic at breakfast day by day. Nature Morte. Louis MacNeice. NoAM

As though an aged person were to wear. Elegy for the Monastery Barn. Thomas Merton. VGW

As though my opaque life were in a tumbler. Message. Norman MacCaig. UsP

As through the wild green hills of Wyre. A. E. Housman. STS

As Toilsome I Wandered Virginia's Woods. Walt Whitman. PAIC

As Tommy Snooks and Bessy Brooks. Mother Goose. MG

As tongueless Echo in the pastoral vale. To the Greek Anthologists. George Rostrevor Hamilton, *after* Satyros. FaBoEE

As t'other night in bed I thinking lay. The Dream of the Cabal: A Prophetical Satire. *Unknown.* APAS

As Tranquil Streams, *with music.* Marion Franklin Ham. AH

As true as I was born into. Halfway. Maxine W. Kumin. PCho

As two men were a-walking, down by the sea-side. The Duke of Grafton. *Unknown.* GBP; PeBB

As virtuous men pass mildly away. A Valediction Forbidding Mourning. John Donne. AnMo; CABA (1972 ed.); ExPo (1973 ed.); FF; HAP; HeIP; HoPM (1975 ed.); ILP (1975 ed.); InPK; InPS; MetP; NIL; NOBE; OAEL-1; PoIA; PoPle; PPoD; PPoe; PPP; SCP-1; SoSe; TT; UnPo (1976 ed.); VoPo; WIF

As we came from the show. *Unknown.* SFF

As we climb to the church of Galilee. The Church of Galilee. Muriel Rukeyser. *Fr.* The Gates. GP

As we get older we do not get any younger. Chard Whitlow. Henry Reed. FaBoCo; FaBoNo; ILP (1975 ed.); NOBL; OxBTC; UnPo (1976 ed.)

As we live, we are transmitters of life. We Are Transmitters. D. H. Lawrence. OxBTC

As we marched down to Fernario. Peggy-O. *Unknown.* FSW

As we stand talking, his eye. An Old Acquaintance. Lewis Turco. CoPAm

As we stood on the crushed stone. A Conversation. Barbara Howes. IHMS

As we were marching to Quebec. Marching to Quebec. *Unknown.* AmFP

As wearied pilgrims, once possessed. His Own Epitaph. Robert Herrick. CaPo

As Weary Pilgrim, Now at Rest. Anne Bradstreet. EAP; PiAm

As when a fragment, from a mountain torn. Virgil, *tr. by* Dryden. *Fr.* The Aeneid, XII. OBVE

As when an architect some palace wall. Homer, *tr. by* William Cowper. *Fr.* The Iliad, XVI. OBVE

As when devouring flames some forest seize. Homer, *tr. by* William Cowper. *Fr.* The Iliad, II. OBVE

As when, down some broad river dropping, we. Frederick Goddard Tuckerman. *Fr.* Sonnets. AmVN

"As When Emotion Too Far Exceeds Its Cause." Gloria C. Oden. AmNP (1974 ed.)

As when far off the warbled strains are heard. La Fayette. Samuel Taylor Coleridge. *Fr.* Sonnets on Eminent Characters. MBPR

As when his first beams tremble in the sky. Dante, *tr. by* Laurence Binyon. Divina Commedia: Purgatorio, XXVII. NAWM-1

As when of frequent bees. Homer, *tr. by* George Chapman. *Fr.* The Iliad, II. OBVE

As When Some Hungry Fledgling Hears and Sees. Vittoria da Colonna, *tr. fr. Italian by* Barbara Howes. BoWoP ("Like a hungry fledgeling that watches and hears," *tr. by* Lynne Lawner.) PBWP

As when the moon hath comforted the night. George Chapman. *Fr.* The Conspiracy of Charles, Duke of Byron. Moon

As when the winds, ascending by degrees. Homer, *tr. by* Pope. *Fr.* The Iliad, IV. OBVE

As when two men have loved a woman well. Lost on Both Sides. Dante Gabriel Rossetti. The House of Life, XCI. VLP

As when you wake before dawn. Borders. Marieve Rugo. PCho

As William and Mary stood by the seaside. William and Mary. *Unknown.* AmFP

As Winter, fleeing. The Fearless. Mortimer J. Adler. PoA

As with/ the new-born. For William Carlos Williams. Geoff Page. FPA

As with Gladness Men of Old. William Chatterton Dix. FaPoR

As with varnish red and glistening. Casualty. W. E. Henley. In Hospital, XIII. VLP

As withereth the primrose by the river. A Palinode. Edmund Bolton. PAIC

As woods whose change appeares. Horace, *tr. by* Ben Jonson. *Fr.* The Art of Poetry. OBVE

As Wulfstan said on another occasion. Speech for the Repeal of the McCarran Act. Richard Wilbur. CMoP (1970 ed.); GOA

As Ye Came from the Holy Land. *Unknown, sometimes at. to* Sir Walter Ralegh. *See* Walsingham.

As Yet. Vicente Rodríguez Nietzche, *tr. from Spanish by* Julio Marzán. InW

As you all know, tonight is the night of the full moon. 12 o'Clock News. Elizabeth Bishop. GP; WeW

As you are walking. Hey Fella Would You Mind Holding This Piano a Moment. William J. Harris. PCho

As You Came from the Holy Land of Walsingham. *Unknown, sometimes at. to* Sir Walter Ralegh. *See* Walsingham.

As you interpret. Interpretations. Beate Goldman. PoUp

As you know, I have not lost you. Orpheus to Eurydice. Frederick Morgan. AMV-80

As You Leave Me. Etheridge Knight. ConAP; FF; NNaP

As you lie there in the shadows of the room. After Love. Vicente Aleixandre, *tr. by* Lewis Hyde. AMV-80

As You Like It, *sels.* Shakespeare. "All the world's a stage," *fr.* II, vii. FaPoR; FF; NIL; PoIA; SFF

Blow, Blow, Thou Winter Wind, *fr.* II, vii. FSFS; GBL; HeIP; ILP (1975 ed.); InPS; IP; NOBE; OAEL-1; PPoe

It Was a Lover, and His Lass, *fr.* V, iii. BiP; FSW; GBL; HeIP; ILP (1975 ed.); InPK; InPS; NOBE; OLR; PPoe

Under the Greenwood Tree, *fr.* II, v. CTV; ECBV; HeIP; HoPM (1975 ed.); ILP (1975 ed.); InPS; OAEL-1; UnPo (1976 ed.)

As You Like It. Theodore Weiss. TAP

As you read, a white bear leisurely. To the Reader. Denise Levertov. VGW

As your cream skin stretched. Poem at Semester's End. Ralph Mecklenburger. SFF

Asbestos-suited Man in Hell, The. Gordon Challis. ATNZ

Ascend my shoulders, firmly keep thy seat. *Unknown, formerly at. to* Homer; *tr. by* Thomas Parnell. *Fr.* The Battle of the Frogs and Mice. OBVE

Ascending Red Cedar Moon. Duane Niatum. CDW

Ascending the hill, we saw the sun as incandescent. Vertical Is Our New Sight. Daisy Aldan. AATT

Ascension. Denis Devlin. BIrV

Ascension Thursday. Saunders Lewis, *tr. fr. Welsh by* Gwyn Thomas. OBW

Ascent. Lynn Strongin. MIT

Ascent into Hell. A. D. Hope. GAS; MAuV

Ascent of T. J. Jackson: A Soldier's Tale. "A. N." BTTM

Ash and the Oak, The. Louis Simpson. ConAP

Ash falls on the roof. Mother. Erica Jong. TV

Ash-Glory. Paul Celan, *tr. fr,. German by* Joachim Neugroschel. VWA

Ash Grove, The, *with music.* Thomas Oliphant. GSB

Ash Grove, The. *Unknown.* FSW

Ash in the air. Ash in everyone's mouth. Wake. Elizabeth Spires. AMV-80

Ash on an old man's sleeve. T. S. Eliot. *Fr.* Four Quartets: Little Gidding. FaBoTw (1975 ed.)

Ash Wednesday. Daniel Burke. AMV-80

Ash-Wednesday. T. S. Eliot. VGW

    *Sels.*

    "Although I do not hope to turn again," VI. BoReV

    "At the first turning of the second stair," III. NoAM; NOBA

    "Because I do not hope to turn again," I. BoReV

    "Lady, three white leopards sat under a juniper-tree," II. UsP

Ash Wednesday. Christina Rossetti. VLP

Ashboughs. Gerard Manley Hopkins. VLP

Ashes. Philip Levine. AMV-80

Ashes, ashes, all fall down. Children's Lenten Wisdom. James A. Houck. AMV-80

Ashes have waited for me in the ash tray, The. Homecoming Blues. Vassar Miller. GP

Ashes, Lord. Nat Turner in the Clearing. Alvin Aubert. CoPAm

Ashes of roses, forsythia bones. Changes of Life. Constance Urdang. VWA

Ashkelon. Anthony Rudolf. VWA

Ashland Tragedy, The, 2 *versions.* Elijah Adams. AmFP

Ashtabula Disaster. Julia A. Moore. OBAL

Ashville Junction, Swannanoa tunnel. Swannonoa Tunnel. *Unknown.* FSW

Asia on the one side. This Narrow Stage. Theodore Weiss. NoAM

Asian Brother, Asian Sister. Lawson Fusao Inada. MPA; SA

Asian Peace Offers Rejected without Publication. Robert Bly. CAPP; NoAM

Asians Dying, The. W. S. Merwin. CAPP; NoBA

Asia's Song. Shelley. *Fr.* Prometheus Unbound, II, v. GrRo

Aside. Alan Dugan. PoA

Aside from ashcans & halljohns & pigeoncoops. Eastside Incidents. Gregory Corso. GP; NYP; SA

Aside to Julie. Sallie Chesham. AATT

Asides and Memoranda. Elton Glaser. NVAP

Ask in one life no more. Word by Night. Charles Brasch. ATNZ

Ask Me. William Stafford. FiCP

Ask me no more: the moon may draw the sea. Tennyson. *Fr.* The Princess, Pt. VI. GBL

Ask [*or* Aske] me no more where Jove bestows. Song. Thomas Carew. CABA (1972 ed.); CaPo; GBL; HAP; HeIP; HoPM (1975 ed.); ILP (1975 ed.); InPS; NOBE; OBP; PoPle; PPP; SCP-2

Ask me why I send you here. The Primrose. Robert Herrick. PF

Ask no return for love that's given. Horace Gregory. *Fr.* Chorus for Survival. VGW

Ask not my name, O friend! A Nameless Epitaph. Matthew Arnold. VLP

Ask not the cause, why sullen spring. Song to a Fair Young Lady Going Out of Town in the Spring. Dryden. CABA (1972 ed.); ILP (1975 ed.)

Ask Not to Know This Man. Ben Jonson. CABA (1972 ed.)

Ask nothing more of me, sweet. The Oblation. Swinburne. VLP

Ask of the sun. Louis Zukofsky. NoAM

Ask the Empress of the night. The Magnet. Thomas Stanley. NOBE

Ask the Mountains. Phillip William George. UsP; VW

Ask what kind of war it is. What Kind of War? Larry Rottman. POL

Ask you what provocation I have had? The Power of Ridicule. Pope. *Fr.* Epilogue to the Satires. NOBE; OBSV

Aske me no more where Jove bestowes. *See* Ask me no more . . .

Asked me to be a woman. Wrists. Alberta Turner. HeS

Askest, "How long thou shalt stay?" The Visit. Emerson. NOBA

Asking for Ruthie. Judy Grahn. GP; NMM

Asking little more than. Ode on Lust. Frank O'Hara. Epi

Asking what, asking what?—all a boy's afternoon. Debate: Question, Quarry, Dream. Robert Penn Warren. VGW

Asleep and Awake. David McCord. ECBV

Asleep he wheezes at his ease. Roger the Dog. Ted Hughes. FPB

Asleep in the Deep, *with music.* Arthur J. Lamb. FSN

Asleep! O sleep a little while, white pearl! Keats. LoAs

Asleep or waking is it? for her neck. Laus Veneris. Swinburne. VLP

Asleep while the children howl and the house burns. Goddess. Judith Johnson Sherwin. BoWoP

Asmodeus. Geoffrey Hill. FaBoTw (1975 ed.)

Asolando, *sels.* Robert Browning.

    Epilogue: "At the midnight in the silence of the sleep-time." NOBE; PAIC; TT; VLP

    Prologue: "Poet's age is sad, The: for why?" OAEL-2; VLP

Aspatia's Song. Beaumont *and* Fletcher. *Fr.* The Maid's Tragedy, II, i. HAP; NOBE; PoPle ("Lay a garland on my hearse.") GBL; ILP (1975 ed.)

Aspect of Love, Alive in the Ice and Fire, An. Gwendolyn Brooks. BPo; CAPP; TAP; TT

Aspecta Medusa. Dante Gabriel Rossetti. VLP

Aspects of Now, *sel.* Gwyn Williams. "Today has it all, sunshine." OBW

Aspects of Robinson. Weldon Kees. AnMo; NYP

Aspects of the World Like Coral Reefs. William Bronk. VGW

Aspens. Edward Thomas. InPS

Aspen's Song, The. Yvor Winters. POL

Asphalt morning found him, The; he was dead. Raccoon on the Road. Joseph Payne Brennan. ECBV

Asphodel, An. Allen Ginsberg. TT

Asphodel, That Greeny Flower, *sels.* William Carlos Williams. "For our wedding too." PoIA
"Of asphodel, that greeny flower." CMoP (1970 ed.); PoIA
"Only the imagination is real!" TT

Aspiring Man, by learned pens. Brief Essay on Man. Arthur Guiterman. OBAL

Asra, The. Heine, *tr. fr. German by* Ernst Feise. NAWM-2

Ass in the Lion's Skin, The. Aesop, *rhymed tr. fr. Greek by* William Ellery Leonard. ECBV

Ass will with his long ears fray, An. Samuel Butler. FaBoEE

Assailant. John Raven. BPo

Assassination, The. Robert Hillyer. OFD

Assassination, The. Donald Justice. CSP

Assassination. Don L. Lee. AmNP (1974 ed.); FF; NeAC; OFD; PoBA

Assassination of President McKinley, The. Paul Blackburn. NYP

Assassination Poems. John Ridland. MAT; OFD

Assassination Raga. Lawrence Ferlinghetti. CAPP

Assassin's Fatal Error, The. Lawrence Raab. AmPA

Assay a Friend. *Unknown.* OxBM

Assemble, all ye maidens, at the door. Elegy on a Lady Whom Grief for the Death of Her Betrothed Killed. Robert Bridges. VLP

Assembly. W. S. Merwin. GP

Assembly of Ladies, The, *sel.* Lady of the Assembly. Palace of Pleasant Regard, The. WPE

Assignation, The. Juana de Ibarbourou, *tr. fr. Spanish by* Brian Swann. PBWP

Assignment. Grace Butcher. RiTi

Assignment: Descriptive Essay. Gary Willis. AMV-81

Assisi. Norman MacCaig. MS

Assistant editor of *Crewel World,* The. The New York Woman. L. E. Sissman. MAT

Assuming the Name of Any Next Child. John Tagliabue. AMV-80

Assumption. Padraic Fallon. BIrV

Assumption, The. *Unknown.* OxBM

Assumptions. Richard Hugo. CNW

Assyrian came down like the wolf on the fold, The. The Destruction of Sennacherib. Byron. AIW; AKE; BTTM; CTV; FaPo; FaPoR; FF; HAP; NIL; PBMP; PIM; PoIA; SFF; WeW

Astapovo, or What Are We to Do, *sels.* Peter Whigham. TwMBP
"Nausicaa's girls."
"Poetry to go."
"Violence swaddles all (love-) acts before and after."

Asteroid Light, The. *Unknown.* FSW

Astigmatic, The. Philip Hobsbaum. LP

Astonished nymphs their flood's strange fate deplore, The. Richard Crashaw. *Fr.* To the Noblest and Best of Ladies, the Countess of Denbigh. OBP

Astrologer Argues Your Death, The. Charles deGravelles. AMV-81

Astronaut. Sean O'Meara. IPM

Astronaut's Choice. M. M. Darcy. QQQ

Astronomer's Journal, An. Jane Shore. PoA

Astronomers of Mont Blanc, The. Edgar Bowers. PoA

Astrophel and Stella. Sir Philip Sidney. AAS; ESO
Sonnets.
I. "Loving in truth, and fain in verse my love to show." CABA (1972 ed.); EBEV; Epi; GBL; HAP; ILP (1975 ed.); LoAs; OAEL-1; OBP; PoIA

II. "Not at the first sight, nor with a dribbed shot." OAEL-1

III. "Let dainty wits cry on the Sisters nine." NIL; OAEL-1

V. "It is most true that eyes are formed to serve." OAEL-1

VII. "When Nature made her chief work, Stella's eyes." CABA (1972 ed.); NIL

XIV. "Alas have I not pain enough my friend." Epi; OAEL-1

XV. "You that do search for every purling spring." ILP (1975 ed.); OAEL-1

XX. "Fly, fly, my friends, I have my death wound; fly." Epi; OAEL-1

XXI. "Your words, my friend, right helpful caustics, blame." CABA (1972 ed.)

XXIV. "Rich fools there be, whose base and filthy heart." Epi

XXV. "The wisest scholar of the wight most wise." OAEL-1

XXVI. "Though dusty wits dare scorn astrology." OAEL-1

XXVIII. "You that with allegory's curious frame." ILP (1975 ed.); InPK; OAEL-1

XXX. "Whether the Turkish new-moon minded be." Epi

XXXI. "With how sad steps, O Moon, thou climb'st the skies!" BoLoP; Epi; GBL; HAP; HeIP; ILP (1975 ed.); InPK; InPS; IPWM; LoAs; MAT; Moon; NIL; OBP; PAIC; PBMP; PPoe; PPP; WeW
(To the Sad Moon.) NOBE

XXXIII. "I might—unhappy word—oh me, I might." OAEL-1

XXXIV. "Come, let me write, and to what end? to ease." Epi

XXXV. "What may words say, or what may words not say." CABA (1972 ed.)

XXXVII. "My mouth doth water, and my breast doth swell." Epi

XXXIX. "Come sleep! O sleep, the certain knot of peace." CABA (1972 ed.); ILP (1975 ed.); LoAs; NIL; PAIC; PoIA; PPP
(To Sleep.) NOBE

XLI. "Having this day my horse, my hand, my lance." HAP; ILP (1975 ed.); PPoD

XLVII. "What, have I thus betrayed my liberty?" GBL; LoAs; NIL

XLIX. "I on my horse, and Love on me, doth try." LFH; OAEL-1

LII. "A strife is grown between Virtue and Love." NIL

LIII. "In martial sports I had my cunning tried." NIL

LIV. "Because I breathe not love to every one." BuTh

LIX. "Dear, why make you more of a dog than me?" GBL; ILP (1975 ed.); LoAs

LXIV. "No more, my dear, no more these counsels try." ILP (1975 ed.)

LXXI. "Who will in fairest book of Nature know." CABA (1972 ed.); Epi; OAEL-1

LXXIV. "I never drank of Aganippe well." CABA (1972 ed.); HeIP

LXXXIII. "Good brother Philip, I have borne you long." Epi

LXXXIV. "Highway, since you my chief Parnassus be." ILP (1975 ed.)

XCIX. "When far-spent night persuades each mortal eye." CABA (1972 ed.)

CVII. "Stella since thou so right a princess art." OBP

CIX. "Thou blind man's mark, thou fool's self-chosen snare." *Sometimes considered part of* Astrophel and Stella. CABA (1972 ed.); Epi; HeIP; PPP
(Desire.) NOBE

CX. "Leave me, O Love, which reachest but to dust." *Sometimes considered part of* Astrophel and Stella. CABA (1972 ed.); GBL; HeIP; NIL; PPP
(Splendidis Longum Valedico Nugis.) LoAs; NOBE
Songs.
Fourth Song: "Only joy, now here you are." GBL; HAP
Eleventh Song: "Who is it that this dark night."
(Voices at the Window.) NOBE; PoPle

Aswelay. Norman Henry Pritchard II. PoBA

Aswell within her billowed skirts. The Mad-Woman. L. A. G. Strong. PFIr

Asylum for War Victims. Robert Morgan. HeHu

At a Bach Concert. Adrienne Rich. CoPAm

At a bend in the Bally-Dale road. The Last Families in the Cabins. Millen Brand. GP

At a Bible House. Robert Lowell. SFF

At a certain hour of the morning of a certain day. Twenty Words/ Twenty Days. Gael Turnbull. TwMBP

At a Concert of Music. Conrad Aiken. ILP (1975 ed.)

At a Cowboy Dance. James Barton Adams. BPAW

At a Danse Macabre. Charles Spear. ATNZ

At a distance, young voices are whooping. On Returning to Teach. Marvin Bell. NowV

At a Fishing Settlement. Alistair Campbell. ATNZ

At a Friends' Meeting. Mary Elizabeth Coleridge. WPE

At a gay reception given in a mansion grand and old. The Moth and the Flame. George Taggart. FSN

At a Georgia Camp Meeting, with music. Kerry Mills. BLSo

At a Hasty Wedding. Thomas Hardy. PAIC; VLP

At a Jewish wedding. The Homeless. Joan Joffe Hall. AMV-81

At a March against the Vietnam War. Robert Bly. EAS; WasP

At a Modernist School. Morris Bishop. TDH

At a Month's End. Swinburne. VLP

At a Motel near O'Hare Airport. Jane Kenyon. TC

At a Pairty. Donald Campbell. MS

At a party of university people. Double Exposure. Ian Young. NeAC

At a pleasant evening party. Ferdinando and Elvira. W. S. Gilbert. FaBoCo; FaBoNo

At a Reading. Thomas Bailey Aldrich. OBAL

At a roundup on the Gily. The Legend of Boastful Bill. Charles Badger Clark, Jr. BPAW

At a show one time—I don't know where we were. Cool Women and Smart Horses Are the Pits. Henry Taylor. Fr. Desperado. PoUp

At a Solemn Music. Milton. AnMo; BoReV; ExPo (1973 ed.); HeIP; NIL; NOBE; PAIC

At a spring well under a thorn. The Virgin. Unknown. GBP

At a suburban yard-sale. Fireflies. David McKain. AAN

At a Summer Hotel. Isabella Gardner. RiTi

At a Watering Place. Thomas Hardy. CMoP (1970 ed.)

At Aberdeen. Unknown. FaBoCo
  (Elgin Cathedral Epitaph.) PoPle
  ("Here lie I, Martin Elginbrod.") FaBoEE

At Akitio. James K. Baxter. ATNZ

At alarming bell daybreak, before. Eilean Ni Chuilleanain. Fr. Site of Ambush. CIP

At all times one low sound rides through the waters. The River. Phyllis Hoge Thompson. PHC

At an Exhibition of Historical Paintings, Hobart. Vivian Smith. GAS; MAuV

At Asqefar. Anthony Thwaite. HeHu

At Baia. Hilda Doolittle ("H. D."). NOBA; PAIC

At Barstow. Charles Tomlinson. NIL; NoAM

At Beautyes barre as I dyd stande. The Arraignment of a Lover. George Gascoigne. AAS

At Beverly Farms, a portly, uncomfortable boulder. Terminal Days at Beverly Farms. Robert Lowell. PSN

At Bickford's. Gerald Stern. NYP

At Breakfast. May Swenson. Psy; SoS

At breakfast I had french toast. On First Knowing God. Reed Whittemore Fr. The Seven Days. GP

At Brill on the Hill. Unknown. GBP
  (Brill.) OBP

At Carmel. Mary Austin. WPW

At Carmel Highlands. Janet Lewis. PoA

At Casterbridge Fair, sels. Thomas Hardy.
  After the Club-Dance, III. VLP
  After the Fair, VII. CMoP (1970 ed.); HAP; VLP
  Ballad-Singer, The, I. BoLoP; OLR; VLP
  Former Beauties, II. NoAM

At Castle Boterel. Thomas Hardy. EBEV; NOBE

At Cheyenne. Eugene Field. BPAW

At Christmas. Robert Duncan. NoAM

At counters where I eat my lunch. Marble-Top. E. B. White. OBAL

At court I met it, in clothes brave enough. On Something That Walks Somewhere. Ben Jonson. SCP-1

At Cove on the Crooked River. William Stafford. CNW; ConAP

At Dante's Grave. Ezra Zussman, tr. fr. Hebrew by D. Shnayorson. VWA

At dawn a knot of sea-lions lies off shore. Animals. Robinson Jeffers. NU

At dawn, caught beneath the rim of light. Beyond Anguish. Milton Kessler. CoPAm

At dawn crowed the cock. Cock. Aharon Amir, tr. by Bernhard Frank. AMV-81

At Dawn he's hunched along the backstretch rail. Old Stomping Grounds: The Half-Mile Track. Henry Taylor. Fr. Desperado. PoUp

At dawn I squat on the garage. Sound. Jim Harrison. VGW

At dawn of the day the Creator. Gaspara Stampa, tr. fr. Italian by J. Vitiello. BoWoP

At dawn she lay with her profile at that angle. Daybreak. Stephen Spender. BoLoP

At dawn the ridge emerges massed and dun. Attack. Siegfried Sassoon. NOBE; OxBTC

At Dawn The Virgin Is Born. Lope de Vega, tr. fr. Spanish by W. S. Merwin. PChr

At dawn today I saw a man come out of a saloon. The Drunkard's Doom. Unknown. FSW

At Dawning, with music. Nelle Richmond Eberhart. BLSo

At day's light. In Autumn. Jon Anderson. AmPA

At dead of night, after an evening ball. The Duchess of York's Ghost. Unknown. APAS

At deep evening, low by the tremulous Hudson. Green in the Halls. Ben Maddow. SPT

At Delphos shrine one did a doubt propound. Upon Master Edmund Spenser. Francis Beaumont. FaBoEE

At Dieppe, sel. Arthur Symons.
  On the Beach, II. VLP

At dinner, she is hostess, I am host. Modern Love, XVII. George Meredith. Epi; HeIP; ILP (1975 ed.)

At Dirty Dick's and Sloppy Joe's. Song of the Master and Boatswain. W. H. Auden. Fr. The Sea and the Mirror. BoLoP; FaBoTw (1975 ed.)

At Dunkeswell Abbey. Anthony Thwaite. HeHu

At Dunwich. Anthony Thwaite. HeHu; MPo

At dusk/ from the island in the river. If the Owl Calls Again. John Haines. BoAnP; CNW; ConAP; HeIP; NCSH; NU; UsP

At dusk and long-distance they are the mouths. Tide Pools. Dave Smith. AMV-81

At dusk I row out to what looks like light or anonymity. Summer Celestial. Stanley Plumly. PCho

At Eagle Farm I stand at the passenger gate. Flights. Roger McDonald. CAAP

At Eighty. Rosamund Stanhope. AMV-80

At eighty/ reading lines. Heavy, Heavy—What Hangs Over? Kenneth Burke. POL

At 85. Richard Ardinger. AMV-81

At eighty they took the scales. At Eighty. Rosamund Stanhope. AMV-80

At eighty-six she takes to pressing flowers. Foxfire. Nancy Willard. IHMS

At Eutaw Springs the valiant died. To the Memory of the Brave Americans. Philip Freneau. BTTM; EAP; ILP (1975 ed.)

At Evans Street. Janet Frame. ATNZ

"At eve should be the time," they said. The Burial Hour. Robert Stephen Hawker. VPC

At evening I pause, neglected pen. "Who Then Is Crazy?" Barry Spacks. GP

At evening, sitting on this terrace. Bat. D. H. Lawrence. HAP; OAEL-1

At evening when I go to bed. Daisies. Frank Dempster Sherman. CTV

At evening when the lamp is lit. The Land of Story-Books. Robert Louis Stevenson. CTV; DuDr

At Every Gas Station There Are Mechanics. Stephen Dunn. NVAP

At every hour I wake. Night. Aldo Camerino, tr. by Anita Barrows. VWA

At Every Major Airport. Patricia Goedicke. AAN

At every stro[a]ke his brazen fin[ne]s do take. The Whale. John Donne. Fr. The Progresse of the Soule. ECS; OBP

At fifty, I approach myself. In a Dream. David Ignatow. GP

At first blush, discomfiting. Diehard. Judith Moffett. PoA

At first he stirs uneasily in sleep. Dog at Night. Louis Untermeyer. MiP

At first I could remove the bandages. Under the Catalpa Trees. Gary Young. AMV-81

At first I was. The Waiting Child. Mel Takahara. PHC

At first I was given centuries. Margaret Atwood. HAP; NMM

At first I was worried about you. When I Held You to My Chest, You Fit. Jack Myers. AmPA

At first it will seem tame. Money. Victor Contoski. GP

At first light. The Print-Out. Howard Nemerov. AMV-80

At first my mother would be shy. In the Ocean. Patricia Goedicke. TV

At first nothing is. Nothing Is. Sun-Ra. PoBA

At First Sight. Robert Graves. FaBoEE

At First Sight. Alastair Reid. SLP

At first was neither Being nor Nonbeing. The Song of Creation. Tr. fr. Sanskrit by Raimundo Panikkar. Fr. Vedic Hymns. ILwL

At five in the afternoon. Lament for Ignacio Sanchez Mejías. Federico García Lorca, tr. by A. L. Lloyd. OBVE

At five in the morning, as jolly as any. The Miner's Doom. Unknown. AmFP

At five of this winter morn the hound and I. Ceremony. Howard Nemerov. AMV-80

At five precisely in the afternoon. Crossing. Archibald MacLeish. POL

At 5:10 a.m. Uncle Henry. Dream 1971. Victor Contoski. GP

At five this morn, when Phoebus raised his head. Tunbridge Wells. Earl of Rochester. OBSV

At Flock Mass. F. R. Higgins. PFIr

At Florence. Wordsworth. VLP

At Flores in the Azores, Sir Richard Grenville lay. The Revenge. [or A Ballad of the Fleet]. Tennyson. BTTM; FaPo; FaPoR

At four a.m. I dreamed of myself on that beach. For You Who Didn't Know. Nancy Willard. RiTi

At four o'clock. Roosters. Elizabeth Bishop. CoPAm

At four o'clock in the afternoon. Surfaces. Jane Mayhall. NYP

At four p.m. small fingers moved the dial to one-six-"O." Riders. Linda Peavy. PH

At 4:30 AM/ she rose. Ntozake Shange. Fr. For Colored Girls Who Have Considered Suicide When the Rainbow Is Enuf. BoWoP

At 14th Street and First Avenue. Strawberries in Mexico. Ron Padgett. EAS

At Francis Allen's on the Christmas-eve. The Epic. Tennyson. VLP

At Galway Races. W. B. Yeats. LiSp

At Gettysburg full anonymity. Yugoslav Cemetery. Celeste Turner Wright. WPE

At Glan-y-Wern. Arthur Symons. Intermezzo: Pastoral, IV. VLP

At Glendalough lived a young saint. St. Kevin. Unknown. WTO

At God's Command. Joseph Rolnik, tr. fr. Yiddish by Keith Bosley. VWA

At Grand Canyon's Edge. David Ray. TAT

At Grass. Philip Larkin. HAP; OxBTC; PSN

At Great Torrington, Devon. Unknown. FaBoCo ("Here lies a man who was killed by lightning.") FaBoEE

At Guaymas I born in this various world. The Pinto. Owen Wister. BPAW

At Hadleigh, Suffolk. Unknown. FaBoCo

At half past summer when the creek. In the Sclaes: II. Madeline DeFrees. Fr. A Catch of Summer. MPA

At Hallowmas, whan nights grow lang. Hallow-Fair. Robert Fergusson. EPC

At Hans Christian Andersen's Birthplace, Odense, Denmark. Maurice Lindsay. MS

At Henry's bier let some thing fall out well. John Berryman. CAPP; ILP (1975 ed.)

At her departure his disdain return'd. Homer, tr. by Dryden. Fr. The Iliad, I. OBVE

At her fair hands how have I grace entreated. Ode. Walter Davison. BoLoP

At His Father's Grave. John Ormond. FaBoTw (1975 ed.); OBW

At Home in Dakar. Margaret Danner. FB

At Home in Heaven. James Montgomery. VLP

At home, in my flannel gown, like a bear to its floe. 90 North. Randall Jarrell. ILP (1975 ed.); NoAM; NOBA; TAP

At home, O Nomades. "Home, Sweet Home," with Variations. H. C. Bunner. OBAL

At 100 Mile House the cowboys ride in rolling. The Cariboo Horses. A. W. Purdy. HeIP

At Hunegg. George MacBeth. TwMBP

At Ithaca. Hilda Doolittle ("H. D."). VGW

At Jesty's Tomb. Edward Lowbury. PMW

At Kenneth Burke's Place. William Carlos Williams. NOBA

At Kilbryde Castle. Lorn M. MacIntyre. SLP

At Last. Melvin DeBruhl. PPoD

At last a juggler is led out under the stars. The Initiate. W. S. Merwin. NNaP

At last I bless the hours. Rosemarie Newcombe. POL

At last I can figure out the nature of that whisking sound. Fate in Incognito. Michael Benedikt. OBAL

At last I found the monastery. A young. Abstinence. Kenneth Rosen. AmPA

"At last I seem to need no time for any journey." Faster than Light. Edward Lowbury. PMW

At last it cannot matter. What You Should Do Each Morning. Brian Patten. BuTh

At last love has come. I would be more ashamed. Sulpicia, tr. fr. Latin by Aliki and Willis Barnstone. BoWoP

At last, my old, inveterate foe. To Melancholy. Countess of Winchilsea. WPE

At last they chanced to meet upon the way. Spenser. *Fr.* Mother Hubberd's Tale. TVS

At Last We Killed the Roaches. Lucille Clifton. GP

At last within my tomb I lie. John Donne Speaks from His Grave. Lord Russell Brain. PMW

At last you yielded up the album, which. Lines on a Young Lady's Photograph Album. Philip Larkin. HAP; HeIP; OAEL-1

At least at night, a streetlight. So Long. William Stafford. Epi

At least 100 seabirds attended my grandmother's funeral. My Grandmother's Funeral. Thomas Lux. WeW

At Leeds. *Unknown.* FaBoCo

At length, my Lord, I have the bliss. Thomas Moore. *Fr.* The Fudge Family in Paris. OBSV

At length old age came on her. Old Poulter's Mare. *Unknown.* PeD

At Length the Busy Day Is Done, *with music.* Francis Hopkinson. AH

At length the crackling noise and dreadful blaze. Dryden. *Fr.* Annus Mirabilis: Fire of London. SCP-1

At length the year, which marks his course, expires. Lines Addressed to Mr. Jefferson. Philip Freneau. EAP

At Length There Dawns the Glorious Day, *with music.* Ozora S. Davis. AH

At length their long kiss severed, with sweet smart. Nuptial Sleep. Dante Gabriel Rossetti. *Fr.* The House of Life. VLP

At length with jostling, elbowing, and the aid. Byron. *Fr.* The Vision of Judgment. OBSV

At Lindos. May Sarton. WPE

At Long Last. Lindsay Patterson. CNA

At Lord's. Francis Thompson. LiSp

At Masada. Ernest Neufeld. AMV-81

At Mass. Vachel Lindsay. VGW

At Max Gate. Siegfried Sassoon. NoAM

At meat, or hearing you deplore. Consumer's Report. X. J. Kennedy. FiCP

At Melville's Tomb. Hart Crane. HAP; ILP (1975 ed.); LFH; NoAM; PoA; TAP; UnPo (1976 ed.); VGW

At midday/ sparrows gossip on. For Years. Ralph J. Mills, Jr. AMV-80

At midday the birds doze. The Hermit Picks Berries. Maxine W. Kumin. RFM

At midnight by the stream I roved. Lewti; or, The Circassian Love-Chaunt. Samuel Taylor Coleridge. MBPR

At midnight I awoke. Clams. Ishigaki Rin, *tr. by* Hiroaki Sato. PBWP

At midnight, in his guarded tent. Fitz-Greene Halleck. *Fr.* Marco Bozzaris. HoPM (1975 ed.)

At midnight in the alley. The Tom-Cat. Don Marquis. BoAnP; SS

At midnight, in the month of June. The Sleeper. Poe. NOBA; TAP

At midnight the heart's. A. M.—P. M. Theodore H. Hirschfield. AMV-81

At midnight they roused us. City of Anguish. Edwin Rolfe. SPT

At mile marker 5 on Highway 89. Armstrong Spring Creek. Lloyd Davis. AMV-81

At minus tide the music. Poke-Pole Fishing. Dennis Schmitz. AmPA

At Mrs. Tyson's farmhouse, the electricity is pumped. The Force. Peter Redgrove. MPo

At moment X. 3 Models of the Universe. May Swenson. Psy

At morn, at noon, at Eve, and Middle Night. The Poet. Keats. TT

At Mount Rushmore I looked up into one. X. J. Kennedy. *Fr.* Edgar's Story. OFD

At my father's wake. Desmet, Idaho, March 1969. Janet Campbell Hall. VoR

At My Mother's Bedside. Marcia Lee Masters. WPE

At Night. Bella Akhmadulina, *tr. fr. Russian by* Daniel Halpern *and* Albert Todd. BoWoP

At Night. Rachel Boimwall, *tr. fr. Yiddish by* Gabriel Preil *and* Howard Schwartz. VWA

At Night. Richard Eberhart. LoAs

At Night. Michael Small. DNGG

At Night. Robley Wilson, Jr. HeS

At night all the maps grow blank. Maps. Howard Schwartz. HeS

At night and in the wind and the rain. Refugees. Chaim Grade, *tr. by* Marc Kaminsky. VWA

At night Babylon is remembered. Apocalypse. Jean Lipkin. VWA

At night, by the fire. Domination of Black. Wallace Stevens. PiAm; PoIA

At night Chinamen jump. Poem. Frank O'Hara. NoAM; NOBA

At night, circling weightless, we dreamed of roses. Roses. Geoffrey Lehmann. CAAP

At night I spurn the coffee cup. Alison Wyrley Birch. PPM

At night I walk right out to the edge of town. Town Boy Yearning. Roger McDonald. FPA

At night in Piazza Navona, I used to lie supine. Going Back. Salvatore Quasimodo, *tr. by* Rina Ferrarelli. AMV-81

At night my shoes look at me. My Mother's Shoes. Rayzel Zychlinska, *tr. by* Marc Kaminsky. VWA

At night, sometimes, when I cannot sleep. The Chosen Light. John Montague. TwMBP

At night, the children came into my room. After His Death. Susan Hartman. AAN

At night the day is constantly woken up. Work. Andrei Codrescu. EAS

At night the factories. Varick Street. Elizabeth Bishop. NYP

At night while. Black Warrior. Norman Jordan. PoBA

At nightfall, as the sea darkens. Ghost Crabs. Ted Hughes. TwMBP

At 9:42 on this May morning. A House of Readers. Jim Wayne Miller. GP

At nine o'clock in the morning. Mother and Son. R. S. Thomas. BuTh

At Nine o'Clock in the Spring. Elissa Bishop. AMV-80

At noon in the desert a panting lizard. At the Bomb Testing Site. William Stafford. CoPAm

At noon, still wearing their white. Friday Lunchbreak. Gregory Orr. PCho

At noon, Tithonus, withered by his singing. The Wedding. Conrad Aiken. CMoP (1970 ed.); TAP

At one glance/ I loved you. Mihri Hatun, *tr. fr. Turkish by* Tâlat S. Halman. PBWP

At one the wind rose. Night-Music. Philip Larkin. InPS

At Our House. William Stafford. Epi

At parties I want to get even. The Odd Woman. Madeline DeFrees. CNW; GP

At Parting. Heine, *tr. fr. German by* Dwight Durling. NAWM-2

At Penshurst ("Had Sacharissa lived when mortals made"). Edmund Waller. OAEL-1

At Poetry Workshop, Winter Semester. Robert A. Martin. AATT

At Pont-Aven, Gauguin's Last Home in France. Andrew Grossbardt. AMV-81

At Potterne, Wiltshire. *Unknown.* FaBoCo

At present I still have. Exit Lines. George Jonas. NeAC

At Queensferry. W. E. Henley. VLP

At Quincey's moat the squandering village ends. Almswomen. Edmund Blunden. OxBTC

At Rochdale. Ian Young. NeAC

At Rushy Lagoon. James McAuley. MAuV

At St. Mary's for the Aged. Eve Shelnutt. TC

At School They Told Us. Ralph Robin. PoUp

At seven in the summer evenings. Plaza Reál with Palmtrees. Paul Blackburn. NoAM

At seven the sun that lit my world blew out. The Astigmatic. Philip Hobsbaum. LP

At seventeen your. Maryuma. Frank Lamont Phillips. AmNP (1974 ed.)

At 79th and Park. Barbara Howes. MiP; NYP

At six, when April chills our hands and feet. Elektra on Third Avenue. Marilyn Hacker. NYP

At 16/ I dreamed of/ a bushy beard. The Vanity of Human Wishes. John Leax. MiP

At Spearfish, S.D. once. Learning. Marie Harris. MMD

At stated .ic times. Composed in the Composing Room. Franklin P. Adams. OBAL

At Staufen. Michael Hamburger. VWA

At Su K'wa K'e there used to bloom a flower. Lost Love. Tr. fr. Tewa Indian by H. J. Spinden. WTO

At such a time, in such a spot. Emily Brontë. VLP

At Summer's End. Saul Hillel Benjamin. AMV-81

At sunset my foot outreached the mounting Pacific's. Swimming in the Pacific. Robert Penn Warren. AMV-80

At sunset, when the night-dews fall. The Snail. James Reeves. ECBV

At Taieri Mouth. James K. Baxter. ATNZ

At Tauba's death I swore. Lamenting Tauba. Laila Akhyaliyya, tr. fr. Arabic by Willis Barnstone. BoWoP

At tea in cocktail weather. Publisher's Party. Phyllis McGinley. OBAL

At ten A.M. the young housewife. The Young Housewife. William Carlos Williams. HeIP; NoAM; PiAm; TAP

At ten I saw a black horse running. Black Horse Running. Noel Maureen Valis. AMV-80

At ten the years made tracks. Biography. Earle Birney. MPA

At That Moment. Raymond R. Patterson. CABA (1972 ed.); PoBA

At that soft pale hour. Encounter in Jerusalem. Fay Lipshitz. VWA

At the age of nineteen I was digging the land. The Kerry Recruit. Unknown. FSW; RDB

At the age of 27. Sketch 48b.11. Ezra Pound. BBGO

At the aged. Thirteen Preludes for Pioneer Square. John Logan. CAAP

At the Airport. Evan Jones. MAuV

At the Airport in Dallas. Stephen Mooney. TAT

At the airport, ready to leave on my little trip. The Fear of Flying. Mona Van Duyn. NMM

At the Altar. Robert Lowell. Between the Porch and the Altar, IV. InPK; InPS

At the Appointed Hour They Came. Michael Smith. CIP

At the "Atlantic" Dinner. Oliver Wendell Holmes. AmVN

At the back of the houses there is the wood. The House in the Wood. Randall Jarrell. UsP

At the Ball! Charles H. Webb. OBAL

At the Ball Game. William Carlos Williams. CMoP (1970 ed.); ExPo (1973 ed.); LiSp; NoAM; NOBA

At the Band Concert. John Malcolm Brinnin. PoA

At the beginning of winter a cold spirit comes. Tr. fr. Chinese by Arthur Waley. BoWoP

At the Beginnings of the Andes. Barbara Ras. AMV-81

At the Birth of a Poet: Amherst, 1830. Larry Rubin. CSP

At the Bomb Testing Site. William Stafford. CoPAm

At the bottom of the twisted. Poem for Lorry. Gerald Hausman. CTBA

At the bowling alley. Pin Ball Angel. Peter Nelson. PHC

At the Cabin. Richard Hugo. CNW

At the Carnival. Anne Spencer. NoAM

At the Cenotaph. "Hugh MacDiarmid." OBP

At the Chairman's Housewarming. William Stafford. AnMo

At the City Park Zoo. R. P Dickey. BCr

At the Confluence of the Soleduck, the Bogachiel and the Quillayute. Beth Bentley. CNW

At the corner of Wood Street, when daylight appears. The Reverie of Poor Susan. Wordsworth. MBPR

At the court of the miracle-working Rabbi of Sadagora. Father. Rose Ausländer, tr. by Ewald Osers. VWA

At the crossroads/ of my gaping dreams. Trembling. Aliza Shenhar, tr. by Linda Zisquit. VWA

At the Crucifixion. Unknown. OxBM

At the Dancing School of the Sisters Schwarz. Judson Jerome. SFF

At the Dark Hour. Paul Dehn. BoLoP

At the dead end of a road twisting snakelike. Party at Bannon Brook. Alden Nowlan. NeAC

At the Discharge of Cannon Rise the Drowned. Hubert Witheford. ATNZ

At the door of Mercy Sighing, with music. Thomas Mackellar. AH

At the Drive-In: "John Wayne vs. God." A. A. Dewey. HeS

At the earliest ending of winter. Not Ideas about the Thing but the Thing Itself. Wallace Stevens. HAP; TAP

At the east end of the horizon. Slade's Anatomy of the Horse. Leon Slade. FPA

At the Eastern Front. Georg Trakl, tr. fr. German by Ingo Seidler. IPWM

At the edge of all the ages. The Song of Finis. Walter de la Mare. ILP (1975 ed.)

At the edge of the macadam parking lot. Getting By on Honesty. Stephen E. Smith. AMV-80

At the edge of the marsh is a church. Church with Long Steeple. Jim Kraus. PHC

At the edge of this pale. Waiting Carefully. Nancy P. Kamm. AMV-80

At the Edge of Town. William Stafford. NNaP

At the end of a freight train rolling away. Late Lights in Minnesota. Ted Kooser. TAT

At the end of a long-walled garden. The Cottage Hospital. John Betjeman. ILP (1975 ed.); NOBE; UnPo (1976 ed.)

At the end of everything, I walk Milwaukee. Walking Milwaukee. Harold Witt. TAT

At the end of his act. Road Show. Geoff Page. FPA

At the end of July, exile. Mediterranean. Muriel Rukeyser. SPT

At the end of our streets is sunrise. The City by the Sea. George Sterling. BPAW

At the End of Spring. Yü Hsüan-chi, tr. fr. Chinese by Geoffrey Waters. BoWoP

At the end of summer. Forty Pounds of Blackberries Equals Thirteen Gallons of Wine. Robert D. Hoeft. AMV-80

At the end of Tarriers' Lane, which was the street. Wm. Brazier. Robert Graves. NOBL

At the End of the Affair. Maxine W. Kumin. CoPAm; TAP

At the end of the bough! Sweet Apple. James Stephens. CMoP (1970 ed.)

At the end of the day. Nothing Strange. Tom Kryss. NeAC

At the end of the road are stone posts. Courland Penders: Going Home. Michael Dransfield. FPA; GAS

At the end of the street,—see? Monkeys from Paradise. Ettore Rella. SPT

At the end of the war I arose. The Driver. James Dickey. VGW

At the equinox when the earth was veiled in a late rain. Continent's End. Robinson Jeffers. TCP

At the far end of a trip north. Nooksack Valley. Gary Snyder. MPA

At the field's edge. The White Hare. Lilian Bowes-Lyon. OxBTC; PoPle

At the Fillmore. Philip Levine. NNaP

At the first peep of dawn she roused me! Paterson—The Strike. William Carlos Williams. *Fr.* The Wanderer: A Rococo Study. Epi

At the first turning of the second stair. Ash Wednesday, III. T. S. Eliot. NoAM; NOBA

At the Fishhouses. Elizabeth Bishop. HAP; ILP (1975 ed.)

At the foot of the Cathedral of Burgos. Autobiography. Gloria Fuertes, *tr. by* Philip Levine. PBWP

At the foot of the stairs. Hope. William Dickey. GDP; POL

At the foot of yonder mountain where the fountains do flow. The Green Briar Shore. *Unknown.* AmFP

At the ford, while grass-green frogs. Charming the Moon. James DenBoer. MAT

At the frontier the long train slows to a stop. The Frontier. John Hewitt. BIrV

At the Gates. Danny Laurino. DNGG

At the gathered ends of rooty paths. The Island in the Evening. Fairfield Porter. PoA

At the Grave of Albert Camus. Barbara F. Lefcowitz. PoUp

At the Grave of Burns, 1803. Wordsworth. MBPR

At the Grave of Henry Vaughan. Siegfried Sassoon. CMoP (1970 ed.); PoPle

At the Gynecologist's. Linda Pastan. RiTi

At the Holi festival of color. Mira Bai, *tr. fr. Hindi by* Willis Barnstone *and* Usha Nilsson. BoWoP

At the hour I slept. Birds in Their Title Work Freeholds of Straw. Les A. Murray. *Fr.* Walking to the Cattle-Place. CAAP

At the Indian Killer's Grave. Robert Lowell. NOBA; VGW

At the instant. Any April. Cathy Beard. AMV-81

At the instant of drowning he invoked the three sisters. The Three Fates. Rosemary Dobson. BoWoP

At the Jewish Cemetery in Prague. Oscar Levertin, *tr. fr. Swedish by* Richard Burns *and* Göran Printz-Pahlson. VWA

At the Jewish Museum. Linda Pastan. VWA

At the kiss of my heel. The Gentled Beast. Dilys Laing. PH

At the lake's edge. Water and Light, Light and Water. Mark Perlberg. HeS

At the large foot of a fair hollow tree. The Country-Mouse. Abraham Cowley, *after* Horace. OBVE

At the last moment I. Elegy for an Android. D. M. Thomas. TwMBP

At the last, tenderly. The Last Invocation. Walt Whitman. PPM

At the long tables of time. The Jugs. Paul Celan, *tr. by* Christopher Middleton. OBVE

At the Loom. Robert Duncan. *Fr.* Passages. PiAm; VGW

At the Manger Mary Sings. W. H. Auden. *Fr.* For the Time Being. BoReV; ILwL

At the merest handshake I feel his blood. Vincent Buckley. *Fr.* Stroke. MAuV

At the Mid Hour of Night. Thomas Moore. NOBE

At the midnight in the silence of the sleep-time. Epilogue. Robert Browning. *Fr.* Asolando. NOBE; PAIC; TT; VLP

At the Moated Grange. Shakespeare. *Fr.* Measure for Measure, IV, i. NOBE

("Take, O! take those lips away.") BiP; EBEV; GBL; HeIP; ILP (1975 ed.); InPS; OAEL-1; STS

At the Mouth of the Ardyne. Maurice Lindsay. MS

At the Museum of Modern Art. May Swenson. NYP

At the Museum of Natural History. Poem for Explorers. Carol Bergé. MMD

At the National Black Assembly. Amiri Baraka. GP

At the Natural History Museum. William Meredith. NYP

At the next vacancy for God, if I am elected. In Place of a Curse. John Ciardi. NowV

At the officers' table, for half an hour afterwards, port. Class Incident from Graves. Alan Brownjohn. OxBTC

At the old concert hall on the Bow'ry. She Is More to Be Pitied, Than Censured. William B. Gray. FSN; FSW

At the Piano. Swinburne. FaBoNo

At the Poem Society a black-haired man stands up to say. Fresh Air. Kenneth Koch. CAPP; NNaP; NoAM

At the point of shining feathers. The Night a Sailor Came to Me in a Dream. Diane Wakoski. TAP; VGW

At the Porno Factory. Jack Thomas. PoW

At the river's edge I study my form and face. Reflections. Merle Molofsky. AMV-81

At the round earth's imagined corners blow. Holy Sonnets, VII. John Donne. BoReV; CABA (1972 ed.); EBEV; Epi; ExPo (1973 ed.); HAP; ILP (1975 ed.); InPS; HeIP; LFH; NOBE; OAEL-1; OBP; PAIC; PoIA; PoPle; PPoe; PPP; SCP-1

At the San Francisco Airport. Yvor Winters. HeIP; InPK; MPA; NIL; NOBA; RRA

At the Seaside. Robert Louis Stevenson. CTV; LCL; OxBChV

At the Seed and Feed. Edgar Simmons. CSP

At the side of the little black crosses. Funeral Notices. Alfonsina Storni, *tr. by* Dorothy Scott Loos. AMV-81

At the Slackening of the Tide. James Wright. CABA (1972 ed.); UnPo (1976 ed.); VGW

At the Smithsonian. Vanessa Haley. AMV-81

At the Spa. James H. Bowden. AMV-81

At the Stilli's Mouth. Richard Hugo. MPA

At the Stronghold. Lawson Fusao Inada. NW

At the Tavern. *Unknown.* OxBM

At the Theatre. John Williams. CoPAm

At the third hour always. Rain. Paul Murray. BIrV

At the time it seemed unimportant: he was lying. The Day. Roy Fuller. OxBTC

At the time of the white dawn. Song of the Fallen Deer. *Tr. fr. Piman by* Frank Russell. OBVE

At the time there were those who said with a wink. The Father. Desmond O'Grady. NoAM

At the time when blossoms *Tr. fr. Chinese by* Arthur Waley *Fr.* Tzu Yeh Songs. BoWoP

At the time when the earth became hot. Birth of Sea and Land Life. Keaulumoku, *tr. by* M. W. Beckwith. *Fr.* The Kumulipo: A Creation Chant. WTO

At the Top. Michael Small. DNGG

At the top of my street the attorneys abound. Conversation in Craven Street, Strand. James Smith *and* Sir George Rose. FaBoCo

At the top of the house the apples are laid in rows. Moonlit Apples. John Drinkwater. FSFS; OxBTC

At the Trieste. Harold Norse. PoW

At the Ukrainian Catholic church. One for the Album. Rhyll McMaster. CAAP

At the Un-National Monument along the Canadian Border. William Stafford. HAP; HeIP; SoSe

At the very beginning of an important symphony. Interruption at the Opera House. Brian Patten. LP

At the Washing of My Son. Su Tung P'o, *tr. fr. Chinese by* Kenneth Rexroth. BBGO

At the Water Zoo. E. V. Knox. BoAnP

At the Wax Museum. Hollis Summers. CoPAm

At the Wedding March. Gerard Manley Hopkins. LoAs

At the week-end conference on Trends. The Subversive Sublime. Tom Buchan. MIS

At the Well. Malka Heifetz Tussman, *tr. fr. Yiddish by* Marcia Falk. VWA

At the Western Shore. Sarah Youngblood. IHMS

At the Western Wall. Barbara F. Lefcowitz. VWA

At the window holding. Saint. Stéphane Mallarmé, *tr. by* Roger Fry. NAWM-2

At the Zoo. Walter de la Mare. BoAnP

At the Zoo. Thackeray. OxBChV

At thieves I bark; at lovers wag my tail. *Unknown, after the Latin of* Joachim du Bellay. FaBoEE

At thirty, when the faiths give out. On When McCarthy Was a Wolf among a Nation of Queer-Queers. Alan Dugan. GP

At this Adonis smiles as in disdain. Shakespeare. *Fr.* Venus and Adonis. EBEV

At this th' impatient hero sowrly smil'd. Homer, *tr. fr. Greek by* Dryden. *Fr.* The Iliad, I. OBVE

At this wharf there are no grand landings to speak of. A Winter Ship. Sylvia Plath. PSN

At Thomas Hardy's Birthplace, 1953. James Wright. ConAP

At three o'clock yesterday afternoon, Jason Quidnunc. Elderly Nobody Erases Self in Central Park. E. S. Forgotson. NowV

"At thy door I'm knocking." Au Clair de la Lune. *Unknown.* BLSH; FSW

At thy nativity a glorious quire. Milton. *Fr.* Paradise Regained, *Bk.* I. PChr

At Times. Kathleen Wiegner. MMD

At Times I Feel Like a Quince Tree. John Robert Quinn. AMV-81

At times I thought the country itself was a cloud. England. Mary Jo Salter. AMV-80

At Timon's Villa. Pope. *Fr.* Moral Essays, Epistle IV. ExPo (1973 ed.)
("At Timon's villa let us pass a day.") OBSV

At Torrey Pines State Park. Jerome Mazzaro. FiCP

At tree level owl and professor blink. The Owl Pellet. Ann Deagon. AAN

At Tripolis. Constance Carrier. WPE

At Trumpingtoun, not fer fro Cantebrigge. The Mill at Trumpington. Chaucer. *Fr.* The Canterbury Tales: The Reeve's Tale. OxBM

At twenty-five he left home. Living with the Fat Man. Michael Delp. TC

At 21. Eugene L. Belisle. AMV-81

At twilight time, when the lamps are lit. Father Coyote. George Sterling. BPAW

At two a.m. Truck Drivers. Terri Haag. CTBA

At 2 a.m. the world is populated. Night Shift. Naomi Shihab. GP

At two-thirty on this bright afternoon. The Longing. William Goodreau. AMV-80

At Upton-on-Severn. *Unknown.* FaBoCo
("Beneath this stone, in hope of Zion.") FaBoEE

At Veronica's. Robert Peterson. NeAC

At Viscount Nelson's lavish funeral. 1805. Robert Graves. OBSV

At War. Russell Atkins. AmNP (1974 ed.)

At Wednesbury there was a cocking. The Wednesbury Cocking. *Unknown.* FaBoBa; PeBB

At White River. John Haines. FiCP

At Woodcombe farm, wi' ground an' tree. Hallowed Pleaces. William Barnes. VPC

At Woodlawn I heard the dead cry. The Lost Son. Theodore Roethke. HAP; VGW

At Woodward's Gardens. Robert Frost. PoA

At words poetic, I'm so pathetic. You're the Top. Cole Porter. OBAL; UnPo (1976 ed.)

At work his arms wave like a windmill. The Secretary. Peter Redgrove. OxBTC

At your burial. In Its Place. Carol Stager. AMV-80

At your entreaty, I at last have writ. Maidenhead. "Ephelia." WPE

At your light side trees shy. Poem. William Knott. EAS

Atalanta. Ovid, *tr. fr. Latin by* Rolfe Humphries. *Fr.* Metamorphoses, X. LiSp

Atalanta in Calydon, *sels.* Swinburne.
"Before the beginning of years." HeIP; PPM
Chorus: "When the hounds of spring are on winter's traces." ExPo (1973 ed.); HAP; HeIP; ILP (1975 ed.); NOBE; OAEL-2; PoPle; SoSe (1977 ed.); VPC
(When the Hounds of Spring.) NIL
Chorus: "Who hath given man speech? or who hath set therein." OAEL-2

Atameros. John Beevers. EAS

Atavism. Richard Lake. NCSH

Atavism. Elinor Wylie. PoA; SBG

Atheists are few; most nymph a godhead own. Edward Young. *Fr.* Satire on Women. SoSe

Atheist's Prayer, The. Miguel de Unamuno, *tr. fr. Spanish.* ILwL

Athelstan King,/ Lord among Earls. Battle of Brunanburh. *Unknown, tr. by* Tennyson. BTTM; OBVE

Athene's Song. Eavan Boland. CIP

Athletes. Walker Gibson. LiSp

Athlete's Prayer, An. Ed Charles. SPo

Athol Brose. Thomas Hood. FaBoCo

Athwart the sky a lowly sigh. London. John Davidson. NOBE

Atlantic is a stormy moat, The; and the Mediterranean. The Eye. Robinson Jeffers. NOBA; PiAm

Atlantis. Conrad Aiken. Priapus and the Pool, XV. EcS

Atlantis. Hart Crane. *Fr.* The Bridge. NYP

Atlantis. Robert Ferguson. BrS

Atlas. Robert Flanagan. HeS

Atlas' Daughter. Polly Mann. NPW

Atmosphere clear and transparent, The. Lewis in Summer. Derick Thomson. MS

Atomic Courtesy. Ethel Jacobson. QQQ

Atop the rock hill, testing the air. Bear (Part Three). Jeffrey Miles. BCr

Atrocious Pun, An. *Unknown.* TDH

Atrocity, The/ Of the great elephant. The Elephant. Sandra Hochman. BoAnP

Attack, The. Leonard Clark. RAE

Attack. Siegfried Sassoon. NOBE; OxBTC

Attack of the Crab Monsters. Lawrence Raab. AmPA

Attainment, The. Coventry Patmore. *Fr.* The Angel in the House, I, iii. FaBoEE

Attempts: 1964. Gray Jacobik. PoUp

Attend, all ye who list to hear our noble England's praise. The Armada. Macaulay. FaPoR

Attend my fable if your ears be clean. Roy Campbell. *Fr.* The Wayzgoose. OBSV

Attend my lays, ye ever honour'd nine. An Hymn to the Morning. Phillis Wheatley. TAP

Attend ye valiant highwaymen and outlaws of disdain. Bold Jack Donohue. *Unknown.* PeBB

Attend, Young Friends, While I Relate. *Unknown.* AmFP

Attending to some inexpressible wish. Nude with Green Chair. Antony Oldknow. AMV–81

Attention. Adrienne Rich. TAP

Attentive eyes, fantastic heed. A Poet. Thomas Hardy. NoAM

Attentively he heard us, while we spoke. Virgil, *tr. by* Dryden. *Fr.* The Aeneid, XI. OBVE

Attic Landscape, The. Herman Melville. NOBA; OBAL

Attic maid! with honey fed. To the Swallow. William Cowper, *after* Euenus. OBVE

Attica. Horace Coleman. SES

Attica. Ron Welburn. NW

Atticus. Pope. *Fr.* An Epistle to Dr. Arbuthnot. InPK; NOBE

Attis. Catullus, *tr. fr. Latin by* Peter Whigham. OBVE

Attis. George Stanley. MIT

Attitude of body may denote the mind, An. Psychological Dissertation. James Boyer May. PoW

Attitudes, *sel.* Richard Eberhart.
New England Protestant. TH

Attraction. Ella Wheeler Wilcox. PeD

Au Clair de la Lune, *with music. Unknown, tr. fr. French by* "C. F. M." BLSH; FSW

Au Jardin des Plantes. John Wain. OxBTC

Au Tombeau de Mon Père. Ronald McCuaig. GAS; MAuV

Aubade: Donna Anna to Juan, Still Asleep. Richard Howard. PoA

Aubade: "Having bitten on life like a sharp apple." Louis MacNeice. NIL; PAIC

Aubade: "Hours before dawn we were woken by the quake." William Empson. FaBoTw (1975 ed.); NIL; OxBTC; PAIC

Aubade: "In the early morning." Linda Pastan. TV

Aubade: "Jane, Jane,/ Tall as a crane." Edith Sitwell. CMoP (1970 ed.); NoAM

Aubade: "Lark now leaves his watery nest, The." Sir William Davenant. NOBE
(Awake! Awake!) PPM
("Lark now leaves his watery nest, The.") LoAs
(Song.) GBL

Aubade: "Long ago when I shouted in red letters." Ruth Lechlitner. AMV–80

Aubade: N.Y.C. Robert Wallace. CoPAm; HoPM (1975 ed.)

Aubade: "Stay, O sweet, and do not rise." *Unknown.* BoLoP; NOBE

Aubade: The Desert. Frederick Bock. PoA

Aubade: "What dawn is it?" Karl Shapiro. GP; VGW

Aube Provençale. Marilyn Hacker. AmPA

Aubrey Bodine's crosswater shot of Menchville. The Perspective and Limits of Snapshots. Dave Smith. PCho

Auburn is a chic color. Christina. Jessica Tarahata Hagedorn. NW

Aucassin and Nicolette. *Unknown, tr. fr. French by* Edward Francis Moyer *and* Carey DeWitt Eldridge. NAWM–1

Auden, MacNeice, Day Lewis, I have read them all. British Leftish Poetry, 1930–40. "Hugh MacDiarmid." CMoP (1970 ed.); FaBoTw (1975 ed.); NoAM

Auditory Hallucinations. Joyce Mansour, *tr. fr. French by* Carol Cosman. PBWP

Audubon, Drafted. Amiri Baraka. PPP

Augur, The. Stephen Tudor. HeS

Auguries for Three Women. Jacquelyne Crews. AMV–81

Auguries of Innocence. Blake. BiP; CABA (1972 ed.); EBEV; FaPoR; LAuP; MBPR; OAEL–1; OBP; PCOP, *much abr.;* VoPo, *much abr.*
*Sels.*
Robin Redbreast in a Cage, A. AKE
(Three Things to Remember.) ECBV
To See a World in a Grain of Sand. InPK; PPoe

August. William Everson. PiAm

August. Louis MacNeice. PoPle

August. William Morris. *Fr.* The Earthly Paradise. VPC

August. Adrienne Rich. NNaP; PBWP

August. Spenser. *Fr.* The Shepheardes Calender. PAIC

August. Celia Thaxter. CTV

August Afternoon. Marion Edey. FPB

August Afternoon. Nancy Remaly. CTBA

August afternoon. Sunday, Guadalajara. Anthony Ostroff. MIT

August, another year and the same. To an Estranged Wife. Gary Young. AMV–81

August, at an Upstairs Window. Harold McCurdy. AMV–80

August at the Lake. David Young. AmPA

August/ Fresno 1973. Roberta Spear. AmPA

August Fugue. Thomas Shapcott. CAAP

August. Hear/ the cicadas. Speaking for Them. Hayden Carruth. GP

August heat. Haiku. Gerald Vizenor. VoR

August is nearly over, the people. Louis MacNeice. *Fr.* Autumn Journal. CMoP (1970 ed.)

August is the windy month. A New England Farm, August 1914. Les A. Murray. GAS

August night thick and black on us, The. Pelvic Meditation. Bruce Smith. AMV–80

August 1914. Isaac Rosenberg. EBEV; NOBE; OxBTC

August 2. Norman Jordan. PoBA

August 13, 1966. Daryl Hine. GP

August 'twas, the twenty-fifth. Bar's Fight, August 28, 1746. Lucy Terry. BPo

August 12, 1952. Charles Fishman. AMV–81

August 24, 1963—1:00 A.M.—Omaha. Donna Whitewing. VW

August 22. John Unterecker. PHC

August Was Foggy. Gary Snyder. NNaP

August Weather. Katharine Tynan. FSFS

August wind rides Spain tonight in a fierce saddle, The. Casa de Pollos. Kathleen Fraser. AmPA

Augustus still survives in Maro's strain. On Colley Cibber. Samuel Johnson. NIL

Augustus was a chubby lad. The Story of Augustus Who Would Not Have Any Soup. Heinrich Hoffmann, *tr. fr. German.* OxBChV; SpRo

Auld Daddy Darkness. James Ferguson. OxBChV

Auld Hunter, The. George Campbell Hay, *tr. fr. Gaelic; Scots version by* "Hugh MacDiarmid." MS

Auld Lang Syne. Burns. AKE; BiP; BLSH, *with music;* BLSo, *with music;* FSW; LAuP; NOBE

Auld Noah was at hame wi' them a'. Parley of Beasts. "Hugh MacDiarmid." BoAnP; NoAM

Auld Robin Gray. Lady Anne Lindsay. WPE

Auld Sanct-Aundrians—Brand the Builder. Tom Scott. MS

Auld sangs soored and cankered, The. The Grave of Love. Heine, *tr. by* Alexander Gray. SLP

Auld Seceder Cat. The. *Unknown.* FaBoCo

Auld wife sat at her ivied door, The. Ballad. Charles Stuart Calverley. FaBoCo; FaBoNo; SpRo; VLP

Auld wumman cam'in, a mere rickle o' banes, An. Old Wife in High Spirits. "Hugh MacDiarmid." CMoP (1970 ed.); ExPo (1973 ed.); OxBTC

Auncient acquaintance, madam, betwen us twayn, The. John Skelton. AAS

Aunt, The. Patrick Galvin. IPM

Aunt Alice in April. William H. Matchett. CTBA

Aunt Dinah's Quilting Party. Francis Kyle. *See* When I Saw Sweet Nelly Home.

Aunt Emma, Uncle Al: A Short History of the South. Marion Montgomery. CSP

Aunt Helen. T. S. Eliot. OBAL; PoA; SoS

Aunt Jane Allen. Fenton Johnson. PoBA

Aunt Jemima of the Ocean Waves. Robert Hayden. PoBA

Aunt Jennifer's Tigers. Adrienne Rich. HeIP; NIL

Aunt Julia. Norman MacCaig. MPo

Aunt Laura Moves toward the Open Grave of Her Father.
Joseph De Roche. HeIP

Aunt Lucrezia. Alistair Campbell. ATNZ

Aunt Mabel. William Stafford. AnMo

Aunt Rhody. *Unknown. See* Old Gray Goose, The.

Aunt Rose—now—might I see you. To Aunt Rose. Allen
Ginsberg. CABA (1972 ed.); VGW

Aunt Sue's Stories. Langston Hughes. DuDa

Aunt Zillah Speaks. Herbert Palmer. FaBoTw (1975 ed.)

Auntie, did you feel no pain. Appreciation. Harry Graham.
PoPle

Aunts, The. Jean Nordhaus. PoUp

Aunts Watching Television. John Pudney. MPo

Aura Lea [*or* Lee], *with music.* W. W. Fosdick. BLSo; PSoN

Aureng-Zebe, *sel.* Dryden.
Prologue: "Our author by experience finds it true." ILP (1975
ed.); LFH

Aurora, *sel.* Earl of Stirling.
"Ile give thee leave my love, in beauties field," Sonnet XXVI.
SLP

Aurora Borealis. Edouard Roditi. EAS

Aurora Leigh, *sel.* Elizabeth Barrett Browning.
"Critics say that epics have died out, The," *fr.* V. PBWP

Auroras of Autumn, The, *sels.* Wallace Stevens.
"Farewell to an idea . . . A cabin stands." CMoP (1970 ed.)
"This is where the serpent lives, the bodiless." CMoP (1970
ed.)
"Unhappy people in a happy world, An." CMoP (1970 ed.)

Auschwitz from Colombo. Anne Ranasinghe. VWA

Auspex. James Russell Lowell. TAP

Auspice of Jewels. Laura Riding. NoAM

Australia. A. D. Hope. GAS

Australian Dream, The. David Campbell. GAS

Austrian Army, An. Alaric A. Watts. FaBoCo; NOBL

Aut Neutrum . . . Vel Duos. Rufinus Domesticus, *tr. fr. Latin by*
Dudley Fitts. OLR

Autant en Emporte le Vent. Marguerite de Navarre, *tr. fr. French
by* Aline Allard. PBWP

Authentic, The! Shadows of it. Matins. Denise Levertov.
IHMS; NoAM; NOBA

Authentic Tidings. Wordsworth. *Fr.* The Prelude, VI. BoReV

Author, The. Charles Churchill. ESaP
*Sels.*
"Gods! with what pride I see the titled slave." OBSV
Pains of Education, The. FaBoCo
"When with much pains this boasted learning's got." OBSV

Author Apologizes to a Lady for His Being a Little Man, The.
Christopher Smart. BoLoP

Author Loving These Homely Meats, Specially, viz.: Cream,
Pancakes, Buttered Pippin-Pies, The. John Davies of
Hereford. FaBoNo

Author, of His Own Fortune, The. Sir John Harington. FaBoEE

Author of light, revive my dying spright. Thomas Campion.
AAS

Author of my talents, only you have I praised. An Athlete's
Prayer. Ed Charles. SPo

Author to Her Book, The. Anne Bradstreet. EAP; ILP (1975
ed.); InPK; NOBA; PiAm; TAP

Author to His Wife, of a Woman's Eloquence, The. Sir John
Harington. BoLoP

Authority is a disease, and cure. Samuel Butler. FaBoEE

Author's Abstract of Melancholy, The. Robert Burton. *See*
Anatomy of Melancholy, The.

Author's Apology, The. T. Carmi, *tr. fr. Hebrew by* Marcia Falk.
VWA

Author's Early Life, The. Julia A. Moore. PeD

Author's Epitaph, An. Written by Himself. Abel Evans.
FaBoEE

Authors—essayist, atheist, novelist, realist, rimester. Tennyson.
*Fr.* Locksley Hall Sixty Years After. PeD

Authors of the Town, The, *sel.* Richard Savage.
"First, let me view what noxious nonsense reigns." OBSV

Author's Reply, The. Sir Carr Scroope. APAS

Auto Icon. John Daniel. TwMBP

Auto Mobile. A. R. Ammons. FF; InPK; OBAL

Auto Wreck. Karl Shapiro. BiP; CMoP (1970 ed.); CoPAm;
FF; ILP (1975 ed.); IP; NIL; SoS; UsP; VGW; VoPo

Autobiographia Literaria. Frank O'Hara. NNaP; NOBA; OSP

Autobiographical Note. Vernon Scannell. HeHu; LP; MPo

Autobiography. Sonja Akesson, *tr. fr. Swedish by* Ingrid Claréus.
BoWoP

Autobiography. Gloria Fuertes, *tr. fr. Spanish by* Philip Levine.
PBWP

Autobiography. Thom Gunn. FoP

Autobiography. Louis MacNeice. BuTh

Autobiography. Dan Pagis, *tr. fr. Hebrew by* Robert Friend.
VWA

Autobiography, Chapter XII: Hearing Montana. Jim Barnes.
AMV–81

Autobiography: Hollywood. Charles Reznikoff. *Fr.* Going To
and Fro and Walking Up and Down. SA; VWA

Autobiography: Last Chapter. Jim Barnes. CDW

Autobiography of a Lungworm. Roy Fuller. NoAM

Autobiography Part Two: Rock and Roll. Jessica Tarahata
Hagedorn. MMD

Autocrat of the Breakfast-Table, The, *sels.* Oliver Wendell
Holmes.
Aestivation [an Unpublished Poem, by My Late Latin Tutor], *fr.
ch.* 11. NOBL; OBAL
(Intramural Aestivation, or Summer in Town, by a Teacher of
Latin.) FaBoNo
Chambered Nautilus, The, *fr. ch.* 4. AmVN; EcS; HoPM (1975
ed.); ILP (1975 ed.); NOBA; PiAm; VoPo
Deacon's Masterpiece, The; or, The Wonderful "One-Hoss
Shay," *fr. ch.* 11. FaPo; NOBA; OBAL; PiAm; SS; TAP

Autograph Book/ Prophecy. Anne Halley. NMM

Autograph Bore, The. Oliver Herford. TDH

Autolycus as Peddler. Shakespeare. *Fr.* The Winter's Tale, IV,
iii. OAEL–1

Autolycus Sings. Shakespeare. *See* Autolycus' Song ("When
daffodils begin to peer.")

Autolycus' Song ("Jog on, jog on . . ."). Shakespeare. *Fr.* The
Winter's Tale, IV, ii. SpRo

Autolycus' Song ("When daffodils begin to peer"). Shakespeare.
*Fr.* The Winter's Tale, IV, ii. OAEL–1
(Autolycus Sings.) NOBE
(Pedlar's Song, The.) BBL
("When daffodils begin to peer.") AIW; OBP; PoPle

Autolycus' Song (In Basic English). Richard L. Greene. SpRo

Automatic fingers write, The. Séance. Francis King. PoA

Autumn. Bella Akhmadulina, *tr. fr. Russian by* Barbara Einzig.
BoWoP

Autumn. Roy Campbell. OxBTC; WIF

Autumn ("The thistledown's flying . . ."). John Clare. HAP;
NU; OBP

Autumn. Walter de la Mare. OxBTC

Autumn. Florence Hoatson. DuDr

Autumn. T. E. Hulme. Moon; PAIC

Autumn. Philip Levine. NNaP

Autumn ("With what a glory comes and goes the year!"). Longfellow. FSFS

Autumn. Itzik Manger, *tr. fr. Yiddish by* Ruth Whitman. VWA

Autumn. Thomas Nashe. *Fr.* Summer's Last Will and Testament. OAEL-1

Autumn. Elizabeth Madox Roberts. PoTa

Autumn. Vernon Scannell. HeHu; MPo; OxBTC

Autumn. Princess Shikishi, *tr. fr. Japanese by* Hiroaki Sato. PBWP

Autumn. Humbert Wolfe. FSFS

Autumn/ autumn fall. Thoughts. Quincy Troupe. SES

Autumn; a Dirge. Shelley. FSFS

Autumn Begins in Martins Ferry, Ohio. James Wright. CAPP; InPS; POL; PPoD

Autumn Change. John Clare. VLP

Autumn Chapter in a Novel. Thom Gunn. OxBTC

Autumn comes to its senses. October. Fredric Koeppel. AMV-80

Autumn Day, An. Sorley MacLean. AMV-81

Autumn Evening. George Anthony. EAS

Autumn—for My Son. Christine Churches. GAS

Autumn Ghost Sounds. *Unknown.* IWK

Autumn hath all the summer's fruitful treasure. Autumn. Thomas Nashe. *Fr.* Summer's Last Will and Testament. OAEL-1

Autumn Horses. Jenne Andrews. HeS

Autumn, I think, now. Fall. Mary Ursula Bethell. ATNZ

Autumn Idleness. Dante Gabriel Rossetti. The House of Life, LXIX. GBL; ILP (1975 ed.); OAEL-2

Autumn Imagined. Donald Davie. PoA

Autumn in Cornwall. Swinburne. PES

Autumn is over the long leaves that love us. The Falling of the Leaves. W. B. Yeats. VLP

Autumn is the blue of the wall: being sheltered by little deaths. Apart from Oneself. Alejandra Pizarnik, *tr. by* Yishai Tobin. VWA

Autumn Journal, *sels.* Louis MacNeice.
  "August is nearly over, the people." CMoP (1970 ed.)
  "Conferences, adjournments, ultimatums." OxBTC
  "Nightmare leaves fatigue." BIrV
  "Shelley and jazz and lieder and love and hymn-tunes." NOBL

Autumn Leaves. Charles H. Webb. OBAL

Autumn light, light of afternoon, the crows. For My Grandfather. Richard Robbins. AMV-81

Autumn made colors burn, The. Venus Khoury-Gata, *tr. fr. French by* Willis Barnstone. BoWoP

Autumn Morning in Shokoku-ji, An. Gary Snyder. HAP

Autumn Music. Gabriel Preil, *tr. fr. Hebrew by* Howard Schwartz. VWA

Autumn on the Wabash. Dave Etter. CoPAm

Autumn Orchard. Catherine Haydon Jacobs. AMV-80

Autumn Poem. Anthony Cronin. CIP

Autumn Rain. Kenneth Rexroth. NU

Autumn Refrain. Wallace Stevens. WeW

Autumn Robin, The. John Clare. DuDr

Autumn Sequence. Adrienne Rich. VGW

Autumn Shade, *sels.* Edgar Bowers.
  "Autumn shade is thin, The. Grey leaves lie faint," I. PiAm
  "In nameless warmth, sun light in every corner," IX. PiAm
  "My shadow moves, until, at noon, I stand," X. PiAm

Autumn Song. Dante Gabriel Rossetti. ILP (1975 ed.)

Autumn Song for Anti-Fascists. Genevieve Taggard. SPT

Autumn swells over the land. Autumn Horses. Jenne Andrews. HeS

Autumn, Thurlby Domain. Charles Brasch. ATNZ

Autumn-time has come, The. My Triumph. Whittier. NOBA

Autumnal, The. John Donne. Elegies, IX. InPS

Autumnal Moon, The. James Thomson. *Fr.* The Seasons: Autumn. NOBE

Autumnal Song. Walter Savage Landor. OAEL-2

Autumn's bright moon. Haiku. Kaga no Chiyo, *tr. by* R. H. Blyth. PBWP

Avalanche. Janet Emig. SPo

Ave atque Vale. Swinburne. NOBE; OAEL-2; VLP

Ave atque Vale. *Malay Oral Tradition, tr. by* R. J. Wilkinson *and* R. O. Winstedt. WTO

Ave Caesar. Robinson Jeffers. NoAM; NOBA

Ave Maria. Hart Crane. *Fr.* The Bridge. NoAM; NOBA

Ave Maria. Frank O'Hara. NNaP

Avenge, O Lord, thy slaughtered saints, whose bones. On the Late Massacre in Piedmont. Milton. AnMo; BiP; CABA (1972 ed.); Epi; FaPo; HAP; HeIP; ILP (1975 ed.); InPK; LFH; NIL; NOBE; OAEL-1; OBP; PPoe; PPP; SoSe; UnPo (1976 ed.); VoPo; WeW

Avenue. Dennis Trudell. AAN

Avenue Bearing the Initial of Christ into the New World, The, *sel.* Galway Kinnell.
  "Fishmarket closed, the fishes gone into flesh, The," II. ConAP

Avenue in Savernake Forest. William Lisle Bowles. PES

Avenue Y. Anita Barrows. VWA

Avenues, The. David St. John. AMV-80

Average, The. W. H. Auden. BBGO

Average Night, The. Paul Nelson. PHC

Aviators, The. William Pillin. SPT

Avis. Ted Morison. AMV-81

Avocado. Gary Snyder. CNW

Avoid the reeking herd. The Eagle and the Mole. Elinor Wylie. BoWoP; PAIC; UnPo (1976 ed.)

Avoidances. Ron Welburn. PoBA

Avoiding News by the River. W. S. Merwin. CoPAm

Avondale. Stevie Smith. RAE

Avondale Mine Disaster, The. *Unknown.* AmFP

Avremele, when will we have our own child? Abraham and Sarah. Itzik Manger, *tr. by* Stephen Garrin. VWA

Aw was young and lusty. Sair Fyel'd, Hinny. *Unknown.* GBP

Awa' wi' your witchcraft o' beauty's alarms. Hey for a Lass wi' a Tocher. Burns. SLP

Awake./ Your youth is passing like smoke. A Lamentation. Carl Rakosi. VWA

Awake, Aeolian lyre, awake. The Progress of Poesy. Thomas Gray. LAuP; LFH

Awake, arise, the hour is come. A Radical War Song. Macaulay. OBSV

Awake, Arise, You Drowsy Sleeper. *Unknown.* AmFP

Awake! Awake! Sir William D'Avenant. *See* Aubade: "Lark now leaves his watery nest, The."

Awake, awake! for my track is red. The Song of the Flume. Anna M. Fitch. BPAW

Awake but not yet up, too early morning. Out of Sleep. Allen Curnow. ATNZ

Awake! for Morning in the Bowl of Night. The Rubáiyát of Omar Khayyám of Naishápúr. Omar Khayyám, *tr. by* Edward Fitzgerald. FaPoR; HAP; HeIP; ILP (1975 ed.); WeW

Awake! Glad Heart! Henry Vaughan. PIM

Awake, my heart, to be loved, awake, awake! Robert Bridges. ILP (1975 ed.); NOBE

Awake, my love, who sleep into the dawn! The Lady's Farewell. Nuno Fernandez Torneol, *tr. by* Yvor Winters. AIW

Awake, My Lute! C. S. Lewis. FaBoNo

Awake, my St. John! leave all meaner things. An Essay on Man, Epistle I. Pope. PAIC

Awake My Soul, Betimes Awake, *with music.* Isaac Chanler. AH

Awake, My Soul! In Grateful Songs, *with music.* Andrew Fowler. AH

Awake now,/ Fully sensible of my own chains. View from the Window. Jane McCoy. AMV–80

Awake, oh Heaven, for (lo) the heavens conspire. Cyril Tourneur. Moon

Awake, O rain, O sun, O night. Ending. *Tr. fr. Hawaiian by* K. Luomala. WTO

Awake or sleeping (for I know not which). An Old-World Thicket. Christina Rossetti. SBG

Awakening. Robert Bly. ConAP; UsP

Awakening. John Haines. EAS

Awakening. David Robinson. AMV–81

Awakening, The. *Unknown, tr. fr. French by* John Attey. NOBE ("On a time the amorous Silvy.") GBL

Awakening—/ Voices of birds. Nelly Sachs, *tr. from German by* Ruth *and* Matthew Mead. PBWP

Awakening like return to Earth from Moon. Brian Coffey. *Fr.* Advent. CIP

Awaking muscle of a race asleep. Maceo. Luis Lloréns Torres, *tr. by* Julio Marzán. InW

Award. Ray Durem. BPo; CABA (1972 ed.); NIL; PoBA

Aware that summer baked the water clear. Skykomish River Running. Richard Hugo. PoA

Awareness. Don L. Lee. PoBA

A-watchin' how the sea behaves. Meditations of a Mariner. Wallace Irwin. OSF

Away! Robert Frost. NOBA

Away. Josephine Miles. GP

Away. Lucien Stark. GP

Away above a Harborful. Lawrence Ferlinghetti. BoLoP; SFF

Away, away from city and street. Away Out West. Sharlot M. Hall. BPAW

Away, birds, away! In a Corn Field. *Unknown.* ECBV

A-way by the river so clear. Little Moses. *Unknown.* FSW

Away, Delights. John Fletcher. *Fr.* The Captain, III, iv. NOBE
(Sad Song, The.) GBL

Away down yonder in the Wahee Mountains. The Oregon Trail. *Unknown.* BPAW

Away, for we are ready to a man! Epilogue. James Elroy Flecker. *Fr.* The Golden Journey to Samarkand. NOBE

Away, four miles, I heard the Santa Fe. 12 o'Clock Freight. Hildegarde Flanner. WPW

Away from friends, away from home. The Wanderer's Grave. Rufus B. Sage. BPAW

Away from You. Cecilia Meireles, *tr. fr. Portuguese by* Harriet Zinnes. AMV–81

Away in a Manger. *Unknown.* AH, *with music;* BLSH, *with music;* FSW; GSB, *with music*
(Cradle Hymn, *at. to* Martin Luther.) CTV

Away, Melancholy. Stevie Smith. OxBTC; PBWP

Away Out West. Sharlot M. Hall. BPAW

Away! the moor is dark beneath the moon. Stanzas—April, 1814. Shelley. MBPR

Away, way down on the old Swaunee. Yale Boola! A. M. Hirsh. FSN

Away with Rum. *Unknown.* FSW

Away with silks, away with lawn. Clothes Do but Cheat and Cozen Us. Robert Herrick. CaPo

Away with your fictions of flimsy romance. The First Kiss of Love. Byron. MBPR

Awful Fix. *Unknown.* BluL

Awful shadow of some unseen Power, The. Hymn to Intellectual Beauty. Shelley. BiP; BoReV; ExPo (1973 ed.); HAP; HeIP; ILP (1975 ed.); MBPR; OAEL–2

Awkward Song for My Sisters. Allan Kornblum. AcAn; EC

Awkward Spring. Anselm Hollo. EC

AW6 May 25, 1974. George Bowering. FoP

Ax. Charles Simic. GP

Ax was sharpe, the stokke was harde, The. Epigram on the year 1390. *Unknown.* NIL

Axe angles, An/ from my neighbor's ashcan. Junk. Richard Wilbur. HAP; InPK; PPoD; WeW

Axe rings in the wood, The. Remembered Morning. Janet Lewis. WPE

Axes/ After whose stroke the wood rings. Words. Sylvia Plath. AnMo; ConAP

Axioms. Gad Hollander. VWA

Axle quits, An. Metal Fatigue. Adam Le Fevre. AMV–81

Axolotl, The. David McCord. OBAL

Ay, Ay, This Is the Day. *Unknown.* OxBM

Ay, besherewe yow, [*or* beshrew you!] be my fay. Manerly Margery Mylk and Ale. John Skelton. AAS; FaBoNo

Ay, every inch a king:/ When I do stare, see how the subject quakes. Shakespeare. *Fr.* King Lear, IV, vi. OBP

Ay me, how many perils doe enfold. Spenser. *Fr.* The Faerie Queene, I, 8. OAEL–1

Ay me! whilst thee the shores and sounding seas. Milton. *Fr.* Lycidas. Prf

Ay, screen thy favourite dove, fair child. A Child Screening a Dove from a Hawk. Letitia Elizabeth Landon. VLP

Ay, so it is in every brain. To a Young Brother. Maria Jane Jewsbury. OxBChV

Ay, tear her tattered ensign down! Old Ironsides. Oliver Wendell Holmes. BTTM; CTV; FaPo; GOA; RhR; TAP

Ay, this is freedom!—these pure skies. The Hunter of the Prairies. Bryant. LiSp

Ay! thou look'st cold on me, pomp-loving Moon. To the Moon. George Darley. Moon

Ayaiyaja/ This why, I wonder. It Is Hard to Catch Trout. Piuvkaq, *tr. fr. Eskimo.* WTO

Aye, back at Leady-Day, you know. Leady-Day, an' Ridden House. William Barnes. VLP

"Aye! I am a poet and upon my tomb." And Thus in Nineveh. Ezra Pound. VGW

Aye, there it is! It wakes to-night. Emily Brontë. VLP

Aye! What a thing is the passing of Cronos, the angular-minded. John Cowper Powys. *Fr.* The Ridge. OBW

Ayee! Ai! This heavy earth on our shoulders. Burying Ground by the Ties. Archibald MacLeish. GOA

Ayii, Ayii,/ I walked on the ice of the sea. *Unknown, tr. fr. Eskimo.* RFM

Ayii, Ayii/ The great sea has set me in motion. *Unknown, tr. fr. Eskimo.* RFM

Aylmer's Field. Tennyson. VLP

Azalea, The. Coventry Patmore. The Unknown Eros, I, vii. GBL

Azaleas are funny plants. Spring Morning: Waking. Emily Seelbinder. AMV–81

Aziola, The. Shelley. EBEV

A-zlay, A-zlay, you who have clambered the mountains, A-zlay. Navajo Song. Maynard Dixon. BPAW

Aztec Figurine. John Beecher. GP

Azure striation swirls beyond the stones. La Fontaine de Vaucluse. Marilyn Hacker. PCho

Azure, 'tis I, come from Elysian shores. Helen, the Sad Queen. Paul Valéry, *tr. by* Janet Lewis. NIL

Azured vault, the crystal circles bright, The. Sonnet. James I, King of England. Moon

# B

B Flat. Douglas Stewart. GAS; MAuV

B is for beautiful Bella. Beautiful Bella. *Unknown*. TDH

B. Negative. X. J. Kennedy. ConAP; WeW

B, taught by Pope to do his good by stealth. A Misconception. James Russell Lowell. OBAL

B was a beggarly bear. A Beggarly Bear Carolyn Wells. TDH

Baa, baa, black sheep, have you any wool? Mother Goose. MG

Baa, baa, black sheep, where'd you leave your lamb? *Unknown*. AmFP

Babe is at peace within the womb, The. Life Rounded with Sleep. Shelley. BuTh

Babe Ruth. Damon Runyon. SPo

Babe, with a cry brief and dismal, The. Edward Gorey. OBAL

Babel. Gary Pacernick. AMV-81

Babes in the Wood. *Unknown*. ECBV; OxBChV; PCOP

Babi Yar. Lev Ozerov, *tr. fr. Russian by* Daniel Weissbort. VWA

Babies. Rick Cannon. PoUp

Babies: Just Babies. Margaret Fishback. ECBV

Babies of the Pioneers. Eunice W. Luckey. BPAW

Baboon, The. Rhydwen Williams, *tr. fr. Welsh by* R. Gerallt Jones. OBW

Baboon. *Zulu Oral Tradition, tr. by* C. *and* W. Leslav. WTO

Baby at my breast, The. Against Dark's Harm. Anne Halley. NMM

Baby, baby, naughty baby. Mother Goose. NOBL

Baby bawling, being sick, The. Old Man's Song. Vernon Scannell. HeHu

Baby, depend upon it. Shade. Charles Lynch. CNA

Baby did you hear about the bad luck. Bad Luck Blues. *Unknown*. BluL

Baby Giraffe. Patricia Ball. PMW

Baby I can see just what's on your mind. Mind Reader Blues. *Unknown*. BluL

Baby I want to see yr. Wildflowers, Smoke. Lyn Lifshin. MMD

Baby, if you love me. Down and Out. Langston Hughes. ExPo (1973 ed.); PiAm

Baby I'm going/ down town. Sic 'Em Dogs On. *Unknown*. BluL

Baby, I'm going up town. Hunkie Tunkie. *Unknown*. BluL

Baby, I'm sick. I need. Night Thoughts. Gwen Harwood. CAAP

Baby is sleeping so cozy and fair. Rock-a-bye Baby. Effie I. Canning. FSN

Baby Mine, *with music*. Charles Mackey. BLSo

Baby Mine. *Unknown*. FSW

Baby moon, a canoe, a silver papoose, The. Early Moon. Carl Sandburg. BPAW

Baby-Movements. D. H. Lawrence. RRA

Baby, Please Don't Go. *Unknown*. FSW

Baby Seeds. *Unknown*. CTV

Baby-Sermon, A. George MacDonald. OxBChV (Lightning and Thunder, The.) DuDr

Baby Toes. Carl Sandburg. LCL

Baby Tortoise. D. H. Lawrence. BoAnP; CMoP (1970 ed.)

Baby you know I get high. Not Quite Spring. Lyn Lifshin. NeAC

Babylon. "Barry Cornwall." PIM

Babylon. Ron Ikan. NVAP

Babylon; or, The Bonnie Banks o' Fordie. *Unknown*. AmFP; PAIC

Babylon Revisited. Amiri Baraka. BPo; NoAM

Babylonian Sorrows. Heine, *tr. fr. German by* Aaron Kramer. NAWM-2

Baby's Dance, The. Ann Taylor. OxBChV ("Dance, little baby, dance up high.") EBCV

Baby's Dress, A. Hazel Hall. WPW

Baby's feet, like sea-shells pink, A. Swinburne. Étude Réaliste, I. WeW

Baccalaureate. David McCord. OBAL; SpRo

Bacchanal. Peter De Vries. NOBL; OBAL

Bacchanalia; or, The New Age, *sel.* Matthew Arnold. "Epoch ends, the world is still, The," II. OAEL-2

Bacchus. Emerson. NOBA; PiAm

Bacchus. William Empson. NoAM

*Sels.*

"God who fled down with a standard yard, The." PoA

"Herm whose length measured degrees of heat, The." PoA

Bacchus in Tuscany, *sel.* Francesco Redi, *tr. fr. Italian by* Leigh Hunt.

Bacchus's Opinion of Wine, and Other Beverages. OBVE

Bachelor. William Meredith. NoAM

Bachelor Bold and Young. *Unknown*. AmFP

Bachelor growls when his peace is, The. A Token of Attachment. J. Adair Strawson. TDH

Bachelor's Complaint, The. *Unknown*. AmFP

Bachelor's Life, A. *Unknown*. OxBM

Back. Angela McCabe. AmPA

Back. Robert Mezey. AmPA

Back Again, Home. Don L. Lee. BPo

Back and forth, back and forth. Fall 1961. Robert Lowell. ExPo (1973 ed.); PSN; VGW

Back and forth cawings between black. Crow. Peter Blue Cloud. NW

Back and Side Go Bare. At. to William Stevenson. Fr. Gammer Gurton's Needle. HeIP; ILP (1975 ed.) (I Cannot Eat but Little Meat.) ExPo (1973 ed.)

Back Behind the Eyes. Leon Stokesbury. NVAP

Back from London. David Meltzer. CPA

Back from the Country. Oliver St. John Gogarty. PFIr

Back Gnawing Blues. *Unknown*. BluL

Back home the black women are all beautiful. W. W. Amiri Baraka. HeIP; NOBA; PiAm; PoBA

Back in a yard where play has grooved a ditch. Old Men Pitching Horseshoes. X. J. Kennedy. AMV-81

Back in back of the back country. Alabama. Judy Dothard Simmons. CNA

Back in Black Mountain a child will smack your face. Black Mountain Blues. *Unknown*. BluL

Back in *tachanka* days, when Red and Green. Makhno's Philosophers. John Manifold. FPA

Back in the dear old thirties' days. The Poet of Bray. John Heath-Stubbs. NOBL

Back in the Return, *sel.* Huw Menai. "Where shall the eyes a darkness find." OBW

Back in the States. Louis Simpson. AMV-81

Back in the years when Phlagstaff, the Dane, was monarch. The Rejected "National Hymns." "Orpheus C. Kerr." OBAL

Back Just below the Shoulder Blades. Coleman Barks. *Fr. Body Poems.* NVAP

Back of Chicago the open fields. Evening Song. Sherwood Anderson. ANTL

Back of the bus. Apartheid. Margo Bohanon. SES

Back of the dam, under. The Town of Hill. Donald Hall. FiCP; TAP

Back of the mind is a small hotel, The. The Small Hotel. Michael Longley. CIP

Back out of all this now too much for us. Directive. Robert Frost. CABA (1972 ed.); CMoP (1970 ed.); HAP; ILP (1975 ed.); MAT; NoAM; NOBA; PiAm; PPP; TT

Back Road. Bruce Guernsey. AMV-81

Back Street. A. R. D. Fairburn. ATNZ

Back through clouds. Train Tune. Louise Bogan. ECBV

Back to Africa. Erica Jong. RiTi

Back to Arizona. Earl Alonzo Brininstool. BPAW

Back to back, old stumps grown together. Mothers. Beth Bentley. CNW

Back to the Angels. William Walter De Bolt. AMV-81

Back to the roots. Vanish. John Oliver Simon. MIT

Back water at Blytheville. High Water Everywhere: 2. *Unknown.* BluL

Back Water Blues. *Unknown.* BluL; FSW

Back water done rose around Sumner, now, The. High Water Everywhere: 1. *Unknown.* BluL

Back water rising: southern people can't make no time. Rising High Water Blues. *Unknown.* BluL

Back when I was still trying. The Fisherman. Will Wells. AMV-80

Back wings, The/ of the. Between Walls. William Carlos Williams. HoPM (1975 ed.); TAP; VGW

Backbitten in the frozen landscape. Chroma. Greg Hannan. PoUp

Backgrounds to Italian Paintings: Fifteenth Century. Anne Ridler. WPE

Backlash Blues, The. Langston Hughes. BPo

Backroad leafmold stonewall chipmunk. Silent Poem. Robert Francis. FiCP

Backstage, eating bananas. Carmen Miranda. Frank Polite. GP

Backward Spring, A. Thomas Hardy. PPP

Bacteria legs, bacteria mouths. World of Bacteria. Sakutaro Hagiwaro, *tr.* by Graeme McD. Wilson. AMV-80

Bad and Good. Alexander Resnikoff. OSF

Bad Bishop Jegon. *Unknown.* GBP

Bad company is a disease. Rowland Watkyns. FaBoEE

Bad Dream. Louis MacNeice. NoAM

Bad Dream in the Commune, A. Robert Hahn. AAN

Bad Dreams, *sel.* Robert Browning.
"This was my dream! I saw a forest," III. OAEL-2; TT; VLP

Bad Dreams. Billy Collins. AAN

Bad Example. Isabella Fey. BoAnP

Bad Girl Blues. *Unknown.* BluL

Bad Habit, The. Charles Henri Ford. EAS

Bad Luck Blues ("Baby did you hear about the bad luck"). *Unknown.* BluL

Bad Luck Blues ("I want to go home and I ain't got sufficient"). *Unknown.* BluL

Bad Man Ballad. *Unknown.* AmFP

Bad Moon Rising. John Fogerty. GrRo

Bad Morning. Langston Hughes. OBAL; PiAm

Bad news has come to town, bad news is carried. Montcalm and Wolfe. *Unknown.* AmFP

Bad Old Days, The. Kenneth Rexroth. NNaP; NoAM

Bad Season Makes the Poet Sad, The. Robert Herrick. CABA (1972 ed.); CaPo; ILP (1975 ed.)

Bad Sir Brian Botany. A. A. Milne. BBL

Bad Thing, The. John Wain. BuTh

Badger ("When midnight comes a host of dogs and men"). John Clare. ExPo (1973 ed.); HAP; LiSp; NU; OAEL-2; PoIA; SoSe (1977 ed.); VLP

Badger ("Badger grunting on his woodland track, The"), *longer version.* InPS

Badger. Michael Longley. IPM

Badgers, The. Seamus Heaney. CIP

Badman of the Guest Professor. Ishmael Reed. BPo

Baedeker for Metaphysicians. Brian Higgins. FaBoTw (1975 ed.)

Baffled Knight, The. *Unknown.* SLP

Bag of the Bee, The. Robert Herrick. SCP-1

Bagatelle, A. James Reeves. POL

Bagel, The. David Ignatow. ConAP; FF; OSP; PPoD; UsP

Baggot Street Deserta. Thomas Kinsella. CIP; CMoP (1970 ed.)

Bagley Wood. Lionel Johnson. VLP

Bagpipe Music. "Hugh MacDiarmid." OAEL-2

Bagpipe Music. Louis MacNeice. CMoP (1970 ed.); ExPo (1973 ed.); ILP (1975 ed.); NoAM; NOBE; NOBL; OAEL-2; OBSV; OxBTC

Bagpipes. *Unknown.* BBL

Bags of Meat. Thomas Hardy. BoAnP

Bags Packed and We Expected This. Ramona Wilson. VoR

Bah! Walter de la Mare. BoAnP

Bah! I have sung women in three cities. Cino. Ezra Pound. VGW

Baha'u'llah in the Garden of Ridwan. Robert Hayden. PoBA

Bahnhofstrasse. James Joyce. NoAM

Bailiff's [*or* Bayliff's] Daughter of Islington, The. *Unknown.* AIW; AmFP; FaBoBa; FSW; PBMP; RDB, *with music*

Bait, The. John Donne. CABA (1972 ed.); HoPM (1975 ed.); ILP (1975 ed.); InPK; InPS; LFH; NIL; OAEL-1

Baja—Outside Mexicali. Michael McClure. GP

Baked potato's, The. Diner. A. R. Ammons. POL

Baker's knuckles are bruised, The. The Town of Bricked Pathways. Roger McDonald. CAAP

Baker's Tale, The. "Lewis Carroll." *Fr.* The Hunting of the Snark. EBEV

Baking Day. Rosemary Joseph. MPo

Balade: "Hide, Absalon, thy gilte tresses clear." Chaucer. *Fr.* The Legend of Good Women: Prologue. GBL; NOBE ("Hide [*or* Hyd], Absalon, thy gilte tresses clere.") EBEV; HAP; OAEL-1; OxBM

Balade Simple. John Lydgate. GBL

Balalaika. Norman Dubie. AmPA

Balance, The. Judith Johnson Sherwin. GP

Balances. Floyd C. Stuart. FAF

Balancing, The. Ross Talarico. AAN

Balancing 'twixt earth and sky. The Pole-Vaulter. *Unknown.* LiSp; SPo

Balboa, the Entertainer. Amiri Baraka. NoAM

Balcony Poems, The. Douglas Smith. AMV-81

Bald-bare, bone-bare, and ivory yellow: skull. The U.S. Sailor with the Japanese Skull. Winfield Townley Scott. ExPo (1973 ed.)

Bald Cavalier, The. *Unknown.* OxBChV

Bald heads forgetful of their sins. The Scholars. W. B. Yeats. CMoP (1970 ed.); IP; OAEL-2; PoA; WIF

Bald Spot, The. Wesley McNair. AMV-81

Balder, *sel.* Sydney Dobell.
"Was this world built for happiness, that man." PeD

Ball Game. Richard Eberhart. LiSp; MiP

Ball once struck off, The. Base-Ball. John Newbery. SPo

Ball Poem, The. John Berryman. FF; LiSp; NoAM; NoBA; SPo; SoSe

Ball we bought in December, The. Handball Players. Paul Goodman. SPo

Ball will bounce, but less and less, A. Juggler. Richard Wilbur. CMoP (1970 ed.); NCSH; TAP

Ballad: "As you came from the holy land." *Unknown, sometimes at. to* Sir Walter Ralegh. *See* Walsingham.

Ballad: "Auld wife sat at her ivied door, The." Charles Stuart Calverley. FaBoCo; FaBoNo; SpRo; VLP

Ballad: "Blackbird has built in the pasture agen, The." John Clare. *Fr.* Child Harold. VLP

Ballad: "He passed by with another." Gabriela Mistral, *tr. fr. Spanish by* Doris Dana. OLR

Ballad: "I dreamed I passed a doorway." John Hall Wheelock. AIW

Ballad: "I put my hat upon my head." Samuel Johnson. NOBL

Ballad: "I want to know the unity in all things." A. R. Ammons. GP

Ballad by Hans Breitmann. Charles Godfrey Leland. NOBL

Ballad Called Perkin's Figary, A. *Unknown.* APAS

Ballad Called the Haymarket Hectors, A. *Unknown.* APAS

Ballad for a Boy, A. William Johnson Cory. OxBChV (Two Captains, The.) FaPoR

Ballad for Katharine of Aragon, A. Charles Causley. FaBoTw (1975 ed.)

Ballad for My Mother Patrick Galvin. IPM

Ballad for Sue Ellen Westerfield, The. Robert Hayden. NoAM

Ballad from the Seven Dials Press, A. *Unknown.* VLP

Ballad Maker, A. Padraic Colum. AIW

Ballad, November 1680, Made upon Casting the Bill against the Duke of York, A. *Unknown.* APAS

Ballad of a Nun, A. John Davidson. PAIC

Ballad of Abbreviations, A. G. K. Chesterton. NOBL

Ballad of Agincourt, The. Michael Drayton. PPoD (Agincourt.) FaPoR (To the Cambro-Britons and Their Harp, His Ballad of Agincourt.) BTTM

Ballad of an Empty Table. Tom Kryss. NeAC

Ballad of Badmen. Owen Dodson. FB

Ballad of Ballymote, The. Tess Gallagher. GP

Ballad of Bath, A, *sel.* Swinburne. "Like a queen enchanted who may not laugh or weep." PES

Ballad of Befana, The. Phyllis McGinley. AIW

Ballad of Benjamin Bones, The. Christopher Ward. BTTM

Ballad of Bigger Thomas, The. E. Curmie Price. WIF

Ballad of Billie Potts, The. Robert Penn Warren. NOBA

Ballad of Billy Rose, The. Leslie Norris. HeHu

Ballad of Billy the Kid, The. Henry Herbert Knibbs. BPAW

Ballad of Birmingham. Dudley Randall. BPo; InPK; NoAM; SoSe (1977 ed.); WIF

Ballad of Bunker Hill, The. *Unknown.* BTTM

Ballad of Calvary Street. James K. Baxter. ATNZ

Ballad of Chocolate Mabbie, The. Gwendolyn Brooks. CAPP; SoS

Ballad of Dead Ladies, The. Villon, *tr. fr. French by* Dante Gabriel Rossetti. PAIC (Ballat o the Leddies o Langsyne, *tr. by* Tom Scott.) OBVE

Ballad of Dead Yankees, The. Donald Petersen. HeIP; LiSp

Ballad of Dreamland, A. Swinburne. ILP (1975 ed.)

Ballad of East and West, The. Kipling. BTTM; FaPoR

Ballad of Eve, A. Julia Randall. CSP

Ballad of Faith. William Carlos Williams. OBAL

Ballad of Father Gilligan, The. W. B. Yeats. PAIC (Father Gilligan.) AIW

Ballad of Father O'Hart, The. W. B. Yeats. VLP

Ballad of Hagensack, The. Wallace Irwin. PoTa

Ballad of Hector in Hades. Edwin Muir. NoAM; NOBE

Ballad of Hell, A. John Davidson. HoPM (1975 ed.); LFH

Ballad of Hiram Hover, The. Bayard Taylor. FaBoCo; OBAL

Ballad of Ho Chi Minh. Ewan MacColl. FSW

Ballad of Ira Hayes. Peter La Farge. MAT

Ballad of Jimmy Governor, The. Les A. Murray. GAS

Ballad of John Cable and Three Gentlemen. W. S. Merwin. NOBA

Ballad of Johnny Appleseed. Helmer O. Oleson. CTV

Ballad of Lager Bier, The. Edmund Clarence Stedman. OBAL

Ballad of Love and Blood. Angel Miguel Queremel, *tr. fr. Spanish by* Rolfe Humphries. LoAs

Ballad of Mary Baldwin, The. Stephen Sandy. MAT

Ballad of Master McGrath, A. *Unknown.* FaBoBa

Ballad of Minepit Shaw, The. Kipling. PoPle; PoTa

Ballad of Mrs. Noah, The. Robert Duncan. MPo; NoAM; NOBA

Ballad of Moll Magee, The. W. B. Yeats. STS

Ballad of Nat Turner, The. Robert Hayden. BPo; VGW

Ballad of New Orleans. Charles G. Wilson. BTTM

Ballad of No Proper Man. Daniel Hoffman. MAT

Ballad of Orpheus, A. Maurice Lindsay. MS; SLP

Ballad of Past Meridian, A. George Meredith. OAEL–2; VLP

Ballad of Persse O'Reilly, The. James Joyce. *Fr.* Finnegans Wake. FaBoBa

Ballad of Pug-nosed Lil, The. Robert H. Fletcher. BPAW

Ballad of Reading Gaol, The, *abr.* Oscar Wilde. OAEL–2 "He did not wear his scarlet coat," *sel.* NOBE

Ballad of Red Fox, The. Melvin Walker LaFollette. BoAnP

Ballad of Remembrance, A. Robert Hayden. AmNP (1974 ed.); BPo; PoBA

Ballad of Rudolph Reed, The. Gwendolyn Brooks. TT

Ballad of Sam Hall. *Unknown. See* Sam Hall.

Ballad of Springhill (The Springhill Mine Disaster). Ewan MacColl *and* Peggy Seeger. FSW

Ballad of Tampa. Joseph Freeman. SPT

Ballad of the Boll Weevil. *Unknown. See* Ballit of de Boll Weevil, De.

Ballad of the Bread Man. Charles Causley. MPo

Ballad of the Cool Fountain. *Unknown, tr. fr. Spanish by* Edwin Honig. BoWoP

Ballad of the Dark Ladie, The. Samuel Taylor Coleridge. MBPR

Ballad of the D-Day Dodgers. *Unknown.* WTO (D-Day Dodgers, The.) FSW

Ballad of the Despairing Husband. Robert Creeley. OBAL

Ballad of the Fleet, A. Tennyson. *See* Revenge, The.

Ballad of the Gold Country, A. Helen Hunt Jackson. BPAW

Ballad of the Goodly Fere. Ezra Pound. CMoP (1970 ed.); Epi; NoAM; OFD; PAIC

Ballad of the Harp-Weaver, The. Edna St. Vincent Millay. PBMP; PoTa

Ballad of the Hidden Dragon, *abr. Unknown, tr. fr. Chinese.* WTO

Ballad of the Hoppy-Toad. Margaret Walker. FB; HoPM (1975 ed.)

Ballad of the Hyde Street Grip. Gelett Burgess. BPAW

Ballad of the Icondic. John Ciardi. OBAL

Ballad of the Landlord. Langston Hughes. NOBA

Ballad of the Light-eyed Little Girl, The. Gwendolyn Brooks. SoS

Ballad of the Long-legged Bait. Dylan Thomas. Epi

Ballad of the Man Who's Gone. Langston Hughes. AIW

Ballad of the Moon, Moon. Federico García Lorca, *tr. fr. Spanish by* Langston Hughes. Epi

Ballad of the Morning Streets. Amiri Baraka. CNA

Ballad of the Mulberry Road, A. Ezra Pound. UsP

Ballad of the Oedipus Complex. Lawrence Durrell. FaBoCo

Ballad of the Old-Time Engine. Eda H. Vines. QQQ

Ballad of the Oysterman, The. Oliver Wendell Holmes. ILP (1975 ed.)

Ballad of the Pigskin. Horace Spencer Fiske. SPo

Ballad of the Sleepwalker, The. Federico García Lorca. *See* Somnambulistic Ballad.

Ballad of the Tempest. James T. Fields. RhR

Ballad of the Ten Casino Dancers. Cecilia Meireles, *tr. fr. Portuguese by* James Merrill. BoWoP

Ballad of the Three Coins. Vernon Watkins. NoAM

Ballad of the Two Grandfathers. Nicolás Guillén, *tr. fr. Spanish by* D. J. Flakoll *and* Claribel Alegria. TVo

Ballad of the Volunteer, The. Dabney Stuart. CSP

Ballad of Tonopah Bill, The. *Unknown.* BPAW

Ballad of Trees and the Master, A. Sidney Lanier. *See* Into the Woods My Master Went.

Ballad of Villon and Fat Madge, The. Villon, *tr. fr. French by* Swinburne. LoAs; OBVE

Ballad of William Bloat, The. *Unknown.* NOBL
(Belfast Linen.) WTO

Ballad on the Times, A. Henry Hall. APAS

Ballad-Singer, The. Thomas Hardy. At Casterbridge Fair, I. BoLoP; OLR; VLP

Ballad to a Traditional Refrain. Maurice James Craig. BIrV

Ballad upon a Wedding, A. Sir John Suckling. CABA (1972 ed.); CaPo; EBEV; FaBoBa; LoAs

Ballad Which Anne Askew Made and Sang When She Was in Newgate, The. Anne Askew. WPE

Ballade: "Brother humans who live on after us." Villon, *tr. fr. French by* Galway Kinnell. NAWM-1
(Ballat o the Hingit, *tr. by* Tom Scott.) OBVE

Ballade against Woman Inconstant, A. Chaucer. CABA (1972 ed.)

Ballade Made in Hot Weather. W. E. Henley. FSFS

Ballade of Beauties. Alexander Scott. MS

Ballade of Dead Actors. W. E. Henley. PPoD

Ballade of Liquid Refreshment. E. C. Bentley. FaBoCo

Ballade of Prose and Rhyme, The. Austin Dobson. PAIC

Ballade of Sayings. W. S. Merwin. NNaP

Ballade of Suicide, A. G. K. Chesterton. PAIC

Ballade of the Armada, A. Austin Dobson. FaPoR

Ballade of the Incompetent Ballade-Monger, The. James Kenneth Stephen. VLP

Ballade of the Scottyshe Kynge, A. John Skelton. FaBoBa

Ballade of Youth and Age. W. E. Henley. VLP

Ballade to His Mistress. Villon, *tr. fr. French by* Norman Cameron. WeW

Ballade Tragique à Double Refrain. Max Beerbohm. OBSV

Ballat o the Hingit. Villon. *See* Ballade: "Brother humans who live on after us."

Ballat o the Leddies o Langsyne. Villon. *See* Ballad of Dead Ladies, The.

Ballatetta. Ezra Pound. VGW

Ballet. Brenda Hillman. AMV-81

Ballet. *Unknown.* TDH

Ballinderry. *Unknown.* WTO

Balliol Rhymes, *sels. Var. authors.*
"First come I. My name is Jowett." Henry Charles Beeching. FaBoCo; FaBoEE; NOBL; PoPle
"I am Branson; Nature's laws." Henry Charles Beeching *and* John Bowyer Nichols. FaBoEE
"I am featly-tripping Lee." Henry Charles Beeching. FaBoEE
"I am rather tall and stately." *Unknown.* FaBoEE; NOBL
"I am the Dean, and this is Mrs. Liddell." *Unknown.* FaBoEE
"I am the Dean of Christ Church, Sir." Cecil Arthur Spring-Rice. FaBoCo; FaBoEE; NOBL
"I'm the great Sir William Anson." *Unknown.* FaBoEE
"My name is George Nathaniel Curzon." John William Mackail *and* Cecil Arthur Spring-Rice. FaBoCo; FaBoEE; NOBL

"Positivists ever talk in s-/Uch an epic style as Dawkins." John William Mackail. FaBoEE

Ballit of de Boll Weevil, De. *Unknown.* NOBA
(Ballad of the Boll Weevil.) FSW
(Boll Weevil Song, The, *with music.*) BLSo

Balloon, A/is a wild. Balloons! Judith Thurman. FPB

Balloon Faces. Carl Sandburg. CMoP (1970 ed.)

Balloon of the Mind, The. W. B. Yeats. POL

Balloons. Sylvia Plath. MPo; NCSH

Balloons! Judith Thurman. FPB

Balloons hang on wires in the Marigold Gardens, The. Balloon Faces. Carl Sandburg. CMoP (1970 ed.)

Ballroom was filled with fashion's throng, The. A Bird in a Gilded Cage. Arthur J. Lamb. BLSo; FSN; FSW

Balls and Chain. Alvin Aubert. CSP

Ballydavid Pier. Thomas Kinsella. BIrV

Ballymurphy. *Unknown.* FSW

Ballynahinch. George Canning. FaBoCo

*Ballyshannon* foundered off the coast of Cariboo, The. Etiquette. W. S. Gilbert. FaBoCo; VLP

Balm. Sandra McPherson. CNW

Balm in Gilead. *Unknown.* FSW

Balmy spring wind, A. Four Haiku. Richard Wright. NoAM

Balthasar. Charles Spear. ATNZ

Baltimore Eclipse. Charles Plymell. MIT

Bambino. Betty Ruth Bird. AATT

Banana boat drifting with the tide, A. Dreams of Lost Atlantis. Alejandro Murguia. CPA

Banana leaves are burning. "Containing Communism." Charlie Cobb. PoBA

Bananas ripe and green, and ginger-root. The Tropics in New York. Claude McKay. AmNP (1974 ed.); ILP (1975 ed.); NIL; NoAM; PBMP; PoBA

Band, The. Carl Dennis. AMV-80

Band of black across his shoulders. Cross Fox. Joseph Bruchac. NW

Band Played On, The, *with music.* John F. Palmer. BLSH; BLSo; FSN; FSW; OBAL

Bandage-white and healthy. A Gift of Trilliums. Sandra McPherson. RiTi

Bandersnatch is a strange affair, The. Wash-Day Wonder. Dorothy Faubion. QQQ

Bang, bang, bang. The History of the Flood. John Heath-Stubbs. OxBTC

Banging around in a cigarette she isn't "in love." Sonnet. Ted Berrigan. CAAP

Banishment, The. Milton. *Fr.* Paradise Lost, XII. NOBE

Banishment from Ur. Enheduanna, *tr. fr. Sumerian; ad. by* Aliki *and* Willis Barnstone. BoWoP

Banjo, The. Robert Winner. FF

Bank. Joseph Kalar. SPT

Bank swallows veer and dip, The. The Siskins. Theodore Roethke. PB

Banker's Daughter, The. Kathryn Ruby. WBN

Banks fou, braes fou. *Unknown.* GBP

Banks o' Doon, The. Burns. BoLoP; NOBE
(Bonie Doon.) HeIP; PoIA
(Ye Banks and Braes.) SLP
(Ye Flowery Banks.) UnPo (1976 ed.)

Banks of a River, The. Abraham Sutskever, *tr. fr. Yiddish by* Ruth Whitman. VWA

Banks of Champlain, The. *Unknown.* AmFP

Banks of Claudy, The. *Unknown.* AmFP

Banks of Dee, The. *Unknown.* AmFP

Banks of Marble. Les Rice. FSW

Banks of Newfoundland, The. *Unknown.* GBP

Banks of Sweet Dundee, The. *Unknown.* AmFP

Banks of the Condamine, The. *Unknown.* FaBoBa; GBP;PeBB

Banks of the Gaspereaux. *Unknown.* AmFP

Banks of the Ohio. *Unknown.* FSW

Banks of the Roses. *Unknown.* FSW

Bannockburn. Burns. *See* Scots Wha Hae.

Banquet Song. W. S. Gilbert. *Fr.* Patience. ECBV

Bantams in Pine-Woods. Wallace Stevens. CMoP (1970 ed.); InPS; NOBA; STS; UnPo (1976 ed.)

Baptism. Alden Nowlan. POL

Bar close as you can, and bolt fast too your door. No Lock against Lechery. Robert Herrick. CaPo

Bar Harbor. Marita Garin. AMV-81

Bar is closed and I come, The. Night on Clinton. Robert Mezey. AmPA

Bar Mitzvah. Isaac Goldemberg, *tr. fr. Spanish by* David Unger. VWA

Bar Mitzvah. Steve Orlen. GP

Bar my girlfield works in is a dive, The. The Lights Go On. Mark McCloskey. AMV-80

Barbara Allen. *Unknown.* CABA (1972 ed.); FaBoBa; FSW; GSB, *with music;* RDB, *with music;* SS; WIF
  (Barbara Allen's Cruelty.) AIW
  (Barbara Ellen.) AIW
  (Barb'ra Allen, *with music.*) BLSo
  (Barb'ry Allen, *with music, ad. by* James Morehead.) BLSH
  (Bonny Barbara Allan.) AmFP; BiP; BoLoP; HeIP; InPK; PAIC; PeBB; PPoD

Barbara Frietchie. Whittier. BTTM; FaPo; FaPoR; NOBA; OBAL; PPM

Barbara's Poem. Jacquelyn Bowman. PoUp

Barbarians. John Fowles. POL

Barbarians, The. Matthew Mead. TwMBP

Barbarossa. Hubert Witheford. ATNZ

Barb'd blossoms of the guarded gorse. A Song of Winter. Emily Jane Davis Pfeiffer. OBW

Barbecue Blues. *Unknown.* BluL

Barber, The. Roy Fuller. NoAM

Barber, barber, shave a pig. Mother Goose. MG

Barber cuts the beard, The. Peter Redgrove. *Fr.* The Barbers. FoP

Barbers, The, *sels.* Peter Redgrove.
  "Barber cuts the beard, The," II. FoP
  "Here is his coffin. And here the barber comes," IX. FoP
  "One clean-shaven like a white grape, The," IV-VI. FoP

Barbie-Doll Goes to College. Ronald Gross. WeW

Barb'ry Allen. *Unknown. See* Barbara Allen.

Bard. Gavin Bantock. FaBoTw (1975 ed.); TwMBP

Bard. Theodore Black. AMV-81

Bard. William Everson. PiAm

Bard, The. Thomas Gray. LAuP; NOBE; OAEL-1

Bard of Armagh, The. *Unknown.* FSW

Bard whom pilf'red pastorals reknown, The. Pope. *Fr.* An Epistle to Dr. Arbuthnot. OBSV

Bards, The. Walter de la Mare. FaBoNo; NOBL

Bards of passion and of mirth. Ode. Keats. ILP (1975 ed.); MBPR

Bare skin is my wrinkled sack. The Shrouded Stranger. Allen Ginsberg. CoPAm

Bare that breathes the northern blast, The. *See* Bear that breathes the northern blast, The.

Bareback in Kansas. F. Eugene Warren. AATT

Barefoot. Luís Omar Salinas. SA

Barefoot. Anne Sexton. SFF

Barefoot Boy, The. Whittier. CTV; OBAL; PCOP

Barefoot I went and made no sound. The Viper. Ruth Pitter. FaBoTw (1975 ed.)

Barefoot tramp on a stone, A. On My Wandering Flute. Abraham Sutskever, *tr. by* Ruth Whitman. VWA

Barefoot, we jumped on midget islands. Pastoral with Visitor. Richard Packer. FPA

Barely a twelvemonth after. The Horses. Edwin Muir. CMoP (1970 ed.); ExPo (1973 ed.); HAP; ILP (1975 ed.); NoAM; NOBE; OAEL-2; OxBTC; PPoe; SoSe; TCP

Barely did the dust settle. Taking Off. Ronald Rogers. VW

Barely literate questions it asks, The. That Bad Music. Robert Harris. CAAP

Barely tolerated, living on the margin. Soonest Mended. John Ashbery. CAAP; Prf

Bargain, The. Sir Philip Sidney. *See* My True Love Hath My Heart.

Bargain. Ruth Stone. GP

Barge Horse, The. Seán Jennett. PH

Barge she sat in, like a burnished throne, The. Shakespeare. *Fr.* Antony and Cleopatra, II, ii. BiP; PPoe

Barges on the Hudson. Babette Deutsch. WPE

Bark. Don Welch. GP

Bark smells like pineapple. Foxtail Pine. Gary Snyder. NU

Barley-Break, A. Sir John Suckling. CaPo

Barley-Break; or, Last in Hell. Robert Herrick. CaPo

Barn, The. Seamus Heaney. HAP; HeHu

Barn, The. Stephen Spender. CMoP (1970 ed.)

Barn Owl. Gwen Harwood. *Fr.* Father and Child. CAAP; MAuV

Barn Owl. Leslie Norris. HeHu

Barn was on fire, The. Snow Is for Tracking the Invisible Man. Sheila Heldenbrand. AcAn

Barnabooth Enters Russia. Paul Hoover. AMV-81

Barney Google. Billy Rose. OBAL

Barney McGee. Richard Hovey. OBAL

Barns grow slowly out of the dark. Lenox Christmas Eve 68. Sam Cornish. CNA

Barnyard, The. *Unknown.* AmFP

Barnyard Melodies. Fred Emerson Brooks. OBAL

Barnyards of Delgaty. *Unknown.* FSW

Barometer. Madeline DeFrees. CNW

Baron has decided to mate the monster, The. The Bride of Frankenstein. Edward Field. HeIP; TPo

Baron of Buchlyvie. Buchlyvie. *Unknown.* GBP

Baroque Image. May Sarton. PPoD

Baroque Wall-Fountain in the Villa Sciarra, A. Richard Wilbur. BiP; CAPP; SoSe

Barracks Apt. 14. Theodore Weiss. TAP

Barracks-square, washed clean with rain, The. In Barracks. Siegfried Sassoon. FaBoTw (1975 ed.)

Barrel-Organ, The, *abr.* Alfred Noyes. SoSe

Barrels of blue potato-spray, The. Spraying the Potatoes. Patrick Kavanagh. BIrV

Barren cross-ties of penny-whistle twigs. Affirmation. Helen Armstead Johnson. AmNP (1974 ed.)

Barren Poem. Michael Ryan. AmPA

Barren Shore, The. Coventry Patmore. GBL

Barren Spring. Dante Gabriel Rossetti. The House of Life, LXXXIII. ILP (1975 ed.); OAEL-2; VLP; VPC

Barren Tree, The, *sel.* Llewelyn Wyn Griffith.
  "From his own solitude to the world unheeding." OBW

Barricades. Michael S. Harper. PoBA

Barriers Burned. Charles K. Field. BPAW

Barriers 1. Gerald Barrax. CSP

Barriers 2. Gerald Barrax. CSP

Barrow, The. Anthony Thwaite. HeHu

Bar's Fight, August 28, 1746. Lucy Terry. BPo

Bars on Eighth Avenue in Harlem, The. Harlem Gallery: From the Inside. Larry Neal. BPo

Bars on my cell have rusted, The. Rust. Michael Hogan. DNGG

Barter. Sara Teasdale. SoSe

Bartley Costello, eighty years old. Gaeltacht. Pearse Hutchinson. BIrV

Base Chapel, Lejeune 4/79. Archie Hobson. AMV-81

Base Details. Siegfried Sassoon. FF; HeIP; NIL; SoSe

Base Stealer, The. Robert Francis. LiSp; NCSH; NIL; PPoD; SPo

Baseball. Tom Clark. LiSp

Base-Ball. John Newbery. SPo

Baseball and Classicism. Tom Clark. LiSp

Baseball and Writing. Marianne Moore. BoWoP; LiSp; SPo

Baseball in spring. Play Ball! Robert Francis. AMV-80

Baseball Pitcher. Mabel M. Kuykendall. LiSp

Basement Watch, The. Thomas Tolnay. AMV-80

Basementmusic: The Love Affair. Angela Jackson. FiCh

Basho, coming. The Snow Party. Derek Mahon. CIP

Basia, *sel.* Johannes Secundus, *tr. fr. Latin by* Thomas Stanley. "Not alwayes give a melting kiss," VIII. OBVE

Basic Rescue. Ann Deagon. CSP

Basic themes of lyric poetry are seven, The. Seven. Nicanor Parra, *tr. by* Miller Williams. POL

Basket of dirty clothes, A. Repetition of Words and Weather. Ruth Stone. BoWoP

Basket-Weaver's Love, The. René Char, *tr. fr. French by* Jackson Mathews. LoAs

Basket-weavers ravel the Republic. Aside and Memoranda. Elton Glaser. NVAP

Basketball. Stephen Vincent. LiSp; NeAC

Basking Shark. Norman MacCaig. BoAnP

Bastard, The. Richard Savage. EPC "In gayer hours, when high my fancy ran," *sel.* OBSV

Bastard King of England, The. *Unknown.* FSW

Bat. D. H. Lawrence. HAP; OAEL-2

Bat, The. Theodore Roethke. ECBV; IWK; RAE; SoS

Bat, The. Roberta Spear. AmPA

Bat and the Scientist, The. J. S. Bigelow. QQQ

Bat Angels. Larry Levis. AmPA

Bat, bat come under my hat. To the Bat. *Unknown.* BBL

Bat in the Monastery, A. John L'Heureux. SFF

Bat is born, A. Bats. Randall Jarrell. BiP; MPo; NU; RAE; RFM; TSWA; UsP

Bat of rather uncertain age, A. The Bat and the Scientist. J S. Bigelow. QQQ

Batches of New Leaves. Jonathan London. AMV

Batellis and the man I will descrive, The. Virgil, *tr. by* Gavin Douglas. *Fr.* The Aeneid, I. OBVE

Bath. Lincoln Kirstein. NoAM

Bath, The. R. C. Lehmann. GDP

Bath, The. Gary Snyder. GP; NNaP; TAP

Bathed in her breath I basked beside her, weak. Duo. William Keys. SLP

Bathing the Aged. Paul Monette. AmPA

Bathing with Father. Doug Fetherling. NeAC

Bathos, The. Richard Porson. FaBoEE

Bathsheba! to whom none ever said scat. Epitaph [*or* For a Little Girl Mourning Her Favorite Cat]. Whittier. ECBV; POL

Bathtub, The. Ezra Pound. NIL

Bats. Randall Jarrell. BiP; MPo; NU; RAE; RFM; TSWA; UsP

Bats. George MacBeth. NoAM

Batt he gets children, not for love to rear 'em. Upon Batt. Robert Herrick. FaBoEE

Batter my heart, three-personed God; for you. Holy Sonnets, XIV. John Donne. AnMo; BiP; BoReV; CABA (1972 ed.); EBEV; Epi; ExPo (1973 ed.); FF; HAP; HeIP; HOPM (1975 ed.); ILP (1975 ed.); ILWL; InPK; InPS; IP; IPWM; LFH; MetP; NOBE; NIL; OAEL-1; OBP; PoIA; PPoD; PPoe; PPP; SCP-1; SoSe (1977 ed.); TT; UsP; WIF

Battery Park, High Noon. Ben Belitt. NYP

Battle-brave king rested on the shore, The. Beowulf's Last Speech. *Unknown, tr. by* Burton Raffel. *Fr.* Beowulf. OBP

Battle-Cry of Freedom, The. George Frederick Root. BTTM; FSW; PSoN, *with music*

Battle-Flag, The. Mary Evelyn Moore Davis. BPAW

Battle Hymn of the Republic, The. Julia Ward Howe. BLSH, *with music*; BLSo, *with music*; BTTM; CTV; FaPo; FaPoR; FSW; NOBA; PSoN, *with music*; TAP; WPE (Mine Eyes Have Seen the Glory.) AH, *with music*

Battle in exact though little shape, The. Gondibert, I, 5. Sir William Davenant. SCP-2

Battle of Antietam Creek, The. *Unknown.* AmFP

Battle of Argoed Llwyfain, The. Taliesin, *tr. fr. Welsh by* Anthony Conran. OBW

Battle of Aughrim, The, *sels.* Richard Murphy. "Deep red bogs divided." CIP Planter. BIrV Rapparees. BIrV

Battle of Blenheim, The. Robert Southey. AKE; FaPoR; PBMP; PCOP

Battle of Brunanburh. *Unknown, tr. fr. Anglo-Saxon by* Tennyson. BTTM; OBVE

Battle of Bull Run, The. *Unknown.* AmFP

Battle of Dunbar, The (1296). *Unknown.* OxBM

Battle of Hohenlinden, The. Thomas Campbell. *See* Hohenlinden.

Battle of Maldon, The. *Unknown,* tr. fr. Anglo-Saxon by Charles W. Kennedy. OAEL-1

Battle of Naseby, The. Macaulay. BTTM

Battle of New Orleans, The. *Unknown.* AmFP

Battle of Otterbourne, The. *Unknown.* BTTM

Battle of Shiloh, The. *Unknown.* AIW; AmFP

Battle of Similes, A. *Malay Oral Tradition, tr. by* R. J. Wilkinson *and* R. O. Winstedt. WTO

Battle of Sole Bay, The. *Unknown.* GBP

Battle of the Baltic. Thomas Campbell. BTTM; FaPoR

Battle of the *Bonhomme Richard* and the *Serapis.* Walt Whitman. Song of Myself, XXXV-XXXVI. UnPo (1976 ed.)

Battle of the Boyne, The. Captain Blacker. BTTM

Battle of the Frogs and Mice, The, *sel. Unknown, formerly at. to* Homer; *tr. fr. Greek by* Thomas Parnell. "Ascend my shoulders, firmly keep thy seat." OBVE

Battle of the Kegs, The. Francis Hopkinson. OBAL

Battle of Waun Gaseg, The. Llywelyn ab y Moel, *tr. fr. Welsh by* H. Idris Bell. OBW

Battle Picture, A. Herman Melville. PiAm

Battle Pledge. *Somali Oral Tradition, tr. by* M. Laurence. WTO

Battle Problem. William Meredith. NoAM

Battle rent a cobweb diamond-strung, The. Range finding. Robert Frost. CABA (1972 ed.); NIL; NoAM; PPoD

Battle Report. Bob Kaufman. AmNP (1974 ed.)

Battle Royal between Dr. Sherlock, Dr. South, and Dr. Burnet, The. William Pittis. APAS

Battle Won Is Lost. Phillip William George. VW

Battlefields. Vernon Scannell. HeHu

Battleship of Maine. *Unknown.* FSW

Batyushkov. Osip Mandelstam, *tr. fr. Russian by* W. S. Merwin *and* Clarence Brown. OBVE

Baucis and Philemon. Katherine Hoskins. PoA

Baucis and Philemon. Ovid, *tr. fr. Latin by* Dryden. *Fr.* Metamorphoses, VIII. OAEL-1

Baucis and Philemon. Swift, *after* Ovid. NIL; OAEL-1

Baudelaire. Delmore Schwartz. VGW

Baudelaire in Brussels. Anthony Cronin. BIrV

Bavarian Gentians. D. H. Lawrence. CMoP (1970 ed.); HAP; ILP (1975 ed.); InPK; InPS; NoAM; NOBE; OAEL-2, 2 *versions;* PoIA; PPoe; TCP; WIF, 2 *versions*

Bawl of a steer, The. The Cowboy's Life. *At. to* James Barton Adams. BPAW; CTV

Bay, The. James K. Baxter. ATNZ

Bay Bridge from Portrero Hill, The. Jack Gilbert. NowV

Bay is as cold, The. Looking for Asia. R. H. W. Dillard. CoPAm

Bay of Biscay, The. *Unknown.* AmFP

Bay of Resolve. Richard Hugo. CNW

Bay Poem. Lance Henson. VoR

Bayliff's Daughter of Islington, The. *Unknown.* *See* Bailiff's Daughter of Islington, The.

Bayonet and the Needle, The. Eliezer Steinbarg, *tr. fr. Yiddish by* Curt Leviant. VWA

Bayonne Turnpike to Tuscarora. Allen Ginsberg. NNaP

"Be alive," they say, when I. On Rape Unattempted. Alan Dugan. NoAM

Be awake mornings. See light spread across the lawn. Crystal. Ted Berrigan. EC

Be Careful! *Unknown.* ECBV ("If you should meet a crocodile.") CaYB; OSF

Be Cool, Baby. Rob Penny. PoBA

Be Daedalus. Nanina Alba. PoBA

Be Frugal. Richard Church. OxBTC

Be Glorified Eternally, *with music.* Balthasar Hoffman, *tr. fr. German by* Sheerna Z. Buehne. AH

Be happy for me, girls,/ my mother-in-law is dead! *Tr. fr. Arabic by* Willis Barnstone. BoWoP

Be kind and tender to the frog. The Frog. Hilaire Belloc. BBL; CTV; LCL; OxBChV

Be kind to yourself, it is only one. Who Be Kind To. Allen Ginsberg. NNaP

Be like the bird, who. Victor Hugo, *tr. fr. French.* CTV; PCOP

Be natural. The Name. Robert Creeley. IPWM; SOS; TCP

Be near me when my light is low. In Memoriam A. H. H., L-LVIII. Tennyson. HAP (L); PFD

Be not dismayed whate'er betide. God Will Take Care of You. Mrs. C. D. Martin. BLSH

Be not proud of your sweet body. *Gond Oral Tradition, tr. by* V. Elwin *and* S. Hivale. WTO

Be not thou so foolish nice. Invitation to Dalliance. *Unknown.* FaBoEE

Be of good cheer, spirit of Myrrha! To a Courtesan a Thousand Years Dead. Paul Eldridge. PoA

Be plain in dress, and sober in your diet. Good Advice. Lady Mary Wortley Montagu. FaBoEE; POL

Be proud be proud whimpers. Bank. Joseph Kalar. SPT

Be proud you people of these graves. City of Monuments. Muriel Rukeyser. SPT; WasP

Be reasonable, my pain, and think with more detachment. Inward Conversation. Baudelaire, *tr. by* Robert Bly. InPK

Be Sad, My Heart. Francis Quarles. NIL

Be still, my soul, be still: the arms you bear are brittle. A. E. Housman. OAEL-2; STS

Be still, while the music rises about us: the deep enchantment. At a Concert of Music. Conrad Aiken. ILP (1975 ed.)

Be Strong. Maltbie D. Babcock. AH, *with music;* CTV; SoSe

Be the mistress of my choice. What Kind of Mistress He Would Have. Robert Herrick. CaPo

Be this the fate. A Curse on a Closed Gate. *Unknown, tr. by* James H. Cousins. PFIr

Be thou then my beauty named. Thomas Campion. AAS

Be True. Horatius Bonar. CTV

Be ware, squier, yeman, and page. Service Is No Heritage. *Unknown.* OxBM

Be wary of the loathsome troll. The Troll. Jack Prelutsky. IWK

Be who you are and will be. For Each of You. Audre Lorde. CNA

Be with me, Beauty, for the fire is dying. On Growing Old. John Masefield. CMoP (1970 ed.); PPM

Be with me, Luis de San Angel, now. Ave Maria. Hart Crane. *Fr.* The Bridge. NoAM; NOBA

Be you to others kind and true. Our Saviour's Golden Rule. Isaac Watts. OxBChV

Beach, The. William Hart-Smith. ECBV

Beach, The. Robert Peters. GP

Beach at Veracruz, The. George Bowering. NeAC

Beach Burial. Kenneth Slessor. GAS; MAuV

Beach Cliff Graffiti. Madeline DeFrees. CNW

Beach House, The. James K. Baxter. ATNZ

Beach in August, The. Weldon Kees. VGW

Beach is a quarter of golden fruit, The. The Beach. William Hart-Smith. ECBV

Beach Talk. Norman MacCaig. PoA

Beaches, The, *sel.* Robin Hyde. "Close under here, I watched two lovers once." ATNZ

Beachhead Preachment. Ahmos Zu-Bolton. AMV-81

Beachy Head, *sels.* Charlotte Smith. "I once was happy, when, while yet a child." WPE "On thy stupendous summit, rock sublime!" SBG

Beacon, The. Arthur Gregor. GP

Bead Work. Hazel Hall. WPW

Beadle's Testimony, The. Jerome Rothenberg. NNaP

Beagles. W. R. Rodgers. FaBoTw (1975 ed.); GDP

Beaks of Eagles, The. Robinson Jeffers. NOBA

Beale Street. Langston Hughes. PPP

Bean Eaters, The. Gwendolyn Brooks. CAPP; CoPAm; HAP; HeIP; IPWM; MAT; PoBA; TAP; TT

Bean Spasms. Ted Berrigan. EAS

Bean Vield, The. William Barnes. VLP

Beans, Bacon and Gravy. *Unknown.* FSW

Beans in Blossom. John Clare. VLP

Bear. D. C. Berry. BCr

Bear. John Ceely. BCr

Bear, The. Robert Frost. BCr; NoAM

Bear. Vi Gale. BCr

Bear, The. William Heyen. BCr

Bear, The. Galway Kinnell. BCr; CoPAm; NNaP; RFM; TAP; VGW

Bear, The. Mark McCloskey. BCr

Bear, The. N. Scott Momaday. CDW; VW

Bear. Kenneth Rexroth. BCr

Bear, The. Judith Rose. BCr

Bear/ was in the back of my mind. Bear. John Ceely. BCr

Bear a Horn and Blow It Not. *Unknown.* OxBM

Bear and Misterwriter. Brendan Galvin. BCr

Bear and the Garden-Lover, The. Marianne Moore. BCr

Bear at the Academy of the Living Arts. Brendan Galvin. BCr

Bear ate the girl, The. Judith W. Steinbergh. BCr

Bear came by, sat down. Bear and Misterwriter. Brendan Galvin. BCr

Bear down under the cliff, A. This Poem Is for Bear. Gary Snyder. *Fr.* Myths and Texts: Hunting. BCr; CNW; NOBA; NU

Bear Hunting. Aua, *tr. fr. Eskimo.* WTO

Bear me to Dictaeus. Acon. Hilda Doolittle ("H. D."). VGW

Bear on the Delhi Road, The. Earle Birney. BCr; BoAnP; HeIP; MPA

Bear (Part Three). Jeffrey Miles. BCr

Bear part with me most straight and pleasant tree. Morea's Sonnet. Mary Sidney Wroth, Countess of Montgomery. *Fr.* Urania. WPE

Bear Paw. Richard Hugo. MPA

Bear puts both arms around the tree above her, The. The Bear. Robert Frost. BCr; NoAM

Bear sang bass, The. The Achromatic Bear. Robert Bloom. AATT

Bear sleeps in a cellar hole, A. New Hampshire. Donald Hall. UsP

Bear Song. John R. Swanton. BPAW

Bear [*or* Bare] that breathes the northern blast, The. Upon a Wasp Chilled with Cold. Edward Taylor. EAP; NOBA; PiAm; SCP-2

Bear That Came to the Wedding, The. Howard McCord. GP

Bear under the snow, A. March. James Wright. BCr; TH

Bear Who Came to Dinner, The. Adrien Stoutenburg. SO

Bear with fur that appeared to have been licked backward, A. The Bear and the Garden-Lover. Marianne Moore. BCr

Bearded goldfish move about the bowl, The. Goldfish. Howard Nemerov. BoAnP

Bearded Oaks. Robert Penn Warren. CoPAm; NoAM; NOBA; PiAm; PoA; TAP

Beardsley Flesh, The. Henry Kanabus. FiCh

Bearer of Evil Tidings, The. Robert Frost. NoAM

Bearing It. Carolyn Stoloff. RiTi

Bearing white myrrh and incense, autumn melts. From a Book of Hours. Charles Spear. ATNZ

Bears. Adrienne Rich. BCr; NCSH

Bears and Waterfalls. May Sarton. GP

Bear's Blessing, The. Victor Contoski. BCr

Bear's Blood. Ileana Malancioiu, *tr. fr. Rumanian by* Stavros Deligiorgis. BoWoP

Bears in the Land-Fill, The. Lewis Turco. BCr

Beast, The. Theodore Roethke. SO

Beast Enough. Robert Billings. AMV-81

Beast in the Space, The. W. S. Graham. FaBoTw (1975 ed.); PoA

Beast Section, The. Welton Smith. PoBA

Beast stands at my eye, A. The Naked Land. Kenneth Patchen. EAS

Beast That Rode the Unicorn, The. Conny Hannes Meyer, *tr. fr. German by* Herbert Kuhner. VWA

Beast, what is love? George Mackay Brown. *Fr.* Lord of the Mirrors. SLP

Beasts. Richard Wilbur. NU; PPoe; PPP

Beasts and Birds. Adelaide O'Keeffe. OxBChV

Beasts Are Very Wise, The. Kipling. BoAnP

Beasts, cattle, have words, neither minor nor many. Death Words. Les A. Murray. *Fr.* Walking to the Cattle-Place. CAAP

Beasts in their major freedom. Beasts. Richard Wilbur. NU; PPoe; PPP

Beasts of Boston, The. Betty Lowry. AMV

Beat! Beat! Drums! Walt Whitman. BiP; InPK; InPS; PoIA

Beat Poem by an Academic Poet. Vassar Miller. WPE

Beat the drum! beat beat the drum! A New Song Made in Honour of His Grace the Duke of Marlborough. Thomas Durfey. SCP-2

Beat the knife on the plate and the fork on the can. Going in to Dinner. Edward Shanks. OxBTC

Beating, The. Ann Stanford. MPA; WPE

Beating, The ("Beating her sensible with a storm of tissues"). Andrew Taylor. FPA

Beatnik Limernik. Norman R. Jaffray. TDH

Beauteous the fleet before the gale. Christopher Smart. *Fr.* A Song to David. PIM

Beauties of Santa Cruz, The. Philip Freneau. EAP

Beautiful, The. W. H. Davies. BBGO

Beautiful American Word, Sure, The. Delmore Schwartz. VGW

Beautiful as the flying legend of some leopard. Judith of Bethulia. John Crowe Ransom. NoAM; NOBA; PiAm

Beautiful, beautiful brown eyes. Beautiful Brown Eyes. *Unknown.* FSW

Beautiful being, you live as do delicate blossoms in winter. To Diotima. Friedrich Hölderlin, *tr. by* Michael Hamburger. LoAs

Beautiful Bella. *Unknown.* TDH

Beautiful Black Men. Nikki Giovanni. BPo; NMM

Beautiful Black Women. Amiri Baraka. BPo

Beautiful Brown Eyes. *Unknown.* FSW

Beautiful cashier's white face has risen once more, The. Before the [*or* a] Cashier's Window in a Department Store. James Wright. MAT; NYP

Beautiful Changes, The. Richard Wilbur. CMoP (1970 ed.); ILP (1975 ed.); InPS; LFH; NIL

Beautiful Contradictions, The, *sels.* Nathaniel Tarn.
"Elders at the zenith of their power look down the sky, The." TwMBP
"When Caesar decided to measure the world." TwMBP

Beautiful Dreamer. Stephen Collins Foster. BiP; BLSH, *with music;* BLSO, *with music.*

Beautiful Evelyn Hope is dead! Evelyn Hope. Robert Browning. TT; VLP

Beautiful face of Paul Delvaux, The. Bruce Beaver. *Fr.* Lauds and Plaints. CAAP

Beautiful is fair, the just is fair, The. Fair and Unfair. Robert Francis. VGW

Beautiful Isle of Somewhere, *with music.* Jessie B. Pounds. FSN

Beautiful ladies through the orchard pass. Les Demoiselles de Sauve. John Gray. VLP

Beautiful lady named Psyche, A. A Lady Named Psyche. *Unknown.* TDH

Beautiful little children. Kyoto Born in Spring Song. Gary Snyder. RRA

Beautiful, lo, the summer clouds. Song of the Blue-Corn Dance. *Tr. by* Natalie Curtis. WTO

Beautiful man and his wife, The. Window Dressing. William Peskett. IPM

Beautiful must be the mountains whence ye come. Nightingales. Robert Bridges. CMoP (1970 ed.); ILP (1975 ed.); NOBE; OAEL-2; PPM; UnPo (1976 ed.); VLP

Beautiful, my delight. To Be Sung on the Water. Louise Bogan. VGW

Beautiful natural blossoms. To a Beautiful Pear Tree. James Wright. HAP

Beautiful new railway bridge of the silvery Tay. An Address to the New Tay Bridge. William McGonagall. PeD; PPoD

Beautiful Night, A. Thomas Lovell Beddoes. PMW

Beautiful Old Age. D. H. Lawrence. TVo

Beautiful Proud Sea. Sara Teasdale. RhR

Beautiful railway bridge of the silvery Tay! The Railway Bridge of the Silvery Tay. William McGonagall. PeD; PPoD

Beautiful railway bridge of the silv'ry Tay! The Tay Bridge Disaster. William McGonagall. PeD; PPoD

Beautiful rain falls, the unheeded angel. In Time. Kathleen Raine. WPE

Beautiful River, *with music.* Robert Lowry. PSoN (Shall We Gather at the River?) AH; BLSH

Beautiful Saviour, *with music. Unknown, tr. fr. German by* J. A. Seiss. BLSH

Beautiful! Sir, you may say so. Chiquita. Bret Harte. BPAW

Beautiful soup, so rich and green. Turtle Soup. "Lewis Carroll." *Fr.* Alice's Adventures in Wonderland. BBL; FaBoNo; SpRo

Beautiful star in heav'n so bright. Star of the Evening. James M. Sayles. SpRo

Beautiful thing/ I saw you. William Carlos Williams. *Fr.* Paterson. CMoP (1970 ed.)

Beautiful Toilet, The. Ezra Pound, *after the Chinese.* OBVE

Beautiful was the appearance of Cormac in that assembly. Cormac Mac Airt Presiding at Tara. *Unknown, tr. by* Douglas Hyde. BIrV

Beautiful Young Nymph Going to Bed, A. Swift. AnMo; NIL

Beautiful Youth. Gottfried Benn, *tr. fr. German by* Joachim Neugroschel. POL

Beautifully Janet slept. Janet Waking. John Crowe Ransom. CABA (1972 ed.); CMoP (1970 ed.); ExPo (1973 ed.); InPK; NCSH; NoAM; PBMP; PiAm; SoS; TAP

Beauty. Paul David Ashley. DNGG

Beauty. Baudelaire, *tr. fr. French by* Elaine Marks. NAWM-2

Beauty. Giovanni Battista Guarini. *See* Of Beauty.

Beauty, The, *sel.* Thomas Hardy. "O do not praise my beauty more." PeD

Beauty. Thomas Stanley, *after the Greek of* Anacreon. OBVE

Beauty. Walt Whitman. WeW

Beauty and Love. Andrew Young. GBL

Beauty Bathing. Anthony Munday. *Fr.* Primaleon of Greece. NOBE

Beauty—be not caused—it is. Emily Dickinson. TAP

Beauty goes into the butcher's shop. A Woman Shopping. Denis Glover. ATNZ

Beauty Imposes. John Shaw Neilson. MAuV

Beauty in the old way of life. New Way, Old Way. David W. Martinez. VW

Beauty Is but a Painted Hell. Thomas Campion. BiP

Beauty is never satisfied. Mythmaking. Kathleen Spivack. NMM

Beauty never visits mining places. Mining Places. Frederick Boden. PES

Beauty no other thing is than a beam. The Definition of Beauty. Robert Herrick. CaPo

Beauty of/ the male face, The. Thanksgiving. Sharon Barba. RiTi

Beauty of Israel is slain upon thy high places, The. David's Lament. Bible, *O.T. Fr.* Second Samuel. FF; OBVE

Beauty of manhole covers, The—what of that? Manhole Covers. Karl Shapiro. GP; MiP; NCSH

Beauty of the Ocean, The. Thomas M. Walker. RhR

Beauty of the world hath made me sad, The. Last Lines—1916. Padraic Pearse. PFIr; WIF

Beauty of Things, The. Robinson Jeffers. PoA

Beauty Rohtraut. Eduard Möricke, *tr. fr. German by* George Meredith. OBVE

Beauty sat bathing by a spring. Beauty Bathing. Anthony Munday. *Fr.* Primaleon of Greece. NOBE

Beauty, Since You So Much Desire. Thomas Campion. OAEL-1

Beauty, sweet love, is like the morning dew. Samuel Daniel. *Fr.* To Delia. NOBE; PAIC

Beauty's a rose, a shining sword, a thief. A Memory, Now Distant. Eric Linklater. SLP

Beauty's Excellency. Henry Noel. SCP-2

Be-Bop Boys. Langston Hughes. OBAL

Because. Paul Johnson. AMV-81

Because. John Lennon *and* Paul McCartney. UsP

Because. James McAuley. GAS; MAuV

Because, *with music.* Edward Teschemacher. FSN

Because a flame wrapped in lonely skies. Eartha. Stanley Burnshaw. SPT

Because dusk comes. Saskatchewan Dusk. C. M. Buckaway. AMV-80

Because everything I build is built on the miracle. The Miracle. Chaim Grade, *tr. by* Ruth Whitman. VWA

Because God put His adamantine fate. Failure. Rupert Brooke. ILwL

Because he had spoken harshly to his mother. Revelation. Robert Penn Warren. NoAM

Because He Liked to Be at Home. Kenneth Patchen. CoPAm

Because he sent a head of cattle on. The Island and the Cattle. Nicholas Moore. EAS

Because he studied texts. The Poor Shammes of Berditchev. Rochelle Ratner. VWA

Because he was a butcher and thereby. Reuben Bright. E. A. Robinson. IPWM; NOBA; PoIA; PPM; STS; TAP

Because he was armored. In Days of New. Elizabeth Bartlett. AMV-81

Because his madness had outgrown the world. The Kabbalist. Deborah Eibel. VWA

Because I am a woman. Muse Poem. Kathryn Van Spanckeren. FF

"Because I am mad about women." The Wild Old Wicked Man. W. B. Yeats. CMoP (1970 ed.); UsP

Because I believe in the community of little children. The Massacre of the Innocents. William Jay Smith. CoPAm

Because I breathe not love to every one. Astrophel and Stella, LIV. Sir Philip Sidney. BuTh

Because I could not stop for Death. Emily Dickinson. AmVN; AnMo; BBGO; BoWoP; CABA (1972 ed.); CMoP (1970 ed.); DL; FF; HAP; HeIP; ILP (1975 ed.); NIL; NoAM; PBMP; PiAm; PPM; SGB; SoSe; TAP; TT; UnPo (1976 ed.); VoPo; WPE

Because I do not hope to turn again. Ash-Wednesday, I. T. S. Eliot. BoReV; VGW

Because I had loved so deeply. Compensation. Paul Laurence Dunbar. AmNP (1974 ed.); BPo

Because I have turned my head for years. The Bittern. Sandra McPherson. CNW

Because I liked you better. A. E. Housman. GBL; OxBTC

Because I Never Learned the Names of Flowers. Roderick Jellema. PoUp

Because I Paced My Thought. John Hewitt. CIP

Because I sit eating cherries. Cherries. Lucien Stryk. PCho

Because I waddle when I walk. The Dachshund. Edward Anthony. GDP

Because I Were Shy. *Unknown.* PoTa

Because I work not, as logicians work. Magic. Lionel Johnson. VLP

Because I'm not sure which. Squint. Edward Lowbury. PMW

Because in Vietnam the vision of a Burning Babe. Advent 1966. Denise Levertov. ILP (1975 ed.); InPS; NNaP; PiAm; Prf

Because it has sunk so low. Holy City. Anne Waldman. RiTi

Because it pleases me I turn to you. The Casketmaker. Ron H. Bayes. AAN

Because my shelter must not be known. Cricket. No Ch'ön-myüng, *tr. by* Ko Won. PBWP

Because of Clothes. Laura Riding. NoAM

Because of long depression and a sudden urge. Midnight and Ten Minutes. Shlomo Vinner, *tr. by* Laya Firestone *and* Howard Schwartz. VWA

Because of your long neck. Deer. No Ch'ŏn-myŭng, *tr. by* Ko Won. PBWP

Because she breathed too wildly in the sun. The Sixth Hell. Jerome Rothenberg. *Fr.* The Seven Hells of Jigoku Zoshi. NNaP

"Because the beetle that lives in the wood." The Beetle in the Wood. Byron Herbert Reece. PoTa

Because the daughters of Zion are haughty. Bible, *O.T. Fr.* Isaiah. OBP

Because the land was shifting, dying. He Left the Pine Ridge Reservation. Carol Cox. MMD

Because the light this morning is recondite. Cold Glow: Icehouses. David Wojahn. AMV-81

Because the pleasure-bird whistles after the hot wires. January 1939. Dylan Thomas. EAS

Because the Savage. Sheila Heldenbrand. AcAn

Because the snow is deep. The Fox. Kenneth Patchen. CoPAm; LP; MPo

Because the Three Moirai Have Become the Three Maries. Constance Urdang. Moon

Because the warden is a cousin, my. Deer Hunt. Judson Jerome. CoPAm; RFM

Because their fathers had been drilled. The Last Republicans. Austin Clarke. CIP

Because there are avenues. After Tonight. Gary Soto. GP

Because there is no time to rest. Hurrying Home. Jim Farrar. DNGG

Because there is safety in derision. The Apparitions. W. B. Yeats. CMoP (1970 ed.)

Because there was a man somewhere in a candystripe silk shirt. Homage to the Empress of the Blues. Robert Hayden. CABA (1972 ed.); CNA; CoPAm; PoBA

Because there was disquiet in the wind. This Poor Man. W. J. Gruffydd. *tr. by* Gwyn Jones. OBW

Because there was no camera. After the Unexpected Answer (Magritte). Paul Hoover. FiCh

Because there was no moon. The Wedding. Roland Gant. BuTh

Because they are coloured usually. Rocks. Richard Packer. FPA

Because this is the way our world goes under. On Why I Would Betray You. Jorie Graham. AMV-81

Because thou canst not see. The Philosopher to His Mistress. Robert Bridges. OBP

Because time is a fiction in the mind. Miklos Radnoti. Willis Barnstone. VWA

Because we are all. Judas, Peter. Luci Shaw. AMV

Because we breathe the same birds of sand. Brotherhood. José Luis Vega, *tr. by* Julio Marzán. InW

Because we suspected/ the pillow would say "I know." Lady Ise, *tr. fr. Japanese by* Etsuko Terasaki *and* Irma Brandeis. BoWoP

Because you are to me a song. Passing Love. Langston Hughes. BiP

Because you come to me with naught save love. Because. Edward Teschemacher. FSN

Because you have thrown off your prelate lord. On the [New] Forcers of Conscience [under the Long Parliament]. Milton. CABA (1972 ed.); NIL; PAIC; PPoD

Because you threw rocks at me on Backbone Mountain. Night Song from Backbone Mountain. Daniel Mark Epstein. TAT

Because your love uncurled my anxious toes. To Leonard and Kerstin, With a Gift of Books. Alberta Turner. HeS

Because your voice was at my side. James Joyce. Chamber Music, XVII. OLR

Because You're You, *with music.* Henry Blossom. BLSo

Becket. Virginia Gilbert. NPW

Becket, *sels.* Tennyson.
   Duet: "Is it the wind of the dawn that I hear." GBL
   Prologue: "Over! the sweet summer closes." GBL

Beckett Kit, The. Linda Gregg. AmPA

Beckoned in Dream to the Unconscious. David Kherdian. FAF

Becky Deem. *Unknown.* BluL

Becoming a Nun. Erica Jong. MMD

Becoming Is Perfection. Tom Johnson. AMV-81

Becoming Real. Barry Goldensohn. AMV-81

Bed, The. A. D. Hope. NoAM

Bed, The. Dennis Saleh. NeAC

Bed, The. Michael Small. DNGG

Bed at Ostend at 5 A.M. Charles Stuart Claverley. *Fr.* Dover to Munich. NOBL

Bed by the Window, The. Robinson Jeffers. PiAm

Bed in Summer. Robert Louis Stevenson. OxBChV

Bedded in tranquility. Voice of the Crocus. Mildred N. Hoyer. AMV-80

Bedelia, *with music.* William Jerome. FSN

Bedouin springs from his horse, A. Into the Book. Martin Grossman. VWA

Bedpost, The. Robert Graves. SO

Bed Time. Peter Davison. UnPo (1976 ed.)

Bedtime. Ian Hamilton Finlay. MS

Bedtime. Denise Levertov. AnMo; IHMS

Bedtime. Hillel Schwartz. AMV-81

Bedtime. J. D. Whitney. NVAP

Bedtime Stories, *sel.* Susan Sonde.
   "Watch out for the Egyptian." PoUp

Bedtime Story. Lou Lipsitz. VGW

Bedtime Story. George MacBeth. LP; MPo; NoAM; PoTa; SoSe

Bedtime Story for My Son. Peter Redgrove. BuTh

Bee, The. James Dickey. LiSp; SoSe

Bee, The ("There is a little gentleman"). *Unknown.* ECBV

Bee, A/ Interestingly. Sandra Ruth Duguid. AATT

Bee, A/ rolls/ in the yellow. A Couple. May Swenson. RiTi

Bee his burnished carriage, A. Emily Dickinson. NOBA

Bee! I'm expecting you! Emily Dickinson. BoAnP; SO

Bee in a bloom on the long hand of a floral, A. Keep in a Cool Place. Allen Curnow. ATNZ

Bee Meeting, The. Sylvia Plath. InPS; PPP; WPE

Bee, the Ant, and the Sparrow, The. Nathaniel Cotton. OxBChV

Bee upon a briar-rose hung, A. The Flesh-Fly and the Bee. Coventry Patmore. FaBoEE

Bee Woman, The. Jim Wayne Miller. CSP

Beech Leaves. James Reeves. RAE

Beechwoods at Knole. V. Sackville-West. PES

Beef. Leon Stokesbury. GP

Beef Sandwich in Randy's on Michigan Ave. Chicago Allegory. Stewart Parker. CIP

Bee-hive, The. Thomas Durfey. SCP-2

Beehive. Jean Toomer. PoBA

Bee-keeper kissed me, The. *Unknown, tr. fr. Spanish by* W. S. Merwin. BoWoP

Beekeeper's Daughter, The. Sylvia Plath. IHMS

Been in the Pen So Long. *Unknown.* FSW

Been working/ on that old. 5/2/75. Darlene Pearlstein. FiCh

Beeny Cliff. Thomas Hardy. LoAs

Beer. George Arnold. OBAL

Beer. Charles Stuart Calverley. FaBoCo

Bees and a honeycomb in the dried head of a horse. In Tall Grass. Carl Sandburg. PoA

Bees build around red liver. A Poor Christian Looks at the Ghetto. Czeslaw Milosz, *tr. by author.* NIL

Bees build in the crevices, The. The Stare's Nest by My Window. W. B. Yeats. Meditations in Time of Civil War, VI. BIrV; NOBE

Beeston, the place, near Nottingham. Autobiographical Note. Vernon Scannell. HeHu; LP; MPo

Beethoven. John Hall Wheelock. PoA

Beethoven's Death Mask. Stephen Spender. OxBTC

Beetle, a Bat, and a Bee, A. The Castaways. E. V. Rieu. PoTa

Beetle in the Wood, The. Byron Herbert Reece. PoTa

Beetle loves his unpretending track, The. Wordsworth. *Fr.* Liberty. FaBoCo; PCOP

Beetle on the Shasta Daylight. Shirley Kaufman. WPE

Befana the Housewife, scrubbing her pane. The Ballad of Befana. Phyllis McGinley. AIW

Before. W. E. Henley. In Hospital, IV. VLP

Before. Ann Stanford. GP

Before/ I opened my mouth. On Reading Poems to a Senior Class at South High. D. C. Berry. SoSe

Before a Cashier's Window in a Department Store. James Wright. *See* Before the Cashier's Window in a Department Store.

Before a Fall. Geoffrey Grigson. EAS

Before a Saint's Picture. Walter Savage Landor. OxBChV

Before an audible sound, an almost recognizable. Prelude to Memorial Song: 100 Years Later. Phillip William George. NW; VoR

Before/ and After. Jewel C. Latimore. JB

Before Battle: [The Lincolns at Villanueva de la Canada]. James Neugass. SPT

Before Bed. Keith Waldrop. InPK

Before Dawn. Ann Darr. MiP

Before dawn i rose thirsty. Other. Lance Henson. VoR

Before Disaster. Yvor Winters. HoPM (1975 ed.); IP

Before Gereint, foe's affliction. Gereint ab Erbin. *Unknown, tr. by* Joseph P. Clancy. OBW

Before I Knocked and Flesh Let Enter. Dylan Thomas. FaBoTw (1975 ed.)

Before I laughed with him. What She Said. Maturai Eruttalan Centamputan, *tr. by* A. K. Ramanujan. BoLoP

Before I melt. The Snowflake. Walter de la Mare. FSFS; LCL; NCSH

Before I opened my mouth they sat as orderly. Fish. D. C. Berry. CSP

Before I see another day. The Complaint of a Forsaken Indian Woman. Wordsworth. MBPR

Before I set sail, I will not fail. Skin the Goat's Curse on Carey. *Unknown.* BIrV

Before I sigh my last gasp, let me breathe. The Will. John Donne. EBEV

Before I slept, I saw the nebula. Sea Otter, a Dream Poem to My Mother. Katherine Doak. NPW

Before man came to blow it right. The Aim Was Song. Robert Frost. SoSe

Before Man's labouring wisdom gave me birth. The Ship and Her Makers. John Masefield. RhR

Before me, it was grandpa's old mad South. My South. Andrew Glaze. CSP

Before mine eye to feede my greedy will. George Gascoigne. AAS

Before morning the dark western valley of the continent. Acts of God. Ben Maddow. SPT

Before morning you shall be here. Alba. Samuel Beckett. BIrV

Before my back was bent I was eloquent. *Unknown, tr. by* Gwyn Jones. *Fr.* Hateful Old Age. OBW

Before my bright window. Winter. Mani Leib, *tr. by* Keith Bosley. VWA

Before my door the box-edg'd border lies. Rural Scenery. John Scott of Amwell. PES

Before my face the picture hangs. Upon the Image of Death. Robert Southwell. BoReV; NOBE

Before My Father before Me. Charles O. Hartman. AAN

Before my feet the ploughshare rolls the earth. Winter Ploughing. William Everson. NU

Before our lives divide for ever. The Triumph of Time. Swinburne. VLP; VPC

Before Parting. Swinburne. OBP

Before she has her floor swept. Portrait by a Neighbor. Edna St. Vincent Millay. TH; UsP

Before she left she took a jug of wine. Eruption. Margaret Reynolds. MIS

Before she sold her life to the asphalt. The Suicide. Joanne Casullo. NPW

Before Sunset. Swinburne. VLP

Before the Actual Cold. Ray A. Young Bear. VoR

Before the beginning of years. Swinburne. *Fr.* Atalanta in Calydon. HeIP; PPM

Before the Bell Rings. Jesús Papoleto Meléndez. NW

Before the Birth of One of Her Children. Anne Bradstreet. BoWoP; EAP; MAT; NOBA; PiAm; SBG; WPE

Before the Breaking. Lee Pennington. AMV-81

Before the bright sun rises over the hill. The Gleaner. Jane Taylor. OxBChV

Before the [*or* a] Cashier's Window in a Department Store. James Wright. MAT; NYP

Before the children say goodnight. The Happy Family. John Ciardi. DuDa

Before the Dark Is Down. Mary Shumway. NVAP

Before the days of duty. The Silver Racer. Joseph Colin Murphey. AMV-80

Before the Dive. Elizabeth Kempf. AMV-81

Before the Fall. Rosemary Daniell. WBN

Before the Fall. Milton. *Fr.* Paradise Lost, IV. NIL

Before the falling summer sun. Musings. William Barnes. HAP; NOBE

Before the Frost. Harley Elliott. HeS

Before the grass could be planted. Building in Nova Scotia. Stephen Dunn. GP

Before the grass is out the people are out. Paterson. William Carlos Williams. PiAm

Before the moon should circlewise close both her horns in one. Medea Casts a Spell to Make Aeson Young Again. Ovid, *tr. by* Arthur Golding. *Fr.* Metamorphoses. Moon

Before the Mountain. Elizabeth Libbey. AmPA

Before the Pacific. Blanca Varela, *tr. fr. Spanish by* Willis Barnstone. BoWoP

Before the Paling of the Stars. Christina Rossetti. PIM

Before the Reincarnation. Bonita Hearn. PoW

Before the Roman came to Rye or out to Severn strode. The Rolling English Road. G. K. Chesterton. NOBE; NOBL; PPoD; OxBTC

Before the starry threshold of Jove's court. Comus. Milton. OAEL-1

Before the Statue of a Laughing Man. William C. Bowie. AMV-81

Before the Storm. Kenneth O. Hanson. MPA

Before the Stuff Comes Down. Gary Snyder. HeIP; PiAm

Before the sun goes down. Astrid Hjertenaes Andersen, *tr. fr. Norwegian by* Nadia Christensen. BoWoP

Before the Thaw. John Gill. NeAC

Before the thing begins we have. Poetry Reading. Vernon Scannell. NOBL

Before the War. Marilyn Hacker. AmPA

Before the War. James Pendergast. AMV-81

Before the war. From Our Album. Lawson Fusao Inada. AmPA

Before, there is water. Water. Edmond Jabès, *tr. by* Anthony Rudolf. VWA

Before, there was one. Birth. Constance Urdang. VWA

Before they ripen into diffused spririts. Katerina Anghelaki-Rooke, *tr. fr. modern Greek by* Kimon Friar. NU

Before this fever of the almost cold. Mirror. Peter De Vries. PoA

Before this longing. Her Longing. Theodore Roethke. NU

Before Trinity Church. The Assassination of President McKinley. Paul Blackburn. NYP

Before we shall again behold. Endimion Porter and Olivia. Sir William Davenant. NOBE

Before you step out. I Hope I Don't Have You Next Semester, But. Edwin S. Godsey. HoPM (1975 ed.)

Before You're a Stranger. Ray Fraser. AKE

Beforehand and Afterward ("Beforehand, liars studied how to lie"). Henry Tim Chambers. AATT

Befriending the Weather. Helena Minton. FAF

Begetting of Cain, The. Hyam Plutzik. VWA

Beggar, The. Adrian Mitchell. FaBoTw (1975 ed.)

Beggar and Poet. Robert A. Martin. AATT

Beggar Boy, The. Cecil Frances Alexander. OxBChV

Beggar Man, The. Lucy Aikin. OxBChV

Beggarman, The, *with music. Unknown.* RDB

Beggarman's Song, A, *sel. Tr. fr. Gaelic by* Frank O'Connor. "Would God that I and my darling." WTO

Beggar shouts his martial wares, The. The Beggar. Adrian Mitchell. FaBoTw (1975 ed.)

Beggar to Beggar Cried. W. B. Yeats. CMoP (1970 ed.); NoAM

Beggar to Mab, the Fairy Queen, The. Robert Herrick. CaPo

Beggarly Bear, A. Carolyn Wells. TDH

Beggars in the stories of old. Fairy Tales. Itzik Manger, *tr. by* Miriam Waddington. VWA

Beggar's Opera, The. John Gay. OAEL-1
  *Sels.*
  "If the heart of a man is depressed with cares," *fr.* II, i. HeIP
  "Man may escape from rope and gun," *fr.* II, ii. ILP (1975 ed.)
  "Modes of the court so common are grown, The" *fr.* III, iv. HeIP
  Over the Hills and Far Away, *fr.* I, i. BLSo, *with music;* NOBE ("Were I laid on Greenland's coast.") ILP (1975 ed.)
  "Through all the employments of life," *fr.* I, i. ILP (1975 ed.)
  Youth and Love, *fr.* II, i. NOBE

Beggar's Serenade. John Heath-Stubbs. BoLoP

Begging-bowl eyes, begging-bowl eyes. You Get Used to It. Adrian Mitchell. NowV

Begging on North Main. Dabney Stuart. AMV-81

Begin by parting your hair. Parting: A Game. Lynn Sukenick. CPA; NMM

Begin, ephebe, by perceiving the idea. Wallace Stevens. *Fr.* Notes toward a Supreme Fiction. NOBA

Begin here; where I began. Poem. Keith Althaus. AAN

Begin to charm, and as thou strok'st mine ears. To Music. Robert Herrick. CaPo

Begin with a kisse. Up Tailes All. Robert Herrick. LoAs

Begin with an unruffled lake. Short Subjects. Carolyn Stoloff. RiTi

Beginner, The. Kipling. *Fr.* Epitaphs of the War. FaBoTw (1975 ed.)

Beginner,/ Perpetual beginner. What Can I Tell My Bones? Theodore Roethke. NOBA

Beginning. Alden Nowlan. NeAC

Beginning. Marcos Rodríguez Frese, *tr. fr. Spanish by* Julio Marzán. InW

Beginning. David Rokeah, *tr. fr. Hebrew by* Robert Mezey. VWA

Beginning, A. David Steingass. CoPAm

Beginning, The. Wallace Stevens. VGW

Beginning, The/ is a circle. Sandra Maria Esteves. NW

Beginning Again as Morning. Eugene Ruggles. MIT

Beginning and an End, A. Edouard Roditi. VWA

Beginning my fortieth year. Beyond the Presidency. Morgan Gibson. FF

Beginning of an Undergraduate Poem. *Unknown.* FaBoCo

Beginning of the End, The. Gerard Manley Hopkins. VLP

Beginning of wisdom, said the Christmas tree, The. Christmas Needles. Albert Howard Carter. AATT

Beginning the Year at Rosebud, S.D. Roberta Hill. CDW

Beginning to Live. Ruth Stone. GP

Beginning to Squall. May Swenson. RFM

Beginnings. Erez Biton, *tr. fr. Hebrew by* Judith Katz. VWA

Beginnings. Robert D. Fitzgerald. GAS; MAuV

Beginnings, *sel.* Robert Hayden.
  "Plowdens, Finns." CNA

Beginnings ("Beginnings of a language"). John Montague. TwMBP

Begins the crying. Guitar. Federico García Lorca, *tr. by* Keith Waldrop. InPK

Begone, begone, my Willie, my Billy. Go from My Window. *Unknown.* AIW

Begot by butchers, but by bishops bred. On Cardinal Wolsey. *Unknown.* FaBoCo

Begun before Easter. . ./ Sign of the Fish. Thomas McGrath. Letter to an Imaginary Friend, Part Two, VI, 4. NNaP

Behind a web of bottles, bales. The Gombeen. Joseph Campbell. BIrV

Behind dept. stores, in/ 3rd st. bars. You See Them in the Alleys. Al Masarik. CPA

Behind her, mesquite and caliche dirt. Yaqui Women: Three Generations. Rick Casillas. GP

Behind her not the quivering of a leaf. Circe. A. D. Hope. PPP

Behind him lay the gray Azores. Columbus. Joaquin Miller. AmVN; BTTM; CTV; RhR

Behind him the hotdogs split and drizzled. Suicide Off Egg Rock. Sylvia Plath. PPP

Behind his dinner jacket. He's Doing Natural Life. Conyus. PoBA

Behind King's Chapel what the earth has kept. At the Indian Killer's Grave. Robert Lowell. NOBA; VGW

Behind me—dips eternity. Emily Dickinson. PBWP

Behind my back I have returned to life. Jim Harrison. *Fr.* Letters to Yesenin. TC

Behind shut doors, in shadowy quarantine. The First Time. Karl Shapiro. VGW

Behind, sun, before, shadow! Silhouette. Annette M'Baye, *tr. by* Kathleen Weaver. PBWP

Behind That Wall My Roommate Fucks His Girl. Geof Hewitt. NeAC; POL

Behind the bar the plates are stacked like silver. The Sea Breathes Quietly, Menelaus. Frank Stewart. PHC

Behind the Falls. William Stafford. RFM

Behind the grille that Easter noon. Reverend Mother Prioress. Betty Ruth Bird. AATT

Behind the Stove. James Hearst. TAT

Behind you/ a riot of pallid orphans. Small Country. Claribel Alegría, *tr. by* Aliki *and* Willis Barnstone. BoWoP

Behold. *Tr. fr. Hawaiian by* M. K. Pukui. WTO

Behold, a silly [or helpless] tender babe. New Prince, New Pomp. Robert Southwell. NOBE; PIM

Behold he comes to make thy people groan. Pasquin to the Queen's Statue at St. Paul's. William Shippen. APAS

Behold her, single in the field. The Solitary Reaper. Wordsworth. AnMo; CABA (1972 ed.); ExPo (1973 ed.); FaPoR; HAP; ILP (1975 ed.); InPS; MBPR; NOBE; OAEL-2; PoPle; PPP; SoSe; UnPo (1976 ed.); WeW

Behold, how eager this our little boy. Of the Boy and Butterfly. John Bunyan. OxBChV

Behold, I have a weapon. Shakespeare. *Fr.* Othello, V, ii. BiP

Behold! in various throngs the scribbling crew. Byron. *Fr.* English Bards and Scotch Reviewers. OAEL-2

Behold, love, thy power how she despiseth! Sir Thomas Wyatt. GBL

Behold me waiting—waiting for the knife. Before. W. E. Henley. In Hospital, IV. VLP

Behold, my dearest, how the fragrant rose. To Her Love. Edward May. FaBoEE

Behold, my Samsons are returning, and the gates of Gaza are on their shoulders. My Samsons. Haim Guri, *tr. by* Mark Elliott Shapiro. VWA

Behold, my servant shall deal prudently. Bible, *O.T. Fr.* Isaiah. NAWM-1

Behold the barren reef, which an earthquake hath just left dry. Martin Farquhar Tupper. *Fr.* Of Invention. VLP

Behold the brand of beauty tossed! The Dancer. Edmund Waller. NIL

Behind the calm famous faces knowledge of what crimes? Collapsible. Tom Raworth. EAS

Behold the child, by Nature's kindly law. Pope. *Fr.* An Essay on Man. POL

Behold the critic, pitched like the castrati. Epigram: Pipling. Theodore Roethke. NIL

Behold the duck. The Duck. Ogden Nash. RAE

Behold the ever-tim'rous hare. April. Samuel Thompson. BIrV

Behold the father is his daughter's son. The Nativity of Christ. Robert Southwell. BoReV

Behold the flag! Is it not a flag? The Rejected "National Hymns." "Orpheus C. Kerr." OBAL

Behold, the Grave of a Wicked Man. Stephen Crane. The Black Riders, XXV. TAP; TT

Behold the house of Sir William Forbes. The Pentland Hills. *Unknown.* GBP

Behold the Mount of Olives and the Greek cloister. Jerusalem. Antoni Slonimski, *tr. by* Isaac Komem. VWA

Behold, the Shade of Night Is Now Receding, *with music.* Gregory the Great, *tr. fr. Latin by* Ray Palmer. AH

Behold the tormented and the fallen angel. Beethoven. John Hall Wheelock. PoA

Behold the worlde, how it is whirled round. Sir John Davies. *Fr.* Orchestra; or, A Poem of Daucing. OBP

Behold this little volume here enrolled. On the Bible. William Strode. SCP-2

Behold those winged images. A Legend of the Hive. Robert Stephen Hawker. VPC

Behold, thou art fair. Bible, *O.T.* The Song of Solomon, IV. BiP

Behold with Joy, *with music.* Elhanan Winchester. AH

Behold, within the leafy shade. The Sparrow's Nest. Wordsworth. MBPR

Behold yon' mountains hoary height. Horace, *tr. by* Dryden. Odes, I, 9. OBVE

Beholde, how good and joyfull a thinge it is. Bible, *O.T.* Psalms, CXXXIII. OBVE

Beholders, The. James Dickey. ILP (1975 ed.)

Being a boy from the hills, brought up. The Welshman in Exile Speaks. T. H. Jones. OBW

Being a burglar, you slip out of doors in the morning. The Burglar. David Wagoner. CoPAm

Being a mammal, I have less care than birds. Displays of Skill: The Bat. Ruth Herschberger. WBN

Being a preacher, he. Blackjack Moses. Ahmos Zu-Bolton. AAN

Being Admired. Grace Cavalieri. PoUp

Being Adult. Bill Zavatsky. POL

Being awake still and not unhappy. Selichos. Francis Landy. VWA

Being Black. Horace Coleman. SES

Being Here (or Anywhere). Charles Doyle. ATNZ

Being his resting place. A Dog Sleeping on My Feet. James Dickey. UsP

Being kissed on the back. Knee Song. Anne Sexton. SFF

Being laid upon her bed she grasped my hand. John Marston. *Fr.* Antonio's Revenge. SCP-2

Being Natural. Carl Rakosi. GP

"Being no longer human, why should I." Paracelsus in Excelsis. Ezra Pound. PiAm

Being on the Edge of Someone Else. Virginia R. Terris. AAN

Being on the road wasn't so bad. Has Been. Alice F. Worsley. AMV–80

Being Somebody. Edwin Honig. TAP

Being to timelessness as it's to time. E. E. Cummings. HAP

Being without quality. Vox Humana. Thom Gunn. ILP (1975 ed.)

Being you, you cut your poetry from wood. The Egg Boiler. Gwendolyn Brooks. PoBA

Being your slave, what should I do but tend. Sonnets, LVII. Shakespeare. HAP; LoAs; STS

Beinn Damph. Paul Mills. MIS

Bel Woman. Roman Adrian. DNGG

Belfast Linen. *Unknown. See* Ballad of William Bloat, The.

Belfast Lough. *Unknown, tr. fr. Irish by* John Montague. BIrV

Belief. A. R. Ammons. GOA; TT

Belief. Josephine Miles. NoAM; TAP

Believe in this couple this day who come. Glen Uig. Richard Hugo. PCho

Believe Me, If All Those Endearing Young Charms. Thomas Moore. BLSH, *with music;* FSW

Believe me, knot of gristle, I bleed like a tree. Give Way, Ye Gates. Theodore Roethke. CMoP (1970 ed.)

Believe me, sir, I'd like to spend whole days. Martial, *tr. fr. Latin by* J. V. Cunningham. OBVE

Believe not, Fair, that I can prove untrue. William Diaper. *Fr.* Eclogue I. PeD

Believing What I Know. William Stafford. Epi

Belinda's Morning. Pope. *See* Toilet, The.

Bell at Midnight. May Miller. PPoD

Bell-bottomed Trousers. *Unknown.* FSW

Bell diphthonging in an atmosphere, A. A Dubious Night. Richard Wilbur. CAPP

Bell-rope that gathers God at dawn, The. The Broken Tower. Hart Crane. CMoP (1970 ed.); ILP (1975 ed.);NoAM; NOBA; PiAm

Bell Speech. Richard Wilbur. CABA (1972 ed.)

Bell Too Heavy to Ring. Tom Kryss. NeAC

Bell Weather. Lewis Turco. AMV–80

Bella and the Golem. Rossana Ombres, *tr. fr. Italian by* Edgar Pauk. VWA

Bella Ciao. *Unknown, tr. fr. Italian.* FSW

Bellair. Van K. Brock. CSP

Belle of the Ball Room, The. Winthrop Mackworth Praed.
FaBoCo

Belle Starr. *Unknown.* BPAW

Bellevue. James Harrison. CoPAm

Belling the Cat. William Langland. *Fr.* The Vision of Piers
Plowman. OxBM

Bellman, The. Robert Herrick. CaPo; PoPle

Bellman's Song, The. *Unknown.* EBEV

Bellows Maker of Oxford, The. John Hoskyns. FaBoEE

Bellringing was another. To My Father. Tony Curtis.
AMV-81

Bells, The. Poe. OBAL; TAP
"Hear the sledges with the bells," *sel.* LFH; SpRo

Bells, The. Lucille F. Travis. AATT

Bells are booming down the bohreens. Ireland with Emily. John
Betjeman. OxBTC

Bells for John Whiteside's Daughter. John Crowe Ransom.
AnMo; CMoP (1970 ed.); FF; HAP; HeIP; HoPM (1975 ed.);
ILP (1975 ed.); InPK; InPS; IP; NIL; NoAM; NOBA; PAIC;
PiAm; PoIA; PPoD; PPP; PSN; RRA; SoS; SoSe; TAP;
UnPo (1976 ed.); VGW; VoPo; WeW; WIF

Bells in their ears; smoke in their lungs. Diggle Mill. Glyn
Hughes. LP

Bells of Heaven, The. Ralph Hodgson. ILP (1975 ed.); NOBE;
PPoD

Bells of London, The. *Unknown.* PoPle
("Gay go up and gay go down.") MG

Bells of Rhymney. Idris Davies *and* Pete Seeger. PoRo

Bells of waiting Advent ring, The. Christmas. John Betjeman.
BoReV; OxBTC

Bells, Ostend, The. William Lisle Bowles. PAIC

Belly Dancer's Daughter, The. Anne Sexton. UsP

Beloved, The. David Roberts, *tr. fr. Welsh by* H. Idris Bell.
OBW

Beloved,/my parents mock me. Freely, from a Song Sung by
Jewish Women of Yemen. Stephen Levy. VWA

Beloved, and he sweetly thus goes on. A Pulpit to Be Let.
*Unknown.* PAAS

Beloved, gaze in thine own heart. The Two Trees. W. B. Yeats.
OAEL-2; VLP

Beloved, it is good. Dream Song. *Tr. by* Francis Densmore.
OBVE

Beloved, let us once more praise the rain. Conrad Aiken.
Preludes for Memnon, VII. UnPo (1976 ed.)

Beloved, may your sleep be sound. Lullaby. W. B. Yeats.
BoLoP; FaBoTw (1975 ed.)

Beloved, my beloved, when I think. Sonnets from the Portuguese,
XX. Elizabeth Barrett Browning. WPE

Beloved, thou hast brought me many flowers. Sonnets from the
Portuguese, XLIV. Elizabeth Barrett Browning. ILP (1975
ed.); VPC; WPE

Beloved's Image, The. *Tr. fr. Hawaiian by* M. W. Beckwith.
WTO

Below Bald Mountain. Janice Townley Moore. AMV-80

Below my father's house lies a river valley. Seeing in the Dark.
Matthew Brennan. AMV-81

Below the down the stranded town. A Cinque Port. John
Davidson. PoPle; VLP

Below the ford, the stream in flood. At Dunkeswell Abbey.
Anthony Thwaite. HeHu

Below the gardens and the darkening pines. At Carmel
Highlands. Janet Lewis. PoA

Below the hawk. South Carolina Baptismal Procession. David
Childers. AAN

Below the ten thousand billionth of a centimeter. The First Day.
Howard Nemerov. AnMo

Below the terrace where he sits. Passage. John Williams. MPA

Below the thunders of the upper deep. The Kraken. Tennyson.
CABA (1972 ed.); EcS; ILP (1975 ed.); OAEL-2; VLP

Below the timberline. For Mantee/My Whole World Came
Falling Down. James Steele. SES

Below thir stanes lie Jamie's banes. On a Noisy Polemic. Burns.
FaBoEE

Belshazzar. "Barry Cornwall." PIM

Ben. Thomas Wolfe. NCSH; TVo

Ben Allah Achmet; or, The Fatal Tum. W. S. Gilbert. VLP

Ben Battle was a soldier bold. Faithless Nellie Gray. Thomas
Hood. FaBoCo; NOBL; VLP

Ben Bolt; or, Ah! Don't You Remember. Thomas Dunn English.
FSW; PSoN; *with music*

Ben Hall was out on the Lachlan side. The Death of Ben Hall.
Will H. Ogilvie. PoTa

Bench of Boors, The. Herman Melville. AmVN; OBAL; SoSe

Benches are broken, the grassplots brown and bare, The. South
End. Conrad Aiken. CMoP (1970 ed.); HoPM (1975 ed.)

Benches round a square of glass. Am Steinplatz. D. J. Enright.
HeHu

Bend as the bow bends, and let fly the shaft. Conrad Aiken.
CMoP (1970 ed.)

Bend low again, night of summer stars. Summer Stars. Carl
Sandburg. RFM

Bendemeer's Stream. Thomas Moore. FSW

Bending down the huddle sprout grass. Rain Sleets Flat.
Besmilr Brigham. Psy

Bending, I bow my head. Combing. Gladys Cardiff. CDW

Bendix. John Updike. SoS

Beneath a grove of stars. Gathering Gems. Ethel Green Russell.
AATT

Beneath a myrtle shade. Song of the Zambra Dance. Dryden.
*Fr.* The Conquest of Granada. ILP (1975 ed.)

Beneath a striped umbrella. Song of the Darkness. John
Bricuth. CSP

Beneath all the statistics. New York. Federico Garcia Lorca, *tr.
by* Robert Bly. EC; NYP; NU

Beneath him with new wonder now he views. Milton. *Fr.*
Paradise Lost, IV. PPP

Beneath my palm-trees, by the river side. The Song of the Indian
Maid. Keats. *Fr.* Endymion. NOBE

Beneath noticing: there is Wyatt lying. Now Is Always the
Miraculous Time. Robert Sargent. PoUp

Beneath Such Rains. James E. Warren, Jr. AATT

Beneath the cement foundations. Washyuma Motor Hotel.
Simon J. Ortiz. GP

Beneath the cloud-topp'd mountain. Song of the Desert. Eliza
R. Snow. WPW

Beneath the silent chambers of the earth. Hell. Abraham
Cowley. *Fr.* Davideis, I. SCP-2

Beneath the snow the broad sad wastelands. Winter Day.
Susannah Fried, *tr. by* Anthony Rudolf. VWA

Beneath the waning moon I walk at night. The Journey of Life.
Bryant. EAP

Beneath the waters of the sea. The Mock Turtle's Song, *early
version.* "Lewis Carroll." *Fr.* Alice's Adventures in
Wonderland. VLP

Beneath the willow wound round with ivy. Hops. Boris
Pasternak, *tr. by* Jon Stallworthy *and* Peter France. BoLoP

Beneath their flames, cities of candelabra. The Chestnut Avenue
at Alton House. Charles Tomlinson. FaBoTw (1975 ed.)

Beneath these alien stars. Pioneer Woman. Vesta Pierce
Crawford. BPAW

Beneath these plains. West of Chicago. John Dimoff. RFM

Beneath these poppies buried deep. Epitaph on Robert Southey.
Thomas Moore. FaBoCo; FaBoEE

Beneath these shades, beside yon winding stream.  On Visiting the Graves of Hawthorne and Thoreau.  Jones Very.  TAP

Beneath this smooth stone by the bone of his bone.  *Unknown.*  FaBoEE

Beneath this sod lie the remains.  Epitaph on a Young Poet Who Died before Having Achieved Success.  Amy Lowell.  OBAL

Beneath this stone a Poet Laureate lies.  Epitaph on William Whitehead.  *Unknown.*  FaBoEE

Beneath this stone does William Hazlitt lie.  W. H. *Eheu!*  Samuel Taylor Coleridge.  FaBoEE

Beneath this stone in hopes of Zion.  At Upton-on-Severn.  *Unknown.*  FaBoCo; FaBoEE

Beneath Time's roaring cannon.  When the Mississippi Flowed in Indiana.  Vachel Lindsay.  CMoP (1970 ed.); ILP (1975 ed.)

Beneath yon birch with silver bark.  The Ballad of the Dark Ladie.  Samuel Taylor Coleridge.  MBPR

Beneath yon larkspur's azure bells.  The Blue-Bird.  Herman Melville.  NOBA

Benedicite! what[e] dreamed I this nyght [*or* night]?  The Dream of a Lover.  *Unknown.*  HAP; LoAs

Benediction.  William Freedman.  VWA

Benediction.  Donald Jeffrey Hayes.  AmNP (1974 ed.)

Benediction.  Bob Kaufman.  IPWM

Benediction.  Stanley Kunitz.  VGW

Benediction.  William R. Mitchell.  AATT

Benediction.  Myra Sklarew.  VWA

Benediction.  Mark Turbyfill.  PoA

Benediction for Danny.  William R. Mitchell.  AATT

Benediction for the Felt.  *Mongol Oral Tradition, tr. by* C. R. Bawden.  WTO

Benediction for the Tent.  *Mongol Oral Tradition, tr. by* C. R. Bawden.  WTO

Benefits of an Education, The.  John Ciardi.  CoPAm

Benign Neglect/ Mississippi, 1970.  Primus St. John.  PoBA

Benjamin Franklin Hazard.  Edgar Lee Masters.  *Fr.* The New Spoon River.  GOA

Benjamin Jones Goes Swimming.  Aileen Fisher.  CTV

Bennie Lynch died in the gutter.  The Laneliest Place in the Warld.  Donald Campbell.  MIS

Bent and knotted as a wintered vine.  The First Generation.  Janice Mirikitani.  MIT

Bent benches, no lockers, nor nowhere near nozzles enough.  Bath.  Lincoln Kirstein.  NoAM

Bent double, like old beggars under sacks.  Dulce et Decorum Est.  Wilfred Owen.  CABA (1972 ed.); CMoP (1970 ed.); DL; FaBoTw (1975 ed.); FF; HeIP; HoPM (1975 ed.); ILP (1975 ed.); InPK; IP; NIL; NoAM; OAEL-2; PPP; SFF; SoSe; UnPo (1976 ed.); VoPo; WIF

Bent over those.  Watching You Draw.  Carol Cox.  MMD

Bent Tree.  Peter Serchuk.  AMV-80

Beowulf.  Kingsley Amis.  FaBoCo

Beowulf.  *Unknown, tr. fr. Anglo-Saxon by* Charles W. Kennedy.  OAEL-1
  *Sels.*

Beowulf's Fight with Grendel's Mother, *tr. by* Michael Alexander.  WTO

Beowulf's Last Speech, *tr. by* Burton Raffel.  OBP

Grendel, *tr. by* Burton Raffel.  NU; OBP

Introductory: "That towering place, gabled and huge," *tr. by* Burton Raffel.  OBP

"Oft in the hall I have heard my people," *tr. by* Charles W. Kennedy.  HeIP

To the Sea, *tr. by* Burton Raffel.  OBP

Beowulf's Fight with Grendel's Mother.  *Unknown, tr. fr. Anglo-Saxon by* Michael Alexander.  *Fr.* Beowulf.  WTO

Beppo: A Venetian Story.  Byron.  MBPR; OBSV
  *Sels.*

"England! with all thy faults I love thee still."  UnPo (1976 ed.)
Italy and England.  PAIC
  (Italy versus England.)  NOBE

"'Tis known, at least it should be, that throughout."  NOBL

Bequest.  S. Gale Gilburt.  AMV-81

Bereaved Swan, The.  Stevie Smith.  FaBoNo; FaBoTw (1975 ed.)

Bereaved years, they've settled to this, The.  Evening Harbour.  Tom Paulin.  AMV-81

Bereavement.  Elizabeth Barrett Browning.  WPE

Bereft.  Robert Frost.  SoSe (1977 ed.)

Bereft.  Thomas Hardy.  BoLoP; NoAM

Bereft Child's First Night.  Frances Bellerby.  POL

Berg, The.  Herman Melville.  AmVN; InPK; LFH; NOBA; PiAm; TAP

Berkeley Pier, The.  John Addiego.  AMV-81

Bermondsey Tragedy, The.  *Unknown.*  VLP

Bermudas.  Andrew Marvell.  AnMo; BoReV; CABA (1972 ed.); ILP (1975 ed.); MetP; NIL; NOBE

Bernard.  Raymond Souster.  POL

Berstein disc jockey.  Ten o'Clock News.  Simon Ortiz.  VW

Bertram Declines.  Thomas Cobb.  FoP

Beryl.  Lyn Lifshin.  NeAC

Beshrew me but I love her heartily.  Shakespeare.  *Fr.* The Merchant of Venice, II, vi.  CTV

Beside a chapel I'd a room looked down.  Dread.  J. M. Synge.  BoLoP

Beside a fall there is a round wood pipe.  Jean Garrigue.  POL

Beside a narrow trail in the blue.  Dream of the Lynx.  John Haines.  NU

Beside a row of gates.  Stray Things.  Dan Johnson.  PPoD

Beside his heavy-shouldered team.  Bullocky.  Judith Wright.  MAuV

Beside me,—in the car,—she sat.  Natura Naturans.  Arthur Hugh Clough.  HAP; VLP; VPC

Beside me she sat, hand hooked and hovering.  An Egyptian Passage.  Theodore Weiss.  TAP

Beside that tent and under guard in majesty alone he stands.  Geronimo.  Ernest McGaffey.  BPAW

Beside the idle summer sea.  Rondel.  W. E. Henley.  NIL

Beside the Bed.  Charlotte Mew.  WPE

Beside the horse troughs, General Grant.  Hens.  Alden Nowlan.  POL

Beside the Road.  Ken Belford.  NeAC

Beside the road to Texas.  The Road to Texas.  Berta Hart Nance.  BPAW

Beside the Seaside, *sels.*  John Betjeman.
  "Green shutters, shut your shutters! Windyridge."  OxBTC
  "On a secluded corner of the beach."  LP

Beside the ungathered rice he lay.  The Slave's Dream.  Longfellow.  FaPoR

Besides the autumn poets sing.  Emily Dickinson.  PPM

Bespoke for weeks, he turned up some morning.  Thatcher.  Seamus Heaney.  HeHu

Bess.  William Stafford.  GP; NNaP

Bessie Bobtail.  James Stephens.  PFIr

Bessie Dreaming Bear.  Marnie Walsh.  VW

Bessie Smith's Funeral.  Alvin Aubert.  CoPAm

Best and brightest, come away.  To Jane: The Invitation.  Shelley.  MBPR

Best dance is the dance of the eastern clans, The.  *Somali Oral Tradition, tr. by* B. W. Andrzejewski *and* I. M. Lewis.  WTO

Best Friends.  Judith Hemschemeyer.  AMV-81

Best Line Yet, The.  Edward Allen.  InPK; POL

Best Loved of Africa.  Margaret Danner.  PoBA

Best of both worlds being got, The. Poets' Corner. Robert Graves. FaBoEE

Best of Show. Barbara Howes. GDP

Best of thy sex! if sacred friendship can. To Philocles [or Phylocles], Inviting Him to Friendship. "Ephelia." SCP-2; WPE

Best of Two Worlds. Basil Boothroyd. BoAnP

Best Old Fellow in the World, The. *Unknown.* AmFP

Best slave, The. Alcestis on the Poetry Circuit. Erica Jong. AmPA; RiTi

Best Thing Going, The. George Mattingly. AcAn

Best thing in the world, The. Biotherm (For Bill Berkson). Frank O'Hara. CAAP

"Best way to go, The," said my muffled-up friend. March Hares. Walter de la Mare. FaBoNo

Best work is made, The. Art. Denise Levertov. CAPP

Bestiary, A. Kenneth Rexroth. OBAL
*Sels.*
  Deer. HoPM (1975 ed.)
  Fox. NNaP
  Herring. HoPm (1975 ed.)
  Horse. NNaP
  Lion. HoPM (1975 ed.)
  Raccoon. NNaP
  Vulture. NNaP
  Wolf. NNaP
  You. HoPM (1975 ed.)

Bestiary for the Fingers of My Right Hand. Charles Simic. AmPA

Beth Appleyard's Verses. Peter De Vries. OBAL

Beth-Gêlert. William Robert Spencer. GDP

Bethsabe's Song. George Peele. *Fr.* David and Bethsabe. NOBE
  ("Hot sun, cool fire, temper'd with sweet air.") GBL

Betjeman, 1984. Charles Causley. FaBoCo; NOBL; OxBTC

Betrayal in Morninside. Donald Campbell. MIS

Betrayed by friend dragged from the garden hailed. Ecce Homunculus. R. A. K. Mason. ATNZ

Betrothal, A. E. J. Scovell. GBL

Better a bug in the dust underfoot. The Child in the Rug. John Haines. GP

Better born than married, misled. The Grandmother. Wendell Berry. GP

Better disguised than the leaf-insect. The Lake. Ted Hughes. FaBoTw (1975 ed.)

Better it were had you borne black earth, o mother, rather than me. Mother of Man. Vesna Param, *tr. by* Mary Coote. PBWP

Better late than never: yea, mate. Of Late and Never. John Heywood. PAIC

Better not go the thee deep woods. The Great Fountains. Anne Hebert, *tr. by* Willis Barnstone. BoWoP

Better not to go back to the village. The Malefic Return. Ramón López Velarde, *tr. by* Samuel Beckett. OBVE

Better Resurrection, A. Christina Rossetti. VLP

Better the book against the rock. Three Poems about Children. Austin Clarke. CIP

Better they never learned to read! The Misogynist. Jean Morgan. FF

Better to be a crow, they said. Biograph. Rodger Kamenetz. AAN

Better to see your cheek grown hollow. Madman's Song. Elinor Wylie. Moon

Better Way, The. Walter Leaf. FaBoCo

Betty and Dupree. Brownie McGhee. FSW

Betty Fuller cried and said, Hit me. A Local Man Remembers Betty Fuller. James Whitehead. GP

Betty Pringle's Pig. *Unknown.* ECBV

Betty told Dupree, "I want a diamond ring." Betty and Dupree. Brownie McGhee. FSW

Bettystown. Sydney Bernard Smith. IPM

Betuix twell houris and ellevin. The Amendis to the Telyouris and Sowtaris for the Turnament Maid on Thame. William Dunbar. OBSV

Between a Good Hat and Good Boots. Kell Robertson. TAT

Between a toasted almond. Cocktails. Susan MacDonald. PoW

Between Appointments. Giles Gordon. SLP

Between dawn and the Opera. Clandestine Work. Yvan Goll, *tr. by* Anthony Rudolf. VWA

Between dinner and death, the crowds shadow the loom of steel. Park Avenue. Robert Fitzgerald. NYP

Between distorted forests, clapped into geometry. Pastoral of the City Streets. A. M. Klein. BBGO

Between extremities. Vacillation. W. B. Yeats. NoAM

Between five and fifty. Praise. Jane Cooper. TAP

Between Life and Death. Frantisek Gottlieb, *tr. fr. Czech by* Ewald Osers. VWA

Between Me and Anyone Who Can Understand. Sharon Scott. JB

Between me and the sunset, like a dome. The Man against the Sky. E. A. Robinson. CMoP (1970 ed.); STS

Between my finger and my thumb. Digging. Seamus Heaney. BIrV; CIP; IPM; MPo

Between my lips the taste of night-time blends. The Realm of Touching. Alan Bold. MS

Between night and this morning's dawn, purple. End of Season. Owen Leeming. ATNZ

Between Our Folding Lips. Thomas Edward Brown. PeD

Between painting a roof yesterday and the hay. Independence Day. Wendell Berry. OFD

Between rebellion as a private study and the public. Last Poem [or Poem]. Charles Donnelly. BIrV; CIP

Between Rivers and Seas. Lance Henson. VoR

Between the dark and the daylight. If. Franklin P. Adams. OBAL

Between the dark and the daylight. The Children's Hour. Longfellow. CTV; OBAL; PCOP

Between the dark and the daylight. Death at Suppertime. Phyllis McGinley. PBMP

Between the dark silent trees. Dionysius. Sophia de Mello Breyner Andresen, *tr. by* Allan Francovich. PBWP

Between the Electric Rhythm and the Melodic Mind. James Schevill. MIT

Between the gardening and the cookery. A Bookshop Idyll. Kingsley Amis. OxBTC; SoSe

Between the green bud and the red. Prelude to "Songs before Sunrise." Swinburne. VLP

Between the moondrawn and the sundown here. On the Cliffs. Swinburne. VLP

Between the Porch and the Altar, sels. Robert Lowell.
  At the Altar, IV. InPK; InPS
  Katherine's Dream, III. ConAP

Between the sewing machine and the kitchen. Two Lives. William Pillin. SPT

Between the Tides. Emily Sargent Councilman. AMV–80

Between the trial for embezzlement and the trial for impiety. The Death of Phidias. Ann Deagon. AAN

Between the turnpike and the avenue. The Road the Crows Own. Susan Astor. AMV–81

Between the two. Eightball. Dave Morice. AcAn

Between the under and the upper blue. Seagulls. Robert Francis. RFM

Between the walls, the brim. Terce. James McMichael. PoA

Between the woods the afternoon. The Mirror. A. A. Milne. ECBV

Between the World and Me. Richard Wright. AmNP (1974 ed.); MiP; NoAM; PoBA; SPT; WIF

Between the World and me. The Meaning of Protest. Michael S. Harper. NW

Between the year of the slump and the sell out, I. Son of a Gun. Padraic Fiacc. IPM

Between them is the land of broken colors. The Black Horse Rider. Pierre Loving. EAS

Between town and the. The Quarry Pool. Denise Levertov. VGW

Between two lines of print. Orpheus. Michael Goldman. NowV

Between Two Prisoners. James Dickey. PAIC

Between two rivers. Island. Langston Hughes. *Fr.* Lenox Avenue Mural. ILP (1975 ed.)

Between Two Wars. R. P. Kingston. NVAP

Between us, a mild river. Translation from Original. Joanne Casullo. NPW

Between us lies the issue clear. Six Poems, 5. Joseph Freeman. SPT

Between us quiet has fallen. Letter V. Robin Skelton. MPA

Between Walls. William Carlos Williams. HoPM (1975 ed.); TAP; VGW

Between winter and spring. Spring Rain. Ettore Rella. SPT

Betweens. Norman MacCaig. EAS

Betwene March and Averil. *See* Bytuene Mersh and Averil.

Betwixt two ridges of ploughed land sat Wat. Margaret Cavendish, Duchess of Newcastle. *Fr.* The Hunting of the Hare. SCP-2

Beulah Land. Edgar Page. BLSH, *with music;* FSW

Beulah Louise. William Jay Smith. TDH

Beverly Fragments. Morgan Sanders. WBN

Beverly Hills, Chicago. Gwendolyn Brooks. VGW

Beware: Do Not Read This Poem. Ishmael Reed. BPo; CNA; Epi; IPWM; NCSH; PoBA; WeW

Beware, My Child. Shel Silverstein. CaYB; IWK

Beware of Benjamin Franklin, he is totally lacking in grace. Sonnet. Ted Berrigan. CAAP

Beware of Dogmas. Ebenezer Elliott. FaBoEE

Beware of the man who denounces ambition. Seventeen [*or* Sixteen] Warnings in Search of a Feminist Poem. Erica Jong. AmPA; NVAP; WBN

Beware of those. Diana DiPrima. *Fr.* Revolutionary Letters. GP

Beware, Oh, Take Care. *Unknown.* FSW

Beware! The Israelite of old, who tore. The Warning. Longfellow. PiAm

Beware the Months of Fire. Patrick Lane. NeAC

Bewick Finzer. E. A. Robinson. CMoP (1970 ed.); PPP; STS

Bewildered in our buying throng. Patrum Propositum. Robert Fitzgerald. GOA

Bewteis of Fute-Ball, The. *Unknown.* FaBoCo

Beyond a low wall. Tortoise. Joanne de Longchamps. BoAnP

Beyond all this, the wish to be alone. Wants. Philip Larkin. PoIA

Beyond Anguish. Milton Kessler. CoPAm

Beyond Belief. Tom Luhrmann. AMV–81

Beyond Breath. Ken Smith. TwMBP

Beyond earshot of others, furtively. The Conspirators. Kenneth Burke. SFF

Beyond her window in October sun. Farm Wife. Matt Field. AMV–81

Beyond Logic. Adrianne Marcus. NPW

Beyond Memory. Monny de Boully, *tr. fr. Serbo-Croat by* Aleksander Nejgebauer. VWA

Beyond Silence (1). Andrew Taylor. CAAP

Beyond Swordale. Derick Thomson, *tr. fr. Gaelic by* author. MS

Beyond that sandbar is the river's turning. Exploration over the Rim. William Dickey. SS

Beyond the Alps. Robert Lowell. NOBA; PiAm

Beyond the Atlas roams a glutton. The Glutton. Robert Graves. CMoP (1970 ed.)

Beyond the bell-post by the door. Winter Morning. Stephen Tudor. HeS

Beyond the bumper cars. Snake Hill. Joseph Bruchac. NW

Beyond the edge of the sepia. Lament for a Cricket Eleven. Kenneth Allott. OxBTC

Beyond the End. Denise Levertov. VGW

Beyond the Firehouse. Patrick Worth Gray. AMV–80

Beyond the hour we counted rain that fell. Old Countryside. Louise Bogan. HAP; WPE

Beyond the Hunting Woods. Donald Justice. ConAP; CSP; NCSH; UsP

Beyond the inmost barriers of the brain. The Owl. Edward Davison. PoA

Beyond the Last Lamp. Thomas Hardy. NOBE

Beyond the Liss. John Montague. TwMBP

Beyond the low marsh-meadows and the beach. The Pines and the Sea. Christopher Pearse Cranch. ILP (1975 ed.)

Beyond the Nigger ("Beyond the outstretched hands"). Sterling Plumpp. PoBA

Beyond the porcelain fence of the pleasure garden. A Year Passes. Amy Lowell. Moon

Beyond the Presidency. Morgan Gibson. FF

Beyond the primitive powers of pain, of love at last. In Praise of Robert Penn Warren. David Lehman. AMV–81

Beyond the shadow of the ship. Water-Snakes. Samuel Taylor Coleridge. *Fr.* The Rime of the Ancient Mariner. EcS

Beyond the smiling and the weeping. A Little While. Horatius Bonar. VLP

Beyond the steady rock the steady sea. The Fable. Yvor Winters. UsP

Beyond the Storm. James Bertolino. HeS

Beyond the sunrise. Ode to Willem de Kooning. Frank O'Hara. Epi

Beyond the turning sea's far foam. At War. Russell Atkins. AmNP (1974 ed.)

Beyond the Window. Joseph P. Darcy. BrS

Beyond the yard the barn is hulking. My Father Dragged by Horses. T. Alan Broughton. AMV–80

Beyond What. Alice Walker. WBN

Bhagavad-Gita, The, *sels. Unknown, tr. fr. Sanskrit.*
"Arjuna said:/How shall I in battle against Bhisma," *tr. by* Franklin Edgerton. DL
One, The, *tr. by* Raimundo Panikkar. ILwL

Biafra. L. V. Mack. PoBA

Biafran, *sertanejo,* Pakistani. Retreat. Amy Bushnell. AMV–80

Bianca, *sel.* Arthur Symons.
Bianca, I. VLP

Bibily Boo and Wollypotump. Laura E. Richards. *See* Bobbily Boo and Wollypotump.

Bible is an antique volume, The. Emily Dickinson. TT

Bible opens then closes real hard, A. Empty Streams of Autumn. Ray A. Young Bear. VW

Bibliotheca Bodleiana. Geoffrey Grigson. GBL

Bibulous eagle behind me at the ball game, The. One to Nothing. Carolyn Kizer. OBAL

Bicause I have the still kept fro lyes and blame. Petrarch, *tr. fr. Italian by* Sir Thomas Wyatt. OBVE

Bicentennial Winter. Linda Pastan. WasP

Bicycle. David Malouf. FPA

Bicycle Built for Two, A (Daisy Bell). Harry Dacre. *See* Daisy Bell.

Bicycle is naturally singular, The. Bicycliary. Robert A. Brooks. PoUp

Bicycle Rider. Eugene McCarthy. SPo

Bicycles go by in twos and threes, The. Inniskeen Road: July Evening. Patrick Kavanagh. NoAM; PFIr

Bicycles! Tricycles! John Banister Tabb. OBAL

Bicycliary. Robert A. Brooks. PoUp

Bid a strong ghost stand at the head. A Prayer for My Son. W. B. Yeats. EBEV

Bid all profane away! Ben Jonson. *Fr.* Hymenaei. SCP-1

Bid me to live, and I will live. To Anthea, Who May Command Him Anything. Robert Herrick. CaPo; ILP (1975 ed.); NOBE; OAEL-1

Bid your Papa Goodnight. Sweet exhibition! Mrs. Hopley, on Seeing Her Children Say Goodnight to Their Father. Gerard Manley Hopkins. FaBoEE

Bidding Prayer, A ("Bidde we with milde stevene"). *Unknown.* OxBM

Big Apple Blues. *Unknown.* BluL

Big Ben is cracked, we needs must own. To Disraeli. Shirley Brooks. NOBL

Big Bessie Throws Her Son into the Street. Gwendolyn Brooks. VGW

Big Billie Potts was big and stout. The Ballad of Billie Potts. Robert Penn Warren. NOBA

Big black Angus bull. Seventh Georgic. George Economou. POL

Big Boy came. Catch. Langston Hughes. NoAM

Big breakers roll over the sea. Breakers over the Sea. *Malay Oral Tradition, tr. by* R. O. Winstedt. WTO

Big brown tin can lyin' in the black sand. Ain't It a Sad Thing? R. Dean Taylor. PoRo

Big Chief Blues. *Unknown.* BluL

Big City Glissando. Nicholas Christopher. NYP

Big Daddy Lipscomb, who used to help them up. Say Goodbye to Big Daddy. Randall Jarrell. LiSp

Big Dog. Philip Booth. BoAnP; GDP

Big doors of the country barn stood open and ready, The. Walt Whitman. *Fr.* Song of Myself. RAE

Big Dream, Little Dream. Louis Simpson. POL; WasP

Big Fanny and stromin vinne deal. Suicide. Bob Kaufman. CPA

Big farm girl with the dumb prophetic body, The. Bitter Harvest. Alistair Campbell. ATNZ

Big Game Hunter. Alexander Resnikoff. OSF

Big Hat or What, A? Pete Morgan. SLP

Big I, The. John Hall Wheelock. IP

Big-jawed Bluefish, ravenous, sleek muscle slamming, The. Night Fishing for Blues. Dave Smith. LiSp

Big Job. William Cole. OSF

Big John Henry. Margaret Walker. WIF

Big mack rolling and rumbling down the long street, A. Timeclock. Herman Spector. SPT

Big Momma. Don L. Lee. BPo; CNA; TPo

Big Muddy, The. Pete Seeger. NIL

Big Night Blues. *Unknown.* BluL

Big old houses have passed away. Sometimes I Think of Maryland. Jodi Braxton. CNA

Big Road Blues. *Unknown.* BluL

Big Rock Candy Mountains, The, *diff. versions. Unknown.* AmFP; DuDr; FSW; GBP; NOBA; OBAL; SoS

Big Rock Jail. *Unknown.* BluL

Big Rocks, The. T. L. Kryss. EC

Big Ship Sailing, A. *Unknown.* FSW

Big star, and that other, The. Leaflets. Adrienne Rich. NIL; NoAM

Big Sunflower, The, *with music.* Bobby Newcomb. BLSo

Big Sur Summer. Delia Chilgren. NPW

Big Wind. Theodore Roethke. AnMo; CMoP (1970 ed.); NCSH; PiAm; PPoe; UsP; VGW

Big with great purposes and proud, they sat. Homer, *tr. by* William Cowper. *Fr.* The Iliad, VIII. OBVE

Big Woman. *Unknown.* BluL

Big young bareheaded woman, A. Proletarian Portrait. William Carlos Williams. MiP; OBAL; OsP; PiAm; TAP

Bigger than your doubt, Thomas. The Ballad of Bigger Thomas. E. Curmie Price. WIF

Biggest Killing, The. Edward Dorn. VGW

Biglow Papers, The, *sels.* James Russell Lowell.
  1st Series, No. VI.
    Pious Editor's Creed, The. PiAm
  1st Series, No. VIII.
    Letter from a Candidate for the Presidency, A. PiAm
  2d Series, Introduction.
    Courtin', The. AmVN; NOBA; OBAL
  2d Series, No. IV.
    Rev. Homer Wilbur's "Festina Lente." OBAL

Bigness of Atoms, The. Margaret Cavendish, Duchess of Newcastle. SCP-2

Bilbea. Carl Sandburg. PiAm

Bile Them Cabbage Down. *Unknown.* AmFP; FSW

Bill/ exists. A Personality Sketch: Bill. Ronda Davis. JB

Bill and Parson Sim. *Unknown.* BPAW

Bill Bailey Won't You Pleases Come Home. Hughie Cannon. BLSo, *with music;* FSN, *with music;* FSW; OBAL

Bill Groggin's Goat. *Unknown.* FSW

Bill learned to play tunes on a comb. A Nuisance at Home. *Unknown.* TDH

Bill Munson's wife was sick, you see. The Cowboy and the Stork. Robert V. Carr. BPAW

Bill of Fare, A, *sel.* William Cartwright.
  "Expect no strange or puzzling meat, no pie." SCP-2

Bill Riley was a cowboy and a quicker shot than him. Bill and Parson Sim. *Unknown.* BPAW

Bill to My Father, A. Edward Field. TPo

Billiards. Laurie Blauner. AMV-81

Billiards. Walker Gibson. LiSp

Billings and Cooings from "The Berkeley Barb." Mona Van Duyn. GP

Billows swell, the winds are high, The. Temptation. William Cowper. PIM

Billy. Harry Graham. FaBoCo

Billy Barlow. *Unknown.* FSW

Billy Batter. Dennis Lee. OSF

Billy Boy. *Unknown.* AmFP; GSB, *with music;* HoPM (1975 ed.)

Billy Budd, Foretopman, *sel.* Herman Melville.
  Billy in the Darbies. ExPo (1973 ed.); HAP; NOBA

Billy Could Ride. James Whitcomb Riley. PH

Billy goat's a handsome gent, The. The Goat. Roland Young. BoAnP

Billy Grimes. *Unknown.* AmFP

Billy, in one of his nice new sashes. Billy. Harry Graham. FaBoCo

Billy in the Darbies. Herman Melville. *Fr.* Billy Budd, Foretopman. ExPo (1973 ed.); HAP; NOBA

Billy is blowing his trumpet. Noise. *Unknown.* DuDr

Billy Lyons and Stack O'Lee. *Unknown.* BluL

Billy Magee Magaw. *Unknown.* FSW

Billy the Kid ("Billy was a bad man"). *Unknown.* BPAW

Billy the Kid ("I'll sing you a true song of Billy the Kid"). *Unknown.* BPAW; FSW

Billy the Kid or William H. Bonney. N. Howard Thorp. BPAW

Billy was a bad man. Billy the Kid. *Unknown.* BPAW

Billy was a marble champion. Champion. Robert Morgan. HeHu

Billy was born for a horse's back! Billy Could Ride. James Whitcomb Riley. PH

Bind your straight hair. Thessalian. Winifred Bryher. PoA

Bingo. *Unknown.* ECBV; FSW

Binni the Meshuggener. Danny Siegel. VWA

Binnorie. *Unknown. See* Two Sisters, The.

Binocular owl, The. Woods at Night, The. May Swenson. DuDa

Binsey Poplars. Gerard Manley Hopkins. ILP (1975 ed.); InPS; NoAM; VLP

Biograph. Rodger Kamenetz. AAN

Biographical Note. Gabriel Preil, *tr. fr. Hebrew by* Howard Schwartz. VWA

Biographical Sketch. Charles S. Bouslog. PHC

Biography. Amiri Baraka. TAP

Biography. Earle Birney. MPA

Biography, *sel.* John Masefield. "Other bright days of action have seemed great." OxBTC

Biography for Beginners. E. C. Bentley. *See* Clerihews.

Biography in the First Person. Stephen Dunn. FoP; NVAP

Biography of Southern Rain. Kenneth Patchen. VGW

Biological, The/ and dynastic phenomenon. The Art of Picasso. Salvador Dali, *tr. by* David Gascoyne. EAS

Biological Light. Primus St. John. MPA

Biology Lesson. John D. Engle, Jr. AMV–80

Biotherm (For Bill Berkson). Frank O'Hara. CAAP

Birch ("Birch tree, you remind me"). Louis Simpson. SFF

Birch-tree trunks are white as plaster casts, The. Lyre. Patrick White. AMV–80

Birch unwraps, The/ its brilliance. Gesture. Mary Swope. PoUp

Birches. Robert Frost. BiP; CMoP (1970 ed.); ILP (1975 ed.) IPWM; LFH; NoAM; STS; TAP

Bird, The. Moishe Leib Halpern, *tr. fr. Yiddish by* John Hollander. PPP

Bird. Agnes Nemes Nagy, *tr. fr. Hungarian by* Bruce Berlind. BoWoP

Bird, The. Charles Simic. AmPA

Bird, The. Henry Vaughan. ILP (1975 ed.); SCP-1

Bird and the Muse. Marya Zaturenska. PoA

Bird Calls. Cathleen Quirk. MMD

Bird calls me, A. The Bird. Charles Simic. AmPA

Bird came down the walk, A. Emily Dickinson. AmVN; BiP; CABA (1972 ed.); CMoP (1970 ed.); FF; ILP (1975 ed.); IPWM; NOBA; OBAL; PB

Bird Cry. Martha Webb. PHC

Bird ecstatic with the spring, A. Verna Tomlinson Baker. AATT

Bird Fancier, The. James Kirkup. ECBV

Bird flying past my head said previous previous, The. Conrad Aiken. *Fr.* Time in the Rock; or, Preludes to Definition, LXII. VGW

Bird in a Cage. *Unknown.* GBP

Bird in a Gilded Cage, A. Arthur J. Lamb. BLSo, *with music*; FSN, *with music*; FSW

Bird in Search of a Cage, A. Robert Pack. SFF

Bird is lost, The. Yardbird's Skull. Owen Dodson. AmNP (1974 ed.); CNA; PoBA; TCP; VGW

Bird is my neighbour, a whimsical fellow and dim, The. The Crane Is My Neighbour. John Shaw Neilson. MAuV

Bird Let Loose, The. Thomas Moore. PIM

"Bird Lives": Charles Parker in St. Louis. Michael S. Harper. AmPA

Bird, most likely a sparrow, A. Two Birds. Kathleen Linnell. AMV–81

Bird Nest Bound. *Unknown.* BluL

Bird of Night, The. Randall Jarrell. CoPAm; DuDa; NCSH; RFM; TSWA

Bird of Power. Jim Tollerud. VoR

Bird on Briar. *Unknown.* OxBM

Bird on Nellie's Hat, The, *with music.* Arthur J. Lamb. FSN

Bird sighs for the air. The Lover's Song. W. B. Yeats. AnMo; PoIA

Bird sings the selfsame song, A. The Selfsame Song. Thomas Hardy. CMoP (1970 ed.)

Bird Song. *See* Birdsong.

Bird swerved dapple-white in the blue sky, The. Winged in Gold. Euros Bowen, *tr. by author.* OBW

Bird Talk. John Malcolm Brinnin. WasP

Bird time of honey, The. Sunflower. Charles Bukowski. VoA

Birdwatchers of America. Anthony Hecht. HoPM (1975 ed.); NoAM; NOBA; PPP

Bird watchers top my honors list. Up from the Egg: The Confessions of a Nuthatch Avoider. Ogden Nash. BoAnP

Bird who for his other sins, A. A Character. Samuel Taylor Coleridge. MBPR

Bird-Window-Flying. Tess Gallagher. PCho

Bird with a big eye, A. The Big I. John Hall Wheelock. IP

Bird-witted. Marianne Moore. CMoP (1970 ed.); ILP (1975 ed.)

Bird-Woman of the ultra-world. Lilith. Yvan Goll. VWA

Birdie with a yellow bill, A. Time to Rise [*or* Time to Get Up]. Robert Louis Stevenson. CTV; DuDr; OxBChV; PCOP

Birds, The. *Aborigine Oral Tradition, tr. by* R. M. Berndt. *Fr.* The Moon-Bone Cycle. WTO

Birds, The. Florence Barbera. PoUp

Birds, The. Blake. *See* Vision of Beulah, The.

Birds. Robinson Jeffers. EcS; MPA; VGW

Birds. D. H. Lawrence. BoAnP

Birds. Rhyll McMaster. FPA

Birds, The. *Unknown, tr. fr. Czechoslovakian.* PChr

Birds against the April wind, The. What the Birds Said. Whittier. NOBA

Birds and bees, flowers and trees. God's Gifts to Me. Thelma Walton. CTV

Birds and Fishes. Robinson Jeffers. PiAm; TCP

Birds and Man. Lindiwe Mabuza. SES

Birds and periodic blood. 5:30 A.M. Adrienne Rich. NMM; NOBA; PiAm; TT

Birds and sunlight. Yellow. De Leon Harrison. PoBA

Birds Are Drowsing on the Branches. Leah Rudnitsky, *tr. fr. Yiddish by* David G. Roskies. VWA

Birds are flowers flying. Mirrorment. A. R. Ammons. OSP

Birds are the life of the skies. Birds. D. H. Lawrence. BoAnP

Birds begin as an isolated shower, The. Elizabeth. Paul Muldoon. IPM

Birds, birds, birds. Beat Poem by an Academic Poet. Vassar Miller. WPE

Birds cannot fly over it. Her Dream House. Marvin Bell. NVAP

Birds drip from the trees. Daybreak. Bert Meyers. EAS

Birds find their way. Migration. Joseph Bruchac. AMV–81

Birds fly in the broken windows. Two Beers in Argyle, Wisconsin. Dave Etter. ANTL

Birds go fluttering in the air, The. The Silent Snake. *Unknown.* CaYB

Birds have come back again early in the morning, in the spring. Homecoming. Wislawa Szymborska, *tr. by* Benjamin Sher. AMV-81

Birds in Snow. Hilda Doolittle ("H. D."). PoA

Birds in the Garden. *Unknown.* DuDr

Birds in the Wood. *Unknown.* HAP

Birds in their little nests agree. Hilaire Belloc. POL

Birds in Their Title Work Freeholds of Straw. Les A. Murray. *Fr.* Walking to the Cattle-Place. CAAP

Birds' mirror and host. Middle River. Keith Althaus. AAN

Birds move from branch to branch. No One to Blame. Laurence Lieberman. CoPAm

Bird's Nest, A. Erez Biton, *tr. fr. Hebrew by* Judith Katz. VWA

Birds' Nests. John Clare. OAEL-2; VLP

Birds' Nests. Edward Thomas. HeIP

Birds of a feather flock together. Mother Goose. MN

Birds of America, The. James Broughton. BoAnP

Birds of Hazard and Prey, *sel.* Nanos Valaoritis. "With great difficulty I managed to get out of my skin." MIT

Birds of the forest are calling for thee, The. Gypsy Love Song. Harry B. Smith. FSN

Birds of Tin, The. Charles Madge. EAS

Birds saw the people walking along, The. The Birds. *Aborigine Oral Tradition, tr. by* R. M. Berndt. *Fr.* The Moon-Bone Cycle. WTO

Birds sleeping gently, The. Alice, Where Art Thou? Wellington Guernsey. VLP

Birds Waking. W. S. Merwin. NOBA

Bird Song. Laura E. Richards. PCOP

Bird Song. Betsy Rosenberg. VWA

Birdsong. Shakespeare. *Fr.* The Merchant of Venice. PB

Birdsong. James Burns Singer. FaBoTw (1975 ed.)

Birdsong, The. William Carlos Williams. TT

Birks of Invermay, The. David Mallet. SLP

Birmingham. Louis MacNeice. CMoP (1970 ed.); ILP (1975 ed.)

Birmingham. Margaret Walker. PoBA

Birmingham Jail. *Unknown. See* Down in the Valley.

Birmingham 1963. Raymond R. Patterson. CNA; GP; PoBA

Birmingham Sunday. Richard Farina. NowV

Birmingham. The city bell tower chimes one. Letters from Birmingham. Harold Bond. TAT

Birth. Edith Bruck, *tr. fr. Italian by* Ruth Feldman *and* Brian Swann. BoWoP

Birth, A. James Dickey. NOBA

Birth, The. Rosemary Dobson. MAuV

Birth. Amir Gilboa, *tr. fr. Hebrew.* OFD, tr. by Robert Mezey *and* Shula Starkman; VWA, *tr. by* Stephen Mitchell

Birth. Gabriela Melinescu, *tr. fr. Rumanian by* Willis Barnstone *and* Matei Calinescu. BoWoP

Birth. Harold Monro. *Fr.* Stange Meetings. PoA

Birth. Judith Smallshaw. PMW

Birth. Constance Urdang. VWA

Birth of a Country. Agnes Gergely, *tr. fr. Hungarian by* Emery George. VWA

Birth of a Genius Among Men. "Hugh MacDiarmid." SLP

Birth of a Poet. Robert Morgan. HeHu

Birth of John Henry, The. Melvin B. Tolson. *Fr.* Harlem Gallery. BPo

Birth of Love. Robert Penn Warren. UnPo (1976 ed.)

Birth of My Drinking Problem, The. Michael McMahon. FAF

Birth of Robin Hood, The. *Unknown.* OAEL-1

Birth of Sea and Land Life. Keaulumoku, *tr. fr. Hawaiian by* M. W. Beckwith. *Fr.* The Kumulipo: A Creation Chant. WTO

Birth of the Foal. Ferenc Juhász, *tr. fr. Hungarian by* David Wevill. BoAnP; PH

Birth of Venus. Constance Urdang. PoA

Birthday, The. Philip Dacey. AmPA

Birthday, The. Morley Jamieson. SLP

Birthday, The. Louis Johnson. ATNZ

Birth Day. Merle Meeter. AATT

Birthday, A. Edwin Muir. LoAs; MS

Birthday, A. Christina Rossetti. ILP (1975 ed.); NOBE; OAEL-2; OLR; UsP; VLP; VPC; WIF; WPE

Birthday Cake. Aileen Fisher. MN

Birthday Card for a Psychiatrist. Mona Van Duyn. IHMS

Birthday Gifts. Herbert Asquith. OFD

Birthday Memorial to Seventh Street, A. Audre Lorde. CNA

Birthday Ode to Mr. Alfred Austin, A. Sir Owen Seaman. NOBL

Birthday of but a single pang. Emily Dickinson. OFD

Birthday Party. Patti Patton. AMV-80

Birthday Poem. Al Young. CSP

Birthday: Tara Regina. George Mosby, Jr. AMV-81

Birthday Verses Written in a Child's Album. James Russell Lowell. OxBChV

Birthdays. Hilde Domin, *tr. fr. German by* Tudor Morris. BoWoP

Birthdays from the ocean one desert april noon. That "Craning of the Neck." Isabella Gardner. WPE

Birthdays? yes, in a general way. Sincere Flattery. James Kenneth Stephen. NOBL

Birthing, The. Beth Bentley. LoAs

Birthplace, The. Robert Frost. OFD

Birthplace Revisited. Gregory Corso. SA; VGW; VoA

Birthright. John Drinkwater. OxBTC

Biscuits with honey running down into the deep crevices. Overweight Poem. Diane Wakoski. CAAP

Bishop Blomfield's First Charge to His Clergy. *At. to* Sydney Smith. FaBoEE

Bishop Blougram's Apology. Robert Browning. PFD; VLP Unfaith and Faith, *sel.* BoReV

Bishop Cody's Last Request. Tom Paxton. GrRo

Bishop Hatto. Robert Southey. PoTa

Bishop of Atlanta, The: Ray Charles. Julian Bond. AmNP (1974 ed.); CNA; NIL

Bishop of Canterbury, The. *Unknown.* AmFP

Bishop of Chester, The. On Dr. Keene, Bishop of Chester. Thomas Gray. FaBoEE

Bishop Orders His Tomb at Saint Praxed's Church, The. Robert Browning. AnMo; CABA (1972 ed.); Epi; GrRo; HAP; HeIP; ILP (1975 ed.); IPWM; LFH; OAEL-2; OBAL; PPoe; PPP; STS

Bishop seduces the world with his voice, The. The Bishop of Atlanta: Ray Charles. Julian Bond. AmNP (1974 ed.); CNA; NIL

Bishop tells us, The: "When the boys come back." "They." Siegfried Sassoon. CMoP (1970 ed.); OBSV

Bishop Winterbourne. Walter de la Mare. FaBoNo

Bison, The. Hilaire Belloc. FaBoNo

Bison Flower Days. Anselm Hollo. TwMBP

Bison is vain, and (I write it with pain), The. The Bison. Hilaire Belloc. FaBoNo

Bison Track, The. Bayard Taylor. AmVN

Bit an apple on its red. Green Red Brown and White. May Swenson. OSP; VGW

Bit of East within a Chinese wall. Chinatown. Anna Blake Mezquida. BPAW

Bite, and the taste of tongues. The Empty Pain-Killer Bottles. Tom Raworth. EAS

Bite-lip brave and militant. The Youngest Schizophrene. Katherine Hoskins. TCP

Bitten to dust are the savage feathers of fire. To a Seaman Dead on Land. Kay Boyle. PoA

Bitter bitter. A Judezmo Writer in Turkey Angry. Stephen Levy. VWA

Bitter Bread. Osip Mandelstam, *tr. fr. Russian by* James Greene. VWA

Bitter for Sweet. Christina Rossetti. GBL

Bitter Harvest. Alistair Campbell. ATNZ

Bitter Herbs. Alta. NMM

Bitter is the wind tonight. The Viking Terror. *Unknown, tr. by* Kuno Meyer. PFIr

Bitter Lemons. Lawrence Durrell. VoPo

Bitter morning, A. Haiku. J. W. Hackett. BoAnP

Bitter Pills for the Dark Ladies. Erica Jong. Psy; RiTi; WBN

Bitter rain in my courtyard. Wu Tsao, *tr. fr. Chinese by* Kenneth Rexroth *and* Ling Chung. BoWoP

Bitter-sweet. George Herbert. BoReV; IPWM; NOBE; PoIA

Bitter the wind tonight. The Vikings. *Unknown, tr. by* John Montague. BIrV

Bitter Withy, The. *Unknown.* FaBoBa; GBP; PeBB

Bitter year it was, A. What woman ever. The Wreath. Robert Graves. BoLoP

Bittern, The. Sandra McPherson. CNW

Bitterness rolls off. Antisong. Phyllis Webb. MMD

Bivouac on a Mountain Side. Walt Whitman. PiAm

Bizarre Apollo, half what Henry dreamed. Apollo 8. John Berryman. Moon

Bizerta. George Campbell Hay, *tr. fr. Gaelic; Scots version by* "Hugh MacDiarmid." MS

Black. Nicholas Rinaldi. AMV-80

Black All Day. Raymond R. Patterson. PoBA

Black an' White. William Barnes. VLP

Black and Gold. Nancy Byrd Turner. CTV

Black and tan—yeah, black and tan. Dancing Gal. Frank Marshall Davis. FB

Black and White. Tom Schmidt. NeAC

Black Angel, The. Michael S. Harper. NVAP

Black Art. Amiri Baraka. BPo; CAPP; NIL

Black Art, The. Anne Sexton. PoA; Psy

Black as the centre of an eye, the centre, a blackness. Marina Tsvetayeva, *tr. by* Elaine Feinstein *and* Angela Livingstone. *Fr.* Insomnia. PBWP

Black Bart. *Unknown.* BPAW

"Black Bart, P08." Ambrose Bierce. BPAW

Black Bear sang, drumming on a log. Moon of Huckleberries. Phillip William George. NW; VoR

Black bear sits alone, A. Galway Kinnell. *Fr.* Lastness. BCr; GP

Black beauty, which, above that common light. Sonnet of Black Beauty. Lord Herbert of Cherbury. PAIC

Black biplane crashes into the window, The. Love Poem. Gregory Orr. MAT

Black Book, The, *sel.* John Berryman. "Grandfather, sleepless in a room upstairs." VGW

Black Bottom Bootlegger, The. Esther M. Leiper. TAT

Black Bourgeoisie. Amiri Baraka. BPo

Black boy/ let me get up from the white man's table of fifty sounds. PSI. Melvin B. Tolson. PoBA

Black brother, think you life so sweet. Time to Die. Ray Garfield Dandridge. PoBA

Black bulge eyes. Kachinas. Lawrence Kearney. PoW

Black-burnin' shame is your garb, quo' they. The Scarlet Woman. "Hugh MacDiarmid." SLP

Black butterflies. Mexico. Barbara Hughes. PoW

Black cat, sweet brother. For James Baldwin. Kay Boyle. NMM

Black cat yawns, The. Cat. Mary Britton Miller. LCL; PCat

Black Cliffs, Ballybunion, The. Brendan Kennelly. PFIr

Black Clouds. Terence Brame. RAE

Black Cottage, The. Robert Frost. ILP (1975 ed.); VGW

Black Crispus Attucks taught. Dark Symphony. Melvin B. Tolson. AmNP (1974 ed.)

Black Day in July. Gordon Lightfoot. IPWM

Black Death, The. Philip Dacey. GP

Black Dog. Ray A. Young Bear. CDW

Black-eyed Susan. John Gay. *See* Sweet William's Farewell to Black-eyed Susan.

Black-eyed Susie. *Unknown.* AmFP; FSW

Black Finger, The. Angelina Weld Grimké. AmNP (1974 ed.); PoBA

Black Flags Are Fluttering. David Vogel, *tr. fr. Hebrew by* A. C. Jacobs. VWA

Black flakes on the quiet wind, The. A Twilight Man. Harry Guest. TwMBP

"Black folks have got to be superhuman." A Poem about Beauty, Blackness, Poetry. Linda Brown Bragg. CNA

Black fool, why winter here? These frozen skies. Advice to a Raven in Russia. Joel Barlow. NOBA

Black Forest. Roderick Watson. MIS

Black gal,/ she took a knife. My Black Gal Blues. *Unknown.* BluL

Black Girl, De. *Unknown.* GBP

Black girl black girl. Blackberry Sweet [*or* Black Magic]. Dudley Randall. CNA; HAP; InPS; NCSH; OLR; PoBA; WeW

Black greyed into white a nightmare of bicycling. That Which We Call a Rose. Michael Dransfield. FPA

Black grows the southern sky, betokening rain. Sudden Shower. John Clare. Epi

Black-haired girl, The. The Yawn. Paul Blackburn. CTBA; VoA

Black hand supports, A. As It Should Be. Tom Meschery. SPo

Black Hat, The. Clayton Eshleman. VGW

Black hen of the night, The. The Four Cardinal Times of Day. Rene Daumal, *tr. by* Jan Pallister. AMV-81

Black Hills are threatening to run dry, The. Western Movies. Jeffry Jensen. AMV-80

Black history. The Living Truth. Sterling Plumpp. PoBA

Black Hole in Space. Heddy Reid. PoUp

Black Horse Blues. *Unknown.* BluL

Black Horse Rider, The. Pierre Loving. EAS

Black Horse Running. Noel Maureen Valis. AMV-80

Black Humor. Archibald MacLeish. NCSH

Black in blazonry means. The Buffalo. Marianne Moore. PoA

Black in Virginia. Grace Cavalieri. AATT

Black Is a Soul. Joseph Blanco White. PoBA

Black Is Beautiful. Philip Appleman. SFF

Black Is Best. Larry Thompson. PoBA

Black Is the Color ("Black is the color of my true love's hair"). *Unknown.* FF; FSW; GBP

Black is the first nail I ever stepped on. Negritude. James A. Emanuel. BPo; CNA

Black is what the prisons are. The African Affair. Bruce McM. Wright. AmNP (1974 ed.); PoBA

Black Jack Davey. *Unknown.* MAT

Black Jackets. Thom Gunn. HeIP; NowV

Black Jam for Dr. Negro. Mari Evans. BPo; PoBA; Psy

Black Job, A, *sel.* Thomas Hood. "History of human-kind to trace, The." VLP

Black Lady in an Afro Hairdo Cheers for Cassius. R. Ernest Holmes. PPoD

Black Lake. Cynthia Nibbelink. TC

Black lambs around his office windows fly. The Dying Dentist. Robert Huff. PoW

Black luggie, lammer bead. Against Witches. *Unknown.* GBP

Black Magic. Dudley Randall. *See* Blackberry Sweet.

Black Magic. Sonia Sanchez. BPo

Black Mail. Alice Walker. AmPA

Black Majesty. Countee Cullen. PoBA; VGW

Black Man, A. Sam Cornish. CNA; PoBA

Blackman/ midway in the night. Midway in the Night: Blackman. Eugene B. Redmond. GP

Black Man Talks of Reaping, A. Arna Bontemps. AmNP (1974 ed.); BPo; FB; LFH; PoBA

Black Man's Feast. Sarah Webster Fabio. PoBA

Black Maps. Mark Strand. PoA

Black men bleeding to death inside themselves. Eulogy for Alvin Frost. Audre Lorde. CNA

Blackmen: Who Make Morning. Angela Jackson. CNA

Black Mesa, The. James Merrill. PoA

Black Mesa Mine No. 1. Gary Snyder. PoW

Black milk of dawn we drink it at dusk. Death Fugue. Paul Celan, *tr. by* Joachim Neugroschel. VWA

Black milk of daybreak we drink it at nightfall. Fugue of Death. Paul Celan, *tr. by* Christopher Middleton. OBVE

Black Mother Woman. Audre Lorde. WBN

Black Mountain Blues. *Unknown.* BluL

Black mountains pricked with pointed pine. The Watershed. Alice Meynell. SBG

Black Narcissus. Gerald W. Barrax. PoBA

Black-nosed kitten will slumber all the day, A. Choosing a Kitten. *Unknown.* CTV

Black November Turkey, A. Richard Wilbur. BoAnP; CoPAm; NCSH

Black one, last as usual, swings her head, The. Fetching Cows. Norman MacCaig. BoAnP; LP

Black Panther, The. John Hall Wheelock. FF

Black Patch on Lucasta's Face, A. Richard Lovelace. CaPo; PAIC

Black People! Amiri Baraka. BPo

Black people think. Awareness. Don L. Lee. PoBA

Black People: This Is Our Destiny. Amiri Baraka. CAPP; CNA

Black people, we rainclouds. We Rainclouds. Marvin Wyche, Jr. AmNP (1974 ed.)

Black Pierrot, A. Langston Hughes. OLR

Black Plateau, The. W. S. Merwin. CAAP; NNaP

Black Poet, White Critic. Dudley Randall. BPo; CABA (1972 ed.); ConAP; UsP

Black poets should live—not leap. For Black Poets Who Think of Suicide. Etheridge Knight. CNA; PoBA

Black Poppies. Wayne Miller. CPA

Black Power. Nikki Giovanni. Psy

Black Power. Alvin Saxon. PoBA

Black Power Poem. Ishmael Reed. BPo

Black Railings. Robert Morgan. HeHu

Black reapers with the sound of steel on stones. Reapers. Jean Toomer. BPo; HAP; InPK; NoAM; PoBA; PPP

Black Riders, The, *sels.* Stephen Crane.
  Behold, the Grave of a Wicked Man, XXV. TAP; TT
  "Black riders came from the sea," I. AmVN; TAP
  Blade of Grass, The, XVIII. PPM
  Book of Wisdom, The, XXXVI. HoPM (1975 ed.)
  God in Wrath, A, XIX. AmVN; IPWM; TAP; TT
  "God lay dead in heaven," LXVII. PiAm; TT
  I Saw a Man Pursuing the Horizon, XXIV. FF; HoPM (1975 ed.); MAT; NOBA; PBMP; PCOP; PiAm; SFF; TT
  I Stood Musing in a Black World, XLIX. TT
  If I Should Cast Off This Tattered Coat, LXVI. PBMP

In the Desert, III. AmVN; FaBoEE; NOBA; PiAm; PoIA; TAP; TT
  (Heart, The.) InPK; HoPM (1975 ed.)
  It Was Wrong to Do This Said the Angel, LIV. PPM
  "Man saw a ball of gold in the sky, A," XXXV. AmVN; PiAm; PPM
  "Many red devils ran from my heart," XLVI. PiAm; TAP
  Many Workman, XXI. TAP
  Ocean Said to me Once, The, XXXVIII. TT
  "Once, I knew a fine song," LXV. PiAm
  "Should the wide world roll away," X. BiP
  "There was, before me," XXI. PiAm
  There Was One I Met upon the Road, XXXIII. TT
  "Think as I Think," XLVII. WeW
  "Well, then, I hate Thee, unrighteous picture," XII. AmVN
  "Youth in apparel that glittered, A," XXVII. PiAm; TT

Black Riders, The. Cesar Vallejo, *tr. fr. Spanish by* Robert Bly. EC

Black Riders Came from the Sea. Stephen Crane. The Black Riders, I. AmVN; TAP

Black Rock of Kiltearn, The. Andrew Young. FaBoTw (1975 ed.)

Black Rook in Rainy Weather. Sylvia Plath. Psy

Black sails knifing through the pitchblende night. Wooden Ships. David Crosby, Paul Kantner, *and* Stephen Stills. GrRo

Black Sheba. Jodi Braxton. WBN

Black Silk Skirts. Elizabeth Brunazzi. PoUp

Black Sketches. Don L. Lee. NeAC

Black skull-caps. Dying under a Fall of Stars. Mark Elliott Shapiro. VWA

Black Snake. *Unknown.* BluL

Black Soldier's Civil War Chant. *Unknown. See* Negro Soldier's Civil War Chant.

Black Soul of the Land. Lance Jeffers. FB

Black Spring Becomes Anonymous, The. Sotère Torregian. MIT

Black Stallion. Michael Small. DNGG

Black Star Line. Henry Dumas. CNA; PoBA

Black-stemmed ax. Parable. Michael S. Harper. NW

Black Stockman. William Hart-Smith. GAS

Black sunshine. No Dice. Kathleen Wiegner. MMD

Black Swan, The. Randall Jarrell. CMoP (1970 ed.); ExPo (1973 ed.)

Black Swan, The. Peter Kostakis. FiCh

Black Sweeper. Joseph Bruchac. NW

Black Taffy. Peggy Susberry Kenner. JB

Black Tambourine. Hart Crane. InPK; NoAM; PAIC; PPP; TAP

Black Tarn. V. Sackville-West. SBG

Black Tomintoul. Ian Hamilton Finlay. MS; SLP

Black Tower, The. W. B. Yeats. BoReV; CMoP (1970 ed.); UsP

Black Trumpeter. Henry Dumas. PoBA

Black Venus of the Dead, what Sun of Night. Elegy for Dylan Thomas. Edith Sitwell. PoA

Black Vulture, The. George Sterling. BPAW; PB

Black walnuts litter the grass. Poem for Dorothy Holt. Susan Irene Rea. AMV-81

Black Warrior. Norman Jordan. PoBA

Black was the color of the peddler's wagon. Needles and Pins. Mark Van Doren. SO

Black Water Crossing. Dennis M. Gaughan. PoUp

Black Wedding Song. A. Gwendolyn Brooks. CNA

Black within and red without. *Unknown.* GBP

Black Woman. Naomi Long Madgett. FB; OLR; PoBA

Black women's feet. These Feet for Rosa Parks. Margo Bohanon. SES

Black Wonder, The. Ambrosia Shepherd. PoUp

Blackberries sweet and dusty. Someplace Else. Marge Piercy NeAC

Blackberry-picking. Seamus Heaney. HeHu

Blackberry Sweet. Dudley Randall. HAP; InPS; NCSH; WeW (Black Magic.) CNA; OLR; PoBA

Blackberry Thicket, The. Ann Stanford. MPA

Blackberry Winter. Peter Huggins. AMV-81

Blackberrying. Sylvia Plath. HAP; MPo; NoAM; NOBA

Blackbird, The. W. E. Henley. *See To A. D.*

Blackbird. Christopher Leach. BoAnP

Blackbird, The. Tennyson. PB

Blackbird, The. Humbert Wolfe. RAE

Blackbird by Belfast Lough, The. *Unknown, tr. fr. Irish by* Frank O'Connor. ECBV

Blackbird has built in the pasture agen, The. Ballad. John Clare. *Fr. Child Harold.* VLP

Blackbird of Derrycairn, The. *Unknown, tr. fr. Irish by* Austin Clarke. BIrV

Blackbird sang, the skies were clear and clean, The. At Queensferry. W. E. Henley. VLP

Blackbird Singing, A. R. S. Thomas. BoAnP; OBW

Blackbird singing in the tree, The. Best of Two Worlds. Basil Boothroyd. BoAnP

Blackbird startles from the homestead hedge, The. John Clare. *Fr. Child Harold.* VLP

Blackbirds and Thrushes. *Unknown.* GBP

Blackbird's Song. *Unknown.* GBP

Blackened trees. Minneapolis. Tom Hennen. HeS

Blackfeet, Blood and Piegan Hunters. James Welch. SA

Blackfish Poem. Milton Acorn. NeAC

Blackfoot Sin-ka-ha. William S. Lewis. BPAW

Blackfriars. Eleanor Farjeon. OxBChV

Blackheads. Knute Skinner. GP

Blackie Thinks of His Brothers. Stanley Crouch. PoBA

Blackjack Moses ("Being a preacher"). Ahmos Zu-Bolton. AAN

Blackjack moses/returning from the war. The Seeker. Ahmos Zu-Bolton. PoUp

Blackleg. Kendrick Smithyman. ATNZ

Blackleg Miners, The. *Unknown.* GBP; VLP

Black'on frowns east on Maidon. After the Club-Dance. Thomas Hardy. At Casterbridge Fair, III. VLP

Blacksmith 1970, The. Sean Clarkin. IPM

Blacksmiths, The. *Unknown.* CABA (1972 ed.); OxBM (Swarte-smeked Smithes.) HAP; WeW

Blacksmith's boy went out with a rifle, The. Legend. Judith Wright. PoTa; SO

Blacksmith's Serenade, The. Vachel Lindsay. PoTa

Blacksmith's Song, The. *Unknown.* GBP

Blackstone Park. Steve Jonas. EC

Blackstone Rangers, The. Gwendolyn Brooks. ExPo (1973 ed.); NoAM; NowV; PoBA

Blackthorn. Euros Bowen, *tr. fr. Welsh by author.* OBW

Blackwater Mountain. Charles Wright. CSP

Blade of Grass, The. Stephen Crane. The Black Riders, XVIII. PPM

Blah, Blah, Blah. Ira Gershwin. OBAL

Blakeney people, The. The People of Blakeney. *Unknown.* GBP

Blame. Gavin Bantock. TwMBP

Blame not my cheeks, though pale with love they be. Thomas Campion. AAS; UnPo (1976 ed.)

Blame not my hart for flieng up too hie. Henry Constable. *Fr. Diana.* ESo

Blame Not My Lute for He Must Sownde [*or* Sound]. Sir Thomas Wyatt. AAS; EBEV; OAEL-1 (Lover's Lute Cannot Be Blamed, The.) NIL

Blanaid's Song ("Blanaid loves roses"). Joseph Campbell. PFIr

Blandly mother. Wild Orphan. Allen Ginsberg. TCP

Blank faced. Vacancy. Daniela Gioseffi. WBN

Blanket Injun, The. Arthur Chapman. BPAW

Blanket loosens, The. Now, before Shaving. Aaron Kramer. AMV-81

Blast of wind, a momentary breath, A. Barnabe Barnes. EBEV

Blasted with sighs, and surrounded with tears. Twicknam [*or* Twickenham] Garden. John Donne. EBEV; SCP-1

Blasts rip newspaper grey Mannahatta's mid day air spires. Friday the Thirteenth. Allen Ginsberg. NNaP

Blatant as factory buildings. Marina Tsvetayeva, *tr. by* Elaine Feinstein *and* Angela Livingstone. *Fr.* Poem of the End. PBWP

Bleached wood massed in bone piles. Kalaloch. Carolyn Forché. AmPA

Bled/ holding on/ to details. Monogram 23. Martina Werner, *tr. by* Rosemarie Waldrop. BoWoP

Bleecker Street. Jean Garrigue. NYP; TAP

Blemishes. James Hart. AMV-81

Bless me, what damps are here! how stiff an air! The Charnel-House. Henry Vaughan. SCP-1

Bless the Lord, o my soul/ And all that is within me. Bible, *O.T.* Psalms, CIII. CTV

Bless the Lord, o my soul/ O Lord my God. Bible, *O.T.* Psalms, CIV. NAWM-1

Bless you God our God. The Fringes. Harris Lenowitz. VWA

Blessed and Resting Uncle. Harley Elliott. NeAC

Blessed angell not a word replies, The. Ariosto, *tr. by* Sir John Harington. *Fr.* Orlando Furioso, XIV. OBVE

Blessed are the poor[e] in spirit: for theirs is the kingdom[e] of heaven. Bible, *N.T. Fr.* St. Matthew. CTV; OBVE

Blessed Are Those Who Sow and Do Not Reap. Avraham Ben-Yitzhak, *tr. fr. Hebrew by* A. C. Jacobs. VWA

Blessed art thou that beholdest the depths, and sittest upon the cherubims. The Song of the Three Holy Children. Bible, *Apocrypha.* ILwL

Blessed Assurance, *with music.* Fanny Crosby. AH; BLSH

"Blesséd be the English and all their ways and works." Jobson's Amen. Kipling. ILP (1975 ed.)

Blessed Be the Paps Which Thou Hast Sucked. Richard Crashaw. *See* Luke XI: Blessed Be the Paps Which Thou Hast Sucked.

Blessed be this place. Blood and the Moon. W. B. Yeats. STS

Blessed Comforter Divine, *with music.* Lydia Sigourney. AH

Blessed Damozel, The. Dante Gabriel Rossetti. ILP (1975 ed.); NIL; NOBE; OAEL-2; VLP; VPC

"Blessed damozel leaned out, The," *sel.* SpRo

Blessed Is Everyone, *with music. Unknown.* AH

Blessed is he who has found the break-weed. Handful of Ashes. Ilya Rubin, *tr. by* Linda Zisquit. VWA

Blessed is the man that walketh not in the counsel of the ungodly. Bible, *O.T.* Psalms, I. BiP; CTV

Blessed Trinity have pity! Childless. Giolla Brighde MacNamee, *tr. by* Frank O'Connor. BIrV

Blessed Virgin Compared to the Air We Breathe, The. Gerard Manley Hopkins. PoIA; VLP

Blessed worm of Eden sang, The. A Ballad of Eve. Julia Randall. CSP

Blessing, The. Ruth Berman. AMV-81

Blessing. Melvin Wilk. VWA

Blessing, A. James Wright. ANTL; ConAP; ILP (1975 ed.); InPK; NoAM; NOBA; PPP; SFF; SoSe; UsP; VoA

Blessing at Kellenberger Road. Maxine Kent Valian. AMV-80

Blessing of the Firstborn. Howard Schwartz. VWA

Blessing on the Cows, A. "Seumas O'Sullivan." BoAnP; PFIr

Blessing without Company. *Unknown.* BPo; POL

Blessings Are. Cid Corman. GP

Blessings in abundance come. The Good-Night, or Blessing. Robert Herrick. CaPo

Blessings on all the kids who improve the signs in the subways. Graffiti. Edward Field. CABA (1972 ed.)

Blessings on thee, little man. The Barefoot Boy. Whittier. CTV; OBAL; PCOP

Blest be Mother bind your hand on my head on the eve. The Poem on the Guilt. Avot Yeshurun, *tr. by* Harold Schimmel. VWA

Blest be the day, and blest the month and year. Petrarch, *tr. by* Joseph Auslander. Sonnets to Laura: To Laura in Life, XLVII. NAWM-1

Blest Be the Tie That Binds, *with music.* John Fawcett. BLSH

Blest Be the Wondrous Grace, *with music.* George Barrell Cheever. AH

Blest, blest and happy he. *Unknown.* GBL

Blest is t' bride at t' sun shines on. Wedding and Funeral. *Unknown.* GBP

Blest is the boy who has a room. Window to the East. Virginia Moran Evans. AMV-80

Blest Is the Man Whose Tender Breast, *with music.* Abijah Davis. AH

Blest pair of Sirens, pledges of heaven's joy. At a Solemn Music. Milton. AnMo; BoReV; ExPo (1973 ed.); HeIP; NIL; NOBE; PAIC

Blest statesman he, whose mind's unselfish will. Wordsworth. VLP

B'lieve I'll take me a walk 'round the corner. Take a Walk around the Corner. *Unknown.* BluL

Blight. Emerson. NOBA; PiAm

Blighted apples will not shine. Apple Blight. Paul Zimmer. VGW

"Blighters." Siegfried Sassoon. CMoP (1970 ed.); FaBoTw (1975 ed.); NoAM

Blind/black. Winnie. Antar S. K. Mberi. SES

Blind Adolphus. Angela McCabe. AmPA

Blind Always Come as Such a Surprise, The. Ted Kooser. HeS

Blind bald-headed blunderer. Hand. Morton Marcus. NVAP

Blind Beggar, The. *Unknown.* AmFP

Blind Boy, The. Colley Cibber. OxBChV

Blind Date. Conrad Aiken. DL

Blind Fiddler, The. *Unknown.* FSW

Blind folding their dollar, The. Braille. Gerald Costanzo. AMV-81

Blind Girl on the Santa Fe. Conrad Hilberry. TC

Blind Hopes. David Lehman. AAN

Blind Leading the Blind, The. Lisel Mueller. IHMS; PCho

Blind Man, The. Ronald Mann. PMW

Blindman, The. May Swenson. MPA; WeW

Blind man draws his curtains for the night, The. Rooming House. Ted Kooser. POL

Blind man, standing on the bridge, as grey, The. Bridge of the Carousel. Rainer Maria Rilke, *tr. by* John Drury. AMV-80

Blind Man Who Sells Brushes, The. David James. TC

Blind Men and the Elephant, The. John Godfrey Saxe. CTV; ECBV; PCOP; PoTa

Blind men on fourteenth street are real, The. Caesar and the Blind Men. Ettore Rella. SPT

Blind Old Woman. Clarence Major. PoBA

Blind, palsied, halting, speechless, mad. An Old Folks Home. Paul Lake. AMV-81

Blind Panorama of New York. Federico García Lorca, *tr. fr. Spanish by* Ben Belitt. NYP

Blind Sheep, The. Randall Jarrell. OBAL

Blind Spot. Alison Wyrley Birch. PPM

Blind Thamyris, and blind Maeonides. Ode to the Human Heart. Laman Blanchard. NOBL

Blind Wish for Randall Jarrell, A. Gibbons Ruark. CSP

Blind with love, my daughter. Pain for a Daughter. Anne Sexton. TV

Blinded Bird, The. Thomas Hardy. BiP; CMoP (1970 ed.); NoAM

Blindfold. Luci Shaw. AATT

Blindman. *See* Blind Man.

Blindness. Delmira Agustini, *tr. fr. Spanish by* D. M. Pettinella. PBWP

Blisful lyf, a paisible and a swete, A. The Former Age. Chaucer. OxBM

Bliss of man (could pride that blessing find), The. Pope. *Fr.* An Essay on Man. NU

Blisters with pride swelled. Dryden. *Fr.* Upon the Death of the Lord Hastings. PeD

Blizzard, The. A. A. Dewey. HeS

Blk/ woman/ speaks, A. Three X Three. Sonia Sanchez. WBN

Blkness No. 2. Mbembe. NW

Bloated, gray-mustachioed crone. Cell Transplants. David Hilton. AcAn

Block City. Robert Louis Stevenson. CTV

Block the cannon; let no trumpets sound! Sunset Horn. Myron O'Higgins. AmNP (1974 ed.)

Blocks. Frank O'Hara. EAS

Blocks, The/ which are the buildings and walls. Comforted by Limestone. Edward Dorn. *Fr.* Oxford. NOBA

Blodwen. Her Name Like the Hours. Gloria Evans Davies. OBW

Blok: Let Me Learn the Poem. Aram Boyajian. NeAC

Blond. Joseph De Roche. HeIP

Blond Hair at the Edge of the Pavement. Michael Smith. CIP

Blond witch, The. The Roots of Revolution in the Vegetable Kingdom. Constance Urdang. GP

Blood. Nina Cassian, *tr. fr. Rumanian by* Herbert Kuhner. VWA

Blood. Les A. Murray. MAuV

Blood and My Brother. Richard Mathews. AATT

Blood and the Moon. W. B. Yeats. STS

Blood Donor. Robert Morgan. HeHu

Blood Donors This Way—the notice broods. Blood Transfusion. S. L. Henderson Smith. PMW

Blood flows in me, but what does it have to do. Living by the Red River. James Wright. NNaP

Blood Horse, The. "Barry Cornwall." PH

Blood Hound Blues. *Unknown.* BluL

Blood Marksman and Kureldei the Marksman. *Tatar (Turkic) Oral Tradition, tr. fr. German and Russian versions by* Norman Cohn. WTO

Blood of the Just London's firm Doome shall fix, The. Nostradamus's Prophecy. Andrew Marvell. TT

Blood on the Saddle. *Unknown.* FSW

Blood Red Roses. *Unknown.* FSW

Blood stains Union Street in Mississippi. May 27, 1971: No Poem. June Jordan. WBN

Blood-strained Banders, The. *Unknown.* AmFP

Blood Supply in New York City Is Low, The. Terry Stokes. NYP

Blood thudded in my ears. I scuffed. First Confession. X. J. Kennedy. ConAP; CoPAm; NCSH; NIL; PPP

Blood to Blood. Alvin Aubert. GP

Blood Transfusion. S. L. Henderson Smith. PMW

Blood will not serve. A Poem for Heroes. Julia Fields. CNA

Bloodhound, The. Edward Anthony. GDP

Bloods and bucks of this lewd town, The. Horace, *tr. fr. Latin*. Odes, I, 25. OBVE

Bloody/ egg yolk, A. A burnt hole. Out of the Sea, Early. May Swenson. RFM

Bloody and a sudden end, A. John Kinsella's Lament for Mrs. Mary Moore. W. B. Yeats. CMoP (1970 ed.); OAEL-2

Bloody Brother, The, *sel.* John Fletcher, *and others*. Drink Today, *fr.* II, ii. PAIC

Bloody Sire, The. Robinson Jeffers. CMoP (1970 ed.); PoA

Bloom. Greg Hannan. PoUp

Bloom Street. Angela McCabe. AmPA

Blooms such as wither at finger-touch. Brian Coffey. *Fr.* Muse, June, Related. BIrV

Blossom, The. Blake. *Fr.* Songs of Innocence. MBPR; PB

Blossom [*or* Blossome], The. John Donne. AnMo; UnPo (1976 ed.)
   "Little think'st thou, poore flower," *sel.* PF

Blossom blows, The/ across the step. There Are Lime Trees in Leaf on the Promenade. Tom Raworth. TwMBP

Blossom is in her hair. Flowers. *Gond Oral Tradition, tr. by* V. Elwin *and* S. Hivale. WTO

Blossom on the plum. March. Nora Hopper. FSFS

Blossome, The. John Donne. *See* Blossom, The.

Blossoms closed into buds, The. Adam's Dream. Howard Schwartz. VWA

Blossoms crowd the branches: too beautiful to endure. Spring-gazing Song. Hsüeh T'ao, *tr. by* Carolyn Kizer. BoWoP

Blossoms have fallen, The. Princess Shikishi, *tr. fr. Japanese by* Donald Keene. BoWoP

Bloudy trunck of him who did possesse, The. A Great Favorit Beheaded. Sir Richard Fanshawe, *after the Spanish of* Gongora. OBVE

Blow Away the Morning Dew. *Unknown. See* Lady's Policy, The.

Blow, blow! The winds are so hoarse they cannot blow. The Winter Storms. Sir William Davenant. SCP-2

Blow, Blow, Thou Winter Wind! Shakespeare. *Fr.* As You Like It, II, vii. FSFS; GBL; HeIP; ILP (1975 ed.); InPS; IP; NOBE; OAEL-1; PPoe

Blow, blow, ye spicy breezes. Ambrose Bierce. *Fr.* The Devil's Dictionary. OBAL

Blow, Bugle, Blow. Tennyson. *See* Splendor Falls on Castle Walls, The.

Blow Gabriel. *Unknown.* BluL

Blow, Northern Wind. *Unknown.* GBL; OxBM

"Blow out the light," they said, they said. Temper. Rose Fyleman. OxBChV

Blow softly down the valley. The King of Ireland's Cairn. "Ethna Carbery." WPE

Blow the Candle Out ("It was late last Saturday evening"). *Unknown.* FaBoBa

Blow the Candle Out (The Jolly Boatsman). *Unknown.* AmFP

Blow the Candles Out ("When I was apprenticed in London"). *Unknown.* FSW; RDB, *with music*

Blow the Man Down. *Unknown.* AmFP; BLSH, *with music;* BLSo, *with music;* FSW

Blow the Winds, I-Ho. *Unknown.* GBP; PeBB

Blow, West Wind. Robert Penn Warren. *Fr.* Notes on a Life to Be Lived. NoAM

Blow, winds, and crack your cheeks! rage! blow! Shakespeare. *Fr.* King Lear, III, ii. OBP; UsP

Blow, Ye Winds [in the Morning]. *Unknown.* AmFP; FSW

Blow Ye Winds Westerly. *Unknown.* FSW

Blowflies Buzz, The. Djalparmiwi, *tr. fr. Aborigine by* C. H. Berndt. WTO

Blown Door, The. Malcolm Cowley. PPoD

Blown out of the prairie in twilight and dew. Coyote. Bret Harte. BPAW

Blows the wind today, and the sun and the rain are flying. To S. R. Crockett. Robert Louis Stevenson. NOBE

Blue. Scott Momaday. *Fr.* The Colors of Night. BCr

Blue/ dis/ tills/ white. Cloud. Martha Webb. PHC

Blue and the Gray, The. Francis Miles Finch. BTTM

Blue Animals, The. Jon Anderson. AmPA

Blue-black flare at the bottom, The. Blue Bottle. Patricia Hampl. AMV-81

Blue-black swallowtail sits on my finger, A. Visitation. Elisavietta Ritchie. AATT

Blue-blooded Mauser's first cousin, The. Guns. Ronald Crowe. AMV-81

Blue, blue is the grass about the river. The Beautiful Toilet. Ezra Pound, *after the Chinese.* OBVE

Blue Bog Children. Roger Weingarten. AmPA

Blue Booby, The. James Tate. AmPA; EAS; NoAM

Blue Bottle. Patricia Hampl. AMV-81

Blue boughs, green fruit. The Furnished Room. James Merrill. NOBA

Blue Bowl of Plums Invention, The. Lyn Lifshin. Psy

Blue Boy on Skates (Twilight). M. L. Rosenthal. SPo

Blue-Butterfly Day. Robert Frost. RFM

Blue calf tethered. *Gond Oral Tradition, tr. by* V. Elwin *and* S. Hivale. WTO

Blue Chairs. Deirdra Baldwin. PoUp

Blue Church, The. Peter Balakian. AMV-80

Blue Closet, The. William Morris. VLP

Blue Coat, A. Gertrude Stein. *Fr.* Tender Buttons. PBWP; RiTi

Blue Day. Alice Corbin. WPW

Blue Day Journey, The. Gwyn Jones. OBW

Blue Duck, The. David Ray. HeS

Blue eagle and the demon of the steppes, The. The Staircase with a Hundred Steps. Benjamin Péret. EAS

Blue-eyed Girl. *Unknown.* AmFP

Blue-eyed Precinct Worker, The. Henri Coulette. MAT

Blue-Fly, The. Robert Graves. CMoP (1970 ed.); ILP (1975 ed.); NoAM

Blue-geese, white-geese, you may say. Hilda Doolittle ("H. D."). *Fr.* The Flowering of the Rod. NOBA

Blue Gift, The. David Perkins. NCSH

Blue Girls. John Crowe Ransom. CMoP (1970 ed.); GBL; LFH; NoAM; SS; TAP; VGW; VoPo; WeW

Blue go up and blue go down. American Lights, Seen from Off Abroad. John Berryman. OBAL

Blue Heron. Don Welch. GP

Blue hill is my desire, The. Hwang Chin-i, *tr. fr. Korean by* Ko Won. PBWP

Blue Horses. Ed Roberson. PoBA

Blue iris, A. Shining. Kathleen Spivack. AMV-81

Blue jay scuffling in the bushes follows, The. On the Move. Thom Gunn. CMoP (1970 ed.); HAP; NIL; NowV; OAEL-2; OBP; OxBTC; PoIA; PPP

Blue Jeaned Rock Queen in Search of Happiness on a Blind Thursday at 1/3 Speed and Crying, A. A. K. Redwing. VoR

Blue jumped a rabbit, run him one solid mile. Rabbit Foot Blues. *Unknown.* BluL

Blue Juniata, *sel.* Malcolm Cowley.
   Streets of Air, The. PoA

Blue landing lights make. Our Ground Time Here Will Be Brief. Maxine W. Kumin. AMV-81

Blue light, morning. This Decoration. Hayden Carruth. NNaP

Blue Like Death. James Welch. CDW

Blue Max. Harvey Shapiro. GP

Blue Moles. Sylvia Plath. BiP

Blue Monday. *Unknown.* AmFP

Blue Mosque, The. Lee Harwood. TwMBP

Blue Mountain. Roberta Hill. VoR

Blue Owl Song. Alfred Kittner, *tr. fr. German by* Herbert Kuhner. VWA

Blue Paisley Shirt, The. Thomas W. Shapcott. FPA; GAS

Blue pickup, A. Landscape, New Mexico. Kell Robertson. TAT

Blue quiet night. Blkness No. 2. Mbembe. NW

Blue Rain. Alistair Campbell. ATNZ

Blue Ridge. Elizabeth Hodges. AMV-81

Blue River Falls. Jordan Smith. AAN

Blue Room, The. Lorenz Hart. OBAL

Blue Ruth: America. Michael S. Harper. PoBA

Blue Sleep. Winifred Bryher. PoA

Blue Stones. Larry Levis. PCho

Blue Swallows, The. Howard Nemerov. AnMo; BiP

Blue-tail Fly, The. *Unknown. See* Jim Crack Corn.

Blue Tanganyika. Lebert Bethune. PoBA

Blue Tattoo, The. Emma Lou Thayne. MPA

Blue Teal's Mother. James Wright. CAAP

Blue! 'Tis the life of heaven,—the domain. Answer to a Sonnet Ending Thus. Keats. MBPR

Blue Tit. John Sjoberg. AcAn

Blue Train for the South—but the Green Train for us, The. The Green Train. E. V. Rieu. SO

Blue unsolid tongue, if you could talk. The Overturned Lake. Charles Henri Ford. EAS

Blue water; upon it two possible movements. The Landfall. James Dickey. PoA

Blue West, The. Dahlia Ravikovich, *tr. fr. Hebrew by* Chana Bloch. PBWP

Blue Whale, The. Robert Watson. MAT

Blue Window. Katha Pollitt. AAN

Blue Wing, The. Donald Hall. ConAP

Blue with Blues. Benjamin Saltman. PoW

Bluebeard's Wife. Daryl Hine. NoAM

Bluebells, The. John Masefield. PF

Blue Bells of Scotland, The. Annie McVicar *and* Dorothy Jordan. FSW

Blueberries. Robert Frost. STS

Blue-Bird, The. Herman Melville. NOBA

Bluebird, Bluebird, Fly through My Window. *Unknown.* FSW

Blueline. Ken Belford. NeAC

Blueness of night, The. The Listening Rock. Ray A. Young Bear. VW

Blues. John Fuller. NOBL

Blues. Derek Walcott. OBP

Blues/ Never climb a hill. Get Up, Blues. James A. Emanuel. AmNP (1974 ed.); PoBA

Blues, The: A Literary Eclogue. Byron. MBPR

Blues and Bitterness. Lerone Bennett, Jr. FF; PoBA

Blues and rum and big fat. The History of Weather. George Mattingly. CPA

Blues at Dawn. Langston Hughes. IlP (1975 ed.)

Blues for a Cello Man. Carol Bergé. MMD

Blues for Benny Kid Paret. Dave Smith. LiSp

Blues for Jimmy. Thomas McGrath. BrS

Blues for John Coltrane, Dead at 41. William Matthews. NVAP

Blues for Sister Sally. Lenore Kandel. NMM; RiTi

Blues meant Swiss-Up, The. Riding across John Lee's Finger. Stanley Crouch. PoBA

Blue's my older brother's color. Mine is brown, you see. Poem for My Brother. John Logan. BrS

Blues Note. Bob Kaufman. CNA; PoBA

Blues Suite. Margo Bohanon. SES

Blues Today, The. Mae Jackson. PoBA

Bluff King Hal was full of beans. Henry VIII. Eleanor *and* Herbert Farjeon. PoTa

Blum. Dorothy Aldis. ECBV; LCL

Blurt, Master Constable, *sel.* Thomas Middleton. Night Sounds. RAE

Blythsome Bridal, The. *Unknown, at. to* Francis Sempill. GBP; PeBB

Boa Constrictor. Shel Silverstein. CaYB

Boadicea. William Cowper. FaPo; FaPoR

Board of War has quelled the mutiny, The. To the Minister Liu. Yu Hsuan-chi, *tr. by* Geoffrey Waters. BoWoP

Boarder, The. Frederick Feirstein. NYP

Boarding, The. Denis Johnson. AMV-80

Boardwalk, like a pier, extends, The. Looking Out To Sea. Anthony Ostroff. MPA

Boar's Head, The. *Unknown.* OxBM

Boast not proud English, of thy birth and blood. Roger Williams. GOA

Boat is chafing at our long delay, The. Song. John Davidson. PoPle

Boat need carry no more than a live man, The. Boats. Norman MacCaig. MS

Boat Poem. Bernard Spencer. FaBoTw (1975 ed.); OxBTC

Boatman's Dance ("Boatman dance, boatman sing"). Daniel Decatur Emmett. FSW

Boats. Norman MacCaig. MS

Boats in a Fog. Robinson Jeffers. LFH; RhR

Boats sail on the rivers. The Rainbow. Christina Rossetti. CTV; OxBChV

Boatswain! The Tempest. Shakespeare. OAEL-1

Bob McKinney. *Unknown.* BluL

Bob, nothing in me wants to tell you again. Homosexual Sonnets. Kenneth Pitchford. GP

Bob Southey! You're a poet—poet-laureate. Dedication. Byron. *Fr.* Don Juan. ILP (1975 ed.); MBPR; OAEL-2; OBSV; PPoe

Bob-tailed Flush, A. John R. Painter. BPAW

Bob White. George Cooper. PCOP

Bobadil. James Reeves. LCL

Bobbie's Cat. Gerald Locklin. GP

Bobbily Boo and Wollypotump. Laura E. Richards. LCL (Bibbily Boo and Wollypotump.) CTV

Bobbing of balloons. Greyhounds. Robert Gray. CAAP

Bobbing with the crowds. The Urban Experience: Part One. Lew Blockcolski. VoR

Bobby Campbell. *Unknown.* FSW

Bobby Shaftoe's gone to sea. Mother Goose. FSW; GBP; GSB, *with music*

Bob-ing split-able heads. Solitary Visions of a Kaufmanoid. James Cunningham. JB

Bock beer in brown bags. You Will Never Get Away No-O. Robert Abney. PoUp

Bodies lift burdens. Bearing It. Carolyn Stoloff. RiTi

Bodily bewildered. A Spastic Child on a Pony. Judith Smallshaw. PMW

Body, The. William Bronk. VGW

Body, The. Robert Herrick. CaPo

Body and Soul: A Meditation. Maxine W. Kumin. FoP

Body black in the rock spine of Quinag. Marry the Lass? Andrew Greig. SLP

Body fat as my forearm, blunt-arrowed head. Snake Handling Religious Service. Charles Wright. *Fr.* Tattoos. GP

Body Fished from the Seine. Gregory Corso. GP

Body full of bees. "I Don't Hear Any Melody Breathing I Hear." John Gill. NeAC

Body is like a November birch facing the full moon, The. Solitude Late at Night in the Woods. Robert Bly. Bip; IPWM; SFF; VGW

Body Is Like Roots Stretching, The. Charles Reznikoff. VWA

Body is the soul's poor house, or home, The. The Body. Robert Herrick. CaPo

Body lies under the ground. Dirge. Gavin Bantock. OxBTC

Body Mechanics. Albert Goldbarth. NVAP

Body my house. Question. Mae Swenson. IPWM; VGW

Body of a woman, white hills, white thigh. Pablo Neruda, *tr. fr. Spanish by* Robert Bly. LoAs

Body of John. R. A. K. Mason. ATNZ

Body perishes, the heart stays young, The. Old Age. *Zulu Oral Tradition, tr. by* H. Tracey. WTO

Body Poems, *sels.* Coleman Barks. NVAP
   Achilles Tendon.
   Adam's Apple.
   Back Just Below the Shoulder Blades.
   Brain.
   Bruises.
   Cheek.
   Dimple.
   Downy Hair in the Shape of Flame.
   Genitals.
   Hair on the Chest.
   Liver.
   Scar.
   Semen.
   Skeleton.
   Skull.
   Tic.
   White Crescents at the Bottoms of Fingernails.

Body Politic, The. Donald Hall. SoS

Body says, The:/ The mind: my moonlight. The Soliloquies. Edward Weismiller. PAIC

Body so carefully, The. At the Gynecologist's. Linda Pastan. RiTi

Body will not reject plastic, The. The Therapeutist. Beth Bentley. AMV-80

Body's Beauty. Dante Gabriel Rossetti. The House of Life, LXXVIII. ILP (1975 ed.); OAEL-2; VLP

Body's products become, The. Dido. John Ashbery. *Fr.* Two Sonnets. CAPP; VGW

Boeotian. Robert Frost. NIL

Bog Queen. Seamus Heaney. HeHu

Bogart. Nicholas Flocos. SA

Bogey. Lee L. Berkson. AMV-81

Bogland. Seamus Heaney. HeHu

Bogs, purgatory, wolves and ease, by fame. Barten Holyday. FaBoEE

Bogus-Boo, The. James Reeves. FPB

Bohannan held on to a birch branch. The Low Road. Tom Buchan. MIS

Bolakins was a very fine mason. Lamkin. *Unknown.* AmFP

Bold, brave crew, on an ocean blue, A. Hurrah for the Sea. *Unknown.* RhR

Bold Fenian Men, The. *Unknown.* FSW; RDB, *with music*

Bold Jack Donahue. *Unknown.* AmFP; FSW; PeBB

Bold Lanty was in love, you see, with lively Rosie Carey. Lanty Leary. Samuel Lover. PFIr

Bold Pedlar and Robin Hood, The. *Unknown.* AIW; AmFP

Bold Robin has robed him in ghostly attire. A Merry Jest of Robin Hood. Thomas Love Peacock. PeBB

Bold Soldier, The. *Unknown.* FSW

Bold Trooper, The. *Unknown.* PeBB

Bold Troubleshooters. Peter Veale. NOBL

Bold Unbiddable Child, The. Winifrid M. Letts. PFIr

Bolding Vedas! Shanks New Nisa! Place-Names of China. Alan Bennett. NOBL

Boldness in Love. Thomas Carew. CaPo (Marigold, The.) PF

Boll Weevil Song, The. *Unknown. See* Ballit of de Boll Weevil, De.

Boll-weevil's coming, and the winter's cold. November Cotton Flower. Jean Toomer. NoAM; UnPo (1976 ed.)

Bomb Disposal, The. Ciaran Carson. CIP

Bombardment of Bristol, R.I., The. *Unknown.* BTTM

Bombers. C. Day Lewis. CMoP (1970 ed.)

Bombers spread out, temperature steady, The. War and Silence. Robert Bly. CAPP

Bombing of Kaho'olawe, The. Marjorie Sinclair. PHC

Bombing of the Cafe de Paris 1941, The. Vernon Scannell. HeHu

Bon jour, bon jour a vous! A Call for a Song. *Unknown.* OxBM

Bon Mot, A. *Unknown.* POL

Bon Voyage. James Steele. SES

Bonac. John Hall Wheelock. PPoD

Bondage. Hubert Witheford. ATNZ

Bonded. Anne Hazlewood Brady. WBN

Bone, The. John Blight. GAS

Bone-aged is my white horse. Talysarn. Brenda Chamberlain. OBW

Bone and Skin, two millers thin. On Two Monopolists. John Byrom. FaBoCo; FaBoEE

Bone and the Baby, The. Ettore Rella. SPT

Bone that has no marrow, The. Emily Dickinson. TAP

Bone Yard. Jim Barnes. CDW

Bones. Brian Lee. FPB

Bones, The. W. S. Merwin. ConAP; UsP

Bones. Charles Simic. NVAP

Bones. S. L. Henderson Smith. PMW

Bones are all there waiting their hour, The. After X-Ray. Linda Pastan. POL

Bones Found in Chalk. Jim Farrar. DNGG

Bones in the Desert. Ned White. BPAW

Bones is good with children. Bones. Brian Lee. FPB

Bones of My Father, The. Etheridge Knight. UsP

Bones of our fathers, The. Talking to the Townsfolk in Ideal, Georgia. Isaac J. Black. CNA

Boney Was a Warrior. *Unknown.* FSW

Bongong Jack and the Trooper. John Manifold. FPA

Bonie Doon. Burns. *See* Banks o' Doon, The.

Bonie Lesley. Burns. *See* Bonnie Lesley.

Bonner's Ferry Beggar. Duane Clark. AMV-81

Bonnets o' Bonnie Dundee, The. Sir Walter Scott. *See* Bonnie Dundee.

Bonnie Black Bess. *Unknown. See* Dick Turpin and Black Bess.

Bonnie Blue Flag, The. Harry Macarthy. BLSo, *with music*; BTTM; PSoN, *with music*

Bonnie Broukit Bairn, The. "Hugh MacDiarmid." HAP; InPS; MS

Bonnie Dundee. Sir Walter Scott. *Fr.* The Doom of Devergoil, II, ii. RDB, *with music* (Bonnets o' Bonnie Dundee, The.) BTTM

Bonnie Earl of Morey [*or* Murray], The. *Unknown. See* Bonny Earl of Murray, The.

Bonnie George Campbell. *Unknown.* AmFP; FaBoBa; GBP; PeBB
(Bonny George Campbell.) AIW; PoPle

Bonnie Lesley. Burns. NOBE
(Bonie Lesley.) SLP

Bonnie Ship *The Diamond,* The. *Unknown.* FSW

Bonny at Morn. *Unknown.* GBP

Bonny Barbara Allan. *Unknown. See* Barbara Allen.

Bonny Bunch of Roses, The. *Unknown.* FaBoBa

Bonny Earl of Murray, The. *Unknown.* AIW; FaBoBa; PoPle
(Bonnie Earl of Morey [*or* Murray], The. FSW; RDB, *with music*

Bonny Eloise. C. W. Elliot *and* J. R. Thomas. FSW

Bonny George Campbell. *Unknown. See* Bonnie George Campbell.

Bonny Grey, The. *Unknown.* GBP

Bonny Keel Laddie, The. *Unknown.* GBP

Bonny Moorhen, The. *Unknown.* GBP

Bony. Simon J. Ortiz. CDW; PoW

Bony black face, The. Esperanza. James Scully. NYP

Bonzai tree, The. A Work of Artifice. Marge Piercy. IHMS

Boo Hoo. Arnold Spilka. OSF

Bood is beabig brighdly, love, The. To Bary Jade. Charles Follen Adams. OBAL

Book, The. Adrienne Rich. RiTi

Book Ends, Immortality Begins, The. Adrianne Marcus. NPW

Book might be the lens of pure hard tears, A. A Coil of Glass (II). Stanley Burnshaw. SPT

Book mites are eating the bindings. The Insect Shuffle Method. Gary Tapp. AMV–80

Book of Hunting, *sels.* Julians Barnes. WPE
"Time of grease beginneth at Midsummer day."
"When ye hunt at the roe, then shall ye see there."
"Wheresoever ye fare by frith or by fell."

Book of Job and a Draft of a Poem to Praise the Paths of the Living, The. George Oppen. NNaP

Book of Kells, The. Padraic Colum. BIrV

Book of Lies, The. James Tate. PPoD

Book of Mysteries, The. Anthony Barnett. VWA

Book of Pilgrimage, The. Rainer Maria Rilke, *tr. fr. German by* Jessie Lemont. ILwL

Book of Songs. *Tr. fr. Chinese. See* Shih Ching.

Book of Stones. Robert Morgan. HeHu

Book of the Dead, Prayer 14. Mei Berssenbrugge. GP; NW; SA

Book of Thel, The. Blake. LAuP; MBPR; OAEL–2

Book of Urizen, The. Blake. MBPR

Book of Verses, A. Mordecai Marcus. AMV–80

Book of verses underneath the bough, A. Omar Khayyám, *tr. by* Edward Fitzgerald. *Fr.* The Rubáiyát of Omar Khayyám. HoPM (1975 ed.); NOBE

Book of Wisdom, The. Stephen Crane. The Black Riders, XXXVI. HoPM (1975 ed.)

Book Reviews. Russell Davies. FaBoEE

Book Rises Out of the Fire, The. Edmond Jabès, *tr. fr. French by* Rosemarie Waldrop. VWA

Book slides from the shelf, pops open, The. A Book of Verses. Mordecai Marcus. AMV–80

Book was writ of late called Tetrachordon, A. On the Detraction Which Followed upon My Writing Certain Treatises. Milton. Epi

Book-Worms, The. Burns. FaBoEE

Book you made, The. Love. Patrick Lane. NeAC

Booker T. and W. E. B. Dudley Randall. NIL; NoAM; TC

Booker Washington Trilogy, The, *sel.* Vachel Lindsay.
Simon Legree—A Negro Sermon, I. TAP

Books. William Baer. AMV–81

Books, lips, hands. Hypodermic Release. Del Corey. AMV–81

Bookshop Idyll, A. Kingsley Amis. OxBTC; SoSe

Boom! Howard Nemerov. NIL; NowV

Boom. Julian Lee Rayford. AMV–80

Boom/ The Shrill whistle of the wolf. Bird of Power. Jim Tollerud. VoR

Boom above my knees lifts, and the boat, The. Sailing to an Island. Richard Murphy. MPo

Boomer Johnson. Henry Herbert Knibbs. BPAW

Boomerang. John Perreault. EAS

Boomerang and kangaroo, The. Up from Down Under. David McCord. ECBV

Boon Nature to the woman bows. The Tribute. Coventry Patmore. *Fr.* The Angel in the House. EBEV

Boot and a shoe and a slipper, A. High and Low. John Banister Tabb. TDH

Booth Killed Lincoln. *Unknown.* AmFP; OFD

Booth led boldly with his big bass drum. General William Booth Enters into Heaven. Vachel Lindsay. CMoP (1970 ed.); ILP (1975 ed.); IP; IPWM; NoAM; NOBA; PoA; TAP

Boothbay Whale, The. *Unknown.* FSW

Bootie Black and the Seven Giants. Mike Cook. JB

Bootlegger, bookie, boxer, tout. Uncles. Harold Norse. PoW

Boots. Kipling. FaPoR

Booty. Eileen Duggan. ATNZ

Bop Lyrics. Allen Ginsberg. OBAL

Bordello, Revisited. Eve Triem. GP

Border, The. Edwin Muir. BoReV

Bordering Manuscript. James Applewhite. PoA

Borders. Marieve Rugo. PCho

Borders slide backwards forwards. Nathaniel Tarn. *Fr.* A Nowhere for Vallejo. TwMBP

Bored lifeguard shrugs, The. Chippewa Lake Park. Warren Woessner. TAT

Bored Ostrich, The. *Unknown.* TDH

Bored with his stall, wanting he knew not what. On Cementing Level the Stable Floor at the Old Manse. Forbes Macgregor. MIS

Bores hed in hands I bring, The. The Boar's Head. *Unknown.* OxBM

Borges. Willis Barnstone. AMV–80

Borgia, thou once wert almost too august. On Seeing a Hair of Lucretia Borgia. Walter Savage Landor. CABA (1972 ed.); HAP; InPK

Boring executors approach their locks, The. Poem against Catholics. James Fenton *and* John Fuller. OBSV

Boris is dead. The fatalist parrot. Obituary. Weldon Kees. BoAnP

Born Again. Forugh Farrokhzad, *tr. fr. Persian by* Jascha Kessler *and* Amin Banani. PBWP

Born from a world of tyrants beneath the western sky. Free America. Joseph Warren. FSW

Born I was to be old. Anacreontic. Robert Herrick. CaPo

Born I was to meet with age. On Himself. Robert Herrick. FaBoEE

Born in the heart of the Institute. Depression Ode (11/23/75). Paul Hoover. FiCh

Born in the quarter night, brash. Delta Traveller. Charles Wright. AmPA

Born new at midpoint in your middle life. Faint Praise on Your Fortieth Birthday. Joanne McCarthy. PoW

Born of my voiceless time, your steps. The Footsteps. Paul Valéry, *tr. by* C. Day Lewis. LoAs

Born over there, in mist, not even God. Grandfather. Willis Barnstone. VWA

Born to these gentle stones and grass. Urn Burial. Ted Hughes. EBEV

Born Tying Knots. Samuel Makidemewabe, *tr. fr. Cree by* Howard Norman. TC

Born was the island. *Tr. fr. Hawaiian.* WTO

Born with a gentle heart, and born to please. John Langhorne. *Fr.* The Country Justice. EPC

Born Yesterday. Philip Larkin. RRA

Borough, The, *sels.* George Crabbe.
"Now it is pleasant in the summer-eve," *fr.* Letter IX. EcS
Peter Grimes; the Outcast, *fr.* Letter XXII. NOBE
Vicar, The, *fr.* Letter III. OBSV

Borrowed light went through the dark, The. Jack Rabbit. Adrien Stoutenburg. BoAnP

Borrowing Days, The. *Unknown.* GBP

Bosky Steer, The. Henry Herbert Knibbs. BPAW

Boss, The. James Russell Lowell. OBAL

Boss comes up to me with a five dollar bill, The. Get Thee behind Me, Satan. Lee Hays, Millard Lampell, *and* Pete Seeger. FSW

Boss he had a yaller gal. Git Along Down to Town. *Unknown.* AmFP

Boss Machine-Tender after Losing a Son, The. Paul Corrigan. AMV-81

Boss's Dream. Herbert Scott. TC

Boston ("I come from the city of Boston"). John Collins Bossidy. FaBoCo; FaBoEE; OBAL (*At. to* Samuel C. Bushnell)

Boston Ballad, A. Walt Whitman. OBAL

Boston Burglar, The. *Unknown.* AmFP; FSW

*Boston Evening Transcript*, The. T. S. Eliot. InPK; PSN

Boston has a festival. In the Public Garden. Marianne Moore. NOBA

Boston, Lincolnshire. *Unknown.* GBP

Boston Nursery Rhymes. Joseph Cook. QQQ

Boston Tea Tax, The. *Unknown.* BTTM

Bot now the haisty, egir, and wild Dido. Virgil, *tr. by* Gavin Douglas. *Fr.* The Aeneid, IV. OBVE

Bot of ane bowrd in to bed I sall yow breif yit. William Dunbar. *Fr.* The Tretis of the Tua Mariit Wemen and the Wedo. EBEV

Botanist's Vision, The. Sydney Dobell. VLP

Botany Bay. *Unknown.* FSW

Botany Lesson. F. D. Reeve. AMV-80

Both my child. Teitoku, *tr. fr. Japanese by* Nobuyuki Yuasa. OFD

Both Plutarch and Pausanius tell a story. Kleomedes. David Wright. NoAM

Both were so shy. Two. Robert Canzoneri. HoPM (1975 ed.)

Bothie of Tober-na-Vuolich, The, *sels.* Arthur Hugh Clough. VLP
"And he continued more firmly, although with stronger emotion," *fr.* Bk. VII.
"Philip returned to his books, but returned to his Highlands after," *fr.* Bk. IX.
"There is a stream, I name not its name," *fr.* Bk. III.

Bottle Up and Go. *Unknown.* FSW

Bottled: New York. Helene Johnson. PoBA

Bottleneck. Louis MacNeice. SFF

Bottomed by tugging combs of water. The Swan. W. R. Rodgers. NoAM

Boudoir Lament. Yü Hsüan-chi, *tr. fr. Chinese by* Geoffrey Waters. BoWoP

Boughs of this pine are spokes that spread. Height. Robert D. Fitzgerald. GAS

Boughs, the boughs are bare enough, The. Winter with the Gulf Stream. Gerard Manley Hopkins. CMoP (1970 ed.); ExPo (1973 ed.); NoAM; VLP

Bought/ from the flower-peddler's tray. Tune: Magnolia Blossom. Li Ching-chao, *tr. by* C. H. Kwôck *and* Vincent McHugh. PBWP

Bought at the drug store, very cheap; and later pawned. Green Light. Kenneth Fearing. ExPo (1970 ed.); VGW

Boulder. Ted Berrigan. FiCh

Bound. Theodore Roethke. PoA

Bound and free. Eudaimon. Kathleen Raine. PBWP

Bound in a moonlight circle. The 49 Stomp. Lew Blockcolski. VoR

Bound lion, almost blind from meeting their gaze and popcorn. Riverdale Lion. John Robert Colombo. LP

Bound No'th Blues. Langston Hughes. AmNP (1974 ed.); BiP

Bound to my heart as Ixion to the wheel. Dirge for the New Sunrise. Edith Sitwell. CMoP (1970 ed.)

Bound with blue where thirteen stars. Dorchester Plate. Gwendolen Haste. WPW

Boundaries. Judith Minty. HeS

Bounty. Josephine Miles. NoAM

Bounty of Jehovah Praise, The, *with music.* George Sandys. AH

Bouquet has mimosas, orchids, roses, The. The Kelly Show. Charles Higham. MAuV

Bouquet of Roses in Sunlight. Wallace Stevens. ILP (1975 ed.)

Bouquets. Robert Francis. GP

Bourbons. Walter Savage Landor. OBSV

Bourne, The. Christina Rossetti. ILP (1975 ed.)

Bourtree, bourtree, crookit rung. The Elder, or Bourtree. *Unknown.* GBP

Bout with Burning. Vassar Miller. CoPAm

Bouzouki. Kenneth O. Hanson. GP

Bouzouki Music. Anselm Hollo. TwMBP

Bow Down, Mountain, *with music.* Norma Farber. AH

Bow down my soul in worship very low. St. Isaac's Church, Petrograd. Claude McKay. AmNP (1974 ed.); PoBA

Bow Down Your Head and Cry. *Unknown.* WTO

Bowed by a torqued and weakened spine. Hunchback Pine. Ethel Green Russell. AATT

Bowed by the weight of centuries he leans. The Man with the Hoe. Edwin Markham. AmVN; WIF

Bower of Bliss, The ("Eftsoones they heard a most melodious sound"). Spenser. *Fr.* The Faerie Queene, II, 12. NOBE

Bower of Bliss, The ("There the most daintie Paradise on ground"). Spenser. *Fr.* The Faerie Queen, II, 12. NIL (Guyon's Temptation.) OBP
("There the most daintie Paradise on ground.") EBEV

Bowery, The, *with music.* Charles Hale Hoyt. FSN

Bowery. David Ignatow. CTBA; MiP

Bowge of Courte, The. John Skelton. AAS

Bowling Green. *Unknown.* FSW

Bows glided down, and the coast, The. Ballad of the Long-legged Bait. Dylan Thomas. Epi

Box Comes Home, A. John Ciardi. CoPAm

Box for Tom, A. James Tate. FiCP

Box of Air, The. Rick Cannon. PoUp

Boxcar Poem, The ("The boxcars drift by"). David Young. AmPA

Boxer. Joseph P. Clancy. SPo

Boxer bitch is pregnant, The. Geisha. Gary Gildner. GP; POL

Boxer Loses Face and Fortune. Lucilius, *tr. fr. Greek by* Tom Dodge. LiSp

Boxes. Toi Derricotte. NPW

Boxes break, The/ At the corners. Christmas Ornaments. Valerie Worth. PChr

Boy. John Ciardi. SFF

Boy, The. Ruth Dallas. ATNZ

Boy, The. Eugene Field. ECBV

Boy, A. Benny Graves. AKE

Boy. Mbembe. NW

Boy, The. Edward Weismiller. PoUp

Boy, The. J. D. Whitney. BCr

Boy Actor, The. Noel Coward. OxBTC

Boy and the Geese, The. Padraic Fiacc. PFIr

Boy and the Lantern, The, *abr.* Evaristo Ribera Chevremont, *tr. fr. Spanish by* Julio Marzán. InW

Boy and the Parrot, The. John Hookham Frere. OxBChV

Boy and the Snake, The. Charles *and* Mary Lamb. OxBChV

Boy at the Window. Richard Wilbur. IP; SoS; TH

Boy balanced on the big root, The. Passing through Virginia. Michael Hogan. DNGG

Boy Breaking Glass. Gwendolyn Brooks. NoAM; NowV

Boy can bring so much outdoors, A. Common Carrier. Richard Armour. ECBV

Boy, Cat, Canary. Stephen Spender. LP

Boy climbed up into the tree, The. The Rescue. Hal Summers. PoTa

Boy Driving His Father to Confession. Seamus Heaney. BuTh

Boy from Tennessee. Gail Killens. PPM

Boy, I detest the Persian pomp. The Preference Declared. Horace, *tr. by* Eugene Field. Odes, I, 38. InPK

Boy, I hate their empty shows. Simplicity. Horace, *tr. by* William Cowper. Odes, I, 38. InPK; OBVE

Boy in the Roman Zoo. Archibald MacLeish. NCSH

Boy is as old as the stars, A. To My God in His Sickness. Philip Levine. NNaP

Boy is perplexed by the sunlight, The. Perplexed by the Sunlight. Grevel Lindop. LP

Boy is writing his first poem in a small, A. The First Poem. James Reiss. CAAP

Boy-Man. Karl Shapiro. SoSe

Boy of Quebec, The. *At. to* Kipling. FaBoNo

Boy, presuming on his intellect, A. At Woodward's Gardens. Robert Frost. PoA

Boy Serving at Table, The. John Lydgate. OxBChV

Boy sits in the classroom, The. Learning Experience. Marge Piercy. FF

Boy stood on the burning deck, The. Casabianca. Felicia Dorothea Hemans. RhR

Boy stoops, picking greens with his mother, A. Greens. David Ray. VGW

Boy that is good, The. The Description of a Good Boy. Henry Dixon. OxBChV

Boy Thirteen, A. Jeff Irish. DL

Boy tried to get killed, A. A Boy. Benny Graves. AKE

Boy was lying upside-down from me, The. Too Dark. Mark McCloskey. PoA

Boy who has crawled, The. Green Pastures. Dick Allen. AMV-80

Boy Who Laughed at Santa Claus, The. Ogden Nash. PoTa

Boy Who Smells Like Cocoa, A. Robert Hershon. NeAC

Boy who throws the ball, The. The Beadle's Testimony. Jerome Rothenberg. NNaP

Boy who was once me, The. The Characters of Forgotten Dirty Jokes. Wesley McNair. FAF

Boy with His Hair Cut Short. Muriel Rukeyser. InPK; SPT; VGW; WPE

Boyne Water, The. *Unknown.* FaPoR

Boys, The. Anthony Thwaite. LP

Boys/ I don't promise you nothing. Admonitions. Lucille Clifton. BPo; InPS; NMM

Boys and Girls Come Out to Play. *Unknown.* BBL; GSB, *with music*

Boys and girls, we pledge allegiance. Dianae Sumus in Fide. Catullus, *tr. by* Horace Gregory. Moon

Boys and the Bubble, The. Samuel Wesley. SCP-2

Boys are comin' to town, The!—Whoop la! Comin' to Town. Robert V. Carr. BPAW

Boys, are ye calling a toast to-night? Admiral Death. Sir Henry Newbolt. VLP

Boys. Black. Gwendolyn Brooks. CNA

Boys Brushed By, The. Catherine Gonick. AMV-80

Boys come round less often, The. Horace, *tr. by* David Malouf. Odes, I, 25. FPA

Boys in sporadic but tenacious droves. The Horse Chestnut Tree. Richard Eberhart. BBGO; CMoP (1970 ed.); TPo

Boys of Mullabaun [Mullaghbawn], The. *Unknown.* BIrV; GBP

Boys of Sanpete County, The. *Unknown.* AmFP

Boys of These Men Full Speed. Muriel Rukeyser. NNaP

Boys play. mind is. Scriptual 1. Anselm Hollo. AcAn

Boy's Song, A. James Hogg. BBL; CTV; FaPoR; OxBChV; PoPle

Bracelets of cold spume wreath my city ankles. Finisterra. Bayla Winters. AMV-81

Bracken fern,/ Why are you so bent? Japanese Folk-song from Hyogo. *Unknown, tr. by* Geoffrey Bownas *and* Anthony Thwaite. RAE

Brackish reach of shoal off Madaket, A. The Quaker Graveyard in Nantucket. Robert Lowell. CMoP (1970 ed.); HAP; ILP; NoAM; NOBA; PiAm; PPoD; TAP; UnPo (1976 ed.)

Brady's Bend. Martha Keller. PoTa

Braemar. Galway Kinnell. PoA

Brag, sweet tenor bull. Basil Bunting. *Fr.* Briggflatts. OBP; TwMBP

Braggin' Bill's Fortytude. *At. to* C. Wiles Hallock. BPAW

Brahma. Emerson. BiP; HAP; ILwL; IPWM; NIL; NOBA; PAIC; PiAm; TAP; UnPo (1976 ed.); VoPo; WIF

Brahma. Andrew Lang. FaBoCo; NOBL

Brahms/ stabbed me in the ear. St. Julien's Eve. James Cunningham. JB

Braided Poem. John Pauker. PoUp

Braille. Gerald Costanzo. AMV-81

Brain. Coleman Barks. *Fr.* Body Poems. NVAP

Brain Cells, The. Donald Hall. TAP

Brain—is wider than the sky, The. Emily Dickinson. NoAM; PoIA

Brain, within its groove, The. Emily Dickinson. NoAM; NOBA

Brainstorm. Howard Nemerov. HAP; NCSH; NoAM; SoSe (1977 ed.)

Bramble, like barbed wire. The Thrush's Nest. Richard Ryan. PFIr

Branch Line, The. Patricia Beer. HeHu

Branch swayed, swerved, The. Windy Boy in a Windswept Tree. Geoffrey Summerfield. LP

Branches Back Into. Ken Belford. NeAC

Branches of blood. Tide. George Mattingly. AcAn

Branches ripped by a storm tide. Walking the Beach. Sarah Youngblood. IHMS

Branded on the bum with. Godspeed to Such Harpoons. L. W. Michaelson. PoW

Brandy Leave Me Alone. *Unknown.* FSW

Branwen's Starling. R. Williams Parry, *tr. fr. Welsh by* Gwyn Jones. OBW

Brass and parrot feathers. Oshun, the River Goddess. *Yoruba Oral Tradition, tr. by* Ulli Beier. WTO

Brass Horse, The. Drummond Allison. FaBoTw (1975 ed.)

Brass Spittoons. Langston Hughes. AmNP (1974 ed.); NoAM

Brasses jangle and the hausers tighten, The. The Barge Horse. Seán Jennett. PH

Brave/ they straddle the animals. Cowboys: One. Rod McKuen. MiP

Brave College is hanged, the chief of our hopes. The Whig's Lamentation for the Death of Their Dear Brother College. *Unknown.* APAS

Brave flowers—that I could gallant it like you. A Contemplation upon Flowers. Henry King. PF

Brave infant of Saguntum, clear. To the Immortal Memory and Friendship of That Noble Pair, Sir Lucius Cary and Sir Henry Morison. Ben Jonson. NOBE; OAEL-1; PAIC

Brave iron! brave hammer! from your sound. Thwick-a-thwack. Thomas Dekker. *Fr.* London's Tempe. SCP-2

Brave Kelso, he's considered great. Julia E. Moore. *Fr.* Grand Rapids Cricket Club. PeD

Brave Knight, A. Mary Mapes Dodge. TDH

Brave Lord Willoughby. *Unknown.* FaPoR

Brave Man, The. Wallace Stevens. PBMP

Brave New World. Archibald MacLeish. NOBA; OFD

Brave Rover. Max Beerbohm. GDP

Brave Teuton, though thy awful name. Schemmelfennig. Bret Harte. OBAL

Brave weathercock, I see thou'lt set thy nose. Upon the Weathercock. John Bunyan. OxBChV

Brave youth, to whom Fate in one hour. For a Picture Where a Queen Laments over the Tomb of a Slain Knight. Thomas Carew. CaPo

Bravely from Fairyland he rode, on furlough. The Broken Girth. Robert Graves. BIrV

Bravery runs in my family. Coward. A. R. Ammons. OBAL

Braving the Wilds All Unexplored, *with music.* Robert Freeman. AH

Brawling of a sparrow in the eaves, The. The Sorrow of Love. W. B. Yeats. OAEL-2; OBP; PoIA

Brazil, January 1, 1502. Elizabeth Bishop. NoAM

Breaching Muse, The. Liam O'Mahony. IPM

Bread. Stanley Burnshaw. SPT

Bread. W. S. Merwin. EAS

Bread. William Pillin. SPT

Bread. Constance Urdang. GP

Bread and a Pension. Louis Johnson. ATNZ

Bread and Music. Conrad Aiken. Discordants, I. VoPo ("Music I heard with you was more than music.") CMoP (1970 ed.); ILP (1975 ed.); NOBA

Bread and Wine, *sel.* Friedrich Hölderlin, *tr. fr. German by* Robert Bly. "Oh friend, we arrived too late." NU

Bread in our mouths. Paradise Is Not a Place. Daniela Gioseffi. WBN

Bread Is Born. Anne Hébert, *tr. fr. French by* Maxine W. Kumin. BoWoP

Bread Loaf to Omaha, Twenty-eight Hours. Patrick Worth Gray. TAT

Bread of heaven, on Thee we feed. Josiah Conder. VLP

Bread of Our Affliction, The. Martin Grossman. VWA

Bread-Word Giver. John Wheelwright. SPT

Breaded Meat, Breaded Hands. Michael S. Harper. NVAP

Breadth. Circle. Desert. Monarch. Month. Wisdom. John Hollander. PoA

Break and trail home. The Girl I Left behind Me. *Unknown.* AmFP

Break, Break, Break. Tennyson. BiP; CABA (1972 ed.); CTV; DL; FaPoR; FF; HAP; HeIP; ILP (1975 ed.); NIL; NOBE; PoIA; PPoe; WeW

Break not the slumbers of the bride. An Hymeneal Song on the Nuptials of the Lady Anne Wentworth and the Lord Lovelace. Thomas Carew. CaPo

Break of Day. John Donne. CABA (1972 ed.); PAIC; PoIA; SoSe (1977 ed.)

Break of Day in the Trenches. Isaac Rosenberg. NOBE; OAEL-2; PoA; PSN; VWA

Break off/ fallen Catullus. Catullus, *tr. fr. Latin by* Peter Whigham. TwMBP

Break the News to Mother, *with music.* Charles Kassell Harris. FSN

Break Thou the Bread of Life, *with music.* Mary Artemisia Lathbury. AH

Breakdown, breakdown, lay me low. Cry. Alexander Scott. MS

Breake now my heart and dye! Oh no, she may relent. Thomas Campion. AAS

Breakers of Broncos. Lew Sarett. BPAW

Breakers over the Sea. *Malay Oral Tradition, tr. by* R. O. Winstedt. WTO

Breakfast. W. W. Gibson. OxBTC

Breakfast. Robin Shectman. AMV-80

Breakfast at Cindy's place. Shawn Wong. *Fr.* Kicking Lego Blocks. NW

Breakfast Song in Time of Diet. Stoddard King. OBAL

Breakfast Time. James Stephens. ECBV

Breakfast with Gerard Manley Hopkins. Anthony Brode. NOBL

Breaking every law except the one. Our City Is Guarded by Automatic Rockets. William Stafford. NowV

Breaking Ground in Me. Tom Kryss. NeAC

Breaking Off from Waiting. Clarisse Nicoïdski, *tr. fr. Judezmo by* Stephen Levy. VWA

Breaking through the first door, he found. Seven Dreams. John Bayliss. EAS

"Breaking Up Is Hard to Do." Hugh Walthall. PoUp

Breaking waves dashed high, The. The Landing of the Pilgrim Fathers in New England. Felicia Dorothea Hemans. BTTM; ECBV; FaPo; PPM; SBG; WPE

Breaklight. Lucille Clifton. OSP

Breakthrough. Philip Roberts. FPA

Breakthrough. Carolyn M. Rodgers. BPo

Breast, The. Anne Sexton. CABA (1972 ed.)

Breastdown fluttering in the breeze. Sparrow in Winter. Shinkichi Takahashi, *tr. by* Lucien Stryk *and* Takashi Ikemoto. NU

Breasts. Tess Gallagher. AmPA

Breasts. Donald Hall. OBAL

Breasts. Charles Simic. NNaP

Breasts of a barmaid of Crale, The. Limerick. *Unknown.* NOBL

Breath. Philip Levine. FoP; MPA

Breath. Arthur Smith. CPA

Breath clamber-short, face sun-peeled, stones. Red-Tail Hawk and Pyre of Youth. Robert Penn Warren. PoIA

Breath in My Nostrils. Lance Jeffers. CNA

Breath of Air, A. James Wright. NOBA

Breath of balm—of orange bloom, A. Retrospect. Ina Coolbrith. WPW

Breathe In Breathe Out. Layle Silbert. NPW

Breathe in experience, breathe out poetry. Poem Out of Childhood. Muriel Rukeyser. NMM

Breathe on the Glass. Raymond Stineford. AMV-81

Breathers, The. James Reiss. AmPA; CAAP; HeS

Breathes there the man, with soul so dead. This Is My Own, My Native Land. Sir Walter Scott. *Fr.* The Lay of the Last Minstrel. BTTM; CTV; FaPoR; NOBE; PBMP; SFF; SoSe

Breathing, The. Denise Levertov. IPWM; RFM; TCP

Breathing, at Last, in the Wichita Art Museum.  D. Clinton. HeS

Breathing in morning.  The Song Turning Back into Itself.  Al Young.  CAAP

Breathing something German at the end.  The Gift to Be Simple. Howard Moss.  SS

Breathless, we flung us on the windy hill.  The Hill.  Rupert Brooke.  OxBTC

Breathless when the breeze deserts them.  Cuban Refugees on Key Biscayne.  Barbara Winder.  TAT

Bredon Hill.  A. E. Housman.  IP; STS; TT; VLP

Breed's described, The: Now, Satire, if you can.  Daniel Defoe. *Fr.* The True-born Englishman, Pt. II.  OBSV

Breeze blows o'er the lake, A.  Herons.  *Unknown, tr. fr. Japanese.*  PCOP

Breeze is blowing, The.  *Tr. fr. Maori by* A. Armstrong *and* R. Ngata.  WTO

Breezes went steadily thro' the tall pines, The.  Nathan Hale. *Unknown.*  BTTM

Breezeways in the tropics winnow the air.  A Letter from the Caribbean.  Barbara Howes.  UnPo (1976 ed.)

Breitmann in Politics, *sel.*  Charles Godfrey Leland.
"Dere's a liddle fact in hishdory vitch few hafe oonershtand." OBAL

Brendan Gone.  Padraic Fiacc.  CIP

Brennan on the Moor.  *Unknown.*  AIW; AmFP; FaBoBa; FSW; GBP

Brent: A Poem to Thomas Palmer Esq., *sels.*  William Diaper. OBSV
"Had mournful Ovid been to Brent condemned."
"Happy are you, whom Quantock overlooks."

Brewer, A.  *Unknown.*  FaBoCo

Brewer's Man, The.  L. A. G.  Strong.  FaBoCo

Brian Boy Magee.  "Ethna Carbery."  PFIr

Brian never makes a real fire.  The Write-off.  Charlotte Alexander.  AAN

Brian O'Linn.  *Unknown.*  FaBoBa; FaBoNo
(Bryan O'Lynn.)  GBP

Bric-a-brac shelf.  Still Life.  Ralph Mecklenburger.  SFF

Brick not used in building, A.  Naomi Replansky.  POL

Bricks of the wall.  The Garden Wall.  Denise Levertov.  PiAm

Brid one brere, brid, brid one brere.  Bird on Briar.  *Unknown.* OxBM

Bridal bed, The.  Above it.  Jenny Mastoraki, *tr. fr. Modern Greek by* Nick Germanacos.  PBWP

Bridal Couch.  Donald J. Lloyd.  NIL

Bridal Day.  Compton Mackenzie.  SLP

Bridal Morn, The.  *Unknown.  See* Maidens Came, The.

Bridal Song.  Thomas Lovell Beddoes.  *Fr.* Death's Jest Book, IV, iii.  GBL

Bridal Song.  George Chapman.  *Fr.* Hero and Leander, Fifth Sestiad.  NOBE

Bridal Song, A.  *At. to* Shakespeare.  *Fr.* The Two Noble Kinsmen, I, i.  NOBE

Bride, The.  Bella Akhmadulina, *tr, fr. Russian by* Stephan Stepanchev.  PBWP; BoWoP

Bride, A.  Harry Fainlight.  BoLoP

Bride, The.  D. H. Lawrence.  NoAM; OxBTC

Bride loved old words, and found her pleasure marred.  J. V. Cunningham.  OBAL

Bride of Frankenstein, The.  Edward Field.  HeIP; TPo

Bride of Lammermoor, The, *sel.*  Sir Walter Scott.
Lucy Ashton's Song, *fr. ch.* 3.  NOBE

Bride Song.  Christina Rossetti.  *Fr.* The Prince's Progress. WPE

Bridegroom, The.  Kipling.  *Fr.* Epitaphs of the War.  FaBoEE

Brides, The.  A. D. Hope.  HAP; InPK; PoIA

Bride's Farewell, The: Two Songs.  *Gond Oral Tradition, tr. by* V. Elwin *and* S. Hivale.  WTO

Bridesmaid.  Robley Wilson, Jr.  AMV–80

Bridge, The, *sels.*  Hart Crane.
Atlantis.  NYP
Ave Maria.  NoAM; NOBA
Cape Hatteras.  PiAm
"Nasal whine of power whips a new universe, The."  NIL
Powhatan's Daughter.
Dance, The.  PiAm
Harbor Dawn, The.  NYP; PiAm; PSN
Indiana.  PiAm
River, The.  CMoP (1970 ed.); GOA; NoAM; NOBA; PiAm
Van Winkle.  PiAm
Three Songs.
National Winter Garden.  InPS
To Brooklyn Bridge.  CABA (1972 ed.); ILP (1975 ed.); InPS; NOBA; NYP
(Proem: to Brooklyn Bridge.)  CMoP (1970 ed.); ExPo (1973 ed.); HAP; HeIP; NoAM; PAIC; PiAm; TAP
Tunnel, The.  CMoP (1970 ed.); MAT; NYP

Bridge, The.  Derek Walcott.  NYP

Bridge, and a hot concrete road, A.  The Desert of Love.  Janos Pilinszky, *tr. by* Ted Hughes *and* János Csokits.  OBVE

Bridge Begins in the Trees, A.  William Stafford.  CNW

Bridge of Heraclitus, The.  George Reavey.  BIrV

Bridge of Sighs, The.  Thomas Hood.  EBEV; FaPoR; PeD
"One more unfortunate," *sel.*  UsP

Bridge of the Carousel.  Rainer Maria Rilke, *tr. fr. German by* John Drury.  AMV–80

Bridge, The, says: Come across, try me; see how good I am. Potomac Town in February.  Carl Sandburg.  LCL

Bridgework.  Annette Lynch.  FF

Brief Autumnal.  *Unknown, tr. fr. Greek by* Dudley Fitts.  NIL; WeW

Brief Essay on Man.  Arthur Guiterman.  OBAL

Brief Explanation.  Claudia Dobkins.  NPW

Brief Journey West, The.  Howard Nemerov.  NoAM

Brief, on a flying night.  Chimes.  Alice Meynell.  SBG; WPE

Brief procession, The.  Bessie Smith's Funeral.  Alvin Aubert. CoPAm

Briefing, The.  David Kirby.  CSP

Briggflatts, *sels.*  Basil Bunting.
"As the player's breath warms the fipple the tone clears," IV. OBP
"Brag, sweet tenor bull," I.  OBP; TwMBP
Coda.  OAEL–2; TwMBP
"Grass caught in willow tells the flood's height," IV.  NoAM
"Light lifts from the water," *fr.* V.  OAEL–2
"Poet appointed dare not decline," II.  OBP

Brigham Young.  *Unknown.*  FSW

Bright are the days which the Fates hold in store for us.  To Willian (Whom We Have Missed).  P. G. Wodehouse. NOBL

Bright as a fallen fragment of the sky.  The Rock Pool.  Alfred Noyes.  EcS

Bright as the day, and like the morning fair.  Cloë.  George Granville.  FaBoCo; FaBoEE; NIL

Bright Be the Place of Thy Soul!  Byron.  HoPM (1975 ed.)

Bright clasp of her whole hand around my finger.  To My Daughter.  Stephen Spender.  RRA

Bright college years with pleasure rife.  Yale Boola!  H. S. Durand.  FSN

Bright-coloured, mirror-plated, strung with lights.  Merry-go-round.  James McAuley.  MAuV

Bright Day, A.  W. H. Davies.  OBW

Bright little buttercup, now you will show.  Buttercup.  Mary Mapes Dodge.  ECBV

Bright little maid in St. Thomas, A.  St. Thomas.  Ferdinand G. Christgau.  TDH

Bright mirror I braved, The: the devil in it.  Cleopatra to the Asp. Ted Hughes.  EBEV

Bright moon illumines the night-prospect, A.  *Tr. fr. Chinese by* Arthur Waley.  BoWoP

Bright oval on a light chain.  Tag, I.D.  John S. Harris.  MPA

Bright scene, A; a summer morning.  A Minor Victorian Painter. John Hewitt.  CIP

Bright Star! Would I Were Steadfast as Thou Art.  Keats. AnMo; CABA (1972 ed.); ExPo (1973 ed.); GBL; HAP; ILP (1975 ed.); InPK; InPS; IPWM; LFH; MBPR; NIL; OAEL-2; PoIA; PPoe; PPP; STS; TT (Last Sonnet.)  NOBE (Written on a Blank Page in Shakespeare's Poems.)  OBP

Bright town, tossed by waves of time to a hill.  Ode to Swansea. Vernon Watkins.  OBW

Bright tulips, we do know.  To a Bed of Tulips.  Robert Herrick. CaPo

Bright was the summer's noon when quickening steps. Wordsworth.  *Fr.* The Prelude, IV.  PES

Bright white street lights, The.  Allegory in Black.  Carl Clark. JB

Bright Winter Morning.  Chris Klein.  AMV-81

Brightest morning of summer, The.  Graveyard Road.  Tom McKeown.  HeS

Brightest of the Bright, The.  Egan O'Rahilly, *tr. fr. Irish by* James Clarence Mangan.  BIrV

Brighton Beach.  Paul Durcan.  IPM

'Brigid is a caution, sure!'—What's that ye say?  Her Sister. Moira O'Neill.  OxBTC

Brignall Banks.  Sir Walter Scott.  *Fr.* Rokeby.  ILP (1975 ed.)

Brill.  *Unknown.  See* At Brill on the Hill.

Brilliant planets float in that black lake.  Retired School-Teacher. Heather McHugh.  PCho

Brineshrimp, The.  Rhyll McMaster.  FPA

Bring a Child Flowers.  Nathaniel Tarn.  RRA

Bring a leaf to me.  Invitation Standing.  Paul Blackburn. IPWM; VGW

Bring 'Em Home.  Barbara Dane *and others.*  FSW

Bring hither the pink and purple columbine.  The Fair Flower Delice.  Spenser.  *Fr.* The Shepheardes Calendar: April.  PF

Bring Me a Little Water, Sylvie.  Leadbelly (Huddie Ledbetter). FSW

"Bring me a long sharp knife for we are in danger."  The Sunflowers.  Douglas Stewart.  POL

Bring me my rose-buds, drawer, come.  A Frolic.  Robert Herrick.  FaBoEE

Bring me to the blasted oak.  Crazy Jane and the Bishop.  W. B. Yeats.  AnMo; CMoP (1970 ed.)

Bring me wine, but wine which never grew.  Bacchus.  Emerson. NOBA; PiAm

Bring now the last flower in to warm this room.  At My Mother's Bedside.  Marcia Lee Masters.  WPE

Bring the good old bugle, boys!  Marching through Georgia. Henry Clay Work.  FaPoR; FSW; PSoN

Bring Us in Good Ale.  *Unknown.*  EBEV; FaBoCo; ILP (1975 ed.); OAEL-1; OxBM

Bring your shears and clip him well.  Vinegaroon.  Witter Bynner.  BPAW

Bringing Flowers.  Roberta Spear.  AmPA

Bringing in the Sheaves.  Knowles Shaw.  BLSH, *with music;* FSW

Brisk methinks I am, and fine.  Anacreontic Verse.  Robert Herrick.  BBL

Brissit brawnis and broken banis.  The Bewteis of the Fute-Ball. *Unknown.*  FaBoCo

Bristol and Clifton.  John Betjeman.  CMoP (1970 ed.)

Britannia and Raleigh.  John Ayloffe.  APAS

Britannia rules the waves.  On a Parisian Boulevard.  James Kenneth Stephen.  NOBL

Britannia's daughters, much more fair than nice.  Edward Young. *Fr.* Love of Fame, the Universal Passion.  OBSV

Britannia's Pastorals, *sels.*  William Browne.
"As that Arabian bird (whom all admire)," *fr.* I, Song 4. OAEL-1
"Glide soft, ye silver floods," *fr.* II, Song 1.  SCP-2
"Muses' friend, grey-eyed Aurora, yet, The," *fr.* II, Song 2. SCP-2
"Now great Hyperion left his golden throne," *fr.* II, Song 1. SCP-2

Brither-men wha eftir us live on.  Ballat o the Hingit.  Villon, *tr. by* Tom Scott.  OBVE

Brither Worm.  Robert Garioch.  MS

British Grenadiers, The.  *Unknown.*  BTTM; FSW

British Leftish Poetry, 1930-40.  "Hugh MacDiarmid."  CMoP (1970 ed.); FaBoTw (1975 ed.); NoAM

British Museum Reading Room, The.  Louis MacNeice.  NOBE

British Prison Ship, The, *sel.*  Philip Freneau.
Hessian Doctor, The.  EAP

British, the Ethiopians, and the Italians are squabbling, The.  Our Country Is Divided.  Faarah Nuur, *tr. fr. Somali by* B. W. Andrzejewski *and* I. M. Lewis.  WTO

Brittle beautie, that nature made so fraile.  The Frailty and Hurtfulness of Beauty.  Earl of Surrey.  AAS; HoPM (1975 ed.)

Brittle Eye, The.  Henry Kanabus.  FiCh

Brittle streets, with midnight walking flung, The.  Sonnet on a Still Night.  J. V. Cunningham.  PoA

Broad-backed hippopotamus, The.  The Hippopotamus.  T. S. Eliot.  AnMo; BoReV; HoPM (1975 ed.); VGW

Broad beach, The.  Afternoon: Amagansett Beach.  John Hall Wheelock.  EcS

Broad field darkens, but, still moving round, The.  Central Park. Howard Nemerov.  NYP

Broad Is the Road.  Isaac Watts.  AH, *with music* ("Broad is the road that leads to death.")  AmFP

Broadminded.  Ray Durem.  *See* Friends.

Broadway.  Walt Whitman.  NYP

Broadway Pageant, A.  Walt Whitman.  NYP

Broccoli.  Tom Schmidt.  GP

Broke and Hungry.  *Unknown.*  BluL

Broken altar, Lord, thy servant rears, A.  The Altar.  George Herbert.  AnMo; HoPM (1975 ed.); ILP (1975 ed.); InPS; NIL; OAEL-1; SCP-1

Broken Appointment, A.  Thomas Hardy.  BiP; GBL; LoAs; NoAM

Broken Arrowheads at Chilmark, Martha's Vineyard.  Ruthven Todd.  MS

Broken Bowl, The.  James Merrill.  PoA

Broken Bowl, The.  Jones Very.  ILP (1975 ed.)

Broken Dreams.  W. B. Yeats.  PSN

Broken-Face Gargoyles.  Carl Sandburg.  ILP (1975 ed.)

Broken Girth, The.  Robert Graves.  BIrV

Broken Gull, A.  John Moore.  NCSH

Broken Heart, The.  John Donne.  EBEV; ILP (1975 ed.)

Broken Heart, The, *sels.*  John Ford.
"List! what sad sounds are these? extremely."  SCP-2
"Oh no more, no more, too late," *fr.* IV, iii.  GBL
(Love's Martyrs.)  NOBE

Broken Heart, Broken Machine.  Richard E. Grant.  PoBA

"Broken heart," A . . . but can a heart break, now?  Sonnet. John Berryman.  Epi

Broken heart does best, A.  Emily Dickinson—in Appreciation. Roy Batt.  PMW

Broken-hearted Gardener, The.  *Unknown.*  GBP

Broken Home, The.  James Merrill.  HAP; NoAM; NOBA; PPP

Broken Home.  William Stafford.  NNaP

Broken in pieces all asunder.  Affliction.  George Herbert. SCP-1

Broken moon on the cold water, A.  Your Birthday in the California Mountains.  Kenneth Rexroth.  PoW

Broken pillar of the wing jags from the clotted shoulder, The. Hurt Hawks.  Robinson Jeffers.  CMoP (1970 ed.); ILP (1975 ed.); NoAM; NOBA; PiAm; SoS; TAP; TPo; UnPo (1976 ed.)

Broken Promise.  James O. Taylor.  BuTh

Broken the pot, there's still the jar.  The Loves of the Birds. *Malay Oral Tradition, tr. by* R. J. Wilkinson *and* R. O. Winstedt.  WTO

Broken Token, The.  *Unknown.*  AmFP

Broken Tower, The.  Hart Crane.  CMoP (1970 ed.); ILP (1975 ed.); NoAM; NOBA; PiAm

Broken Toys, The.  James Kirkup.  FPB

Broken Treaties, *sel.*  Victor Contoski. "Kiss the one you love."  GP

Broken Wedding Ring, The.  *Unknown.*  AIW

Broken Year, The.  Ron Talney.  PoW

Bronco Busting, Event #1.  May Swenson.  LiSp; PH

Broncho That Would Not Be Broken, The.  Vachel Lindsay. BPAW; PH

Broncho versus Bicycle.  John Wallace Crawford.  BPAW

Bronxomania.  Victor Hernández Cruz.  SA

Bronze David of Donatello, The.  Randall Jarrell.  WIF

Bronze Rider, Wellington, The.  Robin Hyde.  ATNZ

Bronze sun blew a long and shimmering call, The.  Epithets of War—I: August 1914.  Vernon Scannell.  HeHu

Bronzeville Man with a Belt in the Back.  Gwendolyn Brooks. PoBA

Bronzeville Woman in a Red Hat.  Gwendolyn Brooks.  TT

Brooding.  David Ignatow.  PBMP; TCP

Brooding Grief.  D. H. Lawrence.  CMoP (1970 ed.); ILP (1975 ed.)

Brooding on the eightieth letter of Fors Clavigera.  Geoffrey Hill. Mercian Hymns, XXV.  HAP

Brooding upon its unexerted power.  Gas and Hot Air.  Morris Bishop.  OBAL

Brook, The.  Tennyson.  PoPle (Song of the Brook, The.)  CTV

Brook, The.  Edward Thomas.  OAEL-2

Brook whose stream so great, so good, A.  An Epitaph upon Doctor Brook.  Richard Crashaw.  WeW

Brooklyn Bridge.  Vladimir Mayakovsky, *tr. fr. Russian by* Vladimir Markov *and* Merrill Sparks.  NYP

Brooklyn Heights.  John Wain.  NYP; OxBTC

Brooklyn Theater Fire, The.  *Unknown.*  AmFP

Broom out the floor now, lay the fender by.  June.  Francis Ledwidge.  BIrV

Broomfield Hill, The.  *Unknown.*  AmFP; PeBB

Brooms.  Charles Simic.  AmPA; NNaP, *early version*

Broomstick Train, The, *sel.*  Oliver Wendell Holmes. "Look out! Lookout, boys! Clear the track!"  IWK

Brother.  R. H. Deutsch.  PoW

Brother, The.  Peter Everwine.  NNaP

Brother, The.  Thomas Hardy.  AIW

Brother.  Jewel C. Latimore.  JB

Brother and Sister.  "Lewis Carroll."  FaBoNo

Brother and Sisters.  Judith Wright.  GAS

Brother at One Week.  Carole Oles.  NPW

Brother Bulleys, let us sing.  The Bullfinches.  Thomas Hardy. PB

Brother, Can You Spare a Dime?  E. Y. Harburg.  AIW

Brother, come!  And What Shall You Say?  Joseph Seamon Cotter, Jr.  PoBA

Brother, consider as you go your way.  Somebody and Somebody Else and You.  Edwin Rolfe.  SPT

Brother Fire.  Louis MacNeice.  NoAM; NOBE

Brother Green.  *Unknown.*  AmFP

Brother, Hast Thou Wandered Far, *with music.*  James Freeman Clarke.  AH

Brother humans who live on after us.  Ballade.  Villon, *tr. by* Galway Kinnell.  NAWM-1

Brother-in-Law, The.  Larry Rubin.  GP

Brother shout your country's anthem.  Hymn for Nations. *Unknown.*  FSW

Brother Simon Calls on Jesus Christ.  Mark Wangberg.  TC

Brother, Though from Yonder Sky, *with music.*  James Henry Bancroft.  AH

Brother to the firefly.  Morning Light (The Dew-Drier).  Mary Effie Lee Newsome.  AmNP (1974 ed.); PoBA

Brother, today I sit on the brick bench outside the house.  To My Brother Miguel: In Memoriam.  César Vallejo, *tr. by* John Knoepfle *and* James Wright.  MiP

Brother told me, A.  Untitled.  Michele Wallace.  WBN

Brotherhood.  José Luis Vega, *tr. fr. Spanish by* Julio Marzán. InW

Brothers, The.  Edwin Muir.  HeIP

Brothers.  Dan Pagis, *tr. fr. Hebrew by* Shirley Kaufman.  VWA

Brothers (I).  James Reiss.  AMV-81

Brothers, The.  Wordsworth.  MBPR

Brothers/ brothers/ everywhere.  Utopia.  Jewel C. Latimore. BPo

Brothers/ i/ under/overstand.  The Revolutionary Screw.  Don L. Lee.  GP

Brothers! between you and me.  To the Republicans of North America.  Shelley.  MBPR

Brothers, celebrate with me this morning.  Ash Wednesday. Daniel Burke.  AMV-80

Brother's cradle/ doesn't rock.  Brother at One Week.  Carole Oles.  NPW

Brothers, my teeth hurt.  Strictly for Posterity.  Charles Simic. NNaP

Brothers Together in Winter.  Harley Elliott.  NeAC

Brought here in slave ships and pitched overboard.  Love Your Enemy.  Yusef Iman.  BPo

Brought this to me today.  The Chronological Ordering of Art Cards.  Robert Sargent.  PoUp

Brought to Amerikkka.  And Now Out of Sight.  Lonnie L. Landrum.  DNGG

Brown and furry.  The Caterpillar.  Christina Rossetti.  CTV; OxBChV; PCOP

Brown Bears of Boston, The.  Roland Pease.  BCr

Brown Bird, The.  Dan Johnson.  PoUp

Brown Boy to Brown Girl.  Countee Cullen.  PoBA

Brown Bug, The.  Michael R. Brown.  SFF

Brown butterfly on the dried leaf, The.  Fauna: March.  David Lake.  FPA

Brown Circles.  Melvin DeBruhl.  PPoD

Brown enormous odor he lived by, The.  The Prodigal.  Elizabeth Bishop.  CoPAm; PPP

Brown-faced nurse has murmured something unintelligible, The. Microcosmos.  Susan Miles.  OxBTC

Brown from the sun's mid-afternoon caress.  Spectrum.  William Dickey.  SoSe

Brown girl chanting Te Deums on Sunday.  Ruth.  Pauli Murray. NMM

Brown Girl Dead, A.   Countee Cullen.   TAP

Brown in the snow, a car with a heater.   Strangers.   William Stafford.   NNaP

Brown is my love, but graceful.   *Unknown, tr. fr. Italian.*   GBL

Brown lived at such a lofty farm.   Brown's Descent.   Robert Frost.   PoTa

Brown o' San Juan.   "Home, Sweet Home," with Variations.   H. C. Bunner.   OBAL

Brown old man with a green thumb, A.   He Was.   Richard Wilbur.   NCSH; SS

Brown owl sits in the ivy bush, The.   The Great Brown Owl.   Jane Euphemia Browne.   OxBChV

Brown Penny.   W. B. Yeats.   BoLoP; CMoP (1970 ed.); OLR; PFIr

Brown River, Smile.   Jean Toomer.   AmNP (1974 ed.); PoBA

Brown Robin.   *Unknown.*   PeBB

Brown Robyn's Confession.   *Unknown.*   GBP; PeBB

Brown Skin Girl.   *Unknown.*   BluL

Brown's Descent.   Robert Frost.   PoTa

Brown's Ferry Blues.   *Unknown.*   FSW

Brownsville Blues.   *Unknown.*   BluL

Bruadar and Smith and Glinn.   *Unknown, tr. fr. Irish by* Douglas Hyde.   PFIr

(Curse, A.)   BIrV

Bruce, The, *sel.*   John Barbour.

Bruce Meets Three Men with a Wether.   OxBM

Bruce to His Men at Bannockburn.   Burns.   *See* Scots Wha Hae.

Bruckner.   James Camp.   MAT

Brueghel's Winter.   Walter de la Mare.   WIF

Bruised by the masseur's final whack.   Health and Fitness.   J. B. Morton.   FaBoCo

Bruises.   Coleman Barks.   *Fr.* Body Poems.   NVAP

Bruno.   *Unknown.*   TDH

Brush Mask.   Linda Parker.   TC

Brush Up Your Shakespeare.   Cole Porter.   OBAL

Brushing back the curls from your famous brow.   The Copulating Gods.   Carolyn Kizer.   Prf

Brussels in Winter.   W. H. Auden.   OxBTC

Brut, The, *sel.*   Layamon.
   Death of Arthur, The, *orig. and mod. English prose.*   OxBM

Bryan, Bryan, Bryan, Bryan.   Vachel Lindsay.   CMoP (1970 ed.)

Bryan O'Lynn.   *Unknown.*   *See* Brian O'Linn.

Bryan's Last Battle.   *Unknown.*   AmFP

Bryant.   James Russell Lowell.   *Fr.* A Fable for Critics.   AmVN; NOBA; TAP

Brynbwrla.   Kingsley Amis.   *Fr.* The Evans Country.   NOBL

Bubba Esther, 1888.   Ruth Whitman.   AMV–81

Bubba Smith.   Ogden Nash.   SPo

Bubble, The: A Song.   Robert Herrick.   CaPo

Bucephalus is neighing me a love song.   Hossolalia.   Mildred Luton.   PH

Buchlyvie.   *Unknown.*   GBP

Buck in the Snow, The.   Edna St. Vincent Millay.   BoAnP

Buckaroo Sandman.   *Unknown.*   BPAW

Buckdancer's Choice.   James Dickey.   NoAM; NOBA

Bucket in the Well.   Connie Wanek.   AMV–80

Buckeye Jim.   *Unknown.*   FSW

Bucking Bronco.   *Unknown.*   AmFP; BPAW (*At.* to Belle Starr); FSW

Buckingham Palace.   A. A. Milne.   OxBChV

Buckinghamshire.   *Unknown.*   GBP

Bucolic Eclogues, sel.   Ethel Anderson.
   "Waking, child, while you slept, your mother took."   WPE

Bud fantasies, dreams of an ear of corn.   Paean to Eve's Apple.   James Liddy.   CIP

Buddha.   Herman Melville.   HeIP; PiAm

Buddha Inherits 6 Cars on His Birthday, The.   Diane Wakoski.   NIL

Buddha is not more strange.   In a Warm Bath.   Carl Rakosi.   TAP

Buddha took some Autumn leaves.   Kenneth Rexroth.   *Fr.* The City of the Moon.   GP

Buddha's Birthday: April 8, 1819.   Issa, *tr. fr. Japanese by* Nobuyuki Yuasa.   *Fr.* Oraga Haru.   OFD

Buddha's Death Day: February 15, 1815.   Issa, *tr. fr. Japanese by* Nobuyuki Yuasa.   *Fr.* Oraga Haru.   OFD

Buddhist Priest, A.   Ho Xuan Huong *tr. fr. Vietnamese by* Nguyen Ngoc Bich *and* Burton Raffel.   PBWP

Buddy.   Langston Hughes.   ILP (1975 ed.)

Budmouth Dears.   Thomas Hardy.   *Fr.* The Dynasts.   PoPle

Buffalo.   Louis Daniel Brodsky.   AMV–80

Buffalo.   Henry Dumas.   PoBA

Buffalo, The.   Marianne Moore.   PoA

Buffalo Bill's.   E. E. Cummings.   CABA (1972 ed.); CMoP (1970 ed.); GrRo; InPK; NOBA; PiAm; PPoD; STS; TAP; UsP; VGW
   (Portrait.)   HeIP; InPS; IP; NIL

Buffalo Boy.   *Unknown.*   AmFP; FSW

Buffalo breathed quietly inside, The.   The Crow-Children Walk My Circles in the Snow.   Ray A. Young Bear.   CDW

Buffalo, buffalo, buffalo, buffalo.   Death Chant.   Peter Blue Cloud.   VoR

Buffalo Dance.   Alice Corbin, *after Chippewa Indian.*   BPAW

Buffalo Dusk.   Carl Sandburg.   BPAW; GOA; MiP; PCOP; RFM; TH

Buffalo Girls.   *Unknown.*   AmFP; ECBV
   (Buffalo Gals.)   BLSH, *with music;* BLSo, *with music;* FSW

Buffalo—Isle of Wight Power Cable.   Anselm Hollo.   TwMBP

Buffalo, Our Sacred Beast, The.   Tom McKeown.   NVAP

Buffalo Skinners, The.   *Unknown.*   AmFP; BPAW; FSW; GBP; PeBB

Buffaloes are gone, The.   Buffalo Dusk.   Carl Sandburg.   BPAW; GOA; MiP; PCOP; RFM; TH

Bugle, The.   Tennyson.   *See* Splendor Falls on Castle Walls, The.

Bugler's First Communion, The ("A bugler boy from barrack").   Gerard Manley Hopkins.   NoAM

Buick.   Karl Shapiro.   BiP; CMoP (1970 ed.); HoPM (1975 ed.)

Buik of Alexander, The, *sel.*   Unknown, *at. to* John Barbour.
   "When I see hir forrow me."   SLP

Build a little fence of trust.   To-Day.   Mary Francis Butts.   CTV

Builder, in building the little house.   The Kitchen Chimney.   Robert Frost.   PPM

Building, The.   Philip Larkin.   PSN

Building in Nova Scotia.   Stephen Dunn.   GP

Building of the Nest, The.   Margaret Sangster.   PCOP

Building of the Ship, The, *sel.* Longfellow.
   Republic, The.   BTTM

Building of the Skyscraper, The.   George Oppen.   GOA

Building Site.   Marian Lines.   FPB

Building Society Blues.   Roger Roughton.   EAS

Building the Bridge.   Will Allen Dromgoole.   WeW

Buildings and Grounds.   Henry Taylor.   CSP

Buladelah-Taree Holiday Song Cycle, The.   Les A. Murray.   GAS

Bulb, A.   Richard Kendall Munkittrick.   POL

Bulbs strung along.   Christmas Lights.   Valerie Worth.   PChr

Bulkeley, Hunt, Willard, Hosmer, Meriam, Flint.   Hamatreya.   Emerson.   AmVN; HeIP; ILP (1975 ed.); IPWM; MAT; NOBA; PiAm; TAP

Bull, A.   Babette Deutsch.   BoAnP; LiSp

Bull, The.   Ralph Hodgson.   OxBTC

Bull, The.   V. Sackville-West.   WPE

Bull, The. William Carlos Williams. LFH

Bull, The. Judith Wright. MAuV

Bull Calf, The. Irving Layton. InPK

Bull Fight, The. Byron. *Fr.* Childe Harold's Pilgrimage, I. LiSp

Bull Moose, The. Alden Nowlan. CABA (1972 ed.)

Bull-voiced young fellow of Pawling, A. Hog-Calling Competition. Morris Bishop. TDH

Bulldog on the Bank, The. *Unknown.* FSW

Bulleted Red is dead, now. The Secret of Seeds. Melvin Dixon. NW

Bullets splat downrange. On Teaching David to Shoot. Walter McDonald. AMV–80

Bullfinches, The. Thomas Hardy. PB

Bullfrog. Ted Hughes. RFM; TSWA

Bullfrog Blues. *Unknown.* BluL

Bullfrog in a Pond Not Far from an Abandoned Farm, A. Duane Locke. CSP

Bullocky. Judith Wright. MAuV

Bullocky Bill. *Unknown.* MAuV

Bull's Eye: the water cries out. Stone and the Obliging Pond. Felix Pollak. POL

Bully, A. *Malay Oral Tradition, tr. by* R. J. Wilkinson. WTO

Bully ship and a bully crew, A. Sacramento. *Unknown.* FSW

Bully Song, The, *with music.* Charles E. Trevathan. BLSo

Bumi. Amiri Baraka. PoBA

Bummer, A. Michael Casey. TSWA

Bumper Sticker, The, on His Pickup Said, "I'm a Lover, I'm a Fighter, I'm a Wild Bull Rider." Eldon Ray Fox. LiSp

Bumpity doun in the corrie gaed whuddran the pitiless whun stane. Sisyphus. Robert Garioch. MS

Bums are the spirit of us parked in ratty old hotels. Bowery. David Ignatow. CTBA; MiP

Bums, on Waking. James Dickey. TSWA

Bunch Grass #37. Robert Sund. NU

Bunch of golden keys is mine, A. Golden Keys. *Unknown.* CTV

Bunch of Grapes, The. George Herbert. AnMo

Bunches of Grapes. Walter de la Mare. LCL; OxBChV

Bundle of orange flames, A. Old Miniatures. Leo Vroman. VWA

Bungaloid Growth. Colin Ellis. FaBoEE

Bunker Hill, *with music.* Nathaniel Niles. BLSo
  (Why Should Vain Mortals Tremble.) AH

Bunky Boy Bunky Boy Who's My Little Bunky Boy. Larry Mollin. NeAC

Bunny. Christopher Fahy. TAT

Bunthorne's Song: The Aesthete. W. S. Gilbert. *Fr.* Patience. OAEL–2
  (Aesthete, The.) VLP

Buoy like a man in a red sou'wester, A. Beginning to Squall. May Swenson. RFM

Buoys begin clanging like churches. The River That Is East. Galway Kinnell. NYP

Burden of Decision, The. Peter Everwine. NNaP

Burden of Tyre, The, *sel.* Christopher Brennan.
  Epilogue: "O life, O radiance, love, delight." MAuV

Bureau of Labor Statistics, The. Bureaucratic Limerick. William Harmon. OBAL

Bureaucrat, The. Arthur J. Bull. HeHu

Bureaucratic Limerick. William Harmon. OBAL

Burglar, The. Sonya Dorman. SFF

Burglar, The. David Wagoner. CoPAm

Burglar came, jimmied a window, A. The Burglar. Sonya Dorman. SFF

Burglars stole my love story, The. Missing MS. Thulani Nkabinde. NW

Burgundy Phase. Ron Welburn. NW

Burial. Robert Francis. NCSH

Burial. May Sarton. GP

Burial, The. Mark Thalman. AMV–80

Burial. Hone Tuwhare. ATNZ

Burial. Alice Walker. AmPA; CSP; WBN

Burial Hour, The. Robert Stephen Hawker. VPC

Burial in the Country, A. Paul Clause. AATT

Burial of a Fisherman in Hydra. Grace Schulman. BoWoP

Burial of an Irish President. Austin Clarke. BIrV

Burial of Sir John Moore after [*or* at] Corunna, The. Charles Wolfe. BTTM; FaPoR; NOBE

Burial of the Linnet, The. Juliana Horatia Ewing. OxBChV

Burials. George Crabbe. *See* Parish Register, The.

Burials. Geoffrey Grigson. PoA

Buried beneath his poems, here lies. The Wandering Jew. Benjamin Fondane, *tr. by* Edouard Roditi. VWA

Buried Lake, The. Allen Tate. PiAm

Buried Life, The. Matthew Arnold. OAEL–2; PFD; VLP

Buried under a flat stone, but beside. Patty, 1949–1961. Sharon Mayer Libera. IHMS

Burke. Samuel Taylor Coleridge. *Fr.* Sonnets on Eminent Characters. MBPR

Burlesque of Lope De Vega. Samuel Johnson. FaBoCo
  (Burlesque Translation of Lines from Lope de Vega's "Arcadia.") EBEV
  (Deduction.) ECBV
  (Epigram: "If a man who turnips cries.") NOBL
  (Turnip Crier, The.) PoPle

Burlesque upon the Great Frost, *sel.* Charles Cotton.
  "Maid compelled to be a gadder, A." SCP–2

Burly, dozing humble-bee. The Humble-Bee. Emerson. FSFS; NOBA

Burn Down the Icons. Grace Schulman. GP

Burn drowns steadily in its own downpour, The. Waterfall. Seamus Heaney. NoAM

Burn me mellow. Basementmusic: The Love Affair. Angela Jackson. FiCh

Burn Ovid with the rest. Lovers will find. Penal Law. Austin Clarke. BoLoP; NoAM

Burn ran blacker for the snow, The. The Mountain. Andrew Young. MS

Burned Bridge, The. Ruth Stone. WPE

Burned in this element. Letter II. W. S. Graham. MS

Burned out by acid, some say. Indian. Martin Laarakker. PoW

Burnet's Character. *Unknown.* APAS

Burning. Galway Kinnell. CoPAm

Burning. Gary Snyder. *See* Myths and Texts.

Burning/ burning/ burning. Crow's Last Stand. Ted Hughes. InPS

Burning Babe, The. Robert Southwell. BoReV; CABA (1972 ed.); HAP; HeIP; ILP (1975 ed.); InPS; NIL; NOBE; OAEL–1; OBP; PPoe; Prf

Burning Love Letters. Howard Moss. HoPM (1975 ed.)

Burning of Paper Instead of Children, The. Adrienne Rich. PiAm

Burning of the Birds, The. Shirley Kaufman. GP

Burning of the Leaves, The. Laurence Binyon. FSFS; NOBE; OxBTC
  "Now is the time for the burning of the leaves," *sel.* PSN

Burning Oneself In. Adrienne Rich. NYP

Burning Sand of Sinai. Nelly Sachs, *tr. fr. German by* Keith Bosley. VWA

Burning the Christmas Greens. William Carlos Williams. NoAM; NOBA; PiAm; TT

Burning the Letters. Gwendolyn Grew. HoPM (1975 ed.)

Burning the Letters. Randall Jarrell. CoPAm

Burning the Small Dead. Gary Snyder. CAPP; NNaP

Burning the Tomato Worms. Carolyn Forché. AmPA

Burning with zeal, whole villages. Theologia Germanica. David Malouf. CAAP

Burnished, burned-out, still burning as the year. The Public Garden. Robert Lowell. ILP (1975 ed.); TAP

Burnished silver mask hangs in white air, The. On a Celtic Mask by Henry Moore. Horace Gregory. PoA

Burns. Sandra Hoben. TV

Burnt. Boris Slutsky, tr. fr. Russian by Daniel Weissbort. VWA

Burnt Bush, The. Jack R. Clemo. FaBoTw (1975 ed.)

Burnt Debris. Thomas Sessler, tr. fr. German by Herbert Kuhner. VWA

Burnt Norton. T. S. Eliot. Fr. Four Quartets. CMoP (1970 ed.); HeIP; ILP (1975 ed.)

Burnt Ship, A. John Donne. EBEV; InPK

Burrowing deep into the earth until the grave is complete. Wolf. Peter Blue Cloud. VoR

Burst, A/ of confidence. Confiding. Answering. Robert Duncan. PiAm

Burst of iris so that, A. Iris. William Carlos Williams. InPS; WeW

Burst of steam from the pipes in the morning startles me, A. The Two of Cups. Emmett Jarrett. NeAC

Bury him deep, down deep. Cat's Funeral. E. V. Rieu. ECBV

Bury Me beneath the Willow. Unknown. FSW

Bury Me in a Free Land. Frances E. W. Harper. BPo

Bury Me Not on the Lone Prairie. Unknown. See O Bury Me Not on the Lone Prairie.

Bury Me Out on the Prairie. Unknown. BPAW

Bury Our Faces. Bob Millard. AMV-80

Bury the Great Duke. Ode on the Death of the Duke of Wellington. Tennyson. VLP

Bury this old Illinois farmer with respect. Illinois Farmer. Carl Sandburg. ANTL

Bury your heart in some deep green hollow. Saturday Market. Charlotte Mew. WPE

Burying Blues for Janis. Marge Piercy. NeAC; WBN

Burying Ground by the Ties. Archibald MacLeish. Frescoes for Mr. Rockefeller's City, III. GOA

Bus, The. Leonard Cohen. HeIP

Bus Ride. Lenore Kandel. NMM

Bus Stop. Donald Justice. TCP

Bush, a gathering smoke, The. Blackthorn. Euros Bowen, tr. by author. OBW

Bush Section, A, sel. B. E. Baughan. "Logs, at the door, by the fence." ATNZ

Bush was on that dump, A. The Burnt Bush. Jack R. Clemo. FaBoTw (1975 ed.)

Bushed. Earle Birney. MPA

Bushes quiver. Shivers. Aileen Fisher. CaYB

Bushfeller, The. Eileen Duggan. ATNZ

Bushrangers, The. Edward Harrington. PoTa

Busie old foole, unruly Sunne. See Busy old fool, unruly Sun.

Business, The. Robert Creeley. CAPP

Business Life, The. David Ignatow. NNaP

Business of Living, The. Ryah Tumarkin Goodman. AAN

Business of the lambing ewes would make me, The. Eagles over the Lambing Paddock. Ernest Moll. MAuV

Business Trips. Laurie Taylor. AMV-80

Busses are bright yellow and have brought, The. The Dream about Junior High School in America. Dick Lourie. NeAC

Buster Keaton. Michael McFee. AMV-81

Bustin' down the canyon. Billy the Kid or William H. Bonney. N. Howard Thorp. BPAW

Bustle in a house, The. Emily Dickinson. HAP; HeIP; IPWM

Busy, curious, thirsty fly. The Fly. William Oldys. PAIC

Busy in study be thou, child. Demeanour. Unknown. OxBChV

Busy Man Speaks, A. Robert Bly. ConAP

Busy [or Busie] old fool, unruly sun. The Sun [or Sunne] Rising. John Donne. AnMo; BiP; BoLoP; CABA (1972 ed.); ExPo (1973 ed.); FF; GBL; HAP; HeIP; ILP (1975 ed.); InPS; IPWM; MetP; NIL; NOBE; OAEL-1; PoPle; PPP; SCP-1; SoSe; TT

Busy with love, the bumble bee. Meleager, tr. fr. Greek by Peter Whigham. BoLoP

But/ he" i/ staring. E. E. Cummings. NoAM

But ae braithless note. Sydney Goodsir Smith, after the French of Tristan Corbière. Fr. The Gangrel Rymour and the Pairdon of Sanct Anne. OBVE

But afar on the headland exalted. Swinburne. By the North Sea, VII. VLP

But are these landscapes to be imagined. Letters to Walt Whitman, IX. Ronald Johnson. VGW

But as she sat allone and thoughte thus. Criseyde Sees Troilus Return from Battle. Chaucer. Fr. Troilus and Criseyde, II. OxBM

But black is the colour of my true love's hair. Black Is the Colour. Unknown. GBP

But do not let us quarrel any more. Andrea del Sarto. Robert Browning. CABA (1972 ed.); ILP (1975 ed.); OAEL-2; SoSe (1977 ed.); TT; VLP

But ere sterne conflict mixt both strengths, faire Paris stept before. Homer, tr. by George Chapman. Fr. The Iliad, III. OBVE

But for a brief/ Moment, a poised minute. A Grasshopper. Richard Wilbur. CoPAm; HAP; HoPM (1975 ed.)

But for Lust. Ruth Pitter. FaBoTw (1975 ed.); OxBTC

But for the steady wash of rain. No Country You Remember. Robert Mezey. FF

But for whom do I look? The Search. John Logan. FoP

But for your Terror. To Death. Oliver St. John Gogarty. FaBoEE

But He Was Cool; or, He Even Stopped for Green Lights. Don L. Lee. AmNP (1974 ed.); BPo; NoAM; PoBA

But Her Eyes Spoke Another Language. William Duncan. PMW

But how shall we this union well express? The Soul and the Body. Sir John Davies. Fr. Nosce Teipsum. NOBE

But I Am Growing Old and Indolent. Robinson Jeffers. ILP (1975 ed.); NoAM; NOBA; TAP

But I Do Not Need Kindness. Gregory Corso. CoPAm; VoA

But I knew it: a verse is a magic helmet. The Seven-League Boots. Ilarie Voronca, tr. by Willis Barnstone and Matei Calinescu. VWA

But I was dead, an hour or more. Escape. Robert Graves. ILP (1975 ed.)

But if I look the ice is gone from the lake. Spring of the Thief. John Logan. BiP; CAPP; NNaP

But if I were a dandelion weed. It's True I'm No Miss America. Stephanie Slowinsky. AMV-80

But in that darkness trees and animals. A Blind Wish for Randall Jarrell. Gibbons Ruark. CSP

But in the crowding darkness not a word did they say. The Old-Marrieds. Gwendolyn Brooks. AmNP (1974 ed.); PoBA

But in the end one tires of the high-flown. About the Phoenix. James Merrill. NoAM

But it could never be true. Devil's Dream. Kenneth Fearing. SPT

But it starts with the picture of my grandfather. The Cloud Unfolding. Ernesto Trejo. CPA

But, John, have you seen the world, said he. Angle of Vision. Robert Rendall. OxBTC

But, knowing now that they would have her speak. The Defence of Guenevere. William Morris. PAIC; VLP; VPC

But let my due feet never fail. Milton. *Fr.* Il Penseroso. SCP-1

But, lo! from forth a copse that neighbours by. Courser and Jennet. Shakespeare. *Fr.* Venus and Adonis. NOBE; PH; PoPle

But man finds means, grant him but place and room. Sonnet. Frederick Goddard Tuckerman. *Fr.* Sonnets. PiAm

But most by numbers judge a poet's song. Pope. *Fr.* An Essay on Criticism. HAP; NIL; WIF

But nearer night than you, my younger. Solomon and Morolph, Their last Encounter. Oscar Levertin, *tr. by* Richard Burns *and* Göran Printz-Pahlson. VWA

But no, the familiar symbol, as that the/ curtain. Time in the Rock, XCII. Conrad Aiken. VGW

But Not Forgotten. Luci Shaw. AATT

But now at thirty years my hair is grey. Growing Old. Byron. *Fr.* Don Juan, I. NOBE

But now lead on. Milton. *Fr.* Paradise Lost, XII. UsP

But now, no longer deaf to honour's call. Homer, *tr. by* Pope. *Fr.* The Iliad, VI. OBVE

But now the wholesome music of the wood. Vivien's Song. Tennyson. *Fr.* Idylls of the King. OAEL-2

But of all the plagues, the greatest is untold. Juvenal, *tr. fr. Latin by* Dryden. *Fr.* Satires, VI. OBSV

But once, oh God, a song comes from my lips. Of the Sea, a Song. E. A. Fielder. RhR

But Perhaps. Nelly Sachs, *tr. fr. German by* Ruth *and* Matthew Mead. BoWoP

But pitie which sometimes doth lyons move. Parthenophil and Parthenophe, XXXVII. Barnabe Barnes. ESo

But please walk softly as you do. Enter This Deserted House. Shel Silverstein. IWK

But pretty though as/ roses is. Three Sayings from Highlands, North Carolina. Jonathan Williams. OBAL

But see here comes they reverend Sire. Milton. *Fr.* Samson Agonistes. EBEV

But she had seen the cattle drop their young. The Birthing. Beth Bentley. LoAs

But, sires, o word forgat I in my tale. Chaucer. *Fr.* The Canterbury Tales: The Pardoner's Tale. EBEV

But, soft! What light through yonder window breaks. Shakespeare. *Fr.* Romeo and Juliet, II, ii. Moon

But some one will ask, "How are the dead raised?" Bible, *N.T. Fr.* First Corinthians. DL

But, Still, He. Henry N. Lucas. AMV-81

"But Still in Israel's Paths They Shine." Carter Revard. VoR

But still the thunder of Los peals loud and thus the thunder's cry. Blake. *Fr.* Jerusalem. OAEL-2

But That Is Another Story. Donald Justice. CoPAm

"But that was nothing to what things came out." Welsh Incident. Robert Graves. CMoP (1970 ed.); NOBE; OxBTC

But the Captain is drunk, and the crew. "I Am the Captain of My Soul." Gwen Harwood. GAS

But the kitten, how she starts. Wordsworth. *Fr.* The Kitten and Falling Leaves. PCat

But the last black horse of all. The Last Ones. Robin Hyde. ATNZ

But the light returns. Dreams. André Breton, *tr. by* Robert Duncan. InPS

But the whole thing is a miracle. Black Power. Nikki Giovanni. Psy

But Then. Ben King. PoTa

But Then and There the Sun Bore Down. N. Scott Momaday. CDW

But they're crazy, I'm telling you. Those Zionists. Crescenzo del Monte, *tr. by* Barbara Garvin. VWA

But this, so feminine? Donald Davie. *Fr.* The Forests of Lithuania. OxBTC

But thou my deere sweet-sounding lute be still. Diella, XVI. Richard Lynche. AAS

But to reach the archimedean point. "Mysticism Has Not the Patience to Wait for God's Revelation." Richard Eberhart. NoAM

But to see now how strangely things sometimes turn out. "Thomas Ingoldsby." *Fr.* A Lay of St. Gengulphus. VLP

But Venus first. Sister Juana Ines de la Cruz, *tr. by* Samuel Beckett. *Fr.* First Dream. BoWoP

But was the language alive? The Test. Robert Friend. GP

But what does it mean? this harmonica. What Does It Mean? This Harmonica. Virginia Gilbert. NVAP

But What I'm Trying to Say Mother Is. Ai. CAAP

But when I looked further. Maps to Nowhere. David Rosenberg. VWA

But when I waked, I saw that I saw not. A Storm at Sea. John Donne. *Fr.* The Storm. NOBE; PoPle

But when it was my turn to wrestle with the angel. Under the Ladder to Heaven. Elizabeth Fenton. NMM

But when the golden-thron'd Aurora made. *Unknown, formerly at. to* Homer; *tr. by* Congreve. *Fr.* The Hymn to Venus. OBVE

But when the next day brake from under ground. Percivale's Quest. Tennyson. *Fr.* Idylls of the King. OAEL-2

But who tipped the sand out of your shoes. Burning Sand of Sinai. Nelly Sachs, *tr. by* Keith Bosley. VWA

But why,/ O fatal Time. George Wither. *Fr.* Rhomboidal Dirge. SCP-2

"But why do you go?" said the lady, while both sate under the yew. Lord Walter's Wife. Elizabeth Barrett Browning. HAP

But You, My Darling, Should Have Married the Prince. Kathleen Spivack. AmPA; NMM

But you, Thomas Jefferson. Brave New World. Archibald MacLeish. NOBA; OFD

"But, you're so/ different," they said of. The Photograph the Cat Licks. Beatrice Walter. NMM

Butch Weldy. Edgar Lee Masters. *Fr.* Spoon River Anthology. PSN

Butcher, A. Thomas Hood. BBL

Butcher, The. Hugo Williams. OxBTC

Butcher, a bald guy, The. Kicking from Centre Field. David McFadden. NeAC

Butcherboy. Tom Schmidt. NeAC

Butcher Boy, The. *Unknown.* AmFP
(Butcher's Boy, The.) FSW

Butcher carves veal for two, The. The Butcher. Hugo Williams. OxBTC

Butcher loved our French maid, The. Movement in Provence. Peter Trias. AAN

Butcher Shop. Charles Simic. AmPA; NNaP; NVAP; PCho

Butcher's Boy, The. *Unknown. See* Butcher Boy, The.

Butcher's Dream. Herbert Scott. TC

Butcher's Wife. Herbert Scott. GP

Buteo Regalis. N. Scott Momaday. VW

Butter. Tom Schmidt. NeAC

Buttercup. Mary Mapes Dodge. ECBV

Buttercup is like a golden cup, The. Golden Glories. Christina Rossetti. PF

Buttercup nodded and said good-bye. August. Celia Laighton Thaxter. CTV

Buttercups. Dolly Radford. PCOP

Buttercups and Daisies.  Mary Howitt.  OxBChV

Butterflies.  Haniel Long.  PCOP

Butterflies.  Clive Sansom.  BoAnP

Butterflies flutter and flit o'er the bay.  Unique among Girls.
  *Malay Oral Tradition, tr. by* R. J. Wilkinson *and* R. O.
  Winstedt.  WTO

Butterflies on an Illinois Road.  Helena Minton.  FAF

Butterfly, The.  Pavel Friedmann, *tr. fr. Czech by* Dennis Silk.
  VWA

Butterfly, a cabbage-white, The.  Flying Crooked.  Robert
  Graves.  UsP

Butterfly, butterfly, butterfly, butterfly.  Butterfly Song.  *Tr. by*
  Frances Densmore.  OBVE

Butterfly in the Fields.  Joseph Campbell.  BoAnP; PFIr

Butterfly maidens.  Lahpu, *tr. fr. Hopi Indian by* Natalie Curtis.
  WTO

Butterfly Song.  *Tr. fr. Acoman Indian by* Frances Densmore.
  OBVE

Butterfly the ancient Grecians made, The.  Psyche.  Samuel
  Taylor Coleridge.  MBPR; PBMP

Butterfly's Ball, The.  William Roscoe.  OxBChV

Butterfly's Ball and the Grasshopper's Feasts, The.  The Peacock
  "At Home."  Catherine Ann Dorset.  OxBChV

Buttermilk Hill.  *Unknown.*  FSW

Buttons.  Walter de la Mare.  FaBoNo

Buttons.  *Unknown.*  CTV

Buy me an ounce and I'll sell you a pound.  E. E. Cummings.
  NCSH

Buy One Now.  D. J. Enright.  NOBL

Buy the paper, take it home.  Coming and Going.  Mitchell
  Goodman.  VGW

Buying a Shop on Dizengoff.  Erez Biton, *tr. fr. Hebrew by* Judith
  Katz.  VWA

Buying Lilies.  Stephen Stepanchev.  SA

Buying wood from Mrs. Lalo Roybal.  Manly Diversion.  Karl
  Kopp.  GP

Buzz.  Jim Tollerud.  VoR

Buzz, quoth the blue fly.  Song of the Satyrs [*or* Elves' Song *or*
  The Satyrs' Catch].  Ben Jonson.  *Fr.* Oberon, the Fairy
  Prince.  BBL; FaBoNo; PoPle

Buzz saw snarled and rattled in the yard, The.  "Out, Out."
  Robert Frost.  AnMo; BuTh; CABA (1972 ed.); DL; FF;
  HAP; ILP (1975 ed.); IP; MiP; NowV; PiAm; PPoe; SoSe;
  TT; UnPo (1976 ed.); VGW; WeW; WIF

Buzzard.  Leslie Norris.  HeHu

Buzzard finds no fault with itself, A.  In Praise of a Guilty
  Conscience.  Wislawa Szymborska, *tr. by* Grazyna Drabik *and*
  Austin Flint.  AMV-81

Buzzing Doubt, The.  Donald L. Hill.  NCSH

Bwagamoyo.  Lebert Bethune.  PoBA

Bwoat, The.  William Barnes.  VLP

By/ birds/ bird flocks.  Divination.  Jerred Metz.  VWA

By a Chapel as I Came.  *Unknown.*  GBP; OxBM

By a flat rock on the shore of the sea.  The Rock.  *Unknown, tr.
  by* Geoffrey Grigson.  GBL

By a forrest as I gan fare.  The Hare.  *Unknown.*  OxBM

By a route obscure and lonely.  Dream-Land.  Poe.  NOBA;
  TAP

By a window in the west.  The Weaver.  John Haines.  MPA

By all the laws.  The Tree Is Father to the Man.  Lou Lipsitz.
  NCSH

By all the published facts in the case.  About Children.  Phyllis
  McGinley.  OBAL

By an alley lined with tumble-down shacks.  Mexican Quarter.
  John Gould Fletcher.  Arizona Poems, II.  BPAW

By and By.  *Unknown.*  FSW

By and by/ God caught his eye.  Epitaph on a Waiter.  David
  McCord.  OBAL

By Babel's Streams, *with music.*  Philip Freneau.  AH

By blind meanders and by crankled ways.  Thomas Nashe.  *Fr.*
  The Choice of Valentines; or, The Merry Ballad of Nashe His
  Dildo.  SCP-2

By Blue Ontario's Shore, *sels.*  Walt Whitman.
  "I swear I begin to see the meaning of these things!"  *fr.* XV.
    (Marches Now the War Is Over.)  InPS
  "I will confront these shows of the day and the night!"  *fr.*
    XVIII.
    (Marches Now the War Is Over.)  InPS
  "Rhymes and rhymers pass away,"  *fr.* XIII.
    (Marches Now the War Is Over.)  InPS

By Candlelight.  Sylvia Plath.  SBG

By constantly tormenting them.  The Poor.  William Carlos
  Williams.  TT

By dark severance the apparition head.  Painted Head.  John
  Crowe Ransom.  NoAM; NOBA; PiAm

By day she woos me, soft, exceeding fair.  The World.  Christina
  Rossetti.  BoWoP; VLP

By day the bat is cousin to the mouse.  The Bat.  Theodore
  Roethke.  ECBV; IWK; RAE; SoS

By day your high gates are closed.  Seal of Fire.  Mordecai
  Temkin, *tr. by* Jeremy Garber.  VWA

By Derwent's side my father's cottage stood.  The Female
  Vagrant.  Wordsworth.  MBPR

By dint of color.  A Dab of Color.  Theodore Weiss.  VGW

By dream or blood transfusion they are recovered.  Evocations.
  Kenyon Alexander.  PMW

By easy slope to west as if it had.  Cheyenne Mountain.  Helen
  Hunt Jackson.  BPAW

By fate, not option, frugal Nature gave.  Xenophanes.  Emerson.
  NOBA

By Ferry to the Island.  Iain Crichton Smith.  MPo

By Frazier Creek Falls.  Gary Snyder.  CNW; GOA

By Hallucination Visited.  Robert Horan.  EAS

By Her Aunt's Grave.  Thomas Hardy.  Satires of Circumstance,
  III.  LFH; SFF

By Heraclides.  *Unknown, tr. fr. Greek by* William Cowper.
  OBVE

By his commandement hee maketh the snow to fall apace.  Bible,
  *Apocrypha.  Fr.* Ecclesiasticus.  OBVE

By landscape reminded once of his mother's figure.  Prologue.
  W. H. Auden.  NoAM

By leave of my eyes that watched the bereaving.  Pledge.
  Avraham Shlonsky, *tr. by* Francis Landy.  VWA

By Loe Pool.  Arthur Symons.  VLP

By love was my eye opened.  How Beautiful You Are: 3.  Elaine
  Edelman.  IHMS

By mid-century there were two quaggas left.  The Quagga.  D. J.
  Enright.  MPo

By mid-day it was warm enough; she climbed.  Aunt Alice in
  April.  William H. Matchett.  CTBA

By nature shy, by nature.  Whispering Clouds.  Mariquita Platov.
  AMV-80

By Night.  Robert Francis.  POL; VGW

By night they haunted a thicket of April mist.  Spectral Lovers.
  John Crowe Ransom.  GBL; HeIP; LoAs; PiAm

By night we lingered on the lawn.  Tennyson.  In Memoriam A.
  H. H., XCV.  HAP

By none but me can the tale be told.  The White Ship.  Dante
  Gabriel Rossetti.  VLP

By now you will have met.  Voice.  W. S. Merwin.  NNaP

By numbers here from shame or censure free.  Samuel Johnson.
  *Fr.* London: A Poem in Imitation of the Third Satire of
  Juvenal.  OBSV

By our first strange and fatal interview. On His Mistress [or Elegy on His Mistress]. John Donne. Elegies, XVI. BoLoP; EBEV; GBL; NOBE; OBP

By pain of stone and wearing down of bronze. Upon This Rock. Ruthven Todd. PoA

By proud New York and its man-piled Matterhorns. Proud New York. John Reed. PoA

By Rail through Istria. Robert Conquest. NoAM

By Rail through the Earthly Paradise, Perhaps Bedfordshire. Denise Levertov. NNaP

By rays sharper than the sharpest angle. Noon Glare. Matthew Brennan. AMV-80

By Saint [or Saynt] Mary, my lady. To Mistress [or Maystres] Isabel Pennell. John Skelton. Fr. The Garlande of Laurell. AAS; NOBE; RRA

By snails, by leaps of frog, I came here, spirit. Unfold! Unfold! Theodore Roethke. STS

By some derision of wild circumstance. Reunion. E. A. Robinson. NoAM; NOBA

By sundown we came to a hidden village. Conquerors. Henry Treece. MPo; OBW

By that dejected city, Arno runs. To My Daughter. Walter Savage Landor. RRA

By that withering oak. Daybreak. Frank Lamont Phillips. CNA

By the banks of the roses my love and I sat down. Banks of the Roses. Unknown. FSW

By the Bivouac's Fitful Flame. Walt Whitman. NoAM

By the blue tapers trembling light. A Night-Piece on Death. Thomas Parnell. EPC

By the blue wooden sea. Switchback. Edith Sitwell. PBWP

By the city dead-house by the gate. The City Dead-House. Walt Whitman. InPK

By the Denali road, facing. Denali Road. John Haines. PPoD

By the dry road the fathers cough and spit. The Brief Journey West. Howard Nemerov. NoAM

By the Exeter River. Donald Hall. AIW; MPo

By the fierce flames of love I'm in a sad taking. A Love Song. Royall Tyler. TAP

By the Fire-Side. Robert Browning. OAEL-2; VLP

By the flow of the inland river. The Blue and the Gray. Francis Miles Finch. BTTM

By the gas-fire, kneeling. Olga Poems. Denise Levertov. NNaP

By the gate with star and moon. Medallion. Sylvia Plath. HeIP

By the high steel hospital bed. Miss Alderman. Robert Winner. GP

By the highway the stream downslope. Runoff. A. R. Ammons. PPP

By the huge dead yards. Harlem River. Herman Spector. SPT

By the impulse of my will. Magnetism. Emma Lazarus. SBG

By the Isar, in the twilight. River Roses. D. H. Lawrence. CMoP (1970 ed.); GBL; OAEL-2

By the margin of the ocean, one pleasant evening in the month of June. The Bonny Bunch of Roses. Unknown. FaBoBa

By the new Boot's, a tool-chest with flagpoles. Aberdarcy: The Main Square. Kingsley Amis. NOBL; OxBTC

By the newly bulldozed logging road, for a hundred yards. Working against Time. David Wagoner. MAT

By the North Gate, the wind blows full of sand. Lament of the Frontier Guard. Li Po, tr. by Ezra Pound. OBVE; PiAm; VGW

By the North Sea, sels. Swinburne. VLP
   "But afar on the headland exalted," VII.
   "Land that is lonelier than ruin, A," I.

By the old bridge in flaring sunlight. In Brisbane. Gwen Harwood. GAS ·

By the old Moulmein Pagoda, lookin' lazy at the sea. Mandalay. Kipling. NOBE; PBMP

By the pale marge of Acheron. Villanelle of Acheron. Ernest Dowson. VLP

By the Pool. Allen Grossman. AMV-80

By the Pool at the Third Rosses. Arthur Symons. In Ireland, II. VLP

By the public hook for the private eye. River Song. Weldon Kees. NoAM; PPP

By the river/ they built huts. Dream Songs of Haka Ancestors. Alan Chong Lau. NW

By the River Ashley, sel. Mary Ursula Bethell.
   "Hour is dark, The. The river comes to its end." ATNZ

By the rivers [or waters] of Babylon [or Babel], there we sat down. Bible, O.T. Psalms, CXXXVII. ExPo (1973 ed.); NAWM-1; OAEL-1, 2 versions; OBVE

By the Riverside. Carolyn Kizer. CNW

By the Road. Geoffrey Grigson. OxBTC

By the road to the contagious hospital. Spring and All. William Carlos Williams. CABA (1972 ed.); CMoP (1970 ed.); ExPo (1973 ed.); HAP; NoAM; NOBA; PiAm; PPoe; PSN; TAP; TCP; UnPo (1976 ed.); UsP

By the roots of my hair some god got hold of me. The Hanging Man. Sylvia Plath. NIL

By the rude bridge that arched the flood. Concord Hymn. Emerson. AmVN; BTTM; CTV; ExPo (1973 ed.); FaPo; FaPoR; GOA; HAP; HeIP; NOBA; PPoD; TAP

By the sad waters of separation. Exile. Ernest Dowson. BoLoP

By the Saltings. Ted Walker. EcS

By the sand between my toes. Summer Song. John Ciardi. ECBV

By the sands of Rio Bravo. The Smugglers. Owen Wister. BPAW

By the Sea. Christina Rossetti. EcS

By the secret that holds the forest up. Reporting Back. William Stafford. CoPAm

By the shore [or shores] of Gitche Gumee. Old Nokomis Sings. Longfellow. Fr. The Song of Hiawatha. CTV; ECBV; SpRo

By the side of a murmuring stream an elderly gentleman sat. The Elderly Gentleman. George Canning. ECBV

By the Statue of King Charles at Charing Cross. Lionel Johnson. NOBE; VLP

By the Swimming. Robert Sward. SPo

By the time you read this. Letter. W. S. Merwin. HAP

By the time you swear you're his. Unfortunate Coincidence. Dorothy Parker. PoIA; SBG

By the wall o'the gearden, a-stannen chalk white. Black an' White. William Barnes. VLP

By the Waters of Babylon. Benjamin Fondane, tr. fr. French by Edouard Roditi. VWA

By the Waters of Babylon, sels. Emma Lazarus.
   Currents. WPE
   Exodus, The (August 3, 1492). WPE

By the waters of Babylon we sat down and wept. Super Flumina Babylonis. Swinburne. VLP

By the waters of Babylon we sat downe and weapte. Bible, O.T. See By the rivers of Babylon, there we sat down.

By the Waters of Minnetonka, with music. J. M. Cavanass. BLSo

By the wells. Zippora Returns to Moses at Rephidim. Rose Drachler. VWA

By thine own tears they song must tears beget. The Song-Throe. Dante Gabriel Rossetti. The House of Life, LXI. VLP

By this cold shuddering fit of fear. The Glen of Silence. "Hugh MacDiarmid." CMoP (1970 ed.)

By this he knew she wept with waking eyes. Modern Love, I. George Meredith. Epi; HeIP; ILP (1975 ed.); LoAs; NIL; OAEL-2; PAIC; PBMP; VLP; VPC

By this, Leander, being near the land. Christopher Marlowe. *Fr.* Hero and Leander, Second Sestiad. EBEV

By this low fire I often sit to woo. Frederick Goddard Tuckerman. *Fr.* Sonnets. AmVN

By this the dreadful beast drew nigh to hand. Spenser. *Fr.* The Faerie Queene, I, ll. LFH

By this time long-gowned Lumen walked abroad. William Rankins. *Fr.* Satyrus Peregrinans. OBSV

By those soft tods of wool. A Conjuration, to Electra. Robert Herrick. GBL

By turning to you. They End It. Dave Morice. AcAn

By two black eyes my heart was won. Rondeau. *Unknown.* FaBoCo

By Vows of Love Together Bound, *with music.* Eleazar Thompson Fitch. AH

By Wauchopeside. "Hugh MacDiarmid." EBEV

By Way of Preface. Edward Lear. *See* How Pleasant to Know Mr. Lear.

By what appalling dim upheaval. Simon Gerty. Elinor Wylie. OBAL

By what sends. Children's Rhymes. Langston Hughes. BPo

By Winter Seas. George Brandon Saul. AMV-80

By yon bonnie banks, and by yon bonnie braes. Loch Lomond. *Unknown.* BLSH; FSW; GSB

By yonder flowing fountain. A La Claire Fontaine (By Yonder Flowing Fountain). *Tr. fr.* French by Arthur Kevess. FSW

By your breasts. Conversation between the Chevalier de Chamilly and Mariana Alcoforado in the Manner of a Song of Regret. The Three Marias, *tr. by* Helen R. Lane. BoWoP

By your unnumbered charities. Hospital for Defectives. Thomas Blackburn. OxBTC

Bye baby bunting. Rhyme for Astronomical Baby. Joseph Cook. QQQ; SpRo

Bye, baby bunting./ Daddy's gone a-hunting. Mother Goose. MG; SpRo

Bye Bye Baby Blues. *Unknown.* BluL

Byre. Norman MacCaig. BoAnP; MS

Byrnies, The. Thom Gunn. NoAM; OxBTC

Byron. J. Gordon Coogler. OBAL

Byron! how sweetly sad thy melody! To Lord Byron. Keats. MBPR

Byron vs. DiMaggio. Peter Meinke. LiSp; SPo

Byron's Address to the Ocean. Byron. *Fr.* Childe Harold's Pilgrimage, IV. RhR ("Roll on, thou deep and dark blue Ocean—roll!") EcS

By's beard the Goat, by his bush-tail the Fox. Of Kate's Baldness. John Davies of Hereford. FaBoEE

Bystander, The. Rosemary Dobson. GAS

Bytuene Mersh [*or* Betwene March] and Averil. Alysoun. *Unknown.* HAP; HeIP; OAEL-1; OxBM

Byways in Biography. Maurice Hare. BBL

Byzantium. W. B. Yeats. CABA (1972 ed.); CMoP (1970 ed.); EBEV; HAP; ILP (1975 ed.); InPS; NIL: NoAm; NOBE; OAEL-2; OxBTC; PPP; STS; UsP

# C

C44. Karen L. Kent. NPW

C is for Curious Charlie. Curious Charlie. Isabel Frances Bellows. TDH

C. L. M. John Masefield. OxBTC

C Stands for Civilization. Kenneth Fearing. SPT

C was papa's gray cat. Edward Lear. PCat

Cabaret lice with clever eyes and loose sucking mouths. A Wreath for Our Murdered Comrade Kobayashi. Michael Gold. SPT

Cabbages catch at the moon. Nocturn Cabbage. Carl Sandburg. DuDa

Cabdriver's Smile, The. Denise Levertov. NYP

Cabin Creek Flood, The. *Unknown.* AmFP

Cabin in Minnesota, A. Marvin Bell. HoPM (1975 ed.)

Cabin in the Clearing, A. Robert Frost. PiAm

Cabin North of It All, The. James McMichael. AmPA

Cable cars swing up the hill, The. San Francisco. Mary Austin. BPAW

Cable Hymn, The. Whittier. PiAm

Cables entangling her. She Is Far from the Land. Thomas Hood. FaBoNo

Caboose Thoughts. Carl Sandburg. CMoP (1970 ed.)

Cackling, smelling of camphor, crumbs of pink icing. Muse. David Wagoner. PoA

Cactus Stem. Clinton F. Larson. MPA

Cactus Tree. Joni Mitchell. GrRo

Cactuses, The. Hubert Witheford. ATNZ

Cadaver. John Stone. CoPAm

Cadenza. Ted Hughes. CMoP (1970 ed.)

Caedmon. Norman Nicholson. FaBoTw (1975 ed.)

Caedmon's Hymn. Caedmon. *tr. fr. Anglo-Saxon.* EBEV, *tr. by* Sally Purcell; OAEL-1

Caelica, *sels.* Fulke Greville.
"Caelica, I overnight was finely used." AAS
"Caelica, when I did see you every day." AAS
"Cynthia, because your horns look diverse ways." Moon
"Downe in the depth of mine iniquity." PPoe
"Earth with thunder torne, with fire blasted, The." AAS
"Farewell sweet boy, complain not of my truth." GBL
Golden Age Was When the World Was Young, The. NIL; OAEL-1
"I offer wrong to my beloved saint." PAIC
"I, with whose colours Myra dress'd her head." GBL; HAP (Myra.) NOBE; PoPle
"In night when colours all to blacke are cast." AAS; OAEL-1
"Love is the peace, whereto all thoughts doe strive." AAS
"Man, dream no more of curious mysteries." (Vain Learning.) BoReV
"Merlin, they say, an English prophet borne." OBP
"Nurse-life wheat within his greene huske growing, The." AAS; PAIC
"O false and treacherous Probability." AAS
"When all this All doth pass from age to age." EBEV
"Whenas man's life, the light of human lust." SCP-2 (Memento Mori.) BoReV
"World, that all contains, is ever moving, The." NIL

Caelius, my Lesbia, that one, that only Lesbia. Catullus, *tr. fr. Latin by* Horace Gregory. NAWM-1

Caernarfon, 2 July 1969. T. Glynne Davies, *tr. fr. Welsh by* Joseph P. Clancy. OBW

Caesar. W. S. Merwin. PPoD

Ceasar and the Blind Men. Ettore Rella. SPT

Caesar is dead, and cannot see the sun. Nominis Umbra. J. A. R. McKellar. MAuV

Cafe in Warsaw. Allen Ginsberg. HAP; TT

Cage, The. John Berryman. PoA

Cage, The. George Garrett. SS

Cage, The. David Gascoyne. EAS

Cage, The. John Montague. CIP; IPM

Cage, The. James Stephens. OxBTC

Cage, The. Avner Treinin, *tr. fr. Hebrew by* A. C. Jacobs. VWA

Caged back of iron grilles. Maiden Lane. Al Lee. NYP

Caged Rats. Ebenezer Elliott. EBEV; VLP

Caged Skylark, The. Gerard Manley Hopkins. AnMo; CMoP (1970 ed.); ILP (1975 ed.); SoSe

Cages. Jane Kenyon. TC

Cain, *sel.* Byron.
Prayer of Abel, The. PIM

Cain's eyes are not gracious to God. Abel. Else Lasker-Schüler, *tr. by* Joachim Neugroschel. VWA

Cain's Song. Donald Finkel. VWA

Caint call your name. The Hermit Cackleberry Brown, on Human Vanity. Jonathan Williams. OBAL

Cairo Hotel. J. R. Rowland. MAuV

Caissons Go Rolling Along, The. Edmund L. Gruber. BLSo, *with music*; BTTM

Calais, August, 1802. Wordsworth. MBPR

Calais, August 15, 1802. Wordsworth. MBPR

Calamiterror, *sel.* George Barker.
"Meandering abroad in the Lincolnshire meadows day," VI. EAS

Calamity Jane Greets Her Dreams. Kathleen Lignell. AMV–80

Calamity of seals begins with jaws, The. Seals at High Island. Richard Murphy. CIP

Calculating Female. Jill Hellyer. POL

Caldwell of Springfield. Bret Harte. BTTM

Caledonia. Anthony Powell. NOBL

Calendar. Cecil Bodker, *tr. fr. Danish by* Nadia Christensen *and* Alexander Taylor. BoWoP

Calendar, The. John Haines. MPA

Calf came two days ago, The. The New Calf. Frances Downing Vaughan. AMV–80

Caliban in the Coal Mines. Louis Untermeyer. SoS

Caliban upon Setebos; or, Natural Theology in the Island. Robert Browning. EBEV; OAEL–2; VLP

Calico Pie. Edward Lear. BBL; LCL; PCOP; RAE

Calidore. Keats. MBPR

California. Joseph Philip Robson. VLP

California Gold Rush. Karoniaktatie. NW

California Idyl, A. Ernest McGaffey. BPAW

California #2. Victor Hernández Cruz. TAT

California Oaks, The. Yvor Winters. GOA; MPA

California Phrasebook, The. Dennis Schmitz. AmPA

California, This Is Minnesota Speaking. Stephen Dunn. GP

California Winter. Karl Shapiro. MPA

Californian, The. *Unknown.* AmFP

Californy Stage. *Unknown.* BPAW

Call, The. Jules Supervielle, *tr. fr. French by* Geoffrey Gardner. NU

Call across the Valley of Not Knowing, The, *sel.* Galway Kinnell. "Of that time in a Southern jail." GP

Call down the hawk from the air. The Hawk. W. B. Yeats. LFH; PoA

Call for a Song, A. *Unknown.* OxBM

Call for the Robin Redbreast and the Wren. John Webster. *Fr.* The White Devil, V, iv. EBEV; HAP; HeIP; ILP (1975 ed.) (Cornelia's Song.) InPS
(Dirge, A: "Call for the robin-redbreast and the wren.") NOBE; OBP

Call from the Afterworld. Jozef Habib Gerez, *tr. fr. Turkish by* Musa Moris Farhi *and* Anthony Rudolf. VWA

Call him drunken Ira Hayes, he won't answer any more. Ballad of Ira Hayes. Peter La Farge. MAT

Call Him the Lover and call me the Bride. The Song the Body Dreamed in the Spirit's Mad Behest. William Everson. PiAm

Call It a Good Marriage Robert Graves. BoLoP; LoAs; NowV

Call it a louse—I'm. Cid Corman. VGW

Call it neither love nor spring madness. Without Name. Pauli Murray. AmNP (1974 ed.); PoBA

Call it our land, our valley, but not ours. Slow Boone. Hildegarde Flanner. WPW

Call me Ishmael and listen. Ishmael. Gabriel Levin. VWA

Call me not false, beloved. The Bridegroom. Kipling. *Fr.* Epitaphs of the War. FaBoEE

Call me the Valiant heading west on Fourteen into the frozen. Ford Pickup. David Allan Evans. NVAP

Call not thy wanderer home as yet. Germinal. "Æ." BIrV

Call of green things to his hand. Nathaniel Tarn. *Fr.* A Nowhere for Vallejo. TwMBP

Call of the Fells, The. Herbert Palmer. PES

Call of the old cock pheasant breaks, The. Boundaries. Judith Minty. HeS

Call out. Call loud: "I'm ready! Come and find me!" Hide and Seek. Vernon Scannell. DuDr; LP

Call Out My Number. Julia de Burgos, *tr. fr. Spanish by* Julio Marzán. InW

Call the roller of big cigars. The Emperor of Ice Cream. Wallace Stevens. AnMo; BiP; CABA (1972 ed.); CMoP (1970 ed.); FF; HAP; ILP (1975 ed.); InPK; NoAM; NOBA; PAIC; PiAm; PoIA; STS; TAP; TT; UsP; WeW

Call to Action, A. Ch'iu Chin, *tr. fr. Chinese by* Kenneth Rexroth *and* Ling Chung. PBWP

Call to Arms. James Welch. MPA; SA

Call to the Wild, A. Lord Dunsany. PFIr

Call to worship said, The. Worship. Elmer F. Suderman. AATT

Called Back. Charles Wright. PCho

Called For. Anthony Thwaite. HeHu

Called from my room to a death. The Stringer. James Brasfield. AMV–81

Called Proud. Walter Savage Landor. GBL

Caller, The. Jim Mulac. AcAn

Caller haar fae lift tae lan', A. Furst Snaw. Billy Kay. MIS

Caller of the Buffalo. Mary Austin. BPAW

Caller rain frae abune. Douglas Young, *after the Greek of* Sappho. OBVE

Calling black people. SOS. Amiri Baraka. BPo; CNA; PoBA

Calling Home the Scientists. Wendy Rose. AMV–81

Calling in the Cat. Elizabeth J. Coatsworth. BoAnP; PCat

Calling Lucasta from Her Retirement. Richard Lovelace. CaPo

Calling Spring VII–MMMC. Ogden Nash. FaBoCo

Calling to mind[e], mine eye [*or* eie] long went about. The Excuse. Sir Walter Ralegh. AAS; LoAs

Calling to mind since first my love begun. Michael Drayton. *Fr.* Idea. NOBE

Calling Trains. *Unknown.* AmFP

Callypso Speaks. Hilda Doolittle ("H. D."). PiAm; RiTi; SBG

Calm. Aldo Camerino, *tr. fr. Italian by* Anita Barrows. VWA

Calm after Storm. Frank Yerby. AmNP (1974 ed.)

Calm as that second summer which precedes. Charleston. Henry Timrod. AmVN; NOBA; TAP

Calm down, my sorrow, we must walk with care. Meditation. Baudelaire, *tr. by* Robert Lowell. InPK; NAWM–2

Calm is the landscape when the storm has passed. Peace in the Welsh Hills. Vernon Watkins. OxBTC

Calm is the morn without a sound. In Memoriam A. H. H., XI. Tennyson. EBEV; NOBE

Calm is unceasing, The. The Old Man in the Autumn. John Shaw Neilson. MAuV

Calm, on the Listening Ear of Night, *with music*. Edmund Hamilton Sears. AH

Calm [*or* Calme] was the day, and through the trembling air [*or* ayre*]. Prothalamion. Spenser. AAS; EBEV; HAP; NIL; PPoe; PPP

Calm was the even, and clear was the sky. Dryden. *Fr.* An Evening's Love, IV, i. FF

Calton Weaver, The. *Unknown.* FSW

Calvary. E. A. Robinson. OFD

Calvary, *with music. Unknown.* AH

Calverly's. E. A. Robinson. NoAM

Calvin in the Attic Cleans. Craig Weeden. AMV-81

Calvin in the Casino. Turner Cassity. NIL

Calvinist in Love, A. Jack R. Clemo. LoAs

Calypso. Richard Kell. CIP

Calypso/ Is a bit of a dipso. Forever Ambrosia. Christopher Morley. OBAL

Calypso for Committed Men. Peter Kostakis. FiCh

Calypsos, *sels.* William Carlos Williams. TH
"Love the sun," II.
"We watched/ a red rooster," III.

Calypso's Island. Archibald MacLeish. PiAm

Calypso's Song to Ulysses. Adrian Mitchell. GBL

Cam Ye By the Salmon Fishers. *Unknown.* GBP

Camas Tuath. Tom Buchan. MIS

Cambrian, *sels.* Eeva-Liisa Manner, *tr. fr. Finnish by* Jaakko A. Ahokas. PBWP
"If they wanted freedom."
"To move over shifting borders."
"Turn the page of stone and there."

Cambrian Swain, The. Edward Davies. *Fr.* Chepstow: A Poem. OBW

Cambric Shirt, The. *Unknown.* FSW

Cambridge Ladies Who Live in Furnished Souls, The. E. E. Cummings. *Fr.* Sonnets—Realities. Epi; HeIP; InPK; NoAM; NOBA; OBAL; TAP; TT; WIF

Cambridge Songs, *sel. Tr. fr. Latin by* Willis Barnstone.
"Wind is thin." BoWoP

Cambridge town is a beleaguered city. The Devourers. Rose Macaulay. PES

Cambridgeshire. Frances Cornford. PES

Came in my full youth to the midnight cave. Ajanta. Muriel Rukeyser. NNaP

Came such a long way. Postcards from Rotterdam. Carolyn Kizer. GP

Came to lakes; came to dead water. A Field of Light. Theodore Roethke. PiAm

Came to me. Rudaki, *tr. fr. Persian by* Basil Bunting. BoLoP; OBVE

Came up that cold sea at Cromer like a running grave. On a Friend's Escape from Drowning off the Norfolk Coast. George Barker. MPo

Came You Not from Newcastle. *Unknown.* GBP

Camel. Laila Akhyaliyya, *tr. fr. Arabic by* Willis Barnstone. BoWoP

Camel. Jon Stallworthy. BoAnP

Camel, with practical views, A. Sole-hungering Camel. Oliver Herford. TDH

Camelopard, The. Hilaire Belloc. FaBoNo

Camels. Jean Nordhaus. PoUp

Camel's Complaint, The. Charles Edward Carryl. OxBChV

Camel's hump is an ugly lump, The. The Hump. Kipling. OxBChV

Camels might never have been here, The. A Visit to the Zoo for the First Kidney Transplant Mothers and Their Children. Daphne Gloag. PMW

Camels, the Kings' Camels, The. Leslie Norris. PChr

Cameo, The. Edna St. Vincent Millay. UnPo (1976 ed.); WPE

Cameo, A. Swinburne. LoAs

Cameo No. II. June Jordan. BPo; WBN

Camera at the crossing sees the city. Gauley Bridge. Muriel Rukeyser. NNaP

Camera records, The. Poem. Diane Kruchkow. FAF

Camerados. Bayard Taylor. PAIC; UnPo (1976 ed.)

Camões, alone, of all the lyric race. Luis de Camões. Roy Campbell. FaBoTw (1975 ed.)

Camoes and the Debt. Sophia de Mello Breyner Andresen, *tr. fr. Portuguese by* Willis Barnstone *and* Nelson Cerqueira. BoWoP

Camouflage. Michael Longley. IPM

Camp in the Prussian Forest, A. Randall Jarrell. CMoP (1970 ed.); NowV; TCP

Camp meeting took place, in a wide open space, A. At a Georgia Camp Meeting. Kerry Mills. BLSo

Camp Site. Denis Glover. ATNZ

Campaign, The. Josephine Miles. WPE

Campaign for Peace in Our Time, The. Jon Anderson. CAAP

Campaign Promise. Henry Taylor. WasP

Campbells Are Comin', The. *Unknown.* BLSH, *with music;* BTTM; FSW

Campers from Fayetteville & Toledo. Reno, 2 A.M. Sam Hamill. TAT

Campidoglio. Robert Garioch, *after the Italian of* Giuseppe Belli. OBVE

Camping at Thunder Bay. David Fedo. AMV-81

Camping Out. William Empson. CMoP (1970 ed.); OxBTC

Camping Out on Rainy Mountain. Jim Barnes. CDW

Camptown Races, The [*or* De]. Stephen Collins Foster. BLSH, *with music;* FSW; PSoN, *with music.*
(Gwine to Run All Night; or, De Camptown Races.) OBAL

Campus on the Hill, The. W. D. Snodgrass. ILP (1975 ed.); NIL; NoAM; NowV; TAP; WIF

Can a mere human brain stand the stress and the strain. Capsule Philosophy. Felicia Lamport. QQQ

Can death be faithful, or the grave be just? The Resurrection. Nathaniel Wanley. SCP-2

Can flame beget white steel. She Contrasts with Herself Hippolyta. Hilda Doolittle ("H. D."). SBG

Can I easily say. Sisters. Adrienne Rich. IHMS

Can I explain this to you? Your eyes. The Knife. Keith Douglas. LoAs

Can I not sing but "hoy." The Jolly Shepherd Wat. *Unknown.* NOBE; OxBM

Can—I—poet. For Some Poets. Mae Jackson. PoBA

Can I see anothers woe. On Anothers Sorrow. Blake. *Fr.* Songs of Innocence. MBPR

"Can I Tempt You to a Pond Walk?" James Schuyler. PoA

Can I, who have for others oft compiled. Of My Dear Son, Gervase Beaumont. Sir John Beaumont. NOBE

Can. Lit. Earle Birney. CABA (1972 ed.)

Can-Opener. David McAleavey. AMV-81

Can the Circle Be Unbroken? *Unknown.* FSW

Can u walk away from ugly. Positives for Sterling Plumpp. Don L. Lee. JB; PoBA

Can we not force from widowed poetry. Elegy upon the Death of the Dean of St. Paul's, Dr. John Donne. Thomas Carew. CABA (1972 ed.); CaPo; OAEL-1

Can we progress? We can, remarked Pellucid. The ABC of Love. O. B. Hardison, Jr. PoUp

Can white birds sing? An ornithologist. No White Bird Sings. John Ciardi. AMV-80

Can ye see the mune, my love? She drives. Ablow the Mune. Donald Campbell. MIS

Can you/ own land, can you. Revolutionary Letter #21. Diane DiPrima. RiTi

Can You Change a Shilling? Toni Del Renzio. EAS

Can you hear the music of the letters of the alphabet? Life of the Letters. Emily Borenstein. VWA

Can you keep it so. Starlings. Norman MacCaig. BoAnP

Can you make me a cambric shirt. Proofs of Love. *Unknown.* ECBV

Can you remember the times. Now That the Buffalo's Gone. Buffy Sainte-Marie. PoRo

Canada-I-O. *Unknown.* AmFP; FSW, *short version*

Canadian Boat-Song. *Unknown, at. to* John Galt, *and also to* "Christopher North." AIW; FaPoR

Canadians. Ivor Gurney. FaBoTw (1975 ed.)

Canal Bank Walk. Patrick Kavanagh. CIP; CMoP (1970 ed.); FaBoTw (1975 ed.); NoAM

Canal Street. John Wheelwright. PoA

Canal Street, Chicago. Clyde Fixmer. TAT

Canary, The. Elizabeth Turner. OxBChV

Canary a piercing pipe of yellow sound. Yellow without Poetry. J. S. Harry. FPA

Canary-birds feed on sugar and seed. The Camel's Complaint. Charles Edward Carryl. OxBChV

Canary, its woe to assuage, A. The Conservative Owl. Oliver Herford. TDH

Cancelled Stanza of the Ode on Melancholy. Keats. MBPR

Cancer Cells, The. Richard Eberhart. HAP

Cancer Match, The. James Dickey. GP

Cancer Patient. Jessica Powers. AMV-81

Cancer's a Funny Thing. J. B. S. Haldane. OxBTC

Candidate, The. Allamae Ezell. AMV-80

Candidate, The. Thomas Gray. PPP

Candle. Jacob Isaac Segal, *tr. fr. Yiddish by* Seymour Mayne. VWA

Candle fit the glass, The. Yahrzeit Candle. Jean Nordhaus. AMV-81

Candle Indoors, The. Gerard Manley Hopkins. ILP (1975 ed.)

Candle lit in darkness of black waters, A. On the Lake. V. Sackville-West. SBG

Candle scratches its nail along the dark panels, A. Ceremony for Cedar: 8. Thomas W. Shapcott. FPA

Candle takes the first desperate, The. Homage to Chagall. Duane Niatum. CDW

Candles. Peter Meinke. AATT

Candles. Sylvia Plath. NMM; PSN

Candles gutter and burn out, The. Winter Night. A. R. D. Fairburn. ATNZ

Candles. Red tulips, ninety cents the bunch. Evening Musicale. Phyllis McGinley. OBAL

Candy/ Is dandy. Reflections on Ice-breaking. Ogden Nash. FaBoCo; IP; OBAL; SFF

Candy Man Blues. *Unknown.* BluL; FSW

Canedolia. Edwin Morgan. FaBoCo

Cang, The. Harry Clifton. IPM

Canibolos de la Montana. Renée Roper. NPW

Canine Amenities. *Unknown.* GDP

Cannas shiny as slag. Flower Dump. Theodore Roethke. PiAm

Canned Heat Blues. *Unknown.* BluL

Cannibal Flea, The. Tom Hood. SpRo

Cannibalee: A Po'em of Passion. C. F. Lummis. SpRo

Cannibals' Grace before Meat, The. Charles Dickens. FaBoNo

Cannily, Cannily. *Unknown.* FSW

Cannon Arrested. Michael S. Harper. CNA

Canny bord ower there. Rape. Tom Pickard. FaBoTw (1975 ed.)

Canoe-hauling Chant. *Tr. fr. Maori by* Apirana Ngata. WTO

Canonical black-coats, like birds of a feather. Vox Clero. *Unknown.* APAS

Canonization, The. John Donne. AnMo; BiP; CABA (1972 ed.); Epi; HAP; ILP (1975 ed.); IPWM; LoAs; MetP; NIL; NOBE; OAEL-1; PoIA; PPoe; PPP; SCP-1; TT; UnPo (1976 ed.)

Canopus. Bert Leston Taylor. NOBL

Canst thou bind the cluster of the Pleiades. Bible, *O.T. Fr.* Job. OBP

Canst thou draw out leviathan with an hook? Leviathan. Bible, *O.T. Fr.* Job. EcS; OBVE

Canst work i' th' ground so fast? Anarchist. Norman Dugdale. BoAnP

Can't make excuses for you, Cinque. Cinque. Janet Campbell Hale. VoR

Can't tell my future/ I can't tell my past. Future Blues. *Unknown.* BluL

Can't Wait. John Kitching. FPB

Can't You Dance the Polka? *Unknown.* FSW

Can't you hear that rooster crowin'? New Morning. Bob Dylan. GrRo

Cantares, *sels.* Leonora Speyer. TH
    "I lied—trusting you knew."
    "Sweet, my sweet!"

Cante Jondo for Soul Brother Jack Spicer. Steve Jonas. EC

Canter has two stride patterns, one on the right, The. The Flying Change. Henry Taylor. CSP

Canterbury Tales, The, *sels.* Chaucer.
  Prologue. ILP (1975 ed.); OAEL-1; PPP, *abr.*
    Clerk of Oxford, The. OxBM
      ("Clerk ther was of Oxenford also, The.") InPS
    "Knyght [*or* Knight] ther was, and that a worthy man, A." BiP; DuDr; InPS
      ("There was a Knight, a most distinguished man," *mod. version by* Nevill Coghill.) BiP
    Persons in the Prologue, *mod. version by* Nevill Coghill. OBP
    Poor Parson, A. BoReV
    Prioress, The. OxBM
      (Madame Eglantine.) NOBE; UsP
    Reeve, The. OxBM
    Wanton Merry Friar, A. BoReV
      ("Frere ther was, a wantowne and a merye, A.") BiP
      ("There was a Friar, a wanton one and merry," *mod. version by* Nevill Coghill.) BiP
    "Whan that April[le] with his shoures soote." DuDr; InPS; LFH; NIL
    Wife of Bath, The. OxBM
      ("Good Wif was ther of biside Bathe, A.") BiP; EBEV; InPS; PPoe
      ("Worthy woman from beside Bath city, A," *mod. version by* Nevill Coghill.) BiP
    "With him ther was his sone, a yong Squyer." DuDr
    "With hym ther rood a gentil Pardoner." BiP
      ("He and a gentle Pardoner rode together," *mod. version by* Nevill Coghill.) BiP
  Franklin's Prologue, The. OAEL-1
  Franklin's Tale, The. OAEL-1
  Friar's Tale, The. PAIC
  Knight's Tale, The.
    "In the third hour after Palamon," *mod. version by* Nevill Coghill. OBP
  Manciple's Tale, The.
    Controlling the Tongue. OxBChV
    Mice before Milk. PCat
  Miller's Prologue, The. OAEL-1
  Miller's Tale, The. OAEL-1
    Carpenter's Young Wife, The. ExPo (1973 ed.)
    "Fair was this yonge wyf, and therwithal." EBEV
  Nun's Priest's Prologue, The. OAEL-1
  Nun's Priest's Tale, The. OAEL-1
    "There liv'd, as authors tell, in days of yore," *mod. version by* Dryden. OBVE

"Oure hoste gan to swere as he were wood." OAEL-1
Pardoner's Prologue, The. OAEL-1
Pardoner's Tale, The. BiP, *mod. version by* Nevill Coghill; HAP, *abr.*; OAEL-1
"But, sires o word forgat I in my tale." EBEV
Three Revellers Search for Death. OxBM
Reeve's Tale, The.
Mill at Trumpington, The. OxBM
Wife of Bath's Prologue, The. OAEL-1
"If poor (you say) she drains her husband's purse," *mod. version by* Pope. OBSV
"If there were no authority on earth," *mod. version by* Nevill Coghill. OBP
Wife's Fifth Husband, The. OxBM
Wife of Bath's Tale, The. ILP (1975 ed.); OAEL-1
Cantica: Our Lord Christ: of Order. St. Francis of Assisi, *tr. fr. Italian by* Dante Gabriel Rossetti. OBVE
Canticle. John Norris. SCP-2
Canticle of the Rose, The. Edith Sitwell. NoAM
Canticle to Apollo, A. Robert Herrick. CaPo
Canticle to the Waterbirds, A. William Everson. PiAm
"Clack your beaks you cormorants and kittiwakes," *sel.* EcS
Canticles to Men. Marya Mannes. AMV-80
Cantico del Sole. Ezra Pound. OBAL
Canto Amor. John Berryman. PAIC; VGW
Canto de Nada. Jessica Tarahata Hagedorn. NW
Canto del Señor Segovia. David Sten Herrstrom. AATT
Canto Llano. Anita Endrezze Probst. CDW
Cantor sings, The. Yom Kippur. Lucille Day. VWA
Cantor was reading Psalms, The. Requiem after Seventeen Years. Dahlia Ravikovitch, *tr. by* Chana Bloch. VWA
Cantor's Dream before the High Holy Days, A. Martin Robbins. VWA
Cantos, *sels.* Ezra Pound.
"And before hell mouth; dry plain," *fr.* XVI. ExPo (1973 ed.)
"And then went down to the ship," I. CMoP (1970 ed.); ExPo (1973 ed.); NoAM; OBVE; PAIC; VGW
"Eleanor (she spoiled in a British climate)," VII. NoAM; NOBA
"'From the colour the nature,'" XC. VGW
"Hang it all, Robert Browning," II. HAP; NoAM; NOBA; PiAm; PoA
"Has he tempered the viol's wood," *fr.* LXXXII. HAP
"I sat on the Dogana's steps," III. Epi; TAP
"Kung walked/ by the dynastic temple," XIII. CMoP (1970 ed.); PiAm
"Oh to be in England now that Winston's out," *fr.* LXXX. PoA
"So that the vines burst from my fingers," XVII. ExPo (1973 ed.)
"Tudor indeed is gone and every rose," *fr.* LXXX. FaBoTw (1975 ed.)
"What thou lovest well remains," *fr.* LXXXI. CMoP (1970 ed.); FaBoTw (1975 ed.); InPS; NOBE
"Who even dead, yet hath his mind entire!" XLVII. CMoP (1970 ed.); PiAm; VGW
"With Usura," XLV. CMoP (1970 ed.); NOBA; PiAm
"Zeus lies in Ceres' bosom," LXXXI. NoAm; NOBA; VGW
Cantos, *sels.* Tom Weatherly. PoBA
Coon Fire, 5.
First Thesis, 7.
Gullfish, 4.
Canyon is deep shade beneath, The. Shasta. Witter Bynner. BPAW
Canzone: Of the Gentle Heart. Guido Guinicelli, *tr. fr. Italian by* Dante Gabriel Rossetti. OBVE
Canzone Pastoral in Honor of Her Majesty, A. Edmund Bolton. PAIC

Canzonetta: A Bitter Song to His Lady. Pier Moronelli da Fiorenza, *tr. fr. Italian by* Dante Gabriel Rossetti. OBVE
Cap and Bells, The. W. B. Yeats. NoAM
Cap for night and, A. Burgundy Phase. Ron Welburn. NW
Cape Ann. T. S. Eliot. Landscapes, V. BiP; UsP
Cape Ann. *Unknown.* BLSo, *with music;* FSW
Cape Cod Girls ("Cape Cod girls they've got no combs"). *Unknown. See* Codfish Shanty, The.
Cape Cod Murders, 1968. Mira Fish. FAF
Cape Cornwall. Paul Mills. MIS
Cape Elizabeth: A Photograph. John Logan. UsP
Cape Hatteras. Hart Crane. *Fr.* The Bridge. PiAm
Cape Horn Gospel—1 ("'I was in a hooker once,' said Karlssen"). John Masefield. PoTa
Capernaum. Lewis Spence. MS
Capital Ship, A ("A capital ship for an ocean trip"). Charles E. Carryl. FSW
(Nautical Ballad, A.) OBAL
(Walloping Window-Blind, The.) RhR
Capitol, The: Spring. Joan LaBombard. PoW
Capped arbiter of beauty in this street. Hart Crane. For the Marriage of Faustus and Helen, III. ILP (1975 ed.)
Caprice. Dorothy Stott Shaw. PoTa
Caprice of the strokes, The. Heirloom. Robert Flanagan. HeS
Capricho. Brian Swann. AAN
Capricious wind stirs Shannon's. An Irish Wind. Zelma S. Dennis. AMV-80
Capsule Philosophy. Felicia Lamport. QQQ
Captain, The, *sel.* John Fletcher.
Away, Delights, *fr.* III, iv. NOBE
(Sad Song, The.) GBL
Captain/ what are you doing. George Simic. Charles Simic. CAAP
Captain bold in Halifax, that dwelt in country quarters, A. Unfortunate Miss Bailey [*or* Miss Bailey's Ghost]. George Colman the Younger. FaBoBa; FSW; GBP; PeBB
Captain Bover. *Unknown.* GBP
Captain Bunker. *Unknown.* AmFP
Captain Captain. *Unknown.* BluL
Captain, captain, what will you give me. The *Turkish Revery.* *Unknown.* RDB
Captain Car. *Unknown. See* Edom o Gordon.
Captain Carpenter. John Crowe Ransom. Epi; HoPM (1975 ed.); LFH; NoAM; NOBA; PPoe
Captain Dobbin. Kenneth Slessor. GAS
Captain Fox was padding along sociably. The Fox and the Goat. La Fontaine, *tr. by* Marianne Moore. AKE
Captain Hall. *Unknown.* GBP
Captain Jinks. William Horace Lingard. BLSo, *with music;* FSW
Captain Kidd. *Unknown.* AmFP; FSW
(Captain Robert Kidd.) PeBB
Captain or colonel, or knight in arms. Sonnet. Milton. OAEL-1; PAIC
Captain Patterson, the folks back home. Americana XIII. Carl Rakosi. InPS
Captain Quiros and Mr. William Lane. Terra Australis. Douglas Stewart. GAS; MAuV
Captain Robert Kidd. *Unknown. See* Captain Kidd.
Captain stood on the carronade, The. The Old Navy. Frederick Marryat. PoTa
Captain! we often heretofore. To Our House-Dog Captain. Walter Savage Landor. OBP
Captain Wedderburn's Courtship. *Unknown.* AmFP; SLP
Caption, Circa 1972. Lawson Fusao Inada. FoP

Captivated by the strange, buzzing. Open Range. Thomas Mitchell. AMV–81

Captive, The. Rochelle Ratner. WBN

Captive Bird. Alison Wyrley Birch. PPM

Captive Stone, The. Jim Barnes. CDW

Captived Bee, The: or, The Little Filcher. Robert Herrick. CaPo; SCP–1

Capture of Major André, The. *Unknown.* BTTM

Caput apri refero. The Boar's Head. *Unknown.* OxBM

Car Cemetery, The. Ciaran Carson. CIP

Car has pulled up outside, A. Alta. MMD

Car loaded. Leaving Home. Shirley Cochrane. AMV–80

Carbreakers. Marian Lines. FPB

Card comes to tell you, A. Non Piangere, Liù. Peter Porter. GAS

Card-Dealer, The. Dante Gabriel Rossetti. VLP

Card-Players, The. David Ray. VGW

Cardigan Bay. John Masefield. EcS

Cardinal and the Dog, The. Robert Browning. VLP

Cardinal Bembo's Epitaph on Raphael. Thomas Hardy, *after the Latin of* Pietro Bembo. FaBoEE

Cardinal Ideograms. May Swenson. Psy

Cards and Kisses. John Lyly. *Fr.* Alexander and Campaspe, III, v. HoPM (1975 ed.); NOBE; PBMP
(Cupid and My Campaspe.) CABA (1972 ed.); HeIP
("Cupid and my Campaspe played.") GBL; ILP (1975 ed.)

Care Away! *Unknown.* OxBM

Care away, away, away. I Am Forsaken. *Unknown.* OxBM

Care-Charmer Sleep. Samuel Daniel. *Fr.* To Delia. IPWM; NIL; OAEL–1
("Care-charmer sleep, son of the sable night.") Epi; ILP (1975 ed.); InPS; NOBE; PAIC
("Care-charmer sleepe, sonne of the sable night.") AAS

Care-charmer sleepe, sweet ease in restles miserie. Fidessa, More Chaste than Kind, XV. Bartholomew Griffin. AAS; ESo; ILP (1975 ed.); NIL

Care-charming Sleep. John Fletcher. *Fr.* The Tragedy of Valentinian, V, ii. ILP (1975 ed.)

Care in Heaven. Spenser. *Fr.* The Faerie Queene, II, 8. BoReV
("And is there care in heaven? and is there love?") OAEL–1

Careering on a downslope from the hill. Blackleg. Kendrick Smithyman. ATNZ

Careful Angler, The. Robert Louis Stevenson. LiSp; SPo

Careful observers may foretell the hour. A Description of a City Shower. Swift. AnMo; ExPo (1973 ed.); HeIP; ILP (1975 ed.); MAT; OAEL–1; OBSV; PCat; PPoD; PPP; UnPo (1976 ed.)

Careless and still. The Rabbit Hunter. Robert Frost. GDP; LiSp; SPo; TH

Careless forever, beautiful proud sea. Beautiful Proud Sea. Sara Teasdale. RhR

Careless Gallant, The. Thomas Jordan. *See* Let Us Drink and Be Merry.

Careless Good Fellow, The. John Oldham. APAS

Careless Love. *Unknown.* BLSH, *with music;* BLSo, *with music;* BluL; FSW; UnPo (1976 ed.)

Careless young driver, McKissen, A. Stop! Lee Blair. TDH

Careless young lad down in Natchez, A. Ouch! *Unknown.* TDH

Careless Zookeeper, The. *Unknown.* TDH

Carelesse Nurse Mayd, The. Thomas Hood. FaBoNo; VLP

Carentan O Carentan. Louis Simpson. MPo; NOBA

Cares o' Love, The. Burns. PBMP

Cargoes. John Masefield. CMoP (1970 ed.); FaPo; FaPoR; ILP (1975 ed.); NOBE; WIF

Carhop floated up, The. Chicken. Dave Etter. MAT

Cariboo Horses, The. A. W. Purdy. HeIP

Carious Exposure. Gladys Cardiff. CDW

Carl Hamblin. Edgar Lee Masters. *Fr.* Spoon River Anthology. CMoP (1970 ed.); OBSV

Carlon the King, our Emperor Charlemayn. The Song of Roland. *Unknown, tr. by* Dorothy L. Sayers. NAWM–1

Carmel Point. Robinson Jeffers. PiAm

Carmen. Victor Hernandez Cruz. PoBA

Carmen Bellicosum. Guy Humphreys McMaster. BTTM

Carmen Miranda. Frank Polite. GP

Carmen Miranda died on my seventh birthday. The Death of Carmen Miranda. Stephen E. Smith. AMV–81

Carmen Saeculare. Charles H. Sisson, *after the Latin of* Horace. OBVE

Carmen Saeculare. John Taylor. NowV

Carmina Burana, *sels. Unknown, tr. fr. Latin.*
"I loved/ secretly," *tr. by* Willis Barnstone. BoWoP
In the Balance. *tr. by* George F. Whicher. OLR
"Let's away with study," *tr. by* Helen Waddell. NAWM–1
"O happy hour," *tr. by* Helen Waddell. NAWM–1

Carnal Knowledge. Thom Gunn. BoLoP

Carnation, The. Paul Hannigan. POL

Carnation Milk is the best in the land. The Virtues of Carnation Milk. David Ogilvy. OBAL

Carnegie Hall: Rescued. Marianne Moore. NYP

Carnival was a sick, The. The Indian Graveyard. Ramona Weeks. TAT

Carol: "My lady went to Canterbury." *Unknown.* FaBoCo; FaBoNo

Carol: "There was a boy bedded in bracken." John Short. FaBoTw (1975 ed.)

Carol of Death, The. Walt Whitman. *Fr.* When Lilacs Last in the Dooryard Bloomed, XIV. DL

Carol of the Brown King. Langston Hughes. CC; LCL; PChr

Carol of the Numbers. *Unknown.* AmFP
(Dilly Song, The.) GBP
(Green Grow the Rushes.) FSW

Carol of the Three Kings. W. S. Merwin. PChr

Carol Took Her Clothes Off. Bill Messenger. CTBA

Carolers. Nancy G. Westerfield. AMV–81

Carolinas, The. David Ray. TAT

Caroline and Her Young Sailor Bold. *Unknown.* AmFP

Caroline of Edinboro' Town. *Unknown.* AmFP

Caroline Pink. *Unknown.* PoPle

Carousel, The. Gloria C. Oden. AmNP (1974 ed.); PoBA

Carp, The. David Malouf. FPA

Carp are secrets, The. Lifting Illegal Nets by Flashlight. William Stafford. NNaP

Carpe Diem. Robert Frost. PAIC

Carpe Diem. C. K. Stead. ATNZ

Carpenter, The. Michael Perkins. POL

Carpenter, The. Primus St. John. FoP

Carpenter. Arthur Smith. BrS

Carpenter is intent on the pressure of his hand, The. El Greco: Espolio. Earle Birney. ExPo (1973 ed.); MPA

Carpenters. Turner Cassity. CSP

Carpenter's made a hole, The. A Hole in the Floor. Richard Wilbur. NoAM; NOBA

Carpenter's Real Anguish, The. Stephen Gardner. AMV–81

Carpenter's Son, The. A. E. Housman. PBMP; SoSe; SpRo; STS

Carpenter's Wife, The. *Unknown. See* Demon Lover, The.

Carpenter's Young Wife, The. Chaucer. *Fr.* The Canterbury Tales: The Miller's Tale. ExPo (1973 ed.)

Carpets cover many floors where I come from. To Vietnam. Charlie Cobb. PoBA

Carrefour. Amy Lowell. BoWoP

Carriage from Sweden, A. Marianne Moore. HAP; SoSe; WeW

Carrickfergus. Louis MacNeice. NoAM

Carried her unprotesting out the door. The Rites for Cousin Vit. Gwendolyn Brooks. *Fr.* The Womanhood. BPo; HAP; WPE

Carrier Letter. Hart Crane. BoLoP

Carriers of the Dream Wheel. N. Scott Momaday. CDW

Carrion Comfort. Gerard Manley Hopkins. AnMo; BoReV; CABA (1972 ed.); HeIP; ILP (1975 ed.); InPK; NoAM; OAEL-2; PFD; PPP
("Not, I'll not, carrion comfort, Despair, not feast on thee.") CMoP (1970 ed.)

Carrion crow sat on an oak, A. Mother Goose. MG

Carrion-eater's nobility calls back from God, The. A Dreamed Realization. Gregory Corso. VGW

Carrots are disappointing. Garden Report. Greg Kuzma. HeS

Carrousel Tune. Tennessee Williams. OBAL

Carry Her over the Water. W. H. Auden. FaBoTw (1975 ed.)

Carry Me Back to Old Virginny, *with music.* James A. Bland. BLSo; PSoN

Carry me back to Ole Virginny. First Families Move Over! Ogden Nash. FaBoCo

Carry your garden. The Serpent Muses. Peggy Henderson. NMM

Carrying a bunch of marigolds. A Negro Woman. William Carlos Williams. IPWM

Carrying a hammer on a quiet street. The Planting. Harley Elliott. NeAC

Carrying Food Home in Winter. Margaret Atwood. TSWA

Carrying generations of lust on his tiny feet. Agent of Love. A. K. Redwing. VoR

Carrying his mandolin in the curve of the afternoon. At the Seed and Feed. Edgar Simmons. CSP

Carrying my world. Father. Myra Cohn Livingston. CC

Cars. Jim Mulac. AcAn

Cars/ In the park. Central Park Tourney. Mildred Weston. MiP

Cars collide and erupt luggage and babies. In Laughter. Ted Hughes. InPS

Cars disappearing from the driveway, carrying. After the Seance. David Clewell. AMV-81

Car's in the Hall, The. Morris Bishop. TDH

Cars once steel and green, now old. Louis Zukofsky. VGW

Carson, turn your coat collar up, throw the cigarette from your hand. The Invitation in It. Kay Boyle. *Fr.* American Citizen. RiTi

Carthusians. Ernest Dowson. VLP

Cartload of Shoes, A. Abraham Sutskever, *tr. fr. Yiddish by* David G. Roskies. VWA

Cartoon. Jim Simmerman. AMV-81

Caruso: a voice. Sleeping with Women. Kenneth Koch. NoAM

Carved on an Areca Nut. Ho Xuan Huong, *tr. fr. Vietnamese by* Nguyen Ngoc Bich *and* Burton Raffel. PBWP

Caryatid. Léonie Adams. LoAs

Caryophyllaceae, The. Spring Coming. A. R. Ammons. InPK

Caryo's sweet smile Dianthus proud admires. Erasmus Darwin. *Fr.* The Loves of the Plants. PeD

Casa de Pollos. Kathleen Fraser. AmPA

Casabianca. Elizabeth Bishop. LoAs

Casabianca. Felicia Dorothea Hemans. RhR

Casanova. Richard Usborne. POL

Cascade, The. Edgell Rickword. FaBoTw (1975 ed.)

Cascadilla Falls. A. R. Ammons. CoPAm; NIL; NOBA

Case, The. H. R. Hays. EAS

Case. Phyllis Janowitz. AMV-81

Case, A. Hughes Mearns. *See* Little Man Who Wasn't There, The.

Case at Sessions, A. Walter Savage Landor. OBSV

Case History. Barbara Drake. TC

Case Notes. Kenyon Alexander. PMW

"Case of Assault," A. Lydia Stephanou, *tr. fr. Modern Greek by* Kimon Friar. BoWoP

Case to the Civilians, A. *Unknown.* FaBoEE

Casey at the Bat. Ernest Lawrence Thayer. LiSp; OBAL; PPoD; SPo

Casey Jones ("Driving that train, high on cocaine"). Robert Hunter. GrRo

Casey Jones ("Come, all you rounders, if you want to hear"). T. Lawrence Seibert. AIW; BLSH, *with music;* DuDr

Casey Jones ("Come all you muckers and gather here"). *Unknown.* AmFP

Casey Jones ("Come all you rounders that want to hear"). *Unknown.* CTV

Casey Jones (Union). Joe Hill. FSW

Casey would waltz with the strawberry blonde. The Band Played On. John F. Palmer. BLSH

Casey's Daughter at the Bat. Al Graham. SPo

Cash In. Sharlot M. Hall. BPAW

Cash on the barrelhead. Hair on the Chest. Coleman Barks. *Fr.* Body Poems. NVAP

Cashel of Munster. *Unknown, at. to* William English, *tr. fr. Irish by* Sir Samuel Ferguson. BIrV; GBL; PFI·

Casi-Gato Aka Carnedechivo Nee Ricardo Sánchez (Sometimes!). Ricardo Sánchez. FoP

Casida of the Rose. Federico García Lorca, *tr. fr. Spanish by* Robert Bly. NU

Casino. W. H. Auden. PSN

Casketmaker, The. Ron H. Bayes. AAN

Cassandra. Louise Bogan. HAP; PBWP; RiTi; SBG; VGW

Cassandra. Robinson Jeffers. HeIP

Cassandra. E. A. Robinson. CMoP (1970 ed.); ExPo (1973 ed.); NoAM; PiAm

Cassinus and Peter. Swift. OAEL-1; PPP

Cassius Hueffer. Edgar Lee Masters. *Fr.* Spoon River Anthology. NoAM

Cast a cold eye. W. B. Yeats. *Fr.* Under Ben Bulben. FaBoEE

Cast on the field from their full height. Second Shadow. Theodore Roethke. PoA

Cast out, amid so many companions. The Comet. Emil Makai, *tr. by* André Ungar. VWA

Cast Thy Bread upon the Waters, *with music.* Phoebe A. Hanaford. AH

Cast thy bread upon the waters. Bible, *O. T. Fr.* Ecclesiastes. NAWM-1; OBVE

Castara, you too fondly court. A Dialogue between Araphil and Castara. William Habington. SCP-2

Castaway, The. William Cowper. CABA (1972 ed.); HeIP; LAuP; NOBE; OAEL-1; PPoe; PPP

Castaway. John Nerber. PoA

Castaways, The. E. V. Rieu. PoTa

Casting a Vote. James DenBoer. PPoD

Casting at Night. Allen Hoey. AMV-80

Castle of Indolence, The, *sel.* James Thomson.
"O mortal Man, who livest here by toil," Canto I. LAuP

Castle of Thorns, The. Yvor Winters. NoAM

Castle Rock. Frederick Morgan. AMV-81

Castle to castle. Caernarfon, 2 July 1969. T. Glynne Davies, *tr. by* Joseph P. Clancy. OBW

Castles. A. Glanz-Leyeles, *tr. fr. Yiddish by* Keith Bosley. VWA

Castles and Candlelight. James Reeves. PoTa

Castles draw in their horns. Highland Portrait. Iain Crichton Smith. MS

Castoff Skin. Ruth Whitman. InPK

Casts from the Antique. David McAleavey. PoUp

Casual at the wheel, blinding rainstorm. Nobody Dies Like Humphrey Bogart. Norman Rosten. PPoD

Casual Man, The. Denis Glover. ATNZ

Casual Meeting. Sam Bradley. AMV–81

Casualty. W. E. Henley. In Hospital, XIII. VLP

Casualty. Michael Longley. IPM

Cat, The. Richard Church. BoAnP; PCat

Cat, The. W. H. Davies. NOBE; PCat

Cat. Eleanor Farjeon. RAE

Cat, The. Faye Kicknosway. TC

Cat, The. William Matthews. AmPA

Cat. Mary Britton Miller. LCL; PCat

Cat. Vernon Scannell. FPB

Cat. Lytton Strachey. PCat

Cat, A. Edward Thomas. BoAnP

Cat. J. R. R. Tolkien. ECBV

Cat, The. Helen Wolfert. RiTi

Cat, A/ I keep, that plays about my. Robert Herrick. PCat

Cat!/ Scat! Cat. Eleanor Farjeon. RAE

Cat and are in love, The. On Reading Lao-tzu. William J. Higginson. AAN

Cat and the Bird, The. George Canning. ECBV

Cat and the Lute, The. Thomas Master. PCat

Cat and the Moon, The. W. B. Yeats. CMoP (1970 ed.); ExPo (1973 ed.); PCat; PFIr; UsP

Cat and the Rain, The. Swift. Fr. A Description of a City Shower. PCat

Cat and the Weather. May Swenson. HAP; MiP; WeW

Cat as Cat, The. Denise Levertov. NOBA; PiAm

Cat at the Cream. Unknown. GBP; POL

Cat bird singing. Air. Robert Creeley. Prf

Cat brushes past, The. Burns. Sandra Hoben. TV

Cat by the fireside, purring, A. Herbs in the Attic. Marilyn Nelson Waniek. AMV–81

Cat, Caged and Shrunken, The. Arthur Freeman. BoAnP

Cat Came Back, The. Harry S. Miller. FSN, with music; FSW

Cat came fiddling out of a barn, A. Mother Goose. ECBV; MN

Cat Heard the Cat-Bird, The. John Ciardi. ECBV; SO

Cat in the cold, so eager to come in. Will You, Won't You. Mark Van Doren. NCSH

Cat into Lady. La Fontaine, tr. fr. French by Edmund Marsh. PCat

Cat is eating the roses, The. The Sage. Denise Levertov. VoA

Cat Morgan Introduces Himself. T. S. Eliot. NOBL

Cat of Cats, The. William Brighty Rands. Fr. The White Princess. DuDr; OxBChV
(Kitten Speaks, The.) PCOP

Cat of Many Years. Gertrude May Lutz. AMV–80

Cat of the House, The. Ford Madox Ford. PCat

Cat on Couch. Barbara Howes. NCSH

Cat on my bosom, The. The Cat as Cat. Denise Levertov. NOBA; PiAm

Cat Poem. Henry Graham. UsP

Cat runs races with her tail, The. The dog. Signs of Winter. John Clare. Epi; OAEL–2

Cat said, A. Vietnam #4. Clarence Major. FF; PoBA

Cat sits on the pavement by the house, A. The Lonely Man. Randall Jarrell. MPo

Cat takes a look at the weather. Cat and the Weather. May Swenson. HAP; MiP; WeW

Cat watches with me, The. Capricho. Brian Swann. AAN

Cat went here and there, The. The Cat and the Moon. W. B. Yeats. CMoP (1970 ed.); ExPo (1973 ed.); PCat; PFIr; UsP

Cat! who has[t] past thy grand climacteric. To a Cat. Keats. MBPR; PCat

Cataclysm, The. Edward Shanks. EcS

Catacombs. István Vas, tr. fr. Hungarian by Jascha Kessler. VWA

Catalogue. Hilde Domin, tr. fr. German by Tudor Morris. VWA

Catalysis. Ann Menebroker. CPA

Cataract. Margoret J. Smith. PPoD

Cataract at Lodore, The. Helen Bevington. SpRo

Cataract of Lodore, The. Robert Southey. OxBChV; SpRo

Catch. Robert Francis. InPK; LiSp; NCSH; WIF

Catch, The. Brewster Ghiselin. HAP; MPA; PoW

Catch. Langston Hughes. NoAM

Catch/ a crawfish/ smell. Secondline for Susan. Jonetta Barras-Abney. PoUp

Catch her and hold her if you can. Defiance. Walter Savage Landor. VLP

Catch him coming off the thing after a state of the union. Strategies. Welton Smith. PoBA

Catch him, crow! Carry him, kite! Swinging the Baby. Unknown. ECBV

Catch me! Love in the Middle of the Air. Lenore Kandel. Fr. Circus. OSP; RiTi

Catch of Shy Fish, A. Gwendolyn Brooks. CAPP

Catch of Summer, A, sels. Madeline DeFrees.
In the Scales: I. MPA
In the Scales: II. MPA

Catch the blues song. Transformation. Quincy Troupe. CNA

Catch What You Can. Jean Garrigue. VGW

Catching a Horse. Barbara Winder. PH

Catechism, 1958. W. M. Ransom. CDW

Caterpillar, The. Christina Rossetti. CTV; OxBChV; PCOP

Caterpillar, The. Miller Williams. CoPAm

Cathedral, A. Stanislav Vinaver, tr. fr. Serbo-Croat by Vasa D. Mihailovich. VWA

Cathedral Close, The. Coventry Patmore. Fr. The Angel in the House, I, i. VPC

Cathedral window was a cliché, The. Lumiere. H. L. Van Brunt. AMV–81

Cathedrals. W. S. Doxey. AMV–80

Cathexis. F. J. Bryant, Jr. PoBA

Cathleen. Unknown, tr. fr. Irish by Thomas MacIntyre. BIrV

Catholic Bells, The. William Carlos Williams. CMoP (1970 ed.); NOBA

Catkin. Christina Rossetti. CTV

Catkins, like caterpillars slung arow. Lost Lane. Dorothy Wellesley. WPE

Cats. Eleanor Farjeon. ECBV; FPB; PCat

Cats. Francis Scarfe. BoAnP
"Those who love cats which do not even purr," sel. PCat

Cats. A. S. J. Tessimond. BoAnP; PCat

Cats and Dogs. Howard Moss. OBAL

Cats and Egypt. Andrew Hudgins. AMV–81

Cats are home tonight, The. Unblinking eyes. On Sitting Up Late, Watching Kittens. Eric W. Paff. AMV–81

Cat's electric fur, The. The Cat, Caged and Shrunken. Arthur Freeman. BoAnP

Cat's Eyes. Francis Scarfe. PCat

Cat's Funeral. E. V. Rieu. ECBV

Cats I scorn, who sleek and fat. A True Cat. Anna Seward. PCat

Cat's Life, A. Eleanor Struthers. CaYB

Cats, no less liquid than their shadows. Cats. A. S. J. Tessimond. BoAnP; PCat

Cats prowl late at night. A Cat's Life. Eleanor Struthers. CaYB

Cat's purr, A. At the Loom. Robert Duncan. *Fr.* Passages. PiAm; VGW

Cats sleep/ Anywhere. Cats. Eleanor Farjeon. ECBV; FPB; PCat

Cat's Song, The. *Unknown.* GBP

Cattails for Bennett. Mary Shumway. HeS

Cattle. Berta Hart Nance. BPAW

Cattle Ghosts, The. David Allan Evans. NVAP

Cattle huddle together. The Blizzard. A. A. Dewey. HeS

Cattle in the common field, The. On the Heights. Walter Savage Landor. FaBoEE

Cattle Show. "Hugh MacDiarmid." HAP; OxBTC

Caught and composed, motionless blue, behind. The Desire of Water. Mark Jarman. PoA

Caught at hanger's ends the limp. Goodwill, Inc. Dennis Schmitz. AmPA

Caught between two streams of traffic, in the gloom. T. S. Eliot. Robert Lowell. NoAM; NOBA

Caught in the centre of a soundless field. Myxomatosis. Philip Larkin. CMoP (1970 ed.); NoAM

Caught in the Pocket. William D. Barney. LiSp

Caught off first, he leaped to run to second, but. Ball Game. Richard Eberhart. LiSp; MiP

Caught Stealing a Dahlia. *Unknown.* TDH

Caught still as Absalom. Chagrin. Isaac Rosenberg. VWA

Caught Up in the Villa. Ralph Storey. SES

Caught without wife and mother, child. Getting Drunk with Daughter. Robert Huff. CNW; CoPAm

Cauld Cornwood. *Unknown.* GBP

Cauliflower, The. John Haines. GP; InPK

Cauliflower-eared Spartan. Reading and Talking. Louis Zukofsky. VGW

Caulker, The. M. A. Lewis. PoTa

Cause nobody deals with Aretha—a mother with four children. Poem for Aretha. Nikki Giovanni. BPo; PoBA

Cause of this stab in my side. The Tryst. *Unknown, tr. by* Joseph P. Clancy. OBW

Causeway. Allan Block. TAT

Caution. *Unknown.* BBL

Cautionary Verses to Youth of Both Sexes. Theodore Hook. OxBChV

Cautious Gunslinger, The. An Idle Visitation. Edward Dorn. *Fr.* Gunslinger. NOBA

Cautious yet unafraid, twirling lightly. Shadow Dirge. R. P. Dexter. LiSp

Cautiously, hoping that nobody sees. In Columbus, Ohio. John Matthias. AMV-80

Cavalier Lyric. James Simmons. InPK; POL

Cavalier Tunes. Robert Browning. BTTM

Cavalry Crossing a Ford. Walt Whitman. AmVN; CABA (1972 ed.); HeIP; ILP (1975 ed.); InPK; InPS; NoAM; PiAm; PPoD; PPP; TAP; UnPo (1976 ed.)

Cavatina. Patricia Ball. PMW

Cave, The. Glenn W. Dresbach. RFM; SOS

Cave, The. A. R. D. Fairburn. ATNZ

Cave, The. Henry Shore. PMW

Cave of Despair, The. Spenser. *Fr.* The Faerie Queene, I, 9. NOBE
("Ere long they come, where that same wicked wight.") OAEL-1

Cave of Night, The, *sel.* John Montague.
Rifled honeycomb, The. CIP

Cave of Staffa, I ("We saw, but surely, in the motley crowd"). Wordsworth. VLP

Cave of Staffa, II ("Ye shadowy beings, that have rights and claims"). Wordsworth. VLP

Cave we found, but vacant all within, The. Homer, *tr. by* Pope. *Fr.* The Odyssey, IX. OBVE

Cave Where Night Sleeps, The. T. Alan Broughton. FAF

Cavern, The. Charles Tomlinson. CMoP (1970 ed.)

Caviar comes from the virgin sturgeon. The Virgin Sturgeon. *Unknown.* FSW

Cavity in the right side of the chest, The. Why Most of Us Are Limping Away from Life. Eugene Ruggles. CPA

Caw, caw, caw. Poem/Ditty-Bop. Carolyn M. Rodgers. JB

Cawsand Bay. *Unknown.* PoPle

Cean Dubh Deelish. *Unknown. See* Dear Dark Head.

Cease rude Boreas blust'ring railers. The Tempest. *Unknown.* AmFP

Cease, Then, My Tongue! Spenser. ILwL

Ceaselessly he watched TV. Addict. Jack Montgomery. QQQ

Cecil County. Ron Welburn. PoBA

Cedar took over an hour of digging, The. In the Dream of the Body. David Keller. AMV-80

Ceiling, The. Theodore Roethke. ECBV; LCL

Ceiling, The/ vibrates in. Portraits of 2 Lonely Women. Ralph Storey. SES

Celan. Asya, *tr. fr. Yiddish by* Gabriel Preil *and* Howard Schwartz. VWA

Celan. Anthony Barnett. VWA

Celandine. Edward Thomas. OxBTC; PF

Celebrated Return. Clarence Major. AmNP (1974 ed.)

Celebration, The. James Dickey. VGW

Celebration. Menke Katz. MN

Celebration. Elizabeth Newton Sachs. AMV-81

Celebration. Ray A. Young Bear. CDW

Celebration for a Young Priest. Barbara Earl Thomson. AATT

Celebration for My Mother. Wendy Rose. CDW

Celebration of Charis, A, *sel.* Ben Jonson.
Triumph of Charis, The. CABA (1972 ed.); ILP (1975 ed.); InPS; NOBE; PoPle
(Her Triumph.) EBEV; LoAs

Celebrity, The. Edward Field. EC

Celemene, pray tell me. A New Dialogue, Sung by a Boy and Girl at the Playhouse. Thomas Durfey. SCP-2

Celery. Gertrude Stein. *Fr.* Tender Buttons. RiTi

Celestial choir, enthron'd in realms of light. To His Excellency, General Washington. Phillis Wheatley. OFD; SBG; WPE

Celestial City, The. Giles Fletcher the Younger. Christ's Victory and Triumph, IV. BoReV; NOBE

Celestial Surgeon, The. Robert Louis Stevenson. PIM; PPM

Celia. Ellen Bass. NMM

Celia. J. S. Harry. FPA

Celia Bleeding: to the Surgeon. Thomas Carew. PeD; SCP-2

Celia Celia. Adrian Mitchell. FaBoEE

Celia, Celia, your name is like cilia. Celia. Ellen Bass. NMM

Celia Singing ("Hark, how my Celia, with the choice"). Thomas Carew. ILP (1975 ed.)

Celibates. Eiléan Ní Chuilleanáin. IPM

Cell by cell the baby made herself, the cells. Sara in her Father's Arms. George Oppen. GP; NNaP

Cell Song. Etheridge Knight. NNaP; PoBA

Cell Transplants. David Hilton. AcAn

Cello Entry. Paul Celan, *tr. fr. German by* Joachim Neugroschel. VWA

Cells Breathe in the Emptiness. Galway Kinnell. VGW

Cells hold mock convention in the brain, The. Lobotomy. Kenneth Pitchford. PoA

Celt in Me, The. Keith Wilson. GP

Celtic Cross. Norman MacCaig. MS

Celtic Fringe, The. Stevie Smith. FaBoNo

Cement house in ruins. Long Haiku No. 7. Louis Cuneo. CPA

Cemetery, A/ is sideways moving. Geoff Page. FPA

Cemetery in New Mexico, A. A. Alvarez. VWA

Cemetery near Burns' Cottage, The. Iain Crichton Smith. MS

"Cemetery stone New England autumn, The." Voices of Heroes. Horace Gregory. OFD

Cenci, The. Shelley. MBPR
"I hardly dare to fear," *fr.* V, iv. LFH

Cenotaph, The. Charlotte Mew. WPE

Censorship. Arthur Waley. OxBTC

Centapod, The. Henry Kanabus. FiCh

Centaur, The. May Swenson. NMM; PH; PoIA; SO

Centaur Overheard, The. Edgar Bowers. ConAP

Centaur, siren, I forgo, The. Another. Richard Lovelace. CaPo

Centaur Song. Hilda Doolittle ("H. D."). VGW

Centaurs, The. James Stephens. PFIr

Centenary Ode, A: Inscribed to Little Crow, Leader of the Sioux Rebellion. James Wright. CoPAm

Centennial Hymn. Whittier. BTTM

Center of America, The. Robert Siegel. AMV–81

Center of Attention, The. Daniel Hoffman. UnPo (1976 ed.)

Centre of equal daughters, equal sons. America. Walt Whitman. GOA

Center of the Garden, The. Ann Stanford. AMV–80

Centipede, A. Julie Holder. FPB

Centipede adown the street, The. Archy at the Zoo. Don Marquis. OBAL

Centipede can run at great speed, A. A Centipede. Julie Holder. FPB

Centipede was happy quite, A. Sad Results of Thinking. *Unknown.* CTV; SFF

Central Maryland, 1963. Gray Jacobik. PoUp

Central Park. Robert Lowell. NYP

Central Park. Howard Nemerov. NYP

Central Park, 1916. Pamela Stewart. NYP

Central Park *Some People (3 P.M.).* Nancy Morejón, *tr. fr. Spanish by* Sylvia Carranza. PBWP

Central Park South. Donald Revell. NYP

Central Park Tourney. Mildred Weston. MiP

Century and eight more years, A. The Four Directions. Emerson Blackhorse Mitchell. VW

Century Farms. Once upon a Nag. Michael Beirne McMahon. PH

Century Piece for Poor Heine, A. John Logan. NNaP

Century was fading fast, A. That Little Hatchet. C. Butler-Andrews. PeD

Ceremonies, The. Van K. Brock. CSP

Ceremonies for Candlemas Day, The. Robert Herrick. ILP (1975 ed.)

Ceremonies for Candlemas Eve, The. Robert Herrick. CaPo; ILP (1975 ed.)

Ceremonies for Christmas, *sel.* Robert Herrick. "Wassail the trees, that they may bear." PChr

Ceremony. Lyn Lifshin. FAF

Ceremony. Howard Nemerov. AMV–80

Ceremony. Richard Wilbur. NoAM

Ceremony/ Judy upstairs. Bedtime. J. D. Whitney. NVAP

Ceremony after a Fire Raid. Dylan Thomas. CMoP (1970 ed.); ExPo (1973 ed.)

Ceremony for Cedar: 8. Thomas W. Shapcott. FPA

Ceremony must be found, The. Speaking of Poetry. John Peale Bishop. NIL

Cerne Giant, The. Paul Mills. MIS

Cernunnos. Hugh Maxton. CIP

Certain dark underground eyes. Picture of Loot. Alan Sillitoe. OxBTC

Certain days wash ashore from the sea. Good Memory. Sotero Rivera-Avilés, *tr. by* Julio Marzán. InW

Certain great statesman, whom all of us know, A. Ballynahinch. George Canning. FaBoCo

Certain Maxims of Archy. Don Marquis. OBAL

Certain moments will never change, nor stop being. Thinking about the Past. Donald Justice. PCho

Certain old party of Moultrie, A. A Strong Feeling for Poultry. Roy Blount, Jr. TDH

Certain Old Women. Brendan Kennelly. IPM

Certain Peace, A. Nikki Giovanni. CNA

Certain portions of the heart. Anatomy. Gilbert Sorrentino. POL

Certain presuppositions are altered. Upland. A. R. Ammons. NOBA

Certain violinist had a beautiful violin, A. Falling Upwards. David Shapiro. AMV–81

Certain women, I think, are born. International Motherhood Assoc. M. L. Hester. AMV–81

Certain World, A. Ruth Herschberger. WBN

Certain Young Gourmet, A. Charles Cuthbert Inge. TDH

Certainly there was something to their stories. Childe Roland, etc. Elder Olson. OBAL

Cervantes, Dostoievsky, Poe. A Poem Intended to Incite the Utmost Depression. Samuel Hoffenstein. FaBoCo

Cerveteri road. Elena Clementelli, *tr. by* Ruth Feldman *and* Brian Swann. *Fr.* Etruscan Notebook. PBWP

Cesar Vallejo/ broken, like slow prey. To the Author of "To My Brother Miguel." Tony Quagliano. PHC

'Cession's stahted on de gospel way, De. A Spiritual. Paul Laurence Dunbar. BPo

C'est un grand Monsieur Pussy-cat. Monsieur Pussy-cat, Blackmailer. Stevie Smith. PCat

Cethegrande is a fis. The Whale. *Unknown.* OxBM

Cézanne. Gertrude Stein. TAP

Cézanne's Ports. Allen Ginsberg. WIF

Cha Till Maccruimein. E. A. Mackintosh. SoSe

Chad. Edward Brathwaite. MPo

Chaff, The. W. S. Merwin. PPP

Chagrin. Isaac Rosenberg. VWA

Chain Gang Blues. *Unknown.* WTO

Chain Gang Trouble. *Unknown.* BluL

Chain Letter. Philip Dacey. AAN

Chain of Pearl, A, *sel.* Lady Diana Primrose. Fourth Pearl, The: Temperance. WPE

Chain Smoking. James Scully. EC

Chains, my good lord: in your raised brows I read. Tennyson. *Fr.* Columbus. OFD

Chair, The. Theodore Roethke. AnMo

Chair:/ It is the name of me. A Splendid Thing Growing. Primus St. John. MPA

Chalk Blue Butterfly, The. Stephen Spender. LP

Chalk mark sex of the nation, on walls we drummers. Three Modes of History and Culture. Amiri Baraka. NoAM

Challenge, The. Longfellow. PiAm

Chamber Music. John Ditsky. AMV–81

Chamber Music. James Joyce. *Poems indexed separately by titles and first lines.*

Chamber-Pot Rhyme. *Unknown.* GBP

Chambered Nautilus, The. Oliver Wendell Holmes. *Fr.* The Autocrat of the Breakfast-Table, *ch.* 4. AmVN; EcS; HoPM (1975 ed.); ILP (1975 ed.); NOBA; PiAm; VoPo

Chambermaid's First Song, The. W. B. Yeats. AnMo

Chambermaid's Second Song, The. W. B. Yeats. AnMo

Chambers of Jerusalem. Yehuda Karni, *tr. fr. Hebrew* by Jeremy Garber. VWA

Chameleon, The. Matthew Prior. OBSV

Chameleons feed on light and air. An Exhortation. Shelley. MBPR

Chameleons saw an arc of color, The. The Lord's Chameleons. Peter Klappert. AmPA

Chamois, The. Hilaire Belloc. FaBoNo

Champagne Charlie, *with music*. *At. to* George Leybourne. BLSo; PSoN

Champion. Robert Morgan. HeHu

Championing heights. Plato. Sandra Ruth Duguid. AATT

Champs d'Honneur. Ernest Hemingway. PoA

Chance adjustment of my car mirror, A. In a Mirror. Marcia Stubbs. MAT

Chance I. Alan Austin. PoUp

Chance You Take, The. Harrison Fisher. PoUp

Chancellor's Nightmare, The. W. S. Gilbert. *See* Nightmare.

Chancery Suit, A. Sir George Rose. FaBoCo

Chances, The, *sel.* John Fletcher.
 "Merciless love, whom nature hath denied," III, ii. GBL

Chances, The. Wilfred Owen. OxBTC

Chances. Brenda S. Stockwell. AMV-81

Chances of Rhyme, The. Charles Tomlinson. PoA

Chandelier as Protagonist, The. William Virgil Davis. AMV-80

Chandeliers hemorrhage, Tritons, The. Figures in a Ruined Ballroom. George Hitchcock. VGW

Chandler's Wife, The. *Unknown.* FSW

Change. John Donne. Elegies, III. EBEV

Change, The. Michael Dransfield. CAAP; FPA

Change. Robert Graves. OxBTC

Change, The. David O'Bruadair, *tr. fr. Irish* by Austin Clarke. BIrV

Change./ like if u were a match I wd light u. A Poem to Complement Other Poems. Don L. Lee. BPo; NoAM

Change Is Not Always Progress. Don L. Lee. TAP

Change, move, dead clock, that this fresh day. Small Prayer. Weldon Kees. PoA; VGW

Change of Address. Kathleen Fraser. WBN

Change of Life. Constance Urdang. VWA

Change of Venue. Jill Clockadale. AMV-80

Change-Up. Don L. Lee. CNA; PoBA

Changeless Changes. Lindiwe Mabuza. SES

Changeling, The. Charlotte Mew. SoSe

Changing a Tire by the Missouri River. Harley Elliott. HeS

Changing guests, each in a different mood, The. Inclusiveness. Dante Gabriel Rossetti. The House of Life, LXIII. VLP

Changing of the Guard. Charles G. Ballard. VW

Changing Water. Adding Aspirin. Nitrogen, potash or. Flowers. Kathleen Fraser. TV

Channel Firing. Thomas Hardy. BiP; CABA (1972 ed.); CMoP (1970 ed.); EBEV; ExPo (1973 ed.); HAP; HeIP; ILP (1975 ed.); InPK; IP; NIL; NoAM; OAEL-2; OBP; OxBTC; PPM; PPoD; SoSe (1977 ed.); UnPo (1976 ed.); VoPo

Channel Passage, A. Swinburne. VLP

Channel Water. Virginia Scott Miner. AMV-80

Chanson: "If they say my furred cloak." Pernette du Guillet, *tr. fr. French* by Joan Keefe *and* Richard Terdiman. PBMP

Chansons Innocentes, *sels.* E. E. Cummings.
 "In Just-/ Spring when the world is mud," I. BBGO; HeIP; InPK; NCSH; NIL; NowV; PiAm; PoIA; SoSe (1977 ed.); STS; TPo; TT; WeW
 "Little tree," II. CC; LCL; PChr

Chant for Dark Hours. Dorothy Parker. SBG

Chant for Young/Brothas and Sistuhs, A. Sonia Sanchez. BPo

Chant-Pagan. Kipling. VLP

Chant to Io. Tiwai Paraone, *tr. fr. Maori* by A. Alpers. WTO

Chanticleer. John Farrar. CTV

Chanting in Tibet has not ceased, The. Moiré. Michael McClure. EAS

Chanting sun, as ever, rivals, The. Prologue in Heaven. Goethe, *tr. by* Louis MacNeice. Fr. Faust. NAWM-2

Chanuke, O Chanuke ("Chanukah, O Chanukah, O holiday so fair"). *Tr. fr. Yiddish.* FSW

"Chaos is purple," you said. Purple Chaos. Alistair Campbell. ATNZ

Chaos Staggered up the Hill. A. R. Ammons. PoIA

Chap has a shark up in Sparkill, A. The Sick Shark. Morris Bishop. TDH

Chapel's cowbell, The. Crusoe's Island. Derek Walcott. NoAM

Chaplinesque. Hart Crane. CMoP (1970 ed.); NoAM; NOBA; VGW

Chapter from Geography, A. William Pillin. SPT

Chapter Heading. Ernest Hemingway. PoA

Character, A. Samuel Taylor Coleridge. MBPR

Character of a Certain Whig, The. William Shippen. APAS

Character of a Happy Life, The. Sir Henry Wotton. FaPoR; NOBE

Character of a landscape stands always in a mysterious relation, The. Poem. Charles Madge. EAS

Character of a Trimmer, The. *Unknown.* APAS

Character of Charles Brown. Keats. MBPR

Character of Holland, The, *abr.* Andrew Marvell. NOBL
 "Holland, that scarce deserves the name of land," *sel.* OBSV

Character of Love Seen as a Search for the Lost, The. Kenneth Patchen. VGW

Character of the Happy Warrior. Wordsworth. MBPR

Characteristics of a Child Three Years Old. Wordsworth. MBPR; RRA

Characters of Forgotten Dirty Jokes, The. Wesley McNair. FAF

Chard Whitlow. Henry Reed. FaBoCo; FaBoNo; ILP (1975 ed.); NOBL; OxBTC; UnPo (1976 ed.)

Charge, The. Anselm Hollo. TwMBP

Charge, The. Jay Wright. FB

Charge of the gallant Three Hundred, the Heavy Brigade, The. The Charge of the Heavy Brigade. Tennyson. BTTM

Charge of the Grid Brigade. George S. Applegarth. SPo

Charge of the Heavy Brigade, The. Tennyson. BTTM

Charge of the Light Brigade, The. Tennyson. BTTM; CTV; FaPo; FaPoR; HoPM (1975 ed.); NIL; PBMP; PPoD; SFF

Charge to mist by spring and midnight luxuries of space. Adultery at the Plaza. John Thompson. WeW

Charge to the Poets, A, *sel.* William Whitehead.
 "If nature prompts you, or if friends persuade." OBSV

Charges I seek, dependent things. Nursing the Hide. Carol Dunne. AMV-81

Chariot rode on the mountain top, The. Great Day. *Unknown.* FSW

Charitas Nimia; or, The Dear Bargain. Richard Crashaw. BoReV; PIM

Charles and Bruce, Geoff and Ron and Nancy. All Friends Together: A Survey of Present-Day Australian Poetry. R. A. Simpson. GAS

Charles Carville's Eyes. E. A. Robinson. CMoP (1970 ed.); TAP

Charles Cavendish to His Posterity. Ben Jonson. SCP-1

Charles Donnelly, *sel.* Donagh MacDonagh.
 "Of what a quality is courage made." CIP

Charles Guiteau. *Unknown.* AmFP, 2 *versions*; FSW

Charles Harpur in his journals long ago. Extinct Birds. Judith Wright. GAS; MAuV; PBWP

Charles river reaps here like a sickle, The. Professor Kelleher and the Charles River. Desmond O'Grady. CIP; IPM; NoAM

Charles II. *Unknown.* FaBoEE (Historical Poem, An.) APAS

Charles XII of Sweden. Samuel Johnson. *Fr.* The Vanity of Human Wishes. NOBE

Charles used to watch Naomi, taking heart. Laboratory Poem. James Merrill. InPK; MAT; PPoD

Charleston. Henry Timrod. AmVN; NOBA; TAP

Charleston Blues ("Charleston, South Carolina, baby is where I was born"). *Unknown.* BluL

Charlie bends to feed the stove. Stone Mountain Face. Peter Blue Cloud. NW

Charlie Cherry. *Unknown.* BluL

Charlie Is My Darling. Lady Caroline Nairne. FSW; GSB, *with music;* RDB, *with music*

Charlie Parker. Morty Sklar. AcAn

Charlie 12. Michael Small. DNGG

Charlie Two-Head. Marnie Walsh. VW

Charlie Wolf used to whittle skinning knives. Halcyon Days. Jim Barnes. CDW

Charlotte Brontë said, "Wow, sister! *What* a man!" Limerick. Victor Gray. NOBL

Charlton Heston. Elliot Fried. AMV–80

Charm a single charm is doubtful, A. Nothing Elegant. Gertrude Stein. *Fr.* Tender Buttons. PBWP

Charm against Pregnancy, A. Harry Stessel. AAN

Charm against the Dumps, A. David Malouf. GAS

Charm against the Toothache, A. John Heath-Stubbs. InPK

Charm against Wens, *orig. and mod. English prose. Unknown.* OxBM

Charm for Our Time, A. Eve Merriam. QQQ

Charm me asleep, and melt me so. To Music, to Becalm His Fever. Robert Herrick. CaPo

Charm of rouge on fragile cheeks, The. Maquillage. Arthur Symons. VLP

Charm'd with a drink which Highlanders compose. Athol Brose. Thomas Hood. FaBoCo

Charmed as a brown wicker nest. Reflections on a Womb Which Is Called "Vacant." Jeanine Hathaway. IHMS

Charming Beauty Bright. *Unknown.* AmFP

Charming the Moon. James DenBoer. MAT

Charming Woman, The. Helen Selina Sheridan. WPE

Charming young woman named Pat, A. Limerick. *Unknown.* NIL

Charms, that call down the moon from out her sphere. To Music, to Becalm a Sweet-Sick Youth. Robert Herrick. CaPo; SCP-1

Charnel-House, The. Henry Vaughan. SCP-1

Charon. Louis MacNeice. FaBoTw (1975 ed.)

Charon! Thou slave! Thou fool! Thou Cavalier! A Mock Charon. Richard Lovelace. CaPo

Chase, The. J. V. Cunningham. LiSp; NoAM

Chasm. A. R. Ammons. OBAL

Chaste Florimel. Matthew Prior. BoLoP

Chaste, pious, prudent Charles the Second. The History of Insipids. John Freke. APAS

Chat/ shah shah. French Persian Cats Having a Ball. Edwin Morgan. MPo

Chatterers in Church. *Unknown.* OxBM ("Tutivillus, the devil of hell.") EBEV

Chattering finch and water-fly. The Skeleton. G. K. Chesterton. FaBoTw (1975 ed.)

Chaucer. Longfellow. AmVN; HeIP; NOBA; PAIC; TAP; UsP

Chaucer, Langland, Douglas, Dunbar with all your. Ode to the Medieval Poets. W. H. Auden. PoA

Chauffeur of Lilacs, The. George Hitchcock. GP

Chaunt of the Brazen Head, The, *sel.* Winthrop Mackworth Praed.
    "I think the thing you call Renown." OBSV

Chauntecleer. Chaucer. *Fr.* The Canterbury Tales: The Nun's Priest's Tale. PB

Cheap Rent. Carl Sandburg. PiAm

Cheat of Cupid, The; or, The Ungentle Guest. Robert Herrick, *after the Greek of* Anacreon. OBVE

Cheating Droone. "T. M." Micro-Cynicon, Satire IV. TVS

Check to Song. "Owen Meredith." FaBoCo

Checker. Herbert Scott. TC

Checking the Firing. R. T. Smith. AMV–80

Checking the traps. The Ice-fishing House: Long Lake, Minnesota. Michael S. Harper. TAT

Chee Lai! (Arise!) *Unknown, tr. fr. Chinese.* FSW

Cheek. Coleman Barks. *Fr.* Body Poems. NVAP

Cheeks as red as the blooming rose. Shady Grove. *Unknown.* FSW

Cheer for the Consumer. Nixon Waterman. OBAL

Cheer Leader, The. Carl Sandburg. SPo

Cheerful old bear at the zoo, A. Limerick. *Unknown.* CTV

Cheerio My Deario. Don Marquis. *Fr.* Archy and Mehitabel. FaBoCo

Cheerios. Peter Meinke. GP

Cheers. Eve Merriam. LiSp; SPo

Cheetah, The. Harold Witt. Pow

Chekhov Comes to Mind at Harvard. William T. Freeman. AMV–81

Chelsea, The. Derek Walcott. NYP

Chelsea Morning. Joni Mitchell. GrRo; PoRo; WIF

Chemist to His Love, The. *Unknown.* QQQ

Chemist's Dream, The. Patricia Beer. HeHu

Chenille. James Dickey. NoAM

Chepstow: A Poem, *sels.* Edward Davies. OBW
    Cambrian Swain, The.
    Tintern Abbey.
    Wily Fox, The.

Cherbourg Airport. Katharine Edgar Cobey. PoUp

Cherries. Lucien Stryk. PCho

Cherries, The, a Parable. Thomas Moore. OBSV

Cherrily carols the lark. Mad Margaret's Song. W. S. Gilbert. *Fr.* Ruddigore. PCOP

Cherry blossoms, The. Spring. Princess Shikishi, *tr. by* Hiroaki Sato. PBWP

Cherry-ripe. Thomas Campion. *See* There Is a Garden in Her Face.

Cherry-ripe. Robert Herrick. CaPo

Cherry Robbers. D. H. Lawrence. OBP; PoIA

Cherry tree blossomed, The. Black was my hair. Tomonori, *tr. fr. Japanese.* TVo

Cherry-Tree Carol, The (*diff. versions*). *Unknown.* AmFP (4 versions); EBEV; FaBoBa; FSW; GBP; HeIP; IPWM; OAEL-1, *with music;* OFD; PChr; PeBB

Cherry trees bend over and are shedding, The. Edward Thomas. PoPle

Cherry trees, mindless of the field, The. The Orchard. Michael Spence. AMV–80

Cherrylog Road. James Dickey. CABA (1972 ed.); CoPAm; CSP; ExPo (1973 ed.); HAP; InPK; InPS; NIL

Cheshire for men. English Counties. *Unknown.* POL

Chester. William Billings. *See* Let Tyrants Shake Their Iron Rod.

Chestnut Avenue at Alton House, The. Charles Tomlinson. FaBoTw (1975 ed.)

Chestnut Casts His Flambeaux, The. A. E. Housman. CMoP (1970 ed.); ILP (1975 ed.); NoAM; PPP; SoSe (1977 ed.); STS; TT

Chestnut tree stands in the line of sight, A. St. Asaph's. Kingsley Amis. OxBTC

Chevaliers de la Table Ronde. *Unknown, tr. fr. French.* FSW

Chevy Chase. *Unknown.* FaBoBa; PeBB

"Chew Mail Pouch." D. L. Klauck. AMV–81

Chewing Chawing Gum. *Unknown.* AmFP (Chewing Gum.) FSW

Cheyenne Mountain. Helen Hunt Jackson. BPAW

Chez Jane. Frank O'Hara. NoAM; NOBA; PoA

Chic Freedom's Reflection. Alice Walker. NMM

Chicago. Lola Ridge. PoA

Chicago. Carl Sandburg. BiP; CMoP (1970 ed.); ILP (1975 ed.); IPWM; NoAM; NOBA; PiAm; PoA; TAP; UnPo (1976 ed.); VGW

Chicago Allegory. Stewart Parker. CIP

Chicago Centennial or: The Town Hall Meeting. Walter Bradford. FiCh

Chicago *Defender* Sends a Man to Little Rock, The. Gwendolyn Brooks. AmNP (1974 ed.); PoBA; Psy

Chicago Morning. Ted Berrigan. FiCh

Chicago: Near West-Side Renewal. Dennis Schmitz. AmPA

Chicago Picasso, The. Gwendolyn Brooks. *Fr.* Two Dedications. BPo; ILP (1975 ed.); Psy

Chicago/ 3 Hours. Victor Hernández Cruz. ANTL

Chicago we could have imagined for ourselves, The. Trading Chicago. Charles O. Hartman. AMV–80

Chickadee, The. Emerson. PCOP

Chickadees/ round suet balls. Winter, New Hampshire. David Kherdian. TAT

Chicken. Dave Etter. MAT

Chicken. How shall I tell you what it is. A Presentation of Two Birds to My Son. James Wright. ILP (1975 ed.); PPP

Chicken-Licken. Maya Angelou. FF

Chicken Unlimited. Peter Meinke. AAN

Chickens, The. *Unknown.* ECBV

Chickens a-crowin' on Sourwood Mountain. Sourwood Mountain. *Unknown.* FSW; GBP

Chickens crowing for midnight. It's Almost Day. Leadbelly (Huddie Ledbetter). FSW

Chickitten Gitten! Ted Joans. GP

Chief, chief, that I am. Bear Song. John R. Swanton. BPAW

Chief defect of Henry King, The. Henry King. Hilaire Belloc. BBL; FaBoNo

Chief Leschi of the Nisqually. Duane Niatum. CDW

Chief of organic numbers! Lines on Seeing a Lock of Milton's Hair. Keats. MBPR; PeD

Chief Petty Officer. Charles Causley. OxBTC

Chieftain Iffucan of Azcan in caftan. Bantams in Pine-Woods. Wallace Stevens. CMoP (1970 ed.); InPS; NOBA; STS; UnPo (1976 ed.)

Chieftain to the Highlands bound, A. Lord Ullin's Daughter. Thomas Campbell. FaPoR

Chiffonier with Glass Flowers, A. Reuel Denney. PHC

Child, A. Katherine Cole. UsP

Child, The. Donald Hall. NCSH

Child. Tom MacIntyre. CIP; IPM

Child, The. W. S. Merwin. NoAM

Child, The. Frank Ormsby. AMV–81

Child. Sylvia Plath. PBWP

Child, The. Lawrence Russ. TC

Child (a boy) bouncing, A. To. William Carlos Williams. OBAL

Child an' the Mowers, The. William Barnes. VLP

Child at Winter Sunset, The. Mark Van Doren. NCSH

Child Bearers, The. Anne Sexton. BoWoP

Child Bearing. Charles Ghigna. AMV–81

Child Beater. Ai. BoWoP

Child Collecting. David James. TC

Child! Do not throw this book about! Dedication on the Gift of a Book to a Child. Hilaire Belloc. EBEV

Child, dream of a pomegranate tree. Winter Garden. Janet Lewis. WPW

Child, dreamer, that I may wind. A Fan for His Daughter. Stéphane Mallarmé, *tr. by* David Paul. RRA

Child Dying, The. Edwin Muir. FaBoTw (1975 ed.)

Child, feverish, frowning, only saw red, The. The Lice-Hunters. Arthur Rimbaud, *tr. by* Robert Lowell. NAWM–2

Child had been struck by two bullets in the head, The. Memory of the Night of the Fourth. Victor Hugo, *tr. by* Mary Ann Caws. NAWM–2

Child Half-asleep, A. Tony Connor. BuTh; UsP

Child Harold, *sels.* John Clare. Ballad: "Blackbird has built in the pasture agen, The." VLP "Blackbird startles from the homestead hedge, The." VLP

Child has a vision of the happy army, The. The Happy Army. Peter Bland. ATNZ

Child I do not have, The. The Second Heart. Ellen Wittlinger. TV

Child, I suffered them, A. Doubts. Elizabeth Jennings. LP

Child, I warn thee in all wise. Symon's Lesson of Wisdom for All Manner of Children. *Unknown.* OxBChV

Child in Adam's field I dreamed away, A. Edwin Muir. *Fr.* Variations on a Time Theme. NoAM

Child in the Rug, The. John Haines. GP

"Child Is Father to the Man, The." Gerard Manley Hopkins. FaBoCo (Triolet.) NOBL

Child is like a rare bird, A. Praise of a Child. *Yoruba Oral Tradition, tr. by* Ulli Beier *and* B. Gbadamosi.

Child is on my shoulders, The. Laughing Child. Carl Sandburg. CTBA

Child Is Singing, A. Adrian Mitchell. BuTh; LP

Child Next Door, The. Robert Penn Warren. TCP

Child of death. Praises of the King of Oyo. *Yoruba Oral Tradition, tr. by* Ulli Beier. WTO

Child of God. *Unknown.* FSW

Child of Mine. Gerry Goffin *and* Carole King. PoRo

Child of Misfortune! Offspring of the Muse! On the Death of Dermody, the Poet. Henry Kirke White. PeD

Child of my winter, born. Heart's Needle. W. D. Snodgrass. CAPP; ConAP; PiAm; RRA

Child of Our Time. Eavan Boland. CIP

Child of patient industry. Invitation to the Bee. Charlotte Smith. OxBChV

Child of silence and shadow. Yvonne Caroutch, *tr. fr. French by* David Cloutier. BoWoP

Child of the clouds! remote from every taint. The River Duddon, II. Wordsworth. MBPR

Child of the Dead and Forgotten Gods. Richard Wright. SPT

Child of the Romans. Carl Sandburg. PiAm

Child on Top of a Greenhouse. Theodore Roethke. BuTh; DuDr; NCSH; PiAm; VGW

Child, A, said *What is the grass*? fetching it. Grass. Walt Whitman. *Fr.* Song of Myself, VI. UsP

Child saw the bombers skate, The. Come to the Stone. Randall Jarrell. VGW

Child Screening a Dove from a Hawk, A. Letitia Elizabeth Landon. VLP

Child should always say what's true, A. Whole Duty of Children. Robert Louis Stevenson. CTV; OxBChV; PCOP

Child that has a cold we may suppose, A.  Thomas Dibdin. FaBoNo

Child, the current of your breath is six days long.  Unknown Girl in the Maternity Ward.  Anne Sexton.  NoAM

Child Unborn, The.  Humbert Wolfe.  BuTh

Child Waters ("Childe Watters in his stable stoode").  Unknown. FaBoBa; LFH

Child Waters ("I warn ye all, ye gay ladies").  Unknown.  PeBB

Child with Six Fingers.  Carol Muske.  AmPA

Child, you were and/you learned to be.  With the Bait of Bread. Helene Pilbosian.  AMV-81

Child, you were conceived in my upstairs room.  To a Child Born in Time of Small War.  Helen Sorrells.  WPE

Childbirth.  Anne S. Perlman.  PoW

Childcity, Aprilcity.  Paris.  Gregory Corso.  VGW

Childe Harold's Pilgrimage, *sels.*  Byron.
  And I Have Loved Thee, Ocean! *fr.* IV.  SPo
  Bull Fight, The. *fr.* I.  LiSp
  "Come, blue-eyed Maid of Heaven!—but thou, alas!" *fr.* II. LFH
  Dying Gladiator, The, *fr.* IV.  NOBE
  Eve of Waterloo, *fr.* III.  NOBE
  (Waterloo.)  PPoD
  "Fair Greece! sad relic of departed worth!," *fr.* II.  ILP (1975 ed.)
  "I stood in Venice on the Bridge of Sighs," *fr.* IV.  LFH
  (Venice and Sunset.)  PAIC
  "Is thy face like thy mother's, my fair child!" III.  MBPR; OAEL-2, *abr.*
  "Lake Leman woos me with its crystal face," *fr.* III.  InPS
  "Oh love! no habitant of earth thou art," *fr.* IV.  OAEL-2
  "Oh! that the Desert were my dwelling-place," *fr.* IV.  ILP (1975 ed.)
  "Roll on, thou deep and dark blue Ocean—roll!" *fr.* IV.  EcS
  (Byron's Address to the Ocean.)  RhR
  "Stop!—for thy tread is on an empire's dust!" *fr.* III.  ILP (1975 ed.); InPS
  (Field of Waterloo, The.)  BTTM
  "There is a pleasure in the pathless woods," *fr.* IV.  LFH
  "There was a sound of revelry by night," *fr.* III.  EBEV; LFH

Childe Roland, etc.  Elder Olson.  OBAL

"Childe Roland to the Dark Tower Came."  Robert Browning. ExPo (1973 ed.); OAEL-2; PPP; VLP

Childe Watters in his stable stoode.  Child Waters.  Unknown. FaBoBa; LFH

Childhood.  Anne Bradstreet.  *Fr.* The Four Ages of Man.  SBG

Childhood.  Edith Bruck, *tr. fr. Italian by* Anita Barrows.  VWA

Childhood.  Frances Cornford.  OxBTC

Childhood.  Jewel C. Latimore.  JB

Childhood.  Edwin Muir.  CMoP (1970 ed.); HeIP

Childhood.  Sherod Santos.  AMV-81

Childhood.  Henry Vaughan.  SCP-1

Childhood.  Margaret Walker.  IHMS; PBWP; PoBA

Childhood and School-Time.  Wordsworth.  *Fr.* The Prelude, I. NOBE
  ("Fair seed-time had my soul, and I grew up.")  ExPo (1973 ed.); HAP; ILP (1975 ed.)

Childhood games.  The Black Angel.  Michael S. Harper. NVAP

Childhood in Jacksonville, Florida.  Jane Cooper.  TAP

Childhood of an Equestrian, The.  Russell Edson.  AmPA

Childhood remembrances are always a drag.  Nikki-Rosa.  Nikki Giovanni.  AmNP (1974 ed.); IHMS; IPWM; NoAM; NYP; PBMP; PoBA; RiTi; TAP

Childish Prank, A.  Ted Hughes.  OAEL-2

Childless.  Giolla Brighde MacNamee, *tr. fr. Irish by* Frank O'Connor.  BIrV

Childless Witch, A.  Raquel Chalfi, *tr. fr. Hebrew by* Alexandra Meiri *and* Myra Glazer Schotz.  VWA

Childlessness.  James Merrill.  ConAP

Children.  Russell Edson.  AmPA

Children, The.  William Heyen.  GP

Children.  Carolyn Kizer.  CNW

Children, The.  Susan MacDonald.  IHMS

Children, The.  Vincent O'Sullivan.  ATNZ

Children, The.  William Soutar.  MS

Children, The.  Constance Urdang.  IHMS

Children, The.  Mark Vinz.  GP

Children, The.  William Carlos Williams.  BBGO

Children/ They teach to walk.  Training on the Shore.  Shlomo Vinner, *tr. by* Laya Firestone *and* Howard Schwartz.  VWA

Children among the Tombstones.  J. R. Hervey.  ATNZ

Children are born with the taste of cotton root, The.  Design in Cotton Fabric.  Norman Macleod.  SPT

Children are dumb to say how hot the day is.  The Cool Web. Robert Graves.  NoAM; OxBTC; PoA; PoIA

Children are singing, The.  Singing.  Peter Shelton.  AKE

Children attend!  Advice to Children and Their Parents. *Unknown.*  DuDr

Children begin at green dawn nimbly to build.  The Altars in the Street.  Denise Levertov.  CAPP

Children believe in clover, magic numbers.  The Sacred Children. H. R. Hays.  EAS

Children, children, come and look.  Jack-in-the-Boat.  Allen Curnow.  ATNZ

Children enter, The.  Sundown at Darlington 1878.  Lance Henson.  VoR

Children go forward with their little satchels, The.  The School Children.  Louise Glück.  AmPA

Children, Go Where I Send Thee.  *Unknown.*  FSW

Children, if you dare to think.  Warning to Children.  Robert Graves.  OAEL-2; SO

Children, It's Time.  Michael Brownstein.  OSP

Children Killed in War.  D. J. Enright.  HeHu

Children know how to do it, The.  Feeding the Fire.  Donald Finkel.  VWA

Children of Auschwitz.  Naum Korzhavin, *tr. fr. Russian by* Daniel Weissbort.  VWA

Children of Darkness.  Robert Graves.  NoAM

Children of Greenock, The.  W. S. Graham.  FaBoTw (1975 ed.)

Children of Light.  Robert Lowell.  CMoP (1970 ed.); ILP (1975 ed.); STS

Children of Night.  Richard Shelton.  FiCP

Children of the cold sun and the broken horizon.  The City.  Ben Maddow.  SPT

Children of the future age.  A Little Girl Lost.  Blake.  *Fr.* Songs of Experience.  MBPR; RRA

Children of the Owl and the Pussy-Cat, The.  Edward Lear. FaBoNo

Children of the Poor, The.  Gwendolyn Brooks.  *Fr.* The Womanhood.  PoA; WPE

Children on the corner, The.  City.  Raymond Biasotti. AMV-80

Children picking up our bones.  A Postcard from the Volcano. Wallace Stevens.  CABA (1972 ed.); HAP

Children play with doll Katchinas, The.  Hopi Woman.  Lillian White Spencer.  BPAW

Children they move stand, The.  Clear.  Angelo Lewis.  PoBA

Children tumbling about the yard, The.  On the Knowledge of Things.  Alexander Taylor.  NowV

Children Visit the Island.  Diane Wakoski.  CAAP

Children walk.  City.  Jane Stembridge.  NMM

Children we have not borne. To My Daughter the Junkie on a Train. Audre Lorde. CNA

Children were spinning, The. Energy Sources. Karren L. Alenier. PoUp

Children, when was/ Napoleon Bonaparte. Napoleon. Miroslav Holub. EC

Children, you are very little. Good and Bad Children. Robert Louis Stevenson. OxBChV; PCOP

Children's Carol, The. Eleanor Farjeon. PChr

Children's Games. William Carlos Williams. NIL

Children's Hour, The. Don Johnson. PCho

Children's Hour, The. Longfellow. CTV; OBAL; PCOP

Children's Lenten Wisdom. James A. Houck. AMV-80

Children's Rhymes. Langston Hughes. BPo; ILP (1975 ed.); InPS

Children's Runes and Omens. *Unknown.* MAT

Children's Song. Arye Sivan, *tr. fr. Hebrew by* David Shevin. VWA

Children's voices in the orchard. New Hampshire. T. S. Eliot. Landscapes, I. BiP; WeW

Child's castle crumbles, The; hot air shimmers. Mercury Bay Eclogue. M. K. Joseph. ATNZ

Child's Creed, A. *Unknown.* CTV

Child's Drawing. Allan Block. FAF

Child's Dream, The. Susan Ludvigson. AMV-80

Child's Evening Prayer, A. Samuel Taylor Coleridge. *See* Pains of Sleep, The.

Child's face at the window, The. The Revenant. Margaret Atwood. Psy

Child's Game. Judson Jerome. DuDa

Child's Nativity, A. John N. Morris. GP

Child's Offering, A. *Unknown.* CTV

Child's Prayer, A. George Meredith. PIM

Child's Present, A. Robert Herrick. OxBChV

Child's Pulse, A. Henry Shore. PMW

Child's Sight, The. Hy Sobiloff. VGW

Child's Song. Thomas Moore. ECBV

Child's Song in Spring. Edith Nesbit. OxBChV

Child's Umbrella, The. Raymond Souster. AKE

Child's Visit to the Biology Lab, A. Kathleen Spivack. AmPA

Child's wisdom is in saying, The. The Child's Sight. Hy Sobiloff. VGW

Chilled by Different Winds. Alice Mackenzie Swaim. AMV-80

Chilled by the Blasts of Adverse Fate, *with music.* Jacob Duché. AH

Chilled by the Present, its gloom and its noise. Sonnets from China, XVIII. W. H. Auden. PPP

Chilled with salt dew, tossed on dark waters deep. A Mermaiden. Thomas Hennell. FaBoTw (1975 ed.)

Chilterns, The. Rupert Brooke. PPM

Chimera, The. Alfred Mombert, *tr. fr. German by* Erna Baber Rosenfeld. VWA

Chimes. Longfellow. PiAm

Chimes. Alice Meynell. SBG; WPE

Chimney Sweeper, The ("A little black thing among the snow"). Blake. CABA (1972 ed.); LAuP; MBPR; OAEL-2; PPoe; PPP; STS; TT

Chimney Sweeper, The ("When my mother died I was very young"). Blake. *Fr.* Songs of Innocence. AnMo; FF; HeIP; ILP (1975 ed.); InPK; LAuP; MBPR; OAEL-2; OxBChV; PPoe; PPP; SoSe; STS; UsP

Chimney Sweeper, The. *Unknown.* AmFP

Chimneys, rank on rank, The. Evening. Richard Aldington. Moon

Ch'in Chia's Wife's Reply. *Tr. fr. Chinese by* Arthur Waley. BoWoP

Chin tucked into collar. The Flowering Cacti. Gene Fowler. CPA

China Lake. John McNally. PoUp

China Shop Vigil. Christopher Middleton. TwMBP

Chinatown. Anna Blake Mezquida. BPAW

Chinese Baby Asleep. Dorothy Donnelly. NCSH

Chinese Checker Players, The. Richard Brautigan. TVo

Chinese Garden, The. Horace Gregory. WasP

Chinese Graves in Beechworth Cemetery, The. Philip Mead. AMV-81

Chinese Serenade for the Ut-Kam and Tong-Koo, *sel.* Thomas Holley Chivers.
"Tu Du,/ Skies blue." PeD

Chinese Vase, A. Edward Hirsch. AMV-80

Chinese Winter. F. R. Higgins. BIrV

Chinese written character, The. Signature. Carol Orlock. AMV-81

Ching a Ring. James Planché. NOBL

Chinoiserie. Charles Wright. AmPA

Chip. George Starbuck. OBAL

Chipmunk's Day, The. Randall Jarrell. NCSH
("In and out the bushes, up the ivy.") BoAnP

Chippewa Lake Park. Warren Woessner. TAT

Chippewa Love Song. *Tr. fr. Chippewa Indian by* Frances Densmore, *ad. by* Willis Barnstone. BoWoP

Chips. Stanley Cook. DuDr

Chiquita. Bret Harte. BPAW

Chiropody instruments, laid out, The. Feet Are Not Funny. William Lindsay. PMW

Chivalrous Shark, The. *Unknown.* FSW

Chloe. Pope. *Fr.* Moral Essays. NOBE
("Yet Cloe sure was formed without a spot.") OBSV

Chloe found Amyntas lying. A Rondelay. Dryden. PAIC

Chloe, why wish you that your years. To Chloe Who Wish'd Her Self Young Enough for Me. William Cartwright. MetP

Chloe's a Nymph. Thomas D'Urfey. PoPle

Chloris, *sels.* William Smith.
"My love, I cannot thy rare beauties place," XVIII. ESo
"Some in their harts their mistris colours bears," XXIX. AAS
"Though you be faire and beautiful withall," XXVI. ESo
To the Most Excellent and Learned Shepheard Collin Cloute, *dedication.* AAS
"Yee wastefull woods beare witnes of my woe," XX. ESo
"You fawnes and silvans, when my Chloris brings," V. ESo

Chloris' Charms Dissolved by Eudora, *sel.* Anne Killigrew.
"Press on till thou descry." SCP-2

Chloris, forbear a while. Song. Henry Bold. GBL

Chloris in the Snow. William Strode. *See* On Chloris Walking in the Snow.

Chock House Blues. *Unknown.* BluL

Chocolate Soldiers, The. Calvin Forbes. MAT

Choctaw Chief Helps Plan a Festival, A. Jim Barnes. TAT

Choeses me boue er plach yoang. Foreign Literature. Thackeray. FaBoNo

Choice. J. V. Cunningham. PiAm; VGW

Choice, The. Winifrid M. Letts. PFIr

Choice, The. Frederick Morgan. AMV-81

Choice, The. Robert Morgan. HeHu

Choice, The. John Pomfret. EPC
"If heaven a date of many years would give," *sel.* PoIA

Choice, The. W. B. Yeats. CMoP (1970 ed.); NoAM; OxBTC

Choice of Valentines, The; or, The Merry Ballad of Nashe His Dildo, *sels.* Thomas Nashe. SCP-2
"By blind meanders and by crankled ways."
"Sweeping she comes, as she would brush the ground."

Choice of Weapons, A. Stanley Kunitz. VGW

Choice of Weapons, A. Phyllis McGinley. SS

Choirs of Heaven are tokened in a harp-string, The. The Counsels of O'Riordan, the Rann Maker. T. D. O'Bolger. PFIr

Chomei at Toyama. Basil Bunting. OxBTC; TwMBP

Choo a choo a choo tooth. The Cannibals' Grace before Meat. Charles Dickens. FaBoNo

Choose me your valentine. To His Mistresse. Robert Herrick. OFD

Choose now among this fairest number. Song. William Browne. GBL

Choose the darkest part o' the grove. Incantation to Oedipus. Dryden. *Fr.* Oedipus, III, i. OFD

Choosing a Kitten. *Unknown.* CTV

Choosing a Mast. Roy Campbell. FaBoTw (1975 ed.); RhR

Choosing a Name. Charles *and* Mary Lamb. OxBChV

Choosing a Name. Anne Ridler. NOBE

Choosing a Stone. John Haines. CNW

Choosing Their Names. Thomas Hood. PCat

Chops. Alan Dixon. BoAnP

Chords knotted together like insane nouns, The. You (IV). Tom Clark. EAS

Choristers Training, *orig. and mod. English prose. Unknown.* OxBM

Chorus: "Dharma law." Jack Kerouac. Mexico City Blues, 66. PiAm

Chorus: "Long ago, the Mountain Mother." Euripides, *tr. fr. Greek by* Richmond Lattimore. *Fr.* Helen. RRA

Chorus: "Praised be man, he is existing in milk." Jack Kerouac. Mexico City Blues, 228. PiAm

Chorus: "Songs that erupt, The." Jack Kerouac. Mexico City Blues, 195. PiAm

Chorus: "Summer holds, The: upon its glittering lake." W. H. Auden. *Fr.* The Dog beneath the Skin. OxBTC

Chorus: "They were singing Old MacDonald in the schoolbus." John Ciardi. SS

Chorus: "We do not wish anything to happen." T. S. Eliot. *Fr.* Murder in the Cathedral. OxBTC

Chorus: "We have not been happy, my Lord, we have not been too happy." T. S. Eliot. *Fr.* Murder in the Cathedral. OxBTC

Chorus: "When the hounds of spring are on winter's traces." Swinburne. *Fr.* Atalanta in Calydon. ExPo (1973 ed.); HAP; HeIP; ILP (1975 ed.); NOBE; OAEL-2; PoPle; SoSe (1977 ed.); VPC
(When the Hounds of Spring.) NIL

Chorus: "Who hath given man speech? or who hath set therein." Swinburne. *Fr.* Atalanta in Calydon. OAEL-2

Chorus: "You are the town and we are the clock." W. H. Auden. *Fr.* The Dog beneath the Skin. OxBTC

Chorus for Survival, *sel.* Horace Gregory.
"Ask no return for love that's given." VGW

Chorus of the Archangels, The. Goethe, *tr, fr.* German by Shelley. *Fr.* Faust. OBVE

Chorus of the Rescued. Nelly Sachs, *tr. fr.* German by Harry Zohn. VWA

Chorus of the Years. Thomas Hardy. *Fr.* The Dynasts, Pt. III, Act VI, sc. viii. CMoP (1970 ed.)

Chorus Sacerdotum. Fulke Greville. *Fr.* Mustapha. NOBE; OAEL-1; PPP
(O Wearisome Condition of Humanity.) HAP

Chosen, The. Carl Dennis. AMV-81

Chosen, The. Thomas Hardy. LoAs

Chosen. W. B. Yeats. BoLoP; CMoP (1970 ed.)

Chosen, The—Kalgoorlie, 1894. Fay Zwicky. VWA

Chosen Light, The. John Montague. TwMBP

Chosen Three, on Mountain Height, The, *with music.* David H. Ela. AH

Chough, The ("The chough, said a dictionary"). James Reaney. CABA (1972 ed.)

Christ, *sel.* Gavin Bantock.
"Rolleth the seventh wave." TwMBP

Christ Climbed Down. Lawrence Ferlinghetti. TCP; VGW

Christ for the World! We Sing, *with music.* Samuel Wolcott. AH

Christ God who savest man, save most. Count Gismond. Robert Browning. VLP

Christ I said aloud. Birth. Judith Smallshaw. PMW

Christ in Alabama. Langston Hughes. PoBA

Christ in the Universe. Alice Meynell. BoReV; NOBE

Christ is a nigger. Christ in Alabama. Langston Hughes. PoBA

Christ made to man a fair present. Divine Love. *Unknown.* OAEL-1

"Christ That Was a Real One," He Said. Hugh Fox. TC

Christ, the Refuge of the Soul. Charles Wesley. *See* Jesus, Lover of My Soul.

Christ Walking on the Water. W. R. Rodgers. NoAM

Christ, wha'd ha'e been Chief Rabbi gin he lik't. Up to Date. "Hugh MacDiarmid." FaBoCo

Christ, whose glory fills the skies. Morning Hymn. Charles Wesley. BoReV

Christabel. Samuel Taylor Coleridge. MBPR; OAEL-2
" 'Tis the middle of night by the castle clock," I. OBP

Christened with scripture, eponymously labelled. Entry. Anthony Thwaite. HeHu

Christening-Day Wishes for My God-Child. Robert P. Tristram Coffin. OFD

Christian, Be Up, *with music.* Robert Nathan. AH

Christian Scientist, high-buttoned mind. Miss Ada. Christopher Fahy. TAT

Christian Year, The, *sels.* John Keble.
Eleventh Sunday after Trinity. VLP
Third Sunday in Lent. VLP

Christians awake, salute the happy morn. A Hymn for Christmas Day. John Byrom. BoReV

Christians have always been pilgriming. "Faith and Practice." John Balaban. GOA

Christina. Jessica Tarahata Hagedorn. NW

Christina. Louis MacNeice. BoLoP

Christine to Her Son. Christine de Pisan, *tr. fr. French by* Barbara Howes. BoWoP

Christmas. Daisy Aldan. AATT

Christmas. John Betjeman. BoReV; OxBTC

Christmas. Grace Cavalieri. AATT

Christmas and Common Birth. Anne Ridler. FaBoTw (1975 ed.)

Christmas Antiphones, *sel.* Swinburne.
Peace-Giver, The. PIM

Christmas at Sea. Robert Louis Stevenson. PoTa

Christmas at Vail: On Staying Indoors. Pat Monaghan. AMV-80

Christmas Bells. Longfellow. *See* I Heard the Bells on Christmas Day.

Christmas bells, awake and ring. Christmas Morning. Harry Behn. CC; PChr

Christmas candles confuse the dusk. Central Park, 1916. Pamela Stewart. NYP

Christmas Carol, A: "Angel told Mary, An." Harry Behn. PChr

Christmas Carol, A: "Close to a quarter of a century since then." Thomas Herbert Parry-Williams, *tr. fr. Welsh by* Joseph P. Clancy. OBW

Christmas Carol: "God bless the master of this house." *Unknown.* CTV

Christmas Carol, A: "In the bleak mid-winter." Christina Rossetti. BoReV
  (In the Bleak Mid-Winter.) GSB, *with music;* PIM
  "What can I give Him," *st.* 5. CC; CTV; LCL; PChr
Christmas Carol: "Thank God, thank God, we do believe." Christina Rossetti. PChr
Christmas Carol Sung to the King [in the Presence] at Whitehall, A. Robert Herrick. PIM
*Sels.*
  "Darling of the world is come, The." PChr
  "What sweeter music can we bring." PChr
Christmas Childhood, A, *sel.* Patrick Kavanagh.
  "My father played the melodion." PChr
Christmas Comes to Moccasin Flat. James Welch. CDW; GP; MAT; MPA; SA; SFF
Christmas day. Robert Dana. *Fr.* Natural Odes/American Elegies. HeS
Christmas Day. John Meade Falkner. OxBTC
Christmas declares the glory of the flesh. Christmas and Common Birth. Anne Ridler. FaBoTw (1975 ed.)
Christmas Eve. A. R. Ammons. TT
Christmas Eve. Patricia Beer. HeHu
Christmas Eve. Ted Kooser. BrS; GP
Christmas Eve. David Mura. *Fr.* A Christmas Package. CC ("My stocking's where.") PChr
Christmas Eve. Anne Sexton. RiTi
Christmas Eve, and twelve of the clock. The Oxen. Thomas Hardy. BiP; CMoP (1970 ed.); EBEV; HAP; InPK; IPWM; NoAM; NOBE; OAEL-2; OxBTC; PChr; PPoe; PPP; SoSe (1977 ed.); VoPo
Christmas Eve in Whitneyville, 1955. Donald Hall. UnPo (1976 ed.)
Christmas Eve Service at Midnight at St. Michael's. Robert Bly. NNaP
Christmas Eve under Hooker's Statue. Robert Lowell. CAPP; ConAP; FF; LFH; PiAm
Christmas Everywhere. Phillips Brooks. CTV; PCOP
Christmas Exchange, The. Arthur Guiterman. CTV
Christmas Family Reunion. Peter De Vries. NOBL
Christmas Gift, A. David Mura. BrS
Christmas Hymn, A. Richard Wilbur. MPo; OFD; PChr
Christmas is coming. The geese are getting fat. *Unknown.* BBL; CC; PChr
Christmas is in the air. Five Days Old. Francis Webb. MAuV
Christmas is my name, for have I gone, have I gone, have I gone. A Song Bewailing the Time of Christmas. *Unknown.* SCP-2
Christmas Letter Home. G. S. Fraser. OxBTC; SLP
Christmas Lights. Valerie Worth. PChr
Christmas Lullaby for a New-born Child. Yvonne Gregory. AmNP (1974 ed.)
Christmas Mass for a Little Atheist Jesus. Claude Maillard, *tr. fr. French by* Maxine W. Kumin *and* Judith Kumin. BoWoP
Christmas Morning. Harry Behn. CC; PChr
Christmas Morning. Steven Lautermilch. AMV–80
Christmas Morning. Elizabeth Madox Roberts. CC; PChr
Christmas Morning, I. Carol Freeman. PChr; PoBA
Christmas Mourning. Vassar Miller. CoPAm
Christmas Mouse. Aileen Fisher. MN
Christmas Needles. Albert Howard Carter. AATT
Christmas 1959 et Cetera. Gerald W. Barrax. OFD; PChr
Christmas: 1924. Thomas Hardy. BuTh; FaBoEE
Christmas Ornaments. Valerie Worth. PChr
Christmas Package, A, *sels.* David McCord.
  "My stocking's where." PChr
  (Christmas Eve.) CC
  "That broken star." PChr
Christmas Poem. David Hilton. AcAn

Christmas Poem. Michael Hogan. DNGG
Christmas Poem. Brian Lynch. IPM
Christmas Prayer, A. George MacDonald. PChr
Christmas Prayer, A. William R. Mitchell. AATT
Christmas Revel, A. Dafydd Bach ap Madog Wladaidd, *tr. fr. Welsh by* Joseph P. Clancy. OBW
Christmas Tree, A. William Burford. SoSe
Christmas Tree, The. Peter Cornelius. PChr
Christmas Trees (A Christmas Circular Letter). Robert Frost. BiP
Christmas was in the air and all was well. Karma. E. A. Robinson. CMoP (1970 ed.); HeIP; ILP (1975 ed.); IPWM; NoAM; OFD; PiAm; STS
Christofo Colombo was a hungry man. Mysterious Biography. Carl Sandburg. CC; OFD
Christographia 35. Eugene Warren. AMV–80
Christoph. Charles Spear. ATNZ
Christopher at Birth. Michael Longley. CIP
Christopher Magisto. Rodger Kamenetz. AAN
Christopher St. Liberation Day, June 28, 1970. Fran Winant. MMD
Christ's Coming. *Unknown. See* Advent.
Christ's Descent into Hell. Rainer Maria Rilke, *tr. fr. German by* James Wright *and* Sarah Youngblood. Prf
Christ's Life Our Code, *with music.* Benjamin Copeland. AH
Christ's Love-Song. *Unknown.* BoReV; OxBM
Christ's Passion. Abraham Cowley. PIM
Christ's Plea to Mankind. *Unknown.* OxBM
Christ's Reply. Edward Taylor. *Fr.* God's Determinations. EAP
Christ's Victory and Triumph, *sels.* Giles Fletcher the Younger.
  Christ's Triumph after Death, IV.
    Celestial City, The. BoReV; NOBE
  Christ's Triumph over Death, III.
    Palm Sunday: Good Friday. BoReV
  Christ's Victory in Heaven, I.
    He Was Made Man. BoReV
  Christ's Victory on Earth, II.
    "Therefore above the rest Ambition sat." SCP-2
Chroma. Greg Hannan. PoUp
Chrome Babies Eating Chocolate Snowmen in the Moonlight. A. K. Redwing. VoR
Chromis! Mnasil! None appear? Ben Jonson. *Fr.* Oberon the Fairy Prince. SCP-1
Chromo. Sarah Webster Fabio. CNA
Chronicle. Edward Dorn. TAT
Chronicle, *sel.* Robert of Gloucester.
  Town Against Gown at Oxford. OxBM
Chronicles: Numbers One and Two. Mei Berssenbrugge. SA
Chronicles: Number Three. Mei Berssenbrugge. GP; SA
Chronological Ordering of Art Cards, The. Robert Sargent. PoUp
Chronology. Turner Cassity. PoA
Chronos, Chronos, mend thy pace. The Secular Masque. Dryden. ExPo (1973 ed.); OBP; PAIC
Chrysalides. Thomas Kinsella. BIrV; NoAM
Chrystal streames, wherein my love did swimme, The. Licia, XXVII. Giles Fletcher the Elder. ESo
Chuck Will's Widow Song. *Unknown.* BPo
Chums, The. Theodore Roethke. NoAM
Chunk off and float she thought. Hibernating in an Old Lost Neighbourhood. Laura Chester. RiTi
Church and State. W. B. Yeats. CMoP (1970 ed.)
Church at little Winwick, The. Winwick, Lancashire. *Unknown.* GBP
Church Bells. Berton Braley. TDH

Church bells in gray air. Sundays. Marieve Rugo. AMV-81

Church bells toll a melancholy round, The. Written in Disgust of Vulgar Superstition. Keats. MBPR

Church Burning: Mississippi. James A. Emanuel. PoBA

Church Calendar of English Flowers, A. *Unknown.* PF

Church-Floor[e], The. George Herbert. EBEV; OAEL-1

Church Going. Philip Larkin. CMoP (1970 ed.); ILP (1975 ed.); InPK; IP; NIL; NoAM; OAEL-2; PPP; PSN; SoSe; UnPo (1976 ed.)

Church is a business, and the rich, The. After Lorca. Robert Creeley. ConAP; InPS; POL; UsP

Church Monuments. George Herbert. CABA (1972 ed.); HAP; ILP (1975 ed.); OAEL-1; SCP-1

Church Mouse, The. Gerald Bullett. BoAnP

Church Mouse commends: tapeworms and slugs grow wings. Critics and Poets. Geoffrey Grigson. FaBoEE

Church of a Dream, The. Lionel Johnson. OAEL-2

Church of England's Glory, The. *Unknown.* APAS

Church of Galilee, The. Muriel Rukeyser. *Fr.* The Gates. GP

Church on Comiaken Hill, The. Richard Hugo. Prf

Church Poem. Joyce Carol Thomas. CNA

Church Porch, The, *sel.* George Herbert. Courage. CTV

Church Romance, A. Thomas Hardy. FaBoTw (1975 ed.); NOBE; OxBTC; VLP

Church with Long Steeple. Jim Kraus. PHC

Church's One Foundation, The. Samuel J. Stone. BLSH, *with music;* VLP

Churchyard on the Sands, The. Lord De Tabley. GBL

Churning Day. Seamus Heaney. HeHu

Churning the compost, dazed. To Earth. James Applewhite. PoA

Chutes are tiny smoke puffs, The. The Schloss. David Kirby. CSP

Cibber! write all thy verses upon glasses. Pope. FaBoEE

Cicada. Adrien Stoutenburg. RFM

Cicadas are dying, The. Homecoming Celebration. Rosemary Catacalos. AMV-80

Cicadas in brambled foliage, The. The House-Builders. Kamala Das. PBWP

Cider and Vesalius. John Peck. AmPA

Cielito Lindo, *with music.* Carlos Fernandez, *tr. fr. Spanish by* James Morehead. BLSH

Cigales. Richard Wilbur. NoAM; NOBA

Cigarette, A. *Mongol Oral Tradition, tr. by* C. R. Bawden. WTO

Cigarette my girl is smoking, A. Jealousy. *Malay Oral Tradition, tr. by* R. J. Wilkinson *and* R. O. Winstedt. WTO

Cigarette Poem, The. Faye Kicknosway. IHMS

Cigarette smoke floated. Milne's Bar. Norman MacCaig. FaBoTw (1975 ed.)

Cincinnati. Cid Corman. GP

Cinco de Mayo, 1862. A. A. Rios. GP

Cinderella. Olga Broumas. PoIA

Cinderella. Anne Sexton. Psy

Cindy. *Unknown.* BLSo, *shorter version, with music;* FSW

Cinéma Vérité. Dorothy Walters. IHMS

Cino. Ezra Pound. VGW

Cinq Ans Après. Gelett Burgess. *See* Sequel to the Purple Cow.

Cinquain: A Warning. Adelaide Crapsey. *See* Warning, The.

Cinque. Janet Campbell Hale. VoR

Cinque Port, A. John Davidson. PoPle; VLP

Circa 1814. David Staudt. AMV-80

Circe. Lord De Tabley. VLP

Circe. Austin Dobson. PoIA

Circe. William Gibson. PoA

Circe. A. D. Hope. PPP

Circle, The. Alan Riddell. SLP

Circle, A/ and, in this circle, another. A Circular Cry. Edmond Jabes, *tr. by* Anthony Rudolf. VWA

Circle, a Square, a Triangle and a Ripple of Water, A. Jane Cooper. TAP

Circle and the Question, The. Josephine Saunders. FoP

Circle on the Grass, The. Jane Kenyon. TC

Circles. Harry Behn. CTV; LCL

Circles. Elizabeth Knies. AMV-80

Circles are praised, not that abound. Long and Short Life. Edmund Waller. NIL

Circles never fully round, but change, The. Perspective of Co-ordination. Arthur Davison Ficke. PoA

Circling. Carole Oles. NPW

Circling shadow on the measured dial, The. Chronology. Turner Cassity. PoA

Circuit Breaker. Sid Gary. QQQ

Circuit Judge, The. Edgar Lee Masters. *Fr.* Spoon River Anthology. FaBoEE

Circular Cry, A. Edmond Jabes, *tr. fr. French by* Anthony Rudolf. VWA

Circular white sun, The. The Apparition. Eiléan Ní Chuilleanáin. IPM

Circumambulation of Mt. Tamalpais. Andrew Hoyem. PoA

Circumcision, The. Linda Zisquit. VWA

Circumference thou bride of awe. Emily Dickinson. PiAm

Circumflex firs. At last the sun. All Souls'. Gwen Harwood. GAS

Circumstance. Laurie Stroblas. AMV-80

Circumstance has estranged my friend. Song. Carl Rakosi. BrS

Circus, *sels.* Lenore Kandel.
  "Catch me!" OSP
  (Love in the Middle of the Air.) RiTi
  Freak Show and Finale. RiTi

Circus, The. Elizabeth Madox Roberts. CC

Circus Animals' Desertion, The. W. B. Yeats. BiP; CMoP (1970 ed.); FaBoTw (1975 ed.); ILP (1975 ed.); MAT; NIL; NoAM; NOBE; OAEL-2; OxBTC; PPoD; PSN; TT

Circus Dancer, A. Celia Dropkin, *tr. fr. Yiddish by* Howard Schwartz. VWA

Circus Elephants. Kathryn Worth. CTV

Circus Lion. C. Day Lewis. BoAnP; MPo; PoPle

Circus of battleships carrying heavy laughter, A. Celebrated Return. Clarence Major. AmNP (1974 ed.)

Circus Song. Patricia Goedicke. TV

Cistercians in Germany. Robert Lowell. NowV

Citadels. Richard Kell. PFIr

Cities and Thrones and Powers. Kipling. *Fr.* Puck of Pook's Hill. NOBE; OxBTC; VLP

Cities are walled. It is a cruel land. Memory. Babette Deutsch. PoA

Cities are washed into time, The. John Oliver Simon. NeAC

Cities Drowned. Sir Henry Newbolt. EcS

Cities of the Plain, The. Whittier. PIM

Citizen, A. Charles Reznikoff. *Fr.* Five Groups of Verse. SA

Citizen. Peter Schjeldahl. CAAP

Citizen Paine. James Daugherty. ECBV

Citizens' Complaint, The. David Allan Evans. HeS

City. Raymond Biasotti. AMV-80

City. Joseph Bruchac. CDW

City. Roy Fisher. TwMBP

City. Langston Hughes. ECBV; LCL

City, The. Ben Maddow. SPT

City. Timothy P. Mocarski. AMV-81

City, The. Linda Pastan. NYP

City.  Jane Stembridge.  NMM

City, The.  James Thomson ("B. V.").  The City of Dreadful
Night, *proem*.  NOBE
(Proem: "Lo, thus, as prostrate, 'In the dust I write.' ")  VLP

City Afternoon.  Barbara Howes.  PPoD

City Bird.  Theda Kenyon.  ECBV

City Boy, The.  Stephen Dunn.  HeS

City Butterfly.  Charles Siebert.  NYP

City by the Sea, The.  George Sterling.  BPAW

City Child, The.  Tennyson.  OxBChV; PCoP

City Corruption.  William Cowper.  *Fr.* The Task, IV.  NIL

City Dead-House, The.  Walt Whitman.  InPK

City grows, The.  Landscapes.  Bert Meyers.  PoW

City had no color for our hearts, The.  Death in the City.
Norman Macleod.  SPT

City had withdrawn into itself, The.  Christmas Trees (A
Christmas Circular Letter).  Robert Frost.  BiP

City in the Sea, The.  Poe.  AmVN; EcS; ILP (1975 ed.); MAT;
NOBA; PiAm; TAP

City is a chaos, The.  Night in New York.  Herman Spector.
SPT

City Is Falling Apart, The.  Diane Kruchkow.  FAF

City is of Night, The; perchance of Death.  James Thomson
("B. V.").  The City of Dreadful Night, I.  VLP

City Life.  D. H. Lawrence.  ILP (1975 ed.); SoSe; UsP

City Limits, The.  A. R. Ammons.  NoAM; NOBA; NYP; PoIA

City, Lord, Where Thy Dear Life, The, *with music*.  William E.
Dudley.  AH

City/Market.  Charlotte A. Raines.  PoUp

City Mouse and the Garden Mouse, The.  Christina Rossetti.
MN; PCOP

City Nights, *sel.*  Arthur Symons.
In the Train, I.  VLP

City of Anguish.  Edwin Rolfe.  SPT

City of ascensions, A.  A Jerusalem Notebook.  Harvey Shapiro.
AMV-81

City of clanging bells.  In the Dim City.  Arthur Salmon.  PES

City of Dreadful Night, The.  James Thomson ("B. V.").  VPC
*Sels.*
"Anear the centre of that northern crest," XXI.  PFD; VLP
(City's Queen, The.)  NOBE
City, The, *proem*.  NOBE
(Proem: "Lo, thus, as prostrate, 'In the dust I write.' ")  VLP
"City is of Night, The; perchance of Death," I.  VLP
"I sat me weary on a pillar's base," XX.  VLP
"Large glooms were gathered in the mighty fane," XIV.  EBEV;
OAEL-2

City of God.  Samuel Johnson.  FaPoR

City of Light.  Nahum Bomze, *tr. fr. Yiddish by* Gabriel Preil *and*
Howard Schwartz.  VWA

City of Monuments.  Muriel Rukeyser.  SPT; WasP

City of Orgies.  Walt Whitman.  NYP

City of Satisfactions, The.  Daniel Hoffman.  Prf

City of tense and stricken faces.  Jackson, Mississippi.  Margaret
Walker.  FB

City of the Moon, The, *sel.*  Kenneth Rexroth.
"Buddha took some Autumn leaves."  GP

City of weathered cloister and worn court.  Lionel Johnson.  *Fr.*
Oxford.  PES

City Pigeons.  Helen Chasin.  WeW

City planners.  To the New Annex to the Detroit County Jail.
Richard W. Thomas.  PoBA

City Psalm.  Denise Levertov.  PiAm

City Rain.  Rachel Field.  ECBV

City Rat and the Country Rat, The.  La Fontaine.  *See* Town
Rat and the Country Rat, The.

City Rises, The.  James Cunningham.  JB

City rises, The.  A Poem for Democrats.  Amiri Baraka.  CAPP

City Shower in Imitation of Virgil's Georgics, A.  Swift.  *See*
Description of a City Shower, A.

City Sparrow.  Jane Mayhall.  TAP

City squats on my back, The.  Route Six.  Stanley Kunitz.
AMV-80

City Summer.  Martin Galvin.  PoUp

City, whose streets are wavering reflections.  Canal Street.  John
Wheelwright.  PoA

City without Smoke.  Edwin Denby.  NYP

City without Walls.  W. H. Auden.  NYP

City's Queen, The.  James Thomson ("B. V.").  The City of
Dreadful Night, XXI.  NOBE
("Anear the centre of that northern crest.")  PFD; VLP

Civic Autobiography, A.  Paul Hoover.  FiCh

Civil Defense.  Kenneth Burke.  OBAL

Civil Riot, *sel.*  G. D. H. Cole.
"And you'll say a nation totters."  OxBTC

Civil Servant, A.  Robert Graves.  InPK

Civile, res ago.  See, Will, 'Ere's a Go.  *Unknown.*  FaBoNo

Civilian.  Josephine Miles.  WPE

Civilization.  Tom Schmidt.  NeAC

Civilization and Its Discontents.  John Ashbery.  CAPP; NIL

Civilization is hooped together, brought.  Meru.  W. B. Yeats.
InPS; NoAM; OAEL-2; PoA

Civilized, crying how to be human again: this will tell you how.
Signpost.  Robinson Jeffers.  TCP

Civilizing the Child.  Lisel Mueller.  CTBA

Clack your beaks you cormorants and kittiwakes.  A Canticle to
the Waterbirds.  William Everson.  EcS; PiAm

Clad in thick mail he stumbles down the floor.  Divers.  Robert
Haven Schauffler.  EcS

Claiming Kin.  Ellen Bryant Voigt.  AAN

Clair de Lune.  Paul Verlaine, *tr. fr. French by* Arthur Symons.
Moon

Clamb ape mountain backwards.  To Be Quicker.  Don L. Lee.
JB

Clamdigger, The.  Dionis Coffin Riggs.  TAT

Clamming.  Reed Whittemore.  IPWM; TAP

Clamour of the wind making music.  Saint Columcille, *tr. fr. Irish
by* John Montague.  BIrV

Clams.  Stanley Moss.  GP

Clams.  Ishigaki Rin, *tr. fr. Japanese by* Hiroaki Sato.  PBWP

Clancy.  David Wagoner.  PH

Clancy of the Overflow.  Andrew Barton Paterson.  MAuV

Clandestine Work.  Yvan Goll, *tr. fr. French by* Anthony Rudolf.
VWA

Clap, clap the double nightcap on!  Walter Savage Landor.
FaBoEE

Claremont.  Robert Peters.  GP

Clarence Mangan.  Thomas Kinsella.  CIP

Clarence Short Bull died.  Sitting Bull's Will versus the Sioux
Treaty of 1868 and Monty Hall.  A. K. Redwing.  VoR

Clarendon had law and sense.  On the Young Statesmen.
Charles Sackville.  APAS

Clari, the Maid of Milan, *sel.*  John Howard Payne.
Home, Sweet Home.  BLSH; BLSo; FSW; PSoN

Claribel.  Tennyson.  PeD

Clarinda's Indifference at Parting with Her Beauty.  Countess of
Winchilsea.  SBG

Claritas.  Denise Levertov.  PiAm; VGW

Claritas.  Gerrye Payne.  NWP

Clarity.  A. R. Ammons.  TAP

Clarity of Apples, The.  Terry M. Perlin.  AMV-80

Clarity of spring, The.  Verna Tomlinson Baker.  AATT

Clark Colven.  *Unknown.*  See Clerk Colvill.

Clark Sanders. *Unknown. See* Clerk Saunders.

Clash with Cliches, A. Vassar Miller. AMV-80

Clashenure Skyline, *sels.* Alfred Allen. IPM
　"Here is a tale of the man who laid."
　"Mad as a hare in spring-time."
　"No one died in this parish when."
　"This is the place where I was born."
　"What do these old stories prove?"

Clasping of Hands. George Herbert. ILwL

Class, The. Josephine Jacobsen. GP

Class Incident from Graves. Alan Brownjohn. OxBTC

Class is judging swine, The. Two for the Hampton Institute.
　David Young. CAAP

Class of thirty student engineers, A. The Pay Is Good. Richard
　Kell. MPo

Classes. Keith Wilson. NowV

Classic. A. R. Ammons. NOBA

Classic Encounter. "Christopher Caudwell." OxBTC

Classic Idyll, A. Avraham Huss, *tr. fr. Hebrew by* Mark Elliott
　Shapiro. VWA

Classic landscapes of dreams are not, The. The Snowfall.
　Donald Justice. CoPAm; VGW

Classic Waits for Me, A. E. B. White. SpRo

Classical Autumn. Robert Clayton Casto. AMV-81

Classical key, A. Cubist Blues in Poltergeist Major. Allan F.
　Kipp. AMV-81

Classical Quatrain, A. Paul Goodman. VGW

Classroom. James Aitchison. MS

Claude Allen. *Unknown.* AmFP

Clausa Germanis Gallia. Millen Brand. GP

Clay Comes Out to Meet Terrell. Muhammed Ali. SPo

Clay is the word and clay is the flesh. Patrick Kavanagh. *Fr.*
　The Great Hunger. NoAM; OxBTC

Clay Jug, The. Kabir, *ad. fr. Hindi by* Robert Bly. NU

Clay, sand, and rock, seem a diff'rent birth. Barten Holyday.
　FaBoEE

Clean birds by sevens. The Dove. *Unknown.* GBP

Clean Curtains. Carl Sandburg. PoIA

Clean, green, windy billows notching out the sky. Cardigan Bay.
　John Masefield. EcS

Clean the spittoons, boy. Brass Spittoons. Langston Hughes.
　AmNP (1974 ed.); NoAM

Clean thin hollow of breast. Reflections. Anita Barrows.
　NMM

Cleaning a Coin. Anthony Thwaite. HeHu

Cleaning Day. José Kozer, *tr. fr. Spanish by* David Unger.
　VWA

Cleaning Ship. Charles Keeler. RhR

Cleaning Stables. William Peskett. IPM

Cleaning the Well. Fred Chappell. CSP

Cleaning Up, Clearing Out. Daniel Ross Bronson. AMV-80

Cleanliness. Charles *and* Mary Lamb. OxBChV

Cleanliness is godliness. The Blessing. Ruth Berman. AMV-81

Cleanly, sir, you went to the core of the matter. A Correct
　Compassion. James Kirkup. FaBoTw (1975 ed.); OxBTC

Clear. Angelo Lewis. PoBA

Clear Air of October, The. Robert Bly. NoAM

Clear and cool, clear and cool. The Tide River. Charles
　Kingsley. *Fr.* The Water Babies. OxBChV

Clear Bright. Li Ch'ing-chao, *tr. fr. Chinese by* Kenneth Rexroth.
　BoWoP

Clear bright morning, with its scented air, The. The Fair
　Morning. Jones Very. NOBA

Clear cool note of the cuckoo which has ousted the legitimate nest
　holder, The. Sincere Flattery of W. W. (Americanus).
　James Kenneth Stephen. NOBL; SpRo

Clear had the day been from the dawn. A Fine Day. Michael
　Drayton. *Fr.* The Muses' Elizium. DuDr

Clear light bulb smashed. Haiku. Louis Cuneo. CPA

Clear Midnight, A. Walt Whitman. HAP

Clear moon arcs, The. Red Rock Ceremonies. Anita Endrezze
　Probst. VoR

Clear nights, the massive. War Bride. Douglas Worth. FF

Clear, noon sky at midsummer is God's eye, A. Cosmic Eye.
　A. K. Redwing. VoR

Clear obsession that holds up the walls, The. Addressing His
　Deaf Wife, Kansas, 1916. William Olsen. AMV-81

Clear ocean seems, The. The Double Vision of Manannan.
　*Unknown, tr. by* John Montague. BIrV

Clear sky may tell it wrong, A. The Choice. Frederick Morgan.
　AMV-81

Clear, the shaken water. After the Swimmer. Robert Wallace.
　LiSp

Clear water of the imperial pond, The. Ise Tayu, *tr. fr. Japanese
　by* Kenneth Rexroth *and* Ikuko Atsumi. BoWoP

Clearing, The. Stewart Conn. MS

Clearing, The. Peter Everwine, *after the Nahuatl.* NNaP

Clearing, The. David Gitin. PoW

Clearing the Air. Nancy Willard. RiTi

Cleator Moor. Norman Nicholson. FaBoTw (1975 ed.); MPo

Cleavage. A. R. Ammons. OBAL

Clement Attlee. Michael Benedikt. CAAP; InPS

Clementine. *Unknown. See* Oh, My Darling Clementine.

Cleombrotus retired from the ring. The Retired Boxer. Lucilius,
　*tr. by* Tom Dodge. LiSP

Cleon. Robert Browning. OAEL-2; VLP

Cleopatra to the Asp. Ted Hughes. EBEV

Cleopatra's Lament. Shakespeare. *Fr.* Antony and Cleopatra, V,
　ii. UnPo (1976 ed.)

Clergyman told from his text, A. Who's Next? *Unknown.*
　TDH

Clerical Cabal, The. *Unknown.* APAS

Clerihew: "Spinoza/Collected curiosa." *Unknown.* NOBL

Clerihews, *sels.* E. C. Bentley.
　"Adam Smith." FaBoCo
　"Art of biography, The." NOBL
　George Hirst. PoPle
　"George the Third." FaBoCo; NOBL
　"I am not Mahomet." NOBL
　"John Stuart Mill." FaBoCo
　" 'No,' said Charles Peace." NOBL
　" 'No, sir,' said General Sherman." NOBL
　Professor James Dewar, F. R. S. PoPle
　"Sir Christopher Wren." FaBoCo; InPk
　"Sir Humphry Davy." FaBoCo
　"There exists no proof as." NOBL
　"What I like about Clive." NOBL
　(Lord Clive.) PoPle

Clerimont's Song. Ben Jonson. *See* Simplex Munditiis.

Clerk Bukashkin is our neighbor, The. Antiworlds. Andrei
　Voznesensky, *tr. by* Richard Wilbur. NIL

Clerk Colvill. *Unknown.* FaBoBa; GBP
　(Clark Colven, *with music.*) Epi

Clerk of Oxford, The. Chaucer. *Fr.* The Canterbury Tales:
　Prologue. OxBM
　("Clerk ther was of Oxenford, A.") InPS

Clerk Saunders. *Unknown.* FaBoBa; ILP (1975 ed.); LoAs; SLP
　(Clark Sanders.) PeBB

Clerk ther was of Oxenford also, A. The Clerk of Oxford.
　Chaucer. *Fr.* The Canterbury Tales: Prologue. InPS;
　OxBM

Clerks, The. E. A. Robinson. CABA (1972 ed.); PiAm; VoPo

Clerk's Dream, The. Herbert Scott. TC

Clerk's Song II. Norman H. Russell. VW

Clerk's Twa Sons o Owsenford, The. *Unknown.* PeBB

Clever Chinese say they read, The. Cat's Eyes. Francis Scarfe. PCat

Clever Skipper, The. *Unknown.* AmFP

Clever Tom Clinch Going to Be Hanged. Swift. FaBoBa; ILP (1975 ed.); NIL

Cliches with worn wit combined. On a Lover of Books. Geoffrey Grigson. FaBoEE

Click Go the Shears, Boys. *Unknown.* MAuV

Clickety-Clack. Paul Blackburn. NoAM

Client meeting at twelve, that lot of layabouts. Nine o'Clock Thoughts on the 73 Bus. Peter Porter. POL

Cliff, The. David Rowbotham. CAAP

Cliff Klingenhagen. E. A. Robinson. IP; PAIC; PiAm; STS

Cliff-Top, The. Robert Bridges. FPB

Cliffside Path, The. Swinburne. A Midsummer Holiday, VI. VLP

Climate of Paradise, The. Louis Simpson. NOBA

Climb at court for me that will. Seneca, *tr. by* Andrew Marvell. *Fr.* Thyestes, II. OBVE

Climbed from the road and found. Latitude, Longitude. George Oppen. CAAP

Climbing. Daniel Mark Epstein. AMV-80

Climbing. Gloria Fuertes, *tr. fr. Spanish by* Philip Levine. PBWP

Climbing from Merthyr through the dew of August mornings. A Small War. Leslie Norris. HeHu

Climbing from the Lethal dead. Orpheus. Yvor Winters. NOBA; PiAm; VGW

Climbing in Glencoe. Andrew Young. LiSp

Climbing in 3rd, then 2nd up N. C. 181. Sitting Bear Mountain. Barbara Lovell. BCr

Climbing mountains. Human Dilemma. Jim Rosemergy. AMV-80

Climbing the last steps to your house, I knew. Light Dying. Brendan Kennelly. PFIr

Climbing the rutted path, the lights of the town. The Phases of Darkness. Paul Petrie. TAP

Climbing the staircase. Simplicity. Louis Simpson. ILP (1975 ed.); InPS; Prf

Climbing the stairway gray with urban midnight. Effort at Speech. William Meredith. NYP; Prf; WeW

Climbing their way through their maternity. The Mountaineers. Christine Bress. PMW

Climbing through the January snow, into the Lobo Canyon. Mountain Lion. D. H. Lawrence. BoAnP; OxBTC; RFM

Climbing You. Erica Jong. PoA

Climbs hobbling. A Very Old Woman. Clayton Eshleman. MAT

Clinging to my breast, no stronger. Spinster's Lullaby. Vassar Miller. BoWoP; CSP; NMM; RiTi

Clinic: Examination. Audrey Conard. AMV-80

Clio's Protest. Sheridan. FaBoEE

Clipper *Dunbar* to the clipper *Cutty Sark,* The. Ethel Anderson. PoTa

Clippety cloppety,/ Cesare Borgia. Chip. George Starbuck. OBAL

Clitta, clatta, clatta, clatter. Thomas Holley Chivers. *Fr.* Railroad Song. PeD

Clock, The. Patricia Beer. HeHu

Clock-a-Clay (The Ladybird). John Clare. OAEL-2; OBP; PCOP; VLP

Clock in the Square, A. Adrienne Rich. HeIP; NIL

Clock of my days winds down, The. The Alligator Bride. Donald Hall. ConAP; EAS

Clock says, The, "When will it be morning?" After Lorca. Ted Hughes. PoA

Clock stopped, A. Emily Dickinson. AmVN

Clock without Hands. John Frederick Nims. PoA

Clocks. Malka Locker, *tr. fr. Yiddish by* Jeremy Garber. VWA

Clockwork. Paul F. Fericano. CPA

Clockwork skating Wordsworth on the ice, A. Xmas for the Boys. Gavin Ewart. OBSV

Clod and the Pebble, The. Blake. *Fr.* Songs of Experience. AnMo; CABA (1972 ed.); ILP (1975 ed.); InPS; LAuP; LoAs; MBPR; NOBE; PoIA; SS; STS

Cloe ("Bright as the day, and like the morning fair"). George Granville. FaBoCo; FaBoEE; NIL

Cloe, by your command, in verse I write. A Letter from Artemisia in the Town to Cloe in the Country. Earl of Rochester. ESaP

Cloe's the wonder of her sex. George Granville. FaBoEE (*At. to* Charles Sackville); POL

Clogged ashtray a dead lung, A. Grass, Grass. George Bowering. NeAC

Cloisonne. Jane Flanders. PoUp

Cloistered afternoons, The. Into Your Hands. Ann Marie Huck. FoP

Cloisters. Anthony Barnett. VWA

Clonakilty. *Unknown.* FaBoEE

Clonfeacle. Paul Muldoon. CIP; IPM

Clonmel Jail. *Unknown, tr. fr. Irish by* Valentin Iremonger. BIrV

Clorinda and Damon. Andrew Marvell. PAIC

Cloris, I cannot say your eyes. To Cloris. Sir Charles Sedley. BoLoP

Clorox Kid, The. Kirk Robertson. GP

Close by those meads for ever crowned with flow'rs. Pope. *Fr.* The Rape of the Lock, III. OBSV

Close his eyes; his work is done! Dirge for a Soldier. George Henry Boker. PeD

Close Quarters. John Banister Tabb. OBAL

Close thine eyes, and sleep secure. On a Quiet Conscience. Charles I, King of England. PoPle

Close to a quarter of a century since then. A Christmas Carol. Thomas Herbert Parry-Williams, *tr. by* Joseph P. Clancy. OBW

Close to nature my brother, your thoughts ring softly. To an Indian Poet. Patty L. Harjo. VoR

Close to the gates a spacious garden lies. The Gardens of Alcinous. Homer, *tr. by* Pope. *Fr.* The Odyssey, VIII. OAEL-1; OBVE

Close to the west the great ocean is singing. Two Rain Songs. *Unknown.* AKE

Close under here, I watched two lovers once. Robin Hyde. *Fr.* The Beaches. ATNZ

Close-Up. A. R. Ammons. PoA

Close up the casement, draw the blind. Shut Out That Moon. Thomas Hardy. CMoP (1970 ed.); ILP (1975 ed.); NoAM; NOBE

Close Your Eyes! Arna Bontemps. AmNP (1974 ed.); FB; IPWM; PoBA

Close your eyes! Feel the. Haiku for Halloween. Myra Cohn Livingston. IWK

Close your sleepy eyes. My Little Buckaroo. *Unknown.* BPAW

Closed like confessionals, they thread. Ambulances. Philip Larkin. FaBoTw (1975 ed.); UsP

Closed System, The. Larry Eigner. VWA

Closed window looks down, A. Ka 'Ba. Amiri Baraka. BPo; CAPP; CNA; PiAm; TAP

Closer First to Earth. Anne Hazlewood-Brady. IHMS

Closet, The. Dave Smith. HeS

Closet. Judith Thurman. FPB

Closing of the Rodeo, The. William Jay Smith. GOA; PPoD

Closing the main door at night is the day's. Doorstep. Frank Ormsby. IPM

Cloth of Gold, the, *sel.* M. Krishnamurti. "Now the last step! Behold." PeD

Cloth-plant grew till it covered the thorn bush, The. Widow's Lament, *tr. fr. Chinese by* Arthur Waley. *Fr. Shih Ching.* BoWoP

Cloth was laid in the Vorkhouse hall, The. The Workhouse Boy. *Unknown.* GBP; PeBB; VLP

Clothes. Elizabeth Jennings. RAE

Clothes, The. Rayzel Zychlinska, *tr. fr. Yiddish by* Marc Kaminsky. VWA

Clothes Do but Cheat and Cozen Us. Robert Herrick. CaPo

Clothes in which you saw me, The. The Clothes. Rayzel Zychlinska, *tr. by* Marc Kaminsky. VWA

Clothes Maketh the Man. Theodore Weiss. NoAM

Clothes Pit, The. Douglas Dunn. OxBTC

Clothesline, The. John Stevens Wade. FAF

Cloud, The. Shelley. MBPR; PPM
Orbed Maiden, *sel.* Moon

Cloud. Martha Webb. PHC

Cloud-backed heron will not move, The. The Heron. Vernon Watkins. UnPo (1976 ed.)

Cloud Burst. Hubert Witheford. ATNZ

Cloud capped peaks fill the eyes. On a Visit to Ch'ung Chen Taoist Temple. Yu Hsüan-chi, *tr. by* Kenneth Rexroth *and* Ling Chung. PBWP

Cloud Factory, The. John Haines. EAS

Cloud-Flower Lullaby, The. *Tr. fr. Tewa Indian by* H. J. Spinden. WTO

Cloud-Mobile, The. May Swenson. SO

Cloud moved close, A. The bulk of the wind shifted. The Visitant. Theodore Roethke. CMoP (1970 ed.); PPoe; UnPo (1976 ed.)

Cloud of Ghosts, A. Russell Grant. PMW

Cloud of witnesses, A. To whom? To what? A Fanfare for the Makers. Louis MacNeice. NOBE

Cloud-piles o'er Kona's sea whet my joy, The. Fathomless Is My Love. Kalola, *tr. fr. Hawaiian by* N. B. Emerson. WTO

Cloud-puffball, torn tufts, tossed pillows. That Nature Is a Heraclitean Fire and of the Comfort of the Resurrection. Gerard Manley Hopkins. AnMo; BiP; CABA (1972 ed.); Epi; OAEL-2; VLP

Cloud Shadows. John Updike. VoPo

Cloud Unfolding, The. Ernesto Trejo. CPA

Cloud walking, A. Native Element. William Jeffrey. MS

Cloudburst and Soaring Moon. "Hugh MacDiarmid." NoAM

Clouded Morning, The. Jones Very. NOBA

Clouded sun on coolin' morn. The Trail Herd. *Unknown.* BPAW

Clouded with snow. Winter. Walter de la Mare. OAEL-2

Clouds. Rupert Brooke. OxBTC

Clouds. Aileen Fisher. FPB

Clouds. Philip Levine. MPA

Clouds, The. Mirabai, *tr. fr. Medieval Hindi; English version by* Robert Bly. NU

Clouds, The. William Carlos Williams. VGW

Clouds are electric in this university, The. Ghazals: Homage to Ghalib. Adrienne Rich. CAAP; NIL

Clouds are giving way: bushes. April. John Linthicum. AMV-80

Clouds darken the plain. Hand. Edouard Roditi. EAS

Clouds fell. Song in White. Anne Le Dressay. AMV-80

Clouds, lingering yet, extend in solid bars. Composed by the Side of Grasmere Lake. Wordsworth. MBPR

Clouds move over. The Park: U.S.A. May Miller. PoUp

Clouds prophesy; the sky portends. Year's End. Jim Barnes. HeS

Clouds raced across the sky like so many buffalos. Sweet Soledad. Alejandro Murguia. CPA

Clouds scattered across the sky all so far away. The Words. Lee Harwood. EAS

Clouds spout upon her. Rain on a Grave. Thomas Hardy. LoAs

Clouds stretch into their. Daybreak on a Pennsylvania Highway. John Daunt. AMV-80

Clouds swollen with rain. Door to the Sun. Ralph J. Molls, Jr. HeS

Clouds That Are So Light, The. Edward Thomas. FaBoTw (1975 ed.)

Clove as Ego. Daniel Halpern. CAAP

Clove, salmon knocking. For Lerida. David St. John. AmPA

Clover. John Banister Tabb. PCOP

Cloverleaf, A. John Fandel. *Fr. Out of Our Blue.* PoIA

Clown, The. Janet Frame. ATNZ

Clown, and All the Sea behind Him. Vincent O'Sullivan. ATNZ

Clownlike, happiest on your hands. You're. Sylvia Plath. FaBoTw (1975 ed.); NCSH

Cloyce Hamilton. My Mother's Milkman. Diane Wakoski. PCho

Club 82: Lisa. Cynthia Kramer Genser. NYP

Clumsy. J. B. Lee. TDH

Clustered in the forest around. Kenneth Rexroth. *Fr. On Flower Wreath Hill.* GP

Clustering up on my Christmas steps. Carolers. Nancy G. Westerfield. AMV-81

Clusters of ruins on vine-shoots of steel. Grave at Cassino. Noah Stern, *tr. by* Harold Schimmel. VWA

Clutter of Mothers, A. Edwin Brock. IPWM

Clydesdale New Town Walk. Duncan Glen. MIS

"C'mon, get out." Sunflower Rock. Paul Blackburn. NoAM

C'mon godamya c'mon gimme that pussy! Chickitten Gitten! Ted Joans. GP

Coal. Audre Lorde. CNA; PoBA; UsP

Coal black woman fry no meat for me. Seven Sister Blues. *Unknown.* BluL

Coal Diggin' Blues. *Unknown.* AmFP

Coal Fire in Winter, A. Thomas McGrath. NU

Coal Loadin' Blues. *Unknown.* AmFP

Coal Mine Disaster's Last Trapped Man Contemplates Salvation, The. William Meissner. AMV-80

Coal Miner's Goodbye, A. *Unknown.* AmFP

Coal Miner's Grace. Jay Divine. AMV-80

Coal Strike. Norman Macleod. SPT

Coarse/jocosity. Archy Confesses. Don Marquis. *Fr. Archy and Mehitabel.* SS

Coast, The: Norfolk. Frances Cornford. OxBTC

Coast of Peru, The. *Unknown.* FSW; RhR

Coasting toward Midnight at the Southeastern Fair. David Bottoms. AMV-81

Coat, A. W. B. Yeats. CABA (1972 ed.); CMoP (1970 ed.); NoAM

Coax Me, *with music.* Andrew Sterling. FSN

"Cobalt and umber and ultramarine." The Paint Box. E. V. Rieu. SO

Cobb Would Have Caught It. Robert Fitzgerald. HAP; WeW

Cobbled with rough stone which rings my tread. Allotments: April. Bernard Spencer. PSN

Cobbler. Karren Alenier. PoUp

Cobwebs and dust have long. Hut near Desolated Plains. Alistair Campbell. ATNZ

Cocaine Blues. *Unknown.* FSW
Cocaine Lil. *Unknown.* MAT; MiP
  (Cocaine Bill and Morphine Sue.) FSW
  (Cocaine Lil and Morphine Sue.) GBP; PeBB
Cock. Aharon Amir, *tr. fr. Hebrew by* Bernhard Frank.
  AMV–81
Cock, The. A. Buttigieg. RAE
Cock, The. Ewa Lipska, *tr. fr. Polish by* Peter Jay *and* Geri
  Lipschultz. VWA
Cock-a-doodle-doo! Mother Goose. MG
Cock-a-doodle-doo the brass-lined rooster goes. Dog. John
  Crowe Ransom. InPS; OBAL
Cock-a-Hoop. Isabella Gardner. UsP; WPE
Cock and the Bull, The. Charles Stuart Calverley. FaBoCo;
  FaBoNo
  "You see this pebble-stone?" *sel.* VLP
Cock Crow. Rosemary Dobson. MAuV
Cock-Crow. Kenneth Slessor. MAuV
Cock-Crow. Edward Thomas. ILP (1975 ed.)
Cock-crow clouds wave like nebulous fingers, The. Morning from
  My Office Window. John A. Wood. AMV–81
Cock-crowing. Henry Vaughan. OAEL–1; SCP–1
Cock Crowing in a Poulterer's Shop, A. John Ferguson. BoAnP
Cock crows, The. Depression before Spring. Wallace Stevens.
  OBAL
Cock doth crow, the wind doth blow, The. Mother Goose. GBP
Cock is crowing, The. Written in March. Wordsworth. CTV;
  MBPR; PBMP; UnPo (1976 ed.)
Cock Lorell's Boat. *Unknown.* TVS
Cock of Glory is the *coq français,* The. The French, 1870–1871.
  *Unknown.* FaBoEE
Cock Robin he got a neat tippet at spring. The Red Robin.
  John Clare. RAE
Cock sparrow with a sweet, The. Rocking. A. R. Ammons. GP
Cockerel. *Unknown. See* I Have a Gentle Cock.
Cockles and Mussels (Molly Malone), *with music. Unknown, ad.*
  *by* James Morehead. BLSH; GSB
  (Molly Malone.) FSW
Cockleshells. *Unknown. See* Waly, Waly ("When cockleshells
  turn silver bells").
Cock's far cry, The. Cock-Crow. Kenneth Slessor. MAuV
Cocktail is a pleasant drink, The. R-e-m-o-r-s-e. George Ade.
  OBAL
Cocktails. Susan MacDonald. PoW
Cocky's Calendar, *sel.* David Campbell.
  To a Ground-Lark. MAuV
Cocoa Morning. Bob Kaufman. AmNP (1974 ed.)
Coconut. Mario Satz, *tr. fr. Spanish by* Willis Barnstone. VWA
Coconut for Katerina, A. Sandra McPherson. FiCP
Cod Liver Oil. *Unknown.* FSW
Coda. Basil Bunting. *Fr. Briggflatts.* OAEL–2; TwMBP
Coda. Fred Johnson. CNA
Coda. Dorothy Parker. SBG
Coda. Ezra Pound. NOBA
Coda. James Tate. AmPA
Coda. William Carlos Williams. NOBA
Code, The. Robert Frost. InPS; PoA; UnPo (1976 ed.)
Code of Morals, A. Kipling. FaBoCo
Codfish Shanty, The. *Unknown.* GBP
  (Cape Cod Girls.) FSW
Codicil. Alvin Aubert. CoPAm
Codicil. Robert Huff. CNW
Codicil. Kenneth Rexroth. MPA
Codicil. Ruth Stone. BoWoP
Codicil. Derek Walcott. NoAM
Co-ed protester named Lil, A. Ogden Nash. SFF

Coelia, *sels.* William Percy.
  "It shall be sayd I dy'de for Coelia," XIX. AAS
  "Relent, my deere, yet unkind Coelia," XVII. AAS
Coffee. J. V. Cunningham. VGW
Coffee-cups cool on the Vicar's harmonium. A Game of
  Consequences. Paul Dehn. NOBL
Coffee Den, Cedar Rapids, The. Jim Mulac. AcAn
Coffee that they give us, The. Gee, but I Want to Go Home.
  *Unknown.* FSW
Cognac and Farewell to My Sanity. Ann Menebroker. PoW
Coil of Glass, A (I). Stanley Burnshaw. SPT
Coil of Glass, A (II). Stanley Burnshaw. SPT
Coin from B.C. Nicholas Flocos. SA
Coins handsome as Nero's; of good substance and weight.
  Geoffrey Hill. Mercian Hymns, XI. HAP
Cokby, Part Two. Jerome Rothenberg. NNaP
Cokkils. Sydney Goodsir Smith. PoA
Cold. Robert Francis. PoA
Cold, The. Lance Henson. CDW
Cold. Glyn Hughes. LP
Cold and Heat. *Tr. fr. Hawaiian by* M. W. Beckwith. WTO
Cold and Married War, A. Marge Piercy. Psy
Cold and the colors of cold: mineral, shell. Cold. Robert
  Francis. PoA
Cold Are the Crabs. Edward Lear. Epi; FaBoNo; VLP
Cold as no love, and wild with all negation. Stevie Smith.
  FaBoEE
Cold as the breath of winds that blow. Lucasta's World.
  Richard Lovelace. CaPo
Cold before the Moonrise, The. W. S. Merwin. CoPAm
Cold blood or warm, crawling or fluttering. Pet Shop. Louis
  MacNeice. BoAnP
Cold-blooded Creatures. Elinor Wylie. SBG
Cold-blooded in warm waters, my Nurse. Among Sharks. Al
  Lee. AmPA
Cold blows the wind to my true-love. The Unquiet Grave.
  *Unknown.* FaBoBa; FSW; ILP (1975 ed.); WIF
Cold Coffee. John Williams. CoPAm
Cold, coiled line of mottled lead, A. Massasauga. Hamlin
  Garland. BPAW
Cold, cold! A Song of Winter. *Unknown, tr. by* Kuno Meyer.
  PFIr
Cold, cold the year draws to its end. *Tr. fr. Chinese by* Arthur
  Waley. BoWoP;
"Cold coming we had of it, A." Journey of the Magi. T. S.
  Eliot. BoReV; CABA (1972 ed.); HAP; HeIP; ILP (1975
  ed.); IP; NIL; OxBTC; PBMP; PChr; PPoe; TAP; TCP; TT;
  UsP
Cold earth slept below, The. To ——. Shelley. MBPR
Cold eyelids that hide like a jewel. Dolores. Swinburne. VLP
Cold Fall. Richard Eberhart. PAIC
Cold Fear. Elizabeth Madox Roberts. WPE
Cold Feet. Brian Lee. FPB
Cold Feet in Columbus. William Heath. TAT
Cold felt cold until our blood, The. Phantasia for Elvira
  Shatayev. Adrienne Rich. LiSp
Cold Front. Peter Sharpe. AMV–80
Cold front:/ The pregnant Arctic pads. From a New and Wild
  Distance. Ted Weiant. BCr
Cold Glow: Icehouses. David Wojahn. AMV–81
Cold grey walls. San Francisco County Jail Cell B-6. Conyus.
  PoBA
Cold had a corpulent pig, A. A Corpulent Pig. Marnie *and*
  Harnie Wood. TDH
Cold has put blue horses where lambs were, The. Blue Horses.
  Ed Roberson. PoBA

Cold Heaven, The. W. B. Yeats. HAP; NoAM; OAEL-2; WeW

Cold in the earth, and the deep snow piled above thee! Remembrance. Emily Brontë. BoLoP; BoWoP; EBEV; HAP; ILP (1975 ed.); NOBE; OBP; PBWP; VLP; WPE

Cold Irish Earth, The. Knute Skinner. InPK

Cold Iron. Kipling. ILP (1975 ed.)

Cold moon hangs to the sky by its horn, The. The Night of the Dance. Thomas Hardy. OBP

Cold morning early. Two Mornings. Lawrence McGaugh. PoBA

Cold night, the sidewalk we walk on icy, A. Christmas Eve Service at Midnight at St. Michael's. Robert Bly. NNaP

Cold nights on the farm, a sock-shod. On the Disadvantage of Central Heating. Amy Clampitt. AMV-80

Cold place, A. Sandra Maria Esteves. NW

Cold Rain Obscures L. A. Tonight, A. Tony Quagliano. PHC

Cold remote islands, The. Night. Louise Bogan. UnPo (1976 ed.)

Cold rises around, The. Midwinter, Presolstice. Margaret Atwood. Psy

Cold slope is standing in darkness, The. December Night. W. S. Merwin. CAPP

Cold Snap. Kathy Mangan. AMV-80

Cold Snap, A. Robert Tait. SLP

Cold Spring, The. Denise Levertov. CAAP; Psy

Cold stings your bare cheeks and arms, The. To a Cactus Seller. Anwar Shaul, tr. by Yoffee Berkovitz. VWA

Cold Term. Amiri Baraka. BPo; CNA

Cold was the night wind, drifting fast the snow fell. The Widow, Sapphics. Robert Southey. ESaP

Cold Water. Donald Hall. NCSH

Cold Water Flat. Philip Booth. NowV

Cold Wave Blues. Unknown. BluL

Colder. Erica Jong. MMD

Colding Nights. Roland Tharp. PHC

Coldly, sadly descends. Rugby Chapel. Matthew Arnold. ILP (1975 ed.); VLP

Coldness, The. Jon Silkin. CABA (1972 ed.); VWA

Coldness that falls upon the hours, The. Cold Fall. Richard Eberhart. PAIC

Cole, that unwearied prince of Colchester. After Lord Tennyson. G. K. Chesterton. NOBL

Cole Younger. Unknown. AmFP; FSW

Coleman lantern light poses the parameter of darkness. Big Sur Summer. Delia Chilgren. NPW

Colenso Rhymes for Orthodox Children. Bret Harte. OBAL

Coleridge received the person from Porlock. Thoughts about the Person from Porlock. Stevie Smith. FaBoCo

Colette, Poor Clare. Colette Inez. AATT

Coleus bloomed, The. I Put the Telephone Back on Its Receiver. Morty Sklar. AcAn

Colin Barnes, Drums. John Smith. Fr. Jazz for Five. MPo

Colin Clout, abr. John Skelton. TVS
  Sels.
    "And if ye stand in doubt." OAEL-1
    "Doctors that learned be." OBSV

Colin Clout's Come Home Again, sels. Spenser.
    "Of loves perfection perfectly to speake." OAEL-1
    "Why, Colin, since thou found'st such grace." TVS

Colin my dear when shall it please thee sing. November. Spenser. Fr. The Shepheardes Calendar. Epi

Coliseum, The. Poe. NOBA

Collaborations. Cathleen Quirk. MMD

Collage for Richard Davis, A—Two Short Forms. De Leon Harrison. PoBA

Collapsible. Tom Raworth. EAS

Collapsible lover, the spider in iniquitousness, The. Anthology of Nouns. Parker Tyler. PoA

Collar, The. George Herbert. AnMo; BiP; BoRev; CABA (1972 ed.); EBEV; ExPo (1973 ed.); HAP; HeIP; ILP (1975 ed.); InPS; IPWM; MetP; NIL; NOBE; OAEL-1; OBP; OBW; PoPle; PPoD; PPoe; PPP; SCP-1

Collar-Bone of a Hare, The. W. B. Yeats. OxBTC

Collective Forces, The. Deirdra Baldwin. PoUp

Collector, The. Richard Behm. AMV-81

Collector, The. Robert F. Whisler. AMV-81

Collector by the sea, The. Sea Known. John Sollid. PoW

Collector of lost beads, buttons, bird bones. The Pack Rat. Robert Pack. CoPAm; PPP; WeW

Collector's Note. Arthur J. Bull. HeHu

Colleen Rue. Unknown. BIrV

College Formal: Renaissance Casino. Langston Hughes. ILP (1975 ed.)

Colley's Run-I-O. Unknown. AmFP

Collie puppies in a dooryard. Wonder. Bernard Raymund. GDP

Collier, The. Vernon Watkins. FaBoTw (1975 ed.); MPo; OBW

Collier's Wife, The. D. H. Lawrence. OxBTC

Collies, The. Edward Anthony. GDP

Collin my deere and most entire beloved. To the Most Excellent and Learned Shepheard Collin Cloute. William Smith. Chloris: Dedication. AAS

Colloquy in Black Rock. Robert Lowell. CAPP; NoAM; PiAm; STS

Colm had a cat. The Pets. Robert Farren. ECBV

Colma—It is night. James Macpherson. Fr. The Songs of Selma. SLP

Cologne. Samuel Taylor Coleridge. FaBoEE; MBPR; PBMP

Cologne. Hilde Domin, tr. fr. German by Tudor Morris. VWA

Colombo. March. The city white fire. Auschwitz from Colombo. Anne Ranasinghe. VWA

Colonel Chartres. John Arbuthnot. See Epitaph on Colonel Francis Chartres.

Colonel Cold strode up the line. Winter Warfare. Edgell Rickword. OxBTC

Colonel Fazackerley. Charles Causley. OSF

Colonel from Cheltenham stopped everyone, A. W. H. Auden. Fr. A Happy New Year. OBSV

Colonel Martin. W. B. Yeats. Epi

Colonels here in solemn manner meet, The. Thomas Brown. FaBoEE

Colonialism ("The colonialist governments"). Cabdullaahi Qarshe, tr. fr. Somali by J. W. Johnson. WTO

Colonus' Praise. Sophocles, tr. fr. Greek by W. B. Yeats. Fr. Oedipus at Colonus. Epi; OBVE

Colophon for Lan-t'ing Hsiu-Hsi. John Peck. AmPA

Color, The. John Haines. GP

Color—caste—denomination. Emily Dickinson. PBMP; TAP

Color in the Wheat. Hamlin Garland. BPAW

Color it/ blue funk. Chromo. Sarah Webster Fabio. CNA

Color of Honey. Anne Waldman. TV

Color of the flowers, The,/ has faded. Ono no Komachi, tr. fr. Japanese by Kenneth Rexroth. BoWoP

Color of the year spills down the street, The. November Walk. Susanne Doyle. AMV-81

Colorado Trail, The. Unknown. FSW

Coloratura. Geoff Page. AMV-81

Coloratura Named Luna, A. J. F. Wilson. TDH

Colored folks work on the Mississippi. Ol' Man River. Oscar Hammerstein II. BLSo

Colored pictures/ of all things to eat: dirty. The Songs of Maximus. Charles Olson. CoPAm; NoAM

Coloring Margarine. William Hathaway. AMV-81

Colours. Frances Evans. RAE

Colours/ painted on you. Dream Songs. Karoniaktatie. NW

Colors for Mama. Barbara Mahone. CNA; PoBA

Colors of Night, The, *sel.* Scott Momaday. Blue. BCr

Colors of the Dark One have penetrated Mira's body, The. Why Mira Can't Go Back to Her Old House. Mirabai, *English version by* Robert Bly. NU

Colors shifting. Time of Fish Dying. Gabriela Melinescu, *tr. by* Stavros Deligiorgis. BoWoP

Colossi. Albert De Pietro. AATT

Colossus, The. Sylvia Plath. AnMo; CAPP; CoPAm; IP; NoAM; NOBA; Psy; TAP

Colt, The. Raymond Knister. AKE

Coltish horseplay of the locker room, The. The Feast of Stephen. Anthony Hecht. HAP

Coltrane must understand how. Soul. D. L. Graham. PoBA

Colts behind their mothers. *Unknown, tr. fr.* Japanese. PCOP

Columbia ("Thus down a lone valley with cedars o'erspread"). *Unknown.* AmFP

Columbia College, 1796. Joseph Shippey. PeD

Columbia, the Gem of the Ocean. David T. Shaw. BTTM; CTV, *1st stanza and chorus only*; FSW

Columbiad, Trust the Lord, *with music. Unknown.* AH

Columbiad, The, *sel.* Joel Barlow. "Now had Columbus well enjoy'd the sight," *fr.* VIII. PiAm

Columbian poet, whom we've all respected. Letter to an American Visitor. Alex Comfort. OxBTC

Columbia's Agony. "Orpheus C. Kerr." OBAL

Columbine, The. Jones Very. NOBA; PiAm

Columbus. Joaquin Miller. AmVN; BTTM; CTV; RhR

Columbus. Ogden Nash. OFD; RhR

Columbus. Muriel Rukeyser. GOA

Columbus. Schiller, *tr. fr.* German *by* Erika Gathmann Koessler. OFD

Columbus. Louis Simpson. MPo

Columbus, *sel.* Tennyson. "Chains, my good lord: in your raised brows I read." OFD

Columbus and the Mermaids. Elizabeth J. Coatsworth. GOA

Columbus Day. Gabrielle Edgcomb. PoUp

Columbus discovered America. A Concise History of the World. Ira Sadoff. AmPA

Columbus is remembered by young men. And of Columbus. Horace Gregory. GOA; OFD

Columbus looks towards the New World. Space. William Hart-Smith. GAS

Columbus Stockade Blues. Woody Guthrie. FSW

Columns and Caryatids. Carolyn Kizer. WPE

Com my swete, com my flowr. The Assumption. *Unknown.* OxBM

Com out, Lazer, what-so befalle! Come Out, Lazarus! *Unknown.* OxBM

Comanche. Gary Gildner. PH

Comanche Ghost Dance: An Impression. Lance Henson. VoR

Comb or womb of what we lay down nightly, A. The People's Choice: The Dream Poems II. Amiri Baraka. BiP

Combat, The. Edwin Muir. CMoP (1970 ed.); NOBE

Combing. Gladys Cardiff. CDW

Come. Bob Kaufman. MIT

Come,/ Let us roam the night together. Harlem Night Song. Langston Hughes. OSP

Come/ with/ me. Barbara Chase-Riboud. *Fr.* Come with Me. OSP

Come a landsman, a pinsman, a tinker or a tailor. Old Maid's Song. *Unknown.* FSW

Come again (Hunter/ Garcia). Atlantis. Robert Ferguson. BrS

Come again to the place. After the Visit. Thomas Hardy. NOBE

Come, all my good people, and listen to my song. Tittery-Irie-Aye. *Unknown.* AmFP

Come all my jolly seamen, likewise the landsmen, too. The *Cumberland* and the *Merrimac. Unknown.* AmFP

Come all New England men. Giles Corey and Goodwyfe Corey—A Ballad of 1692. *Unknown.* PAIC

Come all of you good workers. Which Side Are You On? Florence Reese. FSW

Come all ye bold sailors/ Who sail round Cape Horn. The Coast of Peru. *Unknown.* RhR

Come all ye bold sailors that follow the lakes. Red Iron Ore. *Unknown.* FSW

Come all ye bold undaunted ones who brave the winter's frost. Fifteen Ships on Georges Banks. *Unknown.* AmFP

Come all ye bould Free Staters now and listen to my lay. The Lay of Oliver Gogarty. William Dawson. PeBB

Come All Ye Fair and Tender Ladies. *Unknown.* AmFP

Come all ye foreign strolling gentry. Four Epigrams on the Naturalization Bill. John Byrom. NOBL

Come all ye gentle Christians [*or* you Christian people], wherever you may be. Charles Guiteau. *Unknown.* AmFP; FSW

Come all ye gents vot cleans the plate. Jeames of Buckley Square. Thackeray. VLP

Come, all ye good people, my story to hear. Poor Ellen Smith. *Unknown.* AmFP

Come all ye jolly boatsman boys. Blow the Candle Out. *Unknown.* AmFP

"Come all ye jolly fellows, who delight in a gun." Polly Vaughn (Molly Bawn). *Unknown.* AmFP

Come, all ye jolly sailors bold. The *Arethusa.* Prince Hoare. FaPoR

Come all ye Knights, ye Knights of Molites. The Sons of Levi. *Unknown.* AmFP

Come all ye Lewiston fac'try girls. The Factory Girl's Come-All-Ye. *Unknown.* AmFP; OBAL

Come All Ye Mourning Pilgrims, *with music.* John A. Granade. AH

Come, All Ye People, *with music.* George R. Seltzer. AH

Come all ye young fellows that follow the sea. Blow the Man Down. *Unknown.* BLSH; BLSo.

Come all ye young people and all my relations. Mr. Davis's Experience. *Unknown.* AmFP

Come all ye young sailormen who've rounded the horn. Coast of Peru. *Unknown.* FSW

Come all you blessed Christians dear. A Ballad from the Seven Dials Press. *Unknown.* VLP

Come all you bold fisherman, listen to me. Blow Ye Winds Westerly. *Unknown.* FSW

Come all you booze buyers, if you want to hear. Kentucky Bootlegger. *Unknown.* FSW

Come all you brave Americans and unto me give ear. The Capture of Major André. *Unknown.* BTTM

Come all you Christian people, wherever you may be. *See* Come all ye gentle Christians, wherever you may be.

Come all you cockers, far and near. The Bonny Grey. *Unknown.* GBP

Come All You Fair and Tender Ladies. *Unknown. See* Little Sparrow.

Come all you fair and tender maids. Rue. *Unknown.* FSW

Come all you fair gallants, fair gallants attend. Pretty Polly of Topsham. *Unknown.* FSW

Come all you gallant heroes, I'd have you lend an ear. Major André. *Unknown.* AmFP

Come all you gallant poachers that ramble void of care.  Van Dieman's Land. *Unknown.* FaBoBa; FSW

Come all you girls and all you boys.  Kitty Morey. *Unknown.* AmFP

Come all you good fellows wherever you be.  The Rackets around the Blue Mountain Lake. *Unknown.* FSW

Come all you good people.  Lula Vires. *Unknown.* AmFP

Come all you good people of every degree.  The Bermondsey Tragedy. *Unknown.* VLP

Come all you heroes, where'er you be.  The Dying Sergeant. *Unknown.* AmFP

Come all you jolly [*or* old time] cowboys [*or* skinners] and listen to my song.  The Buffalo Skinners. *Unknown.* BPAW; FSW; GBP; PeBB

Come all you jolly fellows, come listen to my song.  The Shanty Boys and the Pine. *Unknown.* AmFP

Come all you jolly freighters that ever hit the road.  Freighting from Wilcox to Globe. *Unknown.* AmFP

Come all you jolly-hearted sailors.  False Nancy. *Unknown.* AmFP

Come all you jolly highwaymen and outlaws of the land.  Bold Jack Donahue. *Unknown.* AmFP

Come all you jolly husbandmen and listen to my song.  The Honest Ploughman. *Unknown.* GSB

Come all you jolly jokers, if you want to have some fun.  The Great American Bum. *Unknown.* FSW

Come all ye jolly lumbermen and listen to my song.  Canada-I-O. *Unknown.* FSW

Come all you jolly lumbermen, and listen to my song.  Colley's Run-I-O. *Unknown.* AmFP

Come all you jolly lumbermen, I'd have you for to know.  The Banks of the Gaspereaux. *Unknown.* AmFP

Come all you jolly railroad men, and I'll sing you if I can.  Way Out in Idaho. *Unknown.* AmFP; BPAW

Come all you jolly seamen who plough that restless deep.  Jimmy Judge. *Unknown.* AmFP

Come all you jolly shanty boys that work the shanty and go.  Turner's Camp on the Chippewa. *Unknown.* AmFP

Come all you jolly skinners and listen to my song. *See* Come all you jolly cowboys and listen to my song.

Come all you loyal Unionists, wherever you may be.  Virginia's Bloody Soil. *Unknown.* AmFP

Come all you men and maidens.  Rufus Mitchell's Confession. *Unknown.* AmFP

Come all you muckers and gather here.  Casey Jones. *Unknown.* AmFP

Come all you old time cowboys and listen to my song. *See* Come all you jolly cowboys and listen to my song.

Come all you people from every land.  Ellen Flannery. *Unknown.* AmFP

Come all you pretty fair maids.  Green Willow, Green Willow. *Unknown.* AmFP

Come all you pretty fair maids, I pray you attend.  My New Garden Field. *Unknown.* AmFP

Come, all you rounders, if you want to hear.  Casey Jones.  T. Lawrence Seibert. AIW; BLSH; DuDr

Come all you rounders that want to hear.  Casey Jones. *Unknown.* CTV

Come all you sailors bold.  The Death of Admiral Benbow. *Unknown.* GBP; PeBB

Come all you sons of freedom and listen to my theme.  Once More a-Lumbering Go. *Unknown.* AmFP

Come all you Texas Rangers wherever you may be.  The Texas Rangers. *Unknown.* BPAW; FSW

Come all you true-born shanty boys, wherever ye may be.  The Jam on Gerry's Rocks. *Unknown.* AmFP; FaBoBa; FSW

Come all you worthy gentlemen that may be standing by.  Comfort and Tidings of Joy. *Unknown.* FSW

Come all you young and handsome ladies.  Little Sparrow. *Unknown.* AmFP. *See also* Come All You Fair and Tender Ladies.

Come all you young fellows that follow the gun.  Young Molly Ban. *Unknown.* FaBoBa; ILP (1975 ed.); PeBB

Come all you young rebels and list while I sing.  The Patriot Game.  Dominic Behan. FSW

Come all you young people/ That live far and near.  The Murder of Goins. *Unknown.* AmFP

Come all you young people, a story I will tell.  Naomi Wise. *Unknown.* AmFP

Come all young men and ladies, fathers and mothers, too.  The Rowan County Crew.  James William Day. AmFP

Come all young men and maidens, come listen to my rhyme.  Caroline of Edinboro' Town. *Unknown.* AmFP

Come, all young men, taking warning by me.  Married and Single Life. *Unknown.* AmFP

Come along, boys, and listen to my tale.  The Old Chisholm Trail. *Unknown.* BPAW

Come along, fatty-calf.  Prodigal's Return.  Ralph D. Eberly. AMV-80

Come along get you ready.  A Hot Time in the Old Town [*or* There'll Be a Hot Time].  Joe Hayden. BLSo; FSN

Come along girls and listen to my noise.  Kansas Boys. *Unknown.* FSW

Come along in then, little girl!  From a Very Little Sphinx.  Edna St. Vincent Millay. OBAL

Come along, 'tis the time, ten or more minutes past.  Arthur Hugh Clough. *Fr.* Spectator ab Extra. OBSV

Come an' Meet me wi' the Children on the Road.  William Barnes. VLP

Come and Go with Me to That Land. *Unknown.* FSW

Come and let us live my deare.  Catullus, *tr. fr. Latin by* Richard Crashaw. OBVE

Come Anthea, let us two.  The Wake.  Robert Herrick. PAIC

Come at dawn, good friend. *Unknown, tr. fr. Spanish by* Willis Barnstone. BoWoP

Come Away, Come Away, Death.  Shakespeare. *Fr.* Twelfth Night, II, iv.  AIW; GBL; ILP (1975 ed.); NOBE; PoPle; STS (Dirge.)  UsP

Come away, come, sweet love.  To His Love. *Unknown.* GBL

Come Away, My Love.  Joseph Kariuki. BuTh

Come back again and again, the fields no.  Return.  Daniel Halpern. PCho

Come Back Blues.  Michael S. Harper. PoBA

Come Back, Paddy Reilly.  Percy French. PFIr

Come back to me, who wait and watch for you.  Monna Innominata.  Christina Rossetti. VLP

Come back, ye wandering Muses, come back home.  On the Hellenics.  Walter Savage Landor. *Fr.* The Hellenics. ILP (1975 ed.)

Come balmy sleep! tired nature's soft resort.  To Sleep.  Charlotte Smith. WPE

Come, blue-eyed Maid of Heaven!—but thou, alas!  Byron. *Fr.* Childe Harold's Pilgrimage, II. LFH

Come, brethren of the water.  The Powte's Complaint. *Unknown.* GBP

Come, brother, come. Lets lift it.  Cotton Song.  Jean Toomer. BPo

Come buy my fine wares.  Market Women's Cries.  Swift. LoAs; PFIr

Come, chearfull day, part of my life, to mee.  Thomas Campion. AAS

Come child, and with your sunbeam gaze assign. The Green Eye. James Merrill. PoA

Come Christmas. David McCord. PChr

Come, come away. Upon a Delaying Lady. Robert Herrick. PoPle

Come, come Flipote; it's time I left this place. Tartuffe; or, The Impostor. Molière, *tr. by* Richard Wilbur. NAWM-2

Come, come, my love, the bush is growing. With Garments Flowing. John Clare. GBL

"Come, come," said Tom's father, "at your time of life." A Joke Versified. Thomas Moore. FaBoCo

Come Dance with Kitty Stobling. Patrick Kavanagh. NoAM

Come dance with me. South of the Border. Virginia Real Nicholas. AMV-80

Come darling/ be my scapegoat. Lying Down Hungry. Carol Bergé. MMD

Come, dear children, let us away. The Forsaken Merman. Matthew Arnold. EBEV; EcS; FaPoR; ILP (1975 ed.); PoPle; VLP

Come dear sisters and brothers. Ol' Tim Legion. Rubee Dreher Moxley. NPW

Come, Death, I'd have a word with thee. Motley. Walter de la Mare. HoPM (1975 ed.)

Come down from the Cross, my soul, and save thyself. Descent from the Cross. "Michael Field." WPE

Come down, O Christ, and help me! reach thy hand. E Tenebris. Oscar Wilde. CABA (1972 ed.)

Come down, O maid, from yonder mountain height. Tennyson. *Fr.* The Princess, Pt. VII. CABA (1972 ed.); FF; OAEL-2

Come, Every Soul, *with music*. John H. Stockton. AH

Come! fill a fresh bumper, for why should we go. Ode for a Social Meeting. Oliver Wendell Holmes. OBAL

Come follow, follow me. The Fairy Queen. *Unknown.* PoPle

Come, follow me by the smell. Onyons. Swift. *Fr.* Market Women's Cries. BIrV

Come forth from thy oozy couch. Imitation of Julia A. Moore. "Mark Twain." OBAL

Come forth, old lion, from thy den. On Himself. Walter Savage Landor. FaBoEE

Come forth, you workers! Reveille. Lola Ridge. WPE

Come, Friends and Neighbors, Come, *with music*. Lewis Hartsough. AH

Come, friends, if you will listen, a story I will tell. The Sherman Cyclone. *Unknown.* AmFP

Come from thy palace, beauteous Queen of Greece. Invocation. Thomas Randolph. Moon

Come, Gaze with Me upon This Dome. E. E. Cummings. NoAM; TT

Come, gentle sleep, death's image though thou art. Thomas Warton the Younger, *tr. fr. Latin by* Wordsworth. OBVE

Come, gentle Spring, ethereal mildness, come. Spring. James Thomson. *Fr.* The Seasons. LAuP

Come, Happy Children, *with music. Unknown.* AH

Come Harken unto Me, *with music. Unknown.* AH

Come here/ Come near. Phrases for Everyday Use by the British in India. John Daniel. TwMBP

Come here, Denise. Denise. Robert Beverly Hale. GDP

Come here, said my hostess, her face making room. A Literary Dinner. Vladimir Nabokov. OBAL

Come hither all sweet maidens soberly. On a Leander Gem. Keats. MBPR

Come hither, Evan Cameron. The Execution of Montrose. William Edmonstoune Aytoun. BTTM

Come hither my sparrows. The Fairy. Blake. MBPR

Come hither, Topham, come, with a hey, with a hey. A Raree Show. Stephen College. APAS

Come hither ye dreamers of dreams. The Vision. Daniel Defoe. APAS

Come Holy Spirit, Dove Divine, *with music*. Adoniram Judson. AH

Come, holy tortoise shell. Sappho, *tr. fr. Greek by* Willis Barnstone. BoWoP

Come Home, Come Home! Arthur Hugh Clough. HAP

Come, human dogs, interfertilitate. The Eugenist. Robert Graves. FaBoEE

Come In. Robert Frost. ILP (1975 ed.); NOBA; PoIA

Come In. Isaiah Shembe, *tr. fr. Zulu by* H. Tracey. WTO

Come in, come in, you old true love. False True Love. *Unknown.* FSW

Come in, Tom longtail, come short hose and round. Tom Long. *Unknown.* EBEV

Come inside the weather. By Hallucination Visited. Robert Horan. EAS

Come into/ a quiet warm. Sandra Maria Esteves. NW

Come into Animal Presence. Denise Levertov. AnMo; HeIP; InPK; NU

Come into dinner squalls the dame. Snaps for Dinner, Snaps for Breakfast, and Snaps for Supper. George Moses Horton. OBAL

Come into the garden, Maud. Tennyson. *Fr.* Maud, Pt. I. NOBE; OAEL-2

Come into the orchard, Anne. Swinburne. FaBoNo

Come join hand in hand brave Americans all. The Liberty Song. John Dickinson. BLSo

Come ladies and gentlemen, listen to my song. Robert's Farm. *Unknown.* FSW

Come lasses and lads. The Rural Dance about the Maypole. *Unknown.* CC; GBP

Come Laugh with Me. *Gond Oral Tradition, tr. by* V. Elwin *and* S. Hivale. WTO

Come leave the loathed stage. Ode to Himself. Ben Jonson. OAEL-1

Come, lecturer on love, resume your rostrum. Last Letter to the Scholar. Jean Garrigue. LoAs

Come, Lesbia, let us live and love. Catullus, *tr. fr. Latin by* Horace Gregory. NAWM-1

Come, let me write, and to what end? to ease. Astrophel and Stella, XXXIV. Sir Philip Sidney. Epi

Come! let us draw the curtains. Autumn. Humbert Wolfe. FSFS

Come let us journey to. Come. Bob Kaufman. MIT

Come let us mock at the great. W. B. Yeats. Nineteen Hundred and Nineteen, V. ExPo (1973 ed.)

Come, let us pity those who are better off than we are. The Garret. Ezra Pound. PSN

Come, Let Us Tune Our Loftiest Song, *with music*. Robert A. West. AH

Come, let us walk. Spring in Virginia. Ramona Wilson. VoR

Come, let's go climb on that jasmine-mantled rock. What Her Girlfriend[s] Said to Her. Okkur Macatti , *tr. by* A. K. Ramanujan. BoWoP; PBWP

Come, let's to bed. Mother Goose. GBP; MG

Come, list and hark! the bell doth toll. Thomas Heywood. *Fr.* The Rape of Lucrece. SCP-2

Come listen a while and give ear to my song. Hard Times. *Unknown.* AmFP

Come, listen, all you gals and boys. Jump Jim Crow. Thomas D. Rice. BLSo

Come listen, good people, to what I shall say. A Ballad Called Perkins's Figary. *Unknown.* APAS

Come, listen to another song. The Old Scottish Cavalier. William Edmonstoune Aytoun. BTTM

Come listen to me, you gallants so free. Robin Hood and Allen a Dale. *Unknown.* GBP; PEBB

Come, listen to my tragedy, good people, young and old. Mary Wyatt and Henry Green. *Unknown.* AmFP

Come listen, ye Whigs, to my pitiful moan. The Salamanca Doctor's Farewell. *Unknown.* APAS

Come, Little Babe. Nicholas Breton. *See* Cradle Song: "Come, little babe . . ."

Come little infant, love me now. Young Love. Andrew Marvell. RRA; TT

Come, Live with Me and Be My Love. C. Day Lewis. Two Songs, II. BoLoP; HAP; ILP (1975 ed.)
(Song: "Come live with me and be my love.") NIL

"Come live with me and be my love." Bacchanal. Peter De Vries. NOBL; OBAL

Come live with me and be my love. The Bait. John Donne. CABA (1972 ed.); HOPM (1975 ed.); ILP (1975 ed.); InPK; InPS; LFH; NIL; OAEL-1

Come live with me and be my love. The Passionate Shepherd to His Love. Christopher Marlowe. AAS; BiP; BoLoP; CABA (1972 ed.); Epi; FF; HAP; HeIP; HoPM (1975 ed.); ILP (1975 ed.); InPK; InPS; IPWM; LFH; LoAs; NIL; NOBE; OAEL-1; OLR; PAIC; PBMP; PoIA; PPoD; PPoe; PPP; UsP

Come live with me and be my love. Love under the Republicans (or Democrats.) Ogden Nash. IPWM; PBMP

Come, love, for now the night and day. Song for Autumn. Andrew Young. GBL

Come lovely and soothing death. The Carol of Death. Walt Whitman. *Fr.* When Lilacs Last in the Dooryard Bloom'd. DL

Come, madam, come, all rest my powers defy. Going to Bed [*or* To His Mistress Going to Bed]. John Donne. *Fr.* Elegies. AnMo; BoLoP; EBEV; GBL; OAEL-1; OBP; PPP; TT

Come marvel at my ox. Song of Praise for an Ox. Abraham Sutskever, *tr. by* Ruth Whitman. VWA

Come, melt thy soul in mine, that when unite. Song. Sir William Davenant. *Fr.* The Temple of Love. SCP-2

Come, mint me up the golden gorse. The Casual Man. Denis Glover. ATNZ

Come, my brothers. The Only Tourist in Havana Turns His Thoughts Homeward. Leonard Cohen. CABA (1972 ed.); NoAM

Come, My Celia. Ben Jonson. *Fr.* Volpone, III, vii. CABA (1972 ed.); FF; HeIP; ILP (1975 ed.); IPWM; NIL; OBVE (Song: To Celia.) BiP; OAEL-1, *with music*

Come (my dear) whilst youth conspires. Time Recover'd. Thomas Stanley, *after* Girolamo Casone. OBVE

Come my friends come. Call from the Afterworld. Jozef Habib Gerez, *tr. by* Musa Moris Farhi *and* Anthony Rudolf. VWA

Come, my little Robert, near. Cleanliness. Charles *and* Mary Lamb. OxBChV

Come, my Lucasia, since we see. Friendship's Mystery, to My Dearest Lucasia. Katherine Philips. SCP-2

Come, my songs, let us express our baser passions. Ezra Pound. *Fr.* Lustra. PoA

Come, my sweet, whiles every strain. William Cartwright. *Fr.* The Royal Slave. SCP-2

Come Not Near My Songs. *Unknown, tr. fr. Shoshone Indian by* Mary Austin. OLR; WPE
(Song of a Passionate Lover.) BPAW

Come Not, When I Am Dead. Tennyson. BBGO; GBL

Come now! You supercilious detractors of America. Meredith Phyfe. Edgar Lee Masters. *Fr.* The New Spoon River. GOA

Come, O Sabbath Day, *with music.* Gustav Gottheil. AH

Come, O thou traveller unknown. Wrestling Jacob. Charles Wesley. BoReV; NOBE

Come On Home. Sharon Scott. JB

Come On in My Kitchen. *Unknown.* BluL

Come on in now and get in this hip shaking contest. Hip Shakin' Strut. *Unknown.* BluL

Come on, mama/ Out to the edge of town. Bird Nest Bound. *Unknown.* BluL

Come on, my fellow pilgrims, come. *At. to* Sarah Lancaster. AmFP

Come on out of there with your hands up, Charlie. Patriotic Ode on the Fourteenth Anniversary of the Persecution of Charlie Chaplin. Bob Kaufman. PoBA

Come on, ye critics! Find one fault who dare. On Mr. Edward Howard, upon His British Princes. Charles Sackville. OBSV

Come out and climb the garden path. Luriana, Lurilee. Charles Elton. PoPle

Come out come out come out. Moon Eclipse Exorcism. *Unknown, tr. by* Armand Schwerner. Moon

Come Out, Lazarus! *Unknown.* BoReV; OxBM

Come out of Crete/ and find me here. Sappho, *tr. fr. Greek by* Guy Davenport. OBVE

Come out of the shrubs now. Hagar to Ishmael. Deborah Eibel. VWA

Come out, 'tis now September. The Ripe and Bearded Barley. *Unknown.* GBP

Come Painter, you and I, you know, dare do. Old England. Nahum Tate. APAS

Come play with me. To a Squirrel at Kyle-Na-No. W. B. Yeats. LCL; PCOP

Come praise Colonus' horses, and come praise. Colonus' Praise. Sophocles, *tr. by* W. B. Yeats. *Fr.* Oedipus at Colonus. Epi; OBVE

Come, Precious Soul, *with music.* *Unknown.* AH

Come, radishes, rosy against your green. Three from the Market. Sandra McPherson. RiTi

Come 'round by my side and I'll sing you a song. Birmingham Sunday. Richard Farina. NowV

Come round me, little childer. The Ballad of Moll Magee. W. B. Yeats. STS

"Come saddle me my fastest steed." Geordie. *Unknown.* AmFP

Come, Said My Soul. Walt Whitman. NOBA

"Come!" said Old Shellover. Old Shellover. Walter de la Mare. LCL; OxBChV; PoPle

Come Saturday morning, we bring ourselves. Women Hoping for Rain. David Tillinghast. AMV-81

Come, Sleep. Beaumont *and* Fletcher. *Fr.* The Woman-Hater, III, i. ILP (1975 ed.)

Come sleep! O sleep, the certain knot of peace. Astrophel and Stella, XXXIX. Sir Philip Sidney. CABA (1972 ed.); ILP (1975 ed.); LoAs; NIL; NOBE; PAIC; PoIA; PPP

Come slowly—Eden! Emily Dickinson. CMoP (1970 ed.)

Come small creatures of low estate, friskily moving. To the Field Mice. Richard Eberhart. BoAnP

Come Softly to My Wake. Christy Brown. IPM

Come sons of France, march on to victory. La Marseillaise. Claude Joseph Rouget de Lisle, *tr. by* Albert Morehead. BLSH

Come, sons of summer, by whose toil. The Hock-Cart, or Harvest Home. Robert Herrick. CaPo; EBEV; Epi; SCP-1

Come spring, when clouds. Sailing. Susan Murray. NowV

Come, spur away. An Ode to Master Anthony Stafford to Hasten Him into the Country. Thomas Randolph. NOBE; SCP-2

Come, stack arms, men! Pile on the rails. Stonewall Jackson's Way. John Williamson Palmer. BTTM

Come, sweetheart, come. *Unknown, tr. fr. Latin by* Helen Waddell. NAWM-1

Come take up your hats, and away let us haste.    The Butterfly's Ball.    William Roscoe.    OxBChV

Come the little clouds out of the Ice-Caves.    Rain Chant.    Louis Mertins.    BPAW

Come, then, and like two doves with silvery wings.    The Apparition of His Mistress Calling Him to Elysium.    Robert Herrick.    CaPo

Come this way through Autumn streets.    Derelict Valley.    Robert Morgan.    HeHu

Come, Thou Almighty King, *with music.    Unknown.*    BLSH

Come, Thou Fount of Every Blessing, *with music.*    Robert Robinson.    BLSH

Come thou, who art the wine and wit.    His Winding-Sheet.    Robert Herrick.    CaPo

Come to a Wedding.    Grace Cavalieri.    AATT

Come to conquer.    Cold Water Flat.    Philip Booth.    NowV

Come to Jesus.    Frederick William Faber.    VLP

Come to Me.    *Gond Oral Tradition, tr. by* V. Elwin *and* S. Hivale.    WTO

Come to me broken dreams and all.    The Still Voice of Harlem.    Conrad Kent Rivers.    CNA; PoBA

Come to me, Eros, if you needs must come.    To the God of Love.    E. V. Knox.    NOBL

Come to me in the night—we shall sleep closely together.    A Love Song.    Else Lasker-Schüler, *tr. by* Michael Gillespie.    BoWoP

Come to me in the silence of the night.    Echo.    Christina Rossetti.    BoLoP; GBL; NOBE; OAEL-2; VPC

Come to me, my borrowed love.    A Poem for One Who Bares a Pome.    Richard Bastian.    AATT

Come to my door, baby.    Janis Ian.    Society's Child.    WIF

Come to Sunny Prestatyn.    Sunny Prestatyn.    Philip Larkin.    CABA (1972 ed.); NoAM

Come to term the started child shocks.    Mustipara: Gravida 5.    Marie Ponsot.    VGW

Come to the museums, workers; and under every landscape.    To the Museums.    Isidor Schneider.    SPT

Come to the Stone.    Randall Jarrell.    VGW

Come to your heaven, you heavenly choirs!    New Heaven, New War.    Robert Southwell.    BoReV; NOBE

Come touch me baby in his waking dream.    John Berryman.    *Fr.* Dream Songs.    RRA

Come trotting up.    Foal.    Mary Britton Miller.    PH

Come unto me, all ye that are heavvy-laden.    Sabbath.    Alexander Scott.    MS

Come unto Me, When Shadows Darkly Gather, *with music.*    Catharine H. Watterman.    AH

Come unto these yellow sands.    Paul Dehn.    SpRo

Come unto these yellow sands.    Ariel's Song.    Shakespeare.    *Fr.* The Tempest, I, ii.    HeIP; NOBE; PoPle; SpRo

Come Up from the Fields Father.    Walt Whitman.    PPP; UnPo (1976 ed.)

Come, we shepherds, whose blest sight.    An Hymn of the Nativity, Sung as by the Shepherds.    Richard Crashaw.    BoReV; CABA (1972 ed.); HAP

Come, when no graver cares employ.    To the Rev. F. D. Maurice.    Tennyson.    VLP

Come when you're called.    Mother Goose.    MG

Come with Me.    Robert Bly.    CAPP; CoPAm; NoAM; NOBA; SFF

Come with Me, *sel.*    Barbara Chase-Riboud.    "Come/ with/ me."    OSP

Come, worthy Greek! Ulysses, come.    Ulysses and the Siren.    Samuel Daniel.    CABA (1972 ed.); HAP; NOBE; PAIC

Come, Ye Disconsolate.    Thomas Moore.    PIM

Come ye old English huntsmen that love noble sport.    The Old Pack.    *Unknown.*    APAS

Come Ye Sinners, Poor and Needy, *with music.*    Joseph Hart.    BLSH

Come, ye thankful people, come.    Henry Alford.    CTV

Come ye that love the Lord.    We're Marching to Zion.    Isaac Watts.    BLSH

Come you baleened behemoths.    To the Humpback Whales.    Harold J. Morowitz.    RhR

Come you fatall sisters three.    Whipping Cheare.    *Unknown.*    FaBoBa

Come you masters of war.    Masters of War.    Bob Dylan.    GrRo

Comedian, The.    Irving Layton.    AMV-81

Comedians, The.    George Hitchcock.    PoW

Comely and capable one of our race.    On the Portrait of a Woman About To Be Hanged.    Thomas Hardy.    CMoP (1970 ed.)

Comes a brown).    Corkby, Part Two.    Jerome Rothenberg.    NNaP

Comes a crackling noise, a kind of chirping.    From the Direction of the State Mental Institution.    Carol Cox.    MMD

Comes a cry from Cuban water.    Cuba Libre.    Joaquin Miller.    BTTM

Comes a time.    The Poet in Old Age Fishing at Evening.    Desmond O'Grady.    CIP

Comes it will come.    When the Revolution Really.    Peter Michelson.    HeS

Comes the time when it's later.    A Wicker Basket.    Robert Creeley.    CAPP; HAP; NoAM

Comes walking barefoot.    Sojourner Truth.    Robert Hayden.    *Fr.* Stars.    CNA

Comet, The.    Emil Makai, *tr. fr. Hungarian by* André Ungar.    VWA

Comet at Yell'ham, The.    Thomas Hardy.    CMoP (1970 ed.); ExPo (1973 ed.); GBL    (Comet at Yalbury or Yell'ham, The.)    VLP

Comets and Princes.    Samuel Johnson.    FaBoEE

Comfort and Tidings of Joy.    *Unknown.*    FSW

Comfort from Arcadia.    Nicholas Flocos.    SA

Comfort to a Youth That Had Lost His Love.    Robert Herrick.    NOBE

Comfort ye, comfort ye my people, sayth your God.    Bible, *O.T. Fr.* Isaiah.    OBVE

Comforted by Limestone.    Edward Dorn.    *Fr.* Oxford.    NOBA

Comic Adventures of Old Mother Hubbard and Her Dog, The.    Sarah Catherine Martin.    OxBChV

Comin' thro' the Rye.    Burns.    BLSH, *with music;* FSW; SLP; SpRo

Comin' to Town.    Robert V. Carr.    BPAW

Coming.    Philip Larkin.    OxBTC; PSN

Coming and Going.    Mitchell Goodman.    VGW

Coming around the Horn.    John A. Stone.    AmFP

Coming Back.    Joseph Bruchac.    CDW

Coming Back Home.    Ray A. Young Bear.    CDW

Coming back one evening through deserted fields.    Through All Your Abstract Reasoning.    Brian Patten.    FaBoTw (1975 ed.)

Coming back over the col between.    Strength through Joy.    Kenneth Rexroth.    VGW

Coming Back to America.    James Dickey.    NYP

Coming by evening through the wintry city.    At a Bach Concert.    Adrienne Rich.    CoPAm

Coming by night, furtively, one by one.    The Invaders.    A. D. Hope.    CAAP

Coming Down Cleveland Avenue.    James Tate.    PPoD; SFF

Coming down the mountain in the twilight.    Where the Hayfields Were.    Archibald MacLeish.    DuDa

Coming Fall, The, *sel.*    Denise Levertov.    "Down by the fallen fruit in the old orchard."    TSWA

Coming from —— in a Dark Night. Jane Barker. SCP-2

Coming from the south. Six Ten Sixty-Nine. Conyus. PoBA

Coming Home, Detroit, 1968. Philip Levine. TAT

Coming home, I find you still in bed. Abortion. Ai. BoWoP

Coming Home in March. Harold Littlebird. VoR

Coming home to the white. Alba: March. Marilyn Hacker. GP

Coming home with the last load I ride standing. Emergency Haying. Hayden Carruth. NNaP

Coming in again, you know the town by boards it makes eyes touch. Autobiography: Last Chapter. Jim Barnes. CDW

Coming into the store at first angry. The Man Who Finds That His Son Has Become a Thief. Raymond Souster. BBGO

Coming of Age in the County Jail. Carter Revard. VoR

Coming of Dusk upon a Village in Haiti, The. Henry Rago. HoPM (1975 ed.)

Coming of Good Luck, The. Robert Herrick. *See* Good Luck.

Coming of that limpid star is twice, The. Sonnet VI. Louise Labé, *tr. by* Willis Barnstone. BoWoP

Coming of the Plague, The. Weldon Kees. VGW

Coming of the Wee Malkies, The. Stephen Mulrine. MS

Coming of War, The: Actaeon. Ezra Pound. CMoP (1970 ed.); POA

Coming of Wisdom with Time, The. W. B. Yeats. FaBoEE; POL; SoSe

Coming On to Winter. Doug Flaherty. HeS

Coming Out. Jacqueline Lapidus. IHMS

Coming Out Of. Robert Duncan. EAS

Coming out of you. Out of You. Rodney Phillips. POL

Coming over the rise, passing. On the Farm. Barbara Winder. PH

Coming to cottonwoods, an. Prospecting. A. R. Ammons. ConAP

Com[m]ing to kiss[e] her lips [*or* lyps], (such grace I found.) Amoretti, LXIV. Spenser. EBEV; OAEL-1

Coming Up and Falling Down. Stephen Vincent. NeAC

Coming up Buchanan Street, quickly, on a sharp winter evening. Trio. Edwin Morgan. MPo

Coming up England by a different line. I Remember, I Remember. Philip Larkin. NOBL

Command the stones in a loud voice. How to Amuse a Stone. Richard Shelton. AMV-80

Commander Lowell. Robert Lowell. VGW
"Having a naval officer/ for my Father was nothing to shout," *sel.* PoIA

Commanding a Telephone to Ring. Jack Anderson. AMV-81

Commemoration, The. Edwin Muir. SLP

Commemoration. Sir Henry Newbolt. FaBoTw (1975 ed.)

Commemorative of a Naval Victory. Herman Melville. HAP; UnPo (1976 ed.)

Commencement. Constance Carrier. WPE

Commendation of Music, The. William Strode. *See* In Commendation of Music.

Comment. Dorothy Parker. NIL; OBAL

Comment against Lamp Post. Langston Hughes. ILP (1975 ed.)

Commentaries on the Song of Songs. Judith Herzberg, *tr. fr. Dutch by* Shirley Kaufman. VWA

Comments. Peggy Susberry Kenner. JB

Commercial Bank. A. M. Klein. BBGO

Commercial Traveller's Wife, The. Ronald McCuaig. GAS

Comming, The, of K——, *sel. Unknown (Staff of Beeton's Annual).*
"And Sam he looked again, and Sam he saw." VLP

Comming to kisse her lyps, (such grace I found.) *See* Coming to kiss her lips. . .

Commission. Ezra Pound. BoLoP; NIL

Commission Man, The. Robert V. Carr. BPAW

Commitment, A. Jon Anderson. BrS

Commitment in a City. Margaret Tsuda. CTBA

Committee, The. C. Day Lewis. BiP; CMoP (1970 ed.)

Committee's fat, The. Un-American Investigators. Langston Hughes. BPo

Common Bill. *Unknown.* AmFP; FSW

Common Carrier. Richard Armour. ECBV

Common Cormorant, The. Christopher Isherwood. FaBoCo; FaBoNo; RAE; UsP
(Cormorant, The.) PoPle
(Shag, The.) ECBV

Common Dust. Georgia Douglas Johnson. AmNP (1974 ed.); PoBA

Common Form. Kipling. *Fr.* Epitaphs of the War. FaBoEE; FaBoTw (1975 ed.)

Common hands of a girl and, The. Haleiwa Churchyard. Nell Altizer. PHC

Common Poem, A. Carolyn M. Rodgers. CNA

Common Sense. Ogden Nash. SFF

Common Woman, The. Judy Grahn. RiTi
*Sels.*
Ella, in a Square Apron, along Highway 80, II. NMM
Margaret, Seen through a Picture Window, VI. GP
Vera, from My Childhood, VII. GP

Commonplace Day, A. Thomas Hardy. PoPle

Commons' Petition to Charles II, The. Earl of Rochester. FaBoCo

Commonwealth of Toil, The. Ralph Chaplin. FSW

Communards, they are storming heaven, The! What the Thunder Said: A Fire Sermon. Sol Funaroff. SPT

Communication in Whi-te. Don L. Lee. BPo

Communion of Saints: The Poor Bastard under the Bridge. Marie Ponsot. VGW

Communion Portrait in Oil. Larry Weirather. FoP

Communism. Ella Wheeler Wilcox. PeD

Commuters. E. B. White. FaBoCo; SFF

Commuter's Entry in a Connecticut Diary. Robert Penn Warren. AMV-81

Companion, The. E. A. Robinson. NoAM

Companions. Charles Stuart Calverley. FaBoCo; NOBL

Company. Philip Oakes. UsP

Company of vessels on the sea, A. Battle Problem. William Meredith. NoAM

Compare me to the child that plaies with fire. Bartholomew Griffin. Fidessa, More Chaste than Kind, XIII. ESo

Comparison of the Sonnet and the Epigram. Sir John Harington. PAIC

Comparisons. Christina Rossetti. OxBChV

Compassionate Fool, The. Norman Cameron. OxBTC; WIF

Compelled by calamity's magnet. Aftermath. Sylvia Plath. SBG

Compensation. Paul Laurence Dunbar. AmNP (1974 ed.); BPo

Compensation. Emerson. NOBA; TAP

Compensation. Robinson Jeffers. PAIC

Compensation. Virginia Maughan Kammeyer. AMV-80

Competing not so much with one another. Watching Gymnasts. Robert Francis. LiSp; SPo

Competitors, The. Helen Luster. PoW

Complacencies of the peignoir, and late. Sunday Morning. Wallace Stevens. BiP; CABA (1972 ed.); CMoP (1970 ed.); ExPo (1973 ed.); HAP; HeIP; LFH; NIL; NOBA; PiAm; PoA; PoIA; PPoD; PPoe; PSN; TAP; WeW

Complaint. Ian Hamilton. NoAM

Complaint. Rufinus Domesticus, *tr. fr. Greek by* Dudley Fitts. OLR

Complaint. William Carlos Williams. TCP

Complaint, A. Wordsworth. NOBE

Complaint. James Wright. CoPAm; NOBA; TAP; VGW

Complaint, The. Edward Young. *See* Night Thoughts.

Complaint about Exile, A. Mairi MacLeod, *tr. fr. Gaelic by* Joan Keefe. PBWP

Complaint by Night of the Lover Not Beloved, A. Earl of Surrey, *after the Italian of* Petrarch. LoAs; PAIC
("Alas, so all thing[e]s now[e] do[e] hold[e] their peace.")
AAS; EBEV; OAEL-1; OBVE

Complaint of a Forsaken Indian Woman, The. Wordsworth. MBPR

Complaint of a Lover Rebuked. Petrarch. *See* Love That Doth Reign and Live within My Thought.

Complaint of Chaucer to His Purse, The. Chaucer. InPK; OAEL-1; OxBM; PAIC; PPoD
(Complaint to His Purse.) CABA (1972 ed.)
(Compleint of Chaucer to His Empty Purse, The.) ILP (1975 ed.)

Complaint of the Absence of Her Lover Being upon the Sea. Earl of Surrey. GBL
("O happie dames, that may embrace.") AAS; EBEV
(Seafarer, The.) NOBE

Complaint of the Fair Armouress, The. Villon. *See* Old Lady's Lament for Her Youth, The.

Complaint of Troilus, The. Chaucer. *Fr.* Troilus and Criseyde. NOBE

Complaint to His Purse. Chaucer. *See* Complaint of Chaucer to His Purse, The.

Compleint of Chaucer to His Empty Purse, The. Chaucer. *See* Complaint of Chaucer to His Purse, The.

Complete Destruction. William Carlos Williams. TT

Complete in Thee, No Work of Mine, *with music.* Aaron R. Wolfe. AH

Completion of the stretch, The. I-93. Marie Harris. *Fr.* Interstate. AAN

Complicity killed you. I know. I know. Closer First to Earth. Anne Hazlewood-Brady. IHMS

Compline. Debora Greger. AMV-81

Compose compose beds. Sacred Emily. Gertrude Stein. OBAL

Compose for Red a proper verse. For Malcolm, a Year After. Etheridge Knight. NIL

Composed by the Sea-Side, near Calais, August 1802. Wordsworth. MBPR

Composed by the Side of Grasmere Lake. Wordsworth. MBPR

Composed in the Composing Room. Franklin P. Adams. OBAL

Composed in the Tower before his execution. "More Light! More Light!" Anthony Hecht. ConAP; HAP; NoAM; NOBA; SFF; SoSe; UnPo (1976 ed.); UsP; VGW; VWA

Composed in the Valley near Dover, on the Day of Landing. Wordsworth. MBPR

Composed near Calais, on the Road Leading to Ardres. Wordsworth. MBPR

Composed on a May Morning, 1838. Wordsworth. FSFS

Composed upon an Evening of Extraordinary Splendour and Beauty. Wordsworth. OAEL-2

Composed upon Westminster Bridge, September 3, 1802. Wordsworth. AnMo; BiP; CABA (1972 ed.); Epi; FF; HAP; HeIP; ILP (1975 ed.); InPK; InPS; IPWM; MBPR; OAEL-2; OBP; PAIC; PBMP; PES; PoIA; PPoD; PPP; TPo; UnPo (1976 ed.); WeW
(Upon Westminster Bridge.) FaPoR; NOBE; PPM

Composers of Music. Norman MacCaig. MS

Composing scales beside the rails. The Harmonious Heedlessness of Little Boy Blue. Guy Wetmore Carryl. BoAnP

Composition. Peter Blue Cloud. VoR

Composition. Cathleen Quirk. MMD

Composition for Words and Paint. Fleur Adcock. ATNZ

Compound, The. Evan Jones. GAS

Compozishun—to James Herndon and Others. Ronald J. Goba. NCSH

Compromised by sorrow. Elegy for Chief Sealth. Duane Niatum. CDW

Compulsive Qualifications, *sels.* Richard Howard.
"Richard, may I ask a question? What is an episteme? PoA
"Richard, what will it be like when you ask the questions? PoA

Computer. Otto Orban, *tr. fr. Hungarian by* Emery George. VWA

Computer's First Christmas Card, The. Edwin Morgan. FaBoCo; MPo; NIL; PChr; SFF

Comrade—Mister. Isidor Schneider. SPT

Comrades, *with music.* Felix McGlennon. FSN

Comrades, leave me here a little, while as yet 'tis early morn. Locksley Hall. Tennyson. EBEV; OAEL-2; PFD; VLP

Comrades, you may pass the rosy. The Lay of the Lovelorn. William E. Aytoun *and* Sir Theodore Martin. FaBoCo; VLP

Comus. Milton. OAEL-1, *with music*
*Sels.*
Comus Speaks. NOBE
("Star that bids the shepherd fold, The.") PPoe
Lady Sings, The. NOBE
"Neptune, besides the sway." EcS
Sabrina. NOBE
("Sabrina fair.") EBEV
(Song: "Sabrina fair.") Ecs
Spirit Epiloguizes, The. NOBE

Con man in the thirties, A. The Last Ancestor. Gene Fowler. CPA

Concealed within the shady wood. To Cara, after an Interval of Absence. Thomas Moore. PeD

Concealment, The: Ishi, the Last Wild Indian. William Stafford. TCP

Conceited Man, A. *Gond Oral Tradition, tr. by* V. Elwin *and* S. Hivale. WTO

Concentration. Sheila Heldenbrand. AcAn

Concentric. Richard Kostelanetz. TAP

Conception. Josephine Miles. GP

Concerning One Responsible Negro with Too Much Power. Nikki Giovanni. BPo

Concerning the Dead Women: The Munitions Plant Explosion: June, 1918. Elizabeth Libbey. AmPA

Concerning your letter in which you ask. With Mercy for the Greedy. Anne Sexton. CAPP

Concert. Michael Arvey. AMV-81

Concert. Robert Sward. VGW

Concert at Long Melford Church. Patricia Beer. HeHu

Concert at the Station Osip Mandelstam, *tr. fr. Russian by* Andrew Glaze. AMV-81; VWA

Concert Champêtre. Frank O'Hara. VoA

Concert Scene. John Logan. CoPAm

Concertmaster. Richard Burgin. AMV-81

Concise History of the World, A. Ira Sadoff. AmPA

Conclusion: "High in front advanc'd/ The brandist sword of God before them blaz'd." Milton. *Fr.* Paradise Lost, XII. OBP

Conclusion: "If what began (look far and wide) will end." John Frederick Nims. PoA

Concord Hymn. Emerson. AmVN; BTTM; CTV; ExPo (1973 ed.); FaPo; FaPoR; GOA; HAP; HeIP; NOBA; PPoD; TAP

Concordance. Paul Violi. AMV-81

Concrete Cat. Dorthi Charles. InPK

Concrete cold face cased in steel. Pictures of a City. Robert Fripp *and* Peter Sinfield. GrRo

Condemned, The. Edmond Jabès, *tr. fr. French by* Jack Hirschman. VWA

Condemn'd by fate to way-ward curse. The Sot-Weed Factor. Ebenezer Cook. EAP

Condemned to hope's delusive mine. On the Death of Mr. [*or* Dr.] Robert Levet, a Practiser in Physic. Samuel Johnson. BoReV; EBEV; HeIP; InPS; LAuP; NOBE; OAEL-1; PPP

Condemning the Moongod Nanna. Enheduanna, *tr. fr. Sumerian; ad. by* Aliki *and* Willis Barnstone. BoWoP

Condition, The. T. Carmi, *tr. fr. Hebrew by* Peter Everwine *and* Shula Starkman. VWA

Conditions. José Luis Vega, *tr. fr. Spanish by* Julio Marzán. InW

Conductor's cocked twig turns out, The. Orchestra. Reg Saner. AMV-80

Conductor's hands were black with money, The. Charon. Louis MacNeice. FaBoTw (1975 ed.)

Conestoga. George E. Murphy, Jr. AMV-81

Coney Island of the Mind, A, *sels.* Lawrence Ferlinghetti.
"Constantly risking absurdity." CAPP; NowV; PAIC; SoSe; TAP; TPo; UsP; WIF
"Frightened/ by the sound of my own voice." NoAM; TAP
In Golden Gate Park That Day. BBGO; NoAM
In Goya's Greatest Scenes. BBGO; FF: ILP (1975 ed.); HeIP; NoAM; PBMP; TAP
In Woods Where Many Rivers Run. BBGO
"Pennycandystore beyond the El, The." BBGO; BiP; CAPP; CoPAm; CTBA; HeIP; IPWM; SoS; SS; TAP
"See/ it was like this when." CoPAm
"Sometime during eternity." CAPP; NoAM; TPo
"This life is not a circus where." PPP
"What could she say to the fantastic foolybear." CAPP
"Wounded Wilderness of Morris Graves." WIF

Confab. Kenneth Rosen. AmPA

Confederate veterans came to town. John Beecher. *Fr.* To Live and Die in Dixie. GP

Conferences, adjournments, ultimatums. Louis MacNeice. *Fr.* Autumn Journal. OxBTC

Confess We All, before the Lord, *with music.* John Wilson. AH

Confessio Amantis, *sels.* John Gower.
Adrian and Bardus, *fr.* V. OxBM
Ceix and Alceone, *fr.* IV. OxBM
Medea's Magic, *fr.* V. OxBM

Confessio Fidei. Dryden. *See* Revelation.

Confession. Gelett Burgess. *See* Sequel to the Purple Cow.

Confession, The. Peter Cooley. AmPA

Confession. George Herbert. ILP (1975 ed.)

Confession, The. Gary Lawless. FAF

Confession, A. Robert Mezey. AmPA

Confession of a Glutton. Don Marquis. GDP

Confession of a Young Hegelian. Ellen McEvilley Griffin. NPW

Confession of Faith. Elinor Wylie. SBG

Confession Overheard in a Subway. Kenneth Fearing. SoS

Confession to J. Edgar Hoover. James Wright. CAPP; ConAP

Confessional, The ("It is a lie—their Priests, their Pope"). Robert Browning. OBP

Confessions ("What is he buzzing in my ears?"). Robert Browning. NOBE; PoPle; UsP

Confessions of a Born Spectator. Ogden Nash. LiSP

Confessions of the Life Artist. Thom Gunn. CMoP (1970 ed.)

Confidence. Martha Baird. OSP

Confirmation, The. Edwin Muir. SLP

Confirmers, The. A. R. Ammons. TAP

Conflict of Convictions, The. Herman Melville. NOBA

Confounded Nonsense. Tom Hood. FaBoNo

Confrontation. John Hart. MIT; POL

Confrontations of March. H. C. Dillow. AMV-80

Confronting a longing. Poem to My Death. Julia de Burgos, *tr. by* Grace Schulman. BoWoP

Confusion. Kenneth Rexroth. MPA

Congers. Ronald Mann. PMW

Congo, The. Vachel Lindsay. CMoP (1970 ed.); NoAM; NOBA; TAP

Congratulations. Ordinance on Winning. Naomi Lazard. AAN; GP

Congress. Dale Matthews. AAN

Conjergal Rights. Thomas Edward Brown. *Fr.* In the Coach. VLP

Conjugation of the Verb, "To Hope." Lou Lipsitz. FiCP

Conjuration. Agnes Gergely, *tr. fr. Hungarian by* Emery George. VWA

Conjuration, to Electra, A. Robert Herrick. GBL

Conjuring Roethke. James Tate. OBAL

Connecticut summers recede and flow. Vanished. Steve Eng. AMV-81

Connecticut, with much at stake. The Customs of the Country. Phyllis McGinley. *Fr.* New England Pilgrimage. TH

Connection, The. Daniil Kharms, *tr. fr. Russian by* George Gibian. FaBoNo

Conn-Eda hid himself in horse's hide. Dreaming of Conn-Eda. Diane Levenberg. NPW

Connoisseur of Chaos. Wallace Stevens. CABA (1972 ed.)

Connoisseur of pearl, A. African China. Melvin B. Tolson. PoBA

Conqueror Worm, The. Poe. *Fr.* Ligeia, *prose tale.* NOBA; PiAm
(Emperor Worm, The.) DL

Conquerors, The. Phyllis McGinley. PBMP

Conquerors. Henry Treece. MPo; OBW

Conquerors of this paltry decade, strut. Requiem for the '30's. William Pillin. SPT

Conquest. Georgia Douglas Johnson. AmNP (1974 ed.)

Conquest of Canaan, The, *sel.* Timothy Dwight.
"In scenes of distant death bold Hezron stands," *fr.* Bk. VI. EAP

Conquest of Granada, The, *sel.* Dryden.
Song of the Zambra Dance. ILP (1975 ed.)

Conquistador. A. D. Hope. IP; PPoD

Conquistador, *sel.* Archibald MacLeish.
Prologue: "And the way goes on in the worn earth." NoAM

Conrad. Antoni Slonimski, *tr. fr. Polish by* Isaac Komem. VWA

Conscience. Melech Ravitch, *tr. fr. Yiddish by* Keith Bosley. VWA

Conscience, The. Anna Wickham. POL

Conscience Is Instinct Bred in the House. Henry David Thoreau. *Fr.* A Week on the Concord and Merrimack Rivers. HeIP; PiAm

Conscientious Objector. Edna St. Vincent Millay. VoPo

Conscientious Objector, The. Karl Shapiro. SoS

Conscious am I in my chamber. Emily Dickinson. PiAm

Consciousness/ in itself. Who Shall Doubt. George Oppen. CAAP

Consecration, A. John Masefield. NoAM

Consent. Gregory Jerozal. PoUp

Consequence, The. Roger McDonald. CAAP

Consequences. William Meredith. NoAM

Conservancies. Josephine Miles. GP

Conservative. Harold Witt. AMV-80

Conservative, out on his motor, A. On the Wrong Side. A. W. Webster. TDH

Conservative Owl, The. Oliver Herford. TDH

Conserves. David Mus. *Fr.* The Joy of Cooking. PoA

Conserving the Magnitude of Uselessness. A. R. Ammons. NoAM

Consider. W. H. Auden. OBP; TT

Consider Famous Men, Dai Bach. Idris Davies. OBW

Consider fish: magnesium flows, slowly on the whole. Ecological Lecture. Burton Raffel. AMV–81

Consider Icarus, pasting those sticky wings on. To a Friend Whose Work Has Come to Triumph. Anne Sexton. PoIA; SoSe (1977 ed.); TPo

Consider now that Troy has burned. The Second-best Bed. Howard Nemerov. NIL

Consider our Disneyland tour by the Yangtze. Tours. Stephen Shu Ning Liu. AMV–80

Consider the Auk. Ogden Nash. QQQ

Consider the sea's listless chime. The Sea-Limits. Dante Gabriel Rossetti. EcS; ILP (1975 ed.); OAEL–2; VLP

Consider This. Bruce Cutler. BCr

Consider this and in our time. Consider. W. H. Auden. OBP; TT

Consider this barbarian coast. At Akitio. James K. Baxter. ATNZ

Consider your intellect. The Pleasant Evening. Henry Kanabus. FiCh

Considerable Speck, A. Robert Frost. OBAL; PBMP; PPP; STS

Consideration for Others. Christopher Smart. OxBChV

Considerations, sel. Kendrick Smithyman.
  "High in the afternoon the dove." ATNZ

Considered Reply to a Child, A. Jonathan Price. BoLoP

Considering the Bleakness. Moishe Leib Halpern, tr. fr. Yiddish by Richard J. Fein. VWA

Considering the Snail. Thom Gunn. MPA; SoSe (1977 ed.)

Consolatio Nova: For Alan Swallow. J. V. Cunningham. MPA; PiAm

Consolation. Anthony Cronin. IBM

Consolation. Frank Stewart. PHC

Consolation. Earl of Surrey. NOBE
  ("When raging love with extreme pain.") EBEV
  ("When ragyng love with extreme payne.") AAS

Consolation of Philosophy, The, sels. Boethius, tr. fr. Latin.
  "Happy he whose eyes have view'd," fr. III, 12, tr. by Samuel Johnson. OBVE
  "Happy that first white age! when wee," II, 5, tr. by Henry Vaughan. OBVE
  "He that hath set his headlong heart," tr. by Helen Waddell. NAWM–1
  "He who has made his reckoning with life," tr. by Helen Waddell. NAWM–1
  "O Father, give the spirit power to climb," tr. by Helen Waddell. NAWM–1
  "O Maker of the starry world," tr. by Helen Waddell. NAWM–1
  "O thou whose pow'r o'er moving worlds presides," III, 9, tr. by Samuel Johnson. OBVE
  "Though countless as the grains of sand," II, 2, tr. by Samuel Johnson. OBVE

Consolations of Philosophy. Derek Mahon. BIrV; CIP

Consorting with Angels. Anne Sexton. NMM

Conspiracy of Charles, Duke of Byron, The, sel. George Chapman.
  "As when the moon hath comforted the night," fr. III, i. Moon

Conspirators, The. Kenneth Burke. SFF

Constancy. Sir John Suckling. See Constant Lover, The.

Constancy Rewarded. Coventry Patmore. Fr. The Angel in the House, II, xi. VLP

Constancy to an Ideal Object. Samuel Taylor Coleridge. MBPR; OBP

Constant, The. A. R. Ammons. HAP

Constant Cannibal Maiden, The. Wallace Irwin. OBAL

Constant I will be. She Vowed Him This. William Box. BuTh

Constant Labor, A. James W. Thompson. BPo

Constant Love in All Conditions. James I, King of England. SLP

Constant Lover, The. Sir John Suckling. CaPo; HeIP; NOBE; OLR; PBMP; SoSe
  (Constancy.) IP
  (Out Upon It! I Have Loved.) BoLoP; CABA (1972 ed.); FF; ILP (1975 ed.); IPWM; LFH
  (Song: "Out upon it! I have lov'd.") MetP

Constant Lover, The. Aurelian Townsend. BBL

Constant North, The. J. F. Hendry. MS; SLP

Constant Penelope sends to thee, careless Ulysses. Ovid, tr. fr. Latin. GBL; OAEL–1

Constant to none, but ever false to me. An Elegye. Thomas Campion. AAS

Constantly near you, I never in my entire. The Horse Show. William Carlos Williams. CMoP (1970 ed.); NOBA; TAP; VGW

Constantly risking absurdity. Lawrence Ferlinghetti. Fr. A Coney Island of the Mind. CAPP; NowV; PAIC; SoSe; TAP; TPo; UsP; WIF

Constitution and the Guerrière, The. Unknown. AmFP; FSW

Constitution's Last Fight, The. James Jeffrey Roche. BTTM

Constructed Space, The. W. S. Graham. PoA

Construction. Virginia Schonborg. QQQ

Construction #13. Judith Johnson Sherwin. NoAM

Constructions: Upper East Side. Sandra Hochman. NowV

Consultant's Holiday. U. A. Fanthorpe. PMW

Consulting I Ching Smoking Pot Listening to the Fugs Sing Blake. Allen Ginsberg. TT

Consumed. James Tate. MAT

Consumer's Report. X. J. Kennedy. FiCP

Consumer's Report, A. Peter Porter. FaBoCo: NOBL

Contacts with the Past. R. A. Simpson. FPA

Contagiousness of Dreams, The. Diane Middlebrook. AMV–81

Container, The. Cid Corman. VGW

"Containing Communism." Charlie Cobb. PoBA

Containment. Howard Schwartz. HeS

Contemplate all this work of Time. Tennyson. In Memoriam A. H. H., CXVIII. FF

Contemplation upon Flowers, A. Henry King. PF

Contemplation would make a good life, keep it strict, only. The Cruel Falcon. Robinson Jeffers. BiP

Contemplations. Anne Bradstreet. EAP; WPE, abr.
  Sels.
  "I wist not what to wish, yet sure thought I." PBWP
  "O Time the fatal wrack of mortal things." PBWP
  "Shall I then praise the heavens, the trees, the earth." PBWP
  "Silent alone, where none or saw, or heard." PBWP
  "When I behold the heavens as in their prime." PBWP

Contemporania, sel. Ezra Pound.
  Tenzone. PoA

Contemporary. Hortense Flexner. PoA

Contemporary Fear. Don Ober. NowV

Contemporary Muse, The. Edgell Rickword. OBSV

Contemporary Nursery Rhyme. Unknown. SpRo

Contemptuous of his home beyond. A Frog's Fate. Christina Rossetti. VPC

Contend in a sea which the land partly encloses. The Yachts. William Carlos Williams. BiP; CMoP (1970 ed.); HeIP; ILP (1975 ed.); LiSp; NoAM; NOBA; PiAm; PPP; SoS; SPo

Content. George Herbert. SCP–1

Content in her skin she does not challenge. Nude. Robert Siegel. FAF

Content of a river is, The. The River. Richard Kell. IPM

Contention of Ajax and Ulysses, The, sel. James Shirley.
  Glories of Our Blood and State, The, fr. sc. iii. HAP; ILP (1975 ed.); LFH; NIL; PoPle; PPP; SCP–2; SoSe

(Death the Leveller.)  FaPoR; FF; NOBE; PBMP; UnPo (1976 ed.)

(Dirge: "Glories of our blood and state, The.")  OAEL-1; OBP

Contentment.  Nathaniel Cotton.  OxBChV

Contentment.  Lawrence E. Estes.  AMV-80

Contentment.  Burges Johnson.  GDP

Contest of Nerves, The.  Patricia Traxler.  TV

Continent o Venus.  Alexander Scott.  MS; SLP

Continent's End.  Robinson Jeffers.  TCP

Continuance, The.  William Bronk.  GP

Continuing.  Madeline Bass.  WBN

Continuing Story of Bungalow Bill, The.  John Lennon *and* Paul McCartney.  GrRo

Continuous, a medley of old pop numbers.  The Songs.  Martin Bell.  FF

Continuum.  Adrienne Rich.  TT

Contra Mortem.  Hayden Carruth.  PCho
  "Wherever shadow falls wherever the drowning," *sel.*  PoA

Contrapuntalist, A—/ composer of chorales.  Melchior Vulpius.  Marianne Moore.  PiAm

Contretemps, The.  Thomas Hardy.  CMoP (1970 ed.)

Contrite Heart, The.  William Cowper.  WIF

Controlling the Tongue.  Chaucer.  *Fr.* The Canterbury Tales: The Manciple's Tale.  OxBChV

Conundrum.  Carl Clark.  JB

Convalescence.  J. V. Cunningham.  PiAm

Convent, The.  "Seumas O'Sullivan."  PFIr; POL

Convent of Pleasure, The, *sel.*  Margaret Cavendish, Duchess of Newcastle.
  "My cabinets are oyster-shells."  SCP-2
  (Song: "My cabinets are oyster-shells.")  WPE
  (Song by Lady Happy, as a Sea-Goddess.)  EcS

Conventionalist, The.  Stevie Smith.  BBGO

Convergence of the Twain, The.  Thomas Hardy.  AKE; BiP; FaBoTw (1975 ed.); HeIP; ILP (1975 ed.); InPK; LFH; NoAM; OAEL-1; OxBTC; PAIC; PBMP; PoIA

Conversation.  Rose Fyleman.  MN

Conversation.  Nikki Giovanni.  CTBA

Conversation, A.  Barbara Howes.  IHMS

Conversation.  David McCord.  SO

Conversation.  K. Malley.  AMV-80

Conversation.  Gyorgy Raba, *tr. fr.* Hungarian by Jascha Kessler.  VWA

Conversation, A.  Dylan Thomas.  RFM

Conversation between the Chevalier de Chamilly and Mariana Alcoforado in the Manner of a Song of Regret.  The Three Marias, *tr. fr.* Portuguese by Helen R. Lane.  BoWoP

Conversation brings us so close!  Opening.  Looking into a Face.  Robert Bly.  NOBA; TSWA

Conversation confers a sacrament.  Life, the Eternal Sacrament.  Virginia Floyd.  AATT

Conversation Hearts.  Nina Payne.  CC

Conversation in Craven Street, Strand.  James Smith *and* Sir George Rose.  FaBoCo

Conversation in the Bush.  A. R. D. Fairburn.  ATNZ

Conversation in the Drawingroom, The.  Weldon Kees.  EAS

Conversation in the Eighth Street Bookstore.  Honor Moore.  WBN

Conversation of Prayer, The.  Dylan Thomas.  EBEV; STS

Conversation with a Countryman.  Antoni Slonimski, *tr. fr.* Polish by Isaac Komem.  VWA

Conversation with a Giraffe at Dusk in the Zoo.  Douglas Livingstone.  LP; MPo

Conversation with God.  Jeanine Hathaway.  AMV-80

Conversation with Washington.  Myra Cohn Livingston.  OFD

Conversion.  Geof Hewitt.  NeAC

Convert, The.  Margaret Danner.  BPo

Converts, The.  Chana Bloch.  AMV-81

Convert's but a fly, that turns about, A.  Samuel Butler.  FaBoEE

Convex face of the black countries, The.  The First Psalm.  Bertolt Brecht, *tr. by* Robert Bly.  NU

Convict, The.  Wordsworth.  MBPR

Convict of Clonmel, The.  *Unknown, tr. fr. Modern Irish by* Jeremiah Joseph Callanan.  PFIr

Convicted, *sel.*  Harry Edward Mills.
  "Around his open grave from near and far."  PeD

Convicts' Ball, The.  Ambrose Bierce.  BPAW

Convoy, The.  Juan Antonio Corretjer, *tr. fr.* Spanish by Julio Marzán.  InW

Convoy.  James Neugass.  SPT

Cook, The.  Ray A. Young Bear.  CDW

Cooking.  Myra Cohn Livingston.  ECBV

Cooking.  Gertrude Stein.  *Fr.* Tender Buttons.  RiTi

Cook-out.  Dan Masterson.  CoPAm

Cool air just arriving; half moon.  Short Walk Alone.  Alan Stephens.  FoP

Cool beneath melon-colored cloth, your belly.  For Arl in Her Sixth Month.  Al Young.  CPA

Cool black nights thru redwoods.  First Party at Ken Keseys with Hell's Angels.  Allen Ginsberg.  ConAP

Cool, Grey City of Love, The.  George Sterling.  BPAW

Cool in summer's heat.  The Well: Two Songs.  *Gond Oral Tradition, tr. by* V. Elwin *and* S. Hivale.  WTO

Cool it Mag.  Margaret Are You Drug.  George Starbuck.  MAT

Cool Morning Shower in Early Spring.  Larry Levis.  OSP

Cool shades, air-fanning groves.  Ex M. Antonio Flaminio, ad Agellum Suum.  John Ashmore.  SCP-2

Cool shades and dews are round my way.  A Scene on the Banks of the Hudson.  Bryant.  PiAm

Cool shadows blanked dead cities, falling.  Falling.  Bob Kaufman.  PoBA

Cool to the wrist.  Six Divine Circles.  Gail Ghai.  AMV-81

Cool Tombs.  Carl Sandburg.  CMoP (1970 ed.); HAP; HeIP; NoAM; NOBA; PAIC; PiAm; TAP

Cool Web, The.  Robert Graves.  NoAM; OxBTC; PoA; PoIA

Cool Women and Smart Horses Are the Pits.  Henry Taylor.  *Fr.* Desperado.  PoUp

Coole Park and Ballylee, 1931.  W. B. Yeats.  CMoP (1970 ed.); NoAM; PPP; PSN

Coole Park, 1929.  W. B. Yeats.  ILP (1975 ed.); OAEL-2; STS

Coolie Chinee, The.  Septimus Winner.  OBAL

Coon Song.  A. R. Ammons.  NoAM; NOBA

Cooney Potter.  Edgar Lee Masters.  *Fr.* Spoon River Anthology.  CTBA

Cooper.  James Russell Lowell.  *Fr.* A Fable for Critics.  NOBA; TAP

Cooper & Bailey Great London Circus, The.  Robert Hershon.  MAT

Cooper's Hill, *sel.*  Sir John Denham.
  "My eye descending from the hill, surveys."  NIL; OAEL-1; PAIC

Coots are awash, The.  Lake Harriet: Wind.  Laurie Taylor.  AMV-81

Cop, The/ with a cold.  High-cool/2.  James Cunningham.  JB

Cop holds me up like a fish, The.  Fish.  Larry Levis.  AmPA

Cop slumps alertly on his motorcycle, The.  Corner.  Ralph Pomeroy.  NYP

Copa de Oro.  Ina Coolbrith.  WPW

Copenhagen.  Art Lange.  FiCh

Cophetua. "Hugh MacDiarmid." POL

Coplas. *Tr. fr. Spanish.* FSW

Coplas about the Soul Which Suffers with Impatience to See God, *sel.* St. John of the Cross, *tr. fr. Spanish by* Roy Campbell. "I live without inhabiting/ Myself." OBVE

Copper-Beech and Butter-Fingers. Pearse Hutchinson. CIP

Copperhead, The. David Bottoms. AMV–81

Cops and Robbers. Bill Middleton. AMV–80

Coptic Poem. Lawrence Durrell. FaBoCo

Copulate. The Indomitable. Carl Rakosi. GP

Copulating Gods, The. Carolyn Kizer. Prf

Copy. Richard Armour. BBGO

Copy of an Intercepted Despatch from His Excellency Don Strepitoso Diabolo. Thomas Moore. OBSV

Copy of Non Sequitors, A. *Unknown.* FaBoNo

Copying Architecture in an Old Minster. Thomas Hardy. OBP

Coquette. Eugene Field. ECBV

Coquette at Mission Control. Martin Galvin. PoUp

Coquettes with doctors; hoards her breath. The Old Beauty. Phyllis McGinley. FaBoEE

Cor Cordium. Swinburne. VLP

Cora Punctuated with Strawberries. George Starbuck. NCSH

Coral Grove, The. James Gates Percival. EcS

Corbie and the Crow, The. *Unknown.* PoPle

Cordate head meanders through himself, The. Pit Viper. N. Scott Momaday. CDW; VW

Cordoba. Asher Mendelssohn. VWA

Corinna. *Unknown.* FSW

Corinna in Vendome. Pierre de Ronsard, *tr. fr. French by* Robert Mezey. BoLoP

Corinna, pride of Drury Lane. A Beautiful Young Nymph Going to Bed. Swift. AnMo; NIL

Corinna, to Tanagra, from Athens. Walter Savage Landor. *Fr.* Pericles and Aspasia, XLIV. NOBE

Corinnae Concubitus. Ovid, *tr. fr. Latin by* Christopher Marlowe. Amores, I, 5. GBL
(Elegy: "In summer's heat and mid-time of the day.") BoLoP
("In summer's heat, and mid-time of the day.") EBEV; OBVE
(Ovid's Fifth Elegy.) OBP

Corinna's Going a-Maying. Robert Herrick. AnMo; BiP; CABA (1972 ed.); CaPo; Epi; ExPo (1973 ed.); HAP; ILP (1975 ed.); NIL; NOBE; OAEL-1; PoPle; PPP

Cormac Mac Airt Presiding at Tara. *Unknown, tr. fr. Irish by* Douglas Hyde. BIrV

Cormorant, The. Christopher Isherwood. *See* Common Cormorant, The.

Cormorant still screams, The. Late. Louise Bogan. PBWP; VGW

Corn. Sidney Lanier. AmVN

Corn-blossom maidens. Masahongva, *tr. fr. Hopi Indian by* Natalie Curtis. WTO

Corn-grinding Song. *Tr. fr. Tewa Indian.* WPW, *tr. by* Alice Corbin; WTO, *tr. by* N. Barnes

Corn grows up, The. Incantation for Rain. *Unknown, tr. by* Washington Matthews. ExPo (1973 ed.)

Corn Harvest, The. William Carlos Williams. Pictures from Brueghel, VII. PPP

Corn-planting Songs. *Tr. fr. Osage Indian by* Mary Austin. WPW

Corn Rigs Are Bonie. Burns. *See* Rigs o' Barley, The.

Corn-Song, A. Paul Laurence Dunbar. AmVN

Corn swaying in the rhythm of the wind. Death in the Woods. Harold Bird ("Littlebird"). VW

Corncrake, The. James H. Cousins. BoAnP; PFIr

Cornelia's Song. John Webster. *See* Call for the Robin Redbreast . . .

Cornelia's Window. Julie Kane. AMV–81

Corner, The. Rita Johnson. AMV–80

Corner. Ralph Pomeroy. NYP

Cornered and trapped, The. For Mack C. Parker. Pauli Murray. PoBA

Cornhusk bag. Talking Designs. Liz Sohappy Bahe. CDW

Cornish Cliffs. John Betjeman. MPo; PAIC

Cornish Litany, A. *Unknown. See* Litany for Halloween.

Cornwallis' Country Dance. *Unknown.* BTTM

Corona. Paul Celan, *tr. fr. German by* Joachim Neugroschel. VWA

Coronation, *with music.* Edward Perronet. BLSo
(All Hail the Power of Jesus' Name.) BLSH

Coroner's Jury. L. A. G. Strong. OxBTC

Coroner's jury yesterday, A. MD Sewed Wrong Section of Colon. F. R. Scott. AKE

Coronet, The. Andrew Marvell. BoReV; MetP; PoPle

Corporal Pym. Walter de la Mare. FaBoEE

Corporate Entity. Archibald MacLeish. OBAL

Corposant. Peter Redgrove. OxBTC

Corps d'Esprit. Heather McHugh. AmPA

Corpse, clad with carefulness. Of Misery. Thomas Howell. FF

Corpse-Keeper, The. *Unknown, tr. fr. Catalan by* W. S. Merwin. BoWoP

Corpulent Pig, A. Marnie *and* Harnie Wood. TDH

Corpus Christi ("Lully, lulley, lully, lulley"). *Unknown. See* Corpus Christi Carol ("Lully, lullay, lully, lullay").

Corpus Christi Carol, The ("Heron flew east, the heron flew west, The"). *Unknown.* GBP

Corpus Christi Carol ("Lully, lullay [or lulley], lully, lullay [or lulley]"). *Unknown.* BoReV; GBP; ILP (1975 ed.); NOBE; OAEL-1; OxBM
(Corpus Christi.) FaBoBa
(Falcon, The.) NU
(Knight of the Grail, The.) DuDr
(Lully, Lulley, Lully, Lulley.) EBEV; HAP; WeW

Corpus Christi Carol, The ("Over yonder's a park, which is newly begun"). *Unknown.* GBP

Correct Compassion, A. James Kirkup. FaBoTw (1975 ed.); OxBTC

Correspondence:/ when I have sad thoughts. Lady Ise, *tr. fr. Japanese by* Etsuko Terasaki *and* Irma Brandeis. BoWoP

Correspondence between Mr. Harrison in Newcastle and Mr. Sholto Peach Harrison in Hull. Stevie Smith. FaBoNo

Correspondence School Instructor Says Goodbye to His Poetry Students, The. Galway Kinnell. NOBA; TAP

Correspondences. Baudelaire, *tr. fr. French by* Anthony Hartley. NAWM-2

Corridor, The. Thom Gunn. NowV; PPP

Corridors of the soul! Rebirth. Antonio Machado, *tr. by* Robert Bly. NU

Corrs, The. Tom MacIntyre, *tr. fr. Irish.* CIP

Corrupt Man in the French Pub, The. Brian Higgins. OxBTC

Corruption. Henry Vaughan. OAEL-1; Prf; SCP–1

Corsons Inlet. A. R. Ammons. CSP; LFH; NoAM; NOBA; PoIA; PPP

Cortège. Paul Verlaine, *tr. fr. French by* Arthur Symons. OBVE

Cortes. A. A. Rios. GP

Corwin Psychiatric Ward, 1972. Paul Dilsaver. PoW

Cosher Bailey's Engine. *Unknown.* FSW

Cosimo. Andrew Taylor. GAS

Cosmetic. Gretchen Herbkersman. AMV–80

Cosmetic Survival. Ettore Rella. SPT

Cosmic Eye. A. K. Redwing. VoR

Cosmic Leviathan, that monstrous fish. Cosmogony. Edgell Rickword. FaBoTw (1975 ed.)

Cosmic song birds. Franklin Avenue Blues People. Quincy Troupe. SES

Cosmogony. Edgell Rickword. FaBoTw (1975 ed.)

Cosmologists are wrong, The. Creation Myths. Burton Raffel. AMV–80

Cossante. Pero Meogo, *tr. fr. Medieval Galician by* Yvor Winters. AIW

Cost-of-Living Mother Goose, The. Dow Richardson. QQQ

Cosy Cat Nap. James Kirkup. RAE

Cot, The. Grover Amen. NYP

Cottage. "Seumas O'Sullivan." PFIr

Cottage Hospital, The. John Betjeman. ILP (1975 ed.); NOBE; UnPo (1976 ed.)

Cottager to Her Infant, The. Dorothy Wordsworth. OxBChV

Cotter's Saturday Night, The. Burns. LAuP

Cotton blouse you wear, your mother said, The. McDonogh Day in New Orleans. Marcus B. Christian. AmNP (1974 ed.)

Cotton-eyed Joe. *Unknown.* FSW

Cotton Song. Jean Toomer. BPo

Cottonwood, willow, and briar. Leaves like Fish. Gladys Cardiff. CDW

Couch, The. Fred W. Wright, Jr. AMV–80

Cougait Revisited. Donald Campbell. MIS

Coughing in a shady grove. Ipecacuanha. George Canning. FaBoNo

Coughing up blood. Differences. Ray A. Young Bear. NU

Could be Kelly. Namely You. Lawson Fusao Inada. NW

Could I remove the stones from the river? Song of Longing. *Gond Oral Tradition, tr. by* V. Elwin *and* S. Hivale. WTO

Could I Say I Touched You. Harold Littlebird. VoR

Could Man Be Drunk for Ever. A. E. Housman. PPP; STS

Could we but see men as they are! A Window in the Breast. *Unknown, tr. by* Walter Headlam. ECBV

Could you not drink her gaze like wine? The Card-Dealer. Dante Gabriel Rossetti. VLP

Could'st thou resign the park and play content. Samuel Johnson. *Fr.* London. NIL

Councell Given to Master Bartholmew Withipoll. George Gascoigne. AAS

Councils. Marge Piercy. NeAC; RiTi; TSWA

Counsel to Girls. Robert Herrick. *See* To the Virgins, to Make Much of Time.

Counsel to Unreason. Léonie Adams. PoA

Counsels of O'Riordan, the Rann Maker, The. T. D. O'Bolger. PFIr

Count Arnaldos. *Unknown, tr. fr. Spanish by* W. S. Merwin. Epi

Count Gismond. Robert Browning. VLP

Count not his broken pledges as a crime. Lloyd George. *Unknown.* FaBoCo

Count the white horses you meet on the way. White Horses. Eleanor Farjeon. PH

Count this among my heartfelt wishes. Fish Story. Richard Armour. LiSp; SPo

Count up those books whose pages you have read. Indolence. Vernon Watkins. FaBoTw (1975 ed.)

Countdown takeoff. To the Moon and Back. William Plomer. Moon

Counter-Dances of Darkness, The, *sel.* Jerome Rothenberg. "As I dreamed my stature (mad dream!)." FoP

Counterparts. Stephen Dobyns. PoA

Counterpoint, A. Robert Creeley. CoPAm

Countin the Ol One Hundred. Shirley Williams. CPA

Counting. Harry Behn. ECBV

Counting. Fenton Johnson. AmNP (1974 ed.)

Counting-out Rhyme. Helen Adam. PoIA

Counting Out Rhyme ("Round about, round about"). *Unknown.* SpRo

Counting Sheep. Russell Edson. FiCP

Counting Small-boned Bodies. Robert Bly. CAPP; EAS; PPoD; TSWA

Counting the Beats. Robert Graves. GBL; HAP; OxBTC; UsP; WeW

Counting the Mad. Donald Justice. ConAP; FF; LP; NIL; UnPo (1976 ed.); UsP

Countless things escape eaily out of me. Afternoon 3. Saburoh Kuroda. EAS

Country, The/ was back in the hands of the patriots. Poem. Fred Levinson. AmPA

Country Air. Mike Love *and* Brian Wilson. PoRo

Country Alphabet, The. Linda Parker. TC

Country Bedroom, The, *sel.* Frances Cornford. "My room's a square and candle-lighted boat." RAE

Country bumpkin. Clyde Watson. *Fr.* Father Fox's Pennyrhymes. CC

Country Burial. Janet Lewis. WPW

Country Cemetery. Freda Newton Bunner. AMV–80

Country Clergy, The. R. S. Thomas. BoReV; OxBTC; PSN

Country Clergyman's Trip to Cambridge, The. Macaulay. OBSV

Country Club Sunday. Phyllis McGinley. WIF

Country Dance. Edith Sitwell. NoAM

Country Dance, A. Charles Tennyson Turner. VLP; VPC

Country Fiddler, The. John Montague. TwMBP

Country Girl. George Mackay Brown. SLP

Country House, The. Louis Simpson. NOBA

Country Justice, The, *sel.* John Langhorne. "Born with a gentle heart, and born to please," II. EPC

Country Landscape. Sherod Santos. AMV–80

Country Life, A: To His Brother, Master Thomas Herrick. Robert Herrick. CaPo

Country Midwife, The: A Day. Ai. CAAP

Country Morning. Rosemary Dobson. MAuV

Country-Mouse, The. Abraham Cowley, *after the Latin of* Horace. OBVE

Country Mouse and the City Mouse, The. Richard Scrafton Sharpe. MN; OxBChV

Country of desolation between junctions. Junk. William Zaranka. AMV–80

Country of hunchbacks!—where the strong, straight spine. Sonnet to Gath. Edna St. Vincent Millay. BoWoP; CMoP (1970 ed.)

Country of Water. Bernice Ames. WPE

Country Press. Rosemary Dobson. GAS; MAuV

Country Rhyme. *Unknown.* ECBV

Country rings around with loud alarms, The. Lines on a Paid Militia [*or* The Militia]. Dryden. *Fr.* Cymon and Iphigenia. OBSV; SoSe

Country Road. James Taylor. PoRo

Country Roads. Rolf Jacobsen, *tr. by* Robert Bly. NU

Country Singer, The. Carl Rakosi. HeS

Country surrounds the city, The. Revolution in the Revolution in the Revolution. Gary Snyder. PiAm

Country Towns. Kenneth Slessor. MAuV

Country Tunes, *sel.* Elizabeth Riddell. "As I went out to walk." GAS

Country Villa. Jean Garrigue. TAP

Country Walk, A. Thomas Kinsella. CIP; CMoP (1970 ed.)

Country Wedding, The (A Fiddler's Story). Thomas Hardy. UnPo (1976 ed.)

Country-Western Music. Ted Kooser. TAT

Country Words. Wallace Stevens. STS

Countryman's Return, The. Dylan Thomas. OxBTC

Country's Crisis, The. Brian Merriman, *tr. fr. Modern Irish by* David Marcus. *Fr.* The Midnight Court. BIrV

County Ball, The. Coventry Patmore. *Fr.* The Angel in the House, II, iii. VPC

County Mayo, The. Anthony Raftery, *tr. fr. Irish by* James Stephens. PFIr

County of Mayo, The. *Unknown, tr. fr. Irish by* George Fox. BIrV

Coup de Grâce. A. D. Hope. IP; PPP

Couple, The. Sandra Hochman. CTBA

Couple, A. May Swenson. RiTi

Couple. Mary Swope. AMV-81

Couple Overhead, The. William Meredith. CoPAm; HoPM (1975 ed.); NoAM

Couple Upstairs, The. Hugo Williams. POL

Couples sought (enclose photographs please). Billings and Cooings from "The Berkeley Barb." Mona Van Duyn. GP

Couplets for WCW. Martha Christina. AMV-80

Couplets 20. Robert Mezey. NU

Coupling. Cynthia Macdonald. WBN

Courage. Matthew Arnold. OAEL-2

Courage. Karle Wilson Baker. PCOP

Courage! Arthur Hugh Clough. *See* Say Not the Struggle Nought Availeth.

Courage. George Herbert. *Fr.* The Church Porch. CTV

Courage, dear Moll! and drive away despair. À Madame, Madame B, Beauté Sexagenaire. Charles Sackville. APAS

"Courage!" he said, and pointed toward the land. The Lotos-Eaters. Tennyson. CABA (1972 ed.); ExPo (1973 ed.); ILP (1975 ed.); OAEL-2; PoIA; VLP

Courage is armor. Courage. Karle Wilson Baker. PCOP

Courage, my soul, now learn to wield. A Dialogue between the Resolved Soul and Created Pleasure. Andrew Marvell. BoReV; OAEL-1; PAIC

Courage: your tongue has left. Stutterer. Alan Dugan. CAPP

Courland Penders: Going Home. Michael Dransfield. FPA; GAS

Course of a Particular, The. Wallace Stevens. PPoe

Courser and Jennet. Shakespeare. *Fr.* Venus and Adonis. NOBE
("But lo, from forth a copse that neighbours by.") PH; PoPle

Court, The. *Unknown.* APAS

Court considered the country's crisis, The. The Country's Crisis. Brian Merriman, *tr. by* David Marcus. *Fr.* The Midnight Court. BIrV

Court We Live On, The. Bill Tremblay. TAT

Courtesies of good-morning and good-evening. On Dwelling. Robert Graves. CMoP (1970 ed.)

Courtier's Life, The. Sir Thomas Wyatt. FaBoEE

Courtin', The. James Russell Lowell. *Fr.* The Biglow Papers, 2d series, *introd.* AmVN; NOBA; OBAL

Courts wait, wide open, The. Mismatch. Carl Lindner. AMV-80

Courtship. Alice Corbin. BPAW

Courtship. Mark Strand. GP

Courtship of the Yonghy-Bonghy-Bo, The. Edward Lear. FaBoNo; OAEL-2

Cousin Jack Song. *At. to* Charley Tregonning. AmFP

Cousin Nancy. T. S. Eliot. OBAL

Cousins. Paula B. Cullen. AMV-81

Convenant. Paul Auster. VWA

Covenant, The. James Cunningham. JB

Coventry Carol. *Unknown.* GSB, *with music;* OFD; PChr

Cover Her Face. Thomas Kinsella. CIP

Cover me over, clover. Richard Eberhart. CoPAm

Covered Wagon, The. Lena Whittaker Blakeney. BPAW

Covered with yellow leaves. Memory Gardens. Allen Ginsberg. NNaP

Covering the Subject. Richard Armour. CTV

Covetousness. Peter Idley. OxBChV

Coveys of black witches gather. The Witches. Iain Crichton Smith. MS

Cow, The. Theodore Roethke. OBAL

Cow, The. Knute Skinner. PCho

Cow, The. James Stephens. ECBV

Cow, The. Robert Louis Stevenson. CTV; OxBChV

Cow, The. Ann *or* Jane Taylor. OxBChV

Cow and calf. Grandpa's Friend. Roberto Sandoval. TVo

Cow Ate the Piper, The. *Unknown.* GBP; PeBB

Cow belched and invited me, The. Concert Champêtre. Frank O'Hara. VoA

Cow, cow. The Cow. James Stephens. ECBV

Cow in Apple Time, The. Robert Frost. CABA (1972 ed.); PSN

Cow is alone, The. Dread. Dave Morice. AcAn

Cow-Ponies. Maurice Lesemann. BPAW

Cow Slips Away, The. Ben King. ECBV

Coward. A. R. Ammons. OBAL

Coward, The. Kipling. *Fr.* Epitaphs of the War. FaBoEE; FaBoTw (1975 ed.)

Coward, The. Stephen Spender. NoAM

Coward—of heroic size. Grizzly. Bret Harte. BPAW

Cowards die many times before their deaths. Shakespeare. *Fr.* Julius Caesar, II, ii. FF

Cowards fear to die, but courage stout. On the Snuff of a Candle. Sir Walter Ralegh. FaBoEE

Cowboy, The ("Oh, a man there lives on the Western plains"). *Unknown.* BPAW

Cowboy and the Stork, The. Robert V. Carr. BPAW

Cowboy comes to town, The. The Mocker. Gwendolen Haste. WPW

Cowboy has his bunkie, The. The Sheep-Herder's Lament. Arthur Chapman. BPAW

Cowboy hat, and underneath, A. Belle Starr. *Unknown.* BPAW

Cowboy Song. Charles Causley. MiP

Cowboy stands beneath, The. Vaquero. Edward Dorn. VoA

Cowboy with his sweetheart stood beneath a starlit sky, A. The Broken Wedding Ring. *Unknown.* AIW

Cowboys' Christmas Ball, The. William Lawrence Chittenden. BPAW

Cowboys, come and hear a story of Roy Bean in all his glory. Roy Bean. *Unknown.* BPAW; OBAL

Cowboy's Dream, The ("Last night as I lay on the prairie"). *Unknown, at. to* Charles J. Finger. BPAW; FSW, *shorter version*

Cowboy's Lament, The. *Unknown.* BLSo, *with music;* BPAW; GBP; PeBB
(As I Walked Out in the Streets of Laredo.) AIW
(Streets of Laredo, The.) AmFP; FSW

Cowboy's Life, The. *At. to* James Barton Adams. BPAW; CTV

Cowboy's Life Is a Very Dreary Life, The. *Unknown.* AmFP

Cowboy's Love Song. Catherine O'Neill. PoUp

Cowboys: One ("Brave/ they straddle the animals"). Rod McKuen. MiP

Cowboys recline, The/ in their pajamas. Heaven of Cowboys. Edward Gold. PoUp

Cowboys: Three ("They wade through beer cans"). Rod McKuen. MiP

Cowboys: Two ("Huddled in the pits"). Rod McKuen. MiP

Coweta County Courthouse, The. James Miller Robinson. AMV–80

Cowhorn-crowned, shockheaded, cornshuck-bearded. The Knight, Death, and the Devil. Randall Jarrell. WeW

Cowled with a news-sheet in his asphalt cage. At the Zoo. Walter de la Mare. BoAnP

Cows. James Reeves. DuDr

Cows Are Coming Home in Maine. Robert P. Tristram Coffin. DuDa

Cows bring in the last light, The. The Black Plateau. W. S. Merwin. CAAP; NNap

Cows graze. Horses Graze. Gwendolyn Brooks. CNA; FiCh; GP

Cows Grazing at Sunrise. William Matthews. AMV–81

Cows in Vatra Dornii lumber on the grass-wet, The. Hertza. Benjamin Fondane, tr. by Matei Calinescu and Willis Barnstone. VWA

Cows near the Graveyard, The. Howard Nelson. NU

Cowslips. Sacheverell Sitwell. PF

Coyote, The. A. A. Dewey. HeS

Coyote. Bret Harte. BPAW

Coyote, The. Carter Revard. VoR

Coyote/ running. Sweat Song. Peter Blue Cloud. VoR

Coyote and the Star. Arthur Guiterman. BPAW

Coyotes Fighting. Keith Wilson. MPA

Coyote's Song. Peter Blue Cloud. NW

Cozy above us a little airplane chugs. Mail from Home in the Sky. Ernest Sandeen. HeS

Crab, The. Conrad Aiken. BoAnP

Crabbed Age and Youth. Shakespeare. The Passionate Pilgrim, XII. ILP (1975 ed.); InPS; NIL
("Crabbed age and youth cannot live together.") GBL

Crabbing. Marky Daniel. AMV–81

Crack in the Wall Holds Flowers. Adam David Miller. PoBA

Crack Is Moving Down the Wall, The. Weldon Kees. UsP

Crack of Doom. Albert Howard Carter. AATT

Crack ran through our hearthstone long ago, A. The Refugees. Edwin Muir. NoAM

Cracked bell rings to Lenten service over, The. April Landscape. A. L. Rowse. PES

Cracked cedar, The. Elephants. Patrick Lane. NeAC

Cracked Eggs. Herbert Scott. TC

Cracked Looking Glass. Jean Garrigue. LoAs

Cracked Record Blues. Kenneth Fearing. SFF

Cracks, The. Robert Creeley. ConAP

Cracks in eight log buildings, counting sheds. Montana Ranch Abandoned. Richard Hugo. PoW

Cracks on the walls, The. Star Blanket. Ray A. Young Bear. CDW

Cradle Hymn. At. to Martin Luther. See Away in a Manger.

Cradle Hymn. Isaac Watts. OxBChV

Cradle Song, A: "Angels are stooping, The." W. B. Yeats. LCL

Cradle Song, A: "Come, little babe, come, silly soul." Nicholas Breton. NOBE
(Come, Little Babe.) PPoe

Cradle Song, A: "Golden slumbers kiss your eyes." Thomas Dekker. Fr. The Pleasant Comedy of Patient Grissell. OxBChV
(Golden Slumbers.) GSB, with music

Cradle Song: "Imagine lamenting our longing, no." Yona Wallach, tr. fr. Hebrew by Leonore Gordon. VWA

Cradle Song: "Listening/ To the dying voices." Patrick Galvin. IPM

Cradle Song: "Lullaby and good-night," with music. Unknown, tr. fr. German by Natalia Macfarren. BLSH

Cradle Song, A: "Sweet dreams form a shade." Blake. Fr. Songs of Innocence. LAuP; MBPR; PCOP; STS

Cradle Song: "What does little birdie say." Tennyson. See What Does Little Birdie Say.

Cradle-Song of the Fisherman's Wife. Ella Higginson. WPW

Craftsmen. V. Sackville-West. OxBTC

Crafty Farmer, The. Unknown. AmFP

Craigbilly Fair. Unknown. GBP

Cranberry nose and a tin-can hat, A. Mister Snow Man. Bertha Wilcox Smith. CTV

Cranberry Song, The. Barney Reynolds. AmFP

Crane Is My Neighbour, The. John Shaw Neilson. MAuV

Cranes. J. R. S. Davies. POL

Cranes, The. Po Chü-i, tr. fr. Chinese by Arthur Waley. ECBV; OBVE

Crane's Ascent, The. Nick Bozanic. AMV–81

Crankadox leaned o'er the edge of the moon, The. Craqueodoom. James Whitcomb Riley. OBAL

Cranmer. C. H. Sisson. FaBoTw (1975 ed.)

Crapshooters. Carl Sandburg. VGW

Craqueodoom. James Whitcomb Riley. OBAL

Crash/ Take valium. Things to Do in Providence. Ted Berrigan. EC; UsP

Crash, bang! Noisy Boys. Jack Castiglione. BBGO

Crass Times Redeemed by Dignity of Souls, sel. Peter Viereck. "Tenderness of dignity of souls, The." HoPM (1975 ed.)

Craswall. Roland Mathias. OBW

Craving of Samuel Rouse for clearance to create, The. The Slave and the Iron Lace. Margaret Danner. AmNP (1974 ed.); BPo

Crawdad. Unknown. FSW

Crawl, laugh. Issa, tr. fr. Japanese by Nobuyuki Yuasa. OFD

Crawl toward the machine guns. He Said To. Marvin Bell. PCho

Crawlers, The. Keaulumoku, tr. fr. Hawaiian by M. W. Beckwith. Fr. The Kumulipo: A Creation Chant. WTO

Craw's Killed the Poussie, O, The! Unknown. BoAnP

Crayfish, The. Peter Kostakis. FiCh

Crayon World, The. Laurence Lieberman. ILP (1975 ed.)

Crazed by the suck and roar. Calypso. Richard Kell. CIP

Crazed Girl, The. W. B. Yeats. InPS

Crazed Man in Concentration Camp. Agnes Gergely, tr. fr. Hungarian by Edwin Morgan. BoWoP

Crazed Moon, The ("Crazed through much child-bearing"). W. B. Yeats. Moon

Crazy/ old building. Writer's Conference. E. Ethelbert Miller. PoUp

Crazy/ to be alive in such a strange. Lawrence Ferlinghetti. CTBA; FF

Crazy Arithmetic. D'Arcy Thompson. FaBoCo

Crazy Horse Returns to South Dakota. Harley Elliott. NeAC

Crazy Horse: The Last Morning. Lance Henson. VoR

Crazy Jane and Jack the Journeyman. W. B. Yeats. CMoP (1970 ed.)

Crazy Jane and the Bishop. W. B. Yeats. AnMo; CMoP (1970 ed.)

Crazy Jane Grown Old Looks at the Dancers. W. B. Yeats. CMoP (1970 ed.); EBEV

Crazy Jane on God. W. B. Yeats. CMoP (1970 ed.); EBEV; Epi; OxBTC

Crazy Jane on the Day of Judgment. W. B. Yeats. CMoP (1970 ed.)

Crazy Jane on the Mountain. W. B. Yeats. CMoP (1970 ed.)

Crazy Jane Reproved. W. B. Yeats. CMoP (1970 ed.)

Crazy Jane Talks with the Bishop. W. B. Yeats. AnMo; BoLoP; CABA (1972 ed.); CMoP (1970 ed.); EBEV; ExPo (1973 ed.);

ILP (1975 ed.); InPK; NIL; NoAM; OAEL-2; PoIA; PPP; STS; TT

Crazy pier, a roof of splinters, The. The Union Barge on Staten Island. Louis Simpson. NYP

Crazy Soliloquy. Geraldine Kudaka. NW

Creaking by pancake plateaus. Conestoga. George E. Murphy, Jr. AMV-81

Cream sours in this weather. Are You There, Mrs. Goose? John V. Hicks. AMV-80

Creamcheese babies square and downy as bolsters. The Peaceable Kingdom. Marge Piercy. UsP

Created, The. Jones Very. AmVN; PiAm

Created for whose sake? The praying. Don't Sit under the Apple Tree with Anyone Else but Me. Robert Pack. FF

Creation, The. James Weldon Johnson. MiP; PBMP; PoBA

Creation, The. *Maori Oral Tradition, tr. by* Richard Taylor. WTO

Creation, The. Patricia Ramsey. AATT

Creation, The: According to Coyote. Simon J. Ortiz. CDW

Creation Morning. X. J. Kennedy. UsP

Creation Myths. Burton Raffel. AMV-80

Creation of Anguish. Howard Nemerov. AnMo

Creation of Birds, The. Milton. *Fr.* Paradise Lost, VII. PB

Creation of Man, The. *Maori Oral Tradition, tr. by* John White. WTO

Creation of the Child. Susan Litwack. VWA

Creation of the Moon, The. *Unknown, tr. fr. Amazonian Indian by* W. S. Merwin. Moon

Creation of the Sea, The. Milton. *Fr.* Paradise Lost, VII. RhR

Creation: The Fifth Day, Fishes and Birds. Milton. *Fr.* Paradise Lost, VII. SCP-1
("And God said, let the waters generate.") EcS

Creation's and Creator's crowning good. To the Body. Coventry Patmore. OAEL-2; VLP

Creation's Lord, We Give Thee Thanks, *with music.* William deWitt Hyde. AH

Creator of Infinities, *with music.* Chadwick Hansen. AH

Creator Spirit, by whose aid. Veni Creator Spiritus. *Unknown, paraphrased by* Dryden. BoReV; FaPoR; ILwL; PIM

Creature to pet and spoil, A. Kob Antelope. *Yoruba Oral Tradition, tr. by* Ulli Beier. WTO

Creatures. Maxine W. Kumin. BoAnP

Creatures that we met this morning, The. Discovery of the New World. Carter Revard. VoR

Credentials. William Stafford. FoP

Credibility. John Ciardi. InPK; WIF

Credo. Brewster Ghiselin. PoA

Credo. Robinson Jeffers. MPA

Credo. Georgia Douglas Johnson. PoBA

Credo. E. A. Robinson. CMoP (1970 ed.); ILP (1975 ed.); LFH; PiAm; PPM; STS; TAP; VoPo

Creede. Cy Warman. BPAW

Creek Mother Poem. Joy Harjo. SA

Creep into thy narrow bed. The Last Word. Matthew Arnold. CABA (1972 ed.); NOBE; OAEL-2; PBMP; VLP

Creeper, The. Tom Schmidt. NeAC

Creeps in half wanton, half asleep. Wagner. Rupert Brooke. FaBoTw (1975 ed.); NOBL

Cremation of Sam McGee, The. Robert W. Service. PoTa

Crematorium. John Betjeman. PoA

Crepes Flambeau. Tess Gallagher. AMV-81

Crescent Moon, The. *Unknown.* Moon
("In Mornigan's park there is a deer.") GBP

Crescenzio, the Pope's Legate at the High Council, Trent. The Cardinal and the Dog. Robert Browning. VLP

Crew-cuts. Donald Hall. MAT

Crew is changed, the stone's face notched in darkness, The. Weldon Kees. *Fr.* The Hourglass. NYP

Cricket. No Ch'ŏn-myŭng, *tr. fr. Korean by* Ko Won. PBWP

Cricket, The. Frederick Goddard Tuckerman. NOBA; PiAm

Cricket and the greshope wenten hem to fight, The. Nonsense. *Unknown.* EBEV; OxBM

Cricket March. Carl Sandburg. UsP

Crickets. Aram Saroyan. MAT; SFF

Crickets and locusts, cicadas. Rosalía de Castro, *tr. fr. Galician by* Benjamin de Castro. PBWP

Cried the Lip. Wallace Carroll. SPo

Cried the navy-blue ghost. Four in the Morning. Edith Sitwell. NoAM

Crier, The. Michael Drayton. ILP (1975 ed.); PAIC

Crime Club. Weldon Kees. AnMo

Crimes of Lizzie Borden, The. *Unknown.* FaBoCo

Crimes of Lugalanne. Enheduanna, *tr. fr. Sumerian; ad. by* Aliki *and* Willis Barnstone. BoWoP

Crimes of Passion: The Phone Caller. Terry Stokes. AmPA

Crimes of Passion: The Slasher. Terry Stokes. AmPA

Crimes They Got Away With. Harrison Fisher. PoUp

Crimson lute that comest in the dawn. Sister Juana Inés de la Cruz, *tr. fr. Spanish by* Samuel Beckett. Epi

Crimson nor yellow roses, nor. Eros D'Aute. Theodore Wratislaw. GBL

Crimson Tent. John Dos Passos. PoA

Cripple Creek. *Unknown.* AmFP; FSW

Cripple for Life, The; or, The Poor Volunteer. *Unknown.* AmFP

Crippled Child at the Window. Melissa Cannon. AMV-80

Crippler, The. Danny Siegel. VWA

Cripples. Nina Cassian, *tr. fr. Romanian by* Herbert Kuhner. VWA

Cripples. J. D. Reed. NeAC

Cripples. Kathleen Spivack. SFF

Criseyde Sees Troilus Return from Battle. Chaucer. *Fr.* Troilus and Criseyde, II. OxBM

Crisis, The. Robert Creeley. FF; PPP

Crisis is a hair. Emily Dickinson. PiAm

Crisp, The/ pale green. Salad La Raza. Janet Campbell Hale. VoR

Crispus Attucks. Robert Hayden. CNA

Crispus Attucks McCoy. Sterling A. Brown. BPo

Crist made to man a fair present. Divine Love. *Unknown.* OxBM

Criteria. Ruthe T. Spinnanger. AATT

Critic, A. Walter Savage Landor. FaBoEE

Critic, The. Gordon Wharton. IPM

Critic advises, A. Black Poet, White Critic. Dudley Randall. BPo; CABA (1972 ed.); ConAP; UsP

Critic Undefiled. A. Wilber Stevens. MPA

Critical Observations. Archibald MacLeish. OBAL

Critics and Connoisseurs. Marianne Moore. CMoP (1970 ed.); NoAM; NOBA; PSN

Critics and Poets. Geoffrey Grigson. FaBoEE

Critics cry unfair, The. In Defense of Black Poets. Conrad Kent Rivers. BPo

Critics: in your sight. Sister Juana Inés de la Cruz, *tr. by* Judith Thurman. *Fr.* A Satirical Romance. PBWP

Critics say that epics have died out, The. Elizabeth Barrett Browning. *Fr.* Aurora Leigh, V. PBWP

Critique for Our Times. Albert Howard Carter. AATT

Critter. W. M. Ransom. CDW

Croak of a raven hoar, The! A Mammon-Marriage. George Macdonald. BoLoP

"Croak!" said the Toad. The Toad and the Frog. *Unknown.* PCOP

Crockery. Julia Budenz. AMV–80

Crockett. William Jay Smith. TDH

Crocodile, The. Hilaire Belloc. BBL

Crocodile, The. "Lewis Carroll." *See* How Doth the Little Crocodile.

Crocodile ("Once a haughty crocodile left his home upon the Nile"). Kornei Chukovsky, *tr. fr. Russian by* Babette Deutsch. ECBV

Crocodile ("Once there was a crocodile"). Kornei Chukovsky, *tr. fr. Russian by* Richard Coe. ECBV

Crocodile, The. Oliver Herford. TDH

Crocus, The. Walter Crane. PCOP

Crocus. Joan Murray. AMV–80

Crocus, The. Coventry Patmore. PF

Crois was made al of reed, A. Prologue to a Translation. John Trevisa. OxBM

Cromwell. Robert Francis. GP

Cromwell. Paul Mills. MIS

Cromwell, I did not think to shed a tear. The Last Words of Cardinal Wolsey. Shakespeare. *Fr.* King Henry VIII, III, ii. PIM; PoIA

Cromwell, our chief of men, who through a cloud. To the Lord General Cromwell, May 1652 [*or* To Oliver Cromwell]. Milton. CABA (1972 ed.); Epi; OBP

Cronos, Cronos, mend thy pace. Dryden. *Fr.* The Secular Masque. SCP–1

Crooked/ beneath a denim. Dreams. Charles Cooper. PoBA

Crooked Carol. Norma Farber. POL

Crooked gables. In Chagall's Village. Rose Ausländer, *tr. by* Ewald Osers. VWA

Crooked paths go every way, The. The Goat Paths. James Stephens. UnPo (1976 ed.)

Cropped, grey, too-small, bullet, Prussian head, A. Pigeon. Roy Fuller. PB

Croppy Boy, The. *Unknown.* AmFP; FaBoBa; FSW

Crops are all in and the peaches are rotting, The. Plane Wreck at Los Gatos (Deportee). Woody Guthrie. InPK; WTO

Croquet in Childhood. Helena Minton. FAF

Cross. Langston Hughes. AmNP (1974 ed.); CoPAm; PoBA; SoSe; TAP

Cross and the Weathercock, The. James Nolan. AATT

Cross-bars and posts, the echo of distant bells. Football Field: Evening. J. A. R. McKellar. LiSp

Cross-eyed Lover, The. Donald Finkel. Prf

Cross Fox. Joseph Bruchac. NW

Cross is a machine, A. Near the White House. Michael S. Harper. NW

Cross Oceans into My Heart. Ntozake Shange. NW

Cross of boy with man within is an, The. On a Prize Crucifix by a Student Sculptor. Robert Logan. CAPP

Cross of Flame. Robert Gessner. SPT

Cross of Snow, The. Longfellow. AmVN; HeIP; ILP (1975 ed.); IPWM; NOBA; PiAm; TAP

Cross Patch/ Lift [*or* Draw] the latch. Mother Goose. BBL; GBP; MG

Cross, the Cross, The. Tortoise-Shell. D. H. Lawrence. CMoP (1970 ed.); ExPo (1973 ed.); OAEL–2

Cross Ties. X. J. Kennedy. CoPAm; HoPM (1975 ed.); UsP

Crossed Apple, The. Louise Bogan. BiP; HeIP, NIL

Crossedroads. Martin Staples Shockley. FF

Crosses. Robert Herrick. CaPo

Crossing. Anthony Barnett. VWA

Crossing. Philip Booth. GOA

Crossing. Archibald MacLeish. POL

Crossing alone the nighted ferry. A. E. Housman. NOBE

Crossing Brooklyn Ferry. Walt Whitman. CABA (1972 ed.); NoAM; NOBA; NYP; PiAm; TAP

"Crowds of men and women attired in the usual costumes," *sel.* CTBA

Crossing Cook Strait. James K. Baxter. ATNZ

Crossing into the Prairies. Bruce Severy. HeS

Crossing Kansas by Train. Donald Justice. ANTL

"Telephone poles, The," *sel.* OSP

Crossing Over. Dan Johnson. PoUp

Crossing the Atlantic. Anne Sexton. NoAM

Crossing the Bar. Tennyson. BiP; CABA (1972 ed.); DL; FaPoR; FF; HeIP; ILP (1975 ed.); InPK; NOBE; OAEL–2; PBMP; PFD; PIM; PPM; RhR; SoSe (1977 ed.); VLP; VoPo

Crossing the Colorado River into Yuma. Simon J. Ortiz. TAT

Crossing the Plains. Joaquin Miller. AmVN; BPAW

Crossing the shallow holdings high above sea. Hungry Grass. Donagh MacDonagh. BIrV

Crossing the street. The Broken Home. James Merrill. HAP; NoAM; NOBA; PPP

Crossing the Western Ocean to the edge of the world. After the Spanish Chroniclers. William Bronk. GP

Crossing West Texas (1966). Kell Robertson. TAT

Crosspatch. *See* Cross Patch.

Crotchet Castle, *sel.* Thomas Love Peacock. Priest and the Mulberry Tree, The, *fr. ch.* 18. PoTa

Crouched beneath a snowbound sky. The Grey Ones. Louis MacNeice. CMoP (1970 ed.)

Crouched on the pavement close by Belgrave Square. West London. Matthew Arnold. FF

Crow. Peter Blue Cloud. NW

Crow, The. Rita Boumí-Pappás, *tr. fr. Modern Greek by* Kimon Friar. PBWP

Crow, The. James Reaney. AKE

Crow/ settling on a branch. Sunset. Ron Weber. PoUp

Crow and the Birds. Ted Hughes. OBP

Crow-Children Walk My Circles in the Snow, The. Ray A. Young Bear. CDW

Crow doth sing as sweetly as the lark, The. Birdsong. Shakespeare. *Fr.* The Merchant of Venice. PB

Crow flies between your phone and mine, The. Poem. Cathleen Quirk. MMD

Crow goes flopping on from wood to wood, The. The Flight of Birds. John Clare. PCOP

Crow realized God loved him. Crow's Theology. Ted Hughes. UsP

Crow Resting. Ted Hughes. UsP

Crow Sat on the Willow, The. John Clare. VLP

Crow, Straight Flier, but Dark. Laya Firestone. VWA

Crow Voices. Gail Tremblay. AMV–81

Crowd, The. John Masefield. OxBTC

Crowd at the ball game, The. At the Ball Game. William Carlos Williams. CMoP (1970 ed.); ExPo (1973 ed.); LiSp; NoAm; NOBA

Crowd fear: blown paper and uprooted ferns. The Spring Festival on the River. John Peck. AmPA

Crowded balcony and she, A. Big City Glissando. Nicholas Christopher. NYP

Crowded graveyard, the tall solemn trees, The. Haworth in May. Rowland Childe. PES

Crowdieknowe. "Hugh MacDiarmid." InPS; NoAM

Crowds of men and women attired in the usual costumes. Walt Whitman. *Fr.* Crossing Brooklyn Ferry. CTBA

Crown me with roses whilest I live. Abraham Cowley, *after the Greek of* Anacreon. *Fr.* The Epicure. OBVE

Crown of Happiness. Anne Hebert, *tr. fr. French by* Willis Barnstone. BoWoP

Crown of Windflowers, A. Christina Rossetti. OxBChV

Crown Prince of Dullness, The. Dryden. *Fr.* MacFlecknoe. NOBE
("All human things are subject to decay.") LFH; PoIA; SCP-1

Crowned Heart, The. *Unknown.* PoPle

Crowning a bluff where gleams the lake below. Pontoosuce. Herman Melville. NOBA

Crows, The. Louise Bogan. SBG

Crows, The. John Engels. AMV–81

Crows, The. Zulfikar Ghose. BoAnP

Crows. David McCord. RFM

Crows. William Witherup. POL

Crow's Ditty. *Unknown.* GBP

Crow's First Lesson. Ted Hughes. InPS; NoAM

Crow's Last Stand. Ted Hughes. InPS

Crows mark, The. African Day. Gloria de Sant'Ana, *tr. by* Allan Francovich *and* Kathleen Weaver. PBWP

Crows, pheasants, cuckoos, toucans. Sandra Hochman. Three Love Poems, I. UsP

Crow's Theology. Ted Hughes. UsP

Crow's Way. Duane Niatum. CDW

Crows will stick their beaks into anything. The Crows. Zulfikar Ghose. BoAnP

Crowsfeet Splaying round His Eyes. L. Paul Lloyd-Evans. BuTh

Crucified. Anne Sadowski. SES

Crucified upon this cross is black, The. Ebony: Contemporary. Marian Frances Brand. AATT

Crucifix, The. Robert Lowell. NoV

Crucifixion. *Unknown.* BPo; TAP

Crucifixion, The. Whittier. PIM

Crucifixus pro Nobis. Patrick Carey. SCP-2

Cruel arrows gone, The. Fleche. Larry Eigner. VGW

Cruel Brother, The. *Unknown.* AmFP; PeBB

Cruel, but composed and bland. Matthew Arnold. *Fr.* Matthias. POL

Cruel, Clever Cat. Geoffrey Taylor. FaBoEE

Cruel Falcon, The. Robinson Jeffers. BiP

Cruel Frederick. Heinrich Hoffmann, *tr. fr. German.* SpRo

Cruel girls we loved, The. Mothers and Daughters. David Campbell. GAS; POL

Cruel Maid, The. Robert Herrick. CaPo

Cruel Mother, The. *Unknown.* AmFP; FaBoBa; FSW; InPK; PeBB
(Fine Flowers in the Valley.) RDB, *with music;* USP

Cruel War Is Raging, The. *Unknown.* FSW

Cruelty has a human heart. A Divine Image. Blake. MBPR; STS

Cruise for the Prosecution, A. Rodney Hall. FPA

Cruise of the "P. C.," The. *Unknown.* RhR

Cruising for Burgers. George Mattingly. AcAn

Crumbled rock of London is dripping under, The. Sonnet. Roy Fuller. PoA

Crumbling into this world. Venice. James Wright. AMV–81

Crumbling is not an instant's act. Emily Dickinson. NOBA; PPP

Crumbs or the Loaf. Robinson Jeffers. CMoP (1970 ed.)

Crusaders knew the Holy Places, The. Jenny Mastoraki, *tr. fr. Modern Greek by* Nikes Germanakos. BoWoP; PBWP

Crush the manroot, swallow what you desire. Learning the Spells: A Diptych. Anita Endrezze Probst. CDW

Crushed by that just contempt his follies bring. On Poet Ninny. Earl of Rochester. APAS

Crusht cigar, a, The. AW6 May 25, 1974. George Bowering. FoP

Crusoe's Island. Derek Walcott. NoAM

Crust of bread and a corner to sleep in, A. Life. Paul Laurence Dunbar. AmNP (1974 ed.)

Crustaceans. Roy Fuller. NoAM

Crutches. Robert Herrick. CaPo

Cry, The. Grace Cavalieri. AATT

Cry. Alexander Scott. MS

Cry, baby, cry,/ Put your finger in your eye. Mother Goose. MG

Cry, Crow. Sonnet. Hayden Carruth. NNaP

Cry for a Disused Synagogue in Booysens. Mannie Hirsch. VWA

Cry left your mouth, A. Mouth. Clarisse Nicoïdski, *tr. by* Stephen Levy. VWA

Cry Mercy. Charles Brasch. ATNZ

Cry of an Aged One, The. Ray Fraser. NeAC

Cry of Generations, The. Mordechai Husid, *tr. fr. Yiddish by* Seymour Mayne *and* Rivka Augenfeld. VWA

Cry of the Children, The. Elizabeth Barrett Browning. VLP; VPC

Cry of the High Hurdlers, The. Horace Spencer Fiske. SPo

Cry of the Human, The. Elizabeth Barrett Browning. PIM

Cry of the raven rang over the moor, The. Bobby Campbell. *Unknown.* FSW

Cry of those being eaten by America, The. Those Being Eaten by America. Robert Bly. PPoD

Cry out for Sakhr when a dove with necklaces. Elegy for Her Brother Sakhr. Al-Khansa, *tr. fr. Arabic by* Willis Barnstone. BoWoP

Cry, A!—someone is knocked. At 79th and Park. Barbara Howes. MiP; NYP

Cry went through me like a stab of a knife, A. W. H. Auden. *Fr.* A Happy New Year. OBSV

Cryin' ain't goin' down this big road by myself. Big Road Blues. *Unknown.* BluL

Cryin' canned heat. Canned Heat Blues. *Unknown.* BluL

Cryin' I ain't goin' down the dark road by myself. Dark Road Blues. *Unknown.* BluL

Cryin', who's that yonder. Maggie Campbell Blues. *Unknown.* BluL

Crying Asia! that famous place. The Marriage of Hector and Andromache. Sappho, *tr. by* Guy Davenport. OBVE

Cryptology. Ernest Kroll. PoUp

Crystal. Ted Berrigan. EC

Crystal. Faye Kicknosway. IHMS

Crystal Cabinet, The. Blake. AIW; MBPR; OAEL-2; UsP
("Maiden caught me in the wild, The.") Epi

Crystal Moment. Robert P. Tristram Coffin. ECBV; SOS

Crystallization of color spreads, A. Aurora Borealis. Edouard Roditi. EAS

Crystallized Waves, The. Denis Glover. ATNZ

Crystals like Blood. "Hugh MacDiarmid." HAP; InPS

Cu Chuimne in youth. *Unknown, tr. fr. Irish by* John V. Kelleher. BIrV

Cuatro Generales, Los (The Four Insurgent Generals). *Unknown, tr. fr. Spanish.* FSW

Cuba. Lawrence Kearney. AMV–81

Cuba Libre. Joaquin Miller. BTTM

Cuba, 1962. Ai. AmPA

Cuban Refugees on Key Biscayne. Barbara Winder. TAT

Cubical Domes, The. David Gascoyne. EAS

Cubist Blues in Poltergeist Major. Allan F. Kipp. AMV–81

Cubist Portrait. Marjorie Allen Seiffert. PoA

Cubistic Lovers, The. Charles Edward Eaton. AMV–81

Cucaracha, La, *with music. Unknown, tr. fr. Spanish.* BLSH

Cuccu Song. *Unknown. See* Cuckoo Song.

Cuchulain Comforted. W. B. Yeats. CMoP (1970 ed.); OAEL-2

Cuckoo, The. Patrick Reginald Chalmers. BoAnP

Cuckoo. R. P. Lister. BoAnP

Cuckoo, The ("The cuckoo comes in April"). *Unknown.* BBL

Cuckoo, The ("The cuckoo is a bonny [*or* funny] bird"), *diff. versions. Unknown.* AmFP; FSW; GBP; GSB, *with music;* PoPle; RAE

"Cuckoo! The," cried my child, the while I slept. The Oocuck. Justin Richardson. BoAnP

Cuckoo, noisy among the Shenbaka flowers. Andal , *tr. fr. Tamil by* Willis Barnstone. BoWoP

Cuckoo Sings, The. Shakespeare. *See* Spring.

Cuckoo [*or* Cuccu] Song. *Unknown.* DuDr; NOBE; PBMP; PoIA; SpRo
(Now the Summer's Come, *mod. English version.*) HAP
(Sumer Is Icumen In.) BiP; EBEV; FF; GBP; HAP; HeIP; ILP (1975 ed.); InFS; NIL; OAEL–1; OxBM
(Summer Is a-Coming In.) FSW

Cuckoo-throb, the heartbeat of the Spring, The. Ardour and Memory. Dante Gabriel Rossetti. The House of Life, LXIV. OAEL–2

Cuckoo, when the lambkins bleat, The. The Cuckoo. Patrick Reginald Chalmers. BoAnP

Cuckoo's double note, The. Wiltshire Downs. Andrew Young. OxBTC

Cuddie, for shame hold up thy heavye head. October. Spenser. *Fr.* The Shepheardes Calendar. OAEL–1

Cudworth's Undergraduate Ode to a Bare Behind. John Ower. AMV–81

Culbin Sands. Andrew Young. OxBTC

Culloden, the Disruption. Steel? Derick Thomson, *tr. by author.* MS

Culprit, The. A. E. Housman. AIW

Culprit Fay, The, *sel.* Joseph Rodman Drake.
Fairy in Armor, A. PCOP

Cult of the Celtic, The. Anthony C. Deane. NOBL

Cultivating. Janet Kauffman. *Fr.* Tobacco. TC

Cultivation of Christmas Trees, The. T. S. Eliot. OFD

Cultural Exchange. Langston Hughes. BPo; PoBA

Cultural Exchange. Al Masarik. CPA

Cultural Notes. Kenneth Fearing. CMoP (1970 ed.)

Cultural Presupposition, The. W. H. Auden. CABA (1972 ed.)

Cultured Girl Again, The. Ben King. OBAL

*Cumberland* and the *Merrimac,* The, 2 *versions. Unknown.* AmFP

Cumberland Gap. *Unknown.* FSW

Cumberland Gap Drifter. Big John Birkbeck. EC

Cumberland Station. Dave Smith. CSP

*Cumberland's* Crew, The. *Unknown.* AmFP

Cundiyo. Alice Corbin. WPW

Cunning as a woman beautiful as a snake shy as an idol. Another Poem on Absalom. Nathan Yonathan, *tr. by* Richard Flantz. VWA

Cup capsizes along the formica, A. In the Snack-Bar. Edwin Morgan. FF

"Cup for hope, A!" she said. Three Seasons. Christina Rossetti. ILP (1975 ed.)

Cup is bound to spill, a saucer to break, A. Yankee Poet. Robley Wilson, Jr. AMV–81

Cup of tea on a God-swept evening, A. Knell for Insularity. Merle Meeter. AATT

Cup of the Bear, The, *abr.* Siv Cedering Fox. BCr

Cupid a Plowman. Moschus, *tr. fr. Greek by* Matthew Prior. OBVE

Cupid and My Campaspe. John Lyly. *See* Cards and Kisses.

Cupid and Venus. Mark Alexander Boyd. *See* Fra Bank to Bank, Fra Wood to Wood I Rin.

Cupid as he lay among. The Wounded Cupid. Robert Herrick. OBVE; OFD

Cupid-faced hooligan standing on tiptoe, The. Amsterdam Street Scene, 1972. Raphael Rudnik. AMV–81

Cupid Far Gone. Richard Lovelace. CaPo

Cupid's Call. James Shirley. SCP–2

Cur foretells the knell of parting day, The. Ambrose Bierce. *Fr.* The Devil's Dictionary. OBAL

Cure for Poetry, A. *Unknown, after the Latin of* George Buchanan. FaBoEE

Curfew. Paul Eluard, *tr. fr. French by* Quentin Stevenson. BoLoP

Curfew tolls the knell of parting day, The. Elegy Written in a Country Churchyard. Thomas Gray. BiP; CABA (1972 ed.); DL; EBEV; FaPoR; HAP; HeIP; ILP (1975 ed.); InPK; InPS; LAuP; LFH; NIL; NOBE; OAEL–1; OBP; PAIC; PBMP; PES; PPoD; PPoe; PPP; UnPo (1976 ed.); WIF

Curfew tolls the knell of parting day, The. Diversions of the Re-Echo Club. Carolyn Wells. OBAL

Curio, aye me, thy mistress' monkey's dead! Inamorato Curio. John Marston. *Fr.* The Scourge of Villainy. TVS

Curio's rich sideboard seldom sees the light. On a Stingy Beau. John Winstanley. FaBoEE

Curiosity. Alastair Reid. SoSe

Curiosity's not in me head. On Reading: Four Limericks. Myra Cohn Livingston. TDH

Curious business, A. Petty Murder. Albert MacLean, Jr. SFF

Curious Charlie. Isabel Frances Bellows. TDH

Curious is this stonework! The Fates destroyed it. The Ruin. *Unknown, tr. by* Gavin Bone. EBEV

Curious knot God made in Paradise, A. Upon Wedlock, and Death of Children. Edward Taylor. EAP

Curiously, I still remember. After Reading *The First Circle.* Martha Shelley. WBN

Curiously Young like a Freshly-dug Grave. Richard Brautigan. MIT

Curled in his black-ringed tail. The Dance of Gray Raccoon. Arthur Guiterman. BPAW

Curlew, The. Sara Henderson Hay. EcS

Curlew. Leslie Norris. HeHu

Curlew, Scouting for his flock, A. The Curlew. Sara Henderson Hay. EcS

Curly Joe. *Unknown.* BPAW

Curly locks! curly locks! wilt thou be mine? Mother Goose. BBL; MG

Currants on a bush. Fruits. Christina Rossetti. ECBV

Current freed for a while. Listening to Confucius. Henryk Grynberg, *tr. by* Isaac Komem. VWA

Currents. Emma Lazarus. *Fr.* By the Waters of Babylon. WPE

Curricle and hansom, The. The Great Garret, or 100 Wheels. James McMichael. AmPA

Curriculum Vitae. Ingeborg Bachmann, *tr. fr. German by* Jerome Rothenberg. BoWoP

Curriculum Vitae: Incomplete. Elisavietta Ritchie. AATT

Curse, The. John Donne. ILP (1975 ed.)

Curse, The. John Hollander. UnPo (1976 ed.)

Curse, The. J. M. Synge. FaBoCo; FaBoEE

Curse, A. *Unknown. See* Bruadar and Smith and Glinn.

Curse, The: A Song. Robert Herrick. CaPo

Curse for a Nation, A. Elizabeth Barrett Browning. SBG; WPE

Curse of a Fisherman's Wife. Lila Chalpin. AMV–80

Curse of Cromwell, The. W. B. Yeats. BIrV

Curse of the Cat Woman. Edward Field. CABA (1972 ed.); WeW

Curse on a Closed Gate, A. *Unknown, tr. fr. Irish by* James H. Cousins. PFIr

Curse on Uruk, A. Enheduanna, *tr. fr. Sumerian; ad. by* Aliki *and* Willis Barnstone. BoWoP

Curse upon that faithless maid, A. Song. Aphra Behn. *Fr.* Emperor of the Moon. WPE

Curses. Joseph Duemer. AMV-80

Cursor Mundi, *sel. Unknown.* Pound of Flesh, The. OxBM

Curst be the verse, how well so'er it flow. Pope. *Fr.* Epistle to Dr. Arbuthnot. OBP

Curst Wife, The. *Unknown.* AIW

Curtain. Lance Henson. VoR

Curtain Call. Alan Ziegler. AAN

Curtain Speech. Michael Braude. AMV-81

Curtain World. Heather Morse. CaYB

Curtains drawn back, the door ajar. Robinson at Home. Weldon Kees. AnMo

Curtains in the House of the Metaphysician, The. Wallace Stevens. PoA

Curtains in the solemn room, The. Solitude. A. R. D. Fairburn. ATNZ

Curtains Now Are Drawn, The. Thomas Hardy. CMoP (1970 ed.)

Curtains of rock. Orpheus in the Underworld. David Gascoyne. FaBoTw (1975 ed.)

Curtains were half drawn, the floor was swept, The. After Death. Christina Rossetti. GBL; ILP (1975 ed.)

Cushendall. *Unknown.* WTO

Cushie Butterfield. George Ridley. VLP

Cushy Cow, Bonny. *Unknown.* GBP

Cusp/ the little word. How One Thing Leads to Another. David Smith. NVAP

Custer. Edmund Clarence Stedman. BPAW

Custer Lives in Humbolt County. Janet Campbell Hale. UsP; VoR

Custer's Last Charge. Frederick Whittaker. BPAW

Custom of the World, The. Louis Simpson. BoLoP; SFF

Customarily Autumn. F. Eugene Warren. AATT

Customs. Juan Gelman, *tr. fr. Spanish by* Yishai Tobin. VWA

Customs Change. *Unknown.* OxBChV

Customs of the Country, The. Phyllis McGinley. *Fr.* New England Pilgrimage. TH

Cut. David J. Feela. AMV-81

Cut. Sylvia Plath. CABA (1972 ed.); CAPP; InPK; PiAm; TAP

Cut dollars in the shape of men. Dollars. Isidor Schneider. SPT

Cut Flower, A. Karl Shapiro. HAP; WeW

Cut from the green hedge a forked hazel stick. The Diviner. Seamus Heaney. HeHu

Cut the Grass. A. R. Ammons. HAP; PPP; TAP

Cute. Jim Everhard. EC

Cutter risen from the mollusks, it is a god, A. The Memoirs. Carl Rakosi. PoA

Cutting Out a Dress. Dennis Schmitz. PCho

Cutting shade, cool spades and a little last beds. Pastry. Gertrude Stein. *Fr.* Tender Buttons. RiTi

Cutting the Jewish Bride's Hair. Ruth Whitman. RiTi

Cutting Wood: After a Family Photograph. Norbert Krapf. BrS

Cuttings ("Sticks-in-a-drowse droop over sugary loam"). Theodore Roethke. AnMo; NoAM; NOBA; PiAM; TAP; UnPo (1976 ed.)

Cuttings ("This urge, wrestle, resurrection of dry sticks"). Theodore Roethke. AnMo; NoAM; NOBA; PiAM; PPoe; TAP; UnPo (1976 ed.)

Cuttlefish. Ernest Kroll. PoUp

Cutty Wren, The. *Unknown.* FSW; GBP

Cuvier Light. Pat Wilson. ATNZ

Cwa' een like the milk-wort and bog-cotton hair! Milk-Wort and Bog-Cotton. "Hugh MacDiarmid." MS

Cwm above Penrhiwceiber, The. Robert Morgan. HeHu

Cwmrhydyceirw Elegiacs. Vernon Watkins. PoA

Cy Est Pourtraicte, Madame Ste. Ursule, et les Unze Mille Vierges. Wallace Stevens. LoAs

Cycads, The. Judith Wright. MAuV

Cycle, The. Stephen Dunn. HeS

Cycle, A. John Leax. AATT

Cycle. Frank Lonergan. AMV-81

Cycle of Tears, A. Jim Kraus. PHC

Cycle of Women, A. Sharon Barba. RiTi

Cycles, Cycles. Suzanne Berger Rioff. NMM

Cyclist, The. Lawrence Kearney. AMV-80

Cyclists, The. Amy Lowell. WPE

Cymbals clash. Harlem Sounds: Hallelujah Corner. William Browne. AmNP (1974 ed.)

Cymbeline, *sels.* Shakespeare.
Fear No More the Heat o' the Sun, *fr.* IV, ii. AIW; EBEV; FF; GBL; HAP; HeIP; ILP (1975 ed.); InPK; InPS; OAEL-1; OBP; PBMP; PoIA; PoPle; PPoe; SoSe; STS (Dirge for Fidele.) NOBE
"Hark, hark! the lark at heaven's gate sings," *fr.* II, iii. HeIP; ILP (1975 ed.); NIL; OBP; PAIC (Lark, The.) PCOP
"With fairest flowers,/ Whilst summer lasts," *fr.* IV, ii. EBEV

Cymon and Iphigenia, *sel.* Dryden.
Lines on a Paid Militia. SoSe (Militia, The.) OBSV

Cymru. D. Gwenallt Jones, *tr. fr. Welsh by* Gwyn Jones. OBW

Cynara. Ernest Dowson. *See* Non Sum Qualis Eram Bonae sub Regno Cynarae.

Cynddylan on a Tractor. R. S. Thomas. LP; MPo

Cynic, The. St. George Tucker. OBAL

Cynic Satyre, A. John Marston. *Fr.* The Scourge of Villainy, VII. TVS

Cynisca. *Unknown, tr. fr. Greek by* Tom Dodge. LiSp

Cynthia. Edward Benlowes. *Fr.* Theophila; or, Love's Sacrifice. Moon

Cynthia, because your horns look diverse ways. Fulke Greville. *Fr.* Caelica. Moon

Cynthia in the Snow. Gwendolyn Brooks. LCL

Cynthia Matz, with my finger in your cunt. Each Day. David Ignatow. NNaP

Cynthia's Revels, *sels.* Ben Jonson.
Echo's Lament of Narcissus, *fr.* I, ii. SoSe ("Slow, slow fresh fount, keep time with my salt tears.") ExPo (1973 ed.); ILP (1975 ed.); InPK; NIL; OAEL-1; PoIA
Hymn to Diana, *fr.* V, vi. HAP; Moon; NOBE; PoPle ("Queen and huntress, chaste and fair.") CABA (1972 ed.); HeIP; ILP (1975 ed.); OAEL-1; PAIC (Song: To Cynthia.) SoSe (1977 ed.)
"Thou more than most sweet glove," *fr.* IV. GBL

Cypassis, that a thousand ways trimm'st hair. Ovid, *tr. by* Christopher Marlowe. Amores, II, 8. EBEV

Cypress Grove Blues. *Unknown.* BluL

Cyrano De Bergerac, *sel.* Edmond Rostand, *tr. fr. French by* Brian Hooker.
"Love, I love beyond," *fr.* Act III. OLR

Cyriac, this three years' day these eyes, though clear. To Mr. Cyriac Skinner upon His Blindness. Milton. ILP (1975 ed.); SCP-1

Cyriack, Whose Grandsire on the Royal Bench. Milton. PAIC

# D

D Blues. Calvin C. Hernton. PoBA

D-Day Dodgers, The. *Unknown. See* Ballad of the D-Day Dodgers.

D-Day Minus. Edwin Brock. BBGO

D. H. Lawrence and James Joyce. Humbert Wolfe. FaBoEE

D.O.M., A.D. 2167. John Frederick Nims. CoPAm

D-Y Bar. James Welch. CDW

Dab of Color, A. Theodore Weiss. VGW

Daccus is all bedaub'd with golden lace. Against Gaudy-Bragging-Undoughty Daccus. John Davies of Hereford. FaBoEE

Dachau. John Malcolm Brinnin. GP

Dachau, Now: "Roses Grow There, Fat with Blood." Elisavietta Ritchie. AATT

Dachshund, The. Edward Anthony. GDP

Dachshunds ("The dachshund leads a quiet life"). William Jay Smith. OBAL

Dad. Elaine Feinstein. VWA

Daddy. Sylvia Plath. AnMo; BiP; BoWoP; CAPP; CMoP (1970 ed.); ExPo (1973 ed.); InPK; InPS; NMM; NoAM; NOBA; PiAm; Psy; RiTi; TPo; UnPo (1976 ed.)

Daddyboy/ trickster hero. Daring. Carol Konek. IHMS

Dae what ye wull ye canna parry. "Hugh MacDiarmid." *Fr.* A Drunk Man Looks at the Thistle. EBEV

Daedalus. Alastair Reid. NCSH

Daemon Lover, The. *Unknown. See* Demon Lover, The.

Daeth o Brand, The. Tom Scott. MS

Daffadowndilly has come up to town. Mother Goose. *See* Daffy-down-dilly has come up to town.

Daffodil. Waldo Williams, *tr. fr. Welsh by* Gwyn Jones. OBW

Daffodils. Michael Heffernan. AMV-80

Daffodils. Wordsworth. *See* I Wandered Lonely as a Cloud.

Daffy-down-dilly [*or* Daffadowndilly] has come up to town. Mother Goose. CTV; MG; PCOP

Daft Jean. Sydney Dobell. VLP

Dago shovelman sits by the railroad track, The. Child of the Romans. Carl Sandburg. PiAm

Daguerreotype Taken in Old Age. Margaret Atwood. BoWoP

Dai horse neighs against the bleak wind of Etsu, The. South-Folk in Cold Country. Ezra Pound, *after the Chinese.* OBVE

Daily Courage Doesn't Count. Alta. GP

Daily Grind, The. Fenton Johnson. AmNP (1974 ed.)

Daily Growing. *Unknown.* FSW

Daily I Fall in Love with Waitresses. Elliot Fried. GP

Daily News. Tom Clark. EAS

Daily the Ocean between Us. Patricia Goedicke. TAP

Daily the wind-flowers age, and so do I. Weaving Love-Knots. Hsüeh T'ao, *tr. by* Carolyn Kizer. BoWoP

Daily Wages. Amrita Pritam, *tr. fr. Punjabi by author and* Charles Brasch. PBWP

Daily went the Sultan's beauteous. The Asra. Heine, *tr. by* Ernst Feise. NAWM-2

Dainty little maiden, whither would you wander? The City Child. Tennyson. OxBChV; PCOP

Dainty Miss Apathy. Pooh! Walter de la Mare. BBL; HAP

Dainty young heiress of Lincoln's Inn Fields, The. Charles Sackville. POL

Dairymaid and Her Milk-Pot, The. La Fontaine, *tr. fr. French by* Marianne Moore. NAWM-2

Daisies. Alden Nowlan. NeAC

Daisies. Christina Rossetti. PCOP

Daisies. Frank Dempster Sherman. CTV

Daisies. John Stevens Wade. FAF

Daisies. Andrew Young. PF

Daisy, The. Marya Zaturenska. LoAs

Daisy Bell; or, A Bicycle Built for Two, *with music.* Harry Dacre. BLSH; BLSo; FSN
(Bicycle Built for Two, A.) FSW

Daisy Fraser. Edgar Lee Masters. *Fr.* Spoon River Anthology. CMoP (1970 ed.); HAP

Daisy Pinks. Alistair Campbell. *See* O Catch Miss Daisy Pinks.

Dakota Land. *Unknown.* BPAW; FSW

Dakota: October, 1822, Hunkpapa Warrior. Rod Taylor. WeW

Daley's Dorg Wattle. W. T. Goodge. GDP

Dallán Dé! Dallán Dé! Butterfly in the Fields. Joseph Campbell. BoAnP; PFIr

Dalliance of the Eagles, The. Walt Whitman. BiP; BoAnP; CABA (1972 ed.); HAP; HeIP; InPK; LoAs; PiAm; POL, PPoe; PPP; TAP

Dam, The. Patric Dickinson. PoTa

Damages, Two Hundred Pounds. Thackeray. OBSV

Dame. Susan Astor. AMV-80

Dame Wiggins of Lee. *Unknown, at. to* Richard Scrafton Sharpe *and to* Mrs. Pearson. FaBoNo; OxBChV

Dames of France are fond and free, The. The Girl I Left behind Me. Thomas Osborne Davis. BTTM

Damisel, rest thee wel. A Student Courting. *Unknown.* OxBM

Damn blue eyes. Damn the street. Curses. Joseph Duemer. AMV-80

Damn fool feeling her up. Wreck. Noel Polk. AMV-81

Damn Her. John Ciardi. IP

Damn it all! all this our South stinks peace. Sestina: Altaforte. Ezra Pound. CMoP (1970 ed.); FaBoTw (1975 ed.); NOBA

Damnation follows death in other men. On Poets. Pope. FaBoEE

Damned Women. Baudelaire, *tr. fr. French by* Roy Campbell. BoLoP

Damon, come drive thy flocks this way. Clorinda and Damon. Andrew Marvell. PAIC

Damon forbear, and don't disturb your Muse. The Court. *Unknown.* APAS

Damon the Mower. Andrew Marvell. AnMo; OAEL-1

Damp corners are filled, The. For Rent. David James. TC

Damp fallen leaves smell of ripe bananas, The. Walking Home at Night. Daniel Weissbort. VWA

Damp swell of dunes that turn into flour, The. A New Genesis. Avraham Shlonsky, *tr. by* Francis Landy. VWA

Damsels of Time, the hypocritic Days. *See* Daughters of Time, the hypocritic Days.

Dan Ellis's Boys. *Unknown.* AmFP

Dan, the Dust of Masada Is Still in My Nostrils. Ruth Whitman. VWA

Dan the Watchman. John D. Sheridan. FPB

Dana Point. Brewster Ghiselin. AMV-81

Danaë. Barbara Howes. RiTi; WPE

Dance, The. Amiri Baraka. PiAm

Dance, The. Hart Crane. *Fr.* The Bridge: Powhatan's Daughter. PiAm

Dance, The. Gareth Alban Davies, *tr. fr. Welsh by* Gwyn Jones. OBW

Dance. Lynn Sukenick. *See* Death.

Dance, The. William Carlos Williams. CMoP (1970 ed.); ExPo (1973 ed.); HAP; HeIP; ILP (1975 ed.); InPK; NCSH; NIL; NoAM; NOBA; PAIC; PiAm; PoIA; POL; SoSe; TAP; WeW; WIF

Dance, The/ (held up for me by). The Dance. Amiri Baraka. PiAm

Dance and Eye Me (Wicked)ly My Breath a Fixed Sphere. Rochelle Owens. NMM

Dance Figure. Ezra Pound. HeIP

Dance for Ma Rainey, A. Al Young. CSP; SA

Dance for Militant Dilettantes, A. Al Young. CSP; PiAm; PoBA; PPoD; SA

Dance for Rain, A. Witter Bynner. BPAW

Dance grows, The. The Dead. Jay Wright. FB

Dance Hymn. Isaiah Shembe, *tr. fr. Zulu by* B. G. M. Sundkler. WTO

Dance, little baby, dance up high. The Baby's Dance. Ann Taylor. ECBV; OxBChV

Dance Marathon, The. Lee Lally. PoUp

Dance of Burros. Dilys Laing. PCOP

Dance of Gray Raccoon, The. Arthur Guiterman. BPAW

Dance of the Abakweta, The. Margaret Danner. NIL

Dance of the Infidels. Al Young. PoBA

Dance of the Macabre Mice. Wallace Stevens. CMoP (1970 ed.); NOBA; STS

Dance-Song. Jaroslav Seifert, *tr. fr. Czech by* Paul Jagasich *and* Tom O'Grady. AMV–81

Dance Steps. *Unknown.* ECBV
(Lachlan Gorach's Rhyme.) PoPle

Dance there upon the shore. To a Child Dancing in the Wind. W. B. Yeats. BBGO; ILP (1975 ed.); PFIr

Dance, Thumbkin, dance. *Unknown.* MG

Dance to your daddy. Mother Goose. FSW; MG; PoPle

Dancer. Geoff Page. FPA

Dancer, The. Edmund Waller. NIL

Dancer, The. Al Young. PiAm; PoBA; SA

Dancer dips and holds, A. The sun. The Berkeley Pier. John Addiego. AMV–81

Dancer: Four Poems. Paul Engle. AMV–80

Dancer from the Dance, The. Suzanne Juhasz. IHMS

Dancer grins at the ground, The. Picnic. Ted Berrigan. FiCh

Dancer quarrels with solid air, The. Dancer: Four Poems. Paul Engle. AMV–80

Dancers at the Moy. Paul Muldoon. BIrV

Dancers Inherit the Party, The. Ian Hamilton Finlay. FF

Dancers of Colbek, The. Robert Mannyng. *Fr.* Handlyng Synne. OxBM

Dances of Death, *sel.* Alexander Blok, *tr. fr. Russian by* Jon Stallworthy *and* Peter France.
"Night, street, a lamp, a chemist's window." OBVE

Dancing/ to the sound of the night. Sabinas Hidalgo. Diane Kruchkow. FAF

Dancing and drinking go on into the night, The. The New Girls. Douglas Dunn. MS

Dancing Bear, The. Greg Kuzma. BCr

Dancing, bright lady, then began to be. The Praise of Dancing. Sir John Davies. *Fr.* Orchestra; or, A Poem of Dancing. NOBE

Dancing Cabman, The. J. B. Morton. NOBL

Dancing Gal. Frank Marshall Davis. FB

Dancing-Girl's Song. Kshetrayya, *tr. fr. Teluga by* Tambimuttu *and* R. Appalaswamy. BoWoP

Dancing in the Street. Al Young. SA

Dancing Seal, The. W. W. Gibson. EcS

Dancing Teepees. Calvin O'John. VW

Dancing the Shout to the True Gospel; or, The Song Movement Sisters Don't Want Me to Sing. Rita Mae Brown. NMM; WBN

Dandelions. Gerda Mayer. POL

Dane-Geld. Kipling. OxBTC

Danger stalks on such nights, the moon is dangerous. The Lunar Tides. Marya Zaturenska. Moon

"Dangerous Condition": Sign on Inner-City House. Russell Atkins. CNA

Dangling Conversation. Paul Simon. NowV; UsP

Daniel at Breakfast. Phyllis McGinley. BBGO; OBSV

Daniel Boone. Stephen Vincent Benét. GOA

Daniel Boone. Arthur Guiterman. CTV

Daniel Webster's Horses. Elizabeth J. Coatsworth. PH

Danny. Malcolm Cowley. PoA

Danny Boy. *Unknown.* FSW

Danny Deever. Kipling. AIW; BTTM; Epi; FaBoBa; FaPoR; ILP (1975 ed.); InPS; NOBE; OxBTC; PeBB; PBMP; SFF; UnPo (1976 ed.); VLP

Danse Russe. William Carlos Williams. CMoP (1970 ed.); InPK; InPS; NOBA; PoIA; PPP; TAP

Dante Etudes, *sel.* Robert Duncan.
Etude from the Third Epistle, III. CAAP

Danty, baby, diddy. Mother Goose. MG

Danube orchards, The. The Peachtree. Denise Levertov. *Fr.* During the Eichmann Trial. CAPP

Danube to the Severn gave, The. Tennyson. In Memoriam A. H. H., XIX. FF

Danville Girl. *Unknown.* FSW

Daphnaida, *sel.* Spenser.
"She fell away in her first ages spring." PoPle

Daphne. Swift. NOBL

Daphne. Phyllis Hoge Thompson. PHC

Daphne knows, with equal ease. Daphne. Swift. NOBL

Daphne Stillorgan. Denis Devlin. CIP

"Daphne with her thighs in bark." Her Majesty's Ship. Gene Fowler. CPA

Daphnis. Theocritus, *tr. fr. Greek by* Dryden. *Fr.* Idylls, XXVII. SCP–1
("Shepheard Paris bore the Spartan bride, The.") OBVE

Dappled horse stood at the edge of the meadow, A. The Grey Horse. James Reeves. PH

Dar was ole Mister Johnson, he had trouble of his own. The Cat Came Back. Harry S. Miller. FSN

Darby and Joan are dressed in black. *Unknown.* PoPle

Darby Ram, The. *Unknown.* FSW

Dare to be true. Courage. George Herbert. *Fr.* The Church Porch. CTV

Darest Thou Now O Soul. Walt Whitman. PAIC

Daring. Carol Konek. IHMS

Darius Green and His Flying-Machine. John Townsend Trowbridge. OBAL; OxBChV

Dark, The. Roy Fuller. DuDa

Dark. Eloise Klein Healy. AMV–80

Dark accurate plunger down the successive knell. The Subway. Allen Tate. ILP (1975 ed.); NoAM; NOBA; NYP; PiAm

Dark an' stormy may come de wedder. Slave Marriage Ceremony Supplement. *Unknown.* BPo; POL; TAP

Dark and the Fair, The. Stanley Kunitz. LoAs

Dark and Wrinkled. Arthur Rimbaud, *tr. fr. French by* Wallace Fowlie. LoAs

Dark Angel, The. Lionel Johnson. BoReV; NOBE; OAEL–2; PFD; PPM; VLP

Dark are the shrouded hills, and vague, and the rain. Langdale: Nightfall, January 4th. Michael Roberts. PES

Dark Area. Russell Atkins. FB

Dark as the spring river, the earth. Farm Wife. Ellen Bryant Voigt. AAN; CSP

Dark as wells, his eyes. Long Person. Gladys Cardiff. CDW

Dark Aspect and Prospect. *Unknown.* PeD

Dark Birds, The. Bert Meyers. VWA

Dark, black robe. Invitation (To the Night and All Other Things Dark). Ronda Davis. JB

Dark branches. Alaskan Mountain Poem #1. Leslie Marmon Silko. VoR

Dark brother touches me, The. Will Inman. *Fr.* 108 Tales of a Po'Buckra. GP

Dark brown is the river. Where Go the Boats? Robert Louis Stevenson. CTV; LCL; OxBChV

Dark cliff towered up to the stars that flickered, The. The Passage at Night—The Blaskets. Robin Flower. PFIr

Dark Conclusions. Ruth Stone. BoWoP

Dark Corner. Robert Morgan. CSP

Dark Country, A. Derek Mahon. BIrV

Dark, deeply. A red. Inside the River. James Dickey. PoA; SPo

Dark Exciting Days, The. Karl Shapiro. CoPAm

Dark eyed,/ O woman of my dreams. Dance Figure. Ezra Pound. HeIP

Dark-eyed Gentleman, The. Thomas Hardy. UnPo (1976 ed.); VLP

Dark-eyed Sailor, The. *Unknown.* FSW

Dark Eyes, *with music. Unknown, tr. fr. Russian by* Albert Morehead. BLSH

Dark figures, lunged ahead, The. The Moral. Theodore Weiss. Prf

Dark Girl. Arna Bontemps. SoS

Dark Glass, The. Dante Gabriel Rossetti. The House of Life, XXXIV. VPC

Dark-haired girl, who holds my thoughts entirely, The. Peggy Browne. Turlough O'Carolan, *tr. by* Austin Clarke. BIrV

Dark Hand, A. Itzik Manger, *tr. fr. Yiddish by* David G. Roskies *and* Hillel Schwartz. VWA

Dark Hills, The. E. A. Robinson. HAP; ILP (1975 ed.); NoAM; SoSe (1977 ed.); WeW

Dark Hope. Wade Hall. AATT

Dark house, by which once more I stand. In Memoriam A. H. H., VII. Tennyson. EBEV; HAP; InPK; NOBE; PoIA; PPoe; SoSe; UnPo (1976 ed.)

Dark is soft, like fur. Rhyme for Night. Joan Aiken. DuDa

Dark Lady, The. *Unknown.* OxBM

Dark Morning, The. Thomas Merton. PoA

Dark morning turned, The/ into visiting hours. Rituals. Lori Shpunt. PoUp

Dark Night, The. St. John of the Cross, *tr. fr. Spanish by* John Frederick Nims. WeW
 (Upon a Gloomy Night, *tr. by* Roy Campbell.) BoLoP; OBVE
 ("Upon an obscure night," *tr. by* Arthur Symons. ILwL

Dark Planet, The. John Heath-Stubbs. OAEL-2

Dark plume fetch me from yon blasted yew, A. Return. Wordsworth. *Fr.* The River Duddon. HAP

Dark Prophesy: I Sing of Shine. Etheridge Knight. *See* I Sing of Shine.

Dark Reflections. Margo Bohanon. SES

Dark Road Blues. *Unknown.* BluL

Dark Room. Fredrick Zydek. AMV-80

Dark Roots of the Rose, The. William Everson. NIL

Dark Rosaleen. *At. to* Owen Roe MacWard, *tr. fr. Irish by* James Clarence Mangan. BIrV; LoAs; PFIr

Dark Scent of Prayer, The. Rose Drachler. VWA

Dark smoky room, A. Rivage. Hunter Brown. AAN

Dark Song. A. R. Ammons. MAT

Dark Song. Edith Sitwell. CMoP (1970 ed.); FaBoTw (1975 ed.) PBWP

Dark streets are deserted, The. After Midnight. Louis Simpson. NoAM

Dark Symphony. Melvin B. Tolson. AmNP (1974 ed.)

Dark Testament. Pauli Murray. AmNP (1974 ed.)

Dark theme keeps me here, A. In Evening Air. Theodore Roethke. MPA; TAP

Dark thoughts are my companions. I have wined. Epigram. J. V. Cunningham. VGW

Dark Was the Night. *Unknown.* AmFP

Dark Way Home, The: Survivors. Michael S. Harper. CNA

Dark Wings. James Stephens. PoA

Darkened farmhouse is asleep, The. Saving the Harvest. Geoffrey Lehmann. MAuV

Darkened hills around the mine at Coverdale, The. Coal Strike. Norman Macleod. SPT

Darkened in the Soul. Napa, *tr. fr. Eskimo.* WTO

Darkened Windows. Ronald Bottrall. PoA

Darkling Thrush, The. Thomas Hardy. BoReV; CMoP (1970 ed.); FSFS; HAP; ILP (1975 ed.); InPS; NIL; NoAM; NOBE; OAEL-2; PoIA; PPM; PPP; SoSe; UnPo (1976 ed.); UsP; VLP; VoPo

Darkmotherscream. Andrei Voznesensky, *tr. fr. Russian by* Robert Bly *and* Vera Dunham. NU

Darkness. Byron. ILP (1975 ed.); OAEL-2

Darkness. Joseph Campbell. BIrV

Darkness at Noon. Richard Friedman. FiCh

Darkness came o'er like chaos; and the sun. The Hailstorm in June 1831. John Clare. VLP

Darkness Comes to the Woods. Norbert Krapf. HeS

Darkness crumbles away, The. Break of Day in the Trenches. Isaac Rosenberg. NOBE; OAEL-2; PoA; PSN; VWA

Darkness dwells around Dunlathmon. Oithona: A Poem. James Macpherson. EPC; LAuP

Darkness falls like a wet sponge. The Picture of Little J. A. in a Prospect of Flowers. John Ashbery. ConAP; PPP

Darkness has called to darkness, and disgrace. As a Plane Tree by the Water. Robert Lowell. CMoP (1970 ed.); NoAM; NOBA

Darkness in rain. The Meek Shall Disinherit the Earth. Horace Gregory. SPT

Darkness is not dark, nor sunlight the light of the sun. Foal. Vernon Watkins. OxBTC

Darkness let go of hills. In the Middle. Vern Rutsala. MPA

Darkness lifts, imagine, in your lifetime, The. The Undertaking. Louise Glück. NVAP

Darkness Music. Muriel Rukeyser. BoWoP

Darkness presses all around, The. Government! Tuta Nihoniho, *tr. fr. Maori by* A. Armstrong. WTO

Darkness reigned. Sacrifice. Nana Issaia, *tr. by* Helle Tzalopoulou Barnstone. BoWoP

Darkness surrounds us; seeking, we are lost. Uncertainty. Wordsworth. *Fr.* Ecclessiastical Sonnets. MBPR

Darkness wears off and, dawning into daylight. The Figures on the Frieze. Alastair Reid. MS; SLP

Darkroom. Gary Stein. PoUp

Darlin'. *Unknown.* FSW

Darling,/ why couldn't you have told me. End of the Affair. Curtis W. Casewit. AMV-80

Darling, at the beautician's you buy. A Valentine for a Lady. Lucillius, *tr. by* Dudley Fitts. OFD

Darling Cory. *Unknown.* AmFP; FSW

Darling, each morning a blooded rose. Corinna in Vendome. Pierre de Ronsard, *tr. by* Robert Mezey. BoLoP

Darling here's my head. The Balance. Judith Johnson Sherwin. GP

Darling, I am growing old. Silver Threads among the Gold. Eben Eugene Rexford. BLSH; BLSo; FSW; PSoN

Darling, I won't be your hot love. Sulpicia, *tr. fr. Latin by* Aliki *and* Willis Barnstone. BoWoP

Darling Nelly Gray. Benjamin Russel Hanby. BLSo, *with music* FSW; PSoN, *with music*

Darling of Gods and Men, beneath the gliding stars. Basil Bunting. NoAM

Darling of the world is come, The. Robert Herrick. *Fr.* A Christmas Carol, Sung to the King in the Presence at White-Hall. PChr

Darling one was naked and, knowing my wish, The. Jewels. Baudelaire. NAWM-2

Darned Mounseer, The. W. S. Gilbert. *Fr.* Ruddigore. NOBL

Dar'st thou amid the varied multitude. The Solitary. Shelley. MBPR

Dart, The. *Unknown.* GBP

Dart, here's a man. The River Dart. *Unknown.* GBP

Dart of Love, The. *Unknown, tr. fr. Gaelic by* G. R. D. McLean. SLP

Das Schloss. Lincoln Kirstein. NoAM

Dash back that ocean with a pier. Tennyson. *Fr.* Mechanophilus. FaBoCo

Dashing thro' the snow in a one-horse open sleigh. Jingle Bells [*or* The One Horse Open Sleigh]. James S. Pierpont. BLSH; BLSo; FSW; PSoN

Dasius, chucker-out/ at the Turkish Baths. Martial, *tr. fr. Latin by* Peter Porter. OBVE

Dated Valmont 10-16/ october 1849. Eugene Delacroix Says. Edward Dorn. NoAM

Dates on bridges, The. History and Abstraction. Thomas Lux. AmPA

Dauber, *sel.* John Masefield.
"All through the windless night the clipper rolled," VI. CMoP (1970 ed.)

Daughter. Ellen Bryant Voigt. AMV-80

Daughter of Admetus, A. T. Sturge Moore. FaBoTw (1975 ed.)

Daughter of Jairus, The, *sels.* Marina Tsvetayeva, *tr. fr. Russian by* Paul Schmidt. BoWoP
"And now the riverbank. For the last time," VII.
"I catch the movement of his lips," V.
"Our last bridge," VIII.
"Past factory workshops, empty," IX.
"Rain. A heavy mane," XII.
"To lose it all at once," XI.

Daughter of Mendoza, The. Mirabeau Buonaparte Lamar. BPAW

Daughterly. Kathleen Spivack. TV

Daughters of Beulah! Muses who inspire the poets song. Milton. Blake. MBPR

Daughters of the Seraphim led round their sunny flocks. The Book of Thel. Blake. LAuP; MBPR; OAEL-2

Daughters [*or* Damsels] of Time, the hypocritic Days. Days. Emerson. AmVN; HAP; HeIP; ILP (1975 ed.); IPWM; LFH; NOBA; PAIC; PiAm; SoSe; TAP; VoPo

Daughters Will You Marry? *Unknown.* FSW

D'Avalos' Prayer. John Masefield. EcS

Davening. Rochelle Ratner. VWA

David. Josephine Miles. MIT

David and Bethsabe, *sel.* George Peele.
Bethsabe's Song, *fr. sc. i.* NOBE
("Hot sun, cool fire, temper'd with sweet air.") GBL

David and Goliath. Nathaniel Crouch. OxBChV

David and Solomon. James Ball Naylor. PoPle

David before Saul. Christopher Smart. *Fr.* The Song of David. PIM

David Homindae. Marjorie Stamm Rosenfeld. AMV-80

David Hume ate a swinging great dinner. On the Author of the *Treatise of Human Nature.* James Hay Beattie. FaBoCo

David the king was grieved and moved. David's Lamentation. William Billings. AmFP

David, we must have looked comic, sitting. Elegy for David Beynon. Leslie Norris. LP

Davideis, *sels.* Abraham Cowley. SCP-2
Hell, *fr.* I.
Music, *fr.* I.

David's Harp. Gwen Harwood. MAuV

David's Lament. Bible, *O.T.* Second Samuel, I: 19-27. FF ("Beauty of Israel is slaine upon thy high places, The.") OBVE

David's Lament for Jonathan. Peter Abelard, *tr. fr. Latin by* Helen Waddell. NAWM-1

David's Lamentation. William Billings. AmFP

David's Poem. Ben Hiatt. CPA

Davy and the Goblin, *sels.* Charles Edward Carryl.
My Recollectest Thoughts, *fr. ch.* 7. PCOP
Robinson Crusoe's Story, *fr. ch.* 11. ECBV

Dawlish Fair. Keats. PoPle
("Over the hill and over the dale." MBPR

Dawn. Paul Laurence Dunbar. AmNP (1974 ed.)

Dawn. *Malay Oral Tradition, tr. by* R. J. Wilkinson. WTO

Dawn. Octavio Paz. TSWA

Dawn. Alejandra Pizarnik, *tr. fr. Spanish by* Alina Rivero. VWA

Dawn. David Shevin. VWA

Dawn. William Carlos Williams. ILP (1975 ed.)

Dawn, The. W. B. Yeats. GrRo

Dawn/ rose like a hand at the edge of dark. Crazy Horse: The Last Morning. Lance Henson. VoR

Dawn and a high film; the sun burned it. We in the Fields. William Everson. PiAm

Dawn and a Woman. John Logan. PHC

Dawn breeze, The. Sand Paintings. Alice Corbin. BPAW

Dawn cried out: the brutal voice of a bird. In All These Acts. William Everson. PiAm

Dawn. First light tearing. Clouds. Philip Levine. MPA

Dawn Horse, The. William Harmon. CSP

Dawn in Britain, The, *sels.* C. M. Doughty. FaBoTw (1975 ed.)
Gauls Sacrifice, The.
Hymn to the Sun.
Roman Officer Writes, A.

Dawn in January. Lance Henson. CDW

Dawn Is a Feeling. Mike Pinder. GrRo

Dawn is, in essence, sinister as fire. Dew. Jennifer Maiden. CAAP

Dawn of Day, The. Keaulumoku, *tr. fr. Hawaiian by* M. W. Beckwith. *Fr.* The Kumulipo: A Creation Chant. WTO

Dawn of Jaffa Pigeons, A. Eli Bachar, *tr. fr. Hebrew by* Jeremy Garber. VWA

Dawn of Me, The. Jeff Morley. OSP

Dawn of the Space Age. John Ciardi. OBAL

Dawn on the East Coast. Alun Lewis. PSN

Dawn that cares for nobody. February. W. S. Merwin. NNaP; UsP

Dawn was apple-green, The. Green. D. H. Lawrence. GBL; PoA

Dawn Wind on the Islands. Francis Webb. GAS

Dawndrizzle ended dampness steams from. Anglosaxon Street. Earle Birney. CABA (1972 ed.); HeIP

Dawning, The. Henry Vaughan. BoReV

Dawning Fair, Morning Wonderful, *with music. Unknown.* AH

Dawning of morn, the daylight's sinking. Thee, Thee, Only Thee. Thomas Moore. GBL

Dawning sun; The/ Shines down on the dunes. Siilenboor. *Mongol Oral Tradition, tr. by* C. R. Bawden. WTO

Day, The. Roy Fuller. OxBTC

Day, The/ is ready to close. Saturday Night in the Village. Giacomo Leopardi, *tr. by* Robert Lowell. OBVE

Day after day, alone on a hill. The Fool on the Hill. John Lennon *and* Paul McCartney. GrRo; PPoe

Day after day her nest she moulded. The Swallow's Nest. Sir Edwin Arnold. PCOP

Day after decapitation, The. The Head. Padraic Fallon. CIP

Day after Sunday, The. Phyllis McGinley. OBSV; UnPo (1976 ed.)

Day Alvero Pineda Was Killed, The. Ronald Koertge. EC

Day and Night Handball. Stephen Dunn. AmPA; LiSp

Day and night I scan the horizon. Nar-Gad Diack. TVo

Day and night she dances. Shulamit in Her Dreams. Marcia Falk. VWA

Day arrives of the autumn fair, The. A Sheep Fair. Thomas Hardy. Prf

Day at the beach. Littoral. Hjalmar Flax, tr. by Julio Marzán. InW

Day at the Races, A. Louis Phillips. PH

Day before the houses sank beneath the waves, The. The Day the Houses Sank. Constance Urdang. MAT

Day Begins, A. Denise Levertov. AnMo; CoPAm

Day Birth Placard (for Amy), The. Henry Kanabus. FiCh

Day breaks, your mind aches, The. For No One. John Lennon and Paul McCartney. WTO

Day by day I float my paper boats. Rabindranath Tagore. Fr. Paper Boats. RAE

Day by day the manna fell. Josiah Conder. VLP

Day Concludes Burning, The. Desmond O'Grady. CIP

Day creeps down. The moon is creeping up. The Man on the Dump. Wallace Stevens. HAP

Day dawns with scent of must and rain, The. Mirror in February. Thomas Kinsella. CIP; IPM; NoAM

Day Death Comes, The. Faiz Ahmed Faiz, tr. fr. Pakistani by Naomi Lazard. AMV-81

Day dies beautiful, The. Made to See. John Nist. AMV-80

Day draws to an end, The. The Author's Apology. T. Carmi, tr. by Marcia Falk. VWA

Day Dream, A. Emily Brontë. VLP

Day has been washed clean, and so have I, The. Washed in Water. Rayne Mackinnon. MIS

Day I rode throught Devonshire, The. Beneath Such Rains. James E. Warren, Jr. AATT

Day I Stopped Dreaming about Barbara Steele, The. R. H. W. Dillard. PPoD

Day I was born, The. Children, It's Time. Michael Brownstein. OSP

Day in Salamanca, A. Radcliffe Squires. MPA

Day in the Life, A. John Lennon and Paul McCartney. NIL; PPoe; WIF

Day is a woman who loves you, The. Driving Montana. Richard Hugo. MPA

Day is broke, The! Melpomene, begone. Iter Boreale. Robert Wild. APAS

Day is curled about again, The. An Anniversary on the Hymeneals of My Noble Kinsman, Thomas Stanley, Esquire. Richard Lovelace. CaPo

Day is dark and dreary, The. If. Franklin P. Adams. OBAL

Day Is Done, The. Phoebe Cary. OBAL

Day Is Done, The. Longfellow. NOBA; PPM

Day Is Dying in the West, with music. Mary Artemisia Lathbury. AH

Day is found. Vita Silenziosa. Brian Swann. AAN

Day is gone, and all its sweets are gone, The! Keats. LoAs; MBPR

Day is gone, the night is come, The. A Child's Prayer. George Meredith. PIM

Day is past and gone, The. Evening Shade. John Leland. AH; AmFP

Day is past, the sun is set, The. Evening. Thomas Miller. OxBChV

Day is turning ghost, The. A Commonplace Day. Thomas Hardy. PoPle

Day It Was Night, The. Robert Desnos, tr. fr. French by John Frederick Nims. WeW

Day Jayne Mansfield died, The. Bison Flower Days. Anselm Hollo. TwMBP

Day Lady Died, The. Frank O'Hara. CAPP; NoAM; NOBA; NYP

Day like blank paper, The. The Six Hundred Thousand Letters. Harvey Shapiro. VWA

Day of Atonement. Jack Myers. VWA

Day of Days, The. William Morris. VLP

Day of Denial, The. Jones Very. NOBA

Day of Glory! Welcome day! The Fourth of July. John Pierpont. CTV

Day of God! Thou Blessed Day, with music. Hannah Flagg Gould. AH

Day of hunting done. Twilight in California. Philip Dow. AmPA

Day of Judgement [or Judgment], The. Swift. BIrV; ESaP; ILP (1975 ed.); InPK; NOBE; OAEL-1; OBSV; PPP

Day of Judgement [or Judgment], The. Isaac Watts. EPC; HAP; ILP (1975 ed.); NOBE; PAIC

Day of Judgment, The. Thomas of Celano, tr. fr. Latin by Richard Crashaw. OBVE

Day of Love, A. Dante Gabriel Rossetti. The House of Life, XVI. VLP

Day of Notes, A (That Fit into the Puzzle of a Poem). J. Charles Green. DNGG

Day of sunny face and temper, A. Big Bessie Throws Her Son into the Street. Gwendolyn Brooks. VGW

Day of the Circus Horse, The. T. A. Daly. PCOP

Day of the eclipse, I took my daughter, The. About That of Which One Cannot Speak, One Must Be Silent. Rudolph von Abele. PoUp

Day of the Pancreas, The. David McFadden. NeAC

Day of the Wolf. Keith Wilson. MPA

Day pattern pattering trains and so forth. O Viajante. Carol Olivia Herron. PoUp

Day Sailing. David R. Slavitt. CoPAm

Day she visited the dissecting room, The. Two Views of a Cadaver Room. Sylvia Plath. AnMo; CMoP (1970 ed.)

Day Sleeper. James L. White. HeS

Day spread her lap and bade me choose. The Little Searcher. Donna Bowen. AMV-80

Day that I left my home for the rolling sea, The. La Paloma. Sebastian Yradier. BLSH

Day the big tree went, The. The Tree. Pat Wilson. ATNZ

Day the fat woman, The. The Beach in August. Weldon Kees. VGW

Day the father dies, The. Family Getting Back to God. Eve Shelnutt. TC

Day the Houses Sank, The. Constance Urdang. MAT

Day the Old Man Joined the Church (Xmas '66), The. Richard W. Thomas. TC

Day the T.V. Broke, The. Gerald Jonas. QQQ

Day the Weather Broke, The. Alastair Reid. SLP

Day the Winds, The. Josephine Miles. CPA

Day They Ate the Baritone, The. Samuel Hazo. PPoD

Day They Busted the Grateful Dead, The. Richard Brautigan. MAT

Day Thou Gavest, Lord, Is Ended, The. John Ellerton. BLSH, with music; FaPoR

Day Time Sequence/ November. Dalene Stowe. NPW

Day transports fallen snows, muddied, mildewed, ruined, The. Spring over the City. Anne Hébert, tr. by Kathleen Weaver. PBWP

Day turns heavily on its axis, The. Encirclement Mieczyslaw Jastrun, *tr. by* Benjamin Sher. AMV-81

Day waits quietly, The. Still Branches. Jack Simcock. BuTh

Day was here when it was his to know, The. The New Tenants. E. A. Robinson. NoAM

Day was so bright, The. Miroslav Holub, *tr. by* George Theines *and* Ian Milner. *Fr.* A Dog in the Quarry. BoAnP; GDP

Day was when I did not keep myself in readiness, The. Rabindranath Tagore. *Fr.* Gitanjali. ILwL

Day when Charmus ran with five, The. A Mighty Runner. E. A. Robinson. LiSp; OBAL

Day time failed began as usual, The. Burial of a Fisherman in Hydra. Grace Schulman. BoWoP

Day Which Endures Not, A. Arthur Glyn Prys-Jones. OBW

Day will come when I will, The. A Farewell to a Southern Melody. Huang O, *tr. by* Kenneth Rexroth *and* Ling Chung. BoWoP

Day with the Foreign Legion, A. Reed Whittemore. ConAP

Day worth losing, A. The Line. Dan Gerber. HeS

Day you appeared I began to speak, The. To Your Question. Duane Niatum. CDW

Day You Are Reading This, The. William Stafford. PoA

Day you came, The. Breasts. Tess Gallagher. AmPA

Day, you have bruised and beaten me. The New Moon. Sara Teasdale. Moon

Day you shot yourself, The. On a Friend's Suicide. Michael Yots. AMV-81

Daybreak. Bert Meyers. EAS

Daybreak. Frank Lamont Phillips. CNA

Daybreak. Stephen Spender. BoLoP

Daybreak in Alabama. Langston Hughes. CNA

Daybreak on a Pennsylvania Highway. John Daunt. AMV-80

Daybreak: the household slept. Barn Owl. Gwen Harwood. *Fr.* Father and Child. CAAP; MAuV; WPE

Day-Breakers, The. Arna Bontemps. AmNP (1974 ed.); PoBA

Day-Dream, A. Samuel Taylor Coleridge. MBPR

Day-Dream from an Emigrant to His Absent Wife, The. Samuel Taylor Coleridge. MBPR

Day-Dreamer. Louis Untermeyer, *after the German.* CTV

Daylight falls upon the path, the forest falls behind. I Think I Understand. Joni Mitchell. GrRo

Day-long cold hard rain drove, The. Surviving. James Welch. CDW; SA

Daylong this tomcat lies stretched flat. Esther's Tomcat. Ted Hughes. PCat

Days, The. Paul Blocklyn. AMV-80

Days. Emerson. AmVN; HAP; HeIP; ILP (1975 ed.); IPWM; LFH; NOBA; PAIC; PiAm; SoSe; TAP; VoPo

Days, The. Donald Hall. CoPAm

Days. Philip Larkin. EBEV; LP; PSN; UsP

Days are cold, the nights are long, The. The Cottager to Her Infant. Dorothy Wordsworth. OxBChV

Day's End. Sir Henry Newbolt. PCOP

Day's end. A Midas sack of cloud has spilled. Nothing Gold Can Stay. Norma Farber. AMV-81

Days full of sunspots the girl. For a Girl Whose Slow-Dying Called for My Blood. Doug Flaherty. AAN

Days get shorter and. God Is Here Again. Charles Angoff. AMV-80

Days grow and the stars cross over, The. Darkness Music. Muriel Rukeyser. BoWoP

Day's grown old, the fainting sun, The. Evening [*or* Evening Quatrains]. Charles Cotton. ExPo (1973 ed.); SCP-2

Days in White. Ingeborg Bachmann, *tr. fr. German by* Daniel Huws. BoWoP

Days like This. John Stevens Wade. FAF

Days, my grandfather said to me, The. Angle of Vision. Martha Bosworth. AMV-80

Days of Forty-nine, The. *Unknown.* BPAW; FSW

Days of 1956. Robin Magowan. EAS

Days of 1978. Gerald Stern. AMV-81

Days of Re-entry. Patricia Henley. NPW

Days of yore, The—both good and ill. Braggin' Bill's Fortytude. *At. to* C. Wiles Hallock. BPAW

Days pass easy over these ancient hills. We Are a People. Lance Henson. VoR

Day's Ration, The. Emerson. PiAm

Days shuffle together, The. Solitaire. George Garrett. CSP

Days shuttle endlessly, The. Rick's Bag of Tricks. Rick Cannon. PoUp

Days Were Great as Lakes. David Vogel, *tr. fr. Hebrew by* A. C. Jacobs. VWA

Day's Work a-Done. William Barnes. VPC

Daysies. Chaucer. *Fr.* Legend of Good Women. PF

Daysleep. Virginia E. Smith. AMV-81

Daystart: a dusty thunder. Works and Days. V. H. Adair. PoW

Dazzle on the sea, my darling, The. Leaving Barra. Louis MacNeice. EBEV

Dazzled thus with height of place. Upon the Sudden Restraint of the Earl of Somerset, Then Falling from Favour. Sir Henry Wotton. NOBE; SCP-2

De Aegypto. Ezra Pound. VGW

De Civitate Hominum. Thomas MacGreevy. CIP

De Clerico et Puella. *Unknown.* OxBM

"De Gustibus." Robert Browning. InPS

De Gustibus. St. John Emile Clavering Hankin. LiSp

De Gustibus. James Worley. NIL

De Mayor of Harlem. David Henderson. *Fr.* Walk with de Mayor of Harlem. UsP

De Naevo in Facie Faustinae. Thomas Bastard. FaBoEE

De Ponto, *sels.* Ovid, *tr. fr. Latin by* Henry Vaughan. OBVE
"Shall I complain or not? Or shall I mask," *fr.* IV, 3a.
"You have consum'd my language, and my pen," III, 7.

De Profundis. Thomas Campion. BoReV

De Profundis, *sel.* Tennyson.
"Out of the deep, my child, out of the deep," I. ILP (1975 ed.)

De Regimine Principum, *sels.* Thomas Hoccleve.
Anxious Thought. OxBM
Lament for Chaucer and Gower. OxBM
("O maister deere and fader reverent!") EBEV

De Rerum Natura (On the Nature of Things), *sels.* Lucretius, *tr. fr. Latin.*
Against the Fear of Death, *fr.* III, *tr. by* Rolfe Humphries. DL, *abr.*; NAWM-1
*Abr. version, tr. by* Dryden. OAEL-1; OBVE
"Delight of humane kind, and gods above," *fr.* I, *tr. by* Dryden. OBVE
"Now since the members of the world we view," *fr.* V, *tr. by* Thomas Creech. OBVE

De Se. John Weever. FaBoEE

Deacon's Masterpiece, The; or, The Wonderful "One-Hoss Shay." Oliver Wendell Holmes. *Fr.* The Autocrat of the Breakfast-Table, *ch.* 11. FaPo; NOBA; OBAL; PiAm; SS; TAP

Deacon's wife was a bit desirish, The. Pride of Ancestry. Robert Frost. OBAL

Dead, The. Mathilde Blind. SBG

Dead, The ("These hearts were woven"). Rupert Brooke. 1914, IV. PoA

Dead, The. Mark Strand. HeIP

Dead, The. Jones Very. AmVN; HAP; NOBA; PAIC; TAP

Dead, The. Michael Waters. AAN

Dead, The. Jay Wright. FB

Dead abide with us, The! Though stark and cold.   The Dead. Mathilde Blind.   SBG

Dead at Clonmacnoise, The.   *Unknown, tr. fr. Irish by* Thomas William Rolleston.   PFIr

Dead at the pasture edge.   The Dead Calf.   Wendell Berry. PiAm

Dead beast, turned up, The.   The Well-travelled Roadway.   John Newlove.   NeAC

Dead birds fell, but no one had seen them fly, The.   Some Dreams They Forgot.   Elizabeth Bishop.   NoAM

Dead black bear hangs on a weighing pulley, A.   Poem Written in Winter.   Charlotte Gafford.   BCr

Dead Boy.   John Crowe Ransom.   CMoP (1970 ed.); NoAM; PiAm; PoIA

Dead boy living among men as a man, A.   A Head.   James Schuyler.   NoAM

Dead brood over Europe, the cloud and vision descends over chearful France, The.   The French Revolution.   Blake. MBPR

Dead by the Side of the Road, The.   Gary Snyder.   CNW; HAP

Dead Calf, The.   Wendell Berry.   PiAm

Dead Center.   Chester Kallman.   PoA

Dead Cities Speak to the Living Cities, The.   Edmond Fleg, *tr. fr. French by* Anthony Rudolf.   VWA

Dead Cleopatra lies in a crystal casket.   Conrad Aiken. Discordants, IV.   PoA

Dead Crab, The.   Andrew Young.   FaBoTw (1975 ed.)

Dead Drunk Blues.   *Unknown.*   BluL

Dead Fly.   Eilean Ni Chuilleanain.   CIP

Dead Girl.   Anna Hajnal, *tr. fr. Hungarian by* Jascha Kessler. VWA

Dead Hand.   W. S. Merwin.   CAPP; InPK

Dead heat and windless air.   August Weather.   Katharine Tynan. FSFS

Dead Horse, The.   Cecília Meireles, *tr. fr. Portuguese by* James Merrill.   PBWP

Dead in Bloody Snow.   Meridel Le Sueur.   GP

Dead in Europe, The.   Robert Lowell.   CMoP (1970 ed.); STS

Dead in the cold, a song-singing thrush.   Last Rites.   Christina Rossetti.   OxBChV

Dead in the Sierras.   Joaquin Miller.   BPAW

Dead! Is it possible? He, the bold rider.   Custer's Last Charge. Frederick Whittaker.   BPAW

Dead Jews, dead Jews, just points now an underground.   Dime Call.   Albert Goldbarth.   VWA

Dead King, A.   Swinburne.   VLP

Dead Lady Canonized, The.   Amiri Baraka.   CAPP

Dead Leaf, A.   Howard Moss.   NYP

Dead Letter Office, The.   Maxine Chernoff.   FiCh

Dead Liebknecht, The.   "Hugh MacDiarmid," *after the German of* Rudolf Leonhard.   OBVE

Dead, long dead.   Tennyson.   *Fr.* Maud.   OAEL-2

Dead Love.   Swinburne.   LoAs

Dead man, A/ who never caused others to die.   W. H. Auden. *Fr.* Marginalia.   OAEL-2

Dead Man Creek.   Van K. Brock.   NVAP

Dead Man Dragged from the Sea, The.   Carl Gardner.   PoBA

Dead Man's Dump.   Isaac Rosenberg.   VWA

Dead Man's Song, Dreamed by One Who Is Alive.   Paulinaoq, *tr. fr. Eskimo.*   WTO

Dead Men, The.   Sophia de Mello Breyner Andresen, *tr. fr. Portuguese by* Allan Francovich.   PBWP

Dead Neck.   Sue Standing.   AMV-81

Dead of the World, The.   Jeanne Finley.   AMV-81

Dead on the Desert.   Harrison Conrard.   BPAW

Dead on the War Path.   *Tr. fr. Tewa Indian by* H. J. Spinden. WTO

Dead! One of them shot by the sea in the east.   Mother and Poet. Elizabeth Barrett Browning.   SBG

Dead Pan, The.   Elizabeth Barrett Browning.   VLP

Dead Pig, The.   *Unknown.*   FaBoNo

Dead poets, philosophs, priests.   Walt Whitman.   *Fr.* Starting from Paumanok.   InPS

Dead poets stalk the air.   Rainy Night at the Writers' Colony. Josephine Jacobsen.   TAP

Dead Ponies.   Brenda Chamberlain.   OBW; WPE

Dead Prospector, The.   Arthur Chapman.   BPAW

Dead scents I couldn't bear bore.   Year of the Bird.   Brian Swann.   AmPA

Dead Sea, The.   Henryk Grynberg, *tr. fr. Polish by* Isaac Komem. VWA

Dead Seal.   A. W. Purdy.   NoAM

Dead Seal near McClure's Beach, The.   Robert Bly.   NNaP; NU

Dead Shall Be Raised Incorruptible, The.   Galway Kinnell. CAAP; NOBA

"In the Twentieth Century of my trespass on earth," 4.   ExPo (1973 ed.); GP

Dead shall rise again, The.   The Raising of Lazarus.   Lucille Clifton.   CNA

Dead shalt thou lie; and nought.   Sappho, *tr. fr. Greek by* Thomas Hardy.   OBVE

Dead sheep/ beside the highway.   Preparations.   Leslie Silko. NW; VoR

Dead Sparrow, The.   William Cartwright.   BoAnP

Dead Statesman, A.   Kipling.   *Fr.* Epitaphs of the War. FaBoEE

Dead Still.   Andrei Voznesensky, *tr. fr. Russian by* Richard Wilbur.   BoLoP

Dead trees.   Vision of Montezuma Preserve, N.Y.   Ron Welburn.   NW

Deader they die here, or at least.   Fall Comes in Back-Country Vermont.   Robert Penn Warren.   VGW

Deadfall.   Martha Keller.   ECBV

Deadly destructive to my man and me.   The Conscience.   Anna Wickham.   POL

Deaf, giddy, helpless, left alone.   On His Own Deafness.   Swift. AnMo; BIrV; FaBoEE

Deaf—I am/ aware; blind.   Limpet.   Ronald Mann.   PMW

Deaf to the bustle of the street, soporifically.   The Jewish Cemetery.   Cesar Tiempo, *tr. by* Angela McEvan-Alvarado. VWA

Deafening tic-tic-tic of the clock, The.   Loneliness.   Loyal Shegonee.   VW

Deafness.   Richard Ryan.   BIrV

Dealer's Choice and the Dealer Shuffles.   Jonathan Williams. CSP

Dean, The.   Coventry Patmore.   *Fr.* The Angel in the House, I, vi.   VLP

Dean and prebendary, A.   The Battle Royal between Dr. Sherlock, Dr. South, and Dr. Burnet.   William Pittis.   APAS

Dean Inge.   Humbert Wolfe.   FaBoEE

Dean of Paul's did search for his wife, The.   Fragment of a Song on the Beautiful Wife of Dr. John Overall.   *Unknown.* BoLoP

Dear/ Diana.   Andy-Diana DNA Letter.   Andrew Weiman. HAP

Dear Alice! you'll laugh when you know it.   The Talented Man. Winthrop Mackworth Praed.   NOBL

Dear America.   Robert Peterson.   SFF; TPo

Dear Ann, I think I am losing my husband.   Help Is on the Way. Herbert Scott.   GP

Dear as the Moon. *Gond Oral Tradition, tr. by* V. Elwin *and* S. Hivale. WTO

Dear Beatrice Fairfax. Kenneth Fearing. SPT

Dear Bill,/ When I search the past for you. A Letter to William Carlos Williams. Kenneth Rexroth. NNaP

Dear Black Head. *Unknown. See* Dear Dark Head.

Dear boy, you will not hear me speak. Pangloss's Song. Richard Wilbur. NoAM

Dear Brethren, Are Your Harps in Tune? *with music.* Eunice Smith. AH

Dear child of nature, let them rail! To a Young Lady. Wordsworth. MBPR

Dear child, these words which briefly I declare. The Maiden's Best Adorning. *Unknown.* OxBChV; RRA

Dear Chloe, how blubbered is that pretty face! Answer to Chloe Jealous. Matthew Prior. NOBE

Dear Colette. Erica Jong. MMD

Dear common flower, that grow'st beside the way. To the Dandelion. James Russell Lowell. PF

Dear Companion. *Unknown.* FSW

Dear creature by the fire a-purr. Cat. Lytton Strachey. PCat

Dear critic, who my lightness so deplores. To a Captious Critic. Paul Laurence Dunbar. BPo

Dear Dark Head. *Unknown, tr. fr. Irish by* Sir Samuel Ferguson. LoAs; PFIr
(Cean Dubh Deelish.) GBL
(Dear Black Head.) BIrV

Dear Dave: Rain five days and I love it. Letter to Wagoner from Port Townsend. Richard Hugo. NNaP

Dear Denise: Long way from, long time since Boulder. Letter to Levertov from Butte. Richard Hugo. NNaP

Dear Dennice: I'm this close but the pass is tough this year. Letter to Scanlon from Whitehall. Richard Hugo. NNaP

Dear Dr. C. whose talking/ does me no good. Letter to Dr. C. from the Great Divide. Susan Sonde. PoUp

Dear dreamer, that I may plunge. Another Fan. Stéphane Mallarmé, *tr. by* Roger Fry. NAWM-2

Dear Editor. Faye Kicknosway. TC

Dear Emily, my tears would burn your page. To Emily Dickinson. Yvor Winters. PiAm

Dear Eustatio, I write that you may write me an answer. Amours de Voyage, Canto I. Arthur Hugh Clough. VPC

Dear Father, Look Up. "Orpheus C. Kerr." OBAL

Dear father, mother, sister, come listen while I tell. The Ashland Tragedy. Elijah Adams. AmFP

Dear fellow-artist, why so free. To a Young Beauty. W. B. Yeats. CMoP (1970 ed.)

Dear fellow castaway, the cruise ships. Weathering the Depths. Al Lee. AmPA

Dear Female Heart. Stevie Smith. FaBoEE

Dear Folks. Patrick Kavanagh. FaBoTw (1975 ed.)

Dear Fred: I hope this finds you, Marge and children O.K. Letter to Garber from Skye. Richard Hugo. AMV-81.

Dear Friend,/ I hear this town does so abound. An Epistolary Essay from M. G. to O. B. upon Their Mutual Poems. Earl of Rochester. APAS

Dear friend, be silent and with patience see. Michael Drayton. *Fr.* To My Noble Friend Master William Browne: Of the Evil Time. SCP-2

Dear friend, I fear my heart will break. Out of French. Sir Charles Sedley. FaBoEE

Dear Friend, Whose Presence in the House, *with music.* James Freeman Clarke. AH

Dear friends/ (and how). Mr. Whitman to His Friends in the Antipodes. Kris Hemensley. *Fr.* The Poem of the Clear Eye. CAAP

Dear Galway/ it is flooding here, in missouri. A Poem to Galway Kinnell. Etheridge Knight. NNaP

Dear gentle soul, who went so soon away. Luís Camoës, *tr. fr. Portuguese by* Roy Campbell. BoLoP

Dear Girl. Gregory Corso. NoAM

Dear Girl, The. Sylvia Townsend Warner. AIW

Dear girl, you/ you're tough, man. For Heidi, Caving. David Kresh. PoUp

Dear God,/ When someone tries to make me do. Garry Cleveland Myers. CTV

Dear God, give us a flood of water. The Prayer of the Little Ducks. Carmen Bernos de Gasztold. DuDr

Dear God, I keep praying/ For the things I desire. A Prayer for the Young and Lovely. Helen Steiner Rice. CTV

Dear God, the Day Is Grey. Anne Halley. NowV; SoSe (1977 ed.)

Dear Happy Souls, *with music.* Eunice Smith. AH

Dear, I must be gone. Parting. W. B. Yeats. FaBoTw (1975 ed.); PoIA

Dear, if unsocial privacies obsess me. Epigram. J. V. Cunningham. VGW

Dear, if you change, I'll never choose again. *Unknown.* LoAs

Dear ——, I'll gie ye some advice. To an Artist. Burns. PBMP

Dear J. D.: One should think of Chief Joseph here. Letter to Reed from Lolo. Richard Hugo. NNaP

Dear James Wright. Ann Darr. PoUp

Dear Jim: This is as far as I ever chased a girl. Letter to Welch from Browning. Richard Hugo. NNaP

Dear John, Dear Coltrane. Michael S. Harper. AmPA; NVAP

Dear John: This is a Dear John Letter from booze. Letter to Logan from Milltown. Richard Hugo. NNaP

Dear Jonno. A Trip on the Staten Island Ferry. Audre Lorde. CNA

Dear kindly Sergeant Krupke. Gee, Officer Krupke. Stephen Sondheim. OBAL

Dear Kong. Fay Wray to the King. Judith Rechter. NMM

Dear Land of Hope, thy hope is crowned. Land of Hope and Glory. A. C. Benson. FaPoR

Dear, let us two each other spy. Love's Vision. William Cavendish, Duke of Newcastle. SCP-2

Dear little/ Mere little. Mouse. Mary Ann Hoberman. MN

Dear Lord and Father of Mankind, *with music.* Whittier. AH; BLSH

Dear Lord, Behold Thy Servants, *with music.* Hosea Ballou I. AH

Dear Lord, we are afraid. Prayer of the Homesteader. Gwendolen Haste. WPW

Dear Lord, we give Thee thanks for the bright silent moon. Thanks. *Unknown.* CTV

Dear [*or* Deare] love, for nothing less [*or* lesse] than thee. The Dream [*or* Dreame]. John Donne. LoAs; OAEL-1

Dear Lucy, you know what my wish is. Horace, *tr. by* Thackeray. Odes, I, 38. OBVE

Dear Mamma, if you just could be. A Lesson for Mamma. Sydney Dayre. OxBChV

Dear March, come in. Emily Dickinson. FSFS

Dear Martin Folkes, dear scholar, brother, friend. John Byrom. *Fr.* A Full and True Account of a Horrid and Barbarous Robbery. NOBL

Dear Marvin: Months since I left broke down and sobbing. Letter to Bell from Missoula. Richard Hugo. NNaP

Dear Maurice. David Campbell. GAS

Dear me! what signifies a pin. The Pin. Ann Taylor. OxBChV

Dear Men and Women. John Hall Wheelock. Prf

Dear miss, not with a lie to cheat ye. Samuel Wesley. *Fr.* To My Gingerbread Mistress. SCP-2

Dear Mr. Bell. Katie Louchheim. PoUp

Dear Mister Congressman.  Bob Dylan.  MAT

Dear Mr. Noman, does it ever strike you.  On Noman, a Guest.  Hilaire Belloc.  FaBoEE

Dear Molly, why so oft in tears?  Horace, *tr. by* George Stepney.  Odes, III, 7.  OBVE

Dear Mother.  Emmett Jarrett.  NeAC

Dear mother, dear mother, the Church is cold.  The Little Vagabond.  Blake.  *Fr.* Songs of Experience.  MBPR; OBSV

Dear native brook! wild streamlet of the west!  Sonnet to the River Otter.  Samuel Taylor Coleridge.  MBPR; OAEL-2

Dear Oedipus.  Ann Darr.  WBN

Dear Old Girl, *with music.*  Richard Henry Buck.  BLSH; FSN

Dear ones, in those days it was otherwise.  The Woman Who Raised Goats.  Tess Gallagher.  AAN

Dear parents,/ I forgive you my life.  Sorry.  R. S. Thomas.  LP

Dear Passengers, I hate to sound reactionary about this.  At Every Major Airport.  Patricia Goedicke.  AAN

Dear Patty, Dear Tania.  Richard Mathews.  GP

Dear Queenie, though it breaks my heart.  The Handmaid of Religion.  Edgell Rickword.  OBSV

Dear Rabbi Rosenberg.  Do You Need the Gold Ring?  Marc Allen Corren.  PoW

Dear Rat,/ Never in all my life have I seen.  Letters from an Irishman to a Rat.  Christopher Logue.  BoAnP

Dear Reader.  James Tate.  EAS

Dear Reynolds, as last night I lay in bed.  To J. H. Reynolds, Esq.  Keats.  MBPR

Dear Ron: hello. Your name is now a household name.  Sonnet.  Ted Berrigan.  CAAP

Dear Saviour, If These Lambs Should Stray, *with music.*  Abby Bradley Hyde.  AH

Dear Sir:/ Your poem interested us.  God Opens His Mail.  Larry Rubin.  CSP

Dear Sir/ You're a pig.  Letter.  Kenneth "Spider" Nicholson.  DNGG

Dear Sir,—You wish to know my notions.  A Letter from a Candidate for the Presidency.  James Russell Lowell.  *Fr.* The Biglow Papers: 1st Series, No. VII.  PiAm

Dear Sir, your astonishment's odd.  A Reply.  *Unknown.*  FaBoCo; NOBL; PoPle

Dear sister! Dear Ismene! How many evils.  Antigone.  Sophocles, *tr. by* T. H. Banks.  NAWM-1

Dear Sister, my resentment had not been.  Virgil, *tr. fr. Latin by* Sir John Denham.  *Fr.* The Aeneid, IV.  OBVE

Dear Smith, the sleest, paukie thief.  To James Smith.  Burns.  HoPM (1975 ed.)

Dear son:/ when you left us you left.  The Father in Tennessee.  J. Edgar Simmons.  TAT

Dear Thomas, didst thou never pop.  A Simile.  *Unknown.*  ILP (1975 ed.)

Dear, though the night is gone.  W. H. Auden.  BoLoP

Dear, though to part it be hell.  To Dianeme.  Robert Herrick.  CaPo

Dear Uncle Stranger.  Conrad Aiken.  NoAM; NOBA

Dear Vincent.  Elizabeth Bartlett.  PoW

Dear, when on some distant planet.  Love in a Space-Suit.  James Kirkup.  MPo

Dear Whoever-You-Are-That-You-Are.  A Letter from the Pygmies.  Theodore Weiss.  VGW

Dear, why make you more of a dog than me?  Astrophel and Stella, LIX.  Sir Philip Sidney.  GBL; ILP (1975 ed.); LoAs

Dear, why should you command me to my rest.  Michael Drayton.  *Fr.* Idea.  AAS; ILP (1975 ed.); NOBE

"Dear wife, I don't suppose you understand."  The First Goodbye Letter.  James Simmons.  AMV-81

Dear, you are in my hands like dough.  Circus Song.  Patricia Goedicke.  TV

Deare Friend, sit down, the tale is long and sad.  Love Unknown.  George Herbert.  Prf

Deare love, for nothing lesse than thee.  *See* Dear love, for nothing less than thee.

Dearest Evelyn, I often think of you.  The Jungle Husband.  Stevie Smith.  BBL; BuTh

Dearest love, do you remember.  When This Cruel War Is Over [*or* Weeping Sad and Lonely].  Charles C. Sawyer.  AmFP; FSW

Dearest Man-in-the-Moon.  Erica Jong.  MMD; Moon

Death.  Emily Brontë.  VLP

Death.  Howard Byatt.  FF

Death.  Roy Fuller.  NoAM

Death.  *Gond Oral Tradition, tr. by* V. Elwin *and* S. Hivale.  WTO

Death.  Patty L. Harjo.  VoR

Death.  George Herbert.  ILP (1975 ed.); SCP-1

Death.  Mildred Jeffrey.  AMV-80

Death.  L. E. Jones.  POL

Death.  Keats.  *Fr.* The Fall of Hyperion.  OBP

Death.  William Knott.  EAS

Death.  John Stone.  CSP

Death.  Lynn Sukenick.  RiTi (Dance.)  CPA

Death.  *Unknown, tr. fr. Welsh by* Aneirin Talfan Davies.  OBW

Death.  William Carlos Williams.  VGW

Death.  Charles Wright.  FiCP

Death/ Is nothing to us, has no relevance.  Against the Fear of Death.  Lucretius, *tr. by* Rolfe Humphries.  *Fr.* De Rerum Natura, III.  DL; NAWM-1

Death!/ Plop. A Tragedy.  Théophile Marzials.  PeD; PPoD

Death and Co.  Sylvia Plath.  CMoP (1970 ed.); ConAP; FF

Death and darkness, get you packing.  Easter Hymn.  Henry Vaughan.  PoPle

Death and Disfiguration.  Judy Grahn.  *Fr.* A Woman Is Talking to Death.  WBN

Death and Empedocles 444 B.C.  Horace Gregory.  PoA

Death, and it is broken.  The Instrument.  Kathleen Raine.  PoA

Death and Love.  Ben Jonson.  *Fr.* The Sad Shepherd, I, v.  NOBE ("Though I am young and cannot tell.")  ILP (1975 ed.)

Death and Resurrection of the Birds, The.  David Wagoner.  MPA

Death and the Arkansas River.  Frank Stanford.  FiCP

Death and the Cobbler.  *Unknown.*  APAS

Death and the Lover.  *Unknown, tr. fr. Spanish by* W. S. Merwin.  Epi

Death and the Pineapple.  Dan Gerber.  TC

Death and the Plowman.  Sidney Keyes.  OxBTC

Death-angel smote Alexander McGlue, The.  Mr. Slimmer's Funeral Verses for the *Morning Argus.*  "Max Adeler."  OBAL

Death as History.  Jay Wright.  PoBA

Death at Suppertime.  Phyllis McGinley.  PBMP

Death at Winson Green, A.  Francis Webb.  GAS; MAuV

Death, Be Not Proud.  John Donne.  Holy Sonnets, X.  AnMo; BiP; BoReV; CABA (1972 ed.); DL; Epi; ExPo (1973 ed.); FF; HAP; HeIP; ILP (1975 ed.); IP; MetP; NIL; NOBE; OAEL-1; OBP; PAIC; PBMP; PIM; PoIA; PPoe; PPP; SCP-1; TPo; TT; UsP; VoPo

Death be not proud, thy hand gave not this blow.  Elegy.  Lucy Harington, Countess of Bedford.  WPE

Death, become a shewolf.  Crown of Happiness.  Anne Hebert, *tr. by* Willis Barnstone.  BoWoP

Death-Bed, The.  Thomas Hood.  NOBE; PIM, *abr.*

Death Bed.  Thomas Kinsella.  CIP; IPM

Death-Bed, The.  Siegfried Sassoon.  PoPle

Death-Bed Song. *Unknown.* AmFP

Death Bells. *Unknown.* BluL

Death by Aesthetics. Mona Van Duyn. RiTi

Death calls me—Sweet, it might be good. Babylonian Sorrows. Heine, *tr. by* Aaron Kramer. NAWM-2

Death Came Too Late. Alison Wyrley Birch. PPM

Death Chant. Peter Blue Cloud. VoR

Death Comes for the Old Cowboy. Kevin Clark. AMV-81

Death comes in quantity from solved. The Tolerance of Crows. Charles Donnelly. CIP

Death Comes to the Salesman. Louis Daniel Brodsky. AMV-81

Death Dance, The. Marge Piercy. WBN

Death departs and I am drunk. The Duke of York (Courage). Chuck Miller. AcAn

Death designs swirl high above faces that are of disbelief. War Walking Near. Ray A. Young Bear. CDW

Death devours all lovely things. Passer Mortuus Est. Edna St. Vincent Millay. CMoP (1970 ed.); RiTi

Death did not come to my mother. Conception. Josephine Miles. GP

Death for the Dark Stranger. Thomas McGrath. VGW

Death from Cancer. Robert Lowell. In Memory of Arthur Winslow, I. UsP

Death Fugue. Paul Celan. *See* Fugue of Death.

Death has come to visit us today. On the Acequia Madre. Alice Corbin. WPW

Death, I repent. Two Invocations of Death. Kathleen Raine. OxBTC

Death in Duke Street. Edwin Morgan. MS

Death-in-Love. Dante Gabriel Rossetti. The House of Life, XLVIII. VLP

Death in the City. Norman Macleod. SPT

Death in the Desert, A. Charles Tomlinson. FF; TwMBP

Death in the Family. Alison Wyrley Birch. PPM

Death in the Woods. Harold Littlebird. VW

Death in Yorkville. Langston Hughes. PoBA

Death Insurance. Wade Hall. AATT

Death Invited. May Swenson. BoAnP; LiSp; WPE

Death is a country where people wonder. Through the Eye of the Needle. Daniela Gioseffi. AAN

Death is a dialogue between. Emily Dickinson. SoSe (1977 ed.)

Death Is a Door. John Allcock. BuTh

Death is all metaphors, shape in one history. Altarwise by Owl-Light, II. Dylan Thomas. CMoP (1970 ed.); NoAM

Death is another milestone on their way. The Funeral. Stephen Spender. CMoP (1970 ed.); NoAM

Death is asleep. Riddles and Lies. Christine Zawadiwsky. AMV-80

Death Is Awful. *Unknown.* BluL

Death is before me today. Dying. A. Alvarez. VWA

Death is not a period. Thesis. William Walter De Bolt. AMV-80

Death Is Not Evil, Evil is Mechanical. D. H. Lawrence. PBMP

Death is stronger than all the governments. Death Snips Proud Men. Carl Sandburg. BBGO; CMoP (1970 ed.)

Death is the cook of nature, and we find. Margaret Cavendish, Duchess of Newcastle. *Fr.* Nature's Cook. PBWP; SCP-2

Death is the supple suitor. Emily Dickinson. AnMo

Death killed the rich. *Yoruba Oral Tradition, tr. by* W. Abimbola. WTO

Death-Lace. David Ray. MAT

Death makes me love you. Allegiance to Aphrodite. Nicholas Flocos. SA

Death News. Allen Ginsberg. NoAM

Death of a Bird. Jon Silkin. BoAnP

Death of a Cat. Brian Jones. LP

Death of a Cat, The, *sels.* Louis MacNeice.
   "For he was our puck, our miniature lar." PCat
   "To begin with he was a beautiful object." PCat

Death of a Dog. Peter Bland. ATNZ

Death of a Fair Girl. Alpheus Butler. PeD

Death of a Friend. Pauli Murray. PoBA

Death of a Naturalist. Seamus Heaney. HAP; NCSH

Death of a Negro Poet, The. Conrad Kent Rivers. BPo

Death of a Poet. Charles Causley. OxBTC

Death of a Snowman. Vernon Scannell. FPB

Death of a Soldier, The. Wallace Stevens. OFD

Death of a Son. Jon Silkin. BBGO; FF; IPWM; NoAM; OxBTC; PPoD; VWA

Death of a Symbol, The. Ralph Storey. SES

Death of a Toad, The. Richard Wilbur. AnMo; BiP; CABA (1972 ed.); CMoP (1970 ed.) NoAM; PoA; PoIA

Death of a Vermont Farm Woman. Barbara Howes. CoPAm

Death of a Warrior, The. Jenny Mastoraki, *tr. fr. Modern Greek by* Kimon Friar. BoWoP

Death of a Young Son by Drowning. Margaret Atwood. BoWoP

Death of Admiral Benbow, The. *Unknown.* GBP; PeBB

Death of Adonis, The. Philip Ayres, *after the Greek of* Theocritus. OBVE

Death of an Actress. Louis MacNeice. NIL

Death of an Elephant, The. Gianfranco Pagnucci. NU

Death of an Irishwoman. Michael Hartnett. CIP

Death of Arthur, The. Layamon. *Fr.* The Brut. OxBM

Death of Arthur, The. Tennyson. *Fr.* Idylls of the King: Morte d'Arthur. PIM

Death of Ben Hall, The. Will H. Ogilvie. PoTa

Death of Carmen Miranda, The. Stephen E. Smith. AMV-81

Death of Crazy Horse, The. John G. Neihardt. BPAW

Death of Damiens or l'Apres-midi des Lumieres, The. R. F. Brissenden. GAS

Death of Democracy, The. John Sjoberg. AcAn

Death of Dr. King. Sam Cornish. CNA; OFD; PoBA

Death of Justice, The. Walter Everette Hawkins. PoBA

Death of King George V. John Betjeman. NOBE

Death of Kings, The. Shakespeare. King Richard II, *fr.* III, ii. GrRo
   ("Let's talk of graves, of worms, and epitaphs.") PPoe

Death of Lester Brown, House Painter, The. Rod Taylor. WeW

Death of Lincoln, The. Bryant. TAP

Death of mine honor, with the city's fool! Ben Jonson. *Fr.* Volpone, II, iii. SCP-1

Death of Morgan, The. *Unknown.* FaBoBa

Death of My Grandmother, The. G. S. Fraser. MS

Death of Myth-making, The. Sylvia Plath. PoA

Death of Neruda, The. Danny L. Rendleman. TC

Death of Phidias, The. Ann Deagon. AAN

Death of Queen Jane, The, 2 *versions. Unknown.* AmFP (Queen Jane.) FSW

Death of Robin Hood, The. Eugene Field. PoTa

Death of Samuel Adams, The. *Unknown.* AmFP

Death of Sappho, The. Nell Altizer. PHC

Death of Sir Nihil, book the *n*th. Tywater. Richard Wilbur. CMoP (1970 ed.); ConAP

Death of Tammuz, The. Shaul Tchernichovsky, *tr. fr. Hebrew by* Mark Elliott Shapiro. VWA

Death of the Astronomer. Philip Roberts. FPA

Death of the Average Man. Alison Wyrley Birch. PPM

Death of the Ball Turret Gunner, The. Randall Jarrell. BiP; CMoP (1970 ed.); CoPAm; ExPo (1973 ed.) FF; HAP; HoPM (1975 ed.); ILP (1975 ed.); InPK; IPWM; NIL; NoAM;

NOBA; NowV; PoIA; PPP; PSN; SoS; SoSe; TAP; UnPo (1976 ed.); VGW; WIF

Death of the Bird, The. A. D. Hope. MAuV

Death of the Cat. Ian Serraillier. SO

Death of the Craneman, The. Alfred Hayes. NCSH

Death of the Duke of Buckingham, The. Pope. *See* Duke of Buckingham, The.

Death of the Epileptic Poet Yesenin, The. Aram Boyajian. NeAC

Death of the Family, The. John Boland. IPM

Death of the Flowers, The. Bryant. EAP

Death of the Hired Man, The. Robert Frost. CMoP (1970 ed.); HoPM (1975 ed.); IPWM; SoSe (1977 ed.); STS

Death of the Moon. David Wagoner. PoA

Death of the Novel, The. David Young. AmPA

Death of the Sailor's Wife, The. Fred Barton. AMV-80

Death of the Sheriff, The. Robert Lowell. STS

Death of the Sports-Car Driver, The. Jonathan Aaron. MiP

Death of Venus, The. Robert Creeley. NOBA; PiAm

Death of Warren, The. Epes Sargent. BTTM

Death on the Farm. Cary Waterman. GP

Death Penalty, The. Ross Laursen. CPA

Death Piece. Theodore Roethke. STS

Death, Putative Father. Sydney Bernard Smith. IPM

Death Rode a Pinto Pony. Whitney Montgomery. BPAW

Death Seed. Ricarda Huch, *tr. fr. German by* Susan C. Strong. PBWP

Death; She Was Always Here. Yona Wallach, *tr. fr. Hebrew by* Leonore Gordon. VWA

Death Snips Proud Men. Carl Sandburg. BBGO; CMoP (1970 ed.)

Death Song for Owain ab Urien. Taliesin, *tr. fr. Welsh by* Anthony Conran. OBW

Death Songs. L. V. Mack. PoBA

Death Sonnet I. Gabriela Mistral, *tr. fr. Spanish by* David Garrison. BoWoP

Death stands above me, whispering low. On Death. Walter Savage Landor. BBGO; NOBE; OAEL-2

Death Sting Me Blues. *Unknown.* BluL

Death supersedes, but illness conjugates. Two on a Journey. Basil Payne. IPM

Death Takes Only a Minute. Agnes Pratt. VW

Death Terrible in Countenance. Thomas Dekker. *Fr.* Dekker His Dream. SCP-2

Death, that struck when I was most confiding. Death. Emily Brontë. VLP

Death, the friend behind phenomenon. A Game of Chance. Howard Moss. PoA

Death the Leveller. James Shirley. *See* Glories of Our Blood and State, The.

Death, tho I see him not, is near. *See* Death, though I see him not, is near.

Death, thou wast once an uncouth hideous thing. Death. George Herbert. ILP (1975 ed.); SCP-1

Death, though [*or* tho] I see him not, is near. Age. Walter Savage Landor. FaBoEE; InPK

Death to Van Gogh's Ear! Allen Ginsberg. CABA (1972 ed.); VGW

Death took my father. Manos Karastefanís. James Merrill. TAP

Death Valley. Jack H. Lee. BPAW

Death Valley Blues. *Unknown.* BluL

Death was there, sitting by the roadside. Climbing. Gloria Fuertes, *tr. by* Philip Levine. PBWP

Death Watchers, The. Alice Ryerson. AMV-80

Death, where is thy victory! To Death. Shelley. MBPR

Death will come, but not age. Young Revolutionist. Isidor Schneider. SPT

Death will make his entry into your body which is so beautiful. Death. *Gond Oral Tradition, tr. by* V. Elwin *and* S. Hivale. WTO

Death with a Coda. Giuseppe Gioachino Belli, *tr. fr. Italian by* Miller Williams. AMV-81

Death Words. Les A. Murray. *Fr.* Walking to the Cattle-Place. CAAP

Death, you are so much more powerful. Stone Words for Robert Lowell. Richard Eberhart. AMV-80

Deaths and Pretty Cousins. David Campbell. CAAP

Death's Jest Book, *sels.* Thomas Lovell Beddoes.
    Bridal Song ("We have bathed, . . ."), *fr.* IV, iii. GBL
    Sibilla's Dirge, *fr.* V, iv. NOBE
    Song from the Waters, *fr.* I, iv. NOBE
    Song: "Old Adam, the carrion crow," *fr.* V, iv. EBEV; ILP (1975 ed.); OAEL-2; OBP
    Wolfram's Dirge, *fr.* II, ii. NOBE

Deaths of Paragon, The. John Woods. IPWM

Death's the Classic Look. John Ciardi. PoA

Deathward. John Lyle Donaghy. BIrV

Deathwatch. Michael S. Harper. AmPA; PoBA

Debate of the Body and the Soul, The, *abr. Unknown.* PAIC

Debate: Question, Quarry, Dream. Robert Penn Warren. VGW

Deborah Lee. Yvonne. CNA

Debt, The. Paul Laurence Dunbar. AmNP (1974 ed.); CABA (1972 ed.); SS

Debt. *Gond Oral Tradition, tr. by* V. Elwin *and* S. Hivale. WTO

Debt is paid, The. The Past. Emerson. TAP

Decayed Time. Jean Wahl, *tr. fr. French by* Charles Guenther. VWA

Deceased. Cid Corman. VGW

Deceased, The. Keith Douglas. FaBoTw (1975 ed.)

Deceav'd and undeceav'd to be. The Self-Deceaver. Thomas Stanley, *after the Spanish of* Juan Perez de Montalvan. OBVE

Deceitful Brownskin Blues. *Unknown.* BluL

December. Ron Padgett. EAS

December. James Schuyler. NoAM

December. Gary Snyder. InPS

December, and the closing of the year. Christmas Eve in Whitneyville, 1955. Donald Hall. UnPo (1976 ed.)

December and the settling heart remain. The Day Birth Placard (for Amy). Henry Kanabus. FiCh

December 18th. Anne Sexton. *Fr.* Eighteen Days without You. CAPP

December 15, 1811. Poem for My Family: Hazel Griffin and Victor Hernandez Cruz. June Jordan. BPo; RiTi

December Fragments. Richmond Lattimore. PChr

December narrows our day to a thread of light. Song in the Cold Season. Samuel French Morse. PoA

December Night. W. S. Merwin. CAPP

December 1970. John Tagliabue. GP

December Sky, The. A. G. Sobin. HeS

December Stillness. Siegfried Sassoon. CMoP (1970 ed.)

December 24 and George McBride Is Dead. Richard Hugo. HoPM (1975 ed.)

Decent of docent doesn't doze, The. History of Education. David McCord. OBAL

Deception. Alfred Corn. PoA

Deceptions. Philip Larkin. CABA (1972 ed.); CMoP (1970 ed.)

Decidedly the crocus. For the Spring Being. Albert Howard Carter. AATT

Decision. M. P. Flynn. CTV

Decision.  Theodore Roethke.  MPA; VGW

Decision, A.  Edith Södergran, *tr. fr. Swedish by* Jaakko O. Ahokas.  PBWP

Deck out.  You.  John Tagliabue.  GP

Deck the Halls.  *Unknown.*  BLSH, *with music*; FSW

Decks.  Robert Phillips.  NYP

Decks awash,/ Mast-top dipping.  Archilochus, *tr. fr. Latin by* Guy Davenport.  OBVE

Declaration.  Robert Gessner.  SPT

Declaration, The.  Nathaniel Parker Willis.  OBAL

Declaration of Independence.  Wolcott Gibbs.  SoS

Declension.  Stephen Sandy.  PoA

Decline and Fall.  John Frederick Nims.  CoPAm

Decorate the carcass.  Song to Be Attached.  Hollis Summers.  CoPAm

Decorating Problem.  Sonya Dorman.  RiTi

Decoration.  Mary Ursula Bethell.  ATNZ

Decoration Day.  Bennie Lee Sinclair.  TAT

Decoys, The.  W. H. Auden.  CMoP (1970 ed.)

Decrepit old gas man named Peter, A.  Limerick.  *Unknown.*  SoSe

Dede's Return to New Mexico.  Summer Brenner.  RiTi

Dedicated Dancing Bull and the Water Maid, The, *sel.*  Stevie Smith.
"Hop hop, thump thump."  WPE

Dedication, A, *sel.*  Karin Boye, *tr. fr. Swedish by* Nadia Christensen.
"I feel your steps in the hall."  PBWP

Dedication: "Bob Southey! You're a poet—poet-laureate."  Byron.  *Fr. Don Juan.*  ILP (1975 ed.); MBPR; OAEL–2; OBSV
("Bob Southey! You're a poet—poet-laureate.")  PPoe

Dedication: "Had there been peace there never had been riven."  Drummond Allison.  FaBoTw (1975 ed.)

Dedication, The: "Health to great Gloucester—from a man unknown."  Charles Churchill.  OBSV

Dedication: "In my dreams we are always together."  Richard Stull.  AMV–81

Dedication: "Memory of one particular hour, The."  Wordsworth.  *Fr. The Prelude, IV.*  BoReV

Dedication: "Sea gives her shells to the shingle, The."  Swinburne.  VLP

Dedication: "Some nine years gone, as we dwelt together."  Swinburne.  VLP

Dedication: "These to His Memory—since he held them dear."  Tennyson.  *Fr. Idylls of the King.*  CABA (1972 ed.); VLP

Dedication for a Building.  Alan Dugan.  NYP

Dedication for a Plot of Ground.  William Carlos Williams.  TT

Dedication of the Cook.  Anna Wickham.  PPM

Dedication on the Gift of a Book to a Child.  Hilaire Belloc.  EBEV

Dedication to a Book of Stories Selected from the Irish Novelists, The.  W. B. Yeats.  OBP

Dedication to G**** H******* Esq., A, *sel.*  Burns.
"Morality, thou deadly bane."  OBSV

Dedication to Leigh Hunt, Esq.  Keats.  MBPR

Dedication to My Wife, A.  T. S. Eliot.  BoLoP; FF

Dedication to "Songs of the Springtides."  Swinburne.  VLP

Dedication to the Final Confrontation.  Lloyd M. Corbin, Jr.  PoBA

Dedicatory: "Somewhere, sometime, in an April twilight."  Willa Cather.  WPE

Dedicatory Sonnet to S. T. Coleridge.  Hartley Coleridge.  OAEL–2

Deduction.  Samuel Johnson.  *See* Burlseque of Lope de Veaga

Dee dee dee dee dee wee weee eeeeee wee we.  Communication in Whi-te.  Don L. Lee.  BPo

Deed.  Elisabeth Murawski.  PoUp

Deedle, deedle, dumpling, my son John.  Mother Goose.  MG

Deeds of Kindness.  *Unknown.*  CTV

Deep, The.  John G. C. Brainard.  RhR

Deep Blue Sea.  *Unknown.*  FSW

Deep Calleth unto Deep.  Henry Nehemiah Dodge.  RhR

Deep in a vale, a stranger now to arms.  The American Soldier.  Philip Freneau.  TAP

Deep in Deering Oaks.  Hard Edge of Beauty.  Floyd C. Stuart.  FAF

Deep in my soul there roared the crashing thunder.  Calm after Storm.  Frank Yerby.  AmNP (1974 ed.)

Deep in the air the past appears.  The Greeks.  Tom Clark.  PoA

Deep in the back ways of my mind I see them.  My Great-Grandfather's Slaves.  Wendell Berry.  TCP

Deep in the forest there is a pond.  After the Anonymous Swedish.  Jim Harrison.  VGW

Deep in the leafy fierceness of the wood.  Apollo and Daphne.  Yvor Winters.  PiAm

Deep in the hill the gold sand burned.  A Ballad of the Gold Country.  Helen Hunt Jackson.  BPAW

Deep in the olive groves at sunset.  Give Us This Day.  James Neugass.  SPT

Deep in the shady sadness of a vale.  Hyperion; a Fragment.  Keats.  MBPR; OAEL–2

Deep in the wave is a coral grove.  The Coral Grove.  James Gates Percival.  EcS

Deep in the winter plain, two armies.  Two Armies.  Stephen Spender.  OxBTC

Deep in their roots, all flowers keep the light.  Theodore Roethke.  POL

Deep in Winter.  Ted Kooser.  HeS

Deep in your cheeks.  Origins.  Keorapetse Kgositsile.  PoBA

Deep inside me, someone sits at the harp.  Someone Sits at the Harp.  Jon Lang.  AMV–81

Deep lane, poor families; I have few friends.  At the End of Spring.  Yü Hsüan-chi, *tr. by* Geoffrey Waters.  BoWoP

Deep Night.  Juan Ramón Jiménéz, *tr. fr. Spanish by* Robert Bly.  NYP

Deep on the convent-roof the snows.  St. Agnes' Eve.  Tennyson.  ILP (1975 ed.); PIM

Deep red bogs divided.  Richard Murphy.  *Fr. The Battle of Aughrim.*  CIP

Deep River ("Deep river, my home is over Jordan").  *Unknown.*  BLSH, *with music*; BPo; FSW; TAP

Deep Sea Blues.  Joanne Jimason.  PoUp

Deep-Sea Cables, The.  Kipling.  VLP

Deep Spring.  *Unknown.*  AmFP

Deep-sworn Vow, A.  W. B. Yeats.  CMoP (1970 ed.); ExPo (1973 ed.); OAEL–2; PSN; TCP; TPo; UnPo (1976 ed.)

Deep Water.  *Unknown.*  FSW

Deeper into Coleridge.  Melissa Clark.  PoUp

Deeper than sleep but not so deep as death.  Night Feeding.  Muriel Rukeyser.  NMM; UsP; WPE

Deepest Bow, The.  Marie Takvan, *tr. fr. Norwegian by* Harold P. Hansen.  AMV–81

Deepest Sensuality, The.  D. H. Lawrence.  NoAM

Deer, The.  Asya, *tr. fr. Yiddish by* Gabriel Preil *and* Howard Schwartz.  VWA

Deer.  No Ch'ŏn-myŭng, *tr. fr. Korean by* Ko Won.  PBWP

Deer.  Kenneth Rexroth.  *Fr.* A Bestiary.  HoPM (1975 ed.)

Deer, The.  Laurie Sheck.  AMV–80

Deer among Cattle.  James Dickey.  TCP; TSWA

Deer are gentle and graceful. Deer. Kenneth Rexroth. *Fr.* A Bestiary. HoPM (1975 ed.)

Deer carcass hangs from a rafter, The. Gathering the Bones Together. Gregory Orr. AmPA

Deer feed on. Upon Leaving the Parole Board Hearing. Conyus. PoBA

Deer have stood around our house. Deer Stolen. William Stafford. CNW

Deer Hunt. Judson Jerome. CoPAm; RFM

Deer in the Prison, The. Joseph Bruchac. NW

Deer is patience, The. The Deer. Laurie Sheck. AMV–80

Deer Isle. Philip Booth. BiP; VGW

Deer Lay Down Their Bones, The. Robinson Jeffers. PiAm

Deer Song. Leslie Silko. VoR

Deer Stolen. William Stafford. CNW

Deer were bounding like blown leaves, The. Fire on the Hills. Robinson Jeffers. CMoP (1970 ed.)

Deere to my soule, then leave me not forsaken. Henry Constable. *Fr.* Diana. AAS

Deevil's Waltz, The. Sydney Goodsir Smith. FaBoTw (1975 ed.)

Defeat, A. Denise Levertov. PBWP

Defeat may serve as well as victory. Victory in Defeat. Edwin Markham. PPM

Defeated, The. Linda Gregg. PCho

Defeated Victor, The. Horst Bienek, *tr. fr. German.* LP

Defence of Guenevere, The. William Morris. PAIC; VLP; VPC

Defence of the Alamo, The. Joaquin Miller. BPAW; BTTM

Defend Us, Lord, from Every Ill, *with music.* John Hay. AH

Defenses, The. Ben Maddow. SPT

Defiance. Walter Savage Landor. VLP

Defiant One, The. Alice Morrey Bailey. AMV–80

Defiled Is My Name Full Sore. *At. to* Anne Boleyn. WPE

Definition. Edwin Rolfe. SPT

Definition for Blk/ Children. Sonia Sanchez. PoBA

Definition of Beauty, The. Robert Herrick. CaPo

Definition of Blue. John Ashbery. Epi

Definition of Love, The. Andrew Marvell. AnMo; BoLoP; EBEV; GBL; HoPM (1975 ed.); ILP (1975 ed.); InPK; InPS; LoAs; MetP; NOBE; OAEL–1; UnPo (1976 ed.)

Definition of Nature. Eugene Redmond. PoBA

Deflated of flesh,/ like axehafts. Radium Therapy. Peter Dale. PMW

Deftly admiral, cast your fly. Song. W. H. Auden. PSN

Degas. Paul Monette. AmPA

Deid sall ye ligg, and ne'er a memorie. Douglas Young, *after the Greek of* Sappho. OBVE

Deid this day ligs the builder Brand. The Daeth o Brand. Tom Scott. MS

Deil o' Bogie, The. Alexander Gray. MS

Deinosaurs. Arthur J. Bull. HeHu

Deirdre. James Stephens. CMoP (1970 ed.); NoAM

Deity of Love Incorporate, A. Edward Taylor. *Fr.* Preparatory Meditations, First Series. TAP

Deja Vu. J. B. Mulligan. AMV–80

Dejection; an Ode. Samuel Taylor Coleridge. CABA (1972 ed.); Epi; ILP (1975 ed.); MBPR, 3 *versions*; NOBE; OAEL–2; PPP

  New Moon, The, *sel.* FSFS

Dekker His Dream, *sels.* Thomas Dekker.
  Death Terrible in Countenance. SCP–2
  Extremities of Cold in Hell, The. SCP–2

Dekunle, handsome man, hail! Omobayode Arowa, *tr. fr. Yoruba. Fr.* Dirge for Fajuyi. WTO

Delay. Elizabeth Jennings. InPK; OxBTC

Delaying Tactics. Christopher Wiseman. AMV–81

Delfica. Gérard de Nerval, *tr. fr. French by* Andrew Hoyem. NU

Delia. Samuel Daniel. *See* To Delia.

Delia Dalya of the Sponged Stilts. Ron Welburn. NW

Delia Holmes ("Delia, Delia, why didn't you run?"). *At. to* "Whistling Bill" Ruff. AmFP

Delia's Gone. Blind Blake (Blake Alphonso Higgs). FSW

Deliberately, long ago/ the carcasses. From an Old House in America. Adrienne Rich. NNaP

Delicate Balance, A. Laura Schreiber. AMV–80

Delicate Bird Who Is Flying Up Our Asses, The. Marvin Bell. NVAP

Delicate girl was eager to air, The. Princess Elizabeth of Bohemia, as Perdita. Frank O'Hara. PoA

Delicate Impasse, A. Kenneth John Atchity. AMV–80

Delicate, Plummeting Bodies, The. Stephen Dobyns. PCho

Delicate shells lay on the shore, The. Emerson. *Fr.* Each and All. EcS

Delicate the Toad. Robert Francis. DuDa

Delicate young Negro stands, A. Anonymous Drawing. Donald Justice. HeIP

Delicately delineated in pencil's grey. Head. Richard Weber. IPM

Delight in Disorder. Robert Herrick. AnMo; BiP; CABA (1972 ed.); CaPo; FF; HAP; HeIP; ILP (1975 ed.); InPK; InPS; IP; NIL; NOBE; OAEL–1; PBMP; PoIA; PoPle; PPoe; PPP; UsP
  ("Sweet disorder in the dress, A.") EBEV

Delight It Is in Youth and May. A. E. Housman. TT

Delight of humane kind, and gods above. Lucretius, *tr. by* Dryden. *Fr.* De Rerum Natura, I. OBVE

Delight Song of Tsoai-Talee, The. N. Scott Momaday. CDW

Delightful, book, your trip. Aoibhinn, A Leabhrain, Do Thriall. *Unknown, tr. by* Flann O'Brien. BIrV

Delightful change from the town's abode. Barnyard Melodies. Fred Emerson Brooks. OBAL

Delights of the Door, The. Francis Ponge, *tr. fr. French by* Robert Bly. NU

Delineations of the Giants, The. William Carlos Williams. *Fr.* Paterson. NoAM; TAP
  ("Paterson lies in the valley under the Passaic Falls.") TAP

Delirium in Vera Cruz. Malcolm Lowry. FaBoTw (1975 ed.); OxBTC; UsP

Delirium of arms. Apology for the Fall. E. R. Cole. AATT

Deliver Me, O Lord, from My Daily Bread. Jeanne Murray Walker. AMV–80

Deliver us for thy descent. John Donne. *Fr.* A Litany. SCP–1

Deliver us from apple pies. Grandmother's Apple Pies. Bruce Weston Munro. PeD

Deliverance. Geoffrey Holloway. PMW

Deliverance, The. Ralph Knevet. SCP–2

Deliverance from a Fit of Fainting. Anne Bradstreet. TAP

Delivering Lambs. David Campbell. MAuV

Delivery, The. Hollis Summers. CoPAm

Delphic Hymn to Apollo. Swinburne. VLP

Delta Farmer in a Wet Summer. James Whitehead. TAT

Delta lies unchanged, flat, The. View of Louisiana. Cleopatra Mathis. TAT

Delta Ohio CycleRama just broke up a whole, The. Rally. Janet Kauffman. TC

Delta Traveller. Charles Wright. AmPA

Deluge 1939, The. Saunders Lewis, *tr. fr. Welsh by* Gwyn Thomas. OBW

Demagogue, The. Phyllis McGinley. FaBoEE

Demands of the Muse. Vernon Watkins. PoA

Demeanour. *Unknown.* OxBChV

Dementia Praecox. Morris Bishop. PoA

Demeter and Persephone. Tennyson. VLP

Demeter devastated our good land. The Appeasement of Demeter. George Meredith. VLP

Demolition. Victor Borsa. PoW

Demolition. Philip Raisor. AMV–81

Demon, Demon, you have dumped me. Her Love Poem. Lucille Clifton. GP

Demon Lover, The. Adrienne Rich. IHMS

Demon Lover, The. *Unknown.* AIW; CABA (1972 ed.); HAP; MAT; PBMP; UnPo (1976 ed.)
(Carpenter's Wife, The, *with music.*) OAEL–1
(Daemon Lover, The.) NU; SLP
(House Carpenter, The.) AmFP; RDB, *with music*; WIF
(House Carpenter's Wife, The.) FSW
(James Harris.) FaBoBa; PeBB

Demonstration. Margaret Finefrock. AMV–80

Demonstration, A. Coventry Patmore. *Fr.* The Angel in the House, II, xi. VLP

Demonstration, The, *sel.* Thomas Traherne.
"Highest things are easiest to be shown, The." SCP–2

Dempsey, Dempsey. Horace Gregory. SPT

Denali Road. John Haines. PPoD

Denial, A. Elizabeth Barrett Browning. GBL

Denial. George Herbert. BoReV; ILP (1975 ed.); NOBE; OAEL–1

Denials 1. Jane Somerville. AMV–80

Denied the shelter of air and the power. A Broken Gull. John Moore. NCSH

Denise. Robert Beverly Hale. GDP

Denouement. Kenneth Fearing. SPT

Denouement. Ruth Stone. BoWoP

Dented spider like a snow drop white, A. In White. Robert Frost. WIF

Dentist, A. *Unknown.* FaBoCo; FaBoEE

Dentists continue to water their lawns even in the rain. The Great Society. Robert Bly. NoAM; NYP

Denunciation, A. Mahammed Abdille Hassan, *tr. fr. Somali by* B. W. Andrzejewski. WTO

Deo Gracias. *Unknown.* OxBM

Deo gracias, Anglia. The Agincourt Carol. *Unknown.* EBEV; OxBM

Deor. *Unknown, tr. fr. Anglo-Saxon.* EBEV, *tr. by* John Wain; PAIC, *tr. by* Kemp Malone
(Deor's Lament, *tr. by* Charles W. Kennedy.) OAEL–1

Depairt, depairt, depairt. Lament of the Master of Erskine. Alexander Scott. GBL

Departed Friend, The. Salvador Novo. TVo

Departed Friends. Henry Vaughan. *See* They Are All Gone into the World of Light.

Departed—to the judgment. Emily Dickinson. CABA (1972 ed.)

Departmental. Robert Frost. HeIP; HoPM (1975 ed.); InPK; NOBA; NOBL; OBAL; SoSe (1977 ed.); STS; WIF

Departure. Carolyn Forché. AMV–80

Departure. Elizabeth Hanson. NPW

Departure. George Hitchcock. GP

Departure, A. Derek Mahon. CIP

Departure. Coventry Patmore. The Unknown Eros, I, viii. NOBE; VLP

Departure, The. Jeremy Robson. VWA

Departure, The. Reed Whittemore. TAP

Departure in Middle Age. Roland Mathias. OBW

Departure of the Women, The. Nancy Mairs. NPW

Departure's Girl-Friend. W. S. Merwin. ConAP

Deported. John Ennis. IPM

Deposition. Kevin Ireland. ATNZ

Deposition from Love, A. Thomas Carew. CaPo

Depot Blues ("Standing at the station"). *Unknown.* BluL

Depot Blues ("Well look a-here, honey"). *Unknown.* AmFP

Depot in Rapid City. Roberta Hill. BoWoP; UsP

Depressed by a Book of Bad Poetry, I Walk toward an Unused Pasture and Invite the Insects to Join Me. James Wright. ConAP; TH

Depression. Rex Burwell. AMV–80

Depression, *sel.* Charles Reznikoff.
"Simple soul, who so early in the morning." CTBA

Depression. William Witherup. NowV

Depression before Spring. Wallace Stevens. OBAL

Depression before the Solstice. Charles Wright. CSP

Depression: My Father Speaks to My Mother. Dick Allen. FAF

Depression Ode (11/23/75). Paul Hoover. FiCh

Deprived of his enemy, shrugged to a standstill. John Berryman. *Fr.* Dream Songs. CAPP; PiAm

Depths, The. Denise Levertov. NU

Depths of Sorrow, The. *Gond Oral Tradition, tr. by* V. Elwin *and* S. Hivale. WTO

Der Deitcher's Dog, *with music.* Septimus Winner. PSoN

Der noble Ritter Hugo. Ballad by Hans Breitmann. Charles Godfrey Leland. NOBL

Der spring is sprung. Spring in New York. *Unknown.* IP

Deranged. Padraic Fiacc. PFIr

Derby Ram, The. *Unknown.* AmFP; FaBoNo; GBP

Derelict Valley. Robert Morgan. HeHu

Derelict who groaned in the dry gutter, The. Images of Poverty. Ben Maddow. SPT

Dere's a liddle fact in hishdory vitch few hafe onnershtand. Charles Godfrey Leland. *Fr.* Breitmann in Politics. OBAL

Dere's No Hidin' Place Down Dere. *Unknown.* BPo

Derricks. R. R. Cuscaden. ANTL

Derry. Seamus Deane. CIP

Des plu sages de la tere. Four Wise Men on Edward II's Reign. *Unknown.* OxBM

Descend from heav'n Urania, by that name. Milton. *Fr.* Paradise Lost, VII. EBEV; PoIA

Descend, silent spirit. Prayer to the Snowy Owl. John Haines. BoAnP

Descended of an ancient line. Horace, *paraphrased by* Dryden. Odes, III, 29. OBVE

Descent, The. William Carlos Williams. *Fr.* Paterson. HAP; PiAm; WeW
("Descent beckons, The.") TT; UsP

Descent from the Cross. "Michael Field." WPE

Descent of Odin, The; an Ode from the Norse Tongue. Thomas Gray. LAuP

Descent of the Vulture, The. Marya Zaturenska. WPE

Descent of Winter, The (Section 10/30). William Carlos Williams. InPK

Deschutes River. Raymond Carver. NVAP

Description of a City Shower, A. Swift. AnMo; ExPo (1973 ed.); HeIP; ILP (1975 ed.); MAT; OAEL–1; OBSV; PPoD; PPP;
(City Shower in Imitation of Virgil's Georgics, A.) UnPo (1976 ed.)
Cat and the Rain, The, 4 *ll.* PCat

Description of a Good Boy, The. Henry Dixon. OxBChV

Description of a Ninety Gun Ship. William Falconer. PeD

Description of an Author's Bedchamber, A. Goldsmith. BIrV

Description of an Irish-Feast, The. Hugh MacGowran. *See* O'Rourke's Feast.

Description of Elizium, The. Michael Drayton. *Fr.* The Muses' Elizium. OAEL–1

Description of Love, A. Sir Walter Raleigh. OAEL–1

Description of Maidenhead, A. *Unknown.* NOBL

Description of Spring. Earl of Surrey. *See* Soote Season, The.

Description of the Contrarious Passions in a Lover. Petrarch, *tr. fr. Italian by* Sir Thomas Wyatt. Sonnets to Laura: To Laura in Life, CIV. FF; PAIC
("I find [*or* fynde] no peace, and all my war is done.") AAS; ILP (1975 ed.); OAEL–1; OBVE; PPoe

Description of the Morning, A. Swift. AnMo; CABA (1972 ed.); EBEV; FF; HAP; HeIP; ILP (1975 ed.); LFH; NIL; NOBE; OAEL–1; PAIC; PPP; Prf; SoSe; UsP; WeW

Desert. Agnes Gergely, *tr. fr. Hungarian by* Emery George. VWA

Desert, The. Henry Herbert Knibbs. BPAW

Desert. Del Marie Rogers. NPW

Desert around. Desert. Treason of Sand. Hemda Roth, *tr. by* Mariana Potasman. VWA

Desert Bloom. Gertrude Thomas Arnold. BPAW

Desert Flowers. Keith Douglas. FaBoTw (1975 ed.)

Desert Gulls. Dan Gillespie. TAT

Desert Holy Man. John Beecher. TAT

Desert in the Sea. Brian Swann. AmPA

Desert March. Gerda Norvig. VWA

Desert moves out on half the horizon, The. The Supper after the Last. Galway Kinnell. NOBA

Desert Music, The, *sel.* William Carlos Williams.
"How shall we get said what must be said." TT

Desert of Love, The. János Pilinszky, *tr. fr. Hungarian by* Ted Hughes *and* János Csokits. OBVE

Desert Places. Robert Frost. BiP; CABA (1972 ed.); CMoP (1970 ed.); ILP (1975 ed.); IP; IPWM; LFH; NCSH; NoAM; NOBA; PiAm; PPoD; PPP; TAP; TT; UnPo (1976 ed.)

Desert Song ("There's no hiding here in the glare of the desert"). Glenn Ward Dresbach. BPAW

Desert Song ("When I came on from Santa Fe"). John Galsworthy. BPAW

Desert Stone. Miriam Waddington. VWA

Desert Warfare. Michael Longley. CIP

Desert World, The. Tom McKeown. TC

Deserted and scorned, the proud Marlborough sate. The False Favorite's Downfall. *Unknown.* APAS

Deserted Barn, A. Larry Woiwode. WeW

Deserted Beach. Ruth Dallas. ATNZ

Deserted Cabin. John Haines. PCho

Deserted Farm-House, The. Philip Freneau. EAP; NIL

Deserted Farms Poem. Bruce Severy. VW

Deserted Garden. The. Ann Stanford. AMV-81

Deserted Homestead, The. Loren C. Eiseley. PoA

Deserted House, The. Mary Elizabeth Coleridge. RAE

Deserted Mountain, The. *Unknown, tr. fr. Irish by* John Montague. BIrV

Deserted Shrine. Avner Treinin, *tr. fr. Hebrew by* E. A. Levenston. VWA

Deserted Village, The. Goldsmith. ILP (1975 ed.); LAuP; OAEL-1
*Sels.*
"Even now the devastation is begun." EBEV
"Ill fares the land, to hastening ill a prey." OBSV
"O luxury! Thou curst by Heaven's decree." BIrV
Parson,The. PIM
Sweet Auburn. NOBE
"Sweet Auburn! parent of the blissful hour." EBEV
"Yes! let the rich deride, the proud disdain." OBSV

Deserted Village, The. Robin Hyde. ATNZ; WPE

Design. Robert Frost. AnMo; CABA (1972 ed.); CMoP (1970 ed.); ExPo (1973 ed.); HeIP; ILP (1975 ed.); InPK; InPS; NIL; NoAM; NOBA; PiAm; PoIA; PPP; SoSe; STS; TAP; TT; UsP; WIF

Design, The. Clarence Major. PoBA

Design in Cotton Fabric. Norman Macleod. SPT

Desire. "Æ." ILwL

Desire. Isaac de Botton, *tr. fr. Judezmo by* Stephen Levy. VWA

Desire. Samuel Taylor Coleridge. MBPR

Desire. Sir Philip Sidney. *See* Astrophel and Stella: Sonnet CIX

Desire is a witch. C. Day Lewis. CMoP (1970 ed.)

Desire is Dead. D. H. Lawrence. FaBoEE

Desire of Water, The. Mark Jarman. PoA

Desk, The. Cid Corman. VGW

Desmet, Idaho, March 1969. Janet Campbell Hall. VoR

Desnos Reading the Palms of Men on Their Way to the Gas Chambers. Stephen Berg. VWA

Desolate and lone. Lost. Carl Sandburg. CMoP (1970 ed.)

Desolate Rhythm of Dying Recurs, The. Michael Smith. CIP

Desolation. Amy Lowell. PoA

Desolation. *Unknown, tr. fr. Welsh by* Aneirin Talfan Davies. OBW

Desolation Row. Bob Dylan. InPS; WIF

Despair. Richard Eberhart. UsP

Despair. Denise Levertov. NNaP; RiTi

Despair. James F. Mersmann. BCr

Despair. Tennyson. VLP

Despair farms a curse, slackness. The End. Ted Berrigan. FiCh

Despair is big with friends I love. Consequences. William Meredith. NoAM

Despairing Lover, The. William Walsh. NOBL

Desperado, *sels.* Henry Taylor. PoUp
Cool Women and Smart Horses Are the Pits.
He Sees by His Outfit.
Old Stomping Grounds: The Half-Mile Track.

Desperado, The. *Unknown.* FSW

Desperate Measure, A. Nigel Dennis. WIF

Despisals. Muriel Rukeyser. NMM; Prf

Despite All That. Ann Stanford. CPA

Despite someone starving somewhere. Euphoria, Euphoria. Mark DeFoe. AMV-80

Despite the green drapes. Corwin Psychiatric Ward, 1972. Paul Dilsaver. PoW

Despite this learned cult's official. Apollo of the Physiologists. Robert Graves. NIL

Desponding Phyllis was endued. Phyllis; or, The Progress of Love. Swift. OAEL-1; OBSV

Despot's heel is on thy shore, The. Maryland, My Maryland! James Ryder Randall. BTTM; FaPo; PSoN

Destinations. Josephine Jacobsen. WPE

Destiny of the Poet. Claude Vigée, *tr. fr. French by* Anthony Rudolf. VWA

Destroyers, The. Henry Shore. PMW

Destruction of Jerusalem by the Babylonian Hordes, The. Isaac Rosenberg. VWA

Destruction of Letters. Babette Deutsch. WPE

Destruction of Sennacherib, The. Byron. AIW; AKE; BTTM; CTV; FaPo; FaPoR; FF; HAP; NIL; PBMP; PIM; PoIA; SFF; WeW

Destruction of the Bastille. Samuel Taylor Coleridge. MBPR

Destruction of the Pequods, The. Timothy Dwight. Greenfield Hill, Pt. IV. EAP

Detached always detached. Post-Mortem. S. L. Henderson Smith. PMW

Detached by Sarrinen God. Dulles Airport. Eugene McCarthy. WasP

Detail. Mary Ursula Bethell. ATNZ

Determination. Jóhn Henrik Clarke. CNA; PoBA

Determinism. *Unknown.* FaBoCo
(Predestination) PoPle

Detestable race, continue to expunge yourself, die out.
Apostrophe to Man. Edna St. Vincent Millay. PBMP; SBG

Detroit. Donald Hall. ANTL

Detroit City. Jill Witherspoon Boyer. CNA

Detroit Conference of Unity and Art. Nikki Giovanni. HoPM
(1975 ed.)

Detroit Grease Shop Poem. Philip Levine. MPA

Deus ex Machina. Richard Armour. QQQ

Deuteronomy, *sel.* Bible, *O.T., tr. by* William Tyndale.
"For the Lordes parte is his folke," XXXII: 9-15 OBVE

Developers at Crystal River. James Merrill. AMV-81

Developing a Wife. Andrew Taylor. FPA

Developing Curious Survival Patterns against Winter Saltwinds
The. Lyn Lifshin. FAF

Development. Robert Browning. VLP

Devil and The Farmer's Wife, The. *Unknown.* FSW

Devil Got My Woman. *Unknown.* BluL

Devil, having nothing else to do, The. On Lady Poltagrue, a
Public Peril. Hilaire Belloc. FaBoCo; POL

Devil, Maggot and Son. *Unknown, tr. fr. Irish by* Frank
O'Connor. SoSe

Devil now knew his proper cue, The. Shelley. *Fr.* Peter Bell the
Third. OBSV

Devil was given permission one day, The The History of
Arizona: How It Was Made and Who Made It. Charles O.
Brown. BPAW

Devil was more generous than Adam, The. Samuel Butler.
FaBoEE

Devil, we're told, in hell was chained, The. Hell in Texas.
*Unknown.* BPAW

Devilish Mary. *Unknown.* AmFP; FSW

Devils. Norman Mailer. OBAL

Devil's Advice to Story-Tellers, The. Robert Graves. NoAM

Devil's Bag, The. James Stephens. PFIr; PoTa

Devil's Dictionary, The, *sels.* Ambrose Bierce. OBAL
"Blow, blow, ye spicy breezes."
"Cur foretells the knell of parting day, The."
"Fiercely the battle raged and, sad to tell."
"Hail, holy Lead!—of human feuds the great."
"Megaceph, chosen to serve the State."
"Once I seen a human ruin."
"'One night,' a doctor said, 'last fall.'"
"Spelling reformer indicted, A."
"There's a man with nose."

Devil's Dream. Kenneth Fearing. SPT

Devil's Law-Case, The, *sel.* John Webster.
Vanitas Vanitatum, *fr.* V, iv. NOBE; OBP
(All the Flowers of the Spring.) ILP (1975 ed.)

Devil's Nine Questions, The. *Unknown.* AmFP

Devil's Thoughts, The. Robert Southey *and* Samuel Taylor
Coleridge. FaBoCo; OBSV

Devoid [*or* Devoide] of reason, thrall [*or* thrale] to foolish ire.
Thomas Lodge, *after* Pierre de Ronsard. Phillis XXXI.
AAS; NIL

Devotion. Thomas Campion. NOBE
("Follow your saint, follow with accents sweet.") AAS;
EBEV; HAP; OAEL-1

Devourers, The. Rose Macaulay. PES

Devouring Time, blunt thou the lion's paw. Sonnets, XIX.
Shakespeare. EBEV; Epi; MAT; OAEL-1

Devout Lover, A. Thomas Randolph. HoPM (1975 ed.)

Dew. Jennifer Maiden. CAAP

Dew. Charles Reznikoff. *See* Let Other People Come as
Streams.

Dew-Bite. *Unknown.* ECBV

Dew of the rouge-flower, The. Haiku. Kaga no Chiyo, *tr. by*
R. H. Blyth. PBWP

Dew Sat on Julia's Hair. Robert Herrick. ILP (1975 ed.)

Dew was falling fast, the stars began to blink, The. The Pet
Lamb. Wordsworth. OxBChV

Dewdrops. John Clare. VLP

Dexter. Joan Byers Grayston. PH

Dey Got Each and de Udder's Man. *Unknown.* WTO

Dey had a gread big pahty down to Tom's de othah night. The
Party. Paul Laurence Dunbar. AmNP (1974 ed.)

Dey is times in life when Nature. When de Co'n Pone's Hot.
Paul Laurence Dunbar. AmVN

Dey was talkin' in de cabin, dey was talkin' in de hall. When
Dey 'Listed Colored Soldiers. Paul Laurence Dunbar. BPo

Dey's a so't o' threatenin' feelin' in de blowin' of de breeze.
Soliloquy of a Turkey. Paul Laurence Dunbar. BPo

Dharma is like an avocado!, The. Avocado. Gary Snyder.
CNW

Dharma law. Chorus. Jack Kerouac. *Fr.* Mexico City Blues.
PiAm

Diagnosis of our hist'ry proves, A. The Rejected "National
Hymns." "Orpheus C. Kerr." OBAL

Diagnostic Center. Kenneth "Spider" Nicholson. DNGG

Dial Tone, The. Howard Nemerov. NowV

Dialect Quatrain. Marcus B. Christian. AmNP (1974 ed.)

Dialectique. Hugh Maxton. CIP

Dialogue. Agathias Scholasticus, *tr. fr. Greek by* Dudley Fitts.
OLR

Dialogue. George Herbert. BoReV

Dialogue, A. David Ignatow. NNaP

Dialogue, A. Pope. POL

Dialogue. Adrienne Rich. TAP

Dialogue. James Tipton. HeS

Dialogue after Enjoyment. Abraham Cowley. BoLoP

Dialogue between Araphil and Castara, A. William Habington.
SCP-2

Dialogue between Horace and Lydia, A. Horace, *tr. fr. Latin by*
Robert Herrick. Odes, III, 9. OBVE

Dialogue between King William and the Late King James on the
Banks of the Boyne, A. Charles Blount. APAS

Dialogue between Old England and New, A. Anne Bradstreet.
EAP

Dialogue between Sir John Jobson and Harry Homespun. John
Byrom. EPC

Dialogue between the Resolved Soul and Created Pleasure, A.
Andrew Marvell. BoReV; OAEL-1; PAIC

Dialogue between the Soul and Body, A. Andrew Marvell.
HAP; MetP; OAEL-1; PAIC; PPP; SCP-1

Dialogue betwixt [*or* between] Time and a Pilgrim, A. Aurelian
Townsend. NOBE; OAEL-1; SCP-2

Dialogue 4 1 Voice Only. Doug Fetherling. NeAC

Dialogue in Praise of the Owl and Cuckoo. Shakespeare. *See*
Love's Labour's Lost: Spring *and* Winter.

Dialogue of Absence 'twixt Lucasia and Orinda, A. Katherine
Philips. SCP-2

Dialogue of Self and Soul, A. W. B. Yeats. CABA (1972 ed.);
CMoP (1970 ed.); ExPo (1973 ed.); NoAM; PAIC
"Living man is blind and drinks his drop, A," *sel.* PoIA

Dialogue of Watching, A. Kenneth Rexroth. MiP

Dialogue—2 Dollmakers. Gregory Corso. VoA

Diameter of the bomb was thirty centimeters, The. Lament.
Yehuda Amichai, *tr. by* Ruth Nevo. VWA

Diamond, The. Daniel Moore. MIT

Diamond Body. "Hugh MacDiarmid." TwMBP

Diamond Cut Diamond. Ewart Milne. ECBV; PCat

Diamond Cutters, The. Adrienne Rich. NIL

*Diamond, The,* is a ship my lads.  The Bonnie Ship *The Diamond.*
  *Unknown.*  FSW

Diamond of a morning, A.  Morning Song.  Sara Teasdale.
  Moon

Diana, sels.  Henry Constable.
  "Blame not my hart for flieng up too hie."  ESo
  "Deere to my soule, then leave me not forsaken."  AAS
  "Faire sunne, if you would have me praise your light."  ESo
  "Falslie doth envie of your praises blame."  ESo
  "Flie lowe deare love, thy sunne dost thou not see?"  ESo
  "Fouler hides, The. (as closelie as he may)."  ESo
  "Frend of mine, pitieng my helplesse love, A."  ESo
  "If true love might true love's reward obtaine."  ESo
  "It maie be, Love my death doth not pretend."  ESo
  "Ladie in beautie and in favor rare."  ESo
  "Mine eye with all the deadlie sinnes is fraught."  ESo
  "Miracle of the world, I never will deny."  NIL
  "Much sorrow in it selfe my love doth move."  ESo
  "My lady's presence makes the roses red."  ESo; NIL; WIF
  "My Reason absent did mine eyes require."  ESo
  "Pitie refusing my poore love to feed."  ESo
  "Resolv'd to love, unworthie to obtaine."  ESo
  "Sonne his journey ending in the west, The."  ESo
  "Sweete hand, the sweet but creull bowe thou art."  ESo
  "Thine eye the glasse where I behold my hart."  ESo
  To His Absent Diana, *introd.*  ESo
  "To live in hell, and heaven to behold."  AAS; ILP (1975 ed.)
  "Uncivill sickness, hast thou no regard."  ESo
  "When your perfections to my thoughts appeare."  ESo
  "Whilst eccho cryes, what shall become of mee."  AAS
  "Wonder it is, and pitie ist, that shee."  ESo

Dianae Sumus in Fide.  Catullus, *tr. fr. Latin by* Horace Gregory.
  Moon

Diane.  Stewart McIntosh.  SLP

Diapered in hospital linen.  The Recovery Room: Lying-in.
  Helen Chasin.  IHMS

Diaphenia.  Henry Chettle.  NOBE

Diary of a Church Mouse.  John Betjeman.  OxBTC

Diary of the Sailors of the North, A.  David Shulman, *tr. fr.
  Hebrew by author.*  VWA

Diary of the Waning Moon, The, *sel.*  Abutsu the Nun, *tr. fr.
  Japanese by* Edwin O. Reischauer.
  "Shore wind is cold on my travel clothes, The."  PBWP

Diaspora Jews.  Rachel Boimwall, *tr. fr. Yiddish by* Gabriel Preil
  *and* Howard Schwartz.  VWA

Dic Siôn Dafydd.  Thomas Jacob Thomas, *tr. fr. Welsh by*
  H. Idris Bell.  OBW

Dice Player, The.  Dale Matthews.  AAN

Dichterliebe.  Robert Klein Engler.  AMV–81

Dick and Jane.  Judith Kroll.  AmPA

Dick and Will and Charles and I.  Autumn.  Elizabeth Madox
  Roberts.  PoTa

Dick is the one with the weenie.  Dick and Jane.  Judith Kroll.
  AmPA

Dick Powell.  Ronald Koertge.  CPA; PoW

Dick Swash.  John Taylor.  SCP–2

Dick Szymanski.  Ogden Nash.  SPo

Dick Turpin and Black Bess.  *Unknown.*  AmFP
  (Bonnie Black Bess).  BPAW

Dickens Characters.  Robert Morgan.  HeHu

Dickens in Camp.  Bret Harte.  BPAW

Dictionaries cannot.  Luck.  Elaine Epstein.  AMV–81

Dictionary.  Hildegarde Flanner.  WPW

Dictionary Is an *Hist*orian, The: A Found Political Poem.  Judith
  McCombs.  IHMS

Dictum: For a Masque of Deluge.  W. S. Merwin.  NoAM

Did all the lets and bars appear.  The March into Virginia.
  Herman Melville.  HAP; PiAm; TAP

Did any seer of ancient time forbode.  The Steam Threshing
  Machine.  Charles Tennyson Turner.  VLP

Did ever lord such noble house maintain.  Edward Taylor.
  Preparatory Meditations: First Series, IX.  SCP–2

Did he meet Lud at the Fleet Gate?–did he count the top.  David
  Jones.  *Fr.* The Anathemata.  EBEV

Did he strike soundings off Vecta Insula?  Angle-Land.  David
  Jones.  The Anathemata, III.  NoAM; TwMBP

Did I, my lines intend for publick view.  The Introduction.
  Countess of Winchilsea.  SBG

Did my father curse his father for his lust I wonder.  The Young
  Man Thinks of His Sons.  R. A. K. Mason.  ATNZ

Did Not.  Thomas Moore.  BoLoP

Did our best moment last.  Emily Dickinson.  NOBA

Did she mean that much to him that he was.  Achilles.  Phillip
  Corwin.  AMV–80

Did the harebell loose her girdle.  Emily Dickinson.  PiAm

Did the people of Viet Nam.  What Were They Like?  Denise
  Levertov.  HeIP; NIL; PPoD; TCP; VGW; WPE

"Did they dare, did they dare to slay Eoghan Ruadh O'Neill?"
  Lament for the Death of Eoghan Ruadh O'Neill.  Thomas
  Osborne Davis.  PFIr

Did they send me away from my cat and my wife.  Gunner.
  Randall Jarrell.  OFD

Did you ever, ever, ever.  *Unknown.*  FaBoNo; GBP

Did you ever go to meetin', Uncle Joe, Uncle Joe?  Uncle Joe.
  *Unknown.*  FSW

Did you ever have a chipmunk for a friend?  Jessie Orton Jones.
  Secrets, XII.  CTV

Did you ever hear about Cocaine Lil?  Cocaine Lil and Morphine
  Sue.  *Unknown.*  GBP; MAT; MiP; PeBB

Did you ever hear of Editor Whedon.  Daisy Fraser.  Edgar Lee
  Masters.  *Fr.* Spoon River Anthology.  CMoP (1970 ed.);
  HAP

Did you ever hear of good Earl Brand.  Earl Brand.  *Unknown.*
  PeBB

Did you ever hear tell of sweet Betsy from Pike.  Sweet Betsy
  from Pike.  *Unknown.*  FaBoBa; PeBB

Did you ever hear the story 'bout Willy the Weeper?  Willy the
  Weeper.  *Unknown.*  FSW

Did you ever see a muskrat, Sally Ann?  Sally Ann.  *Unknown.*
  FSW

Did you ever see an alligator.  Arlo Will.  Edgar Lee Masters.
  *Fr.* Spoon River Anthology.  PBMP

Did you ever see two Yankees.  Give My Regards to Broadway.
  George M. Cohan.  BLSo; FSN

Did you ever think as a hearse rolls by.  The Hearse Song.
  *Unknown.*  FSW

Did you ever wait for daylight when the stars along the river.
  The Shallows of the Ford.  Henry Herbert Knibbs.  BPAW

Did you exist, ever?  Two Memories.  Cleopatra Mathis.  AAN

Did you go at all to Chicago?  The Stockyard.  J. C. Squire.
  OxBTC

Did you hear?  The Old Warrior Terror.  Alice Walker.  NVAP

Did you hear of the curate who mounted his mare.  The Priest
  and the Mulberry Tree.  Thomas Love Peacock.  *Fr.*
  Crotchet Castle.  PoTa

Did you make the bluebells ring.  The Road to School.  Joy M.
  Lane.  AMV–81

Did you see the sun blotted from sky.  Baltimore Eclipse.
  Charles Plymell.  MIT

Did You See the *Times* Today?  Louis Wyse.  SFF

Did you tackle that trouble that came your way.  How Did You
  Die?  Edmund Vance Cooke.  CTV; PeD

Did you think I was talking about my life?  Adrienne Rich.  *Fr.*
  Ghazals: Homage to Ghalib.  NIL

Did you think you could hide from me?  A Song for Sigmund Freud.  Kelly Cherry.  PPoD

Didactic Sonnet.  Melvin Walker La Follette.  PoA

Diddie Wa Diddie.  *Unknown.*  BluL

Diddlety, diddlety, dumpty.  *Unknown.*  MG

Didn't He Ramble.  Will Handy.  FSW

Didn't I teach you that?  To My Former Student on the Occasion of Birth.  Madeline Bass.  WBN

Didn't It Rain.  *Unknown.*  DuDr

Didn't My Lord Deliver Daniel?  *Unknown.*  AH, *with music*; FSW; WIF

Didn't the water rinse off.  The Drowned Darling.  Danny L. Rendleman.  TC

Didn't you notice/ there were angels around.  Cavatina.  Patricia Ball.  PMW

Didst thou not find the place inspired.  Upon My Lady Carlisle's Walking in Hampton-Court Garden.  Sir John Suckling.  CaPo

Dido.  John Ashbery.  *Fr.* Two Sonnets.  CAPP; VGW

Dido: Swarming.  Kathleen Spivack.  PoA

Didymus.  Louis MacNeice.  LoAs

Die Bauernhochzeit.  Kendrick Smithyman.  ATNZ

Died from fatigue, three laundresses together all.  *Unknown.*  FaBoEE

Died, Sir Charles Wetherell's laundress, honest Sue.  *Unknown.*  FaBoEE

Diehard.  Judith Moffett.  PoA

Diella, *sels.*  Richard Lynche.
    "But thou my deere sweet-sounding lute be still," XVI.  AAS
    "What sugred termes, what all-perswading arte," IV.  AAS; NIL

Difference.  T. H. Jones.  OBW

Difference, The.  Stoddard King.  OBAL

Difference, The.  Tadhg Dall O'Huiginn, *tr. fr. Irish by* Robin Flower.  BIrV

Difference, The.  *Unknown.*  CTV

Difference between despair, The.  Emily Dickinson.  NoAM

Difference between reacting to a storm, The.  Storm and Quiet.  Richard Eberhart.  AMV–81

Difference of Zoos, A.  Gregory Corso.  VGW

Differences.  Ray A. Young Bear.  NU

Different.  Clere Parsons.  FaBoTw (1975 ed.)

Different Image, A.  Dudley Randall.  BPo; CNA; FF; NoAM; TAP

Different Persuasions.  Marge Piercy.  *See* Nothing More Will Happen.

Different wind, taller skies, A.  Footsteps of Spring.  Hayim Nachman Bialik, *tr. by* Ruth Nevo.  VWA

Difficult achievement for true lovers, A.  The Starred Coverlet.  Robert Graves.  BuTh; LoAs

Difficult Guest, A.  Carroll Watson Rankin.  TDH

"Difficult ordinary happiness."  In the Woods.  Adrienne Rich.  PiAm

Difficult to recall an emotion that is dead.  The Patient Is Rallying.  Weldon Kees.  AnMo

Difficulty to think at the end of day, The.  A Rabbit as King of the Ghosts.  Wallace Stevens.  PBMP

Difficulty was, it was, The.  In the Beginning Was a Word.  Robert Graves.  PoA

Diffugere Nives.  Horace, *tr. fr. Latin by* A. E. Housman.  Odes, IV, 7.  OBVE

Dig My Grave.  *Unknown.*  AmFP; FSW

Diggers, The.  W. S. Merwin.  EAS

Digging.  Seamus Heaney.  BIrV; CIP; IPM; MPo

Digging.  Edward Thomas.  FSFS; OxBTC

Digging earth for puddles, she would wake stranded.  Steps.  Roberta Hill.  VoR

Digging for China.  Richard Wilbur.  BuTh; IP; NCSH; PiAm; TH

Digging for Indians.  Gary Gildner.  AmPA

Digging for Singapore.  David James.  TC

Digging through these hill.  Stump Farming.  James Tipton.  TC

Diggle Mill.  Glyn Hughes.  LP

Dignified things, may I your leaves implore.  To the Respective Judges.  *Unknown.*  APAS

Dilemma.  David Ignatow.  VGW

Dilemma of a Dead Man about to Wake Up.  Stanley Burnshaw.  SPT

Diligent in the burnt fields above the sea.  Find.  Josephine Miles.  WPE

Dill.  Marie Harris.  MMD

Dillar, a dollar, A,/ A ten o'clock scholar.  Mother Goose.  MG

Dilly Song, The.  *Unknown.*  *See* Carol of the Numbers.

Dim as the borrowed beams of moon and stars.  Reason and Religion.  Dryden.  *Fr.* Religio Laici.  BoReV; OAEL–1

Dim, gradual thinning of the shapeless gloom.  The Troops.  Siegfried Sassoon.  CMoP (1970 ed.)

Dime Call.  Albert Goldbarth.  VWA

Dimple.  Coleman Barks.  *Fr.* Body Poems.  NVAP

Dimpling in his cheeks.  Smile at the Birdie.  Polly Mann.  NPW

Dinah and Villikens, *with music.*  *Unknown.*  RDB

Dinch me, dark God, having smoked me out.  John Berryman.  *Fr.* Dream Songs.  CAPP

Diner.  A. R. Ammons.  POL

Diner, The.  Gloria Bussel Koster.  NPW

Diners in the Kitchen, The.  James Whitcomb Riley.  GDP; OBAL

Ding, Dong, Bell.  Eve Merriam.  *Fr.* The Inner-City Mother Goose.  IPWM

Ding, dong, bell/ Pussy's in the well!  Mother Goose.  MG

Ding Dong Dollar.  Hamish Henderson.  FSW

Ding Dong Merrily on High, *with music.*  G. R. Woodward, *tr. fr. French.*  GSB

Dingle Bank.  Edward Lear.  FaBoNo

Dingman's Marsh.  John Moore.  NCSH

Dingty diddlety.  My Mammy's Maid.  *Unknown.*  BBL

Dingy donkey, formal and unchanged, A.  A Fable.  John Hookham Frere.  FaBoCo

Dining Out with Doug and Frank.  James Schuyler.  NYP

Dink's Song.  *Unknown.*  FSW

Dinky.  Theodore Roethke.  OBAL

Dinner, The.  Gregory Orr.  POL

Dinner at Lüchow's.  The invisible man.  Lüchow's and After.  L. E. Sissman.  NYP

Dinner Guest: Me.  Langston Hughes.  BPo; SS

Dinograd's Petticoat.  *Unknown, tr. fr. Welsh by* Gwyn Williams.  OBW

Dinoland.  Thomas Reiter.  PPoD

Dinosaur.  Bonnie Hearn.  AMV–80

Dinosaur Bones, The.  Carl Sandburg.  TH

Dinosaur died, was consumed by the soil, The.  Pre-History Repeats.  Robert J. McKent, Jr.  QQQ

Dinosaur Tracks in Beit Zayit.  Shirley Kaufman.  FiCP

Dinosaurs are not all dead, The.  Steam Shovel.  Charles Malman.  DuDr

Dinosaurus courteously, The.  Leaving the Dance.  Alexander Whitaker.  NIL

Dionysius.  Sophia de Mello Breyner Andresen, *tr. fr. Portuguese by* Allan Francovich.  PBWP

Dip, dip, allebadar.  *Unknown.*  GBP

Dip, dip, dip. *Unknown.* GBP

Dipsychus, *sels.* Arthur Hugh Clough.
"As I sat at the café, I said to myself," *fr.* Pt. II, sc. ii. OAEL–2; VPC
(How Pleasant It Is to Have Money.) NOBE
" 'There is no God,' the wicked saith," *fr.* Pt. I, sc. v. VPC
(There Is No God.) NOBE
"Yes, it is beautiful ever, let foolish men rail at it never," *fr.* Pt. II, sc. ii. VLP

Diptych. Velma West Sykes. IHMS

Dirce. Walter Savage Landor. *Fr.* Pericles and Aspasia, CCXXX. EBEV; FaBoEE; GBL; HAP; ILP (1975 ed.); NOBE; OAEL–2; PoPle; VLP; WeW

Dirdum drum. The Cat's Song. *Unknown.* GBP

Direct, The/ connection/ to the sun. Warm Day in Winter. David McAleavey. PoUp

Direction. Barbara Guest. WPE

Direction. Roberta Hill. CDW

Direction. Alonzo Lopez. VW

Direction, The. May Miller. PPoD

Direction/ is in you. The Tree. E. R. Cole. AATT

Directions. William Matthews. AmPA

Directions that you took. Old Haven. Jean Garrigue. UsP; WPE

Directions to the Nomad. James Welch. CDW

Directive. Robert Frost. CABA (1972 ed.); CMoP (1970 ed.); HAP; ILP (1975 ed.); MAT; NoAM; NOBA; PiAm; PPP; TT

Director of the Museum, The. Roderick Watson. MIS

Dirge: "Body lies under the ground." Gavin Bantock. OxBTC

Dirge, A: "Call for the robin-redbreast and the wren." John Webster. *See* Call for the Robin Redbreast and the Wren.

Dirge: "Come away, come away, death." Shakespeare. *See* Come Away, Come Away, Death.

Dirge: "Fear no more the heat o' the sun." Shakespeare. *See* Fear No More the Heat o' the Sun.

Dirge: "Glories of our blood and state, The." James Shirley. *See* Glories of Our Blood and State, The.

Dirge: "He lies in state." Austin Clarke. CIP

Dirge: "I make this dirge for you Miss Mary Binning I miss you." *Unknown, tr. fr. Hawaiian by* Armand Schwerner. BoWoP; RRA

Dirge: "It is the endless dance of the dead." Quincy Troupe. PoBA

Dirge: "1–2–3 was the number he played but today the number came 3–2–1." Kenneth Fearing. FF; HeIP; HoPM (1975 ed.); InPK; NIL; SPT

Dirge, A: "Rough wind, that moanest loud." Shelley. CABA (1972 ed.); GrRo; ILP (1975 ed.); InPK; NOBE; TPo; UsP; VoPo

Dirge, A: "Why were you born when the snow was falling?" Christina Rossetti. SBG; VLP; VPC

Dirge for a Solider. George Henry Boker. PeD

Dirge for Fajuyi, *sel.* Omobayode Arowa, *tr. fr. Yoruba.* "Dekunle, handsome man, hail!" WTO

Dirge for Fidele. Shakespeare. *See* Fear No More the Heat o' the Sun.

Dirge for the New Sunrise. Edith Sitwell. CMoP (1970 ed.)

Dirge for the Year. Shelley. FSFS

Dirge for Three Trumpets. *Unknown (Chainpoem).* EAS

Dirge in "Cymbeline." William Collins.
*See* Song from Shakespeare's Cymbelyne, A.

Dirge in Woods. George Meredith. FF; VLP

Dirge Sung at Death. *Tr. fr. Maori by* John White. WTO

Dirge without Music. Edna St. Vincent Millay. CMoP (1970 ed.); DL; NoAM; SBG

Dirt Dumping. "Mark Twain." TDH
(Limerick: "Man hired by John Smith and Co., A.") FaBoNo

Dirt Road. Tom Hennen. HeS

Dirt road rose abruptly through a wood, The. Snake Hill. Jay Parini. AMV–81

Dirt under the fingernails of the window-ledge. Spring Street in '58. Derek Walcott. NYP

Dirty-billed Freeze Footy, The. Judith Hemschemeyer. TV

Dirty Colours of Her Kiss Have Just, The. E. E. Cummings. Epi

Dirty Dozens, The. *Unknown.* BluL

Dirty money and the sleazy hearts, The. The Matadors. Josephine Jacobsen. TAP

Dirty socks in dirty sneakers. Sorting, Wrapping, Packing, Stuffing. James Schuyler. NoAM

Dirty Word, The. Karl Shapiro. InPK; IP; PoA

Dis Aliter Visum; or, Le Byron de Nos Jours. Robert Browning. VLP

Dis sun are hot. This Sun Is Hot. *Unknown.* BPo

Disabled. Wilfred Owen. BiP; CMoP (1970 ed.); FF; InPS; NoAM; OBW; OxBTC; PoTa; PSN; VoPo

Disabled Debauchee, The. Earl of Rochester. BoLoP; HAP; NOBL; OBSV; PPP; WeW
(Maimed Debauchee, The.) CABA (1972 ed.); NIL

Disappearances. Sean Lucy. IPM

Disappointment, The. Aphra Behn. SBG; SCP–2

Disaster. Charles Stuart Calverley. SpRo

Disasters numb within us, The. Life at War. Denise Levertov. NMM; VGW

Disciple, The. Oscar Wilde. OAEL–2

Discipline. George Herbert. BoReV; ExPo (1973 ed.); NOBE; PAIC; SCP–1

Disco Fever. Barry Schechter. EC

Disconnection, The. Rita Mae Brown. IHMS

Disconsolate I/ from the thinning line. Witness to Death. Richmond Lattimore. VGW

Discontented Satyre, The. Thomas Lodge. TVS

Discontented Student, The. St. George Tucker. OBAL

Discontents in Devon. Robert Herrick. CaPo; ILP (1975 ed.); PAIC; POL

Discordants, *sels.* Conrad Aiken.
"Dead Cleopatra lies in a crystal casket," IV. PoA
"Music I heard with you was more than music, " I. CMoP (1970 ed.); ILP (1975 ed.); NOBA
(Bread and Music.) VoPo

Discovered an old rocking-horse in Woolworth's. You'd Better Believe Him. Brian Patten. LP

Discoveries of Fire, The. Lucille Clifton. TSWA

Discovering. Sharon Scott. JB

Discovering an Island. Edward Lowbury. PMW

Discovering Parts of a Body. Rhyll McMaster. CAAP; GAS

Discovery. Hilaire Belloc. TPo

Discovery, The. Monk Gibbon. PFIr

Discovery. Myra Cohn Livingston. LCL

Discovery, The. J. C. Squire. OFD

Discovery of LSD a True Story, The. Anselm Hollo. AcAn

Discovery of the New World. Carter Revard. VoR

Discovery of the Pacific, The. Thom Gunn. HeIP; MIT

Discrimination. Kenneth Rexroth. MPA

Disdain Returned. Thomas Carew. CaPo; ILP (1975 ed.)
(He That Loves a Rosy Cheek.) PoPle

Disdainful Mistress, The. *Malay Oral Tradition, tr. by* R. J. Wilkinson *and* R. O. Winstedt. WTO

Disdaining butterflies. The Woman Who Loved Worms. Colette Inez. AATT; NMM; RiTi; WBN

Diseases of the Moon. Doug Fetherling. NeAC; POL

Disguises. Thomas Edward Brown. VLP

Dish of Tea, The. Philip Freneau. EAP

Dishonest Mailmen, The. Robert Creeley. PiAm

Dishonest Miller, The. *Unknown.* AmFP

Disillusion. *Tr. fr. Tewa Indian by* H. J. Spinden. WTO

Disillusionment. Claribel Alegria, *tr. fr. Spanish by* Darwin Flakoll. AMV-80

Disillusionment of Ten o'Clock. Wallace Stevens. CMoP (1970 ed.); FF; InPK; InPS; NIL; PoIA; PPod; PPoe; SFF; STS; WeW

Disinherited, The. Charles Spear. ATNZ

Dismantled Ship, The. Walt Whitman. CABA (1972 ed.); NoAM

Dismissing Progress and Its Progenitors. George Reavey. EAS

Dismissing reports and men, he put pressure on the wax. Offa's Laws. Geoffrey Hill. *Fr.* Mercian Hymns. HAP; PSN

Disobedient Statue, The. Marina LaPalma. PoW

Disobliging Bear, The. Carolyn Wells. TDH

Disordering, The. Lynda Yates. AMV-81

Disorientation. Rainer Schulte. SES

Dispart the frost-white boughs, and lo! Promised Land. Charles Spear. ATNZ

Dispatch Number Nine. Doug Fetherling. NeAC

Dispatch Number Sixteen. Doug Fetherling. NeAC

Dispatch Number Sixty. Doug Fetherling. NeAC

Dispensary, The, *sels.* Sir Samuel Garth.
  "As bold Mirmillo the grey dawn descries." PMW
  "How impotent a deity am I!" OBSV
  "Oft has this planet rolled around the sun." OBSV
  Portrait of a Physician. PMW
  "This wight all mercenary projects tries." OBSV

Displacement. Horace Hamilton. AMV-80

Displacement, The. Hubert Witheford. ATNZ

Displacement. Alan Ziegler. AAN

Display thy breasts, my Julia: there let me. Upon Julia's Breasts. Robert Herrick. CaPo; SCP-1

Displays of Skill: The Bat. Ruth Herschberger. WBN

Dispossessed, The. John Berryman. VGW

Dispraise of Absalom, The. *Unknown, tr. fr. Irish by* Robin Flower. BIrV

Dispute of the Heart and Body of François Villon, The. Villon, *tr. fr. French by* Swinburne. OBVE

Disqualification. Elizabeth Brewster. MMD

Disquieting Muses, The. Sylvia Plath. NMM; SBG; TV

Dissatisfaction with Metaphysics. William Empson. CMoP (1970 ed.)

Dissenters' Thanksgiving for the Late Declaration, The. *Unknown.* APAS

Dissipation. Lonnie L. Landrum. DNGG

Dissolution, The. John Donne. ILP (1975 ed.)

Dissonance. Cedric Whitman. AMV-80

Distance. Peter Everwine. NNaP

Distance Anywhere, The. Kenneth O. Hanson. MPA; NIL

Distance back is greater, The. Return. Michael Anania. HeS

Distance brings proportion. From here. Tao in the Yankee Stadium Bleachers. John Updike. LiSp; SPo

Distance comes between us like a knife. Leaving the Prison. Joseph Bruchac. FAF

Distance deceives. Novelists mistake. Day Sailing. David R. Slavitt. CoPAm

Distance doesn't matter, Francisco. Extracts: From the Journal of Elisa Lynch. Maura Stanton. AmPA

Distance drums your words into my ears, The; it's good. Autobiography, Chapter XII: Hearing Montana. Jim Barnes. AMV-81

Distance from the Sea, A. Weldon Kees. NoAM

Distance is swept by the smooth. Radar. Alan Ross. FF; NowV

Distance Spills Itself. Yocheved Bat-Miriam, *tr. fr. Hebrew by* Robert Friend. VWA

Distance strengthens/ my intentions. Disorientation. Rainer Schulte. SES

Distances, The. Jim Carroll. PoA

Distances, The. W. S. Merwin. NOBA

Distances, The. Charles Olson. PiAm

Distances. Linda Pastan. RiTi

Distances They Keep, The. Howard Nemerov. BoAnP

Distant Drum, The. Calvin C. Hernton. CTBA; FF; TPo

Distant fog-horns bicker, the near ones boom, The. Toward Light. Maurice Lindsay. MS

Distant Lover, The. Kraft Rompf. AAN

Distant Orgasm, The. James Tate. AmPA

Distant Runners, The. Mark Van Doren. GOA

Distant Seychelles are not so remote, The. Eireann. Osbert Lancaster. *Fr.* Afternoons with Baedeker. NOBL

Distant Winter, The. Philip Levine. VGW

Distant words, The. Childbirth. Anne S. Perlman. PoW

Distilled Water. M. K. Joseph. ATNZ

Distinction. Charles Tomlinson. CMoP (1970 ed.)

Distinguish carefully between these two. The Justice of the Peace. Hilaire Belloc. OBSV

Distinguished old one-legged colonel, A. The One-legged Colonel. *Unknown.* TDH

Distortions. Pearse Hutchinson. CIP

Distracted with care. The Despairing Lover. William Walsh. NOBL

Distribution of Honours for Literature. Walter Savage Landor. FaBoEE

District, The: Both Sides of Chandler River. Ted Enslin. FAF

Distrust. Robert Herrick. CaPo

Disturb me not, oh bouyant youths! *Tr. fr. Maori by* John White. WTO

Disturb the balance, broken bird. The Birdsong. William Carlos Williams. TT

Disturbances. Anthony Thwaite. MPo

Disturbing the Tarantula. Christopher Middleton. TwMBP

Disused Shed in County Wexford, A. Derek Mahon. CIP; IPM

Disused Temple, The. Norman Cameron. OxBTC

Dithering towards the horizon. Horizon without Landscape. Tom Lowenstein. VWA

Dithyramb, A. John Hall. SCP-2

Ditty. Roger Hecht. NowV

Dive. Langston Hughes. NYP

Dive could come who was its fledgling first, The. Nijinsky. Parker Tyler. PoA

Dive for dreams. E. E. Cummings. OLR

Diver. Robert Francis. EcS; LiSp; SPo

Diver, The. Robert Hayden. BPo; LiSp

Diver, The. Nikos Phocas, *tr. fr. Greek by* Kimon Friar. AMV-81

Diver go down. Diver. Robert Francis. EcS; LiSp; SPo

Divers, The. Peter Quennell. EcS

Divers. Robert Haven Schauffler. EcS

Divers [*or* Dyvers] doth[e] use as I have heard and know. Sir Thomas Wyatt. AAS; ILP (1975 ed.)

Diversions for an Unhappy Princess. *Unknown. Fr.* The Squyer of Lowe Degre. OxBM

Diversions of the Re-Echo Club. Carolyn Wells. OBAL

Diverting History of John Gilpin, The. William Cowper. BBL; LAuP; PoPle

Dives and Lazarus. *Unknown.* AmFP; FaBoBa

Dives, when you and I go down to Hell. To Dives. Hilaire Belloc. OBSV

Divide, The. Kenneth O. Hanson. MPA

Divide your bread in two. Heavenly Jerusalem, of the Earth. Leah Goldberg, *tr. by* Robert Friend VWA

Divided. Jean Ingelow. SpRo; VLP

Dividends. Kenneth Fearing. SPT

Dividing the House. James Richardson. AMV-81

Divina Commedia, *sels.* Dante, *tr. fr. Italian.*
  Inferno, *tr. by* Mark Musa. NAWM-1
    "And now we walked along the solid mire," XV, *tr. by* Robert Lowell. OBVE.
    Canto I, *ll.* 1-21, *tr. fr. Italian by* 5 *diff. trs.* HoPM (1975 ed.)
    Guido da Montefeltro, *fr.* XXVII, *tr. by* Longfellow. Epi
    "Like fire-flies that the peasant on the hill," *fr.* XXVI, *tr. by* Laurence Binyon. Prf
    "Midway the journey of this life I was 'ware," *fr.* I, *tr. by* Laurence Binyon. ExPo (1973 ed.)
    "Now begin wailing notes; the flesh is thrilled," *fr.* V, *tr. by* Laurence Binyon. ExPo (1973 ed.)
    Pier delle Vigne, XII, *tr. by* John Ciardi. HoPM (1975 ed.)
    Ulysses, *fr.* XXVI, *tr. by* Longfellow. Epi
  Paradiso, *much abr., tr. by* Laurence Binyon. NAWM-1
    Vision of God, The, *fr.* XXXIII, *tr. by* Laurence Binyon. ExPo (1973 ed.)
    "Within the deep and luminous subsistence of the High Light," *fr.* XXXIII. ILwL
  Purgatorio
    "As when his first beams tremble in the sky," XXVII, *tr. by* Laurence Binyon. NAWM-1
    "Earnest to explore within and all around," fr. XXVIII, *tr. by* Shelley. OBVE
    "In that hour when the heat of day no more," XIX, *tr. by* Laurence Binyon. NAWM-1
    "Now hoisteth sail the pinnace of my wit," I-II, *tr. by* Laurence Binyon. NAWM-1
    "Now when those Seven of the First Heaven stood still," XXX-XXXI, *tr. by* Laurence Binyon. NAWM-1
    Virgil's Farewell to Dante, *fr.* XXVII, *tr. by* Laurence Binyon. FaBoTw (1975 ed.)

Divina Commedia (*poems introductory to* Longfellow's *tr. of the* Divine Comedy, I–VI). Longfellow. TAP
  (Sonnets on the Divina Commedia.) ILP (1975 ed.)
  "Oft have I seen at some cathedral door," I. HAP; IPWM; LFH; PAIC; PPM

Divination. Jerred Metz. VWA

Divination by a Daffodil. Robert Herrick. CaPo

Divine Blacksmith, The. Matthew Prior. FaBoNo

Divine destroyer, pity me no more. A la Bourbon. Richard Lovelace. CaPo

Divine Image, A ("Cruelty has a human heart"). Blake. MBPR; STS

Divine Image, The ("To mercy pity peace and love"). Blake. *Fr.* Songs of Innocence. BoReV; ILP (1975 ed.); LAuP; MBPR; NOBE; OAEL-2; PoIA; PPP; STS; TT

Divine Insect, The. John Hall Wheelock. PPoD

Divine Love. Michael Benedikt. AmPA; ConAP

Divine Love. *Unknown.* OAEL-1; OxBM

Divine Lover, The. Phineas Fletcher. *Fr.* The Divine Wooer. BoReV

Divine Thalia, strike the harmonious lute. On the Soft and Gentle Motions of Eudora. Anne Killigrew. SCP-2

Divine winds upon the waters, The. Hai. Stuart Z. Perkoff. VWA

Divine Wooer, The, *sel.* Phineas Fletcher.
  Divine Lover, The. BoReV

Divinely Superfluous Beauty. Robinson Jeffers. HeIP; PiAm

Diviner, The. Seamus Heaney. HeHu

Diviners, The. Mary Oliver. WPE

Diving. Shiro Murano, *tr. fr. Japanese by* Ichiro Kono *and* Rikutaro Fukuda. SPo

Diving for wrecks or sunken treasure, see. The Lovely Swimmers. Richmond Lattimore. EcS

Diving into the Wreck. Adrienne Rich. NIL; NoAM; NOBA

Divinities. W. S. Merwin. PoA

Divorce. Kate Jennings. AMV-80

Divorce. Erica Jong. GP

Divorce, The. Adrianne Marcus. CPA

Divorce. Bink Noll. MAT

Divorce. Skaidrite Stelzer. TC

Divorce. Siv Widerberg, *tr. fr. Swedish by* Verne Moberg. CTBA

Divorce Dress, The. Jeanne Finley. AMV-80

Divorce of a Lover, The ("Divorce me nowe good death"). George Gascoigne. AAS

Dixie ("I wish I was in the land of cotton"), *with music.* Daniel Decatur Emmett. BLSH; BLSo; FSW
  (Dixie's Land.) PSoN

Dixie ("Southrons, hear your country call you!"). Albert Pike. BTTM

Dizzy Giraffe, The. *Unknown.* TDH

Djanggawul Song-Cycle, *much abr. Aborigine Oral Tradition, tr. by* R. M. Berndt. WTO

Do all the good you can. John Wesley's Rule. John Wesley. CTV

Do any thing anything you will. Pigeon. Elouise Loftin. CNA

Do as they do in the Isle of Man. The Isle of Man. *Unknown.* GBP

Do but consider this small dust. The Hourglass. Ben Jonson. NIL; OAEL-1

Do diddle di do. Jim Jay Walter de la Mare. SO

Do explain to us, Return to Dachau. B. Z. Niditch. AMV-81

Do Ghouls? Lilian Moore. IWK

"Do I see a hat in the road?" I said. The Old Sussex Road. Ian Serraillier. FPB

Do I sleep? do I dream? Further Language from Truthful James. Bret Harte. FaBoCo; NOBL

Do Li A. *Unknown.* GBP

Do, Lord, Remember Me. *Unknown.* AmFP

Do my Johnny Boker. Johnny Boker. *Unknown.* FSW

Do nettles mar the month of May. Nettles in May. Euros Bowen, *tr. by author.* OBW

Do Not Accompany Me. Shimon Halkin, *tr. fr. Hebrew by* Ruth Nevo. VWA

Do not account that for thine own. Isabella Whitney. *Fr.* A Sweet Nosegay, or Pleasant Posy. WPE

Do not ask: where? We Go. Karl Wolfskehl, *tr. by* Harry Zohn. VWA

Do not bathe her in blood. An Abortion. Frank O'Hara. CoPAm; TAP

Do not be a lost dog. Dogs of Santiago. Eugene McCarthy. BoAnP; GDP

Do not be taken in. Nature. Arthur J. Bull. HeHu

Do not conceal thy radiant eyes. To Cynthia: On Concealment of Her Beauty. Sir Francis Kynaston. NOBE

Do Not Dream. Natan Zach, *tr. fr. Hebrew by* Jon Silkin. BuTh

Do not enforce the tired wolf. Prelude to an Evening. John Crowe Ransom. EAS; ILP (1975 ed.)

Do Not Expect Again. C. Day Lewis. NoAM
  ("Do not expect again a phoenix hour.") CMoP (1970 ed.) OxBTC

Do not fear to put thy feet. Safe Swimming. Beaumont *and* Fletcher. *Fr.* The Faithful Shepherdess. BBL

Do Not Go Gentle into That Good Night. Dylan Thomas. BiP; BuTh; CABA (1972 ed.); DL; FF; HAP; HeIP; HoPM (1975 ed.); InPK; InPS; IP; IPWM; NoAM; NOBE; OAEL-2;

OxBTC; PAIC; PBMP; PoIA; PPM; PPoD; SoSe; TCP; TPo; TT; TVo; UnPo (1976 ed.); UsP; WeW; WIF

Do not hold my few years.   So We've Come at Last to Freud.   Alice Walker.   IHMS

Do not let any woman read this verse!   Deirdre.   James Stephens.   CMoP (1970 ed.); NoAM

Do not lift him from the bracken.   William Aytoun.   *Fr.* The Widow of Glencoe.   SLP

Do not look for him.   Elegy.   Leonard Cohen.   HeIP

Do not look there.   A Child.   Katherine Cole.   UsP

Do not place frill or border or bouquet.   At the Jewish Cemetery in Prague.   Oscar Levertin, *tr. by* Richard Burns *and* Göran Printz-Pahlson.   VWA

Do not stifle me with the strange scent.   Alien.   Donald Jeffrey Hayes.   AmNP (1974 ed.)

Do not suddenly break the branch, or.   Usk.   T. S. Eliot.   Landscapes, III.   BiP

Do Not Think.   Carol Freeman.   CNA

Do not think I am not grateful for your small.   Gratitude.   Louise Glück.   CAAP

Do not tremble, wife.   The Mistress Addresses the Wife.   Naomi Replansky.   GP

Do not weep, maiden, for war is kind.   War Is Kind, I.   Stephen Crane.   BiP; NOBA; PAIC; PiAm; TAP; VoPo; WIF

Do Nothing till You Hear from Me.   David Henderson.   CNA; PoBA

Do skyscrapers ever grow tired.   Skyscrapers.   Rachel Field.   ECBV

Do the Dead Know What Time It Is?   Kenneth Patchen.   CoPAm; HoPM (1975 ed.); PAIC

Do the largest stars terminate the world?   For All the Songs I Sing.   Alice Notley.   FiCh

Do ye hear the children weeping, O my brothers.   The Cry of the Children.   Elizabeth Barrett Browning.   VLP; VPC

Do ye ken hoo to fush for the salmon?   Master and Man.   Sir Henry Newbolt.   OxBTC

Do ye ken John Peel with his coat so gray?   *See* D'ye ken John Peel with his coat so gay?

Do you/ dig ray/ charles.   Ray Charles.   Sam Cornish.   CNA; NVAP

Do you ask me what I think of.   What I Think of Hiawatha.   J. W. Morris.   SpRo

Do you ask what the birds say?   Answer to a Child's Question.   Samuel Taylor Coleridge.   ECBV; OxBChV; PCOP; PoPle

Do you ever hear it?   Afterword: Song of Song.   James Broughton.   GP

Do you ever think of me, Kitty Kline?   Kitty Kline.   *Unknown.*   AmFP

Do you Fear the Wind?   Hamlin Garland.   PPM

Do you give yourself to me utterly.   Sleep.   Kenneth Slessor.   GAS

Do you have a sweet thought, Cerinthus.   Sulpicia, *tr. fr. Latin by* Aliki *and* Willis Barnstone.   BoWoP

Do you have hope for the future?   Thanks, Robert Frost.   David Ray.   PCho

Do you have "my wife" in States?   Two Vietnamese Women.   Herbert Krohn.   AAN

Do you hear, sir?   John Webster.   *Fr.* The White Devil.   SCP–2

Do you hear the blue owl shriek?   Blue Owl Song.   Alfred Kittner, *tr. by* Herbert Kuhner.   VWA

Do you know, I would quietly.   Rainer Maria Rilke, *tr. fr. German by* M. D. Herter Norton.   OLR

Do you know my/ slap-a-hand.   Main Man Blues.   Eugene B. Redmond.   GP

Do you know that once.   Overnight Guest.   Ramona Wilson.   VoR

Do you know that your soul is of my soul such part.   To My Son.   Margaret Johnston Griffin.   SoSe

Do you know what.   Fancy.   Robert Creeley.   NOBA

Do you know what is bad?   Bad and Good.   Alexander Resnikoff.   OSF

Do you know where I got my song?   My Song.   Hayim Nachman Bialik, *tr. by* Ruth Nevo.   VWA

Do you look for a rainbow, Love, in this wet weather.   Wet Weather.   Patricia Low.   VGW

Do You Love Me?   Robert Watson.   POL

"Do you love me?" I asked.   The Toad.   Gerald Locklin.   GP

Do You Need the Gold Ring?   Marc Allen Corren.   PoW

"Do you not find something very strange about him?"   The Assassination.   Robert Hillyer.   OFD

Do you not hear me calling, white deer with no horns!   Mongan Laments the Change That Has Come upon Him and His Beloved.   W. B. Yeats.   VLP

"Do you not hear the aziola cry?"   The Aziola.   Shelley.   EBEV

Do you, now, as the news becomes known.   Pay-off.   Kenneth Fearing.   CMoP (1970 ed.)

Do you remember/ How you won.   To James.   Frank Horne.   *Fr.* Letters Found near a Suicide.   BPo; PAIC

Do you remember a long time ago.   Cotton-eyed Joe.   *Unknown.*   FSW

Do you remember an inn.   Tarantella.   Hilaire Belloc.   SpRo

Do You Remember 1926?   Idris Davies.   OBW

Do You Remember That Night?   *Unknown, tr. fr. Irish by* Eugene O'Curry.   BIrV; PFIr

Do you remember, when you were first a child.   Message from Home.   Kathleen Raine.   WPE

Do you say/ its progesterone.   What Do You Say When a Man Tells You, You Have the Softest Skin.   Mary Mackey.   FF

Do you see that gigantic bone.   The Bone and the Baby.   Ettore Rella.   SPT

Do you think/ you must work signs.   Instructions for the Messiah.   Myra Sklarew.   VWA

Dobbin Dead.   William Barnes.   VLP

Dock-Leaves.   William Barnes.   VLP

Docker.   Seamus Heaney.   HeHu; NoAM

Dockery and Son (" 'Dockery was junior to you' ").   Philip Larkin.   NoAM

Doctor, The.   Dannie Abse.   PMW

Doctor asked him if he dreamed at night, The.   The Patient.   Nicholas Moore.   EAS

Doctor Black.   John Blight.   CAAP

Doctor, doctor, it fits real fine.   Vet's Rehabilitation.   Ray Durem.   PoBA

Dr. Fatt, Instructor.   Donald Hall.   *See* Professor Gratt.

Doctor Faustus.   Christopher Marlowe.   OAEL–1   *Sels.*
   "Ah, Faustus,/ Now hast thou but one bare hour [*or* hower] to live."   HeIP; ILwL; LFH; OBP; PAIC
   "Was this the face that launched a thousand ships?"   EBEV; GBL; HeIP; NIL   (Helen of Troy.)   FF

Doctor Faustus was a good man.   Mother Goose.   MG

Doctor Fell.   Thomas Brown, *after the Latin of* Martial.   BBL; FaBoCo; FaBoEE
   ("I do not love thee, Dr. Fell.")   NIL; OBVE

Doctor Foster went to Glo'ster.   Mother Goose.   MG

Doctor Freud.   David Lazar.   FSW

Doctor, I don't know if I've got the right attitude.   Doctor, I Dream of Sleep.   David Perkins.   AAN

Doctor, I Dream of Sleep.   David Perkins.   AAN

Doctor Johnson.   Soame Jenyns.   FaBoEE; OBSV

Doctor loves the patient, The.   The Bed.   A. D. Hope.   NoAM

Dr. Potatohead Talks to Mothers.  Judith Johnson Sherwin.  NoAM

Doctor punched my vein, The.  Scyros.  Karl Shapiro.  HoPM (1975 ed.); ILP (1975 ed.)

Doctor Rebuilds a Hand, The.  Gary Young.  AMV-80

Doctor said, count to ten, The.  Flight.  Ruth Whitman.  SO

Dr. Sigmund Freud Discovers the Sea Shell.  Archibald MacLeish.  BiP; SoSe

Dr. Unlikely, we love you so.  Horror Movie.  Howard Moss.  MiP; TPo; UsP

Doctor Who Sits at the Bedside of a Rat, The.  Josephine Miles.  CoPAm; VGW

Dr. Wild's Ghost.  *Unknown.*  APAS

Doctor's aseptic popsicle stick, The.  Tonsilectomy.  James W. Rivers.  AMV-81

Doctors attended behind each chair.  W. H. Auden.  *Fr.* A Happy New Year.  OBSV

Doctor's Row.  Conrad Aiken.  HAP; NYP

Doctor's Story, The.  Will M. Carleton.  PoTa

Doctors tender of their fame, The.  Swift.  *Fr.* Verses on the Death of Doctor Swift.  NOBL

Doctors that learned be.  John Skelton.  *Fr.* Colin Clout.  OBSV

Document.  Tuvia Ruebner, *tr. fr. Hebrew by* Harold Schimmel.  VWA

Document, A.  Judith Wright.  MAuV

Documentary on Airplane Glue, A.  David Henderson.  MAT

Dodger, The.  *Unknown.*  AmFP; GBP
(Dodger Song, The.)  FSW

Dodo.  Henry Carlile.  GP

Dodo, The.  Edward Kessler.  PPoD

Dodo, The.  Edward Lucie-Smith.  POL

Dodona's Oaks Were Still.  Patrick MacDonogh.  PFIr

Dodos, The.  Cash Terrell.  DNGG

Doe of the mountains east.  Mother/Deer/Lady.  Harold Littlebird.  VoR

Does Almighty God know about His sneaky competition?  Peek-a-Boo.  Robert Lowenstein.  AMV-81

Does anyone these days respect the artist.  Ovid, *tr. by* Guy Lee.  Amores, III, 8.  NAWM-1

Does It Matter?  Siegfried Sassoon.  VoPo

Does it matter what neat lives we plan.  Lapse of Contract.  Rodney Hall.  FPA

Does it wear a yarmulka?  What Is a Jewish Poem?  Myra Sklarew.  VWA

Does man love Art? Man visits Art, but squirms.  The Chicago Picasso.  Gwendolyn Brooks.  *Fr.* Two Dedications.  BPo; ILP (1975 ed.); Psy

Does morning always *have* to come?  The Second Hymn to the Night.  "Novalis," *tr. by* Robert Bly.  *Fr.* Hymns to the Night.  NU

Does nature bear a tyrant's breast?  John Langhorne.  *Fr.* Owen of Carron.  FaBoCo

Does the elephant remember.  Circus Elephants.  Kathryn Worth.  CTV

Does the road wind up-hill all the way?  Up-Hill.  Christina Rossetti.  ECBV; HAP; IPWM; NOBE; OAEL-2; PPP; SS; VLP; VPC; WPE

Does the Spearmint Lose Its Flavor on the Bedpost Overnight?  Billy Rose.  OBAL

Does the typewriter type.  Truth.  Susan Fromberg Schaeffer.  IHMS

Doesn't he realize/ that I am not/ like the swaying kelp.  Ono no Komachi, *tr. fr. Japanese by* Kenneth Rexroth *and* Ikuko Atsumi.  BoWoP

Doesn't It Seem to You.  Gevorg Emin, *tr. fr. Armenian by* Martin Robbins.  AMV-81

Dog, The.  A. Buttigieg.  RAE

Dog, The.  W. H. Davies.  GDP

Dog.  Lawrence Ferlinghetti.  CoPAm; HoPM (1975 ed.); ILP (1975 ed.)

Dog, The.  Valentin Iremonger.  BIrV

Dog.  Ingrid Jonker, *tr. fr. Afrikaans by* Jack Cope *and* William Plomer.  PBWP

Dog, The.  Ogden Nash.  GDP

Dog.  John Crowe Ransom.  InPS; OBAL

Dog, A.  Charlotte Zolotow.  GDP

Dog Alive.  Harold Witt.  BoAnP

Dog and Tiger.  Eliezer Greenberg, *tr. fr. Yiddish by* Stanley Kunitz.  BoAnP

Dog around the Block.  E. B. White.  GDP

Dog at Night.  Louis Untermeyer.  MiP

Dog beneath the cherry-tree, The.  The Ambiguous Dog.  Arthur Guiterman.  GDP

Dog beneath the Skin, The, *sels.*  W. H. Auden.  OxBTC
Chorus: "The summer holds: upon its glittering lake."
Chorus: "You are the town and we are the clock."

Dog called Sesamë slewed out.  Stray Dog, near Ecully.  Margaret Avison.  PoA

Dog Child, The.  Keaulumoku, *tr. fr. Hawaiian by* M. W. Beckwith.  *Fr.* The Kumulipo: A Creation Chant.  WTO

Dog comes home with a mouth full, The.  Pain.  Robert Wrigley.  AMV-81

Dog Creek Mainline.  Charles Wright.  AmPA; CSP

Dog-Days.  Amy Lowell.  FSFS

Dog Dream.  Ron Welburn.  NW

Dog emerges from the flies, A.  Nino, the Wonder Dog.  Roy Fuller.  FF

Dog fox rolls on his lolling tongue, The.  The Hunt.  Louis Kent.  SoSe

Dog from Malta, The.  Tymnes.  *See* Maltese Dog, The.

Dog gazes back at me, The. The pair of rats.  Another Color.  Frank Stewart.  AMV-81

Dog goes after Cat.  ABC's.  Cinda Kornblum.  AcAn

Dog Hospital.  Peter Wild.  AmPA; GP; MPA

Dog howled and howled, The.  Alison Prince.  POL

Dog in the Fountain.  Raymond Souster.  GDP

Dog in the Quarry, A, *sel.*  Miroslav Holub, *tr. fr. Czech by* George Theiner *and* Ian Milner.
"Day was so bright, The."  BoAnP; GDP

Dog in Us, The.  John Barnie.  AMV-81

Dog is a faithful, intelligent friend, The.  The Song Called "His Hide Is Covered with Hair."  Hilaire Belloc.  FaBoNo

Dog is cousin to the wolf, but more acceptable, The.  Dog and Tiger.  Eliezer Greenberg, *tr. by* Stanley Kunitz.  BoAnP

Dog is the brother.  Who's Who in America.  Mbembe.  NW

Dog loved its churlish life, The.  Lupercalia.  Ted Hughes.  CMoP (1970 ed.)

Dog means dog. And cat means cat.  Blum.  Dorothy Aldis.  ECBV; LCL

Dog, Midwinter.  Raymond Souster.  GDP

Dog of Art, The.  Denise Levertov.  NoAM

Dog Parade, The.  Arthur Guiterman.  BoAnP; GDP

Dog Sacrifice at Lake Ronkonkoma.  William Heyen.  AmPA

Dog Sleeping on My Feet, A.  James Dickey.  UsP

Dog stops barking after Robinson has gone, The.  Robinson.  Weldon Kees.  AnMo; NoAM

Dog Talk.  Albert De Pietro.  AATT

Dog, the lightning frightened us, dark house and both of us.  Jim Harrison.  *Fr.* Ghazals.  InPS

Dog-tired.  D. H. Lawrence.  BuTh

Dog-tired, suisired, will now my body down.  The Poet's Final Instructions.  John Berryman.  VGW

Dog trots freely in the street, The. Dog. Lawrence Ferlinghetti. CoPAm; HoPM (1975 ed.); ILP (1975 ed.)

Dog Wanted. Margaret Mackprang Mackay. GDP

Dog was there, outside her door, The. The Dog. W. H. Davies. GDP

Dog Who Comes from Nowhere, The. Patricia Goedicke. AAN

Dog will come when he is called, The. Beasts and Birds. Adelaide O'Keeffe. OxBChV

Doggerel by a Senior Citizen. W. H. Auden. NOBL

Dogget Gap. *Unknown.* AmFP

Doggin' Me Around Blues. *Unknown.* BluL

Dogs. Frances Cornford. DuDr

Dogs and Wolves. Sorley Maclean, *tr. fr. Gaelic by* Iain Crichton Smith. SLP

Dogs Are Shakespearean, Children Are Strangers. Delmore Schwartz. NoAM

Dogs behind, I'm running for the trees, The. Idyll. John Boland. IPM

Dog's Best Friend Is His Illiteracy, A. Ogden Nash. BoAnP

Dog's Cold Nose, The. Arthur Guiterman. ECBV; GDP; PoTa

Dogs greet me, I descend, The. I Come Home Wanting to Touch Everyone. Stephen Dunn. AMV-81

Dogs of Santiago. Eugene McCarthy. BoAnP; GDP

Dogskin Rug. Adrien Stoutenburg. GP

Dogwood flakes. Variations Done for Gerald van de Wiele. Charles Olson. NoAM; NOBA

Doing, a Filthy Pleasure Is, and Short. Petronius Arbiter, *tr. fr. Latin by* Ben Jonson. BoLoP; CABA (1972 ed.); OBVE; WIF
    (Epigram from Petronius.) OAEL-1
    (Fragment of Petronius Translated, A.) LoAS
    (Fragmentum Petronius Arbiter, Translated.) HeIP

Doing my wash. Wash Day. Larry Mollin. NeAC

Doing 70 on Interstate 94. Bread Loaf to Omaha, Twenty-eight Hours. Patrick Worth Gray. TAT

Dolgelley Hotel, The. Thomas Hughes. FaBoCo

Doll, The. Robert Friend. GP

Doll, The. Gregory Orr. AmPA

Doll House, The. Darlene Button Kitzman. AMV-81

Doll in the doll-maker's house, A. The Dolls. W. B. Yeats. CMoP (1970 ed.); NoAM; PoIA; TT

Doll Poem ("Doll is sitting in a box"). Toi Derricotte. NPW

Doll Thy Ale. *Unknown.* OxBM

Dollar Dog, The. John Ciardi. GDP

Dollars. Isidor Schneider. SPT

Dollmaker, snug in your house. The Doll. Robert Friend. GP

Dolls, The. W. B. Yeats. CMoP (1970 ed.); NoAM; PoIA; TT

Doll's boy's asleep. E. E. Cummings. DuDa

Doll's hair concealing, A. Partial Resemblance. Denise Levertov. CoPAm

Dolls' Wash, The. Juliana Horatia Ewing. OxBChV

Dolly, dolly on our knees, hello etcetera etcetera. Hello Dolly. Leon Slade. FPA

Dolor. Theodore Roethke. AnMo; BiP; CABA (1972 ed.); CMoP (1970 ed.); CoPAm; HeIP; HoPM (1975 ed.); ILP (1975 ed.); InPK; InPS; NoAM; PBMP; PoA; PoIA; PPoD; SFF; TCP; TPo; UsP

Dolores. Swinburne. VLP

Dolorous kno. Koko Oloro. Wole Soyinka. BuTh

Dolphin. Robert Lowell. NOBA

Dolphin plunge, fountain play. Invocation. Louis MacNeice. SO

Dolphin Seen Alone. Richmond Lattimore. BoAnP

*Dom Pedro,* The. *Unknown.* AmFP

Dome, The. Lawrence Lee. WasP

Dome of Sunday, The. Karl Shapiro. CMoP (1970 ed.); NoAM

Dome Poem. Dave Smith. PoA

Domestic Asides; or, Truth in Parentheses. Thomas Hood. BBL

Domestic Didactics by an Old Servant. Thomas Hood. VLP

Domestic Duties. Richard Emil Braun. NoAM

Domestic Life, *sel.* Gregory Orr.
    "You feel heavy and sad as though." OSP

Domestic Man. Augustus Young. IPM

Domestic Scene. Michael Hartnett. BIrV

Domestic Scenes, 2. Charles Reznikoff. WeW

Domestic Stones, The (fragment). Hans Arp, *tr. fr. French by* David Gascoyne. EAS

Domesticating Two Landscapes. Madeline DeFrees. CNW

Domesticity. Rodney Hall. FPA

Domination of Black. Wallace Stevens. PiAm; PoIA

Domineering Eagle and the Inventive Bratling, The. Guy Wetmore Carryl. OBAL

Dominion, *sel.* A. R. D. Fairburn.
    "In the suburbs the spirit of man." ATNZ

Domino players on the yard. Vivisection. Gene Fowler. CPA

Domus Caedet Arborem. Charlotte Mew. PBWP

Don Baty, the Draft Resister. Muriel Rukeyser. NNaP

Don Juan, *abr.* Byron. MBPR
    *Sels.*
    "Alfonso closed his speech, and begged her pardon," *fr.* I. PoIA
    Dedication: "Bob Southey! You're a poet—poet-laureate." ILP (1975 ed.); MBPR; OAEL-2; OBSV
    ("Bob Southey! You're a poet—Poet laureate.") PPoe
    " 'Farewell, my Spain! a long farewell!' he cried," *fr.* II. PoIA
    Fragment: "I would to heaven that I were so much clay." ILP (1975 ed.); MBPR; NIL; NOBL; OAEL-2; OBP
    Growing Old, *fr.* I. NOBE
    "Hail, Muse! et caetera.——We left Juan sleeping," *fr.* III. OAEL-2
    "He who has seen the wild tornado sweep," *fr.* XVII. PeD
    "I know that what our neighbours call *longueurs,*" *fr.* II. OBSV
    "I want a hero: an uncommon want," I. MBPR; NIL, 4 sts. only; OAEL-2, *abr.*
    "I wonder if his appetite was good?" *fr.* V. OAEL-2
    Isles of Greece, The, *fr.* III. BTTM; FaPoR; NOBE
    "Juan knew several languages—as well," *fr.* XI. OAEL-2
    "Man's a phenomenon, one knows not what," *fr.* I. LFH
    "Mighty mass of brick, and smoke, and shipping, A," *fr.* X. PES
    "Milton's the prince of poets—so we say," *fr.* III. NOBL; OAEL-2
    Modern Discoveries, *fr.* I. OBP
    Moon Shot, *fr.* X. OBP
    "Nothing so difficult as a beginning," *fr.* IV. OAEL-2
    "O love! O glory! what are you who fly," *fr.* VII. OAEL-2
    "Oh Wellington! (Or 'Vilainton,' for Fame)," *fr.* IX. OBSV
    "Over the stones still rattling, up Pall Mall," *fr.* XI. NOBL
    Race, fr. XIV. OBP
    "Sagest of women, even of widows, she," *fr.* I. NOBL
    Seduction of Juan, the, *fr.* I. OBP
    "Shore looked wild, without a trace of man, The," *fr.* II. HAP
    Sun Set, and Up Rose the Yellow Moon, The, *fr.* I. Moon
    "They were alone once more; for them to be," *fr.* IV. EBEV
    "Though somewhat large, exuberant, and truculent," *fr.* IX. OAEL-2
    "To our theme.—The man who has stood on the Acropolis," *fr.* XI. InPS; OBSV
    " 'Twas midnight—Donna Julia was in bed," *fr.* I. BiP
    " 'Twas on a summer's day—the sixth of June," *fr.* I. PPP
    "Under the bed they searched, and there they found," *fr.* I. PoIA
    "Why call the miser miserable?" *fr.* XII. UnPo (1976 ed.)

"You know, or you don't know, that great Bacon saith," *fr.* XIV. NOBL

"Young unmarried man, with a good name, A," *fr.* XII. NOBL

Don Juan. D. H. Lawrence. PoA

Don Larsen's Perfect Game. Paul Goodman. LiSp; SPo

Don 1958. Alta. MMD

Don Quixote, *sel.* Thomas Durfey.
"Sleep, sleep, poor youth! sleep, sleep in peace." SCP-2

Don Surly, to aspire the glorious name. On Don Surly. Ben Jonson. FaBoEE

Donal Oge: Grief of a Girl's Heart. *Unknown, tr. fr. Modern Irish* by Lady Gregory. GBL; PFIr
(Grief of a Girl's Heart, The, *shorter version.*) OLR; PBWP

Done Is a Battell on the Dragon Blak. William Dunbar. *See* Lord Is Risen, The.

Doney-Gal ("Traveling up the lonesome trail"). *Unknown.* BPAW

Doney Gal ("We're alone Doney Gal, in the rain and the hail"). *Unknown.* FSW

Dong with a Luminous Nose, The. Edward Lear. BBL; FaBoCo; FaBoNo; VLP

Donibristle Moss Moran Disaster, The. *Unknown.* WTO

Donkey, The. G. K. Chesterton. FaPoR

Donkey, The. Gertrude Hinde. ECBV

Donkey. Vasko Popa, *tr. fr. Serbian* by Anne Pennington. TSWA

Donkey, The. Theodore Roethke. ECBV

Donkey and the Lapdog, The. La Fontaine, *tr. fr. French* by Marianne Moore. OBVE

Donkey Riding. *Unknown.* RAE

Donkey sat down on the roadside, The. Time Out. John Montague. BoAnP; PFIr

Donkey Will Carry You, A. Jakov Steinberg, *tr. fr. Hebrew* by Mark Elliott Shapiro. VWA

Donkeys. Edward Field. BoAnP

Donna Me Prega. Guido Cavalcanti, *tr. fr. Italian* by Ezra Pound. OBVE

Don's Holiday. G. Rostrevor Hamilton. FaBoCo

Don't Answer the Phone for Me the Same. Gerald Locklin. GP

Don't ape what must be born in one. The Donkey and the Lapdog. La Fontaine, *tr. by* Marianne Moore. OBVE

Don't ask a geologist about rocks. No More Soft Talk. Diane Wakoski. FF; IHMS

Don't ask me if these knives are real. Dreaming Winter. James Welch. VW

Don't ask me what to wear. Sappho, *tr. fr. Greek* by Mary Barnard. PBWP

Don't Ask Me Who I Am. James A. Randall, Jr. BPo

Don't be afraid of dying. Couplets 20. Robert Mezey. NU

Don't be polite. How to Eat a Poem. Eve Merriam. OSP

Don't believe the diagrams. Babies. Rick Cannon. PoUp

Don't blame me, ladies, if I've loved. No sneers. Sonnet XXIV. Louise Labé, *tr. by* Willis Barnstone. BoWoP

Don't bother a bit, you are only a dream you are having. A Real Question Calling for a Solution. Robert Penn Warren. PPP

Don't Call. Edward Lowbury. PMW

Don't-Care. *Unknown.* ECBV; GBP

Don't care when you go. Someday Baby. *Unknown.* BluL

Don't dress for it. Chiyo, *tr. fr. Japanese* by David Ray. BoWoP

Don't drive me out of my mind. Second Honeymoon. *Unknown, tr. by* Augustus Young. BIrV

Don't ever grab/ old crusty crab. The Crab. Conrad Aiken. BoAnP

Don't expect smiles on all my faces. Notes toward an Autobiography: The Poet at 41. Richard Shelton. FoP

Don't Fish in My Sea. *Unknown.* BluL

Don't Forget. Stephen Berg. PoA

"Don't get the cart before the horse." Horseplay by Reverse Descartes. Merle Meeter. AATT

Don't Give Up. Phoebe Cary. CTV

Don't hand me over with a word, Toihau. Reply to a Marriage Proposal. Irihapeti Rangi te Apakura, *tr. by* Roger Oppenheim *and* Allen Curnow. PBWP

Don't know why I. Angola Question Mark. Langston Hughes. BPo

Don't let me lose you. How Tuesday Began. Kathleen Fraser. CTBA

Don't Let That Horse. Lawrence Ferlinghetti. TCP

Don't let them die out. Now Poem. For Us. Sonia Sanchez. CNA; PoBA

Don't Let Your Deal Go Down. *Unknown.* FSW

Don't lock me in wedlock, I want. About Marriage. Denise Levertov. NMM

Don't Look Now. J. C. Fogerty. PoRo

Don't love me, my sweet. Song of a Common Lover. Flavien Ranaivo, *tr. by* Alan Ryder. BuTh

Don't Put Me. Stanley Kiesel. HeS

Don't Say. Moshe Yungman, *tr. fr. Yiddish* by Marcia Falk. VWA

Don't scold me, ladies, if I have loved. Sonnet XXIV. Louise Labé, *tr. by* Carol Cosman. PBWP

Don't Send My Boy to Prison. *Unknown.* OSF

Don't shirk/ Your work. Good Advice. Louis Untermeyer, *after the German.* CTV

Don't Shoot! William Wantling. EC

Don't Show Me. Ruth Beker. VWA

Don't sing: a song. Drops of Gall. Gabriela Mistral, *tr. by* David Garrison. BoWoP

Don't Sing Love Songs. *Unknown.* FSW

Don't Sit under the Apple Tree with Anyone Else but Me. Robert Pack. FF

Don't Steal. Ambrose Bierce. POL

Don't step/ so lightly. Break. The Cracks. Robert Creeley. ConAP

Don't suppose that the weightless phantom. The Titans. Betti Alver, *tr. by* Willis Barnstone *and* Felix Oinas. BoWoP

Don't talk to me no words. Relocation. Simon Ortiz. VW

Don't Tell Bad Dreams Says Tita's Mother. John Oliver Simon. NeAC

Don't throw your arms around me in that way. Footnote to John ii. 4. R. A. K. Mason. ATNZ

Don't touch the trees—their soft bark will suck your/ fingers dry. Robin Fulton. *Fr.* Seven Songs for a Cool Man. MS

Don't wait for the wind to blow you through the door. Moving In. Paul Engle. PoA

Don't Wanna Be. Sonia Sanchez. CNA

Don't Want No Hungry Woman. *Unknown.* BluL

Don't worry/ One night we'll find that deserted kinema. If Life's a Lousy Picture, Why Not Leave before the End. Roger McGough. OxBTC

Don't worry baby. Broken Heart, Broken Machine. Richard E. Grant. PoBA

Don't You Be Like the Foolish Virgin, *with music. Unknown.* AH

Don't you care for my love? she said bitterly. Intimates. D. H. Lawrence. BoLoP; PoTa

Don't you ever. Plaint against the Fog. *Unknown.* AKE

Don't you feel sorry. Moles. Aileen Fisher. CTV

Don't you let my good girl catch you here. Ain't No Tellin'. *Unknown.* BluL

Don't you love farce? All those bedroom doors. Adam, Eve and the Big Apple. Edward Watkins. AMV-81

Don't You Weep after Me. *Unknown.* FSW

Don'ts. D. H. Lawrence. NoAM

Dooley Is a Traitor. James Michie. OxBTC

Doom is dark and deeper than any sea-dingle. The Wanderer. W. H. Auden. CMoP (1970 ed.); ILP (1975 ed.); NoAM; WeW

Doom of Devergoil, The, *sel.* Sir Walter Scott. Bonnie Dundee, *fr.* II, ii. RDB, *with music* (Bonnets o' Bonnie Dundee, The.) BTTM

Doom-Well of St. Madron, The. Robert Stephen Hawker. VLP

Dooms menace from tumults. Who's immune. John Berryman. CAAP

Door, The. Robert Creeley. NoAM; VGW

Door, The. Miroslav Holub, *tr. fr. Czech by* Ian Milner *and* George Theiner. LP

Door, A. W. S. Merwin. EAS

Door, The. Mark Strand. NoAM

Door, The. Charles Tomlinson. PoA

Door, The. Lewis Turco. CoPAm

Door, A:/ Per L'Universo. Idyll. Charles Tomlinson. TwMBP

Door a maze, The. Disturbing the Tarantula. Christopher Middleton. TwMBP

Door behind me was you, The. You (I). Tom Clark. EAS

Door is before you again and the shrieking, The. The Door. Mark Strand. NoAM

"Door is shut fast, The." Who's In? Elizabeth Fleming. DuDr

Door it opened slowly, The. The Story of Isaac. Leonard Cohen. GrRo; VWA; WIF

Door opened, The./ She walked towards the waiting seat. But Her Eyes Spoke Another Language. William Duncan. PMW

Door opens apparently by itself, The. Casts from the Antique. David McAleavey. PoUp

Door slam, The. After the First Frost. Lew Blockcolski. VoR

Door still swinging to, and girls revive, The. A Dream of Fair Women. Kingsley Amis. ExPo (1973 ed.); FF; NoAM; OAEL-2

Door sunk in a hillside, with a bolt, A. The Icehouse in Summer. Howard Nemerov. NoAM

Door that someone opened wide, The. The Message. Jacques Prevert, *tr. by* John Frederick Nims. WeW

Door to the Sun. Ralph J. Mills, Jr. HeS

Door was shut, The. I looked between. Shut Out. Christina Rossetti. VLP

Doorbell buzzed, The. It was past three o'clock. The Australian Dream. David Campbell. GAS

Doorbell rang, The. It was Death. Alone in the House. George Bogin. AMV-80

Doorbell rings, The. Crazy Soliloquy. Geraldine Kudaka. NW

Doors. Tom Clark. ConAP

Doors. Therese Plantier, *tr. fr. French by* Willis Barnstone *and* Elene Kolb. BoWoP

Doors. Carl Sandburg. OSP; UsP

Doors flapped open in Ulysses' house, The. The Return. Edwin Muir. CMoP (1970 ed.)

Doors have opened and, The. Feature Time. Jerry Hammond. PPoD

Doors open, The/ and the heat undoes itself. In the Beach House. Anne Sexton. PPP

Doors opened with a silent scream. The Spirit of 34th Street. Peggy Shriver. AMV-80

Doorstep. Frank Ormsby. IPM

Doorway to Time in Three Voices. Luis Palés Matos, *tr. fr. Spanish by* Rachel Benson. InW

Dopey sez to Doc. Snow White. Ed Ochester. GP

Dora versus Rose. Austin Dobson. NOBL

Dora Williams. Edgar Lee Masters. *Fr.* Spoon River Anthology. HAP

Dorchester Plate. Gwendolen Haste. WPW

Doretha wore the short blue lace last night. The Reception. June Jordan. NMM

Doricha. Poseidippus, *tr. fr. Greek by* E. A. Robinson. FaBoEE; OBVE

Dorinda's sparkling wit and eyes. On the Countess of Dorchester. Charles Sackville. APAS

Dorlan's Home Walk. Arthur Guiterman. PoTa

Dorothy Q. Oliver Wendell Holmes. NOBA; PiAm

Dorset. John Betjeman. MPo

"Dorset Nose," The. Clive Sansom. MPo

Dory Miller. Sam Cornish. CNA

Dose of a mere, The. The Discovery of LSD a True Story. Anselm Hollo. AcAn

Don't thou 'ear my 'erse's legs, as they canters awaay? Northern Farmer: New Style. Tennyson. BiP; VLP

Dossier, The. Michael McMahon. FAF

Dost see how unregarded now. Sonnet I. Sir John Suckling. CaPo

"Dost thou hear my horse's feet, as he canters away?" Lord Tennyson and Lord Melchett. D. H. Lawrence. FaBoEE

Dost thou know who made thee? The Lamb. Blake. *Fr.* Songs of Innocence. InPS

Double Axe, The. Anne Hazlewood-Brady. IHMS

Double-conscious sister in the veil. Madimba: Gwendolyn Brooks. Michael S. Harper. MIT

Double Entendre. J. F. Wilson. TDH

Double Exposure. Ian Young. NeAC

"Double flesh/ Double way." Freud: Dying London, He Recalls the Smoke of His Cigar Beginning to Sing. James Schevill. TAP

Double Lent has this your absence been, A. In the Wilderness. Albert Howard Carter. AATT

Double Life. Norman MacCaig. MS

Double Looking Glass, The. A. D. Hope. GAS

Double Mirror. Ann Stanford. MPA

Double mirrors in the dark, The. Introspection. Roger McDonald. FPA

Double Monologue. Adrienne Rich. NIL; Psy

Double Play, The. Robert Wallace. LiSp

Double Shame, The. Stephen Spender. LoAs

Double Standard, The. Franklin P. Adams. OBAL

Double Vision, The. C. Day Lewis. NoAM

Double Vision of Manannan, The. *Unknown, tr. fr. the Irish by* John Montague. BIrV

Doubled Mirrors. Kenneth Rexroth. ExPo (1973 ed.)

Double-Header. John Stone. TAT

Doubt of Future Foes, The. Elizabeth I, Queen of England. PBWP; WPE

Doubt of Martyrdom, A. Sir John Suckling. BoLoP; NOBE ("O for some honest lover's ghost.") PoPle; SCP-2 (Sonnet: "Oh! for some honest lover's ghost.") CaPo; ILP (1975 ed.)

Doubting. Louis Simpson. NNaP

Doubtless, sweet girl! the hissing lead. Lines Addressed to a Young Lady. Byron. MBPR

Doubts. Elizabeth Jennings. LP

Dough Roller Blues. *Unknown.* BluL

Douglas Tragedy, The. *Unknown.* IPWM; PeBB (Earl Brand.) AmFP; FaBoBa; FSW; PeBB

Douglass was someone who. Frederick Douglass: 1817-1895. Langston Hughes. BPo

Doun throu the sea. Cokkils. Sydney Goodsir Smith. PoA

Dove. Norma Farber. PChr

Dove. Keats. PCOP

Dove, The. *Unknown.* GBP

Dove of liberty sat on an egg, The. The American Eagle. D. H. Lawrence. OAEL-2

Dove returns, The; it found no resting place. Where We Must Look for Help. Robert Bly. ConAP

Dover Beach. Matthew Arnold. AnMo; BiP; CABA (1972 ed.); Epi; ExPo (1973 ed.); FF; GrRo; HAP; HeIP; HoPM (1975 ed.); ILP (1975 ed.); InPK; InPS; IP; IPWM; LFH; MAT; NIL; NOBE; NU; OAEL-2; OBP; PAIC; PBMP; PFD; PoIA; PoPle; PPoD; PPoe; PPP; Prf; RhR; SFF; SoSe; TPo; UnPo (1976 ed.); UsP; VLP; VoPo; WeW
"Sea is calm to-night, The," sel. PES

"Dover Beach"—a Note to That Poem. Archibald MacLeish. FF

Dover Bitch, The. Anthony Hecht. CABA (1972 ed.); ILP (1975 ed.); MAT; NOBA; NOBL; NowV; OBAL; PAIC; PPP; SFF; TPo; UnPo (1976 ed.); VGW

Dover to Munich, sels. Charles Stuart Calverley.
"Bed at Ostend at 5 A.M." NOBL
"Farewell, farewell! Before our prow." NOBL
"On, on the vessel steals." NOBL

Doves. Joachim Neugroschel. VWA

Doves flit by in their flocks of thousands. Sick unto Death of Love. Malay Oral Tradition, tr. by R. J. Wilkinson and R. O. Winstedt. WTO

Dove's Song in Winter. Zulu Oral Tradition, tr. by B. W. Vilakazi. WTO

Dovid,/ my twenty-/ three year old son. In the Year of Two Thousand. Menke Katz. AMV-81

Dowie Dens of Yarrow, The. Unknown. FSW

Down/ Down into the fathomless depths. Black Is a Soul. Joseph White. PoBA

Down a blackened alley. La Llorona. Greg Pape. AmPA

Down a broad river of the western wilds. Indian Woman's Death-Song. Felicia Dorothea Hemans. SBG

Down a street in the town where I went. Shapes, Vanishings. Henry Taylor. AMV-81

Down among the Wharves. Eleanore Myers Jewett. RhR

Down and Out. Langston Hughes. ExPo (1973 ed.); PiAm

Down at the Docks. Kenneth Koch. VGW

Down by the fallen fruit in the old orchard. Denise Levertov. Fr. The Coming Fall. TSWA

Down by the ocean side where ships were sailing. The Nightingales of Spring. Unknown. AmFP

Down by the river. Pretty Polly Perkins. Unknown. BBL

Down by the Salley Gardens. W. B. Yeats. CMoP (1970 ed.); FSW; NoAM; RDB, with music; SoSe

Down by the waterside stand a house and a plat. Unknown. GBP

Down by the weeping willow. Florella; or, The Jealous Lover. Unknown. AmFP

Down by the Wild Mustard River. The Wild Mustard River. Unknown. AmFP

Down Dip the Branches. Mark Van Doren. DuDa

Down every passage of the cloister hung. Upon the Death of George Santayana. Anthony Hecht. CoPAm

Down flew the shaft of the god. A Love Affair. Arnold Bennett. OxBTC

Down from the purple mist of trees on the mountain. The Bull Moose. Alden Nowlan. CABA (1972 ed.)

Down here now/ summer's burnt skeins. In Blanco County. Russell T. Fowler. AMV-80

Down in a Coal Mine. J. B. Geoghegan. AmFP

Down in a deep dark ditch sat an old cow munching a beanstalk. Hexameter and Pentameter. Unknown. FaBoNo

Down in a green and shady bed. The Violet. Jane Taylor. PCOP

Down in Alabam'; or, Aint I Glad I Got Out de Wilderness. At. to J. Warner. PSoN

Down in Carlisle there lived a lady. The Lady of Carlisle. Unknown. AmFP; FSW

Down in Dallas. X. J. Kennedy. FF; IPWM; OFD

Down in front of Casey's. The Sidewalks of New York. James W. Blake. BLSo; FSN; FSW

Down in London where I was raised. Barbara Allen. Unknown. FaBoBa

Down in some lone valley, in some lonesome place. Pretty Saro. Unknown. FSW

Down in some lonesome piney grove. Lonesome Dove. Unknown. AmFP

Down in the Bass. Langston Hughes. ILP (1975 ed.)

Down in the deep, dumb worlds are waiting, silent. Letter to My Wife. Miklós Radnóti, tr. by Emery George. VWA

Down in the Field. M. P. Flynn. CTV

Down in the hole we go, boys. Lament while Descending a Shaft. Unknown. AmFP

Down in the jungle/ Living in a tent. Unknown. WTO

Down in the jungle [or jungles] lived a maid. Under the Bamboo Tree. Bob Cole. BLSo; FSN

Down in the Lonesome Garden. Unknown. BPo

Down in the mine, in the dark, dismal drift. Only a Miner. Unknown. AmFP

Down in the silent hallway. Unsatisfied Yearning. Richard Kendall Munkittrick. GDP

Down in the Valley. Unknown. BLSH, with music; BLSo, with music; FSW; RDB, with music; WTO
(Birmingham Jail.) GBP

Down in the water meadows Riley. Riley. Charles Causley. SO

Down in the Willow Garden. Unknown. FSW

Down in Yon Forest. Unknown. FSW

Down in Yonder Meadow. Unknown. PoPle

Down [or Downe] lay the shepherd swain. Hye Nonny Nonny Noe. Unknown. FaBoCo; NOBL

Down mountain roads like scars across a fist. At Tripolis. Constance Carrier. WPE

Down on My Luck. A. R. D. Fairburn. ATNZ

Down on the beach we separate. The Hinge. Sheila Cowing. AMV-81

Down on your knees, boys, holystone the decks. Cleaning Ship. Charles Keeler. RhR

Down Route 2, the farmers. Spring. Linda McCarriston. AMV-81

Down the assembly line they roll and pass. The Brides. A. D. Hope. HAP; InPK; PoIA

Down the Block. John Batki. AcAn

Down the blue night the unending columns press. Clouds. Rupert Brooke. OxBTC

Down the brick divided street. The Orphanage. Grace Cavalieri. PoUp

Down the coast south of here. Earth. Jim Tollerud. VoR

Down the close, darkening lanes they sang their way. The Send-off. Wilfred Owen. InPS; OBW; OxBTC; PSN; SoSe

Down the deep sea, full fourscore fathoms down. The Fatal Ship. Robert Stephen Hawker. VPC

Down the flightline. Beyond the Firehouse. Patrick Worth Gray. AMV-80

Down the hall a bookcase. Lyn Lifshin. Fr. Walking thru Audley End Mansion Late Afternoon. RiTi

Down the long hall she glistens like a star. Venus of the Louvre. Emma Lazarus. SBG

Down the middle. In a Subdivision. Eric Torgersen. TC

Down the Mississippi steamed the Whippoorwill. Steamboat Bill. Unknown. FSW

Down the mud road, between tall bending trees. Soldiers Plundering a Village. Anthony Thwaite. HeHu

Down the road someone is practicing scales. Sunday Morning. Louis MacNeice. HeIP; NIL

Down the rock chute into the tombs of the kings. This Is the Life. Louis MacNeice. NoAM

Down the sky in file the wild geese tack. Harold Stewart. *Fr.* A Flight of Wild Geese. MAuV

Down the soft hillside. The Firstling. Peter Davison. WeW

Down there where I was. The Story of My Life. Carroll Arnett. VoR

Down through the snow-drifts in the street. The Boy. Eugene Field. ECBV

Down through Venetian blinds the morning air. News from Paris. Charles Spear. ATNZ

Down thy valleys, Ireland, Ireland. Ireland, Ireland. Sir Henry Newbolt. FaPoR

Down to the Puritan marrow of my bones. Puritan Sonnet. Elinor Wylie. Wild Peaches, IV. BoWoP; PAIC; SoSe (1977 ed.); VoPo

Down to the Sacred Wave, *with music.* Samuel Francis Smith. AH

Down underground. The Indictment. Frederick Fanning Ayer. PeD

Down valley a smoke haze. Mid-August at Sourdough Mountain Lookout. Gary Snyder. CNW; HAP; MAT; MPA; NCSH; TAP; VoA

Down Wall Street. The Workers Rose on May Day or Postcript to Karl Marx. Audre Lorde. GP

Down, Wanton, Down! Robert Graves. BoLoP; CMoP (1970 ed.); HeIP, FaBoTw (1975 ed.); NoAM; OAEL–2; PoIA

Down Went McGinty, *with music.* Joseph Flynn. FSN

Down with him! chain him! bind him fast! On the Capture and Imprisonment of Crazy Snake, January, 1900. Alexander L. Posey. BPAW

Down with the rosemary and bays. Ceremonies for Candlemas Eve. Robert Herrick. CaPo; ILP (1975 ed.)

Down yonder green valley where streamlets meander. The Ash Grove. Thomas Oliphant. GSB

Downe in the depth of mine iniquity. Fulke Greville. *Fr.* Caelica. PPoe

Downe lay the shepherd swaine. *See* Down lay the shepherd swain.

Downfall of Charing Cross, The. *Unknown.* FaBoCo

Downfall of the Chancellor, The. *Unknown.* APAS

Downhill I came, hungry, and yet not starved. The Owl. Edward Thomas. EBEV; FaBoTw (1975 ed.); FF; NoAM; NOBE; OAEL–2; OBW; PoPle; PPoe; UnPo (1976 ed.)

Downstairs/ lives a small. Juanito's Blues. Antar S. K. Mberi. SES

Downstairs Two Old Lovers Meet. Lyn Lifshin. Psy

Downtown in the city where I was born. The Last Job I Held in Bridgeport. D. W. Donzella. TAT

Downtown Roanoke. R. H. W. Dillard. PPoD

Downwind, he caught the scent. Hunter, Prey. Dabney Stuart. NVAP

Downy Hair in the Shape of a Flame. Coleman Barks. *Fr.* Body Poems. NVAP

Dow's Flat. Bret Harte. PoTa

Doxology. Bert Leston Taylor. OBAL

Doze, The. James Reeves. CTV

Dozen clocks of this courthouse, The. State Message: A Midwestern Small Town. Robert Flanagan. HeS

Dozens of girls would storm up. Embraceable You. Ira Gershwin. BLSo

Drab, The/ concrete walls. "Temporary Escape." Leonard Keller. CPA

Drab skyline, yellowing papers, a fat land. An Allegiance. Chris Wallace-Crabbe. GAS

Draft Dodger, The. Larry Rubin. NIL

Draft Dodger Rag. Phil Ochs. WIF

Draft Horse, The. Robert Frost. CMoP (1970 ed.); HeIP; HoPM (1975 ed.); ILP (1975 ed.); PiAm

Draft of a Reparations Agreement. Dan Pagis, *tr. fr. Hebrew by* Stephen Mitchell. VWA

Drafts for a Quatrain. Edmund Wilson. OBAL

Dragged through doorways of fragrance. The Lynching. Milton Kessler. CoPAm

Dragging in Winter. David McElroy. AmPA

Dragging the Main. David Ray. TAT

Dragon, The. Carolyn Wells. TDH

Dragon Country: To Jacob Boehme. Robert Penn Warren. PPP

Dragon Lesson. James Hearst. AMV–80

Dragon of Wantley, The. *Unknown.* DuDr

Dragon Skate. Gladys Cardiff. CDW

Dragon, who was a great wag, A. The Dragon. Carolyn Wells. TDH

Dragonfly, The. Louise Bogan. HeIP; NIL

Dragonfly, A. Eleanor Farjeon. FPB

Dragonfly, The. Howard Nemerov. PoA

Dragon-fly strives patiently, The. Haiku. José Juan Tablada, *tr. by* Samuel Beckett. PBMP

Dragons. John Ciardi. SFF

Drake he's in his hammock an' a thousand mile away. Drake's Drum. Sir Henry Newbolt. FaPoR; VLP

Drake, who the world hast conquered like a scroll. To the Noble Sir Francis Drake. Thomas Beedome. SCP–2

Drake's Drum. Sir Henry Newbolt. FaPoR; VLP

Drama's vitallest expression is the common day. Emily Dickinson. NOBA

Dramatis Personae, *sel.* Robert Browning. Epilogue: "On the first of the Feast of Feasts." VLP

Draped in white robes and turbans. Your Black Bones Do Not Remember. Stacy Tuthill. PoUp

Drat my hateful birthday. Sulpicia, *tr. fr. Latin by* John Dillon. PBWP

Draw a historical parallel. Entrance Exams. Cuthbert Bede. FaBoNo

Draw me nere, draw me nere. The Juggler and the Baron's Daughter. *Unknown.* EBEV; OxBM

Draw near, young men, and learn of me. McAfee's Confession. *Unknown.* AmFP

Drawing. Roy Fuller. MN

Drawing by Ronnie C., Grade One. Ruth Lechlitner. SoS

Drawn by old Homer's hand, the rose. Helen like the Rose. Evan Lloyd. OBW

Drawn from his refuge in some lonely elm. Squirrel in Sunshine. William Cowper. BoAnP

Dread. Dave Morice. AcAn

Dread. J. M. Synge. BoLoP

Dread of Darkness. George Keithley. PoW

Dread of Death. John Audelay. *See* Passion of Christ Strengthen Me.

Dreadful Dinotherium he, The. Hilaire Belloc. *Fr.* A Moral Alphabet. NOBL

"Dreadful Has Already Happened, The." Mark Strand. NoAM

*Dreadnought,* The. *Unknown.* AmFP

Dream, A. Bella Akhmadulina, *tr. fr. Russian by* Jean Valentine *and* Olga Carlisle. BoWoP

Dream, The [*or* A]. William Allingham. BIrV; PFIr; PoTa

Dream, A. Matthew Arnold. GBL

Dream, The. Aphra Behn. *Fr.* A Voyage to the Isle of Love. PBWP

Dream, A. Blake. *Fr.* Songs of Innocence. LAuP; MBPR; PoPle

Dream, The. Louise Bogan. MAT; SBG

Dream, The, *sel.* Byron.
"Our life is two-fold: Sleep hath its own world," I. GrRo

Dream. Richard Watson Dixon. EBEV; VLP

Dream, The ("Dear love, for nothing less than thee"). John Donne. OAEL-1
(Dreame, The.) LoAs

Dream, The. Stephen Dunn. HeS

Dream. Joseph Eliyia, *tr. fr. Greek by* Rae Dalven. VWA

Dream, The. Robert Herrick. LoAs; SCP-1

Dream, The. David Ignatow. MAT; NNaP; VWA

Dream. Nana Issaia, *tr. fr. Modern Greek by* Helle Tzalopoulou Barnstone. BoWoP

Dream, The. Ben Jonson. NOBE

Dream. Josephine Miles. PoA

Dream, The. Paul Petrie. TAP

Dream. Emilio Prados, *tr. fr. Spanish by* Eleanor L. Turnbull. LoAs

Dream, The. Theodore Roethke. STS; UnPo (1976 ed.)

Dream, A. Michael Small. DNGG

Dream, A, *sels.* Rachel Speght. WPE
"I sought, I found, she asked me what I would."
"My grief, quoth I, is called Ignorance."
"Quoth she, I wish I could prescribe your help."
"Upon a sudden, as I gazing stood."

Dream. D. M. Thomas. FoP

Dream, The ( "Last night I had a dream bad 'cess to my dreaming"). *Unknown.* WTO

Dream, A ("Me thought I was in wildernesse walking al one"). *Unknown. Fr.* Mum and the Sothsegger. OxBM

Dream, a dream is it all—the season, A. Swinburne. *Fr.* A Swimmer's Dream. EcS

Dream about an Aged Humorist, A. Aaron Zeitlin, *tr. fr. Yiddish by* Ruth Whitman. VWA

Dream about Junior High School in America, The. Dick Lourie. NeAC

Dream Barker. Jean Valentine. VGW

Dream Boogie. Langston Hughes. ILP (1975 ed.)

Dream Deferred. Langston Hughes. *See* Harlem ("What happens to a dream deferred.")

Dream Farmer. Jill Witherspoon Boyer. CNA

Dream Feast, The (Three Poems). Anita Endrezze Probst. VoR

Dream-Follower, The. Thomas Hardy. VLP

Dream Girl. Larry Zirlin. AAN

Dream in a dream the heavy soul somewhere. Canto Amor. John Berryman. PAIC; VGW

Dream in Cold, A. Besmilr Brigham. Psy

Dream is a cocktail at Sloppy Joe's, The. Havana Dreams. Langston Hughes. LFH

Dream is that you are half crow, The. The Night You Got Back from the Mountains. Holly Prado. NPW

Dream is vague, The. Beale Street. Langston Hughes. PPP

Dream-Land. Poe. NOBA
(Dreamland.) TAP

Dream Land. Christina Rossetti. VLP

Dream-Love. Christina Rossetti. HAP

Dream 1971. Victor Contoski. GP

Dream of a Baseball Star. Gregory Corso. NoAM; VGW

Dream of a Boy Who Lived at Nine Elms, The. William Brighty Rands. OxBChV

Dream of a Girl Who Lived at Sevenoaks, The. William Brighty Rands. OxBChV

Dream of a Lover, The. *Unknown.* LoAs
(Benedicite, What Dreamèd I This Night?) HAP

Dream of Ascent. James Applewhite. NVAP

Dream of Death, A. W. B. Yeats. GBL

Dream of Dying. Thomas Lovell Beddoes. ILP (1975 ed.)

Dream of Fair Women, A. Kingsley Amis. ExPo (1973 ed.); FF; NoAM; OAEL-2

Dream of Fixing Things, The. Arthur Smith. CPA

Dream of Flying Comes of Age, The. Howard Nemerov. BiP

Dream of Gerontius, The, *sels.* Cardinal Newman.
Angel ("Softly and gently, dearly-ransom'd soul"). PFD
"Now let the golden prison ope its gates," *conclusion.* VLP
"O Lord, how wonderful in depth and height." VLP

Dream of Hanging, A. Patricia Beer. HeHu; MPo

Dream of Jealousy, A. Seamus Heaney. CIP

Dream of Lakes, A. Laurence Lieberman. HeS

Dream of mine flew over the mead, A. The Dream-Follower. Thomas Hardy. VLP

Dream of Rebirth. Roberta Hill. CDW

Dream of Southern Roads. William Claire. PoUp

Dream of the Cabal, The: A Prophetical Satire. *Unknown.* APAS

Dream of the Cross, The. *Unknown. See* Dream of the Rood, The.

Dream of the Forgotten Lover. Lucia Fox, *tr. fr. Spanish by* R. Maghan. BoWoP

Dream of the Lynx. John Haines. NU

Dream of the Rood, The. *Unknown, tr. fr. Anglo-Saxon.* BoReV, *tr. by* Helen Gardner; OAEL-1, *tr. by* Charles W. Kennedy
(Dream of the Cross, The, *tr. by* Sally Purcell.) EBEV

Dream of Washed Hair, A. Rhyll McMaster. CAAP

Dream of Winter. George Mackay Brown. FaBoTw (1975 ed.)

Dream on Women, A. Carolyn Maisel. IHMS

Dream on stone. Afternoon's Angel. Seymour Mayne. VWA

Dream-Pedlary. Thomas Lovell Beddoes. DuDr; HAP; LoAs; NOBE; PMW
("If there were dreams to sell," *st.* 1.) LCL; PCOP

Dream Record: June 8, 1955. Allen Ginsberg. ConAP; NOBA

Dream Sequence, Part 9. Naomi Long Madgett. BPo

Dream Song. Lewis Alexander. PoBA

Dream-Song. Walter de la Mare. PoPle

Dream Song. *Tr. fr. Pawnee Indian by* Frances Densmore. OBVE

Dream Songs. John Berryman. *Poems indexed separately by titles and first lines.*

Dream Songs. Karoniaktatie. NW

Dream Songs of Haka Ancestors. Alan Chong Lau. NW

Dream the small silences clearly. Pantoum. Stephen Shrader. PHC

Dream 3: Night Bear Which Frightened Cattle. Margaret Atwood. BCr

Dream time, The. Out. Ted Hughes. TwMBP

Dream 2: Brian the Still-Hunter. Margaret Atwood. BoWoP

Dream Variation [*or* Variations]. Langston Hughes. AmNP (1974 ed.); HAP; MiP; NOBA; PiAm; PoBA; WeW

Dream Vision. J. V. Cunningham. PiAm

Dream Was of Rabbits, The. Merrill Leffler. PoUp

Dream while Wide Awake. Patricia Garfinkel. PoUp

Dream within a Dream, A. Poe. AmVN; GBL; ILP (1975 ed.); NOBA; PiAm; TAP

Dreame, The. John Donne. *See* Dream, The ("Dear love, for nothing less than thee").

Dreamed Grail found as if in dreams, The. On Finding the Meaning of "Radiance." Alan Dugan. PAIC

Dreamed Realization, A. Gregory Corso. VGW

Dreamed-up for Winter. Arthur Rimbaud, *tr. fr. French by* William Mead. LoAs

Dreamer, The. William Childress. SoS

Dreamer, The. Walter de la Mare. ILP (1975 ed.)

Dreamers. Siegfried Sassoon. NoAM

Dreaming/ I saw a butterfly in the night. God Bless Us. Gaston Bart-Williams. BuTh

Dreaming about Freedom. Jimmy Santiago Baca. AMV-80

Dreaming in the Shanghai Restaurant. D. J. Enright. MPo; PSN; TVo

Dreaming of Conn-Eda. Diane Levenberg. NPW

Dreaming of that place I wake. Green Ash. Jennifer J. Rankin. GAS

Dreaming of the ebony. Brush Mask. Linda Parker. TC

Dreaming the Ancestors. Skaidrite Stelzer. TC

Dreaming Winter. James Welch. VW

Dreamland. *See* Dream Land.

Dreamlike leap, A. For the Record. Roy Blount, Jr. OBAL

Dreams. André Breton, *tr. fr. French by* Robert Duncan. InPS

Dreams. Charles Cooper. PoBA

Dreams. Nikki Giovanni. CNA; PoBA

Dreams. Robert Herrick. CaPo; HAP

Dreams. William Peskett. IPM

Dreams. Poe. TAP

Dreams. Arthur Symons. PoA

Dreams. Thomas Traherne. SCP-2

"Dreams Are the Royal Road to the Unconscious." Paul Goodman. PoA

Dreams come from circular longings. After Drinking Water. Daniela Gioseffi. WBN

Dreams cool. They hold shy looks in awe. Love! Love! Rhoda McMahon. WeW

Dreams fled away, this country bedroom, raw. Another September. Thomas Kinsella. BIrV; CIP; IPM

Dreams from War. Marilyn Krysl. NPW

Dreams in War Time, *sel.* Amy Lowell.
"I dug a grave under an oak-tree." BoWoP

Dreams of Auschwitz. Boris Slutsky, *tr. fr. Russian by* Daniel Weissbort. VWA

Dreams of Eurydice. Margaret Ryan. NPW

Dreams of Lost Atlantis. Alejandro Murguia. CPA

Dreams of the Wars. David Young. CAAP

Dreamscape. Philip Booth. FiCP

Dreamwater. Hilde Domin, *tr. fr. German by* Tudor Morris. VWA

Dreary Black Hills, The. *Unknown.* AmFP; BPAW; FSW

Dreary Change, The. Sir Walter Scott. OAEL-2

Dress goods,/ Silk. Hugh Fox. *Fr.* Apotheosis of Olde Towne. TC

Dress Me, Dear Mother. Avraham Shlonsky, *tr. fr. Hebrew by* Robert Mezey. VWA

Dress me in green. *Unknown, tr. fr. Spanish by* Willis Barnstone. BoWoP

Dress of clouds opens like a flower, The. Diving. Shiro Murano, *tr. by* Ichiro Kono *and* Rikutaro Fukuda. SPo

Dress of Fire, A. Dahlia Ravikovitch, *tr. fr. Hebrew by* Chana Bloch. VWA

Dressed As I Am, a Young Man Once Called Me Names in Spanish. Judy Grahn. *Fr.* A Woman Is Talking to Death. WBN

Dressed in the colours of a country day. From the Painting "Back from Market" by Chardin. Eavan Boland. IPM

Dressed man and a naked man, A. George Orwell. EBEV

Dressed up in my melancholy. Song. M. Carl Holman. AmNP (1974 ed.)

Dresses. Kathleen Fraser. NMM

Dressing for Our Spring Party. Jane Garland Katz. AAN

Dressing Stations, The. Norman Dubie. AmPA

Dried Things Out. Samuel Makidemewabe, *tr. fr. Cree Indian by* Howard Norman. TC

Dried thistles hide his face. Gathering Mushrooms. Alistair Campbell. ATNZ

Drifter off Tarentum, A. Kipling. *Fr.* Epitaphs of the War. FaBoEE; PoPle

Drifters. Bruce Dawe. GAS; MAuV

Drifting. D. Maitland Bushby. BPAW

Drifting, A. Robert Hutchinson. LoAs

Drifting. Kathleen Spivack. IHMS

Drifting and innocent and like snow. Christmas Letter Home. G. S. Fraser. OxBTC; SLP

Drifting night in the Georgia pines. O Daedalus, Fly Away Home. Robert Hayden. BiP; HAP; NCSH; PoBA; WeW

Drifting outside in a pall of smoke. The Wall. Raymond Carver. NVAP

Drifting The. Lyn Lifshin. MMD

Driftwood. Daniel Smythe. RFM

Driftwood Dybbuk. Barbara F. Lefcowitz. VWA

Drill Man Blues. George Sizemore. AmFP; WTO

Drill, Ye Tarriers, Drill! *Unknown. See* Tarrier's Song.

Drink and dance and laugh and lie. The Flaw in Paganism. Dorothy Parker. PoIA

Drink me. Thirst. Musa Moris Farhi. VWA

Drink to Me Only with Thine Eyes. Ben Jonson. *See* To Celia ("Drink to me only. . .").

Drink Today. John Fletcher, *and others. Fr.* The Bloody Brother, II, ii. PAIC

Drink with Something in It, A. Ogden Nash. PPM

Drinker, The. Robert Lowell. SoSe

Drinking. Abraham Cowley, *after the Greek of* Anacreon. CABA (1972 ed.); FF; NOBE; OBVE; PAIC; PMW; PoPle; WeW
(Anacreontics: Drinking.) HeIP; OBP

Drinking Cold Water. Peter Everwine. NNaP

Drinking hot saké. Gary Synder. *Fr.* Hitch Haiku. InPK

Drinking Song. Alexander Brome. PoPle

Drinking Song. Frederick Marryat. RhR

Drinking Song. James Kenneth Stephen. NOBL

Drinking Song ("She tells me with claret she cannot agree"). *Unknown.* NOBL

Drinking Song ("Tappster, fill another ale"). *Unknown.* OxBM

Drinking Song, A. W. B. Yeats. BoLoP; LoAs; OAEL-2; POL

Drinking Time. D. J. O'Sullivan. PFIr

Drinking while Driving. Raymond Carver. NVAP

Drinking with a Dead Bear. D. C. Berry. BCr

Dripping locker room, A. Liver. Coleman Barks. *Fr.* Body Poems. NVAP

Dripping Tap, The. James Kirkup. RAE

Drips surprise, The. They talk too. Fag-End. Philip O'Connor. EAS

Drive Away Blues. *Unknown.* BluL

Drive In Movie. Gary Sange. NVAP; SFF

Drive-ins are out, to start with. One must always be. Movie-going. John Hollander. NYP; PPoD; PPP

Driven out from the centers of population. Steep. Robert Morgan. CSP

Driver, The. James Dickey. VGW

Driver rubbed at his nettly chin, The. To the Four Courts, Please. James Stephens. BIrV; PFIr; UnPo (1976 ed.)

"Driver, what stream is it?" I asked, well knowing. The Lordly Hudson. Paul Goodman. ExPo (1973 ed.); NYP; VGW

Drivers of Boston, The. June Gross. AMV-80

Driving along the eastern shore of Lake Michigan. An Impossibility. Robert Vas Dias. HeS

Driving at Night. John Calvin Rezmerski. HeS

Driving By. Robert Wallace. LiSp

Driving Clock. Hildegarde Flanner. WPW

Driving Down from the Big Horns. Peggy Simson Curry. WPW

Driving down the concrete vein. The White Man Pressed the Locks. James C. Kilgore. InPK

Driving; Driven. David McAleavey. AMV-80

Driving east. Returning from the Funeral. Patricia Henley. NPW

Driving Home. Madeline DeFrees. MPA

Driving Home. Jonathan London. AMV-81

Driving home from the school. All Three of Us. Carol Cox. MMD

Driving, I come for a while. Late at Night. William Stafford. NNaP

Driving in Oklahoma. Carter Revard. VoR

Driving late at night I pass. Sleep. Dana Naone. CDW

Driving Montana. Richard Hugo. MPA

Driving North from Kingsville, Texas. Naomi Shihab. TAT

Driving North from Savannah on My Birthday. Paul Zimmer. AMV-81

Driving that train, high on cocaine. Casey Jones. Robert Hunter. GrRo

Driving the Mule. *Unknown. See* My Sweetie's a Mule in the Mine.

Driving to Town Late to Mail a Letter. Robert Bly. InPK; SFF; TSWA; UsP; VGW

Driving to Winter Park, in Florida. Cages. Jane Kenyon. TC

Driving through New England. Lucille Clifton. GOA

Driving through the Pima Indian Reservation. Paul H. Cook. AMV-80

Driving to Santa Barbara. Light Rain. Christopher Buckley. AMV-81

Driving to Sauk City. Warren Woessner. TAT

Driving toward the Lac Qui Parle River. Robert Bly. ConAP; NCSH

Driving Up to Kokee Park in the Summer. Laban Chang. PHC

Driving with my mother. For My Mother's Mother. Judith McDaniel. TV

Driving Wheels, The. G. E. Murray. HeS

Drizzle shifted, The. The Day I Stopped Dreaming about Barbara Steele. R. H. W. Dillard. PPoD

Drizzling Easter Morning, A. Thomas Hardy. CMoP (1970 ed.)

Droit de Seigneur. Richard Murphy. PFIr

Droll Tale of the Old Woman Who Bought a Pig, The. *Unknown.* BBL

Dromedary. François Dodat, *tr. fr. French by* Bert *and* Odette Meyers. BoAnP

Drone of airplane neared, and dimmed away, The. Immanent. Walter de la Mare. PoA

Drone v. Worker. Ebenezer Elliott. OBSV

Droning a drowsy syncopated tune. The Weary Blues. Langston Hughes. InPK; NoAM; NOBA

Drop. George MacBeth. TwMBP

Drop, Drop, Slow Tears. Phineas Fletcher. NOBE; SCP-2 (Hymn, A: "Drop, drop slow tears.") BoReV

Drop the Wires. Hugh Seidman. AmPA

Drop Thy Still Dews. Whittier. ILwL

Dropped from the air at evening, this desolate call. Curlew. Leslie Norris. HeHu

Dropping back with the ball ripe in my palm. The Passer. George Abbe. LiSp

Dropping toward Stillness. Sharon Barba. RiTi

Drops of Gall. Gabriela Mistral, *tr. fr. Spanish by* David Garrison. BoWoP

Drought. David Holbrook. OxBTC

Drought. Oumar Ba, *tr. fr. French by* Kathleen Weaver. PBWP

Drove away I/ know I'll never go. Leaving Them, Letting the Farm Swallow. Lyn Lifshin. FAF

Drove-Road, The. W. W. Gibson. OxBTC

Drover, A. Padraic Colum. PFIr

Drowned Darling, The. Danny L. Rendleman. TC

Drowning Girl. Beth Bentley. CNW

Drowning in Spanish. Tom Schmidt. NeAC

Drowning is not so pitiful. Emily Dickinson. CMoP (1970 ed.); ExPo (1973 ed.)

Drowsy. Carl Sandburg. OSP

Drug of the incomprehensible. The Bad Habit. Charles Henri Ford. EAS

Drug Store. Karl Shapiro. CMoP (1970 ed.); ILP (1975 ed.); NowV; TCP

Drugged all day, the summer. July the Seventh. Leslie Norris. HeHu

Drugs are a tuition. Going to School in France or America. Tom Clark. ConAP

Drugs made his belly/ break and bleed. Franco. Judith Smallshaw. PMW

Drum. Ricardo Sanchez. NW

Drum, The. John Scott of Amwell. *See* I Hate That Drum's Discordant Sound.

Drum of my people. Drum. Ricardo Sanchez. NW

Drum on your drums, batter on your banjos. Jazz Fantasia. Carl Sandburg. ILP (1975 ed.)

Drum Songs. Joseph Bruchac. TSWA

Drum, The: The Narrative of the Demon of Tedworth. Edith Sitwell. FaBoTw (1975 ed.)

Drumdelgie. *Unknown.* GBP

Drumdrumdrum, A. The Wall. Gwendolyn Brooks. *Fr.* Two Dedications. ILP (1975 ed.); PoBA

Drumlin Woodchuck, A. Robert Frost. ILP (1975 ed.); NoAM; NOBA

Drummer, The. Anne Robinson. PCOP

Drummer Boy of Shiloh, The. *Unknown.* AmFP

Drummer Hodge. Thomas Hardy. EBEV; HAP; ILP (1975 ed.); InPS; NoAM; VLP

Drumming Lightly. Leonard Kubo. PHC

Drums. Martha Chosa. VW

Drums gather and humble us beyond escape. Belief. A. R. Ammons. GOA; TT

Drums of the world, beat! Four Poems, 4. Joseph Freeman. SPT

Drums rap out our cue, The. High Wire Dancers. Ann Hoskins. PPM

Drums, the winter sun overhead. Winter Dance, San Domingo. Wendell B. Anderson. PoW

Drunk. Carroll Arnett. VoR

Drunk, A/ reeking. Dupont Circle. Barbara Berman. PoUp

Drunk as drunk on turpentine. Pablo Neruda, *tr fr. Spanish by* Christopher Logue. BoLoP

Drunk I have been, and drunk I was that night. To Laura Phelan: 1880–1906. Leon Stokesbury. NVAP

Drunk in the Furnace, The. W. S. Merwin. CAPP; MAT; NoAM

Drunk in the kitchen, I ring God. Telephoning God. Gary Soto. AAN; CPA

Drunk Last Night. *Unknown.* FSW

Drunk last night. A Dry Day just before the Rainy Season. Gary Snyder. MIT

Drunk Man Looks at the Thistle, A, *sel.* "Hugh MacDiarmid." "Dae what ye wull ye canna parry." EBEV

Drunkard, A. *Unknown.* OxBM

Drunkard and the Pig, The. *Unknown.* OBAL

Drunkard cannot meet a cork, A. Emily Dickinson. InPS

Drunkards, The ("The drunkards are rolling in slowly"). Jalal ed-Din Rumi, *ad. fr. Persian by* Robert Bly. NU

Drunkard's Doom, The. *Unknown.* FSW

Drunkard's Last Market, The. Charles Tennyson Turner. VPC

Drunken Boat, The. Arthur Rimbaud, *tr. fr. French by* Stepan Stepanchev. NAWM-2

Drunken Fisherman, The. Robert Lowell. AnMo; CMoP (1970 ed.); CoPAm; NOBA; STS; VGW

Drunken Lover. Owen Dodson. AmNP (1974 ed.)

Drunken Man, The. Steven Orlen. AAN

Drunken night in my house with a, A. Dream Record: June 8, 1955. Allen Ginsberg. ConAP; NOBA

Drunken Sailor, The. *Unknown.* *See* What Shall We Do with a Drunken Sailor?

Drunken Stones of Prague, The. David Scheinert, *tr. fr. French by* Edouard Roditi. VWA

Drunken Streets. Malka Locker, *tr. fr. Yiddish by* Jeremy Garber. VWA

Drunkenness of Pain, The. Aliza Shenhar, *tr. fr. Hebrew by* Linda Zisquit. VWA

Dry afternoon scraping the rooftops, The. Summer Street. Ana Ilce, *tr. by* Steven White. AMV-81

Dry brown coughing beneath their feet, The. Beverly Hills, Chicago. Gwendolyn Brooks. VGW

Dry Day just before the Rainy Season, A. Gary Snyder. MIT

Dry Land Blues. *Unknown.* BluL

Dry Loaf. Wallace Stevens. NOBA

Dry-Point. Philip Larkin. CMoP (1970 ed.)

Dry Salvages, The. T. S. Eliot. *Fr.* Four Quartets. CABA (1972 ed.); PiAm

Dry tree with an empty honeycomb, A. The Tomb of Heracles. James McAuley. *Fr.* The Hero and the Hydra. MAuV

Dry vine leaves burn in an angle of the wall. The Thousand Things. Christopher Middleton. TwMBP

Drynaun, Dhun, The. *Unknown.* GBP

Dryness is upon the house, A. In Honor of David Anderson Brooks, My Father. Gwendolyn Brooks. TT

Dtah Dtah. David Kherdian. SA

Du Bartas His Divine Weeks and Works, *sels.* Joshua Sylvester. SCP-2
1st Week 5th Day.
1st Week 6th Day.

Dual, The. Richard Lovelace. CaPo

Dual Site, The. Michael Hamburger. AIW; NowV

Duality. Dannie Abse. NoAM

Dubious Night, A. Richard Wilbur. CAPP

Dublin. Louis MacNeice. CIP; OxBTC; PFIr

Dublin could not tame your tongue. Jack. W. G. McNeice. IPM

Dublin Made Me. Donagh MacDonagh. OxBTC; PFIr

Dubrovnik Poem (Emilio Tolentino). Anthony Rudolf. VWA

Duchess of Malfi, The, *sels.* John Webster.
"Farewell, Cariola./ In my last will I have not much to give," *fr.* IV, ii. LFH
Hark, Now Everything Is Still, *fr.* IV, ii. HAP; InPS (Shrouding of the Duchess of Malfi, The.) NOBE
"I am come to make thy tomb," *fr.* IV, ii. OBP
"O let us howl some heavy note, *fr.* IV, ii. SCP-2

Duchess of York's Ghost, The. *Unknown.* APAS

Duchess Potatoes, The. Diane Wakoski. CAAP

Duchess's Lullaby, The. "Lewis Carroll." *Fr.* Alice's Adventures in Wonderland. FaBoNo; SpRo
("Speak roughly to your little boy.") FaBoCo

Duck. John Lyle Donaghy. BIrV

Duck, The. Ogden Nash. RAE

Duck and the Kangaroo, The. Edward Lear. OxBChV

Duck-chasing. Galway Kinnell. UsP; VGW

Duck Pond at Mini's Pasture, a Dozen Years Later, The. Philip Dow. AmPA

Duck who had got such a habit of stuffing, A. The Notorious Glutton. Ann Taylor. OxBChV

Ducks. Phoebe Hesketh. BoAnP

Ducks' Ditty. Kenneth Grahame. *Fr.* The Wind in the Willows. OxBChV; PoPle

Due Date. Seymour Cain. AMV-80

Duel, The. Eugene Field. CTV; ECBV; OBAL; PCOP

Duel in the Camellias. Charles Doyle. ATNZ

Duellist, The, *sel.* Charles Churchill.
"First, The (entitled to the place)." OBSV

Duelists. Anne Becker. PoUp

Duérmete, Niño Lindo. *Tr. fr. Spanish.* FSW

Duet. Tennyson. *Fr.* Becket. GBL

Dufferin, Simcoe, Grey. Margaret Atwood. AMV-81

Duino Elegies, *sel.* Rainer Maria Rilke, *tr. fr. German by* David Young.
"It's one thing/ to sing the beloved," III. NAWM-2

"Duke" and the "Count," The. Richard Fewell. AMV-81

Duke of Buckingham, The. Pope. *Fr.* Moral Essays. NOBE (Death of the Duke of Buckingham, The.) ExPo (1973 ed.).

Duke of Grafton, The. *Unknown.* GBP; PeBB

Duke of York (Courage), The. Chuck Miller. AcAn

Duke of York's Statue, The. Walter Savage Landor. FaBoEE

Duke upon Duke. Pope. Epi

Duke William was a wench's son. Song of Duke William. Hilaire Belloc. FaBoNo

Duke's Song, The. Mary Sidney Wroth, Countess of Montgomery. *Fr.* Urania. WPE

Dulce et Decorum Est. Wilfred Owen. CABA (1972 ed.); CMoP (1970 ed.); DL; FaBoTw (1975 ed.); FF; HeIP; HOPM (1975 ed.); ILP (1975 ed.); InPK; IP; NIL; NoAM; OAEL-2; PPP; SFF; SoSe; UnPo (1976 ed.); VoPo; WIF

*Dulce* it is, and *decorum,* no doubt, for the country to fall. Arthur Hugh Clough. *Fr.* Amours de Voyage, II, ii. OBP

Dull as an eraser the moon. Rosalie. Danny L. Rendleman. TC

Dull as I was to think that a court fly. A Black Patch on Lucasta's Face. Richard Lovelace. CaPo; PAIC

"Dull day, A." Wait till Then. Mark Van Doren. SO

Dull headaches on dark afternoons. Tony Connor. Twelve Secret Poems, 3. UsP

Dull Love, no more thy senseless arrows prize. An Ode to Love. Aphra Behn. SCP-2

Dull people, A. From Colony to Nation. Irving Layton. CABA (1972 ed.)

"Dull sublunary lovers" Nocturne: Lake Huron. Conor Kelly. AMV-80

Dull to myself, and almost dead to these. The Bad Season Makes the Poet Sad. Robert Herrick. CABA (1972 ed.); CaPo; ILP (1975 ed.)

Dull unwashed windows of eyes. A Poem Some People Will Have to Understand. Amiri Baraka. BPo; NOBA; PiAm

Dulles Airport. Eugene McCarthy. WasP

Dumb,/ Bloodied, the severed. A Grafted Tongue. John Montague. BIrV; CIP

Dumb Soldier, The. Robert Louis Stevenson. OxBChV

Dumb World, The. W. H. Davies. BoAnP; OBW; OxBTC

Dumbarton's Drums. *Unknown.* FSW

Dump, The. Donald Hall. TCP

Dump, The. Greg Kuzma. PoA

Dunbarton. Robert Lowell. ILP (1975 ed.); MPo

Duncan Spoke of a Process. Amiri Baraka. CAPP

Dunce Song 6. Mark Van Doren. DuDa

Dunciad, The, *sels.* Pope.
  "High on a gorgeous seat, that far outshone," *fr.* II.  NIL
  "In vain, in vain—the all-composing hour," *fr.* IV.  EBEV
    (Triumph of Dullness, The.)  NOBE
  "Mighty Mother, and her son who brings, The," *fr.* I.  OBSV
  "Next bidding all draw near on bended knees," *fr.* IV.  OBSV
  "Yet, yet a moment, one dim ray of light," IV.  OAEL-1

Dunderbeck. *Unknown.* FSW

Dunes are graying that were blackest. Aubade: The Desert.
  Frederick Bock. PoA

Dunlavin Green. *Unknown.* FaBoBa

Duns Scotus's Oxford. Gerard Manley Hopkins. EBEV; Epi;
  NoAM; OBP; VLP
  "Towery city and branchy between towers," *sel.* PES

Duo. William Keys. SLP

Dupont Circle. Barbara Berman. PoUp

Durban, Birmingham. Question and Answer. Langston Hughes.
  BPo

Durer would have seen a reason for living. The Steeple-Jack.
  Marianne Moore. *Fr.* Part of a Novel, Part of a Poem, Part
  of a Play. BoWoP; CMoP (1970 ed.); HAP; ILP (1975 ed.);
  NoAM; NOBA; PBWP; SBG; WPE

"Durham," "Devonia," "Allendale,"—their houses, those. A
  Summer Cloud. Waldo Williams, *tr. by* Joseph P. Clancy.
  OBW

Durham Old Women. *Unknown.* GBP

During March while hoeing long rows. Hoeing. Gary Soto.
  NW

During one period I remember. Eveningsong 2. Ramona
  Wilson. VoR

During the dream. Fidelity. Jerry Kass. AMV-80

During the Eichmann Trial, *sel.* Denise Levertov.
  Peachtree, The. CAPP

During the great debates, he tried a joke. Campaign Promise.
  Henry Taylor. WasP

During the holidays. Holidays. Eva Mylonas, *tr. by* Kimon
  Friar. BoWoP

During the Pageant at Medicine Lodge. Charles G. Ballard.
  VoR; VW

During the raids. War Poem. Jim Mulac. AcAn

During the season of cut organs we. Initiation. Jayne Cortez.
  PoBA

During the strike, the ponies were brought up. The Ponies.
  W. W. Gibson. PH

During the Tet offensive, U.S. marines in Hue. News. Robin
  Morgan. WBN

During the War. William Kloefkorn. *Fr.* Loony. GP

During Wind and Rain. Thomas Hardy. CMoP (1970 ed.);
  ExPo (1973 ed.); HAP; ILP (1975 ed.); InPK; NIL; OAEL-2;
  OxBTC; PoPle; PPP

Dusk. Ken Belford. NeAC

Dusk. Gabriela Mistral, *tr. fr. Spanish by* David Garrison.
  BoWoP

Dusk/ Above the/ water. Swan and Shadow. John Hollander.
  PoA; WeW

Dusk/ no dawns, and silver linings. No Dawns. Julianne Perry.
  PoBA

Dusk again at the Old Forge dump. Feeding Time. Janet
  Beeler. BCr

Dusk falters over shelf and chair. God Save the Stock. Charles
  Spear. ATNZ

Dusk-haired and gold-robed o'er the golden wine. For "The Wine
  of Circe" by Edward Burne-Jones. Dante Gabriel Rossetti.
  VLP

Dusk is in the cat. Affinities. Adrien Stoutenburg. TSWA

Dusk of the Gods. Sol Funaroff. SPT

Dusk swirls like a dust of chalk up here, The. Four Postcards
  from Italy. Colman Andrews. PoW

Duskier than the clouds that lie. Willy to Jinny. Joseph Skipsey.
  VLP

Dust. Rupert Brooke. OxBTC

Dust. Kathleen Spivack. BoWoP

Dust. Randolph Stow. GAS

Dust always blowing about the town. A Peck of Gold. Robert
  Frost. BPAW; SO

Dust are our frames; and, gilded dust, our pride. Aylmer's Field.
  Tennyson. VLP

Dust Bowl. Langston Hughes. PoA

Dust of all the saints of the ages, The. Cymru. D. Gwenallt
  Jones, *tr. by* Gwyn Jones. OBW

Dust of Snow. Robert Frost. CMoP (1970 ed.); FSFS; IPWM;
  SoSe; SS; TAP; TSWA; UnPo (1976 ed.); WeW

Dust thou art, but dust carefully. Ralph Hodgson. *Fr.* Flying
  Scrolls. FaBoTw (1975 ed.)

Dustbin Men, The. Gregory Harrison. FPB

Dustless Chalk. James Rankin. MIS

Dustoff: Med Evac. Horace Coleman. SES

Dusty black beetle, A. Robert Sund. BoAnP

Dutch Lover, The, *sels.* Aphra Behn.
  Song: "Ah false Amyntas, can that hour." WPE
  Willing Mistress, The. SBG

Dutch Proverb, A. Matthew Prior. FaBoEE; LFH; POL

Dutchess of Monmouth's Lamentation for the Loss of Her Duke,
  The. *Unknown.* FaBoBa

Duty. Arthur Hugh Clough. VPC

Duty lies in your desk. Hating Your Life. John N. Morris.
  CABA (1972 ed.)

Duty—that's to say, complying. Duty. Arthur Hugh Clough.
  VPC

Duwamish. Richard Hugo. CNW; MPA

Dvonya. Louis Simpson. NNaP; NOBA

Dwarf, The. Gerald Locklin. GP

Dwarf barefooted, chanting, The. The Peasants. Alun Lewis.
  PPP

Dwarf with his hands on backwards, The. Assisi. Norman
  MacCaig. MS

Dwarfed limb, A. The Copperhead. David Bottoms. AMV-81

Dwell, awful Silence, on the shady hills. Pan Piping. Plato, *tr.*
  *by* Thomas Stanley. FaBoEE

Dwelling, The. Moshe Dor, *tr. fr. Hebrew by* Dennis Johnson.
  VWA

Dwellings of Our Dead, The. Arthur H. Adams. ATNZ

D'ye [*or* Do ye] ken John Peel with his coat so gay [*or* gray]?
  John Peel. John Woodcock Greaves. FSW; GSB

D'ye ken the big village of Balmaquhapple. The Village of
  Balmaquhapple. James Hogg. FaBoCo

Dying. A. Alvarez. VWA

Dying. Jascha Kessler. PoW

Dying. Robert Pinsky. AMV-81

Dying Airman, The. *Unknown.* FaBoNo

Dying Californian, The. *Unknown.* AmFP; BPAW

Dying Christian to His Soul, The. Pope. *See* Ode: Dying
  Christian to His Soul, The.

Dying Cowboy, The ("As I rode out by Tom Sherman's bar-
  room"). *Unknown.* FaBoBa; NIL

Dying day pinches the tot. Daily News. Tom Clark. EAS

Dying Dentist, The. Robert Huff. PoW

Dying exaggerates occasional kindness. Flowers in Cellars.
  Conleth Ellis. IPM

Dying Father's Farewell, The. *Unknown.* *See* Time Is Swiftly
  Rolling On, The.

Dying firelight slides along the quirt, A. The End of the Weekend. Anthony Hecht. ConAP; HAP; PSN; WeW

Dying for love is out of fashion. Return to Astolat. Gail White. AMV–81

Dying Gaul, The. Desmond O'Grady. BIrV

Dying Gladiator, The. Byron. *Fr.* Childe Harold's Pilgrimage, IV. NOBE

Dying Goddess, The. Carolyn Kizer. WBN

Dying Hobo, The. *Unknown.* AmFP

Dying is a curious thing. End. Christy Brown. IPM

Dying Is Fine)but Death. E. E. Cummings. TT

Dying Man, The. Theodore Roethke. STS

Dying Mine Brakeman, The. Orville Jenks. AmFP

Dying off Egg Island Bar. David Smith. NVAP

Dying Patriot, The, *sel.* James Elroy Flecker. "Evening on the olden, the golden sea of Wales." EcS

Dying Sergeant, The. *Unknown.* AmFP

Dying Speech of an Old Philosopher. Walter Savage Landor. *See* On His Seventy-fifth Birthday.

Dying sun, shine warm a little longer! Lament for Pasiphae. Robert Graves. FaBoTw (1975 ed.)

Dying Thief. Itzik Manger, *tr. fr. Yiddish by* Stephen Garrin. VWA

Dying tiger, A—moaned for drink. Emily Dickinson. PeD

Dying under a Fall of Stars. Mark Elliott Shapiro. VWA

Dyke, The. Jenny Morgan. PMW

Dykes, The. Kipling. VLP

Dylan Thomas. T. O. Maglow. InPK

Dylan, Who Is Dead. Samuel Allen. PoBA

Dynamite Song. *Unknown.* AmFP

Dynasts, The, *sels.* Thomas Hardy.
Budmouth Dears, *fr.* Pt. III, Act II, sc. i. PoPle
Chorus of the Years ("Yea, the coneys are scared by the thud of hoofs"), *fr.* Pt. III, Act VI, sc. viii. CMoP (1970 ed.)
"Eyelids of eve fall together at last, The," *fr.* Pt. III, Act VI, sc. viii. OAEL–2
Field of Talavera, The, *fr.* Pt. II, Act IV, sc. iv. CMoP (1970 ed.)

Dyvers dothe use as I have hard and kno. *See* Divers doth use as I have heard and know.

Dyvers thy death doo dyverslye bemone. Earl of Surrey. AAS

E

E = mc²: Einstein at Princeton. David Rowbotham. CAAP

E. P. Ode pour l'Election de Son Sepulchre. Ezra Pound. Hugh Selwyn Mauberley, I. HAP; InPS; NoAM; NOBA; PiAm; VGW

E. Tenebris. Oscar Wilde. CABA (1972 ed.)

È, the Feasting Florentines. Daniel Hoffman. VGW

E Uni Que A The Hi A Tho, Father. Roberta Hill. VoR

'E was warned agin 'er. The Sergeant's Weddin'. Kipling. OxBTC

Each and All. Emerson. AmVN; ILP (1975 ed.); NOBA; PiAm; TAP
"Delicate shells lay on the shore, The," *sel.* EcS

Each beat of the drum's a round drop of rain. Santo Domingo Corn Dance. R. P. Dickey. TAT

Each body has its art, its precious prescribed. "Still Do I Keep My Look, My Identity. . ." Gwendolyn Brooks. PoA

Each Day. David Ignatow. NNaP

Each day, a certain hour. In Disguise. Joseph Rolnik, *tr. by* Keith Bosley. VWA

Each day brings its toad, each night its dragon. Jerome. Randall Jarrell. PPP

Each day I live, each day the sea of light. Poem against the Rich. Robert Bly. CAPP; NoAM; NOBA

Each day I lure the hummingbirds. The Ritual. Joy Gwillim. AMV–80

Each Day Is Anxious. "Anna Akhmatova," *tr. fr. Russian by* Judith Hemschemeyer *and* Anne Wilkinson. AMV–81

Each day that summer he walked the avenue. The Last Clean Bough. James Aitchison. MS

Each day the tide withdraws; chills us; pastes. Wreaths. Geoffrey Hill. PoA

Each day was like another. Ballad of the Hidden Dragon. *Unknown, tr. fr. Chinese.* WTO

Each day we settle for a little less. Less Is More. Vern Rutsala. AMV–80

Each dusk I saw, while those I loved the most. The Owl. V. Sackville-West. SBG

Each eve earth falleth down the dark. The Day of Days. William Morris. VLP

Each face in the street is a slice of bread. Bread. W. S. Merwin. EAS

Each for himself is still the rule. In the Great Metropolis. Arthur Hugh Clough. VPC

Each house had its ghost. Sigmund Freud. Howard Nemerov. PoA

Each inmost peece in me is thine. Bible, *O.T., paraphrased by* Countess of Pembroke. *Fr.* Psalms, CXXXIX. OBVE

Each is beautiful. Tell Our Daughters. Besmilr Brigham. IHMS

Each known mile comes late. The Train Runs Late to Harlem. Conrad Kent Rivers. PoBA

Each man has/ his own way. The End Bit. Jim Burns. FF

Each moment of the long-liv'd day. Catullus, *tr. fr. Latin by* Tom Brown. OBVE

Each Morning. Amiri Baraka. *Fr.* Hymn for Lanie Poo. PoBA

Each morning the birds awake me. Morning Vigil. Phillip William George. VoR

Each morning they bring me the condemned man's brekker. Analogy. Brian Higgins. FaBoTw (1975 ed.)

Each morning when I break my buttered toast. Keeping Informed in D. C. Howard Nemerov. WasP

Each morning when I lit the coke furnace. The Morgue. James K. Baxter. ATNZ

Each night/ just before dusk. Elaine H. Jennings. NPW

Each night we hear the sound. Sounds. Paul David Ashley. DNGG

Each of these twigs of tree. In Winter, Elms. Ronald Mann. PMW

Each one had defenses, they said. Continuing. Madeline Bass. WBN

Each one of us has his own likes and dislikes. Painting. Maxine Chernoff. FiCh

Each person lies in their bed, restless. Tonight Everyone in the World Is Dreaming the Same Dream. Susan Litwack. VWA

Each prisoner is so sad in the glare. The Line-up. Joan Swift. FiCP

Each return is a blessing. Gnostology. Sam Hamill. AMV–81

Each storm-soaked flower has a beautiful eye. Rain. Vachel Lindsay. CMoP (1970 ed.)

Each summer, the alien evangelist comes. The Evangelist. Bennie Lee Sinclair. TAT

Each time it rains. Suicide before Coffee in a Furnished Room. Herman Spector. SPT

Each year/ new quotas. New Quotas/ or Brooker T. and Garvey Would Have Loved South Africa. Antar S. K. Mberi. SES

Each year, as spring returns. Grandfather. Joan Aiken. TVo

Each year, the court expands. The Old Pro's Lament. Paul Petrie. LiSp; SPo; TAP

Eachie, peachie, pearie, plum. *Unknown*. GBP

Eadwacer. *Unknown, tr. fr. Anglo-Saxon*. PBWP, *tr. by* Kemp Malone; WPE
(Wulf and Eadwacer, *tr. by* Willis Barnstone *and* Elene Kolb.) BoWoP

Eager note on my door said, "Call me," The. Poem. Frank O'Hara. EAS; NoAM; NOBA

Eager to breathe out. Mocking Song against Qaqortingneq. Piuvkaq, *tr. fr. Eskimo*. WTO

Eagerly/ Like a woman hurrying to her lover. Four Glimpses of Night. Frank Marshall Davis. AmNP (1974 ed.); PoBA

Eagle, The. Richard Blessing. AMV-80

Eagle, The. Tennyson. CABA (1972 ed.); CTV; ExPo (1973 ed.); FF; HeIP; ILP (1975 ed.); InPK; IPWM; LFH; OAEL-2; OBP; PB; PoIA; PPoe; PoPle; SoSe; SS; UnPo (1976 ed.)

Eagle and the Beetle, The. La Fontaine, *tr. fr. French by* Elizur Wright. OBVE

Eagle and the Mole, The. Elinor Wylie. BoWoP; PAIC; UnPo (1976 ed.)

Eagle Converses with Chaucer, The. Chaucer. *Fr*. The House of Fame. OxBM

Eagle Feather [IV]. Phillip William George. NW

Eagle-feather Fan, The ("The Eagle is my power"). N. Scott Momaday. CDW

Eagle into swayback Ganymede. L'Aigle a Deux Jambes. Turner Cassity. GP

Eagle of Pengwern. *Unknown*, tr. fr. Welsh by Gwyn Williams. PBWP

Eagle Sings, The. *Unknown, tr. fr. Papago Indian*. AKE

Eagle Squadron. Vern Rutsala. AMV-80

Eagle, stooping from yon snow-blown peaks, The. Inscription. Whittier. GOA

Eagle That Is Forgotten, The. Vachel Lindsay. CMoP (1970 ed.); NOBA; VoPo

Eagle! why soarest thou above that tomb? Spirit of Plato. *Unknown, tr. by* Shelley. OBVE

Eagles, The. Jones Very. TAP

Eagle's eye is the strongest eye, The. The Great Way of the Man. Norman H. Russell. VW

Eagles gather on the place of death, The. The Eagles. Jones Very. TAP

Eagles have practically left America, The. Inability to Depict an Eagle. Richard Eberhart. GOA

Eagle's nest on the head of an old redwood, An. The Beaks of Eagles. Robinson Jeffers. NOBA

Eagles on a Half. *Unknown*. BluL

Eagles over the Lambing Paddock. Ernest Moll. MAuV

Eagle's shadow runs across the plain, The. Zebra. "Isak Dinesen." Mip; RFM

Eagle's Song, The. Mary Austin. GOA

Eaper Weaper. *Unknown*. FaBoNo

Ear to the earth. Figure and Ground. Elton Glaser. AMV-80

Earbob and the painted carnivores. Parable of the Sidewalk Tellers. Tom House. AAN

Earl Brand. *Unknown*. *See* Douglas Tragedy, The.

Earl Mertoun's Song. Robert Browning. PoPle

Earl Richard. *Unknown*. SLP

Earl the Pearl. Sheila Heldenbrand. AcAn

Earlier in the evening the moon. The Moon. Robert Creeley. VGW

Earliest morning, switching all the tracks. Love Lies Sleeping. Elizabeth Bishop. NYP

Early before the day doth spring. Of Astraea   Sir John Davies. *Fr*. Hymns of Astraea. NIL; PAIC

Early bird got up and whet his beak, The. A Birthday Ode to Mr. Alfred Austin. Sir Owen Seaman. NOBL

Early blossoms—could a single. Permanence in Change. Goethe, *tr. by* John Frederick Nims. HoPM (1975 ed.)

Early blue evening. Wonder. Langston Hughes. ILP (1975 ed.)

Early Copper. Carl Sandburg. HeIP; PiAm

Early, each morning, Martha Blake. Martha Blake at Fifty-one. Austin Clarke. CIP

Early, early in the spring. Early in the Spring. *Unknown*. AmFP

Early electric people had domesticated the wild ass, The. · The Electric Orchard. Paul Muldoon. IPM

Early Electric! With what radiant hope. The Metropolitan Railway. John Betjeman. EBEV; OxBTC

Early Ella   Lynn Sukenick. AAN; RiTi

Early Evening Quarrel. Langston Hughes. UnPo (1976 ed.); USP

Early Fall: The Adirondacks. Carolyne Wright. AMV-81

Early Fix. Andrei Codrescu. PoW

Early Frogs, The. Harry Edward Mills. PeD

Early Frost. Leslie Norris. HeHu

Early in spring the little General came. The Little General. Edwin Muir. MS

Early in the Dawning. Thomas Durfey. SCP-2

Early in the Morning. Louis Simpson. ConAP

Early in the morning at seven o'clock. Drill Ye Tarriers, Drill. *At. to* Thomas F. Casey. FSW

Early in the Spring. *Unknown*. AmFP

Early in the spring when the snow is all gone. A Trip to The Grand Banks. Amos Hanson. AmFP

Early January. W. S. Merwin. VGW

Early June. R. P. Dickey. TAT

Early Lynching. Carl Sandburg. UsP

Early Moon. Carl Sandburg. BPAW

Early Morning, The. Hilaire Belloc. ECBV

Early Morning of Another World. Tom McKeown. AMV-80

Early morning over Rouen, hopeful. Rouen. May Wedderburn Cannan. OxBTC

Early morning quick coffee and bran. "Quick Now, Here, Now, Always." William J. Rewak. AMV-81

Early Morning Song: The Snowstorm. Gloria Bussel Koster. NPW

Early, my God, without delay. Isaac Watts. AmFP

Early on a Sunday morning. Kevin Barry. *Unknown*. FSW

Early One Morning. *Unknown*. FSW; GSB, *with music*

Early one morning. A Girl's Song. Leslie Norris. HeHu

Early one morning. Voodoo on the Un-Assing of Janis Joplin. Carolyn M. Rodgers. JB

Early one morning just about 4 o'clock. Titanic Blues. *Unknown*. BluL

Early one morning, just as the sun was rising. Early One Morning. *Unknown*. FSW; GSB

Early Purges, The. Seamus Heaney. NCSH

Early sun on Beaulieu water. Youth and Age on Beaulieu River, Hants. John Betjeman. FaBoTw (1975 ed. )

Early Supper. Barbara Howes. DuDa; NCSH

Early this morning when you knocked upon my door. Me and the Devil Blues. *Unknown*. BluL

Early thou goest forth, to put to rout. To a "Tenting" Boy. Charles Tennyson Turner. VPC

Early Thoughts of Marriage. Nathaniel Cotton. OxBChV

Early to bed and early to rise. New Proverb. Shirley Brooks. FaBoNo

Early to bed, and early to rise. *Unknown*. MG

Early to meet you, watching a man. The Last Fish. Barry Spacks. AMV-80

Early wagons left no sign, The. The Trail into Kansas. W. S. Merwin. GOA

Early Warning. George MacBeth. TwMBP

Early Warning. Shirley Marks. QQQ

Earlye, Earlye, in the Spring. *Unknown.* AmFP

Earnest, earthless, equal, attuneable. Spelt from Sibyl's Leaves. Gerard Manley Hopkins. CMoP (1970 ed.); OAEL-2

Earnest Liberal's Lament, The. Ernest Hemingway. OBSV (Ernest Liberal's Lament, The.) OBAL

Earnest to explore within and all around. Dante, *tr. by* Shelley. *Fr.* Divina Commedia: Purgatorio, XXVIII. OBVE

Ears cocked wide. Two at Showtime. Suzanne Brabant. PH

Ears in the Turrets Hear. Dylan Thomas. FaBoTw (1975 ed.)

Earth, The. D. Gwenallt Jones, *tr. fr. Welsh by* Dyfnallt Morgan. OBW

Earth. Oliver Herford. MiP

Earth. Jim Tollerud. VoR

Earth (" 'A planet doesn't explode' "). John Hall Wheelock. SFF; SoSe

Earth/ Air/ Fire/ and Water. Mount Tamalpais. Geoffrey Cook. CPA

Earth, The/ is a wonderful. Poem for Friends. Quincy Troupe. PoBA

Earth a flower. For Nothing. Gary Synder. NNaP

Earth and Fire. Wendell Berry. FF; GP

Earth and I Gave You Turquoise. N. Scott Momaday. CDW; UnPo (1976 ed.); VW

Earth and sky black. Camp Site. Denis Glover. ATNZ

Earth around him, The: he within his life. Adam in Love. Stephen Mitchell. VWA

Earth Changes. Kent Shire. AMV-80

Earth darkens and is beaded. "Quod Tegit Omnia." Yvor Winters. BCr

Earth does not understand her child. The Return. Edna St. Vincent Millay. NoAM; PPM

Earth goes on the earth glittering in gold, The. Inscribed in Melrose Abbey. *Unknown.* FaBoEE

Earth grown old, yet still so green. Advent. Christina Rossetti. VLP

Earth grows green; the flowers bloom, The. Song to the Ninth Grade. Pamela Crawford Holahan. AIW

Earth has not any thing to show more fair. Composed upon Westminster Bridge, September 3, 1802. Wordsworth. AnMo; BiP; CABA (1972 ed.); Epi; FaPoR; FF; HAP; HeIP; ILP (1975 ed.); InPK; InPS; IPWM; MBPR; NOBE; OAEL-2; OBP; PAIC; PBMP; PES; PoIA; PPM; PPoD; PPP; TPo; UnPo (1976 ed.); WeW

Earth Has Shrunk in the Wash. William Empson. CMoP (1970 ed. )

Earth is a beautiful place, The. The Third Sermon on the Warpland. Gwendolyn Brooks. BPo

Earth is a place on which England is found, The. Geography. G. K. Chesterton. *Fr.* Songs of Education. OBSV

Earth is the Lord's and the fulness thereof, The  Bible, *O.T.* Psalms, XXIV. CTV

Earth keeps some vibration going, The. Fiddler Jones. Edgar Lee Masters. *Fr.* Spoon River Anthology. CMoP (1970 ed.); NoAM; TAP

Earth, ocean, air, beloved brotherhood! Alastor; or, The Spirit of Solitude. Shelley. MBPR; OAEL-2, *abr.*

Earth Psalm. Denise Levertov. PPP

Earth rais'd up her head. Earth's Answer. Blake. *Fr.* Songs of Experience. InPS; LAuP; MBPR; OAEL-2; STS; TT

Earth, receive an honoured guest. W. H. Auden. *Fr.* In Memory of W. B. Yeats. FaBoTw (1975 ed.)

Earth runs furrows under my skin, The. New Graveyard: Jerusalem. Shirley Kaufman. VWA

Earth Sings Mi-fa-mi, The. Pat Lowther. MMD

Earth smells different here, The. War. Patricia Ramsey. AATT

Earth Song. Thomas Peacock. VoR

Earth, they say, The. The Spinning Earth. Aileen Fisher. FPB

Earth, The: To Marilyn. Judith Johnson Sherwin. WBN

Earth Took of Earth. *Unknown.* HAP

Earth Walk. William Meredith. MAT; PPoD

Earth was green, the sky was blue, The. A Green Cornfield. Christina Rossetti. RAE

Earth was my home, but even there I was a stranger. The Flight of Apollo. Stanley Kunitz. Moon

Earth will be going on a long time, The. Lute Music. Kenneth Rexroth. TAP

Earth with thunder torne, with fire blasted, The. Fulke Greville. *Fr.* Caelica. AAS

Earth Worm, The. Denise Levertov. NOBA

Eartha. Stanley Burnshaw. SPT

Earthly nouris sits and sings, An. *See* Early nourris sits and sings, An.

Earthly Paradise, The, *sels.*     William Morris.
  Apology, An. OAEL-2; PAIC; VPC
    (Prologue: "Of Heaven or Hell I have no power to sing.") VLP
  August. VPC
  February. VPC
  L'Envoi: "Here we are for the last time face to face." VPC
  March ("He ended; and midst those who heard were some"). VLP
  May. VLP
  June. LFH
  October. VLP; VPC
  Outlanders, The. VPC
  "Under a bent when the night was deep." PChr
  Wanderers, The. VPC
  Written in a Copy of "The Earthly Paradise," Dec. 25, 1870. VLP

Earthquake, The. *Tr. fr. Zuni Indian by* K. Kennedy. WTO

Earth's Answer. Blake. *Fr.* Songs of Experience. InPS; LAuP; MBPR; OAEL-2; STS; TT

Earth's Bondman. Betty Page Dabney. ECBV

Earthy Anecdote. Wallace Stevens. CMoP (1970 ed.); RFM

Eartly nourris [*or* Earthly nouris] sits and sings, An. The Great Silkie of Sule Skerry. *Unknown.* FaBoBa; FSW; GBP; MAT; PeBB

Earthworms. Parody. Martha Paley Francescato, *tr. by* Willis Barnstone. BoWoP

Ease It to Me Blues. *Unknown.* BluL

Easier. James Harrison. AMV-80

East Bronx. David Ignatow. ConAP; IPWM

East Coker. T. S. Eliot. *Fr.* Four Quartets. HAP; PPP; VGW

East Hampton: The Structure of Sound. Philip Appleman. NYP

East Kentucky, 1967. Wendell Berry. CSP

East St. Louis Blues. *Unknown.* AmFP

East side, west side, all around the town. The Sidewalks of New York. James W. Blake. BLSH

East to west. Our little township is a lesion. Eyre All Alone. Francis Webb. CAAP

East Virginia. *Unknown.* FSW

East wall's so white, The. My House. Michael Cuddihy. FoP

East Wind asperges Boston with Lynn's sulphurous brine, An. Father. John Wheelwright. UnPo (1976 ed.)

Easter. Hilda Conkling. CC

Easter ("I got me flowers to straw thy way"). George Herbert. NOBE

Easter ("Rise, heart! thy Lord is risen"). George Herbert. SCP-1

Easter. Frank O'Hara. EAS

Easter. Stephen Shrader. PHC

Easter. Spenser. *See* Amoretti, LXVIII.

Easter Bunny Blues Or All I Want for Xmas Is the Loop, The. Ebon Dooley. PoBA

Easter Communion. Gerard Manley Hopkins. OFD

Easter Day. Richard Crashaw. MetP
(Upon Easter Day.) SCP-1

Easter Day, Naples, 1849. Arthur Hugh Clough. PFD; VLP; VPC

Easter Day II. Arthur Hugh Clough. PFD; VLP; VPC

Easter Egg. Alan Kieffaber. AMV-80

Easter Eggs. Harry Behn. CC

Easter Eve. Muriel Rukeyser. VGW

Easter Flood. Brenda S. Stockwell. AMV-81

Easter has come around. W. D. Snodgrass. *Fr.* Heart's Needle. ConAP

Easter Hymn. A. E. Housman. BoReV; CABA (1972 ed.); EBEV; ILP (1975 ed.); OFD; TT

Easter Hymn. Henry Vaughan. PoPle

Easter lilies! Can you hear. On Easter Day. Celia Laighton Thaxter. CTV

Easter Monday. Michael McFee. AMV-80

Easter Morning. David McCord. CC

Easter Night. Alice Meynell. BoReV

Easter 1916. W. B. Yeats. CABA (1972 ed.); CMoP (1970 ed.); Epi; FaPoR; HAP; ILP (1975 ed.); InPS; NIL; NoAM; NOBE; OAEL-2; OBP; OxBTC; PAIC; PPoe; PPP; STS; TT
"I have met them at close of day," *sel.* LFH

Easter Song, An. *Unknown.* OxBM

Easter Sunday. Sedulius Scottus, *tr. fr. Latin by* Helen Waddell. OFD

Easter Sunday: Not the Artist. Ralph Adamo. CoPAm

Easter Wings. George Herbert. AnMo; CABA (1972 ed.); HAP;HeIP; InPK; InPS; NIL; OAEL-1; PAIC; PoIA; PPP; WIF

Easter Zunday. William Barnes. VLP

Eastern guard tower. Haiku. Etheridge Knight. BPo; NeAC; NoAM; TAP

Eastside Chick with Drive. Albert Spector. CTBA

Eastside Incidents. Gregory Corso. GP; NYP; SA

Eastward to Eden. Edgar Bogardus. POL

Easy as a Bat. *Gond Oral Tradition, tr. by* V. Elwin *and* S. Hivale. WTO

Easy as cove-water rustles its pebbles and shells. Part of a Letter. Richard Wilbur. CMoP (1970 ed.)

Easy Boogie. Langston Hughes. ILP (1975 ed.)

Easy Decision, An. Kenneth Patchen. CTBA; OSP; SFF; TPo; UsP

Easy on your drums. Dark Girl. Arna Bontemps. SoS

Easy Poem, An. Terry Kennedy. AMV-80

Easy Rider. *Unknown.* FSW

Easy Rider Blues. *Unknown.* BluL

Eat/ 300 feet. The Anthropophagites See a Sign on NC That Looks like Heaven. Jonathan Williams. OBAL

Eat, eat, while there is bread. Tewa Song of War. *Unknown, tr. by* Daniel G. Brinton. PBMP

Eat 'Em Up Smith Tells All in South Africa. Judith Johnson Sherwin. NoAM

Eaten I have, and though I had good. Meat without Mirth. Robert Herrick. ILP (1975 ed.)

'Eathen, The. Kipling. OxBTC

Eating Bamboo-Shoots. Po Chü-i, *tr. fr. Chinese by* Arthur Waley. OBVE

Eating fire. First Element. Margaret Atwood. MMD

Eating Ground Zero. Alan Austin. PoUp

Eating Out. Alan Wearne. GAS

Eating out alone, one makes solitude. Tokyo West. Alfred Corn. NYP

Eating Poetry. Mark Strand. CoPAm; MAT; NoAM; PPP; TAP

Eating the eggs for a buck eighty. At Grand Canyon's Edge. David Ray. TAT

Eating the same fruit. Marriage. Michael Lopes. PoW

Eaton's Boatyard. Philip Booth. PCho

Eau-Forte. F. S. Flint. OxBTC

Eaves. Ellis Jones, *tr. fr. Welsh by* Anthony Conran. OBW

Ebb and Flow, The. Edward Taylor. ILP (1975 ed.)

Ebb slips from the rock, the sunken, The. Night. Robinson Jeffers. NOBA

Ebb tide has come for me. The Hag of Beare. *Unknown, tr. by* John Montague. BIrV; CIP; PBWP

Ebb-tide to me as of the sea! The Lament of the Old Woman of Beare. *Unknown, tr. by* Kuno Meyer. Epi

Ebb-tide to me as to the sea; old age brings me reproach. The Hag of Beare. *Unknown, tr. by* Lady Gregory. OBVE

Ebony: Contemporary. Marian Frances Brand. AATT

Ecce Homo. David Gascoyne. BoReV

Ecce Homunculus. R. A. K. Mason. ATNZ

Ecce Puer. James Joyce. BIrV; EBEV; NoAM

Ecchoing Green, The. Blake. *See* Echoing Green, The.

Ecclesiastes Derek Mahon. BIrV; CIP; IPM

Ecclesiastes, *sels.* Bible, O.T.
"All things come alike to all," IX: 2-12. NAWM-1
"Cast thy bread upon the waters," XI: 1-8. NAWM-1; OBVE
"I returned, and saw under the sun," IX: 11-12. Prf
"Remember also thy Creator in the days of thy youth," XII: 1-7. OBP
("Remember now thy Creatour in the days of thy youth.") OBVE
To Everything There Is a Season, III: 1-8. FF; NAWM-1; OBVE; PBMP
("For everything there is a season.") DL
"Vanity of vanities, saith the Preacher, vanity of vanities; all is vanity," I:2-II:24. NAWM-1
Vanity of Vanities, I: 2-11. PBMP

Ecclesiastical Chronicle, An, *sel.* John Heath-Stubbs.
"Year of Our Lord two thousand one hundred and seven, The." NOBL

Ecclesiastical Sonnets, *sels.* Wordsworth.
"I, who accompanied with faithful pace," *Introd.* MBPR
Mutability. CABA (1972 ed.); EBEV; HeIP; ILP (1975 ed.); InPK; MBPR; NOBE; OAEL-2; PPoD
Uncertainty. MBPR
"Why sleeps the future, as a snake enrolled," *Conclusion.* MBPR

Ecclesiasticus, *sels.* Bible, Apocrypha.
"All flesh waxeth old as a garment," XIV: 17-18. OBVE
"By his commandement hee maketh the snow to fall apace," XLIII: 13-26. OBVE
"Let us now praise famous men," XLIV: 1-15. OBVE

Ech, Sic a Pairish. *Unknown.* FaBoCo

Eche man me telleth I chaunge moost my devise. Sir Thomas Wyatt. AAS

Echo. Sara Asheron. CaYB

Echo. Walter de la Mare. AKE

Echo. Christina Rossetti. BoLoP; GBL; NOBE; OAEL-2; VPC

Echo always mocks the sound, The. Rabindranath Tagore. *Fr.* Epigrams. PoA

Echo Canyon. *Unknown.* AmFP

Echo Elf Answers, The. Thomas Hardy. LoAs

Echo, I ween, will in the wood reply. A Gentle Echo on Woman. Swift. FaBoCo; NU; OLR; UsP

Echo, the beating of the tide. Prophecy on Lethe. Stanley Kunitz. PoA

Echo to a Rock. Lord Herbert of Cherbury. PAIC

Echoes. Walter de la Mare. EcS

Echoes. W. E. Henley. *Poems indexed separately by titles and first lines.*

Echoes. Emma Lazarus. SBG

Echoing Cliff, The. Andrew Young. EcS; MS

Echoing [*or* Ecchoing] Green, The. Blake. *Fr.* Songs of Innocence. CABA (1972 ed.); FSFS; LAuP; MBPR; UnPo (1976 ed.)

Echo's Lament of Narcissus. Ben Jonson. *Fr.* Cynthia's Revels, I, ii. SoSe
("Slow, slow, fresh fount, keep time with my salt tears.")
ExPo (1973 ed.); ILP (1975 ed.); InPK; NIL; OAEL-1; PoIA

Eclipse. Anita Endrezze Probst. CDW

Eclipse. Tomaz Salamun, *tr. fr. Slovene by* Michael Scammel *and* Veno Taufer. VWA

Eclipses. Nancy Sullivan. TAP

Eclogue: The Common a-Took In. William Barnes. VLP; VPC

Eclogue: "What makes you look so black, so glum, so cross?" Edward Lear. FaBoNo

Eclogue: "Whores are afraid to cross the street, The." David Bergman. AMV-80

Eclogue for Christmas, An. Louis MacNeice. NoAM

Eclogue I, *sel.* William Diaper.
"Believe not, Fair, that I can prove untrue." PeD

Eclogues. Dennis Schmitz. NVAP

Eclogues, *sel.* Virgil, *tr. fr. Latin by* Sir John Beaumont.
"Sicilian Muses, sing we greater things," IV. OBVE

Eco Right. Walt Gavenda. QQQ

Ecole St. Luc. Ray Fraser. NeAC

Ecological Lecture. Burton Raffel. AMV-81

Ecologue. Allen Ginsberg. CAAP

Ecology. X. J. Kennedy. BoAnP

Ecology. James Steele. SES

Ecology. Harold Witt. PoW

Ecstasy, The. Al-Hallaj, *tr. fr. Persian.* ILwL

Ecstasy, The. Abraham Cowley. SCP-2

Ecstasy, The. John Donne. BoLoP; CABA (1972 ed.); ExPo (1973 ed.); HAP; ILP (1975 ed.); InPS; NOBE; OAEL-1; PPoe; SCP-1
(Exstasie, The.) MetP
(Extasie,The.) LoAS; OBP

Ecstasy, *abr.* W. J. Turner. EcS

Ecstasy. *Unknown. See* Oh, When Shall I See Jesus?

Ecstatic bird songs pound. Dawn. William Carlos Williams. ILP (1975 ed.)

Ed and Sid and Bernard. Edward MacDuff. QQQ

Ed Shreckongost. Ed Ochester. TAT

Eddi, priest of St. Wilfrid. Eddi's Service. Kipling. PoPle

Eddie and Eve. Charles Bukowski. GP

Eddington's universe goes phut. Richard Tolman's Universe. Leonard Bacon. PAIC

Eddi's Service. Kipling. PoPle

Eddystone Light, The. *Unknown.* FSW; PoTa
(Keeper of the Eddystone Light, The.) PeBB

Eden. Lev Mak, *tr. fr. Russian by* Daniel Weissbort. VWA

Eden. D. M. Thomas. NCSH

Eden Gate. Allen Curnow. ATNZ

Eden Is a Zoo. Margaret Atwood. WPE
"I keep my parents in a garden," *sel.* OSP

Eden Revisited. Vassar Miller. GP

Edgar A. Guest Considers "The Old Woman Who Lived in a Shoe." Louis Untermeyer. OBAL

Edgar's Story, *sel.* X. J. Kennedy.
"At Mount Rushmore I looked up into one." OFD

Edge, The. James K. Bowen. AMV-80

Edge, The. Ann Chandonnet. AMV-81

Edge. Sylvia Plath. ILP (1975 ed.); PSN; RiTi; TAP; UsP

Edge of/ a coat-of-arms, The. White Crescents at the Bottoms of Fingernails. Coleman Barks. *Fr.* Body Poems. NVAP

Edge of Town, The. William Clamurro. AMV-81

Edge of town disappears, The. The Dream. Stephen Dunn. HeS

Edgehill Fight. Kipling. PoPle

Edinburgh. Margot Robert Adamson. MS

Edinburgh Courtyard in July. Norman MacCaig. MS

Edith Sitwell Assumes the Role of Luna. Robert Francis. Moon

Editor. Glenna Luschei. CPA

Editor Whedon. Edgar Lee Masters. *Fr.* Spoon River Anthology. CMoP (1970 ed.); FaBoEE; NoAM; NOBA; OBSV

Editor's Wooing, The. "Orpheus C. Kerr." OBAL

Edmonton, thy cemetery. Stevie Smith. OxBTC

Edna St. Vincent Millay Exhorts Little Boy Blue. Louis Untermeyer. PAIC

Edom o Gordon. *Unknown.* PeBB
(Captain Car.) FaBoBa

Edser. Spike Milligan. TDH

Educating the Body. Kevin Ireland. ATNZ

Education. Don L. Lee. AmNP (1974 ed.)

Education. Kenneth Rexroth. NowV

Education in Tongues, An. Brian Swann. AAN

Educational Administration Professor's Prayer, The. Gerald Bobango. AMV-80

Educational Music or Erosion. William H. Schubert. AMV-81

Educators, The. D. M. Black. MPo

Edward. *Unknown.* AmFP; BiP; CABA (1972 ed.); EBEV; FaBoBa; FSW, *modern version;* HoPM (1975 ed.); ILP (1975 ed.); InPK; IP; IPWM; LFH; PeBB; PoIA; PPoe; RDB, *with music;* SoSe
(Edward, Edward.) AIW; ExPo (1973 ed.); FaPoR; HAP; InPS; NOBE

Edward Hicks: "The Peaceable Kingdom." Ann Stanford. PPoD

Edward the Second, *sel.* Christopher Marlowe.
"Here, take my crown—the life of Edward too," *fr.* V, i. LFH

Edwardian Hat. Betty Parvin. POL

Edwardus Comes Clarendoniae. Bibliotheca Bodleiana. Geoffrey Grigson. GBL

Edwin in the Lowlands Low. *Unknown.* AmFP

Edy be thou, Hevene-Quene. Queen of Heaven. *Unknown.* OxBM

Eee wah-wah-wah-wah-wah. Talking to Myself. *Unknown.* BluL

E'en so the nipping wind in May doth come. Upon the Decease of My Infant Lady. Clement Barksdale. SCP-2

"Eek/ a nigger." At the National Black Assembly. Amiri Baraka. GP

Eek!/ Her legs are caught in something. The Orlando Commercial. George MacBeth. NOBL

Eel, The. Eugenio Montale, *tr. fr. Italian by* John Frederick Nims. WeW

Eel Grass. Edna St. Vincent Millay. PPM

Eemis-Stane, The. "Hugh MacDiarmid." MS

Eena, deena, dina, duss. *Unknown.* MG

Ees, last Whit-Monday, I an' Meary. Whitsuntide an' Club Walken. William Barnes. VLP

Effect, The. Siegfried Sassoon. BuTh

Effect of Light, An. Vivian Smith. MAuV

Effendi. Michael S. Harper. CNA; PoBA

Effervescence and Evanescence. Keith Preston. OBAL

Efficiency Apartment. Gerald W. Barrax. PoBA

Effingham, Grenville, Raleigh, Drake. Admirals All. Sir Henry Newbolt. FaPoR

Effort at Speech. William Meredith. NYP; Prf; WeW

Effort at Speech between Two People. Muriel Rukeyser. PoIA; UsP; VoPo; WeW

Eftsoones they heard a most melodious sound. The Bower of Bliss. Spenser. *Fr.* The Faerie Queene, II, 12. NOBE

Egan O Rahilly. Egan O'Rahilly, *tr. fr. Irish by* James Stephens. EBEV; NoAM

Egg, The. George Bowering. NeAC

Egg and the Machine, The. Robert Frost. CABA (1972 ed.)

Egg Boiler, The. Gwendolyn Brooks. PoBA

Egg of Nothing, The. John Taylor. AMV–81

Egg sat on the workbench, The. The Egg. George Bowering. NeAC

Egg won't roll well, An. An Airline Breakfast. William Matthews. AMV–80

Egg yolk feels, An. Mandy Ann Fridley. OSP

Eggs. Daniela Gioseffi. AAN

Eggs and Marrowbone. *Unknown.* FSW; RDB, *with music*

Eggs boiling in a pot. Divorce. Erica Jong. GP

Eggstravagance, An. Oliver Wendell Holmes. FaBoNo

Egnatius has fine teeth, and those. Catullus, *tr. fr. Latin by* Walter Savage Landor. OBVE

Ego. Philip Booth. SoS

Ego. Robert Siegel. FAF; PoA

Ego Dominus Tuus. W. B. Yeats. CMoP (1970 ed.)

Ego Tripping. Nikki Giovanni. NoAM

Egocentric. Stevie Smith. FaBoNo

Egotist, The. H. A. C. Evans. POL

Egrets. Judith Wright. NCSH

Egypt flows there. Eighty-third Street Chicago, 1969, Scene at the Salaam Restaurant. Walter Bradford. FiCh

Egyptian Book of the Dead. David Henderson. MIT

Egyptian Passage, An. Theodore Weiss. TAP

Egyptian Pulled Glass Bottle in the Shape of a Fish, An. Marianne Moore. PBWP; PiAm

Egyptians thought the earth. Hurry Hurry. J. S. Harry. FPA

Eheu Fugaces. "Thomas Ingoldsby." FaBoEE

Eichmann. Douglas Blazek. PoW

Eichmann before his death. Construction #13. Judith Johnson Sherwin. NoAM

Eight/ a.m. with the doors. Snow. Kenneth O. Hanson. MPA

Eight and already bored. Indian Mounds. Angela Peace. AMV–80

Eight Frontiers Distant. Pearse Hutchinson. IPM

Eight hands across, form a ring. Mississippi Sawyer. *Unknown.* AmFP

Eight Lines for a Script Girl. George Jonas. NeAC

Eight Miles South of Grand Haven. Dave Kelly. AMV–80

Eight Oars and a Coxswain. Arthur Guiterman. SPo

Eight o'Clock. A. E. Housman. CABA (1972 ed.); CMoP (1970 ed.); ILP (1975 ed.); InPK; IP; NoAM; SoSe (1977 ed.)

Eight o'clock/ The postman's knock! The Postman. Christina Rossetti. CTV

Eight o'Clock Bells. *Unknown.* PoPle

Eight o'clock p.m./ and still Monday. Columbus Day. Gabrielle Edgcomb. PoUp

Eight years ago this May. A Spring Night in Shokoku-Ji. Gary Snyder. VGW

Eight young pigs in a row look at me from the trough. The Laughing Faces of Pigs. Fred Lape. BoAnP

Eightball. Dave Morice. AcAn

Eighteen. Maria Banus, *tr. fr. Rumanian by* Willis Barnstone *and* Matei Calinescu. BoWoP; VWA

Eighteen Days without You, *sel.* Anne Sexton. December 18th. CAPP

1887. A. E. Housman. BTTM; FaPoR; IP; NIL; SoSe (1977 ed.); STS; UnPo (1976 ed.); VLP; VoPo

1805. Robert Graves. OBSV

Eighteen-forty-three. *Unknown.* FaBoCo

1894 in London. Charles Spear. ATNZ

1892-1941. Louis Zukofsky. PoA

1864. Richard Howard. CABA (1972 ed.)

Eighteen sixty nine being the date of the year. A Ballad of Master McGrath. *Unknown.* FaBoBa

1867. Coventry Patmore. *Fr.* The Unknown Eros. VPC

1867. Joseph Mary Plunkett. PFIr

1867: Last Sounds. Gerry O'Egan. POL

1863, my great grandmother. Generations. Judy Dothard Simmons. CNA

1824 Old Bet, bought by a Somers man. America: The Elephant. James Tipton. TC

18 Verses Sung to a Tatar Reed Whistle, *sels.* Ts'ai Yen, *tr. fr. Chinese by* Kenneth Rexroth *and* Ling Chung.
  "I never believed that in my broken life," XIII. BoWoP
  "I was born in a time of peace," I-II. BoWoP; PBWP
  "Sun sets, The. The wind means," VII. BoWoP

18 West 11th. James Merrill. NYP

Eighteen years you beat me over the head. Brothers (I). James Reiss. AMV–81

Eighth Air Force. Randall Jarrell. FF; ILP (1975 ed.); NIL; NoAM; NOBA

Eighth day was the wedding, The. The First Wedding in the World. Joel Rosenberg. VWA

Eighty-four years ago. Birthday Party. Patti Patton. AMV–80

'Eighty-nine was bad. Graves at Elkhorn. Richard Hugo. UnPo (1976 ed.)

Eighty-third Street Chicago, 1969, Scene at the Salaam Restaurant. Walter Bradford. FiCh

Eild comes owre me like a yoke on my craig. The Auld Hunter. George Campbell Hay, *tr. fr. Gaelic; Scots version by* "Hugh MacDiarmid." MS

Einstein's eyes. Relative Sadness. Colin Rowbotham. BuTh

Eire. David O'Bruadair, *tr. fr. Irish by* Austin Clarke. BIrV

Eireann. Osbert Lancaster. *Fr.* Afternoons with Baedeker. NOBL

Eisenhower's Visit to Franco, 1959. James Wright. CAPP; PSN

Either get out of my house or conform to my tastes, woman. Martial, *tr. fr. Latin by* James Michie. FaBoEE

Either she was foule, or her attire was bad. Ovid, *tr. by* Christopher Marlowe. Amores, III, 6. OBVE

Either we're liberals or we truly do. Death with a Coda. Giuseppe Gioachino Belli, *tr. by* Miller Williams. AMV–81

Either you will. Prospective Immigrants Please Note. Adrienne Rich. GOA; VGW

Ejected Wife, The. *Tr. fr. Chinese by* Arthur Waley. OBVE

El Aghir. Norman Cameron. *See* Green, Green Is El Aghir.

El Bosco. Mei Berssenbrugge. NW; SA

El Greco. E. L. Mayo. HoPM (1975 ed.)

El Greco: Espolio. Earle Birney. ExPo (1973 ed.); MPA

El Hombre. William Carlos Williams. CABA (1972 ed.); CMoP (1970 ed.)

Elaine has been in a coma. Girl Clings to Coma. Jim Mulac. AcAn

Elanoy. *Unknown.* FSW

Elbucks on the herbour waa. Mongol Quine. Alastair Mackie. MS

Elder Edda, The, *sels. Unknown, tr. fr. Old Norse by* William Morris *and* Eiriks Magnusson.

First Lay of Gudrun, The: Gudrun Laments over Sigurd.
OBVE
Part of the Lay of Sigrdrifa. OBVE
Short Lay of Sigurd, The ("And now one prayer"). OBVE
Elder, or Bourtree, The. *Unknown.* GBP
Elderly Gentleman, The. George Canning. ECBV
Elderly Nobody Erases Self in Central Park. E. S. Forgotson.
NowV
Elders. J. D. Reed. UsP
Elders at the zenith of their power look down the sky, The.
Nathaniel Tarn. *Fr.* The Beautiful Contradictions. TwMBP
Elder's Reproof to His Wife, An. Abdillaahi Muuse, *tr. fr. Somali
by* B. W. Andrzejewski *and* I. M. Lewis. WTO
Eldest is calling, The. Tip-of-the-Single-Feather. Velema, *tr. by*
B. H. Quain. WTO
Eldest son bestrides him, The. The Undertaker's Horse.
Kipling. FaBoNo
Eldorado. Poe. AmVN; CTV; IPWM; NOBA; PCOP; PiAm;
SS; TAP
El Dorado. Richard Ryan. BIrV
Eleanor Rigby. John Lennon *and* Paul McCartney. ExPo (1973
ed.); InPK; InPS; OBP; PPoe; WIF; WTO
Eleanor (she spoiled in a British climate). Ezra Pound. Cantos,
VII. NoAM; NOBA
Eleazar Wheelock. Richard Hovey. OBAL
Elected silence, sing to me. The Habit of Perfection. Gerard
Manley Hopkins. ILP (1975 ed.); NoAM; PoPle; SoSe; VLP
Election 1960. James K. Baxter. ATNZ
Election Songs. *Yoruba Oral Tradition, tr. by* Ulli Beier. WTO
Elective Affinities. David Malouf. CAAP
Electric Cop, The. Victor Hernandez Cruz. PoBA
Electric Orchard, The. Paul Muldoon. IPM
Electrically, cleanly. January. Richard A. Hawley. AMV-80
Electrocution. Lola Ridge. WPE
Electroencephalogram. Geoffrey Holloway. PMW
Elegant use of foliage and grace, An. More. Gertrude Stein.
*Fr.* Tender Buttons. PBWP
Elegiac. Kenneth O. Hanson. MPA
Elegiac Lines on the Death of a Fiddler, Called Blind Jacob.
Philip Freneau. EAP
Elegiac Stanzas Suggested by a Picture of Peele Castle, in a Storm.
Wordsworth. MBPR; OAEL-2
Elegiac Verses. Wordsworth. MBPR
Elegie: Autumnal, The. John Donne. *See* Elegies.
Elegies, *sels.* John Donne.
Anagram, The, II. PAIC
Autumnal, The, IX. InPS
Change, III. EBEV
Elegy: "Nature's lay idiot, I taught thee to love," VII. SCP-1
Going to Bed, XIX. EBEV; GBL; PPP; TT
(To His Mistress [*or* Mistris] Going to Bed.) AnMo; BoLoP;
OAEL-1;OBP
His Parting from Her, XII. EBEV
Jealousy, I. FF
Love's Progress, XVIII. OAEL-1; SCP-1
On His Mistress, XVI. BoLoP; EBEV
(Elegy on His Mistress.) GBL
(On His Mistris.) OBP
(To His Mistress Desiring to Travel with Him As His Page.)
NOBE
Elegies for the Dead in Cyrenaica, *sels.* Hamish Henderson.
First Elegy, End of a Campaign. MS
Third Elegy, Leaving the City. MS
Elegies for the Hot Season. Sandra McPherson. AmPA; CAAP;
CNW; MPA; RiTi
Elegy: "Death be not proud, thy hand gave not this blow." Lucy
Harington, Countess of Bedford. WPE

Elegy: "Do not look for him." Leonard Cohen. HeIP
Elegy, An: " Friend, whose unnatural early death." David
Gascoyne. FaBoTw (1975 ed.)
Elegy: "Her face like a rain-beaten stone on the day she rolled
off." Theodore Roethke. CTBA; MPA; NCSH; PSN; UsP
Elegy: "Here where the elm trees were." Constance Carrier.
FAF
Elegy XIII: "I got her in the Black Bull." Sydney Goodsir Smith.
*Fr.* Under the Eildon Tree. MS
Elegy: "I know but will not tell." Alan Dugan. CAPP
Elegy: I. M. Orlando Tobias Gordon. Giles Gordon. MS
Elegy: "I must wait for a stranger to knock on my door." David
Ignatow. NNaP
Elegy: "I stood between two mirrors when you died." William
Jay Smith. CoPAm
Elegy: "In summer's heat and mid-time of the day." Ovid. *See*
Corinnae Concubitus.
Elegy: Ise Lamenting the Death of Empress Onshi. Lady Ise, *tr.
fr. Japanese by* Etsuko Terasaki *and* Irma Brandeis. BoWoP
Elegy: "Laundry-basket is still there, The." Anselm Hollo.
AcAn
Elegy, An: "Let me be what I am, as Virgil cold," *abr.* Ben
Jonson. SCP-1
Elegy: "Let them bury your big eyes." Edna St. Vincent Millay.
Memorial to D.C., V. CMoP (1970 ed.); LoAs
Elegy: "Me happy, night, night full of brightness." Ezra Pound.
*Fr.* Homage to Sextus Propertius. PAIC
Elegy: "Morning after death on the bar was calm." Paul
Henderson. ATNZ
Elegy: "Mourn, little harebells owre the lea," *abr.* Burns. PF
Elegy: "My comrade is dead." Salomon de la Selva, *tr. fr.
Spanish by* Donald Walsh. LoAs
Elegy: "My mother in the witness box." Virginia Scott. NPW
Elegy: "My prime of youth is but a frost of cares." Chidiock
Tichborne. EBEV; NOBE; PPoD
(Elegy, Written with His Own Hand in the Tower before His
Execution.) DL; InPK; WIF
(His Elegy.) PPoe
(On the Eve of His Execution.) OBP
(Tichborne's Elegy.) FF; HAP; HeIP; ILP (1975 ed.); InPS;
OAEL-1
(Written the Night before His Execution.) PAIC
Elegy: "Nature's lay idiot, I taught thee to love." John Donne.
Elegies, VII. SCP-1
Elegy: "No more, no more Jewish townships in Poland." Antoni
Slonimski, *tr. fr. Polish by* Isaac Komem. VWA
Elegy, An: "Noon is beautiful, The: the perfect wheel." Yvor
Winters. VGW
Elegy: "Now he is dead, who talked." Alistair Campbell. ATNZ
Elegy: "Our hammock swung between Americas." Derek
Walcott. OBP
Elegy "Pages of history open, The." Sandra M. Gilbert. PoA
Elegy: "These errors loved no less than the saint loves arrows."
George Barker. FaBoTw (1975 ed.)
Elegy: "They are lang deid, folk that I used to ken." Robert
Garioch. MS
Elegy: "Tonight the moon is high, to summon all." William Bell.
FaBoTw (1975 ed.)
Elegy: "Way the hell-bent years consume my pleasure, The."
Pushkin, *tr. fr. Russian by* Robley Wilson, Jr. AMV-81
Elegy 3: "Whatever you call it." Seamus Deane. IPM
(Elegy: Three.) CIP
Elegy: "While walking at dusk in a strange city." Pinhas Sadeh,
*tr. fr. Hebrew by* Gabriel Preil *and* Howard Schwartz. VWA
Elegy: "Wood is bare, The: a river-mist is steeping." Robert
Bridges. ILP (1975 ed.); PoPle

Elegy, An: "You might have died so many kinds of death."
Maurice Lindsay. MS

Elegy and Kaddish. David Rosenmann-Taub, *tr. fr. Spanish by*
Charles Guenther. VWA

Elegy before Death. Edna St. Vincent Millay. CMoP (1970 ed.)

Elegy for a Cricket. J. V. Cunningham. NoAM

Elegy for a Dead Soldier. Karl Shapiro. HAP
Epitaph: "Underneath this wooden cross there lies," *sel.* OFD

Elegy for a Diver. Philip Booth. LiSp; SPo

Elegy for a Forest Clear-cut by the Weyerhaeuser Company.
David Wagoner. CNW

Elegy for a Greenhouse. Shawn Wong. NW

Elegy for a Nature Poet. Howard Nemerov. CoPAm; HoPM
(1975 ed.)

Elegy for a Polish Grandaunt. James Bonk. HeS

Elegy for a Puritan Conscience. Alan Dugan. CAPP; CoPAm;
NoAM

Elegy for a School-Friend. Augustus Young. BIrV

Elegy for a Schoolmate. Vincent O'Sullivan. ATNZ

Elegy for Alfred Hubbard. Tony Connor. MPo; SoSe

Elegy for an Android. D. M. Thomas. TwMBP

Elegy for an Unknown Soldier. James K. Baxter. ATNZ

Elegy for Another Day. Peggy Pond Church. WPW

Elegy for Bella, Sarah, Rosie, and All the Others. Sonya Dorman.
GOA

Elegy for Chief Sealth. Duane Niatum. CDW

Elegy for D. H. Lawrence, An. William Carlos Williams. Epi;
NoAM

Elegy for David Beynon. Leslie Norris. LP

Elegy for Duke Ellington. Jim Mulac. AcAn

Elegy for Dylan Thomas. Edith Sitwell. PoA

Elegy for Former Students. Virginia Scott Miner. AMV-81

Elegy for 41 Whales Beached in Florence, Ore., June, 1979.
Linda Bierds. AMV-81

Elegy for Her Brother Sakhr. Al-Khansa, *tr. fr. Arabic by* Willis
Barnstone. BoWoP

Elegy for His Daughter Ellen. Goronwy Owen, *tr. fr. Welsh by*
Kenneth Jackson. OBW

Elegy for Jack Bowman. Joseph Bruchac. CDW

Elegy for Jane. Theodore Roethke. BiP; CNW; CoPAm; FF;
HAP; ILP (1975 ed.); InPK; InPS; IPWM; LFH; PAIC;
PPM; PPoe; PSN; RRA; SoS; STS; TAP; TCP; VoPo; WIF

Elegy for Lyn James. Leslie Norris. OBW

Elegy for Michael Dransfield. Rodney Hall. FPA

Elegy for My Father. Robert Louthan. AMV-80

Elegy for My Father. Howard Moss. VWA

Elegy for My Father. Mark Strand. CAAP; NVAP; PCho
*Sels.*
Empty Body, The. UnPo (1976 ed.)
New Year, The. UnPo (1976 ed.)
Your Shadow. Prf

Elegy for the Duke of Marmalade. Luis Palés Matos, *tr. fr.
Spanish by* Julio Marzán. InW

Elegy for the Giant Tortoises. Margaret Atwood. BoWoP

Elegy for the Monastery Barn. Thomas Merton. VGW

Elegy for the Wife of a Friend. Yü Hsüan-chi, *tr. fr. Chinese by*
Geoffrey Waters. BoWoP

Elegy for William Soutar. William Montgomerie. MS

Elegy for Yards, Pounds, and Gallons. David Wagoner. PoA;
SoSe (1977 ed.)

Elegy in a Country Churchyard. G. K. Chesterton. FaPoR

Elegy in a Presbyterian Burying-Ground. R. N. D. Wilson.
BIrV

Elegy in the Orongorongo Valley. Hubert Witheford. ATNZ

Elegy Is Preparing Itself, An. Donald Justice. HoPM (1975 ed.)

Elegy of Fortinbras. Zbigniew Herbert, *tr. fr. Polish by* Czeslaw
Milosz. OBVE

Elegy on a Lady Whom Grief for the Death of Her Betrothed
Killed. Robert Bridges. VLP

Elegy on Any Lady by George Moore. Max Beerbohm.
FaBoEE

Elegy on Cynddylan, The, *sel. Unknown, tr. fr. Welsh by* Kenneth
Jackson.
"Stand out, maids, and look on the land of Cynddylan." OBW

Elegy on Herakleitos. Callimachus, *tr. fr. Greek by* Dudley Fitts.
InPK

Elegy on His Mistress. John Donne. *See* On His Mistress.

Elegy on My Father. Allen Curnow. ATNZ

Elegy on That Glory of Her Sex, Mrs. Mary Blaize, An.
Goldsmith. FaBoNo; ILP (1975 ed.); LAuP
(Mrs. Mary Blaize.) FaBoCo

Elegy on the Death of a Mad Dog, An. Goldsmith. *Fr.* The
Vicar of Wakefield, *ch.* 17. AIW; FaBoCo; GDP; ILP (1975
ed.); LAuP; PCOP; PoPle; SS; TPo

Elegy on the Death of Furuhi, An. Yamamoue Okura, *tr. fr.
Japanese.* DL

Elegy on the Death of Her Husband. Anne Howard, Duchess of
Arundel. WPE

Elegy on the Dust. Thom Gunn. NoAM

Elegy on Thomas Hood. Martin Fagg. NOBL

Elegy over a Tomb. Lord Herbert of Cherbury. NOBE

Elegy: Three. Seamus Deane. *See* Elegy 3: "Whatever you call
it."

Elegy to the Memory of an Unfortunate Lady. Pope. NOBE;
OAEL-1; PAIC

Elegy upon His Tomb in Herndon-Hill Church, Erected by His
Wife, Who Speaks, An. James Howell. OBW

Elegy upon the Death of the Dean of St. Paul's, Dr. John Donne.
Thomas Carew. CABA (1972 ed.); CaPo
(Elegy upon the Death of Doctor Donne, Dean of Paul's, An.)
OAEL-1
On the Death of Donne, *sel.* NOBE

Elegy upon the Death of the Most Illustrious Prince Henry, An,
*sel.* John Hagthorpe.
"I do not grieve when some unwholesome air." SCP-2

Elegy while Pruning Roses. David Wagoner. AMV-80

Elegy Written in a Country Churchyard. Thomas Gray. BiP;
CABA (1972 ed.); DL; EBEV; FaPoR; HAP; HeIP; ILP
(1975 ed.); InPK; InPS; LAuP; LFH; NIL; NOBE; OAEL-1;
OBP; PAIC; PBMP; PPoD; PPoe; PPP; UnPo (1976 ed.);
WIF
"Curfew tolls the knell of parting day, The," *sel.* PES

Elegy Written in a Country Coal-Bin. Christopher Morley.
OBAL

Elegy, Written with His Own Hand in the Tower before His
Execution. Chidiock Tichborne. *See* Elegy: "My prime of
youth is but a frost of cares."

Elegye, An: "Constant to none, but ever false to me." Thomas
Campion. AAS

Elektra on Third Avenue. Marilyn Hacker. NYP

Element of air was out of hand, The. Interlude. Theodore
Roethke. STS

Elementary. Jim Tollerud. VoR

Elementary Cosmogony. Charles Simic. NNaP

Elementary Scene, The. Randall Jarrell. CMoP (1970 ed.); ExPo
(1973 ed.); SoS

Elementary School Classroom [*or* Class Room] in a Slum, An.
Stephen Spender. FF; ILP (1975 ed.); IP; MPo; NIL;
PPoD; UnPo (1976 ed.); WIF

Elements. A. R. D. Fairburn. ATNZ

Elements have merged into solicitude, The. The Racer's Widow.
Louise Glück. AmPA; LiSp

Elements of Geometry, The. David Malouf. CAAP

Elements of Night.  Arthur Gregor.  LoAs

Elephant.  Alan Brownjohn.  BBL

Elephant, The.  John Donne.  *Fr.* The Progresse of the Soule.  OBP

Elephant, The.  Sandra Hochman.  BoAnP

Elephant, The.  Louis Phillips.  OSF

Elephant, The/ bogged down.  Song of the Tusk.  Anselm Hollo.  AcAn

Elephant and the Giraffe, The.  Charlotte Osgood Carter.  TDH

Elephant in the Moon, The: A Satire, *sel.*  Samuel Butler.  "Learn'd society of late, A."  SCP-2

Elephant is in love with the millimeter, The.  What the Violins Sing in Their Baconfat Bed.  Jean Arp, *tr. by* John Frederick Nims.  WeW

Elephant Is Slow to Mate, The.  D. H. Lawrence.  InPK; NoAM; PPP

Elephant never forgets, The.  The Zoo.  Anthony Ostroff.  MPA

Elephant of long service to a circus, An.  The Retirement of the Elephant.  Russell Edson.  AmPA

Elephant, The, or the Force of Habit.  A. E. Housman.  NOBL

Elephant Rock.  Primus St. John.  PoBA

Elephant Sat on Some Kegs, An.  J. G. Francis.  TDH

Elephant, the huge old beast, The.  The Elephant Is Slow to Mate.  D. H. Lawrence.  InPK; NoAM; PPP

Elephant to the Girl in Bertram Mills' Circus, The.  Anthony Cronin.  CIP

Elephants.  Patrick Lane.  NeAC

Elephants are born with so much clothing.  Ivory Paper Weight.  Adrien Stoutenburg.  GP

Elephants from the Sea.  Ian Young.  NeAC

Elephants in the Circus.  D. H. Lawrence.  BoAnP

Elephants May Parade before Your House.  *Gond Oral Tradition, tr. by* V. Elwin *and* S. Hivale.  WTO

Eletelephony.  Laura E. Richards.  CTV; ECBV; OxBChV

Elevator Landscapes, *sels.*  Stephen Vincent.  NeAC
  Floor: Five.
  Floor: 0.

Elevator Man Adheres to Form, The.  Margaret Danner.  PoBA

Elevator stops at every floor, The.  Neuteronomy.  Eve Merriam.  QQQ

Eleven.  Archibald MacLeish.  HAP; NCSH; WeW

Eleven Addresses to the Lord, *sels.*  John Berryman.
  "Fearful I peer upon the mountain path," X.  PiAm
  "Master of beauty, craftsman of the snowflake," I.  UnPo (1976 ed.)
  Prayer for the Self, A, VIII.  PiAm; PPP
  "Sole watchman of the flying stars, guard me," III.  PiAm; UnPo (1976 ed.)

"1100 Exposition."  Newsletter from My Mother.  Michael S. Harper.  PoBA

Eleven o'clock, and the curtain falls.  End of the Comedy.  Louis Untermeyer.  PoA

11/16/75.  Darlene Pearlstein.  FiCh

11/22/75.  Darlene Pearlstein.  FiCh

Eleventh Sunday after Trinity.  John Keble.  *Fr.* The Christian Year.  VLP

Elf and the Dormouse, The.  Oliver Herford.  PCOP

Elf Owl.  Mary Austin.  BPAW

Elfin Knight, The.  *Unknown.*  *See* Lady Isabel and the Elf-Knight.

Elgin Cathedral Epitaph.  *Unknown.*  *See* At Aberdeen.

Elgonyi say, there are big dreams and little dreams, The.  Big Dream, Little Dream.  Louis Simpson.  POL; WasP

El-Hajj Malik El-Shabazz.  Robert Hayden.  CNA; PoBA

Eli the Thatcher.  Max Beerbohm *and* William Rothenstein.  FaBoNo

Elinda's Glove.  Richard Lovelace.  SCP-2
  (Ellinda's Glove.)  CaPo

Elinoure and Juga.  Thomas Chatterton.  LAuP

Elisabeth, Elspeth, Betsy, and Bess.  *See* Elizabeth, Elspeth, Betsy, and Bess.

Elisha wroth wi sin and sloth.  Jezebel.  Forbes Macregor.  MIS

Elizabeth.  Robert Lowell.  *Fr.* Harriet.  LoAs

Elizabeth.  Paul Muldoon.  IPM

Elizabeth, Elspeth, Betsy, and Bess.  Mother Goose.  ECBV; MG

Elizabeth, frigidly stretched.  This Houre Her Vigill.  Valentin Iremonger.  CIP; OxBTC; PFIr

Elizabeth in Italy.  Richard Weber.  BoLoP

Elizabeth of Bohemia.  Sir Henry Wotton.  *See* On His Mistress, the Queen of Bohemia.

Ella, in a Square Apron, along Highway 80.  Judy Grahn.  *Fr.* The Comman Woman.  NMM

Ella McStumping.  Michael Dugan.  FPB

Ella Speed.  *Unknown.*  AmFP

Ellas and the Statues.  Gülten Akin, *tr. fr. Turkish by* Nermin Menemencioglu.  PBWP

Ellen enters the pool.  Going Under.  Ann Deagon.  AAN; CSP

Ellen Flannery.  *Unknown.*  AmFP

Ellen Irwin; or, The Braes of Kirtle.  Wordsworth.  PeD

Ellesmereland I ("Explorers say that harebells rise").  Earle Birney.  CABA (1972 ed.)

Ellesmereland II ("And now in Ellesmereland there sits").  Earle Birney.  CABA (1972 ed.)

Ellinda's Glove.  Richard Lovelace.  *See* Elinda's Glove.

Ellora.  Leonard Nathan.  GP

Elm.  Sylvia Plath.  NoAM; NOBA

Elm Buds.  Carl Sandburg.  PiAm

Elms have to fight, The.  Home Movies.  Carter Revard.  VoR

Elms in Winter.  Edward Lowbury.  PMW

Eloquent as stuck drawers, we come out.  Dividing the House.  James Richardson.  AMV–80

Elsa Wertman.  Edgar Lee Masters.  *Fr.* Spoon River Anthology.  NoAM

"Else a Great Prince in Prison Lies."  Denise Levertov.  PPP; VGW

Elsewhere.  Linda Pastan.  VWA

Elsie Marley has grown so fine.  *Unknown.*  BBL; MG

Elves' Song.  Ben Jonson.  *See* Song of the Satyrs.

Elvin's Blues.  Michael S. Harper.  BPo

Elwha River, The.  Gary Snyder.  NoAM

Elysee.  Larry Eigner.  VGW

Elysian glade.  Developers at Crystal River.  James Merrill.  AMV–81

Elysium is as far as to.  Emily Dickinson.  CABA (1972 ed.); LoAs; OLR; WPE

Emancipation of George-Hector (a Colored Turtle), The.  Mari Evans.  AmNP (1974 ed.)

Emancipators, The.  Randall Jarrell.  PoA

Embankment, The.  T. E. Hulme.  EBEV; OxBTC; PPoD

Embarrassing Episode of Little Miss Muffet, The.  Guy Wetmore Carryl.  PoTa

Emblem, An.  Ina Coolbrith.  WPW

Emblem of Two Foxes, An  Barry Spacks.  CoPAm; HoPM (1975 ed.)

Emblems, *sels.*  Francis Quarles.
  Epigram: "My soul, thy love is dear: 'twas thought a good," V, 4.  OAEL-1; SCP-2
  Epigram: "What makes thee, fool, so fat? Fool, thee so bare?" I, 12.  SCP-2
  "Ev'n like two little bank-dividing brooks," V, 3.  PAIC  (My Beloved Is Mine and I Am His.)  NOBE

"Here's your right ground. Wag gently o'er this black," I, 10. SCP-2

"Like to the arctic needle that doth guide," V, 4. EBEV; OAEL–1; SCP-2

"What, never filled? Be thy lips screwed so fast," I, 12. SCP-2

Why Dost Thou Shade Thy Lovely Face? III, 7. BoReV

Emblems. Allen Tate. VGW

Embodied close, the lab'ring Grecian train. Homer, tr. by Pope. Fr. The Iliad, V. OBVE

Embodiment of what, The. Lyric. Arthur Gregor. TAP

Embrace the Blade. Joyce Mansour, tr. fr. French by Carol Cosman. PBWP

Embraceable You, with music. Ira Gershwin. BLSo

Embracing Exile. Lindiwe Mabuza. SES

Embracing low-falutin. The Countryman's Return. Dylan Thomas. OxBTC

Embro my ain, ye are aye meant. Betrayal in Morninside. Donald Campbell. MIS

Embroidery. Maria Jacobs. AMV–80

Embroidery, An. Denise Levertov. BCr; NMM; NU; RiTi

Embryos. Marge Piercy. RiTi

Emerald is as green as grass, An. Flint. Christina Rossetti. OxBChV

Emergency at 8. Geof Hewitt. NeAC

Emergency Gastrectomy. Peter Dale. PMW

Emergency Haying. Hayden Carruth. NNaP

Emergency Room, The. S. L. Henderson Smith. PMW

Emerges daintily, the skunk. The Wood Weasel. Marianne Moore. CMoP (1970 ed.); PiAm

Emerging from the inmost hideout. Splendor. Shin Shalom, tr. by Abraham Birman. VWA

Emerging from the naked labyrinth. August 13, 1966. Daryl Hine. GP

Emerging from the subway station. Grateful Here. Wing Tek Lum. PHC

Emeritus, n. Henri Coulette. FF

Emerson. James Russell Lowell. Fr. A Fable for Critics. AmVN; NOBA; PAIC; TAP

Emerson, strolling through the Louvre. Art in America. Theodore Weiss. AMV–80

Emigrant's Dying Child, The. G. W. Patton. BPAW

Emigration. Anita Barrows. NMM

Emily Dickinson. Inger Hagerup, tr. fr. Norwegian by Harold P. Hansen. AMV–81

Emily Dickinson. Michael Longley. CIP

Emily Dickinson—in Appreciation. Roy Batt. PMW

Emily Dickinson Postage Stamp. Lynn Strongin. NMM

Emily Drowned. William Duncan. PMW

Emily Hardcastle, Spinster. John Crowe Ransom. CMoP (1970 ed.)

Eminence becomes you. Now when the rock is struck. To T. S. Eliot. Emanuel Litvinoff. VWA

Emma. Yvonne. See Premonition.

Emma in My Third Eye. Renée Roper. NPW

Emmeline Grangerford's "Ode to Stephen Dowling Bots, Dec'd." "Mark Twain." Fr. The Adventures of Huckleberry Finn. OBAL

(Ode to Stephen Dowling Bots, Dec'd.) NIL

Emmet Kills-Warrior Turtle Mountain Reservation. Marnie Walsh. VW

Emmett Till. James A. Emanuel. CNA; PoBA; WIF

Emmiline, you were there even before they were cold. Flowers for the Grangerford Girl. William Harrold. HeS

Empathy. Agnes Pratt. VW

Empedocles. George Meredith. VLP

Empedocles came coughing through the smoke. To the Thoughtful Reader. William Meredith. NoAM

Empedocles on Etna. Matthew Arnold. VLP

Song of Callicles ("Through the black, rushing smoke-bursts"), fr. II. NOBE; OAEL–2

Empedocles on Etna. H. B. Mallalieu. PoA

Emperor Hadrian to His Soul, The. Emperor Hadrian. See Hadrian's Address to His Soul When Dying.

Emperor Nap he would set off, The. The March to Moscow. Robert Southey. FaBoCo

Emperor of Ice-Cream, The. Wallace Stevens. AnMo; BiP; CABA (1972 ed.); CMoP (1970 ed.); FF; HAP; ILP (1975 ed.); InPK; NoAM; NOBA; PAIC; PiAm; PoIA; STS; TAP; TT; UsP; WeW

Emperor of the Moon, sels. Aphra Behn.

Song: "All joy to mortals, joy and mirth." WPE

Song: "Curse upon that faithless maid, A." WPE

Song: "When maidens are young, and in their spring." FF

Emperor Worm, The. Poe. See Conqueror Worm, The.

Emperor (you've heard?) went by this road, The. King of Kings. Hubert Witheford. ATNZ

Emperors and kings! in vain you strive. The Republican Genius of Europe. Philip Freneau. VoPo

Empirical History. Charles Doyle. ATNZ

Employed. James Bertolino. HeS

Empress Hotel Poems, The. Anselm Hollo. AcAn

Empress in the Mirror. Colette Inez. WBN

Empresse of townes, exalt in honour. William Dunbar. Fr. In Honour of the City of London. PES

Empryce of prys, imperatrice. William Dunbar. Fr. Ane Ballat of Our Lady. EBEV

Emptiness, An. Passage. Warren Slesinger. HeS

Empty Apartment, The. Aaron Zeitlin, tr. fr. Yiddish by Ruth Whitman. VWA

Empty ashtray, An. In Place of a Phone Call to Arabia. Diane Wakoski. Psy

Empty Bed Blues. Bessie Smith. OBAL; UnPo (1976 ed.)

Empty Body, The. Mark Strand. Fr. Elegy for My Father. UnPo (1976 ed.)

Empty carousel in a deserted place, An. The Carousel. Gloria C. Oden. AmNP (1974 ed.); PoBA

Empty Dwelling Places. Kenneth Patchen. PoA

Empty Glen, The. R. Crombie Saunders. MS

Empty green wine bottles wink. Night Out, Tom Cat. Charles deGravelles. AMV–81

Empty Holds a Question. Pat Folk. NowV

Empty house, The—the empty country—the empty sky. Plato was Right Though. Lee Harwood. TwMBP

Empty, illusory life. The Enchanted Region; or, Mistaken Pleasures. Walter Harte. EBEV

Empty lap, an hour to tea, An. Anno Domini. E. M. Walker. POL

Empty Pain-Killer Bottles, The. Tom Raworth. EAS

Empty Raft. G. C. Dawe. IPM

Empty Saddles. Unknown. BPAW

Empty sky, a world of heather, An. Divided. Jean Ingelow. SpRo; VLP

Empty Streams of Autumn. Ray A. Young Bear. VW

Empty Threat, An. Robert Frost. RFM

Empty Valley, The. J. R. Hervey. ATNZ

Empty Vessel. "Hugh MacDiarmid." FaBoTw (1975 ed.); MS; SLP

Empty winds are creaking and the oak, The. Robert Lowell. Fr. The Quaker Graveyard in Nantucket. UsP

Empty Woman, The. Gwendolyn Brooks. IHMS; SoS

Emus. Mary Fullerton. BoAnP

En Route. Theodore Weiss. PCho

En route to the picnic they drive through their history.  Picnic: The Liberated.  M. Carl Holman.  PoBA

Enacting somone's notion of themselves.  Aunt Jemima of the Ocean Waves.  Robert Hayden.  PoBA

Enamel Girl, The.  Genevieve Taggard.  WPW

Enamoured of the Miniscule.  Michael Hartnett.  BIrV

Encase your legs in nylons.  Inexpensive Progress.  John Betjeman.  LP

Enchanted Island, The, *sel.*  Alfred Noyes.
"Some would dive in the lagoon."  EcS

Enchanted Region, The; or, Mistaken Pleasures.  Walter Harte.  EBEV

Enchanted Shirt, The.  John Hay.  PoTa

Enchantment.  Lewis Alexander.  PoBA

Enchantment, The.  Theocritus, *tr. fr. Greek by* Thomas Creech.  *Fr.* Idylls, II.  OBVE

Enchantress Circe, with a potent wine, The.  To a Lady.  J. B. Morton.  POL

Encirclement.  Mieczyslaw Jastrun, *tr. fr. Polish by* Benjamin Sher.  AMV–81

Enclosed in a circle.  The Pact.  Larry Rubin.  AMV–81

Enclosed you will find the names.  Chain Letter.  Philip Dacey.  AAN

Encomium upon a Parliament, An.  Daniel Defoe.  APAS

Encompass me, my lover.  The Constant North.  J. F. Hendry.  MS; SLP

Encounter.  Denis Devlin.  BIrV

Encounter.  Geraldine Hammond.  IHMS

Encounter.  Dorothy Livesay.  AMV–81

Encounter.  Vassar Miller.  GP

Encounter, The.  Edgell Rickword.  OxBTC

Encounter.  Clarice Short.  MPA

Encounter in Jerusalem.  Fay Lipshitz.  VWA

Encounter in Safed.  Moshe Yungman, *tr. fr. Yiddish by* Gabriel Preil *and* Howard Schwartz.  VWA

Encounter in the Cage Country.  James Dickey.  BiP; CAPP

Encounter with Hunger.  Brian Vanderlip.  AMV–81

Encouragement to a Lover.  Sir John Suckling.  *See* Why So Pale and Wan?

End, The.  Ted Berrigan.  FiCh

End.  Christy Brown.  IPM

End, The.  Allen Ginsberg.  ConAP; TT; UsP

End, The.  Denis Glover.  ATNZ

End, An.  Christina Rossetti.  GBL

End Bit, The.  Jim Burns.  FF

End came as I drove it down the road, The.  Last of the Poet's Car.  Tony Connor.  OxBTC

End came easy for most of us, The.  The Man from Washington  James Welch.  CDW; GP; SA; VW

End Is near the Beginning, The.  David Gascoyne.  EAS

End of a long stillness.  Dawn in January.  Lance Henson.  CDW

End of a Meaningful Relationship, The.  Kurt J. Fickert.  AMV–81

End of a Season.  Vernon Scannell.  HeHu

End of Another Home Holiday.  D. H. Lawrence.  EBEV

End of Clonmacnois, The.  Frank O'Connor, *tr. fr. Irish.*  CIP

End of Fall, The.  Francis Ponge, *tr. fr. French by* Robert Bly.  NU

End of His Work, The.  Robert Herrick.  CaPo

End of history was exactly or so like the end of love, The.  Loss.  Terence Winch.  PoUp

End of Love, The.  Kathleen Raine.  BuTh

End of Man Is His Beauty, The.  Amiri Baraka.  AmNP (1974 ed.)

End of Play.  Robert Graves.  EBEV

End of Season.  Owen Leeming.  ATNZ

End of September.  The Sign.  Paul Blackburn.  TAT

End of Summer.  Stanley Kunitz.  VGW

End of Summer, The.  Judith Minty.  FiCP; HeS

End of Summer.  Berl Pomerantz, *tr. fr. Hebrew by* Harold Schimmel.  VWA

(End) of Summer (1966).  William Knott.  EAS

End of Term.  *Unknown.*  PoPle

End of the Affair.  Curtis W. Casewit.  AMV–80

End of the Affair.  Geoffrey Grigson.  GBL

End of the Comedy.  Louis Untermeyer.  PoA

End of the Indian Poems, The.  Stanley Plumly.  GOA

End of the Weekend, The.  Anthony Hecht.  ConAP; HAP; PSN; WeW

End of the World.  Else Lasker-Schüler, *tr. fr. German by* Willis Barnstone *and* Michael Gillespie.  BoWoP

End of the World, The.  Archibald MacLeish.  CMoP (1970 ed.); HoPM (1975 ed.); ILP (1975 ed.); InPK; IP; MAT; NoAM; NCSH; NOBA; OBAL; PAIC; PBMP; PiAm; SS; TAP; TPo; VGW

End of the World.  Jakov van Hoddis, *tr. fr. German by* Edouard Roditi.  VWA

End of the year fell chilly, The.  New Year's Eve.  A. E. Housman.  VLP

End of World War One, The.  Sharon Olds.  AMV–81

End was quick and bitter, The.  Quick and Bitter.  Yehuda Amichai, *tr. by* Assia Gutmann.  BoLoP

Endimion Porter and Olivia.  Sir William Davenant.  NOBE

Ending.  *Tr. fr. Hawaiian by* K. Luomala.  WTO

Ending an Affair.  Paul David Ashley.  DNGG

Ending is this, The.  A Story.  Eric Torgersen.  TC

Endings.  Daniel Halpern.  CAAP

Endless Chain, An.  Abraham Reisen, *tr. fr. Yiddish by* Keith Bosley.  VWA

Endless line of splendor, An.  Foreign Missions in Battle Array.  Vachel Lindsay.  PIM

Endless Song, The.  Ruth McEnery Stuart.  OBAL

Endlessly searching, we look for the meaning.  Acceptance.  Margaret Reynolds.  MIS

Endlessly, time-honoured irritant.  Dry-Point.  Philip Larkin.  CMoP (1970 ed.)

Ends in a house.  His Third Decade.  Dabney Stuart.  NVAP

Ends of dreams are acts of completion, The.  The Armless.  Don Welch.  AMV–81

Ends of the Hibiscus burgeon, The.  Song of a Sick Child.  *Malay Oral Tradition, tr. by* R. J. Wilkinson *and* R. O. Winstedt.  WTO

Enduring is the bust of bronze.  The Duke of York's Statue.  Walter Savage Landor.  FaBoEE

Endymion [a Poetic Romance], *sels.*  Keats.
Are Then Regalities All Gilded Masks? *fr.* III.  Moon
Song of the Indian Maid, The, *fr.* IV.  NOBE
"Thing of beauty is a joy for ever, A," I.  MBPR
*Brief sels.*  CTV; ILP (1975 ed.); NIL; PMW; PPM; STS; VoPo

Eneas wonderit the greitnes of Cartaige  Virgil, *tr. by* Gavin Douglas.  *Fr.* The Aeneid, I.  OBVE

Enemies, The.  Arthur J. Bull.  HeHu

Enemy, Enemy.  Cecil J. Mullins.  AMV–80

Energetic Women.  D. H. Lawrence.  InPS

Energy.  Victor Hernández Cruz.  PoBA; SA

Energy Sources.  Karren L. Alenier.  PoUp

Enforce we us with all our might.  Love Saint George.  *Unknown.*  ILP (1975 ed.)

Enfranchising cable, silvered by the sea.  Granite and Steel.  Marianne Moore.  PiAm

Engaged. Octavio Paz, *tr. fr. Spanish by* Muriel Rukeyser. PBMP

Engine, The: A Manual. Michael Dobberstein. AMV–81

Engine and tender, old loaf-shaped Pullman. The Old Trip by Dream Train. Brendan Galvin. PCho

Engine and transmission and the wheels, The. The Great Society, Mark X. Howard Nemerov. AnMo

Engine 143. *Unknown. See* George Allen.

Engineer's dream, holding water, an. The Water Tower. James Paul. AMV–81

Engines thrum in their agile wilderness, The. Old World, New World. Harry Roskolenko. AMV–81

England. Walter de la Mare. PES

England. Marianne Moore. Psy

England. Mary Jo Salter. AMV–80

England ("This royal throne of Kings"). Shakespeare. *See* This England ("This royal throne . . .").

England Expects? Sir Owen Seaman. NOBL

England in 1819. Shelley. CABA (1972 ed.); FF; GrRo; MAT; MBPR; NIL; NOBE; OAEL–2; PBMP; PPoD; UnPo (1975 ed.)
    (Sonnet: England in 1819.) ILP (1975 ed.); LFH; PPP

England, my England—you have been my tutrix. W. H. Auden. *Fr.* Letter to Lord Byron. OBSV

England, unlike junior nations. Remember Suez? Adrian Mitchell. OxBTC

"England! with all thy faults I love thee still." Byron. *Fr.* Beppo: A Venetian Story. UnPo (1976 ed.)

England's Difficulty. Seamus Heaney. CIP

England's ingratitude still blots. What Jenner Said on Hearing in Elysium That Complaints Had Been Made of His Having a Statue. Shirley Brooks. FaBoEE

England's lads are miniature men. Boy-Man. Karl Shapiro. SoSe

English. Osbert Lancaster. *Fr.* Afternoons with Baedeker. FaBoCo; NOBL

English, The. *Unknown.* GBP

English Bards, and Scotch Reviewers. Byron. MBPR *Sels.*
    "As Sisyphus against the infernal steep." OBSV
    "Behold! in various throngs the scribbling crew." OAEL–2
    "Illustrious Holland! hard would be his lot." OBSV

English Counties. *Unknown.* POL

English Elegy, An. Daryl Hine. NoAM

English Flag, The. Kipling. BTTM

English Grace, An. Robert Herrick. *See* Grace for Children, A.

English Liberal. Geoffrey Taylor. FaBoEE

English Retort, The. *Unknown.* OxBM

English Succession, The. *Unknown.* OxBChV

English Train, Summer. Ralph Pomeroy. GP

Englishman, The. W. S. Gilbert. NOBL

Englishman in Italy, The. Robert Browning. ExPo (1973 ed.)

Englishman with an Atlas, An; or, America the Unpronounceable. Morris Bishop. GOA

Engraved on the Collar of a Dog Which I Gave to His Royal Highness. Pope. *See* Epigram Engraved on the Collar of a Dog Given to His Royal Highness.

Enigma. Richard Murphy. CIP

Enigmas. Pablo Neruda, *tr. fr. Spanish by* Robert Bly. NU

Enigmatic moon has at long last died, The. Stevedore. Leslie M. Collins. AmNP (1974 ed.)

Enigmatic Traveler, The. Byron Vazakas. AMV–80

Enion's Lament. Blake. *Fr.* The Four Zoas. UsP

Enion's Protest. Blake. *Fr.* The Four Zoas. UsP
    ("I am made to sow the thistle for wheat.") Prf

Enkindled Spring, The. D. H. Lawrence. NoAM

Enlightenment. Robert V. Carr. BPAW

Enlightenment, The. Patricia Sheppard. AMV–81

Enmeshed in steel stands a stone. The Captive Stone. Jim Barnes. CDW

Ennui. Langston Hughes. OBAL

Enoch. Jones Very. HAP

Enormous Sleep. Tom Crawford. NVAP

Enosis. Christopher Pearse Cranch. ILP (1975 ed.)

Enough. Arthur Gregor. TAP

Enough. Tom Masson. OBAL

Enough. Marianne Moore. NOBA

Enough; and leave the rest to fame. Epitaph. Andrew Marvell. PoPle; TT

Enough! Let this season end. Enough. Arthur Gregor. TAP

Enough of a day has come to pass. Inner-City Lullaby. Russell Atkins. CNA

Enough of those who study the oblique. A Good Resolution. Roy Campbell. OBSV

"Enough," she said. But the dust still rained around her. Dust. Randolph Stow. GAS

Enquiry. Denise Levertov. *Fr.* Two Variations. RiTi

Enraptured I Gaze, *with music.* Francis Hopkinson. BLSo

Enrich My Resignation. Hart Crane. PoA

Enriching the Earth. Wendell Berry. PiAm

Ensign and a lady gay, An. Clerk Saunders. *Unknown.* SLP

Enslav'd, the daughters of Albion weep: a trembling lamentation. Visions of the Daughters of Albion. Blake. MBPR; OAEL–2

Enslaved. Claude McKay. BPo

Enter Harlem. Walk with de Mayor of Harlem. David Henderson. PoBA; UsP

Enter the dream-house, brothers and sisters, leaving. Newsreel. C. Day Lewis. ILP (1975 ed.); PPoD

Enter the toney tenement district. Proletarian Visit. Norman Macleod. SPT

Enter This Deserted House. Shel Silverstein. IWK

Entering the darkened room. Fugue. Kathleen Spivack. AMV–80

Entering the hall, she meets the new wife. The Ejected Wife. *Tr. fr. Chinese by* Arthur Waley. OBVE

Entertainers are friendly, The. Saturday Night Out. Jim Mulac. AcAn

Entertainment, or Porch-Verse, at the Marriage of Master Henry Northleigh and the Most Witty Mistress Lettice Yard, The. Robert Herrick. CaPo

Enthusiast, The; or, The Lover of Nature. Joseph Warton. LAuP

Enticer. Richard Armour. SoSe

Entire country is overrun with private property, The. Gypsy. Josephine Miles. NoAM

Entirely. Louis MacNeice. CMoP (1970 ed.)

Entombed in my heart no blood flows to you. Poem. Margery Dodson. AMV–80

Entrance and exit wounds are silvered clean. Recalling War. Robert Graves. CMoP (1970 ed.); NoAM; OAEL–2; OBP

Entrance Exams. Cuthbert Bede. FaBoNo

Entrapped inside a submarine. H. C. Canfield. *Fr.* On the Loss of U.S. Submarine S4. FaBoCo

Entreaties. Rudy Shackelford. AAN

Entrepreneur chicken shed his tail feathers, surplus, The. Josephine Miles. NoAM

Entry. Edwin Rolfe. SPT

Entry. Anthony Thwaite. HeHu

Entwined. *Malay Oral Tradition, tr. by* R. J. Wilkinson *and* R. O. Winstedt. WTO

Entwined on the bed in the dark.  Two Shapes.  Arthur Gregor.
  TAP

Enueg 1.  Samuel Beckett.  CIP

Enueg II.  Samuel Beckett.  NoAM

Envelope, The.  Maxine W. Kumin.  TV

Environs of Vanholt I.  Charles Spear.  ATNZ

Environs of Vanholt II.  Charles Spear.  ATNZ

Envoi: "Fly, white butterflies, out to sea."  Swinburne.  VLP
  (White Butterflies.)  PCOP

Envoi: "Hear me, whom I betrayed."  J. V. Cunningham.  VGW

Envoi: "I am the Prince."  Charles Causley.  FF

Envoi: "Take of me what is not my own."  Kathleen Raine.
  NOBE

Envoi: "What has want to give."  Kathleen Raine.  WPE

Envoi for a Book of Poems.  James McAuley.  GAS

Envoi (1919).  Ezra Pound.  Fr. Hugh Selwyn Mauberly.  CABA
  (1972 ed.); CMoP (1970 ed.); HAP; InPS; NoAM; NOBA;
  TAP; UnPo (1976 ed.)  VGW

Envoy.  Robert Duncan.  Fr. Passages.  VGW

Envy.  Charles and Mary Lamb.  OxBChV

Envy of Poor Lovers, The.  Austin Clarke.  CIP; CMoP (1970
  ed.)

Envy the Old.  Mark Van Doren.  Prf

Envying the Pelican.  Richard Weber.  CIP

Eolian Harp, The.  Samuel Taylor Coleridge.  MBPR; OAEL-2

Ephelia to Bajazet.  Sir George Etherege.  APAS

Ephraim the Grizzly.  Arthur Guiterman.  BPAW

Epic.  Patrick Kavanagh.  BIrV; CIP

Epic, The.  Tennyson.  VLP

Epic of Gilgamesh, The, sels.  Unknown, tr. fr. Babylonian.
  "Gilgamesh washed his grimy hair, polished his weapons," tr. by
  E. A. Speiser.  Prf
  "Hear me, great ones of Uruk," tr. by N. K. Sandars.  DL

Epicoene; or, The Silent Woman, sel.  Ben Jonson.
  Simplex Munditiis, fr. I, i, tr. fr. the Latin of Jean Bonnefons.
  HoPM (1975 ed.); NOBE; OBP; PBMP
  (Clerimont's Song.)  InPS; OAEL-1; PPP
  ("Still to be neat, still to be dressed [or drest].")  CABA
  (1972 ed.); FF; GBL; HAP; HeIP; ILP (1975 ed.); IP;
  NIL; PoPle

Epicure, The, sel.  Abraham Cowley, after the Greek of Anacreon.
  "Crown me with roses whilest I live."  OBVE

Epicure, Dining at Crewe, An.  Unknown.  AKE; MN

Epicure, The, Sung by One in the Habit of a Town Gallant.
  Thomas Jordan.  See Let Us Drink and Be Merry.

Epicurean Reminiscences of a Sentimentalist.  Thomas Hood.
  BBL

Epidermal Macabre.  Theodore Roethke.  NoAM

Epigram: "After some years Bohemian came to this."  J. V.
  Cunningham.  VGW

Epigram: "And what is love? Misunderstanding, pain."  J. V.
  Cunningham.  CoPAm; HAP; HoPM (1975 ed.); PoA

Epigram: "As the body denies the means to look."  Pernette du
  Guillet, tr. fr. French by Joan Keefe and Richard Terdiman.
  PBWP

Epigram: "As Thomas was cudgeled one day by his wife."  Swift.
  FaBoEE; SoSe

Epigram: "Dark thoughts are my companions. I have wined."  J.
  V. Cunningham.  VGW

Epigram: "Dear, if unsocial privacies obsess me."  J. V.
  Cunningham.  VGW

Epigram, An: "Epigram should be, An—if right."  William Walsh.
  NIL

Epigram: For a Woman with Child.  J. V. Cunningham.  PiAm

Epigram: "Golden casket I designed, A."  John Swanick Drennan.
  BIrV

Epigram: "Golden one is gone from the banquets, The."  Hilda
  Doolittle ("H. D.").  PoA

Epigram: "Homer was poor. His scholars live at ease."  J. V.
  Cunningham.  VGW

Epigram: "How we desire desire! Joy of surcease."  J. V.
  Cunningham.  VGW

Epigram: "I am his Highness' dog at Kew."  Pope.  See Epigram
  Engraved on the Collar of a Dog Given to His Royal
  Highness.

Epigram: "I who by day am function of the light."  J. V.
  Cunningham.  See Motto for a Sun Dial.

Epigram: "If a man who turnips cries."  Samuel Johnson.  See
  Burlesque of Lope de Vega.

Epigram: "If wisdom, as it seems it is."  J. V. Cunningham.
  PiAm

Epigram: "In digging up your bones, Tom Paine."  Byron.
  MBPR

Epigram: "In the neat parlor of their honeymoon."  Max Halpern.
  SFF

Epigram: "In whose will is our peace? Thou happiness."  J. V.
  Cunningham.  VGW

Epigram: "King George, observing with judicious eyes."  Joseph
  Trapp.  FaBoCo
  ("King, observing with judicious eyes, The.")  FaBoEE

Epigram: "King to Oxford sent a troop of horse, The."  William
  Browne.  FaBoCo; FaBoEE

Epigram: "Lasses, like nuts at bottom brown."  Allan Ramsay.
  FaBoEE

Epigram: "Life flows to death as rivers to the sea."  J. V.
  Cunningham.  VGW
  ("Life flows to death as rivers to the sea.")  POL

Epigram: "Love signed the contract blithe and leal."  John
  Swanwick Drennan.  BIrV

Epigram: "Member of the modern great, A."  John Cunningham.
  FaBoEE

Epigram: "Midas, they say, possessed the art of old."  "Peter
  Pindar."  NIL

Epigram: "Milo's from home; and, Milo being gone."  Martial, tr.
  fr. Latin by Elijah Fenton.  OBVE

Epigram: Mistake, The.  Theodore Roethke.  NIL

Epigram: "My Soul, sit thou a patient looker-on."  Francis
  Quarles.  NOBE; PoPle
  (My Soul, Sit Thou a Patient Looker-on.)  NIL

Epigram; "My soul, thy love is dear: 'twas thought a good."
  Francis Quarles.  Fr. Emblems, V, 4.  SCP-2

Epigram: "Naked I came, naked I leave the scene."  J. V.
  Cunningham.  See Epitaph for Someone or Other.

Epigram: Night-Piece.  J. V. Cunningham.  PiAm

Epigram: "Oh, God of dust and rainbows."  Langston Hughes.
  SoSe

Epigram: Of Treason.  Sir John Harington.  See Of Treason.

Epigram: "On parent knees, a naked new-born child."  Sir
  William Jones, after the Sanskrit of Kalidasa.  FaBoEE;
  PoPle

Epigram: On Sir Roger Phillimore.  Unknown.  FaBoCo

Epigram: Pipling.  Theodore Roethke.  NIL

Epigram: Political Reflexion.  Howard Nemerov.  See Sparrow in
  the Zoo, The.

Epigram: "Rise not till noon, if life be but a dream."  Matthew
  Prior.  NIL

Epigram: "Scaurus hates Greek, and is become."  Unknown.
  PiAm

Epigram: "Sir, I admit your general rule."  Pope, also at. to
  Matthew Prior.  BBL; FaBoEE
  (Epigram from the French.)  NIL

Epigram: "Some say, compared to Bononcini."  John Byrom.
  See Epigram on Handel and Bononcini.

Epigram: "Swans sing before they die."   Samuel Taylor Coleridge. *See* Swans Sing before They Die.

Epigram: "This Humanist whom no beliefs constrained."   J. V. Cunningham.   VGW

Epigram: "Time heals not: it extends a sorrow's scope."   J. V. Cunningham.   VGW

Epigram: "Thy nags (the leanest things alive)."   Matthew Prior. FaBoEE

Epigram: "To John I ow'd great obligation."   Matthew Prior. FaBoCo; FaBoEE; OBVE

Epigram: "Tom's sickness did his morals mend."   Matthew Prior. FaBoEE

Epigram: "Were I a king, I could command content."   Edward de Vere, Earl of Oxford.   FaBoEE

Epigram: "What makes thee, fool, so fat? Fool, thee so bare?" Francis Quarles.   *Fr.* Emblems, I, 12.   SCP-2

Epigram: "When Bibo thought fit from the world to retreat." Matthew Prior.   FaBoEE

Epigram: "Within this mindless vault."   J. V. Cunningham. VGW

Epigram: "World is full of care, much like unto a bubble, The." Nathaniel Ward.   POL

Epigram: "Yes, every poet is a fool."   Matthew Prior.   FaBoEE (Another.)   FaBoCo

Epigram Engraved on the Collar of a Dog Given to His Royal Highness.   Pope.   FaBoCo; FaBoEE; InPK; IP; PoPle
(Engraved on the Collar of a Dog Which I Gave to His [Royal] Highness.)   AnMo; CABA (1972 ed.); SoSe (1977 ed.)
(Epigram: "I am his Highness' dog at Kew.")   PAIC
(On the Collar of a Dog Presented by Mr. Pope to the Prince of Wales.)   ExPo (1973 ed.)

Epigram from Petronius.   Petronius Arbiter.   *See* Doing, a Filthy Pleasure Is, and Short.

Epigram from the French.   Pope.   *See* Epigram: "Sir, I admit your general rule."

Epigram in a Maid of Honour's Prayer-Book.   Pope.   FaBoEE

Epigram on Fasting.   Swift.   OBVE

Epigram on Florio.   John Winstanley.   FaBoEE

Epigram on Handel and Bononcini.   John Byrom.   FaBoEE (Epigram: "Some say, compared to Bononcini.")   NOBL

Epigram on John Bull.   Byron.   FaBoCo
("World is a bundle of hay, The.")   FF

Epigram on Miltonicks   Samuel Wesley.   POL

Epigram on One Who Made Long Epitaphs.   Pope.   FaBoEE

Epigram on Scolding.   Swift.   FaBoEE

Epigram on the Unknown Inventor of Scissors.   L. E. Jones. POL

Epigram on the Year 1390-1.   *Unknown.*   NIL

Epigram on Two Ladies.   Sophia Burrell.   POL

Epigram on Voltaire.   Edward Young.   FaBoCo

Epigram on Woman, An.   Philip Ayres.   FaBoEE

Epigram should be, An—if right.   An Epigram.   William Walsh. NIL

Epigrams.   Phillip Hey.   NVAP

Epigrams, *sel.*   Rabindranath Tagore.
"Echo always mocks the sound, The."   PoA

Epigrams and Epitaphs, *sel.*   C. S. Lewis.
"Save yourself. Run and leave me. I must go back," *fr.* 6. EBEV

Epigrams must be curt, nor seem.   Walter Savage Landor. FaBoEE

Epigrams on Castlereagh.   Byron.   ExPo (1973 ed.)

Epigrams, I-IX.   Howard Nemerov.   OBAL

Epigraph to the Theme of Love.   Margaret Cavendish, Duchess of Newcastle.   SCP-2

Epilogue: "At the midnight in the silence of the sleep-time." Robert Browning.   *Fr.* Asolando.   NOBE; PAIC; TT; VLP

Epilogue: "Away, for we are ready to a man!"   James Elroy Flecker.   *Fr.* The Golden Journey to Samarkand.   NOBE

Epilogue: "I have just joined a raggedy line."   Dennis Trudell. AAN; NVAP

Epilogue, An: "I have seen flowers come in stony places."   John Masefield.   FaBoEE; OxBTC

Epilogue: "I, too, sing America."   Langston Hughes.   *See* I, Too.

Epilogue: "I too was a little child once."   Joseph Eliyia, *tr. fr. Greek by* Rae Dalven.   VWA

Epilogue: "O life, O radiance, love, delight."   Christopher Brennan.   *Fr.* The Burden of Tyre.   MAuV

Epilogue: "On the first of the Feast of Feasts."   Robert Browning. *Fr.* Dramatis Personae.   VLP

Epilogue: " 'Poets pour us wine, The.' "   Robert Browning.   VLP

Epilogue: "Phoenix on the hot sirocco's breath."   H. B. Mallalieu. PoA

Epilogue: "So she went into the garden."   Samuel Foote.   *See* Great Panjandrum, The.

Epilogue: "That death might not be casual."   James Burns Singer. FaBoTw (1975 ed.)

Epilogue: "There's something in a stupid ass."   Byron.   PAIC

Epilogue: "Truly, my Satan, thou art but a dunce."   Blake.   *See* Gates of Paradise, The.

Epilogue Spoken at Mithridates King of Pontus, *sel.*   Dryden
"Pox on this playhouse! 'Tis an old tired jade."   SCP-1

Epilogue to a Human Drama.   Stephen Spender.   CMoP (1970 ed.)

Epilogue to Alun Mabon.   John Ceiriog Hughes, *tr. fr Welsh by* H. Idris Bell.   OBW

Epilogue to Lessing's Laocoön.   Matthew Arnold.   VLP

Epilogue to the Satires [*or* 1738].   Pope.   OAEL-1
*Sels.*
Power of Ridicule, The, *fr.* Dialogue II.   NOBE
("Ask you what provocation I have had?")   OBSV
"Spare then the person, and expose the vice," *fr.* Dialogue II. OBSV
Triumph of Vice, The, *fr.* Dialogue I.   NOBE
("Virtue may choose the high or low degree.")   NIL; OBSV

Epilogue to "The Sister," *sel.*   Goldsmith.
"Lud! what a group the motley scene discloses!"   OBSV

Epiphany on a Plot of Moonlight.   William R. Mitchell.   AATT

Epipsychidion.   Shelley.   MBPR
*Sels.*
"Let us become the overhanging day."   OAEL-2
"Thy wisdom speaks in me, and bids me dare."   OAEL-2

Epistemologist, over a Brandy, Opining, The.   Robert Sargent. AMV-80

Epistemology   Richard Wilbur.   NoAM; NOBA

Epistle An: "Whether these lines do find you out."   Sir John Suckling.   PAIC

Epistle, An, Containing the Strange Medical Experience of Karshish, the Arab Physician.   Robert Browning.   PFD; VLP

Epistle from Mr. Pope, to Dr. Arbuthnot, An.   Pope.   *See* Epistle to Dr. Arbuthnot.

Epistle of Othea to Hector, The (A Lytil Bibell of Knyghthod), *sel.* Christine de Pisan, *tr. fr. French; adapted by* Joan Keefe.
"Phoebus, the goddess variant and changeable."   PBWP

Epistle to a Friend (Mr. Colby) to Persuade Him to the Wars, An, *sel.*   Ben Jonson.
"Wake, friend, from forth thy lethargy! the drum."   SCP-1

Epistle to a Lady: Of the Characters of Women, *sels.*   Pope.   *Fr.* Moral Essays, Epistle II.
"Men, some to bus'ness, some to pleasure take."   NIL; OBSV
" 'Yet Cloe sure was formed without a spot.' "   OBSV

Epistle to a Young Friend.   Burns.   EBEV

Epistle to a Young Lady, on Her Leaving the Town after the Coronation. Pope. *See* Epistle to Miss Blount, on Her Leaving the Town after the Coronation.

Epistle to Augusta. Byron. MBPR

Epistle to Augustus, *sel.* Pope.
 "Of little use the man you may suppose." EBEV

Epistle to Be Left in the Earth. Archibald MacLeish. CMoP (1970 ed.); NOBA; PAIC

Epistle to Celia, An. D. C. Berry. AAN

Epistle to Dr. Arbuthnot. Pope. CABA (1972 ed.); InPS; OAEL-1
 (Epistle from Mr. Pope, to Dr. Arbuthnot, An.) ESaP; PAIC Sels.
 Apologia pro Vita Sua. NOBE
 "Bard whom pilf'red pastorals reknown, The." OBSV
 Atticus. InPK; NOBE
 "Curst be the verse, how well so'er it flow." OBP
 "Proud, as Apollo on his forked hill." OBSV
 "Shut, shut the door, good John!" HoPM (1975 ed.)
 Sporus. NOBE; OBSV
 "Why did I write? what sin to me unknown." NIL
  ("Why do I write? what sin to me unknown.") EBEV

Epistle to John Hamilton Reynolds. Keats. *See* To J. H. Reynolds, Esq.

Epistle to Katherine, Lady Aubigny, *sel.* Ben Jonson.
 "'Tis grown almost a danger to speak true." SCP-1

Epistle to Miss [*or* Miss Teresa] Blount, on Her Leaving the Town after the Coronation. Pope. BoLoP; EBEV; NOBE; PPP
 (Epistle to a Young Lady, on Her Leaving the Town after the Coronation.) SoSe

Epistle to Peter Pindar. William Gifford. ESaP

Epistle to Richard Boyle, Earl of Burlington, *sel.* Pope. *Fr.* Moral Essays, Epistle IV.
 "At Timon's villa let us pass a day." ExPo (1973 ed.); OBSV

Epistle to the Rapalloon. Archibald MacLeish. PoA

Epistle Written in the Country to the Right Honourable the Lord Lovelace, An, *sel.* Soame Jenyns.
 "In days, my Lord, when mother Time." OBSV

Epistles to Mr. Pope, *sel.* Edward Young.
 "These labouring wits, like paviours, mend our ways." OBSV

Epistolary Briefs to Proclus, *sel.* Jose I. de Diego Padró, *tr. fr. Spanish by* Julio Marzán.
 "Friend Proclus, the world isn't a fantasy," I, II. InW

Epistolary Essay from M. G. to O. B. upon Their Mutual Poems, An. Earl of Rochester. APAS

Epi-Strauss-ium. Arthur Hugh Clough. PAIC; PFD; VPC

Epitaph, An: "All ye that pass by this holy place." *Unknown.* ILP (1975 ed.)

Epitaph: "Bathsheba! to whom none ever said scat." Whittier. ECBV
 (Epitaph for Bathsheba.) PCat
 (For a Little Girl Mourning Her Favorite Cat.) POL

Epitaph, An: "Enough; and leave the rest to fame." Andrew Marvell. PoPle
 (Epitaph upon——, An.) TT

Epitaph: "Even such is Time, which [*or* that] takes in trust." Sir Walter Ralegh. AKE; BoReV; FaBoEE; NOBE
 (Even Such Is Time [*or* Tyme].) BuTh; HAP
 (Verses Found in His Bible.) PoPle
 (Verses Made the Night before He Dyed.) AAS

Epitaph: "For this she starred her eyes with salt." Elinor Wylie. SBG

Epitaph: "Glassblower lies here at rest, A." J. B. Morton. FaBoEE

Epitaph, An: "He worshipped at the altar of Romance." Colin Ellis. OxBTC

Epitaph: "Here he lies moulding." Leslie Mellichamp. QQQ

Epitaph: "Here Johnson lies—a sage by all allow'd." William Cowper. LAuP

Epitaph: "Here lies a greedy girl, Jane Bevan." *Unknown.* OSF

Epitaph: "Here lies a poet, briefly known as Hecht." Anthony Hecht. POL

Epitaph: "Here lies fierce Strephon, whose poetic rage." Anthony Hecht. PPoD

Epitaph: "Here lies her." *Unknown.* IP

Epitaph: "Here lies John Hughes and Sarah Drew." Lady Mary Wortley Montagu. FaBoEE

Epitaph: "Here lies Sir Tact, a diplomatic fellow." Timothy Steele. InPK

Epitaph: "Here, time concurring (and it does)." John Ciardi. BiP

Epitaph: "Hours before my death." Julio Marzán. InW

Epitaph: "I am old." Christopher Logue. OxBTC

Epitaph: Iohannis Sande. Thomas Bastard. FaBoEE

Epitaph, An: Inscription on a Monument at Newstead Abbey. Byron. *See* Epitaph to a Dog.

Epitaph, An: "Interr'd beneath this marble stone." Matthew Prior. FaBoEE; NIL; OAEL-1; OBSV

Epitaph, An: "Meek Francis lies here, friend, without stop or stay." Matthew Prior. FaBoEE

Epitaph: "Mr. Heath-Stubbs as you must understand." John Heath-Stubbs. MPo; OxBTC

Epitaph: "My brother is skull and skeleton now." William Montgomerie. POL

Epitaph, An: "My name—my country—what are they to thee?" Paulus Silentiarius, *tr. fr. Greek by* William Cowper. FaBoEE; OBVE

Epitaph: "Nor practising virtue nor committing crime." Geoffrey Taylor. FaBoEE

Epitaph: "Posterity will ne'er survey." Byron. *See* Epitaph for Castlereagh, An.

Epitaph: "Roots of mankind are tangled in my hair, The." Wendy Rose. CDW

Epitaph: "See here, nice Death, to please his palate." *At. to* Pope. FaBoEE

Epitaph: "Serene descent, as a red leaf's descending." Sara Teasdale. PoA

Epitaph: "Sir, you should notice me: I am the Man." Lascelles Abercrombie. BBGO

Epitaph: Snake River. Lance Henson. VoR

Epitaph: "Stavro's dead. A truant vine." Lawrence Durrell. FaBoCo

Epitaph: "Stop, Christian passer-by!—Stop, child of God." Samuel Taylor Coleridge. MBPR; OAEL-2

Epitaph: "They hanged him on a clement morning, swung." Dennis Scott. SFF

Epitaph: "Tread softly; bid a solemn music sound." J. B. Morton. FaBoEE

Epitaph: "Underneath this wooden cross there lies." Karl Shapiro. *Fr.* Elegy for a Dead Soldier. OFD

Epitaph: "When I shall be without regret." J. V. Cunningham. *See* When I Shall Be without Regret.

Epitaph Ending in And, The. William Stafford. NIL

Epitaph for a Godly Man's Tomb. Robert Wild. FaBoEE

Epitaph for a Horse Thief. *Unknown.* ECBV

Epitaph for a Postal Clerk. X. J. Kennedy. NIL

Epitaph for a Sailor Buried Ashore. Sir Charles G. D. Roberts. RhR

Epitaph for Bathsheba Whittier. *See* Epitaph: "Bathsheba!..."

Epitaph for Castlereagh, An. Byron. NIL
 (Epitaph: "Posterity will ne'er survey.") FaBoEE

Epitaph for Erotion. Martial, *tr. fr. Latin by* James Michie. FaBoEE

Epitaph for G. B. Shaw. Max Beerbohm. FaBoEE

Epitaph for George Moore. Thomas Hardy. FaBoEE

Epitaph for Goliath. David R. Slavitt. CoPAm

Epitaph for James Smith. Burns. EBEV

Epitaph for Mr. Partridge *Unknown.* AKE

Epitaph for My Cat. Jean Garrigue. TAP

Epitaph for One Who Would Not Be Buried in Westminster Abbey. Pope. FaBoEE

Epitaph for Peter Stuyvesant. Henricus Selyns. NYP

Epitaph for Sir Henry Lee. *Unknown.* FaBoEE

Epitaph for Someone or Other. J. V. Cunningham. NIL; OBAL
(Epigram: "Naked I came, naked I leave the scene.") VGW

Epitaph for the Race of Man, *sel.* Edna St. Vincent Millay.
"See where Capella with her golden kids," VI. CMoP (1970 ed.)

Epitaph for the Tomb of Adolfo Baez Bone. Ernesto Cardenal, *tr. fr. Spanish by* Janet Brof. POL

Epitaph for the Unknown Soldier. W. H. Auden. FaBoCo

Epitaph for William Pitt. Byron. FaBoEE; MBPR

Epitaph in St. Olave's, Southwark, on Mr. Munday. *Unknown.* FaBoCo

Epitaph Intended for Sir Isaac Newton. Pope. *See* Intended for Sir Isaac Newton.

Epitaph of a Stripper. William Jay Smith. AMV–80

Epitaph of Cleonicus. Theocritus, *tr. fr. Greek by* Charles Stuart Calverley. FaBoEE

Epitaph of Grande Amoure, The. Stephen Hawes. *Fr.* The Pastime of Pleasure. EBEV
(Epitaphy of la Graunde Amoure.) FaBoEE

Epitaph of Hipponax. Theocritus, *tr. fr. Greek by* Charles Stuart Calverley. FaBoEE

Epitaph of Maister Win Drowned in the Sea, An. George Turberville. FaBoEE

Epitaph of Nearchos. Ammianus, *tr. fr. Greek by* Dudley Fitts. WeW

Epitaph of Pyramus and Thisbe. Abraham Cowley. FaBoEE

Epitaph on a Dog. *Unknown, tr. fr. Greek by* Forrest Reid. ECBV

Epitaph on a Dormouse. *Unknown.* MN (*At.* to J. H. Wynne); OxBChV

Epitaph on a Fir-Tree. Richard Murphy. FaBoTw (1975 ed.)

Epitaph on a Great Sleeper. Sir Aston Cokayne. FaBoEE

Epitaph on a Hare. William Cowper. HAP; HeIP; PoPle

Epitaph on a Jacobite. Macaulay. *See* Jacobite's Epitaph, A.

Epitaph on a Party Girl. Richard Usborne. FaBoEE

Epitaph on a Pessimist. Thomas Hardy. FaBoEE; FF

Epitaph on a Robin-Redbreast, An. Samuel Rogers. FaBoEE

Epitaph on a Schoolmaster. Burns. FaBoCo
("Here lie Willie M——hie's banes.") FaBoEE

Epitaph on a Tuft-Hunter. Thomas Moore. FaBoCo; FaBoEE

Epitaph on a Tyrant. W. H. Auden. HeIP; MiP; NIL; SFF

Epitaph on a Waiter. David McCord. OBAL

Epitaph on a Willing Girl. *At. to* Thomas Rowlandson. FaBoEE

Epitaph on a Young Child. Ivor Gurney. FaBoEE

Epitaph on a Young Poet Who Died before Having Achieved Success. Amy Lowell. OBAL

Epitaph on an Army of Mercenaries. A. E. Housman. BTTM; CMoP (1970 ed.); NIL; NoAM; NOBE; OBP; OxBTC; PPP; PSN; UnPo (1976 ed.)

Epitaph on an Infant. Samuel Taylor Coleridge. MBPR

Epitaph on an Infant Eight Months Old. *Unknown.* SoSe

Epitaph on an Irish Priest. *Unknown.* FaBoEE

Epitaph on an Unfortunate Artist. Robert Graves. FaBoEE; NOBL

Epitaph on Any Man. A. S. J. Tessimond. POL

Epitaph on Charles I. James Graham, Marquess of Montrose. NOBE

Epitaph on Charles II. Earl of Rochester. FaBoCo; OBP
(On Charles II.) ExPo (1973 ed.)

Epitaph on Colonel Francis Chartres. John Arbuthnot. FaBoEE; PMW
(Colonel Chartres.) OBSV

Epitaph on Dr. Keene. Thomas Gray. FaBoEE

Epitaph on Dr. Keene's Wife. Thomas Gray. FaBoEE

Epitaph on Elizabeth, L. H. Ben Jonson. BiP; CABA (1972 ed.); FaBoEE; HAP; HeIP; NIL; SCP-1

Epitaph on Floyd. *Unknown.* POL

Epitaph on Himself. Samuel Taylor Coleridge. FaBoEE

Epitaph on Himself. Pope. FaBoEE

Epitaph on Holy Willie. Burns. ESaP

Epitaph on James Moore Smythe. Pope. FaBoEE

Epitaph on John Dove. Burns. FaBoCo

Epitaph on John Knott. *Unknown.* FaBoEE

Epitaph on Laurence Sterne. David Garrick. FaBoEE

Epitaph on M. H., An. Charles Cotton. EBEV; FaBoEE

Epitaph on Master Philip Gray, An. Ben Jonson. FaBoEE

Epitaph on Newton. Pope. *See* Intended for Sir Isaac Newton.

Epitaph on Prince Henry. Hugh Holland. FaBoEE

Epitaph on Robert Southey. Thomas Moore. FaBoCo; FaBoEE

Epitaph on S. P. [Salomon *or* Salathiel Pavy], a Child of Queen Elizabeth's Chapel. Ben Jonson. CABA (1972 ed.); HeIP; HoPM (1975 ed.); OAEL-1; PoPle; PPP; UnPo (1976 ed.)
(On Solomon Pavy, a Child of Queen Elizabeth's Chapel.) NOBE

Epitaph on Sir Edward Giles and His Wife. Robert Herrick. PoPle

Epitaph on Sir Walter Pye. John Hoskyns. FaBoEE

Epitaph on the Admirable Dramatic Poet, W. Shakespeare, An. Milton. *See* On Shakespeare.

Epitaph on the Countess Dowager of Pembroke. William Browne. *See* On the Countess Dowager of Pembroke.

Eptitaph on the Duke of Grafton. Sir Fleetwood Shepherd. FaBoEE

Epitaph on the Earl of Strafford. John Cleveland. FaBoEE; NOBE; SCP-2

Epitaph on the Fart in the Parliament House. John Hoskyns. FaBoEE

Epitaph on the Favourite Dog of a Politician. Hilaire Belloc. OBSV

Epitaph on the Lady Mary Villiers ("The Lady Mary Villiers lies"). Thomas Carew. CaPo; FaBoEE; SCP-2
(On the Lady Mary Villiers.) NOBE

Epitaph on the Lady Mary Villiers ("This little vault, this narrow room"). Thomas Carew. NIL
(Another.) CaPo

Epitaph on the Monument of Sir William Dyer At Colmworth, 1641. Lady Catherine Dyer. *Fr.* Sir William Dyer, Knight. BoLoP
("My dearest dust, could not thy hasty day.") SCP-2

Epitaph on the Politician Himself. Hilaire Belloc. OBSV
("Here richly, with ridiculous display.") FaBoEE

Epitaph on the Secretary to the Muses. Jane Barker. FaBoCo

Epitaph on the World. Henry David Thoreau. FF; HeIP

Epitaph on William Hogarth. Samuel Johnson. EBEV

Epitaph on William Jones. *Unknown.* FaBoEE

Epitaph on William Whitehead. *Unknown.* FaBoEE

Epitaph to a Dog. Byron. GDP
(Epitaph, An: Inscription on a Monument at Newstead Abbey, first part.) BoAnP
(Inscription on the Monument of a Newfoundland Dog, second part.) MBPR

Epitaph to Thomas Thetcher. *Unknown.* PoPle

Epitaph upon——, An. Andrew Marvell. See Epitaph, An: "Enough; and leave the rest to fame."

Epitaph upon a Child, An ("Virgins promis'd when I died"). Robert Herrick. FaBoEE

Epitaph upon a Sober Matron, An. Robert Herrick. CaPo

Epitaph upon a Virgin, An. Robert Herrick. CaPo; FaBoEE

Epitaph upon a Young Married Couple Dead and Buried Together, An. Richard Crashaw. *See* Epitaph upon Husband and Wife Who Died and Were Buried Together, An.

Epitaph upon Doctor Brook, An. Richard Crashaw. WeW

Epitaph upon Husband and Wife Who Died and Were Buried Together, An. Richard Crashaw. EBEV; NOBE (Epitaph upon a Young Married Couple Dead and Buried Together, An.) FaBoEE; ILP (1975 ed.); NIL

Epitaph upon That Profound and Learned Casuist, The Late Ordinary of Newgate, An. Thomas Brown. OBSV

Epitaph upon the Right Honorable Sir Philip Sidney, An. Fulke Greville. Prf

Epitaphs. Glyn Hughes. LP

Epitaphs of the War, 1914-18, *sels.* Kipling.
Beginner, The. FaBoTw (1975 ed.)
Bridegroom, The. FaBoEE
Common Form. FaBoEE; FaBoTw (1975 ed.)
Coward, The. FaBoEE; FaBoTw (1975 ed.)
Dead Statesman, A. FaBoEE
Drifter off Tarentum, A. FaBoEE; PoPle
Equality of Sacrifice. FaBoTw (1975 ed.)
Refined Man, The. FaBoEE; FaBoTw (1975 ed.)
Son, A. FaBoEE

Epitaphs on Two Piping-Bullfinches of Lady Ossory's. Horace Walpole. FaBoEE

Epitaphy of la Graunde Amoure. Stephen Hawes. *See* Epitaph of Grande Amoure, The.

Epithalamion: "Hark, hearer, hear what I do." Gerard Manley Hopkins. VLP

Epithalamion: "Kingfisher falls through the dry air, The." Charles Wright. CoPAm

Epithalamion: "Singing, today I married my white girl." Dannie Abse. OBW

Epithalamion: "These are the small hours when." Michael Longley. CIP

Epithalamion: "Thou art reprieved old year, thou shalt not die," *abr.* John Donne. SCP-1

Epithalamion: "Ye learned sisters which have oftentimes." Spenser. AAS; BoLoP; CABA (1972 ed.); Epi; ILP (1975 ed.); InPS; LoAs; NOBE; OAEL-1; PAIC
"Wake, now my love, awake; for it is time," *sel.* GBL

Epithalamion Made at Lincoln's Inn. John Donne. PAIC

Epithalamion, An; or, Marriage-Song on the Lady Elizabeth and Count Palatine Being Married on St. Valentine's Day, *abr.* John Donne. SCP-1
"Hail, Bishop Valentine, whose day this is," *sel.* OFD

Epithalamium: "We have found our peace, and move with a turning globe." A. R. D. Fairburn. ATNZ

Epithalamium: "When first my beloved came to my bed." John Peale Bishop. PAIC

Epithalamium upon the Marriage of Captain William Bedloe, An. Richard Duke. APAS

Epithalamy to Sir Thomas Southwell and His Lady, An. Robert Herrick. CaPo

Epithets of War—I: August 1914. Vernon Scannell. HeHu

Epithets of War—III: Casualties. Vernon Scannell. HeHu

Epoch ends, the world is still, The. Matthew Arnold. Bacchanalia: or, The New Age, II. OAEL-2

Epochs. Emma Lazarus. SBG

Epos. Harold Rosenberg. PoA

Eppie Morrie. *Unknown.* PeBB

Equality, Father! Edith Bruck, *tr. fr. Italian by* Anita Barrows. VWA

Equality of Sacrifice. Kipling. *Fr.* Epitaphs of the War. FaBoTw (1975 ed.)

Equator at Quito, The; or, The Will to Die. Rainer Schulte. SES

Equestrian fell from his horse, An. The Childhood of an Equestrian. Russell Edson. AmPA

Equilibrists, The. John Crowe Ransom. CMoP (1970 ed.); HAP; LoAs; NIL; NoAM; NOBA; PPP; TAP

Equinox, The. Dubose Heyward. PoA

Equinox, The. Longfellow. *Fr.* Seaweed. RhR ("When descends on the Atlantic.") EcS

Equinoxial swore by the green leaves on the trees, trees. Little Phoebe. *Unknown.* FSW

Ere I freeze, to sing bravely. Poem of the Frost and Snow. Lewis Morris, *tr. by* Anthony Conran. OBW

Ere I go hence and be no more. My Daughter's Dowry. Robert Herrick. RRA

Ere long they come, where that same wicked wight. The Cave of Despair. Spenser. *Fr.* The Faerie Queene. NOBE; OAEL-1

Ere on my bed my limbs I lay. The Pains of Sleep [*or* A Child's Evening Prayer]. Samuel Taylor Coleridge. MBPR; OxBChV

Ere the cock has crowed. The Forsaken Girl. Randall Jarrell. OLR

Ere You Were Queen of Sheba. Sir Arthur Shipley. FaBoCo

Erect in the movies. Afterword: A Film. Michael S. Harper. NW

Erev Shabbos. Marc Kaminsky. VWA

Erewhile, before the world was old. Jadis. Ernest Dowson. VLP

Ergo Sum. Charles Brasch. ATNZ

Erica. Mary Ursula Bethell. ATNZ

Eric's just left for Washington State. Not a Political Poem. Barbara Berman. PoUp

Erie. *Unknown.* FSW

Erie Canal, The. *Unknown.* BLSo, *with music;* FSW

Erige Cor Tuum ad Me in Caelum. Hilda Doolittle ("H. D."). CMoP (1970 ed.)

Erin Go Braugh! *Unknown.* FSW

Erith, on the Thames. *Unknown.* GBP

Erl-King, The. Goethe, *tr. fr. German by* Sir Walter Scott. OBVE
(Invisible King, The, *tr. by* Robert Bly.) NU

Erl-King's Daughter, The. Johann Gottfried Herder, *tr. fr. German by* James Clarence Mangan. PoTa

Ernest Liberal's Lament, The. Ernest Hemingway. *See* Earnest Liberal's Lament, The.

Ernie Morgan found him. Barn Owl. Leslie Norris. HeHu

Eros. Robert Bridges. CMoP (1970 ed.); ExPo (1973 ed.); ILP (1975 ed.); NOBE

Eros D'Aute. Theodore Wratislaw. GBL

Eros Out of the Sea. Dilys Bennett Laing. PoA

Eros, thou yet behold'st me? Shakespeare. *Fr.* Antony and Cleopatra, IV, xiv. EBEV

Eros Turannos. E. A. Robinson. CMoP (1970 ed.); GBL; HAP; ILP (1975 ed.); IPWM; NoAM; NOBA; PiAm; PoA; PPoe; STS; TAP

Erotic Suite, *sels.* José Luis Vega, *tr. fr. Spanish by* Julio Marzán.
"My love, like the vast majority." InW
"This poem is an erection." InW

Erotion rests here, in the/ Hastening shadows. Kenneth Rexroth, *after the Latin of* Martial. NNaP

Erotion's Death. Peter Whigham. TwMBP

Errata. Charles Simic. NNaP; NVAP

Erthe Toc of Erthe. *Unknown.* HAP

Erudite of literature, The. Alison Wyrley Birch. PPM

Eruption. Margaret Reynolds. MIS

Es war einmal . . . No, it's too heavy. Märchenbilder. John Ashbery. NOBA

Esau. Leib Kwitko, *tr. fr. Yiddish by* Keith Bosley. VWA

Escalator. Patricia Goedicke. AAN

Escape. Robert Graves. ILP (1975 ed.)

Escape. Georgia Douglas Johnson. PoBA

Escape. Ilya Rubin, *tr. fr. Russian by* Linda Zisquit. VWA

Escape. Charles Spear. ATNZ

Escape, The. William Stafford. NNaP

Escape at Bedtime. Robert Louis Stevenson. CTV; ILP (1975 ed.)

Escape to Love, *sel.* Patrick MacDonogh.
  "Alone and Godless, stopped by the sudden edge." BIrV

Escapist's Song. Theodore Spencer. POL; SFF

Eschatology. Heather Banks. PoUp

Eschatology. Wade Hall. AATT

Eshu, the God of Fate ("Eshu turns right into wrong"). *Yoruba Oral Tradition, tr. by* Ulli Beier. WTO

Eskimo Chant. *Unknown, tr. fr. Eskimo by* Knud Rasmussen. RFM

Eskimo Occasion. Judith Rodriguez. GAS

Eskimos in Manitoba. Recital. John Updike. OBAL; OSP

Esope, mine author, makis mentioun. The Two Mice. Robert Henryson. OxBM

ESP. Carter Revard. VoR

Especially he loves. God Poem. Stanley Moss. VGW; VWA

Especially I like the bit where. Sleight-of-Hand. Bruce Dawe. CAAP

Especially When the October Wind. Dylan Thomas. CABA (1972 ed.); OBW; OxBTC; TT

Esperanza. James Scully. NYP

Esplumeoir. "Hugh MacDiarmid." TwMBP

Essay on Criticism, An. Pope. CABA (1972 ed.)
  *Sels.*
  "But most by numbers judge a poet's song," *fr.* Pt. II. HAP; NIL; UsP; WIF
  "First follow Nature, and your judgment frame," *fr.* Pt. I. HAP
  "In wit, as nature, what affects our hearts," *fr.* Pt. II. HAP
  Little Learning, A, *fr.* Pt. II. NOBE
    ("Little learning is a dangerous thing, A.") HAP; HoPM (1975 ed.)
  "Of all the causes which conspire to blind," *fr.* Pt. II. ILP (1975 ed.); PoIA; PPoD; PPoe
  "Some are bewildered in the maze of schools," *fr.* Pt. I. OBSV
  "Some beauties yet no precepts can declare," *fr.* Pt. I. HAP
  "Some ne'er advance a judgment of their own," *fr.* Pt. II. OBSV
  Sound and Sense ("True ease in writing comes from art, not chance"), *fr.* Pt. II. SoSe; UnPo (1976 ed.)
    ("True ease in writing comes from art, not chance.") HAP
  "Such shameless bards we have; and yet 'tis true," *fr.* Pt. III. OBSV
  "'Tis hard to say, if greater want of skill," *fr.* Pt. I. HAP; OAEL-1
  "True wit is Nature to advantage dressed," *fr.* Pt. II. HAP; UsP

Essay on Man, An, *sels.* Pope.
  "Awake, my St. John! leave all meaner things," Epistle I. PAIC
  "Behold the child, by Nature's kindly law," *fr.* Epistle II. POL
  "Bliss of man (could pride that blessing find), The," *fr.* Epistle I. NU
  "For forms of government let fools contest," *fr.* Epistle III. POL
  Great Chain of Being, The, *fr.* Epistles I *and* II. ExPo (1973 ed.)

"Know then thyseif, presume not God to scan," Epistle II. OAEL-1, *ll.*1-18; PoIA, *ll.*1-18; PPoe
  (Know Thyself.) NOBE
"Lo, the poor Indian! whose untutor'd mind," *fr.* Epistle I. NU
"Nor think, in nature's state they blindly trod," *fr.* Epistle III. OAEL-1
"Presumptuous man! the reason wouldst thou find," *fr.* Epistle I. BiP
Vice, *fr.* Epistle II. PPM
"What would this Man? Now upward will he soar," *fr.* Epistle I. HeIP

Essay on Marriage, *sel.* Anne Finch.
  "O, love, in your sweet name enough." FaBoTw (1975 ed.)

Essay on Psychiatrists, *sel.* Robert Pinsky.
  Their Speech, Compared with Wisdom and Poetry. PoA

Essay upon Satire, An. John Sheffield, Duke of Buckingham and Normanby, *formerly at. to* Dryden. APAS

Essential Beauty. Philip Larkin. NowV

Essential oils are wrung. Emily Dickinson. AmVN; PBMP; PiAm; SBG

Essential poem at the center of things, The. A Primitive like an Orb. Wallace Stevens. NOBA

Estate, The, *sel.* Charles Brasch.
  "Once more as I gather about me the cloak of the evening." ATNZ

Estate and an earldom at seventy-four, An! Horace Walpole. FaBoEE

Esther K. Comes to America: 1931. Jerome Rothenberg. NNaP

Esther's Tomcat. Ted Hughes. PCat

Esthete in Harlem. Langston Hughes. BPo; SS

Esthetique du Machiavel. George Starbuck. PAIC

Esthétique du Mal, *sels.* Wallace Stevens.
  "He was at Naples writing letters home." CMoP (1970 ed.); NOBA
  "How red the rose that is the soldier's wound." CMoP (1970 ed.); NOBA
  "Life is a bitter aspic. We are not." CMoP (1970 ed.)
  "Sun, in clownish yellow, but not a clown, The." NOBA

Estienne. Peter Klappert. PCho

Estimable Mable. Gwendolyn Brooks. FB

Estrich, thou feathered fool and easy prey. Lucasta's Fan, with a Looking-Glass in It. Richard Lovelace. CaPo; SCP-2

Estuary, The. Patricia Beer. HeHu

Estuary, The. A. R. D. Fairburn. ATNZ

Esyllt. Glyn Jones. OBW

Et in Arcadia Ego. W. H. Auden. CMoP (1970 ed.)

Et Incarnatus Est. William Langland. *Fr.* The Vision of Piers Plowman. BoReV; NOBE

Et Nox Facta Est. Victor Hugo, *tr. fr. French by* Mary Ann Caws. NAWM-2

État, *sel.* Anne-Marie Albiach, *tr. fr. French by* Paul Auster.
  "Of the unended in the speed of." PBWP

Etched Away From. Paul Celan, *tr. fr. German by* Michael Hamburger. OBVE

Eternal City, The. A. R. Ammons. TT

Eternal Dice, The. César Vallejo, *tr. fr. Spanish by* James Wright. IPWM

Eternal Father, Strong to Save. William Whiting. FaPoR; VLP
  (Navy Hymn, The, *with music*.) BLSH

Eternal Female ground, The! it was heard over all the Earth. A Song of Liberty. Blake. MBPR

Eternal Feminine, The. Oliver Herford. TDH

Eternal gates' terrific porter lifted the northern bar, The. The Secrets of the Earth. Blake. NOBE

Eternal God, How They're Increased, *with music*. Cotton Mather. AH

Eternal God, Whose Power Upholds, *with music*. Henry Hallam Tweedy. AH

Eternal Goodness, The. Whittier. PIM

Eternal Image, The. Ruth Pitter. OxBTC

Eternal Lord! eased of a cumbrous load. Sonnet. Michelangelo, *tr. by* Wordsworth. PIM

Eternal Spirit of the chainless mind! Sonnet on Chillon. Byron. *Fr.* The Prisoner of Chillon. ExPo (1973 ed.); ILP (1975 ed.); LFH; PAIC; PBMP

Eternal Spirit, Source of Light, *with music.* Samuel Davies. AH

Eternity ("He who binds [*or* bends] to himself a joy"). Blake. *Fr.* Several Questions Answered. BoReV; FaBoEE; LAuP; MBPR; NOBE; WIF
    ("He who binds to himself a joy.") EBEV

Eternity is passion, girl or boy. Whence Had They Come? W. B. Yeats. BoLoP

Eternity of Nature, The. John Clare. EBEV

Ethan Boldt. Roger Weingarten. AmPA

Ethelstan, *sel.* George Darley.
    Runilda's Chant. PFIr

Ethereal minstrel! pilgrim of the sky! To a [*or* the] Skylark. Wordsworth. MBPR; PCOP

Ethick. Robert Bridges. *Fr.* The Testament of Beauty. OxBTC

Ethics. Linda Pastan. AMV–81; PCho

Ethics for Everyman. Roger Woddis. NOBL

Ethnic Life, The. Daniel Halpern. AmPA

Ethnogenesis Henry Timrod. NOBA

Etienne de Silhouette Cornelius J. Ter Maat. InPK

Etiquette. W. S. Gilbert. FaBoCo; VLP

Etruscan Notebook, *sels.* Elena Clementelli, *tr. fr. Italian by* Ruth Feldman *and* Brian Swann.
    "Cerveteri road." PBWP
    "From gorge to gorge." PBWP
    "Net rests on the water's surface, The." PBWP

Ettrick. Lady John Scott. SLP; WPE

Etude. Joseph Brodsky, *tr. fr. Russian by* Dimitry Pospielovsky *and* Keith Bosley. VWA

Etude. Richard O'Connell. BCr

Etude. Carlos Pellicer, *tr. fr. Spanish by* H. R. Hays. LoAs

Etude for Voice and Hand. Gabriel Levin. VWA

Etude from the Third Epistle. Robert Duncan. *Fr.* Dante Etudes. CAAP

Etude Géographique. Stoddard King. BPAW

Etude Réaliste, *sel.* Swinburne.
    "Baby's feet, like sea-shells pink, A," I. WeW

Etudes. Laurence W. Thomas. AMV–80

Euch, are you having your period? Alta. NMM

Euclid. Vachel Lindsay. SFF

Euclid Alone Has Looked on Beauty Bare. Edna St. Vincent Millay. CMoP (1970 ed.); ILP (1975 ed.); TAP

Eudaimon. Kathleen Raine. PBWP

Eugene Delacroix Says. Edward Dorn. NoAM

Eugene Onegin, *sel.* Pushkin, *tr. fr. Russian by* Walter Arndt. "Now that he is in grave condition." NAWM–2

Eugenist, The. Robert Graves. FaBoEE

Eulogy for Alvin Frost. Audre Lorde. CNA

Eulogy for Populations. Ron Welburn. PoBA

Eulogy to the Bow and Arrow. *Mongol Oral Tradition, tr. by* C. R. Bawden. WTO

Eunica skornde me, when her I would have sweetly kist. Theocritus, *tr. fr. Greek.* Idylls, XX. OBVE

Eupheme, *sels.* Ben Jonson.
    "I sing the just and uncontrolled descent." SCP–1
    "Truly honoured lady, the Lady Venetia Digby, The." SCP–1

Euphoria, Euphoria. Mark DeFoe. AMV–80

Eureka. Ruth O. Maunders. AMV–80

Euridice. Alta. MMD

Europe and America. David Ignatow. NNaP; PBMP; UnPo (1976 ed.)

Europe overwhelms me! Traveling. Anne Waldman. RiTi

European Night, The. Stanislav Vinaver, *tr. fr. Serbo-Croat by* Vasa D. Mihailovich. VWA

European Shoe, The. Michael Benedikt. AmPA; ConAP

Eurydice. Hilda Doolittle ("H. D."). VGW

Eurydice. Phyllis Thompson. PCho

Eustace and Edith. Charles Tennyson Turner. VPC

Eutaw Springs. Philip Freneau. *See* To the Memory of the Brave Americans.

Eutychides. E. A. Robinson, *after the Greek of* Lucilius. OBAL

Eva, I agree to love, among creation, all the creatures! Alfred de Vigny, *tr. by* Robert Bly. *Fr.* The Shepherd's House. NU

Evacuee, The. R. S. Thomas. MPo

Evadne. Hilda Doolittle ("H. D."). BoWoP; LoAs; RiTi

Evan just had the white birch lined up. Fear and Anger in the Mindless Universe. Hayden Carruth. NNaP

Evangeline, *sels.* Longfellow.
    "Talk not of wasted affection." CTV
    "This is the forest primeval. The murmuring pines and the hemlocks," *fr.* Prologue. SpRo

Evangelist, The. Bennie Lee Sinclair. TAT

Evangelist St. John my patron was, The. Wordsworth. *Fr.* The Prelude, III. HAP

Evans Country, The, *sels.* Kingsley Amis.
    Aberdarcy: The Chaucer Road. NOBL
    Aderdarcy: The Main Square. NOBL; OxBTC
    Aldport (Mystery Tour). NOBL
    Brynbwrla. NOBL
    Fforestfawr. NOBL
    Langwell. NOBL
    Pendydd. NOBL

Evaporation Poems. Kathleen Norris. IHMS

Evasive souls, of whom the wise lose track. The Imaginative Life. Geoffrey Hill. NoAM

Eve. Arthur J. Bull. UnPo (1976 ed.)

Eve. Jakov Fichman, *tr. fr. Hebrew by* Robert Friend. VWA

Eve. Oliver Herford. OBAL

Eve. Ralph Hodgson. ILP (1975 ed.); NIL; PAIC; PoTa; SoSe; UnPo (1976 ed.)

Eve. Christina Rossetti. NIL

Eve, The. Howard Schwartz. VWA

Eve. *Unknown. See* Eve's Lament.

Eve Contemplates Sharing Her Sin. Milton. *Fr.* Paradise Lost, IX. OBP

Eve is angel, though bone of bone. Waiting for Lilith. Jascha Kessler. VWA

Eve: Night Thoughts. Judson Jerome. CoPAm

Eve of Crecy, The. William Morris. VLP

Eve of July Fourth. James Bertolino. HeS

Eve of St. Agnes, The. Keats. AnMo; CABA (1972 ed.); HAP; HoPM (1975 ed.); ILP (1975 ed.); LFH; MBPR; NIL; OAEL–2; PAIC; PoIA; STS

Eve of Saint Mark, The. Keats. MBPR

Eve of Waterloo, The. Byron. *See* Waterloo.

Eve Speaks to Adam ("With thee conversing I forget all time"). Milton. *Fr.* Paradise Lost, IV. GBL

Eve to Her Daughters. Judith Wright. MPo

Eve, with her basket, was. Eve. Ralph Hodgson. ILP (1975 ed.); NIL; PAIC; PoTa; SoSe; UnPo (1976 ed.)

Evelyn Hope. Robert Browning. TT; VLP

Even. Marina Rivera. FoP

Even a cloud. Even If. Rachel Fishman, *tr. by* Gabriel Preil *and* Howard Schwartz. VWA

Even after Confession. On a Catholic Childhood. Janet Campbell Hall. VoR

Even among the deformed. Beauty. Paul David Ashley. DNGG

Even as a dragon's eye that feels the stress. Wordsworth. MBPR

Even as children they were late sleepers. The Undead. Richard Wilbur. CAPP; ConAP

Even as I rest, the road runs through me. Indiana State Highway Patrol. James Beall. PoUp

Even as we kill. On the Birth of My Son, Malcolm Coltrane. Julius Lester. PoBA

Even as your progenitors ran. To a Race Horse at Ascot. Jennie M. Palen. PH

Even at its edge the lake is no miracle. Links. Ricardo Pau-Llosa. AMV-81

Even before the cord is cut, he seems. Interphase. Darcy Cummings. EC

Even for the wind there was no room. The Way the Bird Sat. Ray A. Young Bear. CDW; VoR

Even from the beach I could sense it. Attack of the Crab Monsters. Lawrence Raab. AmPA

Even If. Rachel Fishman, *tr. fr. Yiddish by* Gabriel Preil *and* Howard Schwartz. VWA

Even if the geraniums are artificial. The Geraniums. Genevieve Taggard. VGW

Even if there'd been prayers. Vincent Buckley. *Fr.* Golden Builders. CAAP; GAS

Even in bed I pose: desire may grow. Carnal Knowledge. Thom Gunn. BoLoP

Even in daylight, in murky waters. Feeling for Fish. Leonard Trawick. AMV-81

Even in death they prosper; even in the death. Necropolis. Karl Shapiro. PoA

Even in my dreams/ I must no longer meet you. Lady Ise, *tr. fr. Japanese by* Etsuko Terasaki *and* Irma Brandeis. BoWoP

Even in my dreams you have denied yourself to me. To Kalon. Ezra Pound. PoA

Even in sleep my eyes are on the elements. An Astronomer's Journal. Jane Shore. PoA

Even in the cemetery. Fitzroy, Carlton. Vincent Buckley. *Fr.* Golden Builders. CAAP

Even in the moment of our earliest kiss. Edna St. Vincent Millay. VGW

Even in the worst of times. Easter Flood. Brenda S. Stockwell. AMV-81

Even is come; and from the dark Park, hark. A Nocturnal Sketch. Thomas Hood. BBL; FaBoCo

Even [*or* Ev'n] like two little bank-dividing brooks. My Beloved Is Mine and I Am His. Francis Quarles. Emblems, V, 3. NOBE

Even my dreams are hackneyed. Archetypes. Neal Bowers. AMV-81

Even now, Hippocrates, you can't restore. Time to Kill. Edward Lowbury. PMW

Even now, mid-winter. The Ice Castle. Michael Harris. AMV-80

Even now the devastation is begun. Goldsmith. *Fr. The* Deserted Village. EBEV

Even now there are places where a thought might grow. A Disused Shed in County [*or* Co.] Wexford. Derek Mahon. CIP; IPM

Even now this landscape is assembling. All Hallows. Louise Glück. AmPA; NU

Even now, when the long white hair. In the Fall. Alina Rivero. AMV-81

Even on clear nights, lead the most supple children. The Great Bear. John Hollander. BCr; CoPAm; NoAM

Even on hills by here. Phillips Mill. Terrance Keenan. AAN

Even Sea, The. May Swenson. EcS

Even So. Dante Gabriel Rossetti. NOBE; VLP

Even so distant, I can taste the grief. Deceptions. Philip Larkin. CABA (1972 ed.); CMoP (1970 ed.)

Even Such Is Time [*or* Tyme]. Sir Walter Ralegh. *See* Epitaph: "Even such is Time, which takes in trust."

Even the barflies move to corner tables. Sheepman. Frank Ormsby. IPM

Even the beauty of the rose doth cast. Shadow. Walter de la Mare. ILP (1975 ed.)

Even the sun-clouds this morning cannot manage such skirts. Poppies in October. Sylvia Plath. NoAM

Even the sun, still warm. August/ Fresno 1973. Roberta Spear. AmPA

Even the tips of their fingers. The Loss. Stephen Dunn. NVAP

Even the train is taller than those shacks. Homecoming. John Thompson. MAT

Even the unlived life within us. Like a Beach. Harvey Shapiro. VWA

Even the walls are flowing, even the ceiling. Variation on Heraclitus. Louis MacNeice. NoAM

Even There. Lyn Lifshin. IHMS

Even this is movement. Altars and Sacrifice. Jay Wright. FB

Even Though. John Stone. AMV-81

Even though/ a cat has a kitten. Scat! Skitten! David McCord. ECBV

Even though my hands/ are rough from much rice-pounding. *Unknown, tr. fr. Japanese by* Kenneth Yasuda. BoWoP

Even with its own ax to grind, sometimes. The Mind, Intractable Thing. Marianne Moore. Psy

Evenen in the Village. William Barnes. VPC

Evening. Richard Aldington. Moon

Evening. Alison Wyrley Birch. PPM

Evening. John Clare. VLP

Evening. Charles Cotton. SCP-2 (Evening Quatrains.) ExPo (1973 ed.)

Evening. Hilda Doolittle ("H. D."). CMoP (1970 ed.); IPWM; VGW; WPE

Evening. John Keble. *See* Evening Hymn

Evening. King D. Kuka. VoR

Evening. Itzik Manger, *tr. fr. Yiddish by* Miriam Waddington. VWA

Evening. Thomas Miller. OxBChV

Evening. Edith Sitwell. AIW

Evening. Andrew Taylor. FPA

Evening. Tristan Tzara, *tr. fr. French by* Willis Barnstone *and* Matei Calinescu. VWA

Evening. James Wright. NOBA

Evening and sailboats. Harbors. Judith Minty. TC

Evening: and we/ wait for a train to pass. Evening Song. John Matthias. AMV-81

Evening—another evening—and the lights flare. Thomas McGrath. Letter to an Imaginary Friend, Part Two, V, 2. NNaP

Evening before Rain. L. A. G. Strong. OxBTC

Evening Bread. Jacob Glatstein, *tr. fr. Yiddish by* David G. Roskies *and* Hillel Schwartz. VWA

Evening comes early, and soon discovers. Master's in the Garden Again. John Crowe Ransom. NoAM

Evening cracks. Days of Re-entry. Patricia Henley. NPW

Evening Darkens Over, The. Robert Bridges. CMoP (1970 ed.); HAP

Evening drooped toward owl-call, The. In Italian They Call the Bird Civetta. Robert Penn Warren. PiAm

Evening Ebb. Robinson Jeffers. NoAM; PSN

Evening gathers everything. James Stephens. *Fr.* Hesperus. LCL

Evening Gown, The. Karen Swenson. WBN

Evening Harbour. Tom Paulin. AMV-81

Evening, here, and the gray garden. To One Far Away, Dancing. C. Stephen Finley. AMV-81

Evening Hymn. John Keble. PFD (Evening.) VLP

Evening Hymn, An. Thomas Ken. *See* All Praise To Thee, My God, This Night.

Evening in Eden. Milton. *Fr.* Paradise Lost, IV. OBP (Evening in Paradise.) NOBE (Moon and the Nightingale, The.) Moon.

Evening in Harvest Time, An. Charles Tennyson Turner. VPC

Evening in Paradise. Milton. *See* Evening in Eden.

Evening in the Sanitarium. Louise Bogan. IHMS; SBG

Evening in the Walls. Jean Wahl, *tr. fr. French by* Charles Guenther. VWA

Evening is clogged with gnats as the light fails. Alceste in the Wilderness. Anthony Hecht. ConAP; PoA

Evening is part of the jig-saw truth of her. Ode in Honour. Francis Scarfe. EAS

Evening isnt so much a playland as it is. Groupie. Al Young. NVAP

Evening Musicale. Phyllis McGinley. OBAL

Evening of Home Movies, An. Constance Urdang. UsP

Evening of the Rose. Anthony Rudolf. VWA

Evening on the olden, the golden sea of Wales. James Elroy Flecker. *Fr.* The Dying Patriot. EcS

Evening: Ponte a Mare, Pisa. Shelley. MBPR

Evening Prayer, An. *Unknown.* *See* Now I Lay Me Down to Sleep.

Evening Primrose. John Clare. PF

Evening Quatrains. Charles Cotton. *See* Evening.

Evening Ride Jill Hoffman. PH

Evening Shade. John Leland. AmFP (Day Is Past and Gone, The.) AH

Evening Song. Sherwood Anderson. ANTL

Evening Song. Kenneth Fearing. EAS

Evening Song. Sidney Lanier. UnPo (1976 ed.)

Evening Song. John Matthias AMV-81

Evening Song. Jean Toomer. BPo; ILP (1975 ed.)

Evening Star, The. *Aborigine Oral Tradition, tr. by* R. M. Berndt. *Fr.* The Moon-Bone Cycle. WTO

Evening: To Harriet Shelley. MBPR

Evening traffic homeward burns. Before Disaster. Yvor Winters. HoPM (1975 ed.); IP

Evening Walk, An. Wordsworth. MBPR

Evening Walk in Winter. Mary Ursula Bethell. ATNZ

Evening was in the wood, louring with storm. Haunted. Siegfried Sassoon. CMoP (1970 ed.)

Evening Waterfall. Carl Sandburg. UsP

Evening without Angels. Wallace Stevens. TT; VGW

Evenings a roach of light scrabbling through. The Psychoanalysis of Fire. John Morgan. AAN

Evening's barefoot monk. Evening. Itzik Manger, *tr. by* Miriam Waddington. VWA

Evening's Love, An, *sel.* Dryden. "Calm was the even, and clear was the sky," *fr.* IV, i. FF

Evenings, we call quail. Survival. William Stafford. PoW

Eveningsong. Ramona Wilson. VoR

Evensong. Peter Kane Dufault. AMV-80

Event. Sylvia Plath. NOBA

Event, An. Richard Wilbur. CoPAm

Eventual Music, The ("Eventually someone knocks at your door eventually"). Liam Rector. PoUp

Ever been kidnapped. Kidnap Poem. Nikki Giovanni. AmNP (1974 ed.); BPo; InPK; NoAM; TAP; UsP

Ever-fixed Mark, An. Kingsley Amis. NoAM

Ever heard Bird. Mellowness and Flight. George Barlow. CNA

Ever let the fancy roam. Fancy. Keats. MBPR

Ever myn happe is slack and slo in commyng. Petrarch, *tr. fr. Italian by* Sir Thomas Wyatt. OBVE

Ever since he danced on the ceiling in "Royal Wedding." Fred Astaire. Maxine Chernoff. FiCh

Ever since my daughters started to walk. The Green Tree. James Reiss. AmPA

Ever since our lunch of cheese. Dearest Man-in-the-Moon. Erica Jong. MMD; Moon

Ever since the great planes were murdered at the end of the gardens. Domus Caedet Arborem. Charlotte Mew. PBWP

Ever the green memory. Midway. John D. Engle, Jr. AMV-81

Everett Anderson thinks he'll make. July. Lucille Clifton. CC

Everglade. Anne Cherner. AMV-81

Everlasting Astronauts, The. Tom Buchan. MS

Everlasting Forests, The. Dahlia Ravikovitch, *tr. fr. Hebrew by* Chana Bloch. BoWoP

Everlasting Mercy, The, *sels.* John Masefield. "From '41 to '51." NoAM "O Christ who holds the open gate." ILwL

Everlasting Teamwork in Basketball. H. Victory. SPo

Everlasting universe of things, The. Mont Blanc. Shelley. MBPR; NIL; OAEL-2

Ever-touring Englishmen, The. *Gond Oral Tradition, tr. by* V. Elwin *and* S. Hivale. WTO

Every afternoon at four. Quail Walk. Heather Ross Miller. BoAnP

Every bar on The Block shut down. First Precinct Fourth Ward. Daniel Mark Epstein. TAT

Every branch big with it. Snow in the Suburbs. Thomas Hardy. CMoP (1970 ed.); ILP (1975 ed.); IPWM; OAEL-2; OxBTC; PPP

Every child who has gardening tools. Garden Lore. Juliana Horatia Ewing. OxBChV

Every Christian Born of God, *with music.* Unknown, *tr. fr. German.* AH

Every coin of earthly treasure. Treasure in Heaven. John Godfrey Saxe. PIM

Every critic in the town. Robert Fuller Murray. POL

Every Day. *See also* Everyday.

Every Day. Ingeborg Bachmann, *tr. fr. German.* BoWoP, *tr. by* Christopher Middleton; PBWP, *tr. by* Michael Hamburger.

Every day a bus that says Joy Farm. Joy Farm. Maria Gitin. PoW

Every-Day Characters: Portrait of a Lady. Winthrop Mackworth Praed. NOBL

Every Day I Go to Work. Cinda Kornblum. AcAn

Every day I meet the horses. Horses at Valley Store. Leslie Marmon Silko. NW; VoR

Every day I peruse the box scores for hours. Baseball and Classicism. Tom Clark. LiSp

Every day I see from my window. Wild Oats. Norman MacCaig. OxBTC

"Every day I wake up the world," said the cock. The Cock. A. Buttigieg. RAE

Every day I work a little on my biceps. Muscle Building. Dalene Stowe. NPW

Every day our bodies separate. Villanelle. Marilyn Hacker. AmPA

Every Day Shaggy Man Mushroom. Mary Norbert Körte. CPA

Every day that their sky droops down. Moles. William Stafford. RFM

Every day, walking the city streets. The Nature of Jungles. W. R. Moses. NCSH

Every day when I pursue. History. Alison Wyrley Birch. PPM

Every day Xenoc stood by the city gate. The First Enemy. Steven Goldsberry. PHC

Every dwelling is a desolate hill. By the Pool. Allen Grossman. AMV-80

Every evening, down into the hardweed. Hardweed Path Going. A. R. Ammons. CSP; UnPo (1976 ed.); VGW

Every few years,/ renewing its option. My Family's under Contract to Cancer. Greg Simison. AMV-80

Every hand is open to another's. As Long as the Heart Beats. Christine Zawadiwsky. AMV-81

Every Labor Day the two old guys trot out their flags. Labor Day. Gary Pacernick. TAT

Every lady in the land. *Unknown.* PoPle

Every Land Is Exile. Claude Vigée, *tr. fr. French by* Anthony Rudolf. VWA

Every little nail. Sleepy Song. Arthur Guiterman. ECBV

Every Man. *See also* Everyman.

Every man in the world thinks his banner the best. Pat's Opinion of Flags. Fred Emerson Brooks. InPK

Every man should pride himself on something. Reflections of a Trout Fisherman. Andrew Demon. AMV-80

Every man spins a web of light circles. Webs. Carl Sandburg. TH

Every morning at seven o'clock. Tarrier's Song [*or* Drill, Ye Tarriers, Drill!]. *Unknown.* AIW; RDB

Every morning at six o'clock. Everybody Works but Father. Charles W. McClintock. FSN

Every morning I forget how it is. Poem. Charles Simic. NNaP; NVAP

Every morning I get up/ Beautiful as the Goddess. Huang O, *tr. fr. Chinese by* Kenneth Rexroth *and* Ling Chung. BoWoP

Every morning I look. Where I Am Now. Harvey Shapiro. GP

Every morning I went to her charity and learned. To a Red-headed Do-good Waitress. Alan Dugan. CAPP; NowV

Every morning, in the dust. A Sparrow in the Dust. Ruth Domino, *tr. by* Daniel Hoffman *and* Jerre Mongione. BoWoP

Every night he waits at the window. The Fashion Model at Home. Adrien Stoutenburg. PoW

Every night in the town. Shooting at the Moon. Kim Yo-sop, *tr. by* Ko Won. Moon

Every night when I went to bed. The Lament of the Unmarried Girl. Brian Merriman, *tr. by* Frank O'Connor. *Fr.* The Midnight Court. OBVE

Every Night When the Sun Goes In. *Unknown.* FSW

Every October millions of little fish come along the shore. Birds and Fishes. Robinson Jeffers. PiAm; TCP

Every once in a while. Safely. David Ignatow. BrS

Every planet is a small plane. The Plane: Earth. Sun-Ra. PoBA

Every promised path ends in the Garden. On the Path. A. L. Strauss, *tr. by* Robert Friend. VWA

Every station in the country keeps a pony that was sent. Incognito. John Manifold. FPA

Every stinking son of a bitch. Peace, So That. Greg Kuzma. InPK

Every time I come to town. Stop Kicking My Dog Around. *Unknown.* GDP

Every Time I Feel the Spirit. *Unknown.* FSW

Every time I nudge that spring. The Experiment with a Rat. Carl Rakosi. GP; POL

Every time she tugs the sun across the sky. She Doesn't Want to Bring the Tides in Any More. Ruth Whitman. RiTi

Every time the bucks went clattering. Earthy Anecdote. Wallace Stevens. CMoP (1970 ed.); RFM

Every time the telephone doesn't ring. Telephone Connection. Gabrielle Edgcomb. PoUp

Every time we meet. Embroidery. Maria Jacobs. AMV-80

Every time you hear me sing this song. The Railroad Blues. *Unknown.* AmFP

Every truly beautiful girl needs a lump-type girl as a best friend. One, Annie and Me. Alicia Ostriker. UsP

Every two hours they broke. The Slaughter-Room Picture. David Steingass. CoPAm

Every year without knowing it I have passed the day. For the Anniversary of My Death. W. S. Merwin. CAPP; CoPAm; InPK; NOBA

Everybody but Me. Margaret Burroughs. FB

Everybody give the big boy a hand. Dempsey, Dempsey. Horace Gregory. SPT

Everybody knows by now. Imperialist. A. R. Ammons. GP

Everybody loved Chick Lorimer in our town. Gone. Carl Sandburg. NOBA

Everybody Loves Saturday Night. *Unknown.* FSW

Everybody Ought to Make a Change. *Unknown.* BluL

Everybody wants an intelligent son. At the Washing of My Son. Su Tung P'o, *tr. by* Kenneth Rexroth. BBGO

Everybody wants to know why I sing the blues. Why I Sing the Blues. B. B. King. MAT

Everybody went to bat three times. Don Larsen's Perfect Game. Paul Goodman. LiSp; SPo

Everybody Works but Father, *with music.* Charles W. McClintock. FSN

Everyday between classes intently over coffee in the Union. Academic Affair. Brenda S. Stockwell. AMV-80

Everyday Dirt. *Unknown.* FSW

Everyday I meet the horses. *See* Every day I meet the horses.

Everyman. *Unknown.* OAEL-1

Everyone Begs for Mercy. John Biguenet. CoPAm

Everyone Born in 1926. John Woods. TC

Everyone drinks Havdolah wine. Havdolah Wine. Miriam Ulinover, *tr. by* Seth L. Wolitz. VWA

Everyone in class two at the Grammar School. The French Master. Dannie Abse. LP

Everyone in me is a bird. In Celebration of My Uterus. Anne Sexton. CAPP; RiTi

Everyone is after me to jump through hoops. Fear. Pablo Neruda, *tr. by* Nathanial Tarn. IPWM

Everyone is hungry, no one is safe. Blind Hopes. David Lehman. AAN

Everyone is losing. Hair. Tom McKeown. TC

Everyone now is crowding everyone. Robert Lowell. *Fr.* Long Summer CAPP

Everyone Sang ("Everyone suddenly burst out singing"). Siegfried Sassoon. FSFS; NOBE; OxBTC

Everyone writes of him, myself included. Gunfighter. Gerald Locklin. AMV-80

Everyone's going to ride tomorrow. Gabriel's Blues. Calvin Forbes. PoA

Everything. Philip Levine. AMV-80

Everything as before: blown snow. The Guest. "Anna Akhmatova," *tr. by* Richard McKane. LoAs

Everything: Eloy, Arizona, 1956. Ai. AmPA; FF

Everything formal. Figures near a Bridge. Linda Gregg. AAN

Everything Has Its History. Phillis Levin. AMV-81

Everything in Its Place. Arthur Guiterman. ECBV; OBAL

Everything is a large box—you can't see into it. To Start With. J. S. Harry. CAAP

Everything is black and gold. Black and Gold. Nancy Byrd Turner. CTV

Everything is, once was not. Life after Death. Richard W. Thomas. PoBA

Everything Is Possible. Robert Pack. PPP

Everything Is Round. Gabriela Mistral, *tr. fr. Spanish by* D. M. Pettinella. PBWP

Everything is round. Round. Rachel Boimwall, *tr. by* Gabriel Preil *and* Howard Schwartz. VWA

Everything is stuck together. What Holds the Universe Together. James Broughton. MIT

Everything Is Swimming. Stevie Smith. FaBoNo

Everything Must Go. Tom Crawford. NVAP

Everything shifts here, we agreed. Angle of Repose. Robert A. Brooks. PoUp

Everything That Acts Is Actual. Denise Levertov. NoAM

Everything that lives has its own proper pride. Proper Pride. D. H. Lawrence. FaBoEE

Everything that touched the water died. My Brother Hannu and the Poison Pool. Martha Webb. PHC

Everything We Do. Peter Meinke. AAN

Everytime I leave you. Mother. Stephen Vincent. NeAC

Everywhere, everywhere, Christmas to-night! Christmas Everywhere. Phillips Brooks. CTV; PCOP

Everywhere, everywhere, following me. Camerados. Bayard Taylor. PAIC; UnPo (1976 ed.)

Everywhere I traveled/ there were pine trees. Pines. Heather Banks. PoUp

Everywhere in constancy, He is intoning, Look! Look! Daisy Aldan. AATT

Everywhere in New York City there are factories. Factories. Edward Hirsch. AMV–81

Everywhere of silver, An. Emily Dickinson. SoSe

Eve's Advice to the Children of Israel. Joachim Neugroschel. VWA

Eves Apologie. Emilia Lanier. BoWoP

Eve's Birth. Kim Chernin. VWA

Eve's Lament. *Unknown, tr. fr. Old Irish by* Kuno Meyer. Epi; PFIr

(Eve, *tr. by* Thomas MacDonagh.) BIrV

Eve's Song in the Garden. Lynn Gottlieb. VWA

Eve's Version. James Harrison. AMV–81

Eviction, The. William Allingham. *Fr.* Laurence Bloomfield in Ireland   BIrV

Evidence, The. Van K. Brock. NVAP

Evidence. John Skoyles. AAN

Evidence, like the weather, is from, The. In the Giving Vein. Peter Porter. CAAP

Evidence Read at the Trial of the Knave of Hearts. "Lewis Carroll." *Fr.* Alice's Adventures in Wonderland, *ch.* 12. FaBoNo; PBMP

(Silence in Court.) FaBoCo

("They told me you had been to her.") SS

Evil Devil Woman. *Unknown.* BluL

Evil does not go always. Lines for a Hard Time. Gena Ford. IHMS

Evil Eye, The. John Ciardi. CoPAm

Evil-hearted Man. *Unknown.* FSW

Evil Is No Black Thing. Sarah Webster Fabio. PoBA

Evil Nigger Waits for Lightnin'. Amiri Baraka. NoAM; NOBA

Evil spirit, your beauty haunts me still, An. Michael Drayton. *Fr.* Idea. AAS; GBL; ILP (1975 ed.); NOBE

Evin Dead Behold I Breathe, *sel.* Alexander Montgomerie. "Evin dead behold I breathe!" SLP

Ev'n like two little bank-dividing brooks. *See* Even like two . . .

Evocations. Kenyon Alexander. PMW

Evolution. Edwin Brock. MPo

Evolution. May Swenson. TCP

Evolution. John Banister Tabb. PCOP

Evolution from the Fish. Robert Bly. NoAM; NOBA

Evolution, though a good thing, has. Bathing with Father. Doug Fetherling. NeAC

Evolutionary Hymn. C. S. Lewis. NOBL

Ev'ry Saturday, Willie got his pay. The Bird on Nellie's Hat. Arthur J. Lamb. FSN

Ev'rything is over and I'm feeling bad. My Gal Sal. Paul Dresser. BLSo; FSN

Ewes and lambs, loving the far hillplaces, The. Ad Limina. Joseph Campbell. BIrV

Ex and Squary. *Unknown.* GBP

Ex-Basketball Player. John Updike. BBGO; CTBA; LiSp; MiP; SPo

Ex-Christian and sex-lover, what. YWCA. Heather McHugh. AAN

Ex M. Antonio Flaminio, Ad Agellum Suum. John Ashmore. SCP-2

Ex Ore Infantium. Francis Thompson. OxBChV (Little Jesus.) PeD; PIM

Exactitude: to memorize. From the Bridge. Albert Goldbarth. NVAP

Examination, The. W. D. Snodgrass. CABA (1972 ed.); CAPP; ConAP

Examine my window carefully. Slide Night. Andrew Taylor. FPA

Example, The. W. H. Davies. PCOP

Example of How a Daily Temporary Madness Can Help a Man Get the Job Done, An. John Stone. BCr; TAT

Examples of Created Systems. William Meredith. PCho

Examples of Worker Correspondence. Michael Gold. SPT

Excavation for the new, The. Dedication for a Building. Alan Dugan. NYP

Excelente Balade of Charitie, An. Thomas Chatterton. EBEV; EPC; LAuP

Excellent New Ballad, Called the Brawny Bishop's Complaint, An. Arthur Mainwaring. APAS

Excellent New Ballad Called the Prince of Darkness, An. *Unknown.* APAS

Excellent New Ballad Giving a True Account of the Birth and Conception of a Late Famous Poem Called the Female Nine, An. Charles Sackville. APAS

Excellent New Song, Being the Intended Speech of a Famous Orator against Peace, An. Swift. APAS

Excellent New Song Called "Mat's Peace," An. Arthur Mainwaring. APAS

Excellent Roman knives slip along the ribs. Robert Bly. *Fr.* The Teeth Mother Naked at Last. GP

Excelsior, *sel.* Emerson. "Over his head were the maple buds." PeD

Excelsior. Longfellow. FaPoR; SpRo

Except for me, nobody remembers Clement Attlee. Clement Attlee. Michael Benedikt. CAAP; InPS

Except for the heavy shoes and stout chains. Balls and Chain. Alvin Albert. CSP

Except ourselves, we have no other prayer. Without Ceremony. Vassar Miller. CoPAm

Except the Lord build the house. Bible, *O.T.* Psalms, CXXVII. BiP

Except the Lord, That He for Us Had Been, *with music.* Henry Ainsworth. AH

Except under the cool shadows of pines. To A Wall of Flame in a Steel Mill, Syracuse, New York, 1969. Larry Levis. AMV–81

Excepting the diner. Poem to Be Read at 3 A.M. Donald Justice. CoPAm; HoPM (1975 ed.); MiP

Exceptional. Thelma Lewis. AMV–80

Excerpts from a Diary of a War (1-3). John Daniel. TwMBP

Excerpts from the Notebook of the Poet of Santo Tomas. Richard Shelton. GP

Exchange. George Rostrevor Hamilton, *after the Greek of* Plato. FaBoEE

Exchange. Dabney Stuart. HoPM (1975 ed.)

Exchange in greed the ungraceful signs. Thrust. The Violent Space. Etheridge Knight. BPo

Exchange of Hats, An. Stanley Moss. GP

Excited, they sport high over our valley. Spring Hawks. Jim Thomas. AMV-81

Exclamation points surprise. Rain. Sister Mary Lucina. AMV-80

Exclusive Old Oyster, The. Laura A. Steel. TDH

Excursion, The, *sels.* Wordsworth.
  "All at once, behold!," *fr.* II. PES
  "I have seen/ A curious child," *fr.* IV. EcS

Excuse, The. Sir Walter Ralegh. AAS; LoAs

Excuse me. Do not speak of nerves. To the Upright. Stephen Dunn. NVAP

Excuse me, isn't that you I see concealed underneath there. Thoughts. Michael Benedikt. ConAP

Excuse of Absence, An. Thomas Carew. CaPo

Excuses. Mary Swanson Stroh. NPW

Excuses. Terence Winch. PoUp

Exeat. Stevie Smith. NoAM

Execution. James A. Randall, Jr. BPo

Execution of Cornelius Vane, The. Sir Herbert Read. NoAM

Execution of Montrose, The. William Edmonstoune Aytoun. BTTM

Exeo in a spasm. Enueg 1. Samuel Beckett. CIP

Executive. John Betjeman. NOBL

Exequy, The. Henry King. CABA (1972 ed.); GBL; HAP; ILP (1975 ed.); MetP; PAIC; PPoe
  (Exequy on [*or* upon] His Wife.) BoLoP; NOBE; OBP
  (Exequy, An: To His Matchless Never-to-be-forgotten Friend.) SCP-2
  "Sleep on my love, in thy cold bed," *sel.* PoPle

Exequy, An. Peter Porter. GAS

Exercise. W. S. Merwin. NOBA

Exercise for the Left Hand. Constance Urdang. AMV-81

Exercise in Solitude. William Sprunt. AAN

Exercise No. 2. William Carlos Williams. TH

Exert thy voice, sweet harbinger of Spring! To the Nightingale. Countess of Winchilsea. PAIC; SBG; WPE

Exeunt. Richard Wilbur. HeIP; NCSH

Exhaust the little moment. Soon it dies. Gwendolyn Brooks. *Fr.* The Womanhood. TH

Exhausted now her sighs, and dry her tears. Walter Savage Landor. FaBoEE

Exhortation. Rafael Jesús González. CPA

Exhortation, An. Shelley. MBPR

Exhortation of a Father to His Children, The. Robert Smith. OxBChV

Exhortation to Learn by Others' Trouble. Earl of Surrey. FaBoEE
  ("My Ratclif, when thy retchlesse youth offendes.") AAS

Exigencies. Michael William Gilbert. AMV-80

Exigent Gymnastic, An. Merle Meeter. AATT

Exile. Chana Bloch. GP

Exile. Ernest Dowson. BoLoP

Exile. George Rostrevor Hamilton, *after the Greek of* Isidoros of Aigai. FaBoEE

Exiled. Edna St. Vincent Millay. PPM; RhR

Exiles. "Æ." BIrV

Exiles, The. W. H. Auden. OxBTC

Exiles, The. Robert Gessner. SPT

Exile's Letter. Li Po, *tr. fr. Chinese by* Ezra Pound. TCP

Existence. Sheila Moon. AMV-80

Existence egotistically formed. Homily: Contemporary. Marian Frances Brand. AATT

Existences. William Stafford. UsP

Existing Light. Madeline DeFrees. PoW

Exit Line. John Ciardi. WeW

Exit Lines. George Jonas. NeAC

Exit Molloy. Derek Mahon. PFIr; POL

Exit, Pursued by a Bear. James Tipton. HeS; TC

Exit the fond, the familiar. Enter the strange. In a World of Change. Joseph Awad. AMV-80

Exodus, *sel.* Bible, *O.T., tr. by* William Tyndale.
  "Let us synge unto the Lorde, for he is become glorious," XV: 1-8. OBVE

Exodus. George Oppen. GP; RRA

Exodus. Anita Endrezze Probst. CDW

Exodus. Harvey Shapiro. VWA

Exodus, The (August 3, 1492). Emma Lazarus. *Fr.* By the Waters of Babylon. WPE

Exodus for Oregon. Joaquin Miller. BPAW

Exodus 1940. Alfred Wolfenstein, *tr. fr. German by* Erna Baber Rosenfeld. VWA

Exorcism, The. Theodore Roethke. NoAM; STS

Expanse of fields spreading out, The. Moving. Barbara Crooker. AMV-80

Expect no strange or puzzling meat, no pie. William Cartwright. *Fr.* A Bill of Fare SCP-2

Expect Nothing. Alice Walker. AmPA; FF

Expectancies: The Eleventh Hour. Karla M. Hammond. AMV-80

Expectant Father, The. Simon J. Ortiz. NW

Expectation. Aliza Shenhar, *tr. fr. Hebrew by* Linda Zisquit. VWA

Expecting. Daniel J. Langton. AMV-81

Expense of spirit in a waste of shame, The [*or* Th']. Sonnets, CXXIX. Shakespeare. BiP; CABA (1972 ed.); EBEV; Epi; ExPo (1973 ed.); GBL; HAP; HeIP; ILP (1975 ed.); InPS; LFH; LoAs; NIL; NOBE; OAEL-1; OBP; PoIA; PPoD; PPoe; PPP; UnPo (1976 ed.); WeW

Experience. Emerson. TAP

Experience. Hugo von Hofmannsthal, *tr. fr. German by* John N. Miller. AMV-81

Experience. Dorothy Parker. PPM

Experience. James Simmons. BIrV; CIP

Experience, The ("Oh! that I alwayes breath'd in such an aire"). Edward Taylor. Preparatory Meditations: First Series, III. EAP

Experience, though noon auctoritee. The Wife of Bath's Prologue. Chaucer. *Fr.* The Canterbury Tales. OAEL-1

Experienced men, inured to city ways. John Gay. *Fr.* Trivia; or, The Art of Walking the Streets of London, II. OAEL-1

Experiential Religion. Travis Du Priest. AMV-80

Experiment That Failed, The. John Logan. NU

Experiment to me. Emily Dickinson. PCOP

Experiment with a Rat, The. Carl Rakosi. GP; POL

Expert. *Unknown.* TDH

Expiration, The. John Donne. LoAs

Explanation. Geof Hewitt. NeAC

Explanation of the Grasshopper, An. Vachel Lindsay. PCOP

Explanations of Love. Carl Sandburg. SFF

Exploding before my very eyes. Peyote Vision. Lew Blockcolski. VoR

Exploding, shattering, burning. Helsinki, 1940. Anselm Hollo. EC

Exploiting the medium. Charlie Parker. Morty Sklar. AcAn

Exploration over the Rim. William Dickey. SS

Explorations. Louis MacNeice. ILP (1975 ed.)

Explorer, The. David Ignatow. FoP

Explorers, The. Margaret Atwood. CABA (1972 ed.)

Explorers say that harebells rise. Ellesmereland I. Earle Birney. CABA (1972 ed.)

Explosion, The. Philip Larkin. EBEV; HAP

Explosion of a bomb, The. Perhaps. Stephen Spender. NoAM

Explosions are nearer this evening, The. You Were Wearing Blue. Tom Raworth. TwMBP

Expose yourself! Freak Show and Finale. Lenore Kandel. *Fr.* Circus. RiTi

Expostulation, An. Isaac Bickerstaffe. FaBoCo; NIL; PFIr

Expostulation and Reply. Wordsworth. ILP (1975 ed.); MBPR; OAEL-2

Exposure. Seamus Heaney. CIP

Exposure. Wilfred Owen. InPS; NoAM

Expounding the Torah. Louis Zukofsky. VWA

Express, The. Stephen Spender. CMoP (1970 ed.); ILP (1975 ed.); MPo; NoAM; NowV; WIF

Exquisite torment, dainty Mrs. Hargreaves. Sapphics. D. B. Wyndham Lewis. NOBL

Exstasie [*or* Extasie], The. John Donne. *See* Ecstasy, The.

Extasy of Joy Let in by This Reply Returnd in Admiration. Edward Taylor. *Fr.* God's Determinations. EAP

Extempore Effusion upon the Death of James Hogg. Wordsworth. EBEV; MBPR; NOBE; OAEL-2

Extempore Verses Intended to Allay the Violence of Party-Spirit. John Byrom. *See* Jacobite Toast.

Extensions of Linear Mobility. Jeanine Hathaway. IHMS

Extermination of the Jews, The. Marvin Bell. VWA

External Element, The. David McFadden. NeAC

Extinct Birds. Judith Wright. GAS; MAuV; PBWP

Extinct old ichthyosaurus, An. The Ichthyosaurus. *Unknown.* TDH

Extinct volcanoes are silent. Volcanoes. Bella Akhmadulina, *tr. by* W. H. Auden. PBWP

Extra Joyful Chorus for Those Who Have Read This Far, An. Robert Bly. EAS

Extract. Paul Bowles. PoA

Extracts from a Police Surgeon's Notebook. William Lindsay. PMW

Extracts: From the Journal of Elisa Lynch. Maura Stanton. AmPA

Extraordinary patience of things, The! Carmel Point. Robinson Jeffers. PiAm

Extravagantly your stone gestures. Sentence for Konarak. John Montague. TwMBP

Extreme Unction. Ernest Dowson. BoReV; OAEL-2; VLP

Extreme Unction in PA. David Ray. AMV-81

Extremes. James Whitcomb Riley. ECBV

Extremities of Cold in Hell, The. Thomas Dekker. *Fr.* Dekker His Dream. SCP-2

Exuberance: joy to the last. Open. A. R. Ammons. TT

Exultation. Hywel ab Owain Gwynedd, *tr. fr. Welsh by* Gwyn Williams. OBW

Exultation is the going. Emily Dickinson. AmVN; CABA (1972 ed.); ILP (1975 ed.)

Exulting in his strength, he seems to dare. Virgil, *tr. by* Dryden. *Fr.* The Aeneid, XI. OBVE

Exxon man tugs his CATerpillar cap, The. Trout Fishing in Virginia. Michael Beirne McMahon. AMV-80

Eyaya-eya./ I recognize/ A bit of song. I Should Be Ashamed. Uvlunuaq, *tr. fr. Eskimo.* WTO

Eye, The. Michael Benedikt. ConAP

Eye. Gray Burr. WeW

Eye, The. Robert Herrick. CaPo

Eye, The. Robinson Jeffers. NOBA; PiAm

Eye, The. Richard Wilbur. FiCP

Eye, a viscous eye, with the sight stopped and nothing in the, An. Faye Kicknosway. *Fr.* Janie. PCho

Eye and Tooth. Robert Lowell. CAPP

Eye can hardly pick them out, The. At Grass. Philip Larkin. HAP; OxBTC; PSN

Eye, dark, The. Hut Window. Paul Celan, *tr. by* Joachim Neugroschel. VWA

Eye is lion of these wastes, The. Whose vision. Tears of St. Francis. Robert Duncan. CAAP

Eye Is More or Less Satisfied with Seeing, The. Allen Curnow. ATNZ

Eye of God. Jim Tollerud. VoR

Eye opening is a mouth seeing, The. Eyesight II. Robert Duncan. EAS

Eye standing up eye lying down eye sitting. Making Feet and Hands. Benjamin Péret, *tr. by* David Gascoyne. EAS

Eye-aya/ I call to mind. Ulivfak's Song of the Caribou. *Unknown.* AKE

Eyeglasses. Tom Clark. ConAP; UsP

Eyeglasses, The. William Carlos Williams. NoAM

Eyeless labourer in the night, The. Woman to Man. Judith Wright. GAS; MAuV; WPE

Eyelids fall, the star-charts, The. The Invention of Astronomy. William Matthews. POL

Eyelids glowing, some chill morning, The. Monet: "Les Nymphéas." W. D. Snodgrass. ConAP; TCP

Eyelids meet, The. He'll catch a little nap. In the Smoking Car. Richard Wilbur. ConAP

Eyelids of eve fall together at last, The. Thomas Hardy. *Fr.* The Dynasts. OAEL-2

Eyes. Clarïsse Nicoidski, *tr. fr. Judezmo by* Stephen Levy. VWA

Eyes. Henry Shore. PMW

Eyes always open eyes. Eyewash. Niall Montgomery. EAS

Eyes and Tears. Andrew Marvell. MetP

Eyes blink/ in unequal/ proportions. 11/16/75. Darlene Pearlstein. FiCh

Eyes, hide my love, and do not show. Secrecy. Samuel Daniel. *Fr.* Hymen's Triumph. OLR

Eyes like the morning star. The Colorado Trail. *Unknown.* FSW

Eyes of darkest hue. Dark Eyes. *Unknown, tr. fr. Russian.* BLSH

Eyes of despair, eyes of fire. Ophelia's Song. Marya Zaturenska. OLR

Eyes of Flesh, The. Sandra Hochman. NMM

Eyes of Night-Time. Muriel Rukeyser. BoWoP

Eyes of Texas, The. *Unknown.* FSW

Eyes of the Child Do Not See Me, The. Norman H. Russell. VW

Eyes of the Garden. Laura Chester. RiTi

Eyes of twenty centuries, The. Judas Iscariot. Stephen Spender. ILP (1975 ed.)

Eyes open to a cry of pulleys, The. Love Calls Us to the Things of This World. Richard Wilbur. AnMo; CAPP; CMoP (1970 ed.); ExPo (1973 ed.); HAP; HeIP; InPS; NIL; NoAM; PiAm; PPP; TAP; TCP; VGW; UnPo (1976 ed.); WIF

Eyes shut tight. Madness. Sachiko Yoshihara, *tr. by* James Kirkup *and* Shozo Tokunaga. BoWoP

Eyes that drew from me such fervent praise, The. Petrarch, *tr. by* Edwin Morgan. Sonnets to Laura: To Laura in Death, XXIV. NAWM-1

Eyes that glass fear, though fear on furtive foot. A Hare. Walter de la Mare. EBEV

Eyes that last I saw in tears. T. S. Eliot. NOBE

Eyes that mock me sign the way, The. Bahnhofstrasse. James Joyce. NoAM

Eyes, the Blood, The. David Meltzer. VWA

Eyesight II. Robert Duncan. EAS

Eyewash. Niall Montgomery. EAS

Eyre All Alone. Francis Webb. CAAP

Ezekiel. A. N. Stencl, tr. fr. Yiddish by Joseph Leftwich. VWA

Ezekiel Saw the Wheel. Unknown. FSW

Ezra Pound. Robert Lowell. NoAM; NOBA

Ezra Pound. Jonathan Price. CoPAm

Ezra Pound. Phyllis Webb. MMD

Ezra Pound (his fingers, bones). Postscript, on a Name. Stephen Ratcliffe. AMV–80

Ezra Shank. Unknown. CaYB

Ezra, whom not with eye nor with ear have I ever. Epistle to the Rapalloan. Archibald MacLeish. PoA

Ezry. Archibald MacLeish. NOBA

# F

Fa, mi, fa, re, la, mi. Unknown. InPK

Fa saw the Forty-second. The Forty-second. Unknown. GBP

Fable, The: "Beyond the steady rock the steady sea." Yvor Winters. UsP

Fable, A: "Dingy donkey, formal and unchanged, A." John Hookham Frere. FaBoCo

Fable: "Mountain and the squirrel, The." Emerson. BiP; OBAL; PiAm
   (Mountain and the Squirrel, The.) CTV

Fable: "Once upon a time/ there was a lonely wolf." János Pilinszky, tr. fr. Hungarian by Ted Hughes and János Csokits. OBVE

Fable for Critics, A, sels. James Russell Lowell.
   American Literature. AmVN
   Bryant. AmVN; NOBA; TAP
   Cooper. NOBA; TAP
   Emerson. AmVN; NOBA; PAIC; TAP
   Hawthorne. NOBA; TAP
   Holmes. NOBA
   Irving. TAP
   Lowell. AmVN; NOBA; TAP
   Poe and Longfellow. AmVN, 20 ll. NOBA
   (Poe.) TAP
   "There are truths you Americans need to be told." OBSV
   Whittier. AmVN; NOBA

Fable for When There's No Way Out. May Swenson. MiP; MPA

Fable Merchant, The. Charles Dobzynski, tr. fr. French by Charles Guenther. VWA

Fable of Midas, The. Swift. APAS

Fable of the Airplanes, The. Richard Williams. AAN

Fable of the Mermaid and the Drunks. Pablo Neruda, tr. fr. Spanish by Alastair Reid. LP

Fable of the Piece of Glass and the Piece of Ice, The. John Hookham Frere. OxBChV

Fable of the Talented Mockingbird. Scott Bates. BoAnP

Fable of the Transcendent Tannenbaum. Scott Bates. PoTa

Fables, sel. John Gay.
   Poet and the Rose, The. PAIC

Fables, The. David Malouf. CAAP

Fabrication of Ancestors. Alan Dugan. NoAM

Fabullus I will treat you handsomely. Catullus, tr. fr. Latin by Richard Lovelace. OBVE

Fabulous Teamsters, The. Judith Johnson Sherwin. NYP

Fabulous Wizard of Oz, The. Unknown. QQQ; TDH

Face, A. Robert Browning. LoAs

Face, The. Anthony Euwer. OBAL

Face, A. Marianne Moore. PiAm; Psy

Face. Richard Shelton. PCho

Face, The. Lucien Stryk. GP

Face as It Might Be of Love, The. Toi Derricotte. NPW

Face in the Mirror, The. Robert Graves. LP; PoIA; UsP; WeW

Face Lift. Sylvia Plath. InPK; PPoD

Face of all the world is changed, I think, The. Elizabeth Barrett Browning. Sonnets from the Portuguese, VII. VLP

Face of the precipice is black with lovers, The. Salvador Dali. David Gascoyne. EAS; OxBTC

Face of the Waters, The. Robert D. Fitzgerald. GAS

Face sings, alone, The. A Poem for Willie Best. Amiri Baraka. CAPP

Face, The, you see is but a shadow. Mind Alchemy. David P. Manzo. PoW

Faceless miner. For Laurence Jones. Gary Kizer. CTBA

Faces. John Ciardi. BiP

Faces everwhere! Beautiful ones. Idolatry. Ralph Mecklenburger. SFF

Faces floating in a poolroom fog. Poolroom Faces. Joseph Kalar. SPT

Faces irresolute and unperplexed. In the National Gallery. Siegfried Sassoon. NoAM

Faces may alter, names can't change. Nathaniel Lee to Sir Roger L'Estrange. Nathaniel Lee. FaBoEE

Faces Seen Once. James Dickey. UnPo (1976 ed.)

Facing West from California's Shore. Walt Whitman. NIL; PPoD; TAP

Facing you/ I am not jealous. Always. Pablo Neruda, tr. by Donald D. Walsh. OLR

Fact. Kenneth Rexroth. OBAL

Fact is, The. Some Me of Beauty. Carolyn M. Rodgers. CNA

Fact of this man having made, The. The Lift. Raymond Souster. POL

Factories. Edward Hirsch. AMV–81

Factories are pretending to be closed down for eternity, The. Babylon. Ron Ikan. NVAP

Factory, The. Olga Cabral. GP

Factory Girl, The. Unknown. FSW

Factory Girl's Come-All-Ye, The. Unknown. AmFP; OBAL

Facts. Ken Smith. TwMBP

Facts have no eyes. One must. Observation of Facts. Charles Tomlinson. TwMBP

Facts of Winter. Marie Harris. MMD

Fade in the sound of summer music. Notes for a Movie Script. M. Carl Holman. AmNP (1974 ed.); PoBA; WeW

Fading Beauty. Unknown. FaBoEE

Fado. Edwin Morgan. MS

Faerie Queene, The, sels. Spenser.
   "As pilot well expert in perilous wave," fr. II, 7. OAEL–1
   "Ay me, how many perils doe enfold," fr. I, 8. OAEL–1
   Bower of Bliss, The ("Eftsoones they heard a most melodious sound"), fr. II, 12. NOBE
   "By this the dreadful beast drew nigh to hand," fr. I, 11. LFH
   Care in Heaven, fr. II, 8. BoReV
      ("And is there care in heaven? and is there love.") OAEL–1
   Cave of Despair, The, fr. I, 9. NOBE
      ("Ere long they come, where that same wicked wight.") OAEL–1
   Garden of Adonis, The, fr. III, 6. NOBE
   "Gentle knight was pricking on the plaine, A," fr. I, 1. EBEV; OAEL–1
   Guyon's Temptation, fr. II, 12. OBP
      (Bower of Bliss, The.) NIL
      ("There the most daintie Paradise on ground.") EBEV

"Hard is the doubt, and difficult to deeme," *fr.* IV, 9.  OAEL-1
Hill of the Graces, *fr.* VI, 10.  NOBE
"In such luxurious plentie of all pleasure," *fr.* IV, 10.  OAEL-1
"It fortunèd (as faire it then befell"), *fr.* I, 11.  OAEL-1
"Like as the tide that comes from th' Ocean main," *fr.* IV, 3.  HoPM (1975 ed.)
"Lo! I the man, whose Muse whylome [*or* whilom] did maske," I, *induction.*  OAEL-1; PAIC
Masque of Cupid, The, *fr.* III, 12.  NOBE
Nature's Reply to Mutability, *fr.* VII, 7 *and* VIII, 1.  NOBE
"Nought is on earth more sacred or divine," *fr.* V, 7.  OAEL-1
"Now, at the time that was before agreed," *fr.* VII, 7.  OAEL-1
"Right well I wrote, most mighty Soveraine," II, *induction.*  OAEL-1; PAIC
"Rugged forhead that with grave foresight, The," IV, *proem.*  OAEL-1
"So as they travellèd, the drouping night," *fr.* IV, 5.  OAEL-1
"So forth she comes, and to her coche does clyme," *fr.* I, 4.  OAEL-1
"So oft as I with state of present time," *fr.* V, *proem.*  OAEL-1
Song of Bliss, *fr.* II, 12.  FF
("Whiles some one did chaunt this lovely lay, The.")  OBVE
"Sudden upriseth from her stately place," I, 4.  PPP
"Then said that royall Pere in sober wise," *fr.* I, 12.  OAEL-1
"Thence forward by that painfull way they pas," *fr.* I, 10.  OAEL-1
"They sate to meat, and Satyrane his chaunce," *fr.* III, 9.  OAEL-1
"Tho when as chearelesse night ycovered had," *fr.* III, 12.  OAEL-1
"Thus being entred, they behold around," *fr.* II, 12.  OAEL-1
"Well may I weene, faire ladies, all this while," III, 6.  OAEL-1
"What if some little pain the passage have," *fr.* I, 9.  PoPle
"When I bethinke me on that speech whyleare," VII, 8.  LFH; OAEL-1
"Who now does follow the foule Blatant Beast," *fr.* VI, 10.  OAEL-1

Faery Beam upon You, The.  Ben Jonson.  *Fr.* The Gypsies Metamorphosed.  EBEV; NIL
Fag-End.  Philip O'Connor.  EAS
Failed Fathers.  Lewis Turco.  AMV-81
Failure.  Rupert Brooke.  ILwL
Failure, A.  C. Day Lewis.  NOBE
Fain would I change that note.  No Other Choice.  *Unknown.*  EBEV; GBL; NOBE
Fain would I kiss my Julia's dainty leg.  Her Leg [*or* Legs].  Robert Herrick.  LoAs; SpRo
Faint as a climate-changing bird that flies.  Demeter and Persephone.  Tennyson.  VLP
Faint Falls the Gentle Voice, *with music.*  Henry Timrod.  AH
Faint now in the evening pallor.  Silver Jubilee.  Llewelyn Wyn Griffith.  OBW
Faint Praise on Your Fortieth Birthday.  Joanne McCarthy.  PoW
Faint yet Pursuing.  Coventry Patmore.  The Unknown Eros, I, xxi.  PFD
Fair/ Boy Christian Takes a Break.  Jim Harrison.  NoAM
Fair and fair, and twice so fair.  Oenone and Paris.  George Peele.  *Fr.* The Arraignment of Paris.  NOBE
Fair and Free Elections.  *Unknown.*  FSW
Fair and Unfair.  Robert Francis.  VGW
Fair Annie.  *Unknown.*  FaBoBa; ILP (1975 ed.); PeBB
Fair at Windgap, The.  Austin Clarke.  OxBTC
Fair Beauty Bride, The.  *Unknown.*  AmFP
Fair Cassidy.  *Unknown, tr. fr. Irish by* Donagh MacDonagh.  BIrV
Fair cheek under a merry blue eye, A.  The Beloved.  David Roberts, *tr. by* H. Idris Bell.  OBW
Fair Circassian.  Richard Garnett.  PoTa

Fair copy of my Celia's face.  To T. H., a Lady Resembling My Mistress.  Thomas Carew.  CaPo
Fair daffodils, we weep to see.  To Daffodils.  Robert Herrick.  AKE; CaPo; ExPo (1973 ed.); FSFS; InPS; NOBE; PAIC; PCOP; PPP; SCP-1; SoSe (1977 ed.); UnPo (1976 ed.); WIF
Fair Damsel from London, The.  *Unknown.*  AmFP
Fair Days; or, Dawns Deceitful.  Robert Herrick.  CaPo
Fair Ellen Irwin, when she sate.  Ellen Irwin; or, The Braes of Kirtle.  Wordsworth.  PeD
Fair Ellender.  *Unknown.*  FSW
Fair Flower Delice, The.  Spenser.  *See* Lay to Eliza, The.
Fair flower, that dost so comely grow.  The Wild Honey Suckle.  Philip Freneau.  AmVN; EAP; ILP (1975 ed.); NOBA; PiAm; TAP
Fair girl tripping out to meet her love, A.  The Power of Interval.  Lord de Tabley.  VLP
Fair Golden Age! when milk was the only food.  The Golden Age.  Giovanni Battista Guarini, *tr. by* Sir Richard Fanshawe.  *Fr.* Il Pastor Fido.  OAEL-1; OBVE
Fair, great, and good: since seeing you we see.  To the Countess of Salisbury.  John Donne.  SCP-1
Fair Greece! sad relic of departed worth.  Byron.  *Fr.* Childe Harold's Pilgrimage, II.  ILP (1975 ed.)
Fair gull on the water's bank.  The Seagull.  Siôn Phylip, *tr. by* Joseph F. Clancy.  OBW
Fair insect! that, with threadlike legs spread out.  To a Mosquito.  Bryant.  EAP
Fair Iris I love, and hourly I die.  Mercury's Song to Phaeda.  Dryden.  *Fr.* Amphitryon.  PBMP
Fair[e] is my love, and cruel as she's fair.  Sonnet.  Samuel Daniel.  *Fr.* To Delia.  AAS; HoPM (1975 ed.); ILP (1975 ed.); NOBE
Fair is my love that feeds among the lilies.  Bartholomew Griffin.  *Fr.* Fidessa, More Chaste than Kind.  GBL
Fair is not my face.  A Woman Grows Soon Old.  Larin Paraske, *tr. by* Jaakko A. Ahokas.  PBWP
Fair is the white star of twilight.  The Heart's Friend.  Mary Austin, *after Shoshone Indian.*  BPAW
Fair Isabel, poor simple Isabel!  Isabella; or, The Pot of Basil.  Keats.  MBPR
Fair Isle Pattern.  James Rankin.  MIS
Fair lady Isabel sits in her bower sewing.  Lady Isobel [*or* Isabel] and the Elf-Knight.  *Unknown.*  FaBoBa; PeBB
Fair lady, will you travel.  The Wooing of Etain.  *Unknown, tr. by* John Montague.  BIrV
Fair little girl sat under a tree, A.  Good Night and Good Morning.  Richard Monckton Milnes.  OxBChV
Fair lovely maid, or if that title be.  To the Fair Clarinda, Who Made Love to Me, Imagin'd More than Woman.  Aphra Behn.  SBG
Fair Lucy was sitting in her own cabin door.  Lizie Wan.  *Unknown.*  AmFP
Fair Maid by the Shore, The.  *Unknown.*  AmFP
Fair maid who, [on] the first of May, The.  Mother Goose.  CC; MG
Fair maiden, white and red.  The Voice from the Well.  George Peele.  *Fr.* The Old Wife's Tale.  NOBE
Fair Margaret and Sweet William.  *Unknown.*  AmFP
Fair Mary sat at her father's castle gate.  Willie of Winsbury.  *Unknown.*  AmFP
Fair Morning, The.  Jones Very.  NOBA
Fair Mother Earth lay on her back last night.  Ode to the Spirit of Earth in Autumn.  George Meredith.  VLP
Fair Phoebe and Her Dark-eyed Sailor.  *Unknown.*  AmFP
Fair Phyllis I saw sitting all alone.  *Unknown.*  GBL
Fair Pledges of a fruitful tree.  To Blossoms.  Robert Herrick.  CaPo; PF

Fair princess of the spacious air. The Falcon. Richard Lovelace. CaPo; PB

Fair, rich, and young? how rare is her perfection. Of a Fair Shrew. Sir John Harington, *after* Martial. FaBoEE; NIL

Fair seed-time had my soul, and I grew up. Childhood and School-Time. Wordsworth. *Fr.* The Prelude, I. ExPo (1973 ed.); HAP; ILP (1975 ed.); NOBE

Fair Singer, The. Andrew Marvell. LoAs; NOBE; PoPle

Fair star of evening, splendour of the west. Composed by the Sea-Side, near Calais, August, 1802. Wordsworth. MBPR

Fair stood the wind for France. The Ballad of Agincourt. Michael Drayton. BTTM; FaPoR; PPoD

Fair Summer droops, droop men and beast therefore. Thomas Nashe. *Fr.* Summer's Last Will and Testament. SCP-2

Fair Ursly, in a merry mood. Annibal Cruceius, *tr. fr. Latin.* FaBoEE

Fair Verna! loveliest village of the west. The Flourishing Village. Timothy Dwight. Greenfield Hill, Pt. II. EAP

Fair Virtue, *sel.* George Wither.
  Lover's Resolution, A. BoLoP; NOBE
  ("Shall I, wasting in despair.") PAIC; PoPle; SS

Fair was the dawn, and but e'en now the skies. Fair Days; or, Dawns Deceitful. Robert Herrick. CaPo

Fair was this young wyf, and therwithal. Chaucer. *Fr.* The Canterbury Tales: The Miller's Tale. EBEV

Fair Weather. Dorothy Parker. SGB

Fairbanks under the Solstice. John Haines. CNW

Faire art thou Phillis, I, so faire (sweet mayd). Thomas Lodge. Phillis, XXII. ESo

Faire daffadills, we weep to see. *See* Fair daffodils. . .

Faire is my love, and cruell as she's faire. *See* Fair is my love. . .

Faire sunne, if you would have praise your light. Henry Constable. *Fr.* Diana. ESo

Fairest action of our human life, The. Lady Elizabeth Carey. *Fr.* Mariam, IV. WPE

"Fairest, The!" Aphrodite laughed, and caught. Apple-Logia. Marian Frances Brand. AATT

Fairest day that ever yet has shone, The. The Lost. Jones Very. PiAm; NOBA

Fairest Flower, The. John Audelay. OxBM

Fairest flower, all flowers excelling. To a Child Five Years Old. Nathaniel Cotton. OxBChV; PMW

Fairest Lord Jesus. *Unknown, tr. fr. German.* BLSH, *with music;* CTV

"Fairest o' fair, O, hear my cry." The Fine Fechtin Mouse. Alexander Gray. MS

Fairest of stars, that with your persant light. Balade Simple. John Lydgate. GBL

Fairground. W. H. Auden. LP

Fairies, The. William Allingham. ECBV; LCL; NOBE; OxBChV; PCOP; PoPle

Fairies. Rose Fyleman. OxBChV

Fairies Break Their Dances, The. A. E. Housman. NoAM; TT

Fairies' Farewell, The. Richard Corbet. FaBoBa; NOBE
  Farewell, Rewards and Fairies, *sel.* PoPle; SCP-2

Fairies Have Never a Penny to Spend, The. Rose Fyleman. OxBChV

Fairweill. *Unknown.* SLP

Fairy, The. Blake. MBPR

Fairy in Armor, A. Joseph Rodman Drake. *Fr.* The Culprit Fay. PCOP

Fairy Queen, The ("Come follow me, follow me"). *Unknown.* PoPle
  "When mortals are at rest," *sel.* DuDr

Fairy ring as round's the sun, A. Round Things. William Barnes. VLP

Fairy Song. Shakespeare. *Fr.* A Midsummer Night's Dream, II, i. PCOP
  ("Over hill, over dale.") NOBE; PoPle

Fairy Story. Stevie Smith. DuDr

Fairy Tales. Itzik Manger, *tr. fr.* Yiddish *by* Miriam Waddington. VWA

Fairy Temple, The; or, Oberon's Chapel. Robert Herrick. CaPo

Fairy Thorn, The. Sir Samuel Ferguson. VLP

Fairy Went a-Marketing, A. Rose Fyleman. OxBChV

Faith. Marjorie Dunkels. PH

"Faith and Practice." John Balaban. GOA

Faith Healer Come to Rabun County. David Bottoms. CSP; TAT

Faith Healing. Philip Larkin. NoAM

Faith, Hope, and Charity. Giovanni Battista Guarini, *tr. fr.* Italian *by* Samuel Taylor Coleridge. MBPR

"Faith" is a fine invention. Emily Dickinson. NOBA; PiAm; TAP

Faith of Our Fathers, *with music.* Frederick W. Faber. BLSH

Faith Unfaithful. Siegfried Sassoon. BoReV

Faithful, The. Jane Cooper. CoPAm

Faithful messinger, which is the nicht, The. *At. to* James I, King of Scotland. *Fr.* Sang on Absence. SLP

Faithful Shepherdess, The,*sels.* John Fletcher.
  Hymn to Pan, *fr.* I, ii. NOBE
  Safe Swimming, *fr.* III, i. BBL
  "Shepherds all, and maidens fair," II, i. SCP-2

Faithless Nellie [*or* Nelly] Gray. Thomas Hood. FaBoCo; NOBL; VLP

Faithless Sally Brown. Thomas Hood. BBL; NOBL
  (Sally Brown.) FaBoCo

Faithless Shepherd, A. John Clare. VLP

Faithless Wife, The. Federico García Lorca, *tr. fr.* Spanish *by* A. L. Lloyd. BoLoP

Faithlesse and fond mortality. Upon the Death of a Gentleman. Richard Crashaw. MetP

Faits-divers or News in Brief. Elizabeth Brunazzi. PoUp

Fake,/ I am a thief an honest thief, I lead none. Judas Before. Lucille F. Travis. AATT

Falcon, The. The Knight of Kürenberg, *tr. fr.* German *by* Margarete Münsterberg. LoAs

Falcon, The. Richard Lovelace. CaPo; PB

Falcon, The. *Unknown. See* Corpus Christi Carol ("Lully, lullay, lully, lullay").

Falcon Woman, The. Robert Graves. BuTh; LoAS

Falconers. Lady Luck. Ann Gottlieb. NMM

Fall. Mary Ursula Bethell. ATNZ

Fall. Robert Francis. VGW

Fall. Robert Hass. AmPA

Fall. Gabriela Melinescu, *tr. fr.* Rumanian *by* Michael Impey *and* Brian Swann. AMV-80

Fall, The. Edmund Waller. SCP-2

Fall, The: A Song. Earl of Rochester. SCP-2

Fall Again. H. R. Coursen. AMV-81

Fall Again, The. Howard Nemerov. ConAP

Fall Colors. Jerome Mazzaro. AMV-81

Fall Comes in Back-Country Vermont. Robert Penn Warren. VGW

Fall Down. Calvin C. Hernton. CNA; PoBA

Fall eats its leaf from my hand, The: we are friends. Corona. Paul Celan, *tr. by* Joachim Neugroschel. VWA

Fall In. Lincoln Kirstein. NoAM; PoIA

Fall in Massachusetts. Isabella Gardner. RiTi

Fall, Leaves, Fall. Emily Brontë. FSFS

Fall 1961. Robert Lowell. ExPo (1973 ed.); PSN; VGW

Fall none but angels suddenly to hell? Fulke Greville. *Fr.* Mustapha. SCP-2

Fall of Hyperion, The: A Dream. Keats. MBPR; OAEL-2 Death, *sel.* OBP

Fall of J. W. Beane, The. Oliver Herford. OBAL; PoTa

Fall of Leaves. D. S. Savage. PoA

Fall of Princes, The, *sel.* John Lydgate.
"And semblably, though I go not upright," *fr.* Epilogue. OxBM

Fall of Rome, The. W. H. Auden. AnMo; InPS; MAT; OAEL-2; OxBTC; UnPo (1976 ed.)

Fall of the City, The, *sel.* Archibald MacLeish.
Voice of the Studio Announcer. HoPM (1975 ed.)

Fall of the House of Usher, The, *sel.* Poe.
Haunted Palace, The. NOBA; PiAm; TAP

Fall of the House of Usher, The. Reed Whittemore. GP; InPK

Fall Practice. Dabney Stuart. CoPAm

Fall Song. Daniel David Moses. AMV-81

Fallen flowers rise. Haiku. Arakida Moritake. SoSe

Fallen leaves are scattered by evening rain. Regretful Thoughts.
Yü Hsüan-chi, *tr. by* Geoffrey Waters. BoWoP

Fallen Majesty. W. B. Yeats. PoA

Fallen Tree, The. Robert Bly. PCho

Falling. James Dickey. CAAP

Falling. Bob Kaufman. PoBA

Falling. Reuben Tam. PHC

Falling. John Unterecker. PHC

Falling Asleep. John Ciardi. DuDa

Falling Asleep. Siegfried Sassoon. FSFS; OxBTC

Falling Asleep in a Garden. David Wagoner. AMV-81

Falling Asleep over the Aeneid. Robert Lowell. NIL; NoAM

Falling asleep, the birds are falling. The Death and Resurrection of the Birds. David Wagoner. MPA

Falling chute jammed falling. Falling. John Unterecker. PHC

Falling flower, The. Haiku. Arakida Moritake. SoSe

Falling in Love. David Perkins. NCSH

Falling in Love with Tygers. Thomas Brush. NVAP

Falling Moon. Roberta Hill. CDW

Falling of the Leaves, The. W. B. Yeats. VLP

Falling Out. Helen Chasin. IHMS

Falling separate into the dark. Late at Night. William Stafford. POL; RFM

Falling Sickness, The. Evan Jones. GAS

Falling Snow. *Unknown.* CTV

Falling star, The. "Ping Hsin." *Fr.* Spring Waters. PBWP

Falling Upwards. David Shapiro. AMV-81

Fallingstars/ "a field of/ buttercups." Treblinka Gas Chamber. Phyllis Webb. MMD

Fallow Deer at the Lonely House, The. Thomas Hardy. BoAnP; CMoP (1970 ed.)

Fallow fields, dark pewter sky. Winter Drive. James McAuley. PoA

Falls. Mary Walker. PoUp

Falls from her heaven the Moon, and stars sink burning. Moon-Bathers. John Freeman. EcS

Falls of Falloch, The. Sydney Tremayne. MS

Falls of Glomach, The. Andrew Young. MS

Falltime. Carl Sandburg. PoA

False beauty who, although in semblance fair. Ballade to His Mistress. Villon, *tr. by* Norman Cameron. WeW

False Cadence. Bruce Berger. AMV-80

False Dawn. Walter de la Mare. FaBoNo

False Favorite's Downfall, The. *Unknown.* APAS

False Fox, The. *Unknown.* GBP; OxBM

False Gallop of Analogies, A. Warham St. Leger. FaBoCo

False Heart, The. Hilaire Belloc. FaBoEE

False Knight upon the Road, The. *Unknown.* AmFP; GBP; PeBB

False life! a foil and no more, when. Quickness. Henry Vaughan. BoReV; ILP (1975 ed.); NOBE; SCP-1

False Luve, and Hae Ye Played Me This? *Unknown.* GBP; POL

False Nancy. *Unknown.* AmFP

False places, air flowers, spines. Indian Summer Garden Party. Keith Althaus. AAN

False Prophet. Emanuela O'Malley. AMV-81

False Security. John Betjeman. BBGO; CMoP (1970 ed.); LP

False Sir John a-wooing came. May Colvin. *Unknown.* PBMP

False though she be to me and love. Song. Congreve. BoLoP; NOBE; POL

False True Love. *Unknown.* FSW

Falslie doth envie of your praises blame. Henry Constable. *Fr.* Diana. ESo

Fame. Robert Herrick. FaBoEE

Fame. Charlotte Mew. PBWP; SBG

Fame. Vern Rutsala. GP

Fame is a fickle food. Emily Dickinson. TAP

Fame, like a wayward girl, will still be coy. On Fame. Keats. CABA (1972 ed.); MBPR; TT

Fame Makes Us Forward. Robert Herrick. CaPo

Famed ship *California*, a ship of high renown, The. The Girls around Cape Horn. *Unknown.* AmFP

Fame's pillar here, at last, we set. The Pillar of Fame. Robert Herrick. CaPo; NIL

Familiar. Veneta Nielson. MPA

Familiar Epistle, A. Ann Murry. WPE

Familiar Epistle to J. B. Esq., A, *sel.* Robert Lloyd.
"Mark yon round parson, fat and sleek." OBSV

Families, when a child is born. On the Birth of His Son. Su Tung-p'o, *tr. by* Arthur Waley. BuTh; OBVE; OFD

Family, The. Rose Fyleman. DuDr

Family. Norman MacCaig. FF

Family. Josephine Miles. GP

Family. Eve Shelnutt. TC

Family Album, A. Alter Brody. VWA

Family Circle, A. Beth Joselow. PoUp

Family crowded, The. Blood and My Brother. Richard Mathews. AATT

Family 8. Lyn Lifshin. NeAC

Family Game. Morton Marcus. NVAP

Family Getting Back to God. Eve Shelnutt. TC

Family Goldschmitt, The. Henri Coulette. FF; NowV

Family Group, The. Madeline DeFrees. *Fr.* Figures for a Carrousel. MPA

Family History. Wendy Bishop. AMV-81

Family Man, A. Maxine W. Kumin. CoPAm; IHMS; TAP

Family of Eight, The. Abraham Reisen, *tr. fr. Yiddish by* Marcia Falk. VWA

Family Photograph. Gerald Vizenor. VoR

Family Plot. Sarah Singer. AMV-81

Family Portrait. Rebecca Hood-Adams. AMV-80

Family portrait not too stale to record, A. Father and Son: 1939. William Plomer. NoAM

Family Prime. Mark Van Doren. VGW

Family Reunion. Peter Nelson. PHC

Famine Road, The. Eavan Boland. IPM

Famine Song. *Unknown. See* Praties, The.

Famine Year, The. Lady Wilde. PFIr

"Famous bard, he comes, The! The vision nears!" Visiting Poet. John Frederick Nims. InPK

Famous Hot Pepper Eating Contest, The. Sam Hamod. SA

Famous kingdom of the birds, The.　Somewhere Is Such a Kingdom.　John Crowe Ransom.　CMoP (1970 ed.)

Famous Outlaw Stops in for a Drink, The.　David James.　AMV-81

Famously she descended, her red hair.　A Recollection.　John Peale Bishop.　LoAs; PPoD

Fan for His Daughter, A.　Stéphane Mallarmé, *tr. fr. French by* David Paul.　RRA
(Another Fan, *tr. by* Roger Fry.)　NAWM-2

Fan-mail from foreign countries, is that fame?　John Berryman.　*Fr.* Dream Songs.　ILP (1975 ed.)

Fanaticism?　No.　Writing is exciting.　Baseball and Writing.　Marianne Moore.　BoWoP; LiSp; SPo

Fanatics have their dreams, wherewith they weave.　The Fall of Hyperion: A Dream.　Keats.　MBPR; OAEL-2

Fancy.　Robert Creeley.　NOBA

Fancy.　Keats.　MBPR

Fancy, A.　*Unknown.*　FaBoNo

Fancy's Knell.　A. E. Housman.　PoPle

Fandango.　"Stanley Vestal."　BPAW

Fane Wald I Luve.　John Clerk.　SLP

Fanfare for the Makers, A, *abr.*　Louis MacNeice.　NOBE

Fannie ("Fannie has the sweetest foot").　Thomas Bailey Aldrich.　OBAL

Fanny, *sel.*　Fitz-Greene Halleck.
"We owe the ancients something.　You have read."　OBAL

Fanny Brawne.　James Erickson.　PoW

Fanny!　If in your arms my soul could slip.　Keats to Fanny Brawne.　Edgar Lee Masters.　PoA

Fantasia.　Winifrid M. Letts.　PFIr

Fantasies of old age.　Merced.　Adrienne Rich.　NOBA; TT

Fantastic Collection of Stamps.　John Sjoberg.　AcAn

Fantasy inhabits this house, the stairs.　The Disobedient Statue.　Marina La Palma.　PoW

Fantasy Street.　Andrew Glaze.　NYP

Far above Cayuga's Waters　*Unknown.*　FSW

Far above the dome.　It Pleases.　Gary Snyder.　TAT; WasP

Far and wide as the eye can wander.　Peat Bog Soldiers.　*Unknown.*　FSW

Far as Creation's ample range extends.　The Great Chain of Being.　Pope.　*Fr.* An Essay on Man, Epistles I *and* II.　ExPo (1973 ed.)

Far away across the ocean.　Ballad of Ho Chi Minh.　Ewan MacColl.　FSW

Far away under us, they are mowing on the green steps.　The Beholders.　James Dickey.　ILP (1975 ed.)

Far back when I went zig-zagging.　Orion.　Adrienne Rich.　NIL; NoAM; WPE

Far beyond the sunrise and the sunset rises.　Plus Ultra.　Swinburne.　VLP

Far Brynderwyns heave across the harbour, The.　K. O. Arvidson.　*Fr.* The Last Songs of Richard Strauss at Takahe above the Kaipara.　ATNZ

Far Cry after a Close Call, A.　Richard Howard.　UnPo (1976 ed.)

Far Cry from Africa, A.　Derek Walcott.　NoAM; UnPo (1976 ed.)

"Far enough down is China," somebody said.　Digging for China.　Richard Wilbur.　BuTh; IP; NCSH; PiAm; TH

Far, far down.　City Afternoon.　Barbara Howes.　PPoD

Far far from gusty waves, these children's faces.　An Elementary School Classroom in a Slum.　Stephen Spender.　FF; ILP (1975 ed.); IP; MPo; NIL; PPoD; UnPo (1976 ed.); WIF

Far Field, The.　Theodore Roethke.　ILP (1975 ed.)

Far from a cultural centre he was used.　Sonnets from China, XIII.　W. H. Auden.　CMoP (1970 ed.)

Far from Africa: Four Poems.　Margaret Danner.　AmNP (1974 ed.); PoBA
Garnishing the Aviary, I.　BPo

Far from far.　Bobadil.　James Reeves.　LCL

Far from my dearest friend, 'tis mine to rove.　An Evening Walk.　Wordsworth.　MBPR

Far from Our Friends, *with music.*　Jeremy Belknap.　AH

Far from our garden at the edge of a gulf.　The Gulf.　Denise Levertov.　NNaP

Far from the scent of the crocus.　That's Life?　Alan Bold.　FF

Far from the sea and hard.　The Life Not Given.　David Habercom.　AMV-81

Far from the trouble and toil of town.　Old Man Platypus.　A. B. Paterson.　BoAnP

Far from the vulgar haunts of men.　On the Same.　Roy Campbell.　OxBTC

Far gone in weariness, in oblivion.　Homer, *tr. by* Robert Fitzgerald.　The Odyssey, VI.　NAWM-1

Far greater numbers have been lost by hopes.　Samuel Butler.　FaBoEE

Far have we come to this far spot of earth.　Prometheus Bound.　Aeschylus, *tr. by* Edith Hamilton.　NAWM-1

Far in a western brookland.　A. E. Housman.　PES

Far in the background a blue mountain waits.　Venus and the Lute Player.　Paul Engle.　WIF

Far in the heavens my God retires.　The Incomprehensible.　Isaac Watts.　ILP (1975 ed.)

Far in the sea, to the west of Spain.　The Land of Cokaygne.　*Unknown, tr. by* J. B. Trapp.　OAEL-1

Far inland/ go my sad thoughts.　*Tr. fr. Eskimo by* Knud Rasmussen, *ad. by* Willis Barnstone.　BoWoP

Far North, The.　Terry Savoie.　AMV-80

Far-off/ at the core of space.　Swan.　D. H. Lawrence.　CMoP (1970 ed.)

Far off, above the plain the summer dries.　2nd Air Force.　Randall Jarrell.　CMoP (1970 ed.)

Far off, from the burned fields.　Ashes.　Philip Levine.　AMV-80

Far off, the rumble of freight trains.　The Trestle Bridge.　Carolyne Wright.　AMV-80

Far, oh, far is the Mango island.　The Constant Cannibal Maiden.　Wallace Irwin.　OBAL

Far out as I can see.　Looking from Oregon.　Earle Birney.　MPA

Far out of sight forever stands the sea.　The Slow Pacific Swell.　Yvor Winters.　HeIP; NoAM; NOBA; PiAm

Far Rockaway.　Delmore Schwartz.　NoAM

Far to sea, west from Spain.　The Land of Cockaigne.　*Unknown, tr. by* John Montague.　BIrV

Far Trek.　June Brady.　QQQ

Far under the waves glide in, in rippling lines.　From the Point.　Paul Petrie.　AMV-80

Fara Diddle Dyno.　*Unknown.*　FaBoCo; SCP-2
("Ha ha! ha! ha! This world doth pass.")　FaBoNo
(Madrigal, *at. to* Thomas Weelkes.)　BBL

Fare Thee Well.　Byron.　MBPR

Fare Thee Well.　Eli Siegel.　GOA

Fare Thee Well.　*Unknown, tr. fr. Chippewa Indian by* Frances Densmore.　PBMP

Fare Thee Well Blues.　*Unknown.*　BluL

Fare thee well.　The time is come.　Fare Thee Well.　*Unknown, tr. by* Frances Densmore.　PBMP

Fare wel Advent!　Christmas is cum.　Farewell Advent.　*At. to* James Ryman.　OxBM

Fare Well.　Walter de la Mare.　NOBE

Fare you well, my blue-eyed girl.　Blue-eyed Girl.　*Unknown.*　AmFP

Fare You Well, My Darling.　*Unknown.*　AmFP

Fareweel ye dungeons dark and strong. MacPherson's Farewell. *Unknown.* FSW

Farewel to Worldly Joyes, A ("Farewel to unsubstantial joyes"). Anne Killigrew. BoWoP

Farewell, A: "And if I did, what then?" George Gascoigne. *Fr.* The Adventures of Master F. I. EBEV; GBL; HAP; NOBE

Farewell, The: "And so, one day when the tide was away out." Pat Wilson. ATNZ

Farewell, A: "Farewell, thou little nook of mountain-ground." Wordsworth. MBPR

Farewell, A: "Good-bye!—no, do not grieve that it is over." Harriet Monroe. PoA

Farewell, The: "It was a' for our rightfu' king." Burns. *See* It Was A' for Our Rightfu' King.

Farewell: "My boat goes west, yours east." Chao Li-hua, *tr. fr. Chinese* by J. P. Seaton. BoWoP

Farewell, A: "My cat was a southerner and a lady." Hildegarde Flanner. AMV-81

Farewell, A: "My fairest child, I have no song to give you." Charles Kingsley. OxBChV

Farewell, A: "My horse's feet beside the lake." Matthew Arnold. Switzerland, III. VLP

Farewell, A: "Oft have I mused, but now at length I find." Sir Philip Sidney. GBL; NOBE

Farewell, A: "Partner in the corner bar is high, a grin." Stanley Kiesel. HeS

Farewell: "We were gone from each other." Iain Crichton Smith. SLP

Farewell, A: "What is there left to be said?" A. R. D. Fairburn. ATNZ

Farewell: "What should I say." Sir Thomas Wyatt. NOBE ("What should I say.") LoAs; NOBE

Farewell, A: "With all my will, but much against my heart." Coventry Patmore. The Unknown Eros, I, xvi. BoLoP; NOBE

Farewell: "You sang round-dance songs." Liz Sohappy Bahe. CDW

Farewell, a Welcome, A. Lisel Mueller. Moon

Farewell, Adieu, That Courtly Life. John Pickering. NIL

Farewell Advent. *At. to* James Ryman. OxBM

Farewell, all my welfare. Sir Thomas Wyatt. GBL

Farewell Ballad of Poppies, A. Eva Brudne. VWA

Farewell, Cariola./ In my last will I have not much to give. John Webster. *Fr.* The Duchess of Malfi, IV, ii. LFH

Farewell, dear babe, my heart's too much content. In Memory of My Dear Grandchild Elizabeth Bradstreet. Anne Bradstreet. EAP; WPE

Farewell, dear scenes, for ever closed to me. Lines Written on a Window Shutter at Weston. William Cowper. LAuP

Farewell false friends, farewell ill wine. Farewell to England. *Unknown.* APAS

Farewell false love, the oracle of lies. A Farewell to False Love. Sir Walter Ralegh. BoLoP; ILP (1975 ed.); LoAs

Farewell, farewell! Before our prow. Charles Stuart Calverley. *Fr.* Dover to Munich. NOBL

Farewell Frost; or, Welcome the Spring. Robert Herrick. CaPo

Farewell, Gibson Square. Elizabeth Bartlett. PMW

Farewell! If Ever Fondest Prayer. Byron. VoPo

Farewell, love and all thy laws for ever. A Renoucing of Love. Sir Thomas Wyatt. AAS; GBL; OAEL-1; SoSe

Farewell my friend. Requiem. Martin T. O'Connor. AMV-80

"Farewell, my Spain! a long farewell!" he cried. Byron. *Fr.* Don Juan, II. PoIA

Farewell now, poesy's secret cell, thy ordered grace. Farewell to Hendre Fechan. William Phylip, *tr. by* H. Idris Bell. OBW

Farewell, O eyes which I ne'er saw before. Coming from —— in a Dark Night. Jane Barker. SCP-2

Farewell, Oh sun, Arcadia's clearest light. Sestina. Sir Philip Sidney. *Fr.* Arcadia. NIL; PAIC

Farewell of Clarimonde, The, *sel.* Ella Wheeler Wilcox. "Adieu, Romauld! But thou canst not forget me." PeD

Farewell old year,/ With goodness crowned. The New Year. *Unknown.* CTV

Farewell Poems. Sandra Hochman. RiTi

Farewell, Rewards and Fairies. Richard Corbet. *See* Fairies' Farewell, The.

"Farewell, Romance!" the Cave-men said. The King. Kipling. CABA (1972 ed.); VLP

Farewell sweet boy, complain not of my truth. Fulke Greville. *Fr.* Caelica. GBL

"Farewell, sweet Jane, for I must go across the flowing sea." Sweet Jane. *Unknown.* AmFP

Farewell, Sweet Mary. *Unknown.* AmFP

Farewell this World! *Unknown.* OxBM

Farewell! thou art too dear for my possessing. Sonnets, LXXXVII. Shakespeare. EBEV; InPS; LoAs; NOBE; OAEL-1; PPoD

Farewell, thou child of my right hand, and joy. On My First Son. Ben Jonson. CABA (1972 ed.); EBEV; FaBoEE; FF; HAP; HeIP; HoPM (1975 ed.); IPWM; LoAs; NIL; NOBE; OAEL-1; OBP; PAIC; PBMP; PoIA; PPoe; SCP-1; VoPo

Farewell, thou little nook of mountain-ground. A Farewell. Wordsworth. MBPR

Farewell thou thing, time-past so known, so dear. His Farewell to Sack. Robert Herrick. CaPo

Farewell to a Southern Melody, A. Huang O, *tr. fr. Chinese* by Kenneth Rexroth *and* Ling Chung. BoWoP

Farewell to an idea . . . A Cabin stands. Wallace Stevens. *Fr.* The Auroras of Autumn. CMoP (1970 ed.)

Farewell to Arms. George Peele. *See* His Golden Locks Time Hath to Silver Turned.

Farewell to Barn and Stack and Tree. A. E. Housman. AIW; CMoP (1970 ed.); UnPo (1976 ed.)

Farewell to Bath. Lady Mary Wortley Montagu. WPE

Farewell to Earth, *sel.* Lizzie Doten "I would bear a love Platonic to the souls in earthly life." PeD

Farewell to England. *Unknown.* APAS

Farewell to English, A, *sel.* Michael Hartnett "Gaelic is the conscience of our leaders." CIP

Farewell to Europe. William Pillen. VWA

Farewell to False Love, A. Sir Walter Ralegh. BoLoP; LoAs (Farewell, False Love.) ILP (1975 ed.)

Farewell to Folly, *sel.* Robert Greene. Maesia's Song. ILP (1975 ed.); UnPo (1976 ed.) (Mind Content, A.) PPM ("Sweet are the thoughts that savour of content.") PCOP

Farewell to Hendre Fechan. William Phylip, *tr. fr. Welsh* by H. Idris Bell. OBW

Farewell to Juliet. Wilfrid Scawen Blunt. *Fr.* The Love Sonnets of Proteus. BoLoP ("I see you, Juliet, still, with your straw hat.") OxBTC

Farewell to Kingsbridge. *Unknown.* AIW

Farewell to Kurdistan. Rosemary Tonks. OxBTC

Farewell to Love. John Donne. OAEL-1

Farewell to Love. Michael Drayton. *Fr.* Idea. VoPo ("Since there's no help, come let us kiss and part.") AAS; BoLoP; CABA (1972 ed.); Epi; ExPo (1973 ed.); GBL; HAP; HeIP; ILP (1975 ed.); InPK; InPS; LoAs; NOBE; OAEL-1; PAIC; PBMP; PoIA; PoPle; PPoD; PPoe; SoSe

Farewell to Love. Sir John Suckling. CaPo; SCP-2

Farewell to New Zealand. Wynford Vaughan-Thomas. NOBL

Farewell to old England the beautiful! Botany Bay. *Unknown.* FSW

Farewell to the caterpillars standing in minks. To Paul Eluard. Jorie Graham. AMV-80

Farewell to the Moon, A. Ed Ochester. Moon

Farewell to the world, and to the night farewell. Chikamatsu Monzaemon. *Fr.* The Love Suicides at Sonezaki. DL

Farewell to Van Gogh. Charles Tomlinson. CMoP (1970 ed.)

Farewell to you, my own true love. The Leaving of Liverpool. *Unknown.* FSW

Farewell, too little and too lately known. To the Memory of Mr. Oldham. Dryden. CABA (1972 ed.); EBEV; HAP; HeIP; InPK; InPS; NIL; NOBE; OAEL-1; PAIC; PPoe; PPP; Prf

Farewell, Ungrateful Traitor. Dryden. *Fr.* The Spanish Friar, V, i. BoLoP; HAP; ILP (1975 ed.); NOBE; PoPle

Farewell with a Mischeife. George Gascoigne. AAS

Farm, The. Vassar Miller. NCSH

Farm Boy after Summer. Robert Francis. NCSH

Farm boys wild to couple. The Sheep Child. James Dickey. CAPP; CoPAm; GP; NoAM; NOBA; Prf; TAP

Farm Implements and Rutabagas in a Landscape. John Ashbery. GP

Farm on the Great Plains, The. William Stafford. HAP; VGW

Farm Picture, A. Walt Whitman. InPS; PPoe

Farm Wife. Matt Field. AMV-81

Farm Wife. Ellen Bryant Voigt. AAN; CSP

Farm was abandoned, The. North Dakota Gothic. Mark Vinz. HeS

Farm-Woman's Winter, The. Thomas Hardy. VLP

Farmer, The. Terry Stokes. POL

Farmer and the Shanty Boy, The. *Unknown.* AmFP

Farmer among the Tombs, The. Wendell Berry. CSP

Farmer had a daughter whose beauty ne'er was told, A. The Banks of Sweet Dundee. *Unknown.* AmFP

Farmer in Bungleton, A. Mary Mapes Dodge. ECBV

Farmer Is the Man, The. *Unknown.* FSW

Farmer knew each time a friend went past, The. Hound on the Church Porch. Robert P. Tristram Coffin. GPD

Farmer of Tilsbury Vale, The. Wordsworth. EBEV

Farmer once called his cow "Zephyr," A. Zephyr. *Unknown.* TDH

Farmer Remembers the Somme, The. Vance Palmer. GAS

Farmer went riding [*or* trotting] upon his gray mare, A. Mother Goose. ECBV; MG

Farmers. Hortense Roberta Roberts. AMV-81

Farmer's Boy, A. *Unknown.* PoPle

Farmer's boy, starting to plough, A. "O-U-G-H-"; or, The Cross Farmer. D. S. Martin. TDH

Farmer's Bride, The. Charlotte Mew. BoLoP; OxBTC; PoIA; SBG; WPE

Farmer's Complaint, The, *orig. and mod. English prose. Unknown.* OxBM

Farmer's Curst Wife, The. *Unknown.* AIW; AmFP

Farmer's goose, who in the stubble, The. The Progress of Poetry. Swift. CABA (1972 ed.)

Farmer's in the Dell, The, *with music. Unknown.* GSB

Farmer's Life, A. *Unknown.* RAE
(Rewards of Farming, The.) PoPle

Farmer's Point of View. Alan Brownjohn. BuTh

Farmer's Wife, The. Anne Sexton. CoPAm; HoPM (1975 ed.)

Farmer's Wife, The. Mary Swanson Stroh. NPW

Farrell O'Reilly. Oliver St. John Gogarty. OxBTC

Farther Along. *Unknown.* FSW

Farther and farther from the three Pa Roads. On New Year's Eve. Ts'uei T'u, *tr. by* Witter Bynner. OFD

Farther east it wouldn't be on the map. Midwest Town. Ruth De Long Peterson. ANTL

Farther in summer than the birds. Emily Dickinson. AmVN

Fascination of What's Difficult, The. W. B. Yeats. BIrV; Epi

Fashion me strangely in the human mold. At 21. Eugene L. Belisle. AMV-81

Fashion Model at Home, The. Adrien Stoutenburg. PoW

Fashionable Poet Reading. Tony Connor. PPoD

Fashions in Dogs. E. B. White. GDP

Fashions in the 70's. May Swenson. NYP

Fast rode the knight. War Is Kind, VIII. Stephen Crane. PiAm

Faster, faster,/ O Circe, Goddess. The Strayed Reveller. Matthew Arnold. OAEL-2; VLP

Faster than fairies, faster than witches. From a Railway Carriage. Robert Louis Stevenson. OxBChV

Faster than Light. A. H. Reginald Buller. *See* Relativity.

Faster than Light. Edward Lowbury. PMW

Fastidious Serpent, The. Henry Johnstone. ECBV

Fastidious Yak, The. Oliver Herford. TDH

Fat black bucks in a wine-barrel room. The Congo. Vachel Lindsay. CMoP (1970 ed.); NoAM; NOBA; TAP

Fat Cat. John Ronan. AMV-81

Fat cat on the mat, The. Cat. J. R. R. Tolkien. ECBV

Fat-kneed god! Feeder of mangy leopards! You Also, Gaius Valerius Catullus. Archibald MacLeish. NoAM; TAP

Fat lady came on, The. Landscape of the Vomiting Multitudes. Ferderico García Lorca, *tr. by* Ben Belitt. NYP

Fat Man in the Mirror, The. Robert Lowell. AnMo; PoA

Fat mothering boy that won't. Won't Go to School. James Rankin. MIS

Fat torpedoes in bursting jackets. Fourth of July. Rachel Field. CC; CTV

Fat White Woman Speaks, The. G. K. Chesterton. SpRo

Fatal Love. Matthew Prior. FaBoCo

Fatal Mistake, A. Edward Lear. TDH
("There was an old man of Peru.") EBEV

Fatal Ship, The. Robert Stephen Hawker. VPC

Fatal Sisters, The. Thomas Gray, *after the Icelandic.* LAuP

Fatales Poetae. Henry Parrot. FaBoEE

Fate gave the word, the arrow sped. A Mother's Lament for the Death of Her Son. Burns. HoPM (1975 ed.)

Fate in Incognito. Michael Benedikt. OBAL

Fate of Birds, The. Kenneth Seib. AMV-80

Father. Rose Ausländer, *tr. fr. German by Ewald Osers.* VWA

Father. Paul Carroll. BrS

Father. Sid Gershgoren. BrS

Father. Margit Kaffka, *tr. fr. Hungarian by Laura Schiff.* PBWP

Father. Myra Cohn Livingston. CC

Father. Tom MacIntyre. IPM

Father, The. Desmond O'Grady. NoAM

Father. Lois Reiner. AMV-80

Father. John Wheelwright. UnPo (1976 ed.)

Father,/ Where do giants go to cry? A Small Discovery. James A. Emanuel. LCL

Father/ You are the trunk. Psalm. Howard Schwartz. VWA

Father, and Bard revered! to whom I owe. Dedicatory Sonnet to S. T. Coleridge. Hartley Coleridge. OAEL-2

Father and Child. Gwen Harwood. WPE
Barn Owl, *sel.* CAAP

Father and Child. W. B. Yeats. RRA; TCP

Father and Daughter. Joanne Casullo. NPW

Father and His Children, The. *Unknown.* OxBChV

Father and I in the Woods. David McCord. SO

Father and I went down to camp. Yankee Doodle. *Unknown, at. to* Richard Shuckburg. AIW; AmFP; BLSo; BTTM; CC; PCOP

Father and Son. F. R. Higgins. BIrV; PFIr

Father and Son. Stanley Kunitz. NoAM

Father and Son. William Stafford. GP

Father and Son. Ronald Wallace. AMV-81

Father and Son: 1939. William Plomer. NoAM

Father, be with me still. From Thursday. Barbara Earl Thomson. AATT

Father Coyote. George Sterling. BPAW

Father, Dear Father, Come Home with Me Now. Henry Clay Work. FSW

Father, father, where are you going. The Little Boy Lost. Blake. *Fr.* Songs of Innocence. LAuP; MBPR

Father Fox's Pennyrhymes, *sels.* Clyde Watson.
　"Apples for the little ones." CC
　"Country bumpkin." CC
　"Happy birthday, silly goose!" CC
　"Huckleberry, gooseberry, raspberry pie." CC

Father Gilligan. W. B. Yeats. *See* Ballad of Father Gilligan, The.

Father Grumble. *Unknown.* AmFP
　(Old Man in the Wood.) FSW

Father, Hear the Prayer We Offer, *with music.* Love Maria Willis. AH

Father, His Friend, and Another. William Stafford. BrS

Father Huc lives in the Thyangboche monastery. Two Old Men. David McAleavey. PoUp

Father I cannot tell a lie. A Historical Note (from George Washington to His Father). John L. Sellers. DNGG

Father, I expect your eyes. Before the Mountain. Elizabeth Libbey. AmPA

Father! I Own Thy Voice, *with music.* Samuel Wolcott. AH

Father! I'm hungered! give me bread. The Emigrant's Dying Child. G. W. Patton. BPAW

Father in heaven, after each lost day. Petrarch, *tr. fr. Italian by* Bernard Bergonzi. Sonnets to Laura: To Laura in Life, LXII. NAWM-1

Father in Tennessee, A. J. Edgar Simmons. TAT

Father, in Thy Mysterious Presence Kneeling, *with music.* Samuel Johnson. AH

Father is, dedicatedly. Father. Lois Reiner. AMV-80

Father is hard to live with. Old Storm. David Phillips. NeAC

Father Is Home. *Unknown.* ECBV

Father Mapple's Hymn. Herman Melville. *Fr.* Moby Dick, *ch.* 9. RhR
　(Ribs and Terrors, The.) PPM

Father Mat. Patrick Kavanagh. CMoP (1970 ed.)

Father Missouri takes his own. Foreclosure. Sterling A. Brown. PoBA

Father of all! in every age. The Universal Prayer. Pope. ILP (1975 ed.); ILwL; PIM

Father of heaven, after squandered days. Petrarch, *tr. fr. Italian by* R. G. Barnes. Sonnets to Laura: To Laura in Life, XLVIII. Epi

Father of lights! what sunny seed. Cock-crowing. Henry Vaughan. OAEL-1; SCP-1

Father of My Country, The. Diane Wakoski. NoAM; TAP

Father of Night. Bob Dylan. GrRo

Father of the Victim. Rae Ballard. AMV-80

Father of Women, A. Alice Meynell. SBG; WPE

Father O'Flynn. Alfred Perceval Graves. PFIr

Father, on the first day on the Hunting Moon. The First Day of the Hunting Moon. Patricia Low. VGW

Father once said to his son, A. Punishment. *Unknown.* TDH

Father Out, an' Mother Hwome, A. William Barnes. VPC

Father qua Father. Celebration for a Young Priest. Barbara Earl Thomson. AATT

Father raised words, The. Family. Norman MacCaig. FF

Father Says. Michael Rosen. FPB

Father sees a son nearing manhood, A. What Shall He Tell That Son? Carl Sandburg. SoS

Father Son and Holy Ghost. Audre Lorde. PoBa

"Father, the moon is up and full." The Gatton Tragedy. John Manifold. FPA

Father, the visit/ was so unexpected. To My Father. Susannah Fried, *tr. by* Anthony Rudolf. VWA

Father, the Year Is Fallen. Audre Lorde. PoBA

Father, this year's jinx rides us apart. All My Pretty Ones. Anne Sexton. NoAM; PoIA

Father, thy hand. Bryant. *Fr.* A Forest Hymn. PIM

Father! Thy wonders do not singly stand. The Spirit Land. Jones Very. HAP

Father wears antlers to dinner. The Last Auroch. Maxine Chernoff. FiCh

Father what is that in the sky beckoning to me with long finger? Walt Whitman. *Fr.* Song of the Banner at Daybreak. CC

"Father, what is truelove." Truelove. Mark Van Doren. AIW

Father, who designs his babe a priest, The. William Cowper. *Fr.* Tirocinium; or, A Review of Schools. OBSV

Father, Who Mak'st Thy Suff'ring Sons, *with music.* Arthur C. Coxe. AH

Father, whom I murdered every night but one. Elegy for My Father. Howard Moss. VWA

Father William. "Lewis Carroll." *Fr.* Alice's Adventures in Wonderland, *ch.* 5. BiP; FaBoNo; HoPM (1975 ed.); SpRo; SS; TVo
　(You Are Old, Father William.) OxBChV; UnPo (1976 ed.)
　("You are old, Father William," the young man said.) FaBoCo; NOBL

Fatherless and motherless. *Unknown.* GBP

Fatherless, 250 people. Verigin, Moving in Alone. John Newlove. NeAC

Fathers, The. John N. Morris. GP

Fathers, The. Benjamin Saltman. VWA

Fathers, The. Siegfried Sassoon. NoAM

Father's friend Ray at the planing mill. Father, His Friend, and Another. William Stafford. BrS

Fathers: naked, you stand for their big faces. This Is a Poem for the Dead. Michael Ryan. AmPA

Father's Story. Elizabeth Madox Roberts. CC

Fathers told us, The. Raspberries. Doug Flaherty. HeS

Father's voice. William Stafford. RFM

Father's Whiskers. *Unknown.* FSW

Fathomless Is My Love. Kalola, *tr. fr. Hawaiian by* N. B. Emerson. WTO

Fatigue. Hilaire Belloc. FaBoCo; NOBL; OxBTC

Fatigue, regrets. The lights. The Demon Lover. Adrienne Rich. IHMS

Fatigued, Lily finishes a cigarette. Saigon Tea. Perry Oldham. AAN

Fatima. Tennyson. UnPo (1976 ed.)

Fatted/ on herbs, swollen on crabapples. The Porcupine. Galway Kinnell. CoPAm; NOBA

Fattened sky, The. The Fifth Hell. Jerome Rothenberg. *Fr.* The Seven Hells of Jigoku Zoshi. NNaP

Faun, The. Ezra Pound. FaBoTw (1975 ed.)

Fauna: March. David Lake. FPA

Faust, *sels.* Goethe, *tr. fr. German.*
　Chorus of the Archangels, The, 2 *versions, tr. by* Shelley. OBVE
　"Here stand I, ach, Philosophy," Pt. I, *tr by* Louis MacNeice. NAWM-2
　Prologue in Heaven, *tr. by* Louis MacNeice NAWM-2
　"Stop playing with your melancholy," *tr. by* Walter Kaufman. DL

Faustina hath a spot upon her face. De Naevo in Facie Faustinae. Thomas Bastard. FaBoEE

Faust's Servant. Roy Fuller. OxBTC

Favorite Grandson Braid. Phillip William George. NW; VoR

Fawn's Foster-Mother. Robinson Jeffers. NoAm; NOBA

Fay Wray to the King. Judith Rechter. NMM

Fear. Aldo Camerino, *tr. fr. Italian by* Anita Barrows. VWA

Fear. Stephen Dobyns. AMV-80

Fear, A. Robert Francis. GP

Fear. Anna Hajnal, *tr. fr. Hungarian by* Daniel Hoffman. BoWoP

Fear. Pablo Neruda, *tr. fr. Spanish by* Nathanial Tarn. IPWM

Fear. Thomas Peacock. VoR

Fear. Alejandra Pizarnik, *tr. fr. Spanish by* Lynn Alvarez. AMV-80

Fear. Vittoria Aganoor Pompili, *tr. fr. Italian by* Brenda Webster. PBWP

Fear, The. Margaret Reynolds. MIS

Fear. Roger Stump. AMV-80

Fear and Anger in the Mindless Universe. Hayden Carruth. NNaP

Fear Death by Water. Richard Eberhart. AMV-81

Fear death?—to feel the fog in my throat. Prospice. Robert Browning. BiP; DL; ILP (1975 ed.); PAIC; PFD; STS; TT; VLP; VoPo

Fear falls upon me on the moutain top. The Dog Child. Keaulumoku, *tr. fr. Hawaiian by* M. W. Beckwith. *Fr.* The Kumulipo: A Creation Chant. WTO

Fear Has Cast Out Love. Wilfrid Scawen Blunt. The Love Sonnets of Proteus, XXXVI. VLP

Fear, jealousy and murder are the same. Gamecock. James Dickey. HoPM (1975 ed.); UnPo (1976 ed.)

Fear me, virgin whosoever. After the Pleasure Party. Herman Melville. AmVN

Fear No More the Heat o' the Sun. Shakespeare. *Fr.* Cymbeline, IV, ii. AIW; EBEV; FF; GBL; HAP; HeIP; ILP (1975 ed.); InPK; InPS; OBP; PBMP; PoIA; PoPle; PPoe; SoSe; STS
  (Dirge.) OAEL-1
  (Dirge for Fidele.) NOBE

Fear not, dear love, that I'll reveal. Secrecy Protested. Thomas Carew. CaPo

Fear Not, Poor Weary One, *with music*. Thomas Cogswell Upham. AH

Fear of Death. John Ashbery. TAP

Fear of Flowers, The. John Clare. PF

Fear of Flying, The. Mona Van Duyn. NMM

Fear of Groceries, The. Herbert Scott. TC

Fear of poetry, The, is the/ fear. Reading Time: 1 Minute 26 Seconds. Muriel Rukeyser. PBWP

Fear Test: Integrity of Heroes. James Simmons. CIP

Fear the one who has sharp weapons. Song of the Lioness for Her Cub. *Tr. fr. Hottentot by* Thomas Hahn. BoWoP

Fear thou no more, thou timid flower! The Snowdrop. Samuel Taylor Coleridge. PF

Fear was about me. Hunger. *Tr. fr. Eskimo.* WTO

Feare not, little flocke, for it is your fathers good pleasure to give you the kingdome. Bible, *N.T. Fr.* St. Luke. OBVE

Fearful Finale of the Irascible Mouse, The. Guy Wetmore Carryl. ECBV

Fearful I peer upon the mountain path. Eleven Addresses to the Lord, X. John Berryman. PiAm

Fearful of beauty, I always went. The Enamel Girl. Genevieve Taggard. WPW

Fearful Symmetry. Basil Bunting. PoA

Fearing that Albion should turn his back against the Divine Vision. Blake. *Fr.* Jerusalem. OAEL-2

Fearless, The. Mortimer J. Adler. PoA

Fears in solitude. Samuel Taylor Coleridge. MBPR

Feast and noon grew high, and sacrifice, The. Milton. *Fr.* Samson Agonistes. EBEV

Feast is o'er—the music and the stir, The. After the School-Feast. Charles Tennyson Turner. VPC

Feast of Stephen, The. Anthony Hecht. HAP

Feast of the Monkeys, The. John Philip Sousa. OBAL

Feast of the Ram's Horn. Harvey Shapiro. VGW

Feather, The. Vernon Watkins. FaBoTw (1975 ed.)

Feather plucked out and tossed away, A. Dirt Road. Tom Hennen. HeS

Feather-Stitching. Aileen Fisher. MN

Feathers and Moss. Jean Ingelow. SpRo

Feathers blacken against the sun. Manifest Destiny. Anita Endrezze Probst. CDW

Feathers of Snow. *Unknown.* GBP

Feathers of the willow, The. Song. Richard Watson Dixon. NOBE

Feathers up fast, and steeples; then in clods. The Fountain. Donald Davie. OxBTC

Featherstone's Doom. Robert Stephen Hawker. VPC

Feathery forests are blown back, frost rends, The. Winter. John Lyle Donaghy. BIrV

Feature Time. Jerry Hammond. PPoD

Features frozen in time. Family Portrait. Rebecca Hood-Adams. AMV-80

February. Fred Chappell. CSP

February. John Clare. *Fr.* The Shepherd's Calendar. NOBE

February. W. S. Merwin. NNaP; UsP

February. Larry Moffi. AMV-80

February. William Morris. *Fr.* The Earthly Paradise. VPC

February. John Updike. CC

February. Barbara Winder. PH

February Afternoon. Edward Thomas. NoAM

February 11, 1977. Frederick Morgan. AMV-80

February Evening in New York. Denise Levertov. InPS; NoAM

February I Turn Off the Porch Light and Go Outside. James Tipton. HeS

February Letter to Jack Spicer. Helen Luster. CPA

February Loves. Richmond Lattimore. LoAS

February Morning. King D. Kuka. VoR

February Morning, A. Leslie Norris. HeHu

February Park. Gerald Vizenor. VoR

February Thaw. Arthur J. Bull. HeHu

February 22. John Updike. GOA

Feckless Dinner Party, The. Walter de la Mare. FaBoTw (1975 ed.); PoTa

Fee, faw fum! bubble and squeak! Holy-Cros Day. Robert Browning. VLP

Fee, Fi, Fo, Fum. Eve Merriam. *Fr.* The Inner-City Mother Goose. IPWM

Feeding Cycle of the Catfish, The. Tom Crawford. NVAP

Feeding the Fire. Donald Finkel. VWA

Feeding the Lions. Norman Jordan. CTBA; PoBA

Feeding Time. Janet Beeler. BCr

Feel free. To Bobby Seale. Lucille Clifton. CNA; PoBA

Feel like a Bird. May Swenson. SoSe

Feel Me. May Swenson. GP

Feel of Hands, The. Thom Gunn. PSN

Feel of that leather baby, The. Watching the Jets Lose to Buffalo at Shea. May Swenson. LiSp

Feel the sharpness. The Meeting. Ramona Wilson. VoR

Feeling, The. William Bronk. VGW

Feeling a pain in his breast, when he speaks. Ellas and the Statues. Gülten Akin, *tr. by* Nermin Menemencioglu. PBWP

Feeling all at once imprisoned, I stalk for the door. Fantasy Street. Andrew Glaze. NYP

Feeling for Fish. Leonard Trawick. AMV-81

Feeling Fucked Up. Etheridge Knight. GP; NNaP

Feeling the urge my mother. Birth. Edith Bruck, *tr. by* Ruth Feldman *and* Brian Swann. BoWoP

Feeling You Again. Jim Mulac. AcAn

Feelings go up into the air, The. Some Feelings. Michael Benedikt. ConAP

Feelings I don't have I don't have, The. To Women, as Far as I'm Concerned. D. H. Lawrence. InPS; WeW

Feelings of a Republican on the Fall of Bonaparte. Shelley. MBPR

Feet Are Not Funny. William Lindsay. PMW

Feet of morning the feet of noon and the feet of evening, The. The Domestic Stones (fragment). Hans Arp, *tr. by* David Gascoyne. EAS

Feigned Courage. Charles *and* Mary Lamb. OxBChV

Feld, groes or goers, hus, doeg, dung. Returning to Roots of First Feeling. Robert Duncan. PoA

Feliks Skrzynecki. Peter Skrzynecki. CAAP

Felix Randal. Gerard Manley Hopkins. BoReV; EBEV; Epi; HAP; ILP (1975 ed.); InPS; NoAM; NOBE; OBP; PoIA; PoPle; VLP

Felixstowe; or, The Last of Her Order. John Betjeman. OxBTC

Felled at a Word? Nathaniel Wanley. SCP-2

Felled Plane Tree, The. Anna Hajnal, *tr. fr. Hungarian by* William Jay Smith. BoWoP

Fellow Named Hall, A. J. F. Wilson. TDH

Fellow, you have no flair for art, I fear. The Sitting Bard. Sir Owen Seaman. NOBL

Fellows up in Personnel, The. The Perforated Spirit. Morris Bishop. MiP; QQQ; TPo

Felo de Se. Thomas Blackburn. OxBTC

Female bottom is a sight, The. Cudworth's Undergraduate Ode to a Bare Behind. John Ower. AMV-81

Female, Extinct. Patricia Beer. HeHu

Female Femininity. Pancho Aguila. NW

Female Friend, The. Cornelius Whur. FaBoCo

"Female genital, like the blank page anticipating the poem, The." Sentience. Sandra McPherson. CNW; PoA

Female God, The. Isaac Rosenberg. FaBoTw (1975 ed.)

Female hand puppet refused to let the puppet master put, A. The Little Lady. Russell Edson. GP

Female of the Species Is Hardier than the Male, The. Phyllis McGinley. PPM

Female Parricide, The. *Unknown.* APAS

Female Vagrant, The. Wordsworth. MBPR

Feminine Seal, The. Oliver Herford. TDH

Femme et Chatte. Paul Verlaine, *tr. fr. French by* Arthur Symons. OBVE

Fence, A. Carl Sandburg. WeW

Fence beyond fence from breakfast. The Names of the Humble. Les A. Murray. *Fr.* Walking to the Cattle-Place. CAAP

Fence Wire. James Dickey. VGW

Fer in see by west Spaygne. The Land of Cockayne. *Unknown.* OxBM

Feral Pioneers, The. Ishmael Reed. PoBA; UnPo (1976 ed.)

Ferdinand De Soto lies. The Distant Runners. Mark Van Doren. GOA

Ferdinando and Elvira. W. S. Gilbert. FaBoCo; FaBoNo

Fergus and the Druid. W. B. Yeats. VLP

Fern Hill. Dylan Thomas. BBGO; BiP; CABA (1972 ed.); CMoP (1970 ed.); FSFS; HAP; HeIP; ILP (1975 ed.); InPK; InPS; IPWM; NIL; NoAM; NOBE; NowV; OAEL-2; OBW;

OxBTC; PPM; PPoD; PPoe; PPP; SoS; SoSe (1977 ed.); STS; TCP; TT; VoPo; WeW; WIF

Ferret, The. Lord Alfred Douglas. BBL

Ferry Me across the Water. Christina Rossetti. BiP; ECBV; OxBChV

Fertile Valley of the Nile, The. Eve Merriam. IHMS

Fertilizer plant grinds fish into stink, The. Then the Skins Fall Apart. Dara Wier. TV

Feste's Song ("O mistress mine"). Shakespeare. *Fr.* Twelfth Night, II, iii. BoLoP
    ("O mistress mine, where are you roaming?") BiP; GBL; HAP; HeIP; ILP (1975 ed.); InPS; NIL; NOBE; OAEL-1; OLR
    (Sweet-and-Twenty.) GrRo

Festivals have I seen that were not names. Calais, August 15, 1802. Wordsworth. MBPR

Festus, *sel.* Philip James Bailey.
    Proem: "Poetry is itself a thing of God." VLP

Fetch in the holly from the tree. Holly and Mistletoe. Eleanor Farjeon. PChr

Fetching Cows. Norman MacCaig. BoAnP; LP

Fete confused me, The. Guests played the part of gods. Sigismundo. Linda Gregg. AmPA

Fever, A. John Donne. OAEL-1

Fever 103°. Sylvia Plath. AnMo; CMoP (1970 ed.); NoAM; NOBA; PiAm; VGW

Fever Toy, The. Charles Wright. AmPA

Feverish room and that white bed, The. White Heliotrope. Arthur Symons. BoLoP; EBEV; InPS

Few beds are stonier than one shared by a sleeper. Bed Time. Peter Davison. UnPo (1976 ed.)

Few broken coughs . . . Then blood, a sobbing sigh! Nirvana. Ali S. Hilmi Törel. PeD

Few folk around here have. Credentials. William Stafford. FoP

Few frogs I've kissed/ have come up princes. Frog Prince. Gabrielle Edgcomb. PoUp

Few light flakes of snow, A. Kyoto: March. Gary Snyder. PPP

Few men in any age have second sight. To a Reviewer Who Admired My Book. John Ciardi. OBAL

Few Muddled Metaphors by a Moore-ose Melodist, A. Tom Hood. FaBoNo

Few, of course, could take it seriously. At Jesty's Tomb. Edward Lowbury. PMW

Few originals, but mighty. Primary. Abbie Huston Evans. GP

Few rape men or kill coons so I bat them, A! Mess Occupations. Ted Berrigan. CAAP

Few years later, A. Endings. Daniel Halpern. CAAP

Fforestfawr. Kingsley Amis. *Fr.* The Evans Country. NOBL

Ffrom depth off sinn and from a diepe dispaire. Bible, *O.T.* Psalms, CXXX. OBVE

Fhairshon swore a feud. The Massacre of the Macpherson. William Edmonstoune Aytoun. FaBoCo

Fiametta. John Peale Bishop. LoAs

Fiascherino. Charles Tomlinson. NoAM

Fickle in the Arms of Spring. Susie Fry. AMV-81

Fickle One, The. Pablo Neruda, *tr. fr. Spanish by* Donald D. Walsh. FF; OLR

Fiction and the Reading Public. Philip Larkin. NOBL; OBSV

Fiction of relationship, The. New Potatoes. Ken Belford. NeAC

Fiddle-de-dee, fiddle-de-dee. *Unknown.* MG

Fiddlehead, The. David McFadden. NeAC

Fiddle-I-Fee. *Unknown.* AmFP

Fiddler, The. Martin Buber, *tr. fr. German by* Jawaid Awan. VWA

Fiddler Jones. Edgar Lee Masters. *Fr.* Spoon River Anthology. CMoP (1970 ed.); NoAM; TAP

Fiddler of Dooney, The. W. B. Yeats. PoPle

Fiddler settles in, The. Lament for the O'Neills. John Montague. CIP

Fiddler's Song. George Mackay Brown. MS; SLP

Fidelities. Jean Valentine. NYP

Fidelity. Jerry Kass. AMV-80

Fidelity belongs in the Guinness Book of Records. Graffiti for Lovers. Joan Joffe Hall. AMV-80

Fidessa, More Chaste than Kind, *sels.* Bartholomew Griffin.
  "Care-charmer sleepe, sweet ease in restles miserie," XV. AAS; ESo; ILP (1975 ed.); NIL
  "Compare me to the child that plaies with fire," XIII. ESo
  "Fair is my love that feeds among the lilies," XXXVII. GBL
  "Fly [*or* Flye] to her heart; hover about her heart," XXIII. AAS; LoAs
  "For I have loved long, I crave rewarde," XVI. ESo
  "I have not spent the April of my time," XXXV. AAS; ILP (1975 ed.); LoAs
  "My ladies haire is threeds of beaten gold," XXXIX. AAS; ESo
  "Tongue, never cease to sing Fidessae's praise," XXXI. ESo
  "Venus, and yong Adonis sitting by her," III. ESo

Fie on Eastern Luxury! ("Persicos odi"). Horace, *tr. fr. Latin* by Hartley Coleridge. Odes, I, 38. InPK
  ("Ah child, no Persian—perfect art!" *tr. by* Gerard Manley Hopkins.) InPK; OBVE
  (Preference Declared, The, *tr. by* Eugene Field.) InPK
  (Simplicity, *tr. by* William Cowper.) InPK
  ("Boy, I hate their empty shows.") OBVE

Field, The. Douglas Lawder. PH

Field and Forest. Randall Jarrell. VGW

Field Day. W. R. Rodgers. BIrV

Field Full of Folk, The. William Langland. *See* In a Somer Seson, Whan Softe Was the Sonne.

Field Hospital, The. Paul Muldoon. CIP

Fieldmouse, The. Cecil Frances Alexander. OxBChV

Field Mouse, The. William Sharp. MN; PCoP

Fieldmouse, A/ crouches low. Robert Sund. BoAnP

Field of Autumn. Laurie Lee. NCSH

Field of corn and a bird in flight, A. Sensible People. James Stephens. RAE

Field of Light, A. Theodore Roethke. PiAm

Field of Night, The. Miriam Waddington. VWA

Field of poetry ends here, The. The Dump. Greg Kuzma. PoA

Field of Talavera, The. Thomas Hardy. *Fr.* The Dynasts, Pt. II, Act IV, sc. iv. CMoP (1970 ed.)

Field of Waterloo, The. Byron. *Fr.* Childe Harold's Pilgrimage, III. BTTM
  ("Stop—for thy tread is on an empire's dust.") ILP (1975 ed.); InPS

Field Poem. Gary Soto. NW

Field Trip. Gary Miranda. AMV-81

Field with Figurations. Warren Slesinger. HeS

Fieldmouse. *See* Field Mouse.

Fields are black once more, The. Reading in Fall Rain. Robert Bly. GP

Fields close in on all sides, The. The Road of Birds. Harry Humes. AMV-80

Fields from Islington to Marybone, The. To the Jews. Blake. *Fr.* Jerusalem. MBPR

Fields of the Country, The. Jane Garland Katz. AAN

Fields Where We Slept. Muriel Rukeyser. NNaP

Fiend, The. James Dickey. CoPAm; PPP

Fierce courage his and will straight as a rune. The Pacific. Percy Stickney Grant. RhR

Fierce musical cries of a couple of sparrowhawks, The. Birds. Robinson Jeffers. EcS; MPA; VGW

Fierce they drove on, impatient to destroy. Homer, *tr. by* Pope. *Fr.* The Iliad, XIII. OBVE

Fiercely the battle raged and, sad to tell. Ambrose Bierce. *Fr.* The Devil's Dictionary. OBAL

Fiery mountains answer each other, The. Liberty. Shelley. MBPR

Fiery throb in every star, A. Elizabeth Barrett Browning. *Fr.* A Vision of Poets. PeD

Fife Tune. John Manifold. GAS

Fifteen. William Stafford. SoS

Fifteen Boys. Bella Akhmadulina, *tr. fr. Russian by* George Reavey. BuTh

Fifteen churches lie here. At Dunwich. Anthony Thwaite. HeHu; MPo

Fifteen Million Plastic Bags. Adrian Mitchell. OBSV; OxBTC

Fifteen nights I have lain awake and called you. Elegy for a Cricket. J. V. Cunningham. NoAM

Fifteen or twenty feet below. The Anchorage. Pat Wilson. ATNZ

Fifteen Ships on Georges Banks. *Unknown.* AmFP

Fifteen years ago/ I left this seacoast town. With Due Deference to Thomas Wolfe. Joanne Townsend. AMV-81

Fifteen years ago and twenty. To an Athlete Turned Poet. Peter Meinke. LiSp; SPo

Fifteen years ago, when soldiers. Graduation Day, 1965. Julio Marzán. InW

Fifteen years in the coal mine. Coal Diggin' Blues. *Unknown.* AmFP

Fifteen years up and her tongue's still flapping. Not Her, She Aint No Gypsy. Al Young. GP

Fifteenth day of July, The. Brave Lord Willoughby. *Unknown.* FaPoR

Fifth and 94th. Stanley Plumly. NYP

Fifth Avenue Parade. Anthony Hecht. NYP

Fifth Bedtime Story. Ted Hughes. UsP

Fifth Day. Robert D. Fitzgerald. GAS; MAuV

Fifth-Floor Window, The. Lola Ridge. WPE

Fifth Hell, The. Jerome Rothenberg. *Fr.* The Seven Hells of Jigoku Zoshi. NNaP

5th of July, The. Felice Holman. CC

Fifties, The. Roy Fuller. NIL

Fifties, The. Ira Sadoff. AmPA

Fifty. Kenneth Rexroth. TAP

Fifty Cents. *Unknown.* CTV

50-50. Langston Hughes. NoAM; NOBA

59th Street Bridge Song, The. Paul Simon. TCP

Fifty-seventh Street and Fifth. Alfred Corn. NYP

Fifty times the rose has flower'd and faded. On the Jubilee of Queen Victoria. Tennyson. UnPo (1976 ed.)

Fifty-two years ago. A Short History of the Teaching Profession. Sister Maura. AMV-80

Fifty years and three. My Dad and Mam They Did Agree. *Unknown.* POL

Fig for Momus, A, *sel.* Thomas Lodge.
  "In every land from Gades to Ganges flood." TVS

Fight, The. Sam Hamod. SA

Fight at San Jacinto, The. John Williamson Palmer. BPAW

Fight Fire with Fire. Steve Toth. AcAn

Fight of the Year, The. Roger McGough. DuDr

Fight thou with shafts of silver, and o'ercome. Money Gets the Mastery. Robert Herrick. CaPo

Fight your little fight, my boy. Don'ts. D. H. Lawrence. NoAM

Fighter, The. Dave Etter. TAT

Fighting Her. David Phillips. NeAC

Fighting my dependency. Alta. MMD

Fighting nature of the intellect, The. Vast Light. Richard Eberhart. CMoP (1970 ed.)

Fighting South of the Ramparts. Li Po, *tr. fr. Chinese by* Arthur Waley. NIL

Fighting Talk. Tom Buchan. MIS

Figs. D. H. Lawrence. OAEL-2

Figure. Marcia Lee Masters. HeS

Figure and Ground. Elton Glaser. AMV-80

Figure of Plain Force, A. Michael Heffernan. HeS

Figurehead, The. Léonie Adams. WPE

Figurehead, The. Crosbie Garstin. PoTa

Figurehead, The. Karl Shapiro. MPA

Figures, The. Robert Creeley. UnPo (1976 ed.)

Figures and Ground. Robert Leverant. MIT

Figures for a Carrousel, *sel.* Madeline DeFrees. Family Group, The. MPA

Figures in a Ruined Ballroom. George Hitchcock. VGW

Figures near a Bridge. Linda Gregg. AAN

Figures on the Frieze, The. Alastair Reid. MS; SLP

Filaments of light. In the New Sun. Philip Levine. NNaP

Filing-cabinet of human lives, A. Apartment House. Gerald Raftery. SFF

Fill/ my pants and shirt. Three Friends of Mine. Jimmy Santiago Baca. DNGG

Fill High the Bowl. John Keble. PFD

Fill, lads, fill. Drinking Song. Frederick Marryat. RhR

Fill the Bowl, Butler. *Unknown.* OxBM

Fill up your glass, O comrade true. The Pioneer. Eugene Field. BPAW

Fill your dark glasses with water and toast. Rip-off #1: Hippie Capitalism. Geof Hewitt. NeAC

Fille de Joie: Congo. Michael Jackson. ATNZ

Filling an Order. John Townsend Trowbridge. OBAL

Filling her compact and delicious body. John Berryman. *Fr.* Dream Songs. BoLoP; CAPP; HAP; LoAs; OBAL; PSN; WeW

Filling Station. Elizabeth Bishop. HAP; WeW

Filling the mind. The Clouds. William Carlos Williams. VGW

Film Vermouth: Six o'Clock Show. Magda Portal, *tr. fr. Spanish by* Allan Francovich *and* Kathleen Weaver. PBWP

Filming a motion picture. Cut. David J. Feela. AMV-81

Filtres. Andrew Hoyem. MIT

Final Cut, The. Vern Rutsala. AMV-81

Final end of all but purified souls, The. Your Animal. Gerald Stern. AMV-81

Final Fall, The. Alexandre L. Amprimoz. AMV-81

Final Painting, The. Lee Harwood. EAS

Final Prayer. Enheduanna, *tr. fr. Sumerian; ad. by* Aliki *and* Willis Barnstone. BoWoP

Final Soliloquy of the Interior Paramour. Wallace Stevens. HAP; PiAm

Final Solstice, The. Robert Adamson. CAAP

Final tiny gnash snapped strand from claw, A. Mus Ridiculus Non. Marie De L. Welch. BoAnP

Finale. Carl Sandburg. *Fr.* Prairie. ANTL

Finally. Vittoria Aganoor Pompili, *tr. fr. Italian by* Brenda Webster. PBWP

Finally. Bruce Severy. HeS

Finally/ finally my life has come to this. Deep Sea Blues. Joanne Jimason. PoUp

Finally/ silence. That Silence. Andrew Taylor. FPA

Finally, from your house, there is no view. Water Island. Howard Moss. Prf

Finally retired pensionless. Big Momma. Don L. Lee. BPo; CNA; TPo

Finally the problem is my meaning. Guevara with Minutes to Go. John William Corrington. CoPAm

Finally, to forgo love is to kiss a leaf. Rescue the Dead. David Ignatow. ConAP; VGW

Finally you will grow tired of it all. Gull Lake Reunion. Kelly Ivie. AMV-81

Finch-notes and swallow-notes tell the new year. Spring Thoughts. Huang-fu Jan, *tr. by* Witter Bynner. OFD

Finches, The. Thomas W. Shapcott. BoAnP

Find. Josephine Miles. WPE

Find a good spot and sit there. How to Own Land. Susan Farley. AMV-80

Finder Found, The. Edwin Muir. PoA

Finders Keepers. Donald Finkel. VWA

Finding a Dead Mole with My Sons. Joseph Bruchac. EC

Finding a Friend Home. Timothy Hamm. AMV-80

Finding a Poem. Eve Merriam. RFM

Finding a Teacher. W. S. Merwin. NNap

Finding gold, *A* left. Exchange. George Rostrevor Hamilton, *after* Plato. FaBoEE

Finding is the first act. Emily Dickinson. CABA (1972 ed.); NOBA; Psy

Finding no ghosts we must invent our own. Michael Smith. IPM

Finding Roots. Judith Minty. HeS

Finding Sky Ranch. William Stafford. CNW

Finding the Father. Robert Bly. BrS

Finding the hotel was not the real problem. The Peddler. Hollis Summers. CoPAm

Finding the Pistol. Gibbons Ruark. MAT

Finding Words in Winter. John Judson. HeS

Finding You. Virginia Gilbert. IHMS; NVAP

Fine! S. Omar Barker. BPAW

Fine bright moon and thousands of stars, A! Night Piece. Mark Strand. NYP

Fine Day, A. Michael Drayton. *Fr.* The Muses' Elizium. DuDr

Fine delight that fathers thought, The. To R. B. Gerard Manley Hopkins. CMoP (1970 ed.); OAEL-2; PoIA; VLP

Fine Excess, A. Dan Gerber. FoP

Fine Fechtin Mouse, The. Alexander Gray. MS

Fine feelings under blockade! Cargoes just in from Kamschatka! Winter Coming On. Martin Bell, *after* Jules Laforgue. OBVE; OxBTC

Fine fish to net. Ezra Pound, *after the Chinese.* OBVE

Fine Flowers in the Valley. *Unknown. See* Cruel Mother, The.

Fine Knacks for Ladies. *Unknown. See* Pedlar, A.

Fine Madam Would-Be, wherefore should you fear. To Fine Lady Would-Be. Ben Jonson. FaBoEE

Fine Old English Gentlemen, The; New Version. Charles Dickens. FaBoBa; OBSV

Fine rings of silver dangle. Mandy as Night Bouquet. Henry Kanabus. FiCh

Fine young folly, though you were. Pretty Sport. William Habington. NOBE

Fineness of midnight. Midnight. Gabriela Mistral, *tr. by* David Garrison. BoWoP

Finesse be first, whose elegance deplores. Six Poets in Search of a Lawyer. Donald Hall. SoSe

Finger Points to the Moon, A. R. D. Laing. Moon

Finger Spelling. Kraft Rompf. AAN

Fingers. Uhuru. Mari Evans. CNA

Finis. Waring Cuney. AmNP (1974 ed.)

Finished/ the eye swings like a light. Notes Scribbled on the Last Page of a Novel. Leslie Woolf Hedley. PoW

Finished at last, he escaped from that hideous. Christ's Descent into Hell. Rainer Maria Rilke, *tr. by* James Wright *and* Sarah Youngblood. Prf

Finisterra. Bayla Winters. AMV-81

Finnegans Wake, *sels.* James Joyce.
    Ballad of Persse O'Reilly, The. FaBoBa
    Ondt and the Gracehoper, The. BIrV

Finnegan's Wake. *Unknown.* FaBoBa; FSW

Fir-Tree of Bosnia, The. Dante Gabriel Rossetti. FaBoNo

Fire. Anita Barrows. RiTi

Fire, The. Robert Creeley. NOBA

Fire, The. Robert Duncan. *Fr.* Passages. VGW

Fire, The. Louise Glück. CAAP

Fire. Langston Hughes. NoAM; NOBA; PiAm

Fire. Jose Emilio Pacheco, *tr. fr. Spanish by* Frederick Luciani. AMV-81

Fire! *Unknown.* TDH

Fire./ That is their way of lighting candles in the darkness. Gwendolyn Brooks. *Fr.* The Third Sermon on the Warpland. TT

Fire and brimstone have been modified, The. Seventy. Margaret Reynolds. MIS

Fire and Ice. Robert Frost. AnMo; BiP; CABA (1972 ed.); CMoP (1970 ed.); FaBoEE; FaPo; FF; HeIP; HoPM (1975 ed.); ILP (1975 ed.); InPK; LoAs; MiP; NoAM; NOBA; PoIA; PPP; SoSe; STS; TAP; TT

Fire and Rain. James Taylor. WIF

Fire and sword cavort in her aging body. Cancer Patient. Jessica Powers. AMV-81

Fire and wild light of hope and doubt and fear. A Year's Burden [1870]. Swinburne. VLP

Fire at Alexandria, The. Theodore Weiss. NoAM; PoA; TAP

Fire burns down on winter nights, The. Dark Hope. Wade Hall. AATT

Fire Down Below. *Unknown.* FSW

Fire, fire. Song. Henry Bold. GBL

Fire! Fire! says the town crier. *Unknown.* GBP

Fire, Hair, Meat and Bone. Fred Johnson. PoBA

Fire I praise was once perduring flame, The. Allen Tate. *Fr.* Sonnets of the Blood. PoA

Fire in Enfield. Wesley McNair. FAF

Fire in leaf and grass, The. Living. Denise Levertov. VGW; WPE

Fire in My Meditation Burned, *with music.* Henry Ainsworth. AH

Fire Island. Rita Mae Brown. IHMS

Fire Island. May Swenson. PoA; TAP

Fire Island Poem. Diane Wakoski. BiP

Fire-Mass. Russell Grant. PMW

Fire of Despair Has Been Our Saviour, The. Robert Bly. CoPAm

Fire of Drift-Wood, The. Longfellow. NOBA; PiAm; TAP; VoPo

Fire of London. Dryden. *Fr.* Annus Mirabilis. SCP-1

Fire on the hearth is the woman's fire, The. Indian Song. Willard Johnson. BPAW

Fire on the Hills. Robinson Jeffers. CMoP (1970 ed.)

Fire-Queen. Ruth Fainlight. PoA

Fire runs faster than emus, rams. Staying Ahead. Malcolm Glass. AMV-81

Fire. 10/78. Bart Plantenga. AMV-80

Fire that cancels all that is. Burning Love Letters. Howard Moss. HoPM (1975 ed.)

Fire-Truck, A. Richard Wilbur. NCSH

Fire was first. Genealogy. Donald Finkel. VWA

Fire was furry as a bear, The. Dark Song. Edith Sitwell. CMoP (1970 ed.); FaBoTw (1975 ed.); PBWP

"Fire, water, woman, are man's ruin!" A Dutch Proverb. Matthew Prior. FaBoEE; LFH; POL

Firebird. Alta. MMD

Firebombing, The. James Dickey. CAPP

Firebowl. Sydney Clouts. VWA

Firebrand. Harry Crosby. EAS

Fired Pot, The. Anna Wickham. FaBoTw (1975 ed.); OxBTC

Fireflies. David McKain. AAN

Fireflies. Helena Minton. FAF

Firefly. Kamimura Hajime, *tr. fr. Japanese by* Harry *and* Lynn Guest *and* Kajima Shozo. TSWA

Firefly. Elizabeth Madox Roberts. LCL

Firefly, The. *Unknown, tr. fr. Italian.* RAE

Firefly light. Summer. Ramona Wilson. VoR

Firelight. E. A. Robinson. NoAM

Fireman enters, A. He entertains us. Grief. Sandra Hochman. NowV

Fireship, The. *Unknown.* FSW

Fireworks. Babette Deutsch. OFD

Fireworks. Valerie Worth. CC

Firm of Happiness, Limited, The. Norman Cameron. FaBoTw (1975 ed.)

Firmness. Anthony Hecht. OBAL

1st, The. Lucille Clifton. CAAP; InPS; TSWA

First/ a far thud. Fireworks. Valerie Worth. CC

First a monkey, then a man. Dawn of the Space Age. John Ciardi. OBAL

First and Last. Bruce Severy. VW

First Anniversary, The. John Donne. *See* Anatomy of the World, An.

First, are you our sort of a person? The Applicant. Sylvia Plath. MAT; NMM; NOBA; Psy; SBG; TPo; UsP

First Aspen, *sels.* Lynn Strongin.
    "Apology. Hands shaping air." RiTi
    "Sapphic Love! Sculptress of far more than stone." RiTi
    "Sensuous Latin poet, now I will go off with a thermos, A." IHMS; RiTi

First Autumn leaf: predictable, still, sad. Congers. Ronald Mann. PMW

First Blood. Jon Stallworthy. BoAnP; LiSp

First blow caught me sideways, my jaw, The. The Beating. Ann Stanford. MPA; WPE

First came the primrose. From a Calendar. Sydney Dobell. PCOP

First Camp. Greg Kuzma. NVAP

First Canzone of the Convito, The. Dante, *tr. fr. Italian by* Shelley. OBVE

First Carolina Said-Song. A. R. Ammons. OBAL

First clan of autumn, thistleball on a stem. Thistledown. James Merrill. UnPo (1976 ed.)

First-Class Relics: Letter to Dennis Finnell. Madeline DeFrees. PCho

First cocks begin clearing the throat of morning, The. A Valley Where I Don't Belong. Marge Piercy. IHMS

First cold front came in, The. Winter's Onset from an Alienated Point of View. Alan Dugan. FF

First Cold Night of Autumn. John Stupp. AMV-81

First come I. My name is Jowett. Henry Charles Beeching. *Fr.* Balliol Rhymes. FaBoCo; FaBoEE; NOBL; PoPle

First comes love and then comes marriage. Autograph Book/ Prophecy. Anne Halley. NMM

First Confession. X. J. Kennedy. ConAP; CoPAm; NCSH; NIL; PPP

First Corinthians, *sels.* Bible, *N.T.*
   "But some one will ask, 'How are the dead raised?' " XV:35-57. DL
   "Now I would remind you, brethren," XV:1-8. DL
   Though I Speak with the Tongues of Men and Angels, XIII: 1-13. BiP; OAEL-1; PBMP

First Corinthians at the Crossroads. Bruce Dawe. GAS

First corner, The, has become a/ bodega. The Four Corners. Victor Hernández Cruz. FoP

First country to die was normal in the evening, The. The Last War. Kingsley Amis. OBSV; SoSe (1977 ed.)

First Dance: God Who Walks like a Bear. Judith Johnson Sherwin. *Fr.* Three Power Dances. BCr

First Dandelions, *sel.* Robert Wallace.
   "Sun hangs, The/ medals." OSP

First Dandelions, The. Walt Whitman. PF

First Day, The. Howard Nemerov. AnMo

First Day, The. Christina Rossetti. *Fr.* Monna Innominata. BoLoP; OLR

First Day at School Michael Ivens. OxBTC

First day I shot dope, The. Summer Words of a Sistuh Addict. Sonia Sanchez. BPo; TV; UnPo (1976 ed.)

First day of Christmas my true love sent to me, The. The Twelve Days of Christmas. *Unknown.* AmFP; BBL; PChr

First Day of the Hunting Moon, The. Patricia Low. VGW

First-Day Thoughts. Whittier. AmVN; IPWM; PPoD

First Days. Tuvia Ruebner, *tr. fr. Hebrew by* A. C. Jacobs. VWA

First day's night had come, The. Emily Dickinson. Psy

First Death. Donald Justice. FiCP

First Death in Nova Scotia. Elizabeth Bishop. NCSH; NOBA

First draw the sea, that portion which between. Instructions to a Painter. Edmund Waller. APAS

First Drean, *sel.* Sister Juana Ines de la Cruz, *tr. fr. Spanish by* Samuel Beckett.
   "But Venus first." BoWoP

First Elegy, End of a Campaign. Hamish Henderson. *Fr.* Elegies for the Dead in Cyrenaica. MS

First Element. Margaret Atwood. MMD

First Enemy, The. Steven Goldsberry. PHC

First, The (entitled to the place). Charles Churchill. *Fr.* The Duellist. OBSV

First Epistle of the First Book of Horace Imitated, The, *sel.* Pope.
   "Well, if a King's a lion, at the least." OBSV

First Families Move Over! Ogden Nash. FaBoCo

First, feel, then feel, then. Young Soul. Amiri Baraka. BPo; CNA;TSWA

First Fig. Edna St. Vincent Millay. BBGO; FF; NoAM; PoA; TAP; TH

First Fight. Then Fiddle. Ply the Slipping String. Gwendolyn Brooks. InPK; NIL

First Flame. Samuel Daniel. *Fr.* Hymen's Triumph. VoPo

First follow Nature, and your judgment frame. Pope. *Fr.* An Essay on Criticism. HAP

First, for effusions due unto the dead. Upon His Sister-in-Law, Mistress Elizabeth Herrick. Robert Herrick. CaPo

First forget what time it is. Exercise. W. S. Merwin. NOBA

First Frost. E. Margaret Clarkson. AATT

First full moon of overgrown buffalo. America's Wounded Knee. Phillip William George. NW; VoR

First Generation, The. Janice Mirikitani. MIT

First, Goodbye. John Smith. MPo

First Goodbye Letter, The. James Simmons. AMV-81

First Grade. Phillip William George. VoR

First having read the book of myths. Diving into the Wreck. Adrienne Rich. NIL; NoAM; NOBA

First hear the story of Kaspar the rosy-cheeked. Fraulein Reads Instructive Rhymes. Maxine W. Kumin. SpRo

First Holes Are Fresh. Vivian Shipley. AMV-81

First hour was a word the color of dawn, The. Spring Morning—Sante Fe. Lynn Riggs. BPAW

First Hymn. John Gill. NeAC

First, I am *not* a clown. Not a Clown. Barry Schechter. FiCh

First, I put my. The Power of Love He Wants Shih (Everything). Rochelle Owens. NMM; Psy

First I saw the white bear, then I saw the black. At the Zoo. Thackeray. OxBChV

First Ice of Winter. Michael Shorb. AMV-81

First idea was not our own, The. Wallace Stevens. *Fr.* Notes toward a Supreme Fiction. NOBA

First I'll sing. Later, perhaps, I'll speak. The Condition. T. Carmi, *tr. by* Peter Everwine *and* Shula Starkman. VWA

First in his pride the orient sun's display. Hilaire Belloc. FaBoEE

First in the North. The black sea-tangle beaches. The Mythical Journey. Edwin Muir. ILP (1975 ed.); NoAM

First in the Pentathlon. Lucilius, *tr. fr. Greek by* Tom Dodge. LiSp

First Invasion of Ireland, The *Unknown, tr. fr. Irish by* John Montague. BIrV; ExPo (1973 ed.)

First Kiss of Love, The. Byron. MBPR

First lady of the throne room, The. The Restoration of Enheduanna to Her Former Station. Enheduanna, *tr. fr. Sumerian.* BoWoP

First Lawcase, The. *Unknown, tr. fr. Irish by* John Montague. BIrV

First Lay of Gudrun, The: Gudrun Laments over Sigurd.*Unknown, tr. fr. Old Norse by* William Morris *and* Eiriks Magnusson. *Fr.* The Elder Edda. OBVE

First Lecture. James Whitehead. CoPAm

First Lesson. Philip Booth. BiP; IPWM; LiSp;SFF

First, let me view what noxious nonsense reigns. Richard Savage. *Fr.* The Authors of the Town. OBSV

First Light. Thomas Kinsella. BIrV; CMoP (1970 ed.); ExPo (1973 ed.); NoAm

First light of day in Mississippi. Birthday Poem. Al Young. CSP

First Love. John Clare. BoLoP; GBL; HAP

First Love. "Hugh MacDiarmid." SLP

First Love. Edwin Rolfe. SPT

First Love. *Unknown, tr. fr. Latin by* George F. Whicher. OLR

First Love Poem, The. Myra Glazer Schotz. VWA

First Maccabees, *sel.* Bible, Apocrypha.
   "Then they took whole stones according to the law," IV: 47-59. OFD

First, make a letter like a monument. The Book of Kells. Padraic Colum. BIrV

First Meditation. Theodore Roethke. *Fr.* Meditations of an Old Woman. NOBA

First Menstruation. Ellen Bass. TV

First, Moloch, horrid king, besmeared with blood. Milton. *Fr.* Paradise Lost, I. IP

First Monday Scottsboro Alabama. Tom Weatherly. PoBA

First night when I came home, The. Our Goodman. *Unknown.* AmFP

First night when I come home, drunk as I could be, The. The Four Nights' Drunk. *Unknown.* OBAL

First Nowell [*or* Noel], The. *Unknown.* BLSH, *with music;* FSW; PChr

First of All. Kenneth O. Hanson. GP; MPA

"First of all, it's all true." The Creation: According to Coyote. Simon J. Ortiz. CDW

First of All My Dreams Was of, The. E. E. Cummings. VGW

First of April, some do say, The.  April Fool's Day.  *Unknown.*
CTV

First of God by whom all grace is spread.  Sources of Good
Counsel.  Peter Idley.  OxBChV

First of May, The.  A. E. Housman.  TT

First of the undecoded messages read: "Popeye sits in thunder."
Farm Implements and Rutabagas in a Landscape.  John
Ashbery.  GP

First official version said, The.  He Aint Risen, Baby, Cause He
Aint Gone Nowhere.  Horace Coleman.  SES

First One Drew Me, The.  Rav Abraham Isaac Kook, *tr. fr.
Hebrew by* Ben Zion Bokser.  VWA

First or Last.  Thomas Hardy.  CMoP (1970 ed.)

First Party at Ken Keseys with Hell's Angels.  Allen Ginsberg.
ConAP

First period, The: the epoch of thought.  The Six Periods of
Creation.  *Maori Oral Tradition, tr. by* Richard Taylor.
WTO

First Person Demonstrative.  Phyllis Gotlieb.  MiP

First person I loved, The.  Coming Out.  Jacqueline Lapidus.
IHMS

First Poem, The.  James Reiss.  CAAP

First Practice.  Gary Gildner.  AmPA; InPK; LiSp; PPoD

First Praise.  William Carlos Williams.  VGW

First Prayer.  Margaret Atwood.  MMD

First Precinct Fourth Ward.  Daniel Mark Epstein.  TAT

First Pregnancy.  Alta.  NMM

First Psalm, The.  Bertolt Brecht, *tr. fr. German by* Robert Bly.
NU

First Reader, The.  Winfield Townley Scott.  PoA

First Reading.  Tony Moreno.  NW

First real job I had [*or* got] was delivering drugs, The.  Getting
Experience.  Miller Williams.  CSP; GP; TAT

First Samuel, *sel.*  Bible, O.T.
Hannah's Thanksgiving, II: 1-10.  BoWoP

First Satan's Assault against Those That First Came Up to
Mercy's Terms.  Edward Taylor.  *Fr.* God's Determinations.
EAP

First Satire of the Second Book of Horace, The.  Pope.
OAEL-1; PPP
"There are (I scarce can think it, but I am told)," *sel.*  OBSV

First, scattering rain on the Polish cities, The.  1 September 1939.
John Berryman.  NIL

First Shaman Song.  Gary Snyder.  *Fr.* Myths and Texts:
Hunting, I.  NOBA

First shot out of that sling, The.  After Goliath.  Kingsley Amis.
NOBL; OxBTC

First Sight.  Philip Larkin.  NCSH; TSWA

First sign was your hair, The.  I'm Just a Stranger Here, Heaven
Is My Home.  Carole Gregory Clemmons.  PoBA

First Snow of the Year, The.  Mark Van Doren.  NCSH; TVo

First Snow on an Airfield.  John Ciardi.  PoA

First Snowfall, The.  James Russell Lowell.  TAP

First Solitude, The, *sels.*  Luis de Góngora, *tr. fr. Spanish by*
Edward Meryon Wilson.
River Compared to an Oratorical Sentence, The.  OBVE
Wedding Feast, The.  OBVE
Young Pilgrim Finds Refuge with the Goatherds, The.  OBVE

First Song.  Galway Kinnell.  BiP; CTBA; NCSH

First spasm became the continuous, The.  Recluse.  Aldo
Camerino, *tr. by* Anita Barrows.  VWA

First Star.  Dave Smith.  AMV-81

First Star.  *Unknown.*  ECBV

First star shot up, The.  Between Life and Death.  Frantisek
Gottlieb, *tr. by* Ewald Osers.  VWA

First Steps up Parnassus.  Michael Drayton.  *Fr.* To My Most
Dearly Loved Henry Reynolds.  NOBE

First Story.  Steven Orlen.  AAN

First, suicide notes should be.  Suicide.  Alice Walker.  FF

First temptation is to descend, The.  The True Song.  John
Montague.  IPM

First Test, The.  Susan Fromberg Schaeffer.  IHMS

First Thanksgiving.  Myra Cohn Livingston.  CC

First the canoe.  Portage Poem.  Louis Jenkins.  HeS

First, the dodo disappeared.  The Last Monster.  John Montague.
WIF

First the falls, then the cave.  Behind the Falls.  William Stafford.
RFM

First the heel.  Dance Steps [*or* Lachlan Gorach's Rhyme].
*Unknown.*  ECBV; PoPle

First the melody, clean and hard.  How High the Moon.  Lance
Jeffers.  CNA; PoBA

First the other rooms, then the one.  Privacy.  R. P. Dickey.
PoW

First the soul of our house left, up the chimney.  Tornado.
William Stafford.  AnMo

First, the two men stand pondering.  Verona.  James Wright.
NNaP

First their eyes.  Pulling Out.  Lyn Lifshin.  NeAC

First there is the student.  Ways of Loving.  Theodore Weiss.
GP

First there was nothing.  The White Shark: Notes for a History.
Kirtland Snyder.  AAN

First there was the lamb on knocking knees.  Altarwise by Owl-
Light, III.  Dylan Thomas.  CMoP (1970 ed.); Epi

First there were two of us, then there were three of us.  The
Storm.  Walter de la Mare.  EcS

First they stop speaking.  The Old Women.  Shirley G. Cochrane.
PoUp

First thing I saw in the morning, The.  Mantova.  James Wright.
NNaP

First Things First.  W. H. Auden.  UsP

"First thing to know is."  Who-Tapped-the-Frogs-In.  Samuel
Makidemewabe.  TC

First Time, The.  John Newlove.  NeAC

First Time, The.  Karl Shapiro.  VGW

First Time, The.  James L. White.  BrS

First time death struck her the criticism, The.  The Slabs of Her
Eyes.  Patricia Goedicke.  Psy

First Time Ever I Saw Your Face, The.  Ewan MacColl.  FSW

First time he kissed me, he but only kissed.  Sonnets from the
Portuguese, XXXVIII.  Elizabeth Barrett Browning.  LoAs

First time I ever saw a flying change.  Flying Changes.  Mary
Wood.  PH

First time I met the blues, mama they came walking through the
wood, The.  The First Time I Met You.  *Unknown.*  BluL

First Time I Met You, The.  *Unknown.*  BluL

First time I saw him, he rose, The.  The Morning of the Wolf.
Keith Wilson.  MPA

First time I saw Willa, The.  Willa.  John Haines.  CNW

First time I seen my true love.  Hard, Ain't It Hard.  *Unknown.*
FSW

First time that the sun rose on thine oath, The.  Sonnets from the
Portuguese, XXXII.  Elizabeth Barrrett Browning.  WPE

First to fight for the right.  The Army Goes Rolling Along.
Edmund L. Gruber *and* H. W. Arberg.  BLSH

First, to the feet, as they bear what you have grown to live in.
Praise.  William Matthews.  AmPA; NVAP

First Tooth, The.  Charles *and* Mary Lamb.  OxBChV

First, turn left at the Old Oraibi Bar.  How to Get to New
Mexico.  John Brandi.  TAT

First Vision, The, *sel.*  Tadhg Dall O'Huiginn, *tr. fr. Irish by* the
Earl of Longford.
"Vision of a Queen of Fairyland, A."  BIrV

First Walk in the Park. Ruth Herschberger. WBN

First was Eve. Cain's Song. Donald Finkel. VWA

First was Fancy, like a lovely boy, The. The Masque of Cupid. Spenser. *Fr.* The Faerie Queene, III, 12. NOBE

First Wedding in the World, The. Joel Rosenberg. VWA

First we saw of the high-tone tramp, The. Broncho versus Bicycle. John Wallace Crawford. BPAW

1st Week 5th Day. Joshua Sylvester. *Fr.* Du Bartas His Divine Weeks and Works. SCP-2

1st Week 6th Day. Joshua Sylvester. *Fr.* Du Bartas His Divine Weeks and Works. SCP-2

First week the soil was clean, The. Digging for Indians. Gary Gildner. AmPA

First whimper of the storm, The. A Local Storm. Donald Justice. NCSH

First white hair coils in my hand, The. Sign. Marge Piercy. Psy

First wife floats in memory calmly, The. A Memory. Marvin Bell. GP

First Winter Storm. William Everson. NU

First woman I loved, he said, The. Escapist's Song. Theodore Spencer. POL; SFF

First you bite your fingernails. American Rhapsody (4). Kenneth Fearing. MiP; PAIC; TPo

First, you get some leaves. How to Get a Garden. Andrew Roberts. EC

First, you think they are dead. Lobsters in the Window. W. D. Snodgrass. BiP; BoAnP; HeIP; NCSH; PiAm; TAP

First, you will say goodbye. You will turn. First, Goodbye. John Smith. MPo

Firstborn. Charles Wright. BrS

"Sugar dripping into your vein, The, *sel.* GP

Firstborn Land, The. Ingeborg Bachmann, *tr. fr. German by* Daniel Huws. BoWoP

Firste stok, fader of gentilesse, The. Gentilesse. Chaucer. OAEL-1

Firstling, The. Peter Davison. WeW

Fisbo, *sel.* Robert Nichols.

"Talking of Ezra Pound and long-dead pantos." OBSV

Fish. D. C. Berry. CSP

Fish, The. Elizabeth Bishop. CoPAm; HAP; HeIP; HoPM (1975 ed.); InPK; NoAM; NOBA; NU; WeW

Fish. Edward Gold. PoUp

Fish. Daniel Halpern. AmPA

Fish. Michael Hogan. DNGG; GP

Fish. Larry Levis. AmPA

Fish, The. Paul Mills. MIS

Fish, The. Marianne Moore. NoAM; PBMP; PiAm; UsP

Fish. Mario Satz, *tr. fr. Spanish by* Willis Barnstone. VWA

Fish. Shinkichi Takahashi, *tr. fr. Japanese by* Lucien Stryk. NU

Fish. William Carlos Williams. NoAM

Fish. Sandra Witt. AMV-80

Fish, The. L. L. Zeiger. TV

Fish/ fowl/ flood. Paean to Place. Lorine Niedecker. RiTi

Fish, The/ that fly. Seals. David R. Slavitt. CoPAm

Fish and Chips on the Merry-go-round. K. O. Arvidson. ATNZ

Fish and Swimmers and Lonely Birds Sweep Past Us. Mei Berssenbrugge. NW; SA

Fish and the Shadow. Ezra Pound. ExPo (1973 ed.)

Fish at Mass, The. *Unknown, tr. fr. Latin by* J. F. Webb. BIrV

Fish Does . . . Hip! The. Mba Sholé, *tr. fr. Gabon Pygmy.* AKE

Fish-Dream. Skaidrite Stelzer. TC

Fish (fly-replete, in depth of June). Heaven. Rupert Brooke. EBEV; ExPo (1973 ed.); HoPM (1975 ed.); LFH; NOBE; PoPle

Fish in the unruffled lakes. W. H. Auden. BoLoP; CMoP (1970 ed.); NoAm

Fish of the sea couldn't come. How They Brought the Good News by Sea. Norma Farber. PChr

Fish Peddler and Cobbler. Kenneth Rexroth. NNaP

Fish Replies, A. Leigh Hunt. *Fr.* The Fish, the Man, and the Spirit. NOBL

Fish Story. Richard Armour. LiSp; SPo

Fish Story. B. Jo Kinnick. AMV-81

Fish Story. Sharon Olds. TV

Fish, the Man, and the Spirit, The. Leigh Hunt. HAP
*Sels.*
Fish Replies, A. NOBL
Fish Turns into a Man, and Then into a Spirit, and Again Speaks, The. NOBL
To Fish [*or* a Fish]. EcS; NOBL

Fish Turns into a Man, and Then into a Spirit, and Again Speaks, The. Leigh Hunt. *Fr.* The Fish, the Man, and the Spirit. NOBL

Fish Will Swim as Before, The. Michael Spence. AMV-81

Fishbowl. Margaret Atwood. MMD

Fisherman. Philip Booth. LiSp; SPo

Fisherman, The. Abbie Farwell Brown. RhR

Fisherman, The. George Bruce. MS

Fisherman, The. Sam G. Harrison. AMV-80

Fisherman, The. Jay MacPherson. CABA (1972 ed.)

Fisherman. William Pitt Root. NVAP

Fisherman, The. Dabney Stuart. LiSp; NVAP; SPo

Fisherman, The. Will Wells. AMV-80

Fisherman, The. W. B. Yeats. BiP; CMoP (1970 ed.); HAP; LiSp; NoAM; PSN

Fisherman Casts His Line into the Sea, The. Robert Holland. AMV-80

Fisherman goes out at dawn, The. The Fisherman. Abbie Farwell Brown. RhR

Fisherman's Cross. Ian Hamilton Finlay. WeW

Fisherman's Song. *Unknown.* PoPle

Fisherman's swapping a yarn for a yarn, The. The Flower-Boat. Robert Frost. PoA

Fisherman's Wife, The. Amy Lowell. BoWoP

Fisherman's Wife, The. Nora Mitchell. AMV-80

Fisherman's Wife, The. David Wagoner. CNW

Fishermen. Basil Bunting. PoA

Fishermen. Gabriel Preil, *tr. fr. Hebrew by* Betsy Rosenberg. VWA

Fishermen, The. Theocritus, *tr. fr. Greek by* Charles Stuart Calverley. OBVE

Fishermen among the fireweed, The. By Rail through the Earthly Paradise, Perhaps Bedfordshire. Denise Levertov. NNaP

Fishermen at Ballyshannon. Limbo. Seamus Heaney. CIP; HeHu

Fishermen return with waterstars. Evening. Tristan Tzara, *tr. by* Willis Barnstone *and* Matei Calinescu. VWA

Fishermen say, when your catch is done, The. The Sea Wolf. Violet McDougal. EcS

Fishermen's Wives, The. Elaine Namanworth. AMV-80

Fisher's Life, The. *Unknown.* GBP; RhR

Fishes, The. *Unknown.* GBP

Fishes and the Poet's Hands, The. Frank Yerby. AmNP (1974 ed.)

Fishin' Blues. Valentino Ramirez. AMV-81

Fishing alone in a frail boat. Walking Out. Betty Adcock. CSP

Fishing at Sunrise. Peggy Simson Curry. WPW

Fishing Blues. *Unknown.* BluL

Fishing boats have returned, The! Three Poems. "Ping Hsin." PBWP

Fishing Boats in Martigues. Roy Campbell. FaBoEE

Fishing Harbour towards Evening. Richard Kell. CIP; LP; MPo

Fishing Pole, The ("A fishing pole's a curious thing"). Mary Carolyn Davies. CTV

Fishing Song. *Maori Oral Tradition, tr. by* A. Armstrong *and* R. Ngta. WTO

Fishing with My Daughter in Miller's Meadow. Lucien Stryk. GP

Fishmarket closed, the fishes gone into flesh, The. Galway Kinnell. *Fr.* The Avenue Bearing the Initial of Christ into the New World. ConAP

Fishy Square Dance, A. Eve Merriam. ECBV

Fisk is/ a/ negroid/ institution. Sharon Scott. JB

Fist appears in your fist, A. Sabbath. John Harris. PoW

Fisted, bitten by blizzards. Lava Bed. William Everson. PiAm

Fists. Joseph Hansen. PoW

Fit of Rime against Rime, A. Ben Jonson. MAT; OAEL–1; PAIC

Fitly so named since it doth waste. *Unknown.* SCP-2

Fitting, The. Edna St. Vincent Millay. LoAs

Fitting the labels. Cadaver. John Stone. CoPAm

Fitz Hugh Lane Goes to the Masthead. Wesley McNair. FAF

Fitzroy, Carlton. Vincent Buckley. *Fr.* Golden Builders. CAAP

5. E. E. Cummings. TT

Five. Weldon Kees. PPP

Five, The. Swift. ECBV

5/ derbies-with-men-in-them smoke Helmar. 5. E. E. Cummings. TT

Five A.M. on East Fourteenth I'm out to eat. Sonnet. Tom Clark. Epi

Five Bells. Kenneth Slessor. GAS; MAuV

.05. Ishmael Reed. InPK

Five Days Old. Francis Webb. MAuV

Five dollars, four dollars, three dollars, two. An Inheritance. Naomi Replansky. GP

Five Dreams, The. John Woods. FiCP; TC

Five Eyes. Walter de la Mare. DuDr; PCat

515 Madison Avenue. Rhapsody. Frank O'Hara. NoAM; NYP

5/5/75. Darlene Pearlstein. FiCh

Five for the Grace of Man. Winfield Townley Scott. VGW

5.40. The Bay View. After the office. Aberdarcy: The Chaucer Road. Kingsley Amis. *Fr.* The Evans Country. NOBL

Five Groups of Verse, *sels.* Charles Reznikoff.
  "After I had worked all day at what I earn my living." SA
  Citizen, A, 29. SA
  Ghetto Funeral, 17. SA
  "God saw Adam in a town." SA
  "How difficult for me is Hebrew." SA
  "How shall we mourn you who are killed and wasted." SA
  Samuel. SA
  "Showing a torn sleeve, with stiff and shaking fingers the old man." SA

Five Hens, The. *Unknown.* GBP

Five Horses. May Swenson. PH

Five hours (and who can do it less in?). The Lady's Dressing Room. Swift. AnMo

Five Interior Landscapes. Olga Broumas. CNW

Five jolly rogues of a feather. Johnson's Ale. *Unknown.* FSW

Five Joys, The. *Unknown.* OxBM

Five little monkeys. The Monkeys and the Crocodile. Laura E. Richards. CTV

Five Little Squirrels. *Unknown.* CTV

Five Men against the Theme "My Name Is Red Hot. Yo Name Ain Doodley Squat." Gwendolyn Brooks. CNA

Five Men I Know. Thomas Lux. NVAP

Five-Minute Orlando MacBeth, The. George MacBeth. NOBL

Five Minutes, Oleo. H. H. Lewis. SPT

Five Minutes after the Air Raid. Miroslav Holub, *tr. fr. Czech by* Ian Milner *and* George Theiner. BuTh

Five months after your death, I come like the others. Elegy for a Forest Clear-cut by the Weyerhaeuser Company. David Wagoner. CNW

Five o'clock closes in on another Sunday. View of Vienna from Schonbrunn. Peggy Ruse. NPW

Five o'clock in February. The Prodigal Thinks of His Mother. James Simmons. IPM

Five oxen, grazing in a flow'ry mead. On a Seal. Plato, *tr. by* Thomas Stanley. FaBoEE

Five-past-six of a November dawn. Variations on a Baedecker. Stanley Burnshaw. SPT

Five Poems about Poetry, *sels.* George Oppen.
  From Virgil. NNaP
  Gesture, The. NNaP

Five Psalms of Common Man. Christopher Middleton. TwMBP

Five Reasons, The. Henry Aldrich. FaBoCo
  ("If all be true that I do think.") FaBoEE; FF

Five rings each of five rings. On Flying into Washington over the Pentagon. Alan Austin. PoUp

Five Sense. Marvin Wyche, Jr. AmNP (1974 ed.)

Five soldiers fixed by Mathew Brady's eye. Looking into History. Richard Wilbur. VGW

Five Students, The. Thomas Hardy. CMoP (1970 ed.); ExPo (1973 ed.)

Five summer days, five summer nights. The Blue-Fly. Robert Graves. CMoP (1970 ed.); ILP (1975 ed.); NoAM

Five Things White. Edward May. FaBoEE

5:30. Gray Jacobik. PoUp

5:30 A.M. Adrienne Rich. NMM; NOBA; PiAm; TT

5/30/75. Darlene Pearlstein. FiCh

5:32, The. Phyllis McGinley. *Fr.* I Know a Village. NMM; WPE

Five times a day is what he really likes. A Young Lover. Elizabeth Sargent. WBN

Five times I howled. To a Captain in Sinai. Ada Aharoni. AMV–81

Five Toes. *Unknown.* BBL

527 Cathedral Parkway. Rika Lesser. NYP

5/2/75. Darlene Pearlstein. FiCh

Five Unmistakable Marks, The. David Jones. In Parenthesis, VII. NoAM

Five Vignettes. Jean Toomer. PoBA

Five Ways to Kill a Man. Edwin Brock. DL; IPWM; SFF; TPo; TSWA

Five Were Foolish, *with music.* Arthur J. Hodge. AH

Five years. Anniversary. Philip Dacey. AAN; HeS

Five years after Pastorius had written. Clausa Germanis Gallia. Millen Brand. GP

Five years ago we knew such ecstasies. Interim. Frank Ormsby. CIP

Five years have passed; five summers, with the length. Lines Composed [*or* Written] a Few Miles above Tintern Abbey. Wordsworth. AnMo; BiP; CABA (1972 ed.); ExPo (1973 ed.); FF; HAP; HeIP; ILP (1975 ed.); InPS; IPWM; LFH; MBPR; NIL; OAEL–2; PES; PPP; VoPo

Five years since you died and I am. Letter to a Dead Father. Richard Shelton. BrS; GP

Fivesucked the features of my girl by glory. Nicholas Moore. PoA

Fix me on some bleak precipice. William Habington. *Fr.* Quoniam Ego in Flagella Paratus Sum. David. SCP-2

Fixer of Midnight. Reuel Denney. OBAL

Fixing to Die. *Unknown.* BluL

Fixture, A. May Swenson. RiTi

Flag. Reg Saner. GP

Flag, The/ is folded. The Lowering. May Swenson. TCP

Flag Goes By, The. Henry Holcomb Bennett. BTTM

Flagon in the backyard, A. March Fugue. Thomas Shapcott. CAAP

Flags. Gwendolyn Brooks. AmNP (1974 ed.)

Flags of autumn are mutinous as the tide, The. A Red Dawn in the East. Norman Macleod. SPT

Flame burns in the morning, A. Le Chariot. John Wieners. VGW

Flame-Flower, Day-torch, Mauna Lao. Lines to a Nasturtium (A Lover Muses). Anne Spencer. AmNP (1974 ed.)

Flame-Heart. Claude McKay. AmNP (1974 ed.); ILP (1975 ed.)

Flame of a Candle, The. Howard Nemerov. AnMo

Flame Tree, *sel.* K. O. Arvidson.
  "You might at one time, when you were young perhaps." ATNZ

Flames rising up, The. Dawn. David Shevin. VWA

Flaming Heart, The, *sels.* Richard Crashaw.
  "O Heart! the equal poise of love's both parts." OBP
  "O thou undaunted daughter of desires!" BoReV; HAP
    (Upon the Book and Picture of the Seraphical Saint Teresa.) NOBE
  "Well-meaning readers, you that come as friends." OAEL-1

Flamingos/ with a one leg stance. Catalysis. Ann Menebroker. CPA

Flammonde. E. A. Robinson. CMoP (1970 ed.); NoAM; STS

Flanagan got up on a Saturday morning. Lament for Barney Flanagan. James K. Baxter. ATNZ

Flannan Isle. W. W. Gibson. PoTa

Flannery O'Connor. Dorothy Walters. IHMS

Flashlight. Judith Thurman. FPB

Flashlight, A. Brain. Coleman Barks. *Fr.* Body Poems. NVAP

Flat on the bank I parted. The Trout. John Montague. BoAnP; PFIr; SFF

Flat One, A. W. D. Snodgrass. CAPP

Flat stems of cloud feathering their roots in air. A Cruise for the Prosecution. Rodney Hall. FPA

Flathead and Nez Perce Sin-ka-ha. William S. Lewis. BPAW

Flattered Flying Fish, The. E. V. Rieu. SO

Flattered Lightning Bug, The. Don Marquis. PoTa

Flaubert wanted to write a novel. Style. Howard Nemerov. NoAM

Flavia's a name a deal too free. *Unknown.* FaBoEE

Flavio Gonzales, 72, made jackhammer. The Moon Is a Diamond. Arthur Sze. AMV-81

Flavour the days, tobacco. Tobacco. Robert Harris. CAAP; GAS

Flaw in Paganism, The. Dorothy Parker. PoIA

Flax-pods unload their pollen. At Taieri Mouth. James K. Baxter. ATNZ

Flea, The. John Donne. AnMo; BiP; BoLoP; CABA (1972 ed.); EBEV; FF; HoPM (1975 ed.); ILP (1975 ed.); LFH; MAT; NIL; OAEL-1; PAIC; PoPle;PPoe; SCP-1; SoSe (1977 ed.); TT

Flea and the Fly, The ("A flea and a fly in a flue"). *Unknown.* ECBV
  (Flea and a Fly in a Flue, A.) CTV

Fleadh. Michael Longley. CIP

Fleas, The. Augustus De Morgan. FaBoCo

Fleche. Larry Eigner. VGW

Fled are the frosts, and now the fields appear. Farewell Frost; or, Welcome the Spring. Robert Herrick. CaPo

Flee from the press [*or* fro the prees], and dwell with soothfastness. Truth. Chaucer. BoReV; OAEL-1; OxBM

Fleeing from threatened flood, they sailed. The First Invasion of Ireland. *Unknown, tr. by* John Montague. BIrV; ExPo (1973 ed.)

Fleet ships encountering on the high seas. Good Ships. John Crowe Ransom. WeW

Fleeting birds may soon in ocean swim, The. To Miss Laetitia Van Lewen. Constantia Grierson. WPE

Fleeting pomps of the world are like the green willow trees, The. Song of Nezahualcoyotl. *Unknown.* DL

Fleeting Return. Juan Ramon Jimenez, *ad. fr.* Spanish by William Moritz. AMV-80

Flesh-and-blood does not wear pain. Thoughts on Pain. Sallie Chesham. AATT

Flesh and the Spirit, The. Anne Bradstreet. NOBA; TAP

Flesh-Fly and the Bee, The. Coventry Patmore. FaBoEE

Flesh is sad alas, The! and all books I have read. Sea Breeze. Stéphane Mallarmé, *tr. by* Roger Fry. NAWM-2

Flicker, The. Lew Blockcolski. VoR

Flie lowe deare love, thy sunne dost thou not see? Henry Constable. *Fr.* Diana. ESo

Flies in the buttermilk, skip to my Lou. Skip to My Lou. *Unknown.* ECBV

Flies Love Me. Nuala Archer. AMV-81

Flight. Pamela Alexander. AAN

Flight. Stuart Dybek. TC

Flight, The. John Haines. EAS

Flight. Mary Shumway. HeS

Flight. James Tate. InPK; UsP

Flight. Ruth Whitman. SO

Flight in the Desert, The. William Everson. VGW

Flight is but the Praeparative. The Vision. Thomas Traherne. ILwL

Flight is the bird's value. Aesthetic. Norman Rosten. PoA

Flight of Apollo, The. Stanley Kunitz. Moon

Flight of Birds, The. John Clare. PCOP

Flight of Swans. Robinson Jeffers. MPA

Flight of the Duchess, The. Robert Browning. VLP

Flight of the Earls, The, 1607, *sel.* Fearghal Og MacWard, *tr. fr. Irish by* the Earl of Longford.
  "All Ireland's now one vessel's company." BIrV

Flight of the Roller Coaster. Raymond Souster. PoTa; SO

Flight of Wild Geese, A. Harold Stewart. GAS
  "Down the sky in file the wild geese tack,"*sel.* MAuV

Flight on Naked Wings. Melvin Dixon. NW

Flight songs the way they build their nests. The Burning of the Birds. Shirley Kaufman. GP

Flight 382. Doris Longman. AMV-81

Flight to Italy, *sel.* C. Day Lewis.
  "Winged bull trundles to the wired perimeter, The." OxBTC

Flights. Roger McDonald. CAAP

Flighty Poem. John Pauker. PoUp

Fling Out the Banner! *with music.* George Washington Doane. AH

Fling this useless book away. Written in a Lady's Prayer Book. Earl of Rochester. BoLoP

Flint. Christina Rossetti. OxBChV

Flint Hills, The. Lew Blockcolski. VoR

Flip, clack! The windscreen wipers clear. Seven Rainy Months. William Plomer. OxBTC

Flirtation, The. Michael C. Blumenthal. AMV-81

Flitcraft's Woods. Warren Woessner. HeS

Float up again. Celan. Asya, *tr. by* Gabriel Preil *and* Howard Schwartz. VWA

Floating across the lake. Not Thinking of America. Judith Kroll. AmPA

Floating Bridge. *Unknown.* BluL

Floating Coathangers. Peter Cooley. NVAP

Floating off to Timor. Edwin Morgan. SLP

Floating the Ghost River. Tom McKeown. TC

Floating thru chairs. Nice. Lyn Lifshin. Psy

Floating World Picture: Spring in the Kitagami Mountains. Gary Snyder. ExPo (1973 ed.)

"Flocculations of cirrus hang" morose. To Myself. Art Lange. FiCh

Flock. Lance Henson. VoR

Flock of birds, soaring, twisting, turning, A. Love Is. Ann Darr. MiP; OSP

Flock of birds takes shape, The. A Poem to My Notebook, across Winter. Primus St. John. MPA

Flock of scarlet birds, A. The Ocotillo in Bloom. Marilla Merrimar Guild. BPAW

Flock of winds came winging from the North, A. The Roaring Frost. Alice Meynell. WPE

Flood, The. Ewa Lipska, *tr. fr. Polish by* Peter Jay *and* Geri Lipschultz. VWA

Flood. Roger McGough. FF

Flood, The. Lev Mak, *tr. fr. Russian by* Neil Muhlberger *and* Marvin Misemer. VWA

Flood didn't save me, The. The Flood. Ewa Lipska, *tr. by* Peter Jay *and* Geri Lipschultz. VWA

Flood Disaster in Gallup, New Mexico. Linda Parker. TC

Floodtide. Askia Muhammad Touré. PoBA

Flood-tide below me! I see you face to face! Crossing Brooklyn Ferry. Walt Whitman. CABA (1972 ed.); NOBA; NoAM; NYP; PiAm; TAP

Flooding with a brilliant mist. To the Moon. Goethe, *tr. by* John Frederick Nims. Moon

Floods, by nature enemies to land, The. Ovid, *tr. by* Dryden. *Fr.* Metamorphoses, I. OBVE

Floods of men. All the Spirit Powers Went to Their Dancing Place. Gary Snyder. UnPo (1976 ed.)

Floods Swell around Me, Angry, Appalling, *with music.* Zachary Eddy. AH

Floor: Five. Stephen Vincent. *Fr.* Elevator Landscapes. NeAC

Floor: O. Stephen Vincent. *Fr.* Elevator Landscapes. NeAC

Flora. Ray Fraser. NeAC

Floral Tribute. Sir Charles Jeffries. PoPle

Florella; or, The Jealous Lover. *Unknown.* AmFP

Florence below was an abyss of lights of trembling sordidness. Night Character. Dino Campana, *tr. by* Frank Stewart. AMV-81

Florida. Carl Rakosi. TAP

Florida Road Workers. Langston Hughes. CTBA; SFF; SoS

Florio, one ev'ning, brisk, and gay. Epigram on Florio. John Winstanley. FaBoEE

Floris and Blauncheflour, *sel. Unknown.*
Lover's Stratagem, A. OxBM

Florist was told, cyclamen or azalea, The. Lines to Accompany Flowers for Eve. Carolyn Kizer. BoWoP

Flotsam and Jetsam. E. E. Cummings. NOBA; OBAL

Flourishing Village, The. Timothy Dwight. Greenfield Hill, Pt. II. EAP

Flow at Full Moon. R. A. K. Mason. ATNZ

Flow Gently, Sweet Afton. Burns. *See* Afton Water.

Flow of Them All, The. Vicki Viidikas. FPA

Flower, The. Robert Creeley. CAPP

Flower, The. George Herbert. BoReV; MetP; NIL; NOBE; PPP; SCP-1

Flower. Peter Schjeldahl. CAAP

Flower, The/ fallen. The Loving Dexterity. William Carlos Williams. TH

Flower and the Leaf, The, *sel.* Lady of the Arbour. "And at the last I cast my mine eye aside." WPE

Flower-Boat, The. Robert Frost. PoA

Flower Dump. Theodore Roethke. PiAm

Flower Ensnarer of Psalms. Rossana Ombres, *tr. fr. Italian by* I. L. Salomon. BoWoP

Flower-fed Buffaloes, The. Vachel Lindsay. BPAW; CMoP (1970 ed); ExPo (1973 ed.); NOBA; PCOP; RFM; UsP; VGW

Flower Given to My Daughter, A. James Joyce. RRA

Flower Herding on Mount Monadnock. Galway Kinnell. HeIP; NOBA
(Flower Herding Pictures on Mount Monadnock.) ConAP

Flower—I never fancied, jewel—I profess you! Magical Nature. Robert Browning. VLP

Flower in the Crannied Wall. Tennyson. CTV; InPK; IPWM; LFH; PBMP; PCOP; PF; VoPo

Flower of the flock. On Sweet Killen Hill. Tom MacIntyre. CIP; NCSH

Flower of the race, The. Gentlemen. Geoffrey Taylor. FaBoEE

Flower of waves, A. Lady Ise, *tr. fr. Japanese by* Etsuko Terasaki *and* Irma Brandeis. BoWoP

Flower Piece. Swinburne. PCOP

Flower, that foretell'st a Spring thou ne'er shalt see. The Aconite. Thomas Noel. PF

Flower that smiles to-day, The. Mutability. Shelley. MBPR

Flower was offered to me, A. My Pretty Rose Tree. Blake. *Fr.* Songs of Experience. BoLoP; LAuP; MBPR

Flowering Bars, The. Charles Donnelly. CIP

Flowering Cacti, The. Gene Fowler. CPA

Flowering jungle, where all fauna meet. Commercial Bank. A. M. Klein. BBGO

Flowering Light of the Godhead, The, *sel.* Mechtild of Magdeburg, *tr. fr. German.*
"Ah dearest Love, for how long." ILwL

Flowering of the Rod, The, *sel.* Hilda Doolittle ("H. D."). "Blue-geese, white-geese, you may say." NOBA

Flowering Plum. Louise Glück. CAAP

Flowerpot Is an Ashtray, A. Cinda Kornblum. AcAn

Flowers. W. H. Davies. PF

Flowers. Kathleen Fraser. TV

Flowers. *Gond Oral Tradition, tr. by* V. Elwin *and* S. Hivale. WTO

Flowers always know what they should do. Jessie Orton Jones. Secrets, VI. CTV

Flowers and Men. D. H. Lawrence. FaBoEE

Flowers are beautiful: This opinion. Flower. Peter Schjeldahl. CAAP

Flowers are dead, The. Scenery. Ted Joans. PoBA

Flowers by the Sea. William Carlos Williams. CMoP (1970 ed.); ExPo (1973 ed.); NoAM; TAP

Flowers for a Funeral. Milton. *Fr.* Lycidas. PF

Flowers for the Grangerford Girl. William Harrold. HeS

Flowers have fenced-in. The Clearing. Peter Everwine, *after the Nahuatl.* NNaP

Flowers in Cellars. Conleth Ellis. IPM

Flowers in the Valley. *Unknown.* ECBV; OLR

Flowers in Winter. William Cowper. *Fr.* The Task, VI. PF

Flowers left thick at nightfall in the wood, The. In Memoriam (Easter, 1915). Edward Thomas. NOBE; OBW; OxBTC

Flowers of Darkness. Frank Marshall Davis. AmNP (1974 ed.); PoBA

Flowers of January. Wordsworth. PF

Flowers of mist and silence. Yucca in the Moonlight. Glen Ward Dresbach. BPAW

Flowers of the Forest, The; or, The Battle of Flodden. Jane Elliot. BTTM; SLP; WPE (Lament for Flodden A.) PoPle

Flowers of the willow-herb are wool. Seed-Time. George Meredith. FSFS

Flowers That Bloom in the Spring, The, *with music.* William S. Gilbert. *Fr.* The Mikado. BLSo

Flowers that fringed the waves, The. Under the Moon. George Bruce. MS

Flowers that in thy garden rise, The. Song. Sir Henry Newbolt. FaBoTw (1975 ed.)

Flowers through the window. Nantucket. William Carlos Williams. HAP; TAP; WeW

Floyd has died and few have sobb'd. Epitaph on Floyd. *Unknown.* POL

Flukum couldn't stand the strain. 2 Poems for Black Relocation Centers. Etheridge Knight. NNaP; NoAM

Flush and burn, your fever rose all night. Morning Song. Leon Stokesbury. AMV–80

Flush with the pond the lurid furnace burn'd. The Steam Threshing-Machine. Charles Tennyson Turner. VPC

Flute Girl. Roderick Hunt. FPB

Flute Player. *Gond Oral Tradition, tr. by* V. Elwin *and* S. Hivale. WTO

Flute Song: "Hail, fathers, hail!" *Tr. fr. Hopi Indian by* Natalie Curtis. WTO

Flutes, and the harp on the plain. Home on the Range, February 1962. Edward Dorn. ConAP

Flux. Richard Eberhart. CoPAm; VGW

Fly, The. Philip Ayres, *after the Spanish of* Quevedo. OBVE

Fly, The. Blake. *Fr.* Songs of Experience. LAuP; MBPR; OBP; PBMP; PCOP

Fly, The. Walter de la Mare. PoPle

Fly. W. S. Merwin. CoPAm; NNaP

Fly, The. William Oldys. PAIC

Fly, The. Karl Shapiro. CoPAm; NoAM; NowV; PBMP; PoIA

Fly, A/ sits and/ scrubs his front feet. Mosca. Paul Blackburn. VoA

Fly about a Glass of Burnt Claret, A. Richard Lovelace. CaPo

Fly Around My Blue-eyed Gal. *Unknown.* FSW

Fly away, fly away over the sea. The Swallow. Christina Rossetti. PCOP

Fly-away Horse, The. Eugene Field. PCOP

Fly Caught in a Cobweb, A. Richard Lovelace. CaPo

Fly, envious Time, till thou run out thy race. On Time. Milton. BoReV; CABA (1972 ed.)

Fly, fly, my friends, I have my death wound; fly. Astrophel and Stella, XX. Sir Philip Sidney. Epi; OAEL–1

Fly flying away. Concentration. Sheila Heldenbrand. AcAn

Fly hence those siren charms of wealth and pow'r. Naboth's Vineyard. John Caryll. APAS

Fly is dying hard, The. Mayday. Ed Roberson. PoBA

Fly, Ladybug. Annette Burr Stowman. AMV–80

Fly on the Water, A. Paul Zweig. PCho

Fly That Flew into My Mistress's Eye, A. Thomas Carew. CaPo

Fly[e] to her heart; hover about her heart. Bartholomew Griffin. *Fr.* Fidessa, more Chaste than Kind, XXIII. AAS; LoAs

Fly to the desert, fly with me. Thomas Moore. *Fr.* Lalla Rookh. BIrV

Fly, white butterflies, out to sea. Envoi. Swinburne. PCOP; VLP

"Fly with me then to all's and the world's end." The World's End. William Empson. ILP (1975 ed.)

Flye to her heart, hover about her heart. *See* Fly to her heart . . .

Flyer's Fall. Wallace Stevens. CABA (1972 ed.)

Flying. Henry Carlile. AMV–80

Flying. J. M. Westrup. FPB

Flying Change, The. Henry Taylor. CSP

Flying Changes. Mary Wood. PH

*Flying Cloud*, The. *Unknown.* AmFP

Flying Crooked. Robert Graves. UsP

Flying Crow. *Unknown.* BluL

Flying Dutchman, The. E. A. Robinson. PiAm

Flying Fox. Thomas W. Shapcott. FPA

Flying Home from Utah. May Swenson. MPA; WPE

Flying Horse was in jail. The Urban Experience: Part Two. Lew Blockcolski. VoR

Flying Letters. Zerubavel Gilead, *tr. fr. Hebrew by* Dorothea Krook. VWA

Flying Scrolls, *sels.* Ralph Hodgson. FaBoTw (1975 ed.) "Dust thou Art, but dust carefully." Movement, she explained, would bring poetry to the rich, The."

Flying Trapeze, The. George Leybourne. *See* Man on the Flying Trapeze, The.

Foal. Mary Britton Miller. PH

Foal. Vernon Watkins. OxBTC

Foaming white wave washes over a grave, A. Exultation. Hywel ab Owain Gwynedd, *tr. by* Gwyn Williams. OBW

Focus. Kathleen Norris. GP

Focus. Adrienne Rich. PiAm

Fod. *Unknown.* AmFP

Fodder for the TV cameras. Deported. John Ennis. IPM

Foetal Song. Joyce Carol Oates. IHMS

Fog ("The fog comes/ on little cat feet"). Carl Sandburg. CTV; HeIP; ILP (1975 ed.); InPK; PiAm; RAE; SoSe; TAP

Fog and snow for New Year's greeting. Rhyming Prophecy for a New Year. Leonard Cooper. FaBoCo

Fog Dream, The. Sandra M. Gilbert. PoA

Fog 9/76. Richard Morris Dey. AMV–80

Fog over the base: the beams ranging. A Front. Randall Jarrell. VGW

Fog settles over us, The. Prairie Schooner Poem. Glenna Luschei. CPA

Foggy bottom night, A. Folsom. Ben Hiatt. CPA

Foggy, Foggy Dew, The. *Unknown.* BLSH, *with music;* FSW; GBP; GSB, *with music;* RDB, *with music* (Foggy Dew, The, *diff. vers.*) FSW; PeBB

Foggy Mountain Top. *Unknown.* FSW

Fog-Horn. W. S. Merwin. TCP; TSWA

Fog-horns bellow across the fields of fog, The. Odalisque. Brian Coffey. CIP

Fogless morning but black. Early Morning Song: The Snowstorm. Gloria Bussel Koster. NPW

Fold of my flesh. Sleep Close to Me. Gabriela Mistral, *tr by* D. M. Pettinella. PBWP

Fold those waves away. Fado. Edwin Morgan. MS

Folded Skyscraper, A, *sel.* William Carlos Williams. Hemmed-in Males. MAT

Folding Fan, The. Grey Cohoe. VW

Folding the Panties. Ronald Koertge. AAN

Foliage of light begins to wither, The. The Falling Sickness. Evan Jones. GAS

Foliage of Vision. James Merrill. VGW

Folk group chopped its last note clean, The. Spring Revue. Charlotte Mortimer. NowV

Folk Poet. James Steele. SES

Folk remedy, A. Skull. Coleman Barks. *Fr.* Body Poems. NVAP

Folk Tune. Esther Raab, *tr. fr. Hebrew by* Robert Friend *and* Shimon Sandbank. VWA

Folk Tune. Richard Wilbur. AIW

Folks, I'm telling you. Advice. Langston Hughes. ILP (1975 ed.)

Folks, sex has never been. God Is a Masturbator. Gregory Corso. GP

Folks stopped by our place yestiddy 'bout dinner. All Things Being Equal. J. Lee Humphrey. AMV–81

Follow. Roland Flint. PoUp

Follow a shadow, it still flies you. That Women Are but Men's Shadows [*or* The Shadow]. Ben Jonson. InPS; NOBE

Follow me, follow me, follow and find me! Night Riddle. *Unknown.* ECBV

Follow my Bangelory Man. My Bangelory Man. *Unknown.* ECBV

Follow the Drinkin' Gourd. *Unknown.* WIF

Follow Thy Fair Sun [Unhappy Shadow]. Thomas Campion. NOBE; UnPo (1976 ed.)
(Followe Thy Faire Sunne.) AAS; Prf
(Song: "Follow thy fair sun, unhappy shadow.") PoPle

Follow your saint, follow with accents sweet. Devotion. Thomas Campion. AAS; EBEV; HAP; NOBE; OAEL–1

Followe Thy Faire Sunne. Thomas Campion. *See* Follow Thy Fair Sun.

Followed by his lodge, shabby men stumbling over the cobblestones. Ghetto Funeral. Charles Reznikoff. *Fr.* Five Groups of Verse. SA

Follower. Michael Arvey. AMV–80

Follower. Seamus Heaney. HeHu; ILP; LP; PFIr

Following. William Stafford. BCr

Follows this a narrower bed. Bridal Couch. Donald J. Lloyd. NIL

Folly and error, avarice and vice. To the Reader. Baudelaire, *tr. by* Roy Campbell. GrRo

Folly of Being Comforted, The. W. B. Yeats. GBL; HeIP; LoAs; SoSe; VLP

Folsom. Ben Hiatt. CPA

Folsom, August 11th: A Question of Races. Pancho Aguila. CPA

Fond man, that canst believe her blood. Celia Bleeding: To the Surgeon. Thomas Carew. PeD; SCP–2

Fond woman, which would'st have thy husband die. Jealousy. John Donne. Elegies, I. FF

Fondle me. Marrow of My Bone. Mari E. Evans. BPo

"Fondling," she saith, "since I have hemmed thee here." Shakespeare. *Fr.* Venus and Adonis. OAEL–1

Font, The. Clive Sansom. BuTh

Food drops off a fork, The. Michael Silverton. POL

Food for a Cat. David Starr Jordan. TDH

Food of the North. D. H. Lawrence. FaBoEE

Food Strike. Michael Hogan. GP

Fool much bit by fleas put out the light, A. Richard Lovelace, *after the Greek of* Lucian. FaBoEE

Fool on the Hill, The. John Lennon *and* Paul McCartney. GrRo; PPoe

Fool once caught a crow, A. The Crow. James Reaney. AKE

Fool, to put up four crosses at your door. Swift. FaBoEE

Fooled me once and you fooled me bad. All Night Long Fooling Me. *Unknown.* AmFP

Foolish Boy, The. *Unknown.* RAE

Foolish Flowers. Rupert Sargent Holland. CTV

Foolish impatient apricot trees. Vegetable Destiny. Nina Cassina, *tr. by* Michael Impey *and* Brian Swann. PBWP

Foolish men who accuse. She Proves the Inconsistency of the Desires and Criticism of Men Who Accuse Women of What They Themselves Cause. Sister Juana Ines de la Cruz, *tr. by* Aliki *and* Willis Barnstone. BoWoP

Foolish prater, what dost thou. The Swallow. Abraham Cowley, *after* Anacreon. EBEV

Foolish Questions. *Unknown, ad. by* William Cole. OSF

Foolish rhythm turns in my idle head, A. A Tune. Arthur Symons. BoLoP

Foolproof baby that memorized smile. Dear Beatrice Fairfax. Kenneth Fearing. SPT

Fools. Glenn Hardin. AMV–81

Fool's Blues. *Unknown.* BluL

Foot in the stirrup, A. Indecision Means Flexibility. Elliot Abhau. PH

Foot Race Song. *Unknown, tr. fr. Pima Indian by* Frank Russell. NU; OBVE

Foot-Soldiers. John Banister Tabb. OBAL

Football. F. Scott Fitzgerald. SPo

Football. Walt Mason. SPo

Football Field: Evening. J. A. R. McKellar. LiSp

Football-Player, A. Edward Cracroft Lefroy. LiSp

Footballer in the Small Room, The. Janet Frame. SPo

Foote-Ball. Sebastian Brant. SPo

Foot-folk, The. The Battle of Dunbar (1296). *Unknown.* OxBM

Footnote to a Gray Bird's Pause, A. James Cunningham. JB

Footnote to Howl. Allen Ginsberg. CAPP

Footnote to John ii. 4. R. A. K. Mason. ATNZ

Footnote upon the Construction of the Masses. Charles Bukowski. CoPAm

Footnotes to "The Autobiography of Bertrand Russell," *sel.* Mona Van Duyn.
"This seems, in a world where love must take its chances," II. HAP

Footpaths Cross in the Rice Field. "Lin Ling," *tr. fr. Chinese by* Kenneth Rexroth *and* Ling Chung. PBWP

Footprints I have made. Corn-planting Songs. *Unknown, tr. by* Mary Austin. WPW

Footprints in the Night. Elizabeth J. Coatsworth. CaYB

Footprints on the Glacier. W. S. Merwin. NoAM

Footsteps, The. Paul Valéry, *tr. fr. French by* C. Day Lewis. LoAs

Footsteps of Spring. Hayim Nachman Bialik, *tr. fr. Hebrew by* Ruth Nevo. VWA

For a Bitter Season. George Garrett. CSP

For a Child Expected. Anne Ridler. BuTh

For a College Yearbook. J. V. Cunningham. NoAM

For a Coming Extinction. W. S. Merwin. NNaP; TSWA

For a Dead Lady. E. A. Robinson. CMoP (1970 ed.); DL; HeIP; HoPM (1975 ed.); ILP (1975 ed.); LoAs; NoAM; NOBA; PiAm; STS

For a Father. Anthony Cronin. FaBoTw (1975 ed.)

For a Fatherless Son. Sylvia Plath. TSWA

For a Five-Year-Old. Fleur Adcock. ATNZ

For a fresh start. Issa, *tr. fr. Japanese by* Nobuyuki Yuasa. *Fr.* Oraga Haru. OFD

For a Friend. Lyn Lifshin. NeAC; Psy

For a Girl Whose Slow-Dying Called for My Blood. Doug Flaherty. AAN

For a good decade. The Drunk in the Furnace. W. S. Merwin. CAPP; MAT; NoAM

For a Good Dog. Arthur Guiterman. GDP

For a Homecoming. Julia Randall. NMM

For a Junior School Poetry Book. Christopher Middleton. BBGO; MPo

For a Lady I Know. Countee Cullen. Four Epitaphs, 4. HeIP; InPK; NIL; OBAL; TAP; WIF

For a Lamb. Richard Eberhart. CMoP (1970 ed.); SoS

For a Little Girl Mourning Her Favorite Cat. Whittier. *See* Epitaph: "Bathsheba! to whom none ever said scat."

For a long time I've thought about this body of mine. The Vases of Wombs. Daniela Gioseffi. RiTi

For a long time we thought this boy. Rain Straight Down. Samuel Makidemewabe. TC

For a long time you looked stuffed. Lizard. Alan McLean. BoAnP

For a man that is almost blind. For Sore Eyes. *Unknown.* OxBM

For a Marriage. Erica Jong. CTBA

For a Masseuse and Prostitute. Kenneth Rexroth. NNaP

For a Moment. *Unknown, tr. fr. Burmese by* U Win Pe. PBWP

For a moment I saw a surging river. Impermanence. Lal Ded, *tr. fr. Kashmiri.* BoWoP

For a moment pause. The Mound. Thomas Hardy. OxBTC

For a moment, unaware. For a Moment. *Unknown, tr. by* U Win Pe. PBWP

For a Mouthy Woman. Countee Cullen. OBAL; PoBA

For a Neighbor Girl. Yü Hsüan-chi. *See* Advice to a Neighbour Girl.

For a Picture Where a Queen Laments over the Tomb of a Slain Knight. Thomas Carew. CaPo

For a sense of myself to sing. Sandra Maria Esteves. NW

For a Shetland Pony Brood Mare Who Died in Her Barren Year. Maxine W. Kumin. PH

For A' That and A' That, *parody.* Shirley Brooks. FaBoCo; NOBL

For A' That, and A' That. Burns. BTTM; CABA (1972 ed.); FaPoR; ILP (1975 ed.); LAuP; OAEL-1
("Is there, for honest poverty.") OBP
(Man's a Man for A' That, A.) FSW

For "A Venetian Pastoral" by Giorgione. Dante Gabriel Rossetti. VLP

For a Voice That Is Singing. Aldo Camerino, *tr. fr. Italian by* Anita Barrows. VWA

For a while there we had 25-inch Chinese peasant families. The Not-so-good Earth. Bruce Dawe. GAS

For a Wife in Jizzen. Douglas Young. MS

For a Wine Festival. Vernon Watkins. OxBTC

For a Winnebago Brave. Joseph Bruchac. CDW

For a Woodscolt Miscarried. John William Corrington. CoPAm; CSP

For a year, she walked past my window. Woman through the Window. Marcia Falk. VWA

For a Young Cistercian Monk. Jerome Kiely. IPM

For a Young Friend Seeking "Identity." May Miller. PoUp

For a Young South Dakota Man. Freya Manfred. TAT

For a Young Woman Lying Alone in Bed. Randall Ackley. FoP

For Adolf Eichmann. Primo Levi, *tr. fr. Italian by* Ruth Feldman *and* Brian Swann. VWA

For Alan Blanchard. John Oliver Simon. NeAC

For All the Songs I Sing. Alice Notley. FiCh

For All Things Black and Beautiful. Conrad Kent Rivers. CNA

For All We Have and Are. Kipling. FaPoR

For Allan, Who Wanted to See How I Wrote a Poem. Robert Frost. CC; PChr

For Allen Ginsberg, Who Cut Off His Beard. Sanford Pinsker. AMV-80

For Amy Lowell. Countee Cullen. PoA

For "An Allegorical Dance of Women" by Andrea Mantegna. Dante Gabriel Rossetti. VLP

For an Amulet. A. R. D. Fairburn. ATNZ

For an Epitaph at Fiesole. Walter Savage Landor. FaBoEE

For an Indian Bronc Rider Killed in a Highway Crash near Ethete, Wyoming. Robert Roripaugh. PoW

For an officer/ in the old Capital, fox fur. Ezra Pound, *after the Chinese.* OBVE

For an Old Friend. Norbert Krapf. AMV-81

For Andrew. Fleur Adcock. ATNZ

For Andy Goodman—Michael Schwerner—and James Chaney. Margaret Walker. BPo

For Angela. Zack Gilbert. PoBA

For Anna. Irving Layton. NeAC

For Anne. Leonard Cohen. FF; SoS; TCP

For Anne Gregory. W. B. Yeats. BiP; BuTh; CMoP (1970 ed.); Epi; ExPo (1973 ed.); InPK; PFIr; SFF; SS; TPo

For Anne, Who Doesn't Know. Gail Fox. IHMS

For Annie. Poe. NOBA; PiAm; VoPo

For Anybody's Martyr's Song. Jean Garrigue. LoAs

For Arl in Her Sixth Month. Al Young. CPA

For as the honey of heaven's lovely hives. Joseph Beaumont. *Fr.* Psyche or Love's Mystery. SCP-2

For authorities whose hopes. The Paper Nautilus. Marianne Moore. VGW

For beauty being the best of all we know. Robert Bridges. The Growth of Love, VIII. VLP

For, before Cythna loved it, had my song. Shelley. *Fr.* The Revolt of Islam, II. MBPR

For, Behold the Day Cometh. Rochelle Owens. Psy

For best work. Lorine Niedecker. VGW

For Bill. Geof Hewitt. NeAC

For Bill Hawkins, a Black Militant. William J. Harris. PoBA

For Black folks. The "Duke" and the "Count." Richard Fewell. AMV-81

For Black Poets Who Think of Suicide. Etheridge Knight. CNA; PoBA

For blackmen. Blackmen: Who Make Morning. Angela Jackson. CNA

For Bonfires, *sel.* Edwin Morgan.
"Leaves are gathered, the trees are dying, The." MS

For Bonny Elspeth. Hamish Macbride. SLP

For Borges. Michael Berryhill. AAN

For Both of Us at Fisk. Sharon Scott. JB

For brave comportment, wit without offence. To His Honoured and Most Ingenius Friend, Master Charles Cotton. Robert Herrick. CaPo

For by forged letters he tried to accuse Parnell. William McGonagall. *Fr.* Richard Pigott, the Forger. PeD

For C. Philip Whalen. VGW

For Cal. James Cunningham. JB

For Colored Girls Who Have Considered Suicide When the Rainbow Is Enuf, *sel.* Ntozake Shange.
"At 4:30 AM/ she rose." BoWoP

For Cora Lightbody, R.N. John Glassco. PoA

For Cynara. Charles Plymell. RRA

For Dan Berrigan. Etheridge Knight. NeAC

For David Shapiro. David Lehman. PoA

For days I have been walking around. Letter to a Friend in an Unknown Place. Anita Barrows. NMM; RiTi

For days these curious cardboard buds have lain. Gunpowder Plot. Vernon Scannell. HeHu; MPo

For de Lawd. Lucille Clifton. CNA; PoBA; PPoD; TAP

For dear life some do. Portrait of an Artist. Barbara Howes. IHMS

For deep deer-copse beneath Mount Han. Ezra Pound, *after the Chinese.* OBVE

For Delphine. James Simmons. POL

For Drum Hadley. Harold Littlebird. VoR

For E. C. J.　Emmett Jarrett.　NeAC

For E. J. P.　Leonard Cohen.　NoAM

For E. McC.　Ezra Pound.　LiSp

For Each of You.　Audre Lorde.　CNA

For each one body that i' th' earth is sown.　The Resurrection Possible and Probable.　Robert Herrick.　ILP (1975 ed.)

For Edwin R. Embree.　Owen Dodson.　CNA

For Eleanor and Bill Monahan.　William Carlos Williams.　VGW

For Eleanor Boylan Talking with God.　Anne Sexton.　InPK

For Ellen.　Richard Wilbur.　RRA

For Eusi, Ayi Kwei and Gwen Brooks.　Keorapetse Kgositsile.　PoBA

"For ever with the Lord!"　At Home in Heaven.　James Montgomery.　VLP

For every bird there is this last migration.　The Death of the Bird.　A. D. Hope.　MAuV

For Every Last Batch When the Next One Comes Along.　William Dickey.　GP

For every parcel I stoop down to seize.　The Armful.　Robert Frost.　CMoP (1970 ed.)

For Every Sister in the White Man's Jail.　Rita Mae Brown.　WBN

For everything there is a season.　Bible, *O.T.* *Fr.* Ecclesiastes.　DL

For Fear.　Robert Creeley.　NoAM; PiAm

For Fear of Waking the Alarm Clock.　Liam Murphy.　IPM

For fifty thousand years man has been dreaming of power.　Unnatural Powers.　Robinson Jeffers.　PBMP

For first the abiding.　Bruce Beaver.　*Fr.* Lauds and Plaints.　CAAP

For forms of government let fools contest.　Pope.　*Fr.* Essay on Man, Epistle III.　POL

For Fran.　Philip Levine.　FF

For Freckle-faced Gerald.　Etheridge Knight.　BPo; NeAC

For Fyodor.　Phyllis Webb.　MMD

For Gabriel.　Laya Firestone.　VWA

For Galway.　Ken McCullough.　BrS

For gay bard, barren summer.　Lament for Lleucu Llwyd.　Llywelyn Goch ap Meurig Hen, *tr. by* Joseph P. Clancy.　OBW

For George Oppen.　Darrell Gray.　AcAn

For George Santayana.　Robert Lowell.　CMoP (1970 ed.); VGW (George Santayana.)　CoPAm

For God while Sleeping.　Anne Sexton.　CABA (1972 ed.); CAPP; CoPAm

For Godsake [*or* God's sake] hold your tongue, and let me love.　The Canonization.　John Donne.　AnMo; BiP; CABA (1972 ed.); Epi; HAP; ILP (1975 ed.); IPWM; LoAs; MetP; NIL; NOBE; OAEL-1; PoIA; PPoe; PPP; SCP-1; TT; UnPo (1976 ed.)

For God's sake, let us sit upon the ground.　Shakespeare.　King Richard II, *fr.* III, ii.　HoPM (1975 ed.); IP

For God's sake mark that fly!　Nulla Fides.　Patrick Carey.　SCP-2

For grace in me divined.　Arbor Vitae.　Siegried Sassoon.　PoPle

For Great Grandmother and Her Settlement House.　Ann Darr.　GP

For H. W. Fuller.　Carolyn M. Rodgers.　BPo

For he was our puck, our miniature lar.　Louis MacNeice.　*Fr.* The Death of a Cat.　PCat

For Heidi, Caving.　David Kresh.　PoUp

For her blood runs in my blood.　Rachel.　Rachel, *tr. by* N. N.　VWA

For Her Brother.　Al-Khansa, *tr. fr. Arabic by* E. Powys Mathers.　*Fr.* The Thousand and One Nights.　PBWP

For He's a Jolly Good Fellow.　*Unknown.* BLSo, *with music;* FSW

For Hettie.　Amiri Baraka.　NoAM; NOBA; SoS; SS

For Hidden Mist Pavilion.　Yü Hsüan-chi, *tr. fr. Chinese by* Geoffrey Waters.　BoWoP

For His Own Epitaph　Matthew Prior.　*See* For My Own Monument

For his religion, it was fit.　Samuel Butler.　*Fr.* Hudibras, I, 1.　OBSV; SCP-2

For I am not without authority in my jeopardy.　Christopher Smart.　*Fr.* Jubilate Agno.　LAuP; OBP

For I bless the Prince of Peace and pray that all the guns may be nail'd up.　Christopher Smart.　*Fr.* Jubilate Agno.　InPS

For I complaine not of sic common cace.　James I, King of England.　*Fr.* Ane Metaphoricall Invention of a Tragedie Called Phoenix.　SLP

For I have founde you folk faithful of speche.　Alexander and the Gymnosophists.　*Unknown.* OxBM

For I have learned.　Wordworth.　*Fr.* Lines Composed a Few Miles above Tintern Abbey.　Nu

For I have loved long, I crave rewarde.　Bartholomew Griffin.　Fidessa, More Chaste than Kind, XVI.　ESo

For I inhabit a wood.　Marban, a Hermit Speaks.　*Unknown, tr. by* Michael Hartnett.　BIrV; CIP

For I the ballad will repeat.　Shakespeare.　*Fr.* All's Well That Ends Well, I, iii.　BiP

For I Will Consider My Cat Jeoffry.　Christopher Smart.　*Fr.* Jubilate Agno.　HAP; HeIP; ILP (1975 ed.); InPK; LAuP; OAEL-1; OBW; PCat; PPP; Prf (Of Jeoffry, His Cat.)　AnMo; NU

For if alone thou thinke to waft my love.　Giles Fletcher the Elder.　Licia, XLII.　ESo

For I'm called Little Buttercup—dear Little Buttercup.　Little Buttercup.　W. S. Gilbert.　*Fr.* H.M.S. Pinafore.　PCOP

For Instance.　Robert McAlmon.　PoA

For instance/ if the sea should break.　If Something Should Happen.　Lucille Clifton.　MAT

For Isidore Ducasse.　Paul Hoover.　FiCh

For It Was Early Summer.　James Picot.　GAS

For J. A. R. McKellar.　Geoffrey Lehmann.　MAuV

For Jack Chatham.　Jared Carter.　AMV-81

For James Baldwin.　Kay Boyle.　NMM

For James Dean.　Frank O'Hara.　NNaP

For James Joyce.　Michael C. Ford.　PoW

For Jan, in Bar Maria.　Carolyn Kizer.　RiTi; VGW

For Jane.　Charles Bukowski.　CoPAm; CPA; HoPM (1975 ed.)

For Jane Myers.　Louise Glück.　CAAP

For Jeanette Piccard Ordained at 79.　Renny Golden.　AMV-80

For Jim, Easter Eve.　Anne Spencer.　AmNP (1974 ed.)

For John and Lucy.　Joel Oppenheimer.　BCr

For John Berryman.　Virginia Gilbert.　NPW

For John Berryman, I.　Robert Lowell.　NOBA

For John Chappell.　Gary Snyder.　NNaP

For Josephina.　Wayne Miller.　CPA

For Judy.　Chuck Miller.　AcAn

For Just Men Light Is Sown, *with music.* Michael Wigglesworth.　AH

For Katherine, 1952–1961.　Conrad Hilberry.　TC

For Kelley.　Ken Belford.　NeAC

For Kenneth and Miriam Patchen.　Al Young.　CoPAm

For Kenneth Patchen.　Wayne Miller.　MIT

For King, for Robert Kennedy.　Robert Hayden.　*Fr.* Words in the Mourning Time.　CNA

For Kinte.　Oliver La Grone.　FB

For Kirke on his 34th Birthday.　Kaye McDonough.　CPA

For Kuo Hsiang.　Yü Hsüan-chi, *tr. fr. Chinese by* Geoffrey Waters.　BoWoP

For Laurence Jones.　Gary Kizer.　CTBA

For Leningrad, and My Jewish Ancestors. L. M. Rosenberg. AMV–81

For Leon. Lorraine Sutton. NW

For Lerida. David St. John. AmPA

For Life I Had Never Cared Greatly. Thomas Hardy. CMoP (1970 ed.); NoAM

For Lo! My Jonah How He Slumped, *with music.* John Wilson. AH

For lo! the new Moon winter-bright. The New Moon. Samuel Taylor Coleridge. *Fr.* Dejection; an Ode. FSFS

For, lo, the winter is past. Bible, *O.T.* Song of Solomon, II:11-12. CTV

For Love. Robert Creeley. ConAP; NOBA; PiAm

For love—I would. The Warning. Robert Creeley. CoPAm; TAP; VGW

For love of lovely words, and for the sake. Skerryvore. Robert Louis Stevenson. ILP (1975 ed.)

For love no time has she, or inclination. Soame Jenyns. *Fr.* The Modern Fine Lady. OBSV

For love one must risk. Love Song. Bob Zmuda. AMV–81

For love we all go. The People, the People. George Oppen. GP

For lunch this noon, a mason jar full. Mason Jar. David Steinberg. AMV–81

For Mack C. Parker. Pauli Murray. PoBA

For Malcolm, a Year After. Etheridge Knight. NIL

For Malcolm: After Mecca. Gerald W. Barrax. CNA; OFD; PoBA

For Malcolm Who Walks in the Eyes of Our Children. Quincy Troupe. CNA; PoBA

For Malcolm X. Nanina Alba. PoBA

For Malcolm X. Margaret Walker. BPo; CNA; PoBA

For Malcolm's eyes, when they broke. A Poem for Black Hearts. Amiri Baraka. CAPP; ILP (1975 ed.); PoBA; SFF; UsP

For Mama Streek. Colette Inez. AATT

For Mantee/ My Whole World Came Falling Down. James Steele. SES

For many, many days together. Riding Together. William Morris. NOBE; OAEL-2

For Marianne Moore's Birthday. Kay Boyle. RiTi

For Mariella, in Antrona. Tobey A. Simpson. AMV–80

For Mary. Kenneth Rexroth. SFF

For Masturbation. Alan Dugan. CAPP; NoAM

For Mattie and Eternity. Sterling D. Plumpp. CNA

For Me and My Gal. Edgar Leslie *and* E. Ray Goetz. BLSo

For me, for me, two horses wait. The Wizard's Funeral. Richard Watson Dixon. VLP

For me, the naked and the nude. The Naked and the Nude. Robert Graves. OBP; SoSe; TPo; WIF

For me the night still soughs. After an Eclipse of the Sun. Eugene Heimler, *tr. by* Peter Sherwood *and* Keith Bosley. VWA

For Michael. Karen L. Mitchell. AMV–80

For "Mr. Dudley," a Black Spy. James A. Emanuel. BPo

For moments she didn't recognize me. Elegy: I. M. Orlando Tobias Gordon. Giles Gordon. MS

For months/ my books were stacked. February Park. Gerald Vizenor. VoR

For Muh' Dear. Carolyn M. Rodgers. CNA

For Music. Byron. *See* Stanzas for Music.

For My Brother Henry T. Sutton Jr. Lorraine Sutton. NW

For My Contemporaries. J. V. Cunningham. CoPAm; PiAm

For My Daughter. David Ignatow. RRA

For My Daughter. Weldon Kees. RRA

For My Daughter. Ronald Koertge. GP

For My Daughter in Reply to a Question. David Ignatow. RRA

For My Daughter's 20th Birthday. Walter Lowenfels. RRA

For My Father. David Kherdian. VoA

For My Father. Paul Potts. FaBoTw (1975 ed.)

For My Father: Two Poems. David Kherdian. GP

For my food. St. Ciaran and the Birds. Ciaran Carson. CIP; IPM

For My Friend Michele. Linda Gregg. AAN

For My Funeral. A. E. Housman. BoReV; CMoP (1970 ed.)

For My Grandfather. Richard Robbins. AMV–81

For My Grandfather. Francis Webb. GAS

For My Grandfather in Greenfield Center. Joseph Bruchac. FAF

For My Grandmother. Countee Cullen. Four Epitaphs, 1. VGW

For My Grandmother, Bridgid [*or* Bridget] Halpin. Michael Hartnett. BIrV; CIP; IPM

For My Lover, Returning to His Wife. Anne Sexton. IHMS; NMM; RiTi; UnPo (1976 ed.); WPE

For My Mother. Ellen Bass. TV

For My Mother. Louise Glück. CAAP; UnPo (1976 ed.)

For My Mother. June Jordan. BoWoP; NMM

For My Mother's Mother. Judith McDaniel. TV

For My Own Monument. Matthew Prior. ILP (1975 ed.) (For His Own Epitaph.) FaBoEE

For my part, I never care. Tips Tongueless. Robert Herrick. CaPo

For My People. Wendy Rose. CDW

For My People. Margaret Walker. AmNP (1974 ed.); CNA; PBMP; POBA

For My Pop. Cash Terrell. DNGG

For My Sister Molly Who in the Fifties. Alice Walker. WBN

For My Son. Alan Brownjohn. LP

For My Son Noah, Ten Years Old. Robert Bly. BrS

For My Son on the Highways of His Mind. Maxine W. Kumin. CoPAm; MAT

For My Unborn and Wretched Children. A. B. Spellman. CNA; PoBA

For My Wife. Steven Lautermilch. AMV–80

For Natalya Correia. Irving Layton. NeAC

For nations vague as weed. Nothing to Be Said. Philip Larkin. OxBTC

For Nature daily through her grand design. Frederick Goddard Tuckerman. *Fr.* Sonnets. AmVN; PiAm

For No Clear Reason. Robert Creeley. VGW

For No One. John Lennon *and* Paul McCartney. WTO

For no reason except my evening is to let. Three Greeks. Richard Packer. FPA

For Nothing. Andrés Castro Ríos, *tr. fr. Spanish by* Julio Marzán. InW

For Nothing. Gary Snyder. NNaP

For Once, Then, Something. Robert Frost. NoAM; NOBA; PiAm; TT

For one long term, or e'er her trial came. Inscription. George Canning *and* John Hookham Frere. FaBoCo; FaBoEE

For One Moment. David Ignatow. NNaP; TCP; TVo

For One Who Died Young. H. R. Hays. EAS

For one who says he feels. Petra von Morstein, *tr. fr. German by* Rosemarie Waldrop. BoWoP

For other fruits my father was indifferent. My Father and the Fig Tree. Naomi Shihab. GP

For Our Lady. Sonia Sanchez. IHMS

For "Our Lady of the Rocks" by Leonardo da Vinci. Dante Gabriel Rossetti. PFD; VLP (Sonnets for Pictures: "Our Lady of the Rocks.") EBEV

For our own private reasons. Reasons. Thomas James. PoA

For Our Rising (Warrensong). Angela Jackson. FiCh

For Our Soldiers Who Fell in Russia. Franco Fortini, *tr. fr. Italian by* Ruth Feldman. VWA

For our wedding, too. William Carlos Williams. *Fr.* Asphodel, That Greeny Flower, III. PoIA

For over forty years I'd paid it atlas homage. Hammerfest. W. H. Auden. NIL

For Paddy Mac. Padraic Fallon. CIP

For Paddy O'Sullivan. A. D. Winans. CPA

For Paige. Summer Brenner. RiTi

For parents, the only way. The Way of Pain. Wendell Berry. AMV-80

For Pee Wee. Art Lange. FiCh

For physic and farces his equal there scarce is. On Sir John Hill, M.D., Playwright. David Garrick. FaBoCo; FaBoEE

For Poets. Al Young. CNA; PoBA; RFM

For printed instruction. No Holes Marred. Suzanne Douglass. QQQ

For Prodigal Read Generous. E. E. Cummings. FaBoEE; NoAM; PBMP

For Proserpine. Stanley Kunitz. PAIC

For rage and dignity no words compare. A Classical Quatrain. Paul Goodman. VGW

For Randie. Geof Hewitt. NeAC

For Real. Jayne Cortez. PoBA

For Real Ghetto, The. Lonnie L. Landrum. DNGG

For reasons any/ brigadier/ could tell. Irapuato. Earle Birney. MPA; NIL

For Rent. David James. TC

For Robert Frost. Galway Kinnell. NOBA; VGW

For Ron Tanaka at Stanford. Wendy Rose. NW

For Rosa Yen, Who Lived Here. Greg Pape. AmPA

For "Ruggiero and Angelica" by Ingres. Dante Gabriel Rossetti. VLP

For Saint Peter. U. A. Fanthorpe. PMW

For Sale. Robert Lowell. ConAP; PoIA; PSN

For Sale. Shel Silverstein. CTBA

For Sale. *Unknown.* BPAW

For Sammy Younge. Charlie Cobb. PoBA

For Sapphires. Carolyn M. Rodgers. CNA

For Saturday. Christopher Smart. *Fr.* Hymns for the Amusement of Children. LAuP
(Hymn for Saturday.) OxBChV

For Saundra. Nikki Giovanni. BPo; Psy; RiTi; TPo; WIF

For Scholars and Pupils. George Wither. OxBChV

For seven days it rained that June. Wash. John Updike. TSWA

For seven years I have been here loving your teeth. Serial Monogamy. Michael C. Blumenthal. PoUp

For several days I have been under. The Prisoner. Derek Mahon. PFIr

For several months. P.C. Plod versus the Dale St. Dog Strangler. Roger McGough. NoAM

For shame, thou everlasting wooer. The Antiplatonick. John Cleveland. MetP; SCP-2

For sixty years my mother walked. Ballad for My Mother. Patrick Galvin. IPM

For so long/ We looked into mirrors. Us. Julius Lester. PoBA

For solidarity. South American Sway. Margaretta Byers. ECBV

For Some Poets. Mae Jackson. PoBA

For some strange reason, reading the yellow novel, one/ thinks of Greece. Seascape with Bookends. Charles Edward Eaton. AMV-80

For Some Weeks. Robert Creeley. RRA

For something out of sight. The Summons. James Dickey. LiSp

For Sore Eyes. *Unknown.* OxBM

For Steph. Wendy Rose. CDW

For Stephen. Christopher Brookhouse. AMV-80

For Stephen Dixon. Zack Gilbert. PoBA

For stone that breaks the giant hold, for strength. David Homindae. Marjorie Stamm Rosenfeld. AMV-80

For ten decades this river has crawled. Book of Stones. Robert Morgan. HeHu

For that free Grace bringing us past terrible risks. Minnesota Thanksgiving. John Berryman. GOA

For that I never knew you, I only learned to dread you. St. Roach. Muriel Rukeyser. GP

For the air is purified by prayer which is made aloud. Christopher Smart. *Fr.* Jubilate Agno. Prf

For the Anniversary of My Death. W. S. Merwin. CAPP; CoPAm; InPK; NOBA

For the Book of Love. Jules Laforgue, *tr. fr. French by* Jethro Bithell. LoAs

For the bumps bangs and scratches of. Auto Mobile. A. R. Ammons. FF; InPK; OBAL

For the Centenary. James Simmons. IPM

For the Children. Thomas Peacock. VoR

For the Coming Year. Peter Everwine. OFD

For the Country. Larry Levis. NVAP

For the Crèche. G. K. Chesterton. *Fr.* Songs of Education. FaBoCo

For the Cultural Campaign. Chimedin Jigmed, *Mongol Oral Tradition, tr. by* C. R. Bawden. WTO

For the Death of Vince Lombardi. James Dickey. LiSp

For the dim regions whence my fathers came. Outcast. Claude McKay. AmNP (1974 ed.); CABA (1972 ed.); PoBA

For the doubling of flowers is the improvement of the gardners talent. Christopher Smart. *Fr.* Jubilate Agno. LAuP

For the El Paso Weather Bureau. Peter Wild. MAT

For the Fallen. Laurence Binyon. NOBE; OxBTC

For the Far Edge. Mark Vinz. HeS

For the 5th time. Poem. Diane Kruchkow. FAF

For the first time. A Poem for Positive Thinkers. Barbara Mahone. PoBA

For the first time in 2000 years. The 1950's. Robert Sward. FoP

For the Girls 'cause They Know. Harold Littlebird. VoR

For the Good. Orders, Passages 24. Robert Duncan. CAAP

For the Hippolytus of Euripides. Peggy Pond Church. WPW

For the Last Wolverine. James Dickey. LiSp

For the Lordes parte is his folke. Bible, *O.T.* Deuteronomy, XXXII: 9-15. OBVE

For the Lord's Day Evening. Isaac Watts. OxBChV

For the Market. Jane Mayhall. TAP

For the Marriage of Faustus and Helen. Hart Crane. InPS; NoAM; NOBA
"Capped arbiter of beauty in this street," III. ILP (1975 ed.)

For the Masked Ones. Raymond Ward. ATNZ

For the Minority. Robert Peterson. NeAC

For the Moment. Richard Weber. PFIr

For the most part. Chances. Brenda S. Stockwell. AMV-81

For the Night-Mare. *Unknown.* OxBM

For the Old Highlands. Douglas Young. MS

For the One Who Would Take Man's Life in His Hands. Delmore Schwartz. ILP (1975 ed.); NoAM; VGW

For the Opening of the Hunting Season. Morris Bishop. BoAnP; SPo

For the Passing of Groucho's Pursuer. John Hollander. *See* To the Lady Portrayed by Margaret Dumont.

For the perpetual excuse. W. H. Auden. *Fr.* For the Time Being. TT

For the Poet's Father, on His Taking Up Gardening Late in Life. Philip Dacey. BrS

For the Record. Roy Blount, Jr. OBAL

For the Record. R. S. Thomas. LP; MPo

For the Revolution. Joy Davidman. SPT

For the Running of the New York City Marathon. James Dickey. NYP

For the sin of pride the authorities made me wear this little hat. The Little Hat. Barry Schechter. FiCh

For the sky, blue. Drawing by Ronnie C., Grade One. Ruth Lechlitner. SoS

For the Sleepless. Stephen Dunn. HeS

For the Spring Being. Albert Howard Carter. AATT

For the Suicide's Daughter. Carolyn Stoloff. RiTi

For the Time Being, sels. W. H. Auden.
At the Manger Mary Sings. BoReV; ILwL
"For the perpetual excuse." TT
"Led by the light of an unusual star." PChr
"Our Father, whose creative Will." ILwL
Voice of Caesar, The. AnMo
"Well, so that is that. Now we must dismantle the tree." OAEL-2

For the Union Dead. Robert Lowell. CABA (1972 ed.); ExPo (1973 ed.); HAP; HeIP; InPS; NoAM; NOBA; PiAm; PPoe; PPP; PSN; STS; UnPo (1976 ed.)

For the Unknown Goddess. Elizabeth Brewster. MMD

For the Waiter at Jhonny Pavlovs. Luís Omar Salinas. SA

For "The Wine of Circe" by Edward Burne-Jones. Dante Gabriel Rossetti. VLP

For the woman, a braid of hair lying on the quilt. The Man on the Bed. Cleopatra Mathis. AAN

For the Woman Who Asked Me If I Believed in God and If I Pray. Kathleen Wiegner. MMD

For the Word Is Flesh. Stanley Kunitz. VGW

For the Yiddish Singers in the Lakewood Hotels of My Childhood. Harvey Shapiro. VWA

For thee, O dear dear Country! Jerusalem the Golden. Bernard of Cluny, tr. by John Mason Neale. VLP

For Theodore Roethke. Robert Lowell. STS

For there is hope for a man. South Wind. Nathan Yonathan, tr. by Richard Flantz. VWA

For there is hope for a tree. Bible, O.T. Job, XIV: 7-17. DL

For they who fashion songs must live too close to pain. Weltschmerz. Frank Yerby. AmNP (1974 ed.)

For thirst of power that heaven disowns. Ode on the Installation of His Royal Highness Prince Albert. Wordsworth. MBPR

For this additional declaration. The Dissenters' Thanksgiving for the Late Declaration. Unknown. APAS

For this is not the road against which stand enemy lines. Piyyut for Rosh Hashana. Chaim Guri, tr. by Ruth Finer Mintz. OFD

For this, Old Friend, we burn. In the Time of the Rose. John Savant. AMV-81

For this she starred her eyes with salt. Epitaph. Elinor Wylie. SBG

For this your mother sweated in the cold. To Jesus on His Birthday. Edna St. Vincent Millay. VoPo

For those my unbaptisèd rhymes. His Prayer for Absolution. Robert Herrick. SCP-1

For those who worship Thee there is no death. The Trees of Life. Jones Very. NOBA

For those with empirical. 24 December. John Judson. HeS

For thou art with men here upon the banks. Wordsworth. Fr. Lines Composed a Few Miles above Tintern Abbey. Prf

For three days/ I've wanted to get married. Gerrye Payne. NPW

For three sodden miles. The Priests of Serrabonne. Owen Leeming. ATNZ

For three years, out of key with his time. E. P. Ode pour l'Election de Son Sepulchre. Ezra Pound. Hugh Selwyn Mauberley, I. CABA (1972 ed.); CMoP (1970 ed.); HAP; ILP (1975 ed.); InPS; NoAM; NOBA; PiAm; TAP; UnPo (1976 ed.); VGW

For thus saith the Lord to the men of Judah and Jerusalem. Bible, O.T. Jeremiah, IV: 3-31. OBVE

For Tinkers Who Travel on Foot. Margaret Avison. NoAM

For to a torche or to a taper the Trinité is likened. The Trinity. William Langland. Fr. The Vision of Piers Plowman. OxBM

For Tom (1945-1975). Sheryl Dare. PHC

For Tom Numkena, Hopi/Spokane. Harold Littlebird. VoR

For Travelers Going Sidereal. Robert Frost. OBAL

For twenty years/ she's spent her nights. The Telephone Operator. Pat-Therese Francis. AMV-80

For two days her lineage is in doubt. Life of a Queen. Lisel Mueller. GP; RiTi

For us, born into a still. C. Day Lewis. Overtures to Death, VII. CMoP (1970 ed.)

For Us No Night Can Be Happier, with music. Nicolaus L. Zinzendorf, tr. fr. German at. to John Gambold. AH

For Walter Lowenfels. Wendy Rose. CDW

For want of a nail, the shoe was lost. Mother Goose. BBL; CTV; ECBV; MG

For wars his life and half a world away. A Lullaby. Randall Jarrell. PoIA

For We Are All Madwomen. Barbara Sweeney. AMV-81

For we have thought the longer thoughts. Chapter Heading. Ernest Hemingway. PoA

For weeks I thought of you. Beyond Logic. Adrianne Marcus. NPW

For weeks, of course, the phone still rang for you. One Year Later. Eric Torgerson. POL

For What It's Worth. Stephen Stills. PoRo; WIF

For what the world admires I'll wish no more. The Resolve. Mary Lee, Lady Chudleigh. WPE

For what to-morrow shall disclose. Quid Sit Futurum Cras Fuge Quaerere. Matthew Prior. FaBoEE

For when they meet, the tensile air. The Paradigm. Allen Tate. NOBA

For whole nights—(don't ask how many). In an Alien Place. Leib Neidus, tr. by Ruth Whitman. VWA

For whom the possessed sea littered, on both shores. Requiem for the Plantagenet Kings. Geoffrey Hill. NoAM

For Whosoever Will Save His Life Shall Lose It. Bible, N.T. St. Matthew, XVI: 25-26. PBMP

For why? the gaines doth seldome quitte the charge. George Gascoigne. AAS

For William Carlos Williams. Geoff Page. FPA

For William Edward Burghardt Du Bois on His Eightieth Birthday. Bette Darcie Latimer. PoBA

For Witches. Susan Sutheim. NMM

For X. Louis MacNeice. BoLoP

For Years. Ralph J. Mills, Jr. AMV-80

For years he'd been throwing things down the stairs. In the Basement. Stuart Dybek. TC

For years I had not seen such a town. Reunion. Judith Herzberg, tr. by Shirley Kaufman. BoWoP

For years I have been a coal miner. A Coal Miner's Goodbye. Unknown. AmFP

For years I was known as The Great Profile. Profile. Barry Schechter. FiCh

For years I've watched the corners for signs. Blues for Benny Kid Paret. Dave Smith. LiSp

For years she smiled. The Metamorphosis of Aunt Jemima. William Childress. MAT

For years they came to me, these hurtful wives. The Short Paean of Simon Forman the Astrologer: To Tronco, His Wife. David Kirby. AAN

For years we collected arrowheads. Arrowheads. Leona Gom. AMV-81

For years we've had a little dog. Two Dogs Have I. Ogden Nash. GDP

For You. Calvin Forbes. PHC

For You. Ed Ochester. AAN

For You, Falling Asleep after a Quarrel. Diane Middlebrook. AMV-81

For you I have emptied the meaning. Louis Zukofsky. NoAM

For you, I will be less desperate. Dialogue. James Tipton. HeS

"For you . . . If you live to retire." How I Cancelled My Life Insurance. Joseph Bruchac. FAF

For You, Who Didn't Know. Nancy Willard. RiTi

For Your Inferiority Complex. David O'Rourke. AMV-81

For Yvonne, My Daughter. Tony Moreno. NW

Forbear, bold youth; all's heaven here. An Answer to Another Persuading a Lady to Marriage. Katherine Philips. HAP

Forbear this liquid fire, fly. A Fly about a Glass of Burnt Claret. Richard Lovelace. CaPo

Forbear, thou great good husband, little ant. The Ant. Richard Lovelace. CaPo

Forbearance. Emerson. PCOP; TAP

Force, The. Peter Redgrove. MPo

Force has the best of any argument. The Wolf and the Lamb. La Fontaine, *tr. by* Marianne Moore. NAWM-2

Force That through the Green Fuse Drives the Flower, The. Dylan Thomas. AnMo; BiP; CABA (1972 ed.); CMoP (1970 ed.); EBEV; ExPo (1973 ed.); ILP (1975 ed.); InPS; NIL; NoAM; NOBE; OBW; OxBTC; PAIC; PBMP; PoPle; PPP; STS; UnPo (1976 ed.); UsP

Forced March. Miklós Radnóti, *tr. fr. Hungarian by* Emery George. VWA

Forcing House. Theodore Roethke. PiAm

Ford Hospital. J. D. Reed. UsP

Ford o' Kabul River. Kipling. FaBoTw (1975 ed.)

Ford Pickup. David Allan Evans. NVAP

Fording the River. Seamus Deane. CIP

Foreboding, The. Robert Graves. GBL; PoA

Foreboding. John Haines. ConAP

Foreboding. Rainer Maria Rilke, *tr. fr. German by* Lori Weinstein. InPK

Forecast. Sam Cornish. NVAP

Forecast. Josephine Miles. NoAM

Forecast for a Quiet Night. Robin Fulton. MS

Foreclosure. Sterling A. Brown. PoBA

Forefathers. Edmund Blunden. NOBE; OxBTC

Foreign Affairs. Stanley Kunitz. WasP

Foreign Country, A. Natan Zach, *tr. fr. Hebrew by* Laya Firestone. VWA

Foreign country of the river, The. Poem for Nancy. Stephen Tudor. HeS

Foreign Literature. Thackeray. FaBoNo

Foreign Missions in Battle Array. Vachel Lindsay. PIM

Foreign Policy Commitments; or, You Get into the Catamaran First, Old Buddy. Paul Blackburn. NowV

Foreign Ruler, A. Walter Savage Landor. OBSV

Foreign Streets. Mary Crow. AMV-80

Foreign Student. Barbara B. Robinson. CTBA

Foreigners at the Fair. Fred Emerson Brooks. OBAL

Forerunners, The. George Herbert. BoReV; SCP-1

Foresight. Lincoln Kirstein. NoAM

Forest. Jean Garrigue. NOBA

Forest, The. Judith Wright. MAuV

Forest beyond the Glass, The. Lewis Turco. CoPAm

Forest Fire, The. Arthur W. Monroe. BPAW

Forest Green. Thulani Nkabinde. NW

Forest Hymn, A. Bryant. EAP; TAP
    "Father, thy hand," *sel.* PIM

Forest of Dean, The. Robin Flower. PES

Forest rears on lifted arms, The. The Snake-Charmer. Thomas Gordon Hake. VLP

Forester, The. *Unknown. See* I Have Been a Foster.

Foresters Arms, The. Anthony Thwaite. HeHu

Forests are branches of a tree lying down. Flying Home from Utah. May Swenson. MPA; WPE

Forests of Lithuania, The, *sel.* Donald Davie.
    "But this, so feminine?" OxBTC

"Forever." Charles Stuart Calverley. NOBL

Forever Ambrosia. Christopher Morley. OBAL

Forever—is composed of nows. Emily Dickinson. AnMo

Forever, it comes from the head. Venom. James Dickey. PoA

Forever over now, forever, forever gone. The Cameo. Edna St. Vincent Millay. UnPo (1976 ed.); WPE

Forever the little thud of names, falling. Empty Dwelling Places. Kenneth Patchen. PoA

Forever: 'tis a single word! "Forever." Charles Stuart Calverley. NOBL

Foreword to New Numbers. Christopher Logue. OxBTC

Forge, The. Seamus Heaney. PFIr; SoSe

Forge me a tool, my Seamus. His Request. Owen Roe O'Sullivan, *tr. by* John Keefe. BIrV

Forget about us. Leave Us Alone. Tadeusz Rozewicz, *tr. by* Czeslaw Milosz. BuTh

Forget Me Not. Bob Kaufman. AmNP (1974 ed.)

Forget Not Yet. Sir Thomas Wyatt. AAS; BiP; HAP; LoAs (Lover Beseecheth His Mistress Not to Forget His Steadfast Faith and True Intent, The.) PAIC (Steadfastness.) NOBE

Forget six counties overhung with smoke. The Wanderers. William Morris. *Fr.* The Earthly Paradise. VPC

Forget to mail my letter to my friend Death. Overdue Balance Sheet. Therese Plantier, *tr. by* Maxine *and* Judith Kumin. BoWoP

Forgive? José Montoya. MIT

Forgive/ my sadness. Barefoot. Luís Omar Salinas. SA

Forgive, Lord, Have Mercy! *Tr. fr. Sanskrit by* Raimundo Panikkar. *Fr.* Vedic Hymns. ILwL

Forgive me if I have not sent you. Valentines. Henry Dumas. CC

Forgive me, O Lord. Foul Water. Mordecai Temkin, *tr. by* Jeremy Garber. VWA

Forgive Me, Sire. Norman Cameron. FaBoEE

Forgive me that I pitch your praise too low. Apology for Understatement. John Wain. LoAs; OxBTC

Forgive me, you whom they cast in a name. Prayer. Avraham Shlonsky, *tr. by* Francis Landy. VWA

Forgive, O Lord. Robert Frost. AnMo

Forgive the hours spent listening to the radio [*or* radios]. Looking at a Dead Wren in My Hand. Robert Bly. GP; NNaP

Forgiven Past, The. Laura Riding. NoAM; PBWP

Forgiven, unforgiven, they who drive the nails. Carpenters. Turner Cassity. CSP

Forgotten dryness in the mouth, A. Go Back. Joan Keefe. IPM

Fork. Charles Simic. AmPA; GP

Forlorn and glum the couples go. The Houses. Eden Phillpotts. OxBTC

Form is the woods: the beast. Poem. Jim Harrison. VGW

Form of Women, A. Robert Creeley. CAPP

Form Rejection Letter. Philip Dacey. AAN; AmPA; PCho

Formal Application. Donald W. Baker. FF; SoSe

Formal exercise for withered fingers, A. Old Fisherman with Guitar. George Mackay Brown. MS

Formal World relaxes her cold chain, The. Apology. Wordsworth. *Fr.* Sonnets upon the Punishment of Death. VLP

Formations. William Freedman. VWA

Former Age, The. Chaucer. OxBM

Former Beauties. Thomas Hardy. At Casterbridge Fair, II. NoAM

Former Life. Baudelaire, *tr fr. French by* Roy Campbell. NAWM-2

Former Love, A. Giles Gordon. SLP

"Formerly a Slave." Herman Melville. TAP

Formerly the individual work of a Nuremburg artificer. Watch. John Daniel. TwMBP

Forming Child Poems. Simon J. Ortiz. CDW

Forms of Love, The. George Oppen. NNaP

Forms of the Earth at Abiquiu. N. Scott Momaday. CDW

Forms of the Human. Richard Eberhart. TH

Forsaken, The. Duncan Campbell Scott. PoTa

Forsaken. *Unknown.* AmFP

Forsaken Garden, A. Swinburne. EBEV; NOBE; OAEL-2; VLP

Forsaken Girl, The. Randall Jarrell. OLR

Forsaken Merman, The. Matthew Arnold. EBEV; EcS; FaPoR; ILP (1975 ed.); PoPle; VLP

Forsythia. Mary Ellen Solt. BoWoP

Forsythia Is the Color I Remember. Joseph Cherwinski. AMV-80

Fort of Rathangan, The. *Unknown, tr. fr. Irish by* Kuno Meyer. PFIr

Fort or Castle of Hope, The, *sel.* Margaret Cavendish, Duchess of Newcastle.
"Some with sharp swords, to tell O most accursed!" SCP-2

Fort over against the oak-wook, The. The Fort of Rathangan. *Unknown, tr. by* Kuno Meyer. PFIr

Fort Robinson. Ted Kooser. GP

Fort Wayne, Indiana 1964. Steven Lewis. TAT

Forte: For Tina. David Meltzer. MIT

Forth from Calais, at dawn of night, when sunset summer on autumn shone. A Channel Passage. Swinburne. VLP

Forth from the dark and dismal cell. Mad Tom of Bedlam. *Unknown.* SCP-2

Forth, to the alien gravity. The Launch. Alice Meynell. WPE

Forties Flick. John Ashbery. CAAP

Fortitude. *Somali Oral Tradition, tr. by* B. W. Andrzejewski *and* I. M. Lewis. WTO

Fortitude, endurance, amana: remain faithful. The Amana Colonies. Ken Smith. TwMBP

Fortnight before Christmas Gypsies were everywhere, A. The Gypsy. Edward Thomas. HeIP; NoAM

Fortress, The. Louise Glùck. NVAP

Fortù, Fortù, my beloved one. The Englishman in Italy. Robert Browning. ExPo (1973 ed.)

Fortunate,/ Being articulate. Nocturne of the Self-evident Presence. Thomas MacGreevy. BIrV; CIP

Fortunate Fall, The. A. Alvarez. VWA

Fortunate Isles, and Their Union, The, *sel.* Ben Jonson.
"Now turn, and view the wonders of the deep." SCP-1

Fortune. Lawrence Ferlinghetti. BBGO; SFF
("Fortune/ has its cookies to give out.") SoS; VoA

Fortune favours the brave, old proverbs say. Mr. Cromek to Mr. Stothard. Blake. FaBoEE

Fortunes of War, The. *Unknown.* InPK; POL

45th Parallel Sulks. W. A. Roecker. FoP

Forty-five Minutes from Broadway, *with music.* George M. Cohan. FSN

45 Pistol Blues. *Unknown.* BluL

40-Love. Roger McGough. LiSp; NoAM

49 Stomp, The. Lew Blockcolski. VoR

49th and 5th, December 13. Josephine Jacobsen. NYP

Forty Pounds of Blackberries Equals Thirteen Gallons of Wine. Robert D. Hoeft. AMV-80

Forty-second, The. *Unknown.* GBP

46 and Recalling. Allan Block. FAF

Forty viziers saw I go. The Fair Circassian. Richard Garnett. PoTa

Forty years ago a saloon stood where the church is. The Last Farmer in Queens. Vickie Karp. NYP

Forty Years Peace. Arye Sivan, *tr. fr. Hebrew by* Anthony Rudolf *and* Natan Zach. VWA

Forward abrupt. Night and a Distant Church. Russell Atkins. PoBA

Forward rush by the lamp in the gloom, A. The Contretemps. Thomas Hardy. CMoP (1970 ed.)

Forward! The crackling lashes send. The Wagon Train. Sam L. Simpson. BPAW

Forward youth that would appear, The. An Horatian Ode upon Cromwell's Return from Ireland. Andrew Marvell. EBEV; Epi; HAP; InPS; NIL; NOBE; OAEL-1; OBP; PAIC; TT

Foster-Mother's Tale, The. Samuel Taylor Coleridge. MBPR

Foul ill spirit hath possessed her, A. Ben Jonson. *Fr.* The Sad Shepherd; or, A Tale of Robin Hood. SCP-1

Foul Shot. Edwin A. Hoey. SPo

"Foul vermin they." Rats. Walter de la Mare. BoAnP

Foul Water. Mordecai Temkin, *tr. fr. Hebrew by* Jeremy Garber. VWA

Fouler hides, The (as closelie as he may). Henry Constable. *Fr.* Diana. ESo

Found. Carol Muske. AmPA

Found. Sarah Taylor Shatford. PeD

Found a family, build a state. Fragments of a Lost Gnostic Poem of the 12th Century. Herman Melville. NOBA

Found dead a rat—no case could sure be harder. *Unknown.* FaBoEE

Found in a Storm. William Stafford. RFM

Found in the garden—dead in his beauty. The Burial of the Linnet. Juliana Horatia Ewing. OxBChV

Found out in left hayfield. Poet. Robert Siegel. FAF

Found Poem with Grafts 1866. Christopher Middleton. TwMBP

Found with Chain. Robin Johnson. PoW

Foundation of American Industry, The. Donald Hall. GOA

Founding Fathers, *sel.* Andrea Wyatt.
"In 1843,/ John James Audubon." PoUp

Founding Fathers, Nineteenth-Century Style. Robert Penn Warren. Promises, VIII. NoAM

Fountain, The. Donald Davie. OxBTC

Fountain. Elizabeth Jennings. WPE

Fountain, The　Pavlos Liasides, *tr. by* Edmund Pennant. AMV-80

Fountain, The. Wordsworth. MBPR

Fountain, a Bottle, a Donkey's Ears and Some Books, A. Robert Frost. VGW

Fountain, coolest fountain. Ballad of the Cool Fountain. *Unknown. tr. by* Edwin Honig. BoWoP

Fountain flows, but where the bowl, The. The Broken Bowl. Jones Very. ILP (1975 ed.)

Fountain in the Park, The. Ed Haley. *See* While Strolling through the Park One Day.

Fountains, The. W. R. Rodgers. PFIr; POL

Fountains mingle with the river, The. Love's Philosophy. Shelley. BoLoP; HoPM (1975 ed.); MBPR; OLR; PBMP; VoPo

Fountains that frisk and sprinkle. Ballade Made in the Hot Weather. W. E. Henley. FSFS

Four Ages of Man, The. Anne Bradstreet. *See* Of the Four Ages of Man.

Four Ages of Man, The. W. B. Yeats. BoReV

Four a.m. call to the faithful wakes us, The. Noises in the Dark. Liz Lochhead. MS

Four and Twenty. Stephen Stills. GrRo

Four and twenty bonny boys. Sir Hugh (The Jew's Daughter). *Unknown.* FaBoBa

Four-and-twenty Highland men. Eppie Morrie. *Unknown.* PeBB

Four and Twenty Merulae. J. Moyr Smith. FaBoNo

Four and twenty tailors went to kill a snail. Mother Goose. GBP; MG

Four and twenty white bulls. *Unknown.* GBP

Four and twenty years ago a-comin to this life. Four and Twenty. Stephen Stills. GrRo

Four bright steel crosses. Detroit Grease Shop Poem. Philip Levine. MPA

Four Cardinal Times of Day, The. Rene Daumal, *tr. fr. French by* Jan Pallister. AMV-81

Four Christmas Carols, *sel. Unknown, tr. fr. Spanish by* Cheli Durán.
  "How cold the snow." PChr

Four Corners, The. Victor Hernández Cruz. FoP

4 days till the solstice, the moon. Depression before the Solstice. Charles Wright. CSP

Four Directions, The. Emerson Blackhorse Mitchell. VW

Four Ducks on a Pond. William Allingham. PCOP; PoPle (Memory, A.) FSFS

Four Epigrams on the Naturalization Bill. John Byrom. NOBL

Four Epitaphs. Countee Cullen. AmNP (1974 ed.); ILP (1975 ed.); PoBA
  For a Lady I Know, 4. HeIP; InPK; NIL; OBAL; TAP; WIF
  For My Grandmother, 1. VGW

Four Fawns. Barbara Howes. AMV-80

Four feet up, under the bruise-blue. Small Woman on Swallow Street. W. S. Merwin. ConAP

Four for Sir John Davies. Theodore Roethke. NIL; NoAM; NOBA; PiAm

Four Frescoes of the Future. Genevieve Taggard. SPT

Four gents up and swing Sally Goodin. Sally Goodin. *Unknown.* AmFP

Four Glimpses of Night. Frank Marshall Davis. AmNP (1974 ed.); PoBA

Four Haiku. Richard Wright. NoAM

Four Homages. Allan Block. FAF

Four horsemen rode out from the heart of the range. The Bushrangers. Edward Harrington. PoTa

Four Horses, The. James Reeves. PH

400-Meter Freestyle. Maxine W. Kumin. LiSp; SoSe (1977 ed.); SPo

Four in the Morning. Edith Sitwell. NoAM

4 in 2 goes twice as fast. Crazy Arithmetic. D'Arcy Thompson. FaBoCo

Four insurgent generals, The. Los Cuatro Generales. *Unknown, tr. fr. Spanish.* FSW

Four Japanese Paintings, *sel.* Arthur Davison Ficke.
  Wave Symphony, The. PoA

Four jays (I.) Avis. Ted Morison. AMV-81

Four little children. The Lost Angel. Philip Levine. NOBA

Four Little Foxes. Lew Sarett. RFM

Four Maries, The. *Unknown.* FSW

Four miles out the tide curls in. Poem. Mira Fish. FAF

Four months content. The Spider, Unsurprised. Peter Klappert. AAN

Four Mountain Wolves. Leslie Silko. VoR

Four Nights Drunk. *Unknown.* FSW
  (Four Nights' Drunk, The, *diff. version.*) OBAL

Four o'Clock Flower Blues. *Unknown.* AmFP

Four of Them, The. Yehuda Karni, *tr. fr. Hebrew by* Jeremy Garbers. VWA

Four Pence a Day. *Unknown.* FSW

Four Poems. Joseph Freeman. SPT
  "Drums of the world, beat, " 4.
  "In this black room, midnight and morn are each, " 1.
  "Mankind looks forward, but the hurt look back," 2.
  "Still young, our faces may deceive,"3.

Four Poems. Ray A. Young Bear. Epi

Four Poems for Robin. Gary Snyder. NNaP; NoAM; NOBA

Four Poems from the Strontium Age, *sels.* Louis Johnson.
  "All day the black rain has fallen." ATNZ
  "There were cities here in the hills." ATNZ
  "We have come to a quiet valley in the hills." ATNZ

Four Postcards from Italy. Colman Andrews. PoW

Four Preludes on Playthings of the Wind. Carl Sandburg. CMoP (1970 ed.); NOBA; PAIC; PiAm

Four Quartets, *sels.* T. S. Eliot.
  Burnt Norton. CMoP (1970 ed.); HeIP; ILP (1975 ed.)
  Dry Salvages, The. CABA (1972 ed.); PiAm
  East Coker. HAP; PPP; VGW
  Little Gidding. BoReV; NoAM; NOBA; NOBE; OAEL-2; TAP
  "Ash on an old man's sleeve," II. FaBoTw (1975 ed.)

Four Questions Addressed to His Excellency, the Prime Minister. James P. Vaughn. AmNP (1974 ed.)

Four Saints in Three Acts, *sel.* Gertrude Stein.
  "Pigeons on the grass alas." TAP

Four seasons fill the measure of the year. Keats. MBPR

Four Sheets to the Wind and a One-Way Ticket to France [1933]. Conrad Kent Rivers. AmNP (1974 ed.), *diff. version;* BPo; CABA (1972 ed.), *diff. version;* PoBA

Four Spacious Skies. Susan Astor. AMV-80

Four stiff standers. *Unknown.* GBP

Four sweaters are woven upon me. Springer Mountain. James Dickey. CAPP

Four Tao philosophers as cedar waxwings. Waxwings. Robert Francis. NU

Four Things. Henry van Dyke. PCOP
  ("Four things a man must learn to do.") CTV

Four things are white, the fifth exceeds the rest. Five Things White. Edward May. FaBoEE

Four things in any land must dwell. *Unknown.* CTV

Four Things Make Us Happy Here. Robert Herrick. CaPo

Four Things to See. Ronald Mann. PMW

Four times now I have seen you as another. Boy Driving His Father to Confession. Seamus Heaney. BuTh

Four Translations from the English of Robert Hershon. Robert Hershon. NeAC

4/20/75. Darlene Pearlstein. FiCh

4/22/75. Darlene Pearlstein. FiCh

Four Untitled Poems. Kathleen Wiegner. MMD

Four Victorian Photographs. Roger McDonald. FPA

Four Walls of My Cage, The. George Reavey. FoP

Four white heifers with sprawling hooves. The Orotava Road. Basil Bunting. NoAM

Four Wise Men on Edward II's Reign. *Unknown.* OxBM

Four Women. Nina Simone. MAT

Four-Word Lines. May Swenson. WPE
    "Your eyes are just," *sel.* OSP

Four Years After. Patricia Beer. HeHu

Four years ago, dear old ventriloquist. The Ventriloquist.
    Robert Huff. GP

Four Zoas, The, *sels.* Blake.
    Enion's Lament. UsP
    Enion's Protest. UsP
    ("I am made to sow the thistle for wheat.") Prf
    "Night passd and Enitharmon eer the dawn returnd in bliss."
    OAEL-2
    Vala, Night the Ninth Being the Last Judgment. MBPR
    (Night the Ninth Being the Last Judgment.) OAEL-2

Four-score and seven, so the papers say. The Old Boatman of
    Death's River. R. Williams Parry, *tr. by* Joseph P. Clancy.
    OBW

Four-square Gospel. Roderick Hartigh Jellema. AATT

1492. Emma Lazarus. WPE

Fourteen small broidered berries on the hem. What the Sonnet
    Is. Eugene Lee-Hamilton. HoPM (1975 ed.)

Fourteen-year-old, why must you giggle and dote. The
    Conventionalist. Stevie Smith. BBGO

Fourteen years old, learning the alphabet. The Reading Lesson.
    Richard Murphy. IPM

14th St/New York, *abr.* Patricia Jones. NYP

Fourth, The. Shel Silverstein. CC

Fourth Dance Poem. Gerald W. Barrax. PoBA

Fourth Dimension, The. Leonard Nathan. AMV-81

Fourth Meditation. Theodore Roethke. Meditations of an Old
    Woman, IV. MPA
    ("I was always one for being alone.") STS

Fourth of July. Rachel Field. CC; CTV

Fourth of July, The. John Pierpont. CTV

4th of July. William Carlos Williams. PoA

Fourth of July Drowning, The. Judith Minty. TC

Fourth of July Fireworks. Liz Lochhead. MIS

Fourth of July in Maine. Robert Lowell. CAPP

Fourth of July Night. Dorothy Aldis. CC

Fourth of July Night. Carl Sandburg. OFD

Fourth Option, The. Henry Rasof. AMV-80

Fourth Pearl, The: Temperance. Lady Diana Primrose. *Fr.* A
    Chain of Pearl. WPE

Fourth Psalm: The Cerements. W. S. Merwin. CAAP

Fourth Song: "Only joy, now here you are." Sir Philip Sidney.
    *Fr.* Astrophel and Stella. GBL; HAP

Fourth Song the Night Nurse Sang. Robert Duncan. VGW

Foveran Sands. Roderick Watson. MIS

Fower-an-twenty Heilandmen. *Unknown.* FaBoNo

Fowles in the Frith. *Unknown.* HAP; PoIA

Fowre muckle angels wi their trumpets, stalkin. Judgment Day.
    Robert Garioch, *after* Giuseppe Belli. OBVE

Fox, The. John Clare. BoAnP

Fox, The. C. Day Lewis. BoAnP

Fox, The. Kenneth Patchen. CoPAm; LP; MPo

Fox, The. R. Williams Parry, *tr. fr. Welsh by* Gwyn Williams.
    OBW

Fox. Kenneth Rexroth. *Fr.* A Bestiary. NNaP

Fox, The. *Unknown. See* Fox and the Geese, The.

Fox and the Crow, The. La Fontaine, *tr. fr. French by* Marianne
    Moore. NAWM-2; OBVE; PPP

Fox and the Geese, The. *Unknown.* RDB, *with music*
    (Fox, The.) FSW; PoTa
    ("Fox started out in a hungry plight, A.") MG

Fox and the Goat, The. La Fontaine, *tr. fr. French by* Marianne
    Moore. AKE

Fox and the Goose, The (" 'Pax vobis,' quod the fox"). *Unknown.*
    OxBM

Fox and the Wolf, The. *Unknown.* OxBM

Fox at your neck and snakeskin on your feet, A. Leaving
    Something Behind. David Wagoner. CoPAm

Fox [he] came lolloping, lolloping, The. Hunting Song. Donald
    Finkel. NCSH; SoSe; SPo

Fox Court, Winter. Cathy Colman. NPW

Fox gan out of the wode go, A. The Fox and the Wolf.
    *Unknown.* OxBM

Fox is very clever, The. Fox. Kenneth Rexroth. *Fr.* A Bestiary.
    NNaP

Fox Song. Katherine Doak. NPW

Fox started out in a hungry plight, A. *Unknown.* MG

Fox went out on a chilly night, The. The Fox and the Geese.
    *Unknown.* FSW; PoTa; RDB

Fox woman/ dances, string of blue beads. Second Skins—a
    Peyote Song. Joseph Bruchac. CDW

Foxes, The. Janet Frame. WPE

Foxfire. Nancy Willard. IHMS

Fox's Counsel, The. Huw Llwyd, *tr. fr. Welsh by* Joseph P.
    Clancy. OBW

Foxtail Pine. Gary Snyder. NU

Fra Bank to Bank, Fra Wood to Wood I Rin. Mark Alexander
    Boyd. InPK; PPoe
    (Cupid and Venus.) SLP
    (Sonet: "Fra banc to banc, fra wod to wod, I rin.") ESo
    (Sonet: "Fra bank to bank, fra wood to wood I rin.")
    EBEV; OBP
    (Sonnet: "Fra banc to banc, fra wod to wod, I rin.") GBL;
    NOBE
    (Venus and Cupid.) HAP; Prf

Fra Lippo Lippi. Robert Browning. BiP; OAEL-2; STS; VLP
    "I shall paint/ God in the midst," *sel.* Prf

Frae great Apollo, poet say. The Poet's Wish. Allan Ramsay,
    *after* Horace. OBVE

Fragment: "As if stone Caesar shook." Hugh McCrae. GAS

Fragment, A: "I cannot find my way to Nazareth." Yvor
    Winters. OBSV

Fragment, A: "I have heard a voice of broken seas." James Elroy
    Flecker. EcS

Fragment: "I lived on this earth in an age." Miklós Radnóti, *tr.*
    *fr. Hungarian by* Steven Polgar, Stephen Berg, *and* S. J.
    Martin. VWA

Fragment: "I saw his round mouth's crimson deepen as it fell."
    Wilfred Owen. OAEL-2

Fragment: "I would to heaven that I were so much clay." Byron.
    *Fr.* Don Juan. ILP (1975 ed.); MBPR; NIL; NOBL;
    OAEL-2; OBP

Fragment: Language Has Not the Power. John Clare. FaBoEE;
    OAEL-2

Fragment: "Locke sank into a swoon." W. B. Yeats. ILP (1975
    ed.); NoAM; SoSe

Fragment: "Some pretty face remembered in our youth." John
    Clare. VLP

Fragment: "Strike, churl; hurl, cheerless wind, then; heltering
    hail." Gerard Manley Hopkins. OBP

Fragment: To Byron. Shelley. MBPR

Fragment, The: "Towards the evening of her splendid day."
    Hilaire Belloc. POL

Fragment: "Welcome joy, and welcome sorrow." Keats. MBPR

Fragment: "Where's the poet? show him! show him." Keats.
    MBPR

Fragment from the Elizabethans. W. Bridges-Adams. FaBoCo

Fragment in Imitation of Wordsworth. Catherine Fanshawe.
    FaBoNo

Fragment of a Character. Thomas Moore. FaBoCo

Fragment of a Greek Tragedy.  A. E. Housman.  FaBoNo; NOBL; SpRo

Fragment of a Love Lament.  *Unknown.*  OxBM

Fragment of a Pastoral.  Barry Schwabsky.  AMV–80

Fragment of a Song.  "Lewis Carroll."  FaBoNo

Fragment of a Song on the Beautiful Wife of Dr. John Overall.  *Unknown.*  BoLoP

Fragment of an Ode to Maia.  Keats.  OAEL–2; OBP (Ode to May, Fragment.)  MBPR

Fragment of Bion, A.  Philip Freneau.  EAP

Fragment of Petronius Translated, A.  Petronius Arbiter.  *See* Doing, a Filthy Pleasure Is, and Short.

Fragment 113: "Not honey."  Hilda Doolittle ("H. D.").  PiAm

Fragment Reflection I.  Doris Turner.  JB

Fragment Thirty-six: "I know not what to do."  Hilda Doolittle ("H. D.").  CMoP (1970 ed.); VGW

Fragmentary Blue.  Robert Frost.  NIL

Fragmenti.  Ezra Pound.  PoA

Fragments.  John Cotton.  AMV–80

Fragments, *sels.*  John Masefield.
   "Green and greedy seas have drowned, The."  EcS
   "In some green island of the sea."  EcS

Fragments of a Lost Gnostic Poem of the 12th Century.  Herman Melville.  NOBA

Fragmentum Pertronius Arbiter, Translated.  Petronius Arbiter.  *See* Doing, a Filthy Pleasure Is, and Short.

Fragrances that like a wind disturb.  The Islands Where I Was Born.  Gloria Rawlinson.  ATNZ

Fragrant prayer upon the air, A.  Biddy Crummy, *tr. fr. Gaelic by* Douglas Hyde.  WTO

Fragrant the grasses of high Kane-hoa.  Anklet Song.  *Tr. fr. Hawaiian by* N. B. Emerson.  WTO

Frail as the leaves that quiver on the sprays.  Homer, *tr. by* Samuel Johnson.  *Fr.* The Iliad, VI.  OBVE

Frail scorched grasses are ripped now, The.  Drought.  Oumar Ba, *tr. by* Kathleen Weaver.  PBWP

Frail the white rose and frail are.  A Flower Given to My Daughter.  James Joyce.  RRA

Frailty and Hurtfulness of Beauty, The.  Earl of Surrey.  HoPM (1975 ed.)
   ("Brittle beautie, that nature made so fraile.")  AAS

Frame, The, *sel.*  Judith Johnson Sherwin.
   "There is a frame around my/ words."  OSP

Frame it. Everyone lies, you say.  Portrait in Available Light.  Sara Miles.  NYP

Frames on Bright Faces.  Bruce Severy.  HeS

France: An Ode.  Samuel Taylor Coleridge.  LFH; MBPR

France Blues.  *Unknown.*  BluL

France. Cradle and abstraction.  Wildfire.  Judit Tóth, *tr. by* Emery George.  VWA

Francesca.  Ezra Pound.  PSN; UsP

Francestown Suite.  Carole Oles.  PCho

Francis Marion nudges himself gently into the big blue sky.  Sonnet.  Ted Berrigan.  CAAP

Francisco Coronado rode forth with all his train.  Quivira.  Arthur Guiterman.  BPAW

Franco.  Judith Smallshaw.  PMW

Frank Baker's my name, and a bachelor I am.  Starving to Death on a Government Claim.  *Unknown.*  BPAW

Frank Drummer.  Edgar Lee Masters.  *Fr.* Spoon River Anthology.  NoAM

Frank James, the Roving Gambler.  *Unknown.*  AmFP

Frank, wilt live handsomely? Trust not too far.  Advice to My Best Brother, Colonel Francis Lovelace.  Richard Lovelace.  CaPo

Frankenstein.  Edward Field.  FF

Frankenstein Stagger, The.  Arthur Lane.  PoW

Frankie and Johnny [*or* Johnnie].  *Unknown.*  AmFP; BiP, *2 versions;* BLSo, *with music;* FF; FSW; InPK; LFH; NIL; NOBA; UnPo (1976 ed.)
   (Frankie.)  BluL
   (Frankie and Albert.)  PeBB

Frankie and Johnny [*or* Johnnie] were lovers.  Frankie and Johnny [*or* Johnnie].  *Unknown.*  AmFP; BiP; BLSo; FF; FSW; LFH; NIL; NOBA; UnPo (1976 ed.)

Frankie she was a good woman, Johnny he was her man.  Frankie and Johnny.  *Unknown.*  InPK

Frankie Silvers.  Frances Silvers.  AmFP

Frankie was a good girl.  Frankie.  *Unknown.*  BluL

Frankie was a good woman, everybody knows.  Frankie and Johnny, *second version.*  *Unknown.*  BiP

Frankie wuz a good woman.  Frankie and Albert.  *Unknown.*  PeBB

Franklin Avenue Blues People.  Quincy Troupe.  SES

Franklin D. Roosevelt's Back Again.  *Unknown.*  FSW

Franklin's Prologue, The.  Chaucer.  *Fr.* The Canterbury Tales.  OAEL–1

Franklin's Tale, The.  Chaucer.  *Fr.* The Canterbury Tales.  OAEL–1

Franz Jagesttater's Epistemology.  Mark Halperin.  PCho

Franz Kafka had a nightmare.  Kafka's Other Metamorphosis.  Len Gasparini.  NeAC

Fraser, I think, tells of a Roman.  Charles Reznikoff.  VoA

"Frater Ave atque Vale."  Tennyson.  HAP; InPS

Fraternitas.  Ezra Pound, *after the Chinese.*  OBVE

Frau Bauman, Frau Schmidt, and Frau Schwartze.  Theodore Roethke.  InPK; NoAM; NOBA; PiAm; PSN; TAP

Fraudulent Days.  Michael Benedikt.  PoA

Fräulein Reads Instructive Rhymes.  Maxine W. Kumin.  SpRo

Freak Show, The.  Nancy Willard.  RiTi

Freak Show and Finale.  Lenore Kandel.  *Fr.* Circus.  RiTi

Freckled and frivolous cake there was, A.  The Frivolous Cake.  Mervyn Peake.  *Fr.* Titus Groan.  BBL

Fred Astaire.  Maxine Chernoff.  FiCh

"Fred, where is north?"  West-running Brook.  Robert Frost.  NOBA; PAIC; PiAm; SoSe; TT

Freddy the Rat Perishes.  Don Marquis.  *Fr.* Archy and Mehitabel.  MiP

Frederick Douglass.  Sam Cornish.  NVAP; PoBA

Frederick Douglass.  Paul Laurence Dunbar.  PoBA

Frederick Douglass.  Robert Hayden.  AmNP (1974 ed.); BiP; CNA; CoPAm; GOA; GP; PBMP; PoBA

Frederick Douglass and the Slave Breaker.  Dudley Randall.  TC

Frederick Douglass: 1817-1895.  Langston Hughes.  BPo

Free America.  At. to Joseph Warren.  BTTM; FSW

Free at Last.  *Unknown.*  *See* I Thank God I'm Free at Las'.

Free Coal.  Robert Morgan.  HeHu

Free Enterprise.  Charles Stetler.  GP

Free evening fades, outside the windows, The.  Evening in the Sanitarium.  Louise Bogan.  IHMS; SBG

Free Fall.  Don Gordon.  AMV–81

Free, free, I would run until.  Prison Break.  Michael Hogan.  GP

Free Grace.  Charles Wesley.  BoReV

Free Kirk, The. Eighteen-forty-three.  *Unknown.*  FaBoCo

Free Little Bird.  *Unknown.*  AmFP; FSW

Free One, A.  W. H. Auden.  CMoP (1970 ed.)

Free Silver.  *Unknown.*  AmFP

Free thinker! Do you think you are the only thinker.  Golden Lines.  Gérard de Nerval, *tr. by* Robert Bly.  NU

Free Thoughts on Several Eminent Composers.  Charles Lamb.  FaBoCo

Free Will.  Walter Clark.  NCSH

Free Will and God's Foreknowledge. Milton. *Fr.* Paradise Lost, III. ExPo (1973 ed.)

Free woman, A. At last free! *Tr. fr. Pali by* Willis Barnstone. BoWoP

Freeborn Pindaric never does refuse. A Pindaric on the Grunting of a Hog. Samuel Wesley. NOBL

Freedom. J. Charles Green. DNGG

Freedom. Langston Hughes. PoBA; WIF

Freedom ("Men! whose boast it is that ye"). James Russell Lowell. VoPo

Freedom. William Stafford. MiP

Freedom and dignity have reached us. Independence. *Somali Oral Tradition, tr. by* B. W. Andrzejewski *and* I. M. Lewis. WTO

Freedom Is a Constant Struggle. *Unknown.* FSW

Freedom of Love. André Breton, *tr. fr. French by* Edouard Roditi. EAS

Freedom of the Moon, The. Robert Frost. Moon

Freedom will not come. Freedom. Langston Hughes. PoBA; WIF

Freely, from a Song Sung by Jewish Women of Yemen. Stephen Levy. VWA

Freethinkers. Deborah Eibel. VWA

Freeway. Edward Cardinali. OSP

Freeway Problems. Lawrence P. Spingarn. PoW

Freight Train. *Unknown.* FSW

Freighting from Wilcox to Globe. *Unknown.* AmFP

Freiheit (Freedom). Karl Ernst *and* Peter Daniel, *tr. fr. German.* FSW

Freind! for your epitaphs I'm griev'd. Epigram on One Who Made Long Epitaphs. Pope. FaBoEE

French. Osbert Lancaster. *Fr.* Afternoons with Baedeker. FaBoCo; NOBL

French clocks struck two-thirty, and above, The. Under the Arc de Triomphe: October 17. Marilyn Hacker. PoA

French, The, 1870-1871. *Unknown.* FaBoEE

French Master, The. Dannie Abse. LP

French Mood, The. Abo Stoltzenberg, *tr. fr. Yiddish by* Gabriel Preil *and* Howard Schwartz. VWA

French Persian Cats Having a Ball. Edwin Morgan. MPo

French Revolution, The. Blake. MBPR

Frend of mine, pitieng my helplesse love, A. Henry Constable. *Fr.* Diana. ESo

Frenzy. George Crabbe. *Fr.* Sir Eustace Grey. NOBE

Frequency of bumping, The. There Are in Such Moments. David I. Silverstein. AMV–80

Frère Jacques (Brother John). *Unknown, tr. fr. French.* FSW

Frere ther was, a wantowne and a merye, A. *See* Friar there was, a wanton and a merry, A.

Fresco. Linda Pastan. PoUp

Fresco for A. MacLeish, A. Alfred Hayes. SPT

Frescoes for Mr. Rockefeller's City. Archibald MacLeish. UnPo (1976 ed.)
Burying Ground by the Ties, III. GOA
Landscape as a Nude, I. CMoP (1970 ed.)

Fresh Air. Kenneth Koch. CAPP; NNaP; NoAM

Fresh bread on the table, preganant, whole, A. Evening Bread. Jacob Glatstein, *tr. by* David G. Roskies *and* Hillel Schwartz. VWA

Fresh day cracks, goat's milkspurt. Six-forty-two Farm Commune Struggle Poem. Jay Leifer. MAT

Fresh from the dewy hill, the merry year. Song. Blake. MBPR

Fresh Fruit for Breakfast. Roderick Jellema. PoUp

Fresh I'm cum fra Sandgate Street. Do Li A. *Unknown.* GBP

Fresh peaches, large balls that glow for a princess at night. To Bed. Diane Wakoski. CAAP

Fresh savannas of the Sangamon, The. The Painted Cup. Bryant. EAP

Fresh Spring, the herald of love's mighty king. Amoretti, LXX. Spenser. CABA (1972 ed.); FF; HAP; ILP (1975 ed.)

Fresh strewings allow. The Peter-Penny. Robert Herrick. CaPo

Freshet springs from woodland cleft, The. Postscript to Die Schöne Müllerin. R. P. Lister. POL

Freshmen. Barry Spacks. CoPAm

Fresno Notebook. Neeli Cherkovski. CPA

Fret fools the days away. Life of the Mind, 1934. Genevieve Taggard. SPT

Fretful ladybirds complain, The. The Ladybirds. Edward Lucie-Smith. BoAnP

Freud: Dying in London, He Recalls the Smoke of His Cigar Beginning to Sing. James Schevill. TAP

Friar and the Nun, The. *Unknown.* GBP

Friar had said his paternosters duly, The. Necrological. John Crowe Ransom. PiAm

Friar of Rubygill, The. Thomas Love Peacock. *Fr.* Maid Marian. PeBB

Friar there [*or* Frere ther] was, a wanton and a merry, A. A Wanton Merry Friar. Chaucer. *Fr.* The Canterbury Tales: Prologue. BiP; BoReV

Friars' Retort, The. *Unknown.* OxBM

Friar's Tale, The. Chaucer. *Fr.* The Canterbury Tales. PAIC

Friday afternoon: chicken eggs. Alchemy. Diane Levenberg. NPW

Friday arrives with all its attendant ecstacies. Called Back. Charles Wright. PCho

Friday came and the circus was there. The Circus. Elizabeth Madox Roberts. CC

Friday Evening. Julio Marzán. InW

Friday in berkeley. Untitled I. Ishmael Reed. CNA

Friday Lunchbreak. Gregory Orr. PCho

Friday Morning. Sydney Carter. LP

Friday Night after Bathing. Stephen Levy. VWA

Friday night i stand with spread legs. High. Mbembe. NW

Friday; or, The Dirge. John Gay. *Fr.* The Shepherd's Week. ILP (1975 ed.)

Friday the Thirteenth. Allen Ginsberg. NNaP

Friday. Wet Dusk. Christopher Logue. OxBTC

Friend. Gwendolyn Brooks. CNA

Friend, The. Marge Piercy. IPWM; NMM; RiTi

Friend, A. Marguerite Power. FaBoCo

Friend, A. W. D. Snodgrass. MAT

Friend/ Savior/ woman. Redemption. Stanley Cooperman. AMV–80

Friend—/ your eyes are perforated mirrors. Song for Meeting a Friend. Rafael Jesús González. BrS

Friend Advises Me to Stop Drinking, A. Mei Yao Ch'en, *tr. fr. Chinese by* Kenneth Rexroth. HoPM (1975 ed.)

Friend at a cocktail party tells me, A. Talk to Me, Baby. Michael Dennis Browne. BrS

Friend at a Drug Clinic. John Gonzalez. PMW

Friend Col and I, both full of whim. David Garrick. FaBoEE

Friend, don't be angry. Mirabai, *tr. fr. Hindi by* Willis Barnstone *and* Usha Nilsson. BoWoP

Friend, Hope for the Guest. Kabir, *tr. fr. Hindi by* Robert Bly. EC

Friend, how can I meet my lord? Mirabai, *tr. fr, Hindi by* Willis Barnstone *and* Usha Nilsson. BoWoP

Friend I can trust is the one who will let me have my death, The. Adrienne Rich. *Fr.* Ghazals: Homage to Ghalib. NIL

Friend in the Garden, A. Juliana Horatia Ewing. OxBChV

Friend of Humanity and the Knife-Grinder, The. George Canning *and* John Hookham Frere. ESaP; FaBoCo

Friend of Ronsard, Nashe and Beaumont. On a Birthday. J. M. Synge. GBL

Friend of the albatross. Maidenhead. Michael McMahon. FAF

Friend of the Family, A. Louis Simpson. NNaP

Friend of the wise! and teacher of the good! To William Wordsworth. Samuel Taylor Coleridge. MBPR; OAEL-2

Friend, on this scaffold Thomas More lies dead. J. V. Cunningham. InPK

Friend, Ortho of Syracuse gives thee this charge. Ortho's Epitaph. Theocritus, *tr. by* Charles Stuart Calverley. FaBoEE

Friend Proclus, the world isn't a fantasy. Epistolary Briefs to Proclus. José I. de Diego Padró, *tr. by* Julio Marzán. InW

Friend, whose unnatural early death. An Elegy. David Gascoyne. FaBoTw (1975 ed.)

Friend, with regard to this same hare. To the Rev. Mr. Powell. Christopher Smart. OBW

Friend with Spinning Rod. Napoleon St. Cyr. FAF

Friend, you are wearied. Urbanite Delapidate. Herman Spector. SPT

Friend, you seem thoughtful. I not wonder much. A Sea Dialogue. Oliver Wendell Holmes. OBAL

Friendless and faint, with martyred steps and slow. Calvary. E. A. Robinson. OFD

Friendly Beasts, The. *Unknown.* PChr; RAE

Friendly cow, all red and white, The. The Cow. Robert Louis Stevenson. CTV; OxBChV

Friends. Abbie Farwell Brown. CTV

Friends, The. Robert Creeley. Epi

Friends. Ray Durem. PoBA
(Broadminded.) SoSe (1977 ed.)

Friends. Elizabeth Jennings. LP

Friends. *Unknown.* CTV

Friends. W. B. Yeats. NoAM; WeW

Friends/ we are approaching absolute zero. Approaching Absolute Zero. Joyce Peseroff. PCho

Friends,/ you are lucky you can talk. Vidya, *tr. fr. Sanskrit by* Willis Barnstone. BoWoP

Friends Beyond. Thomas Hardy. VLP

Friends Departed. Henry Vaughan. *See* They Are All Gone into the World of Light.

Friend's Passing, A. Barclay Sheaks. AMV-80

Friends recommmended the new Polish film. A Night Out. Dannie Abse. BuTh

Friends, Romans, countrymen, lend me your ears. Mark Antony Addresses the Mob. Shakespeare. *Fr.* Julius Caesar, III, ii. FaPoR

Friendship. Lucien Stryk. GP

Friendship Game, The. Pier Giorgio Di Cicco. AMV-81

Friendship is like a garden of flowers. Growing Friendship. *Unknown.* CTV

Friendship's Mystery, to My Dearest Lucasia. Katherine Philips. SCP-2

Frigate Jones, the Pussyfooter. Kenneth Burke. OBAL

Frigate Pelican, The. Marianne Moore. Psy

Frightened/ by the sound of my own voice. Lawrence Ferlinghetti. *Fr.* Coney Island of the Mind. NoAM; TAP

Frightened Man, The. Louise Bogan. SBG

Fringes, The. Harris Lenowitz. VWA

Frisco, Denver, Memphis. My Own Brand. Art Cuelho. TAT

'Frisco Town. *Unknown.* BluL

Frisco Whistle Blues. *Unknown.* BluL

Frisco's Defi. H. S. Hooper. BPAW

Frivolous Cake, The. Mervyn Peake. *Fr.* Titus Groan. BBL

Frog, The. Hilaire Belloc. BBL; CTV; LCL; OxBChV

Frog, The. *Unknown.* ECBV

Frog and the Crow, The. *Unknown.* GBP

Frog and the Toad, The. Christina Rossetti. RAE
(Hopping Frog.) PCOP

Frog half fearful jumps across the path, The. Summer Evening. John Clare. PCOP

Frog he would a-wooing go, A. Mother Goose. MG; MN

Frog lay in the step-child's bed, The. The Wooing Frog. James Reeves. SO

Frog Plague, The. Bruce Dawe. CAAP

Frog Prince. Gabrielle Edgcomb. PoUp

Frog Prince, The. Stevie Smith. HAP

Frog Prince, The: A Speculation on Grimm's Fairy Tale. Robert Pack. TPo

Frog Went a-Courting. *Unknown.* RDB, *with music*
(Froggie Went a-Courting.) AmFP; BLSo, *with music;* FSW

Frog Who Would Be an Ox, The. La Fontaine, *tr. fr. French by* Marianne Moore. NAWM-2

Frogs. Norman MacCaig. BoAnP; SFF

Frogs. Louis Simpson. BoAnP; InPS; TH

Frogs and the serpents each had a football team, The. Cheers. Eve Merriam. LiSp; SPo

Frog's Fate, A. Christina Rossetti. VPC

Frog's Lament, The. Aileen Fisher. FPB

Frogs sit more solid. Frogs. Norman MacCaig. BoAnP; SFF

Frogs time out of mind, The. Aesop's Fable of the Frogs. La Fontaine, *tr. by* John Hookman Frere. OBVE

Frolic, A. Robert Herrick. FaBoEE

From. Richard Terrill. AMV-81

From a Book of Hours. Charles Spear. ATNZ

From a Brother Dreaming in the Rye. James Cunningham. JB

From a Calendar. Sydney Dobell. PCOP

From a Cheerful Alphabet. John Updike. FaBoCo

From a Correct Address in a Suburb of a Major City. Helen Sorrells. WPE

From a Diary. Frederick Morgan. NYP

From a Distance. Marvin Bell. HeS

From a distance, I watch. Practical Concerns. William J. Harris. PoBA

From a green sack on a green hill. Here and There. Jon Stallworthy. NoAM

From a gull's oily breath. From All These, You. Harold Norse. CPA

From a height of gargoyles and waterspouts. Lemuel Johnson. *Fr.* Hand on the Navel. AAN

From a high mountain I see how the banks of a river. The Banks of a River. Abraham Sutskever, *tr. by* Ruth Whitman. VWA

From a Lavatory Wall. *Unknown.* FaBoEE

From a Litany. Mark Strand. PPP

From a magician's midnight sleeve. Late Air. Elizabeth Bishop. LoAs

From a Museum Man's Album. John Hewitt. OxBTC

From a New and Wild Distance. Ted Weiant. BCr

From a Plague Year. David Malouf. FPA

From a Print by Maillol. Anne Becker. PoUp

From a Railway Carriage. Robert Louis Stevenson. OxBChV

From a ruler that's a curse. The Litany. Charles Cotton. OBSV

From a Speech Delivered in Freedom Hall on Afrikan Liberation Day: Words from a Welfare Mother. Angela Jackson. FiCh

From a steep driveway the car rolls backward. The Incident. Jim Kraus. PHC

From a Survivor. Adrienne Rich. GP; LoAs

From a Very Little Sphinx. Edna St. Vincent Millay. OBAL

From a Woman to a Greedy Lover. Norman Cameron. Three Love Poems, I. FaBoEE

From across the stream, on the side of the opposite hill. Not Seeing Is Believing. Paul Petrie. TAP

From Age to Age They Gather, *with music.* Frederick Lucian Hosmer. AH

From All These, You. Harold Norse. CPA

From America. James M. Whitfield. BPo

From an Old House in America. Adrienne Rich. NNaP

From an old house shaded with macrocarpas. James K. Baxter. *Fr.* Pig Island Letters. ATNZ

From an old man. Dusk. Ken Belford. NeAC

From an old photo. The Chauffeur of Lilacs. George Hitchcock. GP

From anger into the pit of sleep. Wife to Husband. Fleur Adcock. ATNZ

From Arranmore the weary miles I've come. Mavrone. Arthur Guiterman. SpRo

From Belsen a crate of gold teeth. Riddle. William Heyen. GP

From being anxious, or secure. Good Lord, Deliver Us! John Donne. *Fr.* The Litany. BoReV

From beyond the wooded island. Stenka Razin. *Tr. fr. Russian.* FSW

From bleakness. To Mirikitani. Geraldine Kudaka. NW

From Blenhiem's clocktower a cheerfull bell bangs out. Distilled Water. M. K. Joseph. ATNZ

From Braddon's penniless subornation. A New Litany in the Year 1684. *Unknown.* APAS

From breakfast on through all the day. The Land of Nod. Robert Louis Stevenson. ILP (1975 ed.)

From breasts/ Of Africland. Africland. Oliver LaGrone. FB

From Brooklyn heights a Hessian doctor came. The Hessian Doctor. Philip Freneau. *Fr.* The British Prison Ship. EAP

From Bulgaria thick, wild cannon pounding rolls. Picture Postcards. Miklós Radnóti, *tr. by* Emery George. VWA

From childhood's hour I have not been. Alone. Poe. PiAm; VoPo

From city window, 'way up high. Motor Cars. Rowena Bastin Bennett. FPB

From Clee to heaven the beacon burns. 1887. A. E. Housman. BTTM; FaPoR; IP; NIL; SoSe (1977 ed.); STS; UnPo (1976 ed.); VLP; VoPo

From Colony to Nation. Irving Layton. CABA (1972 ed.)

From Countless Hearts, *with music.* Gail Brook Burket. AH

From Creature to Ghost. Pauline Hanson. TAP

From darkness/ I go onto the road/ of darkness. Izumi Shikibu, *tr. fr. Japanese by* Willis Barnstone. BoWoP

From darkness/ Into the path of darkness. Izumi Shikibu, *tr. fr. Japanese by* Edwin A. Cranston. PBWP

From darkness into darkness. Hoot Owl Shift. Robert Stricklin. AMV-80

From deep sleep. Nightmare. James A. Emanuel. BPo

From dollars to T-shirts. World's Fare. Charles Stetler. GP

From Eastertide to Eastertide. A Ballad of a Nun. John Davidson. PAIC

From Exile. Dafydd Benfras, *tr. fr. Welsh by* Anthony Conran. OBW

From Far Away. Delmira Agustini, *tr. fr. Spanish by* D. M. Pettinella. PBWP

From Far, from Eve and Morning. A. E. Housman. CMoP (1970 ed.); HAP; HeIP

From fairest creatures we desire increase. Sonnets, I. Shakespeare. STS

From Father to Son. Emyr Humphreys. OBW

"From fear to fear, successively betrayed." Reflection from Rochester. William Empson. PoA

From Feathers to Iron, *sel.* C. Day Lewis. Now She Is like the White Tree-Rose. CMoP (1970 ed.); FaBoTw (1975 ed.)

From '41 to '51. John Masefield. *Fr.* The Everlasting Mercy. NoAM

From four walls of/ ivory. Ellen Cooney. NPW

From frozen climes and endless tracks of snow. To the Earl of Dorset. Ambrose Philips. EPC

From garden to garden, ridge to ridge. John Muir. RFM

From Garvey's Farm: Seneca, Wisconsin. Ed Hoeppner. AMV-80

From Generation to Generation. Sir Henry Newbolt. FaBoTw (1975 ed.)

From ghoulies and ghosties. Litany for Halloween. *Unknown, tr. fr. Cornish.* CC; IWK; OFD

From Gloucester Out. Edward Dorn. NoAM; NOBA

From gorge to gorge. Elena Clementelli, *tr. by* Ruth Feldman and Brian Swann. *Fr.* Etruscan Notebook. PBWP

From Grant's grave Galena. Old Dubuque. Dave Etter. ANTL

From Greenland's Icy Mountains. Reginald Heber. BLSH; *with music;* FaPoR; VLP

From harmony, from heavenly harmony. A Song for St. Cecilia's Day, 1687. Dryden. AnMo; BiP; CABA (1972 ed.); HAP; ILP (1975 ed.); InPS; LFH; NIL; OAEL-1; PPP; SCP-1

From Heart to Heart, *with music.* William Channing Gannett. AH

From Heaven High I Come to You. *At. to* Martin Luther, *tr. fr. German.* PChr

From heaven's high embrasure. A Frosty Morning. John Davidson. VLP

From her pool in the muddy shallows. Pregnant Teenager on the Beach. Mary Balazs. AMV-80

From Heraclitus. Alan Dugan. PoA

From here on, all of us will be living. Adrienne Rich. *Fr.* Ghazals: Homage to Ghalib. NIL

From here through tunnelled gloom the track. The Railway Junction. Walter de la Mare. OxBTC

From Here to There. Rachel Korn, *tr. fr. Yiddish by* Seymour Mayne *and* Rivka Augenfeld. VWA

From high windows. Shabbat Morning. Bradley R. Strahan. AMV-81

From his brimstone bed at break of day. The Devil's Thoughts. Robert Southey *and* Samuel Taylor Coleridge. FaBoCo; OBSV

From his library in Surrey. Nothing Sacred. Roger Woddis. NOBL

From his own solitude to the world unheeding. Llewelyn Wyn Griffith. *Fr.* The Barren Tree. OBW

From his shoulder Hiawatha. Hiawatha's Photographing. "Lewis Carroll." FaBoCo; NOBL; SpRo

From his wanderings far to eastward. Longfellow. *Fr.* The Song of Hiawatha. GOA

From holy flower to holy flower. The Study of a Spider. Lord De Tabley. VLP

From hoofbeat to chug-chug to roar of jet. Progress. Suzanne Douglass. QQQ

From inside nothing is plausible. Late Autumn Walk. J. D. McClatchy. AMV-80

From inside the bird a dream hums itself out and turns. These Horses Came. Ray A. Young Bear. CDW

From Jerusalem: A First Poem. Gabriel Preil, *tr. fr. Hebrew by* Robert Friend. VWA

From left to right, she leads the eye. Myth on Mediterranean Beach: Aphrodite as Logos. Robert Penn Warren. HAP

From Life. Lazer Eichenrand, *tr. fr. Yiddish by* Gabriel Preil *and* Howard Schwartz. VWA

From life's grim nightmare he is now released. Jacob Epstein. *Unknown.* FaBoCo

From Lois in London. Angela McCabe. AmPA

From low to high doth dissolution climb. Mutability. Wordsworth. *Fr.* Ecclesiastical Sonnets. CABA (1972 ed.); EBEV; HeIP; ILP (1975 ed.); InPK; MBPR; NOBE; OAEL-2; PPoD

From Mistra: A Prospect. Ted Higgs. AMV-80

From moccasins to shoes. First Grade. Phillip William George. VoR

From Montauk Point. Walt Whitman. RFM

From moonwater, from mirror mist, a slender porcelain. Gift Hour. Maria Banus, *tr. by* Willis Barnstone *and* Matei Calinescu. BoWoP; VWA

From Mount Nebo. Karl Wolfskehl, *tr. fr.* German *by* Erna Baber Rosenfeld. VWA

From my city bed in the dawn. SF. Earnest Leverett. QQQ

From my father's head I sprung. Athene's Song. Eavan Boland. CIP

From my first city bed in the dawn I see a raccoon. Science Fiction. Read Whittemore. GP

From my front wheels the scared rabbits. Iowa, June. Michael Dennis Browne. AmPA

From My Lai the Thunder Went West. Richard Ryan. CIP

From My Mother's Home. Leah Goldberg. *See* My Mother's House.

From my mother's sleep I fell into the State. The Death of the Ball Turret Gunner. Randall Jarrell. BiP; CMoP (1970 ed.); CoPAm; ExPo (1973 ed.); FF; HAP; HoPM (1975 ed.); ILP (1975 ed.); InPK; IPWM; NIL; NoAM; NOBA; NowV; PoIA; PPP; PSN; SoS; SoSe; TAP; UnPo (1976 ed.); VGW; WIF

From my personal album. For Malcolm X. Nanina Alba. PoBA

From my windows on Brodsky street. The Russian Poem IV. Dan Gerber. TC

From near the sea, like Whitman my great predecessor, I call. Ode: Salute to the French Negro Poets. Frank O'Hara. NNaP

From noise of scare-fires rest ye free. The Bellman. Robert Herrick. CaPo; PoPle

From Now On. *Unknown.* BluL

From now on kill America out of your mind. Lyric. James Agee. GOA

From Number Nine, Penwiper Mews. Edward Gorey. TDH

From off his pointed head flies Herr Schmidt's hat. End of the World. Jakov van Hoddis, *tr. by* Edouard Roditi. VWA

From old Fort Walla Walla and the Klickitats. In the Oregon Country. William Stafford. MPA

From one shaft at Cleator Moor. Cleator Moor. Norman Nicholson. FaBoTw (1975 ed.). MPo

From One Who Stays. Amy Lowell. BoWoP

From Orford Ness to Shingle Street. Dawn on the East Coast. Alun Lewis. PSN

From Our Album. Lawson Fusao Inada. AmPA

From out his castle on the sand. The Sea-King. L. Frank Hooker. RhR

From out of a wood did a cuckoo fly. The Birds. *Unknown.* PChr

From out of our/ dwellings have I heard. Desert Stone. Miriam Waddington. VWA

From Paumanok Starting I Fly like a Bird. Walt Whitman. GOA

From Pent-up Aching Rivers. Walt Whitman. BoLoP; CABA (1972 ed.); NOBA

From pitch and catch. Fungo. Stanley Plumly. AmPA

From platforms old, and promising correction. Politicians, 1972. Timothy Clinch. NIL

From pleasure of the bed. The Chambermaid's Second Song. W. B. Yeats. AnMo

From point A a wind is blowing to point B. After the Broken Arm. Ron Padgett. ConAP; EAS; UsP

From prehistoric distance, beyond clocks. Street Fight. Harold Monro. FaBoTw (1975 ed.)

From Rome, for More Public Fountains in New York City. Alan Dugan. NYP; Prf

From Russian Hill. Ina Coolbrith. BPAW; WPW

From St. Luke's Hospital. Madeleine L'Engle. CTBA

From Sappho to myself, consider the fate of women. Pro Femina, I. Carolyn Kizer. NMM; Psy; RiTi; WBN

From scars where kestrels hover. Missing. W. H. Auden. OxBTC

From seeing and seeing the seeing has become so exhausted. The Panther. Rainer Maria Rilke, *tr. by* Robert Bly. NU

From southern isles, on winds of gentlest wing. The Prospect. Timothy Dwight. Greenfield Hill, Pt.I. EAP

From stainless steel basins of water. The Operation. W. D. Snodgrass. InPK; TAP

From Stirling castle we had seen. Yarrow Unvisited. Wordsworth. MBPR

From such old boards. "Dangerous Condition": Sign on Inner-City House. Russell Atkins. CNA

From summer and the wheel-shaped city. Washington Cathedral. Karl Shapiro. WasP

From Sunset to Star Rise. Christina Rossetti. SBG

From that first flash when awful Love took flame. Sonnet IV. Louise Labé, *tr. by* Willis Barnstone. BoWoP

From that first night. Izumi Shikibu, *tr. fr. Japanese by* Edwin A. Cranston. PBWP

From that last acre on oblivion's heap. Edna St. Vincent Millay Exhorts Little Boy Blue. Louis Untermeyer. PAIC

From that last mountain's track. The Last View. Ruthe T. Spinnanger. AATT

From that they found most lovely, most abhorred. Beginning. Alden Nowlan. NeAC

From the balcony you watched her walking. Memory, a Small Brown Bird. Rich Ives. AMV-81

From the bathing machine came a din. Edward Gorey. OBAL

From the Batter's Box. David K. Harford. AMV-80

From the battery of progress and punch-drunk with defeat. The Passing of Joe Williams. Norman Macleod. SPT

From the bed where I lay. The Mirror. John Haines. CNW

From the besieged Ardea all in post. Shakespeare. *Fr.* The Rape of Lucrece. LFH

From the bonny bells of heather. Heather Ale. Robert Louis Stevenson. PoTa

From the Bridge. Albert Goldbarth. NVAP

From the center of the room to the center. Fish. Mario Satz, *tr. by* Willis Barnstone. VWA

From the center of the Sea of Tranquility. The Planet. Josephine Jacobsen. GP

From the cliff-top it appeared a place of defeat. The Cave. A. R. D. Fairburn. ATNZ

"From the colour the nature." Ezra Pound. Cantos, XC. VGW

From the commandant's quarters on Westchester height. Aaron Burr's Wooing. Edmund Clarence Stedman. BTTM

From the converts in Uganda. Grass on the Prayer Path. *Unknown.* PeD

From the Country to the City. Elizabeth Bishop. NYP

From the Crag. Mani Leib, *tr. fr. Yiddish by* David G. Roskies *and* Hillel Schwartz. VWA

From the dark Stygian banks I come. Marvell's Ghost. John Ayloffe. APAS

From the Dark Tower. Countee Cullen. BPo; PoBA

From the dark woods that breathe of fallen showers. The Zebras. Roy Campbell. PoPle

From the dark world I tap, tap, tap. The Blind Man. Ronald Mann. PMW

From the deepest part of a dream the escaped. Doorway to Time in Three Voices. Luis Palés Matos, *tr. by* Rachel Benson. InW

From the depth of the dreamy decline of the dawn. Nephelidia. Swinburne. *Fr.* The Heptalogia. FaBoCo; FaBoNo; HoPM (1975 ed.); SpRo

From the Depths. Otakar Fischer, *tr. fr. Czech.* VWA

From the dire monument of thy black room. Calling Lucasta from Her Retirement. Richard Lovelace. CaPo

From the Direction of the State Mental Institution. Carol Cox. MMD

From the dull confines of the drooping West. His Return to London. Robert Herrick. CaPo; FF; ILP (1975 ed.)

From the Dust. Elaine Dallman. VWA

From the Embassy. Robert Graves. PoA

From the fine nursing home. An Old Man's Lark. Donald Jones. TVo

From the first light we fear falling. Hotel Fire: New Orleans. Paul Ruffin. AMV–81

From the Flats. Sidney Lanier. NOBA

From the forests and highlands. Hymn of Pan. Shelley. ILP (1975 ed.); MBPR

From the four corners of the earth. Carl Sandburg. *Fr.* The People, Yes, Sec. 1. CMoP (1970 ed.)

From the frantic weather into his creaking tomb. His Necessary Darkness. Nancy Sullivan. TAP

From the French. Sir Walter Scott. SLP

From the Gallows Hill to the Tineton Copse. John Masefield. *Fr.* Reynard the Fox, II. OBP

From the great Atlantic Ocean, to the wide Pacific shore. Wabash Cannonball. *Unknown.* BLSo

From the Grove Press. Anthony Hecht. OBAL

From the hag [or hagg] and hungry [or hungrie] goblin. Tom o' Bedlam's Song. *Unknown.* EBEV; HAP; Moon; NOBE; OAEL-1; OBP; WeW

From the half/ Of the sky. The Approach of the Storm. *Tr. by* Frances Densmore. OBVE

From the Halls of Montezuma. The Marines' Hymn. *Unknown.* BLSH; BLSo; BTTM

From the Hazel Bough. Earle Birney. HeIP

From the Head. Louis Zukofsky. VWA

From the heart of a flower. Leave It to Me Blues. Joel Oppenheimer. VGW

From the high deck of Santa Fe's El Capitan. A Siding near Chillicothe. Richmond Lattimore. ANTL

From the hodge porridge. The Farmer's Wife. Anne Sexton. CoPAm; HoPM (1975 ed.)

From the hold of this ship. Mediterranean. Israel Pincas, *tr. by* A. C. Jacobs. VWA

From the Ice Age. Barbara Bloom. AMV–81

From the icy niche where men placed you. Death Sonnet I. Gabriela Mistral, *tr. by* David Garrison. BoWoP

From the immense hemicycle, from the blue fire of the earth. The Tree of Death. Claude Vigée, *tr. by* J. R. Le Master *and* Kenneth L. Beaudoin. VWA

From the land of refuge. Week-Seek. Jim Tollerud. VoR

From the mountains we come. Warrior Nation Trilogy. Lance Henson. VoR

From the Night-Window. Douglas Dunn. SLP

From the north-west a cloud has come up. Prince Sumiya. *Mongol Oral Tradition, tr. by* C. R. Bawden. WTO

From the obscurity of the past, we saw. Nat Turner. Samuel Allen. CNA; FB

From the Observation Deck, Austin. Henry Petroski. AAN

From the old slave shack I chose my lady. Trellie. Lance Jeffers. CNA; FB

From the oracular archives and the parchment. Altarwise by Owl-Light, IX. Dylan Thomas. CMoP (1970 ed.); NoAM

From the other side of the world. To Stanislaw Wyspianski. Katherine Mansfield. ATNZ

From the Painting "Back from Market" by Chardin. Eavan Boland. IPM

From the Point. Paul Petrie. AMV–80

From the Prison House. Adrienne Rich. NNaP

From the quarters of the compass. Catullus, *tr. fr. Latin by* Peter Whigham. TwMBP

From the revenew of thine eyes' exchequer. *Unknown. Fr.* Zepheria. ESo

From the Righteous Man Even the Wild Beasts Run Away. David Bromwich. PoA

From the rodeo's mazy stalls. The Bumper Sticker on His Pickup Said. Eldon Ray Fox. LiSp

From the slopes of the mountain. Clear Bright. Li Ch'ing-chao, *tr. by* Kenneth Rexroth. BoWoP

From the small life that loves with tooth and nail. Coventry Patmore. FaBoEE

From the Stone Age. Alice Corbin. WPW

From the tawny light. Everything That Acts Is Actual. Denise Levertov. NoAM

From the television set comes shots and cries. Goodbye, Old Paint, I'm Leaving Cheyenne. George Garrett. PPoD

From the tracks it appeared. Encounter. Clarice Short. MPA

From the tragic-est novels at Mudie's. Dora versus Rose. Austin Dobson. NOBL

From the Underworld. Howard Blaikley. GrRo

From the very first coming down. The Letter. W. H. Auden. FaBoTw (1975 ed.); NoAM

From the Wash the Laundress Sends. A. E. Housman. InPK; NoAM

From the wild fells I return to my lowland home. Glaramara. R. C. Trevelyan. PES

From the wind I get/ the predicate of plants. Saved. Maria Teresa Horta, *tr. by* Suzette Macedo. PBWP

From the window I can see the corner of a gutter. The Gutter. Franco Fortini, *tr. by* Ruth Feldman. VWA

From the Window of the Beverly Wilshire Hotel. Michael McClure. EAS

From these bare trees. Chinese Winter. F. R. Higgins. BIrV

From these sights/ Take one,—that ancient festival, the Fair. Wordsworth. *Fr.* The Prelude, VII. HAP

From this beach I want to make a poem. Beachhead Preachment. Ahmos Zu-Bolton. AMV–81

From this high place all things flow. Watershed. Robert Penn Warren. PoA

From this moment/ and hence backwards. Joanne Kyger. RiTi

From this sheer tower, as from time's parapet. New York. John Hall Wheelock. NYP

From this mountain's edge, clouds crowd. Beinn Damph. Paul Mills. MIS

From this valley they say you are going. Red River Valley. *Unknown.* BLSH; BLSo; BPAW; FSW

From three dark places Christ came forth this day. Upon Christ's Nativity; or, Christmas. Rowland Watkyns. OBW; SCP-2

From Thursday. Barbara Earl Thomson. AATT

From Travancore to Tripoli. Ballad of the Oedipus Complex. Lawrence Durrell. FaBoCo

From tree to tree ahead of me. Lens for Plum Blossom. Thomas Hornsby Ferril. MPA

From Trollope's Journal. Elizabeth Bishop. GOA

From Tuscan cam my ladies worthi race. Earl of Surrey. AAS

From twenty yards I saw my old love. Art and Reality. James Simmons. CIP

From Venice Was That Afternoon. Jean Garrigue. NOBA

From Venus' breast a bit of greenery grows. On a Statue of Venus. *Unknown.* LoAs

From Virgil. George Oppen. *Fr.* Five Poems about Poetry. NNaP

From watching gulls dive. Advantages. Eve Shelnutt. TC

From what great sleep. Watts. Alvin Saxon. PoBA

From what proud star I know not, but I found. The Giant Puffball. Edmund Blunden. FaBoTw (1975 ed.)

From what strange country do you come, then? Poem. Siv Cedering Fox. NVAP

From whence cometh song? Song. Theodore Roethke. NCSH

From Whence Doth This Union Arise? *with music.* Thomas Baldwin. AH

From where I live, from windows on four sides. Juniper. Robert Francis. VGW

From where I sit, I see. Viewpoint. George Scarbrough. AMV-81

From where I sit I see the stars. Midnight. Archibald Lampman. AKE

From where I stand now. 12 October. Myra Cohn Livingston. CC

From which flow destructions of the Constitution. The Law I Love Is Major Mover. Robert Duncan. PiAm

From winter-sleep. Ladybug's Christmas. Norma Farber. PChr

From witty men and mad. The Poet. Thomas Randolph. POL

From Wynyard's Gap the livelong day. A Trampwoman's Tragedy. Thomas Hardy. VLP

From you have I been absent in the spring. Sonnets, XCVIII. Shakespeare. EBEV; FSFS; ILP (1975 ed.); NOBE; PoPle

From you, Ianthe, little troubles pass. Ianthe's Troubles. Walter Savage Landor. *Fr.* Ianthe. GBL; NOBE

From your high bridge wave and wail. Prayer. Lev Mak, *tr. by* Dan Jaffe. VWA

From your lips I will pluck. Love's Flowers. William Cavendish, Duke of Newcastle. SCP-2

Fronleichnam. D. H. Lawrence. GBL

Front, A. Randall Jarrell. VGW

Front ones I can button fine, The. Buttons. *Unknown.* CTV

Frontier, The. John Hewitt. BIrV

Frontispiece. May Swenson. WPE

Frost. Stella Benson. OxBTC

Frost, The. Tzu Yeh, *tr. fr. Chinese.* TVo

Frost/ lacing/ late summer. Peter Whigham. *Fr.* Love Poems of the VIth Dalai Lama. TwMBP

Frost at Midnight. Samuel Taylor Coleridge. CABA (1972 ed.); EBEV; HAP; ILP (1975 ed.); IPWM; MBPR; NOBE; OAEL-2; PPP
    "Therefore all seasons shall be sweet to thee," *sel.* FSFS

Frost breaks across the dawn. Fall Again. H. R. Coursen. AMV-81

Frost-fallen are the leaves. Insight. Ruthe T. Spinnanger. AATT

Frost Heaves. Michael Dorris. AMV-80

Frost is here, The. Winter. Tennyson. FSFS

Frost on the ground, so still and white. First Frost. E. Margaret Clarkson. AATT

Frost performs its secret ministry, The. Frost at Midnight. Samuel Taylor Coleridge. CABA (1972 ed.); EBEV; HAP; ILP (1975 ed.); IPWM; MBPR; NOBE; OAEL-2; PPP

Frost round the House. Anne B. Murray. MS

Frost Warning. Ron McFarland. AMV-81

Frost's nimble silk. Trahison des Clercs; Against the Perversion of Language. Ezra Pound. PAIC

Frosty Morning, A. John Davidson. VLP

Frosty Night, A. Robert Graves. LP; OxBTC

Froude informs the Scottish youth. A Hymn on Froude and Kingsley. William Stubbs. FaBoEE

Froward Maymond ("Froward knave plainly to descrive, A"). John Lydgate. OxBM

Frowardness of the Elect in the Work of Conversion, The. Edward Taylor. *Fr.* God's Determinations. EAP

Frozen Hands. Joseph Bruchac. CDW

Frozen lemonade, frozen limas. Shopping. Jane Chance Nitzche. AMV-80

Frozen Logger, The. *Unknown.* BPAW (*At. to* James Stevens); FSW; OBAL

Frozen Zone, The; or Julia Disdainful. Robert Herrick. CaPo; SCP-1

Fruit and Vegetables. Erica Jong. CAAP

Fruit itself a giant pinecone, The. Death and the Pineapple. Dan Gerber. TC

Fruit of Loneliness. May Sarton. PoA

Fruit on the trees is aging fast, The. Words to a Song. Agnes Nemes Nagy, *tr. by* Bruce Berlind. BoWoP

Fruit rolled by all day, The. Pickle Belt. Theodore Roethke. AnMo

Fruit that was atop the shelf, The. Till the Sea Runs Dry. *Malay Oral Tradition, tr. by* R. J. Wilkinson. WTO

Fruits. Christina Rossetti. ECBV

Fruits of the Earth. Christopher Smart. *Fr.* A Song to David. OBP

Fruits you give me are more savory than others, The. Marguerite Burnat-Provins, *tr. fr. French by* Cassia Borman. BoWoP

Frutta di Mare. Geoffrey Scott. EcS

Frying Pan Skillet Blues. *Unknown.* BluL

Fuchsia and I seem happy now, The. Cloud Burst. Hubert Witheford. ATNZ

Fudge Family in Paris, The, *sel.* Thomas Moore.
    "After dreaming some hours of the land of Cockaigne." BIrV
    "At length, my Lord, I have the bliss." OBSV

Fudge, Fudge. *Unknown.* OSF

Fueled. Marcie Hans. MiP

Fugato (Coda.) Gad Hollander. VWA

Fugitive Slaves, The. Jones Very. TAP

Fugue. Howard Nemerov. TAP

Fugue. Kathleen Spivack. AMV-80

Fugue and Variations. George Hitchcock. FoP

Fugue of Death. Paul Celan, *tr. fr. German by* Christopher Middleton. OBVE
    (Death Fugue, *tr. by* Joachim Neugroschel.) VWA

Fuimus Fumus. Joshua Sylvester. FaBoEE

Full and True Account of a Horrid and Barbarous Robbery, A. *sel.* John Byrom.
    "Dear Martin Folkes, dear scholar, brother, friend." NOBL

Full be the year, abundant be the grain. Ezra Pound, *after the Chinese.* OBVE

Full cloves, The. A Shallot. Richard Wilbur. GP

Full Consciousness. Juan Ramón Jiménez, *tr. fr. Spanish by* Robert Bly. NU

Full deep green. On Driving behind a School Bus for Mentally Retarded Children. Grace Butcher. RiTi

Full Fathom Five. A. R. D. Fairburn. ATNZ

Full Fanthom Five Thy Father Lies. Shakespeare. *Fr.* The Tempest, I, ii. BiP; EBEV; EcS; ExPo (1973 ed.); HAP; HoPM (1975 ed.); ILP (1975 ed.); InPK; InPS; OBP; PoIA; PoPle; PPoe; STS; WIF
    (Ariel's Song.) AKE; NOBE

("Full fadom five thy father lies.") HeIP (Sea Dirge, A.) RhR

Full many a dreary hour have I past. To My Brother George. Keats. MBPR

Full many a gem of purest ray serene. A "Prize" Poem. Shirley Brooks. FaBoCo; FaBoNo

Full many a glorious morning have I seen. Sonnets, XXXIII. Shakespeare. EBEV; HAP; ILP (1975 ed.); OAEL-1; PPP

Full many sing to me and thee. The Barren Shore. Coventry Patmore. GBL

Full Moon. Walter de la Mare. ECBV

Full Moon. Robert Graves. NOBE

Full Moon. Robert Hayden. BPo

Full Moon. Elinor Wylie. Psy; SBG; VGW

Full moon easterly rising, furious, The. A Love Story. Robert Graves. CMoP (1970 ed.); FaBoTw (1975 ed.)

Full moon half way up the sky, The. Gulls. E. A. Muir. NCSH

Full moon hung above the sea, The. The Play. Charles Otis Judkins. PeD

Full moon rising on the waters of my heart. Evening Song. Jean Toomer. BPo; ILP (1975 ed.)

Full Moonlight in Spring. W. S. Merwin. TH

Full October. Pablo Neruda, tr. fr. Spanish by Stephen Kessler. EC

Full of a nitty-gritty anxiety. Paraders for the Bomb. Sidney Bernard. NowV

Full of her long white arms and milky skin. The Equilibrists. John Crowe Ransom. CMoP (1970 ed.); HAP; LoAs; NIL; NoAM; NOBA; PPP; TAP

Full of superstition. The New Notebook. Maria Banus, tr. by Laura Schiff and Dana Beldiman. PBWP

Full of years and seasoned like a salt timber. Islandman. Brenda Chamberlain. OBW

Full often as I rove by path or stile. Wind on the Corn. Charles Tennyson Turner. VPC

Full rage of Kansas, The. Outside Abilene. Harley Elliott. HeS

Full roses with all their petals like the wrinkles of laughter, The. In Gratitude to Beethoven. Diane Wakoski. Psy

Full Sky. Jules Supervielle, tr. fr. French by Wallace Fowlie. TPo

Full well I know that she is there. Stanzas in Meditation. Gertrude Stein. PoA

Full year since, I took this eager city, A. An Irishman in Coventry. John Hewitt. BIrV; CIP

Fuller and Warren. At. to Moses Whitecotton. AmFP

Fum and Hum, the Two Birds of Royalty. Thomas Moore. OBSV

Fumes from all kinds, The. Coming Down Cleveland Avenue. James Tate. PPoD; SFF

Fun. Leroy F. Jackson. CTV

Fun and Funerals ("Fun street/ Funeral street"). Emilie Glen. EC

Function Room, The. Patrice Phillips. MAT

Funeral, The. Walter de la Mare. CMoP (1970 ed.)

Funeral, The. John Donne. BiP; BoLoP; CABA (1972 ed.); EBEV; HeIP; OAEL-1; PoPle; TT

Funeral, The. Stephen Spender. CMoP (1970 ed.); NoAM

Funeral. Joanna Thompson. AMV-81

Funeral at Ansley. Don Welch. GP; TAT

Funeral Games for Anchises, The: Entellus. Virgil, tr. fr. Latin by Rolfe Humphries. Fr. The Aeneid, V. LiSp

Funeral Games for Patroclus, The: The Boastful Boxer. Homer, tr. fr. Greek by Ennis Rees. Fr. The Iliad, XXIII. LiSp

Funeral Games for Patroclus, The: Wrestling to a Draw. Homer, tr. fr. Greek by Ennis Rees. Fr. The Iliad, XXIII. LiSp

Funeral Home. Margo Bohanon. SES

Funeral Lament (Kommos) from Epiros. Tr. fr. Modern Greek by Elene Kolb. BoWoP

Funeral Notices. Alfonsina Storni, tr. fr. Spanish by Dorothy Scott Loos. AMV-81

Funeral of Martin Luther King, Jr., The. Nikki Giovanni. AmNP (1974 ed.); BPo

Funeral of Paddy Haugh. Jerome Kiely. IPM

Funeral Oration for a Mouse. Alan Dugan. HAP; ILP (1975 ed.); NoAM; PPP

Funeral Poem. Amiri Baraka. CNA

Funeral Rites of the Rose, The. Robert Herrick. CABA (1972 ed.); CaPo; NIL

Funeral stone, A. To Laurels. Robert Herrick. CaPo

Funerall, The. John Donne. See Funeral, The.

Fungi. David Lake. FPA

Fungo. Stanley Plumly. AmPA

Funnels, The. Christian Morgenstern, tr. fr. German by Geoffrey Grigson. FaBoNo

Funny thing about a chair, A. The Chair. Theodore Roethke. AnMo

Funny thing is that he's reading a paper, The. The Sandwich Man. Ron Padgett. ConAP

Furies sink upon their iron beds, The. Pope. Fr. Ode on St. Cecilia's Day. FaBoCo

Furius, Aurelius, bound to Catullus. Catullus, tr. fr. Latin by Horace Gregory. NAWM-1

Furl back black walls with shook Fire! The Diamond. Daniel Moore. MIT

Furnace Monkey. Henry Kanabus. FiCh

Furnace tolls the knell of falling steam, The. Elegy Written in a Country Coal-Bin. Christopher Morley. OBAL

Furnished Lives. Jon Silkin. NoAM

Furnished Room, The. James Merrill. NOBA

Furniture. Chana Bloch. GP

Furniture Factory, The. Vern Rutsala. BrS

Furniture of a Woman's Mind, The. Swift. PPoe

Furniture of the Poem, The. Dennis Saleh. NeAC

Furst Snaw. Billy Kay. MIS

Further Advantages of Learning. Kenneth Rexroth. MPA; TAP

Further Adventures of Charles Simic. Charles Simic. FoP

Further in summer than the birds. Emily Dickinson. NOBA

Further it comes, The. Country-Western Music. Ted Kooser. TAT

Further Language from Truthful James. Bret Harte. FaBoCo; NOBL

Further Notice. Philip Whalen. VGW

Furtively sounding. "It Is Big inside a Man." Kenneth Patchen. VoA

Fury of Abandonment, The. Anne Sexton. UsP

Fury of Aerial Bombardment, The. Richard Eberhart. BiP; CMoP (1970 ed.); CoPAm; ExPo (1973 ed.); FF; HeIP; HoPM (1975 ed.); ILP (1975 ed.); InPK; IP; IPWM; NIL; NoAM; PPoD; PSN; TAP; TCP; UnPo (1976 ed.); VGW; VoPo; WIF

Fury of Flowers and Worms, The. Anne Sexton. BoWoP

Fury of Overshoes, The, sel. Anne Sexton. "Remember when you couldn't." OSP

Fury said to a/ mouse. The Mouse's Tale [or Tail]. "Lewis Carroll." Fr. Alice's Adventures in Wonderland, ch. 3. FaBoNo; MN

Fury this Friday broke through my wall, The. In Memory of a Friend. George Barker. OxBTC

Fury's Field. Cecil Bodker, tr. fr. Danish by Nadia Christensen. PBWP

Fuscara; or, The Bee-Errant. John Cleveland. SCP-2

Fuscus is free, and hath the world at will. In Fuscum. Sir John Davies. FaBoEE

Futile to chide the stinging shower. Perspectives. Dudley Randall. AmNP (1974 ed.)

Futility. Wilfred Owen. BuTh; CMoP (1970 ed.); NoAM; PSN

Future, The. Vahan Tekeyan, *tr. fr. Armenian by* James Russell. AMV-81

Future Blues. *Unknown.* BluL

Future Life, The. Bryant. PIM

Future of the Fishbowl, The. Paul Hoover. FiCh

Future smiles again, The. The Future. Vahan Tekeyan, *tr. by* James Russell. AMV-81

Fuzzy fellow without feet, A. Emily Dickinson. PCOP; TAP

Fuzzy-Wuzzy. Kipling. BTTM

Fuzzy wuzzy, creepy crawly. Lillian Schulz Vanada. CTV

Fy let us a to the bridal. The Blythsome Bridal. *Unknown, at. to* Frances Sempill. GBP; PeBB

# G

G is a grumbler gruff. A Grumbler Gruff. Oliver Herford. TDH

G Is for Gustave. Isabel Frances Bellows. TDH

G. K. Chesterton on His Birth. A. E. Housman. FaBoNo

G stands for Gnu, whose weapons of defense. The Gnu. Hilaire Belloc. BoAnP; FaBoNo

Gaa-a-Muna, a Mountain Flower. Harold Littlebird. VoR

Gabble-Gabble. James Reeves. FPB

Gabriel. Adrienne Rich. Psy; VGW

Gabriel, from Hevene-King. The Annunciation. *Unknown.* OxBM

Gabriel Preil, the Grand Duke of New York. The Grand Duke of New York. Dan Pagis, *tr. by* Robert Friend. VWA

Gabriel's Blues. Calvin Forbes. PoA

Gadfly, The. Keats. MBPR

Gaelic is the conscience of our leaders. Michael Hartnett. *Fr.* A Farewell to English. CIP

Gaeltacht. Pearse Hutchinson. BIrV

Gaeta from wool and weaving first began. In Gaetam. Thomas Bastard. FaBoEE

Gagaku: "Pissed on her chest." Steve Richmond. CPA

Gagaku: "Put my hand through TV screen." Steve Richmond. CPA

Gaggle of Geese, a Pride of Lions, A. John Moore. DuDa

Gaily [*or* Gayly] bedight,/ A gallant knight. Eldorado. Poe. AmVN;CTV; IPWM; NOBA; PCOP; PiAm; SS; TAP

Gaily into Ruislip Gardens. Middlesex. John Betjeman. OxBTC

Gaily the Troubadour, *with music.* Thomas Haynes Bayly. BLSo

Gaily they grow, the quiet throng. Heather Flowers. Eliseus Williams, *tr. by* Kenneth Jackson. OBW

Gaining, with Departure. Neil Baldwin. AAN

Gal I Left Behind Me, The. *Unknown.* BPAW; FSW

Gal, I'm tellin' you, I'm tired fo' true. Lament of the Banana Man. Evan Jones. MPo

Gallant Youth, who may have gained, The. Yarrow Revisited. Wordsworth. VLP

Gallants attend, and hear a friend. The Battle of the Kegs. Francis Hopkinson. OBAL

Galleries, The. Peter Kostakis. FiCh

Gallery of My Heart. King D. Kuka. VoR

Galley Slave, The, *sel. Unknown.*
    "How fortune deceives! I had pleasure in tow." PeD

Galliass, The. Walter de la Mare. FaBoTw (1975 ed.)

Gallop apace, you fiery-footed steeds. Shakespeare. *Fr.* Romeo and Juliet, III, ii. GBL

Galloping. Cordelia Chitty. PH

Galloping away to the farthest pasture. Dexter. Joan Byers Grayston. PH

Galloping collection of boards, The. Somewhere. Robert Creeley. NoAM

Galloway Shore, The. Sydney Tremayne. MS

Gallows, The. Edward Thomas. ILP (1975 ed.); InPS; NoAM; SFF; SoSe (1977 ed.); UnPo (1976 ed.)

Gallows in my garden, people say, The. A Ballade of Suicide. G. K. Chesterton. PAIC

Gallows Pole, The. *Unknown. See* Maid Freed from the Gallows, The.

Galveston with a seawall. Wasn't That a Mighty Storm? *Unknown.* AmFP

Galway is a blackguard place. Clonakilty. *Unknown.* FaBoEE

Gambler, The ("Gambler's life I do admire, du-da, du-da"). *Unknown.* AmFP

Gambler, The ("Good morning Mister Railroad man"). *Unknown.* FSW

Gambler's life I do admire, du-da, du-da. The Gambler. *Unknown.* AmFP

Gamblers they. Farmers. Hortense Roberta Roberts. AMV-81

Gambling. Royall Tyler. TAP

Game. Sean Lucy. IPM

Game, The. Stuart Silverman. CoPAm

Game after Supper. Margaret Atwood. Psy

Game at Salzburg, A. Randall Jarrell. NoAM

Game Called. Grantland Rice. SPo

Game of Chance, A. Howard Moss. PoA

Game of Consequences, A. Paul Dehn. NOBL

Game Resumed. Richmond Lattimore. LiSp; SPo

Game was ended, and the noise, The. Football. Walt Mason. SPo

Gamecock. James Dickey. HoPM (1975 ed.); UnPo (1976 ed.)

Games, hard press and bruise of the flesh. R. G. Vliet. WeW

Gammer Gurton's Needle, *sel. At. to* William Stevenson.
    Back and Side Go Bare. HeIP; ILP (1975 ed.)
    (I Cannot Eat but Little Meat.) Expo (1973 ed.)

Gamorra is a dainty steed. The Blood Horse. "Barry Cornwall." PH

Gang wanted to give Oedipus Rex a going away present, The. Oedipus. Josephine Miles. WPE

Gangrel Rymour and the Pairdon of Sanct Anne, The, *sel.* Sydney Goodsir Smith, *after the French of* Tristan Corbiére. "But ae braithless note." OBVE

Gangrene. Philip Levine. VGW

Gangster's Death, The. Ishmael Reed. PoBA

Gaol Song, The. *Unknown.* GBP

Garbage Disposal Truck, The. Galway Kinnell. AKE

Garden, The, *sel.* Hilda Doolittle ("H. D.").
    Heat, II. CMoP (1970 ed.); FSFS; HeIP; InPK; NoAM; PiAm; TAP; UnPo (1976 ed.); UsP

Garden, The. Nicholas Grimald. OAEL-1

Garden. Minou Drouet, *tr. fr. French by* Margaret Crosland. ECBV

Garden, The. Louise Glück. AmPA; FiCP

Garden, The. Nicholas Grimald. OAEL-1

Garden, The ("How vainly men themselves amaze"). Andrew Marvell. AnMo; BiP; CABA (1972 ed.); ExPo (1973 ed.); HAP; ILP (1975 ed.); InPS; NIL; NOBE; OAEL-1; PAIC; PoPle; PPoD; PPoe; PPP; SCP-1; TT
    "What wondrous life is this I lead!" *sel.* FSFS

Garden, A ("See how the flowers, as at parade"). Andrew Marvell. *See* Garden of Appleton House, The.

Garden, The.   Ezra Pound.   CABA (1972 ed.); HeIP; NIL;
   PiAm; PPP; PSN

Garden, A.   Shelley.   *See* Sensitive Plant, The.

Garden, The.   Stuart Silverman.   CoPAm

Garden, The.   Jones Very.   AmVN; PiAm; TAP

Garden, The.   Robert Penn Warren.   PoA

Garden at Appleton House, The ("See how the flowers, as at
   parade").   Andrew Marvell.   *See* Garden of Appleton House,
   The.

Garden Abstract.   Hart Crane.   PSN

Garden Blooms.   Nicholas Flocos.   SA

Garden by the Sea, A.   William Morris.   *Fr.* The Life and Death
   of Jason, IV.   NOBE; OAEL-2

Garden called Gethsemane, The.   Gethsemene.   Kipling.
   FaBoTw (1975 ed.)

Garden Fancies.   Robert Browning.   VLP
   Sibrandus Schafnaburgensis, *sel.*   OBP

Garden flew round with the angel, The.   The Pleasures of Merely
   Circulating.   Wallace Stevens.   MAT; OBAL; PoIA; TT

Garden Hose, The.   Beatrice Janosco.   POL

Garden in September, The.   Robert Bridges.   PoPle

Garden is a lovesome thing, God wot, A!   My Garden.   Thomas
   Edward Brown.   InPK; PeD

Garden is a *lovesome* thing, A? What rot!   My Garden.   J. A.
   Lindon.   InPK; POL

Garden is only for you, The. It is a shell.   The Center of the
   Garden.   Ann Stanford.   AMV-80

Garden Lore.   Juliana Horatia Ewing.   OxBChV

Garden Lyric, A.   Frederick Locker-Lampson.   PeD

Garden of Adonis, The.   Spenser.   *Fr.* The Faerie Queene, III, 6.
   NOBE

Garden of Appleton House, The.   Andrew Marvell.   *Fr.* Upon
   Appleton House.   NOBE
   Garden at Appleton House, The, *sel.*   PoPle
   (Garden, A.)   PF

Garden of Eden has vanished they say, The.   Come Back, Paddy
   Reilly.   Percy French.   PFIr

Garden of Love, The.   Blake.   *Fr.* Songs of Experience.   CABA
   (1972 ed.); ExPo (1973 ed.); GBL; HAP; ILP (1975 ed.);
   IPWM; LAuP; LoAs; MAT; MBPR; NIL; OBP; PoIA;
   PPoe; SoSe (1977 ed.); SS; STS; TPo; WIF

Garden of mouthings, A. Purple, scarlet-speckled, black.   The
   Beekeeper's Daughter.   Sylvia Plath.   IHMS

Garden of Proserpine, The.   Swinburne.   FaPoR; HAP; ILP
   (1975 ed.); NOBE; PoPle; VLP

Garden of Situations, A.   Jack Anderson.   PoA

Garden Report.   Greg Kuzma.   HeS

Garden Seat, The.   Thomas Hardy.   HAP

Garden Wall, The.   Denise Levertov.   PiAm

Garden Where the Praties Grow, The, *with music.*   Unknown.
   RDB

Gardener, The.   *Unknown.*   GBP

Gardener to His God, The.   Mona Van Duyn.   UnPo (1976 ed.);
   UsP; WPE

Gardener's Song, The.   "Lewis Carroll."   *See* Mad Gardener's
   Song, The.

Gardens No Emblems.   Donald Davie.   OAEL-2

Gardens of Alcinous, The ("Close to the gates a spacious garden
   lies").   Homer, *tr. fr. Greek by* Pope.   *Fr.* The Odyssey, VII.
   OAEL-1; OBVE

Gardens of Alcinous, The ("Without the hall and close upon the
   gate").   Homer, *tr. fr. Greek by* George Chapman.   *Fr.* The
   Odyssey, VII.   OAEL-1; OBVE

Gardens of Proserpine, The.   Turner Cassity.   PoA

Gare du Midi.   W. H. Auden.   PSN

Gargoyle.   Carl Sandburg.   NoAM; NOBA

Garland for a Propagandist.   Ted Pauker.   NOBL

Garland of roses, whether you come.   Martial, *tr. fr. Latin by*
   James Michie.   FaBoEE

Garlande of Laurell, The, *sels.*      John Skelton.
   To Maystres Jane Blenner-Haiset.   AAS
   To Mistress [*or* Maystres] Isabell Pennell.   AAS; NOBE; RRA
   To Mistress [*or* Maystres] Margaret Hussey.   AAS; EBEV;
      HeIP; HoPM (1975 ed.); LoAs; NOBE; OAEL-1; PAIC;
      PPoe; PPP
   To Mistress Margery Wentworth.   EBEV; NOBE; OAEL-1

Garlic.   Marvin Bell.   GP

Garlic, The.   Bert Meyers.   VWA

Garments of inattention, oh mere items.   Teaching Swift to
   Young Ladies.   William Dickey.   PoA

Garnishing the Aviary.   Margaret Danner.   Far from Africa, I.
   BPo

Garret, The.   Ezra Pound.   PSN

Garrisons pent up in a little fort.   Sonnet of Brotherhood.
   R. A. K. Mason.   ATNZ

Gas and Hot Air.   Morris Bishop.   OBAL

Gas flaring on the yellow platform.   The Night-Ride.   Kenneth
   Slessor.   GAS; MAuV

Gas Lamp.   Willis Barnstone.   VWA

Gas-lamps abandoned by the night burn on.   Baudelaire in
   Brussels.   Anthony Cronin.   BIrV

Gas ring's hoarse exhaling wheeze, The.   Twinings Orange Pekoe.
   Judith Moffett.   PoA

Gasbags.   *Unknown.*   NOBL

Gascoignes Good Morrow.   George Gascoigne.   AAS

Gascoigne's Memories.   George Gascoigne.   *See* Memories.

Gascoignes Woodmanship.   George Gascoigne.   AAS

Gascoygnes Good Night.   George Gascoigne.   AAS

Gash, The.   William Everson.   GP

Gasholders, russet among fields.   Geoffrey Hill.   Mercian Hymns,
   VII   HAP

Gaslight.   Michael Burkard.   AAN

Gasoline makes game scarce.   Written on the Stub of the First
   Paycheck.   William Stafford.   *Fr.* The Move to California.
   AnMo; InPK

Gassed going between classes.   Witness.   Josephine Miles.   GP;
   PoW

Gassing the woodchucks didn't turn out right.   Woodchucks.
   Maxine W. Kumin.   HoPM (1975 ed.)

Gastric.   "C. T."   PeD

Gate, The.   C. Day Lewis.   FoP

Gate, The.   Edwin Muir.   CMoP (1970 ed.)

Gate was open, The; the fence under the aspens, fallen.
   Mountain Corral.   Helen Sorrells.   WPE

Gates.   Ted Kooser.   GP

Gates, The, *sel.*   Muriel Rukeyser.
   Church of Galilee, The.   GP

Gates clanged and they walked you into jail, The.   The
   Conscientious Objector.   Karl Shapiro.   SoS

Gates of Paradise, The, *sel.*   Blake.
   "Truly, My Satan, thou art but a Dunce," Epilogue.   HAP;
      OAEL-2
   (Epilogue: "Truly, my Satan, thou art but a dunce.")   CABA
      (1972 ed.)
   (To the Accuser Who Is the God of This World.)   OBP

Gateway, The.   A. D. Hope.   BoLoP

Gateway to the Sea, A (I).   George Bruce.   MS

Gather kittens while you may.   Song.   Oliver Herford.   AKE;
   SpRo

Gather while you may.   Rose.   Kathleen Raine.   WPE

Gather ye rosebuds while ye may.   To the Virgins, to Make Much
   of Time.   Robert Herrick.   AKE, 1 *st.*; AnMo; BoLoP;
   CABA (1972 ed.); CaPo; FF; GBL; HAP; HeIP; ILP (1975

ed.); InPK; InPS; IPWM; LFH; NIL; NOBE; OAEL-1; OLR; PAIC; PBMP; PPoe; SFF; SoSe; SpRo

Gathered in inter-admiration. When the Five Prominent Poets. Josephine Jacobsen. TAP

Gathering, The. Timothy Dwight. *Fr. The Triumph of Infidelity.* EAP

Gathering, The. Dwayne Thorpe. AMV-81

Gathering Gems. Ethel Green Russell. AATT

Gathering Leaves. Robert Frost. VGW

Gathering Mushrooms. Alistair Campbell. ATNZ

Gathering Song of Donald the Black. Sir Walter Scott. *See* Pibroch.

Gathering the Bones Together. Gregory Orr. AmPA

Gathering the Sparks Howard Schwartz. VWA

Gathers/ and gathers. The Gypsy Motorcycle Club of South Minneapolis. Keith Gunderson. Hes

Gatton Tragedy, The. John Manifold. FPA

Gauley Bridge. Muriel Rukeyser. NNaP

Gauley Bridge is a good town for Negroes. George Robinson: Blues. Muriel Rukeyser. NNaP

Gauls Sacrifice, The. C. M. Doughty. *Fr. The Dawn in Britain.* FaBoTw (1975 ed.)

Gauguin's Menhir, Tahiti ("Gauguin's Museum in Papeari bay"). A. D. Hope. CAAP

Gaunt in gloom. Nightpiece. James Joyce. NoAM; PoA

Gaunt kept house with her child for the old man. Montana Fifty Years Ago. J. V. Cunningham. Prf

Gaunt thing, The. Babylon Revisited. Amiri Baraka. BPo; NoAM

Gautama in the Deer Park at Benares Kenneth Patchen. NIL

Gave me things I. Swallow the Lake. Clarence Major. PoBA

Gave proof through the night. Poem to My Sister, Ethel Ennis, Who Sang "The Star-spangled Banner" at the Second Inauguration of Richard Milhous Nixon. June Jordan. TAP; WBN

Gawain and the Lady of the Castle, *orig. and mod. English prose. Unknown. Fr.* Sir Gawain and the Green Knight. OxBM ("Thus laykes this lorde by lunde-wodes eves.") EBEV

Gawain and the Temptress. *Unknown, tr. fr. Middle English by* Burton Raffel. *Fr.* Sir Gawain and the Green Knight. OBP

Gay blade on the gentle hedgerow. Daffodil. Waldo Williams, *tr. by* Gwyn Jones. OBW

Gay go up and gay go down. The Bells of London. *Unknown.* MG; PoPle

Gay Goshawk, The. *Unknown, at. to* Anna Gordon Brown. PeBB; WPE

Gay little Girl-of-the-Diving-Tank. At the Carnival. Anne Spencer. NoAM

Gay Old Hag, The. *Unknown.* BIrV

Gay raftsmen, oh where are they, The? The Raftsmen. *Unknown.* FSW

Gayly bedight,/ A gallant knight. *See* Gaily bedight,/ A gallant knight.

Gaze North-east. *Unknown, tr. fr. Irish by* John Montague. BIrV

Gaze not on swans, in whose soft breast. Beauty's Excellency. Henry Noel. SCP-2

Gaze not on thy beauty's pride. Song: Good Counsel to a Young Maid. Thomas Carew. CaPo

Gazelle Calf, The. D. H. Lawrence. OxBTC

Gazing down upon you I am made aware. The Sleeper. William Soutar. SLP

Gazing upon him now, severe and dead. Edna St. Vincent Millay. SBG

Geans are fleuran whyte i the green Howe o the Mearns, The. Sabbath i the Mearns. Douglas Young. MS

Gebir, *sel.* Walter Savage Landor.
"I have sinuous shells of pearly hue." EcS

Gecko. Noel Lloyd. RAE

Gee, but I Want to Go Home. *Unknown.* FSW

Gee, but it's tough to be broke, kid. I Can't Give You Anything but Love. Dorothy Fields. BLSo

Gee I Like to Think of Dead. E. E. Cummings. HoPM (1975 ed.)

Gee, Officer Krupke. Stephen Sondheim. OBAL

Gee, You're So Beautiful That It's Starting to Rain. Richard Brautigan. PPM; VoA; WeW

Geese, The Richard Peck. SoS

Geese, The. Hyam Plutzik. BiP

Geese are going to live again, The. Dressing for Our Spring Party. Jane Garland Katz. AAN

Geese fly off, but sometimes they don't take, The. Owning a Dead Man. Marcia Southwick. AMV-80

Geese in the pond are drifting, five. Wandsworth Common. David Bromwich. PoA

Geiger, geiger, ticking slow. Paul Dehn. SpRo

Geisha. Gary Gildner. GP; POL

Gemini. Robert Creeley. PiAm

Gems and jewels let them heap. In a Garret. Herman Melville. OBAL

Gemwood. Marvin Bell. FiCP

Genau'r Glyn, Tywyn, each day from these to Rhys's halls. Ode to Rhys ap Maredudd of Tywyn. Dafydd Nanmor, *tr. by* H. Idris Bell. OBW

Genealogical Reflection. Ogden Nash. OBAL

Genealogy. Donald Finkel. VWA

Genealogy. Frank Lamont Phillips. AmNP (1974 ed.)

Genealogy. Eléni Vakaló, *tr. fr. Modern Greek by* Paul Merchant. PBWP

Genealogy of a Generation. Tina Foriyes. PoW

General, The. Siegfried Sassoon. CMoP (1970 ed.); OxBTC

General Communion, A. Alice Meynell. WPE

General Prologue. Chaucer. *See* Canterbury Tales, The: Prologue.

General Secretary's feet whispered over the red carpet, The. Anteroom: Geneva. Denis Devlin. CIP

General Song of Humanity, The. Lawrence Ferlinghetti. CPA

General Song of Praise to Almighty God, A. John Mason. SCP-2

General William Booth Enters into Heaven. Vachel Lindsay. CMoP (1970 ed.); ILP (1975 ed.); IPWM; NoAM; NOBA; PoA; TAP

"Booth led boldly with his bass drum," *sel.* IP

General's Wife, The. Elton Glaser. NVAP

Generation before me departed too soon, The. Generations. Moishe Steingart, *tr. by* Gabriel Preil. VWA

Generation Gap Bronwen Wallace. AMV-80

Generations. Joseph Awad. AMV-81

Generations. Evan Jones. MAuV

Generations. Judy Dothard Simmons. CNA

Generations. Moishe Steingart, *tr. fr. Yiddish by* Gabriel Preil. VWA

Generations 1. Sam Cornish. NVAP

Generations 2. Sam Cornish. NVAP

Generator, The. Rae Desmond Jones. CAAP

"Generosity of her love provides, The." The Grand Guignols of Love. Michael Benedikt. AmPA

Generous Gentleman, The. Allan Ramsay. SLP

Genesis, *sels.* Bible, *O.T.*
"And God saw that the wickedness of man was great," VI: 5-9. NAWM-1
"And the Lord God planted a garden eastward in Eden," II: 8-22. OAEL-1

"And the whole earth was of one language, and of one speech," XI: 1-9 NAWM-1

"And there came two angels to Sodom even," XIX: 1-38 HoPM (1975 ed.)

"In the beginning God created the heaven and the earth," I-IV. NAWM-1

"Joseph, being seventeen years old, was feeding the flock with his brethren," XXXVII-XLVI, abr. NAWM-1

"See, the smell of my sone is as the smell of a feld," XXVII: 27-29, tr. by William Tyndale. OBVE

Genesis. Brian Higgins. FaBoTw (1975 ed.)

Genesis Geoffrey Hill. HAP; OAEL-2

Genesis. Lotte Kramer. VWA

Genesis. Harold Witt. SFF

Genial Grimalkin, The. J. G. Francis. TDH

Genitals. Coleman Barks. Fr. Body Poems. NVAP

Genius Loci of the Morning. Doug Fetherling. NeAC

Genji caught a gray bird, fluttering. Journeys. Gary Snyder. NU

Genteel, elegant once, the place has seen hard times. Gramercy Park Hotel. David Smith. NYP

Gentilesse. Chaucer. OAEL-1

Gentle Alice Brown. W. S. Gilbert. FaBoCo; PeBB

Gentle Ambush, The. George Macadam. SLP

Gentle and smiling as before. The Wheel. Robert Hayden. BPo

Gentle at last, and as clean as ever. Grandfather in the Old Men's Home W. S. Merwin. ConAP; TCP

Gentle blondness and the moray eel go at the same time. On Giving a Son to the Sea. James Dickey. TCP

Gentle Breeze, A. Thomas Durfey. SCP-2

Gentle Echo on Woman, A. Swift. FaBoCo; NU; OLR; UsP

Gentle God is our guest, The. Advent. Clinton F. Larson. MPA

Gentle Heart, A: Two. Judith Johnson Sherwin. BoWoP

Gentle hunter. Leopard. Yoruba Oral Tradition, tr. by Ulli Beier. WTO

Gentle, inaffluent. Eating Out. Alan Wearne. GAS

Gentle Jesus, Meek and Mild. Charles Wesley. OxBChV

Gentle knight was pricking on the plaine, A. Spenser. Fr. The Faerie Queene, I,1. EBEV; OAEL-1

Gentle lady, do not sing. James Joyce. Chamber Music, XXVIII. OLR

"Gentle, modest little flower." To Phoebe. W. S. Gilbert. OLR; WIF

Gentle of hand, the Dean of St. Patrick's guided. A Sermon on Swift. Austin Clarke. BIrV

Gentle sounds rise up to me. From Mount Nebo. Karl Wolfskehl, tr. by Erna Baber Rosenfeld.

"Gentle youth, forbear." Hero Feels the Shaft of Love. Christopher Marlowe. Fr. Hero and Leander. GBL

Gentled Beast, The. Dilys Laing. PH

Gentlemen. Geoffrey Taylor. FaBoEE

Gentlemen, as we take our seats. The Rehearsal. Horace Gregory. VGW

Gentlemen-Rankers. Kipling. BTTM

Gentlemen, we have spoken about these things before. To the Trade. James Neugass. SPT

Gentleness of rain was in the wind, The. Rain. Shelley. POL

Gentlest of women, put your weapons by. Lay Your Arms Aside. Pierce Ferriter, tr. by Eilean Ni Chuilleanain. BIrV

Gentlest poet, with free thoughts endowed, The. Suggested by a Picture of the Bird of Paradise. Wordsworth. VLP

Gently. Christina Rossetti. See Hurt No Living Thing.

Gently dip, but not too deep. The Song at the Well. George Peele. Fr. The Old Wives' Tale. ExPo (1973 ed.); InPS

Gently! Gently! Gently! The Ocean Is like a Wreath. Kuapakaa, tr. fr. Hawaiian. WTO

Gently I wave the visible world away. The Absinthe-Drinker. Arthur Symons. FaBoTw (1975 ed.)

Gently, insistently, all day. In the Park beside the Marina. J. S. Harry. FPA

Gently Johnny, My Jingalo. Unknown. FSW

Gently, O gently, father, do not bruise. On the Circumcision: For the King's Music. William Cartwright. SCP-2

Gently, years, gently! Ralph Hodgson. POL

Geography. G. K. Chesterton. Fr. Songs of Education. OBSV

Geography. Michael Dransfield. CAAP

Geography. Kenneth Koch. NoAM

Geography Lesson. Zulfikar Ghose. LP; MPo

Geography of the Near East. Al Young. NW

Geological Faults. Barbara Unger. AMV-81

Geometry of Motion, The—Crossing the Golden Gate Bridge. Kaye McDonough. CPA

Geordie. Unknown. AmFP; FaBoBa; FSW

(Georgie.) AIW; GSB, with music.

George. Dudley Randall. BPo; ConAP; NoAM; TC

George Allen. Unknown. AmFP

(Engine 143.) FSW

George Collins. Unknown. FSW

George Collins came home last Saturday night. Lady Alice. Unknown. AmFP

George Collins drove home one cold winter night. George Collins. Unknown. FSW

George Crabbe. E. A. Robinson. CMoP (1970 ed.); NOBA; TAP

George Grover was the town looney. Small Town History. John L. Sellers. DNGG

George-Hector. The Emancipation of George-Hector (a Colored Turtle.). Mari Evans. AmNP (1974 ed.)

George Hirst. E. C. Bentley. Fr. Clerihews. PoPle

George Robinson: Blues. Muriel Rukeyser. NNaP

George Santayana. Robert Lowell. See For George Santayana.

George Simic. Charles Simic. CAAP

George I—Star of Brunswick. Thackeray. Fr. The Georges. FaBoEE

George the First was always reckon'd. The Georges. Walter Savage Landor. FaBoCo; FaBoEE; NIL; OBSV

George IV. Thackeray. Fr. The Georges. FaBoEE

George II. Thackeray. Fr. The Georges. FaBoEE

George II and the Chinese Emperor. Robert Graves. BBL

George the Third. E. C. Bentley. Fr. Clerihews. FaBoCo; NOBL

George III. Thackeray. Fr. The Georges. FaBoEE

George the Third's Soliloquy. Philip Freneau. EAP; NOBA

George used to say we all need an hour a day. Morningside Heights: Fragment of a Film. James Reiss. CAAP

George Washington. Unknown. See Washington.

George Washington Goes to a Girlie Movie. Aram Boyajian. NeAC

George Washington Whistler, chief engineer. Whistler's Father. Margaret Ryan. NPW

George Washington, your name is on my lips. Patriotic Poem. Diane Wakoski. OFD; VGW

Georges, The. Walter Savage Landor. FaBoEE; NIL; OBSV (On the Four Georges.) FaBoCo

Georges, The (I-IV). Thackeray. FaBoEE

Georgia Dusk. Jean Toomer. AmNP (1974 ed.); BPo; ILP (1975 ed.); NoAM; PoBA

Georgia dusk/ And the turpentine woods. Mulatto. Langston Hughes. PAIC

Georgia O'Keeffe as a child. Ready. Lynn Strongin. RiTi

Georgiad, The, *sel.* Roy Campbell.
"Next him Jack Squire through his own tear-drops sploshes." OxBTC

Georgian Spring. Roy Campbell. OBSV

Georgics, *sel.* Virgil, *tr. fr. Latin by* Dryden.
"When, after such a length of rolling years," *fr.* III. SCP-1

Georgie. *Unknown.* See Geordie.

Georgie Porgie, pudding and pie. Mother Goose. MG; NIL

Georgie Wedlock. *Unknown.* AmFP

Geraldines, The. Thomas Osborne Davis. BTTM

Geranium The. Theodore Roethke. MPo; UnPo (1976 ed.); WeW

Geranium, The. Sheridan. BoLoP

Geraniums, The. Genevieve Taggard. VGW

Gerard de Nerval. Thomas Brush. NVAP

Gerbil Who Got Away, The. Judith C. Root. AMV-81

Gerda, My Husband's Wife. Eve Triem. GP

Gereint ab Erbin. *Unknown, tr. fr. Welsh by* Joseph P. Clancy. OBW

Geriatric. John Gonzalez. PMW

Geriatric Huts. Michael Smith. IPM

German Legion, The. Sydney Dobell. PeD

German Shepherd. Myra Cohn Livingston. RFM

German steel built like a water-drop. The Death of the Sports-Car Driver. Jonathan Aaron. MiP

German submarines were an idea we watched. The Home Front. Marvin Bell. GP

Germanic. Crossing. Anthony Barnett. VWA

Germans in Greek, The. Porson on German Scholarship. Richard Porson. FaBoCo; FaBoEE

Germinal. "Æ." BIrV

Germination. Arlene Stone. VWA

Geronimo. Ernest McGaffey. BPAW

Gerontion. T. S. Eliot. AnMo; CABA (1972 ed.); CMoP (1970 ed.); EBEV; ExPo (1973 ed.); HAP; InPS; NoAM; NOBA; OAEL-2; PPP; STS; TAP

Gertrude and Gulielma, sister-twins. Frederick Goddard Tuckerman. Sonnets, II, xv. HAP

Gertrude Stein. Philip Roberts. FPA

Gesture. Donald Finkel. InPK

Gesture, The. George Oppen. *Fr.* Five Poems about Poetry. NNaP

Gesture. Mary Swope. PoUp

Gesture by a Lady with an Assumed Name, A. James Wright. ConAP

"Get down, get down, lovin' Henry," she cried. Young Hunting. *Unknown.* AmFP

Get enough food to eat. Karma Repair Kit: Items 1-4. Richard Brautigan. IPWM

Get off my oriental rug, dust I can't shake! Poem for a Hustler. Kathleen Fraser. RiTi

Get on Board, Little Children. *Unknown.* See Gospel Train, The.

Get on, expecting the worst—a mount like a statue. The Trail Horse. David Wagoner. PH

"Get out of my way!" Roosters. Elizabeth J. Coatsworth. SO

Get that man! A Warrant Is Out for the Arrest of Henry Miller. Anselm Hollo. AcAn

Get the children of America out of Troy, New York! Going and Coming: Two Poems. Michael Benedikt. CAAP

Get the Gasworks. David Ignatow. InPK; InPS; VoA

Get Thee behind Me, Satan. Lee Hays, Millard Lampell, *and* Pete Seeger. FSW

Get them new. Jeans. J. V. Brummels. GP

Get Up. Philip Levine. NYP

Get Up! Joseph Skipsey. InPK; VLP

Get Up and Bar the Door. *Unknown.* AIW; AmFP; BiP; DuDr; FaBoBa; HeIP; PAIC; PBMP; PoTa

Get Up, Blues. James A. Emanuel. AmNP (1974 ed.); PoBA

Get up, get up for shame, the blooming morn. Corinna's Going a-Maying. Robert Herrick. AnMo; BiP; CABA (1972 ed.); CaPo; Epi; ExPo (1973 ed.); HAP; ILP (1975 ed.); NIL; NOBE; OAEL-1; PoPle; PPP

Get Up or You'll Be Late for School, Silly! John Ciardi. ECBV

"Get up, our Anna dear, from the weary spinning-wheel." The Fairy Thorn. Sir Samuel Ferguson. VLP

"Get up!" the caller calls, "Get up!" Get Up! Joseph Skipsey. InPK; VLP

Get up under a mule. The Mule. Coleman Barks. POL

"Get ye up from the wrath of God's terrible day!" The Cities of the Plain. Whittier. PIM

Get You Gone. Sir Charles Sedley. ILP (1975 ed.)

Get Your tongue. Poem. Ted Kooser. POL

Gethsemane. Kipling. FaBoTw (1975 ed.)

Getting a Job. Paul Blackburn. NYP

Getting a Poem in the Rain. Dick Lourie. NeAC

Getting Across. Carter Revard. VoR

Getting By on Honesty. Stephen E. Smith. AMV-80

Getting Down to Get Over. June Jordan. TAP

Getting Drunk with Daughter. Robert Huff. CNW; CoPAm

Getting Experience. Miller Williams. CSP; GP; TAT

Getting Fired or "Not Being Retained." Sandra Gilbert. CPA

Getting Home. Judith Rodriguez. FPA

Getting into Focus. Miriam Palmer. RiTi

Getting Loaded. Jim Thomas. AMV-80

Getting Lost in Nazi Germany. Marvin Bell. VWA

Getting Older Here. Barbara Hauk. AMV-80

Getting older, I grow more personal. Cry Mercy. Charles Brasch. ATNZ

Getting the License. Ronald Koertge. AAN

Getting the Mail. Galway Kinnell. UnPo (1976 ed.)

Getting Through the Fifties: The Starkweather Case Revisited. Robert Hahn. AAN

Getting tired of sleeping in this: : low down lonesome cE-Ell. Prison Cell Blues. *Unknown.* BluL

Getting to Emily's. Bernice Ames. PoW

Getting to the End. Cynthia MacDonald. AAN

Getting Under. Alan P. Lightman. AMV-81

Geve place, ye lovers, here before. Earl of Surrey. AAS

Ghazals, *sels.* Jim Harrison.
"After the 'invitation' by the preacher she collapsed in the." NoAM
"Dog, the lightning frightened us, dark house and both of us." InPS
"He sings from the bottom of a well but she can hear him up." NoAM
"I imagined her dead, killed by some local maniac who." InPS
"She climbed the ladder looking over the wall at the party." InPS
"What will I do with seven billion cubic feet of clouds." WeW

Ghazals: Homage to Ghalib. Adrienne Rich. CAAP
*Sels.*
"Clouds are electric in this university, The." NIL
"Did you think I was talking about my life?" NIL
"Friend I can trust is the one who will let me have my death, The." NIL
"From here on, all of us will be living." NIL
"If these are letters, they will have to be misread." NIL
"In Central Park we talked of our own cowardice." NIL
"Last night you wrote on the wall: Revolution is poetry." NIL
"Ones who camped on the slopes, below the bare summit, The." NIL
"Piece of thread ripped-out from a fierce design, A." NIL

"Sapling springs, the milkweed blooms, The: obsolete nature." NIL

"When your sperm enters me, it is altered." CABA (1972 ed.); NIL

Ghetto Funeral. Charles Reznikoff. *Fr.* Five Groups of Verse. SA

Ghetto Lovesong—Migration. Carole Gregory Clemmons. NMM

  (Migration.) PoBA

Ghetto Summer School. Douglas Worth. FF

Ghetto Twilight. Alter Brody. VWA

Ghost. Patricia Beer. HeHu

Ghost, The, *sel.* Charles Churchill.

  "Pomposo (insolent and loud"). OBSV

Ghost, The. Walter de la Mare. CMoP (1970 ed.); NOBE; OAEL-2; OxBTC

Ghost, The. Robert Lowell, *after the Latin of* Sextus Propertius. PoA

Ghost Boy. Mark Van Doren. SO

Ghost Crabs. Ted Hughes. TwMBP

Ghost-grey the fall of night. A Robin. Walter de la Mare. CMoP (1970 ed.); PB

Ghost is someone, A: death has left a hole. The Ghost. Robert Lowell, *after* Sextus Propertius. PoA

Ghost of a mouldy larder is one thing, A: whiskery bread. Corposant. Peter Redgrove. OxBTC

Ghost of Ninon would be sorry now, The. Veteran Sirens. E. A. Robinson. NoAM; NOBA; PiAm

Ghost of the Buffaloes, The. Vachel Lindsay. BPAW

Ghost Poem Five. Mary Norbert Körte. IHMS

Ghost, that loved a lady fair, A. The Phantom Wooer. Thomas Lovell Beddoes. ILP (1975 ed.); PoIA

Ghostly Beast, The. Vassar Miller. CSP

Ghostly Gladness. Richard Rolle of Hampole. HAP

Ghostly Story. Milton Acorn. NeAC

Ghosts of the Living. May Ivimy. PMW

Ghosts on the Strath, The, *sel.* Joseph Gordon Macleod ("Adam Drinan").

  "Long blue shadow of a salmon lying." MS

Ghost's Song, The. *Unknown.* RAE

Ghosts' Stories. Alastair Reid. MS

Ghosts there must be with me in this old house. Solitude. Walter de la Mare. CMoP (1970 ed.)

Giant Decorative Dahlia. Molly Holden. OxBTC; PSN

Giant glares, A—the pages loved before. The Reading. Eve Triem. PoW

Giant Jojo. Michael Rosen. FPB

Giant Norway spruce from Podunk, The. December. James Schuyler. NoAM

Giant Puffball, The. Edmund Blunden. FaBoTw (1975 ed.)

Giant sparkler,/ Lights of the river. "A 4." Louis Zukofsky. VGW

Giant Squid of Tsurai, The. Kirk Robertson. GP

Giant Thunder. James Reeves. DuDa

Giant Tortoise, The. Edward Lucie-Smith. BoAnP

  ("Giant tortoise had a look, The.") POL

Giantess, The. Baudelaire, *tr. fr. French by* Roy Campbell. OBVE

Giaour, The: A Fragment of a Turkish Tale. Byron. MBPR

GIC to HAR. Kenneth Rexroth. VoA

Gie aa, and aa comes back. Luve. Douglas Young. MS

Giffen's Debt. Kipling. VLP

Gift, The. John Ciardi. BiP

Gift. Leonard Cohen. NoAM

Gift, The. Robert Creeley. NOBA

Gift, The. Louise Glück. GP

Gift, The. Dick Lourie. NeAC

Gift, The. Ed Ochester. GP

Gift. Eve Shelnutt. TC

Gift, The. R. A. Simpson. FPA

Gift, The. Robin Skelton. MPA

Gift, The. Ann Stanford. GP

Gift,The. J. D. Whitney. NVAP

Gift, The. William Carlos Williams. IPWM; TCP

Gift comes in a courtly box, The. The Gift. R. A. Simpson. FPA

Gift for Mary MacLane, A. T. Alan Broughton. FAF

Gift Hour. Maria Banus, *tr. fr. Rumanian by* Willis Barnstone *and* Matei Calinescu. BoWoP; VWA

Gift of Fire, The. Lisel Mueller. NowV

Gift of Trilliums, A. Sandra McPherson. RiTi

Gift of Water, The. Hamlin Garland. BPAW

Gift Outright, The. Robert Frost. CMoP (1970 ed.); GOA; IPWM; NoAM; NOBA; PPP; STS

Gift to Be Simple, The. Howard Moss. SS

Gifts. Mary Elizabeth Coleridge. PBWP

Gifts, The. Charles Levendosky. TAT

Gifts. Leon Stokesbury. GP

Gifts/ And words. We'll Never Be the Same (Until Later). Grace Cavalieri. AATT

Gigantic beauty of a stallion, fresh and responsive to my caresses, A. The Stallion. Walt Whitman. *Fr.* Song of Myself, XXXII. PCOP; PH

Gigantic mass, the hard material, The. Shore Leave Lorry. Roy Fuller. NoAM

Gigantic mills stand stark against the sky. Steel Mills. Rachel Albright. ANTL

Gil Brenton. *Unknown.* PeBB

Gilbertus Glanvil, whose heart was a hard as an anvil. *Tr. fr. Latin by* Matthew Prior. FaBoEE

Gilderoy, *sel.* Thomas Campbell.

  "Last, the fatal hour is come, The." SLP

Giles Corey and Goodwyfe Corey—A Ballad of 1692. *Unknown.* PAIC

Giles Johnson, Ph.D. Frank Marshall Davis. BPo; PoBA

Gilgamesh. *Unknown.* See Epic of Gilgamesh, The.

Gimboling. Isabella Gardner. WeW

Gimel. Stuart Z. Perkoff. VWA

Gin a body meet a body. Comin' through the Rye. *Unknown.* FSW

Gin a body meet a body. Rigid Body Sings. James Clerk Maxwell. FaBoCo; SpRo

Gin I Were a Doo. *Unknown.* GBP

Gingerbread House, The. John Ower. AMV-80

Ginger Bread Mama. Doughtry Long. BPo; PoBA

Gingham dog and the calico cat, The. The Duel. Eugene Field. CTV; ECBV; OBAL; PCOP

Ginkgoes in Fall. Howard Nemerov. GP

Giorno dei Morti. D. H. Lawrence. NOBE

Giovanni da Fiesole on the Sublime; or, Fra Angelico's "Last Judgment." Richard Howard. Prf

Gipsies. *See also* Gypsies.

Gipsies ("The snow falls deep; the forest lies alone"). John Clare. Epi; OBP

  (Gypsies.) ILP (1975 ed.)

Gipsy-Night. Richard Hughes. OBW

Giraffe. Stanley Plumly. AmPA

Giraffes, The. Roy Fuller. NoAM

Giraffes already had sea legs, The. In Noah's Wake. Allan Block. FAF  .

Giraffes: The American Version. Stephen Dunn. HeS

Girl. A. W. Purdy. NoAM

Girl at the Center of Her Life, A. Joyce Carol Oates. CoPAm

Girl at the Seaside. Richard Murphy. BIrV

Girl, Boy, Flower, Bicycle. M. K. Joseph. ATNZ; MiP

Girl Clings to Coma. Jim Mulac. AcAn

Girl comes out of a doorway in the morning, A. Back Street. A. R. D. Fairburn. ATNZ

Girl Friends. Rosemary Daniell. WBN

Girl goes dancing there, The. Sweet Dancer. W. B. Yeats. AnMo

Girl Held without Bail. Margaret Walker. BPo; CNA; PoBA

Girl Help. Janet Lewis. WPW

Girl I Call Alma, The. Linda Gregg. AmPA

Girl I left behind Me, The ("The dames of France are fond and free"). Thomas Osborne Davis. BTTM

Girl I Left behind Me, The ("Break and trail home"). *Unknown.* AmFP

Girl I Left behind Me, The ("I'm lonesome since I cross'd the hill"). *Unknown.* BLSo, *with music*; FSW; GSB, *with music*

Girl I Left behind Me, The ("My parents raised me tenderly"). *Unknown.* AmFP

Girl in a Black Bikini. Allan Brown. AMV-80

Girl in a grey frock. A Grey Frock. Zinaida Hippius, *tr. by* Temira Pachmuss. PBWP

Girl in a Library, A. Randall Jarrell. NoAM; NOBA

Girl in a window, eating a melon, A. Oban Girl. Edwin Morgan. MS

Girl in our village makes love in the churchyard, A. RIP. Alan Garner. BuTh

Girl in the lane, that couldn't speak plain, The. *Unknown.* MG

Girl in the Park, The. Hone Tuwhare. ATNZ

Girl in the tea shop, The. The Tea Shop. Ezra Pound. BBGO; HeIP

Girl in the Willow Tree, The. Carolyn Maisel. IHMS

Girl in trousers wheeling a red baby, The. Metamorphoses. Roy Fuller. OxBTC

Girl Marcher. John Frederick Nims. SFF

Girl Next Door, The. Brendan Kennelly. IPM

Girl of Constant Sorrow. Sara Ogan Gunning. FSW

Girl on the Greenbriar Shore, The. *Unknown.* FSW

Girl on the Run. David Kresh. PoUp

Girl, The/The Girlie Magazine. Pat Gray. AMV-81

Girl to Woman. Nixeon Civille Handy. AMV-80

Girl-watching at Grant's Pass. Robert Huff. CNW

Girl, when rejecting me you never guessed. To a Jilt. Martin Armstrong. FaBoEE

Girl who felt my stare and raised her eyes, The. The Invisible Man. T. S. Matthews. POL

Girl Who Had Borne Too Much, The. John Woods. GP

Girl who has seen herself in a mirror, A. The Old Photograph. Dana Naone. PHC

Girl with Car and Guitar. Ralph Mecklenburger. SFF

Girl with Coffee Tray. John Fuller. LP

Girl with 18 Nightgowns, The. Gregory Orr. POL

Girl with orange lips grazes behind the rosebushes, A. Portrait of a Reluctant Passenger. Jeffry Jensen. PoW

Girl with the Green Skirt. Dana Naone. CDW

Girl with the theater hat, The. The Theater Hat. Carolyn Wells. TDH

Girl, your young loveliness. White Swan. A. Glanz-Leyeles, *tr. by* Keith Bosley. VWA

Girls. Pablo Neruda, *tr. fr. Spanish by* Donald D. Walsh. OLR

Girls. Kenneth Rosen. AmPA

Girls and boys, come out to play. Mother Goose. MG

Girls are simply the prettiest things. My Cat and I. Roger McGough. OxBTC; POL

Girls around Cape Horn, The. *Unknown.* AmFP

Girls, at bows, string concentric blooms. On the College Archery Range. Robert Wallace. LiSp

Girls buck the wind in the grooves toward work. The Morning Half-Life Blues. Marge Piercy. WBN

Girl's far treble, muted to the heat, The. Milkmaid. Laurie Lee. BoLoP; FaBoTw (1975 ed.); MPo

Girls from Home. Abraham Reisen, *tr. fr. Yiddish by* Keith Bosley. VWA

Girl's Hair, A. Dafydd ab Edmwnd, *tr. fr. Welsh by* Gwyn Williams. OBW

Girls in Their Seasons. Derek Mahon. BoLoP

Girls of Llanbadarn, The. Dafydd ap Gwilym, *tr. fr. Welsh by* Rolfe Humphries. OBW

Girls on Saddleless Horses. R. G. Vliet. PH

Girls scream,/ Boys shout. School's Out. W. H. Davies. BBGO

Girl's Song, A. Leslie Norris. HeHu

Girl's Song. W. B. Yeats. SS

Girl's Song. Marya Zaturenska. OLR

Girls today in society, The. Brush Up Your Shakespeare. Cole Porter. OBAL

Girls' Voices. Brendan Gill. POL

Girls Who Wave at Cars from Bridges. Harold Bond. NVAP

Girls with fat thighs and no breasts. Before Bed. Keith Waldrop. InPK

Girls Working in Banks. Karl Shapiro. WeW

Girtonian Funeral, A. *Unknown.* FaBoCo

Git Along Down to Town. *Unknown.* AmFP

Git Along Little Dogies. *Unknown.* BPAW; FSW
(As I Walked Out.) BPAW
(Whoopee-Ti-Yi-Yo! *ad. by* James Morehead.) BLSH, *with music*

Git on Board, Little Chillen. *Unknown.* *See* Gospel Train, The.

Git yer little sage hens ready. At a Cowboy Dance. James Barton Adams. BPAW

Gitanjali, *sels.* Rabindranath Tagore.
"Day was when I did not keep myself in readiness, The," XLIII. ILwL
"Thou hast made me endless, such is thy pleasure," I. ILwL

Give a man his. Wait for Me. Robert Creeley. NOBA; PPP

Give All to Love. Emerson. NOBA; PAIC; TAP

Give beauty all her right. Thomas Campion. AAS

Give Ear, O God, to My Loud Cry, *with music.* Thomas Prince. AH

Give Ear, O Heavens, to That Which I Declare, *with music.* Henry Ainsworth. AH

Give God thy heart. Motto for a Sundial. *Unknown.* FaBoEE

Give greatly of your grunts, O pig. Hymn to Joy. Julia Cunningham. PChr

Give him the darkest inch your shelf allows. George Crabbe. E. A. Robinson. CMoP (1970 ed.); NOBA; TAP

Give honour unto Luke Evangelist. Saint Luke the Painter. Dante Gabriel Rossetti. The House of Life, LXXIV. VLP

Give Lucinda pearl nor stone. To the New Year. Thomas Carew. CaPo

Give me a color. America. Wendy Rose. CDW

Give me a death like Buddha's, let me fall. Prayer. Stanley Moss. GP; POL

Give Me a Forty Cent Token or a Gallon of Gas and an Hour to Get There. Jonetta Barras-Abney. PoUp

Give me a good digestion, Lord. An Ancient Prayer. Thomas H. B. Webb. CTV

Give me a harsh land to wring music from. This Land. Ian Mudie. BuTh

Give me a man that is not dull. His Desire. Robert Herrick. CABA (1972 ed.)

Give me a royal niche—it is my due. George III. Thackeray. *Fr.* The Georges. FaBoEE

Give me a thrill, says the reader. Fiction and the Reading Public. Philip Larkin. NOBL; OBSV

Give Me Five. William J. Harris. CNA

Give me, give me Buriano. Bacchus's Opinion of Wine, and Other Beverages. Francesco Redi, *tr. by* Leigh Hunt. OBVE

Give Me Jesus. *Unknown.* BPo

Give me leave, fairest Cynthia, to envy. To Cynthia, on Her Looking-Glass. Sir Francis Kynaston. SCP-2

Give me leave to rail at you. Song. Earl of Rochester. LoAs

Give me more love or more disdain. Song: Mediocrity in Love Rejected. Thomas Carew. CaPo; GBL

"Give me my bow," said Robin Hood. The Death of Robin Hood. Eugene Field. PoTa

Give Me My Infant Now. Te-whaka-io-roa, *tr. fr. Maori by* John White. WTO

Give me my scallop shell of quiet. The Passionate Man's Pilgrimage. Sir Walter Ralegh. AAS; CABA (1972 ed.) BoReV; ILP (1975 ed.); ILwL; IPWM; MetP; NOBE; OBP; PoIA

Give Me Myself. Michael Drayton. *Fr.* Idea. PPM

Give me O indulgent Fate! The Petition for an Absolute Retreat. Countess of Winchilsea. SBG; WPE

Give me one kiss. To Dianeme. Robert Herrick. CaPo; SoSe

Give Me Peace ("Give me quietness and peace"). Andrei Voznesensky, *tr. fr. Russian by* Jean Garrigue *and* Max Hayward. BuTh

Give me sweet nectar in a kiss. *Unknown.* FaBoEE

Give me that man that dares bestride. His Cavalier. Robert Herrick. CaPo

Give Me That Old Time Religion. *Unknown. See* That Old-Time Religion

Give me the crown. Here, cousin, seize the crown. Shakespeare. King Richard II, *fr.* IV, i. LFH

Give me the plains—the barren and sun-beaten plains! The Plains. Maynard Dixon. BPAW

Give me the right of way. Irish. Paul Celan, *tr. by* Michael Hamburger. OBVE

Give Me the Splendid Silent Sun. Walt Whitman. HAP; IPWM; NOBA; NYP; VoPo

Give me time i cannot think. These Dreamings Mine. James O. Taylor. BuTh

Give me truths. Blight. Emerson. NOBA; PiAm

Give me women, wine and snuff. Keats. MBPR

Give me your hand at once. Garden. Minou Drouet, *tr. by* Margaret Crosland. ECBV

Give me your pardon, sir. I have done you wrong. Shakespeare. *Fr.* Hamlet, V, ii. DL

Give me your patience sister while I frame. Acrostic of My Sister's Name. Keats. MBPR

Give money me, take friendship whoso list. Of Money. Barnabe Googe. FF

Give My Regards to Broadway, *with music.* George M. Cohan. BLSo; FSN

Give names to sounds. Out of Blindness. Leslie B. Blades. NowV

Give over, now, red roses. Warning of Winter. Mary Ursula Bethell. ATNZ

Give Peace in These Our Days, O Lord, *with music.* Edmund Grindal. AH

Give Peace, O God, the Nations Cry, *with music.* John W. Norris. AH

Give pensions to the Learned Pig. Blake. FaBoEE

Give store of days, good Jove, give length of years. Juvenal, *tr. fr. Latin by* Henry Vaughan. *Fr.* Satires, X. OBSV

Give Thanks. *Unknown.* CTV

Give the sounds of the curved mated phonographs. Three Found Poems. George Hitchcock. OBAL

Give them my regards when you go to the school reunion. More of a Corpse than a Woman. Muriel Rukeyser. NMM; SPT

Give to Our God Immortal Praise, *with music.* Isaac Watts. BLSH

"Give us a song!" the soldiers cried. The Song of the Camp. Bayard Taylor. BTTM

Give us another poem, he said. Prelude. Patrick Kavanagh. NoAM

Give Us This Day. James Neugass. SPT

Give Us This Day Our Daily Day. Robert J. Levy. AMV-81

Give Way, Ye Gates. Theodore Roethke. CMoP (1970 ed.)

Giveaway, The. Phyllis McGinley. PBMP

Given Note, The. Seamus Heaney. NCSH

Giving the Moon a New Chance. Terry Stokes. Moon

Giving Up on the Shore. Gabriel Preil, *tr. fr. Hebrew by* Gabriel Levin. VWA

Giving, while the rain lasts, soft noises. Eaves. Ellis Jones, *tr. by* Anthony Conran. OBW

Gizzard and some ruby inner parts, A. A. Lament. Margaret Avison. HAP

Glad New Year to all, A! A Wish. Eleanor Farjeon. CC

Glad tidings we bring of peace on earth. Shalom Chaverim. *Unknown.* FSW

Gladdest spaniel who prancing brings the ball, The. Dog Alice. Harold Witt. BoAnP

Gladioli for My Mother. Harriet Bernstein. AMV-81

Gladstone gave his name to the gladstone bag. Christopher Reid. POL

Glamour of the end attic, the smell of old, The. Perdita. Louis MacNeice. PoA

Glance, The. George Herbert. SCP-1

Glance at this fabled page straight from. Historical Society Exhibit: Old Programme. Felix Pollak. HeS

Glanced down at Shannon from the sky-way. Irish-American Dignitary. Austin Clarke. BIrV; PFIr

Glancing back, it all seems different. The Death of the Family. John Boland. IPM

Glaramara. R. C. Trevelyan. PES

Glasgerion. *Unknown.* PeBB

Glasgow. Alexander Smith. VPC

Glasgow Botanic Gardens. James Rankin. MIS

Glasgow Sonnets, *sel.* Edwin Morgan. "Mean wind wanders through the backcourt trash, A." MS; UsP

Glass. Takako Uchino Lento. BoWoP

Glass. W. S. Merwin. EAS

Glass Door, The. Robert Watson. GP

Glass Eaters, The. George Jonas. NeAC

Glass Falling. Louis MacNeice. DuDr; PFIr; RAE

Glass Flowers in a Glass Ball. Robert T. Kasold. DNGG

Glass has been falling all the afternoon, The. Storm Warnings. Adrienne Rich. NIL

Glass is going down, The. Glass Falling. Louis MacNeice. DuDr; PFIr; RAE

Glass I've wanted to live. Through You. Edwin Honig. TAP

Glass of Beer, A. James Stephens, *after the Irish of* David O'Bruaidar. CMoP (1970 ed.); ExPo (1973 ed.); FaBoCo; NCSH; NoAM; OxBTC; SoSe

Glass of Pure Water, The, *sel.* "Hugh MacDiarmid." "Hold a glass of pure water to the eye of the sun!" MS

Glass of Water, The. Wallace Stevens. CABA (1972 ed.); STS; TAP

Glass Snake, The. Francis Coleman Rosenberger. PoUp

Glass World. Dorothy Donnelly. NCSH

Glassblower lies here at rest, A.   Epitaph.   J. B. Morton. FaBoEE

Glassed with cold sleep and dazzled by the moon.   Train Journey. Judith Wright.   GAS; PBWP

Glaze of ice glistens in the manure, A.   The Kiss.   Robert Pack. AMV-81; PCho

Glaze, The. You try to see.   Jonathan Price.   CoPAm

Glazed day crumbles to its fall, The.   Provincetown, Mass. Harvey Shapiro.   PoA

Glazier, The.   Stéphane Mallarmé, *tr. fr. French by* Keith Bosley. OBVE

Gleaming in silver are the hills.   Washed in Silver.   James Stephens.   Moon

Gleaner, The.   Jane Taylor.   OxBChV

Glen Miller's music is a trunk.   Carmen Valle, *tr. fr. Spanish by* Julio Marzán.   InW

Glen of Silence, The.   "Hugh MacDiarmid."   CMoP (1970 ed.)

Glen Uig.   Richard Hugo.   PCho

Glencoe.   Billy Kay.   MIS

Glengormley.   Derek Mahon.   CIP

Glenlogie, *with music. Unknown.*   Epi

Glide soft, ye silver floods.   William Browne.   *Fr.* Britannia's Pastorals, II, Song 1.   SCP-2

Glimpse.   Pearl Cleage Lomax.   PoBA

Glimpse, A.   Walt Whitman.   PPP

Glimpse of a once-loved face, The.   What Do They Say.   Gary Snyder.   NNaP

Glimpsed world, halfway through the film, A.   The Malice of Innocence.   Denise Levertov.   NNaP

Glint of white quartz on the pale cream sand.   Broken Arrowheads at Chilmark, Martha's Vineyard.   Ruthven Todd. MS

Glitter of mica at the windy corners.   Hometown Elegy.   G. S. Fraser.   MS

Glittering, adroit, the Sicilian wonder.   Death and Empedocles 444 B.C.   Horace Gregory.   PoA

Glittering rises in flocks, The.   The Approaches.   W. S. Merwin. NOBA; Prf

Glittering topaz in your glass, The.   At a Danse Macabre. Charles Spear.   ATNZ

Gloat, glittering talmudist.   Talmudist.   Stanley Burnshaw. VWA

Globe, a paper of the Tories, The.   A Suggestion Made by the Posters of the *Globe.*   J. E. Thorold Rogers.   FaBoEE

Gloire de Dijon.   D. H. Lawrence.   CMoP (1970 ed.); GBL; ILP (1975 ed.); IPWM; LoAs; NoAM; TPo

Gloom of death is on the raven's wing, The.   The Raven.   E. A. Robinson, *after* Nicarchus.   FaBoEE; OBAL

Glooms of the live-oaks, beautiful-braided and woven.   The Marshes of Glynn.   Sidney Lanier.   AmVN; NOBA; PiAm; VoPo

Gloomy am I, oppressed and sad.   The Poet's Arbour in the Birchwood.   Edward Williams, *tr. by* Kenneth Jackson. OBW

Gloomy Cathedral, A.   Paris.   Gertrud Kolmar, *tr. by* David Kipp.   PBWP

Gloomy grammarians in golden gowns.   Of the Manner of Addressing Clouds.   Wallace Stevens.   PoA

Gloomy night before us flies, The.   Jefferson and Liberty. *Unknown.*   FSW

Gloomy night embraced the place.   The Shepherds' Hymn. Richard Crashaw.   *Fr.* In the Holy Nativity of Our Lord God.   NOBE; SCP-1

Gloomy Night of Sadness, The, *with music. Unknown.*   AH

Gloomy thought, Ben Bulben, A.   The Deserted Mountain. *Unknown, tr. by* John Montague.   BIrV

Gloria.   Ladislav Novak.   WeW

Gloria.   Christopher Smart.   *Fr.* A Song to David.   OBP (Glory of Christ, The.)   PIM

Gloria Patri, *with music. At. to* St. Thomas Aquinas, *ad. by* John Mason Neale.   BLSH

Glories of Our Blood and State, The.   James Shirley.   *Fr.* The Contention of Ajax and Ulysses.   HAP; ILP (1975 ed.); LFH; NIL; PoPle; PPP; SCP-2; SoSe
(Death the Leveller.)   FaPoR; FF; NOBE; PBMP; UnPo (1976 ed.)
(Dirge.)   OAEL-1; OBP

Glorious it is/ to see long-haired winter caribou.   *Tr. fr. Eskimo. Fr.* Song of Caribou, Musk Oxen, Women, and Men Who Would Be Manly.   RFM

Glorious it is to see/ The caribou flocking down from the forests. Song of Caribou, Musk Oxen, Women, and Men Who Would Be Manly.   *Tr. fr. Eskimo.*   WTO

Glorious people vibrated again, A.   Ode to Liberty.   Shelley. MBPR

Glorious the sun in mid career.   Gloria [*or* The Glory of Christ]. Christopher Smart.   *Fr.* A Song to David.   OBP; PIM

Glorious Virgin, heavenly vision.   O Virgin.   *Tr. fr. Gaelic by* Douglas Hyde.   WTO

Glorious World.   Hermann Hesse, *tr. fr. German by* James Wright. IPWM

Glory.   Harvey Shapiro.   POL

Glory, The.   Edward Thomas.   OxBTC

Glory, *with music.* Joseph Wise.   AH

Glory and a glory, A.   Somewhere.   James E. Warren, Jr. AATT

Glory and loveliness have passed away.   Dedication to Leigh Hunt, Esq.   Keats.   MBPR

Glory be to God for dappled things.   Pied Beauty.   Gerard Manley Hopkins.   AKE; AnMo; BiP; CABA (1972 ed.); CMoP (1970 ed.); Epi; HAP; HeIP; HoPM (1975 ed.); ILP (1975 ed.); InPK; InPS; NIL; NoAM; NOBE; OAEL-2; PAIC; PBMP; PPM; PPoD; PPP; SoSe (1977 ed); SS; VLP; VoPo; WeW; WIF

Glory be to the Father, and to the Son, and to the Holy Ghost. Gloria Patri.   *At. to* St. Thomas Aquinas.   BLSH

Glory of Christ, The.   Christopher Smart.   *See* Gloria.

Glory of evening was spread through the west, The.   The Convict. Wordsworth.   MBPR

Glory of Hanalei is its heavy rain, The.   Alfred Alohikea, *tr. fr. Hawaiian by* S. H. Elbert *and* N. Mahoe.   WTO

Glory of Him who moveth all that is, The.   Dante, *tr. by* Laurence Binyon.   Divina Commedia: Paradiso.   NAWM-1

Glory of the beauty of the morning, The.   The Glory.   Edward Thomas.   OxBTC

Glory of the Day Was in Her Face, The.   James Weldon Johnson. PoBA

Glory of the Garden, The, *sel.* Kipling.
"Oh, Adam was a gardener."   CTV

Glory to you, oh pain, sorrow unending!   The Grey-eyed King. Anna Akhmatova, *tr. by* Robert Tracy.   PBWP

Glory Trail, The.   Charles Badger Clark, Jr.   BPAW; PH; PoTa

Glory's given to the first.   Honorable Mention.   Rebecca Stutsman.   SPo

Gloss.   Padraic Fiacc.   CIP

Gloss.   David McCord.   OBAL

Gloucester Moors.   William Vaughn Moody.   AmVN; NOBA

Glove Glue.   Ken Belford.   NeAC

Glow and beauty of the stars, The.   Sappho, *tr. fr. Greek by* Willis Barnstone.   BoWoP

Glow, little glow-worm, fly of fire.   The Glow-Worm.   Johnny Mercer.   OBAL

Glow of purples at set of sun, A.   Desert Bloom.   Gertrude Thomas Arnold.   BPAW

Glowing gloom of eventide, The. The Monarch's Funeral. Shelley. MBPR

Glowworm. David McCord. ECBV

Glow-Worm, The. Johnny Mercer. OBAL

Glow Worm, *with music.* Lila Cayley Robinson. BLSo

Glow-Worm, The. Wordsworth. MBPR
("Among all lovely things my love had been.") GBL

Glucose. Dabney Stuart. CoPAm

Glutton, The. Robert Graves. CMoP (1970 ed.)

Glutton, The. John Oakman. OxBChV

Glutton in the Tavern. William Langland. *Fr.* The Vision of Piers Plowman. OxBM

Glyn Cynon Wood. *Tr. fr. Welsh by* Gwyn Williams. OBW

Gnarled old apple-tree. Old Sinner. Derek Bowman. MIS

Gnat, The. Joseph Beaumont. SCP-2

Gnat-Psalm. Ted Hughes. NoAM

Gnats and an ant have gnawed your nimble bones. To a Magnificent Spinner, Murdered. Genevieve Taggard. WPW

Gnome. Samuel Beckett. BIrV

Gnome. Harry Behn. IWK

Gnome Matter. Carolyn Wells. TDH

Gnostics on Trial. Linda Gregg. AMV–80

Gnostology. Sam Hamill. AMV–81

Γνωθι σεαντον!—and is this the prime. Self-Knowledge. Samuel Taylor Coleridge. MBPR

Gnu, The. Hilaire Belloc. BoAnP
("G stands for Gnu, whose weapons of defence.") FaBoNo

Gnu, The. Theodore Roethke. ECBV

Go Ahead; Goodbye; Good Luck; and Watch Out. William Bronk. GP

Go and ask Robin to bring the girls over. Vision by Sweetwater. John Crowe Ransom. CMoP (1970 ed.); NOBA; UsP

Go [*or* Goe,] and catch[e] a falling star[re]. Song. John Donne. AnMo; BiP; BuTh; CABA (1972 ed.); EBEV; FF; HAP; HeIP; HoPM (1975 ed.); ILP (1975 ed.); InPK; InPS; IP; NIL; NOBE; OBP; PBMP; PoIA; PoPle; PPoD; PPoe; SoSe; UsP; VoPo

Go and dig my grave both long and narrow. Dig My Grave. *Unknown.* AmFP

Go and lose your way one night. Ahasuerus. Joseph Roth, *tr. by* Erna Baber Rosenfeld. VWA

Go and open the door. The Door. Miroslav Holub, *tr. by* Ian Milner *and* George Theiner. LP

Go Back. Joan Keefe. IPM

Go back, old Devil and look up on your shelf. Old Devil. *Unknown.* BluL

Go Back to the Country. *Unknown.* BluL

Go Bauer praise their patience now. To Otto Bauer. Alfred Hayes. SPT

Go bet, peny, go bet, go! Penny Is a Hardy Knight. *Unknown.* OxBM

"Go Bring Me," Said the Dying Fair, *with music.* William Hunter. AH

Go count the stars! Counting. Fenton Johnson. AmNP (1974 ed.)

Go Down Death. James Weldon Johnson. AmNP (1974 ed.); DL; PoBA

Go Down, Moses. *Unknown.* BPo; FSW; NOBA; RDB, *with music*
(When Israel Was in Egypt's Land.) AH, *with music*

Go Down, Old Hannah. *Unknown.* AmFP

Go down to hell. This end is good to see. A Dead King. Swinburne. VLP

Go Down You Murderers. Ewan MacColl. FSW

Go, dumb-born book. Envoi (1919). Ezra Pound. *Fr.* Hugh Selwyn Mauberly. HAP; UnPo (1976 ed.); VGW

Go fetch to me a pint o'wine. The Silver Tassie [*or* My Bonnie Mary]. Burns. NOBE; PoPle

Go, for they call you, shepherd, from the hill. The Scholar-Gipsy. Matthew Arnold. CABA (1972 ed.); EBEV; HAP; HeIP; ILP (1975 ed.); NOBE; OAEL–2; PoPle; VLP

Go forth and weep. The Death of Tammuz. Shaul Tchernichovsky, *tr. by* Mark Elliot Shapiro. VWA

Go friendly, Go lovely, Go naked. Jealousy. Stephen Vincent. NeAC

Go from me: I am one of those, who fall. Mystic and Cavalier. Lionel Johnson. VLP

Go from me, summer friends, and tarry not. From Sunset to Star Rise. Christina Rossetti. SBG

Go from My Window. *Unknown.* AIW

Go, grieving rimes of mine, to that hard stone. Petrarch, *tr. by* Morris Bishop. Sonnets to Laura: To Laura in Death, LX. NAWM–1

Go, happy rose, and interwove. To the Rose. Robert Herrick. IP

Go Heart, Hurt with Adversity. *Unknown.* ILP (1975 ed.); OxBM

Go, ill-sped book, and whisper to her or. John Berryman. BoLoP; ILP (1975 ed.); LoAs

Go inside a stone. Stone. Charles Simic. NU

Go, let the fatted calf be killed. The Welcome. Abraham Cowley. *Fr.* The Mistress. BoLoP

Go, let us go my friends, go home. Home. *Zulu Oral Tradition, tr. by* H. Tracey. WTO

Go, Little Book ("Go, litel book, go, litel myn tragedy"). Chaucer. *Fr.* Troilus and Criseyde, V. OAEL–1; OxBM
("Go, little book, go, my little tragedy.") OBP

Go, Lovely Rose. Edmund Waller. BoLoP; FF; HAP; HeIP; ILP (1975 ed.); InPK; IP; LFH; NOBE; OLR; PCOP; PoPle; UnPo (1976 ed.)
(Song: "Go lovely rose.") CABA (1972 ed.); ExPo (1973 ed.); GBL; NIL; OAEL–1; OBP; PAIC; PoIA; PPoe

Go, my songs, seek your praise from the young. Ité. Ezra Pound. HAP

Go, my songs, to the lonely and the unsatisfied. Commission. Ezra Pound. BoLoP; NIL

Go on, brave heros, you whose merits claim. An Ironical Encomium. *Unknown.* APAS

Go on, thou noisy one! Praise of a Train. *Zulu Oral Tradition, tr. by* B. W. Vilakazi. WTO

Go out with a small flashlight and a star chart. Things to Do around a Ship at Sea. Gary Snyder. CAPP

Go, perjured man, and if thou e'er return. The Curse: A Song. Robert Herrick. CaPo

Go pretty child, and bear this flower. A Child's Present. Robert Herrick. OxBChV

Go sad or sweet or riotous with beer. The Old Women. George Mackay Brown. MS

Go, said old Lyce, senseless lover, go. Lyce. William Walsh. BoLoP

Go, silly worm, drudge, trudge, and travel. Omnia Somnia. Joshua Sylvester. FaBoEE

Go, solitary wood, and henceforth be. On the Death of a Nightingale. Thomas Randolph. ILP (1975 ed.)

Go, Soul [*or* Goe soule], the body's guest. The Lie. Sir Walter Ralegh. AAS; EBEV; HAP; ILP (1975 ed.); NOBE; PPoD; PPoe

Go soule, go sweetest soule for ever blest. Ariosto, *tr. by* Sir John Harington. *Fr.* Orlando Furioso, XXIX. OBVE

Go, swallow, and tell, now that the summer is dying. Cwmrhydyceirw Elegiacs. Vernon Watkins. PoA

Go tell at Sparta, thou who passest by. On the Spartan Dead at Thermopylae. Simonides, *tr. fr. Greek.* WeW

Go tell Aunt Rhody [or Nancy]. The Old Gray Goose. *Unknown.* AmFP; FSW; GBP; GSB

"Go tell him to clear me one acre of ground." The Elfin Knight. *Unknown.* AmFP

Go tell her to make me a cambric shirt. The Cambric Shirt. *Unknown.* FSW

Go Tell It on the Mountain. *Unknown.* FSW

Go tell the king: the daedal. The Last Utterance of the Delphic Oracle. *Tr. fr. Greek by* Kenneth Rexroth. OBVE

Go tell the Spartans, thou that passest by. Thermopylae. Simonides, *tr. by* William Lisle Bowles. OBVE

Go, Then. Edith Bruck, *tr. fr. Italian by* Anita Barrows. VWA

Go thou forth, my book, though late. To His Book. Robert Herrick. CaPo

Go through the gates with closed eyes. Close Your Eyes! Arna Bontemps. AmNP (1974 ed.); FB; IPWM; PoBA

Go Throw Them Out. Moishe Leib Halpern, *tr. fr. Yiddish by* Ruth Whitman. VWA

Go to Bed First. *Unknown.* GBP

Go to bed late/ Stay very small. *Unknown.* CTV

Go to Old Ireland. *Unknown.* AmFP

Go to sleep, go to sleepy. All the Pretty Little Horses. *Unknown.* AmFP

Go to sleep you weary hobo. Hobo's Lullaby. Goebel Reeves. FSW

"Go to the Ant." Stanley J. Sharpless. NOBL

Go to the ant, thou sluggard. Bible, *O.T.* Proverbs, VI:6–8. CTV

Go to the western gate, Luke Havergal. Luke Havergal. E. A. Robinson. AmVN; GBL; ILP (1975 ed.); LFH; LoAs; NoAM; NOBA; PiAm; UnPo (1976 ed.)

Go 'way from dat window, "My Honey, My Love." Song to the Runaway Slave. *Unknown.* BPo

Goals. Elisavietta Ritchie. AATT

Goat. Siddie Joe Johnson. ECBV

Goat, The. Umberto Saba, *tr. fr. Italian by* Anita Barrows. VWA

Goat, The. Roland Young. BoAnP

Goat Dance. Ron Loewinsohn. GP

Goat-herd follows his flock, The. Juan Quintana. Alice Corbin. BPAW

Goat hungers, The. Everything that lies. Hunger. Conrad Hilberry. TC

Goat Paths, The. James Stephens. UnPo (1976 ed.)

Goat Songs. Ray Drew. VoA

Goat's-Leaf. Marie de France, *tr. fr. Old French by* Aline Allard. PBWP

(Honeysuckle [Chevrefoil], *tr. by* Patricia Terry.) BoWoP

Goblin Market. Christina Rossetti. EBEV; SBG; VLP; VPC

Goblins on the doorstep. This Is Halloween. Dorothy Brown Thompson. IWK

God. Alphonse de Lamartine, *tr. fr. French.* ILwL

God. Isaac Rosenberg. VWA

God. Eugene Ruggles. MIT

God. Boris Slutsky, *tr. fr. Russian by* Dimitry Pospielovsky *and* Keith Bosley. VWA

God—/they fear you, they hold you so. Testimony. Carolyn M. Rodgers. BPo

God almighty's colly cow. The Ladybird. *Unknown.* GBP

God and Man. Samuel Hazo. TPo

God and Nature. Musa Moris Farhi. VWA

God and Saint [or Sanct] Peter was gangand be the way. How the First Hielandman [of God] Was Made. *Unknown.* FaBoCo; GBP; OBSV

God and the devil still are wrangling. For a Mouthy Woman. Countee Cullen. OBAL; PoBA

God and Yet a Man, A? *Unknown.* HAP; IPWM (Wit Wonders.) BoReV

God, Are You There? Helen Steiner Rice. CTV

God banish from your house. Benediction. Stanley Kunitz. VGW

God be with trewthe wher he be! Truth. *Unknown.* OxBM

God Be with You till We Meet Again, *with music.* Jeremiah E. Rankin. AH; BLSH

God bless all policemen. Goodbat Nightman. Roger McGough. BBGO; NoAM

God Bless America. Irving Berlin. BLSo, *with music;* CTV

God Bless America. John Fuller. OBSV

God bless Henry. He lived like a rat. John Berryman. *Fr.* Dream Songs. CAPP

God bless little Danny, where his spirit runs. Benediction for Danny. William R. Mitchell. AATT

God bless our good and gracious King. Impromptu on Charles II. Earl of Rochester. FaBoEE; InPK; NIL; NOBL; OBSV

God Bless the Child. Arthur Herzog, Jr., *and* Billie Holiday. WIF

God bless the field and bless the furrow. The Robin's Song. *Unknown, at. to* Richard Honeywood. ECBV; RAE

God bless the King!—I mean the Faith's Defender. A Jacobite Toast [or Extempore Verses...]. John Byrom. FaBoCo; FaBoEE; NOBL; PPoD

God bless the master of this house. Christmas Carol. *Unknown.* CTV

God Bless Us. Gaston Bart-Williams. BuTh

God broke into my house last night. Scapegoat. W. R. Rodgers. CIP

God Came to a Man, A. Stephen Crane. TT

God, consider the soul's need. Death Song for Owain ab Urien. Taliesin, *tr. by* Anthony Conran. OBW

God created alcohol. Io Baccho! William Carlos Williams. TT

God Don't Never Change. *Unknown.* BluL

God dwells alone, The. Deserted Shrine. Avner Treinin, *tr. by* A. C. Jacobs. VWA

God exists, though he doesn't exist. Phallus. Shiraishi Kazuke, *tr. by* Ikuko Atsumi. BoWoP

God from His Throne with Piercing Eye, *with music.* Joseph Steward. AH

God gave all men all earth to love. Sussex. Kipling. BTTM; PES .

God Give to Men ("God give the yellow man"). Arna Bontemps. BPo

God, God!/ With a child's voice I cry. Elizabeth Barrett Browning. *Fr.* The Soul's Travelling. ILwL

God grant thee thine own wish, and grant thee mine. John Donne, *after* Gazaeus. OBVE

God has a brown voice. For Eleanor Boylan Talking with God. Anne Sexton. InPk

God Has Pity on Kindergarten Children. Yehuda Amichai, *tr. fr. Hebrew by* Stephen Mitchell. VWA

God Hasn't Made Room. Mririda n'Ait Attik, *tr. fr. French version by* Daniel Halpern *and* Paula Paley. PBWP

God! how they plague his life, the three damned sisters. The Little Brother. James Reeves. LoAs; OxBTC

God in Wrath, A. Stephen Crane. The Black Riders, XIX. AmVN; IPWM; TAP; TT

God is a distant, stately lover. Emily Dickinson. SoSe (1977 ed.)

God is a Masturbator. Gregory Corso. GP

God is a screwball. From the Batter's Box. David K. Harford. AMV–80

God Is Everywhere. *Unknown.* CTV

God Is Here Again. Charles Angoff. AMV–80

God is indeed a jealous God. Emily Dickinson. NOBA

God is love. Then by conversion. History of Ideas. J. V. Cunningham. NIL

God Is Mr. Big, Real Big. Carl F. Burke. TPo

God, The, is near, and/ difficult to grasp. Patmos. David Gascoyne, *after* Friedrich Hölderlin. OBVE

God is no botcher, but when God wrought you two. On Botching. John Heywood. FaBoCo; FaBoEE

God is the Old Repair Man. The Old Repair Man. Fenton Johnson. AmNP (1974 ed.); MiP

God Is Working His Purpose Out. A. C. Ainger. FaPoR

God knows how our neighbor managed to breed. Sow. Sylvia Plath. AnMo; CoPAm

God knows it, I am with you. To a Republican Friend, 1848. Matthew Arnold. PAIC; VLP

God knows what it is about Town Halls. Vincent Buckley. Golden Builders, II. CAAP; GAS

God Lay Dead in Heaven. Stephen Crane. The Black Riders, LXVII. PiAm; TT

God love you now, if no one else will ever. Ode for the American Dead in Korea. Thomas McGrath. VGW

God made the wicked grocer. The Song against Grocers. G. K. Chesterton. FaBoCo

God makes sech nights, all white an' still. The Courtin'. James Russell Lowell. *Fr.* The Biglow Papers. AmVN; NOBA; OBAL

God moves in a mysterious way. Light Shining Out of Darkness. William Cowper. BoReV; EBEV; HeIP; NOBE; PIM; PPM

God of Bethel Heard Her Cries, The, *with music.* Richard Allen. AH

God of Judgment, The. Swinburne. PIM

God of mine, I am weeping for the life that I live. The Eternal Dice. César Vallejo, *tr. by* James Wright. IPWM

God of my father discovered at midnight. Oya. Audre Lorde. CNA

God of My Life! *with music.* Benjamin Colman. AH

God of Our Fathers, *with music.* Melancthon W. Stryker. AH

God of Our Fathers, Bless This Our Land, *with music.* John Henry Hopkins, Jr. AH

God of our fathers, known of old. Recessional. Kipling. BLSH; BTTM; CABA (1972 ed.); CTV; FaPo; FaPoR; ILP (1975 ed.); NOBE; UnPo (1976 ed.); VLP

God of our fathers, what is man! The Ways of God. Milton. *Fr.* Samson Agonistes. BoReV

God of Our Fathers, Whose Almighty Hand, *with music.* Daniel C. Roberts. AH

God of Peace, in Peace Preserve Us, *with music.* Ernst W. Olson. AH

God of the golden bow. Hymn to Apollo. Keats. MBPR

God of the Meridian. Keats. MBPR

God of the Nations, *with music.* Walter Russell Bowie. AH

God of the Nations, Near and Far, *with music.* John Haynes Holmes. AH

God of the Prophets! Bless the Prophets' Sons, *with music.* Denis Wortman. AH

God of the Strong, God of the Weak, *with music.* Richard W. Gilder. AH

God of the World, Thy Glories Shine, *with music.* Sewall Sylvester Cutting. AH

God Once Commanded Us, A. Leah Goldberg, *tr. fr. Hebrew by* Robert Friend. VWA

God Opens His Mail. Larry Rubin. CSP

God Poem. Stanley Moss. VGW; VWA

God prosper long our noble king. Chevy Chase. *Unknown.* FaBoBa; PeBB

God Rest You Merry, Gentlemen. *Unknown.* BLSH, *with music;* FSW

God Said to the Angels. Sheila Heldenbrand. AcAn

God Save the King [*or* Queen] ("God save our gracious King [*or* Queen]"). *Unknown, at. to* Henry Carey. BLSH, *with music;* BTTM

(God Save the King ["God save great George our King"].) PeD

God Save the Plough. Lydia Huntley Sigourney. OBAL

God save the Rights of Man! Ode. Philip Freneau. EAP; GOA

God Save the Stock. Charles Spear. ATNZ

God saw Adam in a town. Charles Reznikoff. *Fr.* Five Groups of Verse. SA

God scatters beauty as he scatters flowers. Walter Savage Landor. FaBoEE

God Send Easter. Lucille Clifton. CNA

God send every priest a wife. *Unknown.* TVS

God Set Us Here, *with music.* Nicasius de Sille, *tr. fr. Dutch.* AH

God shepherds me, I have. Psalm XXIII. *Paraphrased by* Harry H. Mayer. SFF

God Speed the Plough! *Unknown.* OxBM

God spoke in a dream. Argument against Metaphor. Gad Hollander. VWA

God spoke once in the dark; dead sound. The Precision. Yvor Winters. EAS

God strengthen me to bear myself. Who Shall Deliver Me? Christina Rossetti. BoReV; PFD

God Supreme! To Thee We Pray, *with music.* Penina Moise *and* Edward N. Calisch. AH

God, That Madest All Things. *Unknown.* SoSe

God, the Port of Peace. John Walton. OxBM

God to Be First Served. Robert Herrick. OxBChV

God to Thee We Humbly Bow, *with music.* George H. Boker. AH

God told Noah about the rainbow sign. Lining Track. *Unknown.* AmFP

God tried to teach Crow how to talk. Crow's First Lesson. Ted Hughes. InPS; NoAM

God Walks among the Dust. Henry Tim Chambers. AATT

God was the first poem ever uttered. In the Beginning. Richard Kell. IPM

God, we don't like to complain. Caliban in the Coal Mines. Louis Untermeyer. SoS

God what a wind! Invader. Shirley G. Cochrane. PoUp

God! What mockery is this life of ours! The Mockery of Life. Wilfrid Scawen Blunt. The Love Sonnets of Proteus, LXXIV. VLP

God who fled down with a standard yard, The. William Empson. *Fr.* Bacchus. PoA

God who mounts the winged winds, The. Homer, *tr. by* Pope. *Fr.* The Odyssey, V. OBVE

God, why have you ruined me. Job's Ancient Lament. Owen Dodson. FB

God Will Take Care of You, *with music.* Mrs. C. D. Martin. BLSH

God Wills It. Gabriela Mistral, *tr. fr. Spanish by* K. G. C. LoAs

God with a Roll of Honour in His hand. The Investiture. Siegfried Sassoon. NoAM

God with honour hang your head. At the Wedding March. Gerard Manley Hopkins. LoAs

God, Woman, Egg. Helena Minton. FAF

God would not let the spheric Lights accost. Hugh Stuart Boyd. Elizabeth Barrett Browning. VLP

God, you could grow to love it. Ecclesiastes. Derek Mahon. BIrV; CIP; IPM

Goddess, The. Denise Levertov. NOBA

Goddess. Judith Johnson Sherwin. BoWoP

Goddess Fortune be praised (on her toothed wheel), The. The Unpredicted. John Heath-Stubbs. BoLoP

Goddess of light, renewer of the mind. Sportsfield. A. D. Hope. MAuV

Goddess of poetry. To the Moon. Yvor Winters. HeIP; MPA

Goddess of rhyme, that didst inspire. An Epithalamium upon the Marriage of Captain William Bedloe. Richard Duke. APAS

Goddess of threads gladly. *Tr. fr. Icelandic by* George Johnston. *Fr.* The Saga of Gisli. OBVE

Goddess stands in front of her cave, The. On the Occasion of Becoming an Echo. Anselm Hollo. TwMBP

Goddesse bade the nymphs remove, The. *Unknown, tr. fr. Latin by* Thomas Stanley. *Fr.* Venus Vigils. OBVE

Godfrey Gordon Gustavas Gore. The Reformation of Godfrey Gore. William Brighty Rands. PCOP

Godfrey of Bulloigne; or, The Recoverie of Jerusalem, *sels.* Tasso, *tr. fr. Italian by* Edward Fairfax.
"Joyous birds, hid under greenewood shade, The," *fr.* XVI. OBVE
"Sweet Armida tooke this charge on hand, The," *fr.* IV. OBVE

Godly Dream, A, *sels.* Elizabeth Melvill, Lady Culross. WPE
"I looked down and saw a pit most black."
"Into that pit when I did enter in."
"Then up I rose, and made no more delay."
"This pit is Hell where through thou now must go."
"Weary I was, and thought to sit at rest."

Gododdin, The, *sels.* Aneirin, *tr. fr. Welsh.*
"Men went to Catraeth, keen their war-band," *tr. by* Joseph P. Clancy. OBW
"To Cattraeth's vale in glitt'ring row," *tr. by* Thomas Gray. OBVE

Godolphin Horne. Hilaire Belloc. FaBoCo

God's Acre. Longfellow. PIM

Gods chase/ Round vase. Ode on a Grecian Urn Summarized. Desmond Skirrow. NOBL

God's collage. Lesson from Jim Crane. Barbara Earl Thomson. AATT

God's Controversy with New-England. Michael Wigglesworth. EAP

God's Determinations, *sels.* Edward Taylor.
Christ's Reply. EAP
Extasy of Joy Let In by This Reply Returned in Admiration, An. EAP
First Satan's Assault against Those That First Came Up to Mercy's Terms. EAP
Frowardness of the Elect in the Work of Conversion, The. EAP
God's Selecting Love in the Decree. EAP
Joy of Church Fellowship Rightly Attended The. EAP
(In Heaven Soaring Up.) AH, *with music*
Our Insufficiency to Praise God Suitably, for His Mercy. PiAm
Preface, The: "Infinity, when all things it beheld." EAP; HAP; ILP (1975 ed.); NOBA; PiAm

God's Education. Thomas Hardy. OBP

God's Gifts. Jakov de Haan, *tr. fr. Dutch by* David Soetendorp. VWA

God's Gifts to Me. Thelma Walton. CTV

God's Grandeur. Gerard Manley Hopkins. AnMo; BiP; BoReV; CABA (1972 ed.); CMoP (1970 ed.); Epi; ExPo (1973 ed.); FF; HAP; ILP (1975 ed.); ILwL; InPK; IP; IPWM; LFH; NoAM; NOBE; OAEL-2; OBP; PAIC; PoIA; PPP; SoSe; UnPo (1976 ed.); VLP; VoPo

Gods have taken alien shapes upon them, The. Exiles. "AE." BIrV

God's head for a paperweight, A. The Desk. Cid Corman. VGW

Gods in Vietnam. Eugene Redmond. PoBA

Gods it is I ask to release me from this watch, The. Agamemnon. Aeschylus, *tr. by* Louis MacNeice. NAWM-1

God's Language. Ruth Fainlight. VWA

Gods live in a micro-world, The. Sonnet for All Greeks Living Now. Darrell Gray. AcAn

God's Measurements. Laurence Lieberman. PCho

Gods, men in straw hats, girls in calico. For J. A. R. McKellar. Geoffrey Lehmann. MAuV

Gods of Hellas, gods of Hellas. The Dead Pan. Elizabeth Barrett Browning. VLP

Gods of the Copybook Headings, The. Kipling. FaPoR; OBP; OBSV; OxBTC

Gods of Washington, D.C., The. Richard Eberhart. WasP

God's Plan for Spring. Nancy Byrd Turner. CTV

God's Selecting Love in the Decree. Edward Taylor. *Fr.* God's Determinations. EAP

Gods, The! The Gods! D. H. Lawrence. CMoP (1970 ed.)

God's Will for You and Me. *Unknown.* IP; SoSe (1977 ed.)

Gods! with what pride I see the titled slave. Charles Churchill. *Fr.* The Author. OBSV

God's Words to the Last Ape. George Mattingly. AcAn

God's World. Edna St. Vincent Millay. CMoP (1970 ed.); ILP (1975 ed.); PPM; VoPo

Gods would have chastened us through confusion, The. The Outrageously Blessed. Barry Spacks. CoPAm

Godspeed to Such Harpoons. L. W. Michaelson. PoW

Goe, and catche a falling starre. *See* Go and catch a falling star.

Goe soule, the bodies guest. *See* Go, Soul, the body's guest.

Goethe in Weimar sleeps, and Greece. Memorial Verses. Matthew Arnold. CABA (1972 ed.); NIL; OAEL-2; VLP

Goggled yellow, the cyclist's face. Stoplight. William Pitt Root. SFF

Goin' Back T'morrer. Hamlin Garland. OBAL

Goin' 'cross the Mountain. *Unknown.* AmFP

Goin' down the road, Lawd. Bound No'th Blues. Langston Hughes. AmNP (1974 ed.); BiP

Goin' down to Cripple Creek, goin' at a run. Cripple Creek. *Unknown.* AmFP

Goin' down to the delta. Mississippi Blues. *Unknown.* AmFP

Goin' up State Street, comin' down Main. Take a Whiff on Me. *Unknown.* NOBA

Going. Peter Everwine. NNaP

Going, The. Thomas Hardy. EBEV; NOBE; UnPo (1976 ed.)

Going. Philip Larkin. CMoP (1970 ed.); NowV; PSN

Going. Richard Ryan. IPM

Going and Coming: Two Poems. Michael Benedikt. CAAP

Going and Staying. Thomas Hardy. CMoP (1970 ed.); NoAM

Going Away. Ann Stanford. GP; PH

Going Away Blues. *Unknown.* BluL

Going Back. Donald Petersen. UsP

Going Back. Salvatore Quasimodo, *tr. fr. Italian by* Rina Ferrarelli. AMV-81

Going Back to Oxford. Eiléan Ní Chuilleanáin. IPM

Going Barefoot. Judith Thurman. FPB

Going Fishing. Lexie Griffiths. RAE

Going Home. Thomas Lux. NVAP

Going Home. Tim Reynolds. NowV

Going Home. Renée Roper. NPW

Going home. The city is being shed behind me. New England: Driving Back in Early April. Frank Stewart. PHC

Going In to Dinner. Edward Shanks. OxBTC

Going into a church my prayers to say. On a Melting Beauty. Margaret Cavendish, Duchess of Newcastle. SCP-2

Going into Breeches. Charles *and* Mary Lamb. OxBChV

Going into the Woods. Tom Hennen. HeS

Going North. Luís Omar Salinas. CPA

Going our halfhappy. Things as [*or* Are as] They Are. Chuck Miller. AcAn; EC

Going the Rounds: A Sort of Love Poem. Anthony Hecht. BoLoP

Going, the wild things of our land. The Passing of the Buffalo. Hamlin Garland. BPAW

Going Through. Bruce P. Woodford. MAT

Going through Changes. Jean Tepperman. NMM

Going through the Old Photos. Michael Rosen. FPB

Going To and Fro and Walking Up and Down, *sels.* Charles Reznikoff.
  Autobiography: Hollywood. SA; VWA
  Kaddish: "In her last sickness, my mother took my hand in hers." SA

Going to Bed. John Donne. Elegies, XIX. EBEV; GBL; PPP; TT
  (To His Mistress [*or* Mistris] Going to Bed.) AnMo; BoLoP; OAEL–1; OBP

Going to bed I bump into the dark. For You. Calvin Forbes. PHC

Going to Boston. *Unknown.* FSW

Going to Cythera. Chris Wallace-Crabbe. CAAP

Going to Germany. *Unknown.* BluL

Going to Hell. *Unknown.* OxBM

Going to Mass Last Sunday. Donagh MacDonagh. BIrV

Going to Norway. Jack Anderson. GP

Going to Press. Judith Moffett. AMV–80

Going to Remake This World. James Welch. CDW; SA

Going to School in France or America. Tom Clark. ConAP

Going to sleep, I cross my hands on my chest. Death. William Knott. EAS

Going to Sleep in the Country. Howard Moss. PPoD

Going to the North. Stanislaw Wygodski, *tr. fr. Polish by* Isaac Komem. VWA

Going to the Wars. Richard Lovelace. *See* To Lucasta, Going to the Wars.

Going to Town. Fred Lape. PH

Going Under. Ann Deagon. AAN; CSP

Going Up and Down. Jim Daniels. AMV–81

Going up for the jump shot. The Poet Tries to Turn In His Jock. David Hilton. AcAn; LiSp; NowV

Going Up the River. *Unknown.* AIW

Going up the river, or down, their tuneless look. Barges on the Hudson. Babette Deutsch. WPE

Going up through the hill called the vineyard. The Vineyard. W. S. Merwin. NNaP

Going Uptown to Visit Miriam. Victor Hernandez Cruz. FF; MAT; NYP

Gold. Donald Hall. ConAP; InPS

Gold-armoured ghost from the Roman road, The. The Youth with Red-gold Hair. Edith Sitwell. FaBoTw (1975 ed.)

Gold-coloured skin of my Lebanese friends, The. A Trip to Four or Five Towns. John Logan. ConAP; NNaP

"Gold is for the mistress—silver for the maid." Cold Iron. Kipling. ILP (1975 ed.)

Gold Leaves. G. K. Chesterton. OxBTC

Gold of a ripe oat straw, gold of a southwest moon. Falltime. Carl Sandburg. PoA

Gold on her head, and gold on her feet. The Eve of Crecy. William Morris. VLP

Gold or iv'ry's not intended. Horace, *tr. by* Christopher Smart. Odes, II, 18. OBVE

Gold pins and pearls of Columbia. Successful Scot. Joseph Gordon Macleod ("Adam Drinan"). MS

Gold savours well, though it be got. Isabella Whitney. *Fr.* A Sweet Nosegay, or Pleasant Posy. WPE

Gold Tooth Blues. Tennessee Williams. OBAL

Gold Watch, The. John Blight. CAAP

Golda. Adrienne Wolfert. AMV–80

Golden. Gérard de Nerval, *tr. fr. French by* Andrew Hoyem. Epi

Golden Age, The. Giovanni Battista Guarini, *tr. fr. Italian by* Sir Richard Fanshawe. *Fr.* Il Pastor Fido. OAEL–1
  ("Fair Golden Age! when milk was th' onely food.") OBVE

Golden Age, The. Ovid, *tr. fr. Latin by* Arthur Golding. *Fr.* Metamorphoses, I. OAEL–1

Golden Age, The. *Unknown.* APAS

Golden Age is come, The. The Newmarket Song. *Unknown.* APAS

Golden Age Restored, The, *sel.* Ben Jonson.
  "We come!/ We come!" SCP-1

Golden Age Was When the World Was Young, The. Fulke Greville. *Fr.* Caelica. NIL; OAEL–1

Golden Bough. Elinor Wylie. PBWP

Golden bridle of Bellerephon. The Fourth Pearl: Temperance. Lady Diana Primrose. *Fr.* A Chain of Pearl. WPE

Golden Builders, *sels.* Vincent Buckley.
  "As the car stooped, seemed to pause," XXVII. CAAP; GAS
  "Even if there'd been prayers," III. CAAP
  (Practising Not Dying.) GAS
  Fitzroy, Carlton, IX. CAAP
  "God knows what it is about Town Halls," II. CAAP; GAS
  "Hammers of iron glow down Faraday, The," I. CAAP; GAS
  "Here, though, the fine cool air," VI. CAAP
  "Purblind walls," V. CAAP; GAS
  Telephones, Muzak, XXV. CAAP
  "They are digging everywhere. From street to street," IV. CAAP; GAS
  "Timid and hot-tempered," VIII. CAAP
  "Traffic glitters towards dull junction, The," XXVI. CAAP
  "With the spring rains, small spiders," VII. CAAP

Golden casket I designed, A. Epigram. John Swanwick Drennan. BIrV

Golden crocus reaches up, The. The Crocus. Walter Crane. PCOP

Golden-eyed Crossbow, The. Claude Pélieu. MIT

Golden Fleece, The. Oscar Williams. PoA

Golden Gate: The Teacher. Lilyan S. Mastrolia. AMV–80

Golden gift that nature did thee geve, The. Earl of Surrey. AAS

Golden Girl. College Formal: Renaissance Casino. Langston Hughes. ILP (1975 ed.)

Golden Glories. Christina Rossetti. PF

Golden Glove, The. *Unknown.* AmFP

Golden goats with lapis eyes. Panegyric. Harris Lenowitz. VWA

Golden Grain. Helen M. Wright. PH

Golden Greats, The. Steve Toth. AcAn

Golden Journey to Samarkand, The, *sels.* James Elroy Flecker.
  "And how beguile you? Death has no repose," II. OxBTC
  Epilogue: "Away, for we are ready to a man!" NOBE
  Prologue: "We who with songs beguile your pilgrimage." FaPoR; OxBTC

Golden Keys. *Unknown.* CTV

Golden Lines. Gérard de Nerval, *tr. fr. French by* Robert Bly. NU

Golden Lot, A. Joseph Skipsey. VLP

Golden Moonrise. William Stanley Braithwaite. PoBA

Golden Net, The. Blake. MBPR; UsP

Golden one is gone from the banquets, The. Epigram. Hilda Doolittle ("H. D."). PoA

Golden Pyramids of the Sun, The. Alden Nowlan. AKE

Golden Sea-Otter, The. Wakarpa, *tr. by* Arthur Waley. *Fr.* Kutune Shirka (The Ainu Epic). WTO

Golden Shower, The, *sel.* Roy Campbell.
  "Here, where relumed by changing seasons, burn." OxBTC

Golden Slippers. James A. Bland. *See* Oh, Dem Golden Slippers!

Golden slumbers kiss your eyes. A Cradle Song. Thomas Dekker. *Fr.* The Pleasant Comedy of Patient Grissell. GSB; OxBChV

Golden Stallion, The. Paul Thompson. BPAW

*Golden Vanity*, The. *Unknown.* AIW; FSW; PBMP; PoPle; RDB, *with music*

Golden Witch, The. Alan Dienstag. MIT

Golden, within this golden hive. Danaë. Barbara Howes. RiTi; WPE

Goldfish. Howard Nemerov. BoAnP

Goldfish Floats, The. Ted Kooser. HeS

Goldfish Wife, The. Sandra Hochman. RiTi; UnPo (1976 ed.)

Golem, The. Shlomo Reich, *tr. fr. French by* Mira Reich. VWA

Golf Ball. John Delaney. AMV–81

Golf Links Lie So Near the Mill, The. Sarah N. Cleghorn. TPo

Golfers. Irving Layton. CABA (1972 ed.)

Golfers. John Updike. LiSp

Golgotha Is a Mountain. Arna Bontemps. AmNP (1974 ed.)

Goliath stood up clear in the assumption of status. David. Josephine Miles. MIT

Golly, it's hard/ To decide what to pick. Decision. M. P. Flynn. CTV

Gombeen, The. Joseph Campbell. BIrV

Gondibert, *sels.* Sir William Davenant. SCP-2
"Battle in exact though little shape, The," I, 5.
"Verona by the port's pencil drawn," II, 1.

Gondoliers, The, *sel.* W. S. Gilbert.
There Lived a King. PoPle; PoTa

Gone. Carl Sandburg. NOBA

Gone. Joanna Thompson. AMV–80

Gone are the days when my heart was young and gay. Old Black Joe. Stephen Collins Foster. PSoN

Gone are the drab monosyllabic days. Tilth. Robert Graves. FaBoEE; OBSV

Gone Away. Denise Levertov. SoS

Gone Dead Train, The. *Unknown.* BluL

Gone, I say, and walk from church. The Truth the Dead Know. Anne Sexton. CoPAm; NoAM; PBWP; Psy; TAP

Gone now the baby's nurse. Home after Three Months Away. Robert Lowell. PBMP; PSN; RRA

Gone she is a long, long way. Upon a Maid. Robert Herrick. CaPo

Gone south, the ice the size of the oven door. Winter 1970, Fox River, Illinois. Ralph Salisbury. MPA

Gone the three ancient ladies. Frau Bauman, Frau Schmidt, and Frau Schwartze. Theodore Roethke. InPK; NoAM; NOBA; PiAm; PSN; TAP

Gone were but the winter. Spring Quiet. Christina Rossetti. FSFS; VoPo; WPE

Gone West. H. H. Lewis. SPT

Gone while your tastes were keen to you. For E. McC. Ezra Pound. LiSp

"Goneys an' gullies an' all o' the birds o' the sea." Sea Change. John Masefield. FaBoTw (1975 ed.); PoTa

Gonna dig my grave both long and narrow. Dig My Grave. *Unknown.* FSW

Gonna Lay My Head Down on Some Railroad Line. *Unknown.* AmFP

Gonna sit around for a while. I Don't Know. *Unknown.* BluL

Goober Peas. *Unknown.* FSW; PSoN, *with music*

Good Advice. Lady Mary Wortley Montagu. POL
("Be plain in dress and sober in your diet.") FaBoEE

Good Advice. Louis Untermeyer, *after the German.* CTV

Good aged Bale, that with thy hoary hairs. To Doctor Bale. Barnabe Googe. PAIC

Good and Bad. Edward Wallis Hoch. CTV

Good and Bad Children. Robert Louis Stevenson. OxBChV; PCOP

Good and Bad Luck. John Milton Hay. *See* Good Luck and Bad.

Good and Clever. Elizabeth Wordsworth. OxBTC

Good and great God! can I not think of Thee. To Heaven. Ben Jonson. ExPo (1973 ed.); HAP; ILP (1975 ed.); ILwL; PPoe; UnPo 1976 ed.)

Good are attracted by mens perceptions, The. Motto to the Songs of Innocence and of Experience. Blake. MBPR

Good bailiff of my farm, that snug domain. Horace, *tr. fr. Latin by* John Conington. OBVE

Good Beasts, The. Willis Barnstone. VWA

Good brother Philip, I have borne you long. Astrophel and Stella, LXXXIII. Sir Philip Sidney. Epi

Good-by and Keep Cold. Robert Frost. CMoP (1970 ed.)

Goodby Betty, Don't Remember Me. E. E. Cummings. CMoP (1970 ed.)

Goodby girls, I'm goin' to Boston. Going to Boston. *Unknown.* FSW

Good-by on an All Day Bean Planter. Nathan Whiting. HeS

Good-by, Steer. Robert V. Carr. BPAW

Goodbye. Bella Akhmadulina, *tr. fr. Russian by* Barbara Einzig. BoWoP

Good-bye. Emerson. TAP; VoPo

Goodbye. William Knott. EAS

Goodbye. Alun Lewis. BoLoP; MPo; OxBTC; PSN

Good-bye,/ try to stay awake now you're dead. Book of the Dead, Prayer 14. Mei Berssenbrugge. GP; NW; SA

Goodbye and Hello. Tim Buckley. WIF

Goodbye David Tamunoemi West. Margaret Danner. BPo

Goodbye, goodbye to summer! Robin Redbreast. William Allingham. OxBChV

Goodbye, he waved, entering the apple. Fruit and Vegetables. Erica Jong. CAAP

Goodbye, lady in Bangor, who sent me. The Correspondence School Instructor Says Goodbye to His Poetry Students. Galway Kinnell. NOBA; TAP

Goodbye, Little Bonnie, Goodbye. *Unknown.* FSW

Goodbye, Little Bonny Blue Eyes. *Unknown.* AmFP

Goodbye 'Liza Jane. *Unknown.* FSW

Good-bye My Fancy! Walt Whitman. TAP

Good Bye, My Lady Love, *with music.* Joseph E. Howard. FSN

Goodbye, My Lover, Goodbye. *Unknown.* FSW

Good-bye!—no, do not grieve that it is over. A Farewell. Harriet Monroe. PoA

Goodbye Old Paint. *Unknown.* FSW

Goodbye, Old Paint, I'm Leaving Cheyenne. George Garrett. PPoD

Goodbye pale cold inconstant. A Farewell, a Welcome. Lisel Mueller. Moon

Good-bye, proud world! I'm going home. Good-bye. Emerson. TAP; VoPo

"Good-bye," said the river, "I'm going downstream." Howard Nemerov. WeW

Goodbye, Sally. James Simmons. BIrV

Goodbye Sonnet. George Mattingly. AcAn

Good-bye to the Mezzogiorno. W. H. Auden. OxBTC

Goodbye to the town!—goodbye! July. Austin Dobson. RAE

Goodbye, winter. Prognosis. Louis MacNeice. CMoP (1970 ed.); NOBE

"Good-bye," you said, and your voice was an echo. Tak for Sidst. Babette Deutsch. PoA

Good children, refuse not these lessons to learn. A Schoolmaster's Admonition. *Unknown.* OxBChV

Good Christian Reader judge me not. God's Controversy with New-England. Michael Wigglesworth. EAP

Good Christians all, both great and small. The Avondale Mine Disaster. *Unknown.* AmFP

Good Counsel. *Unknown, tr. fr. Welsh by* Glyn Jones. OBW

Good Counsel to a Young Maid. Thomas Carew. CaPo

Good dame looked from her cottage, The. The Leak in the Dike. Phoebe Cary. CTV

Good Dream, The. Denise Levertov. NNaP

Good evening/ the time is now 5:55 pm. Rita Valentino. OSP

Good evening, here is the news. The Bridge. Derek Walcott. NYP

Good Father John O'Hart. The Ballad of Father O'Hart. W. B. Yeats. VLP

Good folk, for gold or hire. The Crier. Michael Drayton. ILP (1975 ed.); PAIC

Good Folks at the Camp Meeting, The. William Kloefkorn. *Fr.* Loony. GP

Good folks ever will have their way. The Doctor's Story. Will M. Carleton. PoTa

Good for good is only fair. Good Counsel. *Unknown, tr. by* Glyn Jones. OBW

Good Frend, *sel.* Hilda Doolittle ("H. D."). "Time has an end, they say." NOBA

Good Friday. Richard Bastian. AATT

Good Friday. Arlene De Bevoise. AMV-81

Good Friday. Edwin Morgan. MS

Good Friday. Christina Rossetti. OFD

Good Friday./ Miss Booker's beauty parlor. Rachel and the Truth (c.1945). Yvonne. WBN

Good Friday Explosives. E. R. Cole. AATT

Good Friday, 1613. Riding Westward. John Donne. AnMo; ExPo (1973 ed.); OAEL-1; PPP

Good Friday was the day. The Martyr. Herman Melville. TAP; VoPo

Good Friends and First Impressions. Barbara Drake. TC

Good God! and can it be that such a nook. The Milking Shed. John Clare. VLP

Good God, what a night that was. Petronius Arbiter, *tr. fr. Latin by* Kenneth Rexroth. BoLoP

Good Gossips Mine. *Unknown.* OxBM

Good grey guardians of art, The. Museum Piece. Richard Wilbur. CMoP (1970 ed.); ConAP; NIL; TAP; WIF

Good Harbor Bay, Leland, Michigan. Ellen McEvilley Griffin. NPW

Good Heav'n, I thank thee, since it was design'd. On Myselfe. Countess of Winchilsea. SBG

Good Hours. Robert Frost. PPM

Good King Wenceslas. *Unknown, tr. fr. Latin by* John Mason Neale. BLSH, *with music*; FSW; GSB, *with music*

Good Kosciusko, thy great name alone. To Kosciusko. Keats. MBPR

Good Lady/ I have corn and beets. A Negro Peddler's Song. Fenton Johnson. AmNP (1974 ed.)

Good Life, The. Robert Francis. PoIA

Good Life, The. Mary Alice Gunderson. PoW

Good Life, A. Robert Watson. AMV-81

Good Lord, Deliver Us! John Donne. *Fr.* The Litany. BoReV

Good Lord, what a wicked world is this. *Unknown.* TVS

Good Luck. Robert Herrick. ECBV (Coming of Good Luck, The.) FaBoEE

Good Luck and Bad ("Good luck is the gayest of all gay girls"). John Milton Hay, *after the German of* Heine. FaBoEE (Good and Bad Luck.) OBAL

Good Luck to You Kafka/ You'll Need It Boss. Henry Graham. NowV

Good man was there of religion, A. A Poor Parson. Chaucer. *Fr.* The Canterbury Tales: Prologue. BoReV

Good Memory. Sotero Rivera-Avilés, *tr. fr. Spanish by* Julio Marzán. InW

Good morn t'ye, John. How b'ye? how b'ye? Eclogue: The Common a-Took In. William Barnes. VLP; VPC

Good Mornin', Blues. *Unknown.* InPK

Good Morning. Langston Hughes. *Fr.* Lenox Avenue Mural. WIF

Good Morning. Layle Silbert. NPW

Good Morning. Mark Van Doren. DuDa

Good morning, Algernon: Good morning, Percy. On Mundane Acquaintances. Hilaire Belloc. FaBoEE; OxBTC

Good Morning America, *sel.* Carl Sandburg. "Now it's Uncle Sam sitting on top of the world," XIV. OFD

Good Morning Blues. *Unknown.* FSW

Good morning captain. Mule Skinner Blues. *Unknown.* FSW

Good morning daddy!/ Ain't you heard. Dream Boogie. Langston Hughes. ILP (1975 ed.)

Good morning, daddy/ I was born here, he said. Good Morning. Langston Hughes. *Fr.* Lenox Avenue Mural. WIF

Good morning, fox of the cave. The Fox's Counsel. Huw Llwyd, *tr. by* Joseph P. Clancy. OBW

"Good-morning; good-morning!" the General said. The General. Siegfried Sassoon. CMoP (1970 ed.); OxBTC

Good morning, Judge what may be my fine. Judge Harsh Blues. *Unknown.* BluL

Good Morning Love! Paul Blackburn. NoAM

Good morning, man; good morning, child. World, Hold Me Close. Virginia Floyd. AATT

Good morning Mister Railroad man. The Gambler. *Unknown.* FSW

Good morning to the great trees. Good Morning. Mark Van Doren. DuDa

Good-Morrow, The. John Donne. AnMo; BiP; BoLoP; CABA (1972 ed.); EBEV; FF; HoPM (1975 ed.); ILP (1975 ed.); InPS; LoAs; MetP; NIL; OAEL-1; OLR; PAIC; PoIA; PoPle; PPP; SCP-1; SoSe

Good morrow to the day so fair. The Mad Maid's Song. Robert Herrick. CaPo; OAEL-1; SCP-1

Good Neighbors. May Justus. MN

Good News. *Unknown.* FSW

Good News from New England, *sel. At. to* Edward Johnson. "With hearts revived in conceit, new land and trees they eye." GOA

Good news. It seems he loved them after all. A Song about Major Eatherly. John Wain. NowV; OxBTC

Good news! Nilda Is Back. Colette Inez. RiTi

Goodnight. John Ciardi. OBAL

Good Night, *sel.* Carl Sandburg. "Many ways to spell good night." CC

Goodnight, The. Louis Simpson. MPo; PBMP; SoSe (1977 ed.)

Good night/ Sleep tight. Night Blessing. *Unknown.* CTV

Goodnight and goodbye to the life whose signs denote us. In Harbour. Swinburne. VLP

Good Night and Good Morning. Richard Monckton Milnes. OxBChV

Good Night, at last. Envoy. Robert Duncan. *Fr.* Passages. VGW

Good-night; ensured release. Parta Quies. A. E. Housman. NOBE; TT

Good night for the fireplace to be, A. The Heat in the Room. Weldon Kees. EAS

Goodnight Ladies. *Unknown.* FSW

Good night, my two little cloud ladies.  For the Girls 'cause They Know.  Harold Littlebird.  VoR

Good-Night, or Blessing, The.  Robert Herrick.  CaPo

Good-Night to the Season.  Winthrop Mackworth Praed.  NOBE; NOBL

Good night to the Year Academic.  A Grouchy Good Night to the Academic Year.  Ted Pauker.  NOBL

Good night to thee, Fair Goddess.  Sunset Song.  *Tr. by* N. Barnes.  WTO

Goodnite sun.  Song for Sunsets.  Earle Birney.  MPA

Good of the Chaplain to enter Lone Bay.  Billy in the Darbies.  Herman Melville.  *Fr.* Billy Budd, Foretopman.  ExPo (1973 ed.); HAP; NOBA

Good Old Rebel, The.  Innes Randolph.  *See* Rebel, The.

Good people all, of every sort.  An Elegy on the Death of a Mad Dog.  Goldsmith.  *Fr.* The Vicar of Wakefield.  AIW; FaBoCo; GDP; ILP (1975 ed.); LAuP; PCOP; PoPle; SS; TPo

Good people all, with one accord.  An Elegy on That Glory of Her Sex, Mrs. Mary Blaize.  Goldsmith.  FaBoCo; FaBoNo; ILP (1975 ed.); LAuP

Good people: What? Will you of all be bereft?  A Ballad on the Times.  Henry Hall.  APAS

Good reader! if you e'er have seen.  Nonsense.  Thomas Moore.  FaBoEE

Good Resolution, A.  Roy Campbell.  OBSV

Good Shepherd, The.  Lope de Vega, *tr. fr. Spanish by* Longfellow.  PIM

Good Ships.  John Crowe Ransom.  WeW

Good sirs, be civil, can one man, d'ye think.  The Answer of Mr. Waller's Painter to His Many New Advisers.  *Unknown.* APAS

Good Souls, to Survive.  Brendan Kennelly.  IPM

Good Sportsmanship.  Richard Armour.  LiSp; SPo

Good Start, A.  Larry Moffi.  AMV-81

Good Stuff Cookies.  Anselm Hollo.  AcAn

Good sword and a trusty hand!, A.  The Song of the Western Men.  Robert Stephen Hawker.  BTTM; FaPoR

Good Taste.  Christopher Logue.  RAE

Good Thinking.  *Unknown.*  TDH

Good Time Coming, The.  Charles Mackay.  VLP

Good Times.  Lucille Clifton.  AmNP (1974 ed.); AmPA; BPo; CAAP; CNA; FF; InPS; NCSH; PoBA; SoSe (1977 ed.); TAP

   "My Mama moved among the days," *sel.*  TV

Good Times and No Bread.  Reginald Lockett.  CNA

Good Town, The.  Edwin Muir.  CMoP (1970 ed.)

Good Weather.  Giuseppe Gioachino Belli, *tr. fr. Italian by* Miller Williams.  AMV-81

"Good weather for hay."  Vermont Conversation.  Patricia Hubbell.  CTBA

Good Wif was ther of biside Bathe, A.  The Wife of Bath.  Chaucer.  *Fr.* The Canterbury Tales: Prologue.  BiP; EBEV; InPS; OxBM; PPoe

Goodbat Nightman.  Roger McGough.  BBGO; NoAM

Goodby.  *See* Good-by.

Goodbye.  *See* Good-bye.

Goodly Child, A.  *Unknown.*  OxBChV

Goodly host one day was mine, A.  Mine Host of the "Golden Apple."  Thomas Westwood.  ECBV

Goodnight.  *See* Good Night.

Goodwill, Inc.  Dennis Schmitz.  AmPA

Goody Blake, and Harry Gill.  Wordsworth.  MBPR

Goops they lick their fingers, The.  Table Manners (I-II).  Gelett Burgess.  CTV

Goose.  Richard Emil Braun.  NoAM

Goose, The.  Tennyson.  ECBV

Goose and the Gander, The.  *Unknown.*  GBP

Goose Fish, The.  William Logan.  AAN

Goose Fish, The.  Howard Nemerov.  CMoP (1970 ed.); ExPo (1973 ed.); HeIP; ILP (1975 ed.); InPK; LoAs; NIL; NoAM

Goose, Moose, and Spruce.  David McCord.  ECBV

Goose Pond.  Stanley Kunitz.  PoA

Goose that laid the golden egg, The.  Ars Poetica.  X. J. Kennedy.  NIL

Gooseberries.  Peter Wild.  GP

Gooseberry Wine.  Mary Shumway.  NVAP

Goosegirl, your feet are slow.  The New Leda.  Barbara Howes.  RiTi

Goosey, goosey, gander,/ Whither shall I wander?  Mother Goose.  GSB, *with music*; MG

Gopher remarked to the Prairie Dog, The.  The Prairie Dog.  Arthur Guiterman.  BPAW

Gorilla at Twenty Nine Years, The.  J. D. Reed.  NeAC

Gorilla Gorilla.  Bruce Dawe.  CAAP

Gorilla lay on his back, The.  Au Jardin des Plantes.  John Wain.  OxBTC

Gormley's Laments, *sel.*  Gormley, *tr. fr. Irish by* Joan Keefe.  "I have loved thirty by three."  PBWP

Goshawk, The.  John Haines.  GP

Gospel According to St. John.  Bible, *N.T.*  *See* St. John.

Gospel According to St. Luke.  Bible, *N.T.*  *See* St. Luke.

Gospel According to St. Mark.  Bible, *N.T.*  *See* St. Mark.

Gospel According to St. Matthew.  Bible, *N.T.*  *See* St. Matthew.

Gospel Train, The.  *Unknown.*  BLSo, *with music* (Get on Board, Little Children.)  FSW; PBMP (Git on Board, Little Chillen.)  BPo

Gosport Tragedy, The.  *Unknown.*  AmFP

Gossip.  Nicholas Flocos.  SA

Gossip, The.  Daniel Halpern.  SO

Gossip grows like weeds.  Hitomaro, *tr. fr. Japanese by* Kenneth Rexroth.  OLR

Got a little bitty mama, and a big mama too.  Big Woman.  *Unknown.*  BluL

"Got any boys?" the Marshal said.  The Puzzled Census Taker.  John Godfrey Saxe.  PoTa

Got the Blues, Can't Be Satisfied.  *Unknown.*  BluL

Got there early.  Bear at the Academy of the Living Arts.  Brendan Galvin.  BCr

Got three womens: yellow, brown and black.  Three Women Blues.  *Unknown.*  BluL

Got to pull this timber 'fore the sun goes down.  Timber (Jerry the Mule).  *Unknown.*  FSW

Got up this morning/ The blues, walking like a man.  Preaching Blues.  *Unknown.*  BluL

Gothic Dusk, The.  Frederic Prokosch.  PoA

Gothic looks solemn.  Lines Rhymed in a Letter Received from Oxford.  Keats.  MBPR

Gourd Dancer, The.  N. Scott Momaday.  CDW

Gourmet's Love-Song, The.  P. G. Wodehouse.  NOBL

Government!  Tuta Nihoniho, *tr. fr. Maori by* A. Armstrong.  WTO

Government of your body, sweet, The.  The United States.  William Carlos Williams.  LoAs

Governor loves to go mapping—round and round, The.  Sydney Cove, 1788.  Peter Porter.  GAS

Governor of Ollie Street, The.  Ahmos Zu-Bolton.  AAN

Governor your husband lived so long, The.  John Berryman.  *Fr.* Homage to Mistress Bradstreet.  NoAM; NOBA

Governor's Palace, The.  Linda Pastan.  *Fr.* Williamsburg.  RiTi

Gowa! Gowa!  Crow's Ditty.  *Unknown.*  GBP

Gowan glitters on the sward, The. The Trysting Bush. Joanna Baillie. WPE

Gowk, The. William Soutar. MS

Grabbling in Yokna Bottom. James Seay. CSP

Grace. Emerson. LFH

Grace. Michael Sheridan. HeS

Grace after Dinner. Burns. FaBoEE

Grace for a Child. Robert Herrick. CTV; InPS
(Another Grace for a Child.) CABA (1972 ed.); HeIP; InPK; OxBChV
(Two Graces, I.) PoPle

Grace for Children, A. Robert Herrick. OxBchV
(English Grace, An.) PIM
(Two Graces, II.) PoPle

Grace-Note, The. Denise Levertov. ConAP; UsP

Grace of Cynthia's Maidenhood, The. Vinnie-Marie D'Ambrosio. IHMS

Grace of God and the Meth-Drinker, The. Sydney Goodsir Smith. MS

Grace of the Word immaculate. Raziel. Yvan Goll, *tr. by* Anthony Rudolf. VWA

Grace to Be Said at the Supermarket. Howard Nemerov. AnMo; MPo

Graceful and sure with youth, the skaters glide. The Skaters. John Williams. CoPAm; LiSp

Gracefullest leaper, the dappled fox-cub. Young Reynard. George Meredith. HoPM (1975 ed.)

Gracey Nugent. Austin Clarke, *tr. fr. Irish.* CIP

Gracie. Faye Kicknosway. NMM

Gracing the tide-warmth, this seagull. The Seagull. Dafydd ap Gwilym, *tr. by* Glyn Jones. OBW

Gracious Goodness. Marge Piercy. BoAnP

Gracious Saviour, We Adore Thee, *with music.* Sewall Sylvester Cutting. AH

Gradual bud and bloom and seedfall speeded up. July 4th. May Swenson. PoA

Gradually growing fur. Traveling North. John Woods. POL

Graduate, The. Charles Stetler. GP

Graduate Assistant Tells about His Visit, The. Leon Stokesbury. NVAP

Graduation Day, 1965. Julio Marzán. InW

Graduation Nite. Ntozake Shange. NW

Graecinus, I blame you. Yours that memorable remark. Ovid, *tr. by* Guy Lee. Amores, II, 10. NAWM-1

Graecinus (well I wot) thou told'st me once. Ovid, *tr. by* Christopher Marlowe. Amores, II, 10. EBEV

Graffiti. Edward Field. CABA (1972 ed.)

Graffiti for Lovers. Joan Joffe Hall. AMV-80

Grafted Tongue, A. John Montague. BIrV; CIP

Graham. Sid Gershgoren. BrS

Grail, The. Sidney Keyes. FaBoTw (1975 ed.)

Grain of Moonlight, A. Asya, *tr. fr. Yiddish by* Gabriel Preil *and* Howard Schwartz. VWA

Grain of space holds suns which move like flecks, A. God Walks among the Dust. Henry Tim Chambers. AATT

Grains of snow ride down here as bits. Letter from a Black Soldier. Bill Anderson. VGW

Gramercy Park Hotel. David Smith. NYP

Gramma thinks about her grandchildren. The Way and the Way Things Are. Nila NorthSun. GP

Grammar, A. Andrei Codrescu. EAS

Grammar commences with a 5-line curse. Palladas, *tr. fr. Greek by* Tony Harrison. OBVE

Grammar of the Soul, A. Margaret Gibson. AAN

Grammarian's Funeral, A. Robert Browning. VLP

Grammer's Shoes. William Barnes. VPC

Grand Abacus. John Ashbery. EAS; PoA

Grand attempt some Amazonian dames, A. On a Fortification at Boston Begun by Women. Benjamin Tompson. GOA

Grand Canyon, The. James Merrill. TAP

Grand Duke of New York, The. Dan Pagis, *tr. fr. Hebrew by* Robert Friend. VWA

Grand Guignols of Love, The. Michael Benedikt. AmPA

Grand Hotel, Calcutta. Layle Silbert. AMV-81

Grand Inquisitor Continues, The. John William Corrington. CoPAm

Grand Park, Chicago. William Pillin. SPT

Grand Rapids. Julia A. Moore. OBAL

Grand Rapids Cricket Club, *sel.* Julia A. Moore. "Brave Kelso, he's considered great." PeD

Grand Slammer. R. R. Knudson. SPo

Grandad, I didn't burn it, I. Legacy. Gena Ford. IHMS

Grandeurs of the crazy man alone, The. Theodore Roethke. POL

Granddaddy longlegs did twilight, The. Ohio Valley Swains. James Wright. NNaP

Grandest writer of late ages, The. Distribution of Honours for Literature. Walter Savage Landor. FaBoEE

Grandfather. Joan Aiken. TVo

Grandfather. Willis Barnstone. VWA

Grandfather. Mary Joan Coleman. AMV-80

Grandfather. Michael S. Harper. FiCP; FoP; TAP

Grandfather. Lance Henson. CDW

Grandfather. John Leax. AATT

Grandfather. Katie Louchheim. PoUp

Grandfather. Derek Mahon. LP

Grandfather, *sel.* Lawrence Russ. "Old stick of bitterness, you wanted." TC

Grandfather. Eve Shelnutt. TC

Grandfather, bring me down. Getting Under. Alan P. Lightman. AMV-81

"Grandfather Coyote, sing us a song." Coyote's Song. Peter Blue Cloud. NW

Grandfather! far above on high. Thunder Song. *Tr. fr. Omaha Indian.* TVo

Grandfather in the Old Men's Home. W. S. Merwin. ConAP; TCP

"Grandfather" in Winter. Frederick Feirstein. NYP

Grandfather never went to school. Legacy II. Leroy V. Quintana. FoP; GP

Grandfather Poem, A. William J. Harris. CNA; PoBA; TVo

Grandfather puts down his tea-glass. A Night in Odessa. Louis Simpson. NNaP

Grandfather showed me how stars grow in apples. How Stars and Hearts Grow in Apples. Virginia Elson. AMV-81

Grandfather, sleepless in a room upstairs. John Berryman. *Fr.* The Black Book. VGW

Grandfather Watts's Private Fourth. H. C. Bunner. PoTa

Grandfather, we come to you now. Yahrzeit. Susan Fromberg Schaeffer. VWA

Grandfather Yoneh. Emily Borenstein. AMV-81

Grandfathers. Michael Castro. VWA

Grandfathers, The. Donald Justice. NCSH; PPoD

Grandfather's Clock. Henry Clay Work. BLSo, *with music;* FSW; PSoN, *with music*

Grandma and the children left at night. My Polish Grandma. Edward Field. Prf

Grandma Fire. Charles G. Ballard. VoR

Grandma lit the stove. History. Gary Soto. GP

Grandma sleeps with. Medicine. Alice Walker. NMM

Grandma's picket fence. Spiritual. Michael S. Harper. NW

Grandmither, Think Not I Forget. Willa Cather. WPE

Grandmother, The. Wendell Berry. GP

Grandmother. Henry Carlile. GP

Grandmother and Child. Ruth Dallas. ATNZ

Grandmother Came Down to Visit Us, The. Joseph Bruchac. CDW

Grandmother Grant. Madeline DeFrees. CNW

Grandmother holds my hand so as. Native American Studies, University of California at Berkeley 1975. Wendy Rose. NW

Grandmother, I dreamed of you again. The Visit. Phillip William George. VoR

Grandmother laughs. Progenitor. Skaidrite Stelzer. TC

Grandmother of my mother's mother. Yentel. Emily Leider. PoW

Grandmother, Rocking. Eve Merriam. TVo

Grandmother Sleeps. Liz Sohappy Bahe. CDW

Grandmother Watching at Her Window. W. S. Merwin. VGW

Grandmothers, The. Mary Oliver. UsP; WPE

Grandmother's Apple Pies. Bruce Weston Munro. PeD

Grandmother's love. Love Necessitates. Eugene Redmond. CNA

Grandmother's mother: her age, I guess. Dorothy Q. Oliver Wendell Holmes. NOBA; PiAm

Grandpa. James Rankin. MIS

Grandpa Bear. Susan Eisenberg. AMV-81

Grandpa Dropped His Glasses. Leroy F. Jackson. CTV; OSF

Grandpa, I saw you die in the Indian hospital at Pawnee. Hartico. Anna Walters. VoR

Grandparents. Robert Lowell. PiAm

Grandpa's .45. W. M. Ransom. CDW

Grandpa's Friend. Roberto Sandoval. TVo

Grandson Is a Hoticeberg, A. Margaret Danner. CNA; FB

Granite—/ a granite slab. Charlton Heston. Elliot Fried. AMV-80

Granite and Steel. Marianne Moore. PiAm

Granny and I with dear Dadu. A Very Odd Fish. D'Arcy Wentworth Thompson. OxBChV

Granny Hill—no kin of course—said only sayings. Victory. Eleanor Ross Taylor. CSP

Grant a canoe that shall be swift as a fish! Prayer on Making a Canoe. Tr. by N. B. Emerson. WTO

Grant, I thee pray, such heat into mine heart. A Prayer. Sir Thomas More. BoReV

Grant Wood's American Landscape. Winfield Townley Scott. GOA

Granted that what we summon is absurd. T. R. Donald Hall. PoA

Grape is my mulatto mother. Wino. Ted Hughes. NoAM

Grapefruit at Lights Out. Judith Rodriquez. FPA

Grapes Making. Léonie Adams. UnPo (1976 ed.)

"Graphemics," sels. Jack Spicer. VGW
   "Like a scared rabbit running over and," 1.
   "Love is not mocked whatever use," 10.
   "Walden Pond/ All those noxious gases rising from it," 7.

Grasmere Sonnets. David Wright. NoAM

Grass. Carl Sandburg. LFH; NoAM; NOBA; PiAm

Grass. Walt Whitman. Fr. Song of Myself, VI. UsP

Grass, The. Helen Wolfert. RiTi

Grass, Alas, The. Dick Emmons. QQQ

Grass bends, The: blades crack from a wind. Camping Out on Rainy Mountain. Jim Barnes. CDW

Grass-blades push up between the cobblestones. The Travelling Bear. Amy Lowell. BCr

Grass caught in willow tells the flood's height. Briggflatts, IV. Basil Bunting. NoAM

Grass clutches at the dark dirt with finger holds. Grassroots. Carl Sandburg. RFM

Grass cropped to grass-roots, and a few ewes go down. Lambing. David Campbell. Fr. Works and Days. MAuV

Grass cuts our feet as we wend our way, The. The Young Prince and the Young Princess. John Ashbery. ConAP

Grass fire swooped like a red wolf pack, The. The Wrangler Kid. Unknown. BPAW

Grass, Grass. George Bowering. NeAC

Grass-green and aspen-green. Variables of Green. Robert Graves. FaBoEE

Grass Is a Reasonable Colour, The. John Newlove. NeAC

Grass is half-covered with snow, The. Snowfall in the Afternoon. Robert Bly. CAPP; EAS; NOBA

Grass is so green that, The. Green Grass and Sea. George Woodcock. AMV-81

Grass is very green, my friend, The. A Unison. William Carlos Williams. Epi; NOBA

Grass on the Cliff. Robinson Jeffers. Fr. The Trumpet. PoA

Grass on the Mountain, The. Unknown, tr. fr. Paiute Indian by Mary Austin. GOA

Grass on the Prayer Path. Unknown. PeD

Grass people bow, The. To Turn Back. John Haines. ConAP

Grass was the green of parades when we'd leave, The. Leaving One of the State Parks after a Family Outing. Elizabeth Macklin. AMV-81

Grasse: The Olive Trees. Richard Wilbur. NoAM; NOBA

Grasses, ancient enemies, The. Syria. Keith Douglas. PSN

Grasses green of sweet content, The. Arthur Hugh Clough. VLP

Grasshopper, The. Abraham Cowley, after the Greek of Anacreon. OAEL-l; OBVE

Grasshopper, The. Richard Lovelace. CaPo; EBEV; NOBE; OAEL-1; PPP; SCP-2

Grasshopper. Roger McDonald. CAAP

Grasshopper, The. Thomas Stanley, after the Greek of Anacreon. OBVE

Grasshopper, A. Richard Wilbur. CoPAm; HAP; HoPM (1975 ed.)

Grasshopper and the Ant, The. La Fontaine, tr. fr. French by Marianne Moore. NAWM-2

Grasshopper and the Cricket, The. Leigh Hunt. See To the Grasshopper and the Cricket.

Grasshopper and the Cricket, The. Keats. See On the Grasshopper and Cricket.

Grasshopper and the Elephant, The. Unknown. CTV

Grasshopper clings crazily, A. Grasshopper. Roger McDonald. CAAP

Grasshopper, the Grasshopper, The. An Explanation of the Grasshopper. Vachel Lindsay. PCOP

Grasshopper thrice-happy! who. The Grasshopper. Thomas Stanley, after the Greek of Anacreon. OBVE

Grasshoppers, wheelchairs, rosebuds! An Old Southern Critic Takes a Look at My Poems. Darrell Gray. AcAn

Grassroots. Carl Sandburg. RFM

Grateful Here. Wing Tek Lum. PHC

Gratiana Dancing and Singing. Richard Lovelace. CaPo

Gratitude. Louise Glück. CAAP

Gratitude. Annette Lynch. FF

Gratitude. Christopher Smart. Fr. Hymns for the Amusement of Children. LAuP

Gratitude to Mother Earth, sailing through night and day. Prayer for the Great Family. Gary Snyder. HAP; OFD

Grauballe Man, The. Seamus Heaney. CIP

Grave, A. Marianne Moore. CABA (1972 ed.) CMoP (1970 ed.); ExPo (1973 ed.); HAP; HeIP; InPK; NoAM; NOBA; PPoe; TAP; UnPo (1976 ed.); WPE

Grave, The. Shaul Tchernichovsky, *tr. fr. Hebrew by* Robert Mezey *and* Shula Starkman. VWA

Grave, The. Yvor Winters. NoAM

Grave at Cassino. Noah Stern, *tr. fr. Hebrew by* Harold Schimmel. VWA

Grave charge in Mayfair bathroom case. Headline History. William Plomer. FaBoCo

Grave Clothes. Karen Swenson. AMV-80

Grave House of Commons, by hook or by crook, The. A Ballad, November 1680, Made upon Casting the Bill against the Duke of York. *Unknown.* APAS

Grave of Alexander Hamilton is in Trinity yard, The. Trinity Place. Carl Sandburg. NYP

Grave of Love, The. Heine, *tr. fr. German by* Alexander Gray. SLP

Grave physician, used to write for fees, A. Upon the Author of the "Satire against Wit." Sir Charles Sedley. APAS

Grave wise man that had a great rich lady, A. Of an Heroical Answer of a Great Roman Lady to Her Husband. Sir John Harington. BoLoP

Gravel road rides with a slow gallop, The. So This Is Nebraska. Ted Kooser. EC

Gravelly Run. A. R. Ammons. PoA; Prf

Gravely. James Welch. MPA

Graves Are Made to Waltz On. Peter Viereck. PoA

Graves at Elkhorn. Richard Hugo. UnPo (1976 ed.)

Graves grow deeper, The. The Dead. Mark Strand. HeIP

Graves in Queens. Richard Hugo. NYP

Graves of a Household, The. Felicia Dorothea Hemans. FaPoR; VLP; WPE

Graves the rain makes wet and sleek, The. *Tr. fr. Welsh by* Gwyn Jones. Fr. The Stanzas of the Graves. OBW

Gravestones. Floyd C. Stuart. AMV-80

Graveyard, The. Jane Cooper. CoPAm

Grave-Yard, The. Jones Very. NOBA

Graveyard by the Sea. Thomas Lux. PCho

Graveyard in Oberammergau, 1960, A. Peter Nelson. PHC

Graveyard is wet, The. All Songs. B. Sanford Page. AMV-81

Graveyard Road, The. Tom McKeown. HeS

Gravities. Seamus Heaney. NoAM

Gray. *See also* Grey.

Gray and dingy house in Meudon. House in Meudon. Margarita Aliger, *tr. by* Elaine Feinstein. VWA

Gray and dusty daylight flows, A. Christopher Brennan. *Fr.* The Quest of Silence. MAuV

Gray as a government holiday. Easter Monday. Michael McFee. AMV-80

Gray brick, ash, hand-bent railings, steps so big. Cumberland Station. Dave Smith. CSP

Gray Days. Joanne Lawlor. AMV-80

Gray-eyed huntress in whose hair. Hymn to Artemis, the Destroyer. Marya Zaturenska. Moon

Gray Goose, The. *Unknown.* FSW; OSF

Gray [*or* Grey] goose and gander. Lullaby. *Unknown.* BBL; GBP

Gray gossamer day, A. Afternoon. David Sten Herrstrom. AATT

Gray Hills Taught Me Patience, The, *with music.* Allen Eastman Cross. AH

Gray his head goes his feet green. Sonnet. Ted Berrigan. CAAP

Gray maidservant lets me in, A. Matinees. James Merrill. NOBA; Prf

Gray Mare, The. *Unknown.* AmFP

Gray mist wolf. Four Mountain Wolves. Leslie Marmon Silko. VoR

Gray sea and the long black land, The. *See* Grey sea . . .

Gray [*or* Grey] sheep came, The. I ran. The Exorcism. Theodore Roethke. NoAM; STS

Gray Silk Twisting. Patrick Lane. NeAC

Gray sky, The. It Is Beautiful, It Is Rain. Mark Wangberg. TC

Gray, slow-moving, dust-bepowdered wave, A. Sheep Herding. Sharlot Hall. WPW

Gray smoke rose from the morning ground. Actual Vision of Morning's Extrusion. Alan Dugan. PPP

Gray Squirrel, The. Humbert Wolfe. IP

Gray steel, cloud-shadow-stained. Watch the Lights Fade. Robinson Jeffers. CMoP (1970 ed.); NoAM; NOBA

Gray tiled roof, A. Seeds of Lead. Amir Gilboa, *tr. by* Stephen Mitchell. VWA

Gray Weather. Robinson Jeffers. CMoP (1970 ed.); NoAM

Gray Whale. For a Coming Extinction. W. S. Merwin. NNaP; TSWA

Gray whales are going south, The: I see their fountains. Ocean. Robinson Jeffers. ILP (1975 ed.)

Gray's Anatomy. David Malouf. CAAP

Greasy oysters on friday nights. Cycles, Cycles. Suzanne Berger Rioff. NMM

Greasy snow remnants. Seasons. Hayden Carruth. TVo

Greasy Spoon Blues. Len Gasparini. NeAC

Great A, little a. Mother Goose. MG

Great Alexander sailing was from his true course turned. The Speaking Tree. Muriel Rukeyser. VGW

Great American Bum, The. *Unknown.* FSW

Great and glorious thing it is, A. Arithmetic on the Frontier. Kipling. VLP

Great Auk's Ghost, The. Ralph Hodgson. IWK; PoPle

Great-Aunts. Seán O'Críadáin. PFIr

Great Bacchus: From the Greek. Matthew Prior. FaBoCo

Great Bear, The. John Hollander. BCr; CoPAm; NoAM

Great Bear, The. Dennis Maloney. BCr

Great Bear, The. P. B. Newman. BCr

Great Bear Lake Meditations, The, *sels.* J. Michael Yates.
"Again and again I go away from you." HoPM (1975 ed.)
"*Legend*: The god in the sun made two men." HoPM (1975 ed.)
"Wolves say to the dogs, The." HoPM (1975 ed.)

Great beasts rumble and sway, The. Under the Shawl. Rose Drachler. VWA

"Great Black Music" means. Calypso for Committed Men. Peter Kostakis. FiCh

Great Blue Heron, The. Carolyn Kizer. WPE

Great Brown Owl, The. Jane Euphemia Browne. OxBChV

Great Canzon, The. Kenneth Rexroth. NoAM

Great Chain of Being, The. Pope. *Fr.* An Essay on Man, Epistles I *and* II. ExPo (1973 ed.)

Great cry went up from the stockyards and, A. The Delicate, Plummeting Bodies. Stephen Dobyns. PCho

Great cup tumbled, ringing like a bell, The. The Grail. Sidney Keyes. FaBoTw (1975 ed.)

Great Day ("The chariot rode on the mountain top"). *Unknown.* FSW

Great Day ("One of these mornings bright and fair"). *Unknown.* FSW

Great Day, The. W. B. Yeats. BIrV; CMoP (1970 ed.); FF; WIF

Great Depression, The. Patricia Goedicke. GP

Great Despair of the London Whigs, The. *Unknown.* APAS

Great dream stinks like a whale gone aground, The. Why the Soup Tastes like the Daily News. Marge Piercy. MAT

Great-enough both accepts and subdues. Phenomena. Robinson Jeffers. NoAM; NOBA

Great eucalypti, black amid the flame. The Grave. Yvor Winters. NoAM

Great Explosion, The. Robinson Jeffers. IPWM

Great Favorit Beheaded, A. Sir Richard Fanshawe, *after the Spanish of* Góngora. OBVE

Great female bear, A. First Dance: God Who Walks like a Bear. Judith Johnson Sherwin. *Fr.* Three Power Dances. BCr

Great Figure, The. William Carlos Williams. NoAM

Great fish's eyes never shut, The. Rosario Castellanos, *tr. fr. Spanish by* Willis Barnstone. BoWoP

Great fleas have little fleas. The Fleas. Augustus De Morgan. FaBoCo

Great folks are of a finer mould. Epigram on Scolding. Swift. FaBoEE

Great fool, The. Work Song. Raymond Mazisi Kunene, *tr. by* D. K. Rycroft. WTO

Great Fountains, The. Anne Hebert, *tr. fr. French by* Willis Barnstone. BoWoP

Great Freight, The. Ingeborg Bachmann, *tr. fr. German by* Bill Crisman. PBWP

Great freight truck, A. Gary Snyder. *Fr.* Hitch Haiku. InPK

Great Garret, or 100 Wheels, The. James McMichael. AmPA

Great Getting Up Morning. *Unknown.* FSW

Great God, attend while Zion sings. Isaac Watts. AmFP

Great God, How Frail a Thing Is Man, *with music.* Mather Byles. AH

Great God! I Ask Thee for No Meaner Pelf. Henry David Thoreau. NOBA; PiAm
(My Prayer.) AmVN

Great God, let all my tuneful pow'rs. Ottiwell Heginbothom. AmFP

Great God Paused among Men. Daniel Berrigan. MAT

Great God, Preserver of All Things, *with music.* Francis Daniel Pastorius. AH

Great God, the Followers of Thy Son, *with music.* Henry Ware, Jr. AH

Great God, Thy Works, *with music.* Mather Byles. AH

Great, good and just, could I but rate. Epitaph on Charles I. James Graham, Marquess of Montrose. NOBE

Great grief came over me. Aleqaajik, *tr. fr. Eskimo.* WTO

Great Hunger, The, *sels.* Patrick Kavanagh.
"Clay is the word and clay is the flesh." NoAM; OxBTC
"He gave himself another year." BIrV
"Maguire is not afraid of death, the Church will light him a candle." CIP

Great iron throats offering. The Bells. Lucille F. Travis. AATT

Great is my envy of you, earth, in your greed. Petrarch, *tr. by.* Edwin Morgan. Sonnets to Laura: To Laura in Death, XXXII. NAWM-1

Great is the folly of a feeble brain. Joseph Hall. *Fr.* Virgidemiarum, Bk. I, Satire VII. EBEV; TVS

Great is the likeness of those beauteous two. Morphine. Heine, *tr. by* Ernst Feise. NAWM-2

Great Jack of Lent, clad in a robe of air. A Copy of Non Sequitors. *Unknown.* FaBoNo

Great Lord of All, Whose Work of Love, *with music.* Jacob Duché. AH

Great Lover, The. Rupert Brooke. HoPM (1975 ed.)

Great melech lies waking over Judah, The. Saul. Else Lasker-Schüler, *tr. by* Joachim Neugroschel. VWA

Great men have been among us; hands that penned. Wordsworth. MBPR

Great Merchant, Dives Pragmaticus, Cries His Wares, The, *sel.* Thomas Newbery.

"What lack you, sir? What seek you? What will you buy?" OxBChV

Great Moth, The. Robert Gittings. OxBTC

Great Mother, The. Gary Snyder. CC

Great Nature clothes the soul, which is but thin. The Soul's Garment. Margaret Cavendish, Duchess of Newcastle. WPE

Great Nebula in Andromeda, The. Hugh Seidman. AmPA

Great Northern. Dave Etter. CoPAm

Great Pacific railway, The. The Railroad Cars Are Coming. *Unknown.* BPAW

Great Panjandrum, The. Samuel Foote. FaBoCo
(Epilogue: "So she went into the garden.") ECBV

Great philosopher did choke, A. Samuel Butler. FaBoEE

Great Poet, The. Linda King. GP

Great poets are not in the language but in business, The. Poetry Paper. Andrei Codrescu. EAS

Great queen of shadows, you are pleased to speak. Beaumont *and* Fletcher. *Fr.* The Maid's Tragedy. SCP-2

Great Round-up, The. *Unknown.* BPAW

Great Sad One, The. Uri Zvi Greenberg, *tr. fr. Hebrew by* Robert Mezey *and* Ben Zion Gold. VWA

Great Santa Barbara Oil Disaster OR, The. Conyus. AmPA

Great Sea. Charles Brasch. ATNZ

Great Sea, The. *Unknown, tr. fr. Eskimo by* Knud Johan Rasmussen. NU

Great sea, The/ Has sent me adrift. Song of Joy. Uvavnuk, *tr. fr. Eskimo.* WTO

Great Silkie of Sule Skerry, The. *Unknown.* FaBoBa; FSW; GBP; MAT; PeBB

Great Sir, having just had the good luck to catch. Copy of an Intercepted Despatch from His Excellency Don Strepitoso Diabolo. Thomas Moore. OBSV

Great sir, our poor hearts are ready to burst. The Humble Address. *Unknown.* APAS

Great Society, The. Robert Bly. NoAm; NYP

Great Society, Mark X, The. Howard Nemerov. AnMo

Great Speckled Bird, The. *Unknown.* FSW

Great Spirit, 'tis said, to our forefathers gave, The. The Red Man of the West. Eliza R. Snow. WPW

Great spirits now on earth are sojourning. Addressed to Haydon. Keats. MBPR

Great star has fallen into my lap, A. Reconciliation. Else Lasker-Schüler, *tr. by* Robert Alter. PBWP

Great Talker, A. William Lindsay. PMW

Great Things. Thomas Hardy. NOBE; PPM

Great tiger, The. Folk Tune. Esther Raab, *tr. by* Robert Friend *and* Shiman Sandbank. VWA

Great *Titanic. Unknown.* AmFP

Great trout shone, The. Work of Art. Clarice Short. MPA

Great Wave, The: Hokusai. Donald Finkel. WIF

Great Way of the Man, The. Norman H. Russell. VW

Great, wide, beautiful, wonderful World. The Wonderful World [*or* The World]. William Brighty Rands. CTV; OxBChV

Great wrought-iron gates have been, The. Twilight at the Zoo. Alex Rodger. NCSH

Greate Macedon that out of Persy chased, The. Earl of Surrey. AAS

Greater Cats, The. V. Sackville-West. PoPle

Greater cities are, The. Poem. Victor Hernández Cruz. SA

Greater Country, The. Grace V. Watkins. AMV-80

Greater, he called them, than Homer or Chaucer. The Men of Sudbury. Carlos Baker. GOA

Greater Love. Wilfred Owen. CMoP (1970 ed.); ExPo (1973 ed.); NoAM; OBP; PSN

Greater than memory of Achilles or Ulysses. The Wallabout Martyrs. Walt Whitman. GOA

Greatest in many things, in some the least. On a Distinguished Politician. J. E. Thorold Rogers. FaBoEE

Greatest saints and sinners have been made, The. Samuel Butler. FaBoEE

Greatgrandma's bending to pluck some vegetable. Recipe. Albert Goldbarth. VWA

Greatly shining,/ The autumn moon floats in the thin sky. Wind and Silver. Amy Lowell. BoWoP; IPWM; Moon; RiTi; SoSe

Greed, sel. Diane Wakoski. Turtle, The. NoAM

Greed Song, The. Albert Goldbarth. AMV-80

Greedy Dog. James Hurley. FPB

Greedy Jane. Unknown. ECBV; OxBChV

Greedy little sparrow. Birds in the Garden. Unknown. DuDr

Greedy Richard. Jane Taylor. OxBChV

Greedy small Lassie once said, A. Too Much. Unknown. TDH

Greedy the People, The. E. E. Cummings. SoSe

Greek Athlete, The. Euripides, tr. fr. Greek by Tom Dodge. LiSp

Greek Crazeology. Carolyn M. Rodgers. SA

Greek Islander, being taken to the Vale of, A. Where Is the Sea? Felicia Dorothea Hemans. RhR

Greek Room, The. James W. Thompson. BPo

Greek ship, A/ Sails on the sea. The Couple. Sandra Hochman. CTBA

Greek with your open vowels. I Am. Nanos Valaoritis. PoW

Greeks, The. Tom Clark. PoA

Greeks' chieftains, all irked with the war, The. Virgil, tr. by Earl of Surrey. Fr. The Aeneid, II. OAEL-1

Greeks dismay'd, confus'd disperse or fall, The. Homer, tr. by Pope. Fr. The Iliad, XV. OBVE

Greeks were wrong who said our eyes have rays, The. Lamarck Elaborated. Richard Wilbur. ILP (1975 ed.)

Green. William Barnes. VLP

Green. Walter de la Mare. FaBoNo

Green. D. H. Lawrence. GBL; PoA

Green Afternoon, The. Henry Rago. VGW

Green and greedy seas have drowned, The. John Masefield. Fr. Fragments. EcS

Green and silent spot, amid the hills, A. Fears in Solitude. Samuel Taylor Coleridge. MBPR

Green Apple. Mari Kubo. PHC

Green Apples. Dudley Randall. FB; TC

Green arsenic smeared on an egg-white cloth. L'Art, 1910. Ezra Pound. HeIP

Green as I would have you green. The Ballad of the Sleepwalker. Federico García Lorca, tr. by Langston Hughes. Epi

Green Ash. Jennifer J. Rankin. GAS

Green at Colmar. Daisy Aldan. AATT

Green Autumn Stubble, The. Unknown. WTO

Green Bed, The. Unknown. AmFP

Green Beginning, The. Warren Slesinger. HeS

Green-blue ground, The. On Gay Wallpaper. William Carlos Williams. TAP

Green Briar Shore, The. Unknown. AmFP

Green Broom. Unknown. PoTa

Green Buddhas/ On the fruit stand. Watermelons. Charles Simic. OBAL; OSP

Green Bushes, The. Unknown. AIW

Green Candles. Humbert Wolfe. SO

Green catalpa tree has turned, The. April Inventory. W. D. Snodgrass. BiP; CABA (1972 ed.); CAPP; HAP; NoAM; NowV; PPoe; SFF; TAP; WIF

Green cement has flooded the firehall. Basic Rescue. Ann Deagon. CSP

Green Corn. Unknown. FSW

Green Corn Dance, The. Alice Corbin. BPAW

Green Cornfield, A. Christina Rossetti. RAE

Green elm with the one great bough of gold, The. October. Edward Thomas. NoAM

Green encrusted lump, The. Cleaning a Coin. Anthony Thwaite. HeHu

Green enravishment of human life. Sister Juana Inés de la Cruz, tr. fr. Spanish by Samuel Beckett. Epi

Green Eye, The. James Merrill. PoA

Green Fiddler, The. Rachel Field. PoTa

Green Figs at Table. James K. Baxter. ATNZ

Green Frog at Roadstead, Wisconsin. James Schevill. TAP

Green Frogs. David Rigsbee. AMV-81

Green Gnome, The. Robert Buchanan. PoTa

Green grape, and you refused me. Brief Autumnal. Unknown, tr. by Dudley Fitts. NIL; WeW

Green Grass. Unknown. GBP ("A dis, a dis, a green grass.") PoPle

Green Grass and Sea. George Woodcock. AMV-81

Green Grass Growing All Around, The. Unknown. ECBV (Green Grass Grew All Around, The, diff. version.) FSW

Green, green, I want you green. Somnambulistic Ballad. Federico García Lorca, tr. by Roy and Mary Campbell. TCP

Green, Green Is El Aghir. Norman Cameron. OxBTC (El Aghir.) FaBoTw (1975 ed.)

Green Grow the Lilacs. Unknown. FSW

Green Grow the Rashes [or Rushes], O. Burns. FSW; LAuP; OAEL-1; PBMP; PPoe; PPP; SS

Green Grow the Rushes ("I'll sing you one-o"). Unknown. See Carol of the Numbers.

Green Groweth [or Grow'th] the Holly. At. to Henry VIII, King of England. EBEV; PChr

Green Grows the Rashes. Unknown. GBP

Green-House, The. William Cowper. Fr. The Task, III. PF

Green in the Halls. Ben Maddow. SPT

Green it's your green I love. Sleepwalkers' Ballad. Federico Garcia Lorca, tr. by John Frederick Nims. WeW

Green lady, green lady, come doon for thy tea. Unknown. GBP

Green lamp flares on the table, The. This Life. Rita Dove. AmPA

Green lawn/ a picket fence. Alice Walker. Fr. Once. PoBA

Green leaf that will outlast the winter, The. Louis Zukofsky. VGW

Green Light. Kenneth Fearing. ExPo. (1973 ed.); VGW

Green little vaulter in the sunny grass. To the Grasshopper and the Cricket. Leigh Hunt. ILP (1975 ed.); PCOP

Green Memory. Langston Hughes. ILP (1975 ed.)

Green Mountain Boy. Florida Watts Smyth. ECBV

Green mwold on zummer bars do show. Tokens. William Barnes. VLP

Green Pastures. Dick Allen. AMV-80

Green Plumes of Royal Palms, with music. LeRoy V. Brant. AH

Green points on the shrub. An Elegy for D. H. Lawrence. William Carlos Williams. Epi; NoAM

Green Prose. Thomas Lux. AAN

Green Red Brown and White. May Swenson. OSP, 1st stanza; VGW

Green Refrain, A. Avraham Huss, tr. fr. Hebrew by Mark Elliott Shapiro. VWA

Green River. Bryant. NOBA

Green Roads, The. Edward Thomas. NoAM

Green Room, The. Paul Mills. MIS

Green rushes with red shoots. Plucking the Rushes. *Tr. fr. Chinese by* Arthur Waley. BoLoP; BuTh; OBVE; OLR

Green rustlings, more-than-regal charities. Royal Palm. Hart Crane. CMoP (1970 ed.); NoAM

Green Shag. W. W. Gibson. EcS

Green Shepherd, The. Louis Simpson. NIL; NoAM; PAIC

Green shingles of rest homes unfold revealing, The. The United States Prepare for the Permanent Revolution. George Hitchcock. EAS

Green shutters, shut your shutters! Windyridge. John Betjeman. *Fr.* Beside the Seaside. OxBTC

Green Sleeves ("Green sleeves and tartan ties"). *Unknown.* GBP

Green Snake, when I hung you round my neck. To the Snake. Denise Levertov. NMM; PoA; Psy; SFF

Green snakes in the mulch pile note, The. Neighbors. Charles Malam. AMV-80

Green Tanks and Other Hidden Vehicles of Destruction. Alex Kuo. NW

Green Train, The. E. V. Rieu. SO

Green Tree, The. James Reiss. AmPA

Green Waters. Ian Hamilton Finlay. WeW

Green Willow, Green Willow. *Unknown.* AmFP

Green Willow Tree, The. *Unknown.* AIW

Greenback Dollar, The. *Unknown.* AmFP

Greene's Mourning Garment, *sels.* Robert Greene.
  Hexametra Alexis in Laudem Rosamundi. GBL
  Shepherd's Wife's Song, The. HAP

Greenfield Hill, *sels.* Timothy Dwight.
  Destruction of the Pequods, The, Pt. IV EAP
  Flourishing Village, The, Pt. II EAP
  Prospect, The, Pt. I. EAP

Greenland, 850 A.D. Lyn Lifshin. MMD

Greenland Whale, The. *Unknown.* GBP; PeBB
  (Greenland Fisheries.) FSW
  (Greenland Whale Fishery, The.) AmFP

Greens. Greg Kuzma. HeS

Greens. David Ray. VGW

Greensleeves. *Unknown.* BLSo, *with music;* FSW; RDB, *with music*
  (Lady Greensleeves.) GBL

Greenwich Avenue. James Schuyler. NYP

Greet the bights that gave me shelter. The Old Fisherman. George Campbell Hay. MS

Greeting from a Distance. Hans Sahl, *tr. fr. German by* Erna Baber Rosenfeld. VWA

Grenadier. A. E. Housman. TT

Grenadier, The. *Unknown.* BBL; GBP

Grenadine. Susan Griffin. MMD

Grendel. *Unknown, tr. fr. Anglo-Saxon by* Burton Raffel. *Fr.* Beowulf. OBP; NU

Gresford Disaster, The. *Unknown.* AIW; GBP; PeBB

Gretel in Darkness. Louise Glück. AmPA; GP; NVAP

Grew in Hades. The Creation. *Maori Oral Tradition, tr. by* Richard Taylor. WTO

Grey. *See also* Gray.

Grey as a guinea-fowl is the rain. Two Kitchen Songs. Edith Sitwell. CMoP (1970 ed.)

Grey as a mouse. Oliphaunt. J. R. R. Tolkien. LCL

Grey brick upon brick. Dublin. Louis MacNeice. CIP; OxBTC; PFIr

Grey Cock, The. *Unknown.* FaBoBa

Grey-eyed King, The. Anna Akhmatova, *tr. fr. Russian by* Robert Tracy. PBWP

Grey, flat sky and a flat land, squeezing, A. Midwinter. Leslie Norris. HeHu

Grey friar, The. Cloisters. Anthony Barnett. VWA

Grey Frock, A. Zinaida Hippius, *tr. fr. Russian by* Temira Pachmuss. PBWP

Grey gaunt days dividing us in twain, The. The Minute before Meeting. Thomas Hardy. VLP

Grey Goose and Gander. *Unknown.* GBP
  (Lullaby: "Gray goose and gander.") BBL

Grey grass in the early winter, The. The Stallion. Alan Porter. PH

Grey haunted eyes, absent-mindedly glaring. The Face in the Mirror. Robert Graves. LP; PoIA; UsP; WeW

Grey Horse, The. James Reeves. PH

Grey horse, Death, in profile bears the young Titus, The. The Polish Rider. Derek Walcott. OBP

Grey Ones, The. Louis MacNeice. CMoP (1970 ed.)

Grey over Riddrie the clouds piled up. King Billy. Edwin Morgan. MS

Grey [*or* Gray] sea and the long black land, The. Meeting at Night. Robert Browning. BoLoP; FF; GBL; HeIP; ILP (1975 ed.); InPS; LoAs; NOBE; OLR; PAIC; PoPle; SoSe; SS; STS; UnPo (1976 ed.); VLP; WeW

Grey sheep came, The. I ran. *See* Gray sheep . . .

Grey water tanks in grey mist. Bayonne Turnpike to Tuscarora. Allen Ginsberg. NNaP

Grey Wolf, The. Arthur Symons. FaBoTw (1975 ed.)

Grey Woman. Gladys Cardiff. CDW

Greyhounds. Robert Gray. CAAP

Greyhounds have entered the garden, The. The Marriage of Here and There. Peter Trias. AAN

Grief. Elizabeth Barrett Browning. HeIP; InPK; PPM; SBG; VLP; WPE

Grief. Emery E. George. AAN

Grief. Sandra Hochman. NowV

Grief, The. Rainer Maria Rilke, *tr. fr. German by* Steven Lautermilch. AMV-81

Grief. *Unknown, tr. fr. Welsh by* Aneirin Talfan Davies. OBW

Grief-chewers enter, their shoes hard on the marble, The. Office for the Dead. Thomas Kinsella. IPM

Grief, have I denied thee? A Lamentation. Denise Levertov. PiAm

Grief of a Girl's Heart, The. *Unknown. See* Donal Oge: Grief of a Girl's Heart.

Grief of Our Genitals, The. Henry Carlile. GP

Grief Streams Down My Chest. Lance Jeffers. PoBA

Griesly Wife, The. John Manifold. SoSe

Grieve Not for Beauty ("Grieve not for the invisible, transported brow"). Witter Bynner. PoA

Griffin. Richard Mathews. AATT

Grim Fairy Tale. Lionel Wiggam. TPo

Grim monarch! see, deprived of vital breath. To a Lady on the Death of Her Husband. Phillis Wheatley. TAP

Grim was fishere swithe good. Havelok at Grimsby and Lincoln. *Unknown. Fr.* Havelok. OxBM

Grinder, who serenely grindest. Lines on Hearing the Organ. Charles Stuart Calverley. FaBoCo; NOBL

Grinders, The; or, The Saddle on the Right Horse. *Unknown.* GBP

Grinning, the foreman asked them for a vote. In the Jury Room. Hodding Carter. MAT

Grip, The. Brendan Kennelly. CIP

Grizzel Grimme. *Unknown.* FaBoEE

Grizzly. Bret Harte. BPAW

Grizzly Bear. Mary Austin. BPAW; CTV; ECBV; RAE

Grizzly Bear. *Unknown.* FSW

Grizzly Bear is huge and wild, The. Infant Innocence. A. E. Housman. FaBoCo

Groan of earth in labor pain, A. San Francisco Falling. Edwin Markham. BPAW

Groans of love, The. Coloratura. Geoff Page. AMV-81

Grocery Shopping. John Leax. AATT

Grog-an'-Grumble Steeplechase. Henry Lawson. PH

Groggy fighter on his knees, The. Athletes. Walker Gibson. LiSp

Groins, for his fleshly burglary of late. Upon Groins: Epigram. Robert Herrick. CaPo

Grongar Hill. John Dyer. EPC; LAuP; OBW; PAIC

Groom's Lament, The. Robert Peterson. NeAC

Groping along the tunnel, step by step. The Rear-Guard. Siegfried Sassoon. NoAM

"Gross, Coarse, Hideous" (Police Description of My Pictures). D. H. Lawrence. FaBoEE

Grotesque. Amy Lowell. BoWoP

Grotesque, jumping out. Sky Diver. Adrien Stoutenburg. LiSp; SPo; TSWA

Grotesque, the line of trees, pronged. Outside. Phyllis Beauvais. IHMS

Grotesques. Robert Graves. CMoP (1970 ed.)

Grotto, The. Ray Fraser. NeAC

Grotto, The. Francis Scarfe. PoA

Grouchy Good Night to the Academic Year, A. Ted Pauker. NOBL

Ground is white with snow, The. Resolution. Ted Berrigan. OFD

Ground-Mist, The. Denise Levertov. PiAm

Ground mist moves towards us, The. The Journey. Rhyll McMaster. FPA

Ground twitches and the noble head, The. The Second Coming. Dannie Abse. NoAM

Groundhog, The. Richard Eberhart. CABA (1972 ed.); CMoP (1970 ed.); CoPAm; ExPo (1973 ed.); ILP (1975 ed.); NIL; NoAM; NU; PPoe; TAP; UnPo (1976 ed.); UsP; VoPo

Groundhog. Unknown. FSW

Groundhog Day. Michael Hogan. DNGG

Groundhog Foreshadowed, The. Steven Sher. AMV-80

Group, The. Victor Hernández Cruz. SA

Group of jolly cowboys, discussing plans at ease, A. When the Work's All Done This Fall. Unknown. BPAW; FSW

Groupie. Al Young. NVAP

Groves of Eden, vanished now so long, The. Pope. Fr. Windsor Forest. OAEL-1

Groves were God's first temples, The. A Forest Hymn. Bryant. EAP; TAP

Grow old along with me! Rabbi Ben Ezra. Robert Browning. PBMP; STS

Growing. Kenneth Rexroth. MPA

Growing Friendship. Unknown. CTV

Growing Old. Matthew Arnold. OAEL-2; VLP; VoPo

Growing Old. Byron. Fr. Don Juan, I. NOBE

Growing Old in West Virginia. Michael C. Blumenthal. PoUp

Growing Together. Joyce Carol Oates. IHMS

Growing Up. David Perkins. AAN

Growing Up. Unknown. CTV

Growing weather; enough rain. The Satisfactions of the Mad Farmer. Wendell Berry. PiAm

Growing Wild. Jim Wayne Miller. GP

Growltiger's Last Stand. T. S. Eliot. PoPle

Grown old in love from seven till seven times seven. Blake. FaBoEE; OAEL-2

Grown too big for his skin. Fable for When There's No Way Out. May Swenson. MiP; MPA

Grown-up. Edna St. Vincent Millay. NoAM; TH

Grown-ups are all safe, The. Hard Cheese. Justin St. John. LP

Growth of alder leaves in open light, A. Four Things to See. Ronald Mann. PMW

Growth of Love, The, sels. Robert Bridges
"For beauty being the best of all we know," VIII. VLP
"I will be what God made me, nor protest," LXII. VLP
"Man that sees by chance his picture, made, A," XXXIX. NoAM
"Spring hath her own bright days of calm and peace," XXIV. VLP
"They that in play can do the thing they would," I. NoAM
"Whole world now is but the minister, The," III. VLP

Gr-r-r—there go, my heart's abhorrence! Soliloquy of the Spanish Cloister. Robert Browning. AnMo; CABA (1972 ed.); Epi; FaBoCo; ILP (1975 ed.); InPK; IP; NIL; NOBL; OAEL-2; OBP; PAIC; PoIA; STS

Grudges mend and wear and turn in winter. Household. Laura Jensen. PCho

Grumbler Gruff, A. Oliver Herford. TDH

Grumblers. Leonard Clark. FPB

Grünewald knew that green. Green at Colmar. Daisy Aldan. AATT

Grunion. Myra Cohn Livingston. RFM

Grunion. Wendy Rose. CDW

Gryll's State ("Gryll/ Had his fill"). Roy Blount, Jr. OBAL

Guantanamera. José Martí, ad. fr. Spanish by Pete Seeger and Hector Angulo. FSW

Guard Duty. Tomas Tranströmer, tr. fr. Swedish by May Swenson. FoP

Guarded Wound, The. Adelaide Crapsey. WPE

Guardians consult about the gifts to be, The. At the Birth of a Poet: Amherst, 1830. Larry Rubin. CSP

Guerrilla Handbook, A. Amiri Baraka. PoBA

Guess what I have gone and done. My Invention. Shel Silverstein. QQQ

Guessing. Unknown, tr. fr. Burmese by U Win Pe. PBWP

Guest, The. "Anna Akhmatova", tr. fr. Russian by Richard McKane. LoAs

Guest, The. Unknown. ECBV

Guest, The. Alan Ziegler. AAN

Guests are gathered, The. Fourth of July Fireworks. Liz Lochhead. MIS

Guests in their summer colors have fled, The. The Last Picnic. Stanley Kunitz. NoAM

Guevara with Minutes to Go. John William Corrington. CoPAm

Guid day now, bonnie Robin. Robin Redbreast's Testament. Unknown. GBP

Guide, The. Arthur Gregor. GP

Guide Me, O Thou Great Jehovah. William Williams, tr. fr. Welsh by Peter Williams and John Williams. BLSH, with music; OBW

Guide to Dungeness Spit, A. David Wagoner. CNW

Guide to Familiar American Incest, A, sel. Dennis Saleh. Inventing a Family. NeAC

Guide to Jerusalem. Dennis Silk. VWA

Guide to the Symphony. Weldon Kees. VGW

Guido da Montefeltro. Dante, tr. fr. Italian by Longfellow. Fr. Divina Commedia: Inferno, XXVII. Epi

Guido, I would than Lapo, thou, and I. Sonnet: Dante Alighieri to Guido Cavalcanti. Dante, tr. by Shelley. OBVE

Guilt. Wordsworth. Fr. The Prelude, I. BoReV

Guilty have fewer dreams, The. Solutions. David Barton. AMV-81

Guilty, he does not always like his patients. The Doctor. Dannie Abse. PMW

Guinea-Pig Song, A. Unknown. OxBChV (Precise Guinea-Pig, The.) ECBV

Guitar. Federico García Lorca, *tr. fr. Spanish by* Keith Waldrop. InPK

Guitar Recitativos. A. R. Ammons. TT

Guitarist Tunes Up, The. Frances Cornford. SoSe; UsP

Gulf, The. Denise Levertov. NNaP

Gulf Stream, The. Henry Bellamann. RhR

Gull, ballast of its wings. Stabilities. Anne Stevenson. NCSH

Gull, it is said, The. Nakasuk, *tr. fr. Eskimo.* WTO

Gull Lake Reunion. Kelly Ivie. AMV–81

Gull rides on the ripples of a dream, A. A Walk in Late Summer. Theodore Roethke. MPA

Gull Skeleton. Jonathan Revere. SoSe (1977 ed.)

Gulling Sonnets. Sir John Davies. ESo
Sels.
"Lover, under burden of his mistress' love, The," I. Epi; PAIC
"Mine eye, mine ear, my will, my wit, my heart," V. Epi
"My case is this, I love Zepheria bright," VIII. Epi
"Sacred muse that first made love divine,The," VI. PAIC

Gullion, The. Duncan Glen. MIS

Gulliver. Sylvia Plath. NOBA

Gulls. Barbara Howes. BoAnP

Gulls. Dolores Kendrick. PoUp

Gulls. E. A. Muir. NCSH

Gulls. Leonora Speyer. *Fr.* Sand-pipings. TH

Gulls Land and Cease to Be. John Ciardi. TPo

Gulls wash a dune of stone. Leaving America   Michael Waters. AAN

Gully, The. Douglas Stewart. MAuV

Gulping air, two of them. Why Don't They Go Back to Transylvania? Robert Peters. CPA

Gun full swing the swimmer catapults and cracks, The. 400-Meter Freestyle. Maxine W. Kumin. LiSp; SoSe (1977 ed.); SPo

Gun Teams. Gilbert Frankau. OxBTC

Gun, the trap, the axe are borne, The. Revenge of the Hunted. R. A. D. Ford. LiSp

Gun, White Castle. Peter Klappert. AAN

Gunfighter, The. Alistair Campbell. ATNZ

Gunfighter. Phillip Hey. NVAP

Gunfighter. Gerald Locklin. AMV–80

Gunga Din. Kipling. BTTM; PPM; VLP

Gunner. Randall Jarrell. OFD

Gunpowder Plot. Vernon Scannell. HeHu; MPo

Gunpowder Plot, The. *Unknown.* BBL

Guns. Ronald Crowe. AMV–81

Guns. John Woods. GP

Guns know what is what, but underneath, The. Memories of a Lost War. Louis Simpson. VGW

Guns spell money's ultimate reason, The. Ultima Ratio Regum. Stephen Spender. CMoP (1970 ed.); LP; MPo; OAEL–2; SFF; SoS

Gunslinger, *sels.* Edward Dorn.
"I met in Mesilla." NoAM
Idle Visitation, An. NOBA

Gup, Scot. John Skelton. OBP

Gus is the Cat at the Theatre Door. Gus: The Theatre Cat. T. S. Eliot. OxBTC

Gus the Greek is a short-order cook. Greasy Spoon Blues. Len Gasparini. NeAC

Gus: The Theatre Cat. T. S. Eliot. OxBTC

Gusts of the sun race on the approaching sea. Of Thomas Traherne and the Pebble Outside. Sydney Clouts. VWA

Gut eats all day and lechers all the night. On Gut. Ben Jonson. SCP–1

Guts. Caroline Garrett. PHC

Gutter, The. Franco Fortini, *tr. fr. Italian by* Ruth Feldman. VWA

Guy. Emerson. NOBA

Guy asked two jays at St. Louis, A. Two Jays at St. Louis. Ferdinand G. Christgau. TDH

Guyana. Fern Pankratz Ruth. AMV–80

Guyon's Temptation. Spenser. *See* Bower of Bliss, The.

Guys and Dolls. Frank Loesser. OBAL

G'way an' quit dat noise, Miss Lucy. When Malindy Sings. Paul Laurence Dunbar. ILP (1975 ed.); PoBA

Gwendolyn Brooks. Don L. Lee. NoAM

Gwine to Run All Night; or, De Camptown Races. Stephen Collins Foster. *See* Camptown Races, The.

Gwladys Rhys. W. J. Gruffydd, *tr. fr. Welsh by* D. M. Lloyd. OBW

Gyges Ring they bear about them still, A. Lovers How They Come and Part. Robert Herrick. GBL

Gym teacher was big, The. Always Learning. D. J. Enright. HeHu

Gypsies. *See also* Gipsies.

Gypsies. John Clare. *See* Gipsies ("The snow falls deep; the forest lies alone").

Gypsies. Cynthia Nibbelink. TC

Gypsies. Alden Nowlan. NeAC

Gypsies came to our good lord's gate, The. The Gypsy Laddie. *Unknown.* HAP

Gypsies Metamorphosed, *sel.* Ben Jonson.
Faery Beam upon You, The. EBEV; NIL

Gypsies they came to my lord Cassilis' yett, The. The Gypsy Laddie. *Unknown.* FaBoBa; PeBB

Gypsy. Josephine Miles. NoAM

Gypsy, The. Edward Thomas. HeIP; NoAM

Gypsy Bible, The. Julian Tuwim, *tr. fr. Polish by* Isaac Komem. VWA

Gypsy Countess, The. *Unknown.* PoPle

Gypsy Davey. *Ad. by* Woody Guthrie. FSW

Gypsy Davy, The. *Unknown.* AmFP

Gypsy Eyes. Jimi Hendrix. GrRo

Gypsy Laddie, The. *Unknown.* FaBoBa; HAP; PeBB

Gypsy Love Song, *with music.* Harry B. Smith. FSN

Gypsy Motorcycle Club of South Minneapolis, The. Keith Gunderson. HeS

Gypsy Rover, The. *Unknown.* FSW

Gypsy woman told my mother, The. Hoochie Coochie. *Unknown.* BluL

Gyres, The. W. B. Yeats. HAP; NoAM

Gyre's Galax. Norman Henry Pritchard, II. PoBA

Gyres, The! the gyres! Old Rocky Face, look forth. The Gyres. W. B. Yeats. HAP; NoAM


# H

H.M.S. *Hero.* Michael Roberts. OxBTC

H.M.S. Pinafore, *sels.* W. S. Gilbert.
Little Buttercup. PCOP
Sir Joseph's Song. PPM; RhR

H. Rap Brown. Henry Blakely. CNA

H. S. Beeney Auction Sales. David R. Pichaske. AMV–81

H——[or H(ome)], thou return'st from Thames, whose Naiads long. An Ode on the Popular Superstitions of the Highlands of Scotland. William Collins. LAuP; OAEL–1

Ha ha! Ha ha! This world doth pass. Fara Diddle Dyno. *Unknown.* BBL; FaBoCo; FaBoNo; SCP–2

Ha Ha This-a-Way.   Leadbelly (Huddie Ledbetter).   FSW

Ha! Original Sin.   Ogden Nash.   FaBoCo

Ha! sir, I have seen you sniffing and snoozling.   The Faun.   Ezra Pound.   FaBoTw (1975 ed.)

Ha' we lost the goodliest fere o' all.   Ballad of the Goodly Fere.   Ezra Pound.   CMoP (1970 ed.); Epi; NoAM; OFD; PAIC

Ha! whare ye gaun, ye crowlin' ferlie?   To a Louse.   Burns.   ILP (1975 ed.); PBMP

Haar in Princes Street.   Alexander Scott.   MS

Habakkuk.   Edouard Roditi.   VWA

Habit of Perfection, The.   Gerard Manley Hopkins.   ILP (1975 ed.); NoAM; PoPle; SoSe; VLP

Habitation.   Margaret Atwood.   BoWoP

Habits of the Hippopotamus.   Arthur Guiterman.   BoAnP

Habla Usted Español?   James Reiss.   AmPA

Had a piece of pie an' I had a piece of puddin'.   Sally Goodin.   Unknown.   FSW

Had a whole dream once.   Some Words.   Judith Wright.   CAAP; GAS

Had Cowley ne'er spoke, Killigrew ne'er writ.   Sir John Denham.   FaBoEE

Had everyone Suum.   To the Archbishop of Tuam.   Unknown.   FaBoEE

"Had he and I but met."   The Man He Killed.   Thomas Hardy.   CMoP (1970 ed.); DL; FF; HAP; HeIP; ILP (1975 ed.); InPS; IP; IPWM; PBMP; SFF; SoSe; VoPo; WIF

Had I a Golden Pound.   Francis Ledwidge, after the Irish.   PFIr

Had I a man's fair form, then might my sighs.   To——.   Keats.   MBPR

Had I been mindful of my high descent.   Hadewijch, tr. fr. Dutch by Frans van Rosevelt.   PBWP

Had I but gone some forty days or more.   William R. Mitchell.   AATT

Had I but plenty of money, money enough and to spare.   Up at a Villa—Down in the City.   Robert Browning.   ILP (1975 ed.); NOBE; PPP; STS

Had I lived till now.   Poem for the Year Twenty Twenty.   Al Lee.   AmPA

Had I the Choice.   Walt Whitman.   SoSe

Had I the heavens' embroidered cloths.   Aedh [or He] Wishes for the Cloths of Heaven.   W. B. Yeats.   CMoP (1970 ed.); DuDr; NoAM; OLR

Had me a cat, the cat pleased me.   Fiddle-I-Fee.   Unknown.   AmFP

Had mournful Ovid been to Brent condemned.   William Diaper.   Fr. Brent: A Poem to Thomas Palmer Esq.   OBSV

Had Sacharissa lived when mortals made.   At Penshurst.   Edmund Waller.   OAEL–1

Had she come all the way for this.   The Haystack in the Floods.   William Morris.   CABA (1972 ed.); EBEV; HAP; OAEL–2; OBP; PAIC; VLP

Had there been peace there never had been riven.   Dedication.   Drummond Allison.   FaBoTw (1975 ed.)

Had this effulgence disappeared.   Composed upon an Evening of Extraordinary Splendour and Beauty.   Wordsworth.   OAEL–2

Had we but world enough, and time.   To His Coy Mistress.   Andrew Marvell.   AnMo; BiP; BoLoP; CABA (1972 ed.); EBEV; Epi; ExPo (1973 ed.); FF; GBL; HAP; HeIP: HoPM (1975 ed.); ILP (1975 ed.); InPK; InPS; IP; IPWM; LFH; LoAs; MAT; MetP; NIL; NOBE; OAEL–1; OBP; PAIC; PBMP; PoIA; PoPle; PPoD; PPoe; PPP; SCP–1; SoSe; TT; UnPo (1976 ed.); UsP; VoPo; WeW; WIF

Had we two met, blythe-hearted Burns.   Walter Savage Landor.   FaBoEE

Had you come to me.   Regrets.   Vassar Miller.   RiTi

Had you died when we were together.   The Fire.   Louise Glück.   CAAP

Hadaka De Hanasu.   Jody Manabe.   PHC

Haddock Fishermen.   George Mackay Brown.   MS

Hadrian's Address to His Soul When Dying.   Emperor Hadrian, tr. fr. Latin by Byron.   OBVE
(Adriani Morientis ad Animam Suam, tr. by Matthew Prior.)   OBVE
(Emperor Hadrian to His Soul, The, tr. by Stevie Smith.)   OBVE
("My little soul, my vagrant charmer," tr. by J. V. Cunningham.)   OBVE

Hadst thou liv'd in days of old.   To——.   Keats.   MBPR

Hae ye seen her, ye unco Jew.   Hielant Woman.   Sorley Maclean, tr. fr. Gaelic; Scots version by Douglas Young.   MS

Haemorrhage.   Padraic Fiacc.   CIP

Hag, The ("The hag is astride").   Robert Herrick.   CaPo

Hag, The ("The staff is now greased").   Robert Herrick.   CaPo

Hag and the Slavies, The.   La Fontaine, tr. fr. French by Edward Marsh.   OBVE

Hag of Beare, The.   Unknown.   See Lament of the Old Woman of Beare, The.

Hagar and Ishmael.   Else Lasker-Schüler, tr. fr. German.   BoWoP, tr. by Rosemarie Waldrop; VWA, tr. by Joachim Neugroschel

Hagar to Ishmael.   Deborah Eibel.   VWA

Hagen.   Horace Gregory.   SPT

Hag-ridden.   Robert Graves.   BIrV

Hai.   Stuart Z. Perkoff.   VWA

Haifa.   Dovid Knut, tr. fr. Russian by Daniel Weissbort.   VWA

Haiku: "All the hot night."   Masaoka Shiki, tr. fr. Japanese by Kenneth Rexroth.   VWA

Haiku: "Although he never stirs from home."   José Juan Tablada, tr. fr. Spanish by Samuel Beckett.   PBMP

Haiku: "Ants on inert cricket crawling."   José Juan Tablada, tr. fr. Spanish by Samuel Beckett.   PBMP

Haiku: "August heat."   Gerald Vizenor.   VoR

Haiku: "Autumn's bright moon."   Kaga no Chiyo, tr. fr. Japanese by R. H. Blyth.   PBWP

Haiku: "Bitter morning, A."   J. W. Hackett.   BoAnP

Haiku: "Clear light bulb smashed."   Louis Cuneo.   CPA

Haiku: "Dew of the rouge-flower, The."   Kaga no Chiyo, tr. fr. Japanese by R. H. Blyth.   PBWP

Haiku: "Dragon-fly strives patiently, The."   José Juan Tablada, tr. fr. Spanish by Samuel Beckett.   PBMP

Haiku: "Eastern guard tower."   Etheridge Knight.   BPo; NeAC; NoAM; TAP

Haiku: "Falling flower, The."   Arakida Moritake, tr. fr. Japanese by Babette Deutsch.
(Haiku: "Fallen flowers rise," tr. by Harold G. Henderson.)   SoSe

Haiku: "Halo of the moon, The."   Buson, tr. fr. Japanese.   Moon

Haiku: "He tells us that."   Louis Cuneo.   CPA

Haiku: "Hey, laughing youths."   Louis Cuneo.   CPA

Haiku: "Lightning gleam, A."   Basho, tr. fr. Japanese by Harold G. Henderson.   SoSe
(Haiku: "Lightning flashes, The!" tr. by Earl Miner.)   SoSe

Haiku: "Lumps of mud, the toads."   José Juan Tablada, tr. fr. Spanish by Samuel Beckett.   PBMP

Haiku: "New moon in the sky."   Basho, tr. fr. Japanese by Nobuyuki Yuasa.   PAIC

Haiku: "Oh, the wide world's ways!"   Ryōta, tr. fr. Japanese by Harold G. Henderson.   NIL

Haiku: "Once we talked."   Louis Cuneo.   CPA

Haiku: "Red cold."   José Juan Tablada, tr. fr. Spanish by Samuel Beckett.   PBMP

Haiku: "Spring rain." Kaga no Chiyo, *tr. fr. Japanese by* R. H. Blyth. PBWP

Haiku: "This broken bottle." Elisavietta Ritchie. AATT

Haiku: "Tiny monkey looks at me, The." José Juan Tablada, *tr. fr. Spanish by* Samuel Beckett. PBMP

Haiku Ambulance. Richard Brautigan. InPK

Haiku, for Cinnamon. Lillie D. Chaffin. PH

Haiku for Halloween. Myra Cohn Livingston. IWK

Haiku, you ku, he. The Traditional Grammarian as Poet. Ted Hipple. POL

Hail and beware the dead who will talk life until you are blue. A Newly Discovered "Homeric" Hymn. Charles Olson. CoPAm; NoAM

Hail be thou, Mary, maiden bright. The Five Joys. *Unknown.* OxBM

Hail Bishop Valentine, whose day this is! An Epithalamion; or, Marriage-Song on the Lady Elizabeth and Count Palatine Being Married on St. Valentine's Day. John Donne. OFD; SCP-1

Hail! blessed Virgin, full of heavenly grace. On the Infancy of Our Saviour. Francis Quarles. SCP-2

Hail, Columbia. Joseph Hopkinson. BLSo, *with music*; BTTM; PCOP

Hail, Dionysos. Dudley Randall. BPo

Hail, fathers, hail! Flute Song. *Tr. fr. Hopi Indian by* Natalie Curtis. WTO

Hail, happy bride, for thou art truly blest! On the Death of Mrs. Bowes. Lady Mary Wortley Montagu. BoWoP

Hail, happy day, when, smiling like the morn. To the Right Honourable William, Earl of Dartmouth. Phillis Wheatley. SBG

Hail happy William, thou art strangely great. A Panegyric. *Unknown.* APAS

Hail, Holy Land. Thomas Tillam. *See* Upon the First Sight of New England, June 29, 1638.

Hail, holy Lead!—of human feuds the great. Ambrose Bierce. *Fr.* The Devil's Dictionary. OBAL

Hail, holy light, offspring of Heaven first-born. Holy Light [*or* The Poet's Blindness]. Milton. *Fr.* Paradise Lost, III. NOBE; OBP

Hail, lofty,/ necking quizzically. Conversation with a Giraffe at Dusk in a Zoo. Douglas Livingstone. LP; MPo

Hail Mary!/ Ich am sary. *Unknown.* OxBM

Hail Mary, this is not my body. Translation of an Unwritten Spanish Poem. Steven Goldsberry. PHC

Hail mer-/ry, tricky, and clandestine. Ode to Pornography. Jack Anderson. PoA

Hail, Muse! et caetera.—We left Juan sleeping. Byron. *Fr.* Don Juan, III. OAEL-2

Hail, Oh Hail to the King, *with music*. Beatrice Quickenden. AH

Hail Our Incarnate God! *with music*. William Duke. AH

Hail, pious days! thou most propitious time. On the Sentence Passed by the House of Lords on Dr. Sacheverell. *Unknown.* APAS

Hail! Power Divine, whose soul command. A Hymn on the Power of God. James Thomson. PIM

Hail Saint Michael with thy longe spere! An Irish Satire. *Unknown.* OxBM

Hail, sister springs! Saint Mary Magdalene; or, The Weeper. Richard Crashaw. OAEL-1; SCP-1

Hail the Glorious Golden City, *with music*. Felix Adler. AH

Hail to the Brightness of Zion's Glad Morning, *with music*. Thomas Hastings. AH

Hail to the Joyous Day, *with music*. Royall Tyler. AH

Hail to the Queen, *with music*. *Unknown.* AH

Hail to the Sabbath Day, *with music*. Stephen Greenleaf Bulfinch. AH

Hail to the Town of Limerick. Langford Reed. TDH

Hail to thee. The Carnation. Paul Hannigan. POL

Hail to Thee, Blithe Owl. Ring Lardner. OBAL

Hail to thee, blithe spirit. To a Skylark [*or* Ode to a Skylark]. Shelley. BoAnP; HAP; InPS; MBPR; NOBE; OAEL-2; PB; PBMP; PCOP; VoPo

Hail, Tranquil Hour of Closing Day, *with music*. Leonard Bacon. AH

Hail wedded love, mysterious law, true source. Milton. *Fr.* Paradise Lost, IV. BiP; PAIC

Haill warld waited, The. Problems. Alexander Scott. FF

Hailstorm in June 1831, The. John Clare. VLP

Hain't no use to weep, hain't no use to moan. Down in the Lonesome Garden. *Unknown.* BPo

Hair. Gregory Corso. SFF

Hair. Tom McKeown. TC

Hair. Maxine Silverman. VWA

Hair/ like heather, father would boast. Song. Marie Harris. MMD

Hair and nose and eyes like mine. Living with a Voodoo Doll. John Stone. CoPAm

Hair-bowed Rose, deep in lush grass of the river. Profile of Rose. Glyn Jones. OBW

Hair is heaven's water flowing eerily over us. Hair Poem. William Knott. EAS; PPoD

Hair on the Chest. Coleman Barks. *Fr.* Body Poems. NVAP

Hair ornament of the sun, The. Mitsuhashi Takajo, *tr. fr. Japanese by* Kenneth Rexroth *and* Ikuko Atsumi. BoWoP

Hair Poem. William Knott. EAS; PPoD

Hair-Tonic Bottle, The. Ben King. OBAL

Hairdresser, The. David Hopes. AMV–81

Hairs in My Nose, The. Aram Boyajian. NeAC

Hairy Dog, The. Herbert Asquith. ECBV (My Hairy Dog.) CTV

Hairy Toe, The. *Unknown.* DuDr

Halcyon Days. Jim Barnes. CDW

Haleiwa Churchyard. Nell Altizer. PHC

Halem dud. For "Mr. Dudley," a Black Spy. James A. Emanuel. BPo

Half a century of smoke, burned. Traveling in Europe. Keith Althaus. AAN

Half a league, half a league. The Charge of the Light Brigade. Tennyson. BTTM; CTV; FaPo; FaPoR; NIL; PBMP; PPoD; SFF

Half a yard, half a yard. Charge of the Grid Brigade. George S. Applegarth. SPo

Half asleep on top this bleak landscape. Hunter. Raymond Carver. NVAP

Half Black, Half Blacker. Sterling Plumpp. PoBA

Half-bridge over nothingness. Northanger Ridge. Charles Wright. CSP

Half close your eyelids, loosen your hair. Aedh [*or* He] Thinks of Those Who Have Spoken Evil of His Beloved. W. B. Yeats. NoAM; PFIr; VLP

"Half-cracked" to Higginson, living. "I Am in Danger— Sir." Adrienne Rich. NOBA; PiAm; Psy

Half-door, hall door. Purgatory. W. B. Yeats. CMoP (1970 ed.); ExPo (1973 ed.); PAIC

Half doun the hill, whaur fa's the linn. The Gowk. William Soutar. MS

Half-hidden by trees, the sheer roof of the barn. The Barn. Stephen Spender. CMoP (1970 ed.)

Half-hidden in a graveyard. The Stranger. Walter de la Mare. OxBTC

Half hour for coffee, and at night, A.  To What Strangers, What Welcome, X.  J. V. Cunningham.  PiAm

Half in the dim light from the hall.  To——.  William Stanley Braithwaite.  PoBA

Half loving-kindliness and half disdain.  To My Cat.  Rosamund Marriott Watson.  PCat

Half Moon.  Federico García Lorca, *tr. fr. Spanish by* W. S. Merwin.  RFM

Half-Moon Lake, The.  Ciaran Carson.  IPM

Half Moon Shows a Face of Plaintive Sweetness, The.  Christina Rossetti.  Moon

Half-moon slides by clumsily, as if on tracks, The.  Canal Street, Chicago.  Clyde Fixmer.  TAT

Half my life has passed me by.  The Waters, Indeed, Are to the Palate, Bitter.  Hubert Witheford.  ATNZ

Half Note for the Duke, A.  Karl Carter.  PoUp

Half of death.  In Prague.  Paul Celan, *tr. by* Joachim Neugroschel.  VWA

Half of his/ body hung in.  Spirits.  Victor Hernandez Cruz.  PoBA

Half of Life.  Friedrich Hölderlin, *tr. fr. German by* James Blair Leishman.  OBVE

Half of me is beautiful.  Lilith.  Ruth Feldman.  VWA

Half of my life is gone, and I have let.  Mezzo Cammin.  Longfellow.  AmVN; ILP (1975 ed.); TAP

Half of our borders, rivers and mountains were gone.  In the Home of the Scholar Wu Su-chiang.  Wu Tsao, *tr. by* Kenneth Rexroth *and* Ling Chung.  BoWoP

Half past Four, October.  Anna Hajnal, *tr. fr. Hungarian by* Daniel Hoffman.  BoWoP

Half-shut doors through which we heard that music, The.  Multitudes Turn in Darkness.  Conrad Aiken.  PoA

Half spirit, the older.  The Jest.  Austin Clarke.  BIrV

Half the Story.  Karen Sagstatter.  PoUp

Half the time they munched the grass, and all the time they lay.  Cows.  James Reeves.  DuDr

Half the year has hot nights, like this.  Elegies for the Hot Season.  Sandra McPherson.  AmPA; CAAP; CNW; MPA; RiTi

Half-wild, I hear a wolf.  Existences.  William Stafford.  UsP

Halfwit.  Basil Dowling.  ATNZ

Half-Year Birthday.  Neil Claremon.  FoP

Halfe dead: and rotten at the coare: my Lord!  Edward Taylor.  Preparatory Meditations: Second Series, XIV.  EAP

Halfway.  Maxine W. Kumin.  PCho

Halfway across a bridge one night.  The Swerve.  William Stafford.  GP

Half way between breath and Earth.  The Path.  Joseph Bruchac.  NW

Half way between the house and the barn.  Death on the Farm.  Cary Waterman.  GP

Halfway Down.  A. A. Milne.  LCL; SO

Halidon Hill.  Laurence Minot.  OxBM

Halieutica, *sels.*  William Diaper, *after the Greek of* Oppian.
  "Lamprey, glowing with uncommon fires, The."  OBVE
  "Strange the formation of the eely race."  OBVE
  "When pleasing heat, and fragrant blooms inspire."  PeD
  "When they in throngs a safe retirement seek."  OVBE

Hall of Ifor Hael, The.  Evan Evans, *tr. fr. Welsh by* Gwyn Williams.  OBW

Hall of Ocean Life.  John Hollander.  PoA

Hallaig.  Sorley Maclean.  MS

Halleluja Hardesty, Female Artist.  Hugh Walthall.  PoUp

Hallelujah: A Sestina.  Robert Francis.  PPoD

Hallelujah, Bum Again.  Unknown.  GBP
  (Hallelujah, I'm a Bum.)  FSW

Hallelujah I'm a Bum ("I read in the news, the President said").  Barbara Dane *and* Irwin Silber.  FSW

Hallelujah, I'm a-Travelin'.  Harry Raymond.  FSW

Hallelujah! kneel and sing.  Bible, *O.T., paraphrased by* Christopher Smart.  Psalms, CXLVIII.  OBVE

Hallelujah! Praise the Lord, *with music.*  Edwin Francis Hatfield.  AH

Hallelujah, the thaw!  Metamorphic.  Daniel Mark Fogel.  BCr

"Hallelujah!" was the only observation.  On the Death of a Female Officer of the Salvation Army.  A. E. Housman.  FaBoNo

Hallow-Fair.  Robert Fergusson.  EPC

Hallowed be the Sabbaoth.  Epitaph in St. Olave's, Southwark, on Mr. Munday.  *Unknown.*  FaBoCo

Hallowed be Thy name—Halleluiah!  The Human Cry.  Tennyson.  ILwL

Hallowed Pleaces.  William Barnes.  VPC

Hallowe'en.  Harry Behn.  CC; IWK

Halloween.  Mary Jane Carr.  IWK

Halloween.  Ivy O. Eastwick.  IWK

Halloween.  Myra Cohn Livingston.  OFD

Halloween,/ Halloween.  Trick or Treat.  David McCord.  IWK

Halloween Concert.  Aileen Fisher.  IWK

Hallowe'en 1971.  Michael Dennis Browne.  AmPA

Halloween Witches.  Felice Holman.  CC

Halo, A.  Ralph Salisbury.  MPA

Halo of the moon, The.  Haiku.  Buson.  Moon

Halt in the desert where I have in mind, A.  Hugh Maxton.  *Fr.* Mastrim: A Meditation.  CIP

Halt! Shoulder arms! Recover! As you were!  Sonnet to Britain.  William Edmonstoune Aytoun.  FaBoCo

Ham Hound Crave.  *Unknown.*  BluL

Hamatreya.  Emerson.  AmVN; HeIP; ILP (1975 ed.); IPWM; MAT; NOBA; PiAm; TAP

Hambone Blues.  *Unknown.*  BluL

Hamburger Mary's.  Todd S. J. Lawson.  CPA

Hamden Provision Co.  Barbara Hughes.  CPA

Hamelin Town's in Brunswick.  The Pied Piper of Hamelin.  Robert Browning.  BBL; BiP; FaPo; OxBChV

Hamewith.  Sydney Goodsir Smith.  MS

Hamilton Greene.  Edgar Lee Masters.  *Fr.* Spoon River Anthology.  NoAM

"Hamlet."  Emmett Jarrett.  NeAC

Hamlet, *sels.*  Shakespeare.
  "Air bites shrewdly; it is very cold, The," I, iv.  ExPo (1973 ed.)
  "Angels and ministers of grace defend us!" *fr.* I, iv.  EBEV
  "Give me your pardon, sir. I have done you wrong," *fr.* V, ii.  DL
  "How all occasions do inform against me." *fr.* IV, iv.  BiP; HoPM (1975 ed.)
  "How should I your true love know," *fr.* IV, v.  AIW; EBEV (Ophelia's Song.)  GBL
  "O what a noble mind is here o'erthrown!" *fr.* III, i.  PCOP
  "Some say that ever 'gainst that season comes," *fr.* I, i.  OFD; PChr
  "There,—my blessing with you!" *fr.* I, iii.  PPM
  "To be, or not to be, that is the question," *fr.* III, i.  BiP; FF; HoPM (1975 ed.); STS
  Tomorrow Is Saint Valentine's Day, *fr.* IV, v.  CC; CTV; LCL; OFD; WIF
  "What ceremony else?" *fr.* V, i.  EBEV
  "What man dost thou dig it for?" *fr.* V, i.  DL
  "Whither wilt thou lead me? I'll go no further," I, v.  ExPo (1973 ed.)
  "Who's there?/ Nay, answer me: stand, and unfold yourself," I, i.  ExPo (1973 ed.)

Hamlet's Soliloquy Imitated.  Richard Jago.  FaBoCo

Hammer.  Erica Funkhouser.  AMV-81

Hammer me, let me see. Another Cross. Stephen Gardner. AMV-80

Hammer, Ring. *Unknown.* AmFP

Hammerfest. W. H. Auden. NIL

Hammers, The. Ralph Hodgson. NOBE; OxBTC

Hammers of iron glow down Faraday. Vincent Buckley. *Fr.* Golden Builders. CAAP; GAS

Hamnavoe Market. George Mackay Brown. MS

Hamster, The. Ogden Nash. ILP (1975 ed.)

Ha'nacker Mill. Hilaire Belloc. FaPoR; OxBTC

Hand. Morton Marcus. NVAP

Hand, The. Howard Moss. TAP

Hand. Edouard Roditi. EAS

Hand a shade of moonlight on the pillow, The. Non Ti Fidar. Louis Zukofsky. VGW

Hand and Foot, The. Jones Very. AmVN; PiAm; TAP

Hand by Hand We Shall Us Take. *Unknown.* OxBM

Hand in hand, they are marching. The Children. Mark Vinz. GP

Hand is not always extremity enough, The. Hammer. Erica Funkhouser. AMV-81

Hand Me Down Blues. Calvin Forbes. PHC

Hand Me Down My Walking Cane. *Unknown, ad. by* James Morehead. BLSH, *with music;* FSW

Hand of art here torpid lies, The. Epitaph on William Hogarth. Samuel Johnson. EBEV

Hand of Ms. Fate, The. Cash Terrell. DNGG

Hand on the Navel, *sels.* Lemuel Johnson.
  "Ah, ah." AAN
  "And to what end aim a dry root." AAN
  "And we came caught in the dance." AAN
  "And what price the statue of a victorian man." AAN
  "And what shall I do back in Frankfurt?" AAN
  "And when you have after all this." AAN
  "From a height of gargoyles and waterspouts." AAN
  "How you manage till you reach." AAN
  "Landscape is not an austere one, The." AAN
  "Small finger curves outward, A." AAN
  "*Timmini yimre.*" AAN
  "We have returned too." AAN

Hand Saw. Erica Funkhouser. AMV-81

Hand, The: Spread against the cloudless night. Body Mechanics. Albert Goldbarth. NVAP

Hand That Signed the Paper Felled a City, The. Dylan Thomas. NoAM; NOBE; PBMP; STS; WeW

Hand trembling towards hand; the amazing. Sonnet Reversed. Rupert Brooke. NOBL

Handball Players. Paul Goodman. SPo

Handball Players at Brighton Beach, The. Irving Feldman. NYP

Handbook of Versification. Gilbert Sorrentino. PoA

Handcart Song, The. *Unknown.* AmFP

Handful of Ashes. Ilya Rubin, *tr. fr. Russian by* Linda Zisquit. VWA

Handful of Small Secret Stones, A. Chris Bursk. AMV-81

Handiwork of God, The. *Unknown.* CTV

Handlyng Synne, *sel.* Robert Mannyng.
  Dancers of Colbek, The. OxBM

Handmaid of Religion, The. Edgell Rickword. OBSV

Hands. Donald Finkel. MAT

Hands. Siv Cedering Fox. NVAP
  "When I fall asleep," *sel.* OSP

Hands, The. Tony Harrison. FaBoTw (1975 ed.)

Hands. Robinson Jeffers. GOA

Hands, The. Daniel David Moses. AMV-80

Hands. Peter Young. FPB

Hands are being plated The; they'll be brass. Clock without Hands. John Frederick Nims. PoA

Hands clenched under my shawl. Anna Akhmatova, *tr. fr. Russian by* Robert Tracy. PBWP

Hands, do what you're bid. The Balloon of the Mind. W. B. Yeats. POL

Hands explore tentatively, The. The Feel of Hands. Thom Gunn. PSN

Hands folded like napkins in my lap. Robert Peterson. NeAC

Hands must touch and handle many things, The. The New Man. Jones Very. NOBA

Hands that eased my mother's labor drew, The. Rhyme for the Child as a Wet Dog. Judith Johnson Sherwin. TAP

Hands Up. Anthony Rudolf. VWA

Hands upon hands. Pleading Voices. Shalom Katav, *tr. by* Yoffee Berkovitz. VWA

Hands were yours, the arms were yours, The. Elegy for My Father. Mark Strand. CAAP; NVAP; PCho; UnPo (1976 ed.)

Handsome and self-absorbed young man, The. True Love at Last. D. H. Lawrence. TPo

Handsome Cabin Boy, The. *Unknown.* FSW

Handsome Molly. *Unknown.* FSW

Handsome young airman lay dying, A. The Dying Airman. *Unknown.* FaBoNo

Handsome young gent down in Fla., A. A Helpful Nurse. *Unknown.* TDH

Handsome young rodent named Gratian, A. Ogden Nash. SFF

Handsomely into his instrument his door. Hearing My Son Play. Alvaro Cardona-Hine. BrS

Handwriting on the Wall. *Unknown.* AmFP

Handy Guide, A. *Unknown.* TDH

Handyman. Homer Phillips. QQQ

Hang down your head Tom Dooley. Tom Dooley. *Unknown.* FSW

Hang garlands on the bathroom door. The Bath. R. C. Lehmann. GDP

Hang it all, Robert Browning. Ezra Pound. Cantos, II. HAP; NoAM; NOBA; PiAm; PoA

Hang It on the Wall. *Unknown.* BluL

Hang Me, O Hang Me, and I'll Be Dead and Gone. *Unknown.* AmFP

Hang out our banners on the outward walls. Shakespeare. *Fr.* Macbeth, V, v. EBEV

Hang out your cloth, and let the trumpet sound. The Character of a Trimmer. *Unknown.* APAS

Hang your serious songs. Sipsop's Song. Blake. *Fr.* An Island in the Moon. FaBoNo

Hangar at Sunnydale, The: 1937. Janet Lewis. WPW

Hangar Nine. Ann Darr. WBN

Hanged Man, The. Kenneth Rexroth. MPA

Hanged Man, The. Steve Toth. AcAn

Hanged man, please grow wild and luminous. To Her Dead Mate, Montana, 1966. Elizabeth Libbey. AmPA

Hanging/ out under the bridge. Getting Across. Carter Revard. VoR

Hanging Clothes. Rolly Kent. AAN

Hanging from fresh trees. Lemons, Lemons. Al Young. HeIP; PiAm

Hanging from the beam. The Portent. Herman Melville. AmVN; ILP (1975 ed.); NOBA; TAP

Hanging from the branches of a green/ willow tree. Lady Ise, *tr. fr. Japanese by* Willis Barnstone. BoWoP

Hanging Johnny. *Unknown.* FSW; GBP

Hanging Man, The. Karl Kopp. FoP

Hanging Man, The. Sylvia Plath. NIL

Hanging of Sam Archer, The. *Unknown.* AmFP

Hanging on the walls. Gallery of My Heart. King D. Kuka. VoR

Hangman. Ai. AmPA

Hangman at Home, The. Carl Sandburg. AKE

"Hangman, hangman, slack on the line." The Maid Freed from the Gallows. *Unknown*. AmFP

Hangman, hangman slack your rope. The Gallows Pole. *Unknown*. FSW

Hangman's Love Song, The. Stanley Moss. VGW

Hangman's Tree, The. *Unknown*. *See* Maid Freed from the Gallows, The.

Hangs./ whipped/ blood. Biography. Amiri Baraka. TAP

Hangs, a fat gun-barrel. Trout. Seamus Heaney. CIP

Hangtown Girls. *Unknown*. FSW

Hannah's Thanksgiving. Bible, *O.T.* First Samuel, II: 1-10. BoWoP

Hannibal. Juvenal, *tr. fr. Latin*. *Fr.* Satires, X.
    *Tr. by* William Gifford. OBVE
    *Tr. by* Robert Lowell. OBVE
    *Tr. by* Henry Vaughan. OBVE

Hans Beimler. Ernst Busch, *tr. fr. German*. FSW

Hans Breitmann's Barty. Charles Godfrey Leland. FaBoCo; NOBL; OBAL

Hanukah. Jakov de Haan, *tr. fr. Dutch by* David Soetendorp. VWA

Hap. Thomas Hardy. CABA (1972 ed.); CMoP (1970 ed.); NIL; NoAM; OAEL-2; PBMP; PPP; VLP

Happened like this: it was hot as hell. The Death of the Craneman. Alfred Hayes. NCSH

Happened when he was yawning. The Man Who Swallowed a Bird. David Young. CAAP

Happening, A. Denise Levertov. UsP

Happie is he, that from all businesse cleere. *See* Happy is he that from all business clear.

Happiest Heart, The. John Vance Cheney. PCOP

Happiness. Carl Sandburg. TH; VoPo

Happiness Is a Charlie Chaplin Movie. Luís Omar Salinas. SA

Happiness of a Flea, The. Tasso, *tr. fr. Italian by* William Drummond of Hawthornden. LoAs

Happiness of hedgehogs, The. The Happy Hedgehog. E. V. Rieu. ECBV

Happy? Robert T. Kasold. DNGG

Happy are men who yet before they are killed. Insensibility. Wilfred Owen. CMoP (1970 ed.); ExPo (1973 ed.); FaBoTw (1975 ed.); InPS; OxBTC

Happy are you, whom Quantock overlooks. William Diaper. *Fr.* Brent: A Poem to Thomas Palmer Esq. OBSV

Happy Army, The. Peter Bland. ATNZ

Happy at 40. Peter Meinke. GP

Happy band on the hill slope, A. The Battle of Waun Gaseg. Llywelyn ab y Moel, *tr. by* H. Idris Bell. OBW

Happy Birthday America. Pancho Aguila. NW

Happy birthday, silly goose! Clyde Watson. *Fr.* Father Fox's Pennyrhymes. CC

Happy Birthday to Me. Eve Merriam. CC

Happy Day (or Independence Day). James Cunningham. JB

Happy Day Will Soon Appear, The, *with music*. *Unknown*. AH

Happy Family, The. John Ciardi. DuDa

Happy he whose eyes have view'd. Boethius, *tr. by* Samuel Johnson. *Fr.* The Consolation of Philosophy, III, 12. OBVE

Happy heart hums low, The. Trotting Around. Benjamin Saltman. PoW

Happy Hedgehog, The. E. V. Rieu. ECBV

Happy Hyena, The. Carolyn Wells. TDH

Happy insect, what can be. The Grasshopper. Abraham Cowley, *after the Greek of* Anacreon. OAEL-1; OBVE

Happy is England! I could be content. Keats. MBPR

Happy [*or* Happie] is he that from all business clear. The Praises of a Country Life. Ben Jonson. OBVE; SCP-1

Happy Life, The. Martial, *tr. fr. Latin*. NOBE, *tr. by* Earl of Surrey; OBVE, *tr. by* Sir Richard Fanshawe; PAIC, *tr. by* Sir Edward Sherburne
    ("Marshall, the thinges for to attayne," *tr. by* Earl of Surrey.) OBVE
    (Means to Attain Happy Life, The, *tr. by* Earl of Surrey.) FaBoEE; PPM
    ("My friend, the things that do attain," *tr. by* Earl of Surrey.) CABA (1972 ed.)
    ("Things that make the happier life, are these, The," *tr. by* Ben Jonson.) FaBoEE; OBVE
    ("Would you, my friend, in little room express," *tr. by* Elijah Fenton.) OBVE

Happy Marriage. Thomas Blacklock. SLP

Happy New Year, A, *sels*. W. H. Auden.
    "Colonel from Cheltenham stopped everyone, A." OBSV
    "Cry went through me like a stab of a knife, A." OBSV
    "Doctors attended behind each chair." OBSV
    "In corduroy trousers and seedy black coats." OBSV
    "On a lorry the centre of a gaping crowd." OBSV

Happy Nightingale, The. *Unknown*. OxBChV

Happy Pair, The, *sel*. Sir Charles Sedley.
    Marriage and Money. OBSV

Happy people die whole, they are all dissolved in a moment. Post Mortem. Robinson Jeffers. PiAm

Happy, Saviour, Would I Be, *with music*. Edwin H. Nevin. AH

Happy Sheep, The. Wilfred Thorley. CTV

Happy that first white age! when wee. Boethius, *tr. fr. Latin by* Henry Vaughan. *Fr.* The Consolation of Philosophy, II, 5. OBVE

Happy the hare at morning, for she cannot read. The Cultural Presupposition. W. H. Auden. CABA (1972 ed.)

Happy the Man. Horace, *paraphrased by* Dryden. *Fr.* Odes, III, 29. FaPoR

Happy the man, who free as air. The Widower. Royall Tyler. OBAL

Happy the man who his whole time doth bound. The Old Man of Verona. Claudian, *tr. by* Abraham Cowley. OBVE

Happy the man who, safe on shore. The Hurricane. Philip Freneau. EAP; TAP

Happy the man who, void of cares and strife. The Splendid Shilling. John Philips. EPC; OAEL-1, *abr.*; PAIC

Happy the man whose wish and care. Ode on Solitude [*or* Solitude, an Ode]. Pope. Epi; HeIP; IP; IPWM; LFH; NIL; PAIC; PBMP; PCOP; PoPle; PPoe; Prf

Happy the moment when we are seated in the Palace. Jalal al-Din Rumi, *tr. fr. Persian*. ILwL

Happy the wild birds that can soar. Unfair to Men. *Unknown, tr. by* Gwyn Jones. OBW

Happy those early days [*or* dayes]! when I. The Retreat[e]. Henry Vaughan. CABA (1972 ed.); FF; HAP; HeIP; InPS; MetP; NIL; NOBE; OAEL-1; OBP; OBW; PIM; PoIA; PoPle; PPP; SCP-1

Happy Thought. Robert Louis Stevenson. CTV; PCOP; OxBChV

Happy Time, A. *Unknown*. IP

Happy View, A. C. Day Lewis. CMoP (1970 ed.)

Happy ye leaves! when as those lily hands. Amoretti, I. Spenser. AAS; EBEV; ESo; LoAs; NIL; OAEL-1; PAIC

Harbingers are come, The. See, see their mark. The Forerunners. George Herbert. BoReV; SCP-1

Harbor. Nancy Price. IHMS

Harbor, The. Carl Sandburg. NCSH; TAP

Harbor Dawn, The. Hart Crane. *Fr.* The Bridge: Powhatan's Daughter. NYP; PiAm; PSN

Harbors. Judith Minty. TC

Hard, Ain't It Hard. *Unknown.* FSW

Hard brown bug, maybe a beetle, A. He Faces the Second Winter. Philip Levine. *Fr.* Sierra Kid. PoA

Hard Cheese. Justin St. John. LP

Hard Core, The. D. J. Enright. HeHu

Hard crystals there are hard crystals inside them. Of My Own Flesh. John Newlove. FoP

Hard Edge of Beauty. Floyd C. Stuart. FAF

Hard-edged buildings; cloudless blue enamel. Fifty-seventh and Fifth. Alfred Corn. NYP

Hard eyes glittered ill, the hard voice said, The. The Reichstag Trial. Isidor Schneider. SPT

Hard Heart of Mine, *with music.* Henry Alline. AH

Hard I must listen now. On the Death of Theodore Roethke. Robert Huff. CNW

Hard is the doubt, and difficult to deeme. Spenser. *Fr.* The Faerie Queene, IV, 9. OAEL-1

Hard Is the Fortune of All Womankind. *Unknown.* FSW

Hard Journey, A. Yes. Hayden Carruth. VGW

Hard knowledge to come by. The Music of the Spheres. Marvin Bell. PoA

Hard Lovers, The. George Dillon. PoA

Hard luck poppa, a-countin' his toes. Brown's Ferry Blues. *Unknown.* FSW

Hard Night's Daze, A. Basil Payne. IPM

Hard old grey eyes, no pity. The Rancher. Keith Wilson. GP

Hard Questions. Margaret Tsuda. RFM

Hard Rain's a-Gonna Fall, A. Bob Dylan. PoRo

Hard Rock Returns to Prison from the Hospital for the Criminal Insane. Etheridge Knight. ConAP; NIL; NNaP; NoAM; TAP; UnPo (1976 ed.)

Hard sand breaks, The. Hermes of the Ways. Hilda Doolittle ("H. D."). WPE

Hard Time Killin' Floor Blues. *Unknown.* BluL

Hard Times ("Come listen a while"). *Unknown.* AmFP

Hard Times, but Carrying On. Dave Smith. TAT

Hard times here every, where you go. Hard Time Killin' Floor Blues. *Unknown.* BluL

Hard Traveling. Woody Guthrie. FSW

Hard Way to Learn. James Hearst. AMV-80

Hard-working Miner, The ("The hard-working miners"). *Unknown.* AmFP

Hard-working Miner, The ("To the hard-working miner"). *Unknown.* AmFP

Harden now thy tyred hart with more then flinty rage. Thomas Campion. AAS; OBVE

Hardest thing to imagine is, The. A Valentine for Marianne Moore. Elder Olson. PAIC

Hardest work I ever did, The. Bile Them Cabbage Down. *Unknown.* AmFP

Hardly a Man Is Now Alive. Ring Lardner. OBAL

Hardly spring, with ice. Chiyo, *tr. fr. Japanese by* David Ray. BoWoP

Hardship of Accounting, The. Robert Frost. FaBoCo; OBAL

Hardweed Path Going. A. R. Ammons. CSP; UnPo (1976 ed.); VGW

Hare, A. Walter de la Mare. EBEV

Hare, The. *Unknown.* OxBM

Hare and the Tortoise, The. Ian Serraillier. SO

Hare in the Snow, The. Gloria Rawlinson. ATNZ

Hare in Winter. Marge Piercy. NeAC

Harelip Mary. Ronald Koertge. GP

Hari helps his people. Mirabai, *tr. fr. Hindi by* Willis Barnstone *and* Usha Nilsson. BoWoP

Hari, look at me a while. Mirabai, *tr. fr. Hindi by* Willis Barnstone *and* Usha Nilsson. BoWoP

Hark! ah, the nightingale. Philomela. Matthew Arnold. ILP (1975 ed.); NIL; OAEL-2; PPP; UnPo (1976 ed.); VLP

Hark, All Ye Lovely Saints. *Unknown.* OAEL-1

Hark, All You Ladies. Thomas Campion. Epi, *with music*; SCP-2
("Harke, al you ladies that do sleep.") AAS; EBEV

Hark, and Hear my Trumpet Sounding, *with music. Unknown.* AH

Hark Back. Richard Eberhart. TH

Hark, Celia, hark! but lay thou close thine ear. The Secret. *Unknown.* SCP-2

Hark! from the tombs a doleful sound. Plenary. *Unknown.* AmFP

Hark, hark!/ Bow-wow. Song. Shakespeare. *Fr.* The Tempest, I, ii. SoSe

Hark! hark! that pig—that pig! the hideous note. Ode to a Pig while His Nose Was Being Bored. Robert Southey. NOBL

Hark, hark, the dogs do bark. Mother Goose. GBP; MG

Hark! hark! the lark at heaven's gate sings. Shakespeare. *Fr.* Cymbeline, II, iii. HeIP; ILP (1975 ed.); NIL; OBP; PAIC; PCOP

Hark! Hark! with Harps of Gold, *with music.* Edwin Hubbell Chapin. AH

Hark, hearer, hear what I do. Epithalamion. Gerard Manley Hopkins. VLP

Hark, how my Celia, with the choice. Celia Singing. Thomas Carew. ILP (1975 ed.)

Hark how the mower Damon sung. Damon the Mower. Andrew Marvell. AnMo; OAEL-1

Hark my soul! it is the Lord. Lovest Thou Me? William Cowper. BoReV

Hark, Now Everything Is Still. John Webster. *Fr.* The Duchess of Malfi, IV, ii. HAP; InPS
(Shrouding of the Duchess of Malfi, The.) NOBE

Hark! O hark, you guilty trees. Orpheus to Woods. Richard Lovelace. CaPo

Hark, reader! wilt be learn'd i' th' wars? To My Truly Valiant, Learned Friend, Who in His Book Resolved the Art Gladiatory into the Mathematics. Richard Lovelace. CaPo

Hark! She is calling to her cat. The Cat. Richard Church. BoAnP; PCat

Hark! the cock proclaims the morning. St. Matthias. Christopher Smart. *Fr.* Hymns and Spiritual Songs. LAuP

Hark, the Herald Angels Sing. Charles Wesley. BLSH, *with music*; FSW

Hark! the herald angels sing/ timidly. Dean Inge. Humbert Wolfe. FaBoEE

Hark the sound of holy voices, chanting at the crystal sea. All Saints' Day, Nov. 1. Christopher Wordsworth. VLP

Hark! through the quiet evening air, their song. Emma Lazarus. *Fr.* In Memoriam Rev. J. J. Lyons. SBG

Hark! 'Tis the Saviour of Mankind, *with music.* John Murray. AH

Hark to the rumble of the earthquake god! Ruaumoko—the Earthquake God. Mohi Turei, *tr. by* A. Armstrong. WTO

Hark to the story of Willie the Weeper. Willy the Weeper. *Unknown.* GBP; PeBB

Hark to the welkin ringing at Shea! September Valentine. Frank Sullivan. SPo

Hark to the whimper of the sea-gull. The Sea-Gull. Ogden Nash. SoSe; UsP

Hark, ye sighing sons of sorrow. The Mouldering Vine. *Unknown.* AmFP

Harke, Al You Ladies That Do Sleep. Thomas Campion. *See* Hark, All You Ladies.

Harke how the birds doe sing, and marke then how.   Sir John Davies.   *Fr.* Orchestra; or, A Poeme of Dauncing.   OBP

Harlem ("Here on the edge of hell").   Langston Hughes.   PPP (Puzzled.)   UnPo (1976 ed.)

Harlem ("What happens to a dream deferred").   Langston Hughes.   *Fr.* Lenox Avenue Mural.   BiP; CABA (1972 ed.); HeIP; ILP (1975 ed.); InPS; IP; NIL; PBMP; PoIA (Dream Deferred.)   FF; InPK; PoBA; PPP; SoSe; WIF

Harlem Dancer, The.   Claude McKay.   BPo; FF; ILP (1975 ed.); IPWM; NoAM; TAP

Harlem Freeze Frame.   Lebert Bethune.   PoBA

Harlem Gallery, *sels.*   Melvin B. Tolson.
Birth of John Henry, The.   BPo
Sea-Turtle and the Shark, The.   IP; PoBA; SoSe (1977 ed.)

Harlem Gallery: From the Inside.   Larry Neal.   BPo

Harlem in January.   Julia Fields.   CNA

Harlem is vicious.   Return of the Native.   Amiri Baraka.   BPo

Harlem, Montana: Just Off the Reservation.   James Welch.   CDW; GP; SA; VW

Harlem Night Song.   Langston Hughes.   OSP

Harlem Riot, 1943.   Pauli Murray.   PoBA

Harlem River.   Herman Spector.   SPT

Harlem Sounds: Hallelujah Corner.   William Browne.   AmNP (1974 ed.)

Harlem Sweeties.   Langston Hughes.   CABA (1972 ed.)

Harlots' Catch.   Robert Nichols.   FaBoTw (1975 ed.)

Harlot's House, The.   Oscar Wilde.   InPK; PPoD

Harmonious Heedlessness of Little Boy Blue, The.   Guy Wetmore Carryl.   BoAnP

Harold.   Stephen Tudor.   HeS

Harp and flute and violin, throbbing through the night.   The Hired Man on Horseback.   Eugene Manlove Rhodes.   BPAW

Harp of the North.   Sir Walter Scott.   *Fr.* The Lady of the Lake.   ILP (1975 ed.)

Harp Song of the Dane Women.   Kipling.   *Fr.* Puck of Pook's Hill.   HAP

Harp That Once through Tara's Halls, The.   Thomas Moore.   BTTM; FaPoR; FSW

Harper, The.   *Unknown, tr. fr. Early Modern Irish by* Frank O'Connor.   PFIr

Harpkin.   *Unknown.*   GBP; PeBB

Harpooning, The.   Ted Walker.   EcS

Harpsichord of Nerves, A.   Rainer Schulte.   SES

Harried, The/ earth is swept.   The Wind Increases.   William Carlos Williams.   TT

Harriet, *sel.*   Robert Lowell.
"Unaccustomed ripeness in the wood, An."   CAPP (Elizabeth.)   LoAs

Harriet Beecher Stowe.   Paul Laurence Dunbar.   AmVN; BPo; ILP (1975 ed.)

Harriet! thy kiss to my soul is dear.   To Harriet.   Shelley.   MBPR

Harry.   Francis Webb.   GAS

Harry Houdini, The Hippodrome, New York, January 7, 1918.   Conrad Hilberry.   TC

Harry Parry.   *Unknown.*   GBP

Harry Semen.   "Hugh MacDiarmid."   NoAM; OBP

Harry, you know at night.   To-Night.   Edward Thomas.   PoPle

Harsh bray and hollow, The.   Two Kitchen Songs.   Edith Sitwell.   CMoP (1970 ed.)

Harsh entry I had of it, Grasud, A.   Missionary.   D. M. Thomas.   MPo

Hart Crane.   Julian Symons.   PoA

Hart [He] Loves the High Wood, The.   *Unknown.*   ECBV; GBP

Hartico.   Anna Walters.   VoR

Harum-scarum haze on the Pollock streets.   Sonnet.   Ted Berrigan.   CAAP

Harvard Graduate Speaking to His Troops.   Ed Cox.   PoUp

Harvest.   Jeannette Maino.   AMV-80

Harvest Dawn Is Near, The, *with music.*   George Burgess.   AH

Harvest falls, The.   The Upper Meadows.   Yvor Winters.   PiAm

Harvest Home.   Sir Herbert Read.   RAE

Harvest Hymn.   John Betjeman.   PAIC

Harvest of the Sea.   Máire Mhac an tSaoi.   PBWP

Harvest Song.   Joseph Campbell.   CC; OFD

Harvester, The.   Terry Lawrence.   AMV-80

Harvesting Wheat for the Public Share.   Li Chü, *tr. fr. Chinese by* Kenneth Rexroth *and* Ling Chung.   BoWoP; PBWP

Has a gold tooth, sits long hours.   Black Bourgeoisie.   Amiri Baraka.   BPo

Has a problem he is too old.   The Wolfman.   Greg Kuzma.   GP

Has anybody seen.   Lost—A Lizard.   Irene Gough.   ECBV

Has anybody seen my mouse?   Missing.   A. A. Milne.   MN

Has Been.   Alice F. Worsley.   AMV-80

Has he tempered the viol's wood.   Ezra Pound.   *Fr.* Cantos, LXXXI.   HAP

Has no one said those daring.   Two Years Later.   W. B. Yeats.   ILP (1975 ed.)

Has not altered.   Spenser's Ireland.   Marianne Moore.   NoAM; NOBA; PAIC; TAP

Has thrust his nose under every board.   Ego.   Robert Siegel.   FAF; PoA

Haschish, The.   Whittier.   OBAL

Hasidic Jew from Sadagora.   Rose Ausländer, *tr. fr. German by* Ewald Osers.   VWA

Hasidim Dance.   Nelly Sachs, *tr. fr. German by* Keith Bosley.   VWA

Hast thou a charm to stay the morning-star.   Hymn before Sunrise, in the Vale of Chamouni.   Samuel Taylor Coleridge.   BoReV; MBPR

Hast thou from the caves of Golconda, a gem.   On Receiving a Curious Shell, and a Copy of Verses.   Keats.   MBPR

Hast thou given the horse his might?   Bible, *O.T. Fr.* Job.   OBP

Hast Thou Heard It, O My Brother, *with music.*   Theodore Chickering Williams.   AH

Hast thou named all the birds without a gun?   Forbearance.   Emerson.   PCOP; TAP

Hast thou seen reversed the prophet's miracle.   Frederick Goddard Tuckerman.   *Fr.* Sonnets.   NOBA

Hast thou seen the down i' th' air.   A Song to a Lute.   Sir John Suckling.   CaPo

Hasten on your childhood to the hour when white.   Poem.   Pablo Picasso, *tr. by* David Gascoyne.   EAS

Hastin Dot Klish, just Navajo.   Saddle.   William Haskel Simpson.   BPAW

Hasty Pudding, The.   Joel Barlow.   EAP; OBAL, *abr.*; PiAm; TAP
"Ye Alps audacious, thro' the Heavens that rise," I.   NOBA

Hat in the Ring, A.   John Manifold.   GAS

Hatch, The.   Norma Farber.   SO

Hate.   James Stephens.   VoPo

Hate in the world's hand.   A Proud Lady.   Elinor Wylie.   SBG

Hate-Song, A.   Shelley.   MBPR

Hateful is the dark blue sky.   Tennyson.   *Fr.* The Lotus Eaters.   GrRo

Hateful Old Age, *sel. Unknown, tr. fr. Welsh by* Gwyn Jones.
"Before my back was bent I was eloquent."   OBW

Hater he came and sat by a ditch, A.   A Hate-Song.   Shelley.   MBPR

Hath not the morning dawned with added light?   Ethnogenesis.   Henry Timrod.   NOBA

Hating Your Life. John N. Morris. CABA (1972 ed.)

Hatred. Gwendolyn B. Bennett. AmNP (1974 ed.); PoBA

Hatred, The. Cincinnati. Cid Corman. GP

Hatred and vengeance, my eternal portion. Lines Written during a Period of Insanity [or Lines Written under the Influence of Delirium]. William Cowper. EBEV; HAP; ILP (1975 ed.); OAEL-1; PPP; Prf

Hats. R. H. W. Dillard. CoPAm; GP

Hats off!/ Along the street there comes. The Flag Goes By. Henry Holcomb Bennett. BTTM

Hatshepsut, old girl, old friend. Sister Pharaoh. Ruth Whitman. MAT

Hatteras Calling. Conrad Aiken. NoAM; NOBA; TAP

Haughty Snail-King, The. Vachel Lindsay. SO

Haul Away Joe. Unknown. FSW

Haul Away, My Rosy. Unknown. AmFP

Haul on the Bowline. Unknown. FSW

Haunched like a faun, he hooed. Metamorphosis. Sylvia Plath. PoA

Haunt him, Mona! Haunt him, demon sister! The Brother-in-Law. Larry Rubin. GP

Haunted. Siegfried Sassoon. CMoP (1970 ed.)

Haunted House, The. Thomas Hood. EBEV

Haunted House. Valerie Worth. IWK

Haunted Oak, The. Paul Laurence Dunbar. UnPo (1976 ed.)

Haunted Palace, The. Poe. Fr. The Fall of the House of Usher. NOBA; PiAm; TAP

Haunter, The. Thomas Hardy. LoAs; NOBE; PoPle

Haunting, The. Irving Layton. NeAC

Havana Dreams. Langston Hughes. LFH

Havdolah. Susan Litwack. VWA

Havdolah Wine. Miriam Ulinover, tr. fr. Yiddish by Seth L. Wolitz. VWA

Have angleworms attractive homes? An Alphabet of Questions. Charles Edward Carryl. OSF

Have been turning, have been turning. Holding (After the Nez Perce). Beth Bentley. CNW

Have Courage, My Boy, to Say No! L. M. Hilton. WTO

Have dinosaurs come back again? Highway Construction. Carol Earle Chapin. QQQ

Have done, you men and women all! The Animals in the Ark. Unknown. GBP

Have fair fallen, O fair, fair have fallen, so dear. Henry Purcell. Gerard Manley Hopkins. VLP

Have gentlemen forgotten this? A Poet Speaks from the Visitors' Gallery. Archibald MacLeish. WasP

Have I a wife? Bedam I have! The Brewer's Man. L. A. G. Strong. FaBoCo

Have I ever been other? Exercise for the Left Hand. Constance Urdang. AMV-81

Have I Got Dogs! William Cole. GDP

Have I not blessed thee? Then go forth; nor fear. To His Book. Robert Herrick. CaPo

Have I spent all my life turning. Simon and the Tarantula. James Wright. NNaP

Have I the power to bid the frost not melt. To Barba. Edward May. FaBoEE

Have I, this moment, led thee from the beach. Walter Savage Landor. GBL

Have I told you the name of a lady? Have You Seen the Lady? John Philip Sousa. OBAL

Have learned to burn my hands with fire. Breaking Ground in Me. Tom Kryss. NeAC

"Have mercy, god!" and on the dune sun-curs'd. Dead on the Desert. Harrison Conrard. BPAW

Have no accidents. They loop. Bats. George MacBeth. NoAM

Have No Fear! Eileen Duggan. ATNZ

Have over the Water to Florida. Unknown. AIW

Have Thine Own Way, Lord! with music. Adelaide A. Pollard. BLSH

Have thou no other gods but me. The Ten Commandments. Unknown. OxBChV

Have ye beheld (with much delight). Upon the Nipples of Julia's Breast. Robert Herrick. CaPo; SCP-1

Have ye seen the would-be-not-humble dandy. The Road to Zoagli. Max Beerbohm. FaBoNo

Have You Been at Carrick. Unknown, tr. fr. Irish by Edward Walsh. BIrV

Have you been to that country where the gold. Mignon. Goethe, tr. by Robert Bly. NU

Have you cast your net out over the world? Questions and Answers. Doris Muhringer, tr. by Beth Bjorklund. AMV-80

Have you dug the spill. Harlem Sweeties. Langston Hughes. CABA (1972 ed.)

Have you ever been in love, me boys. The Garden Where the Praties Grow. Unknown. RDB

Have you ever gone visiting for a weekend of ravelry. Tallyho-Hum. Ogden Nash. PH

Have you Ever Had a Witch Bloom like a Highway. Richard Brautigan. InPK

Have you ever heard of Betty Pringle's Pig? Betty Pringle's Pig. Unknown. ECBV

Have you ever heard of the Sugar-Plum Tree? The Sugar-Plum Tree. Eugene Field. CTV; OxBChV; PCOP

Have you ever heard the sun in the sky. Shake Keane, Trumpet. John Smith. Fr. Jazz for Five. MPo

Have you ever held hands with a woman? A Mock Interrogation. Judy Grahn. Fr. A Woman Is Talking to Death. WBN

Have you ever seen a mind. Introspection. Chris Wallace-Crabbe. GAS

Have You Ever Seen the Rain? J. C. Fogerty. PoRo

Have you ever took a trip, baby, on the Mobile Line. France Blues. Unknown. BluL

Have you ever watched the sea go out at Brighton. Brighton Beach. Paul Durcan. IPM

Have you ever woke up with them. Bullfrog Blues. Unknown. BluL

Have you heard about that bully. The Bully Song. Charles E. Trevathan. BLSo

Have you heard of one Humpty Dumpty. The Ballad of Persse O' Reilly. James Joyce. Fr. Finnegans Wake. FaBoBa

Have you heard of the dreadful fate. Ashtabula Disaster. Julia A. Moore. OBAL

Have you heard of the wonderful one-hoss shay. The Deacon's Masterpiece; or, The Wonderful "One-Hoss Shay." Oliver Wendell Holmes. Fr. The Autocrat of the Breakfast-Table. FaPo; NOBA; OBAL; PiAm; SS; TAP

Have you heard? The troubles. Sulpicia, tr. fr. Latin by Aliki and Willis Barnstone. BoWoP

Have you listened for the things I have left out? Unsaid. A. R. Ammons. CSP; NOBA

Have you lived long, sir, in these parts? An Interview. K. W. Grandsen. OxBTC

Have you met Miss Mabel Green. If It Looks like Jelly, Shakes like Jelly, It Must Be Gel-a-tine. Unknown. BluL

Have you no eyes for me? The Intruder. Marya Zaturenska. OLR

Have you not in chimney seen. A Description of Maidenhead. Unknown. NOBL

Have you seen me at all. Before the Thaw. John Gill. NeAC

Have you seen the Hidebehind? The Hidebehind. Michael Rosen. OSF

Have You Seen the Lady? John Philip Sousa. OBAL

Have You Thanked a Green Plant Today. Don Anderson. QQQ

Havelok, *sel. Unknown.*
Havelok at Grimsby and Lincoln. OxBM

Haven. Donald Jeffrey Hayes. AmNP (1974 ed.)

Haven't you wondered. Doesn't It Seem to You. Gevorg Emin, *tr. by* Martin Robbins. AMV-81

Having a fine new suit. Apologue. Tony Connor. BoLoP

Having a naval officer/ for my Father was nothing to shout. Robert Lowell. *Fr.* Commander Lowell. PoIA

Having attained success in business. Robert Whitmore. Frank Marshall Davis. BPo; PoBA

Having been tenant long to a rich Lord. Redemption. George Herbert. BoReV; CABA (1972 ed.); ExPo (1973 ed.); FF; HAP; InPS; MetP; NOBE; SCP-1; SoSe

Having bitten on life like a sharp apple. Aubade. Louis MacNeice. NIL; PAIC

Having come under the baleful, red influence of Mars. Apollo 113. Diderik Finne. AMV-80

Having confused me. A Voice from the Roses. Maxine W. Kumin. NMM

Having crowded once onto the threshold of mortality. Divinities. W. S. Merwin. PoA

Having dreamed a paradise. Chain Smoking. James Scully. EC

Having heard the instruction. One Modern Poet. Carl Sandburg. OBAL

Having interred her infant-birth. An Ode, upon a Question Moved, Whether Love Should Continue Forever? Lord Herbert of Cherbury. NOBE; SCP-2

Having invented a new Holocaust. U. S. 1946 King's X. Robert Frost. NIL

Having learned to play the guitar. On Learning to Play the Guitar. Ray Fraser. NeAC

Having left hard [or solid] ground behind. The Insular Celts. Ciaran Carson. BIrV; CIP

Having lost my leather purse. My Son. Ruth Stone. WPE

Having met as older graduate student and emigrant-prof. When a Body. Gene Dawson. AMV-80

Having never read or wanted to. Below Bald Mountain. Janice Townley Moore. AMV-80

Having no children, I am strange. An Afternoon with a Baby. Susan Snively. AAN

Having no choice but to go down, the sun. Journey into the Eye. David Lehman. AAN

Having No Ear. Donald Davie. AMV-81

Having no past, I invent one. Album. Carol Papenhausen. AMV-81

Having produced lizards eighty feet long. Our Hero. John Frederick Nims. FoP

Having put yourself on the way. Spirits, Dancing. Arthur Gregor. VGW

Having read and written myself almost to sleep, I stretch. Under the Sign of Moth. David Wagoner. AMV-81; PCho

Having so rich a treasury, so fine a hoard. The Daisy. Marya Zaturenska. LoAs

Having stood before the upraised wing of the male fruit fly. On Sunday, the Beginning of the Week, I Make a Religion. Albert Goldbarth. NVAP

Having this day my horse, my hand, my lance. Astrophel and Stella, XLI. Sir Philip Sidney. HAP; ILP (1975 ed.); PPoD

Having tried to use the/ witch cord. It Is Deep. Carolyn M. Rodgers. SA

Having used every subterfuge. A Renewal. James Merrill. CoPAm

Having written several poems which I will not publish. Baedeker for Metaphysicians. Brian Higgins. FaBoTw (1975 ed.)

Hawk, The. Robert Bloom. AATT

Hawk, The. W. B. Yeats. LFH; PoA

Hawk, A/ (I am a hawk). Memoir. David Schaff. MIT

Hawk and Rock. Tony Quagliano. PHC

Hawk and Snake. Leslie Silko. VoR

Hawk free of jess. Elegy for a Diver. Philip Booth. LiSp; SPo

Hawk has haven that is not of man, The. The Hawk. Robert Bloom. AATT

Hawk Is a Woman. Hildegarde Flanner. WPE

Hawk Nailed to a Barn Door. Peter Blue Cloud. VoR

Hawk Roosting. Ted Hughes. CMoP (1970 ed.); ExPo (1973 ed.); HAP; HeIP; ILP (1975 ed.); MPo; OxBTC; PB; PPP; PSN; UnPo (1976 ed.)

Hawk's Eyes. Yvor Winters. PoA

Hawk's sudden weight. Balances. Floyd C. Stuart. FAF

Hawk's Way. Ted Olson. HoPM (1975 ed.)

Haworth in May. Rowland Childe. PES

Hawthorn, The. *Unknown.* GBP; OxBM

Hawthorn Dyke. Swinburne. VLP

Hawthorn Hedge, The. Judith Wright. WPE

Hawthorn morning moving, The. Renewal by Her Element. Denis Devlin. CIP

Hawthorn White. Charles Causley. BuTh

Hawthorne. James Russell Lowell. *Fr.* A Fable for Critics. NOBA; TAP

Hawthorne Garland, A. Richard Harter Fogle. OBAL

Hay, ay, hay, ay. Now Is Yule Come. *Unknown.* OxBM

Hay Derrick. John S. Harris. MPA

Hay for the Horses. Gary Snyder. CNW; ConAP; CTBA; InPS; TVo; UsP

Hay, hay, by this day. A Schoolboy's Complaint. *Unknown.* OxBM

Hay Hotel, The. Oliver St. John Gogarty. BIrV

Haydon! forgive me that I cannot speak. To B. R. Haydon. Keats. MBPR

Haying. Heather Banks. PoUp

Hayle holy-land wherein our holy lord. Uppon the First Sight of New England, June 29, 1638. Thomas Tillam. GOA

Haymaking. Edward Thomas. PES

Hayseed, The. Arthur L. Kellog. FSW

Haystack, The. Andrew Young. POL

Haystack Calhoun. William Heath. AAN

Haystack in the Floods, The. William Morris. CABA (1972 ed.); EBEV; HAP; OAEL-2; OBP; PAIC; VLP

Hazard's friend Elliot is homosexual. Wholesome. William Meredith. TAP

Haze. Henry David Thoreau. *Fr.* A Week on the Concord and Merrimack Rivers. HeIP; PiAm
(Woof of the Sun, Ethereal Gauze.) ILP (1975 ed.); TAP

Haze, and out of it we appear. Eagle Squadron. Vern Rutsala. AMV-80

Haze, char, and the weather of All Souls'. In the Elegy Season. Richard Wilbur. InPK

Haze is on the lake, A; the dipping grasses. August, at an Upstairs Window. Harold McCurdy. AMV-80

Hazy day in Puerto Rico, A. The Last Flight of the Great Wallenda. Barbara Helfgott Hyett. AMV-80

He. Stanley Kunitz. VGW

He/ and she, A. A Pair. May Swenson. RFM

He/ might be plowing. Rowing in Turns. David Swanger. PCho

He accepts the circle, speech and so. Anne-Marie Albiach, *tr. fr. French by* Keith Waldrop. BoWoP

He adored the desk, its brown-oak inlaid with ebony. Geoffrey Hill. Mercian Hymns, X. HAP

He Aint Risen, Baby, cause He Aint Gone Nowhere. Horace Coleman. SES

He all that time among the sewers of Troy. Troy. Edwin Muir. CMoP (1970 ed.)

He and a gentle Pardoner rode together. Chaucer, *mod. version by* Nevill Coghill. *Fr.* The Canterbury Tales: Prologue. BiP

He angled the bright shield. Baroque Image. May Sarton. PPod

He appears from afar. To Wilt Chamberlain. Tom Meschery. SPo

He as O, A. E. E. Cummings. InPS

He asked me what was I fantasizing. Alta. MMD

He ate and drank the precious words. Emily Dickinson. PCOP

He awoke this morning from a strange dream. Chief Leschi of the Nisqually. Duane Niatum. CDW

He bare hym up, he bare hym down. Lully, Lulley, Lully, Lulley. *Unknown.* HAP

He blinks upon the hearth-rug. On a Cat, Ageing. Alexander Gray. MS

He boards the plane. The Hanged Man. Steve Toth. AcAn

He bowed to me when he brought the wine at Mass. For a Young Cistercian Monk. Jerome Kiely. IPM

He brings his ear on a plate. Parable of What You've Always Wanted to Come True. Robert Peters. PoW

He brought a light so she could see. Strains of Sight. Robert Duncan. CMoP (1970 ed.); ExPo (1973 ed.)

He brought our Saviour to the western side. Political Power. Milton. *Fr.* Paradise Regained, IV. SCP-1

He built right on the top of the land. Where She Was Not Born. Yvonne. CNA

He built the ranch house down a little draw. The Ranch in the Coulee. Gwendolen Haste. WPW

He cackled aloud at his mother's funeral. Grief. Emery E. George. AAN

He calls: no answer from his folks. The Carpenter's Real Anguish. Stephen Gardner. AMV-81

He came all so still. *Unknown.* PChr

He came apart in the open. Martin's Blues. Michael S. Harper. CNA; PoBA

He came back and shot. He shot him. When he came. Incident. Amiri Baraka. NoAM

He came down the old road. Ghost Boy. Mark Van Doren. SO

He came from Malta; and Eumelus says. The Maltese Dog. Tymnes, *tr. by* Edmund Blunden. ECBV; FaBoEE; GDP

He came in silver armor, trimmed with black. Sonnet. Gwendolyn B. Bennett. AmNP (1974 ed.); PoBA

He came into the world with showers Assuming the Name of Any Next Child. John Tagliabue. AMV-80

He came like ashes in the burnt leaf fall. Oh, Do You Know the Muffin Man? Richard Mathews. AATT

He came to his love's window at the dead of the night. The Little Drummer. *Unknown.* AmFP

He came to shut/ off the gas. Eichmann. Douglas Blazek. PoW

He came to this unknown town to regain his soul. The Visitor. Duane Niatum. UsP

He Came to Visit Me. Martin Seymour-Smith. FaBoTw (1975 ed.)

He came to Washington secure in tweeds. Curriculum Vitae: Incomplete. Elisavietta Ritchie. AATT

He carries shadows in his face like caves. On the Apparition of Oneself. William Burford. PoA

He chants a boy-chant. The Grace of Cynthia's Maidenhood. Vinnie-Marie D'Ambrosio. IHMS

He clasps the crag with crooked hands. The Eagle. Tennyson. CABA (1972 ed.); CTV; ExPo (1973 ed.); FF; HeIP; ILP (1975 ed.); InPK; IPWM; LFH; OAEL-2; OBP; PB; PoIA; PoPle; PPoe; SoSe; SS; UnPo (1976 ed.)

He climbs the stair. Waterchew! Gregory Corso. VGW

He collects used words. The Word Man. Larry Moffi. AMV-80

He comes from the house as lightning flickers in the sky. Love and Music. *Gond Oral Tradition, tr. by* V. Elwin *and* S. Hivale. WTO

He comes through the door. The Assassin's Fatal Error. Lawrence Raab. AmPA

He comes unknown and heard and stands there. Man into a Churchyard. Bernard Gutteridge. EAS

He Complains to Bishop Hartgar of Thirst. Sedulius Scottus. *See* Nunc Viridant Segetes.

He could hit a blade of grass with his spear. A Skilful Spearman! *Tr. fr. Hawaiian.* WTO

He could not breathe in a crowded place. The Pioneer. William B. Ruggles. ECBV

He could not fall so far. Somnambulist. J. R. Hervey. ATNZ

He could reduce all things to acts. Samuel Butler. *Fr.* Hudibras, I, 1. SCP-2

He counts his blessings who. Dustless Chalk. James Rankin. MIS

He Cracked a Word. Allen Curnow. ATNZ

He crawls to the edge of the foaming creek. Meeting the Mountains. Gary Snyder. NoAM; PiAm; TAP

He darkens the boxes of desired characteristics. The Lecturer Seeks a Wife. Gary Lawless. FAF

He debated whether. Arthur Ridgewood, M.D. Frank Marshall Davis. BPo

He did not come to woo U Nu. Just Dropped In. William Cole. POL

He did not wear his scarlet coat. The Ballad of Reading Gaol. Oscar Wilde. NOBE; OAEL-2

He diddled the ivory keys. Jim Dandy. M. L. Rosenthal. ExPo (1973 ed.)

He didn't know why he nursed the white man back to. Tonto. Ronald Koertge. GP

He died a year ago. Ghost. Patricia Beer. HeHu

He "Digesteth Harde Yron." Marianne Moore. CMoP (1970 ed.); NoAM

He dines alone surrounded by reflections. Witch Doctor. Robert Hayden. AmNP (1974 ed.); MAT; NoAM

He disagrees with Simone de Beauvoir. His Plans for Old Age. William Meredith. TAP

He disappeared in the dead of winter. In Memory of W. B. Yeats. W. H. Auden. CABA (1972 ed.); CMoP (1970 ed.); Epi; HAP; HeIP; HoPM (1975 ed.); ILP (1975 ed.); NIL; NoAM; NOBE; OAEL-2; OxBTC; PAIC; PPoe; PPP; TCP; TT; UnPo (1976 ed.); UsP; WIF

He discovers himself on an old airfield. The Old Pilot's Death. Donald Hall. MPo

He does not have the experiences. The Poster. Lynn Sukenick. AAN; RiTi

He does not think that I haunt here nightly. The Haunter. Thomas Hardy. LoAs; NOBE; PoPle

He doesn't like it, of course. His Body. Sandra McPherson. AmPA; CAAP; CNW; GP; PCho

He Done His Level Best. "Mark Twain." BPAW

He Don't Know the Inside Feel. Herbert R. Adams. MiP

He dreamt that he saw the buffalant. A Quadrupedremian Song. Tom Hood. FaBoNo

He drives onto the grassy shoulder and unfastens. Earth Walk. William Meredith. MAT; PPoD

He drives up shadowed in insect wings. Visit. Eve Shelnutt. TC

He dropped the flannel sleeve. Death of an Average Man. Alison Wyrley Birch. PPM

He drowsed and was aware of silence heaped. The Death-Bed. Siegfried Sassoon. PoPle

He dwelt among "Apartments let." Jacob. Phoebe Cary. OBAL

He eats of the fruits of the great Speckle. Real Life. Ted Berrigan. NoAM

He ended; and midst those who heard were some. March. William Morris. *Fr.* The Earthly Paradise. VLP

He ended; and thus Adam last replied. Milton. *Fr.* Paradise Lost, XII. HeIP

He ended, nor the Argicide refus'd. Homer, *tr. by* William Cowper. *Fr.* The Odyssey, V. OBVE

He erupts from our soil: a grenade. Quaker Hero, Burning. Bink Noll. TCP

He examined the length of his thin body. The Twelve Hotels. George MacBeth. TwMBP

He Faces the Second Winter. Philip Levine. *Fr.* Sierra Kid. PoA

He Fell among Thieves. Sir Henry Newbolt. FaPoR; OxBTC

He fell and was drowned too far. Mastodon. Charles O. Hartman. AAN

He fell in a sweeping arc. Malfunction. Richard E. Albert. MiP

He felt the wild beast in him betweenwhiles. Modern Love, IX. George Meredith. LoAs

He first deceased; she for a little tried. Upon the Death of Sir Albert Morton's Wife. Sir Henry Wotton. BoLoP; FaBoEE; PoPle; PPM; WeW

He Fishes with His Father's Ghost. Lewis Nordan. AMV-81

He flew off to the bottom of the river. The Day It Was Night. Robert Desnos, *tr. by* John Frederick Nims. WeW

He floats a burnt auburn blur. The Animal. Allan Block. FAF

He floats down the Seine. Body Fished from the Seine. Gregory Corso. GP

He followed me up and he followed me down. Lady Isabel and the Elf Knight (Pretty Polly). *Unknown.* AmFP

He found a formula for drawing comic rabbits. Epitaph on an Unfortunate Artist. Robert Graves. FaBoEE; NOBL

He found a rope and picked it up. Epitaph for a Horse Thief. *Unknown.* ECBV

He found her by the ocean's moaning verge. Modern Love, XLIX. George Meredith. LoAS; OAEL-2; PAIC; VPC

He from the wind-bitten North with ship and companions descended. A Drifter off Tarentum. Kipling. *Fr.* Epitaphs of the War. FaBoEE; PoPle

He gave her some kind of elixir. A Mean Trick. *Unknown.* TDH

He gave himself another year. Patrick Kavanagh. *Fr.* The Great Hunger. BIrV

He gave his strength and his loveliness for his country. On a Soldier Killed in the Great War. R. Williams Parry, *tr. by* H. Idris Bell. OBW

He gave the solid rail a hateful kick. The Egg and the Machine. Robert Frost. CABA (1972 ed.)

He gets here and we drink and smoke. Paul. Dennis Saleh. CPA

He gets himself, after a long campaign. The Bureaucrat. Arthur J. Bull. HeHu

He grew up in a bathrobe. Shock. Billy Collins. AAN

He grunted god-i-love-you in. Holy Roller. Harriette Frances. PoW

He had a name. Generations 1. Sam Cornish. NVAP

He had been coming a very long time. For Malcolm Who Walks in the Eyes of Our Children. Quincy Troupe. CNA; PoBA

He had been falling in the abyss some four thousand years. Et Nox Facta Est. Victor Hugo, *tr. by* Mary Ann Caws. NAWM-2

He had driven half the night. Hay for the Horses. Gary Snyder. CNW; ConAP; CTBA; InPS; TVo; UsP

He had got, finally. A Poem for Speculative Hipsters. Amiri Baraka. NoAM; NOBA

He had habits, my grandfather. Zeyde. Roberta Metz. AMV-81

He had hitched a chicken to a cart. The Prophylactic. Russell Edson. GP

He had lived a long time. The Old Man and the Sun. Vicente Aleixandre. EC

He had need of a way. Being Somebody. Edwin Honig. TAP

He had no friend. About to Die. *Gond Oral Tradition, tr. by* V. Elwin *and* S. Hivale. WTO

He had no past and he certainly. Pity Ascending with the Fog. James Tate. NoAM

He had red hair. A Boy Thirteen. Jeff Irish. DL

He had smiled at us. Maximus, to Gloucester, Letter 19. Charles Olson. CMoP (1970 ed.); PAIC

He had to learn the way a staircase. The Child. Lawrence Russ. TC

He hands/ down the gift. The Gift. Robert Creeley. NOBA

He has annihilated the enemies! War Song. *Zulu Oral Tradition, tr. by* D. K. Rycroft. WTO

He has been walking toward me for a thousand miles. The Mailman. Thomas Brush. NVAP

He has been washed and locked in. Someone Gone Away Downstairs. Jeanette Nichols. RiTi

He has finished a day's work. The Pornographer. Robert Hass. CAAP

He has forgone the razor for a year. Fashionable Poet Reading. Tony Connor. PPoD

He has gone. Last Journey. Enrique Gonzales Martinez, *tr. by* Samuel Beckett. PBMP

He has hanged himself—the Sun. November. F. W. Harvey. OxBTC

He has never heard of tides. German Shepherd. Myra Cohn Livingston. RFM

He has not woo'd, but he has lost his heart. A Country Dance. Charles Tennyson Turner. VLP; VPC

He has only to pass by a tree moodily walking head down. The Fiend. James Dickey. CoPAm; PPP

He has the full moon on his breast. The Smoker Parrot. John Shaw Neilson. MAuV

He has the sign. Portrait of Malcolm X. Etheridge Knight. CNA; PoBA

He has the watery desire. Portrait of a False Revolutionist. Isidor Schneider. SPT

He hasn't gone to work. The Poem Circling Hamtramck, Michigan All Night in Search of You. Philip Levine. NNaP

He hated them all one by one but wanted to show them. A Teacher. Reed Whittemore. NCSH; TPo

He Hears the Cry of the Sedge. W. B. Yeats. OxBTC (Aedh Hears the Cry of the Sedge.) VLP

He hears the summer at a distance. Vanishing Point. Peter Cooley. AmPA

He Held Radical Light. A. R. Ammons. NoAM

He held the world upon his nose. Wallace Stevens. *Fr.* The Man with the Blue Guitar. TT

He Hides within the Lily, *with music.* William Channing Gannett. AH

He hie fie finger. The Man. Robert Creeley. OBAL

He hovers at the back door. The Real Muse. Fred Muratori. AMV-81

He hunches into his fur coat. Wolf Dream. Edward Lense. AMV-81

He imagines her. The Modes of Vallejo Street, San Diego, Los Angeles, 3. Hugh Seidman. UnPo (1976 ed.)

He insisted/ on being laid down/ in the foothills.  Lee Mallory. CPA

He invented a rainbow but lightning struck it.  Bushed.  Earle Birney.  MPA

He is a sort of god.  A Snowman in March.  Paul Ramsey.  CSP

He is a tower unleaning. But how will he not break.  Vaunting Oak.  John Crowe Ransom.  VGW

He is all male.  The Defiant One.  Alice Morrey Bailey. AMV-80

He is always right.  The Interrogator.  Elizabeth Jennings.  WPE

He is an Englishman!  The Englishman.  W. S. Gilbert.  NOBL

He is as salt.  Salt.  Lucille Clifton.  GP

He is crying there near the toilet.  Outburst from a Little Face. John Woods.  GP

He is dead, the beautiful youth.  Killed at the Ford.  Longfellow. ILP (1975 ed.)

He is earthed to his girl, one hand fastened.  In the Aran Islands. Derek Mahon.  IPM

He Is Far.  *Unknown.*  OAEL-1; OxBM

He is found with the homeless dogs.  Kid.  Robert Hayden. NCSH

He is green-booting his way through darkness.  Jack Hope. Roger McDonald.  FPA

He is in his room sulked shut. The small.  Boy.  John Ciardi. SFF

He is leading his grandfather under the sun to market.  Niño Leading an Old Man to Market.  Leonard Nathan.  CTBA; NCSH; TVo

He is mad. He is filthy.  Jonah: A Report.  David R. Slavitt. CoPAm

He is making love with his wife on the roof.  The Roof of the World.  Michael Dennis Browne.  AmPA

He is more than a hero.  Sappho, *tr. fr. Greek by* Mary Barnard. PBWP

He is murdered upright in the day.  Vaticide.  Myron O'Higgins. PoBA

He is my God, who maketh all things perfect.  Whatsoever Hath Been Made, God Made.  Dadu.  ILwL

He is my love/ my sweet nutgrove.  *Unknown, tr. fr. Irish by* Michael Hartnett.  BirV

He is no one I really know.  Piccola Commedia.  Richard Wilbur.  FoP; GP

He is not dead, this friend, not dead.  Resurgence.  Robert Louis Stevenson.  PPM

He is not ded that somtyme hath a fall.  Sir Thomas Wyatt. AAS; OBVE

He is not here, the old sun.  No Possum, No Sop, No Taters. Wallace Stevens.  TAP; VGW

He is not John the gardener.  A Friend in the Garden.  Juliana Horatia Ewing.  OxBChV

He is older than the naval side of British history.  Chief Petty Officer.  Charles Causley.  OxBTC

He is patient.  Obatala, the Creator.  *Yoruba Oral Tradition, tr. by* Ulli Beier.  WTO

He is quick, thinking in clear images.  In Broken Images.  Robert Graves.  PPoe

He is stark mad, who ever says.  The Broken Heart.  John Donne.  EBEV; ILP (1975 ed.)

He is that fallen lance that lies as hurled.  The Soldier.  Robert Frost.  ILP (1975 ed.); OFD; WeW

He is the bow, firm.  Telemachus and the Bow.  Randall Colaizzi. AMV-81

He is the pond's old father, its brain.  The Snapper.  William Heyen.  AmPA

He is the primal rock. Gray, wise, and old.  Nation.  Mendel Naigreshel, *tr. by* Joachim Neugroschel.  VWA

He is the victim whom the lean predict.  Die Bauernhochzeit. Kendrick Smithyman.  ATNZ

He is to weet a melancholy carle.  Character of Charles Brown. Keats.  MBPR

He is trying to think.  Teechur.  Dick Higgins.  MiP

He is very busy with his looking.  Young Heroes.  Gwendolyn Brooks.  BPo

He is walking along in his mind.  Avenue.  Dennis Trudell. AAN

He is walking in the road.  A Conceited Man.  *Gond Oral Tradition, tr. by* V. Elwin *and* S. Hivale.  WTO

He is wasted now.  Dylan, Who Is Dead.  Samuel Allen.  PoBA

He jumped me while I was asleep.  Assailant.  John Raven.  BPo

He jumped, seeing an island like a hand.  Hart Crane.  Julian Symons.  PoA

He killed his wife at night.  Wife Killer.  Vernon Scannell. HeHu

"He Killed Many of My Men."  John Bennett.  BuTh

He [*or* When he] killed the [noble] Mudjokivis.  The Modern Hiawatha.  George A. Strong.  AKE; ECBV; FaBoCo; SpRo

He knows he must explain this.  The Modes of Vallejo Street, San Diego, Los Angeles, 9.  Hugh Seidman.  UnPo (1976 ed.)

He knows me before I come.  Dreaming the Ancestors.  Skaidrite Stelzer.  TC

He labors.  For Ron Tanaka at Stanford.  Wendy Rose.  NW

He larved ond he larved on he merd such a nauses.  The Ondt and the Gracehoper.  James Joyce.  *Fr.* Finnegans Wake. BIrV

He lay upon his dying bed.  The Sword of Bunker Hill.  William Ross Wallace.  BTTM

He Leadeth Me, *with music.*  Joseph H. Gilmore.  AH; BLSH

He leaned.  Treaty-trip from Shulus Reservation.  Patrick Lane. NeAC

He leaped. With none to hinder.  Empedocles.  George Meredith. VLP

He led his five senses into dreams.  When Father Slept.  James Anderson.  AMV-80

He left his pants upon a chair.  Epigram: The Mistake. Theodore Roethke.  NIL

He left the kitchen.  Dory Miller.  Sam Cornish.  CNA

He Left the Pine Ridge Reservation.  Carol Cox.  MMD

He lies/ Beside me.  On Death and Love.  Janet Campbell Hale. VoR

He lies in state.  Dirge.  Austin Clarke.  CIP

He lifted up, among the actuaries.  So Long? Stevens.  John Berryman  *Fr.* Dream Songs.  HAP; NOBA

He lifts his hopeful eyes at each new tread.  Lost Dog.  Frances Rodman.  GDP

He Liked the Dead.  Malcolm Lowry.  OxBTC

He lists them.  Yahrzeit.  Dan Jaffe.  VWA

He Lived amidst th' Untrodden Ways.  Hartley Coleridge. FaBoCo; PoIA
(Wordsworth Unvisited.)  NOBL

He lived apart, sometimes in a cave in the mountains.  Shaman. Will Inman.  GP

He lived at Dingle Bank—he did.  Dingle Bank.  Edward Lear. FaBoNo

He lives among a dog.  The Child.  Donald Hall.  NCSH

He lives in the outer land.  Blood Marksman and Kureldei the Marksman.  *Tatar (Turkic) Oral Tradition, tr. fr. German and Russian versions by* Norman Cohn.  WTO

He lives near a grain elevator, farms.  The City Boy.  Stephen Dunn.  HeS

He lives out.  The Giant Squid of Tsurai.  Kirk Robertson.  GP

He lives unsociable, aloof.  The Liftman.  H. A. C. Evans.  POL

He lives, who last night flopped from a log.  Burning.  Galway Kinnell.  CoPAm

He looked and saw a spacious plain, whereon. Vision of the Future; the Flood. Milton. *Fr.* Paradise Lost, XI. SCP-1

He looks like a fat little old man. Dead Seal. A. W. Purdy. NoAM

He looks out the window. In Flight. Patrick Smith. MIT

He loved her and she loved him. Lovesong. Ted Hughes. OBP

He loved her, and through many years. Then and Now. Paul Laurence Dunbar. PBMP

He loved the brook's soft sound. The Peasant Poet. John Clare. OAEL-2

He loved three things in life. Anna Akhmatova, *tr. fr. Russian by* Barbara Einzig. BoWoP

He lumbers from the bed like a. The Great Poet. Linda King. GP

He made his master to cutte his hore. Ipomadon Plays the Fool at Court. *Unknown. Fr.* Ipomadon. OxBM

He Makes a House Call. John Stone. CSP

He May Be Envied, Who with Tranquil Breast. Charlotte Smith. SBG

He met a lady. From the Hazel Bough. Earle Birney. HeIP

He motions me over with a question. Kidnaper. Tess Gallagher. AmPA

He moved among blocked facades. Yiddish Poet. A. C. Jacobs. VWA

He must be coyote. Lame Deer. Joy Harjo. SA

He Must Be Fat. Faye Kicknosway. TC

He never acted well by man or woman. George IV. Thackeray. *Fr.* The Georges. FaBoEE

He Never Expected Much. Thomas Hardy. NoAM; OxBTC

He never felt twice the same about the flecked river. This Solitude of Cataracts. Wallace Stevens. PiAm

He never made the dive—not while I watched. The Springboard. Louis MacNeice. PoA

He never spoke a word to me. Simon the Cyrenian Speaks. Countee Cullen. AmNP (1974 ed.); BPo; HAP

He never talk enough. Blues for a Cello Man. Carol Bergé. MMD

He observes. He has a great black notebook. The Observer. David C. Yates. AMV-81

He, of that greater dread. Dog Talk. Albert De Pietro. AATT

He once did love with fond affection. Forsaken. *Unknown.* AmFP

He outstripped Time with but a bout. Emily Dickinson. PiAm

He owns no car. Drum Songs. Joseph Bruchac. TSWA

He Paid Me Seven. *Unknown.* BPo

He passed by with another. Ballad. Gabriela Mistral, *tr. by* Doris Dana. OLR

He paused on the sill of a door ajar. The Newcomer's Wife. Thomas Hardy. BoLoP; OxBTC

He picks up what he thinks is. My Father: October 1942. William Stafford. CoPAm

He placed the medicine. Wrong Kind of Love. Ray A. Young Bear. VW

He places his hand on her head as a hand placed against pain. Rain. Haim Guri, *tr. by* Mark Elliott Shapiro. VWA

He planked down sixpence and he took his drink. Henry Turnbull. W. W. Gibson. FaBoTw (1975 ed.)

He played by the river when he was young. Washington. Nancy Byrd Turner. CTV; ECBV

He posed her, naked. The Photographer's Wife. Janet Beeler. AMV-81

He praises me, and I praise Him. Ibn al-Arabi, *tr. fr. Arabic.* ILwL

He Praises the Trees. *Unknown, tr. fr. Irish by* Robin Skelton. BIrV

He prayeth best, who loveth best. Samuel Taylor Coleridge. *Fr.* The Rime of the Ancient Mariner. CTV

He preached upon "breadth" till it argued him narrow. Emily Dickinson. CABA (1972 ed.); PAIC; PPoD

He preaches to the crowd that power is lent. Vox Populi. Dryden. *Fr.* The Medal. NOBE; UsP

He preferr'd Hanover to England. George I—Star of Brunswick. Thackeray. *Fr.* The Georges. FaBoEE

He promised to meet me at Linstead Market. Linstead Market. *Unknown.* FSW

He proposed to me on the Ferris wheel. Arches and Shadows. Annie Dillard. CTBA

He pushes behind the words. Waiting. Robert Creeley. VGW

He put his acorn helmet on. A Fairy in Armor. Joseph Rodman Drake. *Fr.* The Culprit Fay. PCOP

He Puts Me to Rest. David Ignatow. VGW

He Raise a Poor Lazarus, *with music. Unknown.* AH

He raised his trombone. The Jazzman. Edelin Coleman Fields. PoUp

He ran in the living air. Laotian Peasant Shot. George Bruce. MS

He ran the course and as he ran he grew. Innocence. Thom Gunn. NoAM; TPo

He rang me up/ In a dream. A Dream of Hanging. Patricia Beer. HeHu; MPo

He received from some thoughtful relations. The Pleasing Gift. *Unknown.* TDH

He Records a Little Song for a Smoking Girl. James Whitehead. GP

He Resigns. John Berryman. PSN; WeW

He roars in the swamp. The Alligator. Beatrice Ravenel. WPE

He rocked the boat. Ezra Shank. *Unknown.* CaYB

He rode forth armed: breast-plate and crest. A Romance. Chester Kallman. PoA

He rose at dawn and, fired with hope. The Sailor Boy. Tennyson. AIW

He rose up on his dying bed. Hope. Langston Hughes. OBAL

He runs before the wise men: he. He. Stanley Kunitz. VGW

He runs like a mad rat seeking. Mazeworks. Elías Hruska Cortés. CPA

He Said. Jean Valentine. TAP

He said:/ "Let's stay here." Party Piece. Brian Patten. BoLoP

He said an old poet, meaning himself. Testing Ground. Karla M. Hammond. AMV-81

He said everything is a struggle. The Augur. Stephen Tudor. HeS

He said he would be back and we'd drink wine together. Waiting for Icarus. Muriel Rukeyser. NNaP

He said he would only kill. Two Byzantine Pieces. Rodney Hall. FPA

He said, I want to be wrapped. Warrior Dreams. Ray A. Young Bear. VW

He Said, Lying There. Alta. GP

He said this/ he said that. Your Friend. Anselm Hollo. TwMBP

He Said To. Marvin Bell. PCho

He said to Patancala Kapya and to the students. *Tr. by* Raimundo Panikkar. *Fr.* Upanishads. ILwL

He said to them, Look at this: you see. The Tall Wind. K. O. Arvidson. ATNZ

He said, unreal the buffalo is standing. Unreal the Buffalo Is Standing. *Unknown.* GOA

He sang of God, the mighty source. David before Saul. Christopher Smart. *Fr.* The Song of David. PIM

He sang of life, serenely sweet. The Poet. Paul Laurence Dunbar. BPo

He sat at the foot of my bed. Father and Son. Ronald Wallace. AMV-81

He sat in a wheeled chair, waiting for dark. Disabled. Wilfred Owen. BiP; CMoP (1970 ed.); FF; InPS; NoAM; OBW; OxBTC; PoTa; PSN; VoPo

He sat in his cell staring. The Baboon. Rhydwen Williams, *tr. by* R. Gerallt Jones. OBW

He sat on a boulder, his miniature. The Lizard. Ruth Lechlitner. AMV–81

He sat upon the rolling deck. Sailor. Langston Hughes. ECBV; PoA

He saw, abandoned to the sand. The Trail beside the River Platte. William Heyen. GOA

He saw her from the bottom of the stairs. Home Burial. Robert Frost. PiAm; SoS; STS; TAP

He saw my/ picture in a/ magazine. Tentacles, Leaves. Lyn Lifshin. RiTi

He saw the gas bubbles. Above the Moving River. David Kherdian. VoA

He saw the grey on black, and that. Rothko. James Moore. AMV–81

He says he wrote by moonlight. Katharyn Machan Aal. AMV–81

He says, "My reign is peace," so slays. A Foreign Ruler. Walter Savage Landor. OBSV

He scans a nocturnal acre for prey. Nightwatchman. Robert Morgan. HeHu

He scarce had ceased when the superior Fiend. Satan and the Fallen Angels. Milton. *Fr.* Paradise Lost, I. SCP-1

He scorned his land, his tongue denied. Dic Siôn Dafydd. Thomas Jacob Thomas, *tr. by* H. Idris Bell. OBW

He sd please/ take it. Here. J. D. Whitney. NVAP

He Sees by His Outfit. Henry Taylor. *Fr.* Desperado. PoUp

He sees the heat give a surge under its tight canopy. The Starer. Rhyll McMaster. CAAP

He sees the ocean. For the Waiter at Jhonny Pavlovs. Luís Omar Salinas. SA

He Sees through Stone. Etheridge Knight. ConAP; NNaP; PoBA

He sells door to door. Salesman. Ruth Roston. AMV–80

He served his God so faithfully and well. On a Puritan. Hilaire Belloc. FaBoEE

He served his master well from youth to age. Old Stephen. Charles Tennyson Turner. VPC

He set out and kept hunting. The Hunter. Frank O'Hara. NNaP

He set two fossil fish/ into the wall. Fish. Edward Gold. PoUp

He shall not hear the bittern cry. Lament for Thomas MacDonagh. Frances Ledwidge. BIrV

He She Because How. Anselm Hollo. TwMBP

He shuddered briefly and stared down the long valley. The Return of Robinson Jeffers. Robert Hass. AmPA

He shudders . . . feeling on the shaven spot. Electrocution. Lola Ridge. WPE

He sings from the bottom of a well but she can hear him up. Jim Harrison. *Fr.* Ghazals. NoAM

He sings in the courtyard, snuggling in his tatters. Jewboy. Julian Tuwim, *tr. by* Isaac Komem. VWA

He sipped at a weak hock and seltzer. The Arrest of Oscar Wilde at the Cadogan Hotel. John Betjeman. AIW; CMoP (1970 ed.); EBEV; ILP (1975 ed.); NoAM; OxBTC

He sits/ among his drums. A Portrait of Rudy. James Cunningham. CNA

He sits at the bar in the Alhambra. Simple. Naomi Long Madgett. FB; PoBA

He sits in a deckchair reading Colette. Villa Thermidor. George Hitchcock. GP

He sits in the chair and does not move. Medicine. Louis Jenkins. HeS

He sleeps in the next room. Nightwalker. Delia Chilgren. NPW

He sleeps on the top of a mast. The Unbeliever. Elizabeth Bishop. NoAM

He slid out of the skin, leaving it. Summer. Diane Wakoski. IPWM; VGW

He slides the cut paper out. The Paper Cutter. David Ignatow. CTBA

He slowly paced his distance off, and turned. The High Jump. *Unknown.* LiSp; SPo

He Smelt the Smell of Death within the Marrow. Louis Johnson. ATNZ

He snuggles his fingers. After Winter. Sterling A. Brown. PoBA

He spake no dream, for as his words had end. Temptation of the Magic Banquet. Milton. *Fr.* Paradise Regained, II. SCP-1

He Spends Time in Southern California. Jonathan Cott. RRA

He spent his childhood hours in a den. The Dreamer. William Childress. SoS

He squats there stolid, brown, and small. Toad School. Merle Meeter. AATT

He stands before the mirror, trying clothes. He Sees by His Outfit. Henry Taylor. *Fr.* Desperado. PoUp

He stared at ruin. Ruin stared straight back. John Berryman. *Fr.* Dream Songs. CAPP

He stares upward at a monstrous face. The Pieta, Rhenish, 14th C., The Cloisters. Mona Van Duyn. Prf

He startles awake. His eyes are full of white light. The Hermit Wakes to Bird Sounds. Maxine W. Kumin. WeW

He stayed, and was imprisoned in possession. Sonnets from China, IV. W. H. Auden. CMoP (1970 ed.)

He steps down from the dark train, blinking; stares. Ten Days Leave. W. D. Snodgrass. UnPo (1976 ed.)

He stood among a crowd at Drumahair. The Man Who Dreamed of Faeryland. W. B. Yeats. CMoP (1970 ed.); NoAM; PoPle

He stood, and heard the steeple. Eight o'Clock. A. E. Housman. CABA (1972 ed.); CMoP (1970 ed.); ExPo (1973 ed.); ILP (1975 ed.); InPK; IP; NoAM; SoSe (1977 ed.)

He stood at the window. Birth of a Poet. Robert Morgan. HeHu

He stood still by her bed. The Goodnight. Louis Simpson. MPo; PBMP; SoSe (1977 ed.)

He stoops down, and crawls on hands and knees. Soil Searcher. J. Joyce. CTBA

He stopped on the irreproachable sidewalk. Elysee. Larry Eigner. VGW

He strides across the grassy corn. The Scarecrow. Andrew Young. FaBoTw (1975 ed.)

He stumbled from the night. Miracle Cure. Edward Lowbury. PMW

He swings down like the flourish of a pen. Skier. Robert Francis. LiSp; NCSH; RFM

He takes the long review of things. To a Certain Most Certainly Certain Critic. David McCord. OBAL

He talked, and as he talked. The Story-Teller. Mark Van Doren. CTBA; ECBV; TH

He talked of Delhi brothels half the night. Long Tom. W. W. Gibson. OxBTC

He talks and talks. Like Ripples on the Water. *Gond Oral Tradition, tr. by* V. Elwin *and* S. Hivale. WTO

He taught Math at the Ecole Centrale. Salomon. Pierre Morhange, *tr. by* Edouard Roditi. VWA

He tells many bad things. Young Training. Lawrence McGaugh. PoBA

He tells us that. Haiku. Louis Cuneo. CPA

He tended his flock. The Village Doctor. Margaret Gillies. PMW

He that had come that morning. Ballad of John Cable and Three Gentlemen. W. S. Merwin. NOBA

He that hath no mistress, must not wear a favour. *Unknown.* GBL

He that hath set his headlong heart. Boethius, *tr. by* Helen Waddell. *Fr.* The Consolation of Philosophy. NAWM-1

He that is down needs fear no fall. The Shepherd Boy Sings in the Valley of Humiliation. Bunyan. *Fr.* The Pilgrim's Progress. EBEV; NOBE

He That Loves a Rosy Cheek. Thomas Carew. *See* Disdain Returned.

He That Ne'er Learns His ABC. *Unknown.* GBP

He That Never Read a Line. *Unknown, tr. fr. Old Irish by* Robin Flower. PFIr

He that will not love must be. Not to Love. Robert Herrick. CaPo

He, the indiscreet agent. Doves. Joachim Neugroschel. VWA

He Thinks of Those Who Have Spoken Evil of His Beloved. W. B. Yeats. *See* Aedh Thinks of Those Who Have Spoken Evil of His Beloved.

He thought he kept the universe alone. The Most of It. Robert Frost. BiP; CABA (1972 ed.); HAP; NU; PiAm; PPoe

He thought he saw a banker's clerk. The Gardener's Song. "Lewis Carroll." *Fr.* Sylvie and Bruno. BBL

He thought he saw an Elephant. The Mad Gardener's Song. "Lewis Carroll." *Fr.* Sylvie and Bruno. FaBoCo; FaBoNo; OxBChV; PBMP

He thought if he could surround himself with quotations. That Man in Manhattan. Shannon Keith Kelley. AMV-80

He thrust his joy against the weight of the sea. The Surfer. Judith Wright. WPE

He Told Me His Name Was Sitting Bull. Joy Harjo. TAT

He told me I drive. Soursobs. Richard Tipping. CAAP

He told me, you'll end up. Marriage. Marea Gordett. AMV-81

He told the barmaid he had things to do. Dodona's Oaks Were Still. Patrick MacDonogh. PFIr

He Took Her. Tom Masson. OBAL

He took the great bunch of letters and kissed it! To the Postmaster General. Peter Redgrove. AMV-81

He tries to forget the crash, to erase a moment. A Phantom Limb. Edward Lowbury. PMW

He turns his truck on its side. Long Lonely Lover of the Highway. Frederic Will. AMV-81

He turns to you, measly immortal page. Page. Sandra McPherson. PoA

He Understands the Great Cruelty of Death. Petrarch, *prose tr. fr. Italian by* J. M. Synge. Sonnets to Laura: To Laura in Death, XLVII. BIrV

He unto whom thou art so partial. Martial, *tr. fr. Latin by* Byron. FaBoEE; NIL; OBVE

He used to come here till he donned gold braid. To a Tyrant. Joseph Brodsky, *tr. by* Alan Myers. VWA

He usually managed to be there when. Because He Liked to Be at Home. Kenneth Patchen. CoPAm

He waits perpetually crouched, teeth. Mean Rufus Throw-Down. David Smith. NVAP

He Wakes Again in Early Light. William Kistler. TVo

He wakes in a new world and wears new eyes. Reformed Drunkard. Vernon Scannell. AMV-80

He wakes to a confused dream of boats, gulls. Murphy in Manchester. John Montague. PFIr

He walks on rubber knees. Oh Lord! Tarzan, Old. Allan Block. FAF

He walks with shopping basket, and an air. Halfwit. Basil Dowling. ATNZ

He wanted/ a pickup truck. Julio. Kell Robertson. TAT

He wanted to pat. A Kind of Love. Jeanette Nichols. RiTi

He Was. Richard Wilbur. NCSH; SS

He was a big man, says the size of his shoes. Abandoned Farmhouse. Ted Kooser. GP

He Was a Friend of Mine. *Unknown.* FSW

He was a gash an' faithful tyke. Luath. Burns. GDP

He was a man and a friend always. My Ramblin' Boy. Tom Paxton. FSW

He was a mighty hunter in his youth. The White Cat of Trenarren. A. L. Rowse. OxBTC; PCat

He was a plain man. Royalty. Luci Shaw. AATT

He was a rat and she was a rat. The Two Rats [*or* What Became of Them?]. *Unknown.* ECBV; OxBChV; PoPle

He was a reprobate I grant. The Deceased. Keith Douglas. FaBoTw (1975 ed.)

He was at Naples writing letters home. Esthétique du Mal. Wallace Stevens. CMoP (1970 ed.); NOBA

He was born as little children are. He Was One of Us. Helen Steiner Rice. CTV

He was born in Alabama. Of De Witt Williams on His Way to Lincoln Cemetery. Gwendolyn Brooks. ANTL; CAPP; NoAM; NOBA

He was born in Deutschland, as you would suspect. The Progress of Faust. Karl Shapiro. ILP (1975 ed.)

He Was Formidable. Robert Penn Warren. LiSp

He was found by the Bureau of Statistics to be. The Unknown Citizen. W. H. Auden. BiP; BuTh; CABA (1972 ed.); FF; HeIP; InPK; IPWM; LP; NIL; NOBL; OBSV; PAIC; PoIA; PPoD; SFF; SoS; SoSe; UnPo (1976 ed.); WIF

He was impoverished, possessing a full island. Castaway. John Nerber. PoA

He was in logick a great critick. Sir Hudibras, His Passing Worth. Samuel Butler. *Fr.* Hudibras, 1. FaBoCo

He was just a young aviator. Lindbergh. *Unknown.* AmFP

He was just back. Vietnam. Clarence Major. PoBA

He was lodging above in Coom. The 'Mergency Man. J. M. Synge. PoPle

He was lost!—not a shade of doubt of that. Little Lost Pup. Arthur Guiterman. CTV

He Was Made Man. Giles Fletcher the Younger. *Fr.* Christ's Victory and Triumph, I. BoReV

He was not bad, as emperors go, not really. Two Pieces after Suetonius. Robert Penn Warren. NOBA

He was once a tiny, helpless thing. Aaron Nicholas, Almost Ten. Janet Campbell Hale. VoR

He Was One of Us. Helen Steiner Rice. CTV

He was one who followed. Sailor Man. H. Sewell Bailey. RhR

He was only a lavender cowboy. The Lavender Cowboy. Harold Hersey. BPAW; FSW

He was picking coal from a tip. Free Coal. Robert Morgan. HeHu

He was protuberant behind, before. Johnson on Pope. David Ferry. NIL

He was reading late, at Richard's, down in Maine. Henry's Understanding. John Berryman. NoAM; NOBA

He was really her favorite. In Spite of His Dangling Pronoun. Lyn Lifshin. IHMS; Psy

He was so compounded. Remembering Him. Joe Reccardi. AMV-80

He was such a curious lover of shells. Full Fathom Five. A. R. D. Fairburn. ATNZ

He was the artist who drew in chalk. Homage to a Homosexual. Leon Slade. FPA

He was the best postilion. The Postilion Has Been Struck by Lightning. Patricia Beer. HeHu

He was the doctor up to Combe. Coroner's Jury. L. A. G. Strong. OxBTC

He was the last. Truly the last. The Butterfly. Pavel Friedmann, *tr. by* Dennis Silk. VWA

He was the only one of us. The Governor of Ollie Street. Ahmos Zu-Bolton. AAN

He was their servant (some say he was blind). Sonnets from China, VII. W. H. Auden. CMoP (1970 ed.)

He was weak, and I was strong—then. Emily Dickinson. PeD

He wasn't my grandpa but we. Grandpa Bear. Susan Eisenberg. AMV-81

He watched the stars and noted birds in flight. Sonnets from China, VI. W. H. Auden. CMoP (1970 ed.)

He watched with all his organs of concern. Poem. W. H. Auden. PoA

He watered the roses. Theodore Roethke. *Fr.* Where Knock Is Open Wide. OSP

He wears a beard to let us see that he is pure within. Sanctimony. *Malay Oral Tradition, tr. by* R. J. Wilkinson. WTO

He wears striped jim-jam pyjamas. Jim-Jam Pyjamas. Gina Wilson. DuDr

He went down to the woodshed. No One Heard Him Call. Dorothy Aldis. CaYB

He went into a grey day. For One Who Died Young. H. R. Hays. EAS

He went out/ the snow was hard packed. And Our Gifts to the Seasons. Thomas Clark. SLP

He went to fix the awning. Fixer of Midnight. Reuel Denney. OBAL

He went to the wood and caught it. Riddle. *Unknown.* GBP

He which hath no stomach to this fight. King Henry the Fifth before Agincourt. Shakespeare. *Fr.* King Henry V. BTTM

He whittled scallops for a hardy thatch. The Thatcher. Brendan Kennelly. CIP

He who becomes his contrary. Shekhina and the Kiddushim. Edouard Roditi. VWA

He who binds [*or* bends] to himself [*or* himself to] a joy. Eternity. Blake. *Fr.* Several Questions Answered. BoReV; EBEV; FaBoEE; LAuP; MBPR; NOBE; WIF

He who but yesterday would roam. Epitaph for a Sailor Buried Ashore. Sir Charles G. D. Roberts. RhR

He who could win the girl I love. A Girl's Hair. Dafydd ab Edmwnd, *tr. by* Gwyn Williams. OBW

He who crosses a park in great and flourishing Havana. Central Park *Some People (3 P.M.).* Nancy Morejón. PBWP

He who has made his reckoning with life. Boethius, *tr. by* Helen Waddell. *Fr.* The Consolation of Philosophy. NAWM-1

He who has lost soul's liberty. Soul's Liberty. Anna Wickham. PPM

He who has seen the wild tornado sweep. Isaac Clason. *Fr.* Don Juan. PeD

He who is my master. The "Word" of a Watch-Dog. Sandag, *tr. by* C. R. Bawden. WTO

He who knows not, and knows not that he knows not, is a fool. *Tr. fr. Persian.* CTV

He, who navigated with success. Death of a Young Son by Drowning. Margaret Atwood. BoWoP

He, who once was my brother, is dead by his own hand. Justice Is Reason Enough. Diane Wakoski. AmPA

He Who Remains. Richard Shelton. MPA

He who wants to hear good rhyme. Aucassin and Nicolette. *Unknown, tr. by* Edward Francis Moyer *and* Carey DeWitt Eldridge. NAWM-1

He who would valiant be. To Be a Pilgrim. Bunyan. *Fr.* The Pilgrim's Progress. FaPoR

He Whose Hand and Eye Are Gentle. *Unknown, tr. fr. Welsh by* Kenneth Jackson. OBW

He will have turned. Old Story. Lance Henson. VoR

He will just do nothing at all. Declaration of Independence. Wolcott Gibbs. SoS

He will know me when we meet, his blade. The Mugger. Robert Pack. GP

He will not see the East catch fire again. A Cock Crowing in a Poulterer's Shop. John Ferguson. BoAnP

He will watch the hawk with an indifferent eye. Icarus. Stephen Spender. NoAM

He wings a slow and watched flight. The Vulture of the Plains. Hamlin Garland. BPAW

He Wishes for the Cloths of Heaven. W. B. Yeats. *See* Aedh Wishes for the Cloths of Heaven.

He with body waged a fight. The Four Ages of Man. W. B. Yeats. BoReV

He withdrew his hand slowly. Open Heart. Michael Salcman. AMV-80

He works/ stone to. Rock Painting. Carroll Arnett. VoR

He worshipped at the altar of Romance. An Epitaph. Colin Ellis. OxBTC

He would declare and could himself believe. Never Again Would Birds' Song Be the Same. Robert Frost. HAP; InPK; NIL; NoAM; VGW

He Would Have His Lady Sing. Digby Mackworth Dolben. EBEV

He would look at the stars. Mark Strand. FoP

He writes again. Friendship. Lucien Stryk. GP

He yelled at me in Greek. John Berryman. *Fr.* Dream Songs. PiAm

Head, The. Padraic Fallon. CIP

Head, A. James Schuyler. NoAM

Head. Richard Weber. IPM

Head Byzantine or from, The. Resting Figure. Denise Levertov. AnMo

Head: egg of all, The. Right Thinking Man. Marge Piercy. RiTi

Head Itself. Laura Riding. PoA

Head like a snake, a neck like a drake, A. How a Good Greyhound Is Shaped. *Unknown.* BoAnP

Head noddling over moist dreams. Bones Found in Chalk. Jim Farrar. DNGG

Head of the congregation here stands at the head, The. The Poem on the Jews. Avot Yeshurun, *tr. by* Harold Schimmel. VWA

Head or Tail, A—which does he lack? The Hippo. Theodore Roethke. VGW

Head pure, sinless quite of brain or soul, A. Burns. FaBoEE

Head thrust in as for the view, A. All Revelation. Robert Frost. CABA (1972 ed.);PiAm

Headland. Brewster Ghiselin. PoA

Headless fountains/ running loose. The Preponderance. William Meredith. PBMP

Headless squirrel, some blood, A. A Day Begins. Denise Levertov. AnMo; CoPAm

Headlights bounce off. The Black Bottom Bootlegger. Esther M. Leiper. TAT

Headlights fading out at dawn, The. A New Day. Philip Levine. MPA

Headlights show that the old, The. Fall Song. Daniel David Moses. AMV-81

Headline History. William Plomer. FaBoCo

Headlines. Foster Robertson. CPA

Headrock. Brian Coffey. CIP

Heads, impenetrable, The.  Oxen: Ploughing at Fiesole.  Charles Tomlinson.  OxBTC

Headstone, like a petrified congregation, The.  In the Old Jewish Cemetery, Prague, 1970.  Edward Lowbury.  VWA

Headstones are thin, The; the trees are thick.  The Cows near the Graveyard.  Howard Nelson.  NU

Healer walks with burning hands, The.  Deliverance.  Geoffrey Holloway.  PMW

Healing from the Beautyway Chant, The.  *Unknown, tr. fr. Navajo Indian.*  TVo

Healing of the Leper, The.  Vernon Watkins.  FaBoTw (1975 ed.)

Healing Song.  *Tr. fr. Papago Indian by* Frances Densmore.  OBVE

Health.  Stewart Parker.  CIP

Health and Fitness.  J. B. Morton.  FaBoCo

Health is the first good lent to men.  Four Things Make Us Happy Here.  Robert Herrick.  CaPo

Health to great Gloucester—from a man unknown.  The Dedication.  Charles Churchill.  OBSV

Health to the Birds, A.  Seumas MacManus.  PFIr

Health to the Tackers, A.  *Unknown.*  APAS

Hear a word, a word in season, for the day is drawing nigh.  All for the Cause.  William Morris.  VLP

Hear, Hear, O Ye Nations, *with music.*  Frederick Lucian Hosmer.  AH

Hear me/ don't you hear me.  Tambourine.  James Cunningham.  JB

Hear me, great ones of Uruk.  *Unknown.  Fr.* The Epic of Gilgamesh.  DL

Hear me, Melissus; I will tell you a dream.  The Terror by Night.  Giacomo Leopardi, *tr. by* John Heath-Stubbs.  Moon

Hear me, O God!  A Hymn to God the Father.  Ben Jonson.  BoReV; PIM

Hear me, whom I betrayed.  Envoi.  J. V. Cunningham.  VGW

Hear my petition you, God who do not exist.  The Atheist's Prayer.  Miguel de Unamuno.  ILwL

Hear my prayer, O Lord, and let my cry come unto thee.  Bible, *O.T.* Psalms, CII.  BiP

Hear now a curious dream I dreamed last night.  My Dream.  Christina Rossetti.  VLP

Hear, O Israel!  André Spire, *tr. fr. French by* Stanley Burnshaw.  VWA

Hear the fluter with his flute.  The Amateur Flute.  *Unknown.*  SpRo

Hear the rumble.  The Pines.  Margaret Mahy.  FPB

Hear the sledges with the bells.  The Bells.  Poe.  LFH; OBAL; SpRo; TAP

Hear the Voice of the Bard (*Introd. to* Songs of Experience).  Blake.  EBEV; NOBE; NU; OBP
(Introduction: "Hear the voice of the bard!")  CABA (1972 ed.); HAP; InPS; LAuP; MBPR; OAEL-2; STS; TT

Hear this and tremble, all.  Upon My Lord Chief Justice's Election of My Lady Anne Wentworth for His Mistress.  Thomas Carew.  CaPo

Hear what Highland Nora said.  Nora's Vow.  Sir Walter Scott.  SLP

Hear, Ye Ladies.  John Fletcher.  *Fr.* The Tragedy of Valentinian.  NOBE

Hear, ye virgins, and I'll teach.  To Virgins.  Robert Herrick.  CaPo

Heard at Dniperstroi.  Robert Gessner.  SPT

Heard in a Violent Ward.  Theodore Roethke.  NoAM

Heard in the Cougate.  Robert Garioch.  OxBTC

Heard'st thou yon universal cry.  Destruction of the Bastille.  Samuel Taylor Coleridge.  MBPR

Hearing.  William Claire.  PoUp

Hearing a sound that may be thy return.  Hildegarde Flanner.  *Fr.* Sonnets in Quaker Language.  WPE

Hearing how tourists, dazed with reverence.  Aldport (Mystery Tour).  Kingsley Amis.  *Fr.* The Evans Country.  NOBL

Hearing James Brown at Café des Nattes (Sidi-bou-Saïd, Tunisia).  Richard A. Long.  AmNP (1974 ed.)

Hearing Men Shout at Night on Macdougal Street.  Robert Bly.  TCP

Hearing My Son Play.  Alvaro Cardona-Hine.  BrS

Hearing of harvests rotting in the valleys.  Paysage Moralisé.  W. H. Auden.  OAEL-2; UnPo (1976 ed.)

Hearing of you, I never lost a brother.  Stepping Outside.  Tess Gallagher.  AmPA

Hearing one saga, we enact the next.  Remembering the 'Thirties.  Donald Davie.  OxBTC

Hearing that you would come who by my love.  Incantatory Poem.  Jean Garrigue.  LoAs

Hearing the cry I looked to see a bird.  As Near to Eden.  Robert Francis.  PoIA

Hearing the twang among the porticoes.  Washington, D.C.  Ernest Kroll.  WasP

Hearing your words, and not a word among them.  Edna St. Vincent Millay.  CMoP (1970 ed.); NoAM; PSN; VGW

Hearken, thou craggy ocean pyramid!  To Ailsa Rock.  Keats.  MBPR

Hears not my Phyllis how the birds.  Phyllis Knotting.  Sir Charles Sedley.  NOBE

Hearse Song, The.  *Unknown.*  FSW; SFF

Hears't thou, my soul, what serious things.  The Day of Judgment.  Thomas of Celano, *tr. by* Richard Crashaw.  OBVE

Heart, The.  Stephen Crane.  *See* In the Desert.

Heart, The.  David Ignatow.  VWA

Heart, The.  Harvey Shapiro.  HoPM (1975 ed.)

Heart and Mind.  Edith Sitwell.  OxBTC

Heart asks pleasure first, The.  Emily Dickinson.  CMoP (1970 ed.); NOBA; PPP; SBG; WPE

Heart Burial.  Geoffrey Grigson.  POL

Heart cold in the breast with terror, grieving.  Lament for Llywelyn ap Gruffudd.  Gruffudd ab yr Ynad Coch, *tr. by* Joseph P. Clancy.  OBW

Heart does not want to go up, The.  The Men like Salmon.  Linda Gregg.  AAN

Heart Flies Up, Erratic as a Kite, The.  Delmore Schwartz.  PoA

Heart goes out ahead, The.  Poem of the Mother.  Myra Sklarew.  AMV-80; PoUp

Heart has need of some deceit, The.  Only the Polished Skeleton.  Countee Cullen.  IP; VGW

Heart is a snail, The.  Catalogue.  Hilde Domin, *tr. by* Tudor Morris.  VWA

Heart leaps up when I behold, A.  Song to Be Sung by the Father of Infant Female Children.  Ogden Nash.  PPM

Heart Mountain Japanese Relocation Camp, The: 30 Years Later.  Charles Levendosky.  TAT

Heart of cleft gold.  Pond Lily.  E. Margaret Clarkson.  AATT

Heart of Gold.  Neil Young.  UsP

Heart of Herakles, The.  Kenneth Rexroth.  *Fr.* The Lights in the Sky Are Stars.  NU

Heart of Midlothian, The, *sel.*  Sir Walter Scott.
Proud Maisie, *fr. ch.* 38.  AIW; Epi; FF; ILP (1975 ed.); InPK; IP; OAEL-2; UnPO (1976 ed.)
(Madge Wildfire's Death Song.)  Hap
(Madge Wildfire's Song.)  NOBE; SLP

Heart of my day holds no, The.  Oh, Say, Mr. Toffler.  Mira Fish.  FAF

Heart of the heartless world.  Huesca [*or* To Margot Heinemann].  John Cornford.  BoLoP; OxBTC

Heart of the rulers is sick, The, and the high-priest covers his head. A Song in Time of Revolution 1860. Swinburne. VLP

Heart/ Song for Christopher Raymond. Bill Pauly. BrS

Heart Surgery. E. Mitter. PMW

Heart, that hideous bear, The. Falling in Love. David Perkins. NCSH

Heart! We will forget him! Emily Dickinson. OLR; PPM; SoSe (1977 ed.)

Heartblow. Michael S. Harper. NW

Heartblow: Messages. Michael S. Harper. NW

Heartbreak Camp. Roy Campbell. OxBTC

Hearth and Home. Stoddard King. OBAL

Heart's Abysses, The. Walter Savage Landor. FaBoEE; OBSV

Hearts and Flowers, *with music*. Mary D. Brine. FSN

Heart's Compass. Dante Gabriel Rossetti. The House of Life, XXVII. PAIC

Heart's Ease. *Unknown. Fr. Misogonus.* WIF

Heart's ease or pansy, pleasure or thought. Flower Piece. Swinburne. PCOP

Heart's Friend, The. Mary Austin, *after Shoshone Indian.* BPAW

Heart's Journey, The, *sel.* Siegfried Sasson.
"What is Stonehenge? It is the roofless past." PES

Hearts, like Doors. Robert Louis Stevenson. CTV

Heart's Needle. W. D. Snodgrass. CAPP; RRA
*Sels.*
"Child of my winter born," I. ConAP; PiAm
"Easter has come around," VI. ConAP
"Here in the scuffled dust," VII. ILP (1975 ed.); NCSH; PiAm
"I thumped on you the best I could," VIII. NoAM
"Late April and you are three; today," II. CoPAm
"No one can tell you why," IV. ConAP; CoPAm; UsP
"Vicious winter finally yields, The," X. PSN
"Winter again and it is snowing," V. ILP (1975 ed.)

Hearts of Gold. Ogden Nash. AKE

Hearty Cook, A. Roy Blount, Jr. TDH

Heat. Hilda Doolittle ("H.D."). The Garden, II. CMoP (1970 ed.); FSFS; HeIP; InPK; NoAM; PiAm; TAP; UnPo (1976 ed.); UsP

Heat acrost the desert was a-swimmin' in the sun, The. Waring of Sonora-Town. Henry Herbert Knibbs. BPAW

Heat, and a dazzle of brichtness. Proem and Inscription for a Hermes. Robert Garioch. MS

Heat in the Room, The. Weldon Kees. EAS

Heat of the oven, The. Breaded Meat, Breaded Hands. Michael S. Harper. NVAP

Heathen Chinee, The. Bret Harte. FaBoCo
(Plain Language from Truthful James.) AmVN; BPAW; NOBL; OBAL

Heathen named Min, passing by, A. Tra-La-Larceny. Oliver Herford. TDH

Heathen Pass-ee, The, *parody.* A. C. Hilton. FaBoCo; NOBL

Heather Ale. Robert Louis Stevenson. PoTa

Heather Flowers. Eliseus Williams, *tr. fr. Welsh by* Kenneth Jackson. OBW

Heat's on, dead wind shoots up, The. John Garfield. Nicholas Christopher. NYP

Heat's on the hooker, The. Translations from the English. George Starbuck. VGW

Heautontimoroumenos. Baudelaire, *tr. fr. French by* Naomi Lewis. NAWM-2

Heaved from the Earth. Besmilr Brigham. CSP; Psy

Heaven. Rupert Brooke. EBEV; ExPo (1973 ed.); HoPM (1975 ed.); LFH; NOBE; PoPle

Heaven. Langston Hughes. NOBA
(Heaven, Heaven, Heaven Is the Place, *longer version, with music.*) AH

Heaven and Hell. *Unknown, tr. fr. Eskimo by* Edward Field. DL; IPWM

Heaven for Railroad Men. David Wojahn. BrS

Heaven-haven. Gerard Manley Hopkins. BuTh; HeIP; ILP (1975 ed.); NoAM; NOBE; SoSe; VLP

Heaven, Heaven, Heaven Is the Place. Langston Hughes. *See* Heaven.

Heaven is/ The place where. Heaven. Langston Hughes. NOBA

Heaven is a great house. Mouse Heaven. Leah Bodine Drake. MN

Heaven Is Here, *with music.* John G. Adams. AH

Heaven is so far of the mind. Emily Dickinson. PiAm

Heaven-murdered one. Poem of Solitude at Columbia University. Federico García Lorca, *tr. by* Ben Belitt. PBMP

Heaven of Animals, The. James Dickey. CAPP; CoPAm; CSP;HeIP; ILP (1975 ed.); NCSH; NoAM; NOBA; TAP; TCP; VoA

Heaven of Cowboys. Edward Gold. PoUp

Heaven, the earth, and all the liquid mayne, The. Virgil, *tr. by* Sir Walter Ralegh. *Fr.* The Aeneid, VI. OBVE

Heavenly bay, ringed round with cliffs and moors, The. In Guernsey. Swinburne. VLP

Heavenly Canaan, The. Isaac Watts. PIM
("There is a land of pure delight.") BoReV

Heavenly City, The. Stevie Smith. FaBoTw (1975 ed.)

Heavenly Eloquence. Samuel Daniel. *Fr.* Musophilus. NOBE

Heavenly Evil, holy One. Hymn to Evil. Louis Ginsberg. PoA

"Heavenly Father"—take to thee. Emily Dickinson. ILwL; PiAm

Heavenly Foreigner, The, *sel.* Denis Devlin.
"Spires, firm on their monster feet rose light and thin, The." CIP

Heavenly Grass. Tennessee Williams. ECBV

Heavenly Jerusalem, Jerusalem of the Earth. Leah Goldberg, *tr. fr. Hebrew by* Robert Friend. VWA

Heavenly Vision. William Billings. AmFP

Heavens are wrath, The—the thunders rattling peal. Written in a Thunder Storm July 15th 1841. John Clare. VLP

Heavens declare the glory of God, The. Bible, *O.T.*
Psalms, XIX. BiP; CTV, 6 *verses*; NAWM-1; OBP; OBVE

Heavens Do Declare, The, *with music. Unknown.* AH

Heaven's power is infinite; earth, air, and sea. Baucis and Philemon. Ovid, *tr. by.* Dryden. *Fr.* Metamorphoses, VIII. OAEL-1

Heaven's Queene. Sir Walter Ralegh. Moon

Heavens themselves, the planets and this centre, The. On Degree [*or* Order and Degree]. Shakespeare. *Fr.* Troilus and Cressida, I, iii. ExPo (1973 ed.); NIL

Heaving the Lead Line. *Unknown.* AmFP

Heavnly frame sets forth the fame, The. Bible, *O.T.* Psalms, XIX, *paraphrased by* Sir Philip Sidney. OBVE

Heavy Bear Who Goes with Me, The. Delmore Schwartz. BCr; NoAM; NOBA; TAP; UnPo (1976 ed.); UsP

Heavy breathing fills all my chamber. August 24, 1963—1:00 A.M.—Omaha. Donna Whitewing. VW

Heavy glacier and the terrifying Alps, The. Long Lines. Paul Goodman. VGW

Heavy heart, Belovéd, have I borne, A. Sonnets from the Portuguese, XXV. Elizabeth Barrett Browning. ILP (1975 ed.)

Heavy, heavy, hangs my head. The Sad Child's Song. Mark Van Doren. SO

Heavy, heavy, heavy, hand and heart. Tenebrae. Denise Levertov. CABA (1972 ed.)

Heavy, Heavy—What Hangs Over? Kenneth Burke. POL

Heavy is my heart. Slowly. Mary Elizabeth Coleridge. SoSe (1977 ed.)

Heavy Water Blues. Bob Kaufman. CPA

Heavy with salt, and warm. The Equinox. Dubose Heyward. PoA

Heavyweight champ of Seattle, The. *Unknown.* OBAL

Hebrew Lesson. Max Brod, *tr. fr. German.* AMV-80

Hebrew Letters in the Trees. J. Rutherford Willems. VWA

Hebrew nation did not write it, The. Blake. OAEL-2

Hebrew of Your Poets, Zion, The. Charles Reznikoff. VGW; VWA

Hebrew Script. Tali Loewenthal. VWA

Hebrew Sibyl, The. Ruth Fainlight. VWA

Hebrides. Archibald MacLeish. FoP

Hector. Valentin Iremonger. CIP

Hector Protector was dressed all in green. Mother Goose. ECBV

Hector the Collector. Shel Silverstein. CTBA

Hector the Dog. Kate Barnes. GDP

"He'd never seen so many dead before." The Effect. Siegfried Sassoon. BuTh

He'd never wrung the. The Husband. Barbara Greenberg. RiTi

He'd play, after the bawdy songs and blues. When de Saints Go Ma'chin' Home. Sterling A. Brown. AmNP (1974 ed.)

He'd seen his blood before, called forth. The Death of Lester Brown, House Painter. Rod Taylor. WeW

Hedge before me, one behind, A. *Unknown, tr. fr. Irish by* Flann O'Brien. BIrV

Hedgehog. Paul Muldoon. BIrV

Hedges are dazed as cock-crow, heaps of leaves, The. Departure in Middle Age. Roland Mathias. OBW

Hedges Freaked with Snow. Robert Graves. OxBTC

Heedless o' My Love. William Barnes. GBL

Heh Nonny No! *Unknown.* BuTh

Heicht o the biggins is happit in rauchens o haar, The. Haar in Princes Street. Alexander Scott. MS

Heifer Clambers Up, A. Gary Snyder. NoAM; NOBA

Heigh-ho on a Winter Afternoon. Donald Davie. OxBTC

Height. Robert D. Fitzgerald. GAS

Height of the Ridiculous, The. Oliver Wendell Holmes. OBAL; PCOP; PPM

Heine in Scots. Alexander Gray. MS

Heine's mother was a monster. A Century Piece for Poor Heine. John Logan. NNaP

Heir, The. *Unknown.* RAE

Heir to Several Yesterdays. Parham J. Kelley. AMV-80

Heir to the office of a man not dead. A Miltonic Sonnet for Mr. Johnson on His Refusal of Peter Hurd's Official Portrait. Richard Wilbur. CAPP; WasP

Heiress and Architect. Thomas Hardy. VLP

Heirloom. Robert Flanagan. HeS

Hekatompathia; or, Passionate Century of Love, *sels.* Thomas Watson. AAS
  "Some that reporte great Alexanders life."
  "Speake gentle heart, where is thy dwelling place?"

Hélas! Oscar Wilde. VLP

Helbatrawss, The. Kingsley Amis. NOBL

Held between wars. Käthe Kollwitz. Muriel Rukeyser. NMM; RiTi

Heledd and Inge, when the torches are red. In Berlin, August 1945: Lehrte Bahnhof. Alun Llywelyn-Williams, *tr. by* Joseph P. Clancy. OBW

Helen. Hilda Doolittle ("H. D."). BoWoP; NIL;NOBA; SBG; TAP

Helen, *sel.* Euripides, *tr. fr. Greek by* Richmond Lattimore. Chorus: "Long ago, the Mountain Mother." RRA

Helen. Paul Valéry, *tr. fr. French by* Robert Lowell. OBVE (Helen, the Sad Queen, *tr. by* Janet Lewis.) NIL

Helen, had I known yesterday. Release. D. H. Lawrence. CMoP (1970 ed.)

Helen in Egypt, *sels.* Hilda Doolittle ("H. D.").
  "Alas, my brothers." NOBA
  "Another shout from the wharves." NOBA
  "Thetis is the moon-goddess." Moon

Helen like the Rose. Evan Lloyd. OBW

Helen of Kirconnell. *Unknown.* ILP (1975 ed.); PoPle

Helen of Troy. Christopher Marlowe. *Fr.* Doctor Faustus. FF ("Was this the face that launched a thousand ships?") EBEV; GBL; HeIP; NIL

Helen, the Sad Queen. Paul Valéry. *See* Helen.

Helen, thy beauty is to me. To Helen. Poe. AmVN; BoLoP; CABA (1972 ed.); ExPo (1973 ed.); FaPo; GBL; HAP; HeIP; HoPM (1975 ed.); ILP (1975 ed.); InPS; LFH; NIL; NOBA; PAIC; PBMP; PiAm; TAP; WIF

Helen's Lamentation. Homer, *tr. fr. Greek by* Congreve. *Fr.* The Iliad, XXIV. OBVE

Helicon. John Hollander. NoAM

Helicopter, The. Ian Serraillier. RAE

Helicopter in the sky, A. Street Scene. Peter Suffolk. PoTa

Heliogabalus. John Hollander. OBAL

Hell. Abraham Cowley. *Fr.* Davideis, I. SCP-2

Hell. *Tr. from Gaelic by* Douglas Hyde. WTO

Hell-bound Train, The. *Unknown.* BPAW

Hell freezing over. To keep sane. Mandelstam. David Young. AmPA

Hell Gate. A. E. Housman. NoAM; UnPo (1976 ed.)

Hell Hath No Fury. Charles Bukowski. GP

Hell in Texas. *Unknown.* BPAW

Hell is a city much like London. Shelley. *Fr.* Peter Bell the Third. OBP; OBSV

Hell whose rains and cold appal. Hell. *Tr. from Gaelic by* Douglas Hyde. WTO

Hellas, *sels.* Shelley.
  World's great age begins anew, The." EBEV; HAP; HeIP; ILP (1975 ed.); NIL; NOBE; OAEL-2
  "Worlds on worlds are rolling ever." HeIP

Hellbabies. Horace Gregory. SPT

Hellenics, The, *sels.* Walter Savage Landor.
  On the Hellenics. ILP (1975 ed.)
  Ternissa. NOBE

Hellhound on My Trail. *Unknown.* BluL

Hello. Robert Creeley. TPo

Hello./ are u the/ suicide man? 221-1424. Sonia Sanchez. NIL

Hello!/ hello! Echo. Sara Asheron. CaYB

Hello darkness my old friend. The Sound of Silence. Paul Simon. PBMP; WIF

Hello Dolly. Leon Slade. FPA

"Hello! Good luck: the trip out west." Letter Back to Oregon. Albert Goldbarth. HeS

Hello, Ma [*or* My] Baby. Joseph E. Howard *and* Ida Emerson. BLSo; *with music;* FSN; *with music;* FSW

Hello mut. When You Blow on Dog. Lorraine Flanders. PHC

Hello, Sister. Mark Saylor. AMV-80

Hell's Pavement. John Masefield. PoTa; RhR

Helmet now an hive for bees becomes, The. The Vote. Ralph Knevet. SCP-2

Helmeted, booted, numbered, horsed, and always at a distance. Polo Match. John Ciardi. LiSp; SPo

Helmsman, The. Hilda Doolittle ("H. D."). CMoP (1970 ed.)

Help from History. William Stafford. AMV-81

Help Is on the Way. Herbert Scott. GP

Help, Lord, because the Godly Man, *with music*. Francis Rous. AH

Help[e] me! help[e] me! now I call. To His Mistresses. Robert Herrick. CaPo; LoAs

Help me now. Song. Emmett Jarrett. NeAC

Help Me to Seek. Sir Thomas Wyatt. FF
("Helpe me to seke for I lost it there.") AAS
(Rondeau: "Help me to seek, for I lost it there.") PAIC

Help Thy Servant, *with music*. Andrew Broaddus. AH

Helpful Nurse, A. *Unknown*. TDH

Helsinki, 1940. Anselm Hollo. EC

Helves Surling Out of Eakspeasies Per (Reel) hapsingly. E. E. Cummings. Epi

Hematite Lake. James Galvin. AMV–80

Hemmed-in Males. William Carlos Williams. *Fr*. A Folded Skyscraper. MAT

Hemorrhage, The. Stanley Kunitz. NYP

Hen: Cock, cock, I have la-a-a-yd. Hen and Cock. *Unknown*. GBP

Hen Dying. Alasdair MacLean. BoAnP

Hen Flower, The. Galway Kinnell. CAAP; NNaP

Hen under Bay-Tree. Ruth Pitter. OxBTC

Hen Woman. Thomas Kinsella. CIP

Hence, all you vain delights. Melancholy. John Fletcher. PoPle

Hence burgundy, claret, and port. Song. Keats. MBPR

Hence Cupid! with your cheating toys. Against Love. Katherine Philips. BoWoP; SBG; WPE

Hence curiosity me led. Thomas Heyrick. *Fr*. The Submarine Voyage: A Pindaric Poem in Four Parts. SCP–2

Hence loathèd Melancholy. L'Allegro. Milton. CABA (1972 ed.); HAP; HoPM (1975 ed.); ILP (1975 ed.); OAEL–1; PPP

Hence vain deluding Joys. Il Penseroso. Milton. CABA (1972 ed.); HAP; HoPM (1975 ed.); ILP (1975 ed.); OAEL–1; PPP

Hence ye prophane; I hate ye all. Horace, *tr. by* Abraham Cowley. *Fr*. Odes, III, 1. OBVE

Henceforth, from the Mind. Louise Bogan. WPE

Henceforth I will not set my love. Sir Arthur Gorges. GBL

Hendecasyllabics. Swinburne. VLP

Hendecasyllabics. Tennyson. EBEV; FaBoCo; NOBL; VLP

Henpecked Husband, A. *Unknown*. OxBM

Henry Adams. W. H. Auden. OBAL

Henry and Mary. Robert Graves. SO

Henry VIII. Eleanor *and* Herbert Farjeon. PoTa

Henry VIII. Shakespeare. *See* King Henry VIII.

Henry V. Shakespeare. *See* King Henry V.

Henry V before Agincourt. Shakespeare. King Henry V, *fr*. IV, iii. FaPoR
(King Henry the Fifth before Agincourt.) BTTM
(St. Crispin's Day.) FF

Henry IV, Pt. I. Shakespeare. *See* King Henry IV, Pt. I.

Henry got me with child. Amanda Barker. Edgar Lee Masters. *Fr*. Spoon River Anthology. NoAM

Henry in transition, transient Henry. John Berryman. *Fr*. Dream Songs. RRA

Henry James at Newport. Weldon Kees. PoA

Henry K. Sawyer. *Unknown*. AmFP

Henry King [Who Chewed Bits of String]. Hilaire Belloc. BBL; FaBoNo

Henry Martin. *Unknown*. FSW

Henry Miller: A Writer. Carol Lem. AMV–80

Henry Purcell. Gerard Manley Hopkins. VLP

Henry Turnbull. W. W. Gibson. FaBoTw (1975 ed.)

Henry was a young king. Henry and Mary. Robert Graves. SO

Henry was every morning fed. The Boy and the Snake. Charles *and* Mary Lamb. OxBChV

Henry's Confession. John Berryman. *Fr*. Dream Songs. NoAM

Henry's Mail. John Berryman. *Fr*. Dream Songs. ILP (1975 ed.)

Henry's mind grew blacker the more he thought. John Berryman. *Fr*. Dream Songs. NOBA

Henry's pelt was put on sundry walls. John Berryman. *Fr*. Dream Songs. NoAM

Henry's Secret. Dorothy Kilner. OxBChV

Henry's Understanding. John Berryman. NoAM; NOBA

Hens. Alden Nowlan. POL

Hens, The. Elizabeth Madox Roberts. LCL

Hens in Winter. Robert P. Tristram Coffin. TH

Hen's Nest. John Clare. AKE

Heptalogia, The, *sels*. Swinburne.
Higher Pantheism in a Nutshell, The. FaBoNo; PAIC; SpRo
Nephelidia. FaBoCo; FaBoNo; HoPM (1975 ed.), *first sixteen lines*; SpRo
Sonnet for a Picture. FaBoNo; OAEL–2

Her/ strong/ white/ legs. Romp. Dave Etter. WeW

Her ambition is to be more shiny. The Common Woman. Judy Grahn. RiTi

Her angel looked upon God's face. The Eternal Image. Ruth Pitter. OxBTC

Her Application to Elysium. Kathleen Norris. IHMS

Her Apron through the Trees. Roger Weingarten. AmPA

Her arms pinned back, impaled against the night. Jacob and the Angel. Stephen Mitchell. VWA

Her Birthday. Harold Witt. AMV–80

Her body dances in my dream, and my body. A Foreign Country. Natan Zach, *tr. by* Laya Firestone. VWA

Her body is not so white as. Queen-Ann's Lace. William Carlos Williams. LoAs; NoAM; NOBA; TAP

Her body is pouchy. The Old Nudists. Joan Colby. AMV–80

Her chaunging lookes no colour longe can holde. Seneca, *tr. by* John Studley. *Fr*. Medea, IV. OBVE

Her cheeks are hot, her cheeks are white. Bianca. Arthur Symons. Bianca, I. VLP

Her cheeks were white, her eyes were wild. The Sea. W. H. Davies. FaBoTw (1975 ed.)

Her Chinese lamps. Just after the Widow's Death. Barbara Greenberg. RiTi

Her day out from the workhouse-ward, she stands. The Ice. W. W. Gibson. OxBTC

Her Dream House. Marvin Bell. NVAP

Her Dwarf. George P. Elliott. MAT

Her Eyes. John Crowe Ransom. OBAL

Her eyes are like forget-me-nots. To a Little Girl. Gustav Kobbé. PCOP

Her eyes are velvet, soft and fine. My Poker Girl. Tom Masson. OBAL

Her eyes are wild, her head is bare. The Mad Mother. Wordsworth. MBPR

Her eyes began to darken when she said she saw it. Familiar. Veneta Nielson. MPA

Her Eyes Don't Shine like Diamonds, *with music*. David Marion. FSN

Her eyes' flood licks his feet's fair stain. Luke VII: She Began to Wash His Feet with Tears. Richard Crashaw. SCP–1

Her eyes the glow-worm lend thee. The Night-Piece, to Julia. Robert Herrick. CaPo; ILP (1975 ed.); NIL; OAEL–1; PoPle; UsP

Her eyes were gentle; her voice was for soft singing. An Old Woman Remembers. Sterling A. Brown. CNA; PoBA

Her face/ Betrays the darkness of storms. Kornelia Woloszczuk. Peter Skrzynecki. CAAP

Her face her tongue her wit. *At. to* Sir Arthur Gorges. GBL

Her face is a scrubbed glove. Clinic: Examination. Audrey Conard. AMV–80

Her face like a rain-beaten stone on the day she rolled off. Elegy. Theodore Roethke. CTBA; MPA; NCSH; PSN; UsP

Her face turned sour. Sensibility. Louis Simpson. GP

Her face was in a bed of hair. Emily Dickinson. NU

Her face was like sad things: was like the lights. A Stranger. Lionel Johnson. VLP

Her face with bones. Welthistorische Perspektiven. Roderick Watson. MIS

Her Fancy Ball, *abr.* Thomas Hood. *Fr.* Miss Kilmansegg and Her Precious Leg. VLP

Her father lov'd me; oft invited me. Shakespeare. *Fr.* Othello, I, iii. EBEV

Her flesh sticks to my hands, something held. Meeting Anais Nin's Elena. Gene Frumkin. AMV–81

Her Gifts. Dante Gabriel Rossetti. The House of Life, XXXI. VLP

Her Going. Shirley Kaufman. RiTi

Her grandmother called her from the playground. Legacies. Nikki Giovanni. CTBA

Her Hair. Baudelaire, *tr. fr. French by* Doreen Bell. NAWM–2

Her hair has a sweet smell of girlhood under his face. Enigma. Richard Murphy. CIP

Her Hair Is Wet. Allan Kornblum. AcAn

Her hand in my hand. Dunce Song 6. Mark Van Doren. DuDa

Her hand that holds. Jesus Drum. Pearl Cleage Lomax. CNA

Her hands established, last time she left my room. Winter Bouquet. W. D. Snodgrass. NowV

Her health is good. She owns to forty-one. Occupation: Housewife. Phyllis McGinley. *Fr.* I Know a Village. WPE

Her heart a bruise on the Christ-flesh suffered out of locked agonies of rebirth. The Rose of Solitude. William Everson. PiAm

Her intentions are to see that blue. Kindergarten Teacher. Stanley Kiesel. NowV

Her Irish maids could never spoon out mush. Mary Winslow. Robert Lowell. ILP (1975 ed.); PPP

Her iron beats. Domestic Scene. Michael Hartnett. BIrV

Her Kind. Anne Sexton. FF; HeIP; NIL; PPP; TAP

Her kiss on the mirror. A Hidden Message. Kevin Ireland. ATNZ

Her—"last poems." Emily Dickinson. SBG

Her Leg [*or* Legs]. Robert Herrick. LoAs; SpRo

Her Lips Are Copper Wire. Jean Toomer. NoAM

Her lips they are redder than coral. *Unknown.* FaBoCo

Her little hot room looked over the bay. Sanary. Katherine Mansfield. ATNZ

Her long brown fingers. Creek Mother Poem. Joy Harjo. SA

Her long with ardent look his eye pursu'd. Milton. *Fr.* Paradise Lost, IX. UnPo (1976 ed.)

Her Longing. Theodore Roethke. NU

Her Love Poem. Lucille Clifton. GP

Her lovely skin is white, like curds new pressed. *Unknown.* SCP-2

Her lute hangs shadowed in the apple-tree. A Sea-Spell. Dante Gabriel Rossetti. VLP

Her Majesty's Ship. Gene Fowler. CPA

Her mind is a stone dull. Dropping toward Stillness. Sharon Barba. RiTi

Her mind lives in a quiet room. Interior. Dorothy Parker. SBG

Her mindful breast perfumes with frankincense. *Unknown.* SCP-2

Her mother died when she was young. Kemp Owyne. *Unknown.* PeBB

Her mouth an O. The Poetess Kō Ōgimi. Helen Chasin. NMM

Her mouth is filled with silver pins. Watching My Daughter Sew. Katharine Privett. AMV–81

Her Muff. Richard Lovelace. SCP-2

Her name is nada. Canto de Nada. Jessica Tarahata Hagedorn. NW

Her Name like the Hours. Gloria Evans Davies. OBW

Her paps like two fair apples in their prime. *Unknown.* SCP-2

Her Place. Liz Lochhead. MS

Her pretty feet. Upon Her Feet. Robert Herrick. CaPo

Her red cloth is like the lightning. Red Beauty. *Gond Oral Tradition, tr. by* V. Elwin *and* S. Hivale. WTO

Her red pump tapping, her ankle-length gown slit at the knee. Mrs. Applebaum's Sunday Dance Class. Philip Schultz. AMV–81

Her Reply. Sir Walter Ralegh. *See* Nymph's Reply to the Shepherd, The.

Her Reticence. Theodore Roethke. AnMo; LoAs

Her ribcage is eked out. Female, Extinct. Patricia Beer. HeHu

Her scarf à la Bardot. Twice Shy. Seamus Heaney. NCSH

Her sense of humor has no gold stop. Telephonist. Janet Frame. WPE

Her shoulder is in your mouth. Some Oral Stanzas. Thomas Lux. NVAP

Her Sister. Moira O'Neill. OxBTC

Her Sleep. Jill Hoffman. TV

Her smiling eyes in the glass. Calculating Female. Jill Hellyer. POL

Her stiffening captor lies in wait. Mercedes, Her Aloneness. Colette Inez. IHMS

Her Story. Naomi Long Madgett. IHMS; PoBA; TPo

Her Strong Enchantments Failing. A. E. Housman. FaBoTw (1975 ed.); MAT; NOBE; OAEL–2

Her that I love, I hate! Catullus, *tr. fr. Latin by* John Frederick Nims. WeW

Her Time. Theodore Roethke. MPA

Her Triumph. Ben Jonson. *See* Triumph of Charis, The.

Her True Body. Jerred Metz. VWA

Her veil was artificial flowers and leaves. Christopher Marlowe. *Fr.* Hero and Leander. HoPM (1975 ed.)

Her veins incised—jagged boulders. Spokane Falls 1874. Phillip William George. NW

Her veins run Mogen David. Lane Is the Pretty One. Lucille Clifton. CAAP

Her Voice. Meleager, *tr. fr. Greek by* Dudley Fitts. NIL

Her voice/ slips through our ears. Early Ella. Lynn Sukenick. AAN; RiTi

Her voice was cold as a bill collector's. The Price of Paper. Lawrence Russ. AMV–81

Her Whole Life Is an Epigram. Blake. FaBoEE; InPK; NIL; OAEL–2

Her window looks upon the lane. Launcelot with Bicycle. Phyllis McGinley. SS

Her Words. Theodore Roethke. LoAs

Her wraithful turnings and her soft answers. Soft Answers. Robert Bagg. FF

Hera, Hung from the Sky. Carolyn Kizer. NMM; WPE

Heraclitus. William Johnson Cory, *paraphrased fr. the Greek of* Callimachus. FaBoEE; FaPoR; InPK; NOBE; VLP

Heraclitus dwelled. Artery of the Sea. Napoleon St. Cyr. FAF

Heralds of Christ, *with music.* Laura S. Copenhaver. AH

Herbaceous Plodd. Michael Dugan. FPB

Herberie. Forbes Macgregor. MIS

Herbert Street Revisited. John Montague. CIP

Herbert, the corner philatelist, tells me. Down the Block. John Batki. AcAn

Herbert White. Frank Bidart. AmPA

Herbs in the Attic. Marilyn Nelson Waniek. AMV-81

Hercules Furens, sel. Seneca, tr. fr. Latin by Jasper Heywood. "Let oken club now strike, and poast of might," fr. IV. OBVE

Hercules Oetaetus, sel. Seneca, tr. fr. Latin by John Studley. "Let other mount aloft, let other sore," fr. II. OBVE

Herded in clinic cattle-cubicles. Town Clinics. Margaret Gillies. PMW

Herdmen, The. *Unknown.* NOBE

Here. Florence Barbera. PoUp

Here. Marvin Bell. AmPA

Here. Robert Creeley. NOBA

Here. Philip Larkin. CMoP (1970 ed.)

Here. R. S. Thomas. PSN

Here. J. D. Whitney. NVAP

Here/ books open themselves. Library. Billy Collins. AAN

Here/ I am cutting you. For Kenneth and Miriam Patchen. Al Young. CoPAm

Here/ where she dropped me. W. S. Wardell. AAN

Here,/ With my beer. Beer. George Arnold. OBAL

Here a little child I stand. Grace [or Another Grace] for a Child. Robert Herrick. CABA (1972 ed.); CTV; HeIP; InPK; InPS; OxBChV; PoPle

Here a pretty baby lies. Upon a Child. Robert Herrick. SCP-1

Here a solemn fast we keep. An Epitaph upon a Virgin. Robert Herrick. CaPo; FaBoEE

Here a wandering seaweed. Anti-Nostalgia. Henryk Grynberg, tr. by Isaac Komem. VWA

Here, above,/ cracks in the buildings are filled with battered moonlight. The Man-Moth. Elizabeth Bishop. ILP (1975 ed.); MAT; NoAM; NOBA; NYP; PPP

Here all is sunny, and when the truant gull. Skerryvore: The Parallel. Robert Louis Stevenson. ILP (1975 ed.)

Here am I, a shape under a cedar. Sitting in the Woods: A Contemplation. W. R. Moses. NCSH

Here am I, little jumping Joan. Mother Goose. MG

Here among long-discarded cassocks. Diary of a Church Mouse. John Betjeman. OxBTC

Here, and here only in an age of iron. Terra Australis. Chris Wallace-Crabbe. MAuV

Here and Human. Vernon Scannell. HeHu

Here and Now. Catherine Cater. AmNP (1974 ed.)

Here and Now. Philip Levine. PoA; VWA

Here and There. Jon Stallworthy. NoAM

Here and there in the searing beam. Deer among Cattle. James Dickey. TCP; TSWA

Here are a dozen wonders of *The Iliad.* Wonders of "The Iliad." Paul Goodman. NIL

Here are all the captivities, the cells are as real. Schoolchildren. W. H. Auden. TT

Here are fine gifts, children. Sappho, tr. fr. Greek by Willis Barnstone. BoWoP

Here are old things. Mending. Hazel Hall. WPW

Here are old trees, tall oaks, and gnarled pines. The Antiquity of Freedom. Bryant. EAP

Here are people and sports of all sizes and sorts. The Mountebank Song. Thomas Durfey. SCP-2

Here are two pictures from my father's head. Wounds. Michael Longley. IPM

Here are weeds about his mouth. Wide Empty Landscape with a Death in the Foreground. N. Scott Momaday. CDW

Here, as in a painting, yellow noon burns [or noon burns yellow]. Natalya Gorbanyevskaya, tr. fr. Russian by Daniel Weissbort. BoWoP; PBWP

Here at last is ending. Ocean on Monday. Richard Hugo. CNW

Here at the edge of nowhere and the sea. August 22. John Unterecker. PHC

Here at the Super Duper, in a glass tank. Lobsters. Howard Nemerov. AnMo; PBMP

Here at the turning of the tide. Tidal Pool. Sara Henderson Hay. EcS

Here at the Vespasian-Carlton, it's just one. Boom! Howard Nemerov. NIL; NowV

Here at the wayside station, as many a morning. The Wayside Station. Edwin Muir. FaBoTw (1975 ed.); PSN

Here Be Dragons. Ginny Friedlander. AMV-80

Here by the windy docks I stand alone. E. A. Robinson. Octaves, XXIII. ILP (1975 ed.)

Here come three dukes a-riding. Ransi-Tansi-Tay. *Unknown.* PoPle

Here come two swans below the Roman bridge. Swans. Morley Jamieson. SLP

Here Comes. Erica Jong. PPoD

Here comes Old Man Adkins with a battle-ax. Coal Loadin' Blues. *Unknown.* AmFP

Here comes the shadow not looking where it is going. Sire. W. S. Merwin. VGW

Here continueth to rot. Epitaph on Colonel Francis Chartres. John Arbuthnot. FaBoEE; OBSV; PMW

Here corpse and soul go bare. The Leader's headpiece. Cistercians in Germany. Robert Lowell. NowV

Here cursing swearing Burton lies. Burns. FaBoEE

Here Dead Lie We. A. E. Housman. OAEL-2 ("Here dead lie we because we did not choose.") FaBoEE

Here Delia's buried at fourscore. Hildebrand Jacob. FaBoEE

Here down my wearied limbs I'll lay. On Himself. Robert Herrick. CaPo

Here envy and lying/ Held me enclosed. On Leaving Prison. Luis de Léon. ILwL

Here evening comes without a welcome. Reilly. Rayne Mackinnon. MIS

Here, ever since you went abroad. What News. Walter Savage Landor. BoLoP

Here, five feet deep, lies on his back. On the Astrologer and Almanac Maker, John Partridge. Swift. FaBoEE

Here Follows Some Verses upon the Burning of Our House. Anne Bradstreet. *See* Upon the Burning of Our House, July 10th, 1666.

Here further up the mountain slope. The Birthplace. Robert Frost. OFD

Here goes a poor old chimney sweeper. The Chimney Sweeper. *Unknown.* AmFP

Here has my salient faith annealed me. Key West. Hart Crane. CMoP (1970 ed.)

Here he lies moulding. Epitaph. Leslie Mellichamp. QQQ

Here he played. Annemarie Ewing. *Fr.* Pine Top Smith. OSP

Here, here I live with what my board. His Content in the Country. Robert Herrick. CaPo

Here, here, oh here Eurydice. Orpheus to Beasts. Richard Lovelace. CaPo

Here Holy Willie's sair worn clay. Epitaph on Holy Willie. Burns. ESaP

Here I am,/ Novice of many years. Two Roads, Etc. Dorothy Walters. IHMS

Here I am, an industry without chimneys. The Perfection of Dentistry. Marvin Bell. AmPA

Here I am, an old man in a dry month. Gerontion. T. S. Eliot. AnMo; CABA (1972 ed.); CMoP (1970 ed.); EBEV; ExPo (1973 ed.); HAP; InPS; NoAM; NOBA; OAEL-2; PPP; STS; TAP

Here I am and forth I must. Prayer for the Journey. *Unknown.* OxBM

Here I am, seated, with all my words. Silence Concerning an Ancient Stone. Rosario Castellanos, *tr. by* George D. Schade. PBWP

Here I am sitting like a side of beef in the middle of Kansas. Three Weeks in the State of Loneliness. Marge Piercy. MMD

Here I am, troubling the dream coast. In California. Louis Simpson. NIL; NoAM; NowV

Here I go again. Starting from San Francisco. Lawrence Ferlinghetti. BiP; CAPP; PiAm

Here I go again. Away. Lucien Stryk. GP

Here I lie at the chancel door. On Elizabeth Ireland. *Unknown.* FaBoEE

Here I lie for the last time. Epitaph on an Irish Priest. *Unknown.* FaBoEE

Here I myself might likewise die. Poetry Perpetuates the Poet. Robert Herrick. FaBoEE

Here I sit. Bad Morning. Langston Hughes. OBAL; PiAm

Here I sit in my infested cubicle. Theresa Greenwood. CTBA

Here I sit in this quiet place. Fair Isle Pattern. James Rankin. MIS

Here I sit on Buttermilk Hill. Buttermilk Hill. *Unknown.* FSW

Here I slept with my face turned. Prospect Beach. Lou Lipsitz. VGW

Here I stand/ For centuries watching. Ask the Mountains. Phillip William George. UsP; VW

Here I stand/ Humble, with outstretched arms. Hymn to the Air Spirit. *Tr. fr. Eskimo.* WTO

Here I will rest beside this hill. Contentment. Lawrence E. Estes. AMV-80

Here I'm supposed to be a great poet. 3:16 and One Half. Charles Bukowski. GP

Here in a crumbled corner of the wall. The Church Mouse. Gerald Bullett. BoAnP

Here in a distant place I hold my tongue. Egan O Rahilly. Egan O'Rahilly, *tr. by* James Stephens. EBEV; NoAM

Here, in a field. In a Field. Robert Pack. CoPAm; MAT

Here in a quiet and dusty room they lie. The Seed Shop. Muriel Stuart. MS

Here in Honolulu a p.a. system squawks. Letter. Geof Hewitt. PHC

Here in Katmandu. Donald Justice. ConAP; HeIP; LiSp; NIL; RFM; UsP

Here, in late spring, the summer is on us already. Hot Afternoons Have Been in West 15th Street. Paul Blackburn. VGW

Here in my careful garden I have nourished. Two Gardens. Arlene De Bevoise. AMV-80

Here in my head, the home that is left for you. Burning the Letters. Randall Jarrell. CoPAm

Here in Nantucket does the tiny soul. Phenomenal Survivals of Death in Nantucket. Louise Glück. AmPA

Here in our cloud we talk. Quiet Town. William Stafford. MAT

Here in Polynia. Tom Raworth. TwMBP

Here, in the/ book. The Book of Mysteries. Anthony Barnett. VWA

Here in the cool and book-infested den. Ulysses' Library. David Daiches. PoA

Here, in the darkness, where this plaster saint. Madeleine in Church. Charlotte Mew. SBG

Here in the dim and the almost dark and the warmth of the truth. The Riding Stable in Winter. John Tagliabue. PH

Here, in the hollow caverns of the rocks. The Wily Fox. Edward Davies. *Fr.* Chepstow: A Poem. OBW

Here, in the most Unchristian basement. The Men's Room in the College Chapel. W. D. Snodgrass. GP; ILP (1975 ed.); PPP

Here in the newspaper—the wreck of the East Bound. It's Here in The. Russell Atkins. AmNP (1974 ed.); PoBA; SoS

Here in the North, our houses and their appointments. How Was Your Trip to L.A.? Philip Whalen. TAT

Here in the open cockpit. Lispy Bails Out. David Barker. GP

Here in the scuffled dust. W. D. Snodgrass. Heart's Needle, VII. ILP (1975 ed.); NCSH; PiAm

Here in the shadow of the Smiths, my forest. Smith Brothers' Lumber Shed. Hildegarde Flanner. WPW

Here, in the thick Carolina darkness. 1965. Gibbons Ruark. NowV

Here in the Uplands. Scotland. Alexander Gray. MS

Here in the wind-shave of prairie land. Inland Sea. Franklin Brainard. HeS

Here in the yellowing. Deserted Cabin. John Haines. PCho

Here in this car is surcease from a thousand dead. Surcease. Patrick Lane. NeAC

Here, in this little Bay. Magna Est Veritas. Coventry Patmore. *Fr.* The Unknown Eros. HAP; ILP (1975 ed.); NOBE; VPC

Here in this world/ I won't live. Izumi Shikibu, *tr. fr. Japanese by* Willis Barnstone. BoWoP

Here in veins of metal and glass. The Dead Sea. Henryk Grynberg, *tr. by* Isaac Komem. VWA

Here is a child who is leaning over a paper. The Mirror. John N. Morris. PoA

Here is a child who presses his head to the ground. The Windows. W. S. Merwin. PHC

Here is a cup left empty in their. Broken Home. William Stafford. NNaP

Here is a face for you, masked ones. For the Masked Ones. Raymond Ward. ATNZ

Here is a fat animal, a bear. Self-Portrait, as a Bear. Donald Hall. SO

Here is a man with a lamp. The House of Light. Dana Naone. PHC

Here is a place that is no place. Madhouse [*or* The Patient: Rockland County Sanitarium]. Calvin C. Hernton. PoBA; TCP; UsP

Here is a poem for the two of us to play. The Newly Pressed Suit. Roger McGough. NoAM

Here is a rarity. Know Thyself. Kenneth Burke. OBAL

Here is a ship you made. The Ship. J. F. Hendry. MS; SLP

Here Is a Song, *with music.* John Peck. AH

Here is a symbol in which. Rock and Hawk. Robinson Jeffers. IPWM; NoAM; NOBA

Here is a tale of the man who laid. Alfred Allen. *Fr.* Clashenure Skyline. IPM

Here is another poem in a picture. Untitled. Daryl Hine. NoAM

Here is cruel Frederick, see! Cruel Frederick. Heinrich Hoffmann, *tr. fr. German.* SpRo

Here is fresh matter, poet. Church and State. W. B. Yeats. CMoP (1970 ed.)

Here is his coffin. And here the barber comes. Peter Redgrove. *Fr.* The Barbers. FoP

Here is Klito's little shack. Kenneth Rexroth, *after the Greek of* Leonidas. NNaP

Here Is Little Effie's Head. E. E Cummings. AnMo; TT

Here is my foot, so small it cannot walk. In Jail. Juan Antonio Corretjer, *tr. by* Julio Marzán. InW

Here is my tail now. Tail. Dennis Saleh. CPA

Here Is the Abattoir Where.   Michael Smith.   CIP

Here is the ancient floor.   The Self-Unseeing.   Thomas Hardy.
EBEV; HAP; NOBE; VLP

Here is the doctor, an abstracted lover.   Death by Aesthetics.
Mona Van Duyn.   RiTi

Here is the foreign cliff and the fabled sea.   On a Picture by
Michele Da Verona, of Arion as a Boy Riding upon a
Dolphin.   Anne Ridler.   PoA

Here is the mirrored image.   Pānini o ka Punahou.   Elizabeth B.
Holmes.   PHC

Here is the old one we can still use.   Utility.   T. R. Jahns.   AAN

Here is the place.   Looking for Maimonides: Tiberias.   Shirley
Kaufman.   VWA

Here is the place; right over the hill.   Telling the Bees.   Whittier.
NOBA; TAP

Here is the reply made by Benny.   Raisin Bread.   Lee Blair.
TDH

Here is this transport.   Scrawled in Pencil in a Sealed Railway
Car.   Dan Pagis, tr. by Anthony Rudolf.   VWA

Here is where people.   Library.   Richard Armour.   ECBV

Here, it is never enough.   February.   Larry Moffi.   AMV-80

Here its like that.   Blue Tanganyika.   Lebert Bethune.   PoBA

Here Johnson lies—a sage by all allow'd.   Epitaph.   William
Cowper.   LAuP

Here lay a fair fat land.   Culbin Sand.   Andrew Young.   OxBTC

Here lie I, Martin Elginbrodde.   At Aberdeen.   Unknown.
FaBoCo; FaBoEE; PoPle

Here lie my old bones: my vexation now ends.   Messenger
Mounsey.   FaBoEE

Here lie the banes o' Tammy Messer.   Tammy Messer.
Unknown.   FaBoEE

Here lie the bones of Elizabeth Charlotte.   On an Aberdeen
Favourite.   Unknown.   FaBoEE

Here lie the relics of a martyred knight.   On Sir John Fenwick.
Henry Hall.   APAS

Here lie two poor lovers, who had the mishap.   Pope.   Fr. Three
Epitaphs on John Hewet and Sarah Drew.   NIL

Here lie Willie Michie's [or M——hie's] banes.   Epitaph on a
Schoolmaster.   Burns.   FaBoCo; FaBoEE

Here Lies. . .   Stevie Smith.   PoA

Here lies,/ A worthy matron of unspotted life.   Anne Bradstreet.
EAP

Here lies a bard, let epitaphs be true.   My Epitaph.   H. J. Daniel.
FaBoEE

Here lies a clerk who half his life had spent.   The Volunteer.
Herbert Asquith.   OxBTC

Here lies a Doctor of Divinity.   On a Doctor of Divinity.
Richard Porson.   FaBoCo; FaBoEE

Here lies a dog: may every dog that dies.   Epitaph on the
Favourite Dog of a Politician.   Hilaire Belloc.   OBSV

Here lies a great sleeper, as everybody knows.   Epitaph on a
Great Sleeper.   Sir Aston Cokayne.   FaBoEE

Here lies a greedy girl, Jane Bevan.   Epitaph.   Unknown.   OSF

Here Lies a Lady.   John Crowe Ransom.   CMoP (1970 ed.);
HAP; NoAM; TAP; VGW

Here lies a man who was killed by lightning.   At Great
Torrington, Devon.   Unknown.   FaBoCo; FaBoEE

Here lies a peer.   Epitaph on the Duke of Grafton.   Sir
Fleetwood Shepherd.   FaBoEE

Here lies a piece of Christ; a star in dust.   Epitaph for a Godly
Man's Tomb.   Robert Wild.   FaBoEE

Here lies a poet, briefly known as Hecht.   Epitaph.   Anthony
Hecht.   POL

Here lies a poet—where's the great surprise!   Z. Z.   FaBoEE

Here lies a poet who would not write.   Here Lies. . .   Stevie
Smith.   PoA

Here lies a poor woman who always was tired.   Unknown.
FaBoEE

Here lies a shoemaker whose knife and hammer.   At His Father's
Grave.   John Ormond.   FaBoTw (1975 ed.); OBW

Here lies Boghead amang the dead.   On James Grieve, Laird of
Boghead, Tarbolton.   Burns.   NIL

Here lies Dr. Keene, the good Bishop of Chester.   Epitaph on Dr.
Keene.   Thomas Gray.   FaBoEE

Here lies dust confusèdly hurled.   On Sight of Some Martyrs'
Sepulchres.   Nahum Tate.   SCP-2

Here lies Factotum Ned at last.   Fragment of a Character.
Thomas Moore.   FaBoCo

Here lies father and mother and sister and I.   In a Staffordshire
Churchyard.   Unknown.   PoPle

Here lies fierce Strephon, whose poetic rage.   Epitaph.   Anthony
Hecht.   PPoD

Here lies Fred.   On Prince Frederick.   Unknown.   FaBoCo;
FaBoEE; NOBL

Here lies free from blood and slaughter.   In Memory of Captain
Underwood Who Was Drowned.   Unknown.   FaBoEE

Here lies her.   Epitaph.   Unknown.   IP

Here lies Hilaire Belloc, who.   Hilaire Belloc.   Humbert Wolfe.
FaBoEE

Here lies I and my three daughters.   Unknown.   FaBoEE

Here lies I, no wonder I'm dead.   Unknown.   FaBoEE

Here lies in death, who living always lied.   On Rÿneveld, an
Unpopular Dutch Judge.   Unknown.   FaBoEE

Here lies intombed/ Beneath these bricks.   Epitaph on a Willing
Girl.   At. to Thomas Rowlandson.   FaBoEE

Here lies John Bun.   John Bun.   Unknown.   FaBoCo; PoPle

Here lies John Hughes and Sarah Drew.   Epitaph.   Lady Mary
Wortley Montague.   FaBoEE

Here lies John Knott.   Epitaph on John Knott.   Unknown.
FaBoEE

Here lies John Trot, the friend of all mankind.   Blake.   FaBoEE

Here lies Johnny Pidgeon.   Epitaph on John Dove.   Burns.
FaBoCo

Here lies Jonson with the rest.   Upon Ben Jonson.   Robert
Herrick.   CaPo; FaBoEE

Here lies Landor.   Walter Savage Landor.   FaBoEE

Here lies Lord Coningsby—be civil.   Lord Coningsby's Epitaph.
Pope.   FaBoEE

Here lies Mary, the wife of John Ford.   At Potterne, Wiltshire.
Unknown.   FaBoCo

Here lies Mistress Keene the Bishop of Chester.   Epitaph on Dr.
Keene's Wife.   Thomas Gray.   FaBoEE

Here lies my dear wife, a sad slattern and a shrew.   Unknown.
FaBoEE

Here lies my poor wife, much lamented.   Unknown.   FaBoEE

Here lies my poor wife, without bed or blanket.   Unknown.
FaBoEE

Here lies my wife.   Susannah Prout.   Walter de la Mare.
FaBoEE

Here lies my wife.   At Leeds.   Unknown.   FaBoCo

Here lies my wife. Eternal peace.   J. V. Cunningham.   NIL;
OBAL

Here lies New Critic who would fox us.   J. V. Cunningham.
OBAL

Here lies Nolly Goldsmith, for shortness call'd Noll.   On Oliver
Goldsmith.   David Garrick.   FaBoEE

Here lies old Forty-five Per Cent.   Old Forty-five Per Cent.
Unknown.   FaBoEE

Here lies old Hobson, Death hath broke his girt.   On the
University Carrier.   Milton.   EBEV; FaBoEE; PoPle

Here lies our good Edmund, whose genius was such.   On Edmund
Burke.   Goldsmith.   Fr. Retaliation.   FaBoEE; PMW

Here lies our Sovereign Lord the King. Epitaph on Charles II. Earl of Rochester. ExPo (1973 ed.); FaBoCo; OBP

Here lies Piron—a man of no position. Alexis Piron, *tr. fr. French.* FaBoEE

Here lies poor Burton. A Brewer. *Unknown.* FaBoCo

Here lies poor Johnson. Reader! have a care. Doctor Johnson. Soame Jenyns. FaBoEE; OBSV

Here lies resting, out of breath. Little Elegy. X. J. Kennedy. ConAP; HoPM (1975 ed.); NCSH

Here lies Sir John Plumpudding of the Grange. *Unknown.* FaBoEE

Here lies Sir Tact, a diplomatic fellow. Epitaph. Timothy Steele. InPK

Here lies Sprawlings, a quarterback. Caught in the Pocket. William D. Barney. LiSp

Here lies that poet, buried in the night. On a Poet. Henry Parrot. FaBoEE

Here lies the author of the "Apparition." An Author's Epitaph. Written by Himself. Abel Evans. FaBoEE

Here lies the best and worst of fate. On the Duke of Buckingham. James Shirley. FaBoEE

Here lies the body of Andrew Gear. Andrew Gear of Sunderland. *Unknown.* FaBoCo

Here lies the body of Daniel Saul. *Unknown.* FaBoEE

Here lies the body of Edith Bone. On Myself. Edith Bone. FaBoEE

Here lies the body of Richard Hind. On Richard Hind. *Unknown.* FaBoCo; FaBoEE

Here lies the body of Sir John Guise. *Unknown.* FaBoEE

Here lies the body of this world. Epitaph on the World. Henry David Thoreau. FF; HeIP

Here lies the body of W. W. On William Wilson, Tailor. *Unknown.* FaBoEE

Here lies the body of William Jones. Epitaph on William Jones. *Unknown.* FaBoEE

Here lies the corpse of Doctor Chard. *Unknown.* FaBoEE

Here lies the corpse of William Prynne. On William Prynne. Samuel Butler. FaBoEE

Here lies the Devil—ask no other name. On a Lord. Samuel Taylor Coleridge. FaBoCo

Here lies the good old knight Sir Harry. Epitaph for Sir Henry Lee. *Unknown.* FaBoEE

Here lies the great. False marble, where? *Unknown.* FaBoEE

Here lies, the Lord have mercy upon her. Upon One of the Maids of Honour to Queen Elizabeth. John Hoskyns. FaBoEE

Here lies the man that madly slain. John Hoskyns. FaBoEE

Here lies the man who in life. On a Contentious Companion. John Hoskyns. FaBoEE

Here lies the man who stripp'd Sin bare. Ebenezer Elliott. FaBoEE

Here lies the preacher, judge and poet, Peter. On Peter Robinson. Francis Jeffrey. FaBoCo; FaBoEE

Here lies the Reverend Jonathan Doe. On the Reverend Jonathan Doe. *Unknown.* FaBoEE

Here lies the stripper stripped, disrobed for good. Epitaph of a Stripper. William Jay Smith. AMV-80

Here lies Thomas Logge—a Rascally Dogge. Thomas Logge. Walter de la Mare. FaBoEE

Here lies [or lyes] to each her parents' ruth. On My First Daughter. Ben Jonson. EBEV; FaBoEE; HoPM (1975 ed.); NOBE; RRA

Here lies Tom Thumb, King Arthur's Knight. Tom Thumb's Epitaph. *Unknown.* DuDr

Here lies what had not birth, nor shape, nor frame. Epitaph on James Moore Smythe. Pope. FaBoEE

Here lies what's left. On Leslie Moore. *Unknown.* CTV

Here lies, whom hound did ne'er pursue. Epitaph on a Hare. William Cowper. HAP; HeIP; PoPle

Her lies Will Smith—and, what's something rarish. On Will Smith. *Unknown.* ECBV; FaBoCo

Here lies wise and valiant dust. Epitaph on the Earl of Strafford. John Cleveland. FaBoEE; NOBE; SCP-2

Here lies with Death auld Grizzel Grimme. Grizzel Grimme. *Unknown.* FaBoEE

Here lies, within his tomb, so calm. On the Clerk of a Country Parish. William Shenstone. FaBoEE

Here lies wrapped up tight in sod. Epitaph for a Postal Clerk. X. J. Kennedy. NIL

Here lieth John Cruker, a maker of bellows. The Bellows Maker of Oxford. John Hoskyns. FaBoEE

"Here lieth One whose name was writ on water!" On Keats. Shelley. FaBoEE; MBPR

Here lieth the worthy warrior/ Who never bloodied sword. On the Earl of Leicester. *Unknown.* FaBoEE

Here lieth Thom Nick's body. Upon a Fool. John Hoskyns. FaBoEE

Here lives a man, who, by relation. Written over a Gate. John Sheffield. NIL

Here, Lord, Retired, I Bow in Prayer, *with music.* Matthew Bolles. AH

Here love delights the wandering thought. *Unknown.* SCP-2

Here luxury's the common lot. The light. Grasse: The Olive Trees. Richard Wilbur. NoAM; NOBA

Here lyes to each her parents ruth. *See* Here lies to each . . .

Here lyeth he, who was born and cried. On One That Lived Ingloriously. John Hoskyns, *after* Simonides. FaBoEE

Here majestic mountains tower. In the Canadian Rockies. Virginia Shearer Hopper. AMV-80

Here might we live in . . . not quite peace, but relative. Fragment of a Pastoral. Barry Schwabsky. AMV-80

Here often, when a child I lay reclined. Lines. Tennyson. CABA (1972 ed.)

Here, on our native soil, we breathe once more. Composed in the Valley near Dover, on the Day of Landing. Wordsworth. MBPR

Here on the earth's brink. The Fiddler. Martin Buber, *tr. by* Jawaid Awan. VWA

Here on the edge of hell. Harlem [*or* Puzzled]. Langston Hughes. PPP; UnPo (1976 ed.)

Here, on this earth soft. As in the Land of Darkness. Robert Miklitsch. AMV-80

Here on your bed I have. January. Deborah Godin. AMV-80

Here or there, some one among the waiting tourists. Going to Cythera. Chris Wallace-Crabbe. CAAP

Here rage the furies that have shaped the world. Land's End. Stanton A. Coblentz. BPAW

Here Reynolds is laid and, to tell you my mind. Goldsmith. *Fr.* Retaliation. FaBoEE

Here richly, with ridiculous display. Epitaph on the Politician Himself. Hilaire Belloc. FaBoEE; OBSV

Here she lies, a pretty bud. Upon a Child That Died. Robert Herrick. CaPo; InPK; SCP-1

Here she lies (in bed of spice). Upon a Maid. Robert Herrick. CaPo; FaBoEE

Here she was wont to go, and here! and here! Ben Jonson. *Fr.* The Sad Shepherd, I, i. ILP (1975 ed.)

Here sits a shepherd and a shepherdess. The Green Shepherd. Louis Simpson. NIL; NoAM; PAIC

Here, six years old, by Destiny's crime. Epitaph for Erotion. Martial, *tr. by* James Michie. FaBoEE

Here sleeps at length poor Col, and without screaming. Epitaph on Himself. Samuel Taylor Coleridge. FaBoEE

Here sleeps in peace a Hampshire Grenadier. Epitaph to Thomas Thetcher. *Unknown.* PoPle

Here something stubborn comes. Seed Leaves. Richard Wilbur. NCSH; PiAm

Here stand I, ach, Philosophy. Goethe, *tr. by* Louis MacNeice. Faust, Pt. I. NAWM-2

Here stand I, for whores as great. *Unknown.* FaBoEE

Here, take my crown—the life of Edward too. Christopher Marlowe. *Fr.* Edward the Second, V, i. LFH

Here tame boys fly down the long light of halls. To a Visiting Poet in a College Dormitory. Carolyn Kizer. PoA

Here the crow starves, here the patient stag. Rannoch, by Glencoe. T. S. Eliot. Landscapes, IV. BiP

Here the foot prints stop. After Twenty Years. Fadwa Tuquan, *tr. fr. Arabic.* PBWP

"Here the hangman stops his cart." The Carpenter's Son. A. E. Housman. PBMP; SoSe; SpRo; STS

Here the jack-hammer jabs into the ocean. Colloquy in Black Rock. Robert Lowell. CAPP; NoAM; PiAm; STS

Here the Messiah lives. Encounter in Safed. Moshe Yungman, *tr. by* Gabriel Preil *and* Howard Schwartz. VWA

Here. The silence echoes. Here. In His Poems Are El Greco's Hands. Robert Leverant. MIT

Here, the sky is colorless and fluid. Separate. Eve Shelnutt. TC

Here the whitest birds. Morning in Gainesville. Karen Whitehill. NPW

Here they are. The soft eyes open. The Heaven of Animals. James Dickey. CAPP; CoPAm; CSP; HeIP; ILP (1975 ed.); NCSH; NoAM; NOBA; TAP; TCP; VoA

Here they come back again, the harriers. Person to Person. Lorine Parks. NowV

Here they lie mottled to the ground unseen. Partridges. John Masefield. LiSp; OxBTC

Here they went with smock and crook. Forefathers. Edmund Blunden. NOBE; OxBTC

Here those of us who really understand. Manhattan. Osbert Lancaster. *Fr.* Afternoons with Baedeker. NOBL

Here, though, the fine cool air. Vincent Buckley. *Fr.* Golden Builders. CAAP

Here, time concurring (and it does). Epitaph. John Ciardi. BiP

Here to the leisured side of life. The Lamplighter. "Seamas O'Sullivan." BIrV

Here to the sweep of the shore. Tides. A. G. Prys-Jones. RhR

Here Together Met. Louis Johnson. ATNZ

Here, too, like in Jerusalem. The Jews. Mieczyslaw Jastrun, *tr. by* Isaac Komem. VWA

Here was raised. The Plain of Adoration. *Unknown, tr. by* John Montague. BIrV

Here was the autumn orchard where now stand. Autumn Orchard. Catherine Haydon Jacobs. AMV-80

Here was the sound of water falling only. The Owl. Robert Penn Warren. CoPAm

Here we are, all, by day; by night we're hurled. Dreams. Robert Herrick. CaPo; HAP

"Here we are at the river" I said to no one. The Gift. Dick Lourie. NeAC

Here we are for the last time face to face. L'Envoi. William Morris. *Fr.* The Earthly Paradise. VPC

Here We Are in the Years. Neil Young. PoRo

Here we are, inside. Glass Flowers in a Glass Ball. Robert T. Kasold. DNGG

Here we are, old chap, at the Café de la Paix. Two Salesmen in Search of a Country. Robert Gessner. SPT

Here we are, picking the first fern-shoots. Song of the Bowmen of Shu. Ezra Pound, *after the Chinese.* OBVE

Here we bring new water from the well so clear. New Year's Water. *Unknown.* CC; GBP; OFD; POL

Here we broached the Christmas barrel. The House of Hospitalities. Thomas Hardy. NoAM

Here we come again, again, and here we come again! The Children's Carol. Eleanor Farjeon. PChr

Here We Come a-Piping. *Unknown.* ExPo (1973 ed.); PoPle

Here We Come a-Wassailing. *Unknown. See* Wassail Song.

Here we come gathering nuts in May. Nuts in May. *Unknown.* GSB

Here we go around this ring. Marriage. *Unknown.* AmFP

Here We Go Looby Loo. *Unknown.* FSW

Here we go round the mulberry bush. Mother Goose. GSB, *with music*; MG

Here we go the jingo-ring. The Merry-ma-Tanzie. *Unknown.* GBP

Here we have thirst. An Egyptian Pulled Glass Bottle in the Shape of a Fish. Marianne Moore. PBWP; PiAm

Here We March All Around in a Ring. *Unknown.* AmFP

Here we see old Uncle Umbert. Uncle Umbert. Shel Silverstein. OSF

Here we see the delicate white curve of the hip. X-Ray. Elizabeth Bartlett. PMW

Here weaves a spider, and here a clock. The Spider and the Clock. Sol Funaroff. SPT

Here, west of winter, lies the ample flower. Prayer for This Day. Hildegarde Flanner. WPW

Here where by all, all saints invoked are. A Letter to the Lady Carey and Mrs. Essex Rich. John Donne. SCP-1

Here Where Coltrane Is. Michael S. Harper. CNA; PoBA

Here where Gary Cooper's figure stands. At the Wax Museum. Hollis Summers. CoPAm

Here where our Lord once laid his head. Upon the Holy Sepulchre. Richard Crashaw. FaBoEE

Here, where relumed by changing seasons, burn. Roy Campbell. *Fr.* The Golden Shower. OxBTC

Here, where the baby paddles in the gutter. Lean Street. G. S. Fraser. MS

Here where the elm trees were. Elegy. Constance Carrier. FAF

Here where the parrots come down. Thomas and Charlie. Peter Wild. AmPA

Here, where the red man swept the leaves away. Frederick Goddard Tuckerman. *Fr.* Sonnets. NOBA; TAP

Here where the river is naming itself. The Sixth Day. Betty Adcock. LiSp

Here where tides come and go. Tides. Will H. Blackwell. AMV-80

Here where the wind is always north-north-east. New England. E. A. Robinson. CABA (1972 ed.); GOA; HeIP; NOBA; PiAm; STS; TAP

Here, where the world is quiet. The Garden of Proserpine. Swinburne. FaPoR; HAP; ILP (1975 ed.); NOBE; PoPle; VLP

Here X. lies dead, but God's forgiving. J. E. Thorold Rogers. FaBoEE

Heredity. Arthur Guiterman. OBAL

Heredity. Thomas Hardy. EBEV; IPWM

Herefor and therefor and therefor I cam. This Pretty Woman. *Unknown.* OxBM

"Here's a fine bag of meat." Bags of Meat. Thomas Hardy. BoAnP

Here's a health to the birds one and all! A Health to the Birds. Seumas MacManus. PFIr

Here's a health to the blacksmith, the best of all fellows. The Blacksmith's Song. *Unknown.* GBP

Here's a health to the Tackers, my boys. A Health to the Tackers. *Unknown.* APAS

Here's a land where all are equal. Creede. Cy Warman. BPAW

Here's a little proverb you surely ought to know. Inspiration on Perspiration. *Unknown.* SoSe (1977 ed.)

Here's a man knows what he's going to shoot. Gunfighter. Phillip Hey. NVAP

Here's a quiet tributary. Tribute. Alice Notley. FiCh

Here's a song. Scel Lem Duib. *Unknown, tr. by* Flann O'Brien. BIrV

Here's an example from/ a butterfly. The Example. W. H. Davies. PCOP

Here's an old lady, almost ninety-one. Two Old Ladies. Siegfried Sassoon. OxBTC

Here's Cooper, who's written six volumes to show. Cooper. James Russell Lowell. *Fr.* A Fable for Critics. NOBA; TAP

Here's Death. Rhyll McMaster. CAAP

Here's flowers for you. Shakespeare. *Fr.* The Winter's Tale, IV, iii. GBL

Here's no more news than virtue: I may as well. To Sir Henry Wotton. John Donne. PAIC

Here's one in whom Nature feared—faint at such vying. Cardinal Bembo's Epitaph on Raphael. Thomas Hardy, *after* Pietro Bembo. FaBoEE

Here's Sulky Sue. Sulky Sue. *Unknown.* BBL

Here's sweet little Sarah Samantha. Sarah Samantha. *Unknown.* TDH

Here's the bus now. All aboard please. Three Fitts. Stewart Parker. CIP

Here's the garden she walked across. Garden Fancies. Robert Browning. VLP

Here's the place: stand still: how fearfull. Shakespeare. *Fr.* King Lear, IV, vi. PES

Here's the spot. Look around you. Above on the height. Caldwell of Springfield. Bret Harte. BTTM

Here's the Tender Coming. *Unknown.* GBP

Here's to "La Canadienne"! Vive la Canadienne. *Tr. fr. French.* FSW

Here's to nick and nora charles. A Toast. Charles Stetler. GP

Here's your right ground. Wag gently o'er this black. Emblems, I, 10. Francis Quarles. SCP-2

Heretic's Tragedy, The. Robert Browning. OAEL-2

Hereto I come to view a voiceless ghost. After a Journey. Thomas Hardy. CMoP (1970 ed.); EBEV; ExPo (1973 ed.); GBL; OxBTC

Heritage. Gwendolyn B. Bennett. AmNP (1974 ed.); PoBA

Heritage. Countee Cullen. AmNP (1974 ed.); BPo; NoAM; PoBA; WIF

Heritage. Augustus Young. CIP; IPM

Herkens to my tale that I shall here shewe. Marvels. *Unknown.* OxBM

Herm whose length measured degrees of heat, The. William Empson. *Fr.* Bacchus. PoA

Herman Melville. Conrad Aiken. NoAM; NOBA; TAP

Hermaphroditus. Swinburne. VLP

Hermes came to me in a dream. I said. Sappho, *tr. fr. Greek by* Willis Barnstone. BoWoP

Hermes of the Ways. Hilda Doolittle ("H. D."). WPE

Hermetic Bird. Philip Lamantia. VGW

Hermit. David Baker. AMV-80

Hermit, The. Daniel Halpern. AMV-80

Hermit, The. Hsü Pên, *tr. fr. Chinese by* Henry H. Hart. RFM

Hermit Cackleberry Brown, on Human Vanity, The. Jonathan Williams. OBAL

Hermit Has a Visitor, The. Maxine W. Kumin. BoWoP

Hermit hoar, in solemn cell. Imitation of the Style of * * * * [*or* Idyll]. Samuel Johnson. FaBoCo; NOBL

Hermit Picks Berries, The. Maxine W. Kumin. RFM

Hermit Wakes to Bird Sounds, The. Maxine W. Kumin. WeW

Hermit's Song, A. *Unknown, tr. fr. Irish by* James Simmons. BIrV

Hermogenes's Song. Ben Jonson. *Fr.* The Poetaster. ILP (1975 ed.)

Hero. Ronald Gross. SPo

Hero, The. Marianne Moore. *Fr.* Part of a Novel, Part of a Poem, Part of a Play. CMoP (1970 ed.); NIL; NOBA; PoA

Hero. William Stafford. WasP

Hero and Leander. Christopher Marlowe (First *and* Second Sestiads), *completed by* George Chapman. AAS; CABA (1972 ed.)

*Sels.*

Amorous Neptune. Marlowe. NOBE

"And now the sun that through the horizon peeps," *fr.* Second Sestiad. Marlowe. OAEL-1

Bridal Song, *fr.* Fifth Sestiad. Chapman. NOBE

"By this, Leander, being near the land," *fr.* Second Sestiad. Marlowe. EBEV

"Her veil was artificial flowers and leaves," *fr.* First Sestiad. Marlowe. HoPM (1975 ed.)

Hero Feels the Shaft of Love. Marlowe. GBL

"Leander to the envious light," Third Sestiad, *argument.* Chapman. OAEL-1

Love at First Sight, *fr.* First Sestiad. Marlowe. NOBE

"New light gives new directions, fortunes new," *fr.* Third Sestiad. Chapman. OAEL-1

"Now from Leander's place she rose, and found," *fr.* Fourth Sestiad. Chapman. EBEV

"On Hellespont, guilty of true love's blood," *fr.* First Sestiad. Marlowe. OAEL-1

Seduction of Hero, The, *fr.* Second Sestiad. Marlowe. NIL

Hero and the Hydra, The, *sel.* James McAuley. Tomb of Heracles, The. MAuV

Hero Feels the Shaft of Love. Christopher Marlowe. *Fr.* Hero and Leander. GBL

Heroes. Robert Creeley. NOBA; PPP

Heroes, The. Louis Simpson. SoS

Heroes, and Kings! your distance keep. Epitaph for One Who Would Not Be Buried in Westminster Abbey. Pope. FaBoEE

Heroes of the Strip. Sheila Cudahy. TAT

Heroes paused upon the plain, The. The Byrnies. Thom Gunn. NoAM; OxBTC

Heroes screamed from my fingertips. Bard. Gavin Bantock. FaBoTw (1975 ed.); TwMBP

Heroic good, target for which the young. Faint yet Pursuing. Coventry Patmore. *Fr.* The Unknown Eros. PFD

Heroic Heart. Charles Donnelly. CIP

Heroides, *sel.* Ovid, *tr. fr Latin by* George Turberville. "To Paris that was once her owne though now it be not so." OBVE

Heron, The. Philip Murray. BoAnP

Heron. Stanley Plumly. AmPA

Heron, The. Theodore Roethke. BoAnP; RFM

Heron, The. Vernon Watkins. UnPo (1976 ed.)

Heron flew east, the heron flew west, The. The Corpus Christi Carol. *Unknown.* GBP

Heron stands in water where the swamp, The. The Heron. Theodore Roethke. BoAnP; RFM

Herons. *Unknown, tr. fr. Japanese.* PCOP

Heron's Bay. Martin Galvin. AMV-81

Hero's Father's Tombs, *sel.* Essex C. Hemphill. "My father is a fist." PoUp

Herr Privatdozent, it is not my way. 1907, A Proposal from Paris. Richard Howard. CAAP

Herrick Hospital, Fifth Floor. Al Young. CPA

Herrick's Julia. Helen Bevington. SpRo

Herring. Kenneth Rexroth. *Fr.* A Bestiary. HoPM (1975 ed.)

Herring and ling! The Red Herring. *Unknown.* FaBoNo

Herring-Girls, The. Derick Thomson, *tr. fr. Gaelic by author.* MS

Herring-Gull. John Hall Wheelock. EcS

Herring Is King. Alfred Perceval Graves. PFIr

Herring is prolific, The. Herring. Kenneth Rexroth. *Fr.* A Bestiary. HoPM (1975 ed.)

Herring Loves the Merry Moonlight, The. *Unknown.* PoPle

Herself. John Holmes. HoPM (1975 ed.)

Hertha. Swinburne. OAEL-2; VLP

Hertza. Benjamin Fondane, *tr. fr. French by* Matei Calinescu *and* Willis Barnstone. VWA

Hervordshir, shild and spere. The Shires. *Unknown.* OxBM

He's a Fool. *Unknown.* FSW

He's asleep, or dead, numb with wind. The Rattlesnake. Robert Wrigley. AMV-80

He's dead/ the dog won't have to. Death. William Carlos Williams. VGW

He's Doing Natural Life. Conyus. PoBA

He's gone, and Fate admits of no return. Epitaph on the Secretary to the Muses. Jane Barker. FaBoCo

He's Gone Away. *Unknown.* FSW

He's Got the Whole World in His Hands. *Unknown.* BLSo, *with music;* FSW

He's howling again, he. Kennel. Beth Bentley. CNW

He's Known His Lesson for Years. R. P. Kingston. NVAP

He's neither Chinese. A Buddhist Priest. Ho Xuan Huong, *tr. by* Nguyen Ngoc Bich. PBWP

He's no Apollo Belvedere. Babe Ruth. Damon Runyon. SPo

He's nothing much but fur. A Kitten. Eleanor Farjeon. RAE

He's on the road again. The Road Again. Tom Matthews. IPM

He's seldom the way anybody wants. Another View of the Beast. R. P. Dickey. FoP

He's very odd, standing on yellow sand. Clown, and All the Sea behind Him. Vincent O'Sullivan. ATNZ

Hesitant door chain, The. Into Blackness Softly. Mari Evans. PoBA

Hesitation Blues. *Unknown.* FSW

Hesperides, The. Tennyson. OAEL-2

Hesperos, you bring home all the bright dawn disperses. Sappho, *tr. fr. Greek by* Willis Barnstone. BoWoP

Hesperus. John Clare. OAEL-2

Hesperus, *sel.* James Stephens.
    "Evening gathers everything." LCL

Hesperus! the day is gone. Hesperus. John Clare. OAEL-2

Hessian Doctor, The. Philip Freneau. *Fr.* The British Prison Ship. EAP

Heth. Carlos Montemayer, *tr. fr. Spanish by* Nigel Grant Sylvester. AMV-81

Hev ye seen owt o' maw bonnie lad. Maw Bonnie Lad. *Unknown.* GBP

Hexameter and Pentameter. *Unknown.* FaBoNo

Hexameters. Samuel Taylor Coleridge. MBPR

Hexametra Alexis in Laudem Rosamundi. Robert Greene. *Fr.* Greene's Mourning Garment. GBL

Hey Animal—Eat This Popcorn. Cinda Kornblum. AcAn; EC

Hey Betty Martin. *Unknown.* FSW

Hey, boys, joint ahead. Track-lining Song. *Unknown.* AmFP

Hey brassy baby whose switched-on hair. The Earth: To Marilyn. Judith Johnson Sherwin. WBN

Hey, Bungalow Bill. The Continuing Story of Bungalow Bill. John Lennon *and* Paul McCartney. GrRo

Hey, Coolidge boy. Brooklyn Bridge. Vladimir Mayakovsky, *tr. by* Vladimir Markov *and* Merrill Sparks. NYP

Hey daddy/ hey daddy/ don't let me cry in vain. Oh Ambulance Man. *Unknown.* BluL

Hey [*or* High] diddle, diddle,/ The cat and the fiddle. Mother Goose. GSB, *with music;* HoPM (1975 ed.); MG

Hey diddle dinketty, poppelty pet. The Merchants of London. *Unknown.* GBP

Hey Fella Would You Mind Holding This Piano a Moment. William J. Harris. GP

Hey for a Lass wi' a Tocher. Burns. SLP

Hey! hey! by this day! The Unhappy Schoolboy. *Unknown.* OxBChV

Hey, hey, hey, hey/ I will have the whetstone. I Will Have the Whetstone. *Unknown.* FaBoNo; GBP

Hey, hey Jane, Jane. Jane, Jane. *Unknown.* FSW

Hey-ho Knave: A Catch. *Unknown.* GBP

Hey, Ho, Nobody Home. *Unknown.* FSW

Hey, how!/ Sely men, God helpe you! An Old Man and His Wife. *Unknown.* OxBM

Hey, laughing youths. Haiku. Louis Cuneo. CPA

Hey, little brand new baby. Little Brand New Baby. Tom Paxton. SoS

Hey look! Hymn for October. Robert Gessner. SPT

Hey, mama/ Tell me what have I. Awful Fix. *Unknown.* BluL

Hey, Mister Tambourine Man, play a song for me. Mister Tambourine Man. Bob Dylan. NIL

Hey Mom! Assignment. Grace Butcher. RiTi

Hey moonface. Only a Little Litter. Myra Cohn Livingston. QQQ

Hey Nellie. Smokey's Gettin' Old. Jessica Tarahata Hagedorn. MMD

Hey, Neruda! Hey, Ritsos! Two Communist Poets. Irving Layton. AMV-81

Hey, nonny no!/ Men are fools that wish to die! *Unknown.* EBEV

Hey there poleece. Poem to a Nigger Cop. Bobb Hamilton. TPo

Hey, this little kid gets roller skates. 74th Street. Myra Cohn Livingston. CTBA

Hey, Walt, you/ should see these lilacs. Late Spring, Sur Coast. Naomi Clark. CPA

Hey, young bride! Teasing Song. Princess Magogo, *tr. by* D. K. Rycroft. WTO

Hi! Walter de la Mare. BBL

Hi, Hi, Curlywig. *Unknown.* PoPle

"Hi," said the little leatherwing bat. Leatherwing Bat. *Unknown.* FSW

Hiatus. Margaret Avison. HAP

Hiawatha and Mudjekeewis. Longfellow. The Song of Hiawatha, IV. AKE

Hiawatha's Photographing. "Lewis Carroll." FaBoCo; NOBL; SpRo

Hibernating in an Old Lost Neighbourhood. Laura Chester. RiTi

Hibernia. Stuart Howard-Jones. NOBL

Hibiscus on the Sleeping Shores. Wallace Stevens. InPS

Hic jacet Tom Shorthose. *Unknown.* FaBoEE

Hickety, Pickety,/ My black hen. Mother Goose. MG

Hickety pickety i sillickety. *Unknown.* GBP

Hickory, dickory, dock. Mother Goose. GSB, *with music;* MG; MN; UsP

Hickory Stick Hierarchy. Len G. Selle. AMV-80

Hid near a lily-spangled stream. Balthasar. Charles Spear. ATNZ

Hidden Bow. Mordecai Temkin, *tr. fr. Hebrew by* Jeremy Garber. VWA

Hidden everywhere. The Two. Irving Feldman. UsP

Hidden Falls. John Minczeski. BrS

Hidden immortal. Near a Waterfall at Ryumon. Lady Ise, *tr. by* Etsuko Terasaki *and* Irma Brandeis. BoWoP

Hidden Message, A. Kevin Ireland. ATNZ

Hidden Things. Ann Stanford. MPA

Hide [*or* Hyd], Absalon [*or* Absolon], thy gilte tresses clear [*or* clere]. Balade. Chaucer. *Fr.* The Legend of Good Women: Prologue. EBEV; GBL; HAP; NOBE; OAEL-1; OxBM; WeW

Hide and Seek. Robert Graves. FPB

Hide and Seek. Dan Pagis, *tr. fr. Hebrew by* Bernhard Frank. AMV-81

Hide and Seek. Vernon Scannell. DuDr; LP

Hide Thou Me. *Unknown.* AmFP

Hidebehind, The. Michael Rosen. OSF

Hiding in the church of an abandoned stone. Confession to J. Edgar Hoover. James Wright. CAPP; ConAP

Hiding Place. Richard Armour. NIL

Hie upon Hielands [*or* High up on highland]. Bonnie [*or* Bonny] George Campbell. *Unknown.* AIW; AmFP; FaBoBa; GBP; PeBB; PoPle

Hieland Laddie. *Unknown.* FSW

Hielant Woman. Sorley Maclean, *tr. fr. Gaelic; Scots version by* Douglas Young. MS

Hieroglyph. Paul Auster. VWA

Hieroglyphs. Ettore Rella. SPT

Hierusalem, My Happy Home. *Unknown.* BoReV; FaPoR; NOBE

Higgledy-piggledy. Twilight's Last Gleaming. Arthur W. Monks. OFD

Higgledy-piggledy/ Andrea Doria. Last Words. John Hollander. OBAL

Higgledy-piggledy,/ Benjamin Harrison. Historical Reflections. John Hollander. OBAL

Higgledy, piggledy/ Gloria Vanderbilt. Poor Kid. William Cole. OBAL

Higgledy-piggledy/ Heliogabalus. Heliogabalus. John Hollander. OBAL

Higgledy-piggledy/ John Simon Guggenheim. No Foundation. John Hollander. OBAL

Higgledy-piggledy/ Josephine Bonaparte. Appearance and Reality. John Hollander. OBAL

Higgledy-piggledy/ Ludwig van Beethoven. E. William Seaman. WeW

Higgledy-piggledy/ Mme. de Maintenon. Firmness. Anthony Hecht. OBAL

Higgledy-piggledy/ Ralph Waldo Emerson. From the Grove Press. Anthony Hecht. OBAL

Higgledy-piggledy/ Thomas Stearns Eliot. Vice. Anthony Hecht. OBAL

High. Mbembe. NW

High and Low. John Banister Tabb. TDH

High and proud on the barnyard fence. Chanticleer. John Farrar. CTV

High are the mountains and low is the plain. When Billy the Kid Rides Again. S. Omar Barker. BPAW

High Are the Winter Rivers. Dave Smith. HeS

High Barbaree. *Unknown. See* Wild Barbaree, The.

High Chair and Low Spirits. Richard Armour. BBGO

High-cool/ 2. James Cunningham. JB

High Country Weather. James K. Baxter. ATNZ

High diddle diddle/ The cat and the fiddle. *See* Hey! diddle, diddle . . . .

High ding a ding, and ho ding a ding. The Parliament Soldiers. *Unknown.* GBP

High Diver. Robert Francis. LiSp

High Fidelity. Thom Gunn. PoA

High Field—First Day of Winter. Gary Eddy. AMV-80

High Frequency. Marge Piercy. MMD

High Germany. *Unknown.* FSW

High grace, the dower of Queens; and therewithal. Her Gifts. Dante Gabriel Rossetti. The House of Life, XXXI. VLP

High in front advanc'd/ The brandisht sword of God before them blaz'd. Conclusion. Milton. *Fr.* Paradise Lost, XII. OBP

High in the afternoon the dove. Kendrick Smithyman. *Fr.* Considerations. ATNZ

High in the breathless hall the minstrel sate. Song at the Feast of Brougham Castle. Wordsworth. MBPR

High in the jacaranda shines the gilded thread. The 90th Year. Denise Levertov. FiCP

High in the mountains of Soviet Armenia. Out of the Deepness. William (Haywood) Jackson. AMV-81

High in the pine, the soft winds sough. The Pine Assessor. Prentice Baker. AATT

High in the trees, small leaves. Wood Fever. Jean Nordhaus. PoUp

High is our calling, friend!—creative art. To B. R. Haydon. Wordsworth. MBPR

High Island. Richard Murphy. CIP

High Jump, The. *Unknown.* LiSp; SPo

High-loping Cowboy, The. Curley W. Fletcher. BPAW

High majesty of Paul's, The. W. E. Henley. *Fr.* London Voluntaries. PES

High o'er the Hills, *with music.* William Walker. AH

High on a gorgeous seat, that far outshone. Pope. *Fr.* The Dunciad, II. NIL

High on a ridge of tiles. Poem. Maurice James Craig. BoAnP

High on a rough and dismal crag. The Miner's Lament. "Mark Twain." BPAW

High on a slope in New Guinea. The Man in the Dead Machine. Donald Hall. CoPAm

High on a throne of royal state, which far. Milton. *Fr.* Paradise Lost, II. NIL

High on his figured couch beyond the waves. Theseus and Ariadne. Robert Graves. HAP

High on his stockroom ladder like a dunce. Playboy. Richard Wilbur. FF; NoAM; NOBA; PoIA; WeW

High on that cliff. Beyond Swordale. Derick Thomson. MS

High on the Hog. Julia Fields. CNA

High on the thrilling strand he dances. Tightrope Walker. Vernon Scannell. NCSH

High over Mecca Allah's prophet's corpse. Dissatisfaction with Metaphysics. William Empson. CMoP (1970 ed.)

High, over the fen. The Windmill. Arthur J. Bull. HeHu

High overhead. Looking Up at Airplanes, Always. Rolfe Humphries. PAIC

High-placed above me the branches quiver. The Lost. *Malay Oral Tradition, tr. by* R. J. Wilkinson *and* R. O. Winstedt. WTO

High Plains Harvest. Bruce Morton. AMV-81

High poetry and low. Wallace Stevens. PoA

High Price Blues. *Unknown.* BluL

High Priests of telescopes and cyclotrons, The. Ode to Terminus. W. H. Auden. HAP

High Renaissance. George Starbuck. OBAL

High-riding kites appear to range quite freely. Gravities. Seamus Heaney. NoAM

High School Band, The. Reed Whittemore. MiP; NCSH

High sheriff been here, The. Big Rock Jail. *Unknown.* BluL

High Sheriff Blues. *Unknown.* BluL

High spirited friend. An Ode. Ben Jonson. PAIC

High stretched upon the swinging yard. Disguises. Thomas Edward Brown. VLP

High Summer. Guy Rotella. AMV-80

High Summer on the Mountains. Idris Davies. OxBTC

High summer's sheen upon all things. The Web. Theodore Weiss. NoAM

High Tension Wires. Allan Block. FAF

High the vanes of Shrewsbury gleam. The Welsh Marches. A. E. Housman. FaBoTw (1975 ed.)

High-toned Old Christian Woman, A. Wallace Stevens. CMoP (1970 ed.); ILP (1975 ed.); NoAM; NOBA; PAIC; PiAm; PPP; SoSe; STS; TAP

High towers the grass where once we'd meet and wander. Parting. *Malay Oral Tradition, tr. by* R. J. Wilkinson *and* R. O. Winstedt. WTO

High up on highland. *See* Hie upon Hielands.

High up on the lonely mountains. A Night with a Wolf. Bayard Taylor. PCOP

High walls . . . of stones. Aran Islands. Irving Layton. NeAC

High Water Everywhere: 1 ("The back water done rose around Sumner, now"). *Unknown.* BluL

High Water Everywhere: 2 ("Back water at Blytheville"). *Unknown.* BluL

High Windows. Philip Larkin. PoIA

High Wire Dancers. Ann Hoskins. PPM

Higher ("The shadows of night were a-comin' down swift"). *Unknown.* SpRo

Higher Empiricism, The. Francis C. Golffing. PoA

Higher Pantheism, The. Tennyson. PAIC; SpRo; VLP

Higher Pantheism in a Nutshell, The, *parody.* Swinburne. *Fr.* The Heptalogia. FaBoNo; PAIC; SpRo

Higher than gull's nests, higher than children go. Rock Climbing. Jane Cooper. NMM

Higher than the handsomest hotel. The Building. Philip Larkin. PSN

Highest things are easiest to be shown, The. Thomas Traherne. *Fr.* The Demonstration. SCP-2

Highland Harry Back Again. *At. to* Burns. EBEV

Highland Portrait. Iain Crichton Smith. MS

Highmindedness, a jealousy for good. Addressed to Haydon. Keats. MBPR

Highway, The. W. S. Merwin. PoA

Highway Blues. *Unknown.* BluL

Highway Construction. Carol Earle Chapin. QQQ

Highway of blood/ volkswagens crushed up. Megalopolis. Victor Hernández Cruz. SA

Highway 101, Seal Beach. Curtis Zahn. NowV

Highway Patrol Stops Me, Going Too Slow. Robert Peterson. NeAC

Highway, since you my chief Parnassus be. Astrophel and Stella, LXXXIV. Sir Philip Sidney. ILP (1975 ed.)

Highway turnpike thruway mall. A Charm for Our Time. Eve Merriam. QQQ

Highwayman's Ghost, The. Richard Garnett. PoTa

Hiking. Joseph Bruchac. CDW

Hiking Santa Fe Baldy on Monday, middle of May. Six Creatures on the Way. Stanley Noyes. PoW

Hilaire Belloc. Humbert Wolfe. FaBoEE

Hilda Lay in Hospital. Judith McCombs. WBN

Hilda's Pelt. Judith McCombs. WBN

Hill, The. Rupert Brooke. OxBTC

Hill, The. Robert Creeley. ConAP; NoAM

Hill, The. Edgar Lee Masters. *Fr.* Spoon River Anthology. CMoP (1970 ed.); NoAM; NOBA; TAP

Hill Farmer Speaks, The. R. S. Thomas. MPo; OBW

Hill flank overlooking the Axe valley, A. Watching Post. C. Day Lewis. MPo

Hill Hunger. John Foster West. TAT

Hill of the Graces, The. Spenser. *Fr.* The Faerie Queene, VI, 10. NOBE

Hill of Zion yields, The. Mount Zion. *Unknown.* AmFP

Hill Pines Were Sighing, The. Robert Bridges. ExPo (1973 ed.)

Hill Summit, The. Dante Gabriel Rossetti. The House of Life, LXX. VLP

Hill was higher every year, The. Model T. Adrien Stoutenburg. CTBA

Hill Wife, The. Robert Frost. CMoP (1970 ed.); HAP
*Sels.*
House Fear. PPM
Impulse, The. AIW; HoPM (1975 ed.); NoAM
"One ought not to have to care." VGW

Hill you may say is a hill, A; take a hill. Object Lesson. Paul Henderson. ATNZ

Hill-billy, hill-billy come to buy. Pedlar. Ezra Pound, *after the Chinese.* OBVE

Hillcrest. E. A. Robinson. PPoe

Hills, The. Frances Cornford. PPM

Hills, The. Rachel Field. LCL

Hills, The/ were never closer. David's Poem. Ben Hiatt. CPA

Hills are high in Caribou, The. The Yellow Witch of Caribou. Clyde Robertson. BPAW

Hills moved. I watched their shadows. Beetle on the Shasta Daylight. Shirley Kaufman. WPE

Hills of God, Break Forth in Singing, *with music.* John Wright Buckham. AH

Hills of Zion, The. The Four of Them. Yehuda Karni, *tr. by* Jeremy Garber. VWA

Hills picking up the/ moonlight like. Nina Cassian, *tr. fr. Rumanian by* Stavros Deligiorgis. BoWoP

Hills shall miss him, The—while the pines. The Dead Prospector. Arthur Chapman. BPAW

Hills step off into whiteness, The. Sheep in Fog. Sylvia Plath. PSN

Hills where I grew up had learned to hide, The. The Hughesville Scythe. Henry Taylor. PPoD

Hill-Side Flowers. Matthew Arnold. *Fr.* Thyrsis. PF

Hillside Thaw, A. Robert Frost. CMoP (1970 ed.); ExPo (1973 ed.)

Hilo, Hanakahi, rain rustling lehua. *Tr. fr. Hawaiian by* S. H. Elbert *and* N. Mahoe. WTO

Himself. Daniel Hoffman. AMV-80

Himself is all he'll talk about to you. The Egotist. H. A. C. Evans. POL

Hind and the Panther, The, *sels.* Dryden.
"Portly prince, and goodly to the sight, A," *fr.* III. OBSV
Revelation, *fr.* I. BoReV
(Confessio Fidei.) NOBE

Hind Etin. *Unknown.* PeBB

Hind Horn. *Unknown.* AmFP

Hinge, The. Sheila Cowing. AMV-81

Hint for the Incomplete Angler. Kendrick Smithyman. ATNZ

Hinx! minx!/ The old witch winks! Children's Runes and Omens. *Unknown.* MAT

Hip Shakin' Strut. *Unknown.* BluL

Hippie Hop. A. R. Ammons. NIL

Hippo, The. Theodore Roethke. VGW

Hippo decided one day, A. Ballet. *Unknown.* TDH

Hippolytus. Euripides, *tr. fr. Greek by* Rex Warner. NAWM-1

Hippolytus Temporizes. Hilda Doolittle ("H. D."). SBG

Hippopotamus, The. Hilaire Belloc. BBL; FaBoNo; InPK

Hippopotamus, The. Georgia Roberts Durston. CTV

Hippopotamus, The. T. S. Eliot. AnMo; BoReV; HoPM (1975 ed.); VGW

Hippopotamus is strong, The. Habits of the Hippopotamus. Arthur Guiterman. BoAnP

Hippopotamuses. Arnold Spilka. OSF

Hips and ass go to an' fro on this good good earth. All Owners of Meat Are Hospitable. Rochelle Owens. WBN

Hiraeth. Unknown, tr. fr. Welsh by Aneirin Talfan Davies. OBW

Hiraeth in N.W.3. Wynford Vaughan-Thomas. NOBL

"Hiram, I think the sump is backing up." Mending Sump. Kenneth Koch. InPK; NoAM

Hiram Powers' "Greek Slave." Elizabeth Barrett Browning. SBG; VLP

Hired Man on Horseback, The. Eugene Manlove Rhodes. BPAW

Hiroshima, sel. Gavin Bantock.
    "There were many of us at the time." TwMBP

Hiroshima. Lord Russell Brain. PMW

His/ name was. A Marriage. Anthony Barnett. VWA

His Age, Dedicated to His Peculiar Friend, Master John Wickes, under the Name of Posthumus. Robert Herrick. CaPo

His aging widow dreams of youth. Memorial Service. Ursula Vaughan Williams. POL

His art is eccentricity, his aim. Pitcher. Robert Francis. LiSp; PoIA; SPo; WIF

His being gone is a gift to my people. Wulf and Eadwacer. Unknown, tr. by Willis Barnstone and Elene Kolb. BoWoP

His Body. Sandra McPherson. AmPA; CAAP; CNW; GP; PCho

His body doubled. On the Swag. R. A. K. Mason. ATNZ

His bridle hung around the post. Horse. Elizabeth Madox Roberts. PH

His broad-brimm'd hat push'd back with careless air. Vaquero. Joaquin Miller. BPAW

His brother after dinner. Uncle Bull-Boy. June Jordan. PoBA

His care-free swagger was a fine invention. Sonnets from China, V. W. H. Auden. CMoP (1970 ed.)

His case inspires interest. A Man of Words. John Ashbery. PoA

His castrating wife is at the controls. Blue Max. Harvey Shapiro. GP

His Cavalier. Robert Herrick. CaPo

His chosen comrades thought at school. What Then? W. B. Yeats. CMoP (1970 ed.)

His coat resembles the snow. The Polar Bear. William Carlos Williams. BCr

His coffin/ knows my shoulder. Father. Tom MacIntyre. IPM

His Coming. Irene Dayton. AATT

His compassionate face, slightly wan. On the Street. C. P. Cavafy, tr. by Rae Dalven. BoLoP

His Confession. "The Archpoet," tr. fr. Latin by Helen Waddell. NAWM-1

His Content in the Country. Robert Herrick. CaPo

His corpse owre a' the city lies. The Dead Liebknecht. "Hugh MacDiarmid," after the German of Rudolf Leonhard. OBVE

His Creed. Robert Herrick. ILP (1975 ed.); PIM

His cry was always sad. Taught to Be Polite. Virginia Brady Young. AMV-81

His daughter Charlotte said to Mr. Brontë. Sampler from Haworth. Frances Minturn Howard. WPE

His Desire. Robert Herrick. CABA (1972 ed.)

His desires, growing. Black Man's Feast. Sarah Webster Fabio. PoBA

His drifter swung in the night. Uncle Roderick. Norman McCaig. MPo

His Elegy. Chidiock Tichborne. See Elegy: "My prime of youth is but a frost of cares."

His enemies: death, suicide, the slow. Consultant's Holiday. U. A. Fanthorpe. PMW

His eyes are quickened so with grief. Lost Love. Robert Graves. ILP (1975 ed.)

His eyes locked in a stare. Griffin. Richard Mathews. AATT

His eyes were once blue and pure. Hard Times, but Carrying On. Dave Smith. TAT

His face is pale and shrunk, his shining hair. November Sun. Elizabeth Daryush. PBWP

His face is streaked with prepared tears. The Clown. Janet Frame. ATNZ

His face was blue, on his fingers. Mourning and Melancholia. A. Alvarez. VWA

His Farewell to Sack. Robert Herrick. CaPo

His father gave him a box of truisms. The Truisms. Louis MacNeice. NOBE; OBSV

His father said: Marry her. She's had a hard life. The Chosen— Kalgoorlie, 1894. Fay Zwicky. VWA

His father said that he had grown. All the Dead Birds. Melvin Walker LaFollette. SFF

His father taught him how to hold the plough. The Ploughman. Nellie Burget Miller. WPW

His figure's not noted for grace. The Wild Boarder. Kenyon Cox. TDH

His finger resembled. The Accident. Len Gasparini. NeAC

His flesh/ fish underwater. The Death of the Epileptic Poet Yesenin. Aram Boyajian. NeAC

His footprints have failed us. Dead in the Sierras. Joaquin Miller. BPAW

His frailty discrete, the rodent turns, looks. Buteo Regalis. N. Scott Momaday. VW

His friends drudged in an airplane factory. Icarus. Irving Layton. BBGO

His friends went off and left Him dead. The Resurrection. Jonathan Brooks. AmNP (1974 ed.)

His fur is matted, plenty of ticks. The Great Bear. P. B. Newman. BCr

His Golden Locks Time Hath to Silver Turned. George Peele. Fr. Polyhymnia. HeIP; PPoe
    (Farewell to Arms.) NIL; NOBE; PoPle
    (Sonnet, A: "His golden locks time hath to silver turned.") InPS

His Good Time. Roland Flint. PoUp

His Grace! impossible! what dead! A Satirical Elegy on the Death of a Late Famous General. Swift. CABA (1972 ed.); ESaP; ExPo (1973 ed.); FF; HoPM (1975 ed.); NIL; OBSV; PAIC; PBMP; SS

His Grange, or Private Wealth. Robert Herrick. CaPo

His great bald head, trembling weightiness. Stone Age. Floyd C. Stuart. FAF

His habit was to counter all her questions. Wife and Mother. Jonathan Sisson. AAN

His hair was yellow and long. A Tale of Last Stands. Fred Red Cloud. VW

His hand came out of the east. Homer, tr. by Christopher Logue. Fr. The Iliad, XVI. OBVE

His hand was a puppet, more wood than flesh. The Doctor Rebuilds a Hand. Gary Young. AMV-80

His hatbrim's full Copernican ellipse. The Portrait of Prince Henry. Sydney Clouts. VWA

His head is tiny because he has few brains. Whippet. Prudence Andrew. GDP

His head like a fist rooted in his abdomen. The Agents. Robert Conquest. EAS

His headstone said. The Funeral of Martin Luther King, Jr. Nikki Giovanni. AmNP (1974 ed.); BPo

His high-boned, young face is so brown. White Pass Ski Patrol. John Logan. BiP; CAPP

His Hope or Sheet-Anchor. Robert Herrick. CaPo

His Immortality. Thomas Hardy. CMoP (1970 ed.); PoPle

His job was. Branches Back Into. Ken Belford. NeAC

His kepi rests on the piano. One for the Fatherland. Leonard Nathan. PoW

His kiss a bristling. Against Winter. Elaine Feinstein. VWA

His lamp his bow and quiver laid aside. Cupid a Plowman. Moschus, *tr. by* Matthew Prior. OBVE

His last days linger in that low attic. The Old Jockey. F. R Higgins. OxBTC

His Late Wife's Wedding-Ring. George Crabbe. *See* Marriage Ring, A.

His life frightened him. The sun in the sky. Fear. Stephen Dobyns. AMV-80

His Litany to the Holy Spirit. Robert Herrick. BoReV (Litany, The: "In the hour of my distress.") ILwL (Litany to the Holy Spirit, *abr.*) PoPle

His logic unperturbed, exacting new. Metaphysician. Robert Fitzgerald. PoA

His lordship's steed. Riding. William Allingham. OxBChV

His mail is brimming with Foundation reports. Henry's Mail. John Berryman. *Fr.* Dream Songs. ILP (1975 ed.)

His mansion in the pool. Emily Dickinson. OBAL

His mither sings to the bairnie Christ. O Jesu Parvule. "Hugh MacDiarmid." MS

His mother loved him. All the world of man. His Mother's Love. Noah Stern, *tr. by* Harold Schimmel. VWA

His mother's eyes. Copy. Richard Armour. BBGO

His Mother's Love. Noah Stern, *tr. fr. Hebrew by* Harold Schimmel. VWA

His name is/ Rubin. Rubin. Charles Cooper. PoBA

His name is levy, daytime. The West, in Drag. Barbara Berman. PoUp

His Necessary Darkness. Nancy Sullivan. TAP

His or her's. David Meltzer. *Fr.* Nature. CPA

His Own Epitaph. Robert Herrick. CaPo

His Own Epitaph, When He Was Sick. John Hoskyns. FaBoEE

His paper propped against the electric toaster. Daniel at Breakfast. Phyllis McGinley. BBGO; OBSV

His Parting from Her. John Donne. Elegies, XII. EBEV

His peasant parents killed themselves with toil. The Average. W. H. Auden. BBGO

His Pilgrimage. Sir Walter Ralegh. *See* Passionate Man's Pilgrimage, The.

His place is before, not in, the National Gallery. London Pavement Artist. James Schevill. TAP

His Plans for Old Age. William Meredith. TAP

His plumage is dun. Jailbird. Vernon Scannell. HeHu

His poems, yellow, torn and fading. Langston Hughes. Lew Blockcolski. VoR

His Poetry His Pillar. Robert Herrick. CaPo

His Prayer for Absolution. Robert Herrick. SCP-1

His Prayer to Ben Jonson. Robert Herrick. CaPo; ILP (1975 ed.)

His pride/ Had cast him out from Heaven, with all his host. Milton. *Fr.* Paradise Lost, I. PPoe

His Reaction to Her Asking for a Divorce. Hugh Fox. TC

His Remedie for Love. Michael Drayton. *Fr.* Idea. AAS

His Request. Owen Roe O'Sullivan, *tr. fr. Irish by* Joan Keefe. BIrV

His Request to Julia. Robert Herrick. CaPo

His Return to London. Robert Herrick. CaPo; FF; ILP (1975 ed.)

His role is to invert the fairy tale. Psychiatrist. Peter DeVries. OBAL

His sad brown bulk rears patient as the hills. A Bull. Babette Deutsch. BoAnP; LiSp

His self-conceit's so swollen by inflation. Positive, a Coxcomb. William Plomer. POL

His shadow monstrous on the palace wall. Oedipus. Thomas Blackburn. FaBoTw (1975 ed.)

His Side/ Her Side. Jeffrey Skinner. AMV-81

His sister named Lucy O'Finner. "Lewis Carroll." FaBoNo

His Sleep. Constance Urdang. AMV-81

His spirit in smoke ascended to high heaven. The Lynching. Claude McKay. PoBA; WIF

His spirit went into the television. When Daddy Died. Duane Ackerson. POL

His sullen kinsmen, by the winter sea. Santa Claus. Dom Moraes. NoAM

His Sweetheart Slain. *Unknown.* OxBM

His teeth are white as curds. The Arrow of Desire. *Gond Oral Tradition, tr. by* V. Elwin *and* S. Hivale. WTO

His Theology. Arthur J. Bull. HeHu

His Third Decade. Dabney Stuart. NVAP

His trousers are wind. Song to a Lover. *Tr. fr. Amharic (Ethiopia) by* Willis Barnstone. BoWoP

His tundra'd mind sprouts leaflets. Senile. Pat Folk. NowV

His two concerns are siege defences. The Medieval. Rodney Hall. FPA

His villa in the mountains was made over. Teahouse. Nicholas Rinaldi. AMV-81

His wet fur, velvet-smooth, was sleek as reeds. Otters. William Hart-Smith. BoAnP

His whiskers didn't come, his mustache is gone. A Mustacheless Bard. J. Gordon Coogler. OBAL

His Winding-Sheet. Robert Herrick. CaPo

Hist, but a word, fair and soft! Master Hugues of Saxe-Gotha. Robert Browning. OAEL-2

Hist Whist. E. E. Cummings. CC; OFD; RAE; SO

Historian, The. Christopher Middleton. TwMBP

Historical Museum, Manitoulin Island. Lisel Mueller. PoA

Historical Note, A (from George Washington to His Father.) John L. Sellers. DNGG

Historical Poem, An. *Unknown.* APAS

Historical Reflections. John Hollander. OBAL

Historical Society Exhibit: Old Programme. Felix Pollak. HeS

History. Alison Wyrley Birch. PPM

History. G. K. Chesterton. *Fr.* Songs of Education. OBSV

History. Arthur Gregor. TAP

History. James Liddy, *tr. fr. Irish.* CIP

History. Robert Lowell. TAP

History. May Miller. PoUp

History. Robin Skelton. MPA

History. Gary Soto. GP

History. Robert Penn Warren. NoAM

History among the Rocks. Robert Penn Warren. GOA

History and Abstraction. Thomas Lux. AmPA

History: arrested for drunken driving. Extracts from a Police Surgeon's Notebook. William Lindsay. PMW

History as Diabolical Maternalism. Michael S. Harper. NW

History has to live with what was here. History. Robert Lowell. TAP

History Lesson, A. Miroslav Holub, *tr. fr. Czech by* Ian Milner *and* George Theiner. BuTh

History Lesson for My Son. Ted Kooser. POL

History of a Literary Movement. Howard Nemerov. PSN

History of Arizona, The: How It Was Made and Who Made It. Charles O. Brown. BPAW

History of blacklife is put down in the motions, The. The Sound of Afroamerican History Chapt I. S. E. Anderson. PoBA

History of Education. David McCord. OBAL

History of human-kind to trace, The. Thomas Hood. *Fr.* A Black Job. VLP

History of Ideas. J. V. Cunningham. NIL

History of Insipids, The. John Freke. APAS

History of Love, A. William Carlos Williams. VGW

History of My Feeling, The. Kathleen Fraser. WBN (Love Poem.) RiTi

History of Samson, The, *sel.* Francis Quarles. "When lusty diet and the frolic cup." SCP-2

History of the Father, A. Charles Buckmaster. CAAP

History of the Flood, The. John Heath-Stubbs. OxBTC

History of the Opera, A. Sandra Hochman. RiTi

History of the Word. Robert Graves. UsP

History of Weather, The. George Mattingly. CPA

History she (Zelda) said stops here. Inside History. Angela McCabe. AmPA

History, the angel, was stirred. Northern Ireland: Two Comments. Seamus Deane. CIP

Hit a huge drive. Hero. Ronald Gross. SPo

Hit it on the rock. Test. Jonathan Price. CoPAm

Hit me! Jab me! Third Degree. Langston Hughes. BPo; BuTh

Hit Tune. *Unknown.* TDH

Hit wes upon a Scere-thorsday that ure loverd aros. Judas. *Unknown.* Epi

Hitch Haiku, *sels.* Gary Snyder. InPK
"After weeks of watching the roof leak."
"Drinking hot saké."
"Great freight truck, A."
"Over the Mindanao Deep."
"They didn't hire him."

Hitchhiker. David McCord. IWK

Hither thou com'st. The busy wind all night. The Bird. Henry Vaughan. ILP (1975 ed.); SCP-1

Hither We Come, Our Dearest Lord, *with music.* Enoch W. Freeman. AH

Hitler, frothy-mouth, wooden-head. *Tr. fr. Maori by* Barry Mitcalfe. WTO

Hits and Runs. Carl Sandburg. SPo

Hitting Fungoes. Michael Ryan. HeS

Ho. Al Young. GP

Ho, Androcles! One Lion, Once. Robert Canzoneri. CoPAm

Ho! brother Teague, dost hear the decree. Lilli Burlero [*or* Lilliburlero.] Thomas, Lord Wharton. APAS; FSW; RDB

Ho, Brother Teig. *Unknown.* GBP

Ho! Cupid calls, come, lovers, come. Cupid's Call. James Shirley. SCP-2

Ho, Everyone That Thirsteth. A. E. Housman. OAEL-2

Ho! in the dawn. Side by Side. Adrienne Rich. CoPAm

Ho, my comrades, see the signal. Hold the Fort. Philip Paul Bliss. FSW

"Ho!" quod the knight, "Good sir, namore of this." The Nun's Priest's Prologue. Chaucer. *Fr.* The Canterbury Tales. OAEL-1

Ho! See the fleet foot hosts of men. Roddy M'Corley. *Unknown.* FSW

Ho! Westward Ho! *with music.* Ossian E. Dodge. BLSo

Ho! who comes here along with bagpipe and drumming? The Morris Dance. *Unknown.* RAE

Hobbes snugly proves that every creature. Swift. *Fr.* On Poetry: A Rhapsody. HAP

Hobbes, 1651. John Hollander. NoAM

Hobo's Lullaby. Goebel Reeves. FSW

Hobson-Jobson children were enamoured of the sciences, The. Ed and Sid and Bernard. Edward MacDuff. QQQ

Hobthrush, The. *Unknown.* GBP

Hock-Cart, or Harvest Home, The. Robert Herrick. CaPo; EBEV; Epi; SCP-1

Hoddesdon. A. S. Wilson. PES

Hoddley, poddley, puddle and fogs. Jingle. *Unknown.* BBL; FaBoNo

Hoeing. Gary Soto. NW

Hoeing. John Updike. TSWA

Hoelderlin's Old Age. Stephen Spender. NoAM

Hog at the Manger. Norma Farber. PChr

Hog Butcher for the World. Chicago. Carl Sandburg. BiP; CMoP (1970 ed.); ILP (1975 ed.); IPWM; NoAM; NOBA; PiAm; PoA; TAP; UnPo (1976 ed.); VGW

Hog-calling. Roy Blount, Jr. TDH

Hog-calling Competition. Morris Bishop. TDH

Hog Drovers. *Unknown.* AmFP

Hogan. Archie Washburn. VW

Hogpen. Robert Morgan. CSP

Hogs in the Sky. Charles Bukowski. EC

Hogyn. *Unknown.* GBP

Hohenlinden. Thomas Campbell. FaPoR; NOBE (Battle of Hohenlinden, The.) BTTM

Hoise up the sail, cried they who understand. A Sea-Voyage from Tenby to Bristol. Katherine Philips. SBG; WPE

Hokku Poems. Richard Wright. AmNP (1974 ed.); PoBA

Hokusai. Jim Farrar. DNGG

"Hold a glass of pure water to the eye of the sun." Robin Fulton. *Fr.* Hung Red. MIS

Hold a glass of pure water to the eye of the sun! "Hugh MacDiarmid." *Fr.* The Glass of Pure Water. MS

"Hold Back the Edges of Your Gowns, Ladies, We Are Going through Hell." Cathleen Quirk. MMD

Hold Back Thy Hours, Dark Night. Beaumont *and* Fletcher. *Fr.* The Maid's Tragedy, I, ii. ILP (1975 ed.)

Hold, hold it tight. Song for a Girl on Her First Menstruation. *Tr. fr. Papuan by* Joe Prentuo. BoWoP

Hold On. *Unknown.* FSW

Hold suffering on a tight leash. Desert. Agnes Gergely, *tr. by* Emery George. VWA

Hold that/ umbrella high over my head. 5/5/75. Darlene Pearlstein. FiCh

Hold the Fort. Philip Paul Bliss. FSW

Hold the Fort. *Unknown.* FSW

Hold the Wind. *Unknown.* GBP

Hold your head high. An Army Buddy Used to Say. John L. Sellers. DNGG

Holdfast, The. George Herbert. Epi

Holding (After the Nez Perce). Beth Bentley. CNW

Holding black whips. Thoughts of Chairman Mao. David Young. AmPA; CAAP

Holding On. Richard Jackson. AMV-80

Holding Pattern. Sandra McPherson. RiTi

Holding the Mirror Up to Nature. Howard Nemerov. PoA

Holding the Sky. William Stafford. RFM

Hole in the Floor, A. Richard Wilbur. NoAM; NOBA

Holes in my arms. For Real. Jayne Cortez. PoBA

Holes of Green. Aileen Fisher. FPB

Holiday. Alan Dugan. CoPAm

Holiday Piece. Denis Glover. ATNZ

Holidays. Eva Mylonas, *tr. fr. Modern Greek by* Kimon Friar. BoWoP

Holiness on the head. Aaron. George Herbert. OAEL-1

Holland, that scarce deserves the name of land. The Character of Holland. Andrew Marvell. NOBL; OBSV

Hollin, Green Hollin. *Unknown.* GBP

Hollo, My Fancy! *Unknown.* SCP-2

Hollow-feeling, empty of sleep and as yet unbreakfasted. Morning. Harry Fainlight. POL

Hollow Flute, The. Avner Strauss. VWA

Hollow Men, The. T. S. Eliot. AnMo; BiP; InPS; OAEL-2; PBMP; STS; TCP; TT

Hollow sea-shell which for years hath stood, The. Sea-Shell Murmurs. Eugene Lee-Hamilton. SoSe

Hollow Thesaurus, The. Roger McDonald. CAAP

Hollow Tree, A. Robert Bly. GP; NNaP

Hollow Wood, The. Edward Thomas. RAE

Holly, The. Walter de la Mare. CMoP (1970 ed.)

Holly and His Merry Men. *Unknown.* OxBM
(Nay! Ivy, Nay!) ILP (1975 ed.)

Holly and Ivy ("Holver and Hivy made a gret party"). *Unknown.* OxBM

Holly and Mistletoe. Eleanor Farjeon. PChr

Holly and the Ivy, The ("The holly and the ivy,/ When they are both full grown"). *Unknown.* FSW; GBP; OFD; PChr

Holly leaves are glinting in the sun, The. Mixed Weather. Sydney Tremayne. MS

Holly's up, the house is all bright, The. The Christmas Tree. Peter Cornelius. PChr

Hollywood Park Race Track is thirty miles. Please. Ronald Koertge. GP

Holmes. James Russell Lowell. *Fr.* A Fable for Critics. NOBA

Holocaust 1944. Anne Ranasinghe. VWA

Holstein cows parked. Black and White. Tom Schmidt. NeAC

Holstenwall. Sidney Keyes. FaBoTw (1975 ed.)

Holver and Hivy made a gret party. Holly and Ivy. *Unknown.* OxBM

Holy angels, in envy I cast no sigh. Gaspara Stampa, *tr. fr. Italian by* J. Vitiello. BoWoP

Holy Baptism ("Since, Lord, to thee/ A narrow way and little gate"). George Herbert. SCP-1

Holy City. Anne Waldman. RiTi

Holy-Cross Day. Robert Browning. VLP

Holy Eye Is Blind, The. Stephen Stepanchev. SA

Holy Fair, The. Burns. LAuP; OBSV

Holy Father, Great Creator, *with music.* Alexander V. Griswold. AH

Holy God, We Praise Thy Name, *with music.* Clarence A. Walworth. AH

Holy, Holy, Holy! Reginald Heber. BLSH, *with music;* VLP

Holy, Holy, Holy. Lawrence Russ. TC

Holy! Holy! Holy! Holy! Holy! Holy! Footnote to Howl. Allen Ginsberg. CAPP

Holy Innocents, The. Robert Lowell. ConAP; NowV

Holy Light. Milton. *Fr.* Paradise Lost, III. NOBE
(Poet's Blindness, The.) OBP

Holy Longing, The. Goethe, *tr. fr. German by* Robert Bly. NU

Holy Matrimony. John Keble. VLP

Holy men. Freethinkers Deborah Eibel. VWA

"Holy Moses!" said the old man Noah. Big Job. William Cole. OSF

Holy Office, The. James Joyce. FaBoTw (1975 ed.); NoAM; OxBTC

Holy Roller. Harriette Frances. PoW

Holy Scriptures, The, I. George Herbert. Epi

"Holy Socrates, why always with deference." Socrates and Alcibiades. Friedrich Hölderlin, *tr. by* Michael Hamburger. LoAs

Holy Sonnets, *sels.* John Donne.
"At the round earth's imagined [*or* imagin'd] corners, blow," VII. BoReV; CABA (1972 ed.); EBEV; Epi; ExPo (1973 ed); HAP; HeIP; ILP (1975 ed.); InPS; LFH; NOBE; OAEL-1; OBP; PAIC; PoIA; PoPle; PPoe; PPP; SCP-1

"Batter my heart, three-personed [*or* person'd] God; for you," XIV. AnMo; BiP; BoReV; CABA (1972 ed.); EBEV; Epi; ExPo (1973 ed.); FF; HAP; HeIP; HoPM (1975 ed.); ILP (1975 ed.); ILwL; InPK; InPS; IP; IPWM; LFH; MetP; NIL; NOBE; OAEL-1; OBP; PoIA; PPoD; PPoe; PPP; SCP-1; SoSe (1977 ed.); TT; UsP; WIF

"Death, be not proud, though some have called thee," X. AnMo; BiP; BoReV; CABA (1972 ed.); DL; Epi; ExPo (1973 ed.); FF; HAP; HeIP; ILP (1975 ed.); IP; MetP; NIL; NOBE; OAEL-1; OBP; PAIC; PBMP; PoIA; PPoe; PPP; SCP-1; TPo; TT; UsP; VoPo
(Death Be Not Proud.) PIM

"I am a little world made cunningly, " V. CABA (1972 ed.); TT

"If poisonous minerals, and if that tree," IX. BiP; CABA (1972 ed.); EBEV; Epi; ILP (1975 ed.); LFH; OAEL-1; PPP; UnPo (1976 ed.)

"O might those sighs and tears return again," III. BiP

"Oh my black [*or* blacke] soul! now thou art summoned," IV. EBEV; OAEL-1; PIM

"O, to vex me contraries meet in one," XIX. BoReV; OAEL-1

"Show me, dear Christ, thy spouse, so bright and clear," XVIII. ExPo (1973 ed.); ILP (1975 ed.); SCP-1; TT

"Since she whom I loved hath paid her last debt," XVII. SCP-1

"This is my play's last scene, here heavens appoint," VI. EBEV; NIL

"Thou hast made me, and shall thy work decay?" I. BoReV; EBEV; ILP (1975 ed.); NOBE

"What if this present were the world's last night?" XIII. BoReV; EBEV; ExPo (1973 ed.); HeIP; ILP (1975 ed.); InPS; PIM

"Why are we by all creatures waited on," XII. CABA (1972 ed.)

Holy Spirit, Faithful Guide, *with music.* Marcus Morris Wells. AH

Holy Spirit, Truth Divine, *with music.* Samuel Longfellow. AH

Holy Spring. Dylan Thomas. STS

Holy Thursday ("Is this a holy thing to see"). Blake. *Fr.* Songs of Experience. FF; ILP (1975 ed.); InPS; LAuP; MBPR; OAEL-2; STS

Holy Thursday ("'Twas on a Holy Thursday"). Blake. *Fr.* Songs of Innocence. BoReV; ILP (1975 ed.); InPS; LAuP; MBPR; NOBE; OAEL-2; OFD; STS; TT

Holy water come and bring. The Spell. Robert Herrick. CaPo

Holy Well, The. *Unknown.* GBP; PeBB

Holy Willie's Prayer. Burns. BoReV; EBEV; ESaP; InPS; LAuP; OAEL-1; OBP; OBSV; PPP
(Prayer of Holy Willie, The.) Epi

Holyhead, Sept. 25th, 1727. Swift. BIrV

Homage and Lament for Ezra Pound in Captivity. Robert Duncan. NOBA

Homage to a Government. Philip Larkin. EBEV

Homage to a Homosexual. Leon Slade. FPA

Homage to Austin Warren. Laurence Lieberman. ILP (1975 ed.)

Homage to Carracci. Tom Disch. PoA

Homage to Chagall. Duane Niatum. CDW

Homage to Chagall. Kathleen Teague. MIT

Homage to Hans Hofmann. Art Lange. FiCh

Homage to Hieronymus Bosch. Thomas MacGreevy. BIrV; EAS

Homage to Marcel Proust. Thomas MacGreevy. CIP

Homage to Mistress Bradstreet, *sels.* John Berryman.
"Governor your husband lived so long, The." NoAM; NOBA

"I trundle the bodies, on the iron bars." NOBA

"O all your ages at the mercy of my loves." NOBA

"So squeezed, wince you I scream? I love you & hate." FF

"Winters close, Springs open, no child stirs, The." NoAM

Homage to René Magritte. George Melly. EAS

Homage to Sextus Propertius, *sels.* Ezra Pound.
"Me happy, night, night full of brightness." VGW
(Elegy VII: "Me happy, night, night full of brightness.")
PAIC
Now if ever it is time to cleanse Helicon." Epi; VGW
"Shades of Callimachus, Coan ghosts of Philetas." CMoP
(1970 ed.); ExPo (1973 ed.); HAP; NoAM; NOBA; OBVE
"When, when, and whenever death closes our eyelids." NoAM;
PoA
"Who, who will be the next man to entrust his girl to a friend?"
NoAM

Homage to the British Museum. William Empson. CMoP (1970
ed.)

Homage to the Empress of the Blues. Robert Hayden. CABA
(1972 ed.); CNA; CoPAm; PoBA

Homage to Theodore Dreiser on the Centennial of His Birth, *sel.*
Robert Penn Warren.
"Who is the ugly one slump-slopping down the street?" GP

Home, The. Susan Axelrod. NMM

Home ("Home's home, although it reachèd be"). Joseph
Beaumont. SCP-2

Home. John Blight. CAAP

Home. Robert V. Carr. BPAW

Home. Sam Cornish. CNA

Home. Edgar A. Guest. OBAL

Home. Steve Kowit. AMV-81

Home. *Zulu Oral Tradition, tr. by* H. Tracey. WTO

Home/ oh/ home. Africa. Lucille Clifton. CNA

Home/ where my/ ground. Home. Sam Cornish. CNA

Home after Three Months Away. Robert Lowell. PBMP; PSN;
RRA

Home Again. Susan Petrykewycz. AMV-81

Home Alone These Last Hours of the Afternoon, Dusk Now, the
Sabbath Setting In, I Sit Back, and These Words Start
Welling Up in Me. Stephen Levy. VWA

Home at Grasmere. Wordsworth. *See* Recluse, The.

Home! at the word, what blissful visions rise. "Home, Sweet
Home," with Variations. H. C. Bunner. OBAL

Home, Boys, Home. *Unknown.* FSW

Home Burial. Robert Frost. PiAm; SoS; STS; TAP

Home for Thanksgiving. W. S. Merwin. NoAM

Home from Guatemala, back at the Waldorf. Arrival at the
Waldorf. Wallace Stevens. NYP

Home from Russia. Dan Gerber. TC

Home from Sea. Burns Singer. MS

Home Front, The. Marvin Bell. GP

Home/Grown. Ralph Storey. SES

Home in Indianapolis. Richard Pflum. AMV-80

Home in That Rock. *Unknown.* FSW

Home is more than just four walls. Hearth and Home. Stoddard
King. OBAL

Home is mysterious: a place to die, a place to breed.
Destinations. Josephine Jacobsen. WPE

Home Is So Sad. Philip Larkin. PSN

Home late, one lamp turned low. At Our House. William
Stafford. Epi

Home Movies. Carter Revard. VoR

Home on the Range. *Unknown.* BLSH, *with music;* BLSo, *with
music;* BPAW; FSW

Home on the Range, February 1962. Edward Dorn. ConAP

Home, Sweet Home. John Howard Payne. *Fr.* Clari, the Maid
of Milan. BLSH, *with music;* BLSo, *with music;* FSW; PSoN,
*with music*

"Home Sweet Home," with Variations. H. C. Bunner. OBAL

H(ome), thou returnest from Thames, whose Naiads long. *See*
H——, thou return'st from Thames, whose Naiads long.

Home Thoughts from Abroad. Robert Browning. FaPoR;
HeIP; ILP (1975 ed.); IPWM; NOBE; OBP; PBMP; STS;
VoPo

Home Thoughts, from the Sea. Robert Browning. ILP (1975
ed.); LFH; NOBE; OBP; STS; OBAL

Homecoming, The. James B. Allen. HeS

Homecoming, The. James K. Baxter. ATNZ

Homecoming. Sean Clarkin. IPM

Homecoming. Bruce Dawe. GAS

Homecoming. Stefan George, *tr. fr. German by* Peter Viereck.
AMV-81

Homecoming. Dan Gerber. HeS; TC

Homecoming, The. Norman Kreitman. PMW

Homecoming. Anna Margolin, *tr. fr. Yiddish by* Keith Bosley.
VWA

Homecoming. Lewis Packer. FPA; GAS

Homecoming. Sonia Sanchez. PoBA

Homecoming. Wislawa Szymborska, *tr. fr. Polish by* Benjamin
Sher. AMV-81

Homecoming. John Thompson. MAT

Homecoming Blues. Vassar Miller. GP

Homecoming Celebration. Rosemary Catacalos. AMV-80

Homecoming Singer, The. Jay Wright. PoBA

Homeless, The. Joan Joffe Hall. AMV-81

Homeless Blues. *Unknown.* BluL

Homely Accommodation, Suit Gent. William Price Turner. MS

Homeowners unite. The Firebombing. James Dickey. CAPP

Homer was poor. His scholars live at ease. Epigram. J. V.
Cunningham. VGW

Homeric Hexameter Described and Exemplified, The. Schiller, *tr.
fr. German by* Samuel Taylor Coleridge. MBPR

Homer's Hymn to Mercury, *sel. Unknown, tr. fr. Greek by*
Shelley.
"Seized with a sudden fancy for fresh meat." OBVE

Homes, The. Anne Pitkin. AMV-80

Home's home, although it reachèd be. Home. Joseph Beaumont.
SCP-2

Homes of England, The. Felicia Dorothea Hemans. FaPoR;
SBG; WPE

Homesick. Else Lasker-Schüler, *tr. fr. German by* Michael
Hamburger. PBWP
(Homesickness, *tr. by* Joachim Neugroschel.) VWA

Homesick Song. William Haskel Simpson. BPAW

Homestead. Horace Gregory. SPT

Homestead in Idaho. Clinton F. Larson. MPA

Home Town W. D. Snodgrass. NowV

Hometown Elegy. G. S. Fraser. MS

Hometown Piece for Messrs. Alston and Reese. Marianne Moore.
OBAL

Homework for Annabelle. Phyllis McGinley. BBGO

Homily: Contemporary. Marian Frances Brand. AATT

Homing. P. C. Bowman. AMV-81

Homo Sapiens. Earl of Rochester. *Fr.* A Satire against
Mankind. NOBE
("Were I who to my cost already am.") SCP-2

Homosexual Sonnets. Kenneth Pitchford. GP

Homosexuality. Frank O'Hara. CoPAm; NYP; PoA; TAP

Honeeeeeeeey, I'm all out and down. All Out and Down.
*Unknown.* BluL

Honest Abe Lincoln. Max Shulman. OBAL

Honest Ploughman, The, *with music. Unknown.* GSB

Honestly I wish I were dead! Sappho, *tr. fr. Greek by* Willis Barnstone. BoWoP

Honey/ When de man. Sister Lou. Sterling A. Brown. AmNP (1974 ed.); PoBA

Honey and Sherry and little Bashaw. Golden Grain. Helen M. Wright. PH

Honey Bee, The. Don Marquis. BoAnP

Honey-Bees. Shakespeare. King Henry V, *fr.* I, ii. PCOP

Honey from silk-worms who can gather. Lines to a Critic. Shelley. MBPR

Honey from the white rose, honey from the red. Sing a Song of Honey. Barbara Euphan Todd. FSFS

Honey-hued beauty, you are. Black Lady in an Afro Hairdo Cheers for Cassius. R. Ernest Holmes. PPoD

Honey people murder mercy U.S.A. In Memoriam: Martin Luther King, Jr. June Jordan. PoBA

Honey, you been gone all day that you may make whoopee all night. Whoopee Blues. *Unknown.* BluL

Honeyflowing moon is on every madman's tongue, The. Moonlight. Guillaume Apollinaire, *tr. by* William Meredith. Moon

Honeymooners, The. Cinda Kornblum. AcAn

Honeystain/ the rhetoricians of blackness. The Anti-Semanticist. Everett Hoagland. BPo

Honeysuckle (Chevrefoil). Marie de France. *See* Goat's-Leaf.

Honeysuckle, nightshade. Poem for L. C. Peter Klappert. AmPA

Honky. Charles Cooper. PoBA

Honour ("Ambitious sir, take heed!"). Joseph Beaumont. SCP-2

Honour. Abraham Cowley. BoLoP

Honor a going thing, goldfinch, corporation, tree. Mechanism. A. R. Ammons. HAP; TT

Honour is flashed off exploit, so we say. In Honour of St. Alphonsus Rodriguez. Gerard Manley Hopkins. EBEV; VLP

Honour is so sublime perfection. To the Countess of Bedford. John Donne. SCP-1

Honor of God and man is not on, The. Trees Once Walked and Stood. Joshua Tan Pai, *tr. by* Yishai Tobin. VWA

Honour, riches, marriage—blessing. Shakespeare. *Fr.* The Tempest, IV, i. PoPle

Honour thy parents; but good manners call. God to Be First Served. Robert Herrick. OxBChV

Honourable Entertainment Given to the Queen's Majesty in Progress at Elvetham, The, 1591, *sel.* Nicholas Breton. Ploughman's Song, The. NOBE
   ("In the merry month of may.") NIL

Honorable Mention. Rebecca Stutsman. SPo

Honored Dead, The. Thomas Doulis. NowV

Hoo-Kee hear me. Blackfoot Sin-ka-ha. William S. Lewis. BPAW

Hoo, Suffolk. *Unknown.* GBP

Hoochie Coochie. *Unknown.* BluL

Hood. C. K. Williams. InPK

Hoofer, The. A. K. Redwing. VoR

Hook. Erica Jong. RiTi

Hooked for two years now on wrinkle creams. Aging. Erica Jong. Psy; WBN

Hooked on the Magic Muscle. Linda King. GP

Hoop, a rolling O, oh those have power, A. Ode on Zero. Phoebe Pettingell. PoA

Hoosen Johnny. *Unknown.* FSW

Hoot Owl Shift. Robert Stricklin. AMV-80

Hop hop, thump thump. Stevie Smith. *Fr.* The Dedicated Dancing Bull and the Water Maid. WPE

Hop-poles stand in cones, The. The Midnight Skaters. Edmund Blunden. FaBoTw (1975 ed.); NOBE; PSN

Hope. Kenneth L. Anderson. AMV-80

Hope. William Dickey. GDP; POL

Hope. George Herbert. WeW

Hope. Langston Hughes. OBAL

Hope. Frank O'Connor, *tr. fr. Irish.* CIP

Hope. F. D. Reeve. PoA

Hope. Edith Södergran, *tr. fr. Swedish by* Jaakko O. Ahokas. PBWP

Hope and Joy. Christina Rossetti. OxBChV

Hope Diamonds. Madeline DeFrees. MPA

Hope for Those Separated by War, A. Sidney Keyes. BuTh

Hope I dreamed of was a dream, The. Mirage. Christina Rossetti. BoLoP

Hope is a crushed stalk. Dark Testament. Pauli Murray. AmNP (1974 ed.)

Hope is a strange invention. Emily Dickinson. WIF

Hope is a subtle glutton. Emily Dickinson. WIF

Hope is like a harebell trembling from its birth. Comparisons. Christina Rossetti. OxBChV

"Hope" is the thing with feathers. Emily Dickinson. NOBA; PCOP; SBG; TAP; WeW; WIF

Hope, whose weak being ruined is. On Hope by Way of Question and Answer between Abraham Cowley and Richard Crashaw. Abraham Cowley *and* Richard Crashaw. NOBE

Hopelessly handcuffed to a mysterious butterfly. A Lost Mohican Visits Hell's Kitchen. A. K. Redwing. VoR

Hopes, The. Dieter Fringell, *tr. fr. German by* A. Leslie Willson. AMV-80

Hopes Are Full of Blisters ("Hopes of night places"). Ron Welburn. NW

Hopi Lament. Charles Beghtol. BPAW

Hopi Prayer. Charles Beghtol. BPAW

Hopi Prayer, A. Harrison Conrard. BPAW

Hopi Woman. Lillian White Spencer. BPAW

Hopi Woman Talking, A. Joy Harjo. SA

Hopping Frog. Christina Rossetti. *See* Frog and the Toad, The.

Hopping on his left. One Leg. William Mohr. PoW

Hoppy. Edwin S. Godsey. PPoD

Hops. Boris Pasternak, *tr. fr. Russian by* Jon Stallworthy *and* Peter France. BoLoP

Hopscotch/ Through patches. Mercedes. Barbara Howes. CoPAm; RiTi

Hop't She. *Unknown.* GBP

Horace, Odes, 1, 5: Surfer's Paradise. J. M. Couper. GAS

Horae Canonica, *sel.* W. H. Auden.
   Sext. TCP

H-óran ó a vee-ó. A Complaint about Exile. Máiri MacLeod, *tr. by* Joan Keefe. PBWP

Horatian Ode. Joseph Warren Beach. PoA

Horatian Ode upon Cromwell's Return from Ireland, An. Andrew Marvell. EBEV; Epi; HAP; InPS; NIL; NOBE; OAEL-1; OBP; PAIC; TT

Horatio, of ideal courage vain. Feigned Courage. Charles *and* Mary Lamb. OxBChV

Horatio Alger Uses Scag. Amiri Baraka. GP

Horatius. Macaulay. *Fr.* Lays of Ancient Rome. BTTM; FaPoR
   (" 'Horatius,' quoth the Consul.") VLP

Hordes that battle for the world's domain, The. Six Poems, 4. Joseph Freeman. SPT

Horizon of Holland, The. Ian Hamilton Finlay. InPK

Horizon without Landscape. Tom Lowenstein. VWA

Horizontal in a deckchair on the bleak ward [*or* Horizontal on a deckchair in the Ward]. Ezra Pound. Robert Lowell. NoAM; NOBA

Horn, The. James Reeves. SO

Horn and Hardart is closing. Samurai and Hustlers. Joe Johnson. CNA

Horn, Mouth, Pit, Fire. William Dickey. AMV-81

Horned Owl, The. "Barry Cornwall." PCOP

Hornes to Buls wise nature lends. Beauty. Thomas Stanley, *after the Greek of* Anacreon. OBVE

Hornets occasionally build their nests near roads. Homer, *tr. by* Christopher Logue. *Fr.* The Iliad, XVI. OBVE

Hornpipe. Edith Sitwell. OAEL-2

Horns crowding toward us. Dream 3: Night Bear Which Frightened Cattle. Margaret Atwood. BCr

Horns weaving an adagio disclose. Symphony. Alfred Dorn. AMV-80

Horrible crime was committed, A. Pearl Bryan. *Unknown.* AmFP

Horrid Voice of Science, The. Vachel Lindsay. PoA

Horror. Henry Treece. EAS

Horror Comic. Robert Conquest. OxBTC

Horror Film. Vernon Scannell. HeHu

Horror Movie. Howard Moss. MiP; TPo; UsP

Horrors, The. Ogden Nash. SFF

Horse. Gerard Benson. PH

Horse. Randy Blasing. PH

Horse, The. A. E. Coppard. BoAnP

Horse. Jim Harrison. BoAnP; PH

Horse, The. W. S. Merwin. GP

Horse, The. Francis Ponge, *tr. fr. French by* Beth Archer. NU

Horse. Kenneth Rexroth. *Fr.* A Bestiary. NNaP

Horse. Elizabeth Madox Roberts. PH

Horse, The. Naomi Royde Smith. FaBoCo

Horse, The. Shakespeare. King Henry V, *fr.* III, vii. PCOP ("I will not change my horse with any that treads.") PH

Horse, A. Shakespeare. *Fr.* Venus and Adonis. ExPo (1973 ed.)

Horse, The. Shel Silverstein. PH

Horse, The. Peter Wild. MPA

Horse and hattock. Witch's Broomstick Spell. *Unknown.* GBP

Horse and the Mule, The. John Huddlestone Wynne. OxBChV

Horse and the Whip, The. Eliezer Steinbarg, *tr. fr. Yiddish by* Curt Leviant. VWA

Horse Chestnut Tree, The. Richard Eberhart. BBGO; CMoP (1970 ed.); TPo

Horse-Girl. Henry Petroski. PH

Horse Graveyard. Fred Lape. PH

Horse, head-swinging, The. February. Barbara Winder. PH

Horse in the Drugstore, The. Tess Gallagher. AmPA

Horse in the grass, The. Poem. Jonathan Sisson. AAN

Horse, Lord Epsom did bestride, A. Lord Epsom. Hilaire Belloc. PH

Horse Named Bill, A. *Unknown.* FSW

Horse Show, The. William Carlos Williams. CMoP (1970 ed.); NOBA; TAP; VGW

Horse Show at Midnight, The. Henry Taylor. PH

Horse skin; hessian or hard hot silk. Horse. Gerard Benson. PH

Horse Thief, The. William Rose Benét. BPAW

Horse Trader's Song, The. *Unknown.* AmFP

Horseplay by Reverse Descartes. Merle Meeter. AATT

Horses. Robert Dana. PH

Horses, The. Ted Hughes. NoAM; PH

Horses. Kipling. BoAnP; POL (Thrown Away.) PH

Horses, The. Maxine W. Kumin. DuDa

Horses. Louis MacNeice. PH

Horses, The ("Barely a twelvemonth after"). Edwin Muir. CMoP (1970 ed.); ExPo (1973 ed.); HAP; ILP (1975 ed.); NoAM; NOBE; OAEL-2; OxBTC; PPoe; SoSe; TCP

Horses ("Those lumbering horses in the steady plough"). Edwin Muir. CMoP (1970 ed.); OAEL-2; PoPle

Horses. Christina Rossetti. PCOP ("Horses of the sea, The.") LCL

Horses. Gwyn Thomas, *tr. fr. Welsh by* Joseph P. Clancy. OBW

Horses. Dorothy Wellesley. OxBTC

Horses/ Are no longer used in the Armed Forces. War Horses. William Cole. PH

Horses Aboard. Thomas Hardy. BoAnP

Horses are going away, The. Going Away. Ann Stanford. GP; PH

Horses at Valley Stores. Leslie Silko. NW; VoR

Horses Chawin' Hay. Hamlin Garland. OBAL

Horses Graze. Gwendolyn Brooks. CNA; FiCh; GP

Horses in front of me. Merry-go-round. Mark Van Doren. SO

Horses in horsecloths stand in a row. Horses Aboard. Thomas Hardy. BoAnP

Horses move sideways to start. Here in Polynia. Tom Raworth. TwMBP

Horses of earth. Horses. Robert Dana. PH

Horses of the sea, The. Horses. Christina Rossetti. LCL; PCoP

Horses on the Camargue. Roy Campbell. PoPle

Horsey Gap. *Unknown.* GBP

Hos Ego Versiculos. Francis Quarles. NIL

Hose and Iron. Greg Kuzma. MAT; NVAP

Hospital, The. Patrick Kavanagh. BIrV; CIP

Hospital. Karl Shapiro. VGW

Hospital Care Authorization. Ronald Gross. UsP

Hospital floors give away, The. Sister Rose. Richard Martin. AMV-81

Hospital for Defectives. Thomas Blackburn. OxBTC

Hospital/ Poem. Sonia Sanchez. BPo; PoBA

Hospital smell, The. Visiting Hour. Norman MacCaig. LP; MS

Hospital Window, The. James Dickey. BiP; HeIP; UsP

Hospitality. John Banister Tabb. ECBV

Hossolalia. Mildred Luton. PH

Host is riding from Knocknarea, The. The Hosting of the Sidhe. W. B. Yeats. NoAM

Hostess of the Ferry Inn, The. Gwerfyl Mechain, *tr. fr. Welsh by* H. Idris Bell. OBW

Hosting of the Sidhe, The. W. B. Yeats. NoAM

Hosts, The. W. S. Merwin. GP; PHC

Hosts of Gods do not know my origin, The. The One. *Tr. fr. Sanskrit by* Raimundo Panikkar. *Fr.* Bhagavadgita. ILwL

Hot Afternoons Have Been in West 15th Street. Paul Blackburn. VGW

Hot cross buns! Mother Goose. MG

Hot Day and Human Nature, The. Gordon Johnston. AMV-81

Hot Day at the Races. Tom Raworth. EAS; TwMBP

Hot days/ the farm does not. Memory of Kuhre. Wesley McNair. FAF

Hot in June a narrow winged. A Nameless One. Margaret Avison. ExPo (1973 ed.); HeIP

Hot light is smeared as thick as paint. Edinburgh Courtyard in July. Norman MacCaig. MS

Hot Line. Louella Dunann. QQQ

Hot midsummer night on Water Street, A. Hot Night on Water Street. Louis Simpson. NowV; SFF

"Hot night makes us keep our bedroom windows open, The." "To Speak of Woe That Is in Marriage." Robert Lowell. CAPP; NoAM

Hot night of the ramparts. Embrace the Blade. Joyce Mansour, tr. by Carol Cosman. PBWP

Hot Night on Water Street. Louis Simpson. NowV; SFF

Hot Poem. Vicki Viidikas. FPA

Hot sun, cool fire, tempered with sweet air. Bethsabe's Song. George Peele. *Fr. David and Bethsabe.* GBL; NOBE

Hot sun. Lizards frolic. Election 1960. James K. Baxter. ATNZ

Hot Time in the Old Town, A, *with music.* Joe Hayden. FSN (There'll Be a Hot Time.) BLSo

Hotbeds of color and an entire language of old. Night and Day. John Batki. AcAn

Hotel. Adam Wazyk, *tr. fr. Polish by* Isaac Komem. VWA

Hotel de l'Univers et Portugal. James Merrill. PoA

Hotel Fire: New Orleans. Paul Ruffin. AMV-81

Hotel in Paris. Dennis Trudell. PoA

Hotel Paradiso e Commerciale. John Malcolm Brinnin. NoAM

Hotel register claims this used to be an exciting town, The. Jefferson, Texas. Naomi Shihab. TAT

Hotels. David Donnell. AMV-81

Hottest Brand Goin'. *Unknown.* BluL

Hound, The. Robert Francis. SoSe

Hound, The. Sidney Lanier. GDP

Hound, The/ Could never be called refined. The Angry Poet. Frank O'Connor, *tr. fr. Irish.* CIP

Hound bays in the blood again, A. Flight. Mary Shumway. HeS

Hound of Heaven, The. Francis Thompson. ILP (1975 ed.); ILwL; VLP

Hound on the Church Porch. Robert P. Tristram Coffin. GDP

Hound twitches, A. Eve of July Fourth. James Bertolino. HeS

Hound was cuffed, the hound was kicked, The. The Hound. Sidney Lanier. GDP

Hounslow Heath. *Unknown.* APAS

Hour, The. Uri Zvi Greenberg, *tr. fr. Hebrew by* Robert Mezey *and* Ben Zion Gold. VWA

Hour at last come round, The. The Dying Gaul. Desmond O'Grady. BIrV

Hour is dark, The. The river comes to its end. Mary Ursula Bethell. *Fr.* By the River Ashley. ATNZ

Hour is very weary, as before sleep, The. The Hour. Uri Zvi Greenberg, *tr. by* Robert Mezey and Ben Zion Gold. VWA

Hour of Concern. Lindley Williams Hubbell. TPo

Hour of midnight met with a gathering of mothers, The. Kariuki. Joseph Gatuira. TVo

Hour of Prayer, The. Albert L. Hoy. AMV-80

Hour of Sleep, The. Robert Ellis, *tr. fr. Welsh by* H. Idris Bell. OBW

Hour-Glass, The. Robert Herrick. CaPo

Hourglass, The. Ben Jonson. NIL; OAEL-1

Hourglass, The, *sel.* Weldon Kees. "Crew is changed, the stone's face notched in darkness, The." NYP

Hour-glass whispers to the lion's roar, The. Our Bias. W. H. Auden. NoAM; PoIA

Hour of Feeling, The. Louis Simpson. FiCP

Hour of the Parting, The. John Shaw Neilson. MAuV

Hour with Thee, An. Sir Walter Scott. BoLoP

Hours, The. Calvin Forbes. CoPAm

Hours after fate had brot us 2gether in. She Employed the Familiar "Tu" Form. Doug Fetherling. NeAC

Hours before dawn we were woken by the quake. Aubade. William Empson. FaBoTw (1975 ed.); NIL; OxBTC; PAIC

Hours before my death. Epitaph. Julio Marzán. InW

Hours I spent with thee, dear heart, The. The Rosary. Robert Cameron Rogers. BLSH; BLSo; FSN

House. Leonard Clark. FPB

House, The. William Carlos Williams. VGW

House across the Way, The. Ralph Hodgson. FaBoTw (1975 ed.)

House All Pictures, A. Emery George. AMV-81

House and Land. Allen Curnow. ATNZ

House Arrest. George Tsongas. CPA

House Beautiful, The. Robert Louis Stevenson. NOBE

House-Builders, The. Kamala Das. PBWP

House by the Tracks, A. Dave Etter. TAT

House Carpenter, The. *Unknown. See* Demon Lover, The.

House Carpenter's Wife, The. *Unknown. See* Demon Lover, The.

House catch on fire and ain't no water 'round. Southern Blues. *Unknown.* BluL

House dawned, The. Reconciliation. David Rosenmann-Taub, *tr. by* Charles Guenther. VWA

House Dog's Grave, The. Robinson Jeffers. GDP

House Fear. Robert Frost. *Fr.* The Hill Wife. PPM

House Guest. Elizabeth Bishop. CoPAm; NCSH; TAP

House Guest, The. Laura Chester. RiTi

House had gone to bring again, The. The Need of Being Versed in Country Things. Robert Frost. NoAM; NOBA; PiAm; UnPo (1976 ed.)

House in Broad Street, red brick, with nine rooms, The. The Things. Conrad Aiken. HAP

House in Chicago, The. Marcia Lee Masters. HeS

House in Meudon. Margarita Aliger, *tr. fr. Russian by* Elaine Feinstein. VWA

House in St. Petersburg. Stanley Burnshaw. VWA

House in the Wood, The. Randall Jarrell. UsP

House is crammed, The: tier beyond tier they grin. "Blighters." Siegfried Sassoon. CMoP (1970 ed.); FaBoTw (1975 ed.); NoAM

House is filled, The. The last heartthrob. Near the Ocean. Robert Lowell. NOBA

House is yours, The. The House. William Carlos Williams. VGW

House leaks and leans, The. The Ancestors. John Peale Bishop. PoA

House lifts off, The. Down below. Night Flight. Ruth Daigon. AMV-81

House nailed up and boarded in, The. Intimacy. Raymond Ward. ATNZ

House o' the Mirror, The. Helen Adam. MAT; NMM

House of a friend. Fresno Notebook. Neeli Cherkovski. CPA

House of Fame, The, *sels.* Chaucer. OxBM
   Eagle Converses with Chaucer, The.
   Jove's Eagle Carries Chaucer into Space.

House of Hospitalities, The. Thomas Hardy. NoAM

House of Life, The, *sels.* Dante Gabriel Rossetti.
   Ardour and Memory, LXIV. OAEL-2
   Autumn Idleness, LXIX. GBL; ILP (1975 ed.); OAEL-2
   Barren Spring, LXXXIII. ILP (1975 ed.); OAEL-2; VLP; VPC
   Body's Beauty, LXXVIII. ILP (1975 ed.); OAEL-2; VLP
   Dark Glass, The, XXXIV. VPC
   Day of Love, A, XVI. VLP
   Death-in-Love, XLVIII. VLP
   Heart's Compass, XXVII. PAIC
   Her Gifts, XXXI. VLP
   Hill Summit, The, LXX. VLP
   Inclusiveness, LXIII. VLP

Kiss, The, VI. VLP
Life-in-Love, XXXVI. HAP; VLP
Lost on Both Sides, XCI. VLP
Love's Last Gift, LIX. VLP
Lovesight, IV. VLP
Not as These, LXXV. VLP
Nuptial Sleep. VLP
One Hope, The, CI. OAEL-2; VLP
Portrait, The ("O Lord of all compassionate control"), X. VLP
Saint Luke the Painter, LXXIV. VLP
Severed Selves, XL. BoLoP; VPC
Silent Noon, XIX. HAP; ILP (1975 ed.); OBP; SoSe (1977 ed.); VLP
Song-Throe, The, LXI. VLP
Sonnet, The ("A sonnet is a moment's monument"), *introd.* HeIP; ILP (1975 ed.); NIL; PAIC; SoSe; VLP
Soul's Beauty, LXXVII. VLP
Superscription, A, XCVII. OAEL-2; VLP; VPC
Transfigured Life, LX. VLP
Vain Virtues, LXXXV. VLP
Willowwood, XLIX-LII. OAEL-2; VLP
Without Her, LIII. GBL; VLP
Youth's Antiphony, XIII. VLP
Youth's Spring-Tribute, XIV. ILP (1975 ed.); VLP
House of Light, The. Dana Naone. PHC
House of Madam Juju, The. Kanai Mieko, *tr. fr. Japanese by* Christopher Drake. BoWoP
House of Night, The, *sel.* Philip Freneau.
    Vision of the Night, The. EAP
House of Readers, A. Jim Wayne Miller. GP
House of the Living. Claude Vigée, *tr. fr. French by* Henry Braun. VWA
House of the Mouse, The. Lucy Sprague Mitchell. MN
House of the Rising Sun. *Unknown.* FSW
House on Buder Street, The. Gary Gildner. TAP
House on the Barge, The. Beth Bentley. CNW
House on the Hill, The. E. A. Robinson. AmVN; TH; UsP; VoPo
House Poem. Jane Cooper. AMV-81
House That Jack Built, The. Samuel Taylor Coleridge. *See On a Ruined House in a Romantic Country.*
House-Top, The. Herman Melville. AmVN; NOBA; NYP; Prf
House-Trailer, The. Lawrence Russ. TC
House was empty and, The. Music in an Empty House. Hugh Sykes Davies. EAS
House Was Quiet and the World Was Calm, The. Wallace Stevens. HAP; UsP; VGW
House was shaken by a rising wind, The. Brainstorm. Howard Nemerov. HAP; NCSH; NoAM; SoSe (1977 ed.)
House We Leave, The. Fredric Matteson. PoW
House we moved into has been landscaped, The. Buildings and Grounds. Henry Taylor. CSP
House where every, A. Louis Zukofsky. *Fr.* Light. NoAM
House-wreckers have left the door and a staircase, The. Charles Reznikoff. WeW
House You Looked For, The. William Pitt Root. NVAP
Housecleaner, The. Gail White. AMV-80
Housed in each other's arms. Song for a Marriage. Vassar Miller. PAIC
Household. Laura Jensen. PCho
Houses, The, *sel.* Robin Hyde.
    "Old nursery chair; its legs, cut down, are broken." ATNZ
Houses, The. Eden Phillpotts. OxBTC
Houses and rooms are full of perfumes. Walt Whitman. *Fr.* Song of Myself, II. UnPo (1976 ed.)
Houses are haunted, The. Disillusionment of Ten o'Clock. Wallace Stevens. CMoP (1970 ed;) FF; InPK; InPS; NIL; PoIA; PPoD; PPoe; SFF; STS; WeW

Houses are swaying, swimming in gray light. Homecoming. Anna Margolin, *tr. by* Keith Bosley. VWA
Houses, Past and Present. Eli Bachar, *tr. fr. Hebrew by* Jeremy Garber. VWA
Housesnake's made her nest in the woodshed, A. This Cold Nothing Else. Dara Wier. CSP
Housewife. Josephine Miles. RiTi
Housewife. William Pillin. PoW
Housewife. Susan Fromberg Schaeffer. IHMS; WBN
Housewife. Anne Sexton. NMM; Psy
Housewife, A. *Unknown.* TDH
Housewifery. Edward Taylor. *See* Huswifery.
Housewife's Lament, The. *Unknown.* FSW; MAT
Housewife's Letter: To Mary. Anne Halley. NMM
Housing Shortage. Naomi Replansky. NMM
Hovering and huge, dark, formless sway, The. The Virgin Mary. Edgar Bowers. PiAm
Hovering in mid-stream. The Moonlit Rock. Morton Marcus. CPA
How? Abraham Sutskever, *tr. fr. Yiddish by* Ruth Whitman. VWA
How/ Then,/ Distinguish. Query. Mildred Weston. POL
How a Girl Was Too Reckless of Grammar. Guy Wetmore Carryl. OBAL
How a Good Greyhound Is Shaped. *Unknown.* BoAnP
How all occasions do inform against me. Shakespeare. *Fr.* Hamlet, IV, iv. BiP; HoPM (1975 ed.)
How and with what will you fill. How? Abraham Sutskever, *tr. by* Ruth Whitman. VWA
How Annandale Went Out. E. A. Robinson. ILP (1975 ed.); NoAM; NOBA; PAIC; PoIA; PPoD
How awfully sad I felt thinking of my sleeping mother in her bed. Sept. 16, 1961, Poem. Jack Kerouac. VoA
How badly and how beautifully she speaks. A Bagatelle. James Reeves. POL
How bald that microscope was. V. D. Clinic. Adrien Stoutenburg. GP
"How bare! How all the lion-desert lies." Macrinus against Trees. "Michael Field." WPE
How Beastly the Bourgeois Is. D. H. Lawrence. NoAM; OBSV
How beautiful and calm how crimson pale. The Spirit Craft. Charles Ballard. VoR
How beautiful are thy feet in sandals, O prince's daughter! Bible, *O.T.* Song of Solomon, VII: 1-9. OBP
How beautiful is the flag. Que Bonita Bandera. *Tr. fr. Spanish.* FSW
How beautiful is the rain! Rain in Summer. Longfellow. FSFS
How beautiful their feet. Martin Tupper. *Fr.* The Train of Religion. FaBoCo
How beautiful things are in a beautiful room. Night Words: The Ravishing. Michael McClure. VoA
How Beautiful You Are: 3. Elaine Edelman. IHMS
How Bill Went East. George S. Bryan. PoTa
How blest [*or* bless'd] art thou, canst love the country, Wroth. To Sir Robert Wroth. Ben Jonson. SCP-1; TVS
How blest is he, who for his country dies. To the Earl of Oxford, Late Lord Treasurer. Swift, *after the Latin of* Horace. OBVE
How blest was the created state. The Fall: A Song. Earl of Rochester. SCP-2
How blowsy the trees are today. June Song. Abby Rosenthal. AMV-81
How bright on the blue. The Kite. Harry Behn. FPB
How brittle are the piers. Emily Dickinson. PiAm
How busie are the sonnes of men? Roger Williams. GOA

How, butler, how! Bevis a tout! Fill the Bowl, Butler. *Unknown.* OxBM

How came this ranger. The Chambermaid's First Song. W. B. Yeats. AnMo

How can a flower stand out. Botany Lesson. F. D. Reeve. AMV-80

How can a long-used body reconstrue. Canticles to Men. Marya Mannes. AMV-80

How can he dare to cross me. Slug. Gwen Head. GP

How can I be wheeled down these white corridors. Multiplication. Lynn Strongin. AAN

How can I call out? How can I shout? At Night. Bella Akhmadulina, *tr. by* Daniel Halpern *and* Albert Todd. BoWoP

How can I care whether you sigh for me. Song: How Can I Care? Robert Graves. GBL

How can I choose but love, and follow her. Another on Her. Robert Herrick. SpRo

How Can I Keep from Singing? *Unknown.* FSW

How Can I Keep My Maidenhead. Burns. LoAs

How Can I Leave Thee? *with music.* Friedrich Wilhelm Kücken, *tr. fr. German.* BLSH

How can I look at my unhappiness. The Displacement. Hubert Witheford. ATNZ

How can I regret my life. The Signal. David Ignatow. NNaP

How Can I Say It Any Other Way. Cynthia Nibbelink. TC

How Can I See You, Love. David Vogel, *tr. fr. Hebrew by* A. C. Jacobs. VWA

How can I sing you when I cannot find you? To Sing the People. Lucille F. Travis. AATT

How can I sustain. Private Pain in Time of Trouble. Kathleen Spivack. AmPA

How can I, that girl standing there. Politics. W. B. Yeats. CMoP (1970 ed.); FF; HeIP; InPS; NIL; OBP; OxBTC; PFIr; POL

How can I turn this wheel that turns my life. The Wheel. Edwin Muir. NoAM

How can it be thought? The Six Days of Creation. James McAuley. CAAP

How can people stand to be around me? I'm always babbling. Alta. MMD

How can they go on, you see them. Another Academy. Charles Bukowski. TAT

How can they write or paint. Observations in a Cornish Teashop. Kenneth Rexroth. OBAL

How can this boyish and uplifted face. Michelangelo: "The Creation of Adam." Gregory Djanikian. AMV-81

How can we stand the soup? Getting a Job. Paul Blackburn. NYP

How can you know, or understand, our loss. Navajo Signs. Winifred Fields Walters. VW

How can you live, how exist. The Likeness. Arthur Gregor. VGW

How can you look at the Neva. "Anna Akhmatova," *tr. fr. Russian by* Stanley Kunitz *and* Max Hayward. BoWoP

How can you set to the table a-dining? The Lost Baby. *Unknown.* AmFP

How can you stand it. The Last Song. Joy Harjo. FoP; TAT

How changed is here each spot man makes or fills. Thyrsis. Matthew Arnold. Epi; NOBE; PES; VLP

How Clouds Move. Barbara Hughes. CPA

How cold the snow. *Unknown. Fr.* Four Christmas Carols. PChr

How Come? Sara Asheron. CaYB

How Come? David Ignatow. NYP

How come nobody is being bombed today? All Quiet. David Ignatow. ConAP

How comes this [*or* that] blood on thy shirt sleeve [*or* all over your shirt]? Edward. *Unknown.* HoPM (1975 ed.); RDB

How could God think of so many kinds of houses? Jessie Orton Jones. Secrets, XXI. CTV

"How could I cheat those lips of their true food?" J. W. Scholl. *Fr.* The Poet's Prothalamion. PeD

How could you be by halves. One of the Chapters. Kathleen Fraser. CPA

How cute is our kitchen. A Man about the Kitchen. Rodney Hobson. QQQ

How dared you die before me? It was not. Elegy for Former Students. Virginia Scott Miner. AMV-81

How dark to my mind are the scenes of my childhood. The Old, Filthy Beer Pail. Katie V. Hall. InPK; PeD

How Daur Ye Call Me Owlet Face. Burns. PoPle ("How daur ye ca' me 'Howlet-face.' ") FaBoEE

How dear to my [*or* this *or* the] heart are the scenes of my childhood. The Old Oaken Bucket. Samuel Woodworth. BLSo; FSW; PSoN

How dear to my heart is the old village drugstore. The Hair-Tonic Bottle. Ben King. OBAL

How dear to my heart was the old-fashioned hurler. The Old-Fashioned Pitcher. George E. Phair. SPo

How dear to this heart are the scenes of my childhood. *See* How dear to my heart are the scenes of my childhood.

How deep is his duplicity who in a flash. High Diver. Robert Francis. LiSp

How delightful to meet Mr. Hodgson! Lines to Ralph Hodgson, Esqre. T. S. Eliot. OBAL

How did a great Red-tailed Hawk. The Dead by the Side of the Road. Gary Snyder. CNW; HAP

How did he die/ O if I told you. The Gangster's Death. Ishmael Reed. PoBA

How Did He Get Here? H. Leivick, *tr. fr. Yiddish by* Ruth Whitman. VWA

How did the Devil come? When first attack? Norfolk. John Betjeman. BBGO

How did the party go in Portman Square. Juliet. Hilaire Belloc. BoLoP

How did they fume, and stamp, and roar, and chafe. Atticus. Pope. *Fr.* Epistle to Dr. Arbuthnot. InPK

How did they kill my grandmother? How They Killed My Grandmother. Boris Slutsky, *tr. by* Daniel Weissbort. VWA

How Did You Die? Edmund Vance Cooke. CTV; PeD

How did your father come down at Lodore? The Cataract at Lodore. Helen Bevington. SpRo

How Different! Ebenezer Elliott. EBEV

How difficult for me is Hebrew. Charles Reznikoff. *Fr.* Five Groups of Verse. SA

How do I know it was a fox? Blue Teal's Mother. James Wright. CAAP

How do I love thee? Let me count the ways. Sonnets from the Portuguese, XLIII. Elizabeth Barrett Browning. BoLoP; FF; HeIP; HoPM (1975 ed.); ILP (1975 ed.); InPS; IPWM; LFH; LoAs; NIL; OLR; PAIC; PPM; SFF; UnPo (1976 ed.); VPC; WPE

How do I love you, beech-trees, in the autumn. Beechwoods at Knole. V. Sackville-West. PES

How do i speak. Ecology. James Steele. SES

How do robins build their nests? What Robin Told. George Cooper. CTV

How do we know, by the bank-high river. The Last Lap. Kipling. OxBTC

How Do You Do, *Alabama*! Fred Wilson. AIW

How do you know that the pilgrim track. The Year's Awakening. Thomas Hardy. CMoP (1970 ed.); ILP (1975 ed.); OxBTC

How do you like to go up in a swing. The Swing. Robert Louis Stevenson. CTV; LCL

How do you make bread talk, this old treasure all wrapped. Bread Is Born. Anne Hébert, *tr. by* Maxine W. Kumin. BoWoP

How do you recognize death? Minor Elegy. Henriqueta Lisboa, *tr. by*. Willis Barnstone *and* Nelson Cerqueira. BoWoP

How do you think I began in the world? The Sow Took the Measles. *Unknown.* FSW

How docile we were, how orderly! Empire Day. Training. D. J. Enright. HeHu

How does it happen, tell me. Judge Somers. Edgar Lee Masters. *Fr.* Spoon River Anthology. FaBoEE; OBSV

How does my royal lord? How fares your Majesty? Shakespeare. *Fr.* King Lear, IV, vii. Prf

How does one tell. Innocence. Irving Layton. BBGO

How does the water. The Cataract of Lodore. Robert Southey. OxBChV; SpRo

How Doth the Little Busy Bee. Isaac Watts. CTV; HoPM (1975 ed.)
(Against Idleness and Mischief.) OxBChV; SpRo

How Doth the Little Crocodile. "Lewis Carroll." *Fr.* Alice's Adventures in Wonderland, *ch.* 2. CTV; ECBV; FaBoCo; FaBoEE; FaBoNo; LCL; NOBL; PCOP; SpRo (Crocodile, The.) HoPM (1975 ed.)

How dry time screaks in its fat axle-grease. The Crucifix. Robert Lowell. NowV

How dull and how insensible a beast. An Essay upon Satire. John Sheffield, Duke of Buckingham and Normanby. APAS

How easily the ripe grain. The Widow. W. S. Merwin. UnPo (1976 ed.); VGW

How easy 'tis to sail with wind and tide! The Medal Reversed. Elkanah Settle. APAS

How empty seems the town now you are gone! From One Who Stays. Amy Lowell. BoWoP

How everything gets tamed. Mountain, Fire, Thornbush. Harvey Shapiro. VGW

How Everything Happens. May Swenson. HAP; Psy; RFM

How fair a flower is sown. Coventry Patmore. FaBoEE

How fair is San Francisco Bay. San Francisco Bay. Joaquin Miller. BPAW

How falls it, oriole, thou hast come to fly. To an Oriole. Edgar Fawcett. PCOP

How far are they deceived who hope in vain. Ephelia to Bajazet. Sir George Etherege. APAS

How Far Is It to Bethlehem? Frances Chesterton. PChr

"How far is St. Helena from a little child at play?" A St. Helena Lullaby. Kipling. EBEV

"How farest thou?" quod he to me. The Eagle Converses with Chaucer. Chaucer. *Fr.* The House of Fame. OxBM

How fashionably sad my early poems are! About My Poems. Donald Justice. PoA

How fever'd is the man, who cannot look. On Fame. Keats. MBPR; NIL

How fierce was I when I did see. Upon Julia Washing Herself in the River. Robert Herrick. CaPo

How foolish men on expeditions go! On Riding to See Dean Swift in the Mist of the Morning. Alexander Pope *and* Thomas Parnell. FaBoEE

"How fortune deceives! I had pleasure in tow." *Unknown. Fr.* The Galley Slave. PeD

How fresh, O Lord, how sweet and clean. The Flower. George Herbert. BoReV; MetP; NIL; NOBE; PPP; SCP-1

How funny you are today, Chicago. A Civic Autobiography. Paul Hoover. FiCh

How funny you are today New York. Steps. Frank O'Hara. CAPP; ConAP

How Glorious Are the Morning Stars, *with music.* Benjamin Keach. AH

How glorious is the hour of secret prayer. The Hour of Prayer. Albert L. Hoy. AMV-80

How God speeds the tax-bribed plough. Drone v. Worker. Ebenezer Elliott. OBSV

How good to lie a little while. Friends. Abbie Farwell Brown. CTV

How good we imagine it would be. Light Morning Snow, We Wait for a Warmer Season. John Garmon. AMV-80

How goodly are the tentes of Jacob and thine habitacions Israel. Bible, *O.T. Tr. by* William Tyndale. *Fr.* Numbers. OBVE

How Goodly Is Thy House, *with music.* Henry S. Jacobs. AH

How! gossip mine, gossip mine. Good Gossips Mine. *Unknown.* OxBM

How Grand and How Bright. *Unknown.* GBP

How grand beneath the feet that company. The Mendip Hills over Wells. Henry Alford. PES

How happier is that flea. The Happiness of a Flea. Tasso, *tr. by* William Drummond of Hawthornden. LoAs

How happy a thing were a wedding. On Marriage. Thomas Flatman. NOBL

How happy are those who know their need for God. Bible, *N.T.* St. Matthew, V: 3-12. CTV

How happy is he born and taught. The Character of a Happy Life. Sir Henry Wotton. FaPoR; NOBE

How hard is my fortune. The Convict of Clonmel. *Unknown, tr. by* Jeremiah Joseph Callanan. PFIr

How hard it is for me, who live. Marriage. Wendell Berry. CSP

How hard it is, we say. Clothes Maketh the Man. Theodore Weiss. NoAM

How hard one has to labor at it. Being Natural. Carl Rakosi. GP

How he thought. Drop the Wires. Hugh Seidman. AmPA

How, hey! It is none les. A Henpecked Husband. *Unknown.* OxBM

How High the Moon. Lance Jeffers. CNA; PoBA

How I Brought the Good News from Aix to Ghent. R. J. Yeatman *and* W. C. Sellar. SpRo

How I Cancelled My Life Insurance. Joseph Bruchac. FAF

How I Escaped from the Labyrinth. Philip Dacey. POL

How I go courting a charming beauty bright. Charming Beauty Bright. *Unknown.* AmFP

How I Got Myself Trapped. Felix Pollak. HeS

How I Got Ovah. Carolyn M. Rodgers. CNA

How I loved one like you when I was little. Slug. Theodore Roethke. CABA (1972 ed.)

How I loved those old movies. Old Movies. John Cotton. FF

How I should like to see great Babylon. Sargon. Arthur J. Bull. HeHu

How I Was Her Kitchen-Boy. Gunter Grass, *tr. fr. German by* Betty Falkenberg. AMV-81

How I wish I had known/ beforehand of this journey. *Tr. fr. Japanese by* Kenneth Yasuda. BoWoP

How I wish I were able to say what I think. Gertrude Stein. *Fr.* Stanzas in Meditation. PBWP

How I wish the Argo had never reached the land. Medea. Euripides, *tr. by* Rex Warner. NAWM-1

How I'd Have It. John Stone. AMV-81

How impotent a deity am I! Sir Samuel Garth. *Fr.* The Dispensary. OBSV

How in the Morning. Chuck Miller. AcAn; EC

How instant joy, how clang. Robert Penn Warren. *Fr.* Mediterranean Beach, Day after Storm. OSP

How intimate was the earth in days gone by. The Earth. D. Gwenallt Jones, *tr. by* Dyfnallt Morgan. OBW

How is it now? Questions [2]. Donald Hall. FF

How is it that I am so careless here. Meditation 62. Philip Pain. NOBA; PiAm

How is man parcelled out! how every hour. The Tempest. Henry Vaughan. SCP-1

How is't, my soul, that thou giv'st eyes their sight. To My Soul in Its Blindness. Phineas Fletcher. SCP-2

How it feels to be touching. We Become New. Marge Piercy. TAP; WBN

How It Goes On. Maxine W. Kumin. FiCP

How It Is. Uri Zvi Greenberg, *tr. fr. Hebrew by* Robert Mezey *and* Ben Zion Gold. VWA

How it is I returned. Childhood. Sherod Santos. AMV-81

How it responds with its heart. For a Voice That Is Singing. Aldo Camerino, *tr. by* Anita Barrows. VWA

How it sits, like a muddle. Jealousy. Rachel de Vries. AMV-81

How It Strikes a Contemporary. Robert Browning. OAEL-2; VLP

How Jack Found That Beans May Go Back on a Chap. Guy Wetmore Carryl. HoPM (1975 ed.)

How joyously the young sea-mew. The Sea-Mew. Elizabeth Barrett Browning. VLP

How kind, how secretly, the sun. The Garden. Robert Penn Warren. PoA

How large unto the tiny fly. The Fly. Walter de la Mare. PoPle

How! Liberty of Conscience! that's a change. Dr. Wild's Ghost. *Unknown.* APAS

How life and death in thee agree? Upon Our Saviour's Tomb Wherein Never Man Was Laid. Richard Crashaw. OAEL-1

"How like a well-kept garden is your soul." The Nineteenth Century as a Song. Robert Hass. CAAP

How like a winter hath my absence been. Sonnets, XCVII. Shakespeare. CABA (1972 ed.); ILP (1975 ed.); NOBE; OAEL-1; PoIA

How like an angel came I down! Wonder. Thomas Traherne. BoReV; HAP; PPoe; SCP-2

How Lilies Came White. Robert Herrick. CaPo

How little does history manage to tell? Lessons in History. Robert Penn Warren. AMV-80

How long ago Hector took off his plume. Parting in Wartime. Frances Cornford. NIL

How long ago she planted the hawthorn hedge. The Hawthorn Hedge. Judith Wright. WPE

How long ago we dreamed. Carol of the Three Kings. W. S. Merwin. PChr

How long, dear Savior, O how long. Isaac Watts. AmFP

"How Long Hast Thou Been a Gravemaker?" David Perkins. NCSH

How long have the cows been gone. Until the Cows Come Home. Michael McMahon. FAF

How long have you been living here? The Arkansas Traveller. Mose Case. PSoN

How Long, Jehovah? *with music.* Henry Ainsworth. AH

How long, O lion, hast thou fleshless lain? The Lion's Skeleton. Charles Tennyson Turner. VLP

How long, O Lord, shall I forgotten be? Bible, *O.T.* Psalms, XIII, *paraphrased by* Sir Philip Sidney. OBVE

How long shall I endure without reply. The Medal of John Bays: A Satire against Folly and Knavery. Thomas Shadwell. APAS; SCP-2, *first 52 lines*

How long shall I pine for love? Pining for Love. Francis Beaumont. POL

"How long shall man be nature's fool?" Man cries. The Sakiyeh. Mathilde Blind. SBG

How long shall we be hunted, like foxes in the chase. The Red Man of the South. Eliza R. Snow. WPW

How long will these graves go on? Graves in Queens. Richard Hugo. NYP

How long will you remain a boy? Meditation. Carl Rakosi. VWA

How lovely is the heaven of this night. A Beautiful Night. Thomas Lovell Beddoes. PMW

How lovely it was, after the official fright. The Phenomenon. Karl Shapiro. CMoP (1970 ed.)

How low when angels fall their black descent. The Promise in Disturbance. George Meredith. VLP

How Man Learned to Walk—and Run. Louis Dudek. AKE

How many bards gild the lapses of time! Keats. MBPR

How many bullets does it take. Death in Yorkville. Langston Hughes. PoBA

How many dawns, chill from his rippling rest. To Brooklyn Bridge [*or* Proem]. Hart Crane. *Fr.* The Bridge. CABA (1972 ed.); CMoP (1970 ed.); ExPo (1973 ed.); HAP; HeIP; ILP (1975 ed.); InPS; NoAM; NOBA; NYP; PAIC; PiAm; TAP

How many days has my baby to play? Mother Goose. MG

How many doors will this man open. Death. Roy Fuller. NoAM

How many evenings in the arbor by the river. Li Ch'ing-chao, *tr. fr. Chinese by* Eugene Eoyang. BoWoP

How many fires. George Reavey. EAS

How many lovers will be caught kissing/ behind the auditorium. Before the Bell Rings. Jesús Papoleto Meléndez. NW

How many men are killed by Power, by Power. Sejanus. Juvenal, *tr. by* Robert Lowell. *Fr.* Satires, X. OBVE

How many miles to Babylon. Mother Goose. GBP; MG

How many moments must (amazing each. E. E. Cummings. PoA

How many morning suns have kissed this glass? Kitchen Window. Ruth N. Ebberts. AMV-80

How many names for what bees see? The Letters of a Name. Colette Inez. AMV-81

How Many Nights. Galway Kinnell. MAT

How many paltry, foolish, painted things. Michael Drayton. *Fr.* Idea. AAS; Epi; GBL; HAP; HeIP; NIL; OAEL-1

How many skies does the earth hold? Ourobouros. Jorge Plescoff, *tr. by* Yishai Tobin. VWA

How many times must I tell. My Angel. Philip Levine. AMV-81

How many times these low feet staggered. Emily Dickinson. CABA (1972 ed.); HAP

How many ways there are of falling into the sea! Falling. Reuben Tam. PHC

How many wise men and heroes. To the Tune "The River Is Red." Ch'iu Chin, *tr. by* Kenneth Rexroth *and* Ling Chung. BoWoP; PBWP

How much are they deceived who vainly strive. Love and Jealousy. William Walsh. BoLoP

How Much Earth. Philip Levine. NNaP

How much living have you done? The Poet Speaks. Georgia Douglas Johnson. AmNP (1974 ed.)

How much longer will I be able to inhabit the divine sepulcher. John Ashbery. NoAM

How much of me is sandwiches radio beer? Lonesome in the Country. Al Young. MAT; SA

How much, preventing God, how much I owe. Grace. Emerson. LFH

How much shall I love her? The Echo Elf Answers. Thomas Hardy. LoAs

How music hungers after him and frightened priests. Stagehand. Phyllis Speros. PoW

How must you be now, old woman.    Words to Remind Me of Grandmother.    Andrés Castro Ríos, *tr. by* Julio Marzán.    InW

How mutable is every thing that here.    Meditation 29.    Philip Pain.    NOBA

How, my dear Mary,—are you critic-bitten.    The Witch of Atlas.    Shelley.    MBPR

How My Father Died.    Nissim Ezekiel.    VWA

How Night Falls in the Courtyard.    Christine Rimmer.    AMV-80

How odd/ Of God.    W. N. Ewer.    FaBoEE

How oft have I, my dere and cruell foo.    Sir Thomas Wyatt.    AAS

How oft when men are at the point of death.    Shakespeare.    *Fr.* Romeo and Juliet, V, iii.    DL

How oft when thou, my music, music play'st.    Sonnets, CXXVIII.    Shakespeare.    Epi; ILP (1975 ed.)

How often hath my pen, mine heart's solicitour.    *Unknown. Fr.* Zepheria.    ESo

How often have I started out.    Inspiration.    Robert W. Service.    WeW

How often have my tears.    In Allusion to the French Song.    Richard Lovelace.    CaPo

How often in the years that close.    A Meditation.    Herman Melville.    GOA

How often, when life's summer day.    Walter Savage Landor.    FaBoEE

How old may Phyllis be, you ask.    Phyllis's Age.    Matthew Prior.    FaBoEE

How Old's the Moon?    *Unknown, tr. fr. Japanese by* Graehme Wilson.    Moon

How One Thing Leads to Another.    David Smith.    NVAP

How Our Forefather Got His Wife.    Eda Lou Walton.    BPAW

How our good king does Papists hate.    Satire on Old Rowley.    *Unknown.*    APAS

How peaceful to have been Li-Po, lying back.    Poet Counterpoet.    Rudolph von Abele.    PoUp

How placidly shine/ The river, the spring, and the sun.    Rosalía de Castro, *tr. fr. Galician by* Benjamin M. Woodbridge, Jr.    PBWP

How Pleasant Is Saturday Night.    *Unknown.*    CTV

How Pleasant It Is to Have Money.    Arthur Hugh Clough.    *Fr.* Dipsychus.    NOBE
("As I sat at the café, I said to myself.")    OAEL-2; VPC

How Pleasant to Know Mr. Lear.    Edward Lear.    EBEV; FaBoCo; HAP; NOBE; NOBL; SpRo; VLP
(By Way of Preface.)    InPS

How poor, how rich, how abject, how august.    Edward Young.    *Fr.* The Complaint; or, Night Thoughts, I.    OAEL-1

How prone we are to sin, how sweet were made.    And Forgive Us Our Trespasses.    Aphra Behn.    EBEV

How pure, how beautiful, how fine.    Reflections Dental.    Phyllis McGinley.    *Fr.* Speaking of Television.    TH

How quickly must she go?    To a Dying Girl.    Clinton F. Larson.    MPA

How quickly the dandelions.    Americana XVII: A Reminder of William Carlos Williams.    Carl Rakosi.    InPS

How rare to be born a human being!    Gary Snyder.    Myths and Texts: Hunting, XVI.    CAPP

How red the rose that is the soldier's wound.    Wallace Stevens.    *Fr.* Esthétique du Mal.    CMoP (1970 ed.); NOBA

How rewarding to know Mr. Smith.    Mr. Smith/ (with Nods to Mr. Lear and Mr. Eliot.)    William Jay Smith.    SpRo

How rich and pleasing thou, my Julia, art.    To Julia.    Robert Herrick.    CaPo

How rich, O Lord, how fresh thy visits are!    Unprofitableness.    Henry Vaughan.    ILP (1975 ed.)

How rich the wave, in front, imprest.    Lines Written near Richmond, upon the Thames, at Evening.    Wordsworth.    MBPR

How rich we were, to know them, exiles.    Priest Lake.    William Stafford.    PoA

How right that you should rise.    New York Skyline.    Ruthe T. Spinnanger.    AATT

How Robin Hood Rescued the Widow's Sons.    *Unknown.*    PoTa

How Roses Came Red.    Robert Herrick.    CaPo

How sad I was then!    "Many Brave Hearts Are Asleep in the Deep."    Morgan Sanders.    WBN

How sad it must be.    A Poem for My Father.    Sonia Sanchez.    BPo; CSP; IHMS; RiTi

How sad, they think, to see him homing nightly.    Academic.    James Reeves.    MPo

How sad to be a casual girl.    For You.    Ed Ochester.    AAN

"How shall I be a poet?"    Poeta Fit, Non Nascitur.    "Lewis Carroll."    FaBoNo; OBSV

How shall I begin my song.    Songs for the Four Parts of the Night.    Owl Woman (Juana Manwell), *tr. by* Frances Densmore.    PBWP

How shall I deck my love in love's habiliment.    *Unknown. Fr.* Zepheria.    ESo

How shall I know thee in the sphere which keeps.    The Future Life.    Bryant.    PIM

How shall I name you, immortal, mild, proud shadows?    W. B. Yeats.    NU

How shall I sing that majesty.    A General Song of Praise to Almighty God.    John Mason.    SCP-2

How shall I withhold my soul so that.    Lovesong.    Rainer Maria Rilke, *tr. by* M. D. Herter Norton.    LoAs; OLR

How shall the wine be drunk, or the woman known?    A Voice from under the Table.    Richard Wilbur.    HAP; NOBA

How shall we adorn.    Angle of Geese.    N. Scott Momaday.    CDW; VW

How shall we get said what must be said?    William Carlos Williams.    *Fr.* The Desert Music.    TT

How Shall We Mourn You Who Are Killed and Wasted.    Charles Reznikoff.    InPK; SA

How shall we please this age? If in a song.    To Nysus.    Sir Charles Sedley.    FaBoEE; OBSV

How She Resolved to Act.    Merrill Moore.    SoS

How should I describe you—eternal.    Koala.    Alan Ross.    BoAnP

How should I praise thee, Lord!    The Temper.    George Herbert.    BoReV

How Should I Rule Me?    *Unknown.*    OxBM

"How should I your true love know."    An Old Song Ended.    Dante Gabriel Rossetti.    BoLoP; VPC

How should I your true love know.    Ophelia's Song.    Shakespeare.    *Fr.* Hamlet, IV, v.    AIW; EBEV; GBL

How should the world be luckier if this house.    Upon a House Shaken by the Land Agitation.    W. B. Yeats.    CMoP (1970 ed.)

How sick/ I get of your ghost.    Father.    Paul Carroll.    BrS

How sick I am!    Marijuana Notation.    Allen Ginsberg.    TT

How silly that soldier is pointing his gun at the wood.    Russians.    Keith Douglass.    OxBTC

How silly were those sages heretofore.    Samuel Butler.    *Fr.* Satire upon the Licentious Age of Charles II.    NOBL

How Singular.    Tom Hood.    FaBoNo

How Sleep the Brave.    William Collins.    NOBE
(Ode: "How sleep the brave, who sink to rest.")    WIF
(Ode Written in 1746.)    PAIC
(Ode, Written in the Beginning of the Year 1746.)    ExPo

(1973 ed.); HAP; HeIP; ILP (1975 ed.); LAuP; NIL; PBMP
(Ode, Written in the Year 1746.)　BTTM

How Slowly Time, the Loathsome Snail.　Heine, *tr. fr. German by* Ernst Feise.　NAWM-2

How smartly the quarters of the hour march by.　Copying Architecture in an Old Minster.　Thomas Hardy.　OBP

How smooth that lake expands its ample breast!　Stanzas.　Anne Radcliffe.　WPE

How soon doth man decay!　Mortification.　George Herbert.　SCP-1

How Soon Hath Time the Subtle Thief of Youth.　Milton. CABA (1972 ed.); ExPo (1973 ed.); FF; HeIP; InPS; IPWM; PAIC; PBMP; PoIA; PPoe
(Sonnet: "How soon hath time, the subtle thief of youth.")　OAEL-1

How soothing sound the gentle airs that move.　Avenue in Savernake Forest.　William Lisle Bowles.　PES

How Stars and Hearts Grow in Apples.　Virginia Elson.　AMV-81

How still.　Sea Calm.　Langston Hughes.　CaYB

How Still, How Happy.　Emily Brontë.　FSFS
("How still, how happy! Those are words.")　PES; VLP

How still the woods were! Not a redbreast whistled.　Sweet Chestnuts.　John Walsh.　DuDr

How straight it flew, how long it flew.　Seaside Golf.　John Betjeman.　LiSp; PPM; SPo

How strange at night to wake.　Night and Sleep.　Coventry Patmore.　VPC

How strange is Love; I am not one.　The Gourmet's Love-Song. P. G. Wodehouse.　NOBL

How strange it seems! These Hebrews in their graves.　The Jewish Cemetery at Newport.　Longfellow.　HAP; HeIP; HoPM (1975 ed.); NOBA; PiAm; TAP

How strange that for a little span.　Post Mortem.　Lord Russell Brain.　PMW

How strange the pride of many Irishmen!　The New Style. David O'Bruadair, *tr. by* John Montague.　BIrV

How strange to awake in a city.　Hearing Men Shout at Night on Macdougal Street.　Robert Bly.　TCP

How strange to be gone in a minute! A man.　Sonnet.　Ted Berrigan.　CAAP

How strange to think of giving up all ambition!　Watering the Horse.　Robert Bly.　NCSH

How strong does my passion flow.　On Her Loving Two Equally. Aphra Behn.　SBG

How struts my love my cavalier.　Cock-a-Hoop.　Isabella Gardner.　UsP; WPE

How sweet a Lord is mine? If any should.　Edward Taylor.　*Fr.* Preparatory Meditations: First Series, III.　PiAm

"How sweet and fit, for fatherland to die."　To Horace.　David Lake.　FPA

How sweet I roamed from field to field.　Song [*or* The Prince of Love].　Blake.　CABA (1972 ed.); LoAS; MBPR; NOBE; OAEL-2; OLR; STS

How Sweet Is the Language of Love, *with music.*　Oliver Holden. AH

How sweet is the shepherds sweet lot.　The Shepherd.　Blake. *Fr.* Songs of Innocence.　MBPR; PIM

How sweet the birds of Avondale.　Avondale.　Stevie Smith. RAE

How sweet the name of Jesus sounds.　The Name of Jesus.　John Newton.　BoReV

How sweet the tuneful bells' responsive peal!　The Bells, Ostend. William Lisle Bowles.　PAIC

How sweet, to see the dells so shady.　An Englishman with an Atlas; *or,* America the Unpronounceable.　Morris Bishop. GOA

How swift along the winding way.　Upon Boys Diverting Themselves in the River.　Thomas Foxton.　OxBChV

How thankful I am.　Demonstration.　Margaret Finefrock. AMV-80

How the days went.　Now That I Am Forever with Child.　Audre Lorde.　PoBA

How the devil do I know.　Truth.　James Hearst.　TPo

How the Doughty Duke of Albany like a Coward Knight Ran away Shamefully, *sel.*　John Skelton.
"O ye wretched Scots."　OBSV

How the elements solidify!　Event.　Sylvia Plath.　NOBA

How the First Hielandman [of God] Was Made.　*Unknown.* FaBoCo; GBP; OBSV

How the Indians Lost the Hot Springs.　Carol Cox.　MMD

How the Invalids Make Love.　Susan Feldman.　AmPA

How the kerosene outlasted.　David Martinson.　*Fr.* Nineteen Sections from a Twenty Acre Poem.　TAT

How the Laws of Physics Love Chocolate!　Reg Saner.　GP

How the light breaks when it does.　Observation.　Derk Wynand. AMV-80

How the place has grown. I hardly recognize it.　Are You Just Back for a Visit or Are You Going to Stay?　Francis Coleman Rosenberger.　AMV-81

How the Ploughman Learned His Paternoster.　*Unknown.*　OxBM

How the red road stretched before us, mile on mile. Independence.　Nancy Cato.　WPE

How the rose lays on.　Song (The Wren).　Henry Kanabus. FiCh

How the Sky Begins to Fall.　Joan Colby.　AMV-81

How the splendour of these veils and of this dress.　Phaedra. Osip Mandelstam, *tr. by* James Greene.　OBVE

How the waters closed above him.　Emily Dickinson.　DL; WIF

How, Then?　Stephen Crane.　TT

How there is anything so old.　Dinosaur Tracks in Beit Zayit. Shirley Kaufman.　FiCP

How They Brought the Good News by Sea.　Norma Farber. PChr

How They Brought the Good News from Ghent to Aix.　Robert Browning.　BTTM; ECBV; FaPoR; HoPM (1975 ed.); PAIC; SpRo; STS

How they enjoyed themselves the military gentlemen.　This and That.　Arthur J. Bull.　HeHu

How They Killed My Grandmother.　Boris Slutsky, *tr. fr. Russian by* Daniel Weissbort.　VWA

How They Sleep.　*Unknown.*　CTV

How thin and sharp is the moon tonight.　Winter Moon. Langston Hughes.　DuDa; PAIC

How Things Fall.　Donald Finkel.　VWA

How things grow upright.　Against Gravity.　Edith E. Cutting. AMV-80

How this woman came by the courage, how she got.　John Berryman.　*Fr.* Dream Songs.　TAP

How this year of years do I best see.　May Trees in a Storm. Geoffrey Grigson.　GBL

How time reverses.　For My Contemporaries.　J. V. Cunningham. CoPAm; PiAm

How to Amuse a Stone.　Richard Shelton.　AMV-80

How to Be Old.　May Swenson.　MAT; UnPo (1976 ed.)

How to Become a Poet.　Mark McCloskey.　PoW

How to behold what cannot be held?　Giovanni da Fiesole on the Sublime; or, Fra Angelico's "Last Judgment."　Richard Howard.　Prf

How to Catch Tiddlers.　Brian Jones.　LP

How to Cure Your Fever.　Thomas Lux.　NVAP

How to do it from the beginning.　Let Me Tell You.　Miller Williams.　CoPAm; CSP

How to Eat a Poem.　Eve Merriam.　OSP

How to End the Summer Alone. Lori Shpunt. PoUp

How to Get a Garden. Andrew Roberts. EC

How to Get On in Society. John Betjeman. NOBL; OBSV; OxBTC

How to Get to New Mexico. John Brandi. TAT

How to keep—is there any any, is there none such. The Leaden Echo and the Golden Echo. Gerard Manley Hopkins. CMoP (1970 ed.); ILP (1975 ed.); PAIC; PoIA

How to Kill. Keith Douglas. NOBE

How to Own Land. Susan Farley. AMV-80

How to Reach the Moon Marsha Pomerantz. VWA

How to Sing or Read. Robert Louis Stevenson. ECBV

How to Start a War Phyllis McGinley. OBSV

How to Tell the Wild Animals. Carolyn Wells. PCoP
"If strolling forth, a beast you view," *sel.* CaYB

How to the invisible. Elementary Cosmogony. Charles Simic. NNaP

How to Treat Elves. Morris Bishop. OBAL

How to Walk in a Crowd. Robert Hershon. FF

How to Write. Anne Waldman. UsP

How to Write a Letter. Elizabeth Turner. OxBChV

How to Write a Poem about the Desert Jefferson Carter. FoP

How totally unpredictable we are to one another. Robert Sward. POL

How Tuesday Began. Kathleen Fraser. CTBA

How unpleasant to meet Mr. Eliot! Lines for Cuscuscaraway and Mirza Murad Ali Beg. T. S. Eliot. OBAL; SpRo

How vainly men themselves amaze. The Garden. Andrew Marvell. AnMo; BiP; CABA (1972 ed.); ExPo (1973 ed.); HAP; ILP (1975 ed.); InPS; NIL; NOBE; OAEL-1; PAIC; PoPle; PPoD; PPoe; PPP; SCP-1; TT

How Violets Came Blue. Robert Herrick. CaPo

How Was Your Trip to L.A.? Philip Whalen. TAT

How we desire desire! Joy of surcease. Epigram. J. V. Cunningham. VGW

How We Drove the Trotter. W. T. Goodge. PH

How we envy their not caring. The Card-Players. David Ray. VGW

How We Heard the Name. Alan Dugan. NoAM

How we lived through that. Depression: My Father Speaks to My Mother. Dick Allen. FAF

How We Must Teach the Children. Richard W. Thomas. TC

How we went around in a/ daze. Growing Up. David Perkins. AAN

How well for the birds that can rise in their flight. *Tr. fr. Gaelic by* Frank O'Connor. WTO

How well her name an army doth present. Ana(Mary-Army)gram. George Herbert. CABA (1972 ed.); OAEL-1

How well I know what I mean to do. By the Fire-Side. Robert Browning. OAEL-2; VLP

How well I remember those days of danger. The Road to Pengya. Tu Fu, *tr. by* Rewi Alley *and* Edward Field. Prf

How well these frozen floods now represent. Sliding on Skates in Very Hard Frost. Nahum Tate. SCP-2

How well we were catered for! Spoilt. D. J. Enright. HeHu

How well you served me above ground. Spirit's Song. Louise Bogan. LoAs

"How will he hear the bell at school." Mutterings over the Crib of a Deaf Child. James Wright. CoPAm

How will you cross the autumn mountain alone? Princess Oku, *tr. fr. Japanese by* Willis Barnstone. BoWoP

How wisely nature did decree. Eyes and Tears. Andrew Marvell. MetP

How wonderful you were, so pious and holy. Sabbath. Jakov de Haan, *tr. by* David Soetendorp. VWA

How you dazzle my mind, panarchaic grandeur. Rebecca. Joseph Eliyia, *tr. by* Rae Dalven. VWA

How You Get Born. Erica Jong. UnPo (1976 ed.); UsP

How you manage till you reach. Lemuel Johnson. *Fr.* Hand on the Navel. AAN

How young I was. Old Age. *Gond Oral Tradition, tr. by* V. Elwin *and* S. Hivale. WTO

Howard. A. A. Milne. *See* Young Puppy, The.

However legendary. The Diamond Cutters. Adrienne Rich. NIL

However much the highway makers want. Wheels. Heather McHugh. AAN

However they talk, whatever they say. Louis Untermeyer, *after the German.* CTV

However we wrangled with Britain awhile. Literary Importation. Philip Freneau. AmVN; TAP

Howl. Allen Ginsberg. CAPP
"I saw the best minds of my generation destroyed by madness," I. AnMo; CoPAm; InPS, *ll.* 1-30; NIL; NoAM; TAP; TT

Howling of Wolves, The. Ted Hughes. OxBTC

Howrah Bridge. James K. Baxter. ATNZ

Hubbard is dead, the old plumber. Elegy for Alfred Hubbard. Tony Connor. MPo; SoSe

*Hubris* was the word I wanted. After He Said. Stephen Dunn. BrS

Huck Finn at Ninety, Dying in a Chicago Boarding House Room. James Schevill. TAP

Huckleberry, gooseberry, raspberry pie. Clyde Watson. *Fr.* Father Fox's Pennyrhymes. CC

Huddle on the greasy street, A. Death in Duke Street. Edwin Morgan. MS

Huddled in the pits. Cowboys: Two. Rod McKuen. MiP

Hudibras, *sels.* Samuel Butler.
"For his religion, it was fit," *fr.* I, 1. OBSV; SCP-2
"He could reduce all things to acts," *fr.* I, 1. SCP-2
"In mathematics he was greater," *fr.* I, 1. NOBL
Independent Squire, *fr.* I, 1. NOBE
Presbyterian Knight, *fr.* I, 1. NOBE
(Sir Hudibras.) NIL
("When civil dudgeon first grew high.") OAEL-1
("When civil fury first grew high.") EBEV; PAIC; SCP-2
"Question then, to state it first, The," *fr.* I, 3. NOBL
"Quoth he, My faith as adamantine," *fr.* II, 1. OBSV
"Quoth he, to bid me not to love," *fr.* II, 1. NOBL
Sir Hudibras, His Passing Worth, *fr.* I, Argument. EBEV; FaBoCo; OAEL-1, SCP-2
"Some were for setting up a king," *fr.* III, 2. EBEV
"There is a tall long-sided dame," *fr.* II, 1. OBSV
"This place (quoth she) they say's enchanted." *fr.* II, 1. NOBL
"What makes a knave a child of God," *fr.* III, 1. NOBL; OBSV

Hudson Ferry. James Schuyler. NYP

Hudson Hornet. William W. Cook. AMV-80

Hue and Cry after Blood and Money, A. *Unknown.* APAS

Huesca. Jim Cornford. BoLoP
(To Margot Heinemann.) OxBTC

Huey. Etheridge Knight. NNaP

Huff the talbot and our cat Tib. The Wars of the Roses. *Unknown.* GBP

Huffy Henry hid the day. John Berryman. *Fr.* Dream Songs. CAPP; PiAm; PoIA

Hug me closer, closer, mother. Little Bessie. *Unknown.* AmFP

Huge/ when she comes back to me. The Mouth That Is a Wound. Holly Prado. NPW

Huge commentators grace my learned shelves. James Bramston. *Fr.* The Man of Taste. FaBoCo

Huge doll of my body, The. My Life. Mark Strand. CAAP

Huge-headed oak. He Praises the Trees. *Unknown, tr. by* Robin Skelton. BIrV

Huge Leviathan, The. Spenser. *Fr.* Visions of the World's Vanity. EcS

Huge red-buttressed mesa over yonder, The. Rain in the Desert. John Gould Fletcher. Arizona Poems, VI. BPAW; NCSH

Huge wound in my head began to heal, The. The Wound. Thom Gunn. PSN

Hugging the ground by the lilac tree. Man and Beast. Clifford Dyment. BoAnP

Hugh Selwyn Mauberley (Life and Contacts). Ezra Pound. CABA (1972 ed.); CMoP (1970 ed.), *complete with* Mauberley; InPS; NoAM, *complete with* Mauberley; NOBA, *complete with* Mauberley; TAP

 "Age demanded an image, The," II. HAP; LFH; PiAm; VGW

 E. P. Ode pour l'Election de Son Sépulchre. HAP; PiAm; VGW

 Envoi (1919). HAP; UnPo (1976 ed.); VGW

 "For three years, out of key with his time." ILP (1975 ed.); UnPo (1976 ed.)

 "Tea-rose tea-gown, etc., The." NOBE

 "There died a myriad." FF; IP; NIL; NOBE; PiAm; TCP

 "These fought in any case." FF; HeIP; NIL; NOBE; PiAm; PPoe; VGW

Hugh Stuart Boyd. Elizabeth Barrett Browning. VLP

Hughie at the Inn. Elinor Wylie. WPE

Hughsville Scythe, The. Henry Taylor. PPoD

Hulk, three masted once, three stubbed now, A. The Benefits of an Education. John Ciardi. CoPAm

Hullabaloo Belay. *Unknown.* FSW

Hulling peas. Seeding. Mary Moore. NPW

Human Abstract, The. Blake. *Fr.* Songs of Experience. BiP; ExPo (1973 ed.); LAuP; MBPR; OAEL-2; PoIA; PPP; STS

Human Animal, The. Jane Mayhall. TAP

Human Condition, The. Howard Nemerov. CoPAm; NowV

Human contours are so easily lost, The. The Human Form Divine. Kathleen Raine. WPE

Human Cry, The. Tennyson. ILwL

Human Dilemma. Jim Rosemergy. AMV-80

Human face becoming locked insect face. Richard Hunt's Arachne. Robert Hayden. FB

Human Firewood Piano, The. Doug Blazek. CPA

Human Form Divine, The. Kathleen Raine. WPE

Human Geography. Gloria Fuertes, *tr. fr. Spanish by* Willis Barnstone. BoWoP

Human Geography. Ruth Whitman. AMV-80

Human Life. Matthew Prior. FaBoEE

Human Life: On the Denial of Immortality. Samuel Taylor Coleridge. IPWM; MBPR

Human Needs. *Unknown.* POL

Human Relations. Emmett Jarrett. NeAC

Human Relations. C. H. Sisson. POL

Human Tragedy, The, *sel.* Alfred Austin.
 "When with staid mothers' milk and sunshine warmed." FaBoCo

Humanities Lecture. William Stafford. NNaP

Humanity of Europe, The. Spring Death. Russell Marano. AMV-81

Humble Address, The. *Unknown.* APAS

Humble-Bee, The. Emerson. CTV; FSFS; NOBA

Humble Petition of Frances Harris, The. Swift. *See* To Their Excellencies the Lords Justices of Ireland, the Humble Petition of Frances Harris.

Humble Petition to the President of Harvard, A. John Beecher. CSP

Humbly to be now walking and talking. After the Storm. Joseph Kalar. SPT

Humbug Steamship Companies. *Unknown.* BPAW

Humidity. R. P. Dickey. HeS

Humiliation Revisited. Nova Trimble Ashley. AMV-80

Humming bee purrs softly o'er his flower, The. The Cricket. Frederick Goddard Tuckerman. NOBA; PiAm

Hummingbird. E. Margaret Clarkson. AATT

Hummingbird, The. Mary Howitt. CTV

Humming Bird, The. Harry Kemp. PCOP

Hummingbird. D. H. Lawrence. CMoP (1970 ed.); InPS; PPP

Hummingbird. Harold Littlebird. VoR

Humorous Ant, The. Oliver Herford. TDH

Hump, The. Kipling. OxBChV

Humpty Dumpty sat on a wall. Mother Goose. MG; NIL

Humpty Dumpty sat on the wall. Mother Goose (Circa 2054). Irene Sekula. QQQ

Humpty Dumpty's Song [*or* Recitation]. "Lewis Carroll." *Fr.* Through the Looking Glass. FaBoCo; FaBoNo; OxBChV

Hunchback, The. John Peale Bishop. PoA

Hunchback Girl: She Thinks of Heaven. Gwendolyn Brooks. IP; SOS

Hunchback in the Park, The. Dylan Thomas. EBEV; FaBoTw (1975 ed.); STS; TCP; TT

Hunchback on the corner, with gum and shoelaces, The. Pursuit. Robert Penn Warren. CoPAm; HAP; PPP

Hunchback Pine. Ethel Green Russell. AATT

Hunchbacked/ by his heart. The Life. Philip Dow. AmPA

Hunchbacked and corrected. Ken Belford. NeAC

Hunchbacked woman, The. Textures. Carol Bergé. MMD

Hunched, The. Douglas Dunn. LP

Hunched forward under rain. Man Holding Boy in the Rain. Melvin Dixon. NW

Hundred buffalo, A. Bone Yard. Jim Barnes. CDW

Hundred-gated Thebes. George Darley. *Fr.* Nepenthe. NOBE

Hundred thousand welcomes, thou Body of the Lord, A. *Tr. from Gaelic by* Douglas Hyde. WTO

Hundred wings are dropt as soft as one, A. On Startling Some Pigeons. Charles Tennyson Turner. PB

Hundreds of stars in the pretty sky. Only One Mother. George Cooper. CTV

Hundreds of yards of woodland. The Forest beyond the Glass. Lewis Turco. CoPAm

Hung from a stone branch of city wall. Beware the Months of Fire. Patrick Lane. NeAC

Hung Red, *sel.* Robin Fulton.
 "Hold a glass of pure water to the eye of the sun," III. MIS

Hungarian, The. Gerald Stern. BrS

Hunger. Nell Altizer. PHC

Hunger. Laurence Binyon. OxBTC

Hunger. Lennart Bruce. MiP

Hunger. Conrad Hilberry. TC

Hunger. Charles Simic. NNaP

Hunger ("Fear was about me"). *Tr. fr.* Eskimo. WTO

Hunger ("You, stranger, who only see us happy and free of care"). *Unknown, tr. fr. Eskimo by* Edward Field. IPWM

Hunger and Thirst. Robert Penn Warren. PoA

Hunger Artist, The. Shirley Kaufman. RiTi

Hunger for Me. Alta. GP

Hunger is beating me. *Yoruba Oral Tradition, tr. by* Ulli Beier *and* B. Gbadamosi. WTO

Hunger makes a person lie down. *Yoruba Oral Tradition,* tr. by Ulli Beier. WTO

Hunger Moon. Jane Cooper. CABA (1972 ed.)

Hungry and thirsty we break these stones in the heat of the sun. The Roadmenders' Song. *Gond Oral Tradition,* tr. by V. Elwin *and* S. Hivale. WTO

Hungry Black Child, The. Adam David Miller. PoBA

Hungry cancer will not let him rest, A.   A Thorn Forever in the Breast.   Countee Cullen.   BiP

Hungry come in a dry time, The.   Grabbling in Yokna Bottom.   James Seay.   CSP

Hungry Grass.   Donagh MacDonagh.   BIrV

Hungry, hungry are we.   Raggedy.   *Unknown.*   FSW

Hunkie Tunkie.   *Unknown.*   BluL

Hunt.   David Childers.   AAN

Hunt, The.   Walter de la Mare.   BoAnP

Hunt, The.   Daniel Halpern.   LiSp

Hunt, The.   Louis Kent.   SoSe

Hunt, The.   Pope.   *Fr.* Windsor Forest.   NIL

Hunt is up, The.   *Unknown.*   GBP

Hunt not, fish not, shoot not.   Bishop Blomfield's First Charge to His Clergy.   *At. to* Sydney Smith.   FaBoEE

Hunt of the Poem, The.   Richard Behm.   AMV-80

Hunter.   Raymond Carver.   NVAP

Hunter, The.   Ogden Nash.   LiSp; SPo

Hunter, The.   Frank O'Hara.   NNaP

Hunter crouches in his blind,The.   The Hunter.   Ogden Nash.   LiSp; SPo

Hunter Named Shephard, A.   *Unknown.*   TDH

Hunter of the Prairies, The.   Bryant.   LiSp

Hunter, Prey.   Dabney Stuart.   NVAP

Hunter Trials.   John Betjeman.   DuDr; PH

Hunters.   Sonya Dorman.   RiTi

Hunters are back, The.   The Woman Thing.   Audre Lorde.   NMM

Hunters in the Snow: Brueghel.   Joseph Langland.   WIF

Hunters of Kentucky, The.   Samuel Woodworth.   BLSo, *with music*; BTTM; FSW

Hunters search out every mountain hollow, Epicydes.   The One Who Runs Away.   Callimachus, *tr. by* Tom Dodge.   LiSp

Hunting.   Gary Snyder.   *See* Myths and Texts.

Hunting Civil War Relics at Nimblewill Creek.   James Dickey.   ConAP; GOA

Hunting Dragons with Fire Tongues and Deep Smoky Throats.   J. S. Harry.   CAAP

Hunting for Blueberries.   Thomas James.   AmPA

Hunting Fragment.   Gary Lawless.   FAF

Hunting of Cupid, The, *sel.*   George Peele.
   What Thing Is Love?   LoAs; NOBE

Hunting of the Hare, The, *sel.*   Margaret Cavendish, Duchess of Newcastle.
   "Betwixt two ridges of ploughed land sat Wat."   SCP-2

Hunting of the Snark, The.   "Lewis Carroll."   FaBoNo
   Baker's Tale, The, *sel.*   EBEV

Hunting Pheasants in a Cornfield.   Robert Bly.   ConAP

Hunting Season.   W. H. Auden.   LiSp

Hunting season.   Long Hair.   Gary Snyder.   NOBA; PiAm

Hunting Song.   Donald Finkel.   NCSH; SoSe; SPo

Hunting Song.   Gene Fowler.   BCr; CPA

Hunting with My Father.   Tom Absher.   AMV-80

Huntsman, What Quarry?   Edna St. Vincent Millay.   LiSp; RiTi

Huntsmen, The.   Walter de la Mare.   BBL; DuDa; PH

Hupa Twined Pendant: A White Woman Speaks.   Wendy Rose.   NW

Huron, The.   Ruth Herschberger.   WPE

Hurrah for revolution and more cannon-shot!   The Great Day.   W. B. Yeats.   BIrV; CMoP (1970 ed.); FF; WIF

Hurrah for the choice of the nation.   Lincoln and Liberty.   Jesse Hutchinson.   FSW

Hurrah for the Sea.   *Unknown.*   RhR

Hurrah! Hurrah!/ Have you heard?   Christmas.   Grace Cavalieri.   AATT

Hurrahing in Harvest.   Gerard Manley Hopkins.   AnMo; BiP; CMoP (1970 ed.); ILP (1975 ed.); OBP; VLP

Hurricane, The.   Bryant, *after the French of* José Maria Heredia.   EAP

Hurricane, The.   Hart Crane.   CMoP (1970 ed.)

Hurricane, The.   Philip Freneau.   EAP; TAP

Hurricane.   Archibald MacLeish.   NCSH

Hurry Home.   Leonard Clark.   FPB

Hurry Hurry.   J S. Harry.   FPA

Hurry On, My Weary Soul, *with music.   Unknown.*   AH

Hurry to bless the hands that play.   The Players Ask for a Blessing on the Psalteries and Themselves.   W. B. Yeats.   VLP

Hurrying Away from the Earth.   Robert Bly.   CoPAm; PoA

Hurrying Home.   Jim Farrar.   DNGG

Hurrying thru eternity.   After the Cries of the Birds.   Lawrence Ferlinghetti.   CAPP

Hurt./ U worried abt a.   To All Sisters.   Sonia Sanchez.   PoBA

Hurt Hawks.   Robinson Jeffers.   CMoP (1970 ed.); ILP (1975 ed.); NoAM; NOBA; PiAm; SoS; TAP; TPo; UnPo (1976 ed.)

Hurt No Living Thing.   Christina Rossetti.   CTV; RAE (Gently.)   ECBV

Hurt people crawl as if they.   These Days.   William Stafford.   NNaP

Hurtful Habits.   Edward Lear.   *See* Limerick: "There was an old person whose habits."

Hurting.   Vi Gale.   GP

Hurtled under the lover-sundering river.   Traveling Boy.   William Meredith.   NoAM

Hurtling between hedges now, I see.   The Limerick Train.   Brendan Kennelly.   IPM

Husband, The.   Barbara Greenberg.   RiTi

Husband and Heathen.   Sam Walter Foss.   OBAL

Husband with No Courage in Him, The.   *Unknown.*   FSW

Husbands.   Virginia R. Terris.   AAN

Husband's Lament, The.   Brian Merriman, *tr. fr. Modern Irish by* Frank O'Connor.   *Fr.* The Midnight Court.   OBVE

Hush and Baloo.   *Unknown.*   GBP

Hush, hush,/ Nobody cares!   Now We Are Sick.   J. B. Morton.   SpRo

Hush, Hush, New House in Charlotte.   E. M. Schorb.   AMV-81

Hush, hush! tread softly! hush, hush, my dear!   Song.   Keats.   MBPR

Hush is over all the teeming lists, A.   Frederick Douglass.   Paul Laurence Dunbar.   PoBA

Hush Little Baby.   *Unknown.*   BLSo, *with music*; FSW; GSB, *with music*

Hush! my dear, lie still and slumber.   Cradle Hymn.   Isaac Watts.   OxBChV

Hush of this place, The.   Turning Forty-five, after Drinks and Dirty Jokes and Talk of Women.   Philip Legler.   TC

Hush, Suzanne!   The Mouse in the Wainscot.   Ian Serraillier.   MN

Hush Thee, Princeling, *with music.*   Anna Elizabeth Bennett.   AH

Hush up, baby,/ Don't say a word.   The Mocking Bird.   *Unknown.*   AmFP

Hush, woman, do not speak to me!   The Tryst after Death.   *Unknown, tr. by* Kuno Meyer.   Epi

Hush-a-ba, Burdie.   *Unknown.*   GBP

Hush-a-bye, baby, on the tree top.   Mother Goose.   MG

Hushabye, don't you cry.   All the Pretty Little Horses.   *Unknown.*   FSW

Hush'd are the winds, and still the evening gloom.   On the Death of a Young Lady, Cousin to the Author.   Byron.   MBPR

Hushed, cruel, amber-eyed.   Pumas.   George Sterling.   BPAW

Huswifery. Edward Taylor. EAP; NOBA; SoSe; TAP
(Housewifery.) ILP (1975 ed.); NIL

Hut, The. Hilda Van Stockum. CTV

Hut near Desolated Pines. Alistair Campbell. ATNZ

Hut Window. Paul Celan, *tr. fr. German by* Joachim Neugroschel.
VWA

Huw's Farm. Robert Morgan. HeHu

Huxley Hall. John Betjeman. OBSV

Huzza! Hodgson, we are going. Lines to Mr. Hodgson. Byron.
MBPR

Hyaenas, The. Kipling. OBSV

Hyd, Absolon, thy gilte tresses clere. *See* Hide, Absalon, thy gilte
tresses clear.

Hyde stamps, and straight upon the ground the swarms. Andrew
Marvell. *Fr.* The Last Instructions to a Painter. SCP-1

Hydrogen Dog and the Cobalt Cat, The. Frederick Winsor. *Fr.*
The Space Child's Mother Goose. QQQ

Hye Nonny Nonny Noe. *Unknown.* FaBoCo; NOBL

Hyena. Carol Muske. AmPA

Hygiene. Perry Oldham. AAN

Hymenaei, *sel.* Ben Jonson.
"Bid all profane away!" SCP-1

Hymeneal Dialogue, An. Thomas Carew. SCP-2

Hymeneal Song on the Nuptials of the Lady Anne Wentworth and
the Lord Lovelace, An. Thomas Carew. CaPo

Hymen's Triumph, *sels.* Samuel Daniel.
First Flame. VoPo
Love Is a Sickness. NOBE
Secrecy. OLR

Hymmnn. Allen Ginsberg. NOBA

Hymn, A: "Drop, drop, slow tears." Phineas Fletcher. *See*
Drop, Drop, Slow Tears.

Hymn: "I know if I find you I will have to leave the earth." A.
R. Ammons. ConAP; CoPAm

Hymn: "I well remember." Alice Walker. CSP

Hymn: "Lord, when the wise men came from far." Sidney
Godolphin. BoReV; HAP
(Wise Men and Shepherds.) NOBE

Hymn: "Some sort of fire leaped out of the dirty and poor and
merciless city." Otto Orban, *tr. fr. Hungarian by* Emery
George. VWA

Hymn: "To those who know the Lord I speak." William Cowper.
PAIC

Hymn: "Whilst I beheld the neck o' the dove." Patrick Carey.
SCP-2

Hymn, A: "Wilt thou forgive that sin where I begun." John
Donne. *See* Hymn to God the Father, A.

Hymn about a Spoonful of Soup, A. Jozef Wittlin, *tr. fr. Polish
by* Isaac Komem. VWA

Hymn before Sunrise in the Vale [*or* Valley] of Chamouni.
Samuel Taylor Coleridge. BoReV; MBPR
"Ye ice-falls! ye that from the mountain's brow," *sel.* PIM

Hymn for Christmas Day, A. John Byrom. BoReV

Hymn for Lanie Poo, *sel.* Amiri Baraka.
Each Morning. PoBA

Hymn for Nations. *Unknown.* FSW

Hymn for October. Robert Gessner. SPT

Hymn for Saturday. Christopher Smart *See* For Saturday.

Hymn in Columbus Circle. Stephen Vincent Benét. OBAL

Hymn of Apollo. Shelley. ILP (1975 ed.); MBPR; OAEL-2

Hymn of Man. Swinburne. VLP

Hymn of Pan. Shelley. ILP (1975 ed.); MBPR

Hymn of the Alamo. Reuben M. Potter. BPAW

Hymn of the City. Bryant. EAP; PiAm

Hymn of the Nativity, Sung as by the Shepherds, An. Richard
Crashaw. BoReV; HAP
(In the Holy Nativity of Our Lord God.) CABA (1972 ed.)

"Gloomy night embraced the place." *sel.* SCP-1
(Shepherds' Hymn, The.) NOBE

Hymn of Trust. Oliver Wendell Holmes. PIM
(O Love Divine, That Stooped to Share, *with music.*) AH

Hymn on Froude and Kingsley, A. William Stubbs. FaBoEE

Hymn on the Morning of Christ's Nativity. Milton. *Fr.* On the
Morning of Christ's Nativity. NOBE

Hymn on the Power of God, A. James Thomson. PIM

Hymn on the Seasons, A. James Thomson. *Fr.* The Seasons.
LAuP; PIM

Hymn to Apollo. Keats. MBPR

Hymn to Artemis, the Destroyer. Marya Zaturenska. Moon

Hymn to Christ, at the Author's Last Going into Germany, A.
John Donne. BoReV; EBEV

Hymn to Death. Bryant. EAP

Hymn to Diana. Ben Jonson. *Fr.* Cynthia's Revels, V, vi.
HAP; Moon; NOBE; PoPle
("Queen and huntress, chaste and fair.") CABA (1972 ed.);
HeIP; ILP (1975 ed.); OAEL-1; PAIC
(Song: To Cynthia.) SoSe (1977 ed.)

Hymn to Evil. Louis Ginsberg. PoA

Hymn to God My God, in My Sickness. John Donne. AnMo;
CABA (1972 ed.); EBEV; HeIP; ILP (1975 ed.); NIL; OAEL-
1; PPP; SCP-1; SoSe
(Hymne to God My God.) MetP

Hymn to God the Father, A. John Donne. BiP; BoReV; EBEV;
HAP; ILP (1975 ed.); InPK; IP; OAEL-1; PAIC; PPoe; WIF
(Hymn: "Wilt Thou forgive that sin where I begun.") NOBE
(Hymne To God the Father.) MetP; TT

Hymn to God the Father, A. Ben Jonson. BoReV; PIM

Hymn to Intellectual Beauty. Shelley. BiP; BoReV; ExPo (1973
ed.); HAP; HeIP; ILP (1975 ed.); MBPR; OAEL-2

Hymn to Joy. Julia Cunningham. PChr

Hymn to Moloch. Ralph Hodgson. OxBTC

Hymn to My God in a Night of My Late Sickness, A. Sir Henry
Wotton. BoReV

Hymn to Pan. John Fletcher. *Fr.* The Faithful Shepherdess, I,
ii. NOBE

Hymn to Priapus. D. H. Lawrence. CMoP (1970 ed.); ExPo
(1973 ed.)

Hymn to Proserpine. Swinburne. ILP (1975 ed.); OAEL-2;
PFD; VLP; VPC

Hymn to St. Teresa. Richard Crashaw. *See* Hymn to the Name
and Honour of the Admirable Saint Teresa, A.

Hymn to the Air Spirit. *Tr. fr. Eskimo.* WTO

Hymn to the Evening, An. Phillis Wheatley. WPE

Hymn to the Morning, An. Phillis Wheatley. TAP

Hymn to the Name and Honour of the Admirable Saint Teresa, A.
Richard Crashaw. BoReV; NOBE; SCP-1
(Hymn to St. Teresa.) EBEV
"Love, thou are absolute sole lord," *sel.* HAP

Hymn to the New Omagh Road. John Montague. TwMBP

Hymn to the Night. Longfellow. AmVN; NOBA; TAP

Hymn to the Sun. C. M. Doughty. *Fr.* The Dawn in Britain.
FaBoTw (1975 ed.)

Hymn to the Sun. Michael Roberts. OxBTC

Hymn to the 10,000 Who Die Each Year on the Abortionist's
Table in Amerika. Rita Mae Brown. WBN

Hymn to the Virgin. *At. to* William of Shoreham. OxBM

Hymn to Venus, The, *sels. Unknown, formerly at. to* Homer; *tr. fr.
Greek by* Congreve.
"Among the springs which flow from Ida's head." OBVE
"But when the golden-thron'd Aurora made." OBVE

Hymn to Zeus. Cleanthes, *tr. fr. Greek by* James Adam. ILwL

Hymn Written after Jeremiah Preached to Me in a Dream. Owen
Dodson. AmNP (1974 ed.); PAIC

Hymne to God My God, in My Sicknesse. John Donne. *See* Hymn to God My God, in My Sickness.

Hymne to God the Father, A. John Donne. *See* Hymn to God the Father.

Hymns and Spiritual Songs, *sels.* Christopher Smart.
Nativity of Our Lord and Saviour Jesus Christ, The. BoReV; EBEV; HAP; LAuP; NOBE; OBP; WeW
St. Mark, XII. LAuP
St. Matthias, VIII. LAuP

Hymns for the Amusement of Children, *sels.* Christopher Smart.
For Saturday, XXXIII. LAuP
(Hymn for Saturday.) OxBChV
Gratitude, XXII. LAuP
Long-Suffering of God, XXIX. LAuP
Mirth, XXV. LAuP; OxBChV

Hymns of Astraea, *sel.* Sir John Davies.
Of Astraea. NIL; PAIC

Hymns to the Night, *sel.* "Novalis," *prose poem version tr. fr German by* Robert Bly.
Second Hymn to the Night, The. NU

Hymns we sing today go straight, The. Sunday Service. Dana Naone. PHC

Hymnus ad Patrem Sinensis. Philip Whalen. VoA

Hyperbole! Can't you arise. Prose for Des Esseintes. Donald Davie, *after Mallarmé.* OBVE

Hyperborean wind, whose rough hand flings, The. The Extremities of Cold in Hell. Thomas Dekker. *Fr.* Dekker His Dream. SCP-2

Hyperion; a Fragment. Keats. MBPR; OAEL-2

Hypnopompic Poem. William Cole. POL

Hypocrisy will serve as well. Samuel Butler. FaBoEE

Hypocrite, The. John Caryll. APAS

Hypocrite. Ann M. Craig. PPoD

Hypocrite Swift. Louise Bogan. PoA; SBG

Hypocrite Women. Denise Levertov. AnMo; CAPP; Epi; MAT; NMM; Psy

Hypocrites shed tears. On Watching Politicians Perform at Martin Luther King's Funeral. Etheridge Knight. NNaP

Hypodermic Release. Del Corey. AMV-81

Hypothesis. Jennifer Maiden. CAAP


# I

I/ am going to rise. Vive Noir! Mari Evans. IHMS; PoBA; Psy

I,/ at one time. The Self-Hatred of Don L. Lee. Don L. Lee. BPo

I/ is the total black, being spoken. Coal. Audre Lorde. PoBA

I/ never liked/ white folks. Alice Walker. *Fr.* Once. PoBA

I/ was five/ when/ mom and dad got married. Black Sketches. Don L. Lee. NeAC

I, a blue wolf. The "Word" of a Wolf Encircled by the Hunt. Sandag, *tr. by* C. R. Bawden. WTO

I abdicate my daily self that bled. Vita Nuova. Stanley Kunitz. VGW

I abhor the slimy kiss. Kisses Loathesome. Robert Herrick. CaPo

I abide and abide and better abide. Sir Thomas Wyatt. BoLoP

I accept the universe, which ranges. Six Poems, 3. Joseph Freeman. SPT

I ache to touch distance into center of light. Versions of Sunlight. James Applewhite. NVAP

I address you only. Letter to My Mother. Dom Moraes. NoAM

I adore you as much as the vault of night. Baudelaire, *tr. fr. French by* Anthony Hartley. NAWM-2

I adore you darling. Complaint. Rufinus Domesticus, *tr. by* Dudley Fitts. OLR

I advocate a semi-revolution. A Semi-Revolution. Robert Frost. NIL; WIF

I advocate a total revolution. A Total Revolution Oscar Williams. WIF

I ain't gonna tell no body 34 have done for me-e-e. 34 Blues. *Unknown.* BluL

I ain't never been to heaven but Ah been told. Swing Low, Sweet Chariot. *Unknown.* GBP

I ain't never loved but three womens in my life. Back Gnawing Blues. *Unknown.* BluL

I almost know you now. You are your name. Eight Lines for a Script Girl. George Jonas. NeAC

I almost walked past without looking. At the Grave of Albert Camus. Barbara F. Lefcowitz. PoUp

I almost went to bed. Song. Leonard Cohen. SoS

I, Alphonso, live and learn. Alphonso of Castile. Emerson. NOBA

I Always Come Home. Alfred Hayes. SPT

I always eat peas with honey. Peas and Honey. *Unknown.* CTV; PoPle

I Always Get Things Right. Louis Phillips. OSF

I always like summer. Knoxville, Tennessee. Nikki Giovanni. AmNP (1974 ed.); BPo; CNA; InPS; OSP; PoBA; SO

I always see—I don't know why. The Knowledgeable Child. L. A. G. Strong. PFIr

I always think of a coffin's quiet. A Poem for a Poet. Audre Lorde. NMM

"I always think that when I see you you." Estimable Mable. Gwendolyn Brooks. FB

I always thought that. Surfaces. David Madden. AMV-80

I always was afraid of Somes's Pond. Atavism. Elinor Wylie. PoA; SBG

I Am. John Clare. EBEV; HAP; ILP (1975 ed.); IPWM; NOBE; OAEL-2; PRF; VLP
(Written in Northampton County Asylum.) PBMP

I Am. Nanos Valaoritis. PoW

I am—/ Excuse me, I was—the Alamo. Last Fall of the Alamo. "O. Henry." BPAW

I am/ look/ ing at/ the Co/ caCola/ bottle. You Too? Me Too— Why Not? Soda Pop. Robert Hollander. NIL

I am a babe of royalty. Royal Education. Winthrop Mackworth Praed. OBSV

I am a beetle in the cabbage soup they serve up for geniuses. For Fyodor. Phyllis Webb. MMD

I am a black Pierrot. A Black Pierrot. Langston Hughes. OLR

I Am a Black Woman. Mari Evans. CNA; NMM

I am a bonded highwayman, Cole Younger is my name. *See* I am a highway bandit man, Cole Younger is my name.

I Am a Book I neither Wrote nor Read. Delmore Schwartz. TAP

I am a bridge. Golden Gate: The Teacher. Lilyan S. Mastrolia. AMV-80

I am a bunch of red roses. *Turkish Love Songs, tr. by* Reza Baraheni *and* Zahra-Soltan Shokoohtaezeh. BoWoP

I am a captain to your will. Christ's Reply. Edward Taylor. *Fr.* God's Determinations. EAP

I am a child/ of six generations here. The Sequence of Generations. Hayim Be'er, *tr. by* Stephen Mitchell. VWA

I am a circus dancer. A Circus Dancer. Celia Dropkin, *tr. by* Howard Schwartz. VWA

I Am a Cowboy in the Boat of Ra. Ishmael Reed. Epi; InPK; NIL; PoBA

I am a crazy woman with a painted face. I Light Your Streets. Meridel LeSueur. GP

I am a deserted barn. A Deserted Barn. Larry Woiwode. WeW

I am a feather on the bright sky. The Delight Song of Tsoai-Talee. N. Scott Momaday. CDW

I am a flag by distant space surrounded. Foreboding. Rainer Maria Rilke, *tr. by* Lori Weinstein. InPK

I am a fool, I can no good. Love. *Unknown.* OxBM

I am a frog. The Frog Prince. Stevie Smith. HAP

I am a gentleman in a dustcoat trying. Piazza Piece. John Crowe Ransom. BoLoP; FoP; HeIP;IP; LFH; NoAM; NOBA; PAIC; PiAm; SFF; TAP; UsP

I am a girl of constant sorrow. Girl of Constant Sorrow. Sara Ogan Gunning. FSW

I am a highway bandit man [*or* bonded highwayman], Cole Younger is my name. Cole Younger. *Unknown.* AmFP; FSW

I Am a Horse. Hans Arp, *tr. fr. French by* Harriet Watts. FaBoNo

I Am a Jew. David Martin. VWA

I am a jolly forester. The Jolly Forester. *Unknown.* RAE

I am a jovial collier lad, as blithe as blithe can be. Down in a Coal Mine. J. B. Geohegan. AmFP

I Am a King. I. Z. Rimon, *tr. fr. Hebrew by* Shlomo Vinner *and* Howard Schwartz. VWA

I am a king's daughter, you a king's wife. A Letter to Her Mother. Eristi-Aya, *tr. fr. Akkadian by* Willis Barnstone. BoWoP

I Am a Leaf. Yehuda Amichai, *tr. fr. Hebrew by* Shlomo Vinner *and* Howard Schwartz. VWA

I am a little world made cunningly. John Donne. Holy Sonnets, V. CABA (1972 ed.); TT

I am a lone, unfathered chick. Orphan Born. Robert Jones Burdette. OBAL

I am a man now. Here. R. S. Thomas. PSN

I am a man of constant sorrow. Man of Constant Sorrow. *Unknown.* FSW

I am a man of few beliefs. Thespian in Jerusalem. Myra Glazer Schotz. VWA

I am a miner. The light burns blue. Nick and the Candlestick. Sylvia Plath. CAPP; PBWP

I am a mirror. Reflecting and. A Slight of Hands. Karren L. Alenier. PoUp

I am a mixture of feelings without beginning. John Perreault. *Fr.* The Mixture. OSP

I am a monster. History. Robin, Skelton. MPA

I Am a Parcel of Vain Strivings Tied. Henry David Thoreau. NOBA; TAP
    (Sic Vita.) AmVN

I Am a Peach Tree. Li Po, *tr. fr. Chinese by* Shigeyoshi Obata. OLR

I am a piece of paper. Paul Green. OSP

I Am a Pilgrim. *Unknown.* FSW

I am a poet of the Hudson River, and the heights above it. America, America! Delmore Schwartz. NYP

I Am a Poor Wayfaring Stranger. *Unknown.* BLSH, *with music* (Poor Wayfaring Stranger, A.) AmFP; BLSo, *with music* (Wayfaring Stranger.) FSW

I Am a Red Slogan. Richard Wright. SPT

I am a restless record. A Harpsichord of Nerves. Rainer Schulte. SES

I am a rich widow, I live all alone. The Rich Widow. *Unknown.* AmFP

I am a river. No More. Carl Clark. JB

I am a roving gambler, I've gambled all around. Roving Gambler Blues *Unknown.* FSW

I am a roving shanty boy, love to sing and dance. The Roving Shanty Boy. *Unknown.* AmFP

I am a sea-shell flung. Frutta di Mare. Geoffrey Scott. EcS

I am a senseless thing, with a hey, with a hey. A New Ballad, to an Old Tune, Called, I Am the Duke of Norfolk, etc. *Unknown.* APAS

I am a skinny girl. The Skinny Girl. Anne Hébert, *tr. by* Willis Barnstone. BoWoP

I am a soul in the world: in. The Invention of Comics. Amiri Baraka. AmNP (1974 ed.); CAPP; PBMP; PoBA

I am a stag: of seven tines. The Alphabet Calendar of Amergin [*or* Song of Amergin]. *Unknown, tr. by* Robert Graves. BIrV; Moon

I am a stranger. The Jewish Woman. Gertrud Kolmar, *tr by* Henry A. Smith. VWA

I am a sundial, and I make a botch. On a Sundial. Hilaire Belloc. FaBoEE; QQQ

I am a sundial. Ordinary words. Hilaire Belloc. FaBoEE

I am a sundial, turned the wrong way round. Hilaire Belloc. FaBoEE; POL

I am a tall chap. Game. Sean Lucy. IPM

I am a traveler. Love Poem. John Batki. AcAn

I am a turtle. The Marriage. James Bertolino. HeS

I am a very mature person. A Decision. Edith Södergran. PBWP

I Am a Victim of the Telephone. Allen Ginsberg. GP; NYP; TT

I am a widow, robed in black, alone. Christine de Pisan, *tr. fr. French by* Willis Barnstone. BoWoP

I am a young executive. No cuffs than mine are cleaner. Executive. John Betjeman. NOBL

I am a young girl. Motet. *Unknown, tr. by* Carol Cosman. PBWP

I am a young girl, gay. *Unknown, tr. fr. French by* Willis Barnstone. BoWoP

I am afraid I may be Ilia. Fear. Anna Hajnal, *tr. by* Daniel Hoffman. BoWoP

I am afraid these verses will not please you, but. Sonnet to Byron. Shelley. MBPR

I am afraid to begin this poem. For My Mother. Ellen Bass. TV

I am afraid to own a body. Emily Dickinson. PiAm

I am alert to these letters in extraordinary numbers. Bordering Manuscript. James Applewhite. PoA

I am alive at night. Moon Song, Woman Song. Anne Sexton. Moon; PPP

I am alive—I guess. Emily Dickinson. NOBA

I am alone. A Dog. Charlotte Zolotow. GDP

I am alone tonight. Report of Health. John Updike. PBMP

I am already quite scarce. For years. The Last Ones. Dan Pagis, *tr. by* Stephen Mitchell. VWA

I am always aware of my mother. Mother. Nagase Kiyoko, *tr. by* Kenneth Roxroth *and* Ikuke Atsumi. BoWoP

I am always happiest in winter. Zimmer in Winter. Paul Zimmer. FoP

I am always meeting him. In his rags. Solo for Clarinet. Raymond Ward. ATNZ

I am Ambassador of Otherwhere. From the Embassy. Robert Graves. PoA

I am an ancient reluctant conscript. Old Timers. Carl Sandburg. NoAM

I am an expectant father. The Expectant Father. Simon J. Ortiz. NW

I am an old man. Crossing into the Prairies. Bruce Severy. HeS

I am an unadventurous man. De Gustibus. St. John Emile Clavering Hankin. LiSp

I am angry at myself said the mirror. Love Poem without Anyone in It. Neeli Cherkovski. CPA

I am as light as any roe. A Woman Is a Worthy Thing. *Unknown.* GBP; OxBM

I am, as you know, Walter Llywarch. Walter Llywarch. R. S. Thomas. PSN

I am ashamed before the earth. Therefore I Must Tell the Truth. Torlino, *tr. by* Washington Matthews. ExPo (1973 ed.)

I am beautiful, O mortals! like a dream of stone. Beauty. Baudelaire, *tr. by* Elaine Marks. NAWM-2

I am become a frightful bloody murtherer. Fragment from the Elizabethans. W. Bridges-Adams. FaBoCo

I am becoming a god! Everything Is Possible. Robert Pack. PPP

I am beside you, now. The Shadow's Song. Yvor Winters. POL

I am black and I have seen black hands. I Have Seen Black Hands. Richard Wright. NoAM; PoBA; SPT

I am blessed with my location. The Lost Pictures. Hollis Summers. HoPM (1975 ed.)

I am blessing two, not one. The Time of Creation Has Come. *Yoruba Oral Tradition, tr. by* Ulli Beier. WTO

I am blood of your ancient blood, bone of your fragile bone. To the Jews in Poland. Jozef Wittlin, *tr. by* Isaac Komen. VWA

I am bound to the bed these colding nights. Colding Nights. Roland Tharp. PHC

I am Branson; Nature's laws. Henry Charles Beeching *and* John Bowyer Nichols. *Fr.* Balliol Rhymes. FaBoEE

I am Brian Boy Magee. Brian Boy Magee. "Ethna Carbery." PFIr

I am broke and hungry. Broke and Hungry. *Unknown.* BluL

I am but a little woman. Kivkarjuk, *tr. fr. Eskimo.* WTO

I am called by name of man. *Unknown.* GBP

I am called Chyldhod, in play is all my mynde. Pageant Verses. Sir Thomas More. AAS

I am caught in the act. The Captive. Rochelle Ratner. WBN

I am caught up in her. Woman. Jane Chambers. IHMS

I am causing a sensation here in the County Clerk's crummy. Getting the License. Ronald Koertge. AAN

I Am Christmas *Unknown.* OxBM

I am closing my window. Tears silence the wind. Sonnet. Ted Berrigan. Epi

I am come into my garden, my sister, my spouse. Bible, *O.T. Fr.* The Song of Solomon. OBVE

I am come to make thy tomb. John Webster. *Fr.* The Duchess of Malfi, IV, ii. OBP

I am complexions of fire. Sandra Maria Esteves. NW

I Am Crying from Thirst. Alonzo Lopez. VW

I am Death, all bone and hair. Pardoner's Tale Blues. Patricia Beer. AIW

I am digging a pit. The Trapper. Peter Klappert. AAN

I Am Disquieted When I See Many Hills. Hyam Plutzik. VGW

I Am Drawn Still to the Desert. Arthur J. Bull. HeHu

I am dreaming about trains, perhaps. Lines Written in Objection, or the Limpopo Express. Phillip Hey. SFF

I am dressed in my old grey running suit. The Work-out. Geoffrey Movius. MAT

I am driving; it is dusk; Minnesota. Driving toward the Lac Qui Parle River. Robert Bly. ConAP; NCSH

I am drunk. Love Poem Beginning with I. David Steingass. CoPAm

I am dying, Egypt, dying! Antony to Cleopatra. William Haines Lytle. FaPo

I am Eve, great Adam's wife. Eve's Lament [*or* Eve]. *Unknown, tr. by* Kuno Meyer. BIrV; Epi; PFIr

I am featly-tripping Lee. Henry Charles Beeching. *Fr.* Balliol Rhymes. FaBoEE

I am fevered with the sunset. The Sea Gypsy. Richard Hovey. RhR

I am filled with fire oaths and utterances. Interpretation. Gloria Bussel Koster. NPW

I am filled with joy. Dead Man's Song, Dreamed by One Who Is Alive. Paulinaoq, *tr. fr. Eskimo.* WTO

I Am Forsaken. *Unknown.* OxBM

I am frightened by ladders, Freud, by ladders. Ladders. Reed Whittemore. PoUp

I Am from Ireland. *Unknown.* HAP

I am furious with myself. Elsa Tio, *tr. fr. Spanish by* Willis Barnstone. BoWoP

"I am Gaspar. I have brought frankincense." The Three Kings. Rubén Darío. PChr

I am getting out of the business of living. The Business of Living. Ryah Tumarkin Goodman. AAN

I am Giuletta, the bird woman. I married. The Freak Show. Nancy Willard. RiTi

I am glad daylong for the gift of song. Rhapsody. William Stanley Braithwaite. AmNP (1974 ed.)

I am glad I'm who I am. Secrets, VIII. Jessie Orton Jones. CTV

I am gloomy; I am the widower. Spook Sheep. Gérard de Nerval, *tr. by* Andrew Hoyem. Epi

I Am Going to California. *Unknown.* AIW

I am going to carry my bed into New York City tonight. 96 Vandam. Gerald Stern. NYP

I am going to make up a legend. The Writer's House. Dick Allen. FAF

I am going to sing you a song, full of muskrats, and guinea hens. Song for Everybody. Robert Paul Smith. ECBV

I Am Going to Sleep (Suicide Poem). Alfonsina Storni, *tr. fr. Spanish by* Aliki *and* Willis Barnstone. BoWoP

I Am Goya. Andrei Voznesensky, *tr. fr. Russian by* Stanley Kunitz. WeW

I am greeting you, Mayor of Lagos. Mayor of Lagos. *Yoruba Oral Tradition, tr. by* Ulli Beier. WTO

I am growing. Troll Songs. Karoniaktatie. NW

I am he as you are he as you are me and we are all together. I Am the Walrus. John Lennon *and* Paul McCartney. PPoe

I am he that walks with the tender and growing night. Walt Whitman. *Fr.* Song of Myself, XXI. ExPo (1973 ed.)

I am hearing the shape of the rain. In the Mountain Tent. James Dickey. CAPP; ILP (1975 ed.)

I am heavy with ancestors. Ancestors. Ryah Tumarkin Goodman. AAN

I Am Here. Robert Mezey. VWA

I am here again. Making an Impression. William (Haywood) Jackson. AMV-80

I am here with my beautiful bountiful womanful child. At a Summer Hotel. Isabella Gardner. RiTi

I am Hermes. I stand in the crossroads by a windy. Anyte, *tr. fr. Greek by* Willis Barnstone. BoWoP

I am his Highness' dog at Kew. Epigram Engraved on the Collar of a Dog Given to His Royal Highness. Pope. AnMo; CABA (1972 ed.); ExPo (1973 ed.); FaBoCo; FaBoEE; InPK; IP; PAIC; PoPle; SoSe (1977 ed.)

I am holding this turquoise. The Serenity in Stones. Simon J. Ortiz. CDW

I am I, old Father Fisheye that begat the ocean, the worm. The End. Allen Ginsberg. ConAP; TT; UsP

"I am Imagination," he said, "I am never idle." The Poet, Rebuked, Responds. William Langland, *tr. by* Selden Rodman *Fr.* The Vision of Piers Plowman, Passus XII. OBP

I am in a long train gliding through England. In the Train. Vivian de Sola Pinto. PES

"I Am in Danger—Sir." Adrienne Rich. NOBA; PiAm; Psy

I am in endless. Incest in Orange. Patricia Garfinkel. PoUp

I am in love with the laughing sickness. Zizi's Lament. Gregory Corso. Epi; VGW

I am in my Eskimo-hunting-song mood. Eskimo Occasion. Judith Rodriguez. GAS

I am in the corner of your eye all day. A Stranger in Your Town. Michael McMahon. FAF

I am in the tub with my body. To My Body. Nancy Sullivan. TAP

I am inside someone. An Agony. As Now. Amiri Baraka. BPo; ExPo (1973 ed.); ILP (1975 ed.); IPWM; LFH; PiAm; PPP

I am interested and amazed: on the building across the way. Dream Song 200. John Berryman. WasP

I am Jojo. Giant Jojo. Michael Rosen. FPB

I am just a weary pilgrim. When the Saints Come Marching In. Edward C. Redding. BLSo

I am leading a quiet life. Autobiography. Sonja Akesson, tr. by Ingrid Claréus. BoWoP

I am learning how to make a horse go left. New Skills. Naomi Shihab Nye. PH

I am leaving. South Wind. Mary Logue. NPW

I Am like a Book. David Rokeah, tr. fr. Hebrew by Robert Mezey. VWA

I am like a field/ waiting. Like a Field Waiting. Raquel Chalfi, tr. by Myra Glazer Schotz. VWA

I am like a jackfruit on the tree. The Jackfruit. Ho Xuan Huong, tr. by Nguyen Ngoc Bich. PBWP

I am like a slip of comet. Gerard Manley Hopkins. VLP

I am listening here in Rome. A Song for the Ragged Schools of London. Elizabeth Barrett Browning. SBG

I am listening to the silence. Sticks and Stones Paulette Dusdall Zachariou. NPW

I am living more alone now than I did. The Last Chapter. Walter de la Mare. CMoP (1970 ed.); ILP (1975 ed.)

I am  locked in a very expensive suit. The Suit. Leonard Cohen. BBGO

I am looking at trees. Trees. W. S. Merwin. GP

I am looking rather seedy now while holding down my claim. The Little Old Sod Shanty on My Claim. Unknown. BPAW; FSW

I am lost and knock on the nearest door. The Guest. Alan Ziegler. AAN

"I am Lot's pillar, caught in turning." Columns and Caryatids. Carolyn Kizer. WPE

I am lying face up on a raft. Dream. David Ignatow. VWA

I am made to sow the thistle for wheat. Enion's Protest. Blake. Fr. The Four Zoas. Prf; UsP

I Am Moved by a Necessity from Within. Daisy Aldan. RiTi

I am my lover's and he desires me. Bible, O.T. Fr. The Song of Solomon, ad. by Willis Barnstone. BoWoP

I am my mammie's ae bairn. I'm Owre Young to Marry Yet. Burns. LoAs

I am my own. As I Am My Father's. Rose Drachler. VWA

I am my prison. Conundrum. Carl Clark. JB

I am named after an old church where boys prayed. Kilbarrack 1969. Finbarr Crowley. IPM

I Am New York City. Jayne Cortez. BoWoP

I am no Norseman, come to plunder. On Devenish Island. Frank Ormsby. CIP; IPM

I am no shepherd of a child's surmises. Montana Pastoral. J. V. Cunningham. CoPAm; MAT; PPoD; VGW

I am no worshiper, but a member. Poem for David Janssen. R. T. Smith. AMV-81

I am nobody/ A red sinking autumn sun. Hokku Poems. Richard Wright. AmNP (1974 ed.); PoBA

I am not a metaphor or symbol. The Distant Drum. Calvin C. Hernton. CTBA; FF; TPo

I am not a painter, I am a poet. Why I Am Not a Painter. Frank O'Hara. ConAP; CoPAm; NoAM; NOBA; PoIA; VoA

I am not ambitious at all. The Ballade of the Incompetent Ballade-Monger. James Kenneth Stephen. VLP

I Am Not as I Wish. Richard Brathwaite. Fr. Nature's Embassy. SCP-2

"I am not as these are," the poet saith. Not as These. Dante Gabriel Rossetti. The House of Life, LXXV. VLP

I am not blind. For Steph. Wendy Rose. CDW

I am not bound to win. Abraham Lincoln. CTV

I am not cousin to thinking brain. Cousins. Paula B. Cullen. AMV-81

I am not going to invite you. Blond. Joseph De Roche. HeIP

I am not Mahomet. E. C. Bentley. Fr. Clerihews. NOBL

I am not one who much or oft delight. Personal Talk. Wordsworth. CABA (1972 ed.); MBPR; NOBE

I am not resigned to the shutting away of loving hearts. Dirge without Music. Edna St. Vincent Millay. DL; CMoP (1970 ed.); NoAM; SBG

I am not sure if I knew the truth. Youth. "Laurence Hope." WeW

I am not surprised. Waking up. Tom Schmidt. GP

"I am not treacherous, callous, jealous, superstitious." A Face. Marianne Moore. PiAm; Psy

I am not yet born; O hear me. Prayer before Birth. Louis MacNeice. BuTh; MPo; PBMP; PFIr; SoS

I am not you. Africa's Plea. Roland Tombekai Dempster. TPo

"I Am Not Yours." Sara Teasdale. VGW

I Am of Ireland. Unknown. GBP
(Icham of Irlaunde.) HAP
(Irish Dancer, The.) BuTh; NOBE; OxBM

"I Am of Ireland." W. B. Yeats. CMoP (1970 ed.); PFIr

I am of puritan and loyalist ancestry. Disqualification. Elizabeth Brewster. MMD

I Am of the Earth. Anna Walters. VoR

I am of the family of the universe, with all of us together. In No Way. David Ignatow. AMV-81

I Am of These. David Curry. HeS

I am of this world. On the Death of Emperor Tenji. Unknown, tr. fr. Japanese by Geoffrey Bownas and Anthony Thwaite. BoWoP

I am old. Epitaph. Christopher Logue. OxBTC

I am on the way. Song of a Child's Spirit. Unknown. AKE

I am one of passion's asses. The Girls of Llanbadarn. Dafydd ap Gwilym, tr. by Rolfe Humphries. OBW

I am only one. Lend a Hand. Edward Everett Hale. CTV

I am oppressed by all the room taken up by the dead. The Farmer among the Tombs. Wendell Berry. CSP

I am ordered out into a pile of stones. Guard Duty. Tomas Tranströmer. FoP

I am, outside. Incredible panic rules. John Berryman. Fr. Dream Songs. CAPP

"I am Pancho Villa," says the truck. Pancho Villa  Lou Lipsitz. NCSH

I am peeling the apples, making a note to. Apples. Margaret Gibson. AAN

I am poetry. Untitled X. Sandra Maria Esteves. NW

I am poor brother Lippo, by your leave! Fra Lippo Lippi. Robert Browning. BiP; OAEL-2; STS; VLP

I am pounding the faces of gods back into the red clay they. The Runner at Sauteurs. Derek Walcott. Fr. Another Life. OBP

I am Prytherch. Forgive me. I don't know.   Invasion on the Farm.
  R. S. Thomas.   POL

I Am Raftery ("I am Raftery, hesitant and confused").   Derek
  Mahon.   CIP

I Am Raftery ("I am Raftery the poet").   Anthony Raftery, *tr. fr.*
  *Irish by* James Stephens.   PFIr

I am rather tall and stately.   *Unknown.   Fr.* Balliol Rhymes.
  FaBoEE

I am reading.   The Distant Orgasm.   James Tate.   AmPA

I am reminded, by the tan man who wings.   The Elevator Man
  Adheres to Form.   Margaret Danner.   PoBA

I am reminded of the vestment.   I'm Not Here / Never Was.
  Constanta Buzea, *tr. by* Stavros Deligiorgis.   BoWoP

I am riding a lion.   Elaine H. Jennings.   NPW

I am riding on a limited express, one of the crack trains of the
  nation.   Limited.   Carl Sandburg.   HAP; PSN

I am rooted to a cliff.   Lighthouse Keeper.   Gary Sange.   NVAP

I am saying goodbye to the trees.   A Departure.   Derek Mahon.
  CIP

I am scorned by patterns which hold.   Moon at Three A.M.
  Lance Henson.   CDW

I am seeing/ other men now.   "Hold Back the Edges of Your
  Gowns, Ladies, We Are Going through Hell."   Cathleen
  Quirk.   MMD

I am shooting a game of pool.   Straightening the Warp.   Douglas
  Blazek.   EC

I am silver and exact. I have no preconceptions.   Mirror.   Sylvia
  Plath.   HAP; SoSe

I am, sir, so to speak, "a Harvard man."   A Humble Petition to
  the President of Harvard.   John Beecher.   CSP

I Am Sitting Here.   Yehuda Amichai, *tr. fr. Hebrew by* Ruth
  Nevo.   VWA

I am sitting here.   The Poor Girl's Meditation.   *Unknown, tr. by*
  Padraic Colum.   BIrV; OLR; PFIr

I am sitting in Mike's Place trying to figure out.   One Thousand
  Fearful Words for Fidel Castro.   Lawrence Ferlinghetti.
  VGW

I am sitting in my room.   House Arrest.   George Tsongas.   CPA

I am sitting on your Indian rock watching the third.   The Wake.
  Madeline DeFrees.   RiTi

I am so close to the skin that.   Green Apple.   Mari Kubo.   PHC

I Am So Glad and Very.   E. E. Cummings.   CMoP (1970 ed.);
  UsP

I am so fragile this morning.   The U.S. Coast and Geodetic
  Survey Ship *Pioneer*.   Robert Hershon.   NeAC

I am so little and gray.   The Prayer of the Mouse.   Carmen
  Bernos De Gasztold.   MN

I am so lonely, I am so blue.   Somebody's Sweetheart I Want to
  Be.   Will D. Cobb.   FSN

I am still bitter about the last place we stayed.   Codicil.   Ruth
  Stone.   BoWoP

I am stuffing this bolster.   Slipping Out of Intensive Care.
  Florence Trefethen.   AMV–80

I am surprised to find today.   The Professor Waking.   James
  Tate.   FF

I am Taliesin. I sing perfect metre.   *Unknown, tr. fr. Welsh by* Ifor
  Williams.   OBW

I am tall and rather stately.   *Unknown. Fr.* Balliol Rhymes.
  NOBL

I am telling you this.   Blue Ruth: America.   Michael S. Harper.
  PoBA

I am ten and no one I love has died.   Deborah Lee.   Yvonne.
  CNA

I am that binge you need.   Tango.   Elena Jordana, *tr. by*
  Kathrine Jason.   AMV–80

I am that Dido which thou here do'st see.   Decimus Magnus
  Ausonius, *tr. fr. Latin by* Sir Walter Ralegh.   OBVE

I am that man more solitary than brandy.   Name Me.   Richard
  Packer.   FPA

I am that which began.   Hertha.   Swinburne.   OAEL–2; VLP

I am the American heartbreak.   American Heartbreak.   Langston
  Hughes.   BPo; CABA (1972 ed.)

I am the bastard in the ragged suit.   Outcast.   Herman Spector.
  SPT

I Am the Beginning.   Isaiah Shembe, *tr. fr. Zulu by* G. C.
  Oosthuizen.   WTO

I am the bird in transit for the winter.   Sandra Maria Esteves.
  NW

I am the bird of the wayside.   Prelude.   Christine Ama Ata
  Aidoo.   PBWP

I am the blue! I come from the lower world.   Helen.   Paul
  Valéry, *tr. by* Robert Lowell.   OBVE

"I Am the Captain of My Soul."   Gwen Harwood.   GAS

I am the cat of cats, I am.   The Cat of Cats [*or* The Kitten
  Speaks].   William Brighty Rands.   *Fr.* The White Princess.
  DuDr; OxBChV; PCOP

I am the chaunt-rann of a Singer.   The Poet.   Padraic Fiacc.
  CIP

I am the child of the Yei-ie.   Yei-ie's Child.   Charles C. Long.
  VW

I am the Dean, and this is Mrs. Liddell.   *Unknown. Fr.* Balliol
  Rhymes.   FaBoEE

I am the Dean of Christ Church, Sir.   Cecil Arthur Spring-Rice.
  *Fr.* Balliol Rhymes.   FaBoCo; FaBoEE; NOBL

I am the dog world's best detective.   The Bloodhound.   Edward
  Anthony.   GDP

I am the drummer's daughter.   Rhythm.   Ruth Stone.   FoP

I Am the Duke of Norfolk.   *Unknown.*   GBP

I am the family face.   Heredity.   Thomas Hardy.   EBEV; IPWM

I am the farmer, stripped of love.   The Hill Farmer Speaks.   R.
  S. Thomas.   MPo; OBW

I am the ghost of Shadwell Stair.   Shadwell Stair.   Wilfred Owen.
  FaBoTw (1975 ed.)

I Am the Great Sun.   Charles Causley.   BuTh

I am the hammer.   Dusk of the Gods.   Sol Funaroff.   SPT

I am the inland man.   Midwestern Man.   Paul Giandi.
  AMV–81

I am the little man who smokes and smokes.   John Berryman.
  *Fr.* Dream Songs.   WeW

I am the longest, the longest, the strongest.   The Longest Tale
  about the Longest Tail.   Alexander Resnikoff.   OSF

I Am the Lord, *with music.*   Alexander Mack, *tr. fr. German by*
  Sheema Z. Buehne.   AH

I am the magical mouse.   The Magical Mouse.   Kenneth Patchen.
  OSP; SO; UsP

I am the man crouched behind a bush.   The Rapist.   Stephen
  Dunn.   POL

I Am the Man Who.   James Moore.   BrS

I am the man who.   The Carpenter.   Michael Perkins.   POL

I am the man who looked for peace and found.   War Poet.
  Sidney Keyes.   BuTh

I am the mother of sorrows.   The Paradox.   Paul Laurence
  Dunbar.   CABA (1972 ed.); PoBA

I am the Muse who sung alway.   Solution.   Emerson.   OBAL

I am the nor'west air nosing among the pines.   Time.   Allen
  Curnow.   ATNZ

I Am the One.   Thomas Hardy.   OxBTC

I am the one they could not conquer.   They Watch Me with
  Radar.   Lee Lally.   PoUp

I am the one who looks the other way.   The Bystander.
  Rosemary Dobson.   GAS

I Am the Only Being Whose Doom.   Emily Brontë.   MAT; VLP

I am the only living thing.   The Stallion.   Boynton Merrill, Jr.
  PH

I am the People, the Mob. Carl Sandburg. TAP

I am the poet of the Body and I am the poet of the Soul. Walt Whitman. Song of Myself, XXI. BiP; WeW

I am the Prince. Envoi. Charles Causley. FF

I am the princess who kissed a frog. Grim Fairy Tale. Lionel Wiggam. TPo

I am the resurrection, and the life. Bible, *N.T.* St. John, XI: 25-26. CTV

I am the rose of Sharon, and the lily of the valleys. Bible, *O.T. Fr.* The Song of Solomon, II. BiP; BoLoP; FF; GBL; OBVE; OLR

I am the ruined queen. Dido: Swarming. Kathleen Spivack. PoA

"I am the sea." Poetry Is. Bruce Bennett. AMV-81

I am the seller and the sold. Criteria. Ruthe T. Spinnanger. AATT

I am the seventh son of the son. Malcolm X—an Autobiography. Larry Neal. AmNP (1974 ed.); BPo

I am the sister of him. Little. Dorothy Aldis. CTV

I am the smoke king. The Song of the Smoke. W. E. B. DuBois. PoBA; UnPo (1976 ed.)

I Am the Soil. Gladstone Yearwood. SES

I am the sorrow in the wheat fields. Ellen Bass. NMM

I am the teacher of athletes. Song of Myself, XLVII. Walt Whitman. AnMo

I am the true vine, and my Father is the husbandman. Bible, *N.T. Fr.* St. John. OBVE

I am the turquoise mechanic's son. The Turquoise Mechanic's Son. Steve Toth. AcAn

I am the unnoticed, the unnoticeable man. The Man in the Bowler Hat. Peter Black. BuTh

I am the very model [*or* pattern] of a modern Major-General. The Modern Major-General. W. S. Gilbert. *Fr.* The Pirates of Penzance. FaPo; NOBL

I Am the Walrus. John Lennon *and* Paul McCartney. PPoe

I Am the Youngest in Our House. Michael Rosen. FPB

I am thin as nail parings. Light as dandruff. Embryos. Marge Piercy. RiTi

I am thinking of Iowa. The Driving Wheels. G. E. Murray. HeS

I am thinking of tents and tentage, tents through the ages. Thinking of Tents. Reed Whittemore. TAP

I am thinking today of that beautiful land I shall reach when the sun goeth down. Will There Be Any Stars in My Crown? E. E. Hewitt. BLSH

I am third in a line of murderers. Shooting Gallery. Martin Galvin. AMV-80

I am 32 years old. Writ on the Eve of My 32nd Birthday. Gregory Corso. SA

I am tired of cursing the Bishop. Crazy Jane on the Mountain. W. B. Yeats. CMoP (1970 ed.)

I am tired of looking at you through this glass. The Flirtation. Michael C. Blumenthal. AMV-81

I am tired of work; I am tired of building up somebody else's civilization. Tired. Fenton Johnson. PoBA

I am to my honey what marijuana is. Skirt Dance. Ishmael Reed. FF

I am too angry to sleep beside you. Love Letter Postmarked Van Beethoven. Diane Wakoski. BiP

I am too near to be dreamt of by him. Wislawa Szymborska, *tr. fr. Polish by* Czeslaw Milosz. BoWoP; PBWP

I am too young to grow a beard. Street Song. Thom Gunn. HeIP

I am trying/ to learn to walk again. Walk. Frank Horne. BPo

I am trying to imagine. Re-forming the Crystal. Adrienne Rich. TAP

I am trying to pry open your casket. Dear Reader. James Tate. EAS

I Am 25. Gregory Corso. CoPAm

I am 25 years old. My Poem. Nikki Giovanni. AmNP (1974 ed.); BPo; PoBA

I am two fools I know. The Triple Fool. John Donne. GBL; ILP (1975 ed.)

I am typing up bills for a firm to be sent to their clients. A Bill to My Father. Edward Field. TPo

"I am unable," yonder beggar cries. A Lame Beggar. John Donne. FF

I am unhappy that I am not God. He Puts Me to Rest. David Ignatow. VGW

I Am Waiting. Lawrence Ferlinghetti. *Fr.* Oral Messages. CAPP; GOA

I am waiting by the canal. The Governor's Palace. Linda Pastan. *Fr.* Williamsburg. RiTi

I am waiting for my honey to return. After the Bombing of Barcelona. Norman Macleod. SPT

I am walking as fast as I can. Foreign Streets. Mary Crow. AMV-80

I am walking rapidly through striations of light and dark. I Dream I'm the Death of Orpheus. Adrienne Rich. NIL; NMM; NoAM; TT

I am watching them churn the last milk. The Mad Yak. Gregory Corso. NoAM

I Am Weary of Straying, *with music.* Sarah E. York. AH

I am weary of these times and their dull burden. Quid Restat. Lucius Beebe. RFM

I Am with Those. Ingrid Jonker, *tr. fr. Afrikaans by* Jack Cope *and* William Plomer. BoWoP

I am within as white as snow. *Unknown.* GBP

I am wondering how I could have changed her blood. Marlow and Nancy. Sandra McPherson. AmPA

I am wondering how these first words will look. American Saturday Afternoon. Ron Ikan. NVAP

I am writing to cancel. Relative Matter. Ann Darr. PoUp

I am writing to you in answer to your letter. The Connection. Daniil Kharms, *tr. by* George Gibian. FaBoNo

I am: yet what I am none [*or* who] cares or knows. I Am [*or* Written in Northampton County Asylum]. John Clare. EBEV; HAP; ILP (1975 ed.); IPWM; NOBE; OAEL-2; PBMP; Prf; VLP

I am your mother, your mother's mother. Jalal Ud Din Rumi, *tr. fr. Persian by* Elizabeth Daryush. OBVE

I am yours and you are mine so. Michael Silverton. POL

I am yours, you are mine. Frau Ava, *tr. fr. German by* Willis Barnstone. BoWoP

I amna' fou' sae muckle as tired—deid dune. Sic Transit Gloria Scotia. "Hugh MacDiarmid." CMoP (1970 ed.)

I and Pangur [*or* Pangor] Ban, my cat. Pangur Ban. *Unknown, tr. by* Robin Flower. MN, *st. 1 only;* PFIr

I and the other intruders. Of Objects Considered as Fortresses in a Baleful Place. Hyam Plutzik. VGW

I argue/ that where the body is concerned. Saddle and Cell. The Three Marias, *tr. by* Helen R. Lane. BoWoP

I arise from dreams of thee. The Indian Serenade. Shelley. ExPo (1973 ed.); HoPM (1975 ed.); MBPR; UsP

I arose early and stepped outside. February Morning. King D. Kuka. VoR

I arrive/ in the unbearable heat. Song for My Father. Jessica Tarahata Hagedorn. NW

I arrive/ Langston. Do Nothing till You Hear from Me. David Henderson. CNA; PoBA

I arrive where an unknown earth is under my feet. Landfall. *Maori Oral Tradition, tr. by* A. S. Thomson. WTO

I arrived in mani. The Music Box Sang. Americo Casiano. NW

I ask but right: let her that caught me late. Ovid, *tr. by* Christopher Marlowe. Amores, I, 3. EBEV

I ask for the strength to follow through my life. Time of Day. Selden Rodman. PoA

I asked a thief to steal me a peach. Blake. CABA (1972 ed.); ExPo (1973 ed.); LAuP; MBPR; STS

I asked if I got sick and died, would you. A Question. J. M. Synge. OxBTC; PFIr; WeW

I asked if I should pray. Mohini Chatterjee. W. B. Yeats. NoAM

I asked my dear friend, Orator Prigg. Orator Prigg. Blake. OBSV

I asked my love to go with me. Banks of the Ohio. *Unknown.* FSW

I asked my mother for fifty cents. Fifty Cents. *Unknown.* CTV

I asked my parents. Going to Norway. Jack Anderson. GP

I asked no other thing. Emily Dickinson. NOBA; PBMP

I asked professors who teach the meaning. Happiness. Carl Sandburg. TH; VoPo

I asked thee oft what poets thou hast read. Upon the Same (Detractor). Robert Herrick. CaPo

I assume the grievous penitence. The Purple Blemish. Par Lagerkvist, *tr. by* Lennart Bruce. AMV-81

I ate everything they put in front of me. My Life. Michael Lally. EC

I attach no importance to life. The Spectral Attitudes. André Breton, *tr. by* David Gascoyne. EAS

I attended the burial of all my rosy feelings. Transaction. A. R. Ammons. PoA

I await his coming. Guessing. *Unknown, tr. by* U Win Pe. PBWP

I awaken to a flow of night. Voyage. Donald G. H. Schramm. AMV-81

I awakened to dryness and the ferns were dead. The Tragedy of Leaves. Charles Bukowski. CoPAm; CPA; HoPM (1975 ed.)

I awoke in profuse sweat. arms aching. Hag-ridden. Robert Graves. BIrV

I awoke in the Midsummer not-to-call night. Moonrise. Gerard Manley Hopkins. Moon

I Awoke with the Room Cold. Marge Piercy. NeAC

"I baited bears and prayed." Testimonies. Weldon Kees. NYP

I banked the five in the side. Kelly. Robert Hershon. NeAC

I bear, in sign of love. Francis Andrewes. *Fr.* Shepherdess' Valentine. OFD

I been drifting and rolling along the road. Rolling Log Blues. *Unknown.* BluL

I been ridin' fer cattle the most of my life. The High-loping Cowboy. Curley W. Fletcher. BPAW

I been scarred and battered. Still Here. Langston Hughes. BPo

I been t'inkin' 'bout de preachah; whut he said de othah night. Philosophy. Paul Laurence Dunbar. BPo

I Been Treated Wrong. *Unknown.* BluL

I been walking all day and all night too. No Job Blues. *Unknown.* BluL

I beg God's grace, guardian of the parish. In Praise of Tenby. *Unknown, tr. by* Joseph P. Clancy. OBW

I beg my bones to be good but. The Poet. Lucille Clifton. GP

I began in Ohio. Stages on a Journey Westward. James Wright. CABA (1972 ed.)

I begin with the hills. This House. Ray A. Young Bear. CDW

I begin with words of air but delightful ones. Sappho, *tr. fr Greek by* Bill Zavatsky. POL

I beheld, and lo a great multitude, which no man could number. Heavenly Vision. William Billings. AmFP

I, being a woman and distressed. Edna St. Vincent Millay. BoLoP; SBG

I Believe. Ardoin Casgrain. PPM

I believe a leaf of grass is no less than the journey-work of the stars. Walt Whitman. *Fr.* Song of Myself, XXXI. InPS

I Believe I'll Dust My Broom. *Unknown.* BluL

I believe in God above. A Child's Creed. *Unknown.* CTV

I believe in laughter. I Believe. Ardoin Casgrain. PPM

I believe in the brook as it wanders. The Handiwork of God. *Unknown.* CTV

I believe in the fitness of surprises. Waiting. Liz Stout. AMV-81

I believe in the flesh and the appetites. Walt Whitman. *Fr.* Song of Myself, XXIV. Prf

I believe in the ultimate justice of Fate. Credo. Georgia Douglas Johnson. PoBA

I believe in the uncarved block and my dark. Translation of a Chinese Tribute to Jade. Alice Notley. FiCh

I believe in this stalled magnificence. The Snowbound City. John Haines. EAS

I believe in you my soul. Walt Whitman. Song of Myself, V. BiP;Prf

I believe it! 'tis Thou, God, that givest, 'tis I who receive. Robert Browning. *Fr.* Saul. ILwL

I believe it was out of the red one that George Washington stepped. The Buddha Inherits 6 Cars on His Birthday. Diane Wakoski. NIL

I believe my old lady's. What? So Soon! Langston Hughes. ILP (1975 ed.)

I believe that if I had my sweet woman's heart in my hand. Drive Away Blues. *Unknown.* BluL

I believe we came together. Past Time. Harvey Shapiro. POL

I believed in Schmidt's piss-ridden. Shaman. Paul Nelson. PHC

I bellowed to the ferryman, methought. Death Terrible in Countenance. Thomas Dekker. *Fr.* Dekker His Dream. SCP-2

I bend over an old hollow cottonwood stump. A Hollow Tree. Robert Bly. GP; NNaP

I bend over the woman. The Country Midwife: A Day. Ai. CAAP

I Bended unto Me. Thomas Edward Brown. PeD

I beseech God's favour, faultless your gift. Petition for Reconciliation. Cynddelw Brydydd Mawr, *tr. by* Joseph P. Clancy. OBW

I bespeak words. Introduction. Clere Parsons. FaBoTw (1975 ed.)

I blame Myrtis. Korinna, *tr. fr. Greek by* John Dillion. PBWP

"I bleed by the black stream." Haemorrhage. Padraic Fiacc. CIP

I bless thee, Lord, because I grow. Paradise. George Herbert. OAEL-1; PAIC

I Bless Thee, Lord, for Sorrows Sent, *with music.* Samuel Johnson. AH

IBM Hired Her. W. J. J. Gordon. QQQ

I bought a dishmop. Youth and Beauty. William Carlos Williams. RRA

I bought a shop on Dizengoff. Buying a Shop on Dizengoff. Erez Biton, *tr. by* Judith Katz. VWA

I bought God in an antique shop. Collector's Note. Arthur J. Bull. HeHu

I bow my forehead to the dust. The Eternal Goodness. Whittier. PIM

I Break the Sky. Owen Dodson. PoBA

I breathe, sweet Gib, the temperate air of Wrest. To My Friend G.N., from Wrest. Thomas Carew. CaPo

I breathed enough to take the trick. Emily Dickinson. NoAM

I breathed upon the aluminum microphone-stand a body's length away. Thus Crosslegged on Round Pillow Sat in Space. Allen Ginsberg. NNaP

I bring fresh showers for the thirsting flowers. The Cloud. Shelley. MBPR; PPM

I bring myself back from the streets that open like long. Home for Thanksgiving. W. S. Merwin. NoAM

I bring ye love. Question. What will love do? Upon Love, by Way of Question and Answer. Robert Herrick. CaPo

I broider the world upon a loom. The Loom of Dreams. Arthur Symons. VLP

I broke bread. Under the Williamsburg Bridge. Galway Kinnell. NYP

I built my hut near where people live. Two Drinking Songs. T'ao Yuan-ming, *ad. by* Robert Bly. NU

I built my soul a lordly pleasure-house. The Palace of Art. Tennyson. VLP

I buried you deeper last night. To a Persistent Phantom. Frank Horne. AmNP (1974 ed.)

I bury my dreams well, under. Awakening. David Robinson. AMV-81

I buy a hamburger. Revelation of the Bare Ass. Doug Blazek. CPA

I buyed me a little dog. Little Brown Dog. *Unknown.* FSW

I call on the sun to strip/ us naked. J. Charles Green. *Fr.* Arioso. DNGG

I call up words that he may write them down. Demands of the Muse. Vernon Watkins. PoA

I called him to come in. Evening. James Wright. NOBA

I called you. You called me. Dream. Emilio Prados, *tr. by* Eleanor L. Turnbull. LoAs

I came/ in the blinding sweep. To Mother. Frank Horne. *Fr.* Letters Found near a Suicide. BPo

I came, a scooped out woman. Desert March. Gerda Norvig. VWA

I came as a shadow. Nocturne Varial. Lewis Alexander. PoBA

I came from Alabama wid my banjo on my knee. *See* I come from Alabama . . .

I came from England into France. The Journey into France. *Unknown.* FaBoBa

I came from ole Kentucky. Jim Crow. Thomas D. Rice. VLP

I came from ole Virginny. Maple Leaf Rag. Sydney Brown. BLSo

I Came from Salem City. *Unknown.* AmFP

I came here often/ Two decades ago. The Library. Margaret Gillies. PMW

I came home the other night as drunk as I could be. Four Nights Drunk. *Unknown.* FSW

I came one day upon a cream-painted wooden house. At Evans Street. Janet Frame. ATNZ

I came then to the city of my brethren. The Shore of Life. Robert Fitzgerald. VGW

I came through autumn forest needing. The Versatile Historian. James Welch. SA

I came to a field. Pastoral. Charles Simic. NNaP

I came to a great door. The Beast. Theodore Roethke. SO

I came to see you in the spring. Remembering Apple Times. John T. Hitchner. AMV-80

I came too late to the hills: they were swept bare. The Wilderness. Kathleen Raine. BoWoP; WPE

I came upon a child of God. Woodstock. Joni Mitchell. GrRo; IPWM; NIL

I came upsouth by way of/ bleeding fingers georgia. Upsouth. Adesanya Alakoye. PoUp

I can change my-/ self more easily. Margaret Atwood. NeAC

I can clear a beach or swimming pool without. Stereo. Don L. Lee. AmNP (1974 ed.); POL

I can climb our apple tree. Secrets, IX. Jessie Orton Jones. CTV

I Can Forget. Michael Small. DNGG

I can get through a doorway without any key. The Wind. James Reeves. ECBV; FPB

I can hear my Saviour calling. Where He Leads Me I Will Follow. E. W. Blandy. BLSH

I can hear you making. Rain. Hone Tuwhare. ATNZ

I can imagine, in some otherworld. Humming-Bird. D. H. Lawrence. CMoP (1970 ed.); InPS: PPP

I can indeed afford a pause of peace. The Asbestos-suited Man in Hell. Gordon Challis. ATNZ

I can look through muddy water. Dry Land Blues. *Unknown.* BluL

I can love both fair and brown. The Indifferent. John Donne. AnMo; BiP; BoLoP; CABA (1972 ed.); PBMP

I can make a sandwich. Recipe. Bobbie Katz. CTV

I can mind the gullion. The Gullion. Duncan Glen. MIS

I can no longer live in Amsterdam, he writes. Return to Prinsengracht. Janice Blue-Swartz. AMV-81

I can only say I have waited for you. Time of Waiting in Amsterdam. Ingrid Jonker, *tr. by* Jack Cope *and* William Plomer. BoWoP

I can prove who I am. I draw my wallet like. Plexus and Nexus. Judson Jerome. AMV-81

I can remember. I can remember. The Boy Actor. Noel Coward. OxBTC

I can remember the fine image. Morning Fog. Quinton Duval. AMV-81

I can see outside the gold wings without birds. The Clear Air of October. Robert Bly. NoAM

I can see you. Not Now. Robert Creeley. Epi

I can shake the wild hay, and wet seed sticks to my hand. Stalks of Wild Hay. H. L. Davis. PoA

I can support it no longer. Flower Herding [Pictures] on Mount Monadnock. Galway Kinnell. ConAP; HeIP; NOBA

I can tell by the way the trees beat, after. The Man Watching. Rainer Maria Rilke, *tr. by* Robert Bly. NU

I Can Tell by the Way You Smell. *Unknown.* BluL

I can tell my dog. Pistol Slapper Blues. *Unknown.* BluL

I can tell you. How I Got Ovah. Carolyn M. Rodgers. CNA

I can tell you. Thin ditches. The Voice. George Chambers. HeS

I can wade grief. Emily Dickinson. NOBA

I canna thole thae fleechin folk. For Bonny Elspeth. Hamish Macbride. SLP

I cannot/ give you words. Deposition. Kevin Ireland. ATNZ

I cannot/ write a poem. The House Guest. Laura Chester. RiTi

I cannot acclaim you. From the Depths. Otakar Fischer, *tr. fr. Czech.* VWA

I cannot be a fish. Skin Song. Laurence Lieberman. CoPAm

I cannot believe that there's any need. Alison Wyrley Birch. PPM

I cannot believe them old, nor believe them dead. Lost Companions. Helen Bryant. AMV-80

I cannot bring a world quite round. Wallace Stevens. The Man with the Blue Guitar, II. CMoP (1970 ed.); SoS

I Cannot Eat but Little Meat. *Unknown. See* Back and Side Go Bare.

I cannot find my way; there is no star. Credo. E. A. Robinson. CMoP (1970 ed.); ILP (1975 ed.); LFH; PiAm; PPM; STS; TAP; VoPo

I cannot find my way to Nazareth. A Fragment. Yvor Winters. OBSV

I cannot forget how in Canton we drank tea. Poem for Liu Ya-tzu. Mao Tse-tung. TVo

I Cannot Forget with What Fervid Devotion. Bryant. EAP

I cannot get to my love if I should dee. The Waters of Tyne. *Unknown.* GBP

I cannot live. Ascent. Lynn Strongin. MIT

I cannot live with you. Emily Dickinson. MAT; NOBA; PiAm; PPoe; Psy; SBG

I cannot move. Malcolm. Welton Smith. BPo

I cannot reach it; and my striving eye. Childhood. Henry Vaughan. SCP-1

I cannot recall you gentle. Black Mother Woman. Audre Lorde. WBN

I cannot rival Helen's face. Compensation. Virgina Maughan Kammeyer. AMV-80

I cannot say it to you, Mother. To a 14 Year Old Girl in Labor and Delivery. John Stone. CoPAm

I cannot see how in time it will be possible to look at. The Altarpiece Finished. John Hollander. NoAM

I cannot see the short, white curls. The Dumb World. W. H. Davies. OBW; OxBTC

I cannot see what flowers are at my feet. Keats. *Fr.* Ode to a Nightingale. FSFS

I cannot sleep or take the air. A Snowy Day. *Unknown, tr. by* H. Idris Bell. OBW

I cannot spare water or wine. Mithridates. Emerson. NOBA

I cannot stand the man who wears. Ringless. Diane Wakoski. Prf

I cannot tell, not I, why she. Poem. Walter Savage Landor. GBL; OAEL-2

I cannot tell who loves the skeleton. La Bella Bona Roba. Richard Lovelace. CaPo; EBEV; LoAs; OAEL-1; OBP; SCP-2

I cannot tell why. The Rustling of Grass. Alfred Noyes. FSFS

I cannot tell you how it was. May. Christina Rossetti. GBL

I cannot think of you. Letter Reaching Out to My Sister, 1600 Miles. Sharon Barba. RiTi

I can't appease Ashimbabbar, the moon god An. Crimes of Lugalanne. Enheduanna, *tr. fr. Sumerian.* BoWoP

"I can't bite." The Frog's Lament. Aileen Fisher. FPB

I can't break with the Dark One. Mirabai, *tr. by Hindi by* Willis Barnstone *and* Usha Nilsson. BoWoP

I can't do it often. Your Woods. Margaret Holley. AMV-80

I can't fall asleep. Falling Asleep. Ian Seraillier. DuDa

I Can't Feel at Home in This World Anymore. *Unknown.* FSW

I Can't Figure You Out. Elliot Fried. AMV-81

I can't forget. Piazza di Spagna, Early Morning. Richard Wilbur. InPS; PSN; VGW

I Can't Give You Anything but Love, *with music.* Dorothy Fields. BLSo

I can't guarantee my name for posterity. As Yet. Vicente Rodríguez Nietzche, *tr. by* Julio Marzán. InW

I Can't Help but Wonder Where I'm Bound. Tom Paxton. FSW

I can't hold it, keep it. Lake. R. A. Simpson. FPA

I can't hold you and I can't leave you. Sister Juana Inés de la Cruz, *tr. fr. Spanish by* Judith Thurman. PBWP

I can't live in this world. Further Notice. Philip Whalen. VGW

I can't move I stand upwind and still. Half-Year Birthday. Neil Claremon. FoP

I can't read any more of this Rich Critical Prose. John Berryman. *Fr.* Dream Songs. CAPP

I can't remember. Smelling a Stone in the Middle of Winter. Tom Hennen. HeS

I can't stand it, said the old man. In the End. Peter Everwine, *after* Natan Sach. NNaP

I can't stand Willy wet-leg. Willy Wet-Leg. D. H. Lawrence. CMoP (1970 ed.)

I can't talk. Give Me Five. William J. Harris. CNA

I care not for these ladies. Thomas Campion. AAS; CABA (1972 ed.); HAP; NIL

I care not what the sailors say. Crazy Jane Reproved. W. B. Yeats. CMoP (1970 ed.)

I Carried Statues. Agnes Nemes Nagy, *tr. fr. Hungarian by* Bruce Berlind. BoWoP

I carried two things around in my mind. Three Things. May Sarton. AMV-80

I carry it on my keychain, which itself. The Ring. Diane Wakoski. PoA

I carry my keys like a weapon. To Nowhere. David Ignatow. NCSH

I carry my poems. March Wardrobe. Charles Potts. FoP

I carry three passengers on a nightly journey. The Trip. Emmett Jarrett. NeAC

I carry you in a glass jar. The Doll. Gregory Orr. AmPA

I Carry Your Heart with Me (I Carry It In. E. E. Cummings. PiAm; TAP

I carve my first head. Then I carve another. Hallowe'en 1971. Michael Dennis Browne. AmPA

I catch myself drifting. Harbor. Nancy Price. IHMS

I catch the movement of his lips. Marina Tsvetayeva, *tr. by* Paul Schmidt. *Fr.* The Daughter of Jairus. BoWoP

I caught a fish and I. What Happened. Dorothy Aldis. ECBV

I caught a tremendous fish. The Fish. Elizabeth Bishop. CoPAm; HAP; HeIP; HoPM (1975 ed.); InPK; NoAM; NOBA; NU; WeW

I caught the American bull. Buffalo. Henry Dumas. PoBA

I Caught This Morning at Dawning. Dennis Neagle. AMV-80

I caught this morning morning's minion. The Windhover. Gerard Manley Hopkins. AnMo; BiP; BoReV; CABA (1972 ed.); CMoP (1970 ed.); Epi; HAP; ILP (1975 ed.); InPK; InPS; NIL; NoAM; NOBE; OAEL-2; PAIC; PoPle; PPoD; PPoe; PPP; UnPo (1976 ed.); VLP; VoPo; WEW

I caught you, sir, having a look at her. Once in Love with Amy. Frank Loesser. BLSo

I celebrate myself and sing myself. Song of Myself. Walt Whitman. AnMo; AmVN; BiP; NOBA; PiAm; TAP; VoPo

I chanced upon a new book yesterday. To Edward Fitzgerald. Robert Browning. ExPo (1973 ed.)

I change, and so do women too. Written on a Looking-Glass. *Unknown.* FaBoEE

I choose not to walk among ghosts. Antigone VI. Herbert Martin. PoBA

I chopped down the house that you had been saving to live in next summer. Variations on a Theme by William Carlos Williams. Kenneth Koch. CAPP; FF; SpRo

I chose the bed downstairs by the sea-window for a good deathbed. The Bed by the Window. Robinson Jeffers. PiAm

I circled on leather paws. The Return. Theodore Roethke. PoA

I clasp in the hot pit and bed. Memorial Couplets for the Dying Ego. George Barker. EBEV

I cleaned the granary off your photo. Jim Harrison. *Fr.* Letters to Yesenin. NNaP

I climb the black rock mountain. Where Mountain Lion Lay Down with Deer. Leslie Marmon Silko. VoR

I climbed the stair in Antwerp church. Antwerp and Bruges. Dante Gabriel Rossetti. VLP

I climbed through woods in the hour-before-dawn dark. The Horses. Ted Hughes. NoAM; PH

I clip coupons from magazines. Yachting in Arkansas. Craig Weeden. AMV-80

I close my eyes and bow my head. Talking to God. Garry Cleveland Myers. CTV

I closed my ears with stinging bugs. Elegy for a Puritan Conscience. Alan Dugan. CAPP; CoPAm; NoAM

I comaunde alle the ratones that are here aboute. Rats Away! *Unknown.* OxBM

I come/ from a long line. My Elbow Ancestry. Larry Mollin. NeAC

I come/ to the White Painted Woman. Puberty Rite Dance Song (Traditional). *Tr. fr. Apache Indian by* Willis Barnstone. BoWoP

I come alone. To surprise you. Visit. James Welch. AmPA

I come among the peoples like a shadow. Hunger. Laurence Binyon. OxBTC

I Come and Stand at Every Door. Nazim Hikmet. FSW

I come back to cold lights. Revisiting the Field. Walter Pavlich. AMV-81

I come back to the cottage in. Only Years. Kenneth Rexroth. TAP

I come back to the geography of it. Maximus to Gloucester, Letter 27. Charles Olson. NOBA

I come every day. It's Me Again, God. Helen Steiner Rice. CTV

I come [*or* came] from Alabama with my banjo on my knee. Oh! Susanna. Stephen Collins Foster. BLSH; BLSo; FSW; OBAL; PSoN

I come from haunts of coot and hern. The Brook [*or* The Song of the Brook]. Tennyson. CTV; PoPle

I come from Salem County. Cowboy Song. Charles Causley. MiP

I come from the city of Boston. Boston. John Collins Bossidy. FaBoCo; FaBoEE; OBAL (*At. to* Samuel C. Bushnell)

I come home from you through the early light of spring. Adrienne Rich. *Fr.* Twenty-one Love Poems. BoWoP

I Come Home Wanting to Touch Everywhere. Stephen Dunn. AMV-81

I come into my dim bedroom. The Stunt Flier. John Updike. BBGO

I come out of a California orange grove. Smudging. Diane Wakoski. AmPA

I come sailing through the Indian Ocean. To a Foreign Friend. Leonard Natham. GP

I Come to Bury Caesar. Sydney Justin Harris. PoA

I come to tell you that my son is dead. The Prince. Edgar Bowers. ConAP

I come to the garden alone. In the Garden. C. Austin Miles. BLSH

I come to town the other night. Old Dan Tucker. Daniel Decatur Emmett. BLSo; PSoN

I come to you from a lonely place. And Why Are All the Voices I Hear Divided into Colors? Alta. MMD

I come to you with the vertigoes of the source. Yvonne Caroutch, *tr. fr. French by* David Cloutier. BoWoP

I confess I get moony. The Divide. Kenneth O. Hanson. MPA

I Consider the Tree. Martin Buber, *tr. fr. German by* Howard Schwartz. VWA

I could bring you jewels—had I a mind to. Emily Dickinson. TAP

I could have a job, but am too lazy to choose it. Lazy Man's Song. Po Chü-i, *tr. by* Arthur Waley. OBVE

I could have let him lash me. Frederick Douglass and the Slave Breaker. Dudley Randall. TC

I could have said makes love. Behind That Wall My Roommate Fucks His Girl. Geof Hewitt. NeAC; POL

I could have painted pictures like that youth's. Pictor Ignotus. Robert Browning. VLP

I could have tried to graduate. The Ballad of the Volunteer. Dabney Stuart. CSP

I could I might. Come to a Wedding. Grace Cavalieri. AATT

I could look at. Joy. Robert Creeley. PPP

I could lose an eyelid and see forever. Checking the Firing. R. T. Smith. AMV-80

I could love her with a love so warm. The World Is a Mighty Ogre. Fenton Johnson. AmNP (1974 ed.)

I could not dig: I dared not rob. A Dead Statesman. Kipling. *Fr.* Epitaphs of the War. FaBoEE

I could not hope/ to touch the sky. Sappho, *tr. fr. Greek by* Willis Barnstone. BoWoP

I could not look on Death, which being known. The Coward. Kipling. *Fr.* Epitaphs of the War. FaBoEE; FaBoTw (1975 ed.)

I could not sleep/ For the sea was so smooth. Walrus Hunting. Aua, *tr. fr. Eskimo.* WTO

I could replace. Earth Psalm. Denise Levertov. PPP

I could ride the Disneyland sky ride forever. He Spends Time in Southern California. Jonathan Cott. RRA

I could take the Harlem night. Juke Box Love Song. Langston Hughes. ILP (1975 ed.); OLR; PoBA

I could tell you. The Farmer's Wife. Mary Swanson Stroh. NPW

I could tell you. Impasse. Langston Hughes. TPo

I couldnt ever tell you. Paris. Al Young. CoPAm

I couldn't find my playground. Letter to My Father. Delia Chilgren. NPW

I Couldn't Hear Nobody Pray. *Unknown.* FSW

I couldn't touch a stop and turn a screw. Thirty Bob a Week. John Davidson. EBEV; FaBoTw (1975 ed.); InPS; NoAM; NOBE; OAEL-2; OBP; OxBTC; VLP

I could've spent my life banging young chicks. Expecting. Daniel J. Langton. AMV-81

I count black-lipped. Come Back Blues. Michael S. Harper. PoBA

I courted pretty Polly the live long night. Pretty Polly. *Unknown.* FSW

I crave an ampler, worthier sphere. Heine, *tr. fr. German by* Charles Stuart Calverley. OBVE

I crawl up the couch leg feeling. Whose Scene? Ruth Stone. BoWoP

I cross them in Macy's. Mask in Macy's. William Kistler. TVo

I cross'd a pynot, an't' pynot cross'd me. Against the Magpie. *Unknown.* GBP

I crouch among the arbor's swollen tongues. Spider in the Grapes. Thomas James. HeS

I crouch over my radio. Speech. Henry Taylor. CSP; MAT

I crushed the brown bug in a blood rage. The Brown Bug. Michael R. Brown. SFF

I cry to be broken open. Multiplicity. Eleanor Berry. AMV-80

I Cry Your Mercy. Keats. *See* To Fanny.

I curse my bearing, childhood, youth. J. M. Synge. FaBoEE

I cut in two/ A long November night. Hwang Chin-i, *tr. fr. Korean by* Peter H. Lee. PBWP

I, Cynisca, who descend from Spartan kings. Cynisca. *Unknown, tr. by* Tom Dodge. LiSp

I Dance and I Have a Fast Hook. Muhammed Ali. SPo

"I dance on all the mountains." This Poem Is for Deer. Gary Snyder. *Fr.* Myths and Texts: Hunting. CAPP; NOBA

I danced in the morning. Lord of the Dance. Sydney Carter. LP

I dare not ask a kiss. To Electra. Robert Herrick. CaPo; HoPM (1975 ed.)

I declare myself. Nu-Plastik Fanfare Red. Judith Rodriguez. FPA

I demand a thatched house. The Poet's Request. *Unknown, tr. by* John Montague. BIrV

I denounce those who are normal. J'Accuse. Peter Klappert. AMV-81

I descended in the evening to the fountain. Saul's Song of Love. Shaul Tchernichovsky, *tr. by* Robert Friend. VWA

I desire that my body be. When I Am Dead. George MacBeth. OxBTC

I did but prompt the age to quit their clogs. On the Detraction Which Followed upon My Writing Certain Treatises. Milton. ExPo (1973 ed.)

I did not know she'd take it so. Under the Mistletoe. Countee Cullen. PChr

I did not know the laws of the land. Trailing My Balloon. Stephen Stepanchev. SA

I did not know where you kept your heart. A "Case of Assault." Lydia Stephanou, *tr. by* Kimon Friar. BoWoP

I did not know you. Celan. Anthony Barnett. VWA

I did not live until this time. To My Excellent Lucasia, on Our Friendship. Katherine Philips. SBG; SCP-2; WPE

I did not look upon her eyes. Penumbra. Dante Gabriel Rossetti. VLP

I Did Not Lose My Heart. A. E. Housman. PPoD

I Did Not See a Mermaid? Siddie Joe Johnson. LCL

I did not see the frigate Constitution. Resurrection. R. P. Blackmur. PoA

I did not think that I should find them there. The Clerks. E. A. Robinson. CABA (1972 ed.); PiAm; VoPo

I did not want to be old Mr. Uncle Dog: The Poet at 9. Robert Sward. VGW

I did not want to go. Speaking: The Hero. Felix Pollak. CTBA

I did not want to grow, but quick-fingered memories. The Tower. Dan Pagis, *tr. by* Stephen Mitchell. VWA

I did nothing—/ Ended my hunger. Poem. Edward Weismiller. PoUp

I didnt choose these things. Hieroglyphs. Ettore Rella. SPT

I Didn't Find Light by Accident. Hayim Nachman Bialik, *tr. fr. Hebrew by* Ruth Nevo. VWA

I didn't get much sleep last night. Underwear. Lawrence Ferlinghetti. OBAL; TPo

I Didn't Know My Soul. Avraham Ben-Yitzhak, *tr. fr. Hebrew by* A. C. Jacobs. VWA

I didn't know you died. On the Death of W. H. Auden. Dave Morice. AcAn

I didn't make you know how glad I was. A Servant to Servants. Robert Frost. CMoP (1970 ed.); Epi

I didn't want this, not. Marina Tsvetayeva, *tr. by* Elaine Feinstein *and* Angela Livingstone. *Fr.* The Poem of the End. OBVE

I didn't want you cosy and neat and limited. To Anybody at All. Margaret Tait. SLP

I died for beauty—but was scarce. Emily Dickinson. AnMo; BoWoP; ILP (1975 ed.); NOBA; PBMP; SBG

I died with the first blow and was buried. Autobiography. Dan Pagis, *tr. by* Robert Friend. VWA

I do believe that die I must. His Creed. Robert Herrick. ILP (1975 ed.); PIM

I do confess, in many a sigh. Lying. Thomas Moore. PFIr

I do confess thou'rt smooth and fair. Inconstancy Reproved. Sir Robert Ayton. GBL

I do not believe in a God. Lost Word. Jean Burden. AMV-80

I do not come alone. The Defeated Victor. Horst Bienek, *tr. fr. German.* LP

I do not count the hours I spend. Waldeinsamkeit. Emerson. NOBA

I do not grieve when some unwholesome air. John Hagthorpe. *Fr.* An Elegy upon the Death of the Most Illustrious Prince Henry. SCP-2

I do not have faith in those. Free Fall. Don Gordon. AMV-81

I do not know/ if you were taught. The Book Rises Out of the Fire. Edmond Jabès, *tr. by* Rosemarie Waldrop. VWA

I do not know/ In what strange far off earth. Holocaust 1944. Anne Ranasinghe. VWA

I do not know much about gods; but I think that the river. The Dry Salvages. T. S. Eliot. *Fr.* Four Quartets. CABA (1972 ed.); PiAm

I do not know what haunts me. Loreley. Heine, *tr. by* Ernst Feise. NAWM-2

I do not like my state of mind. Symptom Recital. Dorothy Parker. SBG

I do not look for love that is a dream. Christina Rossetti. GBL

I do not love [*or* like] thee, Doctor Fell. Doctor Fell. Thomas Brown, *after* Martial. BBL; FaBoCo; FaBoEE; NIL; OBVE

I do not love to wed. The Poet Loves a Mistress, but Not to Marry. Robert Herrick. CaPo

I do not mind symbolism. Symbolism. Karen Swenson. TVo

I do not need a springtime. Morning Song. Henry Blakely. CNA

I do not remember the day you disappeared. Elegy for My Father. Robert Louthan. AMV-80

I do not see you. A Jewish Child Prays to Jesus. Ilse Blumenthal-Weiss, *tr. by* Erna Baber Rosenfeld. VWA

I do not sleep at night. Night-Piece. Raymond R. Patterson. PoBA

I do not Think Grandmother or Grandfather. Favorite Grandson Braid. Phillip William George. NW; VoR

I do not think of you lying in the wet clay. In Memory of My Mother. Patrick Kavanagh. CIP; NoAM

I do not think that skies and meadows are. Reciprocity. John Drinkwater. PoA

I do not think the ending can be right. But That Is Another Story. Donald Justice. CoPAm

I do not think we can save them. The Children. William Heyen. GP

I do not understand. In Memoriam II. Franco Fortini, *tr. by* Ruth Feldman. VWA

I do not want a plain box, I want a sarcophagus. Last Words. Sylvia Plath. RiTi

I do not want to be reflective any more. Wolves. Louis MacNeice. NoAM; OxBTC

I do not want to stand. My Own Hallelujahs. Zack Gilbert. PoBA

I do not want your praises later on. May 1506 (Christopher Columbus Speaking). Winfield Townley Scott. GOA

I do remember an apothecary. Drug Store. Karl Shapiro. NowV

I do seem to zee Grammer as she did use. Grammer's Shoes. William Barnes. VPC

I do tricks in order to know. With My Crowbar Key. William Stafford. ConAP

I do veel vor ye, Thomas, vor I be afear'd. Dobbin Dead. William Barnes. VLP

I do what I have to. Leah. Shirley Kaufman. VWA

I done lose all-a my money. Frying Pan Skillet Blues. *Unknown.* BluL

I don't ask you to tell me the great truths. Words to My Mother. Alfonsina Storni, *tr. by* Marion Hodapp *and* Mary Crow. AMV-80

I don't believe in ristercrats. My Sort o' Man. Paul Laurence Dunbar. AmNP (1974 ed.)

I don't believe the sleepers in this house. A Cabin in the Clearing. Robert Frost. PiAm

I don't bother with rhymes. Alberto Caeiro, *tr. fr. Portuguese by* Jonathan Griffin. TSWA

I Don't Care, *with music.* Jean Lenox. FSN

I don't care at all who died today. This Business of Dying. John Skoyles. AAN

I don't dare start thinking in the morning.  Blues at Dawn. Langston Hughes.  ILP (1975 ed.)

I don't dream anymore about arthritic spiders.  Succubi.  John Newlove.  NeAC

I Don't Eat Animals (And They Don't Eat Me).  Melanie Safka. PoRo

I don't feel well I've never done this.  Excuses.  Terence Winch. PoUp

I don't give a $\sqrt{D^2}$.  A Radical Creed.  Gelett Burgess. FaBoNo

I don't have any medals. I feel their lack.  Jim Harrison.  *Fr.* Letter to Yesenin.  TC

I Don't Have No Bunny Tail on My Behind.  Alta.  GP

"I Don't Hear Any Melody Breathing I Hear."  John Gill. NeAC

I Don't Know.  *Unknown.*  BluL

I don't know.  A Poem against Rats.  Fred Levinson.  AmPA

I don't know/ who you are.  Night Regression Poem.  Robert Peters.  BrS

I don't know about anything sometimes.  Between Me and Anyone Who Can Understand.  Sharon Scott.  JB

I don't know about you, whiteman all dressed in black.  For Dan Berrigan.  Etheridge Knight.  NeAC

I don't know any greatest treat.  The Parterre.  E. Harriet Palmer.  FaBoCo; NOBL

I don't know how he came.  Osawatomie.  Carl Sandburg. CMoP (1970 ed.)

I don't know if he is rare on these northern lakes.  The Pelican. Greg Kuzma.  AmPA

I Don't Know if Mount Zion.  Abba Kovner, *tr. fr. Hebrew by* Shirley Kaufman.  VWA

I don't know my real name I don't know when I was born.  I Been Treated Wrong.  *Unknown.*  BluL

I don't know somehow it seems sufficient.  Gravelly Run.  A. R. Ammons.  PoA; Prf

I don't know the language.  Homesick [*or* Homesickness].  Else Lasker-Schüler, *tr. fr. German.*  PBWP; VWA

I don't know what I'm looking at.  Focus.  Kathleen Norris. GP

I don't know what it is.  It's Raining in Love.  Richard Brautigan.  PPM

I don't know what to think of the years in New York. Homosexual Sonnets.  Kenneth Pitchford.  GP

I don't know whether the gray deer knows.  The Deer.  Asya, *tr. by* Gabriel Preil *and* Howard Schwartz.  VWA

I don't know why but.  Poem: On Moral Leadership as a Political Dilemma.  June Jordan.  WasP

I Don't Let the Girls Worry My Mind.  *Unknown.*  AmFP

I Don't Like Beetles.  Rose Fyleman.  OxBChV

"I don't like the look of little Fan, mother."  Little Fan.  James Reeves.  SO

I don't mind the human race.  Discrimination.  Kenneth Rexroth.  MPA

I don't pretend to drink.  A Welcome for Etheridge.  James Cunningham.  JB

I don't remember your face.  In the Summer of Warren Whitney. David Long.  EC

I don't respect myself.  Jill.  R. D. Laing.  WeW

I don't sleep. All night.  Mirabai, *tr. fr. Hindi by* Willis Barnstone *and* Usha Nilsson.  BoWoP

I don't think it important.  The Beast Section.  Welton Smith. PoBA

I don't use chemical sprays.  Note to a New Lesbian.  Martha Shelley.  WBN

I don't wanna march in the infantry.  I Just Wanna Stay Home. Irwin Silber.  FSW

I don't want a dog that is wee and effeminate.  Dog Wanted. Margaret Mackprang Mackay.  GDP

I don't want no woman if her hair ain't no longer'n mine.  Short Haired Woman.  *Unknown.*  BluL

I don't want none of your weevily wheat.  Weevily Wheat. *Unknown.*  FSW

I don't want to be a nun.  *Unknown, tr. fr. Spanish by* Willis Barnstone.  BoWoP

I don't want to be sheltered here.  For the Yiddish Singers in the Lakewood Hotels of My Childhood.  Harvey Shapiro.  VWA

I don't want to boast.  Vindication.  Daniil Kharms, *tr. by* George Gibian.  FaBoNo

I Don't Want to Get Adjusted.  *Unknown.*  FSW

I don't want to leave.  Lunch and After.  Robert Creeley.  FoP

I Don't Want to Play in Your Yard, *with music.*  Philip Wingate. FSN

I don't want your greenback dollar.  The Greenback Dollar. *Unknown.*  AmFP

I Don't Want Your Millions Mister.  Jim Garland.  FSW

I doubt life is fulfilled, or love let go.  Dichterliebe.  Robert Klein Engler.  AMV-81

I doubt not God is good, well-meaning, kind.  Yet Do I Marvel. Countee Cullen.  AmNP (1974 ed.); BPo; FF; ILP (1975 ed.); IPWM; LFH; NoAM; PBMP; PoBA; SoS; SS; TAP

I drag a boat over the ocean.  Lal Ded, *tr. fr. Kashmiri by* Willis Barnstone.  BoWoP

I drank,/ my arteries filled with fat.  Organ Transplant.  J. D. Reed.  POL

I drank cool water from the fountain.  The Raisin.  James Wright.  TAP

I drank up two glasses of hot tea and milk.  Tuesday.  Zishe Landau, *tr. by* Ruth Whitman.  VWA

I draw a deep breath.  Remembering.  Akjartoq, *tr. fr. Eskimo.* WTO

I dreaded that first robin, so.  Emily Dickinson.  AnMo; HAP

I Dream a World.  Langston Hughes.  AmNP (1974 ed.)

I dream continually of a musical ape.  The Musical Ape.  Darrell Gray.  AcAn

I Dream I'm the Death of Orpheus.  Adrienne Rich.  NIL; NMM; NoAM; TT

I dream millions of buffalo.  The Buffalo, Our Sacred Beast. Tom McKeown.  NVAP

I dream my love goes riding out.  Song for a Dancer.  Kenneth Rexroth.  TAP

I dream my mother.  Generation Gap.  Bronwen Wallace. AMV-80

I dream of Jeanie with the light brown hair.  Jeanie, with the Light Brown Hair.  Stephen Collins Foster.  BLSH; BLSo; FSW

I dream of journeys repeatedly.  The Far Field.  Theodore Roethke.  ILP (1975 ed.)

I dream of making love.  Walter Mitty.  Leonard Bird.  FoP

I dream of the birth of the child.  Creation of the Child.  Susan Litwack.  VWA

I dream of whales. I feel upon my skin.  The Suicides.  George MacBeth.  NoAM

I dreamed [*or* dreamt] a dream the other night.  Lowlands. *Unknown.*  AIW; FSW

I dreamed a dream the other night, when everything was still. Prospecting Dream.  *Unknown.*  AmFP

I dreamed all my fortitude screamed.  Letter across Doubt and Distance.  M. Carl Holman.  AmNP (1974 ed.)

I dreamed I held/ a sword against my flesh.  Lady Kasa, *tr. fr. Japanese by* Kenneth Rexroth.  BoWoP

I dreamed I passed a doorway.  Ballad.  John Hall Wheelock. AIW

I dreamed I saw Joe Hill last night.  Joe Hill.  Alfred Hayes. UnPo (1976 ed.)

I dreamed I saw the crescent moon.  *Unknown.*  POL

I dreamed kind Jesus fouled the big-gun gears. Soldier's Dream. Wilfred Owen. ILwL

I dreamed last night I dreamed, and in that sleep. Le Rêve. Edgar Bowers. ConAP

I dreamed of a shark following us two. Sharks. Dick Lourie. NeAC

I dreamed of my true love last night. Locks and Bolts. *Unknown.* FSW

I dreamed of Ted Williams. Dream of a Baseball Star. Gregory Corso. NoAM; VGW

I dreamed of war-heroes, of wounded war-horoes. The Heroes. Louis Simpson. SoS

I dreamed that/ the gentiles crucified Mozart. Mozart. Jacob Glaststein, *tr. by* Ruth Whitman. VWA

I dreamed [*or* dream'd] that, as I wandered by the way. The Question. Shelley. FSFS; PoPle

I dreamed that I married. Skagway. John Haines. CNW

I dream'd that I walk'd in Italy. Check to Song. Owen Meredith. FaBoCo

I dreamed that one had died in a strange place. A Dream of Death. W. B. Yeats. GBL

I Dreamed That Washington Lay Wreathed in Smoke. Selden Rodman. WasP

I dreamed there was an Emperor Antony. Cleopatra's Lament. Shakespeare. *Fr.* Antony and Cleopatra, V, ii. UnPo (1976 ed.)

I dreamed there would be spring no more. In Memoriam A. H. H., LXIX. Tennyson. NOBE

I dreamed this mortal part of mine. The Vine. Robert Herrick. CaPo

I dream'd we both were in a bed. The Vision to Electra. Robert Herrick. LoAs

I dreamed you were my child, and I had come. The Dream. Paul Petrie. TAP

I dreamt a dream the other night. *See* I dreamed a dream the other night.

I dreamt a dream! what can it mean? The Angel. Blake. *Fr.* Songs of Experience. LAuP; MBPR

I dreamt her sensual proportions. The Death of Venus. Robert Creeley. NOBA; PiAm

I dreamt I dwelt in marble halls. The Palace of Humbug. "Lewis Carroll." FaBoNo

I dreamt last night. For No Clear Reason. Robert Creeley. VGW

I dreamt last night of you, John-John. John-John. Thomas MacDonagh. PFIr; PoTa

I dreamt of the old house. To My Sister. Olga Berggolts, *tr. by* Daniel Weissbort. BoWoP

I dreamt that I was God Himself. Ezra Pound, *after the German of Heine.* FaBoEE

I drew a line/ through yesterday. After a Birthday. Michael Dransfield. FPA

I drink to forget, but whenever I think. Alan Bold. POL

I drink, wherever I go, to the charms. Gracey Nugent. Austin Clarke, *tr. fr. Irish.* CIP

I drive my car to supermarket. Superman. John Updike. BBGO; LiSp; LP

I drive Westward. Tumble and loco weed. To What Strangers, What Welcome. J. V. Cunningham. NoAM

I drove to Little Hunger promontory. Little Hunger. Richard Murphy. BIrV

I drove up to the graveyard, which. The Soul Longs to Return Whence It Came. Richard Eberhart. CMoP (1970 ed.)

I du believe in Freedom's cause. The Pious Editor's Creed. James Russell Lowell. *Fr.* The Biglow Papers. PiAm

I dug a grave under an oak-tree. Amy Lowell. *Fr.* Dreams in War Time. BoWoP

I dug and dug amongst the snow. Christina Rossetti. FaBoEE

I dwell apart. The Hermit. Hsü Pên, *tr. by* Henry H. Hart. RFM

I dwell in Possibility. Emily Dickinson. NoAM; NOBA

I dwell on the misty steppe. The "Word" of an Antelope Caught in a Trap. Sandag, *tr. by* C. R. Bawden. WTO

I eat my cereal with a sliced peach. Getting a Poem in the Rain. Dick Lourie. NeAC

I eat what others throw away. Fight Fire with Fire. Steve Toth. AcAn

I embrace these shoulders and I look. Étude. Joseph Brodsky, *tr. by* Dimitry Pospielovsky *and* Keith Bosley. VWA

I employ the blind mandolin player. A Music. Wendell Berry. VGW

I empty myself of the names of others. I empty my pockets. The Remains. Mark Strand. PPP

I encountered the crowd returning from amusements. Resolution of Dependence. George Barker. FaBoTw (1975 ed.)

I enter, jingling hindu temple bells, deodorant ears. Allen Ginsberg Blesses a Bride and Groom: A Wedding Night Poem. Robert Peters. GP

I entered it before I understood it. Spring at Nant Dywelan. Bobi Jones, *tr. by* Joseph P. Clancy. OBW

I entreat you, Alfred Tennyson. To Alfred Tennyson. Walter Savage Landor. POL

I envy e'en the fly its gleams of joy. Written in Prison. John Clare. Epi; OAEL–2

I envy men who can yearn. Penis Envy. Erica Jong. PoIA

I envy seas, whereon he rides. Emily Dickinson. OLR

I, even I, am he who knoweth the roads. De Aegypto. Ezra Pound. VGW

I examine my wound. The December Sky. A. G. Sobin. HeS

I exchange eyes with the Mad Queen. Vision. Harry Crosby. EAS

I exist that I may say. Document. Tuvia Ruebner, *tr. by* Harold Schimmel. VWA

I expect you're planted somewhere. Living in Another Man's House. Tom O'Grady. AAN

I Explain the Silvered Passing of a Ship at Night. Stephen Crane. War Is Kind, VI. TT

I fasted three canonical hours. The Maiden's Plight. Brian Merriman, *tr. by* Frank O'Connor. *Fr.* The Midnight Court. BIrV

I fear it's very wrong of me. Friends. Elizabeth Jennings. LP

I fear no earthly powers. On Himself. Robert Herrick. CaPo

I fear that appearances are worshipped throughout France. The Rat and the Elephant. La Fontaine, *tr. by* Marianne Moore. OBVE

I fear you letters. The Aleph Bet. Fay Lipshitz. VWA

I feared the darkness as a boy. The Dark. Roy Fuller. DuDa

I feared the fury of my wind. Blake. MBPR

I fed some cheese. Write Me a Verse. David McCord. MN

I feed a flame within, which so torments me. Dryden. *Fr.* The Maiden Queen. PoPle

I feel an apparition. Wallace Stevens, *after the French of* Jean Le Roy. OBVE

I feel I am, I only know I am. John Clare. John Clare. OAEL–2

I feel I know what you have worked through, you. For John Berryman. Robert Lowell. NOBA

I feel it again and again, no matter. Glorious World. Hermann Hesse, *tr. by* James Wright. IPWM

I feel my face being bitten by the tides. The Knowledge That Comes through Experience. Jane Cooper. NMM

I feel my heart melting. Dusk. Gabriela Mistral, *tr. by* David Garrison. BoWoP

I feel my stomach. Not-Knowing. Dawn Hinshaw. AMV–81

I feel remorse for all that time has done. Love's Remorse. Edwin Muir. OxBTC

I feel so awful blue. Teasing; or, I Was Only, Only Teasing You. Cecil Mack. FSN

I feel so lonesome you can hear me when I moan. Terraplane Blues. *Unknown.* BluL

I feel your steps in the hall. Karin Boye, *tr. by* Nadia Christensen. *Fr.* A Dedication. PBWP

I fell in the battle of Ashdod. Since Then. Yehuda Amichai, *tr. by* Shlomo Vinner *and* Howard Schwartz. VWA

I felt a cleaving in my mind. Emily Dickinson. NOBA

I felt a funeral, in my brain. Emily Dickinson. BoWoP; CABA (1972 ed.); CMoP (1970 ed.); NOBA; PBWP; PiAm; Psy; TAP

I felt no pain when they cut it off. Child with Six Fingers. Carol Muske. AmPA

I felt that glance. "The Strength of That Food." Jane Marie Luecke. AATT

I felt the lurch and halt of her heart. Lightning. D. H. Lawrence. CMoP (1970 ed.); ILP (1975 ed.)

I felt the sweet child's pulse. A Child's Pulse. Henry Shore. PMW

I fight all day/ with the other occupant. Purity in What You Do. Harrison Fisher. PoUp

I figure her. Takes All Kinds. R. P. Dickey. POL

I figured/ anything anybody. Mrs. Sadie Grindstaff, Weaver and Factotum. Jonathan Williams. OBAL

I figured you as nude between. The Apostrophe to Vincentine. Wallace Stevens. LoAs

I finally found a way of using the tree. The Beckett Kit. Linda Gregg. AmPA

I finally ran into me one night. And Then What? Dave Kelly. POL

I find it, weakly ticking, at the edge of the yard. The Alarm Clock. Paul Hoover. FiCh

I find my love fishing. Ezra Pound *and* Noel Stock, *fr. Egyptian hieroglyphics.* BoWoP; PBWP

I find [*or* fynde] no peace, and all my war is done. Description of the Contrarious Passions in a Lover. Petrarch, *tr. by* Sir Thomas Wyatt. Sonnets to Laura: To Laura in Life, CIV. AAS; FF; ILP (1975 ed.); OAEL-1; OBVE; PAIC; PPoe

I find you tousled in a bed. Physician, Heal Thyself. S. L. Henderson Smith. PMW

I finish the *Times.* Shut eyes. My head. Commuter's Entry in a Connecticut Diary. Robert Penn Warren. AMV-81

I first adventure, with foolhardy might. Prologue. Joseph Hall. *Fr.* Virgidemiarum, Bk. I. TVS

I first tasted under Apollo's lips. Evadne. Hilda Doolittle ("H. D."). BoWoP; LoAs; RiTi

I fled Him, down the nights and down the days. The Hound of Heaven. Francis Thompson. ILP (1975 ed.); ILwL; VLP

I flee the city, temples, and each place. Sonnet XVII. Louise Labé, *tr. by* Willis Barnstone. BoWoP

I float by woods and rocks. Floating the Ghost River. Tom McKeown. TC

I follow October, that yogi. Follower. Michael Arvey. AMV-80

I follow the scent of a woman. Dancing the Shout to the True Gospel; or, The Song Movement Sisters Don't Want Me to Sing. Rita Mae Brown. NMM; WBN

I followed her to the station, with her suitcase in my hand. Love in Vain. Robert Johnson. UnPo (1976 ed.)

I followed, o splendid season. A Poem to Show the Trouble That Befell Him When He Was at Sea. Thomas Prys, *tr. by* Gwyn Williams. OBW

I followed the narrow cliffside trail half way up the mountain. The Deer Lay Down Their Bones. Robinson Jeffers. PiAm

I forgotten who. Bumi. Amiri Baraka. PoBA

I found a/ hummingbird. The Container. Cid Corman. VGW

I found a ball of grass among the hay. Mouse's Nest. John Clare. InPK; MN; SoSe; VLP

I found a dimpled spider, fat and white. Design. Robert Frost. AnMo; CABA (1972 ed.); CMoP (1970 ed.): ExPo (1973 ed.); HeIP; ILP (1975 ed.); InPK; InPS; NIL; NoAM; NOBA; PBMP; PiAm; PoIA; PPP; SoSe; STS; TAP; TT; UsP; WIF

I Found a Silver Dollar. Dennis Lee. OSF

I Found Her Out There. Thomas Hardy. CMoP (1970 ed.); ILP (1975 ed.); LoAs; NoAM; NOBE; OAEL-2

I found him in the guard-room at the Base. Lamentations. Siegfried Sassoon. OBSV

I found his wool face, I went away. Reading Walt Whitman. Calvin Forbes. PoBA

I found in Munster, unfettered of any. *Unknown, tr. by* James Clarence Mangan. *Fr.* Prince Alfrid's Itinerary. BIrV

I found it in the bottom drawer. The Manual. Larry Rubin. GP

I found my son fallen. Windfall. Joel Arsenault. AMV-81

I found myself one day. The Hatch. Norma Farber. SO

I found that consciousness itself betrays. Convalescence. J. V. Cunningham. PiAm

I found that ivory image there. Crazy Jane Grown Old Looks at the Dancers. W. B. Yeats. CMoP (1970 ed.); EBEV

I found the black bones one day in a trunk. Playing the Bones. Elizabeth Brewster. AMV-81

I found the phrase to every thought. Emily Dickinson. AmVN

I found them there today. Mementos, 2. W. D. Snodgrass. CoPAm; UsP

I found you on a rainy morning. Nansen. Gary Snyder. InPS

I fynde no peace and all my warr is done. *See* I find no peace...

I galloped on a scarlet filly. Absalom. Zerubavel Gilead, *tr. by* Dorothea Krook. VWA

I gather clay and work it with my fingers. Shaman. Esther M. Leiper. AMV-81

I gave my heart to a tin pan bitch. Judas. Andrew Baster. BuTh

I gave my life to learning how to live. Postscript. Sandra Hochman. NMM

I Gave My Love a Cherry (The Riddle), *with music. Unknown.* BLSH
(Riddle Song, The.) BLSo; FSW

I gave myself to him. Emily Dickinson. SoSe (1977 ed.)

I gave to Hope a watch of mine: but he. Hope. George Herbert. WeW

I Gave You My Love. *Unknown, tr. fr. Gaelic by* Derick Thomson. SLP

I gaze across the distant hills. William Williams, *tr. fr. Welsh by* H. Idris Bell. OBW

I gaze out a hundred windows. Lied in Crete. Alvaro Mutis. AMV-80

I gaze where August's sunbeam falls. Newark Abbey. Thomas Love Peacock. NOBE

I Gazed upon the Cloudless Moon. Emily Brontë. Moon

I gently touched her hand: she gave. *Unknown.* BoLoP

I get a cinder in my eye. Walking. Frank O'Hara. TAT

I get into my blue wolf-car. Morning. Marjorie Saiser. AMV-80

I get up. I am sick of/ Rouging my cheeks. Morning. Chu Shu-chen, *tr. by* Kenneth Rexroth. BoWoP

I give praise to thee God for thy kingfisher creeks. One Fragment for God. William Everson. MIT

I give rest to clear words. A Dawn of Jaffa Pigeons. Eli Bachar, *tr. by* Jeremy Garber. VWA

I give you now Professor Twist. The Purist. Ogden Nash. TPo

I gnarled me where the spinster tree. Waterwall Blues. Howard Moss. UsP

I go/ towards the trumpets of light. Tammuz. Nathan Alterman, *tr. by* Robert Friend. VWA

I go a long way back to find that bent tree. Bent Tree. Peter Serchuk. AMV-80

I go back again. Hawk and Snake. Leslie Silko. VoR

I go digging for clams once every two or three years. Clamming. Reed Whittemore. IPWM; TAP

I go inland each afternoon. The Harvester. Terry Lawrence. AMV-80

I go North to cold, to home, to Kinnaird. Kinnaird Head. George Bruce. MS

I go one step forward. Student. Cheng Min, *tr. by* Kenneth Rexroth *and* Ling Ching. PBWP

I go out like a ghost. Home Town. W. D. Snodgrass. NowV

I go out to totem street. Knock on Wood. Henry Dumas. CNA; PoBA

I go through hollyhocks. Las Trampas U.S.A. Charles Tomlinson. TwMBP

I go to concert, party, ball. My Rival. Kipling. OxBTC

I go to say goodbye to the Cailleach. The Wild Dog Rose. John Montague. BIrV; CIP

I go to see my parents. Generations. Evan Jones. MAuV

I go to the Turkish shop, buy a bun. The Turkish Bakery. *Unknown, tr. by* Peter H. Lee. PBWP

I got a gal/ She's got a baker's shop. High Price Blues. *Unknown.* BluL

I got a gal and she loves me. Cripple Creek. *Unknown.* FSW

I Got a Home in Dat Rock. *Unknown.* BPo

I got a letter from my home. Sporting Life Blues. *Unknown.* FSW

I got a shoe [ *or* got-a shoes], you got a shoe [*or* got-a shoes]. All God's Children Got Shoes. *Unknown.* BLSH; FSW

"I got a sunburn on my ass today," you said. Good Friends and First Impressions. Barbara Drake. TC

I got a woman in West Helena, Arkansas. West Helena Blues. *Unknown.* BluL

I got an old tom cat. Tom Cat Blues. *Unknown.* FSW

I got cold feet in Columbus. Cold Feet in Columbus. William Heath. TAT

I got her in the Black Bull. Elegy XIII. Sydney Goodsir Smith. *Fr.* Under the Eildon Tree. MS

I got me flowers to straw thy way. Easter. George Herbert. NOBE

I got one good look. Coon Song. A. R. Ammons. NoAM; NOBA

I got out of bed twice, took down boxes and. Last Night There Was a Cricket in Our Closet. Leroy V. Quintana. GP

I got so I could hear [*or* take] his name. Emily Dickinson. CMoP (1970 ed.); TT

I Got So Old. *Unknown.* BluL

I got stones in my passway. Stones in My Passway. *Unknown.* BluL

I got the blues for my baby. My Crime. *Unknown.* BluL

I got those sad old weary blues. Too Blue. Langston Hughes. SFF

I got to Kansas City on a Frid'y. Kansas City. Oscar Hammerstein II. OBAL

I got up this morning. I Got So Old. *Unknown.* BluL

I got-a shoes, you got-a shoes. *See* I got a shoe, you got a shoe.

I gotta/ buy me a new. Après le Bain. William Carlos Williams. OBAL

I grant indeed that fields and flocks have charms. Rural Life. George Crabbe. *Fr.* The Village. NOBE

I grant you, then, the variants. Joseph Freeman. Six Poems, 6. SPT

I grew/ for you. The Strong Bond. Juana de Ibarbourou, *tr. by* Linda Scheer. PBWP

I grew out of a vicious, viscous swamp. A Reed. Osip Mandelstam, *tr. by* James Greene. VWA

I grew up/ in these blond. How to Write a Poem about the Desert. Jefferson Carter. FoP

I grew up on Humphrey Bogart movies; it was like church. Bogart. Nicholas Flocos. SA

I grieve and dare not show my discontent. On Monsieur's Departure. Elizabeth I, Queen of England. WPE

I grieve for my second daughter. Written on Seeing the Flowers, and Remembering My Daughter. Kao Ch'i. DL

I grieved for Buonaparté, with a vain. Wordsworth. MBPR

I grind the hoofs of broken animals. In the Glue Factory. Allan Block. FAF

I grow. Survivor. Judy Dothard Simmons. CNA

I grow accustomed to a new disguise. Journal. John Ciardi. PoA

I grow together everywhere. Mandelstam. Richard Burns. VWA

I guess because it was Key West. Meeting the Reincarnation Analyst. Gary Gildner. AmPA

I had/ a dream of women, dark. A Dream of Women. Carolyn Maisel. IHMS

I had a brother in the infantry. Put My Name Down. Irwin Silber. FSW

I had a chair at every hearth. The Lamentation of the Old Pensioner [*or* The Old Pensioner]. W. B. Yeats. InPK; NoAM; VLP; WeW

I had [*or* Well, I had] a dog and his name was Blue. Old Blue. *Unknown.* FSW; GDP

I had a dog like a love. Penny Trumpet. Raphael Rudnick. MAT

I had a donkey. Faith. Marjorie Dunkels. PH

I had a donkey, that was all right. The Donkey. Theodore Roethke. ECBV

I had a dove, and the sweet dove died. Dove. Keats. PCOP

I had a dream of purity. Salome. George Garrett. CoPAm; PPoD

I had a dream, which was not all a dream. Darkness. Byron. ILP (1975 ed.); OAEL-2

I Had a Future. Patrick Kavanagh. BIrV; NoAM

I had a good teacher. Education. Don L. Lee. AmNP (1974 ed.)

I had a horse. Full Sky. Jules Supervielle, *tr. by* Wallace Fowlie. TPo

I had a horse, his name was Bill. A Horse Named Bill. *Unknown.* FSW

I had a little dog. Dogs. Frances Cornford. DuDr

I had a little nut tree. Mother Goose. BBL; ECBV; GBP, 2 *sts.*; PCOP

I had a little pony. Mother Goose. MG; PCOP; PH

I had a little sorrow. The Penitent. Edna St. Vincent Millay. PPM

I had a live joy once and pampered her. Joy's Treachery. Wilfrid Scawen Blunt. The Love Sonnets of Proteus, XVII. VLP

I Had a Rooster. *Unknown.* FSW

I had a silver penny. Nursery Rhyme of Innocence and Experience. Charles Causley. LP

I had a sister once, an island sister. A Drifting. Robert Hutchinson. LoAs

I had a vision when the night was late. The Vision of Sin. Tennyson. OAEL-2; VLP

I Had a Wife. *Unknown.* FSW

I had about as much chance, Mother. The Fish. L. L. Zeiger. TV

I had always been told. The Crippler. Danny Siegel. VWA

I had an uncle once who kept a rock in his pocket. I've Got a Home in That Rock. Raymond R. Patterson. FF; PoBA

I had been hungry, all the years. Emily Dickinson. SBG

I had been sitting for days. Long Distance. Dana Naone. CDW; PHC

I had been waiting. First Menstruation. Ellen Bass. TV

I had been watching the child appear. Bedtime. Hillel Schwartz. AMV–81

I had come to the house, in a cave of trees. Medusa. Louise Bogan. BoWoP; HoPM (1975 ed.); RiTi; WPE

I had eight birds hatcht in one nest. In Reference to Her Children, 23 June, 1656. Anne Bradstreet. BoWoP; EAP; SBG; TAP

I had finished my dinner. An Easy Decision. Kenneth Patchen. CTBA; OSP; SFF; TPo; UsP

I had for my winter evening walk. Good Hours. Robert Frost. PPM

I had four brothers over the sea. The Tokens of Love. *Unknown.* GBP

I had heard/ before, of an. Mr. Brodsky. Charles Tomlinson. NoAM; TwMBP

I had just found the bottle opener. Immediate Kindness. Allan Kornblum. AcAn

I had my coronary in Corona. Freeway Problems. Lawrence P. Spingarn. PoW

I had never been to the top of anything. At the Top. Michael Small. DNGG

I had never heard of the whiteness. The Poem. David Schloss. PoA

I Had No Human Speech. Roland Robinson. GAS

I had no mother. Eve's Song in the Garden. Lynn Gottlieb. VWA

I had no thought of violets of late. Sonnet. Alice Dunbar Nelson. PoBA

I had no voice. Lilith's Child. Edward Francisco. DL

I had not minded—walls. Emily Dickinson. CABA (1972 ed.)

I had nothing to do with it. I was not here. A Centenary Ode: Inscribed to Little Crow, Leader of the Sioux Rebellion. James Wright. CoPAm

I had over-prepared the event. Villanelle: The Psychological Hour. Ezra Pound. ExPo (1973 ed.)

I had so little. The Toy. Cid Corman. GP

I had the blues/ Last night. Never Let Your Left Hand Know. *Unknown.* BluL

"I had this dream." My Dream. Lew Blockcolski. VoR

I had thought of the bear in his lair as fiercely free. Part of the Darkness. Isabella Gardner. ANTL; BoAnP

I had three friends. Three Friends. *Tr. fr. Yoruba by* Ulli Beier. BoWoP

I Had to Be Secret. Mark Van Doren. SO

I had to do all that: because. Gaslight. Michael Burkard. AAN

I had to kick their law into their teeth in order to save them. Negro Hero. Gwendolyn Brooks. CAPP

I had twenty-four/ hours/ to erase. Twenty-four Hours. Myra Sklarew. PoUp

I had walked since dawn and lay down to rest on a bare hillside. Vulture. Robinson Jeffers. BoAnP; NOBA; PiAm

I had watched these trees get gradually bigger. The Ravine. James Applewhite. AMV–80

I had written him a letter which I had, for want of better. Clancy of the Overflow. Andrew Barton Paterson. MAuV

I had written to Aunt Maud. Waste. Harry Graham. FaBoCo

I Hae a Wife o' My Ain. Burns. LAuP

I hand you:/ stars, nearer than ever. A Gift for Mary MacLane. T. Alan Broughton. FAF

I hang by my heels from the sky. Hera, Hung from the Sky. Carolyn Kizer. NMM; WPE

I happen to be a veteran. The Significance of a Veteran's Day. Simon J. Oritz. GP

I hardly dare to fear. Shelley. *Fr.* The Cenci, V, iv. LFH

I hardly know you, and already I say to myself. Étude. Carlos Pellicer, *tr. by* H. R. Hays. LoAs

I hardly suppose I know anybody who wouldn't rather be a success than a failure. Kindly Unhitch That Star, Buddy. Ogden Nash. ILP (1975 ed.); PPM

I hate and love./ And if you ask me why. Catullus, *tr. fr. Latin by* Horace Gregory. NAWM–1

I hate and love. Why? You may ask but. Catullus, *tr. fr. Latin by* Ezra Pound. OBVE

I hate and love, wouldst thou the reason know? Catullus, *tr. fr. Latin by* Richard Lovelace. OBVE

I hate hawks. Hawk and Rock. Ton Quagliano. PHC

"I hate my verses, every line, every word." Love the Wild Swans. Robinson Jeffers. HeIP; InPS; PiAm

I Hate That Drum's Discordant Sound. John Scott of Amwell. NIL

(Drum, The.) NOBE

I hate the dreadful hollow behind the little wood. Maud: A Monodrama. Tennyson. VLP

I hate the man who builds his name. The Poet and the Rose. John Gay. *Fr.* Fables. PAIC

I hate these phrases: Of power absolute. Joshua Sylvester, *after the French of* Guy du Faur de Pibrac. FaBoEE

"I hate to lose something." Maya Angelou. *Fr.* No Loser, No Weeper. OSP

I [*or* Ah] hate to see de ev'nin' sun go down. Saint Louis Blues. W. C. Handy. BLSo; FF

I hated the way my sisters looked. My Sisters the Summer of 53. Janet Campbell Hale. NW

I hated thee, fallen tyrant! I did groan. Feelings of a Republican on the Fall of Bonaparte. Shelley. MBPR

I hated to do it, to tell the truth. Wise Guy. William Cole. OSF

I Haue a Yong Suster. *Unknown. See* I Have a Young Sister.

I Have a Big Favour to Ask You, Brothers. Zishe Landau, *tr. fr. Yiddish by* Ruth Whitman. VWA

I have a bone and all dogs chase me. The Bone. John Blight. GAS

I have a bottle and a pen. Thoughts from a Bottle. Carl Clark. JB

I have a bowl of paper whites. Window Ledge in the Atom Age. E. B. White. OBAL

I have a boy of five years old. Anecdote for Fathers. Wordsworth. MBPR

I have a copper penny and another copper penny. Logic. *Unknown.* ECBV

I have a desk job. Shawano Lake, Wisconsin. Robert Gillespie. NVAP

I have a dog with delusions of literature. Literature. Robert A. Brooks. PoUp

I have a dream bone. The Hollow Flute. Avner Strauss. VWA

I have a fairy by my side. My Fairy. "Lewis Carroll." FaBoNo

I have a feeling. The Nets on the Andrea Doria. Karen G. Tepfer. AMV–81

I have a feeling that my boat. Oceans. Juan Ramón Jiménez, *tr. by* Robert Bly. NU

I have a fifth of therapy. Interview with Doctor Drink. J. V. Cunningham. VGW

I have a friend. My Friend. Samuel Allen. FB

I have a friend, she says. The Cross-eyed Lover. Donald Finkel. Prf

I have a friend who would give a price for those long fingers all of one length. Snakes, Mongooses, Snake-Charmers and the Like. Marianne Moore. CMoP (1970 ed.); ExPo (1973 ed.)

I have a garden here, shaped. Letter from an Institution: III. Michael Ryan. AmPA

I have a garden of my own. Child's Song. Thomas Moore. ECBV

I Have a Gentle Cock [or Gentil Cok]. *Unknown.* EBEV; HAP; NOBE; OxBM
(Cockerel.) GBP

I have a gold watch, willed to me by a. The Gold Watch. John Blight. CAAP

I have a good deal of sympathy for you, mate. For Saint Peter. U. A. Fanthorpe. PMW

I have a house where I go. Solitude. A. A. Milne. LCL

I have a life of my own. Maxine W. Kumin. *Fr.* Song for Seven Parts of the Body. POL

I have a little brain. My Brain. Annabel Laurance. AKE

I have a little pussy. Catkin. Christina Rossetti. CTV

I have a little rocking chair. My Rocking Chair. Doris I. Bateman. CTV

I have a little shadow that goes in and out with me. My Shadow. Robert Louis Stevenson. CTV; OxBChV; PCOP

I have a little windmill on my head. Sliding Trombone. Georges Ribemont-Dessaignes, *tr. by* David Gascoyne. EAS

I have a love is Heven-King. The Love of God. John Audelay. OxBM

I have a mistress, for perfections rare. A Devout Lover. Thomas Randolph. HoPM (1975 ed.)

I have a new garden and new is begun. The Pear-Tree. *Unknown.* GBP

I Have a Place. Lily A. De Young. AMV-80

I Have a Rendezvous with Death. Alan Seeger. BTTM; DL
(Rendezvous.) FaPoR

I have a song to sing, O! The Merryman Sings. W. S. Gilbert. ECBV

I have a terrible fear of being an animal. César Vallejo, *tr. fr. Spanish by* Robert Bly. EAS

I have a vague remembrance. The Challenge. Longfellow. PiAm

I have a white cat whose name is Moon. Moon. John Ciardi. CaYB

I have a wide, friendly face. Zimmer Envying Elephants. Paul Zimmer. GP

I have a woman's feel for time. Rearranging My Body. Cleopatra Mathis. AAN

I Have a Young Sister. *Unknown.* ILP (1975 ed.); OAEL–1; OxBM
(I Haue a Yong Suster.) InPS
("I have a young suster.") EBEV
(Tokens of Love, The.) GBP

I have, alas, no taste. Taste. John Updike. AMV–81

I have allowed myself. For Masturbation. Alan Dugan. CAPP; NoAM

I Have Always Heard of These Old Men. *Unknown.* AmFP

I Have Always Known. Narihira, *tr. fr. the Japanese by* Kenneth Rexroth. BBGO

I have always known. The Way It Is. Gloria Oden. CNA; IHMS

I have always loved water, and praised it. Young Women with the Hair of Witches and No Modesty. Peter Redgrove. UsP

I have appropriated the windy twittering of aspen leaves. Plunder. A. R. Ammons. NoAM

I have awakened from the unknowing to the knowing. For William Edward Burghardt Du Bois on His Eightieth Birthday. Bette Darcie Latimer. PoBA

I have become a man to please you. A Long Time Apart. Mari Kubo. PHC

I have become what I am. King of the World. O. B. Hardison, Jr. PoUp

I have been a. Homecoming. Sonia Sanchez. PoBA

I have been a censor for fifteen months. Censorship. Arthur Waley. OxBTC

I Have Been a Foster. *Unknown.* GBP
(Forester, The.) OxBM
("I have been a foster long and many day.") EBEV

I have been asked to write a poem about. A Non Poem about Vietnam. Carolyn M. Rodgers. SA

I have been counselled. The Part of Fortune. Ann Sanfedele. AMV–81

I have been cruel to a fat pigeon. Fly. W. S. Merwin. CoPAm; NNaP

I have been driving. The Cup of the Bear. Siv Cedering Fox. BCr

I have been having an affair. Affair of the Heart. Peter Porter. CAAP

I have been here before. Sudden Light. Dante Gabriel Rossetti. BoLoP; NOBE; OAEL–2; VLP; VPC

I have been here. Dispersed in meditation. Agnosco Veteris Vestigia Flammae. J. V. Cunningham. VGW

I have been in love, and in debt, and in drink. Drinking Song. Alexander Brome. PoPle

I have been in this garden of unripe fruit. First Love. "Hugh MacDiarmid." SLP

I have been introduced to death in bookshops. Thinking of Bookshops. James Liddy. CIP

I have been my arm. Margo Taft. NMM

I have been one acquainted with the night. Acquainted with the Night. Robert Frost. CMoP (1970 ed.); HAP; IP; IPWM; NoAM; NOBA; PoIA; PPP; PSN; SoSe (1977 ed.); STS; TAP VGW; WeW

I have been so great a lover: filled my days. The Great Lover. Rupert Brooke. HoPM (1975 ed.)

I have been standing at the edge. 3 a.m. in New York. Jean Valentine. NYP

I have been thinking here again tonight. Singleman. Alfred Hayes. SPT

I have been treading on leaves all day until I am autumn tired. A Leaf Treader. Robert Frost. BBGO

I have been walking today. Furnished Lives. Jon Silkin. NoAM

I have been warned. It is more than thirty years since I wrote. But I Am Growing Old and Indolent. Robinson Jeffers. ILP (1975 ed.); NoAM; NOBA; TAP

I have been wondering. A Letter. Anthony Hecht. CoPAm

I have been young, and now am not too old. Report on Experience. Edmund Blunden. FaBoTw (1975 ed.); NOBE

I have begun my freedom and it hurts. Stability before Departure. Alan Dugan. NowV

I have begun to die. The Sentry. Alun Lewis. PSN

I have beheld two lovers, in a night. Mr. Robert Herrick, His Farewell unto Poetry. Robert Herrick. SCP-1

I have burst into. The Ritual. Marge Piercy. MMD

I have but one story. Summer Is Gone. *Unknown, tr. by* Sean O'Faolain. PFIr

I have carried my pillow to the windowsill. Summer near the River. Carolyn Kizer. VGW

I have changed nothing but coins. A Pavement Artist. G. E. Murray. HeS

I have come all this way. Ways of Day. Robert Penn Warren. *Fr.* Notes on a Life to Be Lived. NoAM

I have come at last to the short. The Great Canzon. Kenneth Rexroth. NoAM

I have come far enough. A Form of Women. Robert Creeley. CAPP

I have come far to have found nothing. Cid Corman. VGW

I Have Come to Be One Who Cries. Eric Torgersen. TC

I have come to claim. Judy Grahn. RiTi

I have come to the borders of sleep. Lights Out. Edward Thomas. ILP (1975 ed.); NOBE

I Have Come to the Conclusion. Nelle Fertig. FF

I have come to understand my love for you. A Quiet Place. Louis Jenkins. HeS

I have come to you, Babi Yar. Babi Yar. Lev Ozerov, *tr. by* Daniel Weissbort. VWA

I have come upon the visage again. Wood Floor Dreams. Lance Henson. VoR

I have crouched in your kivas by night. Taos Drums. William Haskel Simpson. BPAW

I have desired to go. Heaven-Haven. Gerard Manley Hopkins. BuTh; HeIP; ILP (1975 ed.); NoAM; NOBE; SoSe; VLP

I have discovered that most of. January Morning. William Carlos Williams. InPS

I have done it again. Lady Lazarus. Sylvia Plath. AnMo; CAPP; ConAP; Epi; ILP (1975 ed.); InPK; MAT; NIL; NoAM; NOBA; PiAm; PPoe; Psy; TAP; VGW

I have done one braver thing. The Undertaking. John Donne. NOBE

I have done the deed.—Didst thou not hear a noise? Shakespeare. *Fr.* Macbeth, II, ii. EBEV

I have done what I could but you avoid me. My Life by Somebody Else. Mark Strand. CAAP; GP

I have dreamed so much of you. Poem to the Mysterious Woman. Robert Desnos, *tr. by* Wallace Fowlie. LoAs

I have dreamt it again: standing suddenly still. Wormwood. Thomas Kinsella. CIP; IPM

I have eaten/ the plums. This Is Just to Say. William Carlos Williams. Epi; FF; HoPM (1975 ed.); InPK; InPS; NOBA; OSP; PBMP; PiAm; SoSe; SpRo; SS; TAP; TPo; VoA

I have eaten the city. Manhattan. H. R. Hays. EAS

I have eaten your bread and salt. Prelude to "Departmental Ditties." Kipling. VLP

I have examined a thousand chests. Eyes. Henry Shore. PMW

I Have Exhausted the Delighted Range. Michael Hartnett. CIP

I have fallen in love with American names. American Names. Stephen Vincent Benét. GOA; OBAL

I have fastened everything within a black cloak. The Assignation. Juana de Ibarbourou, *tr. by* Brian Swann. PBWP

"I have finished another year," said God. New Year's Eve. Thomas Hardy. NoAM

I Have Folded My Sorrows. Bob Kaufman. AmNP (1974 ed.); PoBA

I have followed you model. Ode to a Model. Vladimir Nabokov. OBAL; SFF

I have forsworn it while I life. The Wake at the Well. *Unknown.* GBP

I Have Fought the Good Fight, *with music.* Jared B. Waterbury. AH

I have found a way to capture color. The Indian. Thomas Reed. AMV-81

I have found, my dear Miss Ware, a new way of coloring the glass. The Stained Glass Man. Cynthia Macdonald. FiCP

I have found out a gift for my Erin. A Pastoral Ballad by John Bull. Thomas Moore. BIrV; OBSV

I have found out a gig-gig-gift for my fuf-fuf-fair. An Invitation to the Zoological Gardens. *Unknown.* BoAnP

I have found paper. The Old Ladies. Tom O'Grady. AAN

I have gone into the tin can. The Tin Can. William Jay Smith. CoPAm

I have gone out, a possessed witch. Her Kind. Anne Sexton. FF; HeIP; NIL; PPP; TAP

I have good news to bring and that is why I sing. The Old Gospel Ship. *Unknown.* FSW

I have got a new-born sister. Choosing a Name. Charles *and* Mary Lamb. OxBChV

I have grete marvel of a brid. Fragment of a Love Lament. *Unknown.* OxBM

I have grown old. The Old Man's Song. *Tr. fr. Eskimo.* WTO

I have grown past hate and bitterness. Nationality. Mary Gilmore. GAS; MAuV

I have had asthma for a. Visitors. Tu Fu, *tr. by* Kenneth Rexroth. IPWM

I have had playmates, I have had companions. The Old Familiar Faces. Charles Lamb. FaPoR; GrRo; NOBE; PAIC

I have had to learn the simplest things. Maximus, to Himself. Charles Olson. CMoP (1970 ed.); CoPAm; ExPo (1973 ed.); NOBA; VGW

I Have Had to Learn to Live with My Face. Diane Wakoski. FoP

I have had to stop answering yes and no. Diseases of the Moon. Doug Fetherling. NeAC

I have heard a voice of broken seas. James Elroy Flecker. *Fr.* A Fragment. EcS

I have heard of fish. The Sun. Anne Sexton. PBWP

I have heard of this destruction. The Letter. Charles Reznikoff. VWA

"I have heard," said a maid of Montclair. Opportunity's Knock. Morris Bishop. TDH

I have heard some jealous women say. Romantic. George Garrett. CoPAm; HoPM (1975 ed.)

I have heard tell somewhere. The Old Dog in the Ruins of the Graves at Arles. James Wright. NNaP

I have heard that hysterical women say. Lapis Lazuli. W. B. Yeats. AnMo; CMoP (1970 ed.); FaBoTw (1975 ed.); FF; ILP (1975 ed.); InPK; InPS; MAT; NIL; NoAM; NOBE; OAEL-2; OBP; PoIA; PPoe; WIF

I have heard the pigeons of the Seven Woods. In the Seven Woods. W. B. Yeats. CMoP (1970 ed.); NoAM

I Have Heard the Sunset Song of the Birches. Stephen Crane. War Is Kind, VII. TT

I have heard your voice floating, royal and real. To Dinah Washington. Etheridge Knight. PoBA

I have her name, here in my hand, to riddle. The Apples of Sodom and Gomorrah. Barbara A. Holland. WBN

I have hidden something in the inner chamber. Monologue in the Valley of the Kings. Anthony Thwaite. HeHu

I have hunted the first ice. First Ice of Winter. Michael Shorb. AMV-81

I have inherited the universe! Ode to Joy. Michael McClure. GP

I have just been to the Milo. A Thank You Poem for the Andersons. Phillip Hey. NVAP

I have just come down from my father. The Hospital Window. James Dickey. BiP; HeIP; UsP

I have just joined a raggedy line. Epilogue. Dennis Trudell. AAN; NVAP

I have just now. The Young Girl's Song. Alvin J. Gordon. MiP

I have just realized that the stakes are myself. Revolutionary Letter # 1. Diane DiPrima. RiTi

I have just seen a [most] beautiful thing. The Black Finger. Angelina Weld Grimké. AmNP (1974 ed.); PoBA

I have known it from the beginning. Aristophanes' Symposium. Rita Mae Brown. IHMS

I have known nights rain-washed and crystal-clear. Wisdom. Frank Yerby. AmNP (1974 ed.)

I have known the inexorable sadness of pencils.  Dolor.
Theodore Roethke.  AnMo; BiP; CABA (1972 ed.); CMoP
(1970 ed.); CoPAm; HeIP; HoPM (1975 ed.); ILP (1975 ed.);
InPK; InPS; NoAM; PBMP; PoA; PoIA; PPoD; SFF; TCP;
TPo; UsP

I have known the strange nurses of Kindness.  But I Do Not
Need Kindness.  Gregory Corso.  CoPAm; VoA

I Have Labored Sore.  *Unknown.*  WeW

I have learned to go back and walk around.  Time-Travel.
Sharon Olds.  AMV-80

I have led her home, my love, my only friend.  Tennyson.  *Fr.*
Maud.  LoAs

I Have Left You an Empty Room.  Joyce Odam.  CPA

I have lived and died.  The Edge.  James K. Bowen.  AMV-80

I have lived in important places, times.  Epic.  Patrick Kavanagh.
BIrV; CIP

I have lived long enough, having seen one thing, that love hath an
end.  Hymn to Proserpine.  Swinburne.  ILP (1975 ed.);
OAEL-2; PFD; VLP; VPC

I Have Longed to Move Away.  Dylan Thomas.  WIF

I have looked at the Roubaix Cemetery.  Roubaix Cemetery.
Franklin Brainard.  HeS

I have looked him round and looked him through.  Nora Criona.
James Stephens.  PFIr

I have lost, and lately, these.  Upon the Loss of His Mistresses.
Robert Herrick.  CaPo

I have lost my face/ In the night meadow.  For a Young Friend
Seeking "Identity."  May Miller.  PoUp

I have lots of teeth.  A Little Boy.  John Bennett.  PoW

I have loved colours, and not flowers.  Amends to Nature.
Arthur Symons.  FSFS

I have loved coming by the back roads.  Rural Route.  R. T.
Smith.  AMV-81

I have loved flowers that fade.  Song.  Robert Bridges.  VLP

I have loved thirty by three.  Gormley, *tr. by* Joan Keefe.  *Fr.*
Gormley's Laments.  PBWP

I have lucky teeth.  I'm Lucky.  Charlotte Mandel.  AMV-81

I have made tales in verse, but this man made.  The Waggon-
Maker.  John Masefield.  EBEV

I have met a fortunate few.  The Dyke.  Jenny Morgan.  PMW

I have met them at close of day.  Easter, 1916.  W. B. Yeats.
CABA (1972 ed.); CMoP (1970 ed.); Epi; FaPoR; HAP; ILP
(1975 ed.); InPS; LFH; NIL; NoAM; NOBE; OAEL-2; OBP;
OxBTC; PAIC; PPoe; PPP; STS; TT

I have mislaid the torment and the fear.  Success.  William
Empson.  OxBTC

I have more memories than if I had lived a thousand years.
Spleen LXXVI.  Baudelaire, *tr. by* Anthony Hecht.  NAWM-
2

I have moved to Dublin to have it out with you.  John Berryman.
NoAM

I have my heart on my fist.  The Tomb of the Kings.  Anne
Hébert, *tr. by* Kathleen Weaver.  PBWP

I have named you queen.  The Queen.  Pablo Neruda, *tr. by*
Donald D. Walsh.  OLR

I have never been on the cloudy slopes of Olympus.  The Valley
of Men.  Uri Zvi Greenberg, *tr. by* Robert Mezey *and* Ben
Gold Zion.  VWA

I have never beheld you, O pawky Scot.  Who Taught Caddies to
Count? or, A Burnt Golfer Fears the Child.  Ogden Nash.
LiSp

I have never seen/ anything more beautiful.  Baby Giraffe.
Patricia Ball.  PMW

I have never seen that beast.  Rhinoceros.  Adrien Stoutenburg.
BoAnP

I have no brother,—they who meet me now.  Thy Brother's
Blood.  Jones Very.  AmVN; NOBA; TAP

I have no embroidered headband.  Sappho, *tr. fr. Greek by* Willis
Barnstone.  BoWoP

I have no more a golden store.  The Merry Jovial Beggar.  Peter
Casey, *tr. by* Douglas Hyde.  WTO

I have no name.  Infant Joy.  Blake.  *Fr.* Songs of Innocence.
LAuP; MBPR

I Have No Pain.  *Unknown.*  FaBoCo

I have no program for.  Hippie Hop.  A. R. Ammons.  NIL

I have no thumb.  Person.  Alan Jackson.  MS

I have no way of knowing how you tracked me here.  Indian
Autobiographies.  Madeline DeFrees.  CNW; PoW

I have no wit, no words, no tears.  A Better Resurrection.
Christina Rossetti.  VLP

I have not ever seen my father's grave.  Father Son and Holy
Ghost.  Audre Lorde.  PoBA

I have not gone like a pilgrim.  The Tourist.  Garret Keizer.
AMV-81

I have not so much emulated the birds that musically sing.  To
Soar in Freedom and in Fullness of Power.  Walt Whitman.
RFM

I have not spent the April of my time.  Fidessa, More Chaste than
Kind, XXXV.  Bartholomew Griffin.  AAS; ILP (1975 ed.);
LoAs

I have not the purity.  Light.  Jon Silkin.  NoAM

I have not written my poem.  The Experiment That Failed.  John
Logan.  NU

I have not yet begun to relate.  Lune Concrete.  Raymond
Federman.  Moon

I have nothing new to ask of you.  Another Year Come.  W. S.
Merwin.  OFD

I have nothing to say about this garden.  Unexpected Visit.
Fleur Adcock.  ATNZ

"I have often been told," said the horse.  The Thoroughbred
Horse.  Oliver Herford.  TDH

I have opened every drawer.  Hunger.  Nell Altizer.  PHC

I have packed away your clothes.  Relics.  Suzanne Gegna.
AMV-81

I have properly spoken.  A Poem for Anton Schmidt.  William
Pillen.  VWA

I have put my time into the ground.  Melons.  Greg Kuzma.
HeS

I have run out of faces.  Before the Reincarnation.  Bonita
Hearn.  PoW

I have said, "Dear God," under my breath a thousand times.
Raingatherer.  Franklin Brainard.  HeS

I have said I will marry the moon.  The One-eyed Bridegroom.
Constance Urdang.  Moon

I Have Seen.  Kathleen McCracken.  AMV-80

I have seen/ A curious child.  Wordsworth.  *Fr.* The Excursion,
IV.  EcS

I have seen a court, and a dozen courts.  A Christmas Revel.
Dafydd Bach ap Madog Wladaidd, *tr. by* Joseph P. Clancy.
OBW

I Have Seen Black Hands.  Richard Wright.  NoAM; PoBA; SPT

I have seen come on/ slowly as rust.  Death.  John Stone.  CSP

I have seen flowers come in stony places.  An Epilogue.  John
Masefield.  FaBoEE; OxBTC

I have seen old ships sail like swans asleep.  The Old Ships.
James Elroy Flecker.  PoPle

I have seen the hardened innocence.  Repetition.  Wyatt Prunty.
AMV-81

I have seen the poets of the West.  That Poem.  Juan Sáez
Burgos, *tr. by* Julio Marzán.  InW

I have seen the smallest minds of my generation.  Problem in
Social Geometry—the Inverted Square!  Ray Durem.  PoBA

I have seen the soft light flicker.  Message from Ohanapecosh
Glacier.  W. M. Ransom.  CDW

I hear the autumn winds blow down the sky.  The Widow.  Mariana B. Davenport.  AMV-80

I hear the buckles rattle from his bed.  Tyger! Tyger!  James Nolan.  AATT

I hear the clattering of an armed troop.  Psychozoia; or, The First Part of the Song of the Soul, Canto III.  Henry More.  SCP-2

I hear the doctor's loud success.  Waiting for the Doctor.  Colette Inez.  IHMS

I hear the hum of grandfathers in rest homes.  Elders.  J. D. Reed.  UsP

I hear the man downstairs.  The .38.  Ted Joans.  WeW

I hear the shadowy horses, their long manes a-shake.  Michael Robartes Bids His Beloved Be at Peace.  W. B. Yeats.  NoAM

I hear the sound of affliction. They are weeping.  How It Is.  Uri Zvi Greenberg, tr. by Robert Mezey and Ben Zion Gold.  VWA

I hear their signal alert.  Keys.  Glen Rockwell.  AMV-81

I hear them say, There has been too much of rain!  November.  Arthur J. Bull.  HeHu

I Hear You've Let Go.  Rosario Ferre, tr. fr. Spanish by Willis Barnstone.  BoWoP

I heard a bird at dawn.  The Rivals.  James Stephens.  NoAM; PCOP; RAE

I Heard a Bird Sing.  Oliver Herford.  LCL; PCOP

I heard a clash, and a cry.  Middle Ages.  Siegfried Sassoon.  SO

I heard a cow low, a bonnie cow low.  The Queen of Elfan's Nourice.  Unknown.  AIW

I heard a dying man.  The Dying Man.  Theodore Roethke.  STS

I heard a fly buzz—when I died.  Emily Dickinson.  AmVN; AnMo; BoWoP; CABA (1972 ed.); CMoP (1970 ed.); DL; FF; HAP; HoPM (1975 ed.); ILP (1975 ed.); InPK; IP; NIL; NoAm; NOBA; PiAm; PoIA; PPP; Psy; TAP; TT

I heard a mither baing her bairn.  Sealchie Song.  Unknown.  PeBB

I heard a mouse.  The Mouse.  Elizabeth J. Coatsworth.  MN

I Heard a Noise and Wishèd for a Sight.  Unknown.  EBEV; HAP
(Shadow and Substance.)  OAEL-1

I heard a puir deleerit loon.  Newsboy.  Albert D. Mackie.  MS

I heard a thousand blended notes.  Lines Written in Early Spring.  Wordsworth.  ILP (1975 ed.); MBPR; OAEL-2; PBMP; PoIA

I heard a voice from Etna's side.  The Mad Monk.  Samuel Taylor Coleridge.  MBPR

I heard a woman's voice that wailed.  In Ruin Reconciled.  Aubrey Thomas De Vere.  BIrV

I heard an angel speak last night.  A Curse for a Nation.  Elizabeth Barrett Browning.  SBG; WPE

I heard Andrew Jackson say, as he closed his Virgil.  Andrew Jackson's Speech.  Robert Bly.  ConAP

I Heard Christ Sing.  "Hugh MacDiarmid."  NoAM

I heard him faintly, far away.  The Corncrake.  James H. Cousins.  BoAnP; PFIr

I Heard Immanuel Singing.  Vachel Lindsay.  HAP

I heard my love was going to Yang-chou.  Tr. fr. Chinese by Arthur Waley.  Fr. Tzu Yeh Songs.  BoWoP

I heard of gold at Sutter's Mill.  When I Went Off to Prospect.  Unknown.  AmFP

I heard one who said: "Verily."  Cassandra.  E. A. Robinson.  CMoP (1970 ed.); ExPo (1973 ed.); NoAM

I heard the bear in the garbage.  The Bear.  Mark McCloskey.  BCr

I Heard the Bells on Christmas Day.  Longfellow.  AH, with music; CTV
(Christmas Bells, st. 1.)  PChr

I heard the cock at morning crow.  Country Morning.  Rosemary Dobson.  MAuV

I heard the dogs howl in the moonlight night.  The Dream.  William Allingham.  BIrV; PFIr; PoTa

I heard the old, old men say.  The Old Men Admiring Themselves in the Water.  W. B. Yeats.  CMoP (1970 ed.); MiP; TVo

I heard the sea murmur in my ears.  One Goes with Me along the Shore.  Manfred Winkler, tr. by Mary Zilzer.  VWA

I heard the sighing of the reeds.  By the Pool at the Third Rosses.  Arthur Symons.  In Ireland, II.  VLP

I heard the songs.  The Songs.  Tr. fr. Zuni Indian by K. Kennedy.  WTO

I heard the tom-tom.  Jesus Song.  Charley John Greasybear.  PoW

I heard the trailing garments of the night.  Hymn to the Night.  Longfellow.  AmVN; NOBA; TAP

I heard them say I'm ugly.  The Ugly Child.  Elizabeth Jennings.  RAE

I heard this morning.  Summer 1970.  Lindiwe Mabuza.  SES

I heard thy fate without a tear.  Stanzas.  Byron.  PBMP

I Held a Shelley Manuscript.  Gregory Corso.  VGW

I held a tall stump with one hand.  Public Utterance.  Stephen Shrader.  PHC

I held Europe in my hand.  Yonder.  Richard Eberhart.  GOA

I herde a carping of a clerk.  Robin and Gandelein.  Unknown.  OxBM

I, Hermes, have been set up.  Anyte, tr. fr. Greek by Kenneth Rexroth.  OBVE

I hew and hack at Space, at lands and seas.  The Enemies.  Arthur J. Bull.  HeHu

I hid my heart in a nest of roses.  A Ballad in Dreamland.  Swinburne.  ILP (1975 ed.)

I Hid My Love.  John Clare.  GBL; MAT
(Secret Love.)  ILP (1975 ed.); VLP
(Song: "I hid my love when young while I.")  OAEL-2

I hid the peppermint.  I Had to Be Secret.  Mark Van Doren.  SO

I Hid You.  Miklós Radnóti, tr. fr. Hungarian by Steven Polgar and Stephen Berg and S. J. Marks.  VWA

I Hoed and Trenched and Weeded.  A. E. Housman.  UnPo (1976 ed.); VLP; WeW

I hoist the mummy, an armful of frozen plaster.  Floating Coathangers.  Peter Cooley.  NVAP

I hold a newspaper, reading.  Fish.  Shinkichi Takahashi, tr. by Lucien Stryk.  NU

I hold him wise and wel y-taught.  Bear a Horn and Blow It Not.  Unknown.  OxBM

I hold in my hands.  Look Closely.  Morton Marcus.  FF; SFF

I hold it good—as who shall hold it bad?  Columbia's Agony.  "Orpheus C. Kerr."  OBAL

I hold my daughter up to the firelight.  Lilly's Song.  Evan Zimroth.  AMV-81

I hope and feare, I pray and hould my peace.  Thomas Lodge.  Phillis, XXXV.  ESo

I Hope I Don't Have You Next Semester, But.  Edwin S. Godsey.  HoPM (1975 ed.)

I Hope I Never Go There.  Cash Terrell.  DNGG

I hoped/ —the night came anyway.  Conjugation of the Verb, "To Hope."  Lou Lipsitz.  FiCP

I hoped to see the sun today, but ice.  On the Edge.  Frank Dwyer.  AMV-81

I hug you there, moccasins of worn buckskin.  The Moccasins of an Old Man.  Ramona Carden.  VW

I hung like a man on a trapeze, my arms stiffening. Dying off Egg Island Bar. David Smith. NVAP

I hung my verses in the wind. The Test. Emerson. OBAL

I hurry through the lot behind the meat-packing house. Hamden Provision Co. Barbara Hughes. CPA

I hurtle over America's highways. Welcome Home. Charles M. Purcell. EC

I, Icarus. Alden Nowlan. NCSH

I imagine him still with heavy brow. Beethoven's Death Mask. Stephen Spender. OxBTC

I imagine the time of our meeting. Forms of the Earth at Abiquiu. N. Scott Momaday. CDW

I imagine this midnight moment's forest. The Thought-Fox. Ted Hughes. HeIP; NCSH; NoAM

I imagined her dead, killed by some local maniac who. Jim Harrison. Fr. Ghazals. InPS

I, in My Intricate Image. Dylan Thomas. EAS

I inherited forty acres from my father. Cooney Potter. Edgar Lee Masters. Fr. Spoon River Anthology. CTBA

I intended an Ode. Urceus Exit [or Triolet]. Austin Dobson. Fr. Rose-Leaves. PAIC; PoPle

I invite you, child, to dance. You come. I bow my blond head. Song for a Dance. Abraham Sutskever, tr. by Ruth Whitman. VWA

I invited Mozart to dinner. The Dinner. Gregory Orr. POL

I is for Ignorant Ida. Ignorant Ida. Isabel Frances Bellows. TDH

I is uh revolutionist. Yeah, I Is uh Shootin Off at the Mouth. Carolyn M. Rodgers. SA

I, Jim Rogers. Stanley Burnshaw. SPT

I Jocky Bell o'Braikenbrow lyes under this stane. On Jocky Bell. Unknown. FaBoEE

I join a group of women and children. Earl the Pearl. Sheila Heldenbrand. AcAn

I journeyed on a winter's day. Jane Smith. Kipling. SpRo

I jump with terror seeing him. Modes of Pleasure. Thom Gunn. PPP

I just thought. Postcard to a Foetus. Kirk Robertson. GP

I Just Walk Around, Around, Around. Moishe Kulbak, tr. fr. Yiddish by Ruth Whitman. VWA

I Just Wanna Stay Home. Irwin Silber. FSW

I just want to get back to Birmingham. Third Alley Blues. Unknown. BluL

I keep feeling all space as my image. Poem. Sanders Russell. EAS

I keep finding seeds. How Clouds Move. Barbara Hughes. CPA

I keep my parents in a garden. Eden Is a Zoo. Margaret Atwood. OSP, abr.; WPE

I keep telling you. Dark Reflections. Margo Bohanon. SES

I keep the custom of the Ferry, a tavern none can blame. The Hostess of the Ferry Inn. Gwerfyl Mechain, tr. by H. Idris Bell. OBW

I keep the weatherboard facade glossed fresh. Alter Ego. Leon Slade. FPA

I Keep to Myself Such Measures. Robert Creeley. ExPo (1973 ed.); NoAM

I ken these islands each inhabited. Harry Semen. "Hugh MacDiarmid." NoAM; OBP

I kening through astronomy divine. Edward Taylor. Preparatory Meditations: First Series, VIII. EAP; NOBA; PAIC; PiAm; SCP-2; TAP

I kept having to shoo off/ poets. Editor. Glenna Luschei. CPA

I kept my answers small and kept them near. Answers. Elizabeth Jennings. OxBTC

I kicked an Edinbro dug-luver's dug. Nemo Canem Impune Lacessit. Robert Garioch. MS

I killed a gopher. Summer. Ernesto Trejo. CPA

I killed them, but they would not die. The Immortals. Isaac Rosenberg. FaBoTw (1975 ed.)

I kissed a kiss in youth. Scintilla. William Stanley Braithwaite. AmNP (1974 ed.)

I Kissed Pa Twice after His Death. Mattie J. Peterson. PeD

I kissed the friendly brown-eyed cow. Mistake. Unknown. OSF

I kissed them in fancy as I came. Two Lips. Thomas Hardy. BoLoP

I kneel to fasten your shoes. Like Trees, like Islands. Pearse Hutchinson. IPM

I knew a man kept a yellow bird. Bird Talk. John Malcolm Brinnin. WasP

I Knew a Woman. Theodore Roethke. AnMo; BiP; BoLoP; CABA (1972 ed.); CNW; CoPAm; HAP; HeIP; HoPM (1975 ed.); ILP (1975 ed.); InPK; IPWM; MAT; NIL; NoAM; NOBA; PPoe; SoSe; STS; TAP; TCP; UnPo (1976 ed.); UsP ("I knew a woman, lovely in her bones.") LoAs

I knew an old wife lean and poor. The Goose. Tennyson. ECBV

I knew it was too late. One Hook. Ronald Wallace. AAN

I knew not 'twas so dire a crime. Last Words. Emily Brontë. WPE

I knew that porcupines liked to eat trees. Porcupines. Robert Huff. CNW; CoPAm

I knew the dignity of the words. My Grandfather's Funeral. James Applewhite. CSP; NVAP; TAT

I knew the town from nightmares. Christmas at Vail: On Staying Indoors. Pat Monaghan. AMV-80

I knew you forever and you were always old. Some Foreign Letters. Anne Sexton. ILP (1975 ed.)

I know a bank[e] where the wild[e] thyme blows [or time blowes]. Wild Flowers. Shakespeare. Fr. A Midsummer Night's Dream, II, i. PF; PoPle

I know a dim marsh place where tules grow. In the Marsh. Ella Higginson. WPW

I Know a Flower So Fair and Fine, with music. Nicolai F. S. Grundtvig, tr. fr. Norwegian by Olav Lee. AH

I know a funny little man. Mr. Nobody. Unknown. CTV; PCOP

I Know a Lady. Joyce Carol Thomas. CNA

I know a little garden-close. A Garden by the Sea. William Morris. Fr. The Life and Death of Jason. NOBE; OAEL-2

I know a little man both ept and ert. Gloss. David McCord. OBAL

I know a little what it is like, once here at high tide. Seaweeds. Sandra McPherson. AmPA; PoA

I Know a Man. Robert Creeley. CAPP; ConAP; CoPAm; Epi; InPK; InPS; MAT; NOBA; PPoD; PPP; TCP

I know a man. Some Chicks Just Can't Tell a Cézanne from a Sears. Gordon Kirkwood Yates. CPA

I know a man/ Who collects angels. The Angel Collector. Henry Shore. PMW

I know a man in prison. A Prisoner. Arlie "Franko" Durham. DNGG

I Know a Spot Just over the Hill. William Mills. CoPAm

I know a thing that's most uncommon. See I know the thing that's most uncommon.

I Know a Village, sels. Phyllis McGinley.
　5:32, The. NMM; WPE
　Occupation: Housewife. WPE

I know a young girl who can speak. A Warning. Mary A. Webber. TDH

I know, although when looks meet. Crazy Jane and Jack the Journeyman. W. B. Yeats. CMoP (1970 ed.)

I know but will not tell. Elegy. Alan Dugan. CAPP

I Know de Moonlight. *Unknown.* BPo

I know him;/ He'll give no horse for a poem. *Unknown, tr. fr. Irish by* Vivian Mercier. BIrV

I know I am/ The Negro Problem. Dinner Guest: Me. Langston Hughes. BPo; SS

I Know I Am but Summer to Your Heart. Edna St. Vincent Millay. ILP (1975 ed.)

I know I change. Daguerreotype Taken in Old Age. Margaret Atwood. BoWoP

I know I have the best of time and space. Walt Whitman. Song of Myself, XLVI. BiP

I know, I know—though the evidence. Blow, West Wind. Robert Penn Warren. *Fr.* Notes on a Life to Be Lived. NoAM

I know if I find you I will have to leave the earth. Hymn. A. R. Ammons. ConAP; CoPAm

I Know I'm Not Sufficiently Obscure. Ray Durem. BPo; PoBA

I know it is dark; and though I have lain. An Ode to the Rain. Samuel Taylor Coleridge. MBPR

I know I've got a job. The Working Man. Gregory Donovan. AMV-81

I know little about bushes and trees. A Citizen. Charles Reznikoff. *Fr.* Five Groups of Verse. SA

I know monks masturbate at night. The Earnest Liberal's Lament. Ernest Hemingway. OBAL; OBSV

I Know Moonrise. *Unknown.* UnPo (1976 ed.)

I Know My Love. *Unknown.* FSW

I Know My Soul. Claude McKay. BPo

I know not how it may be with others. Old Furniture. Thomas Hardy. OxBTC

I Know Not How That Bethlehem's Babe, *with music.* Harry Webb Farrington. AH

I know not of my forefathers. Lost. Bruce Ignacio. VW

I know not of what we ponder'd. Companions. Charles Stuart Calverley. FaBoCo; NOBL

I know not what to do. Fragment Thirty-six. Hilda Doolittle ("H. D."). CMoP (1970 ed.); VGW

I Know Not Where the Road Will Lead, *with music.* Evelyn Atwater Cummins. AH

I know not who thou art, oh lovely one! To the Lady in the Chemisette with Black Buttons. Nathaniel Parker Willis. OBAL

I know some lonely houses off the road. Emily Dickinson. SO

I know that He exists. Emily Dickinson. ILP (1975 ed.); PiAm; PoIA; Psy

I know that I shall meet my fate. An Irish Airman Foresees His Death. W. B. Yeats. CABA (1972 ed.); Epi; HeIP; HoPM (1975 ed.); ILP (1975 ed.); NoAM; NOBE; PPP; SoS; WeW

I know that life is Jason. The Golden Fleece. Oscar Williams. PoA

I know that mind. ESP. Carter Revard. VoR

I Know That My Redeemer Lives, *with music.* Charles Wesley. BLSH

I know that there are dragons. Serious Omission. John Farrar. PCOP

I know that what our neighbours call *longueurs.* Byron. *Fr.* Don Juan, II. OBSV

I know the barn where they got you. For a Woodscolt Miscarried. John William Corrington. CoPAm; CSP

I know the bottom, she says. I know it with my great tap root. Elm. Sylvia Plath. NoAM; NOBA

I know the colour rose, and it is lovely. Pathology of Colours. Dannie Abse. PMW

I know the injured pride of sleep. Night and Morning. Austin Clarke. CIP; NoAM

I know the story, how. Life Story. J. Kates. AMV-81

I know the [*or* a] thing that's most uncommon. On a Certain Lady at Court. Pope. ILP (1975 ed.); NOBE; PCOP; PoPle

I know the tops of shoes now. The Plant Rhythms. G. E. Murray. HeS

I know the ways [*or* wayes] of learning: both the head. The Pearl. George Herbert. EBEV; HAP; OAEL-1; SCP-1

I know there is a worm in the human heart. John Clare. Jon Anderson. AmPA

I know there is someone. Poem to Be Read And Sung. César Vallejo, *tr. by* James Wright *and* Robert Bly. EAS; LoAs

I know these slopes; who knows them if not I? Hill-Side Flowers. Matthew Arnold. *Fr.* Thyrsis. PF

I know this road like the back of my hand. Ballad of the Three Coins. Vernon Watkins. NoAM

I know those tits. Matisse Tits. David Barker. GP

I know two things about the horse. The Horse. Naomi Royde Smith. FaBoCo

I know two women. The Wife. Robert Creeley. VGW

I know very well, goddess, she is not beautiful. Calypso's Island. Archibald MacLeish. PiAm

I know what the caged bird feels, alas! Sympathy. Paul Laurence Dunbar. AmNP (1974 ed.); ILP (1975 ed.); PoBA

I Know Where I'm Going. *Unknown.* FSW; GBP; OLR; WTO

I know where the destroyers live. The Destroyers. Henry Shore. PMW

I know you got some good apples. Big Apple Blues. *Unknown.* BluL

I know you love me, baby. Guitar Recitativos. A. R. Ammons. TT

I Know You Rider. *Unknown.* FSW

I know you: solitary griefs. The Precept of Silence. Lionel Johnson. VLP

I know your secret, now I've caught you. Six Small Songs for a Silver Flute. Barry Spacks. PCho

I knowed a man, which he lived in Jones. Thar's More in the Man Than Thar Is in the Land. Sidney Lanier. NOBA

I knows a gal that you don't know. Li'l Liza Jane. *Unknown.* BLSo

I Korinna am here to sing the courage. Korinna, *tr. fr. Greek by* Willis Barnstone. BoWoP

I lack the braver mind. Confession of Faith. Elinor Wylie. SBG

I laid me down beside the sea. Lassitude. Mathilde Blind. SBG

I laid me down upon a bank. Blake. GBL; MBPR

I Lais, once an arrow. Kenneth Rexroth, *after the Greek of* Sekundos. NNaP

I laks yo' kin' of lovin'. Long Gone. Sterling A. Brown. BPo

I lang hae thought, my youthfu' friend. Epistle to a Young Friend. Burns. EBEV

I lately vow'd, but 'twas in haste. Song. John Oldmixon. POL

I laughed at sweethearts I met at schools. My Heart Stood Still. Lorenz Hart. BLSo

I laughed when the dawn was a-peepin'. The Night Herder. Charles Badger Clark, Jr. BPAW

I lay at the edge of a well. The Underground Stream. James Dickey. NOBA

I lay down. Children of Night. Richard Shelton. FiCP

I lay i' the bosom of the sun. Palabras Grandiosas. Bayard Taylor. OBAL

I lay my hand. Tribal Cemetery. Janet Campbell Hale. NW; VW

I lay quietly listening to some musical rabbi. Night Poem in an Abandoned Music Room. William Pillen. VWA

I lay waiting. Bog Queen. Seamus Heaney. HeHu

I lay with my heart under me. Cicada. Adrien Stoutenburg. RFM

I leaf through the flat plains.  Poem from "The Revolution."  Ilya Rubin, *tr. by* Linda Zisquit.  VWA

I lean on a lighthouse rock.  Girl at the Seaside.  Richard Murphy.  BIrV

I leant upon a coppice gate.  The Darkling Thrush.  Thomas Hardy.  BoReV; CMoP (1970 ed.); FSFS; HAP; ILP (1975 ed.); InPS; NIL; NoAM; NOBE; OAEL-2; PoIA; PPM; PPP; SoSe; UnPo (1976 ed.); UsP; VLP; VoPo

I learned in my credulous youth.  Why, Some of My Best Friends Are Women.  Phyllis McGinley.  NMM

I learned one kind of thing in the house.  Tracking.  Virginia R. Terris.  AAN

I learned to ride with the Colonel.  Riding.  Florence Grossman.  PH

I learned two things.  Riding Lesson.  Henry Taylor.  PH

I leave here I'm gonna catch that M and O.  M & O Blues.  *Unknown.*  BluL

I leave mortality, and things below.  The Ecstasy.  Abraham Cowley.  SCP-2

I leave my heart in the doorway.  Thank You for the Valentine.  Diane Wakoski.  CoPAm; HoPM (1975 ed.)

I leave this at your ear for when you wake.  W. S. Graham.  LoAs

I Left.  Tuvia Ruebner, *tr. fr. Hebrew by* Betsy Rosenberg.  VWA

I left my hills.  Izumi Shikibu, *tr. fr. Japanese by* Willis Barnstone.  BoWoP

I left my prayers and the kneeling pilgrims.  Fair Cassidy.  *Unknown, tr. by* Donagh MacDonagh.  BIrV

I left my room at last, I walked.  The Monster.  Thom Gunn.  ILP (1975 ed.)

I left my temporary home and set off.  I Left.  Tuvia Ruebner, *tr. by* Betsy Rosenberg.  VWA

I left old Lake Chemo a long way behind me.  Lake Chemo.  James Wilton Rowe.  AmFP

I left the farm I loved. I went.  Exile.  George Rostrevor Hamilton, *after* Isidoros of Aigai.  FaBoEE

I left the valley, no longer heard.  Anabasis.  Rodney Nelson.  AMV-81

I let him find, but never what he sought.  Epitaph on Any Man.  A. S. J. Tessimond.  POL

I let my soul drift with the thistledown.  Soul-Drift.  Mathilde Blind.  SBG

I let the incense grow cold.  Li Ch'ing-chao, *tr. fr. Chinese by* Kenneth Rexroth.  BoWoP

I lie here beside you.  Mount Gilboa.  Malka Heifetz Tussman, *tr. by* Marcia Falk.  PBWP

I lie in bed.  The Way It Is.  Mark Strand.  CAAP

I lie in darkness, as the dead shades gather.  Lament.  Matangi Hauroa, *tr. by* Barry Mitcalfe.  WTO

I lie in wait. It is the in-between.  Expectancies: The Eleventh Hour.  Karla M. Hammond.  AMV-80

I lie under your hand—a cur.  Dog.  Ingrid Jonker, *tr. by* Jack Cope *and* William Plomer.  PBWP

I lied—trusting you knew.  Leonora Speyer.  *Fr.* Cantares.  TH

I lift—lift you five States away your glass.  Sonnet.  John Berryman.  Epi

I Lift My Eyes Up to the Hills, *with music.*  Cotton Mather.  AH

I lift my head and watch.  Thoughts in Exile.  Su Tung P'o, *tr. by* Kenneth Rexroth.  IPWM

I Lift My Heart to Thee, *with music.*  Thomas Sternhold.  AH

I lifted my eyes to the sky.  Twilight Thoughts in Israel.  Melech Ravitch, *tr. by* Seymour Levitan.  VWA

I Light Your Streets.  Meridel Le Sueur.  GP

I like/ dead residue.  Let Us Honor Them.  Rochelle Owens.  Psy

I like a blonde who wears a silver fox.  Tastes.  Arthur J. Bull.  HeHu

I like a church; I like a cowl.  The Problem.  Emerson.  NOBA; TAP

I like a look of agony.  Emily Dickinson.  AmVN; ILP (1975 ed.); InPS; PoIA; TAP

I like a man around.  Hooked on the Magic Muscle.  Linda King.  GP

I, like a slow, morose and shabby fatalist.  The Elephant to the Girl in Bertram Mills' Circus.  Anthony Cronin.  CIP

I like it here just fine.  Girl Held without Bail.  Margaret Walker.  BPo; CNA; PoBA

I like lemon on my salmon.  Women.  *Unknown.*  IP

I like [*or* love] little pussy, her coat is so warm.  Pussy [*or* Kindness].  *Unknown, at. to* Jane Taylor.  BBL; CTV; MG; OxBChV

I like mud.  Mud.  John Smith.  FPB

I Like My Body When It Is with Your Body.  E. E. Cummings.  *Fr.* Sonnets—Actualities.  AnMo; BoLoP; SFF; TT; VGW

I like not tears in tune, nor will [*or* do] I prize.  On the Memory [*or* Upon the Death] of Mr. Edward King, Drowned in the Irish Sea[s].  John Cleveland.  HAP; OAEL-1; SCP-2

I like rust on a nail.  And the Same Words.  David Ignatow.  NNaP

I like that ancient Saxon phrase which calls.  God's Acre.  Longfellow.  PIM

I like that poem, Win. There's a green world in it.  To W. T. Scott.  John Ciardi.  NowV

I like the fall.  The Mist and All.  Dixie Willson.  CTV

I like the hunting of the hare.  The Old Squire.  Wilfrid Scawen Blunt.  FaPoR

I like the park best at evening, on a cool day.  The Park at Evening.  Leslie Norris.  DuDa

I like the streets of New York City, where I was born.  Autobiography: Hollywood.  Charles Reznikoff.  *Fr.* Going To and Fro and Walking Up and Down.  SA; VWA

I like the way.  Ibo Woman.  Mark Wangberg.  TC

I like the way that the world is made.  Contentment.  Burges Johnson.  GDP

I like the wind.  Wind Secrets.  Diane Wakoski.  AmPA

I like to/ pretend.  Closet.  Judith Thurman.  FPB

I like to beat people up.  Sonnet.  Ted Berrigan.  CAAP

I like to find.  Pleasures.  Denise Levertov.  CAPP; NoAM; NOBA

I like to have a home life in the house.  Gertrude Stein.  *Fr.* Afterwards.  OSP

I like to play with many boys.  Friends.  *Unknown.*  CTV

I like to see it lap the miles.  Emily Dickinson.  AmVN; BoWoP; CABA (1972 ed.); CTV; InPK; IP; NOBA; OBAL; PoIA; PPM; PPoD; SoSe; WIF

I like to see the bay filled up with boats.  Fear Death by Water.  Richard Eberhart.  AMV-81

I like to see the cowboys ride.  Silver Screen.  Leonard Clarke.  RAE

I like to think (and/ the sooner the better!).  All Watched Over by Machines of Loving Grace.  Richard Brautigan.  MAT

I Like to Think of Harriet Tubman.  Susan Griffin.  NMM; RiTi

I like to toss him up and down.  My Cats.  Stevie Smith.  FaBoNo

I like to walk/ And hear the black crows talk.  Crows.  David McCord.  RFM

I like to watch an angleworm.  Angleworms.  Marie Louise Allen.  CTV

I like winter, spring, summer, and fall.  Beatrice Schenk de Regnier.  IWK

I like you, bamboo.  Kim Kwang-wuk, *tr. fr. Korean.*  TVo

I likes a woman.  Preference.  Langston Hughes.  NOBA

I listen at night to birds.  Birds.  Rhyll McMaster.  FPA

I listened to the foliage grow at night. What I Did Last Summer. Ron Ikan. AMV–80

I listened to the man and he. Psychometrist. James Stephens. NoAM

I live at a distance. The Hermit. Daniel Halpern. AMV–80

I live but in the present,—where art thou? Today. Jones Very. TAP

I live for the good of my nation. Old Rosin the Beau. *Unknown.* BLSo; FSW

I live, I die, I burn myself and drown. Sonnet VIII. Louise Labé, *tr. by* Willis Barnstone. BoWoP

I live in a beautiful place, a city. New York. Edward Field. NYP

I live in a jungle. Ode to Jibberish. Darrell Gray AcAn; EC

I live my father's old age. My Father. Abraham Chalfi, *tr. by* Shlomo Vinner *and* Howard Schwartz. VWA

I live my life in growing orbits. Rainer Maria Rilke, *tr. fr. German by* Robert Bly. NU

I live on this depraved and lonely cliff. Vittoria da Colonna, *tr. fr. Italian by* Willis Barnstone. BoWoP

I live only to do Thy will. *At. to* Ansari of Herat. ILwL

I live quietly and go nowhere. My Father's House. Calvin Forbes. CoPAm

I live (sweete love) whereas the gentle winde. Licia, XXVI. Giles Fletcher the Elder. ESo

I Live up Here. W. S. Merwin. CAPP

I live where darkness/ is not. Mukta Bai, *tr. fr. Marathi by* Willis Barnstone. BoWoP

I live with the mad woman. The Life. George Chambers. HeS

I live without inhabiting/ Myself. St. John of the Cross, *tr. by* Roy Campbell. *Fr.* Coplas about the Soul Which Suffers with Impatience to See God. OBVE

I lived alone as happy as Larry. The Husband's Lament. Brian Merriman, *tr. by* Frank O'Connor. *Fr.* The Midnight Court. OBVE

I lived among great houses. The Statesman's Holiday. W. B. Yeats. CMoP (1970 ed.); OxBTC

I lived in a very special room once. I Have a Place. Lily A. De Young. AMV–80

I lived in the first century of world wars. Poem (I Lived in the First Century). Muriel Rukeyser. UnPo (1976 ed.)

I lived next door to a big yellow knifethrower who. The Invention of the Gun. John Batki. AcAn

I lived on this earth in an age. Fragment. Miklós Radnóti, *tr. by* Steven Polgar *and* Stephen Berg *and* S. J. Marks. VWA

"I lived with Mr. Punch, they said my name was Judy." Variations. Randall Jarrell. VGW

I loathe that I did love. The Agèd Lover Renounceth Love. Thomas, Lord Vaux. OAEL–1

I long had rack'd my brains to find. A New Simile in the Manner of Swift. Goldsmith. LAuP

I long to talk with some old lover's ghost. Love's Deity. John Donne. GBL; ILP (1975 ed.); LoAs

I longed to love a full-boughed beech. The Ivy-Wife. Thomas Hardy. VLP

I look across the table and think. Incident. Norman MacCaig. FF

I Look at an Old Photo of Myself with Love. May Swenson. FoP

I Look at My Hand. Angel González, *tr. fr. Spanish by* Joel Hancock. AMV–81

I look at my hands. The Carpenter. Primus St. John. FoP

I look down the montainside. Just below my window. In a Mountain Cabin in Norway. Robert Bly. RFM

I look for the way. Poetics. A. R. Ammons. TT

I look into my glass. Thomas Hardy. CABA (1972 ed.); EBEV; FaBoTw (1975 ed.); HAP; NOBE; PoPle; VLP

I look into the eyes of the child. The Eyes of the Child Do Not See Me. Norman H. Russell. VW

I look out at the white sleet covering the still streets. Sleet Storm on the Merritt Parkway. Robert Bly. ConAP; NOBA

I look out of these two holes, or I run. Where I'm Staying Now. William Meredith. FoP

I look out the window: spring is coming. To Robert Lowell and Osip Mandelstam. Frederick Seidel. AMV–81

I look. You look. Over. R. S. Thomas. FF

I looked and I saw. Who but the Lord? Langston Hughes. BPo

I looked down and saw a pit most black. Elizabeth Melvill, Lady Culross. *Fr.* A Godly Dream. WPE

I looked for that which is not, nor can be. A Pause of Thought. Christina Rossetti. NOBE

I looked from the hall to the top of the stair. Talking Nothin'. *Unknown.* FSW

I looked in my heart while the wild swans went over. Wild Swans. Edna St. Vincent Millay. CMoP (1970 ed.); ILP (1975 ed.); PBWP; UnPo (1976 ed.)

I looked in the first glass. The Three Mirrors. Edwin Muir. NoAM

I Looked over Jordan. Lane Dunlop. NowV

I looked over Jordan and [*or* an'] what did I see. Swing Low, Sweet Chariot. *Unknown.* BLSH; BLSo; UnPo (1976 ed.); WIF

I looked to find a man who walked with God. Enoch. Jones Very. HAP

I looked to find Spring's early flowers. The Lament of the Flowers. Jones Very. NOBA

I looked to the east, I looked to the west. Pull Off Your Old Coat. *Unknown.* RDB

I, Lord, of All Mortals! *Malay Oral Tradition, tr. by* R. O. Winstedt. WTO

I lost a world the other day. Emily Dickinson. PCOP

I lost my eyes in the blacksmith shop. The Blind Fiddler. *Unknown.* FSW

I lost my pardner, what'll I do? Skip to My Lou. *Unknown.* AmFP

I lost my temper twice today. To My Four-Year-Old Daughter. Gail Todd. TV

I lost the love of heaven above. A Vision. John Clare. OAEL–2; PPP

I Love. Stevie Smith. FaBoCo

I love Adam. He is brave of Heart. Eve. Jakov Fishman, *tr. by* Robert Friend. VWA

I love all beauteous things. To L. B. C. L. M. Robert Bridges. CMoP (1970 ed.); EBEV; PPM

I love and fear him. Lady Kasa, *tr. fr. Japanese by* Kenneth Rexroth. BoWoP

I love and hate. Ah! never ask why so! Catullus, *tr. fr. Latin by* Walter Savage Landor. OBVE

I love breasts, hard. Breasts. Charles Simic. NNaP

I love crows. Crows. William Witherup. POL

I love flowers too; not for a young girl's reason. The Love of Flowers. Thomas Lovell Beddoes. PF

I love him not; but shew no reason can. Antipathy. Rowland Watkyns, *after* Martial. FaBoEE

"I love, I love, and whom love ye?" Roses. *Unknown.* OxBM

I love it, I love it! and who shall dare. The Old Arm-Chair. Eliza Cook. InPK

I Love Life, *with music.* Irwin M. Cassel. BLSo

I Love Little Pussy. *Unknown. See* Pussy.

I Love My Jean. Burns. BiP; ILP (1975 ed.); LAuP

I Love My Jesus Quite Alone, *with music. At. to* Johannes Kelpius, *tr. fr. German by* Christopher Witt. AH

I love my lady's eyes. Song. Robert Bridges. VLP

I love my little son, and yet when he was ill. The Two Parents. "Hugh MacDiarmid." FaBoTw (1975 ed.); OxBTC

I Love My Love. Helen Adam. NMM

"I love my love with an M," said I. Fantasia. Winifrid M. Letts. PFIr

I love my work and my children. God. Ovid in the Third Reich. Geoffrey Hill. NoAM; POL

I Love Old Women. William Kloefkorn. AMV–80

I love sixpence, pretty [or jolly] little sixpence. Mother Goose. BBL; ECBV; MG

I Love Somebody. *Unknown.* AmFP

I love the butterflies. Menashtash. Alvaro Cardona-Hine. OSP

I love the country air. Mother Pin a Rose on Me. David Lewis, Paul Schindler, *and* Bob Adams. FSN

I love the Deinosaurs, their padded bulk. Deinosaurs. Arthur J. Bull. HeHu

I love the English country scene. I Love. Stevie Smith. FaBoCo

I love the jocund dance. Song. Blake. MBPR

I Love the Lord, *with music. Unknown.* AH

I love the old melodious lays. Proem. Whittier. AmVN; TAP

"I love the sea because it has drowned me." Sea Shanty. Clifford Dyment. POL

I Love the Woods. Leib Neidus, *tr. fr. Yiddish by* Keith Bosley. VWA

I loved thee ere I loved a woman, Love. To Art. Dante Gabriel Rossetti. POL

I love thee, Mary, and thou lovest me. The Chemist to His Love. *Unknown.* QQQ

I love this little house because. Motto for a Dog House. Arthur Guiterman. GDP

I Love Thy Kingdom, Lord, *with music.* Timothy Dwight. AH

I love to rise in a summer morn. The School Boy. Blake. *Fr.* Songs of Experience. MBPR

I love to see a lobster laugh. Fun. Leroy F. Jackson. CTV

I love to see boards lying on the ground in early spring. Old Boards. Robert Bly. CAPP

I love to see the little stars. The Oneness of the Philosopher with Nature. G. K. Chesterton. FaBoNo

I love to see those loving and beloved. Lonely Love. Edmund Blunden. OxBTC

I love to see, when leaves depart. Autumn. Roy Campbell. OxBTC; WIF

I Love to Steal Awhile Away, *with music.* Phoebe Hinsdale Brown. AH

I Love to Tell the Story. Katherine Hankey. BLSH, *with music;* CTV

I love to toy with the Platonic notion. Boeotian. Robert Frost. NIL

I love watching the water. Trinket. Marvin Bell. FoP

I Love What Is Not. Manfred Winkler, *tr. fr. Hebrew by* Mary Zilzer. VWA

I love you/ with my linen heart. The Rag Doll to the Heedless Child. David Harsent. LP

I love you and the rosebush. Armando Uribe, *tr. fr. Spanish by* Miller Williams. HoPM (1975 ed.)

I love you as a sheriff searches for a walnut. To You. Kenneth Koch. CAPP

I love you, as I never loved before. When You Were Sweet Sixteen. James Thornton. BLSH

I love you, baby, I ain't gonna lie. When Things Go Wrong with You. *Unknown.* FSW

I love you, because in my thousand and one nights. Love without Love. Luis Lloréns Torres, *tr. by* Julio Marzán. InW

I love you first because your face is fair. V-Letter. Karl Shapiro. NoAM

I love you for your brownness. To a Dark Girl. Gwendolyn B. Bennett. PoBA

I love you ginger bread mama. Ginger Bread Mama. Doughtry Long. BPo; PoBA

"I love you, Horowitz," he said, and blew his nose. Love in Brooklyn. John Wakeman. AMV–81

I love you, not because I love the guillotine. Ode to Freedom. Aaron Zeitlin, *tr. by* Keith Bosley. VWA

I love you, rotten. Medlars and Sorb-Apples. D. H. Lawrence. OAEL–2

"I love you," said a great mother. Carl Sandburg. *Fr.* The People, Yes. CC

"I love you, sweet: how can you ever learn." Youth's Antiphony. Dante Gabriel Rossetti. The House of Life, XIII. VLP

I Love You Truly, *with music.* Carrie Jacobs Bond. BLSH; BLSo; FSN

"I love you," you said between two mouthfuls of pudding. A Considered Reply to a Child. Jonathan Price. BoLoP

I love you! You say, "I don't believe you." Words Words Words. Marilyn Krysl. AMV–80

I love your hands. Your Hands. Angelina Weld Grimké. PoBA

I loved/ secretly. *Unknown, tr. fr. Latin by* Willis Barnstone. *Fr.* Carmina Burana. BoWoP

I loved a child of this countrie. *Unknown.* GBL; PBWP

I Loved a Lass. George Wither. NOBE; PoPle (Love Sonnet, A.) GBL

I loved her softness, her warm human smell. The Lion's Bride. Gwen Harwood. BoWoP

I loved my country. Ars Poetica: Some Recent Criticism. James Wright. CAAP

I loved thee, though I told thee not. The Secret. John Clare. GBL

I loved to talk of home. Pacific Epitaphs. Dudley Randall. NoAM

I loved you; even now I may confess. Pushkin, *tr. fr. Russian by* Reginald Mainwaring Hewitt. BoLoP

I loved you. I loved your face, like a wellspring. The Basket-Weaver's Love. René Char, *tr. by* Jackson Mathews. LoAs

I Loved You Once. Pushkin, *tr. fr. Russian by* Dudley Randall. AmNP (1974 ed.)

"I loves you porgy" rasps. The Other Side of Town Saturday Night. James Steele. SES

I machine-gunned tourists. Disillusionment. Claribel Alegria, *tr. by* Darwin Flakoll. AMV–80

I made a posie while the day ran by. Life. George Herbert. PoPle

I made a song and placed it far, near God. Fugato (Coda). Gad Hollander. VWA

I made my song a coat. A Coat. W. B. Yeats. CABA (1972 ed.); CMoP (1970 ed.); NoAM

I made up my mind for to change my way. The Trail to Mexico. *Unknown.* AmFP

I made up my mind in the early morn. Trail to Mexico. *Unknown.* FSW

I make a pact with you, Walt Whitman. A Pact. Ezra Pound. NoAM; NOBA; PAIC; PiAm; PSN; TAP

I make a simple assertion. Working with Tools. A. R. Ammons. NoAM

I make a trip to each clock in the apartment. Two Mornings and Two Evenings. Elizabeth Bishop. PoA

I make all the poetic pauses. Dana Naone. CDW

I make seven circles, my love. Country Girl. George Mackay Brown. SLP

I make this dirge for you Miss Mary Binning I miss you. Dirge. *Unknown, tr. by* Armand Schwerner BoWoP; RRA

I make this song about me full sadly. The Wife's Lament. *Unknown, tr. fr. Anglo-Saxon.* IPWM; WPE

I make this song sadly about myself. The Wife's Lament. *Tr. fr. Anglo-Saxon by* Willis Barnstone *and* Elene Kolb. BoWoP

I married me a wife in the month of June. Risselty-Rosselty. *Unknown.* FSW

I marvell'd why a simple child. Only Seven. Henry Sambrooke Leigh. SpRo

I mastered the easy one first. Swallowing. Harold Bond. AMV–81

I, Maximus of Gloucester, to You. Charles Olson. NoAM; NOBA

I may be dead to-morrow, uncaressed. For the Book of Love. Jules Laforgue, *tr. by* Jethro Bithell. LoAs

I may be smelly and I may be old. The River God. Stevie Smith. FaBoNo; FaBoTw (1975 ed.); PBWP

I May, I Might, I Must. Marianne Moore. FF; OBAL; PSN; SoSe

I may look raggy and queer. Scarecrow Independence. James Kirkup. FPB

I mean/ if I didn't know. Discovering. Sharon Scott. JB

I mean/ the fiddleheads have forced their babies. May 10th. Maxine W. Kumin. RFM

I mean by atoms small as small can be. The Bigness of Atoms. Margaret Cavendish, Duchess of Newcastle. SCP-2

I mean, I just slept. Charles Bukowski. *Fr.* Living. OSP

I mean, I'm a no shoes hillbilly an' home. Gracie. Faye Kicknosway. NMM

I mean to penetrate the particular. The Medium IV: Sights. Carl Rakosi. InPS

I Meant to Do My Work Today. Richard Le Gallienne. CTV

I meant to have but modest needs. Emily Dickinson. BiP; Psy

I Meant to Tell You. Sean Haldane. POL

I measured god from side to side. His Theology. Arthur J. Bull. HeHu

I meditate long. She. Manfred Winkler, *tr. by* Mary Zilzer. VWA

I meditate upon a swallow's flight. Coole Park, 1929. W. B. Yeats. ILP (1975 ed.); OAEL–2; STS

I meet Mother on the street. Poem. Lennart Bruce. POL

I meet you in an evil time. An Eclogue for Christmas. Louis MacNeice. NoAM

I member we went to the hospital that day. The Killing of the Birds. Shirley Williams. BoWoP

I mend the fyre and beikit me about. Robert Henryson. *Fr.* The Testament of Cresseid. EBEV

I Met a Genius. Charles Bukowski. OSP

I met a girl from Derrygrave. A New Song. Seamus Heaney. FaBoTw (1975 ed.)

I met a little elf-man, once. The Little Elf. John Kendrick Bangs. CTV; PCOP

I met a little girl in Knoxville. Knoxville Girl. *Unknown.* FSW

I met a man in an onion bed. The Man in the Onion Bed. John Ciardi. SO

I met a seer. The Book of Wisdom. Stephen Crane. *Fr.* The Black Riders. HoPM (1975 ed.)

I met a traveller from an antique land. Ozymandias Revisited. Morris Bishop. PAIC; SpRo

I met a traveller from an antique land. Ozymandias. Shelley. BiP; CABA (1972 ed.); DL; Epi; FaPo; FaPoR; FF; HAP; HeIP; HoPM (1975 ed.); ILP (1975 ed.); InPK; IP; IPWM; LFH; MBPR; NIL; NOBE; OAEL–2; OBP; PAIC; PoIA; PoPle; PPoD; SFF; SoSe; SpRo; WeW

I met an adolescent kitten on Lexington Ave. Eastside Chick with Drive. Albert Spector. CTBA

I met an elf-man in the woods. How to Treat Elves. Morris Bishop. OBAL

I met an old man near a darkened house. A Kind of Good-bye. Theodore Spencer. IP

I met ayont the cairney. Empty Vessel. "Hugh MacDiarmid." FaBoTw (1975 ed.); MS; SLP

I met her as a blossom on a stem. The Dream. Theodore Roethke. STS; UnPo (1976 ed.)

I met him in Venezuela. Venezuela. *Unknown.* FSW

I met in Mesilla. Edward Dorn. *Fr.* Gunslinger. NoAM

I met Louisa in the shade. Louisa. Wordsworth. GBL

I met Murder on the way. Shelley. *Fr.* The Mask of Anarchy. OBP

I met Musette/ In the water-closet. Vague Lyric by G. M. Max Beerbohm. FaBoEE

I met my preacher the other day. Scandalize My Name. *Unknown.* FSW

I met the Bishop on the road. Crazy Jane Talks with the Bishop. W. B. Yeats. AnMo; BoLoP; CABA (972 ed.); CMoP (1970 ed.); EBEV; ExPo (1973 ed.); ILP (1975 ed.); InPK; NIL; NoAM; OAEL–2; PoIA; PPP; STS; TT

I met the Love-Talker one eve in the glen. The Love-Talker. "Ethna Carbery." PFIr; PoTa; WPE

I met with the gnat. The Confession. Gary Lawless. FAF

I might—unhappy word—oh me, I might. Astrophel and Stella, XXXIII. Sir Philip Sidney. OAEL–1

I mind as 'ow the night afore that show. The Chances. Wilfred Owen. OxBTC

I Minded God, *with music.* Henry Ainsworth. AH

I miss the peace and quiet of Chicago. Poem after Apollinaire. Ira Sadoff. AmPA

I Missed His Book, but I Read His Name. John Updike. OBAL

I mock thee not, tho' I by thee am mocked. To Flaxman. Blake. FaBoEE

I move among my pots and pans. Trimming the Sails. Vassar Miller. NMM

I move each fall. Mover. James L. White. HeS

I move on feeling and have learned to distrust those who don't. Poem of Angela Yvonne Davis. Nikki Giovanni. PoBA

I move sharp, not too fancy or nice. The Trees: A Convict Monologue. Thomas W. Shapcott. FPA; GAS

I move the curtain back. After I Have Voted. Laura Jensen. AmPA

I Move the Meeting Be Adjourned. Nicanor Parra, *tr. fr. Spanish by* Miller Williams. *Fr.* Manifesto. HoPM (1975 ed.)

I Move to Random Consolations. William Heyen. AmPA

I moved like a double agent among the big concepts. England's Difficulty. Seamus Heaney. CIP

I moved to the window to wait for somebody. A Suicide. Tom Kryss. NeAC

I murder hate by field or flood. Burns. OBP

I Muriel stood at the altar-table. Don Baty, the Draft Resister. Muriel Rukeyser. NNaP

I must/ Not trust. Anacreontic. Robert Herrick. CaPo

I Must Ask. James E. Warren, Jr. AATT

I must be mad, or very tired. Meeting-House Hill. Amy Lowell. PSN; SBG

I Must Come to Terms with Florida. William E. Taylor. CSP

I must complain, yet doe enjoy my love. Thomas Campion. AAS

"I must eat an apple," said Link. An Apple a Day. Lee Blair. TDH

I must explain why it is that at night, in my own house. Still Life. Reed Whittemore. ConAP; PoUp

I must find a slut tonight. What a Way to Lose the War. Luis Omar Salinas. SA

I must go back to winter. Two Decisions. Vernon Watkins. OxBTC

I must go down to the seas again, to the lonely sea and the sky. Sea-Fever. John Masefield. CTV; FaPoR; ILP (1975 ed.); IPWM; OxBTC; PPM; RhR; SFF

I must go. I must gather my few things. Listening to Her. Natan Zach, *tr. by* Laya Firestone. VWA

I Must Go Walk the Wood So Wild. *Unknown.* ILP (1975 ed.)

I must have passed the crest a while ago. The Long Hill. Sara Teasdale. PPM

I must hide him in my innermost veins. Totem. Léopold Sédar Senghor, *tr. by* Gerald Moore *and* Ulli Beier. BuTh

I must lie down with them all soon and sleep. Thomas Kinsella. *Fr.* Nightwalker. BIrV

I must not grieve my love, whose eyes would read. Sonnet. Samuel Daniel. *Fr.* To Delia. LoAs; PoPle

I must not think of thee; and, tired yet strong. Renouncement. Alice Meynell. BoLoP; NOBE; WPE

I must remember to dismiss. Nature Study, after Dufy. Helen Bevington. CSP

I must tell you. Young Sycamore. William Carlos Williams. TAP

I must wait for a stranger to knock on my door. Elegy. David Ignatow. NNaP

I myself saw furious with blood. Aeneas at Washington. Allen Tate. NoAM; NOBA; PiAm; WasP

I nail Picasso's girl with a mirror. Notes from an Analyst's Couch. Anita Endrezze Probst. CDW

I, named by the tribe, am no rabbi. Axioms. Gad Hollander. VWA

I Need Not Go. Thomas Hardy. NOBE; OxBTC

I need only fall asleep/ to return. Ana Blandiana, *tr. fr. Rumanian by* Stavros Deligiorgis. BoWoP

I ne'er was struck before that hour. First Love. John Clare. BoLoP; GBL; HAP

I never believed that in my broken life. Ts'ai Yen, *tr. fr. Chinese by* Kenneth Rexroth *and* Lin Chung. *Fr.* 18 Verses Sung to a Tatar Reed Whistle. BoWoP

I never cared for Life: Life cared for me. Thomas Hardy. FaBoEE

I never cast a flower away. Partings. Maria Jane Jewsbury. OxBChV

I never drank of Aganippe well. Astrophel and Stella, LXXIV. Sir Philip Sidney. CABA (1972 ed.); HeIP

I never felt so much. A Birthday. Edwin Muir. LoAs; MS

I never gave a lock of hair away. Sonnets from the Portuguese, XVIII. Elizabeth Barrett Browning. HAP; VPC

I never had a barrel of money. Poor Man Blues. *Unknown.* FSW

I never hear the word "escape." Emily Dickinson. CMoP (1970 ed.); NOBA

I never heard a building scream. Demolition. Victor Borsa. PoW

I never learned the names. Santa Caterina. Myra Glazer Schotz. VWA

I never let you come to the games. I never. Basketball. Stephen Vincent. LiSp; NeAC

I never look at himself. Mirror Images. Laurel Speer. AMV-80

I never look upon the sea. Aunt Zillah Speaks. Herbert Palmer. FaBoTw (1975 ed.)

I never lost as much but twice. Emily Dickinson. AmVN; NOBA; PiAm; TAP

I never loved a dear gazelle. Tèma con Variazióni. "Lewis Carroll." FaBoNo; SpRo

"I never nursed a dear gazelle." Thomas Moore. *Fr.* Lalla Rookh. SpRo

I never played for you. You'd have thrown. For the Death of Vince Lombardi. James Dickey. LiSp

I never rear'd a young gazelle. 'Twas Ever Thus. Henry Sambrooke Leigh. FaBoCo; SpRo

I never saw/ a ghost on stilts. Lilian Moore. OSF

I Never Saw a Man in a Negligee. Alta. GP

I never saw a moor. Emily Dickinson. CTV; HeIP; LCL; PCOP; PIM; TAP

I never saw a purple cow. The Purple Cow. Gelett Burgess. CTV; FaBoCo; FaBoNo; OBAL; PCOP

I never saw a wild thing. Self-Pity. D. H. Lawrence. BoAnP; OxBTC

I never saw any point. Alan Dugan. GP

I never saw my father's father's face. Grandfather Yoneh. Emily Borenstein. AMV-81

I never saw that you did painting need. Sonnets, LXXXIII. Shakespeare. STS

I never saw the man whom you describe. The Foster-Mother's Tale. Samuel Taylor Coleridge. MBPR

I Never Saw the Train. Jean Roberts. AMV-80

I never saw you, madam, lay apart. Earl of Surrey. AAS; LoAs

I never shall love the snow again. Robert Bridges. CMoP (1970 ed.)

I never take a cup of tea. The Oceans of Dr. Johnson. Helen Bevington. CSP

I never wake up well. Collaborations. Cathleen Quirk. MMD

I never wanted to be a star. On Earth. Forugh Farrokhzad, *tr. by* Girdhard Tikku. BoWoP

I Never Will Marry. *Unknown.* FSW

I never would 'ave done it if I'd known what it would be. Mules. C. Fox-Smith. BoAnP

I never would have remembered your name. Jimmy Bruder on Quincey Street. Carol Artman Montgomery. AMV-81

I-93. Marie Harris. *Fr.* Interstate. AAN

I no longer want to meet. For a Young South Dakota Man. Freya Manfred. TAT

I, now at Carthage. He, shot dead at Rome. Vale from Carthage. Peter Viereck. CoPAm; SS

I now will throw myself down. A Dialogue. David Ignatow. NNap

I, Oedipus, the club-foot, made to stumble. Oedipus. Edwin Muir. CMoP (1970 ed.)

I offer my back to the silken net. An Allegory. David Ignatow. VGW

I offer wrong to my beloved saint. Fulke Greville. *Fr.* Caelica. PAIC

I offer you the chance to forgive your wounds. Songs from the Maker of Totems. Duane Niatum. VW

I often dream of Auschwitz now. Dreams of Auschwitz. Boris Slutsky, *tr. by* Daniel Weissbort. VWA

I often Pause and Wonder. *Unknown.* CTV

I often sit and wish that I. A Kite. Frank Dempster Sherman. CTV

I often wander on the beach. The Old Swimmer. Christopher Morley. LiSp

I Often Want to Let My Lines Go. Leib Neidus, *tr. fr. Yiddish by* Ruth Whitman. VWA

I on my horse, and Love on me, doth try. Astrophel and Stella, XLIX Sir Philip Sidney. LFH; OAEL-1

I once believed a single line. For E. J. P. Leonard Cohen. NoAM

I once broke evening bread with the brown-faced, white-smiled Prince of Siam. Words of Oblivion and Peace. Gabriel Preil, *tr. fr.* Robert Friend. VWA

I once did an hour-long TV show reading. Osip Mandelshtam. Irving Layton. NeAC

I once did court a damsel most beautiful and bright. A Lover's Lament. *Unknown.* AmFP

I once did know a Turkish man.   Ben Allah Achmet; or, the Fatal
Tum.   W. S. Gilbert.   VLP

I once dressed up and went to town.   Devilish Mary.   *Unknown.*
FSW

I once had a girl.   Norwegian Wood.   John Lennon *and* Paul
McCartney.   OBP

I once had a sweet little doll, dears.   The Lost [*or* Little] Doll.
Charles Kingsley.   *Fr.* The Water Babies.   ECBV; OxBChV

I once knew a fellow named Arthur McBride.   Arthur McBride.
*Unknown.*   GBP; PeBB

I once knew a lass and I loved her to [*or* I've oft heard her] tell.
So I Let Her Go.   *Unknown.*   AmFP

I once knew a little girl, a charming beauty bright.   The Rejected
Lover.   *Unknown.*   AmFP

I once knowed an ole Sexion Boss but he done been laid low.
The Old Section Boss.   *Unknown.*   BPo

I once lov'd a boy, and a bonny, bonny boy.   *Unknown.*   WTO

I Once Loved a Young Man.   *Unknown.*   AmFP

I once loved a young man as dear as my life.   I'm Going to
Georgia.   *Unknown.*   AmFP

I once may see when yeares shall wreck my wrong.   Samuel
Daniel.   *Fr.* To Delia.   AAS

I once spent an evening in a village.   The Man Upright.   Thomas
MacDonagh.   BIrV

I once was a Pirate what sailed the 'igh seas.   Cat Morgan
Introduces Himself.   T. S. Eliot.   NOBL

I once was a seaman stout and bold.   Jolly Soldier.   *Unknown.*
AmFP; OFD

I once was a tool of oppression.   The Hayseed.   Arthur L.
Kellog.   FSW

I once was happy, when, while yet a child.   Charlotte Smith.   *Fr.*
Beachy Head.   WPE

I once wrote a letter as follows.   The Invoice.   Robert Creeley.
VGW

I Only Am Escaped Alone to Tell Thee.   Howard Nemerov.
HeIP; NoAM

I only knew her as a spouse.   At Flock Mass.   F. R. Higgins.
PFIr

I only knew one poet in my life.   How It Strikes a Contemporary.
Robert Browning.   OAEL-2; VLP

I only know that you may lie.   Rupert Brooke.   *Fr.* The Old
Vicarage of Grantchester.   PES

I open an anthology.   On the Dates of Poets.   Michael L.
Johnson.   AMV-80

I open the door and walk in.   Pop.   David McFadden.   NeAC

I opened my door to this nutty witch. I've been suicidal.   After
Reading Sylvia Plath.   Alta.   IHMS

I opened my eyes at the foot of a grey mountain.   Gavin Bantock.
*Fr.* Ichor.   TwMBP

"I order you to operate. I was not made to suffer."   So Going
around Cities.   Ted Berrigan.   FiCh

I ordered this, this clean wood box.   The Arrival of the Bee Box.
Sylvia Plath.   PSN; TCP

I Ovid poet of my wantonnesse.   Ovid, *tr. by* Christopher
Marlowe.   Amores, II, 1.   OBVE

I own certain acre-scraps of woodland, scattered.   Farmer's Point
of View.   Alan Brownjohn.   BuTh

I own, the match, you recommend.   To a Friend, Who
Recommended a Wife to Him.   *Unknown.*   PiAm

I owned a slope full of stones.   The Stones.   Wendell Berry.   GP

I pace the sounding sea-beach and behold.   Milton.   Longfellow.
ILP (1975 ed.); LFH; TAP

I pack the mirrors again and again.   Invitation of the Mirrors.
Tom McKeown.   AMV-81

I painted a picture—green sky—and showed it to my mother.
Accomplishments.   Cynthia MacDonald.   GP

I painted her a gushing thing.   My Fancy.   "Lewis Carroll."
FaBoCo

I painted my eyes wtih black antimony.   Love Song.   *Tr. fr.
Bagirmi by* H. Gaden.   BoWoP

I parted from my life last night.   On the Death of His Wife.
Muireadach O'Dalaigh, *tr. by* Frank O'Connor.   BIrV; CIP

I pass your home in a slow vermilion dawn.   Confusion.
Kenneth Rexroth.   MPA

I passed along the water's edge below the humid trees.   The
Indian upon God.   W. B. Yeats.   IPWM

I passed between the bell and the glass.   49th and 5th, December
13.   Josephine Jacobsen.   NYP

I passed by the beach.   Yamabe no Akahito, *tr. fr. Japanese by*
Kenneth Rexroth.   HoPM (1975 ed.)

I peeled bits of straw and I got switches too.   Song.   John Clare.
VLP

I picked some flowered weeds.   A Visit to My Father-in-Law on
Memorial Day.   Peggy Ruse.   NPW

I picked up a leaf.   Les Etiquettes Jaunes.   Frank O'Hara.
CAPP

I picked up six black stones on the beach today.   Runes.
Emmett Jarrett.   VoA

I picture it as coming.   Divorce.   Kate Jennings.   AMV-80

I pitched my day's leazings in Crimmercrock Lane.   The Dark-
Eyed Gentleman.   Thomas Hardy.   UnPo (1976 ed.); VLP

I pitied one whose tattered dress.   The Vesture of the Soul.
"Æ."   PFIr

I place myself at the edge of thy Grace.   *Tr. from Gaelic by*
Douglas Hyde.   WTO

I place these numbed wrists to the pane.   Nightmare Begins
Responsibility.   Michael S. Harper.   TAP

I placed a jar in Tennessee.   Anecdote of the Jar.   Wallace
Stevens.   CMoP (1970 ed.); ExPo (1973 ed.); HoPM (1975
ed.); ILP (1975 ed.); InPK; NIL; NoAM; NOBA; PoA; PPP;
TAP; TT; UnPo (1976 ed.)

I planned to have a border of lavender.   Paul Goodman.   VGW

"I play a spade.—Such strange new faces."   Arrivals at a
Watering-Place.   Winthrop Mackworth Praed.   NOBL

"I play for seasons; not eternities!"   Modern Love, XIII.   George
Meredith.   PFD; VPC

I play it cool.   Motto.   Langston Hughes.   ILP (1975 ed.); PoBA

I play your furies back to me at night.   High Fidelity.   Thom
Gunn.   PoA

I played with you 'mid cowslips blowing.   Love and Age.
Thomas Love Peacock.   PoPle; PPM

I pledge allegiance to the flag.   The Pledge to the Flag.   Francis
Bellamy.   BLSH

I pledge myself through thick and thin.   Tory Pledges.   Thomas
Moore.   FaBoCo; OBSV

I plucked my soul out of its secret place.   I Know My Soul.
Claude McKay.   BPo

I plucked pink blossoms from mine apple-tree.   An Apple
Gathering.   Christina Rossetti.   OLR

I polish, cook, or clean my nest.   Bruce Holsapple.   FAF

I pondered the cold simplicity.   Rejoinder.   Albert De Pietro.
AATT

I praise a patron high-hearted in strife.   In Praise of Owain
Gwynedd.   Cynddelw Brydydd Mawr, *tr. by* Joseph P.
Clancy.   OBW

I praise Saint Everyman, his house and home.   Here Together
Met.   Louis Johnson.   ATNZ

I praise the disk of the rising sun.   Vidya, *tr. by* Daniel H. H.
Ingalls.   *Fr.* The Sun.   PBWP

I praise those ancient Chinamen.   Hymnus ad Patrem Sinensis.
Philip Whalen.   VoA

I pray for a child-like heart.   A Prayer of Love.   *Unknown.*   CTV

I pray that the great world's flowering stay as it is. The Gardener to His God. Mona Van Duyn. UnPo (1976 ed.); UsP; WPE

I pray thee leave, love me no more. To His Coy Love. Michael Drayton. LoAs

I pray thee Nymph Penaeis stay, I chase not as a fo. Ovid, *tr.* by Arthur Golding. *Fr.* Metamorphoses, I. OBVE

I pray you all give your audience. Everyman. *Unknown.* OAEL-1

I pray you all with one thought. Amend Me. *Unknown.* OxBM

"I pray you, cum kiss me." My Little Pretty Mopsy. *Unknown.* OxBM

I pray you, M, to me be trew. Letter to "M." *Unknown.* OxBM

I press not to the quire, nor dare I greet. To My Worthy Friend Master George Sandys, on His Translation of the Psalms. Thomas Carew. CaPo

I Promise Nothing. A. E. Housman. PPP

I promise to make you more alive than you've ever been. Ordeal. Nina Cassian, *tr.* by Michael Imply *and* Brian Swann. PBWP

I promised I would but I can't. Alta. MMD

I promised once if I got hold of. Written in a Copy of Swift's Poems, for Wayne Burns. James Wright. NOBA

I promised to look out for the child. The Delivery. Hollis Summers. CoPAm

I pull out of the depths of the earth. Etnairis Rivera, *tr. fr. Spanish* by Julio Marzán. InW

I put a lot of stock in the old. Old Age. Rolf Jacobsen, *tr.* by Robert Bly. EC

I put my hand all in her own. Gently Johnny, My Jingalo *Unknown.* FSW

I Put My Hand on His Head. Ted Kooser. HeS

I put my hat upon my head. Ballad. Samuel Johnson. NOBL

I put my nickel. Midnight Raffle. Langston Hughes. PiAm

I put my sweatshirt/ on backwards this morning. Waking Up. J. Charles Green. DNGG

I Put My Two fingers, Pound and Whitman, into a Wall Socket. David Bristol. PoUp

I put my work aside and look. 5:30. Gray Jacobik. PoUp

I Put the Telephone Back on Its Receiver. Morty Sklar. AcAn

I quarrelled with kings till the Sabbath. Song of the Sabbath. Kadia Molodowsky, *tr.* by Jean Valentine. PBWP

I quarrelled with my brother. The Quarrel. Eleanor Farjeon. FPB

I quit after the tenth game of Jacks. Turning. Bonnie Gordon. PoUp

I quit my job this morning. Employed. James Bertolino. HeS

I. R. A. Man Revisits His Hideout, The. Catherine O'Neill. PoUp

I raced to the bluff to drown in the sea. Tarred Gull. Elisavietta Ritchie. AATT

I, Rainey Betha, 22. Plaint. Charles Henri Ford. EAS

I raise the curtains and go out. Alone. Chu Shu-Chen, *tr.* by Kenneth Rexroth. BoWoP

I raised a noble falcon. The Falcon. The Knight of Kürenberg, *tr.* by Margarete Münsterberg. LoAs

I ran along the yellow sand. Pete at the Seashore. Don Marquis. GDP

I ran from you to danger. Round Trip to Chicago. Martha Shelley. WBN

I ran onto Mehitabel again. The Old Trouper. Don Marquis. *Fr.* Archy and Mehitabel. FaBoCo

I ran until lips tripped over. Escape. Ilya Rubin, *tr.* by Linda Zisquit. VWA

I ran upon life unknowing, without or science or art. Tennyson. FaBoEE

I rasp like a sick dog. Theodore Roethke. POL

I Read a Tight-fisted Poem Once. Nancy Woods. RFM

I read about the Blaskets and Dunquin. J. M. Synge. FaBoEE

I read in the news, the President said. Hallelujah I'm a Bum. Barbara Dane *and* Irwin Silber. FSW

I read my sentence—steadily. Emily Dickinson. NoAM

I read or write, I teach or wonder what is truth. Apologia pro Vita Sua. Sedulius Scottus, *tr. by* Helen Waddell. BIrV

I read the news today, oh boy. A Day in the Life. John Lennon *and* Paul McCartney. PPoe; NIL; WIF

I read with him at Hopkins, substituting. Robert Lowell. Richard O'Connell. AMV-81

I read your testimony and I thought. John Beecher. *Fr.* To Alexander Meiklejohn. GOA

I really do not like that cat. What Could It Be? William Cole. BoAnP

"I really take it very kind." Domestic Asides; or, Truth in Parentheses. Thomas Hood. BBL

I reason, earth is short. Emily Dickinson. LFH; TAP

I reckon—when I count at all. Emily Dickinson. PiAm

I recognized you because when I saw the print. Poetry. Juan Ramón Jiménez. LoAs; OLR

I Remember. Mae Jackson. CNA; PoBA

I Remember. Stevie Smith. BoLoP; BoWoP; InPK

I remember a dim evening in Kishinyov. A Woman from the Book of Genesis. Dovid Knut, *tr.* by John Glad. VWA

I remember a house where all were good. The Valley of Elwy. Gerard Manley Hopkins. LoAs

I remember at times. Scholar II. Seamus Deane. CIP

I remember back in hi school. The Art of Enforced Deprivation. Alta. GP; MMD

I remember gestures of infants. To Drink. Gabriela Mistral, *tr.* by Gunda Kaiser. NU

I remember God as an eccentric millionaire. Quite Apart from the Holy Ghost. Adrian Mitchell. OBSV

I remember how, long ago, I found. Crystals like Blood. "Hugh MacDiarmid." HAP; InPS

I Remember How She Sang. Rob Penny. CNA; PoBA

I Remember, I Remember. Thomas Hood. FaPoR; NOBE

I Remember, I Remember. Philip Larkin. NOBL

I remember Longwood. Blind Adolphus. Angela McCabe. AmPA

I remember my father. To My Son, Not Yet Born. William Virgil Davis. AMV-81

I remember my mother, the day that we met. For the Crèche. G. K. Chesterton. *Fr.* Songs of Education. FaBoCo

I remember not knowing. Puberty. Jon Wallace. AMV-80

I remember one September. Billy Lyons and Stack O'Lee. *Unknown.* BluL

I remember one September. Mighty Day. *Unknown.* FSW

I remember partly. Southwest Passage. Dudley Fitts. PoA

I remember reading as a boy, Giotto. The Perfect Symbol. Louis Johnson. ATNZ

I remember rooms that have had their part. Rooms. Charlotte Mew. PBWP

I remember that before. Flying Letters. Zerubavel Gilead, *tr.* by Dorothea Krook. VWA

I remember the August afternoon. August Afternoon. Nancy Remaly. CTBA

I remember the Chillicothe ball players. Hits and Runs. Carl Sandburg. SPo

I remember the day I arrived. Doubting. Louis Simpson. NNaP

I remember the day when I learned to whistle. When I Learned to Whistle. Gordon Lea. AKE

I remember the dread with which I at a quarter past four. False Security. John Betjeman. BBGO; CMoP (1970 ed.); LP

I remember the evening. The Swarming Bees. James Laughlin. VGW

I remember the forehead born. Uncle. Philip Levine. NNaP

I remember the neckcurls, limp and damp as tendrils. Elegy for Jane. Theodore Roethke. BiP; CNW; CoPAm; FF; HAP; ILP (1975 ed.); InPK; InPS; IPWM; LFH; PAIC; PPM; PPoe; PSN; RRA; SoS; STS; TAP; TCP; VoPo; WIF

I remember the night. Somebody Call. Carolyn M. Rodgers. JB

I remember the old joke. The Cliff. David Rowbotham. CAAP

I remember the Roman Emperor, one of the cruellest of them. Exeat. Stevie Smith. NoAM

I remember the schoolgirl under the bus. Large Mercies. D. J. Enright. HeHu

I remember the United States of America. A Box Comes Home. John Ciardi. CoPAm

I remember to this day. Me and You and a Dog Named Boo. Kent LaVoie. PoRo

I remember Wednesday was the day. Two Lean Cats. Myron O'Higgins. PoBA

I remember when a Sunday friend and I. Letter to My Mother. Anita Skeen. IHMS

I remember you as you were that final autumn. Pablo Neruda, tr. fr. Spanish by Robert Bly. LoAs

I remember you in young peaches like jade. Elegy for the Wife of a Friend. Yü Hsüan-chi, tr. by Geoffrey Waters. BoWoP

I remember zoot-suited pimps. 6th and Walnut Street. Rubee Dreher Moxley. NPW

I remembered today. Phil. Ted Kooser. AMV-81

I resemble everyone. Self-Portrait. A. K. Ramanujan. FoP

I reside at Table Mountain and my name is Truthful James. The Society upon the Stanislaus [or Plain Language from Truthful James]. Bret Harte. BPAW; FaBoCo; OBAL

I resist/ my banker. Fire Island Poem. Diane Wakoski. BiP

I resist anything better than my own diversity. Walt Whitman. Fr. Song of Myself, XVI-XVII. UsP

I return from a past that will never enter itself into a book. Back from London. David Meltzer. CPA

I returned, and saw under the sun. Bible, O.T. Ecclesiastes, IX: 11-12. Prf

I Ride an Old Paint. Unknown. AmFP; FSW; RDB

I ride into town. The Famous Outlaw Stops in for a Drink. David James. AMV-81

I ride through Queens. An Invitation to Madison County. Jay Wright. PoBA

I rinse pine soap from my father. Sharktooth Creek. Peter Nelson. PHC

I rip off/ bobtail. Skinning a Rabbit. Norbert Krapf. HeS

I rise at 2 a.m. these mornings, to. The Feral Pioneers. Ishmael Reed. PoBA; UnPo (1976 ed.);

I rise from the sun-deck. Cook-out. Dan Masterson. CoPAm

I rise, I rise I who [or whose tread] makes the earth to rumble. The Rising of the Buffalo Men. Unknown. ANTL; SFF

I rise in the dawn, and I kneel and blow. The Song of the Old Mother. W. B. Yeats. IPWM; PFIr

I rise up from rest. Morning Prayer. Aua, tr. fr. Eskimo. WTO

I rob you gently. Drumming Lightly. Leonard Kubo. PHC

I rode one evening with Count Maddalo. Julian and Maddalo. Shelley. MBPR; OAEL-2, abr.

I Rode Southern, I Rode L. & N. Unknown. AmFP

I rode till I reached the House of Wealth. Rest Only in the Grave. James Clarence Mangan. BIrV

I rode to church last Sunday. My Love She Passed Me By. Unknown. AmFP

I rode with my mother and father. Triad. Donald Foster. AMV-80

I rose at night, and visited. The Unborn. Thomas Hardy. CMoP (1970 ed.)

I rose in joy at the pinking sheared sky. Shattered Sabbath. Roberta B. Goldstein. AMV-81

I rose to catch the early morning. Slanted World. Rhyll McMaster. FPA

I rub my head and find a turtle shell. The Neo-Classical Urn. Robert Lowell. STS

I rub the one bullet. Snake Dance. Lyn Lifshin. FAF; RiTi

I sagh Him with flesh al bi-spred: He cam from Est. See I saw him with flesh all be-spread. . .

I said/ Come up, you breaching thing. The Breaching Muse. Liam O'Mahony. IPM

I said:/ Now will the poets sing. Scottsboro, Too, Is Worth Its Song. Countee Cullen. ILP (1975 ed.); PoBA

I said, Ah! what shall I write? A, a, a, Domine Deus. David Jones. FaBoTw (1975 ed.)

I said, I like our bodies clean. Friday Night after Bathing. Stephen Levy. VWA

I said I splendidly loved you; it's not true. Sonnet. Rupert Brooke. BuTh

I said I will find what is lowly. Still. A. R. Ammons. TT; UsP

I said I'd get her a towel and ran. Girls. Kenneth Rosen. AmPA

I said, "Please send a taxi cab." Taxi Crab. Shel Silverstein. OSF

I said: "The moon is obviously a boat." Nocturnal Landscape. Malcolm Cowley. PoA

I said—Then, dearest, since 'tis so. The Last Ride Together. Robert Browning. BoLoP; TT; UnPo (1976 ed.); VLP

I said, "This horse, sir, will you shoe?" Logical English. Unknown. ECBV

I said to Heart, "How goes it?" Heart replied. The False Heart. Hilaire Belloc. FaBoEE

I Said to Love. Thomas Hardy. GBL; NoAM

I said to my baby. Same in Blues. Langston Hughes. Fr. Lenox Avenue Mural. InPS; WIF

I salute God, asylum's gift. Poem on His Death-Bed. Cynddelw Brydydd Mawr, tr. by Joseph P. Clancy. OBW

I salute the most high lord. The Poet's Loves. Hywel ab Owain Gwynedd, tr. by Gwyn Williams. OBW

I sang a canto in a canton. Country Words. Wallace Stevens. STS

I sat all morning in the college sick bay. Mid-Term Break. Seamus Heaney. NCSH

I sat at the desk for a while fooling with my hair. The Defeated. Linda Gregg. PCho

I sat before my glass one day. The Other Side of a Mirror. Mary Elizabeth Coleridge. BoWoP

I sat behind the glowing grate, fresh heaped. A Meditation on Rhode Island Coal. Bryant. TAP

I sat by a stream in a. Classic. A. R. Ammons. NOBA

I sat by the granite pillar, and sunlight fell. Commemoration. Sir Henry Newbolt. FaBoTw (1975 ed.)

I sat in the cold limbs of a tree. The Man in the Tree. Mark Strand. EAS

I sat me weary on a pillar's base. James Thomson ("B. V."). The City of Dreadful Night, XX. LP

I sat next [to] the duchess at tea. Limerick. Unknown. NIL; SoSe

I sat on the Dogana's steps. Cantos, III. Ezra Pound. Epi; TAP

I sat wi' my love, and I drank wi' my love. Unknown. GBP

I sat with John Brown. That night moonlight framed. Narrative. Russell Atkins. PoBA

I sat with Love upon a woodside well.   Willowwood.   Dante
Gabriel Rossetti.   The House of Life, XLIX-LII.   OAEL-2;
VLP

I sate beside the steersman then, and gazing.   The Revolt of
Islam, VIII.   Shelley.   MBPR

I saw/ a specialist a cook.   To the Heart.   Tadeusz Rozewicz, tr.
by Victor Contoski.   POL

I Saw a Chapel All of Gold.   Blake.   AnMo; CABA (1972 ed.);
LAuP; MBPR; TT

I saw a dead man's finer part.   His Immortality.   Thomas Hardy.
CMoP (1970 ed.); PoPle

I saw a donkey.   The Donkey.   Gertrude Hinde.   ECBV

I saw a doo flee our the dam.   *Unknown.*   GBP

I saw a famous man eating soup.   Soup.   Carl Sandburg.   AKE;
NOBA; TH

I Saw a Fish Pond.   *Unknown.*   ECBV; GBP; NOBL

I saw a fly within a bead.   The Amber Bead.   Robert Herrick.
CaPo

I saw a frieze on whitest marble drawn.   Ecstasy.   W. J. Turner.
EcS

I saw a gardener with a watering can.   The Progress of Poetry.
"Christopher Caudwell."   OxBTC

I saw a gnome.   Gnome.   Harry Behn.   IWK

I saw a hawk devour a screaming bird.   Hawk Is a Woman.
Hildegarde Flanner.   WPE

I saw a hunchback climb over a hill.   The Hunchback.   John
Peale Bishop.   PoA

I Saw a Jolly Hunter.   Charles Causley.   BoAnP; LP

I saw a lang worm snoove throu the space atween twa/ stanes.
Brither Worm.   Robert Garioch.   MS

I saw a little tailor sitting stitch, stitch, stitching.   Tailor.
Eleanor Farjeon.   OxBChV

I saw a maid sit on a bank.   *See* I sawe a mayd. . .

I Saw a Man [Pursuing the Horizon].   Stephen Crane.   The Black
Riders, XXIV.   FF; HoPM (1975 ed.); MAT; NOBA;
PBMP; PCOP; PiAm; SFF; TT

I saw a mouth jeering.   Gargoyle.   Carl Sandburg.   NoAM;
NOBA

I Saw a Peacock with a Fiery Tail.   *Unknown.*   GBP; OBP; PoPle
(Ambiguous Lines, *longer version.*)   ECBV

I saw a querulous old man, the tobacconist of Eighth Street.   The
Tobacconist of Eighth Street.   Richard Eberhart.   NYP

I saw a ship a-sailing.   Mother Goose.   ECBV; MG

I saw a ship a-sailing, a-sailing, a-sailing.   An Old Song Re-sung.
John Masefield.   ECBV; RhR

I saw a ship of martial build.   The Berg.   Herman Melville.
AmVN; InPK; LFH; NOBA; PiAm; TAP

I Saw a Stable.   Mary Elizabeth Coleridge.   PChr
(Salus Mundi.)   BoReV

I saw a staring virgin stand.   Two Songs from a Play, I.   W. B.
Yeats.   *Fr.* The Resurrection.   CABA (1972 ed.); CMoP
(1970 ed.); ExPo (1973 ed.); FaBoTw (1975 ed.); HAP; ILP
(1975 ed.); NIL; NOBE; OAEL-2; OBP; PPoe; PPP

I saw a tree that was greater than all the others.   Edith Södergran,
tr. fr. Swedish by Jaakko A. Ahokas.   PBWP

I saw a t.v. commercial, yesterday.   T.V. Commercial No. 073.
Jesús Papoleto Meléndez.   NW

I saw a vision yesternight.   To the State of Love; or, The Senses'
Festival.   John Cleveland.   PeD; SCP-2

I saw a vulture in the sky.   Life and Death.   W. J. Turner.
FaBoTw (1975 ed.)

I saw a young deer standing.   Moment.   Hildegarde Flanner.
WPW

I saw a young snake glide.   Snake.   Theodore Roethke.   AKE;
ECBV; MPA; NOBA; RFM

I saw a youth and maiden on a lonely city street.   Take Back
Your Gold.   Louis W. Pritzkow.   FSN

I saw about her spotless wrist.   Upon a Black Twist, Rounding
the Arm of the Countess of Carlisle.   Robert Herrick.   CaPo

I saw again in a dream the other night.   Two Girls.   Howard
Nemerov.   AnMo

I saw an aged beggar in my walk.   The Old Cumberland Beggar.
Wordsworth.   MBPR

I Saw an Army.   George Abbe.   FAF

I saw an old black man walk down the road.   Black Soul of the
Land.   Lance Jeffers.   FB

I saw each soul as light, each single body.   Night of Souls.   Ann
Stanford.   WPE

I saw Esau sawing wood.   *Unknown.*   FaBoNo

I saw Eternity the other night.   The World.   Henry Vaughan.
BoReV; CABA (1972 ed.); EBEV; HAP; HeIP; ILP (1975
ed.); ILwL; LFH; MetP; NOBE; OAEL-1; OBP; PPoe; PPP;
SCP-1

I saw fair Chloris walk alone.   On Chloris Walking in the Snow.
William Strode.   ILP (1975 ed.); NOBE; OAEL-1; SCP-2

I saw five birds all in a cage.   Riddle.   *Unknown.*   GBP

I Saw from the Beach.   Thomas Moore.   PFIr

I saw God! Do You doubt it?   What Tomas Said in a Pub.
James Stephens.   CMoP (1970 ed.); NoAM

I saw her amid the dunghill debris.   Tinker's Wife.   Patrick
Kavanagh.   CIP; NoAM

I saw her crop a rose.   Where She Told Her Love.   John Clare.
VLP

I saw her first in gleams.   The Spirit's Odyssey.   M.
Krishnamurti.   PeD

I saw her once, one little while, and then no more.   And Then No
More.   Friedrich Rückert, tr. by James Clarence Mangan.
BIrV

I saw him brought into Emergency.   Empty Holds a Question.
Pat Folk.   NowV

I saw him first lost in the lion cages.   Prisoners.   Eavan Boland.
IPM

I saw him forging link by link his chain.   The Slave.   Jones Very.
TAP

I saw him in Hollywood yesterday and I asked.   Dick Powell.
Ronald Koertge.   CPA; PoW

I saw him in the Airstrip Gardens.   Betjeman, 1984.   Charles
Causley.   FaBoCo; NOBL; OxBTC

I saw him once before.   The Last Leaf.   Oliver Wendell Holmes.
AmVN; PiAm; VoPo

I saw him steal the light away.   God's Education.   Thomas
Hardy.   OBP

I saw [or sagh] him with flesh all be-spread: He came from East.
Advent [or Christ's Coming].   *Unknown.*   BoReV; OxBM

I saw his back.   Wallace Stevens Gives a Reading.   Harriet
Zinnes.   AMV-81

I saw his round mouth's crimson deepen as it fell.   Fragment.
Wilfred Owen.   OAEL-2

I saw in a poet's song.   Symbols.   John Drinkwater.   WIF

I Saw in Louisiana a Live-Oak Growing.   Walt Whitman.
AmVN; InPK; IPWM; MAT; NoAM; NOBA; PPM; TPo

I saw it all, Polly, how when you had call'd for sop.   Poor Poll.
Robert Bridges.   EBEV; OxBTC

I saw it in an empty window.   In an Empty Window.   Ray
Fraser.   NeAC

I saw it jerking as I drove by.   The Coyote.   A. A. Dewey.   HeS

I saw it rise, a stunted, soot-encrusted.   The Honored Dead.
Thomas Doulis.   NowV

I saw magic on a green country road.   Sonnet.   Michael Hartnett.
BIrV

I Saw My Darling.   Frederick Morgan.   UnPo (1976 ed.)

I saw my daughter.   When I Came to Israel.   Bert Meyers.
AMV-80; VWA

I saw my face. Jew. Pierre Morhange, *tr. by* Edouard Roditi. VWA

I saw my grandmother grow weak. First Death. Donald Justice. FiCP

I saw my lady weep. My Lady's Tears. *Unknown.* EBEV; NOBE

I saw my love, younger than primroses. In a Wood. E. J. Scovell. GBL

I saw my soul at rest upon a day. Sestina. Swinburne. VLP

I saw myself leaving. Reflections. Carl Gardner. PoBA

I saw new worlds beneath the water lie. On Leaping over the Moon. Thomas Traherne. Moon

I saw no way—the heavens were stitched. Emily Dickinson. BoWoP; PiAm

I saw old Autumn in the misty morn. Ode: Autumn. Thomas Hood. FSFS; OAEL-2; UnPo (1976 ed.); VLP

I saw old Duchesses with their young loves. Vanity. Anna Wickham. FaBoTw (1975 ed.)

I saw on the slant hill a putrid lamb. For a Lamb. Richard Eberhart. CMoP (1970 ed.); SoS

I Saw Some Lovely Things Today. *Unknown.* CTV

I saw the best minds of my generation. Squeal. Louis Simpson. UnPo (1976 ed.)

I saw the best minds of my generation destroyed by madness, starving hysterical naked. Howl. Allen Ginsberg. AnMo; CAPP; CoPAm; InPS; NIL; NoAM; TAP; TT

I saw the best parts of Iowa covered with New Jersey tea. Touring the Hawkeye State. Gary Gildner. HeS

I saw the black trees leaning. Trees and Evening Sky. N. Scott Momaday. CDW

I saw the Chattahoochee River get a haircut. Dealer's Choice and the Dealer Shuffles. Jonathan Williams. CSP

I saw the dead/ dying a second time. The Pulverized Screen. Edmond Jabes, *tr. by* Anthony Rudolf. VWA

I saw the Devil walking down the lane. The Devil's Bag. James Stephens. PFIr; PoTa

I saw the first pear. Orchard. Hilda Doolittle ("H. D."). CMoP (1970 ed.)

I saw the fox, his red tail beating. Gone. Joanna Thompson. AMV-80

I saw the human millions as the sand. Sydney Dobell. *Fr.* Sonnets on the War. VLP

I Saw the Light Yesterday. Galina V. Ogilvie-Laing. SLP

I saw the long line of the vacant shore. The Tides. Longfellow. EcS

I saw the lovely arch. The Rainbow. Walter de la Mare. CTV

I saw the midlands. Kisses in the Train. D. H. Lawrence. OBP

I saw the moon. Flying. J. M. Westrup. FPB

I saw the pride of all the meadows. Narcissus. William Cowper. PCOP

I Saw the Ramparts of My Native Land. Don Francisco A. Quevedo, *tr. fr. Spanish by* John Masefield. NIL

I saw the salt. Ode to Salt. Pablo Neruda, *tr. by* Robert Bly. NU

I saw the silver morning mist. The Dead Horse. Cecilia Meireles, *tr. by* James Merrill. PBWP

I saw the spiders marching through the air. Mr. Edwards and the Spider. Robert Lowell. AnMo; CABA (1972 ed.); CAPP; CMoP (1970 ed.); HeIP; ILP (1975 ed.); InPS; NIL; NOBA; PSN; SoSe (1977 ed.); STS; UsP

I saw the spot where our first parents dwelt. The Garden. Jones Very. AmVN; PiAm; TAP

I saw the tall bush burn. Fall in Massachusetts. Isabella Gardner. RiTi

I saw the throng, so deeply separate. A General Communion. Alice Meynell. WPE

I Saw the Wind Today. Padraic Colum. Reminiscence, II. CaYB; ECBV; RAE

I saw thee, child, one summer's day. Emily Brontë. VLP

I saw them at games every. Seven Mexican Children. Tom Schmidt. NeAC

I Saw Them Lynch. Carole Freeman. NMM; PoBA; WIF

I saw three Cupids (so I dream'd). The Kites. Coventry Patmore. *Fr.* The Angel in the House. VLP

I saw three ships come sailing by. Mother Goose. MG

I Saw Three Ships Come Sailing In. *Unknown.* CC; FSW

I saw two hares in the corn. The Dance. Gareth Alban Davies, *tr. by* Gwyn Jones. OBW

I saw two trees embracing. All That Time. May Swenson. FF; RiTi; UsP

I saw with open eyes. Stupidity Street. Ralph Hodgson. OxBTC; PCOP; UsP

I saw you/ in the garden. Tolusa. Lués Omar Salinas. CPA

I saw you/ on my walk last. Glimpse. Pearl Cleage Lomax. PoBA

I saw you/ peeking out thru the flower pots. As the World Turns. Larry Mollin. NeAC

I saw you arise from your bed, I saw your door open. All Is Well with the Child. Marya Zaturenska. LoAs

"I saw you take his kiss!" "'Tis true." The Kiss. Coventry Patmore. The Angel in the House, II, viii. BoLoP; PoPle; SoSe

I saw you toss the kites on high. The Wind. Robert Louis Stevenson. CTV

I saw you walking. At Long Last. Lindsay Patterson. CNA

I saw your manager fight. He Was. Elegy for Lyn James. Leslie Norris. OBW

I sawe a mayd sitte on a bank. The Carelesse Nurse Mayd. Thomas Hood. FaBoNo; VLP

I Say. Malka Heifetz Tussman, *tr. fr. Yiddish by* Marcia Falk. VWA

I say I woke up this morning, baby so dark I couldn't hardly see. Y M & V Blues. *Unknown.* BluL

I say now, Fernando, that on that day. Hibiscus on the Sleeping Shores. Wallace Stevens. InPS

I say the oms relating bring into teddy once. A Poem for May Wilson. Michael Cooper. BCr

I say the Rock Island Line is a mighty good road. Rock Island Line. *Unknown.* FSW

I say the women don't sleep right. Explanation. Geof Hewitt. NeAC

I say this evening we'll all get drunk. Suction's Anthem. Blake. *Fr.* An Island in the Moon. FaBoNo

I say to the Almighty, I Say. Malka Heifetz Tussman, *tr. by* Marcia Falk. VWA

I say to the lead. Poem without a Title. Charles Simic. GP; NNaP

I say what Lindbergh's father. Maps for a Son Are Drawn as You Go. Samuel Hazo. AMV-81

I, says the buzzard. From Virgil. George Oppen. *Fr.* Five Poems about Poetry. NNaP

I scarce believe my love to be so pure. Love's Growth; or, Spring. John Donne. SCP-1

I Scattered My Sighs to the Wind. Hayim Nachman Bialik, *tr. fr. Hebrew by* Naomi Nir. VWA

I scream/ You scream. *Unknown.* FaBoNo

I scrub the floor. The Clorox Kid. Kirk Robertson. GP

I search for familiar hair. Out of Body. Janice Townley More. AMV-81

I see a bad moon rising. Bad Moon Rising. John Fogerty. GrRo

I see a man who is dull. *Tr. fr. Arabic by* Willis Barnstone. BoWoP

I see a rabbit drinking at a stream.  The Rabbit.  Philip McIntyre, Jr.  AKE

I see before me now a traveling army halting.  Bivouac on a Mountain Side.  Walt Whitman.  PiAm

I see before me the gladiator lie.  The Dying Gladiator.  Byron. *Fr. Childe Harold's Pilgrimage, IV.*  NOBE

I see black dragons mount the sky.  Shapes and Signs.  James Clarence Mangan.  PFIr

I see bodies in the morning kneel.  Shirley Kaufman.  BoWoP

I see from the paper that Florrie Forde is dead.  Death of an Actress.  Louis MacNeice.  NIL

I see her against the pearl sky of Dublin.  My Mother's Sister. C. Day Lewis.  OxBTC

I see her in my sleep, my red, terrible girl.  Sylvia Plath.  *Fr. Three Women.*  TV

I see her seventeen.  Arizona Highways.  James Welch.  CDW

I see her still, unsteadily riding the edge.  My Grandmother Washes Her Feet.  Fred Chappell.  CSP

"I see herrin'."—I hear the glad cry.  With the Herring Fishers. "Hugh MacDiarmid."  MS

I see I've come a pilgrimage. I didn't.  The *Weepers Tower* in Amsterdam.  Paul Goodman.  VGW

I see no equivalents.  The Poet at Night-Fall.  Glenway Wescott. PoA

I see no single thread.  On Universalism.  Etheridge Knight. UsP

I see nothing of the killing of sparrows.  The Killing of Sparrows. Patricia Beer.  HeHu

I see that you're a poetry lover, sweet Diane.  Sweet Diane. George Barlow.  CNA

I See the Boys of Summer.  Dylan Thomas.  TT

I see the children running out of school.  The Poet Laments the Coming of Old Age.  Edith Sitwell.  NoAM

I See the Moon.  *Unknown.*  CTV; GBP, *diff. version*

I see the sparrow bones folded in their thin shoes.  The Fathers. Benjamin Saltman.  VWA

I see the thin bell-ringer standing at corners.  The Jew at Christmas Eve.  Karl Shapiro.  VGW

I see the wealthy miller yet.  The Miller's Daughter.  Tennyson. VLP

I see them/ Puerto Ricans.  You're Nothing but a Spanish Colored Kid.  Felipe Luciano.  PoBA

I see them, crowd on crowd they walk the earth.  The Dead. Jones Very.  AmVN; HAP; NOBA; PAIC; TAP

I see them illumine.  Fireflies.  Helena Minton.  FAF

I see them working in old rectories.  The Country Clergy.  R. S. Thomas.  BoReV; OxBTC; PSN

I see they worked you over. What you in for?  Coming of Age in the County Jail.  Carter Revard.  VoR

I see you, a child.  The Album.  C. Day Lewis.  BuTh; OxBTC

I see you coming toward the river, a spark.  New Strip.  Peter Wild.  EC

I see you displaced, condensed, within my dream.  Dream. Josephine Miles.  PoA

I see you, Juliet, still, with your straw hat.  Farewell to Juliet. Wilfrid Scawen Blunt.  *Fr. The Love Sonnets of Proteus.* BoLoP; OxBTC

I see you lizard.  What Might Pass a Man as a Survivor.  J. S. Harry.  CAAP

I see you with my inner eye.  Greeting from a Distance.  Hans Sahl, *tr. by* Erna Baber Rosenfield.  VWA

I see your breath.  Going into the Woods.  Tom Hennen.  HeS

I see your father's death.  Taking and Losing.  Martha Webb. PHC

I see'd her in de springtime.  She Hugged Me and Kissed Me. *Unknown.*  BPo

I seek about this world unstable.  Of the Changes of Life. William Dunbar, *tr. by* Andrew Glaze.  OBP

I seem to see.  Queer.  David McCord.  CaYB

I seen a cat once.  Butcher's Dream.  Herbert Scott.  TC

I send my poisoned candies through the mail.  End of the Affair. Geoffrey Grigson.  GBL

I send these wild roses.  Bruce Holsapple.  FAF

I send you here a sort of allegory.  To——with the Following Poem.  Tennyson.  *Fr. The Palace of Art.*  VLP

I Send You Roses.  W. E. Henley.  NIL

I sense that I may someday be assailed.  Arcady Revisited. Robert Funge.  AMV-80

I sent a letter to my love.  George Barker.  *Fr. The True Confession of George Baker.*  FaBoTw (1975 ed.)

I sent for Radcliffe, was so ill.  The Remedy, Worse than the Disease.  Matthew Prior.  FaBoEE

I Sent My Brown Jug Downtown.  *Unknown.*  FSW

I sent my severed self.  To an Old Friend.  Margaret R. Litchfield.  PoUp

I serve a mistress whiter than the snow.  Anthony Munday. HAP; LoAs

"I shall be careful to say nothing at all."  How She Resolved to Act.  Merrill Moore.  SoS

I shall beat you without rage.  Heautontimoroumenos. Baudelaire, *tr. by* Naomi Lewis.  NAWM-2

I shall begin by learning to throw.  Formal Application.  Donald W. Baker.  FF; SoSe

I shall dance, I shall have hope.  Dance Hymn.  Isaiah Shembe, *tr. by* B. G. M. Sundkler.

I shall die, but that is all that I shall do for Death.  Conscientious Objector.  Edna St. Vincent Millay.  VoPo

I Shall Forget You Presently, My Dear.  Edna St. Vincent Millay. TAP

I shall go among red faces and virile voices.  Cattle Show. "Hugh MacDiarmid."  HAP; OxBTC

I shall go as my father went.  The Tenancy.  Mary Gilmore. MAuV

I Shall Go Back.  Edna St. Vincent Millay.  UnPo (1976 ed.)

I shall go to Mamre's oaks.  Abraham.  Eisig Silberschlag. VWA

I shall hate you.  Hatred.  Gwendolyn B. Bennett.  AmNP (1974 ed.); PoBA

I shall kneel weeping when you say.  Letter to Her Son's Commanding Officer.  Ethel Green Russell.  AATT

I shall know why—when time is over.  Emily Dickinson.  NoAM

I shall lie hidden in a hut.  Prophecy.  Elinor Wylie.  BoWoP; RiTi; VGW

I shall never get you put together entirely.  The Colossus.  Sylvia Plath.  AnMo; CAPP; CoPAm; IP; NoAM; NOBA; Psy; TAP

I Shall Never Go.  A. J. Hovde.  AMV-80

I Shall Not Care.  Sara Teasdale.  TPo; UnPo (1976 ed.)

I shall not linger in that draughty square.  French.  Osbert Lancaster.  *Fr. Afternoons with Baedeker.*  FaBoCo; NOBL

I Shall Not Want: In Deserts Wild, *with music.*  Charles F. Deems.  AH

I shall paint/ God in the midst.  Robert Browning.  *Fr. Fra Lippo Lippi.*  Prf

I shall say what inordinate love is.  Inordinate Love.  *Unknown.* EBEV; LoAs (*At. to* John Lydgate.)

I shall see justice done.  Witch.  Patricia Beer.  HeHu

I shall write of the old men I knew.  In These Dissenting Times. Alice Walker.  PoBA

I shipped, d'ye see, in a Revenue sloop.  The Darned Mounseer. W. S. Gilbert.  *Fr. Ruddigore.*  NOBL

I shipped on board of a Liverpool liner.  Sally Brown.  *Unknown.* AmFP

I shiver, spirit fierce and bold. At the Grave of Burns, 1803. Wordsworth. MBPR

I shoot the hippopotamus. The Hippopotamus. Hilaire Belloc. BBL; FaBoNo; InPK

I shot a rocket in the air. Enough. Tom Masson. OBAL

I shot an arrow into the air. A Shot at Random. D. B. Wyndham Lewis. FaBoCo

I shot an arrow into the air. The Arrow and the Song. Longfellow. CTV; PCOP

I shot my friend to save my country's life. The Body Politic. Donald Hall. SoS

I Should Be Ashamed. Uvlunuaq, *tr. fr. Eskimo.* WTO

I should have been a gypsy child. Heir to Several Yesterdays. Parham J. Kelley. AMV-80

I should have died a Trojan or a Spartan. And One Other Thing. A. Wilbur Stevens. MPA

I should have thought. At Baia. Hilda Doolittle ("H. D."). NOBA; PAIC

I should like to rise and go. Travel. Robert Louis Stevenson. CTV

I shouted day and night. Let Zulu Be Heard. Isaiah Shembe, *tr. by* G. C. Oosthuizen. WTO

I shudder thinking. The Cold Irish Earth. Knute Skinner. InPK

I sigh for the heavenly country. The Heavenly City. Stevie Smith. FaBoTw (1975 ed.)

I Sigh When I Sing ("I sike al when I singe"). *Unknown.* OxBM

I sing a song of sixpence, and of rye. An Ode. Anthony C. Deane. NOBL

I sing a song reluctantly. Comtesse de Die, *tr. fr. Provençal by* Carol Cosman *and* Howard Bloch. PBWP

I sing a woeful ditty. A Ballad Called the Haymarket Hectors. *Unknown.* APAS

I Sing No New Songs. Frank Marshall Davis. PoBA

I sing no song. I spin instead. Spider. Norma Farber. PChr

I sing of a captain who's well known to fame. A Nautical Ballad. Keighley Goodchild. ECBV

I sing of a hero, unsung, unrecorded. Crispus Attucks McCoy. Sterling A. Brown. BPo

I Sing of a Maiden [*or* Mayden] That Is Makeless. *Unknown.* BoReV; CABA (1972 ed.); EBEV; FF; ILP (1975 ed.); HAP InPK; InPS; NOBE; OAEL-1; WeW (Maiden That Is Makeless, A.) OFD

I sing of arms and of a man. The Aeneid. Virgil, *tr. by* Allen Mandelbaum. NAWM-1

I sing of brooks, of blossoms, birds, and bowers. The Argument of His Book. Robert Herrick. CaPo; EBEV; HAP; HeIP; ILP (1975 ed.); NIL; OAEL-1; OBP; PoPle

I sing of myself, a sorrowful woman. Wife's Lament. *Unknown, tr. by* Kemp Malone. PBWP

I Sing of Olaf Glad and Big. E. E. Cummings. HeIP; NoAM; NOBA; OBSV; PAIC; STS; VGW; VoPo; WIF

I Sing of Shine. Etheridge Knight. BPo (Dark Prophesy: I Sing of Shine.) GP

I sing of slum scabs on city faces. Today. Margaret Walker. FB

I sing of the decline of Henry Clay. Conquistador. A. D. Hope. IP; PPoD

I sing the brave adventures of two wights. The Voyage Itself. Ben Jonson. TVS

I sing the furious battles of the spheres. Ad Johannuelem Leporem, Lepidissimum, Carmen Heroicum. *Unknown.* FaBoNo

I sing the just and uncontrolled descent. Ben Jonson. *Fr.* Eupheme SCP-1

I sing the praise of honored wars. The Soldier's Song. *Unknown.* NIL

I sing the simplest flower. Karl Shapiro. Six Religious Lyrics, I. CMoP (1970 ed.)

I sing the sofa. I who lately sang. The Sofa. William Cowper. *Fr.* The Task. LAuP

I, singularly moved. Winter. Coventry Patmore. NOBE

I sink into a rare luminous blindness. Blindness. Delmira Agustini, *tr. by* D. M. Pettinella. PBWP

I sink my soft butt in an easy chair. News. Marnie Pomeroy. POL

I sip the dregs, my tongue. Willows. Laura Schreiber. AMV-81

I sit alone late at night. An Extra Joyful Chorus for Those Who Have Read This Far. Robert Bly. EAS

I sit among the hoary trees. The Lizard. Edwin Markham. BPAW

I Sit and Look Out. Walt Whitman. CABA (1972 ed.); CTBA; SFF; TAP

I sit at a gold table with my girl. At the Altar. Robert Lowell. Between the Porch and the Altar, IV. InPK; InPS

I sit at the kitchen tabled with sickness. Breath. Arthur Smith. CPA

I sit at the top of the tree. Crow Resting. Ted Hughes. UsP

I sit back in the city. Wearing Breasts. Daniela Gioseffi. RiTi

I sit beneath the throne of Allah! I, Lord, of All Mortals! *Malay Oral Tradition, tr. by* R. O. Winstedt. WTO

I sit by the window all morning. At a Motel near O'Hare Airport. Jane Kenyon. TC

I sit by the window, reading a book. With a Book at Twilight. Jakov Steinberg, *tr. by* Mark Elliott Shapiro. VWA

I sit clumsy in my flesh, my legs. The Cigarette Poem. Faye Kicknosway. IHMS

I sit down at a table and open a book of poems. Library. Louis Jenkins. HeS; NU

I sit here dreaming. Our Beautiful West Coast Thing. Richard Brautigan. OSP

"I sit here in these stocks." In Weatherbury Stocks. Thomas Hardy. AIW

I sit here with the wind is in my hair. To Helen (of Troy, N.Y.) [*or* The Lyricism of the Weak]. Peter Viereck. CoPAm; WeW

I sit, I sleep, I wait. The Snake. Morton Marcus. CPA

I sit in a huge auditorium. The Return. Dennis Saleh. NeAC

I sit in cubbyhole. Heartblow: Messages. Michael S. Harper. NW

I sit in one of the dives. September 1, 1939. W. H. Auden. CMoP (1970 ed.)

I sit in the marsh. River and Light. Siv Cedering Fox. RiTi

I sit in the top of the wood, my eyes closed. Hawk Roosting. Ted Hughes. CMoP (1970 ed.); ExPo (1973 ed.); HAP; HeIP; ILP (1975 ed.); MPo; OxBTC; PB; PPP; PSN; UnPo (1976 ed.)

I sit musing, ten minutes from the Jap. A Letter for Marian. Thomas McGrath. VGW

I sit on a discarded army bunk that moves toward death. Inside the Wall of My Cell. J. Charles Green. DNGG

I sit poking a small fire. In Memory of Francis Webb. Thomas Shapcott. CAAP

I sit thinking of a rowing-boat I saw. The Waiting-Room. Robin Fulton. PoA

I sit with my toes in the brook. *Unknown.* FaBoNo

I sit with you at the window. Barnabooth Enters Russia. Paul Hoover. AMV-81

I sit within my room and joy to find. The Presence. Jones Very. HAP

I slam the door. Outside I find the day. John Nobody. Dom Moraes. NoAM

I sleep but my heart is awake. Bible, *O.T. Fr.* The Song of Solomon, *ad. by* Willis Barnstone. BoWoP

I sleep, I sleep. Sleeping Beauty. Olga Broumas. CNW

I sleep in your arms. In Your Arms. Miklós Radnóti, *tr. by* Steven Polgar *and* Stephen Berg *and* S. J. Marks. VWA

I sleep with thee, and wake with thee. To Mary: I Sleep with Thee, and Wake with Thee. John Clare. GBL

I slept alone last nite but when you know you dont have to. Alta. MMD

I slept under rhododendron. Four Poems for Robin. Gary Snyder. NNaP; NoAM; NOBA

I slouch down the dark, I am the dark. I Am the Man Who. James Moore. BrS

I slouch in bed. Two Hangovers. James Wright. ILP (1975 ed.)

I smell a smell of death. July, 1964. Donald Davie. ExPo (1973 ed.)

I sneezed a sneeze into the air. Ode to a Sneeze. *At. to* G. Wallace. OSF

I snum I am a Yankee lad, and I guess I'll sing a ditty. The Boston Tea Tax. *Unknown.* BTTM

I So Liked Spring. Charlotte Mew. OxBTC

I sometimes fear the younger generation will be deprived. Hoeing. John Updike. TSWA

I sometimes sleep with other girls. Cavalier Lyric. James Simmons. InPK; POL

I sometimes think. Did You See the Times Today? Lois Wyse. SFF

I sometimes think I'd rather crow. To Be or Not to Be [*or* Rooster Be? Or a Crow?]. *Unknown.* ECBV; FaBoCo

I sought a theme and sought for it in vain. The Circus Animals' Desertion. W. B. Yeats. BiP; CMoP (1970 ed.); FaBoTw (1975 ed.) ILP (1975 ed.); NIL; MAT; NoAM; NOBE; OAEL-2; OxBTC; PPoD; PSN; TT

I sought, I found, she asked me what I would. Rachel Speght. *Fr.* A Dream. WPE

I sought of bishop and priest and judges. On Christians, Mercy Will Fall. *Unknown, tr. by* D. M. Lloyd. OBW

I sowed the seeds of love. The Seeds of Love. *Unknown, at. to* Mrs. Fleetwood Habergham. AIW; GBP

I speak for Erin. The Muse of Amergin. *Unknown, tr. by* John Montague. BIrV

I speak from ignorance. Last of the Chiefs. Nathaniel Tarn. TwMBP

I speak of that great house. Beyond the Hunting Woods. Donald Justice. ConAP; CSP; NCSH; UsP

I speak of the history of the world. Plain Song Talk. Richard Eberhart. PoA

I speak skimpily to. Personal Letter No. 2. Sonia Sanchez. WBN

I speak this poem now with grave and level voice. Immortal Autumn. Archibald MacLeish. BiP; CMoP (1970 ed.)

I spent a nicht amang the cognoscenti. I Was Fair Beat. Robert Garioch. OxBTC

I spent a night turning in bed. The Whip. Robert Creeley. NoAM

I spent the day. Zone. A. R. Ammons. TT

I spied a bear/ On the drifting floe. Bear Hunting. Aua, *tr. fr. Eskimo.* WTO

I spied a very small brown duck. Duck-chasing. Galway Kinnell. UsP; VGW

I spied John Mouldy in his cellar. John Mouldy. Walter de la Mare. NCSH; OxBChV; PoPle

I spoke with a tangle-haired forester from Saskatchewan. A Summing Up. Gabriel Preil, *tr. by* Jeremy Garber. VWA

I spoke without caring. Investigation. Julia Vinograd. IHMS

I spot the hills. Theme in Yellow. Carl Sandburg. LCL

I sprang to the rollocks and Jorrocks and me. How I Brought the Good News from Aix to Ghent. R. J. Yeatman *and* W. C. Sellar. SpRo

I sprang to the stirrup, and Joris, and he. How They Brought the Good News from Ghent to Aix. Robert Browning. BTTM; ECBV; FaPoR; HoPM (1975 ed.); PAIC; SpRo; STS

I Spread Out unto Thee My Hands, *with music.* Henry Ainsworth. AH

I stand and listen, head bowed. Self-employed. David Ignatow. NNaP

I stand and watch for minutes by the pond. This, That & the Other. Howard Nemerov. AnMo

I stand as on some mighty eagle's beak. From Montauk Point. Walt Whitman. RFM

I stand at the back of the room. The Room. Mark Strand. UsP

I stand before you. Position. Carol Bergé. MMD

I stand below the gun tower. The Ritual. Paul David Ashley. DNGG

I stand here in the ditch, my feet on a rock in the water. The Blackberry Thicket. Ann Stanford. MPA

I stand high in the belfry tower. On the Tower. Annette von Droste-Hülshoff, *tr. by* James Edward Tobin. PBWP

I stand in front of the tree. Pre-Positions. Jose Isaacson, *tr. by* Yishai Tobin. VWA

I stand in my door and look over the low field of Drynam. The Widow of Drynam. Patrick MacDonogh. PFIr

I stand in the dark light in the dark street. Birthplace Revisited. Gregory Corso. SA; VGW; VoA

I stand in the late sun. The Reply. Philip Levine. PoA

I stand knee-deep in the ocean. Ancestry. Louis Daniel Brodsky. AMV-81

I stand mute in the moonshine and lights of the moon. The Preparation of the Body. Helen Wolfert. *Fr.* Woman against the Moon. RiTi

I stand on slenderness all fresh and fair. A Cut Flower. Karl Shapiro. HAP; WeW

I stand on the ledge where rock runs into the river. The Wreck of the Thresher. William Meredith. CoPAm

I stand on the mark beside the shore. The Runaway Slave at Pilgrim's Point. Elizabeth Barrett Browning. SBG

I stand on the wharf. Voyage. Stephen Stepanchev. SA

I stand there slapping a house. The Apprentice Painter. Jack Myers. AmPA

I stand upon my miracle hill. Miracle Hill. Emerson Blackhorse Mitchell. VW

I stand washing up, the others have gone out walking. Water a Thousand Feet Deep. Judith Rodriguez. GAS

I stand where water sweeps between my knees. Fishing at Sunrise. Peggy Simson Curry. WPW

I stand within the willowing shadows of Memp-ch-ton. On Hearing the Marsh Bird's Water Cry. Duane Niatum. CDW

I standing on a hill of fancies high. Margaret Cavendish, Duchess of Newcastle. *Fr.* Nature's Landskip. SCP-2

I stare into the dark of night to see. On the Night Express to Madrid. Lora Dunetz. AMV-81

I stared at the printed words. Printed Words. Liz Sohappy Bahe. CDW

I start awake at night afraid of death. Sonnet 21. Paul Goodman. VGW

I start out for a walk at last after weeks at the desk. After Long Busyness. Robert Bly. PoA

I started early, took my dog. Emily Dickinson. AmVN; HAP; InPK; Psy; SBG

I started picking up the stones. Apologia pro Vita Sua. A. R. Ammons. NOBA

I stay;/ But it isn't as if. An Empty Threat. Robert Frost. RFM

I stayed in jail and worked for thirty long days. Nashville Stonewall Blues. *Unknown.* BluL

I stayed the night for shelter at a farm. The Witch of Coös. Robert Frost. *Fr.* Two Witches. CMoP (1970 ed.); ExPo (1973 ed.); NoAM; NOBA; PAIC

I step around a gate of bushes. Cold Water. Donald Hall. NCSH

I stepped from plank to plank. Emily Dickinson. CMoP (1970 ed.); ILP (1975 ed.); NOBA; Psy

I stepped into the elevator. Female Feminity. Pancho Aguila. NW

I stick my tongue in you. Gray Silk Twisting. Patrick Lane. NeAC

I Still Feel You. Marge Piercy. Psy

I still have some money. In Terror of Hospital Bills. James Wright. GP

I stock the cupboards with tomato paste. Settling In. Mary Stroh. EC

I stole forth dimly in the dripping pause. Moon Compasses. Robert Frost. LoAs; Moon; TT

I stood and marveled. About my head. The Washer-Widows. Paul Clause. AATT

I stood and saw my mistress dance. On Her Dancing. James Shirley. PoPle

I stood aside to let the cows. Man and Cows. Andrew Young. EBEV

I stood between two mirrors when you died. Elegy. William Jay Smith. CoPAm

I stood by the old fort's crumbling wall. Sutter's Fort, Sacramento. Lucius Harwood Foote. BPAW

I stood by the river where the flesh of our world. In Bed with a River. George Bradley. AMV-80

I stood by the stone sea-wall at Depoe Bay. The Sprouting Horn. Nelson Bentley. LoAs

I Stood in Jerusalem. Zelda, *tr. fr. Hebrew by* Marcia Falk. VWA

I stood in my mother's kitchen. Ants. Katharyn Machan Aal. AMV-80

I stood in the gloom of a spacious room. Awake, My Lute! C. S. Lewis. FaBoNo

I stood in the shelter of a great tree. Tumbleweed. Ramona Carden. VW

I stood in Venice on the Bridge of Sighs. Venice and Sunset. Byron. *Fr.* Childe Harold's Pilgrimage. LFH; PAIC

I Stood Musing in a Black World. Stephen Crane. The Black Riders, XLIX. TT

I stood on Brocken's sovran height, and saw. Lines Written in the Album at Elbingerode. Samuel Taylor Coleridge. MBPR

I stood on the Atlantic ocean, on the wide Pacific shore. The Wabash Cannonball. *Unknown.* FSW

I stood one day by the breezy bay. A Nautical Extravaganza. Wallace Irwin. PoTa

I stood over myself. A Dream. Michael Small. DNGG

I stood still and was a tree amid the wood. The Tree. Ezra Pound. CMoP (1970 ed.); PBMP; PiAm

I Stood Tiptoe upon a Little Hill. Keats. MBPR
On a Summer's Day, *sel.* FSFS

I stood where real estate, measured in always smaller and more precious. Dana Point. Brewster Ghiselin. AMV-81

I stood within the city disinterred. Ode to Naples. Shelley. PAIC

I Stood within the Heart of God, *with music.* William Vaughn Moody. AH

I stoop to gather a seabird's feather. The Feather. Vernon Watkins. FaBoTw (1975 ed.)

I stopped in a sidestreet surplus shop. The Cot. Grover Amen. NYP

I stopped the doctor busy with his hemps. Lines for a Fifty-fifth Birthday. Jeanne McGahey. MIT

I stopped to pick up the bagel. The Bagel. David Ignatow. ConAP; FF; OSP; PPoD; UsP

I strayed, all alone, where the Autumn. A Rose in October. James Whitcomb Riley. OBAL

I strolled across/ An open field. The Waking. Theodore Roethke. CNW; RFM

I strove with all, for all were worth my strife. Epitaph for G. B. Shaw. Max Beerbohm. FaBoEE

I strove with none, for none was worth my strife. On His Seventy-fifth Birthday [*or* Dying Speech of an Old Philosopher]. Walter Savage Landor. *Fr.* The Last Fruit off an Old Tree. EBEV; FaBoEE; FaPoR; HeIP; NOBE; OAEL-2; PBMP; PCOP; SoSe (1977 ed.); VLP

I struck the board, and cried: No more. The Collar. George Herbert. AnMo; BiP; BoReV; CABA (1972 ed.); EBEV; ExPo (1973 ed.); HAP; HeIP; ILP (1975 ed.); InPS; IPWM; MetP; NIL; NOBE; OAEL-1; OBP; OBW; PoPle; PPoD; PPoe; PPP; SCP-1

I struck the trail in seventy-nine. The Gal I Left behind Me. *Unknown.* BPAW; FSW

I study out a dark similitude. The Swan. Theodore Roethke. VGW

I study the lives on a leaf: the little. The Minimal. Theodore Roethke. BiP; NoAM; NOBA

I subside like a trick cushion. Sleep. Rhyl! McMaster. CAAP

I Substitute for the Dead Lecturer. Amiri Baraka. NOBA

I summon to the winding ancient stair. A Dialogue of Self and Soul. W. B. Yeats. CABA (1972 ed.); CMoP (1970 ed.); ExPo (1973 ed.); NoAM; PAIC

I suppose even molecules are driven to distraction. Swing One, Swing All. George Bradley. AMV-80

I Suppose Her Mother Told Her. Francine Corcos. AMV-80

I suppose it's because we're on foot I'm reminded. Kyran's Christening. Alden Nowlan. NeAC

I suppose it's myself that you're making allusion to. At the "Atlantic" Dinner. Oliver Wendell Holmes. AmVN

I suspect/ They will. Blue Stones. Larry Levis. PCho

I swam the Huron of love, and am not ashamed. The Huron. Ruth Herschberger. WPE

I swear I begin to see the meaning of these things. Walt Whitman. *Fr.* By Blue Ontario's Shore, XV. InPS

I swear it, by love I swear it! Her Voice. Meleager, *tr. by* Dudley Fitts. NIL

I swing round the corner, still alone. Montage. Harry Guest. TwMBP

I switch on the light. Crickets tick. Sleep in the Heat. Laura Jensen. AmPA

I swore I would go back. O Lyric Love. Winfield Townley Scott. VGW

I swore to stab the sonnet with my pen. Karl Shapiro. *Fr.* White-haired Lover. PoA

I take as my theme, "The Independent Woman." Pro Femina, II. Carolyn Kizer. MAT; NMM; Psy; RiTi

I take it he doesn't think at all. The Pike. John Bruce. LiSp

I take my bike. Oregon Landscape with Lost Lover. Olga Broumas. CNW

I take my Aunt out in her pram. My Aunt. Peggy Wood. POL

I take my old clothes out of the cupboard and deck. My Best Clothes. Eli Netser, *tr. by* Bernhard Frank. AMV-81

I take my pen in hand. The Letter. Elizabeth Riddell. BuTh

I take my son outside. What I Tell Him. Simon J. Ortiz. CDW

I take my son to visit in the distant. Sons. Don Polson. AMV-81

I take off my shirt, I show you. Taking Off My Clothes. Carolyn Forché. AmPA

I take their hands. They. R. S. Thomas. OxBTC

I take to this music. The Golden Greats. Steve Toth. AcAn

I take you as I take the moon rising. Death. Charles Wright. FiCP

I take you looking at the statue. The Statue. Kenneth Allott. EAS

I talked to old Lem. Old Lem. Sterling A. Brown. BPo; FB; PoBA

I tarry in days shaped like the high staired street. A Birthday Memorial to Seventh Street. Audre Lorde. CNA

I taste a liquor never brewed. Emily Dickinson. AmVN; AnMo; CABA (1972 ed.); CMoP (1970 ed.); FF; HeIP; IP; IPWM; NOBA; PBMP; PiAm; PoIA; PPM; SBG; SoSe (1977 ed.); TAP; TT; VoPo; WPE

I taught myself to live simply and wisely. "Anna Akhmatova," *tr. fr. Russian by* Richard McKane. PBWP

I teach in a high school. The Wrong Kind of Insurance. John Ashbery. NYP

I Telephoned a Friend. Josephine Miles. MPA

I Tell Her She Is Lovely. Monk Gibbon. PFIr

I tell it to the Freshman. Style 5. William Wantling. CPA

I tell my friend in California. California, This Is Minnesota Speaking. Stephen Dunn. GP

I tell thee, Dick, where I have been. A Ballad upon a Wedding. Sir John Suckling. CABA (1972 ed.); CaPo; EBEV; FaBoBa; LoAs

I tell Therese. Therese. Alden Nowlan. NeAC

I tell words that talk in trees, this hill. Pot Shot. Padraic Fallon. CIP

I tell ye, Sue, it ain't no use! Goin' Back T'morrer. Hamlin Garland. OBAL

I tell yeh whut! The chankin'. Horses Chawin' Hay. Hamlin Garland. OBAL

I tell you, hopeless grief is passionless. Grief. Elizabeth Barrett Browning. HeIP; InPK; PPM; SBG; VLP; WPE

I tell you how dat hypocrite do. That Hypocrite. *Unknown.* BPo

I tell you that I see her still. I Only Am Escaped Alone to Tell Thee. Howard Nemerov. HeIP; NoAM

I Thank God I'm Free at Las'. *Unknown.* BPo; PBMP; TAP (Free at Last.) FSW

I thank you, God. Thanksgiving. Louise Driscoll. CTV

I Thank You God for Most This Amazing. E. E. Cummings. BiP; ILwL; IPWM; PiAm; STS; TAP; TT; VoPo

I thank You, God in Heaven, for friends. In Gratitude for Friends. Margaret Elizabeth Sangster. CTV

I that in health was, and gladness. Lament for the Poets. William Dunbar, *tr. by* Andrew Glaze *and* Selden Rodman. OBP

I That in Heill Wes and Glaidnes. William Dunbar. *See* Timor Mortis Conturbat Me.

I, that with my sword. Shakespeare. *Fr.* Antony and Cleopatra, IV, xiv. IP

I' the how-dumb-deid o the cauld hairst nicht. The Eemis-Stane. "Hugh MacDiarmid." MS

I, the poet William Yeats. To Be Carved on a Stone at Thoor Ballylee. W. B. Yeats. FaBoEE; NoAM

I, therefore, will begin. Soul of the age! Ben Jonson. *Fr.* To the Memory of My Beloved Mr. William Shakespeare. NOBE

I think a time will come when you will understand. For My Father. Paul Potts. FaBoTw (1975 ed.)

I think about where I'd really like to be. Delaying Tactics. Christopher Wiseman. AMV-81

I think all this is somewhere in myself. The Room. W. S. Merwin. NOBA

I think before they saw me the giraffes. The Giraffes. Roy Fuller. NoAM

I Think Continually of Those Who Were Truly Great. Stephen Spender. CMoP (1970 ed.); HAP; ILP (1975 ed.); NOBE; OAEL-2; OBP; OxBTC; UsP; VoPo

I think I could live at seventy miles an hour. Nostalgia for 70. Jim Wayne Miller. AMV-81

I Think I Could Turn and Live with Animals. Walt Whitman. *Fr.* Song of Myself. HAP; NU; TPo (Animals.) POL

I think I grow tensions. The Flower. Robert Creeley. CAPP

I think I have done this before. Spring Cleaning. Sheryl Dare. PHC

I think I have no other home than this. Old Memories of Earth. R. A. K. Mason. ATNZ

I think I hear the angels sing. Shew! Fly Don't Bother Me. *At. to* Billy Reeves, *and to* T. Brigham Bishop. PSoN

I think I heard the belle. The Old Lady's Lament for Her Youth. Villon, *tr. by* Robert Lowell. BoLoP

I think I like this room. Picture of Little Letters. John Koethe. AMV-81

I think I see her sitting bowed and black. Oriflamme. Jessie Redmond Fauset. PoBA

I think I shall live for a while a bit gamely. The Poet Loves from Afar. Desmond O'Grady. NoAM

I think I sing that little song. Union Man. Albert Morgan. AmFP

I think I smell smoke. Il Janitoro. George Ade. OBAL

I Think I Understand. Joni Mitchell. GrRo

"I think I want some pies this morning." Greedy Richard. Jane Taylor. OxBChV

I think I will learn some beautiful language, useless for commercial. Intention to Escape from Him. Edna St. Vincent Millay. SBG

I think if you had loved me when I wanted. Success. Rupert Brooke. OxBTC

I think I'll get a paper. Nerves. "Sagittarius." OxBTC

I think it better that in times like these. On Being Asked for a War Poem. W. B. Yeats. NIL; PFIr

I think it is in Virginia, that place. Low Fields and Light. W. S. Merwin. ConAP

I think it most peculiar. What a Coincidence? *Unknown.* AKE

I think it must be lonely to be God. The Preacher: Ruminates behind the Sermon. Gwendolyn Brooks. PBMP

I think it was Spring—but not certain I am. Epicurean Reminiscences of a Sentimentalist. Thomas Hood. BBL

I think it's worth it today. Souster. Ray Fraser. NeAC

I think mice/ Are rather nice. Mice. Rose Fyleman. CTV; MN

I think not on the state, nor am concerned. Upon the Double Murther of King Charles I. Katherine Philips. SBG

I think of all the women behind locked doors. Winter Mornings. Nancy Mairs. NPW

I think of corner shots, the ball. Day and Night Handball. Stephen Dunn. AmPA; LiSp

I think of God. The Hairs in My Nose. Aram Boyajian. NeAC

I think of him/ Who lives south of the big sea. *Unknown, tr. fr. Chinese by* Wai-lim Yip. BoWoP

I Think of Housman Who Said the Poem Is a Morbid Secretion, like the Pearl. Judith Kroll. UnPo (1976 ed.)

I think of my wife, and I think of Lot. Marriage Couplet. William Cole. OBAL

I Think of Oblivion. Yehuda Amichai, *tr. fr. Hebrew by* Ruth Nevo. VWA

I think of the starved foreign children. The Last Bite. Richard Frost. AMV–80

I think of the things that might have been and were not. Thing That Might Have Been. Jorge Luis Borges, *tr. by* Alastair Reid. AMV–80

I think of the twenty thousand poems of Li Po. Word Drunk. Jim Harrison. IPWM

I think of things like the shadow of a branch. The Shadow of a Branch. Edith Marcombe Shiffert. WPE

I Think of Those. Paul Henderson. ATNZ

I think, old bone, the world's not with us much. To William Wordsworth from Virginia. Julia Randall. CSP; NMM; WPE

"I think," she said, "we shall not see again." The Shadows. Iain Crichton Smith. SLP

I think she sleeps: it must be sleep, when low. Modern Love, XV. George Meredith. Epi

I Think Sometimes. Michael Hartnett. CIP

I think that I shall never see. Trees. Joyce Kilmer. AKE

I think that I shall never see. Song of the Open Road. Ogden Nash. AKE; FaBoCo; ILP (1975 ed.); OBAL; TPo

I think that I shall never ski. Winter Trees. Conrad Diekmann. LiSp

I think that night's our balance. Suite to Fathers. Jim Harrison. AmPA

I think that what he gave us most was pride. Kennedy. Molly Kazan. SoS

I think the dead are tender. Shall we kiss? She. Theodore Roethke. BoLoP

I think the thing you call Renown. Winthrop Mackworth Praed. *Fr.* The Chaunt of the Brazen Head. OBSV

"I think," thought Sam Butler. English Liberal. Geoffrey Taylor. FaBoEE

I think we are being given the same messages. On Reading Another Poet. Elizabeth Brewster. MMD

I think you have to be Catholic to be a nurse. Modern American Nursing. Lucy Hricz. AMV–80

I thirst for violins, as drunkards thirst. Ideal and Reality. Joseph Campbell. BIrV

I thought a horse was "Gee!" and "Whoa!" Learner. J. A. Lindon. PH

I thought he was dumb. Tortoise Shout. D. H. Lawrence. NoAM

I thought I heard the old man say. Leave Her, Johnny. *Unknown.* FSW

I thought I saw an angel flying low. Nocturne at Bethesda. Arna Bontemps. AmNP (1974 ed.)

I thought I was so tough. Tamer and Hawk. Thom Gunn. FaBoTw (1975 ed.)

I thought I woke: the midnight sun. Stanzas. Paul Goodman. PoA

I thought if only I could marry. Unfair to Women. *Unknown, tr. by* Gwyn Jones. OBW

I thought of a house where the stones seemed suddenly changed. Lo! A Child Is Born. "Hugh MacDiarmid." MS

I thought of cards along the mantelpiece. December Fragments. Richmond Lattimore. PChr

I thought of life, the outer and the inner. Scarlett Rocks. Thomas Edward Brown. EcS

I thought of thee, my partner and my guide. After-Thought. Wordsworth. The River Duddon, XXXIV. MBPR; NOBE

I thought once how Theocritus had sung. Sonnets from the Portuguese, I. Elizabeth Barrett Browning. GBL; NOBE; PAIC; VPC; WPE

I thought one spring, just for fun. The Tenderfoot. *Unknown.* FSW

I thought Silver must have snaked logs. Silver. A. R. Ammons. CSP

I thought the dove was the bird of peace. Peace. Charles Bukowski. VoA

I thought the earth. Sleeping in the Forest. Mary Oliver. NU

I thought they stood. I Know a Spot Just over the Hill. William Mills. CoPAm

I thought you loved me. *Zulu Oral Tradition, tr. by* H. Tracey. WTO

"I thought you loved me." "No, it was only fun." In the Orchard. Muriel Stuart. FF; MS; OxBTC

I threat'ned to observe the strict decree. The Holdfast. George Herbert. Epi

I threw the inside of my gizzard out, splashing. Zimmer Drunk and Alone, Dreaming of Old Football Games. Paul Zimmer. MAT

I throw off all the ceremony. Yom Kippur. Eric Chaet. VWA

I thumped on you the best I could. Heart's Needle, VIII. W. D. Snodgrass. NoAM

I tiptoed into her sleep. Mirru. Kenneth Patchen. RRA

I to My Perils. A. E. Housman. PPM; WeW

I to the Hills Will Lift Mine Eyes, *with music.* Francis Rous. AH

I to the Lord from My Distress, *with music. Unknown.* AH

I toke hyr heid atween my hondes. Abasshyd. Pittendrigh MacGillivray. MS

I told him a tale that I adore. Andrew's Bedtime Story. Ian Serraillier. DuDa

I Told Jesus. Sterling Plumpp. PoBA

I told my captain that old Maude was dead. Captain Captain. *Unknown.* BluL

I told the sun that I was glad. The Sun. John Drinkwater. LCL

I told the White House I wanted to write a poem. Just Ask for a Demonstration. Edward Weismiller. WasP

I told them not to ring the bells. Abbey Tomb. Patricia Beer. HeHu

I told you to make me some crazy. Structure. Alberta Turner. HeS

I, Too. Langston Hughes. AmNP (1974 ed.); FF; HeIP; PiAm (Epilogue; "I, too, sing America.") VGW (I, Too, Sing America.) PoBA

I too/ once lived/ in the country. Pachuta, Mississippi/ A Memoir. Al Young. CSP; TAT

I, too, at the mid-point, in a well-lit wood. Ascent into Hell. A. D. Hope. GAS; MAuV

I, too, dislike it: there are things that are important beyond all this fiddle. Poetry. Marianne Moore. AnMo; BiP; BoWoP; CABA (1972 ed.); CMoP (1970 ed.); ExPo (1973 ed.); FF; HAP; HeIP; ILP (1975 ed.); IPWM; LFH; NIL; NoAM; NOBA; PAIC; PiAm; Psy; TAP; TPo; TSWA; UnPo (1976 ed.); UsP; WIF

I, too, have plucked a stalk of grass. Letters to Walt Whitman, V. Ronald Johnson. VGW

I, Too, Sing America. Langston Hughes. *See* I, Too.

I too was a little child once. Epilogue. Joseph Eliyia, *tr. by* Rae Dalven. VWA

I too was born out of a lion's mouth. Let Heroes Account to Love. Alan Dugan. NoAM

I took/ a coney island of the mind. Clickety-Clack. Paul Blackburn. NoAM

I took a piece of the rare cloth of Ch'i. A Present from the Emperor's New Concubine. Lady Pan, *tr. Chinese by* Kenneth Rexroth. BoWoP

I took away the ocean once. The Shell. David McCord. LCL

I took away three pictures. Sandhill People. Carl Sandburg. CMoP (1970 ed.)

I took her to the river. The Unfaithful Married Woman. Federico García Lorca, *tr. by* Rolfe Humphries. LoAs

I took my cat apart. The Secret in the Cat. May Swenson. GP

I took my girl to a ball one night. Accident. *Unknown.* OSF

I took my girlfriend to your last poetry reading. Short Order. Charles Bukowski. HoPM (1975 ed.)

I took my heart in my hand. Twice. Christina Rossetti. BoReV; GBL; NOBE; UsP; VLP

I took my mind a walk. An Ordinary Day. Norman MacCaig. LP

I took my oath I would inquire. The Inquest. W. H. Davies. NOBE; OxBTC

I took one small breath to lift her. The Minyan. Jack Myers. VWA

I took the embankment path. An Advancement of Learning. Seamus Heaney. NCSH

I took you to the clinic today. Physical for My Son. Barbara Smith. AMV–80

I tossed my friend a wreath of roses, wet. Gifts. Mary Elizabeth Coleridge. PBWP

I touch your face. Poems of Night. Galway Kinnell. LoAs

I touch your nose. The Face as It Might Be of Love. Toi Derricotte. NPW

I touched the nothingness of air once. I Read a Tight-fisted Poem Once. Nancy Woods. RFM

I tourist take my coffee. The Tour. Katharine Edgar Cobey. PoUp

I traded a girl. Trader. Jim Harrison. NoAM

I trail and trail along with the mountain range. My Indian Girl. Ali Sedat Hilmi Törel. PeD

I travel in a train. I Am a Horse. Hans Arp, *tr. by* Harriet Watts. FaBoNo

I travel'd thro' a land of men. The Mental Traveller. Blake. Epi; GrRo; ILP (1975 ed.); LAuP; MBPR; OAEL–2; TT

I Traveled among Unknown Men. Wordsworth. *Fr.* Lucy. AnMo; ILP (1975 ed.); MBPR; OAEL–2

I traveled on, seeing the hill, where lay. The Pilgrimage. George Herbert. SoSe

I traveled to the ocean. Prayer to the Pacific. Leslie Silko. CDW; VoR

I travelled the land from Leap to Corbally. The Volatile Kerryman. Owen Roe O'Sullivan, *tr. by* Sean O'Riada. BIrV

I traversed a dominion. Mute Opinion. Thomas Hardy. CMoP (1970 ed.)

I tried each thing, only some were immortal and free. As One Put Drunk into the Packet-Boat. John Ashbery. HAP

I tried to live small. Housing Shortage. Naomi Replansky. NMM

I tried to save those glorious jacarandas. Mrs. Asquith Tries to Save the Jacarandas. Harold Witt. AMV–81

I tried to tell her. Offspring. Naomi Long Madgett. FB

I trundle the bodies, on the iron bars. John Berryman. *Fr.* Homage to Mistress Bradstreet. NOBA

I, trusting that the truly sweet. A Retrospect. Coventry Patmore. VLP

I Try to Turn In My Jock. David Hilton. *See* Poet Tries to Turn In His Jock, The.

I Try to Waken and Greet the World Once Again. James Wright. InPS

I turn on all the lights. My Mother Tries to Visit Me in the Dead of Night. Diane Wakoski. CAAP; TV

I turn round. The Lady's First Song. W. B. Yeats. PSN

I turn to you. To the Divine Neighbor. Judah Leib Teller, *tr. by* Gabriel Preil *and* Howard Schwartz. VWA

I turn you out of doors. Alain Chartier, *tr. fr. French by* Edward Lucie-Smith. BoLoP

I turned aside into the trees, among the shadows. In the Garden of the Turkish Consulate. Pinhas Sadeh, *tr. by* Harris Lenowitz. VWA

I turned to speak to God. Not All There. Robert Frost. FaBoCo

I turned upon the world and inward eye. The Meeting. Jocelyn Hollis. AMV–80

I understand the large heart of heroes. Walt Whitman. *Fr.* Song of Myself, XXXIII. InPS

I understand the ties that are between us. The Summing Up. James Simmons. POL

I upon the first creation. Gratitude. Christopher Smart. *Fr.* Hymns for the Amusement of Children. LAuP

I used to be a drill man. Drill Man Blues. George Sizemore. AmFP; WTO

I used to be a radical. The Radical in the Alligator Shirt. Lou Lipsitz. AMV–80

I used to dream militant. Revolutionary Dreams. Nikki Giovanni. CNA; GP

I used to fall. My Heart Belongs to Daddy. Cole Porter. OBAL

I Used to Love My Garden. C. P. Sawyer. FaBoCo

I used to pray in furnished rooms. Evidence. John Skoyles. AAN

I used to see her daily, we would lie. Mental Health. Elliot Fried. GP

I used to see her in the door. Paul. James Wright. WIF

I used to tell you, "Frances, we grow old." Kenneth Rexroth, *after the Latin of* Ausonius. NNaP

I used to think that grown-up people chose. Childhood. Frances Cornford. OxBTC

I used to walk the morning stream. Walk. Brian Merriman, *tr. by* Brendan Behan. *Fr.* The Midnight Court. BIrV

I Used to Wrap My White Doll Up in. Mae Jackson. PoBA

I usta wonder who i'd be. Adulthood. Nikki Giovanni. NMM

I view the backless rooms. The Doll House. Darlene Button Kitzman. AMV–81

I Visit My Brother. Greg Kuzma. NVAP

I visit them in my dreams: the helpless young. Prayer to Christ and Socrates. James Liddy. IPM

I vow'd unvarying faith, and she. Constancy Rewarded. Coventry Patmore. *Fr.* The Angel in the House. VLP

I wad ha'e gi'en him my lips tae kiss. Mary's Song. Marion Angus. MS; SLP

I wade through sea-green grass. Epitaphs. Glyn Hughes. LP

I wait for her who restores my fingertips. Song of Expectancy. George Hitchcock. EAS; MIT

I wait in the cafe for my wife like a gorilla. Waiting in the Cafe. Stan Rice. MIT

I wait to tangle fear around my hand. Night along the Mackinac Bridge. Roberta Hill. CDW

I wait, with those that rest. Jay MacPherson. *Fr.* The Ark. PoA

I waited for a single flower to blow. An Emblem. Ina Coolbrith. WPW

I waited for you all day in front of the station, 23 degrees. Dream Girl. Larry Zirlin. AAN

I wake/ when lightning cracks. Night Storm. Jane Sherman. CaYB

I wake and feel the city trembling. Lines Written near San Francisco. Louis Simpson. CABA (1972 ed.)

I Wake and Feel the Fell of Dark, Not Day. Gerard Manley Hopkins. BoReV; CMoP (1970 ed.); HAP; ILP (1975 ed.); NoAM; NOBE; OAEL–2; PoIA; PoPle; PPoe; PPP; VLP

I wake and hear it raining. Morning Worship. Mark Van Doren. LoAs

I wake before the clock begins the day. Waking Early. R. L. Barth. AMV-81

I wake, but before I know it it is done. Aging. Randall Jarrell. PoA

I wake despondent. Morning. Tove Ditlevsen, tr. by Nadia Christensen. PBWP

I wake in a dark flat. Afterlives. Derek Mahon. CIP

I wake in New Hampshire. My Horse, Amanda: The Summer of the Watergate Hearings. Maxine W. Kumin. WasP

I wake in the night. Middle of the Way. Galway Kinnell. NU

I Wake, My Friend, I. Faye Kicknosway. IHMS

I wake to sleep, and take my waking slow. The Waking. Theodore Roethke. BiP; CNW; HAP; HeIP; InPS; NoAM; NOBA; PiAm; PPM; PPP; SoSe; STS; TAP; TCP; VoPo

I wake up back aching from soft bed Pat. Sonnet. Ted Berrigan. CAAP

I wake up first and with a sense of. Genius Loci of the Morning. Doug Fetherling. NeAC

I wake up in a morning. Unknown. SFF

I wake up in a room that seems to be snowing. The White Room. Peter Cooley. NVAP

I wake with morning yawning in my mouth. Morning Mood. M. Panegoosho. TVo

I wakened on my hot, hard bed. The Watch. Frances Cornford. InPK; OxBTC

I wakened to love and music; coaxed from the shelter. One Morning. Vassar Miller. AMV-80

I walk/ between the cobblestones. Peripatetic. Robert Lima. AMV-81

I walk along the bustling streets. Girls from Home. Abraham Reisen, tr. by Keith Bosley. VWA

I walk among/ glass tombs. The Indians. Gene Fowler. PoW

I walk among my great-grandfather's trees. Letter from Thurlby Domain. Charles Brasch. ATNZ

I walk at dawn across the hollow hills. Poem. Ruthven Todd. EAS

I walk awkwardly between the beds in row. Just Visiting. Peter Dale. PMW

I walk back. Getting the Mail. Galway Kinnell. UnPo (1976 ed.)

I walk behind you, hand. Days of 1956. Robin Magowan. EAS

I walk beside the prisoners to the road. A Camp in the Prussian Forest. Randall Jarrell. CMoP (1970 ed.); NowV; TCP

I walk by the sea-shore. Psychology. Duncan Glen. MIS

I walk down. Looking for Someone. Michael Small. DNGG

I walk down the garden paths. Patterns. Amy Lowell. BoWoP; DL; NIL; GrRo; PBMP; VoPo

I walk downhill, slow. Roll Call: A Land of Old Folk and Children. Isaac J. Black. CNA

I walk facing against the wind. Walking without Snowshoes. Elizabeth Hanson. NPW

I walk, I trust, with open eyes. Love's Reality. Coventry Patmore. Fr. The Angel in the House. VLP

I walk in loneliness through the greenwood. Unknown, tr. fr. French by Willis Barnstone. BoWoP

I walk in the old street. Louis Zukofsky. VGW

I walk into your house, a friend. A Friend. W. D. Snodgrass. MAT

I walk Main Street, a pelican. Small Town: The Friendly. Stephen Dunn. POL

I walk on the cold mountain above the city. The New Year. Kenneth Rexroth. MPA

I walk on two legs. A Riddle. Cynthia Ozick. VWA

I Walk Out into the Country at Night. Lu Yu, tr. fr. Chinese by Kenneth Rexroth. IPWM

I walk the purple carpet into your eye. Diane Wakoski. Fr. Inside Out. OSP

I walk the tightrope of the heart. Acrobat. Edward Watkins. AMV-80

I walk through the long schoolroom questioning. Among School Children. W. B. Yeats. AnMo; CABA (1972 ed.); CMoP (1970 ed.); Epi; HAP; ILP (1975 ed.); NIL; NoAM; NOBE; OAEL-2; OxBTC; PPoe; PPP; SoSe; STS; WeW

I walk uphill through the snow. Carrying Food Home in Winter. Margaret Atwood. TSWA

I walked about the garden in the evening. Soothsayer. Mary Ursula Bethell. ATNZ

I walked abroad on a snowy day. Soft Snow. Blake. FF; FSFS; SoSe; WeW

I walked all the way from East St. Louis. East St. Louis Blues. Unknown. AmFP

I walked along the winding road. The Prisoner. Charles Spear. ATNZ

I walked in loamy Wessex lanes, afar. The Pity of It. Thomas Hardy. CMoP (1970 ed.)

I walked on the banks of the tincan banana dock. Sunflower Sutra. Allen Ginsberg. MAT; NOBA; PiAm

I walked over the grave of Henry James. Richard Eberhart. VGW

I walked, the first, into a world of whiteness. White Worlds. Jane Marie Luecke. AATT

I walked through Ballinderry in the spring-time. Lament for the Death of Thomas Davis. Sir Samuel Ferguson. BIrV

I walked, when love was gone. A Breath of Air. James Wright. NOBA

I walkit air, I walkit late. Scrievin. Alexander Scott. MS

I wander by the edge. He [or Aedh] Hears the Cry of the Sedge. W. B. Yeats. OxBTC; VLP

I wander through. Accra 8/75. Thulani Nkabinde. NW

I wander through each chartered street. London. Blake. Fr. Songs of Experience. AnMo; CABA (1972 ed.); ExPo (1973 ed.); FF; GrRo; HAP; HeIP; ILP (1975 ed.); InPK; InPS; IP; LAuP; LFH; MAT; MBPR; NIL; NOBE; OAEL-2; OBP; PAIC; PBMP; PoIA; PPoD; STS; TPo; TT; UnPo (1976 ed.); UsP; VoPo; WIF

I wandered angry as a cloud. Paul Dehn. SpRo

I Wandered Lonely as a Cloud. Wordsworth. CABA (1972 ed.); ExPo (1973 ed.); ILP (1975 ed.); InPK; IPWM; MBPR; OAEL-2; PoIA; PPM; SpRo; UnPo (1976 ed.); UsP (Daffodils.) CTV; NOBE; PF

I wandered today to the hill, Maggie. When You and I Were Young, Maggie. George W. Johnson. BLSH; BLSo; FSW; PSoN

I Want. Rosemary Daniell. WBN

I want/ to make a myth of you. Love Poem. Rosemary Aubert. AMV-80

I want a hero: an uncommon want. Don Juan, I. Byron. MBPR; NIL; OAEL-2, abr.

I want a holiday/ From medicine and death. A Mood. E. Mitter. PMW

I want a job as a low cloud. Job Hunting. Tom Hennen. GP; HeS

I want a maid and a bookkeeper. The Weeper. David Bristol. PoUp

I want a typewriter. In Despair He Orders a New Typewriter. Elder Olson. AMV-81

I want all you women to listen to my tale of woe. Death Sting Me Blues. Unknown. BluL

I want free life, and I want fresh air. Lasca. Frank Desprez. BPAW

I want it to be clear for us. On My Stand. Sharon Scott. JB

I want my house with open doors. My House. Saint-Denys Garneau, *tr. by* John Glassco. AKE

I want something suited to my special needs. Needs. A. R. Ammons. NIL; OBAL; UsP

I want the grave to be six by six. One Song. Stanley Plumly. HeS

I want to Be a Cowboy. *Unknown.* BPAW

I want to be beautiful, Mama. The Motive for Metaphor. Cynthia Nibbelink. TC

I want to be buried in an anonymous crater inside the moon. Unholy Missions. Bob Kaufman. CNA

I want to be in a garden with my love. *Tr. fr. Arabic by* Willis Barnstone. BoWoP

I want to be one of those poets. Poem. David Hilton. AcAn

I want to be ready. Walk in Jerusalem, Just like John. *Unknown.* FSW

I want to be with my love in a garden. *Tr. fr. Arabic by* Willis Barnstone. BoWoP

I want to dance. The Deepest Bow. Marie Takvan, *tr. by* Harold P. Hansen. AMV–81

I Want to Die while You Love Me. Georgia Douglas Johnson. AmNP (1974 ed.)

"I want to fight you," he said in a Belfast accent. Experience. James Simmons. BIrV; CIP

I want to forget my manners. Hope. Edith Södergran, *tr. by* Jaakko A. Ahokas. PBWP

"I want to get away somewhere and re-read Proust." Problems of a Journalist. Weldon Kees. NYP

I want to give my babies to the moon. Giving the Moon a New Chance. Terry Stokes. Moon

I want to give you a spoonful of hot soup. A Hymn about a Spoonful of Soup. Jozef Wittlin, *tr. by* Isaac Komem. VWA

I want to give you words. Words. Ulálume González De Leon, *tr. by* Sara Nelson. AMV–81

I want to go home and I ain't got sufficient. Bad Luck Blues. *Unknown.* BluL

I want to hear pitter patter. All La Glory. Robbie Robertson. RRA

I want to help you. The Friends. Robert Creeley. Epi

I want to know the unity in all things. Ballad. A. R. Ammons. GP

I want to learn to whistle. Whistles. Dorothy Aldis. CTV

I want to leave him. Dreams of Eurydice. Margaret Ryan. NPW

I want to live. Heart of Gold. Neil Young. UsP

I want to live in an old adobe house on the outskirts of Sante Fe. Prospectus. Albert Huffstickler. AMV–81

I Want to One Morning. Gordon Turner. AMV–80

I want to see it face to face. Nothing. Charles Simic. NNaP

I want to see the slim palm trees. Heritage. Gwendolyn B. Bennett. AmNP (1974 ed.); PoBA

I want to speak to you while I can. I Am Here. Robert Mezey. VWA

I Want to Tell You. Sandra Hochman. GP

I want to tell you what you are—not for. Landladies. Gerald Locklin. PoW

I want to understand the steep thing. Climbing You. Erica Jong. PoA

I Want to Write a Jewish Poem. Gary Pacernick. VWA

I want to write a poem. Noises. Fred Johnson. CNA

I wanta say just gotta say something. Beautiful Black Men. Nikki Giovanni. BPo; NMM

I wanted a rib sandwich. Rib Sandwich. William J. Harris. CNA

I wanted so ably. The World. Robert Creeley. NoAM

I wanted this morning to bring you a gift of roses. The Roses of Sa'adi. Marceline Desbordes-Valmore, *tr. by* Barbara Howes. BoWoP

I wanted to be a cauliflower. The Cauliflower. John Haines. GP; InPK

I wanted to be more human. Forms of the Human. Richard Eberhart. TH

I wanted to be sure to reach you. To the Harbormaster. Frank O'Hara. RhR

I wanted to bring you this Jap iris. For C. Philip Whalen. VGW

I Wanted to Die in the Desert. *Unknown.* BPAW

I wanted to know my mother when she sat. Leroy. Amiri Baraka. BPo; ILP (1975 ed.); PiAm; PoBA

I wanted to make love with you. A Thought in the Center of a Memory. J. Charles Green. DNGG

I wanted to see you,/ thighs showing. Leila Miccolis, *tr. fr. Portuguese by* Willis Barnstone *and* Nelson Cerqueira. BoWoP

I wanted to take a walk. Walking Past Paul Blackburn's Apt. on 7th St. Diane Wakoski. TAP

I wanted to wear your name religiously for the rest. First-Class Relics: Letter to Dennis Finnell. Madeline DeFrees. PCho

I wanted to write. For Saundra. Nikki Giovanni. BPo; Psy; RiTi; TPo; WIF

I warn ye all, ye gay ladies. Child Waters. *Unknown.* PeBB

I was/ the girl of the chain letter. Love Song. Anne Sexton. NCSH

I was a boy when I heard three red words. Threes. Carl Sandburg. CMoP (1970 ed.)

I Was a Bustlemaker Once, Girls. Patrick Barrington. PoPle

I was a girl waiting by the roadside for my boyfriend to come. The Elwha River. Gary Snyder. NoAM

I was a lady of high renown. Jamie Douglas. *Unknown.* AIW

I was a mere boy in a stone-cutter's shop. Abraham. Delmore Schwartz. VWA

I was a poor groom of thy stable, king. Shakespeare. King Richard II, *fr.* V, v. PoPle

I was a squanderer once of love and days. Conservative. Harold Witt. AMV–80

I was a peasant girl from Germany. Elsa Wertman. Edgar Lee Masters. *Fr.* Spoon River Anthology. NoAM

I was a traveller then upon the moor. Wordsworth. *Fr.* Resolution and Independence. SpRo

I was about to go, and said so. Loneliness. Brooks Jenkins. CTBA; SoS

I Was Afraid of Dying. James Wright. OSP

I was all self-righteous. Shirley 4 Years Later. Alta. MMD

I was alone then looking at the picture of a child. Six Days. Tom Raworth. TwMBP

I was always called in early for dinner. Don't Forget. Stephen Berg. PoA

I was always one for being alone. Theodore Roethke. Meditations of an Old Woman, IV. MPA; STS

I was angry with my friend. A Poison Tree. Blake. *Fr.* Songs of Experience. AnMo; CABA (1972 ed.); HAP; HoPM (1975 ed.); ILP (1975 ed.); IP; IPWM; LAuP; LFH; MBPR; PBMP; PoIA; PPoD; PPoe; PPP; SFF; SoSe (1977 ed.); STS; WIF

I was asking for something specific and perfect for my city. Mannahatta. Walt Whitman. GOA; NYP

I was awake all night. Death of a Snowman. Vernon Scannell. FPB

I was bear huntin. Jim Worley Fries Trout on South Squalla. Jim Wayne Miller. CSP

I was beautiful when we came into Egypt. Sarai. Joseph Sherman. VWA

I was born/ In spittin distance. Moutain Born. Marcia Inzer Bost. AMV–80

I Was Born about Ten Thousand Years Ago. *Unknown.* FSW

I was born and raised in East Virginia. East Virginia. *Unknown.* FSW

I was born conscious, I can't remember. Rino's Song. Lynne Lawner. IHMS

I was born in a drouth year. That summer. Water. Wendell Berry. CSP

I was born in a time of peace. Ts'ai Yen, *tr. by* Kenneth Rexroth *and* Ling Chung. *Fr.* Eighteen Verses Sung to a Tatar Reed Whistle. BoWoP; PBWP

I was born in August, 1942—conceived on a Christmas leave. Requiem of a War-Baby. Joan Watton. PFIr

I was born in Belfast between the mountain and the gantries. Carrickfergus. Louis MacNeice. NoAM

I was born in Boston, a city you all know well. The Boston Burglar. *Unknown.* AmFP

I was born in Cologne. Winter in Another Country. Ai. AMV–81

I was born in the congo. Ego Tripping. Nikki Giovanni. NoAM

I was born in the desert. New Minglewood Blues. *Unknown.* BluL

I was born in the Year of the Horse. The Self-conscious Horse. David Rafael Wang. FoP

I was born long ago. Beans, Bacon and Gravy. *Unknown.* FSW

I was born nowhere. The Dawn of Me. Jeff Morley. OSP

I was born on a street named Joy. Lines on His Birthday. John Logan. CAPP

I was born the year of the gray pennies. 1943. Sandra McPherson. FoP

I was born the year of the loon. Chronicles: Number Three. Mei Berssenbrugge. GP; SA

I was born with a song in my tongue. Ars. Marina Tsvetayeva, *tr. by* Willis Barnstone *and* Edward Brown. BoWoP

I was broke and out of a job in the city of London. Paddy, Get Back. *Unknown.* AmFP

I was brought up in Sheffield, all of a high degree. The Sheffield 'Prentice. *Unknown.* AmFP

I was brought up to believe. Arms. Patricia Beer. HeHu

I was brought up with a myth in my mind. Confession of a Young Hegelian. Ellen McEvilley Griffin. NPW

I was buried near this dyke. Blake. FaBoEE

I was busy, with the normal course of events. On a Death in an Old People's Home. May Ivimy. PMW

I was but seven year auld. The Laily Worm and the Machrel of the Sea. *Unknown.* PeBB

I was considering how. Impressions, Number III. E. E. Cummings. UnPo (1976 ed.)

I was content with the pseudonym. Encounter. Vassar Miller. GP

I was dead and I wanted peace. A Grammar. Andrei Codrescu. EAS

I was directed by my grandfather. Direction. Alonzo Lopez. VW

I was down and I cried. Tin Cup Blues. *Unknown.* BluL

I was drawn to look at an apartment. The Empty Apartment. Aaron Zeitlin, *tr. by* Ruth Whitman. VWA

I Was Driving across the Island. Dennis Trudell. NVAP

I Was Fair Beat. Robert Garioch. OxBTC

I was far forward on the plain, the burning swamp. The Little Girl with Bands on Her Teeth. Genevieve Taggard. VGW

I was foretold that on a certain day. Sonnet XX. Louise Labé, *tr. by* Willis Barnstone. BoWoP

I was foretold your rebel sex. A Deposition from Love. Thomas Carew. CaPo

I was going to say something. Ancestor. Thomas Kinsella. BIrV

I was grass you fell upon. Your Hands. Joan Swift. PoW

I was hangin' round town just a spendin' my time. The Strawberry Roan. *Unknown.* FSW

I was happy I was bubbly drunk. Second Night in N.Y.C. after 3 Years. Gregory Corso. BuTh

"I was in a hooker once," said Karlssen. Cape Horn Gospel—1. John Masefield. PoTa

I was just thinkin' 'bout the way it's s'posed to be. I Don't Eat Animals (And They Don't Eat Me). Melanie Safka. PoRo

I was late for today. On Being Late. Michael Small. DNGG

I was leavin' the Blue Dog on the run. Indigo Pete's J. B. Henry Herbert Knibbs. BPAW

I was led into captivity by the bitch business. Money. C. H. Sisson. POL

I was my own ghost that walked among the hills. About Scotland, and C. Ruthven Todd. MS

I was myself blown. For My People. Wendy Rose. CDW

I was never handsome, always cute. Cute. Jim Everhard. EC

I was never the light lad. The Spawn of Slums. James W. Thompson. BPo

I was never there. A Young Deer/Dust. Hemda Roth, *tr. by* Myra Glazer Schotz. VWA

I was nine years old. Luck. Raymond Carver. PCho

I was no taller than a seedling then. All Men Are . . . Socrates Is. Napoleon St. Cyr. FAF

I was not ready for this world. Bargain. Ruth Stone. GP

I was of delicate mind. I stepped aside for my needs. The Refined Man. Kipling. *Fr.* Epitaphs of the War. FaBoEE; FaBoTw (1975 ed.)

I was on holiday in August. The Director of the Museum. Roderick Watson. MIS

I was on the drive in sixty, working under Silver Jack. Silver Jack's Religion. John P. Jones. BPAW

I was out in the country one beautiful night. The Widow's Old Broom. *Unknown.* AmFP

I was over in Aberdeen on my way to New Orleans. Aberdeen, Mississippi Blues. *Unknown.* BluL

I was playing with my hoop along the road. The Turn of the Road. James Stephens. SO

I was prepared for places. Return. Jane Cooper. UsP

I Was Proud. Jim Harrison. HeS

I was raised up in Louisville, a town you all knew well. Frank James, the Roving Gambler. *Unknown.* AmFP

I was readin' some. What Good Is a Poet? L. X. Lanners. CPA

I Was Riding to Poughkeepsie. Mary Ann Hoberman. ECBV

I was round and small like a pearl. *Unknown.* GBP

I was sewing a seam one day. Seams. Hazel Hall. WPW

I was sick. Jesus Was Crucified or: It Must Be Deep. Carolyn M. Rodgers. PoBA; SA

I Was Sick and in Prison. Jones Very. NOBA

I was sinking deep in sin. Love Lifted Me. James Rowe. BLSH

I was sitting in mcsorley's. E. E. Cummings. NoAM

I was sitting in my study. Papa's Letter. *Unknown.* WeW

I was six when I first saw kittens drown. The Early Purges. Seamus Heaney. NCSH

I was sixteen, a freshman, a former Catholic buddhist. Rissem. Sandra M. Gilbert. AMV–81

I was sixteen years of age. Song Ballet. *Unknown.* AmFP

I was sleeping. A Translation from. Fred Levinson. AmPA

I was sleepless, I was awake all night. Sleepless. Al-Khansa, *tr. fr. Arabic by* Willis Barnstone. BoWoP

I was so sick last night I. Morning After. Langston Hughes. NoAM

I was standing by the window. Can the Circle be Unbroken? *Unknown.* FSW

I was standing by the window yesterday morning. The Letter Edged in Black. *Unknown.* FSW

I was standing in a crap game doing no harm, Baby! You've Been a Good Old Wagon, but You've Done Broke Down. Ben Harney. OBAL

I was the choice of many old men when I was young. The Old Wife. Rolly Kent. AAN; FF

I was the father. The Settlers. Judith Hemschemeyer. SO

I was the first made woman. I first wept. Lilith. Allen Grossman. VWA

I was the first of us, leaving a downtown bar. The Bear. William Heyen. BCr

I was the last passenger of the day. The Bus. Leonard Cohen. HeIP

I was the Moor Moraima. A Lovely Young Moor. *Unknown, tr. by* Willis Barnstone. BoWoP

I was the Mooress, Morayma. The Mooress Morayma. *Unknown, tr. by* W. S. Merwin. Epi

I was the only child of Frances Harris of Virginia. Hamilton Greene. Edgar Lee Masters. *Fr.* Spoon River Anthology. NoAM

I was the patriarch of the shining land. John Sutter. Yvor Winters. MPA; NoAM; NOBA

I was there. Will and Testament. James Neugass. SPT

I was there and I remember the brown brocade. In Memory of V. R. Lang. Mac Hammond. PoA

I was thinking of a son. Menstruation at Forty. Anne Sexton. CAPP

I was three and already. Passing It On. Reg Saner. BrS; GP

I was thy neighbour once, thou rugged pile! Elegiac Stanzas Suggested by a Picture of Peele Castle, in a Storm. Wordsworth. MBPR; OAEL-2

I was tired, cold and already bored. An Occasional Apostrophe. Hugh Walthall. PoUp

I was tired of being a woman. Consorting with Angels. Anne Sexton. NMM

I was traveling fast. Highway Blues. *Unknown.* BluL

I was traveling through South Americas. Travelin' Blues. *Unknown.* BluL

I was walking along, reciting the Lord's Prayer. The Orange Tree. Ellen Pearce. IHMS

I was walking along the Sea of Galilee. Walking along the Sea of Galilee. Dovid Knut, *tr. by* John Glad. VWA

I was walking down by the old/ Santee. Second Carolina Said-Song. A. R. Ammons. OBAL

I was walking downtown. The Man in Black. Mark Strand. EAS

I was walking in a government warehouse. Fifteen Million Plastic Bags. Adrian Mitchell. OSBV; OxBTC

I was watching the great God dance. Ellora. Leonard Nathan. GP

I was Willie Metcalf. Willie Metcalf. Edgar Lee Masters. *Fr.* Spoon River Anthology. IPWM

I was wondering about the gods. The Gods of Washington, D.C. Richard Eberhart. WasP

I was wrapped in black. Us. Anne Sexton. CAPP

I was writing a trenta-sei for the boat-people. An Apology for a Lost Classicism. John Ciardi. AMV–81

I washed my face in water. *Unknown.* GBP

I Wasn't No Mary Ellen. Linda King. GP

I waste my teeming age. I do not know. Abishag. Jakov Fichman, *tr. by* Robert Friend. VWA

I watch airplanes land. Bright Winter Morning. Chris Klein. AMV–81

I watch my concern for the world, how it changes. What Form the World Has. William Bronk. AMV–80

I watch the calligraphy of shadows. Philodendron. Helen Armstead Johnson. AmNP (1974 ed.)

I watch the dung-cart stumble by. In December. Andrew Young. MS

I watch the Indians dancing to help the young corn at Taos pueblo. New Mexico [*or* Mexican] Mountain. Robinson Jeffers. GOA; InPS; NoAM

I watch the jocks come out in the post parade. My Style. Charles Bukowski. AMV–81

I watch the roses float. Requiem. Stephen Vincent. NeAC

I watch the TV close its bleary eye. Sleeping Alone. Kurt J. Fickert. AMV–80

I watch them. Poets. Dana "The Mouse" Merkel. DNGG

I watched a blackbird on a budding sycamore. Thomas Hardy. PB

I watched a bullfrog and entered his dark water. A Bullfrog in a Pond Not Far from an Abandoned Farm. Duane Locke. CSP

I watched a laughing cloud. Evening. King D. Kuka. VoR

I watched a rosebud very long. Symbols. Christina Rossetti. VLP

I watched for years a sidehill farm that died. The Blown Door. Malcolm Cowley. PPoD

I watched last night the rising moon, upon a foreign strand. The Moon behind the Hill. *Unknown.* WTO

I watched old squatting chimpanzee: he traced. Sporting Acquaintances. Siegfried Sassoon. OxBTC

I watched the borrowed children. Intermission. Margaret R. Litchfield. PoUp

I watched the house, and barked agreeably, and. Sudden Assertion. Kenneth Leslie. BoAnP; GDP; POL

I watched the moon around the house. Emily Dickinson. Moon

I watched the rain amaze me again that water. Two Poems Based on Fact. Frank J. Lepkowski. AMV–81

I watched thee when the foe was at our side. Love and Death. Byron. EBEV; MBPR; NOBE

I weave my blanket red. The Marriage Dance. Eda Lou Walton, *after Blackfoot Indian.* BPAW

I weave the night, I cross the weft with stars. In the Flight of the Blue Heron: To Montezuma. Anita Endrezze Probst. CDW

I weep for Adonais—he is dead! Adonais: An Elegy on the Death of John Keats. Shelley. CABA (1972 ed.); EBEV; HoPM (1975 ed.); ILP (1975 ed.); LFH; MBPR; OAEL–2

I weep for my loved one. Song of Despair. Rangiaho, *tr. fr. Maori by* Barry Mitcalfe. WTO

I weep when the gay are around me. Mary and Her Dead Canary. Alexander Kerr. InPK

I welcomed the Spring in romantic Chungking. Lyric to Spring. Joseph W. Stilwell. OBAL

I well remember/ A time when/ "Amazing Grace" was/ All the rage. Hymn. Alice Walker. CSP

I Wende to Dede. *Unknown. See* I Went to Death.

I went a-riding, a-riding. Texas. Amy Lowell. BPAW

I went down a narrow, narrow road, and I lost my cap. The Firefly. *Unknown, tr. fr. Italian.* RAE

I went down by Cascadilla. Cascadilla Falls. A. R. Ammons. CoPAm; NIL; NOBA

I went down in Death Valley. Death Valley Blues. *Unknown.* BluL

I went down the lane to buy a penny whistle. Hi, Hi, Curlywig. *Unknown.* PoPle

I went down to malcolmland. Half Black, Half Blacker. Sterling Plumpp. PoBA

I went down to Saint James this morning. St. James Infirmary. *Unknown.* AmFP

I went down to the river, poor boy. Bow Down Your Head and Cry. *Unknown.* WTO

I went for a walk over the dunes again this morning. Corsons Inlet. A. R. Ammons. CSP; LFH; NoAM; NOBA; PoIA; PPP

I went into a public-'ouse to get a pint o' beer. Tommy. Kipling. BTTM; CABA (1972 ed.); EBEV; FaPoR; OxBTC

I went into my [*or* the ] stable, to see what I might [*or* could] see. Old Wichet. *Unknown.* GBP; PoTa

I went into the chandler's shop some candles for to buy. The Chandler's Wife. *Unknown.* FSW

I went into the flea circus. Small Talk. Don Marquis. PoTa

I Went into the Maverick Bar. Gary Snyder. MAT

I went into the wood one day. Fairy Story. Stevie Smith. DuDr

I went on Friday afternoons. Au Tombeau de Mon Père. Ronald McCuaig. GAS; MAuV

I went out alone. Girl's Song. W. B. Yeats. SS

I went out alone to gather rocks. Prostration. David Semah, *tr. by* Yoffee Berkovitz. VWA

I went out at daybreak and stood on Primrose Hill. Birds Waking. W. S. Merwin. NOBA

I went out on. Saying. A. R. Ammons. TSWA

I went out to the hazel wood. The Song of Wandering Aengus. W. B. Yeats. AKE; CABA (1972 ed.); CMoP (1970 ed.); ILP (1975 ed.); MAT; OBP; PBMP; VLP; WIF

I went to a foreign land to work for money. Sure a Poor Man. *Tr. fr. Hawaiian by* M.K. Pukui *and* A.L. Korn. WTO

I Went to Death. *Unknown.* OxBM
(I Wende to Dede.) HAP

I went to Frankfort and got drunk. Porson's Visit to the Continent. Richard Porson. FaBoCo; FaBoEE

I Went to Noke. *Unknown.* GBP

I went to see "Ane Tryall of Heretiks." And They Were Richt. Robert Garioch. MS

I Went to See Irving Babbitt. Richard Eberhart. OBAL

I went to the animal fair. The Animal Fair. *Unknown.* PoPle

I went to the city. Raising Money. Carla Eugster. PoUp

I went to the dance. Vickie. Marnie Walsh. VW

I went to the dances at Chandlerville. Lucinda Matlock. Edgar Lee Masters. *Fr.* Spoon River Anthology. CMoP (1970 ed.); FF; HAP; IPWM; NoAM; NOBA; PBMP; PPM; UsP; VoPo

I went to the garden of love. The Garden of Love. Blake. *Fr.* Songs of Experience. CABA (1972 ed.); ExPo (1973 ed.); GBL; HAP; ILP (1975 ed.); IPWM; LAuP; LoAs; MAT; MBPR; NIL; OBP; PoIA; PPoe; SoSe (1977 ed.); SS; STS; TPo; WIF

I went to the Hotel Broog. A Difference of Zoos. Gregory Corso. VGW

I Went to the Market, *with music. Unknown.* AKE

I went to the prince of nettles. Entreaties. Rudy Shackelford. AAN

I went to the river: couldn't get across. Keep It Clean. *Unknown.* BluL

I went to the valley. Lucille Clifton. CNA; TAT

I went to turn the grass once after one. The Tuft of Flowers. Robert Frost. IPWM; LFH

I went up to Moses and said to him. Moses. Amir Gilboa, *tr. by* Stephen Mitchell. VWA

I went uptown last Saturday night. Blue Monday. *Unknown.* AmFP

I were unkind unless that I did shed. Lines on His Companions Who Died in the Northern Seas. Thomas James. SCP-2

I, when exposed, will pass the letter on to you. The Rendezvous. Steven Graves. PPoD

I whispered, "I am too young." Brown Penny. W. B. Yeats. BoLoP; CMoP (1970 ed.); OLR; PFIr

I, who accompanied with faithful pace. Ecclesiastical Sonnets: Introduction. Wordsworth. MBPR

I who by day am function of the light. Motto for a Sun Dial. J. V. Cunningham. InPK; VGW

I, who cut off my sorrows. Akazome Emon, *tr. fr. Japanese by* Kenneth Rexroth *and* Ikuke Atsumi. BoWoP

I who was driven mad and cast out. The Hebrew Sibyl. Ruth Fainlight. VWA

I who write here came here to find. Found. Sarah Taylor Shatford. PeD

I widowed my small. Jim—Age 38, 5'10'', W.196, Strapping Goggle-eyed Nordic Bankrupt. Jim Harrison. FoP

I will arise and go now, and go to Innisfree. The Lake Isle of Innisfree. W. B. Yeats. AKE; CMoP (1970 ed.); FaPoR; ILP (1975 ed.); InPS; IPWM; LFH; NoAM; NOBE; OxBTC; PoIA; PPM; STS; TT; UsP; VLP; WeW

I Will Be. E. E. Cummings. VGW

I will be exacting before the closing. Song of the Closing Service. Aliza Shenhar, *tr. by* Linda Zisquit. VWA

I will be the gladdest thing. Afternoon on a Hill. Edna St. Vincent Millay. PPM; PSN

I will be what God made me, nor protest. Robert Bridges. The Growth of Love, LXII. VLP

I will call you. My Friend the Wind. King D. Kuka. VoR

I will carry my coat and not put on my belt. *Tr. fr. Chinese by* Arthur Waley. *Fr.* Tzu Yeh Songs. BoWoP

I will confess to anything that works. I Put My Two Fingers, Pound and Whitman, into a Wall Socket. David Bristol. PoUp

I will confront these shows of the day and night! Walt Whitman. *Fr.* By Blue Ontario's Shore, XVIII. InPS

I will consider the outnumbering dead. Merlin. Geoffrey Hill. POL

I will draw you. Indian Warrior. Mary Logue. NPW

I will drink to your health, sweet Amy. To Amy. J. Gordon. Coogler. OBAL

I will enjoy thee now my Celia, come. A Rapture. Thomas Carew. CaPo; LoAs; OAEL-1; SCP-2

I will found a habitation by the water. Unearthing. Betsy Rosenberg. VWA

I Will Give My Love an Apple. *Unknown.* PBMP

I Will Go Away. Zvi Shargel, *tr. fr. Yiddish by* Gabriel Preil *and* Howard Schwartz. VWA

I will go back to the great sweet mother. Swinburne. *Fr.* The Triumph of Time. SoSe

I will go for a walk before. Around the Block. Keith Waldrop. AMV-80

I Will Go into the Ghetto. Charles Reznikoff. VGW

I Will Go with My Father a-Ploughing. Joseph Campbell. OFD
"I will go with my father a-reaping," *sel.* CC

I will grieve alone. In Response to a Rumor That the Oldest Whorehouse in Wheeling, West Virginia, Has Been Condemned. James Wright. CAPP; NNaP

I will have all my beds blown up, not stuft. Ben Jonson. *Fr.* The Alchemist, II, i. EBEV

I Will Have the Whetstone. *Unknown.* FaBoNo; GBP

I will have to accept women. This Form of Life Needs Sex. Allen Ginsberg. NNaP

I will install windows in my dream. Windows. Mordecai Husid, *tr. by* Seymour Mayne *and* Rivka Augenfeld. VWA

I will kneel at thine altar, will crown thee with bays. Shelley. MBPR

I will lift up mine eyes unto the hills. Bible, *O.T.* Psalms, CXXI. ILwL

I will live Ringsend. Ringsend. Oliver St. John Gogarty. OxBTC

I will make love. *Unknown, tr. fr. Spanish by* Willis Barnstone. BoWoP

I Will Make You Brooches. Robert Louis Stevenson. SLP (My Valentine.) OFD

I will my collection of hats. An Exchange of Hats. Stanley Moss. GP

I will never more deceive you. You Naughty, Naughty Men. T. Kennick. BLSo

I will no longer kiss. On Himself. Robert Herrick. CaPo

I will not be inhabited. The Turtle's Belly. Ellen Pearce. IHMS

I will not change my horse with any that treads. The Horse. Shakespeare. King Henry V, *fr.* III, vi. PCOP; PH

I will not kiss you, country fashion. A Calvinist in Love. Jack R. Clemo. LoAs

I will not let thee go. Robert Bridges. CMoP (1970 ed.)

I will not toy with it nor bend an inch. The White City. Claude McKay. BPo; NoAM; TAP

I will not walk on that road again. The Goshawk. John Haines. GP

"I will put upon you the Telephone Curse," said the witch. The Witch of East Seventy-second Street. Morris Bishop. NYP

I will reach into the grab-bag of unconscious things. Private Pantomime. Ruth Stone. PoA

I will remember you on Bloom Street. Bloom Street. Angela McCabe. AmPA

I will sing a song,/ A song that is strong. My Breath. Orpingalik, *tr. by* K. Rasmussen. WTO

I will sing no more songs! O'Bruadair. David O'Bruadair, *tr. by* James Stephens. BIrV

I Will Sing the Wondrous Story, *with music.* Francis H. Rowley. BLSH

I will sing you a song. Streets of Cairo; or, The Poor Little Country Maid. James Thornton. FSN

I will sleep. December. Ron Padgett. EAS

I will speak about women of letters, for I'm in the racket. Pro Femina, III. Carolyn Kizer. MAT; NMM; Psy; RiTi

I will stuff a small rag of. Winter. Larry Levis. NVAP

I will take nails. Eclipse. Tomaz Salamun, *tr. by* Michael Scammel *and* Veno Taufer. VWA

I will teach you my townspeople. Tract. William Carlos Williams. BiP; DL; FF; MiP; NIL; NoAM; NOBA; PPoD; TAP; TCP; VGW

I will teach you to become American, my students. Notes for a Lecture. David Ignatow. NNaP

I will tell you of a fellow. Common Bill. *Unknown.* FSW

I will tell you of a gallan soldier. The Soldier's Wooing. *Unknown.* AmFP

I will track you down the years. Quest. Naomi Long Madgett. BPo

I Will Turn Your Money Green. *Unknown.* BluL

I will twine and will mingle my raven black hair. Wildwood Flower. *Unknown.* BLSo; FSW

I will visit/Unknown woman. Spirit Song. *Tr. fr. Eskimo.* WTO

I will write a sketch of my early life. The Author's Early Life. Julia A. Moore. PeD

I Will Write Songs against you. Charles Reznikoff. VGW

I wish I could proclaim. The Commemoration. Edwin Muir. SLP

I wish I could remember the [*or* that] first day. The First Day. Christina Rossetti. *Fr. Monna Innominata.* BoLoP; GBL; OLR

I wish I could teach you how ugly. On Flunking a Nice Boy out of School. John Ciardi. NowV; SFF

I wish I had a nickel. Round and Round Hitler's Grave. *Unknown.* FSW

I wish I had the voice of Homer. Cancer's a Funny Thing. J. B. S. Haldane. OxBTC

I wish I had two little mouths. Mouths. Dorothy Aldis. CTV

I wish I knew the names of all the stars. Stars. Alden Nowlan. POL

I wish I lived in a caravan. The Pedlar's Caravan. William Brighty Rands. OxBChV

I wish I loved an honest girl. A Song for an Able Bastard. Eric Linklater. SLP

I wish I loved the Human Race. The Wishes of an Elderly Man. Sir Walter Alexander Raleigh. FaBoCo; FaBoEE; NOBL

I wish I owned a Dior dress. Reflections at Dawn. Phyllis McGinley. NOBL

I Wish I Was a Mole in the Ground. *Unknown.* AmFP

I wish I was in the [*or* de] land of [*or* ob] cotton. Dixie. Daniel Decatur Emmet. BLSH; BLSo; FSW; PSoN

I Wish I Was Single, 2 *versions. Unknown.* AmFP

I wish I were a/ Elephantiaphus. *Unknown.* FaBoNo

I wish I were a jelly fish. Triolet. G. K. Chesterton. LCL

I wish I were as in the years of old. Tiresias. Tennyson. VLP

I wish I were close. Yamabe no Akahito. HoPM (1975 ed); OLR

I Wish I Were [*or* Was] Single Again. *Unknown.* AmFP; FSW

I wish I were where Helen lies. Helen of Kirconnell. *Unknown.* ILP (1975 ed.); PoPle

I wish sometimes, although a worthlesse thing. Licia, XII. Giles Fletcher the Elder. AAS

I wish that I could get in line. They Don't Speak English in Paris. Ogden Nash. OBAL

I wish that when you died last May. May and Death. Robert Browning. NOBE

I wish the rent. Little Lyric (of Great Importance). Langston Hughes. OBAL

I wish there were a touch of these boats about my life. Boat Poem. Bernard Spencer. FaBoTw (1975 ed.); OxBTC

I wish they would hurry up their trip to Mars. A Projection. Reed Whittemore. WIF

"I wish to buy a dog," she said. On Buying a Dog. Edgar Klauber. GDP

I wish to God my child was born. Lullaby. *Unknown.* AmFP

I wish to make a positive statement. Peace. George Jonas. NeAC

I wish to paint my eyes. Willis Barnstone, *fr. Egyptian hieroglyphics.* BoWoP

I wish you triumphs that are yours already. For Marianne Moore's Birthday. Kay Boyle. NMM; RiTi

I wish you were not flying, and I wish. For a Homecoming. Julia Randall. NMM

I wish you would come. Izumi Shikibu, *tr. fr. Japanese by* Willis Barnstone. BoWoP

I wished you awake for the bird song. Bird Song. Betsy Rosenberg. VWA

I wish't I was a mole in the ground. Mole in the Ground. *Unknown.* FSW

I wist not what to wish, yet sure thought I. Anne Bradstreet. *Fr.* Contemplations. PBWP

I, with whose colours Myra dressed her head. Myra. Fulke Greville. *Fr. Caelica.* GBL; HAP; NOBE; PoPle

I woke before the day, when the night bird. Thomas Iron-Eyes. Marnie Walsh. VW

I woke up at night and my language was gone. Nothingness. Aharon Amir, *tr. fr. Hebrew.* VWA

I woke up this mornin'. Sylvester's Dying Bed. Langston Hughes. NoAM; UnPo (1976 ed.)

I woke up this mornin'. Empty Bed Blues. Bessie Smith. OBAL; UnPo (1976 ed.)

I woke up this mornin' with the blues all round my bed. Good Mornin', Blues. *Unknown.* InPK

I Woke Up This Morning. Karla Kuskin. FPB

I woke up this morning feeling around for my shoes. Walking Blues. *Unknown.* BluL

I woke up this morning, four o'clock. Kassie Jones. *Unknown.* BluL

I woke up this morning my good gal was gone. No No Blues. *Unknown.* BluL

I woke up this morning with the blues all 'round my bed. You'll Never Miss Your Jelly. *Unknown.* BluL

I woke up without laws. Poetry. Rainer Schulte. SES

I Wonder. Jeannie Kirby. FPB

I wonder. Jewell Lawton. OSP

I wonder about/ the brother. Come On Home. Sharon Scott. JB

I wonder about the trees. The Sound of Trees. Robert Frost. NoAM

I Wonder as I Wander. *Unknown.* PChr

I wonder, by my troth, what thou and I. The Good-Morrow. John Donne. AnMo; BiP; BoLoP; CABA (1972 ed.); EBEV; FF; HoPM (1975 ed.); ILP (1975 ed.); InPS; LoAs; MetP; NIL; OAEL-1; OLR; PAIC; PoIA; PoPle; PPP; SCP-1; SoSe

I wonder do you feel to-day. Two in the Campagna. Robert Browning. EBEV; ExPo (1973 ed.); LoAs; NOBE; OAEL-2; VLP

I wonder, Duddon, if you still remember. To the River Duddon. Norman Nicholson. PES

I wonder how many old men last winter. The Minneapolis Poem. James Wright. NoAM; UnPo (1976 ed.)

I Wonder How My Home Is. *Tr. fr. Tewa Indian by* H. J. Spinden. WTO

I wonder if his appetite was good? Byron. *Fr. Don Juan, V.* OAEL-2

I wonder if the elephant. Pete at the Zoo. Gwendolyn Brooks. ECBV; UsP

I wonder if they sleep better here. Graveyard by the Sea. Thomas Lux. PCho

I wonder if you ever knew the Freemans. Poem for the 10th Year. Tim Burke. PHC

I wonder: is there no way for us to meet again. Wallada, *tr. fr. Arabic by* A. R. Nykl. PBWP

I wonder poet, can you take it. The Muse to an Unknown Poet. Paul Potts. FaBoTw (1975 ed.)

I wonder, since we are both travelling out. The Traveling Out. Lucile Adler. IHMS

I wonder what to mean by sanctuary, if a real or. Triphammer Bridge. A. R. Ammons. NOBA

I wonder why. Pluvkaq, *tr. fr. Eskimo by* C. M. Bowra. WeW

I wonder why the grass is green. I Wonder. Jeannie Kirby. FPB

"I won't go with you. I want to stay with Grandpa!" My Last Afternoon with Uncle Devereux Winslow. Robert Lowell. VGW

I wore loud ties bought for. A Jig for My Wake. Patrick L. Clary. PoUp

I work all day long for you, until the sun go down. *Unknown.* WTO

I work in a theater. Christopher Magisto. Rodger Kamenetz. AAN

I work like a pump in my own sweat. Song of the Farmworker. T. R. Jahns. AMV-80

I work, roars the sun. The Sun, the Worker. Isidor Schneider. SPT

I worked all the winter. Tired as I Can Be. *Unknown.* BluL

I worked with all aurora at my loom. Archne. Richard Foerster. AMV-80

I worship the greatest first. Hippolytus Temporizes. Hilda Doolittle ("H. D."). SBG

I Worship Thee, O Holy Ghost, *with music.* William F. Warren. AH

I wot not how the world's degenerate. Joseph Hall. *Fr. Virgidemiarum.* TVS

I would be ignorant as the dawn. The Dawn. W. B. Yeats. GrRo

I would be married, but I'd have no wife. On Marriage. Richard Crashaw. FaBoEE

I Would Be True. Howard Arnold Walter. CTV

I would be wandering in distant fields. In Bondage. Claude McKay. PoBA

I would be wearing. Wistful Butch Poem. Rochelle Owens. WBN

I would be with the wind. Theodore Roethke. POL

I would bear a love Platonic to the souls in earthly life. Lizzie Doten. *Fr. Farewell to Earth.* PeD

I would embrace the bear. The Bear. Judith Rose. BCr

I would exorcise you like some common demon. That Is Not Indifference. Howard G. Hanson. AMV-81

I would go around biting my nails. Salvador Villanueva, *tr. fr. Spanish by* Julio Marzán. InW

I would I had some flowers o'th' spring that might. Shakespeare. *Fr. The Winter's Tale, IV, iii.* PoPle

I would in rich and golden coloured raine. Thomas Lodge, *after* Pierre de Ronsard. Phillis, XXXIV. AAS; ESo; NIL

I would like/ to make. Oh---Yeah. Sharon Scott. JB

I would like all things to be free of me. Proof. Brendan Kennelly. CIP

I would like my love to die. Samuel Beckett, *tr. fr. French.* BIrV; CIP

I would like to be as mobile as my mind. Evaporation Poems. Kathleen Norris. IHMS

I would like to be that elderly Chinese gentleman. Dreaming in the Shanghai Restaurant. D. J. Enright. MPo; PSN; TVo.

I Would Like to Describe. Zbigniew Herbert, *tr. fr. Polish by* Czeslaw Milosz. BuTh

I would like to keep this always. Driving Down from the Big Horns. Peggy Simson Curry. WPW

I would like to more than touch you everywhere. More Than. Susan Fitzpatrick. AMV-80

I would like to remind/ the management. The Music Crept by Us. Leonard Cohen. FF

I would like to scream but there is no one to hear. Setting/ Slow Drag. Carolyn Rodgers. JB

I would like to think. Art. Hjalmar Flax, *tr. by* Julio Marzán. InW

I Would Like You for a Comrade. Edward Abbott Parry. OxBChV

I would not be the moon, the sickly thing. In Dispraise of the Moon. Mary Elizabeth Coleridge. Moon

I would not feign a single sigh. Song. John Clare. GBL

I would not have gotten in this boat with you. Revolution. Susan Griffin. RiTi

I Would Not Live Alway, *with music.* William Augustus Mühlenberg. AH

I would not marry a blacksmith. Soldier Boy for Me. *Unknown.* AmFP

I would not paint—a picture. Emily Dickinson. NOBA; PiAm

I would not tell them why I had smashed the window. "In This House, There Shall Be No Idols." Carolyn M. Rodgers. JB

I would not wish to sit. Between Two Prisoners. James Dickey. PAIC

I would play, plucking flowers by the gate. Two Letters from Chang-kan. Li Po, *tr. by* Shigeyoshi Obata. OLR

I would prefer to live quietly in silks. Running through Sleep. Kathleen Norris. IHMS

I would rather be buried/ in some cypress grove. Cypress Grove Blues. *Unknown.* BluL

I would rather sleep. The Weaver. Lisel Mueller. AMV–81

I would say a band. Retreat. Martha Collins. AMV–80

I would send you. The Gift. Robin Skelton. MPA

I would sleep until the mottled jaguar dawn. Auditory Hallucinations. Joyce Mansour, *tr. by* Carol Cosman. PBWP

I would tell a marvelous vision. The Dream of the Cross. *Unknown, tr. by* Sally Purcell. EBEV

I would that folk forgot me quite. Tess's Lament. Thomas Hardy. FaBoTw (1975 ed.)

I would that I were home again. The Call of the Fells. Herbert Palmer. PES

I would to heaven that I were so much clay. Fragment. Byron. *Fr.* Don Juan. ILP (1975 ed.); MBPR; NIL; NOBL; OAEL–2; OBP

I would worry less if she sang. If She Sang. Gerald W. Barrax. CNA

I Wouldn't. John Ciardi. ECBV

I wouldn't coax the plant if I were you. Woman with Flower. Naomi Long Madgett. AmNP (1974 ed.); FB

I wouldn't give a damn if some rum. Whatfor to 3 Who Stole My Shovel. Phyllis Gottlieb. BBGO

I wouldn't like at all to be. Lion Thoughts. Iowna Elizabeth Banker. CTV

I wouldn't marry a bachelor. Old Maid's Song. *Unknown.* AmFP

I wouldn't question the kisses you may offer. For Nothing. Andrés Castro Ríos, *tr. by* Julio Marzán. InW

I Write for Those Unknown. Chuck Miller. AcAn

I write of a cemetery, of the. Funeral at Ansley. Don Welch. GP; TAT

I write to make you suffer. Anne-Marie Kegels, *tr. fr. French by* Willis Barnstone. BoWoP

I write what I know on one side of the paper. Paper II. Carl Sandburg. TH

I wrote him out a check. Country Cemetery. Freda Newton Bunner. AMV–80

I wrote my name on the sidewalk. My Name. Lee Bennett Hopkins. CC

I wrote some lines once on a time. The Height of the Ridiculous. Oliver Wendell Holmes. OBAL; PCOP; PPM

I wrung my hands under my dark veil. "Anna Akhmatova," *tr. fr. Russian by* Max Hayward *and* Stanley Kunitz. BoLoP

I years had been from home. Emily Dickinson. NOBA; Psy

I zot awhile, wi' eyelids down. The Zun a-Lighten Eyes a-Shut. William Barnes. VLP

Iago Prytherch his name, though, be it allowed. A Peasant. R. S. Thomas. OBW

Iambic Feet Considered as Honorable Scars. William Meredith. PoA

Iambicum Trimetrum. Spenser. BoLoP; EBEV

Ianthe, *sels.* Walter Savage Landor.
  "From you, Ianthe, little troubles pass." NOBE (Ianthe's Troubles.) GBL
  "My hopes retire; my wishes as before." GBL
  "Proud word you never spoke, but you will speak." GBL
  "Thou has not rais'd, Ianthe, such desire." GBL
  Your Name upon the Sand. BuTh
  ("Well I remember how you smiled.") HAP

Ibby Damsel. *Unknown.* AmFP

Ibikunle! the Lord of his Quarters. Praise of Ibikunle. *Yoruba Oral Tradition, tr. by* B. Awe. WTO

Ibis, The. Marie De L. Welch. BBL

Ibo Woman. Mark Wangberg. TC

Icarus. Edward Field. TPo

Icarus. Valentin Iremonger. BIrV; CIP

Icarus. Irving Layton. BBGO

Icarus. Stephen Spender. NoAM

Ice. Jack Driscoll. AMV–80

Ice, The. W. W. Gibson. OxBTC

Ice age is here, The. Attention. Adrienne Rich. TAP

Ice-Cart, The. W. W. Gibson. EcS

Ice Castle, The. Michael Harris. AMV–80

Ice comes undone. Thaw. Lyn Lifshin. FAF

Ice Cream. Jonathan Price. SoS

Ice Cream in Paradise. Robert Hollander. AMV–80

Ice-Cream Wars, The. John Ashbery. PoA

Ice-Creepers (for Cid Ricketts Sumner). Eve Merriam. TVo

Ice Eagle, The. Diane Wakoski. InPS

Ice fishers' shacks and tents, The. Point Pelee in March. W. D. Snodgrass. UsP

Ice-fishing House, The: Long Lake, Minnesota. Michael S. Harper. TAT

Ice has been cracking all day. Spring. Michael Hogan. TAT

Ice of heroic heart seals plasmic soil. Heroic Heart. Charles Donnelly. CIP

Ice-Skaters. Elder Olson. LiSp

Ice-Storm, April, 1974. Skaidrite Stelzer. TC

Ice tinkled in glasses. Blues and Bitterness. Lerone Bennett, Jr. FF; PoBA

Icebergs. Samuel Taylor Coleridge. *Fr.* The Rime of the Ancient Mariner. EcS

Icehouse in Summer, The. Howard Nemerov. NoAM

Iceland First Seen. William Morris. VLP

Iceman, The. Gordon Challis. ATNZ

Ich am of Irlaunde. I Am of Ireland [ *or* The Irish Dancer]. *Unknown.* BuTh; GBP; HAP; OxBM

Ich herde men upon mold make muche mone. The Farmer's Complaint. *Unknown.* OxBM

Ich was in one sumere dale. Owl against Nightingale. *Unknown. Fr.* The Owl and the Nightingale. OxBM

Ichabod. Whittier. NOBA; PBMP; TAP; VoPo

Icham of Irlaunde. *Unknown. See* I Am of Ireland.

Ichor, *sel.* Gavin Bantock.
  "I opened my eyes at the foot of a grey mountain." TwMBP

Ich'ot a burde in a bowr as breyl so bright. Annot and John. *Unknown.* OxBM

Ichthyosaurus, The. *Unknown.* TDH

"Ici commence li livres du graunt Caam." Jigsaw Puzzle. Ann Deagon. AAN

Icy evil that struck his father down, The. El-Hajj Malik El-Shabazz. Robert Hayden. CNA; PoBA

Icy touch, Th'. Flowers in Winter. William Cowper. *Fr.* The Task, VI. PF

I'd a dream to-night. The Mother's Dream. William Barnes. NOBE

I'd been away a year, a year. The Ballad of Hagensack. Wallace Irwin. PoTa

I'd been on duty from two till four. Stand-to: Good Friday Morning. Siegfried Sassoon. FaBoTw (1975 ed.)

I'd cut the warp. Where It Appears. Robert Duncan. *Fr.* Passages. PiAm

I'd fill up the house with guests this minute. A Revel. Donagh MacDonagh. PFIr

I'd have no flowers. How I'd Have It. John Stone. AMV–81

I'd Have You, Quoth He. *Unknown.* FF

I'd like to/ pull. The Intelligent Sheepman and the New Cars. William Carlos Williams. OBAL

I'd like to have a word. The Book of Lies. James Tate. PPoD

I'd like to hear the bees again. The Grass, Alas. Dick Emmons. QQQ

I'd like to live with you. Marina Tsvetayeva, *tr. fr. Russian by* Paul Schmidt. BoWoP

I'd Like to Mark Myself. Milton Acorn. NeAC

I'd much rather sit there in the sun. Song. Ruth Krauss. SO

I'd rather/ heave half a brick than say. First Person Demonstrative. Phyllis Gotlieb. MiP

"I'd rather be blind than see this place." Another Life. Philip Levine. CPA

I'd rather be the devil. Devil Got My Woman. *Unknown.* BluL

I'd rather be the devil. Evil Devil Woman. *Unknown.* BluL

I'd rather lie on a rye-grass bed. The Water-Hole. Charles Erskine Scott Wood. BPAW

I'd rather listen to a flute. Samuel Hoffenstein. POL

I'd run about/ on the desert. *Tr. fr. Papago Indian by* Ruth Underhill. BoWoP

I'd sit inside the abandoned shack all morning. About a Year after He Got Married He Would Sit Alone in an Abandoned Shack in a Cotton Field Enjoying Himself. James Whitehead. CSP; GP

I'd wandered all over the country. The Old Settler's Song. Francis Henry. BPAW

I'd Want Her Eyes to Fill with Wonder. Kenneth Patchen. TPo

I'd wed you without herds, without money, or rich array. Cashel of Munster. *At. to* William English, *tr. by* Sir Samuel Ferguson. BIrV; GBL; PFIr

Ida Red. *Unknown.* FSW

Ida, Sweet as Apple Cider, *with music.* Eddie Leonard. BLSo; FSN

Idaho. *Unknown.* BPAW (*At. to* Frank French); GBP

Idaho Jack. *At. to* Jack H. Lee. BPAW

Idea. Michael Drayton. ESo

    *Sels.*

    "Calling to mind since first my love begun." NOBE

    "Deare [*or* Dear], why should you command me to my rest." AAS; ILP (1975 ed.); NOBE

    "Evil [*or* Evill] spirit, your beauty, haunts me still, An." AAS; GBL; ILP (1975 ed.); NOBE

    Give Me Myself. PPM

    "How many paltry, foolish, painted things." AAS; Epi; GBL; HAP; HeIP; NIL; OAEL-1

    "If he, from heav'n that filch'd that living fire." AAS

    "Into these loves, who but for passion lookes," *introd. sonnet.* (To the Reader of These Sonnets.) AAS; ESo

    "Nothing but no and I, and I and no." GBL

    "Since there's [*or* ther's] no help, come let us kiss[e] and part." AAS; BoLoP; CABA (1972 ed.); Epi; ExPo (1973 ed.); GBL; HAP; HeIP; ILP (1975 ed.); InPK; InPS; LoAs; NOBE; OAEL-1; PAIC; PBMP; PoIA; PoPle; PPoD; PPoe; SoSe (Farewell to Love.) VoPo

    "Since to obtaine thee, nothing me will sted." (His Remedie for Love.) AAS

    "There's nothing grieves me, but that age should haste." AAS; OAEL-1

    "Whilst thus my pen strives to eternize thee." AAS; PAIC

    "Witlesse gallant, a young wench that woo'd, A." AAS

Idea can be glazed, captured, brought down, An. The Blue Duck. David Ray. HeS

Idea, The. Made of Alnwick, in His Expedition to Scotland with the Army, 1639. Lord Herbert of Cherbury. SCP-2

Idea of Ancestry, The. Etheridge Knight. BPo; CNA; ConAP; CSP; NNaP; PoBA; PPoe; UsP

Idea of Order at Key West, The. Wallace Stevens. AnMo; CMoP (1970 ed.); FF; HAP; HeIP; ILP (1975 ed.); NIL; NoAM; NOBA; PiAm; PPoD; PPP; TAP; TT

Idea was that Little Louey, The. The Little Louey Comic. Wesley McNair. FAF

Ideal and Reality. Joseph Campbell. BIrV

Ideal Landscape. Adrienne Rich. NIL; NoAM; PoIA

Idealism. Ronald Arbuthnott Knox. FaBoCo; PoPle (Limerick: "There once was a man who said 'God.' " NOBL

Idea's Mirror. Michael Drayton. *See* Idea.

Identities, *sels.* Matthew Mead.

    "After Paeschendale/ After Katyn." TwMBP

    "My verses, Ochkasty, and your music." TwMBP

    "We stand here." TwMBP

Identity. A. R. Ammons. CoPAm

Identity. Robert Friend. GP; VWA

Identity, that spectator. To What Strangers, What Welcome, XV. J. V. Cunningham. PiAm

Idiot, The. John Ashbery. *Fr.* Two Sonnets. VGW

Idiot, The. Dudley Randall. BPo

Idiot Boy. Rowland M. Hill. AMV-81

Idiot Boy, The. Wordsworth. MBPR

"Idle as trout in light, Colonel Jones." The Famine Road. Eavan Boland. IPM

Idle poet, here and there, An. The Revelation. Coventry Patmore. *Fr.* The Angel in the House. GBL; HAP

Idle Visitation, An. Edward Dorn. *Fr.* Gunslinger. NOBA

Idle Words. Walter Savage Landor. OBSV

Idler with a wand for a walking stick, An. Batyushkov. Osip Mandelstam, *tr. by* W. S. Merwin *and* Clarence Brown. OBVE

Idler's Calender, An, *sel.* Wilfrid Scawen Blunt. January: Cover Shooting. VLP

Idly in the sun. Meridian. Brewster Ghiselin. AMV-80

Idolatry. Arna Bontemps. AmNP (1974 ed.)

Idolatry. Ralph Mecklenburger. SFF

Idyll: "Dogs behind, I'm running for the trees, The." John Boland. IPM

Idyll: "Door, A:/ Per L'Universo." Charles Tomlinson. TwMBP

Idyll: "Hermit hoar, in solemn cell." Samuel Johnson. *See* Imitation of the Style of * * * *.

Idylls, *sels.* Theocritus, *tr. fr. Greek.*

    "And so an easier life our Cyclops drew," XI, *tr. by* Elizabeth Barrett Browning. OBVE

    Enchantment, The, II, *abr., tr. by* Thomas Creech. OBVE

    "Eunica skornde me, when her I would have sweetly kist, " XX. OBVE

    "Shepheard Paris bore the Spartan bride, The," XXVII, *tr. by* Dryden. OBVE

    (Daphnis.) SCP-1

    "Whisper of the wind in, The," I, *tr. by* William Carlos Williams. Epi

Idylls of the King, *sels.* Tennyson.

    Dedication: "These to His Memory—since he held them dear." CABA (1972 ed.); VLP

    In Love, If Love Be Love. CABA (1972 ed.)

    Morte d'Arthur. DL; ILP (1975 ed.); NIL; OAEL-2; PAIC; VLP

    (Passing of Arthur, The.)

        "And answer made King Arthur, breathing hard." EBEV

    Death of Arthur, The. PIM

    Percivale's Quest. OAEL-2

    To the Queen ("O loyal to the royal in thyself"). VLP

    Vivien's Song. OAEL-2

If. Franklin P. Adams. OBAL

If. Haroldo de Campos. BBGO

If. Kipling. CTV; FaPoR; OxBChV; OxBTC

If a body meet a body.  Comin' through the Rye.  Burns.  BLSH

If a clear fountain still keeping a sad course.  The Duke's Song.  Mary Sidney Wroth, Countess of Montgomery.  *Fr.* Urania.  WPE

If a gate stands open long enough.  Gates.  Ted Kooser.  GP

If a large heart joined with a noble mind.  Lady Catherine Dyer.  *Fr.* Sir William Dyer, Knight.  SCP-2

If a man can find rich consolation, remembering his good deeds.  Catullus, *tr. fr. Latin by* Horace Gregory.  NAWM-1

If a man who turnips cries.  *See* If the man who turnips cries.

If a man with a shovel came down the road.  The Diggers.  W. S.  Merwin.  EAS

If a person conceives an opinion.  Poeta Loquitur.  Swinburne.  OAEL-2

If a scientist had bred pigeons the size of horses, they.  Pigeons.  Russell Edson.  PCho

If a task is once begun.  Always Finish.  *Unknown.*  CTV

If aa the bluid shed at thy Tron.  Capernaum.  Lewis Spence.  MS

If after rude and boisterous seas.  The Plaudite, or End of Life.  Robert Herrick.  CaPo

If again in the spring.  Seeing the Plum Blossoms by the River.  Lady Ise, *tr. by* Etsuko Terasaki *and* Irma Brandeis.  BoWoP

If (aged Charon), when my life shall end.  Licia, XLI.  Giles  Fletcher the Elder.  ES

If all be true that I do think.  The Five Reasons.  Henry Aldrich.  FaBoCo; FaBoEE; FF

If all the good people were clever.  Good and Clever.  Elizabeth  Wordsworth.  OxBTC

If all the seas were one sea.  Mother Goose.  BBL; CTV; MG

If All the Thermo-nuclear Warheads.  Kenneth Burke.  QQQ

If all the world and love were young.  The Nymph's Reply to the  Shepherd.  Sir Walter Ralegh.  AAS; BiP; BoLoP; CABA  (1972 ed.); Epi; FF; HAP; HeIP; HoPM (1975 ed.); ILP  (1975 ed.); IPWM; LoAs; NIL; NOBE; OAEL-1; OLR;  PoIA; PPoD; PPP; UsP

If all the world was apple-pie.  Mother Goose.  MG

If all the world were candy.  The Ambitious Mouse.  John  Farrar.  MN

If All the World Were Paper.  *Unknown.*  FaBoCo; FaBoNo;  GBP; OBP; PoPle

If an eagle be imprisoned.  America.  Henry Dumas.  PoBA

If angels sung a Savior's birth.  *At. to* John Stephenson.  AmFP

If any ask why there's no great she-poet.  Dedication of the Cook.  Anna Wickham.  PPM

If any man sits up suddenly in the dark at night.  Blame.  Gavin  Bantock.  TwMBP

If any question why we died.  Common Form.  Kipling.  *Fr.*  Epitaphs of the War.  FaBoEE; FaBoTw (1975 ed.)

If anybody ask ye who I am.  Child of God.  *Unknown.*  FSW

If anybody comes to I.  On Dr. Lettsom.  *Unknown.*  FaBoEE

If anyone comes, asking if I am here.  Schizophrenia.  Elizabeth  Bartlett.  PMW

If apples were pears.  To My Valentine.  *Unknown.*  CTV;  ECBV

If at your coming princes disappear.  Comets and Princes.  Samuel Johnson.  FaBoEE

If aught can teach us aught, Affliction's looks.  Affliction.  Sir  John Davies.  *Fr.* Nosce Teipsum.  NOBE

If aught [*or* ought] of oaten stop, or pastoral song.  Ode to  Evening.  William Collins.  CABA (1972 ed.); EBEV; Epi;  ExPo (1973 ed.); HAP; ILP (1975 ed.); LAuP; NOBE;  OAEL-1; OBP; PPP

If Bethlehem were here today.  Christmas Morning.  Elizabeth  Madox Roberts.  CC; PChr

If Birds That Neither Sow nor Reap, *with music.*  Roger Williams.  AH

If Blood Is Black Then Spirit Neglects My Unborn Son.  Conrad  Kent Rivers.  PoBA

If body were not Art.  Open Poetry Reading.  Jesús Papoleto  Meléndez.  AMV-81

If but some vengeful god would call to me.  Hap.  Thomas  Hardy.  CABA (1972 ed.); CMoP (1970 ed.); NIL; NoAM;  OAEL-2; PBMP; PPP; VLP

If by dull rhymes our English must be chain'd.  On the Sonnet.  Keats.  CABA (1972 ed.); ILP (1975 ed.); MBPR; NIL;  OAEL-2; PAIC

If cellos are boys and bass fiddles men.  Afternoon of a Girl.  R. H. Deutsch.  PoW

If "compression is the first grace of style."  To a Snail.  Marianne Moore.  CMoP (1970 ed.); PiAm; UsP

If could some Delius with divided hands.  Daniel Cudmore.  SCP-2

If dead, we cease to be; if total gloom.  Human Life: On the  Denial of Immortality.  Samuel Taylor Coleridge.  IPWM;  MBPR

If death were nothing.  Waking to Snowfall.  Roderick Hartigh  Jellema.  AATT

If death were truly conquered, there would be.  Death.  L. E.  Jones.  POL

If desire is absence—the wind.  Learning to Live without You.  Susan Wood.  AMV-81

If, doubtful of your fate.  The Mark.  Robert Graves.  LoAs

If doughty deeds my ladye please.  O Tell Me How to Woo Thee.  Robert Graham.  SLP

If earthward you could wing your flight.  England Expects?  Sir  Owen Seaman.  NOBL

If e'er in thy sight I found favour, Apollo.  The Poet's Prayer.  *Unknown.*  OBSV

If ever a garden was a Gethsemane.  For Jim, Easter Eve.  Anne  Spencer.  AmNP (1974 ed.)

If Ever Hapless Woman Had a Cause.  Countess of Pembroke.  WPE

If ever I am an old lady.  Survival.  Barbara Greenberg.  RiTi

If ever I had dreamed of my dead name.  To My Friend.  Wilfred Owen.  OBP

If ever I saw blessing in the air.  April Rise.  Laurie Lee.  LP;  MPo

If ever mercy move you murder me.  To the Mercy Killers.  Dudley Randall.  DL

If ever there lived a Yankee lad.  Darius Green and His Flying-  Machine.  John Townsend Trowbridge.  OBAL; OxBChV

If ever this poem is read out loud I pray.  73,000 Days to  Breakthrough.  Julia Watson Barbour.  PoUp

If ever two were one, then surely we.  To My Dear and Loving  Husband.  Anne Bradstreet.  BoWoP; EAP; FF; HAP;  HeIP; ILP (1975 ed.); NOBA; PiAm; SBG; TAP; VoPo;  WPE

If ever you go to Dolgelley.  The Dolgelley Hotel.  Thomas  Hughes.  FaBoCo

If Ever You Go to Dublin Town.  Patrick Kavanagh.  CIP;  CMoP (1970 ed.); MPo

If ever you should go by chance.  How to Tell the Wild Animals.  Carolyn Wells.  PCOP

If Everything Happens That Can't Be Done.  E. E. Cummings.  SoSe; TCP; WeW

If everywhere in the street.  Songs, II.  Denis Glover.  ATNZ

If fansy would favor.  Sir Thomas Wyatt.  AAS

If fired upon, he cannot fire.  Telephone Lineman.  Ernest Kroll.  AMV-81

If from the earth we came, it was an earth.  Anatomy of  Monotony.  Wallace Stevens.  BiP

If from the public way you turn your steps.  Michael: A Pastoral  Poem.  Wordsworth.  ILP (1975 ed.); MBPR; OAEL-2

If fruits are fed on any beast. Epitaph after Reading Ronsard's Lines from Rabelais. J. M. Synge. FaBoEE

If grief come early. First or Last. Thomas Hardy. CMoP (1970 ed.)

If God Exists. Ewa Lipska, *tr. fr. Polish by* Peter Jay *and* Geri Lipshultz. VWA

If Hamlet would betray. Midrash on Hamlet. Francis Landy. VWA

If he chanced to spit, it was whole basketsful of goldfinches. Shrovetide's Countenance. Rabelais, *tr. by* Sir Thomas Urquhart. FaBoNo

If he does not look at her face. The Circumcision. Linda Zisquit. VWa

If he, from heav'n that filch'd that living fire. Michael Drayton. *Fr.* Idea. AAS

If He Let Us Go Now. Shirley Williams. BoWoP

If he were to walk into this cafe. Written on a Girl's Table-Napkin at Wiesbaden. Ronald Duncan. WeW

If heaven a date of many years would give. John Pomfret. *Fr.* The Choice. PoIA

If Heav'n the grateful liberty wou'd give. The Choice. John Pomfret. EPC

If here and now be but a timely span. Here and Now. Catherine Cater. AmNP (1974 ed.)

If hope grew on a bush. Hope and Joy. Christina Rossetti. OxBChV

If hours be years the twain are blest. At a Hasty Wedding. Thomas Hardy. PAIC; VLP

If, husband, I should say. Woman's Complaint. Stephen Mulrine. MS

If I am amazed by anybody. Nothing but Image. Jody Swilky. AMV-81

If I am proud, you surely know. Called Proud. Walter Savage Landor. GBL

If I Ask Whether the Islands. Ellen McEvilley Griffin. NPW

If I believed that my reply were made. Guido da Montefeltro. Dante, *tr. by* Longfellow. *Fr.* Divina Commedia: Inferno. Epi

If I bring back. For My Unborn and Wretched Children. A. B. Spellman. CNA; PoBA

If I can stop one heart from breaking. Emily Dickinson. AH, *with music;* SoSe (1977 ed.)

If I come to you as some bitter herb. Poem. Rachel Loden. UsP

If I could believe that death. Gaspara Stampa. *tr. fr. Italian by* Lynne Lawner. PBWP

If I could choose a role. The Guide. Arthur Gregor. GP

If I Could Grasp a Wave from the Great Sea. John Richard Moreland. RhR

If I could hide in the woods. O, Beautiful They Move. William Pillen. VWA

If I could I surely would. Oh, Mary Don't You Weep. *Unknown.* FSW

If I could, I'd write. Housewife's Letter: To Mary. Anne Halley. NMM

If I could linger on his lovely chest. Sonnet XIII. Louise Labé, *tr. by* Aliki *and* Willis Barnstone. BoWoP

If I Could Meet God. Dennis Schmitz. NVAP

If I Could Only Live at the Pitch That Is Near Madness. Richard Eberhart. FF; MAT

If I could paint you, friend, as you stand there. A Football-Player. Edward Cracroft Lefroy. LiSp

If I could reach you now, in any way. Letter to a Mute. Thomas James. AmPA

If I could send him only. Her Reticence. Theodore Roethke. AnMo; LoAs

If I could start my life again. The Child's Dream. Susan Ludvigson. AMV-80

If I Could Tell You. W. H. Auden. PSN

If I could wish/ I'd be a fish. Wish. Dorothy Brown Thompson. CTV

If I die here in a strange land. Song of a Man about to Die in a Strange Land. *Unknown.* DL; WPW

If I die let my widow go. Jacques Audiberti, *tr. fr. French by* William Mead. LoAs

If I do not look up. The Student. Frederick Eckman. IPWM

If I Forget Thee. Emanuel Litvinoff. VWA

If I freely may discover. Hermogenes's Song. Ben Jonson. *Fr.* The Poetaster. ILP (1975 ed.)

If I give you money. The Sensitive Philanthropist. D. J. Enright. HeHu

If I had a creature's mouth. Suppositions. Margherita Faulkner. AMV-80

If I had a girl child I would tell her to eat. To the Mother from Scarsdale Who Asked about Publishing Her Daughter's Poems. Madeline Bass. WBN

If I had a nickel. .05. Ishmael Reed. InPK

If I Had My Way. *Unknown.* BluL

If I had wings like Noah's dove. Dink's Song. *Unknown.* FSW

If I have faltered more or less. The Celestial Surgeon. Robert Louis Stevenson. PIM; PPM

If I Have Made, My Lady, Intricate. E. E. Cummings. CMoP (1970 ed.); LoAs; NOBA

If I just had a piano. Testimonial. Langston Hughes. ILP (1975 ed.)

If I lived at the time. To Meet Mr. Lincoln. Eve Merriam. CC

If I looked into a mirror. Thru Blue Eyes. Ahmos Zu-Bolton. AAN

If I love you. Thread. Catherine Lucy Czerkawska. SLP

If I must of my senses lose. Prayer. Theodore Roethke. STS

If I needed brandy alone. On Drinking and a New Moon through the Window. Keith Wilson. GP

If I only had something to drink. The Rime of the Ancient Mariner. Bruce Haley. PPoD

If I painted, I'd paint landscapes. Landscapes. Richard Hugo. GP

If I profane with my unworthiest hand. Shakespeare. *Fr.* Romeo and Juliet, II, v. BiP; IP; SoSe

If I reach out. The Balcony Poems. Douglas Smith. AMV-81

If I rest for a moment near The Equestrian. Music. Frank O'Hara. NYP

If I Ride This Train. Joe Johnson. PoBA

If I say to you: "I have given up everything." The One for All Time. Paul Eluard, *tr. by* Wallace Fowlie. LoAs

If I Should Cast Off This Tattered Coat. Stephen Crane. The Black Riders, LXVI. PBMP

If I Should Die. Ben King. OBAL

If I should die, think only this of me. The Soldier. Rupert Brooke. 1914, V. BTTM; FaPoR; FF; HeIP; NOBE; OxBTC; PAIC; PoA; PPM; VoPo

If I Should Ever by Chance. Edward Thomas. OBW; OxBChV; RAE

If I should go away. Postscript: For Gweno. Alun Lewis. BoLoP

If I should pass the tomb of Jonah. Losers. Carl Sandburg. CMoP (1970 ed.); NoAM

If I Should Sleep with a Lady Called Death. E. E. Cummings. BoLoP; VGW

If I should touch her she would shriek and weeping. Secretary. Ted Hughes. InPK; NIL; SFF

If I sing because I must. Signature. Hannah Kahn. IHMS

If I Stand in My Window. Lucille Clifton. BPo; CAAP; RiTi

If I stare at you. The Straits. Valerie Gillies. SLP

If I stay quiet, I am always praying. The Scholar's Wife. Susan Mernit. VWA

If I take silence by the ears. Exercise in Solitude. William Sprunt. AAN

If I told you a rookie. Poker Poem. Michael Pettit. AMV-80

If I waited till September. The Hungarian. Gerald Stern. BrS

If I want to go to pieces. Occupational Hazards. David Young. FiCP

If I was on some foggy mountain top. Foggy Mountain Top. *Unknown.* FSW

If I was the woman who cut/ your hair. Antietam Creek: In the North They Named the Battles after Bodies of Water. Anne Becker. PoUp

If I Went Away. Desmond O'Grady, *tr. fr. Irish.* CIP

If I were a cassowary. Impromptu. Samuel Wilberforce. FaBoNo

If I Were a Queen. Christina Rossetti. PCOP

If I were a song-writer. Thoughts from the Pacific. Lindiwe Mabuza. SES

"If I were a woman," he said. Whore. Linda King. GP

If I were asked to play the part. If I Were on the Stage; or, Kiss Me Again. Henry Blossom. FSN

If I were fierce, and bald, and short of breath. Base Details. Siegfried Sassoon. FF; HeIP; NIL; SoSe

If I Were in Charge of Epiphanies. Stephen Dunn. NVAP

If I were Lord of Tartary. Tartary. Walter de la Mare. OxBChV

If I Were on the Stage. Henry Blossom. *See* Kiss Me Again.

If I were only dafter. Witter Bynner. Spectra: Opus 6. InPK

If I were rich what would I do? Why Thomas Cam Was Grumpy. James Stephens. CMoP (1970 ed.)

If I were Sophocles, brave with truth. Kaire. Richard Eberhart. NoAM

If I were Tickled by the Rub of Love. Dylan Thomas. FF

If I were to make a portrait, it would be of something fragile. Portrait. John Unterecker. PCho

If I when [*or* If when] my wife is sleeping. Danse Russe. William Carlos Williams. CMoP (1970 ed.); InPK; InPS; NOBA; PoIA; PPP; TAP

If I'd a-known my captain was blind, Darlin', Darlin'. Darlin'. *Unknown.* FSW

If I'd as much money as I could spend. Mother Goose. ECBV; MG

If, in an odd angle of the hutment. Eighth Air Force. Randall Jarrell. FF; ILP (1975 ed.); NIL; NoAM; NOBA

If in his study he hath so much care. Antiquary. John Donne. EBEV; FF; InPK; NIL

If in that Syrian garden, ages slain. Easter Hymn. A. E. Housman. BoReV; CABA (1972 ed.); EBEV; ILP (1975 ed.); OFD; TT

If, in the month of dark December. Written after Swimming from Sestos to Abydos. Byron. LiSp; MBPR

If in the scent of violets there came. A Tea-Shop. Ruth Dallas. ATNZ

If, in the silent mind of One all-pure. In Utrumque Paratus. Matthew Arnold. VLP

If, in well-bred society, ("hear! hear!"). Nathaniel Parker Willis. *Fr.* The Lady Jane: A Humorous Novel in Rhyme. OBAL

If in your search. Miracle. Tony Moreno. NW

If injured monarchs may their cause explore. A Dialogue between King William and the Late King James on the Banks of the Boyne. Charles Blount. APAS

If it/ Were lighter touch. The Guarded Wound. Adelaide Crapsey. WPE

If It All Went Up in Smoke. George Oppen. VWA

If it came to change our lives, it didn't want. The Plant. Sandra McPherson. CNW

If It Comes. Philip Booth. NCSH

If it form the one landscape that we, the inconstant ones. In Praise of Limestone. W. H. Auden. CABA (1972 ed.); CMoP (1973 ed.); ExPo (1973 ed.); HAP;NoAM; OAEL-2; PPP

If it is a poem. Sandra Ruth Duguid. AATT

If it is spring, an early warm spring. Photo of a Retired Farmer, Big Bend, Wisconsin. Robert L. McRoberts. HeS

If it is you, there/ in the light boat on the pond. Lady Ise, *tr. fr. Japanese by* Etsuko Terasaki *and* Irma Brandeis. BoWoP

If It Looks like Jelly, Shakes like Jelly, It Must Be Gel-a-tine. *Unknown.* BluL

If it were done when 'tis done, then 'twere well. Shakespeare. *Fr.* Macbeth, I, vii. UnPo (1976 ed.)

If it were evening on a dead man's watch. Blues for Jimmy. Thomas McGrath. BrS

If it were not for these things. The Grand Inquisitor Continues. John William Corrington. CoPAm

If it were set anywhere else but so. Head Itself. Laura Riding. PoA

If It Were Winter. Barry MacSweeney. LP

If It's Ever Spring Again. Thomas Hardy. OxBTC

If it's love, and if, as you say, it's ridiculous. Love's Fool. John Rosenthal. AMV-81

If it's rice-grain, say it's rice-grain. The Lover's Prayer. *Malay Oral Tradition, tr. by* R. J. Wilkinson *and* R. O. Winstedt. WTO

If Langour Makis Men Licht. Lord Darnley. SLP

If life be time that here is spent. Of the Loss of Time. John Hoskyns. FaBoEE

If life is here how stealthily. The Gully. Douglas Stewart. MAuV

If Life's a Lousy Picture, Why Not Leave before the End. Roger McGough. OxBTC

If little mice have birthdays. Birthday Cake. Aileen Fisher. MN

If, Lord, thy love for me is strong. Saint Teresa of Avila, *tr. fr. Spanish by* Arthur Symons. PBWP

If love be strong, hot, mighty and fervent. The Measure of Love. Sir Thomas More. BoReV

If love is the greatest reality. Into Their True Gentleness. Pearse Hutchinson. CIP

If Love's a Yoke. D. C. Berry. AMV-81

If Man Him Bethought. *Unknown.* OxBM

If Mary came would Mary. A Penitent Considers Another Coming of Mary. Gwendolyn Brooks. NoAM; PChr

If meat the gods give, I the steam. Steam in Sacrifice. Robert Herrick. CaPo

If music [*or* musique] and sweet poetry [*or* poetrie] agree. To His Friend, Master R. L., in Praise of Music and Poetry. Richard Barnfield. AAS; ILP (1975 ed.)

If, My Darling. Philip Larkin. EBEV

If My Hands Were Mute. Manfred Winkler, *tr. fr. Hebrew by* Mary Zilzer. VWA

If My Head Hurt a Hair's Foot. Dylan Thomas. NoAM

If my mother had never been the protected child. House in St. Petersburg. Stanley Burnshaw. VWA

If my nipples were to drip milk. Sappho, *tr. fr. Greek by* Willis Barnstone. BoWoP

If my torch goes out it will be dark. Search. Claribel Alegria, *tr. by* Aliki *and* Willis Barnstone. BoWoP

If Nancy Hanks came back as a ghost. Nancy Hanks. Rosemary *and* Stephen Vincent Benét. ECBV

If nature, for a favourite child. Matthew. Wordsworth. MBPR

If nature prompts you, or if friends persuade. William Whitehead. *Fr.* A Charge to the Poets. OBSV

If Nature says to you.  The Daily Grind.  Fenton Johnson.
AmNP (1974 ed.)

If neither brass, nor marble, can withstand.  The Power of Time.
Swift.  FaBoEE

If night takes the form of a whale and.  Isabel Fraire, *tr. fr.
Spanish by* Thomas Hoeksema.  BoWoP

If nine times you your bridegroom kiss.  The Tithe: To The Bride.
Robert Herrick.  CaPo

If no love is, O God, what fele I so.  Chaucer.  *Fr.* Troilus and
Criseyde.  FF; LoAs; OAEL-1

If No One Ever Marries Me.  Laurence Alma-Tadema.
OxBChV; PCOP

If no one sees you, friend.  Poem about Your Face.  Nathan
Alterman, *tr. by* Ruth Nevo.  VWA

If not birds.  Blind Panorama of New York.  Federico Garcia
Lorca, *tr. by* Ben Belitt.  NYP

If not necessary, is essential.  Love.  Anne Stevenson.  NCSH

If, O Maecenas, versed in lore antique.  Horace, *tr. fr. Latin by* Sir
Theodore Martin.  OBVE

If of a beetle you'd make game.  "Oh That My Love Were in My
Arms."  *Malay Oral Tradition, tr. by* R. J. Wilkinson *and*
R. O. Winstedt.  WTO

If on my theme I rightly think.  Why I Drink.  Henry Aldrich.
NIL

If one could have that little head of hers.  A Face.  Robert
Browning.  LoAs

If one should tell them what's clearly seen.  Crumbs or the Loaf.
Robinson Jeffers.  CMoP (1970 ed.)

If one were to describe him, one.  The Man.  Lucille Iverson.
WBN

If one's country is strong, one dreams it is just.  The Dome.
Lawrence Lee.  WasP

If Only.  David Gladish.  SFF

If only I could love.  Before the Dive.  Elizabeth Kempf.  AMV-
81

If only three commuters, one in Tokyo.  The Box of Air.  Rick
Cannon.  PoUp

If only we'd been strangers.  Floating off to Timor.  Edwin
Morgan.  SLP

If only you/ Were night sky.  If Only.  David Gladish.  SFF

If ought of oaten stop, or pastoral song.  *See* If aught of oaten
stop, or pastoral song.

If out of a dire suspicion.  Wet Hair: If Now His Mother Should
Come.  Robert Penn Warren.  *Fr.* Penological Study:
Southern Exposure.  NoAM

If Pigs Could Fly.  James Reeves.  OSF

If Pliny, Lord High Treasurer of all.  Painture.  Richard
Lovelace.  CaPo

If poisonous minerals, and if that tree.  Holy Sonnets, IX.  John
Donne.  BiP; CABA (1972 ed.); EBEV; Epi; ILP (1975 ed.);
LFH; OAEL-1; PPP; UnPo (1976 ed.)

If poor (you say) she drains her husband's purse.  Chaucer, *mod.
version by* Pope.  *Fr.* The Canterbury Tales: The Wife of
Bath's Prologue.  OBSV

If poverty be a title to poetry, I am sure nobody can dispute mine.
The Beggar's Opera.  John Gay.  OAEL-1

If religion was a thing that money could buy.  All My Trials.
*Unknown.*  FSW

If sadly thinking, with spirits sinking.  Let Us Be Merry.  John
Philpot Curran.  PPM

If seasons all were summers.  The Farm-Woman's Winter.
Thomas Hardy.  VLP

If shame can on a soldier's vein-swoll'n front.  King Stephen: A
Fragment of a Tragedy.  Keats.  MBPR

If she had been beautiful, even.  Of a Woman, Dead Young.
Dorothy Parker.  SBG

If she had someplace to run to, she would run.  Couple.  Mary
Swope.  AMV-81

If She Sang.  Gerald W. Barrax.  CNA

If she would come to me here.  Dog-tired.  D. H. Lawrence.
BuTh

If snow falls on the far field.  Mother's Song.  *Unknown, tr. by*
Willis Barnstone.  BoWoP

If so it hap, this of-spring of my care.  Samuel Daniel.  *Fr.* To
Delia.  AAS

If So the Man You Are, *sels.*  D. B. Wyndham Lewis.
"Am I too dangerous, that no man can let."  OBSV
"I'm no He-man you know, I'm not a He."  OBSV
"You now solicit a few enemy thrusts."  OBSV

If someone insults you.  Autant En Emporte le Vent.  Marguerite
de Navarre, *tr. by* Aline Allard.  PBWP

If someone said, Escape.  Longface Mahoney Discusses Heaven.
Horace Gregory.  VGW

If someone was walking across.  A Confession.  Robert Mezey.
AmPA

If Something Should Happen.  Lucille Clifton.  MAT

If spring should rise like a heron.  A Mirage.  Ruth Setterberg.
AMV-80

If stars dropped out of heaven.  Stars and Flowers.  Christina
Rossetti.  PCOP

If strolling forth, a beast you view.  Carolyn Wells.  *Fr.* How to
Tell the Wild Animals.  CaYB

If the autumn would.  Winter Is Another Country.  Archibald
MacLeish.  NCSH

If the Birds Knew.  John Ashbery.  PoA

If the Black Frog Will Not Ring.  Ed Roberson.  PoBA

If the boy or the girl won't keep so much.  The Offer of
Friendship.  Grace Cavalieri.  PoUp

If the butterfly courted the bee.  Topsy-turvy World.  William
Brighty Rands.  ECBV; OxBChV

If the composition of this collection lasted three years.  Michael
Burkard.  AAN

If the Drink.  R. A. K. Mason.  ATNZ

If the heart of a man is depressed with cares.  John Gay.  *Fr.*
The Beggar's Opera, II, i.  HeIP

If the kissing cashier.  Peter.  Albert Howard Carter.  AATT

If the [*or* a] man who turnips cries.  Burlesque of Lope de Vega
[*or* Deduction].  Samuel Johnson.  EBEV; ECBV; FaBoCo;
NOBL; PoPle

If the moon shines.  What Night Would It Be?  John Ciardi.
IWK

If the Owl Calls Again.  John Haines.  BoAnP; CNW; ConAP;
HeIP; NCSH; NU; UsP

If the power of the word is anything, America.  Diane DiPrima.
Revolutionary Letter 40.  GP

If the quick spirits in your eye.  Persuasions to Enjoy.  Thomas
Carew.  CaPo; NOBE; PAIC

If the red slayer think he slays.  Brahma.  Emerson.  BiP; HAP;
ILwL; IPWM; NIL; NOBA; PAIC; PiAm; TAP; UnPo (1976
ed.); VoPo; WIF

If the shack get raided ain't no body run.  Charlie Cherry.
*Unknown.*  BluL

If the speed is open.  A Piano.  Gertrude Stein.  *Fr.* Tender
Buttons.  PBWP

If the Stars Should Fall.  Samuel Allen.  PoBA

If the table was empty before.  Silent Movies.  Pedro Juan Pietri.
InW

If the time ever came.  Poem for Ben Barney.  Leslie Silko.
CDW; VoR

If the victors were magnificent.  The Barbarians.  Matthew Mead.
TwMBP

If the whole of Paris is not quite wholly mine.  The Enigmatic
Traveler.  Byron Vazakas.  AMV-80

If the wild bowler thinks he bowls. Brahma. Andrew Lang. FaBoCo; NOBL

If the wood is good grain. Skin. Roland Flint. PoUp

If There Are Any Heavens. E. E. Cummings. STS ("If there are any heavens my mother will (all by herself) have.") PiAm

If there are wild men. In Iceland. Howard McCord. GP

If There Be Sorrow. Mari Evans. PBMP

If there exists a hell—the case is clear. To Sir Toby. Philip Freneau. ILP (1975 ed.); TAP

If there had been one bird, if there had been. Deserted Beach. Ruth Dallas. ATNZ

If There Is a Perchance. Thomas McAfee. AMV–81

If there is no change in the ocean. No Change in Me. *Unknown.* AmFP

If there must be a god in the house, must be. Less and Less Human, O Savage Spirit. Wallace Stevens. IPWM; VGW

If there was a broken whispering by night. Parting at Dawn. John Crowe Ransom. LoAs

If there was only a road there. The Blue West. Dahlia Ravikovich, *tr. by* Chana Bloch. PBWP

If there were an open way. On One Condition. Charles Madge. EAS

If there were dreams to sell. Dream-Pedlary. Thomas Lovell Beddoes. DuDr; HAP; LCL; LoAs; NOBE; PCOP; PMW

If there were no authority on earth. Chaucer, *tr. by* Nevill Coghill. *Fr.* The Canterbury Tales: The Wife of Bath's Prologue. OBP

If there were, oh! an Hellespont of cream. The Author Loving These Homely Meats, Specially, viz.: Cream, Pancakes, Buttered Pippin-Pies. John Davies of Hereford. FaBoNo

If there were the sound of water only. T. S. Eliot. *Fr.* The Waste Land, V. IP

If there's no wick within the lamp. And Tomorrow Wend Our Ways. *Malay Oral Tradition, tr. by* R. J. Wilkinson *and* R. O. Winstedt. WTO

If these are letters, they will have to be misread. Adrienne Rich. *Fr.* Ghazals: Homage to Ghalib. NIL

If these brief lays, of sorrow born. Tennyson. In Memoriam A. H. H., XLVIII. LFH

If they ask, who here doth lie. Epitaph on Sir Walter Pye. John Hoskyns. FaBoEE

If they had cursed the man. A Part-Sequence for Change. Robert Duncan. VGW

If they say my furred cloak. Chanson. Pernette du Guillet, *tr. by* Joan Keefe *and* Richard Terdiman. PBWP

If they should ask what makes the stuff of us. Edinburgh. Margot Robert Adamson. MS

If they wanted freedom. Eeva-Liisa Manner, *tr. by* Jaakko A. Ahokas. *Fr.* Cambrian. PBWP

If they'd been summoned to worship the God of wine, or Pan, or to visit the Queen of Love. Lysistrata. Aristophanes, *tr. by* Charles T. Murphy. NAWM–1

If Things Grew Down. Robert D. Hoeft. OSF

If this air were to speak to you. Your Air of My Air. Hugo Margenat, *tr. by* Julio Marzán. InW

If this be love, to drawe a wearie breath. Samuel Daniel. *Fr.* To Delia. AAS; GBL

If this country were a sea (that is solid rock). Pennines in April. Ted Hughes. PPP

If this divine quiet. Calm. Aldo Camerino, *tr. by* Anita Barrows. VWA

If this is soccer. Late Game. B. H. Fairchild. AMV–81

If this little world tonight. Earth. Oliver Herford. MiP

If this was our battle, if these were our ends. To a President. Witter Bynner. OBAL

If thou a reason dost desire to know. To Cynthia: On Her Embraces. Sir Francis Kynaston. GBL

If thou be'st ice, I do admire. The Miracle. Sir John Suckling. CaPo

If thou didst feed on western plains of yore. To a Goose. Robert Southey. NOBL

If thou dislik'st the piece thou light'st on first. To the Sour Reader. Robert Herrick. ILP (1975 ed.)

If thou indeed derive thy light from Heaven. Wordsworth. VLP

If thou must love me, let it be for nought. Sonnets from the Portuguese, XIV. Elizabeth Barrett Browning. HeIP; LoAs; NOBE; PBMP; TPo; UnPo (1976 ed.); WPE

If thou survive my well-contented day. Sonnets, XXXII. Shakespeare. ILP (1975 ed.); STS

If thou wert here, these tears were tears of light! The Day-Dream from an Emigrant to His Absent Wife. Samuel Taylor Coleridge. MBPR

If thou wilt ease thine heart. Wolfram's Dirge. Thomas Lovell Beddoes. *Fr.* Death's Jest Book. NOBE

If Thou Wilt Hear, *with music.* John Grave. AH

If through the eyes the heart speaks clear and true. Waiting in Faith. Michelangelo Buonarroti. ILwL

If thy soul check thee that I come so near. Sonnets, CXXXVI. Shakespeare. Epi

If to be absent were to be. To Lucasta, Going beyond the Seas. Richard Lovelace. CaPo; ILP (1975 ed.); PoPle

If to demands of others I agree. Resolving Doubts. William Dickey. CoPAm

If (touched by love's own secret) we, like homing. E. E. Cummings. PoA

If 'Trane had only seen. Poem No. 21. Doughtry Long. CNA

If true love might true love's reward obtaine. Henry Constable. *Fr.* Diana. ESo

If true that notion, which but few contest. *Unknown.* FaBoEE

If 'twere the time of lilies. To the Lady Radegunde, with Violets. Venantius Fortunatus, *tr. by* Helen Waddell. NAWM–1

If U Are a Poet. Gladstone Yearwood. SES

If waker care, if sodayne pale coulor. Sir Thomas Wyatt. AAS

If We Cannot Live as People. Charles Lynch. CNA; PoBA

If we could get the hang of it entirely. Entirely. Louis MacNeice. CMoP (1970 ed.)

If We Didn't Have to Eat. Nixon Waterman. OBAL

If we go back, if we walk into the old darkness. Looking Backward. Robert Bly. UsP

If we had been given names to love. Bird-Window-Flying. Tess Gallagher. PCho

If we hate the rush hour subways. One Year to Life on the Grand Central Shuttle. Audre Lorde. CNA

If we lay bound upon the wheel of change. Sir Edwin Arnold. *Fr.* The Light of Asia, VIII. VLP

If we meet a gorilla. Carl Sandburg. *Fr.* We Must Be Polite. CaYB

If We Must Die. Claude McKay. AmNP (1974 ed.); BPo; CABA (1972 ed.); NoAM; PoBA; PPP; UnPo (1976 ed.)

If we must part. A Valediction. Ernest Dowson. BoLoP

If we must stand alone. As Rocks Rooted. Howard G. Hanson. AMV–80

If we raced a century over hills. Blackfeet, Blood and Piegan Hunters. James Welch. SA

If we shall live, we live. Meeting. Christina Rossetti. GBL

If we square a lump of pemmican. Scientific Proof. J. W. Foley. QQQ

If We Take. Charles Bukowski. EC

If we were in Talisker on the shore. Shores. Sorley MacLean, *tr. by* Iain Crichton Smith. SLP

If what began (look far and wide) will end. Conclusion. John Frederick Nims. PoA

If what you want is jobs. Revolutionary Letter # 9. Diane Di Prima. IHMS

If when Don Cupid's dart. Love's Offence. Sir John Suckling. CaPo

If when I come to Paradise. A Sealess World. Joan Campbell. EcS

If when my wife is sleeping. *See* If I when my wife is sleeping.

If when the wind blows. Daniel Webster's Horses. Elizabeth J. Coatsworth. PH

If, whittler and dumper, gross carver. The Arc Inside and Out. A. R. Ammons. NoAM

If wisdom, as it seems it is. Epigram. J. V. Cunningham. PiAm

If wishes were horses. Mother Goose. MG

If Women Could Be Fair. Edward de Vere, Earl of Oxford. ILP (1975 ed.)

If wrath embitter the sweet mouth of song. Apologia. Swinburne. VLP

If yet I have not all thy love. Lover's Infiniteness. John Donne. OAEL–1

If You. Robert Creeley. NoAM; NOBA

If you/ have seen her. Woman with Finger. Tom McKeown. NVAP

If you all will shut your trap. The Tramp. Joe Hill. FSW

If you and I could ever meet. Monkey. Sylvia Read. RAE

If you and I should chance to meet. The Ordinary Man. Robert Service. BBGO

If you are/ in Spain. Drowning in Spain. Tom Schmidt. NeAC

If you are a revolutionary. The Reactionary Poet. Ishmael Reed. CNA

If you are determined and wishful to go. Railroad to Hell. *Unknown.* VLP

If you are merry sing away. Mirth. Christopher Smart. *Fr.* Hymns for the Amusement of Children. LAuP; OxBChV

If you are still alive when you read this. Goodbye. William Knott. EAS

If you become a nun, dear. The Nun. Leigh Hunt. IP

If You Can Hear My Hooves. Harold Littlebird. VoR

If you can keep your head when all about you. If. Kipling. CTV; FaPoR; OxBChV; OxBTC

If you can lie, Torquatus, when you take. Horace, *tr. fr. Latin by* John Conington. OBVE

If You Can't Eat You Got To. E. E. Cummings. CMoP (1970 ed.); STS

If you c'n keep alive when li'l bleeders. A London Sparrow's If. J. A. Lindon. BoAnP

If you come here and it is barely fall. At Pont-Aven, Gauguin's Last Home in France. Andrew Grossbardt. AMV–81

If You Come Softly. Audre Lorde. AmNP (1974 ed.)

If you could come on the late train for. The Young Ionia. John Frederick Nims. PCho

If you could see, fair brother, how dead beat. Prolonged Sonnet: When the Troops Were Returning from Milan. Niccolo degli Albizzi, *tr. by* Dante Gabriel Rossetti. OBVE

If you desire to paralyze. The Better Way. Walter Leaf. FaBoCo

If you don't know how, why pretend? To the Tune "Red Embroidered Shoes." Huang O, *tr. by* Kenneth Rexroth *and* Ling Chung. PBWP

If you don't know the kind of person I am. A Ritual to Read to Each Other. William Stafford. SoS

If You Don't Like My Apples. *Unknown.* GBP

If You Don't Put Your Shoes On. Michael Rosen. DuDr

If you ever, ever, ever meet a grizzly bear. Grizzly Bear. Mary Austin. BPAW; CTV; ECBV; RAE

If you go away,/ why should I adorn myself? *Tr. fr. Japanese by* Kenneth Yasuda. BoWoP

If you go where cities quake. Percussion Bittersweet. Antar S. K. Mberi. SES

If You Had Known. Thomas Hardy. GBL

If you had not heard of the northward migration. Visitors. Marie Harris. MMD

If You Happy Would Be, *with music.* Abraham Fernández. AH

If you hate the British Army, clap your hands. Ballymurphy. *Unknown.* FSW

If you have formed a circle to go into. To God. Blake. OAEL–2

If you have frost, poinsettias. I Must Come to Terms with Florida. William E. Taylor. CSP

If you have lost the radio beam, then guide yourself by the sun or the stars. Any Man's Advice to His Son. Kenneth Fearing. CMoP (1970 ed.); TPo

If you have no time. Izumi Shikibu, *tr. fr. Japanese by* Willis Barnstone. BoWoP

If you have seen the long lean hound. Aboriginal Sin. William R. Mitchell. AATT

If you haven't made noise enough to warn him, singing, shouting. Meeting a Bear. David Wagoner. BCr; HAP

If you know about the Babylonian Jews. Straus Park. Gerald Stern. NYP

If you listen, I'll sing you a sweet little song. My Wild Irish Rose. Chauncey Olcott. BLSo; FSN; FSW

If you live in the city, you will have. Trapping Bear. John Minczeski. BCr

If you live where I come from. Excerpts from the Notebook of the Poet of Santo Tomas. Richard Shelton. GP

If you love me. Izumi Shikibu, *tr. fr. Japanese by* Willis Barnstone. BoWoP

If you make a revolution, make it for fun. A Sane Revolution. D. H. Lawrence. SFF; TPo

If you must crack it. Easter Egg. Alan Kieffaber. AMV–80

If you never do anything for anyone else. The Immoral Proposition. Robert Creeley. PiAm

If you, O Aynabo, my fleet and fiery horse. Battle Pledge. *Somali Oral Tradition, tr. by* M. Laurence. WTO

If you offer your bag of butterflies. El Bosco. Mei Berssenbrugge. NW; SA

If you plant grain. A Robin's Poem. Nikki Giovanni. AmNP (1974 ed.)

If you press a stone with your finger. Natural Law. Babette Deutsch. RiTi

If you really care for me. *Unknown, tr. fr. Spanish by* Willis Barnstone. BoWoP

If you reject the obvious. Wooden Matches. Robert D. Hoeft. PoW

If You Saw a Negro Lady. June Jordan. IHMS; NMM

If you see my mother, partner, tell her pray for me. Mack Maze. WTO

If You See This Man. Thomas Lux. AmPA; NVAP

If you set out in this world. The Seventh. Attila Jozsef. EC

If You Should Die. A. Wilber Stevens. MPA

If you should meet a crocodile. Be Careful! *Unknown.* CaYB; ECBV; OSF

If you should see/ a man/ walking. Voice in the Crowd. Ted Joans. AmNP (1974 ed.)

If you should seek my footprints you would find. The Inflammable Man. Gordon Challis. ATNZ

If you smoke a cigarette. A Cigarette. *Mongol Oral Tradition, tr. by* C. R. Bawden. WTO

If you stay to school dinners. *Unknown.* WTO

If you stop caressing me. My True Memory. Asya, *tr. by* Gabriel Preil *and* Howard Schwartz. VWA

If you take the moon in your hands. The Moon in Your Hands. Hilda Doolittle ("H. D."). BoWoP

If you visit American city. Pollution. Tom Lehrer. PoRo; WIF

If you wake at midnight, and hear a horse's feet. A Smuggler's Song. Kipling. *Fr.* Puck of Pook's Hill. DuDr; OxBChV; PoPle; PoTa

If you wander far enough. Oh No. Robert Creeley. InPK

If you want higher wages let me tell you what to do. Talking Union. Lee Hays, Millard Lampell, *and* Pete Seeger. FSW

If you want my apartment, sleep in it. Rent. Jane Cooper. TAP

If you want to get to heaven, let me tell you what to do. Talking Blues. *Unknown.* FSW

If you want to go to heaven. The Blood-strained Banders. *Unknown.* AmFP

If You Want to Go to Heben. *Unknown.* GBP

If you want to lead a calf. Hey Animal—Eat This Popcorn. Cinda Kornblum. AcAn; EC

If you want to live in the country. The Power of Maples. Gerald Stern. NU

If you want to write me a letter. Si Me Quieres Escribir (If You Want to Write Me). *Unknown, tr. fr. Spanish.* FSW

If you watch. This Evening, without Blinking. Pattiann Rogers. AMV-80

If you were just in keeping our pact of love. Wallāda, *tr. fr. Arabic by* A. R. Nykl. PBWP

If you watch it long enough you can see the clock move. Cracked Record Blues. Kenneth Fearing. SFF

If you were coming in the fall. Emily Dickinson. NOBA

If you were going to get a pet. If You. Robert Creeley. NoAM

If you were to construct a platform. The Platform Builder. Cynthia MacDonald. AAN

If You Will. Josephine Miles. GP

If you will tell me why the fen. I May, I Might, I Must. Marianne Moore. FF; OBAL; PSN; SoSe

If you wish to pull a cork. Lilliputian's Beer Song. Septimus Winner. OBAL

If you would learn. The Antiquary. Joseph Campbell. OxBTC

If you would run. For the Running of the New York City Marathon. James Dickey. NYP

If you would work one small miracle. Prison. Paul David Ashley. DNGG

If your eyes fall. In Bhaudanath. Mei Berssenbrugge. SA

If your man gets personal. Traveling Riverside Blues. *Unknown.* BluL

If you're anxious for to shine in the high aesthetic line as a man of culture rare. Bunthorne's Song: The Aesthete. W. S. Gilbert. *Fr.* Patience. OAEL-2; VLP

If you're not home, where. Numbers, Letters. Amiri Baraka. BPo; NOBA

If you're so out of love with happiness. John Oldham. *Fr.* A Satire Addressed to a Friend. OBSV

If you've ever been in a car. Stun. James Schuyler. MAT

If you've got to if after tying to. Bitter Pills for the Dark Ladies. Erica Jong. Psy; RiTi; WBN

If you've tried and have not won. Don't Give Up. Phoebe Cary. CTV

Ifa divination was performed for Tiger. Tiger. *Yoruba Oral Tradition, tr. by* B. King. WTO

Ifa speaks in parables. *Yoruba Oral Tradition, tr. by* J. A. Adediji. WTO

Ifor Hael's hall, poorly it looks. The Hall of Ifor Hael. Evan Evans, *tr. by* Gwyn Williams. OBW

Ignacio, Colorado, for You That Time. Joy Harjo. SA

Ignorance of Death. William Empson. CMoP (1970 ed.); NoAM

Ignorant dawn of William Butler Yeats, The. We Love You the Way You Are. David McFadden. NeAC

Ignorant Ida. Isabel Frances Bellows. TDH

Ignorant, in the sense. Death of an Irishwoman. Michael Hartnett. CIP

Ignorant men, who disclaim. Sister Juana Inés de la Cruz, *tr. by* Judith Thurman. *Fr.* A Satirical Romance. PBWP

Ignorant two, we glide. On Minding One's Own Business. James Wright. CoPAm

Il Janitoro. George Ade. OBAL

Il Pastor Fido, *sels.* Giovanni Battista Guarini, *tr. fr. Italian by* Sir Richard Fanshawe.
"Fair Golden Age! when milk was th' onely food." OBVE (Golden Age, The.) OAEL-1
"Learn women all from this housewifery." OBVE
Of Beauty. BoLoP (Beauty.) GBL
"Our beauty is to us that which to men." OBVE
"Well may that kisse be sweet that's giv'n t' a sleek." OBVE

Il Penseroso. Milton. CABA (1972 ed.); HAP; HoPM (1975 ed.); ILP (1975 ed.); OAEL-1; PPP
*Sels.*
"But let my due feet never fail." SCP-1
"Sweet bird, that shunn'st the noise of folly." SCP-1

Il Piccolo Rifiuto. Louis MacNeice. CMoP (1970 ed.)

Ile give thee leave my love, in beauties field. Sonnet. Earl of Stirling. *Fr.* Aurora SLP

Ilex Tree, The. Agnes Lee. PoA

Iliad, The, *much abr.* Homer, *tr. fr. Greek by* Robert Fitzgerald. NAWM-1
*Sels.*
"Ajax the swift swerv'd never from the side," *fr.* XIII, *tr. by* William Cowper. OBVE
"All grave old men, and souldiers they had bene, but for age," *fr.* III, *tr. by* George Chapman. OBVE
"And as in winter time when Jove his cold-sharpe Javelines throwes," *fr.* XII, *tr. by* George Chapman. OBVE
"And as when with the West-wind's flawes the sea thrusts up her waves," *fr.* IV, *tr. by* George Chapman. OBVE
"And now was Paris come/ From his high towres," *fr.* VI, *tr. by* George Chapman. OBVE
"And when they came together in one place," *fr.* IV, *tr. by* Tennyson. OBVE
Andromache's Lamentation, *fr.* XXIV, *tr. by* Congreve. OBVE
"As when an architect some palace wall," *fr.* XVI, *tr. by* William Cowper. OBVE
"As when devouring flames some forest seize," *fr.* II, *tr. by* William Cowper. OBVE
"As when of frequent bees," *fr.* II, *tr. by* George Chapman. OBVE
"As when the winds, ascending by degrees," *fr.* IV, *tr. by* Pope. OBVE
"At her departure his disdain return'd," *fr.* I, *tr. by* Dryden. OBVE
"At this th' impatient hero sowrly smil'd," *fr.* I, *tr. by* Dryden. OBVE
"Big with great purposes and proud, they sat," *fr.* VIII, *tr. by* William Cowper. OBVE
"But ere sterne conflict mixt both strengths, faire Paris stept before," *fr.* III, *tr. by* George Chapman. OBVE
"But now, no longer deaf to honour's call," *fr.* VI, *tr. by* Pope. OBVE
"Embodied close, the lab'ring Grecian train," *fr.* V, *tr. by* Pope. OBVE
"Fierce they drove on, impatient to destroy," *fr.* XIII, *tr. by* Pope. OBVE
"Frail as the leaves that quiver on the sprays," *fr.* VI, *tr. by* Samuel Johnson. OBVE
Funeral Games for Patroclus, The: The Boastful Boxer, *fr.* XXIII, *tr. by* Ennis Rees. LiSp

Funeral Games for Patroclus, The: Wrestling to a Draw, *fr.* XXIII, *tr. by* Ennis Rees. LiSp

"Greeks dismay'd, confus'd disperse or fall, The," *fr.* XV, *tr. by* Pope. OBVE

Helen's Lamentation, *fr.* XXIV, *tr. by* Congreve. OBVE

"His hand came out of the east," *fr.* XVI, *tr. by* Christopher Logue. OBVE

"Hornets occasionally build their nests near roads," *fr.* XVI, *tr. by* Christopher Logue. OBVE

"Like leaves on trees, the race of man is found," *fr.* VI, *tr. by* Pope. OBVE

"Meanwhile the troops beneath Patroclus' care," *fr.* XVI, *tr. by* Pope. OBVE

Nestor, *fr.* XXIII, *tr. by* Ennis Rees. LiSp

"Nor lingered Paris in the lofty house," *fr.* VI, *tr. by* Tennyson. OBVE

"Nor long the trench or lofty walls oppose," *fr.* XII, *tr. by* Pope. OBVE

"Now front to front the hostile armies stand," *fr.* III, *tr. by* Pope. OBVE

"Now hear this," *fr.* XVI, *tr. by* Christopher Logue. TwMBP

"Now side by side, with like unweary'd care," *fr.* XIII, *tr. by* Pope. OBVE

"Now when the solemn rites of pray'r were past," *fr.* I, *tr. by* Dryden. OBVE

"Now, when twelve days complete had run their race," *fr.* I, *tr. by* George Chapman. OBVE

"Oileus by his brother's side stood close," *fr.* XIII, *tr. by* George Chapman. OBVE

"Rat,/ pearl,/ onion,/ honey," *fr.* XIX, *tr. by* Christopher Logue. TwMBP

"So Hector spake; the Trojans roared applause," *fr.* VIII, *tr. by* Tennyson. OBVE

"So saying, light-foot Iris passed away," *fr.* XVIII, *tr. by* Tennyson. OBVE

"Son of Enops, Thestor next he smote, The," *fr.* XVI, *tr. by* William Cowper. OBVE

"Their ardour kindles all the Grecian pow'rs," *fr.* XII, *tr. by* Pope. OBVE

"Their ground they stil made good," *fr.* V, *tr. by* George Chapman. OBVE

"Then first he form'd th' immense and solid shield," *fr.* XVIII, *tr. by* Pope. OBVE

"Then rising in his rage above the shores," *fr.* XXI, *tr. by* Pope. OBVE

"There sate the seniors of the Trojan race," *fr.* III, *tr. by* Pope. OBVE

"This said, he reacht to take his sonne," *fr.* VI, *tr. by* George Chapman. OBVE

"This speech all Troyans did applaud," *fr.* VIII, *tr. by* George Chapman. OBVE

"Thus at the panting dove a falcon flies," *fr.* XXII, *tr. by* Pope. OBVE

"Thus to Glaucus spake/ Divine Sarpedon," *fr.* XII, *tr. by* Sir John Denham. OBVE

"Troops exulting sate in order round, The," *fr.* VIII, *tr. by* Pope. OBVE

"Unweary'd watch their list'ning leaders keep, Th'," *fr.* X, *tr. by* Pope. OBVE

"Why boast we, Glaucus! our extended reign," *fr.* XII, *tr. by* Pope. OBVE

"'Why dost thou so explore,'" *fr.* VI *tr. by* George Chapman. OBVE

"Wrath of Peleus son, O muse, resound, The," Invocation, *tr. by* Dryden. OBVE

Ilkley Moor Baht 'At. *Unknown.* FS

I'll act out a weird dream. Marie-Francoise Prager, *tr. fr. French by* Willis Barnstone *and* Elene Kolb. BoWoP

I'll always dress in black and rave. Christine de Pisan, *tr. fr. French by* Willis Barnstone. BoWoP

I'll be an otter, and I'll let you swim. River-Mates. Padraic Colum. LoAs; PFIr

I'll Be Fourteen Next Sunday. *Unknown.* AmFP; OLR

I'll be going home today. Bunky Boy Bunky Boy Who's My Little Bunky Boy. Larry Mollin. NeAC

I'll Be Polite. Lloyd E. Werth. CTV

I'll build a house of arrogance. Haven. Donald Jeffrey Hayes. AmNP (1974 ed.)

I'll come to thee in all those shapes. To Electra. Robert Herrick. CaPo

I'll come when thou art saddest. Emily Brontë. VLP

I'll do so much for my sweetheart. The Unquiet Grave. *Unknown.* Epi

"Ill fares the land to hastening ills a prey." On Vital Statistics. Hilaire Belloc. POL

Ill fares the land, to hastening ills a prey. Goldsmith. *Fr.* The Deserted Village. OBSV

I'll Find My Self-Belief. Jacob Glatstein, *tr. fr. Yiddish by* Ruth Whitman. VWA

I'll get out of your life," i said. Song for the Nkazi or the Final Ironies. Thulani Nkabinde. NW

"I'll give to you a paper of pins." Paper of Pins. *Unknown.* AmFP; BLSo; FSW

I'll give you the weight of my hands. Tonight When You Leave. Gayle Elen Harvey. AMV-81

I'll go among the dead to see my friend. An Afternoon at the Beach. Edgar Bowers. PiAm

I'll go into the bedroom silently and lie down between the bridegroom and the bride. Love Poem on Theme by Whitman. Allen Ginsberg. CAPP; TT

I'll Go with Her Blues. *Unknown.* BluL

Ill Government. Robert Herrick. PAIC

I'll greet the sun once more. Once More. Forugh Farrokhzad, *tr. by* Jascha Kessler *and* Amin Banani. BoWoP

I'll hang/ them by the neck. The Consequence. Roger McDonald. CAAP

I'll Have a Collier for My Sweetheart. William Oliver. WTO

I'll just take my greenery. No Mixed Green Salad for Me, Thanks. Georgie Starbuck Galbraith. QQQ

I'll keep your shirt white. *Turkish Death Songs, tr. by* Reza Baraheni *and* Zahra-Soltan Shokoohtaezeh. BoWoP

Ill lay he long, upon this last return. John Berryman. *Fr.* Dream Songs. TAP

I'll lay you five hundred pounds. The Broomfield Hill. *Unknown.* AmFP

I'll need a desk that smells of cedar. Letter of Application Long Enough to Indicate Writing Ability. Karen Sagstatter. PoUp

I'll Never Love Thee More. James Graham, Marquess of Montrose. GBL; NOBE; PoPle
To His Mistress, *sel.* SLP

I'll Not Marry at All. *Unknown.* AmFP

I'll not weep that thou art going to leave me. Stanzas. Emily Brontë. IPWM; WPE

I'll prop her, I swear, ankle, butt and chin. The Nude on the Bathroom Wall. Gena Ford. IHMS

I'll Sail upon the Dog-Star. Thomas Durfey. RAE

I'll Say! H. H. Lewis. SPT

I'll sing of heroes, and of kings. Love. Abraham Cowley, *after the Greek of* Anacreon. OBVE

I'll sing of Hildebrand Montrose. I'll Strike You with a Feather. Arthur Lloyd. VLP

I'll sing the searchless depths of the compassion divine. Christ's Passion. Abraham Cowley. PIM

I'll sing you a new ballad, and I'll warrant it first-rate. The Fine Old English Gentleman: New Version. Charles Dickens. FaBoBa; OBSV

I'll sing you a one-O.   Carol of the Numbers [*or* The Dilly Song]. *Unknown*.   AmFP; FSW; GBP

I'll sing you a song and it'll be a sad one.   The Sioux Indians. *Unknown*.   AmFP

I'll sing you a song and it's not very long.   Young Man Who Wouldn't Hoe Corn.   *Unknown*.   FSW

I'll sing you a song of peace and love.   Whack Fol the Diddle. Peadar Kearney.   PFIr

I'll sing you a true song of Billy the Kid.   Billy the Kid. *Unknown*.   BPAW; FSW

I'll sing you one O.   *See* I'll sing you a one-O.

I'll Strike You with a Feather.   Arthur Lloyd.   VLP

I'll take no calls, she says.   The Comedians.   George Hitchcock. PoW

I'll Take You Home Again, Kathleen.   Thomas P. Westendorf. BLSH, *with music*; FSW; PSoN, *with music*

I'll tell all you skinners.   Pete Orman.   *Unknown*.   BPAW

I'll tell thee everything I can.   The White Knight's Song [*or* The Aged Aged Man].   "Lewis Carroll."   *Fr*. Through the Looking-Glass.   ECBV; FaBoCo; FaBoNo; HAP; ILP (1975 ed.); InPS; NOBE; NOBL; OAEL-2; OBP; OxBChV; SpRo; VLP

I'll tell you a story.   Mother Goose.   ECBV; MG

I'll tell you a story about Omie Wise.   Omie Wise.   *Unknown*. FSW

I'll tell you a story of a row in the town.   Erin Go Braugh! *Unknown*.   FSW

I'll tell you everything, I give you my word!   "Shatnes" or Uncleanliness.   Eliezer Steinberg, *tr. by* Seth L. Wolitz. VWA

I'll tell you how the sun rose.   Emily Dickinson.   ILP (1975 ed.); TAP

I'll tell you of a come-lye young lady fair.   Fair Phoebe and Her Dark-eyed Sailor.   *Unknown*.   AmFP

I'll tell you of a sailor now, a tale that can't be beat.   The Story of Samuel Jackson.   Charles Godfrey Leland.   PoTa

I'll tell you of a wild Colloina boy.   The Wild Colloina Boy. *Unknown*.   AmFP

I'll tell you the story of Jimmy Jet.   Jimmy Jet and His TV Set. Shel Silverstein.   CTBA

I'll tell you why I'm afraid of the dark.   Dark.   Eloise Klein Healy.   AMV-80

I'll Twine White Violets.   Meleager, *tr. fr. Greek by* Goldwin Smith.   NIL

I'll Wear Me a Cotton Dress.   *Unknown*.   BPo

I'll write about the world then.   On the Beach.   Anthony Ostroff. MPA

I'll write, because I'll give.   To Critics.   Robert Herrick.   CaPo

I'll write no more of love, but now repent.   On Himself.   Robert Herrick.   CaPo

I'll write no more verses—plague take 'em!   Those Flapjacks of Brown's.   Bert Leston Taylor.   OBAL

Illicit.   D. H. Lawrence.   *See* On the Balcony.

Illinois Farmer.   Carl Sandburg.   ANTL

Illinois, Iowa.   Inventory/ Itinerary.   Ken Smith.   TwMBP

Illness, An, *sel*.   Robert Creeley. "Robinson Crusoe."   UsP

Illness had wanted to kill her, The.   The Smoke Shop Owner's Daughter.   Jean Garrigue.   UsP

Ills of a poet are dull and routine affairs, The.   The Poet in Washington.   John Pauker.   PoUp; WasP

Illuminating lamps, ye orbs christallite.   *Unknown*.   *Fr*. Zepheria. ESo

Illumination, The.   Stanley Kunitz.   GP; TAP

Illumination and Ecstasy.   *Tr. fr. Arabic, at. to* Baba Kuhi of Shiraz.   ILwL

Illusions, The: they fit like an iron lung, and.   Memorandum/ The Accountant's Notebook.   Kathleen Norris.   OBAL

Illustration, The/ is nothing to you.   To a Steam Roller. Marianne Moore.   BoWoP; CMoP (1970 ed.); ILP (1975 ed.); LFH; Psy; VGW

Illustration, The—A Footnote.   Denise Levertov.   PoA

Illustrious Ancestors.   Denise Levertov.   NoAM; NOBA; VGW

Illustrious Holland! hard would be his lot.   Byron.   *Fr*. English Bards and Scotch Reviewers.   OBSV

I'm/ lost.   Supermarket.   Felice Holman.   QQQ

I'm a Baby.   Cid Corman.   GP

I'm a broken-hearted gardener, and don't know what to do.   The Broken-hearted Gardener.   *Unknown*.   GBP

I'm a decent boy just landed.   No Irish Need Apply.   *Unknown*. FSW; WTO

I'm a heartbroken raftsman, from Greenville I came.   Jack Haggerty.   *Unknown*.   AmFP

I'm a lean dog, a keen dog, a wild dog, and lone.   Lone Dog. Irene McLeod.   DuDr; GDP

I'm a peevish old man with a penny-whistle.   Beggar's Serenade. John Heath-Stubbs.   BoLoP

I'm a poor boy, I'm a poor boy.   Payday at Coal Creek. *Unknown*.   RDB

I'm a poor cotton weaver as many one knows.   Jone o' Grinfield. *Unknown*.   VLP

I'm a poor little girl.   The Wagoner's Lad.   *Unknown*.   AmFP

I'm a rabbit's foot.   Susan Legg.   OSP

I'm a riddle in nine syllables.   Metaphors.   Sylvia Plath.   InPK; SoSe

I'm a Roman Jew and I've been Roman.   A Roman Roman. Crescenzo del Monte, *tr. by* Barbara Garvin.   VWA

I'm a snake doctor man.   Snake Doctor Blues.   *Unknown*.   BluL

I'm a Soldier in the Army of the Lord.   *Unknown*.   AmFP

I'm a stable cat, a working cat.   The Stable Cat.   Leslie Norris. PChr

I'm a Stranger Here.   *Unknown*.   FSW

I'm a stranger here just blowed in your town.   Doggin' Me Around Blues.   *Unknown*.   BluL

I'm a stranger to your city and my name is Patty Flynn.   Portland County Jail.   *Unknown*.   FSW

I'm a tiger in the rain.   Sad Day in Berlin.   Sarah Kirsch, *tr. by* Gerda Mayer.   PBWP

I'm a walking down the track.   900 Miles.   *Unknown*.   FSW

I'm a weaver, a Calton weaver.   The Calton Weaver.   *Unknown*. FSW

I'm a young married man that is tired of life.   Cod Liver Oil. *Unknown*.   FSW

I'm Ageing to Lay Down My Sword, *with music*.   *Unknown*.   AH

I'm a-goin' to tell you 'bout the comin' of a new day.   Great Getting Up Morning.   *Unknown*.   FSW

I'm Alabama bound.   Alabama Bound.   *Unknown*.   FSW

I'm a-layin' around, just spendin' muh time.   The Strawberry Roan.   Curley W. Fletcher.   BPAW

I'm all alone in this world, she said.   50—50.   Langston Hughes. NoAM; NOBA

I'm always/ most surprised.   Justice.   Petra von Morstein, *tr. by* Rosemarie Waldrop.   BoWoP

I'm an Old Cowhand.   Johnny Mercer.   OBAL

I'm as free a little bird as I can be.   Free Little Bird.   *Unknown*. AmFP; FSW

I'm as mild-mannered as can be.   The Popular Wobbly.   T-Bone Slim.   FSW

I'm at the edge.   Here Be Dragons.   Ginny Friedlander. AMV-80

I'm beginning to understand that man in old boots.   Beginning to Understand.   Ruth Stone.   GP

I'm bored to extinction with Harrison. Lim'ricks and Puns. *Unknown.* TDH

I'm Bringing You Back. Constance Wright. PHC

I'm Captain Jinks of the Horse Marines. Captain Jinks. William Horace Lingard. BLSo; FSW

I'm ceded—I've stopped being theirs. Emily Dickinson. PiAm; SBG

I'm cold in hand can't get nothing here. No Woman No Nickel. *Unknown.* BluL

I'm coming down the wooded freeway. 45th Parallel Sulks. W.A. Roecker. FoP

"I'm corrupt," he said to me in the French. The Corrupt Man in the French Pub. Brian Higgins. OxBTC

I'm dead drunk this morning, daddy. Dead Drunk Blues. *Unknown.* BluL

I'm determined to be an old maid. I'll Marry Not at All. *Unknown.* AmFP

I'm discontented with homes that are rented. Tea for Two. Irving Caesar. BLSo

I'm dreaming now of Hally [*or* Hallie]. Listen to the Mocking Bird. Septimus Winner. BLSo; FSW; PSoN

I'm driving my car back to you filled. The Furniture of the Poem. Dennis Saleh. NeAC

I'm driving straight and my irons are good. Any Golf Championship. Grantland Rice. SPo

I'm eating alone lately. Things of Late. David Phillips. NeAC

I'm flagging to South Carolina. Long Distance Moan. *Unknown.* BluL

I'm frigid when I wear see thru negligees. I Never Saw a Man in a Negligee. Alta. GP

I'm getting old and feeble and I cannot work no more. The Old Miner's Refrain. *Unknown.* AmFP

I'm glad I walk'd. How fresh the meadows look. Walking to the Mail. Tennyson. VLP

I'm glad our house is a little house. Song for a Little House. Christopher Morley. CTV

I'm glad that I. The Park. James S. Tippett. FPB

I'm glad that I am born to die. Shout for Joy. *Unknown.* AmFP

I'm glad the sky is painted blue. *Unknown.* CTV

I'm goin' away baby take me seven long months to ride. Big Chief Blues. *Unknown.* BluL

I'm goin' away for to stay a little while. He's Gone Away. *Unknown.* FSW

I'm goin' downtown, gonna get me a sack of flour. Keep My Skillet Good and Greasy. *Unknown.* FSW

I'm goin' get up in the morning. I Believe I'll Dust My Broom. *Unknown.* BluL

I'm goin' where de Southern crosses top de C. and O. Tin Roof Blues. Sterling A. Brown. PoUp

I'm going away. Going Away Blues. *Unknown.* BluL

I'm going away for to leave you, love. The Storms Are on the Ocean. *Unknown.* FSW

I'm going back where I come f'm. Old Dog Blue. *Unknown.* BluL

I'm Going Down This Road Feeling Bad. *Unknown.* FSW

I'm Going Down to the River of Jordan, *with music. Unknown.* BLSH

I'm going home/ friends, sitdown. That's No Way to Get Along. *Unknown.* BluL

I'm going out to clean the pasture spring. The Pasture. Robert Frost. BiP; CMoP (1970 ed.); LCL; NOBA; NowV; OSP; RAE; SoSe (1977 ed.)

I'm going over to 3rd Alley lord, but I'm gonna carry my 45. 45 Pistol Blues. *Unknown.* BluL

I'm going to be a pirate with a bright brass pivot-gun. The Tarry Buccaneer. John Masefield. PoTa; RhR

I'm going to be just like you, Ma. A Dance for Ma Rainey. Al Young. CSP; SA

I'm going to break out. Carmen Valle, *tr. fr. Spanish by* Julio Marzán. InW

I'm going to California. Bina Mossman, *tr. fr. Hawaiian by* S.H. Elbert *and* N. Mahoe. WTO

I'm Going to Georgia. *Unknown.* AIW; AmFP

I'm going to Germany—I'll be back some day. Going to Germany. *Unknown.* BluL

I'm Going to Rocky Island. *Unknown.* AmFP

I'm going to save. The Clerk's Dream. Herbert Scott. TC

I'm going to sing you a brand new song. The Other Side of Jordan. *Unknown.* FSW

I'm going to the North on the left rail. Going to the North. Stanislaw Wygodski, *tr. by* Isaac Komem. VWA

I'm gonna get up in the morning do like Buddy Brown. 98 Degree Blues. *Unknown.* BluL

I'm gonna lay down my sword and shield. Study War No More. *Unknown.* FSW

I'm Gonna Move to the Outskirts of Town. *Unknown.* BluL

I'm Gonna Run to the City of Refuge. *Unknown.* BluL

I'm gonna stay around this town. 'Tain't Nobody's Business. *Unknown.* BluL

I'm gonna tell you a story 'bout grizzly bear. Grizzly Bear. *Unknown.* FSW

I'm gonna walk the Streets of Glory. Streets of Glory. *Unknown.* FSW

I'm gonna write me. To Chuck. Sonia Sanchez. UsP

I'm grateful, really grateful. Sulpicia, *tr. fr. Latin by* John Dillon. PBWP

I'm happy/ could a pome be a cup. Anybody Could Write This Poem. All You Have to Say Is Yes. Alta. MMD

I'm having an affair with Hamlet. "Hamlet." Emmett Jarrett. NeAC

I'm Here. David Ignatow. GP

I'm Here. Theodore Roethke. *Fr.* Meditations of an Old Woman. Epi

I'm Honest Abe. Honest Abe Lincoln. Max Shulman. OBAL

I'm in a nice bit of trouble, I confess. Waiting at the Church; or, My Wife Won't Let Me. Fred W. Leigh. FSN

I'm in New York covered by a layer of soap foam. How Come? David Ignatow. NYP

I'm just a poor wayfaring stranger. Poor Wayfaring Stranger. *Unknown.* BLSo; FSW

I'm Just a Stranger Here, Heaven Is My Home. Carole Gregory Clemmons. PoBA

I'm just a typical American boy. Draft Dodger Rag. Phil Ochs. WIF

I'm just like an old rooster. Looking Up at Down. *Unknown.* BluL

I'm Leery of Firms with Easy Terms. C. S. Jennison. QQQ

I'm like the king of a rain-country, rich. Spleen LXXVII. Baudelaire, *tr. by* Robert Lowell. NAWM-2

I'm living in Battersea, July. Old-fashioned Air. Ted Berrigan. FiCh

I'm living with a commercial traveller. The Commercial Traveller's Wife. Ronald McCuaig. GAS

I'm lonesome since I cross'd the hill. The Girl I Left behind Me. *Unknown.* BLSo; FSW; GSB

I'm looking at your lofty head. Pike's Peak. *Unknown.* BPAW

I'm looking funny in my eye, and I. Fixing to Die. *Unknown.* BluL

I'm looking mighty seedy while holding down my claim. Little Old Sod Shanty. *Unknown.* AmFP

I'm lost in my name. Theodore Roethke. POL

I'm Lucky. Charlotte Mandel. AMV-81

I'm made in sport by nature when. On an Indian Tomineios, the Least of Birds. Thomas Heyrick. SCP-2

I'm makin' a road. Florida Road Workers. Langston Hughes. CTBA; SFF; SoS

I'm meeting God in the Mekong Delta. Dustoff: Med Evac. Horace Coleman. SES

I'm melted down into a black ooze. In a Remote Cloister Bordering the Empyrean. Joel Sloman. VGW

I'm more afraid of those I love than dying. A Letter Catches Up with Me. Eric Chaet. VWA

I'm mother. Woman as Artist. Eleanor Ross Taylor. CSP

I'm nine years old! an' you can't guess how much I weigh, I bet. The Little Hunchback. James Whitcomb Riley. PeD

"I'm 92," Joe said. Tom Weber. CTBA

I'm no He-man you know, I'm not a He. D. B. Wyndham Lewis. *Fr. If So the Man You Are.* OBSV

I'm nobody! Who are you? Emily Dickinson. BoWoP; IPWM; NOBA; PPM; SBG; SO; SS; TAP; WPE

I'm not alone. Interior. Joseph Milbauer, *tr. by* Edouard Roditi. VWA

I'm Not Here / Never Was. Constanta Buzea, *tr. fr. Rumanian by* Stavros Deligiorgis. BoWoP

I'm not ready, I shout. Urgency. Betsy Sholl. AMV-80

I'm Not Rich. Joseph Rolnik, *tr. fr. Yiddish by* Keith Bosley. VWA

I'm not scared of dyin. And When I Die. Laura Nyro. WIF

I'm not sure why I touched it. Last Patch of Snow. George Abbe. FAF

I'm not without you. The Place of O. Ray A. Young Bear. VoR

I'm Older than You, Please Listen. A.R.D. Fairburn. ATNZ

I'm on Highway 28 facing the morning. Meditations on Frost's "Stopping by Woods." Albert De Pietro. AATT

I'm on My Way to Canaan, *with music. Unknown.* AH

I'm on my way to Freedom land. *Unknown.* FWS

I'm Only a Broken-down Miner. *Unknown.* AmFP

I'm only a consumer, and it really doesn't matter. Cheer for the Consumer. Nixon Waterman. OBAL

I'm only a merchant of time. The Fable Merchant. Charles Dobzynski, *tr. by* Charles Guenther. VWA

I'm only sorry I've no child to show him. Out after Dark. Geoffrey Lehmann. GAS

I'm Owre Young to Marry Yet. Burns. LoAs

I'm quiet as an old leather belt-lapped snakewise. Quiet. Brian Swann. AmPA

I'm quite the opposite of my clever master. Faust's Servant. Roy Fuller. OxBTC

I'm ready. Sleep. M.R. Doty. AMV-80

I'm ready now to cat-chase those porcelain people, get after them. Imprecation for an Aesthetics Society with Newts, Warts, Waxes and Pins. Rosalie Moore. RiTi

I'm red pepper in a shaker. Sugar in the Cane. Tennessee Williams. OBAL

I'm riding on that new river train. New River Train. *Unknown.* FSW

"I'm rising five," he said. Rising Five. Norman Nicholson. MPo

I'm running from myself down this percolating highway. Percolating Highway. Michael Castro. VWA

I'm Sad. Forugh Farrokhzad, *tr. fr. Persian by* Reza Baraheni. BoWoP

I'm Sad and I'm Lonely. *Unknown.* FSW

I'm scared a lonely. Never see my son. John Berryman. *Fr. Dream Songs.* ILP (1975 ed.)

I'm sick of love; O let me lie. To Sycamores. Robert Herrick. CaPo

I'm sick of you hypocrites babbling about gods! The Sanctimonious Poets. Friedrich Hölderlin, *tr. by* Robert Bly. NU

I'm sister and brotherless. Remember Way Back. *Unknown.* BluL

I'm sitting down here wondering would a, would a matchbox hold my clothes. Packin' Trunk Blues. *Unknown.* BluL

I'm sitting here. Reflections. Dane Knell. TVo

I'm sitting in a cafe. November 3. Richard Brautigan. VoA

I'm sitting in the living room. Sonic Boom. John Updike. QQQ; SoS

I'm sitting on the second floor of my house in West Branch. 3 Days after Father's Day. Allan Kornblum. AcAn

I'm Skeleton. Lilian Moore. IWK

I'm Smith of Stoke, aged sixty-odd. Epitaph on a Pessimist. Thomas Hardy. FaBoEE; FF

I'm so glad good whiskey have made it through. More Good Whiskey Blues. *Unknown.* BluL

I'm so tired of being a Jew, an Arab. Nationalism. Harry Rosolenko. AMV-80

I'm Soaked Through with You. Rachel Korn, *tr. fr. Yiddish by* Ruth Whitman. VWA

I'm speaking again. Speaking. Michael Ryan. AmPA

I'm speaking from the half. To You on the Broken Iceberg. Tess Gallagher. GP

I'm spending my nights in the flop house. Soup Song. Maurice Sugar. FSW

I'm spooked/ and swelled/ with exhaustion. 6/10/75. Darlene Pearlstein. FiCh

I'm such a quiet little ghost. The Superstitious Ghost. Arthur Guiterman. IWK

I'm sure every word that you say is absurd. A Woman's Reason. Gelett Burgess. FaBoNo

"I'm tell j'you what, these sheeps beezness." The Sheep Beezness. S. Omar Barker. BPAW

I'm thankful that the sun and moon. Gasbags. *Unknown.* NOBL

I'm the bloke that's trained to sit behind the public stamp machines. A Song of the GPO. Gerry Hamill. NOBL

I'm the face this side of the microphone. Declaration. Robert Gessner. SPT

I'm the great Sir William Anson. *Unknown. Fr. Balliol Rhymes.* FaBoEE

I'm the kid that's all the candy. The Yankee Doodle Boy. George M. Cohan. BLSo; FSN

I'm the local Skeleton. I'm Skeleton. Lilian Moore. IWK

I'm the man, the very fat man. The Man That Waters the Workers' Beer. Paddy Ryan. FSW

I'm the serpent of somebody else. Sensibility! O La! Theodore Roethke. UsP

I'm the snow on mountains. *Turkish Death Songs, tr. by* Reza Baraheni *and* Zahra-Soltan Shokoohtaezeh. BoWoP

I'm thirty years old. Paris by Night. Gustave Kahn, *tr. by* Edouard Roditi. VWA

I'm Through with You. *Unknown.* WTO

I'm tired of keeping my eyes. The Woman Driving the Country Squire. David Dayton. AMV-81

I'm tired of love: I'm still more tired of rhyme. Fatigue. Hilaire Belloc. FaBoCo; NOBL; OxBTC

I'm tired of murdering children. (End) of Summer (1966). William Knott. EAS

I'm trav'ling to my grave. The Traveler. *Unknown.* AmFP

I'm way down here. God, Are You There? Helen Steiner Rice. CTV

I'm wearin' awa', John. The Land o' the Leal. Lady Nairne. SLP

I'm "wife"—I've finished that. Emily Dickinson. CMoP (1970 ed.); PiAm

I'm with you and you're with me and. Marching to Pretoria. *Unknown.* FSW

I'm writing just after an encounter. Whatever You Say, Say Nothing. Seamus Heaney. IPM

I'm writing this poem with a pencil found in the weeds. Ecology. Harold Witt. PoW

I'm writing this with green ink so you'll believe me. Green Prose. Thomas Lux. AAN

I'm yours, dearest, as are the winter towns. Marceline, to Her Husband. Elizabeth Libbey. AmPA

Image, The. Roy Fuller. OxBTC

Image. T. E. Hulme. InPK; OxBTC

Image. Anna de Noailles, *tr. fr. French by* Carol Cosman. PBWP

Image comes, An. Laser. A. R. Ammons. NOBA

Image from Beckett, An. Derek Mahon. CIP

Image in the Mirror. Peggy Susberry Kenner. JB

Image of City. Lance Henson. VoR

Image of God, The. Francisco de Aldana, *tr. fr. Spanish by* Longfellow. PIM

Image of Lethe, An. The Coming of War; Actaeon. Ezra Pound. CMoP (1970 ed.); PoA

Image the images the great games therefore the locked. The Book of Job and a Draft of a Poem to Praise the Paths of the Living. George Oppen. NNaP

Images. Richard Aldington. PoA

Images. Alastair Campbell. Moon

Images. Andrew Whittaker. IPM

Images drip down my back like sweat. On the Morning of the Third Night above Nisqually. W. M. Ransom. BCr; CDW; NU

Images leap with him from branch to branch. A Poet at Twenty. Donald Hall. EAS

Images of Poverty. Ben Maddow. SPT

Imaginary man, go. Here is your passport. Instructions for Crossing the Border. Dan Pagis, *tr. by* Stephen Mitchell. VWA

Imagination of Necessity, The. Andrei Codrescu. EAS

Imaginative Life, The. Geoffrey Hill. NoAM

Imagine a lost language, imagine a shadow. A Northern Habitat. Robin Fulton. MIS

Imagine coastal spray, far movement, marsh. Now. Robert Huff. CNW

Imagine father that you had a brother were. Landscape with Next of Kin. Olga Broumas. BoWoP; CNW

Imagine for a moment. The Invention of Cuisine. Carol Muske. PCho

Imagine Grass. Knute Skinner. GP; PoW

Imagine his lassoed walk. Cowboy's Love Song. Catherine O'Neill. PoUp

Imagine it, a Sophocles complete. The Fire at Alexandria. Theodore Weiss. NoAM; PoA; TAP

Imagine lamenting our longing, no. Cradle Song. Yona Wallach, *tr. by* Leonore Gordon. VWA

Imagine my surprise when. Unplanned Design. Neal Bowers. AMV-80

Imagine, say, a mediaeval window. The Temptation. Iain Crichton Smith. MS

Imagine that I am the Puerto Rican who. The Translator. Patrick L. Clary. PoUp

Imagine the lake behind your house. Fear. Roger Stump. AMV-80

Imagine the princess's surprise! The Frog Prince: A Speculation on Grimm's Fairy Tale. Robert Pack. TPo

Imagine the shivers on the cold metal. An Old Polish Lesson. Deanna Louise Pickard. AMV-81

Imagine time's like changing neighborhoods. Girl-watching at Grant's Pass. Robert Huff. CNW

Imagine time's tendersweet passions. Sweet Louise. Gladstone Yearwood. SES

Imagine what Mrs. Haessler would say. The Dance of the Abakweta. Margaret Danner. NIL

Imagine your old bow father. Concertmaster. Richard Burgin. AMV-81

(Im)C-A-T(mo). E.E. Cummings. HAP; WeW

Imitation of Julia A. Moore. "Mark Twain." OBAL

Imitation of Spenser. Keats. MBPR

Imitation of the Style of * * * *. Samuel Johnson. FaBoCo (Idyll: "Hermit hoar, in solemn cell.") NOBL

Immanent. Walter de la Mare. PoA

Immeasurable haze. To the Holy Spirit. Yvor Winters. PiAm; VGW

Immeasurable sadness! Sadness. Tennyson. FaBoEE

Immediate Kindness. Allan Kornblum. AcAn

Immediately create. "The Virtue of Uncreatedness." Alice Notley. FiCh

Immense hope, and forbearance, The. Spring Day. John Ashbery. NOBA

Immense room as quiet, An. The Penn Central Station at Beacon, N.Y. Ed Ochester. TAT

Immensity. Gerald Stern. AMV-80

Immensity, cloistered in thy dear womb. Nativity. John Donne. SCP-1

Immersed in night, my senses sharpen, hear. Porch. Alden Nowlan. NeAC

Immersed in the haven of beef flesh. Hamburger Mary's. Todd S.J. Lawson. CPA

Immigrant, The. David Hilton. AcAn

Immigrants. Robert Frost. GOA

Immigrants. Stanley Nelson. AMV-81

Immigrant's Stars, The. Jordan Smith. AAN

Immoderate Death that wouldst not once confer. On the Death of the Lord Treasurer. *Unknown.* FaBoEE

Immoral Proposition, The. Robert Creeley. PiAm

Immorality, An. Ezra Pound. CMoP (1970 ed.); NOBA; OBAL; OLR; VoPo

Immortal Autumn. Archibald MacLeish. BiP; CMoP (1970 ed.)

Immortal clothing I put on. The Transfiguration. Robert Herrick. CaPo

Immortal Hate. Milton. *Fr.* Paradise Lost, I. NOBE

Immortal love, author of this great frame. Love. George Herbert. HoPM (1975 ed.)

Immortal Love, Forever Full, *with music.* Whittier. AH

Immortal Part, The. A. E. Housman. SoSe (1977 ed.); TT; UnPo (1976 ed.); VLP

Immortals, The. Isaac Rosenberg. FaBoTw (1975 ed.)

Immunisation Day. Elizabeth Bartlett. PMW

Immured in thickening walls. The Old Ones. R. E. Sebenthall. HeS

Impact of a dollar upon the heart, The. War Is Kind, XX. Stephen Crane. PiAm

Impartial Inspection, The. *Unknown.* APAS

Impartial Law enrolled a name, The. My Name and I. Robert Graves. NoAM

Impasse. Langston Hughes. TPo

Impasto or washes as a rule. Irish Poetry. Michael Longley. CIP

Impatient with cripples, foreigners, children. Il Piccolo Rifiuto. Louis MacNeice. CMoP (1970 ed.)

Impatiently she tampered with the locks.   Bluebeard's Wife.
   Daryl Hine.   NoAM

Imperfect Enjoyment, The.   Earl of Rochester.   BoLoP; SCP-2

Imperfect enough once for all at thirty.   Last Things, Black Pines
   at 4 a.m.   Robert Lowell.   NOBA

Imperfect pine, An.   On Restoring Verticals.   Sandra Ruth
   Duguid.   AATT

Imperfect Sympathies.   Clarice Short.   PPoD

Imperial.   A. R. D. Fairburn.   ATNZ

Imperial Adam.   A. D. Hope.   GAS; HAP; MAuV; NoAM

Imperial Thumbprint.   Tom Weatherly.   PoBA

Imperialist.   A. R. Ammons.   GP

Imperialists in Retirement.   Edward Lucie-Smith.   MPo

Imperious Muse, your arrows ever strike.   Japanese Beetles.   X. J.
   Kennedy.   OBAL

Imperiously he leaps, he neighs, he bounds.   Shakespeare.   *Fr.*
   Venus and Adonis.   BoAnP

Impermanence.   Lal Ded, *tr. fr. Kashmiri by* Willis Barnstone.
   BoWoP

Impersonal the aim.   Night of Battle.   Yvor Winters.   PoA

Implicated generations made, The.   Celtic Cross.   Norman
   MacCaig.   MS

Imploring Mecca.   Be-Bop Boys.   Langston Hughes.   OBAL

Imponderable the dinosaur.   Cape Hatteras.   Hart Crane.   *Fr.*
   The Bridge.   PiAm

Importance of Mirrors, The.   Helga Sandburg.   IHMS

"Important is the nation's health."   The Double Standard.
   Franklin P. Adams.   OBAL

Important thing is not, The.   Is.   Patrick Kavanagh.   FaBoTw
   (1975 ed.)

Importer, An.   Robert Frost.   FaBoCo

Impossible to tell.   Recovery.   Julie Ball.   PMW

Impossibilities to His Friend.   Robert Herrick.   OLR

Impossibility, The.   Coventry Patmore.   *Fr.* The Angel in the
   House, I, i.   VLP

Impossibility, An.   Robert Vas Dias.   HeS

Impossible Dream, The, *with music*   Joe Darion.   BLSo

Imposture, The, *sel.*   James Shirley.
   "You virgins that did late despair."   SCP-2
   (Piping Peace.)   NOBE

Impotence.   Marvin Bell.   AmPA

Imprecation for an Aesthetics Society with Newts, Warts, Waxes
   and Pins.   Rosalie Moore.   RiTi

Impression du Matin.   Oscar Wilde.   CABA (1972 ed.); VLP

Impressions, Number III.   E. E. Cummings.   UnPo (1976 ed.)

Impressions: II. La Mer.   Oscar Wilde.   VLP

Imprimis he was "broke." Thereafter left.   Giffen's Debt.
   Kipling.   VLP

Imprimis: I forgot all day your face.   Sonnet.   Conrad Aiken.
   LoAs

Imprimis, there's a table blotted.   An Inventory of the Furniture
   of a Collegian's Chamber.   John Winstanley.   OBSV

Impromptu.   *Unknown, wr. at. to* Benjamin Franklin.   *See*
   Quatrain: "Jack, eating rotten cheese, did say."

Impromptu.   Samuel Wilberforce.   FaBoNo

Impromptu Immersion in Tom's Run.   Gibbons Ruark.   CSP

Impromptu on Charles II.   Earl of Rochester.   InPK; NIL;
   NOBL; OBSV
   ("God bless our good and gracious king.")   FaBoEE

Improved Farm Land.   Carl Sandburg.   RFM

Improvisations on Aesop.   Anthony Hecht.   OBAL

Impulse, The.   Robert Frost.   *Fr.* The Hill Wife.   AIW; HoPM
   (1975 ed.); NoAM

Impulse of October, The.   W. R. Moses.   NCSH

In/ The/ Space/ Between.   Separation.   Duane Niatum.   VW

In a Bar.   Ruth Herschberger.   WBN

In a Bar near Shibuya Station, Tokyo.   Paul Engle.   SFF

In a bookstore on the East Side.   Burning Oneself In.   Adrienne
   Rich.   NYP

In a bowl to sea went wise men three.   The Wise Men of Gotham.
   Thomas Love Peacock.   FaBoNo

In a branch of [a] willow hid.   To a Caty-did.   Philip Freneau.
   EAP; TAP

In a Bye-Canal.   Herman Melville.   AmVN

In a cavern [*or* cabin], in a canyon.   Oh, My Darling Clementine.
   *Unknown, at. to* Percy Montross.   AIW; AmFP; BLSo; CTV;
   FSW; GSB; OBAL; PSoN

In a chariot of light from the regions of day.   Liberty Tree.
   Thomas Paine.   BTTM

In a Chinese window.   Elephants from the Sea.   Ian Young.
   NeAC

In a chirche ther I con knel.   Deo Gracias.   *Unknown.*   OxBM

In a Churchyard.   Richard Wilbur.   HeIP; PiAm

In a coffee house at 3 am.   My Son and I.   Philip Levine.   BrS;
   GP; NYP

In a Coffee Pot.   Alfred Hayes.   SPT

In a coign of the cliff between lowland and highland.   A Forsaken
   Garden.   Swinburne.   EBEV; NOBE; OAEL-2; VLP

In a Corn Field.   *Unknown.*   ECBV

In a corner of blue sky.   Daily Wages.   Amrita Pritam, *tr. by*
   *author and* Charles Brasch.   PBWP

In a country without saints or shrines.   The Springs.   Wendell
   Berry.   GP

In a crosshatched 16th-century print, a.   Note from an Exhibition.
   Albert Goldbarth.   AMV-81

In a Curious Way.   John Smith.   UsP

In a dark, dark wood there was a dark, dark house.   In a Dark
   Wood.   *Unknown.*   RAE

In a Dark Time.   Theodore Roethke.   HAP; HeIP; ILP (1975
   ed.); IPWM; MAT; MPA; NoAM; NOBA; PBMP; PiAm;
   PPoD; PPP; TAP; UsP

In a Dark Wood.   *Unknown.*   RAE

In a days-and-nights ghetto.   In a Ghetto.   Jacob Glatstein, *tr. by*
   Ruth Whitman.   VWA

In a dead tree.   The Horse.   W. S. Merwin.   GP

In a dingy kitchen.   Lamentations.   Alter Brody.   VWA

In a Double Rainbow.   Harold Littlebird.   VoR

In a Dream.   David Ignatow.   GP; PoA

In a dream.   Small Favors.   Dale Matthews.   AAN

In a dream I returned to the river of bees.   The River of Bees.
   W. S. Merwin.   HeIP

In a dream last night.   Braided Poem.   John Pauker.   PoUp

In a Dream Ship's Hold.   Suzanne Bernhardt.   VWA

In a Dream, the Automobile.   Adrianne Marcus.   SFF

In a Drear-nighted December.   Keats.   MBPR; NOBE; PBMP;
   PoPle
   (In Drear-nighted December.)   OAEL-2

In a faded grey suit coat.   Black Sweeper.   Joseph Bruchac.   NW

In a fashionable suburb of Santa Barbara.   In Montecito.
   Randall Jarrell.   MAT; VGW

In a few moments.   The Death of a Negro Poet.   Conrad Kent
   Rivers.   BPo

In a few years your arches will fall.   The "Pirushke" Lady Warns
   Me of Going Barefoot.   Skaidrite Stelzer.   TC

In a Field.   Robert Pack.   CoPAm; MAT

In a field.   Keeping Things Whole.   Mark Strand.   CoPAm;
   NIL; NoAM; PPP; SFF; TAP

In a field of swaying grain.   Death Seed.   Ricarda Huch, *tr. by*
   Susan C. Strong.   PBWP

In a frith as I can fare fremede.   The Lady in the Wood.
   *Unknown.*   OxBM

In a frosty sunset.   Winter: East Anglia.   Edmund Blunden.
   LiSp; OxBTC

In a future dynasty of wealth and injustice. Moral Artistry. David McKain. AAN

In a garden shady this holy lady. Song for St. Cecilia's Day. W. H. Auden. FaBoTw (1975 ed.)

In a Garret. Herman Melville. OBAL

In a Ghetto. Jacob Glatstein, *tr. fr. Yiddish by* Ruth Whitman. VWA

In a Gondola, *sels.* Robert Browning.
"Moth's kiss, first, The!" BoLoP; GBL; IP
"Past we glide, and past, and past!" PeD

In a Grave-Yard. William Stanley Braithwaite. PoBA

In a grey rectory a clergyman was reading. Droit de Seigneur. Richard Murphy. PFIr

In a gym in Spanish Harlem. To a Fighter Killed in the Ring. Lou Lipsitz. LiSp; SPo

In a Hard Intellectual Light. Richard Eberhart. CMoP (1970 ed.)

In a herber green, asleep whereas I lay. In Youth Is Pleasure. Robert Wever. *Fr.* Lusty Juventus. GBL; NOBE

In a Home Relief Bureau. Alfred Hayes. SPT

In a Hotel Lobby. Isidor Schneider. SPT

In a Hotel Writing-Room. John Cowper Powys. OxBTC

In a house born of the brown earth. An Adobe House. Witter Bynner. BPAW

In a hundred places in North Dakota. Something Is Dying Here. Thomas McGrath. TAT

In a hut of mud and fire. Gautama in the Deer Park at Benares. Kenneth Patchen. NIL

In a long room that voices sundered. Cold Coffee. John Williams. CoPAm

In a loose robe of tinsel forth she came. George Chapman. *Fr.* Ovid's Banquet of Sense. SCP-2

In a Maple Wood. Pat Schneider. AMV-81

In a meadow/ Beside the chapel three boys were playing football. Father Mat. Patrick Kavanagh. CMoP (1970 ed.)

In a mean abode in [*or* on] the Shankill Road. The Ballad of William Bloat [*or* Belfast Linen]. *Unknown.* NOBL; WTO

In a melancholy fancy. Hollo, My Fancy! *Unknown.* SCP-2

In a Mental Hospital Sitting Room. Elizabeth Jennings. LP

In a milkweed cradle. Baby Seeds. *Unknown.* CTV

In a Mirror. Marcia Stubbs. MAT

In a Mist. Al Young. AMV-80

In a month all those frozen waterfalls. Modern Love. Gerald Stern. AMV-80

In a Moonlit Hermit's Cabin. Allen Ginsberg. Moon

In a Mountain Cabin in Norway. Robert Bly. RFM

In a museum here I saw a Celtic swordblade. The Celt in Me. Keith Wilson. GP

In a nation of one hundred fine, mob-hearted, lynching, relenting, repenting millions. Bryan, Bryan, Bryan, Bryan. Vachel Lindsay. CMoP (1970 ed.)

In a New Year. John McNally. PoUp

In a Night. Ann Marie Savage. AMV-81

In a noon-tide of a sumers day. Turn Again. *Unknown.* OxBM

In a phone booth. Of Human Bondage. Miller Williams. NYP

In a pine tree. I Try to Waken and Greet the World Once Again. James Wright. InPS

In a place of worhip I know, they made a strange mosaic. The Wall. Ludvik Askenazy, *tr. fr. Czech.* VWA

In a plume of sky firelight. Night Teeth. Peter Brett. AMV-80

In a Prominent Bar in Secaucus One Day. X. J. Kennedy. ConAP; HoPM (1975 ed.); NIL; NowV; OBAL; PAIC; PPP; UsP

In a quiet water'd land, a land of roses. The Dead at Clonmacnoise. *Unknown, tr. by* Thomas William Rolleston. PFIr

In a Remote Cloister Bordering the Empyrean. Joel Sloman. VGW

In a Roman tram, where the famous Roman mob. The Thief. Stanley Kunitz. VGW

In a salt ring of moonlight. Moorings. Norman MacCaig. OxBTC

In a season/ the shoots we planted. Peter Whigham. *Fr.* Love Poems of the VIth Dalai Lama. TwMBP

In a semi-circle we toed the line chalked round the master's. The Wanderer. Seamus Heaney. CIP

In a shoe box stuffed in an old nylon stocking. The Meadow Mouse. Theodore Roethke. ExPo (1973 ed.); HeIP; InPk; IPWM; MPA; PPoe; PSN; TSWA

In a sick shade of spruce, moss-webbed, rock-fed. As It Looked Then. E. A. Robinson. CMoP (1970 ed.); NoAM

In a small theodolite of paper. Soluble Noughts and Crosses; or, California, Here I Come. Roger Roughton. EAS

In a small wheelbarrow. A Cathedral. Stanislav Vinaver, *tr. by* Vasa D. Mihailovich. VWA

In a snug little cot lived a fat little mouse. The Country Mouse and the City Mouse. Richard Scrafton Sharpe. MN; OxBChV

In a solitude of the sea. The Convergence of the Twain. Thomas Hardy. AKE; BiP; FaBoTw (1975 ed.); HeIP; ILP (1975 ed.); InPk; LFH; NoAM; OAEL-2; OxBTC; PAIC; PBMP; PoIA

In a Somer Seson, Whan Softe Was the Sonne. William Langland. *Fr.* The Vision of Piers Plowman. EBEV (Field Full of Folk, The.) OxBM (Prologue: "In a summer season, when soft was the sun.") OAEL-1, *mod. by* J. R. Trapp; OBP, *mod. by* Selden Rodman

In a splendid sheath. Burial. Hone Tuwhare. ATNZ

In a Spring Still Not Written of. Robert Wallace. CoPAm; WIF

In a square case. Museum Item 237. Polly Mann. NPW

In a stable of boats I lie still. The Lifeguard. James Dickey. LiSp; NowV; SoS

In a Staffordshire Churchyard. *Unknown.* PoPle

In a Station of the Metro. Ezra Pound. BBGO; CABA (1972 ed.); ExPo (1973 ed.); HAP; HeIP; ILP (1975 ed.); InPK; LFH; NIL; NoAM; NOBA; PiAm; PPoD; TAP; TPo; UnPo (1976 ed.); VGW; WeW; WIF

In a Subdivision. Eric Torgersen. TC

In a Summer Season, When Soft Was the Sun. William Langland. *See* In a Somer Seson, Whan Softe Was the Sonne.

In a tea-garden overhanging Rotha. Grasmere Sonnets. David Wright. NoAM

In a thousand years, if there's History. Ecologue. Allen Ginsberg. CAAP

In a throng,/ A festal company of Maids and Youths. Wordsworth. *Fr.* The Prelude, IV. EBEV

In a time. Sky House. Ralph Storey. SES

In a time of damnation. The Gift of Fire. Lisel Mueller. NowV

In a Time of Pestilence. Thomas Nashe. *See* Adieu, Farewell Earth's Bliss.

In a Train. Robert Bly. CAPP; POL

In a universe infinitely subdividable. Candles. Peter Meinke. AATT

In a valley in Switzerland a brass band marches. Switzerland. Anthony Thwaite. HeHu

In a valley where a stream flows. *Unknown, tr. fr. Korean.* TVo

In a Vermont bedroom closet. A Record Stride. Robert Frost. TT

In a Warm Bath. Carl Rakosi. TAP

In a way, it's more pathetic than the dotage. Old Age of a Clown. Edward Lowbury. PMW

In a wee cot hoose far across the muir. Kate Dalrymple. *Unknown.* GBP

In a weird, forlorn voice. The President Slumming. James Tate. OBAL

In a while they rose and went out aimlessly riding. Merlin Enthralled. Richard Wilbur. CMoP (1970 ed.)

In a white gully among fungus red. Native Born. Eve Langley. WPE

In a windowless room you hold a door open. Feeling You Again. Jim Mulac. AcAn

In a Wood. Thomas Hardy. VLP

In a Wood. E. J. Scovell. GBL

In a World of Change. Joseph Awad. AMV–80

In Absentia. Alastair Mackie. MS

In Adam' fall. An ABC. *Unknown.* GBP

In Aeternum. James McAuley. MAuV

In Agrigentum, earlier in Olympia. Empedocles on Etna. H. B. Mallalieu. PoA

In Agypt's land contaygious to the Nile. Pharao's Daughter. Michael Moran. BIrV

In all humanity, we crave. The Commons' Petition to Charles II. Earl of Rochester. FaBoCo

In All the Days of My Childhood. Russell Edson. AmPA

In all the Eastern hemisphere. The Fall of J. W. Beane. Oliver Herford. OBAL; PoTa

In all the good Greek of Plato. Survey of Literature. John Crowe Ransom. OBAL; TAP; UsP; VGW

In All the Magic of Christmas-Tide, *with music.* John Jacob Niles. AH

In all the midwest. Early June. R. P. Dickey. TAT

In All These Acts. William Everson. PiAm

In all those stories the hero. Heroes. Robert Creeley. NOBA; PPP

IN) all those who got. E. E. Cummings. FaBoEE

In Allusion to the French Song. Richard Lovelace. CaPo

"In America," began. The Student. Marianne Moore. NowV

In Amsterdam there lived a maid. A-Roving. *Unknown.* FSW; GSB

In an age of fops and toys. So Nigh Is Grandeur. Emerson. PCOP

In an Album. James Russell Lowell. OBAL

In an Alien Place. Leib Neidus, *tr. fr. Yiddish by* Ruth Whitman. VWA

In an Artist's Studio. Christina Rossetti. OBP

In an Empty Window. Ray Fraser. NeAC

In an envelope marked. Personal. Langston Hughes. AmNP (1974 ed.); NOBA

In an Indian ditch lies. The World's Last Unnamed Poem. A. K. Redwing. VoR

In an instant, by instinct, I apprehended. An Act. Kenneth Rosen. AmPA

In an island of bitter lemons. Bitter Lemons. Lawrence Durrell. VoPo

In an oak there liv'd an owl. The Owl in the Oak. *Unknown.* FaBoNo

In an orchard a little fountain flows. Song of the Ill-Married. *Unknown, tr. by* Patricia Terry. BoWoP

In an owl cry, night became real night. A Bridge Begins in the Trees. William Stafford. CNW

In an upper room at midnight. The Love Feast. W. H. Auden. SFF

In ancient Egypt. The Fertile Valley of the Nile. Eve Merriam. IHMS

In ancient times, as story tells. Baucis and Philemon. Swift, *after* Ovid. NIL; OAEL–1

In ancient times—'twas no great loss. On a Nomination to the Legion of Honour. *Unknown.* FaBoEE

In and out of the streets. Bruce Beaver. *Fr.* Lauds and Plaints. CAAP

In and out the bushes, up the ivy. The Chipmunk's Day. Randall Jarrell. BoAnP; NCSH

In animalcules, Muse display. The Animalcule, a Tale. Richard Savage. PeD

In another country, black poplars shake themselves over a pond. The North Country. D. H. Lawrence. PES

In another world, there may be utterances. No Such Thing. Marcia Southwick. AMV–81

In Answer to a Request to Write a Poem on World Peace. Elisavietta Ritchie. AATT

In Answer to Your Query. Naomi Lazard. AAN; GP

In Antarctica drooping their little shoulders. The View from Here. William Stafford. RFM

In any element, you are scot-free. Have No Fear! Eileen Duggan. ATNZ

In April we will pierce his body. Letters to a Stranger. Thomas James. AmPA

In Aprill the koocoo can sing her song by rote. The Koocoo. *Unknown.* GBP

In Arizona/ (how many years in the mountains). Louis Zukofsky. NoAM

In Armorik, that called is Britayne. The Franklin's Tale. Chaucer. *Fr.* The Canterbury Tales. OAEL–1

In Autumn. Jon Anderson. AmPA

In Autumn. Barbara Howes. LiSp

In autumn down the beechwood path. Beech Leaves. James Reeves. RAE

In autumn, the bats. The Bat. Roberta Spear. AmPA

In Autumpne, whan the sonne in vyrgyne. The Bowge of Courte. John Skelton. AAS

In Back of the Real. Allen Ginsberg. HeIP; InPK; UsP

In backwards land. I Always Get Things Right. Louis Phillips. OSF

In Baltimore there lived a boy. The Boy Who Laughed at Santa Claus. Ogden Nash. PoTa

In barlight the knuckled men. Night Place. Shirley G. Cochrane. PoUp

In Barracks. Siegfried Sassoon. FaBoTw (1975 ed.)

In Bed. Myra Sklarew. AMV–81

In bed./ My hand on Mark's bare chest. At Rochdale. Ian Young. NeAC

In bed/ with my friend's young brother. A Sugar-Candy Bird. Ian Young. NeAC

In bed, dull man? Upon My Lord Brohall's Wedding. Sir John Suckling. CaPo

In bed I muse on Tenier's boors. The Bench of Boors. Herman Melville. AmVN; OBAL; SoSe

In bed we laugh, in bed we cry. Translation of Lines by Benserade. Samuel Johnson. CABA (1972 ed.); FaBoEE

In Bed with a River. George Bradley. AMV–80

In bed with the stranger who had picked him up. A Bride. Harry Fainlight. BoLoP

In Berlin, August 1945: Lehrte Bahnhof. Alun Llywelyn-Williams, *tr. fr. Welsh by* Joseph P. Clancy. OBW

In Bertram's Garden. Donald Justice. BoLoP; CSP; InPK; SFF; VGW

In Between the Curve. Barbara Bacon. AMV–80

In Bhaudanath. Mei Berssenbrugge. SA

In birth we're fired from our hole. Fox Song. Katherine Doak. NPW

In black core of night, it explodes. African Dream. Bob Kaufman. AmNP (1974 ed.); PoBA

In Blanco County. Russell T. Fowler. AMV–80

In Blessed Weather. Michael Heffernan. HeS

In Bloemfontein. Alan Ross. BoLoP

In Bondage. Claude McKay. PoBA

In Breughel's great picture, The Kermess. The Dance. William Carlos Williams. CMoP (1970 ed.); ExPo (1973 ed.); HAP; HeIP; ILP (1975 ed.); InPk; NCSH; NIL; NoAM; NOBA; PAIC; PiAm; PoIA; POL; SoSe; TAP; WeW; WIF

In Brisbane. Gwen Harwood. GAS

In Broken Images. Robert Graves. PPoe

In Burgundy, beyond Auxerre. Sheep in the Rain. James Wright. AMV-80

In Ca Mau. Horace Coleman. SES

In California. Louis Simpson. NIL; NoAM; NowV

In California you feel as if daylight. The Weights. Lawrence Russ. TC

In calm and cool and silence, once again. First-Day Thoughts. Whittier. AmVN; IPWM; PPoD

In calm fellowship they sleep. In a Grave-Yard. William Stanley Braithwaite. PoBA

In came her sister. Janet (Lady Maisry). Unknown. PeBB

In canary grass insects. Ethan Boldt. Roger Weingarten. AmPA

In candent ire the solar splendor flames. Aestivation [or Intramural Aestivation]. Oliver Wendell Holmes. Fr. The Autocrat of the Breakfast Table. FaBoNo; NOBL; OBAL

In Carpenter's Woods. Gerald Stern. PCho

In Carrowdore Churchyard. Derek Mahon. CIP

In cave like Plato's Harvey saw. Portrait of William Harvey. Lord Russell Brain. PMW

In caves with a single purpose. Fish and Chips on the Merry-go-round. K. O. Arvidson. ATNZ

In Cawsand Bay lying, with the Blue Peter flying. Cawsand Bay. Unknown. PoPle

In Celebration. Ellen Bass. NMM

In Celebration of My Uterus. Anne Sexton. CAPP; RiTi

In Celia's face a question did arise. Lips and Eyes. Giovan Battista Marino, tr. by Thomas Carew. OBVE

In Central Park we talked of our own cowardice. Adrienne Rich. Fr. Ghazals: Homage to Ghalib. NIL

In Chagall's Village. Rose Ausländer, tr. fr. German by Ewald Osers. VWA

In Charles the Second's golden days. See In good King Charles's golden days.

In childhood you think. Thanksgiving. John N. Morris. OFD

In Chu hai, dead machine guns lie frozen in the sun. Chrome Babies Eating Chocolate Snowmen in the Moonlight. A. K. Redwing. VoR

In Church. Thomas Hardy. PoTa

In church he never felt the. The Man Who Invented Las Vegas. Gerald Costanzo. TAT

In Cipres springes (wheras dame Venus dwelt). Earl of Surrey. AAS

In Cnidus born, the consort I became. By Heraclides. Unknown, tr. by William Cowper. OBVE

In Cold Storm Light. Leslie Silko. VoR

In college once I climbed the tree. Sickle Pears. Owen Dodson. AmNP (1974 ed.)

In college when a second language was required. Learning to Speak. Melvin Wilk. AMV-81

In Columbus, Ohio. John Matthias. AMV-80

In Come de Animuls Two by Two. Unknown. GBP

In Commendation of a Solitary Life. Thomas Lodge. TVS

In Commendation of Music. William Strode. ILP (1975 ed.) (Commendation of Music, The.) SCP-2

In Commendation of the Female Sex. Jane Barker. SCP-2

In Cool, Green Haunts. Mahlon Leonard Fisher. WeW

In Cordoba the Caliph's Gardens. Cordoba. Asher Mendelssohn. VWA

In corduroy trousers and seedy black coats. W. H. Auden. Fr. A Happy New Year. OBSV

In costly sheen and gaudy cloak array'd. The Bull Fight. Byron. Fr. Childe Harold's Pilgrimage, I. LiSp

In countries where no birds are alive. For Edwin R. Embree. Owen Dodson. CNA

In Country Sleep. Dylan Thomas. ILP (1975 ed.)

In court to serve decked with fresh array. The Courtier's Life. Sir Thomas Wyatt. FaBoEE

In crimson flood, wave thousands to his tomb. John Danforth. Fr. Pindarick Elegy upon the Renowned Mr. Samuel Willard. PeD

In crossing the Potomac, think twice before arriving. To the President Crossing the Potomac. Grace Cavalieri. WasP

In crow's-foot patterns, like deltas. January Thaw. Allan Block. FAF

In Danger from the Outer World. Robert Bly. CAPP

In dark sockets. Jars. Paul Raboff. VWA

In daydream fantasies of self-indulgence. Personal Column. William Price Turner. SLP

In days, my Lord, when mother Time. Soame Jenyns. Fr. An Epistle Written in the Country to the Right Honourable the Lord Lovelace. OBSV

In Days of New. Elizabeth Bartlett. AMV-81

In days of old,/ So I've been told. The Feast of the Monkeys. John Philip Sousa. OBAL

In days of yore from Britain's shore. The Maple Leaf Forever. Alexander Muir. BLSH

In dear old New York it's remarkable. The Streets of New York. Henry Blossom. FSN

In death the dead remember their spirit. Funeral Poem. Amiri Baraka. CNA

In Death's Field. Al-Khansa, tr. fr. Arabic by Willis Barnstone. BoWoP

In December. Andrew Young. MS

In December predawn. The Fisherman's Wife. Nora Mitchell. AMV-80

In Dedication. John Montague. IPM

In Defense of Black Poets. Conrad Kent Rivers. BPo

In Defense of Satire. Sir Carr Scroope. APAS

In Defiance to the Dutch. Unknown. APAS

In Despair He Orders a New Typewriter. Elder Olson. AMV-81

In Dessexshire as It Befel. Unknown. GBP; PeBB

In desultory walk through orchard grounds. Prelude. Wordsworth. VLP

In Detroit, I walk out Woodward Avenue. R. R. Cuscaden. POL

In digging up your bones, Tom Paine. Epigram. Byron. MBPR

In Discreet Splendor. A. L. Strauss, tr. fr. Hebrew by Robert Friend. VWA

In Disguise. Joseph Rolnik, tr. fr. Yiddish by Keith Bosley. VWA

In Dispraise of the Moon. Mary Elizabeth Coleridge. Moon

In distant countries I have been. The Last of the Flock. Wordsworth. MBPR

In Distrust of Merits. Marianne Moore. NIL; VoPo

In Dives' Dive. Robert Frost. VGW

In Dream: The Privacy of Sequence. Ray A. Young Bear. CDW

In dream the waterfall. The Practice of Absence. Robert Friend. VWA

In dreams my life came toward me. American Dreams. Louis Simpson. GP

In Drear-nighted December. Keats. See In a Drear-nighted December.

In Dublin town I was brought up, a city of great fame. Bold Jack Donahue. *Unknown.* FSW

In Dublin's fair city, where girls are so pretty. Cockles and Mussels (Molly Malone). *Unknown.* BLSH; FSW; GSB

In Due Season. W. H. Auden. Prf

In due season the amphibious crocodile. Amphibious Crocodile. John Crowe Ransom. OBAL

In due time bridges collapse, handsome people get. In the Palms of Ancient Bodhisattvas. John Tagliabue. AMV–81

In Dulci Jubilo, *with music. Unknown, tr. fr. German by* R. L. Pearsall. GSB

In Earliest Morning. James Schuyler. UsP

In early March, before the lark. The Missel-Thrush's Nest. John Clare. VLP

In early morning twilight, raw and chill. The Eviction. William Allingham. *Fr.* Laurence Bloomfield in Ireland. BIrV

In early summer moonlight I have strayed. The Sedge-Warbler. Ralph Hodgson. PB

In early youth's unclouded scene. Thirty-eight. Charlotte Smith. SBG

In Eden,/ everything was all it ought to be. The Way It Really Happened. Lori Shpunt. PoUp

In Egypt. Paul Celan, *tr. fr. German by* Joachim Neugroschel. VWA

In 1843,/ John James Audubon. Andrea Wyatt. *Fr.* Founding Fathers. PoUp

In eighteen hundred and eighty nine. Obituary. Conrad Aiken. OBAL

In eighteen hundred and forty-one, I put my corduroy breeches on. Pat Works on the Railway. *Unknown.* FSW

In 1876/ The Cooper & Bailey Great London Circus. The Cooper & Bailey Great London Circus. Robert Hershon. MAT

In 1867. White Bear. Susan Griffin. GP

In Eternum. Sir Thomas Wyatt. NOBE ("In eternum I was ons determed.") AAS

In ethics class so many years ago. Ethics. Linda Pastan. AMV–81; PCho

In Eundem Macaronicon. John Donne. PAIC

In Evening Air. Theodore Roethke. MPA; TAP

In every brain there do loose atoms lie. Of Loose Atoms. Margaret Cavendish, Duchess of Newcastle. SCP-2

In every dream thy lovely features rise. Sonnet. William Barnes. BoLoP

In every land from Gades to Ganges flood. Thomas Lodge. *Fr.* A Fig for Momus. TVS

In every old lady I chance to meet. Old Ladies. Will Allen Dromgoole. WeW

In every second back yard. Among Old Houses. Ruth Dallas. ATNZ

In Exile. Emma Lazarus. SBG

In fair London city a woman did dwell. The Bold Trooper. *Unknown.* PeBB

In Faith of Rising. X. J. Kennedy. UsP

In fallow college days, Tom Harland. The Ballad of Lager Bier. Edmund Clarence Stedman. OBAL

In Falmouth Harbour. Lionel Johnson. PES

In Fargo, North Dakota, a man. To Flood Stage Again. James Wright. NOBA; Prf

In Favor of One's Time. Frank O'Hara. PoA

In fear of the rich mouth. The Frightened Man. Louise Bogan. SBG

In February, bring them home. Conversation Hearts. Nina Payne. CC

In February there are days. When. Dorothy Aldis. ECBV

In Feng Shan. Searching. Ralph Tabor Williams. PHC

In fiction tales we keep performing. The Collies. Edward Anthony. GDP

In Fields of Summer. Galway Kinnell. RFM; VGW

In fifty-seeven the sweet guitars rang. Minding. Donald Campbell. *Fr.* Sonnets frae Siberia. MIS

In Fine, Transparent Words. David Vogel, *tr. fr. Hebrew by* A. C. Jacobs. VWA

In fire-script. Thou Shalt Not. Malka Heifitz Tussman, *tr. by* Marcia Falk. VWA

In First People's sky there is no moon. Raven/Moon. Anita Endrezze Probst. VoR

In five-score summers! All new eyes. 1967. Thomas Hardy. NoAM

In Flanders Fields. John McCrae. BTTM; CTV; FaPo; FaPoR

In Flanders once there was a company. The Pardoner's Tale. Chaucer, *mod. version by* Nevill Coghill. *Fr.* The Canterbury Tales. BiP

In Flaunders whilom [*or* whylom] was a compaignye [*or* companye]. The Pardoner's Tale. Chaucer. *Fr.* The Canterbury Tales. HAP; OAEL–1

In Flavia's eyes is every grace. On Miss Eleanor Ambrose, a Celebrated Beauty in Dublin. Earl of Chesterfield. FaBoEE

In Flight. Patrick Smith. MIT

In flight in escape. Nelly Sachs, *tr. fr. German by* Arthur Wensinger. BoWoP

In Fond du Lac, Bronxville, Butte, Chicago. Last Year's Discussion: The Nobel Russian. Phyllis McGinley. FaBoEE

In form and feature, face and limb. The Twins. Henry S. Leigh. CTV

In former days we'd both agree. Bhartrihari, *tr. fr. Sanskrit by* John Brough. BoLoP

In former times, when Israel's ancient creed. Absolute and Abitofhell. Ronald Arbuthnott Knox. FaBoCo

In fourteen hundred and ninety-two. *Unknown.* CTV

In fragrant Dixie's arms. Church Burning: Mississippi. James A. Emanuel. PoBA

In frames as large as rooms that face all ways. Essential Beauty. Philip Larkin. NowV

In France, (to baffle thieves and murderers). The Paris Railway-Station. Dante Gabriel Rossetti. VPC

In Francum. Sir John Davies. FaBoEE

In from the roundup and dressed to kill. Love and an Old Western at the Starlite Drive-In Theater. Philip Legler. PPoD

In Front of the Seine, Recalling the Rio de la Plata. Silvina Ocampo, *tr. fr. Spanish by* Jason Weiss. AMV–80

In front of the sombre mountains. On the Balcony [*or* Illicit]. D. H. Lawrence. GBL; PoA

In front the awful Alpine track. Stanzas in Memory of the Author of "Obermann." Matthew Arnold. VLP

In full glare of sunlight I came here, man-tall but thin. The Roundhouse Voices. Dave Smith. AMV–80; LiSp

In Fur. William Stafford. RFM

In Fuscum. Sir John Davies. FaBoEE

In futurity/ I prophetic see. The Little Girl Lost. Blake. *Fr.* Songs of Experience. MBPR; RRA

In Gaetam. Thomas Bastard. FaBoEE

In gayer hours, when high my fancy ran. The Bastard. Richard Savage. EPC; OBSV

In Glasgow. Edwin Morgan. SLP

In Glencullen. J. M. Synge. PFIr; RAE

In gloomy eyes there wells no tear. The Silesian Weavers. Heine, *tr. by* Aaron Kramer. NAWM-2

In God's Eternity, *with music.* Hosea Ballou I. AH

In gold sandals. Sappho, *tr. fr. Greek by* Willis Barnstone. BoWoP

In Golden Gate Park That Day. Lawrence Ferlinghetti. *Fr.* A Coney Island of the Mind. BBGO; NoAM

In good King Charles's [*or* In Charles the Second's] golden days. The Vicar of Bray. *Unknown.* AIW; ESaP; FSW; GBP; NOBE; NOBL; OBSV; RDB

In good old colony times. Old Colony Times. *Unknown.* BLSo

In good old Stalin's early days. Garland for a Propagandist. Ted Pauker. NOBL

In Gosport of late a young damsel did dwell. The Gosport Tragedy. *Unknown.* AmFP

In Goya's Greatest Scenes. Lawrence Ferlinghetti. *Fr.* A Coney Island of the Mind. BBGO; FF; HeIP; ILP (1975 ed.); NoAM; PAIC; PBMP; TAP

In grade school I wondered. Zimmer in Grade School. Paul Zimmer. GP

In Gratitude for Friends. Margaret Elizabeth Sangster. CTV

In Gratitude to Beethoven. Diane Wakoski. Psy

In Guernsey. Swinburne. VLP

In Hans' old mill his three black cats. Five Eyes. Walter de la Mare. DuDr; PCat

In Harbour. Swinburne. VLP

In Hardin County, 1809. Lulu E. Thompson. PoTa

In Hardwood Groves. Robert Frost. HAP

In Harmony with Nature. Matthew Arnold. PFD

In haste, post haste, when first my wandering mind. Memories, IV. George Gascoigne. AAS; PAIC

In Heaven/ Some little blades of grass. The Blade of Grass. Stephen Crane. The Black Riders, XVIII. PPM

In Heaven a spirit doth dwell. Israfel. Poe. AmVN; NOBA; PiAm; TAP

In heaven queene is she among the spheares. Heaven's Queene. Sir Walter Ralegh. Moon

In Heaven Soaring Up. Edward Taylor. *See* Joy of Church Fellowship Rightly Attended, The.

In heaven, too. Heard in a Violent Ward. Theodore Roethke. NoAM

In Heavenly Realms of Hellas Dwelt. E. E. Cummings. NOBA; OBSV; SoSe

In Hebrew "In the beginning." From the Head. Louis Zukofsky. VWA

In her boudoir, the young lady—unacquainted with grief. *Tr. fr. Chinese by* Arthur Waley. OBVE

In her last sickness, my mother took my hand in hers. Kaddish. Charles Reznikoff. *Fr.* Going To and Fro and Walking Up and Down. SA

In Her Praise. Robert Graves. BIrV

In her room at the prow of the house. The Writer. Richard Wilbur. UsP

In her room she is/ small and adrift. The Death of the Sailor's Wife. Fred Barton. AMV-80

In her room that night she looks at herself in the mirror. Randall Jarrell. *Fr.* "The Night before the Night before Christmas." MiP

In here/ the gods have lost all their words. Isolation Cell Poem. J. Charles Green. DNGG

In High Places. Harrie: Monroe. PoA

In high school it was you who wrote darkly well. A Poem for Russell Nowak. Eric Torgersen. TC

In him inexplicably mixed appeared. Byron. Lara, XVII-XIX. OAEL-2

In his chamber, weak and dying. Longfellow. *Fr.* The Norman Baron. PeD

In his chamber, weak and dying. A Strike among the Poets. *Unknown.* FaBoCo

In his dream Jacob was in a wilderness. Jacob. Charles Reznikoff. VWA

In his malodorous brain what slugs and mire. God. Isaac Rosenberg. VWA

In His Poems Are El Greco's Hands. Robert Leverant. MIT

In his sea lit/ distance, the pitcher winding. The Double Play. Robert Wallace. LiSp

In his tall senatorial. The Drum; the Narrative of the Demon of Tedworth. Edith Sitwell. FaBoTw (1975 ed.)

In hollows of the land. The Ground-Mist. Denise Levertov. PiAm

In Hollywood, the air was quiet. Trying to Forget. John Wieners. MIT

In holy books, in church, I hear curses. The Morning of the Red-tailed Hawk. Bettie M. Sellers. AMV-80

In Honor of David Anderson Brooks, My Father. Gwendolyn Brooks. TT

In Honour of St. Alphonsus Rodriguez. Gerard Manley Hopkins. EBEV; VLP

In Honour of St. David's Day. *Unknown.* OBW

In Honour of That High and Mighty Princess Queen Elizabeth of Happy Memory. Anne Bradstreet. SBG
"Now say, have women worth? or have they none?" *sel.* EAP

In Honour of the City of London, *sel.* William Dunbar.
"Empresse of townes, exalt in honour." PES

In Horse Latitudes. Katha Pollitt. AAN

In Hospital. James Elroy Flecker. OxBTC

In Hospital. W. E. Henley. VPC
*Sels.*
Before, IV. VLP
Casualty, XIII. VLP
Waiting, II. ILP (1975 ed.); VLP

In Hospital: Poona (I). Alun Lewis. OBW

In Iceland. Howard McCord. GP

In Imago Dei: Fiat Lux. Roderick Hartigh Jellema. AATT

In Imitation of Anacreon. Matthew Prior. *See* On Critics.

In Ireland, *sel.* Arthur Symons.
By the Pool at the Third Rosses, II. VLP

In Ireland they were put in foundling homes. Orphans. David Ray. FiCP

In Italian They Call the Bird Civetta. Robert Penn Warren. PiAm

In Its Place. Carol Stager. AMV-80

In Jail. Juan Antonio Corretjer, *tr. fr. Spanish by* Julio Marzán. InW

In James Street. Thirty Childbirths. Millen Brand. AMV-80

In Jersey City where I did dwell. The Butcher Boy. *Unknown.* AmFP

In Jerusalem. Elisavietta Ritchie. AATT

In Jerusalem Are Women. Arye Sivan, *tr. fr. Hebrew by* David Shevin. VWA

In Joe Brainard's collage its white arrows. Sonnet. Ted Berrigan. Epi

In Judgment of the Leaf. Kenneth Patchen. VGW

In july of 19 somethin. With All Deliberate Speed. Don L. Lee. JB

In jumping and tumbling. Tumbling. *Unknown.* DuDr; OxBChV

In June. Darrell Gray. AcAn

In June, amid the golden fields. The Groundhog. Richard Eberhart. CABA (1972 ed.); CMoP (1970 ed.); CoPAm; ExPo (1973 ed.); ILP (1975 ed.); NIL: NoAM; NU; PPoe; TAP; UnPo (1976 ed.); USP; VoPo

In Just-/ Spring. E. E. Cummings. Chansons Innocentes, I. BBGO; HeIP; InPK; NCSH; NIL; NowV; PiAm; PoIA; SoSe (1977 ed.); STS; TPo; TT; WeW

In Kansas. *Unknown.* FSW

In Katam. Sir John Davies. *See* Kate Being Pleased.

In Kerem Abraham. Tabernacle of Peace. Hayim Be'er, *tr. by*

Stephen Mitchell. VWA

In Kerry. J. M. Synge. GBL

In Köhln, a town of monks and bones. Cologne. Samuel Taylor Coleridge. FaBoEE; MBPR; PBMP

In Ladbroke Square the light on waxen branches. Pictures in a Gallery Undersea. C. K. Stead. ATNZ

In late autumn the hound. Old Man, Phantom Dog. Frederick Eckman. ANTL

In late winter/ I sometimes glimpse bits of steam. The Bear. Galway Kinnell. BCr; NNaP; RFM; VGW

In Laughter. Ted Hughes. InPS

In Librum. Sir John Davies. FaBoEE

In Lieu. Louis MacNeice. CMoP (1970 ed.)

In life's fair morn, a fiddle, was his choice. Elegiac Lines on the Death of a Fiddler, Called Blind Jacob. Philip Freneau. EAP

In Life's Stable. Kadya Molodovsky, *tr. fr. Yiddish by* Ruth Whitman. VWA

In Lithuania, on the Neman. The Little House in Lithuania. Samuel Marshak, *tr. by* Daniel Weissbort. VWA

In Little Hands. Mani Leib, *tr. fr. Yiddish by* Keith Bosley. VWA

In Little Rock the people bear. The Chicago "Defender" Sends a Man to Little Rock. Gwendolyn Brooks. AmNP (1974 ed.); PoBA; Psy

In London at Bessborough Gardens. Conrad. Antoni Slonimski, *tr. by* Isaac Komem. VWA

In London city was Bicham born. Young Beichan (Lord Bateman). *Unknown.* FaBoBa

In London there I was bent. London Lickpenny. *Unknown.* OBSV

In London Town. Mary Elizabeth Coleridge. RAE

In Long Valley the Finns. Washrags. Vern Rutsala. GP

In Love for Long. Edwin Muir. BoLoP; LoAs

In Love, if Love Be Love. Tennyson. *Fr.* Idylls of the King: Merlin and Vivien. CABA (1972 ed.)

In Love with the Bears. Greg Kuzma. BCr

In Love with You. Kenneth Koch. CAPP

In loving, each one hath free choice. Isabella Whitney. *Fr.* A Sweet Nosegay or Pleasant Posy. WPE

In lungs fresh like honeycomb. Indian. Laura Jensen. AmPA

In Madrid's outlying trenches. Hans Beimler. Ernst Busch, *tr. fr. German.* FSW

In Madurai,/ city of temples and poets. A River. A. K. Ramanujan. MPo

In man, ambition is the common'st thing. Ambition. Robert Herrick. CaPO

In Manchester Square. Alice Meynell. SBG

In marble halls as white as milk. *Unknown.* GBP; PoPle

In March and April, thereabout. Alison. *Unknown.* HAP

In March birds couple, a new birth. The Leaves Come Again. Thomas Stanley. FaBoEE

In Marion, the honey locust trees are falling. Two Poems about President Harding. James Wright. NoAM

In martial sports I had my cunning tried. Sir Philip Sidney. Astrophel and Stella, LIII. NIL

In Masaccio's "Expulsion/ From the Garden." Fresco. Linda Pastan. PoUp

In mathematics he was greater. Samuel Butler. *Fr.* Hudibras. NOBL

In Mather's Magnalia Christi. The Phantom Ship. Longfellow. RhR

In matters of commerce the fault of the Dutch. A Political Despatch. George Canning. FaBoCo

In May, his last time over, he drank too much. Statement and Vision, Two Signs of History. James Whitehead. CoPAm

In May, the sun climbs. May. John Stevens Wade. AMV-80

In May, when sea-winds pierced our solitudes. The Rhodora. Emerson. HeIP; ILP (1975 ed); LFH; NOBA; PiAm; PPM; TAP

In me the Cherokee. Self-Portrait: Microcosm; or, Song of Mixed-Blood. Robert J. Conley. FoP

In me (the worm) clearly. Hilda Doolittle ("H. D."). *Fr.* The Walls Do Not Fall. NoAM

In Memorial. J. Gordon Coogler. OBAL

In Memoriam. "Max Adeler." FaBoCo

In Memoriam. Padraig de Brun. WTO

In Memoriam. W. J. Gruffydd, *tr. fr. Welsh by* R. Gerallt Jones. OBW

In Memoriam A. H. H. Tennyson. ILP (1975 ed.), *much abr.;* OAEL-2, *much abr.;* VLP

*Sels.*

"Again at Christmas did we weave," *fr.* LXXVIII. PChr

"Be near me when my light is low," L-LVIII. HAP; PFD

"By night we lingered on the lawn," XCV. HAP

"Calm is the morn without a sound," XI. EBEV; NOBE

"Contemplate all this work of Time," CXVIII. FF

"Danube to the Severn gave, The," XIX. FF

"Dark house, by which once more I stand," VII. EBEV; HAP; InPK; NOBE; PoIA; PPoe; SoSe; UnPo (1976 ed).

"I dreamed there would be spring no more," LXIX. NOBE

"If these brief lays, of sorrow born," XLVIII-XLIX. LFH

"Love is and was my lord and king," CXXVI. NOBE

"Now fades the last long streak of snow," CXV. FSFS; NOBE

"O sorrow, cruel fellowship!" III. HAP

"O yet we trust that somehow good," LIV. BiP; BoReV; ExPo (1973 ed.); PIM; VoPo

"Old Yew, which graspest at the stones," II. NOBE; UnPo (1976 ed.)

Ring Out, Wild Bells, CVI. FaPoR; OFD (New Year, The.) PIM

" 'So careful of the type?' but no," LVI. BoReV; ExPo (1973 ed.; FF; HAP

"Strong Son of God, immortal Love," Proem. BoReV; HAP; PFD; PIM

"That which we dare invoke to bless," CXXIV. BoReV

"There rolls the deep where grew the tree," CXXIII. BoReV; HAP; NOBE

"Time draws near the birth of Christ, The," XXVIII. LFH; PChr; SoSe

"To-night the winds began to rise," XV. BiP; FSFS; NOBE

"Unwatch'd, the garden bough shall sway," CI. PoPle

"What words are these have fallen from me," XVI. EBEV

"Wish, that of the living whole, The," LV. BoReV; ExPo (1976 ed.) HAP; PoIA (LV-LVI)

In Memoriam Brendan Behan. Paul Durcan. IPM

In Memoriam (Easter, 1915). Edward Thomas. NOBE; OBW; OxBTC

In Memoriam: Gertrud Kolmar, 1943. A. D. Hope. CAAP; GAS

In Memoriam James Joyce, *sel.* "Hugh MacDiarmid."

"World is fast bound in the snares of Varuna, The." TwMBP

In Memoriam: Martin Luther King, Jr. June Jordan. PoBA

In Memoriam I ("You used to ask me once what was wrong"). Franco Fortini, *tr. fr. Italian by* Ruth Feldman. VWA

In Memoriam Paul Celan. Gad Hollander. VWA

In Memoriam: Rev. J. J. Lyons, *sel.* Emma Lazarus. "Hark! through the quiet evening air, their song." SBG

In Memoriam II ("I do not understand"). Franco Fortini, *tr. fr. Italian by* Ruth Feldman. VWA

In Memory of a Child. Vachel Lindsay. PIM

In Memory of a Friend. George Barker. OxBTC

In Memory of Arthur Winslow. Robert Lowell. PAIC; STS Death from Cancer, I. UsP

In Memory of Bryan Lathrop. Edgar Lee Masters. PoA

In Memory of Captain Underwood Who Was Drowned. *Unknown.* FaBoEE

In Memory of Colonel Charles Young. Countee Cullen. PoBA

In Memory of Eva Gore-Booth and Con Markiewicz. W. B. Yeats. CABA (1972 ed.); NoAM; OAEL-2; OxBTC

In Memory of Francis Webb. Thomas Shapcott. CAAP

In Memory of Francois Rabelais. Yunna Moritz, *tr. fr. Russian by* Elaine Feinstein. VWA

In Memory of G. K., for 50 Years the College Carpenter. Robert A. Martin. AATT

In Memory of Jane Fraser. Geoffrey Hill. NoAM; OxBTC

In Memory of Major Robert Gregory. W. B. Yeats. EBEV; OAEL-2

In Memory of My Being Late. Morty Sklar. AcAn

In Memory of My Cat Domino: 1951–1966. Roy Fuller. PSN

In Memory of My Dear Grandchild Anne Bradstreet. Anne Bradstreet. BoWoP

In Memory of My Dear Grandchild Elizabeth Bradstreet. Anne Bradstreet. EAP; WPE

In Memory of My Mother. Patrick Kavanagh. BIrV; CIP; NoAM

In Memory of Patrick Kavanagh. W. G. McNeice. IPM

In Memory of Radio  Amiri Baraka. NIL

In Memory of Sigmund Freud. W. H. Auden. HAP; OAEL-2

In Memory of the Circus Ship *Euzkera.* Walker Gibson. NCSH

In Memory of V.R. Lang. Mac Hammond. PoA

In Memory of W. B. Yeats. W. H. Auden. CABA (1972 ed.); CMoP (1970 ed.); Epi; HAP; HeIP; HoPM (1975 ed.); ILP (1975 ed.); NIL; NoAM; NOBE; OAEL-2; OxBTC; PAIC; PPoe; PPP; TCP; TT; UnPo (1976 ed.); UsP; WIF
"Earth, receive an honoured guest," 4 *sts.* FaBoTw (1975 ed.)

In Mercy, Lord, Incline Thine Ear, *with music.* Isaac M Wise. AH

In merry old England, it once was a rule. On the New Laureate. *Unknown.* FaBoCo

In Mexico. Robert Sward. NowV

In Mexico women have hands strong enough. In the Small Boats of Their Hands. Pamela Kircher. AMV-80

In midnight sleep of many a face of anguish. Old War-Dreams. Walt Whitman. WIF

In midst of the city celestial. The Celestial City. Giles Fletcher, the Younger. *Fr.* Christ's Victory and Triumph, IV. BoReV; NOBE

In Mind. Denise Levertov. Epi; InPS; NMM; RiTi

In Missing. Ray A. Young Bear. CDW

In Mississippi/ balloons of hunger. No New Music. Stanley Crouch. PoBA

In Missoula, Montana, where the townsfolk water. Pendant Watch. Madeline DeFrees. NMM

In mole-blue indolence the sun. The Jungle. Alun Lewis. OBW

In Moncur Street. Dorothy Hewett. GAS

In Montecito. Randall Jarrell. MAT; VGW

In More's Hotel. Robert Nye. SLP

In Morfudd's Arms. Dafydd ap Gwilym, *tr. fr. Welsh by* Rolfe Humphries. OBW

In Mornigan's park there is a deer. The Crescent Moon. *Unknown.* GBP; Moon

In moss-prankt dells which the sunbeams flatter. Lovers, and a Reflection. Charles Stuart Calverley. FaBoCo; SpRo; VLP

In most things I did as my father had done. George II. Thackeray. *Fr.* The Georges. FaBoEE

In Mountjoy jail one Monday morning. Kevin Barry: Died for Ireland, 1st November, 1920. *Unknown.* FaBoBa

In moving-slow he has no Peer. The Sloth. Theodore Roethke. OBAL; SS

In Moynihan's meadow. The Grip. Brendan Kennelly. CIP

In Murasaki's time. Tale of Genji. Hugh Seidman. AmPA

In my arms sometimes I dream he's a woman. My Ice Man Begins to Move. Amanda Powell. AAN

In my bed at night. Bible, *O.T. Fr.* The Song of Solomon, *ad. by* Willis Barnstone. BoWoP

In my bed I turned toward light. Morning Chores. Jim Heynen. PCho

In my beginning is my end. East Coker. T. S. Eliot. *Fr.* Four Quartets. HAP; PPP; VGW

In My Brother's House. Mick Fedullo. BrS

In my childhood trees were green. Autobiography. Louis MacNeice. BuTh

In my country life goes. So Jah Seh. Peter Kostakis. FiCh

In My Craft or Sullen Art. Dylan Thomas. BoLoP; CMoP (1970 ed.); HAP; HeIP; ILP (1975 ed.); IPWM; LoAs; MAT; NIL; NoAM; NowV; OBP; PAIC; PPM; TPo; UsP; WeW; WIF

In my dream, Joey, both of us were alive. Cuba. Lawrence Kearney. AMV-81

In my dreams I always speak Spanish. Sueños. James Reiss. FiCP

In my dreams I hear my tribe. Then and Now. Kath Walker. IHMS

In My Dreams I Searched for You. *Gond Oral Tradition, tr. by* V. Elwin *and* S. Hivale. WTO

In my dreams we are always together. Dedication. Richard Stull. AMV-81

In my dry cell. The Riven Quarry. Gloria C. Oden. PoBA

In my fingers the world can be grasped. Seismograph. Ephraim Auerbach, *tr. by* Howard Schwartz. VWA

In My First Hard Springtime. James Welch. AmPA; CDW; MPA

In my garden, she said, is a private place. Private Places. Fred Caparoso. PHC

In my grandmother's house there was always chicken soup. A Story about Chicken Soup. Louis Simpson. NNaP; NoAM; TAP

In my house I keep green books. The Plants. Michael Dennis Browne. GP

In my kindergarten class. Kindergarten. Ronald Rogers. VW

In My Life. John Lennon *and* Paul McCartney. GrRo

In my life there will be U.S. famine. Good-by on an All Day Bean Planter. Nathan Whiting. HeS

In My Lifetime. James Welch. CDW

In my medicine cabinet. Jack Kerouac. *Fr.* Some Western Haikus. VoA

In My Merry Oldsmobile, *with music.* Vincent Bryan. FSN

In my most spectacular, technicolored dream. Zimmer's Hard Dream. Paul Zimmer. GP

In my own shire, if I was sad. A.E. Housman. STS

In my own twentieth century. Natalya Gorbanyevskaya, *tr. fr. Russian by* Daniel Weissbort. PBWP

In my paintings for they are present. Sonnet. Ted Berrigan. CAAP

In my prison cell I sit, thinking Mother, dear, of you. Tramp! Tramp! Tramp! George F. Root. BLSo

In my shanks. Reb Hanina. Paul Raboff. VWA

In my sleep I was fain of their fellowship, fain. Sunrise. Sidney Lanier. PiAm

In my smoochy corner. In Glasgow. Edwin Morgan. SLP

In my stone eyes I see. What Riddle Asked the Sphinx. Archibald MacLeish. HoPM (1975 ed.)

In my thirtieth year of life/ when I had drunk down all my disgrace. The Testament. Villon, *tr. by* Galway Kinnell. NAWM-1

In my town this week. Faits-divers or News in Brief. Elizabeth Brunazzi. PoUp

In my young days I drank a /Lot of wine. A Friend Advises Me to Stop Drinking. Mei Yao Ch'en, *tr. fr. Chinese by* Kenneth Rexroth. HoPM (1975 ed.)

In my younger years. Dreams. Nikki Giovanni. CNA; PoBA

In my youth the growls. Tennyson. FaBoEE

In nameless warmth, sun light in every corner. Autumn Shade, IX. Edgar Bowers. PiAm

In "nature" there's no choice. Beyond the End. Denise Levertov. VGW

In Neglect. Robert Frost. VGW

In New Hampshire's green paradise this June. Sonnet to Seabrook. David Ray. AMV-80

In New York, it is said. A Place (Any Place) to Transcend All Places. William Carlos Williams. NYP

In Newbern Tennessee he lies awake. The Wake. Wyatt Prunty. AMV-80

In night when colours all to blacke are cast. Fulke Greville. *Fr.* Caelica. AAS; OAEL-1

In 1915 my grandfather's. Grandfather. Michael S. Harper. FiCP; FoP; TAP

In 1945, when the keepers cried kaput. The Gift. John Ciardi. BiP

In nineteen hundred they preferred. Upper Family. Maxwell Bodenheim. OBAL

In 1910 a royal princess. English. Osbert Lancaster. *Fr.* Afternoons with Baedeker. FaBoCo; NOBL

In 1939 the skylark had nothing to say to me. The Ninth of July. John Hollander. CoPAm

In no country. No Offence. D. J. Enright. HeHu; OxBTC

In No Strange Land. Francis Thompson. *See* Kingdom of God, The.

In No Way. David Ignatow. AMV-81

In Noah's Wake. Allan Block. FAF

In North Great George's Street. "Seumas O'Sullivan." BIrV

In Northern Tasmania. James McAuley. MAuV

In Nottamun Town not a soul would look up. Nottamun Town. *Unknown.* FaBoNo.

In November. Harold Norse. CPA

In November, in the days to remember the dead. St. Malachy. Thomas Merton. VGW

In Obitum M. S. x Maij, 1614. William Browne. FaBoEE; NOBE

In Obitum Promi. Henry Parrot. FaBoCo

In Obtuse Angle's Study. Blake. *Fr.* An Island in the Moon. FaBoNo

In Ocean's wide domains. The Witnesses. Longfellow. GOA

In October of the year. Ox Cart Man. Donald Hall. PCho

In Ohio. James Wright. NNaP

In Ohio, where these things happen. The Breathers. James Reiss. AmPA; CAAP; HeS

In Oklahoma. Life Is Motion. Wallace Stevens. WeW

In old commercial Boston down on Milk Street. Gas Lamp. Willis Barnstone. VWA

In Old Tucson. Charles Beghtol. BPAW

In Old Tucson. Harrison Conrard. BPAW

In Old Tucson. Sharlot M. Hall. BPAW

In olden days, a child, I trod thy sands. San Francisco. Ina Coolbrith. WPW

In One Battle. Amiri Baraka. BPo

In one of these excursions, travelling then/ Through Wales on foot. Wordsworth. *Fr.* The Prelude, XIII. EBEV

In one room of the house. The Eve. Howard Schwartz. VWA

In Orangeburg My Brothers Did. A. B. Spellman. BPo; PoBA

In orchard under the hawthorne. Vergier. *Unknown, tr. by* Ezra Pound. GBL

In Order To. Kenneth Patchen. IP; PPoD

In order to breathe, in order. Housewife. Wiliam Pillin. PoW

In order to escape you. Love. Jaime Torres Bodet, *tr. by* Muna Lee de Munoz Marín. LoAs

In Oregon. William Stafford. CNW

In our country, in our country. The Merry Haymakers; or, Pleasant Pastime between the Young Men and Maids in the Pleasant Meadows. *Unknown.* SCP-2

In our old shipwrecked days there was an hour. *Fr.* Modern Love, XVI. George Meredith. BoLoP; LoAs

In our tin-roofed house in the big war's summer. War Summer. James Applewhite. NVAP

In our town, people live in rows. The Fired Pot. Anna Wickham. FaBoTw (1975 ed.); OxBTC

In Oxford there lived a merchant by trade. The Crafty Farmer. *Unknown.* AmFP

In paper case. Epitaph on a Dormouse. *Unknown.* MN; OxBChV

In Parenthesis, *sels.* David Jones.
    "And to Private Ball it came as if a rigid beam." OBW; TwMBP
    Five Unmistakable Marks, The. NoAM
    King Pellam's Launde. NoAM; OAEL-2
    "Lift gently Dai, gentleness befits his gun-shot wound." TwMBP
    "You drop apprehensively—the sun gone out." TwMBP

In Passing. J. Barrie Shepherd. AMV-81

In Paths Untrodden. Walt Whitman. AmVN; NOBA

In-Patients. U. A. Fanthorpe. PMW

In Pennsylvania; it's sort of like losing. Another Night on the Porch Swing. Cathleen Quirk. NMM

In Peterborough Churchyard. Paulus Silentiarius. NOBL ("Reader, pass on, nor idly waste your time.") FaBoEE

In petticoat of green. Of Phyllis. William Drummond of Hawthornden. SoSe (1977 ed.)

In Pilgrim Life Our Rest, *with music.* Edwin Sandys. AH

In Pilsen,/ Twenty-six Station Road. Five Minutes after the Air Raid. Miroslav Holub, *tr. by* Ian Milner *and* George Theiner. BuTh

In pious times, ere priestcraft dd begin. Absalom and Achitophel, Pt. I Dryden. HAP; OAEL-1

In pity for man's darkening thought. Two Songs from a Play, II. W. B. Yeats. *Fr.* The Resurrection. CABA (1972 ed.); CMoP (1970 ed.); ExPo (1973 ed.); FaBoTw (1975 ed.); HAP; ILP (1975 ed.); NIL; NOBE; OAEL–2; OBP; PPoe; PPP

In Place of a Curse. John Ciardi. NowV

In Place of a Phone Call to Arabia. Diane Wakoski. Psy

In placid hours well-pleased we dream. Art. Herman Melville. NOBA; PPM

In Plague Time. Thomas Nashe. *See* Adieu, Farewell Earth's Bliss.

In Pleasant Lands Have Fallen the Lines, *with music.* James Flint. AH

In Pliny, Phoenice, Phoenicians. What Day Is. Robert Penn Warren. PiAm

In poems, our earth's wonders. Poems. Peter Kelso. AKE; TPo

In Poets' Defence. John Wheelwright. SPT

In pools. Cape Elizabeth: A Photograph. John Logan. UsP

In Prague. Paul Celan, *tr. fr. German by* Joachim Neugroschel. VWA

In Praise of a Girl. Huw Morus, *tr. fr. Welsh by* Gwyn Williams. OBW

In Praise of a Guilty Conscience. Wislawa Szymborska, *tr. fr. Polish by* Grazyna Drabik *and* Austin Flint. AMV-81

In Praise of Beverly. Steve Orlen. GP

In Praise of BIC Pens. David Hilton. NowV

In Praise of Fascists. Joy Davidman. SPT

In Praise of Lichen. Mark Perlberg. HeS
In Praise of Limestone. W. H. Auden. CABA (1972 ed.); CMoP (1970 ed.); ExPo (1973 ed.); HAP; NoAM; OAEL-2; PPP
In Praise of Mary. *Unknown.* BoReV; NOBE
(Of One That Is So Fair and Bright.) HAP, 2 *versions;* OxBM
In Praise of Neptune. Thomas Campion. EcS; NOBE
In Praise of Owain Gwynedd. Cynddelw Brydydd Mawr, *tr. fr. Welsh by* Joseph P. Clancy. OBW
In Praise of Robert Penn Warren. David Lehman. AMV-81
In Praise of Tenby. *Unknown, tr. fr. Welsh by* Joseph P. Clancy. OBW
In Praise of Virginity. Hroswitha, *tr. fr. Latin by* John Dillon. PBWP
In Praise of Winchester. *Unknown.* OxBM
In Progress. Christina Rossetti. BoWoP; WPE
In Puerto Vallarta. Anthony Ostroff. MPA; PoW
In Puna's fragrant glades. Puna's Fragrant Glades. Princess Lili'u-o-ka-lani, *tr. fr. Hawaiian by* S. H. Elbert *and* N. Mahoe. WTO
In Pursuit of the Family. Jenne Andrews. HeS
In Pusseyville, where pussies live. Cats and Dogs. Howard Moss. OBAL
In Queen Victoria's early days. The New Vicar of Bray. Colin Ellis. NOBL
In Random Fields of Impulse and Repose. Jeanine Hathaway. AMV-81
In Rattlesnake Gulch of the Skihootch Range. The Ballad of Pug-nosed Lil. Robert H. Fletcher. BPAW
In readin' the story of early days, it's a cause of much personal pain. The Mule-Skinners. *At. to* John Caldwell. BPAW
In red wool jacket and earflaps. The Week-End Indian. Anita Endrezze Probst. VoR
In Reference to Her Children, 23 June, 1656. Anne Bradstreet. BoWoP; EAP; SBG; TAP
In Respect of the Elderly. Thomas Peacock. VoR
In Respectful Memory of Mr. Yarker, *sel.* John Close. "And have we lost another friend?" FaBoCo
In Response to a Rumor That the Oldest Whorehouse in Wheeling, West Virginia, Has Been Condemned. James Wright. CAPP; NNaP
In restaurants we argue. They Eat Out. Margaret Atwood. NeAC; Psy
In Romney Marsh. John Davidson. OxBTC; PES; PoPle
In rooms of stone. Abandoned Copper Refinery. Dan Gillespie. TAT
In rosy-fingered dawn they go. Jersey Cattle. R. N. Currey. OxBTC
In Rousseau's jungle. Poem without the Word Love. Morty Sklar. AcAn
In Ruin Reconciled. Aubrey Thomas De Vere. BIrV
In Sabbath quiet, a street. The Grace-Note. Denise Levertov. ConAP; UsP
In sable weeds the beaux and belles appear. The Mourners. Bevil Higgons. APAS
In sad and ashy weeds I sigh. Elegy on the Death of Her Husband. Anne Howard, Duchess of Arundel. WPE
In St. Louis as at Fountainbleau there is. Letter to Belden. Rosalie Moore. NPW
In Salem. Lucille Clifton. AmPA
In Salem seasick spindrift drifts or skips. Salem. Robert Lowell. CABA (1972 ed.)
In San Juan I wonder how my home is. I Wonder How My Home Is. *Tr. fr. Tewa Indian by* H. J. Spinden. WTO
In Santa Maria del Popolo. Thom Gunn. CMoP (1970 ed.); ExPo (1973 ed.); MPA

In Saturn's reign, at Nature's early birth. Juvenal, *tr. by* Dryden. *Fr.* Satires, VI. OAEL-1; OBSV; OBVE
In Scarlet Town, where I was born. Barbara Allen [*or* Barb'ra Allen]. *Unknown.* BLSo; FSW; GSB; RDB; WIF
In Scarlet Town, where I was bound. Barbara Allen's Cruelty. *Unknown.* AIW
In scenery I like flat country. Passing Remark. William Stafford. GP; VoA
In scenes of distant death bold Hezron stands. Timothy Dwight. *Fr.* The Conquest of Canaan, Bk. VI. EAP
In School Days. Whittier. OxBChV
In Scorching Time. Alex Stevens. AMV-81
In Scotland I was bred and born. Barbara Ellen. *Unknown.* AIW
In Scotland town where I was borned. Hind Horn. *Unknown.* AmFP
In sea-cold Lyonesse. Sunk Lyonesse. Walter de la Mare. EcS
In Search of a Short Poem for My Grandmother. Louise Hardeman. AMV-81
In Search of the Silent Zero. Garrett Kaoru Hongo. EC
In secret/ be quiet say nothing. Poem. Pablo Picasso, *tr. by* David Gascoyne. EAS
In secret/ the out's in. Robert Creeley. PiAm
In secret place where once I stood. The Flesh and the Spirit. Anne Bradstreet. NOBA; TAP
In seed time learn, in harvest teach, in winter enjoy. Blake. *Fr.* The Marriage of Heaven and Hell. FF
In Sepia. Jon Anderson. PoA
In September she appeared. Foreign Student. Barbara B. Robinson. CTBA
In serious jest and jesting seriousness. John Marston. *Fr.* The Scourge of Villainy, Proemium, Bk. III. TVS
In seventeen hundred and forty-four. The Kilruddery Hunt. Thomas Mozeen. BIrV
In seventeen hundred seventy-five. The Bombardment of Bristol, R.I. *Unknown.* BTTM
In Shadow. Hart Crane. NOBA
In shadows fishing sycamores. Autumn on the Wabash. Dave Etter. CoPAm
In Shaka's days we lived well. Those Were the Days. *Zulu Oral Tradition, tr. by* H. Tracey. WTO
In Shame and Humiliation. James Wright. CAPP
In shaping the snow into blossoms. "Ping Hsin," *tr. fr. Chinese by* Kai-yu Hsu. *Fr.* Spring Waters. BoWoP
In shards the sylvan vases lie. The Ravaged Villa. Herman Melville. NOBA; PiAm
In Shining Groups. Mary Thacher Higginson. WeW
In Siberia's wastes. Siberia. James Clarence Mangan. BIrV
In silence I lie. Buddha's Death Day: February 15, 1815. Issa, *tr. by* Nobuyuki Yuasa. *Fr.* Oraga Haru. OFD
In silence I must take my seat. Table Rules for Little Folks. *Unknown.* OxBChV
In silent night when rest I took. Upon the Burning of Our House, July 10th, 1666. Anne Bradstreet. BoWoP; EAP; NOBA; PiAm; SBG; TAP; WPE
In sleep he hunches away from me. His Sleep. Constance Urdang. AMV-81
In sleep made of sleep and remembrance. Rain Quietude. Gary Kissick. PHC
In slow procession. Knockmany. Richard Ryan. CIP; IPM
In slow procession, one by one, silently. From Far Away. Delmira Agustini, *tr. by* D. M. Pettinella. PBWP
In Small Townlands. Seamus Heaney. CIP; NoAM
In smoky outhouses of the court of love. In the Queen's Room. Norman Cameron. Three Love Poems, II. OxBTC
In smoky weather Mal and I strolled the south sector. The American Age. Richard Packer. FPA

In sober mornings do not thou rehearse. When He Would Have His Verses Read. Robert Herrick. CaPo; NOBE

In some green island of the sea. John Masefield. *Fr.* Fragments. EcS

In some places the color. Lyn Lifshin. *Fr.* Walking thru Audley End Mansion Late Afternoon. RiTi

In some unused lagoon, some nameless bay. The Dismantled Ship. Walt Whitman. CABA (1972 ed.); NoAM

In Some Way or Other the Lord Will Provide, *with music.* Mrs. M. A. W. Cook. AH

In somebody's shoes. Halo, A. Ralph Salisbury. MPA

In somer, when the shawes be sheyne. Robin Hood and the Monk. *Unknown.* FaBoBa

In South Australia, I was born. South Australia. *Unknown.* FSW

In South Oregon the Klamath play. The Woyi. Lew Blockcolski. VoR

In Southeast Asia (Viet Nam). J. R. Rowland. GAS

In southeastern Ohio there are porches. Porches. Stanley Plumly. HeS

In Space-Time Aware. Abbie Huston Evans. GP

In spite of all the learned have said. The Indian Burying Ground. Philip Freneau. EAP; HAP; HeIP; IPWM; NOBA; PiAm; TAP

In Spite of His Dangling Pronoun. Lyn Lifshin. IHMS; Psy

In spite of mid-winter, the air is risen. Thaw. T. Alan Broughton. AMV-81

In spite of my sad financial state. I'm Leery of Firms with Easy Terms. C. S. Jennison. QQQ

In Split: Diocletian's Palace. Stephen Stepanchev. SA

In spots/ it is warm enough. Ken Belford. NeAC

In spring from the black branches of the flowering plum tree. Flowering Plum. Louise Glück. CAAP

In Spring I look gay. A Tree. *Unknown.* PCOP

In spring if there are dogs they will bark. Ballade of Sayings. W. S. Merwin. NNaP

In spring the sheep are driven over the mountain. Sheep Country. Margaret Pond. BPAW; WPW

In spring we tried with sharpened spade to dig. Harvest. Jeannette Maino. AMV-80

In spring when everything. Desire. Isaac de Botton, *tr. by* Stephen Levy. VWA

In spring when the honey flows in dandelion. Wild Honey. Aaron Schneider. BCr

In stagnant pools, by disused tennis-courts. The Frog Plague. Bruce Dawe. CAAP

In Stamford, at the edge of town, a giant statue stands. The Best Line Yet. Edward Allen. InPK; POL

In stature the Manlet was dwarfish. The Little Man That Had a Little Gun. "Lewis Carroll." FaBoNo

In stillness, I wait. Softly, White and Pure. Dorothy R. Fulton. AMV-80

In stone settlements when the moon is stone. Peter Levi. EBEV

In strenuous hope I wrought. Vesica Piscis. Coventry Patmore. VLP

In such a night, when every louder wind. A Nocturnal Reverie. Countess of Winchilsea. EBEV; PBWP; SBG; WPE

In such a place. Pond. Fredrick Zydek. AMV-81

In such an armor he may rise and raid. Bronzeville Man with a Belt in the Back. Gwendolyn Brooks. POBA

In such luxurious plentie of all pleasure. Spenser. *Fr.* The Faerie Queene, IV, 10. OAEL-1

In summer/ this red-patch. Peter Whigham. *Fr.* Love Poems of the VIth Dalai Lama. TwMBP

In summer-colored dresses, six young girls. Baptism. Alden Nowlan. POL

In summer-time it was a paradise. The Seaside. Charles Tennyson Turner. VPC

In summertime on Bredon. Bredon Hill. A. E. Housman. IP; STS; TT; VLP

In summer time, when leaves grew green. King Edward the Fourth and a Tanner of Tamworth. *Unknown.* PeBB

In summer time when leaves grow green. Under the Greenwood Tree. *Unknown.* GBP

In summer's heat and mid-time of the day. Corinnae Concubitus [*or* Elegy]. Ovid, *tr. by* Christopher Marlowe. *Fr.* Amores. BoLoP; GBL; EBEV; OBP; OBVE

In summer's mellow midnight. The Night-Wind. Emily Brontë. FSFS; VLP

In sunburnt parks where Sundays lie. Cobb Would Have Caught It. Robert Fitzgerald. HAP; WeW

In sunlight raindrops look like dew. A Battle of Similes. *Malay Oral Tradition, tr. by* R. J. Wilkinson *and* R. O. Winstedt. WTO

In Swarthmore College Ethics Class. John Oliver Simon. CPA

In Sylvia Plath Country. Erica Jong. IHMS

In Tall Grass. Carl Sandburg. PoA

In Tenebris. Thomas Hardy. NOBE
  *Sels.*
  "There have been times when I well might have passed and the ending have come." III. OAEL-2
  "When the clouds' swoln bosoms echo back the shouts," II. CMoP (1970 ed.); NoAM; OxBTC; VLP
  "Wintertime nighs," I. IP; OAEL-2

In terms of some green myth, sailing or drowning. Sailing or Drowning. Allen Curnow. ATNZ

In Terror of Hospital Bills. James Wright. GP

In terror the aches. Shechem. David Shevin. VWA

In Texas Grass. Quincy Troupe. PoBA

In that age, the great anagram of God. The Incarnation of Sirius. James McAuley. GAS; MAuV

In that ancient time—in eternity. Words Spoken by Pasternak during a Bombing. Bella Akhmadulina, *tr. by* Jean Valentine *and* Olga Carlisle. BoWoP

In that building, long and low. The Ropewalk. Longfellow. PiAm

In that corner, where we slept together. Trilce. César Vallejo, *tr. by* James Wright. LoAs

In that dark world the only light. Tick Picking in the Quetico. Don Johnson. PHC

In that desolate land and lone. The Revenge of Rain-in-the-Face. Longfellow. BPAW

In that hotel my life. The Illumination. Stanley Kunitz. GP; TAP

In that hour when the heat of day no more. Dante, *tr. by* Laurence Binyon. Divina Commedia: Purgatorio, XIX. NAWM-1

In that instant. An Image from Beckett. Derek Mahon. CIP

In that November off Tehuantepec. Sea Surface Full of Clouds. Wallace Stevens. CMoP (1970 ed.); VGW

In that repository of auction pots and post-Ark. Homely Accommodation, Suit Gent. William Price Turner. MS

In that same gardin all the goodly flowres. The Garden of Adonis. Spenser. *Fr.* The Faerie Queene, III, 6. NOBE

In that so sudden summer storm they tried. Summer Storm. Louis Simpson. WeW

In that strident summer of battle. Lament. Hone Tuwhare. ATNZ

In that town were hard spaces. Town I Left. Helen Sorrells. IHMS; PoW

In that tribe the priests are chosen. Finders Keepers. Donald Finkel. VWA

In the after-life of speech. Raw Freedom. Arthur Lerner. PoW

In the afternoon, while the wind.  Views from the High Camp. W. S. Merwin.  ConAP

In the alley he lay on what was.  Contemporary Fear.  Don Ober.  NowV

In the Aran Islands.  Derek Mahon.  IPM

In the Art Institute Library.  Alice Notley.  FiCh

In the Aztec design God crowds.  Ultimate Problems.  William Stafford.  NU

In the Backs.  Frances Cornford.  PES

In the back yard.  The Clothesline.  John Stevens Wade.  FAF

In the backyard of the world.  Hide and Seek.  Dan Pagis, *tr. by* Bernhard Frank.  AMV–81

In the bad old days a bewigged old Squire.  Wigs and Beards. Robert Graves.  NOBL

In the Badlands.  David Wagoner.  UnPo (1976 ed.)

In the Baggage Coach Ahead, *with music.*  Gussie L. Davis.  FSN

In the Balance.  *Unknown, tr. fr. Latin by* George F. Whicher. *Fr. Carmina Burana.*  OLR

In the Bar.  Robert Vander Molen.  TAT

In the barn stallions stand.  Summer Solstice.  Marilyn Krysl. NPW

In the bars, the gambling rooms.  The Price of Breast in Las Vegas.  Carole Oles.  NPW

In the Basement.  Stuart Dybek.  TC

In the basement beneath my consciousness.  The Basement Watch.  Thomas Tolnay.  AMV–80

In the basement by the furnace lies.  The New Calf.  James Hearst.  TAT

In the Beach House.  Anne Sexton.  PPP

In the bedroom dense with feathers and smell of sex.  The Death Dance.  Marge Piercy.  WBN

In the Beginning.  Rachel Fishman, *tr. fr. Yiddish by* Gabriel Levin.  VWA

In the Beginning.  Richard Kell.  IPM

In the beginning/ was Sunday.  Prayer.  Rainer Schulte.  SES

In the beginning arose the Golden Germ.  To the One God. *Tr. fr. Sanskrit by* Raimundo Panikkar.  *Fr. Vedic Hymns.* ILwL

In the beginning, at every step, he turned.  The Sickness of Adam. Karl Shapiro.  ILP (1975 ed.)

In the beginning God created the heaven and the earth.  Bible, *O.T.  Fr. Genesis.*  NAWM–1

In the beginning I stood by the window.  Windows in Providence. Aliki Barnstone.  BoWoP

In the beginning of my love wild hearts and trees.  Tele/vision. Amiri Baraka.  UsP

In the Beginning Was a Word.  Robert Graves.  PoA

In the beginning was the/ Kickoff.  Lillian Morrison.  SPo

In the beginning was the air.  Memory Air.  Charles Dobzynski, *tr. by* Anita Barrows.  VWA

In the beginning, your name was never mentioned.  *Unknown.* ILwL

In the bell toll of a clang.  Salt.  Ruth Stone.  NMM

In the big stockyards, where pigs, cows, and sheep.  Lesson. Anthony Thwaite.  HeHu

In the black forest.  Song of the Trees of the Black Forest. Edmond Jabes, *tr. by* Anthony Rudolf.  VWA

In the black forge.  The Cerne Giant.  Paul Mills.  MIS

In the black winter morning.  Bereft.  Thomas Hardy.  BoLoP; NoAM

In the Bleak Midwinter.  Christina Rossetti.  *See* Christmas Carol, A: "In the bleak mid-winter."

In the blue distance.  Nelly Sachs, *tr. by German by* Ruth *and* Matthew Mead.  BoWoP

In the blue hills.  It's Bear Air.  Madeline Tiger Bass.  BCr

In the blue hubbub of the same-through-wealth sky.  Geography. Kenneth Koch.  NoAM

In the blue night.  Pine Tree Tops.  Gary Snyder.  NOBA; OSP; Prf

In the blurring low-blood-pressure.  The Judgment.  Kathleen Spivack.  BoWoP

In the book of the iron angels there is nothing.  Of the Beloved Caravan.  Conny Hannes Meyer, *tr. by* Herbert Kuhner. VWA

In the *Boston Sunday Herald* just three lines.  To an American Poet Just Dead.  Richard Wilbur.  IP

In the boys' room at Macon Elementary.  The Naming.  Terry Hummer.  AMV–81

In the bramble bush shelley slowly eats a lark's heart.  Hot Day at the Races.  Tom Raworth.  EAS; TwMBP

In the bright broad Swiss glare I stand listening.  Recessional. Thomas MacGreevy.  CIP

In the broken box.  The Broken Toys.  James Kirkup.  FPB

In the Cabin of Lost Fir Smells.  Mary Moore.  NPW

In the Cabinet.  Shlomo Vinner, *tr. fr. Hebrew by* Laya Firestone *and* Howard Schwartz.  VWA

In the Cage.  Robert Lowell.  FF; NOBA; PPoD

In the Canadian Rockies.  Virginia Shearer Hopper.  AMV–80

In the Canyon of Echo, there's a railroad begun.  Echo Canyon. *Unknown.*  AmFP

In the Carolinas.  Wallace Stevens.  VGW

In the Case of Lobsters.  Petra von Morstein, *tr. fr. German by* Rosemarie Waldrop.  BoWoP

In the Cellars.  Jiri Gold, *tr. fr. Czech by* Jaroslav Kotan *and* Daniel Weissbort.  VWA

In the cemetery of Lodz.  Mother.  Julian Tuwim, *tr. by* Isaac Komem.  VWA

In the censer the coals are high.  Final Prayer.  Enheduanna, *tr. fr. Sumerian.*  BoWoP

In the center of the field a Lamb.  At Christmas.  Robert Duncan.  NoAM

In the centre, the ancient churchyard, a national.  Sightseeing. Desmond O'Grady.  IPM

In the chapel.  Territory.  Susan Wood-Thompson.  AMV–81

In the Children's Museum in Nashville.  Ralph Salisbury.  MPA

In the chorus of memories a blessing in disguise.  Declension. Stephen Sandy.  PoA

In the Churchyard.  Eleanor Ross Taylor.  UnPo (1976 ed.)

In the Churchyard at Cambridge.  Longfellow.  TAP

In the city, as soon as you fall someone is there to catch you. Not Having a History.  John Vernon.  PPoD

In the city of fire the eyes.  The Pens.  W. S. Merwin.  TH

In the city of Marseilles, there lived a beautiful lady.  The Lowly Peasant.  *Unknown, tr. by* Rina Benmayor.  PBWP

In the city of St. Francis.  Afterwards, They Shall Dance.  Bob Kaufman.  VGW

In the city you had dirt and din.  Alison Wyrley Birch.  PPM

In the clear light that confuses everything.  The Laurel Tree. Louis Simpson.  NNaP

In the close covert of a grove.  The Geranium.  Sheridan. BoLoP

In the Coach, *sel.*  Thomas Edward Brown. Conjergal Rights.  VLP

In the coal-pit, or the factory.  A Golden Lot.  Joseph Skipsey. VLP

In the cold/ and half light.  November.  Samuel S. Turner. AMV–80

In the cold, cold parlor.  First Death in Nova Scotia.  Elizabeth Bishop.  NCSH; NOBA

In the cold compassion.  Forgive?  José Montoya.  MIT

In the cold static of air.  Looking for a Place to be Comfortable. Virginia Gilbert.  NVAP

In the colder climates they.  Mirror Farming.  Robert Morgan. PCho

In the Columbia River Gorge, after a death. Sandra McPherson. CNW

In the common day I find a common fact. Everything Has Its History. Phillis Levin. AMV–81

In the concrete cells of the hatchery. Winter Trout. James Dickey. LiSp

In the Convalescent Hospital. Jean Pumphrey. TPo

In the cool evening the master. A Plum. Mani Leib, *tr. by* David G. Roskies *and* Hillel Schwartz. VWA

In the coolness of the day. Jesus Inter Ubera Mariae. Joseph Beaumont. SCP-2

In the Corn Land. Quentin R. Howard. TAT

In the corner a violet jug the bells the folds of paper. Poem. Pablo Picasso, *tr. by* David Gascoyne. EAS

In the cot beside the water. The German Legion. Sydney Dobell. PeD

In the country down below. Old Dolores. *Unknown.* MiP

In the County Tyrone, in [*or* near] the town of Dungannon. The Old [*or* Ould] Orange Flute. *Unknown.* FaBoBa; FSW; GBP; ILP (1975 ed.); WTO

In the Courtyard. Miriam Ulinover, *tr. fr. Yiddish by* Seth L. Wolitz. VWA

In the cowslip pips [*or* peeps] I lie. Clock-a-Clay (The Ladybird). John Clare. OAEL-2; OBP; VLP

In the crayon world there are waves. The Crayon World. Laurence Lieberman. ILP (1975 ed.)

In the crept hours of our street. The Summons in Indiana. William Stafford. AnMo

In the cross field. Out West. Gary Snyder. NNaP

In the Crypted Way. Thomas Hardy. *See* In the Vaulted Way.

In the curdled afterglow of night. Scott-Moncrieff's Beowulf. Charles Spear. ATNZ

In the custom of the Jews. The Unveiling. Suzanne Bernhardt. VWA

In the Dark. Jane Pridmore. FPB

In the dark/ each sits alone. Train. Ken Smith. EAS

In the dark aisles of Bruckner's symphonies. Bruckner. James Camp. MAT

In the Dark None Dainty. Robert Herrick. CaPo; PoPle

In the dark of night. The Mailman. Victor Contoski. GP

In the dark womb where I began. C. L. M. John Masefield. OxBTC

In the darkness/ of the house of the white brother. Indian School. Norman H. Russell. MAT

In the day of clouds and cold and snow. The Bear's Blessing. Victor Contoski. BCr

In the days before the high tide. A Sea Song. D. M. Dolben. EcS

In the days of Caesar Augustus. Christmas Day. John Meade Falkner. OxBTC

In the Days of Prismatic Color. Marianne Moore. PiAm

In the days that tried our fathers. The Rejected "National Hymns." "Orpheus C. Kerr." OBAL

In the daytime/ I walk in the South Bronx. Change of Venue. Jill Clockadale. AMV-80

In the dead of the afternoon. Fanny Brawne. James Erickson. PoW

In the Dead of the Night. Norman Dubie. AmPA

In the dead of winter, when. Mockingbird in Winter. Ernest Kroll. AMV-80

In the dead screen. While the TV Is Shut Off. Diane Kruchkow. FAF

In the Deep Museum. Anne Sexton. Prf

In the deep rainy morning I cling to sleep. Reluctant. Catherine O'Neill. PoUp

In the Desert. Stephen Crane. The Black Riders, III. AmVN; FaBoEE; NOBA; PiAm; POIA; TAP; TT (Heart, The.) HoPM (1975 ed.); InPK

In the Desert. Herman Melville. PiAm

In the deserted village, sunken down. The Deserted Village. Robin Hyde. ATNZ; WPE

In the diaphanous fall of your gown. Unter der Linde. George Ellenbogen. AMV–81

In the Dim City. Arthur Salmon. PES

In the Distress upon Me, *with music.* Henry Ainsworth. AH

In the doorway. Boy. Mbembe. NW

In the Dordogne. John Peale Bishop. VGW

In the Dream of the Body. David Keller. AMV-80

In the Dry Riverbed. Zelda, *tr. fr. Hebrew by* Marcia Falk. VWA

In the Dumps. *Unknown.* FaBoCo (We're All in the Dumps.) FaBoNo; GBP

In the dust are my father's beautiful hands. At Night. Richard Eberhart. LoAs

In the early morning. Aubade. Linda Pastan. TV

In the early morning, past the shut houses. Scroppo's Dog. May Swenson. GDP

In the earth—the earth—thou shalt be laid. Warning and Reply. Emily Brontë. WPE

In the echo of my deaths. Fear. Alejandra Pizarnik, *tr. by* Lynn Alvarez. AMV-80

In the Egypt of my night. Locusts of Silence. Seymour Mayne. VWA

In the elbow of a macaroni. A Blue Jeaned Rock Queen in Search of Happiness on a Blind Thursday at 1/3 Speed and Crying. A. K. Redwing. VoR

In the Elegy Season. Richard Wilbur. InPK

In the Embers at Midnight. Paulette Dusdall Zachariou. NPW

In the Emptied Rest Home. Bella Akhmadulina, *tr. fr. Russian by* Jean Valentine *and* Olga Carlisle. BoWoP

In the empty lot—a place. The Wild. Wendell Berry. VGW

In the encyclopedia. Fact. Kenneth Rexroth. OBAL

In the End. Peter Everwine, *after* Natan Sach. NNaP

In the end/ there is only color. Matisse's Jazz Cut-Outs at the National Gallery. Barbara F. Lefcowitz. PoUp

In the end, Keats's stone will go. Revelation. Peter Meinke. AATT

In the end you are tired of those places. Locations. Jim Harrison. AmPA

In the evening/ my griefs come to me. Old Woman. Linda Pastan. FiCP

In the evening/ Quiet of the country town. Tanka. Noin Hoshi, *tr. by* Nobuyuki Yuasa. PAIC

In the Evening as from a Cradle. Robert Bloom. AATT

In the Evening by the Moonlight. James A. Bland. FSW; PSoN, *with music*

In the evening, just before. For Mary. Kenneth Rexroth. SFF

In the evening of a brightly. Greenwich Avenue. James Schuyler. NYP

In the evening the dusk. The Poet Is Dead. William Everson. CPA; PiAm

In the evening there is a snail. Talking to the Mule. Laura Jensen. AmPA

In the evening there were flocks of nighthawks. September 2. Wendell Berry. PoA

In the evening when I sit alone a-dreaming. Sweet Adeline. Richard H. Gerard. FSN; FSW

In the evenings the old country old take. In the Gazebo. Nicholas Flocos. SA

In the eye of seafaring man. The Winds of Change. Charles Ballard. VoR

In the eye of the volute, we are. Touristicism. John Batki. AcAn

In the eyes of the brown bear. Casting A Vote. James DenBoer. PPoD

In the faint blue light. Vincent Buckley. *Fr.* Stroke. MAuV

In the fair fields of suburban. Decks. Robert Phillips. NYP

In the Fall. Alina Rivero. AMV-81

In the fall, I believe again in poetry. Still. Aila Meriluoto, *tr. by* Jaakko A. Ahokas. PBWP

In the far corner. The Blackbird. Humbert Wolfe. RAE

In the Field. Phyllis Janik. IHMS

In the Fields. Charlotte Mew. LoAs

In the fields. Pastoral. John William Corrington. CSP

In the Fields of My Father's Youth. W. H. Oliver. ATNZ

In the fields, the silos open their mouths. Hangman. Ai. AmPA

In the first. Ezra Pound. Jonathan Price. CoPAm

In the First Cave. Seymour Mayne. VWA

In the first days, in the forgotten calendars. Imperial. A. R. D. Fairburn. ATNZ

In the first rank of these did Zimri stand. Dryden. *Fr.* Absalom and Achitophel, Pt. I. HAP

In the first ruder age, when love was wild. Love's Force. Thomas Carew. CaPo; SCP-2

In the first taxi he was alone, tra-la. The Taxis. Louis MacNeice. OxBTC

In the first verse I find his skeleton. Gull Skeleton. Jonathan Revere. SoSe (1977 ed.)

In the first year of the last disgrace. News of the World II. George Barker. FaBoTw (1975 ed.)

In the Fleeting Hand of Time. Gregory Corso. SA

In the Flight of the Blue Heron: To Montezuma. Anita Endrezze Probst. CDW

In the Flowering Season. Michael Roberts. FaBoTw (1975 ed.)

In the footsteps of the walking air. Kenneth Patchen. EAS

In the Ford plant. The Foundation of American Industry. Donald Hall. GOA

In the foreground, clots of cream-white flowers. The Gate. Cecil Day Lewis. FoP

In the foreground we see time and life. Cézanne's Ports. Allen Ginsberg. WIF

In the Forest. Pinhas Sadeh, *tr. fr. Hebrew by* Harris Lenowitz. VWA

In the forest hearing. The World Has Many Places Many Ways. Norman H. Russell. VW

In the forest of noyous hevynesse. Lost. Charles d'Orléans. OxBM

In the frightened forest the tree sleeps, the leaves are dead. *Unknown, tr. fr. Gabon Pygmy by* C. M. Bowra. *Fr.* Song for the Elephant Hunt. WeW

In the furrows of the world. Nation. Charlie Cobb. PoBA

In the Garden, *with music.* C. Austin Miles. BLSH

In the Garden. Tom Schmidt. NeAC

In the Garden at Swainston. Tennyson. VLP

In the Garden City Café with its murals on the wall. Huxley Hall. John Betjeman. OBSV

In the Garden of the Turkish Consulate. Pinhas Sadeh, *tr. fr. Hebrew by* Harris Lenowitz. VWA

In the garden. Summer's end. Evening. On a bench. Verses Written on Sand. Melech Ravitch, *tr. by* Seymour Mayne *and* Rivka Augenfeld. VWA

In the garden there strayed. *Unknown.* SoSe

In the garment factory where I work. Cultural Exchange. Al Masarik. CPA

In the gathering dew. Lady Sagami, *tr. fr. Japanese by* Willis Barnstone. BoWoP

In the Gazebo. Nicholas Flocos. SA

In the Generation That Laughed at Me. Susan Hartman. AAN

In the Ghetto. Hugo Sonnenschein, *tr. fr. German by* Edouard Roditi. VWA

In the ghetto of my mouth. The Golem. Shlomo Reich, *tr. by* Mira Reich. VWA

In the Giving Vein. Peter Porter. CAAP

In the Gloaming. Charles Stuart Calverley. NOBL

In the Gloaming. Meta Orred. BLSH, *with music;* BLSo, *with music;* FSW

In the gloom of mighty cities. The Commonwealth of Toil. Ralph Chaplin. FSW

In the gloom of whiteness. Snow. Edward Thomas. FaBoTw (1975 ed.)

In the Glorious Epiphany of Our Lord God, *sel.* Richard Crashaw.
    "We who strangely went astray." SCP-1

In the Glue Factory. Allan Block. FAF

In the golden glade the chestnuts are fallen all. North Wind in October. Robert Bridges. FSFS; VLP

In the Good Old Summertime. Ren Shields. BLSo, *with music;* FSN, *with music;* FSW

In the Grass. Annette von Droste-Hulshoff, *tr. fr. German by* James Edward Tobin. PBWP

In the gray evening. The Garden Hose. Beatrice Janosco. POL

In the great gardens, after bright spring rain. The Innocent Spring. Edith Sitwell. *Fr.* The Sleeping Beauty. NOBE; OxBTC

In the Great Metropolis. Arthur Hugh Clough. VPC

In the great night my heart will go out. Owl Woman's Death Song. *Tr. fr. Papago Indian by* Ruth Underhill. BoWoP

In the great place the great house is gone from. Slave Quarters. James Dickey. CAPP

In the great snowfall before the bomb. Lorine Niedecker. RiTi

In the green light of water, like the day. The Swans. Edith Sitwell. CMoP (1970 ed.); WPE

In the greenest of our valleys. The Haunted Palace. Poe. *Fr.* The Fall of the House of Usher. NOBA; PiAm; TAP

In the grey beginning of years, in the twilight of things that began. Hymn of Man. Swinburne. VLP

In the grey wastes of dread. Horses on the Camargue. Roy Campbell. PoPle

In the grim. Midland. Danny L. Rendleman. TC

In the grooved earth the old grapple. Confrontations of March. H. C. Dillow. AMV-80

In the groves of Africa from their natural wonder. An African Elegy. Robert Duncan. NoAM

In the Half-Point Time of Night. Ann Menebroker. AMV-80

In the halls, in the universities. Cripples. Kathleen Spivack. SFF

In the Hammersmith Public Library. Keith Althaus. AAN

In the Hamptons. John N. Morris. NYP

In the harbor of Askalon. Light of Judea. Claude Vigée, *tr. fr. French.* VWA

In the hazy shape of my mind. Squall. John Moore. NCSH

In the heart of a seed. The Little Plant. Kate Louise Brown. PCOP

In the Heart of the Empire. Harris Schiff. FoP

In the heart of the Hills of Life, I know. My Springs. Sidney Lanier. UnPo (1976 ed.)

In the heart of the hills the rain unabated. *Malay Oral Tradition, tr. by* R. J. Wilkinson *and* R. O. Winstedt. WTO

In the Heartland. Mark Vinz. GP

In the heat-locked room. As a Child Seeing a Cardinal. John Gill. NeAC

In the heat of the day a funnel cloud. For the El Paso Weather Bureau. Peter Wild. MAT

In the heavens' universal alphabet. Joseph Hall. *Fr.* Virgidemiarum. TVS

In the Hellgate Wind. Madeline DeFrees. NYP

In the hexemeter rises the fountain's silvery column. The Ovidian Elegiac Metre Described and Exemplified. Schiller, *tr. by* Samuel Taylor Coleridge. MBPR

In the heydays of 'forty-five. For George Santayana. Robert Lowell. CMoP (1970 ed.); CoPAm; VGW

In the high/ clear air. Joanne Kyger. RiTi

In the high jungle where Assam meets Tibet. Moschus Moschiferus. A. D. Hope. MAuV

In the high leaves of a walnut. Walnut-Leaf Scent. Laurence Binyon. BBGO

In the high seat. Why Log Truck Drivers Rise Earlier than Students of Zen. Gary Snyder. NNaP

In the hollow tree, in the old gray tower. The Horned Owl. "Barry Cornwall." PCOP

In the Holy Nativity of Our Lord God, a Hymn Sung as by the Shepherds. Richard Crashaw. *See* Hymn of the Nativity, Sung as by the Shepherds, An.

In the Home. Marvin Bell. NVAP

In the Home of the Scholar Wu Su-chiang. Wu Tsao, *tr. fr. Chinese by* Kenneth Rexroth *and* Ling Chung. BoWoP

In the Hospital. Laura Jensen. AmPA

In the Hospital of the Holy Physician. Nancy Willard. IHMS

In the hotel room, on tour. Tennis. Nina Nyhart. AMV–81

In the hour of Fresno. California #2. Victor Hernández Cruz. TAT

In the hour of my distress. His Litany to the Holy Spirit [*or* The Litany]. Robert Herrick. BoReV; ILwL; PoPle

In the house/ of Mr. and Mrs. Spouse. Teevee. Eve Merriam. QQQ

In the House of the Dying. Jane Cooper. CoPAm; NMM

In the house of the hangman. The Hangman's Love Song. Stanley Moss. VGW

In the house with the tortoise chair. Poem to Ease Birth. *Unknown, tr. by* Anselm Hollo. BoWoP; IPWM

In the human cities, never again to. Despisals. Muriel Rukeyser. NMM; Prf

In the hungry kitchen. Kitchen Poem. Francis Scarfe. EAS

In the Huon Valley. James McAuley. MAuV

In the inner city. Lucille Clifton. CAAP; CNA; TSWA

In the innermost cavern of labyrinths. Educational Music or Erosion. William H. Schubert. AMV–81

In the Isle of Dogs. John Davidson. VLP
"While the water-wagon's ringing showers," *sel.* PES

In the Jungle. D. J. Enright. HeHu

In the Jury Room. Hodding Carter. MAT

In the kitchen/ making dishes with a brush. A Plea to My Sister. James Cunningham. JB

In the Kitchen of the Old House. Donald Hall. MPo

In the laboratory waiting room. Through a Glass Eye, Lightly. Carolyn Kizer. BoWoP

In the Lake Country. Kay Wissinger. AMV–80

In the lamplight falling. Night. Peter Everwine. NNaP

In the land of dwarfs. Forugh Farrokhzad, *tr. fr. Persian by* Girdhard Tikku. BoWoP

In the land of God. Cecil County. Ron Welburn. PoBA

In the Land of the Bumbley Boo. The Land of the Bumbley Boo. Spike Milligan. OSF

In the land of turkeys in turkey weather. Dance of the Macabre Mice. Wallace Stevens. CMoP (1970 ed.) NOBA; STS

In the landscape that was a saga. Regenerate. Robert Bloom. AATT

In the Last Few Moments Came the Old German Cleaning Woman. Jane Cooper. CoPAm

In the Last Flicker of the Sinking Sun. Peretz Markish, *tr. fr. Yiddish by* Keith Bosley. VWA

In the last ruins of the second fatal war. Some Newly-discovered Prophecies of Nostradamus. David Lake. FPA

In the last storm, when hawks. The Epitaph Ending in And. William Stafford. NIL

In the last village before the frontier. The Republic 1939. James Liddy. CIP

In the late night listening from bed. Thinking for Berky. William Stafford. PPoD; RRA

In the late winter. The Bear. Galway Kinnell. CoPAm; TAP

In the licorice fields at Pontefract. The Licorice Fields at Pontefract. John Betjeman. CMoP (1970 ed.); ILP (1975 ed.); SS

In the life we live together every paradise is lost. Against Botticelli. Robert Hass. AmPA

In the light of the moon. Love Song. Hayim Be'er, *tr. by* Stephen Mitchell. VWA

In the lisping drizzle. Elegy for a Polish Grandaunt. James Bonk. HeS

In the Local Museum. Walter de la Mare. HAP

In the lonesome latter years. The Promissory Note. Bayard Taylor. SpRo

In the long journey out of the self. Journey to the Interior. Theodore Roethke. CABA (1972 ed.); VGW

In the long, sleepless watches of the night. The Cross of Snow. Longfellow. AmVN; HeIP; ILP (1975 ed.); IPWM; NOBA; PiAm; TAP

In the long summer days when I was four. Shells. Medb Mahony. AMV–80

In the lower lands of day. Before Sunset. Swinburne. VLP

In the Madison Zoo. Roberta Hill. CDW

In the market, in the cloister—only God I saw. Illumination and Ecstasy. *Tr. fr. Arabic, at. to* Baba Kuhi of Shiraz. ILwL

In the Marsh. Ella Higginson. WPW

In the marvelling quiet of morning. World Enough. Jeanine Hathaway. AMV–80

In the Men's Room(s). Marge Piercy. MMD

In the merry month of June, when the roses were in bloom. Little Ball of Yarn. *Unknown.* FSW

In the merry month of May. The Ploughman's Song. Nicholas Breton. *Fr.* The Honorable Entertainment Given to the Queen's Majesty in Progress at Elvetham, 1591. NIL; NOBE

In the merry month of May from my home I started. The Rocky Road to Dublin. *Unknown.* FaBoBa

In the Middle. Vern Rutsala. MPA

In the middle life when the skin slackens. Ambulando. Charles Brasch. ATNZ

In the Middle of a Wind Tunnel. Dave Morice. AcAn

In the middle of the afternoon when people turn slowly. The Volunteers. Janet Kauffman. TC

In the middle of the night. Silver Wedding. Ralph Hodgson. OxBTC

In the middle of winter, middle of night. A Middle-aged, Middle-Class Woman at Midnight. Genevieve Taggard. SPT

In the midst of words your wordless image. The Heart. Harvey Shapiro. HoPM (1975 ed.)

In the Mines. John Swett. BPAW

In the monethe of Maye when mirthes been fele. The Poacher. *Unknown. Fr.* The Parlement of the Thre Ages. OxBM

In the month of the long decline of roses. Hendecasyllabics. Swinburne. VLP

In the Moonlight. Thomas Hardy. NoAM

In the Morning. Paul Laurence Dunbar. BPo

In the Morning. Paulette Dusdall Zachariou. NPW

In the morning cool and slender, you. The Hours. Calvin Forbes. CoPAm

In the morning, dark moons. After the Stormy Night. Rolly Kent. FoP

In the morning I am alone in the icy room. The Mountain. Shirley Kaufman. TV

In the morning I went out with my bow. Ambulance Call. Lorrie Goldensohn. AMV-81

In the Morning I Will Pray, *with music.* William Henry Furness. AH

In the morning, in the dark. The Night Hunt. Thomas MacDonagh. GDP; PFIr

In the Morning, in the Morning. A. E. Housman. InPK

In the morning light a line. The Morning Light. Louis Simpson. NNaP; NoAM

In the morning rain. Rainy Morning. Sotero Rivera-Avilés, *tr. by* Julio Marzán. InW

In the morning the city. City. Langston Hughes. ECBV; LCL

In the morning the shadow of the old city falls. Shadow of the Old City. Yehuda Amichai, *tr. by* Shirley Kaufman. VWA

In the morning there is bacon. Camping at Thunder Bay. David Fedo. AMV-81

In the morning when. The Ones You Lost. Liza Gyllenhaal. EC

In the mornings. Loring Johnson. AAN

In the Mountain Cabin. Del Marie Rogers. NPW

In the Mountain Tent. James Dickey. CAPP; ILP (1975 ed.)

In the mountain where you are unworshiped. Inanna and Ebih. Enheduanna, *tr. fr. Sumerian.* BoWoP

In the mountains. First Cold Night of Autumn. John Stupp. AMV-81

In the Mountains, *sel.* Robert Penn Warren. Skiers. LiSp; SPo; TCP

In the mountains o' the west. The Maid o' the West. John Clare. OAEL-2

In the mountains of the Peloponnesus. Gossip. Nicholas Flocos. SA

In the mountains, there is more than slate. Blue Ridge. Elizabeth Hodges. AMV-81

In the Mourning Time. Robert Hayden. BPo

In the museum of antiquities. Glory. Harvey Shapiro. POL

In the Naked Bed, in Plato's Cave. Delmore Schwartz. ExPo (1973 ed.); ILP (1975 ed.); NoAM; NOBA; PAIC; PoA; VGW

In the name of all the gods, tell me, Lydia, why. Horace, *tr. by* C. E. Bennett. Odes, I, 8. LoAs

In the name of Allah, the Merciful the Compassionate! Love Charm. *Malay Oral Tradition, tr. by* R. O. Winstedt. WTO

In the name of God, the merciful, the compassionate! Of Iron Am I. *Malay Oral Tradition, tr. by* W. W. Skeat. WTO

In the narrow/ closet under the stairs, its curved. For the Suicide's Daughter. Carolyn Stoloff. RiTi

In the National Gallery. Siegfried Sassoon. NoAM

In the nativity of time. Love Made in the First Age: To Chloris. Richard Lovelace. CaPo; OAEL-1; SCP-2

In the neat parlor of their honeymoon. Epigram. Max Halpern. SFF

In the Neighborhood. Josephine Miles. MPA

In the news that sails through the air. Los New Yorks. Victor Hernández Cruz. SA

In the New Sun. Philip Levine. NNaP

"In the New World Happiness Is Allowed." Peter Porter. GAS

In the night,/ buildings belching. Trilogy of the Night. Quincy Troupe. SES

In the Night Desert. William Stafford. MPA

In the night in the train pulling out of the city. Among Commuters. Jon Swan. NYP

In the night there was a murder in the street. Of Autumn. Veronica Porumbacu, *tr. by* Willis Barnstone *and* Matei Calinescu. BoWoP; VWA

In the North. The Reach of Winter. Jenne Andrews. HeS

In the north the cloud flower blossoms. The Cloud-Flower Lullaby. *Tr. fr. Tewa Indian by* H. J. Spinden. WTO

In the northern hemisphere. Kangaroo. D. H. Lawrence. EBEV; InPS; OxBTC

In the novels I shall never write. The Right to Life. John N. Morris. AMV-80

In the oasis of the day. Peter Whigham. *Fr.* Love Poems of the VIth Dalai Lama. TwMBP

In the Ocean. Patricia Goedicke. TV

In the Old City. Yehuda Amichai, *tr. fr. Hebrew by* Laya Firestone *and* Howard Schwartz. VWA

In the old days either the plaintiff or the defendant won or lost. Poem. Alan Dugan. NowV

In the old days when we were kids. Roger and Me. Anne Le Dressay. AMV-81

In the old days with married women's stockings. The Libertine. Louis MacNeice. NoAM

In the Old Jewish Cemetery, Prague, 1970. Edward Lowbury. VWA

In the old, old days when the West was young. The Texas Ranger. Margie B. Boswell. BPAW

In the old part of the cemetery. Circa 1814. David Staudt. AMV-80

In the old photograph, my sister and I. Quills. Charlotte Gafford. AMV-81

In the old photograph the two of us. Marginal Music. R. K. Meiners. AMV-81

In the olive darkness of the sally-trees. The Bull. Judith Wright. MAuV

In the one cool room in the house. Developing a Wife. Andrew Taylor. FPA

In the open-faced river. Giving Up on the Shore. Gabriel Preil, *tr. by* Gabriel Levin. VWA

In the Open Fields. Hugo Sonnenschein, *tr. fr. German by* Edouard Roditi. VWA

In the Orchard. Robert Friend. GP

In the Orchard. James Stephens. SO

In the Orchard. Muriel Stuart. FF; MS; OxBTC

In the Orchard. Swinburne. BoLoP

In the Oregon Country. William Stafford. MPA

In the palm. A Guerrilla Handbook. Amiri Baraka. PoBA

In the Palms of Ancient Bodhisattvas. John Tagliabue. AMV-81

In the Pantry. "Hugh MacDiarmid." NoAM

In the pantry the dear dense cheeses, Cheddars and harsh. O Cheese. Donald Hall. TC

In the Park. Gwen Harwood. MAuV

In the Park beside the Marina. J. S. Harry. FPA

In the Past. Trumbull Stickney. NOBA

In the Penile Colony. Erica Jong. MMD

In the Person of Woman Kind. Ben Jonson. NIL

In the pine woods, at the log. Hogpen. Robert Morgan. CSP

In the Pines. *Unknown.* AmFP

In the Pines (Where Did You Sleep Last Night?). Leadbelly (Huddie Ledbetter). FSW

"In the Pink." Siegfried Sassoon. CMoP (1970 ed.)

In the place where the fight was. Where the Fight Was. Alice Corbin, *after Chippewa Indian.* BPAW

In the pleasant pastime of temple viewing. Manners. Edith Marcombe Shiffert. WPE

In the Pocket. James Dickey. LiSp; SPo

In the pond of our new garden. Visiting Hour. Stewart Conn. MS

In the portraits he sits cross-legged on a mat. The Last Frontier. John Thomas. GP

In the prison cell I sit. Tramp! Tramp! Tramp! or, The Prisoner's Hope. George Frederick Root. FSW; PSoN

In the Prison Pen. Herman Melville. TAP

In the Public Garden. Marianne Moore. NOBA

In the purple light, heavy with redwood, the slopes drop seaward. Apology for Bad Dreams. Robinson Jeffers. ILP (1975 ed.); NOBA

In the Quarter of the Negroes. Cultural Exchange. Langston Hughes. BPo; PoBA

In the Queen's Room. Norman Cameron. Three Love Poems, II. OxBTC

In the quiet before cockcrow when the cricket's. Dear Men and Women. John Hall Wheelock. Prf

In the Radiotherapy Unit. Margaret Stanley Wrench. SFF

In the rain, the naked old father is dancing, he will get wet. Natural History. Robert Penn Warren. FF

In the rat race he won by a whisker. Lifelines. Gavin Ewart. EAS

In the reading room in the New York Public Library. Reading Room, The New York Public Library. Richard Eberhart. GP; NYP

In the red water. New Spring. Juan Ramón Jiménez, tr. by H. R. Hays. OLR

In the reference room a man is flipping pages. On My 26th Birthday. Barry Schechter. FiCh

In the region where the roses always bloom. Ida, Sweet as Apple Cider. Eddie Leonard. BLSo; FSN

In the ribs of an ugly school building. Three Brown Girls Singing. M. Carl Holman. NIL

In the Ringwood. Thomas Kinsella. CMoP (1970 ed.); IPM

In the riprap. Mussels. Mary Oliver. NU

In the Room of the Bride-Elect. Thomas Hardy. BuTh

In the rude age when scyence was not so rife. Earl of Surrey. AAS

In the Rue Monsieur le Prince. Song for "Buvez les Vins du Postillion"—Advt. Jean Garrigue. TAP

In the Scales: I. Madeline DeFrees. Fr. A Catch of Summer. MPA

In the Scales: II. Madeline DeFrees. Fr. A Catch of Summer. MPA

In the School of Coquettes. Circe. Austin Dobson. PoIÀ

In the Sea of Tears. Naomi Replansky. GP

In the Season of Wolves and Names. Mariève Rugo. AMV–80

In the Second-best Hotel in Tokyo. Karl Shapiro. TCP

In the Seminole darkness of your singing eyes. Poem to a Redskin. Wendy Rose. CDW

In the Seven Woods. W. B. Yeats. CMoP (1970 ed.); NoAM

In the shabby cafeteria on the lower east side. Circumstance. Laurie Stroblas. AMV–80

In the Shade of the Old Apple Tree, with music. Harry H. Williams. FSN

In the Shadow of the Valley of Death. Abu al-Qasim al-Shabbi, tr. fr. Arabic by Mounah A. Khouri. DL

In the shoppes. Gemwood. Marvin Bell. FiCP

In the Shreve High football stadium. Autumn Begins in Martins Ferry, Ohio. James Wright. CAPP; InPS; POL; PPoD

In the Silence. Stephany Fuller. BPo

In the silence that prolongs the span. Black Jackets. Thom Gunn. HeIP; NowV

In the Silent Midnight Watches, with music. Arthur Cleveland Coxe. AH

In the silent ridges of a late. On the Edge of a Safe Sleep. Teresa D. Cader. AMV–81

In the sixth grade they gave us a belgian nun. Pedagogy. Gerald Locklin. GP

In the sky, clearest blue. Rosalía de Castro, tr. fr. Galician by Benjamin M. Woodbridge, Jr. PBWP

In the sky the bright stars glittered. When I Saw Sweet Nelly Home [or Seeing Nellie Home]. Francis Kyle. BLSH; FSW; PSoN

In the sky there is a moon and stars. Proportion. Amy Lowell. BoWoP

In the slow Mexican air I watched the bull die. The Priest and the Matador. Charles Bukowski. CPA

In the Sly Gardens. Sonya Dorman. RiTi

In the small beauty of the forest. Psalm. George Oppen. NNaP

In the Small Boats of Their Hands. Pamela Kircher. AMV–80

In the Smoking Car. Ruth Whitman. RiTi

In the Smoking Car. Richard Wilbur. ConAP

In the Snack-Bar. Edwin Morgan. FF

In the Snake Park. William Plomer. NoAM; OxBTC

In the Snowfall. Gwerfyl Mechain, tr. fr. Welsh by Willis Barnstone. BoWoP

In the Soul Hour. Robert Mezey. AmPA

In the south, sleeping against. Legacy. Amiri Baraka. NoAM; NOBA; PoBA

In the space of time. Ashkelon. Anthony Rudolf. VWA

In the Spring. William Barnes. GBL

In the spring woods, how good it is to see. Aspects of the World Like Coral Reefs. William Bronk. VGW

In the squdgy river. The Hippopotamus. Georgia Roberts Durston. CTV

In the state of old Kentucky. The Death of Samuel Adams. Unknown. AmFP

In the steadying breadth of day. Poem for My Dead Husband. Sheila Roberts. AMV–80

In the still insanity. Serronydion. Jack Hirshman. CPA

In the still morning when you move. Tropics. Ellen Bryant Voigt. AAN

In the street two children sharpen. East Bronx. David Ignatow. ConAP; IPWM

In the streetcar conductor's uniform. Portrait: The Freedom Fighter. George Jonas. NeAC

In the stump of the old tree, where the heart has rotted out. Poem. Hugh Sykes Davies. EAS

In the Suburbs. Louis Simpson. CoPAm; MAT; SFF; TH

In the suburbs the spirit of man. A. R. D. Fairburn. Fr. Dominion. ATNZ

"In the Subway." Juan Ramón Jiménez, tr. fr. Spanish by Robert Bly. NYP

In the sudden white silence, where are you? Requiem. Jean Garrigue. UsP

In the Summer of Warren Whitney. David Long. EC

In the summer we rode in the clay country. Elements. A. R. D. Fairburn. ATNZ

In the Sun School the mystics of Egypt, our fathers. Order of Service. Amiri Baraka. UsP

In the Surgery. J. M. Ditta. AMV–80

In the swamp in secluded recesses. Walt Whitman. Fr. When Lilacs Last in the Dooryard Bloom'd. RFM

In the Sweet Bye-and-Bye. Sanford Fillmore Bennett. BLSH, with music; FSW
    (Sweet By and By.) PSoN
    (There's a Land That Is Fairer than Day, with music.) AH

In the sweet shire of Cardigan. Simon Lee. Wordsworth. MBPR

In the Tail of the Scorpion. Genevieve Taggard. VGW

In the tall quiet pines of Washington. For Tom Numkena, Hopi/Spokane. Harold Littlebird. VoR

In the Tank. Thom Gunn. NoAM

In the Taxidermist's Shop. Siv Cedering. AMV-81

In the third-class seat sat the journeying boy. Midnight on the Great Western. Thomas Hardy. NOBE; OBP

In the third hour after Palamon. Chaucer, *tr. by* Nevill Coghill. *Fr.* The Canterbury Tales: The Knight's Tale. OBP

In the third month, a sudden flow of blood. The Vow. Anthony Hecht. ConAP; CoPAm; ILP (1975 ed.); Prf

In the thirtieth year of life. J. V. Cunningham. POL

In the time of old sin without sadness. After Swinburne. G. K. Chesterton. NOBL

In the Time of Revolution, *sels.* Julius Lester.
   "It cannot be/ reasoned with," V. PoBA
   "One needs a lyric poet in these," IV. PoBA
   "One needs a lyric poet in this, " VI. PoBA

In the Time of the Rose. John Savant. AMV-81

In the Town. *Unknown, tr. fr. French by* Eleanor Farjeon. PChr

In the town by the sea I walked. Dragging the Main. David Ray. TAT

In the town of Odessa. Dvonya. Louis Simpson. NNaP; NOBA

In the town of Springhill, Nova Scotia. Ballad of Springhill (The Springhill Mine Disaster). Ewan MacColl *and* Peggy Seeger. FSW

In the town where every man is king. Josephine Miles. CoPAm

In the town where I was born. Yellow Submarine. John Lennon *and* Paul McCartney. PPoe

In the Train. Vivian de Sola Pinto. PES

In the Train. Arthur Symons. City Nights, I. VLP

In the Tree House at Night. James Dickey. BrS

In the tunnel/ Light is haloed. The Dark Scent of Prayer. Rose Drachler. VWA

In the tunnel of woods, as the road. Last Things. William Meredith. NoAM

In the twentieth century. Machine Out of the God. Thomas E. Sanders. AMV-81

In the Twentieth Century of my trespass on earth. Galway Kinnell. *Fr.* The Dead Shall Be Raised Incorruptible. ExPo (1973 ed.); GP

In the 2 A.M. Club, a working man's bar. Robert Peterson. NeAC

In the vacant lots. Song of Degrees. Paul Auster. VWA

In the vale [*or* vaile] of restless mind. Quia Amore Langueo. *Unknown.* BoReV; NOBE; OxBM

In the Valley of Cauteretz. Tennyson. BoLoP; NOBE; VLP

In the Vaulted Way. Thomas Hardy. BoLoP; OLR (In the Crypted Way.) VLP

In the very earliest time. Magic Words. *Unknown, tr. fr. Eskimo.* IPWM; NU

In the village churchyard she lies. In the Churchyard at Cambridge. Longfellow. TAP

In the village of the dead. First Shaman Song. Gary Snyder. *Fr.* Myths and Texts: Hunting. NOBA

In the village the children. Then. Gary Gildner. FiCP

In the violet country. Dont Tell Bad Dreams Says Tita's Mother. John Oliver Simon. NeAC

In the visions of sailors. Between Rivers and Seas. Lance Henson. VoR

In the Waiting Room. Elizabeth Bishop. NOBA; Prf

In the waiting room of the psychiatric ward. To a Student Poet, Hospitalized, Having "Broken with Reality." Roderick Hartigh Jellema. AATT

In the waking night. The Cage. David Gascoyne. EAS

In the warm rods of your ears. Elegy for 41 Whales Beached in Florence, Ore., June, 1979. Linda Bierds. AMV-81

In the warm room, cushioned by comfort. Here and Human. Vernon Scannell. HeHu

In the Water. Dave Morice. AcAn

In the water cave, below the root. Howard Nemerov. *Fr.* The Scales of the Eyes. NoAM

In the Week When Christmas Comes. Eleanor Farjeon. LCL; PChr

In the well-fed cage-sound of diesels. Them, Crying. James Dickey. NowV

In the West/ circles a wheel. Wandering Chorus. B. Alquit, *tr. by* Howard Schwartz. VWA

In the West day is drawn into the smelter of sunset. For Judy. Chuck Miller. AcAn

In the Wilderness. Albert Howard Carter. AATT

In the winding folds of old capitals. The Little Old Women. Baudelaire, *tr. by* Barbara Gibbs. LoAs

In the windmill of evening. The Windmill of Evening. Shlomo Reich, *tr. by* Mira Reich. VWA

In the window all the businessmen are. The Coffee Den, Cedar Rapids. Jim Mulac. AcAn

In the Winter of My Thirty-eighth Year. W. S. Merwin. NOBA

In the Winter of Tigers. Tom McKeown. TC

In the wintertime. Toe'osh: A Laguna Coyote Story. Leslie Silko. CDW; NW; VoR

In the winter time we go. White Fields. James Stephens. ECBV

In the wisdom of teeth, you are king. On the Death of My Beard. Peter Frank. AAN

In the wood that dissolves in spark and flame. Fire. Jose Emilio Pacheco, *tr. by* Frederick Luciani. AMV-81

In the Woods. Adrienne Rich. PiAm

In the woods I came on an old friend fishing. Finding a Teacher. W. S. Merwin. NNaP

In the world which He has created. Hymmnn. Allen Ginsberg. NOBA

In the world's mighty gall'ry of pictures. A Picture from Life's Other Side. *Unknown.* FSW

In the worst inn's worst room, with mat half-hung. The Duke of Buckingham. Pope. *Fr.* Moral Essays. ExPo (1973 ed.); NOBE

In the wracks of Walsingham. A Lament for the Priory of Walsingham. *Unknown.* GBP

In the year ninety-eight, when our troubles were great. The Cow Ate the Piper. *Unknown.* GBP; PeBB

In the year of one thousand seven hundred and ninety eight. Dunlavin Green. *Unknown.* FaBoBa

In the year of the great crime. 1867. Coventry Patmore. *Fr.* The Unknown Eros. VPC

In the Year of Two Thousand. Menke Katz. AMV-81

In the Yellow Light of Brooklyn. Al Lee. NYP

In the Yucca Land. Madge Morris. BPAW

In the zero of the night, in the lipping hour. The Approach to Thebes. Stanley Kunitz. PoA

In the zócalo. Three Portraits. George Hitchcock. VGW

In thee, thou valiant man of Persia. The Overreacher. Christopher Marlowe. *Fr.* Tamburlaine the Great, Part I, I. NIL

In their/ limousines the/ teachers come. The Educators. D. M. Black. MPo

In their congealed light. Through Binoculars. Charles Tomlinson. OAEL-2

In their lighted restaurant tank. The Carp. David Malouf. FPA

In their long/ Arabesque, wings ferrying the steady. Gulls. Barbara Howes. BoAnP

In their ragged regimentals. Carmen Bellicosum. Guy Humphreys McMaster. BTTM

In their religion they are so unev'n. Daniel Defoe. *Fr.* The True-born Englishman, Pt. II. OBSV

In their skeletal/ cradle. Kathlyn. Michael Dransfield. FPA

In them days/ they won't hardly no way to know if. First Carolina Said-Song. A. R. Ammons. OBAL

In These Dissenting Times. Alice Walker. PoBA

In these miraculous Catalan streets, yellow. Survivors. Elaine Feinstein. VWA

In these, our first. Theresa. John Pass. AMV-81

In these prayers let us not forget our bodies. First Prayer. Margaret Atwood. MMD

In things a moderation keep. Moderation. Robert Herrick. FaBoEE

In this age we must seek the Byzantine. Severity. Arthur J. Bull. HeHu

In this ancient parable. The Town Rat and the Country Rat. La Fontaine, *tr. by* Marianne Moore. NAWM-2

In this bankers' town of course art would depend. The Elements of Geometry. David Malouf. CAAP

In this black room, midnight and morn are each. Four Poems, 1. Joseph Freeman. SPT

In this book I see your face and in your face. Frontispiece. May Swenson. WPE

In this café Durruti. The Midget. Philip Levine. NoAM

In this city how many masters are clouds. Amsterdam. Jean Garrigue. TAP

In this cold monument lies one. An Epitaph on M. H. Charles Cotton. EBEV; FaBoEE

In this cold room. Temperature Variations. Elisavietta Ritchie. PoUp

In this country I planted not one seed. Sailing from the United States. Stanley Moss. VGW

In this crush around us of a cruel city. Metropole. Forrest Anderson. AATT

In This Deep Darkness ("In this deep heavy darkness"). Natan Zach, *tr. fr. Hebrew by* Peter Everwine *and* Shula Starkman. VWA

In this exploded diagram of my heart, the large. Starship. David McAleavey. AMV-81

In this factory, here the axe-grinders. University Curriculum. William Price Turner. POL

In this green month when resurrected flowers. Memorial Wreath. Dudley Randall. CNA; PoBA

In this high field strewn with stones. The Barrow. Anthony Thwaite. HeHu

In this house, she said, in this high second storey. Under. J. C. Squire. FaBoTw (1975 ed.)

"In This House, There Shall Be No Idols." Carolyn M. Rodgers. JB

In this imperfect, gloomy scene. The Female Friend. Cornelius Whur. FaBoCo

In this little urn is laid. Upon Prew His Maid. Robert Herrick. CaPo; InPK

In this lone, open glade I lie. Lines Written in Kensington Gardens. Matthew Arnold. NIL

In this most foreign of all places. Stateside. R. P. Kingston. NVAP

In this motel where I was told to wait. The Human Condition. Howard Nemerov. CoPAm; NowV

In this nation. Of Being Numerous #24. George Oppen. *Fr.* Of Being Numerous. GOA

In this park of dilapidated times. Blackstone Park. Steve Jonas. EC

In this picture you will see. Snake Sermon. Dave Smith. CSP

In this poem I am fast asleep in bed. Back behind the Eyes. Leon Stokesbury. NVAP

In this poem the bear shambles in. The Bear That Came to the Wedding. Howard McCord. GP

In this small office off the corridor. Ghosts of the Living. May Ivimy. PMW

In this stoned and. Definition of Nature. Eugene Redmond. PoBA

In this vintage season, when the skies are full of movement. I Didn't Know My Soul. Avraham Ben-Yitzhak, *tr. by* A. C. Jacobs. VWA

In this water, clear as air. The Pool in the Rock. Walter de la Mare. EcS

In this woman the earth speaks. Earth and Fire. Wendell Berry. FF; GP

In this world. Flannery O'Connor. Dorothy Walters. IHMS

In this world a tablecloth need not be laid. Tea in a Space-Ship. James Kirkup. MPo

In this world of toil and trouble. I Don't Want to Get Adjusted. *Unknown.* FSW

In this world (the Isle of Dreams). The White Island; or, The Place of the Blest [*or* Blessed]. Robert Herrick. BoReV; OAEL-1; SCP-1

In this Year of Grace. John Hewitt. PFIr

In th'olde dayes of the kyng Arthour. The Wife of Bath's Tale. Chaucer. *Fr.* The Canterbury Tales. ILP (1975 ed.); OAEL-1

In those cold regions which no summers cheer. Prologue to His Royal Highness. Dryden. SCP-1

In those days. The Ancestors. Barbara Drake. TC

In those old days which poets say were golden. Beer. Charles Stuart Calverley. FaBoCo

In those painful days, we knew. Yesterday's Illusion; or, Remembering the Thirties. Alun Llywelyn-Williams, *tr. by* R. Gerallt Jones. OBW

In thriving arts long time had Holland grown. War. Dryden. *Fr.* Annus Mirabilis. SCP-1

In thy western halls of gold. Ode to Apollo. Keats. MBPR

In tight pants, tight skirts. The Young Ones, Flip Side. James A. Emanuel. SS

In Time. Robert Graves. FaBoEE

In Time. Kathleen Raine. WPE

In time all undertakings are made good. In Time. Robert Graves. FaBoEE

In Time of Gold. Hilda Doolittle ("H. D."). PoA

In Time of Need. William Stafford. UnPo (1976 ed.)

In Time of Pestilence. Thomas Nashe. *See* Adieu, Farewell Earth's Bliss.

In Time of "The Breaking of Nations." Thomas Hardy. BoLoP; CMoP (1970 ed.); EBEV; HAP; ILP (1975 ed.); NoAM; NOBE; OAEL-2; POL; PPM; PPoD; PPP; PSN; VoPo

In time [*or* tyme] the strong and stately turrets fall. Licia, XXVIII. Giles Fletcher the Elder. AAS; EBEV; ESo; ILP (1975 ed.); NIL

In time to come, if such a crime should be. To Maecenas. Horace, *tr. by* Thomas Flatman. OBVE

In Time's concatenation and/ Carnal conventicle. Mortmain, I. Robert Penn Warren. NOBA; Prf

In times of calm or hurricane, in days of sun or shower. The Dog Parade. Arthur Guiterman. BoAnP; GDP

In times when princes canceled nature's law. Tarquin and Tullia. Arthur Mainwaring. APAS

In toaster and rotisserie. Try Brillo on the Slimy Stove. Phyllis Gotlieb. BBGO

In town, your friends play hide-and-seek. September. W. D. Snodgrass. PSN

In trellised shed with clustering roses gay. The White Doe of Rylstone; or, The Fate of the Nortons. Wordsworth. MBPR

In tropical climes there are certain times of day. Mad Dogs and Englishmen. Noel Coward. NOBL

In troth, I do myself persuade. Love Enthroned. Richard Lovelace. CaPo

In trust you showed me a photograph. Love among Friends. Shawn Wong. NW

In truth I cannot reach you. Dreams. William Peskett. IPM

In Tupelo, Mississippi. The Tupelo Destruction. *Unknown.* AmFP

In Two Fields. Waldo Williams, *tr. fr. Welsh by* Gwyn Jones. OBW

In tyme the strong and statelie turrets fall. *See* In time the strong and stately turrets fall.

In unexperienced infancy. Shadows in the Water. Thomas Traherne. BoReV; HAP; ILP (1975 ed.); MetP; OAEL–1; SCP–2

In unplowed Maine he sought the lumberers' gang. Emerson. *Fr.* Woodnotes I. TAP

In us and into us and ours. For Eusi, Ayi Kwei and Gwen Brooks. Keorapetse Kgositsile. PoBA

In using there are always two. Song of the Fucked Duck. Marge Piercy. BoWoP; NMM

In Utrumque Paratus. Matthew Arnold. VLP

In vain did Heav'n its miracles produce. A Poem on England's Happiness. *Unknown.* APAS

In vain Her veins incised—jagged boulders. Spokane Falls. Philip William George. VoR

In vain, in vain,—the all-composing hour. The Triumph of Dullness. Pope. *Fr.* The Dunciad. EBEV; NOBE

In vain to me the smiling mornings shine. Sonnet on the Death of [Mr.] Richard West. Thomas Gray. LAuP; NOBE; PAIC

In vain was I born. Nezalhualcoyotl. ILwL

In vain would man his mighty patent show. In Commendation of the Female Sex. Jane Barker. SCP–2

In Valleys Green and Still. A. E. Housman. FaBoTw (1975 ed.); OAEL–2

In view of what is lost, a union, the point. Property Settlement. John Pauker. PoUp

In Virgyne the sweltrie sun gan sheene. An Excelente Balade of Charitie. Thomas Chatterton. EBEV; EPC; LAuP

In Vistas of Stone. Abo Stoltzenberg, *tr. fr. Yiddish by* Gabriel Preil *and* Howard Schwartz. VWA

In Weather. Robert Hass. AmPA

In Weatherbury Stocks. Thomas Hardy. AIW

In Wee-John-Boo the bellies of bloodhounds. Orange Jews. Ted Berrigan *and* Ron Padgett. EAS

In Westminster Abbey. Francis Beaumont. *See* On the Tombs in Westminster Abbey

In Westminster Abbey. John Betjeman. BoReV; CMoP (1970 ed.); FaBoCo; ILP (1975 ed.); InPK; IP; NIL; NOBL; OAEL–2; OBSV

In Westminster not long ago. The Ratcatcher's Daughter. *Unknown.* GBP

In wet and cloudy mists I slowly rise. Night's Song. Sir William Davenant. *Fr.* Luminalia. SCP–2

In wet green midspring, midnight and the wind. Mrs. Walpurga. Muriel Rukeyser. NMM

In wet May, in the months of change. An Exequy. Peter Porter. GAS

In what at least. 18 West 11th Street. James Merrill. NYP

In what estate so ever I be. *See* In what state that ever I be.

In (What Few) Green (Barely) Parks. Horace Coleman. SES

In what state that [*or* estate so] ever I be. The Sparrow-Hawk's Complaint [*or* Timor Mortis]. *Unknown.* FF; OxBM

In what torn ship soever I embark. A Hymn to Christ, at the Author's Last Going into Germany. John Donne. BoReV; EBEV

In which I live hurtles airless a razor's slash. The Present Tense. Joyce Carol Oates. AMV–81

In Which She Satisfies a Fear with the Rhetoric of Tears. Sister Juana Ines de la Cruz, *tr. fr. Spanish by* Aliki *and* Willis Barnstone. BoWoP
("This evening, my love, even as I spoke vainly," *tr. by* Judith Thurman.) PBWP

In White. Robert Frost. WIF

In whose will is our peace? Thou happiness. Epigram. J. V. Cunningham. VGW

In William Rufus's hall the galleries reached. Fifth Day. Robert D. Fitzgerald. GAS; MAuV

In Windsor Castle. Earl of Surrey. NOBE
("So crewell prison, howe could betyde, alas.") AAS
(So Cruel Prison.) HAP; ILP (1975 ed.)

In windy June, the prairie grasses bow. Missouri Town. John Palen. AMV–80

In Winter. Paul Blackburn. NYP

In Winter, Elms. Ronald Mann. PMW

In winter I get up at night. Bed in Summer. Robert Louis Stevenson. OxBChV

In winter in my room. Emily Dickinson. BiP; NoAM; NOBA

In Winter in the Woods Alone. Robert Frost. HeIP; PiAm

In winter my mother goes away. Desert. Del Marie Rogers. NPW

In winter, strangeness stained the fields. Somewhere Farm. Guy Rotella. AMV–81

In winter twilight on a side street. Ghostly Story. Milton Acorn. NeAC

In winter, when the fields are white. Humpty Dumpty's Song [*or* Recitation]. "Lewis Carroll." *Fr.* Through the Looking-Glass. EBEV; FaBoCo; FaBoNo; OxBChV

In winters just returne, when Boreas gan his raigne. Earl of Surrey. AAS

In wit, as nature, what affects our hearts. Pope. *Fr.* An Essay on Criticism. HAP

In wonted walks, since wonted fancies change. Sir Philip Sidney. CABA (1972 ed.)

In Woods Where Many Rivers Run. Lawrence Ferlinghetti. *Fr.* A Coney Island of the Mind. BBGO

In Worcester, Massachusetts. In the Waiting Room. Elizabeth Bishop. NOBA; Prf

In Word and Will I am a friend to you. On Himself. William Oldys. FaBoEE

In wrestling I was pinned first. First in the Pentathlon. Lucilius, *tr. by* Tom Dodge. LiSp

In W.W. II the Japanese. Speech for an Abdication. Harry Stessel. AAN

In Wyoming,/ plain as far as my eye can see. Other Women's Children. Mary Nelson Waniek. AMV–80

In Xanadu did Kubla Khan. Kubla Khan. Samuel Taylor Coleridge. AKE; AnMo; BiP; CABA (1972 ed.); ECBV; ExPo (1973 ed.); FF; HAP; HeIP; HoPM (1975 ed.); ILP (1975 ed.); InPK; InPS; IP; MAT; MBPR; NIL; NOBE; OAEL–2; OBP; PBMP; PCOP; PoIA; PPoD; PPoe; SoSe; UnPo (1976 ed.); UsP; VoPo; WeW

In Yad Vashem, where all vows are renewed. Hands Up. Anthony Rudolf. VWA

In yellow meadows I take no delight. Sir Thomas Browne. FaBoEE

In yonder grave a Druid lies. Ode Occasion'd by the Death of Mr. Thomson. William Collins. LAuP

In yonder marble hero's shade. Italian. Osbert Lancaster. *Fr.* Afternoons with Baedeker. FaBoCo

In Your Arms. Miklós Radnóti, *tr. fr. Hungarian by* Steven Polgar *and* Stephen Berg *and* S. J. Marks. VWA

In your next letter I wish you'd say. Letter to N. Y. Elizabeth Bishop. NYP; TH

In your quiet hand I touch. The Survivors. Miriam Waddington. VWA

In your watercolor, Nely Silvinova. Theresienstadt Poem. Robert Mezey. VWA

In your words. Prologue. Lazer Eichenrand, *tr. by* Gabriel Preil *and* Howard Schwartz. VWA

In youth, gay scenes attract our eyes. The Vanity of Existence. Philip Freneau. EAP

In Youth Is Pleasure. Robert Wever. *Fr.* Lusty Juventus. NOBE
("In a herber green, asleep whereas I lay.") GBL

Inability to Depict an Eagle. Richard Eberhart. GOA

Inadequate Aqua Extremis. Ruth M. Walsh. QQQ

Inamorato Curio. John Marston. The Scourge of Villainy, VIII. TVS

Inamoring rayes, thy sparkles, pearle of price. The Return. Edward Taylor. *Fr.* Preparatory Meditations, First Series. EAP

Inanna and An. Enheduanna, *tr. fr. Sumerian; ad. by* Aliki *and* Willis Barnstone. BoWoP

Inanna and Ebih. Enheduanna, *tr. fr. Sumerian; ad. by* Aliki *and* Willis Barnstone. BoWoP

Inanna and Enlil. Enheduanna, *tr. fr. Sumerian; ad. by* Aliki *and* Willis Barnstone. BoWoP

Inanna and Ishkur. Enheduanna, *tr. fr. Sumerian; ad. by* Aliki *and* Willis Barnstone. BoWoP

Inanna and the Anunna. Enheduanna, *tr. fr. Sumerian; ad. by* Aliki *and* Willis Barnstone. BoWoP

Inanna and the City of Uruk. Enheduanna, *tr. fr. Sumerian; ad. by* Aliki *and* Willis Barnstone. BoWoP

Inanna and the Divine Essences. Enheduanna, *tr. fr. Sumerian; ad. by* Aliki *and* Willis Barnstone. BoWoP

Inapprehensiveness. Robert Browning. VLP

Incantation for Rain. *Unknown, tr. fr. Navajo Indian by* Washington Matthews. ExPo (1973 ed.)

Incantation to Oedipus. Dryden. *Fr.* Oedipus, III, i. OFD

Incantatory Poem. Jean Garrigue. LoAs

Incarnate Devil. Dylan Thomas. TT

Incarnate Love. Christina Rossetti. PIM

Incarnatio Est Maximum Dei Donum. William Alabaster. BoReV

Incarnation of Sirius, The. James McAuley. GAS; MAuV

Incendiary. Vernon Scannell. HeHu

Incest in Orange. Patricia Garfinkel. PoUp

Inchcape Rock, The. Robert Southey. PoPle

Incident. Fleur Adcock. ATNZ

Incident. Amiri Baraka. NoAM

Incident. Countee Cullen. BiP; BPo; CABA (1972 ed.); CTBA; FF; IP; NoAM; NowV; PoBA; SFF; SoSe; VGW

Incident, The. Jim Kraus. PHC

Incident. Norman MacCaig. FF

Incident at Mossel Bay. Mary Balazs. AMV–81

Incident here and there, An. Hilda Doolittle ("H. D."). *Fr.* The Walls Do Not Fall. NoAM

Incident in a Rose Garden. Donald Justice. NCSH

Incident in the Early Life of Ebenezer Jones, Poet, 1828, An. John Betjeman. CMoP (1970 ed.); NoAM

Incident of the French Camp. Robert Browning. AKE; BTTM; FaPo; FaPoR; TT

Incident on a Journey. Thom Gunn. MPo

Incidental Pieces to a Walk. James Cunningham. JB

Incidents in the Life of My Uncle Arly. Edward Lear. FaBoNo; OAEL–2; OBP

Inclusiveness. Dante Gabriel Rossetti. The House of Life, LXIII. VLP

Incognito. John Manifold. FPA

Incoherent in the midst of men. The New Lost Feminist. Rita Mae Brown. WBN

Incomprehensible, The. Isaac Watts. ILP (1975 ed.)

Inconclusive Evening, An. Frances Bellerby. FaBoTw (1975 ed.)

Inconstancy Reproved. Sir Robert Ayton. GBL

Inconvenience, An. John Raven. BPo

Incredible Yachts, The. Philip Booth. GP

Incrusted in his island home that lies beyond the sea. The Neutral British Gentleman. "Orpheus C. Kerr." OBAL

Incurable Home, The. John Haines. CNW

Indecision Means Flexibility. Elliot Abhau. PH

Indeed indeed it is growing very sultry. The Cubical Domes. David Gascoyne. EAS

Indelicate is he who loathes. Epidermal Macabre. Theodore Roethke. NoAM

Independence. Nancy Cato. WPE

Independence. *Somali Oral Tradition, tr. by* B. W. Andrzejewski *and* I. M. Lewis. WTO

Independence Day. Wendell Berry. OFD

Independent, The. Phyllis McGinley. FaBoEE

Independent Squire. Samuel Butler. *Fr.* Hudibras, I, 1. NOBE

Indian. Jeanne Doriot. AMV–81

Indian. Laura Jensen. AmPA

Indian. Martin Laarakker. PoW

Indian, The. Thomas Reed. AMV–81

Indian at the Burial-Place of His Fathers, An. Bryant. HeIP; PiAm

Indian Autobiographies. Madeline DeFrees. CNW; PoW

Indian Burying Ground, The. Philip Freneau. EAP; HAP; HeIP; IPWM; NOBA; PiAm; TAP

Indian chief who, fam'd of yore, The. The Prophecy of King Tammany. Philip Freneau. GOA

Indian Convert, The. Philip Freneau. TAP

Indian Death. Alice Corbin. BPAW

Indian Death. Eda Lou Walton. BPAW

Indian girl, The/ up before sunrise. Advising Anna Doolittle the White Antelope Allusion Will Escape Her Readers. Tom Trusky. PoW

Indian Graves at Jocko. Richard Hugo. MPA

Indian Graveyard, The. Ramona Weeks. TAT

Indian Guys at the Bar. Simon J. Ortiz. NW

Indian Hymn of Thanks to Mother Corn, An. *Unknown, tr. fr.* Pawnee Indian. CC

Indian Love Letter. Soge Track. VW

Indian Love Song. Lew Blockcolski. VoR

Indian Mounds. Angela Peace. AMV–80

Indian Names. Lydia Huntley Sigourney. GOA

Indian Painting, Probably Paiute, in a Cave Near Madras, Oregon. Jarold Ramsey. TAT

Indian Princess, The. The Pet Deer. James Tate. EAS

Indian riding. In the Embers at Midnight. Paulette Dusdall Zachariou. NPW

Indian Rock, Bainbridge Island, Washington. Duane Niatum. CDW

Indian School. Norman H. Russell. MAT

Indian Serenade, The. Shelley. ExPo (1973 ed.); HoPM (1975 ed.); MBPR; UsP

Indian Sky. Alfred Kreymborg. BPAW

Indian Song ("The fire on the hearth is the woman's fire"). Willard Johnson. BPAW

Indian Song, An. W. B. Yeats. VLP

Indian Song: Survival. Leslie Silko. CDW; VoR

Indian Summer. Gray Burr. AMV–80

Indian Summer. Barbara Howes. IHMS

Indian Summer Day on the Prairie, An. Vachel Lindsay. BPAW; RFM

Indian Summer Garden Party. Keith Althaus. AAN

Indian Summer Here, You in Honolulu. Donald Johnson. AMV–80

Indian Summer: Montana, 1956. W. M. Ransom. CDW

Indian Summer, 1927. Anne Hussey. AMV–81

Indian-summer-sun. October–November. Hart Crane. PSN

Indian Summer: Vermont. Anne Stevenson. NCSH

Indian to His Love, The. W. B. Yeats. PBMP; VLP

Indian upon God, The. W. B. Yeats. IPWM

Indian Warrior. Mary Logue. NPW

Indian, who lived at Muskingum, remote, An. The Indian Convert. Philip Freneau. TAP

Indian Woman's Death-Song. Felicia Dorothea Hemans. SBG

Indiana. Hart Crane. *Fr.* The Bridge: Powhatan's Daughter. PiAm

Indiana: no blustering summit or coarse gorge. Midwest. John Frederick Nims. ANTL

Indiana State Highway Patrol. James Beall. PoUp

Indians, The. Gene Fowler. PoW

Indians, The. Peter Wild. MPA

Indians at the Guthrie. Gerald Vizenor. VoR

Indians Come Down from Mixco, The. Miguel Angel Asturias, *tr. fr. Spanish by* Donald Devenish Walsh. TSWA

Indians have mostly gone, The. Like Ghosts of Eagles. Robert Francis. GOA

Indians on Alcatraz, The. Paul Muldoon. CIP

Indictment, The, *abr.* Frederick Fanning Ayer. PeD

Indifferent, The. John Donne. AnMo; BiP; BoLoP; CABA (1972 ed.); PBMP

Indignant at the fumbling wits, the obscure spite. Paudeen. W. B. Yeats. HAP; InPS

Indigo Glass in the Grass, The. Wallace Stevens. PoA

Indigo Pete's J. B. Henry Herbert Knibbs. BPAW

Individual flakes, precise, The. Self Portrait: Women with Children. Pamela Stewart. FoP

Individual spider web, An. Identity. A. R. Ammons. CoPAm

Indolence. Robert Bridges. VLP

Indolence. Vernon Watkins. FaBoTw (1975 ed.)

Indomitable, The. Carl Rakosi. GP

Indoors. George Johnston. PoA

Induction to "A Mirror for Magistrates." Thomas Sackville. *See* Mirror for Magistrates, The.

Indulge thy smiling scorn, if smiling still. The Fish Turns into a Man, and Then into a Spirit, and Again Speaks. Leigh Hunt. *Fr.* The Fish, the Man, and the Spirit. NOBL

Indulgences. Michael Hogan. AMV–80

Indulgent Nature on each kind bestows. On Dr. Evans Cutting Down a Row of Trees. *Unknown.* FaBoEE

Industrious, unfatigued in faction's cause. The Character of a Certain Whig. William Shippen. APAS

Inertia of a warm day. Overdose. Michael Dransfield. FPA

Inexorable. William Drummond of Hawthornden. NOBE

Inexpensive Progress. John Betjeman. LP

Infant Innocence. A. E. Housman. FaBoCo; FaBoNo; NOBL

Infant Joy. Blake. *Fr.* Songs of Innocence. LAuP; MBPR

Infant she played in the shadow. Anne and the Peacock. Noel Welch. FF

Infant Sorrow. Blake. *Fr.* Songs of Experience. InPS; LAuP; MBPR; PoIA: PoPle; STS

Inferno. Dante. *See* Divina Commedia.

Inferno: A New Circle. Frank Ormsby. CIP

Infidelity. Olga Berggolts, *tr. fr. Russian by* Daniel Weissbort. BoWoP

Infinite cosanguinity it bears. Voyages, III. Hart Crane. LoAs

Infinite weariness comes into the faces of the old tenements, An. Ghetto Twilight. Alter Brody. VWA

Infinity, when all things it beheld. The Preface. Edward Taylor. *Fr.* God's Determinations. EAP; HAP; ILP (1975 ed.); NOBA; PiAm

Inflammable Man, The. Gordon Challis. ATNZ

Inflation. Charles O. Hartman. PoA

Informer, art thou in the tree. On the Meetings of the Scotch Covenanters. *Unknown.* FaBoEE

"Ingaborg is the brawest o wemen." Steel on Stane. Alexander Scott. MS

Ingathering of Love, The, *sel.* Peter Whigham. "It was in one of those old houses in Monmouthshire." TwMBP

Ingestion. Barry McDonald. POL

Inglorious friend! most confident I am. Sonnet to a Clam. John Godfrey Saxe. BoAnP

Ingoldsby Legends, The, *sels.* "Thomas Ingoldsby." Jackdaw of Rheims, The. FaBoCo; VLP Not a Sous Had He Got. *Fr.* The Cynotaph. FaBoCo

Ingrateful Beauty Threatened. Thomas Carew. CaPo

Inhabited Emptiness, An. Jiri Gold, *tr. fr. Czech by* Jaroslav Kotan *and* Daniel Weissbort. VWA

Inheritance. George Bruce. MS

Inheritance, An. Naomi Replansky. GP

Inheritance. Kendrick Smithyman. ATNZ

Inheritors, The. William Peskett. IPM

Inimitably quick. Static Autumn. Yvor Winters. PoA

Inis Fal. Egan O'Rahilly, *tr. fr. Irish by* James Stephens. BIrV

Initial Response. Katherine Soniat. AMV–80

Initials. Michael S. Glaser. AMV–81

Initials carved from tenderloin days. Wicked Lady of Gough Street. Todd S. J. Lawson. CPA

Initiate, The. W. S. Merwin. NNaP

Initiation. Jayne Cortez. PoBA

Injured Moon, The. Baudelaire, *tr. fr. French by* Robert Lowell. Moon

Injury to Insured. John Daniel. TwMBP

Ink runs from the corners of my mouth. Eating Poetry. Mark Strand. CoPAm; MAT; NoAM; PPP; TAP

Inky, dinky spider. *Unknown.* CTV

Inland City. John Crowe Ransom. CMoP (1970 ed.)

Inland Lighthouse, The. James McMichael. AmPA

Inland Passages, *sel.* Wendell Berry. Long Hunter, The. GP

Inland Sea. Franklin Brainard. HeS

Inland, within a hollow vale, I stood. September, 1802. Near Dover. Wordsworth. MBPR

Inner-City Lullaby. Russell Atkins. CNA

Inner-City Mother Goose, The, *sels.* Eve Merriam. IPWM Ding, Dong, Bell. Fee, Fi, Fo, Fum. Wino Will.

Inner greet. Greenberg said it. Columbus. Muriel Rukeyser. GOA

Inner Part, The. Louis Simpson. ILP (1975 ed.); InPS; PBMP; SFF

Inner Temple Masque, *sel.* William Browne. Sirens' Song, The. NOBE; PoPle (Syrens' Song, The.) GBL

Inniskeen Road: July Evening. Patrick Kavanagh. NoAM; PFIr

Innocence, The. Robert Creeley. NoAM

Innocence. Thom Gunn. NoAM; TPo

Innocence. Irving Layton. BBGO

Innocence?/ In a sense. A Life. Howard Nemerov. AnMo; PBMP

Innocence is important, and order. Job Description: Medical Records. U. A. Fanthorpe. PMW

Innocent decision: to enjoy. Triple Feature. Denise Levertov. FF

Innocent Spring, The. Edith Sitwell. *Fr.* The Sleeping Beauty. NOBE
("In the great gardens, after bright spring rain.") OxBTC

Innocent to innocent. To What Strangers, What Welcome, IX. J. V. Cunningham. PiAm

Innocent's Song. Charles Causley. MPo

Innominatus. Sir Walter Scott. *See* This Is My Own, My Native Land.

Innumerable Christ, The. "Hugh MacDiarmid." EBEV

Inordinate Love. *Unknown.* EBEV; LoAs (*At. to* John Lydgate)

Inquest, The. W. H. Davies. NOBE; OxBTC

Inquisition, The. Thomas Beedome. SCP-2

Inquisitive Leopard, The. Oliver Herford. TDH

Insatiable Baby, The. Cynthia Macdonald. WBN

Insatiableness. Thomas Traherne. ILP (1975 ed.)

Inscape. Susan Litwack. VWA

Inscribed in Melrose Abbey. *Unknown.* FaBoEE

Inscription: "Eagle, stooping from yon snow-blown peaks, The." Whittier. GOA

Inscription: "For one long term, or e'er her trial came." George Canning *and* John Hookham Frere. FaBoCo; FaBoEE

Inscription, An: "Over the sheer rocks over the gorges." Stanislav Vinaver, *tr. fr. Serbo-Croat by* Vasa D. Mihailovich. VWA

Inscription by the Sea, An. E. A. Robinson, *after the Greek of* Glaucus. FaBoEE

Inscription for a Fountain on a Heath. Samuel Taylor Coleridge. MBPR

Inscription for a Headstone. Austin Clarke. BIrV; CIP

Inscription for Marye's Heights, Fredericksburg. Herman Melville. UnPo (1976 ed.)

Inscription for the Entrance to a Wood. Bryant. AmVN; BiP; EAP; ILP (1975 ed.); PiAm; PPoD; TAP

Inscription in a Book. Gilean Douglas. AMV-81

Inscription on the Monument of a Newfoundland Dog. Byron. *See* Epitaph to a Dog.

Inscriptions. Anthony Thwaite. HeHu

Insect Hunter, The, *sel.* Edward Newman.
"Take thy hat, my little Laura." PPoD

Insect of the Sun/ and of Happiness. True. Phillip William George. NW

Insect or blossom? Fragile, fairy thing. The Mariposa Lily. Ina Coolbrith. BPAW

Insect Shuffle Method, The. Gary Tapp. AMV-80

Insensibility. Wilfred Owen. CMoP (1970 ed.); ExPo (1973 ed.); FaBoTw (1975 ed.); InPS; OxBTC

Inseparable. Philip Bourke Marston. BoLoP

Inseparable from the fire. Coda. William Carlos Williams. NOBA

Inside/ the voices of the boys. Inside, Outside, and Beyond. John Ratti. AMV-80

Inside a cave in a narrow canyon near Tassajara. Hands. Robinson Jeffers. GOA

Inside at the green cafe. Over Coffee. Jennifer Maiden. CAAP

Inside every widow. Portrait of a Widow. Avner Strauss. VWA

Inside History. Angela McCabe. AmPA

Inside or out, the key is pain. It holds. Hospital. Karl Shapiro. VGW

Inside Out, *sel.* Diane Wakoski.
"I walk the purple carpet into your eye." OSP

Inside, Outside, and Beyond. John Ratti. AMV-80

Inside that figure rides opaque malice. The Picador Bit. Bink Noll. LiSp; SFF

Inside the brain they are holding a mass funeral for the dead brain cells. The Brain Cells. Donald Hall. TAP

Inside the child. Night Watch. Margo Magid. NMM

Inside the coconut is Katerina's baby. A Coconut for Katerina. Sandra McPherson. FiCP

Inside the fog that encloses the trees. Trees Lose Parts of Themselves Inside a Circle of Fog. Francis Ponge, *tr. by* Robert Bly. NU

Inside the River. James Dickey. PoA; SPo

Inside the Story, *sel.* Mark Strand.
"She sat in a chair across the room, staring at him." UsP

Inside the veins there are navies setting forth. Waking from Sleep. Robert Bly. CAPP; EAS; InPS; NoAM; NOBA

Inside the Vision of Peace. Tom McKeown. TC

Inside the Wall of My Cell. J. Charles Green. DNGG

Inside these walls. Asylum for War Victims. Robert Morgan. HeHu

Inside this clay jug there are canyons and pine mountains. The Clay Jug. Kabir, *ad. by* Robert Bly. NU

Inside this northern summer's fold. Siena. Swinburne. VLP

Inside this shell. What Is Lived. Carmen Valle, *tr. by* Julio Marzán. InW

Insight. Ruthe T. Spinnanger. AATT

Insistence, The. Gerard Malanga. AAN

Insistent as a whistle, her voice up. Claiming Kin. Ellen Bryant Voigt. AAN

Insistently through sleep—a tide of voices. The Harbor Dawn. Hart Crane. *Fr.* The Bridge: Powhatan's Daughter. NYP; PiAm; PSN

Insomnia. Elizabeth Bishop. TH

Insomnia, *sel.* Marina Tsvetayeva, *tr. fr.* Russian by Elaine Feinstein *and* Angela Livingstone.
"Black as the centre of an eye, the centre, a blackness." PBWP

Insomnia. Elizabeth Zelvin. AMV-80

Insomnia the Gem of the Ocean. John Updike. QQQ

Insomniac Sleeps Well for Once and, The. Hayden Carruth. NNaP

Inspiration. Robert W. Service. WeW

Inspiration. Henry David Thoreau. NOBA

Inspiration on Perspiration. *Unknown.* SoSe (1977 ed.)

Inspire our sons to seek their man-shadows. If We Cannot Live People as People. Charles Lynch. CNA; PoBA

Instalment, The, *sel.* Edward Young.
"Since Brunswick's smile has authoris'd my muse." FaBoCo

Instamatic. Edwin Morgan. FF

Instances. Anselm Hollo. TwMBP

Instans Tyrannus. Robert Browning. EBEV

Instant released, it spins, The. Playing Catch. Keith Moul. AMV-80

Instead of you, I choose the blood. The Unwanted. Mary Gordon. IHMS

Instructed to speak of God with emphasis. Memorial to a Missionary. Keith Sinclair. ATNZ

Instruction. Hazel Hall. WPW

Instruction from Bly. Cynthia Macdonald. NMM

Instruction Manual, The. John Ashbery. HAP; NoAM; NOBA

Instructions. Anita Skeen. IHMS

Instructions for a Park. Brad Walker. AMV-80; AMV-81

Instructions for Crossing the Border. Dan Pagis, *tr. fr. Hebrew by* Stephen Mitchell. VWA

Instructions for the Erection of a Statue to Myself in Central Park. Colette Inez. RiTi

Instructions for the Messiah. Myra Sklarew. VWA

Instructions of King Cormac, The, *sel. Unknown, tr. fr. Irish by* Kuno Meyer.
" 'O Cormac, grandson of Conn,' said Carbery." BIrV

Instructions to a Painter. Edmund Waller. APAS
Instructions to a Princess. Ishmael Reed. CNA; PoBA
Instructor said, The. Theme for English B. Langston Hughes. ILP (1975 ed.); NoAM; NOBA; PoIA
Instrument, The. Kathleen Raine. PoA
Insular Celts, The. Ciaran Carson. BIrV; CIP, *revised version*
Insurance. D. J. Enright. HeHu
Insusceptibles, The. Adrienne Rich. ConAP; HeIP; InPK
Integer Vitae. Thomas Campion. NOBE
    (Man of Life Upright, The.) AAS; ILP (1975 ed.)
Integration. Richard Kell. IPM
Intellect of man is forced to choose, The. The Choice. W. B. Yeats. CMoP (1970 ed.); NoAM; OxBTC
Intellectual, The. Karl Shapiro. CMoP (1970 ed.); LFH
Intellectuals, The. Dudley Randall. PoBA
Intelligent Sheepman and the New Cars, The. William Carlos Williams. OBAL
Intended for Sir Isaac Newton. Pope. InPK; WeW
    (Epitaph Intended for Sir Isaac Newton.) ILP (1975 ed.)
    (Epitaph on Newton.) IP
    ("Nature, and Nature's laws, lay hid in night.") FaBoCo; FaBoEE; QQQ
Intention to Escape from Him. Edna St. Vincent Millay. SBG
Intercessors. Austin Clarke. CMoP (1970 ed.)
Interests of a black man in a cellar, The. Black Tambourine. Hart Crane. NoAM; PAIC; PPP; TAP
Interface. Pamela Alexander. AAN
Interim. Frank Ormsby. CIP
Interior. Padraic Colum. PFIr
Interior. Joseph Milbauer, *tr. fr. French by* Edouard Roditi. VWA
Interior. Dorothy Parker. SBG
Interior. Genevieve Taggard. SPT
Interior Landscape. Gloria Fuertes, *tr. fr. Spanish by* Willis Barnstone. BoWoP
Interlude, An. Robert Duncan. CMoP (1970 ed.)
Interlude. Theodore Roethke. STS
Interlude. Karl Shapiro. PBMP
Interlude. Welton Smith. PoBA
Intermezzo: Pastoral, *sel.* Arthur Symons.
    At Glan-y-Wern, IV. VLP
Intermission. Margaret R. Litchfield. PoUp
Internal Injuries. Robert Penn Warren. NYP
International Chainpoem. *Unknown.* EAS
International Conference. Colin Ellis. FaBoEE
International Hotel. Rapping with One Million Carabaos in the Dark. Al Robles. CPA
International Motherhood Assoc. M. L. Hester. AMV–81
Internationale, The. Eugene Potter *and* Pierre Degeyter. FSW
Interphase. Darcy Cummings. EC
Interplanetary Limericks. Al Graham. QQQ
Interpretation. Gloria Bussel Koster. NPW
Interpretations. Beate Goldman. PoUp
Interred beneath this marble stone. An Epitaph. Matthew Prior. FaBoEE; NIL; OAEL–1; OBSV
Interrogation. Robert Hahn. AAN
Interrogation, The. Edwin Muir. CMoP (1970 ed.)
Interrogator, The. Elizabeth Jennings. WPE
Interrupted, The. Josephine Jacobsen. GP
Interruption at the Opera House. Brian Patten. LP
Intersecting early night. One Gardenia 50C. Ben Maddow. SPT
Intersection. Florence Dolgorukov. AMV–80
Interview, An. K. W. Grandsen. OxBTC
Interview. Laurence Lieberman. AMV–81

Interview with a Tornado Victim on April 16, 1974, An. Philip Legler. TC
Interview with a Tourist. Margaret Atwood. IHMS
Interview with Doctor Drink. J. V. Cunningham. VGW
Interstate, *sels.* Marie Harris. AAN
    I–93.
    "Leaving Ithaca: Buttermilk Falls."
    "Now it's my mother."
    "We came when there were no more horses."
    "We leave layers of ourselves."
    "We live with our mistakes."
    "You imagined the lover I will never be I am."
Intimacy. Raymond Ward. ATNZ
Intimate Associations. Baudelaire, *tr. fr. French by* Robert Bly. NU
Intimate friend of the Czar was I, An. Shootin' with Rasputin. *Unknown.* FSW
Intimates. D. H. Lawrence. BoLoP; PoTa
Intimations. Alma Johanna Koenig, *tr. fr. German by* Edouard Roditi. VWA
Intimations at the Lake, 1963. Helena Minton. FAF
Intimations of Immortality. Wordsworth. *See* Ode: Intimations of Immortality. . .
Intimations of Immortality, Cuttingsville, Vermont, 1880. Constance Carrier. FAF
Into a world where children shriek like suns. On a Child Who Lived One Minute. X. J. Kennedy. HoPM (1975 ed.)
Into Battle. Julian Grenfell. FaPoR; OxBTC
Into Blackness Softly. Mari Evans. PoBA
Into Hell's cave stepped a new guest. Arrival in Hell. Ricarda Huch, *tr. by* Susan C. Strong. PBWP
Into her mother's bedroom to wash the ballooning body. Jessie Mitchell's Mother. Gwendolyn Brooks. BoWoP; NMM
Into love and out again. Theory. Dorothy Parker. SBG
Into my empty head there come. Morning Swim. Maxine W. Kumin. LiSp; NVAP; WPE
Into My Heart an Air That Kills. A. E. Housman. BBGO; CMoP (1970 ed.); EBEV; NoAM; NOBE; OAEL–2; OxBTC; POL
Into My Own. Robert Frost. PPM
Into that pit when I did enter in. Elizabeth Melvill, Lady Culross. *Fr.* A Godly Dream. WPE
Into the Book. Martin Grossman. VWA
Into the clouds the devil lately got. Michael Drayton. *Fr.* To My Noble Friend Master William Browne: Of the Evil Time. SCP–2
Into the Dark. Paul Monette. AmPA
Into the Devil tavern. The Three Troopers. George Walter Thornbury. BTTM
Into the frenzy of falling bodies. Buster Keaton. Michael McFee. AMV–81
Into the gray March light. March Light. Ralph J. Mills, Jr. AMV–81
Into the laps. Mellow. Langston Hughes. ILP (1975 ed.)
Into the night. The Inland Lighthouse. James McMichael. AmPA
Into the playground we went. Black Clouds. Terence Brame. RAE
Into the pool of silence our tears made. The Ancient Couple on Lu Mountain. Mark Van Doren. VGW
Into the quiet of this room. The Room. William Soutar. EBEV
Into the Sky. Sallie Chesham. AATT
Into the spacious bay the sun of the afternoon. Players. Josephine Miles. RiTi
Into the topaz the crystalline signals. Towards a City That Sings. June Jordan. NYP

Into the ward of the whitewashed walls. Somebody's Darling. Marie Ravenel de la Coste. UnPo (1976 ed.)

Into the Woods My Master Went, *with music.* Sidney Lanier. AH; BLSH
   (Ballad of Trees and the Master, A). NOBA; PIM

Into Their True Gentleness. Pearse Hutchinson. CIP

Into these loves, who but for passion lookes. To the Reader of These Sonnets. Michael Drayton. Idea, *introd.* AAS; ESo

Into thir inmost bower. Milton. *Fr.* Paradise Lost, IV. FF

Into your arms I came. To the Anxious Mother. Valente Malangatana, *tr. by* Dorothy Guedes *and* Philippa Rumsey. BBGO

Into Your Hands. Ann Marie Huck. FoP

Intoxicated Rat, The. *Unknown.* FSW

Intramural Aestivation, or Summer in Town, by a Teacher of Latin. Oliver Wendell Holmes. *See* Aestivation.

Introduction, The: "Did I, my lines intend for publick view." Countess of Winchilsea. SBG

Introduction: "Hear the voice of the bard!" Blake. *See* Hear the Voice of the Bard.

Introduction: "I bespeak words." Clere Parsons. FaBoTw (1975 ed.)

Introduction: "Oh, such silliness!" William Cole. OSF

Introduction: "Piping down the valleys wild." Blake. *See* Piping Down the Valleys Wild.

Introduction: "Romance, who loves to nod and sing." Poe. NOBA
   (Romance.) ILP (1975 ed.)

Introduction: "Should you ask me, whence these stories?" Longfellow. *Fr.* The Song of Hiawatha. NOBA; PiAm

Introductory: "That towering place, gabled and huge." *Unknown, tr. fr. Anglo-Saxon by* Burton Raffel. *Fr.* Beowulf. OBP

Introit. Paul Murray. IPM

Introspection. Roger McDonald. FPA

Introspection. Chris Wallace-Crabbe. GAS

Intruder. Susan Feldman. AmPA

Intruder, The. Carolyn Kizer. BoWoP; GP; RiTi

Intruder, The. Marya Zaturenska. OLR

Intry, mintry, cutry corn. Mother Goose. ECBV

Inundation, The. Howard Sergeant. EAS

Invader. Shirley G. Cochrane. PoUp

Invaders, The. John Haines. TAT

Invaders, The. A. D. Hope. CAAP

Invaders, The. Yvor Winters. PiAm

Invariably when wine redeems the sight. The Wine Menagerie. Hart Crane. NoAM; NOBA; VGW

Invasion Exercise on the Poultry Farm. John Betjeman. NOBL

Invasion from Dutchland is all the discourse, An. All Shams. *Unknown.* APAS

Invasion North. Richard Hugo. GP

Invasion of America, The. Celino *and* Steff. EC

Invasion on the Farm. R. S. Thomas. POL

Invective against Ibis, *sel.* Ovid, *tr. fr. Latin by* Thomas Underdowne.
   "While Thracians shal with arrowes war, Iazyges with bowe." OBVE

Inventing a Family. Dennis Saleh. *Fr.* A Guide to Familiar American Incest. NeAC

Inventing a story with grass. A Birth. James Dickey. NOBA

Invention of Astronomy, The. William Matthews. POL

Invention of Comics, The. Amiri Baraka. AmNP (1974 ed.); CAPP; PBMP; PoBA

Invention of Cuisine, The. Carol Muske. PCho

Invention of New Jersey, The. Jack Anderson. InPS; TAT

Invention of the Gun, The. John Batki. AcAn

Invention of the Telephone, The. Peter Klappert. AmPA

Invention of Zero, The. Constance Urdang. VWA

Invention sleeps within a skull. Death Piece. Theodore Roethke. STS

Inventions. Samuel Butler. NIL

Inventory/ Itinerary. Ken Smith. TwMBP

Inventory of the Furniture of a Collegian's Chamber, An. John Winstanley. OBSV

Inverbeg. J. F. Hendry. MS

Inversely, as the Square of Their Distances Apart. Kenneth Rexroth. TSWA

Inversnaid. Gerard Manley Hopkins. CABA (1972 ed.); CMoP (1970 ed.); InPK; NoAM; OAEL-2; UnPo (1976 ed.)

Inverted exclamation point. The Heart Mountain Japanese Relocation Camp: 30 Years Later. Charles Levendosky. TAT

Investigation. Julia Vinograd. IHMS

Investiture, The. Siegfried Sassoon. NoAM

Investment, The. Robert Frost. CMoP (1970 ed.)

Investment. Norman Nathan. MiP

Invictus. W. E. Henley. FaPo; FaPoR; HoPM (1975 ed.); ILP (1975 ed.); PCOP; PPM
   ("Out of the night that covers me.") NOBE; VLP

Invisible hand, An. Sierra. Alfonsina Storni, *tr. by* Rachel Benson. PBWP

Invisible, indivisible spirit. Hilda Doolittle ("H. D."). *Fr.* Tribute to the Angels. BoWoP

Invisible King, The. Goethe. *See* Erl-King, The.

Invisible Man, The. T. S. Matthews. POL

Invisible Playmate, The. Margaret Widdemer. CTV

Invisible Tree. Ryuichi Tamura, *tr. fr. Japanese by* Thomas Fitzsimmons. TSWA

Invisible Woman, The. Robin Morgan. IHMS; NMM

Invitation, The. Robert Herrick. CaPo

Invitation. *Malay Oral Tradition, tr. by* R. J. Wilkinson *and* R. O. Winstedt. WTO

Invitation, The. Goronwy Owen, *tr. fr. Welsh by* George Borrow. OBW

Invitation, The. Nathaniel Wanley. BoReV

Invitation in It, The. Kay Boyle. *Fr.* American Citizen. RiTi

Invitation of the Mirrors. Tom McKeown. AMV-81

Invitation Standing. Paul Blackburn. IPWM; VGW

Invitation to a Spirit. *Malay Oral Tradition, tr. by* W. W. Skeat. WTO

Invitation to Dalliance. *Unknown.* FaBoEE

Invitation to Hsiao Ch'u-shih. Po Chü-i, *tr. fr. Chinese by* Arthur Waley. OBVE

Invitation to Juno. William Empson. CMoP (1970 ed.)

Invitation to Lubberland, An. *Unknown.* FaBoNo; GBP

Invitation to Madison County, An. Jay Wright. PoBA

Invitation to the Bee. Charlotte Smith. OxBChV

Invitation (To the Night and All Other Things Dark). Ronda Davis. JB

Invitation to the Voyage. Baudelaire, *tr. fr. French by* Richard Wilbur. NAWM-2

Invitation to the Zoological Gardens, An. *Unknown.* BoAnP

Invite to Eternity, An. John Clare. OAEL-2

Inviting a Friend to Supper. Ben Jonson, *after the Latin of* Martial. BiP; ILP (1975 ed.); NIL; NOBE; OAEL-1; PPP; TVS

Invocation: "American muse, whose strong and diverse heart." Stephen Vincent Benét. *Fr.* John Brown's Body. BTTM

Invocation: "As pools beneath stone arches take." John Drinkwater. PoA

Invocation: "Come from thy palace, beauteous Queen of Greece." Thomas Randolph. Moon

Invocation: "Dolphin plunge, fountain play." Louis MacNeice. SO

Invocation: "Land earth-root." Nakasuk, *tr. fr. Eskimo.* WTO

Invocation: "Let me be buried in the rain." Helene Johnson. AmNP (1974 ed.)

Invocation: "Of mans first disobedience, and the fruit." Milton. *Fr.* Paradise Lost, I. OBP
("Of man's first disobedience, and the fruit.") EBEV; LFH; NIL; OAEL–2; PAIC; PoIA

Invocation: "Radiant Muse." James McAuley. GAS

Invocation: "Silent, about-to-be-parted-from house." Denise Levertov. PoA

Invocation: "Senator Smoot (Republican, Ut.)." Ogden Nash. OBAL

Invocation: "Ten bloody years with this quill lying." Valentin Iremonger. BIrV

Invocation: "Unwinding the spool of the morning." Vassar Miller. NCSH

Invocation before the Rice Harvest. *Malay Oral Tradition, tr. by* R. O. Winstedt. WTO

Invocation for a Storm. *Tr. fr. Hawaiian.* WTO

Invocation from a Lawn Chair. Mary Jane Irion. AMV–80

Invocation, or the Eternal Father and Mother. Eliza R. Snow. WPW

Invocation to Kali, The, *sels.* May Sarton. RiTi
"It is time for the invocation."
Kingdom of Kali, The.
"There are times when."

Invocation to Sappho. Elsa Gidlow. IHMS

Invocation to the Goddess, An. David Wright. NoAM

Invocation to the Wind. Joseph Kalar. SPT

Invoice, The. Robert Creeley. VGW

Involuntary flex. Jeanetta Jones. MIT

Inward Conversation. Baudelaire, *tr. fr. French by* Robert Bly. InPK

Inward Morning, The. Henry David Thoreau. AmVN; PiAm

Io Baccho! William Carlos Williams. TT

Io dwelt within the breathing-space of immensity. Chant to Io. Tiwai Paraone, *tr. by* A. Alpers. WTO

Iolanthe, *sel.* W. S. Gilbert.
Nightmare. NOBL; PBMP
(Chancellor's Nightmare, The.) FaBoNo

Iowa. Michael Dennis Browne. ANTL

Iowa. Harry Stessel. AAN

Iowa, June. Michael Dennis Browne. AmPA

Ipecacuanha. George Canning. FaBoNo

Iphigeneia in Aulis, *sel.* Euripides, *tr. fr. Greek by* Hilda Doolittle ("H. D.").
"And Pergamos,/ city of the Phrygians." OBVE

Ipomadon, *sel. Unknown.*
Ipomadon Plays the Fool at Court. OxBM

IpsofactopaperAnswerallquesti. Headrock. Brian Coffey. CIP

Iram indeed is gone with all his rose. Omar Khayyám, *tr. by* Edward Fitzgerald. *Fr.* The Rubáiyát. OBVE

Irapuato. Earle Birney. MPA; NIL

Ireland. John Hewitt. CIP

Ireland. Richard Ryan. CIP

Ireland, Ireland. Sir Henry Newbolt. FaPoR

Ireland Lake. Robert Hershon. NeAC

Ireland Never Was Contented. Walter Savage Landor. FaBoCo; FaBoEE

Ireland with Emily. John Betjeman. OxBTC

Iris. William Carlos Williams. InPS; WeW

Irish. Paul Celan, *tr. fr. German by* Michael Hamburger. OBVE

Irish Airman Foresees His Death, An. W. B. Yeats. CABA (1972 ed.); Epi; HeIP; HoPM (1975 ed.); ILP (1975 ed.); NoAM; NOBE; PPP; SoS; WeW

Irish-American Dignitary. Austin Clarke. BIrV; PFIr

Irish Antiquities. Thomas Moore. FaBoEE

Irish Cliffs of Moher, The. Wallace Stevens. NOBA; VGW

Irish Curse on the Occupying English. *Unknown, tr. fr. Modern Irish by* Máire MacEntee. PFIr

Irish Dancer, The. *Unknown. See* I Am of Ireland.

Irish have the thickest ankles in the world, The. John Berryman. *Fr.* Dream Songs. TAP

Irish lady can say, that to-day is every day, The. Cézanne. Gertrude Stein. TAP

Irish Lake, An. W. R. Rodgers. BIrV

Irish Language, The. James Clarence Mangan, *after the Irish of* Philip Fitzgibbon. VLP

Irish Marriage Night, An. Brian Merriman, *tr. fr. Modern Irish by* Frank O'Connor. *Fr.* The Midnight Court. BIrV

Irish nightegale, The. Serenades. Seamus Heaney. HeHu

Irish Poetry. Michael Longley. CIP

Irish Satire, An. *Unknown.* OxBM

Irish Wind, An. Zelma S. Dennis. AMV–80

Irish Wolf-Hound, The. Denis Florence McCarthy. GDP

Irishman in Coventry, An. John Hewitt. BIrV; CIP

Iron. Walter de la Mare. NOBL

Iron flower of the prophet's angry message, The. The Word. Gustave Kahn, *tr. by* Edouard Roditi. VWA

Iron Heaven. Betti Alver, *tr. fr. Estonian by* Willis Barnstone *and* Felix Oinas. BoWoP

Iron horse draweth nigh, with its smoke nostrils high, The. The Utah Iron Horse. *Unknown.* AmFP

Iron Lung, The. Stanley Plumly. AmPA

Iron queen of uncreations. The Gardens of Proserpine. Turner Cassity. PoA

Iron, sulphur, steam: the wastes. Saratoga Ending. Weldon Kees. AnMo

Irondale. Stephen Stepanchev. SA

Ironical Encomium, An. *Unknown.* APAS

Irony of personal loss, The. Poem in the Mirror. Norman Kreitman. PMW

Irresponsive silence of the land, The. Aloof. Christina Rossetti. *Fr.* The Thread of Life. NOBE; UsP

Irritable Song. Russell Atkins. AmNP (1974 ed.)

Irving. James Russell Lowell. *Fr.* A Fable for Critics. TAP

Is. Patrick Kavanagh. FaBoTw (1975 ed.)

Is/ red beans. Energy. Victor Hernandez Cruz. PoBA; SA

Is a caterpillar ticklish? Only My Opinion. Monica Shannon. CTV

Is a monstrance. The Moon Is the Number 18. Charles Olson. CMoP (1970 ed.); UsP

Is a son born into this world of woe? Charles Churchill. *Fr.* The Times. OBSV

Is an enchanted thing. The Mind Is an Enchanting Thing. Marianne Moore. CMoP (1970 ed.); PiAm; PPP

"Is anybody there?" said the Traveller. *See* "Is there anybody there?"...

Is anything central? The One Thing That Can Save America. John Ashbery. NOBA

I's born in Louisiana. Nothing in Rambling. *Unknown.* BluL

Is Charles Simic afraid of death? Further Adventures of Charles Simic. Charles Simic. FoP

Is chasing its tail again. Bobbie's Cat. Gerald Locklin. GP

Is death her wedding dress? Gift. Eve Shelnutt. TC

Is drunken,/ Drunken, drunken. A Drunkard. *Unknown.* OxBM

Is Easter just a day of hats.   Easter Morning.   David McCord.
   CC

Is 5, *sel.*   E. E. Cummings.
   My Sweet Old Etcetera, III.   AnMo; CABA (1972 ed.); CMoP
   (1970 ed.); FF; HeIP; InPS; OBAL; PPP; SoS; STS

Is Football Playing?   A. E. Housman.   *Fr.* Is My Team
   Ploughing?   SPo

I's gonna shine.   *Unknown.*   WTO

Is Is Like Is.   Adrien Stoutenburg.   TSWA

Is it a dream, or not?   During my fever.   The Blue Gift.   David
   Perkins.   NCSH

Is it a Martian creature.   Martian.   Eve Merriam.   CaYB

Is It a Month.   J. M. Synge.   BIrV; PFIr

Is it a reed that's shaken by the wind.   Calais, August, 1802.
   Wordsworth.   MBPR

Is it a sudden thing.   Pause.   Dorothy Livesay.   AMV–81

Is it any better in Heaven, my friend Ford.   To Ford Madox Ford
   in Heaven.   William Carlos Williams.   NoAM; NOBA

Is it as plainly in our living shown.   On Seeing Weather-beaten
   Trees.   Adelaide Crapsey.   SoSe (1977 ed.)

Is it enough?   I'm Here.   Theodore Roethke.   *Fr.* Meditations of
   an Old Woman.   Epi

Is It Far to Go?   C. Day Lewis.   AIW; BBGO

Is it for fear to wet a widow's eye.   Sonnets, IX.   Shakespeare.
   STS

Is it her nature or is it her will.   Amoretti, XLI.   Spenser.   ILP
   (1975 ed.)

Is it illusion? or does there a spirit from perfecter ages.   Arthur
   Hugh Clough.   *Fr.* Amours de Voyage.   EBEV

Is it just like picking a lock.   The Bomb Disposal.   Ciaran
   Carson.   CIP

Is it no dream that I am he.   Walter Savage Landor.   GBL

Is it not better at an early hour.   On Living Too Long.   Walter
   Savage Landor.   PAIC

Is it not fine to fling against loaded dice.   Hughie at the Inn.
   Elinor Wylie.   WPE

Is it possible [*or* Ys yt possyble].   Sir Thomas Wyatt.   AAS; GBL

Is it the wind of the dawn that I hear.   Duet.   Tennyson.   *Fr.*
   Becket.   GBL

Is it time now to go away?   Death of a Vermont Farm Woman.
   Barbara Howes.   CoPAm

Is it true that black birds infinitely dispersed.   To Krishna
   Haunting the Hills.   Andal, *tr. by* Willis Barnstone.   BoWoP

Is it true that you live where there is sorrow, O giver of life?
   *Unknown, tr. fr. Nahuatl.*   ILwL

Is it true, ye gods, who treat us.   Arthur Hugh Clough.   VLP;
   VPC

Is it Ulysses that approaches from the east.   The World as
   Meditation.   Wallace Stevens.   CABA (1972 ed.); HeIP;
   IPWM; NIL; PiAm; PPP

Is it you?   Are you there.   Poem Wondering If I'm Pregnant.
   Kathleen Fraser.   IHMS; NMM

Is it you, that preach'd in the chapel there.   Despair.   Tennyson.
   VLP

Is Juno of the ribbons in gelatin.   The Medusa.   Guy Davenport.
   GP

Is Life Worth Living?   Alfred Austin.   FaPoR

Is like a dull dream.   From time to time.   Summer in Fairbanks.
   Leon Stokesbury.   NVAP

Is love the clang.   Ending an Affair.   Paul David Ashley.
   DNGG

Is my favorite vegetable.   Broccoli.   Tom Schmidt.   GP

Is my favourite.   Who flies.   Owl.   George MacBeth.   MPo

Is My Lover on the Sea?   "Barry Cornwall."   RhH

Is My Team Ploughing?   A. E. Housman.   CMoP (1970 ed.); ILP
   (1975 ed.); LiSp; NoAM; PAIC; SoSe; SS; STS; VLP
   Is Football Playing? *sel.*   SPo

Is poetry always worthy when it's old.   Kalidasa, *tr. fr. Sanskrit by*
   John Brough.   BuTh

Is premature as a dead white cat.   Black in Virginia.   Grace
   Cavalieri.   AATT

Is something like the rest.   The Politics of Rich Painters.   Amiri
   Baraka.   VGW

Is tell you my mind, Annes Tayliur: Dame.   At the Tavern.
   *Unknown.*   OxBM

Is that dance slowing in the mind of man.   Four for Sir John
   Davies.   Theodore Roethke.   NIL; NoAM; NOBA; PiAm

Is that jazz is dead.   Something Else They Say.   Mbembe.   NW

Is that old Father Time.   Scyther.   Liam O'Mahony.   IPM

Is the ball very stupid, *ma mignonne*?   At the Ball!   Charles H.
   Webb.   OBAL

Is the Moon Tired?   Christina Rossetti.   Moon

Is the province of cats.   Living by accident.   Propinquity.
   Alastair Reid.   MS

Is the slide.   Relicts.   Layle Silbert.   NPW

Is the struggle and strife.   Let the Rest of the World Go By.   J.
   Keirn Brennan.   UnPo (1976 ed.)

Is the total black, being spoken.   Coal.   Audre Lorde.   CNA;
   UsP

Is the woman next door.   Love Poem.   Michael Delp.   TC

Is then no nook of English ground secure.   Sonnet on the
   Projected Kendal and Windermere Railway.   Wordsworth.
   MBPR; VLP

Is there a Baltimore fan alive.   Tom Matte.   Ogden Nash.   SPo

Is there a great green commonwealth of Thought.   Sonnet.   John
   Masefield.   ILP (1975 ed.)

Is there any good man here.   A Call for a Song.   *Unknown.*
   OxBM

Is There Any Reward?   Hilaire Belloc.   BuTh

Is there any way I can be sure to remember.   Abiquiu—Thursday
   in Holy Week.   Peggy Pond Church.   WPW

"Is there anybody [*or* Is anybody] there?" said the Traveller.   The
   Listeners.   Walter de la Mare.   CMoP (1970 ed.); HAP;
   HoPM (1975 ed.); ILP (1975 ed.); InPK; NCSH; NoAM;
   NOBE; PoPle; PPoD; SFF; SoSe; SS; UsP; WeW

Is there anything I can do.   The Key to Everything.   May
   Swenson.   IHMS; Psy

Is there anything left on the floor?   Leavetaking.   Lisa Reape.
   AMV–81

Is there, for honest poverty.   For A' That and A' That.   Burns.
   BTTM; CABA (1972 ed.); FaPoR; FSW; ILP (1975 ed.);
   LAuP; OAEL–1; OBP

Is There Life across the Street?   Robert Watson.   GP

Is There No Balm in Christian Lands?   *with music.*   *Unknown.*
   AH

Is There No Love Can Link Us?   Mervyn Peake.   BuTh

Is there still any shadow there, on the rainwet window of the
   coffee pot.   Memo.   Kenneth Fearing.   CMoP (1970 ed.)

Is this a fast, to keep.   To Keep a True Lent [*or* A True Lent].
   Robert Herrick.   BoReV; OFD

Is this a holy thing to see.   Holy Thursday.   Blake.   *Fr.* Songs of
   Experience.   FF; ILP (1975 ed.); InPS; LAuP; MBPR;
   OAEL–2; STS

Is this a time to plant and build.   Eleventh Sunday after Trinity.
   John Keble.   *Fr.* The Christian Year.   VLP

Is this dancing sunlight.   Symphony.   Frank Horne.   AmNP
   (1974 ed.)

Is this God's joke? my father screamed.   Health.   Stewart Parker.
   CiP

Is This Land Your Land?   *Unknown.*   FSW

Is this man turning angel as he stares.   The Messengers.   Thom
   Gunn.   PoA

Is this pain, when my heart.   Gavin Bantock.   *Fr.* Person.
   TwMBP

Is this the gym?. . .Then this must be the wall. Humiliation Revisited. Nova Trimble Ashley. AMV–80

Is this the object. Sestina. Judith Kroll. AmPA

Is this the region, this the soil, the clime. Satan as Rebel-Liberator. Milton. *Fr.* Paradise Lost, I. FF; OBP

Is this the way Attica was. Folsom, August 11th: A Question of Races. Pancho Aguila. CPA

Is thy face like thy mother's, my fair child! Childe Harold's Pilgrimage, III. Byron. MBPR; OAEL–2, *abr.*

"Is water nigh?" The Gift of Water. Hamlin Garland. BPAW

Is without world. The Howling of Wolves. Ted Hughes. OxBTC

Is Wolly's wife now dead and gone? A Jacobite Scot in Satire on England's Unparalleled Loss. *Unknown.* APAS

Is you eye so empty. Signals. Jewel C. Latimore. PoBA

Isaac. Stanley Burnshaw. VWA

Isaac. Amir Gilboa, *tr. fr. Hebrew by* Howard Schwartz. VWA

Isaac. Haim Guri, *tr. fr. Hebrew by* Naomi Tauber *and* Howard Schwartz. VWA

Isaac. Barry Holtz. VWA

Isaac. A. C. Jacobs. VWA

Isaac and Esau. Rose Drachler. VWA

Isaac Babel is riding with bloodthirsty Bolshevik soldiers. Babel. Gary Pacernick. AMV–81

Isaac Leybush Peretz. Moishe Leib Halpern, *tr. fr. Yiddish by* Kathryn Hellerstein. VWA

Isabel met an enormous bear. Adventures of Isabel. Ogden Nash. ECBV; OBAL; OSP; PPM

Isabella; or, The Pot of Basil. Keats. MBPR

Isabella spits at Spain. Bourbons. Walter Savage Landor. OBSV

Isadora, save for the didactic beard. Pounding It Out. Ernest Kroll. PoUp

Isaiah, *sels.* Bible, *O. T.*
  And He Shall Judge among Nations, II:4. PBMP
  "And there shall come forth a rod out of the stemme of Jesse," II:1–11. OBVE
  "Because the daughters of Zion are haughty," III:16–26. OBP
  "Behold, my servant shall deal prudently," LII:13–LIII. NAWM–1
  "Comfort ye, comfort ye my people, sayth your God," XL: 1-8. OBVE
  "Wildernesse and the solitarie place shall be glad for them, The," XXX. OBVE

Iscah. Howard Schwartz. VWA

I'se got a gal in the Sourwood Mountain. Sourwood Mountain. *Unknown.* AmFP

I'se got a little baby, but she's out of sight. Hello! Ma Baby. Joseph E. Howard *and* Ida Emerson. FSN

I'se the b'y that builds the boat. I'se the B'y. *Unknown.* FSW

I'se wild Nigger Bill. Wild Negro Bill. *Unknown.* BPo

Ishmael. Gabriel Levin. VWA

Isidor. Louis Simpson. GP; NNaP

Island, The. Dorothy Aldis. ECBV

Island. Langston Hughes. *Fr.* Lenox Avenue Mural. ILP (1975 ed.)

Island, The. Edwin Muir. OAEL–2

Island, The. Derick Thomson. MS

Island and the Cattle, The. Nicholas Moore. EAS

Island Cemetery, An. W. H. Auden. TT

Island dreams under the dawn, The. The Indian to His Love. W. B. Yeats. PBMP; VLP

Island in the Evening, The. Fairfield Porter. PoA

Island in the Moon, An, *sels.* Blake. FaBoNo
  In Obtuse Angle's Study.
  Quid the Cynic's Song.
  Sipsop's Song.
  Suction's Anthem.

Island is green, The. Spike Island: Convicted Labour. Joan Keefe. IPM

Island Letter. Charles Senior. MIS

Island of Giglio. Harold Norse. GP

Island of the Scots, The, *abr.* William Edmondstoune Aytoun. VLP

Island Quarry. Hart Crane. PPP; PSN

Island Rose. Hamish MacLaren. MS

Island steams under the opening sky, The. Accident at Three Mile Island. Jim Barnes. AMV–81

Island that had flowered to the sun, The. The Coming of Dusk upon a Village in Haiti. Henry Rago. HoPM (1975 ed.)

Island was a word he woke upon, The. Settler. Stewart Lindh. PoA

Island, you mustn't say, had only rocks and scrub pine, The. The Pennacesse Leper Colony for Women. Cape Cod. 1922. Norman Dubie. PCho

Islanders, Inlanders. Michael Mott. PoA

Islandman. Brenda Chamberlain. OBW

Islands, The, *sel.* Charles Brasch.
  "Always, in these islands, meeting and parting," II. ATNZ

Islands, The. Randall Jarrell. EAS

Islands. Muriel Rukeyser. GP

Islands for Seurat. Kraft Rompf. AAN

Islands move inward. The Name of Our Country. Dennis Schmitz. AmPA

Islands Where I Was Born, The. Gloria Rawlinson. ATNZ

Isle of Man, The. *Unknown.* GBP

Isle of Man Shore, The. *Unknown.* AmFP

Isles of Greece, The. Byron. *Fr.* Don Juan, III. BTTM; FaPoR; NOBE

"Isn't the violet a dear little flower? And the daisy, too." The Lay Preacher Ponders. Idris Davies. OxBTC

Isolation Cell Poem. J. Charles Green. DNGG

Isolation: To Marguerite. Matthew Arnold. Switzerland, IV. VLP

Isolation Ward. Robert L. Koenig. AMV–81

Israel. Karl Shapiro. MPA

Israeli Navy, The. Marvin Bell. VWA

Israeli Soldier's Nightmare, An. Alison B. Carb. AMV–80

Israfel. Poe. AmVN; NOBA; PiAm; TAP

Issue of great Jove, draw near you Muses nine, The. The Garden. Nicholas Grimald. OAEL–1

"Issues from the hand of God, the simple soul." Animula. T. S. Eliot. STS

It/ it is here. Ian Hamilton Finlay. UsP

It ain't gonna rain no more, no more. *Unknown.* DuDr

It Ain't Neccessarily So. Ira Gershwin. OBAL

It ain't such a terrible long time ago. Barriers Burned. Charles K. Field. BPAW

It ain't the failures he may meet. The Quitter. *Unknown.* PPM

It all began. Loss. Alex Kuo. NW

It all began so easy. Christina. Louis MacNeice. BoLoP

It All Comes Together outside the Restroom in Hogansville. James Seay. CSP

It all ends in the silence of a second. Barbara's Poem. Jacquelyn Bowman. PoUp

It all fails now. Anderson, Indiana. James L. White. HeS

It all happened so fast. Fenya was in the straight chair. Pastoral. Norman Dubie. AmPA

It appears to be the pampas. The Man in the Dream Is Death. Lynne Butler. IHMS

It baffles the foreigner like an idiom. Drug Store. Karl Shapiro. CMoP (1970 ed.); ILP (1975 ed.); TCP

It beats me. The way. Old People. Myra Cohn Livingston. CTBA

It begins again, the nocturnal pulse. The Assassination. Donald Justice. CSP

It begins to trickle. Darkness Comes to the Woods. Norbert Krapf. HeS

It being lost. The Centapod. Henry Kanabus. FiCh

It bends far over Yell'ham Plain. The Comet at Yell'ham. Thomas Hardy. CMoP (1970 ed.); ExPo (1973 ed.); GBL; VLP

It billows in a gust of wind. The Homes. Anne Pitkin. AMV-80

It blew in on the telephone. Private Hurricane. Elizabeth Bartlett. CPA

It burns in the void. The World. Kathleen Raine. OxBTC

It burns its years into us. The Quiet Sun. James Beall. PoUp

It bursts and holds. Roman Candle. Neil Weiss. LoAs

It came/ Out of the blackness of the spaces between galaxies. The Second Coming. Carl Clark. JB

It came sniffing and nibbling about on the rock terrace. Of a Mouse and Men. A. J. Hovde. AMV-81

It Came upon the [or a] Midnight Clear, with music. Edmund Hamilton Sears. AH; BLSH
(Angels' Song, The.) FaPo

It cannot be/ reasoned with. Julius Lester. Fr. In the Time of Revolution. PoBA

It cannot come. Balboa, the Entertainer. Amiri Baraka. NoAM

It can't be a pocket. The District: Both Sides of Chandler River. Ted Enslin. FAF

It can't happen to me. Age? H. R. Hays. POL

It chanced that Cupid on a season. From the French. Sir Walter Scott. SLP

It comes about that the drifting of these curtains. The Curtains in the House of the Metaphysician. Wallace Stevens. PoA

It comes back. Deceased. Cid Corman. VGW

It comes to this, in plain words. Victory. Eileen Duggan. ATNZ

It consisted of 8 to 10 pages of short essays. Her Application to Elysium. Kathleen Norris. IHMS

It could be Louisiana, attracting rain. Pine Barrens: Letter Home. Cleopatra Mathis. TAT

It could only be seen/ when he closed his eyes. Hebrew Script. Tali Loewenthal. VWA

It Couldn't Be Done. Edgar A. Guest. PPM

It curls in the closet. The Divorce Dress. Jeanne Finley. AMV-80

It curved below the house. Route 29. Catharine Savage Brosman. AMV-81

It dances. The Newborn Colt. Mary Kennedy. PH

It Did Not Last. J. C. Squire. InPK
("It did not last: the Devil howling Ho.") FaBoCo; FaBoEE; QQQ

It does, it does, I have seen it. America Bleeds. Angelo Lewis. PoBA

It does not happen. That love, removes. Audubon, Drafted. Amiri Baraka. PPP

It does not matter. Moonshot. Robert Kelly. Moon

It doesn't exist—the tower where Emily lives. Getting to Emily's. Bernice Ames. PoW

It doesn't look like a finger it looks like a feather of broken glass. Poem. Hugh Sykes Davies. EAS

It doesn't matter. A Fine Excess. Dan Gerber. FoP

It dropped so low—in my regard. Emily Dickinson. CABA (1972 ed.); CMoP (1970 ed.); HAP; InPK; PBMP

It embarrasses. Personal Poem. Ingrid Wendt. NMM

It ended, and the morrow brought the task. Modern Love, II. George Meredith. ILP (1975 ed.); PAIC

It feels good as it is without the giant. Wallace Stevens. Fr. Notes toward a Supreme Fiction. NOBA

It feels so good. One Morning. Ellen Levine. AMV-81

It fell about the Lammas tide. The Battle of Otterbourne. Unknown. BTTM

It fell about the Martinmas. Edom o Gordon [or Captain Car]. Unknown. FaBoBa; PeBB

It fell about the Martinmas time. Get Up and Bar the Door. Unknown. AIW; BiP; DuDr; FaBoBa; HeIP; PBMP; PoTa

It fell about the Martinmas tyde. Jamie Telfer of the Fair Dodhead. Unknown. PeBB

It fell in the ancient periods. Uriel. Emerson. AmVN; NOBA; PiAm

It Fell on a Summer's Day. Thomas Campion. HAP; WeW

It fell upon a holy eve. August. Spenser. Fr. The Shepheardes Calender. PAIC

If fell upon a Wodensday. Brown Robyn's Confession. Unknown. GBP; PeBB

It flows through old hushed Egypt and its sands. The Nile. Leigh Hunt. EBEV; NOBE; PPM

It fortifies my soul to know. Arthur Hugh Clough. VLP

It fortuned (as faire it then befell). Spenser. Fr. The Faerie Queene, I, 11. OAEL-1

It gleamed above our Old Brigade. The Battle-Flag. Mary Evelyn Moore Davis. BPAW

It grows cold in the forest. Choosing a Stone. John Haines. CNW

It had been a good evening. The Lovers. Karen Swenson. WBN

It hangs from heaven to earth. Tapestry. Charles Simic. NVAP

It happended/ in a second. Where Is Justice? Eliezer Steinbarg, tr. by Seth L. Wolitz. VWA

It happened in Jacksboro in the year of 'seventy-three. The Buffalo Skinners. Unknown. AmFP

It happened, it happened all on a Saturday night. Johnny Dyers. Unknown. AmFP

It happended not far away. Clonfeacle. Paul Muldoon. CIP; IPM

It happended so fast. Death Comes to the Salesman. Louis Daniel Brodsky. AMV-81

It happens/ even in my own house. After Your Death. David James. AMV-80

It happens in one of the usual ways. Flight. Stuart Dybek. TC

It happens lonely—no one. The Moment. William Stafford. NNaP

It happens through the blond window, the trees. Ascension. Denis Devlin. BIrV

It has a name. Sleep. Greg Kuzma. NVAP

It has all/ come back today. From Gloucester Out. Edward Dorn. NoAM; NOBA

It has all to be experienced. Between Appointments. Giles Gordon. SLP

It has been/ a long flight. The Pilot. Lewis Turco. CoPAm

It has been many years. Biographical Note. Gabriel Preil, tr. by Howard Schwartz. VWA

It has been well said that quietness. A Dog's Best Friend Is His Illiteracy. Ogden Nash. BoAnP

It has certainty, like the fall of a stone. On the Death of Parents. Alfred Barson. AMV-80

It has happened suddenly. Je Suis une Table. Donald Hall. EAS

It has its place: the extreme right. Nazi Headquarters: El Monte, California. William Burns. PoW

It has no wings. Loneliness and July Ninth. Claribel Alegria, *tr. by* Aliki *and* Willis Barnstone. BoWoP

It has to be the end of the day. Surf-Casting. W. S. Merwin. NOBA

It has turned to snow in the night. The Horses. Maxine W. Kumin. DuDa

It hath been said of old that plays are feasts. To the Reader of Master William Davenant's Play, The Wits. Thomas Carew. CaPo

It holds us, gently. Air. Pamela Alexander. AAN

It Is a Beauteous Evening, Calm and Free. Wordsworth. AnMo; CABA (1972 ed.); Epi; HeIP; ILP (1975 ed.); IPWM; MBPR; OAEL-2; PPP; RRA; WIF

It is a beauteous morning but the air turns sick. Tornado Warning. Karl Shapiro. MPA

It is a beauteous morning, calm and free. Country Club Sunday. Phyllis McGinley. WIF

It is a cave of red stone. The Cave Where Night Sleeps. T. Alan Broughton. FAF

It is a clearing deep in a forest: overhanging boughs. Johnson's Cabinet Watched by Ants. Robert Bly. NoAM; NOBA

It is a cold and snowy night. The main street is deserted. Driving to Town Late to Mail a Letter. Robert Bly. InPK; SFF; TSWA; UsP; VGW

It is a cramped little state with no foreign policy. Shame. Richard Wilbur. ConAP; PPoD; UsP

It is a delusion. Solitary Confinement. Phyllis Webb. *Fr.* The Kropotkin Poems. MMD

It is a God-damned lie to say that these. Another Epitaph on an Army of Mercenaries. "Hugh MacDiarmid." NoAM

It is a good plan, and began with childhood. Monologue of a Deaf Man. David Wright. NoAM; NowV

It is a human universe: and I. Sonnet. Ted Berrigan. Epi

It is a lie—their priests, their pope. The Confessional. Robert Browning. OBP

It is a lost road into the air. An Airstrip in Essex, 1960. Donald Hall. InPS

It is a luxury at my age. Young Widow. Patricia Beer. HeHu

It is a milky morning in San Francisco. Another Given: The Last Day of the Year. William Dickey. AMV-80

It is a new America. Brown River, Smile. Jean Toomer. PoBA

It is a normal day. Poem Found Emptying Out My Pockets. Al Young. CoPAm

It is a Pilgrim village; heavy rain is falling. Pilgram Fish Heads. Robert Bly. UsP

It is a privilege to see so much confusion. Copenhagen. Art Lange. FiCh

It is a summer evening. Lullaby. Anne Sexton. NoAM

It is a thought breaking the granite heart. On the Death of Her Body. James K. Baxter. ATNZ

It is a tide pool, shallow. Looking into a Tide Pool. Robert Bly. MAT

It is a time of hunger. Personal Song. Arnatkoak, *tr. fr. Eskimo.* WTO

It is a universal network. High Tension Wires. Allan Block. FAF

It is a very curious fact. Lines for a Worthy Person Who Has Drifted by Accident into a Chelsea Revel. A. P. Herbert. NOBL

It is a water hand, this right one. Look to the Back of the Hand. Judith Minty. PoA

It is a willow when summer is over. Willow Poem. William Carlos Williams. NCSH

It is a winter's tale. A Winter's Tale. Dylan Thomas. CMoP (1970 ed.)

It is a wonder foam is so beautiful. Spray. D. H. Lawrence. EcS

It is a year of good harvest. Harvesting Wheat for the Public Share. Li Chü, *tr. by* Kenneth Rexroth *and* Ling Chung. BoWoP; PBWP

It is again time when sleek and glossy starlings. Starlings and History. Charles Doyle. ATNZ

It is all a rhythm. The Rhythm. Robert Creeley. UsP

It is all here. The Shad-Blow Tree. Louise Glück. NVAP

It is all right. All they do. To the Muse. James Wright. NNaP

It is almost dark. Crossing the Colorado River into Yuma. Simon J. Ortiz. TAT

It Is Almost the Year Two Thousand. Robert Frost. TH

It is always a temptation to an armed and agile nation. Dane-Geld. Kipling. OxBTC

It is always handled. George MacBeth. *Fr.* A Riddle. TSWA

It is always morning. The fields of Europe begin to dissolve. Gerard de Nerval. Thomas Brush. NVAP

It is always someone else. Destiny of the Poet. Claude Vigée, *tr. by* Anthony Rudolf. VWA

It is an ancestral castle. Life in the Castle. Anne Hébert, *tr. by* Aliki *and* Willis Barnstone. BoWoP

It is an ancient custom. An Ancient Custom. Anatoly Steiger, *tr. by* John Glad. VWA

It is an ancient Mariner. The Rime of the Ancient Mariner. Samuel Taylor Coleridge. CABA (1972 ed.); EBEV; Epi; HAP; HoPM (1975 ed.); ILP (1975 ed.); InPS; MBPR; NOBE; OAEL-2; PPoD; RhR

It is an honorable thought. Emily Dickinson. TT

It is an old stove. Stove. Ken Belford. NeAC

It Is an Outfielder. Ron Loewinsohn. VoA

It is as though someone were peeling away. A View of the Earth from Space. Ron Weber. PoUp

It is August. Drinking while Driving. Raymond Carver. NVAP

It is Beautiful, It is Rain. Mark Wangberg. TC

It is because the sea is blue. The Great Wave: Hokusai. Donald Finkel. WIF

It is best to turn on the set. Violence on Television. Louis Jenkins. NU

It is better this year. If the Birds Knew. John Ashbery. PoA

"It Is Big inside a Man." Kenneth Patchen. VoA

It is blue-butterfly day here in spring. Blue-Butterfly Day. Robert Frost. RFM

It is cold here. The Moths. W. S. Merwin. HeIP

It is colder now. Epistle to Be Left in the Earth. Archibald MacLeish. CMoP (1970 ed.); NOBA; PAIC

It is common knowledge to every schoolboy. Portrait of the Artist as a Prematurely Old Man. Ogden Nash. PoIA; SoSe

It is cool and damp here. Falls. Mary Walker. PoUp

It is dangerous for a woman to defy the gods. Letter to My Sister. Anne Spencer. AmNP (1974 ed.); PoBA

It Is Dangerous to Read Newspapers. Margaret Atwood. HeIP; Psy

It is dangerous to visit you in your woods in May. Reunion. Heather Cadsby. AMV-81

It is dark now. Route 40—Ohio, U.S.A. Milton Kessler. CoPAm

It is day's end; I am thinking of weight. At Night. Robley Wilson, Jr. HeS

It is December in Wicklow. Exposure. Seamus Heaney. CIP

It Is Deep. Carolyn M. Rodgers. SA

It is deep summer. Far out. There. Robert Mezey. TSWA

It Is Difficult Now to Speak of Poetry. George Oppen. *Fr.* Of Being Numerous. MIT; NNaP

It is down/ makes/ up seem/ taller. Of Consolation. Luci Shaw. AATT

It is dusk on the Lost Lagoon. The Lost Lagoon. Pauline Johnson. BPAW

It is early dawn. The city forty miles away draws airplanes. Written Forty Miles South of a Spreading City. Robert Bly. NNaP

It is early, yet. The Grand Canyon. James Merrill. TAP

It is easier to forgive an enemy than to forgive a friend. Blake. *Fr.* Jerusalem. OAEL-2

It is easy enough to love flowers but these. Giant Decorative Dahlias. Molly Holden. OxBTC; PSN

It is easy to be young. How to Be Old. May Swenson. MAT; UnPo (1976 ed.)

It is easy to disturb. As Sun, as Sea. James Sullivan. AMV-81

It is eating me. A Fly on the Water. Paul Zweig. PCho

It is enough for me. Old Man Told Me. Lance Henson. VoR

It is equal to living in a tragic land. Dry Loaf. Wallace Stevens. NOBA

It is essential I remember. Man White, Brown Girl and All That Jazz. Gloria C. Oden. PoBA

It is evening. One bat dances. A Soul. Randall Jarrell. CMoP (1970 ed.)

It is far to Assisi. The Mental Hospital Garden. William Carlos Williams. PiAm

It is finished. The enormous dust-cloud over Europe. Armistice. Paul Dehn. OxBTC

It is fitting that you be here. On Seeing Two Brown Boys in a Catholic Church. Frank Horne. PoBA

It is 5 A.M. everything is the same as it was. Some Lines after the Razing of the Sioux City Armour's Plant. David Allan Evans. HeS

It is from the lips. Sonsito. Victor Hernandez Cruz. MIT

It is fun to ride the horse. Horse. Kenneth Rexroth. *Fr.* A Bestiary. NNaP

It Is Good to Know You. Jim Farrar. DNGG

It is hard, alone is this room at night to remember. The Eagle. Richard Blessing. AMV-80

It is hard going to the door. The Door. Robert Creeley. NoAM; VGW

It is hard not feeling you inside me. Father. Sid Gershgoren. BrS

It is hard to be a man. The Falcon Woman. Robert Graves. BuTh; LoAs

It is hard to beat a good meal. Thomas Kinsella. *Fr.* A Technical Supplement. CIP

It Is Hard to Catch Trout. Piuvkaq, *tr. fr. Eskimo.* WTO

It is here the bones. The Wing Factory. Dona Stein. AMV-80

It is hunter's magic to perform. Magic. Rex Veeder. HeS

It is I in the cities, in the bars, in the. Vanishing Point: Urban Indian. Wendy Rose. NW

It is important to be approximate. Harvard Graduate Speaking to His Troops. Ed Cox. PoUp

It Is Impossible. Ross Falconer. BuTh

It is impossible to see anything. Inversely, as the Square of Their Distances Apart. Kenneth Rexroth. TSWA

It is in captivity. The Bull. William Carlos Williams. LFH

It is Isis the mystery. Don Juan. D. H. Lawrence. PoA

It is January 12. Chronicle. Edward Dorn. TAT

It is June, it is June. Andraitx—Pomegranate Flowers. D. H. Lawrence. NoAM

It is late and the others have turned. Late. Daniel Halpern. AMV-81

It is late at night and still I am losing. In Divés' Dive. Robert Frost. VGW

It is late at night, cold and damp. GIC to HAR. Kenneth Rexroth. VoA

It is late in the year. Night in the House by the River. Tu Fu, *tr. by* Kenneth Rexroth. NIL

It is late last night the dog was speaking of you. The Grief of a Girl's Heart. *Unknown, tr. by* Lady Gregory. OLR

It is like the plot of an ol/ novel. Instructions to a Princess. Ishmael Reed. CNA; PoBA

It is little I repair to the matches of the Southron folk. At Lord's. Francis Thompson. LiSp

It is made of finest linen. A Baby's Dress. Hazel Hall. WPW

It is made to be rolled down. A Poem like a Grenade. John Haines. EAS

It is midnight. Poem at Thirty. Sonia Sanchez. BPo; CNA; NMM; PoBA

It is midnite. The room is blue. Death Songs. L. V. Mack. PoBA

It Is Mine, This Country Wide. *Unknown.* GOA

It is Monday morning. The Goldfish Wife. Sandra Hochman. RiTi; UnPo (1976 ed.)

It is moonlight and white where. Because I Never Learned the Names of Flowers. Roderick Jellema. PoUp

It is morning darling look the sun. Aubade: N.Y.C. Robert Wallace. CoPAm; HoPM (1975 ed.)

It is morning, Senlin says, and in the morning. Morning Song. Conrad Aiken. *Fr.* Senlin; a Biography. CMoP (1970 ed.); NoAM; SoSe

It is most true that eyes are formed to serve. Astrophel and Stella, V. Sir Philip Sidney. OAEL-1

It is my joy in life to find. Make Me Worthy of My Friends. *Unknown.* CTV

It is my white horse, just like the dawn. Mi Caballo Blanco (My White Horse). *Tr. fr. Spanish.* FSW

It is myself. To a Dog Injured in the Street. William Carlos Williams. LFH

It Is Na, Jean, Thy Bonie Face. Burns. SLP

It is never enough to know what you want. "The Wish to Be Believed." Mona Van Duyn. PoA

It is new America. Brown River, Smile. Jean Toomer. AmNP (1974 ed.)

It is New Year's Day. Best Loved of Africa. Margaret Danner. PoBA

It is night and it is the ice storm. February I Turn Off The Porch Light and Go Outside. James Tipton. HeS

It is night. You are asleep. And beautiful tears. Sonnet. Ted Berrigan. CAAP

It is noble country where we dwell. Our Country. Henry David Thoreau. GOA

It is not bad. Let them play. The Bloody Sire. Robinson Jeffers. CMoP (1970 ed.); PoA

It Is Not Beauty I Demand. George Darley. OAEL-2

It is not easy to kill fish. In a Curious Way. John Smith. UsP

It is not enough. The Prophet's Warning or Shoot to Kill. Ebon Dooley. PoBA

It is not far to my place. Visit. A. R. Ammons. VoA

It is not growing like a tree. The Noble Nature. Ben Jonson. *Fr.* To the Immortal Memory and Friendship of That Noble Pair, Sir Lucius Cary and Sir Henry Morison. CABA (1972 ed.); HeIP; PCOP; SoSe; VoPo

It is not human to make demands on other people. The Way It Is. Richard Williams. AAN

It is not in the books. The Three Movements. Donald Hall. NowV

It is not love knowledge to thee. Love Charm. *Unknown, tr. fr. Gaelic.* SLP

It is not my voice, it is not my voice that is tearing. Serenade of Angels. Rina Lasnier, *tr. by* Jan Pallister. AMV-81

It is not raining rain to [or for] me. April Rain. Robert Loveman. CTV; PCOP

It is not so much/ Cooking. Outrage. Lucille Iverson. WBN

It is not so much the image of the man. Photograph of Haymaker, 1890. Molly Holden. OxBTC; PSN

It is not sweet content, be sure. Arthur Hugh Clough. VLP

It is not the earth that I worship. Earth Song. Thomas Peacock. VoR

It is not the still weight. The Jungle. William Carlos Williams. CABA (1972 ed.)

It is not the weight of the jewel or plate. The Perfect Gift. Edmund Vance Cooke. PChr

It is not the words we work with, words we examine. The Collector. Robert F. Whisler. AMV-81

It is not to be thought of that the flood. We Must Be Free or Die. Wordsworth. FaPoR; MBPR; NOBE

It is not youth that intrigues me but suppleness. Michael McClure. MIT

It is nothing I understand any better. Homing. P. C. Bowman. AMV-81

It is of a fearless Irishman a story I will tell. Brennan on the Moor. *Unknown.* AmFP

It is of daffodils. Yellow. Dan Gerber. TC

It is only that this warmth and movement are like. The Woman in Sunshine. Wallace Stevens. BiP

It Is Oregon, The Highway Looms. Harold Bond. NVAP

It is our hand. Patience of a People. F. J. Bryant, Jr. CNA

It is out in the flimsy suburbs. Sunday in Glastonbury. Robert Bly. ConAP

It is past midnight in a thick fog when sirens. Street Fire. Daniel Halpern. AmPA; NYP

It is patience and stalks in the wide house of cattle. The Artery. Les A. Murray. *Fr.* Walking to the Cattle-Place. CAAP

It is people at the edge who say. Sayings from the Northern Ice. William Stafford. BCr; NU

It is pleasant enough here. Voice. Claudia Dobkins. NPW

It is portentous, and a thing of state. Abraham Lincoln Walks at Midnight. Vachel Lindsay. CMoP (1970 ed.); GOA; IPWM; NoAM; NOBA; OFD; TAP; VGW

It is quite unfair to be. Elephant. Alan Brownjohn. BBL

It is raining in her room, rain has all. The Lady in the Water Collection Department. Tom McKeown. TC

It is reported. Sharks in Shallow Water. Fred Levinson. AmPA

It is rough. Poem about a Seashell. Ranice Henderson Crosby. NMM

It is said that certain orientational concepts of an ontological sort. Maxim. Josephine Miles. RiTi

It is said they feed at night. The Feeding Cycle of the Catfish. Tom Crawford. NVAP

It is scary the way I am dreaming of flowers. Van Gogh. Lynn Strongin. RiTi

It is snowing, and/ I can no longer be/ responsible. March 26, 1971. John McNally. PoUp

It Is So Long Since My Heart Has Been with Yours. E. E. Cummings. NoAM; TPo

It is so much easier to forget than to have been Mr. Whittier. Mr. Whittier. Winfield Townley Scott. VGW

It is so pure, so complete. Aesthetics of the Moon. Jack Anderson. Moon

It is so quiet among the leaves. With the Woodnymphs. Michael Smith. IPM

It is so still in the house. The Mother's Song. *Tr. fr. Eskimo.* WTO

It is sometime since I have been. The Hill. Robert Creeley. ConAP; NoAM

It is spring in the mountains. Written on the Wall at Chang's Hermitage. Tu Fu, *tr. fr. Chinese by* Kenneth Rexroth. HoPM (1975 ed.)

It is spring once more in the Coast Range. Yin and Yang. Kenneth Rexroth. MIT; MPA

It is springtime and the ants come into the house. Ants. Lewis Hyde. AMV-80

It is still the tallest building in the world. Looking at the Empire State Building. Ralph Pomeroy. GP

"It is such a beautiful day I had to write you a letter." Thoughts of a Young Girl. John Ashbery. ConAP; RRA; TAP; VGW

It is Tet. Night Flare Drop, Tan Son Nhut. Horace Coleman. SES

It is Thanksgiving, 1964. On Hearing of the Death of Bernard Strempek. Robert Huff. CNW

It is that dream world Anaïs speaks of. A Cycle of Women. Sharon Barba. RiTi

It is the best thing. Pregnancy. Sandra McPherson. BoWoP; NMM

It Is the Cause, It Is the Cause, My Soul. Shakespeare. *Fr.* Othello, V, ii. BiP; EBEV

It is the dark of the moon. Doubled Mirrors. Kenneth Rexroth. ExPo (1973 ed.)

It is the effort of the lie. Upon the Intimations of Love's Mortality. Jean Garrigue. LoAs

It is the endless dance of the dead. Dirge. Quincy Troupe. PoBA

It is the evening hour. To Mary: It Is the Evening Hour. John Clare. BoLoP; GBL

It is the first mild day of March. To My Sister [*or* Lines Written at a Small Distance from My House]. Wordsworth. FSFS; LoAs; MBPR; OAEL-2

It is the football season once more. Autumn. Vernon Scannell. HeHu; MPo; OxBTC

It is the gentle poet's art. Iron. Walter de la Mare. NOBL

It is the Greek waiter. Garden Blooms. Nicholas Flocos. SA

It is the Gulf Stream wind's illusion. Indian Summer Here, You in Honolulu. Donald Johnson. AMV-80

It is the hottest of days. Man on Move Despite Failures. Jeffrey Alan Triggs. AMV-80

It is the light. Aging. Diane Wakoski. AMV-81

It is the man, himself. Aleph. Stuart Z. Perkoff. VWA

It is the moment of twilight. Sowing Season. Evening. Victor Hugo, *tr. by* Mary Ann Caws. NAWM-2

It is the morning of our love. An Aspect of Love, Alice in the Ice and Fire. Gwendolyn Brooks. BPo; CAPP; TAP; TT

It is the nature of man that puzzles me. The Nature of Man. C.H. Sisson. FaBoTw (1975 ed.)

It is the Negro's tragedy I feel. The Negro's Tragedy. Claude McKay. BPo; LFH

It is the Old Man through the sleeping town. The Fall Again. Howard Nemerov. ConAP

It is the orange flower on dark-flushed stem. The Cactuses. Hubert Witheford. ATNZ

It is the pain, it is the pain, endures. Villanelle. William Empson. CMoP (1970 ed.); ILP (1975 ed.); LoAs; NoAM; OAEL-2

It is the picnic with Ruth in the spring. The Picnic. John Logan. ConAP; CTBA; LP; NCSH

It is the quality that most resembles. Yielding. Shellie Keir Robbins. AMV-80

It is the route you took through winter light. Tracking the Sled, Christmas 1951. Jeanne Murray Walker. AMV-81

It is the sea's edge lubbers love. Sailing, Sailing. Gray Burr. SPo

It is the Season. Josephine Jacobsen. TAP

It is the season of the sweet wild rose. Modern Love, XLV. George Meredith. GBL

It is the silver seeking salvation. The Plight. James W. Thompson. BPo

It is the sinners' dust-tongued bell claps me to churches. Dylan Thomas. OxBTC

It is the snow-gum silently. The Snow-Gum. Douglas Stewart. GAS; MAuV

It is the spot I came to seek. An Indian at the Burial-Place of His Fathers. Bryant. HeIP; PiAm

It Is the Stars That Govern Us. Michael Magee. PoA

It is the way of a pleasant path. Green Frog at Roadstead, Wisconsin. James Schevill. TAP

It is the whales that drive. Fish. William Carlos Williams. NoAM

It is this deep blankness is the real thing strange. Let It Go. William Empson. OxBTC; PSN

It is this rainy afternoon that reaches me. This Afternoon. Juan Sáez Burgos, tr. by Julio Marzán. InW

It is three o'clock in the morning. Trials of a Tourist. Anne Tibble. FaBoCo

It Is Time. Ted Joans. PAIC

It is time for the invocation. May Sarton. Fr. The Invocation to Kali. RiTi

It is time for the United States to spend money on education. It Is Time. Ted Joans. PAIC

It is time that I wrote my will. W. B. Yeats. The Tower, III. STS

It is time to be old. Terminus. Emerson. ILP (1975 ed.); NOBA; PAIC; PiAm; TAP

It is time to re-invent life. Moon Walk. Ben Belitt. PPoD

It is to a goodly child well fitting. A Goodly Child. Unknown. OxBChV

It is to my own as if the man made them a gift. Eadwacer. Unknown, tr. by Kemp Malone. PBWP

It is tomorrow now. Morning Star. Thomas Hornsby Ferril. VGW

It is too late for the word. Too Late. Rachel Korn, tr. by Seymour Mayne and Rivka Augenfeld. VWA

It is too simple to turn to the sound. The Cold before the Moonrise. W. S. Merwin. CoPAm

It Is True. Federico García Lorca, tr. fr. Spanish by Harriet de Onís. OLR

It is true-/ I've always loved. Alice Walker. Fr. Once. NMM; NVAP; PoBA

It is true, Martin Heidegger, as you have written. The Envelope. Maxine W. Kumin. TV

It is true, modern life is complicated. For the Market. Jane Mayhall. TAP

It is true, that even in the best-run state. The Murder of William Remington. Howard Nemerov. CMoP (1970 ed.)

It is true that, older than man and ages to oulast him. Gray Weather. Robinson Jeffers. CMoP (1970 ed.); NoAM

It is 12:20 in New York a Friday. The Day Lady Died. Frank O'Hara. CAPP; NoAM; NOBA; NYP

It is twilight as we sit in the two blue chairs. Blue Chairs. Deirdra Baldwin. PoUp

It is very nice to think. A Thought. Robert Lewis Stevenson. CTV

It is well to plant balm about places where bees are. Lemon Balm. Marie Harris. MMD

It is what he does not know. On a Squirrel Crossing the Road in Autumn, in New England. Richard Eberhart. HeIP; TH; VoPo; WIF

It is whatever day, whatever time it is. Sunday Morning. Wayne Moreland. PoBA

It is when I hear Mozart. Deafness. Richard Ryan. BIrV

It is winter and the new year. The New Year. Mark Strand. Fr. Elegy for My Father. UnPo (1976 ed.)

It is winter in California, and outside. California Winter. Karl Shapiro. MPA

It is written in the skyline of the city. Pact. Kenneth Fearing. CMoP (1970 ed.)

It is your last day and hour and you are alone. Who. Edwin Honig. TAP

It isn't any worse than what. Anxiety about Dying. Alicia Ostriker. AMV-80

It isn't freedom, that. That Brings Us to the Woodstove in the Wilds, at Night. Walter Hall. AMV-81

It isn't government that rules. Alison Wyrley Birch. PPM

It isn't that I fear. Turning Thirty. W. D. Ehrhart. AMV-81

It isn't the cough. Unknown. IP

It isn't the thing you do. The Sin of Omission. Margaret Elizabeth Munson Sangster. SoSe

It keeps eternal whisperings around. On the Sea. Keats. CABA (1972 ed.); EcS; ExPo (1973 ed.); FF; MBPR; OAEL-2; RhR

It lay, dark in the corner of the field. Suicide Pond. Kathy McLaughlin. PoA

It little profits that an idle king. Ulysses. Tennyson. AnMo; CABA (1972 ed.); EBEV; Epi; FaPoR; FF; HAP; HeIP; HoPM (1975 ed.); ILP (1975 ed.); InPK; InPS; IP; IPWM; LFH; NIL; NOBE; OAEL-2; PAIC; PoIA; PoPle; PPoe; PPP; SoSe; UnPo (1976 ed.); UsP; VLP

It lives on mere banks and drifts of air. In Praise of Lichen. Mark Perlberg. HeS

It looked extremely rocky for the Mudville five that nite. Lucky Louie Makes a Goal. H. Van Arsdale. SPo

It maie be, Love my death doth not pretend. Henry Constable. Fr. Diana. ESo

It Makes No Difference. Donald Finkel. UsP

It matters not. Be lean as Bengal beef. Poets of My Epoch. Irwin Stark. PAIC

It may be a little different. Blood to Blood. Alvin Aubert. GP

It may be good, like it who list. Sir Thomas Wyatt. AAS

It may be so, my lord./ Hear, Nature, hear! Shakespeare. Fr. King Lear, I, iv. OBP

It may be that a strange dream. Max Jacob, tr. fr. French by Wallace Fowlie. LoAs

It may happen again—this much. The Flight. John Haines. EAS

It may indeed be phantasy, when I. To Nature. Samuel Taylor Coleridge. MBPR; OAEL-2

It May Not Always Be So; and I Say. E. E. Cummings. Fr. Sonnets—Unrealities. BoLoP; TT

It Might Be a Lump of Amber. Walter de la Mare. FaBoNo

It might be good to gather. I Must Ask. James E. Warren, Jr. AATT

It must be done, my soul; but 'tis a strange. The Meditation. John Norris. SCP-2

It Must Be Summer. Sandor Csoori, tr. fr. Hungarian by Nicholas Kolumban. AMV-81

It must have been a Friday. I could hear. Katherine's Dream. Robert Lowell. Fr. Between the Porch and the Altar. ConAP

It must have been a year. Fire, Hair, Meat and Bone. Fred Johnson. PoBA

It must have been one or one-thirty. To Remain. C. P. Cavafy, tr. by Nikos Stangos and Stephen Spender. BoLoP

It must have been summer. Underneath the House. Rhyll McMaster. FPA; GAS

It neither was the words nor yet the tune. Two Girls Singing. Iain Crichton Smith. MS

It never gets dark. Crickets suffocate with little. Luxury Apt. Marie Harris. MMD

It never has failed, and it never will.　God's Plan for Spring. Nancy Byrd Turner.　CTV

It nods.　The Bald Spot.　Wesley McNair.　AMV-81

It occurred to Marshall.　Marshall.　George MacBeth.　NoAM

It ofttimes has been told, that the British seamen bold.　The *Constitution* and the *Guerriére*.　*Unknown.*　AmFP; FSW

It once might have been, once only.　Youth and Art.　Robert Browning.　STS

It ought to be lovely to be old.　Beautiful Old Age.　D. H. Lawrence.　TVo

"It Out-Herods Herod. Pray You, Avoid It."　Anthony Hecht. CoPAm; NCSH; NoAM; NOBA

It Pleases.　Gary Snyder.　TAT; WasP

It rained quite a lot that spring.　Metropolitan Nightmare. Stephen Vincent Benét.　PAIC

It Rains.　Edward Thomas.　OxBTC

It rains/ you knot that goddam gawdy.　A Big Hat or What? Pete Morgan.　SLP

It rains and nothing stirs within the fence.　It Rains.　Edward Thomas.　OxBTC

"It rests me to be among beautiful women."　Tame Cat.　Ezra Pound.　OBAL

It said welcome.　The Second Coming.　John William Corrington. HoPM (1975 ed.)

It Says.　Jon Silkin.　VWA

It says much for your life.　Grandfather.　Mary Joan Coleman. AMV-80

It seemed that out of battle I escaped.　Strange Meeting.　Wilfred Owen.　CMoP (1970 ed.); ExPo (1973 ed.); HeIP; HoPM (1975 ed.); ILP (1975 ed.); NoAM; NOBE; OAEL-2; OBP

It seems a day.　Nutting.　Wordsworth.　MBPR; NU; OAEL-2

It seems a frail mathematics, and ancient.　Robin Fulton.　*Fr.* The Voice of the Surbahar, I.　MIS

It seems I have no tears left.　Tears.　Edward Thomas.　PoPle

It seems now far off and foolish, a memory.　Lot Later.　Howard Nemerov.　CoPAm; HoPM (1975 ed.)

It Seems That God Bestowed Somehow, *with music.*　Amanda Benjamin Hall.　AH

It seems the horse they furnished me.　Enlightenment.　Robert V. Carr.　BPAW

It seems there should be someplace in a poem for black camels. The Loss of Black Camels.　Sam Hamod.　SA

"It seems to me," said Booker T.　Booker T. and W. E. B. Dudley Randall.　NIL; NoAM; TC

It seems to me the kindliness of old men.　Old Men.　Alicia Ostriker.　AMV-81

It seems too enormous just for a man to be.　The Highway. W. S. Merwin.　PoA

It seems vainglorious and proud.　The Conquerors.　Phyllis McGinley.　PBMP

It seems wrong that out of this bird.　A Blackbird Singing.　R. S. Thomas.　BoAnP; OBW

It shall be sayd I dy'de for Coelia.　Coelia, XIX.　William Percy. AAS

It shies from the Appalachians through seven states.　Route 95 North: New Jersey.　P. C. Bowman.　AMV-80

It sifts from leaden sieves.　Emily Dickinson.　SoSe; SS

It sleeps by day!　Lucky Lion!　*Zulu Oral Tradition, tr. by* H. Tracey.　WTO

It snowed hard.　Poem for My Great Grandfather.　Michael Van Walleghen.　HeS

It snowed in New York, I walked on Fifth.　Snow in New York. May Swenson.　NYP; UsP

It so happens I am sick of being a man.　Walking Around. Pablo Neruda, *tr. by* Robert Bly.　EAS

It sometimes happens.　Curse of the Cat Woman.　Edward Field. CABA (1972 ed.); WeW

It soothes the savage doubts.　Apocalypse.　D. J. Enright. OBSV

It sounded as if the streets were running.　Emily Dickinson. PBWP

It sounds unconvincing to say "When I was young."　In the Winter of My Thirty-eighth Year.　W. S. Merwin.　NOBA

"It spreads, " the campaign—carried on.　Carnegie Hall: Rescued. Marianne Moore.　NYP

It starts out.　The Light Year.　John Ridland.　OFD

It struck me every day.　Emily Dickinson.　PPP

It surely is not a natural thing.　Our Decor.　Edward Proffitt. PoIA

It sushes.　Cynthia in the Snow.　Gwendolyn Brooks.　LCL

It takes a fast car.　Lost Parents.　Lawrence Ferlinghetti.　GP

It takes a heap o' children to make a home that's true.　Edgar A. Guest Considers "The Old Woman Who Lived in a Shoe." Louis Untermeyer.　OBAL

It takes a heap o' livin' in a house t' make it home.　Home. Edgar A. Guest.　OBAL

It takes a long.　Trust.　Art Lange.　FiCh

It takes a long time to hear what the sands.　The Bones.　W. S. Merwin.　ConAP; UsP

It takes a worried man to sing a worried song.　Worried Man Blues.　*Unknown.*　FSW

It takes more than wind and sleet to.　Behind the Stove.　James Hearst.　TAT

It takes no courage.　Consolation.　Frank Stewart.　PHC

It took at least a morning.　Sandpile Town.　Aileen Fisher. CTV

It tried to get from out the cage.　The Cage.　James Stephens. OxBTC

It turns out/ You can kill them.　Redwings.　James Wright. NNaP

It used to be said that love is a bird.　The Wishbone.　Fred Bornhauser.　PPoD

It was a big boxy wreck of a house.　The Fall of the House of Usher.　Reed Whittemore.　GP; InPK

It was a bird of Paradise.　In London Town.　Mary Elizabeth Coleridge.　RAE

It was a chilly winter's night.　A Winter Night.　William Barnes. NOBE

It was a cough that carried her off.　*Unknown.*　FaBoNo

It was a day for routine maintenance.　The Couch.　Fred W. Wright, Jr.　AMV-80

It was a dim October day.　Thomas Caulfield Irwin.　*Fr.* Swift. BIrV

It was a dismal and a fearful night.　On the Death of Mr. William Hervey.　Abraham Cowley.　EBEV; NOBE

It was a fiery circus horse.　The Day of the Circus Horse.　T. A. Daly.　PCOP

It Was A' for Our Rightfu' King.　Burns.　AIW (Farewell, The.)　PoPle

It was a foreign ship that sailed.　Newcomers.　Abraham Reisen, *tr. by* Keith Bosley.　VWA

It was a friar of orders free.　The Friar of Rubygill.　Thomas Love Peacock.　*Fr.* Maid Marian.　PeBB

It Was a Funky Deal.　Etheridge Knight.　BPo; PoBA

It was a gingerbread house all right.　"Breaking Up Is Hard to Do."　Hugh Walthall.　PoUp

It was a great pleasure.　Spitting on Ira Rosenblatt.　Robert Hershon.　NeAC

It was a jolly bed in sooth.　Us Idle Wenches.　*Unknown.*　PoPle

It was a kind and northern face.　Praise for an Urn.　Hart Crane. CMoP (1970 ed.); HAP; NoAM; NOBA; PPP

It was a late-blooming/ madrigal.　Eating Ground Zero.　Alan Austin.　PoUp

It was a little captive cat. The Singing Cat. Stevie Smith. OxBTC; PCat

It Was a Lover, and His Lass. Shakespeare. *Fr.* As You Like It, V, iii. BiP; FSW; GBL; HeIP; ILP (1975 ed.); InPK; InPS; NOBE; OLR; PPoe

It was a maid of brenten arse. A Maid of Brenten Arse. *Unknown.* GBP

It was a Maine lobster town. Water. Robert Lowell. CMoP (1970 ed.); ExPo (1973 ed.); HeIP; NOBA; PiAm

It was a mile of greenest grass. The Occasional Yarrow. Stevie Smith. FaBoNo

It was a miniature country once. Japan. Anthony Hecht. InPK

It was a miracle he glimpsed owl swaying. Owl Seen in Rearview Mirror. Duane Niatum. VW

It was a night in winter. Clive Sansom. *Fr.* The Witnesses. PChr

It was a night when all. First Reading. Tony Moreno. NW

It was a place of force. The Rabbit Catcher. Sylvia Plath. SBG

It was a quiet night, you will remember. To My Wife. Edwin Brock. BuTh

It was a refractory gnu. The Refractory Gnu. *Unknown.* TDH

It was a robber's daughter, and her name was Alice Brown. Gentle Alice Brown. W. S. Gilbert. FaBoCo; PeBB

It was a room where everything was strained. The Poolhall. Dan Burt. AMV-80

It was a summer evening. Sentences while Remembering Hiraethog. T. Glynne Davies, *tr. by* R. Gerallt Jones. OBW

It was a summer evening. The Battle of Blenheim. Robert Southey. AKE; FaPoR; PBMP; PCOP

It was a tall young oysterman lived by the riverside. The Ballad of the Oysterman. Oliver Wendell Holmes. ILP (1975 ed.)

It was a tortoise aspiring to fly. Improvisations on Aesop. Anthony Hecht. OBAL

It was a yearlong bloodbath it was. With. Carol Bergé. MMD

It was after a day's rain. Night Herons. Judith Wright. MAuV

It was all technicolor. Reel One. Adrien Stoutenburg. MiP

It Was All Very Tidy. Robert Graves. OxBTC

It was almost post time, the horses were. The Day Alvero Pineda Was Killed. Ronald Koertge. EC

It was always. Hose and Iron. Greg Kuzma. MAT; NVAP

"It was an amazing discovery, like the inside of your head." Esplumeoir. "Hugh MacDiarmid." TwMBP

It was an evening in November. The Pig. *Unknown.* FaBoEE

It was an icy day. Complete Destruction. William Carlos Williams. TT

It was at the very date to which we have come. An Anniversary. Thomas Hardy. OxBTC

It was awful. The Day the T.V. Broke. Gerald Jonas. QQQ

It was back in nineteen forty-two. The Big Muddy. Pete Seeger. NIL

It was better when we were. For My Mother. Louise Glück. CAAP; UnPo (1976 ed.)

It was bright day and all the trees were still. Silence. W. J. Turner. FSFS

It was but now their sounding clamours sung. Palm Sunday: Good Friday. Giles Fletcher the Younger. *Fr.* Christ's Victory and Triumph, III. BoReV

It was cold, and all they gave him to wear. Back in the States. Louis Simpson. AMV-81

It was cold, and we gritted our teeth. Watercress. Janet Kauffman. TC

It was cold then in the cautious hours. Curtain. Lance Henson. VoR

It was daybreak a little while ago. Tuesday, 5 March (Morning) 1963. Pier Paolo Pasolini, *tr. by* Nigel Thompson. AMV-81

It was December. Even There. Lyn Lifshin. IHMS

It was down by the Sally Gardens. Down by the Sally Gardens. W. B. Yeats. FSW

It was down in old Joe's barroom. St. James Infirmary. *Unknown.* FSW

It was down in our far-off village that we heard of the war begun. Sending to War. William Morris. *Fr.* The Pilgrims of Hope. VLP

It was during the winter of 1870. The Black Swan. Peter Kostakis. FiCh

It was early/ fall or late summer. Fog 9/76. Richard Morris Dey. AMV-80

It was early, early in the spring. The Croppy Boy. *Unknown.* AmFP; FaBoBa; FSW

It was early in the season, the fall of 'sixty-three. Michigan-I-O. *Unknown.* AmFP

It was early last December. The Drunkard and the Pig. *Unknown.* OBAL

It was early Monday morning Willie Leonard arose. Willie Leonard; or, The Lake of Cold Finn. *Unknown.* AmFP

It was early morning. Isaac. Amir Gilboa, *tr. by* Howard Schwartz. VWA

It was early springtime that the strike was on. The Ludlow Massacre. Woody Guthrie. FSW

It was early Sunday mornin. Stagolee. *Unknown.* MAT

It Was Easier. Ruthven Todd. MS

It was easy. How I Escaped from the Labyrinth. Philip Dacey. POL

It was easy. How I Got Myself Trapped. Felix Pollak. HeS

It was easy to see. Spassky at Reykjavik. David Fisher. AMV-81

It Was Gentle. Hedva Harkavi, *tr. fr. Hebrew by* Tova Weizman. VWA

It was good for the virgin mary. Poem for Unwed Mothers. Nikki Giovanni. OBAL

It was hard for you to put up with you older brother. A Letter to His Sister. Laurance Wieder. AAN

It was here the boy entered the skylight. The Half-Moon Lake. Ciaran Carson. IPM

It was in and about the Martinmas time. Bonny Barbara Allan. *Unknown.* BiP; BoLoP; CABA (1972 ed.); HeIP; InPK; PAIC; PeBB; PPoD; SS

It was in nineteen-hundred and twenty-nine. Run Come See. Blind Blake. FSW

It was in October, a favorite season. Elegy for a Nature Poet. Howard Nemerov. CoPAm; HoPM (1975 ed.)

It was in one of those old houses in Monmouthshire. Peter Whigham. *Fr.* The Ingathering of Love. TwMBP

It was in the city of Expert. The Oxford Girl; or, Expert Town. *Unknown.* AmFP

It was in the merry month of May. The Trail to Mexico. *Unknown.* BPAW

It was in the Yellow Dog Saloon one sultry summer night. Pizen Pete's Mistake. *At. to* Merrill Honey. BPAW

It was late afternoon, october. Fort Wayne, Indiana 1964. Steven Lewis. TAT

It was just before the last fierce charge, two soldiers drew a-rein. The Last Fierce Charge. *Unknown.* AmFP

It was justice to see her nude haunches. The Return. Stanley Moss. POL

It was late last night when my lord come home. The Gypsy Davy. *Unknown.* AmFP

It was late last night when the boss come home. Gypsy Davey. *Ad. by* Woody Guthrie. FSW

It was late last Saturday evening. Blow the Candle Out. *Unknown.* FaBoBa

It was late, we. Man and Wife. Mitchell Goodman. VGW

It was Leroy Smith we meant to find. The Young Deputy. James Whitehead. CoPAm

It was like a church to me. The Moor. R. S. Thomas. OBW

It was like this once: sprinklers mixed. Memo to the 21st Century. Philip Appleman. PCho; SFF; TAT

It was likely to occur during the happiest story. Preparation. Sandra McPherson. MPA

It was Little Joe, the wrangler, he'll wrangle never more. Little Joe the Wrangler. N. Howard Thorp. FSW

It was Mabbie without the grammar school gates. The Ballad of Chocolate Mabbie. Gwendolyn Brooks. CAPP; SoS

It was Mama who was partial. Premonition [or Emma]. Yvonne. CNA; TV

It was many and many a year ago. Samuel Brown. Phoebe Cary. OBAL

It was many and many a year ago. The Cannibal Flea. Tom Hood. SpRo

It was many and many a year ago. Cannibalee: A Po'em of Passion. C. F. Lummis. SpRo

It was many and many a year ago. Andrew M'Crie. Robert Fuller Murray. FaBoCo

It was many and many a year ago. Annabel Lee. Poe. AmVN; DL; HeIP; NOBA; PCOP; PiAm; RhR; SpRo; TAP

It was meetin' night in Rawhide Town. The Raven Visits Rawhide. Unknown. BPAW

It was morning when we approached. Grand Park, Chicago. William Pillin. SPT

It was my bridal night I remember. I Remember. Stevie Smith. BoLoP; BoWoP; InPK

It was my desert army. no fuss. no incidents. North Africa Breakdown. Tom Raworth. TwMBP

It was my father forced him into the desert. Isaac. A. C. Jacobs. VWA

It was my thirtieth year to heaven. Poem in October. Dylan Thomas. BiP; FSFS; MPo; OBP; PoA; PPM; SoSe; STS; UsP

It was near evening, the room was cold. The Oath. Allen Tate. NoAM; VGW

It was neither his hunger nor mine. Not Being Wise. Virginia Elson. AMV-80

It was night-time! God, the Father Good. What the Devil Said. James Stephens. CMoP (1970 ed.)

It was 1912 when the awful news got around. Sinking of the Titanic. Unknown. PAIC

It was no costume jewellery I sent. With a Gift of Rings. Robert Graves. GBL

It was no polished blade. A Quarrel. John Peck. WeW

It was not death, for I stood up. Emily Dickinson. BiP; ILP (1975 ed.); InPK; NOBA; PoIA

It was not dying; everybody died. Losses. Randell Jarrell. IP; PoA; TAP; UnPo (1976 ed.)

It was not I who began it. Eve to Her Daughters. Judith Wright. MPo

It was not like your great and gracious ways! Departure. Coventry Patmore. Fr. The Unknown Eros. NOBE; VLP

It was not meant for human eyes. The Combat. Edwin Muir. CMoP (1970 ed.); NOBE

It was not "not wanting." Last South Baltimore Poem. David Hilton. AcAn; EC

It was not our duty to question but to guard. Bread and a Pension. Louis Johnson. ATNZ

It was not quite winter. Robert Dana. Fr. Natural Odes/ American Elegies. HeS

It was of a comely young lady fair. The Dark-Eyed Sailor. Unknown. FSW

It was on a Friday morning that they took me from the cell. Friday Morning. Sydney Carter. LP

It was on a May, on a midsummer's day. Sir Hugh; or, The Jew's Daughter. Unknown. AmFP

It was on a Wednesday night, the moon was shining bright. Jesse James. Unknown. AIW; UnPo (1976 ed.)

It was on one Monday morning. Lisbon. Unknown. AmFP

It was on one Monday morning just about one o'clock. The Titanic. Unknown. AmFP

It was on one summer's evening,/ Just about the hour of three. Sailor on the Deep Blue Sea. Unknown. FSW

It was on the banks of the American river. When Running Felt Right. Linda McCloud. PoUp

It was on the twenty-first day of December. Ella Speed. Unknown. AmFP

It was one afternoon when I was young. The Tale the Hermit Told. Alastair Reid. PoTa

It was one Sunday morning of June the eighth day. Henry K. Sawyer. Unknown. AmFP

It was only a film. Two Deaths. Elizabeth Jennings. LP

It was only a small dream of the golden world. John Berryman. Fr. Dream Songs. RRA

It was only important. The Moss of His Skin. Anne Sexton. CABA (1972 ed.); CoPAm; IHMS

It was our best festival. The Ceremonies. Van K. Brock. CSP

It was patent in this ancient city. Pitchfork Department. D. J. Enright. HeHu

It was pneumonia. Lament of the Virtues and Verses on Account of the Death of Don Guido. Antonio Machado, tr. by Charles Tomlinson and Henry Gifford. OBVE

It was poor little Jesus, yes, yes. Poor Little Jesus. Unknown. FSW

It was proper for them, awaking in ordered houses. Apology. Anthony Cronin. CIP; IPM

It was roses, roses, all the way. The Patriot. Robert Browning. PBMP

It was round, orb being most nearly perfect. The Gift. Ann Stanford. GP

It was said at the/ flirting creekwater's birth. To an Imaginary Father. Wendy Rose. CDW

It was said that oranges could not be/ grown in the Soviet Union. The Sweeter Our Fruits. H. H. Lewis. SPT

It was seven years then. Rachel's Lament. Linda Zisquit. VWA

It was simply a dark. The Color. John Haines. GP

It was six men of Indostan. The Blind Men and the Elephant. John Godfrey Saxe. CTV; ECBV; PCOP; PoTa

It was so prety a fole. John Skelton. Fr. Phyllyp Sparrowe. PB

It was some time between the 6th grade. The Widow of a Man Who Is Still Breathing. Michael Small. DNGG

It was sometimes not more than a blemish, or a nervousness. After the Successful Psychotherapy. Michael Ventura. EC

It was somewhere in September, and the sun was going down. Sweeney. Henry Lawson. MAuV

It was strange that morning. Fishin' Blues. Valentino Ramirez. AMV-81

It was summer on Boulevard Raspail. A History of the Opera. Sandra Hochman. RiTi

It was the anniversary of bread. Bread. Constance Urdang. GP

It was the Autumn of her madness. Dark Room. Fredrick Zydek. AMV-80

It was the beginning of me. Look at My Face, a Collage. Carolyn M. Rodgers. JB

It was. The breech smelling of oil. First Blood. Jon Stallworthy. BoAnP; LiSp

It was the country I loved. The Invaders. John Haines. TAT

It was the death of Satan first of all. A Wintry Manifesto. Chris Wallace-Crabbe. GAS

It was the dingiest bird. Robin Redbreast. Stanley Kunitz. Prf

It was the frog in the well. The Marriage of the Frog and the Mouse. *Unknown.* EBEV

It was the hole for looking in. It All Comes Together outside the Restroom in Hogansville. James Seay. CSP

It was the hour of night, when thus the Son. Milton. *Fr.* Paradise Regained, II. EBEV

It was the morning of that blessed day. Petrarch, *tr. by* Joseph Auslander. Sonnets to Laura: To Laura in Life, III. NAWM-1

It was the night of hardly anyone. The No-Night. Irving Feldman. NoAM

It was the rainbow gave thee birth. The Kingfisher. W. H. Davies. NOBE; OBW

It was the schooner *Hesperus.* The Wreck of the *Hesperus.* Longfellow. CTV; FaPoR; RhR

It was the *Stately Southerner*, that carried the Stripes and Stars. The *Stately Southerner. Unknown.* AmFP

It was the time when lilies blow. Lady Clare. Tennyson. PBMP; PoTa

It was the virgin Zennora, who dwelt. John Heath-Stubbs. *Fr.* Artorius. EBEV

It was the west wind caught her up, as. The Ring Of. Charles Olson. NOBA; VGW

It was the wind. Autumn Evening. George Anthony. EAS

It was the winter wild. Hymn on the Morning of Christ's Nativity. Milton. *Fr.* On the Morning of Christ's Nativity. NOBE

It Was the Worm. James Broughton. GP

It was the wrong office. Life and Death among the Xerox People. Olga Cabral. WBN

It was the year the Icondic. Ballad of the Icondic. John Ciardi. OBAL

It was then night: the sound and quiet. Virgil, *tr. by* Earl of Surrey. *Fr.* The Aeneid, IV. OAEL-1

It was there, but I said it couldn't be true in daylight. Nightmare of Mouse. Robert Penn Warren. SO

It was there on the hillside, no tall traveller's story. Pegasus. C. Day Lewis. PoPle

It was Tiny's habit. Sketches of Harlem. David Henderson. CABA (1972 ed.); PAIC

It was too lonely for her there. The Impulse. Robert Frost. *Fr.* The Hill Wife. AIW; HoPM (1975 ed.); NoAM

It was upon a Cristemesse night. The Dancers of Colbek. Robert Mannyng. *Fr.* Handlyng Synne. OxBM

It was upon a Lammas night. The Rigs o' Barley [*or* Corn Rigs Are Bonie *or* Song]. Burns. BoLoP; LoAs; OBP; SLP

It was upon a Shere Thorsday that oure Loverd aras. Judas. *Unknown.* OxBM

It was very late at an empty table. Ballad of an Empty Table. Tom Kryss. NeAC

It was very pleasant. A Certain Peace. Nikki Giovanni. CNA

It was water I was trying to think of all the time. Appoggiatura. Donald Jeffrey Hayes. AmNP (1974 ed.); PoBA

It was way up north in Boothbay Harbor. The Boothbay Whale. *Unknown.* FSW

It was wet and white and swift and where I am. Snow Line. John Berryman. *Fr.* Dream Songs. PoA

It was when I said. On the Road Home. Wallace Stevens. NU

It was wild. Assassination. Don L. Lee. AmNP (1974 ed.); FF; NeAC; OFD; PoBA

It was with resolution that she gave up the. The Ice Eagle. Diane Wakoski. InPS

It Was Wrong to Do This Said the Angel. Stephen Crane. The Black Riders, LIV. PPM

It was you:/ I could have crawled. Watching Salmon Jump. Simon J. Ortiz. CDW

It wasn't always this way for us. A Poem with a Conclusion. Walter Bradford. HeS

It wasn't intended that the cow should find the poppies. Caprice. Dorothy Stott Shaw. PoTa

It wasn't ringworm he. New York. Thom Gunn. NYP

It wasn't the daffodils so much. Daffodils. Michael Heffernan. AMV-80

It went many years. The Lockless Door. Robert Frost. NOBA

It went off in his face. $E = mc^2$: Einstein at Princeton. David Rowbotham. CAAP

It will be in the form of an old man. I Want to Write a Jewish Poem. Gary Pacernick. VWA

It will be like this. Pax Romana. Virginia Gilbert. NPW

It will be Summer eventually. Emily Dickinson. PF

It will darken, stars glimmering, repeating. Tides. Fred Ostrander. MIT

It Will Happen (1). Barbara F. Lefcowitz. PoUp

It will not hurt me when I am old. Moonlight. Sara Teasdale. VGW

It will not resemble the sea. The New Poem. Charles Wright. CoPAm

It winds o'er prairie and o'er crest. The Santa Fe Trail. Arthur Chapman. BPAW

"It would be—/ a mercy if." Phone Call to Rutherford. Paul Blackburn. CTBA

It would be painful to interfere. Memo. Charles Ballard. VoR

It would be snowing back there. Pilgrimage to Hennessey's. Steven Sher. AMV-81

It would be wrong for us. It is not right. Sappho, *tr. fr. Greek by* Willis Barnstone. BoWoP

It would have starved a gnat. Emily Dickinson. SBG

It would not be unfitting. On the Shore of Crete. Clarice Short. MPA

It wouldn't be so damn bad. A Narrow Street. Michael Small. DNGG

It wouldn't do to go crazy. Therapy. Ken Poyner. AMV-81

It wound through strange scarred hills, down cañons lone. The Old Santa Fe Trail. Richard Burton. BPAW

Italia, Io Ti Saluto. Christina Rossetti. WPE

Italian. Osbert Lancaster. *Fr.* Afternoons with Baedeker. FaBoCo

Italian Extravaganza. Gregory Corso. SA

Italian Spring, 1945. Nellie Burget Miller. WPW

Italian women in the back room, The. Excuses. Mary Swanson Stroh. NPW

Italy and England. Byron. *Fr.* Beppo. PAIC (Italy versus England.) NOBE

Itchin, when I behold thy banks again. To the River Itchin, near Winton. William Lisle Bowles. OAEL-2

Ité. Ezra Pound. HAP

Iter Boreale, *sel.* Richard Corbet. "There we crossed Trent and on the other side." SCP-2

Iter Boreale. Robert Wild. APAS

Ithaca last night, Syracuse at noon, Cedar Rapids tonight. Seeing Auden Off. Philip Booth. PoA

It's a daily. Trying to Shovel Out. Philip Legler. TC

It's a Different Story When You're Going into the Wind. David McFadden. NeAC

It's a Funny Thing but True. *Unknown.* CTV

It's a Good Thing to Join a Union. *Unknown.* FSW

It's a little Walden. You All Know the Story of the Other Woman. Anne Sexton. InPK

It's a long and dusty road. I Can't Help but Wonder Where I'm Bound. Tom Paxton. FSW

It's a long walk in the dark. John's Song. Joan Aiken. DuDa

It's a low it's a low low. Eagles on a Half. *Unknown.* BluI.

It's a madman, I said. Dream. Nana Issaia, *tr. by* Helle Tzalopoulou Barnstone. BoWoP

It's a mighty hard row that my poor hands has hoed. Pastures of Plenty. Woody Guthrie. SoS; WTO

It's a still life water color. Dangling Conversation. Paul Simon. NowV; UsP

It's a strange courage. El Hombre. William Carlos Williams. CABA (1972 ed.); CMoP (1970 ed.)

It's a strange, wild force. Wanderlust. Alison Wyrley Birch. PPM

It's a Terrible Thing! Everett Hoagland. BPo

It's a very odd thing. Miss T. Walter de la Mare. BBL

It's a warm wind, the west wind, full of birds' cries. The West Wind. John Masefield. PES

"It's a way to go," I say. November's Lesson. Mel Takahara. PHC

It's a white nest! A Small Bird's Nest Made of White Reed Fiber. Robert Bly. NNaP

"It's a Whole World, the Body. A Whole World!"——Swami Satchidananda. David Young. FF

It's a wonderful world. This Wonderful World. Mary Britton Miller. ECBV

It's about/ the ball,/ the bat,/ and the mitt. Analysis of Baseball. May Swenson. SPo

It's all a trick, quite easy when you know it. Villanelle. W. W. Skeat. FaBoCo

It's all familiar. A Dream. Bella Akhmadulina, *tr. by* Jean Valentine *and* Olga Carlisle. BoWoP

It's all here. In the Hammersmith Public Library. Keith Althaus. AAN

It's all mostly on the ropes now. TKO. Richard Peck. SPo

It's all out on the old railroad. Jubilee. *Unknown.* FSW

It's all right. Things slow down. Five Interior Landscapes. Olga Broumas. CNW

It's all very well for preachin'. The Pledge at Spunky Point. John Hay. OBAL

It's all very well to dream of a dove that saves. Birdwatchers of America. Anthony Hecht. HoPM (1975 ed.); NoAM; NOBA; PPP

It's Almost Day. Leadbelly (Huddie Ledbetter). FSW

It's Almost Done (On a Monday). *Unknown.* FSW

It's always afternoon somewhere. Night Poem. Wayne Dodd. AMV–80

It's always there, like the drone. Exchange. Dabney Stuart. HoPM (1975 ed.)

It's another April, and a day. Landscape with Lapwings. James Aitchison. MS

It's as though/ I had been very happy. When Snow Falls. Katherine Hoskins. TCP

It's autumn in the country I remember. Mnemosyne. Trumbull Stickney. NOBA; PAIC

It's awf'lly bad luck on Diana. Hunter Trials. John Betjeman. DuDr; PH

Its balmy lips the infant blest. Epitaph on an Infant. Samuel Taylor Coleridge. MBPR

It's Bear Air. Madeline Tiger Bass. BCr

It's been a long time comin'. Long Time Gone. David Crosby. WIF

It's been a long time since I wrote poems which dance. Dance-Song. Jaroslav Seifert, *tr. by* Paul Jagasich *and* Tom O'Grady. AMV–81

It's been like fixing a clock, jamming the wheels. Making Up for a Soul. David Wagoner. VGW

It's been like this every morning. Early Fix. Andrei Codrescu. PoW

It's been so long. Alone/ December/ Night. Victor Hernandez Cruz. PBMP

It's been ten years since you tried to kill me. Clearing the Air. Nancy Willard. RiTi

It's been three years of this. The Divorce. Adrianne Marcus. CPA

It's better not to ask, not to deny. Nurse's Song. M. K. Joseph. ATNZ

Its black fur is suddenly still. In the Surgery. J. M. Ditta. AMV–80

It's blackjack town. Wendover. Art Cuelho. PoW

It's bright the icy foam as it flows. From Exile. Dafydd Benfras, *tr. by* Anthony Conran. OBW

It's Christmas Day. I did not get. Otto. Gwendolyn Brooks. CC; PChr

It's Cold in China Blues. *Unknown.* BluL

"It's cold," said the cricket. Halloween Concert. Aileen Fisher. IWK

It's cold, wind gusty. Woman Crossing the Road. Rhyll McMaster. CAAP

It's come to this. David Martinson. *Fr.* Nineteen Sections from a Twenty Acre Poem. TAT

It's Comforting. Judy Dothard Simmons. CNA

Its Curtains. Ted Joans. PoBA

It's dark on purpose. Visiting the Oracle. Lawrence Raab. AmPA

It's Dark Outside. Nancy Chambers. FPB

Its decline was gradual. Casuality. Michael Longley. IPM

Its disguise resides in the commonplace. Stinging Nettle. Gwen Head. GP

Its echoes. Haunted House. Valerie Worth. IWK

It's 8:54 a.m. Brooklyn it's the 28th of July and. Sonnet. Ted Berrigan. CAAP

It's fare thee well, my own true love. Mary Ann. *Unknown.* FSW

It's fine to have a blow-out in a fancy restaurant. The Reckoning. Robert Service. BBGO

Its flat, insect-blackened radiator grill. Buffalo. Louis Daniel Brodsky. AMV–80

It's Food. Cid Corman. GP

Its former green is blue and thin. The Garden Seat. Thomas Hardy. HAP

It's four long years since I reached this land. Lousy Miner. *Unknown.* AmFP

It's funny that smells and sounds return. Scrapbooks. Nikki Giovanni. CNA

It's Funny That You Should Mention That. Nashira N'tosha. NW

It's getting to the point. Suite: Judy Blue Eyes. Stephen Stills. WIF

It's G-L-O-R-Y to Know I'm S-A-V-E-D. *Unknown.* FSW

It's going to be a thick night tonight. Officers' Mess. Gavin Ewart. OxBTC

It's going to come out all right—do you know? Caboose Thoughts. Carl Sandburg. CMoP (1970 ed.)

It's going to rain. The Watchers. Paul Blackburn. PAIC

It's good to do battle with your back. On the Eisenhower Stamp. Sam Pereira. PoW

Its got a good shape. Watermelon. Ted Joans. GP

It's grey/ today. The Time Is Open. Joanne Kyger. RiTi

It's hard to make a j. A Jamboree for J. Eve Merriam. ECBV

It's hard to see but think of a sea. Louis Zukofsky. VGW

It's hard to tell what bird it is. After Frost. Brian Patten. EBEV

It's Here in The. Russell Atkins. AmNP (1974 ed.); PoBA; SoS

It's his eyes. The Owl. Sue Owen. AMV–81

It's holiday night. Riding Westward. Harvey Shapiro. GP; NYP; VWA

It's just no use. Execution. James A. Randall, Jr. BPo

It's Just the Same to Me. Hermann Hesse, *tr. fr. German.* ILwL

It's Lamkin was a mason good. Lamkin. *Unknown.* FaBoBa; PeBB

It's late. Dark. A swatch of moonlight. For the Sleepless. Stephen Dunn. HeS

It's like the riddle Tolstoy. Slow Dance. David St. John. AmPA

It's Little for Glory I Care. Charles Lever. PFIr

Its Lunch. John Hollander. *Fr.* Something about It. GP

It's me/ bathed and ashy. Me, in Kulu Se and Karma. Carolyn M. Rodgers. PoBA

It's Me Again, God. Helen Steiner Rice. CTV

It's Me, Oh Lord. *Unknown.* FSW

Its metal top refused my father's twisting. The Soup Jar. Dabney Stuart. CoPAm; CSP

It's midnight in a drizzling fog. North of Santa Monica. Carter Revard. VoR

It's more than silhouettes tonight. Night of Voyeurs. Stuart Dybek. TC

It's mostly people. Mostly People. Jeanette Nichols. SFF

It's much like stopping travellers to ask directions. Good Harbor Bay, Leland, Michigan. Ellen McEvilley Griffin. NPW

It's my birthday. Happy Birthday to Me. Eve Merriam. CC

It's my lunch hour, so I go. A Step Away from Them. Frank O'Hara. ConAP; NYP; VGW

It's narrow, narrow, make your bed. Fair Annie. *Unknown.* FaBoBa; ILP (1975 ed.); PeBB

It's natural not every Gospel story rings true. Zorba. James Liddy. IPM

It's natural the Boys should whoop it up for. Moon Landing. W. H. Auden. Moon; WeW

Its nature is to look back. Poetry. Carol Rakosi. GP

It's nice that though you are casual about me. Sulpicia, *tr. fr. Latin by* Aliki *and* Willis Barnstone. BoWoP

It's no go the merrygoround, it's no go the rickshaw. Bagpipe Music. Louis MacNeice. CMoP (1970 ed.); ExPo (1973 ed.); ILP (1975 ed.); NoAM; NOBE; NOBL; OAEL-2; OBSV; OxBTC

It's No Good! D. H. Lawrence. InPS

It's no good/ being an actor. Ian Young. NeAC

It's no secret I've failed. Tending. Paula Rankin. AMV-81

It's no use, the Christian thinks of himself first. One Thing to Take, Another to Keep. Crescenzo del Monte, *tr. by* Barbara Garvin. VWA

It's no use trying to find again. The Hunger Artist. Shirley Kaufman. RiTi

It's none too sociable herdin' sheep. Sheep Ranching. Owen Wister. BPAW

It's not because it is. Those Old Zen Blues. James Broughton. GP

It's not celestial music it's the girl in the bathroom singing. Ode on Celestial Music. Brian Patten. OxBTC

It's not exciting to have a bar of soap. Living with Chris. Ted Berrigan. NoAM

It's not from Argos or Messene that I hail. The Spartan Wrestler. Damagetus, *tr. by* Tom Dodge. LiSp

It's not my world, I grant, but I made it. Ride. Josephine Miles. RiTi

It's not that/ unlikely that. Downstairs Two Old Lovers Meet. Lyn Lifshin. Psy

Its not that I hate you. A Prison Bi-Centennial Address. Pancho Aguila. CPA

It's not that I usually try for much. Love. Robert Pack. CoPAm

It's Not the Heat So Much as the Humidity. James Tate. NoAM

It's not true that death is a lump like this, or a blow. Death; She Was Always Here. Yona Wallach, *tr. by* Leonore Gordon. VWA

It's November. The Song of This House. Stephen Vincent. NeAC

It's O! but aw ken well. A, U, Hinny Burd. *Unknown.* GBP

It's of a famous [*or* fearless] highwayman a story I will [*or* now I'll] tell. Brennan on the Moor. *Unknown.* AIW; FaBoBa; GBP

It's of flash packet, a packet of fame. The *Dom Pedro.* *Unknown.* AmFP

It's of a rich squire in Bristol I'll tell. Squire and Milkmaid; or, Blackberry Fold. *Unknown.* InPK

It's OK for the rich and the lucky to keep still. The Voices. Rainer Maria Rilke, *tr. by* Robert Bly. EC

It's on this railroad bank I stand. Careless Love. *Unknown.* UnPo (1976 ed.)

It's one of those storybook days. "You Get the Groceries, I'll Guard the Crib." Dennis Trudell. NVAP

It's one thing/ to sing the beloved. Duino Elegies, III. Rainer Maria Rilke, *tr. by* David Young. NAWM-2

It's Over a (See Just). E. E. Cummings. VGW

Its quick soft silver bell beating, beating. Auto Wreck. Karl Shapiro. BiP; CMoP (1970 ed.); CoPAm; FF; ILP (1975 ed.); IP; NIL; SoS; UsP; VGW; VoPo

It's quiet for me, now that I have buried the child. Ritual Three. David Ignatow. ConAP

It's quiet here among the haunted tenses. The Last of England. Peter Porter. GAS

It's quiet in Hell just now, it's very tame. Lament of an Idle Demon. R. P. Lister. NOBL

It's Raining in Love. Richard Brautigan. PPM

Its red and white/ checkered commonness. The Shirt. Elizabeth Brunazzi. PoUp

It's right to call you son. That cursing alcoholic. Letter to an Absent Son. Madeline DeFrees. CNW; GP; NMM; RiTi

It's so cold in China birds can't hardly sing. It's Cold in China Blues. *Unknown.* BluL

It's so hard to coordinate. Late Again. Gabriel Zaid, *tr. by* Eliot Weinberger. AMV-81

It's so pure in the cemetery. Not Like That. Adrienne Rich. CoPAm

It's Spring Returning, It's Spring and Love. *Unknown.* HAP

It's such a/ Bore. Ennui. Langston Hughes. OBAL

It's such a shock, I almost screech. William Cole. CTV

Its syntax is an arrow. Sentence. Billy Collins. AAN

It's taken many years to find. The One Song. C. G. Hanzlicek. AMV-80

It's ten. Evening. The room is in half light. My Sister. Alfonsina Storni, *tr. by* Aliki *and* Willis Barnstone. BoWoP

It's the anarchy of poverty. The Poor. William Carlos Williams. IPWM; PPP

It's the Buckaroo Sandman. Buckaroo Sandman. *Unknown.* BPAW

It's the day for writing that letter, if one is able. Harry. Francis Webb. GAS

It's the Syme the Whole World Over. *Unknown.* FSW

It's the time of year. The Mini Spooks. Eloise Anderson. IWK

It's the way she moves. The Accomplice. Ron Slate. AMV-80

It's the way you perceive the world I love. The First Love Poem. Myra Glazer Schotz. VWA

It's time to make love: douse the glim. Limerick. Conrad Aiken. FaBoNo

It's to possess more than the skin. Cutting the Jewish Bride's Hair. Ruth Whitman. RiTi

It's to you that I speak, men of the Southern hemisphere.  By the Waters of Babylon.  Benjamin Fondane, *tr. by* Edouard Roditi.  VWA

It's too dark to see black.  A Mother Speaks: The Algiers Motel Incident, Detroit.  Michael S. Harper.  AmPA; BPo

It's too good for them.  Sex and the Over Forties.  Peter Porter.  CAAP

It's too late, too late.  T.B. Blues.  Leadbelly (Huddie Ledbetter).  BluL

It's True I'm No Miss America.  Stephanie Slowinsky.  AMV–80

It's true it can only happen.  Night Atlas.  Luke Breitt.  CPA

It's true Mattie Lee.  Unidentified Flying Object.  Robert Hayden.  NCSH

It's true that days are longer in the country.  Romantic Poem.  Anne Waldman.  RiTi

Its trunk as of dead silver cast.  The Felled Plane Tree.  Anna Hajnal, *tr. by* William Jay Smith.  BoWoP

It's twenty to four.  Linen Town.  Seamus Heaney.  CIP

It's twenty years ago and more.  In Moncur Street.  Dorothy Hewett.  GAS

It's very nice to think of how.  A Kitten's Thought.  Oliver Herford.  PCOP

It's warm wind, the west wind, full of birds' cries.  The West Wind.  John Masefield.  PPM

Its wednesday night baby.  Master Charge Blues.  Nikki Giovanni.  OBAL

It's winter in Paris and women in high heels are strutting.  Paris.  Jane Garnett.  AMV–80

It's wonderful dogs they're breeding now.  Tim, an Irish Terrier.  Winifrid M. Letts.  GDP

It's wonderful how I jog.  Animals Are Passing from Our Lives.  Philip Levine.  NoAM; NOBA; TAP

It's worse than death, that hush.  Miners.  John C. Frohlicher.  BPAW

Itum Paradisum all clothed in green.  *Unknown.*  GBP

Ivan Silen P.R. Poet.  Lorraine Sutton.  NW

Ivanhoe, *sel.*  Sir Walter Scott.
Rebecca's Hymn, *fr. ch.* 40.  PIM

I've a letter from thy sire.  Baby Mine.  Charles Mackey.  BLSo

I've always thought Polonius a dry.  Lines to His Son on Reaching Adolescence.  John Logan.  CAPP

I've always wanted one.  Wanting a Mummy.  Sandra McPherson.  AmPA

I've always wanted to say something of you.  To Teresa.  Iván Silén, *tr. by* Julio Marzán.  InW

I've an ingle, shady ingle, near a dusky bosky dingle.  Newman Levy.  *Fr.* Midsummer Jingle.  OSP

I've been a moonshiner for seventeen [long] years.  Moonshiner.  *Unknown.*  FSW; OBAL

I've been a wandering early and late.  Wandering.  *Unknown.*  FSW

I've been a wild rover for a number of years.  Wild Rover.  *Unknown.*  FSW

I've been a woman.  Poem.  Sonia Sanchez.  WBN

I've been after the exotic.  The Ethnic Life.  Daniel Halpern.  AmPA

I've been all around this whole wide world.  Don't Let Your Deal Go Down.  *Unknown.*  FSW

I've been around a long time.  Curtain Speech.  Michael Braude.  AMV–81

I've been doing some hard traveling.  Hard Traveling.  Woody Guthrie.  FSW

I've been driving for hours.  Looking for a Rest Area.  Stephen Dunn.  AmPA

I've been given this triangular face to wear.  Self-Portrait.  Nina Cassian, *tr. by* Herbert Kuhner.  VWA

I've been going around without any skin.  Josephine Miles.  IHMS

I've been in jail from slander.  The Rocky Mountains.  *Unknown.*  AmFP

I've been in love for long.  In Love for Long.  Edwin Muir.  BoLoP; LoAs

I've been learning to breathe under water.  Learning to Breathe.  Gael Turnbull.  PMW

I've been scarred and battered.  Still Here.  Langston Hughes.  BuTh

I've been to Haarlem, I've been to Dover.  Turn the Glasses Over.  *Unknown.*  FSW

I've been trying to fashion a wifely ideal.  A Plea for Trigamy.  Sir Owen Seaman.  NOBL

I've Been Workin' [*or* Working] on the Railroad.  *Unknown.*  BLSH, *with music*; BLSo, *with music*; FSW

I've changed my ways a little; I cannot now.  The House Dog's Grave.  Robinson Jeffers.  GDP

I've cleaned house.  Saturday Afternoon, When Chores Are Done.  Harryette Mullen.  AMV–81

I've come for your eyes you said.  Dying.  Jascha Kessler.  PoW

I've come this far to freedom and I won't turn back.  Midway.  Naomi Long Madgett.  BPo

I've come to close your door, my handsome, my darling.  Bereft Child's First Night.  Frances Bellerby.  POL

I've come to give you fruit from out my orchard.  The Crossed Apple.  Louise Bogan.  BiP; HeIP; NIL

I've come to see Miss Jennian Jones.  Miss Jennian Jones.  *Unknown.*  AmFP

I've come to town to see you all.  Long Tail Blue.  *Unknown.*  BLSo

I've done what I could. My boys run wild now.  Complaint.  Ian Hamilton.  NoAM

I've ever lost were.  For Both of Us at Fisk.  Sharon Scott.  JB

I've found a small dragon in the woodshed.  A Small Dragon.  Brian Patten.  DuDr; LP

I've Gone and Stained with the Color of Love.  Milton Acorn.  NeAC

I've got a bellyful of whisky.  Long-Line Skinner.  *Unknown.*  FSW

I've got a dog as thin as a rail.  *Unknown.*  GDP

I've got a gal who loves me so.  L'il Liza Jane.  *Unknown.*  FSW

I've Got a Home in That Rock.  Raymond R. Patterson.  FF; PoBA

I've got a home in-a that Rock, don't you see?  Home in That Rock.  *Unknown.*  FSW

I've got a little baby, but she's out of sight.  Hello, Ma Baby.  Joseph E. Howard *and* Ida Emerson.  BLSo; FSW

I've got a mule [and] her name is Sal.  The Erie Canal.  *Unknown.*  BLSo; FSW

I've got a pal.  My Old Dutch: A Cockney Song.  Albert Chevalier.  VLP

I've got a wife and five little children.  Rock About My Saro Jane.  *Unknown.*  FSW

I've Got Connections at the Circus.  Beth Joselow.  PoUp

I've got nasty habits.  Live with Me.  Mick Jagger *and* Keith Richard.  InPK

I've Got No Use for the Women.  *Unknown.*  AmFP

I've Got the World on a String, *with music*.  Ted Koehler.  BLSo

I've got to keep moving.  Hellhound on My Trail.  *Unknown.*  BluL

I've Got to Know.  Woody Guthrie.  FSW; SoS

I've had all of the apple, she said.  Once When She Thought Aloud.  Dorothea MacKellar.  MAuV

I've had tangled feelings lately.  Breakthrough.  Carolyn M. Rodgers.  BPo

I've heard them lilting at loom and belting. Two Songs, I. C. Day Lewis. HAP; NoAM

I've heard them [or the] lilting at our yowe-milking [or the ewe-milking]. The Flowers of the Forest [or A Lament for Flodden]. Jane Elliot. BTTM; PoPle; SLP; WPE

I've Heard Them Talk: For My Main Man. Ralph Storey. SES

I've jumped from myself to dawn. The Tree of Diana. Alejandra Pizarnik, tr. by Yishai Tobin. VWA

I've just got here, through Paris, from the sunny southern shore. The Man Who Broke the Bank at Monte Carlo. Fred Gilbert. FSN; FSW

I've known her too long. A Sequence of Women. James Harrison. CoPAm

I've known rivers. The Negro Speaks of Rivers. Langston Hughes. AmNP (1974 ed.); BPo; CABA (1972 ed.); CoPAm; HAP; HeIP; NIL; NoAM; NOBA; PiAm; PoBA; SoS; TAP; TSWA

I've known you since the time/ you were amphibian. Songs to a Lady Moonwalker. Abraham Sutskever, tr. by Ruth Whitman. VWA

I've learned to recognize angels. Propeller Sleep. Mei Berssenbrugge. SA

I've left the thin autumnal air. Cats and Egypt. Andrew Hudgins. AMV-81

I've lived beneath huge portals where marine. Former Life. Baudelaire, tr. by Roy Campbell. NAWM-2

I've lived by the world's rules. Lines from an Orchard Once Surveyed by Thoreau. Philip Booth. GP

I've made it. Double-Header. John Stone. TAT

I've moved here to the Immortal's place. Staying in the Mountains in Summer. Yü Hsüan-chi, tr. by Geoffrey Waters. BoWoP

I've never felt it true. A Delicate Balance. Laura Schreiber. AMV-80

I've never learned an adequate goodbye. False Cadence. Bruce Berger. AMV-80

I've never seen an abominable snowman. The Abominable Snowman. Ogden Nash. RAE

I've no idea, sense of place. Waiting. Ed Cox. PoUp

I've no tooth to sing you the song. Pat Cloherty's Version of The Maisie. Richard Murphy. IPM

I've oft been told by learned friars. An Argument. Thomas Moore. BoLoP

I've often heard my mother say. The Unknown Color. Countee Cullen. ECBV

I've only sailed through the Mediterranean. Notes to a Biographer. Peter Porter. CAAP

I've poached a pickle paitricks. Poaching in Excelsis. G. K. Menzies. FaBoCo

I've promised that I will not care about things. Alan Dugan. FoP

I've reached the end of my names. In the Season of Wolves and Names. Mariève Rugo. AMV-80

I've Reached the Land of Corn and Wine, with music. Edgar P. Stites. AH

I've reached the land of corn and wine. Beulah Land. Edgar Page. BLSH; FSW

I've [or We've] reached the land of desert sweet. Dakota Land. Unknown. BPAW; FSW

I've rode the Southern, I've rode the L. & N. I Rode Southern, I Rode L & N. Unknown. AmFP

I've seen a deal of gaiety through out my noisy life. Champagne Charlie. At. to George Leybourne. PSoN

I've seen a dying eye. Emily Dickinson. BoWoP; NOBA

Ive seen all the sunrises since u left me. Sex Play in Four Acts. Doug Fetherling. NeAC

I've seen her pass with eyes upon the road. Una Anciana Mexicana. Alice Corbin. WPW

I've seen it drive straw straight through a fence post. Mid-Plains Tornado. Linda Bierds. AMV-80

I've seen the sun sword-slashing hard. Duel in the Camellias. Charles Doyle. ATNZ

I've slept in five houses, but wakened. This Year. Joseph Hutchison. AMV-81

I've sold the old ranch, stock and all. Last Drift. Arthur Chapman. BPAW

I've stayed in the front yard all my life. A Song in the Front Yard. Gwendolyn Brooks. IPWM; NoAM; NOBA; PoBA

I've stitched my dress with continents. Knowledge. Nina Cassian, tr. by Michael Impey and Brian Swann. BoWoP

I've swallowed my mother. Loaded. Mary Swope. PoUp

I've thought of names. Labour of the Brain, Ballad of the Body. Nicole Forman. NMM

I've tossed an apple at you. The Apple. At. to Plato, tr. fr. Greek. WeW

I've traveled all over this country. Acres of Clams. Unknown. FSW

I've traveled 'round this country. Banks of Marble. Les Rice. FSW

I've tried pitying you. Some Scribbles for a Lumpfish. Thomas Johnson. AMV-80

I've tried the new moon tilted in the air. The Freedom of the Moon. Robert Frost. Moon

I've tried to seal it in. The Knot. Stanley Kunitz. HAP

I've watched cars acting like gods. Cars. Jim Mulac. AcAn

I've watched you now a full half-hour. To a Butterfly. Wordsworth. MBPR; PCoP

I've weeded their beds, put down manure and bark dust. Elegy while Pruning Roses. David Wagoner. AMV-80

I've wined and dined on Mulligan stew. The Lady Is a Tramp. Lorenz Hart. OBAL

I've wished a million times. Dissipation. Lonnie L. Landrum. DNGG

I've written you a song. Blah, Blah, Blah. Ira Gershwin. OBAL

Ivory, Coral, Gold, The. William Drummond of Hawthornden. ILP (1975 ed.)

Ivory Gate, The, sel. Thomas Lovell Beddoes. "Mighty thought of an old world, The." ILP (1975 ed.)

Ivory Masks in Orbit. Keorapetse Kgositsile. PoBA

Ivory Paper Weight. Adrien Stoutenburg. GP

Ivry. Macaulay. BTTM

Ivy, Chief of Trees. Unknown. OxBM

Ivy-Wife, The. Thomas Hardy. VLP

Iwa flies heavy to nest in the brush, The. Love by the Water-Reeds. Tr. fr. Hawaiian by M. W. Beckwith. WTO

Iwori wotura. Oracle. Yoruba Oral Tradition, tr. by Ulli Beier. WTO

Ixion. Lex Banning. GAS


# J

J. Alfred Prufrock to. Said. George Starbuck. OBAL

J. J. Walter de la Mare. FaBoNo

Jabber-Whacky. Isabelle Di Caprio. QQQ

Jabberwocky. "Lewis Carroll." Fr. Through the Looking-Glass, ch.1. AnMo; BiP; CABA (1972 ed.); CTV; DuDr; EBEV; FaBoCo; FaBoNo; FF; HeIP; HoPM (1975 ed.); ILP (1975 ed.); InPK; InPS; NIL; NOBE; NOBL; OAEL-2; OBP; OxBChV; PCOP; PoIA; PPoe; PPM; PPP; SpRo; TPo; UsP; VLP; WIF

J'Accuse. Peter Klappert. AMV-81

Jack. W. G. McNeice. IPM

Jack. Charles Henry Ross. OxBChV

Jack and Dinah Want Freedom. *Unknown.* BPo

Jack and His Father. John Heywood. SoSe (1977 ed.)

Jack and His Pony, Tom. Hilaire Belloc. BoAnP; PH

Jack and Jill went up the hill. Mother Goose. MG

Jack and Joan. Thomas Campion. FaPoR; ILP (1975 ed.); NIL ("Jacke and Jone, they thinke no ill.") AAS

Jack be nimble. Mother Goose. MG

Jack, eating rotten cheese, did say. Quatrain [*or* Impromptu]. *Unknown, wr. at. to* Benjamin Franklin. FaBoEE; NOBL; SoSe

Jack Frenchman's Defeat. Congreve. APAS

Jack had a little pony—Tom. Jack and His Pony, Tom. Hilaire Belloc. BoAnP; PH

Jack Haggerty. *Unknown.* AmFP

Jack Hope. Roger McDonald. FPA

Jack-in-the-Boat. Allen Curnow. ATNZ

Jack Is Every Inch a Sailor. *Unknown.* FSW

Jack Monroe. *Unknown.* AmFP

Jack of Diamonds. *Unknown.* AmFP

"Jack," quoth his father, "how shall I ease take?" Jack and His Father. John Heywood. SoSe (1977 ed.)

Jack Rabbit. *See* Jackrabbit.

Jack Sprat could eat no fat. Mother Goose. MG

Jack the Jolly Tar. *Unknown.* AmFP

Jack the Piper. *Unknown.* GBP

Jack Was Every Inch a Sailor. *Unknown.* FSW

Jackdaw, The. William Cowper. PB

Jackdaw. Tom Earley. BoAnP

Jackdaw of Rheims, The. "Thomas Ingoldsby." *Fr.* The Ingoldsby Legends. FaBoCo; VLP

Jacke and Jone, they thinke no ill. Thomas Campion. AAS

Jacket it winsomely in primrose yellow! Ultimate Anthology. Martin Bell. POL

Jackfruit, The. Ho Xuan Huong, *tr. fr. Vietnamese by* Nguyen Ngoc Bich. PBWP

Jackie. King D. Kuka. VoR

Jackie's gone a-sailing with trouble on his mind. Jack Monroe. *Unknown.* AmFP

Jack Rabbit. Adrien Stoutenburg. BoAnP

Jackrabbits. S. Omar Barker. BPAW

Jackson is on sea, Jackson is on shore. Jackson. *Unknown.* FSW

Jackson, Mississippi. Margaret Walker. FB

Jackson Pollock had a quaint. Squeeze Play. Phyllis McGinley. *Fr.* Spectator's Guide to Contemporary Art. FaBoEE; OBSV

Jacksonville Blues. *Unknown.* BluL

Jacob. Phoebe Cary. OBAL

Jacob. Else Lasker-Schüler, *tr. fr. German.* BoWoP, *tr. by* Rosemarie Waldrop; VWA, *tr. by* Joachim Neugroschel

Jacob. Charles Reznikoff. VWA

Jacob. Delmore Schwartz. VWA

Jacob: a bull among his herd. Jacob. Else Lasker-Schüler, *tr. by* Rosemarie Waldrop. BoWoP

Jacob and Esau. Else Lasker-Schüler, *tr. fr. German by* Rosemarie Waldrop. BoWoP

Jacob and the Angel. Stephen Mitchell. VWA

Jacob can have his ladder. Tree Man. Rennie McQuilkin. AMV-81

Jacob Epstein. *Unknown.* FaBoCo

Jacob was the buffalo of his herd. Jacob. Else Lasker-Schüler, *tr. by* Joachim Neugroschel. VWA

Jacobean Merrymaking. Beaumont *and* Fletcher. *Fr.* The Spanish Curate, III, ii. BBL

Jacobite Scot in Satire on England's Unparalleled Loss, A. *Unknown.* APAS

Jacobite Toast, A. John Byrom. FaBoCo (Extempore Verses Intended to Allay the Violence of Party-Spirit.) NOBL; PPoD ("God bless the king—I mean the faith's defender.") FaBoEE

Jacobite's Epitaph, A. Macaulay. FaPoR; NOBE (Epitaph on a Jacobite.) EBEV

Jacob's Ladder, The. Denise Levertov. AnMo; CoPAm; IPWM; PPP

Jacob's Ladder. *Unknown.* FSW

Jacob's Winning. Richard Sherwin. VWA

Jadis. Ernest Dowson. VLP

Jagg'd mountain peaks and skies ice-green. Brueghel's Winter. Walter de la Mare. WIF

Jaguar, The. Ted Hughes. ILP (1975 ed.)

Jailbird. Vernon Scannell. HeHu

Jailhouse Blues ("Thirty days in jail. . ."). *Unknown.* BluL

Jailhouse Blues, The ("When I was lying in jail. . .). *Unknown.* BluL

Jake and Roany was a-chousin' along. The Bosky Steer. Henry Herbert Knibbs. BPAW

Jake Hates All the Girls. E. E. Cummings. CTBA

Jam Fish, The. Edward Abbott Parry. OxBChV

Jam on Gerry's Rock [*or* Rocks], The. *Unknown.* AmFP; FaBoBa; FSW

Jamaican Bus Ride. A. S. J. Tessimond. OxBTC

Jamboree for J, A. Eve Merriam. ECBV

James Alan Park/ Came naked stark. Thomas, Lord Erskine. FaBoEE

James Alley. *Unknown.* BluL

James Bird. *Unknown.* AmFP

James Harris. *Unknown. See* Demon Lover, The.

James Powell on Imagination. Larry Neal. BPo

James Watt. W. H. Auden. InPK

Jamestown. Randall Jarrell. GOA

Jamie Douglas. *Unknown. See* Waly, Waly ("When cockle shells...").

Jamie Telfer of the Fair Dodhead. *Unknown.* PeBB

Jammy. Elizabeth Ripley. TDH

Jane. David Kresh. PoUp

Jane, Jane. *Unknown.* FSW

Jane, Jane,/ Tall as a crane. Aubade. Edith Sitwell. CMoP (1970 ed.); NoAM

Jane Lee told me that in Maine she met a little boy. What Is Truth? James Wright. OSP

Jane looks down at her organdy skirt. In Bertram's Garden. Donald Justice. BoLoP; CSP; InPK; SFF; VGW

Jane Smith. Kipling. SpRo

Janet (Lady Maisry). *Unknown. See* Lady Maisry.

Janet Waking. John Crowe Ransom. CABA (1972 ed.); CMoP (1970 ed.); ExPo (1973 ed.); InPK; NCSH; NoAM; PBMP; PiAm; SoS; TAP

Jangle of the jeering crows, The. Black Humor. Archibald MacLeish. NCSH

Janie, *sel.* Faye Kicknosway. "Eye, An, a viscous eye, with the sight stopped and nothing in the." PCho

Janis Joplin and the Folding Company. Bayla Winters. AMV-80

Janitor, The; Kindergarten, Corinth. Charles Wright. *Fr.* Tattoos. GP

Jankin. *Unknown. See* Jolly Jankin.

Janna. King D. Kuka. VoR

Januar: by this fire I warme my handes. *See* January. By this fire I warm my hands.

Januaries, Nature greets our eyes. Brazil, January 1, 1502. Elizabeth Bishop. NoAM

January. Deborah Godin. AMV–80

January. Richard A. Hawley. AMV–80

January. H. R. Hays. EAS

January brings the snow. The Months [*or* Around the Year]. Sara Coleridge. CTV; OxBChV

January. [*or* Januar:] By this fire I warm my hands. The Months. *Unknown.* EBEV; GBP; OxBM

January: Cover Shooting. Wilfrid Scawen Blunt. *Fr.* An Idler's Calender. VLP

January 15 as a National Holiday. Carter Revard. VoR

January, heat. Raw saplings stand like cattle. SMLE. Les A. Murray. CAAP

January ice drifts downriver. In the Hellgate Wind. Madeline DeFrees. NYP

January Morning. William Carlos Williams. InPS

January 1919. Christopher Middleton. TwMBP

January 1939. Dylan Thomas. EAS

January of 75, The. Alan Chong Lau. NW

January Sky, The. A. G. Sobin. HeS

January sky is deep and calm, The. Reason for Not Writing Orthodox Nature Poetry. John Wain. PAIC

January Thaw. Allan Block. FAF

January 3, 1970. Mae Jackson. PoBA

January wraps up the wound of his arm. Charles Henri Ford. EAS

Japan. Gavin Bantock. TwMBP

Japan. Anthony Hecht. InPK

Japanese Beetles. X. J. Kennedy. OBAL

Japanese Children. James Kirkup. RAE

Japanese Folk-Song from Hyogo. *Unknown, tr. fr. Japanese by* Geoffrey Bownas *and* Anthony Thwaite. RAE

Japanese next to me at the bar, The. In a Bar near Shibuya Station, Tokyo. Paul Engle. SFF

Jarama Valley. *Unknown.* FSW

Jarashow. Morty Sklar. AcAn; BrS

Jars. Paul Raboff. VWA

Jasmine. Thomas Moore. *Fr.* Lalla Rookh: The Light of the Haram. PF

Jaunty traveller that comes to peer, The. Llyn y Gadair. Thomas Herbert Parry-Williams, *tr. by* Anthony Conran. OBW

Javanese Dancers. Arthur Symons. VLP

Jay Gould's Daughter. *Unknown.* FSW

Jaybird ("Jaybird a-sitting on a hickory limb"). *Unknown.* CTV

Jazz. Carolyn M. Rodgers. JB

Jazz Fantasia. Carl Sandburg. ILP (1975 ed.)

Jazz for Five, *sels.* John Smith. MPo
Colin Barnes, Drums, III.
Shake Keane, Trumpet, V.

Jazz notes and Brahms intermittently. To My Contemporaries. Edwin Rolfe. SPT

Jazzman, The. Edelin Coleman Fields. PoUp

Jazzonia. Langston Hughes. AmNP (1974 ed.); CoPAm

"Je Ne Sais Quoi", The. William Whitehead. SoSe

Je Suis une Table. Donald Hall. EAS

Je T'adore. Thomas Kinsella. NoAM

Jealous Brothers, The. *Unknown.* AmFP

Jealous Man, A. Robert Graves. CMoP (1970 ed.)

Jealous Wife, The. Vernon Scannell. HeHu

Jealousy. Rupert Brooke. TPo

Jealousy. Mary Elizabeth Coleridge. WPE

Jealousy. Rachel de Vries. AMV–81

Jealousy. John Donne. Elegies, I. FF

Jealousy. *Malay Oral Tradition, tr. by* R. J. Wilkinson *and* R. O. Winstedt. WTO

Jealousy. Stephen Vincent. NeAC

Jeames of Buckley Square. Thackeray. VLP

Jean ax'd what ribbon she should wear. Jenny's Ribbons. William Barnes. VLP

Jean Charlot. Stefan Baciu. PHC

Jean, death comes close to us all. The Child Bearers. Anne Sexton. BoWoP

Jean, Jean, Jean. Cat at the Cream. *Unknown.* GBP; POL

Jean Richepin's Song. Herbert Trench. ECBV; PFIr; PoTa

Jeanie with the Light Brown Hair. Stephen Collins Foster. BLSH, *with music*; BLSo, *with music*; FSW

Jeans. J. V. Brummels. GP

Jeep. Charles Stetler. GP

Jeff Buckner. Frank Beddo. WTO

Jefferson and Liberty. *Unknown.* FSW

Jefferson, Texas. Naomi Shihab. TAT

Jefferson Valley. John Hollander. PPP

Jehovah, God, Who Dwelt of Old, *with music.* Lewis R. Amis. AH

Jehovah-Jesus. William Cowper. PIM

Jehovah, Lord and Majesty, *with music.* Conrad Weiser, *tr. fr. German by* Sheema Z. Buehne. AH

Jellicle cats are black and white. The Song of the Jellicles. T. S. Eliot. FaBoNo; LCL; PCat; OxBChV; PoPle

Jellon Grame. *Unknown.* EBEV; PeBB

Jelly roll/ Jelly roll/ Jelly roll is so hard to find. Hambone Blues. *Unknown.* BluL

Jellyfish, A. Marianne Moore. TPo

Jellyfish, The. William Pitt Root. BoAnP; NVAP

Jennie clomped on stage. Harry Houdini, The Hippodrome, New York, January 7, 1918. Conrad Hilberry. TC

Jennifer. Howard McCord. FoP

Jenny. Leigh Hunt. *See* Jenny Kiss'd Me.

Jenny. Dante Gabriel Rossetti. VPC

Jenny cold, Jenny darkness. October Ghosts. James Wright. CAAP

Jenny Jenkins. *Unknown.* FSW
(Jinnie Jinkins.) AmFP

Jenny Kiss'd [*or* Kissed] Me. Leigh Hunt. SFF; SpRo
(Jenny.) PCOP
(Rondeau: "Jenny kissed me when we met.") FF; HoPM (1975 ed.); ILP (1975 ed.); InPK; NOBE; PAIC; PPM

Jenny kiss'd me in a dream. Such Stuff as Dreams. Franklin P. Adams. SpRo

Jenny kiss'd me when we met. Paul Dehn. *Fr.* A Leaden Treasury of English Verse. SpRo

Jenny White and Johnny Black. Eleanor Farjeon. CTV

Jenny's Ribbons. William Barnes. VLP

Jerboa, The, *sel.* Marianne Moore.
"Roman, A, had an/ artist, a freedman." CMoP (1970 ed.)

Jeremiah, *sel.* Bible, O.T.
"For thus saith the Lord to the men of Judah and Jerusalem," IV: 3–31. OBVE

Jerome. Randall Jarrell. PPP

Jerome was a dizzy giraffe. The Dizzy Giraffe. *Unknown.* TDH

Jerry Hall. *Unknown.* BBL

Jersey Belle Blues. *Unknown.* BluL

Jersey Cattle. R. N. Currey. OxBTC

Jerusalem. Rose Ausländer, *tr. fr. German by* Ewald Osers. VWA

Jerusalem, *sels.* Blake.
"But still the thunder of Los peals loud and thus the thunder's cry." OAEL–2

"Fearing that Albion should turn his back against the Divine Vision." OAEL–2

"It is easier to forgive an enemy than to forgive a friend." OAEL–2

"Of the sleep of Ulro! and of the passage through." MBPR

"Shuddring the Spectre howls. his howlings terrify the night." OAEL–2

"There is a void, outside of existence, which if enterd into." MBPR

To the Jews. MBPR

Jerusalem. Blake. *Fr. Milton. See* And Did Those Feet in Ancient Time.

Jerusalem. Ruben Kanalenstein, *tr. fr. Spanish by* Yishai Tobin. VWA

Jerusalem. Kadia Molodovski, *tr. fr. Yiddish by* S. F. Chyet. AMV–81

Jerusalem. Jon Silkin. VWA

Jerusalem. Antoni Slonimski, *tr. fr. Polish by* Isaac Komem. VWA

Jerusalem. Shlomo Vinner, *tr. fr. Hebrew by* Laya Firestone *and* Howard Schwartz. VWA

Jerusalem Delivered. Tasso. *See* Godfrey of Bulloigne.

Jerusalem in the Snow. Anath Bental, *tr. fr. Hebrew by* Howard Schwartz. VWA

Jerusalem is a limestone cracked. Guide to Jerusalem. Dennis Silk. VWA

Jerusalem is Sodom's sister city. Sodom's Sister City. Yehuda Amichai, *tr. by* Shirley Kaufman. VWA

Jerusalem Notebook, A. Harvey Shapiro. AMV–81

Jerusalem, Port City. Yehuda Amichai, *tr. fr. Hebrew by* Shirley Kaufman. VWA

Jerusalem the Golden. Bernard of Cluny, *tr. fr. Latin by* John Mason Neale. VLP

Jerusalem's autumn has prepared a text. Autumn Music. Gabriel Preil, *tr. by* Howard Schwartz. VWA

Jesse James. Rosemary *and* Stephen Vincent Benét. BPAW

Jesse James. William Rose Benét. ANTL; BPAW; PoTa

Jesse James ("It was on a Wednesday night, the moon was shining bright"). *Unknown.* AIW; UnPo (1976 ed.)

Jesse James ("Jesse James was a lad that killed many a man"). *Unknown.* AmFP; FSW

Jesse James was a two-gun man. Jesse James. William Rose Benét. ANTL; BPAW; PoTa

Jessie Mitchell's Mother. Gwendolyn Brooks. BoWoP; NMM

Jessie, my cousin, remembers there were gypsies. Gypsies. Alden Nowlan. NeAC

Jest, The. Austin Clarke. BIrV

Jest a worthless blanket Injun. The Blanket Injun. Arthur Chapman. BPAW

Jester walked in the garden, The. The Cap and Bells. W. B. Yeats. NoAM

Jesu Christ, My Leman Swete. *Unknown.* OxBM

Jesu, Come on Board, *with music.* Johann C. Pyrlaeus, *tr. fr. German by* Sheema Z. Buehne. AH

Jesu, Lover of My Soul. Charles Wesley. *See* Jesus, Lover of My Soul.

Jesu, sweete [*or* swete] sone dear [*or* dere]. The Virgin's Song. *Unknown.* BoReV; NOBE; OxBM

Jesu, to Thee My Heart I Bow, *with music.* Nicolaus L. Zinzendorf, *tr. fr. German by* John Wesley. AH

Jesus Christ ("Jesus Christ was a man that travelled through the land"). Woody Guthrie. WTO

Jesus a Child His Course Begun, *with music.* Margaret Fuller. AH

Jesus and His Mother. Thom Gunn. MPo

Jesus Borned in Bethlea. *Unknown.* AmFP

Jesus Calls Us, *with music.* Cecil Frances Alexander. BLSH

Jesus Drum. Pearl Cleage Lomax. CNA

Jesus, Enthroned and Glorified, *with music.* Zachary Eddy. AH

Jesús, Estrella, Esperanza, Mercy. Middle Passage. Robert Hayden. AmNP (1974 ed.); BPo; CoPAm; ILP (1975 ed.); NoAM; PAIC; PoBA; TC

Jesus, Friend of Little Children. Walter J. Mathams. CTV

Jesus got mad one day. A Pun for Al Gelpi. Jack Kerouac. PiAm

Jesus, grant us all a blessing. Shouting Song. *Unknown.* AmFP

Jesus, I Come to Thee, *with music.* Nathan S. S. Beman. AH

Jesus, I Live to Thee, *with music.* Henry Harbaugh. AH

Jesus, in Sickness and in Pain, *with music.* Thomas H. Gallaudet. AH

Jesus Inter Ubera Mariae. Joseph Beaumont. SCP-2

Jesus Is Coming Soon. *Unknown.* BluL

Jesus, Keep Me Near the Cross, *with music.* Fanny J. Crosby. AH

Jesus, Lord, Welcome Thou Be. *Unknown.* ILP (1975 ed.)

Jesus, Lover of My Soul. Charles Wesley. BLSH, *with music* (Christ, the Refuge of the Soul.) ILwL (Jesu, Lover of My Soul.) FaPoR

Jesus Loves Me, This I Know, *with music.* Anna B. Warner. AH

Jesus Make Up My Dying Bed. *Unknown.* BluL

Jesus, Master, O Discover, *with music. Unknown.* AH

Jesus, Merciful and Mild! *with music.* Thomas Hastings. AH

Jesus never turned on me. The Boys Brushed By. Catherine Gonick. AMV–80

Jesus our brother, strong and good. The Friendly Beasts. *Unknown.* PChr; RAE

Jesus, Saviour, Pilot Me, *with music.* Edward Hopper. AH

Jesus, Shepherd of Thy Sheep, *with music.* George Washington Bethune. AH

Jesus Song. Charley John Greasybear. PoW

Jesus Spreads His Banner o'er Us, *with music* Roswell Park. AH

Jesus, These Eyes Have Never Seen, *with music.* Ray Palmer. AH

Jesus, thou art the sinner's friend. 'Tis Sweet to Rest in Lively Hope. *Unknown.* AmFP

Jesus, Thou Divine Companion, *with music.* Henry Van Dyke. AH

Jesus Was Crucified or: It Must Be Deep. Carolyn M. Rodgers. PoBA; SA

Jesus' Wounds So Wide. *Unknown.* ILP (1975 ed.)

Jet Must Be Hunting for Something, The. Robert Penn Warren. CoPAm

Jew. Pierre Morhange, *tr. fr. French by* Edouard Roditi. VWA

Jew. James A. Randall, Jr. BPo

Jew, The. Isaac Rosenberg. VWA

Jew. Karl Shapiro. VWA

Jew at Christmas Eve, The. Karl Shapiro. VGW

Jew, in the painting by Chagall, The. Painting. A. C. Jacobs. VWA

Jew was always treated, The. Dubrovnik Poem (Emilio Tolentino). Anthony Rudolf. VWA

Jewboy. Julian Tuwim, *tr. fr. Polish by* Isaac Komem. VWA

Jewel, The. James Wright. CAPP; FoP; ILP (1975 ed.); OSP

Jewel Stairs' Grievance, The ("The jewelled steps are already quite white with dew"). Li Po, *tr. fr. Chinese by* Ezra Pound. InPK; NOBA; OBVE; PiAm; PoIA

Jeweled crown for an old man's brow, A. The Occultation of Venus. Sharlot Hall. WPW

Jewels, The. Baudelaire, *tr. fr. French.* BoLoP, *tr. by* Roy Campbell; NAWM–2, *tr. by* David Paul

Jewish Cemetery, The. Cesar Tiempo, *tr. fr. Spanish by* Angela McEvan-Alvarado. VWA

Jewish Cemetery at Newport, The. Longfellow. HAP; HeIP; HoPM (1975 ed.); NOBA; PiAm; TAP

Jewish Cemetery near Leningrad, A. Joseph Brodsky, *tr. fr. Russian by* Dimitry Pospielovsky *and* Keith Bosley. VWA

Jewish Child Prays to Jesus, A. Ilse Blumenthal-Weiss, *tr. fr. German by* Erna Baber Rosenfeld. VWA

Jewish extremities—cold. In Bed. Myra Sklarew. AMV–81

Jewish Family, The. Steven Orlen. AAN

Jewish Main Street. Irving Layton. VWA

Jewish Woman, The. Gertrud Kolmar, *tr. fr. German by* Henry A. Smith. VWA

Jews, The. Mieczyslaw Jastrun, *tr. fr. Polish by* Isaac Komem. VWA

Jews, The. Likewise. Langston Hughes. ILP (1975 ed.)

Jews in Hell, The. Isaac Goldemberg, *tr. fr. Spanish by* David Unger. VWA

Jezebel. Forbes Macgregor. MIS

Jig. C. Day Lewis. PFIr

Jig for My Wake, A. Patrick L. Clary. PoUp

Jig Tune: Not for Love. Thomas McGrath. VGW

Jigsaw Puzzle. Ann Deagon. AAN

Jill. R. D. Laing. WeW

Jim. Hilaire Belloc. BBL

Jim. Barbara Howes. GP

Jim—Age 38, 5'10", W.196, Strapping Goggle-eyed Nordic Bankrupt. Jim Harrison. FoP

Jim and I as children played together. Oh Lucky Jim. *Unknown.* GBP

Jim Crack Corn; or, The Blue Tail Fly. *Unknown.* PSoN, *with music*
(Blue-tail Fly, The.) BLSH, *with music*; BLSo, *with music*; FSW; GBP

Jim Crow. Thomas D. Rice. VLP

Jim Dandy. M. L. Rosenthal. ExPo (1973 ed.)

Jim Desterland. Hyam Plutzik. VGW

Jim-Jam Pyjamas. Gina Wilson. DuDr

Jim Jay. Walter de la Mare. SO

Jim Jones at Botany Bay. *Unknown.* GBP; PeBB

Jim, Who Ran Away from His Nurse, and Was Eaten by a Lion. Hilaire Belloc. OxBChV

Jim Worley Fries Trout on South Squalla. Jim Wayne Miller. CSP

"Jiminy Whillikers/ Admiral Samuel." Monarch of the Sea. George Starbuck. OBAL

Jimmie's Got a Goil. E. E. Cummings. TT

Jimmy Bruder on Quincey Street. Carol Artman Montgomery. AMV–81

Jimmy Jet and His TV Set. Shel Silverstein. CTBA

Jimmy Judge. *Unknown.* AmFP

Jimmy Jupp, Who Died of Over-eating. H. A. C. Evans. OSF

Jimmy's Enlisted; or, The Recruited Collier. *Unknown.* EBEV

Jimson lives in a new. A Call to the Wild. Lord Dunsany. PFIr

Jindrichuv Hradec. Christopher Middleton. TwMBP

Jingle. *Unknown.* BBL
("Hoddley, poddley, puddle and fogs.") FaBoNo

Jingle Bells. James S. Pierpont. BLSH, *with music*; BLSo, *with music*; FSW
(One Horse Open Sleigh, The, *with music*.) PSoN

Jinnie Jinkins. *Unknown. See* Jenny Jenkins.

Jinny the Just. Matthew Prior. NOBE

Jinx Blues, The. *Unknown.* BluL

Jitterbugging in the Streets. Calvin C. Hernton. PoBA

Joachim of Flora. Charles Spear. ATNZ

Joan Miró ("After that war, when death had gone away"). Ruthven Todd. EAS

Joan Miró ("Once there were peasant pots and a dry brown hare"). Ruthven Todd. EAS

Job, *abr.* Bible, *O.T.* NAWM–1
*Sels.*
"Canst thou bind the cluster of the Pleiades," XXXVIII: 31-34. OBP
"Canst thou draw out Leviathan with an hooke?" XLI. OBVE (Leviathan, *abr.*) EcS
"For there is hope for a tree," XIV: 7-17 DL
"Hast thou given the horse his might?" XXXIX: 19-25. OBP (War Horse, The.) PH
"Knowest thou the time when the wild goates of the rocke bring forth?" XXXIX. OBVE
"Let the day perish, wherein I was borne," III: 3-26. OBVE
"Man that is borne of a woman is of a few dayes, and full of trouble," XIV. OBVE
"Moreover the Lord answered Job, and said," XL. OBVE
"Then the Lord answered Job out of the whirlewind, and sayd," XXXVIII. OBVE

Job Description: Medical Records. U. A. Fanthorpe. PMW

Job Hunting. Tom Hennen. GP; HeS

Job's Ancient Lament. Owen Dodson. FB

Jobson's Amen. Kipling. ILP (1975 ed.)

Jock of Hazeldean. Sir Walter Scott. ILP (1975 ed.)

Joe Bowers. *Unknown.* AmFP; FSW

Joe Green Joe Green O how are you doing today? An Old Inmate. Kenneth Mackenzie. GAS

Joe Hill. Alfred Hayes. UnPo (1976 ed.)

Joe Hill Listens to the Praying. Kenneth Patchen. SPT

Joe Was the Best of Them. Judith McCombs. WBN

Jog on, Jog on, the Footpath Way. *Unknown.* GBP

Jog on, jog on the footpath way. Autolycus' Song. Shakespeare. *Fr.* The Winter's Tale, IV, ii. SpRo

Jog-Trot Pair, A *sel.* Thomas Hardy.
"Trite usages in tamest style." PeD

Jogging. Gary Stein. AMV–81

Jogging at Dusk. Andrew Grossbardt. AMV–80

Johannes Agricola in Meditation. Robert Browning. OAEL–2

Johannes Milton, Senex. Robert Bridges. BoReV; CMoP (1970 ed.); OBP

John. Bible, *N.T. See* St. John.

John Adkins' Farewell. *Unknown.* AmFP

John and Karl. *Unknown. Fr.* On Visiting the Graves of Keats and Marx in Hampstead Churchyard. PeD

John Anderson. Keith Douglas. SoSe

John Anderson, My Jo ("John Anderson my jo, John,/ When we were first acquent"). Burns. BoLoP; CABA (1972 ed.); FF; HeIP; InPK; IPWM; LAuP; LoAs; NOBE; SLP

John Anderson My Jo ("John Anderson my jo, John,/ I wonder what you mean"). At. to Burns. FSW; LAuP

John Anderson, My Jo ("John Anderson, my Jo, John,/ When Nature first began"). *After* Burns. FSW

*John B.* Sails. *Unknown.* FSW

John Barleycorn [a Ballad]. Burns. AIW; Epi

John Barley-Corn, My Foe. Charles Follen Adams. OBAL

John begins like Genesis. The Word Is Deed. John Wheelwright. SPT

John Brown's Body, *sels.* Stephen Vincent Benét.
Invocation: "American muse, whose strong and diverse heart." BTTM
Melora's Song. AIW

John Brown's Body. *Unknown.* BLSo, *with music*; BTTM; FSW

John Bun. *Unknown.* FaBoCo; PoPle

John Cabot, out of Wilma, once a Wycliffe. Riot. Gwendolyn Brooks. BPo; CAPP; FiCh; PoBA; Psy; TAP; TT

John Cherokee. *Unknown.* GBP

John Clare. Jon Anderson. AmPA

John Clare. John Clare. OAEL–2

John Coltrane: An Impartial Review. A. B. Spellman. CNA; NIL; PoBA

John Day, Frontiersman. Yvor Winters. MPA

John Deere, Allis Chalmers, Farm-All, Oliver. On the Land. Ray Lindquist. TAT

John Doe and Mary Smith. Podunk, 1941. Dick Allen. CoPAm

John Donne. James Simmons. CIP

John Donne Speaks from His Grave. Lord Russell Brain. PMW

John Evereldown. E. A. Robinson. CMoP (1970 ed.)

John, founder of towns,—dweller in none. Bread-Word Giver. John Wheelwright. SPT

John Garfield. Nicholas Christopher. NYP

John Gilpin was a citizen. The Diverting History of John Gilpin. William Cowper. BBL; LAuP; PoPle

John Gorham. E. A. Robinson. NoAM; SoSe (1977 ed.)

John Grumlie. Unknown. GBP

John Hardy. Unknown. AmFP; FaBoBa; FSW

John Harralson, John Harralson, you are a wretched creature. Two Appeals to John Harralson, Agent. Unknown. OBAL

John Henry, with music. Unknown, ad. by James Morehead. BLSH

John Henry (diff. versions). Unknown. AIW; AmFP; BPo; FaBoBa; FSW; NOBA; PeBB; WIF

John Hielandman. Unknown. GBP

John in the desert. Bellevue. James Harrison. CoPAm

John J. Curtis. Joseph Gallagher. AmFP

John Jacob Jingleheimer Schmidt. Unknown. FSW

John-John. Thomas MacDonagh. PFIr; PoTa

John Keats. Byron. FaBoEE; MBPR

John Kinsella's Lament for Mrs. Mary Moore. W. B. Yeats. CMoP (1970 ed.); OAEL-2

John Littlehouse the redhead was a large ruddy man. The Blacksmith's Serenade. Vachel Lindsay. PoTa

John McCormack, you are riding again the air. Upon Hearing His High Sweet Tenor Again. Joseph Langland. AMV-81

John Mouldy. Walter de la Mare. NCSH; OxBChV; PoPle

John Muir on Mt. Ritter. Gary Snyder. Myths and Texts: Burning, VIII. Epi; NOBA; TCP

John Nobody. Dom Moraes. NoAM

John of Gaunt Speaks. Shakespeare. See This England ("This royal throne of Kings, this sceptered isle").

John Oswald McGuffin he wanted to die. But Then. Ben King. PoTa

John Peel. John Woodcock Greaves. FSW; GSB, with music

John Rabbit, by Dame Eagle chased. The Eagle and the Beetle. La Fontaine, tr. by Elizur Wright. OBVE

John Riley. Unknown. FSW; GSB, with music

John Stuart Mill. E. C. Bentley. Fr. Clerihews. FaBoCo

John Sutter. Yvor Winters. MPA; NoAM; NOBA

John, Tom, and James ("John was a bad boy"). Charles Henry Ross. OxBChV

John Weber/ built this house. Re-forming a Monument. Douglas Musella. PoW

John Wesley's Rule. John Wesley. CTV

John Without Heaven. John Malcolm Brinnin. NoAM

Johnie Armstrong. Unknown. BiP; FaBoBa; HoPM (1975 ed.), cond.

Johnie Cam to Our Toun. Unknown. GBP

Johnie Cock. Unknown. FaBoBa
(Johny Cock.) PeBB

Johnnie Crack and Flossie Snail. Dylan Thomas. Fr. Under Milk Wood. LCL; RAE

Johnny Boker. Unknown. FSW

Johnny Bull, My Jo, John. Unknown. FSW

Johnny Carroll's Camp. Unknown. AmFP

Johnny Dow. Unknown. FaBoCo
(Johnny Doo.) FaBoEE

Johnny Dyers. Unknown. AmFP

Johnny Gallagher. Unknown. AmFP

Johnny Germany. Unknown. AmFP

Johnny Get Your Gun, with music. Monroe H. Rosenfeld. PSoN

Johnny, I Hardly Knew Ye. Unknown. BIrV; FaBoBA; FSW; GBP; InPK; OBP; PeBB

Johnny is a long-haired Blue. Three Cheers for the Black, White and Blue. Ruth Pitter. BoAnP

Johnny reading in his comic. Any Day Now. David McCord. QQQ

Johnny Rich, sel. Will Carleton. "Raise the light a little, Jim." PeD

Johnny Sands. Unknown. AmFP

Johnny shall have a new bonnet. Mother Goose. MG

Johnny Thomson, so they say. Mrs. Vickers' Daughter. Unknown. AmFP

Johnny Todd. Unknown. FSW

Johnny's in the basement. Subterranean Homesick Blues. Bob Dylan. InPK

Johnny's the Lad I Love. Unknown. AIW

John's my name, John Everyone, citizen. John Without Heaven. John Malcolm Brinnin. NoAM

John's Song. Joan Aiken. DuDa

John's words were the words. After the Rain. Stanley Crouch. CNA

Johnshaven. Unknown. GBP

Johnson. Unknown. FSW
(Johnson-Jinkson.) AmFP

Johnson Boys, The. Unknown. FSW

Johnson, he was riding along [or out], as fast as he could ride. Johnson. Unknown. AmFP; FSW

Johnson on Pope. David Ferry. NIL

Johnson's Ale. Unknown. FSW

Johnson's Cabinet Watched by Ants. Robert Bly. NoAM; NOBA

Johnson's Motor Car. Unknown. FSW

Johny he has risen up i' the morn. Johnie [or Johny] Cock. Unknown. FaBoBa; PeBB

Joining, The. Gerda Norvig. VWA

Jojina, My Love. Zulu Oral Tradition, tr. by H. Tracey. WTO

Joke and the Stars, The. Ted Berrigan. FiCh

Joke Versified, A. Thomas Moore. FaBoCo

Jolly Beggars, The. Burns. LAuP

Jolly Forester, The. Unknown. RAE

Jolly Jankin. Unknown. GBP; OxBM
(Jankin.) NOBE

Jolly old sow once lived in a sty, A. The Three Little Pigs. Sir Alfred Scott Gatty. DuDr; OxBChV

Jolly Plowboy, The. Unknown. AmFP

Jolly Shepherd Wat, The. Unknown. NOBE; OxBM

Jolly Soldier ("I once was a seaman stout and bold"). Unknown. AmFP; OFD

Jolly Soldier, The (" 'Tis of jolly soldier that lately came from war"). Unknown. AmFP

Jolly Thresherman, The. Unknown. AmFP

Jolly young artist called Bruno, A. Bruno. Unknown. TDH

Jolly Young Waterman, The. Charles Dibdin. PoPle

Jollymerry/ hollyberry. The Computer's First Christmas Card. Edwin Morgan. FaBoCo; MPo; NIL; PChr; SFF

Jonah. Bible, O.T. NAWM-1

Jonah. Randall Jarrell. CoPAm

Jonah: A Report. David R. Slavitt. CoPAm

Jonah Is Cast into the Sea. *Unknown. Fr.* Patience. OxBM

Jonathan Swift/ Had the gift. Lines on Swift's Ancestors. Pope. FaBoCo

Jonathan Swift Somers. Edgar Lee Masters. *Fr.* Spoon River Anthology. OBAL

Jone o'Grinfield. *Unknown.* VLP

Jones! as from Calais southward you and I. Composed near Calais, on the Road Leading to Ardres. Wordsworth. MBPR

Jordan ("When first my lines of heavenly joy made mention"). George Herbert. OAEL-1; OBW; PPP

Jordan ("Who says that fictions only and false hair"). George Herbert. CABA (1972 ed.); HAP; ILP (1975 ed.); NIL; OAEL-1; OBP; PAIC; PoPle; PPP

Joseph and Mary walked one day. The Cherry-Tree Carol. *Unknown.* AmFP

"Joseph, being seventeen years old, was feeding the flock with his brethren." Bible, *O.T. Fr.* Genesis. NAWM-1

Joseph, Dearest Joseph Mine, *with music. Unknown, tr. fr. German.* GSB

Joseph Mica. *Unknown.* GrRo

Joseph was an old man. The Cherry-Tree Carol. *Unknown.* AmFP; EBEV; FaBoBa; GBP; HeIP; IPWM; OAEL-1; OFD; PeBB

Joseph were a young man, a young man were he. The Cherry-Tree Carol. *Unknown.* AmFP

Joshua Fit De [*or* Fought the] Battle of [*or* ob] Jericho. *Unknown.* BPo; FSW; NOBA; TAP

Joshua's Face. Amir Gilboa, *tr. fr. Hebrew by* Shirley Kaufman. VWA

Journal. John Ciardi. PoA

Journal Entry: April 5, 1974. Dan Gerber. TC

Journal for My Daughter. Stanley Kunitz. RRA

Journal Literary Gazette says dozens of irate, The. Women Called Bossy Cowboys. Beth Jankola. AMV-80

Journal of Society, The. Godfrey Turner. NOBL

Journal of the Storm. Greg Kuzma. AmPA

Journal to Stella. Morton Dauwen Zabel. PoA

Journey, The. Rhyll McMaster. FPA

Journey. Diane Wakoski. IHMS

Journey Begins, The. Vern Rutsala. MPA

Journey in the Orient. Maria Luisa Spaziani, *tr. fr. Italian by* Ruth Feldman. BoWoP

Journey into France, The. *Unknown.* FaBoBa

Journey into the Eye. David Lehman. AAN

Journey of a Poem Compared to All the Sad Variety of Travel, The. Delmore Schwartz. NowV

Journey of Life, The. Bryant. EAP

Journey Nears the Road-End, The. Rabindranath Tagore, *tr. fr. Bengali by* Amiya Chakravarty. DL

Journey of the Magi. T. S. Eliot. BoReV; CABA (1972 ed.); HAP; HeIP; ILP (1975 ed.); IP; NIL; OxBTC; PBMP; PChr; PPoe; TAP; TCP; TT; UsP

Journey round the World. Ingrid Jonker, *tr. fr. Afrikaans by* Jack Cope *and* William Plomer. PBWP

Journey to Iceland. W. H. Auden. PoA

Journey to the Insane Asylum, The. Alfred Lichtenstein, *tr. fr. German by* Mary Zilzer. VWA

Journey to the Interior. Theodore Roethke. CABA (1972 ed.); VGW

Journey with Hands and Arms, The. Benjamin Saltman. VWA

Journeys. Gary Snyder. NU

Jousting of Jesus, The. William Langland. *Fr.* The Vision of Piers Plowman. BoReV

Jove for Europa's [*or* Europaes] love, took shape of bull. Parthenophil and Parthenope, LXIII. Barnabe Barnes. AAS; Epi; ESo; LoAs; NIL

Jove, grant me length of life, and years' good store. Juvenal, *tr. fr. Latin by* Dryden. *Fr.* Satires, X. SCP-1

Jove's Eagle Carries Chaucer into Space. Chaucer. *Fr.* The House of Fame. OxBM

Jovial Hunter of Bromsgrove, The. *Unknown.* PeBB

Joy. Gavin Bantock. OxBTC

Joy. Robert Creeley. PPP

Joy. Robinson Jeffers. CMoP (1970 ed.)

Joy—a beginning. Anguish, ardor. Relearning the Alphabet. Denise Levertov. NOBA

Joy Farm. Maria Gitin. PoW

Joy, I did lock thee up, but some bad man. The Bunch of Grapes. George Herbert. AnMo

Joy of a Singer, The. Piuvkaq. *See* Wonderful Occupation, A.

Joy of Church Fellowship Rightly Attended, The. Edward Taylor. *Fr.* God's Determinations. EAP
(In Heaven Soaring.) AH, *with music*

Joy of Cooking, The, *sel.* David Mus.
Conserves. PoA

Joy of my life, full oft for loving you. Amoretti, LXXXII. Spenser. HeIP

Joy of the springtime! How the sun. Sisyphus. Robert J. Burdette. PoTa

Joy, Shipmate, Joy. Walt Whitman. TAP; VoPo

Joy Sonnet in a Random Universe. Helen Chasin. NIL

Joy to Philip, he this day. Going into Breeches. Charles *and* Mary Lamb. OxBChV

Joy to the bridegroom and the bride. The Milkmaid's Epithalamium. Thomas Randolph. BoLoP

Joy to the World. Isaac Watts. BLSH, *with music*; FSW

Joyful ants nest on the roof of my tree. Sonnet. Ted Berrigan. CAAP

Joyful Sound It Is, A, *with music*. George Strebeck. AH

Joyfully, Joyfully Onward I Move, *with music*. William Hunter. AH

Joyless/ what I have [*or* have I] done. Liadan Laments Cuirithir. Liadan, *tr. by* John Montague. BIrV; PBWP

Joyous birds, hid under greenwood shade, The. Tasso, *tr. by* Edward Fairfax. *Fr.* Godfrey of Bulloigne; or, The Recoverie of Jerusalem, XVI. OBVE

Joys of Mary, The. *Unknown.* AmFP
(Seven Blessings of Mary, The, *diff. version.*) FSW

Joy's Treachery. Wilfrid Scawen Blunt. The Love Sonnets of Proteus, XVII. VLP

Juan de Juni the priest said. Aodh Ruadh O'Domhnaill. Thomas MacGreevy. CIP

Juan de Pareja: Painted by Velázquez. Richard A. Long. AmNP (1974 ed.)

Juan knew several languages—as well. Byron. *Fr.* Don Juan, XI. OAEL-2

Juan Quintana. Alice Corbin. BPAW

Juan, the moron next door. Report from the Correspondent They Fired. David McElroy. AmPA

Juanita. Caroline Norton. BLSH, *with music*; FSW

Juanito's Blues. Antar S. K. Mberi. SES

Jubilate Agno, *sels.* Christopher Smart.
"For I am not without authority in my jeopardy." LAuP; OBP
"For I bless the Prince of Peace and pray that all the guns may be nail'd up." InPS
"For I will consider my Cat Jeoffry." AnMo; HAP; HeIP; ILP (1975 ed.); InPK; LAuP; OAEL-1; OBW; PCat; PPP; Prf
(Of Jeoffry, His Cat.) NU
"For the air is purified by prayer which is made aloud." Prf
"For the doubling of flowers is the improvement of the gardners talent." LAuP
"Let Elizure rejoice with the partridge." OAEL-1

"Rejoice in god, O ye tongues; give the glory to the Lord, and the Lamb." LAuP

Jubilate Herbis. Norma Farber. PChr

Jubilation T. Cornpone. Johnny Mercer. OBAL

Jubilee. *Unknown.* FSW

Judah in Exile Wanders, *with music.* George Sandys. AH

Judas. Andrew Baster. BuTh

Judas. Vassar Miller. CoPAm

Judas. *Unknown.* Epi; OxBM

Judas Before. Lucille F. Travis. AATT

Judas Iscariot. R.A.K. Mason. ATNZ

Judas Iscariot. Stephen Spender. ILP (1975 ed.)

Judas, Joyous Little Son. Norma Farber. AMV-80

Judas, Peter. Luci Shaw. AMV-80

Judas Touch, The. David Malouf. FPA

Judean Summer. Fay Lipshitz. VWA

Judeebug's Country. Joe Johnson. PoBA

Judezmo Writer in Turkey Angry, A. Stephen Levy. VWA

Judge, The. Karl Kopp. TAT

Judge, The. Kenneth A. McClane. AMV-81

Judge Bean's court, knowed near and far. Fine! S. Omar Barker. BPAW

Judge gimme life this morning. Parchman Farm Blues. *Unknown.* BluL

Judge Harsh Blues. *Unknown.* BluL

Judge Kroll. Barbara L. Greenberg. AMV-81

Judge Me, O God, *with music.* Joel Barlow. AH

Judge Roy Bean of Vinegarroon. The Law West of the Pecos. S. Omar Barker. BPAW

Judge said "Stand up, boy, and dry up your tears," The. Twenty-one Years. *Unknown.* AmFP

Judge Somers. Edgar Lee Masters. *Fr.* Spoon River Anthology. FaBoEE; OBSV

Judge, who lives impeccably upstairs, The. Upstairs Downstairs. Hervey Allen. PoA

Judge with the Sore Rump, The. St. George Tucker. OBAL

Judgement Day. *Unknown.* WTO

Judges, *sel.* Bible, *O.T.*
    Song of Deborah, The, V:1–31. BoWoP; PBWP

Judging Distances. Henry Reed. Lessons of the War, II. BoLoP; NIL; NOBE; PSN; SoSe

Judgment, The. Kathleen Spivack. BoWoP

Judgment Day. Robert Garioch, *after the Italian of* Giuseppe Belli. OBVE

Judgment of Paris, The. W. S. Merwin. NNaP; UsP

Judith of Bethulia. John Crowe Ransom. NoAM; NOBA; PiAm

Judith Recalls Holofernes. Maura Stanton. AmPA

Judy-One. Don L. Lee. TAP

Jug-jug! Fair fall the nightingale. I Am Not as I Wish. Richard Brathwaite. *Fr.* Nature's Embassy. SCP-2

Jug of Punch, The. Francis McPeake. FSW

Juggle of Myrtle Twigs, A. Edward Codish. VWA

Juggler. Richard Wilbur. CMoP (1970 ed.); NCSH; TAP

Juggler and the Baron's Daughter, The. *Unknown.* OxBM ("Draw me nere, draw me nere.") EBEV

Juggling Jerry. George Meredith. VLP

Jugs, The. Paul Celan, *tr. fr. German by* Christopher Middleton. OBVE

JuJu. Askia Muhammad Touré. PoBA

Juju of My Own, A. Lebert Bethune. InPS; PoBA

Jukebox has a big square face, The. Kenneth Fearing. *Fr.* King Juke. OSP

Juke Box Love Song. Langston Hughes. ILP (1975 ed.); OLR; PoBA

Julia, how Irishly you sacrifice. Reproach to Julia. Robert Graves. FaBoEE

Julia, I Bring. A Ring Presented to Julia. Robert Herrick. BBL

Julia, if I chance to die. His Request to Julia. Robert Herrick. CaPo

Julia, when thy Herrick dies. To Julia. Robert Herrick. CaPo

Julian and Maddalo. Shelley. MBPR; OAEL-2, *much abr.*

Julia's Petticoat. Robert Herrick. CaPo; SCP-1

Juliet. Hilaire Belloc. BoLoP

Juliet. Shakespeare. *Fr.* Romeo and Juliet, II, ii. PCOP

Julio. Kell Robertson. TAT

Julius Caesar, *sels.* Shakespeare.
    "Cowards die many times before their deaths," *fr.* II, ii. FF
    Mark Antony Addresses the Mob, *fr.* III, ii. FaPoR

Julius Caesar. *Unknown.* InPK

July. John Clare. *See* Shepherd's Calendar, The.

July. Lucille Clifton. CC

July. Austin Dobson. RAE

July. W. Ralph Johnson. AMV-81

July dust covers the ever-/ greens where I lie. In the Scales: I. Madeline DeFrees. *Fr.* A Catch of Summer. MPA

July 4th. May Swenson. PoA

July ghost, aghast at the strange winter, A. Midsummer Frost. Isaac Rosenberg. UsP

July in Indiana. Robert Fitzgerald. ANTL

July in Washington. Robert Lowell. Prf; WasP

July, 1964. Donald Davie. ExPo (1973 ed.)

July Noon in Dupont Circle. Ann Darr. PoUp

July Storm, A: Johnson, Nemaha County, Nebraska. Steve Hahn. AMV-81

July the first, in Oldbridge town, there was a grievous battle. The Battle of the Boyne. Captain Blacker. BTTM

July the first, of a morning clear, one thousand six hundred and ninety. The Boyne Water. *Unknown.* FaPoR

July the Seventh. Leslie Norris. HeHu

July 31. Norman Jordan. PoBA

July 12. Simon J. Ortiz. NW

Jumblies, The. Edward Lear. BBL; CTV; EBEV; FaBoNo; OxBChV; SS

Jump bigness upward. Mwilu/ or Poem for the Living. Don L. Lee. JB

Jump Jim Crow, *with music.* Thomas D. Rice. BLSo

Jump over the wall and come to me. Come to Me. *Gond Oral Tradition, tr. by* V. Elwin *and* S. Hivale. WTO

Jump Shot. Richard Peck. MiP; SPo

Jump Shooter, The. Dennis Trudell. LiSp

Jump stone hand leaf shadow sun. The Fire. Robert Duncan. *Fr.* Passages. VGW

Jump-to-Glory Jane. George Meredith. VLP

Jumped his cage. The Gerbil Who Got Away. Judith C. Root. AMV-81

June. Francis Ledwidge. BIrV

June. William Morris. *Fr.* The Earthly Paradise. LFH

June. Bink Noll. TCP

June. Spenser. *Fr.* The Shepheardes Calender. PAIC

June Bracken and Heather. Tennyson. PPoe

June first we spoke. We Talked. Americo Casiano. NW

June Fugue. Thomas W. Shapcott. CAAP; GAS

June Is Bustin' Out All Over, *with music.* Oscar Hammerstein II. BLSo

June 1967 at Buchenwald. Alan Bold. UsP

June Rain. W. S. Merwin. PHC

June Song. Abby Rosenthal. AMV-81

June Thunder ("Junes were free and full"). Louis MacNeice. CMoP (1970 ed.); MPo

Jungle, The. Arthur J. Bull. HeHu

Jungle, The. Alun Lewis. OBW

Jungle, The. William Carlos Williams. CABA (1972 ed.)

Jungle Husband, The. Stevie Smith. BBL; BuTh

Jungle is about me, The: I am content. The Jungle. Arthur J. Bull. HeHu

Junglegrave. S. E. Anderson. PoBA

Junior Addict. Langston Hughes. BPo; CNA; TCP

Junior's just a little tot. On His Marks. Richard Armour. PPM

Juniper. Eileen Duggan. PChr

Juniper. Robert Francis. VGW

Juniper ("Juniper, Juniper/ Green in the snow"). Unknown. RAE

Junk. Richard Wilbur. HAP; InPK; PPoD; WeW

Junk. William Zaranka. AMV-80

Junkies Is. Horace Coleman. SES

Junkman's Obbligato. Lawrence Ferlinghetti. WIF

Jupiter and Ten. James Thomas Fields. OBAL

Just. Judith Johnson Sherwin. TAP

Just a Closer Walk with Thee. Unknown. FSW

Just a line to remind my friends that after much trouble. Dear Folks. Patrick Kavanagh. FaBoTw (1975 ed.)

Just a little more. Mythistorema. George Seferis, tr. by Rex Warner. BuTh

Just a little rain falling all around. What Have They Done to the Rain. Malvina Reynolds. FSW; PoRo

Just a Smack at Auden. William Empson. FaBoCo; UnPo (1976 ed.)

Just a While. Frantisek Gottlieb, tr. fr. Czech by Ewald Osers. VWA

Just a worried old rounder. Lowdown Rounder's Blues. Unknown. BluL

Just about now. To a Woman Half a World Away. Dick Allen. CoPAm

Just after the Widow's Death. Barbara Greenberg. RiTi

Just an Old Sweet Song. Donagh MacDonagh. CIP

Just and fit actions Ptolemy (he saith). Lucan, tr. by Ben Jonson. Fr. Pharsalia, VII. OBVE

Just and Unjust. At. to Lord Bowen. See Rain, The ("The rain it raineth every day").

Just as eventide draws near. Song of Longing. Tr. fr. Maori by John White. WTO

Just as I Am, with music. Charlotte Elliott. BLSH ("Just as I am—without one plea."). VLP

Just as I'd sucked in wind to take. A Monstrous Mouse. X. J. Kennedy. CC

Just as my fingers close about the pen. The Spider. Kenneth Mackenzie. BoAnP

Just as my fingers on these keys. Peter Quince at the Clavier. Wallace Stevens. AnMo; CABA (1972 ed.); CMoP (1970 ed.); ExPo (1973 ed.); InPK; InPS; LoAs; NOBA; PAIC; PPP; SoSe; STS; TAP; TCP; TT; UsP

Just as the day is about to die. Dog in the Fountain. Raymond Souster. GDP

Just as the signal tower lights flash. Night at an Airport. David Ignatow. NNaP

Just as the Small Waves Came Where No Waves Were. Pamela Millward. NU

Just as Thou Art, with music. Russell Sturgis Cook. AH

Just Ask for a Demonstration. Edward Weismiller. WasP

Just at that moment the Wolf. Coup de Grâce. A. D. Hope. IP; PPP

Just back of the beach at Cannes, the afternoon blue as angels swimming. Afternoon. Paul Davis. AMV-81

Just Because. Moishe Leib Halpern, tr. fr. Yiddish by Ruth Whitman. VWA

Just Because. David McCord. ECBV

Just because you wear a natural baby. Dancing in the Street. Al Young. SA

Just before I sleep. Out of the Gaping Distance. Cynthia Nibbelink. TC

Just before the Battle, Mother. George Frederick Root. FSW; PSoN, with music.

Just broke from school, pert, impudent, and raw. The Modern Fine Gentleman. Soame Jenyns. ESaP; OBSV

Just California. John S. McGroarty. BPAW

Just down around the corner of the street where I reside. Sweet Rosie O'Grady. Maude Nugent. FSN

Just Dropped In. William Cole. POL

Just for a handful of silver he left us. The Lost Leader. Robert Browning. BTTM; PBMP; PPoD; VLP

Just for Propaganda. H. H. Lewis. SPT

Just get up. The Empress Hotel Poems. Anselm Hollo. AcAn

Just hand me my old Martin, for soon I will be startin'. Franklin D. Roosevelt's Back Again. Unknown. FSW

Just inside the bark the tree's charm slides. Tree Animals. Laurence Lieberman. CoPAm

Just Italian, The, sel. Sir William Davenant. "This lady, ripe and calm and fresh." SCP-2

Just keep/ inflating/ and patching. 11/22/75. Darlene Pearlstein. FiCh

"Just keep quiet and we're not going to hurt you." Getting Through the Fifties: The Starkweather Case Revisited. Robert Hahn. AAN

Just like a penitent that doth prepare. Love's Preparation. William Cavendish, Duke of Newcastle. SCP-2

Just look out there in the lot, dozens. The Poet Finds an Ephemeral Home in a Truck Stop on the New Jersey Turnpike, ca. 1970. James Baker Hall. CSP

Just lookee here mama don't treat pigmeat the way you do. Pigmeat. Unknown. BluL

Just lost, when I was saved! Emily Dickinson. NOBA; Prf

Just man followed then his angel guide, The. Lot's Wife. "Anna Akhmatova," tr. by Richard Wilbur. BoWoP; PBWP

Just now/ Out of the strange. The Warning [or Cinquain]. Adelaide Crapsey. OSP; WeW; WPE

Just now the lilac is in bloom. The Old Vicarage, Grantchester. Rupert Brooke. OxBTC

Just off the highway to Rochester, Minnesota. A Blessing. James Wright. ANTL; ConAP; ILP (1975 ed.); InPK; NoAM; NOBA; PPP; SFF; SoSe; UsP; VoA

Just out of San Francisco one cold December day. The Dying Hobo. Unknown. AmFP

Just over the border. Montana. Kenneth O. Hanson. MPA

Just Passing Through. Philip Roberts. FPA

Just past the clockhouse is a building of cinder. Letter to My Kinder. Bob Gaskin. AMV-81

Just so it goes—the day, the night. An Ordinary evening in Cleveland. Lewis Turco. ANTL

Just Taking Note. Sharon Scott. JB

Just Tell Them That You Saw Me, with music. Paul Dresser. FSN

"Just the place for a Snark!" the Bellman cried. The Hunting of the Snark. "Lewis Carroll." FaBoNo

Just then, forgetful of the strict command. Homer, tr. by William Cowper. Fr. The Odyssey, XII. OBVE

Just Think. Paul Celan, tr. fr. German by Joachim Neugroschel. VWA

Just This. István Vas, tr. fr. Hungarian by Jascha Kessler. VWA

Just this morning I signed the contract. Pearl Harbor Day 1970. Dick Lourie. NeAC

Just three days old. The New Moon. Issa, tr. by Harold G. Henderson. Moon

Just to be tender, just to be true. God's Will for You and Me. *Unknown.* IP; SoSe (1977 ed.)

Just two hours after. Senryu. Les A. Murray. GAS

Just Visiting. Peter Dale. PMW

Just weeks ago dead. Poppies. Greg Kuzma. HeS

Just when you're able to admit. Corps d'Esprit. Heather McHugh. AmPA

Just where my long road started out, it ends. Going Back. Donald Petersen. UsP

Just yesterday morning they let me know you were gone. Fire and Rain. James Taylor. WIF

Justice. Langston Hughes. BPo

Justice. Petra von Morstein, *tr. fr. German by* Rosemarie Waldrop. BoWoP

Justice corrupts/All those years of spying. The Watergate Elegy. Robert Dana. WasP

Justice Denied in Massachusetts. Edna St. Vincent Millay. GOA; RiTi; SBG

Justice Has Become a Woman. Anne Hazlewood Brady. WBN

Justice Is Reason Enough. Diane Wakoski. AmPA

Justice is the Man's statue. Justice Has Become a Woman. Anne Hazlewood Brady. WBN

Justice of the Peace, The. Hilaire Belloc. OBSV

Justshakeityoucanbreakityoucanhangitonthewall. Hang It on the Wall. *Unknown.* BluL

Justus Quidem Tu Es, Domine. Gerard Manley Hopkins. *See* Thou Art Indeed Just, Lord, If I Contend.

# K

Ka 'Ba. Amiri Baraka. BPo; CAPP; CNA; PiAm; TAP

Kabbalist, The. Deborah Eibel. VWA

Kabul town's by Kabul river. Ford o' Kabul River. Kipling. FaBoTw (1975 ed.)

Kachinas. Lawrence Kearney. PoW

Kaddish. Allen Ginsberg. VWA
   *Sels.*
   "O Russian faced, woman on the grass." TPo
   "Strange now to think of you gone without corsets & eyes." ExPo (1973 ed.); NOBA

Kaddish. David Ignatow. NU; VWA

Kaddish ("In her last sickness, my mother took my hand in hers"). Charles Reznikoff. *Fr.* Going To and Fro and Walking Up and Down. SA

Kaddish ("Upon Israel and upon the rabbis"). Charles Reznikoff. *Fr.* Separate Way. SA

Kaddish for Naomi Ginsberg. Allen Ginsberg. *See* Kaddish.

Kafka's Other Metamorphosis. Len Gasparini. NeAC

Kag the Porcupine (The Misanthrope). Arthur Guiterman. ECBV

Kaho'olawe! A thrust of land. The Bombing of Kaho'olawe. Marjorie Sinclair. PHC

Kaire. Richard Eberhart. NoAM

Kalahari. Luis Palés Matos, *tr. fr. Spanish by* Rachel Benson. InW

Kalahari Bushman fires flowing. Firebowl. Sydney Clouts. VWA

Ka-la-kaua, a great name. Praise Song for King Kalakaua. *Tr. fr. Hawaiian by* N. B. Emerson. WTO

Kalaloch. Carolyn Forché. AmPA

Kaleidoscopic memories fall in and out. Memory Movie. Diane Webster. AMV-81

Kalorama Triangle, The. Terence Winch. PoUp

Kangaroo. D. H. Lawrence. EBEV; InPS; OxBTC

Kangaroo, The. *Unknown.* ECBV

Kansa, The. Victor Contoski. HeS

Kansas Boy. Ruth Lechlitner. ANTL

Kansas Boys. *Unknown.* FSW

Kansas City. Oscar Hammerstein II. OBAL

Kansas City Blues. *Unknown.* FSW

Kansas City West Bottoms. Edward Dahlberg. PoA

Karen can canter, Karen can. Horse-Girl. Henry Petroski. PH

Kariuki. Joseph Gatuira. TVo

Karl ("All day he stood at Weeping Cross"). Charles Spear. ATNZ

Karl ("Outside among the talking criss-cross reeds"). Charles Spear. ATNZ

Karl Marx. Al Lee. AmPA

Karl Marx is a comic novelist, almost. John Tranter. The Alphabet Murders, XI. GAS

Karl, my friend, caught the crabs. Policy of the House. Charles Stetler. GP

Karma. E. A. Robinson. CMoP (1970 ed.); HeIP; ILP (1975 ed.); IPWM; NoAM; OFD; PiAm; STS

Karma Repair Kit: Items 1-4. Richard Brautigan. IPWM

Karshish, the picker-up of learning's crumbs. An Epistle Containing the Strange Medical Experience of Karshish, the Arab Physician. Robert Browning. PFD; VLP

Kashrut. Edouard Roditi. VWA

Kassie Jones. *Unknown.* BluL

Kate and the Cowhide. *Unknown.* AmFP

Kate Being Pleased. Sir John Davies. POL
   (In Katam.) FaBoEE

Kate Dalrymple. *Unknown.* GBP

Kate meets me at the top of the stairs. At Veronica's. Robert Peterson. NeAC

Kathaleen Ny-Houlahan. James Clarence Mangan, *after the Irish of* William Heffernan. VLP

Käthe Kollwitz. Muriel Rukeyser. NMM; RiTi

Katherine. Paul F. Fericano. CPA

Katherine's Dream. Robert Lowell. *Fr.* Between the Porch and the Altar. ConAP

Kathleen Mavourneen. Mrs. A. B. Crawford *and* F. Nicholls Crouch. FSW

Kathleen ni Houlihan. The Celtic Fringe. Stevie Smith. FaBoNo

Kathlyn. Michael Dransfield. FPA

Katie May. *Unknown.* BluL

Kato's Poem. David Kherdian. FAF

Katrina. Bruce Dawe. CAAP

Katy Cline. *Unknown.* FSW

Katy Cruel. *Unknown.* FSW

Katydids. Amy Lowell. PBWP

Katzenjammer Kids, The. James Reaney. AKE

Kayumangi. Jessica Tarahata Hagedorn. MMD

Kearney at Seven Pines. Edmund Clarence Stedman. BTTM

Keats. Longfellow. ILP (1975 ed.); TAP

Keats to Fanny Brawne. Edgar Lee Masters. PoA

Keel Row, The. *Unknown.* PoPle

Keelhauled across the star-wrecked death of God. George Barker. *Fr.* Sonnets of the Triple-headed Manichee. PoA

Keen, fitful gusts are whisp'ring here and there. Keats. CABA (1972 ed.); MBPR

Keener tempests come, The: and, fuming dun. James Thomson. *Fr.* The Seasons: Winter. EBEV

Keep Hidden from Me ("Keep from me all that I might comprehend!"). Rachel Korn, *tr. fr. Yiddish by* Carolyn Kizer. PBWP

Keep in a Cool Place. Allen Curnow. ATNZ

Keep in the heart the journal nature keeps. Conrad Aiken. Preludes for Memnon, XLII. CMoP (1970 ed.)

Keep It Clean. *Unknown.* BluL

Keep It under Your Hat. Gary Margolis. CoPAm

Keep me as your servant, O Girdhar. Mirabai, *tr. fr. Medieval Hindi by* Usha Nilsson. PBWP

Keep me clean. Chamber-Pot Rhyme. *Unknown.* GBP

Keep My Skillet Good and Greasy. *Unknown.* FSW

Keep on Pushing. David Henderson. PoBA

Keep the commandments, Trapp, and go no further. Abel Evans. FaBoEE

Keep the Sea. *Unknown. Fr.* The Libelle of Englyshe Polycye. OxBM

Keep thy tunge, thy tunge, thy tunge. Wicked Tongues. *Unknown.* OxBM

Keep to yourself your kisses. Taisigh Agat Fein Do Phog. *Unknown, tr. by* Maire Cruise O'Brien. BIrV

Keep your back door locked baby, keep your windows pinned. Keep Your Windows Pinned. *Unknown.* BluL

Keep your distance, Stranger Death, and call. Unwelcome. Irma Dovey. AMV–80

Keep Your Eyes on the Prize. *Unknown.* FSW

Keep your eyes open when you kiss: do: when. John Berryman. BoLoP

Keep Your Face. George Tsongas. CPA

Keep Your Lamp Trimmed and Burning. *Unknown.* FSW

Keep Your Windows Pinned. *Unknown.* BluL

Keeper, The. *Unknown.* FSW

Keeper, The. Living There. James Dickey. UsP

Keeper did a hunting go, The. The Keeper. *Unknown.* FSW

Keeper of the Eddystone Light, The. *Unknown. See* Eddystone Light, The.

Keeper unlocks the cage, The. Performance. Raymond R. Patterson. FoP

Keepers. Roger McDonald. FPA

Keeping Hair. Ramona Wilson. VoR

Keeping Informed in D.C. Howard Nemerov. WasP

Keeping Things Whole. Mark Strand. CoPAm; NIL; NoAM; PPP; SFF; TAP

Keeping Watch on the Heart. Vicki Viidikas. FPA

Keeping You Alive. Tess Gallagher. GP

Kelly. Robert Hershon. NeAC

Kelly Show, The. Charles Higham. MAuV

Kelly's kept an unlicensed bull, well away. The Outlaw. Seamus Heaney. NoAM

Kemp Owyne. *Unknown.* PeBB

Kennack Sands. Laurence Binyon. EcS

Kennedy. Michael Heffernan. AMV–80

Kennedy. Molly Kazan. SoS

Kennedy Airport. Aaron Kramer. AMV–80

Kennel. Beth Bentley. CNW

Kenst doo hoo. The Miller's Wife's Lullaby. *Unknown.* GBP

Kent State Massacre, The. Jack Warshaw *and* Barbara Dane. FSW

Kent State, May 4, 1970. Paul Goodman. MAT; TSWA

Kentish Sir Byng stood for his King. Cavalier Tunes. Robert Browning. BTTM

Kentucky Babe, *with music.* Richard Henry Buck. BLSH; FSN

Kentucky Belle. Constance Fenimore Woolson. PH; PoTa

Kentucky Blues. *Unknown.* BluL

Kentucky Bootlegger. *Unknown.* FSW

Kentucky Moonshiner. *Unknown. See* Moonshiner.

Kentucky water, clear springs: a boy fleeing. The Swimmers. Allen Tate. InPS; NOBA

Kepe well x and flee fro vii. Ten Commandments, Seven Deadly Sins, and Five Wits. *Unknown.* FaBoEE

Kerry Recruit, The. *Unknown.* FSW; RDB, *with music*

Kevin Barry [Died for Ireland, 1st November, 1920]. *Unknown.* FaBoBa; FSW

Key of the Kingdom, The. Ed Reed. BBGO

Key of the Kingdom, The. *Unknown. See* This Is the Key of the Kingdom.

Key to Everything, The. May Swenson. IHMS; Psy

Key West. Hart Crane. CMoP (1970 ed.)

Keys. Glen Rockwell. AMV–81

Keys of Canterbury, The. *Unknown.* AmFP

Keys turning. The Liberator. Emily Holmes Coleman. EAS

Khwa! Ye! O! Rainbow, O rainbow! The Rainbow. *Unknown.* AKE

Kick at the rock, Sam Johnson, break your bones. Epistemology. Richard Wilbur. NoAM; NOBA

Kicking from Centre Field. David McFadden. NeAC

Kicking Lego Blocks, *sels.* Shawn Wong. NW
  "Breakfast at Cindy's place."
  "Two hours after I saw her."
  "Wherever we are in this country."

Kicking Mule, The. *Unknown.* AmFP

Kicking the Leaves. Donald Hall. FoP; TC

Kid. Robert Hayden. NCSH

Kid Stuff. Frank Horne. AmNP (1974 ed.); PChr; PoBA

Kidnap Poem. Nikki Giovanni. AmNP (1974 ed.); BPo; InPK; NoAM; TAP; UsP

Kidnaper. Tess Gallagher. AmPA

Kids are asleep, The. It's a Different Story When You're Going into the Wind. David McFadden. NeAC

Kids are left out late tonight, The. New Year 1974. Rae Desmond Jones. CAAP

Kid's Last Fight, The. *Unknown.* SPo

Kid's packed the last five months, The. Fish. Michael Hogan. DNGG; GP

Kilbarrack 1969. Finbarr Crowley. IPM

Kilcash. *Unknown, tr. fr. Irish by* Frank O'Connor. BIrV; PFIr

Kill or be killed, the sergeant cried. The Killer Too. Walker Gibson. FF

Killed at the Ford. Longfellow. ILP (1975 ed.)

Killed by an omnibus—why not? On a Man Run Over by an Omnibus. Henry Luttrell. FaBoEE

Killer Diller. *Unknown.* BluL

Killer Too, The. Walker Gibson. FF

Killigrew Wood, The. Norman Dubie. AmPA

Killing, The. Arthur Smith. AAN

Killing a Whale. David Gill. BoAnP

Killing Kiss, The. Thomas Stanley. SCP–2

Killing of the Birds, The. Shirley Williams. BoWoP

Killing of the Sparrows, The. Patricia Beer. HeHu

Killings continue, each second, The. City Psalm. Denise Levertov. PiAm

Kilroy. Eugene McCarthy. NIL

Kilroy. Peter Viereck. FF; NIL

Kilroy Turtle. D. C. Berry. CSP

Kilruddery Hunt, The. Thomas Mozeen. BIrV

Kind[e] are her answers [*or* answeres]. Thomas Campion. BoLoP; LoAs; SCP–2

Kind Armadillo, The. Oliver Herford. TDH

Kind friends, you must pity my horrible tale [*or* won't you listen to my pitiful tale]. The Dreary Black Hills. *Unknown.* AmFP; FSW

Kind kinderpark. Bears and Waterfalls. May Sarton. GP

Kind o'er the kinderbank leans Myfanwy. Myfanwy. John Betjeman. BoLoP

Kind of an Ode to Duty. Ogden Nash. IP

Kind of change came in my fate, A. Byron. *Fr.* The Prisoner of Chillon. NOBE

Kind of Good-bye, A. Theodore Spencer. IP

Kind of Love, A. Jeanette Nichols. RiTi

Kind of Palmistry, A. Paul Murray. IPM

Kind of Poetry I Want, The, *sels.* "Hugh MacDiarmid." InPS
"And, constantly, I seek/ A poetry of facts."
"Poetry of one the Russians call 'a broad nature,' The."

Kind old face, the egg-shapped head, The. On a Portrait of a Deaf Man. John Betjeman. NoAM

Kind pity chokes my spleen; brave scorn forbids. Satires, III. John Donne. CABA (1972 ed.); EBEV; PAIC; OAEL-1; SCP-1

Kind Words Can Never Die, *with music.* Abby Hutchinson. AH

Kinde are her answeres. *See* Kind are her answers.

Kindergarten. Ronald Rogers. VW

Kindergarten children first come forth, The. The May Day Dancing. Howard Nemerov. NoAM

Kindergarten Teacher. Stanley Kiesel. NowV

Kindertotenlieder. Michael Longley. CIP

Kindle the Christmas brand and then. The Ceremonies for Candlemas Day. Robert Herrick. ILP (1975 ed.)

Kindle the Taper, *with music.* Emma Lazarus. AH

Kindly Unhitch That Star, Buddy. Ogden Nash. ILP (1975 ed.); PPM

Kindness. Sylvia Plath. Psy

Kindness. *Unknown. See* Pussy.

Kindness to Animals. *Unknown.* CTV

Kindred. Douglas Stewart. MAuV

King, The. Kipling. CABA (1972 ed.); VLP

King, The. Douglas Livingstone. BoAnP

King, The. *Unknown.* TDH

King and Queen of the Pelicans we. The Pelican Chorus. Edward Lear. FaBoNo; PB

King Arthur Growing Very Tired Indeed. Mortimer Collins. FaBoCo

King asked, The. The King's Breakfast. A. A. Milne. OxBChV

King Billy. Edwin Morgan. MS

King but an his nobles a', The. Brown Robin. *Unknown.* PeBB

King can move a single square, The. The Powers of the Pawn. David Solway. AMV-81

King Charles the First. *Unknown.* GBP

King David and King Solomon. David and Solomon. James Ball Naylor. PoPle

King Edward the Fourth and a Tanner of Tamworth. *Unknown.* PeBB

King Fisher courted Lady Bird. The King-Fisher Song. "Lewis Carroll." *Fr.* Sylvie and Bruno Concluded. FaBoNo

King George [*or* The King], observing with judicious eyes. Epigram. Joseph Trapp. FaBoCo; FaBoEE

King had three little sons, The. Lanzarote. *Unknown, tr. by* W. S. Merwin. Epi

King Harald's Trance. George Meredith. VLP

King he hath been a prisoner, The. Willie o Winsbury. *Unknown.* PeBB

King he sits in Dumferling town, The. *See* King sits in Dunfermline town, The.

King he wrote a love-letter, The. Lord Derwentwater. *Unknown.* AmFP

King Henry IV, Pt. I, *sel.* Shakespeare.
"O Harry, thou hast robb'd me of my youth!" *fr.* V, iv. LFH

King Henry V, *sels.* Shakespeare.
Henry V before Agincourt, *fr.* IV, iii. FaPoR
(King Henry the Fifth before Agincourt.) BTTM
Honey-Bees, *fr.* I, ii. PCOP
"I will not change my horse with any that treads," *fr.* III, vi. PH

(Horse, The) PCOP

King Henry the Fifth before Harfleur, *fr.* III, i. BTTM
("Once more unto the breach, dear friends, once more.") PPoe

"Now entertain conjecture of a time," *fr.* IV, Prologue. EBEV

St. Crispin's Day, *fr.* IV, iii. FF

"Thus with imagin'd wing our swift scene flies," *fr.* III, Prologue. EBEV

"We few, we happy few, we band of brothers," *fr.* IV, iii. UnPo (1976 ed.)

King Henry VIII, *sels.* Shakespeare *and probably* John Fletcher.
Last Words of Cardinal Wolsey, The, *fr.* III, ii. PIM
("Cromwell, I did not think to shed a tear.") PoIA
Sweet Music's Power, *fr.* III, i. Fletcher. NOBE

King I Sit. *Unknown.* OxBM

King Juke, *sel.* Kenneth Fearing.
"Jukebox has a big square face, The." OSP

King Lear, *sels.* Shakespeare.
"And my poor fool is hang'd! No, no, no life!" *fr.* V, iii. LFH
"Ay, every inch a king:/ When I do stare, see how the subject quakes," *fr.* IV, vi. OBP
"Blow, winds, and crack your cheeks! rage! blow! *fr.* III, ii. OBP; UsP
"Here's the place: stand still: how fearfull," *fr.* IV, vi. PES
"How does my royal lord? How fares your Majesty?" *fr.* IV, vii. Prf
"It may be so, my lord./ Hear, Nature, hear!" *fr.* I, iv. OBP
"Let it be so; thy truth then be thy dower," *fr.* I, i. OBP
"No, no, no, no! Come, let's away to prison," *fr.* V, iii. OBP
"Please you, draw near.—Louder the music there!" *fr.* IV, vii. EBEV
"Thou art a lady;/ If only to go warm were gorgeous," *fr.* II, iv. OBP
"Thou thinkst 'tis much that this contentious storm," *fr.* III, iv. OBP
"We are not the first," *fr.* V, iii. PoPle

King Lives. Jill Witherspoon Boyer. CNA

King Midas. Howard Moss. TAP

King's Speech, The, *sel.* PoA

King Midas Has Asses' Ears. Donald Finkel. CoPAm

King Must Die, The. Bernie Taupin. GrRo

King, observing with judicious eyes, The. *See* King George, observing with judicious eyes.

King of Ai, The. Hyam Plutzik. VWA

King of Beasts. Oliver Herford. PCOP

King of China's Daughter, The. Edith Sitwell. RAE

King of Harlem, The. Federico García Lorca, *tr. fr. Spanish by* Ben Belitt. NYP

King of Ireland's Cairn, The, *abr.* "Ethna Carbery." WPE

King of Kings. Hubert Witheford. ATNZ

King of rock 'n roll, The. Painkillers. Thom Gunn. AMV-81

King of the perennial holly-groves, the riven sandstone. Geoffrey Hill. Mercian Hymns, I. HAP

King of the World. O. B. Hardison. PoUp

King Oliver of New Orleans. Satchmo. Melvin B. Tolson. BPo

King, on assuming his reign, A. The King. *Unknown.* TDH

King Pellam's Launde. David Jones. In Parenthesis, IV. NoAM; OAEL-2

King Philip had vaunted his claims. A Ballade of the Armada. Austin Dobson. FaPoR

King Richard II, *sels.* Shakespeare.
"And nothing can we call our own but death," *fr.* III, ii. DL
Death of Kings, The, *fr.* III, ii. GrRo
("Let's talk of graves, of worms, and epitaphs.") PPoe
"For God's sake, let us sit upon the ground," *fr.* III, ii. HoPM (1975 ed.); IP
"Give me the crown. Here, cousin, seize the crown," *fr.* IV, i. LFH
"I was a poor groom of thy stable, king," *fr.* V, v. PoPle

This England ("This royal throne of kings, this sceptered isle"),
*fr.* II, i.  VoPo
(England.)  BTTM
(John of Gaunt Speaks.)  FaPoR
"Where is the duke my father with his power?" *fr.* III, ii.  PoPle
King Richard III, *sel.*  Shakespeare.
"Lord, lord! methought what pain it was to drown," *fr.* I, iv.
EcS
King Saul.  Allan Kolski Horvitz.  VWA
King sent his lady on the first Yule day, The.  The Yule Days.
*Unknown.*  GBP
King Shall Reign in Righteousness, A, *with music.*  Sebastian
Streeter.  AH
King Siegfried sat in his lofty hall.  The Three Songs.  Bayard
Taylor.  PoTa
King [he] sits in Dunfermline [*or* Dumferling] town [*or* toune], The.
Sir Patrick Spens [*or* Spence].  *Unknown.*  AIW; AmFP; BiP;
CABA (1972 ed.); DuDr; EBEV; Epi; ExPo (1973 ed.);
FaBoBa; FaPoR; FF; HAP; HoPM (1975 ed.); ILP (1975
ed.); InPK; InPS; IP; NIL; NOBE; OAEL-1; PAIC; PBMP;
PeBB; PoIA; PPP; SoSe (1977 ed.); UnPo (1976 ed.); WeW
King Stephen: A Fragment of a Tragedy.  Keats.  MBPR
King still lives.  King Lives.  Jill Witherspoon Boyer.  CNA
King to Oxford sent a troop of horse, The.  Epigram.  Sir
William Browne.  FaBoCo; FaBoEE
King was not to think of other days, The.  Larder.  John Blight.
CAAP
King was on his throne, The.  Vision of Belshazzar.  Byron.
FaPo; PIM
King was sick, The.  His cheek was red.  The Enchanted Shirt.
John Hay.  PoTa
King will take the Queen, The.  Tom Brown.  *Unknown.*  FSW
King William Was King George's Son.  *Unknown.*  AmFP
King William's Dispatch to Queen Augusta.  Coventry Patmore.
FaBoEE
King Wind.  Mark Van Doren.  NCSH
Kingdom Coming, *with music.*  Henry Clay Work.  BLSo; PSoN
Kingdom of God, The.  Francis Thompson.  FaPoR; ILP (1975
ed.); ILwL; IP; PoPle
(In No Strange Land.)  HAP; NOBE
Kingdom of Kali, The.  May Sarton.  *Fr.* The Invocation to Kali.
RiTi
Kingdoms.  Oliver St. John Gogarty.  RAE
Kingfisher, The.  W. H. Davies.  NOBE; OBW
Kingfisher, The.  Andrew Marvell.  *Fr.* Upon Appleton House.
PB
Kingfisher blue along a tangled bank.  Poem to the Tune
"Riverbank Willows."  Yu Hsuan-chi, *tr. by* Geoffrey Waters.
BoWoP
Kingfisher falls through the dry air, The.  Epithalamion.  Charles
Wright.  CoPAm
King-Fisher Song, The.  "Lewis Carroll."  *Fr.* Sylvie and Bruno
Concluded.  FaBoNo
Kingfishers, The.  Charles Olson.  CMoP (1970 ed.); ILP (1975
ed.); NOBA; PiAm
Kingis Quair, The, *sels.*  James I, King of Scotland.
"And therewith kest I doun myn eye ageyne."  SLP
Nightingale's Song, The.  OxBM
("Now was there maid fast by the towris wall.")  EBEV
Kings/ like golden gleams.  A History Lesson.  Miroslav Holub,
*tr. by* Ian Milner *and* George Theiner.  BuTh
Kings and Tyrants.  Robert Herrick.  ILP (1975 ed.)
King's Breakfast, The.  A. A. Milne.  OxBChV
King's Dochter Lady Jean, The.  *Unknown.*  AmFP
Kings don't touch doors.  The Delights of the Door.  Francis
Ponge, *tr. by* Robert Bly.  NU
King's Highway, The.  John S. McGroarty.  BPAW

King's Highway to the Dare-Not-Know, The.  "Dreams Are the
Royal Road to the Unconscious."  Paul Goodman.  PoA
Kings kill their messengers.  Song to Accompany the Bearer of
Bad News.  David Wagoner.  PPoD
King's Men, The.  William Heyen.  PoA
Kings of the world are growing old, The.  Rainer Maria Rilke, *tr.*
*fr. German by* Robert Bly.  NU
King's poet was his captain of horse in the wars, The.  Mount
Badon.  Charles Williams.  FaBoTw (1975 ed.)
King's Son, The.  Thomas Boyd.  AIW
King's Speech, The.  Howard Moss.  *Fr.* King Midas.  PoA
Kinmont Willie.  *Unknown.*  PeBB
Kinnaird Head.  George Bruce.  MS
Kinneret.  Judith Herzberg, *tr. fr. Dutch by* Shirley Kaufman.
VWA
Kirk of the Birds, Beasts and Fishes, The.  *Unknown.*  GBP
Kirkyaird by the Sea, The, *sel.*  Douglas Young, *after the French*
*of* Paul Valéry.
"Steekit, consecrat, fou o fire but fuel."  OBVE
Kirov was shot, Solon will rot in jail.  Once More.  George
Jonas.  NeAC
Kiss, A.  Austin Dobson.  *Fr.* Rose-Leaves.  PPoD
Kiss, A.  Robert Herrick.  CaPo
Kiss, The.  Robert Pack.  AMV-81; PCho
Kiss, The.  Coventry Patmore.  *Fr.* The Angel in the House, II,
viii.  BoLoP; PoPle; SoSe
Kiss, The.  Dante Gabriel Rossetti.  The House of Life, VI.
VLP
Kiss.  Al Young.  PoBA
Kiss, The: A Dialogue.  Robert Herrick.  PAIC
"Kiss Grandpa!" you said.  Grandpa.  James Rankin.  MIS
Kiss in the Morning Early, A.  *Unknown.*  GBP
Kiss in the Rain, A.  Samuel Minturn Peck.  OBAL
Kiss Me Again, *with music.*  Henry Blossom.  BLSo
(If I Were on the Stage, *longer version.*)  FSN
Kiss me again, rekiss me, kiss me more.  Sonnet XVIII.  Louise
Labé, *tr. by* Willis Barnstone.  BoWoP
Kiss me and hug me.  *Unknown, tr. fr. Spanish by* Willis
Barnstone.  BoWoP
Kiss Me Quick and Go, *with music.*  Silas S. Steele.  BLSo
Kiss [*or* Kisse] me, sweet; the wary [*or* warie] lover.  To the Same.
Ben Jonson.  BiP; OAEL-1; OBVE
Kiss the one you love.  Victor Contoski.  *Fr.* Broken Treaties.
GP
Kiss'd Yestreen.  *Unknown.*  GBP; POL; SLP
Kisse me, sweet; the warie lover.  *See* Kiss me, sweet; the wary
lover.
Kisses.  *Malay Oral Tradition, tr. by* R. J. Wilkinson *and* R. O.
Winstedt.  WTO
Kisses in the Train.  D. H. Lawrence.  OBP
Kisses Loathesome.  Robert Herrick.  CaPo
Kissie Lee.  Margaret Walker.  NMM
Kissing, *sel.*  Fred Emerson Brooks.
"Those lustrous eyes but tell met this."  PeD
Kissing and Bussing.  Robert Herrick.  SoSe
Kissing Helena.  Plato, *tr. fr. Greek by* Shelley.  OBVE
Kissing her hair I sat against her feet.  Rondel.  Swinburne.
PAIC
Kissing of My Dame.  *Unknown.*  GBP
Kissinger has made it, yall.  Horatio Alger Uses Scag.  Amiri
Baraka.  GP
Kit Carson might be surprised.  Imperfect Sympathies.  Clarice
Short.  PPoD
Kit Carson's Ride.  Joaquin Miller.  BPAW
Kitchen Chimney, The.  Robert Frost.  PPM
Kitchen Door Blues.  Tennessee Williams.  OBAL

Kitchen patio in snowy, The. One A.M. Denise Levertov. CAPP

Kitchen Poem. Francis Scarfe. EAS

Kitchen today is so full of appliances, The. Deus ex Machina. Richard Armour. QQQ

Kitchen Window. Ruth N. Ebberts. AMV-80

Kitchenette Building. Gwendolyn Brooks. BPo; FF; UnPo (1976 ed.)

Kite, The. Harry Behn. FPB

Kite. R. H. W. Dillard. CSP

Kite, The. Adelaide O'Keeffe. OxBChV

Kite, A. Frank Dempster Sherman. CTV

Kite Day at the Washington Monument. Greg Orfalea. WasP

Kite holds in the April air, A. Kite. R. H. W. Dillard. CSP

Kite Is a Victim, A. Leonard Cohen. AKE

Kites, The. Coventry Patmore. *Fr.* The Angel in the House, II, i. VLP

Kites/ Kites/ Kites/ Cars are obsolete today. Kite Day at the Washington Monument. Greg Orfalea. WasP

Kithairon sang of cunning Kronos. Korinna, *tr. fr. Greek by* Willis Barnstone. BoWoP

Kitten, A. Eleanor Farjeon. RAE

Kitten and [the] Falling Leaves, The. Wordsworth. PCOP *Sels.*
   "But the kitten, how she starts." PCat
   "See the kitten on the wall." PCat

Kitten can, A. Where Knock Is Open Wide. Theodore Roethke. HAP; VGW

Kittens have paws they don't have pawses. Just Because. David McCord. ECBV

Kitten Speaks, The. William Brighty Rands. *See* Cat of Cats, The.

Kitten's Thought, A. Oliver Herford. PCOP

Kitty-Cat Bird, The. Theordore Roethke. OBAL

Kitty Kline. *Unknown.* AmFP

Kitty Morey. *Unknown.* AmFP

Kitty of Coleraine. *Unknown.* PoTa

Kleomedes. David Wright. NoAM

Klunder, people of sensibility. A Necessary Bucket. Peter Meinke. AATT

Knave of darkness, limber in the leaves, The. Death for the Dark Stranger. Thomas McGrath. VGW

Knedneuch land. In the Pantry. "Hugh MacDiarmid." NoAM

Knee Deep. Ted Joans. GP

Knee-deep in coldness, muzzle buried white. Wisdom. Linda Peavy. PH

Knee on Its Own, The. Christian Morgenstern, *tr. fr. German by* Geoffrey Grigson. FaBoNo

Knee Song. Anne Sexton. SFF

Kneegrows niggas. Be Cool, Baby. Rob Penny. PoBA

Kneeling Here, I Feel Good. Marge Piercy. NeAC

Kneeling in the sheepshit. Mountain Oysters. Patrick Lane. NeAC

Knell for Insularity. Merle Meeter. AATT

Knew a poet. W. C. W. David Ray. POL

Knickers Fisher has been at work again. Inscriptions. Anthony Thwaite. HeHu

Knife, The. Keith Douglas. LoAs

Knife, The. Juan Gelman, *tr. fr. Spanish by* Yishai Tobin. VWA

Knife, The. Judith Smallshaw. PMW

Knife and Sap. Kenneth Leslie. POL

Knight, The. Adrienne Rich. ILP (1975 ed.); PiAm

Knight, The. Rainer Maria Rilke, *tr. fr. German by* John N. Miller. AMV-81

Knight and a Lady, A. *Unknown.* ECBV

Knight and the Lady, The. William Cornish. NOBE

Knight and the Shepherd's Daughter, The. *Unknown.* AmFP

Knight, Death, and the Devil, The. Randall Jarrell. WeW

Knight in the Wood, The. Lord De Tabley. VLP

Knight knocked at the castle gate, The. The Knight and the Lady. William Cornish. NOBE

Knight of the Burning Pestle, The, *sel.* Francis Beaumont. Mirth, *fr.* II, viii. PPM

Knight of the Grail, The. *Unknown.* *See* Corpus Christi Carol ("Lully, lullay, lully, lullay").

Knight of the Sad Face, The. Rafael Jesús González. MIT

Knight rides into the noon, A. The Knight. Adrienne Rich. ILP (1975 ed.); PiAm

Knight ther was, and that a worthy man, A. *See* Knyght ther was . . .

"Knight there is, A," a lady said. Reward of Service. *Unknown, tr. by* F. C. Nicholson. LoAs

Knight's Leap, The. Charles Kingsley. PoTa

Knight's Tale, The, *sel.* Chaucer, *tr. fr. Middle English by* Nevill Coghill. *Fr.* The Canterbury Tales.
   "In the third hour after Palamon." OBP

Knight's Tomb, The. Samuel Taylor Coleridge. MBPR

Knock here's where I live. Message. Gyorgy Raba, *tr. by* Jascha Kessler. VWA

Knock last night's softness. Loving. Kathleen Fraser. WBN

Knock on Wood. Henry Dumas. CNA; PoBA

Knockmany. Richard Ryan. CIP; IPM

Knolege, aquayntance, resort, favour with grace. John Skelton. AAS

Knot, The. Stanley Kunitz. HAP

Know, Celia (since thou art so proud). Ingrateful Beauty Threatened. Thomas Carew. CaPo

Know, that I would accounted be. To Ireland in the Coming Times. W. B. Yeats. NoAM

Know then:/ Toward summer when the sun is in Hyades. Ezra Pound, *tr. fr. Chinese.* OBVE

Know then, my brethren, heaven is clear. Song. *Unknown. Fr.* The Song of Anarchus. FaBoCo

Know Thyself. Kenneth Burke. OBAL

Know Thyself. Pope. *Fr.* An Essay on Man, Epistle II. NOBE ("Know then thyself, presume not God to scan.") OAEL-1; PPoe

Know Yourself. John Arbuthnot. PMW

Knowest thou the time when the wild goates of the rocke bring forth? Bible, *O.T. Fr.* Job. OBVE

Knowing her is not knowing her. An Afterword: For Gwen Brooks. Don L. Lee. JB

Knowing no peace but war. Domestic Man. Augustus Young. IPM

Knowing this man, who calls himself comrade. Definition. Edwin Rolfe. SPT

Knowledge. Louise Bogan. PoA

Knowledge. Nina Cassian, *tr. fr. Rumanian by* Michael Impey *and* Brian Swann. BoWoP

Knowledge. Harold M. Grutzmacher. AMV-81

Knowledge of Light, The. Henry Rago. VGW

Knowledge That Comes through Experience, The. Jane Cooper. NMM

Knowledgeable Child, The. L. A. G. Strong. PFIr

Know'st thou not at the fall of the leaf. Autumn Song. Dante Gabriel Rossetti. ILP (1975 ed.)

Knoxville Girl. *Unknown.* FSW

Knoxville, Tennessee. Nikki Giovanni. AmNP (1974 ed.); BPo; CNA; InPS; OSP; PoBA; SO

Knuckles over the flame. Paradigms of Fire. Brian Swann. AmPA

Knyght [or Knight] ther was, and that a worthy man, A. Chaucer. *Fr.* The Canterbury Tales: Prologue. BiP; DuDr; InPS

Koala. Alan Ross. BoAnP

Kob Antelope. *Yoruba Oral Tradition, tr. by* Ulli Beier. WTO

Kohoutek. Richard Ryan. CIP

Ko-jin goes West from Ko-keku-to. Separation on the River Kiang. Ezra Pound. UnPo (1976 ed.)

Koko Oloro. Wole Soyinka. BuTh

Kona Sea, The. *Tr. fr. Hawaiian by* N. B. Emerson. WTO

Koocoo, The. *Unknown.* GBP

Kookaburra. *Unknown.* FSW

Kore. Robert Creeley. ConAP; InPK; InPS

Korf's Clock. Christian Morgenstern, *tr. fr. German by* Geoffrey Grigson. FaBoNo

Kornelia Woloszczuk. Peter Skrzynecki. CAAP

Kraken, The. Tennyson. CABA (1972 ed.); EcS; ILP (1975 ed.); OAEL-2; VLP

Kral Majales. Allen Ginsberg. GP; PiAm

Kropotkin Poems, The, *sel.* Phyllis Webb.
Solitary Confinement. MMD

Ku Klux. Langston Hughes. BPo

Kubla Kahn; or, A Vision in a Dream. Samuel Taylor Coleridge. AKE; AnMo; BiP; CABA (1972 ed.); ECBV; ExPo (1973 ed.); FF; HAP; HeIP; HoPM (1975 ed.); ILP (1975 ed.); InPK; InPS; IP; MAT; MBPR; NIL; NOBE; OAEL-2; OBP; PBMP; PCOP; PoIA; PPoD; PPoe; SoSe; UnPo (1976 ed.); VoPo; WeW

Kum Ba Yah (Come By Here). *Unknown.* FSW

Kumara God. Peter Bland. ATNZ

Kumulipo, The: A Creation Chant, *sels.* Keaulumoku, *tr. fr. Hawaiian by* M. W. Beckwith. WTO
Birth of Sea and Land Life.
Crawlers, The.
Dawn of Day, The.
Dog Child, The.

Kung walked/ by the dynastic temple. Canto XIII. Ezra Pound. CMoP (1970 ed.); PiAm

Kutune Shirka (The Ainu Epic), *sel.* Wakarpa, *tr. by* Arthur Waley.
Golden Sea-Otter, The. WTO

Kyoto Born in Spring Song. Gary Snyder. RRA

Kyoto: March. Gary Snyder. PPP

Kyng Jamy/ Jamy your Joye is all go. A Ballade of the Scottyshe Kynge. John Skelton. FaBoBa

Kypros! Andromache's Wedding. Sappho, *tr. by* Willis Barnstone. BoWoP

Kyran's Christening. Alden Nowlan. NeAC

"Kyrie," so "Kyrie." Jolly Jankin. *Unknown.* GBP; NOBE; OxBM

**L**

L(a. E. E. Cummings. BBGO; LFH; NIL; TT

La Bella Bona Roba. Richard Lovelace. CaPo; EBEV; LoAs; OAEL-1; OBP; SCP-2

La Belle Confidante. Thomas Stanley. SCP-2

La Belle Dame sans Merci. Keats. AIW; AnMo; CABA (1972 ed.); Epi; ExPo (1973 ed.); HAP; ILP (1975 ed.); InPK; InPS; IP; IPWM; LFH; LoAs; MBPR; NIL, 2 versions; NOBE; OAEL-2; OLR; PAIC; PBMP; PoIA; PoPle; PPoD; PPoe; Prf; SoSe (1977 ed.); STS; UnPo (1976 ed.); WeW

La Chute. Charles Olson. InPK

La Condition Botanique. Anthony Hecht. NoAM

La Divina Commedia. David Malouf. CAAP

La Figlia Che Piange. T. S. Eliot. AnMo; BuTh; FaBoTw (1975 ed.); GBL; HeIP; MAT; OxBTC; PiAm; PoA; PSN; UnPo (1976 ed.); VGW

La Fontaine de Vaucluse. Marilyn Hacker. PCho

La Llorona. Greg Pape. AmPA

La Marche des Machines. A. S. J. Tessimond. MPo

La Pesadilla. Gerda Penfold. GP

La Selva. Cid Corman. VGW

La Vie En Rose. Peter Schjeldahl. CAAP

La Vita Nuova. Weldon Kees. VGW

Label, The. Ruthe T. Spinnanger. AATT

Labor. Lucille Day. VWA

Labor Camp, The. John Pijewski. AMV-81

Labor Day. Gary Pacernick. TAT

Labour of the Brain, Ballad of the Body. Nicole Forman. NMM

Labor Room: three handed. Oblique Birth Poem. Ann Darr. GP

Laboratory, The: Ancien Régime. Robert Browning. LoAs

Laboratory Poem. James Merrill. InPK; MAT; PPoD

Labourer, The. Iolo Goch, *tr. fr. Welsh by* Gwyn Williams. OBW

Laborers, domestics, blue. Annunciation. Sister Maura. TAT

Labourer's Noon-Day Hymn, The. Wordsworth. PIM

Laborers of Christ! Arise, *with music.* Lydia Sigourney. AH

Laboring and Heavy Laden, *with music.* Jeremiah E. Rankin. AH

Laboring men, please all attend. Free Silver. *Unknown.* AmFP

Labouring poor, in spite of double pay, The. Daniel Defoe. *Fr.* The True-born Englishman, II. NOBL

Labours of the Months, The. *Unknown. See* Months, The.

Labors of Thor, The. David Wagoner. GP; MPA

Labyrinth, The. Edwin Muir. CMoP (1970 ed.); NoAM

Lace curtain stands effaced, A. Stéphane Mallarmé, *tr. fr. French by* Roger Fry. NAWM-2

Lace grows in her eyes like. Waiting, the Hallways under Her Skin Thick with Dreamchildren. Lyn Lifshin. FAF; NeAC

Lachlan Gorach's Rhyme. *Unknown. See* Dance Steps.

Lack of Steadfastness. Chaucer. *See* Lak of Stedfastnesse.

Lack Wit. *Unknown.* BBL

Lackying my loue I go from place to place. Amoretti, LXXVIII. Spenser. LoAs

Lacking Sense, The. Thomas Hardy. CMoP (1970 ed.)

Lacrimas or There Is a Need to Scream. K. Curtis Lyle. PoBA

Lad came to the door at night, The. The True Lover. A. E. Housman. LoAs

Lad of Athens, faithful be. Emily Dickinson. FaBoEE

Ladder ascends and descends, A. The Drunkenness of Pain. Aliza Shenhar, *tr. by* Linda Zisquit. VWA

Ladder Has No Steps, The. Jorge Plescoff, *tr. fr. Spanish by* Yishai Tobin. VWA

Ladder sticking up at the open window, A. Dog-Days. Amy Lowell. FSFS

Ladders. Reed Whittemore. PoUp

Ladie in beautie and in favor rare. Henry Constable. *Fr.* Diana. ESo

Ladies, The. Karen Bunting. PoW

Ladies and gentlemen:/ I have only one question. I Move the Meeting Be Adjourned. Nicanor Parra, *tr. by* Miller Williams. *Fr.* Manifesto. HoPM (1975 ed.)

Ladies and gentlemen:/ This broadcast comes to you from the city. Voice of the Studio Announcer. Archibald MacLeish. *Fr.* The Fall of the City. HoPM (1975 ed.)

Ladies and gentlemen/ This is our final word.  Nicanor Parra, *tr. by* Miller Williams.  *Fr.* Manifesto.  TSWA

Ladies and gentlemen, my mother is.  Honor Moore.  *Fr.* Mourning Pictures.  TV

Ladies and Gentlemen This Little Girl.  E. E. Cummings.  CMoP (1970 ed.)

Ladies at the Troy Laundry pressed, The.  One for the Ladies at the Troy Laundry Who Cooled Themselves for Zimmer.  Paul Zimmer.  GP

Ladies in Love.  Paul David Ashley.  DNGG

Ladies Prayer to Cupid, A.  Thomas Carew.  *See* Lady's Prayer to Cupid, A.

Ladies rose, The. I held the door.  The Dean.  Coventry Patmore.  *Fr.* The Angel in the House.  VLP

Ladies should never fall in love.  Ladies in Love.  Paul David Ashley.  DNGG

Lads in their hundreds to Ludlow come in for the fair, The.  A. E. Housman.  OxBTC; STS; VLP

Lady,/ how long you been driving a bus?  Interview.  Laurence Lieberman.  AMV-81

Lady A. L., My Asylum in a Great Extremity, The.  Richard Lovelace.  CaPo

Lady Alice, *4 versions. Unknown.*  AmFP

Lady Alice, Lady Louise.  The Blue Closet.  William Morris.  VLP

Lady and Gentleman.  Richard Weber.  IPM

Lady and the Bear, The.  Theodore Roethke.  BCr; CNW; ECBV; SO

Lady and Tiger.  Edward Lear.  ECBV; SoSe ("There was a young lady of Niger.")  DuDr

Lady asks me, A.  Donna Me Prega.  Guido Cavalcanti, *tr. by* Ezra Pound.  OBVE

Lady-Bird. *See* Ladybird.

Lady-Bug. *See* Ladybug.

Lady, by yonder blessed moon I swear.  Shakespeare.  *Fr.* Romeo and Juliet, II, ii.  Moon

Lady came to a bear by a stream, A.  The Lady and the Bear.  Theodore Roethke.  BCr; CNW; ECBV; SO

Lady Clare.  Tennyson.  PBMP; PoTa

Lady Comes to an Inn, A.  Elizabeth J. Coatsworth.  PoTa; SO

Lady comes to the gate, The.  Albatross.  Judy Collins.  GrRo

Lady Diamond. *Unknown.*  PeBB

Lady Feeding the Cats, *sel.*  Douglas Stewart. "Shuffling along in her broken shoes from the slums."  BoAnP

Lady Fortune, The. *Unknown.*  HeIP; NIL

Lady Greensleeves. *Unknown. See* Greensleeves

Lady, help! Jesu, [*or* Hesu] mercy!  Passion of Christ Strengthen Me [*or* Dread of Death].  John Audelay.  BoReV; OxBM

Lady, I Thank Thee. *Unknown.*  OxBM

Lady in a Distant Face.  James Welch.  AmPA

Lady in the Water Collection Department, The.  Tom McKeown.  TC

Lady in the Wood, The. *Unknown.*  OxBM

Lady Is a Tramp, The.  Lorenz Hart.  OBAL

Lady is smarter than a gentleman, maybe, A.  Trial and Error.  Phyllis McGinley.  BBL

Lady Isabel and the Elf-Knight. *Unknown.*  FaBoBa; FSW; PeBB; SLP (Elfin Knight, The.)  AmFP; FaBoBa; GBP; PeBB

Lady Isabel and the Elf-Knight (Pretty Polly). *Unknown.*  AmFP

Lady Isabella's Tragedy, The. *Unknown.*  GBP

Lady Jane, The: A Humorous Novel in Rhyme, *sels.*  Nathaniel Parker Willis.  OBAL "If, in well-bred society, ('hear! hear!')." "Some men, 'tis said, prefer a woman fat."

Lady, Lady.  Anne Spencer.  PoBA

Lady, lady, lady fair.  The Suffolk Miracle. *Unknown.*  AmFP

Lady Lazarus.  Sylvia Plath.  AnMo; CAPP; ConAP; Epi; ILP (1975 ed.); InPK; MAT; NIL; NoAM; NOBA; PiAm; PPoe; Psy; TAP; VGW

Lady lived in Lancaster, A.  Kate and the Cowhide. *Unknown.*  AmFP

Lady Lost.  John Crowe Ransom.  UnPo (1976 ed.)

Lady Love.  Paul Eluard, *tr. fr. French by* Samuel Beckett.  OBVE

Lady Luck.  Ann Gottlieb.  NMM

Lady Maisery, *with music. Unknown.*  Epi (Janet [Lady Maisry], *diff. version.*)  PeBB

Lady Margaret. *Unknown.*  FSW

Lady Mary Villiers lies, The.  Epitaph on the Lady Mary Villiers.  Thomas Carew.  CaPo; FaBoEE; NOBE; SCP-2

Lady Moon.  Richard Monckton Milnes.  OxBChV

Lady Moon.  Christina Rossetti. *See* O Lady Moon.

Lady Moon, Lady Moon, where are you roving?  Lady Moon.  Richard Monckton Milnes.  OxBChV

Lady Murasaki says.  Murasaki Shikibu, *tr. fr. Japanese by* Kenneth Rexroth *and* Ikuko Atsumi.  *Fr.* The Tale of Genji.  BoWoP

Lady My Treasure.  Sir Philip Sidney.  GBL

Lady Named Psyche, A. *Unknown.*  TDH

Lady of all the essences, full light.  Inanna and the Divine Essences.  Enheduanna, *tr. fr. Sumerian.*  BoWoP

Lady, of anonymous flesh and face.  J. V. Cunningham.  CoPAm; HoPM (1975 ed.)

Lady of Carlisle, The. *Unknown.*  AmFP; FSW

Lady of dusk-wood fastnesses.  First Praise.  William Carlos Williams.  VGW

Lady of light, I would admit a dream.  The Buried Lake.  Allen Tate.  PiAm

Lady of Shalott, The.  Tennyson.  NOBE; OAEL-2; PCOP; VLP, *2 versions*

Lady of the bright coils and curlings.  Eire.  David O'Bruadair, *tr. by* Austin Clarke.  BIrV

Lady of the Castle, The.  John Hollander.  GP

Lady of the crescent moon.  Indian Love Letter.  Soge Track.  VW

Lady of the Ferry Inn.  Gwerfyl Mechain, *tr. fr. Welsh by* Willis Barnstone.  BoWoP

Lady of the Lake, The, *sels.*  Sir Walter Scott. Harp of the North.  Prologue.  ILP (1975 ed.) Soldier, Rest! *fr.* I.  NOBE

Lady of the Manor, The.  George Crabbe.  *Fr.* The Parish Register: Burials, Pt. III.  NOBE

Lady Prayeth the Return of Her Lover Abiding on the Seas, The. *Unknown.*  GBL

Lady Queen Anne she sits in the sun.  Queen Anne. *Unknown.*  BBL

Lady Sings, The.  Milton.  *Fr.* Comus.  NOBE

Lady stands in her bower door, The.  The Twa [*or* Two] Magicians. *Unknown.*  GBP; OAEL-1; PeBB

Lady Sweet and Kind, A. *Unknown. See* There Is a Lady Sweet and Kind.

Lady, take care; for in the diamond eyes.  Light and Dark.  Barbara Howes.  CoPAm; RiTi

Lady, the unknown goddess.  For the Unknown Goddess.  Elizabeth Brewster.  MMD

Lady, this measure of time accept with serene eye.  To Eliza, with a Tulip-fashioned Watch.  Robert Baron.  SCP-2

Lady, three white leopards sat under a juniper-tree.  T. S. Eliot.  *Fr.* Ash Wednesday, II.  UsP

Lady Track Star, A.  Roy Blount, Jr.  TDH

Lady walked down a roadbed, A.  A Gentle Heart: Two.  Judith Johnson Sherwin.  BoWoP

Lady Weeping at the Crossroads.  W. H. Auden.  AIW

Lady, When I Behold the Roses Sprouting. *Unknown.* InPK

Lady Who Lived at Bordeaux, A. *Unknown.* TDH

Lady who lived in Uganda, A. The Panda. William Jay Smith. TDH

Lady Who Loved a Swine, The. *Unknown.* RDB, *with music* (There Was a Lady Loved a Swine.) GBP

Lady Who Offers Her Looking-Glass to Venus, The. Matthew Prior, *after the Greek of* Plato. FaBoEE

Lady who signs herself "Vexed," The. Edward Gorey. OBAL

Lady whose name was Miss Hartley, A. Miss Hartley. William Jay Smith. TDH

Lady with a Falcon on Her Fist, A. Richard Lovelace. CaPo

"Lady, you're a poet, do you think about death?" No Signal for a Crossing. Rhoda Donovan. AMV-80

Ladybird, The, *sel.* John Clare.
"Ladybird! Ladybird! Where art thou gone?" RAE

Ladybird, The. *Unknown.* GBP

Lady-bird! Lady-bird! Fly away home. To the Lady-Bird. Caroline Anne Bowles. PPM

Lady bird, lady bird, fly away home. Mother Goose. MG

Ladybird! Ladybird! Where art thou gone? John Clare. *Fr.* The Ladybird. RAE

Ladybirds, The. Edward Lucie-Smith. BoAnP

Ladybug. François Dodat, *tr. fr. French by* Bert *and* Odette Meyers. BoAnP

Lady-bug, lady-bug. Mother Goose. PCOP

Ladybug, ladybug, fly away home. Fly, Ladybug. Annette Burr Stowman. AMV-80

Ladybug's Christmas. Norma Farber. PChr

Lady's Dressing Room, The. Swift. AnMo

Lady's Farewell, The. Nuño Fernández Torneol, *tr. fr. Medieval Galician by* Yvor Winters. AIW

Lady's First Song, The. W. B. Yeats. PSN

Lady's Policy, The. *Unknown.* RDB, *with music* (Blow Away the Morning Dew.) FSW

Lady's Prayer to Cupid, A. Thomas Carew, *after the Italian of* Giovanni Battista Guarini. CaPo
(Ladies Prayer to Cupid, A.) OBVE

Lady's Resolve, The. Lady Mary Wortley Montagu. BoWoP

Lady's Song in Leap Year, The. *Unknown.* GBP

Lady's Third Song, The. W. B. Yeats. *Fr.* The Three Bushes. FaBoTw (1975 ed.)

La Fayette. Samuel Taylor Coleridge. *Fr.* Sonnets on Eminent Characters. MBPR

Laguna Perdida. Maynard Dixon. BPAW

Laid in My Quiet Bed. Earl of Surrey. PBMP

Laid with papyrus to catch fire. Martial, *tr. fr. Latin by* James Michie. FaBoEE

Laieikawai's Lament after Her Husband's Death. *Tr. fr. Hawaiian by* M. W. Beckwith. WTO

L'Aigle A Deux Jambes. Turner Cassity. GP

Laila Boasting. Laila Akhyaliyya, *tr. fr. Arabic by* Willis Barnstone. BoWoP

Laily Worm and the Machrel of the Sea, The. *Unknown.* PeBB

Laird o' Cockpen, The. Lady Nairne. PoTa; WPE

Lais now old, that erst attempting lass. Plato, *tr. fr. Greek.* FaBoEE

Lais to Aphrodite. E. A. Robinson, *after the Greek of* Plato. FaBoEE

Lak of Stedfastnesse. Chaucer. ILP (1975 ed.)
(Lack of Steadfastness.) PBMP

Lake, The. Ted Hughes. FaBoTw (1975 ed.)

Lake. R. A. Simpson. FPA

"Lake, The/ is not encumbered by the swan." The Mutabilities. Vincent McHugh. MIT

Lake above Santos, The. Keith Wilson. GP

Lake Chelan. William Stafford. BiP; ILP (1975 ed.)

Lake Chemo. James Wilton Rowe. AmFP

Lake Flies of Winnebago, The. Doug Flaherty. HeS

Lake Harriet: Wind. Laurie Taylor. AMV–81

Lake is sky, The. To the Other Side. T. Alan Broughton. FAF

Lake Isle, The. Ezra Pound. CABA (1972 ed.); FaBoCo; PoA

Lake Isle of Innisfree, The. W. B. Yeats. AKE; CMoP (1970 ed.); FaPoR; ILP (1975 ed.); InPS; IPWM; LFH; NoAM; NOBE; OxBTC; PoIA; PPM; STS; TT; UsP; VLP; WeW

Lake Leman woos me with its crystal face. Byron. *Fr.* Childe Harold's Pilgrimage, III. InPS

Lake Michigan. David Kherdian. FAF

Lake Michigan Blues. *Unknown.* BluU

Lake of Gaube, The. Swinburne. OAEL–2; VLP; VPC

Lake of night is still in the valley, The. The Pine. Saunders Lewis, *tr. by* Gwyn Thomas. OBW

Lake of the Caogama, The. *Unknown.* WTO

Lake on the map of Canada, A. Believing What I Know. William Stafford. Epi

Lake sunken among, A. Woman Skating. Margaret Atwood. IHMS

Lake Walk at New Year's. Leigh Perez-Diotima. AMV–81

Lalla Halima! Protect abandoned girls! Like Smoke. Mririda n'Ait Attika, *tr. by* Daniel Halpern *and* Paula Paley. PBWP

Lalla Rookh, *sels.* Thomas Moore.
"Fly to the desert, fly with me," *fr.* The Story of the Sultana Nourmahal. BIrV
" 'I never nursed a dear gazelle,' " *fr.* The Fire-Worshippers. SpRo
Jasmine, *fr.* The Light of the Haram. PF

Lalla Rookh/ Is a naughty book. On T. Moore's Poems. *Unknown.* FaBoCo

L'Allegro. Milton. CABA (1972 ed.); HAP; HoPM (1975 ed.); ILP (1975 ed.); OAEL–1; PPP
*Sels.*
"And ever against eating cares." SCP–1
"And, if I give thee honour due." PoPle
"While the cock with lively din." SCP–1

Laly, Laly. Mark Van Doren. SO

Lama, The. Ogden Nash. RAE

Lamarck Elaborated. Richard Wilbur. ILP (1975 ed.)

Lamb, The. Blake. *Fr.* Songs of Innocence. CABA (1972 ed.); ExPo (1973 ed.); HeIP; ILP (1975 ed.); InPS; LAuP; LCL; LFH; MBPR; NIL; OAEL–2; OxBChV; PAIC; PCOP; PIM; PoIA; RAE; SoSe; STS; TT; UnPo (1976 ed.)

Lamb. Michael Dennis Browne. NU

Lamb. James Rankin. MIS

Lamb, The. Theodore Roethke. LCL

Lamb Was Bleating Softly, The. Juan Ramón Jiménez, *tr. fr. Spanish by* Robert Bly. NU; PChr

Lambing. David Campbell. *Fr.* Works and Days. MAuV

Lambs Frolicking Home. Fred Lape. BoAnP

Lambs that learn to walk in snow. First Sight. Philip Larkin. NCSH; TSWA

Lambton Worm, The. *Unknown.* DuDr; PeBB

Lame Angel. Donald Finkel. VWA

Lame Beggar, A. John Donne. FF

Lame Deer. Joy Harjo. SA

Lamed-Vov, The. Rose Ausländer, *tr. fr. German by* Ewald Osers. VWA

Lament: "Diameter of the bomb was thirty centimeters, The." Yehuda Amichai, *tr. fr. Hebrew by* Ruth Nevo. VWA

Lament, A: "Gizzard and some ruby inner parts, A." Margaret Avison. HAP

Lament: "I lie in darkness, as the dead shades gather." Matangi Hauroa, *tr. fr. Maori by* Barry Mitcalfe. WTO

Lament: "In that strident summer of battle." Hone Tuwhare. ATNZ

Lament: "Listen, children:/ Your father is dead." Edna St. Vincent Millay. DL

Lament: "My man is a bone ringed with weed." Brenda Chamberlain. WPE

Lament, A: "O world! O life! O time!" Shelley. MBPR; NOBE

Lament: "Someone is dead." Anne Sexton. ConAP; UsP; WPE

Lament: "We who are left, how shall we look again." W. W. Gibson. OxBTC

Lament: "What face, in the water." William Carlos Williams. VGW

Lament: "When I was a windy boy and a bit." Dylan Thomas. PPP; TT

Lament: "You did not suck at my mother's breast." Yonathan Ratosh, *tr. fr. Hebrew by* Howard Schwartz. VWA

Lament after Her Husband Bishr's Murder. Al-Khirniq, *tr. fr. Arabic by* Willis Barnstone. BoWoP

Lament City. Thomas Lux. AmPA

Lament for a Cricket Eleven. Kenneth Allott. OxBTC

Lament for a Dead Lover. Siraad Haad, *tr. fr. Somali by* B. W. Andrzejewski *and* I. M. Lewis. WTO

Lament for a Husband. *Tr. fr. Papuan by* Don Laycock. BoWoP

Lament for a Leg. John Ormond. OBW

Lament for Adonis. Bion, *tr. fr. Greek by* John Addington Symonds. Epi

Lament for Apirana Ngata. Arnold Reedy, *tr. fr. Maori by* Barry Mitcalfe. WTO

Lament for Art O'Leary. Eibhlin Dubh O'Connell, *tr. fr. Irish by* Eilis Dillon *and* John Montague. BIrV
(Lament for Arthur O'Leary, The, *abr.*) PBWP

Lament for Azazel. Francis Landy. VWA

Lament for Barney Flanagan. James K. Baxter. ATNZ

Lament for Chaucer and Gower. Thomas Hoccleve. *Fr.* De Regimine Principum. OxBM
("O maister deere and fader reverent!") EBEV

Lament for Flodden, A. Jane Elliot. *See* Flowers of the Forest, The.

Lament for Glasgerion. Elinor Wylie. PoA

Lament for Ignacio Sánchez Mejías. Federico García Lorca, *tr. fr. Spanish by* A. L. Lloyd. OBVE

Lament for Lleucu Llwyd. Llywelyn Goch ap Meurig Hen, *tr. fr. Welsh by* Joseph P. Clancy. OBW

Lament for Llywelyn ap Gruffudd. Gruffudd ab yr Ynad Coch, *tr. fr. Welsh by* Joseph P. Clancy. OBW

Lament for Lost Lodgings. Phyllis McGinley. SpRo

Lament for Mafukuzela. *Zulu Oral Tradition, tr. by* H. Tracey. WTO

Lament for Pasiphae. Robert Graves. FaBoTw (1975 ed.)

Lament for Siôn y Glyn. Lewis Glyn Cothi, *tr. fr. Welsh by* Joseph P. Clancy. OBW

Lament for Taramoana. Makere, *tr. fr. Maori by* Barry Mitcalfe. WTO

Lament for the Cuckoo. Alcuin, *tr. fr. Latin by* Helen Waddell. NAWM-1

Lament for the Death of Eoghan Ruadh O'Neill. Thomas Osborne Davis. PFIr

Lament for the Death of Thomas Davis. Sir Samuel Ferguson. BIrV

Lament for the European Exile. A. L. Strauss, *tr. fr. Hebrew by* A. C. Jacobs. VWA

Lament for the Great Music, *sel.* "Hugh MacDiarmid."
"Yet there is no great problem in the world today." OxBTC

Lament for the Makaris [*or* Makers]. William Dunbar. *See* Timor Mortis Conturbat Me.

Lament for the O'Neills. John Montague. CIP

Lament for the Poets. William Dunbar. *See* Timor Mortis Conturbat Me.

Lament for the Priory of Walsingham, A. *Unknown.* GBP

Lament for Thomas MacDonagh. Francis Ledwidge. BIrV

Lament for Una, A, *sel.* Tomas Costello, *tr. fr. Gaelic by* Frank O'Connor.
"Young Una, you were a rose in a garden." WTO

Lament him, Mauchline husbands a' Epitaph for James Smith. Burns. EBEV

Lament, lament, Sir Isaac Heard. Epitaph on Tuft-Hunter. Thomas Moore. FaBoCo; FaBoEE

Lament my losse, my labor, and my payne. Sir Thomas Wyatt. AAS

Lament of a Last Letter. Janet E. Harrison. AMV-80

Lament of a Man for His Son. *Unknown, tr. fr. Paiute Indian by* Mary Austin. BPAW
(Lament of a Young Man for His Son.) DL

Lament of a Young Man for His Son. *Unknown, tr. fr. Piute Indian.* DL

Lament of an Idle Demon. R. P. Lister. NOBL

Lament of Barbara Douglas, The. *Unknown. See* Waly, Waly ("O waly, waly up the bank").

Lament of Hsi-chün. Hsi-chün, *tr. fr. Chinese by* Arthur Waly. BoWoP

Lament of My Father, Lakota. Paula Gunn Allen. VW

Lament of the Banana Man. Evan Jones. MPo

Lament of The Border Widow, The. *Unknown.* GBP; PeBB; SLP

Lament of the Cherokee Reservation Indian, The. John D. Loudermilk. PoRo

Lament of the Flowers, The. Jones Very. NOBA

Lament of the Frontier Guard. Li Po, *tr. fr. Chinese by* Ezra Pound. OBVE; PiAm; VGW

Lament of the Jewish Women for Tammuz. Charles Reznikoff. VWA

Lament of the Master of Erskine. Alexander Scott. GBL

Lament of the Old Woman of Beare, The. *Unknown, tr. fr. Irish by* Kuno Meyer. Epi
(Hag of Beare, The, *tr. by* John Montague.) BIrV; CIP; PBWP, *abr.*; OBVE, *tr. by* Lady Gregory

Lament of the Unmarried Girl, The. Brian Merriman, *tr. fr. Modern Irish by* Frank O'Connor. *Fr.* The Midnight Court. OBVE

Lament of the Virtues and Verses on Account of the Death of Don Guido. Antonio Machado, *tr. fr. Spanish by* Charles Tomlinson *and* Henry Gifford. OBVE

Lament while Descending a Shaft. *Unknown.* AmFP

Lamentation, A: "Awake./ Your youth is passing like smoke." Carl Rakosi. VWA

Lamentation, A: "Grief, have I denied thee?" Denise Levertov. PiAm

Lamentation: "My lips lack prophecy." Nissim Ezekiel. VWA

Lamentation of Glumdalclitch, The. Pope. Epi

Lamentation of the Old Pensioner, The. W. B. Yeats. HAP; InPK; NoAM; PFIr; VLP; WeW, *2 versions*
(Old Pensioner, The, *diff. version.*) InPK

Lamentations. Alter Brody. VWA

Lamentations. Louise Glück. BoWoP; PCho

Lamentations. Siegfried Sassoon. OBSV

Lamentations of an Au Pair Girl. Susan Feldman. AmPA

Lamenting Tauba. Laila Akhyaliyya, *tr. fr. Arabic by* Willis Barnstone. BoWoP

Lamia. Keats. MBPR

L'Amitié et l'Amour. John Swanwick Drennan. BIrV

Lamkin ("Bolakins was a very fine mason"). *Unknown.* AmFP

Lamkin ("It's Lamkin was a mason good"). *Unknown.* FaBoBa; PeBB

Lammermuir Lilt, The. Forbes Macgregor. MIS

Lamp, The. A. Buttigieg. RAE

Lamp are you, above all stars of night, A. The Pole Star. Coslett Coslett, *tr. by* Kenneth Jackson. OBW

Lamp, don't moan. The Air Vision. Jakov van Hoddis, *tr. by* Charles Guenther. VWA

Lamp in the West, The. Ella Higginson. WPW

Lamp must be replenished, but even then, The. Manfred: A Dramatic Poem. Byron. MBPR

Lamp Now Flickers, The. Alfred Grünewald, *tr. fr. German by* Edouard Roditi. VWA

Lamplight from our kitchen window-pane. Again. Glyn Jones. OBW

Lamplighter, The. "Seamus O'Sullivan." BIrV

Lamplighter, The. Robert Louis Stevenson. OxBChV

Lamp-post pokes out of the dark street, The. Uprooted. Sol Funaroff. SPT

Lamprey, glowing with uncommon fires, The. William Diaper, *after the Greek of* Oppian. *Fr.* Halieutica. OBVE

Lamps hung like a lynching, The. All the Way Home. Primus St. John. MPA

L'An Trentiesme de Mon Eage [*or* Age]. Archibald MacLeish. NoAM; NOBA; PAIC

Lana Turner has collapsed! Poem. Frank O'Hara. CAPP; CoPAm; VGW

Lancashire Born. *Unknown.* GBP

Lancashire Winter. Tony Connor. OxBTC

Lancaster County Tragedy. W. Lowrie Kay. CaYB

Lancelot of the Laik, *sel. Unknown.*
    Lancelot's Soliloquy in Prison. SLP

Land. Carroll Arnett. VoR

Land, The, *sel.* V. Sackville-West.
    "Only a bold man ploughs the Weald for corn." PES

Land and sea. Wordsworth. *Fr.* Ode: Intimations of Immortality from Recollections of Early Childhood. FSFS

Land earth-root. Invocation. Nakasuk, *tr. fr. Eskimo.* WTO

Land floats by under us, The. Love Making. James Tate. EAS

Land has sunk to black, The. Pilot. Floyd C. Stuart. FAF

Land I came thro' last was dumb with night, The. Christopher Brennan. *Fr.* The Wanderer. MAuV

Land I plowed last fall, The. Sun and I. Ken Mammone. AMV–81

Land is an ark, full of things waiting, The. A Wet Time. Wendell Berry. PiAm

Land lies in water; it is shadowed green. The Map. Elizabeth Bishop. NOBA

Land not mine, still, A. "Anna Akhmatova," *tr. fr. Russian by* Jane Kenyon. NU

Land o' the Leal, The. Lady Nairne. SLP

Land of Cockayne, The. *Unknown.* OAEL–1, *paraphrased fr. Middle English by* J.B. Trapp; OxBM
    (Land of Cockaigne, The, *tr. fr. Middle English by* John Montague.) BIrV

Land of Counterpane, The. Robert Louis Stevenson. CTV; EBEV; ECBV; ILP (1975 ed.); OxBChV

Land of Heart's Desire, The, *sel.* W. B. Yeats.
    "Wind blows out of the gates of the day, The." PPM

Land of Hope and Glory. A. C. Benson. FaPoR

Land of leaning ice, A. North Labrador. Hart Crane. CMoP (1970 ed.); POL

Land of Nod, The. Robert Louis Stevenson. ILP (1975 ed.)

Land of Story-Books, The. Robert Louis Stevenson. CTV; DuDr

Land of the Bumbley Boo, The. Spike Milligan. OSF

Land of the Horizontal Yellow. Indian Death. Eda Lou Walton. BPAW

Land of the Old Fields, The. Van K. Brock. CSP

Land of the Silver Birch, *with music. Unknown.* AKE

Land that is lonelier than ruin, A. Swinburne. By the North Sea, I. VLP

Land wants me to come back, The. Dust Bowl. Langston Hughes. PoA

Land was ours before we were the land's, The. The Gift Outright. Robert Frost. CMoP (1970 ed.); GOA; NoAM; NOBA; PPP; STS

Landed: A Valentine. Richard Howard. PoA

Landfall, The. James Dickey. PoA

Landfall. *Maori Oral Tradition, tr. by* A. S. Thomson. WTO

Landfall in Unknown Seas. Allen Curnow. ATNZ

Landing, The. Daniel Halpern. AmPA

Landing of the Pilgrim Fathers in New England, The. Felicia Dorothea Hemans. BTTM; ECBV; FaPo; PPM; SBG; WPE

Landing on the Moon. May Swenson. Moon; TAP

Landladies. Gerald Locklin. PoW

Landlady, The. Margaret Atwood. Psy

Landlord Fill the Flowing Bowl. *Unknown.* FSW

Landlord, landlord. Ballad of the Landlord. Langston Hughes. NOBA

Landlord's coat is tulip red, The. Wild Sports of the West. John Montague. CIP

Land's End. Stanton A. Coblentz. BPAW

Land's End. Daniel J. Langton. MIT

Landscape. Octavio Paz, *tr. fr. Spanish by* Charles Tomlinson. OBVE

Landscape, The. David Ray. EC

Landscape. R. A. Simpson. GAS

Landscape. Abraham Sutskever, *tr. fr. Yiddish by* Ruth Whitman. VWA

Landscape as a Nude. Archibald MacLeish. Frescoes for Mr. Rockefeller's City, I. CMoP (1970 ed.)

Landscape by Cezanne, A. Art Lange. FiCh

Landscape, Deer Season. Barbara Howes. LiSp; MiP; POL

Landscape 4. Robert Gray. CAAP

Landscape here is Africa, The. Sand Hill Road. Morton Grosser. SoS

Landscape is not an austere one, The. Lemuel Johnson. *Fr.* Hand on the Naval. AAN

Landscape near an Aerodrome, The. Stephen Spender. IPWM; NoAM; OxBTC

Landscape, New Mexico. Kell Robertson. TAT

Landscape of the Star. Adrienne Rich. TT

Landscape of the Vomiting Multitudes. Federico García Lorca, *tr. fr. Spanish by* Ben Belitt. NYP

Landscape I ("The character of a landscape stands always in a mysterious relation"). Charles Madge. EAS

Landscape was, The. Canto 5: Coon Fire. Tom Weatherly. PoBA

Landscape with Lapwings. James Aitchison. MS

Landscape with Leaves and Figure. Olga Broumas. BoWoP; CNW

Landscape with Minute Wildflowers. Hugh Maxton. CIP

Landscape with Next of Kin. Olga Broumas. BoWoP; CNW

Landscape with One Figure. Douglas Dunn. MS

Landscape with Pervert. Bink Noll. PPoD

Landscape with Poets. Olga Broumas. CNW

Landscape with the Fall of Icarus. William Carlos Williams. Pictures from Brueghel, II. BBGO; NIL; PPP; TT; WIF

Landscape without Touch. Olga Broumas. CNW

Landscapes, *sels.* T. S. Eliot.
    Cape Ann, V. BiP; UsP
    New Hampshire, I. BiP; WeW
    Rannoch, by Glencoe, IV. BiP

Usk, III. BiP

Virginia, II. BiP

Landscapes. Richard Hugo. GP

Landscapes. Bert Meyers. PoW

Lane Is the Pretty One. Lucille Clifton. CAAP

Laneliest Place in the Warld, The. Donald Campbell. MIS

Lanely Müne, The. William Soutar. MS

Lanes of England never end, The. Hoddesdon. A. S. Wilson. PES

Langdale: Nightfall, January 4th. Michael Roberts. PES

Langston. Mari Evans. CNA

Langston Blues. Dudley Randall. CNA; FB

Langston Hughes. Lew Blockcolski. VoR

Language, The. Robert Creeley. CAPP; IPWM; LoAs; PiAm; TAP

Language has not the power to speak what love indites. Fragment. John Clare. FaBoEE; OAEL-2

Language is the first perversion of the senses. Genesis. Brian Higgins. FaBoTw (1975 ed.)

Language of Ancients. Hayim Lenski, tr. fr. Hebrew by Pearl Grodensky. VWA

Language of Erin is brilliant as gold, The. The Irish Language. James Clarence Mangan. VLP

Language of walls, The. Hieroglyph. Paul Auster. VWA

Language on which the sun flows, A. Epos. Harold Rosenberg. PoA

Language, Talk to Me. Evan Jones. GAS

Langwell. Kingsley Amis. Fr. The Evans Country. NOBL

Lanky hank of a she in the inn over there, The. A Glass of Beer. James Stephens, after O'Bruaidar. CMoP (1970 ed.); ExPo (1973 ed.); FaBoCo; NCSH; NoAM; OxBTC; SoSe

Lantern. Frank Polite. GP

Lantern Out of Doors, The. Gerard Manley Hopkins. AnMo; CMoP (1970 ed.); VLP

Lanty Leary. Samuel Lover. PFIr

Lanzarote. Unknown, tr. fr. Spanish by W. S. Merwin. Epi

Laodamia. Wordsworth. MBPR

Laotian Peasant Shot. George Bruce. MS

Lapful of Nuts, The. Unknown, tr. fr. Irish by Sir Samuel Ferguson. VLP

Lapidary. Bonnie L. Alexander. AMV-80

Lapis Lazuli. W. B. Yeats. AnMo; CMoP (1970 ed.); FaBoTw (1975 ed.); FF; ILP (1975 ed.); InPK; InPS; MAT; NIL; NoAM; NOBE; OAEL-2; OBP; PoIA; PPoe; WIF

Lapse of Contract. Rodney Hall. FPA

Lapsus Linguae. Richard Howard. NoAM

Lapsus Linguae. Keith Preston. OBAL

Lara, sel. Byron.
"In him inexplicably mixed appeared," XVII–XIX. OAEL-2

Laramie Trail. Joseph Mills Hanson. BPAW

Larder. John Blight. CAAP

Large, calm harbour lies below, The. In Falmouth Harbour. Lionel Johnson. PES

Large glooms were gathered in the mighty fane. James Thomson ("B. V."). The City of Dreadful Night, XIV. EBEV; OAEL-2

Large Mercies. D. J. Enright. HeHu

Large Red Man Reading. Wallace Stevens. HAP

Large, waxen backyard tomato, A. Family Reunion. Peter Nelson. PHC

Largest stock of armaments allows me, The. Civilian. Josephine Miles. WPE

Largo. Sydney Goodsir Smith. MS

Lariat snaps, The; the cowboy rolls. The Closing of the Rodeo. William Jay Smith. GOA; PPoD

Lark, The. Shakespeare. See Cymbeline.

Lark, The ("Liverockie, liverockie lee"). Unknown. GBP

Lark, The ("Malisons, malisons more than ten"). Unknown. GBP

Lark begins to go up, The. Skylarks. Ted Hughes. HAP

Lark now leaves his watery [or wat'ry] nest, The. Aubade [or Song]. Sir William Davenant. GBL; LoAs; NOBE; PPM

Lars Porsena of Clusium. Horatius. Macaulay. Fr. Lays of Ancient Rome. BTTM; FaPoR

L'Art, 1910. Ezra Pound. HeIP

Las Trampas U.S.A. Charles Tomlinson. TwMBP

LaSalle Street. Rachel Albright. ANTL

Lasca. Frank Desprez. BPAW

Laser. A. R. Ammons. NOBA

Lashes of my eye are clipped away, The. Cataract. Margoret J. Smith. PPoD

Lass from Bally-na-Lee, The. Anthony Raftery, tr. fr. Irish by Desmond O'Grady. BIrV

Lass of Richmond Hill, The, with music. Leonard McNally. BLSo

Lass of Roch Royal, The. Unknown. AmFP; FSW

Lass That Made the Bed to Me, The. Burns. OBP

Lasses, like nuts at bottom brown. Epigram. Allan Ramsay. FaBoEE

Lassie, can ye say. For a Wife in Jizzen. Douglas Young. MS

Lassie, think lang, think lang. Think Lang. Marion Angus. MS

Lassitude. Mathilde Blind. SBG

Last, The. Ezra Zussman, tr. fr. Hebrew by D. Shnayorson. VWA

Last Ancestor, The. Gene Fowler. CPA

Last and greatest herald of Heaven's King. Saint John Baptist. William Drummond of Hawthornden. NOBE; OBP; PIM

Last Auroch, The. Maxine Chernoff. FiCh

Last Bite, The. Richard Frost. AMV-80

Last Boat of the Season, The. Robin Fulton. MS

Last century took its courage in both hands, The. The New Coventry Cathedral. Arthur J. Bull. HeHu

Last Chapter, The. Walter de la Mare. CMoP (1970 ed.); ILP (1975 ed.)

Last Christmas, Father. Lines for My Father. Patrick Worth Gray. AMV-81

Last Chrysanthemum, The. Thomas Hardy. CMoP (1970 ed.)

Last Clean Bough, The. James Aitchison. MS

Last Confession, A. W. B. Yeats. BoLoP; CMoP (1970 ed.); HAP; OAEL-2; STS; WeW

Last Covenant, The. Naomi Lazard. AAN

Last dark violet, The. Poetry. Abraham Sutskever, tr. by Ruth Whitman. VWA

Last Day and the First, The. Theodore Weiss. LoAs, VGW

Last Day of the Year, The. Su Tung P'o, tr. fr. Chinese by Kenneth Rexroth. CC

Last Day of the Year, The (New Year's Eve). Annette von Droste-Hülshoff, tr. fr. German by Willis Barnstone. BoWoP

Last Days. Richard Hugo. PoA

Last Days of Alice. Allen Tate. NoAM; NOBA; PiAm; UnPo (1976 ed.)

Last decent man alive, The. Across to the Peloponnese. James Welch. CDW; MPA

Last Drift. Arthur Chapman. BPAW

Last Drink, A. Unknown. OxBM

Last Easter I was married, that night I went to bed. The Lowlands of Holland. Unknown. AmFP

Last Easter Jim put on his blue. Easter Zunday. William Barnes. VLP

Last evening I entered a pool. To My Father. John Haines. CNW

Last Fall of the Alamo. "O. Henry." BPAW

Last Families in the Cabins, The.  Millen Brand.  GP

Last Farmer in Queens, The.  Vickie Karp.  NYP

Last Fierce Charge, The.  *Unknown.*  AmFP

Last Fire, The.  Moishe Steingart, *tr. fr. Yiddish by* Gabriel Preil.  VWA

Last Fish, The.  Barry Spacks.  AMV-80

Last Flight of the Great Wallenda, The.  Barbara Helfgott Hyett.  AMV-80

Last Frontier, The.  John Thomas.  GP

Last Fruit off an Old Tree, The, *sel.*  Walter Savage Landor.
On His Seventy-Fifth Birthday.  EBEV; OAEL-2; PBMP; SoSe (1977 ed.)
(Dying Speech of an Old Philosopher.)  FaBoEE; HeIP; VLP ("I strove with none, for none was worth my strife.")  NOBE; PCOP

Last full moon of February, The.  Hunger Moon.  Jane Cooper.  CABA (1972 ed.)

Last Gangster, The.  Gregory Corso.  CoPAm; SA

Last Grizzly Bear in the State.  Richard E. Lee.  PoW

Last hour nears, The.  Pshytik.  Nahum Bomze, *tr. by* Gabriel Preil.  VWA

Last Instructions to a Painter, The.  Andrew Marvell.  APAS *Sels.*
"After two sittings, now our Lady State."  OBSV
"Hyde stamps, and straight upon the ground the swarms."  SCP-1
"Monk from the bank the dismal sight does view."  SCP-1
"Paint Castlemaine in colours that will hold."  OBSV; SCP-1
"Paint last the King, and a dead shade of night."  OBSV
"Ruyter the while, that had our ocean curbed."  SCP-1

Last Invocation, The.  Walt Whitman.  PPM

Last Job I Held in Bridgeport, The.  D. W. Donzella.  TAT

Last Journey.  Enrique Gonzales Martinez, *tr. fr. Spanish by* Samuel Beckett.  PBMP

Last Lap, The.  Kipling.  OxBTC

Last Lauch.  Douglas Young.  FaBoCo; MS

Last Leaf, The.  Oliver Wendell Holmes.  AmVN; PiAm; VoPo

Last Leaves.  Leslie Norris.  HeHu

Last Letter to the Scholar.  Jean Garrigue.  LoAs

Last Light.  Robert Kelly.  VGW

Last light has gone out of the world, except, The.  Liberty.  Edward Thomas.  OAEL-2

Last light muffles itself in cloud and goes, The.  Mise en Scène.  Robert Fitzgerald.  VGW

Last Lines.  Emily Brontë.  BoReV; ILwL; NOBE; OAEL-2; OBP;PoPle
(No Coward Soul Is Mine.)  HeIP; PIM; PFD; VLP; VoPo

Last Lines.  X. J. Kennedy.  OBAL

Last Lines—1916.  Padraic Pearse.  PFIr; WIF

Last Longhorn, The.  R. W. Hall.  BPAW

Last Longhorn's Farewell, The.  John P. Sjolander.  BPAW

Last Look at La Plata, Missouri.  Jim Barnes.  CDW

Last Look Round St. Martin's Fair.  Thomas Hardy.  OBP

Last Love.  Fyodor Tyutchev, *tr. fr. Russian by* Vladimir Nabokov.  BoLoP

Last Man, The.  Thomas Hood.  VLP

Last minutes of light, The. My slow Shadow.  Jogging at Dusk.  Andrew Grossbardt.  AMV-80

Last Monster, The.  John Montague.  WIF

Last Month.  John Ashbery.  CAPP

Last month in your little Roman house, The.  On the Death of Keats.  John Logan.  Prf

Last Night.  David Ignatow.  VGW

Last night.  After Selecting the Wedding Invitations.  Diane Levenberg.  NPW

Last night a baby gargled in the throes.  A Widow in Wintertime.  Carolyn Kizer.  CNW; NIL

Last night a freezing cottontail.  Twin Lakes Hunter.  A. B. Guthrie, Jr.  PoTa

Last night a storm howled outside.  Triptych.  Greg Hannan.  PoUp

Last night, ah, yesternight, betwixt her lips and mine.  Non Sum Qualis Eram Bonae sub Regno Cynarae.  Ernest Dowson.  BoLoP; CABA (1972 ed.); GBL; HAP; HeIP; LoAs; NIL; NOBE; OAEL-2; UnPo (1976 ed.); VLP; VoPo

Last night, among his fellow roughs.  The Private of the Buffs.  Sir Hastings Doyle.  VLP

Last night and the night before.  Robbers.  *Unknown.*  ECBV

Last night as I lay on the prairie.  The Cowboy's Dream.  *Unknown, at. to* Charles J. Finger.  BPAW; FSW

Last night at black midnight I woke with a cry.  The Ghost of the Buffaloes.  Vachel Lindsay.  BPAW

Last night came calling out of the dark.  Mother.  Peter Bland.  ATNZ

Last night did Christ the Sun rise from the dark.  Easter Sunday.  Sedulius Scottus, *tr. by* Helen Waddell.  OFD

Last night for the first time since you were dead.  To L. H. B.  Katherine Mansfield.  ATNZ

Last night I did not fight for sleep.  In Hospital: Poona.  Alun Lewis.  OBW

Last night I dreamed.  The Night-Apple.  Allen Ginsberg.  NoAM

Last night I dreamed a dream.  Death and the Lover.  *Unknown, tr. by* W. S. Merwin.  Epi

Last night I dreamed of an old lover.  Grandmother, Rocking.  Eve Merriam.  TVo

Last night I had a dream.  A Dream about an Aged Humorist.  Aaron Zeitlin, *tr. by* Ruth Whitman.  VWA

Last night I had a dream bad 'cess to my dreaming.  The Dream.  *Unknown.*  WTO

Last night I heard wolves howling.  Wolves.  John Haines.  BoAnP

Last night I lay on the prairie.  *See* Last night as I lay on the prairie.

Last night I licked.  In Celebration.  Ellen Bass.  NMM

Last night I saw a face riding out on.  What We Move Thru.  Stephen Shrader.  PHC

Last night I saw the monster near.  The White Monster.  W. H. Davies.  PPM

Last night I saw the savage world.  Song for a Birth or a Death.  Elizabeth Jennings.  EBEV

Last night I saw your corpse.  Joyce Mansour, *tr. fr. French by* Willis Barnstone.  BoWoP

Last night I spoke to a dead woman with green face.  Last Night.  David Ignatow.  VGW

Last night I watched my brother play.  The Brothers.  Edwin Muir.  HeIP

Last Night in Calcutta.  Allen Ginsberg.  NoAM

Last night in the rain I was frightened.  Sabine.  John Batki.  AcAn

Last night it rained.  Amy Lowell.  TH

Last night returning from my twilight walk.  A Ballad of Past Meridian.  George Meredith.  OAEL-2; VLP

Last night she danced with her lover.  Islands for Seurat.  Kraft Rompf.  AAN

Last night that she lived, The.  Emily Dickinson.  BoWoP; CMoP (1970 ed.); ILP (1975 ed.)

Last night the first light frost, and now sycamore.  Long Walks in the Afternoon.  Margaret Gibson.  AMV-81

Last night the wind came into the yard.  The Circle on the Grass.  Jane Kenyon.  TC

Last Night There Was a Cricket in Our Closet.  Leroy V. Quintana.  GP

Last night there were four Maries. The Four Maries. *Unknown.* FSW

Last Night They Heard the Woman Upstairs. Leslie Ullman. AMV-80

Last night thin rain, gusty wind. Li Ch'ing-chao, *tr. fr. Chinese by* Willis Barnstone *and* Sun Chu-chin. BoWoP

Last night thou didst invite me home to eat. Upon Showbread: Epigram. Robert Herrick. CaPo

Last night watching the Pleiades. An Autumn Morning in Shokoku-ji. Gary Snyder. HAP

Last night we anchored in. Arrival, New York Harbor. Robert Peters. GOA

Last night we sat with the stereopticon. Readings of History. Adrienne Rich. ConAP

Last night we slept in Miami in the house of. September 30. Dick Lourie. NeAC

Last night we started with some dry vermouth. Ballade of Liquid Refreshment. E. C. Bentley. FaBoCo

Last night we talked about God. Furniture. Chana Bloch. GP

Last night when the sun went down. Evensong. Peter Kane Dufault. AMV-80

Last night you would not come. Love Poem. John Logan. CAPP; CoPAm

Last night you wrote on the wall: Revolution is poetry. Adrienne Rich. *Fr.* Ghazals: Homage to Ghalib. NIL

Last of England, The. Peter Porter. GAS

Last of the Chiefs. Nathaniel Tarn. TwMBP

Last of the Flock, The. Wordsworth. MBPR

Last of the Light Brigade, The. Kipling. BTTM

Last of the Poet's Car. Tony O'Connor. OxBTC

Last of the poets, first of the undead. The Mole. Dennis Schmitz. AmPA

Last on legs, last on sax. "Bird Lives": Charles Parker in St. Louis. Michael S. Harper. AmPA

Last One, The. W. S. Merwin. CoPAm; NoAM; VGW

Last one, The/ to die here. Nelly Sachs, *tr. fr. German by* Arthur Wensinger. BoWoP

Last Ones, The. Robin Hyde. ATNZ

Last Ones, The. Dan Pagis, *tr. fr. Hebrew by* Stephen Mitchell. VWA

Last out in the raining weather, a girl and I. The Day the Weather Broke. Alastair Reid. SLP

Last Page but One, The. Charles Edward Eaton. WasP

Last Patch of Snow. George Abbe. FAF

Last Picnic, The. Stanley Kunitz. NoAM

Last Poem. Charles Donnelly. BIrV
   (Poem: "Between rebellion as a private study and the public.") CIP

Last Poems. A. E. Housman. *Poems indexed separately by titles and first lines.*

Last Quarter. John Hollander. Moon

Last Quatrain of the Ballad of Emmet Till, The. Gwendolyn Brooks. CAPP; CNA; PoBA; WPE

Last Refuge, The. Augustus Young. BIrV

Last Republicans, The. Austin Clarke. CIP

Last Ride Together, The. Robert Browning. BoLoP; TT; UnPo (1976 ed.); VLP

Last Ride Together, The (From Her Point of View). James Kenneth Stephen. FaBoCo; UnPo (1976 ed.)

Last Rite. John V. Hicks. AMV-81

Last Rites. David Citino. AMV-80

Last Rites. Christina Rossetti. OxBChV

Last Rose of Summer, The. Thomas Moore. FSW

Last seeds, The. Flitcraft's Woods. Warren Woessner. HeS

Last settlement scraggled out with a barbed wire fence, The. The Flight in the Desert. William Everson. VGW

Last Snow. Andrew Young. OxBTC

Last Song, The. Joy Harjo. FoP; TAT

Last Songs of Richard Strauss at Takahe above the Kaipara, The, sel. K. O. Arvidson.
   "Far Brynderwyns heave across the harbour, The." ATNZ

Last Sonnet. Keats. *See* Bright Star! Would I Were Steadfast as Thou Art.

Last South Baltimore Poem. David Hilton. AcAn; EC

Last summer, in the blue heat. La Vita Nuova. Weldon Kees. VGW

Last summer was hot and dry, a better time. Delta Farmer in a Wet Summer. James Whitehead. TAT

Last Sunday petrified. Wingwalking in Oregon. Robert Peterson. MIT; NeAC

Last Superstition, The. Sol Funaroff. SPT

Last Supper, The. Rainer Maria Rilke, *tr. fr. German by* M. D. Herter Norton. OFD

Last, the fatal hour is come, The. Thomas Campbell. *Fr.* Gilderoy. SLP

Last Things. William Meredith. NoAM

Last Things, Black Pines at 4 a.m. Robert Lowell. NOBA

Last time around the forest floor. Rainier. Jim Tollerud. VoR

Last time I kissed her, The. Almost Ninety. Ruth Whitman. TVo

Last time I left/ Bill's Twilight Lounge. Sensational Relatives. Alexis Krasilovsky. AMV-80

Last time I left, you pulled your chair. In Search of a Short Poem for My Grandmother. Louise Hardiman. AMV-81

Last time I saw Donald Armstrong, The. The Performance. James Dickey. ConAP; CSP; ExPo (1973 ed.); NoAM; NOBA

Last time I saw my hometown, The. Just Passing Through. Philip Roberts. FPA

Last time i was home, The. Mothers. Nikki Giovanni. CNA; CTBA; TV; UnPo (1976 ed.)

Last Trail, The. Stanton A. Coblentz. BPAW

Last Turn, The. William Carlos Williams. NYP

Last Utterance of the Delphic Oracle, The. *Tr. fr. Greek by* Kenneth Rexroth. OBVE

Last View, The. Ruthe T. Spinnanger. AATT

Last War, The. Kingsley Amis. OBSV; SoSe (1977 ed.)

Last Warmth of Arnold, The. Gregory Corso. NoAM; SA

Last week/ my mother died. Two Poems. Don L. Lee. UsP

Last week a new dentist. Loyal Citizen. Richard Lyons. HeS

Last Week I Took a Wife, *with music.* M. Kelly. BLSo

Last week my old cat fell to the worms. Poem Ending with an Old Cliché. Paul Zimmer. AMV-81

Last Will and Testament. Alvin Aubert. CoPAm

Last Will and Testament, A. John Winstanley. OBSV

Last Will and Testament of Anthony, King of Poland, The. *Unknown.* APAS

Last Word, The. Matthew Arnold. CABA (1972 ed.); NOBE; OAEL-2; PBMP; VLP

Last Word, The. Peter Davison. InPK

Last Word, A. Ernest Dowson. VLP

Last Word, A. W. R. Rodgers. Epi

Last Word of a Bluebird, The. Robert Frost. LCL; PCOP; RAE; SO

Last Words. Emily Brontë. WPE

Last Words. John Hollander. OBAL

Last Words. James Merrill. TAP

Last Words. Sylvia Plath. RiTi

Last Words, 1968. Lance Henson. CDW

Last Words of Cardinal Wolsey, The. Shakespeare. King Henry VIII, *fr.* III, ii. PIM ("Cromwell, I did not think to shed a tear.") PoIA

Last words of Shaw, The: "I'm going to die." Alan Bold. POL

Last Words to a Dumb Friend. Thomas Hardy. PCat

Last year at the Feast of Lanterns. Lost. Chu Shu-chen, *tr. by* Kenneth Rexroth. BoWoP

Last year, Orlando. The Political Orlando. George MacBeth. NOBL

Last year we were fighting at the source of the Sang-kan. Fighting South of the Ramparts. Li Po, *tr. by* Arthur Waley. NIL

Last year when I accompanied you. To a Traveler. Su Tung P'o, *tr. fr. Chinese by* Kenneth Rexroth. HoPM (1975 ed.)

Last year's decencies. Odysseus. Padraic Fallon. CIP

Last Year's Discussion: The Nobel Russian. Phyllis McGinley. FaBoEE

Lastly, stood War, in glittering arms yclad. The Shield of War. Thomas Sackville. *Fr.* Mirror for Magistrates. NOBE

Lastness. Galway Kinnell. NNaP "Black bear sits alone, A," *sel.* BCr; GP

Lat take a cat and fostre hym wel with milk. Mice before Milk. Chaucer. *Fr.* The Canterbury Tales: The Manciple's Tale. PCat

Late. Louise Bogan. PBWP; VGW

Late. Daniel Halpern. AMV-81

Late Abed. Archibald MacLeish. NCSH

Late Advisory for Intergalactic Travellers Such as Poets. Will Inman. FoP

Late afternoon and we arrive. Last Grizzly Bear in the State. Richard E. Lee. PoW

Late afternoon, summer on the prairie. Bucket in the Well. Connie Wanek. AMV-80

Late Again. Gabriel Zaid, *tr. fr. Spanish by* Eliot Weinberger. AMV-81

Late Air. Elizabeth Bishop. LoAs

Late April and you are three; today. W. D. Snodgrass. *Fr.* Heart's Needle. CoPAm

Late at Night. William Stafford. NNaP; POL; RFM

Late at night. First Camp. Greg Kuzma. NVAP

Late at night, their sow rooted open the door of their cabin. Domestic Scenes, 2. Charles Reznikoff. WeW

Late Aubade, A. Richard Wilbur. PAIC; SoSe

Late August. Margaret Atwood. MMD

Late August at the Game Refuge. William Stafford. CNW

Late August, given heavy rain and sun. Blackberry-picking. Seamus Heaney. HeHu

Late Autumn Walk. J. D. McClatchy. AMV-80

Late-born and woman-souled I dare not hope. Echoes. Emma Lazarus. SBG

Late Fair. Sean Lucy. IPM

Late fall finishes the season for marketing. Tobacco Men. James Applewhite. CSP

Late-flowering Lust. John Betjeman. CMoP (1970 ed.); PAIC

Late Game. B. H. Fairchild. AMV-81

Late in Fall. Ramona Wilson. VoR

Late Lark Twitters, A. W. E. Henley. *See* Margaritae Sorori.

Late Last Night. Arthur Gregor. VGW

Late Last Night. Langston Hughes. NoAM

Late last night I killed my wife. Necessity. Harry Graham. FaBoCo

Late last night I was a-making my rounds. Bad Man Ballad. *Unknown.* AmFP

Late last night, the moon in puddles, I walked the lane. Last Leaves. Leslie Norris. HeHu

Late lies the wintry sun a-bed. Winter Time. Robert Louis Stevenson. OxBChV

Late Lights in Minnesota. Ted Kooser. TAT

Late Manuscript at the Schocken Institute, A. Gabriel Preil, *tr. fr. Hebrew by* Gabriel Levin. VWA

Late Miss H. came to us Wednesday at four, The. Swansong. Carol Muske. AmPA

Late Morning: Oahu. Dolores Kendrick. *Fr.* Rice and Mats. PoUp

Late Movie, A. William Matthews. PCho

Late, my grandson! half the morning have I paced these sandy tracts. Locksley Hall, Sixty Years After. Tennyson. PFD

Late Night at the Hamburg Inn. Cinda Kornblum. AcAn

Late night, with my bundle of new straws. The Burden of Decision. Peter Everwine. NNaP

Late November in a Field. James Wright. CAPP; NNaP

Late November, Madison. David Hilton. AcAn

Late, of late summer night, almost white. Night-Piece. Kendrick Smithyman. ATNZ

Late of the jungle, wild and dim. Billiards. Walker Gibson. LiSp

Late on a summer night maybe twenty years from now. Midnight, Walking the Wakeful Daughter. Joseph Meredith. AMV-81

Late Saturday afternoons in Emeryville. Butcherboy. Tom Schmidt. NeAC

Late Sewing. Hazel Hall. WPW

Late Show, The. David McKain. AAN

Late Snow and Lumber Strike of the Summer of Fifty-Four, The. Gary Snyder. CNW; MPA

Late Spring: A Heaving, a Turning. John Gill. NeAC

Late Spring Day in My Life, A. Robert Bly. NCSH

Late Spring, Sur Coast. Naomi Clark. CPA

Late that mad Monday evening. Madness One Monday Evening. Julia Fields. NIL; UsP

Late Visitor, The. Ann Stanford. MPA; PPoD

Lately I become. Names. Lyn Lifshin. FAF

Lately I saw a sight most quaint. "Gross, Coarse, Hideous" (Police Description of My Pictures). D. H. Lawrence. FaBoEE

Lately, I've become accustomed to the way. Preface to a Twenty Volume Suicide Note. Amiri Baraka. AmNP (1974 ed.); CABA (1972 ed.); CAPP; ILP (1975 ed.); InPK; InPS; IPWM; PAIC; PoBA; PPP; SoS; TCP; VoA

Lately I've felt a grave concern. Countess Beatritz de Die, *tr. fr. Provençal by* Willis Barnstone. BoWoP

Lately Our Poets. Walter Savage Landor. OAEL-2 ("Lately our poets loitered in green lanes.") CABA (1972 ed.); FaBoEE

Lately the wind burns. Everything. Philip Levine. AMV-80

Later there would be miles, hills, a country, a world. Under Way. Bruce Dawe. CAAP

Later, when the scent of early leaves. A Wish for Waving Goodbye. Roberta Hill. AMV-80

Latest Decalogue, The. Arthur Hugh Clough. BiP; BoReV; CABA (1972 ed.); EBEV; ExPo (1973 ed.); FaBoCo; FaBoEE; FF; HAP; HoPM (1975 ed.); ILP (1975 ed.); IPWM; NIL; NOBE; OAEL-2; OBSV; PBMP; PPP; SoSe; SS; VLP; VPC

Latest poems, like the most recent, The. Dispatch Number Sixteen. Doug Fetherling. NeAC

Latin for Today ("Latin is a dead tongue"). *Unknown.* PoPle

Latitude, Longitude. George Oppen. CAPP

Latter-Day Geography Lesson. R. A. K. Mason. ATNZ

Latter Purification, A. Haim Guri, *tr. fr. Hebrew by* Mark Elliott Shapiro. VWA

Lauds. John Berryman. HAP

Lauds and Plaints, *sels.* Bruce Beaver. CAAP
  "Beautiful face of Paul Delvaux, The."
  "For first the abiding."
  "In and out of the streets."

Laugh and Be Merry. John Masefield. PPM

Laugh, my friends, and without blame. A Memory-Picture. Matthew Arnold. VLP

Laughing Child. Carl Sandburg. CTBA

Laughing Faces of Pigs, The. Fred Lape. BoAnP

Laughing god born of a startling answer, The. Bacchus. William Empson. NoAM

Laughing Song. Blake. *Fr.* Songs of Innocence. LAuP; MBPR; OxBChV
  (Laughter.) ECBV

Laughs not the heart, when giants, big with pride. The Apology Addressed to the Critical Reviewers. Charles Churchill. LAuP

Laughter. Blake. *See* Laughing Song.

Laughter of children brings. Early Supper. Barbara Howes. DuDa; NCSH

Launcelot with Bicycle. Phyllis McGinley. SS

Launch, The. Alice Meynell. WPE

Laundrette. Liz Lochhead. MIS

Laundromat. David McCord. QQQ

Laundry-basket is still there, The. Elegy. Anselm Hollo. AcAn

Laura. Thomas Campion. *See* Rose-cheeked Laura, Come.

Laureate, The. Robert Graves. BIrV; FaBoTw (1975 ed.); OBSV

Laurel and Hardy. John Bricuth. CSP

Laurel leaf, which you this day do wear, The. Amoretti, XXVIII. Spenser. CABA (1972 ed.)

Laurel Tree, The. Louis Simpson. NNaP

Laurence Bloomfield in Ireland, *sel.* William Allingham. Eviction. The. BIrV

L'Aurore Grelottante. Peter Levi. UsP

Laus Deo. Robert Bridges. VLP

Laus Veneris. Swinburne. VLP

Lausanne. Thomas Hardy. FaBoTw (1975 ed.)

Lava Bed. William Everson. PiAm

Lava Tubes. John Unterecker. PHC

Lavender Blue. *Unknown.* FSW
  (Lavender's Blue, *with music.*) GSB
  (Love Song: "Lavender's blue, diddle, diddle.") BBL

Lavender Cowboy, The. Harold Hersey. BPAW; FSW

Lavender Kitten, The. Alonzo Lopez. VW

Lavinia at Church. Edward Young. *Fr.* Love of Fame, the Universal Passion. BoReV

Law, The. Grace Schulman. GP

Law, A/ removing from use the monosyllable love. There Is Good News. Josephine Jacobsen. AMV-80

Law against Lovers, The, *sel.* Sir William Davenant.
  "Wake all the dead! what ho! what ho!" HAP; ILP (1975 ed.); OBP; SCP-2

Law I Love Is Major Mover, The. Robert Duncan. PiAm

Law in the Country of the Cats. Ted Hughes. NowV

Law like Love. W. H. Auden. CMoP (1970 ed.); PBMP

Law makes long spokes of the short stakes of men. Legal Fiction. William Empson. CMoP (1970 ed.); ExPo (1973 ed.); ILP (1975 ed.); InPK; NoAM

Law of Falling and Catching Up, The. Cathleen Quirk. MMD

Law, say the gardeners, is the sun. Law like Love. W. H. Auden. CMoP (1970 ed.); PBMP

Law there is of ancient fame, A. Tit for Tat: A Tale. John Aikin. OxBChV

Law West of the Pecos, The. S. Omar Barker. BPAW

Lawd, I'm broke and hungry, ragged and dirty, too. Ragged and Dirty. *Unknown.* AmFP

Lawn, The. Robert Herrick. LoAs

Lawn as white as driven snow. Autolycus as Peddler. Shakespeare. *Fr.* The Winter's Tale, IV, iii. OAEL-1

Lawrence here for ever blames. D. H. Lawrence and James Joyce. Humbert Wolfe. FaBoEE

Lawrence—not the bearded one—the one. Any Complaints? Vernon Scannell. OxBTC

Lawrence, of virtuous father virtuous son. Milton. CABA (1972 ed.)

Laws of God, the Laws of Man, The. A. E. Housman. ILP (1975 ed.); OBP; OBSV; STS; TT
  (Laws of God, The.) PPP

Laws of the bronze gods, The. Cheap Rent. Carl Sandburg. PiAm

Lawyer Clark Blues. *Unknown.* BluL

Lawyer Dickinson's spinsterly daughter. Occupation: Spinster. Olga Cabral. WBN

Lawyers Know Too Much, The. Carl Sandburg. BiP; CMoP (1970 ed.)

Lay a garland on my hearse of the dismal yew. Aspatia's Song. Beaumont *and* Fletcher. *Fr.* The Maid's Tragedy. HAP; ILP (1975 ed.); GBL; NOBE; PoPle

Lay down boys, take a little nap. Cumberland Gap. *Unknown.* FSW

Lay down these words. Riprap. Gary Snyder. NOBA; PPoD

Lay her and lea her here i the gantan grund. The Shepherd's Dochter. Douglas Young. MS; SLP

Lay me on an anvil, O God. Prayers of Steel. Carl Sandburg. CMoP (1970 ed.)

Lay not up for yourselves treasures upon earth. Bible, *N.T.* St. Matthew, VI: 19-21. CTV

Lay of Oliver Gogarty, The. William Dawson. PeBB

Lay of St. Gengulphus A, *sel.* "Thomas Ingoldsby."
  "But to see now how strangely things sometimes turn out." VLP

Lay of the Honeysuckle, The. Marie de France, *tr. fr. French by* Robin Johnson. WPE

Lay of the Last Minstrel, The, *sel.* Sir Walter Scott.
  "Breathes there the man, with soul so dead," *fr.* VI SoSe
  (Innominatus.) PBMP
  (Native Land.) SFF
  (Patriot, The.) FaPoR
  (Patriotism.) CTV; NOBE
  (This Is My Own, My Native Land.) BTTM

Lay of the Lovelorn, The. William E. Aytoun *and* Sir Theodore Martin. FaBoCo
  "Comrades, you may pass the rosy," *sel.* VLP

Lay Preacher Ponders, The. Idris Davies. OxBTC

Lay to Eliza, The. Spenser. *Fr.* The Shepheardes Calender: April. NOBE
  Fair Flower Delice, The. PF, *one stanza*

Lay up nearer, brother, nearer. The Dying Californian. *Unknown.* BPAW

Lay Your Arms Aside. Pierce Ferriter, *tr. fr. Irish by* Eilean Ni Chuilleanain. BIrV

Lay Your Head on My Shoulder. Yehuda Amichai, *tr. fr. Hebrew by* Robert Friend. VWA

Lay your sleeping head, my love. Lullaby. W. H. Auden. BoLoP; CMoP (1970 ed.); ExPo (1973 ed.); HAP; NoAM; NOBE; OAEL-2; OxBTC; PPP; PSN; UnPo (1976 ed.); UsP

Layer-out, The. S. L. Henderson Smith. PMW

Layer upon layer, with clay and bricks and hard work. A Witch Going Down to Egypt. Raquel Chalfi, *tr. by* Alexandera Meiri *and* Myra Glazer Schotz. VWA

Layers, The. Stanley Kunitz. AMV-80

Laying By. Randall Williams. AMV-80

Laying here alone tonight. Rebirth. A. D. Winans. CPA

Laying in the hospital. Little Red Riding Hood. Nila NorthSun. GP

Lays of Ancient Rome, *sel.* Macaulay.
Horatius. BTTM; FaPoR
"Horatius,' quoth the Consul." VLP

Lazarus. Stuart Dybek. TC

Laziness and Silence. Robert Bly. PPP

Lazy laughing languid Jenny. Jenny. Dante Gabriel Rossetti. VPC

Lazy loop of loozenged gray, A. The Sidewinder. Charles F. Lummis. BPAW

Lazy Man's Song. Po Chü-i, *tr. fr. Chinese by* Arthur Waley. OBVE

Lazy Mary. *Unknown.* AmFP

Lazy sheep, pray tell me why. The Sheep. Ann *or* Jane Taylor. OxBChV

Le Chariot. John Wieners. VGW

Le Livre Est sur la Table. John Ashbery. EAS

Le Médecin Malgré Lui. William Carlos Williams. PoA

Le Monocle de Mon Oncle. Wallace Stevens. NoAM

Le Rêve. Edgar Bowers. ConAP

Lead. Jayne Cortez. PoBA

Lead, Kindly Light. Cardinal Newman. *See* Pillar of the Cloud, The.

Lead On, O King Eternal, *with music.* Ernest W. Shurtleff. AH

Lead the black bull to slaughter, with the boar. Upon Master Walter Montagu's Return from Travel. Thomas Carew. CaPo

Lead us, Evolution, lead us. Evolutionary Hymn. C. S. Lewis. NOBL

Lead Us, O Father, in the Paths of Peace, *with music.* William Henry Burleigh. AH

Leadbelly Gives an Autograph. Amiri Baraka. CNA

Leaden Echo and the Golden Echo, The. Gerard Manley Hopkins. CMoP (1970 ed.); ILP (1975 ed.); PAIC
Leaden Echo, The, *sel.* PoIA

Leaden-eyed, The. Vachel Lindsay. CMoP (1970 ed.); FaBoEE; PBMP; SFF; TPo

Leaden Treasury of English Verse, A, *sels.* Paul Dehn.
"Jenny kiss'd me when we met." SpRo
"Ring-a-ring o' neutrons." QQQ; SpRo

Leaders of the Crowd, The. W. B. Yeats. EBEV; SFF

Leading a goat to pasture like playing with a toy. Maybe You Cannot Comprehend. Salvador Villanueva, *tr. by* Julio Marzán. InW

Leading poor Delmore's bear up here. An Old High Walk. Robert Huff. CNW

Leads nowhere, cannot be entered. The Street. Ken Smith. TwMBP

Leady-Day, an' Ridden House. William Barnes. VLP

Leaf after Leaf. Walter Savage Landor. PPM

Leaf floats in endless space, A. Seeking a Mooring. Wang Wei, *tr. by* Kenneth Rexroth *and* Ling Chung. BoWoP

Leaf knows sorrow in this time of thorns, The. Anglo-American Chainpoem. *Unknown.* EAS

Leaf membranes lid the window. Seamus Heaney. *Fr.* A Northern Hoard. CIP

Leaf of lehua and noni-tint, the Kona Sea. The Kona Sea. *Tr. fr. Hawaiian by* N. B. Emerson. WTO

Leaf Out of a Rhyming Diary. Hugh McCrae. MAuV

Leaf Treader, A. Robert Frost. BBGO

Leafe gold, Lord of thy golden wedge o'relaid. Edward Taylor. Preparatory Meditations, First Series, XVI. EAP

Leafing through. Looking for Lola. Morgan Sanders. WBN

Leaflets. Adrian Mitchell. NowV

Leaflets. Adrienne Rich. NIL; NoAM
"Your face/ stretched like a mask," *sel.* TT

Leaflight. Dorothy Donnelly. NCSH

Leafy-with-love banks and the green waters of the canal. Canal Bank Walk. Patrick Kavanagh. CIP; CMoP (1970 ed.); FaBoTw (1975 ed.); NoAM

League of Selves, The. Alvin Toffler. AMV-80

Leagues, leagues over. Mermaids. Walter de la Mare. EcS

Leah. Shirley Kaufman. VWA

Leak in the Dike, The. Phoebe Cary. CTV

Lean Day in a Convict's Suit, A. Jean Wahl, *tr. fr. French by* Charles Guenther. VWA

Lean Gaius, who was thinner than a straw. Lucilius, *tr. fr. Greek by* Peter Porter. OBVE

Lean, lanky son of desert sage. To a Jack Rabbit. S. Omar Barker. BPAW

Lean out of the window. James Joyce. Chamber Music, V. PCOP; UsP

Lean Street. G. S. Fraser. MS

Leander to the envious light. George Chapman. *Fr.* Hero and Leander, Third Sestiad. OAEL-1

Leaning/ over the footbridge the Willamette. Landscape with Poets. Olga Broumas. CNW

Leaning into the edge of the earth. Summer's Darkness. Elizabeth Hanson. NPW

Leaning on a Limerick, *sel.* Eve Merriam.
"Let the limerick form be rehoised." TDH

Leaning on the Everlasting Arms, *with music.* Elisha A. Hoffman. BLSH

Leaning on the unpainted rail. Over the Green Sands. Peggy Bennett. EcS

Leap-Centuries. Paul Celan, *tr. fr. German by* Michael Hamburger. OBVE

Lear. William Carlos Williams. NOBA; PoA

Learn women all from this housewifery. Giovanni Battista Guarini, *tr. by* Sir Richard Fanshawe. *Fr.* Il Pastor Fido. OBVE

Learn'd lapidaries say the diamond. To Cynthia: Learn'd Lapidaries. Sir Francis Kynaston. SCP-2

Learn'd society of late, A. Samuel Butler. *Fr.* The Elephant in the Moon: A Satire. SCP-2

Learner. J. A. Lindon. PH

Learning. Marie Harris. MMD

Learning bad grammar, then getting blamed for it. Two Bad Things in Infant School. D. J. Enright. HeHu

Learning by Doing. Howard Nemerov. HAP; NowV

Learning Experience. Marge Piercy. FF

Learning the Spells: A Diptych. Anita Endrezze Probst. CDW

Learning to Breathe. Gael Turnbull. PMW

Learning to Keep a Low Profile. Elisavietta Ritchie. PoUp

Learning to Live with Friends. Cleopatra Mathis. AAN

Learning to Live without You. Susan Wood. AMV-81

Learning to Speak. Peter Everwine. NNaP

Learning to Speak. Melvin Wilk. AMV-81

Leather belt white shirt black pants. Telegram. Dick Lourie. NeAC

Leatherette relic smelling of musk and camphor falls, A. Homage to Austin Warren. Laurence Lieberman. ILP (1975 ed.)

Leatherwing Bat. *Unknown.* FSW

Leathery, wry and rough. Rodeo. Edward Lueders. MPA; SPo

Leave go my hands, let me catch breath and see. In the Orchard. Swinburne. BoLoP

Leave Helen to her lover. Draw away. The White Isle of Leuce. Sir Herbert Read. FaBoTw (1975 ed.)

Leave Her, Johnny. *Unknown.* FSW

Leave it for the papers. Keep It under Your Hat. Gary Margolis. CoPAm

Leave It to Me Blues. Joel Oppenheimer. VGW

Leave Krete and come to this holy temple. Sappho, *tr. fr. Greek by* Willis Barnstone. BoWoP

Leave Me, O Love. Sir Philip Sidney. *Sometimes considered Sonnet CX of* Astrophel and Stella. CABA (1972 ed.); HeIP; NIL; PPP

    ("Leave me, O Love, which reachest but to dust.") GBL (Splendidis Longum Valedico Nugis.) BoReV; LoAs; NOBE

Leave my eyes. And Who Are You? June Jordan. RiTi

Leave-taking, A. Swinburne. NOBE; VLP

Leave the bars lying in the grass. Fall. Robert Francis. VGW

Leave the sluice and "tom" untended. In the Mines. John Swett. BPAW

Leave the Top Plums. Janet Carncross Chandler. AMV-80

Leave the window open. *Turkish Death Songs, tr. by* Reza Baraheni *and* Zahra-Soltan Shokoohtaezeh. BoWoP

Leave Us Alone. Tadeusz Rozewicz, *tr. fr. Polish by* Czeslaw Milosz. BuTh

Leave your home behind, lad. The Recruit. A. E. Housman. FaPoR

Leaves. Sam Hamod. SA

Leaves. Ted Hughes. BBL

Leaves, The. Ron Loewinsohn. GP

Leaves. Ross Shideler. PoW

Leaves and Ashes. John Haines. MPA

Leaves and Ashes. Michael Waters. AAN

Leaves are gathered, the trees are dying, The. Edwin Morgan. *Fr.* For Bonfires. MS

Leaves as red as rowanberries ride. Romantics. Maurice Lindsay. MS

Leaves bed the woods. Near Caledonia. Patricia Henley. NPW

Leaves Come Again, The. Thomas Stanley. FaBoEE

Leaves come down with little grieving, The. Autumn Song for Anti-Fascists. Genevieve Taggard. SPT

Leaves Compared with Flowers. Robert Frost. NOBA

Leaves from eternity are simple things. The Eternity of Nature. John Clare. EBEV

Leaves from the ancient forest gleam. The Princes' Land. Les A. Murray. MAuV

Leaves hang like fruit in your eyes, autumn cat, The. The Cat. Helen Wolfert. RiTi

Leaves have fallen. On the Inside Strong. Antar S. K. Mberi. SES

Leaves like Fish. Gladys Cardiff. CDW

Leaves looked in at the window, The. The House across the Way. Ralph Hodgson. FaBoTw (1975 ed.)

Leaves of autumn drop by two and threes, The. Autumn Change. John Clare. VLP

Leaves that rustled on this oak-crowned hill, The. Wordsworth. VLP

Leaves were everywhere in air. In a Maple Wood. Pat Scheider. AMV-81

Leaves, wind-torn, sun-smoothed in passage. The Wind. Ruth Stephan. FoP

Leavetaking. Lisa Reape. AMV-81

Leaving America. Michael Waters. AAN

Leaving aside then for all time the songs. Poem. Anthony Cronin. IPM

Leaving Barra. Louis MacNeice. EBEV

Leaving beer and apples. For a Friend. Lyn Lifshin. NeAC; Psy

Leaving Buffalo. Charles Martin. PoA

Leaving Here. Stephen Philbrick. AMV-81

Leaving Home. Shirley Cochrane. AMV-80

Leaving Home. Amanda Powell. AAN

Leaving Ithaca: Buttermilk Falls. Marie Harris. *Fr.* Interstate. AAN

Leaving Mexico One More Time. Constance Urdang. AMV-80

Leaving of Liverpool, The. *Unknown.* FSW

Leaving One of the State Parks after a Family Outing. Elizabeth Macklin. AMV-81

Leaving School. Roy Fuller. BBL

Leaving Something Behind. David Wagoner. CoPAm

Leaving the Atocha Station. John Ashbery. CAPP

Leaving the bird house. Responses. Robert Hershon. POL

Leaving the Country House to the Landlord, Five Years Later. Wesley McNair. FAF

Leaving the Dance. Alexander Whitaker. NIL

Leaving the Flag Out All Night. Napoleon St. Cyr. FAF

Leaving the island, she believes, to go to the child. Monique Laederach, *tr. by* Charles Guenther. *Fr.* Penelope. BoWoP

Leaving the Motel. W. D. Snodgrass. FF; PiAm; WeW

Leaving the Prison. Joseph Bruchac. FAF

Leaving them, children of the Sun, to their perpetual. Perseus. James K. Baxter. ATNZ

Leaving Them, Letting the Farm Swallow. Lyn Lifshin. FAF

Leaving them, running. 28 VIII 69. Laura Chester. IHMS

Leaving, to where it was that. The Way It Happens to You. Harold Bond. NVAP

Leaving Town Blues. *Unknown.* BluL

Leaving us behind. After the Death of Her Daughter in Childbirth. Izumi Shikibu, *tr. by* Edwin A. Cranston. PBWP

Leavings. Barbara A. Holland. WBN

Lecture before a Lecture on Pushkin. George M. Young, Jr. FAF

Lecture Hall. Patrick Kavanagh. FaBoTw (1975 ed.); NoAM

Lecture upon the Shadow, A. John Donne. CABA (1972 ed.); Epi; InPK; UnPo (1976 ed.)

Lecture with Slides, Film Clips and Tape. Marilyn Krysl. NPW

Lecturer Seeks a Wife, The. George M. Young, Jr. FAF

Lectures on the Biology of the Shadow. George M. Young, Jr. FAF

Led by the light of an unusual star. W. H. Auden. *Fr.* For the Time Being. PChr

Leda. Rainer Maria Rilke, *tr. fr. German by* Robert Bly. NU

Leda. Mona Van Duyn. NMM

Leda and the Swan. Oliver St. John Gogarty. HAP

Leda and the Swan. W. B. Yeats. AnMo; CABA (1972 ed.); CMoP (1970 ed.); EBEV; Epi; ExPo (1973 ed.); FF; HAP; HeIP; ILP (1975 ed.); InPK; LFH; NIL; NoAM; NOBE; NowV; OAEL-2; OBP; PAIC; PoIA; PPoD; PPoe; PPP; PSN; SoSe; STS; TCP; WeW

Leda Reconsidered. Mona Van Duyn. NMM

L'Education Sentimentale. David Malouf. CAAP

Lee Handley's dead. Jeep. Charles Stetler. GP

Lee-ers of Hew. James Cunningham. JB

Leering across Pearl Street. Trouble. James Wright. FF; InPK

Leesome Brand. *Unknown.* PeBB

Left/ Forward! He's the leanest in the shower. Soccer. Andrei Voznesensky, *tr. by* Anselm Hollo. LiSp; SPo

Left Folkestone 5 p.m. Excerpts from a Diary of a War. John Daniel. TwMBP

Left leg flung out, head cocked to the right. Poet. Karl Shapiro. CMoP (1970 ed.); NoAM

Left like water in glasses overnight. Love from My Father. Carole Gregory Clemmons. CNA; PoBA

Left side of her world is gone, The. Strokes. William Stafford. ConAP

Left to themselves people. Revolutionary Letter # 4. Diane DiPrima. GP; RiTi

Leg, The. Karl Shapiro. HAP; MPA; UnPo (1976 ed.)

Leg over leg. *Unknown.* MG

Legacies. Nikki Giovanni. CTBA

Legacy. Amiri Baraka. NoAM; NOBA; PoBA

Legacy. Gena Ford. IHMS

Legacy, The. *Unknown.* BBL
("My father died a month ago.") PoPle

Legacy:/ the estate, the tools. Cosmetic Survival. Ettore Rella. SPT

Legacy for a Beboppin Gentle Giant: DuBois. Antar S. K. Mberi. SES

Legacy: My South. Dudley Randall. PoBA

Leg-acy of a Blue Capricorn. James Cunningham. JB

Legacy II. Leroy V. Quintana. GP
("Grandfather never went to school.") FoP

Legal children of a literary man, The. Relationships. Mona Van Duyn. GP; RiTi

Legal Fiction. William Empson. CMoP (1970 ed.); ExPo (1973 ed.); ILP (1975 ed.); InPK; NoAM

Legend. Hart Crane. CABA (1972 ed.); NoAM

Legend. Jules Laforgue, *tr. fr. French by* Louis Simpson. Prf

Legend. Frederick Morgan. PoIA

Legend. Judith Wright. PoTa; SO

Legend of Boastful Bill, The. Charles Badger Clark, Jr. BPAW

Legend of Good Women, The: Prologue, *sels.* Chaucer.
"And as for me, though that I konne but lyte." HeIP
Balade: "Hide [*or* Hyd], Absalon [*or* Absalom], thy gilte tresses clear." EBEV; GBL; NOBE; OAEL-1
("Hide [*or* Hyd], Absalon, thy gilte tresses clere.") HAP; OxBM
(Hyd, Absolon.) WeW
Daysies. PF
Old Books. OxBM

Legend of Lake Okeefinokee, The. Laura E. Richards. ECBV

Legend of Paper Plates, The. John Haines. GP; PPoD

Legend of the Crossbill, The. Julius Mosen, *tr. fr. German by* Longfellow. PIM

Legend of the Hive, A. Robert Stephen Hawker. VPC

Legend of the Raindrop, The. Helen Steiner Rice. CTV

Legend of Versailles, A. Melvin B. Tolson. BPo

*Legend*: The god in the sun made two men. J. Michael Yates. *Fr.* The Great Bear Lake Meditations. HoPM (1975 ed.)

Legende. Hart Crane. PSN

Legion Club, The, *sel.* Swift.
"As I strole the city, oft I." BIrV

Legree's big house was white and green. Simon Legree—a Negro Sermon. Vachel Lindsay. The Booker Washington Trilogy, I. TAP

Legs, The. Robert Graves. NoAM

Legs. Vernon Scannell. HeHu

Legs!/ How we have suffered each other. Poem in Which My Legs Are Accepted. Kathleen Fraser. AmPA; NMM; RiTi

Legs of the elk punctured the snow's crust, The. To Christ Our Lord. Galway Kinnell. InPK; MiP; NIL; RFM

Legsby, Lincolnshire. *Unknown.* GBP

Leisure. W. H. Davies. CTV; ECBV; NOBE; PPM; WIF

Leit. Marcos Rodríguez Frese, *tr. fr. Spanish by* Julio Marzán. InW

L'Elisir d'Amore. Dallas E. Wiebe. MAT

Lem Catlett had one pretty gal. Hill Hunger. John Foster West. TAT

Lemmings, The. John Masefield. CMoP (1970 ed.); ILP (1975 ed.); NoAM

Lemon. Mario Satz, *tr. fr. Spanish by* Willis Barnstone. VWA

Lemon Balm. Marie Harris. MMD

Lemon Pie. Edgar A Guest. OBAL

Lemonade. *Unknown.* GBP
(Picnic Rhyme.) FaBoNo

Lemons. Patricia Hubbell. ECBV

Lemons, Lemons. Al Young. HeIP; PiAm

Lemuel's Blessing. W. S. Merwin. CAPP; TCP

Lend a Hand. Edward Everett Hale. CTV; PCOP

L'Enfant Glacé. Harry Graham. FaBoCo

Lenora. *Unknown.* TDH

Lenore, 3 *versions.* Poe. WIF

Lenox Avenue/ by daylight. Dive. Langston Hughes. NYP

Lenox Avenue is a big street. Keep on Pushing. David Henderson. PoBA

Lenox Avenue Mural. Langston Hughes. AmNP (1974 ed.); CoPAm; HoPM (1975 ed.)
*Sels.*
Good Morning. WIF
Harlem ("What happens to a dream deferred"). BiP; CABA (1972 ed.); HeIP; ILP (1975 ed.); InPS; IP; NIL; PBMP; PoIA
(Dream Deferred.) FF; InPK; PoBA; PPP; SoSE; WIF
Island. ILP (1975 ed.)
Same in Blues. InPS; WIF

Lenox Christmas Eve 68. Sam Cornish. CNA

Lens for Plum Blossom. Thomas Hornsby Ferril. MPA

Lens is not an eye, The. It will not leave you. On Being Photographed. William H. Gass. AMV-81

Lent in a Year of War. Thomas Merton. EAS

Lent Lily, The. A. E. Housman. FSFS

Lent Tending. J. Barrie Shepherd. AMV-80

Lenten Ys Come with Love to Toune. *Unknown.* HAP
("Lenten is come with love to towne.") EBEV
(Spring.) OAEL-1; OxBM
(Spring Has Come to Town with Love.) CABA (1972 ed.)

Lentinus! thou dost nought but fume, and fret. Martial, *tr. fr. Latin by* Sir Edward Sherburne. OBVE

L'Envoi: "Here we are for the last time face to face." William Morris. *Fr.* The Earthly Paradise. VPC

L'Envoi: "When Earth's last picture is painted, and the tubes are twisted and dried." Kipling. *See* When Earth's Last Picture Is Painted.

Leonardo's Secret. Robert Bly. NNaP

Leopard. *Yoruba Oral Tradition, tr. by* Ulli Beier. WTO

Leopard when told that benzine, A. The Inquisitive Leopard. Oliver Herford. TDH

Leoun, *abr.* Jean Cocteau, *tr. fr. French by* Alan Neame. OBVE

Lepanto. G. K. Chesterton. BTTM; FaPo; FaPoR
"Strong gongs groaning as the guns boom far," *sel.* IP

Leper, The. Ka-'ehu, *tr. fr. Hawaiian by* M. K. Pukui *and* A. L. Korn. WTO

Leper, The. Swinburne. GBL

Leroy. Amiri Baraka. BPo; ILP (1975 ed.); PiAm; PoBA

Les Demoiselles de Sauve. John Gray. VLP

Les Etiquettes Jaunes. Frank O'Hara. CAPP

Les Luths. Frank O'Hara. NoAM; NOBA

Les Sylphides. Louis MacNeice. BoLoP; BuTh; PSN

Les Vaches. Arthur Hugh Clough. PeD

Lesbia Forever on Me Rails. Catullus, *tr. fr. Latin by* Swift. NIL; OBVE

Lesbia loads me night and day with her curses. Catullus, *tr. fr. Latin by* Peter Whigham. BoLoP

Lesbia speaks evil of me with her husband near. Catullus, *tr. fr. Latin by* Horace Gregory. NAWM-1

Lesbian Poem. Robin Morgan. IHMS

Lesbian girl of Khartoum, A. Limerick. *Unknown.* NOBL

Lesbia's sparrow. Catullus, *tr. fr. Latin by* Peter Whigham. TwMBP

Lesbos. Lawrence Durrell. EBEV

Lesbos. Sylvia Plath. RiTi

Leslie. Marvin Wyche, Jr. AmNP (1974 ed.)

Less and Less Human, O Savage Spirit. Wallace Stevens. IPWM; VGW

Less Is More. Vern Rutsala. AMV-80

Less Nonsense. A. P. Herbert. OxBTC

Less passionate the long war throws. The Long War. Laurie Lee. BuTh

Less said the better. Missing. John Pudney. OxBTC

Less than Love. Aileen Campbell Nye. SLP

Lesson, The. Miroslav Holub, tr. fr. Czech by Ian Milner and George Theiner. LP

Lesson, The. Robert Lowell. CMoP (1970 ed.)

Lesson, The. Edward Lucie-Smith. BuTh; LP; MPo; NCSH; OxBTC

Lesson, The. Elizabeth Peterson. AMV-80

Lesson, A. Christina Rossetti. PCOP

Lesson. Anthony Thwaite. HeHu

Lesson, The. David Wagoner. MPA

Lesson for Mamma, A. Sydney Dayre. OxBChV

Lesson from Jim Crane. Barbara Earl Thomson. AATT

Lesson in Detachment, A. Vassar Miller. CSP

Lesson in Love, A. Philip Hobsbaum. OxBTC

Lesson in Oblivion, A. Dabney Stuart. GP

Lesson in Translation, A. Gabriel Preil, tr. fr. Hebrew by Howard Schwartz. VWA

Lesson of the Master. William Dickey. CoPAm

Lessons in History. Robert Penn Warren. AMV-80

Lessons of the War. Henry Reed. HeIP
*Sels.*
Judging Distances, II. BoLoP; NIL; NOBE; PSN; SoSe
Naming of Parts, I. ExPo (1973 ed.); FF; HoPM (1975 ed.); ILP (1975 ed.); InPK; InPS; MPo; NOBE; OxBTC; PoIA; PPoD; SoS; SoSe; UnPo (1976 ed.); UsP; VoPo

Lest men suspect your tale to be untrue. The Devil's Advice to Story-Tellers. Robert Graves. NoAM

Lester Young. Ted Joans. AmNP (1974 ed.)

Let all chaste matrons, when they chance to see. Upon a Young Mother of Many Children. Robert Herrick. CaPo

Let All Created Things, *with music.* Artis Seagrave. AH

Let all the fish that swim the sea. Herring Is King. Alfred Perceval Graves. PFIr

Let all the little poets be gathered together in classes. To School! Stevie Smith. FaBoEE

Let all who will. Militant. Langston Hughes. PoBA

Let Bachus to Venus libations pour forth. "Vive la Compagnie." *Unknown.* PSoN

Let but thy voice engender with the string. Upon Her Voice. Robert Herrick. CaPo

Let by Rain. Edward Taylor. NOBA

Let Christian Hearts Rejoice Today, *with music. Unknown, tr. fr. French by* Francis X. Curley. AH

Let Christmas celebrate greenly. For the fir is king. Jubilate Herbis. Norma Farber. PChr

Let Cynics bark, and the stern Stagirite. The Paradox. *Unknown.* APAS

Let dainty wits cry on the Sisters nine. Astrophel and Stella, III. Sir Philip Sidney. NIL; OAEL-1

Let dogs delight to bark and bite. Against Quarrelling and Fighting. Isaac Watts. OxBChV

Let due civilities be strictly paid. John Gay. *Fr.* Trivia; or, The Art of Walking the Streets of London, II. OAEL-1

"Let Earth give thanks," the deacon said. Simon Sogg's Thanksgiving. W. A. Croffut. PoTa

Let Elizure rejoice with the partridge. Christopher Smart. *Fr.* Jubilate Agno. OAEL-1

Let 'em censure: what care I? On Critics [*or* In Imitation of Anacreon]. Matthew Prior. FaBoEE; LFH

Let every good fellow now fill up his glass. Vive la Compagnie (Vive l'Amour). *Unknown.* FSW

Let fools great Cupid's yoke disdain. Song: The Willing Prisoner to His Mistress. Thomas Carew. CaPo

Let go of the present and death. Once Again. Liz Sohappy Bahe. CDW; VW

Let go of the unicorn's reins. The Beast That Rode the Unicorn. Conny Hannes Meyer, *tr. by* Herbert Kuhner. VWA

Let Go: Once. Gerald Fleming. AMV-81

Let grass grow, and waters flow. Real Old Mountain Dew. *Unknown.* FSW

Let happy throats be mute. Threnody. Donald Jeffrey Hayes. AmNP (1974 ed.)

Let her lie naked here, my hand resting. News of the World III. George Barker. FaBoTw (1975 ed.)

Let Heroes Account to Love. Alan Dugan. NoAM

Let him answer as he will. The Companion. E. A. Robinson. NoAM

Let him rail on, let his invective Muse. Dryden. *Fr.* Absalom and Achitophel, Pt. II. OBP

Let him that will, ascend the tottering seat. Seneca, *tr. by* Sir Matthew Hale. *Fr.* Thyestes, II. OBVE

Let Him with Kisses of His Mouth, *with music. Unknown.* AH

Let him who may. To Be Recited to Flossie on Her Birthday. William Carlos Williams. VGW

Let holy saints, now safely out. After Bad Dreams. George Garrett. CoPAm

Let it age. I think of you and. Request. Stephen Shrader. PHC

Let it be alleys. Let it be a hall. A Lovely Love. Gwendolyn Brooks. BPo; TT

Let it be forgotten, as a flower is forgotten. Song. Sara Teasdale. PoA

Let it be so; thy truth then be thy dower. Shakespeare. *Fr.* King Lear, I, i. OBP

Let it disturb no more at first. Fountain. Elizabeth Jennings. WPE

Let It Go. William Empson. OxBTC; PSN

Let it no longer be a forlorn hope. On the Baptized Ethiopian. Richard Crashaw. FaBoEE; PeD

Let kings command, and do the best they may. The Power in the People. Robert Herrick. CaPo

Let man's soul be a sphere, and then in this. Good Friday, 1613. Riding Westward. John Donne. AnMo; ExPo (1973 ed.); OAEL-1; PPP

Let me alone, I prithee, in this cell. Everard Guilpin. *Fr.* Skialetheia. TVS

Let me ask you, Mind. *Unknown, tr. fr. Korean.* TVo

Let me be a little kinder. My Daily Creed. *Unknown.* CTV

Let me be at the place of the castle. Psalm Concerning the Castle. Denise Levertov. PiAm; WPE

Let me be buried in the rain. Invocation. Helene Johnson. AmNP (1974 ed.)

Let me be formed with stone. Instructions for the Erection of a Statue of Myself in Central Park. Colette Inez. RiTi

Let Me Be Held When the Longing Comes. Stephany Fuller. BPO

Let me be my own fool. A Counterpoint. Robert Creeley. CoPAm

Let me be the mane that swings. Poem for a Singer. Milton Acorn. NeAC

Let me be to Thee as the circling bird. Gerard Manley Hopkins. VLP

Let me be what I am, as Virgil cold. An Elegy. Ben Jonson. SCP-1

Let me be your salty dog. Salty Dog Blues. *Unknown.* FSW

Let me be your wiggler until your wobbler comes.  Jacksonville Blues.  *Unknown.*  BluL

Let me break down foundations of the earth.  To the Dead of the International Brigade.  Sol Funaroff.  SPT

Let me call a ghost.  Song of Three Smiles.  W. S. Merwin.  NOBA; VGW

Let me celebrate you.  A Dialogue of Watching.  Kenneth Rexroth.  MiP

Let Me Die a Youngman's Death.  Roger McGough.  BuTh; LP

Let Me Enjoy.  Thomas Hardy.  NoAM; PPM

Let me fall down about your feet oh Christ.  Oils and Ointments.  R. A. K. Mason.  ATNZ

Let Me Fly.  *Unknown.*  FSW

Let Me for Once.  Bobby Byrd.  FoP

Let Me Go.  *Gond Oral Tradition, tr. by* V. Elwin *and* S. Hivale.  WTO

Let Me Go Where Saints Are Going, *with music.*  Lewis Hartsough.  AH

Let me go where'er I will.  Music.  Emerson.  CTV; PCOP

Let me just finish off my slender fiddle.  My Fiddle.  Leib Kwitko, *tr. by* Keith Bosley.  VWA

Let me look at what I was, before I die.  Jamestown.  Randall Jarrell.  GOA

Let me not be unfair Lord to New York that sink that sewer.  Ode to New York.  Reed Whittemore.  NYP

Let me not die for ever, when I'm gone.  A Wish.  Fanny Kemble.  WPE

Let me not go anywhere.  Poem Composed in Rogue River Park . . .  Tom Wayman.  POL

Let me not live, if I not love.  On Himself.  Robert Herrick.  CaPo

Let me not pass to the house of clay.  Forgive, Lord, Have Mercy!  *Tr. fr. Sanskrit by* Raimundo Panikkar.  *Fr.* Vedic Hymns.  ILwL

Let me not to the marriage of true minds.  Sonnets, CXVI.  Shakespeare.  CABA (1972 ed.); ExPo (1973 ed.); Epi; GBL; HAP; HeIP; ILP (1975 ed.); InPK; InPS; IPWM; LFH; NIL; NOBE; OAEL-1; OBP; PBMP; PoIA; PPoe; PPP; SoSe; STS; UnPo (1976 ed.); VoPo

Let me obtain forgiveness of thee, Samson.  Milton.  *Fr.* Samson Agonistes.  EBEV

Let Me Out.  Michael Benedikt.  CAAP

Let me play to you tunes without measure or end.  Bagpipe Music.  "Hugh MacDiarmid."  OAEL-2

Let me pour [*or* powre] forth.  A Valediction: Of Weeping.  John Donne.  CABA (1972 ed.); HAP; HeIP; ILP (1975 ed.); MetP; OAEL-1; SCP-1; TT

"Let me put an edge on that hoe."  The Whetstone.  Clarice Short.  MPA

Let me put it this way.  George Jonas.  NeAC

Let me say (in anger) that since the day we were married.  The Crisis.  Robert Creeley.  FF; PPP

Let me see if Philip can.  The Story of Fidgety Philip.  Heinrich Hoffmann, *tr. fr. German.*  OxBChV

Let me see you.  Mirabai, *tr. fr. Hindi by* Willis Barnstone *and* Usha Nilsson.  BoWoP

Let me strap/ the baby in the seat.  If He Let Us Go Now.  Shirley Williams.  BoWoP

Let me take this other glove off.  In Westminster Abbey.  John Betjeman.  BoReV; CMoP (1970 ed.); FaBoCo; ILP (1975 ed.); InPK; IP; NIL; NOBL; OAEL-2; OBSV

Let me take you down.  Strawberry Fields Forever.  John Lennon *and* Paul McCartney.  GrRo

Let me tell to you the story.  Edith Agnew.  PChr

Let Me Tell You.  Miller Williams.  CoPAm; CSP

Let me tell you a little story.  Miss Gee.  W. H. Auden.  OxBTC

Let me tell you about our land.  The Judge.  Karl Kopp.  TAT

Let me tell you where I have walked.  Places I Have Been.  Joyce M. Volk.  AMV-80

Let no blasphemer till the sacred earth.  Benediction.  Mark Turbyfill.  PoA

Let No Charitable Hope.  Elinor Wylie.  PBWP; Psy; SBG; VGW

Let no girl wait on you on that day when you bind your wild.  The Alchemy of Day.  Anne Hébert, *tr. by* A. Poulin, Jr.  BoWoP

Let no man boste of cunning nor vertù.  Like a Midsummer Rose.  John Lydgate.  OxBM

Let not young souls be smothered out before.  The Leaden-eyed.  Vachel Lindsay.  CMoP (1970 ed.); FaBoEE; PBMP; SFF; TPo

Let nothing disturb thee/ Nothing affright thee.  St. Theresa of Avila, *tr. fr. Spanish by* Longfellow.  ILwL

Let observation with extensive view.  The Vanity of Human Wishes: The Tenth Satire of Juvenal, Imitated.  Samuel Johnson.  CABA (1972 ed.); EBEV; ESaP; HeIP; LAuP; OAEL-l; PoIA

Let oken club now strike, and poast of might.  Seneca, *tr. by* Jasper Heywood.  *Fr.* Hercules Furens, IV.  OBVE

Let other mount aloft, let other sore.  Seneca, *tr. by* John Studley.  *Fr.* Hercules Oetaetus, II.  OBVE

Let Other People Come as Streams.  Charles Reznikoff.  VGW (Dew.)  VWA

Let others draw from smiling skies their theme.  The Vision of the Night.  Philip Freneau.  *Fr.* The House of Night.  EAP

Let others pray for the passenger pigeon.  Elegy for the Giant Tortoises.  Margaret Atwood.  BoWoP

Let others sing of knights and palladin[e]s.  Samuel Daniel.  *Fr.* To Delia.  AAS; NIL; NOBE

Let poetry be/ like an air conditioner.  Ars Poetica.  Arturo Trías, *tr. by* Julio Marzán.  InW

Let poets praise the softer winds of spring.  J. B. Morton.  FaBoEE

Let praise devote they work, and skill employ.  Laus Deo.  Robert Bridges.  VLP

Let school-masters puzzle their brain.  Song [*or* The Three Pigeons].  Goldsmith.  *Fr.* She Stoops to Conquer.  BIrV; ILP (1975 ed.)

Let shrieking steel and gray stone be set.  Psalmodist.  Mani Leib, *tr. by* David G. Roskies *and* Hillel Schwartz.  VWA

Let sleep take her, let sleep take her, let sleep.  Fourth Song the Night Nurse Sang.  Robert Duncan.  VGW

Let some in beer place their delight.  The Dish of Tea.  Philip Freneau.  EAP

Let Sporus tremble—"What? That thing of silk."  Sporus.  Pope.  *Fr.* Epistle to Dr. Arbuthnot.  NOBE; OBSV

Let the bells ring, and let the boys sing.  Jacobean Merrymaking.  Beaumont *and* Fletcher.  *Fr.* The Spanish Curate, III, ii.  BBL

Let the bird of loudest lay.  The Phoenix and the Turtle.  Shakespeare.  NOBE; OAEL-1

Let the boy try along this bayonet-blade.  Arms and the Boy.  Wilfred Owen.  CABA (1972 ed.); CMoP (1970 ed.); HAP; ILP (1975 ed.); IP; LFH; OAEL-1; OBP; PBMP; PoIA; WeW

Let the Brothels of Paris Be Opened.  Blake.  Epi; MBPR

Let the crows go by hawking their caw and caw.  River Roads.  Carl Sandburg.  VGW

Let the damned ride their earwigs to Hell, but let me not join them.  Rock Pilgrim.  Herbert Palmer.  OxBTC

Let the day glare: O memory, your tread.  Ode to Fear.  Allen Tate.  PAIC

Let the day perish, wherein I was borne.  Bible, *O.T.*  *Fr.* Job.  OBVE

Le the Dead Depart in Peace. *Yoruba Oral Tradition, tr. by* Ulli Beier. WTO

Let the Deep Organ Swell, *with music.* Constantine Pise. AH

Let the exiles in-gather. Evening of the Rose. Anthony Rudolf. VWA

Let the flowers make a journey. The Fury of Flowers and Worms. Anne Sexton. BoWoP

Let the knowing speak. Adjuration. Charles Enoch Wheeler. AmNP (1974 ed.)

Let the limerick form be rehoised. Leaning on a Limerick. Eve Merriam. TDH

Let the men be free. Monument. E. M. de Melo e Castro. UsP

Let the pines rock in torment of the storm. Horatian Ode. Joseph Warren Beach. PoA

Let the rain kiss you. April Rain Song. Langston Hughes. LCL

Let the rain plunge radiant. The Way Through. Denise Levertov. CoPAm

Let the Rest of the World Go By. J. Keirn Brennan. UnPo (1976 ed.)

Let the robed kings march in the mind. A Letter from a Friend. John N. Morris. CABA (1972 ed.)

Let the shark keep to the shelves and closets of coral. From a litany. Mark Strand. PPP

Let the sloughs back up and history. Spring for All Seasons. James Welch. SA

Let the snake wait under. A Sort of a Song. William Carlos Williams. BiP; HoPM (1975 ed.); PoIA; TAP

Let the still yellow goldenrod, hot with sun, come back. You Are More than I Need. Rebbekka Kaplan. AMV-80

Let the tale's sailor from a Christian voyage. Altarwise by Owl-Light, X. Dylan Thomas. CMoP (1970 ed.); Epi; NoAM; OAEL-2

Let the wealthy and great. A Farmer's Life [*or* The Rewards of Farming]. *Unknown.* PoPle; RAE

Let the world's sharpness like a clasping knife. Sonnets from the Portuguese, XXIV. Elizabeth Barrett Browning. VLP

Let them bestow on every airth a limb. On Himself, upon Hearing What Was His Sentence. James Graham, Marquis of Montrose. FaBoEE; SCP-2

Let them bury your big eyes. Elegy. Edna St. Vincent Millay. *Fr.* Memorial to D. C. CMoP (1970 ed.); LoAs

Let them count scalps under the barroom wall. Lying in a Yuma Saloon. Jim Barnes. CDW

Let them keep it. And Was Not Improved. Lerone Bennett, Jr. CNA; PoBA

Let There Be Light, *with music.* William M. Vories. AH

Let there be light in all the nightmare places. Benediction. William R. Mitchell. AATT

Let There Be New Flowering. Lucille Clifton. GP

Let there be no flowery banks. A Garden of Situations. Jack Anderson. PoA

Let there be ripeness, said the Lord. Their Mouths Full. David Ignatow. GP

Let this book as it ends. The Calendar. John Haines. MPA

Let those whose low delights to earth are given. Faith, Hope, and Charity. Giovanri Battista Guarini, *tr. by* Samuel Taylor Coleridge. MBPR

Let Thy Kingdom, *with music. Unknown.* AH

Let Tyrants Shake Their Iron Rod. William Billings. AH, *with music*
(Chester.) BLSo, *with music*

Let uh revolution come. uh. U Name This One. Carolyn M. Rodgers. NMM; PoBA

Let us abandon then our gardens and go home. Justice Denied in Massachusetts. Edna St. Vincent Millay. GOA; RiTi; SBG

Let Us All be Unhappy on Sunday. Lord Neaves. FaBoCo

Let us arise, and watch by night. Matins—Sunday. Cardinal Newman. VLP

Let us, as by this verdant bank we float. A Water-Party. Robert Bridges. PoPle

Let us await the great American novel! Critical Observations. Archibald MacLeish. OBAL

Let Us Be Merry. John Philpot Curran. PPM

Let us become the overhanging day. Shelley. *Fr.* Epipsychidion. OAEL-2

Let us begin and carry up this corpse. A Grammarian's Funeral. Robert Browning. VLP

Let us begin and portion out these sweets. A Girtonian Funeral. *Unknown.* FaBoCo

Let Us Believe. Hildegarde Flanner. WPE

Let Us Break the Bread Together. *Unknown.* AH, *with music*; FSW

Let us bring out those heavy dice. Birth. Gabriela Melinescu, *tr. by* Willis Barnstone *and* Matei Calinescu. BoWoP

Let us celebrate the single-cloaked beings. Psalm to the Creatures. Gwilym R. Jones, *tr. by* Joseph P. Clancy. OBW

Let Us Cheer the Weary Traveler, *with music. Unknown.* AH

Let us come in to worship Jehovah. Come In. Isaiah Shembe, *tr. by* H. Tracey. WTO

Let us consider the skeleton inside the body. Three Lectures on the Skeleton. George M. Young, Jr. FAF

Let Us Drink and Be Merry. Thomas Jordan. PoPle
(Careless Gallant, The.) HAP
(Epicure, The, Sung by One in the Habit of a Town Gallant.) NOBE

Let us drink knights of the round table. Chevaliers de la Table Ronde. *Unknown.* FSW

Let us for this love. Paradox. Tom McGrath. SLP

Let us forgive Ty Kendricks. Southern Cop. Sterling A. Brown. SoSe (1977 ed.); WIF

Let us give up our trips. Direction. Barbara Guest. WPE

Let us go hence, my songs; she will not hear. A Leave-taking. Swinburne. NOBE; VLP

Let us go hence: the night is now at hand. A Last Word. Ernest Dowson. VLP

Let us go then, you and I. The Love Song of J. Alfred Prufrock. T. S. Eliot. AnMo; BiP; CABA (1972 ed.); CMoP (1970 ed.); EBEV; Epi; ExPo (1973 ed.); FF; HAP; HeIP; HoPM (1975 ed.); ILP (1975 ed.); InPK; InPS; IPWM; LFH; NIL; NoAM; NOBA; NOBE; OAEL-2; OxBTC; PAIC; PoA; PoIA; PPP; PSN; SoSe; STS; TAP; TT; UsP; WIF

"Let Us Have Madness Openly." Kenneth Patchen. SPT

Let us have winter loving that the heart. Winter Love. Elizabeth Jennings. BoLoP

Let Us Honor Them. Rochelle Owens. Psy

Let Us Laugh. Zvi Shargel, *tr. fr. Yiddish by* Gabriel Preil. VWA

Let Us Learn. Melech Ravitch, *tr. fr. Yiddish by* Seymour Mayne *and* Rivka Augenfeld. VWA

Let us leave behind this city. City of Light. Nahum Bomze, *tr. by* Gabriel Preil *and* Howard Schwartz. VWA

Let us leave this place, brother. The Romanies in Town. Anne Beresford. LP; MPo

Let us make death masks. Hymn to the 10,000 Who Die Each Year on the Abortionist's Table in Amerika. Rita Mae Brown. WBN

Let us make the test. Say God wants you. Gnostics on Trial. Linda Gregg. AMV-80

Let us not live with Lear. Ripeness Is All. J. V. Cunningham. PiAm

Let us not make apologies. Instructions. Anita Skeen. IHMS

"Let Us Now Praise Famous Men." C. Day Lewis. BiP; CMoP (1970 ed.); ILP (1975 ed.)

Let us now praise famous men.  Bible, Apocrypha.  *Fr.*
  Ecclesiasticus.  OBVE
Let us quit the leafy arbour.  The Longest Day.  Wordsworth.
  RRA
Let us rejoice on our cots, for His nocturnal miracles.  Lauds.
  John Berryman.  HAP
Let us say good-bye.  Bags Packed and We Expected This.
  Ramona Wilson.  VoR
Let us say my drinking problem hangs.  The Birth of My
  Drinking Problem.  Michael McMahon.  FAF
Let us sing of it ever and long.  Song of Sukkaartik, The Assistant
  Spirit.  Ajukutooq, *tr. fr. Eskimo*.  WTO
Let us sing of the unsung hero.  Mel Allen, Mel Allen, Lend Me
  Your Cliché.  Ogden Nash.  SPo
Let us stiffen.  The Covenant.  James Cunningham.  JB
Let us suppose the mind.  Barbara Moraff.  IHMS
Let us suppose, valley and such ago.  John Berryman.  *Fr.* Dream
  Songs.  PPP
Let us synge unto the Lorde, for he is become glorious.  Bible,
  *O.T. Fr.* Exodus.  OBVE
Let us tunnel.  Letters to Walt Whitman, I.  Ronald Johnson.
  VGW
Let us use it while we may.  Of Beauty [*or* Beauty].  Giovanni
  Battista Guarini, *tr. by* Sir Richard Fanshawe.  *Fr.* Il Pastor
  Fido.  BoLoP; GBL
Let us walk in the white snow.  Velvet Shoes.  Elinor Wylie.
  FSFS; IP; PPM
Let who so lyst with mighty mace to raygne.  Seneca, *tr. by* Jasper
  Heywood.  *Fr.* Thyestes, II.  OBVE
Let wits contest.  The Posy.  George Herbert.  SCP-1
Let X Equal Half.  J. F. Wilson.  TDH
Let Y stand for you who says.  You.  Kenneth Rexroth.  *Fr.* A
  Bestiary.  HoPM (1975 ed.)
Let your eyes look at old people.  In Respect of the Elderly.
  Thomas Peacock.  VoR
Let your longing for me, my love.  Sulpicia, *tr. fr. Latin by* John
  Dillon.  PBWP
Let your song be delicate.  Song Be Delicate.  John Shaw
  Neilson.  GAS; MAuV
Let Zulu Be Heard.  Isaiah Shembe, *tr. fr. Zulu by* G. C.
  Oosthuizen.  WTO
Lethe.  Hilda Doolittle ("H.D.").  CMoP (1970 ed.); PiAm;
  VGW
Let's All Meet and Have a Party Sometime.  John Birkby.  BuTh
Let's away with study.  *Unknown, tr. by* Helen Waddell.  *Fr.*
  Carmina Burana.  NAWM-1
Let's count the bodies over again.  Counting Small-boned Bodies.
  Robert Bly.  CAPP; EAS; PPoD; TSWA
Let's Do It.  Cole Porter.  OBAL
Let's get going.  Leylâ Hanim, *tr. fr. Turkish by* Tâlat S. Halman.
  PBWP
Let's go/ Come on.  Junkman's Obbligato.  Lawrence
  Ferlinghetti.  WIF
Let's go hunting, says Risky Rob.  Billy Barlow.  *Unknown.*
  FSW
Let's go—much as that dog goes.  Overland to the Islands.
  Denise Levertov.  ConAP; UnPo (1976 ed.)
Let's go see Old Abe.  Lincoln Monument: Washington.
  Langston Hughes.  CC; OFD
Let's go up to the hillside today.  Play Song.  Peter Kumalo.
  SPo
Let's have less nonsense from the friends of Joe.  Less Nonsense.
  A. P. Herbert.  OxBTC
Let's let the good man sign the bill.  The Man of Property.
  Charles G. Ballard.  VW
Let's not use eyes anymore.  Dialogue—2 Dollmakers.  Gregory
  Corso.  VoA

Let's paddle, dear, by yonder fort.  Invitation.  *Malay Oral
  Tradition, tr. by* R. J. Wilkinson *and* R. O. Winstedt.  WTO
Let's say it's not language.  Finger Spelling.  Kraft Rompf.
  AAN
Let's Send a Rocket.  Kit Patrickson.  FPB
Let's sing the new ministry's praise.  The Procession: A New
  Protestant Ballad.  *Unknown.*  APAS
Let's step on daddy's head shout.  Step on His Head.  James
  Laughlin.  VGW
Let's take a trip somewhere, we say.  Sand and Snow.  Laurence
  Lieberman.  ILP (1975 ed.)
Let's Talk, Mother.  Edith Bruck, *tr. fr. Italian by* Anita Barrows.
  VWA
Let's talk of graves, of worms, and epitaphs.  The Death of Kings.
  Shakespeare.  King Richard II, *fr.* III, ii.  GrRo; PPoe
Let's think of eggs.  The Poultries.  Ogden Nash.  RAE
Letter, The.  W. H. Auden.  FaBoTw (1975 ed.); NoAM
Letter, A.  Anthony Hecht.  CoPAm
Letter.  Geof Hewitt.  PHC
Letter, A.  Rachel Korn, *tr. fr. Yiddish by* Ruth Whitman.  VWA
Letter.  W. S. Merwin.  HAP
Letter.  Kenneth "Spider" Nicholson.  DNGG
Letter, The.  Charles Reznikoff.  VWA
Letter, The.  Elizabeth Riddell.  BuTh
Letter, A.  Burns Singer.  MS; SLP
Letter.  Mark Strand.  NoAM
Letter across Doubt and Distance.  M. Carl Holman.  AmNP
  (1974 ed.)
Letter Back to Oregon.  Albert Goldbarth.  HeS
Letter came in the mail from the Vice President of Crucial Events,
  A.  Getting Fired or "Not Being Retained."  Sandra Gilbert.
  CPA
Letter Catches Up with Me, A.  Eric Chaet.  VWA
Letter Edged in Black, The.  *Unknown.*  FSW
Letter V.  W. S. Graham.  OxBTC
Letter V.  Robin Skelton.  MPA
Letter for Marian, A.  Thomas McGrath.  VGW
Letter from a Black Soldier.  Bill Anderson.  VGW
Letter from a Candidate for the Presidency, A.  James Russell
  Lowell.  *Fr.* The Biglow Papers, 1st Series, No. VII.  PiAm
Letter from a Death Bed.  John Ciardi.  NCSH
Letter from a Friend, A.  Carolyn Maisel.  IHMS
Letter from a Friend, A.  John N. Morris.  CABA (1972 ed.)
Letter from a Girl to Her Own Old Age, A.  Alice Meynell.
  SBG
Letter from a Working Girl.  Herbert Scott.  GP
Letter from an Institution: III.  Michael Ryan.  AmPA
Letter from an Island.  John Malcolm Brinnin.  TAP
Letter from Artemisia in the Town to Cloe in the Country, A.
  Earl of Rochester.  ESaP
Letter from Berlin, A.  Jon Stallworthy.  NoAM
Letter from Brooklyn, A.  Derek Walcott.  OxBTC
Letter from Des Moines.  Thomas Swiss.  AMV–81
Letter from Germany.  Emily Grosholz.  AMV–81
Letter from Li Po, A, *sel.*  Conrad Aiken.
  "Winds of doctrine blow both ways at once, The."  VGW
"Letter from my love today, A!"  A Ballad of Hell.  John
  Davidson.  HoPM (1975 ed.); LFH
Letter from My Son.  Michael Hogan.  AAN
Letter from Olga, Declaiming.  Danny L. Rendleman.  TC
Letter from the Caribbean, A.  Barbara Howes.  UnPo (1976 ed.)
Letter from the North Atlantic.  John Williams.  CoPAm
Letter from the Pygmies, A.  Theodore Weiss.  VGW
Letter from Thurlby Domain.  Charles Brasch.  ATNZ
Letter from Town: The Almond Tree.  D. H. Lawrence.  PAIC

Letter Home, A. Kenneth "Spider" Nicholson. DNGG

Letter in my mailbox says you've made it, A. To a Girl Who Lives in a Tree. Audré Lorde. WBN

Letter in Winter. Raymond R. Patterson. PoBA

Letter of Advice, A. Winthrop Mackworth Praed. NOBL

Letter of Application Long Enough to Indicate Writing Ability. Karen Sagstatter. PoUp

Letter on the Use of Machine Guns at Weddings, A. Kenneth Patchen. SPT

Letter Out of the Gray. Gabriel Preil, tr. fr. Hebrew by Shirley Kaufman and Howard Schwartz. VWA

Letter Reaching Out to My Sister, 1600 Miles. Sharon Barba. RiTi

Letter 6. Charles Olson. Fr. The Maximus Poems. PiAm

Letter 60. Mary Norbert Körte. CPA

Letter to a Chinese Poet, sel. Ruth Dallas.
"Warming a set of new bones." ATNZ

Letter to a Conceivable Great-Grandson. Earle Birney. BBGO

Letter to a Dead Father. Richard Shelton. BrS; GP

Letter to a Friend. Jon Stallworthy. NoAM

Letter to a Friend in an Unknown Place. Anita Barrows. NMM; RiTi

Letter to a Jealous Friend. James Simmons. CIP

Letter to a Librarian. Irving Layton. MAT

Letter to a Mute. Thomas James. AmPA

Letter to a Policeman in Kansas City, A. Kenneth Patchen. SPT

Letter to a Teacher of English, A. Robert Hillyer. PAIC

Letter to a Young Father in Exile. John Logan. CAPP

Letter to a Young Friend. Alden Nowlan. AKE

Letter to Alex Comfort. Dannie Abse. FaBoTw (1975 ed.)

Letter to an Absent Son. Madeline DeFrees. CNW; GP; NMM; RiTi

Letter to an American Visitor. Alex Comfort. OxBTC

Letter to an Imaginary Friend, Part One, sels. Thomas McGrath. NNaP
"And I hear the pad of feet to the union hall," II, 2.
"We go out in the stony midnight," VIII, 4.

Letter to an Imaginary Friend, Part Two, sels. Thomas McGrath.
"Begun before Easter.../ Sign of the Fish." VI, 4. NNaP
"Evening—another evening—and the lights flare," V, 2. NNaP
"Road outside the window was 'our' road, The," V, 1. GP
"Windless city built on decaying granite, loose ends," II, 2-5. NNaP

Letter to Auden, A. Robert Phillips. AMV-81

Letter to Be Disguised as a Gas Bill. Marge Piercy. MMD; WPE

Letter to Belden. Rosalie Moore. NPW

Letter to Bell from Missoula. Richard Hugo. NNaP

Letter to Dafnis, A. Countess of Winchilsea. SBG

Letter to Dr. C. from the Great Divide. Susan Sonde. PoUp

Letter to E. Franklin Frazier. Amiri Baraka. BPo; PoBA

Letter to Eve. Alan Dugan. PAIC

Letter to Evelyn Baring, A. Edward Lear. FaBoNo

Letter to Garber from Skye. Richard Hugo. AMV-81

Letter to Her Father, A. Inib-sarri, tr. fr. Akkadian by Willis Barnstone. BoWoP

Letter to Her Husband, Absent upon Public Employment, A ("As loving hind..."). Anne Bradstreet. SCP-2; WPE
(Another.) SBG

Letter to Her Husband, Absent upon Publick Employment, A ("My head, my heart, mine eyes,..."). Anne Bradstreet. EAP; HAP; HeIP; PiAm

Letter to Her Mother, A. Eristi-Aya, tr. fr. Akkadian by Willis Barnstone. BoWoP

Letter to Her Son's Commanding Officer. Ethel Green Russell. AATT

Letter to His Sister, A. Laurance Wieder. AAN

Letter to Kafka. Maura Stanton. AmPA

Letter to Kathy from Wisdom. Richard Hugo. CNW

Letter to Lady Margaret Cavendish Holles-Harley, When a Child, A. Matthew Prior. See Letter to the Honourable Lady Miss Margaret Cavendish Holles-Harley.

Letter to Levertov from Butte. Richard Hugo. NNaP

Letter to Logan from Milltown. Richard Hugo. NNaP

Letter to Lord Byron, sels. W. H. Auden.
"England, my England—you have been my tutrix." OBSV
"I like your muse because she's gay and witty." NOBL
"Ottava Rima would, I know, be proper." NOBL
"Thought of writing came to me today, The." NOBL
"You lived and moved among the best society." OBSV

Letter to "M." Unknown. OxBM

Letter to Maria Gisborne. Shelley. MBPR
Sels.
To Maria Gisborne in England, from Italy. NOBE
"You are now/ In London, that great sea, whose ebb and flow." EBEV

Letter to My Father. Delia Chilgren. NPW

Letter to My Kinder. Bob Gaskin. AMV-81

Letter to My Mother. Dom Moraes. NoAM

Letter to My Mother. Anita Skeen. IHMS

Letter to My Sister. Anne Spencer. AmNP (1974 ed.); PoBA

Letter to My Wife. Miklós Radnóti, tr. fr. Hungarian by Emery George. VWA

Letter to N.Y. Elizabeth Bishop. NYP; TH

Letter to Paul Celan in Memory, A. Jerome Rothenberg. VWA

Letter to Reed from Lolo. Richard Hugo. NNaP

Letter to Robert. Mary Fabilli. IHMS

Letter to Sara Hutchinson, A. Samuel Taylor Coleridge. See Dejection: An Ode.

Letter to Scanlon from Whitehall. Richard Hugo. NNaP

Letter to the Child Lady Margaret Cavendish Holles-Harley, A. Matthew Prior. See Letter to the Honourable Lady Miss Margaret Cavendish Holles-Harley.

Letter to the Chronicle. Bob Kaufman. UsP

Letter to the Countess of Denbigh against Irresolution and Delay in Matters of Religion, A. Richard Crashaw. See To the Noblest and Best of Ladyes.

Letter to the Honourable Lady Miss Margaret Cavendish Holles-Harley, A. Matthew Prior. PAIC
(Letter to Lady Margaret Cavendish Holles-Harley, When a Child, A.) NOBE
(Letter to the Child Lady Margaret Cavendish Holles-Harley, A.) OxBChV

Letter to the Lady Carey and Mrs. Essex Rich, A, sel. John Donne.
"Here where by all, all saints invokèd are." SCP-1

Letter to Three Irish Poets, A. Michael Longley. BIrV

Letter to Wagoner from Port Townsend. Richard Hugo. NNaP

Letter to Welch from Browning. Richard Hugo. NNaP

Letter to William Carlos Williams, A. Kenneth Rexroth. NNaP

Letter II. W. S. Graham. MS

Lettering on the window. The Big Rocks. T. L. Kryss. EC

Letters. Charles Bukowski. GP

Letters [or Notes] Found near a Suicide. Frank Horne. AmNP (1974 ed.); PoBa
Sels.
To "Chick." BPo
To James. BPo; PAIC
To Mother. BPo
To You. BPo

Letters from an Irishman to a Rat. Christopher Logue. BoAnP

Letters from Birmingham. Harold Bond. TAT

Letters of a Name, The. Colette Inez. AMV-81

Letters of Summer, The. Christopher Buckley. AMV-80

Letters of the Book, The. Rose Drachler. VWA

Letters of the Jews as strict as flames, The. The Alphabet. Karl Shapiro. MPA; NoAM; PoA; VWA

Letters, Returned. Adrianne Marcus. NPW

Letters she left to clutter up the desk. A Gesture by a Lady with an Assumed Name. James Wright. ConAP

Letters still come for Mrs. Watters, The. Mrs. G. Watters. Frank Ormsby. IPM

Letters to a Stranger. Thomas James. AmPA

Letters to Live Poets, *sels.* Bruce Beaver.
   "Our street is known as the street of widows," XVI. GAS
   "Three anti-depressants and one diuretic a day," XII. MAuV

Letters to My Daughters, 11. Judith Minty. AMV-81

Letters to My Daughters, 3. Judith Minty. TV

Letters to Walt Whitman, *sels.* Ronald Johnson. VGW
   "But are these landscapes to be imagined," IX.
   "I, too, have plucked a stalk of grass," V.
   "Let us tunnel," I.
   "Slant sheen/ wrinkled silver," II.

Letters to Yesenin, *sels.* Jim Harrison. TC
   "Behind my back I have returned to life."
   "I cleaned the granary dust off your photo."
   "I don't have any medals. I feel their lack."
   "Naturally we would prefer seven epiphanies."
   "This matted and glossy photo of Yesenin."
   "Thus the poet is a beached gypsy."
   "What if I own more paper clips than I'll ever use."

Letting Go. Richard Shelton. AMV-81

Letting his wisdom be the whole of love. The World and the Child. James Merrill. CoPAm; PAIC

Letting My Feelings Out. Yü Hsüan-chi, *tr. fr. Chinese by* Geoffrey Waters. BoWoP

Letting of Humour's Blood in the Head-Vein, The, *sels.* Samuel Rowlands. TVS
   "Melfluvious, sweet, rose-watered eloquence," Satire IV.
   "Oh let the gentlewoman have the wall," Satire III.
   "Who have we here? Behold him and be mute!" Satire I.

Levedy, ich thanke thee. Lady, I Thank Thee. *Unknown.* OxBM

Levee Camp Moan. *Unknown.* BluL

Level slope of colored sea, The. Metaphysical. Robert Fitzgerald. PoA

Levelled Churchyard, The. Thomas Hardy. NOBL; OBP

Lever de Rideau. Mary Ursula Bethell. ATNZ

Levi Yitzhok:/ binding tefillin on. The Morning Prayers of the Hasid, Rabbi Levi Yitzhok. Phyllis Gotlieb. VWA

Leviathan. Bible, *O.T.* Job, XLI, *abr.* EcS
   ("Canst thou draw out Leviathan with an hooke.") OBVE

Leviathan. W. S. Merwin. ConAP; NoAM; NOBA; TCP

Leviathan. Peter Quennell. EcS

Leviathan, or a Hymn to Poor Brother Ben. *Unknown.* APAS

Leviathan the ocean, spiked and mailed. Off Cape Leeuwen. M. K. Joseph. ATNZ

Levin, on his way to Kitty's love. Secular Games. Richard Howard. PoA

Levitation. Alvin Aubert. GP

Lewis. Derick Thomson, *tr. fr. Gaelic by author.* MS

Lewis and Clark. Rosemary *and* Stephen Vincent Benét. BPAW

Lewis Carrol. Eleanor Farjeon. OxBChV

Lewis in Summer. Derick Thomson, *tr. fr. Gaelic by author.* MS

Lewti; or, The Circassian Love-Chaunt. Samuel Taylor Coleridge. MBPR

Lexington, dear heart, you old whore. The Old Athens of the West Is Now a Blue Grass Tour. James Baker Hall. TAT

L'Homme Moyen Sensuel, *sels.* Ezra Pound. OBSV
   "Alas, eheu, one question that sorely vexes."
   " 'Tis of my country that I would endite."

Li Po. Mary Moore. NPW

Liadan Laments Cuirithir. Liadan, *tr. fr. Irish by* John Montague. BIrV; PBWP

Liar, The. Amiri Baraka. NOBA; WIF

Liard Hot Springs. Gordon Massman. CTBA

'Lias! 'Lias! Bless de Lawd! In the Morning. Paul Laurence Dunbar. BPo

Libation. Denise Levertov. GP

Libelle of Englyshe Polycye, The, *sel. Unknown.* Keep the Sea. OxBM

Liber doth vaunt how chastely he hath liv'd. In Librum. Sir John Davies. FaBoEE

Liberal, blue-eyed, shivering, trying not. The Blue-eyed Precinct Worker. Henri Coulette. MAT

Liberation. Ruth Stone. BoWoP

Liberation. Mary Swanson Stroh. NPW

Liberator, The. Emily Holmes Coleman. EAS

Liberator, The. Lucien Stryk. GP

Liberia? On the Founding of Liberia. Melvin B. Tolson. *Fr.* Libretto for the Republic of Liberia. UnPo (1976 ed.)

Libertine, The. Louis MacNeice. NoAM

Liberty. Archibald MacLeish. GOA

Liberty. Shelley. MBPR

Liberty. Edward Thomas. OAEL-2

Liberty, *sel.* Wordsworth.
   "Beetle loves his unpretending track, The." FaBoCo; PCOP

Liberty and Peace. Phillis Wheatley. SBG

Liberty Song, The, *with music.* John Dickinson. BLSo

Liberty Tree. Thomas Paine. BTTM

Library. Richard Armour. ECBV

Library. Billy Collins. AAN

Library, The. Margaret Gillies. PMW

Library. Louis Jenkins. HeS; NU

Library, The. John Logan. AMV-80

Library, The. Henry Shore. PMW

Libretto for the Republic of Liberia, *sel.* Melvin B. Tolson. On the Founding of Liberia. UnPo (1976 ed.)

Lice-Hunters, The. Arthur Rimbaud, *tr. fr. French by* Robert Lowell. NAWM-2
   (Lice-Hunters, *tr. by* Ezra Pound.) NAWM-2
   (Seekers of Lice, The, *tr. by* Wallace Fowlie.) NAWM-2

Licia, *sels.* Giles Fletcher the Elder.
   "As are the sandes (faire Licia) on the shore," XVII. ESo
   "Chrystal streames, wherein my love did swimme, The," XXVII. ESo
   "For if alone thou thinke to waft my love," XLII. ESo
   "I live (sweete love) whereas the gentle winde," XXVI. ESo
   "I wish sometimes, although a worthlesse thing," XII. AAS
   "If (aged Charon), when my life shall end," XLI. ESo
   "In time [*or* tyme] the strong and stately [*or* statelie] turrets fall," XXVIII. AAS; EBEV; ILP (1975 ed.); NIL
   "Like [*or* Lyke] Memnons rock, touched [*or* rocke toucht] with the rising sun[ne]," XLVII. AAS; FF
   "Sadde all alone, not long I musing satte," I. ESo
   "When as her lute is tuned to her voyce," XXXI. ESo

Lick your lips, X. darling, it may be the last. The Summer Ending. Glenway Wescott. PoA

Licorice Fields at Pontefract, The. John Betjeman. CMoP (1970 ed.); ILP (1975 ed.); MPo; SS

Lie, The. Kipling. NOBL

Lie, The. Al Lee. AmPA

Lie, The. Sir Walter Ralegh. AAS; EBEV; HAP; ILP (1975 ed.); NOBE; PPoD; PPoe

Lie back, daughter, let your head. First Lesson. Philip Booth. BiP; IPWM; LiSp; SFF

Lie Closed, My Lately Loved. John Woods. ConAP

"Lie still, my newly married wife." The Griesly Wife. John Manifold. SoSe

Lie up nearer, brother, nearer, for my limbs are growing cold. The Dying Californian. *Unknown.* AmFP

Lie where you fell and longed. Letter V. W. S. Graham. OxBTC

Lied in Crete. Alvaro Mutis. AMV-80

Liefer would I turn and love. Deranged. Padraic Fiacc. PFIr

Lies. Yevgeny Yevtushenko, *tr. fr. Russian by* Robin Milner-Gulland *and* Peter Levi. LP

Lies have been told about this American blood. Twentieth-Century Americanism. Joy Davidman. SPT

Lies on the same couch that he used to. My Father. Ronald Koertge. BrS

Lif of this world, The. The Life of This World. *Unknown.* OxBM

Life, The. George Chambers. HeS

Life, The. Philip Dow. AmPA

Life. Paul Laurence Dunbar. AmNP (1974 ed.)

Life. George Herbert. PoPle

Life, A. Howard Nemerov. AnMo; PBMP

Life, A. Sylvia Plath. NOBA; UsP

Life. James Steele. SES

Life. Grace Treasone. InPK; PeD

Life/ anthology of bewilderments. Violins in Repose. Jorge Plescoff, *tr. by* Yishai Tobin. VWA

Life/ is at 2 playing. Childhood. Jewel C. Latimore. JB

Life after Death. Richard W. Thomas. PoBA

Life and Death. W. J. Turner. FaBoTw (1975 ed.)

Life and Death among the Xerox People. Olga Cabral. WBN

Life and Death of Jason, The, *sel.* William Morris. Garden by the Sea, A, IV. NOBE; OAEL-2

Life and Death of the Cantata System, The. Alan Dugan. ILP (1975 ed.)

Life and Genuine Character of Dean Swift, The, *sel.* Swift. "Wise Rochefoucault a maxim writ." NOBL

Life at War. Denise Levertov. NMM; VGW

Life breathes its first in gasps. Birth Day. Merle Meeter. AATT

Life contracts and death is expected. The Death of a Soldier. Wallace Stevens. OFD

Life-Cycle. Bruce Dawe. MAuV

Life Cycle of Common Man. Howard Nemerov. MPo; NIL; TPo

Life Dance. Jim Farrar. DNGG

Life drains out, The. In drops and spurts it flows. The Arena. Hubert Witheford. ATNZ

Life-Drama, A, *sel.* Alexander Smith. "What hope is that?" VLP

Life flows to death as rivers to the sea. Epigram. J. V. Cunningham. POL; VGW

Life, friends, is boring. We must not say so. John Berryman. *Fr.* Dream Songs. CAPP; HAP; HeIP; ILP (1975 ed.); InPK; IPWM; NoAM; NOBA; PoIA; PPoD; TAP

Life from the Lifeless. Robinson Jeffers. CMoP (1970 ed.)

Life has conquered, the wind has blown away. Hope. Frank O'Connor, *tr. fr. Irish.* CIP

Life has loveliness to sell. Barter. Sara Teasdale. SoSe

Life in a day: he took his girl to the ballet. Les Sylphides. Louis MacNeice. BoLoP; BuTh; PSN

Life-in-Love. Dante Gabriel Rossetti. The House of Life, XXXVI. HAP; VLP

Life in the Boondocks. A. R. Ammons. HAP

Life in the Castle. Anne Hébert, *tr. fr. French by* Aliki *and* Willis Barnstone. BoWoP

Life in the cellars. In the Cellars. Jiri Gold, *tr. by* Jaroslav Kotan *and* Daniel Weissbort. VWA

Life is a bitter aspic. We are not. Wallace Stevens. *Fr.* Esthétique du Mal. CMoP (1970 ed.)

Life Is a Dream. Pedro Calderón de la Barca, *tr. fr. Spanish by* Roy Campbell. NAWM-1

Life is a jest, and all things show it. My Own Epitaph. John Gay. FaBoEE; FF; NIL

Life is a long discovery, isn't it? Discovery. Hilaire Belloc. TPo

Life Is a Platform, *sel.* Peter Levi. "Smoke when the sun fell and when it rose." FaBoTw (1975 ed.)

Life Is All Right. Mark Wangberg. TC

Life is butter, life is butter. *Unknown.* FaBoNo

Life is full of horrors and hormones. Kenneth Koch. *Fr.* The Art of Love. GP

Life is like a jagged tooth. Life. Grace Treasone. InPK; PeD

Life Is Like a Mountain Railroad. *Unknown.* FSW

Life Is Motion. Wallace Stevens. WeW

Life is ours like the real. Theme One: The Variations. August Wilson. PoBA

Life is suspended over foreign countries, A. Over Asia. Anne Waldman. RiTi

"Life! length of life!" for this, with earnest cries. Juvenal, *tr. by* William Gifford. *Fr.* Satires, X. OBVE

Life Not Given, The. David Habercom. AMV-81

Life of a lone comrade, The. Strength. Richard Wright. SPT

Life of a Queen. Lisel Mueller. GP; RiTi

Life of a Tar, The. *Unknown.* RhR

Life of Ages, Richly Poured, *with music.* Samuel Johnson. AH

Life of an offensive center, The. Dick Szymanski. Ogden Nash. SPo

Life of Hard Times, The. Joshua Tan Pai, *tr. fr. Hebrew by* Yishai Tobin. VWA

Life of Life! thy lips enkindle. Shelley. *Fr.* Prometheus Unbound. NOBE

Life of Lincoln West, The. Gwendolyn Brooks. FB; FiCh

Life of my life, take not so soon thy flight. To His Dying Brother, Master William Herrick. Robert Herrick. CaPo; PoPle

Life of the Blessed, The. Luis Ponce de León, *tr. fr. Spanish by* Bryant. PIM

Life of the Letters. Emily Borenstein. VWA

Life of the Mannings. *Unknown.* FaBoBa

Life of the Mind, 1934. Genevieve Taggard. SPT

Life of the snail is a fight against odds, The. The Snail. A. P. Herbert. BoAnP

Life of the Wolf, The. Gary Gildner. AmPA

Life of This World, The. *Unknown.* OxBM

Life on Earth, *sel.* Frank O'Hara. "Shine, 'O world!' don't weary the gulping Pole." UnPo (1976 ed.)

Life on the Ocean Wave, A. Epes Sargent. BLSH, *with music*; FSW; RhR

Life pours out images, the accidental. The Rokeby Venus. Robert Conquest. NoAM

Life Rounded with Sleep. Shelley. BuTh

Life smitten with a feverish chill. The Wedding. Coventry Patmore. *Fr.* The Angel in the House. VLP

Life Story. J. Kates. AMV-81

Life Style, The. Edwin Brock. IPWM

Life-Style. Jenny Morgan. PMW

Life, the Eternal Sacrament. Virginia Floyd. AATT

Life the hound. The Hound. Robert Francis. SoSe

Life to Let. Liam Murphy. IPM

Life with yon lambs, like day, is just begun. Composed on a May Morning, 1838. Wordsworth. FSFS

Life would be an easy matter. If We Didn't Have to Eat. Nixon Waterman. OBAL

Lifeguard, The. James Dickey. LiSp; NowV; SoS

Lifeguard is a man of brawn, The. Seasonal Phenomenon. Richard Armour. BBGO

Lifeless solitude—an angry waste, A. On the Telescopic Moon. John Swanick Drennan. BIrV

Lifelines. Gavin Ewart. EAS

Lifelines. T. R. Hummer. AMV-80

Lifelong. Rachel Boimwall, tr. fr. Yiddish by Gabriel Preil and Howard Schwartz. VWA

Lifers file into the hall, The. In the Cage. Robert Lowell. FF; NOBA; PPoD

Life's Evil. Eugenio Montale, tr. fr. Italian by Jan Pallister. AMV-81

Life's Morning. Howell Elvet Lewis, tr. fr. Welsh by H. Idris Bell. OBW

Life's Work. Maxine W. Kumin. GP

Lifesize in a car. Drive In Movie. Gary Sange. NVAP; SFF

Lift, The. Raymond Souster. POL

Lift Every Voice and Sing. James Weldon Johnson. FSW

Lift gently Dai, gentleness befits his gunshot wound. David Jones. Fr. In Parenthesis. TwMBP

Lift latch, step in, be welcome, Sir. A Luncheon. Max Beerbohm. FaBoCo; NOBL; OxBTC; OBSV

Lift not the painted veil which those who live. Sonnet. Shelley. MBPR

Lift up thy lips, turn round, look back for love. Hermaphroditus. Swinburne. VLP

Lift up your eyes on high. Erige Cor Tuum ad Me in Caelum. Hilda Doolittle ("H. D."). CMoP (1970 ed.)

Lift up your heads, rejoice. Thomas Toke Lynch. VLP

Lift up your heads, ye gates of brass! James Montgomery. VLP

Lift Your Glad Voices in Triumph on High, with music. Henry Ware, Jr. AH

Lifting, both hands pulling whitely. Grandpa's .45. W. M. Ransom. CDW

Lifting his slowly trickling jaws. Tête-á-Tête. Edwin Honig. NoAM

Lifting Illegal Nets by Flashlight. William Stafford. NNaP

Lifting my fingers. Frozen Hands. Joseph Bruchac. CDW

Lifting their guns easily. Working the Skeet House. Jon Eastman. AMV-80

Liftman, The. H. A. C. Evans. POL

Ligeia, prose tale, sel. Poe.
Conqueror Worm, The. NOBA; PiAm
(Emperor Worm, The.) DL

Light. Brewster Ghiselin. MPA

Light. Jon Silkin. NoAM

Light, sels. Louis Zukofsky. NoAM
"House where every, A."
"These are not my sentiments."

Light, The/ drains me of what I might be. A Nude by Edward Hopper. Lisel Mueller. RiTi

Light a Candle. Zelda, tr. fr. Hebrew by Marcia Falk. VWA

Light across the courtyard. Saint's Bridge. Lola Ridge. WPE

Light and Dark. Barbara Howes. CoPAm; RiTi

Light and Glory of the Word, The. William Cowper. PIM

Light are the spinning favours, intangible tonight. An English Elegy. Daryl Hine. NoAM

Light as petals, white as daisies. Butterflies. Clive Sansom. BonAnP

Light at this hour, The. Circles. Elizabeth Knies. AMV-80

Light became her grace and dwelt among, The. Ballatetta. Ezra Pound. VG

Light Breaks Where No Sun Shines. Dylan Thomas. CMoP (1970 ed.); OxBTC; PAIC

Light breezes, drifting through the window. Morning. M. A. George. AMV-80

Light comes into the house and a few flies, The. In Blessed Weather. Michael Heffernan. HeS

Light Dying. Brendan Kennelly. PFIr

Light elegant wall waves down, A. The Estuary. Patricia Beer. HeHu

Light exists in spring, A. Emily Dickinson. BoWoP; ExPo (1973 ed.); FSFS; NOBA; VoPo

Light falling into my kitchen. Words from Storms and Geese in the Morning. Jenne Andrews. HeS

Light feet, dark violet eyes, and parted hair. Keats. MBPR

Light fell from the window and the day was done, The. "The Truth Is Blind." David Gascoyne. EAS

Light flows our war of mocking words, and yet. The Buried Life. Matthew Arnold. OAEL-2; PFD; VLP

Light foot hears you and the brightness begins, The. A Poem Beginning with a Line by Pindar. Robert Duncan. ConAP; Epi; NNaP

Light, glinting off the bracelet, The. Claritas. Gerrye Payne. NPW

Light glows bright, The. The Parade. Liz Sohappy Bahe. VW

Light going out in the forehead, A. Swimming by Night. James Merrill. VGW

Light in the window seemed perpetual, The. The Room above the Square. Stephen Spender. NOBE

Light into the olive entered. After Greece. James Merrill. ConAP; NOBA

Light is around the petals, and behind them. Looking at Some Flowers. Robert Bly. NOBA

Light is burning late, A. Herbert Street Revisited. John Montague. CIP

Light keeps on breaking. Breaklight. Lucille Clifton. OSP

Light lifts from the water. Basil Bunting. Fr. Briggflatts, V. OAEL-2

Light Listened. Theodore Roethke. AnMo; BiP; NowV

Light little zephyr came flitting, A. Morning Compliments. Sydney Dayre. OxBChV

Light making patterns. The Creation. Patricia Ramsey. AATT

Light mist, then dense fog. Li Ch'ing-chao, tr. fr. Chinese by Kenneth Rexroth. BoWoP

Light Morning Snow, We Wait for a Warmer Season. John Garmon. AMV-80

Light of Asia, The, sels. Sir Edwin Arnold. VLP
"If we lay bound upon the wheel of change," fr. VIII.
"So they rode/ Into a land of wells and gardens, where," fr. I.

Light of dimmed stars goes on, The. The Life of Hard Times. Joshua Tan Pai, tr. by Yishai Tobin. VWA

Light of evening, Lissadell, The. In Memory of Eva Gore-Booth and Con Markiewicz. W. B. Yeats. CABA (1972 ed.); NoAM; OAEL-2; OxBTC

Light of four suns, five moons, The. May I Be Beautiful. Malay Oral Tradition, tr. by W. W. Skeat. WTO

Light of Judea. Claude Vigée, tr. fr. French. VWA

Light of Life, The. "Hugh MacDiarmid." CMoP (1970 ed.)

Light of Other Days, The. Thomas Moore. See Oft in the Stilly Night.

Light of the World, The. B. Alquit, tr. fr. Yiddish by Howard Schwartz. VWA

Light on his pins. Roethke Plain. John Malcolm Brinnin. NoAM; TAP

Light passes, The. Evening. Hilda Doolittle ("H.D."). CMoP (1970 ed.); IPWM; VGW; WPE

Light pulling away from trees, The. Distance. Peter Everwine. NNaP

Light Rain. Christopher Buckley. AMV-81

Light rides the wings of heron. Passage. Mary Shumway. NVAP

Light Shining Out of Darkness. William Cowper. BoReV; EBEV; HeIP; NOBE; PIM; PPM

Light Showers of Light. Kathryn Lindskoog. AMV-80

Light, so low upon earth. Marriage Morning. Tennyson. GBL

Light the candle I will return. Near. Abba Kovner, tr. by Shirley Kaufman. VWA

Light the first light of evening, as in a room. Final Soliloquy of the Interior Paramour. Wallace Stevens. HAP; PiAm

Light the prime work of God to me is extinct. Milton. Fr. Samson Agonistes. SCP-1

Light white, a disgrace, an ink spot, a rosy charm. A Petticoat. Gertrude Stein. Fr. Tender Buttons. RiTi

Light-winged Smoke, Icarian Bird. Henry David Thoreau. See Smoke.

Light Woman, A. Robert Browning. VLP

Light Woman's Song, The. Judith Johnson Sherwin. TAP

Light Year, The. John Ridland. OFD

Light-years in the dark. Kohoutek. Richard Ryan. CIP

Light you down, light you down, love Henry, she said. Young Hunting. Unknown. FaBoBa

Light young man lay with a lighter woman, A. On Tom Holland and Nell Cotton. Unknown. FaBoEE

Lighthearted William. William Carlos Williams. SO; VoA

Lighthouse, The. John Seller Anson. AMV-80

Lighthouse. Merle Meeter. AATT

Lighthouse in the Night. Alfonsina Storni, tr. fr. Spanish by Aliki and Willis Barnstone. BoWoP

Lighthouse Keeper. Gary Sange. NVAP

Lighthouses. Dorothy Wellesley. WPE

Lighting a spill late in the afternoon. A Winter Talent. Donald Davie. OAEL-2

Lightkeeper, The. Michael McPherson. PHC

Lightly forsaking/ the spring mist as it rises. Seeing the Returning Geese. Lady Ise, tr. by Etsuko Terasaki and Irma Brandeis. BoWoP

Lightly stepped a yellow star. Emily Dickinson. SoSe (1977 ed.)

Lightning. D. H. Lawrence. CMoP (1970 ed.); ILP (1975 ed.)

Lightning and Thunder, The. George MacDonald. See Baby-Sermon, A.

Lightning bug got, A. The Flattered Lightning Bug. Don Marquis. PoTa

Lightning Flash, The. Unknown. AmFP

Lightning flashes, The! Haiku. Basho, tr. by Earl Miner. SoSe

Lightning gleam, A. Haiku. Basho, tr. by Harold G. Henderson. SoSe

Lightning hits the roof. Woman to Man. Ai. GP

Lightning in the sky! Basho, tr. fr. Japanese. WeW

Lightning is a yellow fork, The. Emily Dickinson. InPK

Lightning, like an Arab, cross'd, The. The Tree of Rivelin. Ebenezer Elliot. VLP

Lightning slices above Texas City. Tornado Watch. Paul Shuttleworth. AMV-80

Lightnings slaughtered. After Derry, 30 January 1972. Seamus Deane. IPM

Lights, along the tidal reaches. Approaching Washington. Charles G. Bell. WasP

Lights are burning. Bus Stop. Donald Justice. TCP

Lights, Flowers. Judith Johnson Sherwin. WBN

Lights from the parlour and kitchen shone out, The. Escape at Bedtime. Robert Louis Stevenson. CTV; ILP (1975 ed.)

Lights Go On, The. Mark McCloskey. AMV-80

Lights in the Hallway, The. James Wright. CAPP

Lights in the Sky Are Stars, The. Kenneth Rexroth. RRA Heart of Herakles, The, sel. NU

Lights Out. Edward Thomas. ILP (1975 ed.); NOBE

Like a Beach. Harvey Shapiro. VWA

Like a bird in the butcher's palm you flutter in my hand. Revolt. Rachel, tr. by Robert Friend. VWA

Like a blind boy. Song Three: A Search for Taiping Ghosts. Alan Chong Lau. NW

Like a blind man, with eyes habituated to the darkness. The Diver. Nikos Phocas, tr. by Kimon Friar. AMV-81

Like a Bulwark. Marianne Moore. PiAm

Like a caught breath. Pause between Clock Ticks. James Hearst. AMV-81

Like a curlew giving depth. Aelred of Rievaulx. Liam Lynch. IPM

Like a dog before the dog-catcher's sling. Conscience. Melech Ravitch, tr. by Keith Bosley. VWA

Like a dragon you have filled the land. Inanna and An. Enheduanna, tr. fr. Sumerian. BoWoP

Like a drummer's brush. Rain. Emanuel diPasquale. InPK; POL

Like a dry fish flung inland far from shore. Lost Anchors. E. A. Robinson. CMoP (1970 ed.); PiAm

Like a Field Waiting. Raquel Chalfi, tr. fr. Hebrew by Myra Glazer Schotz. VWA

Like a first coat of whitewash when it's wet. Twelfth Morning; or, What You Will. Elizabeth Bishop. PSN

Like a fishbone in my throat. I Still Feel You. Marge Piercy. Psy

Like a flat sea. Population. George Oppen. PoA

Like a flight of arrows the wind. Stormy Night in Autumn. Chu Shu-chen, tr. by Kenneth Rexroth. BoWoP

Like a fruit wine with earth. Cider and Vesalius. John Peck. AmPA

Like a gaunt pillar wreathed in weeping flowers. For the Hippolytus of Euripides. Peggy Pond Church. WPW

Like a glum cricket. Flight. James Tate. InPK; UsP

Like a gondola of green scented fruits. Images. Richard Aldington. PoA

Like a hungry fledgeling that watches and hears. Vittoria da Colonna, tr. fr. Italian by Lynne Lawner. PBWP

Like a lit-up Christmas Tree. The Lover and the Syringa-Bush. Herman Melville. OBAL

Like a lizard in the sun, though not scuttling. The Laureate. Robert Graves. BIrV; FaBoTw (1975 ed.); OBSV

Like a lone Arab, old and blind. Love's Apparition and Evanishment. Samuel Taylor Coleridge. MBPR

Like a loose island on the wide expanse. To a Deaf and Dumb Little Girl. Hartley Coleridge. VLP

Like a madwoman and almost alone. Interior Landscape. Gloria Fuertes, tr. by Willis Barnstone. BoWoP

Like a Midsummer Rose. John Lydgate. OxBM

Like a mountain whirlwind. Sappho, tr. fr. Greek by Willis Barnstone. BoWoP

Like a pair of companionable porcupines. Baucis and Philemon. Katherine Hoskins. PoA

Like a Pearl. Hayim Naggid, tr. fr. Hebrew by Shlomo Vinner and Howard Schwartz. VWA

Like a private eye she searches. The Jealous Wife. Vernon Scannell. HeHu

Like a queen enchanted who may not laugh or weep. Swinburne. Fr. A Ballad of Bath. PES

Like a rainstorm, he said, the braided colors.  Worsening Situation.  John Ashbery.  NOBA

Like a ravaged sea/ this bed.  Lady Ise, *tr. fr. Japanese by* Etsuko Terasaki *and* Irma Brandeis.  BoWoP

Like a river she was.  The Memory.  Robert Creeley.  CAPP; VGW

Like a scared rabbit running over and.  "Graphemics," 1.  Jack Spicer.  VGW

Like a Shabbos Goy.  Elsewhere.  Linda Pastan.  VWA

Like a she-camel with a large bell.  Fortitude.  *Somali Oral Tradition, tr. by* B. W. Andrzejewski *and* I. M. Lewis.  WTO

Like a silkworm weaving.  Mahādēviyakka, *tr. fr. Kannada by* A. K. Ramanujan.  PBWP

Like a skein of loose silk blown against a wall.  The Garden. Ezra Pound.  CABA (1972 ed.); HeIP; NIL; PiAm; PPP; PSN

Like a skeleton, the old woman who has kept.  Balm.  Sandra McPherson.  CNW

Like a sleeping swine upon the skyline.  Muckish Mountain (The Pig's Back).  Shane Leslie.  PFIr

Like a small gray/ coffeepot.  Th Gray Squirrel.  Humbert Wolfe.  IP

Like a spider that leaves its wind-torn web.  To My Wife Asleep. Edward Tick.  AMV–80

Like a spider through ink, someone says, mocking: see it.  Arabic Script.  Anthony Thwaite.  HeHu

Like a sweet apple reddening on the high.  Sappho, *tr. fr. Greek by* Willis Barnstone.  BoWoP

Like a tower above the tortuous.  The Pilgrimage to Testour. Ryvel, *tr. by* Edouard Roditi.  VWA

Like a white wall whereon forever breaks.  E. A. Robinson. Octaves, XVIII.  ILP (1975 ed.)

Like a Woman.  Uri Zvi Greenberg, *tr. fr. Hebrew by* Robert Mezey *and* Ben Zion Gold.  VWA

Like a woman you've longed to make love to, and finally did. Pennsylvania Winter Indian 1974.  Harold Littlebird.  VoR

Like a Young Levite.  Osip Mandelstam, *tr. fr. Russian by* Daniel Weissbort.  VWA

Like Abraham and Sarah by the trees of Mamre.  Song at the Skirts of Heaven.  Uri Zvi Greenberg, *tr. by* Zvi Jagendorf. VWA

Like America, his art consists.  Politics of a Pornographer. Robert Hass.  CAAP

Like an adventurous sea-farer am I.  Idea.  Michael Drayton. ESo

Like an elephant.  Mahādēviyakka, *tr. fr. Kannada by* A. K. Ramanujan.  PBWP

Like an home-reared animal in a quiet nook.  King Pellam's Launde.  David Jones.  *Fr.* In Parenthesis.  OAEL–2

Like an Ideal Tenant.  Ruth Daigon.  AMV–81

Like an older sister who wasn't quite as pretty.  Los Angeles. Eloise Klein Healy.  GP

Like an overdone acrobat you keep.  Brother.  R. H. Deutsch. PoW

Like ancient shrunken dolls they shuffle by.  Certain Old Women. Brendan Kennelly.  IPM

Like Any Other Man.  Gregory Orr.  FF

Like apoplectic fur balloons.  Babies: Just Babies.  Margaret Fishback.  ECBV

Like [*or* Lyke] as a huntsman after weary chace.  Amoretti, LXVII.  Spenser.  Epi; GBL; HeIP; ILP (1975 ed.); NIL

Like as the armed knight.  The Ballad Which Anne Askew Made and Sang When She Was in Newgate.  Anne Askew.  WPE

Like as the culver on the bared bough.  Amoretti, LXXXIX. Spenser.  FF; GBL

Like as the fountain of all light created.  Incarnatio Est Maximum Dei Donum.  William Alabaster.  BoReV

Like as the tide that comes from th' Ocean main.  Spenser.  *Fr.* The Faerie Queene, IV.  HoPM (1975 ed.)

Like as the waves make towards the pebbled shore.  Sonnets, LX. Shakespeare.  EBEV; Epi; ILP (1975 ed.); NIL; NOBE; UnPo (1976 ed.)

Like as, to make our appetites more keen.  Sonnets, CXVIII. Shakespeare.  CABA (1972 ed.)

Like Attracts Like.  Emmett Williams.  WeW

Like bats they flew night's corridors.  The Night Sisters. Margaret Gillies.  PMW

Like beheaded geese plucked to their yellow skin.  Squashes. Charles Edward Eaton.  CSP

Like chapters of prophecy my days burn, in all the revelations. With My God, the Smith.  Uri Zvi Greenberg, *tr. by* Robert Mezey *and* Ben Zion Gold.  VWA

Like Children of the Summertime Playing at Cards.  Julie Herrick White.  AMV–80

Like children, when it's sunny they behave.  In-Patients.  U. A. Fanthorpe.  PMW

Like cutting the dry rot out of a potato.  Dark Conclusions. Ruth Stone.  BoWoP

Like David.  Gabriel Preil, *tr. fr. Hebrew by* Laya Firestone. VWA

Like Dolmens round My Childhood, the Old People.  John Montague.  EBEV

Like drunken seamen bunched upon the ground.  They Slept while Jesus Prayed.  Henry Tim Chambers.  AATT

Like, everyone wants to look black.  Fashions in the 70's.  May Swenson.  NYP

Like everything else.  Poetry.  Al Masarik.  CPA

Like eyes coming out of the wood.  Some Knots.  Edwin Honig. NoAM

Like Fire Spreadin/ the Joylessness.  Thulani Nkabinde.  NW

Like Ghosts of Eagles.  Robert Francis.  GOA

Like Gulliver.  Nina Cassian, *tr. fr. Rumanian by* Willis Barnstone *and* Matei Calinescu.  BoWoP; VWA

Like lamps between the trees.  Firefly.  Kamimura Hajime, *tr. by* Harry *and* Lynn Guest *and* Kajima Shozo.  TSWA

Like leaves on trees the race of man is found.  Homer, *tr. by* Pope.  *Fr.* The Iliad, VI.  OBVE

Like lips behind a veil.  The Poppies.  Richard Church.  PF

Like liquid gold the wheat-field lies.  Color in the Wheat. Hamlin Garland.  BPAW

Like mail order brides.  Seedlings in the Mail.  Marge Piercy. MMD

Like me are you still searching.  Communion Portrait in Oil. Larry Weirather.  FoP

Like [*or* Lyke] Memnon's rock[e], touched [*or* toucht] with the rising sun[ne]."  Licia, XLVII.  Giles Fletcher the Elder. AAS; FF

Like Mistress, Like Maid.  Samuel Rowlands.  SCP–2

Like Musical Instruments.  Tom Clark.  PPoe (Poem.)  ConAP; UsP

Like my father I'm.  The Final Cut.  Vern Rutsala.  AMV–81

Like new waters that form nightly.  Blessing of the Firstborn. Howard Schwartz.  VWA

Like Noah's Weary Dove, *with music*.  William Augustus Mühlenberg.  AH

Like Odysseus under the ram.  Archilochus, *tr. fr. Latin by* Guy Davenport.  OBVE

Like one who in her third widowhood doth profess.  To Mr. Rowland Woodward.  John Donne.  PAIC

Like our father Abraham.  With My Grandfather.  Zelda, *tr. by* Marcia Falk.  VWA

Like plump green floor plans.  Rotation.  Julian Bond.  FF; NIL

Like porches they trust their attachments.  Rhododendrons.  Tess Gallagher.  AAN

Like priests in a strange town. Public House Cinematics. Michael Smith. IPM

Like Ripples on the Water. *Gond Oral Tradition, tr. by* V. Elwin *and* S. Hivale. WTO

Like Rousseau. Amiri Baraka. PoA

Like Sieur Montaigne's distinction. Golfers. Irving Layton. CABA (1972 ed.)

Like Smoke. Mririda n'Ait Attik, *tr. fr. French version by* Daniel Halpern *and* Paula Paley. PBWP

Like snooker balls thrown on the table's faded green. A Poet's Progress. Michael Hamburger. WIF

Like some ripe, old couple. Growing Old in West Virginia. Michael C. Blumenthal. PoUp

Like sweet brother Johnny Hodges dying alone. Elegy for Duke Ellington. Jim Mulac. AcAn

Like the beat, beat, beat of the tom-tom. Night and Day. Cole Porter. BLSo

Like the fey goose-girl in the enchanted wood. Horror. Henry Treece. EAS

Like the Idalian queen. Madrigal. William Drummond of Hawthornden. GBL; ILP (1975 ed.); NOBE; OAEL-1; SCP-2

Like the Poets of Ancient China. Vern Rutsala. MPA

Like the rusty bronze of a copper kettle. Spring in the Desert. Arthur Truman Merrill. BPAW

Like the soldier, like the sailor, like the bib and tuck and bailer. A Letter on the Use of Machine Guns at Weddings. Kenneth Patchen. SPT

Like the stones. 3 A.M. Mbembe. NW

Like the sun on February ice dazzling. Snow, Snow. Marge Piercy. AMV-81

Like the Touch of Rain. Edward Thomas. BoLoP; GBL

Like the universe. Science as Art. Hugh Seidman. AmPA

Like the vicious cartoon innocent. Roadrunner and Coyote. Sharon Leiter. AAN

Like the white whale, born black, myself grows brighter. Pervigilium Veneris. Suzanne Noguere. PoA

Like the wild organs of winter storms. At the Eastern Front. Georg Trakl, *tr. by* Ingo Seidler. IPWM

Like the yu'ub wood bell tied to gelded camels that are running away. Poet's Lament on the Death of His Wife. Raage Ugaas, *tr. fr. Somali by* B. W. Andrzejewski *and* I. M. Lewis. WTO

Like This Together. Adrienne Rich. PiAm; VGW

Like thousands, I took just pride and more than just. Reading Myself. Robert Lowell. TAP

Like thunder they run out, like Holstein thunder. The New Cows. Charles Waterman. GP

Like to a baker's oven is the grave. *Unknown.* FaBoEE

Like to a Hermit Poor. *At. to* Sir Walter Ralegh. GBL

Like to Diana in her summer weed. Samela. Robert Greene. *Fr.* Menaphon. GBL; NOBE

Like to the arctic needle that doth guide. Emblems, V, 4. Francis Quarles. EBEV; OAEL-1; SCP-2

Like to the damask rose you see. Hos Ego Versiculos. Francis Quarles. NIL

Like to the falling of a star. Sic Vita. Henry King. BBGO; FF; ILP (1975 ed.); NIL; NOBE; WIF

Like to the Grass That's Green Today, *with music.* Peter Bulkeley the Younger. AH

Like to the thund'ring tone of unspoke speeches. Nonsense. Richard Corbet. FaBoNo

Like to these unmesurable montayns. Jacopo Sannazaro, *tr. fr. Italian by* Sir Thomas Wyatt. AAS; CABA (1972 ed.)

Like torn-up newsprint in the nonchalant snow. 1894 in London. Charles Spear. ATNZ

Like trains of cars on tracks of plush. Emily Dickinson. PiAm

Like Trees, Like Islands. Pearse Hutchinson. IPM

Like twilight bleeding on a winter day. Villanelle. John Nist. AMV-81

Like two cathedral towers these stately pines. My Cathedral. Longfellow. PBMP

Like two somnambulists we entered the dawn sun. Hunting for Blueberries. Thomas James. AmPA

Like Venus. Sputin. Ishmael Reed. CPA

Like waking in the small room, looking out. Wren: Three Mirrors. Michael Burkard. AAN

Like Weary Trees. Jacob Glatstein, *tr. fr. Yiddish by* Ruth Whitman. VWA

Like when/ I drove one of my students. Sparkling Water. Richard Schaaf. TAT

Like women who are loved very much and are still not sated. Years. Anna Margolin, *tr. by* Ruth Whitman. VWA

Like you, your house had a beauty. Learning to Live with Friends. Cleopatra Mathis. AAN

Likeness, A. Robert Browning. InPS; VLP

Likeness, The. Arthur Gregor. VGW

Likeness, The. Leonard Nathan. GP

Likewise. Langston Hughes. ILP (1975 ed.)

Li'l Liza Jane. *Unknown.* BLSo, *with music*; FSW

Lilac. Mary Ellen Solt. WeW

Lilacs. Amy Lowell. PF
  *Sels.*
  "Lilacs,/ False blue,/ White." PCOP
  "May is lilac here in New England." FSFS

Lilacs. Bill Pruitt. EC

Lilacs,/ False blue,/ White. Amy Lowell. *Fr.* Lilacs. PCOP

Lilacs wither in the Carolinas, The. In the Carolinas. Wallace Stevens. VGW

Lilian. Tennyson. PeD

Lilies Are White. *Unknown.* PoPle

Lilies of the Field, The. Bible, *N.T.* St. Matthew, VI: 28-30. PF

Lilies of the Valley. Jon Silkin. NoAM

Lilies will languish; violets look ill. The Sadness of Things for Sappho's Sickness. Robert Herrick. PoPle

Lilith, *sel.* Christopher Brennan.
  "She is the night: all horror is of her." MAuV

Lilith. Ruth Fainlight. VWA

Lilith. Ruth Feldman. VWA

Lilith. Donald Finkel. VWA

Lilith. Yvan Goll. VWA

Lilith. Allen Grossman. VWA

Lilith. Primo Levi, *tr. fr. Italian by* Ruth Feldman *and* Brian Swann. VWA

Lilith, Adam's first companion. Lilith. Ruth Fainlight. VWA

Lilith our second kinswoman. Lilith. Primo Levi, *tr. by* Ruth Feldman *and* Brian Swann. VWA

Lilith's Child. Edward Francisco. DL

Lillian's Chair ("Lillian had just arisen from her chair"). Olga Cabrall. GP

Lilliburlero (A New Song). Thomas, Lord Wharton. APAS (Lilli Burlero.) FSW; RDB, *with music*

Lilliputian's Beer Song. Septimus Winner. OBAL

Lilly, The. Blake. *Fr.* Songs of Experience. MBPR

Lilly Dale, *with music.* H. S. Thompson. BLSo

Lilly's Song. Evan Zimroth. AMV-81

Lily Adair. Thomas Holley Chivers. OBAL

Lily and the Rose, The. *Unknown.* See Maidens Came, The.

Lily-Bell. Roger Wescott. PCOP

Lily, Germander, and Sops-in-Wine. *Unknown. Fr.* Robin Goodfellow, Pt. II. ECBV

Lily of a Day, A. Ben Jonson. *See* Noble Nature, The.

Lily of the Valley.  Hartley Coleridge.  PF

Lily of the West, The.  *Unknown.*  AmFP; FSW

Limb of forests rises up, The.  Yvonne Caroutch, *tr. fr. French by* David Cloutier.  BoWoP

Limbo.  Samuel Taylor Coleridge.  MBPR; OAEL-2; OBP

Limbo.  Seamus Heaney.  CIP; HeHu

Limbo.  Marieve Rugo.  AMV-81

Lime condensed on the ceiling, or maybe.  Living in the Boneyard.  John Oliver Simon.  NeAC

Lime-Tree, The.  Edward Lucie-Smith.  BuTh

Limeraiku.  Ted Pauker.  NOBL

Limerick: "Ambitious gay boy of Khartoum, An."  *Unknown.* NIL

Limerick: "Animula vagula blandula."  Conrad Aiken.  FaBoNo; OBAL

Limerick: "Argentine gaucho named Bruno, An."  *Unknown.* NOBL

Limerick: "Breasts of a barmaid of Crale, The."  *Unknown.* NOBL

Limerick: "Charlotte Brontë said, 'Wow, sister! *What* a man!' " Victor Gray.  NOBL

Limerick: "Charming young woman named Pat, A."  *Unknown.* NIL

Limerick: "Cheerful old bear at the zoo, A."  *Unknown.*  CTV

Limerick: "Dear Sir, your astonishment's odd."  *Unknown.* See Reply, A.

Limerick: "Decrepit old gas man named Peter, A."  *Unknown.* SoSe

Limerick: "I sat next the duchess at tea."  *Unknown.*  NIL; SoSe

Limerick: "It's time to make love: douse the glim."  Conrad Aiken.  FaBoNo

Limerick: "Lesbian girl of Khartoum, A."  *Unknown.*  NOBL

Limerick: "Man hired by John Smith and Co., A."  "Mark Twain."  See Dirt Dumping.

Limerick: "Old East End worker called Jock, An."  Victor Gray. NOBL

Limerick: "On the deck of a ship called the Masm."  Conrad Aiken.  FaBoNo

Limerick: "One morning old Wilfrid Scawen Blunt."  Victor Gray.  NOBL

Limerick: "Staid schizophrenic named Struther, A."  *Unknown.* NIL

Limerick: "Taxi-cab whore out at Iver, A."  Victor Gray.  NOBL

Limerick: "There once was a bright young physician."  *Unknown.* NIL

Limerick: "There once was a man who said, 'Damn!' "  M. E. Hare.  NOBL

Limerick: "There once was a man who said 'God.' "  Ronald Arbuthnott Knox.  See Idealism.

Limerick: "There once was a pious young priest."  *Unknown.* NIL
    (Pious Young Priest, The.)  TDH
    ("There was once a pious young priest.")  BBL

Limerick: "There once was a spinster of Ealing."  *Unknown.* NIL

Limerick: "There once was a wonderful wizard."  Conrad Aiken. FaBoNo

Limerick: "There was a young fellow called Crouch."  Victor Gray.  NOBL

Limerick: "There was a young Fellow of Caius."  *Unknown.* NOBL

Limerick: "There was a young Fellow of King's."  *Unknown.* NOBL

Limerick: "There was a young Fellow of Waldham."  *Unknown.* NOBL

Limerick: "There was a young lady named Bright."  Arthur Buller.  See Relativity.

Limerick: "There was a young lady of Corsica."  Edward Lear. FaBoNo

Limerick: "There was a young lady of Lynn."  *Unknown.*  CTV; SoSe

Limerick: "There was a young lady of Riga."  *Unknown.*  CTV; FaBoCo

Limerick: "There was a young lady of Trent."  *Unknown.*  NIL

Limerick: "There was a young maid who said, 'Why'."  *Unknown.* SoSe

Limerick: "There was a young person of Crete."  Edward Lear. FaBoNo

Limerick: "There was a young woman called Starky."  *Unknown.* See Mendelian Theory.

Limerick: "There was an old man in a boat."  Edward Lear. EBEV; FaBoNo

Limerick: "There was an old man in a tree."  Edward Lear. FaBoNo; OxBChV

Limerick: "There was an old man of Dundee."  Edward Lear. FaBoNo

Limerick: "There was an old man of El Hums."  Edward Lear. FaBoNo

Limerick: "There was an old man of Girgenti."  Edward Lear. FaBoNo

Limerick: "There was an old man of Hong Kong."  Edward Lear. FaBoCo

Limerick: "There was an old man of Kamschatka."  Edward Lear. NOBL

Limerick: "There was an old man of Khartoum."  W. R. Inge. NOBL

Limerick: "There was an old man of Madras."  Edward Lear. FaBoNo

Limerick: "There was an old man of Peru/ Who dreamt he was eating his shoe."  *Unknown.*  SoSe
    (Old Man from Peru, An.)  TDH

Limerick: "There was an old man of Spithead."  Edward Lear. FaBoNo

Limerick: "There was an old man of the Dee."  Edward Lear. FaBoNo

Limerick: "There was an old man of Thermopylae."  Edward Lear.  EBEV; FaBoNo; NOBL

Limerick: "There was an old man of Three Bridges."  Edward Lear.  FaBoNo

Limerick: "There was an old man of Vesuvius."  Edward Lear. FaBoNo

Limerick: "There was an old man who said, 'Hush!' "  Edward Lear.  FaBoCo; NOBL; OxBChV

Limerick: "There was an old man whose despair."  Edward Lear. FaBoNo; VLP

Limerick: "There was an old man with a beard."  Edward Lear. CTV; FaBoCo; FaBoNo; NOBL; OxBChV
    (Nesting.)  ECBV

Limerick: "There was an old man with a ribbon."  Edward Lear. FaBoCo

Limerick: "There was an old person of Anerley."  Edward Lear. FaBoCo

Limerick: "There was an old person of Bar."  Edward Lear. FaBoNo

Limerick: "There was an old person of Brussels."  Edward Lear. FaBoNo

Limerick: "There was an old person of Crowle."  Edward Lear. FaBoNo

Limerick: "There was an old person of Dover."  Edward Lear. FaBoNo

Limerick: "There was an old person of Grange."  Edward Lear. FaBoNo

Limerick: "There was an old person of Harrow."  Edward Lear. FaBoNo

Limerick: "There was an old person of Hove." Edward Lear. FaBoNo

Limerick: "There was an old person of Philae." Edward Lear. FaBoNo

Limerick: "There was an old person of Twickenham." Edward Lear. FaBoNo

Limerick: "There was an old person of Wick." Edward Lear. FaBoNo

Limerick: "There was an old person whose habits." Edward Lear. FaBoNo
(Hurtful Habits.) TDH

Limerick: "There's a notable family named Stein." Unknown. NOBL

Limerick: "Tutor who tooted the flute, A." Carolyn Wells. CTV; SoSe

Limerick: "Vice most obscene and unsavory, A." Unknown. NOBL

Limerick: "Well, it's partly the shape of the thing." Unknown. SoSe

Limerick: "When Gauguin was visiting Fiji." Victor Gray. NOBL

Limerick: "When our dean took a pious young spinster." Victor Gray. NOBL

Limerick: "Whenever a fellow called Rex." Unknown. NOBL

Limerick: "While Titian was grinding rose madder." Unknown. NOBL

Limerick: "While visiting Arundel Castle." Victor Gray. NOBL

Limerick: "Young engine-driver called Hunt, A." Victor Gray. NOBL

Limerick: "Young things who frequent picture-palaces, The." Unknown. NOBL

Limerick of Frankness, A. "X. Y. Z." TDH

Limerick Train, The. Brendan Kennelly. IPM

Lim'ricks and Puns. Unknown. TDH

Limestone and pine: a dry country. By Rail through Istria. Robert Conquest. NoAM

Limited. Carl Sandburg. HAP; PSN

Limited, The. Robert Penn Warren. PoA

Limits of Departure, The. Bruce Weigl. AMV-81

Limits of Equitation, The. Barbara Winder. AMV-81

Limits of Submission, The. Faarah Nuur, tr. fr. Somali by B. W. Andrzejewski and I. M. Lewis. WTO

Limp as unwatered flowers, the grey limbs. Homage to the Carracci. Tom Disch. PoA

Limpet. Ronald Mann. PMW

Limping among the hookers and drunks. No Quarter. Steven Orlen. AAN; FoP

Limping past the Guthrie theater. Indians at the Guthrie. Gerald Vizenor. VoR

Limping to this spreading portrait. Portrait of a Negative. Alex Kuo. NW

Limpopo and Tugela churned. The Scorpion. William Plomer. NoAM

L'Imprévisibilité. Zinaida Hippius, tr. fr. Russian by Temira Pachmuss. PBWP

Lincoln, sel. John Gould Fletcher.
"There was a darkness in this man," II. OFD

Lincoln and Liberty. Jesse Hutchinson. FSW

Lincoln Monument: Washington. Langston Hughes. CC; OFD

Lincoln, the Man of the People, sel. Edwin Markham.
"Up from the log cabin to the capitol." OFD

Lincoln was a long man. Abraham Lincoln. Rosemary and Stephen Vincent Benét. CC

Lincolnshire Poacher, The. Unknown. FSW; GBP

Linda. John Stone. CoPAm

Lindamira's Complaint. Mary Sidney Wroth, Countess of Montgomery. Fr. Urania. WPE

Lindbergh. Unknown. AmFP

Lindeman. Mary Jane White. AMV-81

Line, The. Dan Gerber. HeS

Line forms early each Sunday, The. The Sitting. Maxine Chernoff. FiCh

Line in long array where they wind betwixt green islands, A. Cavalry Crossing a Ford. Walt Whitman. AmVN; CABA (1972 ed.); HeIP; ILP (1975 ed.); InPK; InPS; NoAM; PiAm; PPoD; PPP; TAP; UnPo (1976 ed.)

Line Like. Nelly Sachs, tr. fr. German by Michael Hamburger. BoWoP

Line of the cut must be clean, The. Lapidary. Bonnie L. Alexander. AMV-80

Line-Storm Song, A. Robert Frost. ILP (1975 ed.)

Line to heaven by Christ was made, The. Unknown. PeD

Line-up, The. Joan Swift. FiCP

Lineage. Reba Terry. AMV-81

Lineage. Margaret Walker. CNA; NMM; PBWP; PoBA; TVo

Linear, encircled youth, The. On Alexander and Aristotle, on a Black-on-Red Greek Plate. Alan Dugan. PPP

Linebacker at Forty, The. Jon Wallace. AMV-81

Linen Town. Seamus Heaney. CIP

Lines. Brian Swann. AMV-81

Lines: "Here often, when a child I lay reclined." Tennyson. CABA (1972 ed.)

Lines: Inspired by the Controversy on the Value or Otherwise of Old English Studies. Anthony Burgess. FaBoCo

Lines: "Lines which are the imitation of imagined veins." Anne Waldman. CAAP

Lines: "Other day I was loving a sweet little fruitpie-and-cream, The." Gavin Ewart. EAS

Lines: "Singularly and in pairs the decade has been ripped by bullets." Herbert Martin. PoBA

Lines: "Though all the Fates should prove unkind." Henry David Thoreau. See Though All the Fates Should Prove Unkind.

Lines: "Unfelt, unheard, unseen." Keats. MBPR

Lines: "We meet not as we parted." Shelley. MBPR

Lines: "When the lamp is shattered." Shelley. See When the Lamp Is Shattered.

Lines: "Wheresoe'er I turn my view." Samuel Johnson. See Lines Written in Ridicule of Certain Poems Published in 1777.

Lines Addressed to a Young Lady. Byron. MBPR

Lines Addressed to Mr. Jefferson. Philip Freneau. EAP

Lines are keen against today's bad sky, The. The Church on Comiaken Hill. Richard Hugo. Prf

Lines Composed a Few Miles above Tintern Abbey. Wordsworth. BiP; CABA (1972 ed.); ExPo (1973 ed.); FF; HeIP; ILP (1975 ed.); InPS; IPWM; LFH; NIL; OAEL-2; PPP; VoPo
(Lines Written a Few Miles above Tintern Abbey.) AnMo; HAP; MBPR
Sels.
"Five years have past; five summers with the length." PES
"For I have learned." NU
"For thou art with me here upon the banks." Prf

Lines for a Christmas Card. Hilaire Belloc. IP; SFF; SoSe

Lines for a Fifty-fifth Birthday. Jeanne McGahey. MIT

Lines for a Hard Time. Gena Ford. IHMS

Lines for a President. Robert Watson. PPoD

Lines for a Worthy Person Who Has Drifted by Accident into a Chelsea Revel. A. P. Herbert. NOBL

Lines for a Young Wanderer in Mexico. John Logan. PoA

Lines for an Interment. Archibald MacLeish. CMoP (1970 ed.); NOBA

Lines for an Old Man. T. S. Eliot. FaBoTw (1975 ed.)

Lines for Cuscuscaraway and Mirza Murad Ali Beg. T. S. Eliot. OBAL; SpRo

Lines for Marking Time. Roberta Hill. BoWoP; CDW

Lines for Michael in the Picture. John Logan. CAPP

Lines for My Father. Patrick Worth Gray. AMV-81

Lines for the Ancient Scribes. Harvey Shapiro. VWA

Lines for Those to Whom Tragedy Is Denied. Joyce Carol Oates. CoPAm; IHMS

Lines Found on an Envelope. Adrianne Marcus. NPW

Lines from an Orchard Once Surveyed by Thoreau. Philip Booth. GP

Lines in Ridicule of Certain Poems Published in 1777. Samuel Johnson. *See* Lines Written in Ridicule of Certain Poems Published in 1777.

Lines Inscribed upon a Cup Formed from a Skull. Byron. InPK; MBPR

Lines Left upon a Seat in a Yew-Tree. Wordsworth. MBPR

Lines of history. Lines of defiance. John Montague. *Fr.* A New Siege: An Historical Meditation. CIP

Lines of this new song are nothing, The. Louis Zukofsky. VGW

Lines on a Paid Militia. Dryden. *Fr.* Cymon and Iphigenia. SoSe
(Militia, The.) OBSV

Lines on a Young Lady's Photograph Album. Philip Larkin. HAP; HeIP; OAEL-2

Lines on Brueghel's Icarus. Michael Hamburger. NIL

Lines on Hearing That Lady Byron Was Ill. Byron. EBEV; MBPR

Lines on Hearing the Organ. Charles Stuart Calverley. FaBoCo; NOBL

Lines on His Birthday. John Logan. CAPP

Lines on His Companions Who Died in the Northern Seas. Thomas James. SCP-2

Lines on Milton. Dryden. *See* Lines Printed under the Engraved Portrait of Milton.

Lines on Seeing a Lock of Milton's Hair. Keats. MBPR; PeD

Lines on Swift's Ancestors. Pope. FaBoCo

Lines on the Back of a Leary Bailfund Card. Mary Norbert Körte. MIT

Lines on the Mermaid Tavern. Keats. ILP (1975 ed.); MBPR; TT

Lines on Thomas Warton's Poems. Samuel Johnson. *See* Lines Written in Ridicule of Certain Poems Published in 1777.

Lines parallel. The Room. De Leon Harrison. PoBA

Lines Printed under the Engraved Portrait of Milton. Dryden. HeIP; InPK
(Lines on Milton.) OAEL-1

Lines Rhymed in a Letter Received from Oxford. Keats. MBPR

Lines Supposed to Have Been Addressed to Fanny Brawne. Keats. *See* This Living Hand, Now Warm and Capable.

Lines to a Critic. Shelley. MBPR

Lines to a Don. Hilaire Belloc. FaBoCo; OBSV

Lines to a Nasturtium (A Lover Muses). Anne Spencer. AmNP (1974 ed.)

Lines to a Tree. Judah Leib Teller, *tr. fr. Yiddish by* Gabriel Preil *and* Howard Schwartz. VWA

Lines to a World-famous Poet Who Failed to Complete a World-famous Poem; or, Come Clean, Mr. Guest! Ogden Nash. OBAL

Lines to Accompany Flowers for Eve. Carolyn Kizer. BoWoP

Lines to Do with Youth. Witter Bynner. PoA

Lines to García Lorca. Amiri Baraka. TCP

Lines to His Son on Reaching Adolescence. John Logan. CAPP

Lines to Mr. Hodgson. Byron. MBPR

Lines to My Father. Sam Hamod. SA

Lines to Nefertiti. Peter Kostakis. FiCh

Lines to Ralph Hodgson, Esqre. T. S. Eliot. OBAL

Lines to the South. John William Corrington. CSP

Lines Where Beauty Lingers. Franklin P. Adams. OBAL

Lines which are the imitation of imagined veins. Lines. Anne Waldman. CAAP

Lines with a Gift of Herbs. Janet Lewis. WPW

Lines Written a Few Miles above Tintern Abbey. Wordsworth. *See* Lines Composed a Few Miles above Tintern Abbey.

Lines Written among the Euganean Hills. Shelley. MBPR

Lines Written at a Small Distance from My House. Wordsworth. *See* To My Sister.

Lines Written beneath an Elm in the Churchyard of Harrow. Byron. MBPR

Lines Written but Never Mailed from Hawaii. William Meredith. PHC

Lines Written by a Bear of Very Little Brain. A. A. Milne. FaBoNo

Lines Written during a Period of Insanity. William Cowper. EBEV; HAP; OAEL-1; PPP; Prf
(Lines Written under the Influence of Delirium.) ILP (1975 ed.)

Lines Written in a Blank Leaf of the Prometheus Unbound. Thomas Lovell Beddoes. OAEL-2

Lines Written in Dejection. W. B. Yeats. STS

Lines Written in Early Spring. Wordsworth. MBPR; OAEL-2; PoIA; PBMP
(Written in Early Spring.) ILP (1975 ed.)

Lines Written in Kensington Gardens. Matthew Arnold. NIL

Lines Written in Objection, or the Limpopo Express. Phillip Hey. SFF

Lines Written in Ridicule of Certain Poems Published in 1777. Samuel Johnson. PAIC
(Lines: "Wheresoe'er I turn my view.") PPoD
(Lines in Ridicule of Certain Poems Published in 1777.) FaBoCo
(Lines on Thomas Warton's Poems.) FaBoEE

Lines Written in the Album at Elbingerode. Samuel Taylor Coleridge. MBPR

Lines Written in the Bay of Lerici. Shelley. MBPR; OAEL-2

Lines Written in the Highlands after a Visit to Burns's Country. Keats. MBPR

Lines Written in Windsor Forest. Pope. EBEV

Lines Written near Richmond, upon the Thames, at Evening. Wordsworth. MBPR

Lines Written near San Francisco. Louis Simpson. CABA (1972 ed.)

Lines Written on a Seat on the Grand Canal, Dublin. Patrick Kavanagh. BIrV; CIP; CMoP (1970 ed.)

Lines Written on a Window Shutter at Weston. William Cowper. LAuP

Lines Written on Hearing the News of the Death of Napoleon. Shelley. MBPR

Lines Written under the Influence of Delirium. William Cowper. *See* Lines Written during a Period of Insanity.

Lingam and the Yoni, The. A. D. Hope. MAT; NoAM; WeW

Linger longer, Olga. Molly Fitton. POL

Lingerie. Hazel Hall. WPW

Lining Track. *Unknown.* AmFP

Links. Ricardo Pau-Llosa. AMV-81

Links of fear. The Sacrifice. Moshe Yungman, *tr. by* Marcia Falk. VWA

Linnet in the rocky dells, The. Song. Emily Brönte. HAP; VLP

Linstead Market. *Unknown.* FSW

Lion, The. Lord Alfred Douglas. ECBV

Lion. Kenneth Rexroth. *Fr.* A Bestiary. HoPM (1975 ed.)

Lion and lioness are intractable, The. Letter to Eve. Alan Dugan. PAIC

Lion and the Mouse, The. Jeffreys Taylor. MN

Lion and the unicorn, The. Mother Goose. BBL, 2 *versions*; MG

Lion dishonoured bids death come, The. Reversionary. Stevie Smith. FaBoEE

Lion Hunts. Patricia Beer. OxBTC

Lion is an awful bore, The. The Lion. Lord Alfred Douglas. ECBV

Lion is called the king, The. Lion. Kenneth Rexroth. *Fr.* A Bestiary. HoPM (1975 ed.)

Lion is never a lion in a royal hunt, A. Lion Hunts. Patricia Beer. OxBTC

Lion ramps around the cage, The. King of Beasts. Oliver Herford. PCOP

Lion roars at the rose, A. Parable of the Garden. Robert Peters. PoW

Lion Skin, The. James K. Baxter. ATNZ

Lion Thoughts. Iowna Elizabeth Banker. CTV

Lion with the heat oppress'd, A. The Lion and the Mouse. Jeffreys Taylor. MN

Lions. Sandra McPherson. CAAP

Lion's Bride, The. Gwen Harwood. BoWoP

Lions in Sweden. Wallace Stevens. BiP

Lions of fire, The. Kenneth Patchen. VGW

Lion's Skeleton, The. Charles Tennyson Turner. VLP

Lions who ate the Christians on the sands of the arena, The. Sunt Leones. Stevie Smith. SBG

*Lip* was a man who used his head. J. V. Cunningham. OBAL

Lip which had once been stolid, now moving, A. Divine Love. Michael Benedikt. AmPA; ConAP

Lips and Eyes. Giovanni Battista Marino, *tr. fr. Italian by* Thomas Carew. OBVE

Lips caked with lipstick. Fille de Joie: Congo. Michael Jackson. ATNZ

Lips of the one I love are my perpetual pleasure, The. Hafiz, *tr. fr. Persian by* Peter Avery *and* John Heath-Stubbs. BoLoP

Lips Tongueless. Robert Herrick. CaPo

Liquor, you turn us into kings. What Matter? *Gond Oral Tradition, tr. by* V. Elwin *and* S. Hivale. WTO

Lisbon. *Unknown.* AmFP

Lisnagade. *Unknown.* WTO

Lispy Bails Out. David Barker. GP

List, The. Michael McClure. NU

List! what sad sounds are these? extremely. John Ford. *Fr.* The Broken Heart. SCP-2

List while the poet trolls. The Rival Curates. W. S. Gilbert. BBL; VLP

Listen. Ogden Nash. ILP (1975 ed.)

Listen,/ listen to me, fellow members of the company. An Angry Sermon for Any Day in the Week. F. Eugene Warren. AATT

Listen,/ she spent her days. Death. Mildred Jeffrey. AMV-80

Listen.../ With faint dry sound. November Night. Adelaide Crapsey. PAIC

Listen, and when thy hand this paper presses. A Letter from a Girl to Her Own Old Age. Alice Meynell. SBG

Listen Children. Lucille Clifton. CNA; PoBA

Listen, children:/ Your father is dead. Lament. Edna St. Vincent Millay. DL

"Listen, children, listen, won't you come into the night?" Who Calls? Frances Clarke. LCL

Listen, for example, to the thudding of the winter stream. An Inconclusive Evening. Frances Bellerby. FaBoTw (1975 ed.)

Listen here, Joe. Without Benefit of Declaration. Langston Hughes. AmNP (1974 ed.); IP

Listen! I will tell the most treasured of dreams. The Dream of the Rood. *Unknown, tr. by* Helen Gardner. BoReV

Listen: in the distance delicate hooves of sable antelope. Phylogeny. Marilyn Thompson. UsP

Listen, let me explain, it was not the fire. The Late Visitor. Ann Stanford. MPA; PPoD

Listen listen/ There's walking in the world. Colin Barnes, Drums. John Smith. *Fr.* Jazz for Five. MPo

Listen, Lonnie, I saw that ad. Ted Speaking. Lynn Steele. BCr

Listen, Lord—a Prayer. James Weldon Johnson. BPo

Listen, my children, and you shall hear. Paul Revere's Ride. Longfellow. *Fr.* Tales of a Wayside Inn. BTTM; CTV; FaPo; FaPoR; OBAL

Listen, my dearest, once this flesh of mine. "Two Hearts Divided." R. Williams Parry, *tr. by* Joseph P. Clancy. OBW

Listen natives of a dry place. The Old Boast. W. S. Merwin. NOBA

Listen, Put on Morning. W. S. Graham. FaBoTw (1975 ed.)

Listen Sally. Phone Call. Tom Crawford. AMV-81

Listen! The garbage pouring down the chutes. For David Shapiro. David Lehman. PoA

Listen, the hay-bells tinkle as the cart. The Holy Innocents. Robert Lowell. ConAP: NowV

Listen. The wind is still. Spring Thunder. Mark Van Doren. TH

Listen to me, as when ye heard our father. Canadian Boat-Song. *Unknown, at. to* John Galt. AIW; FaPoR

Listen to me there have. Freddy the Rat Perishes. Don Marquis. *Fr.* Archy and Mehitabel. MiP

Listen to the Bird. Laya Firestone. VWA

Listen to the call of the muezzin. A Denunciation. Mahammed Abdille Hassan, *tr. fr. Somali by* B. W. Andrzejewski. WTO

Listen to the Mocking Bird. Septimus Winner. BLSo, *with music*; FSW; PSoN, *with music*

Listen to the mournful drums of a strange funeral. A Strange Funeral in Braddock. Michael Gold. SPT

Listen to the music. Pro Musica Antiqua. O. B. Hardison. WasP

Listen to the story of Willie the Weeper. Willie the Weeper. *Unknown.* OBAL

Listen, you drawing men. Snapshots of the Cotton South. Frank Marshall Davis. PoBA

"Listen," you said. Rainbow. Liz Lochhead. MIS

Listenen to Big Black at S. F. State. Sonia Sanchez. BPo

Listeners, The. Walter de la Mare. CMoP (1970 ed.); HAP; HoPM (1975 ed.); ILP (1975 ed.); InPK; NCSH; NoAM; NOBE; PoPle; PPoD; SoSe; SS; SFF; UsP; WeW

Listening. Alice Corbin, *after Chippewa Indian.* BPAW

Listening. Hanny Michaelis, *tr. fr. Dutch by* Marjolijn de Jager. VWA

Listening. Nancy Passy. AMV-81

Listening. William Stafford. RFM; TSWA; VoA

Listening/ To the dying voices. Cradle Song. Patrick Galvin. IPM

Listening Back. Ina Coolbrith. WPW

Listening, listening; it is never still. The Märchen. Randall Jarrell. CMoP (1970 ed.)

Listening Macaws, The. Hazel Hall. WPW

Listening-Post. Martin C. Rosner. AMV-80

Listening Rock, The. Ray A. Young Bear. VW

Listening to Confucius. Henryk Grynberg, *tr. fr. Polish by* Isaac Komem. VWA

Listening to Foxhounds. James Dickey. InPS; LiSp; PPoD

Listening to hard bop. Zimmer's Last Gig. Paul Zimmer. AMV-80

Listening to Her. Natan Zach, *tr. fr. Hebrew by* Laya Firestone. VWA

Listening to Mbaqanga. Lindiwe Mabuza. SES

Listening to Miss Anthony, our lovely Miss. And Two Good Things. D. J. Enright. HeHu

Listening to rock 'n roll. Bouzouki. Kenneth O. Hanson. GP

Listening to the man. Poem for Otis Redding. Joyce Carol Thomas. CNA

Listening to the music. Listening. Hanny Michaelis, *tr. by* Marjolijn de Jager. VWA

Listless he eyes the palisades. In the Prison Pen. Herman Melville. TAP

Litany, A, *sels.* John Donne.
"Deliver us for thy descent." SCP-1
Good Lord, Deliver Us! BoReV
"O Holy Ghost, whose temple I." SCP-1

Litany, The: "From a ruler that's a curse." Charles Cotton. OBSV

Litany, The: "In the hour of my distress." Robert Herrick. *See* His Litany to the Holy Spirit.

Litany, A: "Ring out your bells, let mourning shows be spread." Sir Philip Sidney. UnPo (1976 ed.)
("Ring out your bells, let mourning shows be spread.") CABA (1972 ed.); GBL

Litany for Halloween. *Unknown, tr. fr. Cornish.* IWK
(Cornish Litany, A.) CC
("From ghoulies and ghosties.") OFD

Litany in Time of Plague, A. Thomas Nashe. *See* Adieu, Farewell Earth's Bliss.

Litany of Sleep, *sel.* Tristan Corbière, *tr. fr. French by* Christopher Pilling.
"You who snore with your sleeping wife so near." OBVE

Litany to the Holy Spirit. Robert Herrick. *See* His Litany to the Holy Spirit.

Litel wot it any mon. An Unfortunate Lover. *Unknown.* OxBM

Literacy: An Abandoned Ode. William Harmon. CSP

Literary Dinner, A. Vladimir Nabokov. OBAL

Literary Importation. Philip Freneau. AmVN; TAP

Literature. Robert A. Brooks. PoUp

Lithe, quicker than the ball itself. Jump Shot. Richard Peck. MiP; SPo

Little. Dorothy Aldis. CTV

Little Americano children are, The. Self-Portrait. Orlando Romero. FoP

Little anna brown anna. Anna. Joe Johnson. CNA

Little Annie Rooney, *with music.* Michael Nolan. FSN

Little Ball of Yarn. *Unknown.* FSW

Little Benny sat one evening. Misplaced Sympathy. Charles Follen Adams. OBAL

Little Bessie. *Unknown.* AmFP

Little Betty Blue. Mother Goose. MG

Little Billee. Thackeray. BBL; ECBV; FaBoCo; NOBL; PoPle

Little Billy. *Unknown.* GBP

Little bird whispers in their ear, A. Parable for Our Time. Peter Michelson. HeS

Little Birdie. *Unknown.* FSW

Little Birds. "Lewis Carroll." FaBoNo

Little Black Boy, The. Blake. *Fr.* Songs of Innocence. AnMo; BiP; CABA (1972 ed.); HeIP; ILP (1975 ed.); InPK; LAuP; LFH; MBPR; OAEL-2; OBP; OxBChV; SoSe (1977 ed.); STS

Little black bull came down the meadow, The. Hoosen Johnny. *Unknown.* FSW

Little Black Rose, The. Aubrey Thomas De Vere. BIrV

Little black thing among the snow, A. The Chimney Sweeper. Blake. *Fr.* Songs of Experience. CABA (1972 ed.); LAuP; MBPR; OAEL-2; PPoe; PPP; STS; TT

Little Black Train. *Unknown.* AmFP

Little boat at anchor, The. Fourth of July Night. Carl Sandburg. OFD

Little Bo-Peep. Frederick Winsor. *Fr.* The Space Child's Mother Goose. QQQ

Little Bo-Peep has lost her sheep. Mother Goose. MG; SpRo

Little bo-peepals. Rhyme for Botanical Baby. Joseph Cook. QQQ; SpRo

Little Boxes. Malvina Reynolds. FSW; SoS

Little Boy, A. John Bennett. PoW

Little boy, The. Junior Addict. Langston Hughes. BPo; CNA; TCP

Little Boy Blue. Eugene Field. CTV; OBAL; PCOP; SoSe

Little Boy Blue. *Unknown.* BluL

Little Boy Blue, come, blow [up] your horn. Mother Goose. GSB, *with music*; MG

Little Boy Found, The. Blake. *Fr.* Songs of Innocence. LAuP; MBPR

Little boy kneels at the foot of the bed. Vespers. A. A. Milne. OxBChV; SpRo

Little boy, little boy, where wast thou born? Lancashire Born. *Unknown.* GBP

Little Boy Lost, The ("Father, father, where are you going"). Blake. *Fr.* Songs of Innocence. LAuP; MBPR

Little Boy Lost, A ("Nought loves another as itself"). Blake. *Fr.* Songs of Experience. ILP (1975 ed.); MBPR; OBP; STS

Little Boy Lost, A. Jerome Rothenberg. VoA

Little Boy Lost, The. Stevie Smith. FaBoTw (1975 ed.); UsP

Little boy lost in the lonely fen, The. The Little Boy Found. Blake. *Fr.* Songs of Innocence. LAuP; MBPR

Little boy once played so loud, A. Extremes. James Whitcomb Riley. ECBV

Little boy stopped in the middle of the haystack, The. Railroad Reverie. E. R. Young. ECBV

Little Boy, to show his might and power, The. The Metamorphosis. Sir John Suckling. CaPo; FaBoEE

Little boys and little maidens. Little Catkins. Alexander Blok, *tr. by* Babette Deutsch. CC; OFD

Little Brand New Baby. Tom Paxton. SoS

Little Brass Wagon. *Unknown.* FSW

Little Brother, The. James Reeves. LoAs; OxBTC

Little brown boy. Poem. Helene Johnson. AmNP (1974 ed.); PoBA

Little Brown Bulls, The. *Unknown.* AmFP

Little Brown Church in the Vale, The, *with music.* William S. Pitts. BLSH

Little Brown Dog. *Unknown.* FSW

Little Brown Jug. At. to Joseph E. Winner. BLSH, *with music*; BLSo, *with music*; FSW; GSB, *with music*; OBAL; PSoN, *with music*

Little brown squirrel hops in the corn, The. The Rejected "National Hymns." "Orpheus C. Kerr." OBAL

Little bunches of/ grass pretend they are bushes. Stories from Kansas. William Stafford. RFM

Little Bush. Elizabeth Madox Roberts. LCL

Little Buttercup. W. S. Gilbert. *Fr.* H.M.S. Pinafore. PCOP

Little by little and also in large amounts. Full October. Pablo Neruda. EC

Little Carol of the Virgin, A. Lope de Vega, *tr. fr. Spanish by* Denise Levertov. PChr

Little Catkins. Alexander Blok, *tr. fr. Russian by* Babette Deutsch. CC; OFD

Little cats walk with their tails up. Confidence. Martha Baird. OSP

Little Cheat, A. *Malay Oral Tradition, tr. by* R. J. Wilkinson *and* R. O. Winstedt. WTO

Little child, I counsel you that ye. Customs Change. *Unknown.* OxBChV

Little child is kneeling by his mother's chair, A.  Lost after All.  Charlie D. Tillman.  PeD

Little children here ye may lere.  Manners at Table When Away from Home.  *Unknown.*  OxBChV

Little children, never give.  Kindness to Animals.  *Unknown.*  CTV

Little circle/ big circle.  Blue Boy on Skates (Twilight).  M. L. Rosenthal.  SPo

Little cock-sparrow sat on a green tree, A.  Mother Goose.  MG

Little colt, A—broncho, loaned to the farm.  The Broncho That Would Not Be Broken.  Vachel Lindsay.  BPAW; PH

Little cousin is dead, by foul subtraction, The.  Dead Boy.  John Crowe Ransom.  CMoP (1970 ed.); NoAM; PiAm; PoIA

Little Cradle Rocks Tonight in Glory, The.  *Unknown.*  AmFP

Little Dame Crump.  *Unknown.*  RAE

Little Dancers, The.  Laurence Binyon.  BBGO; OxBTC

Little David.  *Unknown.*  FSW

Little Death.  Gwyn Thomas, *tr. fr. Welsh by* Joseph P. Clancy.  OBW

Little Dicky Dilver.  Mother Goose.  SoSe (1977 ed.)

Little Doll, The.  Charles Kingsley.  *See* Lost Doll, The.

Little Donkey, The.  Francis Jammes, *tr. fr. French by* Lloyd Alexander.  PChr

Little Dove, The.  *Unknown.*  AmFP

Little drops of water.  Little Things.  Julia A. Carney.  CTV; OxBChV

Little Drummer, The.  *Unknown.*  AmFP

Little Dunkeld.  *Unknown.*  GBP

Little Elegy.  X. J. Kennedy.  ConAP; HoPM (1975 ed.); NCSH

Little Elegy.  Elinor Wylie.  LoAs; UsP

Little Elf, The.  John Kendrick Bangs.  CTV  ("I met a little Elf-man, once.")  PCOP

Little Exercise.  Elizabeth Bishop.  NCSH; UnPo (1976 ed.)

Little Fan.  James Reeves.  SO

Little Fish.  D. H. Lawrence.  AKE; OxBTC

Little fish swim in the river, big fish swim in the sea.  I Don't Let the Girls Worry My Mind.  *Unknown.*  AmFP

Little fly/ Thy summers play.  The Fly.  Blake.  *Fr.* Songs of Experience.  LAuP; MBPR; OBP; PBMP; PCOP

Little fogs were gathered in every hollow.  The Country Wedding (A Fiddler's Story).  Thomas Hardy.  UnPo (1976 ed.)

Little Fugue.  Sylvia Plath.  ILP (1975 ed.)

Little General, The.  Edwin Muir.  MS

Little ghost.  No TV.  Lilian Moore.  IWK

Little Gidding.  T. S. Eliot.  *Fr.* Four Quartets.  BoReV; FaBoTw (1975 ed.); NoAM; NOBA; NOBE; OAEL-2; OxBTC; TAP

Little Giffen.  Francis Orray Ticknor.  GOA

Little girl crouches with her little brother, A.  The Journey to the Insane Asylum.  Alfred Lichtenstein, *tr. by* Mary Zilzer.  VWA

Little girl dressed, The.  Celebration.  Ray A. Young Bear.  CDW

Little Girl Found, The.  Blake.  *Fr.* Songs of Experience.  MBPR; RRA

Little girl I'd known, The.  Flora.  Ray Fraser.  NeAC

Little Girl Lost, A ("Children of the future age").  Blake.  *Fr.* Songs of Experience.  MBPR; RRA

Little Girl Lost, The ("In futurity/ I prophetic see").  Blake.  *Fr.* Songs of Experience.  MBPR; RRA

Little girl marched around her Christmas tree, A.  Ogden Nash.  *Fr.* The New Nutcracker Suite.  PChr

Little Girl, My String Bean, My Lovely Woman.  Anne Sexton.  RiTi; WBN

Little girl running in the street.  The Lizards of La Brea.  Marc De Baca.  AMV–80

Little Girl Saw Her First Troop Parade, The.  Carl Sandburg.  PBMP

Little Girl with Bands on Her Teeth, The.  Genevieve Taggard.  VGW

Little Girl's Heart.  Reginald Holmes.  CTV

Little girls smearing.  Schoolyard in April.  Kenneth Koch.  PoA

Little goat/ crops/ new grass lying down, The.  April.  Yvor Winters.  RFM

Little gold in law will make, A.  Isabella Whitney.  *Fr.* A Sweet Nosegay, or Pleasant Posy.  WPE

Little Grenade, The.  J. S. Harry.  CAAP; FPA

Little Hat, The.  Barry Schechter.  FiCh

Little hedge-row birds, The.  Old Man Travelling; Animal Tranquillity and Decay, a Sketch.  Wordsworth.  MBPR

Little Horse.  W. S. Merwin.  TH

Little House in Lithuania, The.  Samuel Marshak, *tr. fr. Russian by* Daniel Weissbort.  VWA

Little Hunchback, The.  James Whitcomb Riley.  PeD

Little Hunger.  Richard Murphy.  BIrV

Little Indian, Sioux, or Crow.  Other Children.  Robert Louis Stevenson.  PCOP

Little Ink More or Less, A.  War Is Kind, II.  Stephen Crane.  VoPo

Little Jack Horner/ Sat in a corner.  Mother Goose.  MG; SoSe

Little Jenny Wren.  *Unknown.*  PoPle

Little Jesus.  Francis Thompson.  *See* Ex Ore Infantium.

Little joe gould has lost his teeth and doesn't know where.  E. E. Cummings.  NoAM

Little Joe, the Wrangler.  *Unknown.*  BPAW

Little Joe the Wrangler.  N. Howard Thorp.  FSW

Little Johnny-jump-up said.  Wise Johnny.  Edwina Fallis.  CTV

Little Johnny's Final Letter.  Brian Patten.  LP

Little Johnny's Foolish Invention.  Brian Patten.  BuTh

Little Keats' Soliloquy.  Leon Stokesbury.  NVAP

Little Kingdom I Possess, A.  Louisa May Alcott.  AH, *with music*  (My Kingdom.)  CTV

Little Lady, The.  Russell Edson.  GP

Little Lamb, who made thee?  The Lamb.  Blake.  *Fr.* Songs of Innocence.  CABA (1972 ed.); ExPo (1973 ed.); HeIP; ILP (1975 ed.); LAuP; LCL; LFH; MBPR; NIL; OAEL-2; OxBChV; PAIC; PCOP; PIM; PoIA; RAE; SoSe; STS; TT; UnPo (1976 ed.)

Little-League Baseball Fan.  W. R. Moses.  LiSp; NCSH

Little League Women.  Deena Metzger.  RiTi

Little Learning, A.  Pope.  *Fr.* An Essay on Criticism, Pt. II.  NOBE  ("Little learning is a dangerous thing, A.")  HAP; HoPM (1975 ed.)

Little Lemlem was married, at last.  The Marital Journey.  Hailu Araaya.  MiP

Little Libbie.  Julia A. Moore.  OBAL; PeD

Little light is going by, A.  Firefly.  Elizabeth Madox Roberts.  LCL

Little lonely child am I, A.  The Moon-Child.  William Sharp.  EcS

Little Lost Pup.  Arthur Guiterman.  CTV

Little Louey Comic, The.  Wesley McNair.  FAF

Little lute, when I am gone.  Richard Corbet.  FaBoEE

Little Lyric (of Great Importance).  Langston Hughes.  OBAL

Little madness in the spring, A.  Emily Dickinson.  TAP

Little Maggie.  *Unknown.*  FSW

Little maiden climbed [on] an old man's knee, A.  After the Ball Is Over.  Charles K. Harris.  BLSo; FSN; FSW

Little maidens when you look.  Acrostic.  "Lewis Carroll."  NIL

Little Man That Had a Little Gun, The. "Lewis Carroll." FaBoNo

Little Man Who Wasn't There, The. Hughes Mearns. CTV (Case, A.) FaBoCo

Little Marg'et sitting in her high hall door. Fair Margaret and Sweet William. *Unknown.* AmFP

Little marsh-plant, yellow green, A. The Sundew. Swinburne. VLP

Little Mary Bell had a fairy in a nut. Long John Brown and Little Mary Bell. Blake. InPK

Little masters, hat in hand. Clover. John Banister Tabb. PCOP

Little Militant, The. John Shaw Neilson. MAuV

Little Miss and Her Parrot. John Marchant. OxBChV

Little Miss Limberkin. Mary Mapes Dodge. MN

Little Miss Muffett. Mother Goose. MG

Little Miss Muffet discovered a tuffet. The Embarrassing Episode of Little Miss Muffet. Guy Wetmore Carryl. PoTa

Little Mrs. Whitefoot Mouse. Winter Mouse. Aileen Fisher. MN

Little Mohea, The. *Unknown.* AmFP (Little Mohee.) FSW

Little More About the Brothers and Sisters, A. Sharon Scott. JB

Little Moses. *Unknown.* FSW

Little moths are creeping, The. Interior. Padraic Colum. PFIr

Little Musgrave and Lady Barnard, *diff. versions. Unknown.* AmFP; FaBoBa; PeBB

Little Nancy Etticoat. Mother Goose. IP; MG

Little nearer, this time, A. After the Second Operation. Patricia Goedicke. AAN; TAP

Little Ode. Paul Goodman. PoA

Little Old Man. Charlotte Zolotow. TVo

Little old shack. Home. Robert V. Carr. BPAW

Little Old Sod Shanty. *Unknown.* AmFP (Little Old Sod Shanty on My Claim, The.) FSW (Little Old Sod Shanty on the Claim, The.) BPAW

Little old woman, A. Good Neighbors. May Justus. MN

Little Old Women, The. Baudelaire, *tr. fr. French by* Barbara Gibbs. LoAs

Little onion lay by the fireplace, A. Song. Nicholas Moore. EAS

Little onward lend thy guiding hand, A. Samson Agonistes. Milton. OAEL-1

Little Orphant Annie. James Whitcomb Riley. OBAL; OxBChV

Little oxenfaced girls bump down together, The. Shabbytown Fugue. Thomas W. Shapcott. FPA

Little Papoose. Arthur Chapman. BPAW

Little Peach, The. Eugene Field. OBAL

Little Phoebe. *Unknown.* FSW

Little Pig, The. Zishe Landau, *tr. fr. Yiddish by* Ruth Whitman. VWA

Little Piggy. Thomas Hood. ECBV

Little Pigs Lie in the Best of Straw, *with music. Unknown.* RDB

Little Plant, The. Kate Louise Brown. PCOP

Little plant that never sang before, The. Lydia H. Sigourney. *Fr.* On the Death of Mrs. Felicia Hemans. PeD

Little Political Poem. Edward Hirsch. AMV-81

Little Poll Parrot/ Sat in his garret. Mother Goose. MN

Little Pollie Pillikins. A-Apple Pie. Walter de la Mare. MN

Little Polly Flinders. Mother Goose. MG

Little priest of Felton, The. Mother Goose. MN

Little ragged girl, our ball-boy, A. A Game at Salzburg. Randall Jarrell. NoAM

Little Raindrops. Jane Euphemia Browne. OxBChV

Little Red Riding Hood. Nila NorthSun. GP

Little robber girl, you sleep. The Story of Good. Phyllis Janik. IHMS

Little Robin Red-breast sat upon a tree. Mother Goose. CTV

Little Rosewood Casket. *Unknown.* FSW

Little saint best fits a little shrine, A. A Ternarie of Littles, upon a Pipkin of Jelly Sent to a Lady. Robert Herrick. ECBV

Little Sally Racket. *Unknown.* FSW

Little Sally Waters, 2 *versions. Unknown.* AmFP (Little Sally Walker.) FSW

Little Scraping, A. Robinson Jeffers. NoAM

Little Searcher, The. Donna Bowen. AMV-80

Little Shon a Morgan, shentleman of Wales. Shon a Morgan. *Unknown.* GBP

Little Sis. David Kherdian. AMV-80

Little Sleep's-Head Sprouting Hair in the Moonlight. Galway Kinnell. RRA

Little slice of humanity, A. Tied under My Heart. Judith Smallshaw. PMW

Little soul so sleek and smiling. The Emperor Hadrian to His Soul. Emperor Hadrian, *tr. by* Stevie Smith. OBVE

Little Sparrow. *Unknown.* AmFP (Come All You Fair and Tender Ladies, *diff. version.*) FSW

Little squirrel/ In the tree. Mirror for Myself. Roger Wescott. PCOP

Little Star, The. *Unknown.* SpRo

Little Stone in the Middle of the Road, in Florida, A. Muriel Rukeyser. RiTi

Little Things. Julia A. Carney. CTV; OxBChV

Little Things. James Stephens. ECBV; PCOP

Little thinks, in the field, yon red-cloaked clown. Each and All. Emerson. AmVN; ILP (1975 ed.); NOBA; PiAm; TAP

Little think'st thou, poor flower. The Blossom. John Donne. AnMo; PF; UnPo (1976 ed.)

Little tiny puppy dog. Spike Milligan. GDP

Little to write about. Sea Variations. R. A. Simpson. CAAP

Little toe, big toe, three toes between. Close Quarters. John Banister Tabb. OBAL

Little Tom Tucker. Mother Goose. MG

Little Tommy Tittlemouse. *Unknown.* MG

Little toy dog is covered with dust, The. Little Boy Blue. Eugene Field. CTV; OBAL; PCOP; SoSe

Little train called 29, A. Number 29. *Unknown.* BluL

Little tree. E. E. Cummings. Chansons Innocentes, II. CC; LCL; PChr; RAE

Little Trotty Wagtail. John Clare. PB; UnPo (1976 ed.)

Little Turtle, The. Vachel Lindsay. CTV; LCL; OBAL; PCOP; RAE;

Little Vagabond, The. Blake. *Fr.* Songs of Experience. MBPR; OBSV

Little Wee Man, The. *Unknown, at. to* Ian Serraillier. *See* Wee Wee Man, The.

Little While, A. Horatius Bonar. VLP

Little While, A, *sel.* Emily Brontë. "There is a spot, 'mid barren hills." PES

Little While, A. Dante Gabriel Rossetti. ILP (1975 ed.); VLP

Little White Rose, The. Compton Mackenzie. MS

Little Willie from his mirror. *Unknown.* PoPle

Little Wind. Kate Greenaway. CTV; RAE

Little word in kindness spoken, A. *Unknown.* CTV

Little Wren of tender mind, The. The Wren. *Unknown.* OxBChV

Little Yellow Leaf. James Tate. NoAM

Littoral. Hjalmar Flax, *tr. fr. Spanish by* Julio Marzán. InW

Liu Ch'e. Ezra Pound. OBVE; VGW

Live and Let Live. Langston Hughes. ILP (1975 ed.)

Live fowl squatting on the grapefruit and bananas, The. Jamaican Bus Ride. A. S. J. Tessimond. OxBTC

Live, live with me, and thou shalt see. To Phyllis [or Phillis], to Love and Live with Him. Robert Herrick. CaPo; LoAs

Live lizard, dead lizard. Witches' Menu. Sonja Nikolay. IWK

Live Man's Epitaph. Francis Hope. BuTh

Live so that you. Certain Maxims of Archy. Don Marquis. OBAL

Live thy life,/ Young and old. The Oak. Tennyson. CTV; PPM; SoSe

Live with Me. Mick Jagger and Keith Richard. InPK

Live you by love confined. C. Day Lewis. Fr. The Magnetic Mountain. PoPle

Liver. Coleman Barks. Fr. Body Poems. NVAP

Liverockie, liverockie lee. The Lark. Unknown. GBP

Liverpool. Unknown. AmFP

Lives. Gerald Dawe. AMV-81

Lives. Lawrence Russ. TC

Lives of great men all remind us. After Emerson. Unknown. NOBL

Lives of the Poet. Ron Miles. AMV-81

Lives of the Poets, The, sel. George Mattingly. "After a long evening waiting For John Wayne." AcAn

Lives of the Saints. Jon Anderson. FiCP

Lives of the Saints. Paul Muldoon. IPM

Livid sky on London, A. The Old Song. G. K. Chesterton. FaBoTw (1975 ed.)

Living, sel. Charles Bukowski. "I mean, I just slept." OSP

"Living, A." W. S. Di Piero. AMV-80

Living, A. D. H. Lawrence. RFM

Living. Denise Levertov. VGW; WPE "Red salamander, A," sel. OSP

Living, The. Raymond Ward. ATNZ

Living, A. Making a living. "A Living." W. S. Di Piero. AMV-80

"Living a life." A Man. Denise Levertov. TVo

Living ahead of people—a dangerous habit. In the Evening as from a Cradle. Robert Bloom. AATT

Living being, the Temple was killed, A. The Temple. Gustave Kahn, tr. by Edouard Roditi. VWA

Living by the Red River. James Wright. NNaP

Living/Dying. Peter Steele. GAS

Living in a wide landscape are the flowers. Desert Flowers. Keith Douglas. FaBoTw (1975 ed.)

Living in an old house. Great-Aunts. Séan O'Críadáin. PFIr

Living in Another Man's House. Tom O'Grady. AAN

Living in Sin. Adrienne Rich. FF; IHMS; RiTi; SoSe (1977 ed.); TAP; UnPo (1976 ed.)

Living in the Boneyard. John Oliver Simon. NeAC

Living in the earth-deposits of our history. Power. Adrienne Rich. TAP

Living in the Moment. Marilyn Hacker. NYP

Living in the Present. Clarinda Harriss Lott. AMV-81

Living man is blind and drinks his drop, A. W. B. Yeats. Fr. A Dialogue of Self and Soul. PoIA

Living Marble. Arthur O'Shaughnessy. VLP

Living on the river I am able to dip my feet in darkness. One Foot in the River. Gerald Stern. NYP

Living paradise of flowers. Merioneth. John Machreth Rees, tr. by Kenneth Jackson. OBW

Living Poetry. Hugo Margenat, tr. fr. Spanish by Julio Marzán. InW

Living room walks softly on Bukara, The. Oriental. Napoleon St. Cyr. FAF

Living someplace else is wrong. The Spring Offensive of the Snail. Marge Piercy. TAP; WBN

Living swim through their photographs, The. Profile. Bronwen Wallace. AMV-81

Living Tenderly. May Swenson. BoAnP

Living There. James Dickey. UsP

Living Truth, The. Sterling Plumpp. PoBA

Living Values, The. Stephen Spender. NIL

Living with a Voodoo Doll. John Stone. CoPAm

Living with Chris. Ted Berrigan. NoAM

Living with the Fat Man. Michael Delp. TC

Living with You. Angela Langfield. FF

Lizard. D. H. Lawrence. BoAnP

Lizard, The. Ruth Lechlitner. AMV-81

Lizard. Alan McLean. BoAnP

Lizard, The. Edwin Markham. BPAW

Lizard. Paul Mills. MIS

Lizard and the Yellow Dandelion, The ("The lizard is wearing a dandelion"). Mark Wangberg. TC

Lizard, lover of heat, of high. The Old Man to the Lizard. Archibald MacLeish. PiAm

Lizard ran out on a rock and looked up, listening, A. Lizard. D. H. Lawrence. BoAnP

Lizards and Snakes. Anthony Hecht. NCSH; PPoD

Lizards of La Brea, The. Marc De Baca. AMV-80

Lizie Wan. Unknown. AmFP; PeBB

Lizzie Borden with an axe. The Crimes of Lizzie Borden. Unknown. FaBoCo

Llama, The. Hilaire Belloc. FaBoNo

Llanberis Summer. Marianne Loyd. AMV-81

Lloyd George. Unknown. FaBoCo

Lloyd George and Woodrow Wilson and Clemenceau. A Legend of Versailles. Melvin B. Tolson. BPo

Llyn y Gadair. Thomas Herbert Parry-Williams, tr. fr. Welsh by Anthony Conran. OBW

Lo! A Child Is Born. "Hugh MacDiarmid." MS

Lo, alas, I look and seek. The Ageing Hunter. Avane, tr. fr. Eskimo. WTO

Lo, as a careful housewife runs to catch. Sonnets, CXLIII. Shakespeare. BiP; ILP (1975 ed.); InPK

Lo as I pause in the alien vale of the airport. Twenty-third Flight. Earle Birney. HeIP

Lo, between the myrtles standing. Ann Griffiths, tr. fr. Welsh by H. Idris Bell. OBW

Lo, Collin, here the place whose pleasaunt syte. June. Spenser. Fr. The Shepheardes Calender. PAIC

Lo! Death has reared himself a throne. The City in the Sea. Poe. AmVN; EcS; ILP (1975 ed.); MAT; NOBA; PiAm; TAP

Lo, for I to myself am unknown. Jalal al-Din Rumi, tr. fr. Persian. ILwL

Lo freedom comes. Th' prescient muse foretold. Liberty and Peace. Phillis Wheatley. SBG

Lo from our loitering ship a new land at last to be seen. Iceland First Seen. William Morris. VLP

Lo here I sit at holy head. Holyhead, Sept. 25th, 1727. Swift. BIrV

Lo, how it gleams and glistens in the sun. The New Cake of Soap. Ezra Pound. PAIC

Lo! I am come to autumn. Gold Leaves. G. K. Chesterton. OxBTC

Lo! I have learned of the loveliest lands. Unknown, tr. by Charles W. Kennedy. Fr. The Phoenix. OAEL-1

Lo! I must tell a tale of chivalry. Specimen of an Induction to a Poem. Keats. MBPR

Lo! I the man, whose Muse whylome did maske. The Faerie Queene, I, Induction. Spenser. OAEL-1; PAIC

Lo! I will tell the dearest of dreams. The Dream of the Rood. *Unknown, tr. by* Charles W. Kennedy. OAEL-1

Lo! in the middle of the wood. Tennyson. *Fr.* The Lotus-Eater. GrRo

Lo! lemman swete, now may thou see. Christ's Plea to Mankind. *Unknown.* OxBM

Lo, Lord, Thou ridest! The Hurricane. Hart Crane. CMoP (1970 ed.)

Lo, Love's obey'd by all. 'Tis right. The Impossibility. Coventry Patmore. *Fr.* The Angel in the House. VLP

Lo now four other act upon the stage. Of the Four Ages of Man. Anne Bradstreet. EAP

Lo now he shineth yonder. Epitaph on Prince Henry. Hugh Holland. FaBoEE

Lo! now with red rent cloak and bonnet black. George Crabbe. *Fr.* Phoebe Dawson. EBEV

Lo, quhat it is to love. *See* Lo! what it is to lufe.

Lo, the moon's self! Phases of the Moon. Robert Browning. *Fr.* One Word More. Moon

Lo, the poor Indian! whose untutor'd mind. Pope. *Fr.* An Essay on Man. NU

Lo! the Sun, among the daughters. Sunset in the Sea. Tom Hood. FaBoNo

Lo, thus, as prostrate, "In the dust I write." The City of Dreadful Night. James Thomson ("B. V."). NOBE; VLP; VPC

Lo! 'tis a gala night. The Conqueror Worm. Poe. *Fr.* Ligeia. DL; NOBA; PiAm

Lo! we have listened to many a lay. Beowulf. *Unknown, tr. by* Charles W. Kennedy. OAEL-1

Lo, What Enraptured Songs of Praise, *with music.* Sebastian Streeter. AH

Lo! what [*or* quhat] it is to lufe [*or* love]. A Rondel of Luve [*or* Love]. Alexander Scott. BoLoP; SLP

Lo! where the four mimosas blend their shade. For an Epitaph at Fiesole. Walter Savage Landor. FaBoEE

Lo! where the rosy-bosom'd hours. Ode on the Spring. Thomas Gray. LAuP

Lo worms enjoy the seat of bliss. Burns. FaBoEE

Loaded. Mary Swope. PoUp

Loaded Hearts. Vicki Viidikas. FPA

Loaded questions, The. Genitals. Coleman Barks. *Fr.* Body Poems. NVAP

Loam and lungs of dreams, The. There Are Many Things That Please Me. Thomas Lux. AAN

Loan that buildt the barn, The. Tom Ball's Barn. Ted Kooser. GP

Lobotomy. Kenneth Pitchford. PoA

Lobster, The. "Lewis Carroll." *See* Alice's Recitation.

Lobster Quadrille, The. "Lewis Carroll." *Fr.* Alice's Adventures in Wonderland, *ch.* 10. OxBChV; PoPle
(Mock Turtle's Song, The.) FaBoNo; VLP, 2 *versions*

Lobsters. Howard Nemerov. AnMo; PBMP

Lobsters in the Window. W. D. Snodgrass. BiP; BoAnP; HeIP; NCSH; PiAm; TAP

Local Destruction. Perry Oldham. AAN

Local groceries are all out of broccoli, The. Against Broccoli. Roy Blount, Jr. OBAL

Local I'll bright my tale on, how. The Children of Greenock. W. S. Graham. FaBoTw (1975 ed.)

Local Man Goes to the Killing Ground, A. James Whitehead. *See* Local Man Remembers the Killing Ground, A.

Local Man Remembers Betty Fuller, A. James Whitehead. GP

Local Man Remembers the Killing Ground, A. James Whitehead. CoPAm
(Local Man Goes to the Killing Ground, A.) CSP

Local Storm, A. Donald Justice. NCSH

Locale, A. Dennis Trudell. AAN

Locate I/ love you. The Language. Robert Creeley. CAPP; IPWM; LoAs; PiAm; TAP

Location. Knute Skinner. MAT

Location of Things, The. Barbara Guest. NYP

Locations. Jim Harrison. AmPA

*Loch Achray* was a clipper tall, The. The Yarn of the *Loch Achray.* John Masefield. PoTa

Loch Brandy. Andrew Young. MS

Loch Leven. Sydney Goodsir Smith. MS

Loch Lomond. *Unknown, at. to* Lady John Scott. BLSH, *with music;* FSW; GSB, *with music*

Loch Ness Monster, The. Tom Buchan. SLP

Lochinvar. Sir Walter Scott. *Fr.* Marmion, V. AIW; BTTM; ECBV; ILP (1975 ed.); NOBE; PoTa; PPM; SLP

Lock, The. Pope. *Fr.* The Rape of the Lock, V. Moon

Locke sank into a swoon. Fragment. W. B. Yeats. ILP (1975 ed.); NoAM; SoSe

Locked arm in arm they cross the way. Tableau. Countee Cullen. PoBA

Locked In. Ingemar Gustafson, *tr. fr. Swedish by* May Swenson. PoTa

Locked in a Home for Les Enfants Dérangés en Dieu. James Nolan. AATT

Lockless Door, The. Robert Frost. NOBA

Locks and Bolts. *Unknown.* FSW

Locksley Hall. Tennyson. EBEV; OAEL-2; PFD; VLP

Locksley Hall, Sixty Years After. Tennyson. PFD
"Authors—essayist, atheist, novelist, realist, rimester," *sel.* PeD

Locus, The. Cid Corman. VGW

Locust Tree in Flower, The. William Carlos Williams. PiAm

Locusts of Silence. Seymour Mayne. VWA

Locusts or Appolyonists, The, *sel.* Phineas Fletcher.
"Now are they met: this armèd with a spade." SCP-2

Lodestoned salmon, hurtling, The. Weir Bridge. Padraic Fallon. CIP

Lodged firmly in my jaw a little tombstone, memorial. Gray's Anatomy. David Malouf. CAAP

Lodged in a flake of bone. Songs. David Steingass. HeS

Lodgers. Julian Tuwim, *tr. fr. Polish by* Isaac Komem. VWA

Lodging, The. George Mackay Brown. MS

Loe! formest of a rout that followd him. Virgil, *tr. by* Earl of Surrey. *Fr.* The Aeneid, II. OBVE

Loftiest spirit that ever flamed in flesh, The. Paul Clause. AATT

Lofty ship from Salcombe came, A. The Salcombe Seaman's Flaunt to the Proud Pirate. *Unknown.* PeBB

Lofty young squire from Portsmouth he came, A. The Golden Glove. *Unknown.* AmFP

Log: 19N 72E. Horace Coleman. SES

Logging. Gary Snyder. *See* Myths and Texts.

Logic. *Unknown.* ECBV

Logic does well at school. Scholars. Walter de la Mare. NoAM

Logical English. *Unknown.* ECBV

Logs, at the door , by the fence. B. E. Baughan. *Fr.* A Bush Section. ATNZ

Lois in Concert. Charles Moorman. AMV-81

Loitering with a Vacant Eye. A. E. Housman. SoSe; WeW

Lollay, Lollay, Little Child! *Unknown.* OxBM

Lolly-Too-Dum. *Unknown. See* Rolly Trudum.

London ("I wander through each chartered street"). Blake. *Fr.* Songs of Experience. AnMo; CABA (1972 ed.); ExPo (1973 ed.); FF; GrRo; HAP; HeIP; ILP (1975 ed.); InPK; InPS; IP; LAuP; LFH; MAT; MBPR; NIL; NOBE; OAEL-2;

OBP; PAIC; PBMP; PoIA; PPoD; STS; TPo; TT; UnPo (1976 ed.); UsP; VoPo; WIF

London. John Davidson. NOBE

London: A Poem in Imitation of the Third Satire of Juvenal. Samuel Johnson. LAuP

*Sels.*
"By numbers here from shame or censure free." OBSV
"Could'st thou resign the park and play content." NIL
"Prepare for death, if here at night you roam." OAEL-1

London after the Great Fire, 1666. Dryden. *Fr.* Annus Mirabilis. NOBE

London Beautiful. Richard Le Gallienne. PES

London Bridge Is a-Burning Down. *Unknown.* AmFP

London Bridge [is broken down]. *Unknown.* BBL; GBP; MG; NIL

London Bridge was built. Stranger than the Worst. Babette Deutsch. WPE

London, 1802 ("Milton! thou shouldst be living..."). Wordsworth. BiP; CABA (1972 ed.); Epi; ExPo (1973 ed.); FF; HAP; HeIP; ILP (1975 ed.); IPWM; LFH; MBPR; NIL; OBP; PAIC; PBMP (Milton.) FaPoR

London Fete, A. Coventry Patmore. HAP; VPC

London, hast thow accused me. Earl of Surrey. AAS

London, I heard one say, no more is fair. London Beautiful. Richard Le Gallienne. PES

London is full of chickens, on electric spits. Peter Porter. *Fr.* Annotations of Auschwitz. OxBTC

"London: John Lane, The Bodley Head." On the Imprint of the First English Edition of "The Works of Max Beerbohm." Max Beerbohm. InPK

London Lickpenny. *Unknown.* OBSV; OxBM

London Pavement Artist. James Schevill. TAP

London Rain. Louis MacNeice. HeIP

London Snow. Robert Bridges. CMoP (1970 ed.); EBEV; FSFS; ILP (1975 ed.); NoAM; NOBE; OAEL-2; OxBTC; VLP

London Sparrow's If, A. J. A. Lindon. BoAnP

London, thou art of townes A *per se.* To the City of London. William Dunbar. EBEV

London Tom-Cat. Michael Hamburger. BoAnP

London Voluntaries, *sels.* W. E. Henley.
"High majesty of Paul's, The." PES
"Out of the poisonous East." VLP

Londoners Gent to the King do present, The. On the Lord Mayor and Court of Aldermen, Presenting the Late King and Duke of York Each with a Copy of Their Freedoms. Andrew Marvell. APAS; FaBoBa

London's Tempe; or, The Field of Happiness, *sel.* Thomas Dekker.
Thwick-a-thwack. SCP-2

Lone Dog. Irene Rutherford McLeod. DuDr; GDP

Lone flower, hemmed in with snows, and white as they. Flowers of January. Wordsworth. PF

Lone heart, learning. Vigils. Siegfried Sassoon. CMoP (1970 ed.)

Lone knee wanders through the world, A. The Knee on Its Own. Christian Morgenstern, *tr. by* Geoffrey Grigson. FaBoNo

Lone plunge, The/ Of the hawk. Near Ganado. Lucile Adler. PoW

Lone Striker. Robert Frost. PPM

Lone Wild Fowl, The, *with music.* H. R. MacFayden. AH

Loneliness. Hayden Carruth. FiCP

Loneliness. Brooks Jenkins. CTBA; SoS

Loneliness. Sandra McPherson. AMV-80

Loneliness. Loyal Shegonee. VW

Loneliness. Al Young. NVAP; PoBA

Loneliness and July Ninth. Claribel Alegria, *tr. fr. Spanish by* Aliki *and* Willis Barnstone. BoWoP

Loneliness leapt in the mirrors, but all week. Departure's Girl-Friend. W. S. Merwin. ConAP

Lonely and big. First Pregnancy. Alta. NMM

Lonely Boy. John Kitching. FPB

Lonely caravan a- rollin' through the night. Star of the Western Skies. *Unknown.* BPAW

Lonely Love. Edmund Blunden. OxBTC

Lonely Man, The. Randall Jarrell. MPo

Lonely rock above a midnight plain, A. Te Whetu Plains. Edward Tregear. ATNZ

Lonely, save for a few faint stars, the sky. The Little Dancers. Laurence Binyon. BBGO; OxBTC

Lonely Scarecrow, The. James Kirkup. RAE

Lonely Street, The. William Carlos Williams. PoA

Lonesome Dove ("Down in some lonesome piney grove"), 3 *versions. Unknown.* AmFP

Lonesome Dove, The ("Ye weary, heavy laden souls"). *Unknown.* AmFP

Lonesome in the Country. Al Young. MAT; SA

Lonesome on the cliffside. Legend. Frederick Morgan. PoIA

Lonesome scenes of winter incline to frost and snow, The. The Rejected Lover. *Unknown.* AmFP

Lonesome Valley, The. *Unknown.* FSW; RDB, *with music*

Long after dark. Scroll. Stanley Moss. VWA

Long after his great carapace was wrenched. Sea Turtle. Liston Pope. AMV-80

Long after the sun has gone down. Before Battle: [The Lincolns at Villanueva de la Canada]. James Neugass. SPT

Long after we are gone. Lupine Ridge. Peggy Simson Curry. WPW

Long after you have swung back. Losing Track. Denise Levertov. AnMo; ExPo (1973 ed.); HeIP; NoAM; NOBA; SoSe

Long afterward, Oedipus, old and blinded. Myth. Muriel Rukeyser. IHMS; NNaP

Long afterwards/ the intelligent could deduce. The Judgment of Paris. W. S. Merwin. NNaP; UsP

Long ago he had walked. Rimbaud in Abyssinia. Ellen McEvilley Griffin. NPW

Long ago how fine was everything! Disillusion. *Tr. fr. Tewa Indian by* H. J. Spinden. WTO

Long ago in the north. Songs in the Turtle Dance at Santa Clara. *Tr. fr. Tewa Indian by* H. J. Spinden. WTO

Long ago some one carved me in the semblance of a god. From the Stone Age. Alice Corbin. WPW

Long ago, the Mountain Mother. Chorus. Euripides, *tr. by* Richmond Lattimore. *Fr.* Helen. RRA

Long ago when I shouted in red letters. Aubade. Ruth Lechlitner. AMV-80

Long and Lazy. Robert Herrick. FaBoEE

Long and Shadowy Habits. Gene Frumkin. PoW

Long and Short Life. Edmund Waller. NIL

Long as the Darkening Cloud Abode, *with music.* George Richards. AH

Long Barren. Christina Rossetti. PBWP; VLP

Long Beach, 1975. Merrill Leffler. PoUp

Long beardes heartles. The English. *Unknown.* GBP

Long before a woman knows she's pregnant. Progression of the Species. Brian W. Aldiss. FF

Long before morning they waked me to say. The Lunar Probe. Maxine W. Kumin. Moon

Long before the sun cast a shadow. Gathering the Sparks. Howard Schwartz. VWA

Long blue shadow of a salmon lying. Joseph Gordon Macleod ("Adam Drinan"). *Fr.* The Ghosts of the Strath. MS

Long canoe, The. Lullaby. Robert Hillyer. DuDa

Long curved room, the walls, The. Monet's Les Nymphéas. Lyn Lifshin. FAF

Long desired, the dead return. They Return. Jay MacPherson. *Fr.* The Way Down. PoA

Long-Distance. Carol Burns. AMV-81

Long Distance. Patrick L. Clary. PoUp

Long Distance. Dana Naone. CDW; PHC

Long Distance. William Stafford. CoPAm; SO

Long distance information, get me Memphis, Tennessee. Memphis, Tennessee. Chuck Berry. RRA

Long Distance Moan. *Unknown.* BluL

Long, Dodington, in debt, I long have sought. Edward Young. *Fr.* Love of Fame, the Universal Passion: Satire III. LAuP

Long-expected one and twenty. A Short Song of Congratulation [*or* To a Young Heir]. Samuel Johnson. CABA (1972 ed.); EBEV; HAP; ILP (1975 ed.); InPK; InPS; IP;LAuP; NOBE; OBSV; UnPo (1976 ed.)

"Long Fox led against the Sioux a war-party that captured seven." The Landscape. David Ray. EC

Long Gone. Sterling A. Brown. BPo

Long had passed the hour of midnight. Dawn. *Malay Oral Tradition, tr. by* R. J. Wilkinson. WTO

Long had this nation been amused in vain. The Spanish Descent. Daniel Defoe. APAS

Long Haiku No. 7. Louis Cuneo. CPA

Long Hair. Gary Snyder. NOBA; PiAm

Long hair tangled. Sedna. Lyn Lifshin. MMD

Long-haired preachers come out every night. The Preacher and the Slave. Joe Hill. FSW; GBP; WTo

Long Harbour, The. Mary Ursula Bethell. ATNZ

Long has he been of that amphibious fry. Portrait of a Physician. Sir Samuel Garth. *Fr.* The Dispensary. PMW

Long hast thou, friend! been absent from thy soil. Mr. Pope's Welcome from Greece. John Gay. EBEV

Long hath my sufferance labored to inforce. Thomas Lodge. Phillis, IV. ESo

Long have I beat with timid hands upon life's leaden doors. The Suppliant. Georgia Douglas Johnson. PoBA

Long Hill, The. Sara Teasdale. PPM

Long Hunter, The. Wendell Berry. *Fr.* Inland Passages. GP

Long I Thought That Knowledge Alone Would Suffice. Walt Whitman. NOBA

Long in thy shackles, liberty. To Lucasta, from Prison. Richard Lovelace. CaPo

Long is the night. Curriculum Vitae. Ingeborg Bachmann, *tr. by* Jerome Rothenberg. BoWoP

Long Island Night, The. Howard Moss. PCho

Long Island Springs. Howard Moss. GP; UnPo (1976 ed.)

Long John  *Unknown.* FSW

Long John Brown and Little Mary Bell. Blake. InPK

Long lane of black timber huts, The. Geriatric Huts. Michael Smith. IPM

Long-legged Fly. W. B. Yeats. AnMo; CMoP (1970 ed.); FaBoTw; (1975 ed.); InPK; InPS; NoAM; NOBE; PPoe; PSN; TT

Long legs, crooked thighs. Mother Goose. GBP; MG

Long lilies in a blue jug. Crockery. Julia Budenz. AMV-80

Long-Line Skinner. *Unknown.* FSW

Long Lines. Paul Goodman. VGW

Long live our dear and noble Queen. Edward Edwin Foot. *Fr.* On the Inauguration of the Memorial Statue. FaBoCo

Long Live the Weeds. Theodore Roethke. NoAM; NOBA; PoA; PoIA

Long Lonely Lover of the Highway. Frederic Will. AMV-81

Long, Long Ago. Thomas Haynes Bayly. BLSH, *with music;* BLSo, *with music;* FSW; PSoN, *with music*

Long, Long Ago. *Unknown.* CTV (*At. to* Katherine Parker); PChr; RAE

Long long ago when the world was a wild place. Bedtime Story. George MacBeth. LP; MPo; NoAM; PoTa; SoSe

Long, long legs, The. From the Country to the City. Elizabeth Bishop. NYP

Long[e] love, that in my thought doth harbour, The. The Lover for Shamefastnesse Hideth His Desire within His Faithfull Hart. Petrarch, *tr. by* Sir Thomas Wyatt. Sonnets to Laura: To Laura in Life, CIX. AAS; CABA (1972 ed.); Epi; ILP (1975 ed.); NIL; OAEL-1; OBVE

Long May. Rosalía de Castro, *tr. fr. Galician by* Benjamin M. Woodbridge, Jr. PBWP

Long Melford church is built of flint and glass. Concert at Long Melford Church. Patricia Beer. HeHu

Long morning covered in fog, The. Waiting. Fay Enos. PHC

Long Overdue Thankyou Note to the Girl Who Taught Me Loving, A. Tom Schmidt. NeAC

Long Person. Gladys Cardiff. CDW

Long placid evening. Tune: The Butterfly Woos the Blossoms. Li Ching-chao, *tr. by* C. H. Kwock *and* Vincent McHugh. PBWP

Long Prologue to a Short Play, A. Sir Henry Sheers. APAS

Long red underwear of Randolph Scott, The. Ride the High Country. David Slavitt. PPoD

Long River, The. Donald Hall. ConAP

Long Road West, The. Henry Herbert Knibbs. BPAW

Long-rolling, The. The Main-Deep. James Stephens. EcS; UnPo (1976 ed.)

Long schoolroom days, drowsy with chanting voices. Photograph of an Actress, c. 1860. Nan McDonald. MAuV

Long Season, The. James Haug. AMV-81

Long steel grass. Trio for Two Cats and a Trombone. Edith Sitwell. PBWP

Long straggling lines. Wild Geese. William Hart-Smith. BoAnP

Long Summer, sel. Robert Lowell.
"Everyone now is crowding everyone." CAPP

Long-Suffering of God. Christopher Smart. *Fr.* Hymns for the Amusement of Children. LAuP

Long Tail Blue, with music. *Unknown.* BLSo

Long Term Suffering. Richard Eberhart. GP

Long they pine in weary woe, the nobles of our land. Kathaleen Ny-Houlahan. James Clarence Mangan. VLP

Long tides shudder over hidden rock, The. By Winter Seas. George Brandon Saul. AMV-80

Long Time Ago, A. *Unknown.* AmFP

Long Time Apart, A. Mari Kubo. PHC

Long Time Gone. David Crosby. WIF

Long time he lay upon the sunny hill. Childhood. Edwin Muir. CMoP (1970 ed.); HeIP

Long time Plain Dealing in the haughty town. Plain Dealing's Downfall. *Unknown.* OBSV

Long time since it seems to-day, A. W. H. Auden. *Fr.* A New Year Letter. GOA

Long time you have been making the trip, A. Of Hartford in a Purple Light. Wallace Stevens. ILP (1975 ed.)

Long Tom. W. W. Gibson. OxBTC

Long, Too Long America. Walt Whitman. GOA; NoAM

Long Voyage, The. Malcolm Cowley. SoSe

Long Walks in the Afternoon. Margaret Gibson. AMV-81

Long War, The. Laurie Lee. BuTh

Long Waters, The. Theodore Roethke. CNW

Long Way outside Yellowstone, A. Thomas McGrath. VGW

Long ways, A. A Remembrance of a Color inside a Forest. Ray A. Young Bear. CDW

Long whip lingers, the. Horses. Louis MacNeice. PH

Long white barn, A. *Unknown.* GBP

Long Will in London. William Langland. *Fr.* The Vision of Piers Plowman. OxBM

Long Word, The. Deirdre Ballantyne. AMV-80

Long years ago I wandered here. On Recrossing the Rocky Mountains after Many Years. John Charles Frémont. BPAW

Longe love that in my thought doth harbour, The. *See* Long love...

Longest and much the dearest. Book Review. Russell Davies. FaBoEE

Longest Day, The. Wordsworth. RRA

Longest days are those spent at sea, The. Home from Sea. Burns Singer. MS

Longest Tale about the Longest Tail, The. Alexander Resnikoff. OSF

Longface Mahoney Discusses Heaven. Horace Gregory. VGW

Longfellow's Visit to Venice. John Betjeman. NOBL

Longford Legend, A. *Unknown.* PoTa

Longing, The. William Goodreau. AMV-80

Longing. Rachel Korn, *tr. fr. Yiddish by* Ruth Whitman. VWA

Longing, The. Theodore Roethke. PiAm

Longing. *Gond Oral Tradition, tr. by* V. Elwin *and* S. Hivale. WTO

Longing at twilight the lovesick Adam saw. The Begetting of Cain. Hyam Plutzik. VWA

Longing for speed the Pontiac ascends the land in dusk. For an Indian Bronc Killed in a Highway Crash near Ethete, Wyoming. Robert Roripaugh. PoW

Longing for the Emperor. Empress Iwa no Hime, *tr. fr. Japanese by* Geoffrey Bownas *and* Anthony Thwaite. BoWoP

Longing for the Persimmon Tree. Millen Brand. TAT

Longing that moves me in a second, heavier body, The. The Apartment Hunter. Philip Schultz. NYP

Longjaunes His Periplus, *sel.* Howard McCord. "My father gave me the freedom of love." GP

Longshore Intellectual. Sean Lucy. CIP

Look, The. Elizabeth Daryush. PoA

Look at him there in his stovepipe hat. American Primitive. William Jay Smith. CoPAm; FF; InPK; SFF; TPo; UsP; WIF

Look at it! The Photo. Lennart Bruce. MIT

Look at it well. This was the good town once. The Good Town. Edwin Muir. CMoP (1970 ed.)

Look at me. Caption, Circa 1972. Lawson Fusao Inada. FoP

Look at me 8th. Poem. Sonia Sanchez. PoBA

Look at me move. The Amputee Soldier. Philip Dacey. NVAP

Look at me: my mouth unlearned complaining early. Mother of Fishermen. Henriëtte Roland-Holst, *tr. by* Ria Leigh-Loohuizen. PBWP

Look at my continent containing. Human Geography. Gloria Fuertes, *tr. by* Willis Barnstone. BoWoP

Look at My Face, a Collage. Carolyn M. Rodgers. JB

Look at that Mountain Jalgumbun standing up The Myth and the Mountain. Roland Robinson. GAS

Look at the gentle savage, monstrous gentleman. London Tom-Cat. Michael Hamburger. BoAnP

Look at the mare of Farmer Giles! The Mare. Herbert Asquith. DuDr; PH

Look at the stars! look, look up at the skies! The Starlight Night. Gerard Manley Hopkins. ExPo (1973 ed.); ILP (1975 ed.); InPS;PoPle; PPP; VLP

Look at the steady rifles, Joe. Joe Hill Listens to the Praying. Kenneth Patchen. SPT

Look at this man in the room before you. Room with Revolutionists. Edwin Rolfe. SPT

"Look at us now, destroyed." The Dead Cities Speak to the Living Cities. Edmond Fleg, *tr. by* Anthony Rudolf. VWA

Look at wealth through warm, misty rain. Looking at Wealth in Newport. James Schevill. TAT

Look between the bow and the bowstring, beneath. Backgrounds to Italian Paintings: Fifteenth Century. Anne Ridler. WPE

Look, bored middle mania. Other Books by the Author? Mbembe. NW

Look Closely. Morton Marcus. FF; SFF

Look, Delia, how we esteem the half-blown rose. Samuel Daniel. *Fr.* To Delia. HeIP; ILP (1975 ed.)

Look Down Fair Moon. Walt Whitman. Moon

Look Down That Lonesome Road, *with music. Unknown.* BLSo

Look for a place in my skin that may not have been. That Which You Call "Love Me." Luis Rosales, *tr. by* Lynn C. Jacox. AMV-81

Look! From my window there's a view. There Is. Louis Simpson. ConAP

Look how evening comes and around us the barbed-wire-hemmed, wild. Seventh Eclogue. Miklós Radnóti, *tr. by* Emery George. VWA

Look how he shakes for cold! Crucifixus pro Nobis. Patrick Carey. SCP-2

Look how the pale Queen of the silent night. A Sonnet of the Moon. Charles Best. Moon; SoSe

Look in my face; my name is Might-have-been. A Superscription. Dante Gabriel Rossetti. The House of Life, XCVII. NOBE; OAEL-2; VLP; VPC

Look in the glass and tell the face thou viewest. Sonnets, III. Shakespeare. CABA (1972 ed.)

"Look, it's a fox!"—their two hearts spoke. The Fox. C. Day Lewis. BoAnP

Look, it's morning, and a little water gurgles in the tap. Morning Song. Alan Dugan. NowV

Look, Loig, behind. The Only Jealousy of Emer. *Unknown, tr. by* John Montague. BIrV

Look, look! rejoice and wonder! The Return of Astraea. Ben Jonson. NOBE

Look, my love, on the wall, and here, at this Eastern picture. Morning. Henry Reed. LoAs

Look not thou on beauty's charming. Lucy Ashton's Song. Sir Walter Scott. *Fr.* The Bride of Lammermoor, *ch.* 3. NOBE

Look Not Too Deep, *sel.* Laurence Binyon. "Sleeplessly circle the waves." EcS

Look now, bride of God. In Praise of Virginity. Hroswitha, *tr. by* John Dillon. PBWP

Look off, dear Love, across the sallow sands. Evening Song. Sidney Lanier. UnPo (1976 ed.)

Look one way and the sun is going down. The Mockingbird. Randall Jarrell. DuDa; RFM

Look out how you use proud words. Primer Lesson. Carl Sandburg. OSP; SFF; TH

Look out! Look out, boys! Clear the track! Oliver Wendell Holmes. *Fr.* The Broomstick Train. IWK

Look, stranger, on this island now. On This Island. W. H. Auden. CMoP (1970 ed.); ExPo (1973 ed.); InPS; MPo; PSN

Look, the eucalyptus, the atlas pine. Any Night. Philip Levine. AMV-80

Look there at the star! Shepherd's Song at Christmas. Langston Hughes. PChr

Look to the Back of the Hand. Judith Minty. PoA

Look up! Eagle Feather IV. Phillip William George. NW

Look up! and not down. Lend a Hand. Edward Everett Hale. PCOP

Look up into the dome. Altitudes. Richard Wilbur. CMoP (1970 ed.)

Look up, old stranger. Two: Long After. Alfons Korn. PHC

Look up, you men. Men there at the fire. Rainer Maria Rilke. *Fr.* Annunciation over the Shepherds. PChr

Look! We are the depression bastards! Upsurge. Robert Gessner. SPT

Look where the mist. The Mist over Pukehina. *Maori Oral Tradition, tr. by* E. Shortland. WTO

Look you, my simple friend, 'tis one of those. Arthur Hugh Clough. VLP

Looke how the woods, where enterlaced trees. Bible, *O.T., paraphrased by* Countess of Pembroke. *Fr.* Psalms. OBVE

Looked stitched together and. Reuben's Cabin. Robert Morgan. TAT

Looking as I've looked before, straight down the heart. The Stranger. Adrienne Rich. NNaP

Looking at a Dead Wren in My Hand. Robert Bly. GP; NNaP

Looking at a Dry Canadian Thistle Brought In from the Snow. Robert Bly. NNaP

Looking at Each Other. Muriel Rukeyser. NNaP

Looking at Kapiti. Alistair Campbell. ATNZ

Looking at Models in the Sears Catalogue. Philip Dacey. HeS

Looking at Pictures to Be Put Away. Gary Snyder. CoPAm; FF; InPS; NNaP

Looking at Power. Warren Woessner. AMV-80

Looking at Some Flowers. Robert Bly. NOBA

Looking at the Empire State Building. Ralph Pomeroy. GP

Looking at Wealth in Newport. James Schevill. TAT

Looking back in my mind I can see. The Elementary Scene. Randall Jarrell. CMoP (1970 ed.); ExPo (1973 ed.); SoS

Looking Backward. Robert Bly. UsP

Looking Both Ways before Crossing. John Woods. ConAP; IPWM

Looking by chance in at the open window. The Foreboding. Robert Graves. GBL; PoA

Looking cross-country I suddenly saw. Company. Philip Oakes. UsP

Looking Down on West Virginia. John Dickson. AMV-81

Looking eastward from Tablerock. Tablerock. Darryl Wally. AMV-81

Looking for a Place to Be Comfortable. Virginia Gilbert. NVAP

Looking for a Rest Area. Stephen Dunn. AmPA

Looking for Asia. R. H. W. Dillard. CoPAm

Looking for Lola. Morgan Sanders. WBN

Looking for love, she read cookbooks. The Woman Who Loved to Cook. Erica Jong. TAP; WBN

Looking for Maimonides: Tiberias. Shirley Kaufman. VWA

Looking for Mountain Beavers. David Wagoner. VGW

Looking for Mushrooms at Sunrise. W. S. Merwin. NOBA

Looking for Someone. Michael Small. DNGG

Looking for Something? Edward Lowbury. PMW

Looking for the Buckhead Boys. James Dickey. LiSp

Looking Forward. Robert Louis Stevenson. OxBChV

Looking from Oregon. Earle Birney. MPA

Looking-Glass, A. Thomas Carew. CaPo

Looking Glass, The. Kipling. FaBoTw (1975 ed.)

Looking Glass. Martha Webb. PHC

Looking inside the bony plate, perceive. The Salt Lesson. Carol Frost. AAN

Looking into a Face. Robert Bly. NOBA; TSWA

Looking into a Tide Pool. Robert Bly. MAT

Looking into History. Richard Wilbur. VGW

Looking into my daughter's eyes I read. For My Daughter. Weldon Kees. RRA

Looking Out. Helen Chasin. NMM

Looking Out to Sea. Anthony Ostroff. MPA

Looking through the clean lens of sunlight. The Aviators. William Pillin. SPT

Looking to the sea, it is a line. The Innocence. Robert Creeley. NoAM

Looking Up. John Allcock. BuTh

Looking up/ I find myself written. The Paisley Ceiling. Lila Arnold. IHMS

Looking Up at Airplanes, Always. Rolfe Humphries. PAIC

Looking Up at Down. *Unknown.* BluL

Looking up at the stars, I know quite well. The More Loving One. W. H. Auden. HoPM (1975 ed.)

Lookout, The. William Collins. RhR

Loom of Dreams, The. Arthur Symons. VLP

Loon, A? No. Chippewa Love Song. *Tr. by* Frances Densmore, *ad. by* Willis Barnstone. BoWoP

"Loon Call, A." Richard Eberhart. AMV-80

Loon I Thought It Was, A. *Tr. fr. Chippewa Indian by* Frances Densmore. OBVE

Loony, *sels.* William Kloefkorn. GP
　During the War.
　Good Folks at the Camp Meeting, The.

Loose knot of geese crossed the road, vain and squabbling, A. Driving, Driven. David McAleavey. AMV-80

Loose Saraband, A. Richard Lovelace. CaPo

Loose Woman. X. J. Kennedy. WeW

Lopsided love in hotel rooms. Adolescent's Song. Howard Moss. LoAs

Lord/ forgive me/ if I twist the sunset. The Hungry Black Child. Adam David Miller. PoBA

Lord/ We come. A Maze of the Magi. Sandra Ruth Duguid. AATT

Lord,/ we have been watching over him. Act of Faith. Arturo Trías, *tr. by* Julio Marzán. InW

Lord Abbott. Hilaire Belloc. FaBoNo

Lord Apollo, who has never died, The. Many Are Called. E. A. Robinson. PiAm

Lord Arnaldos. James Elroy Flecker. PoTa

Lord, at This Closing Hour, *with music.* Eleazar Thompson Fitch. AH

Lord Barrenstock. Stevie Smith. FaBoNo; OBSV

Lord Bateman. *Unknown.* AmFP; FSW

Lord Bless You and Keep You, The. Bible, *O.T. Fr.* Numbers. BLSH, *with music*
　("Lorde blesse the and kepe the, The," *tr. by* William Tyndale.) OBVE

"Lord Byron" was an Englishman. Sketch of Lord Byron's Life. Julia A. Moore. OBAL

Lord, can a crumb of dust the earth outweigh. Prologue. Edward Taylor. *Fr.* Preparatory Meditations, First Series. EAP

Lord Clive. E. C. Bentley. *Fr.* Clerihews. PoPle
　("What I like about Clive.") NOBL

Lord, confound this surly sister. The Curse. J. M. Synge. FaBoCo; FaBoEE

Lord Coningsby's Epitaph. Pope. FaBoEE

Lord Cozens Hardy. John Betjeman. OxBTC

Lord, Dear God! to Thy Attending, *with music.* Heinrich Otto, *tr. fr. German by* Sheema Z. Buehne. AH

Lord, Deliver, Thou Canst Save, *with music.* Eliza Lee Follen. AH

Lord Derwentwater. *Unknown.* AmFP

Lord Descended from Above, The, *with music.* Thomas Sternhold. AH

Lord, dub my tongue with a new tier of words. Edward Taylor. Preparatory Meditations: Second Series, XIX. SCP-2

Lord Epsom. Hilaire Belloc. PH

Lord Finchley.  Hilaire Belloc.  FaBoCo; FaBoEE; NOBL

Lord Fluting Dreams of America on the Eve of His Departure from Liverpool.  Paul Zimmer.  VGW

Lord God of Hosts, *with music.*  Shepherd Knapp.  AH

Lord god of wings, forgive this hand.  Early Warning.  George MacBeth.  TwMBP

Lord God! this was a stone.  The Stone.  Thomas Vaughan.  OBW

Lord Gorbals.  Harry Graham.  FaBoCo

Lord Has a Child, The, *with music.*  Langston Hughes.  AH

Lord, heavy hip mama she done moved to piney wood.  Piney Wood Money Mama.  *Unknown.*  BluL

Lord here my prayre and let my crye passe.  Bible, *O.T.*  Psalms, CII.  OBVE

Lord, how can man preach thy eternal word?  The Windows.  George Herbert.  AnMo; CABA (1972 ed.); ILP (1975 ed.); NIL; SCP-1

Lord, how delightful 'tis to see.  For the Lord's Day Evening.  Isaac Watts.  OxBChV

Lord how many are my foes.  Bible, *O.T., paraphrased by* Milton.  Psalms, III.  OBVE

Lord, how sholde I roule me.  How Should I Rule Me?  *Unknown.*  OxBM

Lord, I am not one of the just.  Seder, 1944.  Friedrich Torberg, *tr. by* Erna Baber Rosenfeld.  VWA

Lord, I Am Thine, *with music.*  Samuel Davies.  AH

Lord I can't see how these hungry women please.  Don't Want No Hungry Woman.  *Unknown.*  BluL

Lord I hate to hear that Frisco whistle blow.  Frisco Whistle Blues.  *Unknown.*  BluL

Lord, I have leaped my zenith, passed my noon.  The Old Tiger and the God of the Water-Hole.  Margaret Reynolds.  MIS

Lord, I Know Thy Grace Is Nigh Me, *with music.*  Hervey Doddridge Ganse.  AH

Lord, I lie here.  Prayer from a Stryker Frame.  E. Margaret Clarkson.  AATT

Lord, I Want to Be a Christian, *with music.*  Unknown.  AH

Lord, I'm Troublin', *with music.*  Unknown.  BLSH

Lord, in Thy Presence Here, *with music.*  Jesse L. Holman.  AH

Lord into His Garden Comes, The, *with music.*  Unknown.  AH

Lord is my external-internal integrative mechanism, The.  The Twenty-third Psalm.  Alan Simpson.  SFF

Lord is my shepherd, I shall not, The.  Neo-Thomist Poem.  Ernest Hemingway.  OBAL

Lord is my shepherd, I shall not want.  Bible, *O.T.*  Psalms, XXIII.  BiP; CTV; ExPo (1973 ed.); IP; NAWM-1; SFF

Lord[e] is my shepherd[e], The: therefore can I lack nothing.  Bible, *O.T., tr. by* Miles Coverdale.  Psalms, XXIII.  ILwL; OBVE

Lord Is Risen, The.  William Dunbar.  BoReV; NOBE  (Done Is a Battell on the Dragon Blak.)  HAP

Lord Jesus bring your peace to fathers with no luck.  A Christmas Prayer.  William R. Mitchell.  AATT

Lord Jesus Christ, We Humbly Pray, *with music.*  Henry Eyster Jacobs.  AH

Lord! Lead the Way the Saviour Went, *with music.*  William Crosswell.  AH

Lord, Listen.  Else Lasker-Schüler, *tr. fr. German by* Edouard Roditi.  VWA

Lord, lord! methought what pain it was to drown.  Shakespeare.  King Richard III, *fr.* I, iv.  EcS

Lord Lovel.  *Unknown.*  AmFP; FSW  (Tale of Lord Lovell, The.)  NOBL

Lord Lundy.  Hilaire Belloc.  FaBoCo; OBP; OBSV

Lord, make me an instrument of Your peace.  A Simple Prayer.  St. Francis of Assisi.  CTV

"Lord make me the co-ordinator of Thy implementation."  The Educational Administration Professor's Prayer.  Gerald Bobango.  AMV-80

Lord, Many Times Thou Pleased Art, *with music.*  George Wither.  AH

Lord, may it be my choice.  My Choice.  *Unknown.*  CTV

Lord, mind your trees today!  The Bushfeller.  Eileen Duggan.  ATNZ

Lord, mine eye offended.  Matthew V. 29-30.  Derek Mahon.  CIP; IPM

Lord, My Weak Thought in Vain Would Climb, *with music.*  Ray Palmer.  AH

Lord of All Being, Throned Afar, *with music.*  Oliver Wendell Holmes.  AH

Lord of all, himself through all diffused, The.  William Cowper.  *Fr.* The Task, VI.  OAEL-1

Lord of Each Soul, *with music.*  Paul Engle.  AH

Lord of Life, All Praise Excelling, *with music.*  Clement Clarke Moore.  AH

Lord of My Heart's Elation, *with music.*  Bliss Carman.  AH

Lord of Rosslyn's daughter gaed through the wud her lane, The.  Captain Wedderburn's Courtship.  *Unknown.*  SLP

Lord of Sea and Earth and Air.  Prayer for a Pilot.  Cecil Roberts.  CTV

Lord of the Dance.  Sydney Carter.  LP

Lord of the Isles, The, *sel.*  Sir Walter Scott.  "No! sum thine Edith's wretched lot."  SLP

Lord of the Mirrors, *sel.*  George Mackay Brown.  "Beast, what is love?"  SLP

Lord of the Mountain.  Prayer to the Mountain Spirit.  Mary Austin, *after Navajo Indian.*  BPAW

Lord of the winds! I feel thee nigh.  The Hurricane.  Bryant.  EAP

Lord of the Worlds Below! *with music.*  James Freeman.  AH

Lord Our God Alone Is Strong, The, *with music.*  Caleb T. Winchester.  AH

Lord Rameses of Egypt sighed.  Birthright.  John Drinkwater.  OxBTC

Lord Randal.  *Unknown.*  AIW; AmFP; CABA (1972 ed.); EBEV; FaBoBa; FF; HAP; HeIP; HoPM (1975 ed.); ILP (1975 ed.); LFH; NIL, 2 *versions;* OAEL-1, *with music;* PAIC; PoIA; SLP; WeW  (Lord Randall.)  FSW; WIF  (Lord Rendal, *with music.*)  RDB

Lord, serene on your symbol.  Accepting.  Vassar Miller.  FiCP

Lord, shall I find it in Thy Holy Church.  Truth.  Claude McKay.  BPo

Lord, she won't pick cotton girl won't pull no corn.  No More Women Blues.  *Unknown.*  BluL

Lord she's gone done left me done packed/up and split.  Feeling Fucked Up.  Etheridge Knight.  GP; NNaP

Lord Tennyson and Lord Melchett.  D. H. Lawrence.  FaBoEE

Lord, the Roman hyacinths are blooming in bowls.  A Song for Simeon.  T. S. Eliot.  BuTh

Lord they accused me of murder.  Levee Camp Moan.  *Unknown.*  BluL

Lord, this woman who fell into many sins.  Mary Magdalene.  Kassia, *tr. by* Aliki *and* Willis Barnstone *and* Elene Kolb.  BoWoP

Lord Thomas and Fair Annet, *diff. versions.*  *Unknown.*  AmFP; FaBoBa; PeBB  (Lord Thomas and Fair Ellender.)  AmFP

Lord, Thou art mine, and I am Thine.  Clasping of Hands.  George Herbert.  ILwL

Lord, thou hast been our dwelling place in all generations.  Bible, *O.T.* Psalms, XC.  DL

Lord, Thou hast given me a cell. A Thanksgiving to God, for His House. Robert Herrick. HAP; OFD

Lord, Thou hast made this world below the shadow of a dream. McAndrew's Hymn. Kipling. OxBTC; VLP

Lord, Thou Hast Promised, *with music.* Samuel K. Cox. AH

Lord Ullin's Daughter. Thomas Campbell. FaPoR

Lord Walter's Wife. Elizabeth Barrett Browning. HAP

Lord Waterford. *Unknown.* GBP

Lord, we look to once for all, The. The Heretic's Tragedy. Robert Browning. OAEL-2

Lord! what a goodly thing is want of shirts. John Cleveland. *Fr.* The Rebel Scot. OBSV

Lord, what a thoughtless wretch was I. *Unknown.* AmFP

Lord, what am I, that, with unceasing care. To-Morrow. Lope de Vega, *tr. by* Longfellow. PIM

Lord, what is man? Meditation. Carl Rakosi. AMV-80

Lord, what is man? why should he cost thee. Charitas Nimia: or, The Dear Bargain. Richard Crashaw. BoReV;PIM

Lord! What these weathers are cold, and I am ill happed. The Wakefield Second Shepherds' Play. *Unknown.* OAEL-1

Lord, what unvalued pleasures crowned. The Invitation. Nathaniel Wanley. BoReV

Lord, when I look at lovely things which pass. In the Fields. Charlotte Mew. LoAs

Lord, when the sense of thy sweet grace. A Song. Richard Crashaw. IPWM

Lord, When the Wise Men Came from Far. Sidney Godolphin. *See* Hymn: "Lord, when the wise men came from far."

Lord, who createdst man in wealth and store. Easter Wings. George Herbert. AnMo; CABA (1972 ed.); HAP; HeIP; InPK; InPS; NIL; OAEL-1; PoIA; PPP; WIF

Lord, who hast formed me out of mud. Trinity Sunday. George Herbert. PAIC

Lord, Who's the Happy Man, *with music.* Nahum Tate *and* Nicholas Brady. AH

Lord will happiness divine, The. The Contrite Heart. William Cowper. WIF

Lord, with what bounty and rare clemency. Ungratefulness. George Herbert. ILP (1975 ed.)

Lord, with what care hast Thou begirt us round! Sin. George Herbert. Epi

Lord, You may not recognize me. The Gift. Louise Glück. GP

Lord, you've sent both. The Cancer Match. James Dickey. GP

Lorde, thou hast bene oure refuge. Bible, *O.T., tr. by* Miles Coverdale. Psalms, XC. OBVE

"Lordings," quod he, "in chirches whan I preche." The Pardoner's Prologue. Chaucer. *Fr.* The Canterbury Tales. OAEL-1

Lordly Hudson, The. Paul Goodman. ExPo (1973 ed.); NYP; VGW

Lord's Chameleons, The. Peter Klappert. AmPA

Lords have been made whose hired robes have hidden. On the Relinquishment of a Title. Geoffrey Grigson. FaBoEE

Lords, knights, and squires, the numerous band. To a Child of Quality Five Years Old. Matthew Prior. NIL; NOBE; RRA

Lord's lost Him His mockingbird. Mourning Poem for the Queen of Sunday. Robert Hayden. PoBA

Lord's My Shepherd, I'll Not Want, The, *with music.* Francis Rous. AH

Lords of life, the lords of life, The. Experience. Emerson. TAP

Lord's Prayer, The. Bible, *N.T.* St. Matthew, VI: 9-13. CTV (Our Father Which in Heaven Art, *with music.*) AH

Lorelei, The. Heine, *tr. fr. German by* James Morehead. BLSH, *with music* (Loreley, *tr. by* Ernst Feise.) NAWM-2

Lorena. Henry De Lafayette Webster. FSW; PSoN, *with music*

Lorenzo dwelt at Heighington. Fragment of a Song. "Lewis Carroll." FaBoNo

Los Alamos: Manhattan. David Rowbotham. CAAP

Los Angeles. Eloise Klein Healy. GP

Los New Yorks. Victor Hernández Cruz. SA

Los Sedentarios. Anselm Hollo. AcAn

Loser, The. Charles Bukowski. MiP

Losers. Carl Sandburg. CMoP (1970 ed.); NoAM

Losing Track. Denise Levertov. AnMo; ExPo (1973 ed.); HeIP; NoAM; NOBA; SoSe

Loss. A. R. Ammons. ConAP

Loss, The. Stephen Dunn. NVAP

Loss. Alex Kuo. NW

Loss. Terence Winch. PoUp

Loss! Loss! Rhoda McMahon. WeW

Loss, my molester, at last patient be. Pamphilia's Sonnet. Mary Sidney Wroth, Countess of Montgomery. *Fr.* Urania. WPE

Loss of Black Camels, The. Sam Hamod. SA

Loss of control, parquet, paraqueets, The. Spring Poem. Bin Ramke. AMV-81

Loss of the *Due Dispatch*, The. *Unknown.* AmFP

Loss of the *New Columbia*, The. *Unknown.* AmFP

Losses. Randall Jarrell. IP; PoA; TAP; UnPo (1976 ed.)

Lost. A. Alvarez. UsP

Lost. Chu Shu-chen, *tr. fr. Chinese by* Kenneth Rexroth. BoWoP

Lost. Patricia Goedicke. EC

Lost. Bruce Ignacio. VW

Lost, The. *Malay Oral Tradition, tr. by* R. J. Wilkinson *and* R. O. Winstedt. WTO

Lost. Charles d'Orléans. OxBM

Lost. Carl Sandburg. CMoP (1970 ed.)

Lost. *Unknown.* CTV

Lost, The. Jones Very. NOBA; PiAm

Lost. David Wagoner. GP; PoA

Lost—A Lizard. Irene Gough. ECBV

Lost Acres. Robert Graves. NoAM

Lost after All. Charlie D. Tillman. PeD

Lost Aisles, The. Herbert Scott. TC

Lost among secrets in a tangle. First Days. Tuvia Ruebner, *tr. by* A. C. Jacobs. VWA

Lost Anchors. E. A. Robinson. CMoP (1970 ed.); PiAm

Lost Angel, The. Philip Levine. NOBA

Lost Baby, The. *Unknown.* AmFP

Lost Baby Poem, The. Lucille Clifton. InPK; RiTi; WPE

Lost Children, The. Randall Jarrell. PBMP; RRA; TAP

Lost Chord, A. Adelaide Anne Procter. VLP

Lost Companions. Helen Bryant. AMV-80

Lost Contact. William Cole. POL

Lost Country. Warren Woessner. HeS

Lost Dancer, The. Jean Toomer. PoBA

Lost, Dancing, The. Edward Field. GP

Lost Deer, The. Joseph Bruchac. FAF

Lost Desire. Meleager, *tr. fr. Greek by* William M. Hardinge. LoAs

Lost Dog. Frances Rodman. GDP

Lost Doll, The. Charles Kingsley. *Fr.* The Water Babies. ECBV
(Little Doll, The.) OxBChV

Lost Egg, The. Percy Illot. ECBV

Lost Girl, The. *Unknown.* TDH

Lost Heifer, The. Austin Clarke. BIrV

Lost in a Norther. Hamlin Garland. BPAW

Lost in Oregon, hunting my bearings. Atlas. Robert Flanagan. HeS

Lost in the words. Davening. Rochelle Ratner. VWA

Lost Jewel, A. Robert Graves. LoAs

Lost Jimmie Whalen. *Unknown.* AmFP

Lost Johnny. *Unknown.* AmFP

Lost Lagoon, The. Pauline Johnson. BPAW

Lost Lane. Dorothy Wellesley. WPE

Lost Leader, The. Robert Browning. BTTM; PBMP; PPoD; VLP

Lost Love. Robert Graves. ILP (1975 ed.)

Lost Love. Andrew Lang. SLP

Lost Love. Clive Turnbull. GAS

Lost Love. *Tr. fr. Tewa Indian by* H. J. Spinden. WTO

Lost Lover Blues. *Unknown.* BluL

Lost manor where I walk continually. The Pier-Glass. Robert Graves. CMoP (1970 ed.); NoAM

Lost Mistress, The. Robert Browning. BoLoP; NOBE; PoPle

Lost Mohican Visits Hell's Kitchen, A. A. K. Redwing. VoR

Lost Moment. Hoyt W. Fuller. PoBA

Lost my partner what'll do. Skip to My Lou. *Unknown.* FSW

Lost Objects. Diana O Hehir. AMV-80

Lost Occasion, The. Whittier. NOBA

Lost on a fogbound spit of sand. W. H. Auden. FaBoEE

Lost on Both Sides. Dante Gabriel Rossetti. The House of Life, XCI. VLP

Lost Orchard, The. Edgar Lee Masters. CMoP (1970 ed.)

Lost Parasol, The, *sel.* Sándor Weöres, *tr. fr. Hungarian by* Edwin Morgan.
    "Where metalled road invades light thinning air." OBVE

Lost Parents. Lawrence Ferlinghetti. GP

Lost Picture. Ray Fraser. NeAC

Lost Pictures, The. Hollis Summers. HoPM (1975 ed.)

Lost Pilot, The. James Tate. UnPo (1976 ed.)

Lost Range, The. Henry Herbert Knibbs. BPAW

Lost Son, The. Theodore Roethke. HAP; VGW
    "Shape of a rat, The?"*sel.* OSP

Lost Street, The. David Wagoner. MPA

Lost: The Original, Its Reason and Its Rhyme. Translation. Rika Lesser. PoA

Lost Weekend Bar, The. Joy Harjo. SA

Lost Will. Roger McDonald. FPA

Lost Word. Jean Burden. AMV-80

Lost, yesterday, somewhere. Lost. *Unknown.* CTV

Lot Later. Howard Nemerov. CoPAm; HoPM (1975 ed.)

Lot of Hearts Are Pounding in the Universe, A. Allan Kornblum. AcAn

Lot of love is chosen, The. I learnt that much. Chosen. W. B. Yeats. BoLoP; CMoP (1970 ed.)

Lot of men and armies stand to take, A. A Letter to a Policeman in Kansas City. Kenneth Patchen. SPT

Lot of the old folks here—all that's left, A. Reflections in a Slum. "Hugh MacDiarmid." FaBoTw (1975 ed.)

Lotos-Eaters, The. Tennyson. CABA (1972 ed.); ILP (1975 ed.); OAEL-2; VLP
    *Sels.*
    "'Courage!' he said, and pointed toward the land." ExPo (1973 ed.); PoIA
    "Hateful is the dark blue sky." GrRo
    "Lo! in the middle of the wood." GrRo
    Song of the Lotos-Eaters. NOBE
    ("There is sweet music here that softer falls.") HeIP

Lots of truisms don't have to be repeated. The Anatomy of Happiness. Ogden Nash. PAIC; TAP

Lot's Wife. "Anna Akhmatova," *tr. fr. Russian by* Richard Wilbur. BoWoP; PBWP

Lotus Eaters, The. Tennyson. *See* Lotos-Eaters, The.

Loud he sang the psalm of David! The Slave Singing at Midnight. Longfellow. GOA

Loud is the summer's busy song. John Clare. *Fr.* The Shepherd's Calendar: July. FSFS

Loud o'er my head though awful thunders roll. On a Thunder Storm. Sir Walter Scott. PIM

Loud report through Lybian cities goes, The. Virgil, *tr. by* Dryden. *Fr.* The Aeneid, IV. OBVE

Loudest thing in our car, The. Vacation Trip. William Stafford. CTBA

Loudspeaker screamed, The. The Akedah. Aliza Shenhar, *tr. by* Linda Zisquit. VWA

Lough Derg. Denis Devlin. BIrV; CIP

Louisa. Wordsworth. GBL

Louisa, when I offered. The Clamdigger. Dionis Coffin Riggs. TAT

Louisburg. *Unknown.* BTTM

Louise. Stevie Smith. SBG

Louisiana Weekly # 4, The. David Henderson. PoBA

Lounge in the shade of the luxuriant laurel's. Anyte, *tr. fr. Greek by* Willis Barnstone. BoWoP

Louse Hunting. Isaac Rosenberg. EBEV; OxBTC

Louse of a german p w, A. News from Other Small Worlds. Jonathan Williams. UsP

Lousy Miner. *Unknown.* AmFP

Love. Samuel Taylor Coleridge. MBPR

Love ("I'll sing of heroes, and of kings"). Abraham Cowley, *after the Greek of* Anacreon. OBVE

Love. George Granville. BoLoP

Love. Pauline Hanson. LoAs

Love ("Immortal love, author of this great frame"). George Herbert. HoPM (1975 ed.)

Love ("Love bade me welcome; yet my soul drew back"). George Herbert. BoReV; CABA (1972 ed.); EBEV; HeIP; ILwL; InPK; IP; LoAs; MAT; MetP; NOBE; OAEL-1; OBW; PBMP; PoPle; PPP; Prf; SCP-1; VoPo

Love. Patrick Lane. NeAC

Love. "Hugh MacDiarmid." CMoP (1970 ed.)

Love. Pablo Neruda, *tr. fr. Spanish by* Alastair Reid. LP

Love. Robert Pack. CoPAm

Love. Shelley. MBPR

Love. Anne Stevenson. NCSH

Love. Jaime Torres Bodet, *tr. fr. Spanish by* Muna Lee de Munoz Marín. LoAs

Love ("I am a fool, I can no good"). *Unknown.* OxBM

Love ("My love is no short year's sentence"). *Unknown, tr. fr. Irish by* John Montague. BIrV

Love ("She stood in her snood and arasaid"). *Unknown, tr. fr. Gaelic by* G. R. D. McLean. SLP

Love ("There's the wonderful love of a beautiful maid"). *Unknown.* SFF; SoSe

Love, *sel.* Alice Walker.
    "Old man in White, An." NMM

Love/ landing easily, easily caught. Another Love Poem. Jimmy Santiago Baca. DNGG

Love a woman? You're an ass! Song. Earl of Rochester. GBL; NOBL

Love Affair, A. Arnold Bennett. OxBTC

Love among Friends. Shawn Wong. NW

Love among the Ruins. Robert Browning. HAP; NOBE; OAEL-2; STS; VLP

Love and a Question. Robert Frost. LoAs

Love and Age. Walter Savage Landor. GBL

Love and Age. Thomas Love Peacock. PoPle; PPM

Love and an Old Western at the Starlite Drive-In Theater. Philip Legler. PPoD

Love and Death. Byron. EBEV; MBPR; NOBE

Love and Death. John Frederick Nims. CoPAm; HoPM (1975 ed.); WeW

Love and forgetting might have carried them. Two Look at Two. Robert Frost. ILP (1975 ed.); NU

Love and Friendship. Emily Brontë. VLP

Love and harmony combine. Song. Blake. MBPR

Love and Jealousy. William Walsh. BoLoP

Love and Liberty (The Jolly Beggars), *sel.* Burns. "See the smoking bowl before us." OBP

Love and Life. Earl of Rochester. BoLoP; GBL; HAP; NOBE ("All my past life is mine no more.") FF

Love and Music. *Gond Oral Tradition, tr. by* V. Elwin *and* S. Hivale. WTO

Love and Poetry. Louis Simpson. PPoe

Love and Sleep. Swinburne. BoLoP; LoAs; VLP

Love Arm'd. Aphra Behn. *See* Song: "Love in fantastic triumph sate."

Love at First Sight. Christopher Marlowe. *Fr.* Hero and Leander, First Sestiad. NOBE

"Love at first sight," some say, misnaming. At First Sight. Robert Graves. FaBoEE

Love at Large. Coventry Patmore. *Fr.* The Angel in the House, I, ii. VPC

Love at Stress-Point. Ruthe T. Spinnanger. AATT

Love at the closing of our days. Last Love. Fyodor Tyutchev, *tr. by* Vladimir Nabokov. BoLoP

Love at the lips was touch. To Earthward. Robert Frost. BiP; CABA (1972 ed.); LoAs; NoAM; NOBA; PPoe; TAP

Love bade me welcome; yet my soul drew back. Love. George Herbert. BoReV; CABA (1972 ed.); EBEV; HeIP; ILwL; InPK; IP; LoAs; MAT; MetP; NOBE, OAEL-l; OBW; PBMP; PoPle; PPP; Prf; SCP-1; VoPo

Love—bittersweet, irrepressible. Sappho, *tr. fr. Greek by* Willis Barnstone. BoWoP

Love brought by night a vision to my bed. Lost Desire. Meleager, *tr. by* William M. Hardinge. LoAs

Love by the Water-Reeds. *Tr. fr. Hawaiian by* M. W. Beckwith. WTO

Love Calls Us to the Things of This World. Richard Wilbur. AnMo; CAPP; CMoP (1970 ed.); ExPo (1973 ed.); HAP; HeIP; InPS; NIL; NoAM; PiAm; PPP; TAP; TCP; UnPo (1976 ed.); VGW; WIF

Love came by from the riversmoke. Melora's Song. Stephen Vincent Benét. *Fr.* John Brown's Body. AIW

Love came down at Christmas. Incarnate Love. Christina Rossetti. PIM

Love Charm. *Malay Oral Tradition, tr. by* R. O. Winstedt. WTO

Love Charm. *Unknown, tr. fr. Gaelic.* SLP

Love-Charms. Thomas Campion. *See* Thrice Toss These Oaken Ashes in the Air.

Love-charms were loud and joy said all! Loss! Loss! Rhoda McMahon. WeW

Love Child—a Black Aesthetic. Everett Hoagland. BPo

Love comes back to his vacant dwelling. Rondel: The Wanderer. Austin Dobson. PAIC

Love Day, The. Douglas Dunn. MS

Love (Dialogue) Poem. Michael Dransfield. FPA

Love Dirge. *Tr. fr. Maori by* John White. WTO

Love Divine, *with music.* Charles Wesley. BLSH

Love, drunk the other day, knocked at my breast. The Dual. Richard Lovelace. CaPo

Love Enthroned. Richard Lovelace. CaPo

Love ere he bleeds, an eagle in high skies. Modern Love, XXVI. George Meredith. PAIC

Love Feast, The. W. H. Auden. SFF

Love flies with bow unstrung when Time appears. Love and Age. Walter Savage Landor. GBL

Love from My Father. Carole Gregory Clemmons. CNA; PoBA

Love God—/ my mother said. The Will's Love. Besmilr Brigham. IHMS

Love goddess, alas, grows frailer, The. The Dying Goddess. Carolyn Kizer. WBN

Love guards the roses of thy lips. Thomas Lodge. Phillis, XIII. ILP (1975 ed.)

Love has seven names. Hadewijch, *tr. fr. Dutch by* Willis Barnstone *and* Elene Kolb. BoWoP

Love, I love beyond. Edmond Rostand, *tr. by* Brian Hooker. *Fr.* Cyrano de Bergerac, Act III. OLR

Love I love whose lips I love, A. The Accomplices. Conrad Aiken. LoAs; NOBA

Love? I'd rather be condemned to Grand Opera. Do You Love Me? Robert Watson. POL

Love, if nothing solid rises like wood. Song: The Organic Years. Marvin Bell. NVAP

Love! if Thy destined sacrifice am I. The Acquiescence of Pure Love. William Cowper, *after* Madame Guyon. ILwL

Love in a Life. Robert Browning. NOBE

Love in a Space-Suit. James Kirkup. MPo

Love in a Warm Room in Winter. James Wright. OBAL

Love in Age. George Bruce. MS

Love in America. Marianne Moore. GOA

Love in Brooklyn. John Wakeman. AMV-81

Love in Edinburgh. Nicholas Fairbairn. SLP

Love in fantastic [*or* fantastique] triumph sate. Song [*or* Love Arm'd]. Aphra Behn. *Fr.* Abdelazer. NOBE; SBG; WPE

Love in Labrador. Carl Sandburg. VGW

Love in Magnolia Cemetery. Paula Rankin. AMV-80

Love in my bosom like a bee. Rosalind's Madrigal. Thomas Lodge. *Fr.* Rosalynde; or, Euphues' Golden Legacy. NOBE

Love in Particular. John Malcolm Brinnin. NYP

Love in the Asylum. Dylan Thomas. LoAs

Love in the Middle of the Air. Lenore Kandel. *Fr.* Circus. RiTi
("Catch me!") OSP

Love in the peaceful u.s.a. Love u.s.a. Kathleen Spivack. BoWoP

Love in the Valley. George Meredith. NOBE; OAEL-2; VLP, 2 *versions*; VPC

Love in Vain. Robert Johnson. UnPo (1976 ed.)

Love Is. Ann Darr. MiP; OSP

Love is a circle that doth restless move. Love What It Is. Robert Herrick. FaBoEE; CaPo

"Love is a law, a discord of such force." *Unknown, at. to* John Webster *and* William Rowley. *Fr.* The Thracian Wonder. GBL

Love is a place. E. E. Cummings. FaBoEE; OLR; OSP

Love is a queer little elfin sprite. Because You're You. Henry Blossom. BLSo

Love Is a Shark. *Tr. fr. Hawaiian by* N. B. Emerson. WTO

Love Is a Sickness. Samuel Daniel. *Fr.* Hymen's Triumph. NOBE

Love is a universal migraine. Symptoms of Love. Robert Graves. BoLoP

Love is a well that never runs dry. No Fear. Mary Doyle Curran. AMV-80

"Love is all/ Unsatisfied." Crazy Jane on the Day of Judgment. W. B. Yeats. CMoP (1970 ed.)

Love is and was my lord and king. In Memoriam A. H. H., CXXVI. Tennyson. NOBE

Love is begot by fancy, bred. Love. George Granville. BoLoP

Love Is Enough, *sel.* William Morris.
"Love is enough: though the world be a waning." VLP

Love Is Life, *orig. and mod. English prose.*   Richard Rolle of
Hampole.   OxBM

Love Is like a Dizziness.   James Hogg.   SLP

Love is like butter, Evans mused, and stuck.   Pendydd.   Kingsley
Amis.   *Fr.* The Evans Country.   NOBL

Love is like the wild rose-briar.   Love and Friendship.   Emily
Brontë.   VLP

Love Is Loathing & Why.   Dan Ford.   AMV-81

Love Is More Thicker than Forget.   E. E. Cummings.   AnMo

Love is no more.   Amor Vincit Omnia.   Edgar Bowers.   PiAm

Love is not all; it is not meat nor drink.   Edna St. Vincent Millay.
CMoP (1970 ed.); HAP; ILP (1975 ed.); NoAM; TAP; UsP

Love is not blind. I see with single eye.   Edna St. Vincent Millay.
SBG

Love is not mocked whatever use.   "Graphemics," 10.   Jack
Spicer.   VGW

Love is not worth so much.   Coda.   James Tate.   AmPA

Love is soft, love is swete, love is good sware.   Love Is Weal,
Love Is Wo.   *Unknown.*   OxBM

Love is something some people do not know about.   *Unknown.*
SFF

Love is the peace, whereto all thoughts doe strive.   Fulke Greville.
*Fr.* Caelica.   AAS

Love is the plant of peace and most precious of virtues.   Et
Incarnatus Est.   William Langland.   *Fr.* The Vision of Piers
Plowman.   BoReV; NOBE

Love is too young to know what conscience is.   Sonnets, CLI.
Shakespeare.   BiP; EBEV; HeIP

Love Is Weal, Love Is Wo.   *Unknown.*   OxBM

Love is where the glory falls.   Hafiz, *tr. fr.* Persian.   ILwL

Love-Joy.   George Herbert.   OAEL-1

Love Letter.   Brewster Ghiselin.   MPA

Love Letter.   Sylvia Plath.   NOBA; UsP

Love Letter Postmarked Van Beethoven   Diane Wakoski.   BiP

Love Lies Sleeping.   Elizabeth Bishop.   NYP

Love Lifted Me, *with music.*   James Rowe.   BLSH

Love lives beyond.   John Clare.   NOBE

Love-lorn microbe met by chance, A.   The Microbe's Serenade.
George Ade.   OBAL

Love! Love!   Rhoda McMahon.   WeW

Love, love, a lily's my care.   Words for the Wind.   Theodore
Roethke.   LoAs; NoAM; NOBA; STS

Love Made in the First Age: To Chloris.   Richard Lovelace.
CaPo; OAEL-1; SCP-2

Love made me such that I live in fire.   Gaspara Stampa, *tr. fr.*
*Italian by* Lynne Lawner.   PBWP

Love Making.   James Tate.   EAS

Love Me.   Maria Wine, *tr. fr. Swedish by* Nadia Christensen.
PBWP

Love me and leave me; what love bids retrieve me?   At the Piano.
Swinburne.   FaBoNo

Love Me and Never Leave Me.   Ronald McCuaig.   POL

Love me brought[e].   Christ's Love-Song.   *Unknown.*   BoReV;
OxBM

Love me—I love you.   Lullaby.   Christina Rossetti.   PoPle

Love Me Little, Love Me Long.   Robert Herrick.   CaPo; LoAs

Love me, love my dog: by love to agree.   Of Loving a Dog.   John
Heywood.   PAIC

Love me with the left hand.   The Light Woman's Song.   Judith
Johnson Sherwin.   TAP

Love Medicine.   Eda Lou Walton.   BPAW

"Love my heart for an hour, but my bone for a day."   Street
Song.   Edith Sitwell.   CMoP (1970 ed.)

Love Necessitates.   Eugene Redmond.   CNA

Love now no fire hath left him.   Madrigal.   Giovanni Battista
Marino, *tr. by* Richard Crashaw.   OBVE

Love, oh, love, oh, careless love.   Careless Love.   *Unknown.*
BLSH; BLSo; BluL; FSW

Love, oh my love, it will come.   Geoffrey Hill.   *Fr.* The Songbook
of Sebastian Arrurruz.   PSN

Love of a woman, The.   Air.   Robert Creeley.   VGW

Love of Fame, the Universal Passion, *sels.*   Edward Young.
"Britannia's daughter's, much more fair than nice," *fr.* Satire V.
OBSV

Lavinia at Church, *fr.* Satire VI.   BoReV

"Long, Dodington, in debt, I long have sought," Satire III.
LAuP

"Love of praise, howe'er concealed by art, The," *fr.* Satire I.
OBSV

"See commons, peers, and ministers of state," *fr.* Satire III.
OBSV

"These all their care expend on outward show," *fr.* Satire II.
OBSV

"With what, O Codrus! is thy fancy smit?" *fr.* Satire II.   OBSV

Love of Flowers, The.   Thomas Lovell Beddoes.   PF

Love of God, The.   John Audelay.   OxBM

Love of praise, howe'er concealed by art, The.   Edward Young.
*Fr.* Love of Fame, the Universal Passion.   OBSV

Love on a day (wise poets tell).   How Violets Came Blue.
Robert Herrick.   CaPo

Love on the Farm.   D. H. Lawrence.   CMoP (1970 ed.); FF;
OBP

Love Pictures You as Black and Long-faced.   Lance Jeffers.   FB

Love Poem: "Black biplane crashes into the window, The."
Gregory Orr.   MAT

Love Poem: "History of My Feeling, The."   Kathleen Fraser.
*See* History of My Feeling, The.

Love Poem: "I am a traveler."   John Batki.   AcAn

Love Poem: "I want/ to make a myth of you."   Rosemary
Aubert.   AMV-80

Love Poem: "Is the woman next door."   Michael Delp.   TC

Love Poem: "Last night you would not come."   John Logan.
CAPP; CoPAm

Love Poem: "Morning settles in."   Cary Waterman.   PCho

Love Poem: "My clumsiest dear, whose hands shipwreck vases."
John Frederick Nims.   CoPAm; FF; HoPM (1975 ed.);
InPK; SoSe; TCP; UsP; VoPo

Love Poem: "Rain smell comes with the wind."   Leslie Silko.
UnPo (1976 ed.); VoR

Love Poem: "She coils her body around me."   Howard Schwartz.
HeS

Love Poem: "Six o'clock and/ the sun rises..."   Miller Williams.
MAT

Love Poem: "These words are all of me."   Lewis Turco.   NowV

Love Poem: "Thrust of your body, The."   Mark Wangberg.   TC

Love Poem: "Warned, warned for years."   Susan Irene Rea.
AMV-80

Love Poem: "When we are in love, we love the grass."   Robert
Bly.   BiP; InPS; OSP

Love Poem Beginning with I.   David Steingass.   CoPAm

Love Poem for All the Women I Have Known, A.   Charles
Bukowski.   PCho

Love Poem Investigation for A. T.   Frank Frate.   AMV-80

Love Poem on Theme by Whitman.   Allen Ginsberg.   CAPP; TT

Love Poem, I.   Elizabeth Wray.   PoUp

Love Poem 3.   Laughton Johnston.   SLP

Love Poem without Anyone in It.   Neeli Cherkovski.   CPA

Love Poems of the VIth Dalai Lama, *sels.*   Peter Whigham.
TwMBP

"Frost/ lacing/ late summer."

"In a season/ the shoots we planted."

"In summer/ this reed-patch."

"In the oasis of the day."

"Old dog, The/ at the west poster."

"Pattern of birds, A."

"This country girl."

"Why does this pretty boy from Kong-po."

Love poems they read. Uses of Poetry. Winfield Townley Scott. PoA

Love Pursued. *Unknown. Fr.* The Thracian Wonder. GBL

Love, Reason, Hate, did once bespeak. A Barley-Break. Sir John Suckling. CaPo

Love Rejected. Lucille Clifton. BPo

Love Saint George. *Unknown.* ILP (1975 ed.)

"Love seeketh not itself to please." The Clod and the Pebble. Blake. *Fr.* Songs of Experience. AnMo; CABA (1972 ed.); ILP (1975 ed.); InPS; LAuP; LoAs; MBPR; NOBE; PoIA; SS; STS

Love sells off a wilderness in which. About That. Marvin Bell. HeS

Love set you going like a fat gold watch. Morning Song. Sylvia Plath. BoWoP; HeIP; ILP (1975 ed.); IHMS; InPK; InPS; LoAs; NOBA; PSN; SBG

Love should grow up like a wild iris in the fields. Susan Griffin. RiTi

Love should intend realities: good-bye! Exit Line. John Ciardi. WeW

Love signed the contract blithe and leal. Epigram. John Swanwick Drennan. BIrV

Love Sleeping. Plato, *tr. fr. Greek by* Thomas Stanley. FaBoEE

Love Somebody, Yes I Do. *Unknown.* FSW

Love Song. Hayim Be'er, *tr. fr. Hebrew by* Stephen Mitchell. VWA

Love Song. Patricia Beer. HeHu

Love Song. Kosrof Chantikian. AMV-81

Love Song. Gavin Ewart. OxBTC

Lovesong. Ted Hughes. OBP

Love Song, A. Else Lasker-Schüler, *tr. fr. German by* Michael Gillespie. BoWoP

Love Song. Edward Lear. *Fr.* The Owl and the Pussy-Cat. PCat

Love Song. Joseph Macleod. SLP

Love Song. Dorothy Parker. TPo

Lovesong. Rainer Maria Rilke, *tr. fr. German by* M. D. Herter Norton. LoAs; OLR

Love Song. Anne Sexton. NCSH

Love Song, A. Royall Tyler. TAP

Love Song ("I painted my eyes with black antimony"). *Tr. fr. Bagirmi by* H. Gaden. BoWoP

Love Song ("Lavender's blue, diddle, diddle"). *Unknown. See* Lavender Blue.

Love Song. Bob Zmuda. AMV-81

Love Song for a Tyrant. Marion Brimm Rewey. AMV-81

Love Song for the Future. Vassar Miller. NCSH

Love Song: I and Thou. Alan Dugan. BuTh; CAPP; CoPAm; FF; HoPM (1975 ed.); ILP (1975 ed.); InPK; LoAs; NoAM; SFF; SoSe

Love Song of J. Alfred Prufrock, The. T. S. Eliot. AnMo; BiP; CABA (1972 ed.); CMoP (1970 ed.); EBEV; Epi; ExPo (1973 ed.); FF; HAP; HeIP; HoPM (1975 ed.); ILP (1975 ed.); InPK; InPS; IPWM; LFH; NIL; NoAM; NOBA; NOBE; OAEL-2; OxBTC; PAIC; PoA; PoIA; PPP; PSN; SoSe; STS; TAP; TT; UsP; WIF

Love Songs. Mina Loy. VGW; WPE, *abr.*

Love-Songs, at Once Tender and Informative. Samuel Hoffenstein. OBAL

Love Songs (Dadaria). *Gond Oral Tradition, tr. by* V. Elwin *and* S. Hivale. WTO

Love Songs in Age. Philip Larkin. PPP; PSN

Love Sonnet, A. George Wither. *See* I Loved a Lass.

Love Sonnets of Proteus, The, *sels.* Wilfrid Scawen Blunt.

"And then fate strikes us. First our joys decay," LXXV. VLP

Farewell to Juliet ("I see you, Juliet, still, with your straw hat"), XLVII. BoLoP; OxBTC

Fear Has Cast Out Love, XXXVI. VLP

Joy's Treachery, XVII. VLP

Mockery of Life, The, LXXIV. VLP

St. Valentine's Day, LV. LoAs

Love still has something of the sea. Song. Sir Charles Sedley. GBL; NOBE

Love Story, A. Robert Graves. CMoP (1970 ed.); FaBoTw (1975 ed.)

Love, strong as death, is dead. An End. Christina Rossetti. GBL

Love Suicides at Sonezaki, The, *sel.* Chikamatsu Monzaemon, *tr. fr. Japanese.*

"Farewell to the world, and to the night farewell." DL

Love-Talker, The. "Ethna Carbery." PFIr; PoTa; WPE

Love That Doth Reign and Live within My Thought. Petrarch, *tr. fr. Italian by* the Earl of Surrey. Sonnets to Laura: To Laura in Life, CIX. HeIP; ILP (1975 ed.); NIL; OAEL-1 (Complaint of a Lover Rebuked.) CABA (1972 ed.) ("Love that doth raine and live within my thought.") AAS; OBVE

("Love that liveth and reigneth in my thought.") Epi

Love that drained her drained him she'd loved, though each. The Turtle Dove. Geoffrey Hill. FaBoTw (1975 ed.)

Love that is not pardoned, A. Doors. Tom Clark. ConAP

Love That's Pure, Itself Disdaining, *with music.* Johann A. Gruber, *tr. fr. German by* Sheema Z. Buehne. AH

Love, the delight of all well-thinking minds. Fulke Greville. GBL

Love the Ruins. Malka Heifetz Tussman, *tr. fr. Yiddish by* Marcia Falk. VWA

Love the sun. William Carlos Williams. *Fr.* Calypsos. TH

Love the unholy, that frost which quickens summer. Didactic Sonnet. Melvin Walker La Follette. PoA

Love the Wild Swan. Robinson Jeffers. HeIP; InPS; PiAm

Love, thou art absolute, sole Lord. A Hymn to the Name and Honour of the Admirable Saint Teresa. Richard Crashaw. BoReV; EBEV; HAP; NOBE; SCP-1, *abr.*

Love Tight. Ted Joans. CNA

Love to his singer held a glistening leaf. Love's Last Gift. Dante Gabriel Rossetti. The House of Life, LIX. VLP

Love to My Electric Handmixer. Diane Wakoski. CoPAm

Love, 20¢ the First Quarter Mile. Kenneth Fearing. HAP; WeW

Love twists. The Pressures. Amiri Baraka. BPo

Love Undeclared. *Unknown.* OxBM

Love under the Republicans (or Democrats). Ogden Nash. IPWM; PBMP

Love Unfeigned. Chaucer. *Fr.* Troilus and Criseyde. BoReV; NOBE
(O Yonge Freshe Folkes.) ExPo (1973 ed.); OxBM

Love Unknown. George Herbert. Prf

Love u.s.a. Kathleen Spivack. BoWoP

Love, we are a small pond. We Are. Maxine W. Kumin. WBN

Love, we curve downwards, we are set to night. After Midsummer. E. J. Scovell. OxBTC

Love we define for ourselves, The. Prothalamion. Michael Ryan. AmPA

Love What It Is. Robert Herrick. FaBoEE; GBL

Love who points the swallow home. Who Points the Swallow. David Campbell. MAuV

Love Will Find Out the Way. *Unknown.* GBL

Love without Hope. Robert Graves. BoLoP; FaBoEE; GBL; OAEL-2

Love without Love. Luis Lloréns Torres, *tr. fr. Spanish by* Julio Marzán. InW

Love Your Enemy. Yusef Iman. BPo

Love your toys, my darling. Toys. Abraham Sutskever, *tr. by* Seymour Levitan. VWA

Love, You've Been a Villain. James Planché. NOBL

Loveliest of Pies. Peter De Vries. OBAL

Loveliest of Trees [the Cherry Now]. A. E. Housman. BiP; CMoP (1970 ed.); FF; FSFS; HAP; HeIP; ILP (1975 ed.); InPK; IPWM; NoAM; OAEL-2; OxBTC; PCOP; PPoD; SoSe (1977 ed.); STS; TT; VLP; VoPo; WIF

Loveliest of what I leave. Adonis, Dying. Praxilla, *tr. by* John Dillon. PBWP

Lovelight. Georgia Douglas Johnson. AmNP (1974 ed.)

Lovely! all the essential parts. These Purists. William Carlos Williams. OBAL

Lovely Big Cow. J. B. Morton. RAE

Lovely body of the dead, The. Lament for Glasgerion. Elinor Wylie. PoA

Lovely Fia was the summer queen. A Mare. Kate Barnes. PH

Lovely form there sate beside my bed, A. Phantom or Fact. Samuel Taylor Coleridge. MBPR

Lovely girl, you look at me through the window. Praxilla, *tr. fr. Greek by* John Dillon. PBWP

Lovely Love, A. Gwendolyn Brooks. BPo; TT

Lovely Pamela, who found. Epitaph on a Party Girl. Richard Usborne. FaBoEE

Lovely Shall Be Choosers, The. Robert Frost. NOBA

Lovely Swimmers, The. Richmond Lattimore. EcS

Lovely Tear of Lovely Eye. *Unknown.* OxBM

Lovely whore though. Cathleen. *Unknown, tr. by* Thomas MacIntyre. BIrV

Lovely Young Moor, A. *Unknown. See* Mooress Morayma, The.

Lovelye William, 2 *versions. Unknown.* AmFP

Lover and the Syringa-Bush, The. Herman Melville. OBAL

Lover Beseecheth His Mistress Not to Forget His Steadfast Faith and True Intent, The. Sir Thomas Wyatt. *See* Forget Not Yet.

Lover Compareth His State to a Ship in Perilous Storm Tossed on the Sea, The. Petrarch, *tr. fr. Italian by* Sir Thomas Wyatt. Sonnets to Laura: To Laura in Life, CLVI. GBL; HeIP; PAIC
  (My Galley Charged with Forgetfulness.) BiP; CABA (1972 ed.); Epi; HAP; ILP (1975 ed.); LFH; OAEL-1; PPP; WeW
  ("My galy charged with forgetfulnes.") AAS; OBVE

Lover Complaineth the Unkindness of His Love, The. Sir Thomas Wyatt. GBL
  ("My lute, awake! perform the last.") AAS; CABA (1972 ed.); EBEV; HAP; ILP (1975 ed.); LoAs; OAEL-1
  (To His Lute.) BoLoP; NIL; NOBE

Lover Deceived Writes to His Lady, The, *sel.* Thomas Howell. "Who would have thought that face of thine." POL

Lover for Shamefastnesse Hideth His Desire within His Faithfull Hart, The. Petrarch, *tr. fr. Italian by* Sir Thomas Wyatt. Sonnets to Laura: To Laura in Life, CIX. AAS, 2 *versions*
  ("Long[e] love that in my thought doth harbour, The.") CABA (1972 ed.); Epi; ILP (1975 ed.); NIL; OAEL-1; OBVE

Lover Having Dreamed Enjoying of His Love, Complaineth That the Dream Is Not either Longer or Truer, The. Sir Thomas Wyatt. AAS, 2 *versions*

Lover in Winter Plaineth for the Spring, The. *Unknown. See* Western Wind.

Lover Mourns for the Loss of Love, The. W. B. Yeats. PoIA; WeW

Lover of mine, if upland you journey. Ave atque Vale. *Malay Oral Tradition, tr. by* R. J. Wilkinson *and* R. O. Winstedt. WTO

Lover of swamps. To the Snipe. John Clare. Epi

Lover of the Lord. *Unknown.* AmFP

Lover Proved False, The. *Unknown.* AmFP

Lover Showeth [*or* Sheweth] How He Is Forsaken of Such as He Sometime Enjoyed, The. Sir Thomas Wyatt. AAS, 2 *versions*; GBL; HoPM (1975 ed.); InPS; UsP (Remembrance.) BoLoP; NOBE; PoPle
  (They Flee from Me That Sometime Did Me Seek [*or* Seke].) BiP; CABA (1972 ed.); ExPo (1973 ed.); FF; HAP; HeIP; ILP (1975 ed.); InPK; LoAs; NIL; OAEL-1; PoIA; PPP; SoSe; WeW
  (Vixi Puellis Nuper Idoneus.) OBP

Lover Tells of the Rose in His Heart, The. W. B. Yeats. CMoP (1970 ed.); ILP (1975 ed.); PFIr
  (Aedh Tells of the Rose in His Heart.) VLP

Lover That I Hope You Are. Milton Acorn. NeAC

Lover to Himself, The. David Phillips. NeAC

Lover to His Lady, The. At. to Plato, *tr. fr. Greek by* George Turberville. FaBoEE; FF; LoAs

Lover under burden of his mistress' love, The. Gulling Sonnets, I. Sir John Davies. Epi; ESo; PAIC

Lover, upon an Accident Necessitating His Departure, Consults with Reason, A. Thomas Carew. CaPo

Loverd, thou clepedest me. Wait a Little! *Unknown.* BoReV; OxBM

Lovers, The. Conrad Aiken. LoAs

Lovers, The. Alex Comfort. PoA

Lovers, The. W. R. Rodgers. BIrV

Lovers, The. Karen Swenson. WBN

Lovers, The. Marya Zaturenska. PPM

Lovers, and a Reflection. Charles Stuart Calverley. FaBoCo; SpRo; VLP

Lovers and madmen have such seething brains. Shakespeare. *Fr.* A Midsummer Night's Dream, V, i. UsP

Lover's Confession, A. Charles d'Orléans. *See* My Ghostly Father, I Me Confess.

Lovers everywhere are bringing babies into the world. Make Love Not War. Howard Nemerov. NoAM

Lover's eyes will gaze an eagle blind, A. Shakespeare. *Fr.* Love's Labour's Lost, IV, iii. GBL

Lovers Go Fly a Kite, The. W. D. Snodgrass. NowV

Lovers How They Come and Part. Robert Herrick. GBL

Lovers in ladies' magazines. Song. Thomas McGrath. VGW

Lovers in the act dispense. The Thieves. Robert Graves. BoLoP; CMoP (1970 ed.); ExPo (1973 ed.); OAEL-2; WeW

Lovers in Winter. Robert Graves. FaBoEE

Lovers' Infiniteness. John Donne. OAEL-1

Lover's Invitation, The. John Clare. VLP

Lover's Lament, A, 3 *versions. Unknown.* AmFP

Lover's Lament for Her Sailor, The. *Unknown.* AmFP

Lover's Lute Cannot Be Blamed, The. Sir Thomas Wyatt. *See* Blame Not My Lute for He Must Sownde.

Lovers may find similitudes. The Cascade. Edgell Rickword. FaBoTw (1975 ed.)

Lovers of pleasure more than God. Lover of the Lord. *Unknown.* AmFP

Lovers of the Poor, The. Gwendolyn Brooks. BiP; CAPP; NoAM; NOBA

Lover's Plea, A. Thomas Campion. NOBE
  ("Shall I come sweet love to thee.") AAS; EBEV; GBL; HAP; LoAs

Lover's Prayer, The. *Malay Oral Tradition, tr. by* R. J. Wilkinson *and* R. O. Winstedt. WTO

Lover's Resolution, A.   George Wither.   *Fr. Fair Virtue.*
BoLoP; NOBE
("Shall I wasting in despair.")   PAIC; PoPle; SS
Lover's Shirt, The.   *Unknown, tr. fr. Welsh by* Gwyn Williams.
BuTh
Lover's Song, The.   W. B. Yeats.   AnMo; PoIA
Lover's Stratagem, A.   *Unknown. Fr.* Floris and Blauncheflour.
OxBM
Lovers who/ came to me.   Ghost Poem Five.   Mary Norbert
Körte.   IHMS
Lovers who are young indeed, and wish to know the sort of life.
Love, You've Been a Villain.   James Planché.   NOBL
Lovers whose lifted hands are candles in winter.   For a Child
Expected.   Anne Ridler.   BuTh
Love's Alchemy.   John Donne.   AnMo; CABA (1972 ed.); NIL;
OAEL-1
Loves and Lays of William J. Higginson, The.   William J.
Higginson.   AAN
Loves and sorrows of those who lose an orchard.   The Lost
Orchard.   Edgar Lee Masters.   CMoP (1970 ed.)
Love's Apparition and Evanishment.   Samuel Taylor Coleridge.
MBPR
Love's Clock.   Sir John Suckling.   CaPo
Love's Commission.   William Cavendish, Duke of Newcastle.
SCP-2
Love's Deity [*or Deitie*].   John Donne.   GBL; ILP (1975 ed.);
LoAs
Love's Diet.   John Donne.   ILP (1975 ed.)
Love's domain, supernal Zion.   Brynbwrla.   Kingsley Amis.   *Fr.*
The Evans Country.   NOBL
Love's Emblems.   John Fletcher.   *Fr.* The Tragedy of
Valentinian, II, iv.   BoLoP; NOBE
(Now the Lusty Spring.)   FF
Love's Flowers.   William Cavendish, Duke of Newcastle.   SCP-2
Love's Fool.   John Rosenthal.   AMV-81
Love's Force.   Thomas Carew.   CaPo; SCP-2
Love's Good-Morrow.   Thomas Heywood.   *Fr.* The Rape of
Lucrece.   LoAs
("Pack, clouds, away, and welcome, day!")   GBL
Love's Growth; or, Spring.   John Donne.   SCP-1
Love's Immaturity.   E. J. Scovell.   BuTh
Love's Labour's Lost, *sels.*   Shakespeare.
"Lover's eyes will gaze an eagle blind, A," *fr.* IV, iii.   GBL
Spring, *fr.* V, ii.   FSFS; HAP; ILP (1975 ed.); NIL; OAEL-1;
SoSe; UnPo (1976 ed.)
(Cuckoo Sings, The.)   PoPle
("When daisies pied and violets blue.")   BiP; FF; HeIP;
InPK; IPWM; NOBE; OBP
When Icicles Hang by the Wall, *fr.* V, ii.   BiP; FF; HeIP;
InPK; InPS; NOBE; OBP
(Winter.)   AKE; FSFS; HAP; ILP (1975 ed.); IPWM; NIL;
OAEL-1; SoSe; UnPo (1976 ed.); UsP; WeW
Love's Last Gift.   Dante Gabriel Rossetti.   The House of Life,
LIX.   VLP
Love's Martyrs.   John Ford.   *Fr.* The Broken Heart, IV, iii.
NOBE
("Oh no more, no more, too late.")   GBL
Love's Matrimony.   William Cavendish, Duke of Newcastle.
SCP-2
Love's night and a lamp.   Meleager, *tr. fr. Greek by* Peter
Whigham.   BoLoP
Loves of the Birds, The.   *Malay Oral Tradition, tr. by* R. J.
Wilkinson *and* R. O. Winstedt.   WTO
Loves of the Plants, The, *sel.*   Erasmus Darwin.
"Caryo's sweet smile Dianthus proud admires."   PeD
Loves of the Puppets.   Richard Wilbur.   LoAs
Loves of the Triangles, The, *sel.*   John Hookham Frere.
"Stay your rude steps, or e'er your feet invade."   FaBoNo

Love's Offence.   Sir John Suckling.   CaPo
Love's Old Sweet Song, *with music.*   G. Clifton Bingham.   BLSH;
BLSo; FSN
Love's own form.   R. G. Vliet.   POL
Love's Philosophy.   Shelley.   BoLoP; HoPM (1975 ed.); MBPR;
OLR; PBMP; VoPo
Love's Preparation.   William Cavendish, Duke of Newcastle.
SCP-2
Love's Progress.   John Donne.   Elegies, XVIII.   OAEL-1; SCP-1
Love's Reality.   Coventry Patmore.   *Fr.* The Angel in the House,
I, i.   VLP
Love's Remorse.   Edwin Muir.   OxBTC
Love's Secret.   Blake.   OLR; PPoe
(Never Seek to Tell Thy Love.)   InPS; LoAs; NOBE; OBP;
PoPle
(Song: "Never seek to tell thy love.")   ExPo (1973 ed.)
Love's Siege.   Sir John Suckling.   CaPo
Love's strength, like the tiger's smile.   Second Wind.   Ruth
Stephan.   FoP
Love's the boy stood on the burning deck.   Casabianca.
Elizabeth Bishop.   LoAs
Loves upturned faces, laves everybody.   My Party the Rain.
William Stafford.   CNW
Love's Vision.   William Cavendish, Duke of Newcastle.   SCP-2
Loves who many years held all my mind, The.   Walter Savage
Landor.   GBL
Love's Witness.   Aphra Behn.   BoWoP
Lovesight.   Dante Gabriel Rossetti.   The House of Life, IV.
VLP
Lovest Thou Me?   William Cowper.   BoReV
Loving.   Kathleen Fraser.   WBN
Loving.   Shirley Kaufman.   VWA
Loving.   Wendy Rose.   NW
Loving.   Jane Stembridge.   NMM
Loving and Beloved.   Sir John Suckling.   CaPo
Loving and Liking.   Dorothy Wordsworth.   OxBChV
Loving Dexterity, The.   William Carlos Williams.   TH
Loving in truth, and fain in verse my love to show.   Astrophel
and Stella, I.   Sir Philip Sidney.   AAS; CABA (1972 ed.);
EBEV; Epi; ESo; GBL; HAP; ILP (1975 ed.); LoAs;
OAEL-1; OBP; PoIA
Loving looks the large-eyed cow.   A Christmas Prayer.   George
MacDonald.   PChr
Loving Mad Tom.   *Unknown.   See* Tom o' Bedlam's Song.
Loving me with my shoes off.   Barefoot.   Anne Sexton.   SFF
Loving she is, and tractable, though wild.   Characteristics of a
Child Three Years Old.   Wordsworth.   MBPR; RRA
Loving She Stood Apart.   Patrick Lane.   NeAC
Loving the rituals that keep men close.   Palladas, *tr. fr. Greek by*
Tony Harrison.   OBVE
Loving you is a warm room.   A Cold and Married War.   Marge
Piercy.   Psy
Lovingly I turn me down.   After Mass.   "Michael Field."   WPE
Low along the River.   Ralph Adamo.   CoPAm
Low Barometer.   Robert Bridges.   CMoP (1970 ed.); NoAM
Low Fields and Light.   W. S. Merwin.   ConAP
Low in thy grave with thee.   David's Lament for Jonathan.   Peter
Abelard, *tr. by* Helen Waddell.   NAWM-1
Low lies the land upon the sea.   The Lookout.   William Collins.
RhR
Low prayer, a high prayer, I send through space, A.   *Tr. from
Gaelic by* Douglas Hyde.   WTO
Low Road, The.   Tom Buchan.   MIS
Low...the Violence Begins Low.   Ann Darr.   WBN
Low-Tide.   Edna St. Vincent Millay.   RhR

Low was our pretty cot: our tallest rose. Reflections on Having Left a Place of Retirement. Samuel Taylor Coleridge. MBPR

Low ye hills in ocean lie. My Heart Is in Merioneth. *Unknown, tr. by* Richard Llwyd. OBW

Lowdown Dirty Blues. *Unknown.* AmFP

Lowdown Rounder's Blues. *Unknown.* BluL

Lowell. James Russell Lowell. *Fr.* A Fable for Critics. AmVN; NOBA; TAP

Lower the flags. Special Bulletin. Langston Hughes. PoBA

Lower the Standard: That's My Motto. Karl Shapiro. NoAM

Lowering, The. May Swenson. TCP

Lowest Trees Have Tops, The. Sir Edward Dyer. *See* Silent Love, A.

Lowlands ("I dreamt [*or* dreamed] a dream the other night"). *Unknown.* AIW; FSW

Lowlands Away ("Lowlands, Lowlands away, my John"). *Unknown.* GBP; PeBB

Lowlands of Holland, The ("Last Easter I was married"). *Unknown.* AIW; AmFP, *diff. version*

Lowly Peasant, The. *Unknown, tr. fr. Ladino by* Rina Benmayor. PBWP

Lowshot Light. William Barnes. VLP

Lowson. John Blight. CAAP

Loyal Citizen. Richard Lyons. HeS

"Loyal Hearts of London City, come I pray, and sing my ditty." The Dutchess of Monmouth's Lamentation for the Loss of Her Duke. FaBoBa

Loyal Sins. Jacob Glatstein, *tr. fr. Yiddish by* Ruth Whitman. VWA

Luath. Burns. GDP

Luau, The. Genevieve Taggard. WPW

Lucas Park (Saint Louis). Paul Southworth Bliss. ANTL

Lucasta, frown and let me die. To Lucasta: Her Reserved Looks. Richard Lovelace. CaPo

Lucasta Taking the Waters at Tunbridge: Ode. Richard Lovelace. SCP-2

Lucasta's Fan, with a Looking-Glass in It. Richard Lovelace. CaPo; SCP-2

Lucasta's World. Richard Lovelace. CaPo

Lüchow's and After. L. E. Sissman. NYP

Lucifer in Starlight. George Meredith. CABA (1972 ed.); Epi; ExPo (1973 ed.); FF; HAP; ILP (1975 ed.); InPK; IPWM; LFH; NOBE; OAEL–2; OBP; PAIC; PBMP; PoIA; PPoe; SoSe; UnPo (1976 ed.); VLP; VPC; WeW

Lucilia, wedded to Lucretius, found. Lucretius. Tennyson. OAEL–2; VLP

Lucina Schynning in Silence of the Night. Eilean Ni Chuilleanain. CIP

Lucinda Matlock. Edgar Lee Masters. *Fr.* Spoon River Anthology. CMoP (1970 ed.); FF; HAP; IPWM; NoAM; NOBA; PBMP; PPM; UsP; VoPo

Luck. Raymond Carver. PCho

Luck. Elaine Epstein. AMV–81

Luck. W. W. Gibson. ECBV; RAE

Luck has no songs, luck has no thoughts, luck has nothing. Pain. Edith Södergran. PBWP

Luck is not smiling upon us. Smile at Me. Musa Moris Farhi. VWA

Luck of Edenhall, The. Longfellow. PoTa

Luckes, my faire falcon, and your fellowes all. Sir Thomas Wyatt. AAS

Lucky Chance, The, *sel.* Aphra Behn.
Song: "Oh! Love, that stronger art than wine." WPE

Lucky Lion! *Zulu Oral Tradition, tr. by* H. Tracey. WTO

Lucky Louie Makes a Goal. H. Van Arsdale. SPo

Lucky Spence's Last Advice. Allan Ramsay. EPC

Lucky the husband. Mabel Kelly. Turlough O'Carolan, *tr. by* Austin Clarke. BIrV; CIP

Lucretius. Tennyson. OAEL–2; VLP

Lucretius could not credit centaurs. Invitation to Juno. William Empson. CMoP (1970 ed.)

Lucy. Walter de la Mare. CMoP (1970 ed.)

Lucy, *complete, in 5 parts.* Wordsworth. AnMo; MBPR; NOBE; OAEL–2

*Sels.*
I Traveled among Unknown Men. AnMo; ILP (1975 ed.); MBPR; NOBE; OAEL–2
She Dwelt among the Untrodden Ways. AnMo; BoLoP; CABA (1972 ed.); FF; HAP; HeIP; ILP (1975 ed.); IP; MBPR; NOBE; OAEL–2; PBMP; PCOP; PoIA; PPP; SpRo; UnPo (1976 ed.); WIF, 2 *versions*
Slumber Did My Spirit Seal, A. AnMo; BiP; CABA (1972 ed.); ExPo (1973 ed.); HAP; HeIP; ILP (1975 ed.); InPK; InPS; IP; MBPR; NIL; NOBE; OAEL–2; PAIC; PBMP; PoIA; PoPle; PPP
Strange Fits of Passion Have I Known. AnMo; EBEV; Epi; GBL; ILP (1975 ed.); LoAs; MBPR; NOBE; OAEL–2; PPP; SoSe
Three Years She Grew in Sun and Shower. AnMo; HAP; ILP (1975 ed.); MBPR; NOBE; OAEL–2

Lucy Ashton's song. Sir Walter Scott. *Fr.* The Bride of Lammermoor, *ch.* 3. NOBE

Lucy Gray; or, Solitude. Wordsworth. Epi; ILP (1975 ed.); MBPR; OAEL–2; OxBChV

Lucy in the Sky with Diamonds. John Lennon *and* Paul McCartney. NIL; SoS

Lucy Lake. Newton Mackintosh. SpRo

Lucy Lockett lost her pocket. Mother Goose. GSB, *with music*

Lud! what a group the motley scene discloses! Goldsmith. *Fr.* Epilogue to "The Sister." OBSV

Ludlow Massacre, The. Woody Guthrie. FSW

Ludwig's Death Mask. Ted Hughes. NoAM

Lugete O Veneres. R. A. K. Mason. ATNZ

Luini in porcelain! Medallion. Ezra Pound. PSN

Luis de Camões. Roy Campbell. FaBoTw (1975 ed.)

Luke. Bible, *N.T. See* St. Luke.

Luke and John. Handwriting on the Wall. *Unknown.* AmFP

Luke XI: Blessed Be the Paps Which Thou Hast Sucked. Richard Crashaw. CABA (1972 ed.); SCP–1
(Blessed Be the Paps Which Thou Hast Sucked.) PeD

Luke Havergal. E. A. Robinson. AmVN; GBL; ILP (1975 ed.); LFH; LoAs; NoAM; NOBA; PiAm; UnPo (1976 ed.)

Luke VII: She Began to Wash His Feet with Tears. Richard Crashaw. SCP–1

Lula Vires. *Unknown.* AmFP

Lullabie of a Lover, The. George Gascoigne. *See* Lullaby of a Lover, The.

Lullaby: "Beloved, may your sleep be sound." W. B. Yeats. BoLoP; FaBoTw (1975 ed.)

Lullaby, A: "For wars his life and half a world away." Randall Jarrell. PoIA

Lullaby: "Gray goose and gander." *Unknown. See* Grey Goose and Gander.

Lullaby: "I wish to God my child was born." *Unknown.* AmFP

Lullaby: "It is a summer evening." Anne Sexton. NoAM

Lullaby: "Lay your sleeping head, my love." W. H. Auden. CMoP (1970 ed.); ExPo (1973 ed.); HAP; NoAM; NOBE; OAEL–2; OxBTC; PPP; PSN; UnPo (1976 ed.); UsP
("Lay your sleeping head, my love.") BoLoP

Lullaby: "Long canoe, The." Robert Hillyer. DuDa

Lullaby: "Love me—I love you." Christina Rossetti. PoPle

Lullaby: "O Men from the fields." Padraic Colum. WTO

Lullaby: "O my son, born on a winter's morn." Nohomaiterangi, *tr. fr. Maori by* Barry Mitcalfe. WTO

Lullaby: "Rook's nest do rock on the tree-top, The." William Barnes. VLP

Lullaby: "Sleep now." Shlomo Vinner, *tr. fr. Hebrew by* Laya Firestone. VWA

Lullaby: "This is where/ the light sleeps." Sue Owen. AMV-80

Lullaby: "Though the world has slipped and gone." Edith Sitwell. CMoP (1970 ed.)

Lullaby: "Wide as this night, old as this night is old and young as it is young." Kenneth Fearing. CMoP (1970 ed.)

Lullaby and good-night. Cradle Song. *Unknown.* BLSH

Lullaby for an Emigrant. Benjamin Fondane, *tr. fr. French by* Keith Bosley. VWA

Lullaby for Ann-Lucian. Calvin Forbes. PoBA

Lullaby for Miriam. Richard Beer-Hofmann, *tr. fr. German by* Jonathan Griffin. VWA

Lullaby for My Dead Child. Denise Jallais, *tr. fr. French by* Maxine Kumin *and* Judith Kumin. BoWoP

Lullaby for the Christ Child. Anna Elizabeth Bennett. *See* Hush Thee, Princeling.

Lullaby in Auschwitz. Pierre Morhange, *tr. fr. French by* Edouard Roditi. VWA

Lullaby [*or* Lullabie] of a Lover, The. George Gascoigne. AAS; EBEV; HAP

Lullaby of an Infant Chief. Sir Walter Scott. OxBChV

Lullabye! "Snow is lying on my roof." Kathryn Stripling. AMV-80

Lullay, By-by, Lullay. *Unknown.* OxBM ("This endris night.") EBEV

Lullay, Lullay, Little Child. *Unknown.* BoReV

Lullay, My Child. *Unknown.* OxBM

Lulled, at silence, the spent attack. Baggot Street Deserta. Thomas Kinsella. CIP; CMoP (1970 ed.)

Lulls swears he is all heart, but you'll suppose. Upon Lulls. Robert Herrick. CaPo

Lully, lulla, thou little tiny child. Coventry Carol. *Unknown.* GSB; OFD; PChr

Lully, lullay [*or* lulley], lully, lullay [*or* lulley]. Corpus Christi Carol. *Unknown.* BoReV; DuDr; EBEV; FaBoBa; GBP; HAP; ILP (1975 ed.); NOBE; NU; OAEL-1; OxBM; WeW

Lumber of a London-going dray, The. An Incident in the Early Life of Ebenezer Jones, Poet, 1828. John Betjeman. CMoP (1970 ed.); NoAM

Lumbering haunches, pussyfoot tread, a pride of. Circus Lion. C. Day Lewis. BoAnP; MPo; PoPle

Lumberman's Alphabet, The. *Unknown.* AmFP

Lumberyard, The. Ruth Herschberger. WPE

Lumiere. H. L. Van Brunt. AMV-81

Luminalia, *sel.* Sir William Davenant. Night's Song. SCP-2

Luminous almonds have. Anne Sexton. Hans Juergensen. AMV-81

Luminous blaze! An Ode on Gas. *Unknown.* OBAL

Lump. Robert Phillips. AMV-80

Lumps of mud, the toads. Haiku. José Juan Tablada, *tr. by* Samuel Beckett. PBMP

Lumumba's Grave. Langston Hughes. CNA

Lunar Baedeker. Mina Loy. VGW

Lunar Paraphrase. Wallace Stevens. Moon

Lunar Probe, The. Maxine W. Kumin. Moon

Lunar Stanzas. Henry Coggswell Knight. FaBoNo

Lunar Tides, The. Marya Zaturenska. Moon

Lunatic, the Lover, and the Poet, The. Shakespeare. *Fr.* A Midsummer Night's Dream, V, i. PAIC

Lunch and After. Robert Creeley. FoP

Luncheon, A. Max Beerbohm. FaBoCo; NOBL; OBSV; OxBTC

Lunching with you at a restaurant on Commonwealth Ave. Letters to My Daughters. Judith Minty. AMV-81

Lunchroom Bus Boy Who Looked like Orson Welles, The. Horace Gregory. *Fr.* The Passion of M'Phail. NYP

Lune Concrete. Raymond Federman. Moon

Lunes. Margaret Gibson. AAN

Lupercalia. Ted Hughes. CMoP (1970 ed.)

Lupine Ridge. Peggy Simson Curry. WPW

Luriana, Lurilee. Charles Elton. PoPle

Lusiads, The, *sels.* Luis de Camoëns, *tr. fr. Portuguese by* Sir Richard Fanshawe.
"Now through the ocean in great haste they flunder." OBVE
"Shores are crown'd with people, The." OBVE

Luss Village. Iain Crichton Smith. MS

Lust for Murder, The. Gerda Penfold. GP

Lustra, *sels.* Ezra Pound.
"Come, my songs, let us express our baser passions." PoA
"O helpless few in my country." PoA
(Rest, The.) NoAM; NOBA

Lusty Juventus, *sel.* Robert Wever.
In Youth Is Pleasure. NOBE
("In a herber green, asleep whereas I lay.") GBL

Lute, companion of my calamity. Sonnet XII. Louise Labé, *tr. by* Aliki *and* Willis Barnstone. BoWoP

Lute Music. Kenneth Rexroth. TAP

Luther B——stepped from his air-conditioned house. I Hear America Griping. Morris Bishop. QQQ

Lutra, the Fisher. James McMichael. AmPA

Luve. Douglas Young. MS

Luvin' wumman is a licht, A. Love. "Hugh MacDiarmid." CMoP (1970 ed.)

Luxurious man, to bring his vice in use. The Mower against Gardens. Andrew Marvell. AnMo; EBEV; ILP (1975 ed.); NIL; OAEL-1; PPP

Luxury. Donald Justice. HeIP

Luxury Apt. Marie Harris. MMD

Luxury, then, is a way of. Political Poem. Amiri Baraka. NoAM

Luzzato. Charles Reznikoff. VWA

Lyarde Is an Old Horse. *Unknown.* OxBM

Lyce. William Walsh. BoLoP

Lycidas. Milton. AnMo; BiP; CABA (1972 ed.); EBEV; Epi; ExPo (1973 ed.); HAP; ILP (1975 ed.); InPK; InPS; LFH; NIL; NOBE; OAEL-1; OBP; PAIC; PPoD; PPoe; PPP; SCP-1; UnPo (1976 ed.); WeW
*Sels.*
"Ay me! whilst thee the shores and sounding seas." Prf
Flowers for a Funeral. PF

Lycoris darling, once I burned for you. Martial, *tr. fr. Latin by* Peter Porter. BoLoP

Lydia, in Heavens bane. Horace, *tr. by* Sir Richard Fanshawe. Odes, I, 8. OBVE

Lydlinch Bells. William Barnes. VCP

Lyell's Hypothesis Again. Kenneth Rexroth. NoAM

Lying. Thomas Moore. PFIr

Lying apart now, each in a separate bed. One Flesh. Elizabeth Jennings. MPo; OxBTC; PBWP

Lying asleep between the strokes of night. Love and Sleep. Swinburne. BoLoP; LoAs; VLP

Lying Awake. W. D. Snodgrass. HoPM (1975 ed.); ILP (1975 ed.)

Lying awake. White. Marguerite Bouvard. AMV-81

Lying close to your heart-beat, my lips. Fleur Adcock. *Fr.* Night-Piece. ATNZ

Lying Down Hungry. Carol Bergé. MMD

Lying Down with Men and Women. John Woods. GP; TC

Lying here alone. Izumi Shikibu, *tr. fr. Japanese.* WeW

Lying here, everything in me. Margaret Atwood. NeAC

Lying in a Hammock at William Duffy's Farm. James Wright. ANTL; CAPP; ConAP; HAP; HoPM (1975 ed.); InPS; IPWM; NOBA; PSN; SFF

Lying in a Yuma Saloon. Jim Barnes. CDW

Lying in bed in the dark, I hear the bray. Weather Ear. Norman Nicholson. MPo

Lying in the middle of our bed. For Galway. Ken McCullough. BrS

Lying is an occupation. Song. Laetitia Pilkington. WPE

Lying Muslims, The. *Yoruba Oral Tradition, tr. by* Ulli Beier. WTO

Lying on a Bridge. Van K. Brock. NVAP

Lying under the stars. The Heart of Herakles. Kenneth Rexroth. *Fr.* The Lights in the Sky are Stars. NU

Lyke as a huntsman, after weary chace. *See* Like as a huntsman. . .

Lyke as a ship that through the Ocean wyde. Amoretti, XXXIV. Spenser. ILP (1975 ed.)

Lyke Memnons rocke toucht, with the rising sunne. *See* Like Memnon's rock. . .

Lyke-Wake Dirge, The. *Unknown.* GBP; HAP; HoPM (1975 ed.); NOBE

Lynching, The. Milton Kessler. CoPAm

Lynching, The. Claude McKay. PoBA; WIF

Lynching and Burning. Primus St. John. PoBA

Lynching of Jesus, The. Muriel Rukeyser. SPT

Lynton Verses, *sel.* Thomas Edward Brown. "Milk! milk! milk!" PeD

Lyon. Herman Melville. PeD

Lyre. Patrick White. AMV-80

Lyre! though such power do in thy magic live. Wordsworth. VLP

Lyrebirds. Judith Wright. BoAnP

Lyric: "Embodiment of what, The." Arthur Gregor. TAP

Lyric: "From now on kill America out of your mind." James Agee. GOA

Lyric by Nine. *Unknown.* EAS

Lyric night of the lingering Indian Summer. September Midnight. Sara Teasdale. PoA

Lyric to Mirth, A. Robert Herrick. CaPo

Lyric to Spring. Joseph W. Stilwell. OBAL

Lyricism of the Weak, The. Peter Viereck. *See* To Helen (of Troy, N.Y.).

Lysidike dedicates. Kenneth Rexroth, *after the Greek of* Asklepiades. NNaP

Lysistrata. Aristophanes, *tr. fr. Greek by* Charles T. Murphy. NAWM-1

Lyve thowe gladly, yff so thowe may. Sir Thomas Wyatt. AAS

# M

M and A, R and I. *Unknown.* OxBM

M & O Blues. *Unknown.* BluL

MD Sewed Wrong Section of Colon. F. R. Scott. AKE

MJQ, The. Joyce Carol Thomas. CNA

Ma. Morty Sklar. AcAn

Ma and I were at Louise's house. The Contest of Nerves. Patricia Traxler. TV

Ma Canny Hinny. *Unknown.* GBP

Ma Rainey. Sterling A. Brown. PoUp

Ma'am dear, did ye never hear of pretty Molly Brannigan. Molly Brannigan. *Unknown.* FSW

Mabel cried as she stood by the window. Boo Hoo. Arnold Spilka. OSF

Mabel Kelly. Turlough O'Carolan, *tr. fr. Irish by* Austin Clarke. BIrV

(Mable Kelly.) CIP

Mabel—when is the bomb set to. An Anarchist's Letter. Harald Wyndham. POL

Macadam, gun-grey as the tunny's belt. Van Winkle. Hart Crane. *Fr.* The Bridge: Powhatan's Daughter. PiAm

McAfee's Confession. *Unknown.* AmFP

McAndrew's Hymn. Kipling. OxBTC; VLP

Macao. W. H. Auden. TT

Macavity: The Mystery Cat. T. S. Eliot. BiP; FaBoCo; ILP (1975 ed.); InPS; NOBL; OxBChV; STS

Macbeth, *sels.* Shakespeare.
  "Hang out our banners on the outward walls."*fr.* V, v. EBEV
  "I have done the deed—Didst thou not hear a noise?" *fr.* II, ii. EBEV
  "If it were done when 'tis done, then 'twere well," *fr.* I, vii. UnPo (1976 ed.)
  "Queen, my lord, is dead, The," *fr.* V, v. STS
  "She should have died hereafter," *fr.* V, v. DL; IP; SoSe
  "Thrice the brinded cat hath mew'd," *fr.* IV, i. OFD
  Tomorrow, and Tomorrow, and Tomorrow, *fr.* V, v. FF; TPo

McCoy Tyner at Slugs. Quincy Troupe. SES

McDonogh Day in New Orleans. Marcus B. Christian. AmNP (1974 ed.)

Maceo. Luis Lloréns Torres, *tr. fr. Spanish by* Julio Marzán. InW

M'Fingal, *sel.* John Trumbull.
  "Rise then, ere ruin swift surprize." GOA

MacFlecknoe; or, A Satire upon the True-Blue Protestant Poet T. S. Dryden. CABA (1972 ed.); ESaP; HAP, *abr.;* NIL; OAEL-1; OBSV; PPP
  *Sels.*
  "All human things are subject to decay." LFH; PoIA; SCP-1
  (Crown Prince of Dullness, The.) NOBE
  "Now Empress Fame had published the renown." SCP-1
  Shadwell Anatomized. OBP

Macha. Paul Muldoon. IPM

Machine Out of the God. Thomas E. Sanders. AMV-81

Machines/ like mothers. Steamer on the Seedbed. Janet Kauffman. *Fr.* Tobacco. TC

Machines of death from east to west. Revelation. William Soutar. MS

Machismo. Martin Steingesser. AAN

Machu Picchu, Peru. Fred Red Cloud. VW

McKinley called for volunteers. Battleship of Maine. *Unknown.* FSW

McKinley hollered, McKinley squalled. White House Blues. *Unknown.* FSW

MacPherson's Farewell. *Unknown.* FSW

Macramé. Michael D. Riley. AMV-81

Macrinus against Trees. "Michael Field." WPE

Macy's Poem, The. James Reiss. POL

Mad Answer of a Madman, A. Robert Hayman. FF; SoSe

Mad as a hare in spring-time. Alfred Allen. *Fr.* Clashenure Skyline. IPM

Mad Dog. Robert Siegel. FAF

Mad Dogs and Englishmen. Noel Coward. NOBL

Mad Farmer Revolution, The. Wendell Berry. CSP

Mad Farmer Stands Up in Kentucky for What He Thinks Is Right, The. James Baker Hall. TAT

Mad Farmer, the thirsty one, The. The Mad Farmer Revolution. Wendell Berry. CSP

Mad Fight Song for William S. Carpenter, 1966, A. James Wright. LiSp

Mad Gardener's Song, The. "Lewis Carroll." *Fr.* Sylvie and Bruno. BBL, 5 sts.; FaBoCo; OxBChV; PBMP

Mad girl with the staring eyes and long white fingers, The. Cassandra. Robinson Jeffers. HeIP; PiAm

Mad Hatter's Song. "Lewis Carroll." *Fr.* Alice's Adventures in Wonderland, ch. 7. FaBoNo; SpRo ("Twinkle, twinkle, little bat!") CTV; NOBL

Mad have black roots in their brains, The. Sequence. James Harrison. CoPAm

Mad is like touching the devil. Shawn Randolph. OSP

Mad Lover, The, *sels.* John Fletcher.
"O divine star of heaven," *fr.* IV, i. GBL
"Orpheus I am, come from the deeps below," *fr.* IV, i. GBL

Mad Maid's Song, The. Robert Herrick. CaPo; OAEL-1; SCP-1

Mad male-hearted woman in a prouder age, A. Desmond O'Grady. NoAM

Mad Margaret's Song. W. S. Gilbert. *Fr.* Ruddigore. PCOP

Mad Meg on my mantelpiece. Three Women. Liz Lochhead. MIS

Mad Monk, The. Samuel Taylor Coleridge. MBPR

Mad Mother, The. Wordsworth. MBPR

Mad paper, stay! and grudge not here to burn. To Mrs. Magdalen Herbert. John Donne. SCP-1

Mad Poem Addressed to My Nephews and Nieces, A. Po Chü-i, *tr. fr. Chinese by* Arthur Waley. BBGO; BuTh

Mad Queen Aeronautical Corporation . . Cyclone . 3030. Telephone Directory. Harry Crosby. EAS

Mad Scene, The. James Merrill. CoPAm; NoAM; NOBA; PoA; TAP

Mad Song. Blake. ILP (1975 ed.); MBPR; OAEL-2; STS

Mad Song. Denise Levertov. Psy; TAP

Mad Tom of Bedlam. *Unknown.* SCP-2

Mad-Woman, The. L. A. G. Strong. PFIr

Mad Yak, The. Gregory Corso. NoAM

Madam,/ If you're deceived, it is not by my cheat. A Very Heroical Epistle in Answer to Ephelia. Earl of Rochester. APAS

Madam and the Minister. Langston Hughes. NOBA

Madam and the Rent Man. Langston Hughes. UsP

Madam Eglantine. Chaucer. *See* Prioress, The.

Madam, he thinks you've become his lover. Ode to the Muse on Behalf of a Young Poet. David Wagoner. AMV-80

Madam Life's a Piece in Bloom. W. E. Henley. CABA (1972 ed.); ILP (1975 ed.); InPK
(To W. R.) VLP

Madam Mouse Trots. Edith Sitwell. MN
(Madame Mouse Trots.) UsP

Madam would speak with me. So, now it comes. George Meredith. Modern Love, XXXIV. ILP (1975 ed.)

Madam, your beauty and your lovely parts. Platonic Love. Lord Herbert of Cherbury. SCP-2

Madame, for your newefangelnesse. A Ballade against Woman Inconstant. Chaucer. CABA (1972 ed.)

Madame, I Have Come a-Courting. *Unknown.* AmFP

Madame Mouse Trots. Edith Sitwell. *See* Madam Mouse Trots.

Madame, withouten many wordes. Sir Thomas Wyatt. AAS; CABA (1972 ed.); LoAS; OBVE

Madame, ye been [*or* ben] of alle [*or* al] beautee [*or* beaute] shrine [*or* shryne] To Rosemond [*or* Rosemounde.] Chaucer. CABA (1972 ed.); ILP (1975 ed.); OAEL-1

Madam's Past History. Langston Hughes. NoAM

Made in his maker's image? Tree of Knowledge. Edward Lowbury. VWA

Made Shine. Josephine Miles. NoAM

Made to See. John Nist. AMV-80

Madeleine came running up the stair. For It Was Early Summer. James Picot. GAS

Madeleine in Church. Charlotte Mew. SBG

Mademoiselle from Armentières. *Unknown.* BLSo, *with music;* FSW; OBAL

Madge Wildfire's [Death] Song. Sir Walter Scott. *See* Proud Maisie.

Madhouse. Calvin C. Hernton. TCP; UsP
(Patient, The: Rockland County Sanitarium.) PoBA

Madimba: Gwendolyn Brooks. Michael S. Harper. MIT

Madison Square. A. Glanz-Leyeles, *tr. fr. Yiddish by* Keith Bosley. VWA

Madman ("A madman/ in a stream/ provokes me"). Dan Johnson. PoUp

Madman's Song. Elinor Wylie. Moon

Madness. Laura Lee Carter. PoW

Madness. Sachiko Yoshihara, *tr. fr. Japanese by* James Kirkup *and* Shozo Tekunaga. BoWoP

Madness is my sidekick. Whats My Name if Not Everyone Elses. Luís Omar Salinas. SA

Madness One Monday Evening. Julia Fields. NIL; UsP

Madonna and Daughter. Carol Bergé. MMD

Madonna of the Evening Flowers. Amy Lowell. RiTi

Madonna over the pool table. Locked in a Home for Les Enfants Dérangés en Dieu. James Nolan. AAT

Madrid. "Pai Wei," *tr. fr. Chinese by* Kenneth Rexroth *and* Ling Chung. PBWP

Madrigal: "Ha ha! ha ha! This world doth pass." *Unknown. See* Fara Diddle Dyno.

Madrigal: "Like the Idalian queen." William Drummond of Hawthornden. GBL; ILP (1975 ed.); NOBE; OAEL-1

Madrigal: "Love now no fire hath left him." Giovanni Battista Marino, *tr. fr. Italian by* Richard Crashaw. OBVE

Madrigal: "My love in her attire doth show her wit." *Unknown. See* My Love in Her Attire.

Madrigal: "My mistress is as fair as fine." Thomas Ravenscroft. BBL

Madrigal: "This life which seems so fair." William Drummond of Hawthornden. OAEL-1
("This life which seems so fair.") SCP-2

Madrigal: "To be a whore, despite of grace." Charles Cotton. FaBoEE

Madrigal: "Your love is dead, lady, your love is dead." R. S. Thomas. BoLoP

Maesia's Song. Robert Greene. *Fr.* Farewell to Folly. ILP (1975 ed.); UnPo (1976 ed.)
(Mind Content, A.) PPM
("Sweet are the thoughts that Savour of content.") PCOP

Mafukuzela, rain-giving clouds. Lament for Mafukuzela. *Zulu Oral Tradition, tr. by* H. Tracey. WTO

Mag. Patricia Hubbell. CaYB

Magalu. Helene Johnson. PoBA

Magdalene, Afterward. Karen Whitehill. NPW

Magdalene Silver Mine, The. Gene Frumkin. CoPAm

Magellan braved all seas that roll. The Windham Thaw. Arthur Guiterman. ECBV

Maggie and Milly and Molly and May. E. E. Cummings. BuTh; NOBA

Maggie Campbell Blues. *Unknown.* BluL

Maggie Lauder. *At. to* Francis Sempill of Beltrees. SLP

*Maggie Mac. Unknown.* AmFP

Magi, The. Louise Glück. PoA

Magi, The. W. B. Yeats. BiP; CABA (1972 ed.); CMoP (1970 ed.); HAP; InPK; InPS; NIL; NoAM; OAEL-2; OFD; PChr; PoA; PPoe; PSN; TT

Magic. Lionel Johnson. VLP

Magic. Rex Veeder. HeS

Magic/ my man. Black Magic. Sonia Sanchez. BPo

Magic Children. Barbara Drake. TC

Magic Fox. James Welch. CDW

Magic of the day is the morning, The. Ballad of the Morning Streets. Amiri Baraka. CNA

Magic Sam. Steve Toth. AcAn

Magic Seeds, The. James Reeves. ECBV

Magic Wood, The. Henry Treece. DuDa; EAS

Magic Words, The. Ronald Koertge. AMV-81

Magic Words. *Unknown, tr. fr. Eskimo.* IPWM; NU

Magic Words for Hunting Seal. *Unknown, tr. fr. Netsilik Eskimo by* Edward Field ExPo (1973 ed.)

Magical Mouse, The. Kenneth Patchen. OSP; SO; UsP

Magical Nature. Robert Browning. VLP

Magical prognosticator. Halloween Witches. Felice Holman. CC

Magician, The. Diane Wakoski. Psy

Magna Est Veritas. Coventry Patmore. *Fr.* The Unknown Eros. HAP; ILP (1975 ed.); NOBE; VCP

Magnet, The. Thomas Stanley. NOBE

Magnetic Mountain, The, *sels.* C. Day Lewis.
"Live you by love confined." PoPle
Nearing Again the Legendary Isle, VI. FaBoTw (1975 ed.)
"Tempt me no more; for I," XXIV PoA

Magnetism. Emma Lazarus. SBG

Magnets. Countee Cullen. PBMP

Magnificat, The. Bible, *N.T.* St. Luke, I: 46-56. BoWoP; ILwL
("And Marie said, My soule doth magnife the Lord.")
OBVE

Magnificent to tourists and to tradesmen come. The Port of New York. Alfred Hayes. SPT

Magnolia trees, The. Genealogy. Frank Lamont Phillips. AmNP (1974 ed.)

Magnolias of the south were a silver fragrance. Newsreel. Norman Macleod. SPT

Magpie and Pines. Louis Johnson. ATNZ

Magpie Rhyme, Northumberland, A. *Unknown.* GBP

Magpie Song. *Tr. fr. Navajo Indian by* Washington Matthews. OBVE

Magpies, The. Denis Glover. ATNZ

Maguire is not afraid of death, the Church will light him a candle. Patrick Kavanagh. *Fr.* The Great Hunger. CIP

Magus, A. John Ciardi. CoPAm; MAT

Mahabalipuram. Louis MacNeice. NoAM

Mahabharata, The, *sel. Unknown, tr. fr. Sanskrit by* Franklin Edgerton.
"So, pure and dutiful, she sought that place." DL

Mahler, *sel.* Jonathan Williams.
Symphony No. 3, in D Minor. VGW

Mahratta Ghats, The. Alun Lewis. OBW

Maid and the Palmer, The. *Unknown.* PeBB

Maid compelled to be a gadder, A. Charles Cotton. *Fr.* Burlesque upon the Great Frost. SCP-2

Maid Freed from the Gallows, The. *Unknown.* AIW; AmFP, 2 *versions*; ECBV
(Gallows Pole, The.) FSW
(Hangman's Tree, The.) ExPo (1973 ed.)

Maid going to Comber, her markets to larn, A. The Next Market Day. *Unknown.* FSW

Maid in the Mill, The, *sel.* John Fletcher *and* William Rowley.
"Now having leisure, and a happy wind," *fr.* V, i. GBL

Maid Marian, *sel.* Thomas Love Peacock.
Friar of Rubygill, The. PeBB

Maid Mars Me, A. *Unknown.* OxBM

Maid of Athens Ere We Part. Byron. EBEV; MBPR

Maid of Brenten Arse, A. *Unknown.* GBP

Maid of Monterey, The. *Unknown.* AmFP

Maid of Neidpath, The. Sir Walter Scott. SLP

Maid of the Moor, The. *Unknown.* NOBE; OAEL-1; OxBM

Maid o' the West, The. John Clare. OAEL-2

Maid shee went to the well to washe, The. The Maid and the Palmer. *Unknown.* PeBB

Maid, where's my lawrel? Oh my rageing soul! The Enchantment. Theocritus, *tr. by* Thomas Creech. *Fr.* Idylls, II. OBVE

Maiden caught me in the wild, The. The Crystal Cabinet. Blake. AIW; Epi; MBPR; OAEL-2; UsP

Maiden caught stealing a dahlia, A. Caught Stealing a Dahlia. *Unknown.* TDH

Maiden in the moor [*or* mor] lay. The Maid of the Moor. *Unknown.* NOBE; OAEL-1; OxBM

Maiden Lane. Al Lee. NYP

Maiden Queen, The. *sel.* Dryden.
"I feed a flame within, which so torments me." PoPle

Maiden That Is Makeless, A. *Unknown. See* I Sing of a Maiden That Is Makeless.

Maiden There Lived, A. *Unknown.* NOBL

Maidenhead. "Ephelia." WPE

Maidenhead. Michael McMahon. FAF

Maiden's Best Adorning, The. *Unknown.* OxBChV; RRA

Maidens Came, The. *Unknown.* BuTh; GBL
(Bridal Morn, The.) NOBE
(Lily and the Rose, The.) UsP

Maiden's Complaint, The. *Unknown.* OLR

Maiden's Plight, The. Brian Merriman, *tr. fr. Modern Irish by* Frank O'Connor. *Fr.* The Midnight Court. BIrV .

Maidens shall weep at merry morn. The Summer Malison. Gerard Manley Hopkins. CMoP (1970 ed.); NoAM

Maidens who this bursting May. A Young Man's Song. William Bell. FaBoTw (1975 ed.)

Maids to bed and cover coal. The Bellman's Song. *Unknown.* EBEV

Maid's Tragedy, The, *sels.* Beaumont *and* Fletcher.
Aspatia's Song, *fr.* II, i. HAP; NOBE; PoPle
("Lay a garland on my hearse.") GBL; ILP (1975 ed.)
"Great queen of shadows, you are pleased to speak." SCP-2
Hold Back Thy Hours, Dark Night, *fr.* I, ii. ILP (1975 ed.)

Maids When You're Young, Never Wed an Old Man. *Unknown.* FSW

Mail from Home in the Sky. Ernest Sandeen. HeS

Mailman, The. Thomas Brush. NVAP

Mailman, The. Victor Contoski. GP

Mailman Is Coming, The. Josephine Miles. MPA

Maimed Debauchee, The. Earl of Rochester. *See* Disabled Debauchee, The.

Main-Deep, The. James Stephens. EcS; UnPo (1976 ed.)

Main Man Blues. Eugene B. Redmond. GP

Main Problem in Portraiture, The. Elisavietta Ritchie. AATT

Main-Sheet Song, The. Thomas Fleming Day. RhR

Maine Sea Gulls. Russell Hoban. BoAnP

Mainline. John Ditsky. AMV-80

Major abstraction is the idea of man, The. Wallace Stevens. *Fr.* Notes toward a Supreme Fiction. NOBA

Major André. *Unknown.* AmFP

Major Macroo. Stevie Smith. SBG

Major, with wonderful force, A. An Atrocious Pun. *Unknown.* TDH

Make a joyful noise unto the Lord, all ye lands. Bible, *O.T.* Psalms, C. CTV; OFD

Make Love Not War. Howard Nemerov. NoAM

Make me a grave where'er you will. Bury Me in a Free Land. Frances E. W. Harper. BPo

Make me a heaven, and make me there. The Eye. Robert Herrick. CaPo

Make Me a Pallet on Your Floor. *Unknown.* BluL

Make me, O Lord, thy spinning [or spining] wheel complete [or compleate]. Huswifery [or Housewifery.] Edward Taylor. EAP; ILP (1975 ed.); NIL; NOBE; SoSe; TAP

Make me one, my Only One, in such true God-is-One. The Ecstasy. Al-Hallaj. ILwL

Make Me Worthy of My Friends. *Unknown.* CTV

Make Music with Your Life. Bob O'Meally. CNA

Make no mistake. This is not. The Seven-Year Body Cycle: To My Cells Replacing Themselves for the Fourth Time. David Steingass. NVAP

Make this assumption. Rearrangement for the Brain. Gary Margolis. CoPAm

Make Way! Ada Negri, *tr. fr. Italian by* Lynne Lawner. PBWP

Make we mery, both more and lass. Now Is the Time of Christmas. *Unknown.* OxBM

Make Ye a Joyful Sounding Noise, *with music. Unknown.* AH

Maker of Heaven and Earth. Cecil Frances Alexander. *See* All Things Bright and Beautiful.

Maker-of-Sevens in the scheme of things. The Wife-Woman. Anne Spencer. NoAM

Makers, The. Richard Kell. CIP; PFIr

Making a meaning out of everything that has happened. Ramble on What in the World Why. Ralph Gustafson. AMV-81

Making an Impression. William (Haywood) Jackson. AMV-80

Making Feet and Hands. Benjamin Péret, *tr. fr. French by* David Gascoyne. EAS

Making his advances. Tortoise Gallantry. D. H. Lawrence. CMoP (1970 ed.); NoAM

Making It Simple December 8, 1969. David McElroy. AmPA

Making Love to Myself. James L. White. BrS

Making Miso. Lawson Fusao Inada. GP

Making Money. John Woods. TC

Making of Color, The. Hugh Seidman. AmPA

Making of the Cross, The. William Everson. VGW

Making Out. Leatrice W. Emeruwa. RiTi

Making the Jam without You. Maxine W. Kumin. TV

Making Up for a Soul. David Wagoner. VGW

Making Yourself at Home. David James. TC

Malacoda. Samuel Beckett. CIP

Malaga. Pearse Hutchinson. BIrV

Malcolm. Lucille Clifton. CNA

Malcolm. Welton Smith. BPo

Malcolm, a Thousandth Poem. Conrad Kent Rivers. CNA

Malcolm X. Gwendolyn Brooks. CNA; NowV; OFD; PoBA; TT

Malcolm X—An Autobiography. Larry Neal. AmNP (1974 ed.); BPo

Maldive Shark, The. Herman Melville. EcS; ILP (1975 ed.); NOBA; PiAm; TAP

Malediction. Barry Spacks. InPK

Malefic Return, The. Ramón López Velarde, *tr. fr. Spanish by* Samuel Beckett. OBVE

Malfunction. Richard E. Albert. MiP

Malice of Innocence, The. Denise Levertov. NNaP

Malison of the Stone-chat. *Unknown.* GBP

Malisons, malisons more than ten. The Lark. *Unknown.* GBP

Mallarme on July 14, 1889 ("Mallarme liked his wine"). John Batki. AcAn

Mallow evenings on the shallow lake. The Heron. Philip Murray. BoAnP

Maltese Dog, The. Tymnes, *tr. fr. Greek by* Edmund Blunden. ECBV

(Dog from Malta, The.) GDP

("He came from Malta, and Eumelus says.") FaBoEE

Malum Opus. James Appleton Morgan. FaBoCo

Malvern Hill. Herman Melville. AmVN; TAP

Malvern Waters. *Unknown.* FaBoEE

Malvolio in San Francisco. Jack Gilbert. NowV

Mama/ eats death/ tastes like fish. Monogram 4. Martina Werner, *tr. by* Rosemarie Waldrop. BoWoP

Mama,/ papa,/ and us. An Inconvenience. John Raven. BPo

Mama and Daughter. Langston Hughes. UnPo (1976 ed.)

Mama Don't 'Low. *Unknown.* FSW

Mama Knows. Sharon Scott. JB

Mama, please brush off my coat. Mama and Daughter. Langston Hughes. UnPo (1976 ed.)

Mama sent me to the spring. *See* Mamma sent me to the spring, she told me not to stay.

Mama was a friendly mountain. For Mama Streek. Colette Inez. AATT

Mama writes. Under Your Voice, among Legends. Phyllis Beauvais. NMM

Mama, you turn from the sink, shaking water. To My Mother. L. M. Rosenberg. AMV-81

Mama's God. Carolyn Rodgers. GP

Mamma! Frank Horne. BPo

Mamma sent me to the spring, she told me not to stay. Chewing Chewing Gum. *Unknown.* AmFP; FSW

Mammon-Marriage, A. George MacDonald. BoLoP

Mammoth morning moved grey flanks and groaned, A. Walking Wounded. Vernon Scannell. HeHu

Man, The. Michael Dennis Browne. GP

Man, The. Robert Creeley. OBAL

Man. George Herbert. CABA (1972 ed.); MetP

Man, The. Lucille Iverson. WBN

Man, A. Denise Levertov. TVo

Man, The. Judith McCombs. BCr

Man. Henry Vaughan. ILP (1975 ed.); MetP; NOBE; PMW; SCP-1

"Man, a man, a kingdom for a man, A." A Cynic Satyre. John Marston. *Fr.* The Scourge of Villainy, VII. TVS

Man, A (a Tom, a Dick, or some such epithet). The Bayonet and the Needle. Eliezer Steinbarg, *tr. by* Curt Leviant. VWA

Man about the Kitchen, A. Rodney Hobson. QQQ

Man adrift on a slim spar, A. Stephen Crane. AmVN

Man against the Sky, The. E. A. Robinson. CMoP (1970 ed.); STS

Man All Grown Up Is Supposed To, A. Terry Stokes. AmPA

Man and a woman, A. The Origin of Hot and Cold According to the Delawares. Lyn Lifshin. FAF

Man and Bat. D. H. Lawrence. BoAnP

Man and Beast. Clifford Dyment. BoAnP

Man and Cows. Andrew Young. EBEV

Man and His Image, The. La Fontaine, *tr. fr. French by* Elizur Wright. OBVE

Man and Wife. Mitchell Goodman. VGW

Man and Wife. Robert Lowell. BoLoP; ConAP; PSN

Man and Wife. Anne Sexton. CAPP

Man and Woman. Robert Conquest. OxBTC

Man and Woman. Don L. Lee. NeAC

Man at the end. Hamewith. Sydney Goodsir Smith. MS

Man at the moment of departure, turning, A. Ritual of Departure. Thomas Kinsella. CIP; CMoP (1970 ed.)

Man Awakened by a Song above His Roof, The. Tomas Tranströmer, *tr. fr. Swedish by* Robert Bly. EAS

Man, be ware and wise in dede. Assay a Friend. *Unknown.* OxBM

Man before me stands, black muscles, The. Base Chapel, Lejeune 4/79. Archie Hobson. AMV-81

Man behind the book may not be man, The. The Intellectual. Karl Shapiro. CMoP (1970 ed.); LFH

Man behind the counter is young and blond, The.   Conversation in the Eighth Street Bookstore.   Honor Moore.   WBN

Man bent over his guitar, The.   The Man with the Blue Guitar.   Wallace Stevens.   CMoP (1970 ed.); NoAM; SoS

Man bows out of the employment office, A.   The Long Season.   James Haug.   AMV-81

Man-brained and man-handed ground-ape, physically, The.   Original Sin.   Robinson Jeffers.   MPA; PiAm

Man builds boxes, A.   Boxes.   Toi Derricotte.   NPW

Man came running faceless over earth.   Two Eskimo Songs.   Ted Hughes.   ExPo (1973 ed.)

Man comes in the door, A.   The Man.   Michael Dennis Browne.   GP

Man could love the city he detested, The.   Ovid.   Richard Pevear.   AMV-81

Man cut his throat and left his head there, The.   The Creation of the Moon.   Unknown, tr. by W. S. Merwin.   Moon

Man, dream no more of curious mysteries.   Vain Learning.   Fulke Greville.   Fr. Caelica.   BoReV

Man Flammonde, from God knows where, The.   Flammonde.   E. A. Robinson.   CMoP (1970 ed.); NoAM; STS

Man found the escape river, A.   Crossing Over.   Dan Johnson.   PoUp

Man, free-thinker, think you yourself alone possessed of thought?   Golden.   Gérard de Nerval, tr. by Andrew Hoyem.   Epi

Man from Moscow, The.   H. H. Lewis.   SPT

Man from Snowy River, The.   Andrew Barton Paterson.   MAuV; PH

Man from the finance company, The.   Good Luck to You Kafka/ You'll Need It Boss.   Henry Graham.   NowV

Man from the Woods, The.   John Ciardi.   SO

Man from Washington, The.   James Welch.   CDW; GP; SA; VW

Man goes to a grocery store, A.   The Fear of Groceries.   Herbert Scott.   TC

Man growing old is going, A.   Shalom.   Denise Levertov.   NoAM

Man has been standing, A.   The Tunnel.   Mark Strand.   HeIP; WeW

Man has separated lust and sorrow.   All Is God's.   Jakov de Haan, tr. by David Soetendorp.   VWA

Man He Killed, The.   Thomas Hardy.   CMoP (1970 ed.); DL; FF; HAP; HeIP; ILP (1975 ed.); InPS; IP; IPWM; PBMP; SFF; SoSe; VoPo; WIF

Man hired by John Smith and Co., A.   Dirt Dumping [or Limerick].   "Mark Twain."   FaBoNo; TDH

Man Holding Boy in the Rain.   Melvin Dixon.   NW

Man, husband existence: ne'er launch on the sea.   Epitaph of Cleonicus.   Theocritus, tr. by Charles Stuart Calverley.   FaBoEE

Man I married twice, The.   Reject Jell-o.   Lucille Day.   AMV-81

Man I saw in the forest, The.   Dream 2: Brian the Still-Hunter.   Margaret Atwood.   BoWoP

Man, if I said once, 'I know.'   The Islands.   Randall Jarrell.   EAS

Man, if you gonna love your woman.   You Got to Love Her with a Feeling.   Unknown.   BluL

Man in armor, A.   Touch.   Erica Jong.   RiTi

Man in Black, The.   Mark Strand.   EAS

Man in his secret shrine.   Hymn in Columbus Circle.   Stephen Vincent Benét.   OBAL

Man in life wherever placed, The.   Paraphrase of the First Psalm.   Burns.   PIM

Man in Our Village, A.   Leslie Norris.   GDP

Man in Overalls, The.   Edward Lueders.   MPA

Man in righteousness array'd, The.   To Sally.   John Quincy Adams.   OBAL

Man in the Bowler Hat, The.   Peter Black.   BuTh

Man in the Dead Machine, The.   Donald Hall.   CoPAm

Man in the Dream Is Death, The.   Lynne Butler.   IHMS

Man in the feed store called them mountain beavers, The.   Looking for Mountain Beavers.   David Wagoner.   VGW

Man in the Moon, The ("Man in the moone stand and strit"), orig. and mod. English prose.   Unknown.   OxBM

Man in the moon came tumbling down, The.   Unknown.   Moon

Man in the moon was caught in a trap, The.   Unknown.   Moon

Man in the moone stand and strit.   The Man in the Moon.   Unknown.   OxBM

Man in the Onion Bed, The.   John Ciardi.   SO

Man in the red scarf comes—from five split places, The.   The Raspberry in the Pudding.   Philip O'Connor.   EAS

Man in the Street.   Robert Penn Warren.   OBAL

Man in the Tree, The.   Mark Strand.   EAS

Man in the wilderness asked [of] me, The [or A].   Mother Goose.   BBL; ECBV; FaBoCo; FaBoNo; GBP; MG

Man in the womb is but a zoophyte.   The Progress.   Ralph Knevet.   SCP-2

Man in this lapst estate at very best.   God's Selecting Love in the Decree.   Edward Taylor.   Fr. God's Determinations.   EAP

Man into a Churchyard.   Bernard Gutteridge.   EAS

Man, introverted man, having crossed.   Science.   Robinson Jeffers.   MPA; NU; WIF

Man Is a Snow.   Earle Birney.   MPA

Man is clothed, The.   And When the Green Man Comes.   John Haines.   ConAP; NCSH

Man is flesh and blood and brittle bones.   Bones.   S. L. Henderson Smith.   PMW

Man is in terror of impotence, A.   The Ninth Symphony of Beethoven Understood at Last as a Sexual Message.   Adrienne Rich.   TAP

Man is killing time—there's nothing else, The.   The Drinker.   Robert Lowell.   SoSe

"Man is mad, The" they said.   We Are All a Little Mad.   John Gonzalez.   PMW

Man is mind.   Progress.   Peter Meinke.   POL; SoSe (1977 ed.)

Man Is Nothing But.   Shaul Tchernichovsky, tr. fr. Hebrew by Robert Friend.   VWA

Man knows where first he ships himself, but he.   Man's Dying-Place Uncertain.   Robert Herrick.   CaPo

Man laughing on the steep hill, The.   Trifles.   William Everson.   CoPAm

Man lies down to sleep, A.   Pull of the Earth.   Stanley Plumly.   HeS

Man, like others, formed by God, A.   The Saxons of Flint.   Unknown, tr. by Mary C. Llewelyn.   OBW

Man looking into the sea.   A Grave.   Marianne Moore.   CABA (1972 ed.); CMoP (1970 ed.); ExPo (1973 ed.); HAP; HeIP; InPK; NoAM; NOBA; PPoe; TAP; UnPo (1976 ed.); WPE

Man Lying on a Wall.   Michael Longley.   CIP

Man, Man, Man Is for the Woman Made.   Unknown.   PAIC; Prf

Man may escape from rope and gun.   John Gay.   Fr. The Beggar's Opera, II, ii.   ILP (1975 ed.)

Man Meeting Himself.   Howard Sergeant.   EAS

Man Missing.   Charles Brasch.   ATNZ

Man-Moth, The.   Elizabeth Bishop.   ILP (1975 ed.); MAT; NoAM; NOBA; NYP; PPP

Man moves toward himself as old, A.   In Random Fields of Impulse and Repose.   Jeanine Hathaway.   AMV-81

Man, My Father, The.   Marcia Lee Masters.   HeS

Man, my friend, whose conscious heart, The.   To Aristius Fuscus.   Horace, tr. by Samuel Johnson.   Odes, I, 22.   OBVE

Man next to me has a box, The.   UA Flight to Chicago.   Duane Ackerson.   PoW

Man next to me with the gray hair, The. In the Bar. Robert Vander Molen. TAT

Man of bone confirms his throne, The. The New Ancient of Days. Herman Melville. OBAL

Man of Calvary, The, *sel.* "Sin-Killer" Griffin. "Roman soldiers come riding in full speed." AmFP

Man of Constant Sorrow. *Unknown.* FSW

Man of Experience, A. Laoiseach Mac an Bhaird, *tr. fr. Irish by* Frank O'Connor. PFIr

Man of Glass, The. Gordon Challis. ATNZ

Man of himself's a little world, but join'd. The Microcosm. Giovanni Battista Guarini, *tr. by* Sir Edward Sherburne. LoAs

Man of independent means, A. No Occupation. George Rostrevor Hamilton. FaBoEE

Man of Letters. Warren Knox. QQQ

Man of Life Upright, The. Thomas Campion. *See* Integer Vitae.

Man of massive meditation, A. Analogue of Unity in Multeity. Richard Eberhart. NoAM

Man of Prayer, The. Christopher Smart. *Fr.* A Song to David. PIM

Man of Property, The. Charles G. Ballard. VW

Man of Taste, The, *sel.* James Bramston. "Huge commentators grace my learned shelves." FaBoCo

Man of Thessaly, The. *Unknown.* FaBoCo ("There was a man of Thessaly.") FaBoNo; MG

Man of Words, A. John Ashbery. PoA

Man of Words, A. *Unknown.* ECBV; FF ("Man of words and not of deeds, A.") CTV

Man on a Raft. J. R. Hervey. ATNZ

Man on his own in a car, A. Meditation on the A30. John Betjeman. BBGO

Man on Move Despite Failures. Jeffery Alan Triggs. AMV–80

Man on My Back, The. Pradip Sen. BuTh

Man on the Bed, The. Cleopatra Mathis. AAN

Man on the Dump, The. Wallace Stevens. HAP

Man on the Flying Trapeze, The. George Leybourne. BLSH, *with music*; BLSo, *with music*; FSW; PoTa (Flying Trapeze, The.) PSoN

Man one out of his head, A. A Week in Paradise. John Ridland. NowV

Man or woman walking today, A. To Xanadu, Which Is Beth Shaul. Arye Sivan, *tr. by* Anthony Rudolf *and* Natan Zach. VWA

Man out walking alone in the snow, A. Winter Exercise. Howard Nemerov. NowV

Man plays harmonica at midnight, The. Ruston, Louisiana: 1952. Cleopatra Mathis. AMV–80

Man possessed a cat on which he doted, A. Cat into Lady. La Fontaine, *tr. by* Edmund Marsh. PCat

Man proposes, God in His time disposes. On a Dead Child. Richard Middleton. SoSe

Man riding on the meaning of rivers, A. Are You Born?—I. Muriel Rukeyser. LoAs

Man runs across the ceiling, A. In the Dark. Jane Pridmore. FPB

Man said to me at the fair, A. The Market. James Stephens. AIW

Man said to the universe, A. War Is Kind, XXI. Stephen Crane. AmVN; FaBoEE; FF; NIL; OBAL; OBSV; PiAm; PoIA; SFF; TAP; TT; WeW

Man sat in the felon's tank, alone, A. In the Tank. Thom Gunn. NoAM

Man saw a ball of gold in the sky, A. The Black Riders, XXXV. Stephen Crane. AmVN; PiAm; PPM

Man say I had something look like new, A. Stew Meat Blues. *Unknown.* BluL

Man seasick with drink. Brendan Gone. Padraic Fiacc. CIP

Man shapes the patterns of his mind. To Sir Charles Sherrington. Lord Russell Brain. PMW

Man should never earn his living, A. A Living. D. H. Lawrence. RFM

Man sits in a timelessness, The. The Rescue. Robert Creeley. CAPP

Man-sized Job. Sharlot Hall. WPW

Man so sick that the sexual soup, A. Sexual Soup. Erica Jong. GP

Man, standing in the shadows of a, A. For H. W. Fuller. Carolyn M. Rodgers. BPo

Man steps in out of the blizzard with his Klootch, The. The Sweet. Ai. GP

Man stood in the laurel tree, A. Things. Louis Simpson. TCP

Man that had six mortal wounds, a man, A. Cuchulain Comforted. W. B. Yeats. CMoP (1970 ed.); OAEL-2

Man that hails you Tom or Jack, The. William Cowper. *Fr.* On Friendship. POL

Man that hath great griefs I pity not, The. Thomas Edward Brown. *Fr.* Pain. PeD

Man that is borne of woman, is of a few dayes, and full of trouble. Bible, *O.T.* Job, XIV. OBVE

Man that sees by chance his picture made, A. The Growth of Love, XXXIX. Robert Bridges. NoAM

Man That Waters the Workers' Beer, The. Paddy Ryan. FSW

Man, the egregious egoist. Cold-blooded Creatures. Elinor Wylie. SBG

Man, them revolutionary niggers is all. Just Taking Note. Sharon Scott. JB

Man Thinking about Woman. Don L. Lee. CNA; IPWM; NoAM

Man to the Wound in Christ's Side. Robert Southwell. PIM

Man under the Bed, The. Erica Jong. AmPA; NVAP; OSP, 5 *ll.*

Man Upright, The. Thomas MacDonagh. BIrV

Man Upstairs, The. David Hilton. AcAn

Man Walked under a Plastic Decoration, A. Ralph Robin. PoUp

Man walks quietly through the bank, A. Papa Doc Is Dead. Carol Cox. MMD

Man walks through a district, A. Animation and Ego. Jody Swilky. AMV–80

"Man wants but little here below." The Wants of Man. John Quincy Adams. OBAL

Man was forever haunted by his head, The. O Metaphysical Head. Horace Gregory. SPT

Man was sitting underneath a tree, A. Seumas Beg. James Stephens. OxBTC

Man Watching, The. Rainer Maria Rilke, *tr. fr. German by* Robert Bly. NU

Man went forth with gifts, A. Martin Luther King, Jr. Gwendolyn Brooks. CNA; PoBA; WIF

Man went walking up and down, A. One Fish Ball. *Unknown.* FSW

Man White, Brown Girl and All That Jazz. Gloria C. Oden. PoBA

Man Who Broke the Bank at Monte Carlo, The. Fred Gilbert. FSN, *with music*; FSW

Man Who Closes Himself, The. Peter Cooley. NVAP

Man Who Dreamed of Faeryland, The. W. B. Yeats. CMoP (1970 ed.); NoAM; PoPle

Man Who Finds That His Son Has Become a Thief, The. Raymond Souster. BBGO

Man who for his race might supersede, The. Richard Henry Horne. *Fr.* Orion. VLP

Man who found the aardvark, The. A Bestiary. Kenneth Rexroth. OBAL

Man Who Had Fallen among Thieves, A.　E. E. Cummings.
HAP; IP; NoAM; NOBA; NowV; PiAm; TAP

Man, who had no rivals in the love, A.　The Man and His Image.
La Fontaine, *tr. by* Elizur Wright.　OBVE

Man who, having collapsed, rises, takes steps, is insane, The.
Forced March.　Miklós Radnóti, *tr. by* Emery George.
VWA

Man who holds fear, A.　The Underground Parking.　Gary Soto.
AAN; CPA

Man Who Invented Las Vegas, The.　Gerald Costanzo.　TAT

Man Who Knew the Colt Boy, The.　Gene Keller.　TVo

Man who loves hiking, A.　Hiking.　Joseph Bruchac.　CDW

Man Who Married Magdalene, The.　Louis Simpson.　NoAM;
TAP

Man Who Prayed, The.　John Shaw Neilson.　MAuV

Man who sold his lawn to standard oil, The.　The War against the
Trees.　Stanley Kunitz.　HAP; NoAM

Man Who Spilled Light, The.　David Wagoner.　MPA

Man Who Swallowed a Bird, The.　David Young.　CAAP

Man who told the hawk, The.　Much of Me.　Chuck Eggerth.
AMV-80

Man Who Wasn't There, The.　Brian Lee.　FPB

Man whom many held for wise, A.　Memo.　Hans Sahl, *tr. by*
Edouard Roditi.　VWA

Man whose height his fear improved he, The.　Medgar Evers.
Gwendolyn Brooks.　NowV; PoBA

Man Whose Pharynx Was Bad, The.　Wallace Stevens.　PiAm

Man with a leaf in his head, A.　The Mulch.　Stanley Kunitz.
GP

Man with a scythe: the torrent of his swing.　Gardens No
Emblems.　Donald Davie.　OAEL-2

Man with the Blue Guitar, The, *sels*.　Wallace Stevens
"He held the world upon his nose," XXV.　TT
"I cannot bring a world quite round," II.　CMoP (1970 ed.);
SoS
"Man bent over his guitar, The," I.　CMoP (1970 ed.); NoAM;
SoS
"Tom-tom, c'est moi. The blue guitar," XII.　CMoP (1970 ed.)
"Tune beyond us as we are, A," VI.　CMoP (1970 ed.)

Man with the camera comes, The.　Reservation Special.　Lew
Blockcolski.　VoR

Man with the Hoe, The.　Edwin Markham.　AmVN; WIF

Man with the Wooden Leg, The.　Katherine Mansfield.　ATNZ

Man, you got a bird where your brain.　The One That Got Away.
Gary Miranda.　AAN

Man you know, assured and kind, The.　Almost Human.　C. Day
Lewis.　NoAM

Manchester by Night.　Mathilde Blind.　SBG

Manchild.　Margo Bohanon.　SES

Manchild.　Emma Lou Thayne.　MPA

Manciple's Tale, The, *sels*.　Chaucer.　*Fr.* The Canterbury Tales.
Controlling the Tongue.　OxBChV
Mice before Milk.　PCat

Mandalay.　Kipling.　NOBE; PBMP

Mandarin/ in a silent film.　The Yellow Bird.　James W.
Thompson.　PoBA

Mandelstam.　Richard Burns.　VWA

Mandelstam.　David Young.　AmPA

Mandrake Hairt, The.　Sydney Goodsir Smith.　SLP

Mandy as Night Bouquet.　Henry Kanabus.　FiCh

Manerly Margery Mylk and Ale.　John Skelton.　AAS
(Mannerly Margery Milk and Ale.)　FaBoNo

Manfred: A Dramatic Poem.　Byron.　MBPR
"Stars are forth, the moon above the tops, The," *fr.* III, iv.
OAEL-2

Mango on the Mango Tree, The.　Robert Penn Warren.　Mexico
Is a Foreign Country: Four Studies in Naturalism, IV.
NoAM

Mangoes grow in clusters, The.　So Close Should Be Our Love.
*Gond Oral Tradition, tr. by* V. Elwin *and* S. Hivale.　WTO

Manhattan.　Lorenz Hart.　OBAL

Manhattan.　H. R. Hays.　EAS

Manhattan.　Osbert Lancaster.　*Fr.* Afternoons with Baedeker.
NOBL

Manhattan is no island, it.　Under.　George Bowering.　NeAC

Manhole Covers.　Karl Shapiro.　GP; MiP; NCSH

MANICdepressant.　Kim Dammers.　POL

Manichaeans, The.　Gary Snyder.　VGW

Manifest Destiny.　Anita Endrezze Probst.　CDW

Manifestation, The.　Theodore Roethke.　CNW

Manifesto, *sels*.　Nicanor Parra, *tr. fr. Spanish by* Miller Williams.
I Move the Meeting Be Adjourned.　HoPM (1975 ed.)
"Ladies and gentlemen/ This is our final word."　TSWA

Mankho's Philosophers.　John Manifold.　FPA

Mankind looks forward, but the hurt look back.　Four Poems, 2.
Joseph Freeman.　SPT

Manless Society, The.　Pierre Unik, *tr. fr. French by* David
Gascoyne.　EAS

Manly Diversion.　Karl Kopp.　GP

Man-made bay, its fat weeds, The.　Mission Bay.　John Koethe.
PoA

Mannahatta.　Walt Whitman.　GOA; NYP

Manner of your going, The.　Poem for Eric Barker.　Jean Burden.
PoW

Mannerly Margery Milk and Ale.　John Skelton.　*See* Manerly
Margery Mylk and Ale.

Manners.　Elizabeth Bishop.　CTBA; NCSH

Manners.　Edith Marcombe Shiffert.　WPE

Manners at Table When Away from Home.　*Unknown.*　OxBChV

Manor Farm, The.　Edward Thomas.　ExPo (1973 ed.)

Manor Water.　*Unknown.*　GBP

Manos Karastefanis.　James Merrill.　TAP

Manresa and the mango trees and the sterile landscape.　St.
Ignatius Loyola, Founder of the Jesuits: His Autobiography.
John L'Heureux.　PAIC

Man's a man, A.　Rat Fever: History as Hallucination.　Michael
S. Harper.　NW

Man's a Man for A' That, A.　Burns.　*See* For A' That and A'
That.

Man's a phenomenon, one knows not what.　Byron.　*Fr.* Don
Juan, I.　LFH

Man's and woman's bodies lay without souls.　A Childish Prank.
Ted Hughes.　OAEL-2

Man's been pitying himself all Sunday long, The.　The Apron.
Stuart Friebert.　FiCP

Man's Days.　Eden Phillpotts.　OxBTC

Man's Dying-Place Uncertain.　Robert Herrick.　CaPo

Man's left leg, The/ is torn away at last.　The Death of Damiens
or l'Apres-midi des Lumieres.　R. F. Brissenden.　GAS

Man's life is like a rose, that in the spring.　Meditation 9.　Philip
Pain.　NOBA

Man's mind is larger than his brow of tears.　To the Victor.
William Ellery Leonard.　PPM

Man's Need, A.　*Gond Oral Tradition, tr. by* V. Elwin *and* S.
Hivale.　WTO

Man's parts tell us such a lot!, A.　Parts.　Zishe Landau, *tr. by*
Ruth Whitman.　VWA

Man's work, A.　The Stone Poems.　Ken Smith.　TwMBP

Manservants on the last trains.　North to Milwaukee.　Gerald
Vizenor.　VoR

Mantis.　David McCord.　OBAL

"Mantis." Louis Zukofsky. PoA

Mantis with translucent grin, The. Confontation. John Hart. MIT; POL

Mantle So Green, The. *Unknown.* AmFP

Mantova. James Wright. NNaP

Manual, The. Larry Rubin. GP

Many a curious mortal have I seen. The Aquarium, San Francisco. V. Sackville-West. SBG

Many a green isle needs must be. Lines Written among the Euganean Hills. Shelley. MBPR

Many a hearth upon our dark globe sighs after many a vanish'd face. Vastness. Tennyson. VLP

Many a long, long year ago. The Alarmed Skipper. James Thomas Fields. RhR

Many a Long Year. *Unknown.* PoPle

Many a night I pulled up a chair. Their Strange Evaluation. Deirdra Baldwin. PoUp

Many Are Called. E. A. Robinson. PiAm

Many arrivals make us live: the tree becoming. The Manifestation. Theodore Roethke. CNW

"Many Brave Hearts Are Asleep in the Deep." Morgan Sanders. WBN

Many-clothed and smelling of cheap soap. A Clutter of Mothers. Edwin Brock. IPWM

Many days of sorrow, many nights of woe. Chain Gang Blues. *Unknown.* WTO

Many desire, but few or none deserve. The Advice. Sir Walter Ralegh. AAS

Many ingenious lovely things are gone. Nineteen Hundred and Nineteen. W. B. Yeats. BIrV; ExPo (1973 ed.)

Many liberals don't just. Respectabilities. Jon Silkin. NoAM

Many-maned scud-thumper, tub. Winter Ocean. John Updike. InPK; OSP; SoSe

Many, many welcomes. The Snowdrop. Tennyson. FSFS

Many nicknames. On Nicknames. Louis Phillips. OSF

Many paths lead. Paths to God. Musa Moris Farhi. VWA

Many people have gathered together. Foot Race Song. *Unknown, tr. by* Frank Russell. NU; OBVE

Many people seem to think. Parisian Nectar. Gelett Burgess. FaBoNo

Many people watch the fire. Still Life. Henry Kanabus. FiCh

Many red devils ran from my heart. The Black Riders, XLVI. Stephen Crane. PiAm; TAP

Many sewing days ago. The Listening Macaws. Hazel Hall. WPW

Many the wonders I this day have seen. To My Brother George. Keats. MBPR

Many things I might have said today. Aprons of Silence. Carl Sandburg. NoAM; NOBA

Many Thousand Gone. *Unknown. See* No More Auction Block.

Many times the size of man. The Horse. Francis Ponge, *tr. by* Beth Archer. NU

Many Voices. Samuel Makidemewabe, *tr. fr. Cree Indian by* Howard Norman. TC

Many ways to spell good night. Carl Sandburg. *Fr.* Good Night. CC

Many women call on me to sleep with them. A Mourning-Song for Rangiaho. Te Heuheu Herea, *tr. by* Barry Mitcalfe. WTO

Many Workmen. Stephen Crane. The Black Riders, XXI. TAP

Many years ago my mother and I skated. My Grandmother and the Voice of Tolstoy. Steve Orlen. AMV-81

Manzanita, The. Yvor Winters. VGW

Map, The. Elizabeth Bishop. NOBA

Map, The. Gloria C. Oden. AmNP (1974 ed.)

Map, The/ takes me back. Passover. Rose Ausländer, *tr. by* Ewald Osers. VWA

Map of Places, The. Laura Riding. NoAM

Map of the Western Part of the County of Essex in England, A. Denise Levertov. ConAP

Map Reading. David Citino. AMV-81

Map shows me where it is you are, The. A Private Letter to Brazil. Gloria C. Oden. AmNP (1974 ed.)

Maple buds were blossoming reddish tufts, The. The Grotto. Ray Fraser. NeAC

Maple in November. Ethel Green Russell. AATT

Maple Leaf Forever, The, *with music.* Alexander Muir. BLSH

Maple Leaf Rag, *with music.* Sydney Brown. BLSo

Maps. Robert Hass. CAAP

Maps. Howard Schwartz. HeS

Maps for a Son Are Drawn as You Go. Samuel Hazo. AMV-81

Maps to Nowhere. David Rosenberg. VWA

Maquillage. Arthur Symons. VLP

Maratea Porto: Saying Goodbye to the Vitolos. Richard Hugo. MAT

Marauder, The. Robley Wilson, Jr. BCr

Marban, a Hermit Speaks. *Unknown, tr. fr. Irish by* Michael Hartnett. BIrV; CIP

Marble. A. R. Ammons. WasP

Marble-Top. E. B. White. OBAL

Marceline, to Her Husband. Elizabeth Libbey. AmPA

March. Nora Hopper. FSFS

March ("He ended; and midst those who heard were some"). William Morris. *Fr.* The Earthly Paradise. VLP

March, The ("Under the too white marmorial Lincoln Memorial"). Robert Lowell. NowV

March, The ("Where two or three were heaped together, or fifty"). Robert Lowell. NowV

March. *Unknown.* GBP

March. William Carlos Williams. NCSH

March. James Wright. BCr; TH

March Bee, The. Edmund Blunden. PoPle

March Fugue. Thomas Shapcott. CAAP

March Hares. Walter de la Mare. FaBoNo

March has come to the bridge head. Poem by the Bridge at Ten-shin. Li Po, *tr. by* Ezra Pound. OBVE

March into Virginia, The. Herman Melville. HAP; PiAm; TAP

March Light. Ralph J. Mills, Jr. AMV-81

March on the Delta. Art Berger. NowV

March on Washington, A. Radcliffe Squires. WasP

March Rite: Getting It Up. A. G. Sobin. HeS

March said to Averil. The Borrowing Days. *Unknown.* GBP

March Sound. Harry Thurston. AMV-81

March 10th and the snow flees like eloping brides. May You Always Be the Darling of Fortune. Jane Miller. AMV-80

March to Moscow, The. Robert Southey. FaBoCo

March 26th, 1971. John McNally. PoUp

March Wardrobe. Charles Potts. FoP

March went out like a lion. June Is Bustin' Out All Over. Oscar Hammerstein II. BLSo

March winds and April showers. *Unknown.* MG

March with All Drums Muffled, A. Reuel Denney. NYP

March yeans the lammie. March. *Unknown.* GBP

Märchen, The. Randall Jarrell. CMoP (1970 ed.)

Märchenbilder. John Ashbery. NOBA

Marches Now the War Is Over. Walt Whitman. *See* By Blue Ontario's Shore.

Marching 'round the Levee. *Unknown.* AmFP

Marching through Georgia. Henry Clay Work. FaPoR; FSW; PSoN, *with music*

Marching to Pretoria. *Unknown.* FSW

Marching To Quebec. *Unknown.* AmFP

Marching to Utah. *Unknown.* AmFP

Marco Bozzaris, *sel.* Fitz-Greene Halleck.
  "At midnight, in his guarded tent." HoPM (1975 ed.)

Mardi Gras. Miller Williams. TAT

Mare, The. Herbert Asquith. DuDr; PH

Mare, A. Kate Barnes. PH

Mare. Judith Thurman. FPB; PH

Mare, The. Vernon Watkins. OBW

Mare, dead since November, is still, The. The January Sky. A.
  G. Sobin. HeS

Mare lathers the wind, The. Bareback in Kansas. F. Eugene
  Warren. AATT

Mare lies down in the grass where the nest of the skylark is
  hidden, The. The Mare. Vernon Watkins. OBW

Mare roamed soft about the slope, The. Orchard. Ruth Stone.
  PH

Mares of Night. Virginia Long. AMV-81

Marezle toats. *Unknown.* FaBoNo

Margaret Are You Drug. George Starbuck. MAT

Margaret, are you grieving. Spring and Fall. Gerard Manley
  Hopkins. AnMo; BBGO; BiP; CMoP (1970 ed.); EBEV;
  FF; HAP; HeIP; HoPM (1975 ed.); ILP (1975 ed.); InPK;
  InPS; IP; MAT; NIL; NOBE; PAIC; PoPle; PPoe; PPP;
  VLP; VoPo; WeW; WIF

Margaret had a very low I.Q. Mother. William Duncan. PMW

Margaret Nash Got Wet but I Don't Know How. John Ciardi.
  OSF

Margaret, Seen through a Picture Window. Judy Grahn. *Fr.*
  The Common Woman, VI. GP

Margaritae Sorori. W. E. Henley. *Fr.* Echoes. NOBE
  (Late Lark Twitters, A.) ILP (1975 ed.)

Margie Silver. Henry Kanabus. FiCh

Marginal Field, The. Stephen Spender. PoA

Marginal Music. R. K. Meiners. AMV-81

Marginalia, *sel.* W. H. Auden.
  "Dead man, A/ who never caused others to die." OAEL-2

Marginalia. Richard Wilbur. CMoP (1970 ed.); PoA

Maria intended a letter to write. How to Write a Letter.
  Elizabeth Turner. OxBChV

Maria Wentworth. Thomas Carew. CaPo; MetP; SCP-2

Mariam, *sels.* Lady Elizabeth Carey.
  "Fairest action of our human life, The," *fr.* IV. WPE
  "'Tis not enough for one that is a wife," *fr.* III. WPE

Mariana. Tennyson. BiP; InPS; NOBE; OAEL-2; PoIA; PoPle;
  UnPo (1976 ed.); VLP

Mariana in the South. Tennyson. VLP

Marie Hamilton's to the kirk gane. The Queen's Marie.
  *Unknown.* PoPle

Marigold, The. Thomas Carew. *See* Boldness in Love.

Marigold. Richard Garnett. PCat

Marigold. John Haines. POL

Marigold, The. George Wither. PF

Marigolds. Bliss Carman. AKE

Marijuana Notation. Allen Ginsberg. TT

Marijuana Patch on the State Hospital's Former Grounds.
  Nathan Whiting. HeS

Marilyn Monroe. Paul Ramsey. PPoD

Marina. T. S. Eliot. BoReV; CMoP (1970 ed.); HeIP; NOBE;
  PiAm; PSN; RRA; TCP; UsP

Marin-An. Gary Snyder. PoIA; TAT; WeW

Marine. Rolfe Humphries. EcS

Mariners. David Morton. RhR

Mariners' Compass, The. *Unknown.* RhR

Mariners, seabirds, sailing-ships of the lustrous early annals.
  Thalassa, Thalassa. James Neugass. SPT

Marines' Hymn, The. *Unknown.* BLSH, *with music*; BLSo, *with
music*; BTTM

Mariposa Lily, The. Ina Coolbrith. BPAW

Marital Journey, The. Hailu Araaya. MiP

Mark. Bible, *N.T. See* St. Mark.

Mark, The. Robert Graves. LoAs

Mark. Steve Toth. AcAn

Mark Anthony would now rouse fears. Transplantitis. Lester A.
  Sobel. QQQ

Mark Antony. John Cleveland. OAEL-1; SCP-2

Mark Antony Addresses the Mob. Shakespeare. *Fr.* Julius
  Caesar, III, ii. FaPoR

Mark [*or* Marke] but this flea, and mark [*or* marke] in this. The
  Flea. John Donne. AnMo; BiP; BoLoP; CABA (1972 ed.);
  EBEV; FF; HoPM (1975 ed.); ILP (1975 ed.); LFH; MAT;
  NIL; OAEL-1; PAIC; PoPle; PPoe; SCP-1; SoSe (1977 ed.);
  TT

Mark how the bashful morn in vain. Boldness in Love [*or* The
  Marigold]. Thomas Carew. CaPo; PF

Mark how the lanterns cloud mine eyes! A Non Sequitor.
  Richard Corbet. FaBoNo

Mark how the lark and linnet sing. An Ode: On the Death of
  Mr. Purcell. Dryden. ILP (1975 ed.)

Mark how yon eddy steals away. To My Mistress Sitting by a
  River's Side: An Eddy. Thomas Carew. CaPo

Mark the dark rook, on pendent branches hung. George
  Canning. *Fr.* The Progress of Man. FaBoNo

Mark the note that rises, mark the notes that fall. How to Sing or
  Read. Robert Louis Stevenson. ECBV

Mark This. Sallie Chesham. AATT

Mark Van Doren. James Worley. AMV-81

Mark where the pressing wind shoots javelin-like. Modern Love,
  XLIII. George Meredith. GBL; ILP (1975 ed.); NOBE;
  OBP; VPC

Mark yon round parson, fat and sleek. Robert Lloyd. *Fr.* A
  Familiar Epistle to J. B. Esq. OBSV

Mark you the floor [*or* floore]? that square and speckled stone.
  The Church-Floor [*or* Floore.] George Herbert. EBEV;
  OAEL-1

Marke but this flea, and marke in this. *See* Mark but this flea. . .

Marker slants, flowerless, day's almost done, The. John
  Berryman. *Fr.* Dream Songs. CAPP

Market, The. James Stephens. AIW

Market Women's Cries. Swift. LoAs; PFIr
  Onyons, *sel.* BIrV

Marl white road, the Dorée rushing cool, The. Tales of the
  Islands. Derek Walcott. OxBTC

Marlin. Brewster Ghiselin. MPA; PPoD

Marlow and Nancy. Sandra McPherson. AmPA

Marmion, *sel.* Sir Walter Scott.
  Lochinvar, *fr.* V. AIW; BTTM; ECBV; ILP (1975 ed.); NOBE;
  PoTa; PPM; SLP

Marriage, A. Anthony Barnett. VWA

Marriage. Wendell Berry. CSP

Marriage, The. James Bertolino. HeS

Marriage. Austin Clarke. BIrV

Marriage. Gregory Corso. CABA (1972 ed.); CoPAm; InPS;
  NoAM; OBAL; PPoD; PPP; TAP

Marriage. Marea Gordett. AMV-81

Marriage. Michael Lopes. PoW

Marriage. Marianne Moore. NOBA; RiTi

Marriage. John L. Sellers. DNGG

Marriage. Mary Ellen Solt. BoWoP

Marriage, The. Mark Strand. EAS; NoAM

Marriage ("Here we go around this ring"). *Unknown.* AmFP

Marriage ("Put your hand in the creel"). *Unknown.* GBP

Marriage. William Carlos Williams. IPWM; PoA

Marriage à la Mode, *sels.* Dryden.
Song: "Why should a foolish marriage vow," *fr.* I, i. BuTh; LoAs
(Why Should a Foolish Marriage Vow.) HeIP; ILP (1975 ed.); NIL
"Whil'st Alexis lay prest [*or* press'd]," *fr.* IV, ii. FF; LoAs
(Song: "Whilst Alexis lay pressed.") BoLoP

Marriage Amulet. Nancy Willard. RiTi

Marriage and Money. Sir Charles Sedley. *Fr.* The Happy Pair OBSV

Marriage Couplet. William Cole. OBAL

Marriage Dance, The. Eda Lou Walton, *after Blackfoot Indian.* BPAW

Marriage in Eden, The. William Williams, *tr. fr. Welsh by* Saunders Lewis *and* Gwyn Jones. *Fr.* A View of Christ's Kingdom. OBW

Marriage is not/ a house or even a tent. Habitation. Margaret Atwood. BoWoP

Marriage Morning. Tennyson. GBL

Marriage of Heaven and Hell, The. Blake. LAuP; MBPR; OAEL-2
*Sels.*
"In seed time learn, in harvest teach, in winter enjoy." FF
Memorable Fancy, A ("An angel came to me and said"). NU
Memorable Fancy, A ("As I was walking . . ."). NU
"Pride of the peacock is the glory of God, The." FF
Voice of the Devil, The. NU

Marriage of Hector and Andromache, The. Sappho, *tr. fr. Greek by* Guy Davenport. OBVE

Marriage of Here and There, The. Peter Trias. AAN

Marriage of the Frog and the Mouse, The. *Unknown.* EBEV

Marriage Ring, A. George Crabbe. BoLoP
(His Late Wife's Wedding-Ring.) NOBE

Marriage Wig, The. Ruth Whitman. IHMS

Marriage within the group is endogamy. Marriage. John L. Sellers. DNGG

Marrie dear. When in Rome. Mari Evans. AmNP (1974 ed.); NIL; SoSe

Married academic woman ten. My Mother's Novel. Marge Piercy. TV

Married and Single Life. *Unknown.* AmFP

Married for one year. Making It Simple December 8, 1969. David McElroy. AmPA

Married Lover, The. Coventry Patmore. *Fr.* The Angel in the House, II, xii. VLP

Married Man Blues. *Unknown.* BluL

Married man comes nearest to the dead, A. Samuel Butler. FaBoEE

Married man who begs his friend, A. Enticer. Richard Armour. SoSe

Married to rural goldmines. The Dark Way Home: Survivors. Michael S. Harper. CNA

Marrog, The. R. C. Scriven. DuDr; FPB

Marrow of My Bone. Mari Evans. BPo

Marry and love thy Flavia, for she. The Anagram. John Donne. *Fr.* Elegies. PAIC

Marry the Lass? Andrew Greig. SLP

Mars is braw in crammasy. The Bonnie Broukit Bairn. "Hugh MacDiarmid." HAP; InPS; MS

Marseillaise, La. Claude Joseph Rouget de Lisle, *tr. fr. French by* Albert Morehead. BLSH, *with music;* FSW

Marsh, The. W. D. Snodgrass. PiAm

Marsh Leaf. David Wagoner. PoA

Marsh, New Year's Day, The. Peter Everwine. NNaP

Marsh Song—At Sunset. Sidney Lanier. NOBA

Marshall. George MacBeth. NoAM

Marshall, the thinges for to attayne. *See* Martial, the things for to attain.

Marshes, The. Jane Mayhall. TAP

Marshes of Glynn, The. Sidney Lanier. AmVN; NOBA; PiAm; VoPo

Marston. Stephen Spender. FaBoTw (1975 ed.)

Marten flew to the finch's nest, The. Feathers and Moss. Jean Ingelow. SpRo

Martha/ Mary passed this morning. Mary Passed This Morning. Owen Dodson. PoBA

Martha Blake at Fifty-one. Austin Clarke. CIP

Martha rows me from the bleeding horror. Black Water Crossing. Dennis M. Gaughan. PoUp

Martial Cadenza. Wallace Stevens. NIL; VGW

Martial [*or* Marshall], the things for to attain. The Happy Life. Martial, *tr. by* Earl of Surrey. NOBE; OBVE

Martial [*or* My Friend], the things that do attain. The Means to Attain Happy Life. Martial, *tr. by* Earl of Surrey. CABA (1972 ed.); FaBoEE; PPM

Martial, thou gavest far nobler epigrams. To the Ghost of Martial. Ben Jonson. PAIC

Martian. Eve Merriam. CaYB

Martian named Harrison Harris, A. Interplanetary Limericks. Al Graham. QQQ

Martin Luther King, Jr. Gwendolyn Brooks. CNA; PoBA; WIF

Martin said to his man. *Unknown.* FaBoNo

Martin's Blues. Michael S. Harper. CNA; PoBA

Martyr, The. Herman Melville. TAP; VoPo

Martyr and the Army, The. Jock Henderson. AMV-81

Martyrdom. Richard W. Thomas. PoBA

Martyrdom of Saint Sebastian, The. Rosemary Dobson. MAuV

Martyred Earth, The. Ewart Milne. BIrV

Maru Mori brought me. Ode to My Socks. Pablo Neruda, *tr. by* Robert Bly. Epi

Marvaill no more all tho. Sir Thomas Wyatt. AAS

Marvel of Marvels. Christina Rossetti. BoReV; NOBE

Marvell! I think you'd neither seen nor smelt. Hibernia. Stuart Howard-Jones. NOBL

Marvell's Ghost. John Ayloffe. APAS

Marvelous. Allan Kaplan. POL

Marvels. *Unknown.* OxBM

Marvoil. Ezra Pound. Epi

Marx the Sign Painter. Edgar Lee Masters. *Fr.* The New Spoon River. NoAM; TAP

Mary. Blake. MBPR

Mary—A Reminiscence. Charles Tennyson Turner. VPC

Mary and Her Dead Canary. Alexander Kerr. InPK

Mary and Her Son Alone. *At. to* James Ryman. OxBM

Mary and the Baby, Sweet Lamb. *Unknown.* AmFP

Mary Ann ("It's fare thee well, my own true love"). *Unknown.* FSW

Mary Ann ("Mary Ann has gone to rest"). *Unknown.* FaBoCo

Mary Arnold the Female Monster. *Unknown.* GBP; PeBB

Mary Gulliver to Captain Lemuel Gulliver, *abr.* John Gay *and* Alexander Pope. OAEL-1

Mary Had a Baby. *Unknown.* FSW

Mary had a baby. Crooked Carol. Norma Farber. POL

Mary had a little bird. The Canary. Elizabeth Turner. OxBChV

Mary had a little lamb. Mary's Lamb. Sara Josepha Hale. CTV; MG; OxBChV

Mary Hamilton. *Unknown.* AIW; AmFP; FaBoBa; NOBE; PAIC; PeBB

Mary hath born alone. Mary and Her Son Alone. *At. to* James Ryman. OxBM

Mary Hines. Padraic Fallon, *after the Irish of* Anthony Raftery. SoSe

Mary Lifted from the Dead, *with music.* William Alfred. AH

Mary Magdalene. Kassia, *tr. fr. Byzantine Greek by* Aliki *and* Willis Barnstone *and* Elene Kolb. BoWoP

Mary Magdalene. Saunders Lewis, *tr. fr. Welsh by* Gwyn Thomas. OBW

Mary, Mary. Peter Viereck. CoPAm

Mary, Mary, quite contrary. Mother Goose. MG

"Mary mother, dost thou sleep?" Mary's Dream. *Unknown, tr. by* C. C. Bell. OBW

Mary, Mother of Christ. Countee Cullen. PChr

Mary Passed This Morning. Owen Dodson. PoBA

Mary sat musing on the lamp-flame at the table. The Death of the Hired Man. Robert Frost. CMoP (1970 ed.); HoPM (1975 ed.); IPWM; SoSe (1977 ed.); STS

Mary sat on a long brown bench. Song about Mary. Adrian Mitchell. PeBB

Mary stood in the kitchen. Ballad of the Bread Man. Charles Causley. MPo

Mary Stuart. Edwin Muir. MS

Mary to Her Savior's Tomb. John Newton. PIM

Mary wears them. Overalls. John Sjoberg. AcAn

Mary, will you ever grow? Water, blessed by bishops. Song for Healing. Roberta Hill. CDW

Mary Winslow. Robert Lowell. ILP (1975 ed.); PPP

Mary wore three links of chain. Hold On. *Unknown.* FSW

Mary Wyatt and Henry Green. *Unknown.* AmFP

Marye, maide milde and free. Hymn to the Virgin. *At. to* William of Shoreham. OxBM

Maryland Battalion, The. John Williamson Palmer. BTTM

Maryland, My Maryland! James Ryder Randall. FaPo; PSoN, *with music*
  (My Maryland.) BTTM

Maryland, Virginia, Caroline. Emblems. Allen Tate. VGW

Maryland Yellow-Throat, The. Henry Van Dyke. PCOP

Mary's a Grand Old Name, *with music.* George M. Cohan. BLSo; FSN

Mary's Dream. Unknown, *tr. fr. Welsh by* C. C. Bell. OBW

Mary's Ghost. Thomas Hood. PoTa

Mary's Lamb. Sarah Josepha Hale. CTV; MG; OxBChV

Mary's Song. Marion Angus. MS; SLP

Mary's Song. Sylvia Plath. CAPP

Maryuma. Frank Lamont Phillips. AmNP (1974 ed.)

Masada. Isaac Elchanan Mozeson. AMV-81

Masai warrior is not, The. Outbreak. Bill Anderson. VGW

Mask, The. Patty L. Harjo. VoR

Mask, The. Valery Larbaud, *tr. fr. French by* William Jay Smith. LoAs

Mask and the Poem, The. Alejandra Pizarnik, *tr. fr. Spanish by* Alina Rivero. VWA

Mask in Macy's. William Kistler. TVo

Mask of Anarchy, The. Shelley. MBPR
  *Sels.*
  "As I lay asleep in Italy." OBSV
  "I met Murder on the way." OBP

Mask of Love. Thomas Kinsella. CMoP (1970 ed.)

Mask the Wearer of the Mask Wears, The. William Bronk. GP

Masks. Elizabeth Fenton. NMM

Masks. Brian Swann. AMV-81

Masochist, The. Maxine W. Kumin. IHMS; POA

Mason Jar. David Steinberg. AMV-81

Masons, when they start upon a building. Scaffolding. Seamus Heaney. IPM; LP

Masque of Cupid, The. Spenser. *Fr.* The Faerie Queene, III, 12. NOBE

Masque of Flowers, The, *sel. Unknown.*
  "Thrice happy flowers!" SCP-2

Masque of Queens, The, *sels.* Ben Jonson.
  "What our Dame bids us do." OFD
  Witches' Charm, The. NOBE; UsP
  ("Owl is abroad, the bat and the toad, The.") PoPle, 6 *ll.*; SCP-1

Mass media I adore you. To R—— before Leaving to Fight in Unknown Terrain. Nina Serrano. MIT

Massacre of the Innocents, The, *sel.* Giovanni Battista Marino, *tr. fr. Italian by* Richard Crashaw.
  "Yet on the other side, faine would he start." OBVE

Massacre of the Innocents, The. William Jay Smith. CoPAm

Massacre of the Macpherson, The. William Edmonstoune Aytoun. FaBoCo

Massada, *sel.* Yitzhak Lamdan, *tr. fr. Hebrew by* A. C. Jacobs.
  "On an autumn night, lying restless, far from her broken homeland." VWA

Massasauga. Hamlin Garland. BPAW

Massive engines lift beautifully from the deck. The Teeth Mother Naked at Last. Robert Bly. CAAP; NNaP

Massive trembling of late dusk air, The. Night Riders. Jean Farley. NowV

Master and Boatswain. W. H. Auden. *See* Song of the Master and Boatswain.

Master and Man. Sir Henry Newbolt. OxBTC

Master Charge Blues. Nikki Giovanni. OBAL

Master Hugues of Saxe-Gotha. Robert Browning. OAEL-2

Master, No Offering, *with music.* Edwin Pond Parker. AH

Master of Arts. Cosmo Monkhouse. TDH

Master of beauty, craftsman of the snowflake. Eleven Addresses to the Lord, I. John Berryman. UnPo (1976 ed.)

Master of blood I am yours. Nocturnal Heart. Anne-Marie Kegels, *tr. by* W. S. Merwin. BoWoP

Master of discords John. The Harper. *Unknown, tr. by* Frank O'Connor. PFIr

Master, the swabber, the boatswain and I, The. Song. Shakespeare. *Fr.* The Tempest, II, ii. FF; NOBL; OBP; PoPle; RhR

Mastering the Craft. Vernon Scannell. HeHu

Masterly lens-polisher, A. The Spectacle of Truth. John Hewitt. CIP

Masters, be kind to the old house that must fall. Rockland. Julia Randall. CSP; WPE

Master's in the Garden Again. John Crowe Ransom. NoAM

Masters in This Hall. William Morris. FSW

Masters of War. Bob Dylan. GrRo

Mastodon. Charles O. Hartman. AAN

Mastrim: A Meditation, *sel.* Hugh Maxton.
  "Halt in the desert where I have in mind, A." CIP

Matadors, The. Josephine Jacobsen. TAP

Match, The. Andrew Marvell. EBEV

Match with the Moon, A. Dante Gabriel Rossetti. VLP

Materialism. C. E. M. Joad. FaBoCo

Maternity. Alice Meynell. BBGO

Maternity Gown. David Holbrook. OxBTC

Math. It's deliberately solutionless. "Titus, Son of Rembrandt: 1665." Richard J. Lyons. AMV-81

Mathematician named Bath, A. Let X Equal Half. J. F. Wilson. TDH

Mathematician named Rose, A. IBM Hired Her. W. J. J. Gordon. QQQ

Matilda Maud Mackenzie frankly hadn't any chin. How a Girl Was Too Reckless of Grammar. Guy Wetmore Carryl. OBAL

Matilda Who Told Lies, and Was Burned to Death. Hilaire Belloc. NOBE; OxBChV; PoTa

Matinees. James Merrill. NOBA; Prf

Mating Answer. Ronald Bottrall. PoA

Mating Swans. James McAuley. MAuV

Mating the Goats. Aliki Barnstone. AMV-81; BoWoP

Matins. Denise Levertov. IHMS; NoAM; NOBA

Matins—Friday. Cardinal Newman. VLP

Matins, or Morning Prayer. Robert Herrick. CaPo

Matins—Sunday. Cardinal Newman. VLP

Matisse: "The Red Studio." W. D. Snodgrass. WIF

Matisse Tits. David Barker. GP

Matisse's Jazz Cut-Outs at the National Gallery. Barbara F. Lefcowitz. PoUp

Matrilineal Descent. Robin Morgan. WBN

Matron of Jedborough and Her Husband, The, *sel.* Wordsworth. "More I looked, I wondered more, The." PeD

Matron well known in Montclair, A. Uncertain What to Wear. William Jay Smith. TDH

Matronita. Dennis Silk. VWA

Matsushima. Harry Guest. TwMBP

Matt Casey formed a social club that beat the town for style. The Band Played On. John F. Palmer. BLSo; FSN; FSW; OBAL

Matter is palsy: the land heaving, water. From Heraclitus. Alan Dugan. PoA

Matter of Urgency. Louis Johnson. ATNZ

Matthew. Bible, *N.T. See* St. Matthew.

Matthew. Wordsworth. MBPR

Matthew and Mark and Luke and holy John. Epi-Strauss-ium. Arthur Hugh Clough. PAIC; PFD; VPC

Matthew V. 29-30. Derek Mahon. CIP; IPM

Matthew, Mark, Luke and John. The White Paternoster. *Unknown.* GBP; MG

Matthew met Richard; when or where. Alma; or, The Progress of the Mind. Matthew Prior. EPC

Matthias, *sels.* Matthew Arnold.
"Cruel, but composed and bland." POL
"Rover, with the good brown head." PCat

Matty Groves. *Unknown.* FSW

Mauberley. Ezra Pound. *See* Hugh Selwyn Mauberley.

Maud: A Monodrama. Tennyson. VLP
*Sels.*
"Come into the garden, Maud," Pt. I, xxii. NOBE; OAEL-2
"Dead, long dead," Pt. II, v. OAEL-2
"I have led her home, my love, my only friend," Pt. I, xviii. LoAs
"My life has crept so long on a broken wing," Pt. III, vi. OAEL-2
"Oh! that 'twere possible," Pt. II, iv. BoLoP; NOBE; OAEL-2
Shell, The, Pt. II, ii. EcS

Maud Muller. Whittier. TAP

Maud Muller all that summer day. Mrs. Judge Jenkins (Being the Only Genuine Sequel to "Maud Muller"). Bret Harte. CABA (1972 ed.)

Maud went to college. Sadie and Maud. Gwendolyn Brooks. CoPAm; NoAM; NOBA; TAP

Maude Clare. Christina Rossetti. VPC

Mavrone. Arthur Guiterman. SpRo

Maw Bonnie Lad. *Unknown.* GBP

Maxim. Josephine Miles. RiTi

Maxims of a Park Vagrant. Nicholas Swift. AMV-80

Maximus, to Gloucester, Letter 19. Charles Olson. CMoP (1970 ed.); PAIC

Maximus, to Gloucester, Letter 6. Charles Olson. PiAm

Maximus to Gloucester, Letter 27. Charles Olson. NOBA

Maximus to Gloucester, Letter 2. Charles Olson. NoAM

Maximus, to Himself. Charles Olson. CMoP (1970 ed.); CoPAm; ExPo (1973 ed.); NOBA; VGW

Maxixe. Sir Osbert Sitwell. PoA

Maxwelton['s] braes are bonnie. Annie Laurie. William Douglas *and* Lady John Scott. BLSH; FSW; PoPle

May ("O love, this morn when the sweet nightingale"). William Morris. *Fr.* The Earthly Paradise. VLP

May. John Shaw Neilson. GAS; MAuV

May. Christina Rossetti. GBL

May. John Stevens Wade. AMV-80

May All Earth Be Clothed in Light. George Hitchcock. VGW

May all my enemies go to hell. Lines for a Christmas Card. Hilaire Belloc. IP; SFF; SoSe

"May an unforeseen disaster." The Horse and the Whip. Eliezer Steinbarg, *tr. by* Curt Leviant. VWA

May and Death. Robert Browning. NOBE

May, and the air is light. The Road's End. John Montague. TwMBP

May! Be thou never graced with birds that sing. In Obitum M. S. x Maij, 1614. William Browne. FaBoEE; NOBE

May Colvin. *Unknown.* PBMP

May Day. *Unknown.* CTV

May Day Carol, A. *Unknown.* RDB, *with music* ("Moon shines bright, The.") GBL

May Day Dancing, The. Howard Nemerov. NoAM

May Day Rounds: Renfrew County, *sel.* Joan Finnigan. "Stoop on the log-house is brown with sweet rain-rot, The." IPWM; WPE

May 1506 (Christopher Columbus Speaking). Winfield Townley Scott. GOA

May-Fly. John Heath-Stubbs. SoSe

May God be praised for woman. On Woman. W. B. Yeats. BiP; CMoP (1970 ed.); STS

May have killed the cat; more likely. Curiosity. Alastair Reid. SoSe

May he have new life like the fall. John Coltrane: An Impartial Review. A. B. Spellman. CNA; NIL; PoBA

May he lose his way on the cold sea. Archilochus, *tr. fr. Latin by* Guy Davenport. OBVE

May His Body make me safer. Thanksgiving after Communion. *Tr. fr. Gaelic by* Douglas Hyde. WTO

May his lines lose their lures. Curse of a Fisherman's Wife. Lila Chalpin. AMV-80

May I Ask You a Question. Kenneth Patchen. CoPAm

May I Be Beautiful. *Malay Oral Tradition, tr. by* W. W. Skeat. WTO

May I Feel Said He. E. E. Cummings. BoLoP; FF; HeIP; NOBE; SFF

May I for my own self song's truth reckon. The Seafarer. *Unknown, tr. by* Ezra Pound. ExPo (1973 ed.); FaBoTw (1975 ed.); HeIP

May I never be afraid. 30th Birthday. Alice Notley. FiCh

May I slobber over you. Third Day in a Strange City. Carol Bergé. MMD

May is lilac here in New England. Amy Lowell. *Fr.* Lilacs. FSFS

May is Mary's month, and I. The May Magnificat. Gerard Manley Hopkins. VLP

May Janet. Swinburne. VLP

May Magnificat, The. Gerard Manley Hopkins. VLP

May Margret stood in her bouer door. Hind Etin. *Unknown.* PeBB

May Mobilization. Allen Ginsberg. MIT

May Morn. Michael McClure. EAS

May No Man Sleep in Your Hall. *Unknown.* GBP

May Poem ("O lusty May with Flora quene"). *Unknown.* SLP

May Poem ("When flora had ourfret the firth"). *Unknown.* SLP

May Queen, The, *sel.* Tennyson.
"You must wake and call me early, call me early, mother dear." CC

May seven tears in every week. A Wish. J. M. Synge. FaBoEE

May 10th. Maxine W. Kumin. RFM

May The dread Three in One, who sways. Matins—Friday. Cardinal Newman. VLP

May the man who gained my trust yet did not come. Ryojin Hisho, *tr. fr. Japanese by* Geoffrey Bownas *and* Anthony Thwaite. BoWop

May the spirit of contentment. Acrostic for Anna Geen. Eliza R. Snow. WPW

May they stumble [*or* wander], stage by stage. Traveller's Curse after Misdirection. Robert Graves. CMoP (1970 ed.); ExPo (1973 ed.); HoPM (1975 ed.); NCSH

May Trees in a Storm. Geoffrey Grigson. GBL

May 27, 1971: No Poem. June Jordan. WBN

May we never taste of death nor quit this vale of tears. Irish Curse on the Occupying English. *Unknown, tr. by* Máire MacEntee. PFIr

May with its light behaving. W. H. Auden. EBEV

May You Always Be the Darling of Fortune. Jane Miller. AMV-80

May you live long and be well. Vigndig A Fremd Kind (Babysitter's Song). *Unknown.* FSW

May your sleep be calm as snow in the pleats of clouds. For You, Falling Asleep after a Quarrel. Diane Middlebrook. AMV-81

Maya. E. A. Robinson. PiAm

Mayakovsky was right. Kiss. Al Young. PoBA

Maybe I should go back to the white leather. Desnos Reading the Palms of Men on Their Way to the Gas Chambers. Stephen Berg. VWA

Maybe it ain't right. Live and Let Live. Langston Hughes. ILP (1975 ed.)

Maybe it is true we have to return. Obsessions. Denise Levertov. PAIC

Maybe it was the way. Finding You. Virginia Gilbert. IHMS; NVAP

Maybe morning lightens over. For My Grandmother, Bridget [*or* Bridgid] Halpin. Michael Hartnett. BIrV; CIP; IPM

Maybe the Birds. June Jordan. TSWA

Maybe the dead are asleep. The Dead. Michael Waters. AAN

Maybe You Cannot Comprehend. Salvador Villanueva, *tr. fr. Spanish by* Julio Marzán. InW

Maybe you ranted in the grove. Ezry. Archibald MacLeish. NOBA

Maybe you've noticed that around here. Redwings. William Heyen. PCho

Mayday. Ed Roberson. PoBA

Mayers' Song, The. *Unknown.* AIW; GBP

Mayor of Lagos. *Yoruba Oral Tradition, tr. by* Ulli Beier. WTO

Maytime, loveliest season. Sadness in Spring. *Unknown, tr. by* Gwyn Jones. OBW

Maze, The. Norman Kreitman. PMW

Maze of the Magi, A. Sandra Ruth Duguid. AATT

Mazeworks. Elías Hruska Cortés. CPA

Mbuyazi of the Bay! Praises of Henry Francis Fynn. *Zulu Oral Tradition, tr. by* T. Cope. WTO

Me. Walter de la Mare. CTV

Me,/ i'm just. Log: 19N 72E. Horace Coleman. SES

Me Again. Kenneth Rexroth. VoA

Me and My Chauffeur Blues. *Unknown.* BluL

Me and Samantha. Pyke Johnson, Jr. GDP

Me and the Devil Blues. *Unknown.* BluL

Me and You and a Dog Named Boo. Kent LaVoie. PoRo

Me clairvoyant. After Walt Whitman. G. K. Chesterton. NOBL

Me [*or* My] father was the keeper of the Eddystone Light. The Eddystone Light [*or* The Keeper of the Eddystone Light]. *Unknown.* FSW; PeBB; PoTa

Me first/ you all. Mardi Gras. Miller Williams. TAT

Me from myself—to banish. Emily Dickinson. NoAM; SBG

Me happy, night, night full of brightness. Elegy VII. Ezra Pound. *Fr.* Homage to Sextus Propertius. PAIC; VGW

Me Imperturbe. Walt Whitman. NOBA

Me, in Kulu Se and Karma. Carolyn M. Rodgers. PoBA

Me liketh ever the lengere the bet. In Praise of Winchester. *Unknown.* OxBM

Me list no more to sing. Sir Thomas Wyatt. AAS

Me, Lord? Canst thou mispend. The Divine Lover. Phineas Fletcher. *Fr.* The Divine Wooer. BoReV

Me mother kept a boarding house. Hullabaloo Belay. *Unknown.* FSW

Me. My poems don't ride/ underground. Give Me a Forty Cent Token or a Gallon of Gas and an Hour to Get There. Jonetta Barras-Abney. PoUp

Me nappy hair dream child. Image in the Mirror. Peggy Susberry Kenner. JB

Me Rueth, Mary. *Unknown.* GBP
(Now Goth Sonne under Wode.) HAP
("Now goeth sun under wood.") BoReV
(Under the Wood, *mod. English.*) HAP

Me that 'ave been what I've been. Chant-Pagan. Kipling. VLP

Me thinks [*or* Methinks], I see, with what a busie hast. On Zacheus [*or* Zacchaeus]. Frances Quarles. HAP; MetP

Me thought I was in wildernesse walking al one. A Dream. *Unknown. Fr.* Mum and the Sothsegger. OxBM

Me thought, (last night) love in an anger came. *See* Methought (last night) . . .

Me Up at Does. E. E. Cummings. WeW

Meadow and the mountain with desire, The. Attraction. Ella Wheeler Wilcox. PeD

Meadow Grass. Michael Mott. AMV-80

Meadow Mouse, The. Theodore Roethke. ExPo (1973 ed.); HeIP; InPK; IPWM; MPA; PPoe; PSN; TSWA

Meadowland. *Tr. fr. Russian.* FSW

Meadows with yellow cowslips all aglow. The Wood-Dove's Note. Emily Huntington Miller. PCOP

Meal Piece. Elton Glaser. NVAP

Mean grimy houses, shades drawn. May I Ask You a Question Kenneth Patchen. CoPAm

Mean Mistreater Mama. *Unknown.* BluL

Mean Old Twister. *Unknown.* BluL

Mean Rufus Throw-Down. David Smith. NVAP

Mean Song. Eve Merriam. CaYB

Mean while. *See* Meanwhile.

Mean Trick, A. *Unknown.* TDH

Mean wind wanders through the backcourt trash, A. Edwin Morgan. *Fr.* Glasgow Sonnets. MS; UsP

Meandering abroad in the Lincolnshire meadows day. George Barker. *Fr.* Calamiterror, VI. EAS

Meaning of Love, The. *Malay Oral Tradition, tr. by* R. O. Winstedt. WTO

Meaning of Protest, The. Michael S. Harper. NW

Means Test. D. J. Enright. HeHu

Means to Attain Happy Life, The. Martial. *See* Happy Life, The.

Meanwhile surely there must be something to say. The Constructed Space. W. S. Graham. PoA

Meanwhile [*or* mean while] the adversary of God and man. Milton. *Fr.* Paradise Lost, II. DL; EBEV

Meanwhile, the Baron Albert. At Hunegg. George MacBeth. TwMBP

Mean while the tepid caves, and fens and shoares. The Creation of Birds. Milton. *Fr.* Paradise Lost, I. PB

Meanwhile the troops beneath Patroclus' care. Homer, *tr. by* Pope. *Fr.* The Iliad, XVI. OBVE

Meares' milk, and deers' milk. Witch's Milking Charm. *Unknown.* GBP

Measles in the Ark. "Susan Coolidge." OxBChV

Measure for Measure, *sels.* Shakespeare.
  At the Moated Grange, *fr.* IV, i. NOBE
    ("Take, O take those lips away,") BiP; EBEV;GBL; HeIP; ILP (1975 ed.); InPS; OAEL-1; STS
  "Our doubts are traitors," *fr.* I, iv. CTV
  "What says my brother?/ Death is a fearful thing," *fr.* III, i. LFH

Measure is a guess the mind makes about itself. Telemann. Helen Chasin. TV

Measure of Love, The. Sir Thomas More. BoReV

Measures. Joseph Gordon Macleod ("Adam Drinan"). MS

Measuring, The. Jared Carter. AMV-80

Meat Epitaph, The. Michael Benedikt. FiCP

Meat without Mirth. Robert Herrick. ILP (1975 ed.)

Meat Works, The. Robert Gray. CAAP

Mechanic, The. Diane Wakoski. AmPA

Mechanical/ Oracles dot the sky. Gods in Vietnam. Eugene Redmond. PoBA

Mechanism. A. R. Ammons. HAP; TT

Mechanophilus, *sel.* Tennyson.
  "Dash back that ocean with a pier." FaBoCo

Medal, The, *sel.* Dryden.
  Vox Populi. NOBE; USP

Medal of John Bays, The: A Satire against Folly and Knavery. Thomas Shadwell. APAS
  "How long shall I endure without reply,"*sel.* SCP-2

Medal Reversed, The. Elkanah Settle. APAS

Medallion. Sylvia Plath. HeIP

Medallion. Ezra Pound. PSN

Meddlesome Matty. Ann Taylor. OxBChV

Medea. Euripides, *tr. fr. Greek by* Rex Warner. NAWM-1

Medea, *sels.* Seneca, *tr. fr. Latin by* John Studley.
  "Her chaunging lookes no colour longe can holde, " *fr.* IV. OBVE
  "That Orpheus Calliops sonne who stayde the running brooke," *fr.* III. OBVE

Medea Casts a Spell to Make Aeson Young Again. Ovid, *tr. fr. Latin by* Arthur Golding. *Fr.* Metamorphoses, VII. Moon

Medea's Magic. John Gower. *Fr.* Confessio Amantis. OxBM

Medgar Evers. Gwendolyn Brooks. NowV; PoBA

Medicine. Louis Jenkins. HeS

Medicine. Alice Walker. NMM

Medieval, The. Rodney Hall. FPA

Meditatio. Ezra Pound. OBAL; OSP; PBMP

Meditation. Baudelaire, *tr. fr. French by* Robert Lowell. InPK; NAWM-2

Meditation. Anne Bradstreet. EAP
  (As Spring the Winter Doth Succeed, *with music.*) AH

Meditation, A. Herman Melville. GOA

Meditation, The. John Norris. SCP-2

Meditation ("How long will you remain a boy?"). Carl Rakosi. VWA

Meditation ("Lord, what is a man?"). Carl Rakosi. AMV-80

Meditation ("Men are children of this world"). Carl Rakosi. VWA

Meditation ("Three things remind me of you"). Carl Rakosi. VWA

Meditation. Beyle Schaechter-Gottesman, *tr. fr. Yiddish by* Gabriel Preil. VWA

Meditation at Kew. Anna Wickham. BuTh; FaBoTw (1975 ed.)

Meditation at Oyster River. Theodore Roethke. CMoP (1970 ed.); CNW; MPA

Meditation 8 ("Scarce do I pass a day but that I hear"). Philip Pain. NOBA; PiAm

Meditation for a Pickle Suite. R. H. W. Dillard. CoPAm; HoPM (1975 ed.)

Meditation for His Mistress, A. Robert Herrick. CaPo; NOBE

Meditation in My Favorite Position. Marge Piercy. *Fr.* Walking into Love. RiTi

Meditation 9 ("Man's life is like a rose, that in the spring"). Philip Pain. NOBA

Meditation on a Bone. A. D. Hope. MAuV

Meditation on Statistical Method. J. V. Cunningham. NIL; VGW

Meditation on the A30. John Betjeman. BBGO

Meditation on the Rhode Island Coal, A. Bryant. TAP

Meditation 62 ("How is it that I am so careless here"). Philip Pain. NOBA; PiAm

Meditation 10 ("Alas, what is the world? A sea of glass"). Philip Pain. NOBA; PiAm

Meditation 29 ("How mutable is every thing that here"). Philip Pain. NOBA

Meditations. Edward Taylor. *See* Preparatory Meditations.

Meditations in an Emergency. Frank O'Hara. TAP

Meditations in Time of Civil War, *sels.* W. B. Yeats.
  Ancestral Houses, I. OAEL-2
  Road at My Door, The, V. BIrV; NOBE
  Stare's Nest by My Windows, The, VI. BIrV; NOBE

Meditations of a Mariner. Wallace Irwin. OSF

Meditations of an Old Woman, *sels.* Theodore Roethke.
  First Meditation. NOBA
  "I was always one for being alone," IV. STS
    (Fourth Meditation.) MPA
  I'm Here, II. Epi

Meditations on Frost's "Stopping by Woods." Albert De Pietro. AATT

Mediterranean. Israel Pincas, *tr. fr. Hebrew by* A. C. Jacobs. VWA

Mediterranean. Muriel Rukeyser. SPT

Mediterranean, The. Allen Tate. GOA; HAP; VGW; WeW

Mediterranean. Ruth Whitman. VWA

Mediterranean Beach, Day after Storm, *sel.* Robert Penn Warren. "How instant joy, how clang." OSP

Medium IV, The: Sights. Carl Rakosi. InPS

Medium white onion, The. John Fandel. *Fr.* Out of Our Blue. PoIA

Medlars and Sorb-Apples. D. H. Lawrence. OAEL-2

Medora, N.D. Richard Lyons. HeS

Medusa. Louise Bogan. BoWoP; HoPM (1975 ed.); RiTi; WPE

Medusa, The. Guy Davenport. GP

Medusa. Vincent O'Sullivan. ATNZ

Medusa. Sylvia Plath. CAPP

Meek Francis lies here, friend, without stop or stay. Epitaph. Matthew Prior. FaBoEE

Meek, sang the crickets, wheat, meet, creek. A Small Score. Delmore Schwartz. PBMP

Meek Shall Disinherit the Earth, The. Horace Gregory. SPT

Meekly the sea. The Even Sea. May Swenson. EcS

Meet Me in St. Louis, Louis. Andrew B. Sterling. FSN, *with music;* FSW; OBAL

Meet me tonight. Jackie. King D. Kuka. VoR

Meet Rabbi Shatz in his correct black homburg. Tales of Shatz. Dannie Abse. VWA

Meet was at 'The Cock and Pye,' The. John Masefield. *Fr.* Reynard the Fox. OxBTC

Meeting. Matthew Arnold. Switzerland, I. VLP

Meeting, The. Jocelyn Hollis. AMV-80

Meeting. Christina Rossetti. GBL

Meeting, The. Kathleen Spivack. NMM

Meeting, The. Ramona Wilson. VoR

Meeting a Bear. David Wagoner. BCr; HAP

Meeting after Separation. Marula, *tr. fr. Sanskrit by* Tambimuttu *and* G. V. Vaidya. BoWoP

Meeting Anais Nin's Elena. Gene Frumkin. AMV-81

Meeting at Night. Robert Browning. BoLoP; FF; GBL; HeIP; ILP (1975 ed.); InPS; LoAs; NOBE; OLR; PAIC; PoPle; SoSe; SS; STS; UnPo (1976 ed.); VLP; WeW

Meeting at the Building. *Unknown.* FSW

Meeting by chance and speaking. The Judas Touch. David Malouf. FPA

Meeting-House Hill. Amy Lowell. PSN; SBG

Meeting-house is not what it used to be, The. Elegy in a Presbyterian Burying-Ground. R. N. D. Wilson. BIrV

Meeting me it was love at first sight. Escalator. Patricia Goedicke. AAN

Meeting the Mountains. Gary Snyder. NoAM; PiAm; TAP

Meeting the Reincarnation Analyst. Gary Gildner. AmPA

Meeting when all the world was in the bud. Loves of the Puppets. Richard Wilbur. LoAs

Meetings meetings meetings. Yuh Lookin Good. Carolyn M. Rodgers. BPo

Meg Merrilies. Keats. OxBChV; PoPle ("Old Meg she was a gipsey.") MBPR; TT

Megaceph, chosen to serve the State. Ambrose Bierce. *Fr.* The Devil's Dictionary. OBAL

Megalomaniac/ midgets. Strange Encounter. Anselm Hollo. AcAn

Megalopolis. Victor Hernández Cruz. SA

Mel Allen, Mel Allen, Lend Me Your Cliché. Ogden Nash. SPo

Melampus. George Meredith. VLP

Melancholia. Robert Bridges. CMoP (1970 ed.)

Melancholy ("Hence, all you vain delights"). John Fletcher. PoPle

Melancholy days have come, The. Autumn Leaves. Charles H. Webb. OBAL

Melancholy days have come, the saddest of the year, The. The Death of the Flowers. Bryant. EAP

Melancholy face Charles Carville had, A. Charles Carville's Eyes. E. A. Robinson. CMoP (1970 ed.); TAP

Melancholy Summer. Kris Hemensley. *Fr.* A Mile from Poetry. CAAP

Melchior Vulpius. Marianne Moore. PiAm

Melfluvious, sweet, rose-watered eloquence. Samuel Rowlands. *Fr.* The Letting of Humour's Blood in the Head-Vein. TVS

Melissa. Carolyn D. Redl-Hlus. AMV-80

Melissa didn't tell people, I'm Illegitimate. The Belly Dancer's Daughter. Anne Sexton. UsP

Mellifluous as bees, these brittle men. On First Looking in on Blodgett's *Keats's "Chapman's Homer."* George Starbuck. NIL; OBAL

Mellow. Langston Hughes. ILP (1975 ed.)

Mellow the moonlight to shine is beginnning. The Spinning Wheel. John Francis Waller. PFIr; PoTa

Mellow year is hastening to its close, The. November. Hartley Coleridge. FSFS

Mellowness and Flight. George Barlow. CNA

Melody. Shmuel Moreh, *tr. fr. Arabic by* Yoffee Berkovitz. VWA

Melody. Edward Proffitt. PoIA

Melody for Lute and Ocarina. Morris Bishop. ECBV

Melon on the table, The. Self-Portrait as Still Life. Donald Justice. FoP

Melons. Greg Kuzma. HeS

Melons. Moshe Yungman, *tr. fr. Yiddish by* Gabriel Preil *and* Howard Schwartz. VWA

Melora's Song. Stephen Vincent Benét. *Fr.* John Brown's Body. AIW

Melting in thin mist and heavy clouds. Li Ch'ing-chao, *tr. fr. Chinese by* J. P. Seaton. BoWoP

Melting Pot, The. Dudley Randall. BPo

Member of the modern great, A. Epigram. John Cunningham. FaBoEE

Members of the Family. Derek Bowman. MIS

Memento for Mortality, A. *At. to* William Basse. *See* On the Tombs in Westminster Abbey.

Memento Mori. Fulke Greville. *Fr.* Caelica. BoReV ("Whenas man's life, the light of human lust.") SCP-2

Memento Mori. Moishe Leib Halpern, *tr. fr. Yiddish by* Ruth Whitman. VWA

Memento Vivendi. Eva Brudne. VWA

Mementos, *sel.* Charlotte Brontë. "And heaven did curse—they found him laid." PeD

Mementos, 1 ("Sorting out letters and piles of my old"). W. D. Snodgrass. CABA (1972 ed.); CoPAm; FF; HeIP; ILP (1975 ed.); PiAm; PPP; TPo; UnPo (1976 ed.)

Mementos, 2 ("I found them there today"). W. D. Snodgrass. CoPAm; UsP

Memo. Charles G. Ballard. VoR

Memo. Kenneth Fearing. CMoP (1970 ed.)

Memo. Charles Lynch. PoBA

Memo. Hans Sahl, *tr. fr. German by* Edouard Roditi. VWA

Memo to the 21st Century. Philip Appleman. PCho; SFF; TAT

Memoir. David Schaff. MIT

Memoir. Roger Weingarten. AMV-80

Memoirs, The. Carl Rakosi. PoA

Memorabilia. Robert Browning. CABA (1972 ed.); ILP (1975 ed.); OAEL-2; STS

Memorable Fancy, A ("An Angel came to me and said"). Blake. *Fr.* The Marriage of Heaven and Hell. NU

Memorable Fancy, A ("As I was walking among the fires of hell"). Blake. *Fr.* The Marriage of Heaven and Hell. NU

Memoranda. William Dickey. CoPAm

Memorandum/ The Accountant's Notebook. Kathleen Norris. OBAL

Memorial Couplets for the Dying Ego. George Barker. EBEV

Memorial Day. Laureen Ching. AMV-80

Memorial Day: A Collaboration, *sel.* Anne Waldman *and* Ted Berrigan "And now the book is closed." EAS

Memorial for Mr. Jefferson, A. Francis Coleman Rosenberger. WasP

Memorial Ode. Chief John Buck. GOA

Memorial Pillar, The. Felicia Dorothea Hemans. SBG

Memorial Poem. Jacob Glatstein, *tr. fr. Yiddish by* Ruth Whitman. VWA

Memorial Rain. Archibald MacLeish. CMoP (1970 ed.); NoAM

Memorial Service. Ursula Vaughan Williams. POL

Memorial to a Missionary. Keith Sinclair. ATNZ

Memorial to D. C., *sel.* Edna St. Vincent Millay. Elegy: "Let them bury your big eyes," V. CMoP (1970 ed.); LoAs

Memorial Verses. Matthew Arnold. CABA (1972 ed.); NIL; OAEL-2; VLP

Memorial Wreath. Dudley Randall. CNA; PoBA

Memories, *sel.* George Gascoigne.
"In haste, post haste, when first my wandering mind," IV.
AAS; PAIC

Memories. Tony Moreno. NW

Memories of a good life are not enough. A Good Life. Robert
Watson. AMV-81

Memories of a Lost War. Louis Simpson. VGW

Memories of President Lincoln. Walt Whitman. *See* When
Lilacs Last in the Dooryard Bloomed *and* O Captain, My
Captain!

Memories of West Street and Lepke. Robert Lowell. CAPP;
CMoP (1970 ed.); ConAP; CoPAm; InPS; NOBA; PiAm;
PSN

Memoriter. Charles Spear. ATNZ

Memory. Thomas Bailey Aldrich. CTV; PCOP

Memory, A. William Allingham. *See* Four Ducks on a Pond.

Memory, A. Marvin Bell. GP

Memory, The. Robert Creeley. CAPP; VGW

Memory. Babette Deutsch. PoA

Memory. Michael Hamburger. OxBTC

Memory, A. Manfred Jurgensen. FPA

Memory. Walter Savage Landor. EBEV; OAEL-2

Memory, A. L. A. G. Strong. FaBoCo; NOBL; PFIr

Memory, A. Mona Van Duyn. *Fr.* Recovery. RiTi

Memory. W. B. Yeats. BIrV

Memory, a Small Brown Bird. Rich Ives. AMV-81

Memory Air. Charles Dobzynski, *tr. fr. French by* Anita Barrows.
VWA

Memory comes, like the shadow of fog. Deja Vu. J. B.
Mulligan. AMV-80

Memory: farfields of morning. Persephone. Robert Duncan.
NoAM; NOBA

Memory Gardens. Allen Ginsberg. NNaP

Memory, hither come. Song. Blake. MBPR; STS

Memory: I can take my head and strike it on a wall. The Shark's
Parlor. James Dickey. CSP

Memory Movie. Diane Webster. AMV-81

Memory, Now Distant, A. Eric Linklater. SLP

Memory of a Porch. Donald Justice. NCSH

Memory of Another Climate. Gabriel Preil, *tr. fr. Hebrew by*
Jeremy Garber. VWA

Memory of Kreisler once, A. The Musician. R. S. Thomas.
BoReV

Memory of Kuhre. Wesley McNair. FAF

Memory of one particular hour, The. Dedication. Wordsworth.
*Fr.* The Prelude, IV. BoReV

Memory of the face, A. After the War. Hayim Naggid, *tr. by*
Shlomo Vinner *and* Howard Schwartz. VWA

Memory of the Night of the Fourth. Victor Hugo, *tr. fr. French
by* Mary Ann Caws. NAWM-2

Memory of the Players in a Mirror at Midnight, A. James Joyce.
NoAM

Memory of you may be. Night Song for an Old Lover. Susan
Glickman. AMV-81

Memory, out of the mist, in a long slow ripple. Seagulls on the
Serpentine. Alfred Noyes. EcS

Memory pales in the face of the moon. On Leaving Baltimore.
Duane Niatum. CDW

Memory parachutes in. Birthday: Tara Regina. George Mosby,
Jr. AMV-81

Memory-Picture, A. Matthew Arnold. VLP

Memphis Minnie-Jitis Blues. *Unknown.* BluL

Memphis, Tennessee. Chuck Berry. RRA

Men/ dropped children. After the Fact. Grace Cavalieri.
AATT

Men and women long ago, The. Old Laughter. Gwendolyn
Brooks. TH

Men are children of this world. Meditation. Carl Rakosi.
VWA

Men Are Coming Back, The. Barry Cole. OxBTC

Men are running across a field. Letter. Mark Strand. NoAm

Men at Forty. Donald Justice. GP; PPP; Prf

Men, bloody, approach the house. Dreams from War. Marilyn
Krysl. NPW

Men en masse. Observation. Richard Weber. POL

Men heard this roar of parleying starlings, saw. February
Afternoon. Edward Thomas. NoAM

Men if you love us, play no more. In the Person of Woman
Kind. Ben Jonson. NIL

Men in/ miles of mud. Building Site. Marian Lines. FPB

Men in Black. Robert Morgan. HeHu

Men in Green. David Campbell. GAS

Men in her department envied her, The. Sayre. Lynn Strongin.
IHMS; RiTi

Men in the City. Alfonsina Storni, *tr. fr. Spanish by* Rachel
Benson. PBWP

Men lean toward the wood. Lynching and Burning. Primus St.
John. PoBA

Men like Salmon, The. Linda Gregg. AAN

Men Loved Wholly beyond Wisdom. Louise Bogan. PBWP;
VGW

Men Made Out of Words. Wallace Stevens. NOBA; TAP;
VGW

Men may leve all games. Pilgrims to St. James. *Unknown.*
OxBM

Men might put their hands. This Woman Will Not Bear
Children. Toi Derricotte. NPW

Men of England, wherefore plough. Song to the Men of England.
Shelley. ExPS (1973 ed.); ILP (1975 ed.); InPS; MBPR;
PBMP; SFF

Men of Sudbury, The. Carlos Baker. GOA

Men of the Alamo, The. James Jeffrey Roche. BPAW

Men of the East, The. Feathers of Snow. *Unknown.* GBP

Men of the Rocks, The, *sel.* Joseph Gordon Macleod ("Adam
Drinan").
"Our pastures are bitten and bare." MS

Men seldom make passes. News Item. Dorothy Parker. OBAL

Men, some to bus'ness, some to pleasure take. Pope. *Fr.* Moral
Essays, Epistle II. NIL; OBSV

Men That Once Were, The, *sel.* Owen Gruffydd, *tr. fr. Welsh by*
Anthony Conran.
"Old, old/ To live on, wretched to behold." OBW

Men that worked for England, The. Elegy in a Country
Churchyard. G. K. Chesterton. FaPoR

Men tortured children. Children of Auschwitz. Naum
Korzhavin, *tr. by* Daniel Weissbort. VWA

Men trample the earth, The. The Departure of the Women.
Nancy Mairs. NPW

Men wear wigs, The. Congress. Dale Matthews. AAN

Men went to Catraeth, keen their war-band. Aneirin, *tr. by*
Joseph P. Clancy. *Fr.* The Gododdin. OBW

Men went up on these sands along the sea. Children's Song.
Arye Sivan, *tr. by* David Shevin. VWA

Men who have loved the ships they took to sea. Mariners.
David Morton. RhR

Men! whose boast it is that ye. Freedom. James Russell Lowell.
VoPo

Men Whose Tongues, The. Dana Naone. PHC

Men with crew-cuts. Crew-cuts. Donald Hall. MAT

Men with ventilators of black straw, The. Confab. Kenneth
Rosen. AmPA

Men worked, men loafed, men sired. Ulster. Hans Adler. AMV-81

Men worry, or. Nightfall. Richard Ryan. IPM

Men would never have come to need an attic. Up There. W. H. Auden. OxBTC

Menaphon, *sels.* Robert Greene.
Samela. GBL; NOBE
Sephestia's Song to Her Childe. ILP (1975 ed.); OBP (Sephestia's Lullaby.) NOBE

Menashtash. Alvaro Cardona-Hine. OSP

Mendacious Mole, The. Oliver Herford. TDH

Mendelian Theory. *Unknown.* FaBoCo
(Limerick: "There was a young woman called Starkey.") NOBL

Mending. Hazel Hall. WPW

Mending ("The mending pillow is set against the wall"). Morty Sklar. AcAn

Mending Sump. Kenneth Koch. InPK; NoAM

Mending Wall. Robert Frost. CMoP (1970 ed.); ExPo (1973 ed.); HAP; HoPM (1975 ed.); ILP (1975 ed.); InPS; IP; IPWM; LFH; NoAM; NOBA; NowV; PiAm; PoIA; PPoD; SoSe (1977 ed.); STS; TAP; VGW

Mendip Hills over Wells, The. Henry Alford. PES

Meningitis killing me, The. Memphis Minnie-Jitis Blues. *Unknown.* BluL

Mennonite Farm Wife. Janet Kauffman. TC

Men's Impotence. *Tr. fr. Eskimo.* WTO

Men's Room in the College Chapel, The. W. D. Snodgrass. GP; ILP (1975 ed.); PPP

Men's Voices. Inger Christensen, *tr. fr. Danish by* Nadia Christensen. BoWoP

Menstruation at Forty. Anne Sexton. CAPP

Mental Cases. Wilfred Owen. BiP; CMoP (1970 ed.); NoAM

Mental Health. Elliot Fried. GP

Mental Hospital Garden, The. William Carlos Williams. PiAm

Mental Traveller, The. Blake. Epi; GrRo; ILP (1975 ed.); LAuP; OAEL-2; MBPR; TT

Menu. Edward Lear. FaBoNo

Menzi son of Ndaba! Senzangakhona. *Zulu Oral Tradition, tr. by* T. Cope. WTO

Mercado. Greg Pape. AmPA

Merced. Adrienne Rich. NOBA; TT

Mercedes. Barbara Howes. CoPAm; RiTi

Mercedes, Her Aloneness. Colette Inez. IHMS

Merchant addressing a debtor, A. Persuasive Go-Gebtor. "R. C." TDH

Merchant Marine. Josephine Miles. TAP; VGW

Merchant of Venice, The, *sels.* Shakespeare.
"Beshrew me but I love her heartily," *fr.* II, vi. CTV
Birdsong, *fr.* V, i. PB
"Moon shines bright, The. In such a night as this," *fr.* V, i. GBL; PoPle
Quality of Mercy, The, *fr.* IV, i. AKE; PIM
(Portia's Speech.) PCOP
"Tell me where is fancy bred," *fr.* III, ii. ILP (1975 ed.); OAEL-1; STS

Merchant, to secure his treasure, The. An Ode [*or* Song]. Matthew Prior. CABA (1972 ed.); PoPle

Merchants of London, The. *Unknown.* GBP

Mercian Hymns, *sels.* Geoffrey Hill.
"Brooding on the eightieth letter of *Fors Clavigera*," XXV. HAP
"Coins handsome as Nero's; of good substance and weight," XI. HAP
"Dismissing reports and men, he put pressure on the wax," XIV. HAP
(Offa's Laws.) PSN

"Gasholders, russet among fields," VII. HAP

"He adored the desk, its brown-oak inlaid with ebony," X. HAP

"King of the perennial holly-groves, the riven sandstone," I. HAP

" 'Not strangeness, but strange likeness,' " XXIX. HAP

"On the morning of the crowning we chorused our remission from school," III. HAP

"Princes of Mercia were badger and raven, The," VI. HAP

"We ran across the meadow scabbed with the cow-dung," XXII. HAP

Merciless Beauty. Chaucer. OxBM; PAIC
(Merciles Beautee.) EBEV; HAP
"Your eyen two will slay me suddenly," *sel.* BoLoP

Merciless love, whom nature hath denied. John Fletcher. *Fr.* The Chances. GBL

Mercury Bay Eclogue. M. K. Joseph. ATNZ

Mercury's Song to Phaedra. Dryden. *Fr.* Amphitryon, IV, i. PBMP

Mercy ("Mercy is hendest where sinne is mest"). *Unknown.* OxBM

Mercy is whiter than laundry. Angels in Winter. Nancy Willard. FiCP

Mercy Mercy Me. Marvin Gaye. PoRo

Mercy o' Gode. Pittendrigh MacGillivray. MS

Mercy of God may often come to a homeless hermit, The. The Wanderer. *Unknown, tr. by* Andrew Hoyem. Epi

Mercy to Animals: A Ballad of Humanity. Martin Farquhar Tupper. PeD

Meredith Phyfe. Edgar Lee Masters. *Fr.* The New Spoon River. GOA

'Mergency Man, The. J. M. Synge. PoPle

Meridian. Brewster Ghiselin. AMV-80

Meridians are a net. Objects. Richard Wilbur. FF

Merioneth. John Machreth Rees, *tr. fr. Welsh by* Kenneth Jackson. OBW

Merlin (I-II). Emerson. AmVN; NOBA; PiAm

Merlin. Geoffrey Hill. POL

Merlin. Edwin Muir. FaBoTw (1975 ed.)

Merlin and the Gleam. Tennyson. OAEL-2; VLP
"Not of the sunlight," IX. CTV

Merlin and Vivien. *See* Idylls of the King.

Merlin Enthralled. Richard Wilbur. CMoP (1970 ed.)

Merlin, they say, an English prophet borne. Caelica, XXIII. Fulke Greville. OBP

Mermaid, The. Ben King. OBAL

Mermaid. Helena Minton. FAF

Mermaid, The. Lisel Mueller. RiTi

Mermaid, The. Tennyson. EcS
"Who would be/ A mermaid fair," *sel.* LCL

Mermaid, The, 2 *versions. Unknown.* AmFP
(" 'Twas Friday morn when we set sail.") FSW

Mermaid, The ("The mermaid found a swimming lad"). W. B. Yeats. EcS; PoIA

Mermaiden, A. Thomas Hennell. FaBoTw (1975 ed.)

Mermaidens' Vesper-Hymn, The. George Darley. *Fr.* Syren Songs, VI. GBL
(Siren Chorus.) BIrV

Mermaids. Walter de la Mare. EcS

Mermaids six or seven. Gerard Manley Hopkins. *Fr.* The Vision of the Mermaids. EcS

Merman, The. Tennyson. EcS

Merrie world did on a day, The. *See* Merry world did on a day, The.

Merrily swinging on brier and weed. Robert of Lincoln. Bryant. EAP

Merry Christmas, A. *Unknown. See* We Wish You a Merry Christmas.

Merry Crocodile, The. Gertrude E. Heath. TDH

Merry Cuckow, messenger of Spring, The. Amoretti, XIX. Spenser. ILP (1975 ed.)

Merry-go-round. Rachel Field. CTV; PCOP

Merry-go-round. Langston Hughes. CTBA

Merry-go-round. James McAuley. MAuV

Merry-go-round. Sean O'Meara. IPM

Merry-go-round. Gloria Rawlinson. ATNZ

Merry-go-round, The. Rainer Maria Rilke, *tr. fr. German by* C. F. MacIntyre. WeW

Merry-go-round. Mark Van Doren. SÖ

Merry Haymakers, The; or, Pleasant Pastimes between the Young Men and Maids in the Pleasant Meadows. *Unknown.* SCP-2

Merry [*or* Mery] it is in May morning. By a Chapel as I Came. *Unknown.* GBP; OxBM

Merry it is, while the summer last. *Unknown.* HAP

Merry Jest of Robin Hood, A. Thomas Love Peacock. PeBB

Merry Jovial Beggar, The. Peter Casey, *tr. fr. Gaelic by* Douglas Hyde. WTO

Merry-ma-Tanzie, The. *Unknown.* GBP

Merry [*or* Mirry] Margaret,/ As midsummer flower. To Mistress Margaret Hussey. John Skelton. *Fr.* The Garlande of Laurell. AAS; EBEV; HeIP; HoPM (1975 ed.); LoAs; NOBE; OAEL-1; PAIC; PPoe; PPP

Merry May the Keel Row. *Unknown.* GBP

Merry merry sparrow. The Blossom. Blake. *Fr.* Songs of Innocence. MBPR; PB

Merry month of May, sunny skies of blue. I've Got the World on a String. Ted Koehler. BLSo

Merry the green, the green hill shall be merry. Another Song. Donald Justice. ConAP; VGW

Merry Window, The. Francis Scarfe. EAS

Merry [*or* Merrie] world did on a day, The. The Quip. George Herbert. ILP (1975 ed.); LFH; SCP-1

Merryman Sings, The. W. S. Gilbert. ECBV

Merthe of all this land, The. God Speed the Plough! *Unknown.* OxBM

Meru. W. B. Yeats. InPS; NoAM; OAEL-2; PoA

Mery Gest How a Sergeaunt Wolde Lerne to Be a Frere, A. Sir Thomas More. AAS

Mery it is in May morning. *See* Merry it is in May morning.

Mery [*or* Mirie] it is while sumer y-last [*or* ilast]. Winterfall. *Unknown.* HAP; OxBM

Meseemeth I heard cry and groan. The Complaint of the Fair Armouress. Villon, *tr. by* Swinburne. OBVE; VLP

Mesh cast for mackerel. Fishermen. Basil Bunting. PoA

Mess Occupations. Ted Berrigan. CAAP

Mess of Love, The. D. H. Lawrence. OAEL-2

Message, The. John Donne. PAIC

Message. Allen Ginsberg. ConAP; VGW

Message. Norman MacCaig. UsP

Message, The. Jacques Prevert, *tr. fr. French by* John Frederick Nims. WeW

Message. Gyorgy Raba, *tr. fr. Hungarian by* Jascha Kessler. VWA

Message. Dorothy M. Richardson. PoA

Message Clear. Edwin Morgan. NIL

Message from Home. Kathleen Raine. WPE

Message from Ohanapecosh Glacier. W. M. Ransom. CDW

Message to the Editor. Patrick Galvin. IPM

Messages for Herod. Charles Doyle. ATNZ

Messed Damozel, The. Charles Hanson Towne. SpRo

Messenger, The. Thom Gunn. PoA

Messengers. Louise Glück. CAAP

Messiah, The. Moshe Yungman, *tr. fr. Yiddish by* David G. Roskies *and* Hillel Schwartz. VWA

Messiah will not come. The Field of Night. Miriam Waddington. VWA

Messias. Karl Shapiro. MPA

Metal Fatigue. Adam Le Fevre. AMV-81

Metal smokestack, The. Exercise No. 2. William Carlos Williams. TH

Metamorphic. Daniel Mark Fogel. BCr

Metamorphoses. Roy Fuller. OxBTC

Metamorphoses. Vassar Miller. RiTi

Metamorphoses, *sels.* Ovid, *tr. fr. Latin.*
"And from the Citie Tegea there came the Paragone," *fr.* X, *tr. by* Arthur Golding. OBVE
Atalanta, *fr.* X, *tr. by* Rolfe Humphries. LiSp
Baucis and Philemon, *fr.* VIII, *tr. by* Dryden. OAEL-1
"Floods, by nature enemies to land, The," *fr.* I, *tr. by* Dryden. OBVE
Golden Age, The, *fr.* I, *tr. by* Arthur Golding. OAEL-1
"I pray thee Nymph Penaeis stay, I chase not as a fo," *fr.* I, *tr. by* Arthur Golding. OBVE
Medea Casts a Spell to Make Aeson Young Again, *fr.* VII, *tr. by* Arthur Golding. Moon
"More whyght thou art then primrose leaf my Lady Galatee," *fr.* XIII, *tr. by* Arthur Golding. OBVE
"Near the Cymmerians, in his dark abode," *fr.* XI, *tr. by* Dryden. OBVE
"Neare Enna walles there standes a Lake Pergusa is the name," *fr.* V, *tr. by* Arthur Golding. OBVE
"Northern breath, that freezes floods, he binds, The," *fr.* I, *tr. by* Dryden. OBVE
"Not Pallas, not ev'n Spleen it self could blame," *fr.* VI, *tr. by* John Gay. OBVE
"Now have I brought a woork too end which neither Joves feerce wrath," *fr.* XV, *tr. by* Arthur Golding. OBVE
"Now in this while gan Daedalus a wearinesse to take," *fr.* VIII, *tr. by* Arthur Golding. OBVE
"Now whyle Hippomenes/ Debates theis things," *fr.* X, *tr. by* Arthur Golding. OBVE
Of the Pythagorean Philosophy, *fr.* XV, *tr. by* Dryden. OBVE
Orpheus and Eurydice, *fr.* X, *tr. by* Rolfe Humphries. GrRo
"Pygmalion seeing these to spend their times," *fr.* X, *tr. by* George Sandys. OAEL-1
Pygmalion's Statue Comes to Life, *fr.* X, *tr. by* Arthur Golding. OAEL-1
"Soon as the father saw the rosy morn," *fr.* II, *tr. by* Joseph Addison. OBVE
"Stones (a miracle to mortal view), The," *fr.* I, *tr. by* Dryden. OBVE
"Then Lelex rose, an old experienc'd man," *fr.* VIII, *tr. by* Dryden. OBVE
"To thee obeyeth all the East as far as Ganges goes," *fr.* IV, *tr. by* Arthur Golding. OBVE
"Ye ayres and windes, ye elves of hilles," *fr.* VII, *tr. by* Arthur Golding. OBVE

Metamorphoses, The. Edward Weismiller. PoUp

Metamorphosis. Sylvia Plath. PoA

Metamorphosis. Peter Porter. OxBTC

Metamorphosis. Wallace Stevens. InPK; VGW

Metamorphosis, The. Sir John Suckling. CaPo; FaBoEE

Metamorphosis of Aunt Jemima, The. William Childress. MAT

Metamorphosis of Pygmalion's Image, The, *sel.* John Marston. "O gracious gods, take compassion." OAEL-1

Metaphors. Sylvia Plath. InPK; SoSe

Metaphors. Miklós Radnóti, *tr. fr. Hungarian by* Steven Polgar *and* Stephen Berg *and* S. J. Marks. VWA

Metaphysic of Snow. Donald Finkel. PoA

Metaphysical. Robert Fitzgerald. PoA

Metaphysical Amorist, The.   J. V. Cunningham.   VGW

Metaphysical Paintings, The.   John Perreault.   EAS

Metaphysician.   Robert Fitzgerald.   PoA

Meteorologists, like old lovers, know.   Spring.   Frederick Feirstein.   AMV-81

Methinks already from this chymic flame.   London after the Great Fire, 1666.   Dryden.   *Fr.* Annus Mirabilis.   NOBE

Methinks I hear, methinks I see.   Robert Burton.   *Fr.* The Anatomy of Melancholy: The Author's Abstract of Melancholy.   SCP-2

Me thinks I see our mighty monarch stand.   *Unknown.   Fr.* The Royal Angler.   OBSV

Methinks I see, with what a busy haste.   *See* Me thinks . . .

Methinks I spy Almighty holding in.   Edward Taylor.   *Fr.* Preparatory Meditations, Second Series, LXVIII.   HAP

Method must be purest meat, The.   On Burroughs' Work.   Allen Ginsberg.   NoAM; NOBA

Methodist, The, *sel.*   Evan Lloyd.
   "Sons of War sometimes are known, The."   OBSV

Methought I saw (as I did dream in bed).   The Vision.   Robert Herrick.   CaPo

Methought I saw my late espoused saint.   On His Deceased Wife.   Milton.   BoLoP; CABA (1972 ed.); EBEV; Epi; ExPo (1973 ed.); GBL; HAP; ILP (1975 ed.); LFH; LoAs; NOBE; OAEL-1; OBP; PoIA; PoPle; PPP; SCP-1

Methought I Saw the Grave Where Laura Lay.   Sir Walter Ralegh.   ILP (1975 ed.)

Methought [*or* Me thought,] (last night), love in an anger came.   The Dream.   Robert Herrick.   LoAs; SCP-1

Methuselah ("Methuselah ate what he found on his plate").   *Unknown.*   QQQ

Meticulous, past midnight in clear rime.   Voyages, V.   Hart Crane.   PSN

Metonymy as an Approach to a Real World.   William Bronk.   VGW

Metre Columbian, The.   *Unknown.*   SpRo

Metric Figure.   William Carlos Williams.   AKE

Metrical Feet.   Samuel Taylor Coleridge.   NIL; OxBChV

Metroliner.   Jack DuVall.   AMV-80

Metropole.   Forrest Anderson.   AATT

Metropolitan Night.   Jorge Guillén, *tr. fr. Spanish by* Barbara Howes.   NYP

Metropolitan Nightmare.   Stephen Vincent Benét.   PAIC

Metropolitan Railway, The.   John Betjeman.   EBEV; OxBTC

Mewlips, The.   J. R. R. Tolkien.   SO

Mews Flat Mona.   William Plomer.   FaBoTw (1975 ed.)

Mexican/ Flea powder.   In Mexico.   Robert Sward.   NowV

Mexican bandits.   Caught Up in the Villa.   Ralph Storey.   SES

Mexican dwarfs can dance for miles, The.   Maxixe.   Sir Osbert Sitwell.   PoA

Mexican Quarter.   John Gould Fletcher.   Arizona Poems, II.   BPAW

Mexican Village.   Rainer Schulte.   SES

Mexico.   Barbara Hughes.   PoW

Mexico, *sel.*   Robert Lowell.
   "No artist perhaps, you go beyond their phrases."   BiP

Mexico City Blues, *sels.*   Jack Kerouac.
   Chorus: "Dharma law," 66.   PiAm
   Chorus: "Praised be man, he is existing in milk," 228.   PiAm
   Chorus: "Songs that erupt, The," 195.   PiAm

Mexico Is a Foreign Country: Four Studies in Naturalism, *sel.*   Robert Penn Warren.
   Mango on the Mango Tree, The, IV.   NoAM

Meyer and I, we drove.   Herman Nibbelink.   AMV-80

Mezzo Cammin.   Longfellow.   AmVN; ILP (1975 ed.); TAP

Mi Caballo Blanco (My White Horse.).   *Tr. fr. Spanish.*   FSW

Mi Corazón.   Gordon W. Norris.   BPAW

Mi Y'Malel (Who Can Retell?).   *Tr. fr. Hebrew.*   FSW

Mica shines on the beach.   Extract.   Paul Bowles.   PoA

Mice.   Rose Fyleman.   CTV; MN

Mice before Milk.   Chaucer.   *Fr.* The Canterbury Tales: The Manciple's Tale.   PCat

Mice Celebrate Christmas, The.   Alf Prøysen, *tr. fr. Norwegian by* Mrs. A. H. Sevig.   MN

Mice in the garbage.   For Rosa Yen, Who Lived Here.   Greg Pape.   AmPA

Mice in the Hay.   Leslie Norris.   PChr

Michael: A Pastoral Poem.   Wordsworth.   ILP (1975 ed.); MBPR; OAEL-2

Michael Finnigan.   *Unknown.*   FSW; GSB, *with music.*

Michael from Mountains.   Joni Mitchell.   WIF

Michael Robartes and the Dancer.   W. B. Yeats.   OAEL-2

Michael Robartes Bids His Beloved Be at Peace.   W. B. Yeats.   NoAM

Michael, Row the Boat Ashore.   *Unknown.*   BLSo, *with music;* FSW

Michael wakes you up with sweets.   Michael from Mountains.   Joni Mitchell.   WIF

Michael's Room.   Reginald Gibbons.   AMV-81

Michelangelo: "The Creation of Adam."   Gregory Djanikian.   AMV-81

Michigan-I-O.   *Unknown.*   AmFP

Mick.   James Reeves.   GDP; RAE

Microbe's Serenade, The.   George Ade.   OBAL

Microcosm, The.   Giovanni Battista Guarini, *tr. fr. Italian by* Sir Edward Sherburne.   LoAs

Microcosmos.   Susan Miles.   OxBTC

Micro-Cynicon, *sel.*   "T. M."
   Cheating Droone, Satire IV.   TVS

Microscope, The.   Maxine W. Kumin.   PoTa; QQQ

Microscope.   Gwyn Thomas.   OBW

Mid-August at Sourdough Mountain Lookout.   Gary Snyder.   CNW; HAP; MAT; MPA; NCSH; TAP; VoA

Mid Century Love Letter.   Phyllis McGinley.   PPM

Mid-Plains Tornado.   Linda Bierds.   AMV-80

Mid pleasures and palaces though we *or* I] may roam.   Home, Sweet Home.   John Howard Payne.   *Fr.* Clari, the Maid of Milan.   BLSH; BLSo; FSW; PSon

'Mid pleasures and palaces though we may roam.   "Home, Sweet Home," with Variations.   H. C. Bunner.   OBAL

Mid-afternoons.   Daysleep.   Virginia E. Smith.   AMV-81

Midas, they say, possessed the art of old.   Epigram.   "Peter Pindar."   NIL

Midas, we are in story told.   The Fable of Midas.   Swift.   APAS

Midday, midsummer, the field is watercolor green.   Five Horses.   May Swenson.   PH

Middle [aged.   40-Love.   Roger McGough.   LiSp; NoAM

Middle-aged Conversation.   A. S. J. Tessimond.   POL

Middle-aged king, The.   King Saul.   Allan Kolski Horvitz.   VWA

Middleaged Man, The.   Louis Simpson.   NNaP

Middle-aged, Middle-Class Woman at Midnight, A.   Genevieve Taggard.   SPT

Middle Aged Midwesterner at Waikiki Again.   John Logan.   PHC

Middle Ages.   Siegfried Sassoon.   SO

Middle class fortress in which to hide, A!   Interior.   Genevieve Taggard.   SPT

Middle of the Night, The.   Karla Kuskin.   IWK

Middle of the Way.   Galway Kinnell.   NU

Middle of the World.   D. H. Lawrence.   HAP

Middle of the World, The.   Kathleen Norris.   GP; PHC

Middle Passage. Robert Hayden. AmNP (1974 ed.); BPo; CoPAm; ILP (1975 ed.); NoAM; PAIC; PoBA; TC

Middle River. Keith Althaus. AAN

Middleness of the Road, The. Robert Frost. NOBA

Middlesex. John Betjeman. OxBTC

Middleton's Rouseabout. Henry Lawson. MAuV

Midget, The. Philip Levine. NoAM

Midland. Danny L. Rendleman. TC

Midnight. Mary Ursula Bethell. ATNZ

Midnight. Weldon Kees. NoAM

Midnight. Archibald Lampman. AKE

Midnight. Gabriela Mistral, tr. fr. Spanish by David Garrison. BoWoP

Midnight. R. A. Simpson. FPA

Midnight. Tennyson. VLP

Midnight and Ten Minutes. Shlomo Vinner, tr. fr. Hebrew by Laya Firestone and Howard Schwartz. VWA

Midnight, and three women. Auguries for Three Women. Jacquelyne Crews. AMV-81

Midnight at midwinter: the dead land laid. Turning Point. W. L. Holshouser. AMV-81

Midnight Court, The, sels. Brian Merriman, tr. fr. Modern Irish.
  Country's Crisis, The, tr. by David Marcus. BIrV
  Husband's Lament, The, tr. by Frank O'Connor. OBVE
  Irish Marriage Night, An, tr. by Frank O'Connor. BIrV
  Lament of the Unmarried Girl, The, tr. by Frank O'Connor. OBVE
  Maiden's Plight, The, tr. by Frank O'Connor. BIrV
  Now God Stand Up for Bastards, tr. by Arland Ussher. BIrV
  Old Man's Tale, The, tr. by David Marcus. BIrV
  Solution, The, tr. by Arland Ussher. BIrV
  Walk, tr. by Brendan Behan. BIrV

Midnight Dancer. Langston Hughes. FF

Midnight in Bonnie's Stall. Siddie Joe Johnson. PChr

Midnight is no time for. No Time for Poetry. Julia Fields. AmNP (1974 ed.)

Midnight Lamentation. Harold Monro. OxBTC

Midnight March, The. Fred Gilbert. VLP

Midnight on Front Street. Roberta Hill. CDW

Midnight on my ladders, FM blasting, and three beers. Painting an Old Apartment. James Bonk. HeS

Midnight on the Great Western. Thomas Hardy. NOBE; OBP

Midnight Raffle. Langston Hughes. PiAm

Midnight Skaters, The. Edmund Blunden. FaBoTw (1975 ed.); NOBE; PSN

Midnight Special. Leadbelly (Huddie Ledbetter). FSW

Midnight Special. Kenneth Patchen. VGW

Midnight Tennis Match, The. Thomas Lux. AmPA

Midnight. The wind yawing nor-east. Haddock Fishermen. George Mackay Brown. MS

Midnight. The words start out, walking. Tracks. Peter Cooley. HeS

Midnight, Walking the Wakeful Daughter. Joseph Meredith. AMV-81

Midnight's bell goes ting, ting, ting, ting, ting. Night Sounds. Thomas Middleton. Fr. Blurt, Master Constable. RAE

Midrash. David Meltzer. CPA
  "Rabbi is before me, The," sel. GP

Midrash on Hamlet. Francis Landy. VWA

Midstream they met. Challenger and champion. The Swans. Clifford Dyment. BoAnP

Midsummer. Robert Fitzgerald. PoA

Midsummer Frost. Isaac Rosenberg. UsP

Midsummer Holiday, A, sel. Swinburne.
  Cliffside Path, The. VI. VLP

Midsummer Jingle, sel. Newman Levy.
  "I've an ingle, shady ingle, near a dusky bosky dingle." OSP

Midsummer Night's Dream, A, sels. Shakespeare.
  "Lovers and madmen have such seething brains," fr. V, i. UsP
  Lunatic, the Lover, and the Poet, The, fr. V, i. PAIC
  "My gentle Puck, come hither," fr. II, i. EcS
  "My hounds are bred out of the Spartan kind," fr. IV, i. GDP; PoPle
  "Ousel-cock, so black of hue, The," fr. III, i. PB
  "Over hill, over dale," fr. II, i. NOBE; PoPle
  (Fairy Song.) PCOP
  Puck's Night Song, fr. V, ii. ECBV
  ("Now the hungry lion roars.") DuDr; OBP
  Wild Flowers, fr. II, i. PF
  ("I know a bank where the wild thyme blows.") PoPle
  "You spotted snakes with double tongue," fr. II, ii. ECBV; NOBE

Mid-Term Break. Seamus Heaney. NCSH

Midway. John D. Engle, Jr. AMV-81

Midway. Naomi Long Madgett. BPo

Midway along the journey of our life. Inferno. Dante, tr. by Mark Musa. Fr. Divina Commedia. NAWM-1

Midway in the Night: Blackman. Eugene B. Redmond. GP

Midway the journey of this life I was 'ware. Dante, tr. by Lawrence Binyon. Fr. Divina Commedia: Inferno, I. ExPo (1973 ed.)

Midweek. Josephine Miles. RiTi

Midwest. John Frederick Nims. ANTL

Midwest Town. Ruth De Long Peterson. ANTL

Midwest U. F. O. David Steingass. NVAP

Midwestern in the heat, this river's. Duwamish. Richard Hugo. CNW; MPA

Midwestern Man. Paul Giandi. AMV-81

Midwinter. Leslie Norris. HeHu

Midwinter, Presolstice. Margaret Atwood. Psy

Midwinter spring is its own season. Little Gidding. T. S. Eliot. Fr. Four Quartets. BoReV; NoAM; NOBA; NOBE; OAEL-2; OxBTC; TAP

Might have been. This Place Rumord to Have Been Sodom. Robert Duncan. NOBA; PPP

Might I, if you can find it, be given. Saint Nicholas. Marianne Moore. WPE

Might souls converse with souls by angel-way. Edward Benlowes. Fr. Theophila; or, Love's Sacrifice, Canto I. SCP-2

Mighty Brahma, Lord Almighty. The Pariah's Prayer. Goethe. ILwL

Mighty change it is, and ominous, A. The Winter Shore. Thomas Wade. OAEL-2

Mighty Day. Unknown. FSW

Mighty Fortress, A, with music. Martin Luther, tr. fr. German by Frederick H. Hedge. BLSH

Mighty Lak' a Rose, with music. Frank L. Stanton. BLSo; FSN

Mighty mass of brick, and smoke, and shipping, A. Byron. Fr. Don Juan, X. PES

Mighty Mother, and her son who brings, The. Pope. Fr. The Dunciad, I. OBSV

Mighty One, before Whose Face, with music. Bryant. AH

Mighty Runner, A (Variation of a Greek Theme.) E. A. Robinson. LiSp; OBAL

Mighty thought of an old world, The. Thomas Lovell Beddoes. Fr. The Ivory Gate. ILP (1975 ed.)

Mighty wave rush'd o'er him as he spoke, A. Homer, tr. by Pope. Fr. The Odyssey, V. OBVE

Mignon. Goethe, tr. fr. German by Robert Bly. NU

Mignonette. H. C. Bunner. PCOP

Migrant Hostel. Peter Skrzynecki. CAAP

Migrants, The. Wendell Berry. CSP

Migration. Joseph Bruchac. AMV-81

Migration. Carole Gregory Clemmons. *See* Ghetto Lovesong— Migration.

Migration of the Grey Squirrels, The. William Howitt. OxBChV

Migrations of People, The. Dorothy Leiser. AMV-80

Migratory Rats, The. Heine, *tr. fr. German by* Ernst Feise. NAWM-2

Mikado, The, *sels.* W. S. Gilbert.
Flowers That Bloom in the Spring, The, *with music.* BLSo
Suicide's Grave, The. VLP
They'll None of 'Em Be Missed. VLP
"Wandering minstrel I, A." AIW

Mike 65. Lennox Raphael. PoBA

Miklos Radnoti. Willis Barnstone. VWA

Mikveh, The. Blu Greenberg. AMV-80

Mild and slow and young. Girl Help. Janet Lewis. WPW

Mild-spoken Citizen Finally Writes to the White House, A. William Meredith. WasP

Mild yoke of Christ, most harsh to me not bearing. Paradox. Vassar Miller. WIF

Mile behind is Gloucester town, A. Gloucester Moors. William Vaughn Moody. AmVN; NOBA

Mile below Blue Canyon on the lonely Pinon Trail, A. Curly Joe. *Unknown.* BPAW

Mile from Poetry, A, *sel.* Kris Hemensley.
Melancholy Summer. CAAP

Mile out in the marshes, under a sky, A. The Town Dump. Howard Nemerov. BiP; CMoP (1970 ed.); ILP (1975 ed.); MAT; NIL

Miles and miles of giraffes galloping. Serengeti Sunset. Andrew Oerke. POL

Miles and miles of pasture. The Lavender Kitten. Alonzo Lopez. VW

Miles away, the dome. Looking at Power. Warren Woessner. AMV-80

Miles from here, in the mountains. Lost. Patricia Goedicke. EC

Miles is so sufficient. At the Stronghold. Lawson Fusao Inada. NW

Miles of pram in the wind and Pam in the gorse track. Pot Pourri from a Surrey Garden. John Betjeman. NOBL

Militant. Langston Hughes. PoBA

Military Harpist, The. Ruth Pitter. FaBoTw (1975 ed.)

Military officers from Prussia. The Dossier. Michael McMahon. FAF

Militia, The. Dryden. *See* Lines on a Paid Militia.

Milkcow Blues. *Unknown.* BluL

Milkcow's Calf Blues. *Unknown.* BluL

Milk for the Cat. Harold Monro. PCat

Milk! milk! milk! Thomas Edward Brown. *Fr.* Lynton Verses. PeD

Milken Time. William Barnes. VPC

Milking Shed, The. John Clare. VLP

Milking Time. Elizabeth Madox Roberts. RAE

Milkmaid. Laurie Lee. BoLoP; FaBoTw (1975 ed.); MPo

Milkmaid, The. *Unknown.* AmFP; BBL
("Where are you going to, my pretty maid?") MG

Milkmaid's Epithalamium, The. Thomas Randolph. BoLoP

Milkman's broken bottles are just, The. Words from the Housewife. Robert Hahn. AAN

Milkweed. Charles O. Hartman. AAN

Milkweed. James Wright. NOBA; NU

Milkweed is pertinent now; so in the air. Milkweed. Charles O. Hartman. AAN

Milk-Wort and Bog-Cotton. "Hugh MacDiarmid." MS

Milky Way, The. Jon Anderson. BrS

Milky Way above, The. Fire Island. May Swenson. PoA; TAP

Mill, A. William Allingham. FaBoEE; POL

Mill, The. E. A. Robinson. CMoP (1970 ed.); DL; HAP; NoAM; SoSe; STS; WeW
(Miller's Wife, The.) TAP

Mill, The. Richard Wilbur. SoSe (1977 ed.)

Mill at Romesdal. Richard Hugo. AMV-80

Mill at Trumpington, The. Chaucer. *Fr.* The Canterbury Tales: The Reeve's Tale. OxBM

Mill Town. Genevieve Taggard. SPT

Mill Valley. Myra Cohn Livingston. RFM

"Millennium," yes; "pandemonium"! Hometown Piece for Messrs. Alston and Reese. Marianne Moore. OBAL

Miller, The. *Unknown.* FSW

Miller of Dee, The ("There dwelt a miller hale and bold"). *Unknown.* GBP

Miller of the Dee, The ("There was a jolly miller once"). *Unknown.* GSB, *with music*
(Miller of Dee, The, *st. 1.*) BBL
(Song: "There was a jolly miller once," *st. 1, at. to* Isaac Bickerstaffe.) PFIr

Miller's Daughter, The. Tennyson. VLP

Miller's Daughter, The. *Unknown.* PeBB

Miller's daughter, The. Spinning Song. Edith Sitwell. DuDr

Miller's mill-dog lay at the mill door, The. Bingo. *Unknown.* ECBV

Miller's Prologue, The. Chaucer. *Fr.* The Canterbury Tales. OAEL-1

Miller's Tale, The. Chaucer. *Fr.* The Canterbury Tales. OAEL-1

Miller's Wife, The. E. A. Robinson. *See* Mill, The.

Miller's wife had waited long, The. The Mill. E. A. Robinson. CMoP (1970 ed.); DL; HAP; NoAM; SoSe; STS; TAP; WeW

Miller's Wife's Lullaby, The. *Unknown.* GBP

Mill-stream, now that noises cease, The. A. E. Housman. GBL

Milne's Bar. Norman MacCaig. FaBoTw (1975 ed.)

Milord, how beautifully you write! To Li Po from Tu Fu. Carolyn Kizer. GP

Milo's from home; and, Milo being gone. Epigram. Martial, *tr. by* Elijah Fenton. OBVE

Milton. Blake. MBPR
*Sels.*
And Did Those Feet in Ancient Time, *fr.* Preface. CABA (1972 ed.); HAP; HeIP; InPS; IP; MAT; NIL; OAEL-2; OBP; STS
(Jerusalem.) FaPoR; NOBE; PIM
(New Jerusalem, A.) FSW; VoPo
(Preface: "And did those feet in ancient time.") ILP (1975 ed.); PPoe
Birds, The, *fr.* II. PB
Odours of Flowers, The, *fr.* II. PF
"Then Milton rose up from the heavens of Albion ardorous!" *fr.* I. OAEL-2
"This Wine-press is call'd War on Earth," *fr.* I. EBEV
Vision of Beulah, The, *fr.* II. NOBE; OAEL-2

Milton. Longfellow. ILP (1975 ed.); LFH; TAP

Milton. Tennyson. Epi; PAIC; VLP

Milton! Wordsworth. *See* London, 1802 ("Milton! thou shouldst be living...").

Milton by Firelight. Gary Snyder. CAPP; CNW; ConAP; ILP (1975 ed.); InPK; InPS; PPP

Milton! thou shouldst be living at this hour. London, 1802. Wordsworth. BiP; CABA (1972 ed.); Epi; ExPo (1973 ed.); FaPoR; FF; HAP; HeIP; ILP (1975 ed.); IPWM; LFH; MBPR; NIL; OBP; PAIC; PBMP

Miltonic Sonnet for Mr. Johnson on His Refusal of Peter Hurd's Official Portrait, A. Richard Wilbur. CAPP; WasP

Milton's the prince of poets—so we say. Byron. *Fr.* Don Juan, III. NOBL; OAEL-2

Milton's Wife on Her Twenty-third Birthday. Jane Conant-Bissell. AMV–80

Milwaukee Fire, The. *Unknown.* AmFP

Mime. Dick Allen. AMV–81

Mimnermus in Church. William Johnson Cory. NOBE; VLP

Min. *Unknown.* ECBV

Mind. Richard Wilbur. CMoP (1970 ed.); CoPAm; HoPM (1975 ed.); ILP (1975 ed.); LFH; NCSH; PPP

Mind Alchemy. David P. Manzo. PoW

Mind and Matter. *Unknown.* FaBoCo ("There was a faith healer of Deal.") BBL

Mind Content, A. Robert Greene. *See* Maesia's Song.

Mind Flying Afar. Edgar Lee Masters. PoA

Mind has shown itself at times, The. For the Marriage of Faustus and Helen. Hart Crane. InPS; NoAM; NOBA

Mind in its [*or* the] purest play is like some bat. Mind. Richard Wilbur. CMoP (1970 ed.); CoPAm; HoPM (1975 ed.); ILP (1975 ed.); LFH; NCSH; PPP

Mind, Intractable Thing, The. Marianne Moore. Psy

Mind invented daily on premise (early). Hallelujah Hardesty, Female Artist. Hugh Walthall. PoUp

Mind Is an Ancient and Famous Capital, The. Delmore Schwartz. NoAM; TAP

Mind Is an Enchanting Thing, The. Marianne Moore. CMoP (1970 ed.); PiAm; PPP

Mind Is Still, The. Ursula K. Le Guin. AMV–80

Mind Reader Blues. *Unknown.* BluL

Mind would like to get out of here, The. Winter Insomnia. Raymond Carver. NVAP

Minding. Donald Campbell. *Fr.* Sonnets frae Siberia. MIS

Mind's eye aches from Henry James, The. Satie, at the End of Term. Simon Curtis. NOBL

Mine. Andrew Hudgins. AMV–80

Mine be a cot beside the hill. A Wish. Samuel Rogers. FaPoR; NOBE

Mine—by the right of the white election. Emily Dickinson. LoAs

Mine enemy is growing old. Emily Dickinson. WIF

Mine eye, mine ear, my will, my wit, my heart. Gulling Sonnets, V. Sir John Davies. Epi

Mine eye with all the deadlie sinnes is fraught. Henry Constable. *Fr.* Diana. ESo

Mine eyes have seen the glory of the coming of the Lord. The Battle Hymn of the Republic. Julia Ward Howe. AH; BLSH; BLSo; BTTM; CTV; FaPo; FaPoR; FSW; NOBA; PSoN; TAP; WPE

Mine eyes have seen the guru. *Unknown.* POL

Mine eyes were dim with tears unshed. To Mary Wollstonecraft Godwin. Shelley. MBPR

Mine Host of the "Golden Apple." Thomas Westwood. ECBV

Mine is a dark and twisting place. Coal Miner's Grace. Jay Divine. AMV–80

Mine own John Poyntz, since ye delight to know. *See* Myne owne John Poyntz...

Mine owne good Bat, before thou hoyse up saile. Councell Given to Master Bartholmew Withipoll. George Gascoigne. AAS

Mine was a Midwest home—you can keep your world. One Home. William Stafford. IPWM; VGW; VoA

Miner Boy, The. *Unknown.* AmFP

Miner Coming Home One Night, A. *Unknown.* GBP

Miners. John C. Frohlicher. BPAW

Miners. Wilfred Owen. NOBE; OBW

Miners. James Wright. ConAP; CTBA; TCP

Miner's Doom, The. *Unknown.* AmFP

Miner's Helmet, The. George MacBeth. OxBTC

Miner's Lament, The ("High on a rough and dismal crag"). *At. to* "Mark Twain." BPAW

Miner's Lament, The ("When the gold fever raged I was doing very well"). *Unknown.* AmFP

Miner's Lifeguard ("Miner's life is like a sailor's"). *Unknown.* FSW

Miner's Progress, The. *At. to* Alanzo Delano. BPAW

Mines/ concealed/ in the flesh. Good Friday Explosions. E. R. Cole. AATT

Mingled the moonlight with daylight. Thomas Hardy. Walter de la Mare. NoAM

Mingram Mo. David McCord. ECBV

Mingus. Bob Kaufman. PoBA

Mini Spooks, The. Eloise Anderson. IWK

Miniatures IV. Lynn Strongin. IHMS

Minimal, The. Theodore Roethke. BiP; NoAM; NOBA

Mining Places. Frederick Boden. PES

Minister said it wad [*or* wald] dee, The. Last Lauch. Douglas Young. FaBoCo; MS

Ministers who've sold the King. Are You Glad? *Mongol Oral Tradition, tr. by* C. R. Bawden. WTO

Miniver Cheevy. E. A. Robinson. CABA (1972 ed.); CMoP (1970 ed.); FaPo; FF; HeIP; NIL; NoAM; NOBA; OBSV; PiAm; PPM; SpRo; SS; STS; TAP; WIF

Miniver Cheevy, Jr. David Fisher Parry. SpRo

Minneapolis. Tom Hennen. HeS

"Minneapolis, Midwest." Wisconsin Farm Auction. David Steingass. NVAP

Minneapolis Poem, The. James Wright. NoAM; UnPo (1976 ed.)

Minneapolis White Castle, Winter '72. James L. White. HeS

Minnesota Thanksgiving. John Berryman. GOA

Minnie and Winnie. Tennyson. OxBChV

Minnie, I canna caa my wheel. Douglas Young, *after the Greek of* Sappho. OBVE

Minnie Morse. Kaye Starbird. PH

Minnows sheer out, The. Blue River Falls. Jordan Smith. AAN

Minor Bird, A. Robert Frost. CMoP (1970 ed.); PB

Minor Elegy. Henriqueta Lisboa, *tr. fr. Portuguese by* Willis Barnstone *and* Nelson Cerqueira. BoWoP

Minor Key. Judah Leib Teller, *tr. fr. Yiddish by* Gabriel Preil *and* Howard Schwartz. VWA

Minor Victorian Painter, A. John Hewitt. CIP

Minority Report. John Updike. GOA

Minstrel Boy, The. Thomas Moore. FSW; GSB, *with music*

Minstrel's Last Lay, The. John Barth. OBAL

Minstrel's Song, The. Thomas Chatterton. *Fr.* Aella. HAP; OBP ("O! Synge untoe mie roundelaie.") NOBE (Song from Aella.) LoAs

Minute before Meeting, The. Thomas Hardy. VLP

Minute flowers harden. Depend. Lilies of the Valley. Jon Silkin. NoAM

Minutes are flying swiftly, and as yet. On Receiving a Laurel Crown from Leigh Hunt. Keats. MBPR

Minyan, The. Jack Myers. VWA

Mira is dancing with bells tied on her ankles. Mirabai, *tr. fr. Hindi by* Willis Barnstone *and* Usha Nilsson. BoWoP

Mirabeau Bridge, The. Guillaume Apollinaire, *tr. fr. French.* BoLoP, *tr. by* Quentin Stevenson; OBVE, *tr. by* W. S. Merwin

Miracle, The. Walter de la Mare. UnPo (1976 ed.)

Miracle, The. Chaim Grade, *tr. fr. Yiddish by* Ruth Whitman. VWA

Miracle. Tony Moreno. NW

Miracle. William Soutar. MS

Miracle, The. Sir John Suckling. CaPo

Miracle Cure. Edward Lowbury. PMW

Miracle Hill. Emerson Blackhorse Mitchell. VW

Miracle of the children the brilliant. Exodus. George Oppen. GP; RRA

Miracle of the world, I never will deny. Henry Constable. *Fr.* Diana. NIL

Miracle Worker. Claudia Dobkins. NPW

Miracles ("Why, who makes much of a miracle?"). Walt Whitman. PBMP; UsP

Miracles offend because they lack proportion. Why I Am Offended by Miracles. David Bergman. AMV–80

Miraculous Dawn. R. Williams Parry, *tr. fr. Welsh by* Joseph P. Clancy. OBW

Miraculously in the autumn twilight, out of. The Boy. Ruth Dallas. ATNZ

Mirage. Christina Rossetti. BoLoP

Mirage, A. Ruth Setterberg. AMV–80

Miramar Beach. J. V. Cunningham. To What Strangers, What Welcome, VIII. PoA ("Night is still, The. The unfailing surf.") PiAm

Miramichi Fire, The. *Unknown.* AmFP

Mirie It Is while Sumer Ilast. *Unknown.* *See* Winterfall.

Mirror. Tada Chimako, *tr. fr. Japanese by* Kenneth Rexroth *and* Ikuko Atsumi. BoWoP

Mirror. Peter De Vries. PoA

Mirror, The. Louise Glück. GP

Mirror, The. John Haines. CNW

Mirror, The. A. A. Milne. ECBV

Mirror, The. John N. Morris. PoA

Mirror. Sylvia Plath. HAP; SoSe

Mirror Farming. Robert Morgan. PCho

Mirror for Magistrates, A, *sel.* William Baldwin *and others.* Induction, The. Thomas Sackville. AAS; PAIC, 56 *ll.* Shield of War, The. NOBE

Mirror for Myself. Roger Wescott. PCOP

Mirror for the Barnyard. Jack Myers. AmPA

Mirror hung on the broken, A. The Mirror in the Woods. Kenneth Rexroth. MPA

Mirror Images. Laurel Speer. AMV–80

Mirror in February. Thomas Kinsella. CIP; IPM; NoAM

Mirror in the Woods, The. Kenneth Rexroth. MPA

Mirror in Which Two Are Seen as One, The. Adrienne Rich. NIL; NNaP; RiTi; WBN

Mirror-mad. Narcissus, Photographer. Erica Jong. SoSe (1977 ed.)

Mirrorment. A. R. Ammons. OSP

Mirrors, The. Sophia de Mello Breyner Andresen, *tr. fr. Portuguese by* Allan Francovich. PBWP

Mirrors of Jerusalem, The. Barbara F. Lefcowitz. AMV–80; VWA

Mirru. Kenneth Patchen. RRA

Mirry Margaret,/ As mydsomer flowre. *See* Merry Margaret . . .

Mirth. Francis Beaumont. *Fr.* The Knight of the Burning Pestle, II, viii. PPM

Mirth. Christopher Smart. *Fr.* Hymns for the Amusement of Children. LAuP; OxBChV

Mirth and Melancholy. Margaret Cavendish, Duchess of Newcastle. WPE

Misapprehended Goose, The. Oliver Herford. TDH

Misapprehension. Paul Laurence Dunbar. BPo

Miscarriage. Michael Longley. POL

Miscegenous Zebra, The. Roland Young. BoAnP

Miscellaneous screaming that comes from nowhere, A. The Geese. Hyam Plutzik. BiP

Mischievous, they say, as a monkey. Jackdaw. Tom Earley. BoAnP

Misconception, A. James Russell Lowell. OBAL

Misdemeanor. Eve Triem. GP

Mise en Scène. Robert Fitzgerald. VGW

Miser and the Mouse, The. Christopher Smart. MN; RAE

Miserable Catullus, stop being foolish. Catullus, *tr. fr. Latin by* Louis Zukofsky. NoAM

Miserable change now at my end, The. Shakespeare. *Fr.* Antony and Cleopatra, IV, xiii. EBEV; PoPle

Miserable shower those Corrs. The Corrs. Tom MacIntyre, *tr. fr. Irish.* CIP

Misericordia. Teresa A. McCarthy. NPW

Misericordia. Margaret Mead. PoA

Misery of Mechanics, The. Philip Booth. MAT

Misfortune is as huge/ and heavy as this cold. Snow-Girl. Yunna Moritz, *tr. by* Elaine Feinstein. VWA

Misfortunes of Elphin, The, *sel.* Thomas Love Peacock. War Song of Dinas Vawr, The. CABA (1972 ed.); ExPo (1973 ed.); FaPoR; HAP; NOBE; OAEL-2; PoPle; PoTa

Misgivings. Herman Melville. ILP (1975 ed.); NOBA; PiAm

Mishka. John Gray. VLP

Mishnah says I blind you with my hair, The. The Marriage Wig. Ruth Whitman. IHMS

Mismatch. Carl Lindner. AMV–80

Misnomer really, A. With a few exceptions. Squares. Michael Hamburger. FF

Misogonus, *sel. Unknown.* Heart's Ease. WIF

Misogynist, The. Jean Morgan. FF

Misplaced Sympathy. Charles Follen Adams. OBAL

Misplacing—Mistaking. On Sir Nathaniel Wraxall the Historian. George Colman the Younger. FaBoEE

Miss Ada. Christopher Fahy. TAT

Miss Alderman. Robert Winner. GP

Miss America. Anne Sadowski. SES

Miss Bailey's Ghost. George Colman the Younger. *See* Unfortunate Miss Bailey.

Miss Buss and Miss Beale. *Unknown.* FaBoEE; PoPle

Miss Cecily Finch. Patrick Galvin. IPM

Miss Cho Composes in the Cafeteria. James Tate. WeW

Miss Dickinson is gone. A New England Sampler. John Malcolm Brinnin. GOA

Miss Ellen Gee of Kew. *Unknown.* FaBoNo

Miss Euphemia. John Crowe Ransom. CMoP (1970 ed.)

Miss Finch is dead. Miss Cecily Finch. Patrick Galvin. IPM

Miss Flora McFlimsey, of Madison Square. Nothing to Wear. William Allen Butler. OBAL

Miss Gee. W. H. Auden. OxBTC

Miss Hartley. William Jay Smith. TDH

Miss Helen Slingsby was my maiden aunt. Aunt Helen. T. S. Eliot. OBAL; PoA; SoS

Miss her, Catullus? don't be so inept to rail. Catullus, *tr. fr. Latin by* Celia *and* Louis Zukofsky. OBVE

Miss Hewett's Shenanigans. Dorothy Hewett. GAS

Miss Hocket. *Unknown.* TDH

Miss Israel Nineteen-sixty-eight is new. Ballade of Beauties. Alexander Scott. MS

Miss J. Hunter Dunn, Miss J. Hunter Dunn. A Subaltern's Love-Song. John Betjeman. BoLoP; HAP; LiSp; NOBL; OxBTC; PPoD

Miss Jane. *Unknown.* MN

Miss Jennian Jones. *Unknown.* AmFP

Miss Kilmansegg and Her Precious Leg, *sel.* Thomas Hood. Her Fancy Ball, *abr.* VLP

Miss Loo. Walter de la Mare. CMoP (1970 ed.); OxBTC

Miss Maime. Jodi Braxton. WBN

Miss Nancy Ellicott. Cousin Nancy. T. S. Eliot. OBAL

Miss Pheasant. Walter de la Mare. FaBoNo

Miss Rafferty wore taffeta. The Private Dining Room. Ogden Nash. UsP

Miss Rosie. Lucille Clifton. AmPA; CAPP; CNA; NMM; PoBA; RiTi

Miss T. Walter de la Mare. BBL

Miss Tillie McLush. Joseph S. Newman. TDH

Miss Twye. Gavin Ewart. NOBL

Missel-Thrush's Nest, The. John Clare. VLP

Misshapen, black, unlovely to the sight. A Bulb. Richard Kendall Munkittrick. POL

"Mis-shapen Time, copesmate of ugly Night." Shakespeare. Fr. The Rape of Lucrece. OAEL-1

Missing. W. H. Auden. OxBTC

Missing. A. A. Milne. MN

Missing. John Pudney. OxBTC

Missing Beat. Carolyn M. Rodgers. JB

Missing Dates. William Empson. CMoP (1970 ed.); HAP; ILP (1975 ed.); NIL; NoAM; NOBE; OAEL-2; PAIC; PSN; UnPo (1976 ed.)

Missing from the map, the abandoned roads. Old Roads. Eilean Ni Chuilleanain. CIP

Missing MS. Thulani Nkabinde. NW

Missing My Daughter. Stephen Spender. RRA

Mission. Unknown. AmFP

Mission Bay. John Koethe. PoA

Mission Bells of Monterey, The. Bret Harte. PeD

Mission Uncontrolled. Richard Peck. MiP

Missionary. D. M. Thomas. MPo

Missionary from the Mau Mau told me, A. A Magus. John Ciardi. CoPAm; MAT

Mississippi Blues. Unknown. AmFP

Mississippi Born. Pearl Cleage Lomax. CNA

Mississippi Sawyer. Unknown. AmFP

Missouri Sequence, sel. Brian Coffey. "Our children have eaten supper." CIP

Missouri Town. John Palen. AMV-80

Misspelt scrawl, upon the wall, The. In an Album. James Russell Lowell. OBAL

Mist and All, The. Dixie Willson. CTV

Mist came up thick this morning, The. November Birthday. Mary Swanson Stroh. NPW

Mist drenched, moonlit, the sculpture. Kenneth Rexroth. Fr. On Flower Wreath Hill. GP

Mist Forms. Carl Sandburg. CMoP (1970 ed.)

Mist-moist, past the rainbow, we make a small row. Niagara. Richard Emil Braun. NoAM

Mist over Pukehina, The. Maori Oral Tradition, tr. by E. Shortland. WTO

Mistakable Identity. Elaine V. Emans. AMV-80

Mistake. Unknown. OSF

Mistaken./ take. en. The Trick Is Consciousness. Paula Gunn Allen. FoP

Mistaken fair, lay Sherlock by. Verses Written in a Lady's Sherlock upon Death. Earl of Chesterfield. EBEV

Mistaken Identity. Joanne Casullo. NPW

Mr. and Mrs. Spikky Sparrow. Edward Lear. OxBChV

Mr. and Mrs. Vite's Journey. Unknown. NOBL

Mr. Apollinax. T. S. Eliot. PoA

Mr. Artesian's Conscientiousness. Ogden Nash. SS

Mister Backlash, Mister Backlash. The Backlash Blues. Langston Hughes. BPo

Mister Beedle Baddlebug. Tea Party. Harry Behn. LCL

Mr. Bidery's Spidery Garden. David McCord. DuDr

Mr. Bleaney. Philip Larkin. BuTh; HoPM (1975 ed.); InPS; PPoe

Mr. Brodsky. Charles Tomlinson. NoAM; TwMBP

Mister Charlie. Unknown. BluL

Mr. Cherry. Paul Baker Newman. AMV-81

Mr. Clean. John William Corrington. PPoD

"Mr. Colwell"/ says Sharon the nurse. The Cry of an Aged One. Ray Fraser. NeAC

Mr. Con, Mr. Can. Unknown. ECBV

Mr. Cooper. Anthony Thwaite. OxBTC

Mr. Cromek to Mr. Stothard. Blake. FaBoEE

Mr. Davis's Experience. Unknown. AmFP

Mr. Edwards and the Spider. Robert Lowell. AnMo; CABA (1972 ed.); CAPP; CMoP (1970 ed.); HeIP; ILP (1975 ed.); InPS; NIL; NOBA; PSN; SoSe (1977 ed.); STS; UsP

Mr. Finney's Turnip. Unknown. ECBV

Mr. Flood's Party. E. A. Robinson. BiP; CABA (1972 ed.); CMoP (1970 ed.); FF; HAP; HoPM (1975 ed.); ILP (1975 ed.); InPK; IP; IPWM; MAT; MiP; NIL; NoAM; NOBA; PAIC; PiAm; PoTa; PPoD; PPoe; PPP; SoSe; STS; TAP; UnPo (1976 ed.)

Mr. Heath-Stubbs as you must understand. Epitaph. John Heath-Stubbs. MPo; OxBTC

Mr. Housman's Message. Ezra Pound. FaBoEE; PAIC

Mister Johnson. Ben Harney. OBAL

Mr. Jones. Harry Graham. FaBoCo

Mr. Leach made a speech. A Chancery Suit. Sir George Rose. FaBoCo

Mr. Macklin's Jack-o'-Lantern. David McCord. CaYB; IWK

Mr. Mine. Anne Sexton. SFF

Mr. Nobody. Unknown. CTV; PCOP

"Mr. Nowlan, are you asleep?" Semi-Private Room. Alden Nowlan. NeAC

Mr. Ody met a body. Edith Nesbit. FaBoNo

Mr. P.—I have heard it rumored. Letter to a Librarian. Irving Layton. MAT

Mr. Pope. Allen Tate. CABA (1972 ed.); NIL; NoAM; NOBA; PAIC; VGW

Mr. Pope's Welcome from Greece. John Gay. EBEV

Mr. Pratt, your sheep are very fat. The Norfolk Rebellion. Unknown. GBP

Mr. Punchinello. Unknown. ECBV

Mr. Rhind is very kind. The Schoolmaster. Unknown. GBP

Mr. Robert Herrick, His Farewell unto Poetry. Robert Herrick. SCP-1

Mr. Rockefeller's Hat. Helen Bevington. OBAL

Mr. Roosevelt Regrets. Pauli Murray. PoBA

Mr. Slimmer's Funeral Verses for the Morning Argus. "Max Adeler." OBAL

Mr. Smith/ (With Nods to Mr. Lear and Mr. Eliot.) William Jay Smith. SpRo

Mister Snow Man. Bertha Wilcox Smith. CTV

Mr. T./ bareheaded. The Artist. William Carlos Williams. InPS; TPo

Mister Tambourine Man. Bob Dylan. NIL

Mister, things ain't never been all stirred up this way befo'! Ah Feels It in Mah Bones. Richard Wright. SPT

Mr. Todd is maudlin now. Lost Love. Clive Turnbull. GAS

Mr. Tom Narrow. James Reeves. SO

Mr. Tubbe's Morning Service. Stanley Burnshaw. SPT

Mr. U Will Not Be Missed. E. E. Cummings. FaBoEE; VGW

Mr. Walter de la Mare Makes the Little Ones Dizzy, sel. Samuel Hoffenstein. "Speckled with glints of star and moonshine." SpRo

Mr. Whitman to His Friends in the Antipodes. Kris Hemensley. Fr. The Poem of the Clear Eye. CAAP

Mr. Whittier. Winfield Townley Scott. VGW

Mister Williams/ lets youn me move. Uncle Iv Surveys His Domain from His Rocker. Jonathan Williams. OBAL

Mr. Z. M. Carl Holman. SoSe

Mistletoe. Walter de la Mare. SO

Mistletoe Bough, The. Thomas Haynes Bayly. VLP

Mistral blows, the plane leaves, The. On the Eve of the Plebiscite. Kenneth Rexroth. NNaP

Mistress, The. Joan Barton. OxBTC

Mistress, The, *sels.* Abraham Cowley.
  Spring, The. HAP; MetP
  Welcome, The. BoLoP
  Wish, The. ILP (1975 ed.); NOBE
  Written in Juice of Lemon. CABA (1972 ed.)

Mistress, The. Earl of Rochester. EBEV; NOBE

Mistress Addresses the Wife, The. Naomi Replansky. GP

Mrs. Albion You've Got a Lovely Daughter. Adrian Henri. OxBTC

Mrs. Alfred Uruguay. Wallace Stevens. InPS; PiAm

Mrs. Applebaum's Sunday Dance Class. Philip Schultz. AMV-81

Mrs. Asquith Tries to Save the Jacarandas. Harold Witt. AMV-81

Mrs. Brown. Rose Fyleman. OxBChV

Mrs. Busk. Sir Osbert Sitwell. OxBTC

Mrs. Chub was rich and portly. Jupiter and Ten. James Thomas Fields. OBAL

Mrs. Coley's three-flat brick. The Vacant Lot. Gwendolyn Brooks. NoAM; NOBA

Mrs. Evans fach, you want butter again. Idris Davies. OBW

Mrs. G. Watters. Frank Ormsby. IPM

Mrs. Golightly. James Reeves. OSF

Mrs. Hamer. Jane Stembridge. NMM

Mrs. Hopley, on Seeing Her Children Say Goodnight to Their Father. Gerard Manley Hopkins. FaBoEE

Mrs. Jaypher. Edward Lear. FaBoNo

Mrs. Jaypher on Lemons. Edward Lear. FaBoNo

Mrs. Judge Jenkins (Being the Only Genuine Sequel to "Maud Muller"). Bret Harte. CABA (1972 ed.)

Mrs. Lombardi's month-old son is dead. Italian Extravaganza. Gregory Corso. SA

Mrs. McGrath. *Unknown.* FaBoBa; FSW

Mrs. Malone. Eleanor Farjeon. OxBChV

Mrs. Mary Blaize. Goldsmith. *See* Elegy on That Glory of Her Sex. . .

Mistress Murphy gave a party just about a week ago. Who Threw the Overalls in Mistress Murphy's Chowder? George L. Geifer. FSN

Mrs. Noah in the Ark. The Ballad of Mrs. Noah. Robert Duncan. MPo; NoAM; NOBA

Mrs. Sadie Grindstaff, Weaver and Factotum. Jonathan Williams. OBAL

Mrs. Saunder's Experience. *Unknown.* AmFP

Mistress, Since You So Much Desire. Thomas Campion. OAEL-1

Mrs. Snipkin and Mrs. Wobblechin. Laura E. Richards. OxBChV

Mrs. Someone's been to Asia. An Importer. Robert Frost. FaBoCo

Mistress Towl. *Unknown.* FaBoNo
  ("There was an old woman named Towl.") OxBChV

Mrs. Trollope in America. Helen Bevington. OBAL

Mrs. Vickers' Daughter. *Unknown.* AmFP

Mrs. Walpurga. Muriel Rukeyser. NMM

Mists rise over, The. Yamabe no Akahito, *tr. fr. Japanese by* Kenneth Rexroth. HoPM (1975 ed.)

Misty and dim, a bush in the wilds of Kapa's. Song. Kaiama, *tr. fr. Hawaiian by* N. B. Emerson. WTO

Misty-Moisty Was the Morn. *Unknown.* GBP

Mithras, God of the Morning, our trumpets waken the wall! A Song to Mithras. Kipling. BTTM

Mithridates. Emerson. NOBA

Mix a pancake. Christina Rossetti. LCL

Mixed Brews. Clive Sansom. FPB

Mixed Feelings. John Ashbery. GP; HAP

Mixed Media. James Schevill. AMV-81

Mixed Sketches. Don L. Lee. BPo; TAP

Mixed Weather. Sydney Tremayne. MS

Mixer, The. Louis MacNeice. FaBoTw (1975 ed.)

Mixture, The, *sel.* John Perreault.
  "I am a mixture of feelings without beginning." OSP

Mixture, always, A. Mud. William Sprunt. AAN

Mmenson. Edward Brathwaite. MPo

Mmmmmmmm lordy lordy lord. Savannah Mama. *Unknown.* BluL

Mnemosyne. Trumbull Stickney. NOBA; PAIC

Mnemosyne Lay in Dust, *sels.* Austin Clarke.
  "One night he heard heart-breaking sound." VI. CIP; CMoP (1970 ed.)
  "Past the house where he was got," I. CMoP (1970 ed.)
  "Rememorised, Maurice Devane," XVIII. CMoP (1970 ed.
  "Straight-jacketing sprang to every lock," II. CMoP (1970 ed.)

Moaning. They lay in bed. Last Night They Heard the Woman Upstairs. Leslie Ullman. AMV-80

Moby Christ. Gerald Barrax. CSP

Moby Dick, *sel.* Herman Melville.
  Father Mapple's Hymn, *fr. ch.* 9. RhR
  (Ribs and Terrors, The.) PPM

Moccasins of an Old Man, The. Ramona Carden. VW

Mock Charon, A. Richard Lovelace. CaPo

Mock Interrogation, A. Judy Grahn. *Fr.* A Woman Is Talking to Death. WBN

Mock Miracle, A. Oliver Herford. TDH

Mock On, Mock On, Voltaire, Rousseau. Blake. AnMo; BiP;BoReV; CABA (1972 ed.); HAP; ILP (1975 ed.); IP; LAuP; MBPR; OAEL-2; PPoe; PPP; STS; TT (Scoffers, The.) UnPo (1976 ed.)

Mock Song, A. Richard Lovelace. CaPo

Mock Turtle's Song, The. "Lewis Carroll." *See* Lobster Quadrille, The.

Mock up again, summer, the sooty altars. Spectacular Blossom. Allen Curnow. ATNZ

Mockado, Fustian, and Motley. John Taylor. FaBoNo

Mocker, The. Gwendolen Haste. WPW

Mockery of Life, The. Wilfrid Scawen Blunt. The Love Sonnets of Proteus, LXXIV. VLP

Mocking Song against Qaqortingneq. Piuvkaq, *tr. fr. Eskimo.* WTO

Mockingbird, The. Randall Jarrell. DuDa; RFM

Mocking Bird, The. *Unknown.* AmFP

Mocking-Bird, The. Walt Whitman. *Fr.* Out of the Cradle Endlessly Rocking. PB

Mockingbird, Copy This. Jack Myers. AMV-81

Mockingbird in Winter. Ernest Kroll. AMV-80

Mockingbird, I've been working hard. Mockingbird, Copy This. Jack Myers. AMV-81

Mockingbird shrieks and dives again and again at the squirrel, A. Can-Opener. David McAleavey. AMV-81

Model for the Laureate, A. W. B. Yeats. CMoP (1970 ed.)

Model T. Adrien Stoutenburg. CTBA

Moderation. Robert Herrick. FaBoEE

Modern American Nursing. Lucy Hricz. AMV-80

Modern Architecture. Norman Nathan. AMV-81

Modern Chinese History Professor Plays Pool Every Tuesday and Thursday, The. James Baker Hall. TAT

Modern Critics. Samuel Taylor Coleridge. FaBoEE

Modern Discoveries. Byron. *Fr.* Don Juan. OBP

Modern Fine Gentleman, The. Soame Jenyns. ESaP
"Just broke from school, pert, impudent, and raw," *sel.* OBSV

Modern Fine Lady, The, *sel.* Soame Jenyns.
"For love no time has she, or inclination." OBSV

Modern Hiawatha, The, *parody.* George A. Strong. AKE; ECBV; FaBoCo; SpRo

Modern Kabbalist. Marcia Falk. UsP; VWA

Modern Leader, A. R. A. Simpson. FPA

Modern Love. J. V. Cunningham. POL

Modern Love. Keats. LoAs; MBPR

Modern Love. George Meredith. VLP
*Sels.*
"All other joys of life he strove to warm," IV. PAIC
"Am I failing? For no longer can I cast," XXIX. CABA (1972 ed.); GBL
"At dinner, she is hostess, I am host," XVII. Epi; HeIP; ILP (1975 ed.)
"By this he knew she wept with waking eyes," I. Epi; HeIP; ILP (1975 ed.);LoAs; NIL; OAEL-2; PAIC; PBMP; VPC
"He felt the wild beast in him betweenwhiles," IX. LoAs
"He found her by the ocean's moaning verge," XLIX. LoAs; OAEL-2; PAIC; VPC
"I play for seasons; not eternities!" XIII. PFD; VPC
"I think she sleeps; it must be sleep, when low," XV. Epi
"In our old shipwrecked days there was an hour," XVI. BoLoP; LoAs
"It ended, and the morrow brought the task," II. ILP (1975 ed.); PAIC
"It is the season of the sweet wild rose," XLV. GBL
"Love ere he bleeds, an eagle in high skies," XXVI. PAIC
"Madam would speak with me. So, now it comes," XXXIV. ILP (1975 ed.)
"Mark where the pressing wind shoots javelin-like," XLIII. GBL; ILP (1975 ed.); NOBE; OBP; VPC
"My lady unto madam makes her bow," XXXVI. VPC
"Not solely that the future she destroys," XII. GBL; VPC
"Out in the yellow meadows, where the bee," XI. GBL
"Their sense is with their senses all mixed in," XLVIII. LoAs; OAEL-2
"This was the woman; what now of the man?" III. PAIC
"Thus piteously love closed what had begat," L. EBEV; HAP; ILP (1975 ed.); NOBE; OAEL-2; PAIC; PFD; VPC
" 'Tis Christmas weather, and a country house," XXIII. PAIC
"We saw the swallows gathering in the sky," XLVII. NOBE; OAEL-2
"What are we first? First, animals; and next," XXX. GBL; HAP; VPC
"What may the woman labor to confess?" XXII. ILP (1975 ed.)
"What soul would bargain for a cure that brings," XIV. PAIC
"Yet it was plain she struggled, and that salt," VIII. LoAs

Modern Love. Gerald Stern. AMV-80

Modern Love Poems. *Somali Oral Tradition, tr. by* B. W. Andrzejewski *and* M. Laurence. WTO

Modern Major-General, The. W. S. Gilbert. *Fr.* The Pirates of Penzance. FaPo; NOBL

Modern malady of love is nerves, The. Nerves. Arthur Symons. FaBoTw (1975 ed.)

Modern Poetry. Anita Skeen. IHMS

Modern Romance. William J. Harris. GP

Modern Times. Morty Sklar. AcAn

Modern World, The. Colin Ellis. FaBoEE

Modernismus; or, Prayer for Standstill. Arthur J. Bull. HeHu

Modes of Pleasure. Thom Gunn. PPP

Modes of the court so common are grown, The. John Gay. *Fr.* The Beggar's Opera, III, iv. HeIP

Modes of Vallejo Street, San Diego, Los Angeles, The, *sels.* Hugh Seidman.
"He imagines her," 3. UnPo (1976 ed.)
"He knows he must explain this," 9. UnPo (1976 ed.)

Modest Couple, The. W. S. Gilbert. PoTa

Modest rose puts forth a thorn, The. The Lilly. Blake. *Fr.* Songs of Experience. MBPR

Modifications. Ron Koertge. MiP

Modigliani's paintings are being shipped by train. The Weather Gallery. Liam Rector. PoUp

Mohammed Ibrahim Speaks. Martha Beidler. FF

Mohini Chatterjee. W. B. Yeats. NoAM

Moiré. Michael McClure. EAS

Moishe Leib stood up. Just Because. Moishe Leib Halpern, *tr. by* Ruth Whitman. VWA

Mojo Hiding Woman. *Unknown.* BluL

Mole, The. John Haines. NCSH

Mole, The. Morton Marcus. PoW

Mole, The. Dennis Schmitz. AmPA

Mole in the Ground *Unknown.* FSW

Mole the cats killed. The Mole. Morton Marcus. PoW

Molecatcher. Albert D. Mackie. MS

Moles. Aileen Fisher. CTV

Moles. William Stafford. RFM

Molly Brannigan, *Unknown.* FSW; RDB, *with music*

Molly Malone. *Unknown.* *See* Cockles and Mussels.

Molly Means. Margaret Walker. AmNP (1974 ed.); NMM; PoTa; SS

Moloney Remembers the Resurrection of Kate Finucane. Brendan Kennelly. PoTa

Moly. Thom Gunn. HAP; NoAM

Mom really knows how to pick 'em. Portrait. Carol Merrill. FoP

Moment. Hildegarde Flanner. WPW

Moment. Howard Nemerov. CoPAm

Moment, The. William Stafford. NNaP

Moment of silence, first, then there it is, A. The Dial Tone. Howard Nemerov. NowV

Moment Please, A. Samuel Allen. AmNP (1974 ed.); PoBA; SS

Moments of Vision. Thomas Hardy. OAEL-2

Moment's patience, gentle Mistress Anne, A. William Shakespeare to Mrs. Anne, Regular Servant to the Rev. Mr. Precentor of York. Thomas Gray. ILP (1975 ed.)

Momma Momma Momma. Getting Down to Get Over. June Jordan. TAP

Mommie. Sarah Kennedy. CPA

Monadnock, The. John Gould Fletcher. PoA

Monarch of gods and daemons, and all spirits. Prometheus Unbound. Shelley. MBPR; OAEL-2

Monarch of the Sea. George Starbuck. OBAL

Monarch's Funeral, The. Shelley. MBPR

Monasteries Lift Gold Domes, The. Yocheved Bat-Miriam, *tr. fr. Hebrew by* Robert Friend. VWA

Monday Night in Winter. Ellen Cooney. NPW

Monday's child [*or* bairn] is fair of face. Mother Goose. CC; CTV; ECBV; MG

Monet: "Les Nymphéas." W. D. Snodgrass. ConAP; TCP

Monet's Les Nymphéas. Lyn Lifshin. FAF

Money. Victor Contoski. GP

Money. Howard Nemerov. WeW

Money. C. H. Sisson. POL

Money Gets the Mastery. Robert Herrick. CaPo

Money Is King. *Unknown.* FSW

Money Isn't Everything! Oscar Hammerstein II. OBAL

Money Makes the Marriage. *Unknown.* TDH

Money Makes the Mirth. Robert Herrick. CaPo

Money men collect in high rise, The. Thumbing Old Magazines. Gerald Vizenor. VoR

Money! Money! *Yoruba Oral Tradition, tr. by* O. Ogunba. WTO

Money thou ow'st me; prithee fix a day. Upon Bunce: Epigram. Robert Herrick. CaPo

Mongan Laments the Change That Has Come upon Him and His Beloved. W. B. Yeats. VLP

Mongol Quine. Alastair Mackie. MS

'Mongst all the hard names that denote reproach. Burnet's Character. *Unknown.* APAS

Monk from the bank the dismal sight does view. Andrew Marvell. *Fr.* The Last Instructions to a Painter. SCP-1

Monk sat in his den, The. The Weak Monk. Stevie Smith. BoWoP; FaBoTw (1975 ed.)

Monkey. Sylvia Read. RAE

Monkey Difference. Barbara Howes. GP

Monkey-flower, or mimulus, The. Floral Tribute. Sir Charles Jeffries. PoPle

Monkeys. Padraic Colum. OxBTC

Monkeys, The. Marianne Moore. CMoP (1970 ed.); NoAM; NOBA; UsP

Monkeys and the Crocodile, The. Laura E. Richards. CTV

Monkeys from Paradise. Ettore Rella. SPT

Monkeys on Mt. Hiei. Edith Marcombe Shiffert. WPE

Monkshood. Marie Harris. MMD

Monna Innominata. Christina Rossetti. VLP
   *Sels.*
   First Day, The, II. BoLoP
      ("I wish I could remember that first day.") GBL
   "Youth gone, and beauty gone if ever there," XIV. GBL

Monody on a Tea-Kettle. Samuel Taylor Coleridge. MBPR

Monody on the Death of Chatterton. Samuel Taylor Coleridge. MBPR

Monody to the Sound of Zithers. Kay Boyle. PoA

Monogamy, *sel.* Gerald Gould.
   "You were young—but that was scarcely to your credit." OxBTC

Monogram 4. Martina Werner, *tr. fr. German by* Rosemarie Waldrop. BoWoP

Monogram 29. Martina Werner, *tr. fr. German by* Rosemarie Waldrop. BoWoP

Monogram 23. Martina Werner, *tr. fr. German by* Rosemarie Waldrop. BoWoP

Monologue in the Valley of the Kings. Anthony Thwaite. HeHu

Monologue of a Deaf Man. David Wright. NoAM; NowV

Monologue of the Rating Morgan in Rutherford County. C. F. MacIntyre. PH

Monologue of Two Moons, Nudes with Crests. 1938. Norman Dubie. FiCP

Monologue through Bars. Nelson Hubbell. AMV-81

Monsieur Etienne de Silhouette. Some Frenchmen. John Updike. FaBoCo

Monsieur Pussy-Cat, Blackmailer. Stevie Smith. PCat

Monsieur Qui Passe. Charlotte Mew. SBG

Monster, The. Thom Gunn. ILP (1975 ed.)

Monster, The. Greg Kuzma. AmPA

Monster, The. Henry Rago. PoA

Monster has escaped from the dungeon, The. Frankenstein. Edward Field. FF

Monster rests upon my roof, A. The Chimera. Alfred Mombert, *tr. by* Erna Baber Rosenfeld. VWA

Monsters Do Not Scare Me Much. Beatrice Schenk de Regnier. IWK

Monstrous Mouse, A. X. J. Kennedy. CC

Mont Blanc. Shelley. MBPR; NIL; OAEL-2

Montage. Harry Guest. TwMBP

Montalbert, *sel.* Charlotte Smith.
   "Swift fleet the billowy clouds along the sky." BoWoP; WPE

Montana. Kenneth O. Hanson. MPA

Montana Fifty Years Ago. J. V. Cunningham. Prf

Montana Pastoral. J. V. Cunningham. CoPAm; MAT; PPoD; VGW

Montana Ranch Abandoned. Richard Hugo. PoW

Montcalm and Wolfe. *Unknown.* AmFP

Montezuma. A. F. Alderson. ECBV

Montgomery. Sam Cornish. CNA; PoBA

Montgomery. H. A. C. Evans. GDP

Month of the drowned dog, The. After long rain the land. November. Ted Hughes. CMoP (1970 ed.)

Month or twain to live on honeycomb, A. Before Parting. Swinburne. OBP

Month to the hour, A. The Next Moon. W. S. Merwin. PHC

Months, The. Sara Coleridge. OxBChV
   (Around the Year.) CTV

Months, The. *Unknown.* OxBM
   ("Januar: By this fire I warme my handes.") EBEV
   (Labours of the Months.) GBP

Months after the Muse. The Illustration—a Footnote. Denise Levertov. PoA

Months of waiting: then everyone. At Summer's End. Saul Hillel Benjamin. AMV-81

Monticello. May Sarton. GOA

Montrachet-le-Jardin. Wallace Stevens. UsP

Monument. Milton Acorn. NeAC

Monument, The. Elizabeth Bishop. NoAM; NOBA; PPoe

Monument. E. M. de Melo e Castro. UsP

Monument in Bone. Phillip William George. UsP

Monument Mountain. Bryant. EAP

Monument to a Boxer. Lucilius, *tr. fr. Greek by* Tom Dodge. LiSp

Monument to Pushkin. Joseph Brodsky, *tr. fr. Russian by* Dimitry Pospielovsky *and* Keith Bosley. VWA

Monuments of Hiroshima, The. D. J. Enright. HeHu

Monumentum Aere, Etc. Ezra Pound. NOBA

Moo! Robert Hillyer. OBAL; TH

Mood, A. E. Mitter. PMW

Mood, The. Quandra Prettyman. PoBA

Moods, The. W. B. Yeats. VLP

Moon. Elizabeth Brewster. MMD

Moon, The. Robert Creeley. VGW

Moon, The. Robert Duncan. *Fr.* Passages. PiAm

Moon, The. Donald Hall. NCSH

Moon. William Jay Smith. CaYB

Moon, The. Charles Upton. MIT

Moon. Derek Walcott. NoAM

Moon, The/ is a white/ bull. Images. Alastair Campbell. Moon

Moon and I a-tiptoe peer within, The. The Old Casa. Torrey Connor. BPAW

Moon and the Night and the Men, The. John Berryman. VGW

Moon and the Nightingale, The. Milton. *See* Evening in Eden.

Moon and the satellite orbit together, The. The Travelers. Patricia Hubbell. CTV

Moon and the Yew Tree, The. Sylvia Plath. Moon; MPo; PPP; VGW; WPE

Moon as Medusa. Vinnie-Marie D'Ambrosio. IHMS

Moon at the full. Europe has burst its banks. The Inundation. Howard Sergeant. EAS

Moon at Three A.M. Lance Henson. CDW

Moon-Bathers. John Freeman. EcS

Moon beams and yams. Rapping Along with Ronda Davis. James Cunningham. JB

Moon behind the Hill, The. *Unknown.* WTO

Moon bloats full and white, The. Omalos. Rosanna Warren. AMV-80

Moon-Bone Cycle, The, *sels. Aborigine Oral Tradition, tr. by* R. M. Berndt.
Birds, The. WTO
Evening Star, The. WTO
New Moon. WTO

Moon came to the forge, The. Ballad of the Moon, Moon. Fererico García Lorca, *tr. by* Langston Hughes. Epi

Moon-Child, The. William Sharp. EcS

Moon-cold could awe joy's proud star? Moon Mission. Ron Baxter. WeW

Moon Compasses. Robert Frost. LoAs; Moon; TT

Moon dangling wet like a half-plucked eye, The. Summer Night. Leonard Cohen. TCP

Moon Deer, how near. By the Waters of Minnetonka. J. M. Cavanass. BLSo

Moon Eclipse Exorcism. *Unknown, tr. fr. American Indian by* Armand Schwerner. Moon

Moon-faced baby with cocaine arms. Blues for Sister Sally. Lenore Kandel. NMM; RiTi

Moon goes over the water, The. Half Moon. Federico García Lorca, *tr. by* W. S. Merwin. RFM

Moon Going Down. *Unknown.* BluL

Moon Ground, The. James Dickey. Moon

Moon had climbed the highest hill, The. The Banks of Dee. *Unknown.* AmFP

Moon had risen on the eastern hill, The. The Sailor and His Bride. *Unknown.* AmFP

Moon hangs in the air, A. Starting from Central Station. David Campbell. MAuV

Moon holds nothing in her arms, The. Target. R. P. Lister. SoS; SoSe

Moon, in her pride, once glanced aside, The. The Moon Sings. *Unknown.* Moon

Moon in the bureau mirror, The. Insomnia. Elizabeth Bishop. TH

Moon in your eyes is best, The. Tracking Rabbits: Night. Jim Barnes. CDW

Moon in Your Hands, The. Hilda Doolittle ("H. D."). BoWoP

Moon Is a Diamond, The. Arthur Sze. AMV-81

Moon is a sow, The. Song for Ishtar. Denise Levertov. AnMo; NMM; NoAM; PiAm; Psy

Moon is an eye under pondweed of trees, The. The Fish. Paul Mills. MIS

Moon is an usurer, whose gain. Upon Moon. Robert Herrick. Moon

Moon is at her full, and, riding high, The. The Tides. Bryant. TAP

Moon is balking its bleached skin from the November night, The. Sunday Evening with Elizabeth, Age 5. Martha Yoak. NPW

Moon is on the little trail that, The. Reply of the Free Woman. Sharlot Hall. WPW

Moon is so high it is, The. I Walk Out into the Country at Night. Lu Yu, *tr. by* Kenneth Rexroth. IPWM

Moon Is Teaching Bible, The. Zelda, *tr. fr. Hebrew by* Marcia Falk. VWA

Moon is the mother of pathos and pity, The. Lunar Paraphrase. Wallace Stevens. Moon

Moon Is the Number 18, The. Charles Olson. CMoP (1970 ed.); UsP

Moon, The? It is a griffin's egg. Yet Gentle Will the Griffin Be. Vachel Lindsay. ECBV; Moon

Moon labours through black cloud, The. Lionel Johnson. Sancta Silvarum, II-IV. VLP

Moon Landing. W. H. Auden. Moon; WeW

Moon like a flower, The. Blake. *Fr.* Songs of Innocence: Night. Moon

Moon made a double circle around itself, The. Christmas. Daisy Aldan. AATT

Moon Man. Jean Valentine. Moon

Moon Mattress. Diane DiPrima. NMM

Moon mentions, The. Grunion. Myra Cohn Livingston. RFM

Moon Mission. Ron Baxter. WeW

Moon more indolently dreams tonight, The. The Sadness of the Moon. Baudelaire, *tr. by* F. P. Trurm. Moon

Moon moved over last night, The. The 5th of July. Felice Holman. CC

Moon of Huckleberries. Phillip William George. NW; VoR

Moon of Id came, The. Empress Nur Jahan, *tr. fr. Persian by* Willis Barnstone. BoWoP

Moon of Mobile, The. Thomas Holley Chivers. OBAL

Moon of the Earth. *Gond Oral Tradition, tr. by* V. Elwin *and* S. Hivale. WTO

Moon on the one hand, the dawn on the other, The. The Early Morning. Hilaire Belloc. ECBV

Moon Poem. Saundra Sharp. QQQ

Moon Poems. John Wieners. VGW

Moon rises, The, a vengeance on anguish. Sleepwalkers. Bella Akhmadulina, *tr. by* Barbara Einzig. BoWoP

Moon Rock. E. Louise Mally. POL

Moon, The: she shakes off her cloaks. Promontory Moon. Galway Kinnell. Moon

Moon shines bright, The. In such a night as this. Shakespeare. *Fr.* The Merchant of Venice, V, i. GBL; PoPle

Moon shines bright, The; [and] the stars give a light. A May Day Carol. *Unknown.* GBP; RDB

Moon shining in silence of the night. Lucina Schynning in Silence of the Night. Eilean Ni Chuilleanain. CIP

Moon Shot. Byron. *Fr.* Don Juan, X. OBP

Moonshot. Robert Kelly. Moon

Moonshot Sonnet. Mary Ellen Solt. BoWoP

Moon Sings, The. *Unknown.* Moon

Moon, Son of Heaven. Miyazawa Kenji, *tr. fr. Japanese by* Gary Snyder. Moon

Moon Song. Hildegarde Flanner. AMV-81

Moon Song, Woman Song. Anne Sexton. Moon; PPP

Moon, Sun, Sleep, Birds, Live. Kenneth Patchen. WeW

Moon that is a cow, being horned like her. Because the Three Moirai Have Become the Three Maries. Constance Urdang. Moon

Moon Tiger. Denise Levertov. Moon

Moon Travels Slow, The. Faye Kicknosway. TC

Moon Walk. Ben Belitt. PPoD

Moonwalk. John Engels. MAT

Moon Was a-Waning, The. James Hogg. SLP

Moon was born grey, and Beethoven was weeping, The. Nudes. Juan Ramón Jiménez. LoAs

Moon was but a chin of gold, The. Emily Dickinson. Moon

Moon was shining brightly upon the battle plain, The. The Maid of Monterey. *Unknown.* AmFP

Moon, worn thin to the width of a quill. Moon's Ending. Sara Teasdale. Moon

Moonlight. Guillaume Apollinaire, *tr. fr. French by* William Meredith. Moon

Moonlight. Longfellow. Moon

Moon Light. Freya Manfred. PH

Moonlight. Sara Teasdale. VGW

Moonlight, *sel.* W. G. Vincent.
"And in the cold, bleak winter time." ANTL

Moonlight among the Pines. "Hugh MacDiarmid." OAEL-2

Moonlight, The: Juice flowing from an overripe pomegranate.
Enchantment. Lewis Alexander. PoBA

Moonlight through my gauze curtains. The Skein. Carolyn
Kizer. LoAs; VGW

Moonlight washes the west side of the house. Winter Verse for
His Sister. William Meredith. TAP

Moonlit Apples. John Drinkwater. FSFS; OxBTC

Moonlit Doorway, The. Kenneth Mackenzie. GAS

Moonlit Night in Kansas. Victor Contoski. TAT

Moonlit Rock, The. Morton Marcus. CPA

Moonmoth and grasshopper that flee our page. A Name for All.
Hart Crane. VGW

Moonrise. Hilda Doolittle ("H. D."). PoA

Moonrise. Gerard Manley Hopkins. Moon

Moonrise. D. H. Lawrence. Moon; PoA

Moonrise in the Rockies. Ella Higginson. WPW

Moon's a steaming chalice, The. What Semiramis Said. Vachel
Lindsay. Moon

Moon's Ending. Sara Teasdale. Moon

Moon's glow by seven fold multiplied, turned red. After Reading
St. John the Divine. Gene Derwood. WPE

Moon's my constant mistress, The. Tom o' Bedlam. *Unknown.*
PoPle

Moon's the North Wind's Cooky, The. Vachel Lindsay. LCL

Moon's up-riding makes a line, The. Night Scenes. Robert
Duncan. VGW

Moonsheep, The. Christian Morgenstern, *tr. fr. German.*
FaBoNo, *tr. by* Geoffrey Grigson; Moon, *tr. by* E. M. Valk

Moonshine. Walter de la Mare. TDH

Moonshine. *Unknown.* BluL

Moonshiner. *Unknown.* FSW
(Kentucky Moonshiner.) OBAL

Moor, The. R. S. Thomas. OBW

Moored wes i Cornwale and somnede cnihtes feole: The Death of
Arthur. Layamon. *Fr.* The Brut. OxBM

Mooress Morayma, The. *Unknown, tr. fr. Spanish by* W. S.
Merwin. Epi
(Lovely Young Moor, A, *tr. by* Willis Barnstone.) BoWoP

Moorhen Pond, The. Tom Earley. BoAnP

Moorings. Norman MacCaig. OxBTC

Moorish King Who Lost Granada, The. *Unknown, tr. fr. Spanish
by* W. S. Merwin. Epi

Moorland sheep is frightened and amazed, The. Philosophy Is
Born. Christian Morgenstern, *tr. by* Geoffrey Grigson.
FaBoNo

Moose. Robert Wiljer. AMV-81

Moral, The. Theodore Weiss. Prf

Moral Alphabet, A, *sel.* Hilaire Belloc.
"Dreadful Dinotherium he, The." NOBL

Moral Artistry. David McKain. AAN

Moral Essays, *sels.* Pope.
Death of the Duke of Buckingham, The, *fr.* Epistle III. ExPo
(1973 ed.)
Duke of Buckingham, The, *fr.* Epistle III. NOBE
Sad Story, A, *fr.* Epistle III. BoReV
To a Lady: Of the Characters of Women, Epistle II. OAEL-1
"Men, some to bus'ness, some to pleasure take." OBSV
" 'Yet Cloe sure was formed without a spot.' " OBSV
(Chloe.) NOBE
To Richard Boyle, Earl of Burlington: Of the Use of Riches,
Epistle IV. OAEL-1; PPP
"At Timon's villa let us pass a day." ExPo (1973 ed.); OBSV

Moral Ode. David Rosenmann-Taub, *tr. fr. Spanish by* Charles
Guenther. VWA

Moral Poem, A. J. V. Cunningham. VGW

Moralists, The. Yvor Winters. PiAm

Morality Play. Pat Lowther. MMD

Morality, thou deadly bane. Burns. *Fr.* A Dedication to G****
H******* Esq. OBSV

More. Gertrude Stein. *Fr.* Tender Buttons. PBWP

More Ancient Mariner, A. Bliss Carman. OBAL

More beautiful and soft than any moth. The Landscape near an
Aerodrome. Stephen Spender. IPWM; NoAM; OxBTC

More beautiful than any gift you gave. The Token. F. T. Prince.
FaBoTw (1975 ed.); OxBTC

More bombs and planes/ than birds and clouds. And Doves
Were Nowhere to Be Found. Jesús Papoleto Meléndez.
NW

More Clues. Muriel Rukeyser. IHMS

More discontents I never had. Discontents in Devon. Robert
Herrick. CaPo; ILP (1975 ed.); PAIC; POL

More distant than the dead sea. Nadia Tuéni, *tr. fr. French by*
Carol Cosman. PBWP

More gaily, dance. Quick-Step. Robert Creeley. VGW

More Good Whiskey Blues. *Unknown.* BluL

More grotesque than a row of laundromats. The Novelty Shop.
Duane Niatum. CDW

More I chew this stuff, The. O'Connor the Bad Traveler. Peter
Klappert. FiCp

More I looked, I wondered more, The. Wordsworth. *Fr.* The
Matron of Jedborough and Her Husband. PeD

More kicks than pence. To Hell with Commonsense. Patrick
Kavanagh. CIP; FaBoTw (1975 ed.)

"More Light! More Light!" Anthony Hecht. ConAP; HAP;
NoAM; NOBA; SFF; SoSe; UnPo (1976 ed.); UsP; VGW;
VWA

More Love, *with music. Unknown.* AH

More Love to Thee, O Christ, *with music.* Elizabeth Payson
Prentiss. AH

More Loving One, The. W. H. Auden. HoPM (1975 ed.)

More luck to honest poverty. For A' That and A' That. Shirley
Brooks. FaBoCo; NOBL

More of a Corpse than a Woman. Muriel Rukeyser. NMM;
SPT

More Power. Egan O'Rahilly, *tr. fr. Irish by* John Montague.
BIrV

More Reformation, *sel.* Daniel Defoe.
"To sin's a vice in nature, and we find." OBSV

More Self-conscious. Steve Toth. AcAn

More shower than shine. Valentines to My Mother, 1880.
Christina Rossetti. OFD

More Than. Susan Fitzpatrick. AMV-80

More than moon-measure. Between the Tides. Emily Sargent
Councilman. AMV-80

More than most fair, full of the living fire. Amoretti, VIII.
Spenser. CABA (1972 ed.)

More than the ash stays you from nothingness! The Phoenix. J.
V. Cunningham. MPA; NoAM

More than the gems/ locked away and treasured. Sent from the
Capital to Her Elder Daughter. Lady Otomo of Sakanone,
*tr. by* Geoffrey Bownas *and* Anthony Thwaite. BoWoP

More to It than Riding. J. A. Lindon. PH

More whyght thou art then primrose leaf my Lady Galatee. Ovid,
*tr. by* Arthur Golding. *Fr.* Metamorphoses, XIII. OBVE

More Wisdom. Edward Hersey Richards. *See* Wise Old Owl, A.

Morea's Sonnet. Mary Sidney Wroth, Countess of Montgomery.
*Fr.* Urania. WPE

Morels. William Jay Smith. MAT; PPoD; RFM

Moreover the Lord answered Job, and said. Bible, *O.T.* Job, XL. OBVE

Morgan's Country. Francis Webb. GAS

Morgans in October. Suzanne Brabant. PH

Morgue, The. James K. Baxter. ATNZ

Morley's light went out. Power Failure. Michael Dennis Browne. AmPA

Mormons, led by Colonel Cooke, The. On the Road to California; or, The Buffalo Bullfight. *Unknown.* AmFP

Morn of life is past, The. Old Dog Tray. Stephen Collins Foster. FSW; GDP

Morn when first it thunders in March, The. Old Pictures in Florence. Robert Browning. VLP

Morning. Blake. OAEL-2; STS

Morning. Chu Shu-chen, *tr. fr. Chinese by* Kenneth Rexroth. BoWoP

Morning. Tove Ditlevsen, *tr. fr. Danish by* Nadia Christensen. PBWP

Morning. Harry Fainlight. POL

Morning. M. A. George. AMV-80

Morning. Henry Reed. LoAs

Morning. Marjorie Saiser. AMV-80

Morning./ and she awoke to. Five Sense. Marvin Wyche, Jr. AmNP (1974 ed.)

Morning, The/ island light begins. Dawn and a Woman. John Logan. PHC

Morning After, The. Walter Clark. NCSH

Morning After. Langston Hughes. NoAM

Morning after death on the bar was calm. Elegy. Paul Henderson. ATNZ

Morning after. Get moving. Cheerio. Third Elegy, Leaving the City. Hamish Henderson. *Fr.* Elegies for the Dead in Cyrenaica. MS

Morning and evening. Goblin Market. Christina Rossetti. EBEV; SBG; VLP; VPC

Morning and evening a heron flies. Neighbor. Charles Waterman. GP

Morning and evening, drunk and singing. For Kuo Hsiang. Yu Hsuah-chi, *tr. by* Geoffrey Waters. BoWoP

Morning, and the poet up again and out and about. The Poet's Day. Richard Weber. CIP

Morning and the snow might fall forever. Going to Remake This World. James Welch. CDW; SA

Morning Assignment. Mark Van Doren. OSP

Morning at the Window. T. S. Eliot. CABA (1972 ed.); PiAm; PoA; PSN; TT

Morning Bright, with Rosy Light, The, *with music.* Thomas O. Summers. AH

Morning Chores. Jim Heynen. PCho

Morning comes, and thickening clouds prevail, The. The Clouded Morning. Jones Very. NOBA

Morning comes with milk and bread. Morning Voluntary. James McAuley. MAuV

Morning Compliments. Sydney Dayre. OxBChV

Morning Dialogue. Conrad Aiken. NoAM

Morning Duke Ellington Praised the Lord, The. Owen Dodson. FB

Morning Fog. Quinton Duval. AMV-81

Morning from My Office Window. John A. Wood. AMV-81

Morning-glory, climbing the morning long, The. Indiana. Hart Crane. *Fr.* The Bridge: Powhatan's Daughter. PiAm

Morning Half-Life Blues, The. Marge Piercy. WBN

Morning Has No House. Rosemarie Waldrop. MAT

Morning he had gone. My Face Is My Own, I Thought. Tom Raworth. EAS

Morning Hymn, A. Christopher Smart. OxBChV

Morning Hymn. Charles Wesley. BoReV

Morning in Gainesville. Karen Whitehill. NPW

Morning in Spring. Louis Ginsberg. ECBV

Morning Letter, A. Robert Duncan. PoA

Morning Light. Louis Dudek. AMV-80

Morning Light, The. Louis Simpson. NNaP; NoAM

Morning Light Is Breaking, The, *with music.* Samuel Francis Smith. AH

Morning Light (The Dew-Drier). Mary Effie Lee Newsome. AmNP (1974 ed.); PoBA

Morning man came in to report, The. People Who Went By in Winter. William Stafford. GP

Morning, May rain. The Man Awakened by a Song above His Roof. Tomas Tranströmer, *tr. by* Robert Bly. EAS

Morning mists still haunt the stony street, The. In Hospital. W. E. Henley. VPC

Morning Mood. M. Panegoosho. TVo

Morning of the Red-tailed Hawk, The. Bettie M. Sellers. AMV-80

Morning of the Wolf, The. Keith Wilson. MPA

Morning opened/ Like a rose. Song. Donald Justice. NCSH

Morning ought not/ to be complex. Pas de Deux for Lovers. Michael Dransfield. FPA

Morning Poem. Jennivien-Diana Beenen. AMV-81

Morning Prayer. Aua, *tr. fr. Eskimo.* WTO

Morning Prayer. Ogden Nash. OxBChV

Morning Prayers of the Hasid, Rabbi Levi Yitzhok, The. Phyllis Gotlieb. VWA

Morning settles in. Love Poem. Cary Waterman. PCho

Morning sky glitters, The. De Civitate Hominum. Thomas MacGreevy. CIP

Morning Smallfire in Lukachukai Mountains. Simon J. Ortiz. FoP

Morning Song. Conrad Aiken. *Fr.* Senlin; a Biography, II, ii. CMoP (1970 ed.); SoSe ("It is morning, Senlin says, and in the morning.") NoAM

Morning Song. Henry Blakely. CNA

Morning Song. Alan Dugan. NowV

Morning Song. Sylvia Plath. BoWoP; HeIP; IHMS; ILP (1975 ed.); InPK; InPS; LoAs; NOBA; PSN; SBG

Morning Song. Leon Stokesbury. AMV-80

Morning Song. Sara Teasdale. Moon

Morning spreads over. May All Earth Be Clothed in Light. George Hitchcock. VGW

Morning Star. Thomas Hornsby Ferril. VGW

Morning Star, The. Primus St. John. PoBA

Morning Star, O Cheering Sight! *with music. Unknown.* AH

Morning sun, The. Poem for Myself and Mei: Abortion. Leslie Silko. VoR

Morning Swim. Maxine W. Kumin. LiSp; NVAP; WPE

Morning: the soft release. Meditation for a Pickle Suite. R. H. W. Dillard. CoPAm; HoPM (1975 ed.)

Morning, this morning wakes me. Elegiac. Kenneth O. Hanson. MPA

Morning to Remember, A; or, E Pluribus Unum. Edward Dorn. NoAM

Morning trickles over the bruised vegetables. The Manless Society. Pierre Unik, *tr. by* David Gascoyne. EAS

Morning uptown, quiet on the street. Song Form. Amiri Baraka. CTBA

Morning Vigil. Phillip William George. VoR

Morning Voluntary. James McAuley. MAuV

Morning wakens on time. Get Up. Philip Levine. NYP

Morning-Watch, The. Henry Vaughan. BoReV; GrRo; MetP; PiAm; SCP-1; UsP

Morning Workout. Babette Deutsch. LiSp

Morning Worship. Mark Van Doren. LoAs

Mornings. Suzanne E. Berger. PCho

Mornings/ I got up early. The Way It Was. Lucille Clifton. WPE

Mornings/ I slip as a dull blade. X2s and 42s (Into Northeast Washington). Ken Forde. PoUp

Mornings/ of an Impossible Love. Alice Walker. NVAP

Mornings, after leg lifts and knee bends. Body and Soul: A Meditation. Maxine W. Kumin. FoP

Mornings everything is grey. Morning Has No House. Rosemarie Waldrop. MAT

Morningside Heights: Fragment of a Film. James Reiss. CAAP

Morns are meeker than they were, The. Emily Dickinson. FSFS

Morphine. Heine, *tr. fr. German by* Ernst Feise. NAWM-2

Morrigan, The. *Unknown, tr. fr. Irish by* Thomas Kinsella. BIrV

Morris Dance, The. *Unknown.* RAE

Mort aux Chats. Peter Porter. CAAP

Mortal flesh is full of grief. The Vanity of the World. Siôn Cent, *tr. by* Joseph P. Clancy. OBW

Mortal mixed of middle clay. Guy. Emerson. NOBA

Mortal Prudence, handmaid of divine Providence. The Testament of Perpetual Change. William Carlos Williams. GOA

Mortality. Naomi Long Madgett. PoBA

Mortality, behold, and fear. On the Tombs in Westminster Abbey. At. to Francis Beaumont, *also to* William Basse. FaPoR; HAP; NOBE; OBP; PoPle

Mortality grows all over them. Old Men during a Fall of Government. Chris Wallace-Crabbe. GAS

Morte d'Arthur. Tennyson. *Incorporated in* Idylls of the King, *with changes, as* The Passing of Arthur. DL; ILP (1975 ed.); NIL; OAEL-2; PAIC; VLP
*Sels.*
"And answer made King Arthur, breathing hard." EBEV
Death of Arthur, The. PIM

Mortification. George Herbert. SCP-1

Mortmain, *sel.* Robert Penn Warren.
"In Time's concatenation and/ Carnal conventicle," I. NOBA; Prf

Morty calls from a halfway house. While the Garden Grows. Cinda Kornblum. AcAn

Mosca. Paul Blackburn. VoA

Moschus Moschiferus. A. D. Hope. MAuV

Moscow Nights. M. Matusovskii *and* V. Solovyov-Sedoi, *tr. fr. Russian.* FSW

Moses. Amir Gilboa, *tr. fr. Hebrew by* Stephen Mitchell. VWA

Moses' Account. Milan Fuest, *tr. fr. Hungarian by* Andrè Ungar. VWA

Moses and Joshua. Else Lasker-Schüler, *tr. fr. German by* Joachim Neugroschel. VWA

Moses, from whose loins I sprung. The Jew. Isaac Rosenberg. VWA

Moses on Mount Nebo. Abraham Regelson, *tr. fr. Hebrew by* Richard Flantz. VWA

Moshudi. Mark Wangberg. TC

Mosquito, The. D. H. Lawrence. BoAnP; PoPle

Mosquito. John Updike. BoAnP

Mosquito Knows, The. D. H. Lawrence. FaBoEE; OxBTC

Moss-gathering. Theodore Roethke. ILP (1975 ed.); PiAm; RFM; VGW

Moss of His Skin, The. Anne Sexton. CABA (1972 ed.); CoPAm; IHMS

Mossbawn: Two Poems in Dedication. Seamus Heaney. CIP
Mossbawn Sunlight, I. BIrV

Most are innocent, shy, will not undress. Angels. Dannie Abse. PoA

Most artists are known to turn the other cheek. Tragicomic Conceit. Miguel González-Gerth. FoP

Most Beautiful Girl in the World, The. Lorenz Hart. OBAL

Most beautiful of things I leave is sunlight. Praxilla, *tr. fr. Greek by* Willis Barnstone. BoWoP

Most beautiful! the red flowering eucalyptus. The Torso: Passages 18. Robert Duncan. GP

Most chivalrous fish of the ocean, The. The Chivalrous Shark. *Unknown.* FSW

Most Days. Elisavietta Ritchie. AATT

Most days/ the barn stands. Fire in Enfield. Wesley McNair. FAF

Most glorious Lord of life [*or* lyfe], that on this day. Amoretti, LXVIII [*or* Easter]. Spenser. BoReV; CABA (1972 ed.); Epi; ExPo (1973 ed.); HAP; NOBE

Most Gracious Queen, we thee implore. On Queen Caroline. *Unknown.* FaBoEE

Most is your name the name of this dark stone. Rainy Mountain Cemetery. N. Scott Momaday. CDW

Most kissed, The. Back Just Below the Shoulder Blades. Coleman Barks. *Fr.* Body Poems. NVAP

Most Like an Arch This Marriage. John Ciardi. WeW

Most Lovely Shade. Edith Sitwell. FaBoTw (1975 ed.)

Most Men Know Love. Henry Timrod. LFH

Most men use/ their eyes. The Mechanic. Diane Wakoski. AmPA

"Most music is beneath me." Deeper into Coleridge. Melissa Clark. PoUp

Most near, most dear, most loved and most far. Sonnet to My Mother [*or* To My Mother]. George Barker. FF; IP; LoAs; LP; NCSH; OxBTC; PAIC; SoS

Most of It, The. Robert Frost. BiP; CABA (1972 ed.); HAP; NU; PiAm; PPoe

Most of the time we sit down. Los Sedentarios. Anselm Hollo. AcAn

Most of the world's poetry. Codicil. Kenneth Rexroth. MPA

Most of them worked around the slaughtering. The Meat Works. Robert Gray. CAAP

Most people from Idaho are crazed rednecks. Running Away from Home. Carolyn Kizer. CNW

Most people, of which I am. The Graduate Assistant Tells about His Visit. Leon Stokesbury. NVAP

Most people think. Initials. Michael S. Glaser. AMV-81

Most prefer not to know, proceed by faith and chance. Matter of Urgency. Louis Johnson. ATNZ

Most reverend lords, the church's joy and wonder. On Calamy's Imprisonment and Wild's Poetry. *Unknown.* APAS

Most stupendous show they ever gave, The. In Memory of the Circus Ship *Euzkera*. Walker Gibson. NCSH

Most sweet it is with unuplifted eyes. Wordsworth. VLP

Most Vital Thing in Life, The. Granville Kleiser. SoSe (1977 ed.)

Mostly, I remember all the books. The House in Chicago. Marcia Lee Masters. HeS

Mostly People. Jeanette Nichols. SFF

Motet: "I am a young girl." *Unknown, tr. fr. Old French by* Carol Cosman. PBWP
("I am a young girl, gay.") BoWoP

Motet: "My love, how could your heart consider." *Unknown, tr. fr. Old French by* Carol Cosman. PBWP

Moth, The. Prentice Baker. AATT

Moth. Lance Henson. VoR

Moth and the Flame, The, *with music.* George Taggart. FSN

Moth is a shadow without a source, The. Getting Older Here. Barbara Hauk. AMV-80

Mother. Peter Bland. ATNZ

Mother, The. Gwendolyn Brooks. BPo; CAPP; GP; ILP (1975 ed.); NMM; TT

Mother. Aldo Camerino, *tr. fr. Italian by* Anita Barrows. VWA

Mother. Barry Dempster. AMV-80

Mother, The. Babette Deutsch. RiTi

Mother. William Duncan. PMW

Mother. Seamus Heaney. IPM

Mother. Erica Jong. TV

Mother. Sharon Mayer Libera. IHMS

Mother. Nagase Kiyoko, *tr. fr. Japanese by* Kenneth Rexroth *and* Ikuko Atsumi. BoWoP

Mother. Anwar Shaul, *tr. fr. Arabic by* Yoffee Berkovitz. VWA

Mother. Julian Tuwim, *tr. fr. Polish by* Isaac Komem. VWA

Mother. Stephen Vincent. NeAC

Mother, among the Dustbins. Stevie Smith. PBWP

Mother and child! whose blending tears. The Memorial Pillar. Felicia Dorothea Hemans. SBG

Mother and daughter German refugees. Schwiegermutterlieder. Tony Harrison. InPS

Mother and I. Martha Yoak. NPW

Mother and listener she is, but she does not listen. The Question. Muriel Rukeyser. IHMS

Mother and Poet. Elizabeth Barrett Browning. SBG

Mother and Son. Allen Tate. PiAm

Mother and Son. R. S. Thomas. BuTh

Mother and the Moon. Martha Yoak. NPW

Mother at her novenas. Puritan Poet Reel. Vincent Buckley. MAuV

Mother, because you never spoke to me. More Clues. Muriel Rukeyser. IHMS

Mothe, close your eyes. A Someday Song for Sophia. Rochelle Ratner. PCho

Mother darling, I cannot work the loom. Sappho, *tr. fr. Greek by* Willis Barnstone. BoWoP

Mother Dear, I am being careful. Letter from a Working Girl. Herbert Scott. GP

"Mother dear, may I go downtown." Ballad of Birmingham. Dudley Randall. BPo; InPK; NoAM; SoSe (1977 ed.); WIF

Mother Dear, O! Pray for Me, *with music. Unknown.* AH

Mother/Deer/Lady. Harold Littlebird. VoR

Mother, don't read. Preface. Carol Shauger. AMV-80

Mother Earth. Anna Margolin, *tr. fr. Yiddish by* Keith Bosley. VWA

Mother Earth: Her Whales, *sel.* Gary Snyder. "Owl winks int the shadow, An." OSP

Mother Goose (Circa 2054). Irene Sekula. QQQ

Mother Goose's Garland. Archibald MacLeish. OBAL

Mother Hubberd's Tale, *sel.* Spenser. "At last they chanced to meet upon the way." TVS

Mother, I am something more. Looking Out. Helen Chasin. NMM

Mother, I Cannot Mind My Wheel. Walter Savage Landor, *first st. par. fr. the Greek of* Sappho. BoLoP; CABA (1972 ed.); GBL; InPK; NOBE; OBVE

Mother, I have loved you long. Misericordia. Teresa A. McCarthy. NPW

Mother, I long to get married. Whistle, Daughter, Whistle. *Unknown.* AmFP

Mother, I may do violence to you. Mother. Sharon Mayer Libera. IHMS

Mother, I want to go. *Unknown, tr. fr. Spanish by* Willis Barnstone. BoWoP

Mother, I won't be home this evening, so. Little Johnny's Final Letter. Brian Patten. LP

Mother, I would marry, yes I would be a bride. Whistle, Daughter, Whistle. *Unknown.* FSW

Mother in old Alabama, A. Beulah Louise. William Jay Smith. TDH

Mother, in the 45¢ Bottle. Paul Blackburn. NYP

Mother, is this the darkness of the end. For "Our Lady of the Rocks." Dante Gabriel Rossetti. EBEV; PFD; VLP

Mother, it is time. Rimbaud's Farewell to Europe. Anthony Glavin. IPM

Mother, may I go out to swim? Caution. *Unknown.* BBL

"Mother, may I stay up tonight?" Conversation. David McCord. SO

Mother Mother shave me. Song. *Tr. fr. Nyasa by* Ulli Beier. BoWoP

Mother, mother, what illbred aunt. The Disquieting Muses. Sylvia Plath. NMM; SBG; TV

Mother, mother, what is that. *Unknown.* OSF

Mother, my eyes wait on you, unfulfilled. Mother. Anwar Shaul, *tr. by* Yoffee Berkovitz. VWA

Mother my good girl. Life's Work. Maxine W. Kumin. GP

Mother of Fisherman. Henriëtte Roland-Holst, *tr. fr. Dutch by* Ria Leigh-Loohuizen. PBWP

Mother of God, The. W. B. Yeats. ExPo (1973 ed.)

Mother of God, in this brazen sun. A Prayer. Denis Glover. ATNZ

Mother of God! no lady thou. Our Lady. Mary Elizabeth Coleridge. WPE

Mother of God! Our Lady! For Eleanor and Bill Monahan. William Carlos Williams. VGW

"Mother of heaven, regina of the clouds." Le Monocle de Mon Oncle. Wallace Stevens. NoAM

Mother of Hermes! and still youthful Maia! Fragment of an Ode to Maia. Keats. MBPR; OAEL-2; OBP

Mother of Man. Vesna Parun, *tr. fr. Croatian by* Mary Coote. PBWP

Mother of musings, contemplation sage. The Pleasures of Melancholy. Thomas Warton, the Younger. LAuP

Mother of my birth, for how long were we together. Kaddish. David Ignatow. NU; VWA

Mother of Samson to Manoah, Her Husband, The. Whittier. PIM

Mother of the Muses, we are taught, The. Memory. Walter Savage Landor. EBEV; OAEL-2

Mother Pin a Rose on Me, *with music.* David Lewis, Paul Schindler, *and* Bob Adams. FSN

Mother rock is black basalt, The. Human Geography. Ruth Whitman. AMV-80

Mother Rosarine. Maxine W. Kumin. RiTi

Mother said to call her if the H bomb exploded. Belief. Josephine Miles. NoAM; TAP

Mother Speaks, A: The Algiers Motel Incident, Detroit. Michael S. Harper. AmPA; BPo

Mother Tabbyskins. Elizabeth Anna Hart. OxBChV

Mother the Wardrobe Is Full of Infantrymen. Roger McGough. BuTh; MAT

Mother, they say you looked Irish. Summer Brenner. RiTi

Mother to Son. Langston Hughes. AmNP (1974 ed.); CABA (1972 ed.); CC; CTBA; IPWM; SO; SoS

Mother told me the directions. Memorial Day. Laureen Ching. AMV-80

Mother Was a Lady; or, If Jack Were Only Here, *with music.* Edward B. Marks. FSN

Mother watched her daughter kneeling, The. Fish Story. Sharon Olds. TV

Mother Wept. Joseph Skipsey. VLP

Mother your children give you. Karen L. Kent. NPW

Motherhood. Susan Ludvigson. AMV-81

Motherless Child Blues. *Unknown.* BluL

Motherless Children. *Unknown.* BluL; FSW

"Motherless mite," the women bill. Lamb. James Rankin. MIS

Mothers. Beth Bentley. CNW

Mothers. Nikki Giovanni. CNA; CTBA; TV; UnPo (1976 ed.)

Mothers. Anne Sexton. IPWM

Mothers. Tristan Tzara, *tr. fr. French by* Willis Barnstone *and* Matei Calinescu. VWA

Mother's Advice. *Unknown.* AmFP

Mothers and Daughters. David Campbell. GAS; POL

Mothers are waiting in the yard, The. For a Junior School Poetry Book. Christopher Middleton. BBGO; MPo

Mothers, Daughters. Shirley Kaufman. BoWoP; GP; NMM; RiTi; TPo; TV

Mother's Day. Sam Hamod. SA

Mother's Dream, The. William Barnes. NOBE

Mother's got salve. Color of Honey. Anne Waldman. TV

Mother's hardest to forgive, A. The Adversary. Phyllis McGinley. FaBoEE

Mother's home early, out of bed. After Illness. Vi Gale. GP

Mother's Lament for the Death of Her Son, A. Burns. HoPM (1975 ed.)

Mother's Nerves. X. J. Kennedy. OSF

Mothers of America/ let your kids go to the movies! Ave Maria. Frank O'Hara. NNaP

Mothers of sailors, I hope you will draw nigh. Johnny Gallagher. *Unknown.* AmFP

Mother's on her bed playing solitaire. The Jewish Family. Steven Orlen. AAN

Mother's Song, The. *Tr. fr. Eskimo.* WTO

Mother's Song. *Unknown, tr. fr. Japanese by* Willis Barnstone. BoWoP

Moths, The. W. S. Merwin. HeIP

Moth's kiss, first, The! Robert Browning. *Fr.* In a Gondola. BoLoP; GBL; IP

Mothsong. William Harmon. CSP

Motion, The. Theodore Roethke. MPA

Motionless—His sons. Death Bed. Thomas Kinsella. CIP; IPM

Motionless Swaying. Yannis Ritsos, *tr. fr. Greek by* Nikos Stangos. TSWA

Motions and means, on land and sea at war. Steamboats, Viaducts, and Railways. Wordsworth. VLP

Motion's the dead giveaway. Viable. A. R. Ammons. TAP

Motive. Cecilia Meireles, *tr. fr. Portuguese by* Don Wilson. AMV-81

Motive. Muriel Rukeyser. PoA

Motive for Metaphor, The. Cynthia Nibbelink. TC

Motive of all of it was loneliness, The. Motive. Muriel Rukeyser. PoA

Motley. Walter de la Mare. HoPM (1975 ed.)

Motor Bus. Alfred Denis Godley. FaBoCo; NOBL (On the Motor Bus.) FaBoNo

Motor Cars. Rowena Bastin Bennett. FPB

Motorcycle Irene. Skip Spence. MAT

Motorcyclist's Song, The. DeWitt Bell. MiP

Motto. Langston Hughes. ILP (1975 ed.); PoBA

Motto for a Dog House. Arthur Guiterman. GDP

Motto for a Sun Dial. J. V. Cunningham. InPK (Epigram: "I who by day am function of the light.") VGW

Motto for a Sundial. *Unknown.* FaBoEE

Motto to the Songs of Innocence and of Experience. Blake. MBPR

Moulded in cobweb, horse-hair, cow-hair. The Wagtail's Nest. Kenneth Mackenzie. MAuV

Mouldering Vine, The. *Unknown.* AmFP

Mound, The. Thomas Hardy. OxBTC

Mounds of humped rust-colored hills. Safed. Dovid Knut, *tr. by* Daniel Weissbort. VWA

Mount Badon. Charles Williams. FaBoTw (1975 ed.)

Mount Gilboa. Malka Heifetz Tussman, *tr. fr. Yiddish by* Marcia Falk. PBWP

Mount, mount for the chase! let your lassos be strong. The White Steed of the Prairies. J. Barber. BPAW

Mount of the Muses, The. Robert Herrick. CaPo

Mount Tamalpais. Geoffrey Cook. CPA

Mount Vernon. *Unknown.* AmFP; OFD

Mount Zion. *Unknown.* AmFP

Mountain, The. Shirley Kaufman. TV

Mountain, The. W. S. Merwin. VGW

Mountain, The. Andrew Young. MS

Mountain Afterglow, The. James Laughlin. IPWM; VGW

Mountain and the Squirrel, The. Emerson. *See* Fable: "Mountain and the squirrel, The."

Mountain Born. Marcia Inzer Bost. AMV-80

Mountain Bride. Robert Morgan. GP

Mountain Cemetery, The. Edgar Bowers. ConAP; CSP

Mountain Corral. Helen Sorrells. WPE

Mountain Day. W. S. Merwin. PHC

Mountain Dew. *Unknown.* FSW

Mountain, Fire, Thornbush. Harvey Shapiro. VGW

Mountain Greenery. Lorenz Hart. OBAL

Mountain Heritage, A. Joan Wyrick Ellison. AMV-80

Mountain is streaked white, the air is cold, The. St. John's Park. James McAuley. MAuV

Mountain is wild with men, The. Matronita. Dennis Silk. VWA

Mountain Liar. A. R. Ammons. TT

Mountain Lion. D. H. Lawrence. BoAnP; OxBTC; RFM

Mountain moving day is coming, The. Yosano Akiko *and* Naomi Weisstein. MMD

Mountain Oysters. Patrick Lane. NeAC

Mountain road ends here, The. Lyell's Hypothesis Again. Kenneth Rexroth. NoAM

Mountain road is steep, the stone steps are dangerous, The. Spring Thoughts Sent to Tzu-an. Yü Hsüan-chi, *tr. by* Geoffrey Waters. BoWoP

Mountain sheep are sweeter, The. The War Song of Dinas Vawr. Thomas Love Peacock. *Fr.* The Misfortunes of Elphin. CABA (1972 ed.); ExPo (1973 ed.); FaPoR; HAP; NOBE; OAEL-2; PoPle; PoTa

Mountain Stream, The. John Ceiriog Hughes, *tr. fr. Welsh by* Kenneth Jackson. OBW

Mountain tips are white and dead, The. The River. Leo Vroman. VWA

Mountain Whippoorwill, The. Stephen Vincent Benét. PoTa

Mountaineers, The. Christine Bress. PMW

Mountains. Besmilr Brigham. RiTi

Mountains, The. W. S. Merwin. UsP

Mountains and cold places on the earth. The Cloud Factory. John Haines. EAS

Mountains are moving, rivers. The Redwoods. Louis Simpson. TH

Mountains are steadfast but the mountain streams. Hwang Chin-i, *tr. fr. Korean by* Peter H. Lee. PBWP

Mountain's green and shining, The. Summer Solstice. Alan Garner. BuTh

Mountains have gathered in the distance. Sleep on the Fraser. Patrick Lane. NeAC

Mountains high seem to hide the sky. Cielito Lindo. Carlos Fernandez. BLSH

Mountains nuzzle mountains. The Scene. Denis Glover. ATNZ

Mountains of Mourne, The. Percy French. PFIr

Mountains said they were, The. Mountain Liar. A. R. Ammons. TT

Mountains stand, and stare around, The. The Paps of Dana. James Stephens. NoAM

Mountebank Song, The. Thomas Durfey. SCP-2

Mounting Summer, Brilliant and Ominous, The. Delmore Schwartz. TPo

Mourn for Yourself. Geoffrey Keating, *tr. fr. Irish by* Sean Lucy. BIrV

Mourn, little harebells owre the lea. Elegy. Burns. PF

Mourn Not for Adonais. Shelley. *Fr. Adonais.* BoReV; NOBE

Mourn Not the Dead. Ralph Chaplin. TPo

Mourners, The. Bevil Higgons. APAS

Mournful Dove, The. *Unknown.* AmFP

Mourning. Andrew Marvell. CABA (1972 ed.); SCP-1

Mourning and Melancholia. A. Alvarez. VWA

Mourning Dove, The. Myra Cohn Livingston. ECBV

Mourning Letter from Paris, A. Conrad Kent Rivers. BPo

Mourning Letter, March 29 1963. Edward Dorn. ConAP

Mourning Picture. Adrienne Rich. UsP

Mourning Pictures, *sel.* Honor Moore.
"Ladies and gentlemen, my mother is." TV

Mourning Poem for the Queen of Sunday. Robert Hayden. PoBA

Mourning-Song for Rangiaho, A. Te Heuheu Herea, *tr. fr. Maori by* Barry Mitcalfe. WTO

Mourning Women. Mathilde Blind. SBG

Mouse, The. Elizabeth J. Coatsworth. MN

Mouse. Mary Ann Hoberman. MN

Mouse, The. Sandra McPherson. CNW

Mouse and the Cake, The. Eliza Cook. OxBChV

Mouse Heaven. Leah Bodine Drake. MN

Mouse in the cupboard repeats himself, The. A Ritual Mouse. William Meredith. PBMP

Mouse in the Wainscot, The. Ian Serraillier. MN

Mouse Night: One of Our Games. William Stafford. MN; NCSH

Mouse That Gnawed the Oak-Tree Down, The. Vachel Lindsay. ILP (1975 ed.)

Mouse, the Frog, and the Little Red Hen, The. *Unknown.* ECBV

Mousemeal. Howard Nemerov. NCSH; NowV; UsP

Mouse's Courting Song, The. *Unknown.* AIW

Mouse's Nest. John Clare. InPK; MN; SoSe; VLP

Mouse's Petition, The. Anna Laetitia Barbauld. MN; OxBChV

Mouse's Tale, The. "Lewis Carroll." *Fr. Alice's Adventures in Wonderland, ch. 3.* FaBoNo
(Mouse's Tail). MN

"Mousie, mousie,/ Where is your little wee housie?" Conversation. Rose Fyleman. MN

Mouth. Clarisse Nicoïdski, *tr. fr. Judezmo by* Stephen Levy. VWA

Mouth, A. Can blow or breathe. Cardinal Ideograms. May Swenson. Psy

Mouth of a girl who had been lying, The. Beautiful Youth. Gottfried Benn, *tr. by* Joachim Neugroschel. POL

Mouth of the Amazon. R. P. Gira. AMV-80

Mouth of the Hudson, The. Robert Lowell. NYP; PSN; STS

Mouth That Is a Wound, The. Holly Prado. NPW

Mouth to mouth joined we lie, her naked breasts. Tantalos. Paulus Silentarius, *tr. by* Dudley Fitts. LoAs

Mouths. Dorothy Aldis. CTV

Mouth's disfurnished eyes. Three. John N. Morris. GP

Mouths of the Poor, The. Jon Anderson. CAAP

Move Continuing, The. Al Young. PoBA

Move him into the sun. Futility. Wilfred Owen. BuTh; CMoP (1970 ed.); NoAM; PSN

Move objects we desire. The Truckers. Allan Kornblum. AcAn

Move On, Yiddish Poet. Jacob Glatstein, *tr. fr. Yiddish by* Ruth Whitman. VWA

Move over, ham. Hiding Place. Richard Armour. NIL

Move to California, The, *sel.* William Stafford.
Written on the Stub of the First Paycheck. AnMo; InPK

Move your head and the view undulates. Through Old Farmhouse Windows. Allan Block. FAF

Moved to forward position at Lovidina. Excerpts from a Diary of a War (2). John Daniel. TwMBP

Movement. Gary Lawless. FAF

Movement,/ Feet hit pavement. Running under Street Lights. Christy White. AMV-80

Movement in Provence. Peter Trias. AAN

Movement of Fish, The. James Dickey. VGW

Movement, she explained, would bring poetry to the rich, The. Ralph Hodgson. *Fr. Flying Scrolls.* FaBoTw (1975 ed.)

Movement Song. Audre Lorde. CNA

Mover. James L. White. HeS

Movie Actors Scribbling Letters Very Fast in Crucial Scenes. Jean Garrigue. TAP

Movie-going. John Hollander. NYP; PPoD; PPP

Movie House. John Updike. PPoD

Movies. Langston Hughes. ILP (1975 ed.)

Movies are badder. Saturday Afternoon at the Movies. John Logan. NNaP

Movies, she told me, The. Grenadine. Susan Griffin. MMD

Movin amang thae stanes, I ken. Cougait Revisited. Donald Campbell. MIS

Moving. Barbara Crooker. AMV-80

Moving. James Harrison. CoPAm

Moving. William Matthews. POL

Moving Ahead. Rainer Maria Rilke, *tr. fr. German by* Robert Bly. NU

Moving Away. Gary Soto. *See* Remember.

Moving from Cheer to Joy, from Joy to All. Next Day. Randall Jarrell. HAP; NoAM; PPoD

Moving from left to left, the light. View of the Capitol from the Library of Congress. Elizabeth Bishop. WasP

Moving In. Paul Engle. PoA

Moving Inland. Gregory Jerozal. PoUp

Moving North. Ann Deagon. CSP

Moving Out. Joyce Carol Oates. AMV-81

Moving out. Thing Poem. Petra von Morstein, *tr. by* Rosemarie Waldrop. BoWoP

Moving over the hills, crossing the irrigation. Some San Francisco Poems. George Oppen. NNaP

Moving sun-shapes on the spray, The. Going and Staying. Thomas Hardy. CMoP (1970 ed.); NoAM

Moving through the Silent Crowd. Stephen Spender. LP; MPo; NOBE; UsP

Moving thru the drifting mist. Poem. William Pillin. SPT

Mower against Gardens, The. Andrew Marvell. AnMo; EBEV; ILP (1975 ed.); NIL; OAEL-1; PPP

Mower to the Glow-Worms, The. Andrew Marvell. AnMo; ILP (1975 ed.); NOBE; OAEL-1; PoPle; PPP

Mower's Song, The. Andrew Marvell. AnMo; ILP (1975 ed.); PoIA; PPP

Mowing. Robert Frost. CMoP (1970 ed.); HoPM (1975 ed.); LFH; NOBA; PPP; VGW

Mowing His Crew-cut. Manfred Jurgensen. FPA

Mozart. Jacob Glatstein, *tr. fr. Yiddish by* Ruth Whitman. VWA

Mozart. John Heath-Stubbs. EBEV

Ms. Minnie McFinney. *Unknown.* TDH

Much Ado about Nothing, *sel.* Shakespeare.
"Sigh no more, ladies, sigh no more," *fr.* II, iii. FF; SS; STS

Much as he left it when he went from us.  Why He Was There. E. A. Robinson.  CMoP (1970 ed.); NOBA

Much did I rage when young.  Youth and Age.  W. B. Yeats. FaBoEE

Much have I traveled in the realms of gold.  On First Looking into Chapman's Homer.  Keats.  AnMo; BiP; CABA (1972 ed.); ExPo (1973 ed.); FaPo; FF; HAP; HeIP; HoPM (1975 ed.); ILP (1975 ed.); InPK; IP; LFH; MBPR; NIL; NOBE; OAEL-2; OBP; PAIC; PoIA; PPoD; PPoe; PPP; SoSe; STS; TT; WIF

Much here is historical.  In the Hamptons.  John N. Morris. NYP

Much madness is divinest sense.  Emily Dickinson.  AmVN; BoWoP; CMoP (1970 ed.); HeIP; ILP (1975 ed.); MAT; NoAM; NOBA; PBMP; PiAm; SS; WPE

Much Obliged.  Dave Morice.  AcAn

Much of Me.  Chuck Eggerth.  AMV-80

Much of what is seen is best avoided.  Running Back.  Dave Smith.  LiSp

Much on my early youth I love to dwell.  To a Young Lady with a Poem on the French Revolution.  Samuel Taylor Coleridge. MBPR

Much sorrow in it selfe my love doth move.  Henry Constable. Fr. Diana.  ESo

Much suspected by me.  Written with a Diamond on Her Window at Woodstock.  Elizabeth I, Queen of England. PBWP; WPE

Muckers.  Carl Sandburg.  CTBA

Muckers drive muckers' cars.  Heroes of the Strip.  Sheila Cudahy.  TAT

Muckish Mountain (The Pig's Back).  Shane Leslie.  PFIr

Mud.  John Smith.  FPB

Mud.  William Sprunt.  AAN

Mud turkle settin' on de end of a log.  The Turtle's Song. Unknown.  BPo

Mugger, The.  Robert Pack.  GP

Mulatto.  Langston Hughes.  PAIC

Mulberry Mountain.  Unknown.  AmFP

Mulch, The.  Stanley Kunitz.  GP

Mule, The.  Coleman Barks.  POL

Mule Skinner Blues.  Unknown.  FSW

Mule-Skinners, The.  At. to John Caldwell.  BPAW

Mules.  C. Fox-Smith.  BoAnP

Mules.  Paul Muldoon.  CIP

Mules, I think, will not be here this hour, The.  Empedocles on Etna.  Matthew Arnold.  VLP

Mulligan Guard, The, with music.  Ned Harrigan.  BLSo

Multipara: Gravida 5.  Marie Ponsot.  VGW

Multiple I.  Richard Tipping.  FPA

Multiplication.  Lynn Strongin.  AAN

Multiplicity.  Eleanor Berry.  AMV-80

Multitude and no tumult: a maze on march.  Four Frescoes of the Future.  Genevieve Taggard.  SPT

Multitude of masts in the harbour, A.  The Victim of Aulis. Dannie Abse.  NoAM

Multitudes Turn in Darkness.  Conrad Aiken.  PoA

Multitudinous Stars, sel.  "Ping Hsin," tr. fr. Chinese by Kenneth Rexroth and Ling Chung. "Void only."  PBWP

Mum and the Sothsegger, sel.  Unknown. Dream, A.  OxBM

Mummy, A.  Primavera.  Frank Lima.  UsP

Mummy of a Lady Named Jemutesonekh XXI Dynasty.  Thomas James.  AmPA

Munching a plum on.  To a Poor Old Woman.  William Carlos Williams.  OBAL; PoIA; TAP; TVo

Mundus Qualis.  Joshua Sylvester.  FaBoEE

Municipal Gallery Revisited, The.  W. B. Yeats.  OxBTC

Mural, sel.  Vicente Rodríguez Nietzche, tr. fr. Spanish by Julio Marzán. "We must burn up."  InW

Muramoto knew all this as a child.  Making Miso.  Lawson Fusao Inada.  GP

Murder in the Cathedral, sels.      T. S. Eliot.  OxBTC Chorus: "We do not wish anything to happen." Chorus: "We have not been happy, my Lord, we have not been too happy."

Murder Mystery.  Timothy Steele.  AMV-81

Murder of a Community.  Daniel Weissbort.  VWA

Murder of Goins, The.  Unknown.  AmFP

Murder of William Remington, The.  Howard Nemerov.  CMoP (1970 ed.)

Murder self slowly.  And die like ants shuffling up under. Reckoning A.M. Thursday.  Doris Turner.  JB

Murderers/ of Emmett Till.  Salute.  Oliver Pitcher.  PoBA

Murderous owls off Malo bay, The.  Owls.  John Fuller.  POL

Murphy.  Patrick Williams.  IPM

Murphy in Manchester.  John Montague.  PFIr

Mus Ridiculus Non.  Marie De L. Welch.  BoAnP

Musa, Musae,/ The Gods were at tea.  The Muses.  Unknown. FaBoNo

Muscle and Bone of Song.  Hone Tuwhare.  ATNZ

Muscle Building.  Dalene Stowe.  NPW

Muse.  M. Deiter Keyishian.  BCr

Muse, The.  Barry Spacks.  MAT; POL

Muse.  David Wagoner.  PoA

Muse, disgusted at an age and clime, The.  On the Prospect of Planting Arts and Learning in America.  George Berkeley. ILP (1975 ed.); NIL; OBP; PAIC; PPoD

Muse Elektrique.  Paul Mariah.  CPA

Muse, June, Related, sel.  Brian Coffey. "Blooms such as wither at finger-touch."  BIrV

Muse of Amergin, The.  Unknown, tr. fr. Irish by John Montague. BIrV

Muse of the many-twinkling feet! whose charms.  Byron.  Fr. The Waltz.  OBSV

Muse of Water, A.  Carolyn Kizer.  NMM

Muse Poem.  Kathryn Van Spanckeren.  FF

Muse that stirs my blood, The.  Bird and the Muse.  Marya Zaturenska.  PoA

Muse to an Unknown Poet, The.  Paul Potts.  FaBoTw (1975 ed.)

Muse! twang the powerful harp and brush each string.  Edward Benlowes.  Fr. Theophila; or, Love's Sacrifice, Canto III. SCP-2

Musée des Beaux Arts.  W. H. Auden.  AnMo; BiP; CABA (1972 ed.); CMoP (1970 ed.); ExPo (1973 ed.); FF; HAP; HeIP; ILP (1975 ed.); InPK; InPS; IP; MPo; NIL; NoAM; NOBE; OBP; PBMP; PPoD; PPP; PSN; TCP; TT; VoPo; WeW; WIF

Muses, The.  Unknown.  FaBoNo

Muses' Elizium, The, sels.      Michael Drayton. Description of Elizium, The.  OAEL-1 Fine Day, A.  DuDr

Muses' friend, grey-eyed Aurora, yet, The.  William Browne.  Fr. Britannia's Pastorals, II, Song 2.  SCP-2

Muses' garden, with pedantic weeds, The.  On the Death of Donne.  Thomas Carew.  Fr. Elegy upon the Death of the Dean of St. Paul's, Dr. John Donne.  NOBE

Museum is gone from my bones now, The.  Calling Home the Scientists.  Wendy Rose.  AMV-81

Museum Item 237.  Polly Mann.  NPW

Museum Piece.  Richard Wilbur.  CMoP (1970 ed.); ConAP; NIL; TAP; WIF

Museum Piece No. 16228.  Elaine Watson.  AMV-81

Museum with Chinese Landscapes. Walter Cybulski. AMV-81

Museums. Louis MacNeice. ILP (1975 ed.); SOS

Musgrove. *Unknown.* AmFP

Mushroom was beautiful, The. A Story for a Child. Cynthia MacDonald. AAN

Mushrooms. Basil Dowling. ATNZ

Mushrooms. Sylvia Plath. PBMP; Psy; SS; WeW

Music, A. Wendell Berry. VGW

Music. Abraham Cowley. *Fr.* Davideis, I. SCP-2

Music. Emerson. CTV; PCOP

Music. Robert Herrick. CaPo

Music, The. Everett Hoagland. CNA

Music. Amy Lowell. RiTi
"Neighbour sits in his window and plays the flute, The," *sel.* OSP

Music. *Malay Oral Tradition, tr. by* R. O. Winstedt. WTO

Music. Frank O'Hara. NYP

Music Alone Shall Live. *Unknown.* FSW

Music and Drum. Archibald MacLeish. TH

Music and its harmony, The. The Design. Clarence Major. PoBA

Music Box Sang, The. Americo Casiano. NW

Music by the Waters. John Hay. AMV-81

Music Crept by Us, The. Leonard Cohen. FF

"Music for a while." Song at Night. Norman Nicholson. FaBoTw (1975 ed.)

Music I heard with you was more than music. Bread and Music. Conrad Aiken. Discordants, I. CMoP (1970 ed.); ILP (1975 ed.); NOBA; VoPo

Music in a Dark Room. Elizabeth Bartlett. PMW

Music in an Empty House. Hugh Sykes Davies. EAS

Music in my mind. Blues Suite. Margo Bohanon. SES

Music Lesson, A. Ann Ward. PMW

Music of ancient Greece, The. At the Trieste. Harold Norse. PoW

Music of His Steps, The, *with music.* Samuel Wakefield. AH

Music of the Spheres, The. Marvin Bell. PoA

Music stirs me, for you. Ricarda Huch, *tr. fr. German by* Susan C. Strong. PBWP

Music, thou queen of heaven, care-charming spell. To Music: A Song. Robert Herrick. CaPo

Music, thou soul of heaven, care-charming spell. Music. Robert Herrick. CaPo

Music touches me with your hands, The. Leit. Marcos Rodríguez Frese, *tr. by* Julio Marzán. InW

Music was going on, The. At the Fillmore. Philip Levine. NNaP

Music, when soft voices die. To ——. Shelley. ExPo (1973 ed.); HeIP; ILP (1975 ed.); MBPR; NOBE

Musical Ape, The. Darrell Gray. AcAn

Musical Instrument, A. Elizabeth Barrett Browning. ILP (1975 ed.); OAEL-2; OBP; VPC; WPE

Musical Lion, The. Oliver Herford. TDH

Musical Maiden, The. *Unknown.* TDH

Musical poet, collector of basset-horns, A. An Addition to the Family. Edwin Morgan. MPo; MS

Musical Shuttle. Harvey Shapiro. VWA

Musician, The. R. S. Thomas. BoReV

Musician Returning from a Cafe Audition, A. Michael D. Minard. AMV-80

Musicians, calling in your circles and phases. Composers of Music. Norman MacCaig. MS

Music's Duel. Richard Crashaw. OAEL-1; SCP-1

Musing on roses and revolution. Roses and Revolutions. Dudley Randall. BPo; CNA; ConAP; NoAM; PoBA; TAP

Musing upon the restless bisynesse. Anxious Thought. Thomas Hoccleve. *Fr.* De Regimine Principum. OxBM

Musings. William Barnes. HAP; NOBE

Musings. Patty Harjo. VW

Musk-ox smells, The. The Long River. Donald Hall. ConAP

Musk Oxen. Igjugarjuk, *tr. fr. Eskimo.* WTO

Musk Rose, The. Keats. *See* To a Friend Who Sent Me Some Roses.

Muskrat. *Unknown.* FSW

Muskrats, The. Winter Pond. Mary Logue. NPW

Muslims are still lying, The. The Lying Muslims. *Yoruba Oral Tradition, tr. by* Ulli Beier. WTO

Musophilus, *sel.* Samuel Daniel.
Heavenly Eloquence. NOBE

Muss I Denn (Must I Then). *Tr. fr. German.* FSW

Mussels. Mary Oliver. NU

Must all successful rebels grow. 1912–1952, Full Cycle. Peter Viereck. OBAL

Must I go bound and you go free. *Unknown.* WTO

Must I shoot the. Watts. Conrad Kent Rivers. PoBA

Must I then, must I then leave the village today. Muss I Denn (Must I Then). *Tr. fr. German.* FSW

Must I then see, alas! eternal night. Elegy over a Tomb. Lord Herbert of Cherbury. NOBE; OBW

Must then my crimes become thy scandal too? To Antenor. Katherine Philips. SBG

Must we part, Von Hügel, though much alike, for we. W. B. Yeats. *Fr.* Vacillation. BoReV

Mustacheless Bard, A. J. Gordon Coogler. OBAL

Mustapha, *sels.* Fulke Greville.
Chorus Sacerdotum. NOBE; OAEL-1; PPP
(O Wearisome Condition of Humanity.) HAP
"Fall none but angels suddenly to hell?" SCP-2

Mutabilities, The. Vincent McHugh. MIT

Mutability ("The flower that smiles to-day"). Shelley. MBPR

Mutability ("We are as clouds that veil the midnight moon"). Shelley. MBPR

Mutability. Wordsworth. Ecclesiastical Sonnets, Pt. III, Sonnet XXXIV. CABA (1972 ed.); EBEV; HeIP; ILP (1975 ed.); InPK; MBPR; NOBE; OAEL-2; PPoD

Mutant, The. Anita Barrows. RiTi

Mutation. Bryant. EAP

Mutations of the Phoenix, *sel.* Sir Herbert Read.
"Phoenix, bird of terrible pride." FaBoTw (1975 ed.)

Mute/ the hand moves from the heart. Miniatures IV. Lynn Strongin. IHMS

Mute City, The. Lazer Eichenrand, *tr. fr. Yiddish by* Gabriel Preil *and* Howard Schwartz. VWA

Mute Is Thy Wild Harp, Now, O Bard Sublime! Charlotte Smith. SBG

Mute Opinion. Thomas Hardy. CMoP (1970 ed.)

Mute, with signs I speak. Faith Unfaithful. Siegfried Sassoon. BoReV

Muted Screen of Graham Greene, The. Phyllis McGinley. FaBoEE

Mutes, The. Denise Levertov. AnMo; IHMS; NOBA; Psy; RiTi

Mutterings over the Crib of a Deaf Child. James Wright. CoPAm

Mutual Congratulations of the Poets Anna Seward and Hayley, The. Richard Porson. FaBoEE; OBSV

Mutual magnetism of love, The. Physics of Love. Charles Brasch. ATNZ

Mutual Problem. William Cole. OBAL; POL

Muzzle and jowl and beastly brow. Fearfull Symmetry. Basil Bunting. PoA

Mwilu/ or Poem for the Living. Don L. Lee. JB

My/ father/ dreams. The Eyes of Flesh. Sandra Hochman. NMM

My adored statue. The Arid Husband. E. L. T. Mesens. EAS

My age fallen away like white swaddling. Age. Philip Larkin. CMoP (1970 ed.)

My aged friend, Miss Wilkinson. The Bards. Walter de la Mare. FaBoNo; NOBL

My Aim. Alexander Seymour. CTV

My Alba. Allen Ginsberg. NoAM; NOBA

My Angel. Philip Levine. AMV-81

My annals have it so. Emus. Mary Fullerton. BoAnP

My arm sweeps down. Gesture. Donald Finkel. InPK

My arms smell good. Think. Please Forward. James Welch. CDW

My aspens dear, whose airy cages quelled. Binsey Poplars. Gerard Manley Hopkins. ILP (1975 ed.); InPS; NoAM; VLP

My Atlas Poet. George Bowering. NeAC

My Atthis, although our dear Anaktoria. Sappho, tr. fr. Greek by Willis Barnstone. BoWoP

My Auld Wife. Unknown. GBP

My Aunt. Oliver Wendell Holmes. TAP

My Aunt. Peggy Wood. POL

My Aunt Bibi. The Aga Khan. Steve Orlen. PCho

My aunt she died a month ago. The Heir. Unknown. RAE

My Aunt's Spectre. Mortimer Collins. PoTa

My Babe My Babe. Unknown. BluL

My baby ain't good looking and she don't dress fine. Robbing and Stealing Blues. Unknown. BluL

My baby done quit me. Squabbling Blues. Unknown. BluL

My Baby Has No Name Yet. Kim Nam-jo, tr. fr. Korean by Ko Won. PBWP

My baby's face is a. To the White Critics. Carolyn M. Rodgers. SA

My bands of silk and miniver. Full Moon. Elinor Wylie. Psy; SBG; VGW

My Bangelory Man. Unknown. ECBV

My barefoot steps lie broad and big. Spring. Moishe Kulbak, tr. by Ruth Whitman. VWA

My Baseland. Unknown. OxBM

My beautiful hair is dead. Hair. Gregory Corso. SFF

My Beauty, My Love, You Have Bound Me. Heine, tr. fr. German by Meno Spann. NAWM-2

My belly joined the Belly Potential Movement. Psychology Today. Judson Jerome. AMV-81

My Beloved Is Mine and I Am His. Francis Quarles. Emblems, V, 3. NOBE
("Ev'n like two little bank-dividing brooks.") PAIC

My beloved land. Minority Report. John Updike. GOA

My Best Clothes. Eli Netser, tr. fr. Hebrew by Bernhard Frank. AMV-81

My birthday is coming tomorrow. Growing Up. Unknown. CTV

My black-eyed lover broke my back. The Masochist. Maxine W. Kumin. IHMS; PoA

My Black Gal Blues. Unknown. BluL

My black hills have never seen the sun rising. Shancoduff. Patrick Kavanagh. BIrV; CIP; FaBoTw (1975 ed.)

My Black Mama. Unknown. BluL

My black mothers I hear them singing. Black Star Line. Henry Dumas. CNA

My Blackness Is the Beauty of This Land. Lance Jeffers. PoBA

My blessed Lord, art thou a lilly flower? Edward Taylor. Fr. Prepatory Meditations: First Series, V. PiAm

My blessing on the patient cows. A Blessing on the Cows. "Seumas O'Sullivan." BoAnP; PFIr

My Blindness. Eric Torgersen. TC

My boat goes west, yours east. Farewell. Chao Li-hua, tr. by J. P. Seaton. BoWoP

My Body. Rachel Korn, tr. fr. Yiddish by Ruth Whitman. VWA

My body a rounded stone. Living Tenderly. May Swenson. BoAnP

My body being dead, my limbs unknown. The Preparative. Thomas Traherne. SCP-2

My body holds crazed messages I can't remember. Surviving the Wreck. Betty Adcock. CSP

My body holds its shape. The genius is intact. Mummy of a Lady Named Jemutesonekh XXI Dynasty. Thomas James. AmPA

My body I give. Auto Icon. John Daniel. TwMBP

My body is like/ a field wasted by winter. On Seeing the Field Being Singed. Lady Ise, tr. by Etsuko Terasaki and Irma Brandeis. BoWoP

My body is made of waves and foam. Sea-Games. Aliza Shenhar, tr. by Linda Zisquit. VWA

My body is weary to death of my mischievous brain. Nebuchadnezzar. Elinor Wylie. SBG

My body knows it will never bear children. Waiting. Jane Cooper. TAP

My body's like a tree trunk in the wood. My Body. Rachel Korn, tr. by Ruth Whitman. VWA

My body's passion-hide. Two Times Two is Four. H. Leivick, tr. by Ruth Whitman. VWA

My Bonnie Lies over the Ocean. Unknown. BLSH, with music; FSW

My Bonnie Mary. Burns. See Silver Tassie, The.

My bonny keel laddie, my canny keel laddie. The Bonny Keel Laddie. Unknown. GBP

My bonny moorhen, my bonny moorhen. The Bonny Moorhen. Unknown. GBP

My Boots. Henry David Thoreau. PeD

My Bounding Bark. Unknown. RhR

My boy was scarcely ten years auld. Leesome Brand. Unknown. PeBB

My Brain. Annabel Laurance. AKE

My Breath. Orpingalik, tr. fr. Eskimo by K. Rasmussen. WTO

My broken bones cry out for love. The Ghostly Beast. Vassar Miller. CSP

My Brother. Dave Morice. AcAn

My Brother Ben's face, thought Eugene. Ben. Thomas Wolfe. NCSH; TVo

My Brother Bert. Ted Hughes. DuDr

My brother came back from the field. My Brother was Silent. Amir Gilboa, tr. by Shirley Kaufman. VWA

My brother came home from a Princeton club. Eastward to Eden. Edgar Bogardus. POL

My brother comes home from work. You Can Have It. Philip Levine. BrS

My Brother Hannu and the Poison Pool. Martha Webb. PHC

My brother has on/ a thin robe. Lady Otomo of Sakanone, tr. fr. Japanese by Willis Barnstone. BoWoP

My brother is skull and skeleton now. Epitaph. William Montgomerie. POL

My brother Jamie lost me all. Mary Stuart. Edwin Muir. MS

My brother knows the man. An Example of How a Daily Temporary Madness Can Help a Man Get the Job Done. John Stone. BCr; TAT

My brother stands among his friends. I Visit My Brother. Greg Kuzma. NVAP

My brother the air in this room: I was not. A Locale. Dennis Trudell. AAN

My brother was killed. My Brother. Dave Morice. AcAn

My brother was not a camel driver. On Her Brother. Al-Khansa, *tr. by* Willis Barnstone. BoWoP

My Brother Was Silent. Amir Gilboa, *tr. fr. Hebrew by* A. C. Jacobs. VWA

My Brothers. Anna Walters. VoR

My Brother's Braces. Robert Hutchinson. BrS

My bully boys of Liverpool. The Banks of Newfoundland. *Unknown.* GBP

My Buried Firends. *Unknown.* AmFP

My Busconductor. Roger McGough. LP

My business is words. Words are like labels. Said the Poet to the Analyst. Anne Sexton. Psy

My cabinets are oyster-shells. Song. Margaret Cavendish, Duchess of Newcastle. *Fr.* The Convent of Pleasure. EcS; SCP-2; WPE

My camel kneels at Ibn Marwan's door. Camel. Laila Akhyaliyya, *tr. by* Willis Barnstone. BoWoP

My candle burns at both ends. First Fig. Edna St. Vincent Millay. BBGO; FF; NoAM; PoA; TAP; TH

My candle burns up lank and fair. Resurrection. Margiad Evans. OBW

My canoe slowly drifting downriver. Moose. Robert Wiljer. AMV-81

My case is this, I love Zepheria bright. Gulling Sonnets, VIII. Sir John Davies. Epi

My Cat. Lesley Syrett. RAE

My Cat and I. Roger McGough. OxBTC; POL

My cat has got no name. Cat. Vernon Scannell. FPB

My cat is a blackish-brown Persian. My Cat. Lesley Syrett. RAE

My cat jumps to the window sill. Waiting for It. May Swenson. BoAnP

My cat was a southerner and a lady. A Farewell. Hildegarde Flanner. AMV-81

My cat, washing her tail's tip, is a whorl. Cat on Couch. Barbara Howes. NCSH

My Cathedral. Longfellow. PBMP

My Cats. Stevie Smith. FaBoNo

My cellpartner quick. Freedom. J. Charles Green. DNGG

My child and I hold hands on the way to school. September, the First Day of School. Howard Nemerov. PPoD

My child, my sister, dream. Invitation to the Voyage. Baudelaire, *tr. by* Richard Wilbur. NAWM-2

My child, we were two children. Heine, *tr. fr. German by* Elizabeth Barrett Browning. OBVE

My childhood all a myth. The Myth. Edwin Muir. CMoP (1970 ed.)

My childhood was like a dark passage. Intimations. Alma Johanna Koenig, *tr. by* Edouard Roditi. VWA

My Childhood's Bedroom. Charles Tisdale. AMV-80

My children haul me there. Visit to the Museum. R. A. Simpson. GAS

My children, you grow so. Magic Children. Barbara Drake. TC

My Children's Book. John N. Morris. AMV-80

My Chinese uncle, gouty, deaf, half-blinded. Grotesques. Robert Graves. CMoP (1970 ed.)

My Choice. *Unknown.* CTV

My city, my beloved, my white! Ah slender. N.Y. Ezra Pound. NYP

My Clothes. Barry Spacks. NIL

My clumsiest dear, whose hands shipwreck vases. Love Poem. John Frederick Nims. CoPAm; FF; HoPM (1975 ed.); InPK; SoSe; TCP; UsP; VoPo

My clutch and your clutch. Gary Snyder. Myths and Texts: Burning, VI. Epi

My Cobra Girl. *Gond Oral Tradition, tr. by* V. Elwin *and* S. Hivale. WTO

My comforts drop and melt away like snow. The Answer. George Herbert. Epi

My comrade is dead. Elegy. Salomón de la Selva, *tr. by* Donald Walsh. LoAs

My conscience has given me several twitches. To My Cousin Mary, for Mending My Tobacco Pouch. Francis Scott Key. OBAL

My country need not change her gown. Emily Dickinson. GOA

My country, 'tis of thee. America. Samuel Francis Smith. BLSH; BLSo; BTTM; CTV; PSoN

My Country 'Tis of Thy People You're Dying. Buffy Sainte-Marie. WIF

My Country, to Thy Shore, *with music.* Theodore Chickering ·Williams. AH

My countrymen have now become too base. April 1962. Paul Goodman. VGW

My Cousin Agueda. Ramón López Velarde, *tr. fr. Spanish by* Samuel Beckett. OBVE

My cousin Max is being married. Plan. Rod McKuen. MiP

My Cow. Howard McCord. GP

My Crime. *Unknown.* BluL

My Dad and Mam They Did Agree. *Unknown.* POL

My daddy come home this morning drunk as he could be. Don't Fish in My Sea. *Unknown.* BluL

My daddy don't know. For Sapphires. Carolyn M. Rodgers. CNA

My Daddy has paid the rent. Good Times. Lucille Clifton. AmNP (1974 ed.); AmPA; BPo; CAAP; CNA; FF; InPS; NCSH; PoBA; SoSe (1977 ed.); TAP

My daddy went a-huntin'. The Gray Goose. *Unknown.* OSF

My daddy's fingers move among the couplers. Lucille Clifton. CAAP

My Daily Creed. *Unknown.* CTV

My Dark Fathers. Brendan Kennelly. BIrV; CIP

My Darling Dear, My Daisy Flower. John Skelton. HAP; LoAs ("With, Lullay, lullay, lyke a chylde.") AAS

My Darling's on the Deep Blue Sea. *Unknown.* AmFP

My Daughter. Robert Pack. CoPAm

My daughter, at eleven. Little Girl, My String Bean, My Lovely Woman. Anne Sexton. RiTi; WBN

My daughter has given me a grandchild. Celebration. Elizabeth Newton Sachs. AMV-81

My daughter is a mystic about cats. Waiting for the Transformation. Judith Minty. TV

My Daughter Very Ill. Paul Goodman. RRA

My Daughter's Dowry. Robert Herrick. RRA

My daughter' heavier. Light leaves are flying. John Berryman. *Fr.* Dream Songs. CAPP; RRA

My Daughter's Ring. Barbara Eve. TV

My Days are Gliding Swiftly By, *with music.* David Nelson. AH

My Dead. Rachel, *tr. fr. Hebrew by* Robert Mezey. VWA

My dear,/ Today a letter from Berlin. A Letter from Berlin. Jon Stallworthy. NoAM

My dear and only love, I pray. I'll Never Love Thee More. James Graham, Marquess of Montrose. GBL; NOBE; PoPle; SLP

My dear child, first thyself enable. The Boy Serving at Table. John Lydgate. OxBChV

My dear deaf father, how I loved him then. John Betjeman. *Fr.* Summoned by Bells. OxBTC

My dear, deare, Lord I do thee Saviour call. Edward Taylor. *Fr.* Preparatory Meditations: First Series, II. PiAm

My dear [*or* dears], do you know. The Babes in the Wood. *Unknown.* ECBV; OxBChV; PCOP

My dear, do you remember that country. Remember That Country. Jean Garrigue. VGW

My dear, I wonder if before the end. To D——, Dead by Her Own Hand. Howard Nemerov. PoA

My dear, my dear, I know. To a Young Girl. W. B. Yeats. EBEV; OLR; PSN; SoSe

My dear son whom I put to bed each evening. Graham. Sid Gershgoren. BrS

My dear, when I was very young. To a Lady on Her Marriage. William Bell. PAIC

My dearest dust, could not thy hasty day. Epitaph on the Monument of Sir William Dyer at Colmworth, 1641. Lady Catherine Dyer. Fr. Sir William Dyer, Knight. BoLoP; SCP-2

My dearest Kathy: When I heard your tears. Letter to Kathy from Wisdom. Richard Hugo. CNW

My dearly loved friend, how oft have we. First Steps Up Parnassus. Michael Drayton. Fr. To My Most Dearly Loved Henry Reynolds. NOBE

My dears, do you know. See My dear, do you know.

My dears, 'tis said in days of old. The Bee, the Ant, and the Sparrow. Nathaniel Cotton. OxBChV

My Death. Mark Strand. CAAP

My death was arranged by special plans in Heaven. A New England Bachelor. Richard Eberhart. NoAM

My delight and thy delight. Robert Bridges. CMoP (1970 ed.); NOBE

My desire for revenge, the bitterness. Till Death Do Us Part. Leila Miccolis, tr. by Willis Barnstone and Nelson Cerqueira. BoWoP

My desk's at the back of the class. The Marrog. R. C. Scriven. DuDr; FPB

"My deth I love, my lif ich hate, for levedy shene." De Clerico et Puella. Unknown. OxBM

My dog lay dead five days without a grave. The Pardon. Richard Wilbur. ILP (1975 ed.); NoAM; NOBA; PoIA

My dog's so furry, I've not seen. The [or My] Hairy Dog. Herbert Asquith. CTV; ECBV

My Dolphin, you only guide me by surprise. Dolphin. Robert Lowell. NOBA

My Doves. Elizabeth Barrett Browning. PCOP; VLP

My Dream. Lew Blockcolski. VoR

My Dream. Christina Rossetti. VLP

My dream a drink with Lonnie Johnson. Sonnet. Ted Berrigan. CAAP; NoAM

"My Dream of Pure Invention." Madeline DeFrees. MPA

My dreams are so full of longing. Longing. Rachel Korn, tr. by Ruth Whitman. VWA

My dreams come to me in pairs. Two. Dana Naone. PHC

My drooping eyelids veil waking. To Sleep. Barbara Fialkowski. AMV-81

My drum, hollowed out thru the thin slit. La Chute. Charles Olson. InPK

My ear, still keyed to summer, failed to label. Partial Draft. Robert B. Shaw. AMV-81

My Een Are Nae on Calvary. Sorley Maclean, tr. fr. Gaelic; Scots version by Douglas Young. MS

My eight spring in England I walk among. This Landscape, These People. Zulfikar Ghose. MPo

My Elbow Ancestry. Larry Mollin. NeAC

My electric handmixer of 87 bloodstone finches. Love to My Electric Handmixer. Diane Wakoski. CoPAm

My enemy came high. Hate. James Stephens. VoPo

My enemy had bidden me as guest. The Compassionate Fool. Norman Cameron. OxBTC; WIF

My enemy is dead. The news arrived. Enemy, Enemy. Cecil J. Mullins. AMV-80

My Epitaph. H. J. Daniel. FaBoEE

My ex-wife Acid, my children Brood and Shout. The Only Leap That Matters. Mark McCloskey. PoW

My eye cried and woke me. The Night. Al-Khansa, tr. by Willis Barnstone. BoWoP

My eye descending from the hill, surveys. Sir John Denham. Fr. Cooper's Hill. NIL; OAEL-l; PAIC

My eyes are thirsty. Mirabai, tr. fr. Hindi by Willis Barnstone and Usha Nilsson. BoWoP

My eyes make pictures, when they are shut. A Day-Dream. Samuel Taylor Coleridge. MBPR

My eyes welcome high grass. Some Good Things Left after the War with the Sioux. John Calvin Rezmerski. HeS

My eyes went away from me. The Fickle One. Pablo Neruda, tr. by Donald D. Walsh. FF; OLR

My Face. Unknown. RAE

My face is black. See the moon? My eyes. Crystal. Faye Kicknosway. IHMS

My Face Is My Own, I Thought. Tom Raworth. EAS

My face is on fire. Speeding. Arlie "Franko" Durham. DNGG

My face isn't pretty. My Face. Unknown. RAE

My fairest child, I have no song to give you. A Farewell. Charles Kingsley. OxBChV

My Fairy. "Lewis Carroll." FaBoNo

My Fairy Steed. Laura Benét. PCOP

My Faith Looks Up to Thee, with music. Ray Palmer. AH; BLSH; BLSo

My Faither. Duncan Glen. MIS; MS

My faithful friend, if you can see. Impossibilities to His Friend. Robert Herrick. OLR

My family, in Christian pantomime. Grace. Michael Sheridan. HeS

My Family's under Contract to Cancer. Greg Simison. AMV-80

My Fancy. "Lewis Carroll." FaBoCo

My Father. Abraham Chalfi, tr. fr. Hebrew by Shlomo Vinner and Howard Schwartz. VWA

My Father. Judy Collins. WIF

My Father. David Kherdian. SA

My Father. Ronald Koertge. BrS

My Father. William Logan. AAN

My father/ who is my blood and water. Remnants. Cathy Song. PHC

My Father after Work. Gary Gildner. AMV-80; EC

My father always promised us. My Father. Judy Collins. WIF

My father and his muscles. My Father Toured the South. Jeanette Nichols. RiTi

My father and my mother never quarrelled. Because. James McAuley. GAS; MAuV

My Father and the Fig Tree. Naomi Shihab. GP

My father brings whiskey home. Tradition. David James. TC

My father brought that dog home. Bony. Simon J. Ortiz. CDW; PoW

My father brought the emigrant bundle. Europe and America. David Ignatow. NNaP; PBMP; UnPo (1976 ed.)

My father by some strange conjuction had mice for sons. In All the Days of My Childhood. Russell Edson. AmPA

My father comes to see me on Friday night. Bar Mitzvah. Issac Goldemberg, tr. by David Unger. VWA

My father could go down a mountain faster than I. That Dark Other Mountain. Robert Francis. CC; LiSp; NCSH; SoS

My father could hear a little animal step. Listening. William Stafford. RFM; TSWA; VoA

My father didn't really belong in history. Parentage. William Stafford. BiP

My father died a month ago. The Legacy. Unknown. BBL; PoPle

My father died, and I cannot tell how. The Foolish Boy. *Unknown.* RAE

My Father Dragged by Horses. T. Alan Broughton. AMV-80

My Father Dreams of Baseball. Laurence Lieberman. LiSp; SPo

My father entered the kingdom of roots. 1933. Philip Levine. VWA

My father found it after the war. The House on Buder Street. Gary Gildner. TAP

My father gave me the freedom of love. Howard McCord. *Fr.* Long jaunes His Periplus. GP

My father goes to Africa. Big Game Hunter. Alexander Resnikoff. OSF

My father had a glass eye. My Father's Eye. Eleni Vakalo, *tr. by* Kimon Friar. BoWoP

My father, his mouth full of nails. Nails. Gary Gildner. TAP

My father hurried. Chronicles: Numbers One and Two. Mei Berssenbrugge. SA

My father in his. Beryl Lyn Lifshin. NeAC

My Father in the Night Commanding No. Louis Simpson. ConAP; HeIP; ILP (1975 ed.); NoAM; NOBA; TAP; VGW

My father is a fist. Essex C. Hemphill. *Fr.* Hero's Father's Tombs. PoUp

My father is a fugitive/ from the villages of Chagall. Two Refugees. Mordecai Marcus. VWA

My Father is watching over his Mosque, silently. Lines to My Father. Sam Hamod. SA

My father is with some other. My Father. William Logan. AAN

My Father, it is surely a blue place. Hunchback Girl: She Thinks of Heaven. Gwendolyn Brooks. IP; SoS

My Father Kept a Horse. *Unknown.* GBP

My father lies black and hushed. The Worker. Richard W. Thomas. PoBA; TC

My father made a synagogue of a boat. Two Fishermen. Stanley Moss. VWA

My Father Moved through Dooms of Love. E. E. Cummings. AnMo; CMoP (1970 ed.); HAP; IPWM; NoAM; NOBA; STS; TAP; TT; UnPo (1976 ed.); WIF

My father moves through the South hunting duck. Treetops. Marvin Bell. AmPA

My father: October 1942. William Stafford. CoPAm

My Father Paints the Summer. Richard Wilbur. NCSH; NOBA

"My father planted those fields." The Wheat District. Ted Enslin. FAF

My father played the melodion. Patrick Kavanagh. *Fr.* A Christmas Childhood. PChr

My father preached full, powerful. Hudson Hornet. William W. Cook. AMV-80

My father returned. The Return. Shmuel Mareh, *tr. by* Yoffee Berkovitz. VWA

My father sang the songs. Yiddish. Judith Herzberg, *tr. by* Shirley Kaufman. VWA

My father sleeps in the sun porch. When at Night. Mark Perlberg. AMV-80

My father talked too much. How My Father Died. Nissim Ezekiel. VWA

My father talked with ghosts. Story from Another World. Paul Petrie. AMV-81

My father, the least happy. The Cage. John Montague. CIP; IPM

My Father Toured the South. Jeanette Nichols. RiTi

My father used to say. Silence. Marianne Moore. CMoP (1970 ed.); LFH; NOBA; PiAm; PPM; PSN; Psy; SBG

My father used to say. The Seed of Reality. Max von Hartmann. AMV-80

My father used to show off by putting his forefinger. Fire. 10/78. Bart Plantenga. AMV-80

My father was a farmer gay. One-and-Twenty. *Unknown.* AmFP

My Father was a scholar and knew Greek. Development. Robert Browning. VLP

My father was a working man. Red-Herring. D. H. Lawrence. NoAM

My father was hung from a star. Song of the Last Jewish Child. Edmond Jabès, *tr. by* Anthony Rudolf. VWA

My father was not inarticulate. False Prophet. Emanuela O'Malley. AMV-81

My father was the first to hear. The Geese. Richard Peck. SoS

My father was the keeper of the Asteroid Light. The Asteroid Light. *Unknown.* FSW

My father was the keeper of the Eddystone Light. *Unknown.* *See* Me father was the keeper of the Eddystone Light.

My father wears a light on his head. There is No Light. Lindiwe Mabuza. SES

My Father, Who's Still Alive. Jose Kozer, *tr. fr. Spanish by* Jorge Guitart. VWA

My father wore it working coal at Shotts. The Miner's Helmet. George MacBeth. OxBTC

My father worked with a horse plough. Follower. Seamus Heaney. HeHu; IPM; LP; PFIr

My father would walk about for hours with a lit cigarette. The Stranger. Juan Gelman, *tr. by* Yishai Tobin. VWA

My father's cluttered workbench stands, heaped up. Cleaning Up, Clearing Out. Daniel Ross Bronson. AMV-80

My fathers come to me in an old film. The Worm. Willis Barnstone. VWA

My Father's Eye. Eleni Vakalo, *tr. fr. Modern Greek by* Kimon Friar. BoWoP

My Father's House. Calvin Forbes. CoPAm

My Father's House. Peter Nicoletta. PoW

My Father's House. Steven Orlen. AAN

My Father's Leaving. Ira Sadoff. AmPA

My father's white uncle became. Todd. Stewart Conn. MS

My Feet. Louis Jenkins. GP

My feet and limbs, young friend, are no longer. Nestor. Homer, *tr. by* Ennis Rees. *Fr.* The Iliad, XXIII. LiSp

My feet fall in step with absent whores. Amelia Street. Frank Ormsby. CIP; IPM

My feet have felt the sands. Determination. John Henrik Clarke. CNA; PoBA

My feet taste funny. Why I Didn't Go to Delphi. James Welch. CDW; MPA

My feet took a walk in heavenly grass. Heavenly Grass. Tennessee Williams. ECBV

My feets is so sore can't hardly wear my shoes. Big Night Blues. *Unknown.* BluL

My female friends, whose tender hearts. Swift. *Fr.* Verses on the Death of Doctor Swift. NOBL

My Fiddle. Leib Kwitko, *tr. fr. Yiddish by* Keith Bosley. VWA

My fiftieth year had come and gone. W. B. Yeats. *Fr.* Vacillation. BoReV; IP

My First Cigar. Robert J. Burdette. PoTa

My first thought was, he lied in every word. "Childe Roland to the Dark Tower Came." Robert Browning. ExPo (1973 ed.); OAEL-2; PPP; VLP

My first vivid memory of you. To Jesus Villanueva, with Love. Alma Villanueva. NW

My flashlight sends its message. The Lightkeeper. Michael McPherson. PHC

My flashlight tugs me. Flashlight. Judith Thurman. FPB

My flesh is racked by plague. The New Ahasuerus. Jozsef Kiss, *tr. by* André Ungar. VWA

My flowery and green age was passing away.  He Understands the Great Cruelty of Death.  Petrarch, *tr. by* J. M. Synge.  Sonnets to Laura: To Laura in Death, XLVII.  BIrV

My Flute.  Herbert Krohn.  AAN

My Flying Machine.  Louis Daniel Brodsky.  AMV-80

My Folk, What Have I Done Thee?  William Herebert.  OxBM

My food was pallid till I heard it ring.  King Midas.  Howard Moss.  TAP

My foot in the stirrup, my pony won't stand.  Old Paint.  *Unknown.*  BPAW

My foster-brother and foster-sister.  The Golden Sea-Otter.  Wakarpa, *tr. by* Arthur Waley.  *Fr.* Kutune Shirka (The Ainu Epic.)  WTO

My freshmen/ settle in.  Achilles.  Freshmen.  Barry Spacks.  CoPAm

My Friend.  Samuel Allen.  FB

My friend from Asia has powers and magic.  Credo.  Robinson Jeffers.  MPA

My friend must be a bird.  Emily Dickinson.  TAP

My friend tells me I don't understand women.  The Perfect One.  Steven Orlen.  AAN

My friend the blue paisley shirt is always assured.  The Blue Paisley Shirt.  Thomas W. Shapcott.  FPA; GAS

My Friend, the Doctor.  George Abbe.  FAF

My friend, the things that do attain.  *See* Martial, the things that do attain.

My Friend the Wind.  King D. Kuka.  VoR

My friend, this body is made of bone.  The Origin of the Praise of God.  Robert Bly.  NU

My friend who married the girl I.  Watts.  Shirley Kaufman.  NMM

My friends,/ I am amazed.  Acceptance Speech.  Marvin Bell.  AmPA

My friends are on vacation.  Mothers.  Tristan Tzara, *tr. by* Willis Barnstone *and* Matei Calinescu.  VWA

My friends have left.  Far away, my darling is asleep.  A Small Elegy.  Jiri Orten, *tr. by* Lyn Coffin.  AMV-81

My Gal Sal, *with music.*  Paul Dresser.  BLSo; FSN

My Galley Charged with Forgetfulness.  Petrarch.  *See* Lover Compareth His State to a Ship . . .

My garage is a structure of excessive plainness.  Detail.  Mary Ursula Bethell.  ATNZ

My Garden.  Thomas Edward Brown.  InPK; PeD

My Garden, *parody.*  J. A. Lindon.  InPK; POL

My Garden.  Janice Appleby Succorsa.  HoPM (1975 ed.)

My gentle child, behold this horse.  The Racing-Man.  A. P. Herbert.  BoAnP; PH

My gentle father.  Feliks Skrzynecki.  Peter Skrzynecki.  CAAP

My gentle Puck, come hither.  Shakespeare.  *Fr.* A Midsummer Night's Dream, II, i.  EcS

My Ghostly Father, I Me Confess.  Charles d'Orléans.  BoLoP; SoSe

(Lover's Confession, A.)  NOBE; OxBM

("My ghostly fadir I me confess.")  GBL

My girl the voluptuous creature.  Love and Poetry.  Louis Simpson.  PPoe

My girl, thou gazest much.  The Lover to His Lady.  *At. to* Plato, *tr. by* George Turberville.  FaBoEE; FF; LoAs

My girlfriend, at my urging.  Domestic Duties.  Richard Emil Braun.  NoAM

My glittering sky, high, clear, profound.  The Lovers.  Marya Zaturenska.  PPM

My god,/ the joke's on you.  Good Friday.  Richard Bastian.  AATT

My God, how gracious art thou!  The Relapse.  Henry Vaughan.  PAIC

My God, How the Money Rolls In.  *Unknown.*  FSW

My God, I heard this day.  Man.  George Herbert.  CABA (1972 ed.); MetP

My God, I Thank Thee, *with music.*  Andrews Norton.  AH

My God is just, yes he is.  *Unknown, tr. fr. Pashto by* Saduddin Shpoon.  PBWP

My God most glad to look, most prone to hear.  Bible, *O.T., paraphrased by* Countess of Pembroke.  Psalms, LV.  OBVE; WPE

My God, my God, have mercy on my sin.  Ash Wednesday.  Christina Rossetti.  VLP

My God, my God, what queer corner am I in?  In the Deep Museum.  Anne Sexton.  Prf

My God, when I walk in those groves.  Religion.  Henry Vaughan.  BoReV; OAEL-1

My God, where is that ancient heat towards thee.  To His Mother [*or* Sonnet].  George Herbert.  ILP (1975 ed.); OAEL-1

My God, you have wounded me with love.  Paul Verlaine, *tr. fr. French.*  *Fr.* Sagesse.  ILwL

My god you shall not thus forsake me, you.  Prayer of a Little Hope.  Jean Wahl, *tr. by* Charles Guenther.  VWA

My godmother invited my cousin.  My Cousin Agueda.  Ramón López Velarde, *tr. by* Samuel Beckett.  OBVE

My gracious Lord, I would thee glory doe.  Edward Taylor.  Preparatory Meditations: Second Series, IV.  EAP; PiAm

My Grandfather.  Roman Adrian.  DNGG

My Grandfather/ the Hajj Abbass Habhab.  The Fight.  Sam Hamod.  SA

My Grandfather Always Promised Us.  Liam Rector.  AMV-80

My grandfather found.  Dunbarton.  Robert Lowell.  ILP (1975 ed.)

My grandfather kept his face.  Keep Your Face.  George Tsongas.  CPA

My grandfather leads me through snow.  Blessing.  Melvin Wilk.  VWA

My grandfather said to me.  Manners.  Elizabeth Bishop.  CTBA; NCSH

My grandfather's beard/ Was blacker than God's.  On the Photograph of a Man I Never Saw.  Hyam Plutzik.  VWA

My grandfather's clock was too large for the shelf.  Grandfather's Clock.  Henry Clay Work.  BLSo; FSW; PSoN

My Grandfather's Funeral.  James Applewhite.  CSP; NVAP; TAT

My grandfather's hands were wise and hard.  Rivets.  N. S. Olds.  RhR

My grandfather's mind was a covered ark.  The Law.  Grace Schulman.  GP

My Grandmother.  Elizabeth Jennings.  LP; MPo

My Grandmother.  Karl Shapiro.  VGW

My Grandmother and the Voice of Tolstoy.  Steve Orlen.  AMV-81

My Grandmother at her farm table.  Apple Scoop.  Emilie Glen.  OSP; TVo

My Grandmother Green.  *Unknown.*  AmFP

My grandmother had braids.  Keeping Hair.  Ramona Wilson.  VoR

My grandmother, I've discovered.  The Smile.  Joan Aiken.  TVo

My grandmother lived on yonder green.  My Grandmother Green.  *Unknown.*  AmFP

My grandmother (Lord, love her jackdaw soul!).  Touchstone.  James Worley.  AMV-80

My grandmother moves to my mind in context of sorrow.  My Grandmother.  Karl Shapiro.  VGW

My Grandmother Sifting.  Jeff Daniel Marion.  CSP

My grandmother was a wrinkled little girl.  Genealogy.  Eléni Vakaló, *tr. by* Paul Merchant.  PBWP

My Grandmother Washes Her Feet.  Fred Chappell.  CSP

My Grandmother's Funeral.  Thomas Lux.  WeW

My grandmother's grave. Threads to Be Woven Later. Linda Pastan. PoUp

My Grandmother's Love Letters. Hart Crane. CMoP (1970 ed.); NoAM; NOBA; PSN; UsP

My grandmothers were strong. Lineage. Margaret Walker. CNA; NMM; PBWP; PoBA; TVo

My Grandpa lives in a wonderful house. The Painted Ceiling. Amy Lowell. OBAL

My grandpa used to say "much obliged." Much Obliged. Dave Morice. AcAn

My great brother. A Psalm Praising the Hair of Man's Body. Denise Levertov. AnMo; CAPP

My Great-Grandfather's Slaves. Wendell Berry. TCP

My Great Great etc. Uncle Patrick Henry. James Tate. GP; OBAL

My grief on the sea. Biddy Cussrooee, *tr. fr. Gaelic by* Douglas Hyde. WTO

My grief, quoth I, is called Ignorance. Rachel Speght. *Fr. A Dream.* WPE

My growing up. Enormous Sleep. Tom Crawford. NVAP

My hair has dried. Self Dirge. Wendy Rose. CDW

My hair is grey, but not with years. The Prisoner of Chillon. Byron. MBPR

My hair is springy like the forest grasses. Black Woman. Naomi Long Madgett. FB; OLR; PoBA

My Hairy Dog. Herbert Asquith. *See* Hairy Dog, The.

My hand has a pain from writing. *Unknown, tr. fr. Irish by* Flann O'Brien. BIrV

My hand on your breasts the kitchen. The Knife. Juan Gelman, *tr. by* Yishai Tobin. VWA

My hand plunged into the waters of night. Memory of Another Climate. Gabriel Preil, *tr. by* Jeremy Garber. VWA

My hands/ Open the curtains of your being. Touch. Octavio Paz, *tr. by* Charles Tomlinson. BoLoP

My hands are in the garden. Song of Ceres. Katherine Doak. NPW

My hands are tender feathers. Calypso's Song to Ulyssess. Adrian Mitchell. GBL

My hands did numb to beauty. I Held a Shelley Manuscript. Gregory Corso. VGW

My hands get all the abuse. Case History. Barbara Drake. TC

My hands have developed eyes! Conversion. Geof Hewitt. NeAC

My hands have not touched water since your hands. Carrier Letter. Hart Crane. BoLoP

My hands, my fists, my small bells. Oh Yes. William Matthews. AmPA

My hands that guide a needle. Instruction. Hazel Hall. WPW

My Harry was a gallant gay. Highland Harry Back Again. *At. to* Burns. EBEV

My hated birthday is here, and I must go. Sulpicia, *tr. fr. Latin by* Aliki *and* Willis Barnstone. BoWoP

My hazard wouldn't be yours, not ever. Advice. Ruth Stone. NMM

My head aches. Going through Changes. Jean Tepperman. NMM

My head and shoulders, and my book. The Signature of All Things. Kenneth Rexroth. NNaP; NU

My head is bald, my breath is bad. Late-flowering Lust. John Betjeman. CMoP (1970 ed.); PAIC

My head is drawing closer to the bar again. Indian Guys at the Bar. Simon J. Ortiz. NW

My head is green. Porch Window. John Sjoberg. AcAn

My head, my heart, mine eyes, my life, nay more. A Letter to Her Husband, Absent upon Publick Employment. Anne Bradstreet. EAP; HAP; HeIP; PiAm

My heart aches, and a drowsy numbness pains. Ode to a Nightingale. Keats. AnMo; BiP; CABA (1972 ed.); EBEV; Epi; ExPo (1973 ed.); HAP; HeIP; ILP (1975 ed.); InPK; InPS; IPWM; MBPR; NIL; NOBE; OAEL-2; OBP; PAIC; PB; PoIA; PPoe; PPP; SoSe; SpRo; STS; TT; UnPo (1976 ed.); UsP; VoPo; WeW

My heart beating, my blood running. Time's Dedication. Delmore Schwartz. VGW

My heart beats to the feet of the first faithful. An Interlude. Robert Duncan. CMoP (1970 ed.)

My Heart Belongs to Daddy. Cole Porter. OBAL

My Heart Burns for Him. *Gond Oral Tradition, tr. by* V. Elwin *and* S. Hivale. WTO

My heart grows sick before the wide-spread death. The Grave-Yard. Jones Very. NOBA

My heart has an opening that discharges blood. The Heart. David Ignatow. VWA

My heart has become capable of every form. Ibn al-Arabi, *tr. fr. Arabic.* ILwL

My heart has grown rich with the passing of years. The Solitary. Sara Teasdale. IPWM; PPM

My heart has thank'd thee, Bowles! for those soft strains. To the Rev. W. L. Bowles. Samuel Taylor Coleridge. MBPR

My Heart, How Very Hard It's Grown, *with music.* Cotton Mather. AH

My heart, I cannot still it. Auspex. James Russell Lowell. TAP

My heart is an oil lamp. A Rapier of Treason. *Tr. fr. Arabic by* Willis Barnstone. BoWoP

My Heart Is in Merioneth. *Unknown, tr. fr. Welsh by* Richard Llwyd. OBW

My heart is just as heavy. Grief. *Unknown, tr. by* Aneirin Talfan Davies. OBW

My heart is like a singing bird. A Birthday. Christina Rossetti. ILP (1975 ed.); NOBE; OAEL-2; OLR; UsP; VLP; VPC; WIF; WPE

My heart is like one asked to dine. An Unexpected Pleasure. *Unknown.* FaBoCo

My heart is on my fist. The Tomb of the Kings. Anne Hébert, *tr. by* Aliki *and* Willis Barnstone. BoWoP

My Heart Is Set upon a Lusty Pin. Queen Elizabeth of York. WPE

My Heart Is Woe. *Unknown. See* O, My Heart Is Woe!

My Heart Leaps Up When I Behold. Wordsworth. AKE; CTV; ILP (1975 ed.); InPK; NOBE; PBMP
   (My Heart Leaps Up.) BiP; CABA (1972 ed.); OAEL-2; SoSe (1977 ed.); TPo
   (Rainbow, The.) MBPR
   (Rainbow in the Sky.) PCOP

My heart stirs quietly now to think. A Hermit's Song. *Unknown, tr. by* James Simmons. BIrV

My Heart Stood Still, *with music.* Lorenz Hart. BLSo

My heart, thinking/ "How beautiful he is.' Lady Otomo of Sakanoe, *tr. fr. Japanese by* Arthur Waley. PBWP

My heart's friend, will you tell me who this mischievous youngster is? Dancing-Girl's Song. Kshetrayya, *tr. fr. Teluga.* BoWoP

My Heart's in the Highlands. Burns. BTTM; PoPle

My history crucified, buried under the muddy flood of time. The Rusted Chain. Yosef Damana ben Yeshaq, *tr. by* Ephraim Isaac. VWA

My home over there, my home over there. That Mountain Far Away. *Unknown, tr. by* Herbert Joseph Spinden. PBMP

My Home's Across the Smoky Mountains. *Unknown.* AmFP; FSW

My homestead's with lightning aflame. The Meaning of Love. *Malay Oral Tradition, tr. by* R. O. Winstedt. WTO

My homeward barque is stocked with treasure. Homecoming. Stefan George, *tr. by* Peter Viereck. AMV-81

My Hope, My Love. *Unknown, tr. fr. Irish by* Edward Walsh. BIrV

My hopes retire; my wishes as before. Walter Savage Landor. *Fr.* Ianthe. GBL

My horny feet are cutting through the fog. Satyr. Charles Gullans. PoA

My Horse, Amanda: The Summer of the Watergate Hearings. Maxine W. Kumin. WasP

My Horses Ain't Hungry. *Unknown.* FSW

My horse's feet beside the lake. A Farewell. Matthew Arnold. Switzerland, III. VLP

My hounds are bred out of the Spartan kind. Shakespeare. *Fr.* A Midsummer Night's Dream, IV, i. GDP; PoPle

My hour switched on the cameras take. The Voice of America, 1961. James Liddy. CIP

My House. Michael Cuddihy. FoP

My House. Saint-Denys Garneau, *tr. fr. French by* John Glassco. AKE

My House. Robert Louis Stevenson. ILP (1975 ed.)

My house also has/ an oversized room. Possible Love Poem to the Usurer. Octavio Armand, *tr. by* Carol Maier. AMV–81

My house, I say. But hark to the sunny droves. My House. Robert Louis Stevenson. ILP (1975 ed.)

My house was an infinite series of houses. Poem to my Twin Possibility. Dalene Stowe. NPW

My humanoid friend, myself, a limited animal. The Week-End Naturalist. Tom Buchan. MIS; MS

My husband calls them "The Nomads." Black Lake. Cynthia Nibbelink. TC

My husband is the same [man] who took my maidenhead [or who first pierced me]. Silabhattarika, *tr. fr. Sanskrit. Fr.* The Wanton. BoWoP, *tr. by* Willis Barnstone; PBWP, *tr. by* Daniel H. H. Ingalls

My Ice Man Begins to Move. Amanda Powell. AAN

My Indian Girl. Ali Sedat Hilmi Törel. PeD

My Infundibuliform Hat. Charles Follen Adams. OBAL

My innocent my animal. Before the Fall. Rosemary Daniell. WBN

My Invention. Shel Silverstein. QQQ

My, it's nice. Tea Party. Mary R. Hurley. CTV

My Jack Spratt parents, full of spite and bile. Family History. Wendy Bishop. AMV–81

My ketch must lead into the fray. Parting at Dawn. *Malay Oral Tradition, tr. by* R. J. Wilkinson *and* R. O. Winstedt. WTO

My kid says I. Playing. Philip Dow. MIT

My Kin Talk. Anna Margolin, *tr. fr. Yiddish by* Keith Bosley. VWA

My Kingdom. Louisa May Alcott. *See* Little Kingdom I Possess.

My kite is three feet broad, and six feet long. The Kite. Adelaide O'Keeffe. OxBChV

My kitten walks on velvet feet. Night. Lois Weakley McKay. CTV

My knee against the ground. The Ladder Has No Steps. Jorge Plescoff, *tr. by* Yishai Tobin. VWA

My Knees Go before the Firing Squad at Dawn. Diane Wakoski. CAAP

My ladies haire is threads [or threeds] of beaten gold. Bartholomew Griffin. *Fr.* Fidessa, More Chaste than Kind. AAS; ESo

My ladie's presence makes the roses red. *See* My lady's presence. . .

My lady/ fair with. A Token. Robert Creeley. VGW

My Lady Carenza of the lovely body. *Unknown, tr. fr. Provençal by* Willis Barnstone. BoWoP

My lady unto madam makes her bow. Modern Love, XXXVI. George Meredith. VPC

My lady went to Canterbury. Carol. *Unknown.* FaBoCo; FaBoNo

My Lady Wind. *Unknown.* ECBV

My lady's presence makes the roses red. Henry Constable. *Fr.* Diana. ESo; NIL; WIF

My Lady's Tears. *Unknown.* NOBE ("I saw my Lady weep.") EBEV

My Last Afternoon with Uncle Devereux Winslow. Robert Lowell. VGW

My last defense. Old Mary. Gwendolyn Brooks. CoPAm

My Last Duchess. Robert Browning. BiP; CABA (1972 ed.); ExPo (1973 ed.); FF; HAP; HoPM (1975 ed.); ILP (1975 ed.); InPS; IPWM; LFH; MAT; NIL; NOBE; OAEL–2; PAIC; PBMP; PoIA; PoPle; PPP; SoSe; SS; STS; TT; VLP; WeW; WIF

My Latest Sun Is Sinking Fast, *with music.* Jefferson Haskell. AH

My lefe is faren in londe. Separated Lovers. *Unknown.* OAEL–1; OxBM

My left eye is blind and jogs like. Sketch for a Job Application Blank. Jim Harrison. AmPA; NoAM

My left upper. After the Dentist. May Swenson. GP

My Lesbia let us love and live. Catullus, *tr. fr. Latin by* Wordsworth. OBVE

My letters! all dead paper, mute and white! Sonnets from the Portuguese, XXVIII. Elizabeth Barrett Browning. HAP

My Life. Michael Lallay. EC

My Life. Mark Strand. CAAP

My life/ is/ a/ bald headed match. Black Taffy. Peggy Susberry Kenner. JB

My Life by Somebody Else. Mark Strand. CAAP; GP

My life closed twice before its close. Emily Dickinson. BoLoP; BoWoP; GBL; HeIP; ILP (1975 ed.); NoAM; NOBA; OLR; PAIC; PPP; SBG

My life flows on in endless song. How Can I Keep from Singing? *Unknown.* FSW

My life had stood—a loaded gun. Emily Dickinson. HAP; ILP (1975 ed.); PiAm; Psy; SBG; SoSe; TT; WeW

My life has crept so long on a broken wing. Tennyson. *Fr.* Maud, III, vi. OAEL–2

My life is engraved on my poems. Of Myself. Leah Goldberg, *tr. by* Ramah Commanday. BoWoP

My life is like a music-hall. Prologue to "London Nights." Arthur Symons. VLP

My life is measured by this glass, this glass. On an Hour-Glass. John Hall. SCP-2

My Life like Any Other. Philip Levine. AMV–81

My life, my love, you say our love will last forever. Catullus, *tr. fr. Latin by* Horace Gregory. NAWM–1

My Life, the Quality of Which. Etheridge Knight. NNaP

My life—to Discontent a prey. Rhymes (?). Henry S. Leigh. NOBL

My life was rescued like a bird from the fowler's snare. Psalm for a New Nun. Madeline DeFrees. CNW

My life, your light green eyes. Last Words. James Merrill. TAP

My light will tip tankards of fire in the sky. A Costant Labor. James W. Thompson. BPo

My lines falter. Arriving. Gabriel Preil, *tr. by* Robert Friend. VWA

My lips lack prophecy. Lamentation. Nissim Ezekiel. VWA

My lips murmur. The Vigil. Shlomo Reich, *tr. by* Mira Reich. VWA

My little Ben, whilst thou art young. To His Son Bennet. John Hoskyns. FaBoEE

My little bird, how canst thou sit. Of the Child with the Bird on the Bush. John Bunyan. OxBChV

My little boy/ takes an imaginary thing. The Silver Bullet. Constance Fowlkes. PoUp

My little boy, no longer small. Letter from My Son. Michael Hogan. AAN

My little breath, under the willows by the water side we used to sit. The Willows by the Water Side. *Tr. fr. Tewa Indian by* H. J. Spinden. WTO

My Little Buckaroo. *Unknown.* BPAW

My little cousin, if you'll be. To My Youngest Kinsman, R. L. Abraham Chear. OxBChV

My little darling looked so pale today. My Daughter Very Ill. Paul Goodman. RRA

My little dears, who learn to read. Cautionary Verses to Youth of Both Sexes. Theodore Hook. OxBChV

My little doves have left a nest. My Doves. Elizabeth Barrett Browning. PCOP; VLP

My Little Love Lies on the Ground. Larin Paraske, *tr. fr. Finnish by* Jaakko A. Ahokas. PBWP

My Little Pretty Mopsy. *Unknown.* OxBM

My little scholar, to thy book inclined. A Schoolmaster's Precepts. John Penkethman. OxBChV

My little sister likes to try my shoes. Poem for My Sister. Liz Lochhead. MS

My little son, I have cast you out. Choosing a Name. Anne Ridler. NOBE

My little son, who looked from thoughtful eyes. The Toys. Coventry Patmore. *Fr.* The Unknown Eros. BoReV; EBEV; ILP (1975 ed.); PAIC; PIM; SoSe; VPC

My little soul, my vagrant charmer. Emperor Hadrian, *tr. fr. Latin by* J. V. Cunningham. OBVE. *See also* Hadrian's Address to His Soul When Dying.

My little stone. Letters [*or* Notes] Found near a Suicide. Frank Horne. AmNP (1974 ed.); PoBA

My lizard, my lively writher. Wish for a Young Wife. Theodore Roethke. AnMo; LoAs; NoAM; STS; TAP

My locker, green steel. Game Resumed. Richmond Lattimore. LiSp; SPo

My long strong bamboo fishing pole. Goals. Elisavietta Ritchie. AATT

My long two-pointed ladder's sticking through a tree. After Apple-picking. Robert Frost. CMoP (1970 ed.); Epi; NoAM; NOBA; NU; PPP; PSN; STS; TAP; TT; UnPo (1976 ed.)

My Lord has departed. Longing for the Emperor. Empress Iwa no Hime, *tr. by* Geoffrey Bownas *and* Anthony Thwaite. BoWoP

My Lord: Poor wretched states, pressed by extremities. To the Right Honourable the Lord High Treasurer. Ben Jonson. SCP-1

My Lord Tomnoddy. Robert Brough. VLP

My Lord, what a morning when de stars begin to fall. Judgement Day. *Unknown.* WTO

My Lord, What a Mourning. *Unknown.* FSW

My Lost Youth. Longfellow. AmVN; FaPoR; IPWM; NOBA; TAP

My loud machine for making hay. An Old Field Mowed for Appearances' Sake. William Meredith. PPoD

My lov'd, my honor'd, much respected friend. The Cotter's Saturday Night. Burns. LAuP

My Love. E. E. Cummings. VGW

My Love. Richard Shelton. MPA

My love and I for kisses play'd. William Strode. FaBoEE

My love came back to me. All Souls' Night. Frances Cornford. OxBTC

My Love for All Things Warm and Breathing. William Kloefkorn. AMV-81

My love forever! The Lament for Art [*or* Arthur] O'Leary. Eibhlin Dubh O'Connell, *tr. by* Eilis Dillon *and* John Montague. BIrV; PBWP

My love has gone down to his garden. Bible, *O.T. Fr.* The Song of Solomon, *ad. by* Willis Barnstone. BoWoP

My love has left me has gone from me. Souvenirs. Dudley Randall. BPo

My love he built me a bonny bower. The Lament of the Border Widow. *Unknown.* GBP; PeBB; SLP

My love he is fairer than a summer day. The Drynaun Dhun. *Unknown.* GBP

My love, how could your heart consider. Motet. *Unknown, tr. by* Carol Cosman. PBWP

My love, I cannot thy rare beauties place. William Smith. Chloris, XVIII. ESo

My Love I Gave for Hate. *Unknown, tr. fr. Irish by* George Hay. BIrV

My love, I have betrayed you seventy times. Sonnet. Conrad Aiken. LoAs

My Love in Her Attire. *Unknown.* FF; HeIP (Madrigal: "My love in her attire doth show her wit.") BoLoP; ILP (1975 ed.); NOBE; PAIC

My love is a rider, wild broncos he breaks. *See* My lover's a cowboy, wild broncos he breaks.

My love is as a fever, longing still. Sonnets, CXLVII. Shakespeare. EBEV; HoPM (1975 ed.)

My love is in my house. Mirabai, *tr. fr. Hindi by* Willis Barnstone *and* Usha Nilsson. BoWoP

My love is lessened and must soon be past. The Beginning of the End. Gerard Manley Hopkins. VLP

My Love Is like a Red, Red Rose. Burns. *See* Red, Red Rose, A.

My love is like to ice, and I to fire. Amoretti, XXX. Spenser. FF

My love is living. South of the Great Sea. *Unknown, tr. by* Arthur Waley. OLR

My love is no short year's sentence. Love. *Unknown, tr. by* John Montague. BIrV

My love is o' comely height, an' straight. White an' Blue. William Barnes. GBL

My love is of a birth as rare. The Definition of Love. Andrew Marvell. AnMo; BoLoP; EBEV; GBL; HoPM (1975 ed.); ILP (1975 ed.); InPK; InPS; LoAs; MetP; NOBE; OAEL-1; UnPo (1976 ed.)

My love is playing on a fiddle. *Gond Oral Tradition, tr. by* V. Elwin *and* S. Hivale. WTO

My love is tasting the fragrance. *Unknown, tr. fr. Pashto by* Saduddin Shpoon. PBWP

My love is the maid ov all maidens. In the Spring. William Barnes. GBL

My love is the red sky before a rain. Signals. Keith Waldrop. AMV-81

My Love Is to the Light of Lights. "Hugh MacDiarmid." SLP

My love is white and ruddy. Bible, *O.T. Fr.* The Song of Solomon, *ad. by* Willis Barnstone. BoWoP

My Love Late Walking. James K. Baxter. ATNZ

My love lies in the gates of foam. The Churchyard on the Sands. Lord De Tabley. GBL

My love lies underground. Hymn to Priapus. D. H. Lawrence. CMoP (1970 ed.); ExPo (1973 ed.)

My love, like the vast majority. Erotic Suite. José Luis Vega, *tr. by* Julio Marzán. InW

My love looks like a girl tonight. The Bride. D. H. Lawrence. NoAM; OxBTC

My Love Must Be as Free. Henry David Thoreau. PiAm

My Love, She Passed Me By. *Unknown.* AmFP

My love, this is the bitterest, that thou. Any Wife to Any Husband. Robert Browning. VLP

My love to you is so much—nay, 'tis more. The Unexpressible Love. William Cavendish, Duke of Newcastle. SCP-2

My love tonight is far away. Harry Edward Mills. *Fr.* On a Rainy Night. PeD

My Love Wants to Park. Eloise Klein Healy. GP

My Love Was Light. Tennessee Williams. PoA

My Love When This Is Past. Stephany Fuller. BPo

My love, while we talked. In Dedication. John Montague. IPM

My lovely child all clothed in blue. Lullaby in Auschwitz. Pierre Morhange, *tr. by* Edouard Roditi. VWA

My lovely friend, that long hast been content. Prosopopoeia Corporis Animae Valedicturi: Adios: Arrivederci. William Lathum. SCP-2

My lover capable of terrible lies. Kaccipettu Nannakaiyar, *tr. fr. Tamil by* A. K. Ramanujan. BoWoP; PBWP

My lover is ridiculous. Nocturnal Visitor. Carolyn Miller. AMV-80

My lover's [*or* love is] a cowboy [*or* rider], wild broncos he breaks. Bucking Bronco. *Unknown.* AmFP; BPAW; FSW

My lovers suffocate me. Walt Whitman. *Fr.* Songs of Myself, XLV. LoAs

My love's eyes are red as the sargasso. The Talking Fish. Ruth Stone. BoWoP

My Love's Guardian Angel. William Barnes. GBL

My love's manners in bed. The Way. Robert Creeley. BoLoP; PPP

My loyal sins. Loyal Sins. Jacob Glatstein, *tr. by* Ruth Whitman. VWA

My Lucia in the dew did go. Upon Lucia Dabbled in the Dew. Robert Herrick. SCP-1

My lute, awake! perform the last. The Lover Complaineth the Unkindness of His Love [*or* To His Lute]. Sir Thomas Wyatt. AAS; BoLoP; CABA (1972 ed.); EBEV; GBL; HAP; ILP (1975 ed.); LoAs; NIL; NOBE; OAEL-1

My Luve Is like a Red, Red Rose. Burns. *See* Red, Red Rose, A.

My madman bathes in the golden tank. The Right True End. *Gond Oral Tradition, tr. by* V. Elwin *and* S. Hivale. WTO

My madness is dear to me. Mad Song. Denise Levertov. Psy; TAP

"My magic is dead," said the witch. "I'm astounded." The Witch's Cat. Ian Serraillier. SO

My male ancestors. The Touch of Moonlight. Keith Wilson. FoP

My Mall, I mark that when you mean to prove me. The Author to His Wife, of a Woman's Eloquence. Sir John Harington. BoLoP

My Mama Moved among the Days. Lucille Clifton. *Fr.* Good Times. CAAP; PoBA; TV

My mamma is dead and she's buried. My Darling's on the Deep Blue Sea. *Unknown.* AmFP

My mammy she told me to open the door. Old Gray Beard a-Shaking. *Unknown.* AmFP

My Mammy Was a Wall-eyed Goat. *Unknown.* FaBoNo

My Mammy's Maid. *Unknown.* BBL

My man is a bone ringed with weed. Lament. Brenda Chamberlain. WPE

My man loved me so much. So Long. Jayne Cortez. BoWoP

My Maryland. James Ryder Randall. *See* Maryland, My Maryland!

My mattress floats in an ocean of newspapers. Depression. William Witherup. NowV

My meaning passes like wild nightbirds. Credo. Brewster Ghiselin. PoA

My mind is so evil and unjust. Human Relations. C. H. Sisson. POL

My mind is stuffed with tablecloths. Poland/ 1931. Jerome Rothenberg. Prf

My mind lets go a thousand things. Memory. Thomas Bailey Aldrich. CTV; PCOP

My mind shrugs off his threadbare winter poems. Time Out. Donald Finkel. HoPM (1975 ed.)

My Mind to Me a Kingdom Is. Sir Edward Dyer. ILP (1975 ed.); NIL; NOBE

My Mind to Me a Kingdom Is. Antonia Fraser. SLP

My mind was once the true survey. The Mower's Song. Andrew Marvell. AnMo; ILP (1975 ed.); PoIA; PPP

My mirror is always a little taller than I am. Mirror. Tada Chimako, *tr. by* Kenneth Rexroth *and* Ikuko Atsumi. BoWoP

My mistress' eyes are nothing like the sun. Sonnets, CXXX. Shakespeare. BiP; BoLoP; CABA (1972 ed.); EBEV; Epi; FF; HAP; HoPM (1975 ed.); ILP (1975 ed.); InPK; InPS; IP; IPWM; LFH; NIL; OAEL-1;PBMP; PoIA; PoPle; PPoD; PPP; SoSe; STS; VoPo; WeW; WIF

My mistress is a hive of bees in yonder flowery garden. The Bee-hive. Thomas Durfey. SCP-2

My mistress is as fair as fine. Madrigal. Thomas Ravenscroft. BBL

My mistress sayes she'll marry none but me. Catullus, *tr. fr. Latin by* Richard Lovelace. OBVE

My misunderstandings: for years I thought "muso bello" meant. Taking a Walk with You. Kenneth Koch. CABA (1972 ed.); CAPP

My mither sent me to the well. Whistle o'er the Lave o't. *Unknown.* GBP

My moccasins are black obsidian. Song of the Black Bear. *Unknown.* BCr

My Mommy Told Me. *Unknown.* EC

My money! O, my money! Mavimbela, *tr. fr. Zulu by* H. Tracey. WTO

My Morose Master-Sergeants. Ray Holt. PPoD

My most distinguished guest and learnèd friend. Edna St. Vincent Millay. VGW

My most honoured father. William Cartwright. *Fr.* The Siege; or, Love's Convert. SCP-2

My most pious songs I have written. God's Gifts. Jakov de Haan, *tr. by* David Soetendorp. VWA

My Mother. Alistair Campbell. ATNZ

My Mother. Hayim Naggid, *tr. fr. Hebrew by* Rose Drachler. VWA

My Mother. Ann Taylor. OxBChV

My mother/ a snail in black velvet. That Life, on Film. Lynn Sukenick. RiTi

My mother/ the magician. Tricks. Sharon Olds. TV

My mother, a great believer in presences. Keeping You Alive. Tess Gallagher. GP

My mother always said. Sappho, *tr. fr. Greek by* Willis Barnstone. BoWoP

My Mother and My Sisters. Simon J. Ortiz. GP

My Mother and the Americans. David Kherdian. FAF; SA

My Mother and the Bed. Lyn Lifshin. TV

My mother bore me in the heat of summer. On Approaching My Birthday. Vassar Miller. CSP; IHMS; NMM

My mother bore me in the southern wild. The Little Black Boy. Blake. *Fr.* Songs of Innocence. AnMo; BiP; CABA (1972 ed.); HeIP; ILP (1975 ed.); InPK; LAuP; LFH; MBPR; OAEL-2; OBP; OxBChV; SoSe (1977 ed.); STS

My mother calls it. The City. Linda Pastan. NYP

My mother came/ From a village of grasses. Beginnings. Erez Biton, *tr. by* Judith Katz. VWA

My Mother came again, her. Mother's Day. Sam Hamod. SA

My mother gathered balls of dust. The Housecleaner. Gail White. AMV-80

My mother groaned! my father wept. Infant Sorrow. Blake. *Fr.* Songs of Experience. InPS; LAuP; MBPR; PoIA; PoPle; STS

My mother had a maid call'd Barbara. Shakespeare. *Fr.* Othello, IV, iii. AIW

My mother in the witness box. Elegy. Virginia Scott. NPW

My mother keeps on telling me. Clothes. Elizabeth Jennings. RAE

My mother makes beer in the bathtub. My God, How the Money Rolls In. *Unknown.* FSW

My mother, moving among improving books. The Story of My Life. Hollis Summers. TPo

My mother never forgave my father. The Portrait. Stanley Kunitz. CTBA; GP; TPo

My mother of the blue/ Anglo-saxon eyes. The Eyes, the Blood. David Meltzer. VWA

My mother once was a doe. My Nightingale. Rose Ausländer, *tr. by* Ewald Osers. VWA

My mother—preferring the strange to the tame. The Intruder. Carolyn Kizer. BoWoP; GP; RiTi

My Mother Said. *Unknown.* BBL; PoPle; RAE

My mother said. Warning. *Unknown.* ECBV

My mother said I must not have a collier. I'll Have a Collier for My Sweetheart. William Oliver. WTO

My mother said I'd inherit a moustache and I did. My Mother's Moustache. Honor Moore. WBN

My mother said: "If just once more." Mother's Nerves. X. J. Kennedy. OSF

My mother saw the green tree toad. Lorine Niedecker. VGW

My mother sliced the south for us. Lullaby for Ann-Lucian. Calvin Forbes. PoBA

My Mother Takes My Wife's Side. David Kherdian. SA

My mother taught me purple. Taught Me Purple. Evelyn Tooley Hunt. SoS

My mother told me just before she died. Motherless Child Blues. *Unknown.* BluL

My mother took care of my father's shirts. Tracing Back. Jane Mayhall. WBN

My Mother Tries to Visit Me in the Dead of Night. Diane Wakoski. CAAP; TV

My mother twice in her life on worn feet. Frederick Douglass. Sam Cornish. NVAP; PoBA

My mother was a romantic girl. Papa Love Baby. Stevie Smith. SBG

My Mother Was Always Dressed. Abigail Luttinger. TV

My mother was born in England. *Unknown.* OSF

My mother was old. Piccante. Mary Di Michele. AMV-81

My mother wept loudly. Austin Clarke. *Fr.* Tiresias. CIP

My mother, who. My Mother and the Americans. David Kherdian. FAF; SA

My Mother Would Be a Falconress. Robert Duncan. CAAP

My mother-in-law hates. Li Po. Mary Moore. NPW

My Mother's/ My/ Death/ Birthday. Patricia Goedicke. Psy

My Mother's Breakfront. Janet Sternburg. TV

My mother's brother hauled me to the big-boys' club. Fall In. Lincoln Kirstein. NoAM; PoIA

My Mother's Childhood. Barry Spacks. GP

My mother's Council house is occupied. Ornaments. Frank Ormsby. CIP

My mother's fingers that have decorated cakes. I Am of These. David Curry. HeS

My Mother's House, *sel.* Leah Goldberg, *tr. fr. Hebrew.* "My mother's mother died," *tr. by* Robert Alter. PBWP (From My Mother's Home, *tr. by* Robert Friend.) VWA

My Mother's Life. William Meredith. AMV-81

My mother's maids [*or* maydes], when they did sew and spin [*or* sowe and spynne]. Sir Thomas Wyatt. Satires, II. AAS; TVS

My Mother's Milkman. Diane Wakoski. PCho

My mother's mother died. Leah Goldberg. *Fr.* My Mother's House. PBWP; VWA

My mother's mother painted her. Before My Father before Me. Charles O. Hartman. AAN

My Mother's Moustache. Honor Moore. WBN

My mother's name was Mary. Mary's a Grand Old Name. George M. Cohan. BLSo; FSN

My Mother's Novel. Marge Piercy. TV

My Mother's Shoes. Rayzel Zychlinska, *tr. fr. Yiddish by* Marc Kaminsky. VWA

My Mother's Sister. C. Day Lewis. OxBTC

My mother's strongest religious feeling. Sunday. D. J. Enright. HeHu

My mountains, God has company in heaven. In High Places. Harriet Monroe. PoA

My mournful Muse Melpomene, draw near. Truth's Complaint over England. Thomas Lodge. TVS

My mouth doth water, and my breast doth swell. Astrophel and Stella, XXXVII. Sir Philip Sidney. Epi

My muse in meads has spent her many hours. To Mistress Katherine Bradshaw, the Lovely, That Crowned Him with Laurel. Robert Herrick. CaPo

My muse, what ails this ardour? Sappho, *tr. fr. Greek by* Sir Philip Sidney. OBVE

My naked foot was sheeted with blood. My Friend, the Doctor. George Abbe. FAF

My Name. Edward Gold. PoUp

My Name. Lee Bennett Hopkins. CC

My Name and I. Robert Graves. NoAM

My Name Is a Name. James Steele. SES

My Name Is Afrika. Keorapetse Kgositsile. PoBA

My name is Captain Hall. Captain Hall. *Unknown.* GBP

My name is Edgar Poe and I was born. On the Edge. Philip Levine. TAP

My name is Edward Hollander, as you may understand. The *Flying Cloud. Unknown.* AmFP

My name is Frank Taylor [*or* Tom Hight], a [*or* an old] bachelor I am. Starving to Death on a Government Claim. *Unknown.* AmFP; FSW; OBAL

My name is George Nathaniel Curzon. John William Mackail *and* Cecil Arthur Spring-Rice. *Fr.* Balliol Rhymes. FaBoCo; FaBoEE; NOBL

My name is John J. Curtis. John J. Curtis. Joseph Gallagher. AmFP

My name is Johnson. Madam's Past History. Langston Hughes. NoAm

My name is Peter Emily, as you might understand. Peter Amberley. *Unknown.* AmFP

My name is Phyllis Janik. In the Field. Phyllis Janik. IHMS

My name is Samuel Hall, Samuel Hall. Sam Hall. *Unknown.* AmFP

My name is Sanford Barney [*or* Stamford Barnes], and I came from Little Rock [*or* Nobleville] town. Sanford Barney [*or* The State of Arkansas]. *Unknown.* AmFP; FSW

My name is Solomon Levi. An Old Cracked Tune. Stanley Kunitz. GP

My name is sweet Jenny, my age is sixteen. A Song. *Unknown.* POL

My name is Tom Hight, an old bach'lor I am. *See* My name is Frank Taylor, a bachelor I am.

My name it is Joe Bowers, I have [*or* I've got] a brother Ike. Joe Bowers. *Unknown.* AmFP; FSW

My name—my country—what are they to thee? An Epitaph. Paulus Silentiarius, *tr. by* William Cowper. FaBoEE; OBVE

My name was a heavy stone. My Name. Edward Gold. PoUp

My namesake, old Bill Norris, standing beneath a tree. Nightingales. Leslie Norris. HeHu

My Native Land, thy Puritanic stock. The Rejected "National Hymns." "Orpheus C. Kerr." OBAL

My neighbor, a lady from Fu-kien. The Distance Anywhere. Kenneth O. Hanson. MPA; NIL

My neighbor, a scientist and art-collector, telephones me in a. The Burning of Paper Instead of Children. Adrienne Rich. PiAm

My neighbor puts steakbones. Steakbones. Peter Wild. MPA

My nephew sleeping in a basement room. Rain on the Roof. Janet Frame. ATNZ

My New Garden Field. *Unknown.* AmFP

My new province is a land of bamboo-groves. Eating Bamboo-Shoots. Po Chü-i, *tr. by* Arthur Waley. OBVE

My Nightingale. Rose Ausländer, *tr. fr. German by* Ewald Osers. VWA

My nights is so lonely days is so doggone long. Jersey Belle Blues. *Unknown.* BluL

My Nkosi you loved me. I Am the Beginning. Isaiah Shembe, *tr. by* G. C. Oosthuizen. WTO

My noble, lovely, little Peggy. A Letter to the Honourable Lady Miss Margaret Cavendish Holles-Harley. Matthew Prior. NOBE; OxBChV; PAIC

My normal dwelling is the lungs of swine. Autobiography of a Lungworm. Roy Fuller. NoAM

My Old Cat. Hal Summers. OxBTC; PCat

My Old Dutch: A Cockney Song. Albert Chevalier. VLP

My old flame, my wife! The Old Flame. Robert Lowell. BoLoP; NoAM; NOBA

My old friend Jake. Thin Jake. Michael Dugan. FPB

My old friend, Lord O., owned a parcel of land. False Dawn. Walter de la Mare. FaBoNo

My Old Kentucky Home. Stephen Collins Foster. BLSH; *with music;* BLSo; *with music;* FSW; PSoN, *with music*

My old lady died of a common cold. Kitchen Door Blues. Tennessee Williams. OBAL

My old love for the water has come back again. Sea Call. Margaret Widdemer. RhR

My old man's a white old man. Cross. Langston Hughes. AmNP (1974 ed.); CoPAm; PoBA; SoSe; TAP

My old massa he's got the dropser. Down in Alabam'; or, Aint I Glad I Got Out de Wilderness. *At. to* J. Warner. PSoN

My old master promised me. Raise a Ruckus Tonight. *Unknown.* FSW

My old Mistiss promise me. Promises of Freedom. *Unknown.* BPo

My oldest sister wears thick glasses. My Mother and My Sisters. Simon J. Ortiz. GP

My Olson Elegy. Irving Feldman. Prf

My once dear love; hapless that I no more. The Surrender. Henry King. BoLoP; EBEV; SCP-2

My only son, more God's than mine. Jesus and His Mother. Thom Gunn. MPo

My Own Brand. Art Cuelho. TAT

My own dear love, he is strong and bold. Love Song. Dorothy Parker. TPo

My Own Epitaph. John Gay. FaBoEE; FF; NIL

My own family. Immigrants. Stanley Nelson. AMV-81

My Own Hallelujahs. Zack Gilbert. PoBA

My Own Heart Let Me More Have Pity On. Gerard Manley Hopkins. InPS; VLP

My Own House. David Ignatow. AMV-80; PCho

My own musk. The Tropics. Holly Prado. NPW

My own voice brings you back. Peninsular. Madeline DeFrees. CNW

My Packard Bell was set up in the vacant lot near the stump. The Campaign. Josephine Miles. WPE

My Papa's Waltz. Theodore Roethke. AnMo; CMoP (1970 ed.); CTBA; FF; HAP; HeIP; HoPM (1975 ed.); ILP (1975 ed.); InPK; InPS; IP; NCSH; NIL; NoAM; NOBA; NowV; PBMP; PoIA;PPoe; PPP; PSN; SoS; STS; TAP; VGW; WeW

My parents are making the journey. Spirit-like before Light. Arthur Gregor. VWA

My Parents Kept Me from Children Who Were Rough. Stephen Spender. BBGO; SoS; TPo (Rough.) LP; NoAM; PBMP

My parents raised me tenderly. The Girl I Left behind Me. *Unknown.* AmFP

My parents stand beside my bed. Scenario. Barbara Eve. TV

My Party the Rain. William Stafford. CNW

My passion is as mustard strong. A New Song of New Similies. John Gay. FaBoCo; NOBL

My passion is like turbulence at the head of waters. *Tr. fr. Arabic by* Willis Barnstone. BoWoP

My patent pardouns ye may see. Sir David Lyndsay. *Fr.* Ane Satyre of the Thrie Estaitis. OBSV

My pathway lies through worse than death. Conquest. Georgia Douglas Johnson. AmNP (1974 ed.)

My Penis. Ed Ochester. GP

My pensive Sara! thy soft cheek reclined. The Eolian Harp. Samuel Taylor Coleridge. MBPR; OAEL-2

My peonies have lovely leaves. What Ails My Fern? James Schuyler. UsP

My People. Margery Himel. IHMS

My people are as a people of grass. The Exiles. Robert Gessner. SPT

My people grew potatoes. The Duchess Potatoes. Diane Wakoski. CAAP

My people have married me. Lament of Hsi-chün. Hsi-chün, *tr. by* Arthur Waley. BoWoP

My Picture. Adelaide Anne Procter. PeD

My pillow won't tell me. The Apparition. Theodore Roethke. AIW; LoAs

My "place of clear water." Anahorish. Seamus Heaney. HeHu

My plaid awa, my plaid awa. Lady Isabel and the Elf-Knight [*or* The Elfin Knight]. *Unknown.* FaBoBa; GBP; SLP

My Playmate. Whittier. NOBA

My pocket book was empty. Danville Girl. *Unknown.* FSW

My Poem. Nikki Giovanni. AmNP (1974 ed.); BPo; PoBA

My poem is full of joy. My Poem. Ethel Hewell. AKE

My poem would eat nothing. The Poem You Asked For. Larry Levis. AmPA; NVAP

My poems/ are the sounds. Poems. Bruce Severy. VW

My poet, thou canst touch on all the notes. Sonnets from the Portuguese, XVII. Elizabeth Barrett Browning. VLP

My Poetry. Kotaro Takamura. IPWM

My Poker Girl. Tom Masson. OBAL

My Polish Grandma. Edward Field. Prf

My poor body is alas unworthy. Ch'in Chia's Wife's Reply. *Tr. fr. Chinese by* Arthur Waley. BoWoP

My poor old bones—I've only two. The Lonely Scarecrow. James Kirkup. RAE

My poor Pegasus must go on foot. In Life's Stable. Kadya Molodovsky, *tr. by* Ruth Whitman. VWA

My Prayer. Henry David Thoreau. *See* Great God, I Ask Thee for No Meaner Pelf.

My Pretty Pink. *Unknown.* AmFP

My Pretty Rose Tree. Blake. *Fr.* Songs of Experience. BoLoP; LAuP; MBPR

My prime of youth is but a frost of cares. Elegy [*or* On the Eve of His Execution]. Chidiock Tichborne. DL; EBEV; FF; HAP; HeIP; ILP (1975 ed.); InPK; InPS; NOBE; OAEL-1; OBP; PAIC; PPoD; PPoe; WIF

My purpose is to tell my own true tale. The Seafarer. *Unknown, tr. by* John Wain. EBEV

My Purse. *Unknown.* OxBM ("Singe we alle and say we thus.") EBEV

My quiet kin, must I affront you. Preliminary to Classroom Lecture. Josephine Miles. NoAM

My railwayman father voted. One Man One Vote. Patricia Beer. HeHu

My Ramblin' Boy. Tom Paxton. FSW

My Ratclif [*or* Ratcliffe], when thy retchlesse [*or* rechless] youth offendes. Exhortation to Learn by Others' Trouble. Earl of Surrey. AAS; FaBoEE

My Reason absent did mine eyes require. Henry Constable. *Fr.* Diana. ESo

My Recollectest Thoughts. Charles Edward Carryl. *Fr.* Davy and the Goblin, *ch.* 7. PCOP

My Relatives for the Most Part. Frederick B. Hudson. AMV-80

My report is not of schools. Return from Luluabourg. Michael Jackson. ATNZ

My Rival. Kipling. OxBTC

My rival's house. Her Place. Liz Lochhead. MS

My Rocking Chair. Doris I. Bateman. CTV

My roof is covered with pigeon bones. Bones. Charles Simic. NVAP

My room is dark. Cognac and Farewell to My Sanity. Ann Menebroker. PoW

My room is so small. Leah Goldberg, *tr. by* Ramah Commanday. *Fr.* Nameless Journey. BoWoP

My room's a square and candle-lighted boat. Frances Cornford. *Fr.* The Country Bedroom. RAE

My room's bigger than a coffin. On Saint-Urbain Street. Milton Acorn. NeAC

My rug is red. My couch, whereon I deal. The Map. Gloria C. Oden. AmNP (1974 ed.)

My Sad Captains. Thom Gunn. CMoP (1970 ed.); InPS

My Sad Self. Allen Ginsberg. ILP (1975 ed.); IPWM; NoAM; UnPo (1976 ed.)

My Sadness Sits around Me. June Jordan. BPo

My Samsons. Haim Guri, *tr. fr. Hebrew by* Mark Elliott Shapiro. VWA

My Savior, Hear My Prayer. Henry L. Jenner. CTV

My scarlet coat lies on the ground. The Martyrdom of Saint Sebastian. Rosemary Dobson. MAuV

My secrets cry aloud. Open House. Theodore Roethke. AnMo; NoAM; NOBA; STS

My serious son! I see thee look. Before a Saint's Picture. Walter Savage Landor. OxBChV

My Shadow. Robert Louis Stevenson. CTV; OxBChV; PCOP

My shadow moves, until, at noon, I stand. Autumn Shades, X. Edgar Bowers. PiAm

My shag-hair Cyclops, come, let's ply. John Lyly. *Fr.* Sapho and Phao. EBEV

My shattred phancy stole away from mee. Edward Taylor. *Fr.* Preparatory Meditations: First Series, XXIX. EAP; PiAm

My Shepherd Is the Living Lord, *with music.* Thomas Sternhold. AH

My shoes are almost dead. Caesar. W. S. Merwin. PPoD

My signs are a rain-proof coat, good shoes, and a staff cut from the woods. Walt Whitman. *Fr.* Song of Myself, XLVI. Prf

My Silks and Fine Array. Blake. *See* Song: "My silks and fine array."

My sin! my sin, my God, these cursed dregs. Edward Taylor. Preparatory Meditations: First Series, XXXIX. EAP

My Sister. Alfonsina Storni, *tr. fr. Spanish by* Aliki *and* Willis Barnstone. BoWoP

My sister/ we are lying in a large bed by the sea. Monday Night in Winter. Ellen Cooney. NPW

My sister Betty. Charlie Two-Head. Marnie Walsh. VW

My sister had a slumber party. Slumber Party. Carson McCullers. CTV

My Sister Jane. Ted Hughes. SO

My Sister Laura. Spike Milligan. FPB; OSF

My sister! my sweet sister! if a name. Epistle to Augusta. Byron. MBPR

My sister was quicker at everything than I. The Paper Lantern. Tennessee Williams. *Fr.* Recuerdo. CTBA

My sister writes, "Come out, I need you." Seal Rock. Sue Baugh. AMV-81

My sister, you are a stranger to this place. God Hasn't Made Room. Mririda n'Ait Attik, *tr. by* Daniel Halpern *and* Paula Paley. PBWP

My Sister's Sleep. Dante Gabriel Rossetti. VLP

My Sisters the Summer of 53. Janet Campbell Hale. NW

My skin is black, my arms are long. Four Women. Nina Simone. MAT

My skin is comfortably loose. Old Age. Mura Dehn. TVo

My skin is so thin. And Yet. Kadya Molodovsky, *tr. by* Seymour Levitan. VWA

My sleep falters and the good dreams. Lost. A. Alvarez. UsP

My Son. Ruth Stone. WPE

My Son. Rex Veeder. HeS

My son aged three fell in the nettle bed. Nettles. Vernon Scannell. HeHu

My Son and I. Philip Levine. BrS; GP; NYP

My son and I go walking in the garden. New Season. Philip Levine. NNaP

My son as a child saying. A Little Stone in the Middle of the Road, in Florida. Muriel Rukeyser. RiTi

My son, forget not my law. Bible, *O.T.* Proverbs, III: 1-4. CTV

My Son, Forsake Your Art. Mahon O'Heffernan, *tr. fr. Irish by* Maire Cruise O'Brien. BIrV

My son has birds in his head. Daedalus. Alastair Reid. NCSH

My son invites me to witness with him. Mousemeal. Howard Nemerov. NCSH; NowV; UsP

My son, keep well thy tongue, and keep thy friend. Controlling the Tongue. Chaucer. *Fr.* The Canterbury Tales: The Manciple's Tale. OxBChV

My son kept wanting a snake. The Evidence. Van K. Brock. NVAP

My son leaps across my back. Still Wrestling. Phil Boiarski. AMV-81

My Son, My Executioner. Donald Hall. BrS; CoPAm; InPK

My Son, My Son. Seymour Cain. AMV-81

My son tells his aunt. A San Diego Poem. Simon J. Ortiz. CDW

My son was killed while laughing at some jest. A Son. Kipling. *Fr.* Epitaphs of the War. FaBoEE

My Song. Hayim Nachman Bialik, *tr. fr. Hebrew by* Ruth Nevo. VWA

My Song. King D. Kuka. VoR

My Song Is Love Unknown. Samuel Crossman. OxBChV

My song shall bless the Lord of all. Jehovah-Jesus. William Cowper. PIM

My song today is the storm-cock's song. The Storm-Cock's Song. "Hugh MacDiarmid." OxBTC

My sons/ sometimes I can. Efficiency Apartment. Gerald W. Barrax. PoBA

My Sort o' Man. Paul Laurence Dunbar. AmNP (1974 ed.)

My Soul before Thee Prostrate Lies, *with music.* C. F. Richter, *tr. fr. German by* John Wesley. AH

My soul doth magnify the Lord. The Magnificat. Bible, *N.T.* St. Luke I: 46-56. ILwL

My Soul Hovers over Me. Joshua Tan Pai, *tr. fr. Hebrew by* Yishai Tobin. VWA

My Soul is an enchanted boat. Asia's Song. Shelley. *Fr.* Prometheus Unbound, II, v. GrRo

My soul is covered by layers. The Recognitions: Seedtime. Rosemary Christoph. UsP

My soul is like a well of dead, deep water. The Well. Luis Palés Matos, *tr. by* Donald Walsh. InW

My soul looked down from a vague height, with Death. The Show. Wilfred Owen. NoAM; OBP; OBW; OxBTC

My soul magnifies the Lord. The Magnificat. Bible, *N.T.* St. Luke, I: 46-56. BoWoP

My Soul, Sit Thou a Patient Looker-on. Francis Quarles. *See* Epigram: "My soul, sit thou a patient looker-on."

My soul stands at the window of my room. Nostalgia. Karl Shapiro. CMoP (1970 ed.)

My soul, there is a country. Peace. Henry Vaughan. BoReV; EBEV; HAP; IPWM; NOBE; PIM

My soul, thy love is dear: 'twas thought a good. Epigram. Francis Quarles. *Fr.* Emblems, V, 4. OAEL-1; SCP-2

My soul was an old horse. Pegasus. Patrick Kavanagh. PFIr

My Soul was as if free and. Etude from the Third Epistle. Robert Duncan. *Fr.* Dante Etudes. CAAP

My Soul, Weigh Not Thy Life, *with music.* Leonard Swain. AH

My soul, what's lighter than a feather? Wind. Francis Quarles. FaBoEE

My Soul Would Fain Indulge a Hope, *with music.* Joseph Steward. AH

My South. Andrew Glaze. CSP

My Specialty Is Living Said. E. E. Cummings. NOBA

My Spectre around Me Night and Day. Blake. OAEL-2

My spirit is too weak—mortality. On Seeing the Elgin Marbles. Keats. CABA (1972 ed.); ILP (1975 ed.); MBPR; NIL; PAIC; STS

My Spirit Longeth for Thee. John Byrom. BoReV; NOBE

My spouse, Chunaychunay. *Tr. fr. Quechua (Peru) by* W. S. Merwin. BoWoP

My Spring Thing. Everett Hoagland. BPo

My Springs. Sidney Lanier. UnPo (1976 ed.)

My Star. Robert Browning. HeIP; SoSe

My Star Spangled–Red Striped Socks. Abelardo Delgado. FoP

My stare like God's in space. The Well-aimed Stare. Hugo Margenat, *tr. by* Julio Marzán. InW

My Stars. Abraham Ibn Ezra, *tr. fr. Spanish by* Robert Mezey. OFD

My steps are wet from the cold death. Old Jewish Cemetery in Worms. Alfred Kittner, *tr. by* Herbert Kuhner. VWA

My stick fingers click with a snicker. Player Piano. John Updike. WeW

My stocking's where. Christmas Eve. David McCord. *Fr. A* Christmas Package. CC; PChr

My stomach is of many minds. Stomach. Kathleen Norris. OBAL

My Strawlike Hair. Asya, *tr. fr. Yiddish by* Gabriel Preil *and* Howard Schwartz. VWA

My straying thoughts, reduced stay. Song. Anne Collins. WPE

My street is holy. The Street Where I Live. Virginia Floyd. AATT

"My strength is failing fast." The Sea-King's Burial. Charles MacKay. RhR

My stutter, my cough, my unfinished sentences. The Second-fated. Robert Graves. NoAM

My Style. Charles Bukowski. AMV-81

My suite is just, just lord to my suite hark. Bible, *O.T.* Psalms, XVII, *paraphrased by* Sir Philip Sidney. OBVE

My sweet deare Lord, for thee I'le live, dy, fight. An Extasy of Joy Let in by This Reply Returnd in Admiration. Edward Taylor. *Fr.* God's Determinations. EAP

My sweet-faced, tattle-tale brother was born blind. The Twins. Mona Von Duyn. GP

My sweet, let me tell you about the Shark. The Shark. John Ciardi. MiP

My Sweet Old Etcetera. E. E. Cummings. *Fr.* Is 5. AnMo; CABA (1972 ed.); CMoP (1970 ed.); FF; HeIP; InPS; OBAL; PPP; SoS; STS

My sweet Parthenophe, within thy face. Parthenophil and Parthenophe, LXXXIV. Barnabe Barnes. ESo

My Sweetest Lesbia [Let Us Live and Love]. Thomas Campion, *after the Latin of* Catullus. AAS; BiP; CABA (1972 ed.); FF; GBL; HAP; HeIP; LoAs; NIL; OAEL-1; OBVE; PAIC; SoSe (1977 ed.)
(Vivamus, Mea Lesbia, atque Amemus.) EBEV

My sweetheart in the rippling hills of sand. *Tr. fr. Hawaiian by* S. H. Elbert *and* N. Mahoe. WTO

My Sweetie's a Mule in the Mine. *Unknown.* AmFP; BPAW (Driving the Mule.) GBP
(My Sweetheart's the Mule in the Mines.) FSW

My swirling wants. Your frozen lips. A Valediction Forbidding Mourning. Adrienne Rich. NIL; NoAM; PoIA; TT

My tailor is against parting. Against Parting. Natan Zach, *tr. by* Jon Silkin. VWA

My tap is run; then Baxter, tell me why. The Last Will and Testament of Anthony, King of Poland. *Unknown.* APAS

My tea is nearly ready and the sun has left the sky. The Lamplighter. Robert Louis Stevenson. OxBChV

My teacher fish! He Don't Know the Inside Feel. Herbert R. Adams. MiP

My tears were Orion's splendor with sextuple suns. Tears. Edith Sitwell. CMoP (1970 ed.)

My Teeth. Ed Ochester. GP

My teeth dare not trust you. Bridgework. Annette Lynch. FF

My temples throb, my pulses boil. To Minerva. Thomas Hood. FaBoCo; FaBoNo; NOBL

My tender age in sorrow did begin. Easter Wings. George Herbert. PAIC

My tender parents brought me here. The Wexford Girl. *Unknown.* AmFP

My thoughts are winged with hopes, my hopes with love. *At. to* Sir Walter Ralegh. GBL

My thoughts hold mortal strife. Inexorable. William Drummond of Hawthornden. NOBE

My three sisters are sitting. Women. Adrienne Rich. NMM; Psy

My Three Wives. *Unknown, after the Latin of* Etienne Pasquier. FaBoEE

"My towers at last!" Herman Melville. Conrad Aiken. NoAM; NOBA; TAP

My towers at last! These rovings end. The Return of the Sire de Nesle A. D. 16—. Herman Melville. NOBA

My trade takes me frequently into decaying houses. From a Museum Man's Album. John Hewitt. OxBTC

My trembling song, awake! arise! A Song on New Year's Day before the King. Thomas Flatman. SCP-2

My Trewth Is Plicht. Sir John Fethy. SLP

My Triumph. Whittier. NOBA

"My True Love Hath My Heart and I Have His." Mary Elizabeth Coleridge. BoLoP

My True Love Hath My Heart [And I Have His.] Sir Philip Sidney. *Fr.* Arcadia. BoLoP; GBL; ILP (1975 ed.); LoAs; PoPle
(Bargain, The.) NOBE

My True Memory.  Asya, *tr. fr. Yiddish by* Gabriel Preil *and* Howard Schwartz.  VWA

My Twelve Oxen.  *Unknown.*  OxBM

My twenty-six-year-old ensign.  To a Portrait of Lermontov.  Margarita Aliger, *tr. by* Elaine Feinstein.  VWA

My two older sisters went suddenly wide/ in the hips.  Sisters, Daughters.  Roderick Jellema.  PoUp

My Ulick.  Charles J. Kickham.  PFIr

My uncle, a craftsman of hammers and wood.  Willy Lyons.  James Wright.  NNaP

My Uncle Al on Saturday night lay warmly in the ditch.  Aunt Emma, Uncle Al: A Short History of the South.  Marion Montgomery.  CSP

My uncle believed he had.  Parity.  Kenneth Rexroth.  GP

My uncle died a month ago.  My Uncle.  *Unknown.*  ECBV

My uncle James.  Uncle James.  Margaret Mahy.  FPB

My Uncle Jehoshaphat.  Laura E. Richards.  OxBChV

My uncle played the fiddle—more elegantly the violin.  The Country Fiddler.  John Montague.  TwMBP

My urine smells of smoke.  Desert in the Sea.  Brian Swann.  AmPA

My Valentine.  Robert Louis Stevenson.  *See* I Will Make You Brooches.

"My verses, Ochkasty, and your music."  Matthew Mead.  *Fr.* Identities.  TwMBP

My verses please—I thank you, friend.  A Fragment of Bion.  Philip Freneau.  EAP

My verses will never stop bombs.  Most Days.  Elisavietta Ritchie.  AATT

My voice has been imprisoned.  Voice.  Stanley Moss.  AMV-80

My walls tonight are lined with ancestors.  Ancestors.  Harold Schimmel.  VWA

My wavering mind resembles.  In the Balance.  *Unknown, tr. by* George Whicher.  *Fr.* Carmina Burana.  OLR

My Way Is Not Thy Way.  D. H. Lawrence.  CMoP (1970 ed.)

My wearied bark, O let it now be crowned!  To Crown It.  Robert Herrick.  CaPo

My well-beloved was stripped. Knowing my whim.  The Jewels.  Baudelaire, *tr. by* Roy Campbell.  BoLoP

My whining lover, what needs all.  Against Absence.  Sir John Suckling.  CaPo

My White Book of Poems.  Rachel, *tr. fr. Hebrew by* N. N.  VWA

My whole eye was sunset red.  Eye and Tooth.  Robert Lowell.  CAPP

My whole life.  At the Well.  Malka Heifetz Tussman, *tr. by* Marcia Falk.  VWA

My whole life coming to this place.  Port Jefferson.  Louis Simpson.  IPWM

My whole life has been a chronology of—changes.  For Malcolm: After Mecca.  Gerald W. Barrax.  OFD

My whole life has led me here.  Woolworth's.  Donald Hall.  WeW

My Wife.  Robert Louis Stevenson.  DL

My wife and I have asked a crowd of craps.  Vers de Société.  Philip Larkin.  PSN

My wife and I lived all alone.  Ballad of the Despairing Husband.  Robert Creeley.  OBAL

My wife and I lived [*or* live] all alone.  Little Brown Jug.  *At. to* Joseph E. Winner.  BLSH; BLSo; FSW; GSB; OBAL; PSoN

My wife comes home.  Refusing What Would Bind You to Me Irrevocably.  Ronald Koertge.  GP

My wife is left-handed.  For Hettie.  Amiri Baraka.  NoAM; NOBA; SoS; SS

My Wife Is My Shirt.  Stephen Tropp.  InPK; PeD

My wife reads them.  The Personals.  Alan Feldman.  PCho

My wife saw it first.  Blackbird.  Christopher Leach.  BoAnP

My wife sits reading in a garden chair.  October.  Barry Spacks.  PoA

My Wife Who Is American.  John Daniel.  TwMBP

My wife with the hair of a wood fire.  Freedom of Love.  André Breton.  EAS

My wife's new pink slippers.  The Thinker.  William Carlos Williams.  TT

My Wild Irish Rose.  Chauncey Olcott.  BLSH, *chorus only, with music*; BLSo, *with music;*  FSN, *with music*; FSW

My wind is turned to bitter north.  Arthur Hugh Clough.  VLP

My window opens out into the trees.  Solace.  Clarissa Scott Delany.  AmNP (1974 ed.); PoBA

My window shows the travelling clouds.  The Alchemist in the City.  Gerard Manley Hopkins.  IPWM

My windows now are giant drops of dew.  A Bright Day.  W.H. Davies.  OBW

My wives do not write.  Memory.  Michael Hamburger.  OxBTC

My Woman.  A.D. Winans.  AMV-80

My Woman/ she look at me.  Brown Circles.  Melvin DeBruhl.  PPoD

My woman said to me.  Dream.  D. M. Thomas.  FoP

My woman says that she would rather wear the wedding-veil for me.  Catullus, *tr. fr. Latin by* Horace Gregory.  NAWM-1

My woman weeping under a brush of stars.  Simple Ode.  Kendrick Smithyman.  ATNZ

My woorthy Lord, I pray you wonder not.  Gascoignes Woodmanship.  George Gascoigne.  AAS

My words and thoughts do both express this notion.  Our Life Is Hid with Christ in God.  George Herbert.  OAEL-1

My young comrade.  Letter to a Young Friend.  Alden Nowlan.  AKE

My young love said to me, "My brothers won't mind."  She Moved through the Fair.  Padraic Colum.  AIW; BIrV

My Young Mother.  Jane Cooper.  NMM

My young son pushes a football into my stomach.  Out-and-Down Pattern.  William Kloefkorn.  BrS

Mye love toke skorne my servise to retaine.  Sir Thomas Wyatt.  AAS

Myfanwy.  John Betjeman.  BoLoP

Myne [*or* Mine] owne John Poyntz, sins [*or* since] ye delight to know.  Sir Thomas Wyatt.  Satires, I.  AAS; OBSV; OBVE

Myra.  Fulke Greville.  *Fr.* Caelica.  NOBE; PoPle  ("I, with whose colours Myra dress'd her head.")  GBL; HAP

Myrtilla, early on the lawn.  Sweet Slug-a-Bed.  *Unknown.*  FaBoCo

Myrtle.  Theodore Roethke.  OSP; RAE

Myrtle bush grew shady, The.  Jealousy.  Mary Elizabeth Coleridge.  WPE

Myself unto myself will give.  The Holy Office.  James Joyce.  FaBoTw (1975 ed.); NoAM; OxBTC

Myself When I Am Real.  Al Young.  CNA; PoBA

Myself when young did eagerly frequent.  Omar Khayyam, *tr. by* Edward Fitzgerald.  *Fr.* The Rubaiyat.  ILwL

Myselves/ The grievers/ Grieve.  Ceremony after a Fire Raid.  Dylan Thomas.  CMoP (1970 ed.); ExPo (1973 ed.)

Mysteries Remain, The.  Hilda Doolittle ("H. D.").  NOBA; TAP; VGW

Mysterious Biography.  Carl Sandburg.  CC; OFD

Mysterious Britain.  Amy Clampitt.  AMV-81

Mysterious East.  William Cole.  OBAL

Mysterious Night! when our first parent knew.  To Night.  Joseph Blanco White.  EBEV; PPM; SoSe

Mysterious Presence! Source of All, *with music.*  Seth Curtis Beach.  AH

Mystery Baseball.  Philip Dacey.  AAN

" 'Mystery Boy' Looks for Kin in Nashville."  Robert Hayden.  NoAM

Mystery of a kind, A. Planting a Magnolia. W. D. Snodgrass. NoAM

Mystic. D. H. Lawrence. WeW

Mystic, The. Tennyson. VLP

Mystic and Cavalier. Lionel Johnson. VLP

Mystic in the morning, half asleep, A. Bachelor. William Meredith. NoAM

Mystic Lake. R. P. Kingston. NVAP

Mysticism, but let us have no words. Conrad Aiken. *Fr.* Time in the Rock, XI. VGW

"Mysticism Has Not the Patience to Wait for God's Revelation." Richard Eberhart. NoAM

Myth, The. Edwin Muir. CMoP (1970 ed.)

Myth. Muriel Rukeyser. IHMS; NNaP

Myth lilies. A smog-edge sky blurs his eyes. Crow's Way. Duane Niatum. CDW

Myth of the Blaze. George Oppen. CAAP

Myth of the Spanish moss. Of Jayne Mansfield, Flannery O'Connor, My Mother and Me. Rosemary Daniell. CSP

Myth on Mediterranean Beach: Aphrodite as Logos. Robert Penn Warren. HAP

Mythical Journey, The. Edwin Muir. ILP (1975 ed.); NoAM

Mythics. Helen Chasin. IHMS

Mythistorema. George Seferis, *tr. fr. Modern Greek by* Rex Warner. BuTh

Mythmaking. Kathleen Spivack. NMM

Mythology. Lawrence Durrell. OxBTC

Myths and Texts, *sels.* Gary Snyder.
  Burning.
    John Muir on Mt. Ritter, VIII. Epi; NOBA; TCP
    "My clutch and your clutch," VI. Epi
    Second Shaman Song, I. NOBA
      ("Squat in swamp shadows.") Epi
    "Spikes of new smell driven up nostrils," XIII. FoP
    Text, The, XVII. Epi
  Hunting.
    First Shaman Song, I. NOBA
    "How rare to be born a human being! XVI. CAPP
    This Poem Is for Bear, VI. BCr; CNW; NOBA; NU
    This Poem Is for Deer, VIII. CAPP; NOBA
  Logging.
    "Again the ancient, meaningless," V. CAPP
    "Stood straight/ holding the choker high," III. NOBA

Myth and the Mountain, The. Roland Robinson. GAS

Myxomatosis. Philip Larkin. CMoP (1970 ed.); NoAM

# N

N. Hugh Seidman. PoA

N. B. A. Prelim, Boston Garden. Thomas Whitbread. PPoD

NFL/ Going backward. In the Pocket. James Dickey. LiSp; SPo

NHR. Jack Hirschman. VWA

N is for Naughty Young Nat. Naughty Young Nat. Isabel Frances Bellows. TDH

N.Y. Ezra Pound. NYP

N.Y. to L.A. by Jet Plane. Sonya Dorman. GOA

NYC. Art Lange. FiCh

Naboth's Vineyard. John Caryll. APAS

Naighbour Playmeates. William Barnes. VPC

Nails. Gary Gildner. TAP

Nails and a Cross. R. A. K. Mason. ATNZ

Naked/ I have lain in beastly days. Dawn. Alejandra Pizarnik, *tr. by* Alina Rivero. VWA

Naked all night the field. Sports Field. Judith Wright. LiSp; MAuV

Naked and grey the Cotswolds stand. Edgehill Fight. Kipling. PoPle

Naked and the Nude, The. Robert Graves. OBP; SoSe; TPo; WIF

Naked blondhead/ dolls do not. Peace. Jonetta Barras-Abney. PoUp

Naked children play. Mexican Village. Rainer Schulte. SES

Naked earth is warm with Spring, The. Into Battle. Julian Grenfell. FaPoR; OxBTC

Naked Eve shared the last bite. Like Weary Trees. Jacob Glatstein, *tr. by* Ruth Whitman. VWA

Naked house, a naked moor, A. The House Beautiful. Robert Louis Stevenson. NOBE

Naked I Came. Palladas, *tr. fr. Greek by* A. J. Butler. NIL

Naked I came, naked I leave the scene. Epitaph for Someone or Other. J. V. Cunningham. NIL; OBAL; VGW

Naked I came, when I began to be. Nudus Redibo. Thomas Flatman. SCP-2

Naked I reached the world at birth. Naked I Came. Palladas, *tr. by* A. J. Butler. NIL

Naked in snowdrifts, we've made love. Windy Nights. David Campbell. MAuV

Naked Land, The. Kenneth Patchen. EAS

Naked out of the dark we came. Kenneth Rexroth, *after the Persian.* FaBoEE

Naked she lay, clasped in my longing arms. The Imperfect Enjoyment. Earl of Rochester. BoLoP; SCP-2

Naked Woman and a Dead Dwarf, A. Stephen Crane. TT

Nakedness of women, The. Blake. POL

Namby-Pamby. Henry Carey. FaBoNo; OBSV

Name, The. Robert Creeley. IPWM; SoS; TCP

Name, The. Jalal ed-Din Rumi, *ad. fr. Persian by* Robert Bly. NU

Name, The/ never left his lips. Scribe. Paul Auster. VWA

Name for All, A. Hart Crane. VGW

Name Giveaway. Phillip William George. NW; VoR

Name in a footnote. Faceless name. Crispus Attucks. Robert Hayden. CNA

Name is immortal but only the name, for the rest, The. Jew. Karl Shapiro. VWA

Name of a fact, The: at home in that leafy world. Thoughts on Looking into a Thicket. John Ciardi. PoIA

Name—of it—is "Autumn," The. Emily Dickinson. InPS

Name of Jesus, The. John Newton. BoReV

Name of Our Country, The. Dennis Schmitz. AmPA

Name of the product I tested is "Life," The. A Consumer's Report. Peter Porter. FaBoCo; NOBL

Name of this poem is, The. Cameo No. II. June Jordan. BPo; WBN

Name Me. Richard Packer. FPA

Name they gave me is lost, The. Privilege. Alejandra Pizarnik, *tr. by* Yishai Tobin. VWA

Name, wide on banners, The. A Modern Leader. R. A. Simpson. FPA

Nameless Doon, The. William Larminie. BIrV

Nameless Epitaph, A. Matthew Arnold. FaBoEE; VLP

Nameless Journey, *sel.* Leah Goldberg, *tr. fr. Hebrew by* Ramah Commanday.
  "My room is so small." BoWoP

Nameless One, A. Margaret Avison. ExPo (1973 ed.); HeIP

Nameless One, The. James Clarence Mangan. BIrV

Nameless presence on the paling green, A. The Child. Frank Ormsby. AMV-81

Nameless Recognition, A. Arthur Gregor. GP

Namely You.  Lawson Fusao Inada.  NW

Names.  G. C. Dawe.  IPM

Names.  D. J. Enright.  FaBoCo

Names.  Lyn Lifshin.  FAF

Names for everything I touch.  The Hollow Thesaurus.  Roger McDonald.  CAAP

Names in Monterchi: To Rachel.  James Wright.  NNaP

Names of Georgian Women, The.  Bella Akhmadulina, *tr. fr. Russian by* Stanley Noyes *and* Olga Carlisle.  BoWoP

Names of Horses.  Donald Hall.  HAP; PH

Names of the Humble, The.  Les A. Murray.  *Fr.* Walking to the Cattle-Place.  CAAP

Names of those who fought and died, The.  Sitting in Bib Overalls, Workshirt.  Louis Daniel Brodsky.  AMV-81

Naming, The.  Terry Hummer.  AMV-81

Naming of Cats, The.  T. S. Eliot.  AnMo; OSP; TPo

Naming of Parts.  Henry Reed.  Lessons of the War, I.  ExPo (1973 ed.); InPK; InPS; FF; HoPM (1975 ed.); ILP (1975 ed.); MPo; NOBE; OxBTC; PoIA; PPoD; SoS; SoSe; UnPo (1976 ed.); UsP; VoPo; WIF

Naming the State Bird.  Keith Gunderson.  HeS

Nancy Hanks.  Rosemary *and* Stephen Vincent Benét.  ECBV

Nancy Hanks, Mother of Abraham Lincoln.  Vachel Lindsay.  CMoP (1970 ed.)

Nancy Lee, *with music.*  Frederick E. Weatherly.  BLSH

Nancy, the hogs don't know us.  Mirror for the Barnyard.  Jack Myers.  AmPA

Nancy, You Dance.  Michael L. Johnson.  AMV-81

Nani.  A. A. Rios.  GP

Nansen.  Gary Snyder.  InPS

Nantucket.  William Carlos Williams.  HAP; TAP; WeW

Nantucket's Widows.  Richard Foerster.  AMV-81

Naomi Wise.  *Unknown.*  AmFP

Napoleon.  Walter de la Mare.  FaBoTw (1975 ed.); NOBE

Napoleon.  Miroslav Holub, *tr. fr. Czechoslovakian by* Kaca Polackova.  EC

Napoleon hoped that all the world would fall beneath his sway.  *Unknown.*  FaBoCo

Napoleon is standing with his pants upon the floor.  The Poor Old Prurient Interest Blues.  John Hartford.  MAT

Napoleon writes me.  The Departed Friend.  Salvador Novo.  TVo

Nappy Head Blues.  *Unknown.*  BluL

Narcissist's eye is blue, fringed with white and covered, The.  The Eye.  Michael Benedikt.  ConAP

Narcissus.  William Cowper.  PCOP

Narcissus, Photographer.  Erica Jong.  SoSe (1977 ed.)

Narcissus: To Himself.  David Galler.  PoA

Narrative.  Russell Atkins.  PoBA

Narrative Hooper and L.D.O. Sestina with a Long Last Line, The.  James Whitehead.  HoPM (1975 ed.); TAT

Narrator's Trance, The, *sels.*  James Cunningham.  JB
  "And birds came crying."
  "Song thumbed down a cruiser for a ride, A."
  "There were blood spots on the skirt."
  "Woods are overhead over everywhere, The."

Narrow Door, The.  Charlotte Mew.  SBG

Narrow fellow in the grass, A.  Emily Dickinson.  AnMo; BoWoP; CABA (1972 ed.); CMoP (1970 ed.); HAP; HoPM (1975 ed.); ILP (1975 ed.); IP; IPWM; NIL; NOBA; PBMP; PiAm; PoIA; PPM; PPoe; PPP; SoSe (1977 ed.); TAP; TT; VoPo; WeW

Narrow paths branch every way up here, The.  On Holmbury Hill.  Edward Shanks.  PES

Narrow Sea, The.  Robert Graves.  FaBoEE

Narrow Street, A.  Michael Small.  DNGG

Narrow water, channel water.  Channel Water.  Virginia Scott Miner.  AMV-80

Narrowing of knowledge to one window to a door, A.  Elegy for William Soutar.  William Montgomerie.  MS

Nasal whine of power whips a new universe, The.  Hart Crane.  *Fr.* The Bridge, IV.  NIL

Nashville Stonewall Blues.  *Unknown.*  BluL

Nat Turner.  Samuel Allen.  CNA; FB

Nat Turner in the Clearing.  Alvin Aubert.  CoPAm

Nathan Hale.  Francis Miles Finch.  BTTM

Nathan Hale.  *Unknown.*  BTTM

Nathaniel Lee to Sir Roger L'Estrange.  Nathaniel Lee.  FaBoEE

Nation.  Charlie Cobb.  PoBA

Nation.  Mendel Naigreshel, *tr. fr. Yiddish by* Joachim Neugroschel.  VWA

Nation of trees, drab green and desolate grey, A.  Australia.  A. D. Hope.  GAS

Nation Wrapped in Stone, A.  Roberta Hill.  BoWoP; CDW

National Animal, The.  Barry Schechter.  FiCh

National Cold Storage Company.  Harvey Shapiro.  MAT; NYP; VGW

National Miner, The.  *Unknown.*  AmFP

National Security.  Archibald MacLeish.  GOA

National Shrine.  X. J. Kennedy.  CoPAm

National Winter Garden.  Hart Crane.  *Fr.* The Bridge: Three Songs.  InPS

Nationalism.  Harry Roskolenko.  AMV-80

Nationality.  Mary Gilmore.  GAS; MAuV

Nations That Long in Darkness Walked, *with music.*  John Barnard.  AH

Native African Revolutionaries.  Paul Jones.  AMV-80

Native American Studies, University of California at Berkeley 1975.  Wendy Rose.  NW

Native Born.  Eve Langley.  WPE

Native Companions Dancing.  John Shaw Neilson.  GAS

Native Element.  William Jeffrey.  MS

Native Land.  Sir Walter Scott.  *See* This Is My Own, My Native Land.

Nativity.  John Donne.  SCP-1

Nativity, The.  William Drummond of Hawthornden.  SCP-2

Nativity of Christ, The.  Robert Southwell.  BoReV

Nativity of Our Lord and Saviour Jesus Christ, The.  Christopher Smart.  *Fr.* Hymns and Spiritual Songs.  BoReV; EBEV; HAP; LAuP; NOBE; OBP; WeW

Natura Naturans.  Arthur Hugh Clough.  HAP; VLP; VPC

Natural Grace, A.  C. K. Stead.  ATNZ

Natural History.  Richard Howard.  TAP

Natural History.  Robert Penn Warren.  FF

Natural History of Dragons and Unicorns My Daughter and I Have Known, A.  William Pitt Root.  AMV-81

Natural Law.  Babette Deutsch.  RiTi

Natural Magic.  Robert Browning.  VLP

Natural Mother, The.  Jay MacPherson.  CABA (1972 ed.)

Natural Odes/ American Elegies, *sels.*  Robert Dana.  HeS
  "Christmas day," 39.
  "It was not quite winter," 42
  "We had known from the beginning this could happen," 38.

Natural Order of Things, The.  Harley Elliott.  NeAC

Natural pussy.  Bitter Herbs.  Alta.  NMM

Natural world is a spiritual house, The.  Intimate Associations.  Baudelaire, *tr. by* Robert Bly.  NU

Naturalist, The.  Margaret Reynolds.  MIS

Naturally.  Audre Lorde.  CNA

Naturally it is night.  Air.  W. S. Merwin.  CAPP

Naturally it was the naked moon.  Moon Song.  Hildegarde Flanner.  AMV-81

Naturally we would prefer seven epiphanies. Jim Harrison. *Fr.* Letters to Yesenin. TC

Nature. Arthur J. Bull. HeHu

Nature, ("The rounded world is fair to see"). Emerson. ILP (1975 ed.)

Nature ("A subtle chain of countless rings"). Emerson. ILP (1975 ed.)

Nature. Longfellow. AmVN; TAP

Nature, *sel.* David Meltzer. "His or her's." CPA

Nature/ leaks like a tub and not a boat. Samuel Butler. *Fr.* Arts and Sciences. SCP-2

Nature and Art. Oliver Herford. TDH

Nature and Nature's laws lay hid in night. Intended for Sir Isaac Newton. Pope. FaBoCo; FaBoEE; ILP (1975 ed.); InPK; IP; QQQ; WeW

Nature, Creation's law, is judged by sense. Upon Love Fondly Refused for Conscience's Sake. Thomas Randolph. OAEL-1

Nature had long a treasure made. The Match. Andrew Marvell. EBEV

Nature had made them hide in crevices. New Hampshire, February. Richard Eberhart. SS

Nature herself doth Scotchmen beasts confess. John Cleveland. *Fr.* The Rebel Scot. OBSV

Nature is a temple where living pillars. Correspondences. Baudelaire, *tr. by* Anthony Hartley. NAWM-2

Nature Lover. John Frederick Nims. CoPAm

Nature might chicken out, but "I love you." X. J. Kennedy. PeD

Nature Morte. Louis MacNeice. NoAM

Nature of Jungles, The. W. R. Moses. NCSH

Nature of Man, The. C. H. Sisson. FaBoTw (1975 ed.)

Nature of the beast is the, The. Small Comment. Sonia Sanchez. NIL

Nature Study, after Dufy. Helen Bevington. CSP

Nature that day a woman was in weakness. A Storm in Summer. Wilfrid Scawen Blunt. FaBoTw (1975 ed.)

Nature that washed [*or* washt] her hands in milk[e]. A Poem of Sir Walter Rawleighs. Sir Walter Ralegh. AAS; CABA (1972 ed.)

Nature the gentlest mother is. Emily Dickinson. SoSe (1977 ed.)

Nature, which is the vast creation's soul. To Mr. Henry Lawes. Katherine Philips. SBG; WPE

Nature, with endless being rife. A Demonstration. Coventry Patmore. *Fr.* The Angel in the House. VLP

Nature withheld Cassandra in the skies. Pierre de Ronsard, *tr. fr. French by* Keats. OBVE

Nature's confectioner, the bee. Fuscara; or, The Bee-Errant. John Cleveland. SCP-2

Nature's Cook, *sel.* Margaret Cavendish, Duchess of Newcastle. "Death is the cook of nature, and we find." PBWP; SCP-2

Nature's Dessert, *sel.* Margaret Cavendish, Duchess of Newcastle. "Sweet marmalade of kisses newly gathered." SCP-2

Nature's Embassy, *sel.* Richard Brathwaite. I Am Not as I Wish. SCP-2

Nature's first green is gold. Nothing Gold Can Stay. Robert Frost. AnMo; ILP (1975 ed.); NCSH; NIL; NOBA; PPP; SoSe (1977 ed.); STS; TAP; TSWA; VGW

Nature's great masterpiece, an elephant. The Elephant. John Donne. *Fr.* The Progresse of the Soule. OBP

Nature's Hymn to the Deity. John Clare. VLP

Nature's Landskip, *sel.* Margaret Cavendish, Duchess of Newcastle. "I standing on a hill of fancies high." SCP-2

Nature's lay idiot, I taught thee to love. Elegy VII. John Donne. *Fr.* Elegies. SCP-1

Nature's Lineaments. Robert Graves. FaBoTw (1975 ed.)

Nature's Prospect. Margaret Cavendish, Duchess of Newcastle. SCP-2

Nature's Questioning. Thomas Hardy. IPWM; PBMP; VLP

Nature's Reply to Mutability. Spenser. *Fr.* The Faerie Queene, VII, 7. NOBE

Naught loves another as itself. *See* Nought loves another as itself.

Naughty Boy. Robert Creeley. NoAM; NOBA; VoA

Naughty Boy, The. Keats. *See* Song about Myself.

Naughty Paughty Jack-a-Dandy. Namby-Pamby. Henry Carey. FaBoNo

Naughty Young Nat. Isabel Frances Bellows. TDH

Nausicaa with Some Attendants. Tom Lowenstein. VWA

Nausicaa's girls. Peter Whigham. *Fr.* Astapovo, or What Are We to Do. TwMBP

Nautical Ballad, A. Charles E. Carryl. *See* Capital Ship, A.

Nautical Ballad. Keighley Goodchild. ECBV

Nautical Extravaganza, A. Wallace Irwin. PoTa

Nautilus Island's hermit. Skunk Hour. Robert Lowell. BiP; CAPP; CMoP (1970 ed.); ConAP; HAP; HeIP; ILP (1975 ed.); InPK; LFH; NIL; NoAM; NOBA; PiAm; PPP; STS; TAP; TCP; WeW

Nauvoo. Bayard Taylor. OBAL

Navajo. William Haskel Simpson. BPAW

Navajo Girl of Many Farms. Charles G. Ballard. VW

Navajo Poem. Warren Woessner. HeS

Navajo Signs. Winifred Fields Walters. VW

Navajo Song. Maynard Dixon. BPAW

Navy Hymn, The, William Whiting. *See* Eternal Father, Strong to Save.

Nay but you, who do not love her. Song. Robert Browning. VoPo

Nay! Ivy, Nay! *Unknown. See* Holly and His Merry Men.

Nay, lady, one frown is enough. To Helen in a Huff. Nathaniel Parker Willis. OBAL

Nay, Lord, not thus! white lilies in the spring. Sonnet on Hearing the Dies Irae Sung in the Sistine Chapel. Oscar Wilde. PIM

Nay, nay, my boy—'tis not for me. Fie on Eastern Luxury! Horace, *tr. by* Hartley Coleridge. Odes, I, 38. InPK

Nay, painter, if thou dar'st design that fight. The Second Advice to a Painter. Andrew Marvell. APAS

Nay, prithee dear, draw nigher. A Loose Saraband. Richard Lovelace. CaPo

Nay, *that*, furini, never I at least. With Francis Furini. Robert Browning. *Fr.* Parleyings with Certain People of Importance in Their Day. VLP

Nay, traveller! rest. This lonely yew-tree stands. Lines Left upon a Seat in a Yew-Tree. Wordsworth. MBPR

Nazi Headquarters: El Monte, California. William Burns. PoW

Ndaaya's Kàsàlà, *sel.* Citèkù Ndaaya, *tr. after French-Luba texts by* Judith Gleason. "Ndaaya, I, am so poor." PBWP

Ne Plus Ultra. Samuel Taylor Coleridge. MBPR; OAEL-2

Neaera when I'm there is adamant. J. V. Cunningham, *after the Latin of* George Buchanan. OBVE

Neap-tide and the ebbing days slide. A Song of Sickness. Hine Tangikuku, *tr. by* Barry Mitcalfe. WTO

Neaps are ow'er champit, The. Love in Edinburgh. Nicholas Fairbairn. SLP

Near. Abba Kovner, *tr. fr. Hebrew by* Shirley Kaufman. VWA

Near. William Stafford. ConAP; UsP

Near a Waterfall at Ryumon. Lady Ise, *tr. fr. Japanese by* Etsuko Terasaki *and* Irma Brandeis. BoWoP

Near and Far. Harry Behn. LCL

Near Avalon. William Morris. OAEL-2

Near Caledonia. Patricia Henley. NPW

Near Catalonia. Joy Davidman. SPT

Near Ganado. Lucile Adler. PoW

Near Hampton Court there lies a common. Hounslow Heath. *Unknown.* APAS

Near Kyoto, around 1900. Cloisonne. Jane Flanders. PoUp

Near Lanivet, 1872. Thomas Hardy. CMoP (1970 ed.); ILP (1975 ed.); NoAM

Near Midnight. Norman MacCaig. SLP

Near Rhydcymerau. Rhydcymerau. D. Gwenallt Jones, *tr. by* Anthony Conran. OBW

Near the Border of Insanities. Dannie Abse. PoA

Near the celebrated Lido where the breeze is fresh and free. Longfellow's Visit to Venice. John Betjeman. NOBL

Near the Cymmerians, in his dark abode. Ovid, *tr. by* Dryden. *Fr.* Metamorphoses, XI. OBVE

Near the Death of Ovid. Robert Conquest. NoAM

Near the mountain's summit, when the bells. The Fox. R. Williams Parry, *tr. by* Gwyn Williams. OBW

Near the Ocean. Robert Lowell. NOBA

Near the Old Slave Fort. Joseph Bruchac. FAF

Near the Vipsanian columns where the aqueduct. Martial, *tr. fr. Latin by* Peter Porter. OBVE

Near the White House. Michael S. Harper. NW

Near this spot. Epitaph to a Dog [*or* An Epitaph: Inscription on a Monument at Newstead Abbey]. Byron. BoAnP; GDP

Near to me as my flesh, my flesh and blood. Allen Tate. *Fr.* Sonnets of the Blood. PoA

Near to the Rose where punks in numbers flock. The Play-House. Joseph Addison. APAS

Near to the silver Trent. Michael Drayton. *Fr.* The Shepherd's Sirena. SCP-2

Near yonder copse, where once the garden smiled. The Parson. Goldsmith. *Fr.* The Deserted Village. PIM

Neare Enna walles there standes a Lake Pergusa is the name. Ovid, *tr. by* Arthur Golding. *Fr.* Metamorphoses, V. OBVE

Nearer. Judith Herzberg, *tr. fr. Dutch by* Shirley Kaufman. BoWoP; VWA

Nearer, My God, to Thee. Sarah Flower Adams. BLSH, *with music*; FSW; VLP

Nearer the pulse than other themes. A True Picture Restored. Vernon Watkins. NoAM

Nearing Again the Legendary Isle. C. Day Lewis. *Fr.* The Magnetic Mountain. FaBoTw (1975 ed.)

Nearing the Snow-Line. Oliver Wendell Holmes. PiAm

Nearly dark; warm stones of the wall in the woods. The Owl. Thorkild Bjornvig, *tr. by* Robert Bly. NU

Nearly Everybody Loves Harvey Martin. William D. Barney. LiSp

Nearly right, The. To the Tune of the Coventry Carol. Stevie Smith. FaBoTw (1975 ed.)

Nebraska. Jon Swan. RFM

Nebraskan Childhood. Daniel Halpern. CAAP

Nebuchadnezzar. Elinor Wylie. SBG

Necessary Bucket, A. Peter Meinke. AATT

Necessitarian's Epitaph, A. Thomas Hardy. FaBoEE

Necessities of Life. Adrienne Rich. NIL; NoAM; NOBA; Psy

Necessity. Harry Graham. FaBoCo

Necessity. Langston Hughes. NOBA

Necrological. John Crowe Ransom. PiAm

Necropolis. Karl Shapiro. PoA

Nectar, puff of sails, lily. To a Young Girl. David Rosenmann-Taub, *tr. by* Charles Guenther. VWA

Ned Bratts. Robert Browning. VLP

Ned Vaughan. Walter de la Mare. FaBoEE

Neddy Nibble'm and Biddy Finn. *Unknown.* GBP

Need five bucks to Boston. On My Way to Boston Need Five Bucks. Jack Micheline. CPA

Need of Being Versed in Country Things, The. Robert Frost. NoAM; NOBA; PiAm; UnPo (1976 ed.)

Need to Love, The. Shlomo Vinner, *tr. fr. Hebrew by* Laya Firestone *and* Howard Schwartz. VWA

Needing nothing, not lonely nor bored. Creation Morning. X. J. Kennedy. UsP

Needle of dawn has drugged them, life and death, The. Dawn Wind on the Islands. Francis Webb. GAS

Needles and Pins. Mark Van Doren. SO

Needles and pins, needles and pins. Mother Goose. MG

Needle's Eye, The. *Unknown.* AmFP

Needs. A. R. Ammons. NIL; OBAL; UsP

Needs no introduction. My Woman. A. D. Winans. AMV-80

"Needy Knife-grinder! whither are you going?" The Friend of Humanity and the Knife-Grinder. George Canning *and* John Hookham Frere. FaBoCo

Needy were lined up by order of famine, The. The Offended. Anne Hébert, *tr. by* Willis Barnstone. BoWoP

Neep-Fields by the Sea, The. Violet Jacob. MS

Negative Passage. Michael Newman. PoA

Negative tree, you are belief. Bound. Theodore Roethke. PoA

Negatives. Charles Wright. PoA

Negotiations. John T. Zaremba. DNGG

Negritude. James A. Emanuel. BPo; CNA

Negro, The. James A. Emanuel. HoPM (1975 ed.); IP

Negro Dreams. Doughtry Long. PoBA

Negro Hero. Gwendolyn Brooks. CAPP

Negro in a Chesterfield, A. Street Scenes from All Over. Elisavietta Ritchie. AATT

Negro Love Song, A. Paul Laurence Dunbar. ILP (1975 ed.)

Negro Peddler's Song, A. Fenton Johnson. AmNP (1974 ed.)

Negro Servant. Langston Hughes. AmNP (1974 ed.)

Negro Soldier's Civil War Chant. *Unknown.* BPo (Black Soldier's Civil War Chant.) TAP

Negro Soldier's Viet Nam Diary, A. Herbert Martin. PoBA

Negro Speaks of Rivers, The. Langston Hughes. AmNP (1974 ed.); BPo; CABA (1972 ed.); CoPAm; HAP;HeIP; NIL; NoAM; NOBA; PiAm; PoBA; SoS; TAP; TSWA

Negro sprouts from the pavement like an asparagus, A. Stumpfoot on 42nd Street. Louis Simpson. NNaP; NYP; TCP; UnPo (1976 ed.); VGW

Negro Woman. Lewis Alexander. PoBA

Negro Woman, A. William Carlos Williams. IPWM

Negroes/ Sweet and docile. Warning. Langston Hughes. BPo

Negroes turned black overnight. The Sixties. Thomas Listmann. AMV-80

Negro's Tragedy, The. Claude McKay. BPo; LFH

Negrun. Lucille F. Travis. AATT

Nehi Blues. *Unknown.* BluL

Neighbor. Charles Waterman. GP

Neighbor, The. Miller Williams. GP

Neighbour sits in his window and plays the flute, The. Music. Amy Lowell. OSP; RiTi

Neighbor thought that they, A. The Planetary Arc-Light. August Derleth. ECBV

Neighbors. David Allan Evans. HeS

Neighbours. Patrick King. IPM

Neighbors. Charles Malam. AMV-80

Neïla. Yvan Goll, *tr. fr. French by* Anthony Rudolf. VWA

Neither earth nor sky. Hashin, *tr. fr. Japanese.* WeW

Neither Hook nor Line. Bunyan. LiSp

Neither in idleness consume thy days. Walter Savage Landor. FaBoEE

Neither of us/ could do much. The Competitors. Helen Luster. PoW

Neither on horseback nor seated. Walt Whitman at Bear Mountain. Louis Simpson. ConAP; ILP (1975 ed.)

Neither our vices nor our virtues. Poetry, a Natural Thing. Robert Duncan. NoAM; NOBA

Neither Out Far nor In Deep. Robert Frost. CABA (1972 ed.); HAP; NoAM; NOBA; PoIA; PSN; TAP; TT; WeW

Neither Spirit nor Bird. Mary Austin, *after Shoshone Indian.* BPAW

Neither This nor That. Luis Palés Matos, *tr. fr. Spanish by* Julio Marzán. InW

Neither Up nor Down. Judith Rodriguez. FPA

Nelly Bly. Stephen Collins Foster. FSW

Nelly Kelly loved baseball games. Take Me Out to the Ball Game. Jack Norworth. OBAL

Nemea. Lawrence Durrell. FaBoTw (1975 ed.)

Nemesis. Emerson. NOBA

Nemo Canem Impune Lacessit. Robert Garioch. MS

Neo-Classical Urn, The. Robert Lowell. STS

Neo-Thomist Poem. Ernest Hemingway. OBAL

Neon glow escapes from, The. West End Blues. John Hollander. NYP

Nepenthe, *sels.* George Darley.
　Hundred-gated Thebes. NOBE
　"O blest unfabled incense tree." BIrV
　(Phoenix, The.) NOBE; OAEL-2

Nephelidia. Swinburne. *Fr.* The Heptalogia. FaBoCo; FaBoNo; HoPM (1975 ed.); SpRo

Neptune. Eleanor Farjeon. EcS

Neptune. Milton. *Fr.* Comus. EcS

Neptune and Mars in council sate. Louisburg. *Unknown.* BTTM

Neptune, besides the sway. Neptune. Milton. *Fr.* Comus. EcS

Neptune—Polka. Edith Sitwell. NOBE

Neptune sat in his chariot high. Thomas Heyrick. *Fr.* The Submarine Voyage: A Pindaric Poem in Four Parts. SCP-2

Nerve to make a high toss and the sense, The. Tennis. Robert Pinsky. PCho

Nerves. "Sagittarius." OxBTC

Nerves. Arthur Symons. FaBoTw (1975 ed.)

Nervous hose is dribbling on the tar, A. The Roof Garden. Howard Moss. MAT; NYP

Nervous poet sings again, The. Ode to Mexican Experience. Luís Omar Salinas. SA

Nervy with neons, the main drag. At Barstow. Charles Tomlinson. NIL; NoAM

Nesting. Edward Lear. *See* Limerick: "There was an old man with a beard."

Nesting. Dennis Saleh. NeAC

Nesting Time. Arthur Guiterman. ECBV

Nesting Time. Douglas Stewart. BoAnP

Nestor. Homer, *tr. fr. Greek by* Ennis Rees. *Fr.* The Iliad, XXIII. LiSp

Nests. Bruce Weber. PoUp

Net, The. W. R. Rodgers. BoLoP; CIP

Net rests on the water's surface, The. Elena Clementelli, *tr. by* Ruth Feldman *and* Brian Swann. *Fr.* Etruscan Notebook. PBWP

Nets on the Andrea Doria, The. Karen G. Tepfer. AMV-81

Nettles. Vernon Scannell. HeHu

Nettles in May. Euros Bowen. OBW

Neuteronomy. Eve Merriam. QQQ

Neutral British Gentlemen, The. "Orpheus C. Kerr." OBAL

Neutral Tones. Thomas Hardy. CABA (1972 ed.); CMoP (1970 ed.); HAP; HeIP; ILP (1975 ed.); InPK; LoAs; NoAM; OAEL-2; PPP; SS; UnPo (1976 ed.); VLP

Nevada. Stanley Noyes. PH

Never. George Reavey. BIrV

Never a careworn wife but shows. Wives in the Sere. Thomas Hardy. NOBE; VLP

Never Again, The. Charles Dobzynski, *tr. fr. French by* Anita Barrows. VWA

Never again, Orpheus. Antipater of Sidon, *tr. fr. Greek by* Kenneth Rexroth. OBVE

Never Again Would Birds' Song Be the Same. Robert Frost. HAP; InPK; NIL; NoAM; VGW

Never and never, my girl riding far and near. In Country Sleep. Dylan Thomas. ILP (1975 ed.)

Never ask of money spent. The Hardship of Accounting. Robert Frost. FaBoCo; OBAL

Never be fool enough to think. Love Song. Patricia Beer. HeHu

Never believe all you hear. Wolf. Kenneth Rexroth. *Fr.* A Bestiary. NNaP

Never, believe me/ Appear the Immortals. The Visit of the Gods. Schiller, *tr. by* Samuel Taylor Coleridge. OBVE

Never could I think/ Our love a worldly commonplace. Izumi Shikibu, *tr. fr. Japanese by* Edwin A. Cranston. PBWP

Never did get down there to Washington. Marble. A. R. Ammons. WasP

Never forget the moors. Summer Song for Me and My Aunts. Patricia Beer. HeHu

Never Give All the Heart. W. B. Yeats. BoLoP; CMoP (1970 ed.); LoAs

Never going off, always here, I. Away. Josephine Miles. GP

Never in This World You Will Drop a Yellow Sponge. Rochelle Owens. WBN

Never Let Your Left Hand Know. *Unknown.* BluL

Never Love Unless[e] You Can. Thomas Campion. AAS; ILP (1975 ed.)

Never May the Fruit Be Plucked. Edna St. Vincent Millay. SBG

Never pain to tell thy love. Blake. MBPR; OAEL-2; STS

Never pass a nun. How to Walk in a Crowd. Robert Hershon. FF

Never Pharaoh's night. In the Desert. Herman Melville. PiAm

Never presume that in this marble stable. The Brass Horse. Drummond Allison. FaBoTw (1975 ed.)

Never said/ a word. Adam's Apple. Coleman Barks. *Fr.* Body Poems. NVAP

Never Said a Mumbalin' Word. *Unknown.* GBP

Never saw him. The Negro. James A. Emanuel. HoPM (1975 ed.); IP

Never say that there is only death for you. Zog Nit Keynmol (Tell Us No More). *Unknown, tr. fr. Yiddish.* FSW

Never Seek to Tell Thy Love. Blake. *See* Love's Secret.

"Never shall a young man." For Anne Gregory. W. B. Yeats. BiP; BuTh; CMoP (1970 ed.); Epi; ExPo (1973 ed.); InPK; PFIr; SFF; SS; TPo

Never so strong as to fly unassisted, I have left. The Red/White Blues. Wendy Rose. NW

Never Such Love. Robert Graves. BoLoP

Never take her away. Song. Vinícius de Moraes, *tr. by* Richard Wilbur. RRA

Never talk down to a glowworm. Glowworm. David McCord. ECBV

Never Tell. *Unknown, tr. fr. Welsh by* Anthony Conran. OBW

Never think you fortune can bear the sway. On Fortune. Elizabeth I, Queen of England. PBWP; WPE

Never to fight unless from a pure motive. Bottleneck. Louis MacNeice. SFF

Never to remember. Accident. Sydney Lea. NYP

Never to see a nation born. James Russell Lowell. *Fr.* Under the Old Elm. GOA

Never until the mankind making. A Refusal to Mourn the Death, by Fire, of a Child in London. Dylan Thomas. AnMo; BuTh; CABA (1972 ed.); CMoP (1970 ed.); EBEV; FF; HeIP; HoPM (1975 ed.); IP; LFH; MPo; NIL; NoAM; NOBE; OAEL-2; OBW; OxBTC; TT; UnPo (1976 ed.); VoPo

Never was there a man much uglier. Vain Gratuities. E. A. Robinson. SS

Never Weather-beaten Sail. Thomas Campion. *See* O Come Quickly!

Nevertheless. Marianne Moore. CMoP (1970 ed.)

Nevertheless I prefer . . .1968. . . Petra von Morstein, *tr. by* Rosemarie Waldrop. BoWoP

New Ahasuerus, The. Jozsef Kiss, *tr. fr. Hungarian by* André Ungar. VWA

New air has come around us. Dakota: October, 1822, Hunkpapa Warrior. Rod Taylor. WeW

New Ancient of Days, The. Herman Melville. OBAL

New and Old Gospel. Nate Mackey. CNA

New Antigone, The, *sel.* Thomas Parkinson. "Twenty five years of the endless war." MIT

New Approach Needed. Kingsley Amis. OxBTC; TPo

New Arm, The. Tom Hennen. HeS

New Ballad, A. Arthur Mainwaring. APAS

New Ballad, A. *Unknown.* APAS

New Ballad, to an Old Tune, Called, I Am the Duke of Norfolk, etc., A. *Unknown.* APAS

New Birth, The. Jones Very. AmVN; NOBA; PiAm

New Block. Patric Dickinson. LP

New blue notebook can make anyone a poet, A. Late Night at the Hamburg Inn. Cinda Kornblum. AcAn

New Cake of Soap, The. Ezra Pound. PAIC

New Calf, The. James Hearst. TAT

New Calf, The. Frances Downing Vaughan. AMV-80

New Catch in Praise of the Reverend Bishops, A. *Unknown.* APAS

New Cecilia, The. Thomas Lovell Beddoes. OAEL-2

New-Chum's First Trip, The. *Unknown.* FaBoBa

New Coasts and Poseidon's Son. Homer, *tr. fr. Greek by* Robert Fitzgerald. The Odyssey, IX. WTO

New Colossus, The. Emma Lazarus. FaPo; SBG; WPE

New Coventry Cathedral, The. Arthur J. Bull. HeHu

New Cows, The. Charles Waterman. GP

New Day, A. Philip Levine. MPA

New Dialogue, Sung by a Boy and Girl at the Playhouse, A. Thomas Durfey. SCP-2

New diet, A. Figures and Ground. Robert Leverant. MIT

New Direction, The. Emerson Blackhorse Mitchell. VW

New Dolores Leather Bar, The. Turner Cassity. CSP

New Dress, A. Rachel Korn, *tr. fr. Yiddish by* Ruth Whitman. VWA

New Emigration, The. Kay Boyle. WPE

New England. E. A. Robinson. CABA (1972 ed.); GOA; HeIP; NOBA; PiAm; STS; TAP

New England Bachelor, A. Richard Eberhart. NoAM

New England: Driving Back in Early April. Frank Stewart. PHC

New England Farm, August 1914, A. Les A. Murray. GAS

New England Greenhouse. Rennie McQuilkin. AMV-80

New England Pilgrimage, *sel.* Phyllis McGinley. Customs of the Country, The. TH

New England Protestant. Richard Eberhart. *Fr.* Attitudes. TH

New England Sampler, A. John Malcolm Brinnin. GOA

New England's mytilus, its old-blue tidal shell. Traits: Inner Portrait. Jeremy Ingalls. FoP

New Every Morning. John Keble. FaPoR

New Excavations. Leonora Speyer. *Fr.* Pompeii. TH

New Farm Tractor. Carl Sandburg. AKE

New Fashions. George Moses Horton. OBAL

New Formalists, The. Marvin Bell. AMV-81

New Genesis, A. Avraham Shlonsky, *tr. fr. Hebrew by* Francis Landy. VWA

New Girls, The. Douglas Dunn. MS

New Graveyard: Jerusalem. Shirley Kaufman. VWA

New Hampshire. T. S. Eliot. Landscapes, I. BiP; WeW

New Hampshire. Donald Hall. UsP

New Hampshire, February. Richard Eberhart. SS

New Heaven and Earth. D. H. Lawrence. CMoP (1970 ed.)

New Heaven, New War. Robert Southwell. BoReV; NOBE

New House, The. Edward Thomas. EBEV; NOBE; OBW

New Houses, New Clothes. D. H. Lawrence. BBGO

New Icarus, The. Vassar Miller. TPo

New Jail. *Unknown.* AmFP

New Jerusalem, A. Blake. *See* And Did Those Feet in Ancient Time.

New Kelso. Roderick Watson. MIS

New Leda, The. Barbara Howes. RiTi

New light gives new directions, fortunes new. George Chapman. *Fr.* Hero and Leander, Third Sestiad. OAEL-1

New Lines for Cuscuscaraway and Mirza Murad Ali Beg. Louis Simpson. OBAL

New Litany in the Year 1684, A. *Unknown.* APAS

New Little Boy, The. Harry Behn. LCL

New Lost Feminist, The. Rita Mae Brown. WBN

New Man, The. Jones Very. NOBA

New man flies in from Manchester, A. A New Poet Arrives. Gavin Ewart. OxBTC

New Mexican Desert. Witter Bynner. BPAW

New Mexican Mountain. Robinson Jeffers. GOA; InPS; NoAM

New Mexico Sky. Bill Pearlman. FoP

New Minglewood Blues. *Unknown.* BluL

New Mistress, The. A. E. Housman. SoSe

New Moon. *Aborigine Oral Tradition,* tr. by R. M. Berndt. *Fr.* The Moon-Bone Cycle. WTO

New Moon, The. Samuel Taylor Coleridge. *Fr.* Dejection; an Ode. FSFS

New Moon, The. Issa, *tr. fr. Japanese by* Harold G. Henderson. Moon

New Moon, The. Sara Teasdale. Moon

New moon in the sky. Haiku. Basho, *tr. by* Nobuyuki Yuasa. PAIC

New Morality, *sel.* George Canning *and* John Hookham Frere. "Sweet sensibility, that dwells enshrined." ESaP

New Morning. Bob Dylan. GrRo

New Mystic, The. Al Young. NW

New neighbors came to the corner house at Congress and Green streets. Clean Curtains. Carl Sandburg. PoIA

New Notebook, The. Maria Banus, *tr. fr. Rumanian by* Laura Schiff and Dana Beldiman. PBWP

New Nutcracker Suite, The, *sel.* Ogden Nash. "Little girl marched around her Christmas tree, A." PChr

New Philosophy, The. John Donne. *Fr.* An Anatomy of the World: The First Anniversary. ExPo (1973 ed.)

New Pietà, The: For the Mothers and Children of Detroit. Clarence Major. PoBA

New Poem, A. Robert Duncan. NNaP

New Poem, The. Charles Wright. CoPAm

New Poet Arrives, A.   Gavin Ewart.   OxBTC

New Potatoes.   Ken Belford.   NeAC

New Prince, New Pomp.   Robert Southwell.   NOBE; PIM

New professional group, A.   Stacking Up.   Rita Rosenfeld.
    AMV-81

New Proverb.   Shirley Brooks.   FaBoNo

New Quotas/ or Booker T. and Garvey Would Haved Loved
    South Africa.   Antar S. K. Mberi.   SES

New River Train.   *Unknown.*   FSW

New road runs into, The.   Directions.   William Matthews.
    AmPA

New Season.   Philip Levine.   NNaP

New servant maid named Maria, A.   Fire!   *Unknown.*   TDH

New Siege, A: An Historical Meditation, *sel.*   John Montague.
    "Lines of history. Lines of defiance."   CIP

New Simile in the Manner of Swift, A.   Goldsmith.   LAuP

New Skills.   Naomi Shihab Nye.   PH

New Song, A.   Seamus Heaney.   FaBoTw (1975 ed.)

New Song Made in Honour of His Grace the Duke of
    Marlborough, A.   Thomas Durfey.   SCP-2

New Song of New Similies, A.   John Gay.   FaBoCo; NOBL

New Song on the Birth of the Prince of Wales, A.   *Unknown.*
    FaBoBa; VLP

New Song on the Taxes, A.   *Unknown.*   WTO

New Spoon River, The, *sels.*   Edgar Lee Masters.
    Benjamin Franklin Hazard.   GOA
    Marx the Sign Painter.   NoAM; TAP
    Meredith Phyfe.   GOA
    Rhoda Pitkin.   NoAM
    Unknown Soldiers.   NoAM; TAP

New Spring.   Juan Ramón Jiménez, *tr. fr. Spanish by* H. R. Hays.
    OLR

New Storefront.   Russell Atkins.   FB

New Streets.   F. A. Nettelbeck.   EC

New Strip.   Peter Wild.   EC

New Style, The.   David O'Bruadair, *tr. fr. Irish by* John
    Montague.   BIrV

New Tenants, The.   E. A. Robinson.   NoAM

New Territory.   Eavan Boland.   CIP

New Uses for Old Utensils.   Edward Proffitt.   PoIA

New Vestments, The.   Edward Lear.   RAE

New Vicar of Bray, The.   Colin Ellis.   NOBL

New Way, Old Way.   David W. Martinez.   VW

New Wife, The.   *Gond Oral Tradition, tr. by* V. Elwin *and* S.
    Hivale.   WTO

New World, The.   Amiri Baraka.   NoAM

New World, The.   Jones Very.   AmVN; ILP (1975 ed.)

New Worlds for Old.   Louis Johnson.   ATNZ

New Year, The.   Kenneth Rexroth.   MPA

New Year, The.   Mark Strand.   *Fr.* Elegy for My Father.   UnPo
    (1976 ed.)

New Year, The.   Tennyson   *See* Ring Out, Wild Bells.

New Year, The.   *Unknown.*   CTV

New Year for Trees, The.   Howard Schwartz.   VWA

New Year Letter, *sels.*   W. H. Auden.
    "Long time since it seems to-day, A."   GOA
    "O Unicorn among the cedars."   BoReV; NoAM

New Year 1974.   Rae Desmond Jones.   CAAP

New Year's.   Charles Reznikoff.   VGW
    "This is the autumn and our harvest," *sel.*   OFD

New Year's Day.   Robert Lowell.   CABA (1972 ed.); ConAP;
    PPoe

New Year's Eve.   Thomas Hardy.   NoAM

New Year's Eve.   A. E. Housman.   VLP

New Year's Eve.   D. H. Lawrence.   BoLoP

New Year's Eve in Solitude.   Robert Mezey.   VWA

New-Year's Gift Sent to Sir Simeon Steward, A.   Robert Herrick.
    CaPo

New Year's Sacrifice, A: To Lucinda.   Thomas Carew.   CaPo

New Year's Song.   Ted Hughes.   OFD

New Year's Water.   *Unknown.*   CC; GBP; OFD; POL

New York.   Edward Field.   NYP

New York.   Federico García Lorca, *tr. fr. Spanish by* Robert Bly.
    EC; NU; NYP

New York.   Thom Gunn.   NYP

New York.   Marianne Moore.   NYP

New York.   Léopold Sédar Senghor, *tr. fr. French by* Ellen Conroy
    Kennedy.   NYP

New York.   John Hall Wheelock.   NYP

New York! At first I was confused by your beauty.   New York.
    Léopold Sédar Senghor, *tr. by* Ellen Conroy Kennedy.   NYP

New York Bird.   Andrei Voznesensky, *tr. fr. Russian by* William
    Jay Smith.   NYP

New York deserted—without a person!   Deep Night.   Juan
    Ramón Jiménez, *tr. by* Robert Bly.   NYP

New York 1962: Fragment.   Robert Lowell.   *See* Picture, The.

New York Skyline.   Ruthe T. Spinnanger.   AATT

*New York Times* I buy from him each day, The.   Weatherman of
    Sorrows.   Emery E. George.   AAN

New York Woman, The.   L. E. Sissman.   MAT

New York's lovely weather.   Bean Spasms.   Ted Berrigan.   EAS

New Youngfellow.   Stanley Burnshaw.   SPT

Newark Abbey.   Thomas Love Peacock.   NOBE

Newark, for Now (68).   Carolyn M. Rodgers.   PoBA

Newberry.   *Unknown.*   AmFP

Newborn Colt, The.   Mary Kennedy.   PH

Newborn, on the naked sand.   Song for the Newborn.   *Unknown,*
    *tr. by* Mary Austin.   OFD; WPE

Newcastle Beer.   John Cunningham.   EPC

Newcomers.   Abraham Reisen, *tr. fr. Yiddish by* Keith Bosley.
    VWA

Newcomer's Wife, The.   Thomas Hardy.   BoLoP; OxBTC

Newest Banana Plant Leaf, The.   Ingrid Wendt.   NMM

Newgate's Garland.   John Gay.   FaBoBa

Newly Born, The.   *Unknown.   Fr.* The Pricke of Conscience.
    OxBM

Newly Discovered "Homeric" Hymn, A.   Charles Olson.
    CoPAm; NoAM

Newly Pressed Suit, The.   Roger McGough.   NoAM

Newmarket Song, The.   *Unknown.*   APAS

Newport Railway, The.   William McGonagall.   PeD

News.   Robin Morgan.   WBN

News.   Marnie Pomeroy.   POL

News.   Thomas Traherne.   *Fr.* The Third Century.   NOBE;
    PoPle
    (On News.)   BoReV; MetP

News for the Delphic Oracle.   W. B. Yeats.   CMoP (1970 ed.);
    NoAM

News from a foreign [*or* forrein] country came.   News.   Thomas
    Traherne.   *Fr.* The Third Century.   BoReV; MetP; NOBE;
    PoPle

News from abroad does a secret reveal, The.   An Excellent New
    Song Called "Mat's Peace."   Arthur Mainwaring.   APAS

News from Other Small Worlds.   Jonathan Williams.   UsP

News from Paris.   Charles Spear.   ATNZ

News from the heavens! All wars are at an end.   Rare News.
    Nicholas Breton.   NIL

News from the V. A.   A. D. Winans.   PoW

News Item.   Dorothy Parker.   OBAL

News! News!   Eleanor Farjeon.   CC

News of the palace.   Lady Ise, *tr. fr. Japanese by* Etsuko Terasaki
    *and* Irma Brandeis.   BoWoP

News of the Phoenix. A. J. M. Smith. ExPo (1973 ed.)

News of the World. Philip Levine. AMV-81

News of the World II ("In the first year of the last disgrace"). George Barker. FaBoTw (1975 ed.)

News of the World III ("Let her lie naked here, my hand resting"). George Barker. FaBoTw (1975 ed.)

Newsboy. Albert D. Mackie. MS

Newsletter from My Mother. Michael S. Harper. PoBA

Newspaper Hats. Jim Howard. AMV-81

Newspaper Is a Collection of Half-Injustices, A. Stephen Crane. War Is Kind, XII. TT

Newspapers rise high in the air over Maryland. At a March against the Vietnam War. Robert Bly. EAS; WasP

Newsreel. C. Day Lewis. ILP (1975 ed.); PPoD

Newsreel. Norman Macleod. SPT

Newton's Third. Jake T. W. Hubbard. AMV-80

Newtown. Ted Berrigan. FiCh

Next after comes coyote, Stretched-out-in-Dew. Scalp Dance Song. Tr. fr. Tewa Indian by H. J. Spinden. WTO

Next bidding all draw near on bended knees. Pope. Fr. The Dunciad, IV. OBSV

Next came one/ Who mourn'd in earnest. Milton. Fr. Paradise Lost, I. EBEV

Next Day. Randall Jarrell. HAP; NoAM; PPoD

Next died the Lady who yon Hall possessed. The Lady of the Manor. George Crabbe. Fr. The Parish Register: Burials, Pt. III. NOBE

Next-door Mother Rosarine. Mother Rosarine. Maxine W. Kumin. RiTi

Next door they've finally brought home the new baby. For Every Last Batch When the Next One Comes Along. William Dickey. GP

Next Door to Monica's Dance Studio. Barbara Smith. AMV-81

Next Heaven, my vows to thee, O sacred Muse! Upon the Saying That My Verses Were Made by Another. Anne Killigrew. WPE

Next him Jack Squire through his own tear-drops sploshes. Roy Campbell. Fr. The Georgiad. OxBTC

Next is your lot, fair, to be numbered one. To His Kinswoman, Mistress Penelope Wheeler. Robert Herrick. CaPo

Next Market Day, The. Unknown. FSW

Next Moon, The. W. S. Merwin. PHC

Next, Please. Philip Larkin. HeIP; ILP (1975 ed.)

Next these, a troop of busy spirits press. Dryden. Fr. Absalom and Achitophel, Pt. II. PPP

Next Time We Meet. Binnie Klein. AAN

Next to me is a radiator. Rita Rio. Richard Williams. AAN

Next to of Course God America I. E. E. Cummings. BiP; CABA (1972 ed.); Epi; ExPo (1973 ed.); ILP (1975 ed.); InPK; IPWM; NCSH; NowV; OFD; PPoD; SoS; TAP; VGW

Next to will/ I value reason. Swimming Pool. Maria Teresa Horta, tr. by Suzette Macedo. PBWP

Next year grave grass will cover us. Street Corner College. Kenneth Patchen. SPT

Next year, I'm forty years old. Lantern. Frank Polite. GP

Next Year, in Jerusalem. Shirley Kaufman. VWA

Next year we are to bring the soldiers home. Homage to a Government. Philip Larkin. EBEV

Ngh. R. S. Themes. UsP

Niagara. Richard Emil Braun. NoAM

Niagara Falls. Alan Dugan. PoA

Niagara Falls Nocturne. Len Gasparini. NeAC

Niantic River pauses, The. Saunders Point. Henry Combellick. BrS

Nice. Lyn Lifshin. Psy

Nice Old Couple, The. Dorothy Aldis. TVo

Nice place ya got here. Instances. Anselm Hollo. TwMBP

Nice place you have here, Jabez Holmes. Francestown Suite. Carole Oles. PCho

"Nicest Phantasies Are Shared, The." Brian Coffey. CIP

Nicholas Nye. Walter de la Mare. DuDr

Nichols, my better self, forbear. An Answer to an Invitation to Cambridge. Abraham Cowley. PAIC

Nicht we stood on Snawdon Hill, The. Snawdon Wood. Forbes Macgregor. MIS

Nick and the Candlestick. Sylvia Plath. CAPP; PBWP

Nick could hardly wait. The Graduate. Charles Stetler. GP

Nickleplate moon, The. Kansas City West Bottoms. Edward Dahlberg. PoA

Nicodemus, the slave, was of African birth. Wake Nicodemus. Henry Clay Work. FSW

Nigerian Unity/ or Little Niggers Killing Little Niggers. Don L. Lee. NeAC

Nigga Section, The. Welton Smith. BPo

Nigger. Sonia Sanchez. BPo

Nigger/ Can you kill. The True Import of Present Dialogue, Black vs. Negro. Nikki Giovanni. BPo; PoBA

Nigger: as if it were not. Internal Injuries. Robert Penn Warren. NYP

Nigger Song: An Odyssey. Rita Dove. AmPA

Nigguhs with naturrals. So This Is Our Revolution. Sonia Sanchez. GP

Nigh seated where the river flows. Bible, O.T., paraphrased by Countess of Pembroke. Psalms, CXXXVII. OAEL-1

Night, The. Al-Khansa, tr. fr. Arabic by Willis Barnstone. BoWoP

Night. Blake. Fr. Songs of Innocence. MBPR; OxBChV

Night. Louise Bogan. UnPo (1976 ed.)

Night. Aldo Camerino, tr. fr. Italian by Anita Barrows. VWA

Night. Peter Everwine. NNaP

Night. Robinson Jeffers. NOBA

Night. Richard Lovelace. CaPo

Night. Lois Weakley McKay. CTV

Night. Anne Radcliffe. WPE

Night. Sara Teasdale. FSFS

Night, The ("Through that pure virgin shrine"). Henry Vaughan. BoReV; EBEV; MetP; NOBE; OAEL-1; OBW; SCP-1

Night/ and in the warm blackness. Upon Your Leaving. Etheridge Knight. NeAC; NNaP

Night, The/ empty as a condemned house. The Bed. Michael Small. DNGG

Night, a grey sky, a ghostly sea. On the Beach. Arthur Symons. At Dieppe, II. VLP

Night a Sailor Came to Me in a Dream, The. Diane Wakoski. TAP; VGW

Night after night. The Survivors. Judith Hemschemeyer. TV

Night after night I dream about my losses. Lost Object. Diana O Hehir. AMV-80

Night after summer night the drift of pipe-talk. Figure. Marcia Lee Masters. HeS

Night airs that make tree-shadows walk, and sheep. On Grey Cliffs. Walter Savage Landor. VLP

Night along the Mackinac Bridge. Roberta Hill. CDW

Night; an Epistle to Robert Lloyd, sel. Charles Churchill. "Spectators only on this bustling stage." OBSV

Night and a Distant Church. Russell Atkins. PoBA

Night and Day. John Batki. AcAn

Night and Day, with music. Cole Porter. BLSo

Night and day arrive, and day after day goes by. For My Son Noah, Ten Years Old. Robert Bly. BrS

Night and day under the rind of me.  Parodies of Cole Porter's "Night and Day."  Ring Lardner.  OBAL

Night and Morning.  Austin Clarke.  CIP; NoAM

Night and Morning.  *Unknown, tr. fr. Welsh by* R. S. Thomas.  OBW

Night, and one single ridge of narrow path.  Robert Browning.  *Fr.* Pauline  VLP

Night and Sleep.  Coventry Patmore.  VPC

Night, and the hill to me!  From Russian Hill.  Ina Coolbrith.  BPAW; WPN

Night and the hood.  Prelude.  Conrad Kent Rivers.  PoBA

Night-Apple, The.  Allen Ginsberg.  NoAM

Night at an Airport.  David Ignatow.  NNaP

Night at the Napi in Browning, A.  Richard Hugo.  TAT

Night Atlas.  Luke Breitt.  CPA

Night attendant, a B.U. sophomore, The.  Waking in the Blue.  Robert Lowell.  CoPAm; PiAm; PPP; PSN; UnPo (1976 ed.)

Night before Larry Was Stretched, The.  *Unknown.*  BIrV; FaBoBa; GBP; NOBL; PeBB

Night before my uncle Carter got shot, The.  Support Your Local Police Dog.  Carter Revard.  VoR

"Night before the Night before Christmas, The," *sel.*  Randall Jarrell.
   "In her room that night she looks at herself in the mirror."  MiP

Night before you left, as you lay, The.  Lawrence Russ.  *Fr.* The Wedding Poem.  AMV-80

Night Blessing.  Phillip William George.  VW

Night Blessing.  *Unknown.*  CTV

Night-blooming Cereus, The.  Robert Hayden.  FB; NU

Night breathes in the window.  Death Comes for the Old Cowboy.  Kevin Clark.  AMV-81

Night breaths, short ones.  In the Hospital.  Laura Jensen.  AmPA

Night by a river.  Tree.  Florence Barbera.  PoUp

Night Catch.  Heather McHugh.  AmPA

Night Character.  Dino Campana, *tr. fr. Italian by* Frank Stewart.  AMV-81

Night, children.  Grandfather.  Eve Shelnutt.  TC

Night Clouds.  Amy Lowell.  TH

Night comes.  Day runs for its life into my eyes.  Gil Orlovitz.  *Fr.* Art of the Sonnet.  PoA

Night comes to the man who can pray.  New Year's Eve in Solitude.  Robert Mezey.  VWA

Night covers the pond with its wing.  The Pond.  Louise Glück.  CAAP

Night Crow.  Theodore Roethke.  CoPAm; HoPM (1975 ed.); InPK; NCSH; STS; VGW

Night, Death, Mississippi.  Robert Hayden.  FF; VGW

Night draws itself as tight.  Lord, Listen.  Else Lasker-Schüler, *tr. by* Edouard Roditi.  VWA

Night Driving.  Sharyn November.  AMV-80

Night Duty.  Kenneth Mackenzie.  MAuV

Night Duty.  Jill Thomas.  PMW

Night, expositor of love.  Musical Shuttle.  Harvey Shapiro.  VWA

Night Feeding.  Muriel Rukeyser.  NMM; UsP; WPE

Night Fight.  Marge Piercy.  PCho

Night filled, A:/ Light pinning the dark.  Verna Tomlinson Baker.  AATT

Night Fishing.  Gary Stein.  PoUp

Night Fishing.  Michael Waters.  AAN

Night Fishing for Blues.  Dave Smith.  LiSp

Night Flare Drop, Tan Son Nhut.  Horace Coleman.  SES

Night Flight.  Ruth Daigon.  AMV-81

Night Flight.  Don Johnson.  AMV-81

Night flutters.  Hasidim Dance.  Nelly Sachs, *tr. by* Keith Bosley.  VWA

Night folded itself about me like a woman's hair, The.  Birth of a Genius Among Men.  "Hugh MacDiarmid."  SLP

Night from a railroad car window.  Window.  Carl Sandburg.  OSP

Night Funeral in Harlem.  Langston Hughes.  InPS

Night Harvest.  Susan Pence.  AMV-80

Night Has a Thousand Eyes, The.  Francis William Bourdillon.  BoLoP; CTV; PCOP

Night has come on like a woman sleeping, The.  Moon Poems.  John Wieners.  VGW

Night has secreted us.  Amen.  Richard W. Thomas.  PoBA

Night Has Twenty-four Hours, The.  Pedro Juan Pietri.  InW

Night he died, earth's images all came, The.  Poet.  Peter Viereck.  CoPAm; HoPM (1975 ed.)

Night he died, they sent me out for candles, The.  The Runaway.  Larry Rubin.  CSP

Night held me as I scrawled and scrambled near.  The Turkish Trench Dog.  Geoffrey Dearmer.  GDP

Night Herder, The.  Charles Badger Clark, Jr.  BPAW

Night-herding Song.  Harry Stephens.  BPAW

Night Herons.  Judith Wright.  MAuV

Night hides our thefts; all faults then pardoned be.  In the Dark None Dainty.  Robert Herrick.  CaPo; PoPle

Night hides outside.  City.  Timothy P. Mocarski.  AMV-81

Night his/ house I don't remember.  The Blue Bowl of Plumbs Invention.  Lyn Lifshin.  Psy

Night Hunt, The.  Thomas MacDonagh.  GDP; PFIr

Night, I know you are powerful and artistic.  For Bill Hawkins, a Black Militant.  William J. Harris.  PoBA

Night in a rainbow pool.  Rachel at Twenty-three.  Yvonne.  WBN

Night in June, a lovely moon, A.  Coax Me.  Andrew Sterling.  FSN

Night in Nevada with a Friend from Italy, A.  Luciano Mezzetta.  PoW

Night in New York.  Herman Spector.  SPT

Night in Odessa, A.  Louis Simpson.  NNaP

Night in the Forest.  Galway Kinnell.  CoPAm; TAP

Night in the House by the River.  Tu Fu, *tr. fr. Chinese by* Kenneth Rexroth.  NIL

Night in the Royal Ontario Museum, A.  Margaret Atwood.  PBWP

Night, in the sweetness of his murky dominion.  Nocturnal Thoughts.  Avraham Huss, *tr. by* Mark Elliott Shapiro.  VWA

Night is a furrow, a queasy, insistent wound, The.  Nightletter.  Charles Wright.  PoA

Night is black swan wholly adrift.  Hotel in Paris.  Dennis Trudell.  PoA

Night is cloudy, The.  The Middle of the World.  Kathleen Norris.  GP; PHC

Night is come.  Day's End.  Sir Henry Newbolt.  PCOP

Night is covered with signs, The.  Akiba.  Muriel Rukeyser.  VWA

Night is dark and stormy, and the sky is clouded o'er, The.  The Sandy Maranoa.  *At. to* A. W. Davis.  MAuV

Night Is Darkening round Me.  Emily Brontë.  VoPo (Spellbound.)  NOBE

Night Is Freezing Fast, The.  A. E. Housman.  CMoP (1970 ed.); PoPle; STS

Night is full of stars, full of magnificence, The.  Bagley Wood.  Lionel Johnson.  VLP

Night is my sister, and how deep in love.  Edna St. Vincent Millay.  HAP

Night Is No More or Less Important than Bad Circles or "Ksing." Carol Frost. AAN

Night is o'er England, and the winds are still. Peace. Walter de la Mare. ILP (1975 ed.)

Night is still silky, The. Curtains are drawn. Observation at Dawn. Abba Kovner, *tr. by* Shirley Kaufman. VWA

Night is still, The. The unfailing surf. Miramar Beach. J. V. Cunningham. To What Strangers, What Welcome, VIII. PiAm; PoA

Night is very dark, The. Assassination Poems. John Ridland. MAT; OFD

Night it was horribly dark, The. Measles in the Ark. "Susan Coolidge." OxBChV

Night John Henry is born an ax, The. The Birth of John Henry. Melvin B. Tolson. *Fr.* Harlem Gallery. BPo

Night Journey. Theodore Roethke. ECBV; GOA; InPS

Night Landscape. Joan Aiken. DuDa

Night Las Vegas caught fire, The. The Case. H. R. Hays. EAS

Night last night was strange and shaken, The. At a Month's End. Swinburne. VLP

Night Letter. Marge Piercy. NMM

Nightletter. Charles Wright. PoA

Night lies beside me. Amy Lowell. TH

Night lies blue and white, The. Minor Key. Judah Leib Teller, *tr. by* Gabriel Preil *and* Howard Schwartz. VWA

Night! loathèd jailor of the locked-up sun. Night. Richard Lovelace. CaPo

Night Mail. W. H. Auden. OxBTC

Night makes no difference 'twixt the priest and clerk. No Difference in the Dark. Robert Herrick. CaPo

Night-March, The. Herman Melville. PiAm

Night Mirror, The. John Hollander. Prf

Night moves in fast. Across the Charles. Nocturne: Homage to Whistler. Ruth Feldman. AMV-81

Night-Music. Philip Larkin. InPS

Night music slanted. Cell Song. Etheridge Knight. NNaP; PoBA

Night my father got me, The. The Culprit. A. E. Housman. AIW

Night of Battle. Yvor Winters. PoA

Night of Dreams. Laura Beausoleil. NPW

Night of Frost in May. George Meredith. VLP

Night of Souls. Ann Stanford. WPE

Night of the Dance, The. Thomas Hardy. OBP

Night of Voyeurs. Stuart Dybek. TC

Night on Clinton. Robert Mezey. AmPA

Night on Hatchet Cove. Denise Levertov. PiAm; Psy

Night on the Prairies, *sel.* Walt Whitman. "Night on the prairies." RFM

Night opens like an almond. Yvonne Caroutch, *tr. fr. French by* Elene Kolb. BoWoP

Night Out, A. Dannie Abse. BuTh

Night Out, Tom Cat. Charles deGravelles. AMV-81

Night passd and Enitharmon eer the dawn returnd in bliss. Blake. *Fr.* The Four Zoas. OAEL-2

Night Patrol. Josephine Jacobsen. WasP

Night Piece, *sel.* Fleur Adcock. "Lying close to your heart-beat, my lips." ATNZ

Nightpiece. James Joyce. NoAM; PoA

Night-Piece. Raymond R. Patterson. PoBA

Nightpiece. Judith Johnson Sherwin. WBN

Night-Piece. Kendrick Smithyman. ATNZ

Night Piece. Mark Strand. NYP

Night-Piece, A. Wordsworth. Moon

Night-Piece on Death, A. Thomas Parnell. EPC

Night-Piece, to Julia, The. Robert Herrick. CaPo; ILP (1975 ed.); NIL; OAEL-1; PoPle (To Julia.) UsP

Night Place. Shirley Cochrane. PoUp

Night Poem. Wayne Dodd. AMV-80

Night Poem in an Abandoned Music Room. William Pillen. VWA

Night rattles with nightmares, The. From the Night-Window. Douglas Dunn. SLP

Night Regression Poem. Robert Peters. BrS

Night Riddle. *Unknown.* ECBV

Night-Ride, The. Kenneth Slessor. GAS; MAuV

Night Riders. Jean Farley. NowV

Night saw the crew like pedlars with their packs. Lunar Stanzas. Henry Coggswell Knight. FaBoNo

Night, say all, was made for rest, The. Upon Visiting His Lady by Moonlight. "A. W." Moon

Night Scenes. Robert Duncan. VGW

Night sea quickens, The. On the shoal or rock. Lighthouses. Dorothy Wellesley. WPE

Night sends this white eye. Full Moonlight in Spring. W. S. Merwin. TH

Night set softly. The. Patterns. Paul Simon. NIL

Night shakes loose, The. Fish-Dream. Skaidrite Stelzer. TC

Night-Shift. Joseph Kalar. SPT

Night Shift. Naomi Shihab. GP

Night Shift at the Plating Division of Keeler Brass. James B. Allen. HeS

Night Shift at the Poetry Factory, The. James Magorian. EC

Night should be fuller than this. Now and Again. Roo Borson. AMV-81

Night Sisters, The. Margaret Gillies. PMW

Night-sky bird's world. Myth of the Blaze. George Oppen. CAAP

Night sky edges our roof with stars, The. The Nighthawk. Dennis Gaughan. PoUp

Night-sky red, crackle and roar of flame, The. In This Year of Grace. John Hewitt. PFIr

Night Song. Frances Cornford. GDP

Night Song. Lisel Mueller. AMV-80

Night Song for an Old Lover. Susan Glickman. AMV-81

Night Song from Backbone Mountain. Daniel Mark Epstein. TAT

Night Sounds. Thomas Middleton. *Fr.* Blurt, Master Constable. RAE

Night Sowing. David Campbell. MAuV

Night still lingers. To My Wife. Jack Simcock. BuTh

Night Storm. Jane Sherman. CaYB

Night, street, a lamp, a chemist's window. Alexander Blok, *tr. by* Jon Stallworthy *and* Peter France. *Fr.* Dances of Death. OBVE

Night Sweat. Robert Lowell. TAP; VGW

Night Teeth. Peter Brett. AMV-80

Night that ends so soon. The Short Night. Buson, *tr. by* Harold G. Henderson. Moon

Night that has no star lit up by God, The. The New World. Jones Very. AmVN; ILP (1975 ed.)

Night that lives protectively, The. Stone. Juliet Chayat. AMV-80

Night, the black summer, simplifies her smells. Nights in the Gardens of Port of Spain. Derek Walcott. OBP

Night the Ninth Being the Last Judgment. Blake. *See* Vala, Night the Ninth Being the Last Judgment

Night Thoughts. Richard Bastian. AATT

Night Thoughts. Gwen Harwood. CAAP

Night Thoughts [The Complaint], *sels.* Edward Young.
Art of Happiness, The, *fr.* VIII. POL
"How poor, how rich, how abject, how august," *fr.* I. OAEL-1
Night the First ("Tir'd nature's sweet restorer, balmy Sleep!").
EPC; LAuP
"Where, thy true treasure? Gold says, 'Not in me,'" *fr.* VI.
OAEL-1

Night tinkles like ice in glasses, The. November Night,
Edinburgh. Norman MacCaig. MS

Night Train. Mary C. Fineran. AMV-81

Night Train. Robert Francis. DuDa

Night Visitor. Alison Wyrley Birch. PPM

Night Visitors. Kadya Molodovsky, *tr. fr. Yiddish by* Ruth
Whitman. VWA

Nightwalker. Delia Chilgren. NPW

Night-Walker, The. Horace Gregory. Moon

Nightwalker, *sel.* Thomas Kinsella.
"I must lie down with them all soon and sleep." BIrV

Night was as sweet, The. The Airwaves. Warren Woessner. TAT

Night was clear, sea calm, The; I came on deck. Crossing Cook
Strait. James K. Baxter. ATNZ

Night was coming very fast, The. The Hens. Elizabeth Madox
Roberts. LCL

Night was faint and sheer, The. A Nocturne for October 31st.
Yvor Winters. PoA

Night was growing old, The. *Unknown.* FaBoNo

Night Was Smooth, The. James Bertolino. POL

Night was stormy and dark, The. The Speculators. Thackeray.
OBSV

Night was thick and hazy, The. Robinson Crusoe's Story.
Charles Edward Carryl. *Fr.* Davy and the Goblin. ECBV

Night Watch. Margo Magid. NMM

Night Watch. Adrienne Rich. TT

Night Watch. Patricia Torrington. PMW

Nightwatchman. Robert Morgan. HeHu

Night we went up into the rising hills, The. The Moon. Charles
Upton. MIT

Night Will Never Stay, The. Eleanor Farjeon. FPB; OxBChV

Night-Wind, The. Emily Brontë. FSFS; VLP

Night Wind in Fall. W. R. Moses. NCSH

Night with a Wolf, A. Bayard Taylor. PCOP

Night without Sleep. Robinson Jeffers. PiAm

Nightwood. William Jay Smith. PoA

Night Words: The Ravishing. Michael McClure. VoA

Night you got away, I dreamed you rose, The. To a Fugitive.
James Wright. TH

Night You Got Back from the Mountains, The. Holly Prado.
NPW

Nightbreak. Adrienne Rich. IHMS; PiAm

Nightfall. Walter Davies, *tr. fr. Welsh by* Anthony Conran.
OBW

Nightfall. Richard Ryan. IPM

Nightfishing, The, *sels.* W. S. Graham.
"Very gently struck/ The quay night bell," I. MS
"We are at the hauling then hoping for it," III. MS

Nighthawk, The. Dennis Gaughan. PoUp

Nighthawks circle/ through the midwestern elms. For a
Winnebago Brave. Joseph Bruchac. CDW

Nightingale, The. Samuel Taylor Coleridge. MBPR

Nightingale, The. Marie de France, *tr. fr. French by* Patricia
Terry. BoWoP

Nightingale, The. Sir Philip Sidney. *See* Philomela.

Nightingale, The. William Strode, *after the Latin of* Famianus
Strada. OBVE

Nightingale, The ("One morning, one morning, one morning in
May"). *Unknown. See* One Morning in May.

Nightingale and the Glowworm, The. William Cowper. CTV

Nightingale, as soon as April bringeth, The. Philomela. Sir
Philip Sidney. EBEV; ILP (1975 ed.); NOBE

Nightingale has a lyre of gold, The. To A. D. [*or* The Blackbird].
W. E. Henley. Echoes, XVIII. HoPM (1975 ed.); LoAs;
PCOP

Nightingale, in dead of night, The. The Happy Nightingale.
*Unknown.* OxBChV

Nightingale that all day long, A. The Nightingale and the
Glowworm. William Cowper. CTV

Nightingale, whose happy noble hart, The. The Steele Glas.
George Gascoigne. AAS

Nightingales. Robert Bridges. CMoP (1970 ed.); ILP (1975 ed.);
NOBE; OAEL-2; PPM; UnPo (1976 ed.); VLP

Nightingales. Leslie Norris. HeHu

Nightingales Are Not Singing. Moshe Dor, *tr. fr. Hebrew by*
Dennis Johnson. VWA

Nightingales of Spring, The. *Unknown.* AmFP

Nightingale's Song, The. James I, King of Scotland. *Fr.* The
Kingis Quair. OxBM
("Now was there maid fast by the towris wall.") EBEV

Nightingales warbled without. In the Garden at Swainston.
Tennyson. VLP

Nightlines. Paul Clause. AATT

Nightlong you lie and mock the idle moon. Moon Rock. E.
Louise Mally. POL

Nightly off Route 50. Stars Shine So Faithfully. Jane Flanders.
AMV-80

Nightly tormented by returning doubt. The Struggle. Sully-
Prudhomme, *tr. by* Arthur O'Shaughnessy. PPM

Nightmare. James A. Emanuel. BPo

Nightmare. W. S. Gilbert. *Fr.* Iolanthe. NOBL; PBMP
(Chancellor's Nightmare, The.) FaBoNo

Nightmare Abbey, *sel.* Thomas Love Peacock.
Song by Mr. Cypress. OAEL-2

Nightmare Begins Responsibility. Michael S. Harper. TAP

Nightmare Factory, The. Maxine W. Kumin. NVAP

Nightmare leaves fatigue. Louis MacNeice. *Fr.* Autumn Journal.
BIrV

Nightmare of beasthood, snorting, how to wake. Moly. Thom
Gunn. HAP; NoAM

Nightmare of Mouse. Robert Penn Warren. SO

Nightmare, with Angels. Stephen Vincent Benét. MAT

Nightmares have told me. 46 and Recalling. Allan Block. FAF

Nightmares: Part Three. Lynn Moskowitz. AMV-81

Nights and days we stumble over each other. Stumbling. Dick
Lourie. NeAC

Nights are drawing in, The; the daylight dies. End of a Season.
Vernon Scannell. HeHu

Nights bring you the fever. Prometheus. Jenny Mastoraki, *tr. by*
Nikos Germanakos. BoWoP

Nights hang heavy on the winter air, The. Winter Nights. Lora
Dunetz. AMV-80

Nights here are usually clear and the shadows, The. Addio a la
Mamma. Noe Jitrik, *tr. by* Yishai Tobin. VWA

Nights in the Gardens of Port of Spain. Derek Walcott. OBP

Nights on the Indian Ocean. Cale Young Rice. RhR

Nights Passed on Ward's Island, Toronto Harbour. Doug
Fetherling. NeAC

Night's Song. Sir William Davenant. *Fr.* Luminalia. SCP-2

Nights we spend apart. Hook. Erica Jong. RiTi

Nights we spent, The/ Watching her cross. Night Watch.
Patricia Torrington. PMW

Nighttime. The faithful prison guard. Bedtime Story. Lou
Lipsitz. VGW

Nijinsky. Parker Tyler. PoA

Nike. Adam Wazyk, *tr. fr. Polish by* Isaac Komem. VWA

Nikki-Rosa. Nikki Giovanni. AmNP (1974 ed.); IHMS; IPWM; NoAM; NYP; PoBA; RiTi; TAP (Nikki-Roasa.) PBMP

Nil Pejus Est Caelibe Vita. Samuel Taylor Coleridge. MBPR

Nile, The. Leigh Hunt. EBEV; NOBE; PPM

Nimble as dolphins to. Gimboling. Isabella Gardner. WeW

Nimphs Reply to the Sheepheard, The. Sir Walter Ralegh. See Nymph's Reply to the Shepherd, The.

Nina Simone. Lance Jeffers. CNA

Nine, The. John Sheffield, Duke of Buckingham and Normanby. APAS

Nine adulteries, 12 liaisons, 64 fornications and something approaching a rape. The Temperaments. Ezra Pound. BoLoP; NoAM; NOBA

Nine Bean-Rows on the Moon. A. W. Purdy. Moon

Nine Birds. E. E. Cummings. UnPo (1976 ed.)

Nine drops of water bead the jessamine. A Wet August. Thomas Hardy. PPP

Nine grenadiers, with bayonets in their guns. The Dream of a Boy Who Lived at Nine Elms. William Brighty Rands. OxBChV

900 Miles. Unknown. FSW

Nine Men out of a Minyan. Haim Guri, tr. fr. Hebrew by Mark Elliott Shapiro. VWA

Nine meshes of the net enclose. Jonathan Price. CoPAm

9:00. Patricia Hooper. AMV-81

Nine o'Clock Thoughts on the 73 Bus. Peter Porter. POL

Nine Parts of Speech, The. Unknown. ECBV

Nine Pound Hammer. Unknown. FSW

Nine swallows sat on a telephone wire. The Swallows. Elizabeth J. Coatsworth. LCL

9/3/76. Laban Chang. PHC

Nine white chickens come. A Black November Turkey. Richard Wilbur. BoAnP; CoPAm; NCSH

Nine Years after Viet Nam. Leroy V. Quintana. AMV-80

Nine years ago, early winter. Waiting. Philip Levine. CPA

1915: A Pre-Raphaelite Ending, London. Richard Howard. NoAM

1950's. The. Robert Sward. FoP

1945. Sir Herbert Read. OxBTC

1946. Yvonne. AAN

1943. Sandra McPherson. FoP

1914, sels. Rupert Brooke.
   Dead, The ("These hearts were woven"), IV. PoA
   Peace, I. BTTM; PoA
   Soldier, The, V. BTTM; FaPoR; FF; HeIP; NOBE; OxBTC; PAIC; PoA;VoPo
   ("If I should die, think only this of me.") PPM

MCMXIV. Philip Larkin. EBEV

19??. Dan Georgakas. NowV

Nineteen Hundred and Nineteen. W. B. Yeats. BIrV
   Sels.
   "Come let us mock at the great," V. ExPo (1973 ed.)
   "Many ingenious lovely things are gone," I. ExPo (1973 ed.)

1905. David Ignatow. VWA

1907, a Proposal from Paris. Richard Howard. CAAP

Nineteen Sections from a Twenty Acre Poem, sels. David Martinson.
   "All morning I watched," 12. TAT
   "How the kerosene outlasted," 1. TAT
   "It's come to this," 8. TAT
   "Sharpening grandpa's scythe," 19. TAT
   "Where pollen crusts the pine bough," 4. TAT

. . .1968. . . Petra von Morstein, tr. fr. German by Rosemarie Waldrop. BoWoP

1965. Gibbons Ruark. NowV

1967. Thomas Hardy. NoAM

1913 Massacre, The. Woody Guthrie. FSW

Nineteen Thirty-nine, sel. Charles Brasch.
   "Walls divide us from water and from light, The." ATNZ

1939. Alan Brownjohn. LP

1937 Ford Convertible. Tom McKeown. NVAP

1933. Philip Levine. VWA

1912-1952, Full Cycle. Peter Viereck. OBAL

Nineteenth Century and After, The. W. B. Yeats. FaBoEE

Nineteenth Century as a Song, The. Robert Hass. CAAP

90th Year, The. Denise Levertov. FiCP

Ninety and Nine, The. Elizabeth Cecilia Clephane. BLSH, with music; FSW
   ("There were ninety and nine that safely lay.") VLP

90 North. Randall Jarrell. ILP (1975 ed.); NoAM; NOBA; TAP

98 Degree Blues. Unknown. BluL

Ninety-fifth. Isaac Watts. AmFP

97th Kentucky Derby, The. Geoff Young. PoW

96 Vandam. Gerald Bickford. NYP

Niño Leading an Old Man to Market. Leonard Nathan. CTBA; NCSH; TVo

Nino, the Wonder Dog. Roy Fuller. FF

Ninth, The; last half; the score was tied. Dorlan's Home Walk. Arthur Guiterman. PoTa

Ninth of July, The. John Hollander. CoPAm

Ninth Symphony of Beethoven Understood at Last as a Sexual Message. Adrienne Rich. TAP

Nirvana. Ali S. Hilmi Törel. PeD

No! Thomas Hood. PBMP
   (November.) CTV

No. Natan Zach, tr. fr. Hebrew by Laya Firestone. VWA

No. E. M. Schorb. AMV-80

No,/ I never could talk with my father. Love Song for a Tyrant. Marion Brimm Rewey. AMV-81

No/ No/ No/ I am not doing. Our Lives. Sharon Scott. JB

No argument, no anger, no remorse. Hedges Freaked with Snow. Robert Graves. OxBTC

No artist perhaps, you go beyond their phrases. Robert Lowell. Fr. Mexico. BiP

No Bargains Today. Peggy Susberry Kenner. JB

No bars are set too close, no mesh too fine. The Sparrow in the Zoo [or Epigram: Political Reflexion]. Howard Nemerov. NIL; NoAM

No bird, no fabled fowl it is. A Little Cheat. Malay Oral Tradition, tr. by R. J. Wilkinson and R. O. Winstedt. WTO

No bitterness: our ancestors did it. Ave Caesar. Robinson Jeffers. NoAM; NOBA

No bottom,/ Mark four. Unknown. AmFP

No boy chooses war. Sailors on Leave. Owen Dodson. AmNP (1974 ed.)

No breath of air to break the wave. The Giaour: A Fragment of a Turkish Tale. Byron. MBPR

No butler, no second maid, no blood upon the stair. Crime Club. Weldon Kees. AnMo

No camellia. Yosano Akiko, tr. fr. Japanese by Geoffrey Bownas and Anthony Thwaite. PBWP

No cedar dares a roothold in the stone. LaSalle Street. Rachel Albright. ANTL

No Change in Me. Unknown. AmFP

No Change of Place. W. H. Auden. OxBTC

No changes of support—only. Last Month. John Ashbery. CAPP

No charm can stay, no medicine can assuage. Walter Savage Landor. FaBoEE

No closer the glove clings to the sweaty hand. Little-League Baseball Fan. W. R. Moses. LiSp; NCSH

No cloud, no relique of the sunken day.  The Nightingale. Samuel Taylor Coleridge.  MBPR

No Cold Approach.  *At. to* Burns.  EBEV

No considerable picture.  All Too Little on Pictures.  Charles Black.  AMV-80

No Country You Remember.  Robert Mezey.  FF

No Coward Soul Is Mine.  Emily Brontë.  *See* Last Lines.

No Credit.  Kenneth Fearing.  CMoP (1970 ed.); SPT

No crooked leg, no bleared eye.  Written in Her French Psalter. Elizabeth I, Queen of England.  PBWP; WPE

No crowd that has occurred.  Emily Dickinson.  PiAm

No Dawns.  Julianne Perry.  PoBA

No day was sad as the day Sakhr.  On Her Brother Sakhr.  Al-Khansa, *tr. by* Willis Barnstone.  BoWoP

No days but these.  Matthew Mead.  *Fr.* The Administration of Things.  TwMBP

No Dice.  Kathleen Wiegner.  MMD

No Difference.  Keats.  *See* Song about Myself.

No Difference.  Beverly Lawn.  AMV-81

No Difference in the Dark.  Robert Herrick.  CaPo

No dignity without a chromium.  Ballad of Faith.  William Carlos Williams.  OBAL

No doubt this way is best.  No Use.  W. D. Snodgrass.  BoLoP

No doubt to-morrow I will hide.  At Mass.  Vachel Lindsay. VGW

No dust have I to cover me.  An Inscription by the Sea.  E. A. Robinson, *after* Glaucus.  FaBoEE

No earthquake. Chapped, a lifting in this field.  Dead Center. Chester Kallman.  PoA

No egg on Friday Alph will eat.  Of Alphus.  John Parkhurst, *tr. by* Timothe Kendall.  SoSe

No fabulous warrior came hunting.  The Gentle Ambush. George Macadam.  SLP

No "fan is in his hand" for these.  The Threshing-Machine. Alice Meynell.  WPE

No Fear.  Mary Doyle Curran.  AMV-80

No first-class war can now be fought.  Civil Defense.  Kenneth Burke.  OBAL

No, for I'll save it! Seven years since.  Apparent Failure.  Robert Browning.  NOBE

No for you, my queyn, will I prepare.  The Real Muse.  Tom Scott.  PoA

No Foundation.  John Hollander.  OBAL

No Ghost Is True.  Leslie A. Fiedler.  PoA

No Great Matter.  David Lawson.  VGW

No haste but good, where wisdome makes the waye.  George Gascoigne.  AAS

No hawk hangs over in this air.  The Snow Storm.  Edna St. Vincent Millay.  PoA

No hay nada nuevo en nueva york.  There Is Nothing New in New York.  Miguel Piñero.  NYP

No heralding daffodils.  Row of Houses.  John Robert Quinn. AMV-80

No hesitation.  Mourning Letter, March 29 1963.  Edward Dorn. ConAP

No Hiding Place ("There's no hiding place down there"). *Unknown.*  FSW

No Hiding Place Down There ("A sinner man sat on the gates of hell").  *Unknown.*  GBP

No Holes Marred.  Suzanne Douglass.  QQQ

"No home, no home," cried an orphan girl.  The Orphan Girl. *Unknown.*  AmFP

No, I have never found.  Places, Loved Ones.  Philip Larkin. CMoP (1970 ed.); SoS

No, I would not like to meet Bob Dylan.  Citizen.  Peter Schjeldahl.  CAAP

No—I'll endure ten thousand deaths.  Chaste Florimel.  Matthew Prior.  BoLoP

No Images.  Waring Cuney.  AmNP (1974 ed.); MAT

No, in the New World, happiness is enforced.  "In the New World Happiness Is Allowed."  Peter Porter.  GAS

No Irish Need Apply.  *Unknown.*  FSW; WTO

No, it's a tenement.  "It's a Whole World, the Body. A Whole World!"—Swami Satchidananda.  David Young.  FF

No. It's an impudent falsehood. Men did not.  On a Vulgar Error. C. S. Lewis.  OxBTC

No Job Blues.  *Unknown.*  BluL

No John.  *Unknown.*  FSW
  (O, No John, *with music.*)  GSB

No landscape ever fancies or delights me.  In Front of the Seine, Recalling the Rio de la Plata.  Silvina Ocampo, *tr. by* Jason Weiss.  AMV-80

No leaf moves. The weather.  The Shirt.  Hilda Morley.  AMV-81

No light except the stars, but from the cliff.  The Sea Birds.  Van K. Brock.  NVAP

No Loath[e]someness in Love.  Robert Herrick.  BBL; GBL; PBMP

No Lock against Lechery.  Robert Herrick.  CaPo

No longer a real thing.  Still Life.  Regina M. Austin.  AMV-80

No longer can we sit.  The Transparent Closet.  Martha Shelley. WBN

No longer itself.  Six Kisses.  Nancy Sullivan.  LoAs

No longer mourn for me when I am dead.  Sonnets, LXXI. Shakespeare.  EBEV; Epi; GBL; HAP; ILP (1975 ed.); PPoe; SoSe; STS

No longer throne of a goddess to whom we pray.  Full Moon. Robert Hayden.  BPo

No longer to lie reading "Tess of the d'Urbervilles."  The Lesson. Robert Lowell.  CMoP (1970 ed.)

No longer torn by what she knows.  The Poor Relation.  E. A. Robinson.  STS

No longer will I close an opaque door.  Daisy Aldan.  AATT

No Loser, No Weeper, *sel.*  Maya Angelou.
  "'I hate to lose something.'"  OSP

No lovelier hills than thine have laid.  England.  Walter de la Mare.  PES

No McTavish.  Genealogical Reflection.  Ogden Nash.  OBAL

No Madam Butterfly.  Louise Hajek.  AMV-80

No man can serve two masters.  Bible, *N.T.* St. Matthew, VI: 24-29.  OBVE

No man e'er found a happy life by chance.  The Art of Happiness.  Edward Young.  *Fr.* Night Thoughts, VIII. POL

No Man, If Men Are Gods.  E. E. Cummings.  VGW

No man in the West ever won such renown.  The Ballad of Billy the Kid.  Henry Herbert Knibbs.  BPAW

"No man may him hyde."  Sun.  Marianne Moore.  PiAm

No man's a jester playing Shakespeare.  The King Must Die. Bernie Taupin.  GrRo

No Man's Good Bull.  James Seay.  PPoD

No man's trust let woman claim.  The Roman Earl.  *Unknown, tr. by* Douglas Hyde.  OBVE

No Matter How Her Thighs.  James Mecklenburger.  SFF

No matter how tough the job.  Handyman.  Homer Phillips. QQQ

No Matter If You Remain Unaffected by.  Brian Patten.  BuTh

No matter what I say.  Eel Grass.  Edna St. Vincent Millay. PPM

No matter who is using the body.  Estienne.  Peter Klappert. PCho

No Mean City.  Patrick MacDonogh.  BIrV

No Meaning.  Terence Brame.  RAE

No memory but this new day, dark wings. City Butterfly. Charles Siebert. NYP

No Mixed Green Salad for Me, Thanks. Georgie Starbuck Galbraith. QQQ

No mo meetings. Listenen to Big Black at S. F. State. Sonia Sanchez. BPo

No money to bury him. Ballad of the Man Who's Gone. Langston Hughes. AIW

No More. Carl Clark. JB

No More Auction Block. *Unknown.* BPo (Many Thousand Gone). FSW

No more be grieved at that which thou hast done. Sonnets, XXXV. Shakespeare. CABA (1972 ed.); UnPo (1976 ed.)

No More beneath the Oppressive Hand, *with music. Unknown.* AH

No More Booze. *Unknown.* OBAL

No more exercises of style for him. A Younger Poet. Peter Schjeldahl. PoA

No More Good Water. *Unknown.* BluL

No more let Greece her bolder fables tell. On the Famous Voyage. Ben Jonson. PAIC; TVS

No more, my dear, no more these counsels try. Astrophel and Stella, LXIV. Sir Philip Sidney. ILP (1975 ed.)

No more my visionary soul shall dwell. Pantisocracy. Samuel Taylor Coleridge. MBPR; PAIC

No more, no more Jewish townships in Poland. Elegy. Antoni Slonimski, *tr. by* Isaac Komem. VWA

No more no more to be. I Want. Rosemary Daniell. WBN

No more of your titled acquaintances boast. Burns. FaBoEE

No more phrases, Swenson: I was once. Lions in Sweden. Wallace Stevens. BiP

No more shall I, since I am driven hence. To Lar. Robert Herrick. CaPo

No more shall I work in the factory. The Factory Girl. *Unknown.* FSW

No More Soft Talk. Diane Wakoski. FF; IHMS

No More than Five. Fred Levinson. AmPA

No more the swanboat on the artificial lake. Blind Date. Conrad Aiken. DL

No more violets. Pastorale. Hart Crane. PSN

No more wine? Then we'll push back chairs and talk. Bishop Blougram's Apology. Robert Browning. PFD; VLP

No more with overflowing light. For a Dead Lady. E. A. Robinson. CMoP (1970 ed.); DL; HeIP; HoPM (1975 ed.); ILP (1975 ed.); LoAs; NoAM; NOBA; PiAm; STS

No More Women Blues. *Unknown.* BluL

No more words! To the field, to arms. Veronica Franco, *tr. fr. Italian by* Lynne Lawner. PBWP

"No mortal man beneath the sky." Epitaph for George Moore. Thomas Hardy. FaBoEE

No movement on the hill: the old soldiers. Old Soldiers Home at Marshalltown, Iowa. Jim Barnes. AMV-80

No name but a number. Number 1 by Jackson Pollack (1948). Nancy Sullivan. WIF

No Need for, the Computer Concern Error Letter, The. Lyn Lifshin. EC

"No need to get home early." Father's Voice. William Stafford. RFM

No new delights to our desire. Singers to Come. Alice Meynell. WPE

No new moon in its arms. Last Quarter. John Hollander. Moon

No New Music. Stanley Crouch. PoBA

No New Thing. Vincent Buckley. MAuV

No news of navies burnt at seas. A New-Year's Gift Sent to Sir Simeon Steward. Robert Herrick. CaPo

No-Night, The. Irving Feldman. NoAM

No No Blues. *Unknown.* BluL

No, no, don't, please. Crimes of Passion: The Phone Caller. Terry Stokes. AmPA

No, no, fair heretic, it needs must be. Song. Sir John Suckling. *Fr. Aglaura.* CABA (1972 ed.); CaPo

No, no; for my virginity. A True Maid. Matthew Prior. FaBoCo; FaBoEE; NIL

No, no! Go from me. I have left her lately. A Virginal. Ezra Pound. CMoP (1970 ed.); ILP (1975 ed.); NIL; NoAM; NOBA; TAP

No, no, go not to Lethe, neither twist. Ode on Melancholy. Keats. CABA (1972 ed.); Epi; ExPo (1973 ed.); HAP; ILP (1975 ed.); InPS; MAT; MBPR; NIL; NOBE; OAEL-1; OBP; PMW; PoIA; PoPle: PPP; STS

No, no, my friend, we're off! Six months have passed. Phaedra (Phèdre). Racine, *tr. by* Robert Lowell. NAWM-2

No, no, no, I know I was not important as I moved. Come Dance with Kitty Stobling. Patrick Kavanagh. NoAM

No, no, no, no! Come, let's away to prison. Shakespeare. *Fr.* King Lear, V, iii. OBP

No noise is here, or none that hinders thought. William Cowper. *Fr.* The Robin in Winter. BoAnP

No, not far beneath some foreign sky then. Requiem. "Anna Akhmatova," *tr. by* Robin Kemble. NAWM-2

No not that way she'd. My Mother and the Bed. Lyn Lifshin. TV

No, not the last Last Supper, and yet. Extreme Unction in PA. David Ray. AMV-81

No, not this leaf haunts me. Some year I might. Not This Leaf Haunts Me. Tony Cosier. AMV-81

No, not under the vault of another sky. Requiem 1935—1940. "Anna Akhmatova," *tr. by* Richard McKane. BoWoP

No notice in the papers. Tombstone with Cherubim. Horace Gregory. TPo

No Occupation. George Rostrevor Hamilton. FaBoEE

No Offence. D. J. Enright. HeHu; OxBTC

No one but him. Swimmer in the Rain. Robert Wallace. FiCP; LiSp

No one can come here for the first time. Limbo. Marieve Rugo. AMV-81

No one can die twice of the same fever? Twice of the Same Fever. Robert Graves. LoAs

No one can hurt me. They've tried to kill me. Alone. "Anna Akhmatova," *tr. by* Stephen Berg. BoWoP

No one can tell you why. Heart's Needle, IV. W. D. Snodgrass. ConAP; CoPAm; UsP

No one comes. The Old Place. Hone Tuwhare. ATNZ

No one could find his grave for relic-plunder. Casanova. Richard Usborne. POL

No one could have a blacker tail. Othello Jones Dresses for Dinner. Ed Roberson. PoBA

No one died in this parish when. Alfred Allen. *Fr.* Clashenure Skyline. IPM

No one ever walking this our only earth. Muriel Rukeyser. NNaP

No one has ever said he goes "out" into the city. Storm in the Desert. Radcliffe Squires. MPA

No one has sung "Let the world know!" Antiphonal Hymn in Praise of Inanna. Enheduanna, *tr. fr. Sumerian.* BoWoP

No One Heard Him Call. Dorothy Aldis. CaYB

No one is as acquainted with pain as I am. W. S. Wardell. AAN

No one is snug against the heart's disasters. Lines Written but Never Mailed from Hawaii. William Meredith. PHC

No one is the homeland. Not even the horseman. Ode Written in 1966. Jorge Luis Borges, *tr. by* Lynn C. Jacox. AMV-81

No one kept count. Migrant Hostel. Peter Skrzynecki. CAAP

No one kneads us again of earth and clay. Psalm. Paul Celan, *tr.* by Joachim Neugroschel. VWA

No one knows the man who throws out the season's first ball. Mystery Baseball. Philip Dacey. AAN

No one knows us here. Love in Magnolia Cemetery. Paula Rankin. AMV-80

No one knows what the banging is all about. The Neighbor. Miller Williams. GP

No one moulds us again out of earth and clay. Psalm. Paul Celan, *tr.* by Michael Hamburger. OBVE

No one remembered when she first discovered God. Grandmother. Henry Carlile. GP

No One Remembers Abandoning the Village of White Fir. Duane Niatum. CDW

No One So Much as You. Edward Thomas. GBL; PSN

No One Talks about This. Carl Rakosi. GP

No One to Blame. Laurence Lieberman. CoPAm

No one told them about the disease. How the Indians Lost the Hot Springs. Carol Cox. MMD

No one was in the fields. Tom's Angel. Walter de la Mare. AIW

No one wondered that I could love this. Orphee at Rest. Frank Stewart. PHC

No One Would Believe. Charlotte Zolotow. TVo

No one writes to me. Letter Out of the Gray. Gabriel Preil, *tr.* by Shirley Kaufman *and* Howard Schwartz. VWA

No one's going to read. A Dance for Militant Dilettantes. Al Young. CSP; PiAm; PoBA; PPoD; SA

No Other Choice. *Unknown.* NOBE
("Fain would I change that note.") EBEV; GBL

No pavement chalks the plain with memories. Beginning the Year at Rosebud, S. D. Roberta Hill. CDW

No people are uninteresting. People. Yevgeny Yevtushenko, *tr.* by Robin Milner-Gulland *and* Peter Levi. DL

No photographs exist. This man. Crazy Horse Returns to South Dakota. Harley Elliott. NeAC

No Place like Home. Llawdden, *tr. fr. Welsh by* Gwyn Jones. OBW

No place seemed farther than your death. And I Am Old to Know. Pauline Hanson. TAP

No Place So Grand. *Unknown.* WTO

No Platonic Love. William Cartwright. CABA (1972 ed.); GBL; ILP (1975 ed.); OAEL-1; SCP-2

No porter guards the passage of your door. To My Honour'd Kinsman, John Driden, of Chesterton. Dryden. EBEV

No Possum, No Sop, No Taters. Wallace Stevens. TAP; VGW

No private grudge they need, no personal spite. Modern Critics. Samuel Taylor Coleridge. FaBoEE

No Quarter. Steven Orlen. AAN; FoP

No Remedy. Drummond Allison. OxBTC

No Reparation. Charles Brasch. ATNZ

No Respect for Authority. Marisha Chamberlain. AAN

No Road. Philip Larkin. EBEV; ILP (1975 ed.)

No rock along the road but knows. Poet. Donald Jeffrey Hayes. AmNP (1974 ed.)

No rooftops to rest on. Madison Square. A. Glanz-Leyeles, *tr.* by Keith Bosley. VWA

No Room at the Inn. *Unknown.* FSW

No room for mourning: he's gone out. William Wordsworth. Sidney Keyes. OxBTC

No rooster wakes them. A donkey brays. In the Madison Zoo. Roberta Hill. CDW

"No," said Charles Peace. E. C. Bentley. *Fr.* Clerihews. NOBL

No saint on a disc of snow. Emily Dickinson Postage Stamp. Lynn Strongin. NMM

No Second Troy. W. B. Yeats. CABA (1972 ed.); CMoP (1970 ed.); NoAM; NOBE; OAEL-2; OxBTC; PPP; TT; WeW

No Sense Grieving. Ilya Rubin, *tr. fr. Russian by* Linda Zisquit. VWA

No, she's not lying down there now for love. In the Radiotherapy Unit. Margaret Stanley Wrench. SFF

No ship of all that under sail or steam. Immigrants. Robert Frost. GOA

No Signal for a Crossing. Rhoda Donovan. AMV-80

No, Sir, No. *Unknown.* AmFP

"No, sir," said General Sherman. E. C. Bentley. *Fr.* Clerihews. NOBL

No sleep in the sky; nobody, nobody. Unsleeping City. Federico García Lorca, *tr.* by Ben Belitt. NYP

No sleep. The sultriness pervades the air. The House-Top. Herman Melville. AmVN; NOBA; NYP; Prf

No sleep tonight. Summary. Sonia Sanchez. BPo

No Smiles. Frank Lamont Phillips. AmNP (1974 ed.)

No sooner came, but gone, and fall'n asleep. On My Dear Grandchild Simon Bradstreet. Anne Bradstreet. EAP

No sorrows or plagues popped. Hope. Kenneth L. Anderson. AMV-80

No sound—a spell—on, on out. Father and Son. William Stafford. GP

No sound of any storm that shakes. Hillcrest. E. A. Robinson. PPoe

No Speech from the Scaffold. Thom Gunn. OxBTC

No spot of earth where men have so fiercely for ages of time. Antrim. Robinson Jeffers. BIrV; NOBA; VGW

No Spring. Alice Corbin. WPW

No spring, nor summer beauty hath such grace. The Autumnal. John Donne. Elegies, IX. InPS

No Stewart art thou, Galloway. On Lord Galloway. Burns. FaBoEE

No stir in the air, no stir in the sea. The Inchcape Rock. Robert Southey. PoPle

No straight lines but drooping shoulders. Miss Maime. Jodi Braxton. WBN

No Such Thing. Marcia Southwick. AMV-81

No! sum thine Edith's wretched lot. Sir Walter Scott. *Fr.* The Lord of the Isles. SLP

No sun—no moon! No! [*or* November]. Thomas Hood. CTV; PBMP

No Swan So Fine. Marianne Moore. PoA; PoIA; UnPo (1976 ed.)

No Talking Shop. Minnie Leona Upton. TDH

No telling his age. The Piano Tuner. W. Atmar Smith II. AMV-80

No Thank You. John Skoyles. AAN

No, the serpent did not. Theology. Ted Hughes. NoAM

No, the serpent was not. Reveille. Ted Hughes. PPP

No Theory. David Ignatow. NNaP

No; there he moves, the thoughtful engineer. Ebenezer Elliott. *Fr.* Steam. VLP

No thing/ no-thing. Cathexis. F. J. Bryant, Jr. PoBA

No this time it is not the Avon Lady. The Sacred Heart of Jesus Bleeds for You. Elton Glaser. NVAP

No! those days are gone away. Robin Hood. Keats. MBPR

No, thou hast never griev'd but I griev'd too. Walter Savage Landor. GBL

No Time for Poetry. Julia Fields. AmNP (1974 ed.)

No time, no time. The Suburb. Anne Stevenson. NMM

No trees in sight except thin spindly things. The Foresters Arms. Anthony Thwaite. HeHu

No trust to metals nor to marbles, when. Epitaph on Sir Edward Giles and His Wife. Robert Herrick. PoPle

No TV. Lilian Moore. IWK

No unemployed in Russia now. Just for Propaganda. H. H. Lewis. SPT

No Use. W. D. Snodgrass. BoLoP

No use trying to hurry it. The Wait. Phyllis Janowitz. AMV-80

No use waiting for it to stop. Apples. Shirley Kaufman. NMM; RiTi

No wake, please. Codicil. Robert Huff. CNW

No water is still, on top. The Movement of Fish. James Dickey. VGW

"No water so still as the/ dead fountains of Versailles." No Swan So Fine. Marianne Moore. PoA; PoIA; UnPo (1976 ed.)

No Way of Knowing. John Ashbery. CAAP

No White Bird Sings. John Ciardi. AMV-80

No woman has ever lost her man. Nine Bean-Rows on the Moon. A. W. Purdy. Moon

No woman, if she is honest, can say that she's/ been blessed with greater love, my Lesbia. Catullus, tr. fr. Latin by Horace Gregory. NAWM-1

No Woman No Nickel. *Unknown.* BluL

No, worlding, no, 'tis not thy gold. The Second Rapture. Thomas Carew. CaPo

No Worst, There Is None. Gerard Manley Hopkins. BoReV; CABA (1972 ed.); CMoP (1970 ed.); HeIP; InPS; NoAM; NOBE; OAEL-2; PFD; PoIA; PPP; VLP (Sonnet.) OBP

No You. Robert Tait. SLP

Noah. Chana Bloch. VWA

Noah in New England. Tom Lowenstein. VWA

Noah sailed his ark and skimmed his inner world. Proust on Noah. Eisig Silberschlag. VWA

Noah's Ark. Marguerite Young. WPE

Noah's daughter. Sibyl of the Waters. Ruth Fainlight. VWA

Noah's Raven. W. S. Merwin. ILP (1975 ed.); NIL

Noble Duke of York, The. *Unknown.* CTV; FSW

Noble lady, in whose light. With an Antique Crystal Cup and Ring. John Sobieski Stuart. SLP

Noble Nature, The. Ben Jonson. *Fr.* To the Immortal Memory and Friendship of That Noble Pair, Sir Lucius Cary, and Sir Henry Morison. VoPo
("It is not growing like a tree.") CABA (1972 ed.); HeIP; SoSe
(Lily of a Day, A.) PCOP

Noble Soldier, The, *sel.* Thomas Dekker.
"O Sorrow, Sorrow, say where dost thou dwell?" SCP-2

Nobles, and heralds by your leave. On Himself. Matthew Prior. FaBoEE

Noblest bodies are but gilded clay. Samuel Harding. *Fr.* Sicily and Naples; or, The Fatal Union: A Tragedy. SCP-2

Nobly, nobly Cape Saint Vincent to the North-West died away. Home-Thoughts, from the Sea. Robert Browning. ILP (1975 ed.); LFH; NOBE; OBP; STS

Nobody at the edge of the firepit. Floating World Picture: Spring in the Kitagami Mountains. Gary Snyder. ExPo (1973 ed.)

Nobody Comes. Thomas Hardy. BiP

Nobody Dies like Humphrey Bogart. Norman Rosten. PPoD

Nobody else makes doors like the poet's wife. The Poet's Wife Makes Him a Door So He Can Find the Way Home. Nancy Willard. RiTi

Nobody ever told my grandmother Eleni. Comfort from Arcadia. Nicholas Flocos. SA

Nobody heard him, the dead man. Not Waving but Drowning. Stevie Smith. BuTh; ExPo (1973 ed.); FF; HAP; HeIP; NoAM; NOBE; OAEL-2; OxBTC; POL; PPP; SS

Nobody in the lane, and nothing, nothing but blackberries. Blackberrying. Sylvia Plath. HAP; MPo; NoAM; NOBA

Nobody interfered. My two uncles stood. The Life Style. Edwin Brock. IPWM

Nobody know what i got inside. Emmet Kills-Warrior Turtle Mountain Reservation. Marnie Walsh. VW

Nobody Knows the [*or* de] Trouble I've Seen. *Unknown.* AH, *with music;* BLSH, *with music;* BLSo, *with music;* FSW

Nobody knows what I say. Alone. Itzik Manger, *tr.* by Ruth Whitman. VWA

Nobody knows what love is anymore. For a Masseuse and Prostitute. Kenneth Rexroth. NNaP

Nobody Loses All the Time. E. E. Cummings. CMoP (1970 ed.); DL; FaBoCo; FF; IPWM; NOBA; STS

Nobody may grow old now, grandfathers are out. Modernismus; or, Prayer for Standstill. Arthur J. Bull. HeHu

Nobody mentioned war. Malcolm. Lucille Clifton. CNA

Nobody noogers the shaff of a sloo. On a Flimmering Floom You Shall Ride. Carl Sandburg. ECBV; OBAL

Nobody planted roses, he recalls. "Summertime and the Living." Robert Hayden. BPo; NCSH; PoBA; PPP; UsP

Nobody Riding the Roads Today. June Jordan. BPo

Nobody said Apples for nearly a minute. Political Intelligence. A. J. M. Smith. EAS

Nobody told her it was time to go. Time Out. Patricia Henley. NPW

Nobody will open the door for you. Blanca Varela, *tr. fr. Spanish by* Willis Barnstone. BoWoP

Nobody will quarrel with the woodcock. Quarrel. *Yoruba Oral Tradition, tr. by* Ulli Beier. WTO

Nobody would have guessed. Sixes and Sevens. Roderick Hartigh Jellema. AATT

Nobody's Business. James Tate. PCho

Nocturn Cabbage. Carl Sandburg. DuDa

Nocturnal Heart. Anne-Marie Kegels, *tr. fr. French by* W. S. Merwin. BoWoP

Nocturnal Landscape. Malcolm Cowley. PoA

Nocturnal Reverie, A. Countess of Winchilsea. EBEV; PBWP; SBG; WPE

Nocturnal Sketch, A. Thomas Hood. BBL; FaBoCo

Nocturnal Thoughts. Avraham Huss, *tr. fr. Hebrew by* Mark Elliott Shapiro. VWA

Nocturnal[l] upon St Lucy's [*or* S. Lucies] Day, Being the Shortest Day, A. John Donne. AnMo; EBEV; GBL; MetP; NOBE; OAEL-1; OBP; PoPle; PPP; SCP-1

Nocturnal Visitor. Carolyn Miller. AMV-80

Nocturne: "Three-toed tree toad, The." Arthur Guiterman. ECBV

Nocturne II: "You who have listened to the heart of the night." Ruben Dario. *tr. fr. Spanish by* Jan Pallister. AMV-81

Nocturne at Bethesda. Arna Bontemps. AmNP (1974 ed.)

Nocturne, Central Park South. L. E. Sissman. NYP

Nocturne for October 31st, A. Yvor Winters. PoA

Nocturne for the U.S. Congress. Victor Contoski. GP

Nocturne: Homage to Whistler. Ruth Feldman. AMV-81

Nocturne in a Deserted Brickyard. Carl Sandburg. ILP (1975 ed.)

Nocturne in the Corner Phonebox, The. Andrew Taylor. FPA; GAS

Nocturne: Lake Huron. Conor Kelly. AMV-80

Nocturne of the Self-evident Presence. Thomas MacGreevy. BIrV; CIP

Nocturne of the Wharves. Arna Bontemps. BPo

Nocturne Varial. Lewis Alexander. PoBA

Nocturnes I. Dan Gerber. TC

Nod. Walter de la Mare. OxBTC

Nodding against. Jack Kerouac. *Fr.* Some Western Haikus. VoA

Nodding, its great head rattling like a gourd. Original Sin: A Short Story. Robert Penn Warren. CoPAm; HoPM (1975 ed.); PPP; TAP

Nodding oxeye bends before the wind, The. The Fear of Flowers. John Clare. PF

Noel of the marvelous night. To Noel. Gabriela Mistral. PChr

Nofretete. Felix Pollak. HeS

Noise. *Unknown.* DuDr

Noise of hammers once I heard. The Hammers. Ralph Hodgson. NOBE; OxBTC

Noise of passing feet, The. Listening. Alice Corbin, *after Chippewa Indian.* BPAW

Noise of the Village, The. *Tr. fr. Chippewa Indian by* Frances Densmore. OBVE

Noise of water teased his literal ear, The. Persistent Explorer. John Crowe Ransom. PiAm

Noiseless Patient Spider, A. Walt Whitman. BiP; CABA (1972 ed.); FF; HAP; HeIP; ILP (1975 ed.); InPK; IPWM; LFH; NIL; NOBA; PAIC; PBMP; PiAm; SoSe; TAP; VoPo; WIF, 2 *versions*

Noises. Fred Johnson. CNA

Noises from underground made gibber some. John Berryman. *Fr.* Dream Songs. CAPP

Noises in the Dark. Liz Lochhead. MS

Noises of the harbour die, the smoke is petrified, The. The Statue. Roy Fuller. NOBE

Noisy Boys. Jack Castiglione. BBGO

Noisy politicians confuse the world. Rhyming with a Friend. Yü Hsüan-chi, *tr. by* Geoffrey Waters. BoWoP

Nokes went, he thought, to Styles's wife to bed. A Case to the Civilians. *Unknown.* FaBoEE

Nomads gather in autumn. Assembly. W. S. Merwin. GP

Nomine Domini/ Theotocopoulos. High Renaissance. George Starbuck. OBAL

Nominis Umbra. J. A. R. McKellar. MAuV

Non Piangere, Liú. Peter Porter. GAS

Non Poem about Vietnam, A. Carolyn M. Rodgers. SA

Non Sequitor, A. Richard Corbet. FaBoNo

Non Sum Qualis Eram Bonae sub Regno Cynarae. Ernest Dowson. BoLoP; CABA (1972 ed.); GBL; HAP; HeIP; NIL; NOBE; OAEL-2; VLP; VoPo (Cynara.) UnPo (1976 ed.) ("Last night ah, yesternight, betwixt her lips and mine.") LoAs

Non Ti Fidar. Louis Zukofsky. VGW

Nona poured oil on the water and saw the eye. The Evil Eye. John Ciardi. CoPAm

Nondescript express in from the South, A. Gare du Midi. W. H. Auden. PSN

None. Josephine Miles. VGW

None could ever say that she. Catullus, *tr. fr. Latin by* Walter Savage Landor. OBVE

None ever was in love with me but grief. "My True Love Hath My Heart and I Have His." Mary Elizabeth Coleridge. BoLoP

None other fame mine unambitious muse. Samuel Daniel. *Fr.* To Delia. AAS

None Other Lamb, None Other Name. Christina Rossetti. PFD

Nonsense. Richard Corbet. FaBoNo

Nonsense. Thomas Moore. FaBoEE

Nonsense ("The cricket and the greshope. . ."). *Unknown.* OxBM ("Cricket and the greshope wenten hem to fight, The.") EBEV

Nonsense ("Oh that my lungs. . ."). *Unknown. See* Odd but True.

Nonsense Rhyme. Elinor Wylie. PBMP; Psy

Nonsense Song, A. Stephen Vincent Benét. OBAL

Nooksack Valley. Gary Snyder. MPA

Noon. Thomas Hornsby Ferril. MPA

Noon—and the north-west sweeps the empty road. February. William Morris. *Fr.* The Earthly Paradise. VPC

Noon Glare. Matthew Brennan. AMV-80

Noon heat in the yard, The. Hen Woman. Thomas Kinsella. CIP

Noon Hour. Joan Finnigan. BuTh

Noon is beautiful, The: the perfect wheel. An Elegy. Yvor Winters. VGW

Noon is half the passion of light. Noon. Thomas Hornsby Ferril. MPA

Noon of the Sunbather. Marge Piercy. NMM

Noon on Alameda Street. Hildegarde Flanner. WPW

Noon on the mountain! Walt Whitman. Emanuel Carnevali. PoA

Noon sets the tips of pines on fire. To Shadow. Charles O. Hartman. AAN

Noon sun beats down the leaf; the noon. Grapes Making. Léonie Adams. UnPo (1976 ed.)

Noon. The luminous tide. Ballydavid Pier. Thomas Kinsella. BIrV

Nor happiness, nor majesty, nor fame. Sonnet: Political Greatness. Shelley. NIL; OBP

Nor lingered Paris in the lofty house. Homer, *tr. by* Tennyson. *Fr.* The Iliad, VI. OBVE

Nor long the trench or lofty walls oppose. Homer, *tr. by* Pope. *Fr.* The Iliad, XII. OBVE

Nor looks that backward life so bare to me. Frederick Goddard Tuckerman. *Fr.* Sonnets. AmVN

Nor practising virtue nor committing crime. Epitaph. Geoffrey Taylor. FaBoEE

Nor shall you for your fields neglect your stock. Young Stock. V. Sackville-West. OxBTC

Nor skin nor hide nor fleece. Lethe. Hilda Doolittle ("H. D."). CMoP (1970 ed.); PiAm; VGW

Nor think, in nature's state they blindly trod. Pope. *Fr.* An Essay on Man, III. OAEL-1

Nor truth nor good did they know. Gloss. Padraic Fiacc. CIP

Nor, will anyone dare say to. Sharon Will Be No/Where on Nobody's Best-Selling List. Sharon Scott. JB

Nor yet do I, your knowing lover. Portrait. John Lyle Donaghy. BIrV

Nora. Fran Winant. WBN

Nora Criona. James Stephens. PFIr

Nora's Vow. Sir Walter Scott. SLP

Norfolk. John Betjeman. BBGO

Norfolk Rebellion, The. *Unknown.* GBP

Norfolk sprang thee, Lambeth holds thee dead. Earl of Surrey. AAS

Normal as Two Ships in the Night. Walta Borawski. AMV-81

Normal Lives. Dick Allen. FAF

Norman Baron, The, *sel.* Longfellow. "In his chamber, weak and dying." PeD

Norman conquest all historians fix, The. The English Succession. *Unknown.* OxBChV

Norman Morrison. David Ferguson. NowV

Norman Morrison. Adrian Mitchell. FF; NowV

North Africa Breakdown. Tom Raworth. TwMBP

North Beach Poem. A. D. Winans. CPA

North Coast Town. Robert Gray. CAAP

North Country, The. D. H. Lawrence. PES

North Country maid up to London had strayed, A. The Oak and the Ash. *Unknown.* FSW

North Dakota Gothic. Mark Vinz. HeS

North Infiinity Street. Conrad Aiken. ILP (1975 ed.)

North Labrador. Hart Crane. CMoP (1970 ed.); POL

North, near the tip, where the island. Approaching Washington Heights. James Reiss. NYP

North of Berwick. Sydney Tremayne. MS

North of Chillicothe. Blessing at Kellenberger Road. Maxine Kent Valian. AMV-80

North of 96th where the tracks come out from under. From a Diary. Frederick Morgan. NYP

North of north, citizens were holding. The Metamorphoses. Edward Weismiller. PoUp

North of Santa Monica. Carter Revard. VoR

North of the house there was a graveled range of hills. Prairie Wolf. Gwendolen Haste. WPW

North Pole Story, A. Menella Bute Smedley. OxBChV

North Sea Undertaker's Complaint, The. Robert Lowell. LFH

North Star, The. John Morris-Jones, tr. fr. Welsh by Anthony Conran. OBW

North to Milwaukee. Gerald Vizenor. VoR

North Wales girl was once my passion, A. Two-faced Too. Tr. fr. Welsh by Glyn Jones. OBW

North wind doth blow, The. Mother Goose. MG

Northwind fallen, in the newstarrèd night, The. The Hesperides. Tennyson. OAEL-2

North Wind in October. Robert Bridges. FSFS; VLP

Northern breath, that freezes floods, he binds, The. Ovid, tr. by Dryden. Fr. Metamorphoses, I. OBVE

Northern Cobbler, The. Tennyson. EBEV

Northern Farmer: New Style. Tennyson. BiP; VLP

Northern Farmer: Old Style. Tennyson. VLP

Northern Habitat, A. Robin Fulton. MIS

Northern Pike. James Wright. CAAP

Northern Hoard, A, sel. Seamus Heaney.
    "Leaf membranes lid the window." CIP

Northern Ireland: Two Comments. Seamus Deane. CIP

Northhanger Ridge. Charles Wright. CSP

Northward. Dominick J. Lepore. AMV-80

Northwest Airlines (My Emergency Instructions Were in Chinese). Fred Chappell. HoPM (1975 ed.)

Norwegian Wood. John Lennon and Paul McCartney. OBP

Nosce Teipsum, sels. Sir John Davies. NOBE
    Affliction.
    Soul and the Body, The.

Nose becomes a triangular history, The. Terra Cotta. K. Curtis Lyle. CNA

Noses are running at our house, The. A Winter Scene. Reed Whittemore. NCSH

Nostalgia. D. H. Lawrence. PoA

Nostalgia. Gertrude Millard. BPAW

Nostalgia. Karl Shapiro. CMoP (1970 ed.)

Nostalgia for 70. Jim Wayne Miller. AMV-81

Nostalgia's a rough trip. Mainline. John Ditsky. AMV-80

Nostradamus's Prophecy. Andrew Marvell. TT

Not a breath of air. Airey-Force Valley. Wordsworth. VLP

Not a Clown. Barry Schechter. FiCh

Not a drum was heard, not a funeral note. The Burial of Sir John Moore after [or at] Corunna. · Charles Wolfe. BTTM; FaPoR; NOBE

Not a line of her writing have I. Thoughts of Phena. Thomas Hardy. OxBTC

Not a Political Poem. Barbara Berman. PoUp

Not a Sous Had He Got. "Thomas Ingoldsby." Fr. The Ingoldsby Legends: The Cynotaph. FaBoCo

Not a thing on the river McCluskey did fear. The Little Brown Bulls. Unknown. AmFP

Not a tree but the tree. There Is Only One of Everything. Margaret Atwood. MMD

Not a viper with milk beneath its tongue. Who Will Give Cover? Anadad Eldan, tr. by Ruth Nevo. VWA

Not Aladdin magian. On Visiting Staffa. Keats. MBPR

Not all of them were human. The Village of Tudda. Kenneth Patchen. VGW

Not All There. Robert Frost. FaBoCo

Not all those who pass. The Great Mother. Gary Snyder. CC

Not all thy flushing suns are set. An Ode to Master Endymion Porter, upon His Brother's Death. Robert Herrick. CaPo; SCP-1

Not Alone for Mighty Empire, with music. William Pierson Merrill. AH

Not always give a melting kiss. Johannes Secundus, tr. fr. Latin by Thomas Stanley. Fr. Basia, VIII. OBVE

Not an unhappy man. Norman Morrison. David Ferguson. NowV

Not as height rises into lightness. Breadth. Circle. Desert. Monarch. Month. Wisdom. John Hollander. PoA

Not as These. Dante Gabriel Rossetti. The House of Life, LXXV. VLP

Not at midnight, not at morning, O sweet city. Caryatid. Léonie Adams. LoAs

Not at night, no, altogether, tomorrow. No. Natan Zach, tr. by Laya Firestone. VWA

Not at the first sight, nor with a dribbled shot. Astrophel and Stella, II. Sir Philip Sidney. OAEL-1

Not because of victories. Te Deum. Charles Reznikoff. VWA

Not because of you, not because of me, just that. Natalya Gorbanyevskaya, tr. fr. Russian by Daniel Weissbort. BoWoP

Not because your body is lovely or your hair. To X. Tom Scott. SLP

Not Being Wise. Virginia Elson. AMV-80

Not believing that igneous dream. Nothing Inside and Nothing Out. Ray Amorosi. FiCP

Not Blindly in the Dark. Robert M. Stanley. AMV-81

Not but they die, the teasers and the dreams. The Teasers. William Empson. OxBTC

Not by chance/ the cock sparrow. Christographia 35. Eugene Warren. AMV-80

Not by hammering the furious word. Harlem Riot, 1943. Pauli Murray. PoBA

Not by lost killers stranded. The Biggest Killing. Edward Dorn. VGW

Not Canaan and its cities, the splendor of towers. Moses on Mount Nebo. Abraham Regelson, tr. by Richard Flantz. VWA

Not, Celia, that I juster am. To Celia. Sir Charles Sedley. NOBE

Not Dead but Sleeping. Elizabeth Bartlett. PMW

Not diverted by this windowful. Blind Girl on the Santa Fe. Conrad Hilberry. TC

Not easy to state the change you made. Love Letter. Sylvia Plath. NOBA; UsP

Not envying Latian shades—if yet they throw. The River Duddon, I. Wordsworth. MBPR

Not even dried-up leaves. Thesis, Antithesis, and Nostalgia. Alan Dugan. NowV

Not even for a moment. He knew, for one thing, what he was. Leda. Mona Van Duyn. NMM

Not even my pride will suffer much. Theme and Variations. Edna St. Vincent Millay. SBG

Not even the angels could bring a breath of air. The Old Biograph Girl. Margaret Benbow. AMV-81

Not even when the early birds. The Rabbit. W. H. Davies. BoAnP

Not ever to talk when merely requested. For My Son. Alan Brownjohn. LP

Not every man has gentians in his house. Bavarian Gentians. D. H. Lawrence. CMoP (1970 ed.); HAP; ILP (1975 ed.); InPK; InPS; NoAM; NOBE; OAEL-2, 2 versions; PoIA; PPoe; TCP; WIF, 2 versions

Not falling/ but curling up. The Children's Hour. Don Johnson. PCho

Not far beyond the town wild flowers grow. Sanctuary. Clifford Dyment. PoA

Not far from the Cooper River Bridge. One Summer in Charleston. Michael Hogan. DNGG

Not fighting it for once. Insomnia. Elizabeth Zelvin. AMV-80

Not for the promise of the laboured field. Ode to the Poppy. Henrietta Oneil. WPE

Not for these lovely blooms that prank your chambers did I come. Rendezvous. Edna St. Vincent Millay. RiTi

Not for us this shell grew like a lily. A Striped Shell. Ruth Dallas. ATNZ

Not Fortune's worshipper, nor Fashion's fool. Apologia pro Vita Sua. Pope. Fr. Epistle to Dr. Arbuthnot. NOBE

Not from the unmapped valleys of darkness, nor. Hall of Ocean Life. John Hollander. PoA

Not from this anger, anticlimax after. Dylan Thomas. PoA

Not Going with It. Zali Gurevitch, tr. fr. Hebrew by Gabriel Levin. VWA

Not guns, not thunder, but a flutter of clouded drums. Fireworks. Babette Deutsch. OFD

Not Having a History. John Vernon. PPoD

Not having found your way out of the woods, begin. Sleeping in the Woods. David Wagoner. MPA

Not having much fun. Can't Wait. John Kitching. FPB

Not having spoken for years now. Matrilineal Descent. Robin Morgan. WBN

Not he who holds the sceptre high atop the eagle's throne. Why the Resurrection Was Revealed to Women. Catharina Regina von Greiffenberg, tr. by Michael Hamburger. PBWP

Not hell but a street, not. 209 Canal. Richard Howard. NYP; TAP

Not Her, She Aint No Gypsy. Al Young. GP

Not Here. Edmund Wilson. PoA

Not honey,/ not the plunder of the bee. Fragment 113. Hilda Doolittle ("H.D."). PiAm

Not I. Robert Louis Stevenson. NOBL

Not I myself know all my love for thee. The Dark Glass. Dante Gabriel Rossetti. The House of Life, XXXIV. VPC

Not I, not I, but the wind that blows through me! The Song of a Man Who Has Come Through. D. H. Lawrence. CMoP (1970 ed.); InPS; NoAM; OxBTC

Not Ideas about the Thing but the Thing Itself. Wallace Stevens. HAP; TAP

Not, I'll not, carrion comfort, Despair, not feast on thee. Carrion Comfort. Gerard Manley Hopkins. AnMo; BoReV; CABA (1972 ed.); CMoP (1970 ed.); HeIP; ILP (1975 ed.); InPK; NoAM; OAEL-2; PFD; PPP

Not in a silver casket cool with pearls. Edna St. Vincent Millay. CMoP (1970 ed.); VGW

Not in India, where fire rivers are. Jalal al-Din Rumi, tr. fr. Persian. ILwL

Not in my saddle, but above it. Indian Summer: Montana, 1956. W. M. Ransom. CDW

Not in our time, O Lord. Hilda Doolittle ("H. D."). Fr. Tribute to the Angels. NOBA

Not in the crises of events. The Spirit's Epochs. Coventry Patmore. Fr. The Angel in the House. EBEV; GBL

Not in the days of Adam and Eve, but when Adam. In the Days of Prismatic Color. Marianne Moore. PiAm

Not in the solitude. Hymn of the City. Bryant. EAP; PiAm

Not in thy body is thy life at all. Life-in-Love. Dante Gabriel Rossetti. The House of Life, XXXVI. HAP; VLP

Not it. She. The one with eggs. Moving North. Ann Deagon. CSP

Not just one night but all the nights. Land's End. Daniel J. Langton. MIT

Not Just Yet. Carter Revard. VoR

Not-Knowing. Dawn Hinshaw. AMV-81

Not knowing in what season this again. Parting: 1940. John Frederick Nims. PoA

Not large, not fierce, and in distress. The White Bear. Paula Goff. BCr

Not Leaving the House. Gary Snyder. IPWM; NIL

Not less because in purple I descended. Tea at the Palaz of Hoon. Wallace Stevens. PoA

Not Like a Cypress. Yehuda Amichai, tr. fr. Hebrew by Stephen Mitchell. VWA

Not like Jesus pinned. Crucified. Anne Sadowski. SES

Not like That. Adrienne Rich. CoPAm

Not like the brazen giant of Greek fame. The New Colossus. Emma Lazarus. FaPo; SBG; WPE

Not long this transport held its place. The Third Voice. "Lewis Carroll." Fr. The Three Voices. VLP

Not Lost in the Stars. Bruce Bliven. QQQ

"Not Marble nor the Gilded Monuments." Archibald MacLeish. BoLoP; CMoP (1970 ed.); HoPM (1975 ed.); NIL; WIF

Not marble, not the gilded monuments. Sonnets, LV. Shakespeare. CABA (1972 ed.); Epi; FF; HeIP; ILP (1975 ed.); InPK; NIL; NOBE; OAEL-1; PAIC; PPoe; STS; WIF

Not Marching Away to Be Killed. Jean Overton Fuller. FF

Not marching in the fields of Thrasimene. Doctor Faustus. Christopher Marlowe. OAEL-1

Not Men Alone. Edwin Rolfe. SPT

Not mine own fears nor the prophetic soul. Sonnets, CVII. Shakespeare. CABA (1972 ed.); EBEV; HAP; OAEL-1; PPoe

Not Now. Robert Creeley. Epi

Not now the sun yellows the vine. Sparrows in College Ivy. Edgar Wolfe. AMV-81

Not of all my eyes see, wandering on the world. Ashboughs. Gerard Manley Hopkins. VLP

Not, of course, the monster hunched downtown. Dome Poem. Dave Smith. PoA

Not of the princes and prelates with periwigged charioteers. A Consecration. John Masefield. NoAM

Not of the sunlight. Tennyson. Fr. Merlin and the Gleam, IX. CTV

Not Often. Ray Fraser. NeAC

Not often con brio, but andante, andante. Stanley Matthews. Alan Ross. LiSp; OxBTC

Not one of them has seen it, but the fox. Field Trip. Gary Miranda. AMV-81

Not only how far away, but the way that you say it. Judging Distances. Henry Reed. Lessons of the War, II. BoLoP; NIL; NOBE; PSN; SoSe

Not Only Where God's Free Winds Blow, with music. Shepherd Knapp. AH

Not only with no sense of shame. Tennyson. FaBoEE

Not out of the war, not out of the agitated. Man on a Raft. J. R. Hervey. ATNZ

Not Palaces, an Era's Crown. Stephen Spender. CMoP (1970 ed.); ExPo (1973 ed.); ILP (1975 ed.); NoAM

Not Pallas, not ev'n Spleen it self could blame. Ovid, tr. by John Gay. Fr. Metamorphoses, VI. OBVE

Not picnics or pageants or the improbable. Terror. Robert Penn Warren. PoA

Not power nor the storied hand of God. Allen Tate. *Fr.* Sonnets of the Blood. PoA

Not proud of station nor in worldly pelf. Frederick Goddard Tuckerman. *Fr.* Sonnets. AmVN

Not-quiet touchable air, A. The State in Indian Language Was Called "Running Water." Besmilr Brigham. Psy

Not quite/ spherical. At Breakfast. May Swenson. Psy; SOS

Not quite alone from night to night you'll find them. The New Dolores Leather Bar. Turner Cassity. CSP

Not Quite Spring. Lyn Lifshin. NeAC

Not quite yet. Dining Out with Doug and Frank. James Schuyler. NYP

Not Ragged-and-Tough. *Unknown.* FaBoNo

Not realizing. Six Feet Under. Janet Campbell Hale. VoR

Not Seeing Is Believing. Paul Petrie. TAP

Not Singing. Linda Gregg. AAN

Not-so-good Earth, The. Bruce Dawe. GAS

Not so long ago my Lord a child lay manger-cradled. Bambino. Betty Ruth Bird. AATT

Not solely that the future she destroys. Modern Love, XII. George Meredith. GBL; VPC

Not Speaking. Lawrence Russ. TC

Not Steel Alone. Norman Macleod. SPT

"Not strangeness, but strange likeness." Geoffrey Hill. Mercian Hymns, XXIX. HAP

Not that by this disdain. The Repulse. Thomas Stanley. MetP

Not that God's dead. Jacob's Winning. Richard Sherwin. VWA

Not that he promised not to windowshop. One Man's Wife. Philip Booth. VGW

Not that I cared about the other women. Colder. Erica Jong. MMD

Not that I would attribute. An Interview with a Tornado Victim on April 16, 1974. Philip Legler. TC

Not that the earth is changing, O my God! On Refusal of Aid between Nations. Dante Gabriel Rossetti. EBEV; VLP

Not that the pines were darker there. The Long Voyage. Malcolm Cowley. SoSe

Not the attendance of stones. Black Maps. Mark Strand. PoA

Not the beautiful youth with features of bloom and brightness. Beauty. Walt Whitman. WeW

Not the branch that taps at the widow. Leaving Mexico One More Time. Constance Urdang. AMV-80

Not the cougar leaping to myth. Man Is a Snow. Earle Birney. MPA

Not the divine rising up from earth as dew. Forte: For Tina. David Meltzer. MIT

Not the official ones, who have been. Patients. U. A. Fanthorpe. PMW

Not the rejected lies of the New York Foundling. Grandmother Grant. Madeline DeFrees. CNW

Not the normal natural world, not the deep mind. Frederick Goddard Tuckerman. *Fr.* Sonnets. AmVN; PiAm; PPoD

Not Thinking of America. Judith Kroll. AmPA

Not This Leaf Haunts Me. Tony Cosier. AMV-81

Not those who have lived here and gone. Moving. James Harrison. CoPAm

Not time in a rush but whole time. June. Bink Noll. TCP

Not to be believed, this blunt savage wind. Papermill. Joseph Kalar. SPT

Not to be the mother of solitude will I give myself. A Busy Man Speaks. Robert Bly. ConAP

Not to have known the hard-bitten. Beginnings. Robert D. Fitzgerald. GAS; MAuV

Not to Keep. Robert Frost. CMoP (1970 ed.)

Not to Love. Robert Herrick. CaPo

Not to March. Kris Hackleman. AMV-80

Not to say what everyone else was saying. Different. Clere Parsons. FaBoTw (1975 ed.)

Not to sigh and to be tender. Aphra Behn. BoWoP

Not to Sleep. Robert Graves. BuTh

Not to the butcher did he pass. The Old Ox. George Rostrevor Hamilton, *after* Addaios of Makedon. FaBoEE

Not to the fury of the storm, though loud. The Pine of Whiting Wood. John P. Sjolander. BPAW

Not to the I-80 where. Where I Walk in Nebraska. Nancy G. Westerfield. AMV-80

Not to touch, she said to me, anything sticky. Nightpiece. Judith Johnson Sherwin. WBN

Not to Us, Not unto Us, Lord, *with music. Unknown.* AH

Not too far north from where I write set dawn. Hint for the Incomplete Angler. Kendrick Smithyman. ATNZ

Not twice a twelvemonth you appear in print. Epilogue to the Satires. Pope. OAEL-1

Not Ulysses, no, nor any other man. Sonnet I. Louise Labé, *tr. fr. Italian by* Willis Barnstone. BoWoP

Not under a stone. Breathe In Breathe Out. Layle Silbert. NPW

Not under Holly or Green Boughs. Tom Raworth. TwMBP

Not upon earth, as you suppose. Tu Non Se' in Terra, Si Come Tu Credi. Kathleen Raine. WPE

Not walking, in my dreams, my dreams. Infidelity. Olga Berggolts, *tr. by* Daniel Weissbort. BoWoP

Not Waving but Drowning. Stevie Smith. BuTh; ExPo (1973 ed.); FF; HAP; HeIP; NoAM; NOBE; OAEL-2; OxBTC; POL; PPP; SBG; SS

Not weaned yet, without comprehension loving. Love's Immaturity. E. J. Scovell. GBL

Not what you get, but what you give. Of Giving. Arthur Guiterman. CTV

Not with more glories, in the ethereal plain. The Voyage on the Thames. Pope. *Fr.* The Rape of the Lock. EBEV; NOBE

Not with my hands. Benediction. Donald Jeffrey Hayes. AmNP (1974 ed.)

Not working, not breathing. Autumn. Bella Akhmadulina, *tr. by* Barbara Einzig. BoWoP

Not yet can she bear the yoke on submissive neck. Odes II, 5. Horace, *tr. by* C. E. Bennett. LoAs

Not yet dawn. Asian Brother, Asian Sister. Lawson Fusao Inada. MPA; SA

Not yet dead, not yet alone. Osip Mandelstam, *tr. fr. Russian by* James Greene. OBVE

Not yet forsaken (gentle muse) draw near. In Commendation of a Solitary Life. Thomas Lodge. TVS

Not yet half-drest. To a Late Poplar. Patrick Kavanagh. PFIr

Not yet, not yet. The Tree. Joel Sloman. VGW

Not yet will those measureless fields be green again. The Cenotaph. Charlotte Mew. WPE

Not you, lean quarterlies and swarthy periodicals. To the Film Industry in Crisis. Frank O'Hara. CAAP; NoAM; NOBA; OBAL

Note Delivered by a Female Impersonator. Heather McHugh. AmPA

Note from an Exhibition. Albert Goldbarth. AMV-81

Note from my dying sister stirs up, The. Bordello, Revisited. Eve Triem. GP

Note how the desert takes form, easily as wax. In Scorching Time. Alex Stevens. AMV-81

Note on Lizard's Feet, A. James Van Rensselaer. BPAW

Note on Local Flora. William Empson. EBEV; PSN

Note on Master Crow, A. Jean Garrigue. BoAnP

Note on Propertius 1.5. Fleur Adcock. ATNZ; BoLoP

Note on the Latin Gerunds, A. Richard Porson. FaBoCo ("When Dido found Aeneas would not come.") FaBoEE

Note on the Social Arts, A. Kendrick Smithyman. ATNZ

Note on Wyatt, A. Kingsley Amis. WeW

Note the stump, a peach tree. Places and Ways to Live. Richard Hugo. GP

Note this survivor, bearing the mark of the violator. Swendenborg's Skull. Vernon Watkins. FaBoTw (1975 ed.)

Note to a New Lesbian. Martha Shelley. WBN

Note to Olga (1966), A. Denise Levertov. CAPP

Notes for a History of Poetry. David Daiches. PoA

Notes for a Lecture. David Ignatow. NNaP

Notes for a Movie Script. M. Carl Holman. AmNP (1974 ed.); PoBA; WeW

Notes Found near a Suicide. Frank Horne. *See* Letters Found near a Suicide.

Notes from an Analyst's Couch. Anita Endrezze Probst. CDW

Notes from the Delivery Room. Linda Pastan. RiTi

Notes of schoolmates, The. For Isidore Ducasse. Paul Hoover. FiCh

Notes on a Life to Be Lived, *sels.* Robert Penn Warren. NoAM
Blow, West Wind.
Small White House.
Ways of Day.

Notes on a Long Evening. David Phillips. NeAC

Notes on My Father, *sel.* Katerina Anghelaki-Rooke. "Old man moved into his night, The." PBWP

Notes Scribbled on the Last Page of a Novel. Leslie Woolf Hedley. PoW

Notes to a Biographer. Peter Porter. CAAP

Notes toward a Supreme Fiction, *sels.* Wallace Stevens. NOBA
"And for what, except for you, do I feel love?"
"Begin, ephebe, by perceiving the idea."
"First idea was not our own, The. Adam."
"It feels good as it is without the giant."
"Major abstraction is the idea of man, The."

Notes toward an Autobiography: The Poet at 41. Richard Shelton. FoP

Nothin very bad happen to me lately. Henry's Confession. John Berryman. *Fr.* Dream Songs. NoAM

Nothing. Julia de Burgos, *tr. fr. Spanish by* Aliki *and* Willis Barnstone. BoWoP

Nothing. Walter de la Mare. ECBV

Nothing. Charles Simic. NNaP

Nothing/substance utters or time. The Word. Basil Bunting. PoA

Nothing as miserable has happened before. The Long Island Night. Howard Moss. PChO

Nothing at all more delicate and charming. Dance of Burros. Dilys Laing. PCOP

Nothing but a hovel now. The Ruin. Dafydd ap Gwilym, *tr. by* Rolfe Humphries. OBW

Nothing but a man. Nadia Tueni, *tr. fr. French by* Willis Barnstone. BoWoP

Nothing but Death. Pablo Neruda, *tr. fr. Spanish by* Robert Bly. EAS

Nothing but Image. Jody Swilky. AMV-81

Nothing but no and I, and I and no. Michael Drayton. *Fr.* Idea. GBL

Nothing comes to a halt sleeping off. "My Dream of Pure Invention." Madeline DeFrees. MPA

Nothing could/ prevent her from being photographed. Rested near Nefertete. Carol Bergé. MMD

Nothing doing here. New England Greenhouse. Rennie McQuilkin. AMV-80

Nothing Elegant. Gertrude Stein. *Fr.* Tender Buttons. PBWP

Nothing False and Possible Is Love. E. E. Cummings. Epi

Nothing Gold Can Stay. Norma Farber. AMV-81

Nothing Gold Can Stay. Robert Frost. AnMo; ILP (1975 ed.); NCSH; NIL; NOBA; PPP; SoSe (1977 ed.); STS; TAP; TSWA; VGW

Nothing if not utterly in death. So? James P. Vaughn. AmNP (1974 ed.)

Nothing in Heaven Functions as It Ought. X. J. Kennedy. CoPAm; ExPo (1973 ed.)

Nothing in Rambling. *Unknown.* BluL

Nothing in the sky is high. Asleep and Awake. David McCord. ECBV

Nothing in thick clothes is. In the Home. Marvin Bell. NVAP

Nothing Inside and Nothing Out. Ray Amorosi. FiCP

Nothing Is. Sun-Ra. PoBA

Nothing is better, I well think. The Leper. Swinburne. GBL

Nothing is easy! Pity then. Variations: # 21. James Stephen. WIF

Nothing is getting up now in my life. Packer City Poem. Peter Cooley. HeS

Nothing is happening after all. Codicil. Alvin Aubert. CoPAm

Nothing Is Lost. Anne Ridler. WPE

Nothing is new: we walk where others went. Nothing New. Robert Herrick. CaPo

Nothing is pacified. It will be. Written. Mary Ruelfe. AMV-81

Nothing is plumb, level or square. Love Song: I and Thou. Alan Dugan. BuTh; CAPP; CoPAm; FF; HoPM (1975 ed.); ILP (1975 ed.); InPK; LoAs; NoAM; SFF; SoSe

Nothing is so beautiful as spring. Spring. Gerard Manley Hopkins. FSFS; HAP; ILP (1975 ed.); NoAM; NOBE; OAEL-2; OBP; SoSe; VLP

Nothing is the same to anyone. After Reading Takahashi. Jim Harrison. HeS

Nothing is too small for my sarcasm. Immensity. Gerald Stern. AMV-80

Nothing like Grog. Charles Dibdin. RhR

Nothing like that road runs from me. A Cabin in Minnesota. Marvin Bell. HoPM (1975 ed.)

Nothing more impermanent, it appears. Young Girl. Iain Crichton Smith. MS

Nothing More than a Sister. *Unknown.* TDH

Nothing More Will Happen. Marge Piercy. NeAC (Different Persuasions.) InPK

Nothing move thee. Poem. St. Theresa of Avila, *tr. by* Arthur Symons. PBMP

"Nothing moves," you say, and stare across the lawn. The Recruits. Ian Hamilton. NoAM

Nothing New. Robert Herrick. CaPo

Nothing, not the hotel's beige darkness, not. The Chelsea. Derek Walcott. NYP

Nothing of ours there now. Selling the House. Sandra McPherson. CNW

Nothing out of which to create a new, A. None. Josephine Miles. VGW

Nothing remained: Nothing, the wanton name. The Annihilation of Nothing. Thom Gunn. NoAM

Nothing Sacred. Roger Woddis. NOBL

Nothing so difficult as a beginning. Byron. *Fr.* Don Juan, IV. OAEL-2

Nothing so startles us as tumbleweeds in December. Weeds. Ann Stanford. MPA

Nothing so true as what you once let fall. To a Lady: Of the Characters of Women. Pope. Moral Essays, Epistle II. OAEL-1

Nothing Strange. Tom Kryss. NeAC

Nothing! thou elder brother even to Shade. Upon Nothing. Earl of Rochester. OBSV; SCP-2

Nothing to Be Said. Philip Larkin. OxBTC

Nothing to be said about it, and everything. Dying. Robert Pinsky. AMV-81

Nothing to do but work. The Pessimist. Ben King. FaBoCo; FaBoNo; OBAL

Nothing to Lose. Joseph Kalar. SPT

Nothing to Wear. William Allen Butler. OBAL

Nothing Will Die. Tennyson. PBMP

Nothing will fill the salt caves our youth wore. Alone. E. J. Scovell. GBL

Nothing will keep. Personal Letter # 3. Sonia Sanchez. RiTi

Nothing would sleep in that cellar, dank as a ditch. Root Cellar. Theodore Roethke. HeIP; PiAm; PoIA; PPP

Nothingness. Aharon Amir, tr. fr. Hebrew. VWA

Nothing's going to become of anyone. Play. A. R. Ammons. PoA

Notice how he has numbered the blue veins. Mr. Mine. Anne Sexton. SFF

Notice the Convulsed Orange Inch of Moon. E. E. Cummings. VGW

Noticing winter I can't stop thinking. Winter Sonnet. Anne Waldman. CAAP

Notify someone of authority. If You See This Man. Thomas Lux. AmPA; NVAP

Notorious Glutton, The. Ann Taylor. OxBChV

Notre Dame. Osip Mandelstam, tr. fr. Russian by James Greene. OBVE

Nottamun Town. Unknown. FaBoNo

Nottingham Fair. Unknown. AmFP

Nou Goth Sonne under Wode. Unknown. See Me Rueth, Mary.

Nought is on earth more sacred or divine. Spenser. Fr. The Faerie Queene, V, 7. OAEL-1

Nought [or Naught] loves another as itself. A Little Boy Lost. Blake. Fr. Songs of Experience. ILP (1975 ed.); MBPR; OBP; STS

Nova. Robinson Jeffers. CMoP (1970 ed.); HAP

Novel, The. Denise Levertov. ILP (1975 ed.); NoAM

Novella. Adrienne Rich. PPP

Novelty Shop, The. Duane Niatum. CDW

November. Arthur J. Bull. HeHu

November. John Clare. FSFS

November. Hartley Coleridge. FSFS

November. F. W. Harvey. OxBTC

November. Thomas Hood. See No!

November. Ted Hughes. CMoP (1970 ed.)

November. Spenser. Fr. The Shepheardes Calendar. Epi

November. Frederick Goddard Tuckerman. NOBA

November. Samuel S. Turner. AMV-80

November Birthday. Mary Swanson Stroh. NPW

November Blue. Alice Meynell. PES

November Cotton Flower. Jean Toomer. NoAM; UnPo (1976 ed.)

November Day at McClure's. Robert Bly. NU

November Morning. Mary Ann Larkin. PoUp

November Night. Adelaide Crapsey. PAIC

November Night, Edinburgh. Norman MacCaig. MS

November 1968. Adrienne Rich. NMM

November on Lake Michigan. Tom McKeown. HeS

November Snow. E. J. Carson. AMV-81

November Sun. Elizabeth Daryush. PBWP

November 3. Richard Brautigan. VoA

November through a Giant Copper Beech. Edwin Honig. NoAM

November Walk. Susanne Doyle. AMV-81

Novembers, half a stalk high. Cattails for Bennett. Mary Shumway. HeS

November's Lesson. Mel Takahara. PHC

Novus Ordo Seclorum. Grace Cavalieri. AATT

Now. Robert Browning. VLP

Now. Robert Huff. CNW

Now. William Stafford. NNaP

Now,/ asked sweet mama, let me. Milkcow Blues. Unknown. BluL

Now/ Change in the ocean. Everybody Ought to Make a Change. Unknown. BluL

Now/ Got offices in town. Lawyer Clark Blues. Unknown. BluL

Now/ I know the people. Street Car Blues. Unknown. BluL

Now, after a party with the consul and our best friend. Summer, 1970. Daniel Halpern. AmPA

Now, age came on, and all the dismal traine. Clarinda's Indifference at Parting with Her Beauty. Countess of Winchilsea. SBG

Now Ain't That Love? Carolyn M. Rodgers. BPo

Now air is air and thing is thing: no bliss. E. E. Cummings. PBMP

Now all aloud the wind and rain. The Watercress Seller. Thomas Miller. OxBChV

Now all day long the man who is not dead. Mother and Son. Allen Tate. PiAm

Now all that sound of laughter, sound of singing. Rosalia de Castro, tr. fr. Galician by John Frederick Nims. BoWoP

Now all the truth is out. To a Friend Whose Work Has Come to Nothing. W. B. Yeats. BiP; IP; OAEL-2; PoA; PoIA; SoSe (1977 ed.)

Now almost everything I ever imagined. My Mother's/ My/ Death/ Birthday. Patricia Goedicke. Psy

Now and Again. Roo Borson. AMV-81

Now and it's moon shine. Moonshine. Unknown. BluL

Now and Then. Ian Hamilton. NoAM

Now and then there will arise. Song. Tr. fr. Chippewa Indian by Frances Densmore. OBVE

Now another day is breaking. Morning Prayer. Ogden Nash. OxBChV

Now are the bells unlimbered from their spires. Pilgrimage. Eileen Duggan. ATNZ

Now are they met: this armed with a spade. Phineas Fletcher. Fr. The Locusts or Appolyonists. SCP-2

Now Arethusa from her snow couches arises. Shelley's "Arethusa" Set to New Measures. Robert Duncan. CMoP (1970 ed.)

Now as at all times I can see in the mind's eye. The Magi. W. B. Yeats. BiP; CABA (1972 ed.); CMoP (1970 ed.); HAP; InPK; InPS; NIL; NoAM; OAEL-2; OFD; PChr; PoA; PPoe; PSN; TT

Now as I was young and easy under the apple boughs. Fern Hill. Dylan Thomas. BBGO; BiP; CABA (1972 ed.); CMoP (1970 ed.); FSFS; HAP; HeIP; ILP (1975 ed.); InPK; InPS; IPWM; NIL; NoAM; NOBE; NowV; OAEL-2; OBW; OxBTC; PPM; PPoD; PPoe; PPP; SoS; SoSe (1977 ed.); STS; TCP; TT;VoPo; WeW; WIF

Now as the train bears west. Night Journey. Theodore Roethke. ECBV; GOA; InPS

Now as we cross this white page together. The Escape. William Stafford. NNaP

Now at the end I smell the smells of spring. Exit Molloy. Derek Mahon. PFlr; POL

Now at the road's quick turn. Edwin Muir. Fr. Variations on a Time Theme. NoAM

Now, at the time that was before agreed. Spenser. Fr. The Faerie Queene, VII, 7. OAEL-1

Now austere lips are laid. The Hard Lovers. George Dillon. PoA

Now *Ban the Bomb!* I'm with you, though we fail.   Girl Marcher.
John Frederick Nims.   SFF

Now Barbie's/ a co-ed!   Barbie-Doll Goes to College.   Ronald
Gross.   WeW

Now Be the Gospel Banner, *with music.*   Thomas Hastings.   AH

Now be ye lords or commoners.   The Tod's Hole.   *Unknown.*
GBP

Now, before Shaving.   Aaron Kramer.   AMV-81

Now begin wailing notes; the flesh is thrilled.   Dante, *tr. by*
Laurence Binyon, *Fr.* Divina Commedia: Inferno, V.   ExPo
(1973 ed.)

Now Behold the Saviour Pleading, *with music.*   John Leland.   AH

Now, being invisible, I walk without mantilla.   The Souls of
Women at Night.   Wallace Stevens.   CMoP (1970 ed.)

Now Bekotsidi, that am I. For them I make.   The Song of
Bekotsidi.   *Tr. fr. Navajo Indian by* Washington Matthews.
OBVE

Now bethink thee, gentilman.   Adam Driven from Eden.
*Unknown.*   OxBM

Now biginneth Glotoun for to go to shrifte.   Glutton in the
Tavern.   William Langland.   *Fr.* The Vision of Piers
Plowman.   OxBM

Now boys you all can say what you want to.   Shirley McDaniel
Ain't Dead.   Lee Howard.   PoUp

Now burley's curing in the high-tiered barn.   Squirrel Stand.   Jim
Wayne Miller.   CSP

Now burst above the city's cold twilight.   Six o'Clock.   Trumbull
Stickney.   PPoD

Now, by the verdure on thy thousand hills.   Adequacy.
Elizabeth Barrett Browning.   SGB

Now call to mind Edom, remember well.   The Church of
England's Glory.   *Unknown.*   APAS

Now came still evening on, and twilight gray.   Evening in Eden
[*or* The Moon and the Nightingale].   Milton.   *Fr.* Paradise
Lost, IV.   Moon; NOBE; OBP

Now can you see the monument? It is of wood.   The Monument.
Elizabeth Bishop.   NoAM; NOBA; PPoe

Now chaos has pitched a tent.   Revival.   George Garrett.   CSP

Now Christmas is come.   *Unknown.*   PChr

Now cometh alle ye that been y-brought.   God, the Port of Peace.
John Walton.   OxBM

Now conscience wakes despair.   Satan's Address to the Sun.
Milton.   *Fr.* Paradise Lost, IV.   BiP

Now corn pushes past the foam.   Ode to a Dead Dodge.   David
McElroy.   AmPA

Now do you suppose that bee.   The Buzzing Doubt.   Donald L.
Hill.   NCSH

Now doeth disdainfull Saturne sadd and olde.   Constant Love in
All Conditions.   James I, King of England.   SLP

Now don't you see a little turtle dove.   Turtle Dove.   *Unknown.*
FSW

Now dreams.   Oppression.   Langston Hughes.   CNA

Now Dreary Dawns the Eastern Light.   A. E. Housman.   CMoP
(1970 ed.); TT

Now Empress Fame had published the renown.   Dryden.   *Fr.*
MacFlecknoe; or, A Satire upon the True-Blue Protestant
Poet.   SCP-1

Now entertain conjecture of a time.   Shakespeare.   Henry V, *fr.*
IV, prologue.   EBEV

Now especially, each flower moves.   Variation on the Gothic
Spiral.   W. S. Merwin.   PoA

Now Evening Puts Amen to Day, *with music.*   Paul Horgan.   AH

Now every day the braken browner grows.   September.   Mary
Elizabeth Coleridge.   FSFS

Now Everyone Is Writing Poems about Indians.   James Tipton.
HeS; TC

Now ev'ning fades! her pensive step retires.   Night.   Anne
Radcliffe.   WPE

Now fades the last long streak of snow.   In Memoriam A. H. H.,
CXV.   Tennyson.   FSFS; NOBE

Now first, as I shut the door.   The New House.   Edward
Thomas.   EBEV; NOBE; OBW

Now first of all he means the night.   A Song for the Middle of the
Night.   James Wright.   ILP (1975 ed.); WeW

"Now for a brisk and a cheerful fight!"   The Fight at San Jacinto.
John Williamson Palmer.   BPAW

Now for a little I have fed on loneliness.   Fruit of Loneliness.
May Sarton.   PoA

Now friends if you'll listen to a horrible tale.   The Dreary Black
Hills.   *Unknown.*   BPAW

Now from Labor and from Care, *with music.*   Thomas Hastings.
AH

Now from Leander's place she rose, and found.   George
Chapman.   *Fr.* Hero and Leander, Fourth Sestiad.   EBEV

Now from the dark, a deeper dark.   Calling in the Cat.   Elizabeth
J. Coatsworth.   BoAnP; PCat

Now from the east.   Masahongva, *tr. fr. Hopi Indian by* Natalie
Curtis.   WTO

Now front to front the hostile armies stand.   Homer, *tr. by* Pope.
*Fr.* The Iliad, III.   OBVE

Now gently winding up the fair ascent.   Homer, *tr. by* Pope.   *Fr.*
The Odyssey, XXI.   OBVE

Now glory to the Lord of Hosts, from whom all glories are!   Ivry.
Macaulay.   BTTM

Now, God be thanked Who has matched us with His hour.
Peace.   Rupert Brooke.   1914, I.   BTTM; PoA

Now God Stand Up for Bastards.   Brian Merriman, *tr. fr. Modern
Irish by* Arland Ussher.   *Fr.* The Midnight Court.   BIrV

Now goth son [*or* goeth sun] under wod [*or* wood].   Me Rueth,
Mary.   *Unknown.*   BoReV; GBP

Now gowans sprout, an' lavrocks sing.   Ode to Mr. F——.   Allan
Ramsay, *after* Horace.   OBVE

Now great Hyperion left his golden throne.   William Browne.
*Fr.* Britannia's Pastorals.   SCP-2

Now had Columbus well enjoy'd the sight.   Joel Barlow.   *Fr.* The
Columbiad, Book VIII.   PiAm

Now had th' Almighty father from above.   Milton.   *Fr.* Paradise
Lost, III.   NIL

Now handy high and handy low.   So Handy, Me Boys, So Handy.
*Unknown.*   AmFP

Now hardly here and there a[n] hackney-coach.   A Description of
the Morning.   Swift.   AnMo; CABA (1972 ed.); EBEV; FF;
HAP; HeIP; ILP (1975 ed.); InPS; LFH; NIL; NOBE;
OAEL-1; PAIC; PPP; Prf; SoSe; UsP; WeW

Now have good day, now have good day!   I Am Christmas.
*Unknown.*   OxBM

Now have I brought a woork too end which neither Joves feerce
wrath.   Ovid, *tr. by* Arthur Golding.   *Fr.* Metamorphoses,
XV.   OBVE

Now have I thereto this condicioun.   Daysies.   Chaucer.   *Fr.*
Legend of Good Women.   PF

Now having leisure, and a happy wind.   John Fletcher *and*
William Rowley.   *Fr.* The Maid in the Mill.   GBL

Now he is content.   The Afternoon Nap.   Joan White.   PoW

Now he is dead.   The End of Love.   Kathleen Raine.   BuTh

Now he is dead, who talked.   Elegy.   Alistair Campbell.   ATNZ

Now he roars through an unlit stadium of silence.   The Footballer
in the Small Room.   Janet Frame.   SPo

Now hear this.   Homer, *tr. by* Christopher Logue.   *Fr.* The Iliad,
XVI.   TwMBP

Now Help Us, Lord, *with music.*   *Unknown, ad. by* Charles E. Ives.
AH

Now here is this man mending his nets. Follow. Roland Flint. PoUp

Now his nose's bridge is broken, one eye. On Hurricane Jackson. Alan Dugan. LiSp; MiP; NCSH; NowV; POL; PPoD; SPo

Now hoisteth sail the pinnace of my wit. Dante, *tr. by* Laurence Binyon. Divina Commedia: Purgatorio, I-II. NAWM-1

Now homing tradesmen scatter through the streets. Place Pigalle. Richard Wilbur. HeIP

Now how I came to get this hat 'tis very strange and funny. Where Did You Get That Hat? Joseph J. Sullivan. FSN

Now I ain't no butcher. All Around Man. *Unknown.* BluL

Now I Am a Man. Russell Marano. AMV-80

"Now I am going to give you a perm, " she says. Electroencephalogram. Geoffrey Holloway. PMW

Now I am slow and placid, fond of sun. With Child. Genevieve Taggard. LoAs; PPM; WPW

Now I am sure. Beast Enough. Robert Billings. AMV-81

Now I can be sure of my sleep. On the Hill below the Lighthouse. James Dickey. PAIC

Now I can straighten your wires. Brownsville Blues. *Unknown.* BluL

Now I come home to you. The Homecoming. James B. Allen. HeS

Now I go, do not weep, woman. Parting. Alice Corbin. BPAW

Now I got a brown skin girl. Brown Skin Girl. *Unknown.* BluL

Now I have a son. To My Father. Charles Waterman. BrS

Now I have come to reason. C. Day Lewis. CMoP (1970 ed.)

Now I Have Forgotten All. David Vogel, *tr. fr. Hebrew by* A. C. Jacobs. VWA

Now I Have Nothing. Stella Benson. OxBTC

Now I know/ why God ordered Abe. On Living with Children for a Prolonged Time. Mark Lowey. AMV-81

Now I Lay Me Down to Sleep. *Unknown.* CTV; GBP (Evening Prayer, An, *sl. diff.*) CTV

Now I lay me down to sleep. Now I Set Me. Reinhold W. Herman. QQQ

Now I lay (with everywhere around). E. E. Cummings. PiAm

Now I never will forget that floating bridge. Floating Bridge. *Unknown.* BluL

Now I out walking. Away! Robert Frost. NOBA

Now I see their faces stamped forever. Why I Can't Write a Poem about Lares. Iván Silén, *tr. by* Julio Marzán. InW

Now I Set Me. Reinhold W. Herman. QQQ

Now I tell you mama now I'm sure gonna leave this town. Leaving Town Blues. *Unknown.* BluL

Now I will do nothing but listen. Walt Whitman. Song of Myself, XXVI. HoPM (1975 ed.); LFH

Now I woke up this morning, mama. You Can't Keep No Brown. *Unknown.* BluL

Now I would remind you, brethren. Bible, *N.T.* First Corinthians, XV: 1-8. DL

Now ich see blostme springe. Of Jesu Christ I Sing. *Unknown.* OxBM

Now if a man has money today. Money Is King. *Unknown.* FSW

Now if ever it is time to cleanse Helicon. Ezra Pound. *Fr.* Homage to Sextus Propertius. Epi; VGW

Now if thou hast one dram of grace. Nahum Tate, *after the Latin of* Catullus. OBVE

Now if you stop/ & think. God's Words to the Last Ape. George Mattingly. AcAn

Now if you will listen I'll tell you a story. The New-Chum's First Trip. *Unknown.* FaBoBa

Now I'm going to sing to you. Sheep-skin and Beeswax. *Unknown.* RAE

Now in golden glory goes. Songs. Lionel Johnson. VLP

Now in my/ heart I/ see clearly. Sappho, *tr. fr. Greek by* Willis Barnstone. BoWoP

Now in my Samarkand of blue enamels. Journey in the Orient. Maria Luisa Spaziani, *tr. by* Ruth Feldman. BoWoP

Now in old age, quiet in his tent. Isaac. Barry Holtz. VWA

Now in the after play. Blackheads. Knute Skinner. GP

Now in the dawn before it dies, the eagle swings low. The Story of a Well-made Shield. N. Scott Momaday. CDW

Now in the patron's mansion see the wight. Richard Savage. *Fr.* The Progress of a Divine. OBSV

Now in the perfumed dusk. Sadly They Perish. Herman Spector. SPT

Now in the suburbs and the falling light. Father and Son. Stanley Kunitz. NoAM

Now in the summer of life sweet-heart. Will You Love Me in December as You Do in May? J. J. Walker. FSN

Now in the window. Four Untitled Poems. Kathleen Wiegner. MMD

Now in this while gan Daedalus a wearinesse to take. Ovid, *tr. by* Arthur Golding. *Fr.* Metamorphoses, VIII. OBVE

Now is a bursting in me. Argent Solipsism. Howard Blake. PoA

Now is Albano's marriage-bed new hung. John Marston. *Fr.* What You Will: A Comedy. SCP-2

Now is Always the Miraculous Time. Robert Sargent. PoUp

Now is Ingland all in fight. On the Times. *Unknown.* OxBM

Now is my misery full, and namelessly. Pieta. Rainer Maria Rilke, *tr. by* M. D. Herter Norton. OFD

Now is the month of maying. *Unknown.* EBEV

Now is the season when myriad leaves are. Maple in November. Ethel Green Russell. AATT

Now is the time for mirth. To Live Merrily, and to Trust to Good Verses. Robert Herrick. CaPo

Now is the time for the burning of the leaves. The Burning of the Leaves. Laurence Binyon. FSFS; NOBE; OxBTC; PSN

Now Is the Time of Christmas. *Unknown.* OxBM

Now is the time when all the lights wax dim. To Anthea. Robert Herrick. SCP-1

Now Is Yule Come. *Unknown.* OxBM

Now Israel May Say, and That Truly, *with music.* William Whittingham. AH

Now It Can Be Told. Philip Levine. VWA

Now it is autumn and the falling fruit. The Ship of Death. D. H. Lawrence. CMoP (1970 ed.); ExPo (1973 ed.); FaBoTw (1975 ed.); NoAM; OAEL-2

Now it is fifteen years you have lain in the meadow. Lines for an Interment. Archibald MacLeish. CMoP (1970 ed.); NOBA

Now it is pleasant in the summer-eve. Goerge Crabbe. *Fr.* The Borough, Letter IX. EcS

Now it was that the Morrigan settled in bird shape. The Morrigan. *Unknown, tr. by* Thomas Kinsella. BIrV

Now It's Happened. D. H. Lawrence. OBP

Now it's my mother. Marie Harris. *Fr.* Interstate. AAN

Now it's stingy mama. Mojo Hiding Woman. *Unknown.* BluL

Now it's Uncle Sam sitting on top of the world. Carl Sandburg. *Fr.* Good Morning America. OFD

Now, I've got no use for the women. Bury Me Out on the Prairie. *Unknown.* BPAW

Now Jack he had a ship in the North Counterie. The *Golden Vanity. Unknown.* AIW

Now Jentil Belly Down. *Unknown.* GBP

Now John come home all in a wonder. Everyday Dirt. *Unknown.* FSW

Now Johnson would go up to join the great simulacra of men. Up Rising. Robert Duncan. *Fr.* Passages. NNaP

Now Jones had left his new-wed bride. A Code of Morals. Kipling. FaBoCo

Now leave the check-reins slack. To the Man after the Harrow. Patrick Kavanagh. CIP

Now let my thoughts be like the Arrow, wherein was gold. Holiday Piece. Denis Glover. ATNZ

Now let no charitable hope. Let No Charitable Hope. Elinor Wylie. PBWP; Psy; SBG; VGW

Now Let Our Hearts Their Glory Wake, *with music*. Elizabeth Scott. AH

Now let the cycle sweep us here and there. Sigil. Hilda Doolittle ("H. D."). VGW

Now let the golden prison ope its gates. Cardinal Newman. *Fr.* The Dream of Gerontius. VLP

Now let the wife look up from her stove, the husband. The Voice of Caesar. W. H. Auden. *Fr.* For the Time Being. AnMo

"Now life alone is left me, to maintain." Near the Death of Ovid. Robert Conquest. NoAM

Now light the candles; one; two; there's a moth. Repression of War Experience. Siegfried Sassoon. CMoP (1970 ed.); NoAM

Now listen closely, children. The Hand of Ms. Fate. Cash Terrell. DNGG

Now, listen, Ye who established the Great League. Memorial Ode. Chief John Buck. GOA

Now Little Billy is gone to the kirk. Little Billy. *Unknown*. GBP

Now manhood and garbroyls I chaunt. Virgil, *tr. by* Richard Stanyhurst. *Fr.* The Aeneid, I. BIrV; OBVE

Now may we turn aside and dry our tears. Inis Fal. Egan O'Rahilly, *tr. by* James Stephens. BIrV

Now me and my baby we talked last night. Welfare Store. *Unknown*. BluL

Now, miners, if you'll listen, I'll tell you quite a tale. Coming around the Horn. John A. Stone. AmFP

Now Mr. Boomer Johnson was a gettin' old in spots. Boomer Johnson. Henry Herbert Knibbs. BPAW

Now Mrs. Sallie. Gwendolyn Brooks. UsP

Now more and more on my concern with the lifted waves of genius gaining. On the Ocean Floor. "Hugh MacDiarmid." HAP

Now (more near ourselves than we). E. E. Cummings. UsP

Now morning from her orient chamber came. Imitation of Spenser. Keats. MBPR

Now, morphine, now. Shot. Emma Lou Thayne. MPA

Now must I lerne to lyve at rest. Sir Thomas Wyatt. AAS

Now must I these three praise. Friends. W. B. Yeats. NoAM; WeW

Now must we praise of heaven's kingdom the keeper. Caedmon's Hymn. Caedmon, *tr. fr. Anglo-Saxon*. OAEL-1

"Now, my dear friend, what is our plan?" America Is Darken'd. R. H. W. Dillard. CoPAm

Now, my dear, we're getting down. A Delicate Impasse. Kenneth John Atchity. AMV-80

Now, my fair'st friend. Spring Garland. Shakespeare. *Fr.* The Winter's Tale, IV, iii. PF

Now my father carries his old heart. Christmas Eve. Ted Kooser. BrS; GP

Now my legs begin to walk. Thaw in the City. Lou Lipsitz. MAT; NCSH

Now my mind's been brought to such extremes. Catullus, *tr. fr. Latin by* John Frederick Nims. WeW

Now, My Usefulness Over. Edwin Honig. NoAM

Now 'neath the silver moon. Santa Lucia. Teodoro Cottrau. BLSH; FSW

Now, not a tear begun. A Woman Mourned by Daughters. Adrienne Rich. IHMS; NCSH; Psy; TV

Now—now, as low I stooped, thought I. The Snowdrop. Walter de la Mare. PF

Now, now's the time so oft by Truth. An Epithalamy to Sir Thomas Southwell and His Lady. Robert Herrick. CaPo

Now old Dan Tucker's a fine old man. Old Dan Tucker. Daniel Decatur Emmett. FSW

Now on this out of season afternoon. Original Sin on the Sussex Coast. John Betjeman. BBGO

Now ore the sea from her old love comes she. Ovid, *tr. by* Christopher Marlowe. Amores, I, 13. OBVE

Now our joy. A Sad Song, This Time. Rolfe Humphries. PAIC

Now over the map that took ten million years. It Was Easier. Ruthven Todd. MS

Now over there across the sea they've got another war. That Crazy War. *Unknown*. FSW

Now Phillipa Is Gone. Anne Ridler. FaBoTw (1975 ed.)

Now Phoebus did the world with frowns survey. Abigail's Lamentation for the Loss of Mr. Harley. William Walsh. APAS

Now Poem. For Us. Sonia Sanchez. CNA; PoBA

Now prompts the muse poetic lays. Monody on the Death of Chatterton. Samuel Taylor Coleridge. MBPR

Now rock the boat to a fare-thee-well. Rite of Passage. Audre Lorde. CNA; PoBA

Now roses grow there, fat with blood. Dachau, Now: "Roses Grow There, Fat with Blood." Elisavietta Ritchie. AATT

Now Sam McGee was from Tennessee, where the cotton blooms. The Cremation of Sam McGee. Robert W. Service. PoTa

Now say, have women worth? or have they none? Anne Bradstreet. *Fr.* In Honour of That High and Mighty Princess Queen Elizabeth of Happy Memory. EAP

Now shall the adventurous muse attempt a theme. Philip Freneau. *Fr.* The Rising Glory of America. AmVN

Now She Is like the White Tree-Rose. C. Day Lewis. *Fr.* From Feathers to Iron. CMoP (1970 ed.); FaBoTw (1975 ed.)

Now Shrinketh Rose and Lily-Flower. *Unknown*. OxBM

Now side by side, with like unweary'd care. Homer, *tr. by* Pope. *Fr.* The Iliad, XIII. OBVE

Now since the members of the world we view. Lucretius, *tr. by* Thomas Creech. *Fr.* De Rerum Natura, V. OBVE

Now sinks another day to rest. The Bull. V. Sackville-West. WPE

Now Sleep My Little Child So Dear, *with music*. Casper Kriebel, *tr. fr. German by* Sheema Z. Buehne. AH

Now Sleeps the Crimson Petal. Tennyson. *Fr.* The Princess, Pt. VII. BoLoP; CABA (1972 ed.); EBEV; GBL; ILP (1975 ed.); LoAs; NIL; NOBE; PPoe; PPP (Song: "Now sleeps the crimson petal, now the white.") ExPo (1973 ed.)

Now Snow Descends. Jean Garrigue. WPE

Now so many people that are in this place. *Unknown, tr. by* Richard Johnny John. *Fr.* Thank You, Part I. IPWM

Now south and south and south the mallard heads. The North Sea Undertaker's Complaint. Robert Lowell. LFH

Now spears lift them by their ribs. Dog Sacrifice at Lake Ronkonkoma. William Heyen. AmPA

Now Springs the Spray. *Unknown*. OAEL-1; OxBM

Now, starflake frozen on the windowpane. Moment. Howard Nemerov. CoPAm

Now stoops the sun, and dies day's cheerful light. The Gauls Sacrifice. C. M. Doughty. *Fr.* The Dawn in Britain. FaBoTw (1975 ed.)

Now stop your noses, readers, all and some. Portrait of "Og." Dryden. *Fr.* Absalom and Achitophel, Pt. II. NIL

Now, suddenly, they show up. My Morose Master-Sergeants. Ray Holt. PPoD

Now supposing the French or the Neapolitan soldier. Arthur Hugh Clough. *Fr.* Amours de Voyage. OBP

Now tell me where my easy rider gone.   Easy Rider Blues.
*Unknown.*   BluL

Now that black ground and bushes.   Winter Sketches.   Charles
Reznikoff.   PoA

Now that guy was a real fruit. A peach.   A Musician Returning
from a Cafe Audition.   Michael D. Minard.   AMV-80

"Now that he is in grave condition."   Pushkin, *tr. by* Walter
Arndt.   *Fr.* Eugene Onegin.   NAWM-2

Now that he's left the room.   Univac to Univac.   Louis B.
Salomon.   FF; QQQ

Now that high, oft-affronted bosom heaves.   To the Lady
Portrayed by Margaret Dumont.   John Hollander.   OBAL;
PoA

Now that I am fifty-six.   Rondel.   Muriel Rukeyser.   FF

Now That I Am Forever with Child.   Audre Lorde.   PoBA

Now that I have lighted my smoke.   Smoking My Prayers.
Simon Ortiz.   VW

Now that I have your face by heart, I look.   Song for the Last
Act.   Louise Bogan.   LoAs; UnPo (1976 ed.); WPE

Now that I know.   Knowledge.   Louise Bogan.   PoA

Now that I live no longer among mountains.   Among Friends.
Greg Kuzma.   AMV-80

Now that I, tying thy glass mask tightly.   The Laboratory: Ancien
Régime.   Robert Browning.   LoAs

Now that I've nearly done my days.   The Things That Matter.
Edith Nesbit.   OxBTC

Now that I've taken a wife.   The Groom's Lament.   Robert
Peterson.   NeAC

Now that I've wasted.   My Alba.   Allen Ginsberg.   NoAM;
NoBA

Now that my father telephones long distance.   Grocery Shopping.
John Leax.   AATT

Now that our love has drifted.   Finis.   Waring Cuney.   AmNP
(1974 ed.)

Now That Snow Is Falling.   Joseph Kalar.   SPT

Now that the barbarians have got as far as Picra.   Translation.
Roy Fuller.   NOBE; OxBTC

Now That the Buffalo's Gone.   Buffy Sainte-Marie.   PoRo

Now that the causeway spans the channel.   Causeway.   Allan
Block.   TAT

Now that the day is done.   Centaur Song.   Hilda Doolittle
("H. D.").   VGW

Now that the days are growing light and long.   Cuckoo.   R. P.
Lister.   BoAnP

Now that the holidays have come.   Here We Are in the Years.
Neil Young.   PoRo

Now that the others are gone, all of them, forever.   Tomorrow.
Kenneth Fearing.   CMoP (1970 ed.)

Now that the winter's gone, the earth hath lost.   The Spring.
Thomas Carew.   CaPo; ILP (1975 ed.); OBP; PPoe

Now that we have had our day, you.   Love in Age.   George
Bruce.   MS

Now that we're almost settled in our house.   In Memory of Major
Robert Gregory.   W. B. Yeats.   EBEV; OAEL-2

Now that we're alone we can talk prince man to man.   Elegy of
Fortinbras.   Zbigniew Herbert, *tr. by* Czeslaw Milosz.
OBVE

Now that you have lost.   Ordinance on Failure.   Naomi Lazard.
AAN

Now that your big eyes have finally opened.   My Country 'Tis of
Thy People You're Dying.   Buffy Sainte-Marie.   WIF

Now the bat circles on the breeze of eve.   Sonnet.   Anne
Radcliffe.   WPE

Now the bright morning star, day's harbinger.   Song on May
Morning.   Milton.   FSFS

Now the Day Is Over.   Sabine Baring-Gould.   OxBChV

Now the declining sun 'gan downwards bend.   The Nightingale.
William Strode, *after* Famianus Strada.   OBVE

Now the golden morn aloft.   Ode on the Pleasure Arising from
Vicissitude.   Thomas Gray.   LAuP

Now the heart sings with all its thousand voices.   The Gateway.
A. D. Hope.   BoLoP

Now the Holy Lamp of Love.   Patrick MacDonogh.   BIrV

Now the hungry lion roars.   Puck's Night Song.   Shakespeare.
*Fr.* A Midsummer Night's Dream, V, ii.   DuDr; ECBV; OBP

Now the ice lays its smooth claws on the sill.   Scotland's Winter.
Edwin Muir.   MS; OxBTC

Now the last day of many days.   To Jane: The Recollection.
Shelley.   MBPR

Now the last step! Behold.   M. Krishnamurti.   *Fr.* The Cloth of
Gold.   PeD

Now the late fruits are in.   For a Wine Festival.   Vernon
Watkins.   OxBTC

Now the leaves are falling fast.   W. H. Auden.   CMoP (1970 ed.)

Now the light o' the west is a-turn'd to gloom.   Evenen in the
Village.   William Barnes.   VPC

Now the lotuses in the imperial lake.   Wang Ch'ing-hui, *tr. fr.
Chinese by* Kenneth Rexroth *and* Ling Chung.   BoWoP

Now the Lusty Spring.   John Fletcher.   *See* Love's Emblems.

Now the narrowing track.   The Look.   Elizabeth Daryush.   PoA

Now the New Moon is hanging, having cast away his bone.   New
Moon.   *Aborigine Oral Tradition, tr. by* R. M. Berndt.   *Fr.*
The Moon-Bone Cycle.   WTO

Now the People Have the Light.   Charles G. Ballard.   VoR; VW

Now the pines lift.   Burning the Tomato Worms.   Carolyn
Forché.   AmPA

Now, the showground is quiet.   The Horse Show at Midnight.
Henry Taylor.   PH

Now the snow/ lies on the ground.   Winter.   William Carlos
Williams.   NCSH

Now the stone house on the lake front is finished.   A Fence.
Carl Sandburg.   WeW

Now the storm begins to lower.   The Fatal Sisters.   Thomas
Gray.   LAuP

Now the Summer's Come.   *Unknown.   See* Cuckoo Song.

Now the time of year has come for the leaves to be burning.
October 1954.   Kay Boyle.   RiTi

Now the trumpet of the atomic gale.   Hiroshima.   Lord Russell
Brain.   PMW

Now the wheat is in the ear, and the rose is on the brere.   The
Lover's Invitation.   John Clare.   VLP

Now the white roses, wilted and yellowing fast.   Lament of the
Jewish Women for Tammuz.   Charles Reznikoff.   VWA

Now the word of the Lord came unto Jonah.   Jonah.   Bible, *O.T.*
NAWM-1

Now then, for love of Crist and of His joye.   Keep the Sea.
*Unknown.   Fr.* The Libelle of Englyshe Polycye.   OxBM

"Now then, what are you up to, Dai?"   Langwell.   Kingsley
Amis.   *Fr.* The Evans Country.   NOBL

Now there are gold reflections on the water.   In Time of Gold.
Hilda Doolittle ("H. D.").   PoA

Now there are no walls.   Passover Dachau.   B. Z. Niditch.
AMV-81

Now there comes/ The Christmas rose.   New Year's Song.   Ted
Hughes.   OFD

Now there is a love of which Dante does not speak unkindly.
Sonnet I.   Robert Duncan.   GP

Now there's many fool things a woman will do.   Gold Tooth
Blues.   Tennessee Williams.   OBAL

Now they are loading the old Ford in the evening.   The Journey
Begins.   Vern Rutsala.   MPA

Now they're pillaging the last coast.   The Vandals.   Jenny
Mastoraki, *tr. by* Nikos Germanakos.   BoWoP

Now they're ready, now they're waiting.  Football.  F. Scott Fitzgerald.  SPo

Now thin mists temper the slow-ripening beams.  The Garden in September.  Robert Bridges.  PoPle

Now this dark cloud is rising.  Mean Old Twister.  *Unknown.* BluL

Now this is my first counsel.  Part of the Lay of Sigrdrifa. *Unknown, tr. by* William Morris *and* Eiriks Magnusson.  *Fr.* The Elder Edda.  OBVE

Now this particular girl.  Spinster.  Sylvia Plath.  CoPAm

Now through the ocean in great haste they flunder.  Luis de Camoëns, *tr. by* Sir Richard Fanshawe.  *Fr.* The Lusiads. OBVE

Now Time's Andromeda on this rock rude.  Andromeda.  Gerard Manley Hopkins.  EBEV; VLP

Now to be clean he must abandon himself.  The Swan Bathing. Ruth Pitter.  BoAnP

Now to dispose the dead, the care remains.  Homer, *tr. by* Pope. *Fr.* The Odyssey, XXII.  OBVE

Now to pick wild plums.  Leave the Top Plums.  Janet Carncross Chandler.  AMV-80

Now to the banquet we press.  Banquet Song.  W. S. Gilbert. *Fr.* Patience.  ECBV

Now to the dry hillside.  Education.  Kenneth Rexroth.  NowV

Now toils the heroe; trees on trees o'erthrown.  Homer, *tr. by* Pope.  *Fr.* The Odyssey, V.  OBVE

Now touch the air softly.  A Pavane for the Nursery.  William Jay Smith.  DuDa; OSP

Now turn, and view the wonders of the deep.  Ben Jonson.  *Fr.* The Fortunate Isles, and their Union.  SCP-1

Now, 'twas twenty-five or thirty years.  Jack Was Every Inch a Sailor.  *Unknown.* FSW

Now upon sale, a bankrupt island.  Four Epigrams on the Naturalization Bill.  John Byrom.  NOBL

Now upon this piteous year.  The Stranger.  Jean Garrigue. NOBA

Now war is all the world about.  An Ode upon Occasion of His Majesty's Proclamation in the Year 1630 [*or* Ode on His Majesty's Proclamation].  Sir Richard Fanshawe.  NOBE; SCP-2

Now was there maid fast by the towris wall.  The Nightingale's Song.  James I, King of Scotland.  *Fr.* The Kingis Quair. EBEV; OxBM

Now watch this autumn that arrives.  Song at the Beginning of Autumn.  Elizabeth Jennings.  OxBTC

Now we are at peaceful war.  Testimonies for a School Prayer. Serge Gavronsky.  NowV

Now We Are Sick.  J. B. Morton.  SpRo

Now we enter a strange world, where the Hessian Christmas. After the Industrial Revolution, All Things Happen at Once. Robert Bly.  ConAP

Now we have in our group a lot.  Should We Legalize Abortion? Frank O'Hara.  NoAM

Now we must get up quickly.  Two Lines from the Brothers Grimm.  Gregory Orr.  AmPA

Now Welcom[e], Summer [*or* Somer].  Chaucer.  *Fr.* The Parliament of Fowls.  HAP; OxBM
  (Roundel: "Now welcome, somer, with thy sunne softe.") OAEL-1

Now we're stuck there.  Heaving the Lead Line.  *Unknown.* AmFP

Now westward Sol had spent the richest beams.  Music's Duel. Richard Crashaw.  OAEL-1; SCP-1

Now we've made a child.  And What About the Children.  Audre Lorde.  PoBA

Now, what did you do with the gun in your hand.  Take a Drink on Me.  *Unknown.* FSW

Now What Good That Do?  H. H. Lewis.  SPT

Now what is he after below in the street?  The Bold Unbiddable Child.  Winifrid M. Letts.  PFIr

Now what is love? I pray, tell.  A Description of Love.  Sir Walter Ralegh.  OAEL-1

Now when I drove to the sand pit, the horizon.  Red Wing Hawk. James Applewhite.  AMV-81

Now when I walk around at lunchtime.  Personal Poem.  Frank O'Hara.  CAPP; NYP

Now when the solemn rites of pray'r were past.  Homer, *tr. by* Dryden.  *Fr.* The Iliad, I.  OBVE

Now when those Seven of the First Heaven stood still.  Dante, *tr. by* Laurence Binyon.  Divina Commedia: Purgatorio, XXX-XXXI.  NAWM-1

Now, when twelve days complete had run their race.  Homer, *tr. by* Dryden.  *Fr.* The Iliad, I.  OBVE

Now when we leave the windows of hay.  To a Horse.  Jill Hoffman.  PH

Now, while the birds thus sing a joyous song.  Wordsworth.  *Fr.* Ode: Intimations of Immortality from Recollections of Early Childhood.  Prf

Now Whitehall's in the grave.  A Mock Song.  Richard Lovelace. CaPo

Now whyle Hippomenes/ Debates theis things.  Ovid, *tr. by* Arthur Golding.  *Fr.* Metamorphoses, X.  OBVE

Now Winter as a shrivelled scroll.  Winter.  Katharine Tynan. FSFS

Now winter downs the dying of the year.  Year's End.  Richard Wilbur.  CAPP; HeIP

Now Winter Nights Enlarge.  Thomas Campion.  AAS; EBEV;HeIP; NOBE; PPoD

Now with the coming in of the spring the days will stretch a bit. The County Mayo.  Anthony Raftery, *tr. by* James Stephens. PFIr

Now, with your palms on the blades of my shoulders.  Dead Still. Andrei Voznesensky, *tr. by* Richard Wilbur.  BoLoP

Now wolde I faine sum merthes make.  An Absent Lover. *Unknown.* OxBM

Now Wu Tao-tzu, continuing his stroll.  A Flight of Wild Geese. Harold Stewart.  GAS

Now you/ tell me mama, do you.  Saturday Blues.  *Unknown.* BluL

Now you are dead.  Broken Promise.  James O. Taylor.  BuTh

Now you are going, what can I do but wish you.  The Poet's Farewell to His Teeth.  William Dickey.  GP; PoA

Now you are the gay familiar.  Island Letter.  Charles Senior. MIS

Now you clown with your grocery man.  Go Back to the Country. *Unknown.* BluL

Now you depart, and though your way may lead.  To a Friend Going on a Journey.  Mahammed Abdille Hassan, *tr. fr. Somali by* M. Laurence.  WTO

Now you done spent all my 1940 rent.  Working Man Blues. *Unknown.* BluL

Now, you great stanza, you heroic mould.  Single Sonnet.  Louise Bogan.  NIL

Now you have freely giv'n me leave to love.  To a Lady That Desired I Would Love Her.  Thomas Carew.  CaPo

"Now you must die," the young one said.  The Rite.  Dudley Randall.  HoPM (1975 ed.)

Now you take ol Rufus. He beat drums.  For Freckle-faced Gerald.  Etheridge Knight.  BPo; NeAC

Now your cheeks are as old and bald.  For Allen Ginsberg, Who Cut Off His Beard.  Sanford Pinsker.  AMV-80

Now you've been an Abbess for years.  Abelard at Cluny. Grover Rees III.  AMV-80

Nowhere are we safe.  Hymn Written after Jeremiah Preached to Me in a Dream.  Owen Dodson.  AmNP (1974 ed.); PAIC

Nowhere around him.  The Perfectionist.  Philip Dacey.  NVAP

Nowhere can flesh feel more limp. Voting Machine. Norman Nathan. AMV-80

Nowhere for Vallejo, A, *sels.* Nathaniel Tarn. TwMBP
"And he passed around midnight."
"And they went down into the king-city."
"Borders slide backwards forwards."
"Call of green things to his hand."
"On the train to the ruins."

Now's the time for mirth and play. For Saturday. Christopher Smart. *Fr.* Hymns for the Amusement of Children. LAuP; OxBChV

Nox Nocti Indicat Scientiam. William Habington. NOBE

Nuances of a Theme by Williams. Wallace Stevens. CMoP (1970 ed.)

Nubs Lilly liked to use his fists. The Fighter. Dave Etter. TAT

Nuclear Land. Ellen Tifft. AMV-81

Nuclear Physicists, The. Peggy Pond Church. WPW

Nude. Robert Siegel. FAF

Nude Beneath the Willows, leaves hanging down. Art Gallery. John Dickson. AMV-81

Nude bodies like peeled logs. Sonnet in Search of an Author. William Carlos Williams. Epi

Nude by Edward Hopper, A. Lisel Mueller. RiTi

Nude Climbing a Flagpole. Tom McKeown. TC

Nude Descending a Staircase. X. J. Kennedy. ConAP; HeIP; HoPM (1975 ed.); NIL; PoA; POL; PPoD; WIF

Nude on the Bathroom Wall, The. Gena Ford. IHMS

Nude Poet, The. Charles Edward Eaton. CSP

Nude Swim, The. Anne Sexton. WPE

Nude with Green Chair. Antony Oldknow. AMV-81

Nudes. Juan Ramón Jiménez, *tr. fr. Spanish.* LoAs

Nudes—stark and glistening. Louse Hunting. Isaac Rosenberg. EBEV; OxBTC

Nudities. Andre Spire, *tr. fr. French by* Stanley Burnshaw. VWA

Nudus Redibo. Thomas Flatman. SCP-2

Nuisance at Home, A. *Unknown.* TDH

Nulla Fides. Patrick Carey. SCP-2

Number Four. Doughtry Long. CNA; PoBA; SO

Number 14. Keith Bosley. LP

Number 1 by Jackson Pollock (1948). Nancy Sullivan. WIF

Number One Daughter of the Wang Family, The. Chen Hsieh, *tr. fr. Chinese by* C. H. Kwock. MIT

Number Twelve Train. *Unknown.* FSW

Number 29. *Unknown.* BluL

Numbers, *sels.* Bible, *O.T.*
"How goodly are the tentes of Jacob and thine habitacions Israel," XXIV: 5-9, *tr. by* William Tyndale. OBVE
Lord Bless You and Keep You, The, VI: 24-26. BLSH
("Lorde blesse the and kepe the, The," VI: 24-27, *tr. by* William Tyndale.) OBVE

Numbers. Elizabeth Madox Roberts. LCL

Numbers, Letters. Amiri Baraka. BPo; NOBA

Numbers of employees them. Richard Hofstadter and Michael Wallace, a Documentary History of American Violence. Jim Rosenberg. Epi

Numerous Celts. J. C. Squire. SpRo

Numerous host of dreaming Saints succeed, A. Zimri: The Duke of Buckingham. Dryden. *Fr.* Absalom and Achitophel, Pt. I. NOBE; OBSV

Nummum et secalis sacculum cantate! Four and Twenty Merulae. J. Moyr Smith. FaBoNo

Nun, The. Leigh Hunt. IP

Nun bent shameless, The. In the Art Institute Library. Alice Notley. FiCh

Nun walked on her prayer, The. The Friar and the Nun. *Unknown.* GBP

Nunc Viridant Segetes. Sedulius Scottus, *tr. fr. Medieval Latin by* Helen Waddell. BIrV

(He Complains to Bishop Hartgar of Thirst.) NAWM-1

Nunnery. Katherine Doak. NPW

Nuns at Eve. John Malcolm Brinnin. PPoD

Nuns fret not at their convent's narrow room. Wordsworth. CABA (1972 ed.); EBEV; ILP (1975 ed.); MBPR; NIL; OBP; PAIC; PPM

Nuns, his nieces, bring the priest in next. A Far Cry after a Close Call. Richard Howard. UnPo (1976 ed.)

Nuns in the Wind. Muriel Rukeyser. NNaP

Nun's Priest's Prologue, The. Chaucer. *Fr.* The Canterbury Tales. OAEL-1

Nun's Priest's Tale, The. Chaucer. *Fr.* The Canterbury Tales. OAEL-1; OBVE, *mod. version by* Dryden.
Chauntecleer, *sel.* PB

Nu-Plastik Fanfare Red. Judith Rodriguez. FPA

Nuptial Sleep. Dante Gabriel Rossetti. *Fr.* The House of Life. VLP

Nuptial Song, or Epithalamy, on Sir Clipesby Crew and His Lady, A. Robert Herrick. CaPo; SCP-1
"To bed, to bed, kind turtles, now, and write," *sel.* OBP

Nuremberg. Kenneth Slessor. MAuV

Nurse. May Ivimy. PMW

Nurse carried him up the stair, The. At Thomas Hardy's Birthplace, 1953. James Wright. ConAP

Nurse in the rainbow, The/ Dress. Kilroy Turtle. D. C. Berry. CSP

Nurse-life wheat within his green husk growing, The. Fulke Greville. *Fr.* Caelica. AAS; PAIC

Nurse No Long Grief. Mary Gilmore. MAuV

Nurse Sharks. William Matthews. FiCP

Nurse, who is neither young nor pretty, The. Rivalry. Alden Nowlan. POL

Nursery Rhyme. Kenneth Burke. OBAL

Nursey Rhyme Alphabet, A. *Unknown.* ECBV

Nursery Rhyme of Innocence and Experience. Charles Causley. LP

Nursery Song in Pidgin English. *Unknown.* SpRo

Nurse's Dole in the Medea, The. Byron. OBVE

Nurse's Song ("When the voices of children are heard on the green/ And laughing is heard on the hill"). Blake. *Fr.* Songs of Innocence. LAuP; MBPR; OxBChV; STS

Nurse's Song ("When the voices of children are heard on the green/ And whisprings are in the dale"). Blake. *Fr.* Songs of Experience. CABA (1972 ed.); FF; LAuP; MBPR; STS

Nurse's Song. M. K. Joseph. ATNZ

Nursing Home. Linda Parker. HeS

Nursing the Hide. Carol Dunne. AMV-81

Nursing your nerves. The Afterwake. Adrienne Rich. NOBA; Prf

Nutcrackers and the Sugar-Tongs, The. Edward Lear. PoPle

Nuts in May, *with music. Unknown.* GSB

Nutting. Wordsworth. MBPR; NU; OAEL-2

Nymph Complaining for the Death of Her Fawn, The. Andrew Marvell. Epi; HeIP; OAEL-1; PAIC; SCP-1

Nymph, nymph, what are your beads? Overheard on [*or* in] a Saltmarsh. Harold Monro. ECBV; LCL; SO

Nymph of the downward smile, and sidelong glance. To G. A. W. Keats. MBPR

Nymph turnd home, The. He fell to felling downe. Homer, *tr. by* George Chapman. *Fr.* The Odyssey, V. OBVE

Nympholept, A. Swinburne. VLP

Nymphs and shepherds dance no more. Song. Milton. *Fr.* Arcades. LoAs

Nymph's Reply to the Shepherd, The. Sir Walter Ralegh. BiP; CABA (1972 ed.); Epi; FF; HAP; HeIP; HoPM (1975 ed.);

ILP (1975 ed.); IPWM; LoAs; NIL; NOBE; OLR; PoIA; PPoD; PPP
(Answer to Marlowe.) OAEL-1
(Her Reply.) BoLoP; UsP
(Nimphs Reply to the Sheepheard, The.) AAS

# O

Oh/ Crash! The Fourth. Shel Silverstein. CC

O/ Out of a bed of love. Holy Spring. Dylan Thomas. STS

Oh a high holiday, on a high holiday. Little Musgrave and Lady Barnard. *Unknown.* AmFP

Oh, a man there lives on the Western plains. The Cowboy. *Unknown.* BPAW

Oh, a ship she was rigged and ready for sea. The Fishes. *Unknown.* GBP

Oh, a wonderful horse is the Fly-away Horse. The Fly-away Horse. Eugene Field. PCOP

O a year from tomorrow I left my own people. Clonmel Jail. *Unknown, tr. by* Valentin Iremonger. BIrV

Oh Achilles of the moleskins. To "Chick." Frank Horne. *Fr.* Letters Found near a Suicide. BPo

Oh, Adam was a gardener. Kipling. *Fr.* The Glory of the Garden. CTV

O all down within the pretty meadow. Kenneth Patchen. HAP; WeW

O all ye fair ladies with your colours and your graces. The Revenant. Walter de la Mare. GBL

O all ye who pass by, whose eyes and mind. The Sacrifice. George Herbert. SCP-1

O all your ages at the mercy of my loves. John Berryman. *Fr.* Homage to Mistress Bradstreet. NOBA

O Allison Gross, that lives in yon towr. Allison Gross. *Unknown.* PeBB

O amiable prospect! New Lines for Cuscuscaraway and Mirza Murad Ali Beg. Louis Simpson. OBAL

Oh Ambulance Man. *Unknown.* BluL

O an old King in a story. After W. B. Yeats. G. K. Chesterton. NOBL

Oh, answer me a question, love, I pray. The Sweetest Story Ever Told. R. M. Stults. BLSo; FSN, *with music*

O apple into ant and beard. And With the Sorrows of This Joyousness. Kenneth Patchen. ECBV

O Artemis and your virgin girls. Telesilla, *tr. fr. Greek by* Willis Barnstone. BoWoP

Oh, as I went down to Derby Town. The Derby Ram. *Unknown.* AmFP

O Atthis. Ezra Pound. PoA

O Autumn, laden with fruit, and stained. To Autumn. Blake. FSFS; MBPR

Oh, away down South where I was born. Roll the Cotton Down. *Unknown.* AmFP

O, aye! they had woone child bezide. The Child an' the Mowers. William Barnes. VLP

Oh, Babe, It Ain't No Lie. Elizabeth Cotton. FSW

O battalions! O disaster! Ode. William Pillin. SPT

O, Be Not Too Hasty, My Dearest. "Orpheus C. Kerr." OBAL

O be swift. The Helmsman. Hilda Doolittle ("H. D."). CMoP (1970 ed.)

O beautiful bones. The Tough Ones. Errol Miller. AMV-80

O beautiful calm. Tu-kehu *and* Wetea, *tr. fr. Maori by* J. C. Andersen. WTO

O beautiful for spacious skies. America the Beautiful. Katherine Lee Bates. BLSH; BTTM; CTV; FSW; GOA; TAP

O Beautiful My Country, *with music.* Frederick Lucian Hosmer. AH

O, Beautiful They Move. William Pillen. VWA

O bells that rang, O bells that sang. The Mission Bells of Monterey. Bret Harte. PeD

Oh Beverly, do you remember. September 7. Ellen Bass. NMM

Oh, bid my tongue be still. Song. Richard Watson Dixon. VLP

O billows bounding far. Profoundly True Reflections on the Sea. A. E. Housman. FaBoNo

O Black and Unknown Bards. James Weldon Johnson. AmNP (1974 ed.); BPo; HeIP; NIL; PAIC; PoBA; UnPo (1976 ed.)

O blackbird! sing me something well. The Blackbird. Tennyson. PB

O blazing Sun, how happy you are there. Sonnet XXII. Louise Labé, *tr. by* Willis Barnstone. BoWoP

O blessed body! Whither art thou thrown? Sepulchre. George Herbert. SCP-1

O Blest Estate, Blest from Above, *with music.* George Sandys. AH

O blest unfabled incense tree. The Phoenix. George Darley. *Fr.* Nepenthe. BIrV; NOBE; OAEL-2

O blithe new-comer! I have heard. To the Cuckoo. Wordsworth. MBPR; PB

O blithely shines the bonnie sun. Fisherman's Song. *Unknown.* PoPle

Oh blow the man down bullies, blow the man down. Blow the Man Down. *Unknown.* FSW

O blush not so! O blush not so! Song. Keats. MBPR

Oh blythely shines the bonnie sun. We'll Go to Sea No More. *Unknown.* GBP

Oh, Bonnie is the little cow. Midnight in Bonnie's Stall. Siddie Joe Johnson. PChr

Oh Book! infinite sweetness! let my heart. The Holy Scriptures, I. George Herbert. Epi

Oh, Boston, Boston, thou hast nought to boast on. Boston, Lincolnshire. *Unknown.* GBP

Oh, Boston's a fine town with ships in the bay. Home, Boys, Home. *Unknown.* FSW

O Boswell, Bozzy, Bruce, what'er thy name. A Poetical and Congratulatory Epistle to James Boswell, Esq. "Peter Pindar." ESaP

Oh, bow your head, Tom Dooley. Tom Dooley. *Unknown.* AmFP

O Boy God, Muse of Poets. Ode to Fidel Castro. Edward Field. CABA (1972 ed.)

Oh boy Ken the smiling mountain is playing his guitar. Loaded Hearts. Vicki Viidikas. FPA

O boys and men of British mould. Mercy to Animals: A Ballad of Humanity. Martin Farquhar Tupper. PeD

O Boys! O Boys! Oliver St. John Gogarty. PFIr

Oh, Brandy leave me alone. Brandy Leave Me Alone. *Unknown.* FSW

O, Brignall banks are wild and fair. Brignall Banks. Sir Walter Scott. *Fr.* Rokeby. ILP (1975 ed.)

Oh! bring me one sweet orange bough. The Orange Bough. Felicia Dorothea Hemans. VLP

O brother, as you've given me so much. The Bride's Farewell: Two Songs. *Gond Oral Tradition, tr. by* V. Elwin *and* S. Hivale. WTO

"Oh, brother, oh, brother, can you play ball." The Two Brothers. *Unknown.* AmFP

O, brothers, you oughta been there. Roll, Jordan, Roll. *Unknown.* FSW

"O! bury me not in the deep, deep sea." The Ocean Burial. Edwin H. Chapin. PSoN

O Bury Me Not on the Lone Prairie. *Unknown.* BLSH, *with music*
(Bury Me Not on the Lone Prairie.) BPAW; FSW

Oh, but it is dirty! Filling Station. Elizabeth Bishop. HAP; WeW

Oh but It Was Good. Harold Littlebird. VoR

O Cambridge, attend. Satire upon the Heads. Thomas Gray. FaBoCo

O Canada! Adolphe Routhier, *tr. fr. French by* Robert Stanley Weir. BLSH, *with music;* FSW

O Captain! My Captain! Walt Whitman. *Fr.* Memories of President Lincoln. BTTM; FaPo; FaPoR; GOA; InPK; PBMP; RhR; TAP

O Carib Isle! Hart Crane. NoAM; PoA; VGW

O Catch Miss Daisy Pinks. Alistair Campbell. MiP
(Daisy Pinks.) ATNZ

O Cedar-tree, Cedar, my Mother. Song of Basket-weaving. Constance Lindsay Skinner. BPAW

Oh, Charlie, he's my darling. Charlie Is My Darling. *Unknown.* FSW; GSB

Oh, Charlie's sweet and Charlie's neat. Weevily Wheat. *Unknown.* AmFP

O Chatterton! how very sad thy fate! To Chatterton. Keats. MBPR

O Cheese. Donald Hall. TC

O Child of Lowly Manger Birth, *with music.* Ferdinand Q. Blanchard. AH

O Children, Would You Cherish? *with music.* Christopher Dock, *tr. fr. German by* Samuel W. Pennypacker. AH

O child's tremble. Forming Child Poems. Simon J. Ortiz. CDW

O Christ of Bethlehem, *with music.* H. Glenn Lanier. AH

O Christ who holds the open gate. John Masefield. *Fr.* The Everlasting Mercy. ILwL

O Christmas Night, *with music.* Henricus Selyns, *tr. fr. Dutch by* Howard Murphy. AH

Oh Christmas Tree. *Unknown. See* Oh Tannenbaum.

O cloud that wants to be the sky's arrow. Rosario Castellanos, *tr. fr. Spanish by* Willis Barnstone. BoWoP

O Columbia, the gem of the ocean. Columbia, the Gem of the Ocean. David T. Shaw. BTTM; CTV; FSW

O Come, All Ye Faithful. *Unknown, at. to* John Francis Wade, *tr. fr. Latin by* Frederic Oakeley. BLSH, *with music;* FSW
(Adeste Fideles.) PSoN

O come, my body is alone. Come Laugh with Me. *Gond Oral Tradition, tr. by* V. Elwin *and* S. Hivale. WTO

O Come Quickly! Thomas Campion. BoReV; NOBE
(Never Weather-beaten Sail.) OAEL-1

O! Come, soft rest of cares, come Night. Bridal Song. George Chapman. *Fr.* Hero and Leander, Fifth Sestiad. NOBE

O come to me, my brother Green, for I am shot and bleeding. Brother Green. *Unknown.* AmFP

O commemorate me where there is water. Lines Written on a Seat on the Grand Canal. Patrick Kavanagh. BIrV; CIP; CMoP (1970 ed.)

O comrades, come gather and join in my ditty. The *Cumberland's* Crew. *Unknown.* AmFP

"O Cormac, grandson of Conn," said Carbery. *Unknown, tr. by* Kuno Meyer. *Fr.* The Instructions of King Cormac. BIrV

O, could clock hands be moved in either way. The Process. Marguerite Young. FoP

O Could I Find from Day to Day, *with music.* Benjamin Cleavland. AH

Oh! could I hope the wise and pure in heart. Hymn to Death. Bryant. EAP

Oh, could we weep. Nurse No Long Grief. Mary Gilmore. MAuV

O Country People. John Hewitt. PFIr

"O cruel day, accusour of the joie." Chaucer. *Fr.* Troilus and Criseyde, III. PAIC

Oh Cruel Was the Press-Gang. *Unknown.* GBP

O Cuckoo! shall I call thee Bird. To the Cuckoo. F. H. Townsend. FaBoNo

O cuckoo that sang to us and art fled. Lament for the Cuckoo. Alcuin, *tr. by* Helen Waddell. NAWM-1

"O.D." Zack Gilbert. CNA

O Daedalus, Fly Away Home. Robert Hayden. BiP; HAP; NCSH; PoBA; WeW

Oh Danny boy, the pipes, the pipes are calling. Danny Boy. *Unknown.* FSW

O David, if I had. That Harp You Play So Well. Marianne Moore. PoA

Oh, Day of Days, *with music.* LeRoy V. Brant. AH

O Day of God, Draw Nigh, *with music.* Robert B. Y. Scott. AH

O Day of Light and Gladness, *with music.* Frederick Lucian Hosmer. AH

Oh, de ole sheep, dey know de road. De Ole Sheep Dey Know de Road. *Unknown.* BPo

Oh, de white gal ride in a automobile. De Black Girl. *Unknown.* GBP

O dear! I cannot choose but write. Eve. Oliver Herford. OBAL

O dear sweet rosy. An Asphodel. Allen Ginsberg. TT

Oh, Dear! What Can the Matter Be? *Unknown.* FSW; PoPle

Oh, dear, what can the matter be?/ Two old women got up in an apple-tree. *Unknown.* FaBoNo

Oh! dearer by far than the land of our birth. Richard Henry Wilde. GOA

Oh! Death. *Unknown.* AmFP

O Death, Rock Me Asleep. *At. to* Anne Boleyn. FF; WPE

O death, thy certainty is such. Henry Luttrell. FaBoEE

O deep-blue sea, O god Uli! Prayer of the Fishing Net. *Tr. fr. Hawaiian by* N. B. Emerson. WTO

Oh, Dem Golden Slippers! James A. Bland. PSoN, *with music*
(Golden Slippers.) FSW

O depth sufficient to desire. Adam's Song to Heaven. Edgar Bowers. ConAP

Oh, dey whupped him up de hill, up de hill, up de hill. Never Said a Mumbalin' Word. *Unknown.* GBP

Oh, did you go to see the show. The Orange Lily. *Unknown.* GBP

O discoveries!/ the landscape developing. In Southeast Asia (Viet Nam). J. R. Rowland. GAS

Oh, ditch of all ditches. Ode to a Ditch. *Unknown.* PeD

O divine star of heaven. John Fletcher. *Fr.* The Mad Lover, IV, i. GBL

Oh do not die, for I shall hate. A Fever. John Donne. OAEL-1

Oh do not wanton with those eyes. Song. Ben Jonson. LoAs

Oh, Do You Know the Muffin Man? Richard Mathews. AATT

Oh, do [*or* don't] you remember sweet Betsy from Pike. Sweet Betsy from Pike. *Unknown.* AmFP; BLSo; BPAW; FSW; OBAL

O Doctor Dear My Love. Anne Halley. NMM

O Donal Oge, if you go across the sea. Donal Oge: Grief of a Girl's Heart. *Unknown, tr. by* Lady Gregory. GBL; PBWP; PFIr

O don't, don't ever ask me for alms. Death and the Plowman. Sidney Keyes. OxBTC

Oh! don't you remember sweet Alice, Ben Bolt. Ben Bolt; or, Ah! Don't You Remember. Thomas Dunn English. FSW; PSoN

Oh, don't you remember sweet Betsey from Pike. *See* Oh, do you remember sweet Betsy from Pike.

O dream from the blackness. Sappho, *tr. fr. Greek by* Willis Barnstone. BoWoP

Oh! Dublin sure there is no doubtin'. No Place So Grand. *Unknown.* WTO

Oh, Dunderbeck, oh Dunderbeck. Dunderbeck. *Unknown.* FSW

O Duty,/ Why hast thou not the visage of a sweetie or a cutie? Kind of an Ode to Duty. Ogden Nash. IP

Oh, early in the evenin', just after dark. The Blackleg Miners. *Unknown.* GBP; VLP

O early one morning I walked out like Agag. The Streets of Laredo. Louis MacNeice. AIW; MPo; PeBB

O Earnest Be, *with music. Unknown.* AH

O Earth, lie heavily upon her eyes. Rest. Christina Rossetti. NOBE; OAEL-2

Oh, East is East, and West is West, and never the twain shall meet. The Ballad of East and West. Kipling. BTTM; FaPoR

Oh effervescent palisades of ferns in drippage. From Rome, for More Public Fountains in New York City. Alan Dugan. NYP; Prf

Oh, Eleazar Wheelock was a very pious man. Eleazar Wheelock. Richard Hovey. OBAL

O elephant, possessor of a savings-basket full of money. Salute to the Elephant. Odeniyi Apolebieji, *tr. by* S. A. Babalola. WTO

Oh, England. Sick in head and sick in heart. *Unknown.* FaBoEE

O eternal grass. On the Meadow. "Katri Vala," *tr. by* Jaakko A. Ahokas. PBWP

Oh, Eve, where's Adam? Adam in the Garden Pinning Leaves. *Unknown.* FSW

Oh, ever thus, from childhood's hour. A Few Muddled Metaphors by a Moore-ose Melodist. Tom Hood. FaBoNo

Oh, every year hath its winter. When the Birds Go North Again. Ella Higginson. WPW

O eye, weep for a rider. Rain to the Tribe. Al-Khansa, *tr. by* Willis Barnstone *and* Tony Nawfal. BoWoP

O eyes clear with beauty, O tender gaze. Sonnet XI. Louise Labé, *tr. by* Willis Barnstone. BoWoP

Oh, factious viper! whose envenom'd tooth. On the Death of Mr. Fox. Byron. MBPR

Oh, Fair to See. Christina Rossetti. ECBV

O fair young land, the youngest, fairest far. On Leaving California. Bayard Taylor. AmVN

Oh, Fairest of the Rural Maids. Bryant. EAP; TAP

O faithless thorn. *Gond Oral Tradition, tr. by* V. Elwin *and* S. Hivale. WTO

O fare ye weel, my auld wife! My Auld Wife. *Unknown.* GBP

Oh, fare you well, my darling. Fare You Well, My Darling. *Unknown.* AmFP

"O fare you well, my darling." Ten Thousand Miles. *Unknown.* AmFP

O fare you well, sweet Ireland, whom I shall see no more. The Sons of Liberty. *Unknown.* AIW

Oh Father. Wendy Rose. CDW

O Father, give the spirit power to climb. Boethius, *tr. by* Helen Waddell. *Fr.* The Consolation of Philosophy. NAWM-1

O Father, God! to whom, in happier days. Frederick Goddard Tuckerman. *Fr.* Sonnets. AmVN

Oh, father, oh, father, come riddle to me. Fair Ellender. *Unknown.* FSW

O Father, O Supreme of heav'nly Thrones. Milton. *Fr.* Paradise Lost, VI. ILwL

O Felix Culpa! *Unknown. See* Adam Lay I-bowndyn.

Oh flame falling, as shaken, as the stories. The Fire. Robert Creeley. NOBA

O fleece, that down the neck waves to the nape! Her Hair. Baudelaire. NAWM-2

O flowers of Mekhmekh, give us peace! Ezra Pound *and* Noel Stock, *fr. Egyptian hieroglyphics.* BoWoP

O fond, but fickle and untrue. Walter Savage Landor. GBL

O fondest, and O frailest fair. Ode to Popularity. Winthrop Mackworth Praed. VLP

O! for a bowl of fat canary. A Serving-Men's Song. John Lyly. *Fr.* Alexander and Campaspe. NOBE

Oh! for a closer walk with God. Walking with God. William Cowper. BoReV; ILP (1975 ed.); PIM

O for a muse of fire, a sack of dough. Sonnet with a Different Letter at the End of Every Line. George Starbuck. OBAL

Oh for a poet—for a beacon bright. Sonnet. E. A. Robinson. ILP (1975 ed.)

O for a toe, such as the funeral pyre. Sir Thomas Browne. FaBoEE

O for God's sake. Islands. Muriel Rukeyser. GP

O for our upland meads. Shepherd and Shepherdess. Thomas Hennell. FaBoTw (1975 ed.)

O for some honest lover's ghost. A Doubt of Martyrdom. Sir John Suckling. BoLoP; CaPo; ILP (1975 ed.); NOBE; PoPle: SCP-2

O for ten years, that I may overwhelm. Keats. *Fr.* Sleep and Poetry. OAEL-2; TT

O for the Happy Hour, *with music.* George Washington Bethune. AH

Oh forlorn fancy, whereto dost thou live. A Solemn Farewell to the World. Nicholas Breton. TVS

Oh fortune, thy wresting wavering state. Written on a Wall at Woodstock. Elizabeth I, Queen of England. PBWP; WPE

Oh Freedom. *Unknown.* FSW

O Friend! I know Not Which Way I Must Look. Wordsworth. BBGO; VoPo
(Written in London, September, 1802.) ILP (1975 ed.); MBPR

Oh friend, we arrived too late. Friedrich Hölderlin, *tr. by* Robert Bly. *Fr.* Bread and Wine. NU

O friends! who have accompanied thus far. Walter Savage Landor. GBL

O Friendship! Friendship! the shell of Aphrodite. Walter Savage Landor. GBL

O, Frisco was a strumpet. Nostalgia. Gertrude Millard. BPAW

Oh, Frog Prince, Frog Prince. The Princess Addresses the Frog Prince. Elizabeth Brewster. MMD

Oh, Froggie went a'courtin' and he did ride. Froggie Went a Courtin'. *Unknown.* BLSo

O Future bards. A Prophecy. Allen Ginsberg. TAP

Oh Galuppi, Baldassaro, this is very sad to find! A Toccata of Galuppi's. Robert Browning. HAP; LFH; NOBE; OAEL-2; PAIC; TT

O generation of the thoroughly smug. Salutation. Ezra Pound. HeIP; NOBA; PiAm; TAP; VGW

Oh Genevieve, I'd give the world. Sweet Genevieve. George Cooper. BLSH; BLSo; FSW; PSoN

O gentle, gentle land. Night Sowing. David Campbell. MAuV

O gentle Love, do not forsake the guide. Upon Some Alterations in My Mistress, after My Departure into France. Thomas Carew. CaPo

Oh, gentle one, thy birthday sun should rise. The Twenty-seventh of March. Bryant. EAP

O gentle, restless earth. Night Harvest. Susan Pence. AMV-80

O gentle sleep! do they belong to thee. To Sleep. Wordsworth. MBPR

"Oh, Georgie Wedlock is my name." Georgie Wedlock. *Unknown.* AmFP

Oh gin I were a doo. Gin I Were a Doo. *Unknown.* GBP

O Gin My Love Were Yon Red Rose. *Unknown.* GBP; SLP

O girl, you torment me, you are so deceiving. *Gond Oral Tradition, tr. by* V. Elwin *and* S. Hivale. WTO

Oh, give me a home, where the buffalo roam. Home on the Range. *Unknown.* BLSH; BLSo; BPAW; FSW

Oh give me a pup. Poetic Tale. Grace Maddock Miller. GDP

Oh, Give Me the Hills. *Unknown.* AmFP

Oh, give thanks to Him who made. Give Thanks. *Unknown.* CTV

Oh, Give Us Pleasure in the Flowers Today. Robert Frost. *See* Prayer in Spring, A.

Oh, go to old Ireland and then you will know. Go to Old Ireland. *Unknown.* AmFP

O god. Obit Page. Paul Blackburn. VoA

Oh, God!/ Who made us. The Prayer of Abel. Byron. *Fr.* Cain. PIM

O God, above the Drifting Years, *with music.* John Wright Buckham. AH

O God, Accept the Sacred Hour, *with music.* Samuel Gilman. AH

O God, beneath Thy Guiding Hand, *with music.* Leonard Bacon. AH

O God, Great Father, Lord, and King, *with music.* E. Embree Hoss. AH

O God, I Cried, No Dark Disguise, *with music.* Edna St. Vincent Millay. AH

O God, in the dream the terrible horse began. The Dream. Louise Bogan. MAT; SBG

O God, in Whom the Flow of Days, *with music.* Donald C. Babcock. AH

O God, in Whose Great Purpose, *with music.* James G. Gilkey. AH

Oh god, let's go. Please. Robert Creeley. VoA

O God, make this age great that we may be. To Poesy. Tennyson. VLP

O God most glorious, called by many a name. Hymn to Zeus. Cleanthes, *tr. by* James Adam. ILwL

O God! My God! have mercy now. Supposed Confessions of a Second-rate Sensitive Mind. Tennyson. VLP

O God! O Montreal! Samuel Butler. FaBoCo (Psalm of Montreal.) OBSV

O God, O Venus, O Mercury, patron of thieves. The Lake Isle. Ezra Pound. CABA (1972 ed.); FaBoCo; PoA

O God of Bethel. Philip Doddridge *and* John Logan. WTO

Oh, God of dust and rainbows, help us see. Epigram. Langston Hughes. SoSe

O God of global battle-lines. Italian Spring, 1945. Nellie Burget Miller. WPW

O God of My Salvation, Hear, *with music.* Joel Barlow. AH

O God of Stars and Distant Space, *with music.* John Franzen. AH

O God of Youth, *with music.* Bates G. Burt. AH

O God, Our Help in Ages Past. Isaac Watts. FaPoR

O God, Send Men, *with music.* Elizabeth Burrowes. AH

Oh God, she said. Song My. Susan Griffin. NMM

O God, though Countless Worlds of Light, *with music.* James D. Knowles. AH

O God, who made me. The Prayer of the Donkey. Carmen Bernos de Gasztold. PChr

O God Whose Presence Glows in All, *with music.* Nathaniel L. Frothingham. AH

O God, whose thunder shakes the sky. On Resignation. Thomas Chatterton. PIM

O Goddess! hear these tuneless numbers, wrung. Ode to Psyche. Keats. CABA (1972 ed.); InPS; MBPR; NIL; NOBE; OAEL-2; PPP; STS

O goddess Laka! Altar Prayers. *Tr. fr. Hawaiian by* N. B. Emerson. WTO

O golden tongued romance, with serene lute! On Sitting Down to Read King Lear Once Again. Keats. EBEV; MBPR

O Gongyla, my darling rose. Sappho, *tr. fr. Greek by* Willis Barnstone. BoWoP

Oh! Good, good, good, my Lord. What more love yet. Edward Taylor. Preparatory Meditations: Second Series, CXII. NOBA

"O good Lord Judge, and sweet Lord Judge." The Maid Freed from the Gallows. *Unknown.* ECBV

Oh Goofy. Modern Times. Morty Sklar. AcAn

O Gracious Father of Mankind, *with music.* Henry Hallam Tweedy. AH

O gracious gods, take compassion. John Marston. *Fr.* The Metamorphosis of Pygmalion's Image. OAEL-1

O Gracious Jesus, Blessed Lord! *with music.* Andrew Fowler. AH

O great humming nymphet and mother and moth and. 25 Spontaneous Lines Greeting the World. Jim Tyack. AMV-80

O handsome chestnut eyes, evasive gaze. Sonnet II. Louise Labé, *tr. by* Willis Barnstone. BoWoP

Oh, hang down your head, Tom Dooley. Tom Dooley. *Unknown.* GSB

"Oh, hangman, hangman, slacken your rope." The Sycamore Tree. *Unknown.* AmFP

O happy [*or* happie] dames, that may embrace. Complaint of the Absence of Her Lover Being upon the Sea. Earl of Surrey. AAS; EBEV; GBL; NOBE

O Happy Day, *with music.* Philip Doddridge. BLSH

Oh happy golden age. A Pastoral. Tasso, *tr. by* Samuel Daniel. *Fr.* Aminta. OAEL-1

O happy hour. *Unknown, tr. by* Helen Waddell. *Fr.* Carmina Burana. NAWM

O, happy is the craw. The Lammermuir Lilt. Forbes Macgregor. MIS

Oh happy shades—to me unblest. The Shrubbery. William Cowper. NOBE

O happy souls, that mingle with your kind. "Social Science." Thomas Edward Brown. PeD

Oh, hard is the fortune of all womankind. Hard Is the Fortune of All Womankind. *Unknown.* FSW

Oh, hark the dogs are barking, love. The Banks of the Condamine. *Unknown.* FaBoBa; GBP; PeBB

O Harry Heine, curses be. Translator to Translated. Ezra Pound. FaBoEE

O Harry, thou hast robb'd me of my youth! Shakespeare. King Henry IV, Pt. I, *fr.* V, iv. LFH

O have ye na heard o the fause Sakelde? Kinmont Willie. *Unknown.* PeBB

O Have You Caught the Tiger? A. E. Housman. FaBoNo; SpRo

Oh Have You Heard. Shel Silverstein. CC

Oh, have you heard de lates'. De Ballit of de Boll Weevil. *Unknown.* NOBA

Oh have you heard it's time for vaccinations? Oh Have You Heard. Shel Silverstein. CC

"Oh, have you heard the gallant news." Stephen Vincent Benét. *Fr.* Western Star. AIW

Oh have you heard the story 'bout Aimee McPherson? Aimee McPherson. *Unknown.* FSW

O have you seen my fairy steed? My Fairy Steed. Laura Benét. PCOP

O, have you seen the leper healed. The Healing of the Leper. Vernon Watkins. FaBoTw (1975 ed.)

Oh, have you seen the *Tattlesnake.* The Journal of Society. Godfrey Turner. NOBL

Oh, he was a handsome trotter, and he couldn't be completer. How We Drove the Trotter. W. T. Goodge. PH

Oh, he was old and he was spare. The Swagman. C. J. Dennis. ECBV

O hear a pensive prisoner's prayer. The Mouse's Petition. Anna Laetitia Barbauld. MN; OxBChV

O Hear My Prayer, Lord, *with music.* John Craig. AH

"Oh, hear you a horn, mother, behind the hill?" The Horn. James Reeves. SO

O heart of hearts, the chalice of love's fire. Cor Cordium. Swinburne. VLP

O Heart! the equal poise of love's both parts. Richard Crashaw. *Fr.* The Flaming Heart. OBP

O Heaven Indulge, *with music.* Stephen Tilden. AH

O heavenly colour, London town. November Blue. Alice Meynell. PES

Oh, heavens! the weakness of my unkind father! The Obscured Prince; or, The Black Box Boxed. *Unknown.* APAS

O Hector, thou wert rooted in my heart. Helen's Lamentation. Homer, *tr. by* Congreve. *Fr.* The Iliad, XXIV. OBVE

"Oh hell, what do mine eyes." Milton by Firelight. Gary Snyder. CAPP; CNW; ConAP; ILP (1975 ed.); InPK; InPS; PPP

O helpless few in my country. The Rest. Ezra Pound. *Fr.* Lustra. NoAM; NOBA; PoA

Oh, here you see old Tom Moore. The Days of Forty-nine. *Unknown.* FSW

O hermitage well found. The Young Pilgrim Finds Refuge with the Goatherds. Luis de Góngora, *tr. by* Edward Meryon Wilson. *Fr.* The First Solitude. OBVE

Oh he's God. God Don't Never Change. *Unknown.* BluL

O hideous little bat, the size of snot. The Fly. Karl Shapiro. CoPAm; NoAM; NowV; PBMP; PoIA

O hill-hung city of my West. San Francisco Arising. Edwin Markham. BPAW

Oh hinny, Geordie, canny man. California. Joseph Philip Robson. VLP

Oh, Hollow! Hollow! Hollow! W. S. Gilbert. FaBoNo

O Holy City Seen of John, *with music.* Walter Russell Bowie. AH

O Holy Ghost, whose temple I. John Donne. *Fr.* A Litany. SCP-1

O Holy, Holy, Holy, Lord, *with music.* James Wallis Eastburn. AH

Oh how comely it is and how reviving. Milton. *Fr.* Samson Agonistes. BoReV; NOBE; SCP-1

Oh, how far away things are. The Grief. Rainer Maria Rilke, *tr. by* Steven Lautermilch. AMV-81

Oh, How He Lied. *Unknown.* FSW

Oh, how I love, on a fair summer's eve. Keats. MBPR

O, how I remember the pain of it. Blood. Nina Cassian, *tr. by* Herbert Kuhner. VWA

Oh how I wish that an embargo. The Nurse's Dole in the Medea. Byron. OBVE

Oh, How Lovely Is the Evening. *Unknown.* FSW

O, how much more doth beauty beauteous seem. Sonnets, LIV. Shakespeare. STS

Oh, how my love/ With a whirling power. Tu-kehu *and* Wetea, *tr. fr. Maori by* J. C. Andersen. WTO

O how this sullen, careless world. The Idiot. John Ashbery. *Fr.* Two Sonnets. VGW

O hurry where by water among the trees. The Ragged Wood. W. B. Yeats. GBL

Oh! hush thee, my baby, the night is behind us. The White Seal's Lullaby. Kipling. EcS

O hush thee, my baby, thy sire was a knight. Lullaby of an Infant Chief. Sir Walter Scott. OxBChV

Oh, I am a poor girl, my fortune is sad. The Wagoner's Lad. *Unknown.* FSW

Oh, I am a Texas cowboy, just off the Texas plains. The Texas Cowboy. *Unknown.* AmFP

O I am sick for the sagebrush. Sagebrush. Charles Erskine Scott Wood. BPAW

Oh, I am the living God. Novus Ordo Seclorum. Grace Cavalieri. AATT

Oh, I couldn't hear nobody pray. I Couldn't Hear Nobody Pray. *Unknown.* FSW

Oh I do love thee, meek Simplicity! To Simplicity. Samuel Taylor Coleridge. *Fr.* Sonnets Attempted in the Manner of Contemporary Writers. Epi

O I forbid you, maidens a'. Tam Lin. *Unknown.* AIW; Epi; FaBoBa; NOBE; PeBB

Oh I got up and went to work. On a Seven-Day Diary. Alan Dugan. OBAL

Oh, I had a bird and the bird pleased me. The Barnyard. *Unknown.* AmFP

O I had a future. I Had a Future. Patrick Kavanagh. BIrV; NoAM

Oh I had my fantasies when I worked at Grosvenor Square. Pigeon Pie. Carl Bode. PoUp

O, I hae come from far away. The Witch's Ballad. William Bell Scott. VLP

Oh I have grown so shrivelled and sere. Body of John. R. A. K. Mason. ATNZ

O, I love to hear the frogs. The Early Frogs. Harry Edward Mills. PeD

Oh, I never had but one true love. The Unquiet Grave. *Unknown.* AmFP

O I remember in Duncan's Mills. Kato's Poem. David Kherdian. FAF

Oh I suppose I should. Le Médecin Malgré Lui. William Carlos Williams. PoA

O, I tell you. Lament of a Last Letter. Janet E. Harrison. AMV–80

Oh, I used to sing a song. The Endless Song. Ruth McEnery Stuart. OBAL

Oh! I vu'st know'd o' my true love. Heedless o' My Love. William Barnes. GBL

Oh I was born in Boston, a city you all know well. The Boston Burglar. *Unknown.* FSW

Oh, I was born in Mobile town. I've Been Workin' on the Railroad. *Unknown.* BLSH

Oh I went down South for to see my Sal. Polly Wolly Doodle. *Unknown.* FSW

Oh, I went to California in the spring of seventy-six. Root, Hog, or Die. *Unknown.* FSW

O I will sing to you a sang. The Clerk's Twa Sons o Owsenford. *Unknown.* PeBB

Oh, I Wish I Were Single Again. *Unknown.* AmFP

Oh, I wonder where my lost Johnny's gone. Lost Johnny. *Unknown.* AmFP

O if all the young maidens was blackbirds and thrushes. Blackbirds and Thrushes. *Unknown.* GBP

Oh, if but a single hour. Permanence in Change. Goethe, *tr. by* Mark Doyle. HoPM (1975 ed.)

Oh, I'm a good old Rebel. The Rebel [*or* The Good Old Rebel]. Innes Randolph. FSW; OBAL

Oh I'm being eaten by a boa constrictor. Boa Constrictor. Shel Silverstein. CaYB

Oh, I'm goin' round the world, baby mine. Baby Mine. *Unknown.* FSW

Oh, I'm goin' to sing a song, and I won't detain you long. How Do You Do, *Alabama!* Fred Wilson. AIW

Oh, I'm gonna get me a religion. Preachin' the Blues. *Unknown.* BluL

Oh, in the merry month of May. Bonny Barbara Allan. *Unknown.* AmFP

O interminable desires, O futile hope. Sonnet III. Louise Labé, *tr. by* Willis Barnstone. BoWoP

Oh it happen'd in Vienna not so very long ago. Doctor Freud. David Lazar. FSW

Oh, it will be fine. Valentine for Earth. Frances Frost. QQQ

Oh, it's beer, beer, that makes you feel so queer. The Quartermaster Store. *Unknown.* FSW

O It's Nice to Get Up in, the Slipshod Mucous Kiss. E. E. Cummings. Epi

Oh, It's Nine Years Ago I Was Digging in the Land. *Unknown.* AmFP

Oh it's nonsense, nonsense. "Hugh MacDiarmid." *Fr.* Second Hymn to Lenin. MS

Oh, I've got no use for the women. I've Got No Use for the Women. *Unknown.* AmFP

O jay betide the dear wold mill. Naighbour Playmeates. William Barnes. VPC

O Jean Baptiste, pourquoi. Pourquoi? *Unknown.* ECBV; GDP

O Jean, my Jean, when the bell ca's the congregation. Tam i' the Kirk. Violet Jacob. GBL; MS; SLP

O Jellon Grame sat in Silver Wood. Jellon Grame. *Unknown.* EBEV; PeBB

O Jenny, don't sobby! vor I shall be true. A Zong. William Barnes. BoLoP

O Jesu Parvule. "Hugh MacDiarmid." MS

O Jesus Christ, True Light of God, *with music.* John F. Ernst. AH

O Jesus, My Savior, I Know Thou Art Mine, *with music.* Caleb J. Taylor. AH

O, Johnny Bull, my jo, John, I wonder what you mean. Johnny Bull, My Jo, John. *Unknown.* FSW

O Joie. Song. Paul Mariah. BrS

O Jojina my love, I always miss you. Jojina, My Love. Zulu Oral Tradition, tr. by H. Tracey. WTO

O joy of creation. What the Bullet Sang. Bret Harte. PeD

O Joy of Love's Renewing. Andrew Lang. SLP

O joy! that in our embers. Wordsworth. *Fr.* Ode: Intimations of Immortality. PoPle

O Joyes! Infinite sweetness! with what flowres. *See* O joys! Infinite sweetness! with what flowers.

Oh, Joyous House. Richard Janzen. AKE

O joys! Infinite sweetness! with what flowers. The Morning-Watch. Henry Vaughan. BoReV; GrRo; MetP; SCP-1; UsP

O June, O June, that we desired so. June. William Morris. *Fr.* The Earthly Paradise. LFH

O Kane, O Ku-ka-Pao. Old Creation Chant. *Tr. fr. Hawaiian.* WTO

O Kane, O Lono of the blue sea. *Tr. fr. Hawaiian by* N. B. Emerson. WTO

O Kentucky! my parents were driving. A Poem of the Forty-eight States. Kenneth Koch. NNaP; OBAL

Oh, kind friend you may ask me what makes me sad and still. Utah Carroll. *Unknown.* FSW

O King, I know you gave me poison. Mirabai, *tr. fr. Medieval Hindi by* Usha Nilsson. PBWP

O King of Saints, We Give Thee Praise and Glory, *with music.* Mary A. Thomson. AH

Oh, King of the fiddle, Wilhelmj. Wilhelmj. Robert J. Burdette. TDH

O King of the Friday. *Unknown, tr. fr. Irish by* Douglas Hyde. BIrV

O King of the World. *Tr. fr. Gaelic by* Douglas Hyde. WTO

O kiss me yet again, O kiss me over. Sonnet. Louise Labé, *tr. by* Frederic Prokosch. LoAs

O know you what I have done. The Brother. Thomas Hardy. AIW

O Lady amorous,/ Merciless lady. Canzonetta: A Bitter Song to His Lady. Pier Moronelli da Fiorenza, *tr. by* Dante Gabriel Rossetti. OBVE

O! Lady dear, fair is thy noon. The Song. James Hogg. *Fr.* The Queen's Wake. SLP

O Lady Moon. Christina Rossetti. Moon (Lady Moon.) OxBChV

O lady, rock never your young son young. Young Hunting. *Unknown.* PeBB

Oh, lance of lightning. My Grandfather. Roman Adrian. DNGG

O land of Empire, art and love! Resignation—to Faustus. Arthur Hugh Clough. VLP

O, land of mud and mist, where man is wet and shivers. Such Is Holland! Petrus Augustus de Genestet, *tr. by* Adriaan Barnouw. POL

O Lapwing, thou fliest around the heath. Blake. FaBoEE

Oh last Thursday morning while playing at ball. Willie. *Unknown.* AmFP

Oh Lawd have mussy now upon us. Blessing without Company. *Unknown.* BPo; POL

Oh, lead me to a quiet cell. Portrait of the Artist. Dorothy Parker. PPM

Oh Leaden heeld. Lord, give, forgive I pray. Edward Taylor. *Fr.* Preparatory Meditations: Second Series, I. PiAm

"O leaders and counselors." Odysseus and the Phaeacian Games. Homer, *tr. by* Ennis Rees. *Fr.* The Odyssey, VIII. LiSp

O leafy yellowness you create for me. October. Patrick Kavanagh. CIP

Oh leave his body broken on the rocks. On a Dying Boy. William Bell. WIF

Oh, leave me! It's time for the horizon to. Reverie. Victor Hugo, *tr. by* Mary Ann Caws. NAWM–2

Oh! leave the past to bury its own dead. To One Who Would Make a Confession. Wilfrid Scawen Blunt. PPM

O lend to me, sweet nightingale. The Daughter of Mendoza. Mirabeau Buonaparte Lamar. BPAW

Oh let the gentlewoman have the wall. Samuel Rowlands. *Fr.* The Letting of Humour's Blood in the Head-Vein. TVS

O let the seeds be planted. Rogation Sunday. William Carlos Williams. TT

O let us howl some heavy note. John Webster. *Fr.* The Duchess of Malfi. SCP-2

O life is a game of poker. Cash In. Sharlot M. Hall. BPAW

Oh, life is a glorious cylce of song. Comment. Dorothy Parker. NIL; OBAL

O life, O radiance, love, delight. Epilogue. Christopher Brennan. *Fr.* The Burden of Tyre. MAuV

O Life That Maketh All Things New, *with music.* Samuel Longfellow. AH

O Light. Allan Kornblum. AcAn

O Light Invisible, we praise Thee! T. S. Eliot. *Fr.* The Rock. ILwL

O lightning! slice the sky. Thunder in a Moment of Calm. Joseph Kalar. SPT

Oh! List to the tale of a poor Irish harper. The Bard of Armagh. *Unknown.* FSW

O listen for a moment, lads.   Jim Jones at Botany Bay.   *Unknown.*   GBP; PeBB

O Little Town of Bethlehem.   Phillips Brooks.   AH, *with music;* BLSH, *with music;* FSW

O little well, you give no water.   *Gond Oral Tradition, tr. by* V. Elwin *and* S. Hivale.   WTO

O Living Always, Always Dying.   Walt Whitman.   NOBA

O living pine, be still!   Sleep.   Yvor Winters.   POL

O lonely bay of Trinity.   The Cable Hymn.   Whittier.   PiAm

O lonely workman, standing there.   In the Moonlight.   Thomas Hardy.   NoAM

O lonesome sea-gull, floating far.   Sea-Birds.   Elizabeth Akers Allen.   EcS

Oh, long, long.   The Grass on the Mountain.   *Unknown, tr. by* Mary Austin.   GOA

O, Look at the Moon.   Eliza Lee Follen.   CTV

Oh look outside the window.   Outside of a Small Circle of Friends.   Phil Ochs.   NowV

O Lord, Almighty God, *with music.*   *Unknown.*   AH

O Lord, Bow Down Thine Ear, *with music.*   Thomas Prince.   AH

Oh Lord Cozens Hardy.   Lord Cozens Hardy.   John Betjeman.   OxBTC

O Lord, How Lovely Is the Place, *with music.*   *Ad. by* Francis Hopkinson.   AH

O Lord, how wonderful in depth and height.   Cardinal Newman.   *Fr.* The Dream of Gerontius.   VLP

O Lord, I been a-working.   Trifling Women.   *Unknown.*   AmFP

O lord, I dred, and that I did not dred.   Bible, *O.T.*   Psalms, VI.   OBVE

Oh Lord, I have been staring into a mirror.   Psalm.   Eugene Heimler, *tr. by* Anthony Rudolf.   VWA

O Lord in me there lieth nought.   Psalm CXXXIX: Domine, Probasti.   Countess of Pembroke.   WPE

O Lord, it was all night.   Sun.   James Dickey.   CAPP

O Lord of all compassionate control.   The Portrait.   Dante Gabriel Rossetti.   The House of Life, X.   VLP

O Lord of Life, *with music.*   Washington Gladden.   AH

O Lord Our God, Thy Mighty Hand, *with music.*   Henry Van Dyke.   AH

O Lord, our Lord, how excellent is thy name.   Bible, *O.T.*   Psalms, VIII.   AKE; NAWM-1; PBMP

O Lord, since we have feasted thus.   Grace after Dinner.   Burns.   FaBoEE

O Lord, That Art My God and King, *with music.*   John Craig.   AH

O Lord, that rul'st the human heart.   Bible, *O.T., paraphrased by* Christopher Smart.   Psalms, VIII.   OBVE

O Lord, Thou Hast Been to the Land, *with music.*   *Unknown.*   AH

O Lord, Turn Not Away Thy Face, *with music.*   *At. to* John Marckant.   AH

O Lord, we come this morning.   Listen, Lord—a Prayer.   James Weldon Johnson.   BPo

O Lord! who seest from yon starry height.   The Image of God.   Francisco de Aldana, *tr. by* Longfellow.   PIM

O Lorde oure governoure, howe excellent is thy name.   Bible, *O.T.*   Psalms, VIII.   OBVE

Oh lordy, lord, oh lordy, lord.   Worried Life Blues.   *Unknown.*   AmFP

Oh, Lordy, pick a bale of cotton.   Pick a Bale of Cotton.   *Unknown.*   FSW

O Love, be fed with apples while you may.   Sick Love.   Robert Graves.   BoLoP; CMoP (1970 ed.); EBEV; ExPo (1973 ed.); HAP; NoAM; NOBE; OAEL-2

O Love, bringer of fire.   Aut Neutrum . . . Vel Duos.   Rufinus Domesticus, *tr. by* Dudley Fitts.   OLR

O Love Divine, That Stooped to Share.   Oliver Wendell Holmes.   *See* Hymn of Trust.

O love, how thou art tired out with rhyme!   Epigraph to the Theme of Love.   Margaret Cavendish, Duchess of Newcastle.   SCP-2

O, love, in your sweet name enough.   Anne Finch.   *Fr.* Essay on Marriage.   FaBoTw (1975 ed.)

O, Love, love, love!   Love Is like a Dizziness.   James Hogg.   SLP

O love, love, love!   O withering might!   Fatima.   Tennyson.   GBL; UnPo (1976 ed.)

Oh love!   no habitant of earth thou art.   Byron.   *Fr.* Childe Harold's Pilgrimage, IV.   OAEL-2

O Love That Lights the Eastern Sky, *with music.*   Louis F. Benson.   AH

Oh!   Love, that stronger art than wine.   Song.   Aphra Behn.   *Fr.* The Lucky Chance.   WPE

O Love That Wilt Not Let Me Go, *with music.*   George Matheson.   BLSH

O love, the interest itself in thoughtless heaven.   Prologue.   W. H. Auden.   EBEV

O love, this morn when the sweet nightingale.   May.   William Morris.   *Fr.* The Earthly Paradise.   VLP

O love, turn from the unchanging sea, and gaze.   October.   William Morris.   *Fr.* The Earthly Paradise.   VPC

O lovely age of gold!   Tasso, *tr. by* Leigh Hunt.   *Fr.* Aminta.   OBVE

O lovely O most charming pug.   A Sonnet.   Marjory Fleming.   FaBoCo

O lovely pussy!   O pussy my love.   Love Song.   Edward Lear.   *Fr.* The Owl and the Pussy-Cat.   PCat

Oh, Lovely Rock.   Robinson Jeffers.   NoAM; NU

O lovely wheel that weds along the groove.   Driving Clock.   Hildegarde Flanner.   WPW

O lovers' eyes are sharp to see.   The Maid of Neidpath.   Sir Walter Scott.   SLP

O loyal to the royal in thyself.   To the Queen.   Tennyson.   *Fr.* Idylls of the King.   VLP

Oh Lucky Jim.   *Unknown.*   GBP

O, lucky poet tone-deaf.   Poet.   Conrad Hilberry.   PPoD

O luely, luely, cam she in.   The Tryst [*or* Trysting Place].   William Soutar.   BoLoP; EBEV; MSL; SLP

O lusty May with Flora quene.   May Poem.   *Unknown.*   SLP

O luxury!   Thou curst by Heaven's decree.   Goldsmith.   *Fr.* The Deserted Village.   BIrV

O Lyric Love.   Winfield Townley Scott.   VGW

O madam, I will give to you the keys of Canterbury.   The Keys of Canterbury.   *Unknown.*   AmFP

O maister deer and fader reverent!   Lament for Chaucer and Gower.   Thomas Hoccleve.   *Fr.* De Regimine Principum.   EBEV; OxBM

O make me a mask and a well to shut from your spies.   Dylan Thomas.   PoA

Oh, make me, sphere-descended Queen.   A Wykehamist's Address to Learning.   P. N. Shuttleworth.   FaBoCo

O Maker of the infinite starry spaces.   Petition.   Harold McCurdy.   AMV-81

O Maker of the starry world.   Boethius, *tr. by* Helen Waddell.   *Fr.* The Consolation of Philosophy.   NAWM-1

"Oh, Mammy, Mammy, now I'm married."   Will the Weaver.   *Unknown.*   AmFP

O Man Unkind.   *Unknown.*   OxBM

Oh, many a day have I made good ale in the glen.   The Outlaw of Loch Lene.   *Unknown, tr. by* Jeremiah Joseph Callanan.   BIrV; GBL; PFIr

O many-petaled light where.   Lament of My Father, Lakota.   Paula Gunn Allen.   VW

Oh, Marcia. Gee, You're So Beautiful That It's Starting to Rain. Richard Brautigan. PPM; VoA; WeW

Oh, Mary and the Baby, sweet Lamb. Mary and the Baby, Sweet Lamb. *Unknown.* AmFP

O Mary, Don't You Weep, Don't You Mourn. *Unknown.* AH; *with music;* FSW

"O Mary, go and call the cattle home." The Sands of Dee. Charles Kingsley. FaPoR; PoPle; VLP

O Mary Hamilton to the kirk is gane. Mary Hamilton. *Unknown.* NOBE

Oh, Mary, this London's a wonderful sight. The Mountains of Mourne. Percy French. PFIr

O Mary's lovelier than anything that grows. Prisoner's Song. Horace Gregory. OLR

O Master, Let Me Walk with Thee, *with music.* Washington Gladden. AH

O Master Workman of the Race, *with music.* Jay T. Stocking. AH

O Matre Pulchra. Charles Spear. ATNZ

O May I Join the Choir Invisible. "George Eliot." PFD

O me, oh my, oh you. Does the Spearmint Lose Its Flavor on the Bedpost Overnight? Billy Rose. OBAL

Oh, meet me tonight in the moonlight. New Jail. *Unknown.* AmFP

"O 'Melia, my dear, this does everything crown!" The Ruined Maid. Thomas Hardy. BoLoP; CABA (1972 ed.); CMoP (1970 ed.); HeIP; InPK, NOBL; OBP; OxBTC; PoIA; PPoD; PPoe; WeW; WIF

O melon-bellied (I talk/ to my gut). Lunes. Margaret Gibson. AAN

O Memory, could I but loose thee now. Lindamira's Complaint. Mary Sidney Wroth, Countess of Montgomery. *Fr.* Urania. WPE

O men from the fields. Lullaby. Padraic Colum. WTO

O men, the beautiful world is going to be spoiled. The Suez Crisis. *Somali Oral Tradition, tr. by* B. W. Andrzejewski. WTO

O merciful God, hear this our request. A Prayer to Be Said When Thou Goest to Bed. Francis Seager. OxBChV

O Merlin in your crystal cave. Merlin. Edwin Muir. FaBoTw (1975 ed.)

O Metaphysical Head. Horace Gregory. SPT

O might/ I but touch. On the Daughter of Lykambes. Archilochos, *tr. by* Jonathan Cott. RRA

O might those sighs and tears return again. Holy Sonnets, III. John Donne. BiP

Oh, mighty America, hast thou come to this? Fare Thee Well. Eli Siegel. GOA

O mighty mind, in whose deep stream this age. Fragment: To Byron. Shelley. MBPR

O mighty-mouth'd inventor of harmonies. Milton. Tennyson. Epi; PAIC; VLP

Ohhhhhhh Mister Charlie your rolling mill is burning down. Mister Charlie. *Unknown.* BluL

"Oh, Mrs. McGrath," the sergeant said. Mrs. McGrath. *Unknown.* FaBoBa; FSW

O mistress mine, where are you roaming? Feste's Song [*or* Sweet-and-Twenty]. Shakespeare. *Fr.* Twelfth Night, II, iii. BoLoP; GBL; GrRo; HAP; HeIP; InPS; NOBE; OLR

Oh, Molly, oh, Molly, I've told you before. Red Whiskey. *Unknown.* AmFP

"O monstrous, dead, unprofitable world." Written in Emerson's Essays. Matthew Arnold. ILP (1975 ed.)

Oh Moon, discreetly worshipped by our sires. The Injured Moon. Baudelaire, *tr. by* Robert Lowell. Moon

Oh moon, oh moon! *Tr. fr. Papuan by* Mari Marase. BoWoP

O Moon, When I Gaze on Thy Beautiful Face. *Unknown.* InPK

O mortal[l] folk[e]! you may behold and see. The Epitaph of Grande Amoure. Stephen Hawes. *Fr.* The Pastime of Pleasure. EBEV; FaBoEE

O mortal man, that lives by bread. *At. to* Julius Caesar Ibbetson. FaBoEE

O mortal Man, who livest here by toil. The Castle of Indolence, Canto I. James Thomson. LAuP

Oh mother,/ here in your lap. Mothers. Anne Sexton. IPWM

Oh, Mother, I shall be married to Mr. Punchinello. Mr. Punchinello. *Unknown.* ECBV

O mother, mother, where is happiness? The Sonnet-Ballad. Gwendolyn Brooks. SoS; TT; WeW

Oh mother my mouth is full of stars. Song of the Dying Gunner A.A.1. Charles Causley. AIW

Oh Mother of a Mighty Race. Bryant. EAP

Oh! mourn not for Anacreon dead. On Tom Moore's Translation of Anacreon. Thomas, Lord Erskine. FaBoEE

O muse who sangest late another's pain. Monody on a Tea-Kettle. Samuel Taylor Coleridge. MBPR

Oh, Musgrove, he persuaded me. Musgrove. *Unknown.* AmFP

O my aged Uncle Arly. Incidents in the Life of My Uncle Arly. Edward Lear. FaBoNo; OAEL-2; OBP

O My America. D. M. Thomas. TwMBP

O My Belly. *Unknown.* GBP; POL

Oh my black soul! now thou art summoned. John Donne. Holy Sonnets, IV. EBEV; OAEL-1; PIM

Oh! my boat can swiftly float. The Queen of Connemara. Francis A. Fahy. PFIr

O My Bonny, Bonny May. *Unknown.* GBP

O my brother I heard u. Before/ and After. Jewel C. Latimore. JB

O my chief good! The Passion. Henry Vaughan. PIM

O my comrade, it is cold. Cold and Heat. *Tr. fr. Hawaiian by* M. W. Beckwith. WTO

O my dark Rosaleen. Dark Rosaleen. *Unknown, at. to* Owen Roe MacWard, *tr. by* James Clarence Mangan. BIrV; LoAs; PFIr

Oh, My Darling Clementine. *Unknown, at. to* Percy Montross. AIW; PSoN, *with music*
(Clementine.) AmFP; BLSo, *with music*; CTV; FSW; GSB, *with music*; OBAL

O my father, thou that dwellest. Invocation, or the Eternal Father and Mother. Eliza R. Snow. WPW

Oh my fine, my honey-colored Duke of Marmalade! Elegy for the Duke of Marmalade. Luis Palés Matos, *tr. by* Julio Marzán. InW

O my first love! You are in my life forever. Of My First Love. "Hugh MacDiarmid." SLP

Oh, my golden slippers am [*or* are] laid away. Oh, Dem Golden Slippers. James A. Bland. FSW; PSoN

O my heart is the unlucky heir of the ages. Personal History. Ruthven Todd. MS

O, My Heart Is Woe! *Unknown.* BoReV
(My Heart Is Woe.) OxBM

O my hornbill husband, you have a bad smell. Lament for a Husband. *Tr. fr. Papuan by* Don Laycock. BoWoP

O my lady, the Anunna, the great gods. Inanna and the Anunna. Enheduanna, *tr. fr. Sumerian.* BoWoP

O my life is so simple and the world. The Fiddlehead. David McFadden. NeAC

O my Lord, if I worship you from fear of Hell. Rabi'a the Mystic, *tr. fr. Arabic by* Willis Barnstone. BoWoP

O my Lord, the stars glitter and eyes of men are closed. Rabi'a the Mystic, *tr. fr. Arabic by* Willis Barnstone. BoWoP

O my lost husband! let me ever mourn. Andromache's Lament. Homer, *tr. by* Congreve. *Fr.* The Iliad, XXIV. OBVE

O my love/ The pretty towns. Kenneth Patchen. VGW

O, My Luve Is like a Red, Red Rose. Burns. *See* Red, Red Rose, A.

Oh, my name is Captain Kidd. Captain Kidd. *Unknown.* FSW

Oh my name it is Benjamin Bones. The Ballad of Benjamin Bones. Christopher Ward. BTTM

Oh, my name it is Sam Hall, it is Sam Hall. Sam Hall. *Unknown.* FSW; PeBB; UnPo (1976 ed.); VLP

Oh My People I Remember. Wendy Rose. CDW

O my sinner, let us spend this night together. Tonight, at Least, My Sinner. *Gond Oral Tradition, tr. by* V. Elwin *and* S. Hivale. WTO

O my son,/ Only your name remains. Lament for Taramoana. Makere, *tr. fr. Maori by* Barry Mitcalfe. WTO

O my son, born on a winter's morn. Lullaby. Nohomaiterangi, *tr. fr. Maori by* Barry Mitcalfe. WTO

O my songs. Coda. Ezra Pound. NOBA

O my soul be patient, she is very beautiful. She Is Not for Me. *Gond Oral Tradition, tr. by* V. Elwin *and* S. Hivale. WTO

O my thoughts' sweet food, my only owner. Lady My Treasure. Sir Philip Sidney. GBL

Oh, my wandering melody. Melody. Shmuel Moreh, *tr. by* Yoffee Berkovitz. VWA

Oh, neighbors! I'll have such a quest shortly. Cops and Robbers. Bill Middleton. AMV-80

Oh Neïla/ borne away by evening. Neïla. Yvan Goll, *tr. by* Anthony Rudolf. VWA

Oh never in this hard world was such an absurd. Nesting Time. Douglas Stewart. BoAnP

O! Never say that I was false of heart. Sonnets, CIX. Shakespeare. ILP (1975 ed.); NOBE; STS

O Night! O jealous Night, repugnant to my pleasures! To Night. *Unknown.* Moon

O Night of the Crying Children. Nelly Sachs, *tr. fr. German by* Keith Bosley. VWA

O Nightingale, That on Yon Bloomy Spray. Milton. ILP (1975 ed.); PB
(Sonnet: "O nightingale, that on yon bloomy spray.") OAEL-1

Oh nimber, nimber Will-o! Chuck Will's Widow Song. *Unknown.* BPo

Oh No. Robert Creeley. InPK

O, No John. *Unknown. See* No John.

Oh no more, no more! too late. Love's Martyrs. John Ford. *Fr.* The Broken Heart, IV, iii. GBL; NOBE

Oh, no one can deny. Self's the Man. Philip Larkin. NOBL

Oh, not to be in England. Abroad Thoughts. Edward Blishen. NOBL

"Oh, now I've come back to you, Mother." The Cripple for Life; or, The Poor Volunteer. *Unknown.* AmFP

O Now the Drenched Land Wakes. Kenneth Patchen. PoA

Oh, now we're leaving home, me boys; to Ottawa we're goin'. The Lake of the Caogama. *Unknown.* WTO

O now you come in rut. To Frighten a Storm. Gladys Cardiff. CDW

O nuclear wind, when wilt thou blow. Paul Dehn. SpRo

Oh - ohh/ Smokestack lightnin'. Smokestack Lightnin'. *Unknown.* BluL

Oh Oh Blues. *Unknown.* BluL

Oh—oh: death is awful. Death Is Awful. *Unknown.* BluL

Oh, oh, you will be sorry for that word! Edna St. Vincent Millay. BoWoP; SoSe (1977 ed.)

O ole Zip Coon he is a larned skoler. Zip Coon. *Unknown.* PSoN

Oh, on an early morning I think I shall live forever! Poem in Three Parts. Robert Bly. CAPP; ConAP; NOBA; OSP

Oh, once I lived in Cottonwood and owned a little farm. Once I Lived in Cottonwood. *Unknown.* AmFP

Oh, once I was happy but now I'm forlorn. The Man on the Flying Trapeze. George Leybourne. BLSH; BLSo; FSW

Oh, once upon a time in Arkansas. The Arkansas Traveler. *Unknown.* FSW

O only Source of all our light and life. Qui Laborat, Orat. Arthur Hugh Clough. VLP; VPC

Oh, open the door, my hinnie, my heart. The Padda Song. *Unknown.* GBP

"O opportunity! thy guilt is great." An Outcry upon Opportunity. Shakespeare. *Fr.* The Rape of Lucrece. NOBE

Oh our Mother the Earth oh our Father the Sky. Song of the Sky Loom. *Unknown, tr. by* Herbert J. Spinden. TSWA; WTO

O Paddy, dear, and did you hear the news that's going 'round? The Wearing of [*or* Wearin' o'] the Green. *Unknown.* AIW; BLSH; BTTM; FaPoR; FSW; GBP; WTO

"O palace, whilom crown of houses all." The Complaint of Troilus. Chaucer. *Fr.* Troilus and Criseyde. NOBE

O parent of each lovely Muse. Ode to Fancy. Joseph Warton. PAIC

"O Passenger, pray list and catch." The Levelled Churchyard. Thomas Hardy. NOBL; OBP

O peace! and dost thou with thy presence bless. On Peace. Keats. MBPR

O people who live in the world. Andal, *tr. fr. Tamil by* Willis Barnstone. BoWoP

O piano I heard at evening. Piano at Evening. Palea, *tr. fr. Hawaiian by* M. K. Pukui *and* A. L. Korn. WTO

O, Pioneers! John Peale Bishop. VGW

Oh, pity Reuben Ranzo! Reuben Ranzo. *Unknown.* FSW

O pleasant exercise of hope and joy! Wordsworth. *Fr.* The Prelude, XI. HAP

O pleasant spot! O place of rest! Man to the Wound in Christ's Side. Robert Southwell. PIM

O plump head-waiter at The Cock. Will Waterproof's Lyrical Monologue. Tennyson. VLP

O, po' sinner, O, now is yo' time. What Yo' Gwine to Do When Yo' Lamp Burn Down? *Unknown.* BPo

O poet strutting from the sandbagged portal. As One Non-Combatant to Another. George Orwell. OxBTC

O Polly dear, O Polly, the rout has now begun. High Germany. *Unknown.* FSW

O prairie mother, I am one of your boys. Finale. Carl Sandburg. *Fr.* Prairie. ANTL

O praise God in his holiness: praise him. Bible, *O.T.* Psalms, CI. ILwL; RAE

Oh, Promise Me, *with music.* Clement Scott. BLSH; BLSo; FSN

O pumpkins! O periwinkles! Wet Weather at Cannes. Edward Lear. FaBoNo

Oh, pure is the poppy on the prairie. Melody for Lute and Ocarina. Morris Bishop. ECBV

O quick quick quick, quick here the song-sparrow. Cape Ann. T. S. Eliot. Landscapes, V. BiP; UsP

O, Rachel, your very gait. A Vilna Puzzle. Sasha Chorny, *tr. by* Daniel Weissbort. VWA

O radiant luminary of light interminable. A Prayer to the Father of Heaven. John Skelton. HoPM (1975 ed.)

O Rare! W. Dale Nelson. PoUp

O rare circle. Americana XV: Simplicity. Carl Rakosi. GP; InPS

O rare Harry Parry. Harry Parry. *Unknown.* GBP

O reapers and gleaners. Harvest Song. Joseph Campbell. CC; OFD

O rich red wheat! thou wilt not long defer. To a Red-Wheat Field. Charles Tennyson Turner. VPC

O Ride On, Jesus, *with music. Unknown.* AH

O Risen Lord upon the Throne, *with music.* Louis F. Benson. AH

Oh Roberta honey where you been so long. Roberta. *Unknown.* BluL

Oh, rock-a my soul in the bosom of Abraham. Rock-a My Soul. *Unknown.* FSW

O, Rose, thou art sick! The Sick Rose. Blake. *Fr.* Songs of Experience. BoLoP; CABA (1972 ed.); ExPo (1973 ed.); HAP; HeIP; ILP (1975 ed.); InPK; InPS; LAuP; LFH; MBPR; NIL; NOBE; OAEL-2; PAIC; PoIA; PPP; STS; WeW

O Rose, thou flower of flowers, thou fragrant wonder. The Rose. Christina Rossetti. PF

Oh, row me cross the river. Rock 'n' Row Me Over. *Unknown.* FSW

O ruddier than the cherry. Song. John Gay. *Fr.* Acis and Galatea. NOBE

O ruined father dead, long sweetly rotten. For the Word Is Flesh. Stanley Kunitz. VGW

O Russian faced, woman on the grass. Allen Ginsberg. *Fr.* Kaddish. TPo

Oh, Sally, my dear, I wish I could wed you. Sally My Dear. *Unknown.* FSW

Oh, San-ty Ana won th' day. Santy Ana. *Unknown.* AIW

O sassafras, your portrait in a book. Dictionary. Hildegarde Flanner. WPW

O Saviour of a World Undone, *with music.* Leonard Withington. AH

O saw ye bonnie [*or* bonie] Lesley. Bonnie Lesley. Burns. NOBE; SLP

Oh say! can you see, by the dawn's early light. The Star-spangled Banner. Francis Scott Key. BLSH; BLSo; BTTM; CTV; FaPo; FaPoR; FSW; NIL; TAP

Oh, Say, Mr. Toffler. Mira Fish. FAF

O, Say My Jolly Fellow. *Unknown.* AIW

Oh, say were you ever in Rio Grande? Rio Grande. *Unknown.* FSW

O say, what is that thing called light. The Blind Boy. Colley Cibber. OxBChV

O scapegoats! How you grew chaste. Poem for my Hands. Carole Oles. NPW

O sea born and obscene. An Invocation to the Goddess. David Wright. NoAM

O sea goddess Nuliajuk. Magic Words for Hunting Seal. *Unknown, tr. by* Edward Field. ExPo (1973 ed.)

Oh see how thick the goldcup flowers. A. E. Housman. SoSe (1977 ed.); STS

Oh sharp diamond my mother! Christmas Eve. Anne Sexton. RiTi

O she has the best tri-level avacado-tufted wall-to-wall. The Good Life. Mary Alice Gunderson. PoW

Oh, she walked unaware of her own increasing beauty. She Walked Unaware. Patrick MacDonogh. BoLoP; FaBoTw (1975 ed.); PFIr

"O she was the handsome corpse," he said. Moloney Remembers the Resurrection of Kate Finucane. Brendan Kennelly. PoTa

Oh, shed no tears for Jimmy Jupp. Jimmy Jupp, Who Died of Over-eating. H. A. C. Evans. OSF

Oh, Shenandoah, I long to hear [*or* see] you. Shenandoah [*or* Across the Wide Missouri]. *Unknown.* BLSH; BLSo; FSW

O shut your bright eyes that mine must endanger. At the Manger Mary Sings. W. H. Auden. *Fr.* For the Time Being. BoReV; ILwL

"Oh, sick I am to see you, will you never let me be?" The New Mistress. A. E. Housman. SoSe

Oh, silver tree! Jazzonia. Langston Hughes. AmNP (1974 ed.); CoPAm

O Simplicitas. Madeleine L'Engle. *Fr.* Three Songs of Mary. PChr

Oh, sing a song of phosphates. Rhyme for a Chemical Baby. Joseph Cook. QQQ; SpRo

Oh, Sing to God, *with music.* Jacob Steendam, *tr. fr. Dutch.* AH

O Sing to Me of Heaven, *with music.* Mary Stanley Bunce Dana. AH

Oh! sing unto my roundelay [*or* O! Synge untoe mie roundelaie]. The Minstrel's Song. Thomas Chatterton. *Fr.* Aella. LoAs; HAP; NOBE; OBP

O singer of Persephone! Theocritus. Oscar Wilde. NOBE

Oh, sinner man, where you gonna run to? Sinner Man. *Unknown.* FSW

O Sion, Haste, Thy Mission High Fulfilling, *with music.* Mary A. Thomson. AH

Oh, sister Phoebe, how merry were we. Tom Jones's Plum Tree. *Unknown.* AmFP

O sixteen hundred and ninety one. The Two Witches. Robert Graves. SO

Oh, sleep forever in the Latmian cave. Edna St. Vincent Millay. CMoP (1970 ed.); NoAM

Oh sleep, thou holy baby. Duérmete, Niño Lindo. *Tr. fr. Spanish.* FSW

O sleeper rise, if thou would'st see. Sleeper Rise. *Gond Oral Tradition, tr. by* V. Elwin *and* S. Hivale. WTO

O sleepy city of reeling wheelchairs. The Wheelchair Butterfly. James Tate. NoAM

Oh, slow to smite and swift to spare. The Death of Lincoln. Bryant. TAP

Oh, slow up, dogies, quit your roving round. Night-herding Song. Harry Stephens. BPAW

O small-feac'd flow'r that now dost bloom. The Water Crowvoot. William Barnes. VPC

O smooth flatterers, go over sea. Reflection and Advice. Ezra Pound. OBSV

O so gay, The. Children among the Tombstones. J. R. Hervey. ATNZ

O soft embalmer of the still midnight. To Sleep. Keats. MBPR; NIL; OBP; PMW; PPM; STS

"O soldier, O soldier, won't you marry me now." Soldier, Won't You Marry Me? *Unknown.* AmFP; OLR

O Sole Mio, *with music.* Eduardo di Capua, *tr. fr. Italian by* James Morehead. BLSH

O solitude! if I must with thee dwell. Keats. MBPR

O Solitude, romantic maid. James Grainger. *Fr.* Solitude, an Ode. LFH

Oh! some folks boast of quail on toast. The Abalone Song. George Sterling. BPAW

O Son of Man, Thou Madest Known, *with music.* Milton S. Littlefield. AH

O Son of mine, when dusk shall find thee bending. From Generation to Generation. Sir Henry Newbolt. FaBoTw (1975 ed.)

O sorrow, cruel fellowship! Tennyson. In Memoriam A. H. H., III. HAP

O Sorrow, Sorrow, say where dost thou dwell? Thomas Dekker. *Fr.* The Noble Soldier. SCP-2

O spare a tear for poor Tom Hood. Elegy on Thomas Hood. Martin Fagg. NOBL

O sprinting of the wind over land. Invocation to the Wind. Joseph Kalar. SPT

O Star (the fairest one in sight). Take Something like a Star. Robert Frost. STS

O! Start a Revolution. D. H. Lawrence. FaBoEE

Oh stay at home, my lad, and plough. A. E. Housman. STS

O stay that covetous hand! First turn all eye. Upon the Curtain of Lucasta's Picture It Was Thus Wrought. Richard Lovelace. CaPo

O stony grey soil of Monaghan. Stony Grey Soil. Patrick Kavanagh. CIP

Oh, Stormy's dead an' gone to rest. Stormalong. *Unknown.* AIW

Oh strong ridged and deeply hollowed. Smell! William Carlos Williams. TAP; WeW

Oh, such silliness! Introduction. William Cole. OSF

O Suen, the usurper Lugalanne means nothing to me! Appeal to the Moongod Nanna-Suen to Throw Out Lugalanne. Enheduanna, *tr. fr. Sumerian.* BoWoP

O suitably-attired-in-leather-boots. Fragment of a Greek Tragedy. A. E. Housman. FaBoNo; NOBL; SpRo

O sun, and moonlight shining in the woods. Carmen Saeculare. Charles H. Sisson, *after the Latin of* Horace. OBVE

O sun, be his protection. Branwen's Starling. R. Williams Parry, *tr. by* Gwyn Jones. OBW

O supreme Light, who dost thy glory assert. The Vision of God. Dante, *tr. by* Laurence Binyon. *Fr.* Divina Commedia: Paradiso, XXXIII. ExPo (1973 ed.)

Oh! Susanna. Stephen Collins Foster. BLSH, *with music;* BLSo, *with music;* FSW; OBAL; PSoN, *with music*

O swan, come slowly from the sky. Song of Poverty. *Gond Oral Tradition, tr. by* V. Elwin *and* S. Hivale. WTO

O, sweet is the vale where the Mohawk gently glides. Bonny Eloise. C. W. Elliott *and* J. R. Thomas. FSW

O Sweet Spontaneous Earth. E. E. Cummings. NoAM; PAIC

O sweetheart, hear you. James Joyce. GBL

O Sylvia, Sylvia. Sylvia's Death. Anne Sexton. WBN

O! Synge untoe mie roundelaie. *See* Oh! sing unto my roundelay.

O take me to the sullen flats. From the Righteous Man Even the Wild Beasts Run Away. David Bromwich. PoA

Oh, talk not to me of a name great in story. Stanzas Written on the Road between Florence and Pisa. Byron. ILP (1975 ed.)

Oh Tannenbaum (Oh Christmas Tree). *Unknown, tr. fr. German.* FSW

(Oh Christmas Tree, *with music.*) GSB

O Taste and See. Denise Levertov. PBWP; PiAm; PPP; TAP

Oh, Teddy wants a nine-dollar shawl. I Wish I Was a Mole in the Ground. *Unknown.* AmFP

O Tell Me How to Woo Thee. Robert Graham. SLP

Oh, tell me the reason I sorrow. The Lorelei. Heine. BLSH

O tender-heartedness right bitter grown. Fragmenti. Ezra Pound. PoA

O terrible is the highest thing. Kenneth Patchen. VGW

O Terry why is sex so quick. Ruth Herschberger. POL

Oh thank you cowboy with four-wheel drive. For Drum Hadley. Harold Littlebird. VoR

Oh! that I always breath'd in such an aire. The Experience. Edward Taylor. Preparatory Meditations: First Series, III. EAP

Oh that I had no hart, as I have none. Parthenophil and Parthenophe, LXV. Barnabe Barnes. ESo

O, That I Had Some Secret Place. *Unknown.* AmFP

Oh, that last day in Lucknow fort! The Relief of Lucknow. Robert Traill Spence Lowell. BTTM; PoTa

Oh that moon is going down, baby. Moon Going Down. *Unknown.* BluL

"O That My Love Were in My Arms." *Malay Oral Tradition, tr. by* R. J. Wilkinson *and* R. O. Winstedt. WTO

Oh that my lungs could bleat like butter'd pease. Odd but True. *Unknown.* FaBoCo; FaBoNo; NOBL

Oh that my soul a marrow-bone might seize! Sonnet Found in a Deserted Mad-House. *Unknown.* FaBoCo; FaBoNo

Oh! That my young life were a lasting dream. Dreams. Poe. TAP

O that our dreamings all, of sleep or wake. Keats. *Fr.* Epistle to John Hamilton Reynolds. OAEL-2

Oh! that the Desert were my dwelling-place. Byron. *Fr.* Childe Harold's Pilgrimage, IV. ILP (1975 ed.)

Oh! that 'twere possible. Tennyson. *Fr.* Maud, Pt. II, iv. BoLoP; NOBE; OAEL-2

Oh, the boll weevil is a little black bug. The Boll Weevil Song [*or* Ballad of the Boll Weevil]. *Unknown.* BLSo; FSW

Oh, the bosses' tricks of '76. Two-Cent Coal. *Unknown.* AmFP

Oh, the Camptown ladies sing this song. Camptown Races. Stephen Collins Foster. FSW

Oh, the candidate's a dodger. The Dodger Song. *Unknown.* FSW

O the Chimneys. Nelly Sachs, *tr. fr. German by* Keith Bosley. VWA

O the cuckoo she's a pretty bird. The Cuckoo. *Unknown.* GBP

Oh, the Deacon went down. Ain't Gonna Grieve My Lord No More. *Unknown.* FSW

O the French are on the sea. The Shan Van Vocht. *Unknown.* FSW; GBP

Oh, the full-back bows to the cheering crowd. To the Men Who Hold the Line. W. F. Barron. SPo

Oh, the Funniest Thing. *Unknown.* CTV

O the goose and the gander walk'd over the green. The Goose and the Gander. *Unknown.* GBP

O, the grand old Duke of York. Mother Goose. GBP; MG

Oh! The King's gane gyte. Cophetua. "Hugh MacDiarmid." POL

Oh, the minstrels sing of an English king of many long years ago. The Bastard King of England. *Unknown.* FSW

Oh, the moonlight's fair tonight along the Wabash. On the Banks of the Wabash. Paul Dresser. BLSH

Oh! the night that I struck New York. The Bowery. Charles Hale Hoyt. FSN

Oh, the noble duke of York. The Noble Duke of York. *Unknown.* FSW

Oh, the old gray mare, she ain't what she used to be. Old Gray Mare. *Unknown.* GBP

O the opal and the sapphire of that wandering western sea. Beeny Cliff. Thomas Hardy. LoAs

Oh, the outlook isn't pretty for the Orioles today. Ode to the New York Mets. John Vliet Lindsay. SPo

Oh, the praties they grow small. The Praties. *Unknown.* FSW; WTO

O the Raggedy Man! He works fer Pa. The Raggedy Man. James Whitcomb Riley. OxBChV

Oh, the rain is slanting sharply, and the Norther's blowing cold. Ballad of the Hyde Street Grip. Gelett Burgess. BPAW

Oh, the revenue men is riding. Revenue Man Blues. *Unknown.* BluL

O the sky shall crack with laughter. Now That Snow Is Falling. Joseph Kalar. SPT

Oh, the slimy, squirmy, slithery eel! Song of Hate for Eels. Arthur Guiterman. OBAL

O the snows last so long. Despair. Richard Eberhart. UsP

Oh, the streams of lovely Nancy are divided in three parts. The Streams of Lovely Nancy. *Unknown.* FaBoBa

Oh, the summer time is coming. Will You Go, Lassie, Go? *Unknown.* FSW

Oh! the time that is past. *Unknown.* BoLoP

Oh the times are hard and the wages low. Across the Western Ocean. *Unknown.* FSW

Oh, the train's off the track. The Train Is off the Track. *Unknown.* AmFP

O the vexation. Lost Contact. William Cole. POL

Oh the white seagull, the wild seagull. The Seagull. Mary Howitt. OxBChV

Oh, the wide world's ways! Haiku. Ryōta, *tr. by* Harold G. Henderson. NIL

Oh the wiggley-woggley men. The Wiggley-Woggley Men. Spike Milligan. OSF

Oh, the wild joys of living! A Psalm of David. Robert Browning. *Fr.* Saul. PIM

Oh the wold, the wold. Wind. Sydney Dobell. PeD

O the wonder man rides his space ship. African Things. Victor Hernández Cruz. InW; SA

Oh, then a wreath! William Carlos Williams. *Fr.* Promenade. TT

O, then I see Queen Mab hath been with you. Shakespeare. *Fr.* Romeo and Juliet, I, iv. STS

"Oh! then tell me, Sean O'Farrell." The Rising of the Moon. *Unknown.* FSW

Oh! There are spirits of the air. To——. Shelley. MBPR

O there is blessing in this gentle breeze. The Prelude; or, Growth of a Poet's Mind. Wordsworth. MBPR; OAEL–2

Oh, there once was a merry crocodile. The Merry Crocodile. Gertrude E. Heath. TDH

Oh, there once was a puffin. There Once Was a Puffin. Florence Page Jacques. CTV

Oh there was a woman and she was a widow. Flowers in the Valley. *Unknown.* ECBV; OLR

Oh, there was a youth and a noble youth. The Bailiff's Daughter of Islington. *Unknown.* AmFP

Oh, there was once a tree. The Green Grass Grew All Around. *Unknown.* FSW

Oh they built the ship Titanic to sail the ocean blue. The Titanic. *Unknown.* FSW

Oh, they call me Hanging Johnny. Hanging Johnny. *Unknown.* FSW

O Thirsty Wind. *Tr. fr. Hawaiian by* N. B. Emerson. WTO

Oh, this is the place where fishermen gather. The Squid-jiggin' Ground. *Unknown.* FSW

Oh, this is the tale of John Cherokee. John Cherokee. *Unknown.* GBP

O this worlds Theatre in which we stay. Amoretti, LIV. Spenser. ILP (1975 ed.)

O Thou bright jewel in my aim I strive. On Virtue. Phillis Wheatley. TAP

O thou bright sun! beneath the dark blue line. Evening: To Harriet. Shelley. MBPR

O thou by Nature taught. Ode to Simplicity. William Collins. LAuP; NOBE

O thou great Power, in whom I move. A Hymn to My God in a Night of My Late Sickness. Sir Henry Wotton. BoReV

Oh, thou immortal bard! Byron. J. Gordon Coogler. OBAL

O Thou Most High Who Rulest All. Anne Bradstreet. *See* Upon My Dear and Loving Husband. . .

O Thou my monster, Thou my guide. Prayer in Mid-Passage. Louis MacNeice. BoReV

O thou that from thy mansion. For My Funeral. A. E. Housman. BoReV; CMoP (1970 ed.)

O thou that [or wha] in the heavens does [or dost] dwell! Holy Willie's Prayer [or The Prayer of Holy Willie]. Burns. BoReV; EBEV; Epi; ESaP; InPS; LAuP; OAEL–1; OBP; OBSV; PPP

O thou that sit'st upon a throne. A Song to David. Christopher Smart. BoReV; EBEV; EPC; LAuP; NOBE; OAEL–1; OBW

O thou that swing'st upon the waving hair. The Grasshopper. Richard Lovelace. CaPo; EBEV; NOBE; OAEL–1; PPP; SCP–2

O thou, the friend of man assign'd. Ode to Pity. William Collins. LAuP

O Thou to Whom the Musical White Spring. E. E. Cummings. STS

O thou undaunted daughter of desires! Upon the Book and Picture of the Seraphical Saint Teresa. Richard Crashaw. *Fr.* The Flaming Heart. BoReV; HAP; NOBE

O thou, wha in the heavens does dwell. *See* O thou that in the heavens does dwell!

O thou, whatever title suit thee! Address to the Deil. Burns. LAuP; OAEL–1

O thou who didst furnish. Hymn to Moloch. Ralph Hodgson. OxBTC

O Thou, Who Didst Ordain the Word, *with music.* Edwin Hubbell Chapin. AH

O Thou Who Dry'st the Mourner's Tear. Thomas Moore. PIM

O thou who giving helm and sword. The Dreamer. Walter de la Mare. ILP (1975 ed.)

O thou, who lately closed my eyes. A Morning Hymn. Christopher Smart. OxBChV

O thou, who passest thro' our vallies in. To Summer. Blake. LAuP; MBPR

O thou, who plumed with strong desire. The Two Spirits: An Allegory. Shelley. MBPR; OAEL–2; Prf

O thou, who sit'st a smiling bride. Ode to Mercy. William Collins. LAuP

O thou whom Poetry [or Poesy] abhors. On Elphinston's Translation of Martial. Burns. FaBoCo; FaBoEE

O thou whose face hath felt the winter's wind. What the Thrush Said. Keats. EBEV; MBPR; NIL; OBP

O thou! whose fancies from afar are brought. To H. C. Wordsworth. MBPR

O Thou Whose Feet Have Climbed Life's Hill, *with music.* Louis F. Benson. AH

O Thou Whose Gracious Presence Shone, *with music.* Marion Franklin Ham. AH

O thou whose name shatters the universe. Eli the Thatcher. Max Beerbohm *and* William Rothenstein. FaBoNo

O Thou Whose Own Vast Temple Stands, *with music.* Bryant. AH

O thou whose pow'r o'er moving worlds presides. Boethius, *tr. by* Samuel Johnson. The Consolation of Philosophy, III, 9. OBVE

O Thou! Whose Presence Went Before, *with music.* Whittier. AH

O thou, whose radiant eyes and beamy smile. Sonnet to Harriet on Her Birthday. Shelley. MBPR

O thou, with dewy locks, who lookest down. To Spring. Blake. LAuP; MBPR; OAEL–2; PPP

O Time the fatal wrack of mortal things. Anne Bradstreet. *Fr.* Contemplations. PBWP

"O Time, whence comes the Mother's moody look amid her labours." The Lacking Sense. Thomas Hardy. CMoP (1970 ed.)

O times most bad. Upon the Troublesome Time. Robert Herrick. CaPo

Oh! 'tis of a bold major a tale I'll relate. A Longford Legend. *Unknown.* PoTa

Oh! 'tis of a rich merchant, in London did dwell. *See* 'Tis of a rich merchant who in London did dwell.

Oh! 'tis pretty to be in Ballinderry. Ballinderry. *Unknown.* WTO

Oh to be a bride. The Bride. Bella Akhmadulina, *tr. by* Stephen Stepancehv. BoWoP; PBWP

Oh to be at Crowdieknowe. Crowdieknowe. "Hugh MacDiarmid." InPS; NoAM

Oh, to be in England. Home-Thoughts, from Abroad. Robert Browning. FaPoR; HeIP; ILP (1975 ed.); IPWM; NOBE; OBP; PBMP; STS; VoPo

Oh to be in England now that Winston's out. Ezra Pound. *Fr.* Cantos, LXXX. PoA

Oh, to be in Oleanna! Oleanna. Pete Seeger. FSW

O to be "in the news" again—now as fashion runs. Sonnets to Be Written from Prison. Robert Adamson. CAAP; GAS

Oh to be moving as we once were. After Sex. Greg Kuzma. GP

O to break loose, like the chinook. Waking Early Sunday Morning. Robert Lowell. NOBA

Oh, to those who know no better. That Little Lump of Coal. *Unknown.* AmFP

O, to vex me, contraries meet in one. Holy Sonnets, XIX. John Donne. BoReV; OAEL-1

Oh, Tommy's gone, what shall I do? Tommy's Gone to Hilo. *Unknown.* FSW

O tremble, all ye earthly Princes. The Revolutionaries. R. P. Lister. NOBL

O. T.'s Blues. Waring Cuney. MAT

O Turn Ye, O Turn Ye, *with music.* Josiah Hopkins. AH

Oh 'twas a poor country, in autumn it was bare. The Poor, Poor Country. John Shaw Neilson. MAuV

O Unicorn among the cedars. W. H. Auden. *Fr.* New Year Letter. BoReV; NoAM

O Viajante. Carol Olivia Herron. PoUp

O Virgin. *Tr. from Gaelic by* Douglas Hyde. WTO

O Visionary who adjust your lens. The Higher Empiricism. Francis C. Golffing. PoA

O Waly, Waly, up the Bank. *Unknown. See* Waly, Waly.

Oh wanderer in the southern weather. An Indian Song. W. B. Yeats. VLP

O was an ossified oyster. An Ossified Oyster. Carolyn Wells. TDH

O wastfull riot, never well content. Lucan, *tr. by* Sir Walter Ralegh. *Fr.* Pharsalia, IV. OBVE

Oh! water for me! Bright water for me! The Water-Drinker. Edward Johnson. PeD

O water-girl! with tinkling anklets. Water-girl. *Gond Oral Tradition, tr. by* V. Elwin *and* S. Hivale. WTO

O we can wait no longer. Walt Whitman. *Fr.* Passage to India. ILwL

O, we loved long and happily, God knows! The Custom of the World. Louis Simpson. BoLoP; SFF

O, we must visit the sea again. Two and the Sea. Jacqueline M. Fitzgerald. PPM

O Wearisome Condition of Humanity. Fulke Greville. *See* Chorus Sacerdotum.

Oh well it's our Father who art in Heaven. You Shall. *Unknown.* BluL

Oh, we'll rally 'round the flag, boys, we'll rally once again. The Battle Cry of Freedom. George Frederick Root. FSW

Oh Wellington! (Or " 'Vilainton," for Fame). Byron. *Fr.* Don Juan, IX. OBSV

"O well's me o my gay goss-hawk." The Gay Goshawk. *Unknown, at. to* Anna Gordon Brown. PeBB; WPE

Oh were I at the moss house, where the birds do increase. The Streams of Bunclody. *Unknown.* BIrV

O, Were I on Parnassus Hill. Burns. SLP

O Were My Love Yon Lilac Fair. Burns. GBL

Oh, we're up in the morning ere breaking of day. The Railroad Corral. *Unknown.* FSW

O, Wert Thou in the Cauld Blast. Burns. EBEV; HAP; HeIP; ILP (1975 ed.); NOBE

O Western Wind. *Unknown. See* Western Wind.

O wha my babie-clouts will buy. The Rantin Dog the Daddie o't. Burns. PPP

"O whare are ye gaun?" The False Knight upon the Road. *Unknown.* GBP; PeBB

O whare hae ya been, my dearest dear. The Carpenter's Wife. *Unknown.* OAEL-1

O Wha's the Bride? "Hugh MacDiarmid." BoLoP; CMoP (1970 ed.); ExPo (1973 ed.); NoAM; TwMBP (O Wha's Been Here Afore Me, Lass.) FaBoTw (1975 ed.), *shorter version*; MS

Oh, what a beautiful city. Twelve Gates to the City. *Unknown.* FSW

O what a cunning guest. Confession. George Herbert. ILP (1975 ed.)

Oh, what a drear dark close to my poor day! Robert Browning. *Fr.* Pippa Passes, sc. iv. PeD

Oh, what a dreary place this was when first the Mormons found it. St. George. Charlie Walker. AmFP

O what a lovely poem, Mrs. Jones. The Teacher of Poetry. William Packard. PPoD

O, what a noble mind is here o'erthrown! Ophelia. Shakespeare. *Fr.* Hamlet, III, i. PCOP

O what a physical effect it has on me. In Love with You. Kenneth Koch. CAPP

O what a tangled web we weave. A Word of Encouragement. J. R. Pope. NOBL

Oh! What a thing is man? Lord, who am I? Edward Taylor. *Fr.* Preparatory Meditations: First Series, XXXVIII. NOBA; PiAM

Oh, what an effort it is. It Is True. Federico García Lorca, *tr. by* Harriet de Onís. OLR

O what are heroes, prophets, men. Pan. Emerson. ILP (1975 ed.); PiAm

O [*or* Ah,] what can ail thee, knight-at-arms. La Belle Dame sans Merci. Keats. AIW; AnMo; CABA (1972 ed.); Epi; ExPo (1973 ed.); HAP; ILP (1975 ed.); InPK; InPS; IP; IPWM; LFH; LoAs; MBPR; NIL; NOBE; OAEL-2; OLR; PAIC; PBMP; PoIA; PoPle; PPoD; PPoe; Prf; SoSe (1977 ed.); STS; UnPo (1976 ed.); WeW

O what could be more nice. Light Listened. Theodore Roethke. AnMo; BiP; NowV

O what harper could worthily harp it. The Schoolmaster Abroad with His Son. Charles Stuart Calverley. NOBL

Oh, what if the Easter Bunny. What If. Myra Cohn Livingston. CC

Oh, what is Jeanie weeping for. All on a Summer's Day. *Unknown.* PoPle

Oh, what is that I see yonder coming. Union Train. Lee Hays, Millard Lampell, *and* Pete Seeger. FSW

O What Is That Sound [Which So Thrills the Ear]. W. H. Auden. AIW; BiP; ExPo (1973 ed.); MPo; SS; UsP (Quarry, The.) CMoP (1970 ed.); MiP

O what transparent waves, what a tranquil sea. Vittoria da Colonna, *tr. fr. Italian by* Lynne Lawner. PBWP

"Oh, what will you give me?" say the sad bells of Rhymney. Bells of Rhymney. Idris Davies *and* Pete Seeger. PoRo

Oh! what's befallen Bessy Brown. As It Fell upon a Day. Thomas Hood. BBL

"Oh, what's that stain on your shirt sleeve?" Edward. *Unknown.* AmFP

Oh! what's the matter? what's the matter? Goody Blake, and Harry Gill. Wordsworth. MBPR

Oh, what's the matter wi' you, my lass. Jimmy's Enlisted; or, The Recruited Collier. *Unknown.* EBEV

O What's the Rhyme to Porringer. *Unknown.* GBP

O what's the weather in a Beard? Dinky. Theodore Roethke. OBAL

Oh, when I come to die. Give Me Jesus. *Unknown.* BPo

Oh when I think of my long-suffering race. Enslaved. Claude McKay. BPo

Oh, When I Was in Love with You. A. E. Housman. BoLoP; MiP; OLR; PPM; STS

Oh, when I was single, oh then, oh then! I Wish I Were Single Again. *Unknown.* AmFP

Oh, when I'm in trouble. Do, Lord, Remember Me. *Unknown.* AmFP

O, when our clergy, at the dreadful day. On Those That Deserve It. Francis Quarles. BoReV

Oh, When Shall I See Jesus? *with music. Unknown.* AH (Ecstasy, 1 *st., at. to* John Leland.) AmFP

Oh! when shall the grave hide for ever my sorrow? To Caroline. Byron. MBPR

Oh, when the Saints go marching in. When the Saints Go Marching In. *Unknown.* FSW

"Oh, when we going to marry, to marry, to marry." Buffalo Boy. *Unknown.* AmFP

"Oh whence do you come, my dear friend, to me." The Poor Ghost. Christina Rossetti. GBL

O Where Are You Going? W. H. Auden. *Fr.* The Orators. CMoP (1970 ed.); IP; NOBE; OBP; SoSe (1977 ed.); TT (Song: "O Where Are You Going?") ILP (1975 ed.); OAEL-2

"O, where are you going?" Scarborough Fair. *Unknown.* GSB

Oh, where are you going, my good old man? Where Are You Going, My Good Old Man? *Unknown.* FSW

"Oh, where are you going, my kind old husband." The Best Old Fellow in the World. *Unknown.* AmFP

"Oh, where are you going, my little maiden fair." The Milkmaid. *Unknown.* AmFP

"O where are you going?" said reader to rider. O Where Are You Going? W. H. Auden. *Fr.* The Orators. CMoP (1970 ed.); ILP (1975 ed.); IP; NOBE; OAEL-2; OBP; SoSe (1977 ed.); TT

O where are you going? says [or said] Milder to Malder. The Cutty Wren. *Unknown.* FSW; GBP

Oh, where do you come from. Little Raindrops. Jane Euphemia Browne. OxBChV

"O where ha[e] you been, Lord Randal, my son?" *See* "O where have you been, Lord Randal my son?"

'O where hae ye been, my long, long love. *See* "O where have you been, my dear, dear love."

"Oh, where have you been, Billy boy, Billy boy?" Billy Boy. *Unknown.* AmFP; HoPM (1975 ed.)

"O where have [or ha or hae] you been, Lord Randal my son?" Lord Randal. *Unknown.* AmFP; CABA (1972 ed.); EBEV; FaBoBa; FF; FSW; HAP; HeIP; HoPM (1975 ed.); ILP (1975 ed.); LFH; NIL; OAEL-1; PAIC; PoIA; SLP; WeW; WIF

Oh, where have you been, my blue-eyed son? A Hard Rain's a-Gonna Fall. Bob Dylan. PoRo

"O where have you [or hae ye] been, my dear, dear [or long, long] love." The Demon [or Daemon] Lover [or James Harris]. *Unknown.* AIW; CABA (1972 ed.); FaBoBa; HAP; HoPM (1975 ed.); MAT; NU; PBMP; PeBB; SLP; UnPo (1976 ed.)

O where is the dwelling I love the most. Ruth Pitter. LoAs

Oh where, Oh where ish mine little dog gone. Der Deitcher's Dog. Septimus Winner. PSoN

Oh where, please tell me where. The Blue Bells of Scotland. Annie McVicar *and* Dorothy Jordan. FSW

O, where, where are the winter grounds of angels. The Angels. Marguerite Young. WPE

O! Wherefore. Robert Peter. PPoD

Oh! wherefore come ye forth in triumph from the north. The Battle of Naseby. Macaulay. BTTM

O! wherefore pensive heaves that sigh? O! Wherefore. Robert Peter. PPoD

O, while beneath the fervent heat. The Mother of Samson to Manoah, Her Husband. Whittier. PIM

Oh, whisky here, and whisky there. Whisky Johnny. *Unknown.* AmFP

O whisper, O my soul! The afternoon. The Tired Worker. Claude McKay. BPo

O Whistle, and I'll Come to You, My Lad. Burns. InPS (Song: "O whistle, and I'll come to ye, my lad.") BoLoP

"O whither are you faring to, my sweetheart?" The Tryst. Walter de la Mare. AIW

O who can ever praise enough. Poem. W. H. Auden. PoA

Oh, Who Can Make a Flower? Grace W. Owens. CTV

Oh Who Is That Young Sinner. A. E. Housman. FaBoTw (1975 ed.); SoSe (1977 ed.)

Oh! who is there of us that has not felt. November. Frederick Goddard Tuckerman. NOBA

O who rides by night tro' the woodland so wild? The Erl-King. Goethe, *tr. by* Sir Walter Scott. OBVE

O who shall, from this dungeon, raise. A Dialogue between the Soul and [the] Body. Andrew Marvell. HAP; MetP; OAEL-1; PAIC; PPP; SCP-1

"O who will shoe my little feet." The Lass of Roch Royal. *Unknown.* AmFP

"Oh, who will shoe your feet, my love." The Mournful Dove. *Unknown.* AmFP

Oh, who will shoe your pretty little foot. Kenneth Rexroth. AIW

"Oh, why did God,/ Creator wise." Adam Speaks. Milton. *Fr.* Paradise Lost, X. NU

O why do you walk through the field in gloves. To a Fat Lady Seen from the Train. Frances Cornford. SpRo; WeW

Oh, why don't I work like other men do? Hallelujah, Bum Again. *Unknown.* GBP

O why was I born with a different face? Blake. POL

O Wilberforce! thou man of black renown. Race. Byron. *Fr.* Don Juan, XIV. OBP

O wild West Wind, thou breath of autumn's being. Ode to the West Wind. Shelley. BiP; CABA (1972 ed.); EBEV; Epi; ExPo (1973 ed.); FSFS; HAP; HeIP; ILP (1975 ed.); InPS; IPWM; LFH; MBPR; NIL; NOBE; OAEL-2; OBP; PAIC; PBMP; PoIA; PPoe; PPP; VoPo

Oh, will you wear red? I'll Wear Me a Cotton Dress. *Unknown.* BPo

Oh, will you wear white, oh my dear, oh my dear? Jenny Jenkins. *Unknown.* FSW

O Willie Brew'd a peck o' maut. Willie Brew'd a Peck o' Maut. Burns. ILP (1975 ed.)

O Willie's large o' limb and lith. The Birth of Robin Hood. *Unknown.* OAEL-1

O wind, rend open the heat. Heat. Hilda Doolittle ("H. D."). *Fr.* The Garden. CMoP (1970 ed.); FSFS; HeIP; InPK; NoAM; PiAm; TAP; UnPo (1976 ed.); UsP

O winds, that ripple the long grass! With a Wreath of Laurel. Ina Coolbrith. WPW

O Winter! bar thine adamantine doors. To Winter. Blake. MBPR

O, winter, your gesture. Winter. Bella Akhmadulina, *tr. by* Barbara Einzig. BoWoP

Oh, with the hunger of the sea, forever born anew. Song. John Hall Wheelock. LoAs

O with what key. Skeleton Key. John Hollander. InPK

O woe, woe,/ People are born and die. Mr. Housman's Message. Ezra Pound. FaBoEE; PAIC

O woman of Three Cows, agra! don't let your tongue thus rattle! The Woman of Three Cows. *Unknown, tr. by* James Clarence Mangan. PFIr

O Woman, Shapely as the Swan. *Unknown, tr. fr. Irish by* Padraic Colum. BIrV

Oh women/ the oyster in me responds. To the Dead Ladies. David Bristol. PoUP

"O words are lightly spoken." The Rose Tree. W. B. Yeats. CMoP (1970 ed.)

O world, I cannot hold thee close enough! God's World. Edna St. Vincent Millay. CMoP (1970 ed.); ILP (1975 ed.); PPM; VoPo

O world invisible, we view thee. The Kingdom of God [or In No Strange Land.] Francis Thompson. FaPoR; HAP; ILP (1975 ed.); ILwL; IP; NOBE; PoPle

O world! O life! O time! A Lament. Shelley. MBPR; NOBE

O worthy of belief I hold it was. Pan and Luna. Robert Browning. VLP

O ye that put your trust and confidence. A Rueful Lamentation. Sir Thomas More. AAS

O ye wha are sae guid yoursel. Address to the Unco Guid. Burns. ILP (1975 ed.); NOBE

O ye wretched Scots. John Skelton. Fr. How the Doughty Duke of Albany like a Coward Knight Ran Away Shamefully. OBSV

Oh---Yeah! Sharon Scott. JB

O year, grow slowly. Exquisite, holy. Slow Spring. Katharine Tynan. FSFS

O yee, whome lorde of lande and waters wyde. Seneca, tr. by Jasper Heywood. Fr. Thyestes, III. OBVE

Oh Yes. William Matthews. AmPA

Oh yes/ We got Mr. President Roosevelt. President Roosevelt. Unknown. BluL

O yes, I love you, book of my confessions. Water under the Earth. Robert Bly. NNaP

O yes, the Chinese Garden! Do you remember. The Chinese Garden. Horace Gregory. WasP

Oh yesterday I was married, last night I went to bed. The Lowlands of Holland. Unknown. AIW

O yet we trust that somehow good. In Memoriam A. H. H., LIV. Tennyson. BiP; BoReV; ExPo (1973 ed.); PIM; VoPo

O Yonge Freshe Folkes. Chaucer. See Love Unfeigned.

O you,/ Who came upon me once. Carrefour. Amy Lowell. BoWoP

O You among Women. F. R. Higgins. BIrV

Oh, you are a kilt which a young dandy set out to choose. A Woman Sings of Her Love. Somali Oral Tradition, tr. by B. W. Andrzejwski and I. M. Lewis. WTO

Oh you canna spend a dollar when you're dead. Ding Dong Dollar. Hamish Henderson. FSW

O you chorus of indolent reviewers. Hendecasyllabics. Tennyson. EBEV; FaBoCo; NOBL; VLP

O you clouds. Callypso Speaks. Hilda Doolittle ("H. D."). PiAm; RiTi; SBG

Oh, you come along, boys, you listen to my tale. The Old Chisholm Trail. Unknown. AmFP

O you hollow-cheeked offspring. Baboon. Zulu Oral Tradition, tr. by C. and W. Leslav. WTO

O you innocent liberal! Child of the Dead and Forgotten Gods. Richard Wright. SPT

"Oh, you must answer my questions nine." The Devil's Nine Questions. Unknown. AmFP

Oh, you tall traveler. A Friend's Passing. Barclay Sheaks. AMV-80

Oh you used to told me you could drive me like a cow. From Now On. Unknown. BluL

O you who come to me—alas! Laieikawai's Lament after Her Husband's Death. Tr. fr. Hawaiian by M. W. Beckwith. WTO

O Young and Fearless Prophet, with music. Samuel Ralph Harlow. AH

O, young Lochinvar is come out of the west. Lochinvar. Sir Walter Scott. Fr. Marmion, V. AIW; BTTM; ECBV; NOBE; ILP (1975 ed.); PoTa; PPM; SLP

O young Mariner. Merlin and the Gleam. Tennyson. OAEL-2; VLP

O younge [or yonge] freshe folkes, he or she. Love Unfeigned. Chaucer. Fr. Troilus and Criseyde. BoReV; ExPo (1973 ed.); NOBE; OxBM

Oh Zlotchev, my home, my town. Zlotchev, My Home. Moishe Leib Halpern, tr. by Richard J. Fein. VWA

Oa! hoy! awe! ba! mey! Canedolia. Edwin Morgan. FaBoCo

Oak, The. Tennyson. CTV; PPM; SoSe

Oak and the Ash, The. Unknown. FSW

Oak and the Reed, The. La Fontaine, tr. fr. French by Marianne Moore. NAWM-2

Oak is called the king of trees, The. Trees. Sara Coleridge. OxBChV

Oak leaf fell from the tree, An. The One Leaf. Leslie Norris. LP

Oak tree in my front yard dies, The. For a Bitter Season. George Garrett. CSP

Oaks, how subtle and marine, The. Bearded Oaks. Robert Penn Warren. CoPAm; NoAM; NOBA; PiAm; PoA; TAP

Oath, The. Joseph Beaumont. SCP-2

Oath, The. Allen Tate. NoAM; VGW

Oatmeal Deluxe. Stephen Dobyns. AMV-81

Oban Girl. Edwin Morgan. MS

Obatala, the Creator. Yoruba Oral Tradition, tr. by Ulli Beier. WTO

Oberon, the Fairy Prince, sels. Ben Jonson.
    "Chromis! Mnasil! None appear?" SCP-1
    Song of the Satyr. PoPle
    (Elves' Song.) BBL
    (Satyrs' Catch, The.) FaBoNo

Oberon's Feast. Robert Herrick. CaPo; SCP-1

Oberon's Palace. Robert Herrick. CaPo

Obit Page. Paul Blackburn. VoA

Obituary. Kenneth Fearing. VGW

Obituary. Weldon Kees. BoAnP

Obituary in Bitcherel. Conrad Aiken. OBAL

Object among dreams, you sit here with your shoes off, An. A Girl in a Library. Randall Jarrell. NoAM; NOBA

Object Lesson. Paul Henderson. ATNZ

Objects. Richard Wilbur. FF

Objets d'Art. Cynthia Macdonald. NMM; WBN

Oblation, The. Swinburne. VLP

Oblique Birth Poem. Ann Darr. GP

Obliterate/ mythology. The Cavern. Charles Tomlinson. CMoP (1970 ed.)

Oblivion! Skin. Nelly Sachs, tr. fr. German by Michael Roloff. PBWP

O'Bruadair. David O'Bruadair, tr. fr. Irish by James Stephens. BIrV

Obscene Caller, The. Philip Dacey. AmPA

Obscured Prince, The; or, The Black Box Boxed. Unknown. APAS

Obscurely yet most surely called to praise. Praise in Summer. Richard Wilbur. CAPP

Obscuring the hieroglyphs. Poem while Reading The Naked Lunch by William Burroughs. Charles Senior. MIS

Obscurity has its tale to tell. Focus. Adrienne Rich. PiAm

Observant of the way she told. Tact. E. A. Robinson. NoAM

Observation, The. Donovan Leitch. GrRo

Observation. Richard Weber. POL

Observation. Derk Wynand. AMV-80

Observation at Dawn. Abba Kovner, *tr. fr. Hebrew by* Shirley Kaufman. VWA

Observation Car. A. D. Hope. NoAM

Observation of Facts. Charles Tomlinson. TwMBP

Observations in a Cornish Teashop. Kenneth Rexroth. OBAL

Observe how he negotiates his way. Swimmer. Robert Francis. LiSp

Observe how it will be at last. Summing Up in Italy. Elizabeth Barrett Browning. VLP

"Observe the young and tender frond." Conversation in the Bush. A. R. D. Fairburn. ATNZ

Observe these pirates bold and gay. On the Dangers Attending Altruism on the High Seas. G. K. Chesterton. FaBoNo

Observer, The. David C. Yates. AMV-81

Obsession, The. Rosy Liggett. AMV-80

Obsessions. Denise Levertov. PAIC

Obstetrician, The. Henry Shore. PMW

Obtuse Angle, Scopprell, Aradobo, and Tilly Lally. In Obtuse Angle's Study. Blake. *Fr.* An Island in the Moon. FaBoNo

Occasion. Roger Pfingston. SFF

Occasional Apostrophe, An. Hugh Walthall. PoUp

Occasional mornings when an early fog. Housewife. Josephine Miles. RiTi

Occasional Poem. A. E. Housman. NOBL

Occasional Yarrow, The. Stevie Smith. FaBoNo

Occultation of Venus, The. Sharlot Hall. WPW

Occupation: Housewife. Phyllis McGinley. *Fr.* I Know a Village. WPE

Occupation: Spinster. Olga Cabral. WBN

Occupational Hazards. David Young. FiCP

Ocean. Robinson Jeffers. ILP (1975 ed.)

Ocean Burial, The, *with music.* Edwin H. Chapin. PSoN

Ocean has not been so quiet for a long while, The. Evening Ebb. Robinson Jeffers. NoAM; PSN

Ocean is a strange, The. Laura St. Martin. FF

Ocean Is like a Wreath, The. Kuapakaa, *tr. fr. Hawaiian.* WTO

Ocean Lullaby, An. Charles Keeler. RhR

Ocean, mother of all living. Riptide. Marge Piercy. MMD

Ocean on Monday. Richard Hugo. CNW

Ocean Said to Me Once, The. Stephen Crane. The Black Riders, XXXVIII. TT

Oceana and Britannia. John Ayloffe. APAS

Oceans. Juan Ramón Jiménez, *tr. fr. Spanish by* Robert Bly. NU

Oceans of Dr. Johnson, The. Helen Bevington. CSP

Och, we shall never want, witch, you and I. We Shall Never Want. Sydney Goodsir Smith. SLP

Och, what was it got me at all that time. The Rachray Man. Moira O'Neill. PFIr

Och! what will [*or* shall] we do for linen? What Will We Do for Linen? *Unknown.* GBP; WTO

Ock Gurney and old Pete were there. John Masefield. *Fr.* Reynard the Fox. CMoP (1970 ed.)

O'Connor the Bad Traveler. Peter Klappert. FiCP

Ocotillo in Bloom, The. Marilla Merrimar Guild. PBAW

Octaves, *sels.* E. A. Robinson.
"Here by the windy docks I stand alone," XXIII. ILP (1975 ed.)
"Like a white wall whereon forever breaks," XVIII. ILP (1975 ed.)
"Prophet of dead words defeats himself, The," XX. ILP (1975 ed.)

October. Judith Goren. AMV-81

October. Ella Higginson. WPW

October. Patrick Kavanagh. CIP

October. Frederic Koeppel. AMV-80

October ("Ah, these, with life so done with now, might deem"). William Morris. *Fr.* The Earthly Paradise. VLP

October ("O love, turn from the unchanging sea, and gaze"). William Morris. *Fr.* The Earthly Paradise. VPC

October. Greg Pape. AmPA

October. Barry Spacks. PoA

October. Spenser. *Fr.* The Shepheardes Calender. OAEL-1

October. Edward Thomas. NoAM

October, and a rain-blurred face. At a Fishing Settlement. Alistair Campbell. ATNZ

October and November. Robert Lowell. MAT

October Dawn. Ted Hughes. TwMBP

October Dusk. C. Stephen Finley. AMV-80

October 1. Karl Shapiro. PoA

October Ghosts. James Wright. CAAP

October in the Lane. Leslie Norris. HeHu

October is marigold, and yet. October Dawn. Ted Hughes. TwMBP

October Journey. Margaret Walker. AmNP (1974 ed.); PoBA

October Morning. Mary Ursula Bethell. ATNZ

October nights, wild geese string. The Impulse of October. W. R. Moses. NCSH

October 1954. Kay Boyle. RiTi

October-November. Hart Crane. PSN

October 16: The Raid. Langston Hughes. PoBA

October. The sumach sheds the crimson light. St. Luke's Little Summer. Edward Lowbury. PMW

October walks these beautiful days. October. Ella Higginson. WPW

Octobering. Margaret Gibson. AAN

Octobers. Christopher Middleton. TwMBP

October's end. A day of sunny still. Indian Summer. Gray Burr. AMV-80

Octopus. A. C. Hilton. FaBoCo

Octopus, The. James Merrill. GP

Octopus, The. Ogden Nash. CTV; ILP (1975 ed.)

Octopus. Sam Reavin. CaYB

Odalisque. Brian Coffey. CIP

Odd but True. *Unknown.* FaBoCo
(Nonsense.) FaBoNo
(Oh That My Lungs.) NOBL

Odd, friendless boy raised by four aunts, The. Thumb. Philip Dacey. POL

Odd Old Man in Hackensack, An. *Unknown.* TDH

Odd old woman named Georgetown. Pride of Place. Katie Loucheim. WasP

Odd way you comb your hair, The. Lady in a Distant Face. James Welch. AmPA

Odd Woman, The. Madeline DeFrees. CNW; GP

Ode: Acme and Septimius. Catullus, *tr. fr. Latin by* Abraham Cowley. OBVE

Ode: "At her fair hands how have I grace entreated." Walter Davison. BoLoP

Ode: Autumn. Thomas Hood. FSFS; OAEL-2; UnPo (1976 ed.); VLP

Ode: "Bards of passion and of mirth." Keats. ILP (1975 ed.); MBPR

Ode: Dying Christian to His Soul, The. Pope. ILP (1975 ed.)

Ode: "God save the Rights of Man!" Philip Freneau. EAP; GOA

Ode, An: "High spirited friend." Ben Jonson. PAIC

Ode: "How sleep the brave, who sink to rest." William Collins. *See* How Sleep the Brave.

Ode, An: "I sing a song of sixpence, and of rye." Anthony C. Deane. NOBL

Ode: Infinity. Ralph Storey. SES

Ode: Intimations of Immortality from Recollections of Early Childhood. Wordsworth. BiP; CABA (1972 ed.); HAP; HeIP; ILP (1975 ed.); LFH; MBPR; NOBE; OAEL-2;OBP; PAIC; PBMP; PoIA; PPoD; PPoe; PPP; TPo
*Sels.*
   "Land and sea." FSFS
   "Now, while the birds thus sing a joyous song." Prf
   "O joy! that in our embers." PoPle; Prf
   "Our birth is but a sleep and a forgetting." ILwL

Ode, An: "Merchant, to secure his treasure, The." Matthew Prior. CABA (1972 ed.)
   (Song: "Merchant, to secure his treasure, The.") PoPle

Ode: "O battallions! O disaster!" William Pillin. SPT

Ode: Of Wit. Abraham Cowley. OAEL-1; PAIC

Ode: "Old tumbril rolling with me till I die." X. J. Kennedy. PCho

Ode, An: On the Death of Mr. Purcell. Dryden. ILP (1975 ed.)

Ode: "People in the middle ages didn't think they were living." David Lehman. AMV-81

Ode: Salute to the French Negro Poets. Frank O'Hara. NNaP

Ode: "Sleep sweetly in your humble graves." Henry Timrod. AmVN; GOA; NOBA; TAP
   (Sleep Sweetly.) AH, *with music*

Ode: "Spacious firmament on high, The." Joseph Addison. *See* Spacious Firmament on High, The.

Ode: "There is a door in these hands that has been." James Tipton. TC

Ode: "We are the music-makers." Arthur O'Shaughnessy. FaPoR; PFIr; PPM; VLP; WIF

Ode against St. Cecilia's Day. George Barker. PoA

Ode for a Social Meeting. Oliver Wendell Holmes. OBAL

Ode for Him, An. Robert Herrick. CaPo

Ode for the American Dead in Korea. Thomas McGrath. VGW

Ode in Honour. Francis Scarfe. EAS

Ode Inscribed to W. H. Channing. Emerson. HAP; ILP (1975 ed.); NOBA; PAIC; PiAm; TAP

Ode Occasion'd by the Death of Mr. Thomson. William Collins. LAuP

Ode of Odium on Aquariums. Arthur Guiterman. BoAnP

Ode on a Decision to Settle for Less. William Pillen. VWA

Ode on a Distant Prospect of Eton College. Thomas Gray. CABA (1972 ed.); HeIP; ILP (1975 ed.); LAuP; NOBE; OAEL-1; PAIC
   "Ye distant spires, ye antique towers," 2 *sts.* PES

Ode on a Grecian Urn. Keats. AnMo; BiP; CABA (1972 ed.); EBEV; ExPo (1973 ed.); FF; HAP; HeIP; HoPM (1975 ed.); ILP (1975 ed.); InPK; InPS; IP; LFH; MBPR; NIL; NOBE; OAEL-2; OBP; PAIC; PBMP; PPoD; PPoe; PPP; SoSe; STS; TT; UnPo (1976 ed.); WIF

Ode on a Grecian Urn Summarized. Desmond Skirrow. NOBL

Ode on a Jar of Pickles. Bayard Taylor. SpRo

Ode on Celestial Music. Brian Patten. OxBTC

Ode on Gas, An. *Unknown.* OBAL

Ode on His Majesty's Proclamation, Commanding the Gentry to Reside on Their Estates. Sir Richard Fanshawe. *See* Ode, An, upon Occasion of His Majesty's Proclamation in the Year 1630.

Ode on Indolence. Keats. MBPR

Ode on Lust. Frank O'Hara. Epi

Ode on Melancholy. Keats. CABA (1972 ed.); Epi; ExPo (1973 ed.); HAP; ILP (1975 ed.); InPS; MAT; MBPR; NIL; NOBE; OAEL-2; OBP; PMW; PoIA; PoPle; PPP; STS

Ode on St. Cecilia's Day, *sel.* Pope.
   "Furies sink upon their iron beds, The." FaBoCo

Ode on Solitude. Pope. HeIP; IP; IPWM; LFH; NIL; PAIC; PCOP; PoPle; PPoe; Prf
   (Solitude, an Ode.) Epi; PBMP

Ode on the Death of a Favourite Cat, Drowned in a Tub of Gold Fishes. Thomas Gray. EBEV; Epi; HoPM (1975 ed.); ILP (1975 ed.); LAuP; NOBE; NOBL; OAEL-1; PCat; PPP
   (On a Favorite Cat Drowned in a Tub of Goldfishes.) FaBoCo; PBMP; PoPle

Ode on the Death of the Duke of Wellington. Tennyson. VLP

Ode on the Despoilers of Learning in an American University, An. Yvor Winters. ExPo (1973 ed.)

Ode on the Installation of His Royal Highness Prince Albert. Wordsworth. MBPR

Ode on the Morning of Christ's Nativity. Milton. *See* On the Morning of Christ's Nativity.

Ode on the Pleasure Arising from Vicissitude. Thomas Gray. LAuP

Ode on the Poetical Character. William Collins. LAuP; OAEL-1

Ode on the Popular Superstitions of the Highlands of Scotland, An. William Collins. LAuP; OAEL-1
Stormy Hebrides, The, *sel.* NOBE

Ode on the Spring. Thomas Gray. LAuP

Ode on Zero. Phoebe Pettingell. PoA

Ode Recited at the Harvard Commemoration. James Russell Lowell. NOBA; PiAm

Ode Sung at the Opening of the International Exhibition. Tennyson. VLP

Ode to a Beautiful Woman. Carl Clark. JB

Ode to a Dead Dodge. David McElroy. AmPA

Ode to a Ditch. *Unknown.* PeD

Ode to a Fat Cat. Annabel Farjeon. PCat

Ode to a Homemade Coffee Cup. Marine Robert Warden. AMV-81

Ode to a Lebanese Crock of Olives. Diane Wakoski. GP

Ode to a Model. Vladimir Nabokov. OBAL; SFF

Ode to a Nightingale. Keats. AnMo; BiP; CABA (1972 ed.); EBEV; Epi; ExPo (1973 ed.); HAP; HeIP; ILP (1975 ed.); InPK; InPS; IPWM; MBPR; NIL; NOBE; OAEL-2; OBP; PAIC; PB; PoIA; PPoe; PPP; SoSe; SpRo; STS; TT; UnPo (1976 ed.); UsP; VoPo; WeW
   "I cannot see what flowers are at my feet," *sel.* FSFS

Ode to a Pig while His Nose Was Being Bored. Robert Southey. NOBL

Ode to a Skylark. Shelley. *See* To a Skylark.

Ode to a Sneeze. *Unknown, at. to* G. Wallace. OSF

Ode to a Vanished Operator in an Automatized Elevator. Loyd Rosenfield. QQQ

Ode to a Young Dog. Vicki Viidikas. FPA

Ode to a Violin. Luís Omar Salinas. SA

Ode to an Urban Day. Raymond Ward. ATNZ

Ode to Anactoria. Sappho, *tr. fr. Greek by* William Ellery Leonard. LoAS
   ("Peer of the gods is that man, who, " *tr. by* William Carlos Williams.) OBVE

Ode to Apollo. Keats. MBPR

Ode to Autumn. Keats. *See* To Autumn.

Ode to Delmore Schwartz. Paul Carroll. FiCh

Ode to Duty. Wordsworth. BiP; MBPR; OAEL-2

Ode to Evening. William Collins. CABA (1972 ed.); EBEV; Epi; ExPo (1973 ed.); HAP; ILP (1975 ed.); LAuP; NOBE; OAEL-1; OBP; PPP

Ode to Fancy. Philip Freneau. EAP

Ode to Fancy. Joseph Warton. PAIC

Ode to Fanny. Keats. MBPR

Ode to Fear. William Collins. ILP (1975 ed.); LAuP; PAIC

Ode to Fear. Allen Tate. PAIC

Ode to Fidel Castro. Edward Field. CABA (1972 ed.)

Ode to Freedom. Aaron Zeitlin, *tr. fr. Yiddish by* Keith Bosley. VWA

Ode to Himself ("Come leave the loathèd stage"). Ben Jonson. OAEL-1

Ode to Himself, An ("Where dost thou careless lie"). Ben Jonson. Epi; ExPo (1973 ed.); HAP; ILP (1975 ed.); NOBE; PAIC; SCP-1

Ode to Jibberish. Darrell Gray. AcAn; EC

Ode to Joy. Daniel Hoffman. AMV-81

Ode to Joy. Miroslav Holub, *tr. fr. Czech by* Ian Milner *and* George Theiner. BuTh

Ode to Joy. Michael McClure. GP

Ode to Joy. Frank O'Hara. PPP

Ode to Liberty. Shelley. MBPR

Ode to Love, An. Aphra Behn. SCP-2

Ode to Master Anthony Stafford to Hasten Him into the Country, An. Thomas Randolph. NOBE; SCP-2

Ode to Master Endymion Porter, upon His Brother's Death, An. Robert Herrick. CaPo; SCP-1

Ode to May. Fragment. Keats. *See* Fragment of an Ode to Maia.

Ode to Memory. Tennyson. VLP

Ode to Mercy. William Collins. LAuP

Ode to Mexican Experience. Luís Omar Salinas. SA

Ode to Mr. F——. Allan Ramsay, *after* Horace. OBVE

Ode to My Socks. Pablo Neruda, *tr. fr. Spanish by* Robert Bly. Epi

Ode to Naples. Shelley. PAIC

Ode to Napoleon Buonaparte. Byron. MBPR

Ode to New York. Reed Whittemore. NYP

Ode to Pity. William Collins. LAuP

Ode to Popularity. Winthrop Mackworth Praed. VLP

Ode to Pornography. Jack Anderson. PoA

Ode to Psyche. Keats. CABA (1972 ed.); InPS; MBPR; NIL; NOBE; OAEL-2; PPP; STS

Ode to Rhys ap Maredudd of Tywyn. Dafydd Nanmor, *tr. fr. Welsh by* H. Idris Bell. OBW

Ode to Salt. Pablo Neruda, *tr. fr. Spanish by* Robert Bly. NU

Ode to Simplicity. William Collins. LAuP; NOBE

Ode to Spring. Burns. OBP

Ode to Stephen Dowling Bots, Dec'd. "Mark Twain." *See* Emmeline Grangerford's "Ode to Stephen Dowling Bots, Dec'd."

Ode to Swansea. Vernon Watkins. OBW

Ode to Terminus. W. H. Auden. HAP

Ode to the Cameleopard. Thomas Hood. FaBoNo

Ode to the Confederate Dead. Allen Tate. CABA (1972 ed.); HeIP; ILP (1975 ed.); LFH; NoAM; NOBA; TAP; UnPo (1976 ed.)

Ode to the Departing Year. Samuel Taylor Coleridge. MBPR

Ode to the Human Heart. Laman Blanchard. NOBL

Ode to the Maguire. Eochaidh O'Hussey, *tr. fr. Irish by* James Clarence Mangan. BIrV

Ode to the Medieval Poets. W. H. Auden. PoA

Ode to the Muse on Behalf of a Young Poet. David Wagoner. AMV-80

Ode to the New York Mets. John Vliet Lindsay. SPo

Ode to the North-east Wind. Charles Kingsley. FaPoR

Ode to the Norther. William Lawrence Chittenden. BPAW

Ode to the Poppy. Henrietta Oneil. WPE

Ode to the Rain, An. Samuel Taylor Coleridge. MBPR

Ode to the Spirit of Earth in Autumn. George Meredith. VLP

Ode to the Watermelon. Pablo Neruda, *tr. fr. Spanish by* Robert Bly. EAS; NU

Ode to the West Wind. Shelley. BiP; CABA (1972 ed.); EBEV; Epi; ExPo (1973 ed.); FSFS; HAP; HeIP; ILP (1975 ed.); InPS; IPWM; LFH; MBPR; NIL; NOBE; OAEL-2; OBP; PAIC; PBMP; PoIA; PPoe; PPP; VoPo

Ode to Tobacco. Charles Stuart Calverley. FaBoCo

Ode to Tranquillity. Samuel Taylor Coleridge. MBPR

Ode to Tropical Skiing. John Forbes. GAS

Ode to Walt Whitman. Michael Gold. SPT

Ode to Willem de Kooning. Frank O'Hara. Epi

Ode upon a Question Moved, Whether Love Should Continue Forever? Lord Herbert of Cherbury. NOBE; SCP-2

Ode, An, upon Occasion of His Majesty's Proclamation in the Year 1630. Sir Richard Fanshawe. SCP-2
(Ode on His Majesty's Proclamation, Commanding the Gentry to Reside on Their Estates.) NOBE

Ode Written in 1966. Jorge Luis Borges, *tr. fr. Spanish by* Lynn C. Jacox. AMV-81

Ode Written in the Beginning of the Year 1746. William Collins. *See* How Sleep the Brave.

Odes, *sels.* Horace, *tr. fr. Latin.*
I, 4. Solvitur Acris Hiems, *tr. by* Louis MacNeice. Epi
I, 5. "What slender youth bedewed with liquid odours" ("Quis multa gracilis"), *tr. by* Milton. EBEV; OBVE; SCP-1
(To Pyrrha.) LoAs
("Pyrrha, what slender well-shap'd beau," *tr. by* Anthony Horneck.) OBVE
("Say what slim youth, with moist perfumes, " *tr. by* Christopher Smart.) OBVE
("Tell me, Pyrrha, what fine youth," *tr. by* William Browne.) OAEL-1
("To whom now, Pyrrha, art thou kind?" *tr. by* Abraham Cowley.) OBVE
("What stripling now thee discomposes," *tr. by* Sir Richard Fanshawe.) OBVE
I, 8. "In the name of all the gods, tell me, Lydia, why" ("Lydia, dic, per omnes"), *tr. by* C. E. Bennett. LoAs
("Lydia, in Heavens Name," *tr. by* Sir Richard Fanshawe.) OBVE
I, 9. To Thaliarchus ("Vides ut alta"), *tr. by* Sir Richard Fanshawe. OBVE
("Behold yon' mountains hoary hieght," *tr. by* Dryden.) OBVE
I, 21. To Apollo and Diana ("Dianam tenerae dicite virgines"), *tr. by* Branwell Brontë. OBVE
I, 22. "Virtue, dear friend, needs no "defence" ("Integer vitae"), *tr. by* Earl of Roscommon. OBVE
(To Aristius Fuscus, *tr. by* Samuel Johnson.) OBVE
I, 23. To Chloe ("Vitas hinnuleo"). LoAs, *tr. by* Austin Dobson; OBVE, *tr. by* Branwell Brontë
I, 25. Ribald Romeos Less and Less Berattle ("Parcius iunctas quatiunt fenestras"), *tr. by* John Frederick Nims. MAT
("Bloods and bucks of this lewd town, The, " *tr. by* the Young Gentlemen of Mr. Rule's Academy at Islington.) OBVE
("Boys come round less often, The," *tr. by* David Malouf.) FPA
(To Lydia, *tr. by* Philip Francis.) OBVE
("Young bloods come round less often now, The," *tr. by* James Michie.) BoLoP
I, 38. Fie on Eastern Luxury! ("Persicos odi"), *tr. by* Hartley Coleridge. InPK
("Ah child, no Persian—perfect art!" *tr. by* Gerard Manley Hopkins.) InPK; OBVE
("Dear Lucy, you know what my wish is," *tr. by* Thackeray.) OBVE
("Persian pomps, boy, ever I renounce them," *tr. by* Christopher Smart.) OBVE
(Preference Declared, The, *tr. by* Eugene Field.) InPK
(Simplicity, *tr. by* William Cowper.) InPK
("Boy, I hate their empty shows.") OBVE

II, 5. "Not yet can she bear the yoke on submissive neck" ("Nondum subacta"), *tr. by* C. E. Bennett. LoAs

II, 10. "Receive, dear friend, the truths I teach" ("Rectius vives"), *tr. by* William Cowper. OBVE
("Of thy lyfe, Thomas, this compass well mark," *tr. by* Earl of Surrey.) OBVE
("You better sure shall live, not evermore," *tr. by* Sir Philip Sidney.) OBVE

II, 18. "Gold or iv'ry's not intended" ("Non ebur neque aureum"), *tr. by* Christopher Smart. OBVE

III, 1. "Tread back—and back, the lewd and lay!" ("Odi profanum vulgus"), *tr. by* Gerard Manley Hopkins. OBVE
("Hence ye prophane; I hate ye all," *tr. by* Abraham Cowley.) OBVE, 2 *sts.*

III, 7. "Dear Molly, why so oft in tears?" ("Quid sles, asterie"), *tr. by* George Stepney. OBVE

III, 9. A Dialogue between Horace and Lydia ("Donec gratus eram", *tr. by* Robert Herrick. OBVE

III, 29. "Descended of an ancient line" ("Tyrrhena regum progenies"), *paraphrased by* Dryden. OBVE
Happy the Man, *st.* 8 *only.* FaPoR

III, 9. A Dialogue between Horace and Lydia ("Donec gratus eram", *tr. by* Robert Herrick. OBVE

IV, 1. To Venus ("Intermissa, Venus"), *tr. by* Ben Jonson. OBVE

IV, 2. The Praise of Pindar ("Pindarum quisquis studet aemulari"), *tr. by* Abraham Cowley. Epi; OAEL–1; PAIC

IV, 7. "The snow dissolv'd no more is seen" ("Diffugere nives"), *tr. by* Samuel Johnson. LAuP; OBVE
(Diffugere Nives, *tr. by* A. E. Housman.) OBVE

Odes, *sel.* Pindar, *tr. fr. Greek.*
Seventh Olympic Hymn, *tr. by* Robin Blaser. Epi

Odiham. John Gray. FaBoCo

O'Donnell Aboo. M. J. McCann. FSW

Odor of algaroba, lure of release. The Luau. Genevieve Taggard. WPW

Odor of limp leaves, The. My Daughter. Robert Pack. CoPAm

Odours of Flowers, The. Blake. Fr. Milton, II. PF

Odysseus. Padraic Fallon. CIP

Odysseus. W. S. Merwin. NOBA

Odysseus/ once I was ready to split. Penelope. Karen Whitehill. NPW

Odysseus was/ ein Sitzriese. Bouzouki Music. Anselm Hollo. TwMBP

Odysseus and the Phaeacian Games. Homer, *tr. fr. Greek by* Ennis Rees. *Fr.* The Odyssey, VIII. LiSp

Odysseus has come home, to the gully farm. The Homecoming. James K. Baxter. ATNZ

Odysseus, twenty years gone, was recognized. Advice to a Prizefighter. Lucilius, *tr. fr. Greek by* Tom Dodge. LiSp

Odyssey, The, *sels.* Homer, *tr. fr. Greek.*
"And now Eurynome had bath'd the king," *fr.* XXIII, *tr. by* George Chapman. OBVE
"And now his well-known bow the master bore," *fr.* XXI, *tr. by* Pope. OBVE
"And now man-slaughtering Pallas took in hand," *fr.* XXII, *tr. by* George Chapman. OBVE
"And now the Queere of women had intent," *fr.* XXI, *tr. by* George Chapman. OBVE
"Cave we found, but vacant all within, The," *fr.* IX, *tr. by* Pope. OBVE
"Close to the gates a spacious garden lies," *fr.* VII, *tr. by* Pope. OBVE
"Far gone in weariness, in oblivion," VI, *tr. by* Robert Fitzgerald. NAWM-1
Gardens of Alcinous, The ("Close to the gates a spacious garden lies"), *fr.* VII, *tr. by* Pope. OAEL–1
Gardens of Alcinous, The ("Without the hall, and close upon the gate"), *fr.* VII, *tr. by* George Chapman. OAEL–1

"God who mounts the winged winds, The," *fr.* V, *tr. by* Pope. OBVE
"He ended, nor the Argicide refus'd," *fr.* V, *tr. by* William Cowper. OBVE
"Just then, forgetful of the strict command," *fr.* XII, *tr. by* William Cowper. OBVE
"Mighty wave rush'd o'er him as he spoke, A," *fr.* V, *tr. by* Pope. OBVE
New Coasts and Poseidon's Son, IX, *tr. by* Robert Fitzgerald. WTO
"Now gently winding up the fair ascent, " *fr.* XXI, *tr. by* Pope. OBVE
"Now to dispose of the dead, the care remains," *fr.* XXII, *tr. by* Pope. OBVE
"Now toils the Heroe; trees on trees o'erthrown," *fr.* V, *tr. by* Pope. OBVE
"Nymph turnd home, The. He fell to felling downe," *fr.* V, *tr. by* George Chapman. OBVE
Odysseus and the Phaeacian Games, *fr.* VIII, *tr. by* Ennis Rees. LiSp
" 'She thus; when I had great desire to prove,' " *fr.* X!, *tr. by* George Chapman. OBVE
Sirens' Song, The, *fr.* XII, *tr. by* Robert Fitzerald. GrRo
"There grew two olives, closest of the grove," *fr.* V, *tr. by* Pope. OBVE
"This spoke, a huge wave tooke him by the head," *fr.* V, *tr. by* George Chapman. OBVE
"Thus charg'd he; nor Argicides denied," *fr.* V, *tr. by* George Chapman. OBVE
"Trembling the spectres glide, and plaintive vent," *fr.* XXIV, *tr. by* Pope. OBVE
"Under the opening fingers of the dawn," *fr.* VIII–XI, *tr. by* Robert Fitzgerald. NAWM-1
"While thus he thought, a monst'rous wave up-bore," *fr.* V, *tr. by* Pope. OBVE
"Without the hall, and close upon the gate," *fr.* VII, *tr. by* George Chapman. OBVE
"Youth there was, Elpenor was he nam'd, A," *fr.* X, *tr. by* Pope. OBVE

Oedipus. Thomas Blackburn. FaBoTw (1975 ed.)

Oedipus, *sel.* Dryden.
Incantation to Oedipus, *fr.* III, i. OFD

Oedipus. Josephine Miles. WPE

Oedipus. Edwin Muir. CMoP (1970 ed.)

Oedipus at Colonus, *sel.* Sophocles, *tr. fr. Greek.*
Colonus' Praise, *tr. by* W. B. Yeats. Epi; OBVE

Oedipus, Pentheus. David Bromwich. AMV-81

Oedipus Tyrannus; or, Swellfoot the Tyrant. Shelley. MBPR

Oedipus Tyrannus. Sophocles, *tr. fr. Greek by* Luci Berkowitz *and* Theodore F. Brunner. NAWM-1

Oenone. Tennyson. VLP

Oenone and Paris. George Peele. *Fr.* The Arraignment of Paris. NOBE

O'er a small suburban borough. The Domineering Eagle and the Inventive Bratling. Guy Wetmore Carryl. OBAL

O'er all the hill tops. Wanderer's Night Song. Goethe, *tr. by* Longfellow. PPM

O'er Continent and Ocean, *with music.* John Haynes Holmes. AH

O'er the men of Ethiopia she would pour her cornucopia. Husband and Heathen. Sam Walter Foss. OBAL

O'er the wild gannet's bath. Runilda's Chant. George Darley. *Fr.* Ethelstan. PFIr

O'er this huge town, rife with intestine wars. Manchester by Night. Mathilde Blind. SBG

O'er Waiting Harp-Strings of the Mind, *with music.* Mary Baker Eddy. AH

Of a Fair Shrew. Sir John Harington, *after the Latin of* Martial. FaBoEE
("Fair, rich, and young? How rare is her perfection.") NIL

Of a pendulum's mildness, with her feet up. A Timepiece. James Merrill. HoPM (1975 ed.); NoAM; UsP

Of a Rose, a Lovely Rose. *Unknown.* OxBM

Of a sudden and sharp I arise from the loam. Where the Mind Meets the Body in Revolt. Helen Wolfert. *Fr.* Woman against the Moon. RiTi

Of a tall stature and of sable hue. Charles II [*or* An Historical Poem]. *Unknown.* APAS; FaBoEE

Of a' the airts the wind can blaw. I Love My Jean. Burns. BiP; ILP (1975 ed.); LAuP

Of a Woman, Dead Young. Dorothy Parker. SBG

Of a Zealous Lady. Sir John Harington, *after the Latin of* Martial. FaBoEE

Of Adam's first wife, Lilith, it is told. Body's Beauty. Dante Gabriel Rossetti. The House of Life, LXXVIII. ILP (1975 ed.); OAEL-2; VLP

Of all her appalling virtues, none. Damn Her. John Ciardi. IP

Of All Plants, the Tree. Mary Jane White. AMV-80

Of all that Orient lands can vaunt. The Haschish. Whittier. OBAL

Of all the birds I love. Reincarnation. John L. Sellers. DNGG

Of all the bonny buds that blow. Pansy. Mary E. Bradley. PCOP

Of all the causes which conspire to blind. Pope. *Fr.* An Essay on Criticism, Pt. II. ILP (1975 ed.); PoIA; PPoD, PPoe

Of all the creatures, in the world, that be. John Oldham, *after the French of* Boileau. *Fr.* Satires, VIII. OBVE

Of all the facts about mammals. The Elephant. Louis Phillips. OSF

Of all the girls that are so smart. Sally in Our Alley. Henry Carey. BLSo; BoLoP; FSW; NOBE; PCOP; PoPle

Of all the grain our nation yields. A Panegyric upon Oates. Richard Duke. APAS

Of all the problems no one's solved. Minnie Morse. Kaye Starbird. PH

Of all the rides since the birth of time. Skipper Ireson's Ride. Whittier. NOBA; OBAL

Of all the seas that's coming. *Unknown.* EBEV

Of all the souls that stand create. Emily Dickinson. LoAs

Of all the tales of human struggle, hear this one from Tennessee. Bryan's Last Battle. *Unknown.* AmFP

Of all the tales was ever told. Mary Arnold the Female Monster. *Unknown.* GBP; PeBB

Of all the weathers wind is king. King Wind. Mark Van Doren. NCSH

Of all the wives as e'er you know. Nancy Lee. Frederick E. Weatherly. BLSH

Of Alphus. John Parkhurst, *tr. fr. Latin by* Timothe Kendall. SoSe

Of an Ancient Spaniel in Her Fifteenth Year. Christopher Morley. GDP

Of an Heroical Answer of a Great Roman Lady to Her Husband. Sir John Harington. BoLoP

Of asphodel, that greeny flower. William Carlos Williams. *Fr.* Asphodel, That Greeny Flower, I. CMoP (1970 ed.); PoIA

Of Astraea. Sir John Davies. *Fr.* Hymns of Astraea. NIL; PAIC

Of Autumn. Veronica Porumbacu, *tr. fr. Rumanian by* Willis Barnstone *and* Matei Calinescu. BoWoP; VWA

Of Battel: whereat Michael bid sound. War in Heaven. Milton. *Fr.* Paradise Lost, VI. OBP

Of Beauty. Sir Richard Fanshawe. BoLoP

Of Being Numerous, *sels.* George Oppen.
"In this nation." GOA
It Is Difficult Now to Speak of Poetry. MIT; NNaP

Of Birthright. Eric Torgersen. TC

Of Bombs and Boys. Richard Corbin. SoS

Of bricks . . . Who built it? Like some crazy balloon. Our Youth. John Ashbery. CAPP; ConAP; VGW

Of bright cities/ and citrus. Florida. Carl Rakosi. TAP

Of bronze and blaze. Emily Dickinson. AmVN

Of Commerce and Society. Geoffrey Hill. PPoe

Of Consolation. Luci Shaw. AATT

Of Course I Know. Zishe Landau, *tr. fr. Yiddish by* Ruth Whitman. VWA

Of course—I prayed. Emily Dickinson. BoWoP

Of course I tried to tell him. Poets Hitchhiking on the Highway. Gregory Corso. NoAM

Of course, we'll do the Physical Anthropology Hall. Spring Vacation: The Smithsonian. Elisavietta Ritchie. PoUp

Of course when someone leaves you forever. Back. Angela McCabe. AmPA

Of Curious Questions. Martin Farquhar Tupper. VLP

Of De Witt Williams on His Way to Lincoln Cemetery. Gwendolyn Brooks. ANTL; CAPP; NoAM; NOBA

Of diverse monsters I have sometimes read. Strange Monsters. Rowland Watkyns. FaBoEE

Of Dying Beauty. Louis Zukofsky. PoA

Of Eden lost, in ancient days. Rondeau. George Ellis. PAIC

Of Edenhall, the youthful Lord. The Luck of Edenhall. Longfellow. PoTa

Of English Verse. Edmund Waller. OAEL-1; OBP

Of every kinne [*or* everykune] tree, of every kinne tree. The Hawthorn. *Unknown.* GBP; OxBM

Of every vice pursued by those. Gambling. Royall Tyler. TAP

Of Giving. Arthur Guiterman. CTV

Of Hartford in a Purple Light. Wallace Stevens. ILP (1975 ed.)

Of Heaven Considered as a Tomb. Wallace Stevens. PoA

Of Heaven or Hell I have no power to sing. An Apology. William Morris. *Fr.* The Earthly Paradise. OAEL-2; PAIC; VLP; VPC

Of her friends at the textile mill. The Labor Camp. John Pijewski. AMV-81

Of himself to think this: she does not. Lady and Gentleman. Richard Weber. IPM

Of how your poems. A Letter to Paul Celan in Memory. Jerome Rothenberg. VWA

Of Human Bondage. Miller Williams. NYP

Of interest to John Calvin and Thomas Aquinas. Why God Permits Evil: For Answers to This Question of Interest to Many Write Answers Dept. E-7. Miller Williams. CSP

Of Invention, *sel.* Martin Farquhar Tupper.
"Behold the barren reef, which an earthquake hath just left dry." VLP

Of inviting to dine, in Epirus. A Difficult Guest. Carroll Watson Rankin. TDH

Of Iron Am I. *Malay Oral Tradition, tr. by* W. W. Skeat. WTO

Of Jayne Mansfield, Flannery O'Connor, My Mother and Me. Rosemary Daniell. CSP

Of Jeoffry, His Cat. Christopher Smart. *See* For I Will Consider My Cat Jeoffry.

Of Jesu Christ I Sing. *Unknown.* OxBM

Of John Cabanis' wrath and of the strife. The Spooniad. Edgar Lee Masters. OBAL

Of Kate's Baldness. John Davies of Hereford. FaBoEE

Of Kings and Things. Lillian Morrison. NCSH

Of Late. George Starbuck. NowV; VGW

Of Late and Never. John Heywood. PAIC

Of lead and emerald. A Note to Olga (1966). Denise Levertov. CAPP

Of life the darkest part is solitude. From Mistra: A Prospect. Ted Higgs. AMV-80

Of little use the man you may suppose. Pope. *Fr.* Epistle to Augustus. EBEV

Of Loose Atoms. Margaret Cavendish, Duchess of Newcastle. SCP-2

Of loves perfection perfectly to speake. Spenser. *Fr.* Colin Clouts Come Home Againe. OAEL-1

Of Loving a Dog. John Heywood. PAIC

Of M, A, R, I,/ Sing I will a new song. M and A, R and I. *Unknown.* OxBM

Of mans first disobedience, and the fruit. Invocation. Milton. *Fr.* Paradise Lost, I. EBEV; LFH; NIL; OAEL-1; OBP; PAIC; PoIA

Of Misery. Thomas Howell. FF

Of Modern Poetry. Wallace Stevens. CABA (1972 ed.); ILP (1975 ed.); LFH; NIL; NoAM; PAIC; PoIA; TAP; WIF

Of Money. Barnabe Googe. FF

Of Mouse and Men. A. J. Hovde. AMV-81

Of My Dear Son, Gervase Beaumont. Sir John Beaumont. NOBE

Of My First Love. "Hugh MacDiarmid." SLP

Of My Lady Isabella Playing on the Lute. Edmund Waller. HAP

Of My Own Flesh. John Newlove. FoP

Of Myself. Abraham Cowley. ILP (1975 ed.)

Of Myself. Leah Goldberg, *tr. fr. Hebrew by* Ramah Commanday. BoWoP

Of Nelson and the North. Battle of the Baltic. Thomas Campbell. BTTM; FaPoR

Of Neptune's empire let us sing. In Praise of Neptune. Thomas Campion. EcS; NOBE

Of 91 Men Leaving an Underground Station. John Daniel. TwMBP

Of Objects Considered as Fortresses in a Baleful Place. Hyam Plutzik. VGW

Of Old Sat Freedom on the Heights. Tennyson. ILP (1975 ed.)

Of old when Nature, in her verve defiant. The Giantess. Baudelaire, *tr. by* Roy Campbell. OBVE

Of old, when Scarron his companions invited. Retaliation. Goldsmith. ESaP

Of One That Had a Great Nose. George Turberville, *after the Greek of* Trajan. FaBoEE

Of One That Is So Fair and Bright. *Unknown. See* In Praise of Mary.

Of people running down the street. A Picture. Howard Nemerov. NowV

Of Phyllis. William Drummond of Hawthornden. SoSe (1977 ed.)

Of priests we can offer a charmin' variety. Father O'Flynn. Alfred Perceval Graves. PFIr

Of Robert Frost. Gwendolyn Brooks. NoAM; NOBA

Of Salvador the Celery King I sing. Sonnet for Salvador; or, One Could Do Worse than Be a Celery King. Gary Miranda. AAN

Of Suicide. John Berryman. NoAM

Of that time in a Southern jail. Galway Kinnell. *Fr.* The Call across the Valley of Not Knowing. GP

Of that world, having returned from it, I may say. Voyage to the Moon. William Dickey. CoPAm; Moon

Of the Beloved Caravan. Conny Hannes Meyer, *tr. fr. German by* Herbert Kuhner. VWA

Of the Birth and Bringing Up of Desire. Edward de Vere, Earl of Oxford, *after the Latin of* George Buchanan. FaBoEE

Of the Boy and Butterfly. John Bunyan. OxBChV

Of the Changes of Life. William Dunbar, *tr. fr. Middle English by* Andrew Glaze. OBP

Of the Child with the Bird on the Bush. John Bunyan. OxBChV

Of the dark past. Ecce Puer. James Joyce. BIrV; EBEV; NoAM

Of the Elmira Wood. Her Apron through the Trees. Roger Weingarten. AmPA

Of the first paradise there's nothing found. On St. James's Park as Lately Improved by His Majesty. Edmund Waller. NIL; SCP-2

Of the five waiters, white, stiff-shirt fronted. George Bruce. *Fr.* Visitation from a Wartime Childhood. MS

Of the Four Ages of Man. Anne Bradstreet. EAP

Four Ages of Man: Childhood. SBG

Of the goddess there is only the marble shoulder and one. The Interrupted. Josephine Jacobsen. GP

Of the Last Verses in the Book. Edmund Waller. EBEV; HAP; MetP; PAIC; SCP-2

Old Age ("The seas are quiet"), *sel.* NOBE

Of the Loss of Time. John Hoskyns. FaBoEE

Of the Manner of Addressing Clouds. Wallace Stevens. PoA

Of the many ills afflicting Greece. The Greek Athlete. Euripides, *tr. fr. Greek by* Tom Dodge. LiSp

Of the million or two, more or less. Instans Tyrannus. Robert Browning. EBEV

Of the Moon. Charles Best. *See* Sonnet of the Moon, A.

Of the primeval priests assum'd power. The Book of Urizen. Blake. MBPR

Of the Progress of the Soul; the Second Anniversary, *sels.* John Donne.

"Poor soul, in this thy flesh what dost thou know?" OAEL-1

"Think further on thyself, my soul, and think." SCP-1

"Think then, my soul, that Death is but a groom." BoReV

Of the Pythagorean Philosophy. Ovid, *tr. fr. Latin by* Dryden. *Fr.* Metamorphoses, XV. OBVE

Of the Sea, a Song. E. A. Fielder. RhR

Of the sleep of Ulro! and of the passage through. Blake. Jerusalem, *ch.* 1. MBPR

Of the three Wise Men. Carol of the Brown King. Langston Hughes. CC; LCL; PChr

Of the unended in the speed of. Anne-Marie Albiach, *tr. by* Paul Auster. *Fr.* État. PBWP

Of thee, kind boy, I ask no red and white. Sonnet II. Sir John Suckling. CaPo

Of these the false Achitophel was first. Dryden. *Fr.* Absalom and Achitophel, Pt. I. HAP; InPS

Of this blot. Spiritus Sanctus. Betty Ruth Bird. AATT

Of this house I know the backwindow. Eyeglasses. Tom Clark. ConAP; UsP

Of this world's theater in which we stay. Amoretti, LIV. Spenser. NIL; OAEL-1

Of Thomas Traherne and the Pebble Outside. Sydney Clouts. VWA

Of those rebellions that we start in jest. Fear Test: Integrity of Heroes. James Simmons. CIP

Of those who muck in Mammon's total mess. Unholy Roller. H. H. Lewis. SPT

Of Three or Four in a Room. Yehuda Amichai, *tr. fr. Hebrew by* Stephen Mitchell. VWA

Of thy lyfe, Thomas, this compasse well mark. Horace, *tr. by* Earl of Surrey. Odes, II. 10. OBVE

Of Time. Lindiwe Mabuza. SES

Of Treason. Sir John Harington. ExPo (1973 ed.); FaBoEE; FF; InPK

(Epigram: Of Treason.) NIL

(Treason.) FaBoCo

Of Tyndarus, That Frumped a Gentlewoman. *Unknown, tr. fr. Latin by* Richard Stanyhurst. BIrV

Of Use. John Heywood. FaBoEE

Of vitures I most warmly bless. Gerard Manley Hopkins. FaBoEE

Of waterbirds that in my youth I did admire. The Little Militant. John Shaw Neilson. MAuV

Of well-fed babies activate. Legs. Vernon Scannell. HeHu

Of what a quality is courage made. Donagh MacDonagh. *Fr.* Charles Donnelly. CIP

Of what mould did Nature frame me? The Tinder. Thomas Carew. CaPo

Of whom 100,000 are to be drafted by MacNamara. Poem for the Subterranean Poor. Diane di Prima. VoA

Of woods, of plains, of hills and dales. Upon a Rich Country Gentleman. *Unknown.* FaBoEE

Of your lives and of your love. Love. Pauline Hanson. LoAs

Off Cape Leeuwen. M. K. Joseph. ATNZ

Off Crane's Neck the sun. The Spirit of Wrath. William Heyen. AmPA

Off Highway 106. Cherrylog Road. James Dickey. BiP; CABA (1972 ed.); CoPAm; CSP; ExPo (1973 ed.); HAP; InPK; InPS; NIL

Off that landspit of stony mouth-plugs. Medusa. Sylvia Plath. CAPP

Off the coast of Hispaniola. Columbus and the Mermaids. Elizabeth J. Coatsworth. GOA

Off the Ground. Walter de la Mare. PoTa

Off the track/ I blew. Phoenix. Carolyn M. Rodgers. JB

Off to Patagonia. Theodore Weiss. TAP

Off with your shoes, forget those blues. Walking through the Country. Dennis Provisor. PoRo

Offa's Laws. Geoffrey Hill. Mercian Hymns, XIV. PSN ("Dismissing reports and men, he put pressure on the wax.") HAP

Offended, The. Anne Hébert, *tr. fr. French by* Willis Barnstone. BoWoP

Offer of Friendship, The. Grace Cavalieri. PoUp

Offered a sexless heaven I'd say "No thank you." Ovid, *tr. by* Guy Lee. Amores, II, 9b. NAWM-1

Offering. *Unknown, tr. fr. Zuni Indian by* Ruth Bunzel, *ad. by* Robert Bly. NU

Offering, The: Part One. Mary Lee, Lady Chudleigh. WPE

Office for the Dead. Thomas Kinsella. IPM

Office Party. Phyllis McGinley. OBSV

Officers' Mess. Gavin Ewart. OxBTC

Offshore Breeze. Milton Acorn. NeAC

Off-shore, by islands hidden in the blood. I, Maximus of Gloucester, to You. Charles Olson. NoAM; NOBA

Offspring. Naomi Long Madgett. FB

Oft do I return/ To my little song. The Song of the Trout Fisher. Ikinilik, *tr. fr. Eskimo.* WTO

Oft has this planet rolled around the sun. Sir Samuel Garth. *Fr.* The Dispensary. OBSV

Oft have I brooded on defeat and pain. Success. Emma Lazarus. SBG

Oft have I heard my lief Corydon. Hexametra Alexis in Laudem Rosamundi. Robert Greene. *Fr.* Greene's Mourning Garment. GBL

Oft have I heard thee mourn the wretched lot. Charles Churchill. *Fr.* The Prophecy of Famine. OBSV

Oft have I mused, but now at length I find. A Farewell. Sir Philip Sidney. GBL; NOBE

Oft have I played at cards and dice. The Rantin Laddie. *Unknown.* AmFP

Oft have I seen at some cathedral door. Divina Commedia, I. Longfellow. HAP; ILP (1975 ed.); IPWM; LFH; PAIC; PPM; TAP

Oft have I seen, when that renewing breath. Resurrection and Immortality. Henry Vaughan. SCP-1

Oft have we heard of impious sons before. The Female Parricide. *Unknown.* APAS

Oft have you seen a swan superbly frowning. To Charles Cowden Clarke. Keats. MBPR

Oft I had heard of Lucy Gray. Lucy Gray; or, Solitude. Wordsworth. Epi; ILP (1975 ed.); MBPR; OAEL-2; OxBChV

Oft I string the Lydian lyre. To Sylvia. An Imitation of Anacreon. *Unknown.* PiAm

Oft in danger yet alive. To Mrs. Thrale on Her Thirty-fifth Birthday. Samuel Johnson. FaBoEE

Oft in the hall I have heard my people. *Unknown, tr. fr. Anglo-Saxon by* Charles W. Kennedy. *Fr.* Beowulf. HeIP

Oft, in the Stilly Night. Thomas Moore. PFIr; Prf; RDB, *with music*
(Light of Other Days, The.) NOBE

Oft to the Wanderer, weary of exile. The Wanderer. *Unknown, tr. by* Charles W. Kennedy. OAEL-1

Oft when I'm sitting without anything to read. Lines to a World-famous Poet Who Failed to Complete a World-famous Poem; or, Come Clean, Mr. Guest! Ogden Nash. OBAL

Often/ he wears my son's face. Child. Tom MacIntyre. CIP; IPM

Often beneath the wave, wide from this ledge. At Melville's Tomb. Hart Crane. HAP; ILP (1975 ed.); LFH; NoAM; PoA; TAP; UnPo (1976 ed.); VGW

Often called man's half/ brother and beast-self. Bear. Vi Gale. BCr

Often I Am Permitted to Return to a Meadow. Robert Duncan. CMoP (1970 ed.); HeIP; NOBA; NU; PiAm

Often I compare my lord to heaven. Gaspara Stampa, *tr. fr. Italian by* Lynne Lawner. PBWP

Often I have stumbled on life's evil. Life's Evil. Eugenio Montale, *tr. by* Jan Pallister. AMV-81

Often I think of my Jewish friends. The Pripet Marshes. Irving Feldman. NoAM; VWA

Often I think of the beautiful town. My Lost Youth. Longfellow. AmVN; FaPoR; IPWM; NOBA; TAP

Often in summer, on a tarred bridge plank standing. Wild Bees. James K. Baxter. ATNZ

Often, in these blue meadows. Pursuit from Under. James Dickey. HAP; PPP

Often I've wished that I'd been born a woman. A Wish. Laurence Lerner. FF; OxBTC

Often rebuked, yet always back returning. Stanzas. Emily Brontë. OAEL-2; PBWP

Often the sudden smell of "home." Remembering England. Peter Bland. ATNZ

Often when alone I liken my lord/ to the cosmos. Gaspara Stampa, *tr. fr. Italian by* J. Vitiello. BoWoP

Often when the moon is full. Wife of the Moon Man Who Never Came Back. Grace Butcher. RiTi

Often you walked at night, houselights made. In Sepia. Jon Anderson. PoA

Oftener seen, the more I lust, The. Out of Sight, Out of Mind. Barnabe Googe. InPS

Ogres and Pygmies. Robert Graves. CABA (1972 ed.); CMoP (1970 ed.); NoAM

Ohio. John Updike. AMV-80

Ohio Valley Swains. James Wright. NNaP

Ohms. Irving Layton. NeAC

Oil. Hansjörg Mayer. WeW

Oil, came, The. NHR. Jack Hirschman. VWA

Oil Lamp, The. William Jay Smith. TDH

Oil Spots in Every Parking Place. Cinda Kornblum. AcAn

Oil Trucks. The Season of Despair, Your Grass. Faye Kicknosway. TC

Oil wells and blue narcissus brighter than an oak leaf. Margie Silver. Henry Kanabus. FiCh

Oileus by his brother's side stood close. Homer, *tr. by* George Chapman. *Fr.* The Iliad, XIII. OBVE

Oils and Ointments. R. A. K. Mason. ATNZ

Oithona: A Poem. James Macpherson. EPC; LAuP

Okamura's greenhouse fell down today. Elegy for a Greenhouse. Shawn Wong. NW

Okay. Sharon Scott. JB

Okay, my starsick beauty! Unknown Shores. D. M. Thomas, *after* Théophile Gautier. MPo

Okay "Negroes." June Jordan. BPo; RiTi

Okay, so the wheel bit was a grinding bore. Eve: Night Thoughts. Judson Jerome. CoPAm

Okinawa Kanashii Monogatari. Geraldine Kudaka. NW

Oklahoma Ligno and Lithograph Co, The. Corporate Entity. Archibald MacLeish. OBAL

Ol' Bunk's Band. William Carlos Williams. NOBA

Ol' Dynamite. Phil Le Noir. BPAW

Ol' Hannah. *Unknown.* BluL

Ol' Man River, *with music.* Oscar Hammerstein II. BLSo

Ol' Tim Legion. Rubee Dreher Moxley. NPW

Olaf and Sigurd ("Olaf the Viking, arriving by the eastern way"). Robert Sargent. PoUp

Old Abe Lincoln Came Out of the Wilderness. *Unknown.* FSW

Old Acquaintance, An. Lewis Turco. CoPAm

Old Adam, The. Denise Levertov. UnPo (1976 ed.)

Old Adam, the carrion crow. Song. Thomas Lovell Beddoes. *Fr.* Death's Jest Book, V, iv. EBEV; ILP (1975 ed.); OAEL-2; OBP

Old Age. E. E. Cummings. BBGO

Old Age. Mura Dehn. TVo

Old Age. *Gond Oral Tradition, tr. by* V. Elwin *and* S. Hivale. WTO

Old Age. Rolf Jacobsen, *tr. fr. Norwegian by* Robert Bly. EC

Old Age. John Morris-Jones, *tr. fr. Welsh by* Anthony Conran. OBW

Old Age. Edmund Waller. *Fr.* Of the Last Verses in the Book. NOBE

Old Age. *Zulu Oral Tradition, tr. by* H. Tracey. WTO

Old Age Compensation. James Wright. NNaP

Old age has come, my head is shaking. Once I played and Danced in My Parents' Kingdom. *Gond Oral Tradition, tr. by* V. Elwin *and* S. Hivale. WTO

Old Age in His Ailing. Herman Melville. TAP

Old age is. To Waken an Old Lady. William Carlos Williams. HAP; InPK; PSN

"Old age never comes alone"—it brings sighs. Old Age. John Morris-Jones, *tr. by* Anthony Conran. OBW

Old Age of a Clown. Edward Lowbury. PMW

Old Age Sticks. E. E. Cummings. InPS

Old, and abandon'd by each venal friend. On Lord Holland's Seat near Margate, Kent. Thomas Gray. CABA (1972 ed.); LAuP; OAEL-1

Old and longhairs in crome light. Minneapolis White Castle, Winter '72. James L. White. HeS

Old and the New Masters, The. Randall Jarrell. ExPo (1973 ed.); InPK

Old Anguish, The. Chu Shu-chen, *tr. fr. Chinese by* Kenneth Rexroth. BoWoP

Old Argonaut. Sara Saper Gauldin. AMV-81

Old Ark's a-Moverin', The. *Unknown.* FSW

Old Arm-Chair, The. Eliza Cook. InPK

Old Athens of the West Is Now a Blue Grass Tour, The. James Baker Hall. TAT

Old Bangum. *Unknown.* FSW

Old barns let in the rain that always. In Oregon. William Stafford. CNW

Old Beauty, The. Phyllis McGinley. FaBoEE

Old Beebe had three full grown sons, Buster, Bill and Bee. Didn't He Ramble. Will Handy. FSW

Old Ben Golliday. Mark Van Doren. SO

Old Biograph Girl, The. Margaret Benbow. AMV-81

Old bitch labrador swims, The. The End of Summer. Judith Minty. FiCP; HeS

Old Black Joe, *with music.* Stephen Collins Foster. PSoN

Old Black ladies. Weeksville Women. Elouise Loftin. PoBA

Old Black Men. Georgia Douglas Johnson. PoBA

Old Black Men Say. James A. Emanuel. PoBa

Old Blue. *Unknown. See* Old Dog Blue.

Old Boards. Robert Bly. CAPP

Old Boast, The. W. S. Merwin. NOBA

Old Boatman of Death's River, The. R. Williams Parry, *tr. fr. Welsh by* Joseph P. Clancy. OBW

Old Books. Chaucer. *Fr.* The Legend of Good Women: Prologue. OxBM

Old bottle, mauled by the fire, An. William Carlos Williams. *Fr.* Paterson. TT

Old brown thorn-trees break in two high over Cummen Strand, The. Red Hanrahan's Song about Ireland. W. B. Yeats. CMoP (1970 ed.)

Old canoe in, The. Sunrise. Jim Tollerud. VoR

Old Casa, The. Torrey Connor. BPAW

Old Chalky face/ Mr. Teacher Sir. Sir of the C Stream. Valerie Sinason. PMW

Old Charley Garber delivered ice. Desert Holy Man. John Beecher. TAT

Old Chartist, The. George Meredith. VPC

Old Chisholm Trail, The. *Unknown.* AmFP; BLSH, *with music;* BPAW; FSW

Old cloud passes mourning her daughter. Sunset after Rain. W. S. Merwin. PoA

Old Codger's Lament, The. Carl Rakosi. HeS

Old Colonist, The. Andrew Taylor. FPA

Old Colony Times, *with music. Unknown.* BLSo

Old cottonwood has jeweled, my piece, An. Pietas: The Petrified Wood. Dave Smith. HeS

Old Countryside. Louise Bogan. HAP; WPE

Old Couple, The. F. Pratt Green. OxBTC

Old couple living in Gloucester, An. The Lost Girl. *Unknown.* TDH

Old Cow Died, The. *Unknown.* FSW

Old Cowboy's Lament, The. Robert V. Carr. BPAW

Old Cracked Tune, An. Stanley Kunitz. GP

Old Creation Chant. *Tr. fr. Hawaiian.* WTO

Old Cumberland Beggar, The. Wordsworth. MBPR

Old Dan Tucker. Daniel Decatur Emmett. BLSo, *with music;* FSW; PSoN, *with music*

Old daughter, small traveler. Making the Jam without You. Maxine W. Kumin. TV

Old Davis owned a solid mica mountain. A Fountain, a Bottle, a Donkey's Ears and Some Books. Robert Frost. VGW

Old decrepit city like London, An. Roaches. Edward Field. NYP

Old Devil. *Unknown.* BluL

Old Devil he came to a woodsman one day, The. The Curst Wife. *Unknown.* AIW

Old Dog, The. Alasdair MacLean. LP

Old Dog. Raymond Souster. GDP

Old Dog. William Stafford. BoAnP; GDP

Old dog, The/ at the west postern. Peter Whigham. *Fr.* Love Poems of the VIth Dalai Lama. TwMBP

Old dog barks backward without getting up, The. The Span of Life. Robert Frost. GDP; HoPM (1975 ed.); IP; SoSe

Old Dog Blue. *Unknown.* BluL (Old Blue.) FSW; GDP

Old Dog in the Ruins of the Graves at Arles, The. James Wright. NNaP

Old Dog lay in the summer sun. Sunning. James S. Tippett. ECBV; GDP

Old Dog Tray. Stephen Collins Foster. FSW; GDP

Old dogged ways of writing poems, The. Wearing White. Sandra McPherson. MPA

Old Dolores. *Unknown.* MiP

Old Dubuque. Dave Etter. ANTL

Old Eben Flood, climbing alone one night. Mr. Flood's Party. E. A. Robinson. BiP; CABA (1972 ed.); CMoP (1970 ed.); FF; HAP; HoPM (1975 ed.); ILP (1975 ed.); InPK; IP; IPWM; MAT; MiP; NIL; NoAM; NOBA; PAIC; PiAm; PoTa; PPoD; PPoe; PPP; SoSe; STS; TAP; UnPo (1976 ed.)

Old East End worker called Jock, An. Limerick. Victor Gray. NOBL

Old Ego Song ("Old ego climbing out of the trap door on the top of my head"). John Minczeski. AMV-80

Old Egyptians hid their wit, The. On Mr. Nash's Picture at Full Length. Jane Brereton. WPE

Old enemies. Safed and I. Molly Myerowitz Levine. VWA

Old England. Nahum Tate. APAS

Old England Forever and Do It No More. *Unknown.* GBP

Old Ernie Anderson eating peanuts. Peanuts. Ken Belford. NeAC

Old Euclid drew a circle. Euclid. Vachel Lindsay. SFF

Old fabulous rendering up. The Flame of a Candle. Howard Nemerov. AnMo

Old Familiar Faces, The. Charles Lamb. FaPoR; GrRo; NOBE; PAIC

Old Farmer and His Young Wife, The. *Unknown. See* Old Wichet.

Old farmer, nearing death, asked, The. Field Day. W. R. Rodgers. BIrV

Old-fashioned Air. Ted Berrigan. FiCh

Old-fashioned Pitcher, The. George E. Phair. SPo

Old Fence Post. Leigh Hanes. ECBV

Old Field Mowed for Appearances' Sake, An. William Meredith. PPoD

Old, Filthy Beer Pail, The. Katie V. Hall. InPK; PeD

Old Fisherman, The. George Campbell Hay. MS

Old Fisherman with Guitar. George Mackay Brown. MS

Old Flame, The. Robert Lowell. BoLoP; NoAM; NOBA

Old Florist. Theodore Roethke. CTBA; NCSH; PiAm

Old Folk, The. Tove Ditlevsen, *tr. fr. Danish by* Nadia Christensen. PBWP

Old Folk Tale. Barbara Drake. TC

Old Folks at Home, The. Stephen Collins Foster. BLSH, *with music;* BLSo, *with music;* FSW; PSoN, *with music*

Old Folks Home. Tom Hennen. HeS

Old Folks Home, An. Paul Lake. AMV-81

Old forms are like birdhouses that, The. Poetry. Greg Kuzma. PoA

Old Forty-five Per Cent. *Unknown.* FaBoEE

Old friend/ I saw one brown ricepaper print. Hokusai. Jim Farrar. DNGG

Old friend, kind friend! lightly down. To My Old Schoolmaster. Whittier. NOBA

Old Fritz, on this rotating bed. A Flat One. W. D. Snodgrass. CAPP

Old Furniture. Thomas Hardy. OxBTC

Old Glory Lord/ Old Glory! Changeless Changes. Lindiwe Mabuza. SES

Old Gospel Ship, The. *Unknown.* FSW

Old Grandpaw Yet. *Unknown.* AmFP

Old Gray Beard a-Shaking. *Unknown.* AmFP

Old Gray Goose, The. *Unknown.* GBP (Aunt Rhody.) FSW; GSB, *with music.* ("Go tell Aunt Rhody.") AmFP

Old gray hearse goes rolling by, The. The Hearse Song. *Unknown.* SFF

Old gray hen is dying, The. Hen Dying. Alasdair MacLean. BoAnP

Old Gray Mare. *Unknown.* FSW; GBP

Old Grey. Fred Lape. BoAnP

Old greybeard dozing, The. On the Death of God. Roderick Hartigh Jellema. AATT

Old guy put down his beer, The. Do the Dead Know What Time It Is? Kenneth Patchen. CoPAm; HoPM (1975 ed.); PAIC

Old Hannah. *Unknown.* FSW

Old Haven. Jean Garrigue. UsP; WPE

Old High Walk, An. Robert Huff. CNW

Old homes and human lives—both. Reflections. David R. Pichaske. AMV-80

Old House Place. Velma Sanders. AMV-80

Old house with trees and twisting river, An. A Visit to Bridge House. Richard Weber. BIrV

Old houses were scaffolding once. Images. T. E. Hulme. InPK; OxBTC

Old Humpy. *Unknown.* AmFP

Old Hundredth. William Kethe. BLSo, *with music;* FaPoR (Old Hundred.) FSW

Old Inmate, An. Kenneth Mackenzie. GAS

Old Ironsides. Oliver Wendell Holmes. BTTM; CTV; FaPo; GOA; RhR; TAP

Old Jew, The. Paradise. Willis Barnstone. VWA

Old Jew asked me by the Jaffa Gate, An. Conversation with a Countryman. Antoni Slonimski, *tr. by* Isaac Komem. VWA

Old Jewish Cemetery in Worms. Alfred Kittner, *tr. fr. German by* Herbert Kuhner. VWA

Old Jockey, The. F. R. Higgins. OxBTC

Old Joe Clark. *Unknown.* FSW

Old John is foolish. Epigrams. Phillip Hey. NVAP

Old Jumpety-Bumpety-Hop-and-Go-One. The Kangaroo. *Unknown.* ECBV

Old Kimball. *Unknown.* AmFP

Old King, The. Walter de la Mare. AIW

Old King Cole. Mother Goose. FSW; GSB, *with music;* MG

Old Ladies. Will Allen Dromgoole. WeW

Old Ladies, The. Colin Ellis. OxBTC

Old Ladies, The. Tom O'Grady. AAN

Old Lady from Dover, The. Carolyn Wells. TDH

Old Lady of Harrow, An. *Unknown.* TDH

Old Lady of London, The. *Unknown.* AmFP

Old Lady Sitting in the Dining Room. *Unknown.* AmFP

Old lady, when last year I sipped your tea. To an Old Lady Dead. Siegfried Sassoon. PoPle

Old lady writes me in a spidery style, An. A Letter from Brooklyn. Derek Walcott. OxBTC

Old Lady's Lament for Her Youth, The. Villon, *tr. fr. French by* Robert Lowell. BoLoP

(Complaint of the Fair Armouress, The, *tr. by* Swinburne.) OBVE; VLP

Old Laughter. Gwendolyn Brooks. *Fr.* The Womanhood. TH

Old Lem. Sterling A. Brown. BPo; FB; PoBA

Old Looney, An. *Unknown.* TDH

Old Love. William Morris. PeD; VLP

Old MacDonald Had a Farm. *Unknown.* FSW; GSB, *with music*

Old, mad, blind, despised, and dying king, An. England in 1819. Shelley. CABA (1972 ed.); FF; GrRo; ILP (1975 ed.); LFH; MAT; MBPR; NIL; NOBE; OAEL-2; PBMP; PPoD; PPP; UnPo (1976 ed.)

Old Maggie's sweat would drip and sizzle. John Beecher. *Fr.* To Live and Die in Dixie. GP

Old Maid Factory, The. Constance Urdang. GP

Old Maids. *Unknown.* AmFP

Old Maid's Song. *Unknown.* AmFP; FSW

Old Man. Philip Booth. AMV-80

Old Man. Alan J. Carr. AMV-80

Old Man. David E. Stern. AMV-81

Old Man. Edward Thomas. PSN

Old man/ man black man. Tony Get the Boys. D. L. Graham. PoBA

Old man, An/ on st catherine street. For Your Inferiority Complex. David O'Rourke. AMV-81

Old man, The/ sits. Navajo Poem. Warren Woessner. HeS

Old man alone in the dark, muttering, An. Girls' Voices. Brendan Gill. POL

Old man and a boy, An. An Answer to Allegory. Basil Payne. IPM

Old Man and His Wife, An. *Unknown.* OxBM

Old Man and Jim, The. James Whitcomb Riley. PoTa

Old Man and the Sun, The. Vicente Aleixandre, *tr. fr. Spanish by* Robert Bly *and* Lewis Hyde. EC

Old man bending I come among new faces, An. The Wound-Dresser. Walt Whitman. NOBA; TAP

Old Man by Salt Lake, An. William Jay Smith. TDH

Old man came a-courting me, An. Maids When You're Young, Never Wed an Old Man. *Unknown.* FSW

Old Man from Peru, An. *Unknown. See* Limerick: "There was an old man of Peru/ Who dreamt he was eating his shoe.

Old man from the North, immaculate liar. Borges. Willis Barnstone. AMV-80

Old man gets up turns, An. Zeimbekiko. Robin Magowan. EAS

Old man, going a lone highway, An. Building the Bridge. Will Allen Dromgoole. WeW

Old man in a lodge within a park, An. Chaucer. Longfellow. AmVN; HeIP; NOBA; PAIC; TAP; UsP

Old Man in a Moon Loft. T. Glynne Davies. OBW

Old Man in the Autumn, The. John Shaw Neilson. MAuV

Old man in the crystal morning after snow. Poem. Delmore Schwartz. PoA

Old Man in the Wood. *Unknown. See* Father Grumble.

Old man in white, An. Alice Walker. *Fr.* Love. NMM

Old man is a greyer stone this year, The. The Birthday. Louis Johnson. ATNZ

Old Man Jeremy. James K. Baxter. ECBV

Old Man Know-All. *Unknown.* BPo

Old Man Let's Go Fishing in the Yellow Reeds of the Bay. Mei Berssenbrugge. SA

Old man, listening to the careful, The. The First Snow of the Year. Mark Van Doren. NCSH; TVo

Old man moved into his night, The. Katerina Anghelaki-Rooke. *Fr.* Notes on My Father. PBWP

Old man never had much to say. The Old Man and Jim. James Whitcomb Riley. PoTa

Old man of eighty. Hasidic Jew from Sadagora. Rose Ausländer, *tr. by* Ewald Osers. VWA

Old Man of Hawaii, An. *Unknown.* TDH

Old Man of the Hague, The. Edward Lear. TDH

Old Man of the Nile, An. Edward Lear. TDH ("There was an old man of the Nile.") VLP

Old Man of the Sea. Donal Murphy. IPM

Old Man of Toulon, An. William Jay Smith. TDH

Old Man of Verona, The. Claudian, *tr. fr. Latin by* Abraham Cowley. OBVE

Old man of wise sayings. Profetizador/ Old Prophet. Henry L. Pachece. PoW

Old man, old father, old argonaut. Old Argonaut. Sara Saper Gauldin. AMV-81

Old Man, or Lad's-love, —in the name there's nothing. Old Man. Edward Thomas. PSN

Old Man, Phantom Dog. Frederick Eckman. ANTL

Old Man Platypus. A. B. Paterson. BoAnP

Old man raises his bones, The. Levitation. Alvin Aubert. GP

Old man Sargent, sittin' at the desk. Winnsboro Cotton Mill Blues. *Unknown.* FSW

Old man selling charms in a cranny of the town wall, An. The Peddler of Spells. Lu Yu. TVo

Old Man, the Sweat Lodge. Phillip William George. VW

Old Man to the Lizard, The. Archibald MacLeish. PiAm

Old Man Told Me. Lance Henson. VoR

Old Man Travelling; Animal Tranquillity and Decay, a Sketch. Wordsworth. MBPR

Old man was cold, The. Translating. Ruth Whitman. VWA

Old man who had dug the small pit, The. Burial. May Sarton. GP

Old man who seined. Lorine Niedecker. VGW

Old man whose black face, An. The Rainwalkers. Denise Levertov. CTBA; PPP

Old Man with a Gong, The. Edward Lear. TDH

Old man with a yellow flower on his coat, The. The Lion Skin. James K. Baxter. ATNZ

Old man—your great eyes show the simple truth. Death Came Too Late. Alison Wyrley Birch. PPM

Old man's been deadlocked there, The. A Quiet, Orderly Life. Michael Hogan. AAN; DNGG

Old Man's Comforts and How He Gained Them, The. Robert Southey. HoPM (1975 ed.); OxBChV; SpRo; UnPo (1976 ed.)

Old Man's Counsel, The. Bryant. EAP

Old Man's Lark, An. Donald Jones. TVo

Old Man's Song. Vernon Scannell. HeHu

Old Man's Song, The. *Tr. fr. Eskimo.* WTO

Old Man's Tale, The. Brian Merriman, *tr. fr. Modern Irish by* David Marcus. *Fr.* The Midnight Court. BIrV

Old Man's Winter Night, An. Robert Frost. AnMo; HAP; NoAM; PiAm; TT; VGW

Old Mansion. John Crowe Ransom. NOBA

Old-Marrieds, The. Gwendolyn Brooks. AmNP (1974 ed.); PoBA

Old Mary. Gwendolyn Brooks. CoPAm

Old master yourself now, Auden, An. As You Like It. Theodore Weiss. TAP

Old Meg she was a gipsy. Meg Merrilies [*or* Old Meg]. Keats. MBPR; OxBChV; PoPle; TT

Old Memories of Earth. R. A. K. Mason. ATNZ

Old Men, The. Kipling. OBSV

Old Men. Ogden Nash. SFF

Old Men. Alicia Ostriker. AVM-81

Old men/ in Lucas Park. Lucas Park (St. Louis). Paul Southworth Bliss. ANTL

Old Men Admiring Themselves in the Water, The. W. B. Yeats. CMoP (1970 ed.); MiP; TVo

Old Men during a Fall of Government. Chris Wallace-Crabbe. GAS

Old Men in a Home. May Ivimy. PMW

Old men in blue: and heavily encumbered. Pihsien Road. Robin Hyde. ATNZ; WPE

Old men live in a life. Hebrides. Archibald MacLeish. FoP

Old Men Pitching Horseshoes. X. J. Kennedy. AMV-81

Old men sleeping. The List. Michael McClure. NU

Old men sit on park benches. Perspective. Robert L. Vorpahl. AMV-80

Old Men Working Concrete. Phillip Hey. FiCP

Old Mill, Newton St. Cyres. Ken Smith. TwMBP

Old Miniatures. Leo Vroman. VWA

Old Miner's Refrain, The. Unknown. AmFP

Old Miser Named Quince, An. John Ciardi. TDH

Old Mr. Hardy, upright in his chair. At Max Gate. Siegfried Sassoon. NoAM

Old Mister Johnson had troubles of his own. The Cat Came Back. Harry S. Miller. FSW

Old Moke. Harold Littlebird. VoR

Old Molly Means was a hag and a witch. Molly Means. Margaret Walker. AmNP (1974 ed.); NMM; PoTa; SS

Old moon is tarnished. Sea Lullaby. Elinor Wylie. PBMP

Old moon my eyes are new moon with human footprint. Poem Rocket. Allen Ginsberg. CoPAm; VGW

Old Mother Goose, when. Mother Goose. MG

Old Mother Hubbard. The Comic Adventures of Old Mother Hubbard and Her Dog. Sarah Catherine Martin. MG; OxBChV

Old Mother turns blue and from us. Lorine Niedecker. RiTi

Old Movies. John Cotton. FF

Old Navy, The. Frederick Marryat. PoTa

Old Noah he built himself an ark. One More River to Cross. Unknown. FSW

Old Noah he had an ostrich farm and fowls. Wine and Water. G. K. Chesterton. FaBoCo

Old Nokomis Sings. Longfellow. Fr. The Song of Hiawatha. ECBV
("By the shores of Gitche Gumee.") CTV; SpRo

Old Nudists, The. Joan Colby. AMV-80

Old nursery chair; its legs, cut down, are broken. Robin Hyde. Fr. The Houses. ATNZ

Old Oaken Bucket, The. Samuel Woodworth. BLSo, with music FSW; PSoN, with music

Old ocean, lulled by thee. Deep Calleth unto Deep. Henry Nehemiah Dodge. RhR

Old, old/ To live on, wretched to behold. Owen Gruffydd, tr by Anthony Conran. Fr. The Men That Once Were. OBW

Old One and the Wind, The. Clarice Short. IHMS; MPA

Old Ones, The. R. E. Sebenthall. HeS

Old ones go to each other's funerals. The. Burials. Geoffrey Grigson. PoA

Old one's to the side. Psalm. Charles Simic. AmPA

Old [or Ould] Orange Flute, The. Unknown. FaBoBa; FSW; GBP; ILP (1975 ed.); WTO (At. to Nugent Bohen)

Old Ox, The. George Rostrevor Hamilton, after the Greek of Addaios of Makedon: FaBoEE

Old Pack, The. Unknown. APAS

Old Paint. Unknown. BPAW

Old Penobscot Indian, The. Flux. Richard Eberhart. CoPAm; VGW

Old Pensioner, The. W. B. Yeats. See Lamentation of the Old Pensioner, The.

Old People. Myra Cohn Livingston. CTBA

Old people are like birds. City Pigeons. Helen Chasin. WeW

Old People Speak of Death, The. Quincy Troupe. CNA

Old Person of Cromer, An. Edward Lear. TDH

Old Person of Tring, An. Unknown. TDH

Old Peter led a wretched life. The Perils of Invisibility. W. S. Gilbert. PoTA

Old Peter Prairie-Dog. Prairie-Dog Town. Mary Austin. BPAW

Old Photo in an Old Life, An. Daniel Hoffman. SoSe

Old Photograph, The. Dana Naone. PHC

Old photograph shows you, An. The Opposite Field. Dabney Stuart. PCho

Old Photographs. David Harsent. POL

Old piano was just a torso, The. The Human Firewood Piano. Doug Blazek. CPA

Old Pictures in Florence. Robert Browning. VLP

Old Pilot's Death, The. Donald Hall. MPo

Old Pines, The. Cid Corman. GP

Old Place, The. B. E. Baughan. ATNZ

Old Place, The. Hone Tuwhare. ATNZ

Old Plum tree blossom, one time I knew. Springtime. Drummond Hadley. FoP

Old Pluvius, month of rains, in peevish mood. Spleen LXXV. Baudelaire, tr. by Kenneth O. Hanson. NAWM-2

Old Polish Lesson, An. Deanna Louise Pickard. AMV-81

Old Poulter's Mare. Unknown. PeD

Old priest Peter Gilligan, The. The Ballad of Father Gilligan [or Father Gilligan]. W. B. Yeats. AIW; PAIC

Old Prison, The. Judith Wright. MAuV

Old professor of zoology, The. The Parrot. James Elroy Flecker. FaBoTw (1975 ed.)

Old Pro's Lament, The. Paul Petrie. LiSp; SPo; TAP

Old Provincial Council Buildings, Christchurch, The. Allen Curnow. ATNZ

Old Rattler. Unknown. FSW

Old Reilly (In Dem Long Hot Summer Days). Leadbelly (Huddie Ledbetter). FSW

Old Repair Man, The. Fenton Johnson. AmNP (1974 ed.); MiP

Old Roads. Eilean Ni Chilleanain. CIP

Old Roger. Unknown. RAE

Old Rosin the Beau. Unknown. BLSo, with music; FSW; PSoN, with music

Old rude church, The, with bare, bald tower, is here. Wordsworth's Grave. Sir William Watson. VLP

Old Rugged Cross, The, with music. George Bennard. AH; BLSH

Old Ruralities. Charles Tennyson Turner. VPC

Old rusty-belly thing will soon be gone. The Sappa Creek. Gary Snyder. NCSH

Old Santa Fe Trail, The. Richard Burton. BPAW

Old Scottish Cavalier, The. William Edmonstoune Aytoun. BTTM

Old sea dog on a sailor's log, An. The Powerful Eyes o' Jeremy Tait. Wallace Irwin. PoTa

Old Section Boss, The. Unknown. BPo

Old Settler's Song, The. Francis Henry. BPAW

Old Shellover. Walter de la Mare. LCL; OxBChV; PoPle

Old Shepherd's Prayer. Charlotte Mew. OxBTC; WPE

Old Ship of Zion. Unknown. FSW
(What Ship Is This? with music.) AH

Old Ship Riggers. H. A. Cody. RhR

Old Ships, The. James Elroy Flecker. PoPle

Old Ships. David Morton. CTV

Old Shoe, an old pot, an old skin, An. Autumn Sequence. Adrienne Rich. VGW

Old Sinner. Derek Bowman. MIS

Old Sir Robert Bolton had three sons. The Jovial Hunter of Bromsgrove. *Unknown.* PeBB

Old smiling woman, you have had all the lessons. Salt. Nicholas Flocos. SA

Old Smoky. *Unknown. See* On Top of Old Smoky.

Old Soldiers Home at Marshalltown, Iowa. Jim Barnes. AMV-80

Old Soldiers Never Die. *Unknown.* FSW

Old Song, The. G. K. Chesterton. FaBoTw (1975 ed.)

Old Song Ended, An. Dante Gabriel Rossetti. BoLoP; VPC

Old Song Re-sung, A. John Masefield. ECBV; RhR

Old South Boston Aquarium stands, The. For the Union Dead. Robert Lowell. CABA (1972 ed.); ExPo (1973 ed.); HAP; HeIP; InPS; NOBA; NoAM; PiAm; PPoe; PPP; PSN; STS; UnPo (1976 ed.)

Old Southern Critic Takes a Look at My Poems, An. Darrell Gray. AcAn

Old spoon, An. The Spoon. Charles Simic. NNaP

Old squaw, The. Indian Sky. Alfred Kreymborg. BPAW

Old Squire, The. Wilfrid Scawen Blunt. FaPoR

Old Stephen. Charles Tennyson Turner. VPC

Old stick of bitterness, you wanted. Lawrence Russ. *Fr.* Grandfather. TC

Old Stoic, The. Emily Brontë. FaPoR; NOBE

Old Stomping Grounds: The Half-Mile Track. Henry Taylor. *Fr.* Desperado. PoUp

Old Stone Cross, The. W. B. Yeats. PBMP

Old Stories, The. Gene Frumkin. AMV-80

Old stories of a Tyler sing. Tom Tiler; or, The Nurse. *Unknown.* APAS

Old Storm. David Phillips. NeAC

Old Story. Lance Henson. VoR

Old Story, An. Rena Lee. VWA

Old Story, The. Louis MacNeice. GBL

Old Story, An. E. A. Robinson. TH

Old Summerhouse, The. Walter de la Mare. CMoP (1970 ed.)

Old Susan. Walter de la Mare. CMoP (1970 ed.)

Old Sussex Road, The. Ian Serraillier. FPB

Old Swimmer, The. Christopher Morley. LiSp

Old Tailor, The. Walter de la Mare. ECBV

Old Tawny's mane is moth. The King. Douglas Livingstone. BoAnP

Old Tennis Player. Gwendolyn Brooks. LiSp

Old Testament, a bygone age, The. The Flood. Lev Mak, *tr. by* Neil Muhlberger *and* Marvin Misemer. VWA

Old Tiger and the God of the Water-Hole, The. Margaret Reynolds. MIS

Old Timbrook Blues. *Unknown.* BluL

Old-time Yanks, becoming poor, oppressed, The. Gone West. H. H. Lewis. SPT

Old Timers. Carl Sandburg. NoAM

Old Toby. Keith Wilson. MPA

Old Trail Town, Cody Wyoming. John Garmon. TAT

Old Trip by Dream Train, The. Brendan Galvin. PCho

Old troll, The. For a Young Woman Lying Alone in Bed. Randall Ackley. FoP

Old Trouper, The. Don Marquis. *Fr.* Archy and Mehitabel. FaBoCo

Old tumbril rolling with me till I die. Ode. X. J. Kennedy. PCho

Old Uncle Fred could squint along forty-foot beams. Four-square Gospel. Roderick Hartigh Jellema. AATT

Old Upright I Did Not Learn to Play, The. Nicholas Flocos. SA

Old Vicarage, Grantchester, The. Rupert Brooke. OxBTC

"I only know that you may lie," *sel.* PES

Old Walking Song, The. J. R. R. Tolkien. RFM

Old Walt. Langston Hughes. HeIP; PiAm

Old War-Dreams. Walt Whitman. WIF

Old Warrior Terror, The. Alice Walker. NVAP

Old watch, The: their. Vapor Trail Reflected in the Frog Pond. Galway Kinnell. SoS; VGW

Old West, the old time, The. Spanish Johnny. Willa Cather. BPAW

Old Wichet. *Unknown.* PoTa

(Old Farmer and His Young Wife, The.) GBP

Old Wife, The. Rolly Kent. AAN; FF

Old Wife and the Ghost, The. James Reeves. ECBV; IWK; RAE

Old Wife in High Spirits. "Hugh MacDiarmid." CMoP (1970 ed.); ExPo (1973 ed.); OxBTC

Old Wife's Tale, The. George Peele. *See* Old Wives' Tale, The.

Old Witherington. Dudley Randall. ConAP; NoAM

Old Wives' [*or* Wife's] Tale, The, *sels.* George Peele.

"Gently dip, but not too deep." InPS

(Song at the Well, The.) ExPo (1973 ed.)

Summer Song, A. NOBE

("When as the rye reach to the chin.") GBL

Voice from the Well, The. NOBE

Old Woman, The. Joseph Campbell. OxBTC; WIF

Old Woman. Elizabeth Jennings. BuTh

Old Woman, An. D. Gwenallt Jones, *tr. fr. Welsh by* H. Idris Bell. OBW

Old Woman. Linda Pastan. FiCP

Old Woman, An. Charles Henry Ross. OxBChV

Old Woman ("And she, being old, fed from a mashed plate"). Iain Crichton Smith. FaBoTw; MS; OxBTC; PSN

Old Woman ("Your thorned back"). Iain Crichton Smith. MS

Old Woman. *Unknown.* AmFP

Old woman/ in black shawl. Jarashow. Morty Sklar. BrS

Old woman across the way, The. The Whipping. Robert Hayden. GP; MiP; NCSH; POBA; SFF

Old Woman Awaiting the Greyhound Bus. Duane Niatum. CDW

Old woman, naked, An. Near the Old Slave Fort. Joseph Bruchac. FAF

Old Woman of Harrow. *Unknown.* FaBoNo

"Old woman, old woman, are you fond of carding?" Old Woman. *Unknown.* AmFP

"Old woman, old woman, shall we go shearing?" Mother Goose. ECBV

Old Woman on a Broom. *Unknown.* ECBV

Old Woman Remembers, An. Sterling A. Brown. CNA; PoBA

Old woman sits, The. Leasa Davis. CTBA

Old woman sits on a bench before the door and quarrels, The. Fawn's Foster-Mother. Robinson Jeffers. NoAM; NOBA

Old Woman Speaks of the Moon, An. Ruth Pitter. WPE

Old woman was sweeping her house, An. *Unknown.* MG

Old woman went to market and bought a pig, An. The Droll Tale of the Old Woman Who Bought a Pig. *Unknown.* BBL

Old Women, The. George Mackay Brown. MS

Old Women, The. Shirley G. Cochrane. PoUp

Old women all their lives, they're a mixture of whitelime and brine. Women at the Market. Angela Figueroa Aymerich, *tr. by* Hardie St. Martin. PBWP

Old women in this town never sleep. Cold Front. Peter Sharpe. AMV-80

Old Women Still Sing, The. Charles H. Rowell. CNA

Old World, New World. Harry Roskolenko. AMV-81

Old-World Thicket, An. Christina Rossetti. SBG

Old wound in my ass, The. Fabrication of Ancestors. Alan Dugan. NoAM

Old Year Now Away Is Fled, The, *with music.* Percy Dearmer. GSB

Old yellow stucco, The. Winter Nightfall. J. C. Squire. OxBTC

Old Yew, which graspest at the stones. In Memoriam, A. H. H., II. Tennyson. NOBE; UnPo (1976 ed.)

Old Young who sleeps by day by night. Night Duty. Kenneth Mackenzie. MAuV

Older ones have gone to school, The. The Dustbin Men. Gregory Harrison. FPB

Older poets are showing the new ones, The. The Night Shift at the Poetry Factory. James Magorian. EC

Older than the ancient Greeks. Pigeons. Marianne Moore. PoA

Oldest clock we have, The. The Clock. Patricia Beer. HeHu

Oldest of us burst into tears and cried, The. Tomb of an Ancestor. Allen Curnow. ATNZ

Ole Abe (God bless 'is ole soul!). Negro [*or* Black] Soldier's Civil War Chant. *Unknown.* BPo; TAP

Ole Aunt Dinah, she's jes lak me. Jack and Dinah Want Freedom. *Unknown.* BPo

Ole Olson. Five Minutes, Oleo. H. H. Lewis. SPT

Ole Sheep Dey Know de Road, De. *Unknown.* BPo

Oleanna. Pete Seeger, *after the Norwegian.* FSW

Olga Poems. Denise Levertov. NNaP

Oliphaunt. J. R. R. Tolkien. LCL

Olive, The. A. E. Housman. NoAM

Olive journeys. Journey round the World. Ingrid Jonker, *tr. by* Jack Cope *and* William Plomer. PBWP

Oliver Ames is a stalwart man. The Female of the Species Is Hardier than the Male. Phyllis McGinley. PPM

Oliver Wiggins. "Stanley Vestal." BPAW

Olympic torch. Legacy for a Beboppin Gentle Giant: DuBois. Antar S. K. Mberi. SES

Om. *Malay Oral Tradition, tr. by* R. O. Winstedt. WTO

Omalos. Rosanna Warren. AMV–80

Omen of Victory Mina Loy. InPK

Omie Wise. *Unknown.* FSW

Omnes gentes plaudite. A Last Drink. *Unknown.* OxBM

Omnia Somnia. Joshua Sylvester. FaBoEE

Omnipresence of the Deity, The, *sel.* Robert Montgomery. "Stupendous God! how shrinks our bounded sense." VLP

Omnivorous Bookworm, The. Oliver Herford. TDH

On a Bad Singer. Samuel Taylor Coleridge. *See* Swans Sing before They Die.

On a Bicycle, *sel.* Yevgeny Yevtushenko, *tr. fr. Russian by* Robin Milner-Gulland *and* Peter Levi. "Under the dawn I wake my two-wheel friend." SPo

On a Birthday. J. M. Synge. GBL

On a Bright and Summer's Morning. *Unknown.* AmFP

On a Cat, Ageing. Alexander Gray. MS

On a Catholic Childhood. Janet Campbell Hall. VoR

On a Celtic Mask by Henry Moore. Horace Gregory. PoA

On a Certain Alderman. John Cunningham, *after the Greek of* Simonides. FaBoEE

On a Certain Effeminate Peer. John Winstanley. FaBoEE

On a Certain Lady at Court Pope. ILP (1975 ed.); NOBE; PCOP; PoPle

On a Child Who Lived One Minute. X. J. Kennedy. HoPM (1975 ed.)

On a Clergyman's Horse Biting Him. *Unknown.* FaBoCo; FaBoEE; SoSe

On a clothesline hangs the moon. Room Poems. Eli Bachar, *tr. by* Jeremy Garber. VWA

On a Cock at Rochester. Sir Charles Sedley. FaBoEE; POL

On a cold night I came through the cold rain. J. V. Cunningham. HAP

On a Contentious Companion. John Hoskyns. FaBoEE

On a Country Road. Harley Elliott. NeAC

On a dark/ and lonely street. Witch? Sam Reavin. CaYB

On a dark and stormy night. The Wreck of the Royal Palm. *Unknown.* AmFP

On a dark stormy night, as the train rattled on. In the Baggage Coach Ahead. Gussie L. Davis. FSN

On a dark winter morning, I couldn't see. Unseen Horses. Joan Byers Grayston. PH

On a day in June. An Unripe Peach. Rebecca Fein. OSP

On a day long and wet we fall upon. Arriving. Daniel Halpern. HoPM (1975 ed.)

On a day of grief. Misdemeanor. Eve Triem. GP

On a day when smoke lies down in alleys. Looking Both Ways before Crossing. John Woods. ConAP; IPWM

On a Dead Child. Robert Bridges. CMoP (1970 ed.); EBEV; NoAM; NOBE

On a Dead Child. Richard Middleton. SoSe

On a Death in an Old People's Home. May Ivimy. PMW

On a Distant Prospect of an Absconding Bookmaker. G. Rostrevor Hamilton. FaBoCo

On a Distinguished Politician. J. E. Thorold Rogers. FaBoEE

On a Doctor of Divinity. Richard Porson. FaBoCo ("Here lies a Doctor of Divinity.") FaBoEE

On a Drawing by Flavio. Philip Levine. VWA

On a Dream. Keats. LoAs

On a Drop of Dew. Andrew Marvell. AnMo; BoReV; HAP; ILP (1975 ed.); MetP; NIL; PAIC

On a Dying Boy. William Bell. WIF

On a Favorite Cat Drowned in a Tub of Goldfishes. Thomas Gray. *See* Ode on the Death of a Favourite Cat . . .

On a fine Morning. Thomas Hardy. VLP

On a flat road runs the well-train'd runner. The Runner. Walt Whitman. InPS; LiSp; MiP; PPoD; SPo

On a Flimmering Floom You Shall Ride. Carl Sandburg. ECBV; OBAL

On a Fortification at Boston Begun by Women. Benjamin Thompson. GOA

On a Friend's Escape from Drowning off the Norfolk Coast. George Barker. MPo

On a Friend's Suicide. Michael Yots. AMV–81

On a General Election. Hilaire Belloc. FaBoCo; FaBoEE; NOBE; NOBL; OBSV; OxBTC

On a Gentleman Marrying His Cook. Colin Ellis. FaBoEE

On a Girdle. Edmund Waller. CABA (1972 ed.); FF; HeIP; InPK; SoSe

On a Great Hollow Tree. William Strode. SCP–2

On a green island in the Main Street traffic. Pro Patria. Constance Carrier. WPE

On a highly polished table. Portrait. Ryah Tumarkin Goodman. AAN

On a hill far away stood an old rugged cross. The Old Rugged Cross. George Bennard. BLSH

On a hill there grows a flower. A Pastoral of Phillis and Coridon. Nicholas Breton. PAIC

On a holy day when sails were blowing southward. The Straying Student. Austin Clarke. BIrV; CIP

On a Honey Bee. Philip Freneau. TAP

On a ladder, in an old checkered shirt. Washing Windows. Barry Spacks. NCSH

On a Leander Gem. Keats. MBPR

On a Little Boy's Endeavouring to Catch a Snake. Thomas Foxton. OxBChV

On a little piece of wood. Mr. and Mrs. Spikky Sparrow. Edward Lear. OxBChV

On a Lord. Samuel Taylor Coleridge. FaBoCo

On a lorry the centre of a gaping crowd. W. H. Auden. *Fr.* A Happy New Year. OBSV

On a Lover of Books. Geoffrey Grigson. FaBoEE

On a Magazine Sonnet. Russell Hillard Loines. OBAL

On a Man Run Over by an Omnibus. Henry Luttrell. FaBoEE

On a Mandrake. Thomas Heyrick. SCP-2

On a Melting Beauty. Margaret Cavendish, Duchess of Newcastle. SCP-2

On a mid-December day. Since. W. H. Auden. InPS

On a Monday I was arrested. It's Almost Done (On a Monday). *Unknown.* FSW

On a Monday morning early as my wandering steps did lead me. The Boys of Mullabaun [*or* Mullaghbawn]. *Unknown.* BIrV; GBP

On a morning such as this. Veteran. Lola Ridge. WPE

On a mountain of sugar-candy. Arno Holz. *Fr.* Phantasus. PChr

On a mule you find two feet behind. *Unknown.* CTV

On a New Duke. *Unknown.* FaBoEE

On a Night like This. Jody Bolz. PoUp

On a Noisy Polemic. Burns. FaBoEE

On a Nomination to the Legion of Honour. *Unknown.* FaBoEE

On a North British Devolutionary. Douglas Young. MS

On a Painted Woman. Shelley. FaBoCo

On a Painting by Patient B of the Independence State Hospital for the Insane. Donald Justice. ConAP

On a Parisian Boulevard. James Kenneth Stephen. NOBL

On a patrician evening in Ireland. The Woman of the House. Richard Murphy. IPM

On a Peacock. Thomas Heyrick. PB

On a Photo of Sgt. Ciardi a Year Later. John Ciardi. CoPAm

On a Picture by Michele da Verona, of Arion as a Boy Riding upon a Dolphin. Anne Ridler. PoA

On a Poet. Henry Parrot. FaBoEE

On a Political Prisoner. W. B. Yeats. OAEL-2

On a Portrait of a Deaf Man. John Betjeman. NoAM

On a Portrait of Wordsworth by B. R. Haydon. Elizabeth Barrett Browning. HeIP

On a Prize Crucifix by a Student Sculptor. Robert Logan. CAPP

On a Professional Couple in a Side-Show. Alan Dugan. GP

On a Puritan. Hilaire Belloc. FaBoEE

On a Quaker's Tankard. Walter Savage Landor. FaBoEE

On a Quiet Conscience. Charles I, King of England. PoPle

On a Rainy Night, *sel.* Harry Edward Mills. "My love tonight is far away." PeD

On a Rhine Steamer. James Kenneth Stephen. NOBL

On a Rose in December. Ebenezer Elliott. FaBoEE

On a Ruined House in a Romantic Country. Samuel Taylor Coleridge. *Fr.* Sonnets Attempted in the Manner of Contemporary Writers. Epi
(House That Jack Built, The.) AKE

On a Saturday afternoon in the football season. Laziness and Silence. Robert Bly. PPP

On a Seal. Plato, *tr. fr. Greek by* Thomas Stanley. FaBoEE

On a secluded corner of the beach. John Betjeman. *Fr.* Beside the Seaside. LP

On a Seven-Day Diary. Alan Dugan. OBAL

On a snug evening I shall watch her fingers. Piano after War. Gwendolyn Brooks. AmNP (1974 ed.)

On a Soldier Fallen in the Philippines. William Vaughn Moody. AmVN; LFH; NOBA

On a Soldier Killed in the Great War. R. Williams Parry, *tr. fr. Welsh by* H. Idris Bell. OBW

On a squeaking cart, they push the usual stuff. A Removal from Terry Street. Douglas Dunn. LP; POL

On a Squinting Poetess. Thomas Moore. FaBoCo

On a Squirrel Crossing the Road in Autumn, in New England. Richard Eberhart. HeIP; TH; VoPo; WIF

On a starred [*or* starr'd] night Prince Lucifer uprose. Lucifer in Starlight. George Meredith. CABA (1972 ed.); Epi; ExPo (1973 ed.); FF; HAP; ILP (1975 ed.); InPK; IPWM; LFH; NOBE; OAEL-2; OBP; PAIC; PBMP; PoIA; PPoe; SoSe; UnPo (1976 ed.); VLP; VPC; WeW

On a Statue of Sir Arthur Sullivan. G. Rostrevor Hamilton. FaBoCo

On a Statue of Venus. *Unknown.* LoAs

On a stiff morning I raise the greasy shade and see the magic. Aladdin's Lamp. Charles Cantrell. AAN

On a Stingy Beau. John Winstanley. FaBoEE

On a summer day in the month of May. The Big Rock Candy Mountains. *Unknown.* DuDr; NOBA

On a Summer's Day. Keats. *Fr.* I Stood Tiptoe upon a Little Hill. FSFS

On a summer's day when the wave was rippled. The Ship That Never Returned. Henry Clay Work. FSW

On a Sunday Afternoon, *with music.* Andrew B. Sterling. FSN

On a Sunday morn, sat a maid forlorn. Wait till the Sun Shines, Nellie. Andrew B. Sterling. BLSo; FSN; FSW

On a Sundial ("I am a sundial, and I make a botch"). Hilaire Belloc. FaBoEE; QQQ

On a Sundial ("Save on the rare occasion when the sun"). Hilaire Belloc. POL

On a sunny brae alone I lay. A Day Dream. Emily Brontë. VLP

On a Thunder Storm. Sir Walter Scott. PIM

On a time the amorous Silvy. The Awakening. *Unknown, tr. by* John Attey. GBL; NOBE

On a tree by a river a little tomtit. The Suicide's Grave. W. S. Gilbert. *Fr.* The Mikado. VLP

On a two-seated cultivator, we sniffed exhaust. Cultivating. Janet Kauffman. *Fr.* Tobacco. TC

On a Virtuous Young Gentlewoman That Died Suddenly. William Cartwright. HAP

On a Visit to Ch'ung Chen Taoist Temple. Yü Hsüan-chi, *tr. fr. Chinese by* Kenneth Rexroth *and* Ling Chung. PBWP

On a Vulgar Error. C. S. Lewis. OxBTC

On a Wednesday. Jody Aliesan. AMV-80

On a wet night, laden with books for luggage. The Poet on the Island. Richard Murphy. CIP

On a Whore. John Hoskyns. FaBoEE

On a Windy Day. Gene Frumkin. CoPAm

On a withered branch. Basho, *tr. fr. Japanese.* WeW

On Alexander and Aristotle, on a Black-on-Red Greek Plate. Alan Dugan. PPP

On alien ground I dwelt and also. The Dwelling. Moshe Dor, *tr. by* Dennis Johnson. VWA

On All Soul's Night. The Aunt. Patrick Galvin. IPM

On all the channels,/ Nothing but panels! Almost Any Evening. Phyllis McGinley. *Fr.* Speaking of Television. TH

On all the whole nacyon. Anathema of Cats. John Skelton. *Fr.* Phyllyp Sparowe. PCat

On an Aberdeen Favourite. *Unknown.* FaBoEE

On an Anniversary. J. M. Synge. FaBoEE; POL

On an autumn night, lying restless, far from her broken homeland. Yitzhak Lamdan, *tr. by* A. C. Jacobs. *Fr.* Massada. VWA

On an early winter night. The Great Bear. Dennis Maloney. BCr

On an Ecdysiast. John Ciardi. IP

On an Hour-Glass. John Hall. SCP-2

On an Indian Tomineios, the Least of Birds. Thomas Heyrick. SCP-2

On an Island, *abr.* "Ethna Carbery." WPE

On an Island. J. M. Synge. BIrV

On an oak in autumn. Survivor. Archibald MacLeish. NCSH

On Anothers Sorrow. Blake. *Fr.* Songs of Innocence. MBPR

On Apis the Prizefighter. Lucilius, *tr. fr. Latin by* Dudley Fitts. WeW

On Approaching My Birthday. Vassar Miller. CSP; IHMS; NMM

On Arrival. Richard Howard. TAP

On Arthur Hugh Clough. Swinburne. FaBoEE

On August nights. Driving By. Robert Wallace. LiSp

On Authors and Booksellers. Pope. FaBoEE

On beaches washed by seas. What She Said to Her Girl-Friend. Venmanipputi, *tr. by* A. K. Ramanujan. PBWP

On Being Asked for a War Poem W. B. Yeats. NIL; PFIr

On Being Brought from Africa to America. Phillis Wheatley. FF; GOA; HeIP; IPWM; NOBA; PiAm; SBG; TAP; WPE

On Being Late. Michael Small. DNGG

On Being Photographed. William H. Gass. AMV–81

On Ben Jonson. Robert Herrick. FaBoEE

On Bertrand Russell's "Portraits from Memory." Donald Davie. FaBoTw (1975 ed.)

On black bare trees a stale cream moon. Eau-Forte. F. S. Flint. OxBTC

On Botching. John Heywood. FaBoCo; FaBoEE

On Burroughs' Work. Allen Ginsberg. NoAM; NOBA

On Butler who can think without just rage. John Oldham. *Fr.* A Satire. OBSV

On Button the Grave-Maker. *Unknown.* FaBoEE

On Buying a Dog. Edgar Klauber. GDP

On Buying a Horse. *Unknown.* PH

On Calamy's Imprisonment and Wild's Poetry. *Unknown.* APAS

On Calvary Street are trellises. Ballad of Calvary Street. James K. Baxter. ATNZ

On Cardinal Wolsey. *Unknown.* FaBoCo

On Cementing Level the Stable Floor at the Old Manse. Forbes Macgregor. MIS

On Certain Days of the Year. Nancy Simpson. AMV–81

On Certain Ladies. Pope. FaBoCo
("When other ladies to the groves go down.") FaBoEE

On Charles II. Earl of Rochester. *See* Epitaph on Charles II.

On Children. Kahlil Gibran. *Fr.* The Prophet. SFF

On Chloris Walking in the Snow. William Strode. ILP (1975 ed.); OAEL–1; SCP–2
(Chloris in the Snow.) NOBE

On Christians, Mercy Will Fall. *Unknown, tr. fr. Welsh by* D. M. Lloyd. OBW

On Christmas Day I weep. Christmas Mourning. Vassar Miller. CoPAm

On Christmas Eve. W. S. Di Piero. AMV–81

On Christmas Eve we drove. Angels We Have Heard on High. R. T. Smith. AAN

On Christopher Wordsworth, Master of Trinity. Benjamin Hall Kennedy. FaBoCo; FaBoEE

On Christ's Birth (To Sisters). Jane Marie Luecke. AATT

On clear May evenings the old sheep. Lambs Frolicking Home. Fred Lape. BoAnP

On cold days/ it is easy to be reasonable. Becoming a Nun. Erica Jong. MMD

On Colley Cibber. Samuel Johnson. NIL

On coming to this sprawled and lazy city. How Night Falls in the Courtyard. Christine Rimmer. AMV–80

On coming up on deck Palm Sunday morning, oh. Sailing to Jerusalem. Alan Dugan. ILP (1975 ed.)

On Communists. Ebenezer Elliott. NOBL

On Corwen Road. Jay Ames. AMV–80

On Courtworm. Ben Jonson. SCP–1

On Critics. Matthew Prior. LFH, *wr. at. to* Swift
(In Imitation of Anacreon.) FaBoEE

On Cromek Blake. FaBoCo; PoPle

On dark days the clouds. Sarentino-South Tyrol. Philip Brantingham. AMV–80

On Death. Anne Killigrew. BoWoP

On Death. Walter Savage Landor. BBGO
("Death stands above me, whispering low.") NOBE

On Death and Love. Janet Campbell Hale. VoR

On Degree. Shakespeare. *Fr.* Troilus and Cressida, I, iii. ExPo (1973 ed.)
(Order and Degree.) NIL

On Dennis. Pope. FaBoEE

On Devenish Island. Frank Ormsby. CIP; IPM

On Dr. Evans Cutting Down a Row of Trees. *Unknown.* FaBoEE

On Dr. Isaac Letsome. *Unknown.* FaBoCo
(On Dr. Lettsom.) FaBoEE

On Dr. Keene, Bishop of Chester. Thomas Gray. FaBoEE

On Dr. Lettsom. *Unknown. See* On Dr. Isaac Letsome.

On Dr. Samuel Ogden. R. P. Arden. FaBoCo

On Don Surly. Ben Jonson. FaBoEE

On Donne's Poetry. Samuel Taylor Coleridge. CABA (1972 ed.); MBPR; OAEL–2; PAIC; PPoD

On Drawing-Room Amenities. Gelett Burgess. FaBoNo

On Dreams. Swift. BIrV

On Dressing to Go Hunting. *Unknown.* PH

On Drinking and a New Moon through the Window. Keith Wilson. GP

On Driving behind a School Bus for Mentally Retarded Children. Grace Butcher. RiTi

On dull mornings. Mrs. Busk. Sir Osbert Sitwell. OxBTC

On Dwelling. Robert Graves. CMoP (1970 ed.)

On ear and ear two noises too old to end. The Sea and the Skylark. Gerard Manley Hopkins. LFH

On Earth. Forugh Farrokhzad, *tr. fr. Persian by* Girdhard Tikku. BoWoP

On Earth There Is a Lamb So Small, *with music.* Nicolaus L. Zinsendorf, *tr. fr. German by* Sheema Z. Buehne. AH

On Easter Day. Celia Laighton Thaxter. CTV

On Easter morn. Easter. Hilda Conkling. CC

On Edges. Adrienne Rich. Psy

On Edmund Burke. Goldsmith. *Fr.* Retaliation. PMW
("Here lies our good Edmund, whose genius was such.") FaBoEE

On either side the river lie. The Lady of Shalott. Tennyson. NOBE; PCOP; OAEL–2; VLP

On Elizabeth Ireland. *Unknown.* FaBoEE

On Elphinston's Translation of Martial. Burns. FaBoCo
("O thou, whom Poesy abhors.") FaBoEE

On Enclosures. *Unknown. See* On Inclosures.

On eves of cold, when slow coal fires. Town Owl. Laurie Lee. PB

On Evolution. John Ciardi. OBAL

On eyes embarked for sleep the only light. For Ellen. Richard Wilbur. RRA

On fair Augusta's towers and trees. A Tale of Drury Lane. Horace Smith. FaBoCo

On Falling Asleep by Firelight. William Meredith. NoAM

On Fame ("Fame, like a wayward girl, will still be coy"). Keats. CABA (1972 ed.); MBPR; TT

On Fame ("How fever'd is the man, who cannot look"). Keats. MBPR; NIL

On Finding the Meaning of "Radiance." Alan Dugan. PAIC

On First Knowing God. Reed Whittemore. *Fr.* The Seven Days. GP

On First Looking in on Blodgett's Keats's "Chapman's Homer." George Starbuck. NIL; OBAL

On First Looking into Chapman's Homer. Keats. AnMo; BiP; CABA (1972 ed.); ExPo (1973 ed); FaPo; FF; HAP; HeIP; HoPM (1975 ed.); ILP (1975 ed.); InPK; IP; LFH; MBPR; NIL; NOBE; OAEL-2; OBP; PAIC; PoIA; PPoD; PPoe; PPP; SoSe; STS; TT; WIF

On Flower Wreath Hill, *sels.* Kenneth Rexroth.
 "Aging pilgrim on a, An," GP
 "Clustered in the forest around." GP
 "Mist drenched, moonlit, the sculpture." GP

On Flunking a Nice Boy out of School. John Ciardi. NowV; SFF

On Flying into Washington over the Pentagon. Alan Austin. PoUp

On Forelands High in Heaven. A. E. Housman. InPS

On Fortune. Elizabeth I, Queen of England. PBWP; WPE

On Friendship, *sel.* William Cowper
 "Man that hails you Tom or Jack, The." POL

On Galtymore. Joan Keefe. IPM

On gay Anacreon's joy-inspiring line. On the Translation of Anacreon. Horace Walpole. FaBoEE

On Gay Wallpaper. William Carlos Williams. TAP

On getting a card. Poem. William Carlos Williams. VGW

On Getting a Natural. Dudley Randall. FB; PoBA

On Giles and Joan. Ben Jonson. NOBL

On Giving a Son to the Sea. James Dickey. TCP

On glossy wires artistically bent. Waspish. Robert Frost. BoAnP

On goes the age with footsteps fleet and strong. An Evening in Harvest Time. Charles Tennyson Turner. VPC

On Grey Cliffs. Walter Savage Landor. VLP

On Growing Old. John Masefield. CMoP (1970 ed.)
 ("Be with me, Beauty, for the fire is dying.") PPM

On Gustavus Adolphus, King of Sweden. Sir Thomas Roe. FaBoEE

On Gut. Ben Jonson. SCP-1

On gypsum slabs of preternatural whiteness. Animal, Vegetable and Mineral. Louise Bogan. SBG

On Haiti two years ago he stalled. A Late Movie. William Matthews. PCho

On Halloween. Shel Silverstein. IWK

On Halloween, what bothers some. Witch's Broom Notes. David McCord. IWK

On Hardscrabble Mountain. Galway Kinnell. RFM

On Harting Down. T. Sturge Moore. OxBTC

On Having Piles. Sir Walter Scott. FaBoEE

On Hearing a Beautiful Young Woman Describe Her Class in Physical Anthropology. A. J. Hovde. AMV-81

On Hearing a Symphony of Beethoven. Edna St. Vincent Millay. VoPo

On Hearing of the Death of Bernard Strempek. Robert Huff. CNW

On Hearing That the Students of Our New University Have Joined the Agitation against Immoral Literature. W. B. Yeats. NoAM

On Hearing the Airlines Will Use a Psychological Profile to Catch Potential Skyjackers. Stephen Dunn. AmPA; SoSe (1977 ed.)

On Hearing the Marsh Bird's Water Cry. Duane Niatum. CDW

On Hellespont, guilty [*or* guiltie] of true love's blood. Hero and Leander. Christopher Marlowe. AAS; CABA (1972 ed.); OAEL-1

On her beautiful face there are smiles of grace. A Pretty Girl. J. Gordon Coogler. OBAL

On Her Brother. Al-Khansa, *tr. fr. Arabic by* Willis Barnstone. BoWoP

On Her Brother Sakhr. Al-Khansa, *tr. fr. Arabic by* Willis Barnstone. BoWoP

On Her Dancing. James Shirley. PoPle

On Her Loving Two Equally. Aphra Behn. SBG

On her side, reclining on her elbow. So-and-so Reclining on Her Couch. Wallace Stevens. NOBA

On Himself ("Born I was to meet with age"). Robert Herrick. FaBoEE

On Himself ("Here down my wearied limbs I'll lay"). Robert Herrick. CaPo

On Himself ("I fear no earthly powers"). Robert Herrick. CaPo

On Himself ("I will no longer kiss"). Robert Herrick. CaPo

On Himself ("I'll write no more of love, but now repent"). Robert Herrick. CaPo

On Himself ("Let me not live, if I not love"). Robert Herrick. CaPo

On Himself ("Weep for the dead, for they have lost this light"). Robert Herrick. FaBoEE

On Himself ("The work is done. Young men and maidens, set"). Robert Herrick. CaPo

On Himself. Walter Savage Landor. FaBoEE

On Himself. William Oldys. FaBoEE

On Himself. Matthew Prior. FaBoEE

On Himself. Dante Gabriel Rossetti. FaBoEE

On Himself. Swift. PFIr

On Himself, upon Hearing What Was His Sentence. James Graham, Marquis of Montrose. SCP-2
 (Verses Composed on the Eve of His Execution.) FaBoEE

On his airy perch among the branches. The Fox and the Crow. La Fontaine, *tr. by* Marianne Moore. NAWM-2; OBVE; PPP

On His Blindness. Milton. BoReV; Epi; FaPoR; HAP; HeIP; InPS; IP; IPWM; NOBE; PBMP; PIM; PPM; PPoe; SoSe; TPo; WIF
 (Sonnet: "When I consider how my light is spent.") AnMo; EBEV; LFH; OAEL-1; SCP-1
 (When I Consider How My Light Is Spent.) BiP; CABA (1972 ed.); ExPo (1973 ed.); FF; ILP (1975 ed.); InPK; MAT; NIL; OBP; PAIC; PoIA; PPoD; PPP

On His Books. Hilaire Belloc. FaBoCo; FaBoEE; PoIA; WeW

On His Dead Wife. Milton. *See* On His Deceased Wife.

On his deathbed my Grandfather. Gooseberries. Peter Wild. GP

On his deathbed poor Lubin lies. A Reasonable Affliction. Matthew Prior. PoIA

On His Deceased Wife. Milton. Epi; ExPo (1973 ed.); LoAs; PoPle
 ("Methought I saw my late espoused saint.") BoLoP; CABA (1972 ed.); ILP (1975 ed.); OBP; PoIA; PPP
 (On His Dead Wife.) GBL; HAP; NOBE
 (Sonnet: "Methought I saw my late espoused saint.") EBEV; LFH; OAEL-1; SCP-1

On His Marks. Richard Armour. PPM

On His Mistress [*or* Mistris]. John Donne. Elegies, XVI. BoLoP; EBEV; OBP
 (Elegy on His Mistress.) GBL
 (To His Mistress Desiring to Travel with Him as His Page.) NOBE

On His Mistress Looking in a Glass. Thomas Carew. CaPo

On His Mistress, [*or* Mistris], the Queen of Bohemia. Sir Henry Wotton. GBL; HAP; MetP
 (Elizabeth of Bohemia.) BoLoP; NOBE; PoPle

On His Own Deafness. Swift. AnMo; BIrV; FaBoEE

On His Queerness. Christopher Isherwood. OxBTC

On His Seventy-fifth Birthday.  Walter Savage Landor.  *Fr.* The Last Fruit off an Old Tree.  EBEV; OAEL-2; PBMP; SoSe (1977 ed.)
(Dying Speech of an Old Philosopher.)  FaBoEE; HeIP; VLP ("I strove with none, for none was worth my strife.")  FaPoR; NOBE; PCOP

On Holmbury Hill.  Edward Shanks.  PES

On Hope by Way of Question and Answer between Abraham Cowley and Richard Crashaw.  Abraham Cowley *and* Richard Crashaw.  NOBE

On Hot Days.  James Reiss.  AmPA

On hot September nights, when sleep is scarce.  My Father Dreams of Baseball.  Laurence Lieberman.  LiSp; SPo

On hot summer mornings my aunt set glasses.  Water.  Leslie Norris.  HeHu; OBW

On humming rubber along this white concrete.  Driving in Oklahoma.  Carter Revard.  VoR

On Hurricane Jackson.  Alan Dugan.  LiSp; MiP; NCSH; NowV; POL; PPoD; SPo

On Inclosures.  *Unknown.*  FaBoCo
(On Enclosures.)  FaBoEE

On Inhabiting an Orange.  Josephine Miles.  NoAM; PoA

On Its Way.  May Swenson.  WPE

On J. M. S. Gent.  Pope.  FaBoEE

On Jacob Tonson, His Publisher.  Dryden.  FaBoEE; OBSV

On James Grieve, Laird of Boghead, Tarbolton.  Burns.  NIL

On Jocky Bell.  *Unknown.*  FaBoEE

On John So.  *Unknown.*  FaBoEE

On Jordan's stormy banks I stand.  The Promised Land.  Samuel Stennett.  AmFP

On Keats.  Shelley.  FaBoEE; MBPR

On Kennack Sands the sun.  Kennack Sands.  Laurence Binyon.  EcS

On King Richard the Third, Who Lies Buried under Leicester Bridge.  Sir John Suckling.  CaPo

On Lady Anne Hamilton.  Sheridan.  FaBoEE

On Lady Poltagrue, a Public Peril.  Hilaire Belloc.  FaBoCo; POL

On Lake Michigan—1972.  John Matthias.  HeS

On Late-acquired Wealth.  *Unknown, tr. fr. Greek by* William Cowper.  OBVE

On Leander's Swimming over the Hellespont to Hero.  Thomas Warton the Younger, *after the Latin of* Martial.  FaBoEE

On Leaping over the Moon.  Thomas Traherne.  Moon

On Learning to Play the Guitar.  Ray Fraser.  NeAC

On Leaving.  Gertrudis Gomez de Avellaneda, *tr. fr. Spanish by* Frederick Sweet.  PBWP

On Leaving Baltimore.  Duane Niatum.  CDW

On Leaving California.  Bayard Taylor.  AmVN

On Leaving London for Wales.  Shelley.  MBPR

On Leaving Newstead Abbey.  Byron.  MBPR

On Leaving Prison.  Luis de Leon, *tr. fr. Spanish.*  ILwL

On Leslie Moore.  *Unknown.*  CTV

On Lieutenant Shift.  Ben Jonson.  OBSV

On Linden Street.  Shelley Ehrlich.  AMV-80

On Linden, when the sun was low.  Hohenlinden [*or* The Battle of Hohenlinden].  Thomas Campbell.  BTTM; FaPoR; NOBE

On Listening to a Death-of-God Theologian Lecture in the Chapel.  Elmer F. Suderman.  AATT

On Listening to the Spirituals.  Lance Jeffers.  PoBA

On Living Too Long.  Walter Savage Landor.  PAIC

On Living with Children for a Prolonged Time.  Mark Lowey.  AMV-81

On London fell a clearer light.  Summer in England, 1914.  Alice Meynell.  SBG; WPE

On longer evenings.  Coming.  Philip Larkin.  OxBTC; PSN

On Looking at a Copy of Alice Meynell's Poems.  Amy Lowell.  SBG

On Looking into the Spilled Ink on the Porcelain.  Wayne Andrews.  PHC

On Looking Up by Chance at the Constellations.  Robert Frost.  CMoP (1970 ed.)

On Lord Chesterfield and His Son.  *Unknown.*  FaBoCo

On Lord Galloway.  Burns.  FaBoEE

On Lord Holland's Seat near Margate, Kent.  Thomas Gray.  CABA (1972 ed.); LAuP; OAEL-1

On love's worst ugly day.  First Meditation.  Theodore Roethke.  *Fr.* Meditations of an Old Woman.  NOBA

On Lucy, Countess of Bedford.  Ben Jonson.  ILP (1975 ed.)

On man, on nature, and on human life.  Wordsworth.  *Fr.* The Recluse.  OAEL-2; PoIA

On Marriage.  Richard Crashaw.  FaBoEE

On Marriage.  Thomas Flatman.  NOBL

On Mary Magdalene.  William Drummond of Hawthornden.  OAEL-1

On Meeting a Gentlewoman in the Dark.  *Unknown.*  FaBoEE

On Mike O'Day.  *Unknown.*  FaBoEE
("This is the grave of Mike O'Day.")  IP

On Minding One's Own Business.  James Wright.  CoPAm

On miserable Nearchos' bones lie lightly, earth.  Last Lines.  X. J. Kennedy.  OBAL

On Miss Eleanor Ambrose, a Celebrated Beauty in Dublin.  Earl of Chesterfield.  FaBoEE

On Mr. Edward Howard, upon His British Princes.  Charles Sackville.  OBSV

On Mr. Milton's Paradise Lost.  Andrew Marvell.  TT

On Mr. Nash's Picture at Full Length.  Jane Brereton.  WPE

On Mr. Pitt's Hair-Powder Tax.  Burns.  FaBoEE

On Mr. Pricke.  *Unknown.*  FaBoEE

On Mrs. E. Montague's Blushing in the Cross-bath.  Thomas Flatman.  SCP-2

On Monday, when the sun is hot.  Lines Written by a Bear of Very Little Brain.  A. A. Milne.  FaBoNo

On Monsieur's Departure.  Elizabeth I, Queen of England.  WPE

On moonlit heath and lonesome bank.  A. E. Housman.  CMoP (1970 ed.); SoSe; STS

On moony nights the dogs bark shrill.  Night Song.  Frances Cornford.  GDP

On Mundane Acquaintances.  Hilaire Belloc.  FaBoEE; OxBTC

On my desk lies a photo.  Surfer and Others.  Sonya Dorman.  SPo

On My 18th Birthday.  John William Corrington.  CoPAm

On My First Daughter.  Ben Jonson.  EBEV; FaBoEE; HoPM (1975 ed.); NOBE; RRA

On My First Son [*or* Sonne].  Ben Jonson.  CABA (1972 ed.); EBEV; FaBoEE; FF; HAP; HeIP; HoPM (1975 ed.); IPWM; LoAs; NIL; OAEL-1; OBP; PAIC; PBMP; PoIA; PPoe; SCP-1; VoPo
(On My Son.)  NOBE

On My Grandchild Simon Bradstreet.  Anne Bradstreet.  EAP

On My Joyful Departure.  Samuel Taylor Coleridge.  FaBoCo

On my knees.  In the Garden.  Tom Schmidt.  NeAC

On My Son.  Ben Jonson.  *See* On My First Son.

On My Stand.  Sharon Scott.  JB

On My Thirty-third Birthday.  Byron.  BBGO; FaBoEE

On My 26th Birthday.  Barry Schechter.  FiCh

On My Wandering Flute.  Abraham Sutskever, *tr. fr. Yiddish by* Ruth Whitman.  VWA

On my way home from school.  The Testing-Tree.  Stanley Kunitz.  MAT; UnPo (1976 ed.)

On My Way to Boston Need Five Bucks.  Jack Micheline.  CPA

On my way to Mass. The Lass from Bally-na-Lee. Anthony Raftery, *tr. by* Desmond O'Grady. BIrV

On my windowsill. New York Bird. Andrei Voznesensky, *tr. by* William Jay Smith. NYP

On Myself. Edith Bone. FaBoEE

On Myselfe. Countess of Winchilsea. SBG

On New Year's Eve. Ts'uei T'u, *tr. fr. Chinese by* Witter Bynner. OFD

On News. Thomas Traherne. *See* News.

On Nicknames. Louis Phillips. OSF

On nights when hail/ falls noisily. Izumi Shikibu, *tr. fr. Japanese by* Willis Barnstone. BoWoP

On Noman, a Guest. Hilaire Belloc. FaBoEE

On November 2nd 1965. Norman Morrison. Adrian Mitchell. FF; NowV

On ochre walls in ice-formed caves shaggy Neanderthals. To My Son Parker, Asleep in the Next Room. Bob Kaufman. PoBA; VGW

On old slashed spruce boughs. On Hardscrabble Mountain. Galway Kinnell. RFM

On Oliver Goldsmith. David Garrick. FaBoEE

On, on the vessel steals. Charles Stuart Calverley. *Fr.* Dover to Munich. NOBL

On One Condition. Charles Madge. EAS

On one fixed point all nature moves. On the Uniformity and Perfection of Nature. Philip Freneau. EAP; ILP (1975 ed.); IPWM

On one of my long walks. Louis Zukofsky. UsP

On one of the steep slopes. City. Roy Fisher. TwMBP

On one of those days with the Legion. A Day with the Foreign Legion. Reed Whittemore. ConAP

On one summer [*or* summer's] day, sun was shining fine. Bill Bailey, Won't You Please Come Home. Hughie Cannon. BLSo; FSN; OBAL

On One That Lived Ingloriously. John Hoskyns, *after the Greek of* Simonides. FaBoEE

On Our Crucified Lord, Naked and Bloody. Richard Crashaw. CABA (1972 ed.); HoPM (1975 ed.); OAEL-1; SCP-1 (Upon the Body of Our Blessèd Lord, Naked and Bloody.) ILP (1975 ed.)

On parent knees, a naked new-born child. Epigram. Sir William Jones, *after* Kalidasa. FaBoEE; PoPle

On Paunch, a Parasite. Hilaire Belloc. POL

On pavements wet with the misty wind of spring. Anchorage in Time (I). Stanley Burnshaw. SPT

On payday, after the rent. After the Rent. Ed Cox. PoUp

On Peace. Keats. MBPR

On Peter Robinson. Francis Jeffrey. FaBoCo; FaBoEE

On Philosophy. Jonas Goldstein. AMV-81

On pianos and organs she lbs. The Musical Maiden. *Unknown.* TDH

On Poet Ninny. Earl of Rochester. APAS

On Poetry: A Rhapsody. Swift. OBSV
*Sels.*
"All human race would fain be wits." HAP
"Hobbes clearly proves that every creature." HAP

On Poets. Pope. FaBoEE

On Prince Frederick. *Unknown.* FaBoCo; FaBoEE; NOBL

On Pure Sudden Days like Innocence. Richard Brautigan. MIT

On Queen Caroline. *Unknown.* FaBoEE

On Rachmaninoff's Birthday. Frank O'Hara. CAPP

On rainy days alone I dine. On Himself. Swift. PFIr

On Rape Unattempted. Alan Dugan. NoAM

On Reading Aloud My Early Poems. John Williams. WeW

On Reading Another Poet. Elizabeth Brewster. MMD

On Reading: Four Limericks. Myra Cohn Livingston. TDH

On Reading Lao-tzu. William J. Higginson. AAN

On Reading Mr. Ytche Bashes' Stories in Yiddish. Lester Ehrlichman. AMV-80

On Reading Poems to a Senior Class at South High. D. C. Berry. SoSe

On Rears. Mary Hedin. PH

On Receiving a Curious Shell, and a Copy of Verses. Keats. MBPR

On Receiving a Laurel Crown from Leigh Hunt. Keats. MBPR

On Recrossing the Rocky Mountains after Many Years. John Charles Frémont. BPAW

On Refusal of Aid between Nations. Dante Gabriel Rossetti. EBEV; VLP

On Resignation. Thomas Chatterton. PIM

On Restoring Verticals. Sandra Ruth Duguid. AATT

On Returning to Teach. Marvin Bell. NowV

On Richard Hind. *Unknown.* FaBoCo
("Here lies the body of Richard Hind.") FaBoEE

On Richmond Hill there lives a lass. The Lass of Richmond Hill. Leonard McNally. BLSo

On Riding to See Dean Swift in the Mist of the Morning. Alexander Pope *and* Thomas Parnell. FaBoEE

On Robert Buchanan, Who Attacked Him under the Pseudonym of "Thomas Maitland." Dante Gabriel Rossetti. FaBoEE

On Roofs of Terry Street. Douglas Dunn. OxBTC

On Rÿneveld, an Uppopular Dutch Judge. *Unknown.* FaBoEE

On St. James's Park as Lately Improved by His Majesty. Edmund Waller. NIL
"Of the first paradise there's nothing found," *sel.* SCP-2

On St. Martin's evening green. Nuns at Eve. John Malcolm Brinnin. PPoD

On Saint-Urbain Street. Milton Acorn. NeAC

On sale everywhere: Spicer's Instant Poetry. Spicer's Instant Poetry. James Reeves. MPo

On Sannazar's Being Honoured, *sel.* Richard Lovelace.
"There is not in my mind one sullen fate." SCP-2

On Saturday on Saturday. Saturday in New York. Anne Beresford. MPo

On Scott's "The Field of Waterloo." Thomas, Lord Erskine. FaBoCo

On Seeing a Hair of Lucretia Borgia. Walter Savage Landor. CABA (1972 ed.); HAP; InPK

On Seeing a Stamp from the Democratic Republic of Vietnam. Leslie Woolf Hedley. NowV

On Seeing a Torn Out Coin Telephone. Martin Robbins. MAT

On Seeing Films of the War. Louis Coxe. PPoD

On Seeing Francis Jeffrey Riding on a Donkey. *At. to* Sydney Smith. FaBoEE

On Seeing the Elgin Marbles [for the First Time]. Keats. CABA (1972 ed.); ILP (1975 ed.): MBPR; NIL; PAIC; STS

On Seeing the Field Being Singed. Lady Ise, *tr. fr. Japanese by* Etsuko Terasaki *and* Irma Brandeis. BoWoP

On Seeing Two Brown Boys in a Catholic Church. Frank Horne. PoBA

On Seeing Weather-beaten Trees. Adelaide Crapsey. SoSe (1977 ed.)

On shadowy back porches. Old Folks Home. Tom Hennen. HeS

On Shakespeare. Milton. ILP (1975 ed.)
(Epitaph on the Admirable Dramatic Poet, W. Shakespeare, An.) FaBoEE

On shallow straw, in shadeless glass. Take One Home for the Kiddies. Philip Larkin. OxBTC

On Shiloh's dark and bloody ground. The Drummer Boy of Shiloh. *Unknown.* AmFP

On Sight of a Gentlewoman's Face in the Water. Thomas Carew. CaPo

On Sight of Some Martyrs' Sepulchres. Nahum Tate. SCP-2

On Sir John Calf. *Unknown.* FaBoEE

On Sir John Fenwick. Henry Hall. APAS

On Sir John Hill, M.D., Playwright. David Garrick. FaBoCo ("For physic and farces.") FaBoEE

On Sir John Vanbrugh, Architect. Abel Evans. FaBoCo; FaBoEE

On Sir Nathaniel Wraxall the Historian. George Colman the Younger. FaBoEE

On Sir Voluptuous Beast. Ben Jonson. SCP-1

On Sitting Down to Read King Lear Once Again. Keats. EBEV; MBPR

On Sitting Up Late, Watching Kittens. Eric W. Paff. AMV-81

On sloping, shattered granite, the snake man. Snake Hunt. David Wagoner. GP

On small donkeys they bring in suns. Melons. Moshe Yungman, *tr. by* Gabriel Preil *and* Howard Schwartz. VWA

On soft puff of satin he now lies. Cat of Many Years. Gertrude May Lutz. AMV-80

On Solomon Pavy, a Child of Queen Elizabeth's Chapel. Ben Jonson. *See* Epitaph on S.P., a Child of . . .

On some island I long to be. Saint Columcille, *tr. fr. Irish by* John Montague. BIrV

On some mad magnificent mornings. Tidying Up. Nancy Weber. AMV-80

On Some Shells Found Inland. Trumbull Stickney. EcS

On Some South African Novelists. Roy Campbell. FaBoCo; FaBoEE; InPK; NOBL; OxBTC

On some Vermont road. Mating the Goats. Aliki Barnstone. AMV-81; BoWoP

On Something That Walks Somewhere. Ben Jonson. SCP-1

On Springfield Mountain[s] there did dwell. Springfield Mountain. *Unknown.* AIW; AmFP; BLSo; FSW

On Squire Neale's Projects. *Unknown.* APAS

On starry heights. The Conflict of Convictions. Herman Melville. NOBA

On Startling Some Pigeons. Charles Tennyson Turner. PB

On Stella's Birthday ("Stella this day is thirty-four"). Swift. InPK; NIL; OAEL-1 (Stella's Birthday.) SoSe

On still days when country telephone. Trouble-shooting. William Stafford. AMV-80

On Such a Windy Afternoon. Theodore Enslin. AMV-80

On Sunday Afternoons. Sunday Afternoons. Anthony Thwaite. OxBTC

On Sunday, the Beginning of the Week, I Make a Religion. Albert Goldbarth. NVAP

On Sunday, when she visits him, she must come prepared. Erev Shabbos. Marc Kaminsky. VWA

On Sundays I ran my mare past. Sketch from Loss of Memory. Sonya Dorman. SoS

On sunny summer Sunday afternoon in Harlem. Passing. Langston Hughes. ILP (1975 ed.)

On Sweet Killen Hill. Tom MacIntyre. CIP; NCSH

On T. Moore's Poems. *Unknown.* FaBoCo

On Teaching David to Shoot. Walter McDonald. AMV-80

On Teaching the Young. Yvor Winters. NoAM; NOBA

On that slope. An Autumn Day. Sorley MacLean. AMV-81

On that vacant day. One-Eye. W. S. Merwin. ILP (1975 ed.)

On the/ dashboard. September Butterfly. Mollie Boring. AMV-80

On the Acequia Madre. Alice Corbin. WPW

On the Amazon. C. Gray *and* G. Newman. UsP

On the Apparition of Oneself. William Burford. PoA

On the Astrologer and Almanac Maker, John Partridge. Swift. FaBoEE

On the athletic field. A Day of Notes (That Fit into the Puzzle of a Poem). J. Charles Green. DNGG

On the Author of the *Treatise of Human Nature.* James Hay Beattie. FaBoCo

On the avenue the faces change each day. Hope. F. D. Reeve. PoA

On the back of the toilet at my doctor's. Smells. Ronald Koertge. PoW

On the back porch. The Passport. Luis Garcia. MIT

On the Balcony. D. H. Lawrence. GBL (Illicit.) PoA

On the Banks of Salee. *Unknown.* AmFP

On the Banks of the Little Eau Pleine. *Unknown.* AmFP

On the banks of the Potomac there's an army so grand. The Red, White and Red. *Unknown.* AmFP

On the Banks of the Wabash, Far Away. Paul Dresser. BLSH, *with music;* BLSo, *with music;* FSN, *with music;* FSW

On the Baptized Ethiopian. Richard Crashaw. PeD (On the Baptized Aethiopian.) FaBoEE

On the bare veld where nothing ever grows. A Veld Eclogue: The Pioneers. Roy Campbell. OBSV

On the Beach. Frances Cornford. BoAnP

On the Beach. Anthony Ostroff. MPA

On the Beach. Arthur Symons. At Dieppe, II. VLP

On the beach among the sunbathers. Practicing My Death. Barry Schechter. FiCh

On the Beach at Fontana. James Joyce. PoA; SoSe

On the Beach at Night. Walt Whitman. InPS; NOBA

On the Beach at Night Alone. Walt Whitman. TAP

On the beach where we had been idly. Gracious Goodness. Marge Piercy. BoAnP

On the beryl-rimmed rebecs of Ruby. Lily Adair. Thomas Holley Chivers. OBAL

On the Bible. William Strode. SCP-2

On the Birth of Good and Evil during the Long Winter of '28. Philip Levine. PoW

On the Birth of His Son. Su Tung-po, *tr fr. Chinese by* Arthur Waley. BuTh; OBVE; OFD

On the Birth of My Son, Malcolm Coltrane. Julius Lester. PoBA

On the Blessed Virgin's Bashfulness. Richard Crashaw. HAP; ILP (1975 ed.)

On the blue corner's top rope. Ripper Collins' Legacy. Don Johnson. LiSp

On the blue plains in wintry days. Native Companions Dancing. John Shaw Neilson. GAS

On the bog road the blackthorn flowers, the turf-stacks. Anthony Cronin. *Fr.* R.M.S. *Titanic.* BIrV

On the Border of Impossibility. Laura Beausoleil. NPW

On the boulder a lizard. Recognition. Georgette Perry. AMV-80

On the bridge at Avignon. Sur le Pont d'Avignon (On the Bridge at Avignon). *Tr. fr. French.* FSW

On the Bright Side. Carter Revard. VoR

On the Building of a New Church. *Unknown.* FaBoEE

On the Candidates for the Laurel. Pope. FaBoEE

On the Capture and Imprisonment of Crazy Snake, January, 1900. Alexander L. Posey. BPAW

On the chalk cliff edge struggles the final field. The Marginal Field. Stephen Spender. PoA

On the Circuit. W. H. Auden. NOBL; OxBTC

On the Circumcision: For the King's Music. William Cartwright. SCP-2

On the Clerk of a Country Parish. William Shenstone. FaBoEE

On the Cliffs. Swinburne. VLP

On the Closing of Millom Ironworks. Norman Nicholson. FaBoTw (1975 ed.)

On the coast of Chile where Neruda lived. The General Song of Humanity. Lawrence Ferlinghetti. CPA

On the coast of Coromandel. The Courtship of the Yonghy-Bonghy-Bo. Edward Lear. FaBoNo; OAEL-2

On the Collar of a Dog Presented by Mr. Pope to the Prince of Wales. Pope. See Epigram Engraved on the Collar of a Dog Given to His Royal Highness.

On the Collar of Mrs. Dingley's Lap-Dog. Swift. FaBoEE

On the College Archery Range. Robert Wallace. LiSp

On the Completion of the Pacific Telegraph. Jones Very. ILP (1975 ed.); TAP

On the cool porch of "Wannamasset." Vignette: 1922. Lawrence P. Spingarn. AMV-81

On the corner—116th and Lenox. Harlem Freeze Frame. Lebert Bethune. PoBA

On the corner where s. klien's used to be. 14th St/New York. Patricia Jones. NYP

On the Countess of Dorchester. Charles Sackville. APAS

On the Countess Dowager of Pembroke. William Browne. CABA (1972 ed.); HAP; ILP (1975 ed.); OBP; WeW (Epitaph on the Countess Dowager of Pembroke.) FaBoEE; NOBE (On the Death of Marie [or Mary], Countess of Pembroke.) NIL; OAEL-1; SCP-2 (Underneath This Sable Hearse.) PoPle

On the cover of the book of 19th-century. The Cyclists. Lawrence Kearney. AMV-80

On the crooked arm of Columbus, on his cloak. Pigeons. Alastair Reid. NYP

On the cross the dying Saviour. The Legend of the Crossbill. Julius Mosen, tr. by Longfellow. PIM

On the Dangers Attending Altruism on the High Seas. G. K. Chesterton. FaBoNo

On the Dates of Poets. Michael L. Johnson. AMV-80

On the Daughter of Lykambes. Archilochos, tr. fr. Greek by Jonathan Cott. RRA

On the day I was born. My Stars. Abraham Ibn Ezra, tr. by Robert Mezey. OFD

On the Day of Atonement. Yehuda Amichai, tr. fr. Hebrew by Shirley Kaufman. VWA

On the Day of Atonement we fasted. Day of Atonement. Jack Myers. VWA

On the day of the explosion. The Explosion. Philip Larkin. EBEV; HAP

On the Death of a Cat. Christina Rossetti. PCat

On the Death of a Female Officer of the Salvation Army. A. E. Housman. FaBoNo

On the Death of a Metaphysician. George Santayana. PAIC

On the Death of a Nightingale. Thomas Randolph. ILP (1975 ed.)

On the Death of a Young Lady, Cousin to the Author. Byron. MBPR

On the Death of Anne Brontë. Charlotte Brontë. WPE

On the Death of Dermody, the Poet. Henry Kirke White. PeD

On the Death of Dr. Robert Levet. Samuel Johnson. See On the Death of Mr. Robert Levet.

On the Death of Donne. Thomas Carew. Fr. Elegy upon the Death of the Dean of St. Paul's, Dr. John Donne. NOBE

On the Death of Echo. Hartley Coleridge. BoAnP; GDP

On the Death of Edward III. Unknown. OxBM

On the Death of Emperor Tenji. Unknown, tr. fr. Japanese by Geoffrey Bownas and Anthony Thwaite. BoWoP

On the Death of Friends in Childhood. Donald Justice. ConAP; NCSH

On the Death of God. Roderick Hartigh Jellema. AATT

On the Death of Her Body. James K. Baxter. ATNZ

On the Death of His Wife. Muireadach O'Dalaigh, tr. fr. Irish by Frank O'Connor. BIrV; CIP

On the Death of Keats. John Logan. Prf

On the Death of Marie, Countess of Pembroke. William Browne. See On the Countess Dowager of Pembroke.

On the Death of Mr. Fox. Byron. MBPR

On the Death of Mr. [or Dr.] Robert Levet, a Practiser in Physic. Samuel Johnson. BoReV; EBEV; HeIP; InPS; LAuP; NOBE; OAEL-1; PPP

On the Death of Mr. William Harvey [or Hervey]. Abraham Cowley. EBEV
"It was a dismal and a fearful night," sel. NOBE

On the Death of Mrs. Bowes. Lady Mary Wortley Montagu. BoWoP

On the Death of Mrs. Felicia Hemans, sel. Lydia H. Sigourney. "Little plant that never sang before, The." PeD

On the Death of Mrs. Throckmorton's Bullfinch. William Cowper. PPP (On the Lamented Death of Mrs. Throckmorton's Bullfinch.) LAuP

On the Death of My Beard. Peter Frank. AAN

On the Death of Parents. Alfred Barson. AMV-80

On the Death of Richard West. Thomas Gray. See Sonnet on the Death of Richard West.

On the Death of Sylvia Plath. Judith Herzberg, tr. fr. Dutch by Shirley Kaufman. VWA

On the Death of the Dearly Beloved and Much Lamented Father. Eliza R. Snow. WPW

On the Death of the Evansville University Basketball Team in a Plane Crash, December 13, 1977. Robert W. Hamblin. AMV-80

On the Death of the Giraffe. Thomas Hood. FaBoEE

On the Death of the Great Chef Alexis Soyer. Unknown. FaBoEE

On the Death of the Lord Treasurer. Unknown. FaBoEE

On the Death of Theodore Roethke. Robert Huff. CNW

On the Death of W. H. Auden. Dave Morice. AcAn

On the Death of William Edward Burghardt Du Bois by African Moonlight and Forgotten Shores. Conrad Kent Rivers. PoBA

On the Debt My Mother Owed to Sears Roebuck. Edward Dorn. ConAP

On the deck of a ship called the Masm. Limerick. Conrad Aiken. FaBoNo

On the deck of Patrick Lynch's boat I sat in woeful plight. The County of Mayo. Unknown, tr. by George Fox. BIrV

On the Departure of Sir Walter Scott from Abbotsford, for Naples. Wordsworth. EBEV

On the Departure Platform. Thomas Hardy. NOBE; OxBTC

On the Deputy of Ireland's Child. Sir John Davies. FaBoEE

On the Desert. Stephen Crane. War Is Kind, XI. TT

On the Detraction Which Followed upon My Writing Certain Treatises ("A book was writ of late called Tetrachordon"). Milton. Epi

On the Detraction Which Followed upon My Writing Certain Treatises ("I did but prompt the age to quit their clogs"). Milton. ExPo (1973 ed.)

On the Disadvantages of Central Heating. Amy Clampitt. AMV-80

On the distant prairie, where the heather wild. Rosalie, the Prairie Flower. George Frederick Root. BLSo

On the Duke of Buckingham. James Shirley. FaBoEE

On the Earl of Kildare. Unknown. FaBoEE

On the Earl of Leicester. Unknown. FaBoEE

On the Eclipse of the Moon of October 1865. Charles Tennyson Turner. VPC

On the Edge. Alison Wyrley Birch. PPM

On the Edge. Frank Dwyer. AMV-81

On the Edge. Philip Levine. TAP

On the Edge at Santorini. Michael C. Blumenthal. AMV-80

On the Edge of a Safe Sleep. Teresa D. Cader. AMV-81

On the edge of the eye. Here. Florence Barbera. PoUp

On the Eisenhower Stamp. Sam Pereira. PoW

On the Emigration to America. Philip Freneau. PiAm; TAP (Stanzas on the Emigration to America, and Peopling the Western Country.) GOA

On the Erection of Shakespeare's Statue in Westminster Abbey. Pope. FaBoEE

On the Erie Canal, it was. The Aged Pilot Man. "Mark Twain". OBAL

On the Eve of His Execution. Chidiock Tichborne. See Elegy: "My prime of youth is but a frost of cares."

On the Eve of the Plebiscite. Kenneth Rexroth. NNaP

On the Extinction of the Venetian Republic. Wordsworth. FaPo; MBPR; NOBE; OBP; PPoD

On the Famous Voyage. Ben Jonson. PAIC; TVS

On the far edge of a plain. The Watcher. John Peck. AmPA

On the far rock. Lives. Gerald Dawe. AMV-81

On the Farm. R. S. Thomas. OxBTC

On the Farm. Barbara Winder. PH

On the Farther Wall, Marc Chagall. Phyllis McGinley. Fr. Spectator's Guide to Contemporary Art. OBSV

On the Fen: A Stormy Day near Heckington. Arthur J. Bull. HeHu

On the 15th day of November in the year of the motorcar. Sonnet. Ted Berrigan. VW

On the Fifth Anniversary of Bluma Sach's Death. Vinnie-Marie D'Ambrosio. IHMS

On the Fine Arts Garden, Cleveland. Russell Atkins. PoBA

On the fine wire of his whine he walked. Mosquito. John Updike. BoAnP

On the first day/ malcolm. The Easter Bunny Blues Or All I Want for Xmas Is the Loop. Ebon Dooley. PoBA

On the first day of Christmas. The Twelve Days of Christmas. Unknown. BLSH; FSW

On the first hour of my first day. The Beginner. Kipling. Fr. Epitaphs of the War. FaBoTw (1975 ed.)

On the first morning of the moon, in land. The Good Beasts. Willis Barnstone. VWA

On the first of March. The Rooks. Unknown. GBP

On the first of May. Mountain Greenery. Lorenz Hart. OBAL

On the first of the Feast of Feasts. Epilogue. Robert Browning. Fr. Dramatis Personae. VLP

On the floodis of Babiloyne there we saten. Bible, O.T. (Second Wycliffite Version). Psalms, CXXXVII. OAEL-1

On the Fly-Leaf of Pound's Cantos. Basil Bunting. FaBoTw (1975 ed.); NoAM; OxBTC

On the Forcers of Conscience. Milton. See On the New Forcers of Conscience. . .

On the Founding of Liberia. Melvin B. Tolson. Fr. Libretto for the Republic of Liberia. UnPo (1976 ed.)

On the Four Georges. Walter Savage Landor. See Georges, The.

On the fourth floor. Ford Hospital. J. D. Reed. UsP

On the front of the envelope. Lines Found on an Envelope. Adrianne Marcus. NPW

On the Grasshopper and [the] Cricket. Keats. BiP; Epi; FSFS; ILP (1975 ed.); MBPR; NIL; OAEL-2; OBP; TT (Grasshopper and the Cricket, The.) ECBV

On the gray days, when the sky. Gray Days. Joanne Lawlor. AMV-80

On the green lawn of a city park. The Will to Live. Mekeel McBride. PCho

On the grey sand beside the shallow stream. Ego Dominus Tuus. W. B. Yeats. CMoP (1970 ed.)

On the ground are my sketches of the contours. The Painter in the Lion Cage. Betti Alver, tr. by Willis Barnstone and Felix Oinas. BoWoP

On the ground there was a tree. The Tree in the Wood. Unknown. AmFP

On the Hall at Stowey. Charles Tomlinson. CMoP (1970 ed.); NoAM

On the Happy Corydon and Phyllis. At. to Sir Charles Sedley. BoLoP; SCP-2 ("Young Coridon and Phillis.") SFF

On the Hazards of Smoking. Leah Goldberg, tr. fr. Hebrew by Bernhard Frank. AMV-81

On the headland's grassed and sheltered side. Storm. Judith Wright. WPE

On the hearth a little fire burns. Oyfn Pripetshuk (On the Hearth). Mark Warshawsky. FSW

On the Heart's Beginning to Cloud the Mind. Robert Frost. CMoP (1970 ed.)

On the Heights. Walter Savage Landor. FaBoEE

On the Hellenics. Walter Savage Landor. Fr. The Hellenics. ILP (1975 ed.)

On the hill above the pond. October Dusk. C. Stephen Finley. AMV-80

On the Hill below the Lighthouse. James Dickey. PAIC

On the hills behind the dunes. November on Lake Michigan. Tom McKeown. HeS

On the hilltop, close to the house of the empress. The Mother. Babette Deutsch. RiTi

On the Historians Freeman and Stubbs. J. E. Thorold Rogers. FaBoEE

On the holiest day we fast till sundown. The Converts. Chana Bloch. AMV-81

On the holy day of your going out to war. Mohodahi, tr. fr. Sanskrit by Willis Barnstone. BoWoP

On the Homefront. James Applewhite. CSP

On the Ice Islands Seen Floating in the German Ocean. William Cowper. OAEL-1

On the idle hill of summer. A. E. Housman. ILP (1975 ed.); NOBE; OAEL-2; STS

On the Imprint of the First English Edition of "The Works of Max Beerbohm." Max Beerbohm. InPK

On the Inauguration of the Memorial Statue, sel. Edward Edwin Foot. "Love live our dear and noble Queen." FaBoCo

On the Industrial Highway. Daniel Gerard Hoffman. PCho

On the Ineffable Inspiration of the Holy Spirit. Catharina Regina von Greiffenberg, tr. fr. German by Michael Hamburger. PBWP

On the Infancy of Our Saviour. Francis Quarles. SCP-2

On the Inside Strong. Antar S. K. Mberi. SES

On the Irish Club. Swift. OBSV

On the Isle of Man shore, I carelessly wandered. The Isle of Man Shore. Unknown. AmFP

On the isle of Penang there is 'stablished a city. Regret. Malay Oral Tradition, tr. by R. J. Wilkinson. WTO

On the Jewish Day of Judgment in the Year 1942 (5703). Jozef Wittlin, tr. fr. Polish by Issaac Komem. VWA

On the Jubilee of Queen Victoria, abr. Tennyson. UnPo (1976 ed.)

On the kitchen wall a flash. The World Outside. Denise Levertov. ConAP

On the Knowledge of Things. Alexander Taylor. NowV

On the Lady Mary Villiers. Thomas Carew. See Epitaph on the Lady Mary Villiers.

On the Lake. V. Sackville-West. SBG

On the lake-bottom near. Petoskey Stone. Robert Vas Dias. HeS

On the Lake Poets. Charles Townsend. FaBoEE

On the Lakes of Ponchartrain. *Unknown.* AmFP

On the Lamented Death of Mrs. Throckmorton's Bullfinch. William Cowper. *See* On the Death of Mrs. Throckmorton's Bullfinch.

On the Land. Ray Lindquist. TAT

On the Last Page of the Last Yellow Pad in Rome before Taking Off for Dacca on Air Bangladesh. Miller Williams. AMV-80

On the last year's trip I enjoyed this place. On the Road through Chang-te. Sun Yün-feng, *tr. by* Kenneth Rexroth *and* Ling Chung. BoWoP

On the Late Massacre in Piedmont. Milton. BiP; CABA (1972 ed.); Epi; FaPo; HAP; HeIP; ILP (1975 ed.); InPK; NIL; NOBE; OBP; PPoe; PPP; SoSe; UnPo (1976 ed.); VoPo; WeW
  (Sonnet: "Avenge, O Lord, thy slaughtered saints, whose bones.") LFH; OAEL-1
  (Sonnet: On the Late Massacre in Piedmont.) AnMo

On the Late Metamorphosis of an Old Picture of Oliver Cromwell's. *Unknown.* APAS

On the Lawn at the Villa. Louis Simpson. GOA; OBAL; PPoD; PPP

On the ledges of Newbury Street. The Beasts of Boston. Betty Lowry. AMV-80

On the levee the Saarinen Arch. Riverfront, St. Louis. John Knoepfle. TAT

On the Life of Man. Sir Walter Ralegh. *See* What Is Our Life? A Play of Passion.

On the lips a taste of tolling we are blind. (Poem) (Chicago) (The Were-Age). William Knott. EAS

On the long shore, lit by the moon. The Goose Fish. Howard Nemerov. CMoP (1970 ed.); ExPo (1973 ed.); HeIP; ILP (1975 ed.); InPK; LoAs; NIL; NoAM

On the Lord Mayor and Court of Aldermen, Presenting the Late King and Duke of York Each with a Copy of Their Freedoms. Andrew Marvell. FaBoBa
  (Upon His Majesty's Being Made Free of the City.) APAS

On the Loss of the *Royal George*. William Cowper. EBEV; NOBE
  (*Royal George*, The.) FaPoR

On the Loss of U.S. Submarine S4, *sel.* H. C. Canfield. "Entrapped inside a submarine." FaBoCo

On the Marginal Way. Richard Wilbur. CAPP; NOBA

On the Margins of a Poem. Jiri Mordecai Langer, *tr. fr. Hebrew by* Gabriel Preil *and* Howard Schwartz. VWA

On the Marriage of a Virgin. Dylan Thomas. STS

On the Marriage of T. K. and C. C., the Morning Stormy. Thomas Carew. BoLoP

On the Meadow. "Katri Vala," *tr. fr. Finnish by* Jaakko A. Ahokas. PBWP

On the Meetings of the Scotch Covenanters. *Unknown.* FaBoEE

On the Memory of Mr. Edward King, Drowned in the Irish Seas. John Cleveland. OAEL-1; SCP-2
  (Upon the Death of Mr. King Drowned in the Irish Seas.) HAP

On the Merry, Merry-go-round. Dorothy McGrath Martin. CTV

On the Morning of Christ's Nativity. Milton. Epi; ILP (1975 ed.); SCP-1
  (Ode on the Morning of Christ's Nativity.) BoReV
Hymn on the Morning of Christ's Nativity, *sel.* NOBE

On the morning of the crowning we chorused our remission from school. Geoffrey Hill. Mercian Hymns, III. HAP

On the Morning of the Third Night above Nisqually. W. M. Ransom. BCr; CDW; NU

On the morning you woke beside me. Mornings/of an Impossible Love. Alice Walker. NVAP

On the most westerly Blasket. The Given Note. Seamus Heaney. NCSH

On the Motor Bus. Alfred Denis Godley. *See* Motor Bus, The.

On the Mountain. Ruth Stone. BoWoP

On the Move. Thom Gunn. CMoP (1970 ed.); HAP; NIL; NowV; OAEL-2; OBP; OxBTC; PoIA; PPP

On the Murder of Sir Edmund Berry Godfrey. *Unknown.* APAS

On the Naming Day. Jewel C. Latimore. CNA

On the Nature of Things. Lucretius. *See* De Rerum Natura.

On the New Forcers of Conscience under the Long Parliament. Milton. CABA (1972 ed.); NIL; PPoD
  (On the Forcers of Conscience.) PAIC

On the New Laureate. *Unknown.* FaBoCo

On the New Road. Lyn Lifshin. FAF; NeAC; RiTi

On the Night Express to Madrid. Lora Dunetz. AMV-81

On the Night in Question. Patricia Goedicke. TAP

On the night of the Belgian surrender the moon rose. The Moon and the Night and the Men. John Berryman. VGW

On the ninth of November by the dawning of the day. Farewell to Kingsbridge. *Unknown.* AIW

On the Occasion of Becoming an Echo. Anselm Hollo. TwMBP

On the Ocean Floor. "Hugh MacDiarmid." HAP

On the other side/ of my world. To the Man I Live With. Ann Menebroker. IHMS

On the other side of the one-way mirror. In Search of the Silent Zero. Garrett Kaoru Hongo. EC

On the other side of the world I heard. Elegy for a Schoolmate. Vincent O'Sullivan. ATNZ

On the Painter Val Prinsep. Dante Gabriel Rossetti. FaBoEE

On the Passion. *Unknown.* OxBM

On the Path. A. L. Strauss, *tr. fr. Hebrew by* Robert Friend. VWA

On the path. Under the Maud Moon. Galway Kinnell. CAAP; NNaP

On the path winding. The Path among the Stones. Galway Kinnell. NNaP; NOBA; Prf

On the pathway mica glints. Water and Worship: An Open-Air Service on the Gatineau River. Margaret Avison. HAP

On the Pavement. David A. Sam. AMV-80

On the phonograph, the voice. Reunion. Carolyn Forché. PCho

On the Photograph of a Man I Never Saw. Hyam Plutzik. VWA

On the Plains, crows speak in raucous caws. Crow Voices. Gail Tremblay. AMV-81

On the Planet of Flies. Christian Morgenstern, *tr. fr. German by* Geoffrey Grigson. FaBoNo

On the Pole. Uri Zvi Greenberg, *tr. fr. Hebrew by* Robert Mezey *and* Ben Zion Gold. VWA

On the Portrait of a Woman about to Be Hanged. Thomas Hardy. CMoP (1970 ed.)

On the Power of Sound. Wordsworth. VLP

On the Projected Kendal and Windermere Railway. Wordsworth. *See* Sonnet on the Projected Kendal and Windermere Railway.

On the Prorogation. *Unknown.* APAS

On the Prospect of Establishing a Pantisocracy in America. Samuel Taylor Coleridge. MBPR

On the Prospect of Planting Arts and Learning in America. George Berkeley. NIL; OBP
  (Verses on the Prospect of Planting Arts and Learning in America.) ILP (1975 ed.); PAIC; PPoD

On the proud banks of great Euphrates' flood. Bible, *O.T.*, *paraphrased by* Richard Crashaw. Psalms, CXXXVII. OAEL-1

On the prow. The Landing. Daniel Halpern. AmPA

On the Queen's Visit to London, the Night of the Seventeenth of March, 1789, *sel.* William Cowper.
"When, long sequester'd from his throne." PeD

On the Religion of Nature. Philip Freneau. EAP

On the Relinquishment of a Title. Geoffrey Grigson. FaBoEE

On the Reverend Jonathan Doe. *Unknown.* FaBoEE

On the Road Home. Wallace Stevens. NU

On the Road There Stands a Tree. Itzik Manger, *tr. fr. Yiddish by* Stephen Griffin. VWA

On the Road through Chang-te. Sun Yün-feng, *tr. fr. Chinese by* Kenneth Rexroth *and* Ling Chung. BoWoP

On the Road to California; or, The Buffalo Bullfight. *Unknown.* AmFP

On the road to the bay was a lake of rushes. The Bay. James K. Baxter. ATNZ

On the roads at night I saw the glitter of eyes. Eyes of Night-Time. Muriel Rukeyser. BoWoP

On the roof cloudy sky fading sun rays. Allen Ginsberg. *Fr.* Waking in New York. NYP

On the Run. William Sprunt. AAN

On the run is the Otoe County corn rootworm. Otoe County in Nebraska. William Kloefkorn. GP

On the Same [Some South African Novelists]. Roy Campbell. OxBTC

On the Saviour's Wounds. Richard Crashaw. PAIC

On the Sea. Keats. CABA (1972 ed.); EcS; ExPo (1973 ed.); FF; MBPR; OAEL-2; RhR

On the secret map the assassins. Rivers and Mountains. John Ashbery. NoAM; NOBA

On the Sentence Passed by the House of Lords on Dr. Sacheverell. *Unknown.* APAS

On the Setting Sun. Sir Walter Scott. PIM

On the shining china white and gold. Its Lunch. John Hollander. *Fr.* Something about It. GP

On the Shore of Crete. Clarice Short. MPA

On the sicilian strand a hare well wrought. Decimus Magnus Ausonius, *tr. fr. Latin by* Richard Lovelace. OBVE

On the side of the road. Song. Edmond Jabès, *tr. by* Anthony Rudolf. VWA

On the sidewalk the people are bustling. The Observation. Donovan Leitch. GrRo

On the sixteenth day of September, nineteen twenty-eight. The West Palm Beach Storm. *Unknown.* AmFP

On the smooth brow and clustering hair. Walter Savage Landor. GBL

On the snow I found prints. Invisible Tree. Ryuichi Tamura, *tr. by* Thomas Fitzsimmons. TSWA

On the Snuff of a Candle. Sir Walter Ralegh. FaBoEE

On the Soft and Gentle Motions of Eudora. Anne Killigrew. SCP-2

On the soft white snow. Christmas Mouse. Aileen Fisher. MN

On the Sonnet. Keats. CABA (1972 ed.); ILP (1975 ed.); MBPR; NIL; OAEL-2; PAIC

On the southwest side of Capri. The Nude Swim. Anne Sexton. WPE

On the southwest up-escalator. The Macy's Poem. James Reiss. POL

On the Spartan Dead at Thermopylae. Simonides, *tr. fr. Greek.* WeW
("Stranger, when you come to/ Lakedaimon," *tr. by* Kenneth Rexroth.) OBVE
("Tell them in Lakedaimon, passer-by.") FaBoEE
(Thermopylae, *tr. by* William Lisle Bowles.) OBVE

On the stage, mirrored many times. The Stripper. Anita Endrezze Probst. CDW

On the steep road. Dreamscape. Philip Booth. FiCP

On the steps of the bright madhouse. In the Fleeting Hand of Time. Gregory Corso. SA

On the stiff twig up there. Black Rook in Rainy Weather. Sylvia Plath. Psy

On "The Story of Rimini." Keats. MBPR

On the Street. C. P. Cavafy. *tr. fr. Greek by* Rae Dalven. BoLoP

On the street/ Slung on his shoulder. The Shovel Man. Carl Sandburg. HAP

On the street at dusk. Visitations. Jennifer Crewe. AMV-80

On the street-corner. What It Means, Living in the City. William Dickey. POL

On the street we two pass. Commitment in a City. Margaret Tsuda. CTBA

On the Suicide of a Friend. Reed Whittemore. ConAP

On the summer road that ran by our front porch. Lizards and Snakes. Anthony Hecht. NCSH; PPoD

On the supposed Author of a Late Poem "In Defense of Satire." Earl of Rochester. APAS

On the Swag. R. A. K. Mason. ATNZ

On the Telescopic Moon. John Swanwick Drennan. BIrV

On the third day after her unexpected death. A Ballad of Orpheus. Maurice Lindsay. MS; SLP

On the threshold of heaven, the figures in the street. To an Old Philosopher in Rome. Wallace Stevens. NoAM; NOBA; TT

On the threshold of the stable smelling. The Stable. Jill Hoffman. PH

On the Times. *Unknown.* OxBM

On the Tombs in Westminster Abbey. *At. to* Francis Beaumont, *also at. to* William Basse. NOBE; OBP; PoPle
(In Westminster Abbey, *shorter version.*) FaPoR
(Memento for Mortality, A.) HAP

On the top of the Crumpetty Tree. The Quangle Wangle's Hat. Edward Lear. EBEV; PCOP

On the top step with soft kitchen light. Coloring Margarine. William Hathaway. AMV-81

On the Tower. Annette von Droste-Hülshoff, *tr. fr. German by* James Edward Tobin. PBWP

On the train/ old ladies playing football. Going Uptown to Visit Miriam. Victor Hernandez Cruz. FF; MAT; NYP

On the train to the ruins. Nathaniel Tarn. *Fr.* A Nowhere for Vallejo. TwMBP

On the Translation of Anacreon. Horace Walpole. FaBoEE

On the Triumph of Rationalism. Alfred Ainger. FaBoCo

On the twenty-sixth of August, our fatal moss gave way. The Donibristle Moss Moran Disaster. *Unknown.* WTO

On the 26th of October, in the evening. Winter Journey. Stanislaw Wygodski, *tr. by* Isaac Komen. VWA

On the Uniformity and Perfection of Nature. Philip Freneau. EAP; ILP (1975 ed.); IPWM

On the Universality and Other Attributes of the God of Nature. Philip Freneau. EAP

On the University Carrier ("Here lies old Hobson, Death hath broke his girt"). Milton. EBEV; FaBoEE; PoPle

On the University of Cambridge's Burning the Duke of Monmouth's Picture. George Stepney. APAS

On the Use of Jayshus. Oliver St. John Gogarty. FaBoEE

On the Vanity of Earthly Greatness. Arthur Guiterman. HoPM (1975 ed.); InPK; NIL

On the verge of the infinite. Jerusalem. Kadia Molodovski, *tr. by* S. F. Chyet. AMV-81

On the "Vita Nuova" of Dante. Dante Gabriel Rossetti. VLP

On the Wall. *Unknown.* BluL

On the wave-washed scarp of crag. Green Shag. W. W. Gibson. EcS

On the Way. Mordechai Husid, *tr. fr. Yiddish by* Seymour Mayne *and* Rivka Augenfeld. VWA

On the way down. The Way Down. Philip Levine. NOBA

On the wet sand the queen emerged from forest. Theseus: A Trilogy. Yvor Winters. NOBA

On the Wide Heath. Edna St. Vincent Millay. CMoP (1970 ed.); WPE

On the wide level of a mountain's head. Time, Real and Imaginary. Samuel Taylor Coleridge. MBPR; NOBE; PBMP

On the Wide Stairs. Yehuda Amichai, *tr. fr. Hebrew by* Laya Firestone *and* Howard Schwartz. VWA

On the wide veranda white. A Corn-Song. Paul Laurence Dunbar. AmVN

On the window-sill across the alley. A Prayer for Violets. Charles O. Hartman. AAN

On the Wing. Christina Rossetti. SBG

On the Wings of a Dove. Jim Wayne Miller. AMV-80

On the World. Francis Quarles. HAP

On the Wrong Side. A. W. Webster. TDH

On the Young Statesmen. Charles Sackville. APAS

On their highest bluff. The Citizen's Complaint. David Allan Evans. HeS

On these sunny steps. View from the Planetarium. David Barker. GP

On things asleep, no balm. The Longing. Theodore Roethke. PiAm

On Third Street there's a naked spot. The Ballad of Mary Baldwin. Stephen Sandy. MAT

On this black night of rain. The Son, Condemned. Larry Rubin. GP

On This Day I Complete My Thirty-sixth Year. Byron. CABA (1972 ed.); ILP (1975 ed.); MBPR; NIL; OAEL-2

On this day of longed-for peace. Armistice. Elizabeth Daryush. AMV-81

On this dishonored, this perverted globe. Port Townsend, 1974. Richard Hugo. CNW

On this feast day, oh, cursed day and hour! Love at First Sight. Christopher Marlowe. *Fr.* Hero and Leander, First Sestiad. NOBE

On this floor. Floor: O. Stephen Vincent. *Fr.* Elevator Landscapes. NeAC

On this hotel their rumpled royalties. The West Forties: Morning, Noon and Night. L. E. Sissman. NYP

On This Island. W. H. Auden. CMoP (1970 ed.); ExPo (1973 ed.); InPS; MPo; PSN

On this jungle gym. Skeleton. Coleman Barks. *Fr.* Body Poems. NVAP

On this, my thirtyfirst detachment. A Memory. Manfred Jurgensen. FPA

On this piece of earth I seize a knife. Conversation. Gyorgy Raba, *tr. by* Jascha Kessler. VWA

On this side of the tapestry. The Tapestry. Howard Nemerov. PCho; Prf

On this sweet bank your head thrice sweet and dear. Youth's Spring-Tribute. Dante Gabriel Rossetti. The House of Life, XIV. ILP (1975 ed.); VLP

On this tree thrown up. Spindrift. Galway Kinnell. IPWM

On this winter night. Izumi Shikibu, *tr. fr. Japanese by* Willis Barnstone. BoWoP

On Thomas, Second Earl of Onslow. *Unknown.* FaBoCo (On Tom Onslow, Earl of Onslow.) FaBoEE

On those chill days, the lumped, steaming. Guts. Caroline Garrett. PHC

On Those That Deserve It. Francis Quarles. BoReV

On thrones from China to Peru. A Model for the Laureate. W. B. Yeats. CMoP (1970 ed.)

On Throwing a Copy of the New Statesman into the Coorong. Max Harris. GAS

On thy stupendous summit, rock sublime! Charlotte Smith. *Fr.* Beachy Head. SBG

On Time. Milton. BoReV; CABA (1972 ed.)

On Tintock-Tap there is a mist. Tintock. *Unknown.* GBP

On to the beach the quiet waters crept. The Quiet Tide near Ardrossan. Charles Tennyson Turner. VPC

On Tobacco. Charles Cotton. OBSV

On Tom Holland and Nell Cotton. *Unknown.* FaBoEE

On Tom Moore's Translation of Anacreon. Thomas, Lord Erskine. FaBoEE

On Tom-o-Combe. *Unknown.* FaBoEE

On Tom Onslow, Earl of Onslow. *Unknown. See* On Thomas, Second Earl of Onslow.

On Top of Old Smoky. *Unknown.* BLSH, *with music;* BLSo, *with music;* FSW; InPK (Old Smoky.) AmFP

On Trinity Sunday, *sel.* John Byrom. "One Divinity of Father, Son, The." PeD

On Trust in the Heart. Seng-ts'an, *tr. fr. Chinese.* ILwL

On Two Monopolists. John Byrom. FaBoCo ("Bone and Skin.") FaBoEE

On Universalism. Etheridge Knight. UsP

On Venus, time passes slowly because. Here. Marvin Bell. AmPA

On Virtue. Phillis Wheatley. TAP

On Visiting Central Park Zoo. Alan Dugan. NYP

On Visiting My Son, Port Angeles, Washington. Duane Niatum. CDW

On Visiting Staffa. Keats. MBPR

On Visiting the Graves of Hawthorne and Thoreau. Jones Very. TAP

On Visiting the Graves of Keats and Marx in Hampstead Churchyard, *sel. Unknown.* "John and Karl." PeD

On Visiting the Tomb of Burns. Keats. MBPR; NIL

On Vital Statistics. Hilaire Belloc. POL

On wan dark night on Lac St. Pierre. The Wreck of the *Julie Plante.* William Henry Drummond. PoTa

On warm days in September the high school band. The High School Band. Reed Whittemore. MiP; NCSH

On Watching Pimps. Quincy Troupe. SES

On Watching Politicians Perform at Martin Luther King's Funeral. Etheridge Knight. NNaP

On Waterloo's ensanguined plain. On Scott's "The Field of Waterloo." Thomas, Lord Erskine. FaBoCo

On Wednesday night. Wednesday Night Prayer Meeting. Jay Wright. PoBA

On Wenlock Edge the wood's in trouble. A. E. Housman. CABA (1972 ed.); ILP (1975 ed.); IP; NOBE; OxBTC; PES; SoSe (1977 ed.); STS; VLP

On Westwell Downs. William Strode. SCP-2

On what foundation stands the warrior's pride. Charles XII of Sweden. Samuel Johnson. *Fr.* The Vanity of Human Wishes. NOBE

On what pure mission do the seagulls fly. On the Beach. Frances Cornford. BoAnP

On When McCarthy Was a Wolf amoung a Nation of Queer-Queers. Alan Dugan. GP

On Why I Would Betray You. Jorie Graham. AMV-81

On Will Smith. *Unknown.* ECBV; FaBoCo

On William Prynne. Samuel Butler. FaBoEE

On William Wilson, Tailor. *Unknown.* FaBoEE

On windy days the mill. The Unfortunate Miller. A. E. Coppard. FaBoTw (1975 ed.); PoTa

On winter days, about the gloamin hour. Auld Sanct-Aundrians—Brand the Builder. Tom Scott. MS

On winter nights. The Car Cemetery. Ciaran Carson. CIP

On Woman. W. B. Yeats. BiP; CMoP (1970 ed.); STS

On wool-soft feet he peeps and creeps. Santa Claus. Walter de la Mare. PChr

On yonder hill there is a red deer. *Unknown.* GBP

On yonder hill there stands a creature [*or* maiden]. No John. *Unknown.* FSW; GSB

On your dazzling throne, Aphrodite. Sappho, *tr. fr. Greek by* Willis Barnstone. BoWoP

On your midnight pallet lying. A. E. Housman. STS

On your pale aged face. Funeral Home. Margo Bohanon. SES

On your slender body/ Your jade and coral girdle ornaments chime. Wu Tsao, *tr. fr. Chinese by* Kenneth Rexroth *and* Ling Chung. BoWoP

On your way home you stopped to shop. A Nameless Recognition. Arthur Gregor. GP

On Zacheus. Francis Quarles. MetP (On Zacchaeus.) HAP

On Zion and on Lebanon, *with music.* Henry Ustic Onderdonk. AH

Once, *sels.* Alice Walker.
    "Green lawn/ a picket fence." PoBA
    "I/ never liked/ white folks." PoBA
    "It is true—/ I've always loved." NMM; NVAP; PoBA

Once,/ I was afraid of dying. I Was Afraid of Dying. James Wright. OSP

Once a dream did weave a shade. A Dream. Blake. *Fr. Songs of Innocence.* LAuP; MBPR; PoPle

Once a Frenchman. *Unknown.* TDH

Once a grasshopper (food being scant). The Humorous Ant. Oliver Herford. TDH

Once a haughty crocodile left his home upon the Nile. Crocodile. Kornei Chukovsky, *tr. by* Babette Deutsch. ECBV

Once a jolly swagman camped by a billabong. Waltzing Matilda. Andrew Barton Paterson. FSW; GBP; PeBB; PoTa; RDB

Once a man is born he has to die. All Intents. Larry Eigner. VGW

Once a mouse, a frog, and a little red hen. The Mouse, the Frog, and the Little Red Hen. *Unknown.* ECBV

Once a pound-keeper chanced to impound. The Ounce of Detention. Oliver Herford. TDH

Once a raven from Pluto's dark shore. The True Facts of the Case. Anthony Euwer. OBAL

Once a snowflake fell. Winter Poem. Nikki Giovanni. OSP

Once a winter bayou child knew the green music. Troubador. J. Edgar Simmons. TAT

Once, a woman sat in a white room. Gertrude Stein. Philip Roberts. FPA

Once a young "Canadien." Un Canadien Errant (An Exiled Canadien). *Tr. fr. French.* FSW

Once, after a rotten day at school. The Place's Fault. Philip Hobsbaum. LP; MPo

Once after he'd come back from Ohio. On the Wings of a Dove. Jim Wayne Miller. AMV-80

Once again I'm integrated with machinery. My Flying Machine. Louis Daniel Brodsky. AMV-80

Once again the best foot. The Balancing. Ross Talarico. AAN

Once again the scurry of feet—those myriads. The Face of the Waters. Robert D. Fitzgerald. GAS

Once again they've quarreled on a tram. Two. Margarita Aliger, *tr. by* Elaine Feinstein. VWA

Once again your twittering notes. Listening to Mbaqanga. Lindiwe Mabuza. SES

Once Alien Here. John Hewitt. CIP

Once Again. Liz Sohappy Bahe. CDW; VW

Once an old man was an only. Something like an Apple. James Reiss. CAAP

Once, as a child, I ate raspberries. And forgot. Raspberries. Laurence Lerner. EBEV

Once as a child I loved to hop. Adam's Footprint. Vassar Miller. NIL

Once as I travelled through a quiet evening. Egrets. Judith Wright. NCSH

Once as methought Fortune me kissed. Sir Thomas Wyatt. BoLoP
("Ons as me thought fortune me Kyst.") AAS

Once, as old Lord Gorbals motored. Lord Gorbals. Harry Graham. FaBoCo

Once as we were sitting by. Spring 1942. Lawrence Durrell. OxBTC

Once at imagination's windows I. Nature's Prospect. Margaret Cavendish, Duchess of Newcastle. SCP-2

Once by a mountain lake high in the wilds. Mystic Lake. R. P. Kingston. NVAP

Once by mishap two poets fell a-squaring. Comparison of the Sonnet and the Epigram. Sir John Harrington. PAIC

Once by the Pacific. Robert Frost. BPAW; CMoP (1970 ed.); HAP; HeIP; ILP (1975 ed.); NOBA; PiAm; RhR; VGW; WeW

Once did my thoughts both ebb and flow. *Unknown.* EBEV

Once did she hold the gorgeous east in fee. On the Extinction of the Venetian Republic. Wordsworth. FaPo; MBPR; NOBE; OBP; PPoD

Once every so often the risible makes me think of my friends. The Friendship Game. Pier Giorgio Di Cicco. AMV-81

Once, far over the breakers. Tanka. Akiko No Yosano, *tr. by* Kenneth Rexroth. PAIC

Once Fondly Lov'd. Burns. SLP

Once from a big, big building. A Visit to the Asylum. Edna St. Vincent Millay. SO

Once he puts out the light. The Hermit Has a Visitor. Maxine W. Kumin. BoWoP

Once I am sure there's nothing going on. Church Going. Philip Larkin. CMoP (1970 ed.); InPK; IP; ILP (1975 ed.); NIL; NoAM; OAEL-2; PPP; PSN; SoSe; UnPo (1976 ed.)

Once I courted a fair beauty bride. The Fair Beauty Bride. *Unknown.* AmFP

Once I cried for new songs to sing. I Sing No New Songs. Frank Marshall Davis. PoBA

Once I did have a dear companion. Dear Companion. *Unknown.* FSW

Once I followed horses. Thistledown. Denis Glover. ATNZ

Once I heard a hobo, singing by the tie-trail. The Long Road West. Henry Herbert Knibbs. BPAW

Once I heard an old bachelor say. The Bachelor's Complaint. *Unknown.* AmFP

Once, I knew a fine song. The Black Riders, XLV. Stephen Crane. PiAm

Once I lived at a Riverside. By the Riverside. Carolyn Kizer. CNW

Once I Lived in Cottonwood. *Unknown.* AmFP

Once I lived with my brothers, images. The Centaur Overheard. Edgar Bowers. ConAP

Once I loved a maiden fair. A Ballad Maker. Padraic Colum. AIW

Once I loved a spider. The Spider and the Ghost of the Fly. Vachel Lindsay. VGW

Once I Pass'd through a Populous City. Walt Whitman. MiP

Once I Played and Danced in My Parents' Kingdom. *Gond Oral Tradition, tr. by* V. Elwin *and* S. Hivale. WTO

Once I saw a little bird. Mother Goose. CTV

Once I saw a wolf tread a circle in his cage. Traverse City Zoo. Jim Harrison. BoAnP

Once I seen a human ruin. Ambrose Bierce. *Fr.* The Devil's Dictionary. OBAL

Once I stood in a green bough. Portrait of the Father. Lindy Hough. IHMS

Once I was a lady's maid way down in Drury Lane. Bell-bottomed Trousers. *Unknown.* FSW

Once I was good like the Virgin Mary and the Minister's wife. The Scarlet Woman. Fenton Johnson. PoBA

Once I was happy, but now I'm forlorn. The Man on the Flying Trapeze [*or* The Flying Trapeze]. George Leybourne. PoTa; PSoN

Once I woke up in the dark and thought I was blind. My Blindness. Eric Torgensen. TC

Once in a dream (for once I dreamed of you). On the Wing. Christina Rossetti. SBG

Once in a hundred years the Lemmings come. The Lemmings. John Masefield. CMoP (1970 ed.); ILP (1975 ed.); NoAM

Once in a Saintly Passion. James Thomson ("B. V."). FF

Once in a while. The Children. William Carlos Williams. BBGO

Once in an adolescent sweat. The Campaign for Peace in Our Time. Jon Anderson. CAAP

Once in an Ancient Book. Marya Zaturenska. GP

Once in Canandaigua, hitchhiking from Ann Arbor. Faces. John Ciardi. BiP

Once, in finesse of fiddles found I ecstasy. The Embankment. T. E. Hulme. EBEV; OxBTC; PPoD

Once in Love with Amy, *with music.* Frank Loesser. BLSo

Once in our lives,/ Let us drink to our wives. *Unknown.* FaBoEE

Once in Royal David's City. Cecil Frances Alexander. OxBChV

Once in the dark of night. The Dark Night. St. John of the Cross, *tr. by* John Frederick Nims. WeW

Once in the dear dead days beyond recall. Love's Old Sweet Song. G. Clifton Bingham. BLSH; BLSo; FSN

Once in the Jurassic, about 150 million years ago. Smokey the Bear Sutra. ·*Unknown.* MAT

Once in the winter. The Forsaken. Duncan Campbell Scott. PoTa

Once it was Africa, now it is/ jazz. Hot Poem. Vicki Viidikas. FPA

Once, Lily and I fell from a ladder. Monologue of Two Moons, Nudes with Crests. 1938. Norman Dubie. FiCP

Once looked Gudrun. The First Lay of Gudrun: Gudrun Laments over Sigurd. *Unknown, tr. by* William Morris *and* Eiriks Magnusson. OBVE

Once made a fairy rooster from. For My Sister Molly Who in the Fifties. Alice Walker. WBN

Once More. Forugh Farrokhzad, *tr. fr. Persian by* Jascha Kessler *and* Amin Banani. BoWoP

Once More. George Jonas. NeAC

Once More a-Lumbering Go. *Unknown.* AmFP

Once more around should do it, the man confided. Flight of the Roller Coaster. Raymond Souster. PoTa; SO

Once more as I gather about me the cloak of the evening. Charles Brasch. *Fr.* The Estate. ATNZ

Once more, before I move on. To the Unknown God. Friedrich Nietzsche. ILwL

Once more by the brook the alder leaves. Hayden Carruth. NNaP

Once more I came to Sarum Close. The Cathedral Close. Coventry Patmore. *Fr.* The Angel in the House. VPC

Once more, if you want, make many. Landscape with Pervert. Bink Noll. PPoD

Once more it seems. Zohara. Jack Hirschman. VWA

Once more, listening to the wind and rain. The Return. Arna Bontemps. PoBA; WIF

Once more my deeper life goes on with more strength. Moving Ahead. Rainer Maria Rilke, *tr. by* Robert Bly. NU

Once More, O Lord, *with music.* George Washington Doane. AH

Once More, Our God, Vouchsafe to Shine! *with music.* Samuel Sewall. AH

Once more the changed year's turning wheel returns. Barren Spring. Dante Gabriel Rossetti. The House of Life, LXXXIII. ILP (1975 ed.); OAEL-2; VLP; VPC

Once more the storm is howling, and half hid. A Prayer for My Daughter. W. B. Yeats. CABA (1972 ed.); CMoP (1970 ed.); HAP; NoAM; OxBTC; PoA; RRA; SoSe

Once more unto the breach, dear friends, once more. King Henry the Fifth before Harfleur. Shakespeare. King Henry V, *fr.* III, i. BTTM; PPoe

Once my heart was a summer rose. Song. Edith Sitwell. UsP

Once my parents were older. Chiyo, *tr. fr. Japanese by* David Ray. BoWoP

Once neighbor to the dinosaur. The Star-nosed Mole. Robert Wallace. BoAnP

Once new, you rolled easy and maroon. Packard. David Barker. GP

Once on a time, a monarch, tired with whooping. The Apple Dumplings and a King. "Peter Pindar." OBSV

Once on a time I used to be. Harlots' Catch. Robert Nichols. FaBoTw (1975 ed.)

Once on a time, it came to pass. The Fable of the Piece of Glass and the Piece of Ice. John Hookham Frere. OxBChV

Once on a time there lived a man. Peter Gray. *Unknown.* BLSo; FSW

Once on a time there was a pool. Rev. Homer Wilbur's "Festina Lente." James Russell Lowell. *Fr.* The Biglow Papers. OBAL

Once on a time—'twas long ago. The Youth and the Northwind. John Godfrey Saxe. PoTa

Once, once, in Washington. Patriotic Tour and Postulate of Joy. Robert Penn Warren. WasP

Once Only. Gary Snyder. CoPAm

Once only by the garden gate. Youth and Love. Robert Louis Stevenson. SLP

Once or twice this side of death. Crystal Moment. Robert P. Tristram Coffin. ECBV; SoS

Once, Paumanok. The Mocking-Bird. Walt Whitman. *Fr.* Out of the Cradle Endlessly Rocking. PB

Once people believed the blood. Why Fires Are Lit December 21st. Michael McMahon. FAF

Once riding in old Baltimore. Incident. Countee Cullen. BiP; BPo; CABA (1972 ed.); CTBA; FF; IP; NoAM; NowV; PoBA; SoSe; SFF; VGW

Once, so long ago. For Paddy Mac. Padraic Fallon. CIP

Once somebody walked this Piney Mountain. Impromptu Immersion in Tom's Run. Gibbons Ruark. CSP

Once the basic skills have been mastered. Another Attempt at the Trick. Cynthia Macdonald. WBN

Once the Days. Denis Glover. ATNZ

Once the family meeting place. Fish Story. B. Jo Kinnick. AMV-81

Once the poet goes behind the shades. For Cynara. Charles Plymell. RRA

Once There Came a Man. Stephen Crane. TT

Once there lived side by side. I Don't Want to Play in Your Yard. Philip Wingate. FSN

Once there was a crocodile. Crocodile. Kornei Chukovsky, *tr. by* Richard Coe. ECBV

Once there was a house with the ceiling on the floor. Time Upon a Once. Robert Paul Smith. ECBV

Once there was a man named Mr. Artesian and his. Mr. Artesian's Conscientiousness. Ogden Nash. SS

Once there was a Quaker lover. The Quaker Lover. *Unknown.* RDB

Once there was a woman went out to pick beans. The Hairy Toe. *Unknown.* DuDr

Once there was an elephant. Eletelephony. Laura E. Richards. CTV; ECBV; OxBChV

Once there were peasant pots and a dry brown hare. Joan Miró. Ruthven Todd. EAS

Once There Were Three Fishermen. *Unknown.* FSW

Once there would have been the woman standing. The Railings. Alan Brownjohn. LP

Once to Every Man and Nation. James Russell Lowell. FaPoR

Once to the verge of yon steep barrier came. The Recluse; or, Home at Grasmere. Wordsworth. MBPR

Once up u hurl a stone. Mike 65. Lennox Raphael. PoBA

Once upon a midnight dreary, while I pondered, weak and weary. The Raven. Poe. NOBA; PiAm; TAP

Once upon a Nag. Michael Beirne McMahon. PH

Once upon a time/ a freeway came through my life. Freeway. Edward Cardinali. OSP

Once upon a time/ I composed a witty rhyme. The Minstrel's Last Lay. John Barth. OBAL

Once upon a time,/ In the realm of Dewajing. Zong Belegt Baatar. *Mongol Oral Tradition, tr. by* C. R. Bawden. WTO

Once upon a time/ there was a lonely wolf. Fable. Janos Pilinszky, *tr. by* Ted Hughes *and* János Csokits. OBVE

Once upon a time I spent a summer. Remembering Kevan MacKenzie. Henry Taylor. InPK

Once upon a time in California. A Friend of the Family. Louis Simpson. NNaP

Once upon a time there was a person. Fifth Bedtime Story. Ted Hughes. UsP

Once upon a time there was an Italian. Columbus. Ogden Nash. OFD; RhR

Once upon a time there were three little foxes. The Three Foxes. A. A. Milne. OxBChV

Once we dreamed of eagles. Reading Indian Poetry. Ramona Wilson. VoR

Once we felt at home with Nature if we knew the nomenclature. Progress. Felicia Lamport. QQQ

Once we rode. The Number One Daughter of the Wang Family. Chen Hsieh, *tr. by* C. H. Kwock. MIT

Once we talked. Haiku. Louis Cuneo. CPA

Once we'd packed up your clothes. Partial Eclipse. W. D. Snodgrass. Moon; PSN

Once When She Thought Aloud. Dorothea MacKellar. MAuV

Once when the snow of the year was beginning to fall. The Runaway. Robert Frost. ECBV; PH; PPM; VGW

Once, when their hearts were wild with joy. On Harting Down. T. Sturge Moore. OxBTC

Once when you were a star. A Poem for Foster. Walter Bradford. HeS

Once white with bells, and blithe, but now a mast. Cactus Stem. Clinton F. Larson. MPA

Once, with a whirl of thought oppressed. The Day of Judgment. Swift. InPK. *See also* With a whirl of thought oppres'd.

Once you said joking slyly. The Faithful. Jane Cooper. CoPAm

Oncoming Industrial Revolution, The. George Crabbe. *Fr.* The Village. OBP

Ondt and the Gracehoper, The. James Joyce. *Fr.* Finnegans Wake. BIrV

One. Carolyn M. Rodgers. BPo

One, The. *Tr. fr. Sanskrit by* Raimundo Panikkar. *Fr.* Bhagavadgita. ILwL

One/ poem. Poem. Mbembe. NW

One A.M. Denise Levertov. CAPP

One a.m./ and she has been sleeping. He She Because How. Anselm Hollo. TwMBP

One afternoon as I was wandering around. A Lesson in Oblivion. Dabney Stuart. GP

One alone is God; there cannot be a second. *Tr. fr. Sanskrit by* Raimundo Panikkar. *Fr.* Upanishads. ILwL

One amber dextrous day. Negotiations. John T. Zaremba. DNGG

One-and-Twenty. Samuel Johnson. *See* Short Song of Congratulation, A.

One-and-Twenty. *Unknown.* AmFP

One, Annie and Me. Alicia Ostriker. UsP

One arch of the sky. Love in Labrador. Carl Sandburg. VGW

One Art. Elizabeth Bishop. HAP

One asked a madman if a wife he had. A Mad Answer of a Madman. Robert Hayman. FF; SoSe

One Beauty Still. George Dillon. PPM

One blindfold went upon the narrow ridge. The Deliverance. Ralph Knevet. SCP-2

One block away from my house is an office building. Tie Your Tongue, Sir? Robert Paul Smith. ECBV

One born to hardship in his place and station. Vidya, *tr. by* Daniel H. H. Ingalls. *Fr.* Substantiations. PBWP

One boy, Saint Dwyn, my bauble. Lament for Sion y Glyn. Lewis Glyn Cothi, *tr. by* Joseph P. Clancy. OBW

One brought me the news of your death, O Herakleitos my friend. Elegy on Herakleitos. Callimachus, *tr. by* Dudley Fitts. InPK

One by one, the ancient. Next Year, in Jerusalem. Shirley Kaufman. VWA

One by one they appear in. My Sad Captains. Thom Gunn. CMoP (1970 ed.); InPS

One can do one begins to one can only. Reincarnation (II). James Dickey. CAPP

One cannot now help thinking. Now It's Happened. D. H. Lawrence. OBP

One cannot possess. Heritage. Augustus Young. CIP; IPM

One chain-smoked cigarettes. Grandfathers. Michael Castro. VWA

One chance, The. Scar. Coleman Barks. *Fr.* Body Poems. NVAP

One Chip of Human Bone. Ray A. Young Bear. VW

One chop uncovered. Chops. Alan Dixon. BoAnP

One Chord. Nelly Sachs, *tr. fr. German by* Keith Bosley. VWA

One Christmas eve my lovers and I. Death and Disfiguration. Judy Grahn. *Fr.* A Woman Is Talking to Death. WBN

One Christmas eve, when Santa Claus. Santa Claus and the Mouse. Emilie Poulsson. MN

One clean-shaven like a white grape, The. Peter Redgrove. *Fr.* The Barbers. FoP

One cop holds the spic delicately between thumb and forefinger. The Jet Must Be Hunting for Something. Robert Penn Warren. CoPAm

One crunch of fangs is all the thanks I'd get. The Sleepdancers. Peter Viereck. BCr

One dark world is all I am. Born Again. Forugh Farrokhzad, *tr. by* Jascha Kessler *and* Amin Banani. PBWP

One day/ as I was lying on the lawn. The Gift. Ed Ochester. GP

One day/ Marilyn marched. Chic Freedom's Reflection. Alice Walker. NMM

One day/ the apolitical/ intellectuals. Apolitical Intellectuals. Otto Rene Castillo. EC

One day/ two people decide to build a bed. The Bed. Dennis Saleh. NeAC

One day/ while playing with old junk in the attic. Little Johnny's Foolish Invention. Brian Patten. BuTh

One day/ You gonna walk in this house. Seduction. Nikki Giovanni. NMM; RiTi

One day, a fine day, a high-flying-sky day. The Cat Heard the Cat-Bird. John Ciardi. ECBV; SO

One day a wag—what would the wretch be at? Art. Ambrose Bierce. InPK

One day a week I stay home. When You Are Gone. Nance Van Winckel. AMV-81

One day across the lake where echoes come now. The Animal That Drank Up Sound. William Stafford. VGW

One day after school. Tanya. Jay Parini. AMV-80

One day as I rambled, down by the seashore. I Never Will Marry. Unknown. FSW

One day as I unwarily did gaze. Amoretti, XVI. Spenser. OAEL-1

One day as I was a-rambling around. Will Bill Jones. Unknown. AmFP

One day as I was sitting still. The Battle of Sole Bay. Unknown. GBP

One-Day Diary. John Biguenet. CoPAm

One day I complained about the periphery. Periphery. A. R. Ammons. NOBA

One day I was out walking on the mountain. The Wild Lumberjack. Unknown. AIW

One day I was walking, I heard a complaining. The Housewife's Lament. Unknown. FSW; MAT

One day I went down in the golden harvest field. Unknown. GBP

One day I wrote her name upon the strand. Amoretti, LXXV. Spenser. BoLoP; CABA (1972 ed.); EBEV; GBL; HAP; HeIP; ILP (1975 ed.); IPWM; LFH; LoAs; NIL; OAEL-1; PBMP; WeW

One day in the Library. Further Advantages of Learning. Kenneth Rexroth. MPA; TAP

One day Mamma said "Conrad dear." The Story of Little Suck-a-Thumb. Heinrich Hoffmann, tr. fr. German. SpRo

One day, one day, (one day, one day). Long John. Unknown. FSW

One day ringing men will be a race gone. The Ringers. John Peck. AmPA

One day soon he'll tell her it's time to start packing. Drifters. Bruce Dawe. GAS; MAuV

One day Sun found a new canyon. People of the South Wind. William Stafford. NNaP

One day the amorous Lysander. The Disappointment. Aphra Behn. SBG; SCP-2

One day the Chinese Bird of Royalty, Fum. Fum and Hum, the Two Birds of Royalty. Thomas Moore. OBSV

One day the Earth will be. Prophecy. Jules Supervielle, tr. by Jan Pallister. AMV-81

One day the Nouns were clustered in the street. Permanently. Kenneth Koch. CAPP; OSP; PoA; PPP

One day the sun was rising high. The Peddler and His Wife. Unknown. AmFP

One day the thing to do/ is quit your job. Love Poem, I. Elizabeth Wray. PoUp

One day the tired sea will open to the sun. Like a Pearl. Hayim Naggid, tr. by Shlomo Vinner and Howard Schwartz. VWA

One day when I was a child, long ago. Grace Paley. NMM

One day when I was studying with Stan Musial. Baseball. Tom Clark. LiSp

One day, while in a lonesome grove. Newberry. Unknown. AmFP

One day while walking down Thirty Fifth Street. He's a Fool. Unknown. FSW

One day you look at the mirror and it's open. Glass. W. S. Merwin. EAS

One day you trip and jar yourself. Tracks. Mei Berssenbrugge. NW

One day you'll have to go to the City of the Dead. Elephants May Parade before Your House. Gond Oral Tradition, tr. by V. Elwin and S. Hivale. WTO

One dignity delays for all. Emily Dickinson. SoSe (1977 ed.)

One Divinity of Father, Son, The. John Byrom. Fr. On Trinity Sunday. PeD

One dolphin./ Strongly curved, watertight. Dolphin Seen Alone. Richmond Lattimore. BoAnP

One dot/ Grainily shifting. The Bee. James Dickey. LiSp; SoSe

One dream of passion and of beauty more! Properzia Rossi. Felicia Dorothea Hemans. SBG

One effort more, one cheerful sally more. Mark Akenside. Fr. The Pleasures of Imagination, IV. EPC

One-Eleven Grape Street. Dan Masterson. CoPAm

One evenin' in de month of May. Johnny Get Your Gun. Monroe H. Rosenfeld. PSoN

One evening a goose, for a treat. The Misapprehended Goose. Oliver Herford. TDH

One evening a young lady fair, her estate rode out to see. On the Banks of Salee. Unknown. AmFP

One evening as the sun went down. The Big Rock Candy Mountains. Unknown. AmFP; FSW; OBAL; SoS

One evening bright stars they were shining. The Brooklyn Theater Fire. Unknown. AmFP

One evening, coming home when I should. Winter Evening. Harry Behn. CaYB

One evening in November I happened for to stray. Johnny Carroll's Camp. Unknown. AmFP

One evening last June as I rambled. On the Banks of the Little Eau Pleine. Unknown. AmFP

One evening (surely I was led by her). Guilt. Wordsworth. Fr. The Prelude, I. BoReV

One evening when the sun was low. The Big Rock Candy Mountains. Unknown. GBP

One-Eye. W. S. Merwin. ILP (1975 ed.)

One eye open. Polar Bear. Diana Der Hovanessian. BCr

One eye without a head to wear it. On the Farther Wall, Marc Chagall. Phyllis McGinley. Fr. Spectator's Guide to Contemporary Art. OBSV

One Eyed Black Man in Nebraska. Sam Cornish. PoBA

One-eyed Bridegroom, The. Constance Urdang. Moon

One face looks out from all his canvases. In an Artist's Studio. Christina Rossetti. OBP

One fall not far from Ozark, Arkansas. The Narrative Hooper and L.D.O. Sestina with a Long Last Line. James Whitehead. HoPM (1975 ed.) TAT

One feather is a bird. The Voice. Theodore Roethke. NowV; VGW

One fine green line precedes another. We Don't Know What to Plan or Say or Do. Lee Lally. PoUp

One Fish Ball. Unknown. FSW

One Fixed Star. Ardoin Casgrain. PPM

One Flesh. Elizabeth Jennings. MPo; OxBTC; PBWP

One flower at a time, please. Bouquets. Robert Francis. GP

One flutter of memory, then all becomes. Burning the Letters. Gwendolyn Grew. HoPM (1975 ed.)

One Foot in Eden. Edwin Muir. BoReV; CMoP (1970 ed.); NoAM; NOBE

One foot in front of the other, heel to toe. Highway Patrol Stops Me, Going Too Slow. Robert Peterson. NeAC

One Foot in the River.  Gerald Stern.  NYP

One for All Time, The.  Paul Eluard, *tr. fr. French by* Wallace Fowlie.  LoAs

One for the Album.  Rhyll McMaster.  CAAP

One for the Fatherland.  Leonard Nathan.  PoW

One for the Ladies at the Troy Laundry Who Cooled Themselves for Zimmer.  Paul Zimmer.  GP

One forfeit more from life the current claimed.  At the Discharge of Canon Rise the Drowned.  Hubert Witheford.  ATNZ

One Fragment for God.  William Everson.  MIT

One Furrow, The.  R. S. Thomas.  HoPM (1975 ed.)

One Gardenia 50C.  Ben Maddow.  SPT

One gets inured to having the wrong face.  Two Faces.  Anthony Thwaite.  HeHu

One girl in a red dress leaves the shopping center.  Suburban Dusk.  Bert Meyers.  EAS

One-gloved beasts in cleats, they come clattering.  Golfers.  John Updike.  LiSp

One Goes with Me along the Shore.  Manfred Winkler, *tr. fr. Hebrew by* Mary Zilzer.  VWA

One granite ridge.  Piute Creek.  Gary Snyder.  CAPP; ConAP; MPA; NOBA

One great vision unites us.  World Youth Song.  *Unknown.*  FSW

One had a lovely face.  Memory.  W. B. Yeats.  BIrV

One has a feeling it is all coming to an end.  The Feeling.  William Bronk.  VGW

One has fallen drunk.  Five Men I Know.  Thomas Lux.  NVAP

One hay-wire sawmill, nice new location.  For Sale.  *Unknown.*  BPAW

One high, one high, one high holiday.  Matty Groves.  *Unknown.*  FSW

One Hogmany, at Glesca Fair.  Rothesay, O.  *Unknown.*  FSW

One Home.  William Stafford.  IPWM; VGW; VoA

One Hook.  Ronald Wallace.  AAN

One Hope, The.  Dante Gabriel Rossetti.  The House of Life, CI.  OAEL-2; VLP

One-horned Ewe, The.  *Unknown.*  GBP

One Horse Open Sleigh, The.  James S. Pierpont.  *See* Jingle Bells.

One hot Bengali night returning home.  Grand Hotel, Calcutta.  Layle Silbert.  AMV-81

One house in my walk holds a corner.  The Corner.  Rita Johnson.  AMV-80

One hue of our Flag is taken.  The Rejected "National Hymns."  "Orpheus C. Kerr."  OBAL

108 Tales of a Po'Buckra, *sel.*  Will Inman.  "Dark brother touches me, The."  GP

One hundred feet from off the ground.  Long-Suffering of God.  Christopher Smart.  *Fr.* Hymns for the Amusement of Children.  LAuP

151st Psalm, The.  Karl Shapiro.  VWA

One hundred fifty miles down, these uncut.  Hope Diamonds.  Madeline DeFrees.  MPA

112 at Presidio.  Virginia Long.  AMV-80

100 Year Old Woman at Christmas Dinner.  Colin Style.  AMV-80

One if by land.  Early Warning.  Shirley Marks.  QQQ

One infant grows up and becomes a jockey.  Confessions of a Born Spectator.  Ogden Nash.  LiSp

One job she had was to dry fish.  Dried Things Out.  Samuel Makidemewabe.  TC

One kick/ of Cossack's boots.  Golda.  Adrienne Wolfert.  AMV-80

One Kingfisher and One Yellow Rose.  Eileen Brennan.  PFIr

One-l lama, The.  The Lama.  Ogden Nash.  RAE

One late afternoon I hitched from Galway down to Kinvara.  Kennedy.  Michael Heffernan.  AMV-80

One Leaf, The.  Leslie Norris.  LP

One Leg.  William Mohr.  PoW

One-legged Colonel, The.  *Unknown.*  TDH

One-legged Man, The.  Siegfried Sassoon.  CMoP (1970 ed.)

One Lion, Once.  Robert Canzoneri.  CoPAm

One little noise of life remain'd—I heard.  On the Eclipse of the Moon of October 1865.  Charles Tennyson Turner.  VPC

One look at this mill and the adjacent croft.  Mill at Romesdal.  Richard Hugo.  AMV-80

One looks from the train.  The Orient Express.  Randall Jarrell.  CMoP (1970 ed.); NOBA

One Man One Vote.  Patricia Beer.  HeHu

One Man Went to Mow, *with music.*  *Unknown.*  GSB

One Man's Wife.  Philip Booth.  VGW

1,000,001 Starlings.  Karoniaktatie.  NW

One Mr. B——,/ A joker he.  Repartée.  Charles Follen Adams.  OBAL

One misty, moisty morning.  Mother Goose.  MG

One Modern Poet.  Carl Sandburg.  OBAL

One month after my tenth birthday.  August 12, 1952.  Charles Fishman.  AMV-81

One More Day's Work for Jesus, *with music.*  Anna B. Warner.  AH

One more little spirit to Heaven has flown.  Little Libbie.  Julia A. Moore.  OBAL; PeD

One more march.  March on the Delta.  Art Berger.  NowV

One More New Botched Beginning.  Stephen Spender.  CMoP (1970 ed.); NoAM

One More Night.  Bob Dylan.  UsP

One More River to Cross.  *Unknown.*  FSW

One More Time.  Alvin Aubert.  GP

One More Time.  Patricia Goedicke.  AMV-80

One More Time.  Richard Shelton.  GP

One More Time.  James Welch.  VW

One more unfortunate.  The Bridge of Sighs.  Thomas Hood.  EBV; FaPoR; PeD; UsP

One morn as through Hyde Park we walk'd.  Epilogue to Lessing's Laocoön.  Matthew Arnold.  VLP

One morn before me were three figures seen.  Ode on Indolence.  Keats.  MBPR

One Morning.  Ellen Levine.  AMV-81

One Morning.  Vassar Miller.  AMV-80

One morning as I rambled.  The Miner Boy.  *Unknown.*  AmFP

One morning, as we travelled in the fields.  The Riders Held Back.  Louis Simpson.  ConAP

One Morning in May.  *Unknown.*  AIW; FSW (Nightingale, The.)  AmFP

One Morning in May; or, The Young Girl Cut Down in Her Prime.  *Unknown.*  AmFP

One morning in St. Thomas, when I tried.  The Eye.  Richard Wilbur.  FiCP

One morning in spring.  Fife Tune.  John Manifold.  GAS

One Morning, Oh, So Early!  Jean Ingelow.  OxBChV

One morning old Wilfrid Scawen Blunt.  Limerick.  Victor Gray.  NOBL

One morning, one morning, one morning in May.  One Morning in May [*or* The Nightingale].  *Unknown.*  AIW; AmFP; FSW

One morning, one morning, one morning in spring.  I'll Be Fourteen Next Sunday.  *Unknown.*  AmFP; OLR

One Morning We Brought Them Order.  Al Lee.  FF; WIF

One morning when I went downtown.  Morning in Spring.  Louis Ginsberg.  ECBV

One morning when you went.  Breakthrough.  Philip Roberts.  FPA

One mos' ___ self is not this mirror's, The. Himself. Daniel Hoffman. AMV–80

One Music. Edwin Markham. *See* There Is a High Place.

One must have a mind of winter. The Snow Man. Wallace Stevens. CABA (1972 ed.); CMoP (1970 ed.); HAP; HeIP; InPK; MAT; NU; PiAm; STS; TT; UsP

One need not be a chamber—to be haunted. Emily Dickinson. AmVN; PiAm; Psy

One needs a lyric poet in these. Julius Lester. In the Time of Revolution, IV. PoBA

One needs a lyric poet in this. Julius Lester. In the Time of Revolution, VI. PoBA

One night/ as I lay. Old Folk Tale. Barbara Drake. TC

One night a bird came to me. Night Visitors. Kadya Molodovsky, *tr. by* Ruth Whitman. VWA

"One night," a doctor said, "last fall." Ambrose Bierce. *Fr.* The Devil's Dictionary. OBAL

One night, all tired with the weary day. The Gnat. Joseph Beaumont. SCP-2

One night as Dick lay half asleep. Full Moon. Walter de la Mare. ECBV

One night as I lay on my bed. Death. *Unknown, tr. by* Aneirin Talfan Davies. OBW

One Night Away from Day. John Digby. EAS

One night, being pressed by his old friend Chubb. The Undertakers' Club. *Unknown.* GBP

One night came on a hurricane. The Sailor's Consolation. William Pitt, *wr. at. to* Charles Dibdin. FaBoCo; PoPle

One night, crossing a muddy field. The House-Trailer. Lawrence Russ. TC

One night from the stern I thought, as I watched. Braemar. Galway Kinnell. PoA

One night he dreamed he was a. The Young Man Who Loved the Girl Who Took Care of Her Aged Father. Greg Kuzma. AmPA

One night he heard heart-breaking sound. Austin Clarke. *Fr.* Mnemosyne lay in Dust. CIP; CMoP (1970 ed.)

One night I reached a cave: I slept, my head. Incident on a Journey. Thom Gunn. MPo

One night in the year, my dearest beauties, come. To His Lovely Mistresses. Robert Herrick. CaPo; ILP (1975 ed.)

One night of tempest I arose and went. Night and Morning. *Unknown, tr. by* R. S. Thomas. OBW

One night there appeared a child in the camp. Blue. Scott Momaday. *Fr.* The Colors of Night. BCr

One night when I was in the House of Death. Birth. Harold Monro. *Fr.* Strange Meetings. PoA

One night, your mother is listening to the walls. How You Get Born. Erica Jong. UnPo (1976 ed.); UsP

One nostril means latin. Queer Things. Emanuel Carnevali. EAS

One of my father; he stands. Photographs. Charles Wright. HoPM (1975 ed.)

One of my wishes is that those dark trees. Into My Own. Robert Frost. PPM

One of the Chapters. Kathleen Fraser. CPA

One of the numb ones, hating. Fighting Talk. Tom Buchan. MIS

One of the other things. Toad Suck Ferry. H. R. Stoneback. TAT

One of their horses was Nancy Hanks. Going to Town. Fred Lape. PH

One of them seems to offer her breasts. Two Women with Mangoes. Steven Cramer. AMV–80

One of them undid your blouse, then. For the Country. Larry Levis. NVAP

One of these days under the white. The Boarding. Denis Johnson. AMV–80

One of these last summer nights. Finding a Friend Home. Timothy Hamm. AMV–80

One of these mornings bright and fair. Great Day. *Unknown.* FSW

One of us/ will/ be. Devils. Norman Mailer. OBAL

One of you is a major made of cord and catskin. Lent in a Year of War. Thomas Merton. EAS

One Old Ox. *Unknown.* FaBoNo

One old woman, Lord, in this town. Oh, Babe, It Ain't No Lie. Elizabeth Cotton. FSW

One ought not to have to care. The Hill Wife. Robert Frost. CMoP (1975 ed.); HAP; VGW

One ounce of truth benefits. Nikki Giovanni. CNA

One peers over test tubes, samples soils. Projects. Emery E. George. AAN

One Perfect Rose. Dorothy Parker. OBAL; OLR; PAIC; PoIA; PPM

One person present steps on his pedal of speech. The Talker. Mona Van Duyn. POL

One Saturday night as we set sail. The Mermaid. *Unknown.* AmFP

One scene as I bow to pour her coffee. Vacation. William Stafford. POL; SFF

One seem'd all dark and red—a tract of sand. Tennyson. *Fr.* The Palace of Art. UnPo (1976 ed.)

1 September 1939. John Berryman. NIL

One should not neglect one's chin-ups. An Exigent Gymnast. Merle Meeter. AATT

One side of his world is always missing. Riding a One-eyed Horse. Henry Taylor. PH

One Sided Shoot-out. Don L. Lee. BPo; PoBA

One silent night of late. The Cheat of Cupid; or, The Ungentle Guest. Robert Herrick, *after* Anacreon. OBVE

One sister for sale! For Sale. Shel Silverstein. CTBA

One Snowy Night in December. John N. Morris. NYP

One Song, The. C. G. Hanzlicek. AMV–80

One Song. Stanley Plumly. HeS

One sound. Then the hiss and whir. The Garden. Louise Glück. AmPA; FiCP

One spot of cheer in the Midlands gloom. Insurance. D. J. Enright. HeHu

One still dark night I sat alone and wrote. Sonnet. Frederick Goddard Tuckerman. *Fr.* Sonnets. PiAm

One stone sufficeth (lo what death can do). On a Whore. John Hoskyns. FaBoEE

One stood still, looking stupid. The other. The Willets. May Swenson. WPE

One stormy morn I chanced to meet. A Kiss in the Rain. Samuel Minturn Peck. OBAL

One Summer Evening. Wordsworth. *Fr.* The Prelude, I. OBP ("One summer evening (led by her) I found.") NU; UsP

One summer, high in Wyoming. Before the Storm. Kenneth O. Hanson. MPA

One Summer in Charleston. Michael Hogan. DNGG

One summer morning the sun fell gold. Waking Up. Edward Lense. AMV–80

One Sunday, Dad was feeling bad. When Dad Felt Bad. Charles Causley. FPB

One Sunday mornin' Lambton went. The Lambton Worm. *Unknown.* DuDr; PeBB

One sure hand. Skipping Stones. Allan D. Farber. SoSe

One Sweetly Solemn Thought, *with music*. Phoebe Cary. AH

One That Got Away, The. Gary Miranda. AAN

One that is ever kind said yesterday. The Folly of Being Comforted. W. B. Yeats. GBL; HeIP; LoAs; SoSe; VLP

One, The Other, And. Wendy Wieber. NMM

One thing has a shelving bank. A Drumlin Woodchuck. Robert Frost. ILP (1975 ed.); NoAM; NOBA

One thing I waited for always. The Smile Was. Dannie Abse. PMW

One Thing That Can Save America, The. John Ashbery. NOBA

One thing that literature would be greatly the better for. Very like a Whale. Ogden Nash. HAP; InPK; PoIA; UsP; WeW

One Thing to Take, Another to Keep. Crescenzo del Monte, tr. fr. Judeo-Romanesque by Barbara Garvin. VWA

One thing you left with us, Jack Johnson. Strange Legacies. Sterling A. Brown. CNA; PoBA

One thing you taught me I'm grateful for. The Lesson. Elizabeth Peterson. AMV-80

One thought the recurring "image" in the poet's song. Handbook of Versification. Gilbert Sorrentino. PoA

One thousand eight hundred and twenty-four. The Greenland Whale Fishery. Unknown. AmFP

One Thousand Fearful Words for Fidel Castro. Lawrence Ferlinghetti. VGW

One thousand saxophones infiltrate the city. Battle Report. Bob Kaufman. AmNP (1974 ed.)

One Time Henry Dreamed the Number. Doughtry Long. BPo; CNA; PoBA

One-time liaison officer in Babel's tower. The Oracle. Gordon Challis. ATNZ

One to destroy, is murder by the law. Edward Young. FF

One to make ready. Unknown. MG

One to Nothing. Carolyn Kizer. OBAL

One train was the last. The Branch Line. Patricia Beer. HeHu

One translucent magenta leaf on a hot house plant is. Filtres. Andrew Hoyem. MIT

One tree might take seventy years to produce this round. Acorns. Paul Mills. MIS

One, two/ Buckle my shoe. Mother Goose. MG

One, two, three, four. Mother Goose. MG

One, two, three, four, five. Unknown. MG

1-2-3 was the number he played but today the number came 3-2-1. Dirge. Kenneth Fearing. FF; HeIP; HoPM (1975 ed.); InPK; NIL; SPT

One ugly trick has often spoiled. Meddlesome Matty. Ann Taylor. OxBChV

One wading a Fall meadow finds on all sides. The Beautiful Changes. Richard Wilbur. CMoP (1970 ed.); ILP (1975 ed.); InPS; LFH; NIL

One wants a Teller in a time like this. Gwendolyn Brooks. Fr. The Womanhood. WPE

One wants to be sitting in. The Sky-splitting Pink Rubber Bistro. Rochelle Owens. RiTi

One was kicked in the stomach. Gangrene. Philip Levine. VGW

One wave/ sucking the shingle. Evolution. Edwin Brock. MPo

One Way Gal. Unknown. BluL

One We Knew. Thomas Hardy. VLP

One wept whose only child was dead. Maternity. Alice Meynell. BBGO

One white foot, try him. On Buying a Horse. Unknown. PH

One who does not love me, The. Song of Abuse. Yoruba Oral Tradition, tr. by Ulli Beier and B. Gbadamosi. WTO

One Who Is Missing, The. Abraham Chalfi, tr. fr. Hebrew by Shlomo Vinner and Howard Schwartz. VWA

One, who is not, we see: but one, whom we see not, is. The Higher Pantheism in a Nutshell. Swinburne. Fr. The Heptalogia. FaBoNo; PAIC; SpRo

One Who Runs Away, The. Callimachus, tr. fr. Greek by Tom Dodge. LiSp

One who sees giant Orion, the torches of wi   midnig   Fligl of Swans. Robinson Jeffers. MPA

One Whose Reproach I Cannot Evade, The. George H hcock. EAS

One winter afternoon. E. E. Cummings. NCSH

One without looks in to-night. The Fallow Deer at the Lonely House. Thomas Hardy. BoAnP; CMoP (1970 ed.)

One word is too often profaned. To ——. Shelley. BoLoP; ILP (1975 ed.); MBPR; NOBE; PPP

One Word More. Robert Browning. VLP
Phases of the Moon, sel. Moon

One writer needs something to cloak him. Plot. Laurie Stroblas. BCr

One year a deer ran through the prison gate. The Deer in the Prison. Joseph Bruchac. NW

One Year Later. Eric Torgerson. POL

One year there were too many/ frogs. Calendar. Cecil Bodker, tr. by Nadia Christensen and Alexander Taylor. BoWoP

One Year to Life on the Grand Central Shuttle. Audre Lorde. CNA

Oneness of the Philosopher with Nature, The. G. K. Chesterton. FaBoNo

One's grand flights, one's Sunday baths. The Sense of the Sleight-of-Hand Man. Wallace Stevens. CABA (1972 ed.); HAP; ILP (1975 ed.); NOBA; PoA

One's-Self I Sing. Walt Whitman. NOBA

Ones who camped on the slopes, below the bare summit, The. Adrienne Rich. Fr. Ghazals: Homage to Ghalib. NIL

Ones who hammer the air with fists, The. Cripples. J. D. Reed. NeAC

Ones You Lost, The. Liza Gyllenhaal. EC

Onion Bucket. Lorenzo Thomas. PoBA

Only/ a little/ yellow/ school bus. Snow Country. David Etter. SFF

Only/ the gray wind. Something for Supper. Carroll Arnett. VoR

Only a bold man ploughs the Weald for corn. V. Sackville-West. Fr. The Land. PES

Only a dish of blueberries could pull me. It's Not the Heat So Much as the Humidity. James Tate. NoAM

Only a few could understand his ways and his outfit queer. The Lost Range. Henry Herbert Knibbs. BPAW

Only a few top-heavy hollyhocks, wilting in arid beds. The Public Gardens. Alun Lewis. PSN

Only a few will really understand. One Sided Shoot-out. Don L. Lee. BPo; PoBA

Only a green hill. A Last Word. W. R. Rodgers. Epi

Only a Little Litter. Myra Cohn Livingston. QQQ

Only a little more. His Poetry His Pillar. Robert Herrick. CaPo

Only a man harrowing clods. In Time of "The Breaking of Nations." Thomas Hardy. BoLoP; CMoP (1970 ed.); EBEV; HAP; ILP (1975 ed.); NoAM; NOBE; OAEL-2; POL; PPM; PPoD; PPP; PSN; VoPo

Only a Miner. Unknown. AmFP

Only Bar in Dixon, The. James Welch. AmPA; FF

Only begotten Son, seest thou what rage. Free Will and God's Foreknowledge. Milton. Fr. Paradise Lost, III. ExPo (1973 ed.)

Only brooms. Brooms. Charles Simic. AmPA; NNaP

Only difference, I said, The. Poetry Workshop in a Reform School. Betty Adcock. AMV-80

Only for Me. Mark Van Doren. NCSH

Only head in the sky, The. Giraffe. Stanley Plumly. AmPA

Only Jealousy of Emer, The. Unknown, tr. fr. Irish by John Montague. BIrV

Only joy now, her ... are. Fourth Song. Sir Philip Sidney. *Fr.* Astrophel and Stella. GBL; HAP

Only last week, walking the hushed fields. Father and Son. F. R. Higgins. BIrV; PFIr

Only Leap That Matters, The. Mark McCloskey. PoW

Only moment held, The. Night Train. Mary C. Fineran. AMV-81

Only monument, The. On the Pavement. David A. Sam. AMV-80

Only My Opinion. Monica Shannon. CTV

Only on the rarest occasions, when the blue air. The Mountain. W. S. Merwin. VGW

Only One Mother. George Cooper. CTV

Only quiet death. Threnody. Waring Cuney. AmNP (1974 ed.)

Only response, The. Poem. William Knott. InPK

Only revolution is among the oaks, The. Bicentennial Winter. Linda Pastan. WasP

Only Seven. Henry Sambrooke Leigh. SpRo

Only Sign, The/ advertises Tire Ale. Thinking about Carnevale's Wife. Wesley McNair. FAF

Only snake writes, a coil sprung in my fingers. Yetzer ha Ra. Edward Codish. VWA

Only teaching on Tuesdays, book-worming. Memories of West Street and Lepke. Robert Lowell. CAPP; CMoP (1970 ed.); ConAP; CoPAm; InPS; NOBA; PiAm; PSN

Only Teasing. *Unknown.* TDH

Only the air-spirits know. Solitary Song. *Tr. fr. Eskimo.* WTO

Only the city's people understand four-thirty. American City. Joyce Carol Oates. IPMW

Only the deep well. I Break the Sky. Owen Dodson. PoBA

Only the eye can drink. Eye. Gray Burr. WeW

Only the feathers floating around the hat. Icarus. Edward Field. TPo

Only the human being, absolved from kissing and strife. Death Is Not Evil, Evil Is Mechanical. D. H. Lawrence. PBMP

Only the Illegitimate are beautiful. Thesis. Edward Dorn. NOBA

Only the imagination is real! William Carlos Williams. *Fr.* Asphodel, That Greeny Flower. TT

Only the lion and the cock. After Galen. Oliver St. John Gogarty. FaBoEE

Only the Polished Skeleton. Countee Cullen. IP; VGW

Only the Sky. Pete Winslow. MIT

Only their hands are living, to the wheel attracted. Casino. W. H. Auden. PSN

Only thing that can be relied on, The. The Snow on Saddle Mountain. Kenji Miyazawa, *tr. by* Gary Snyder. IPWM; NoAM; NOBA

Only this evening I saw again low in the sky. Martial Cadenza. Wallace Stevens. NIL; VGW

Only to have a grief. Peeling Onions. Adrienne Rich. BoWoP; TAP

Only totems protrude. An Inhabited Emptiness. Jiri Gold, *tr. by* Jaroslav Kotan *and* Daniel Weissbort. VWA

Only Tourist in Havana Turns His Thoughts Homeward, The. Leonard Cohen. CABA (1972 ed.); NoAM

Only two beds. The Family of Eight. Abraham Reisen, *tr. by* Marcia Falk. VWA

Only Years. Kenneth Rexroth. TAP

Onne Ruddeborne bank twa pynynge maydens sate. Elinoure and Juga. Thomas Chatterton. LAuP

Ons as me thought fortune me kyst. Sir Thomas Wyatt. *See* Once as methought Fortune me kissed.

Onset, The. Robert Frost. CMoP (1970 ed.); PBMP; PPP; TT

Onto the hallowit steid bryng in, thai cry. Virgil, *tr. by* Gavin Douglas. *Fr.* The Aeneid, II. OBVE

Ontology of Accident, The, *sel.* Carlo Parcelli. "Young begin with generalizations, The." PoUp

Onward, Christian Soldiers. Sabine Baring-Gould. BLSH, *with music;* FaPoR; FSW; VLP

"Onward Christian Soldiers!" Frank Marshall Davis. FB

Onward led the road again. Hell Gate. A. E. Housman. NoAM; UnPo (1976 ed.)

Onward, Onward, Men of Heaven, *with music.* Lydia H. Sigourney. AH

Onyons. Swift. *Fr.* Market Women's Cries. BIrV

Oo oo ah, mercy mercy me. Mercy Mercy Me. Marvin Gaye. PoRo

Oocuck, The. Justin Richardson. BoAnP

Ootower the grey-broon mairs. Glencoe. Billy Kay. MIS

Opal. Josephine Miles. PAIC

Open. A. R. Ammons. TT

Open and Closed Space. Tomas Tranströmer, *tr. fr. Swedish by* Robert Bly. EAS

Open Door, The. Elizabeth J. Coatsworth. DuDa; ECBV

Open door says, "Come in," An. Doors. Carl Sandburg. OSP; VsP

Open Earth. Clarisse Nicoïdski, *tr. by* Stephen Levy. VWA

Open Heart. Michael Salcman. AMV-80

Open House. Theodore Roethke. AnMo; NoAM; NOBA; STS

Open Letter from a Constant Reader. Mona Van Duyn. GP; PoA

Open, love. Unclench Yourself. Marge Piercy. NeAC

Open me. Close me. The Swimming Pool. Sandra Hochman. RiTi

Open me like a meadow lily. The Seduction. Suzanne Berger Rioff. NMM

Open Poetry Reading. Jesús Papoleto Meléndez. AMV-81

Open Range. Thomas Mitchell. AMV-81

Open Sea, The. William Meredith. CoPAm; TAP; UnPo (1976 ed.)

Open the Door. *Malay Oral Tradition, tr. by* R. J. Wilkinson *and* R. O. Winstedt. WTO

Open the door, who's there within? *Unknown.* GBL

Open the Heart. Charles Brasch. ATNZ

Open Your Hand. Dorothy R. Fulton. AMV-81

Opened, clear as a child's geography. The Summer Countries. Henry Rago. VGW

Opening Day. Bruce Severy. VW

Opening of Eyes. Laura Riding. NoAM

Opening the Cage: 14 Variations on 14 Words. Edwin Morgan. NIL

Opening up the house. After Death. Patricia Beer. HeHu

Operatic Olivia. Isabel Frances Bellows. TDH

Operation, The. S. L. Henderson Smith. PMW

Operation, The. W. D. Snodgrass. InPK; TAP

Ophelia's Song. Shakespeare. *Fr.* Hamlet, IV, v. GBL ("How Should I your true love know.") AIW

Ophelia's Song. Marya Zaturenska. OLR

Opinion is not worth a rush. Michael Robartes and the Dancer. W. B. Yeats. OAEL-2

Opium-Den, The. *Malay Oral Tradition, tr. by* R. J. Wilkinson *and* R. O. Winstedt. WTO

Opportunistically now I'll begin. Learning to Keep a Low Profile. Elisavietta Ritchie. PoUp

Opportunity. Harry Graham. FaBoCo

Opportunity. Edward Rowland Sill. PCOP

Opportunity's Knock. Morris Bishop. TDH

Opposite Field, The. Dabney Stuart. PCho

Opposite House, The. Robert Lowell. CMoP (1970 ed.); NYP

Opposites. Carolyn Stoloff. RiTi

Oppression. Langston Hughes. CNA

Opulent oracle—it's a terrible thing! It's a Terrible Thing! Everett Hoagland. BPo

Opus virtuoso, the piano grand, The. A Questionnaire for Walter Mitty. Michael Longley. IPM

Opusculum paedagogum. Study of Two Pears. Wallace Stevens. InPK; InPS; NU

Or/ did he make the estuary? Redriff. David Jones. *Fr.* The Anathemata. TwMBP

Or/ hoodoo ecology vs. the judeo. Al Capone in Alaska. Ishmael Reed. MIT

Or a ship's mast. Speak like Rain. Jerred Metz. VWA

Or Ever God Created Adam. *Malay Oral Tradition, tr. by* R. J. Wilkinson. WTO

Or scorn or pity on me take. The Dream. Ben Jonson. NOBE

Oracle, The. Gordon Challis. ATNZ

Oracle ("Iwori wotura"). *Yoruba Oral Tradition, tr. by* Ulli Beier. WTO

Oracles, The. A. E. Housman. BTTM; HAP

Oraga Haru, *sels.* Issa, *tr. fr. Japanese by* Nobuyuki Yuasa. OFD
    Buddha's Birthday: April 8, 1819.
    Buddha's Death Day: February 15, 1815.
    "For a fresh start."

Oral Messages, *sel.* Lawrence Ferlinghetti.
    I Am Waiting. CAPP; GOA

Orange and purple, shot with white and mauve. Orchids. Theodore Wratislaw. VLP

Orange Bears, The. Kenneth Patchen. BCr; IPWM; VoA

Orange Bough, The. Felicia Dorothea Hemans. VLP

Orange devours, An. In Earliest Morning. James Schuyler. UsP

Orange fish are swimming. Watching the Sun Rise over Mount Zion. Ruth Whitman. VWA

Orange in the middle of a table. Against Still Life. Margaret Atwood. NMM

Orange Jews. Ted Berrigan *and* Ron Padgett. EAS

Orange Juice Song. David Phillips. NeAC

Orange leaves are gone. Izumi Shikibu, *tr. fr. Japanese by* Willis Barnstone. BoWoP

Orange Lily, The. *Unknown.* GBP

Orange line splits the sky, An. The Flint Hills. Lew Blockcolski. VoR

Orange on its way. On Its Way. May Swenson. WPE

Orange on the table, An. Alicante. Jacques Prévert, *tr. by* Lawrence Ferlinghetti. BoLoP

Orange Tree, The. John Shaw Neilson. GAS; MAuV

Orange Tree, The. Ellen Pearce. IHMS

Orange Tree Dream. Judith Serin. NPW

Oranges and Lemons, *with music. Unknown.* GSB

Oration on the Toes. Edward Brynes. AMV-81

Orator dismal of Nottinghamshire, An. An Excellent New Song, Being the Intended Speech of a Famous Orator against Peace. Swift. APAS

Orator from rhetorick gardens picks, The. Edward Taylor. Preparatory Meditations: Second Series, XLIV. EAP

Orator Prigg. Blake. OBSV

Oratorical Crab, The. Oliver Herford. TDH

Orators, The, *sel.* W. H. Auden.
    O Where Are You Going? CMoP (1970 ed.); IP; NOBE; OBP; SoSe (1977 ed.); TT
    (Song: "O Where Are You Going?") ILP (1975 ed.); OAEL-2

Orbed Maiden. Shelley. *Fr.* The Cloud. Moon

Orchard. Hilda Doolittle ("H. D."). CMoP (1970 ed.)

Orchard, The. Michael Spence. AMV-80

Orchard. Ruth Stone. PH

Orchard Is Not Cut Down, The ("The orchard is gone. A space"). Peter Whigham. TwMBP

Orchard-Pit, The. Dante Gabriel Rossetti. OAEL-2; VLP

Orchard Snow. J. B. Goodenough. AMV-81

Orchards half the way, The. The First of May. A. E. Housman. TT

Orchestra. Reg Saner. AMV-80

Orchestra, The. William Carlos Williams. HAP

Orchestra; or, A Poeme of Dauncing, *sels.* Sir John Davies.
    "And merry Bacchus practiced dancing too." NIL
    "Behold the worlde, how it is whirled round." OBP
    "Harke how the birds doe sing, and marke then how." OBP
    Praise of Dancing, The. NOBE

Orchids. Theodore Roethke. AnMo; CMoP (1970 ed.); ExPo (1973 ed.); PF; PiAm; PPoe

Orchids. Theodore Wratislaw. VLP

Ordeal. Nina Cassian, *tr. fr. Rumanian by* Michael Impey *and* Brian Swann. PBWP

Order and Degree. Shakespeare. *See* On Degree.

Order of Service. Amiri Baraka. UsP

Ordered to strip prior to execution. Murder of a Community. Daniel Weissbort. VWA

Orders. Robert Duncan. *Fr.* Passages. CAAP

Ordinance on Failure. Naomi Lazard. AAN

Ordinance on Winning. Naomi Lazard. AAN; GP

Ordinarily I call it "my cock but." My Penis. Ed Ochester. GP

Ordinary Day, An. Norman MacCaig. LP

Ordinary Evening in Cleveland, An. Lewis Turco. ANTL

Ordinary Man, The. Robert Service. BBGO

Ore is waiting in the tubs; the snow's upon the fell, The. Four Pence a Day. *Unknown.* FSW

Oread. Hilda Doolittle ("H. D."). CMoP (1970 ed.); ExPo (1973 ed.); LFH; NoAM; NOBA; PiAm; RiTi; SBG; TAP; UsP; WeW

Oregon Landscape with Lost Lover. Olga Broumas. CNW

Oregon Message, An. William Stafford. Moon

Oregon Trail, The. Arthur Guiterman. BPAW

Oregon Trail, The. *Unknown.* BPAW

Oregon Trail: 1851. James Marshall. BPAW

Oreti Beach. Charles Brasch. ATNZ

Organ Cactus, The. Dorothy Scarborough. BPAW

Organ Solo. Knute Skinner. GP

Organ Transplant. J. D. Reed. POL

Organizer's Bogeymen, The. Marge Piercy. Psy

Orgasm completely, The. Sonnet. Tom Clark. PPoD

Orient Express, The. Randall Jarrell. CMoP (1970 ed.); NOBA

Oriental. Napoleon St. Cyr. FAF

Orientale. W. E. Henley. PeD

Oriflamme. Jessie Redmond Fauset. PoBA

Origin of Baseball, The. Kenneth Patchen. IPWM; LiSp; TPo

Origin of Cities, The. Robert Hass. PCho

Origin of Hot and Cold According to the Delawares, The. Lyn Lifshin. FAF

Origin of Species, The. Myra Sklarew. PoUp

Origin of the Praise of God, The. Robert Bly. NU

Original./ Ragged-round. Malcolm X. Gwendolyn Brooks. CNA; NowV; OFD; PoBA; TT

Original Epitaph on a Drunkard. Royall Tyler. OBAL

Original family rock is three parts restored, The. Anniversary. Daniel Weissbort. VWA

Original man lies down to be copied, The. Xerox. Ben Belitt. NYP

Original Sequence. Philip Booth. SFF

Original Sin. Robinson Jeffers. MPA; PiAm

Original Sin: A Short Story. Robert Penn Warren. CoPAm; HoPM (1975 ed.); PPP; TAP

Original Sin on the Sussex Coast. John Betjeman. BBGO

Origins. Keorapetse Kgositsile. PoBA

Origins of Escape, The. Charles P. R. Tisdale. AMV-81

Orinda to Lucasia Parting, October 1661, at London. Katherine Philips. SCP-2

"Oriole, questing." Nesting Time. Arthur Guiterman. ECBV

Oriole with joy was sweetly singing, The. In the Shade of the Old Apple Tree. Harry H. Williams. FSN

Orion, *sels*. Richard Henry Horne.
"Man who for his race might supersede, The." VLP
"There was a slumbrous silence in the air." VLP

Orion. Adrienne Rich. NIL; NoAM; WPE

Orison to the Blessed Virgin, An. William Herebert. BoReV

Orlando Commercial, The. George MacBeth. NOBL

Orlando Furioso, *sels*. Ariosto, *tr. fr. Italian by* Sir John Harington.
"Alcyna met them at the outer gate," *fr*. VII. OBVE
"Blessed angell not a word replies, The," *fr*. XIV. OBVE
"Go soule, go sweetest soule for ever blest," *fr*. XXIX. OBVE

Ornaments. Frank Ormsby. CIP

Ornithology. Siv Cedering Fox. NVAP

Ornithology in Florida. Arthur Guiterman. BoAnP

Oro Stage, The. Henry Herbert Knibbs. BPAW

Orotava Road, The. Basil Bunting. NoAM

O'Rourke's Feast. Hugh MacGowran, *tr. fr. Irish by* Charles Wilson. BIrV
(Description of an Irish-Feast, The, *tr. by* Swift.) OBVE

Orphan, The. *Unknown, tr. fr. Chinese by* Arthur Waley. PoA

Orphan beat of my heart, The. "Ping Hsin," *tr. fr. Chinese by* Kenneth Rexroth *and* Ling Chung. BoWoP

Orphan Born. Robert Jones Burdette. OBAL

Orphan Girl, The. *Unknown*. AmFP

Orphan hours, the year is dead. Dirge for the Year. Shelley. FSFS

Orphan, The; or, The Unhappy Marriage, *sels*. Thomas Otway. SCP-2
"Then thus let's go together," *fr*. IV, ii.
"Where am I? Sure I wander 'midst enchantment," *fr*. V, ii.

Orphan, yes, An. But not. Fragment Reflection I. Doris Turner. JB

Orphanage, The. Grace Cavalieri. PoUp

Orphans. David Ray. FiCP

Orphee at Rest. Frank Stewart. PHC

Orpheus. Michael Goldman. NowV

Orpheus. Robert Herrick. CaPo

Orpheus. Yvor Winters. NOBA; PiAm; VGW

Orpheus and Eurydice. Ovid, *tr. fr. Latin by* Rolfe Humphries. *Fr*. Metamorphoses. GrRo

Orpheus he went (as poets tell). Orpheus. Robert Herrick. CaPo

Orpheus I am, come from the deeps below. John Fletcher. *Fr*. The Mad Lover, IV, i. GBL

Orpheus in Greenwich Village. Jack Gilbert. POL

Orpheus in the Underworld. David Gascoyne. FaBoTw (1975 ed.)

Orpheus to Beasts. Richard Lovelace. CaPo

Orpheus to Eurydice. Frederick Morgan. AMV-80

Orpheus to Woods. Richard Lovelace. CaPo

Orpheus with his lute made trees. Sweet Music's Power. John Fletcher. *Fr*. King Henry VIII (*by* Shakespeare). NOBE

Orthodoxy's staunch adherent. To Dr. Kipling. Richard Porson. FaBoCo

Ortho's Epitaph. Theocritus, *tr. fr. Greek by* Charles Stuart Calverley. FaBoEE

O's Operatic Olivia. Operatic Olivia. Isabel Frances Bellows. TDH

Osawatomie. Carl Sandburg. CMoP (1970 ed.)

Oscar Robertson: Peripheral Vision. William Matthews. PPoD

Oshun, the River Goddess. *Yoruba Oral Tradition, tr. by* Ulli Beier. WTO

Osip Mandelshtam. Irving Layton. NeAC

Osprey's Nest, The. David Wagoner. CNW

Ossified Oyster, An. Carolyn Wells. TDH

Ostrich, The. Lord Alfred Douglas. BBL

Ostrich Is a Silly Bird. Mary E. Wilkins Freeman. CTV

Ostrich who lived at the zoo, An. The Bored Ostrich. *Unknown*. TDH

Othello, *sels*. Shakespeare.
"And let me the canakin clink, clink," *fr*. II, iii. AIW
"Behold, I have a weapon," *fr*. V, ii. BIP
"Her father lov'd me; oft invited me," *fr*. I, iii. EBEV
"It is the cause, it is the cause, my soul," *fr*. V, ii. BIP; EBEV
"My mother had a maid call'd Barbara," *fr*. IV, iii. AIW

Othello Jones Dresses for Dinner. Ed Roberson. PoBA

Other, The. Peter Cooley. AMV-80

Other. Lance Henson. VoR

Other Books by the Author? Mbembe. NW

Other bright days of action have seemed great. John Masefield. *Fr*. Biography. OxBTC

Other Children. Robert Louis Stevenson. PCOP

Other day I chanced to meet, The. The Angry Man. Phyllis McGinley. SoS

Other day I was loving a sweet little fruitpie-and-cream, The. Lines. Gavin Ewart. EAS

Other Fabrics, Other Mores! Anna Maria Lenngren, *tr. fr. Swedish by* Nadia Christensen *and* Mariann Tiblin. PBWP

Other Lives. Patricia Hooper. AMV-81

Other Lives. Vern Rutsala. MPA

Other men are thorn. Mahadevi, *tr. fr. Kannada by* A. K. Ramanujan. BoWoP

Other night, The. Visions of You. Tim Burke. PHC

Other night while I was sparking sweet Terlina Spray, The. Kiss Me Quick and Go. Silas S. Steele. BLSo

Other one, The. Rumor You Called My Name. Susan North. FoP

Other props are gone, The. Je t'adore. Thomas Kinsella. NoAM

Other ranchers came this morning, The. Day of the Wolf. Keith Wilson. MPA

Other Side, The. Thomas Reiter. AMV-80

Other Side of a Mirror, The. Mary Elizabeth Coleridge. BoWoP

Other Side of Jordan, The. *Unknown*. FSW

Other Side of Town Saturday Night, The. James Steele. SES

Other states were carved or born. Cattle. Berta Hart Nance. BPAW

Other Woman. Judith Moffett. AAN

Other Women's Children. Marilyn Nelson Waniek. AMV-80

Others abide our question. Thou art free. Shakespeare. Matthew Arnold. BiP; CABA (1972 ed.); LFH

Others always skip over the word. In Praise of BIC Pens. David Hilton. NowV

Others are tunneled in sleep, The. Night Flight. Don Johnson. AMV-81

Others because you did not keep. A Deep-sworn Vow. W. B. Yeats. CMoP (1970 ed.); ExPo (1973 ed.); OAEL-2; PSN; TCP; TPo; UnPo (1976 ed.)

Others have sought publicity. Lives of the Saints. Paul Muldoon. IPM

Others, I am not the first. A. E. Housman. CMoP (1970 ed.); OBP; OxBTC; PPM; PPP; SoSe (1977 ed.); STS

Others, many others, must have known. Leaving Buffalo. Charles Martin. PoA

Others taunt me with having knelt at well-curbs. For Once, Then, Something. Robert Frost. NoAM; NOBA; PiAm; TT

Others would think I was walking somewhere. Friday Evening. Julio Marzán. InW

Otoe County in Nebraska. William Kloefkorn. GP

Ottava Rima would, I know, be proper. W. H. Auden. *Fr.* Letter to Lord Byron. NOBL

Otter, An. Ted Hughes. CMoP (1970 ed.); NoAM

Otter is known, The. Lutra, the Fisher. James McMichael. AmPA

Otters. William Hart-Smith. BoAnP

Otto. Gwendolyn Brooks. CC; PChr

Ouch! *Unknown.* TDH

"O-U-G-H-"; or, The Cross Farmer. D. S. Martin. TDH

Ould Orange Flute, The. *Unknown. See* Old Orange Flute, The.

Ounce of Detention, The. Oliver Herford. TDH

Our age has Caesars, though they wear silk hats. Six Poems, 2. Joseph Freeman. SPT

Our Angels. Howard Schwartz. VWA

Our Annual Return to the Lake. Robert D. Hoeft. AMV-81

Our author, by experience, finds it true. Prologue. Dryden. *Fr.* Aureng-Zebe. ILP (1975 ed.); LFH

Our Backs Are to the Cypress. Leah Goldberg, *tr. fr. Hebrew by* Ramah Commanday. BoWoP

Our band is few, but true and tried. Song of Marion's Men. Bryant. BTTM

Our Beautiful West Coast Thing. Richard Brautigan. OSP

Our beauty is to us that which to men. Giovanni Battista Guarini, *tr. by* Sir Richard Fanshawe. *Fr.* Il Pastor Fido. OBVE

Our Bias. W. H. Auden. NoAM; PoIA

Our birth is but a sleep and a forgetting. Wordsworth. *Fr.* Ode: Intimations of Immortality from Recollections of Early Childhood. ILwL

Our Blackheath Comprehensive School (for mice). Leaving School. Roy Fuller. BBL

Our Blackness Did Not Come to Us Whole. Linda Brown Bragg. CNA

Our Bodies. Denise Levertov. AnMo; PPP

Our Bodies Young and Running in the Sun. Lynn Strongin. PoW

Our Bog Is Dood. Stevie Smith. FaBoNo; WeW

Our Bondage It Shall End, *with music. At. to* Peter Cartwright. AH

Our boots and clothes are all in pawn. Blood Red Roses. *Unknown.* FSW

Our brains ache, in the merciless iced east winds that knive us. Exposure. Wilfred Owen. InPS; NoAM

Our bugles sang truce, for the night-cloud had lower'd. The Soldier's Dream. Thomas Campbell. FaPoR

Our captain stood upon the deck, a spyglass in his hand. Captain Bunker. *Unknown.* AmFP

Our cherished dualism gone? Journal to Stella. Morton Dauwen Zabel. PoA

Our Childhood Spilled into Our Hearts. David Vogel, *tr. fr. Hebrew by* A. C. Jacobs. VWA

Our children have eaten supper. Brian Coffey. *Fr.* Missouri Sequence. CIP

Our church had no theology. Woods Gets Religion. John Woods. GP

Our City Is Guarded by Automatic Rockets. William Stafford. NowV

"Our couch shall be roses all spangled with dew." A Sensible Girl's Reply to Moore's. Walter Savage Landor. FaBoEE

Our Country. Henry David Thoreau. GOA

Our Country Is Divided. Faarah Nuur, *tr. fr. Somali by* B. W. Andrzejewski *and* I. M. Lewis. WTO

Our daughter, Alicia. Hot Line. Louella Dunann. QQQ

Our day was composed of resemblances, take. Sail Away. Robert Adamson. CAAP

Our Decor. Edward Proffitt. PoIA

Our dog Fred. The Diners in the Kitchen. James Whitcomb Riley. GDP; OBAL

Our doubts are traitors. Shakespeare. *Fr.* Measure for Measure, I, iv. CTV

Our earth in 1969. Doggerel by a Senior Citizen. W. H. Auden. NOBL

Our Earth Mother. *Tr. fr. Zuni Indian by* R. Bunzel. WTO

Our faces/ looked up at us. In the Water. Dave Morice. AcAn

"Our Fadder, Which are in Heaben!" He Paid Me Seven. *Unknown.* BPo

Our Family. Leonard Clark. RAE

Our Father, by Whose Name, *with music.* F. Bland Tucker. AH

Our Father, God, *with music.* Adoniram Judson. AH

Our Father in Heaven, *with music.* Sarah Josepha Hale. AH

Our Father which art in heaven. The Lord's Prayer. Bible, *N.T. Fr.* St. Matthew. CTV

Our Father Which in Heaven Art. Bible, *N.T. See* Lord's Prayer, The.

Our Father! While Our Hearts Unlearn, *with music.* Oliver Wendell Holmes. AH

Our Father, whose creative Will. W. H. Auden. *Fr.* For the Time Being. ILwL

Our father works in us. A Father of Women. Alice Meynell. SBG; WPE

Our Fathers' God, *with music.* Benjamin Copeland. AH

Our fathers' God! from out whose hand. Centennial Hymn. Whittier. BTTM

Our fathers took oaths as of old they took wives. Thomas Brown. FaBoEE

Our fathers wrung their bread from stocks and stones. Children of Light. Robert Lowell. CMoP (1970 ed.); ILP (1975 ed.); STS

Our Fear. Zbigniew Herbert, *tr. fr. Polish by* Czeslaw Milosz. BuTh

Our flat bottomed boat. Old Man Let's Go Fishing in the Yellow Reeds of the Bay. Mei Berssenbrugge. SA

Our forefather once wished a wife. How Our Forefather Got His Wife. Eda Lou Walton. BPAW

Our Gaelic poets, going about the west. Consolation. Anthony Cronin. IPM

Our gang/ laid for the kids from niggertown. To Live and Die in Dixie. John Beecher. CSP

Our glances spin silver threads. Empathy. Agnes Pratt. VW

Our God and soldiers we alike adore. Francis Quarles. FaBoEE

Our God, Our Help in Ages Past. Isaac Watts. BLSH, *with music;* BoReV; OBVE

Our golden age was then, when lamp and rug. Family Prime. Mark Van Doren. VGW

Our Goodman. *Unknown.* AmFP

Our Ground Time Here Will Be Brief. Maxine W. Kumin. AMV-81

Our guttural muse. Traditions. Seamus Heaney. IPM

Our hammock swung between Americas. Elegy. Derek Walcott. OBP

Our Hands in the Garden. Anne Hébert, *tr. fr. French by* A. Poulin, Jr. BoWoP

Our happiness is easily wronged by speech. Writing. Anthony Cronin. IPM

Our hearts knelt down in wonder. Alston Chapel. James E. Warren, Jr. AATT

Our Hero. John Frederick Nims. FoP

Our homes are eaten out by time. The Town Betrayed. Edwin Muir. CMoP (1970 ed.)

Our Hunting Fathers. W. H. Auden. NoAM

Our Insufficiency to Praise God Suitably, for His Mercy. Edward Taylor. *Fr.* God's Determinations. PiAm

Our journey had advanced. Emily Dickinson. AmVN; GrRo; ILwL

Our Kind. William Stafford. AMV-81

Our Kind Creator, *with music.* Solomon Howe. AH

Our King went forth to Normandy. The Agincourt Carol. *Unknown.* OAEL-1; OxBM

Our Lady. Mary Elizabeth Coleridge. WPE

Our last bridge. Marina Tsvetayeva, *tr. by* Paul Schmidt. *Fr.* The Daughter of Jairus. BoWoP

Our last free summer we mooned about at odd hours. Chrysalides. Thomas Kinsella. BIrV; NoAM

Our last morning in that long room. In the Last Few Moments Came the Old German Cleaning Woman. Jane Cooper. CoPAm

Our Life Is Hid with Christ in God. George Herbert. OAEL-1

Our life is not life, save in the fleeting. Responding Voice. Francisco A. De Icaza, *tr. by* Samuel Beckett. PBMP

Our life is two-fold: Sleep hath its own world. The Dream, I. Byron. GrRo

Our little fleet in July first. The Armada, 1588. John Wilson. OxBChV

Our Lives. Sharon Scott. JB

Our lives are sketched in the simplest lines. Cartoon. Jim Simmerman. AMV-81

Our lives are Swiss. Emily Dickinson. NOBA; POL; TAP

Our Love Was a Grim Citadel. R. A. K. Mason. ATNZ

Our love was conceived in silence and must live silently. At the Dark Hour. Paul Dehn. BoLoP

Our love was pure. Song of Snow-white Heads. Cho Wen-chün, *tr. by* Arthur Waley. BoWoP

Our low cabin above the river is lost. Staying Up on Jack's Fork near Eminence, Missouri. Albert Salsich. AMV-80

Our Lucy (1956-1960). Paul Goodman. GDP

Our mother knew our worth. Our Kind. William Stafford. AMV-81

Our mother was the pussy-cat, our father was the owl. The Children of the Owl and the Pussy-Cat. Edward Lear. FaBoNo

Our Mother's Body Is the Earth. Mary McAnally. AMV-80

Our moulting days are in their twilight stage. Garnishing the Aviary. Margaret Danner. Far from Africa, I. AmNP (1974 ed.); BPo; PoBA

Our mournful Philomel. Michael Drayton. *Fr.* The Shepherd's Sirena. SCP-2

Our name burn in the air. Fame. Vern Rutsala. GP

Our Needy Neighbours. William Langland. *Fr.* The Vision of Piers Plowman. OxBM

Our new clothes fool no one. Yom Kippur. Chana Bloch. VWA

Our Norman betters. Lines: Inspired by the Controversy on the Value or Otherwise of Old English Studies. Anthony Burgess. FaBoCo

Our nuns come out to shop in the afternoon. Intercessors. Austin Clarke. CMoP (1970 ed.)

Our objections to the war. For the Minority. Robert Peterson. NeAC

Our old cat has kittens three. Choosing Their Names. Thomas Hood. PCat

Our old new house climbs a hill. Hush, Hush, New House in Charlotte. E. M. Schorb. AMV-81

Our old tomcat, with his weak heart. The Old Colonist. Andrew Taylor. FPA

Our orange wood and lemon glade. Cowslips. Sacheverell Sitwell. PF

Our passions are most like to floods and streams. Sir Walter Ralegh to the Queen. Sir Walter Ralegh. AAS

Our pastures are bitten and bare. Joseph Gordon Macleod ("Adam Drinan"). *Fr.* The Men on the Rocks. MS

Our perverse old *pisatel'* Vladimir. Something for My Russian Friends. Edmund Wilson. OBAL

Our Photograph. Frederick Locker-Lampson. NOBL

Our portion of fire. The Manichaeans. Gary Snyder. VGW

Our private foliage has unscrolled. Early Fall: The Adirondacks. Carolyne Wright. AMV-81

Our purple tongues that testify. For Proserpine. Stanley Kunitz. PAIC

Our revels now are ended. These our actors. Postscript. Shakespeare. *Fr.* The Tempest, IV, i. TPo

Our roads are ridden. For Sammy Younge. Charlie Cobb. PoBA

Our roofs are adjacent. *Turkish Love Songs, tr. by* Reza Baraheni *and* Zahra-Soltan Shokoohtaezeh. BoWoP

"Our saints are poets, Milton and Blake." Encounter. Denis Devlin. BIrV

Our sardine fishermen work at night in the dark of the moon. The Purse-Seine. Robinson Jeffers. CMoP (1970 ed.); HAP; NoAM; NOBA; PoIA; WeW

Our Saviour's Golden Rule. Isaac Watts. OxBChV

Our School Now Closes Out, *with music.* Edmund Dumas. AH

Our ship is a cradle on ocean's blue billow. An Ocean Lullaby. Charles Keeler. RhR

Our short fat, lord bishop. Bad Bishop Jegon. *Unknown.* GBP

Our single purpose was to walk through snow. Polar Exploration. Stephen Spender. NoAM

Our Smoke Has Gone Four Ways. Lance Henson. CDW

Our Sobbing Must Be Heard. Grace Cavalieri. AATT

Our Stars Come from Ireland. Wallace Stevens. GOA

Our stars, ourselves. W. S. Wardell. AAN

Our States, O Lord, *with music.* John Mycall. AH

Our stony island, Spain's laconic child. Silence in Mallorca. Genevieve Taggard. SPT

Our street is known as the street of widows. Bruce Beaver. Letters to Live Poets, XVI. GAS

Our Sunday morning when dawn-priests were applying. Sonnet. John Berryman. BoLoP; Epi

Our tarin' Dan O'Connell sure he was a mighty man. Cushendall. *Unknown.* WTO

Our Tense and Wintry Minds, *with music.* Hayden Carruth. AH

Our toes touched stone. Sleeping in a Cave. Naomi Shihab Nye. AMV-81

Our Town. Ann Stanford. CPA

Our towns decayed, our gardens overgrown. Camouflage. Michael Longley. IPM

Our trivial fights over spading. For My Father: Two Poems. David Kherdian. GP; VoA

Our Two Worthies. John Crowe Ransom. OBAL

Our Vegetable Love Shall Grow. Elaine Feinstein. POL

Our Vicar. *Unknown.* TDH

Our Village—by a Villager. Thomas Hood. OBSV; PoPle

Our Visit to the Zoo. Jessie Pope. PoPle

Our whistling son called his canary Hector. Boy, Cat, Canary. Stephen Spender. LP

Our Whole Life. Adrienne Rich. TT; UsP

Our Youth. John Ashbery. CAPP; ConAP; VGW

Our youth was happy: why repine. Walter Savage Landor. FaBoEE

Our zummer way to church did wind about. Green. William Barnes. VLP

Oure hoste gan to swere as he were wood. Chaucer. *Fr.* The Canterbury Tales. OAEL-1

Ourobouros. Jorge Plescoff, *tr. fr. Spanish by* Yishai Tobin. VWA

Ours are the streets where Bess first met her. Bess. William Stafford. GP; NNaP

Ourselves we do inter with sweet derision. Emily Dickinson. FaBoEE

Ousel-cock, so black of hue, The. Shakespeare. *Fr. A Midsummer Night's Dream III, i.* PB

Out. Ted Hughes. TwMBP

Out after Dark. Geoffrey Lehmann. GAS

Out amongst the flowers sweet. Hearts and Flowers. Mary D. Brine. FSN

Out-and-Down Pattern. William Kloefkorn. BrS

Out beside the highway, first thing in the morning. North Coast Town. Robert Gray. CAAP

Out beyond the grasses growing. Drifting. D. Maitland Bushby. BPAW

Out Fishing. Barbara Howes. LiSp; PPoD; WPE

Out for a walk, after a week in bed. An Urban Convalescence. James Merrill. NOBA; NowV; NYP

Out for a walk on the ice. Ice. Jack Driscoll. AMV-80

Out from Lobster Cove. J. D. Reed. NeAC

Out Goes She. *Unknown.* PoPle

Out here where the summer air. Driving through the Pima Indian Reservation. Paul H. Cook. AMV-80

Out in Arizona where the bad men are. Rag Time Cowboy Joe. Grant Clarke, Lewis F. Muir, *and* Maurice Abrahms. FSW

Out in the Dark. Edward Thomas. ILP (1975 ed.); NOBE; OBW; PoPle

Out in the far distance away. Unknown Smoke. Archie Washburn. VW

Out in the late amber afternoon. In Shadow. Hart Crane. NOBA

Out in the sun the goldfinch flits. The Hollow Wood. Edward Thomas. RAE

Out in the yellow meadows, where the bee. George Meredith. *Fr. Modern Love.* GBL

Out in this desert we are testing bombs. Trying to Talk with a Man. Adrienne Rich. NIL; RiTi; WBN

Out into/ the harsh night into. North Beach Poem. A. D. Winans. CPA

Out into Essex. John Betjeman. PES

Out-island once, on a South slope. Deer Isle. Philip Booth. BiP; VGW

Out of/ the 60's. The Poet's Appeal. Larry Goodell. FoP

Out of a cell into this darkened space. Frank Drummer. Edgar Lee Masters. *Fr. Spoon River Anthology.* NoAM

Out of a fired ship which by no way. A Burnt Ship. John Donne. EBEV; InPK

Out of a gothic North, the pallid children. Good-bye to the Mezzogiorno. W. H. Auden. OxBTC

Out of a War of Wits. Dylan Thomas. PoA

Out of all the wild horse bands. The Golden Stallion. Paul Thompson. BPAW

Out of Blindness. Leslie B. Blades. NowV

Out of blue nowhere came guns. Indian Death. Alice Corbin. BPAW

Out of Body. Janice Townley Moore. AMV-81

Out of burlap sacks, out of bearing butter. They Feed They Lion. Philip Levine. MAT; NNaP; NoAM; NOBA; Prf

Out of chaos. Star. Joanie Whitebird. GP

Out of childhood into manhood. Hiawatha and Mudjekeewis. Longfellow. The Song of Hiawatha, IV. AKE

Out of every hundred of us. American Commencement. Aram Boyajian. NeAC

Out of French. Sir Charles Sedley. FaBoEE

Out of friendship and a slow retreat of the blood. Ascending Red Cedar Moon. Duane Niatum. CDW

Out of gas south. Autumn. Philip Levine. NNaP

Out of her house she crept. Miss Euphemia. John Crowe Ransom. CMoP (1970 ed.)

Out of him that I loved. Our Stars Come from Ireland. Wallace Stevens. GOA

Out of hunger/ or out of great love. To My Child. Abraham Sutskever, *tr. by* David G. Roskies *and* Hillell Schwartz. VWA

Out of me unworthy and unknown. Anne Rutledge. Edgar Lee Masters. *Fr. Spoon River Anthology.* CMoP (1970 ed.); FaPo; HAP; NoAM; NOBA; OFD

Out of Mobile I saw a 60 Ford. Plain. Miller Williams. TAT

Out of Mourning. Anthony S. Abbott. AMV-81

Out of my heart, one day, I wrote a song. Misapprehension. Paul Laurence Dunbar. BPo

Out of my soul's depth to thee my cries have sounded. De Profundis. Thomas Campion. BoReV

Out of Our Blue, *sels.* John Fandel.
"Cloverleaf, A." PoIA
"Medium white onion, The." PoIA

Out of Palestine, out of Babylon. Wandering Jews. Nancy Keesing. VWA

Out of Sight, Out of Mind. Barnabe Googe. InPS

Out of Sleep. Allen Curnow. ATNZ

Out-of-the-Body Travel. Stanley Plumly. AmPA

Out of the bosom of the air. Snow-Flakes. Longfellow. FSFS; NOBA; TAP; UnPo (1976 ed.)

Out of the breath of Gehennah. Germination. Arlene Stone. VWA

Out of the broken/ morning. To Redistort a Weltanschauung. Matthew Mead. TwMBP

Out of the church she followed them. Maude Clare. Christina Rossetti. VPC

Out of the complicated house, come I. The Hills. Frances Cornford. PPM

Out of the corner of my eye. Shadow Life. Robert F. Reid III. AMV-81

Out of the corpse-warm vestibule of heaven steps the sun. Ingeborg Bachmann, *tr. fr. German by* Janice Orion. BoWoP

Out of the Cradle Endlessly Rocking. Walt Whitman. AmVN; CABA (1972 ed.); Epi; ExPo (1973 ed.); HAP; HeIP; ILP (1975 ed.); IPWM; NOBA; PiAm; PPoe; SoSe (1977 ed.); TAP; WeW
Mocking-Bird, The, *sel.* PB

Out of the dark. The Open Door. Elizabeth J. Coatsworth. DuDa; ECBV

Out of the dark raw earth. Alabama. Julia Fields. PoBA

Out of the deep have I called unto thee, O Lord. Bible, *O.T.* Psalms, CXXX. ILwL

Out of the deep, my child, out of the deep. Tennyson. *Fr. De Profundis.* ILP (1975 ed.)

Out of the Deepness. William (Haywood) Jackson. AMV-81

Out of the Desert. Diane Levenberg. NPW

Out of the dusk a shadow. Evolution. John Banister Tabb. PCOP

Out of the earth, out of the air, out of the water. Rapparees. Richard Murphy. *Fr. The Battle of Aughrim.* BIrV

Out of the Earth We Come. Rodney Hall. FPA

Out of the focal and foremost fire. Little Giffen. Francis Orray Ticknor. GOA

Out of the fog. The Fog Dream. Sandra M. Gilbert. PoA

Out of the Gaping Distance. Cynthia Nibbelink. TC

Out of the hurt left standing in his eyes. A Requiem for Innocence. William R. Mitchell. AATT

Out of the lamplight. Mice in the Hay. Leslie Norris. PChr

Out of the land of shadows and darkness. From the Underworld. Howard Blaikley. GrRo

Out of the marbled underwaters. Music by the Waters. John Hay. AMV-81

Out of the mud two strangers came. Two Tramps in Mud Time. Robert Frost. CMoP (1970 ed.); NoAM; STS

Out of the night and the north. The Train Dogs. Pauline Johnson. GDP

Out of the night that covers me. Invictus. W. E. Henley. FaPo; FaPoR; HoPM (1975 ed.); ILP (1975 ed.); NOBE; PCOP; PPM; VLP

Out of the paper bag. Chips. Stanley Cook. DuDr

Out of the Past. Robert Wallace. POL

Out of the poisonous East. W. E. Henley. London Voluntaries, IV. VLP

Out of the rolling ocean the crowd came a drop gently to me. Walt Whitman. LoAs

Out of the scraped surface of the land. The End of World War One. Sharon Olds. AMV-81

Out of the Sea, Early. May Swenson. RFM

Out of the shadow, I am come in to you whole a black holy man. Study Peace. Amiri Baraka. PoBA

Out of the Strong, Sweetness. Charles Reznikoff. VWA

Out of the western chaparral. Road Runner. Sharlot M. Hall. BPAW

Out of the wine-pot cry'd the fly. The Fly. Philip Ayres, *after the Spanish of* Quevedo. OBVE

Out of the wood of thoughts that grows by night. Cock-Crow. Edward Thomas. ILP (1975 ed.)

Out of their slumber Europeans spun. Snow in Europe. David Gascoyne. LP; MPo

"Out of this thoughtless, formless, swarming life." Self to Self. Charles Brasch. ATNZ

Out of wild roses down from the switching road between pools. A Guide to Dungeness Spit. David Wagoner. CNW

Out of You. Rodney Phillips. POL

Out of your whole life give but a moment! Now. Robert Browning. VLP

Out on Santa Fe—Blues. *Unknown.* BluL

Out on the board the old shearer stands. Click Go the Shears, Boys. *Unknown.* MAuV

Out on the desert. A Note on Lizard's Feet. James Van Rensselaer. BPAW

Out on the Hillside. Mary Gilmore. MAuV

Out on the lawn I lie in bed. A Summer Night. W. H. Auden. PSN

Out on the ocean, great wide ocean. Great *Titanic. Unknown.* AmFP

Out on the wide marsh at Malheur. Late August at the Game Refuge. William Stafford. CNW

"Out, Out." Robert Frost. AnMo; BuTh; CABA (1972 ed.); DL; FF; HAP; ILP (1975 ed.); IP; MiP; NowV; PiAm; PPoe; SoSe; TT; UnPo (1976 ed.); VGW; WeW; WIF

Out rides the knight in dusky steel. The Knight. Rainer Maria Rilke, *tr. by* John N. Miller. AMV-81

Out they came from Liberty, out across the plains. Oregon Trail: 1851. James Marshall. BPAW

Out through the fields and the woods. Reluctance. Robert Frost. CMoP (1970 ed.); NOBA

Out Upon It! I Have Loved. Sir John Suckling. *See* Constant Lover, The.

Out upon you California. Pennsylvania Places. T. A. Daly. OBAL

Out walking in the frozen swamp one gray day. The Wood-Pile. Robert Frost. AnMo; CABA (1972 ed.); ILP (1975 ed.); IP; NoAM; STS; VGW

Out walking ties left over from a track. Cross Ties. X. J. Kennedy. CoPAm; HoPM (1975 ed.); UsP

Out West. Gary Snyder. NNaP

Out West, they say, a man's a man; the legend still persists. Étude Géographique. Stoddard King. BPAW

Out where the hand-clasp's a little stronger. Out Where the West Begins. Arthur Chapman. BPAW

Out where the talk is a little stronger. Out Where the West Begins: A Parody. Ernest Douglas. BPAW

Out Where the West Begins. Arthur Chapman. BPAW

Out Where the West Begins: A Parody. Ernest Douglas. BPAW

Out with the mountain moon, stinging clear. Mill Valley. Myra Cohn Livingston. RFM

Outbreak. Bill Anderson. VGW

Outburst from a Little Face. John Woods. GP

Outcast. Claude McKay. AmNP (1974 ed.); CABA (1972 ed.); PoBA

Outcast, The. Frank Elwood Sanford. PeD

Outcast. Herman Spector. SPT

Outcry upon Opportunity, An. Shakespeare. *Fr.* The Rape of Lucrece. NOBE

Outlanders, The. William Morris. *Fr.* The Earthly Paradise. VPC

Outlaw, The. Seamus Heaney. NoAM

Outlaw of Loch Lene, The. *Unknown, tr. fr. Modern Irish by* Jeremiah Joseph Callanan. BIrV; GBL; PFIr

Outlaw stands with blindfold eyes, The. Ol' Dynamite. Phil Le Noir. BPAW

Outlook wasn't brilliant for the Mudville nine that day, The. Casey at the Bat. Ernest Lawrence Thayer. LiSp; OBAL; PPoD; SPo

Outlook wasn't brilliant for the Mudvillettes, it seems, The. Casey's Daughter at the Bat. Al Graham. SPo

Outposts. J. S. Harry. CAAP

Outrage. Lucille Iverson. WBN

Outrageously Blessed, The. Barry Spacks. CoPAm

Outside. Phyllis Beauvais. IHMS

Outside, a delicate arch. The Curse. John Hollander. UnPo (1976 ed.)

Outside Abilene. Harley Elliott. HeS

Outside, affectionate eyes. Ursula. David Ray. VGW

Outside among the talking criss-cross reeds. Karl. Charles Spear. ATNZ

Outside Bristol Rovers' Football Ground. The Ballad of Billy Rose. Leslie Norris. HeHu

Outside cool July half an hour from morning. Goodbye Sonnet. George Mattingly. AcAn

Outside Every Window Is a Flowering Thing. Anita Skeen. AMV-81

Outside Fargo, North Dakota. James Wright. NNaP; VoA

Outside it is cold. Inside. Winter: For an Untenable Situation. Alan Dugan. NIL; NowV

Outside my cheap candle. To Myself, Late, in a Myrtle Grove. Robert Peterson. NeAC

Outside my window. A Good Start. Larry Moffi. AMV-81

Outside my window. A Proper Place. Robert Nye. OSP

Outside New York, a high place where with one glance. Schubertiana. Tomas Tranströmer, *tr. by* Robert Bly. NU

Outside of a Small Circle of Friends. Phil Ochs. NowV

Outside, ponies pound. The Average Night. Paul Nelson. PHC

Outside soft and sidling, white as June, snow. At Poetry Workshop, Winter Semester. Robert A. Martin. AATT

Outside the cats are wailing. Leah Goldberg, *tr. by* Robert Alter. *Fr.* The Symposium. PBWP

Outside the cold, the rain, the happy dogs. This Is Not a Poem. Luís Omar Salinas. SA

Outside the Holy City, *with music.* James G. Gilkey. AH

Outside, the landlord undertakes the landscape. Leaving the Country House to the Landlord, Five Years Later. Wesley McNair. FAF

Outside, the last kids holler. Leaving the Motel. W. D. Snodgrass. FF; PiAm; WeW

Outside the plasma supermarket. Leaflets. Adrian Mitchell. NowV

Outside, the rain, pinafore of gray water, dresses the town. Child Beater. Ai. BoWoP

Outside the U.S. Consulate. The Earth Sings Mi-fa-mi. Pat Lowther. MMD

Outside the window, at the top. Starlings. Laura Jensen. AMV-81

Outspoken buttocks in pink beads. National Winter Garden. Hart Crane. *Fr.* The Bridge: Three Songs. InPS

Outward Bound. James Simmons. IPM

"Ouu/ gee whiz." Moon Poem. Saundra Sharp. QQQ

Ovals of opal on dislustred seas. Memoriter. Charles Spear. ATNZ

Oven Bird, The. Robert Frost. HeIP; NoAM; NOBA; PiAm; PoIA; PPP; TAP; TT; VoPo

Over. R. S. Thomas. FF

Over a mountain-slope with lentisk, and with abounding. Actaeon. Arthur Hugh Clough. VLP

Over a trail glinting with flakes. Indian Painting, Probably Paiute, in a Cave near Madras, Oregon. Jarold Ramsey. TAT

Over all the face of Earth. The Creation of the Sea. Milton. *Fr.* Paradise Lost, VII. RhR

Over all the hilltops. The Second Poem the Night-Walker Wrote. Goethe, *tr. by* Robert Bly. NU

Over an ash-fawn beach fronting a sea which keeps. Fiascherino. Charles Tomlinson. NoAM

Over and back. At Ithaca. Hilda Doolittle ("H. D."). VGW

Over and over again he remembers that huge black sound. The Coal Mine Disaster's Last Trapped Man Contemplates Salvation. William Meissner. AMV-80

Over and over again to people. The Limits of Submission. Faarah Nuur, *tr. by* B. W. Andrzejewski *and* I. M. Lewis. WTO

Over and under. Stitches. Hazel Hall. WPW

Over Asia. Anne Waldman. RiTj

Over back where they speak of life as staying. The Investment. Robert Frost. CMoP (1970 ed.)

Over Coffee. Jennifer Maiden. CAAP

Over deep cushions, drenched with drowsy scents. Damned Women. Baudelaire, *tr. by* Roy Campbell. BoLoP

Over hill, over dale. Fairy Song. Shakespeare. *Fr.* A Midsummer Night's Dream, II, i. NOBE; PCOP; PoPle

Over hill, over dale, we have hit the dusty trail. The Caissons Go Rolling Along. Edmund L. Gruber. BLSo; BTTM

Over his head were the maple buds. Emerson. *Fr.* Excelsior. PeD

Over logs jammed between rocks. The Fish Will Swim as Before. Michael Spence. AMV-81

Over Manhattan island when gales subside. City without Smoke. Edwin Denby. NYP

Over my head, I see the bronze butterfly. Lying in a Hammock at William Duffy's Farm. James Wright. ANTL; CAPP; ConAP; HAP; HoPM (1975 ed.); InPS; IPWM; NOBA; PSN; SFF

Over rock and wrinkled ground. Beagles. W. R. Rodgers. FaBoTw (1975 ed.); GDP

Over Sir John's Hill. Dylan Thomas. TT

Over that morn hung heaviness, until. Seascape. Francis Brett Young. OxBTC

Over the Arafura sea, the China sea. For John Chappell. Gary Snyder. NNaP

Over the barbered lawn a great. Glasgow Botanic Gardens. James Rankin. MIS

Over the bleak and barren snow. Tony O. Colin Francis. FaBoCo

Over the deep sea Love came flying. The Two Burdens. Philip Bourke Marston. VLP

Over the eye behind the moon's cloud. Raison d'Etre. Oliver Pitcher. AmNP (1974 ed.)

Over the fence. Emily Dickinson. SBG

Over the Green Sands. Peggy Bennett. EcS

Over the half-finished houses. The Roofwalker. Adrienne Rich. PiAm; PPP; Psy

Over the hearth with my 'minishing eyes I muse. The Cat of the House. Ford Madox Ford. PCat

Over the hill and over the dale. Dawlish Fair. Keats. MBPR; PoPle

Over the Hills and Far Away. John Gay. *Fr.* The Beggar's Opera, I, i. BLSo, *with music;* NOBE ("Were I laid on Greenland's coast.") ILP (1975 ed.)

Over the hills I went one day, a lovely maid I spied. The Foggy Dew. *Unknown.* FSW

Over the hiss of the coffee urns. Next Door to Monica's Dance Studio. Barbara Smith. AMV-81

Over the land freckled with snow half-thawed. Thaw. Edward Thomas. EBEV; FaBoTw (1975 ed.); OxBTC

Over the low, barnacled, elephant-colored rocks. Meditation at Oyster River. Theodore Roethke. CMoP (1970 ed.); CNW; MPA

Over the mantel in the settlement house in Gary. For Great Grandmother and Her Settlement House. Ann Darr. GP

Over the Mindanao Deep. Gary Snyder. *Fr.* Hitch Haiku. InPK

Over the monstrous shambling sea. Marsh Song—At Sunset. Sidney Lanier. NOBA

Over the mountains. Love Will Find Out the Way. *Unknown.* GBL

Over the rainy day mountain. Wishes. Patty L. Harjo. VoR

Over the river, and through the wood. Thanksgiving Day. Lydia Maria Child. CTV; ECBV

Over the sheer rocks over the gorges. An Inscription. Stanislav Vinaver, *tr. by* Vasa D. Mihailovich. VWA

Over the stones still rattling, up Pall Mall. Byron. *Fr.* Don Juan. NOBL

Over! the sweet summer closes. Prologue. Tennyson. *Fr.* Becket. GBL

Over the warts on the bumpy. Sadie's Playhouse. Margaret Danner. PoBA

Over the west side of the mountain. Lyrebirds. Judith Wright. BoAnP

Over the western sea hither from Niphon come. A Broadway Pageant. Walt Whitman. NYP

Over the wreck of winter another season. Barometer. Madeline DeFrees. CNW

Over there in your fields you have. Rains for the Harvest. *Tr. fr. Tewa Indian by* H. J. Spinden. WTO

Over Three Nipple-Stones. Paul Celan, *tr. fr. German by* Joachim Neugroschel. VWA

Over 2000 Illustrations and a Complete Concordance. Elizabeth Bishop. NoAM

Over yonder's a park, which is newly begun. The Corpus Christi Carol. *Unknown.* GBP

Over your body the clouds go. Gulliver. Sylvia Plath. NOBA

Overalls. John Sjoberg. AcAn

Overcoats. Larry Kramer. AMV-80

Overcoats are gone from Central Park, The. "Grandfather" in Winter. Frederick Feirstein. NYP

Overdose. Michael Dransfield. FPA

Overdue Balance Sheet. Therese Plantier, *tr. fr. French by* Maxine W. Kumin *and* Judith Kumin. BoWoP

Overflowing eyes. Meditation. Beyle Schaechter-Gottesman, *tr. by* Gabriel Preil. VWA

Overheard in a Saltmarsh. Harold Monro. ECBV; LCL; SO

Overheard in an Orchard. Elizabeth Cheney. CTV

Overheard over S.E. Asia. Denise Levertov. BoWoP

Overland to the Islands. Denise Levertov. ConAP; UnPo (1976 ed.)

Overlooking the River Stour. Thomas Hardy. PES

Overnight Guest. Ramona Wilson. VoR

Overnight, very. Mushrooms. Sylvia Plath. PBMP; Psy; SS; WeW

Overreacher, The. Christopher Marlowe. *Fr.* Tamburlaine the Great, Part I, I. NIL

Overtures to Death, *sel.* C. Day Lewis.
"For us, born into a still," VII. CMoP (1970 ed.)

Overturned Lake, The. Charles Henri Ford. EAS

Overweight Poem. Diane Wakoski. CAAP

Ovid. Richard Pevear. AMV–81

Ovid in the Third Reich. Geoffrey Hill. NoAM; POL

Ovid is the surest guide. Written in an Ovid. Matthew Prior. FaBoEE

Ovidian Elegiac Metre Described and Exemplified, The. Schiller, *tr. fr. German by* Samuel Taylor Coleridge. MBPR

Ovid's Banquet of Sense, *sel.* George Chapman.
"In a loose robe of tinsel forth she came." SCP–2

Ovid's Fifth Elegy. Ovid. *See* Corinnae Concubitus.

Owen of Carron, *sel.* John Langhorne.
"Does nature bear a tyrant's breast?" FaBoCo

Owl, The. Thorkild Bjornvig, *tr. fr. Danish by* Robert Bly. NU

Owl, The. Edward Davison. PoA

Owl. George MacBeth. MPo

Owl, The. W. S. Merwin. PPP

Owl, The. Sue Owen. AMV–81

Owl, The. V. Sackville-West. SBG

Owl, The. Tennyson. ECBV; PoPle
(Song—the Owl.) PB

Owl, The. Edward Thomas. EBEV; FaBoTw (1975 ed.); FF; NoAM; NOBE; OAEL–2; OBW; PoPle; PPoe; UnPo (1976 ed.)

Owl, The. Robert Penn Warren. CoPAm

Owl, The. David Young. CAAP

Owl and the Nightingale, The, *sel. Unknown, at. to* Nicholas de Guildford.
Owl against Nightingale, *orig. and mod. English prose.* OxBM

Owl and the Pussy-Cat, The. Edward Lear. BBL; CTV; FaBoNo; NOBE; OxBChV; PCOP; RhR; SFF
Love Song, *sel.* PCat

Owl-Critic, The. James Thomas Fields. ECBV; OBAL; PoTa

Owl in the Oak, The. *Unknown.* FaBoNo

Owl in the Rabbi's Barn, The. Dan Jaffe. VWA

Owl is abroad, the bat, and the toad, The. The Witches' Charm. Ben Jonson. *Fr.* The Masque of Queens. NOBE; PoPle; SCP–1; UsP

Owl Pellet, The. Ann Deagon. AAN

Owl Seen in Rearview Mirror. Duane Niatum. VW

Owl swoops, An. The Visit. William J. Rewak. AMV–80

Owl winks in the shadow, An. Gary Snyder. *Fr.* Mother Earth: Her Whales. OSP

Owl Woman's Death Song. *Tr. fr. Papago Indian by* Ruth Underhill. BoWoP

Owl Woman's years and twisted hands lie. Hupa Twined Pendant: A White Woman Speaks. Wendy Rose. NW

Owls. John Fuller. POL

Owls. Leslie Norris. HeHu

Owls. W. D. Snodgrass. BoAnP

Owls are flying, The. Owls. Leslie Norris. HeHu

Owner of My Face, The, *sel.* Rodney Hall.
"You are coming to me in the rain." CAAP

Owning a Dead Man. Marcia Southwick. AMV–80

Owt of thise blake wawes for to saylle. Chaucer. *Fr.* Troilus and Criseyde, II. ILP (1975 ed.)

Ox Cart Man. Donald Hall. PCho

Ox carts/ huge wooden wheels. Para Olga. Charles Potts. EC

Ox-Driver, The. *Unknown.* FSW

Ox, long fed with musty hay, An. Recantation Illustrated in the Story of the Mad Ox. Samuel Taylor Coleridge. MBPR

Oxen, The. Thomas Hardy. BiP; CMoP (1970 ed.); EBEV; HAP; InPK; IPWM; NoAM; NOBE; OAEL–2; OxBTC; PChr; PPoe; PPP; SoSe (1977 ed.); VoPo

Oxen: Ploughing at Fiesole. Charles Tomlinson. OxBTC

Oxford, *sel.* Edward Dorn.
Comforted by Limestone. NOBA

Oxford, *sel.* Lionel Johnson.
"City of weathered cloister and worn court." PES

Oxford Barber's Verses on the Queen's Death. *Unknown.* APAS

Oxford Canal. James Elroy Flecker. OxBTC

Oxford Commination. Paris Leary. AMV–81

Oxford Girl, The; or, Expert Town. *Unknown.* AmFP

Oya. Audre Lorde. CNA

Oyfn Pripetshuk (On the Hearth). Mark Warshawsky, *tr. fr. Yiddish.* FSW

Oyster, The ("The oyster, about as large as a medium-sized stone"). Francis Ponge, *tr. fr. French by* Robert Bly. NU

Oyster boats are moored. Boom. Julian Lee Rayford. AMV–80

Oyster shuts his gates to form the pearl, The. The Precious Pearl. Pat Wilson. ATNZ

Oyster that went to bed x-million years ago. An. Goodnight. John Ciardi. OBAL

Oystercatchers. Christopher Middleton. FaBoTw (1975 ed.)

Oystering. Richard Howard. NoAM

Ozymandias. Shelley. BiP; CABA (1972 ed.); DL; Epi; FaPo; FaPoR; FF; HAP; HeIP; HoPM (1975 ed.); ILP (1975 ed.); InPK; IP; IPWM; LFH; MBPR; NIL; NOBE; OAEL–2; OBP; PAIC; PoPle; PoIA; PPoD; SFF; SoSe; SpRo; WeW

Ozymandias Revisited. Morris Bishop. PAIC; SpRo

# P

P. C. Plod Versus the Dale St Dog Strangler. Roger McGough. NoAM

P.S. 42. Gregory Corso. SA

Pa. Leo Dangel. AMV–81

Pa, Pa, Build Me a Boat. *Unknown.* AmFP

Pa would often have to fetch you home. To My Sister. David Kherdian. SA

Pablo Anytime. John Sjoberg. AcAn

Pacelli and the Ethiop. Turner Cassity. GP

Pachuta, Mississippi/ A Memoir. Al Young. CSP; TAT

Pacific, The. Percy Stickney Grant. RhR

Pacific Dawn. Alison Wyrley Birch. PPM

Pacific Epitaphs. Dudley Randall. NoAM

Pacing with Bag-Pipe in a bosky Square. Caledonia. Anthony Powell. NOBL

Pack, clouds, away! and welcome day! Love's Good-Morrow. Thomas Heywood. *Fr.* The Rape of Lucrece. GBL; LoAs

Pack Rat, The. Robert Pack. CoPAm; PPP; WeW

Packard. David Barker. GP

Packed in my mind lie all the clothes. The Inward Morning. Henry David Thoreau. AmVN; PiAm

Packed streets, humbled by the/ Mercy of music. Valley. Robert Morgan. HeHu

Packer City Poem. Peter Cooley. HeS

Packin' Trunk Blues. *Unknown.* BluL

Pact. Kenneth Fearing. CMoP (1970 ed.)

Pact, A. Ezra Pound. NoAM; NOBA; PAIC; PiAm; PSN; TAP

Pact, The. Larry Rubin. AMV-81

Pact that we made was the ordinary pact, The. From a Survivor. Adrienne Rich. GP; LoAs

Padda Song, The. *Unknown.* GBP

Paddy, Get Back. *Unknown.* AmFP

Paddy, I have but stol'n your living. Ebenezer Elliott. FaBoEE

Paddy O'Rafther. Samuel Lover. PFIr; PoTa

Paddy O'Sullivan. For Paddy O'Sullivan. A. D. Winans. CPA

Padraic O'Conaire, Gaelic Storyteller. F. R. Higgins. PFIr

Padstow Night Song, The. *Unknown.* GBP

Paean to Eve's Apple. James Liddy. CIP

Paean to Place. Lorine Niedecker. RiTi

Paffer Jocker. John Sjoberg. AcAn

Pagan Isms, The. Claude McKay. BPo

Page. Sandra McPherson. PoA

Page from a Diary. Desmond O'Grady. NoAM

Page from the Koran. James Merrill. PCho

Pageant Verses. Sir Thomas More. AAS

Pages of history open, The. Elegy. Sandra M. Gilbert. PoA

Pagget, a schoolboy, got a sword, and then. Upon Pagget. Robert Herrick. CaPo

Pain, *sel.* Thomas Edward Brown. "Man that hath great griefs I pity not, The." PeD

Pain. Edith Södergran, *tr. fr. Swedish by* Jaakko A. Ahokas. PBWP

Pain. Robert Wrigley. AMV-81

Pain—expands the time. Emily Dickinson. PiAm

Pain for a Daughter. Anne Sexton. TV

Pain has an element of blank. Emily Dickinson. PPP; SBG

Pain is the cutting edge, the skim of a wave. The Cave. Henry Shore. PMW

Pain of loving you, The. A Young Wife. D. H. Lawrence. PBMP; VoPo

Pain visits me. My Knees Go before the Firing Squad at Dawn. Diane Wakoski. CAAP

Painkillers. Thom Gunn. AMV-81

Painlessly Out of Ourselves. William Page. AMV-81

Pains of Education, The. Charles Churchill. *Fr.* The Author. FaBoCo

Pains of insecurity surround me. Back Again, Home. Don L. Lee. BPo

Pains of Sleep, The. Samuel Taylor Coleridge. MBPR (Child's Evening Prayer, A.) OxBChV

Paint Box, The. E. V. Rieu. SO

Paint Castlemaine in colours that will hold. Andrew Marvell. *Fr.* The Last Instructions to a Painter. OBSV; SCP-1

Paint last the King, and a dead shade of night. Andrew Marvell. *Fr.* The Last Instructions to a Painter. OBSV

Paint me a cavernous waste shore. Sweeney Erect. T. S. Eliot. AnMo; OxBTC; STS; VGW

Paint samples. Bruises. Coleman Barks. *Fr.* Body Poems. NVAP

Painted Ceiling, The. Amy Lowell. OBAL

Painted Cup, The. Bryant. EAP

Painted Head. John Crowe Ransom. NoAM; NOBA; PiAm

Painted Hills of Arizonas, The. Edwin Curran. BPAW

Painted Lady, The. Margaret Danner. BPo

Painted stars. Pictures on the Wall. Zvi Shargel, *tr. by* Gabriel Preil *and* Howard Schwartz. VWA

Painter, The. John Ashbery. NOBA

Painter in the Lion Cage, The. Betti Alver, *tr. fr. Estonian by* Willis Barnstone *and* Felix Oinas. BoWoP

Painter of Dante's awful ferry-ride, The. The Poem. Babette Deutsch. PoA

Painting. Maxine Chernoff. FiCh

Painting. A. C. Jacobs. VWA

Painting an Old Apartment. James Bonk. HeS

Paintings with stiff. Primitives. Dudley Randall. BPo; CABA (1972 ed.)

Painture. Richard Lovelace. CaPo

Pair, A. May Swenson. RFM

Pair of black swans on the lake, A. Mating Swans. James McAuley. MAuV

Pair of funnels stroll by night, A. The Funnels. Christian Morgenstern, *tr. by* Geoffrey Grigson. FaBoNo

Pair of muscular calves, A. Harold Norse. *Fr.* You Must Have Been a Sensational Baby. GP

Paired Lives. W. R. Rodgers. CIP

Paisley Ceiling, The. Lila Arnold. IHMS

Pait, pieet, pweat, the ivory-bill's. Bellair. Van K. Brock. CSP

Paiute Ponies. Jim Barnes. CDW

Pal, in the Pals of Death Club. This Is a Poem for the Fathers and for Michael Ryan. Thomas Lux. AmPA

Palabras Grandiosas. Bayard Taylor. OBAL

Palace clocks are stiff as coats of mail, The. The King's Speech. Howard Moss. *Fr.* King Midas. PoA

Palace for Teeth, The. Abigail Luttinger. AMV-80

Palace of Art, The. Tennyson. VLP "One seem'd all dark and red—a tract of sand," *sel.* UnPo (1976 ed.)

Palace of humbug, The. "Lewis Carroll." FaBoNo

Palace of Pleasant Regard, The. Lady of the Assembly. *Fr.* The Assembly of Ladies. WPE

Palace with revolving doors, was mine, The. Atameros. John Beevers. EAS

Pale as cold moons in retreat. History. May Miller. PoUp

Pale beech and pine so blue. In a Wood. Thomas Hardy. VLP

Pale Blue Casket, The. Oliver Pitcher. PoBA

Pale brown Moses went down to Egypt land. Benediction. Bob Kaufman. IPWM

Pale brows, still hands, and dim hair. The Lover Mourns for the Loss of Love. W. B. Yeats. PoIA; WeW

Pale, drooping girl and the swaggering soldier, The. Just an Old Sweet Song. Donagh MacDonagh. CIP

Pale faced, tight laced. Margaret Southgate. POL

Pale gold of the walls, gold. Gold. Donald Hall. ConAP; InPS

Pale grey, her guns hooded, decks clear of all impediment. H. M. S. *Hero.* Michael Roberts. OxBTC

Pale moon was rising above the green mountain, The. The Rose of Tralee. C. Mordaunt Spencer. BLSH; FSW

Pale morning in June 4 AM, A. Country Roads. Rolf Jacobsen, *tr. by* Robert Bly. NU

Palindrome. Lisel Mueller. IHMS

Palinode, A. Edmund Bolton. PAIC

Palladium. Matthew Arnold. OAEL-2; PPP; VLP

Palm of my hand bleeds, The. Stigmata. Virginia R. Terris. AAN

Palm of the Hand. Rainer Maria Rilke, *tr. fr. German by* Robert Bly. NU

Palm of the hand, The,/ is not aware of dying. Fumi Saito, *tr. fr. Japanese by* Edith Marcombe Shiffert *and* Yuki Sawa. BoWoP

Palm Sunday: Good Friday. Giles Fletcher the Younger. *Fr.* Christ's Victory and Triumph, III. BoReV

Palm tree grows in the far bush, The. Election Songs. *Yoruba Oral Tradition, tr. by* Ulli Beier. WTO

Palm Willow, The. Robert Bridges. VLP

Palmistry for Blind Mariners. Judith Minty. TC

Paloma, La, *with music.* Sebastian Yradier, *tr. fr. Spanish.* BLSH

Palomino Stallion, The. Alden Nowlan. BoAnP; PH; POL

Pampered steed, of swiftness proud. The. The Horse and the Mule. John Huddlestone Wynne. OxBChV

Pamphilia to Amphilanthus. Mary Sidney Wroth, Countess of Montgomery. *Fr.* Urania. WPE

Pamphilia's Sonnet. Mary Sidney Wroth, Countess of Montgomery. *Fr.* Urania. WPE

Pan. Emerson. ILP (1975 ed.); PiAm

Pan and Luna. Robert Browning. VLP

Pan, grant that I may never prove. Song by the Wavering Nymph. Aphra Behn. SBG

Pan loved his neighbour Echo—but that child. Moschus, *tr. fr. Greek by* Shelley. OBVE

Pan Piping. Plato, *tr. fr. Greek by* Thomas Stanley. FaBoEE

Panama Limited, The. *Unknown.* BluL

Pancho Villa. Lou Lipsitz. NCSH

Panda, The. Harley Elliott. *Fr.* Animals That Stand in Dreams. NeAC

Panda, The. William Jay Smith. TDH

Panegyric. Harris Lenowitz. VWA

Panegyric, A ("Hail happy William, thou art strangely great"). *Unknown, at. to* Henry Hall *and to* John Grubham Howe. APAS

Panegyric, A ("Of a great heroine I mean to tell"). *Unknown.* APAS

Panegyric on the Author of "Absalom and Achitophel," A. *Unknown.* APAS

Panegyric to My Lord Protector, A, *sel.* Edmund Waller. "While with a strong and yet a gentle hand." SCP-2

Panegyric to Sir Lewis Pemberton, A. Robert Herrick. CaPo

Panegyric upon Oates, A. Richard Duke. APAS

Panes of light cracking. A Wet Night. Richard Ryan. CIP

Pangloss's Song. Richard Wilbur. NoAM

Pangolin, The. Marianne Moore. HAP; NoAM; NOBA; PBWP

Pangur Ban. *Unknown, tr. fr. Old Irish by* Robin Flower. PFIr "I and Pangor Ban, my cat," *st.* 1. MN

Pānini o ka Punahou. Elizabeth B. Holmes. PHC

Pan's/ spring rain. Symphony No. 3, in D Minor. Jonathan Williams. *Fr.* Mahler. VGW

Pan's Syrinx ("Pan's Syrinx was a girl indeed"). John Lyly. ILP (1975 ed.)

Pansies, lilies, kingcups, daisies. To the Small Celandine. Wordsworth. MBPR; PCOP

Pansy. Mary E. Bradley. PCOP

Panteater, The. William Cole. OSF

Panther. Sam Cornish. PoBA

Panther, The. Ogden Nash. OBAL

Panther, The. Rainer Maria Rilke, *tr. fr. German by* Robert Bly. NU

Panther is like a leopard, The. The Panther. Ogden Nash. OBAL

Panther Man. James A. Emanuel. BPo

Panting, immobile, his head lies flat. The Polar Bear at Crandon Park Zoo, Miami. Barbara Winder. BCr

Pantisocracy. Samuel Taylor Coleridge. MBPR; PAIC

Pantomime Diseases. Dannie Abse. PMW

Pantoum. Stephen Shrader. PHC

Papa above! Emily Dickinson. PiAm

Papa Doc Is Dead. Carol Cox. MMD

Papa finally left us. Divorce. Siv Widerberg, *tr. by* Verne Moberg. CTBA

Papa . . . here are the $7. Happiness Is a Charlie Chaplin Movie. Luis Omar Salinas. SA

Papa Love Baby. Stevie Smith. SBG

Papa's Letter. *Unknown.* WeW

Paper boat sank to the bottom of the garden, The. Eden Gate. Allen Curnow. ATNZ

Paper Boats, *sel.* Rabindranath Tagore. "Day by day I float my paper boats." RAE

Paper come out—done strewed de news. Scottsboro. *Unknown.* InPK

Paper Cutter, The. David Ignatow. CTBA

Paper Lantern, The. Tennessee Williams. *Fr.* Recuerdo. CTBA

Paper Nautilus, The. Marianne Moore. VGW

Paper of Pins. *Unknown.* AmFP; BLSo, *with music*; FSW

Paper tiger throw H-bomb in south pole. Pepsi Generation. Walasse Ting. MAT

Paper II. Carl Sandburg. TH

Papermill. Joseph Kalar. SPT

Papers that clear him tucked in his inside pocket, The. Two Figures from the Movies. William Meredith. PPoD

Paps of Dana, The. James Stephens. NoAM

Para Olga. Charles Potts. EC

Parable. W. H. Auden. FaBoCo

Parable. Michael S. Harper. NW

Parable for Our Time. Peter Michelson. HeS

Parable of the Garden. Robert Peters. PoW

Parable of the Old Man [*or* Men] and the Young, The. Wilfred Owen. GrRo; OBP; WIF

Parable of the Sidewalk Tellers. Tom House. AAN

Parable of Two Talents. Kendrick Smithyman. ATNZ

Parable of What You've Always Wanted to Come True. Robert Peters. PoW

Parabola. A. D. Hope. PoA

Paracelsus in Excelsis. Ezra Pound. PiAm

Parachutist, The. Jon Anderson. AmPA; LiSp

Parachutist. Samuel Hazo. SPo

Parade, The. Liz Sohappy Bahe. VW

Parade: Liberation Day. Kevin Ireland. ATNZ

Paraders for the Bomb. Sidney Bernard. NowV

Paradigm, The. Allen Tate. NOBA

Paradigms of Fire. Brian Swann. AmPA

Paradise. Willis Barnstone. VWA

Paradise. Chana Bloch. VWA

Paradise. George Herbert. OAEL-1; PAIC

Paradise Is Not a Place. Daniela Gioseffi. WBN

Paradise Lost, *abr.* Milton. OAEL-1

*Sels.*

Adam and Eve in Paradise, Bk. IV, *ll.* 223–319, 736–775. SCP-1

Adam Speaks ("Oh, why did God,/ Creator wise"), Bk. X, *ll.* 888-908. NU

"And God created the great whales, and each," Bk. VII, *ll.* 391-416. RhR

Banishment, The, Bk. XII, *ll.* 624–649. NOBE

Before the Fall, Bk. IV, *ll.* 304-355. NIL

"Beneath him with new wonder now he views," Bk. IV, *ll.* 205–268. PPP

"But now lead on," Bk. XII, *ll.* 614-649.  UsP

Conclusion: "High in front advanc'd/ The brandisht sword of God before them blaz'd," Bk. XII, *ll.* 632-649.  OBP

Creation of the Sea, The, Bk. VII, *ll.* 278-308.  RhR

Creation: The Fifth Day, Fishes and Birds, Bk. VII, *ll.* 387-449. SCP-1

("And God said, let the waters generate," *ll.* 387-417.)  EcS

(Creation of Birds, The. *ll.* 418-447.)  PB

"Descend from Heaven, Urania, by that name," Bk. VII, *ll.* 1-39. EBEV; PoIA

Eve Contemplates Sharing Her Sin, Bk. IX, *ll.* 811-833.  OBP

Eve Speaks to Adam ("With thee conversing I forget all time"), Bk. IV, *ll.* 639-656.  GBL

Evening in Paradise, Bk. IV, *ll.* 598-656.  NOBE

(Evening in Eden, *ll.* 598-609.)  OBP

(Moon and the Nightingale, The, *ll.* 598-609.)  Moon

"First Moloch, horrid king, besmeared with blood," Bk. I, *ll.* 392-399.  IP

Free Will and God's Foreknowledge, Bk. III, *ll.* 80-134.  ExPo (1973 ed.)

"Hail wedded love, mysterious law, true source," Bk. IV.  BiP, *ll.* 750-755; PAIC, *ll.* 750-770

"He ended; and thus Adam last replied," Bk. XII, *ll.* 552-649. HeIP

"Her long with ardent look his eye pursu'd," Bk. IX, *ll.* 397-470. UnPo (1976 ed.)

"High on a throne of royal state, which far," Bk. II, *ll.* 1-42. NIL

"His pride/ Had cast him out from Heaven, with all his host," Bk. I, *ll.* 37-236, *abr.* PPoe

Holy Light, Bk. III, *ll.* 1-55.  NOBE

(Poet's Blindness, The.)  OBP

Immortal Hate, Bk. I, *ll.* 76-124.  NOBE

"Into thir inmost bower," Bk. IV, *ll.* 738-757.  FF

"Is this the region, this the soil, the clime," Bk. I, *ll.* 242-255. FF

"Meanwhile the adversary of God and man," Bk. II.  DL, *ll.* 629-841; EBEV, *ll.* 629-734

"Next came one/ Who mourn'd in earnest," Bk. I, *ll.* 457-489. EBEV

"Now had th'Almighty Father from above," Bk. III, *ll.* 56-76. NIL

"O Father, O Supreme of heav'nly Thrones," Bk. VI, *ll.* 723-745. ILwL

"Of man's first disobedience, and the fruit," Bk. I.  EBEV, *ll.* 1-270; LFH, *ll.* 1-363; NIL, *ll.* 1-49; PAIC, *ll.* 1-83; PoIA, *ll.* 1-26

(Invocation.)  OBP, *ll.* 1-26

Satan and the Fallen Angels, Bk. I, *ll.* 283-376, 492-507. SCP-1

Satan as Rebel-Liberator, Bk. I, *ll.* 242-262.  OBP

Satan Discovers Eden, Bk. IV, *ll.* 131-196, *abr.*  ExPo (1973 ed.)

Satan Flies to the Sun, Bk. III, *ll.* 552-630.  SCP-1

Satan's Address to the Sun, Bk. IV, *ll.* 23-113.  BiP

"Thee, Father, first they sung Omnipotent," Bk. III, *ll.* 372-415. ILwL

"Thus saying, from her side the fatal key," Bk. II, *ll.* 871-1055 EBEV

"Thus talking hand in hand alone they pass'd," Bk. IV, *ll.* 689-775.  EBEV

"Thus they in Heav'n above the starry sphear," Bk. III, *ll.* 416-515.  EBEV

Vision of the Future; the Flood, Bk. XI, *ll.* 556-700, 738-756, 829-835.  SCP-1

War in Heaven, Bk. VI, *ll.* 202-219.  OBP

"When Adam thus to Eve: 'Fair consort, the hour,'" Bk. IV, *ll.* 610-656  UsP

Paradise on earth is found, A.  The Description of Elizium. Michael Drayton.  *Fr.* The Muses' Elizium.  OAEL-1

Paradise Regained, *sels.*  Milton.

"At thy nativity a glorious quire," Bk. I, *ll.* 242-254.  PChr

"It was the hour of night, when thus the Son," Bk. II, *ll.* 260-389.  EBEV

Political Power ("He brought our Saviour to the western side"), Bk. IV, *ll.* 25-143.  SCP-1

Temptation of the Magic Banquet, Bk. II, *ll.* 337-392.  SCP-1

"Therefore let pass, as they are transitory," Bk. IV, *ll.* 209-364. OAEL-1

Paradise Rug, The.  Laurance Wieder.  AAN

Paradiso.  Dante.  *See* Divina Commedia.

Paradox.  Benjamin K. Bennett.  POL

Paradox, The.  Paul Laurence Dunbar.  CABA (1972 ed.); PoBA

Paradox.  Tom McGrath.  SLP

Paradox.  Vassar Miller.  WIF

Paradox, The.  *Unknown.*  APAS

Parakeet, The.  Keith Sinclair.  ATNZ

Paralytic man has dropped in death, The.  In Manchester Square. Alice Meynell.  SBG

Paranoia.  Michael Dennis Browne.  AmPA; SoSe (1977 ed.)

Paraphrase of the First Psalm.  Burns.  PIM

Parasitosis.  Ronda Davis.  JB

Parcae, The, or Three Dainty Destinies: The Armillet.  Robert Herrick.  CaPo

Parched with age, in the quiet mist.  The Advent Images.  Paul Ramsey.  CSP

Parchman Farm Blues.  *Unknown.*  BluL

Parchment and paper left clean.  The Making of Color.  Hugh Seidman.  AmPA

Pardon, The.  Richard Wilbur.  ILP (1975 ed.); NoAM; NOBA; PoIA

Pardon my omissions.  Prologue.  Michael Hartnett.  IPM

Pardoner's Prologue, The.  Chaucer.  *Fr.* The Canterbury Tales. OAEL-1

Pardoner's Tale, The.  Chaucer.  *Fr.* The Canterbury Tales. BiP, *mod. version by* Nevill Coghill; HAP; OAEL-1

Pardoner's Tale Blues.  Patricia Beer.  AIW

Pare a willow.  Peeled Wand.  Derek Bowman.  MIS

Parentage.  Alice Meynell.  SBG

Parentage.  William Stafford.  BiP

Parents are sinful now, for they must whisper.  Marriage.  Austin Clarke.  BIrV

Pariah's Prayer, The.  Goethe, *tr. fr. German.*  ILwL

Paring the Apple.  Charles Tomlinson.  CMoP (1970 ed.); OxBTC, TwMBP

Paris.  Gregory Corso.  VGW

Paris.  Jane Garnett.  AMV-80

Paris.  Gertrud Kolmar, *tr. fr. German by* David Kipp.  PBWP

Paris.  Al Young.  CoPAm

Paris by Night.  Gustave Kahn, *tr. fr. French by* Edouard Roditi. VWA

Paris Railway-Station, The.  Dante Gabriel Rossetti.  VPC

Parish Register, The, *sels.*  George Crabbe.

Burials, Pt. III, *abr.*  OAEL-1

Lady of the Manor, The.  NOBE

Parisian Nectar.  Gelett Burgess.  FaBoNo

Parity.  Kenneth Rexroth.  GP

Park, The.  James S. Tippett.  FPB

Park at Evening, The.  Leslie Norris.  DuDa

Park Avenue.  Robert Fitzgerald.  NYP

Park lamp in reverie, The.  Unemployed: 2 A.M.  Sol Funaroff. SPT

Park, the heart, you see at town's center is soft, The.  Last Look at La Plata, Missouri.  Jim Barnes.  CDW

Park, The: U. S. A.  May Miller.  PoUp

Parked in the fields. The Forms of Love. George Oppen. NNaP

Park's beautiful, The. On the Fine Arts Garden, Cleveland. Russell Atkins. PoBA

Parlement of the Thre Ages, The, sel. Unknown. Poacher, The, orig. and mod. English prose. OxBM

Parley of Beasts. "Hugh MacDiarmid." BoAnP; NoAM

Parleyings with Certain People of Importance in Their Day, sel. Robert Browning. With Francis Furini. VLP

Parliament Dissolved at Oxford, The. Unknown. APAS

Parliament Hill Fields. John Betjeman. FaBoTw (1975 ed.); NOBE

Parliament of England, Ye. Unknown. See Ye Parliament of England.

Parliament of Fowls, The, sels. Chaucer.
Now Welcome, Summer. OxBM
(Now Welcom, Somer.) HAP
(Roundel: "Now welcome, somer, with thy sunne softe.") OAEL-1
Seynt Valentynes Day. PB

Parliament Soldiers, The. Unknown. GBP

Parlour Piece. Ted Hughes. BuTh

Parnell. W. B. Yeats. CMoP (1970 ed.)

Parodies of Cole Porter's "Night and Day." Ring Lardner. OBAL

Parody. Martha Paley Francescato, tr. fr. Spanish by Willis Barnstone. BoWoP

Parole Denial. J. Charles Green. DNGG

Paros. Robin Magowan. EAS

Parrot. Alan Brownjohn. BBL

Parrot, The. Thomas Campbell. PB

Parrot, The. James Elroy Flecker. FaBoTw (1975 ed.)

Parrot, The. Edward Lucie-Smith. BoAnP; SO

Parrot, The/ Is eating a carrot. Who Killed Lawless Lean? Stevie Smith. BBGO

Parrot and Dove. Walter Savage Landor. PB

Parrot Fish, The. James Merrill. NOBA

Parrot, from the Spanish main, A. The Parrot. Thomas Campbell. PB

Parrot, if I had your wings. The Boy and the Parrot. John Hookham Frere. OxBChV

Parrot is a thief, The. The Parrot. Edward Lucie-Smith. BoAnP; SO

Parrots have richly color'd wings. Parrot and Dove. Walter Savage Landor. PB

Parry, of all my friends the best. The Invitation. Goronwy Owen, tr. by George Borrow. OBW

Parson, The. Goldsmith. Fr. The Deserted Village. PIM

Part fenced by man, part by a rugged steep. A Place of Burial in the South of Scotland. Wordsworth. VLP

Part for the Whole. Robert Francis. PoA

Part of a Letter. Richard Wilbur. CMoP (1970 ed.)

Part of a Novel, Part of a Poem, Part of a Play, sels. Marianne Moore.
Hero, The. CMoP (1970 ed.); NIL; NOBA; PoA
Steeple-Jack, The. BoWoP; CMoP (1970 ed.); HAP; ILP (1975 ed.); NoAM; NOBA; PBWP; SBG; WPE

Part of Fortune, The. Ann Sanfedele. AMV-81

Part of Plenty. Bernard Spencer. GBL

Part of the Darkness. Isabella Gardner. ANTL; BoAnP

Part of the Doctrine. Amiri Baraka. PiAm

Part of the Lay of Sigrdrifa. Unknown, tr. fr. Old Norse by William Morris and Eiriks Magnusson. Fr. The Elder Edda. OBVE

Part of the Vigil. James Merrill. NoAM

Part of the work remains; one part is past. The End of His Work. Robert Herrick. CaPo

Part of the world is dying. To Whom It May Concern. Anne Sadowski. SES

Part-Sequence for Change, A. Robert Duncan. VGW

Parta Quies. A. E. Housman. NOBE; TT

Parterre, The. E. Harriet Palmer. FaBoCo; NOBL

Parthenophil and Parthenophe, sels. Barnabe Barnes.
"Ah sweet content, where is thy mylde abode?" LXVI. AAS; ESo
"And thus continuing with outrageous fier," XXXVI. ESo
"But pitie which sometimes doth lyons move," XXXVII. ESo
"Jove for Europaes [or Europa's] love took[e] shape of bull," LXIII. AAS; Epi; ESo: LoAs; NIL
"My sweet Parthenophe, within thy face," LXXXIV. ESo
"Oh that I had no hart, as I have none," LXV. ESo
"When I was yong, indewd'd with nature's graces, " LIV ESo
"Whilst some the Troiane warres in verse recount," LX. ESo
"Write! write! help! help, sweet Muse! and never cease!" XVIII. Epi
"Yea, but uncertain hopes are anchors feeble," XXI. Epi

Partholan went out one day. The First Lawcase. Unknown, tr. by John Montague. BIrV

Partial Comfort. Dorothy Parker. FaBoCo; OBAL

Partial Draft. Robert B. Shaw. AMV-81

Partial Eclipse. W. D. Snodgrass. Moon; PSN

Partial Explanation, The. Charles Simic. FiCP

Partial Resemblance. Denise Levertov. CoPAm

Parting. Matthew Arnold. Switzerland, II. VLP

Parting. Alice Corbin. BPAW

Parting. Lady Heguri, tr fr. Japanese by Geoffrey Bownas and Anthony Thwaite. OLR
("Thousand years, you said, A.") BoLoP

Parting. Michael Hogan. GP

Parting ("High towers the grass where once we'd meet and wander"). Malay Oral Tradition, tr. by R. J. Wilkinson and R. O. Winstedt. WTO

Parting. Gabriel Preil, tr. fr. Hebrew by Laya Firestone. VWA

Parting. Shlomo Vinner, tr. fr. Hebrew by Laya Firestone and Howard Schwartz. VWA

Parting. W. B. Yeats. FaBoTw (1975 ed.); PoIA

Parting: A Game. Lynn Sukenick. CPA; NMM

Parting, a thousand cups won't wash away the sorrow. To Tzu-an. Yü Hsüan-chi, tr. by Geoffrey Waters. BoWoP

Parting as Descent. John Berryman. CoPAm

Parting at Dawn. Malay Oral Tradition, tr. by R. J. Wilkinson and R. O. Winstedt. WTO

Parting at Dawn. John Crowe Ransom. LoAs

Parting at Morning. Robert Browning. FF; HeIP; ILP (1975 ed.); LoAs; NOBE; PAIC; SoSe; STS; UnPo (1976 ed.); VLP

Parting Chores, The. Danny L. Rendleman. TC

Parting from My Son. Evangeline Paterson. AMV-80

Parting Hymn We Sing, A, with music. Aaron R. Wolfe. AH

Parting in Wartime. Frances Cornford. NIL

Parting Is Hard. Unknown, tr. fr. Chinese by Geoffrey Waters. BoWoP

Parting: 1940. John Frederick Nims. PoA

Parting with——. Jane Barker. SCP-2

Parting, without a Sequel. John Crowe Ransom. SoSe

Partings. Maria Jane Jewsbury. OxBChV

Partly to My Cat. Ellen Bass. NMM

Partner in the corner bar is high, a grin. A Farewell. Stanley Kiesel. HeS

Partners. Jaime Castiello. ECBV

Partnership dissolved. Sale. Miller Williams. WeW

Partridge and quail, of course. Occasional woodcock. The Sportsman. David McCord. LiSp; SPo

Partridges. John Masefield. LiSp; OxBTC

Parts. Zishe Landau, *tr. fr. Yiddish by* Ruth Whitman. VWA

Party, The. Margaret Avison. PoA

Party, The. Paul Laurence Dunbar. AmNP (1974 ed.)

Party. Donald Justice. GP

Party, The. W. R. Rodgers. BIrV

Party, The. Reed Whittemore. BBGO; ConAP; LP; NCSH

Party at Bannon Brook. Alden Nowlan. NeAC

Party at the Contessa's House, The. Brian Robertson. AMV-80

Party is going strong, The. Tribute to Kafka for Someone Taken. Alan Dugan. CAPP; CoPAm; NoAM; WeW

Party Piece. Brian Patten. BoLoP

Partying by a river near Ellwood City, Pennsylvania. Coming Home in March. Harold Littlebird. VoR

Pas de Deux for Lovers. Michael Dransfield. FPA

Pascal's abyss went with him, yawned in the air. The Abyss. Baudelaire, *tr. by* Jackson Matthews. GrRo

Paso por Aqui. Wade Hall. AATT

Pasquin to the Queen's Statue at St. Paul's. William Shippen. APAS

Pass Me Not, O Gentle Saviour, *with music.* Fanny Crosby. BLSH

Pass of Kirkstone, The. Wordsworth. MBPR

Passage. Hart Crane. CMoP (1970 ed.); ExPo (1973 ed.); NoAM; NOBA

Passage. Mary Shumway. NVAP

Passage. Warren Slesinger. HeS

Passage. John Williams. MPA

Passage at Night, The—The Blaskets. Robin Flower. PFIr

Passage over Water. Robert Duncan. NoAM; NOBA

Passage to godhead, fitfully glared upon. The Lynching of Jesus. Muriel Rukeyser. SPT

Passage to India, *sel.* Walt Whitman.
    "O we can wait no longer." ILwL

Passages, *sels.* Robert Duncan.
    At the Loom. PiAM; VGW
    Envoy. VGW
    Fire, The. VGW
    Moon, The. PiAm
    Orders. CAAP
    Tribal Memories. NOBA; PiAm
    Up Rising. NNaP
    Where It Appears. PiAm

Passages. David Walker. AMV-80

Passed through the dark well. The Long Hunter. Wendell Berry. *Fr.* Inland Passages. GP

Passer, The. George Abbe. LiSp

Passer Mortuus Est. Edna St. Vincent Millay. CMoP (1970 ed.); RiTi

Passer-by, A. Robert Bridges. CMoP (1970 ed.); OAEL-2; OxBTC; PoPle

Passes are blocked by snow, The. Persia. V. Sackville-West. WPE

Passing. Langston Hughes. ILP (1975 ed.)

Passing and passing. Love Letter. Brewster Ghiselin. MPA

Passing Away. Christina Rossetti. OAEL-2; PIM; WPE

Passing By. *Unknown. See* There Is a Lady Sweet and Kind.

Passing Illness, A. Peter Wild. MPA

Passing It On. Reg Saner. BrS; GP

Passing like a Strauss waltz. The Hoofer. A. K. Redwing. VoR

Passing Love. Langston Hughes. BiP

Passing of Arthur, The. Tennyson. *See* Morte d'Arthur.

Passing of Joe Williams, The. Norman Macleod. SPT

Passing of the Buffalo, The. Hamlin Garland. BPAW

Passing of the Shee, The. J. M. Synge. BIrV; FaBoEE

Passing Remark. William Stafford. GP; VoA

Passing Stockyards Where They Killed the Buffalo. Harley Elliott. HeS

Passing stranger! you do not know how longingly I look upon you. To a Stranger. Walt Whitman. NoAM; NOBA

Passing the American graveyard, for my birthday. Poem for My Twentieth Birthday. Kenneth Koch. PoA

Passing through huddled and ugly walls. The Harbor. Carl Sandburg. NCSH; TAP

Passing through Virginia. Michael Hogan. DNGG

Passing Visit to Helen. D. H. Lawrence. CMoP (1970 ed.)

Passion, The. Henry Vaughan. PIM

Passion Drinker, The. Anita Endrezze Probst. VoR

"Passion o' me!" cried Sir Richard Tyrone. The Sally from Coventry. George Walter Thornbury. BTTM

Passion of Christ Strengthen Me. John Audelay. BoReV (Dread of Death.) OxBM

Passion of M'Phail, The, *sel.* Horace Gregory.
    Lunchroom Bus Boy Who Looked like Orson Welles, The. NYP

Passionate love is temporary. Landscape with Leaves and Figure. Olga Broumas. BoWoP; CNW

Passionate Man's Pilgrimage, The. Sir Walter Ralegh. AAS; BoReV; CABA (1972 ed.); ILP (1975 ed.); IPWM; MetP; NOBE; OBP; PoIA; (His Pilgrimage.) ILwL

Passionate Pilgrim, The, *sels.* Shakespeare, *and others.*
    Crabbed Age and Youth, XII. Shakespeare. ILP (1975 ed.); InPS; NIL
    ("Crabbed age and youth cannot live together.") GBL
    Philomel. Richard Barnfield. NOBE
    ("As it fell upon a day.") GBL
    "Venus, with young Adonis sitting by her," XI. Bartholomew Griffin. LoAs

Passionate Shepherd to His Love, The, 6 *sts.* Christopher Marlowe. AAS; BiP; BoLoP; CABA (1972 ed.); Epi; FF; HAP; HeIP; HoPM (1975 ed.); ILP (1975 ed.); InPK; InPS; IPWM; LFH; LoAs; NIL; NOBE; OAEL-1; OLR; PAIC; PBMP; PoIA; PPoD; PPoe, 7 *sts.;* PPP; UsP, 5 *sts.*

Passions. Sir Walter Ralegh. *Fr.* Sir Walter Ralegh to the Queen. PoPle

Passions, The; an Ode to Music. William Collins. LAuP

Passions are liken'd best to floods and streams. Passions. Sir Walter Ralegh. *Fr.* Sir Walter Ralegh to the Queen. PoPle

Passover. Rose Ausländer, *tr. fr. German by* Ewald Osers. VWA

Passover Dachau. B. Z. Niditch. AMV-81

Passport, The. Luis Garcia. MIT

Past, The. Emerson. TAP

Past a swim-by of deep sea fish. At the Natural History Museum. William Meredith. NYP

Past and present wilt, The. Song of Myself, LI. Walt Whitman. AnMo

Past arenas, sanctuaries. Pilgrims. Joseph Brodsky, *tr. by* Dimitry Pospielovsky *and* Keith Bosley. VWA

Past comes back, The. Ralph Hodgson. POL

Past crag and scarp. History. Robert Penn Warren. NoAM

Past exchanges have left orbits of rain around my face. An Apology. Diane Wakoski. TAP

Past factory workshops, empty. Marina Tsvetayeva, *tr. by* Paul Schmidt. *Fr.* The Daughter of Jairus. BoWoP

Past Is Dark with Sin and Shame, The, *with music.* Thomas Wentworth Higginson. AH

Past Mogollon River. Arizona Ruins. Lyn Lifshin. RiTi

Past Ruined [*or* Ruin'd] Ilion Helen Lives. Walter Savage Landor. GBL; HAP; HeIP; ILP (1975 ed.); NIL; POL (To Ianthe.) NOBE; VLP

Past sends images to beach, The. Lines for the Ancient Scribes. Harvey Shapiro. VWA

Past the house where he was got. Austin Clarke. *Fr.* Mnemosyne Lay in Dust. CMoP (1970 ed.)

Past the school and down. Directions to the Nomad. James Welch. CDW

Past the Tin Butterflies and Plaster Gnomes. Peter Bland. ATNZ

Past Time. Harvey Shapiro. POL

Past we glide, and past, and past! Robert Browning. *Fr.* In a Gondola. PeD

Pastel the flowers, the wreaths in the pastel gardens. Moon Mattress. Diane Di Prima. NMM

Pastime. Henry VIII, King of England. EBEV

Pastime of Pleasure, The, *sel.* Stephen Hawes.
Epitaph of Graunde Amoure, The. EBEV
(Epitaphy of la Graunde Amoure.) FaBoEE

Pastime with good company. Pastime. Henry VIII, King of England. EBEV

Pastoral: "I came to a field." Charles Simic. NNaP

Pastoral: "In the fields." John William Corrington. CSP

Pastoral: "It all happened so fast. Fenya was in the straight chair." Norman Dubie. AmPA

Pastoral, A: "Oh happy golden age." Tasso, *tr. fr. Italian by* Samuel Daniel. *Fr.* Aminta. OAEL-1
("O lovely age of gold!" *tr. by* Leigh Hunt.) OBVE

Pastoral: "Shuddering geography pulls the dead sentences, A." James Tipton. HeS

Pastoral: "This is a place of ease." Marion Strobel. PoA

Pastoral: "Today in Peru, this first day of summer." Lawrence Raab. AmPA

Pastoral: "When I was younger." William Carlos Williams. SoS; TVo

Pastoral Ballad by John Bull, A. Thomas Moore. BIrV; OBSV

Pastoral Dialogue, A.: Shepherd. Nymph. Chorus. Thomas Carew. CaPo; GBL; SCP-2

Pastoral of Phillis and Coridon, A. Nicholas Breton. PAIC

Pastoral of the City Streets. A. M. Klein. BBGO

Pastoral Poesy. John Clare. OAEL-2

Pastoral with Visitor. Richard Packer. FPA

Pastorale: "No more violets." Hart Crane. PSN

Pastorals, *sel.* Robert Hillyer.
"So soft in the hemlock wood." PAIC

Pastorals, *sels.* Pope.
Summer.
Sylvan Delights. NOBE
Winter. PAIC

Pastourelle. Donald Jeffrey Hayes. AmNP (1974 ed.)

Pastry. Gertrude Stein. *Fr.* Tender Buttons. RiTi

Pasture, The. Robert Frost. BiP; CMoP (1970 ed.); LCL; NOBA; NowV; OSP; RAE; SoSe (1977 ed.)

Pasture, stone wall, and steeple. Question in a Field. Louise Bogan. SBG

Pastures of Plenty. Woody Guthrie. SoS; WTO

Pat Cloherty's Version of *The Maisie*. Richard Murphy. IPM

Pat Works on the Railway. *Unknown.* FSW

Pat your foot. Leadbelly Gives an Autograph. Amiri Baraka. CNA

Pat-a-cake, pat-a-cake, baker's man! Mother Goose. GSB, *with music;* MG

Patapan. Bernard de la Monnoye, *tr. fr. French.* PChr

Patch of Old Snow, A. Robert Frost. CMoP (1970 ed.)

Patch-Shaneen. J. M. Synge. PFIr

Patchwork. Lindiwe Mabuza. SES

Pater Filio. Robert Bridges. CMoP (1970 ed.)

Paternosters/ flow from facile worshipers. Thy Kingdom Come. Elmer F. Suderman. AATT

Pater's Bathe. Edward Abbott Parry. OxBChV

Paterson, *sels.* William Carlos Williams.
"Beautiful thing/ I saw you." CMoP (1970 ed.)
Delineaments of the Giants, The. NoAM
Descent, The. HAP; PiAm; WeW
("Descent beckons, The.") TT; UsP
"Old bottle, mauled by the fire, An." TT
"Paterson lies in the valley under the Passaic Falls." NoAM; TAP
Preface: "To make a start." CMoP (1970 ed.); ILP (1975 ed.); NoAM; NOBA
"There is a woman in our town." CMoP (1970 ed.)

Paterson ("Before the grass is out the people are out"). William Carlos Williams. PiAm

Paterson lies in the valley under the Passaic Falls. The Delineaments of the Giants. William Carlos Williams. *Fr.* Paterson. NoAM; TAP

Paterson—The Strike. William Carlos Williams. *Fr.* The Wanderer: A Rococo Study. Epi

Path, The. Joseph Bruchac. NW

Path, The. Bryant. EAP

Path, The. Edward Thomas. NoAM

Path among the Stones, The. Galway Kinnell. NNaP; NOBA; Prf

Path crossed green closes and went down the lane, The. We Passed by Green Closes. John Clare. VLP

Path I Must Travel, The. Emerson Blackhorse Mitchell. VW

Path of the Old Spells, The. Donald Sinclair, *tr. fr. Gaelic; Scots version by* "Hugh MacDiarmid." MS

Path we planned beneath October's sky, The. The Path. Bryant. EAP

Pathology of Colours. Dannie Abse. PMW

Paths. Vern Rutsala. MPA

Paths become accustomed to the feel. In Memory of Patrick Kavanagh. W. G. McNeice. IPM

Paths of Prayer, The. Edouard Roditi. VWA

Paths They Kept Barren. John Garmon. AMV-81

Paths to God. Musa Moris Farhi, *tr. fr. Turkish by the author.* VWA

Patience. Bartola Cattafi, *tr. fr. Italian by* Rina Ferrarelli. AMV-81

Patience, *sels.* W. S. Gilbert.
Banquet Song. ECBV
Bunthorne's Song: The Aesthete. OAEL-2
(Aesthete, The.) VLP

Patience. Frank Horne. BPɔ

Patience, *sel. Unknown.*
Jonah Is Cast into the Sea, *orig. and mod. English prose.* OxBM

Patience! coy singers of the Delphic wood. To Poets. Walter Savage Landor. FaBoEE

Patience Hard Thing. Gerard Manley Hopkins. Prf

Patience, No Speed. George Mattingly. AcAn

Patience of a People. F. J. Bryant, Jr. CNA

Patience . . . patience. Patience. Frank Horne. BPo

Patient, The. Nicholas Moore. EAS

Patient Is Rallying, The. Weldon Kees. AnMo

Patient, The: Rockland County Sanitarium. Calvin C. Hernton. *See* Madhouse.

Patients. U. A. Fanthorpe. PMW

Patient's Surname. Hospital Care Authorization. Ronald Gross. UsP

Patmos. David Gascoyne, *after the German of* Friedrich Hölderlin. OBVE

Patna-Benares Express. Allen Ginsberg. TT

Patriarch in black takes, The. The Sacrifice. Chana Bloch. VWA

Patrick Casey is sitting on the beach. Jack Anderson. *Fr.* This Is a Poem for Patrick Casey. OSP

Patriot, The. Robert Browning. PBMP

Patriot, A. Langford Reed. TDH

Patriot, The. Sir Walter Scott. *See* This Is My Own, My Native Land.

Patriot Game, The. Dominic Behan. FSW

Patriotic Ode on the Fourteenth Anniversary of the Persecution of Charlie Chaplin. Bob Kaufman. PoBA

Patriotic Poem. Diane Wakoski. OFD; VGW

Patriotic Tour and Postulate of Joy. Robert Penn Warren. WasP

Patriotism. Sir Walter Scott. *See* This Is My Own, My Native Land.

Patrum Propositum. Robert Fitzgerald. GOA

Pat's Opinion of Flags. Fred Emerson Brooks. InPK

Patter, patter, little feet. To Beatrice Stuart Wortley: Aetat 2. Alfred Austin. PeD

Pattern, The. Robert Creeley. PPoD

Pattern of birds, A. Peter Whigham. *Fr.* Love Poems of the VIth Dalai Lama. TwMBP

Pattern Poem with an Elusive Intruder. Reinhard Döhl. WeW

Patterns. Amy Lowell. BoWoP; DL; GrRo; NIL; PBMP; VoPo

Patterns. Ruth Setterberg. AMV-81

Patterns. Paul Simon. NIL

Patty, 1949–1961. Sharon Mayer Libera. IHMS

Patty-cake, patty-cake. Tact. Paul Pascal. WeW

Paucity is gathering at the real places, A. For Pee Wee. Art Lange. FiCh

Paudeen. W. B. Yeats. HAP; InPS

Paul. Dennis Saleh. CPA

Paul. James Wright. WIF

Paul and Silas bound in jail. Keep Your Eyes on the Prize. *Unknown.* FSW

Paul grounded at Braga, a gull on his shoulder. Shipwreck. George Mackay Brown. LP

Paul Jones's Victory. *Unknown.* AmFP

Paul Klee. Ruthven Todd. EAS

Paul Revere's Ride. Longfellow. *Fr.* Tales of a Wayside Inn: The Landlord's Tale, Pt. I. BTTM; CTV; FaPo; FaPoR; OBAL

Paul Robeson. Gwendolyn Brooks. CNA; PoBA

Pauline, *sels.* Robert Browning.
"Night, and one single ridge of narrow path." VLP
"Sun-treader, life and light be thine for ever!" VLP
"Thou wilt remember. Thou art not more dear." OAEL-2

Paunch talks against good liquor to excess. On Paunch, a Parasite. Hilaire Belloc. POL

Pause. Mary Ursula Bethell. ATNZ

Pause. Dorothy Livesay. AMV-81

Pause a Moment. Asya, *tr. fr. Yiddish by* Gabriel Preil *and* Howard Schwartz. VWA

Pause before anything ordinary. Poem in Two Parts. Michael Brownstein. OSP

Pause between Clock Ticks. James Hearst. AMV-81

Pause in this desert! Here, men say, of old. Babylon. "Barry Cornwall." PIM

Pause of Thought, A. Christina Rossetti. NOBE

Pause stranger at the porch: nothing beyond. A Gateway to the Sea (I). George Bruce. MS

Pavane for the Nursery, A. William Jay Smith. DuDa
"Now touch the air softly," *sel.* OSP

Pavane for the Passing of a Child. Laura Chester. FiCP

Pavement Artist, A. G. E. Murray. HeS

Pavlov. Naomi Long Madgett. BPo

Pawnbroker, The. Maxine W. Kumin. NVAP

Pawn-shop man knows hunger, The. Street Window. Carl Sandburg. SFF

Paw-Paw Patch. *Unknown.* FSW

Pax. D. H. Lawrence. BoReV

Pax Romana. Virginia Gilbert. NPW

Pax vobis', quod the fox. The Fox and the Goose. *Unknown.* OxBM

Pay Day at Coal Creek. *Unknown. See* Payday at Coal Creek.

Pay Is Good, The. Richard Kell. MPo

Pay Me My Money Down. Lydia A. Parrish. FSW

Payday at Coal Creek. *Unknown.* AmFP; ExPo (1973 ed.); FSW; RDB, *with music*

Pay-off. Kenneth Fearing. CMoP (1970 ed.)

Paysage Moralisé. W. H. Auden. OAEL-2; UnPo (1976 ed.)

Peabody Bird, The. Rachel Field. ECBV

Peace. Jonetta Barras-Abney. PoUp

Peace. Rupert Brooke. 1914, I. BTTM; PoA

Peace. Charles Bukowski. VoA

Peace. Walter de la Mare. ILP (1975 ed.)

Peace. George Herbert. SoSe (1977 ed.)

Peace. Langston Hughes. BPo

Peace. George Jonas. NeAC

Peace. Michael Longley. CIP

Peace. Henry Vaughan. BoReV; EBEV; HAP; IPWM; NOBE; PIM

Peace, Be at Peace, O Thou My Heaviness. Baudelaire, *tr. fr. French by* Lord Alfred Douglas. InPK

Peace be unto you, Penglima Lenggang Laut! Invitation to a Spirit. *Malay Oral Tradition, tr. by* W. W. Skeat. WTO

Peace be with you, O Tin-ore. Tin-Ore. *Malay Oral Tradition, tr. by* W. W. Skeat. WTO

Peace-Giver, The. Swinburne. *Fr.* Christmas Antiphones. PIM

Peace in the valley will sing to me like a choir, The. A Clash with Cliches. Vassar Miller. AMV-80

Peace in the Welsh Hills. Vernon Watkins. OxBTC

Peace is made with a warlike man. *Unknown, tr. fr. Irish by* John Montague. BIrV

Peace is the men not marching away to be killed. Not Marching Away to Be Killed. Jean Overton Fuller. FF

Peace Is the Mind's Old Wilderness, *with music.* John Holmes. AH

Peace, muttering thoughts! and do not grudge to keep. Content. George Herbert. SCP-1

Peace of Wild Things, The. Wendell Berry. CSP; HeIP; IPWM; NU; PiAm; VGW

Peace, peace! he is not dead, he doth not sleep. Mourn Not for Adonais. Shelley. *Fr.* Adonais. BoReV; NOBE

Peace Prospect. Daniela Gioseffi. RiTi

Peace, So That. Greg Kuzma. InPK

Peace, the wild valley streaked with torrents. The Straw. Robert Graves. OxBTC

Peace to all such! But were there one whose fires. Atticus. Pope. *Fr.* Epistle to Dr. Arbuthnot. NOBE

"Peace upon earth!" was said. We sing it. Christmas: 1924. Thomas Hardy. BuTh; FaBoEE

Peace, war, religion. This Tokyo. Gary Snyder. CAPP

Peace, we have arrived. Meditation in My Favorite Position. Marge Piercy. *Fr.* Walking into Love. RiTi

Peaceable Kingdom, The. Marge Piercy. UsP

Peaceful Song, A. Natan Zach, *tr. fr. Hebrew by* Peter Everwine *and* Shula Starkman. VWA

Peach, The. Abbie Farwell Brown. TDH

Peach Orchard Mama. *Unknown.* BluL

Peaches in, and pears late. Orchard Snow. J. B. Goodenough. AMV-81

Peaches so sweet this summer. Indulgences. Michael Hogan. AMV-80

Peachtree, The.   Denise Levertov.   *Fr.* During the Eichmann Trial.   CAPP

Peacock "At Home," The.   Catherine Ann Dorset.   OxBChV

"Peacock colored tears and rotten oranges."   Midnight on Front Street.   Roberta Hill.   CDW

Peacock-eye of the half-moon long since up, The.   The Moonlit Doorway.   Kenneth Mackenzie.   GAS

Peacock Room, The.   Robert Hayden.   FB; WasP

Peanuts.   Ken Belford.   NeAC

Peanuts.   Gerald Locklin.   CPA

Pear Tree.   Hilda Doolittle ("H. D.").        BoWoP; CMoP (1970 ed.); NOBA; UnPo (1976 ed.)

Pear-Tree, The.   *Unknown.*   GBP

Pear Tree, the sun has reached the corner.   Strawberries.   Dorothy Hughes.   AMV-81

Pearl, The.   Hans Christian Andersen, *tr. fr. Danish by* Charles Wharton Stork.   LoAs

Pearl, The.   George Herbert.   EBEV; HAP; OAEL-1; SCP-1

Pearl, *sels.   Unknown.*
   "Pearl all-pleasing, prince's treasure," *tr. fr. Middle English by* Sir Israel Gollancz.   RRA, *sts.* 1-32
   "Perle, plesaunte to prynces paye."   OxBM, *sts.* 1-15, *orig. and mod. English prose;*   EBEV, *sts.* 1-5, *orig. only*

Pearl Avenue runs past the high-school lot.   Ex-Basketball Player.   John Updike.   BBGO; CTBA; LiSp; MiP; SPo

Pearl Bryan, 2 *versions.   Unknown.*   AmFP

Pearl Harbor Day 1970.   Dick Lourie.   NeAC

Pearl Seed.   Charles Kingsley.   PCOP

Pearly Beads.   *Gond Oral Tradition, tr. by* V. Elwin *and* S. Hivale.   WTO

Pears.   Linda Pastan.   VWA

Peas and Honey.   *Unknown.*   PoPle
   (Peas.)   CTV

Peasant, A.   R. S. Thomas.   OBW

Peasant Poet, The.   John Clare.   OAEL-2

Peasants, The.   Alun Lewis.   PPP

Pease-pudding hot.   Mother Goose.   MG

Peat Bog Soldiers.   *Unknown.*   FSW

Pebbles.   Herman Melville.   AmVN

Peck of Gold, A.   Robert Frost.   BPAW; SO

Pedagogy.   Gerald Locklin.   GP

Peddler, The.   Hollis Summers.   CoPAm

Peddler and His Wife, The.   *Unknown.*   AmFP

Peddler of Spells, The.   Lu Yu, *tr. fr. Chinese by* Arthur Waley.   TVo

Peddler's Song, A.   *Unknown. See* Pedlar, A.

Pedigree of honey, The.   Emily Dickinson.   NoAM; NOBA; PCOP

Pedlar.   Sharon Nelson.   VWA

Pedlar.   Ezra Pound, *after the Chinese.*   OBVE

Pedlar, A.   *Unknown.*   NOBE; PoPle
   (Fine Knacks for Ladies.)   HAP
   ("Fine knacks for ladies, cheap, choice, brave and new.")   EBEV
   (Pedler's Song, A.)   OAEL-1

Pedlar of Small-Wares, A ("A pedlar I am, that take great care").   Sir John Suckling.   CaPo

Pedlar's Caravan, The.   William Brighty Rands.   OxBChV

Pedlar's Song, The.   Shakespeare.   *Fr.* The Winter's Tale, IV, ii.   BBL

Pedro.   Luis Omar Salinas.   FF

Peek-a-Boo.   Robert Lowenstein.   AMV-81

Peeled Wand.   Derek Bowman.   MIS

Peeler's Lament, The.   *Unknown.*   WTO

Peeling Onions.   Adrienne Rich.   BoWoP; TAP

Peepers in Our Meadow, The.   Archibald MacLeish.   NCSH

Peer of the gods is that man, who.   Sappho, *tr. fr. Greek by* William Carlos Williams.   OBVE

Peer of the golden gods is he to Sappho.   Ode to Anactoria.   Sappho, *tr. by* William Ellery Leonard.   LoAs

Peerless yet hopeless maid of Q.   Miss Ellen Gee of Kew.   *Unknown.*   FaBoNo

Pegasus.   C. Day Lewis.   PoPle

Pegasus.   Patrick Kavanagh.   PFIr

Peggy Browne.   Turlough O'Carolan.   BIrV

Peggy-O.   *Unknown.*   FSW

Pelican, The.   Greg Kuzma.   AmPA

Pelican Chorus, The.   Edward Lear.   FaBoNo
   "King and Queen of the Pelicans we," *sel.*   PB

Pelvic Meditation.   Bruce Smith.   AMV-80

Penal Law.   Austin Clarke.   BoLoP; NoAM

Pendant Watch.   Madeline DeFrees.   NMM

Pendulum.   John Updike.   BBGO

Pendydd.   Kingsley Amis.   *Fr.* The Evans Country.   NOBL

Penelope.   Mary Gilmore.   MAuV

Penelope, *sels.*   Monique Laederach, *tr. fr. French by* Charles Guenther.   BoWoP
   "And so I speak/ in place of that primordial cry."
   "(Leaving the island, she believes, to go to the child.)"

Penelope.   Karen Whitehill.   NPW

Penelope, for her Ulysses' sake.   Amoretti, XXIII.   Spenser.   NIL

Penetration and Trust.   George Meredith.   VLP

Penguins in the Home ("A penguin hailed me at the door").   Helen Bevington.   OBAL

Penguins must have had it once, The.   Teaching Penguins to Fly.   Barry Spacks.   GP

Peninsular.   Madeline DeFrees.   CNW

Penis Envy.   Erica Jong.   PoIA

Penitence.   Richard Schramm.   PoW

Penitent, The.   Edna St. Vincent Millay.   PPM

Penitent Considers Another Coming of Mary, A.   Gwendolyn Brooks.   NoAM; PChr

Penn Central Station at Beacon, N.Y., The.   Ed Ochester.   TAT

Penn Station at three in the morning.   One Snowy Night in December.   John N. Morris.   NYP

Pennacesse Leper Colony for Women, The.   Cape Cod. 1922.   Norman Dubie.   PCho

Pennines in April.   Ted Hughes.   PPP

Pennsylvania Academy of Fine Arts.   Ernest Kroll.   AMV-80

Pennsylvania Dutch Mouse.   Lancaster County Tragedy.   W. Lowrie Kay.   CaYB

Pennsylvania Places.   T. A. Daly.   OBAL

Pennsylvania Station.   Langston Hughes.   AmNP (1974 ed.); NIL

Pennsylvania Winter Indian 1974.   Harold Littlebird.   VoR

Penny Fiddle, The.   Robert Graves.   ECBV

Penny for a ball of thread, A.   Pop Goes the Weasel.   *Unknown.*   CTV

Penny Is a Hardy Knight.   *Unknown.*   OxBM

Penny Trumpet.   Raphael Rudnik.   MAT

Pennycandystore beyond the El, The.   Lawrence Ferlinghetti.   *Fr.* A Coney Island of the Mind.   BBGO; BiP;CAPP; CoPAm; CTBA; HeIP; IPWM; SoS; SS; TAP

Penological Study: Southern Exposure, *sel.*   Robert Penn Warren.   Wet Hair: If Now His Mother Should Come.   NoAM

Pens, The.   W. S. Merwin.   TH

Pensioners fondle the books in the sidewalk bins.   The Band.   Carl Dennis.   AMV-80

Pensive they sit, and roll their languid eyes.   Keats.   MBPR

Pentachromatic.   Julia de Burgos, *tr. fr. Spanish by* Julio Marzán.   InW

Pentagonia. G. E. Bates. SpRo

Pentecost. Ai. PCho

Pentecost Castle, The, *abr.* Geoffrey Hill. HAP

Pentland Hills, The. *Unknown.* GBP

Penumbra. Dante Gabriel Rossetti. VLP

Penus envy, they call it. Alta. NMM

People, The. Robert Creeley. VGW

People, The. Joy Harjo. SA

People, The. W. B. Yeats. CMoP (1970 ed.)

People. Yevgeny Yevtushenko, *tr. fr. Russian by* Robin Milner-Gulland *and* Peter Levi. DL

People,/ male and female. Mahadevi, *tr. fr. Kannada by* A. K. Ramanujan. BoWoP

People along the sand, The. Neither Out Far nor In Deep. Robert Frost. CABA (1972 ed.); HAP; NoAM; NOBA; PoIA; PSN; TAP; TT; WeW

People are eating dinner in that country north of Legge's Lake, The. The Buladelah-Taree Holiday Song Cycle. Les A. Murray. GAS

People are putting up storm windows now. Storm Windows. Howard Nemerov. ConAP

People are saying that I am your enemy, The. To Julia de Burgos. Julia de Burgos, *tr. by* Grace Schulman. BoWoP; PBWP

People are standing, as if out of the rain. Fifth and 94th. Stanley Plumly. NYP

People Cannot Speak, The. T. Alan Broughton. FAF

People chained to aurora, A. Civilization and Its Discontents. John Ashbery. CAPP; NIL

People die from loneliness. One. Carolyn M. Rodgers. BPo

People do gossip. Sappho, *tr. fr. Greek by* Mary Barnard. PBWP

People expect old men to die. Old Men. Ogden Nash. SFF

People Hide Their Love. Emperor Wu Ti, *tr. fr. Chinese by* Arthur Waley. OLR

People in the middle ages didn't think they were living. Ode. David Lehman. AMV-81

People know, The. A Little More about the Brothers and Sisters. Sharon Scott. JB

People living round the place. Thief Jones. Robert P. Tristram Coffin. MiP

People made a ring, The. The Hemorrhage. Stanley Kunitz. NYP

People of Blakeney, The. *Unknown.* GBP

People of the South Wind. William Stafford. NNaP

People say they have a hard time. For de Lawd. Lucille Clifton. CNA; PoBA; PPoD; TAP

People south of Gibbon call him, The. Blue Heron. Don Welch. GP

People spoiled by too many masters. Poetics. André Spire, *tr. by* Edouard Roditi. VWA

People, the People, The. George Oppen. GP

People were bathing and posturing themselves on the beach. The Gods! The Gods! D. H. Lawrence. CMoP (1970 ed.)

People who have no children can be hard. The Children of the Poor. Gwendolyn Brooks. *Fr.* The Womanhood. PoA; WPE

People who have what they want. The Terrible People. Ogden Nash. TAP

People who remain flabergasting for a lifetime. Staying Married. Dick Allen. FAF

People Who Went By in Winter. William Stafford. GP

People, Yes, The, *sels.* Carl Sandburg.
  "From the four corners of the earth," *fr.* Sec. 1. CMoP (1970 ed.)
  " 'I love you,'/ said a great mother," *fr.* Sec. 8 CC
  "People will live on, The," Sec. 107. NoAM; NOBA; PiAm
  "People, yes, the people, The," *fr.* Secs. 86–107. WIF

"What the people learn out of lifting and hauling," Sec. 32. OBAL

" 'Why did the children,' " Sec. 41. OBAL

"Why repeat? I heard you the first time," Sec. 42. OBAL

People's Choice, The: The Dream Poems II. Amiri Baraka. BiP

People's [*or* Worker's] flag is deepest red, The. The Red Flag. Jim Connell. FSW; VLP

Peopleshaped Toomany-ness Far Too, A. E. E. Cummings. ILP (1975 ed.)

Pepita, my paragon, bright star of Arragon. Saragossa. Henry Sambrooke Leigh. FaBoCo

Pepsi Generation. Walasse Ting. MAT

Pepys Bar, West Forty-eighth Street, 8 a.m. L. E. Sissman. NYP

Perambulator Poem. David McCord. CC; OFD

Perception of an object costs. Emily Dickinson. NOBA

Perched on my city office stool. The Ice-Cart. W. W. Gibson. EcS

Percivale's Quest. Tennyson. *Fr.* Idylls of the King. OAEL-2

Percolating Highway. Michael Castro. VWA

Perculator. Magic Sam. Steve Toth. AcAn

Percussion Bittersweet. Antar S. K. Mberi. SES

Percussions. Ron Welburn. CNA

Perdita. Louis MacNeice. PoA

Perennial fluctuation. Cuvier Light. Pat Wilson. ATNZ

Perfect Day, A, *with music.* Carrie Jacobs Bond. BLSo

Perfect Gift, The. Edmund Vance Cooke. PChr

Perfect little body, without fault or stain on thee. On a Dead Child. Robert Bridges. CMoP (1970 ed.); EBEV; NoAM; NOBE

Perfect One, The. Steven Orlen. AAN

Perfect Poem Trumpets, The. James E. Warren, Jr. AATT

Perfect Symbol, The. Louis Johnson. ATNZ

Perfect Way is only difficult for those who pick and choose, The. On Trust in the Heart. Seng-ts'an, *tr. fr. Chinese.* ILwL

Perfection, of a kind, was what he was after. Epitaph on a Tyrant. W. H. Auden. HeIP; MiP; NIL; SFF

Perfection of Dentistry, The. Marvin Bell. AmPA

Perfectionist, The. Philip Dacey. NVAP

Perfectly happy now, he looked at his estate. Voltaire at Ferney. W. H. Auden. PoA

Perfervid Roc, sitting on candle light, The. The Roc. Richard Eberhart. CMoP (1970 ed.)

Perforated Spirit, The. Morris Bishop. MiP; QQQ; TPo

Performance, The. James Dickey. ConAP; CSP; ExPo (1973 ed.); NoAM; NOBA

Performance. Raymond R. Patterson. FoP

Performance at Hog Theater, A. Russell Edson. AmPA

Performances, assortments, résumés. The Tunnel. Hart Crane. *Fr.* The Bridge. CMoP (1970 ed.); MAT; NYP

Performer numbs toward the moribund, The. The Martyr and the Army. Jock Henderson. AMV–81

Perfume, The. Robert Herrick. CaPo

Perfume of the iris, sweet citron, The. The Words, the Words, the Words. William Carlos Williams. BiP

Perhaps. Rachel, *tr. fr. Hebrew by* A. C. Jacobs. VWA

Perhaps. Stephen Spender. NoAM

Perhaps/ This is the way. Antigone I. Herbert Martin. PoBA

Perhaps/ You will remember/ John Brown. October 16: The Raid. Langston Hughes. PoBA

Perhaps Eve in the garden knew the sun. The Fortunate Fall. A. Alvarez. VWA

"Perhaps I may allow, the Dean." Swift. *Fr.* Verses on the Death of Doctor Swift. NOBE

Perhaps I'll find God someday. Search. Elisavietta Ritchie. AATT

Perhaps I'm kidding myself about. How to Write. Anne Waldman. UsP

Perhaps it makes more. Letter to a Conceivable Great-Grandson. Earle Birney. BBGO

Perhaps it was never so. Perhaps. Rachel, *tr. by* A. C. Jacobs. VWA

Perhaps it was usual. Into the Sky. Sallie Chesham. AATT

Perhaps It's as You Say. Peter Everwine. NNaP

Perhaps It's Only Music. Natan Zach, *tr. fr. Hebrew by* Peter Everwine *and* Shula Starkman. VWA

Perhaps the children of a future day. Unless We Guard Them Well. Jane Merchant. QQQ

Perhaps they wonder who the tall man is. Riding with Some North Vietnamese Students in a Polish Elevator, 1966. Roger Mitchell. PAIC

Perhaps this day the sun may waken her. Unconscious Woman. Jill Thomas. PMW

Perhaps this valley too leads into the head of long-ago days. Grand Abacus. John Ashbery. EAS; PoA

Perhaps—well/ It may not matter! Men's Impotence. *Tr. fr. Eskimo.* WTO

Perhaps when I am gaunt. To Drift Down. Janet Carncross Chandler. AMV–81

Pericles, *sels.* Shakespeare.
Shakespeare on the Sea ("Thou God of this great vast, rebuke these surges"), *fr.* III, I. RhR
"Terrible childbed hast thou had, my dear, A," *fr.* III, i. EBEV

Pericles and Aspasia, *sels.* Walter Savage Landor.
Corinna, to Tanagra, from Athens, *fr.* XLIV. NOBE
Dirce, *fr.* CCXXX. EBEV; FaBoEE; GBL; HAP; ILP (1975 ed.); NOBE; OAEL–2; PoPle; VLP; WeW

Perils of Invisibility, The. W. S. Gilbert. PoTa

Peripatetic. Robert Lima. AMV–81

Periphery. A. R. Ammons. NOBA

Periphery. Ruth Stone. GP

Perle, pleasaunte to prynces paye. *Unknown. Fr.* Pearl. EBEV; OxBM

Permanence in Change. Goethe, *tr. fr. German by* John Frederick Nims; *diff. tr. by* Mark J. Doyle. HoPM (1975 ed.)

Permanently. Kenneth Koch. CAPP; PoA; PPP
"One day the Nouns were clustered in the street," *sel.* OSP

Permit me here a simple brief aside. To Calliope. Robert Graves. CMoP (1970 ed.)

Permit Us, Lord, to Consecrate, *with music.* Joseph Green. AH

Permitted to assist you, let me see. St. Valentine. Marianne Moore. OFD

Peron is back and wants to make you chicken inspector. For Borges. Michael Berryhill. AAN

Perplexed by the Sunlight. Grevel Lindop. LP

Perrette's milk-pot fitted her head-mat just right. The Dairymaid and Her Milk-Pot. La Fontaine, *tr. by* Marianne Moore. NAWM–2

Persephone. Robert Duncan. NoAM; NOBA

Persepolis is great with pomp and pride. On the Fen: A Stormy Day near Heckington. Arthur J. Bull. HeHu

Perseus. James K. Baxter. ATNZ

Persia. V. Sackville-West. WPE

Persian Miniature. Jane Shore. PCho

Persian pomps, boy, ever I renounce them. Horace, *tr. by* Christopher Smart. Odes, I, 38. OBVE

Persian Version, The. Robert Graves. CMoP (1970 ed.); ExPo (1973 ed.); FaBoCo; NIL; NoAM; NOBL; WeW

Persimmon Tree, The. *Unknown.* GBP

Persimmon Trees, She Remembers, Not Far Away. David Baker. AMV–81

Persistency of Poetry. Matthew Arnold. VLP

Persistent Explorer. John Crowe Ransom. PiAm

Persistent Narrative. Ken Smith. TwMBP

Person, *sel.* Gavin Bantock.
"Is this pain, when my heart." TwMBP

Person. Alan Jackson. MS

Person after person. Buddha's Birthday: April 8, 1819. Issa, *tr. by* Nobuyuki Yuasa. *Fr.* Oraga Haru. OFD

Person is very self-conscious about his head, A. Thoughts on One's Head. William Meredith. HAP

Person of Note, A. Walter Parke. TDH

Person to Person. Gwen Harwood. GAS

Person to Person. Elisabeth Murawski. PoUp

Person to Person. Lorine Parks. NowV

Person who can do, The. Poem. Alan Dugan. NoAM

Personal. Langston Hughes. AmNP (1974 ed.); NOBA

Personal Column. William Price Turner. SLP

Personal Helicon. Seamus Heaney. HeHu; IPM

Personal History. Ruthven Todd. MS

Personal Letter No. 3. Sonia Sanchez. RiTi

Personal Letter No. 2. Sonia Sanchez. WBN

Personal Poem. Frank O'Hara. CAPP; NYP

Personal Poem. Ingrid Wendt. NMM

Personal Song. Arnatkoak, *tr. fr. Eskimo.* WTO

Personal Talk. Wordsworth. CABA (1972 ed.); MBPR; NOBE

Personality Sketch, A: Bill. Ronda Davis. JB

"Personals." Leatrice W. Emeruwa. RiTi

Personals, The. Alan Feldman. PCho

Persons of the Prologue. Chaucer, *tr. fr. Middle English by* Nevill Coghill. *Fr.* The Canterbury Tales: Prologue. OBP

Perspective. Adrianne Marcus. MIT

Perspective. Coventry Patmore. *Fr.* The Angel in the House, II, i. FaBoEE; GBL

Perspective. Robert L. Vorpahl. AMV–80

Perspective and Limits of Snapshots, The. Dave Smith. PCho

Perspective of Co-ordination. Arthur Davison Ficke. PoA

Perspectives. Dudley Randall. AmNP (1974 ed.)

Persuasions to Enjoy. Thomas Carew. NOBE; PAIC
(Song: Persuasions to Enjoy.) CaPo

Persuasive Go-Gebtor. "R. C." TDH

Perversion interests me. Note Delivered by a Female Impersonator. Heather McHugh. AmPA

Pervigilium Veneris. Suzanne Noguere. PoA

Pesci Misti. Leonard Aaronson. FaBoTw (1975 ed.)

Pessimist, The. Ben King. FaBoCo; FaBoNo; OBAL

Pessimist and Optimist. Frederick Langbridge. SoSe (1977 ed.)

Pet Deer, The. James Tate. EAS

Pet Lamb, The. Wordsworth. OxBChV

Pet Shop. Louis MacNeice. BoAnP

Pet was never mourned as you. Last Words to a Dumb Friend. Thomas Hardy. PCat

Petals of the Tulips, The. Judith Hemschemeyer. TV

Pete at the Seashore. Don Marquis. GDP

Pete at the Zoo. Gwendolyn Brooks. ECBV; UsP

Pete Orman. *Unknown.* BPAW

Pete Petersen, before this bit, a professional entertainer. Vaudeville. Lincoln Kirstein. NoAM

Peter. Albert Howard Carter. AATT

Peter. Marianne Moore. CMoP (1970 ed.)

Peter Amberley. *Unknown.* AmFP

Peter Bell. Wordsworth. MBPR

Peter Bell the Third. Shelley. MBPR
*Sels.*
"Devil now knew his proper cue, The." OBSV
"Hell is a city much like London." OBP; OBSV

Peter Gray. *Unknown.* BLSo, *with music;* FSW

Peter Grimes; the Outcast. George Crabbe. *Fr.* The Borough, Letter XXII. NOBE

Peter Hath Lost His Purse. *At. to* Henry Parrot. FF

Peter-Penny, The. Robert Herrick. CaPo

Peter Piper picked a peck of pickled pepper. Mother Goose. MG

Peter Quince at the Clavier. Wallace Stevens. AnMo; CABA (1972 ed.); CMoP (1970 ed.); ExPo (1973 ed.); InPK; InPS; LoAs; NOBA; PAIC; PPP; SoSe; STS; TAP; TCP; TT; UsP

Peterhead in May. Burns Singer. MS

Peter's Little Daughter Dies. Kenneth Patchen. RRA

Peter's not friendly. He gives me sideways looks. John Berryman. *Fr.* Dream Songs. CAPP

Pete's Error. Arthur Chapman. BPAW

Petit, the Poet. Edgar Lee Masters. *Fr.* Spoon River Anthology. CMoP (1970 ed.); InPK; NoAM; NOBA; TAP

Petition. W. H. Auden. CMoP (1970 ed.)

Petition. Harold McCurdy. AMV-81

Petition for an Absolute Retreat, The. Countess of Winchilsea. SBG; WPE, *abr.*

Petition for Reconciliation. Cynddelw Brydydd Mawr, *tr. fr. Welsh by* Joseph P. Clancy. OBW

Petoskey Stone. Robert Vas Dias. HeS

Petrified bones. The Desert World. Tom McKeown. TC

Pets, The. Robert Farren. ECBV

Pets are the hobby of my brother Bert. My Brother Bert. Ted Hughes. DuDr

Petticoat, A. Gertrude Stein. *Fr.* Tender Buttons. RiTi

Pettigrew Museum. John Calvin Rezmerski. HeS

Pettitoes are little feet, The. Five Toes. *Unknown.* BBL

Petty Murder. Albert McLean, Jr. SFF

Petty sneaking knave I knew, A. On Cromek. Blake. FaBoCo; PoPle

Petulance is purple. Spectrum. Mari Evans. BPo

Peveril of the Peak, *sel.* Sir Walter Scott.
" 'Speak not of niceness, when there's chance of wreck,' " *fr. ch.* 38. FaBoEE

Pew, The/ across from mine. On Listening to a Death-of-God Theologian Lecture in Chapel. Elmer F. Suderman. AATT

Pew, pew,/My minny me slew. Song of the Murdered Child. *Unknown.* GBP

Peyote Vision. Lew Blockcolski. VoR

Phaedra. Hilda Doolittle ("H. D."). SBG

Phaedra. Osip Mandelstam, *tr. fr. Russian by* James Greene. OBVE

Phaedra (Phèdre). Racine, *tr. fr. French by* Robert Lowell. NAWM-2

Phallus. Shiraishi Kazuko, *tr. fr. Japanese by* Ikuko Atsumi. BoWoP

Phantasia for Elvira Shatayev. Adrienne Rich. LiSp

Phantasus, *sel.* Arno Holz, *tr. fr. German by* Babette Deutsch.
"On a mountain of sugar-candy." PChr

Phantom. Samuel Taylor Coleridge. MBPR; OAEL-2

Phantom Bark, The. Hart Crane. CMoP (1970 ed.)

Phantom Horsewoman, The. Thomas Hardy. CMoP (1970 ed.); LoAs; NOBE

Phantom Limb, A. Edward Lowbury. PMW

Phantom or Fact. Samuel Taylor Coleridge. MBPR

Phantom Ship, The. Longfellow. RhR

Phantom to me. Second Sapphic Fragment/Fainetai Moi. Sappho, *tr. by* Harvey Bialy. MIT

Phantom Wooer, The. Thomas Lovell Beddoes. ILP (1975 ed.); PoIa

Phantoms. Nashira N'tosha. NW

Pharaoh and Joseph ("Pharaoh rejects his blossoming wives"). Else Lasker-Schüler, *tr. fr. German by* Joachim Neugroschel. VWA

Pharao's Daughter. Michael Moran. BIrV

Pharisees come bloom. Egyptian Book of the Dead. David Henderson. MIT

Pharsalia, *sels.* Lucan, *tr. fr. Latin.* OBVE
"Just and fit actions Ptolemy (he saith)," *fr.* VII, *tr. by* Ben Jonson.
"O wastfull riot, never well content," *fr.* IV, *tr. by* Sir Walter Ralegh.
"Thee Pompey thy past deeds by turns infest," *fr.* I, *tr. by* Nicholas Row.

Phases of Darkness, The. Paul Petrie. TAP

Phases of the Moon. Robert Browning. *Fr.* One Word More. Moon.

Pheasant, The. Robert P. Tristram Coffin. TH

Pheasant Hunter and the Arrowhead, The. Julian Gitzen. AMV-80

Phèdre. Racine. *See* Phaedra.

Phenomena. Robinson Jeffers. NoAM; NOBA

Phenomenal Survivals of Death in Nantucket. Louise Glück. AmPA

Phenomenon, The. Karl Shapiro. CMoP (1970 ed.)

Phil. Ted Kooser. AMV-81

Philadelphia ("Philadelphia is a handsome town"). *Unknown.* AmFP

Philadelphia Airport, The. Ron H. Bayes. AAN

Philarete to His Mistress, *sel.* George Wither.
"Thee entirely I have loved." PeD

Philatelist Royal. Robert Graves. FaBoCo

Philip returned to his books, but returned to his Highlands after. Arthur Hugh Clough. *Fr.* The Bothie of Tober-na-Vuolich. VLP

Philip Sparrow. John Skelton. *See* Phyllyp Sparowe.

Philippus, for his pleadings famed afar. Horace, *tr. fr. Latin by* Francis Howes. OBVE

Phillip Michael Irving. Chicago Centennial or: The Town Hall Meeting. Walter Bradford. FiCh

Phillips Mill. Terrance Keenan. AAN

Phillis, *sels.* Thomas Lodge.
"Devoide of reason, thrale to foolish ire," XXXI, *after the French of* Pierre de Ronsard. AAS; NIL
"Faire art thou Phillis, I, so faire (sweet mayd)," XXII. ESo
"I hope and feare, I pray and hould my peace," XXXV. ESo
"I would in rich and golden coloured raine," XXXIV, *after the French of* Pierre de Ronsard. AAS; ESo; NIL
"Long hath my sufferance labored to inforce," IV. ESo
"Love guards the roses of thy lips," XIII. ILP (1975 ed.)

Phillis was a fair maid. The Maiden's Complaint. *Unknown.* OLR

Philodendron. Helen Armstead Johnson. AmNP (1974 ed.)

Philomel. Richard Barnfield. *Fr.* The Passionate Pilgrim. NOBE
("As it fell upon a day.") GBL

Philomela. Matthew Arnold. ILP (1975 ed.); NIL; OAEL-2; PPP; UnPo (1976 ed.); VLP

Philomela. John Crowe Ransom. CMoP (1970 ed.); ILP (1975 ed.); NoAM; NOBA; OBAL; OBSV

Philomela. Sir Philip Sidney. NOBE
(Nightingale, The.) EBEV; ILP (1975 ed.)

Philon the Shepherd. *Unknown.* NOBE

Philosopher, A. Sam Walter Foss. OBAL

Philosopher, The. Edna St. Vincent Millay. CMoP (1970 ed.)

Philosopher and the Birds, The. Richard Murphy. CIP

Philosopher and the Lover, The: To a Mistress Dying. Sir William Davenant. NOBE; Prf

Philosopher to His Mistress, The. Robert Bridges. OBP

Philosophers have measured mountains. The Agony. George Herbert. SCP-1

Philosophic Taed, The. William Soutar. MS

Philosophy. Paul Laurence Dunbar. BPo

Philosophy Is Born. Christian Morgenstern, *tr. fr. German by* Geoffrey Grigson. FaBoNo

Philosophy, the love of wisdom. On Philosophy. Jonas Goldstein. AMV-81

Phineas Within and Without. Paul Zimmer. VGW

Phizzog. Carl Sandburg. UsP

Phlebas the Phoenician, a fortnight dead. Death by Water. T. S. Eliot. *Fr.* The Waste Land, IV. IP; OBVE

Phoebe Dawson, *sel.*. George Crabbe.
    "Lo! now with red rent cloak and bonnet black." EBEV

Phoebus, the goddess variant and changeable. Christine de Pisan, *tr. fr. French: ad. by* Joan Keefe. *Fr.* The Epistle of Othea to Hector (A Lytil Bibell of Knyghthod). PBWP

Phoebus with Admetus. George Meredith. NOBE

Phoenix. Rose Ausländer, *tr. fr. German by* Ewald Osers. VWA

Phoenix, The. J. V. Cunningham. MPA; NoAM

Phoenix, The. George Darley. *Fr.* Nepenthe. NOBE; OAEL-2 ("O blest unfabled incense tree.") BIrV

Phoenix, The. Matti Megged, *tr. fr. Hebrew by* Howard Schwartz. VWA

Phoenix. Carolyn M. Rodgers. JB

Phoenix, The, *sel. Unknown, tr. fr. Anglo-Saxon by* Charles W. Kennedy.
    "Lo! I have learned of the loveliest of lands." OAEL-1

Phoenix and [the] Turtle, The. Shakespeare. NOBE: OAEL-1

Phoenix, bird of terrible pride. Sir Herbert Read. *Fr.* Mutations of the Phoenix. FaBoTw (1975 ed.)

Phoenix of Mozart, The. Claude Vigée, *tr. fr. French by* Anthony Rudolf. VWA

Phoenix on the hot sirocco's breath. Epilogue. H. B. Mallalieu. PoA

Phone Call. Tom Crawford. AMV-81

Phone Call to Rutherford. Paul Blackburn. CTBA

Phone duet over the radio, A. The Louisiana Weekly #4. David Henderson. PoBA

Phone for the fish-knives, Norman. How to Get On in Society. John Betjeman. NOBL; OBSV; OxBTC

Phone shivers interrupting, The/ your nerves. Half the Story. Karen Sagstatter. PoUp

Phoning My Son Long Distance. Ted Kooser. HeS

Photo, The. Lennart Bruce. MIT

Photo of a Retired Farmer, Big Bend, Wisconsin. Robert L. McRoberts. HeS

Photo of someone else's childhood, A. The Old Adam. Denise Levertov. UnPo (1976 ed.)

Photograph. Quandra Prettyman. PoBA

Photograph: an empty house, the windows intact. Seizure. James E. Warren, Jr. AMV-81

Photograph at the Cloisters: April 1972. Helen Chasin. NMM

Photograph of a Baby. Charles Brasch. ATNZ

Photograph of an Actress, c. 1860. Nan McDonald. MAuV

Photograph of Haymaker, 1890. Molly Holden. OxBTC; PSN

Photograph of Miranda, A. Snapshots. Ron McCurdy. PHC

Photograph of Myself, The. Jon Anderson. AmPA

Photograph of the Back of My House. Del Marie Rogers. NPW

Photograph of the Hanging Pianos. Jane Garland Katz. AAN

Photograph of you at the edge, A. At 85. Richard Ardinger. AMV-81

Photograph the Cat Licks, The. Beatrice Walter. NMM

Photographed at midday. To Boris Pasternak. Aleksandr Kushner, *tr by* Dimitry Pospielovsky *and* Keith Bosley. VWA

Photographer's Wife, The. Janet Beeler. AMV-81

Photographing the Facade—San Miguel de Allende. Betsy Colquitt. AMV-80

Photographs. William Peskett. AMV-81

Photographs. Charles Wright. HoPM (1975 ed.)

Photographs: A Vision of Massacre. Michael S. Harper. PoBA

Photographs of China. Donald Hall. TC

Phrase which was to be the axis of my poem's crystallization, The. Ars Poetica. Adam Wazyk, *tr. by* Isaac Komem. VWA

Phrases for Everyday Use by the British in India. John Daniel. TwMBP

Phryne. John Donne. FaBoEE

Phyllidula. Ezra Pound. FaBoTw (1975 ed.)

Phyllis. Thomas Lodge. *See* Phillis.

Phyllis. Thomas Randolph. BoLoP

Phyllis Corydon clutched to him. Catullus, *tr. fr. Latin by* Peter Whigham. BoLoP

Phyllis Knotting. Sir Charles Sedley. NOBE

Phyllis; or, The Progress of Love. Swift. OAEL-1; OBSV

Phyllis, why should we delay. To Phyllis. Edmund Waller. ILP (1975 ed.)

Phyllis's Age. Matthew Prior. FaBoEE

Phyllyp Sparowe [*or* Philip Sparrow]. John Skelton. AAS
    *Sels.*
    Anathema of Cats. PCat
    "And prytily he wolde pant." ECBV
    "It was so prety a fole." PB
    "Pla ce bo!/ Who is there, who?" NOBE; OAEL-1

Phylogeny. Marilyn Thompson. UsP

Physical Fitness. Alison Wyrley Birch. PPM

Physical for My Son. Barbara Smith. AMV-80

Physical Imperfections of Old Films, The. Paul Ramsey. PPoD

Physician, Heal Thyself. S. L. Henderson Smith. PMW

Physician Nature! let my spirit blood! Ode to Fanny. Keats. MBPR

Physics of Love. Charles Brasch. ATNZ

Piano ("Softly, in the dusk, a woman is singing to me"). D. H. Lawrence. CMoP (1970 ed.); HAP; HeIP; ILP (1975 ed.); InPK; NIL; NoAM; NOBE; OAEL-2; PoPle; PPM; PPP; UnPo (1976 ed.); WeW

Piano, The ("Somewhere beneath the piano's superb sleek black"). D. H. Lawrence. WeW

Piano, A. Gertrude Stein. *Fr.* Tender Buttons. PBWP

Piano after War. Gwendolyn Brooks. AmNP (1974 ed.)

Piano at Evening. Palea, *tr. fr. Hawaiian by* M. K. Pukui *and* A. L. Korn. WTO

Piano hums, The. Effendi. Michael S. Harper. CNA; PoBA

Piano Practice. Derek Walcott. NYP

Piano Tuner, The. W. Atmar Smith II. AMV-80

Piano tuner spoke to me, that tenderest, The. Pyrargyrite Metal, 9. Cecilia Meireles, *tr. by* James Merrill. PBWP

Piazza di Spagna, Early Morning. Richard Wilbur. InPS; PSN; VGW

Piazza Piece. John Crowe Ransom. BoLoP; FoP; HeIP; IP; LFH; NoAM; NOBA; PAIC; PiAm; SFF; TAP; UsP

Pibroch. Ted Hughes. OAEL-2; TwMBP

Pibroch ("Pibroch of Donuil Dhu, pibroch of Donuil"). Sir Walter Scott. FaPoR
    (Gathering Song of Donald the Black.) BTTM

Picador Bit, The. Bink Noll. LiSp; SFF

Piccante. Mary Di Michele. AMV-81

Piccola Commedia. Richard Wilbur. FoP; GP

Pick a Bale of Cotton. *Unknown.* FSW

Pick a fern, pick a fern, ferns are high.   Ezra Pound, *after the Chinese.* OBVE

Pick up my pen.   The World Is a Stubbed Toe.   Mbembe.   NW

Picked up where.   Attica.   Ron Welburn.   NW

Picked you said.   Every Day Shaggy Man Mushroom.   Mary Norbert Körte.   CPA

Pickers.   Peter Brett.   AMV-81

Picket fence of steeples to the east, A.   From the Observation Deck, Austin.   Henry Petroski.   AAN

Picket Line Song, The.   *Unknown.* FSW

Pickety Fence.   David McCord.   ECBV

Pickle Belt.   Theodore Roethke.   AnMo

Picnic.   Ted Berrigan.   FiCh

Picnic, The.   John Logan.   ConAP; CTBA; LP; NCSH

Picnic.   Adrienne Rich.   CoPAm

Picnic Rhyme.   *Unknown. See* Lemonade.

Picnic on the Lawn.   Vernon Scannell.   HeHu

Picnic: The Liberated.   M. Carl Holman.   PoBA

Pictor Ignotus.   Robert Browning.   VLP

Picture, The.   Robert Lowell.   NoAM
   (New York 1962: Fragment, *diff. version.*) NYP

Picture, A.   Howard Nemerov.   NowV

Picture and book remain.   An Acre of Grass.   W. B. Yeats.   CMoP (1970 ed.); NoAM; OBP

Picture-frame for you to fill, A.   To Minnie.   Robert Louis Stevenson.   SLP

Picture from Life's Other Side, A.   *Unknown.* FSW

Picture is worth a thousand words, A.   Existing Light.   Madeline DeFrees.   PoW

Picture of a Nativity.   Geoffrey Hill.   NoAM

Picture of J. T. in a Prospect of Stone, The.   Charles Tomlinson.   PPP

Picture of Little J. A. in a Prospect of Flowers, The.   John Ashbery.   ConAP; PPP

Picture of Little Letters.   John Koethe.   AMV-81

Picture of Little T. C. in a Prospect of Flowers, The.   Andrew Marvell.   ExPo (1973 ed.): NOBE; OAEL-1; PPP

Picture of Loot.   Alan Sillitoe.   OxBTC

Picture of the Times, A.   Philip Freneau.   EAP; PiAm

Picture of Workers Resting.   Patricia Beer.   HeHu

Picture, The; or, The Lover's Resolution.   Samuel Taylor Coleridge.   MBPR

Picture Postcards.   Miklós Radnóti, *tr. fr. Hungarian by* Emery George.   VWA

Picture-Show.   Siegfried Sassoon.   CMoP (1970 ed.)

Picture: the energy of rest.   From a Print by Maillol.   Anne Becker.   PoUp

Picture yourself in a boat on a river.   Lucy in the Sky with Diamonds.   John Lennon *and* Paul McCartney.   NIL; SoS

"Pictures are my friends."   Books.   William Baer.   AMV-81

Pictures from Brueghel, *sels.*   William Carlos Williams.
   Corn Harvest, The, VII.   PPP
   Landscape with the Fall of Icarus, II.   BBGO; NIL; PPP; TT; WIF

Pictures in a Gallery Undersea.   C. K. Stead.   ATNZ

Pictures of a City.   Robert Fripp *and* Peter Sinfield.   GrRo

Pictures on the Wall.   Zvi Shargel, *tr. fr. Yiddish by* Gabriel Preil *and* Howard Schwartz.   VWA

Pie in the Sky.   Joe Hill.   *See* Preacher and the Slave, The.

Pie sat on a pear tree, A.   Hop't She.   *Unknown.* GBP

Piece by piece I seem.   Necessities of Life.   Adrienne Rich.   NIL; NoAM; NOBA; Psy

Piece of blank paper, A/ Is a uterine lining.   The Obstetrician.   Henry Shore.   PMW

Piece of flesh gives off, A.   The Dead Shall Be Raised Incorruptible.   Galway Kinnell.   CAAP; NOBA

Piece of green pepper, A.   Haiku Ambulance.   Richard Brautigan.   InPK

Piece of thread ripped-out from a fierce design, A.   Adrienne Rich.   *Fr. Ghazals:* Homage to Ghalib.   NIL

Piecemeal the summer dies.   Exeunt.   Richard Wilbur.   HeIP; NCSH

Pieces of memory stick together.   Remembering.   Judit Tóth, *tr. by* Emery George.   VWA

Pied Beauty.   Gerard Manley Hopkins.   AKE; AnMo; BiP; BoReV; CABA (1972 ed.); CMoP (1970 ed.); Epi; HAP; HeIP; HoPM (1975 ed.); ILP (1975 ed.); InPK; InPS; NIL; NoAM; NOBE; OAEL-2; PAIC; PBMP; PPM; PPoD; PPP; SoSe (1977 ed.); SS; VLP; VoPo; WeW; WIF

Pied Piper of Hamelin, The.   Robert Browning.   BBL; BiP; FaPo; OxBChV

Pier delle Vigne.   Dante, *tr. fr. Italian by* John Ciardi.   *Fr. Divina Commedia:* Inferno, XIII.   HoPM (1975 ed.)

Pier-Glass, The.   Robert Graves.   CMoP (1970 ed.); NoAM

Piercing, The.   Pat Lowther.   MMD

Piercing Chill I Feel, The.   Buson, *tr. fr. Japanese by* Harold G. Henderson.   InPK

Pierrot le Fou.   Adrienne Rich.   PiAm

Piers are pummelled by the waves, The.   The Fall of Rome.   W. H. Auden.   AnMo; InPS; MAT; OAEL-2; OxBTC; UnPo (1976 ed.)

Piers Plowman.   William Langland.   *See* Vision of Piers Plowman, The.

Pietà.   James McAuley.   MAuV

Pieta.   Rainer Maria Rilke, *tr. fr. German by* M. D. Herter Norton.   OFD

Pieta, The, Rhenish, 14th C., The Cloisters.   Mona Van Duyn.   Prf

Pietas: The Petrified Wood.   Dave Smith.   HeS

Pig, The.   *Unknown.* FaBoEE

Pig-crowds in successive, screaming pens.   Blood.   Les A. Murray.   MAuV

Pig Island Letters, *sel.*   James K. Baxter.
   "From an old house shaded with macrocarpas."   ATNZ

Pig lay on a barrow dead, The.   View of a Pig.   Ted Hughes.   BoAnP; CABA (1972 ed.); OxBTC; SoSe

Pig Poem.   Cary Waterman.   GP

Pig Tale, The, *abr.*   "Lewis Carroll."   *Fr. Sylvie and Bruno Concluded.*   RAE

Pig Woman, *sel.*   Carolyn Maisel.
   "She wants to seduce a homosexual Jesuit."   FoP

Pigeon.   Roy Fuller.   PB

Pigeon.   Elouise Loftin.   CNA

Pigeon Pie.   Carl Bode.   PoUp

Pigeons.   Russell Edson.   PCho

Pigeons.   Richard Kell.   BoAnP

Pigeons.   James Mecklenburger.   SFF

Pigeons.   Bert Meyers.   EAS

Pigeons.   Marianne Moore.   PoA

Pigeons.   Alastair Reid.   NYP

Pigeons.   Robert F. Whisler.   AMV-80

Pigeons on the grass alas.   Gertrude Stein.   *Fr. Four Saints in Three Acts.*   TAP

Pigeons on the roof puzzle me.   Pigeons.   Robert F. Whisler.   AMV-80

Pigmeat.   *Unknown.* BluL

Pigs.   John Cotton.   BoAnP

Pig's ears blossom and fold, The.   Pig Poem.   Cary Waterman.   GP

Pigs o' Pelton.   *Unknown.* GBP

Pihsien Road.   Robin Hyde.   ATNZ; WPE

Pike, The.   John Bruce.   LiSp

Pike. Ted Hughes. CMoP (1970 ed.); ExPo (1973 ed.); HAP; HeIP; MAT; MPo; NCSH; OBP; OxBTC; PSN; SoSe (1977 ed.)

Pike, The. Theodore Roethke. STS

Pike, three inches long, perfect. Pike. Ted Hughes. CMoP (1970 ed.); ExPo (1973 ed.); HAP; HeIP; MAT; MPo; NCSH; OBP; OxBTC; PSN; SoSe (1977 ed.)

"Pikes him/ And dikes him." The English Retort. *Unknown.* OxBM

Pike's Peak. *Unknown.* BPAW

Pile the bodies high at Austerlitz and Waterloo. Grass. Carl Sandburg. LFH; NoAM; NOBA; PiAm

Piled deep below the screening apple branch. The Orchard-Pit. Dante Gabriel Rossetti. OAEL-2; VLP

Pilgrim, The. Bunyan. *Fr.* The Pilgrim's Progress. CTV
(To Be a Pilgrim, *sl. diff. version.*) FaPoR
("Who would true valour see.") EBEV

Pilgrim Fathers, The. John Pierpont. BTTM

Pilgrim Fish Heads. Robert Bly. UsP

Pilgrim from the Eastern shore, A. The Miner's Progress. *At. to* Alanzo Delano. BPAW

Pilgrimage. Austin Clarke. CIP

Pilgrimage. Eileen Duggan. ATNZ

Pilgrimage, The. George Herbert. SoSe

Pilgrimage Song. *Unknown, tr. fr. Pueblo Indian by* Mary Austin. WPE

Pilgrimage to Hennessey's. Steven Sher. AMV-81

Pilgrimage to Testour, The. Ryvel, *tr. fr. French by* Edouard Roditi. VWA

Pilgrims. Joseph Brodsky, *tr. fr. Russian by* Dimitry Pospielovsky *and* Keith Bosley. VWA

Pilgrims. Jean Valentine. TAP

Pilgrims of Hope, The, *sel.* William Morris. Sending to the War. VLP

Pilgrim's Progress, The, *sels.* Bunyan.
Pilgrim, The. CTV
(To Be a Pilgrim, *sl. diff. version.*) FaPoR
("Who would true valour see.") EBEV
Shepherd Boy Sings in the Valley of Humiliation, The. NOBE
("He that is down needs fear no fall.") EBEV
"What danger is the pilgrim in." EBEV

Pilgrims to St. James. *Unknown.* OxBM

Pill versus the Springhill Mine Disaster, The. Richard Brautigan. NowV

Pillar of Fame, The. Robert Herrick. CaPo; NIL

Pillar of [*or* and] the Cloud, The. Cardinal Newman. ILP (1975 ed.); ILwL; PFD; VLP
(Lead, Kindly Light.) BLSH, *with music;* FaPoR

Piller pearisht is whearto I lent, The. Sir Thomas Wyatt, *after the Italian of* Petrarch. AAS; OBVE

Pillows swell with confession, The. Leaving Home. Amanda Powell. AAN

Pillows wet our faces with, The. New and Old Gospel. Nate Mackey. CNA

Pilot. Floyd C. Stuart. FAF

Pilot, The. Lewis Turco. CoPAm

Pilpul. Rodger Kamenetz. VWA

Pin, The. Ann Taylor. OxBChV

Pin Has a Head, A. Christina Rossetti. CTV

Pin Ball Angel. Peter Nelson. PHC

Pinball Queen of South Illinois St., The. Stephen Tietz. AMV-80

Pindar is imitable by none. The Praise of Pindar. Horace, *tr. by* Abraham Cowley. Odes, IV, 2. Epi; OAEL-1; PAIC

Pindaric Ode, A. Ben Jonson. *See* To the Immortal Memory and Friendship of That Noble Pair, Sir Lucius Cary and Sir Henry Morison.

Pindaric on the Grunting of a Hog, A. Samuel Wesley. NOBL

Pindarick Elegy upon the Renowned Mr. Samuel Willard, *sel.* John Danforth.
"In crimson flood, wave thousands to his tomb." PeD

Pine, The. Saunders Lewis, *tr. fr. Welsh by* Gwyn Thomas. OBW

Pine Assessor, The. Prentice Baker. AATT

Pine at Timber-Line, The. Harriet Monroe. PoA

Pine Barrens: Letter Home. Cleopatra Mathis. TAT

Pine boat a-shift. Ezra Pound, *fr. the Chinese.* OBVE

Pine Cones. Dave Smith. AMV-80

Pine cones on the ground of the park. Home in Indianapolis. Richard Pflum. AMV-80

Pine Needles. Warren Slesinger. HeS

Pine of Whiting Wood, The. John P. Sjolander. BPAW

Pine Top Smith, *sel.* Annemarie Ewing.
"Here he played." OSP

Pine Tree. Geoff Page. FPA

Pine-tree boy breathing late-afternoon fireflies. Arkansas. Jackman Young. TAT

Pine Tree Tops. Gary Snyder. NOBA; OSP; Prf

Pine trees were stripped red, The. Black Forest. Roderick Watson. MIS

Pines. Heather Banks. PoUp

Pines, The. Margaret Mahy. FPB

Pines and the Sea, The. Christopher Pearse Cranch. ILP (1975 ed.)

Pines are black on Sierra's slope, The. Winter in the Sierras. Mary Austin. BPAW

Pines were dark on Ramoth hill, The. My Playmate. Whittier. NOBA

Piney Woods Money Mama. *Unknown.* BluL

Pining for Love. Francis Beaumont. POL

Pink confused with white. The Pot of Flowers. William Carlos Williams. PiAm

Pink sand and sandpipers pink in the setting. Camas Tuath. Tom Buchan. MIS

Pinkletinks. Grace Elisabeth Allen. ECBV

Pinsheel's Song, The. John Ciardi. SO

Pinto, The. Owen Wister. BPAW

Pin wheels whirling round. Fourth of July Night. Dorothy Aldis. CC

Pioneer, The. Eugene Field. BPAW

Pioneer, The. William B. Ruggles. ECBV

Pioneer Woman. Vesta Pierce Crawford. BPAW

Pioneers, The. Charlotte Mortimer. NowV

Pious Editor's Creed, The. James Russell Lowell. *Fr.* The Biglow Papers, 1st Series, No. VI. PiAm

Pious Selinda. Congreve. *See* Song: "Pious Selinda goes to prayers."

Pious Young Priest, The. *Unknown. See* Limerick: "There once was a pious young priest."

Piped a tiny voice hard by. The Chickadee. Emerson. PCOP

Piper, The. Blake. *See* Piping Down the Valleys Wild.

Piper, A. "Seumas O'Sullivan." PFIr

Piper's Progress, The. Francis Sylvester Mahony. PFIr

Piper's Song, The. Blake. *See* Piping Down the Valleys Wild.

Pipes in the street were playing bravely, The. Cha Till Maccruimein. E. A. Mackintosh. SoSe

Piping Down the Valleys Wild (*Introd. to* Songs of Innocence). Blake. NIL; NOBE; PoPle
(Introduction: "Piping down the valleys wild.") ILP (1975 ed.); InPS; LAuP; MBPR; OAEL-2; STS; TPo; TT
(Piper, The.) LCL; OxBChV
(Piper's Song, The.) PCOP
(Songs of Innocence: Introduction.) CABA (1972 ed.); HeIP

Piping Peace. James Shirley. *Fr.* The Imposture. NOBE ("You virgins that did late despair.") SCP-2

Pippa Passes, *sels.* Robert Browning.
"Oh, what a drear dark close to my poor day!" *fr.* sc. iv. PeD
Year's at the Spring, The, *fr.* sc. i. CTV; InPK; PCOP; PIM; PPM
(Pippa's Song.) LCL; UnPo (1976 ed.)
(Song: "Year's at the spring, The.") GrRo
(Spring Song.) DuDr
You'll Love Me Yet! *fr.* sc. iii. OLR

Pirates of Penzance, The, *sels.* W. S. Gilbert. NOBL
Modern Major-General, The.
Policeman's Lot, The.

"Pirushke" Lady Warns Me of Going Barefoot, The. Skaidrite Stelzer. TC

Pisan Cantos, The. Ezra Pound. *See* Cantos.

Pisces Child. Sandra McPherson. NMM

Pissed on her chest. Gagaku. Steve Richmond. CPA

Pistol Slapper Blues. *Unknown.* BluL

Pistyll Rhaeadr and Wrexham steeple. The Seven Wonders of North Wales. *Unknown.* OBW

Pit Viper. N. Scott Momaday. CDW; VW

Pitch here the tent, while the old horse grazes. Juggling Jerry. George Meredith. VLP

Pitch Piles Up in Part, The. Desmond O'Grady. CIP

Pitch pine/ often stops. Developing Curious Survival Patterns against Winter Saltwinds The. Lyn Lifshin. FAF

Pitch pines fade, The. The Quiet Fog. Marge Piercy. UnPo (1976 ed.); UsP

Pitch was lowered, slowed, decoded, The. Whale Song. Francis Maguire. BoAnP; POL

Pitcher. Robert Francis. LiSp; PoIA; SPo; WIF

Pitcher of mignonette, A. Mignonette. H. C. Bunner. PCOP

Pitchfork Department. D. J. Enright. HeHu

Pithecanthropus erectus. On Evolution. John Ciardi. OBAL

Pitie refusing my poore love to feed. Henry Constable. *Fr.* Diana. ESo

Pittsburgh. Peggy Ruse. NPW

Pity. William Mills. CoPAm; CSP

Pity Ascending with the Fog. James Tate. NoAM

Pity beyond all telling, A. The Pity of Love. W. B. Yeats. CMoP (1970 ed.); PBMP; VLP

Pity cry of love. Life to Let. Liam Murphy. IPM

Pity for him who suffers from his waste. Suffer the Children. Audre Lorde. PoBA

Pity Me Not because the Light of Day. Edna St. Vincent Millay. CMoP (1970 ed.); PPM

Pity of It, The. Thomas Hardy. CMoP (1970 ed.)

Pity of Love, The. W. B. Yeats. CMoP (1970 ed.); PBMP; VLP, 2 *versions*

Pity poor lovers who may not do what they please. The Envy of Poor Lovers. Austin Clarke. CIP; CMoP (1970 ed.)

Pity the Down-trodden Landlord. B. Woolf *and* Arnold Clayton. FSW

Pity This Busy Monster, Manunkind. E. E. Cummings. ILP (1975 ed.); NOBA; PPP; SoS; TAP

Pity this girl. The Stranger. William Everson. CoPAm; FF

Pity, A; We Were Such a Good Invention. Yehuda Amichai, *tr. fr. Hebrew by* Assia Gutmann. BoLoP; LoAs

Pity would be no more. The Human Abstract. Blake. *Fr.* Songs of Experience. BiP; ExPo (1973 ed.); LAuP; MBPR; OAEL; PoIA; PPP; STS

Piute Creek. Gary Snyder. CAPP; ConAP; MPA; NOBA

Piyyut for Rosh Hashana. Chaim Guri, *tr. fr. Hebrew by* Ruth Finer Mintz. OFD

Pizen Pete's Mistake. *At. to* Merrill Honey. BPAW

Place, The. Kenneth Rexroth. MPA

Place, The. Robert Wallace. CoPAm

Place a custard stand in a garden. The Invention of New Jersey. Jack Anderson. InPS; TAT

Place (Any Place) to Transcend All Places. William Carlos William. NYP

Place at Albert Bay, The. Muriel Rukeyser. PoA

Place by the River, A. William Keens. TAT

Place in Kansas, A. Ted Kooser. HeS

Place Me under Your Wing. Hayim Nachman Bialik, *tr. fr. Hebrew by* Gabriel Levin. VWA

Place-Names of China. Alan Bennett. NOBL

Place of Backs, The. W. S. Merwin. HoPM (1975 ed.)

Place of Burial in the South of Scotland, A. Wordsworth. VLP

Place of O, The. Ray A. Young Bear. VoR

Place of the Damned, The. Swift. FaBoEE; OBSV

Place of V, The. Ray A. Young Bear. VoR

Place Pigalle. Richard Wilbur. HeIP

Place to Live, A. Martin Grossman. AMV-80

Place your hand. Love Tight. Ted Joans. CNA

". . . place your name in a time." Hangar Nine. Ann Darr. WBN

Pla ce bo,/ Who is there, who? Phyllyp Sparowe. John Skelton. AAS; NOBE; OAEL-1

Places and Ways to Live. Richard Hugo. GP

Place's Fault, The. Philip Hobsbaum. LP; MPo

Places I Have Been. Joyce M. Volk. AMV-80

Places, Loved Ones. Philip Larkin. CMoP (1970 ed.); SoS

Placid Pew, The. Elmer F. Suderman. AATT

Placing a $2 Bet for a Man Who Will Never Go to the Horse Races Any More. Diane Wakoski. UnPo (1976 ed.)

Plague, The. Gordon Wharton. IPM

Plague of Dead Sharks. Alan Dugan. NoAM

Plague of those musty old lubbers, A. Nothing like Grog. Charles Dibden. RhR

Plague take all your pedants, say I! Sibrandus Schafnaburgensis. Robert Browning. *Fr.* Garden Fancies. OBP

Plague walked on the wrong side of the mountain, The. The Plague. Gordon Wharton. IPM

Plain. Miller Williams. TAT

Plain as the Glistering Planets Shine. Robert Louis Stevenson. SLP

Plain be the phrase, yet apt the verse. A Utilitarian View of the *Monitor's* Fight. Herman Melville. UnPo (1976 ed.)

Plain Dealing's Downfall. *Unknown.* OBSV

Plain, Humble Letters. David Vogel, *tr. fr. Hebrew by* A. C. Jacobs. VWA

Plain it is to you that I am tir'd. The Midnight March. Fred Gilbert. VLP

Plain Language from Truthful James ("I reside at Table Mountain"). Bret Harte. *See* Society upon the Stanislaus, The.

Plain Language from Truthful James ("Which I wish to remark"). Bret Harte. *See* Heathen Chinee, The.

Plain of Adoration, The. *Unknown, tr. fr. Irish by* John Montague. BIrV

Plain Sense of Things, The. Wallace Stevens. InPS

Plain Song. Benjamin Fondane, *tr. fr. French by* Matei Calinescu *and* Willis Barnstone. VWA

Plain Song Talk. Richard Eberhart. PoA

Plainer Dubliners amaze us, The. On the Use of Jayshus. Oliver St. John Gogarty. FaBoEE

Plains, The. Maynard Dixon. BPAW

Plains of Kansas stretch out, The. Moonlit Night in Kansas. Victor Contoski. TAT

Plaint. Charles Henri Ford. EAS

Plaint against the Fog. *Unknown, tr. fr. Nootka Indian.* AKE

Plainview: 3. N. Scott Momaday. CDW

Plan. Rod McKuen. MiP

Plan was to go after the city, The. Photograph of the Hanging Pianos. Jane Garland Katz. AAN

Plane, The: Earth. Sun-Ra. PoBA

Plane Geometry. Emma Rounds. QQQ; SpRo

Plane meets, The. Arrivals. Stuart Conn. SLP

Plane tilts in to Nashville, The. The Homecoming Singer. Jay Wright. PoBA

Plane wheels lurch, leave, The. Parting from My Son. Evangeline Paterson. AMV-80

Plane Wreck at Los Gatos (Deportee). Woody Guthrie. InPK; WTO

Planet, The. Josephine Jacobsen. GP

"Planet doesn't explode of itself, A," said drily. Earth. John Hall Wheelock. SFF; SoSe

Planet Dream. T. Alan Broughton. FAF

Planet of Nothing fills the sky, The. The Day You Are Reading This. William Stafford. PoA

Planet on the Table, The. Wallace Stevens. HAP

Planet that we plant upon, The. Imagine Grass. Knute Skinner. GP; PoW

Planetarium. Adrienne Rich. NIL; NoAM; NOBA; RiTi

Planetary Arc-Light, The. August Derleth. ECBV

Plant, The. Sandra McPherson. CNW

Plant Rhythms, The. G. E. Murray. HeS

Plant the 'ahi'a and cause it to propagate. The Crawlers. Keaulumoku, tr. by M. W. Beckwith. Fr. The Kumulipo: A Creation Chant. WTO

Plant without moisture sweet, A. Rising in the Morning. Hugh Rhodes. OxBChV

Planter. Richard Murphy. Fr. The Battle of Aughrim. BIrV

Planter's Daughter, The. Austin Clarke. CIP; OxBTC; PFIr

Planting, The. Harley Elliott. NeAC

Planting. Gary Snyder. BrS

Planting a Magnolia. W. D. Snodgrass. NoAM

Plants, The. Michael Dennis Browne. GP

Plaque in the Reading Room for My Classmates Killed in Korea, The. F. D. Reeve. GOA

Plashes the Fountain. Paul Celan, tr. fr. German by Michael Hamburger. OBVE

Plashes the tree-trunk lost in the river. Remember Thou Me. Malay Oral Tradition, tr. by R. J. Wilkinson and R. O. Winstedt. WTO

Plastic Jesus. Unknown. FSW

Plastic surgeon who has, The. Poem. William Carlos Williams. NIL

Plate-glass doors form a dangerous duo. Roy Fuller. OSF

Plate glass gazed on the depot. Auto parts wholesale. On the Homefront. James Applewhite. CSP

Platform Builder, The. Cynthia MacDonald. AAN

Platform I stood upon began to move, The. A Visit Home. Joseph Glazer. VWA

Plath said, "Perfection is terrible." A Room of Her Own. Rita Garitano. FoP

Plato. Sandra Ruth Duguid. AATT

Plato, despair! Meditation on Statistical Method. J. V. Cunningham. NIL; VGW

Plato in London. Lionel Johnson. VLP

Plato Told Him. E. E. Cummings. AnMo; ExPo (1973 ed.); IP; NoAM; NOBA; NYP; STS

Plato Was Right Though. Lee Harwood. TwMBP

Platonic Love. Lord Herbert of Cherbury. SCP-2

Platonic Love. Coventry Patmore. Fr. The Angel in the House, II, xi. VLP

Plaudite, or End of Life, The. Robert Herrick. CaPo

Play. A. R. Ammons. PoA

Play, The. Charles Otis Judkins. PeD

Play Ball! Robert Francis. AMV-80

Play I could once; but, gentle friend, you see. To His Friend, on the Untunable. Robert Herrick. CaPo

Play it one more time, Bix, so I can cascade down. In a Mist. Al Young. AMV-80

Play, let the cards and light fall. The Late Show. David McKain. AAN

Play of Nature underground, The. On a Mandrake. Thomas Heyrick. SCP-2

Play, Phoebus, on thy lute. A Canticle to Apollo. Robert Herrick. CaPo

Play Song. Peter Kumalo. SPo

Play the tune again; not watching. To a Child at the Piano. Alastair Reid. MS

Playboy. Richard Wilbur. FF; NoAM; NOBA; PoIA; WeW

Playboy of the Demi-World, The: 1938. William Plomer. OxBTC

Player Piano. John Updike. WeW

Players. Josephine Miles. RiTi

Players Ask for a Blessing on the Psalteries and Themselves, The. W. B. Yeats. VLP

Playground, The. Michael Bedard. BBGO

Playground is so filled with kids, The. It Is an Outfielder. Ron Loewinsohn. VoA

Play-House, The. Joseph Addison. APAS

Playing. Philip Dow. MIT

Playing Catch. Keith Moul. AMV-80

Playing Pocahontas. Lew Blockcolski. VoR

Playing the Bones. Elizabeth Brewster. AMV-81

Playing upon the hill three centaurs were! The Centaurs. James Stephens. PFIr

Plaza Reál with Palmtrees. Paul Blackburn. NoAM

Plea for a Captive. W. S. Merwin. NoAM

Plea for Trigamy, A. Sir Owen Seaman. NOBL

Plea to My Sister, A. James Cunningham. JB

Plea to Those Who Matter. James Welch. AmPA; SA

Pleading Voices. Shalom Katav, tr. fr. Arabic by Yoffe Berkovitz. VWA

Pleasant Changes. Jane Euphemia Browne. OxBChV

Pleasant Comedy of Patient Grissell, The, sels. Thomas Dekker, and others.
    "Art thou poor, yet hast thou golden slumbers?" fr. I, i. HAP; InPS; UnPo (1976 ed.)
    Cradle Song, A: "Golden slumbers kiss your eyes," fr. IV, ii. OxBChV
    (Golden Slumbers.) GSB, with music

Pleasant Evening, The. Henry Kanabus. FiCh

Pleasant it was, when woods were green. Prelude. Longfellow. Fr. Voices of the Night. FSFS

Pleasant place I was at today, A. The Woodland Mass. Dafydd ap Gwilym. tr. by Gwyn Williams. OBW

Pleasant smell of frying sausages, A. Mixed Feelings. John Ashbery. GP; HAP

Pleasant the House. Unknown, tr. fr. Irish by John Montague. BIrV

Pleasantry of the sea bells, and I talk to myself alone, The. Sea Bells. Richard Eberhart. AMV-80

Please. Robert Creeley. VoA

Please. Ronald Koertge. GP

Please Forward. James Welch. CDW

Please God, forsake your water and dry bread. To a Nun. John Ormond, after the Welsh. EBEV; FaBoTw (1975 ed.)

Please help me know it happened. Help from History. William Stafford. AMV-81

Please keep an eye on my house for a few moments. Vidya, *tr. fr. Sanskrit by* Willis Barnstone. BoWoP

Please let my hair grow, mother. *Unknown, tr. fr. Pashto by* Saduddin Shpoon. PBWP

Please open your hearts and your purses. Pity the Down-trodden Landlord. B. Woolf *and* Arnold Clayton. FSW

Please read this when you are alone. A Mild-spoken Citizen Finally Writes to the White House. William Meredith. WasP

Please to remember. The Gunpowder Plot. *Unknown.* BBL

Please you, draw near.—Louder the music there! Shakespeare. *Fr.* King Lear, IV, vii. EBEV

Please your grace, from out your store. The Beggar to Mab, the Fairy Queen. Robert Herrick. CaPo

Pleased am I, and more than willing. The Lay of the Honeysuckle. Marie de France, *tr. by* Robin Johnson. WPE

Pleasing Gift, The. *Unknown.* TDH

Pleasure and pride are not, as duty knows. A Vulgar Error. J. E. Thorold Rogers. FaBoEE

Pleasure of Ruins, The. J. D. McClatchy. PoA

Pleasure Reconciled to Virtue (A Masque). Ben Jonson. OAEL-1

Pleasures. Denise Levertov. CAPP; NoAM; NOBA

Pleasures newly found are sweet. To the Same Flower. Wordsworth. MBPR

Pleasures of Imagination, The, *sel.* Mark Akenside. "One effort more, one cheerful sally more," *fr.* IV. EPC

Pleasures of Melancholy, The. Thomas Warton, the Younger. LAuP

Pleasures of Merely Circulating, The. Wallace Stevens. MAT; OBAL; PoIA; TT

Pledge. Avraham Shlonsky, *tr. fr. Hebrew by* Francis Landy. VWA

Pledge at Spunky Point, The. John Hay. OBAL

Pledge me: I had the hangman for a father. Secret Policeman. Vincent Buckley. GAS

Pledge to the Flag, The, *with music.* Francis Bellamy. BLSH

Pleiades are sinking calm as paint, The. Lesbos. Lawrence Durrell. EBEV

Plenary. *Unknown.* AmFP

Plentiful people went to the Cadillac drawing. Midweek. Josephine Miles. RiTi

Plentiful sacrifice and believers in redemption. When the Saints Come Marching In. Audre Lord. NYP

Plexus and Nexus. Judson Jerome. AMV-81

Plight, The. James W. Thompson. BPo

Pliny Jane. Mildred Luton. PH

Plot. Laurie Stroblas. BCr

Plot against the Giant, The. Wallace Stevens. CMoP (1970 ed.); FF

Plot to Assassinate the Chase Manhattan Bank, The. Carl Larsen. FF; TPo

Ploughing on Sunday. Wallace Stevens. NCSH; RAE

Ploughman, The. Nellie Burget Miller. WPW

Ploughman, The ("The ploughman he comes home at night"). *Unknown.* GBP

Ploughman's [*or* Plowman's] Song, The. Nicholas Breton. *Fr.* The Honourable Entertainment Given to the Queen's Majesty in Progress at Elvetham, 1591. NIL; NOBE

Plow pares the thin afternoon into ribbon furrows. A Winter Wait. Charlotte A. Raines. PoUp

Plowdens, Finns. Robert Hayden. *Fr.* Beginnings. CNA

Plowin' undah cotton. I'll Say! H. H. Lewis. SPT

Plowing at Full Moon. Leo Dangel. AMV-80

Plowman, The ("As Ralph and Nick i' th' field were plowing"). *Unknown.* APAS

Plowman plows, the fisherman dreams of fish, The. Lines on Brueghel's *Icarus.* Michael Hamburger. NIL

Plowman's song, The. Nicholas Breton. *See* Ploughman's Song, The.

Plucking Out a Rhythm. Lawson Fusao Inada. AmPA

Plucking the Rushes. *Unknown, tr. fr. Chinese by* Arthur Waley. BoLoP; BuTh; OBVE; OLR

Plum, A. Mani Leib, *tr. fr. Yiddish by* David G. Roskies *and* Hillel Schwartz. VWA

Plum Blossoms. Chu Shu-chên, *tr. fr. Chinese by* Kenneth Rexroth *and* Ling Chung. PBWP

Plum Gatherer, The. Edna St. Vincent Millay. NoAM

Plumber Arrives at Three Mile Island, The. Robert Stewart. AMV-81

Plumber may be a poet, but a poet is not likely, A. The Difference. Stoddard King. OBAL

Plumber's price is high because he uses, A. The Plumber Arrives at Three Mile Island. Robert Stewart. AMV-81

Plums on the ground. Conservancies. Josephine Miles. GP

Plunder. A. R. Ammons. NoAM

"Plunge thy right hand in St. Madron's spring." The Doom-Well of St. Madron. Robert Stephen Hawker. VLP

Plunging limbers over the shattered track, The. Dead Man's Dump. Isaac Rosenberg. VWA

Plunging towards Phrygia over violent water. Attis. Catullus, *tr. by* Peter Whigham. OBVE

"Plus Ça Change." Philip Whalen. WeW

Plus Ultra. Swinburne. VLP

Pneumonia Blues. *Unknown.* BluL

Po Chu-i, balding old politician. As I Step over a Puddle at the End of Winter, I Think of an Ancient Chinese Governor. James Wright. CAPP; NIL; TCP; VoA

Poacher, The. *Unknown. Fr.* The Parlement of the Thre Ages. OxBM

Poaching *in Excelsis.* G. K. Menzies. FaBoCo

Pobble Who Has No Toes, The. Edward Lear. ECBV; FaBoCo; FaBoNo; OxBChV

Pockets of our greatcoats full of barley, The. Requiem for the Croppies. Seamus Heaney. BIrV; CIP

Pockmarked like a little moon, the golf ball. Golf Ball. John Delaney. AMV-81

Pocomania. Derek Walcott. NoAM

Pods split their seams. Melody. Edward Proffitt. PoIA

Podunk, 1941. Dick Allen. CoPAm

Poe and Longfellow. James Russell Lowell. *Fr.* A Fable for Critics. AmVN, *shorter version*; NOBA

(Poe.) TAP

Poem: "After your death." William Knott. EAS

Poem: "Always loving or blithe." Charles Senior. MIS

Poem: "As the cat." William Carlos Williams. CABA (1972 ed.); InPK; InPS; PiAm

Poem: "At night Chinamen jump." Frank O'Hara. NoAM; NOBA

Poem: "At your light side trees shy." William Knott. EAS

Poem: "Begin here; where I began." Keith Althaus. AAN

Poem: "Between rebellion as a private study and the public." Charles Donnelly. *See* Last Poem.

Poem: "By the road to the contagious hospital." William Carlos Williams. *See* Spring and All.

Poem: "Camera records, The." Diane Kruchkow. FAF

Poem: "Country, The/ was back in the hands of the patriots." Fred Levinson. AmPA

Poem: "Crow flies between your phone and mine, The." Cathleen Quirk. MMD

Poem: "Eager note on my door said, 'Call me,' The." Frank O'Hara. EAS; NoAM; NOBA

Poem: "Entombed in my heart no blood flows to you." Margery Dodson. AMV–80

Poem: "Every morning I forget how it is." Charles Simic. NNaP; NVAP

Poem: "For the 5th time." Diane Kruchkow. FAF

Poem: "Form is the woods: the beast." Jim Harrison. VGW

Poem: "Four miles out the tide curls in." Mira Fish. FAF

Poem: "From what strange country do you come, then?" Siv Cedering Fox. NVAP

Poem: "Get your tongue." Ted Kooser. POL

Poem: "Greater cities are, The." Victor Hernández Cruz. SA

Poem: "Hasten on your childhood to the hour when white." Pablo Picasso, tr. fr. French by David Gascoyne. EAS

Poem: "He watched with all his organs of concern." W. H. Auden. PoA

Poem: "High on a ridge of tiles." Maurice James Craig. BoAnP

Poem: "Horse in the grass, The." Jonathan Sisson. AAN

Poem: "I cannot tell, not I, why she." Walter Savage Landor. GBL; OAEL–2

Poem: "I did nothing—/ Ended my hunger." Edward Weismiller. PoUp

Poem, The: "I had never heard of the whiteness." David Schloss. PoA

Poem: "I keep feeling all space as my image." Sanders Russell. EAS

Poem: "I lived in the first century of world wars." Muriel Rukeyser. See Poem (I Lived in the First Century).

Poem: "I meet Mother on the street." Lennart Bruce. POL

Poem: "I walk at dawn across the hollow hills." Ruthven Todd. EAS

Poem: "I want to be one of those poets." David Hilton. AcAn

Poem: "If I come to you as some bitter herb." Rachel Loden. UsP

Poem: "In secret." Pablo Picasso, tr. fr. French by David Gascoyne. EAS

Poem: "In the corner a violet jug the bells the folds of paper." Pablo Picasso, tr. fr. French by David Gascoyne. EAS

Poem: "In the old days either the plaintiff or the defendant won or lost." Alan Dugan. NowV

Poem: "In the stump of the old tree, where the heart has rotted out." Hugh Sykes Davies. EAS

Poem: "It doesn't look like a finger it looks like a feather of broken glass." Hugh Sykes Davies. EAS

Poem: "I've been a woman." Sonia Sanchez. WBN

Poem: "Lana Turner has collapsed!" Frank O'Hara. CAPP; CoPAm; VGW

Poem: "Leaving aside then for all time the songs." Anthony Cronin. IPM

Poem: "Like musical instruments." Tom Clark. See Like Musical Instruments.

Poem: "Little brown boy." Helene Johnson. AmNP (1974 ed.); PoBA

Poem: "Look at me 8th." Sonia Sanchez. PoBA

Poem: "Moving thru the drifting mist." William Pillin. SPT

Poem: "Nothing move thee." St. Theresa of Avila, tr. fr. Spanish by Arthur Symons. PBWP

Poem: "O who can ever praise enough." W. H. Auden. PoA

Poem: "Old man in the crystal morning after snow." Delmore Schwartz. PoA

Poem: "On getting a card." William Carlos Williams. VGW

Poem: On Moral Leadership as a Political Dilemma. June Jordan. WasP

Poem: "One/ poem." Mbembe. NW

Poem: "Only response, The." William Knott. InPK

Poem, The: "Painter of Dante's awful ferry-ride, The." Babette Deutsch. PoA

Poem: "Person who can do, The." Alan Dugan. NoAM

Poem: "Plastic surgeon who has, The." William Carlos Williams. NIL

Poem: "Rose fades, The." William Carlos Williams. NIL

Poem: "She didn't know it yet." Diane Kruchkow. FAF

Poem: "So many pigeons at Columbus." Arthur Gregor. VGW

Poem: "Something broke the dream." John Gill. NeAC

Poem: "There I could never be a boy." Frank O'Hara. NNaP

Poem: "There is a wailing baby under every stone." Norman MacCaig. EAS

Poem: "Thing, The/ To do/ Is organize." Kenneth Koch. CAPP

Poem: "This beauty that I see." James Schuyler. PoA

Poem: "This life like no other." Gregory Orr. AmPA

Poem: "Time and the weather wear away." Donald Justice. PoA

Poem: "Tiny new emotions, The." Tom Clark. ConAP

Poem: "To be sad in the morning." William Pillen. VWA

Poem: "Upended, it crouches on broken limbs." Charles Tomlinson. CMoP (1970 ed.)

Poem: "Walls of the maelstrom are painted with trees, The." Charles Madge. EAS

Poem: "What's the balm." Alan Dugan. CAPP

Poem: "When he came home." Sonia Sanchez. WBN

Poem: "While we were walking under the top." John Ashbery. EAS

Poem: "Yo/ smile." Sonia Sanchez. WBN

Poem: "You can look into my face." Mike Todachine. CTBA

Poem: "You jam your arm into the white air." Mira Fish. FAF

Poem: "You said./ don't write me/ a love poem." Pearl Cleage Lomax. CNA

Poem: "Your face,/so pale now it is blue." David St. John. AmPA

Poem, The/ exists. A Cycle. John Leax. AATT

Poem, The/ that I chose for you. On the Margins of a Poem. Jiri Mordecai Langer, tr. by Gabriel Preil and Howard Schwartz. VWA

Poem about a Poem about a Poem. Robert Conquest. WIF

Poem about a Seashell. Ranice Henderson Crosby. NMM

Poem about Beauty, Blackness, Poetry, A. Linda Brown Bragg. CNA

Poem about Birth. Anne Sadowski. SES

Poem about Breasts, A. James Wright. CAAP; TAP

Poem about Poems about Vietnam, A. Jon Stallworthy. NoAM

Poem about Your Face. Nathan Alterman, tr. fr. Hebrew by Ruth Nevo. VWA

Poem after a Speech by Chief Seattle, 1855. Charles Brasher. AMV–81

Poem after Apollinaire. Ira Sadoff. AmPA

Poem against Catholics. James Fenton and John Fuller. OBSV

Poem against Rats, A. Fred Levinson. AmPA

Poem against the British. Robert Bly. ConAP; InPS

Poem against the Rich. Robert Bly. CAPP; NoAM; NOBA

Poem as Mask, The. Muriel Rukeyser. RiTi

Poem at Semester's End. Ralph Mecklenburger. SFF

Poem at Thirty. Sonia Sanchez. BPo; CNA; NMM; PoBA

Poem before Birth. George MacBeth. SLP

Poem before Birth. Alexander Scott. MS

Poem before Departure. Jean Burden. UsP; WPE

Poem Beginning with a Line by Pindar, A. Robert Duncan. ConAP; Epi; NNaP

Poem Beginning with a Line Memorized at School. Roderick Hartigh Jellema. AATT

Poem begins, The. Beginnings. David Rokeah, tr. by Robert Mezey. VWA

Poem by the Bridge at Ten-shin. Li Po, *tr. fr. Chinese by* Ezra Pound. OBVE

(Poem) (Chicago) (The Were-Age). William Knott. EAS

Poem Circling Hamtramck, Michigan All Night in Search of You, The. Philip Levine. NNaP

Poem Composed in Rogue River Park . . . Tom Wayman. POL

Poem/ Ditty-Bop. Carolyn M. Rodgers. JB

Poem Ending with an Old Cliché. Paul Zimmer. AMV-81

Poem for a Goodbye. Norman MacCaig. SLP

Poem for a Hustler. Kathleen Fraser. RiTi

Poem for a Neighbor. Pat Therese Francis. AMV-81

Poem for a Poet, A. Don L. Lee. PoBA

Poem for a Poet, A. Audre Lorde. NMM

Poem for a Singer. Milton Acorn. NeAC

Poem for a Son. Heather Cadsby. AMV-80

Poem for Anton Schmidt, A. William Pillen. VWA

Poem for Aretha. Nikki Giovanni. BPo; PoBA

Poem for Ben Barney. Leslie Silko. CDW; VoR

Poem for Bhain, A. John Berryman. CoPAm

Poem for Black Boys. Nikki Giovanni. BPo

Poem for Blackboys in Floppy Tie-Dye Hats. Jodi Braxton. WBN

Poem for Black Hearts, A. Amiri Baraka. CAPP; ILP (1975 ed.); PoBA; SFF; UsP

Poem for Carroll, Descendant of Chiefs. Lance Henson. VoR

Poem for David Janssen. R. T. Smith. AMV-81

Poem for Deep Thinkers, A. Amiri Baraka. EC

Poem for Democrats, A. Amiri Baraka. CAPP

Poem for Diane Wakoski, A. Ray A. Young Bear. CDW

Poem for Dorothy Holt. Susan Irene Rea. AMV-81

Poem for Easter. Robert Kelly. VGW

Poem for Eric Barker. Jean Burden. PoW

Poem for Etheridge. Sonia Sanchez. BPo

Poem for Explorers. Carol Bergé. MMD

Poem for Flora. Nikki Giovanni. PoBA

Poem for Foster, A. Walter Bradford. HeS

Poem for Friends. Quincy Troupe. PoBA

Poem for Half White College Students. Amiri Baraka. BPo; CAPP; TAP; UnPo (1976 ed.)

Poem for Heroes, A. Julia Fields. CNA

Poem for Integration, A. Alvin Saxon. PoBA

Poem for Jan. Joseph Bruchac. CDW

Poem for L. C. Peter Klappert. AmPA

Poem for Liu Ya-tzu. Mao Tse-tung, *tr. fr. Chinese*. TVo

Poem for Lorry. Gerald Hausman. CTBA

Poem for May Wilson, A. Michael Cooper. BCr

Poem for Mother's Day. Stanley Kiesel. HeS

Poem for My Brother. John Logan. BrS

Poem for My Dead Husband. Sheila Roberts. AMV-80

Poem for My Eighth Year in Prison. Michael Hogan. DNGG

Poem for My Family. June Jordan. BPo; RiTi

Poem for My Father. Michael Delp. TC

Poem for My Father, A. Sonia Sanchez. BPo; CSP; IHMS; RiTi

Poem for My Grandfather. A. C. Jacobs. VWA

Poem for My Great Grandfather. Michael Van Walleghen. HeS

Poem for My Hands. Carole Oles. NPW

Poem for My Mother. Siv Cedering Fox. TV

Poem for My Mother. Lowell Jaeger. AMV-80

Poem for My Sister. Liz Lochhead. MS

Poem for My Students. Robert L. McRoberts. HeS

Poem for My Twentieth Birthday. Kenneth Koch. PoA

Poem for Myself and Mei: Abortion. Leslie Silko. VoR

Poem for Nancy. Stephen Tudor. HeS

Poem for One Who Bares a Pome, A. Richard Bastian. AATT

Poem for Otis Redding. Joyce Carol Thomas. CNA

Poem for Players, A. Al Young. GP

Poem for Positive Thinkers, A. Barbara Mahone. PoBA

Poem for Richard Speck, A. Michael McMahon. FAF

Poem for Rupert Weber, 85 Years Too Late. Ed Lipman. CPA

Poem for Russell Nowak, A. Eric Torgersen. TC

Poem for Speculative Hipsters, A. Amiri Baraka. NoAM; NOBA

Poem for Susan. Barbara Greenberg. RiTi

Poem for the Subterranean Poor. Diane DiPrima. VoA

Poem for the 10th Year. Tim Burke. PHC

Poem for the Year Twenty Twenty. Al Lee. AmPA

Poem for Unwed Mothers. Nikki Giovanni. OBAL

Poem for Valerie. Luke Breitt. CPA

Poem for Vladimir. G. Ripley. AMV-81

Poem for Willie Best, A. Amiri Baraka. CAPP

Poem Found Emptying Out My Pockets. Al Young. CoPAm

Poem from the Empire State. June Jordan. BPo

Poem from "The Revolution." Ilya Rubin, *tr. fr. Russian by* Linda Zisquit. VWA

Poem, A—Good or Bad—a Thing—with One Attribute—Flat. Melech Ravitch, *tr. fr. Yiddish by* Ruth Whitman. VWA

Poem H. Vicente Rodríguez Nietzche, *tr. fr. Spanish by* Julio Marzán. InW

Poem (I Lived in the First Century). Muriel Rukeyser. UnPo (1976 ed.)

Poem in Hungarian. Beth Joselow. PoUp

Poem in October. Dylan Thomas. BiP; FSFS; MPo; OBP; PoA; PPM; SoSe; STS; UsP

Poem in the Matukituki Valley. James K. Baxter. ATNZ

Poem in the Mirror. Norman Kreitman. PMW

Poem in Three Parts. Robert Bly. CAPP; ConAP; NOBA
"Oh, on an early morning I think I shall live forever!" *sel.* OSP

Poem in Translation, A. Tess Gallagher. AAN

Poem in Two Parts. Michael Brownstein. OSP

Poem in Which My Legs Are Accepted. Kathleen Fraser. AmPA; NMM; RiTi

Poem Intended to Incite the Utmost Depression, A. Samuel Hoffenstein. FaBoCo

Poem Is Mightier than the Switchblade, The. Richard W. Thomas. TC

Poem Is Not, A. Gary Catalano. GAS

Poem like a Grenade, A. John Haines. EAS

Poem makes truth a little more disturbing, The. Hands. Donald Finkel. MAT

Poem moves down a page, A. Richard Meltzer. POL

Poem moves forward, A. The Journey of a Poem Compared to All the Sad Variety of Travel. Delmore Schwartz. NowV

Poem No. 21. Doughtry Long. CNA

Poem of Angela Yvonne Davis. Nikki Giovanni. PoBA

Poem of Distant Childhood. Noémia da Sousa, *tr. fr. Portuguese by* Allan Francovich *and* Kathleen Weaver. PBWP

Poem of Explanations. Dahlia Ravikovitch, *tr. fr. Hebrew by* Chana Bloch. BoWoP

Poem of Sir Walter Rawleighs, A. Sir Walter Ralegh. AAS
("Nature, that washed her hands in milk.") CABA (1972 ed.)

Poem of Solitude at Columbia University. Federico García Lorca, *tr. fr. Spanish by* Ben Belitt. PBMP

Poem of the Clear Eye, The, *sel.* Kris Hemensley.
Mr. Whitman to His Friends in the Antipodes. CAAP

Poem of the End, *sels.* Marina Tsvetayeva, *tr. fr. Russian by* Elaine Feinstein *and* Angela Livingstone.
"Blatant as factory buildings." PBWP
"I didn't want this, not." OBVE

Poem of the Forty-eight States, A. Kenneth Koch. NNaP;
    OBAL
Poem of the Frost and Snow. Lewis Morris, *tr. fr. Welsh by*
    Anthony Conran. OBW
Poem of the Intimate Agony. Julia de Burgos, *tr. fr. Spanish by*
    Julio Marzán. InW
Poem of the mind in the act of finding, The. Of Modern Poetry.
    Wallace Stevens. CABA (1972 ed.); ILP (1975 ed.); LFH;
    NIL; NoAM; PAIC; PoIA; TAP; WIF
Poem of the Mother. Myra Sklarew. AMV-80; PoUp
Poem of the Year of the Bear, The, *sel.* Russell Banks.
    "You really can't count on the bastard." BCr
Poem on England's Happiness, A. *Unknown.* APAS
Poem on His Death-Bed. Cynddelw Brydydd Mawr, *tr. fr. Welsh*
    *by* Joseph P. Clancy. OBW
Poem on His Death-Bed. Meilyr Brydydd, *tr. fr. Welsh by* Joseph
    P. Clancy. OBW
Poem on Inter-uterine Device, A. A. Rasheed Ghazi. PeD
Poem on Our Mother, Our Mother Rachel, The. Avot Yeshurun,
    *tr. fr. Hebrew by* Harold Schimmel. VWA
Poem on the End of Sensation. Ken Stange. AMV-80
Poem on the Guilt, The. Avot Yeshurun, *tr. fr. Hebrew by* Harold
    Schimmel. VWA
Poem on the Jews, The. Avot Yeshurun, *tr. fr. Hebrew by* Harold
    Schimmel. VWA
Poem, or Beauty Hurts Mr. Vinal. E. E. Cummings. InPS; NIL;
    OBAL; PAIC; PiAm; PPoe
Poem out of Childhood. Muriel Rukeyser. NMM
Poem quietly goes aside to weep, A. A Note on the Social Arts.
    Kendrick Smithyman. ATNZ
Poem Rising by Its Own Weight, The. Denise Levertov. GP
Poem Rocket. Allen Ginsberg. CoPAm; VGW
Poem should be palpable and mute, A. Ars Poetica. Archibald
    MacLeish. BiP; CMoP (1970 ed.); HAP; HeIP; HoPM (1975
    ed.); ILP (1975 ed.); InPK; IPWM; NIL; NOBA; PAIC;
    PiAm; PoA; PoIA; SFF; SoSe; TAP; TH; WIF
Poem Some People Will Have to Understand, A. Amiri Baraka.
    BPo; NOBA; PiAm
Poem That Took the Place of a Mountain, The. Wallace Stevens.
    PiAm
Poem to a Mule, Dead Twenty Years. Guy Owen. BoAnP; POL
Poem to a Nigger Cop. Bobb Hamilton. TPo
Poem to a Potted Plant. Steve Toth. AcAn
Poem to a Redskin. Wendy Rose. CDW
Poem to Be Read and Sung. César Vallejo, *tr. fr. Spanish by*
    James Wright *and* Robert Bly. EAS; LoAs
Poem to Be Read at 3 A.M. Donald Justice. CoPAm; HoPM
    (1975 ed.); MiP
Poem to Complement Other Poems, A. Don L. Lee. BPo;
    NoAM
Poem to Delight My Friends Who Laugh at Science-Fiction, A.
    Edwin Rolfe. TPo
Poem to Ease Birth. *Unknown, tr. fr. Nahuatl (Aztec) by* Anselm
    Hollo. BoWoP; IPWM
Poem to Galway Kinnell, A. Etheridge Knight. NNaP
Poem to My Creditors. Thomas Lux. AAN
Poem to My Death. Julia de Burgos, *tr. fr. Spanish by* Grace
    Schulman. BoWoP
Poem to My New Jacket. Fran Winant. MMD
Poem to My Notebook, A. Primus St. John. MPA
Poem to My Sister, Ethel Ennis, Who Sang "The Star-spangled
    Banner" at the Second Inauguration of Richard Milhous
    Nixon. June Jordan. TAP; WBN
Poem to My Twin Possibility. Dalene Stowe. NPW
Poem to Show the Trouble That Befell Him When He Was at Sea,
    A. Thomas Prys, *tr. fr. Welsh by* Gwyn Williams. OBW

Poem to the Mysterious Woman. Robert Desnos, *tr. fr. French by*
    Wallace Fowlie. LoAs
Poem to the Tune "Riverbank Willows." Yü Hsüan-chi, *tr. fr.*
    *Chinese by* Geoffrey Waters. BoWoP
Poem upon the Imprisonment of Mr. Calamy in Newgate, A.
    Robert Wild. APAS
Poem was entitled "The Streets of Hanoi," The. Streets. D. J.
    Enright. HeHu
Poem while Reading "The Naked Lunch" by William Burroughs.
    Charles Senior. MIS
Poem with a Conclusion, A. Walter Bradford. HeS
Poem with the Final Tune. Julia de Burgos, *tr. fr. Spanish by*
    Julio Marzán. InW
Poem without a Metaphor. David Allan Evans. NVAP
Poem without a Title. Charles Simic. GP; NNaP
Poem without the Word Love. Morty Sklar. AcAn
Poem Wondering If I'm Pregnant. Kathleen Fraser. IHMS;
    NMM
Poem Written after Contemplating the Adverb "Primarily."
    Christopher Middleton. TwMBP
Poem Written in Winter. Charlotte Gafford. BCr
Poem You Asked For, The. Larry Levis. AmPA; NVAP
Poems. Peter Kelso. AKE; TPo
Poems (I-XI). Philip O'Connor. EAS
Poems. Bruce Severy. VW
Poems about Playmates. Ronda Davis. JB
Poems are bullshit unless they are. Black Art. Amiri Baraka.
    BPo; CAPP; NIL
Poems: Birmingham 1962-1964. Julia Fields. PoBA
Poems for My Brother Kenneth, *sel.* Owen Dodson.
    "Sleep late with your dream." PoBA
Poems for the New. Kathleen Fraser. IHMS; NMM; RiTi
Poems have become so boring to me. Literacy: An Abandoned
    Ode. William Harmon. CSP
Poems of Night. Galway Kinnell. LoAs
Poems of the Condemned Man, The. Stuart Dybek. TC
Poems to My Father. Rae Desmond Jones. CAAP
Poet, The. George Mackay Brown. MS
Poet, The. Elizabeth Barrett Browning. VLP
Poet, The. Bryant. EAP; TAP
Poet, The. Lucille Clifton. GP
Poet, The. Paul Laurence Dunbar. BPo
Poet, The. Padraic Fiacc. CIP
Poet, A. Thomas Hardy. NoAM
Poet. Donald Jeffrey Hayes. AmNP (1974 ed.)
Poet. Conrad Hilberry. PPoD
Poet, The. Keats. TT
Poet, The. Thomas Randolph. POL
Poet. Karl Shapiro. CMoP (1970 ed.); NoAM
Poet. Robert Siegel. FAF
Poet, The. Tennyson. VLP
Poet. Peter Viereck. CoPAm; HoPM (1975 ed.)
Poet and the Rose, The. John Gay. *Fr. Fables.* PAIC
Poet appointed dare not decline. Basil Bunting. *Fr. Briggflatts.*
    OBP
Poet at Night-Fall, The. Glenway Wescott. PoA
Poet at Twenty, A. Donald Hall. EAS
Poet because his hand goes first, A. Spitballer. Fred Chappell.
    LiSp; PPoD
Poet Counterpoet. Rudolph von Abele. PoUp
Poet doesn't speak in paradigms, A. Critique for Our Times.
    Albert Howard Carter. AATT
Poet felt the rain, The. Rain. Margiad Evans. OBW
Poet Finds an Ephemeral Home in a Truck Stop on the New
    Jersey Turnpike, ca. 1970, The. James Baker Hall. CSP

Poet hath the child's sight in his breast, The.   The Poet.
Elizabeth Barrett Browning.   VLP

Poet, A!—He Hath Put His Heart to School.   Wordsworth.   ILP
(1975 ed.); NIL; VLP

Poet! I like not mealy fruit; give me.   Walter Savage Landor.
FaBoEE

Poet in a golden clime was born, The.   The Poet.   Tennyson.
VLP

Poet in his lone yet genial hour, The.   Apologia pro Vita Sua.
Samuel Taylor Coleridge.   MBPR

Poet in Need, A.   John Heath-Stubbs.   SFF

Poet in Old Age Fishing at Evening, The.   Desmond O'Grady.
CIP

Poet in Washington, The.   John Pauker.   WasP

Poet Is Dead, The.   William Everson.   CPA; PiAm

Poet is hunter, The.   Poem prey.   The Hunt of the Poem.
Richard Behm.   AMV-80

Poet is Priest.   Death to Van Gogh's Ear!   Allen Ginsberg.
CABA (1972 ed.); VGW

Poet is the dreamer, The.   Loneliness.   Al Young.   NVAP;
PoBA

Poet Laments the Coming of Old Age, The.   Edith Sitwell.
NoAM

Poet Lives, The.   Jacob Glatstein, tr. fr. Yiddish by Ruth
Whitman.   VWA

Poet Loves a Mistress, but Not to Marry, The.   Robert Herrick.
CaPo

Poet Loves from Afar, The.   Desmond O'Grady.   NoAM

Poet of Bray, The.   John Heath-Stubbs.   NOBL

Poet of nature, thou hast wept to know.   To Wordsworth.
Shelley.   MBPR

Poet of One Mood, A.   Alice Meynell.   SBG

Poet on the Island, The.   Richard Murphy.   CIP

Poet, Rebuked, Responds, The.   William Langland, tr. fr. Middle
English by Selden Rodman.   Fr. The Vision of Piers
Plowman, Passus XII.   OBP

Poet Recognizing the Echo of the Voice, A.   Diane Wakoski.
NIL; Psy

Poet Speaks, The.   Georgia Douglas Johnson.   AmNP (1974 ed.)

Poet Speaks from the Visitors' Gallery, A.   Archibald MacLeish.
WasP

Poet spilled my gin, The.   Tropisms on John Berryman.   Gerald
Vizenor.   VoR

Poet told me if I was serious, The.   Instruction from Bly.
Cynthia Macdonald.   NMM

Poet Tries to Turn In His Jock, The.   David Hilton.   LiSp;
NowV
(I Try to Turn In My Jock.)   AcAn

Poet was busted by a topless judge, A.   Sermonette.   Ishmael
Reed.   PoBA

Poet, whoe'er thou art, God damn thee.   Earl of Rochester.
FaBoEE

Poeta Fit, Non Nascitur.   "Lewis Carroll."   FaBoNo; OBSV

Poeta Loquitur.   Swinburne.   OAEL-2

Poetaster, The, sel.   Ben Jonson.
Hermogenes's Song.   ILP (1975 ed.)

Poetess Kō Ōgimi, The.   Helen Chasin.   NMM

Poetic Tale.   Grace Maddock Miller.   GDP

Poetical and Congratulatory Epistle to James Boswell, Esq., A.
"Peter Pindar."   ESaP

Poetical and Philosophical Essay on the French Revolution . . . ,
A, sel.   John Courtenay.
"Ye Nuns and Capuchins, begin the song."   ESaP

Poetical Economy.   Harry Graham.   FaBoCo

Poetics.   A. R. Ammons.   TT

Poetics.   André Spire, tr. fr. French by Edouard Roditi.   VWA

Poetry.   Alison Wyrley Birch.   PPM

Poetry.   Juan Ramón Jiménez, tr. fr. Spanish.   LoAs
("I recognized you because when I saw the print.")   OLR

Poetry.   Greg Kuzma.   PoA

Poetry.   Al Masarik.   CPA

Poetry.   Marianne Moore.   AnMo; BiP; BoWoP; CABA (1972
ed.); CMoP (1970 ed.); ExPo (1973 ed.); FF; HAP; HeIP;
ILP (1975 ed.); IPWM; LFH; NIL; NoAM; NOBA; PAIC;
PiAm; Psy; TAP; TPo; TSWA; UnPo (1976 ed.); UsP; WIF

Poetry.   Carl Rakosi.   GP

Poetry.   Rainer Schulte.   SES

Poetry.   Abraham Sutskever, tr. fr. Yiddish by Ruth Whitman.
VWA

Poetry.   Claude Vigée, tr. fr. French by Anthony Rudolf.   VWA

Poetry, a Natural Thing.   Robert Duncan.   NoAM; NOBA

Poetry and Revolution.   William Pitt Root.   NVAP

Poetry and the Poet.   H. C. Bunner.   OBAL

Poetry Concert.   Michael S. Harper.   TAP

Poetry does not complicate the arrangement of words.   Poetry.
Alison Wyrley Birch.   PPM

Poetry has opened all my pores.   After Reading Nelly Sachs.
Linda Pastan.   VWA

Poetry Is.   Bruce Bennett.   AMV-81

Poetry is a projection across silence.   Ten Definitions of Poetry.
Carl Sandburg.   WIF

Poetry is a way of counting.   Holding Pattern.   Sandra
McPherson.   RiTi

Poetry is in the Darkness.   Aram Boyajian.   NeAC

Poetry is itself a thing of God.   Proem.   Philip James Bailey.   Fr.
Festus.   VLP

Poetry is the supreme fiction, madame.   A High-toned Old
Christian Woman.   Wallace Stevens.   CMoP (1970 ed.); ILP
(1975 ed.); NoAM; NOBA; PAIC; PiAm; PPP; SoSe; STS;
TAP

Poetry? It's a hobby.   What the Chairman Told Tom.   Basil
Bunting.   OxBTC; TwMBP

Poetry Liberation.   Jean Pumphrey.   TPo

Poetry of Departures.   Philip Larkin.   CMoP (1970 ed.); FF;
HeIP; ILP (1975 ed.); LP; NowV; SS; UsP

Poetry of earth is never dead, The.   On the Grasshopper and [the]
Cricket.   Keats.   BiP; ECBV; Epi; FSFS; ILP (1975 ed.);
MBPR; NIL; OAEL-2; OBP; TT

Poetry of one the Russians call "a broad nature," The.   "Hugh
MacDiarmid."   Fr. The Kind of Poetry I Want.   InPS

Poetry Paper.   Andrei Codrescu.   EAS

Poetry Perpetuates the Poet.   Robert Herrick.   FaBoEE

Poetry Reading.   Vernon Scannell.   NOBL

Poetry, sir.   Poetry Liberation.   Jean Pumphrey.   TPo

Poetry to go.   Peter Whigham.   Fr. Astapovo, or What Are We to
Do.   TwMBP

Poetry Today.   John Heath-Stubbs.   POL

Poetry Workshop in a Reform School.   Betty Adcock.   AMV-80

Poetry's a tree.   Yes, the Secret Mind Whispers.   Al Young.
PoBA

Poets.   Dana "The Mouse" Merkel.   DNGG

Poets/ die/ reading that last poem.   Answers for Ethelbert.
Ahmos Zu-Bolton II.   PoUp

"Poet's age is sad, The: for why?"   Prologue.   Robert Browning.
Fr. Asolando.   OAEL-2; VLP

Poets Agree to Be Quiet by the Swamp, The.   David Wagoner.
CoPAm; VGW

Poets and parents say he cannot die.   Yet Another Poem about a
Dying Child.   Janet Frame.   ATNZ

Poet's Appeal, The.   Larry Goodell.   FoP

Poet's Arbour in the Birchwood, The.   Edward Williams, tr. fr.
Welsh by Kenneth Jackson.   OBW

Poet's Blindness, The.   Milton.   See Holy Light.

Poet's cat, sedate and grave, A. The Retired Cat. William Cowper. PCat

Poets, come out of your closets. Populist Manifesto. Lawrence Ferlinghetti. EC

Poet's Complaint of His Muse, The, *sel.* Thomas Otway. "To a high hill where never yet stood tree." SCP-2

Poet's Confidence, The. Coventry Patmore. *Fr.* The Angel in the House, I, i. VLP

Poet's Corner. Robert Graves. FaBoEE

Poet's Day, The. Richard Weber. CIP

Poet's Epitaph, A. Wordsworth. MBPR

Poet's Farewell to His Teeth, The. William Dickey. GP; PoA

Poet's Final Instructions, The. John Berryman. VGW

Poets have been writing about the death of flowers. Roses, Revisited, in a Paradoxical Autumn. J. W. Cullum. AMV-81

Poets Hitchhiking on the Highway. Gregory Corso. NoAM

Poet's Household, A. Carolyn Kizer. POL

Poet's Lament on the Death of His Wife. Raage Ugaas, *tr. fr. Somali by* B. W. Andrzejewski *and* I. M. Lewis. WTO

Poets light but lamps, The. Emily Dickinson. HeIP; PiAm

Poets, like elephants, when they are dying. The Critic. Gordon Wharton. IPM

Poets Love Nature. John Clare. OAEL-2

Poet's Loves, The. Hywel ab Owain Gwynedd, *tr. fr. Welsh by* Gwyn Williams. OBW

Poets may boast, as safely vain. Of English Verse. Edmund Waller. OAEL-1; OBP

Poets Observed. F. C. Rosenberger. AMV-80

Poets of My Epoch. Irwin Stark. PAIC

"Poets pour us wine, The." Epilogue. Robert Browning. VLP

Poet's Prayer. M. L. Sussman. AMV-80

Poet's Prayer, The. *Unknown.* OBSV

Poet's Prayer para Yukio Mishima. Pancho Aguila. NW

Poet's Progress, A. Michael Hamburger. WIF

Poet's Prothalamion, The, *sel.* J. W. Scholl. " 'How could I cheat those lips of their true food?' " PeD

Poet's Request, The. *Unknown, tr. fr. Irish by* John Montague. BIrV

Poet's Song, The. Tennyson. VLP

Poets to Come. Walt Whitman. FF

Poet's Welcome to His Love-begotten Daughter, A. Burns. RRA

Poets who are veterans of the wars, The. The Draft Dodger. Larry Rubin. NIL

Poet's Wife, A. Amy Lowell. RiTi

Poet's Wife Makes Him a Door So He Can Find the Way Home, The. Nancy Willard. RiTi

Poet's Wish. Valery Larbaud, *tr. fr. French by* William Jay Smith. LoAs

Poet's Wish, The. Allan Ramsay, *after* Horace. OBVE

Poggio. Lawrence Durrell. OxBTC

Pogroms. André Spire, *tr. fr. French by* Stanley Burnshaw. VWA

Point of Love, The. Alan Bold. SLP

Point of No Return. Robert Graves. BIrV

Point of Noon Is Past, The. Christopher Brennan. GAS

Point Pelee in March. W. D. Snodgrass. UsP

Pointed clouds have become fixed in the heaven, The. A Stormy Day. *Tr. fr. Hawaiian.* WTO

Pointless old miser named Quince, A. An Old Miser Named Quince. John Ciardi. TDH

Poised between going on and back, pulled. The Base Stealer. Robert Francis. LiSp; NCSH; NIL; PPoD; SPo

Poised impossibly on the high tight-rope. Acrobats. Robert Graves. PSN

Poised, relaxed, as a cat that waits. Boxer. Joseph P. Clancy. SPo

Poison. Nancy Mairs. NPW

Poison Tree, A. Blake. *Fr.* Songs of Experience. AnMo; CABA (1972 ed.); HAP; HoPM (1975 ed.); ILP (1975 ed.) IP; IPWM; LAuP; LFH; MBPR; PBMP; PoIA; PPoD; PPoe; PPP; SFF; SoSe (1977 ed.); STS; WIF

Poke-Pole Fishing. Dennis Schmitz. AmPA

Poker Poem. Michael Pettit. AMV-80

Poland/ 1931. Jerome Rothenberg. Prf

Polar Bear. Diana Der Hovanessian. BCr

Polar Bear. Ramon Guthrie. ExPo (1973 ed.)

Polar Bear, The. Edward Lucie-Smith. OSF

Polar Bear, The. William Carlos Williams. BCr

Polar Bear at Crandon Park Zoo, Miami, The. Barbara Winder. BCr

Polar DEW has just warned that, The. Your Attention Please. Peter Porter. LP; OxBTC

Polar Expedition. George M. Young, Jr. FAF

Polar Exploration. Stephen Spender. NoAM

Pole Star, The. Coslett Coslett, *tr. fr. Welsh by* Kenneth Jackson. OBW

Pole Vaulter. David Allan Evans. NVAP

Pole-Vaulter, The. *Unknown.* LiSp; SPo

Poled high on his cactus over a cliff of desert island. Song at San Carlos Bay. Brewster Ghiselin. MPA

Polemical Elegy for Reinhardt Heydrich. Tom Buchan. MIS

Police are dragging for the bodies, The. Miners. James Wright. ConAP; CTBA; TCP

Police sirens die. Midnight. R. A. Simpson. FPA

Police Station Ditties. Max Beerbohm. NOBL

Policeman, A/ is a pig. Definition for Blk/Children. Sonia Sanchez. PoBA

Policeman's Lot, The. W. S. Gilbert. *Fr.* The Pirates of Penzance. NOBL

Policemen Laughing. Ray Fraser. NeAC

Policy of the House. Charles Stetler. GP

Polis is/ eyes. Maximus, to Gloucester, Letter 6. Charles Olson. PiAm

Polish Rider, The. Derek Walcott. OBP

Political Despatch, A. George Canning. FaBoCo

Political Greatness. Shelley. *See* Sonnet: Political Greatness.

Political Intelligence. A. J. M. Smith. EAS

Political Orlando, The. George MacBeth. NOBL

Political Poem. Amiri Baraka. NoAM

Political Power. Milton. *Fr.* Paradise Regained, IV. SCP-1

Politician, A. E. E. Cummings. InPK; NIL (Politician Is an Arse Upon, A.) FaBoEE; OBAL

Politician, The. Michael McMahon. FAF

Politician Is an Arse Upon, A. E. E. Cummings. *See* Politician, A.

Politicians, 1972. Timothy Clinch. NIL

Politics. W. B. Yeats. CMoP (1970 ed.); FF; HeIP; InPS; NIL; OBP; OxBTC; PFIr; POL

Politics of a Pornographer. Robert Hass. CAAP

Politics of Rich Painters, The. Amiri Baraka. VGW

Poll. Ed Roberson. PoBA

Pollution. Tom Lehrer. PoRo; WIF

Polly put the kettle on. Mother Goose. MG

Polly Vaughn (Molly Bawn). *Unknown. See* Young Molly Bán.

Polly Wolly Doodle. *Unknown.* FSW

Polo Grounds. Rolfe Humphries. HoPM (1975 ed.); LiSp

Polo Match. John Ciardi. LiSp; SPo

"Polo season would start early in April, The." Animal Days. Lee Harwood. TwMBP

Polyhymnia, *sel.* George Peele.
  His Golden Locks Time Hath to Silver Turned. HeIP; PPoe
  (Farewell to Arms, A.) NIL; NOBE; PoPle
  (Sonnet, A: "His golden locks time hath to silver turned.")
  InPS

Pomander. Edwin Morgan. NIL

Pomegranate speaks, The. Ezra Pound *and* Noel Stock, *fr.*
  *Egyptian hieroglyphics.* BoWoP

Pomegranate Tree in Jerusalem ("The pomegranate tree in my
  garden adorns itself"). Zerubavel Gilead *tr. fr. Hebrew by*
  Dorothea Krook. VWA

Pompeii, *sel.* Leonora Speyer.
  New Excavations. TH

Pomposo (insolent and loud). Charles Churchill. *Fr.* The Ghost.
  OBSV

Ponce de León: A Morning Walk. Al Young. HoPM (1975 ed.)

Pond, The. Louise Glück. CAAP

Pond, The. Anthony Thwaite. LP; MAT

Pond. Fredrick Zydek. AMV-81

Pond Lily. E. Margaret Clarkson. AATT

Ponder, darling, these busted statues. E. E. Cummings. CMoP
  (1970 ed.); ExPo (1973 ed.); NIL; NoAM

Pond'rous projectiles, hurl'd by heavy hands. The Rejected
  "National Hymns." "Orpheus C. Kerr." OBAL

Ponies, The. W. W. Gibson. PH

Pont and Blyth. *Unknown.* GBP

Pont y Caniedydd. Alun Llywelyn-Williams, *tr. fr. Welsh by*
  Joseph P. Clancy. OBW

Pontoosuce. Herman Melville. NOBA

Pony air, wild wheat, The. The End of the Indian Poems.
  Stanley Plumly. GOA

Pony Blues, The. *Unknown.* BluL

Pony Girl. Jane P. Moreland. PH

Poodles are in the basement again so my aunt, The. Summer
  Visitors. Stephen Clark. AMV-81

Pooh! Walter de la Mare. BBL; HAP

Pool, The. Hilda Doolittle ("H. D."). CMoP (1970 ed.); ExPo
  (1973 ed.)

Pool glitters, the fishes leap in the sun, The. By Loe Pool.
  Arthur Symons. VLP

Pool in the Rock, The. Walter de la Mare. EcS

Pool-Shootin' Roy. Damon Runyon. SPo

Poolhall, The. Dan Burt. AMV-80

Poolroom Faces. Joseph Kalar. SPT

Poor, The. William Carlos Williams. IPWM; PPP; TT

Poor, and the dazed, and the idiots, The. Hurrying Away from
  the Earth. Robert Bly. CoPAm; PoA

Poor Boy ("When I went down to the river, poor boy").
  *Unknown.* FSW

Poor Boy Blues ("Poor boy. Poor boy. Poor boy long way from
  home"). *Unknown.* BluL

Poor Can Feed the Birds, The. John Shaw Neilson. MAuV

Poor Christian Looks at the Ghetto, A. Czeslaw Milosz, *tr. fr.*
  *Polish by author.* NIL

Poor clerk, "Arnaut the less" they call me, A. Marvoil. Ezra
  Pound. Epi

Poor credulous and simple maid! Phyllis. Thomas Randolph.
  BoLoP

Poor Dad he got five years or more as everybody knows. Stir the
  Wallaby Stew. *Unknown.* FaBoBa

Poor damned Catullus, here's no time for nonsense. Catullus, *tr.*
  *fr. Latin by* Horace Gregory. NAWM-1

Poor dear dead have been laid out in vain, The. Thomas Hood.
  FaBoEE

Poor devil that I am, being so attacked. Palladas, *tr. fr. Greek by*
  Tony Harrison. OBVE

Poor Doctor Blow went out of church. Queen Anne's Musicians.
  Thomas Hennell. FaBoTw (1975 ed.)

Poor drunkards, poor drunkards, take warning by me. John
  Adkins' Farewell. *Unknown.* AmFP

Poor Ellen Smith. *Unknown.* AmFP

Poor fawn about to die. Image. Anna de Noailles, *tr. by* Carol
  Cosman. PBWP

Poor fellow, what is it to you. Verses. Sir Charles Hanbury
  Williams. OBW

Poor fountain, dusty, clogged with pebbles. The Fountain.
  Pavlos Liasides, *tr. by* Edmund Pennant. AMV-80

Poor Ghost, The. Christina Rossetti. GBL

Poor Girl's Meditation, The. *Unknown, tr. fr. Irish by* Padraic
  Colum. BIrV; PFIr; OLR

Poor Grandma's hair hung all awry. Ruthless Rhyme. J. A.
  Lindon. OSF

Poor Hal caught his death standing under a spout. Fatal Love.
  Matthew Prior. FaBoCo

Poor have hands, and feet, and eyes, The. The Poor Man and His
  Parish Church. Robert Stephen Hawker. VPC

Poor Howard. Leadbelly (Huddie Ledbetter). FSW

Poor in my youth, and in life's later scenes. On Late-acquired
  Wealth. *Unknown, tr. by* William Cowper. OBVE

Poor in spirit on their rosary rounds, The. Lough Derg. Denis
  Devlin. BIrV; CIP

Poor Ivan. Ivan Silen P. R. Poet. Lorraine Sutton. NW

Poor john, who joined in make of wrong. Welcome the Wrath.
  Stanley Kunitz. VGW

Poor Kid. William Cole. OBAL

Poor lad once and a lad so trim, A. Jean Richepin's Song.
  Herbert Trench. ECBV; PFIr; PoTa

Poor legendary princess! The Princess of Dreams. Ernest
  Dowson. VLP

Poor little foal of an oppressed race! To a Young Ass. Samuel
  Taylor Coleridge. MBPR

Poor Little Jesus. *Unknown.* FSW

Poor Little Johnny. *Unknown.* AmFP

Poor little, pretty, flutt'ring thing. Adriani Morientis ad Animam
  Suam. Emperor Hadrian, *tr. by* Matthew Prior. OBVE

Poor little Timothy Grady. Timothy Grady. Leroy F. Jackson.
  OSF

Poor Lucy Lake was overgrown. Lucy Lake. Newton
  Mackintosh. SpRo

Poor malkin, why hast thou been left behind? To a Scarecrow;
  or, Malkin Left Long after Harvest. Charles Tennyson
  Turner. VPC

Poor Man, The. *Unknown, tr. fr. Swahili.* SFF

Poor Man and His Parish Church, The. Robert Stephen Hawker.
  VPC

Poor Man Blues ("And it's never mind, never mind baby").
  *Unknown.* BluL

Poor Man Blues ("I never had a barrel of money"). *Unknown.*
  FSW

Poor man knows not how to eat with the rich man, The. The
  Poor Man. *Unknown, tr. fr. Swahili.* SFF

"Poor man, oh, poor man, come tell to me true." The Jolly
  Thresherman. *Unknown.* AmFP

Poor man's sins are glaring, The. Rich and Poor; or, Saint and
  Sinner. Thomas Love Peacock. FaBoCo; NOBE; NOBL;
  OBSV

Poor Mouse. Mei Berssenbrugge. NW

Poor Old Lady. *At. to* Pamela Smith. CTV

Poor old Mr. Bidery. Mr. Bidery's Spidery Garden. David
  McCord. DuDr

Poor Old Prurient Interest Blues, The. John Hartford. MAT

Poor old Reuben Ranzo. Reuben Ranzo. *Unknown.* AmFP

Poor old Robinson Crusoe! Mother Goose. MG

Poor Parson, A. Chaucer. *Fr.* The Canterbury Tales: Prologue. BoReV

Poor Poll. Robert Bridges. EBEV; OxBTC

Poor, Poor Country, The. John Shaw Neilson. MAuV

Poor Relation, The. E. A. Robinson. STS

Poor rocking-horse! Eustace, and Edith too. Eustace and Edith. Charles Tennyson Turner. VPC

Poor savage, doubting that a river flows. Watching the Dance. James Merrill. NIL

Poor Shammes of Berditchev, The. Rochelle Ratner. VWA

Poor sheepish plaything. For Sale. Robert Lowell. ConAP; PoIA; PSN

Poor soul, in this thy flesh what dost thou know? John Donne. *Fr.* The Second Anniversary. OAEL-1

Poor soul, the centre [*or* center] of my sinful earth. Sonnets, CXLVI. Shakespeare. BiP; CABA (1972 ed.); Epi; ExPo (1973 ed.); HAP; InPK; NIL; NOBE; OAEL-1; OBP; PoIA; PPoe; PPP

Poor South! Her books get fewer and fewer. J. Gordon Coogler. FaBoCo

Poor spineless things, the clothes I've shed. My Clothes. Barry Spacks. NIL

Poor tired Tim! It's sad for him. Tired Tim. Walter de la Mare. LCL

Poor Unfortunate Hottentot, The. Laura E. Richards. CTV

"Poor wanderer," said the leaden sky. The Subalterns. Thomas Hardy. CMoP (1970 ed.); NoAM; OAEL-2; PPP; VLP

Poor Wayfaring Stranger, A. *Unknown. See* I Am a Poor Wayfaring Stranger.

Poor wayside white. Queen Anne's Lace. Ruthe T. Spinnanger. AATT

Poor weaver, with the hopeless brow. How Different! Ebenezer Elliott. EBEV

Poor William did what could be done. William Brown. Joaquin Miller. BPAW

Poor Wolf Speaks. Poor Wolf. NU

Pop. David McFadden. NeAC

Pop! Goes the [*or* de] Weasel, *diff. versions. Unknown.* BLSo, *with music;* CTV; FaBoNo; FSW, *longer version;* PoPle; PSoN, *with music*

Pop my whip and I bring the blood. The Ox-Driver. *Unknown.* FSW

Popcorn-Popper, The ("The popcorn man"). Dorothy Baruch. CTV

Pope from penance purgatorial, The. J. V. Cunningham, *after the Latin of* George Buchanan. OBVE

Pope He Leads a Happy Life, The. Charles Lever. PFIr

Poplar-Field, The ("The poplars are felled, farewell to the shade"). William Cowper. HAP; ILP (1975 ed.); LAuP; NOBE; VoPo

Poplars. Henryk Grynberg, *tr. fr. Polish by* Isaac Komem. VWA

Poplars are standing there still as death. Southern Mansion. Arna Bontemps. AmNP (1974 ed.); CNA; FB; FF; PoBA; SoSe; UsP

Poppa left no will. Bequest. S. Gale Gilburt. AMV-81

Poppies, The. Richard Church. PF

Poppies. Greg Kuzma. HeS

Poppies in October. Sylvia Plath. NoAM

Poppies on the Wheat. Helen Hunt Jackson. BPAW

Popular ("Popular, popular, unpopular!"). Tennyson. NOBL

Popular Romance, A. Kevin Ireland. ATNZ

Popular Wobbly, The. T-Bone Slim. FSW

Popularity. Robert Browning. OAEL-2

Population. George Oppen. PoA

Population of Attica is 2,900, The. Attica. Horace Coleman. SES

Populist Manifesto. Lawrence Ferlinghetti. EC

Porch, The. Gary Gildner. AMV-80

Porch. Alden Nowlan. NeAC

Porch, The. Philip Pain. PiAm

Porch Window. John Sjoberg. AcAn

Porches. Stanley Plumly. HeS

Porcupine, The. Galway Kinnell. CoPAm; NOBA

Porcupine, The. Karla Kuskin. CC

Porcupine, The. Ogden Nash. ECBV

Porcupine looks somewhat silly, A. The Porcupine. Karla Kuskin. CC

Porcupines. Robert Huff. CNW; CoPAm

Porcupines. Robley Wilson, Jr. AMV-81

Porno Love. Philip Dacey. NVAP

Pornographer, The. Robert Hass. CAAP

Porphyria's Lover. Robert Browning. AnMo; CABA (1972 ed.); ExPo (1973 ed.); HAP; ILP (1975 ed.); IP; LoAs; PoIA; STS; TT

Porson on German Scholarship. Richard Porson. FaBoCo ("Germans, in Greek, The.") FaBoEE

Porson on His Majesty's Government. Richard Porson. FaBoCo

Porson's Visit to the Continent. Richard Porson. FaBoCo; FaBoEE

Port Jefferson. Louis Simpson. IPWM

Port of New York, The. Alfred Hayes. SPT

Port Townsend, 1974. Richard Hugo. CNW

Portage Poem. Louis Jenkins. HeS

Portent, The. Herman Melville. AmVN; ILP (1975 ed.); NOBA; TAP

Portentous change when history can appear. Sonnet in Allusion to Various Recent Histories and Notices of the French Revolution. Wordsworth. MBPR

Porter thoughte what to rede, The. A Lover's Stratagem. *Unknown. Fr.* Floris and Blauncheflour. OxBM

Portholes. Conrad Hilberry. TC

Portia's Speech. Shakespeare. *See* Quality of Mercy, The.

Portion of this yew. Transformations. Thomas Hardy. NoAM; PPP

Portland County Jail. *Unknown.* FSW

Portly prince, and goodly to the sight, A. Dryden. *Fr.* The Hind and the Panther, III. OBSV

Portrait. E. E. Cummings. *See* Buffalo Bill's.

Portrait, A. Walter de la Mare. NoAM

Portrait. John Lyle Donaghy. BIrV

Portrait. Ryah Tumarkin Goodman. AAN

Portrait, The. Robert Graves. CABA (1972 ed.); CMoP (1970 ed.); LoAs; PBMP

Portrait, The. Stanley Kunitz. CTBA; GP; TPo

Portrait. Carol Merrill. FoP

Portrait, The ("O Lord of all compassionate control"). Dante Gabriel Rossetti. The House of Life, X. VLP

Portrait, The ("This is her picture as she was"). Dante Gabriel Rossetti. VLP

Portrait. John Unterecker. PCho

Portrait by a Neighbor. Edna St. Vincent Millay. TH; UsP

"Portrait de Femme." Irving Feldman. NoAM

Portrait d'une Femme. Ezra Pound. CABA (1972 ed.); CMoP (1970 ed.); FF; ILP (1975 ed.); NoAM; NOBA; PPP; SoSe; TAP

Portrait in Available Light. Sara Miles. NYP

Portrait of a False Revolutionist. Isidor Schneider. SPT

Portrait of a Girl with Comic Book. Phyllis McGinley. CTBA; IPWM; SoS; SoSe (1977 ed.)

Portrait of a Jew Old Country Style. Jerome Rothenberg. NNaP

Portrait of a Lady. T. S. Eliot. PSN

Portrait of a Lady. William Carlos Williams. CMoP (1970 ed.); NoAM; NOBA; PoIA; VoA

Portrait of a Machine. Louis Untermeyer. MiP

Portrait of a Marriage. Dannie Abse. NoAM

Portrait of a Negative. Alex Kuo. NW

Portrait of a Nun. Bobi Jones, *tr. fr. Welsh by* Joseph P. Clancy. OBW

Portrait of a Physician. Sir Samuel Garth. *Fr.* The Dispensary. PMW

Portrait of a Pregnant Woman. Bobi Jones, *tr. fr. Welsh by* Joseph P. Clancy. OBW

Portrait of a Reluctant Passenger. Jeffry Jensen. PoW

Portrait of a Widow. Avner Strauss. VWA

Portrait of a Woman. Kathryn Ruby. WBN

Portrait of a Woman I Won't Know. Carol Orlock. PoW

Portrait of a Young Girl Raped at a Suburban Party. Brian Patten. OxBTC

Portrait of a Younger Twin. Thomas W. Shapcott. FPA

Portrait of an Artist. Barbara Howes. IHMS

Portrait of an Engine Driver. Bobi Jones, *tr. fr. Welsh by* Joseph P. Clancy. OBW

Portrait of Malcolm X. Etheridge Knight. CNA; PoBA

Portrait of Mary Stuart, Holyrood. Lewis Spence. MS

Portrait of My Mother on Her Wedding Day. Celia Gilbert. AMV-81

Portrait of "Og." Dryden. *Fr.* Absalom and Achitophel, Pt. II. NIL

Portrait of Prince Henry, The. Sydney Clouts. VWA

Portrait of Rudy, A. James Cunningham. CNA

Portrait of the Artist. Dorothy Parker. PPM

Portrait of the Artist as a Prematurely Old Man. Ogden Nash. PoIA; SoSe

Portrait of the Father. Lindy Hough. IHMS

Portrait of William Harvey. Lord Russell Brain. PMW

Portrait: The Freedom Fighter. George Jonas. NeAC

Portraits of 2 Lonely Women. Ralph Storey. SES

Porwigles. Julie Holder. FPB

Position. Carol Bergé. MMD

Position is where you. The Window. Robert Creeley. CAPP; CoPAm; NoAM; NOBA; TAP; VGW

Positions of the angles, The. Billiards. Laurie Blauner. AMV-81

Positive, a Coxcomb. William Plomer. POL

Positive Movement Will Be Difficult but Necessary. Don L. Lee. FiCh

Positives. Jewel C. Latimore. PoBA

Positives for Sterling Plumpp. Don L. Lee. JB; PoBA

Positivists ever talk in s-/ Uch an epic style as Dawkins. John William Mackail. *Fr.* Balliol Rhymes. FaBoEE

Possessed, The. John Berryman. UsP

Possessed of this city, we are born. The Washingtonian. May Miller. WasP

Possession. Marie Ponsot. VGW

Possession palls. Prophecy of the Grecian Urn. Ruthe T. Spinnanger. AATT

Possessions. Ai. CAAP

Possessions. Ken Smith. EAS

Possessor. Things. W. S. Merwin. HAP

Possibility of New Poetry, The. Robert Bly. ConAP

Possible/ that I lift this hand. Pavane for the Passing of a Child. Laura Chester. FiCP

Possible Love Poem to the Usurer. Octavio Armand, *tr. fr. Spanish by* Carol Maier. AMV-81

Possibly to say every. Letter 60. Mary Norbert Körte. CPA

Possum Tree, The. Irene Gough. ECBV

Post Alcoholum Tristis. James Liddy. IPM

Post-boy drove with fierce career, The. Alice Fell. Wordsworth. MBPR; SpRo

Post Mortem. Lord Russell Brain. PMW

Post Mortem. Robinson Jeffers. PiAm

Post-Mortem, A. Siegfried Sassoon. PBMP

Post-Mortem. S. L. Henderson Smith. PMW

Postcard from the Volcano, A. Wallace Stevens. CABA (1972 ed.); HAP

Post Card out of Panama, A. William D. Barney. LiSp

Postcard to a Foetus. Kirk Robertson. GP

Postcard to Send to Sumer, A. William Bronk. VGW

Postcards from Rotterdam. Carolyn Kizer. GP

Poster, The. Lynn Sukenick. AAN; RiTi

Poster with my picture on it, The. Unwanted. Edward Field. SS

Posterity will ne'er survey. An Epitaph for Castlereagh. Byron. FaBoEE; NIL

Postilion Has Been Struck by Lightning, The. Patricia Beer. HeHu

Postman, The. Gordon Challis. ATNZ

Postman, The. Christina Rossetti. CTV

Postman Cheval. André Breton, *tr. fr. French by* David Gascoyne. EAS

Postman comes when I am still in bed, The. A Sick Child. Randall Jarrell. SO; VGW

Postscript. Sandra Hochman. NMM

Postscript. Shakespeare. *Fr.* The Tempest, IV, i. TPo

Postscript: For Gweno. Alun Lewis. BoLoP

Postscript, on a Name. Stephen Ratcliffe. AMV-80

Postscript to Die Schöne Müllerin. R. P. Lister. POL

Posture of the tree, The. Lovers in Winter. Robert Graves. FaBoEE

Posturing to wake lust/ In the mirror. The Boy. Edward Weismiller. PoUp

Posy, The. George Herbert. SCP-1

Pot-bellied Anachronism, The. Ann Darr. GP

Pot of Flowers, The. William Carlos Williams. PiAm

Pot Shot. Padraic Fallon. CIP

Potage au Petit Puss. Menu. Edward Lear. FaBoNo

Potato. Richard Wilbur. CAPP

Potato was deep in the dark under ground. The Tryst. John Banister Tabb. OBAL

Potomac Town in February. Carl Sandburg. LCL

Pot Pourri from a Surrey Garden. John Betjeman. NOBL

Potted fern, A. Two Takes from Love in Los Angeles. Al Young. CoPAm

Pottery goodness, The. Loving. Wendy Ross. NW

Pouch, The. Thom Swiss. AAN

Poultries, The. Ogden Nash. RAE

Pound of Flesh, The. *Unknown. Fr.* Cursor Mundi. OxBM

Pounding It Out. Ernest Kroll. PoUp

Pour, O pour that parting soul in song. Song of the Son. Jean Toomer. AmNP (1974 ed.); ILP (1975 ed.); NIL; PoBA

Pour out your light, O stars, and do not hold. Requiem. Ivor Gurney. FaBoEE; FaBoTw (1975 ed.)

Pourquoi? *Unknown.* ECBV; GDP

Poverty. Margaret Reynolds. MIS

Poverty. Charles Simic. MAT

Poverty. Thomas Traherne. Prf

Poverty Knock. *Unknown.* VLP

Povre widwe, somdel stape in age, A. The Nun's Priest's Tale. Chaucer. *Fr.* The Canterbury Tales. OAEL-1

Power. Adrienne Rich. TAP

Power above powers, O heavenly Eloquence. Heavenly Eloquence. Samuel Daniel. *Fr.* Musophilus. NOBE

Power and Peace. Robert Herrick. CaPo

Power Failure. Michael Dennis Browne. AmPA

Power Failure. Dabney Stuart. NVAP

Power glides in the root. Root. Miklós Radnóti, *tr. by* Steven Polgar *and* Stephen Berg *and* S. J. Marks. VWA

Power in the People, The. Robert Herrick. CaPo

Power of armies is a visible thing, The. Wordsworth. MBPR

Power of Interval, The. Lord De Tabley. VLP

Power of Love He Wants Shih (Everything), The. Rochelle Owens. NMM; Psy

Power of Maples, The. Gerald Stern. NU

Power of Music, The. Thomas Lisle. NOBL

Power of Prayer, The. Samuel Johnson. *Fr.* The Vanity of Human Wishes. NOBE
(Prayer: "Where then shall Hope and Fear their objects find?") BoReV

Power of Ridicule, The. Pope. *Fr.* Epilogue to the Satires. NOBE
("Ask you what provocation I have had?") OBSV

Power of the Dog, The. Kipling. BoAnP; GDP

Power of Time, The. Swift. FaBoEE

Power of Women. Barbara Sobol. PoUp

Power Station, The. James Merrill. ConAP

Power, that gives with liberal hand, The. On the Religion of Nature. Philip Freneau. EAP

Power to the People. Howard Nemerov. POL

Powerful Eyes o' Jeremy Tait, The. Wallace Irwin. PoTa

Powers of the Pawn, The. David Solway. AMV-81

Powhatan's Daughter. Hart Crane. *See* Bridge, The.

Powte's Complaint, The. *Unknown.* GBP

Powwow. W. D. Snodgrass. SoS

Powwow Remnants. Lew Blockcolski. VoR

Pox of this fooling and plotting of late, A. The Careless Good Fellow. John Oldham. APAS

Pox on this playhouse! 'Tis an old tired jade. Dryden. *Fr.* Epilogue Spoken at Mithridates King of Pontus. SCP-1

Pox on't, says Time to Thomas Hearne. *Unknown.* FaBoEE

Practical Concerns. William J. Harris. PoBA

Practice of Absence, The. Robert Friend. VWA

Practices/ silence, they way of wind. As a Possible Lover. Amiri Baraka. AmNP (1974 ed.)

Practicing. Sonia Gernes. AMV-80

Practicing My Death. Barry Schechter. FiCh

Prairie, The. William Pillin. SPT

Prairie, *sel.* Carl Sandburg.
Finale. ANTL

Prairie Dog, The. Arthur Guiterman. BPAW

Prairie-Dog Town. Mary Austin. BPAW

Prairie grass:/ new sprouts. Struggle for the Roads. Bruce Severy. VW

Prairie Lullaby. *Unknown.* BPAW

Prairie Melts, The. Thomas Hornsby Ferril. MPA

Prairie Schooner, The. Edward Everett Dale. BPAW

Prairie Schooner Poem. Glenna Luschei. CPA

Prairie Sunset, A. Walt Whitman. PiAm

Prairie Town. William Stafford. PPoD

Prairie wind blew harder than it could, The. Swallows. Thomas Hornsby Ferril. MPA; RFM

Prairie Wolf. Gwendolen Haste. WPW

Prairie Wolves. Robert V. Carr. BPAW

Prairies, The. Bryant. AmVN; EAP; NOBA; PiAm; TAP

Praise. Jane Cooper. TAP

Praise. William Matthews. AmPA; NVAP

Praise. Christopher Smart. OxBChV

Praise above all—for praise prevails. Adoremus. Christopher Smart. *Fr.* A Song to David. OBP

Praise be to those who gave it birth. A Soldier's Plea for the Y.M.C.A. Joseph Samuel Reed. PeD

Praise for an Urn. Hart Crane. CMoP (1970 ed.); HAP; NoAM; NOBA; PPP

Praise for the Fountain Opened. William Cowper. PIM

Praise God for this little scrap of light. Epiphany on a Plot of Moonlight. William R. Mitchell. AATT

Praise Hearst, from whom all blessings flow! Doxology. Bert Leston Taylor. OBAL

Praise Him Who Makes Us Happy, *with music.* Mark Van Doren. AH

Praise in Summer. Richard Wilbur. CAPP

Praise Now Your God, *with music.* H. P. Brucker. AH

Praise of a Child. *Yoruba Oral Tradition, tr. by* Ulli Beier *and* B. Gbadamosi. WTO

Praise of a Train. *Zulu Oral Tradition, tr. by* B. W. Vilakazi. WTO

Praise of Dancing, The. Sir John Davies. *Fr.* Orchestra; or, A Poem of Dancing. NOBE

Praise of Ibikunle. *Yoruba Oral Tradition, tr. by* B. Awe. WTO

Praise of Pindar, The. Horace, *tr. fr. Latin by* Abraham Cowley. Odes, IV, 2. Epi; OAEL-1; PAIC

Praise of Zeus. Aratus of Soli, *tr. fr. Greek.* ILwL

Praise Song for King Kalakaua. *Tr. fr. Hawaiian by* N. B. Emerson. WTO

Praise to God for things we see. M. M. Penstone. CTV

Praise we the Lord/ of Heaven's kingdom. Caedmon's Hymn. Caedmon, *tr. by* Sally Purcell. EBEV

Praise Ye the Lord. O Celebrate His Fame, *with music.* Peleg Folger. AH

Praise ye the Lord. Praise God in his sanctuary. Bible, *O.T.* Psalms, CL. CTV

"Praise ye the Lord!" The psalm to-day. The Thanksgiving in Boston Harbor. Hezekiah Butterworth. BTTM

Praised be man, he is existing in milk. Chorus. Jack Kerouac. *Fr.* Mexico City Blues. PiAm

Praised beyond all Enids be. In Morfudd's Arms. Dafydd ap Gwilym, *tr. by* Rolfe Humphries. OBW

Praisers of women in their proud and beautiful poems, The. "Not Marble nor the Gilded Monuments." Archibald MacLeish. BoLoP; CMoP (1970 ed.); HoPM (1975 ed.); NIL; WIF

Praises, The. Charles Olson. VGW

Praises of a Country [*or* Countrie] Life, The. Ben Jonson, *after* Epodes, II, *by* Horace. OBVE; SCP-1

Praises of Henry Francis Fynn. *Zulu Oral Tradition, tr. by* T. Cope. WTO

Praises of the King of Oyo. *Yoruba Oral Tradition, tr. by* Ulli Beier. WTO

Praties, The. *Unknown.* FSW
(Famine Song.) WTO

Praxis in midwinter. Site. Harry Clifton. IPM

Pray Billy Pitt explain thy rigs. On Mr. Pitt's Hair-Powder Tax. Burns. FaBoEE

Pray but one prayer for me 'twixt thy closed lips. Summer Dawn. William Morris. NOBE; OAEL-2

Pray for you, my darling? Aside to Julie. Sallie Chesham. AATT

Pray how did she look? Was she pale, was she wan? On Lady Anne Hamilton. Sheridan. FaBoEE

Pray in May. James J. Metcalfe. SoSe

Pray steal me not, I'm Mrs. Dingley's. On the Collar of Mrs. Dingley's Lap-Dog. Swift. FaBoEE

Pray to What Earth Does This Sweet Cold Belong. Henry David Thoreau. UnPo (1976 ed.)

Pray who lies here? why don't you know. Original Epitaph on a Drunkard. Royall Tyler. OBAL

Pray why are you so bare, so bare. The Haunted Oak. Paul Laurence Dunbar. UnPo (1976 ed.)

Prayer: "Forgive me, you whom they cast in a name." Avraham Shlonsky, *tr. fr. Hebrew by* Francis Landy. VWA

Prayer: "From your high bridge wave & wail." Lev Mak, *tr. fr. Russian by* Dan Jaffe. VWA

Prayer: "Give me a death like Buddha's, let me fall." Stanley Moss. GP; POL

Prayer, A: "Grant, I thee pray, such heat into mine heart." Sir Thomas More. BoReV

Prayer: "If I must of my senses lose." Theodore Roethke. STS

Prayer: "In the beginning/ was Sunday." Rainer Schulte. SES

Prayer, A: "Mother of God, in this brazen sun." Denis Glover. ATNZ

Prayer: "Prayer the church's [*or* churches] banquet, angels' age." George Herbert. BoReV; CABA (1972 ed.); EBEV; Epi; ILP (1975 ed.); InPS; LFH; NOBE; OAEL-1; OBW; PAIC

Prayer, A: "Searcher of souls, you who in heaven abide." Samuel Butler. FaBoEE

Prayer: "Sign that I might, A." Patrick King. IPM

Prayer, A: "Sun, my relative." *Unknown, tr. fr. Havasupai Indian.* AKE

Prayer, A: "Teach me, Father, how to go." Edwin Markham. CTV

Prayer: "Where then shall Hope and Fear their objects find?" Samuel Johnson. *See* Power of Prayer, The.

Prayer, The: "Wilt thou not visit me?" Jones Very. AmVN

Prayer: "Your golden loins slake my lust for treasures." Mike Newell. AMV-80

Prayer after World War. Carl Sandburg. VGW

Prayer against Indifference. Joy Davidman. SPT

Prayer before Birth. Louis MacNeice. BuTh; MPo; PBMP; PFIr; SoS

Prayer for a Pilot. Cecil Roberts. CTV

Prayer for a Second Flood, A. "Hugh MacDiarmid." EBEV

Prayer for Faith, A. Michelangelo Buonarroti, *tr. fr. Italian by* John Addington Symonds. ILwL

Prayer for Fine Weather. Shane Leslie. PFIr; POL

Prayer for Fish. Ronald Wallace. AMV-80

Prayer for Good Dreams. *Unknown.* OxBM

Prayer for Kafka and Ourselves. Anthony Rudolf. VWA

Prayer for Love, A. *Unknown.* CTV

Prayer for My Daughter, A. W. B. Yeats. CABA (1972 ed.); CMoP (1970 ed.); HAP; NoAM; OxBTC; PoA; RRA; SoSe

Prayer for My Son, A. W. B. Yeats. EBEV

Prayer for Rain. Sheikh Aqub Abdullahi Jama, *tr. fr. Somali by* B. W. Andrzejewski. WTO

Prayer for Rain. *Unknown, tr. fr. Zuni Indian.* AKE

Prayer for the Great Family. Gary Snyder. HAP; OFD

Prayer for the Journey. *Unknown.* OxBM

Prayer for the Self, A. John Berryman. Eleven Addresses to the Lord, VIII. PiAm; PPP

Prayer for the Young and Lovely, A. Helen Steiner Rice. CTV

Prayer for This Day. Hildegarde Flanner. WPW

Prayer for Violets, A. Charles O. Hartman. AAN

Prayer from a Stryker Frame. E. Margaret Clarkson. AATT

Prayer in Mid-Passage. Louis MacNeice. BoReV

Prayer in Sickness, A. "Barry Cornwall." PIM

Prayer in Spring, A. Robert Frost. SoSe
    (Oh, Give Us Pleasure in the Flowers Today, *with music.*) AH

Prayer of a Little Hope. Jean Wahl, *tr. fr. French by* Charles Guenther. VWA

Prayer of Abel, The. Byron. *Fr.* Cain. PIM

Prayer of Holy Willie, The. Burns. *See* Holy Willie's Prayer.

Prayer of Thanksgiving, *with music. Unknown, tr. fr. Dutch by* Theodore Baker. BLSo
    (Thanksgiving Hymn.) CTV

Prayer of the Donkey, The. Carmen Bernos de Gasztold, *tr. fr. French by* Rumer Godden. PChr

Prayer of the Fishing Net. *Tr. fr. Hawaiian by* N. B. Emerson. WTO

Prayer of the Homesteader. Gwendolen Haste. WPW

Prayer of the Little Ducks, The. Carmen Bernos de Gasztold, *tr. fr. French by* Rumer Godden. DuDr

Prayer of the Mouse, The. Carmen Bernos de Gasztold, *tr. fr. French by* Rumer Godden. MN

Prayer on Making a Canoe. *Tr. fr. Hawaiian by* N. B. Emerson. WTO

Prayer the church's [*or* churches] banquet, angels' age. Prayer. George Herbert. BoReV; CABA (1972 ed.); EBEV; Epi; ILP (1975 ed.); InPS; LFH; NOBE; OAEL-1; OBW; PAIC

Prayer to Be Said When Thou Goest to Bed, A. Francis Seager. OxBChV

Prayer to Christ and Socrates. James Liddy. IPM

Prayer to St. Helena. *Unknown.* OxBM

Prayer to the Father of Heaven, A. John Skelton. HoPM (1975 ed.)

Prayer to the Lord Ramakrishna, A. James Wright. NNaP

Prayer to the Mothers. Diane DiPrima. RiTi

Prayer to the Mountain Spirit. Mary Austin, *after Navajo Indian.* BPAW

Prayer to the Pacific. Leslie Silko. CDW; VoR

Prayer to the Snowy Owl. John Haines. BoAnP

Prayer unsaid, and Mass unsung. The Sea-Ritual. George Darley. Syren Songs, V. BIrV; EcS

Prayerbooks return to Jerusalem. A Late Manuscript at the Schocken Institute. Gabriel Preil, *tr. by* Gabriel Levin. VWA

Prayers, The. Howard Schwartz. VWA

Prayers, Dorcas, Fellowship, and Children's Groups! Gwladys Rhys. W. J. Gruffydd, *tr. by* D. M. Lloyd. OBW

Prayers of Steel. Carl Sandburg. CMoP (1970 ed.)

Prayers to Liberty. Anwar Shaul, *tr. fr. Arabic by* Yoffee Berkovitz. VWA

Praying mantis doesn't pray, The. Mantis. David McCord. OBAL

Praying to the Stars. Patrocinio Barela. PoW

Preacher and the Slave, The. Joe Hill. FSW; WTO
    (Pie in the Sky.) GBP

Preacher Considers His Sermon, The. Elmer F. Suderman. AATT

Preacher, The: Ruminates behind the Sermon. Gwendolyn Brooks. PBMP

Preacher, Said the General. Peter Meinke. AATT

Preachin' the Blues. *Unknown.* BluL

Preaching Blues. *Unknown.* BluL

Precept of Silence, The. Lionel Johnson. VLP

Precious Child, So Sweetly Sleeping, *with music.* Anna Hoppe. AH

Precious, mouldering pleasure 'tis, A. Emily Dickinson. PCOP

Precious Pearl, The. Pat Wilson. ATNZ

Precise counterpart, The. The Orchestra. William Carlos Williams. HAP

Precise Guinea-Pig, The. *Unknown. See* Guinea-Pig Song, A.

Precision, The. Yvor Winters. EAS

Precocious, impulsive young Mr., A. Nothing More than a Sister. *Unknown.* TDH

Predestination. *Unknown. See* Determinism.

Predicter of Famine, The. William Carlos Williams. VGW

Prediction, The. Mark Strand. EAS; NVAP

Preest ne monk ne yet canoun. Against Friars. *Unknown.* OxBM

Preface: "And did those feet in ancient time." Blake. *See* And Did Those Feet in Ancient Time.

Preface, The: "Infinity, when all things it beheld." Edward Taylor. *Fr.* God's Determinations. EAP; HAP; ILP (1975 ed.); NOBA; PiAm

Preface: "Mother, don't read/ my poems." Carol Shauger. AMV-80

Preface: " 'Sonja Henie,' the young girl." Theodore Weiss. VGW

Preface: "To make a start." William Carlos Williams. *Fr.* Paterson. CMoP (1970 ed.); ILP (1975 ed.); NoAM; NOBA

Preface to a Twenty Volume Suicide Note. Amiri Baraka. AmNP (1974 ed.); CABA (1972 ed.); CAPP; ILP (1975 ed.); InPK; InPS; IPWM; PAIC; PoBA; PPP; SoS; TCP; VoA

Preface to the Memoirs, A. James Merrill. NOBA

Preface to the Picture of Dorian Gray. Oscar Wilde. WIF

Preface: Topping. Janet Kauffman. *Fr.* Tobacco. TC

Preference. Langston Hughes. NOBA

Preference. Elinor Wylie. Psy

Preference Declared, The ("Persicos odi"). Horace. *See* Fie on Eastern Luxury!

Pregnancy. Mira Fish. FAF

Pregnancy. Sandra McPherson. BoWoP; NMM

Pregnant girl, under sorrow's sign, A. Under Sorrow's Sign. Gofraidh Fionn O'Dalaigh, *tr. by* John Montague. BIrV

Pregnant Teenager on the Beach. Mary Balazs. AMV-80

Pre-History Repeats. Robert J. McKent, Jr. QQQ

Prejudice. Georgia Douglas Johnson. AmNP (1974 ed.); PoBA

Preliminary to Classroom Lecture. Josephine Miles. NoAM

Prelude, The [or, Growth of a Poet's Mind]. Wordsworth. MBPR; OAEL-2, *much abr.*

*Sels.*

"And in the frosty season, when the sun," *fr.* I. FSFS (Skaters, The.) LiSp; SPo

"As the black storm upon the mountain top," *fr.* VII. HAP Authentic Tidings, *fr.* VI. BoReV

"Bright was the summer's noon when quickening steps," *fr.* IV. PES

Childhood and School-Time, *fr.* I. NOBE ("Fair seed-time had my soul, and I grew up.") ExPo (1973 ed.); HAP; ILP (1975 ed.)

Dedication: "Memory of one particular hour, The," *fr.* IV. BoReV

"Evangelist St. John my patron was, The," *fr.* III. HAP

"From these sights/ Take one,—that ancient festival, the Fair," *fr.* VII. HAP

"In a throng/ A festal company of Maids and Youths," *fr.* IV. EBEV

"In one of these excursions, travelling then/ Through Wales on foot," *fr.* XIII. EBEV

"O pleasant exercise of hope and joy!" *fr.* XI. HAP

"One summer evening (led by her) I found," *fr.* I. NU; OBP; UsP (Guilt, *diff. version.*) BoReV

"Rise up, thou monstrous ant-hill on the plain," *fr.* VII. HAP

"There are in our existence spots of time," *fr.* XII. PoIA There Was a Boy, *fr.* V. SoSe (1977 ed.)

"Thus did my days pass on, and now at length," *fr* II. BoReV

"Wisdom and Spirit of the universe!" *fr.* I. NOBE

Prelude: "Afterwards, afterwards the wind between two mountains." David Rosenmann-Taub, *tr. fr. Spanish by* Charles Guenther. VWA

Prelude: "Give us another poem, he said." Patrick Kavanagh. NoAM

Prelude: "I am the bird of the wayside." Christine Ama Ata Aidoo. PBWP

Prelude: "In desultory walk through orchard grounds." Wordsworth. VLP

Prelude: "Night and the hood." Conrad Kent Rivers. PoBA

Prelude: "Pleasant it was, when woods were green." Longfellow. *Fr.* Voices of the Night. FSFS

Prelude to an Evening. John Crowe Ransom. EAS; ILP (1975 ed.)

Prelude to "Departmental Ditties." Kipling. VLP

Prelude to Memorial Song: 100 Years Later. Phillip William George. NW; VoR

Prelude to "Songs before Sunrise." Swinburne. VLP

Preludes (I–IV). T. S. Eliot. HeIP; ILP (1975 ed.); InPS; IP; PoIA; PPoD; PPP; PSN; UnPo (1976 ed.); VGW; WeW "Winter evening settles down, The," I. ExPo (1973 ed.)

Preludes for Memnon, *sels.* Conrad Aiken. "Beloved, let us once more praise the rain," VII. UnPo (1976 ed.) "Keep in the heart the journal nature keeps," XLII. CMoP (1970 ed.) "Rimbaud and Verlaine, precious pair of poets," LVI. NoAM "Two coffees in the Español, the last," II. NoAM "Watch long enough, and you will see the leaf," XIX. CMoP (1970 ed.)

Preludes to Definition. Conrad Aiken. *See* Time in the Rock.

Premonition. Yvonne. TV (Emma.) CNA

Premonition of Winter. Hugh Maxton. IPM

Prenegard, prenegard! My Baselard. *Unknown.* OxBM

'Prentice Boy, The.' *Unknown.* AmFP

Preparation. Sandra McPherson. MPA

Preparation of the Body, The. Helen Wolfert. *Fr.* Woman against the Moon. RiTi

Preparations. Leslie Silko. NW; VoR

Preparations. *Unknown.* NOBE; PoPle

Preparative, The. Thomas Traherne. SCP-2

Preparatory Meditations, *sels.* Edward Taylor. *First Series.* "Am I thy gold? Or purse, Lord, for thy wealth," VI. EAP; ILP (1975 ed.); TAP; VoPo "Deity of Love Incorporate, A," XI. TAP "Did ever lord such noble house maintain," IX. SCP-2 Experience The ("Oh! that I always breath'd in such an aire"), III. EAP "How sweet a Lord is mine? If any should," III. PiAm "I kenning [*or* kening] through astronomy divine," VIII. EAP; NOBA; PiAm; SCP-2; TAP (Sacramental Meditations.) PAIC "Leafe gold, Lord of thy golden wedge o'relaid," EAP "My blessed Lord, art thou a lilly flower?" V. PiAm "My dear, deare Lord I do thee Savior call," II. PiAm "My shattred phancy stole away from mee," XXIX. EAP; PiAm "My sin! my sin, my God, these cursed dregs," XXXIX. EAP "Oh! What a thing is man? Lord, who am I?" XXXVIII. NOBA; PiAm Prologue: "Lord, can a crumb of dust the earth outweigh." EAP Return, The ("Inamoring rayes, thy sparkles, pearle of price"). EAP "Stupendous love! All saints astonishment!" X. EAP "Thy grace, dear Lord's my golden wrack, I finde," XXXII. EAP "Thy humane frame, my glorious Lord, I spy," VII. PiAm "What glory's this, my Lord? Should one small point," XXI. EAP "What love is this of thine, that cannot bee," I. PiAm "Would God I in that Golden City were," XXIII. EAP; PiAm *Second Series.* "All dull, my lord, my spirits flat, and dead," VII. EAP

"Halfe dead: and rotten at the coare: my Lord!" XIV.   EAP

"Lord, dub my tongue with a new tier of words," XIX.   SCP-2

"Methinks I spy Almighty holding in," LXVIII.   HAP

"My gracious Lord, I would thee glory doe," IV.   EAP; PiAm

"Oh! Good, good, good, my Lord. What more love yet," CXII.   NOBA

"Oh leaden heeld. Lord, give, forgive I pray," I.   PiAm

"Orator from rhetorick gardens picks, The," XLIV.   EAP

"Should I with silver tooles delve through the hill," LVI.   EAP

"State, a state, oh! dungeon state indeed A," LXXVII.   EAP

"What shall a mote up to a monarch rise?" XCV.   EAP

"What shall I say, my deare deare Lord? most deare," CXLII.   EAP

"What shall I say, my Lord? With what begin?" XXIX.   HAP

"Ye angells bright, pluck from your wings a quill," LX.   PiAm

Prepare for death. But how can you prepare.   Speculation. Howard Nemerov.   TAP

Prepare for death, if here at night you roam.   Samuel Johnson. *Fr.* London: A Poem in Imitation of the Third Satire of Juvenal.   OAEL-1

Prepare for gypsies.   Palmistry for Blind Mariners.   Judith Minty. TC

Preparing for Exile.   Derek Walcott.   OBP

Preponderance, The.   William Meredith.   PBMP

Pre-Positions.   Jose Isaacson, *tr. fr. Spanish by* Yishai Tobin. VWA

Preposterous is that government, and rude.   Ill Government. Robert Herrick.   PAIC

Presbyterian Knight.   Samuel Butler.   *Fr.* Hudibras, I, 1.   NOBE (Sir Hudibras.)   NIL
("When civil dudgeon first grew high.")   OAEL-1
("When civil fury first grew high.")   EBEV; PAIC; SCP-2

Presence, The.   Maxine W. Kumin.   RFM; TSWA; WPE

Presence, The.   Dana Naone.   CDW

Presence, The.   Jones Very.   HAP

Presence among us.   Voyage to the Moon.   Archibald MacLeish. Moon; PBMP

Presences.   Zoë Karélli, *tr. fr. Modern Greek by* Kimon Friar. PBWP

Present, The.   Dick Allen.   FAF

Present.   Sonia Sanchez.   CNA

Present day we cannot spend, The.   Isabella Whitney.   *Fr.* A Sweet Nosegay, or Pleasant Posy.   WPE

Present from the Emperor's New Concubine, A.   Lady Pan, *tr. fr. Chinese by* Kenneth Rexroth.   BoWoP

Present is such a lovely place, The.   The Present.   Dick Allen. FAF

Present of Butter, A.   Tadhg Dall O'Huiginn, *tr. fr. Irish by* the Earl of Longford.   BIrV

Present Tense, The.   Joyce Carol Oates.   AMV-81

Present Time, The.   Congreve.   NIL

Presentation of Two Birds to My Son, A.   James Wright.   ILP (1975 ed.); PPP

Presentation Piece.   Marilyn Hacker.   AmPA

Presentiment—is that long shadow—on the lawn.   Emily Dickinson.   CABA (1972 ed.)

Presently at our touch the teacups stirred.   Voices from the Other World.   James Merrill.   GP

Preserve jar, A.   In Memory of My Being Late.   Morty Sklar. AcAn

Preserve thy sighs, unthrifty girl.   The Soldier [*or* Souldier] Going to the Field.   Sir William Davenant.   MetP; NOBE

President is a welfare-chiseler, The.   From a Speech Delivered in Freedom Hall on Afrikan Liberation Day: Words from a Welfare Mother.   Angela Jackson.   FiCh

President Is Not Funny, The.   Sheila Heldenbrand.   AcAn

President Langton.   Daniel J. Langton.   TPo

President Roosevelt.   *Unknown.*   BluL

President says, The/eat fish.   Virginia Scott.   NPW

President Slumming, The.   James Tate.   OBAL

Press of the Spoon River *Clarion* was wrecked, The.   Carl Hamblin.   Edgar Lee Masters.   *Fr.* Spoon River Anthology. CMoP (1970 ed.); OBSV

Press on till thou descry.   Anne Killigrew.   *Fr.* Chloris' Charms Dissolved by Eudora.   SCP-2

Pressed between the flat sides of the buildings.   The Dog Who Comes from Nowhere.   Patricia Goedicke.   AAN

Press'd by the Moon, Mute Arbitress of Tides.   Charlotte Smith. SBG
(Sonnet Written in the Church-Yard at Middleton, in Sussex.) WPE

Pressure.   Anne Waldman.   CAAP

Pressures, The.   Amiri Baraka.   BPo

Prestidigitator, The.   Al Young.   MIT

Preston.   *Unknown.*   GBP

Presumptuous man! the reason wouldst thou find.   Pope.   *Fr.* An Essay on Man, Epistle I.   BiP

Pretences, discontents.   Ergo Sum.   Charles Brasch.   ATNZ

Pretending Not to Sleep.   Ian Hamilton.   NoAM

Prettiest girl, The.   Sucking [*or* Sipping] Cider through a Straw. *Unknown.*   FSW; GBP

Prettiest Little Baby in the County-O.   *Unknown.*   FSW

Pretty a Day, A.   E. E. Cummings.   CMoP (1970 ed.)

Pretty fair maid all in the garden, A.   The Broken Token. *Unknown.*   AmFP

Pretty Girl, A.   J. Gordon Coogler.   OBAL

Pretty Ploughboy, The.   *Unknown.*   AIW; GBP

Pretty Polly ("I courted pretty Polly the live long night"). *Unknown.*   FSW

Pretty Polly ("Pretty Polly, pretty Polly, come and go [*or* come go 'long] with me").   *Unknown.*   AmFP, 2 *versions*

Pretty Polly of Topsham.   *Unknown.*   AmFP

Pretty Polly Perkins.   *Unknown.*   BBL

Pretty prating poll.   Little Miss and Her Parrot.   John Marchant. OxBChV

Pretty, pretty, pretty!   Sings a Bird.   John Nist.   AMV-80

Pretty Saro.   *Unknown.*   AmFP; FSW

"Pretty, say when."   The Dear Girl.   Sylvia Townsend Warner. AIW

Pretty sneaking knave I knew, A.   Blake.   FaBoEE

Pretty Sport.   William Habington.   NOBE

Pretty white lady.   Stuff.   H. B. Johnson.   AMV-80

Pretty Woman, A.   Simon J. Ortiz.   CDW; PoW

Pretty young school mistress named Beauchamp, A.   A Young School Mistress.   *Unknown.*   TDH

Pretzel man ugly with warts and a crippled hand, The.   I Always Come Home.   Alfred Hayes.   SPT

Pretzels.   E. Ethelbert Miller.   PoUp

Previsioning death in advance, our doom is delayed.   Foresight. Lincoln Kirstein.   NoAM

Priapupation of Queen Pasiphaë, The.   Jonathan Williams.   CSP

Priapus and the Pool, *sels.*   Conrad Aiken.
Atlantis, XV.   EcS
"This is the shape of the leaf, and this of the flower," IV. CMoP (1970 ed.); NOBA
"When trout swim down Great Ormond Street," III.   NoAM; NOBA

Price of Breast in Las Vegas, The.   Carole Oles.   NPW

Price of Paper, The.   Lawrence Russ.   AMV-81

Price seemed reasonable, location, The.   Telephone Conversation. Wole Soyinka.   SFF; SoSe; TPo

Priceless Mr. Waldo Tubbe, The.   Mr. Tubbe's Morning Service. Stanley Burnshaw.   SPT

Pricke of Conscience, The, *sel. Unknown.* Newly Born, The. OxBM

Prickle a lamb. Conjuring Roethke. James Tate. OBAL

Pride cannot see itself by mid-day light. Barten Holyday. FaBoEE

Pride is his pity, artifice his praise. *Unknown.* FaBoEE

Pride, lust, ambition, and the people's hate. The Downfall of the Chancellor. *Unknown.* APAS

Pride of Ancestry. Robert Frost. OBAL

Pride of Ladies, A. Anne Halley. NMM

Pride of Place. Katie Louchheim. WasP

Pride of the peacock is the glory of God, The. Blake. *Fr.* The Marriage of Heaven and Hell. FF

Priest and the Matador, The. Charles Bukowski. CPA

Priest and the Mulberry Tree, The. Thomas Love Peacock. *Fr.* Crotchet Castle. PoTa

Priest Lake. William Stafford. PoA

Priestley. Samuel Taylor Coleridge. *Fr.* Sonnets on Eminent Characters. MBPR

Priests of Serrabonne, The. Owen Leeming. ATNZ

Primaleon of Greece, *sel.* Anthony Munday. Beauty Bathing. NOBE

Primary. Abbie Huston Evans. GP

Primary Ground, A. Adrienne Rich. NNaP; WBN

Primary Lesson: The Second Class Citizens. Sun-Ra. PoBA

Primary Numbers. Edvard Kocbek, *tr. fr. Slovakian by* Herbert Kuhner *and* Peter Kersche. AMV-81

Primavera. Frank Lima. UsP

Prime. W. H. Auden. CMoP (1970 ed.)

Prime. Langston Hughes. PoBA

Primer for Schoolchildren, A. Richard Weber. CIP

Primer Lesson. Carl Sandburg. OSP; SFF; TH

Primer Lesson. Mark Vinz. TAT

Primer of Plato. Jean Garrigue. NOBA

Primer of the Daily Round, A. Howard Nemerov. WeW

Primitive, The. Don L. Lee. BPo

Primitive like an Orb, A. Wallace Stevens. NOBA

Primitive Man. Woods Night. Tom Hennen. GP

Primitive Pithecanthropus erectus, The. Heredity. Arthur Guiterman. OBAL

Primitives. Dudley Randall. BPo; CABA (1972 ed.)

Primrose, The. Robert Herrick. PF

Primrose, Being at Montgomery Castle, The. John Donne. GBL

Primula Scotica. Charles Senior. MIS

Prince, The. Edgar Bowers. ConAP

Prince Absalom and Sir Rotherham Redde. Evening. Edith Sitwell. AIW

Prince Alfrid's Itinerary, *sel. Unknown, tr. fr. Irish by* James Clarence Mangan. "I found in Munster, unfettered of any." BIrV

Prince George of Hanover was thirty-one. George II and the Chinese Emperor. Robert Graves. BBL

Prince Jernikidze. Joseph Freeman. SPT

Prince of Love, The. Blake. *See* Song: "How sweet I roamed from field to field."

Prince of Peace His Banner Spreads, The, *with music.* Harry Emerson Fosdick. AH

Prince Robert. *Unknown.* AmFP

Prince Sumiya. *Mongol Oral Tradition, tr. by* C. R. Bawden. WTO

Prince, with wonder, sees the stately tow'rs, The. Virgil, *tr. by* Dryden. *Fr.* The Aeneid, I. OBVE

Princes and kings decay and die. Stanzas. Philip Freneau. GOA

Princes' Land, The. Les A. Murray. MAuV

Princes of Mercia were badger and raven, The. Geoffrey Hill. Mercian Hymns, VI. HAP

Prince's Progress, The, *sel.* Christina Rossetti. Bride Song. WPE

Princess, The, *sels.* Tennyson.
"Ask me no more: the moon may draw the sea," *fr.* Pt. VI. GBL
"Come down, O maid, from yonder mountain height," *fr.* Pt. VII. CABA (1972 ed.); FF; OAEL-2
"Now sleeps the crimson petal, now the white," *fr.* Pt. VII. BoLoP; CABA (1972 ed.); EBEV; GBL; ILP (1975 ed.); LoAs; NIL; NOBE; PPoe; PPP
(Song: "Now sleeps the crimson petal, now the white.") ExPo (1973 ed.)
Splendor [*or* Splendour] Falls on Castle Walls, The, *fr.* Pt. III. CTV; HeIP; ILP (1975 ed.); InPK; OAEL-2; PoIA
(Blow, Bugle, Blow.) NOBE; UnPo (1976 ed.)
(Bugle, The.) PoPle
Sweet and Low, *fr.* Pt. II. BiP; BLSH; CTV; FSW; ILP (1975 ed.); OxBChV
"Tears, idle tears, I know not what they mean," *fr.* Pt. IV. CABA (1972 ed.); FaPoR; HAP; InPK; InPS; NIL; NOBE; OAEL-2; PoIA; PPoe; PPP; UnPo (1976 ed.); VoPo; WeW

Princess Addresses the Frog Prince, The. Elizabeth Brewster. MMD

Princess and the Gypsies, The. Frances Cornford. PoTa

Princess Elizabeth of Bohemia, as Perdita. Frank O'Hara. PoA

Princess of Dreams, The. Ernest Dowson. VLP

Princess Who Fled to the Castle, The. Francis Landy. VWA

Print-out, The. Howard Nemerov. AMV-80

Printed Words. Liz Sohappy Bahe. CDW

Printing Jenny ("Printing Bibles is Jenny's daily chore"). Matthew Mitchell. OxBTC

Prioress, The. Chaucer. *Fr.* The Canterbury Tales: Prologue OxBM
(Madam Eglantine.) NOBE; UsP

Pripet Marshes, The. Irving Feldman. NoAM; VWA

Prison. Paul David Ashley. DNGG

Prison Bi-Centennial Address, A. Pancho Aguila. CPA

Prison Break. Michael Hogan. GP

Prison Cell Blues. *Unknown.* BluL

Prison Dorm. Robert T. Kasold. DNGG

Prison sleeps, The! Tom Mooney Walks at Midnight. Michael Gold. SPT

Prison Song. Alan Dugan. PoA

Prisoner, The. Emily Brontë. BoReV; NOBE

Prisoner, The. Keith Douglas. PSN

Prisoner, A. Arlie "Franko" Durham. DNGG

Prisoner, The. Derek Mahon. PFIr

Prisoner, The. Charles Spear. ATNZ

Prisoner between the Panes of Glass. Silvina Ocampo, *tr. fr. Spanish by* Jason Weiss. AMV-81

Prisoner of Chillon, The. Byron. MBPR
*Sels.*
"Kind of change came in my fate, A." NOBE
Sonnet on Chillon. ExPo (1973 ed); ILP (1975 ed.); LFH; PAIC; PBMP

Prisoners. Eavan Boland. IPM

Prisoner's Prayer, A. *Unknown.* OxBM

Prisoner's Song. Horace Gregory. OLR

Prithee die and set me free. Martial, *tr. fr. Latin by* Sir John Denham. OBVE

Prithee forgive me,/ I did but chide in jest. Thomas Middleton. *Fr.* Women Beware Women: A Tragedy. SCP-2

Prithee, say aye or no. The Resolute Courtier. Thomas Shipman. GBL

Prithee stand awhile and view this tree. On a Great Hollow Tree. William Strode. SCP-2

Privacy. R. P. Dickey. PoW

Private Dining Room, The. Ogden Nash. UsP

Private faces in public places. W. H. Auden. FaBoEE

Private Hurricane. Elizabeth Bartlett. CPA

Private Letter to Brazil, A. Gloria C. Oden. AmNP (1974 ed.)

Private of the Buffs, The. Sir Francis Hastings Doyle. VLP

Private Pain in Time of Trouble. Kathleen Spivack. AmPA

Private Pantomime. Ruth Stone. PoA

Private Places. Fred Caparoso. PHC

Private Transport. Adrian Mitchell. FaBoEE

Privately, your pencil makes. Snapshot of a Pedant. George Garrett. WIF

Privilege. Alejandra Pizarnik, *tr. fr.* Spanish *by* Yishai Tobin. VWA

Prize Cat, The. E. J. Pratt. NoAM

"Prize" Poem, A. Shirley Brooks. FaBoCo; FaBoNo

Pro, The. Karen Swenson. AMV-81

Pro Basketball Players. Tom Meschery. SPo

Pro Femina, *sels.* Carolyn Kizer.
    "From Sappho to myself, consider the fate of women," I. NMM; Psy; RiTi; WBN
    "I take as my theme, 'The Independent Woman,' " II. MAT; NMM; Psy; RiTi; WBN
    "I will speak about women of letters, for I'm in the racket," III. MAT; NMM; Psy; RiTi; WBN

Pro Musica Antiqua. O. B. Hardison. WasP

Pro Patria, *abr.* Constance Carrier. WPE

Probability and Birds in the Yard. Russell Atkins. CNA; FB

Probable-Possible, my black hen. Frederick Winsor. *Fr.* The Space Child's Mother Goose. QQQ

Problem, The. Emerson. NOBA; TAP

Problem in Social Geometry—The Inverted Square! Ray Durem. PoBA

Problem of Wild Horses, The. Barbara Winder. PH

Problem, surely, is to live with Here, The. Revelation. Jerald Bullis. AMV-81

Problem with Dreams, The. Thomas Brush. NVAP

Problems. Alexander Scott. FF

Problems of a Journalist. Weldon Kees. NYP

Procedure is habit. I affirm it. David Meltzer. VoA

Process, The. Marguerite Young. FoP

Procession, The: A New Protestant Ballad. *Unknown.* APAS

Proclaim the Lofty Praise, *with music.* Sarah Judson. AH

Proclamation/ From Sleep, Arise. Carolyn M. Rodgers. JB

Proclitic in the wind he walks. Prophet. Henry Tim Chambers. AATT

Procne, Philomela, and Itylus. Philomela. John Crowe Ransom. CMoP (1970 ed.); ILP (1975 ed.); NoAM; NOBA; OBAL; OBSV

Prodigal, The. Elizabeth Bishop. CoPAm; PPP

Prodigal Son, The. E. A. Robinson. LFH

Prodigal Thinks of His Mother, The. James Simmons. IPM

Prodigal's Return. Ralph D. Eberly. AMV-80

Produce the urn that Hannibal contains. Hannibal. Juvenal, *tr. by* William Gifford. *Fr.* Satires, X. OBVE

Proem: "I love the old melodious lays." Whittier. AmVN; TAP

Proem: "Lo, thus, as prostrate, 'In the dust I write.' " James Thomson ("B. V."). *See* City, The.

Proem: "Poetry is itself a thing of God." Philip James Bailey. *Fr.* Festus. QQQ

Proem: "Strong Son of God, immortal Love." Tennyson. *See* In Memoriam A.H.H.: "Strong Son of God. . ."

Proem and Inscription for a Hermes. Robert Garioch. MS

Proem: To Brooklyn Bridge. Hart Crane. *See* To Brooklyn Bridge.

Professional, The. David Ignatow. NNaP

Professionals, The. Geoffrey Grigson. PoA

Professor Burke's symphony, "Colorado Vistas." Cultural Notes. Kenneth Fearing. CMoP (1970 ed.)

Professor Called Chesterton, A. W. S. Gilbert. TDH

Professor Gratt. Donald Hall. OBAL
    (Dr. Fatt, Instructor, *sl. diff.*) TPo

Professor James Dewar, F. R. S. E. C. Bentley. *Fr.* Clerihews (Biography for Beginners). PoPle

Professor Kelleher and the Charles River. Desmond O'Grady. CIP; IPM; NoAM

Professor Robinson each summer beats. Don's Holiday. G. Rostrevor Hamilton. FaBoCo

Professor Waking, The. James Tate. FF

Professor's Song, A. John Berryman. HeIP; NoAM; NOBA

Profetizador/ Old Prophet. Henry L. Pacheco. PoW

Profile. Barry Schechter. FiCh

Profile. Bronwen Wallace. AMV-81

Profile of a Day. Ruthe T. Spinnanger. AATT

Profile of Rose. Glyn Jones. OBW

Profile on the Pillow, The. Dudley Randall. BPo; PoBA; TAP

Profligate, The. John T. Zaremba. DNGG

Profoundest of all sensualities, The. The Deepest Sensuality. D. H. Lawrence. NoAM

Profoundly True Reflections on the Sea. A. E. Housman. FaBoNo

Progenitor. Skaidrite Stelzer. TC

Prognosis. Louis MacNeice. CMoP (1970 ed.); NOBE

Progress. Suzanne Douglass. QQQ

Progress, The. Ralph Knevet. SCP-2

Progress. Felicia Lamport. QQQ

Progress. Peter Meinke. POL; SoSe (1977 ed.);

Progress of a Divine, The, *sel.* Richard Savage.
    "Now in the patron's mansion see the wight." OBSV

Progress of Beauty, The. Swift. AnMo; CABA (1972 ed.)

Progress of Faust, The. Karl Shapiro. ILP (1975 ed.)

Progress of Learning, The, *sel.* Sir John Denham.
    "Then darkness Europe's face did overspread." SCP-2

Progress of Man, The, *sel.* George Canning.
    "Mark the dark rook, on pendent branches hung." FaBoNo

Progress of Poesy, The. Matthew Arnold. VLP

Progress of Poesy, The. Thomas Gray. LAuP; LFH

Progress of Poetry, The. "Christopher Caudwell." OxBTC

Progress of Poetry, The. Swift. CABA (1972 ed.)

Progress of the Soul, The ("Nothing could make me sooner to confess"). John Donne. *See* Of the Progress of the Soul; the Second Anniversary.

Progresse of the Soule, The ("I sing the progress of a deathless soul"), *sels.* John Donne.
    Elephant, The. OBP
    Whale, The. EcS; OBP

Progression of the Species. Brian W. Aldiss. FF

Projection, A. Reed Whittemore. WIF

Projectionist's Nightmare, The. Brian Patten. LP

Projections for an Eagle Escaped in This City, March 1965. Nathaniel Tarn. TwMBP

Projects. Emery E. George. AAN

Proletarian Portrait. William Carlos Williams. MiP; OBAL; OSP; PiAm; TAP

Proletarian Visit. Norman Macleod. SPT

Prologue: "And the way goes on in the worn earth." Archibald MacLeish. *Fr.* Conquistador. NoAM

Prologue: "By landscape reminded once of his mother's figure." W. H. Auden. NoAM

Prologue: "I first adventure, with foolhardy might." Joseph Hall. *Fr.* Virgidemiarum, Bk. I. TVS

Prologue: "In a summer season, when soft was the sun." William Langland. *See* In a Somer Seson, Whan Softe Was the Sonne.

Prologue: "In your words." Lazer Eichenrand, *tr. fr. Yiddish by* Gabriel Preil *and* Howard Schwartz. VWA

Prologue: "Lord, can a crumb of dust the earth outweigh." Edward Taylor. *Fr.* Preparatory Meditations, First Series. EAP

Prologue: "O love, the interest itself in thoughtless heaven." W. H. Auden. EBEV

Prologue: "Of Heaven or Hell I have no power to sing." William Morris. *See* Apology, An.

Prologue: "Our author by experience finds it true." Dryden. *Fr.* Aureng-Zebe. ILP (1975 ed.); LFH

Prologue: "Over! the sweet summer closes." Tennyson. *Fr.* Becket. GBL

Prologue: "Pardon my omissions." Michael Hartnett. IPM

Prologue: " 'Poet's age is sad, The: for why?' " Robert Browning. *Fr.* Asolando. OAEL-2; VLP

Prologue, The: "To sing of wars, of captain[e]s, and of kings." Anne Bradstreet. BoWoP; EAP; NOBA; SBG; TAP; WPE

Prologue: "We who with songs beguile your pilgrimage." James Elroy Flecker. *Fr.* The Golden Journey to Samarkand. FaPoR; OxBTC

Prologue: "Whan that April with his showres soote." Chaucer. *See* Canterbury Tales, The.

Prologue in Heaven. Goethe, *tr. fr. German by* Louis MacNeice. *Fr.* Faust. NAWM-2

Prologue Spoken [by Mr. Garrick] at the Opening of the Theatre in Drury-Lane, 1747. Samuel Johnson. EBEV; LAuP

Prologue to a Translation. John Trevisa. OxBM

Prologue to "A Word to the Wise." Samuel Johnson. FaPoR (Prologue to Hugh Kelly's "A Word to the Wise.") EBEV

Prologue to His Royal Highness. Dryden. SCP-1

Prologue to Hugh Kelly's "A Word to the Wise." Samuel Johnson. *See* Prologue to "A Word to the Wise."

Prologue to "London Nights." Arthur Symons. VLP

Prologue to "Rhymes and Rhythms." W. E. Henley. VLP

Prologue to "The Canterbury Tales." Chaucer. *See* Canterbury Tales, The.

Prolonged Sonnet: When the Troops Were Returning from Milan. Niccolò degli Albizzi, *tr. fr. Italian by* Dante Gabriel Rossetti. OBVE

Promenade, *sel.* William Carlos Williams. "Oh, then a wreath," III. TT

Promenading their/ skirted galleons of sex. The Return to Work. William Carlos Williams. CTBA

Prometheus. Byron. InPS; MBPR; NOBE; OAEL-2

Prometheus. Jenny Mastoraki, *tr. fr. Modern Greek by* Nikos Germanakos. BoWoP

Prometheus! Titanic Litany. John Wheelwright. SPT

Prometheus Bound. Aeschylus, *tr. fr. Greek by* Edith Hamilton. NAWM-1

Prometheus Unbound. Shelley. MBPR; OAEL-2 *Sels.* Asia's Song, *fr.* II, v. GrRo "Life of Life! thy lips enkindle," *fr.* II, v. NOBE

Prominent lady in Brooking, A. Expert. *Unknown.* TDH

Promise, The. Phyllis Hoge Thompson. PHC

Promise in Disturbance, The. George Meredith. VLP

Promised Land. Mary Engel. AMV-80

Promised Land. Charles Spear. ATNZ

Promised Land, The. Samuel Stennett. AmFP

Promises, *sel.* Robert Penn Warren. Founding Fathers, Nineteenth-Century Style, VIII. NoAM

Promises of Freedom. *Unknown.* BPo

Promising a river of grass, you guided me. Everglade. Anne Cherner. AMV-81

Promissory Note, The. Bayard Taylor. SpRo

Promontory Moon. Galway Kinnell. Moon

Prompt, executive bird is the jay, A. Emily Dickinson. SoSe (1977 ed.)

Promptly along the wave-length'd air. Life-Style. Jenny Morgan. PMW

Promptress of unnumber'd sighs. To Fortune on Buying a Ticket in the Irish Lottery. Samuel Taylor Coleridge. MBPR

Prone couple still sleeps, A. First Light. Thomas Kinsella. BIrV; CMoP (1970 ed.); ExPo (1973 ed.); NoAM

Proof, The. W. H. Auden. OAEL-2

Proof. Brendan Kennelly. CIP

Proofs of Love. *Unknown.* ECBV

Prope ripam fluvii solus. Malum Opus. James Appleton Morgan. FaBoCo

Propeller Sleep. Mei Berssenbrugge. SA

Proper New Ballad, A, Intituled The Fairies Farewell. Richard Corbet. *See* Fairies Farewell, The.

Proper Place, A. Robert Nye. OSP

Proper Pride. D. H. Lawrence. FaBoEE

Proper scale would pat you on the head, The. The Scales. William Empson. CMoP (1970 ed.); LFH

Proper way to eat a fig, in society, The. Figs. D. H. Lawrence. OAEL-2

Properties of the Shires of England, The ("The properte of every shire"). *Unknown.* GBP

Property Settlement. John Pauker. PoUp

Properzia Rossi. Felicia Dorothea Hemans. SBG

Prophecy, A. Allen Ginsberg. TAP

Prophecy. Jules Supervielle, *tr. fr. French by* Jan Pallister. AMV-81

Prophecy. Elinor Wylie. BoWoP; RiTi; VGW

Prophecy of Famine, The, *sels.* Charles Churchill. "Oft have I heard thee mourn the wretched lot." OBSV "Two boys, whose birth beyond all question springs." OBSV

Prophecy of King Tammany, The. Philip Freneau. GOA

Prophecy of the Grecian Urn. Ruthe T. Spinnanger. AATT

Prophecy of This Present Year 1600, A. John Weever. TVS

Prophecy on Lethe. Stanley Kunitz. PoA

Prophet. Henry Tim Chambers. AATT

Prophet, The, *sels.* Kahlil Gibran. "And a woman who held a babe against." PPM On Children. SFF "Then Almitra spoke again and said, "And what of Marriage, Master?" PPM "Then Almitra spoke, saying, We would ask now of Death." DL

Prophet digs with iron hands, The. Transfiguration. Djuna Barnes. EAS

Prophet of dead words defeats himself, The. E A. Robinson. Octaves, XX. ILP (1975 ed.)

Prophet of the body's. Walt Whitman. Edwin Honig. PAIC; TAP

Prophet speaks, The. Saint Malcolm. Jewel C. Lattimore. BPo

Prophets for a New Day. Margaret Walker. BPo

Prophets have died in the desert, The. Fall. Gabriela Melinescu, *tr. by* Michael Impey *and* Brian Swann. AMV-80

Prophet's Warning or Shoot to Kill, The. Ebon Dooley. PoBA

Prophylactic, The. Russell Edson. GP

Propinquity. Alastair Reid. MS

Proportion. Amy Lowell. BoWoP

Proposal for Recycling Wastes, A. Marge Piercy. GP

Proposal of Marriage, The. *Unknown.* BBL

Propped boughs are heavy with apples. In the Huon Valley. James McAuley. MAuV

Propped in a cave of pillows. 100 Year Old Woman at Christmas Dinner. Colin Style. AMV-80

Propped on a stick he viewed the August weald. The One-legged Man. Siegfried Sassoon. CMoP (1970 ed.)

Propped on second, dropping ever so slowly. Neither Up nor Down. Judith Rodriguez. FPA

Prorogued on prorogation—damned rogues and whores! On the Prorogation. *Unknown.* APAS

Prose for Des Esseintes. Donald Davie, *after the French of* Stéphane Mallarmé. OBVE

Prose Poem. Humphrey Jennings. EAS

Proserpine may pull her flowers. Song of the Stygian Naiades. Thomas Lovell Beddoes. OAEL-2

Prosopopoeia Corporis Animae Valedicturi: Adios: Arrivederci. William Lathum. SCP-2

Prospect, The. Timothy Dwight. Greenfield Hill, Pt. I. EAP

Prospect Beach. Lou Lipsitz. VGW

Prospecting. A. R. Ammons. ConAP

Prospecting Dream. *Unknown.* AmFP; FSW

Prospective Immigrants Please Note. Adrienne Rich. GOA; VGW

Prospectus. Albert Huffstickler. AMV-81

Prospice. Robert Browning. BiP; DL; ILP (1975 ed.); PAIC; PFD; STS; TT; VLP; VoPo

Prostitutes at Les Halles, The. Jane Mayhall. WBN

Prostration. David Semah, *tr. fr. Arabic by* Yoffee Berkovitz. VWA

Protect Me. Hans Adler. AMV-80

Protective Colors. William Logan. AMV-81

Protective Grigri, The. Ted Joans. PoBA

Protestant Courts Catholic. James Simmons. IPM

Proteus. Kathleen Wiegner. MMD

Prothalamion. Michael Ryan. AmPA

Prothalamion. Spenser. AAS; EBEV; HAP; NIL; PPoe; PPP

Prothalamium. Donagh MacDonagh. BIrV

Protocols. Randall Jarrell. VGW

Proud, as Apollo on his forked hill. Pope. *Fr.* An Epistle to Dr. Arbuthnot. OBSV

Proud Engine, The. *Unknown.* TDH

Proud Lady, A. Elinor Wylie. SBG

Proud Maisie. Sir Walter Scott. *Fr.* The Heart of Midlothian, *ch.* 38. AIW; Epi; FF; ILP (1975 ed.); InPK; IP; OAEL-2; UnPo (1976 ed.)
(Madge Wildfire's Death Song.) HAP
(Madge Wildfire's Song.) NOBE; SLP

Proud New York. John Reed. PoA

Proud of his hump. Dromedary. François Dodat, *tr. by* Bert *and* Odette Meyers. BoAnP

Proud Preston, poor people. Preston. *Unknown.* GBP

Proud Songsters. Thomas Hardy. NoAM; PB; UsP

Proud word you never spoke, but you will speak. Walter Savage Landor. *Fr.* Ianthe. GBL

Proudly swept the rain cloud by the cliff. Aloha Oe. Queen Lydia Liliuokalani. BLSH

Proudly the note of the trumpet is sounding. O'Donnell Aboo. M. J. McCann. FSW

Proust on Noah. Eisig Silberschlag. VWA

Proust's Madeleine. Kenneth Rexroth. NoAM

Proverbial. John Seller Anson. AMV-80

Proverbial Man. Martin Galvin. PoUp

Proverbial Philosophy: Of Reading. Charles Stuart Calverley. FaBoCo

Proverbs, *sels.* Bible, *O.T.*
"As snow in summer, and as rain in harvest," XXVI. BiP

"Go to the ant, thou sluggard," VI: 6-8. CTV

"My son, forget not my law," III: 1-4. CTV

"Soft answer turneth away wrath, A," XV. BiP

"Strength and dignity are her clothing," XXXI: 25-29. CTV

"There be four things which are little upon the earth," XXX: 24-28 CTV

Proverbs. Morton Marcus. NVAP

Proverbs of Alfred, The, *sel. At. to* Alfred, King of England. Wealth and Wisdom. OxBM

Provide, Provide. Robert Frost. CABA (1972 ed.); CMoP (1970 ed.); HAP; InPK; IPWM; NIL; NoAM; NOBA; PPP; SS; STS; TAP; UnPo (1976 ed.)

Provincetown, Mass. Harvey Shapiro. PoA

Provincial Obituary. Michael Coady. IPM

Provisions. Margaret Atwood. IHMS

Prowling the Ridge. Judith Minty. TC

Prowling wolf, whose shaggy skin, A. The Wolf and the Dog. La Fontaine, *tr. by* Elizur Wright. OBVE

Prudence. Emerson. OBAL

Prudent Simplicity. William Cowper. FaBoEE

Pruners are quick and cruel, The. Knife and Sap. Kenneth Leslie. POL

Psalm: "Father/ You are the trunk." Howard Schwartz. VWA

Psalm: "In the small beauty of the forest." George Oppen. NNaP

Psalm: "No one kneads us again of earth and clay." Paul Celan, *tr. fr. German by* Joachim Neugroschel. VWA
(Psalm: "No one moulds us again out of earth and clay," *tr. by* Michael Hamburger.) OBVE

Psalm: "Oh Lord, I have been staring into a mirror." Eugene Heimler, *tr. fr. Hungarian by* Anthony Rudolf. VWA

Psalm: "Old ones to the side." Charles Simic. AmPA

Psalm: "There are a very few moments when you." Avraham Ben-Yitzhak, *tr. fr. Hebrew by* A. C. Jacobs. VWA

Psalm, The: "While Northward the hot sun was sinking o'er the trees." Robert Bridges. FaBoTw (1975 ed.)

Psalm Concerning the Castle. Denise Levertov. PiAm; WPE

Psalm for a New Nun. Madeline DeFrees. CNW

Psalm of David, A. Robert Browning. *Fr.* Saul, IX. PIM

Psalm of Life, A. Longfellow. AmVN; CABA (1972 ed.); CTV; PiAm; TAP
(Tell Me Not in Mournful Numbers, *with music.*) AH

Psalm of Montreal, A. Samuel Butler. *See* O God! O Montreal!

Psalm of Onan for Harp, Flute and Tambourine, A. Alden Nowlan. NeAC

Psalm of the Jealous God. Henry Abramovitch. VWA

Psalm Praising the Hair of Man's Body, A. Denise Levertov. AnMo; CAPP

Psalm III: "To God: to illuminate all men. Beginning with Skid Row." Allen Ginsberg. CAPP

Psalm to the Creatures. Gwilym R. Jones, *tr. fr. Welsh by* Joseph P. Clancy. OBW

Psalmen Gezangen. Irene Dayton. AATT

Psalmodist. Mani Leib, *tr. fr. Yiddish by* David G. Roskies *and* Hillel Schwartz. VWA

Psalms, *sels.* Bible, *O.T.*
Psalm I ("Blessed is the man that walketh not in the counsel of the ungodly"). BiP; CTV (1-3)
Psalm II ("Why do the heathen rage . . .").
(Psalm II: "Why do the Gentiles tumult," *paraphrased by* Milton.) OBVE
Psalm III ("Lord, how are they increased that trouble me!").
(Psalm III: "Lord how many are my foes," *paraphrased by* Milton.) OBVE
Psalm VI ("O Lord rebuke me not in thine anger . . .").
(Psalm VI: "O lord, I dred, and that I did not dred," *freely ad. and expanded by* Sir Thomas Wyatt.) OBVE

Psalm VIII ("O Lord our Lord, how excellent is thy name in all the earth!").   AKE; NAWM-1; PBMP
   (Psalm VIII: "O Lord, that rul'st the human heart," *paraphrased by* Christopher Smart.) OBVE
   (Psalm VIII: "O Lorde oure governoure, howe excellent is thy name," *tr. by* Miles Coverdale.) OBVE
Psalm XI ("In the Lord put I my trust . . .").
   (Psalm XI: "Since I do trust Jehova still," *paraphrased by* Sir Philip Sidney.) OBVE
Psalm XIII ("How long wilt thou forget my O Lord . . .").
   (Psalm XIII: "How long, O Lord, shall I forgotten be?" *paraphrased by* Sir Philip Sidney.) OBVE
Psalm XVII ("Hear the right O Lord, attend unto my cry . . .").
   (Psalm XVII: "My suite is just, just lord to my suite hark," *paraphrased by* Sir Philip Sidney.) OBVE
Psalm XIX ("The Heavens declare the glory of God").   BiP; CTV (1-6); NAWM-1; OBP; OBVE, *tr. by* Miles Coverdale
   (Psalm XIX: "The heavenly frame sets forth the fame," *paraphrased by* Sir Philip Sidney.) OBVE
Psalm XXIII ("The Lord is my shepherd; I shall not want"). BiP; CTV; ExPo (1973 ed.); NAWM-1; SFF
   (Psalm XXIII: "God shepherds me," *paraphrased by* Harry H. Mayer.) SFF
   (Psalm XXIII: "Lorde is my shepherde, The; therfore can I lack nothing, *tr. by* Miles Coverdale.) ILwL, *mod. version*; OBVE
   (Psalm XXIII: "Yahweh is my shepherd," *Jerusalem Bible.*) SFF
   (Twenty-third Psalm.)  IP
Psalm XXIV ("The earth is the Lord's, and the fulness thereof"). CTV
Psalm LII ("Why boastest thou thyself in mischief, O mighty man?").
   (Psalm LII: "Tyrant, why swel'st thou thus," *paraphrased by* the Countess of Pembroke.) OBVE
Psalm LV ("Give ear to my prayer. . .").
   (Psalm LV: Exaudi, Deus: "My God most glad to look, most prone to hear," *paraphrased by* the Countess of Pembroke.) OBVE (1-4); WPE
Psalm LVIII ("Do ye indeed speak righteousness . . .").
   (Psalm LVIII: Si Vere Utique: "And call ye this to utter what is just," *paraphrased by* the Countess of Pembroke.) BoWoP; WPE
Psalm LXII ("Truly my soul waiteth . . .").
   (Psalm LXII: "Yet shall my soule in silence still," *paraphrased by* the Countess of Pembroke.) PBWP
Psalm LXXII ("Give the king thy judgments . . .").
   (Psalm LXXII: "Looke how the woods, where enterlaced trees," *paraphrased by* the Countess of Pembroke.) OBVE
Psalm LXXVIII ("Give ear, O my people, to my law . . .").
   (Psalm LXXVIII: "There where the deepe did show his sandy flore," *paraphrased by* the Countess of Pembroke.) OBVE
Psalm XC ("Lord, thou hast been our dwelling place in all generations"). DL
   (Psalm XC: "Lorde, thou hast bene oure refuge," *tr. by* Miles Coverdale.) OBVE
Psalm C ("Make a joyful noise unto the Lord, all ye lands"). CTV; OFD
Psalm CII ("Hear my prayer, O Lord, and let my cry come unto thee").  BiP
   (Psalm CII: "Lord here my prayre and let my crye passe," *paraphrased by* Sir Thomas Wyatt.) OBVE
Psalm CIII ("Bless the Lord, O my soul: and all that is within me").  CTV (1-5)
Psalm CIV ("Bless the Lord, O my soul. O Lord my God, thou art very great").  NAWM-1
Psalm CVII ("O give thanks . . .").
   "They that go down to the sea in ships, that do business in great waters," *sel.* CTV (23-31); RhR (23-30)
Psalm CXIV ("When Israel went out of Egypt . . .".
   (Psalm CXIV: "When Israel came from Egypt's coast," *paraphrased by* Christopher Smart.) OBVE

Psalm CXXI ("I will lift up mine eyes unto the hills").  ILwL
Psalm CXXVII ("Except the Lord build the house").  BiP
Psalm CXXX ("Out of the depths . . .").
   (Psalm CXXX: 'Ffrom depth off sinn and from a diepe dispaire," *paraphrased by* Sir Thomas Wyatt.) OBVE
   (Psalm CXXX: "Out of the deep have I called unto thee, O Lord.")  ILwL
Psalm CXXXIII ("Behold, how good and how pleasant . . .").
   (Psalm CXXXIII: "Beholde, how good and joyfull a thinge it is," *tr. by* Miles Coverdale.) OBVE
Psalm CXXXVII ("By the rivers of Babylon, there we sat down").  ExPo (1973 ed.); NAWM-1; OAEL-1
   (Psalm CXXXVII: "As by the streams of Babylon," *paraphrased by* Thomas Campion.) OAEL-1
   (Psalm CXXXVII: "By the rivers of Babel we sate," *The Geneva Bible.*) OAEL-1
   (Psalm CXXXVII: "By the waters of Babylon we sat downe and weapte," *tr. by* Miles Coverdale.) OBVE
   (Psalm CXXXVII: "Nigh seated where the river flows," *paraphrased by* the Countess of Pembroke.) OAEL-1
   (Psalm CXXXVII: "On the floodis of Babiloyne there we saten," *Second Wycliffite Version.*) OAEL-1
   (Psalm CXXXVII: "On the proud banks of great Euphrates' flood," *paraphrased by* Richard Crashaw.) OAEL-1
   (Psalm CXXXVII: "Sitting by the streams that glide," *paraphrased by* Thomas Carew.) OAEL-1
   (Psalm CXXXVII: "Upon the rivers of Babylon, there we sat and wept," *The Douay-Rheims Version.*) OAEL-1
   (Psalm CXXXVII: "When as we sat all sad and desolate," *paraphrased by* Francis Bacon.) OAEL-1
   (Psalm CXXXVII: "When on Euphrates' banks we sate," *paraphrased by* Sir John Denham.) OAEL-1
   (Psalm CXXXVII: "When we, our weary limbs to rest," *paraphrased by* Nahum Tate *and* Nicholas Brady.) OAEL-1
   (Psalm CXXXVII: "Whenas we sat in Babylon," *paraphrased by* Thomas Sternhold *and* John Hopkins.) OAEL-1
Psalm CXXXIX ("O Lord, thou hast searched me . . .").
   (Psalm CXXXIX: Domine, Probasti: "O Lord in me there lieth nought," *paraphrased by* the Countess of Pembroke.) OBVE (7-10); WPE
Psalm CXLVIII ("Praise ye the Lord. Praise ye the Lord from the heavens . . .").
   (Psalm CXLVIII: "Hallelujah! kneel and sing," 1-10, *paraphrased by* Christopher Smart.) OBVE
Psalm CL ("Praise ye the Lord. Praise God in his sanctuary"). CTV
   (Psalm CL: "O praise God in his holiness: praise him," *Book of Common Prayer.*) ILwL; RAE
Pshytik.   Nahum Bomze, *tr fr. Yiddish by* Gabriel Preil.   VWA
PSI.   Melvin B. Tolson.   PoBA
Psychathanasia; or, The Second Part of the Song of the Soul, *sel.* Henry More.
"World's great soul knows by protópathy, The," Bk. III. SCP-2
Psyche.   Samuel Taylor Coleridge.   MBPR; PBMP
Psyche; or, Love's Mystery, *sels.* Joseph Beaumont.   SCP-2
"All things at first was God, who dwelt alone," *fr.* Canto VI
"For as the honey of heaven's lovely hives," *fr.* Canto II.
"Stately mirror's all-enamelled case, A," *fr.* Canto V.
Psychiatrist.   Peter DeVries.   OBAL
Psychiatrist works below the cliff, The.   Loneliness.   Sandra McPherson.   AMV-80
Psychiatrists in Los Angeles.   The Frankenstein Stagger.   Arthur Lane.   PoW
Psychoanalysis of Fire, The.   John Morgan.   AAN
Psychological Dissertation.   James Boyer May.   PoW
Psychology.   Duncan Glen.   MIS
Psychology Today.   Judson Jerome.   AMV-81
Psychometrist.   James Stephens.   NoAM

Psychozoia; or, The First Part of the Song of the Soul, *sels.*
Henry More.   SCP-2
"I hear the clattering of an armèd troop," Canto III.
"There you may see the eyelids of the morn," Canto I.
Pterodactyl and Powhatan's Daughter, The.   Donald Macrae.
MS
Puberty.   Jon Wallace.   AMV-80
Puberty Rite Dance Song.   *Tr. fr. Apache Indian by* Willis
Barnstone.   BoWoP
Public Bar   D. J. Enright.   LP
Public Garden, The.   Robert Lowell.   ILP (1975 ed.); TAP
Public Gardens, The.   Alun Lewis.   PSN
Public House Cinematics.   Michael Smith.   IPM
Public-House Confidence.   Norman Cameron.   BBGO
Public Nuisance, A.   Reginald Arkell.   LiSp
Public Utterance.   Stephen Shrader.   PHC
Publisher's Party.   Phyllis McGinley.   OBAL
Puck of Pook's Hill, *sels.* Kipling.
Cities and Thrones and Powers.   NOBE; OxBTC; VLP
Harp Song of the Dane Women.   HAP
Puck's Song ("See you the ferny ride that steals").   OxBChV;
PoPle
Smuggler's Song, A.   DuDr; OxBChV; PoPle
Puckering in the speckled porcelain.   1946.   Yvonne.   AAN
Puck's Night Song.   Shakespeare.   *Fr.* A Midsummer Night's
Dream.   ECBV
("Now the hungry lion roars.")   DuDr; OBP
Puck's Song ("See you the ferny ride that steals").   Kipling.   *Fr.*
Puck of Pook's Hill.   OxBChV; PoPle
"Pudding and pie."   Greedy Jane.   *Unknown.*   ECBV; OxBChV
Puddy and the Mouse, The.   *Unknown.*   GBP
Puerto Ricans in New York, (I & II).   Charles Reznikoff.
CTBA; VoA
Pu-Heter Pu-Huligan.   *Unknown.*   ECBV
Pull in the net!   Fishing Song.   *Maori Oral Tradition, tr. by* A.
Armstrong *and* R. Ngata.   WTO
Pull my arm back, Seymour.   Seymour and Chantelle or Un Peu
de Vice.   Stevie Smith.   SBG
Pull of the Earth.   Stanley Plumly.   HeS
Pull Off Your Old Coat, *with music.   Unknown.*   RDB
Pull up the bell-flow'rs of the spring.   St. Mark.   Christopher
Smart.   *Fr.* Hymns and Spiritual Songs.   LAuP
Pull your bed aside and dig.   How to Cure Your Fever.   Thomas
Lux.   NVAP
Pulley, The.   George Herbert.   HAP; HeIP; ILP (1975 ed.);
InPK; InPS; IP; MetP; NOBE; OAEL-1; PPP
Pullin me in off the corner to wash my face an.   Black Jam for
Dr. Negro.   Mari Evans.   BPo; PoBA; Psy
Pulling Out.   Lyn Lifshin.   NeAC
Pulling the last tie rope taut, I pause.   Getting Loaded.   Jim
Thomas.   AMV-80
Pulling up in my car, I went into the cottage.   After Five Years.
Augustus Young.   BlrV
Pulpit to Be Let, A.   *Unknown.*   APAS
Pulverized Screen, The.   Edmond Jabes, *tr. fr. French by* Anthony
Rudolf.   VWA
Pumas.   George Sterling.   BPAW
Pumpkin, The.   Robert Graves.   CaYB
Pumpkin.   Valerie Worth.   CC; IWK
Pumpkin Pie.   Sharlot Hall.   WPW
Pun for Al Gelpi, A.   Jack Kerouac.   PiAM
Puna's Fragrant Glades.   Queen Lydia Liliuokalani, *tr. fr.
Hawaiian by* S. H. Elbert *and* N. Mahoe.   WTO
Punctual as bad luck.   The Family Goldschmitt.   Henri Coulette.
FF; NowV
Punctually at Christmas the soft plush.   White Christmas.   W. R.
Rodgers.   PFIr

Punishment.   *Unknown.*   TDH
Punkin Pie.   Harry Edward Mills.   PeD
Puppy.   Fred Lape.   BoAnP; GDP
Purblind walls.   Vincent Buckley.   *Fr.* Golden Builders, V.
CAAP; GAS
Purcell in many victories of his.   Bounty.   Josephine Miles.
NoAM
Pure/ Every day there's the bridge.   The Bay Bridge from
Portrero Hill.   Jack Gilbert.   NowV
Pure blood domestic, guaranteed.   The Prize Cat.   E. J. Pratt.
NoAM
Pure fasted faces draw unto this feast.   Easter Communion.
Gerard Manley Hopkins.   OFD
Pure flame of one taper fall, The.   Plato in London.   Lionel
Johnson.   VLP
Pure gold, they said in her praise.   Around Thanksgiving.   Rolfe
Humphries.   OFD
Pure products of America, The.   To Elsie.   William Carlos
Williams.   CABA (1972 ed.); CMoP (1970 ed.); InPs; NOBA
Pure spite, wanting.   View.   Christian J. Van Gell, *tr. by* Emilie
Peech *and* W. S. Di Piero.   AMV-81
Pure sun dazzled, The.   The Glazier.   Stéphane Mallarmé, *tr. by*
Keith Bosley.   OBVE
Pure? What does it mean?   Fever 103°.   Sylvia Plath.   AnMo;
CMoP (1970 ed.); NoAM; NOBA; PiAm; VGW
Pure white bodies of my friends, The.   Verigin 3.   John Newlove.
NeAC
Purer than Purest Pure, *with music.*   E. E. Cummings.   AH
Purest soul that e'er was sent, The.   Another [Epitaph on the
Lady Mary Villiers].   Thomas Carew.   CaPo
Purgatorio.   Dante.   *See* Divina Commedia.
Purgatory.   Maxine W. Kumin.   CoPAm
Purgatory.   W. B. Yeats.   CMoP (1970 ed.); ExPo (1973 ed.);
PAIC
Purified, I struggle.   Heth.   Carlos Montemayor, *tr. by* Nigel
Grant Sylvester.   AMV-81
Purist, The.   Ogden Nash.   TPo
Puritan Hacking Away at Oak, The.   Todd Gitlin.   AMV-80
Puritan on His Honeymoon, The.   Robert Bly.   FF
Puritan Poet Reel.   Vincent Buckley.   MAuV
Puritan Sonnet.   Elinor Wylie.   Wild Peaches, IV.   PAIC; SoSe
(1977 ed.)
("Down to the Puritan marrow of my bones.")   BoWoP;
VoPo
Purity.   Hayim Lenski, *tr. fr. Hebrew by* Pearl Grodzensky.
VWA
Purity/ Is obscurity.   Reflection on a Wicked World.   Ogden
Nash.   SFF
Purity in What You Do.   Harrison Fisher.   PoUp
Purple Blemish, The.   Pär Lagerkvist, *tr. fr. Swedish by* Lennart
Bruce.   AMV-81
Purple blot against the dead white door, A.   Monsieur Qui Passe.
Charlotte Mew.   SBG
Purple-blotched and red-haired.   March Sound.   Harry Thurston.
AMV-81
Purple Chaos.   Alistair Campbell.   ATNZ
Purple Cow, The.   Gelett Burgess.   CTV; FaBoCo; FaBoNo;
OBAL; PCOP
Purple horses with orange manes.   Merry-go-round.   Rachel
Field.   CTV; PCOP
Purple Indians pas de bourrée.   Lord Fluting Dreams of America
on the Eve of His Departure from Liverpool.   Paul Zimmer.
VGW
Purpose for Radishes, *sel.*   Martha Baird.
"What is the silly radish doing."   OSP
Purse-Seine, The.   Robinson Jeffers.   CMoP (1970 ed.); HAP;
NoAM; NOBA; PoIA; WeW

Pursuit. Hilda Doolittle ("H. D."). WPE

Pursuit. Robert Penn Warren. CoPAm; HAP; PPP

Pursuit from Under. James Dickey. HAP; PPP

Push hard across the sand. A Song in Time of Order 1852. Swinburne. VLP

Pushed to the Scroll. Winifred Hamrick Farrar. AMV-80

Pushing the wedge of his body. Badger. Michael Longley. IPM

Puss came dancing out of a barn. Bagpipes. *Unknown.* BBL

Pussy. *Unknown, at. to* Jane Taylor. OxBChV
    (I Love Little Pussy.) CTV; MG
    (Kindness.) BBL

Pussy-cat, pussy-cat, where have you been? Mother Goose. CTV; MG; PCOP

Pussy-kitten, pussy-cat. Cosy Cat Nap. James Kirkup. RAE

Put a rocket up the man in the moon. Nocturne, Central Park South. L. E. Sissman. NYP

Put-down Come On, The. A. R. Ammons. TT

Put down the pen. The Tale. Charles Simic. CAAP

Put Forth, O God, Thy Spirit's Might, *with music.* Howard Chandler Robbins. AH

Put forth thy leaf, thou lofty plane. Arthur Hugh Clough. EBEV

Put Hannibal i'th' scale. Hannibal. Juvenal, *tr. by* Henry Vaughan. *Fr.* Satires, X. OBVE

Put his head. Odiham. John Gray. FaBoCo

Put my hand through tv screen. Gagaku. Steve Richmond. CPA

Put My Name Down. Irwin Silber. FSW

Put off the deference that this sea compels. Beach Talk. Norman MacCaig. PoA

Put off your public faces. The Last Superstition. Sol Funaroff. SPT

Put on the skillet, put on the led. Short'nin' Bread. *Unknown.* BLSo

Put on your silks, and piece by piece. To His Mistresses. Robert Herrick. CaPo

Put things in their place. The Sky Is Blue. David Ignatow. FF; NNaP

Put your/ self out. Chasm. A. R. Ammons. OBAL

Put your arms on your back. Bird Calls. Cathleen Quirk. MMD

Put your hand in the creel. Marriage. *Unknown.* GBP

Put your hand on my heart, say that you love me as. A Betrothal. E. J. Scovell. GBL

Put your head, darling, darling, darling. Dear Dark Head [*or* Cean Dubh Deelish]. *Unknown, tr. by* Sir Samuel Ferguson. BIrV; GBL; LoAs; PFIr

Put your man down somewhere. After. Kendrick Smithyman. ATNZ

Put Your Word to My Lips. Rachel Korn, *tr. fr. Yiddish by* Seymour Mayne *and* Rivka Augenfeld. VWA

Putting in the Seed. Robert Frost. NoAM

Putting on the Style. *Unknown.* FSW

Putting out the candles. My Father after Work. Gary Gildner. AMV-80; EC

Putting the Croutons Back into the Jar. Diane Kruchkow. FAF

Putting to Sea. Louise Bogan. PoA

Puzzle faces in the dying elms. " 'Mystery Boy' Looks for Kin in Nashville." Robert Hayden. NoAM

Puzzled. Langston Hughes. *See* Harlem ("Hard on the edge of hell").

Puzzled Census Taker, The. John Godfrey Saxe. PoTa

Pygmalion. Hans Brockerhoff. AMV-80

Pygmalion. Kathryn Ruby. WBN

Pygmalion seeing these to spend their times. Ovid, *tr. by* George Sandys. *Fr.* Metamorphoses, X. OAEL-1

Pygmalion's Statue Comes to Life. Ovid, *tr. fr. Latin by* Arthur Golding. *Fr.* Metamorphoses, X. OAEL-1

Pylon for some incomplete gateway. The Monadnock. John Gould Fletcher. PoA

Pylons, The. Stephen Spender. LP; NoAM

Pyrargyrite Metal, 9. Cecília Meireles, *tr. fr. Portuguese by* James Merrill. PBWP

Pyre of My Indian Summer, The. Mani Leib, *tr. fr. Yiddish by* Keith Bosley. VWA

Pyrrha, what slender well-shap'd beau. Horace, *tr. by* Anthony Horneck. Odes, I, 5. OBVE

Pythagoras ("Pythagoras knew the world is symbols"). O. B. Hardison, Jr. PoUp

Pythagoras planned it. Why did the people stare? The Statues. W. B. Yeats. NoAM; OAEL-2; WeW

Pythagorean Razzle-Dazzle. Sid Gary. QQQ

Python, The. Hilaire Belloc. BBL; OxBChV

Python. *Yoruba Oral Tradition, tr. by* Ulli Beier. WTO

Python I should not advise, A. The Python. Hilaire Belloc. BBL; OxBChV

# Q

Q:dwo. E. E. Cummings. OBAL

Q is a quoter who'll cite. A Quoter. Oliver Herford. TDH

Qua Cursum Ventus. Arthur Hugh Clough. VLP; VPC

Quadroon mermaids, Afro angels, black saints. A Ballad of Remembrance. Robert Hayden. AmNP (1974 ed.); BPo; PoBA

Quadrupedremian Song, A. Tom Hood. FaBoNo

Quagga, The. D. J. Enright. MPo

Quai de l'Horloge. Peter Nelson. PHC

Quail and rabbit hunters with tawny hounds. Hunters in the Snow: Brueghel. Joseph Langland. WIF

Quail Walk. Heather Ross Miller. BoAnP

Quaker Graveyard in Nantucket, The. Robert Lowell. CMoP (1970 ed.); HAP; ILP (1975 ed.); NoAM; NOBA; PiAm; PPoD; TAP; UnPo (1976 ed.)
    "Empty winds are creaking and the oak, The," *sel.* UsP

Quaker Hero, Burning. Bink Noll. TCP

Quaker Lover, The, *with music. Unknown.* RDB

Quaker Widow, The. Bayard Taylor. AmVN

Quality of Mercy, The. Shakespeare. *Fr.* The Merchant of Venice, IV, i. AKE; PIM
    (Portia's Speech.) PCOP

Quality of Pain, A. Barbara D. Holender. TVo

Quality of these trees, green height, The; of the sky, shining. Shine, Republic. Robinson Jeffers. GOA

Quangle Wangle's Hat, The. Edward Lear. EBEV; PCOP

Quarrel, The. Conrad Aiken. LoAs

Quarrel, The. Diane DiPrima. NMM; RiTi

Quarrel, The. Eleanor Farjeon. FPB

Quarrel, A. John Peck. WeW

Quarrel. *Yoruba Oral Tradition, tr. by* Ulli Beier. WTO

Quarrel of the sparrows in the eaves, The. The Sorrow of Love. W. B. Yeats. NoAM; OAEL-2; PoIA; VLP

Quarrelsome Bishop, A. Walter Savage Landor. FaBoEE; OBSV

Quarry, The. W. H. Auden. *See* O What Is That Sound.

Quarry, The. Vassar Miller. WPE

Quarry Pool, The. Denise Levertov. VGW

Quarter century ago and, A. H. S. Beeney Auction Sales. David R. Pichaske. AMV-81

Quarter horse, no rider, A. Horse. Jim Harrison. BoAnP; PH

Quarter less four,/ Half twain. *Unknown.* AmFP

Quartermaster Store, The. *Unknown.* FSW

Quatrain: "Jack, eating rotten cheese, did say." *Unknown, wr. at. to* Benjamin Franklin. SoSe
(Impromptu.) NOBL
(Sampson Imitated.) FaBoEE

Quatrain: "Strictly mathematic God, A." Arthur J. Bull. HeHu

Quavering cry, A. Screech-owl? Night, Death, Mississippi. Robert Hayden. FF; VGW

Que Bonita Bandera. *Tr. fr. Spanish.* FSW

Quechua Song: When You Find Yourself Alone. *Unknown, tr. fr. Spanish by* Ruth Stephan. RRA

Queen, The. Pablo Neruda, *tr. fr. Spanish by* Donald D. Walsh. OLR

Queen, The. Kenneth Pitchford. NYP

Queen [*or* Queene] and huntress, chaste and fair. Hymn to Diana [*or* Song: To Cynthia]. Ben Jonson. *Fr.* Cynthia's Revels, V, vi. CABA (1972 ed.); HAP; HeIP; ILP (1975 ed.); Moon; NOBE; OAEL-1; PAIC; PoPle; SoSe (1977 ed.)

Queen Anne. *Unknown.* BBL

Queen Anne's Lace. June Jordan. TAP

Queen Anne's Lace. Ruthe T. Spinnanger. AATT

Queen Anne's Musicians. Thomas Hennell. FaBoTw (1975 ed.)

Queen-Ann's-Lace. William Carlos Williams. LoAs; NoAM; NOBA; TAP

Queen Bess was Harry's daughter. Stand forward partners all! The Looking Glass. Kipling. FaBoTw (1975 ed.)

Queen declares, The: "The evening wears." Lullaby for an Emigrant. Benjamin Fondane, *tr. by* Keith Bosley. VWA

Queen Elenor's Confession. *Unknown.* PeBB

Queen has lately lost a part, The. Verses Said to Be Written on the Union. Swift. APAS

Queen Jane ("Queen Jane lay in labour for six weeks and some more"). *Unknown. See* Death of Queen Jane, The.

Queen Jane sat at her window one day. The King's Dochter Lady Jean. *Unknown.* AmFP

Queen Jane was [*or* lay] in labor. The Death of Queen Jane. *Unknown.* AmFP; FSW

Queen Mab, *sel.* Shelley.
War Is the Statesman's Game, *fr.* IV. FF

Queen Mother to New Queen. Robert Graves. OBSV

Queen, my lord, is dead, The. Shakespeare. *Fr.* Macbeth, V, v. STS

Queen of Cheese. James McIntyre. PeD

Queen of Connemara, The. Francis A. Fahy. PFIr

Queen of Elfan's Nourice, The. *Unknown.* AIW

Queen of Hearts, The. *Unknown.* FSW

Queen of Hearts, The/ She made some tarts. Mother Goose. MG

Queen of Heaven. *Unknown.* OxBM

Queen of Paphos, Erycine, The. *Unknown.* GBL

Queen of the double sea, beloved of him. To Corinth. Walter Savage Landor. ILP (1975 ed.)

Queen of the Orkney Islands, The. Laura E. Richards. OSF

Queen of the silver bow!—by thy pale beam. To the Moon. Charlotte Smith. Moon

Queen she sent to look for me, The. Grenadier. A. E. Housman. TT

Queen Victoria and Me. Leonard Cohen. NoAM

Queen was in the parlour, The. Contemporary Nursery Rhyme. *Unknown.* SpRo

Queene and huntress, chaste and faire. *See* Queen and huntress. . .

Queens. J. M. Synge. GBR

Queen's Marie, The. *Unknown.* PoPle

Queen's Speech, The. Arthur Mainwaring. APAS

Queen's Wake, The, *sel.* James Hogg.
Song, The: "O! lady dear, fair is thy noon." SLP

Queer. David McCord. CaYB

Queer are the ways of a man I know. The Phantom Horsewoman. Thomas Hardy. CMoP (1970 ed.); LoAs; NOBE

Queer Fellow Named Woodin, A. Edward Bradley. TDH

Queer thing about those waters, A: there are no. Across the Bay. Donald Davie. PSN

Queer Things. Emanuel Carnevali. EAS

Quem Queritis. Albert Howard Carter. AATT

Query. Ebon Dooley. PoBA

Query. Mildred Weston. POL

Query, a question, A. The Water of Kane. *Tr. fr. Hawaiian by* N. B. Emerson. WTO

Quest. Naomi Long Madgett. BPo

Quest of Silence, The, *sel.* Christopher Brennan.
"Gray and dusty daylight flows, A." MAuV

Quest of the Sangraal, The, *sel.* Robert Stephen Hawker.
"Then saw they that the mighty Quest was won!" VLP

Question, The. James Beattie. FaBoCo

Question, A. William Cole. BoAnP

Question. Norma Craig. POL

Question, A. Robert Frost. TH

Question, The. F. T. Prince. BoLoP

Question, The. Muriel Rukeyser. IHMS

Question, The ("I dream'd that, as I wander'd by the way"). Shelley. FSFS; PoPle

Question. May Swenson. IPWM; VGW

Question, A. J. M. Synge. OxBTC; PFIr; WeW

Question. Lucille F. Travis. AATT

Question and Answer. Langston Hughes. BPo

Question Answer'd, The. Blake. *Fr.* Several Questions Answered. FaBoEE; GBL
("What is it men in women do require?") MBPR; NIL; OAEL-2

Question in a Field. Louise Bogan. SBG

Question is, The. These Two. Howard Schwartz. VWA

Question is, The: how does one hold an apple. The Gesture. George Oppen. *Fr.* Five Poems about Poetry. NNaP

Question, Is It, The? Alfred G. Bailey. AMV-81

Question not, but live and labour. Adam Lindsay Gordon. CTV

Question of Balance, A. Fay Enos. PHC

Question then, to state it first. The. Samuel Butler. *Fr.* Hudibras. NOBL

Question was an academic one, The. Tomorrows. James Merrill. OBAL

Questioning Faces. Robert Frost. NCSH

Questionnaire for Walter Mitty, A. Michael Longley. IPM

Questions [1] ("Why do you love her"). Donald Hall. FF

Questions [2] ("How is it now"). Donald Hall. FF

Questions. Dagmar Hilarova, *tr. fr. Czech by* Ewald Osers. VWA

Questions and Answers. Doris Muhringer, *tr. fr. German by* Beth Bjorklund. AMV-80

Questions of Travel. Elizabeth Bishop. NOBA

Quhen thou art careit to that cuntree. Virgil, *tr. by* Gavin Douglas. *Fr.* The Aeneid, III. OBVE

Qui Laborat, Orat. Arthur Hugh Clough. VLP; VPC

Quia Amore Langueo ("In the vale of restless mind"). *Unknown.* BoReV; NOBE; OxBM

Quick! a last poem before I go. On Rachmaninoff's Birthday. Frank O'Hara. CAPP

Quick and Bitter. Yehuda Amichai, *tr. fr. Hebrew by* Assia Gutmann. BoLoP

Quick and the Dead, The. Ilarie Voronca, *tr. fr. French by* Edouard Roditi. VWA

Quick cold hands. Dawn. Octavio Paz. TSWA

Quick, Henry, the Flit! James Schuyler. NoAM

Quick little mouse, A. Feather-Stitching. Aileen Fisher. MN

Quick night. The World Is Full of Remarkable Things. Amiri Baraka. NIL

"Quick Now, Here, Now, Always." William J. Rewak. AMV-81

Quick on my feet in those Novembers of my loneliness. A Mad Fight Song for William S. Carpenter, 1966. James Wright. LiSp

Quick sea shone, The. Sunrise at Sea. Swinburne. RhR

Quick-Step. Robert Creeley. VGW

Quick, woman, in your net. The Net. W. R. Rodgers. BoLoP; CIP

Quickly. What is being forgotten? What Is Being Forgotten. Eloise Klein Healy. GP

Quickness. Henry Vaughan. BoReV; ILP (1975 ed); NOBE; SCP-1

Quicksilver Thing. Philip Legler. TC

Quickview. Antar S.K. Mberi. SES

Quickview #2. Antar S.K. Mberi. SES

Quid Restat, *abr.* Lucius Beebe. RFM

Quid Sit Futurum Cras Fuge Quaerere. Matthew Prior. FaBoEE

Quid the Cynic's Song. Blake. *Fr.* An Island in the Moon. FaBoNo

¿Quien Sabe? Madge Morris. BPAW

Quiescent, a Person Sits Heart and Soul. Ring Lardner. OBAL

Quiet. Brian Swann. AmPA

Quiet by Hillsides in the Afternoon. Martha Lifson. AMV-80

Quiet congregation of the trees, The. The Forest of Dean. Robin Flower. PES

Quiet Days in Sutherland. Robin Fulton. MIS

Quiet deepens, The. You will not persuade. Farewell to Van Gogh. Charles Tomlinson. CMoP (1970 ed.)

Quiet domestic round proceeds, The. Domesticity. Rodney Hall. FPA

Quiet-eyed Cattle, The. Leslie Norris. PChr

Quiet faces. Bruce Holsapple. FAF

Quiet Fog, The. Marge Piercy. UnPo (1976 ed.); UsP

Quiet Glades of Eden, The. Robert Graves. BoLoP

Quiet House, The. Charlotte Mew. EBEV; SBG

Quiet Light of Flies, The. Natan Zach, *tr. fr. Hebrew by* Peter Everwine *and* Shula Starkman. VWA

Quiet, my horse, be quiet. Alexander to His Horse. Eleanor Farjeon. PH

Quiet Orderly Life, A. Michael Hogan. AAN; DNGG

Quiet Place, A. Louis Jenkins. HeS

Quiet Sun, The. James Beall. PoUp

Quiet Tide near Ardrossan, The. Charles Tennyson Turner. VPC

Quiet Town. William Stafford. MAT

Quiet until now. Mornings. Suzanne E. Berger. PCho

Quieter the people are, The. The Signboard. Robert Creeley. ConAP

Quietly at our side the dead. The Dead Men. Sophia de Mello Breyner Andresen, *tr. by* Allen Francovich. PBWP

Quills. Charlotte Gafford. AMV-81

Quilt, The. Karen Swenson. WBN

Quinquireme of Nineveh from distant Ophir. Cargoes. John Masefield. CMoP (1970 ed.); FaPo; FaPoR; ILP (1975 ed.); NOBE; WIF

Quintana Lay in the Shallow Grave of Coral. Karl Shapiro. VGW

Quip, The. George Herbert. ILP (1975 ed.); LFH; SCP-1

Quite a country, back and forth. The U.S.A. Grantland Rice. SPo

Quite Apart from the Holy Ghost. Adrian Mitchell. OBSV

Quite apropos that we should visit here. Family Plot. Sarah Singer. AMV-81

Quite horfen, fer a lark, coves on a ship. The Helbatrawss. Kingsley Amis. NOBL

Quite often, when I look out. English Train, Summer. Ralph Pomeroy. GP

Quite unexpectedly as Vasserot. The End of the World. Archibald MacLeish. CMoP (1970 ed.); HoPM (1975 ed.); ILP (1975 ed.); InPK; IP; MAT; NCSH; NoAM; NOBA; OBAL; PAIC; PBMP; PiAm; SS; TAP; TPo; VGW

Quitter, The. *Unknown.* PPM

Quitting is out of the question yet. Dispatch Number Sixty. Doug Fetherling. NeAC

Quivira. Arthur Guiterman. BPAW

"Quod Tegit Omnia." Yvor Winters. BCr

Quondam was I in my leady's grace. Sir Thomas Wyatt. GBL

Quoniam Ego in Flagella Paratus Sum. David, *sel.* William Habington.
  "Fix me on some bleak precipice." SCP-2

Quotation from Shakespeare with Slight Improvements, A. "Lewis Carroll." FaBoNo

Quotations. George Oppen. NNaP

Quotations from Charwoman Me. Robin Morgan. WBN

Quoter, A. Oliver Herford. TDH

Quoth a cat to me once: "Pray relieve." Tact. Oliver Herford. TDH

Quoth Cibber to Pope, tho' in verse you foreclose. Pope. FaBoEE.

Quoth he, My faith as adamantine. Samuel Butler. *Fr.* Hudibras. OBSV

Quoth he, to bid me not to love. Samuel Butler. *Fr.* Hudibras. NOBL

Quoth she, I wish I could prescribe your help. Rachel Speght. *Fr.* A Dream. WPE

Quoth the bookworm, "I don't care one bit." The Omnivorous Bookworm. Oliver Herford. TDH

# R

RIP. Alan Garner. BuTh

R.M.S. *Titanic, sel.* Anthony Cronin.
  "On the bog road the blackthorn flowers, the turf-stacks." BIrV

R.S.V.P. Peter Klappert. AAN

Rabbi Ben Ezra. Robert Browning. PBMP; STS

Rabbi, if a child is born with two heads. Pilpul. Rodger Kamenetz. VWA

Rabbi is before me, The. David Meltzer. *Fr.* A Midrash. GP

Rabbi of condiments. The Garlic. Bert Meyers. VWA

Rabbi Pinhas:/ From true prayers. Expounding the Torah. Louis Zukofsky. VWA

Rabbinic/ The cynic. Sandra Ruth Duguid. AATT

Rabbit, The. Alan Brownjohn. MPo

Rabbit, The. W. H. Davies. BoAnP

Rabbit, The. Philip McIntyre, Jr. AKE

Rabbit, The. *Unknown.* FaBoCo

Rabbit as [*wr.* Is] King of the Ghosts, A. Wallace Stevens. PBMP

Rabbit Catcher, The. Sylvia Plath. SBG

Rabbit crossed and dodged and turned, The. The Chase. J. V. Cunningham. LiSp; NoAM

Rabbit Foot Blues. *Unknown.* BluL
Rabbit has a charming face, The. The Rabbit. *Unknown.* FaBoCo
Rabbit Hunter, The. Robert Frost. GDP; LiSp; SPo; TH
Rabbit Leaves, The. Dennis Schmitz. NVAP
Rabbits. Dennis Schmitz. FiCP
Rabid or dog dull. Let me tell you how. A Professor's Song. John Berryman. HeIP; NoAM; NOBA
Raccoon. Kenneth Rexroth. *Fr.* A Bestiary. NNaP
Raccoon on the Road. Joseph Payne Brennan. ECBV
Raccoon Poem. Miriam Palmer. NMM
Raccoon Skeleton at Long Plain Creek. Helena Minton. FAF
Raccoon wears a black mask, The. Raccoon. Kenneth Rexroth. *Fr.* A Bestiary. NNaP
Raccoons are selectively polygamous. Raccoon Poem. Miriam Palmer. NMM
Raccoon's Got a Bushy Tail. *Unknown.* FSW
Race. Byron. Don Juan, XIV. OBP
Race Question, The. Naomi Long Madgett. BPo
Racer's Widow, The. Louise Glück. AmPA; LiSp
Racetrack, The. Jane Cooper. LoAs
Rachel. Linda Pastan. TV
Rachel. Rachel, *tr. fr. Hebrew by* N. N. VWA
Rachel and the Truth (c.1945). Yvonne. WBN
Rachel at Thirteen. Yvonne. WBN
Rachel at Twenty-three. Yvonne. WBN
Rachel Goes to the Well for Water ("Rachel stands by the mirror and plaits"). Itzik Manger, *tr. fr. Yiddish by* Ruth Whitman. VWA
Rachel's Lament. Linda Zisquit. VWA
Rachray Man, The. Moira O'Neill. PFIr
Racialism. John Blight. CAAP
Racing-Man, The. A. P. Herbert. BoAnP; PH
Racing, reckoning fingers flick. Palladas, *tr. fr. Greek by* Tony Harrison. OBVE
Racist Delicious. Lonnie L. Landrum. DNGG
Rackets around the Blue Mountain Lake, The. *Unknown.* FSW
Racoon up the 'simmon tree. The Persimmon Tree. *Unknown.* GBP
Radar. Alan Ross. FF; NowV
Radiance of Extinct Stars, The. Allan Kolski Horvitz. VWA
Radiance of that star that leans on me, The. Delay. Elizabeth Jennings. InPK; OxBTC
Radiant Heat. Rochelle Owens. WBN
Radiant Is the World Soul. Rav Abraham Isaac Kook, *tr. fr. Hebrew by* Ben Zion Bokser. VWA
Radiant Muse, my childhood's nurse. Invocation. James McAuley. GAS
Radiant soda of the seashore fashions, The. Far Rockaway. Delmore Schwartz. NoAM
Radical Creed, A. Gelett Burgess. FaBoNo
Radical in the Alligator Shirt, The. Lou Lipsitz. AMV-80
Radical War Song, A. Macaulay. OBSV
Radio. Frank O'Hara. PoA
Radio brings whole cities, The. Driving at Night. John Calvin Rezmerski. HeS
Radio exploded without a sound, The. Cruising for Burgers. George Mattingly. AcAn
Radio is teaching my goldfish Jujuitsu, The. Heavy Water Blues. Bob Kaufman. CPA
Radio Men, The. Elizabeth Jennings. FPB
Radio said, Go to your shelters, The. I'm Here. David Ignatow. GP
Radio under the Bed, The. Reed Whittemore. PoUp
Radium Therapy. Peter Dale. PMW

Raffaele Minichiello. Sandra McPherson. CAAP
Raft of *The Medusa*, The. T. E. Porter. AAN
Raftsmen, The. *Unknown.* FSW
Rag Doll to the Heedless Child, The. David Harsent. LP
Rag Time Cowboy Joe. Grant Clarke, Lewis F. Muir, *and* Maurice Abrahms. FSW
Ragged and Dirty. *Unknown.* AmFP
Ragged and gray as the salt-cedars. Windmill in March. Katharine Privett. AMV-80
Ragged-and-Tough. Not Ragged-and-Tough. *Unknown.* FaBoNo
Ragged Robin Opens, The. Miklos Radnoti, *tr. fr. Hungarian by* Emery George. AMV-80
Ragged, unheeded, stooping, meanly shod. The Poor Can Feed the Birds. John Shaw Neilson. MAuV
Ragged Wood, The. W. B. Yeats. GBL
Raggedy. *Unknown.* FSW
Raggedy Man, The. James Whitcomb Riley. OxBChV
Raid, The. William Everson. NoAM; PiAm; TCP
Rail on, poor feeble scribbler, speak of me. The Author's Reply. Sir Carr Scroope. APAS
Rail Splitting. Gary Lawless. FAF
Railing up New Jersey. Metroliner. Jack DuVall. AMV-80
Railings, The. Alan Brownjohn. LP
Railroad Bill. *Unknown.* FSW
Railroad Blues, The. *Unknown.* AmFP
Railroad Cars Are Coming, The. *Unknown.* BPAW
Railroad Corral, The. *Unknown.* FSW
Railroad look so pretty. Two Hoboes. *Unknown.* WTO
Railroad Reverie. E. R. Young. ECBV
Railroad Song, *sel.* Thomas Holley Chivers. "Clitta, clatta, clatta, clatter." PeD
Railroad suddenly hops out of the, A. Machu Picchu, Peru. Fred Red Cloud. VW
Railroad to Hell. *Unknown.* VLP
Railroad track is miles away, The. Travel. Edna St. Vincent Millay. PPM
Railroad yard in San Jose. In Back of the Real. Allen Ginsberg. HeIP; InPK; UsP
Railroader for Me, A. *Unknown.* AmFP
Rails rise through dimness. Three Sunrises from Amtrak. Florence Dolgorukov. AMV-81
Railway Bridge of the Silvery Tay, The. William McGonagall. PeD; PPoD
Railway Junction, The. Walter de la Mare. OxBTC
Railway official at Crewe, A. The Proud Engine. *Unknown.* TDH
Rain, The ("The rain it raineth every day [*or* on the just]"). *At. to* Lord Bowen. ECBV; FaBoCo
(Just and Unjust.) PoPle
(Rain it Raineth, The.) OSF
Rain, The. Robert Creeley. CAPP; ConAP; UsP; VGW
Rain, The. W. H. Davies. FSFS; OxBTC
Rain. Emanuel diPasquale. InPK; POL
Rain. Margiad Evans. OBW
Rain. Haim Guri, *tr. fr. Hebrew by* Mark Elliott Shapiro. VWA
Rain. Lance Henson. VoR
Rain. Vachel Lindsay. CMoP (1970 ed.)
Rain. Sister Mary Lucina. AMV-80
Rain. Paul Murray. BIrV
Rain. "Seumas O'Sullivan." PFIr
Rain. Peter Sears. AMV-80
Rain. Shelley. POL
Rain. Adrian Keith Smith. AKE
Rain. Robert Louis Stevenson. CTV; ECBV

Rain. Edward Thomas. OxBTC

Rain. Hone Tuwhare. ATNZ

Rain, The (" 'Twas in Koolau I met with the rain"). *Tr fr. Hawaiian by* N. B. Emerson. WTO

Rain, / Million-footed requiem of the rain. Atavism. Richard Lake. NCSH

Rain. A heavy mane. Marina Tsvetayeva, *tr. by* Paul Schmidt. *Fr. The Daughter of Jairus.* BoWoP

Rain all over the cornfields. Butterfly Maidens. Lahpu, *tr. by* Natalie Curtis. WTO

Rain Chant. Louis Mertins. BPAW

Rain Down. Mary Ellen Solt. BoWoP

Rain drifts forever in this place. The Falls of Glomach. Andrew Young. MS

Rain fails, The; the rice birds come out. Easter. Stephen Shrader. PHC

Rain falls and then vanishes, The. A Green Refrain. Avraham Huss, *tr. by* Mark Elliott Shapiro. VWA

Rain falls in my face, The. Rain-in-the-Face. Mary Crow. PH

Rain Falls. It Dries. Miklos Radnoti, *tr. fr. Hungarian by* Emery George. AMV-81

Rain fell this Memorial Day. Grandfather. Katie Louchheim. PoUp

Rain had fallen, the Poet arose, The. The Poet's Song. Tennyson. VLP

Rain has been reciting, The. Fishermen. Gabriel Preil, *tr. by* Betsy Rosenberg. VWA

Rain Has Fallen on the History Books. David Rosenberg. VWA

Rain has filled, The. Jack Kerouac. *Fr.* Some Western Haikus. VoA

Rain has passed, The. Birth. Amir Gilboa, *tr. by* Stephen Mitchell. VWA

Rain in Summer. Longfellow. FSFS

Rain in the city! City Rain. Rachel Field. ECBV

Rain in the Desert. John Gould Fletcher. Arizona Poems, VI. BPAW; NCSH

Rain-in-the-Face. Mary Crow. PH

Rain is over, The. Birth. Amir Gilboa, *tr. by* Robert Mezey *and* Shula Starkman. OFD

Rain is plashing on my sill, The. The Unknown Dead. Henry Timrod. AmVN

Rain is raining all around, The. Quick, Henry, the Flit! James Schuyler. NoAM

Rain is raining all around, The. Rain. Robert Louis Stevenson. CTV; ECBV

Rain it raineth every day [*or* on the just], The. The Rain [*or* Just and Unjust]. *At. to* Lord Bowen. ECBV; FaBoCo; OSF; PoPle

Rain, it streams on stone and hillock, The. A. E. Housman. CMoP (1970 ed.)

Rain, lean down. Hopi Prayer. Charles Beghtol. BPAW

Rain Magic Song. *Tr. fr. Tewa Indian by* H. J. Spinden. WTO

Rain makes little cuts on the window, The. Dialogues 4 1 Voice Only. Doug Fetherling. NeAC

Rain, midnight rain, nothing but the wild rain. Rain. Edward Thomas. OxBTC

Rain of a night and a day and a night, The. After Rain. Edward Thomas. NCSH

Rain of London pimples, The. London Rain. Louis MacNeice. HeIP

Rain of Rites, A. Jayanta Mahapatra. PoA

Rain of the white valley the clear rain, The. June Rain. W. S. Merwin. PHC

Rain on a Grave. Thomas Hardy. LoAs

Rain on a night like this. On a Night like This. Jody Bolz. PoUp

Rain on a spring day. Spring Rain. Issa, *tr. by* Harold G. Henderson. NIL

Rain on the far tip of the grove. Scattered Leaves. Lance Henson. VoR

Rain on the Roof. Janet Frame. ATNZ

Rain Poem. Elizabeth J. Coatsworth. ECBV

Rain Quietude. Gary Kissick. PHC

Rain! rain!/ For the growing grain. A Hopi Prayer. Harrison Conrard. BPAW

Rain, rain, go to Spain. *Unknown.* MG

Rain Rain on the Splintered Girl. Ishmael Reed. PoBA

Rain, said the first, as it falls in Venice. Song Tournament: New Styles. Louis Untermeyer. OBAL

Rain screws up its face, The. Rain. Adrian Keith Smith. AKE

Rain seeps through the olives. Sabbath. Jean Burden. AMV-81

Rain set early in tonight, The. Porphyria's Lover. Robert Browning. AnMo; CABA (1972 ed.); ExPo (1973 ed.); HAP; ILP (1975 ed.); IP; LoAs; PoIA; STS; TT

Rain Sleets Flat. Besmilr Brigham. Psy

Rain smell comes with the wind. Love Poem. Leslie Silko. UnPo (1976 ed.); VoR

Rain Straight Down. Samuel Makidemewabe, *tr. fr. Cree Indian by* Howard Norman. TC

Rain sweeps in as the gale begins to blow. Wet Day. James McAuley. MAuV

Rain to the Tribe. Al-Khansa, *tr. fr. Arabic by* Willis Barnstone *and* Tony Nawfal. BoWoP

Rain touches your face just at daylight. Sleeping on the Sisters Land. William Stafford. CNW

Rain Trip. Diane Wakoski. CABA (1972 ed.)

Rain was like a little mouse, The. Rain Poem. Elizabeth J. Coatsworth. ECBV

Rain was raining cheerfully, The. The Vulture and the Husbandman. A. C. Hilton. FaBoCo

Rain, with a silver flail. Whale. William Rose Benét. EcS

Rainbow, The. Walter de la Mare. CTV

Rainbow. Robert Huff. CoPAm

Rainbow. Liz Lochhead. MIS

Rainbow, The. Christina Rossetti. OxBChV ("Boats sail on the rivers.") CTV

Rainbow, The ("Khwa! Ye! O! Rainbow, O rainbow!"). *Unknown, tr. fr. Gabon Pygmy.* AKE

Rainbow, The ("Yonder, yonder see the fair rainbow"). *Tr. fr. Hopi Indian by* Natalie Curtis. WTO

Rainbow, The. Wordsworth. *See* My Heart Leaps Up When I Behold.

Rainbow at Night. *Unknown.* ECBV

Rainbow stands red o'er the ocean, The. *Tr. fr. Hawaiian by* N. B. Emerson. WTO

Rainbows all lie crumpled on these hills, The. The Painted Hills of Arizona. Edwin Curran. BPAW

Raingatherer. Franklin Brainard. HeS

Rainier. Jim Tollerud. VoR

Rain's all right. The boys who physic. Biography of Southern Rain. Kenneth Patchen. VGW

Rains, already old, The. Okkur Macatti, *tr. fr. Tamil by* A. K. Ramanujan. PBWP

Rains for the Harvest. *Tr. fr. Tewa Indian by* H. J. Spinden. WTO

Rain's grey buckshot spatters the windshield. Stopped in Memphis. Steven Bauer. AMV-80

Rains on the Island. Gabriel Preil, *tr. fr. Hebrew by* Robert Friend. VWA

Rain's unassuaging fountains multiply. The Waking Bird Refutes. Allen Curnow. ATNZ

Rainwalkers, The. Denise Levertov. CTBA; PPP

Rainy mid-morning. Haiku, for Cinnamon. Lillie D. Chapin. PH

Rainy Morning. Sotero Rivera-Avilés, *tr. fr. Spanish by* Julio Marzán. InW

Rainy morning. Don't get up. Don't even smoke. On the Hazards of Smoking. Leah Goldberg, *tr. by* Bernhard Frank. AMV-81

Rainy Mountain Cemetery. N. Scott Momaday. CDW

Rainy Night at the Writers' Colony. Josephine Jacobsen. TAP

Rainy Pleiads Wester, The. A. E. Housman. BoLoP; NoAM

Rainy skies, misty mountains. Fifty. Kenneth Rexroth. TAP

Rainy Summer, The. Alice Meynell. OxBTC; SBG

Raise a "Rucus" To-Night. *Unknown.* BPo; FSW; TAP

Raise Me Up, Lord. Miguel de Guevara, *tr. fr. Spanish by* Samuel Beckett. PBMP

Raise the light a little, Jim. Will Carleton. *Fr.* Johnny Rich. PeD

Raise the race raise the rays the raze raise it race raise. Part of the Doctrine. Amiri Baraka. PiAm

Raise the Shade. E. E. Cummings. VGW

Raisin, The. Donald Hall. TAP

Raisin Bread. Lee Blair. TDH

Raising Money. Carla Eugster. PoUp

Raising of Lazarus, The. Lucille Clifton. CNA

Raising our glasses, smilingly. Libation. Denise Levertov. GP

Raising the blind, she said. The Green Room. Paul Mills. MIS

Raising the Flag. Gerald Vizenor. VoR

Raisins and Nuts. Charles Reznikoff. VWA

Raison d'Etre. Oliver Pitcher. AmNP (1974 ed.)

Raja, my heart is mad for you. My Heart Burns for Him. *Gond Oral Tradition, tr. by* V. Elwin *and* S. Hivale. WTO

Rake. Dorothy Una Ratcliffe. BoAnP; GDP

Raleigh Was Right. William Carlos Williams. NoAM

Rally. Janet Kauffman. TC

Ram came last, The. Isaac. Haim Guri, *tr. by* Naomi Tauber *and* Howard Schwartz. VWA

Ram, the Bull, the Heavenly Twins, The. The Zodiac Rhyme. *Unknown.* GBP

Ramble, The: An Anti-heroic Poem, *much abr.* Alexander Radcliffe. SCP-2

Ramble on What in the World Why. Ralph Gustafson. AMV-81

Rambling, Gambling Man. Gil Houston. FSW

Ram's Horn, The. John Hewitt. BIrV

Ramshackles, archipelagoes, loose constellations. The Unifying Principle. A. R. Ammons. NOBA

Ran out of tear gas and became panicky. Kent State, May 4, 1970. Paul Goodman. MAT; TSWA

Rana, I know you gave me poison. Mirabai, *tr. fr. Hindi by* Willis Barnstone *and* Usha Nilsson. BoWoP

Rana, why do you treat me as your enemy? Mirabai, *tr. fr. Hindi by* Willis Barnstone *and* Usha Nilsson. BoWoP

Ranch, The. Lawrence P. Spingarn. PoW

Ranch at Twilight. *Unknown.* BPAW

Ranch in the Coulee, The. Gwendolen Haste. WPW

Rancher, The. Keith Wilson. GP

Ranchers. Maurice Lesemann. BPAW

Ranchers are selling their wheat early this year, The. Bunch Grass #37. Robert Sund. NU

Ranching country. Crossing West Texas (1966). Kell Robertson. TAT

Random Generation of English Sentences; or, The Revenge of the Poets. William Jay Smith. OBAL

Range-finding. Robert Frost. CABA (1972 ed.); NIL; NoAM; PPoD

Range in the Desert, The. Randall Jarrell. NOBA

Range's filled up with farmers and, The. The Old Cowboy's Lament. Robert V. Carr. BPAW

Rannoch, by Glencoe. T. S. Eliot. Landscapes, IV. BiP

Ransi-Tansi-Tay. *Unknown.* PoPle

Ransomed from darkness and released in Time. Edwin Muir. *Fr.* Variations on a Time Theme. NoAM

Ransomed Spirit to Her Home, The, *with music.* William B. Tappan. AH

Rant Block. Michael McClure. EAS

Rantin Dog the Daddie o't, The. Burns. PPP

Rantin Laddie, The. *Unknown.* AmFP

Rape. Tom Pickard. FaBoTw (1975 ed.)

Rape. Adrienne Rich. GP; TT

"Rape?" he says. Father of the Victim. Rae Ballard. AMV-80

Rape of Lucrece, The, *sels.* Thomas Heywood.
 "Come, list and hark! the bell doth toll." SCP-2
 "Pack, clouds, away, and welcome, day!" GBL
 (Love's Good-morrow.) LoAs

Rape of Lucrece, The, *sels.* Shakespeare.
 "From the besieged Ardea all in post." LFH
 "Mis-shapen Time, copesmate of ugly Night." OAEL-1
 Outcry upon Opportunity, An. NOBE

Rape of the Lock, The. Pope. AnMo; BiP; CABA (1972 ed.); HAP; ILP (1975 ed.); OAEL-1
 *Sels.*
 "Close by those meads for ever crowned with flow'rs," *fr.* III. OBSV
 Lock, The, *fr.* V. Moon
 Toilet, The, *fr.* I. NOBE
 (Belinda's Morning.) ExPo (1973 ed.)
 Voyage on the Thames, The, *fr.* II. NOBE
 ("Not with more glories, in th' etherial plain.") EBEV

Rapidly cruising or lying on the air there is a bird. The Frigate Pelican. Marianne Moore. Psy

Rapids shake the low hung limbs like hair. Where Mission Creek Runs Hard for Joy. Richard Hugo. CNW

Rapier of Treason, A. *Tr. fr. Arabic by* Willis Barnstone. BoWoP

Rapist, The. Stephen Dunn. POL

Rapparees. Richard Murphy. *Fr.* The Battle of Aughrim. BIrV

Rapping Along with Ronda Davis. James Cunningham. JB

Rapping with One Million Carabaos in the Dark. Al Robles. CPA

Rapture, A. Thomas Carew. CaPo; LoAs; OAEL-1; SCP-2

Rapture. Randolph Carlson. AMV-80

Rapunzel. Anne Sexton. RiTi

Rapunzel, Rapunzel. Mark Van Doren. AIW

Rare, crystalline and cloudless. After the Locust. Rene Gascou. PoW

Rare News. Nicholas Breton. NIL

Rare temples thou hast seen, I know. The Fairy Temple; or, Oberon's Chapel. Robert Herrick. CaPo

Rare Willie Drowned in Yarrow. *Unknown.* AIW; GBP; PeBB

Raree Show, A. Stephen College. APAS

Rarely, rarely, comest thou. Song. Shelley. MBPR

Rarity. Ralph Robin. PoUp

Raspberries. Doug Flaherty. HeS

Raspberries. Laurence Lerner. EBEV

Raspberries splash, redly. What He Says. Robert Wallace. CoPAm

Raspberry in the Pudding, The. Philip O'Connor. EAS

Rasslers, The. William D. Barney. LiSp

Rat, The. W. H. Davies. OBW; OxBTC

Rat,/ pearl,/ onion,/ honey. Homer, *tr. by* Christopher Logue. *Fr.* The Iliad, XIX. TwMBP

Rat and the Elephant, The. La Fontaine, *tr. fr. French by* Marianne Moore. OBVE

Rat Fever: History as Hallucination. Michael S. Harper. NW

Rat is in the trap, it is in the trap, The. Song of a Rat. Ted Hughes. CMoP (1970 ed.)

Rat Riddles. Carl Sandburg. SO

Rat-a-tat-tat. The Drummer. Anne Robinson. PCOP

Ratcatcher's Daughter, The. *Unknown.* GBP

"Rather dead than spotted"; and believe it. Then the Ermine. Marianne Moore. PoA

Rather notice, mon cher. To a Solitary Disciple. William Carlos Williams. VGW

Rather slender. Rather tiny. Emily Dickinson. Inger Hagerup, *tr. by* Harold P. Hanson. AMV-81

Rather tired at the Philadelphia airport. The Philadelphia Airport. Ron H. Bayes. AAN

Ration Card, The. Liz Sohappy Bahe. CDW

Rationalists, wearing square hats. Wallace Stevens. *Fr.* Six Significant Landscapes, VI. PoIA

Rats. Walter de la Mare. BoAnP

Rats Away! *Unknown.* OxBM

Rats, Ducks, Dogs, Cats, Pigs. *Unknown. See* Three Young Rats.

Rattan bed, paper netting. I wake from morning sleep. Li Ch'ing-chao, *tr. fr. Chinese by* Willis Barnstone *and* Sun Chu-chin. BoWoP

Rattler, Alert. Brewster Ghiselin. HAP;WeW

Rattler was a good old dog. Old Rattler. *Unknown.* FSW

Rattlesnake, The. Robert Wrigley. AMV-80

Rattlesnakes have begun to come out, The. Snakes. Peter Wild. AmPA; GP

Rattling his orange cartons. The Dream of Fixing Things. Arthur Smith. CPA

Rav, The/ of Northern White Russia declined. Illustrious Ancestors. Denise Levertov. NoAM; NOBA; VGW

Ravaged Villa, The. Herman Melville. NOBA; PiAm

Raven, The. Poe. NOBA; PiAm; TAP

Raven, The. E. A. Robinson, *after the Greek of* Nicarchus. FaBoEE; OBAL

Raven/Moon. Anita Endrezze Probst. VoR

Raven sat upon a tree, A. The Sycophantic Fox and the Gullible Raven. Guy Wetmore Carryl. PBMP

Raven Visits Rawhide, The. *Unknown.* BPAW

Ravenna. David Ray. HeS

Ravine, The. James Applewhite. AMV-80

Raving warre, begot. Thomas Campion. AAS

Ravished arms. Boy in the Roman Zoo. Archibald MacLeish. NCSH

Raw Freedom. Arthur Lerner. PoW

Ray. Otto Orban, *tr. fr. Hungarian by* Emery George. VWA

Ray Charles. Sam Cornish. CNA; NVAP

Ray Charles is the black wind of Kilimanjaro. Blues Note. Bob Kaufman. CNA; PoBA

"Ray-hee-nah!" Aztec Figurine. John Beecher. GP

Ray John. Honky. Charles Cooper. PoBA

Raya Brenner. Pinhas Sadeh, *tr. fr. Hebrew by* Gabriel Preil *and* Howard Schwartz. VWA

Raziel. Yvan Goll, *tr. fr. French by* Anthony Rudolf. VWA

Razors pain you. Résumé. Dorothy Parker. DL; InPK; OBAL; SS

Razorsharp wind, A. Valentine. Len Gasparini. NeAC

Razzle dazzle maggots are summary, The. Easter. Frank O'Hara. EAS

Re. Vito Hannibal Acconci. PAIC

Reach for arrows of falling light. A man once sang. Falling Moon. Roberta Hill. CDW

Reach like you never reached before past Night's somber robes. Tauhid. Askia Muhammad Touré. PoBA

Reach of Silence, The. Charles Black. AMV-81

Reach of Winter, The. Jenne Andrews. HeS

Reach, with your whiter hands, to me. To the Water Nymphs, Drinking at the Fountain. Robert Herrick. CaPo; ILP (1975 ed.)

Reaching our deep exquisite splendor. Haying. Heather Banks. PoUp

Re-act for Action ("Re-act to Animals"). Don L. Lee. BPo

Reactionary Poet, The. Ishmael Reed. CNA

Read me a lesson, muse, and speak it loud. Sonnet Written upon Ben Nevis. Keats. MBPR

Read not Milton, for he is dry; no Shakespeare. Proverbial Philosophy: Of Reading. Charles Stuart Calverley. FaBoCo

Read, sweet, how others strove, *with music.* Emily Dickinson. AH

Read yr/ exile. A Poem for a Poet. Don L. Lee. PoBA

Reader, behold! this monster wild. Infant Innocence. A. E. Housman. FaBoNo; NOBL

Reader, beneath this turf I lie. Thomas Brown. FaBoEE

Reader, I was born and cried. Epitaph on the Fart in the Parliament House. John Hoskyns. FaBoEE

Reader, I would not have thee mistake. His Own Epitaph, When He Was Sick. John Hoskyns. FaBoEE

Reader, pass on, nor idly waste your time. In Peterborough Churchyard. Paulus Silentiarius, *tr. fr. Greek.* FaBoEE; NOBL

Reader, stay,/ And if I had no more to say. An Epitaph on Master Philip Gray. Ben Jonson. FaBoEE

Readers of the *Boston Evening Transcript.* The *Boston Evening Transcript.* T. S. Eliot. InPK; PSN

Reading, The. Eve Triem. PoW

Reading a Medal. Terence Tiller. FaBoTw (1975 ed.)

Reading about Machado. Facts. Ken Smith. TwMBP

Reading and Talking. Louis Zukofsky. VGW

Reading Faust. Judah Goldin. AMV-81

Reading how even the Swiss had thrown the sponge. Beyond the Alps. Robert Lowell. NOBA; PiAm

Reading in Fall Rain. Robert Bly. GP

Reading in Li Po. After the Last Dynasty. Stanley Kunitz. TAP

Reading Indian Poetry. Ramona Wilson. VoR

Reading Lesson, The. Richard Murphy. IPM

Reading Myself. Robert Lowell. TAP

Reading Room, The New York Public Library. Richard Eberhart. GP; NYP

Reading the shorthand on a barber's sheet. The Barber. Roy Fuller. NoAM

Reading through your work tonight. Negative Passage. Michael Newman. PoA

Reading Time: 1 Minute 26 Seconds. Muriel Rukeyser. PBWP

Reading Today's Newspaper. Steve Abbott. AMV-80

Reading Walt Whitman. Calvin Forbes. PoBA

Readings of History. Adrienne Rich. ConAP

Ready. Lynn Strongin. RiTi

Ready we stand in San Juan town. Rain Magic Song. *Tr. fr. Tewa Indian by* H. J. Spinden. WTO

Readymade. John Perreault. EAS

Real Jane Flanders, The. Jane Flanders. PoUp

Real Life. Ted Berrigan. NoAM

Real Muse, The. Fred Muratori. AMV-81

Real Muse, The. Tom Scott. PoA

Real Old Mountain Dew. *Unknown.* FSW

Real People Loves One Another, The. Rob Penny. CNA; PoBA

Real Question Calling for Solution, A. Robert Penn Warren. PPP

Real Thing, The. Ronald Wallace. AMV-81

Realities. Shirley Kaufman. MIT

Really, what a shocking scene! A Man of Experience. Laoiseach Mac an Bhaird, *tr. by* Frank O'Connor. PFIr

Realm of Touching, The. Alan Bold. MS

Reaper, The. L. H. Allen. MAuV

Reapers. Mathilde Blind. SBG; WPE

Reapers. Jean Toomer. BPo; HAP; InPK; NoAM; PoBA; PPP

Reaping. Amy Lowell. SBG

Rear-Guard, The. Siegfried Sassoon. NoAM

Rearmament. Robinson Jeffers. PSN

Rearrangement for the Brain. Gary Margolis. CoPAm

Rearranging My Body. Cleopatra Mathis. AAN

Reason, The. Gwendolen Haste. WPW

Reason. Josephine Miles. InPK; NCSH; NoAM; PoIA; PPoD; SS; TAP

Reason, The/ we got rid. Modern Romance. William J. Harris. GP

Reason and Nature. J. V. Cunningham. PiAm

Reason and Religion. Dryden. *Fr.* Religio Laici. BoReV ("Dim as the borrowed beams of moon and stars.") OAEL-1

Reason for Not Writing Orthodox Nature Poetry. John Wain. PAIC

Reason I am leaning over, The. Ngh. R. S. Themes. UsP

Reason I fall apart easily. The. The Stained Glass Woman. Cynthia MacDonald. AAN

Reason I Stay on Job So Long. *Unknown.* GBP

Reason is our soul's left hand, faith her right. To the Countess of Bedford. John Donne. PAIC

Reason of Numbers, A. Josephine Jacobsen. IPWM

Reasonable Affliction, A. Matthew Prior. PoIA

Reasons. Thomas James. PoA

Reasons. Tom McGrath. SLP

Reasons for Attendance. Philip Larkin. BiP; NowV; OBP

Reasons for Music. Archibald MacLeish. PiAm

Reb Hanina. Paul Raboff. VWA

Reb of ruins My father. Zealot without a Face. Charles Dobzynski, *tr. by* Anita Barrows. VWA

Rebecca. Joseph Eliyia, *tr. fr. Greek by* Rae Dalven. VWA

Rebecca, Who Slammed Doors for Fun and Perished Miserably. Hilaire Belloc. NOBL; SO

Rebecca's Hymn. Sir Walter Scott. *Fr.* Ivanhoe, *ch.* 40. PIM

Rebecca's maid: a girl come from afar. Jacob and Esau. Else Lasker-Schüler, *tr. by* Rosemarie Waldrop. BoWoP

Rebel, The. Mari Evans. AmNP (1974 ed.); IHMS; PoBA; SoS; TPo

Rebel, The. Innes Randolph. OBAL (Good Old Rebel, The.) FSW

Rebel as the betrayed. Post Alcoholum Tristis. James Liddy. IMP

Rebel Girl, The. Joe Hill. FSW

Rebel poets, who've given vicar aid. In Poets' Defence. John Wheelwright. SPT

Rebel Scot, The, *sels.* John Cleveland. "Lord! what a goodly thing is want of shirts." OBSV "Nature herself doth Scotchmen beasts confess." OBSV "Ring the bells backward; I am all on fire." PeD

Rebellion was in her character. My Mother. Alistair Campbell. ATNZ

Rebels from Fairy Tales. Hyacinthe Hill. SO

Rebel's Progress. Tom Earley. OBW

Rebirth. Antonio Machado, *tr. fr. Spanish by* Robert Bly. NU

Rebirth. A. D. Winans. CPA

Rebolushinary X-mas. Carolyn M. Rodgers. JB

Recalling War. Robert Graves. CMoP (1970 ed.); NoAM; OAEL-2; OBP

Recantation Illustrated in the Story of the Mad Ox. Samuel Taylor Coleridge. MBPR

Receipt for the Vapours. Lady Mary Wortley Montagu. PBWP

Receive, dear friend, the truths I teach. Horace, *tr. by* William Cowper. Odes, II, 10. OBVE

"Receive Thy Sight." Bryant. PIM

Recently I heard a friend was mad. First Lecture. James Whitehead. CoPAm

Reception, The. June Jordan. NMM

Recessional. Kipling. BLSH, *with music*; BTTM; CABA (1972 ed.); CTV; FaPo; FaPoR; ILP (1975 ed.); NOBE; UnPo (1976 ed.); VLP

Recessional. Thomas MacGreevy. CIP

Recipe. Albert Goldbarth. VWA

Recipe. Bobbi Katz. CTV

Recipe for an Ocean in the Absence of the Sea. Richard Howard. TAP

Recipe for Toothache. *Unknown.* SCP-2

Recipe: To Mak a Ballant. Alexander Scott. MS

Reciprocity. John Drinkwater. PoA

Reciprocity. Vassar Miller. IHMS

Recital. John Updike. OBAL; OSP

Recklessly/ I cast myself away. Izumi Shikibu, *tr. fr. Japanese by* Edwin A. Cranston. PBWP

Reckoning, The. Alice Friman. AMV-81

Reckoning, The. Theodore Roethke. PoA

Reckoning, The. Robert W. Service. BBGO

Reckoning A. M. Thursday. Doris Turner. JB

Reclaimed Area. Jon Silkin. NoAM

Reclining Figure. Donald Hall. ConAP

Recluse. Aldo Camerino, *tr. fr. Italian by* Anita Barrows. VWA

Recluse, The; or, Home at Grasmere. Wordsworth. MBPR "On man, on nature, and on human life," *sel.* OAEL-2; PoIA

Recognition, The. Denise Levertov. VGW

Recognition. Georgette Perry. AMV-80

Recognitions, The: Seedtime. Rosemary Christoph. UsP

Recollection, A. John Peale Bishop. LoAs; PPoD

Recollection. Dorothy Donnelly. NCSH

Recollection. Marilyn R. Mumford. AMV-80

Recollection of First Love. William Soutar. SLP

Recollections of "Lalla Rookh." John Townsend Trowbridge. OBAL

Recollections of the Arabian Nights. Tennyson. VLP

Reconcilable Differences. Roger Sauls. AMV-81

Reconciliation. C. Day Lewis. NoAM

Reconciliation. Else Lasker-Schüler, *tr. fr. German by* Robert Alter. PBWP

Reconciliation. David Rosenmann-Taub, *tr. fr. Spanish by* Charles Guenther. VWA

Reconciliation. Walt Whitman. HAP

Reconnaissance. Arna Bontemps. AmNP (1974 ed.); BPo

Record Stride, A. Robert Frost. TT

Record with deep regret. Provincial Obituary. Michael Coady. IPM

Recovery. Julie Ball. PMW

Recovery, *sel.* Mona Van Duyn. Memory, A. RiTi

Recovery Room, The: Lying-in. Helen Chasin. IHMS

Recruit, The. A. E. Housman. FaPoR

Recruiting Drive. Charles Causley. OxBTC

Recruits, The. Ian Hamilton. NoAM

Rector's pallid neighbor at The Firs, The. The Villagers and Death. Robert Graves. HeIP

Recuerdo. Edna St. Vincent Millay. CTBA; NoAM; PoA; PPM; TAP

Recuerdo, *sel.* Tennessee Williams.
Paper Lantern, The. CTBA

Red and Blue a property, The. Red and Blue Noon. Morty
Sklar. EC

Red and blue and delicate green. *Unknown.* GBP

Red and Blue Noon. Morty Sklar. EC

Red ants in a bamboo—the passion. *Malay Oral Tradition, tr. by*
R. J. Wilkinson *and* R. O. Winstedt. WTO

Red Apple Juice. *Unknown.* FSW

Red as the guardroom lamp. Heartbreak Camp. Roy Campbell.
OxBTC

Red Beauty. *Gond Oral Tradition, tr. by* V. Elwin *and* S. Hivale.
WTO

Red Bird. *Unknown.* FSW

Red brick in the suburbs, white horse on the wall. Ballad to a
Traditional Refrain. Maurice James Craig. BIrV

Red brick monastery in, The. The Semblables William Carlos
Williams. ILP (1975 ed.); NOBA

Red Butte in Autumn. Peggy Simson Curry. WPW

Red carpet-ing, The. While Cecil Snores: Mom Drinks Cold
Milk. James Cunningham. JB

Red Cloud. John G. Neihardt. BPAW

Red cold. Haiku. José Juan Tablada, *tr. by* Samuel Beckett.
PBMP

Red Dawn in the East, A. Norman Macleod. SPT

Red Dress, The. James Bertolino. HeS

Red Dust. Philip Levine. NNaP

Red Eagle. Janet Campbell Hale. UsP

Red Earth. Alice Corbin. WPW

Red Eyes Lick the Night. T. L. Kryss. EC

Red eyes of rabbits, The. The Springtime. Denise Levertov.
ConAP

Red Flag, The. Jim Connell. FSW; VLP

Red flag is up, The. We Meet in the Lives of Animals. Peter
Everwine. NNaP

Red Flowers. Tanya Felix. PHC

Red fool, my laughing comrade. To a Comrade in Arms. Alun
Lewis. FaBoTw (1975 ed.)

Red for danger and for rage. No Meaning. Terence Brame.
RAE

Red fox, the vixen, The. Abnegation. Adrienne Rich. WPE

Red Glow in the Sky, A. Alexander Blok, *tr. fr. Russian by* Jon
Stallworthy *and* Peter France. OBVE

Red Haired Man's Wife, The. James Stephens. PPM

Red Hanrahan's Song about Ireland. W. B. Yeats. CMoP (1970
ed.)

Red head, red head. Blackbird's Song. *Unknown.* GBP

Red-Herring. D. H. Lawrence. NoAM

Red Herring, The. George MacBeth. SO

Red Herring, The. *Unknown.* FaBoNo

Red Iron Ore. *Unknown.* FSW

Red is a sunset. What Is Red? Mary O'Neill. FPB

Red is death, for people who are dying. Colours. Frances
Evans. RAE

Red lips are not so red. Greater Love. Wilfred Owen. CMoP
(1970 ed.); ExPo (1973 ed.); NoAM; OBP; PSN

Red lotus incense fades on/ the jewelled curtain. Li Ch'ing-chao,
*tr. fr. Chinese by* Kenneth Rexroth. BoWoP

Red Man of the South, The. Eliza R. Snow. WPW

Red Man of the West, The. Eliza R. Snow. WPW

Red Movie. John Tranter. CAAP

Red on sun sky sail. Six Eagles. Thomas Peacock. VoR

Red, Red Rose, A. Burns. BiP; BoLoP; CABA (1972 ed.); FF;
GBL; HAP; ILP (1975 ed.); IPWM; LAuP; NIL; NOBE;
OAEL-1; OBP; OLR; PAIC; PoIA; SLP; SoSe; WIF
(My Love Is like a Red, Red Rose.) FSW; PCOP

(My Luve Is like a Red, Red Rose.) HoPM (1975 ed.); IP
(O, My Luve Is like a Red, Red Rose.) InPS; UsP

Red river, red river. Virginia. T. S. Eliot. Landscapes, II. BiP

Red River Valley. *Unknown.* BLSH, *with music;* BLSo, *with
music;* BPAW; FSW

Red Robin, The. John Clare. RAE

Red Rock Ceremonies. Anita Endrezze Probst. CDW; VoR

Red Rose, proud Rose, sad Rose of all my days! To the Rose
upon the Rood of Time. W. B. Yeats. ILP (1975 ed.);
NoAM; VLP

Red rose whispers of passion, The. A White Rose. John Boyle
O'Reilly. SoSe

Red salamander, A. Denise Levertov. *Fr.* Living. OSP

Red sky at night is a shepherd's delight, A. *Unknown.* MG

Red sumac presses. On the New Road. Lyn Lifshin. FAF;
NeAC; RiTi

Red sun breaks through muddy lakes of haze and rifted cloud,
The. The Stampede. Arthur I. Caldwell. BPAW

Red-Tail Hawk and Pyre of Youth. Robert Penn Warren. PoIA

Red-tailed hawk, The. Air War. Linda Pastan. PoUp

Red-tiled ships you see reflected, The. Five Vignettes. Jean
Toomer. PoBA

Red Wheelbarrow, The. William Carlos Williams. CMoP (1970
ed.); HoPM (1975 ed.); InPK; NIL; NoAM; NOBA; NowV;
OSP; PiAm; SFF; SoSe (1977 ed.); TAP; TSWA; TT; UnPo
(1976 ed.); UsP; WIF
("So much depends.") HAP

Red Whiskey. *Unknown.* AmFP

Red, White and Red, The. *Unknown.* AmFP

Red/White Blues, The. Wendy Rose. NW

Red Wing Hawk. James Applewhite. AMV-81

Redemption. Stanley Cooperman. AMV-80

Redemption. George Herbert. BoReV; CABA (1972 ed.); ExPo
(1973 ed.); FF; HAP; InPS; MetP; NOBE; SCP-1; SoSe

Redmen come. In Autumn. Barbara Howes. LiSp

Redriff. David Jones. *Fr.* The Anathemata. TwMBP

Redwing, The. Patric Dickinson. BoAnP

Redwings. William Heyen. PCho

Redwings. James Wright. NNaP

Redwoods, The. Louis Simpson. TH

Reed, A. Osip Mandelstam, *tr. fr. Russian by* James Greene.
VWA

Reeds give, The. Small Song. A. R. Ammons. POL

Reefing Topsails. Walter Mitchell. RhR

Reeking of unsolved crimes, the cop. Two Hookers. A. K.
Redwing. VoR

Reel One. Adrien Stoutenburg. MiP

Reeve, The. Chaucer. *Fr.* The Canterbury Tales: Prologue.
OxBM

Reeving. Michael Anania. HeS

Refined Man, The. Kipling. *Fr.* Epitaphs of the War.
FaBoEE; FaBoTw (1975 ed.)

Reflected in a venetian mirror, heavy-framed. Soho. Joseph
Brodsky, *tr. by* Alan Myers. VWA

Reflection, A. Thomas Hood. FaBoEE

Reflection and Advice. Ezra Pound. OBSV

Reflection from Rochester. William Empson. PoA

Reflection from Sea and Sky. Walter Savage Landor. FaBoEE

Reflection in a Green Arena. Gregory Corso. VGW

Reflection Kiss, one given, The. Some Kisses from *The Kama
Sutra.* Hugo Williams. BoLoP

Reflection on a Wicked World. Ogden Nash. SFF

Reflections. Anita Barrows. NMM

Reflections. Antoinette Deshoulières, *tr. fr. French by* Yvor
Winters. PBWP

Reflections. Carl Gardner. PoBA

Reflections. Lary H. Gibson. PoW

Reflections. Dane Knell. TVo

Reflections. Merle Molofsky. AMV-81

Reflections. David R. Pichaske. AMV-80

Reflections at Dawn. Phyllis McGinley. NOBL

Reflections Dental. Phyllis McGinley. *Fr.* Speaking of Television. TH

Reflections in a Slum. "Hugh MacDiarmid." FaBoTw (1975 ed.)

Reflections of a Trout Fisherman. Andrew Demon. AMV-80

Reflections on a Small Parade. Bob Kaufman. VoA

Reflections on a Womb Which Is Called "Vacant." Jeanine Hathaway. IHMS

Reflections on Having Left a Place of Retirement. Samuel Taylor Coleridge. MBPR

Reflections on Ice-Breaking. Ogden Nash. FaBoCo; IP; OBAL; SFF

Reflections on Limitations. Albert Howard Carter. AATT

Reflexions on suicide, and on my father, possess me. Of Suicide. John Berryman. NoAM

Reformation of Godfrey Gore, The. William Brighty Rands. PCOP

Reformation of Manners, *sels.* Daniel Defoe. OBSV
　"Search all the Christian climes from pole to pole."
　"Yet Ostia boasts of her regeneration."

Reformed Drunkard. Vernon Scannell. AMV-80

Reformer to His Father, A. James Simmons. BIrV

Re-forming a Monument. Douglas Musella. PoW

Re-forming the Crystal. Adrienne Rich. TAP

Refractory Gnu, The. *Unknown.* TDH

Refreshing rest, ecstatic dream. In the Grass. Annette von Droste-Hülshoff, *tr. by* James Edward Tobin. PBWP

Refrigerator, The. Howard Moss. GP

Refugee, The. Dabney Stuart. GP

Refugee in America. Langston Hughes. CC; GOA
　(Words like Freedom.) BPo

Refugees. Chaim Grade, *tr. fr. Yiddish by* Marc Kaminski. VWA

Refugees, The. Edwin Muir. NoAM

Refusal, A. Thomas Hardy. FaBoCo

Refusal to Mourn the Death, by Fire, of a Child in London, A. Dylan Thomas. AnMo; BuTh; CABA (1972 ed.); CMoP (1970 ed.); EBEV; FF; HeIP; HoPM (1975 ed.); IP; LFH; MPo; NIL; NoAM; NOBE; OAEL-2; OBW; OxBTC; TT; UnPo (1976 ed.); VoPo

Refuses/ to refuse the racket. Old Tennis Player. Gwendolyn Brooks. LiSp

Refusing to fall in love with God, he gave. Didymus. Louis MacNeice. LoAs

Refusing What Would Bind You to Me Irrevocably. Ronald Koertge. GP

Regard the motion of the villanelle. The Villanelle. Donald Harington. AMV-81

Regard to Neruda. Pat Lowther. MMD

Regarding Wave, II. Gary Snyder. CAAP

Regenerate. Robert Bloom. AATT

Regeneration. Henry Vaughan. CABA (1972 ed.); SCP-1

Regiment of Princes, The. Thomas Hoccleve. *See* De Regimine Principum.

Region of life and light! The Life of the Blessed. Luis Ponce de León, *tr. by* Bryant. PIM

Regret. *Malay Oral Tradition, tr. by* R. J. Wilkinson. WTO

Regret. Vassar Miller. RiTi

Regret and Refusal. *Tr. fr. Tewa Indian by* H. J. Spinden. WTO

Regret Not Me. Thomas Hardy. PoPle

Regretful Thoughts. Yü Hsüan-chi, *tr. fr. Chinese by* Geoffrey Waters. BoWoP

Rehearsal, The. Horace Gregory. VGW

Reichstag Trial, The. Isidor Schneider. SPT

Reilly. Rayne Mackinnon. MIS

Reilly's Daughter. *Unknown.* FSW

Reincarnation (I). James Dickey. CoPAm; HoPM (1975 ed.)

Reincarnation (II). James Dickey. CAPP

Reincarnation. Mae Jackson. PoBA

Reincarnation. John L. Sellers. DNGG

Reindeer and Engine. Josephine Jacobsen. WPE

Reject Jell-o. Lucille Day. AMV-81

Rejected Lover, The ("I once knew a little girl"). *Unknown.* AmFP

Rejected Lover, The ("The lonesome scenes of winter"). *Unknown.* AmFP

Rejected Member's Wife, The. Thomas Hardy. VLP

Rejected "National Hymns," The. "Orpheus C. Kerr." OBAL

Rejoice in God, O ye tongues; give the glory to the Lord, and the Lamb. Christopher Smart. *Fr.* Jubilate Agno. LAuP

Rejoice in the Lamb. Christopher Smart. *See* Jubilate Agno.

Rejoice, Let Alleluias Ring, *with music.* Sister M. Cherubim Schaefer. AH

Rejoice you sots, your idol's come again. Upon the King's Return from Flanders. Henry Hall. APAS

Rejoicing/ because we had met again. The Good Dream. Denise Levertov. NNaP

Rejoinder. Albert De Pietro. AATT

Relapse, The. Henry Vaughan. PAIC

Relating to Robinson. Weldon Kees. AnMo; NYP

Relationship, The. Stephen Vincent. NeAC

Relationships. Mona Van Duyn. GP; RiTi

Relative Matter. Ann Darr. PoUp

Relative Sadness. Colin Rowbotham. BuTh

Relatives are leaning over, staring expectantly, The. "The Dreadful Has Already Happened." Mark Strand. NoAM

Relativity. Kathleen Millay. QQQ

Relativity. *Unknown, at. to* Arthur Buller. FaBoCo; PoIA
　(Faster than Light.) QQQ
　(Limerick: "There was a young lady named Bright.") NOBL

Relaxed, nothing to do. Letting My Feelings Out. Yü Hsüan-chi, *tr. by* Geoffrey Waters. BoWoP

Relaxing here with brandy and certitude. The Epistemologist, over a Brandy, Opining. Robert Sargent. AMV-80

Relearning the Alphabet. Denise Levertov. NOBA

Release. D. H. Lawrence. CMoP (1970 ed.)

Released from the noise of the butcher and baker. Jinny the Just. Matthew Prior. NOBE

Relent, my deere, yet unkind Coelia. Coelia, XVII. William Percy. AAS

Relic, The. John Donne. CABA (1972 ed.); GBL; HAP; ILP (1975 ed.); NIL; NOBE; OAEL-1; PPP; SCP-1
　(Relique, The.) MetP; PoPle; TT

Relics. Suzanne Gegna. AMV-81

Relicts. Layle Silbert. NPW

Relief of Lucknow, The. Robert Traill Spence Lowell. BTTM; PoTa

Relieved, I let the book fall behind a stone. Depressed by a Book of Bad Poetry. James Wright. ConAP; TH

Religio Laici, *sel.* Dryden.
　Reason and Religion. BoReV
　("Dim as the borrowed beams of moon and stars.") OAEL-1

Religion. Henry Vaughan. BoReV; OAEL-1

Religion Back Home. William Stafford. OBAL
　"When my little brother chanted," *sel.* CC

Religion? Huh! Whenever I hear the word. Two Memories. "Hugh MacDiarmid." MS

Religion of Sweet Jesus, The. "Onward Christian Soldiers!" Frank Marshall Davis. FB

Religious Musings. Samuel Taylor Coleridge. MBPR

Reliquary. Hart Crane. PoA

Relique, The. John Donne. See Relic, The.

Relish honey. If you please. To a Swallow. John Peale Bishop, after Euenus. OBVE

Relish of the Muse, The. Sir John Beaumont. POL

Relocation. Simon Ortiz. VW

Reluctance. Robert Frost. CMoP (1970 ed.); NOBA

Reluctant. Catherine O'Neill. PoUp

Remain, Ah Not in Youth Alone. Walter Savage Landor. HAP

Remains, The. Mark Strand. PPP

Remains of blue bog children, The. Blue Bog Children. Roger Weingarten. AmPA

Remarkable Art. Gelett Burgess. FaBoNo

Remarks from the Pup. Burges Johnson. GDP

Remedy, Worse than the Disease, The. Matthew Prior. FaBoEE

Remember. Christina Rossetti. BoLoP; IPWM; NOBE; OAEL-2; PAIC; PoPle; PPM; SBG; VPC

Remember. Gary Soto. NW
(Moving Away.) AAN

Remember. Steve Toth. AcAn

Remember/ when the skin of your fingers healed. The Discoveries of Fire. Lucille Clifton. TSWA

Remember also thy Creator in the days of thy youth. Bible, O.T. Ecclesiastes, XII: 1-7. OBP

Remember always to eat with both eyes open. Meal Piece. Elton Glaser. NVAP

Remember Dear Mary. John Clare. WeW

Remember me, I was a celebrity. A Voice from Out of the Night. Lisel Mueller. GP

Remember me? I was the one. Hood. C. K. Williams. InPK

Remember me when I am dead. Simplify Me When I'm Dead. Keith Douglas. OxBTC

Remember me when I am gone away. Remember. Christina Rossetti. BoLoP; IPWM; NOBE; OAEL-2; PAIC; PoPle; PPM; SBG; VPC

Remember now my Creatour in the days of thy youth. Bible, O.T. Ecclesiastes, XII: 1-8. OBVE

Remember past ugly to memories of the once. Positive Movement Will Be Difficult but Necessary. Don L. Lee. FiCh

Remember, poet, while gallivanting across the sky. Forget Me Not. Bob Kaufman. AmNP (1974 ed.)

Remember Sabbath Days. Larry Eigner. VWA

Remember, Sinful Youth, with music. Unknown. AH

Remember Suez? Adrian Mitchell. OxBTC

Remember That Country. Jean Garrigue. VGW

Remember that old love song, Daphne? Delfica. Gérard de Nerval, tr. by Andrew Hoyem. NU

Remember that Saturday morning. The Dirty-billed Freeze Footy. Judith Hemschemeyer. TV

Remember that we are moving away brother. Remember. Gary Soto. AAN; NW

Remember thee! remember thee! Byron. BoLoP

Remember there is someone who loves you terribly. To the Stolen Children. Robert Hahn. AAN

Remember those wingovers and loops and spins? The Dream of Flying Comes of Age. Howard Nemerov. BiP

Remember those X-ray machines in shoe stores. On Hot Days. James Reiss. AmPA

Remember Thou Me. Malay Oral Tradition, tr. by R. J. Wilkinson and R. O. Winstedt. WTO

Remember Thy Creator Now, with music. Peter Long. AH

Remember Times for Sandy. Carolyn M. Rodgers. JB

Remember us poor Mayers all. The Mayers' Song. Unknown. AIW; GBP

Remember Way Back. Unknown. BluL

Remember what I promised you. Way Out in Idaho. Unknown. FSW

Remember when. Among Strangers. William Stafford. NNaP

Remember when I draped. Poem for My Mother. Siv Cedering Fox. TV

Remember when you couldn't. Anne Sexton. Fr. The Fury of Overshoes. OSP

Remember Whistling Willie's market. Whistling Willie. Kaye Starbird. QQQ

Remembered Morning. Janet Lewis. WPE

Remembered summers are the smell of nettles. Fragments. John Cotton. AMV-80

Remembering. Akjartoq, tr. fr. Eskimo. WTO

Remembering. Clarisse Nicoïdski, tr. fr. Judezmo by Stephen Levy. VWA

Remembering. Judit Tóth, tr. fr. Hungarian by Emery George. VWA

Remembering Apple Times. John T. Hitchner. AMV-80

Remembering Day. Mary Wright Saunders. CTV

Remembering England. Peter Bland. ATNZ

Remembering Him. Joe Reccardi. AMV-80

Remembering Home. Susan Petrykewycz. AMV-80

Remembering How. Pat Lowther. MMD

Remembering Kevan MacKenzie. Henry Taylor. InPK

Remembering Lutsky. Rayzel Zychlinska, tr. fr. Yiddish by Marc Kaminsky. VWA

Remembering Nat Turner. Sterling A. Brown. PoBA

Remembering the 'Thirties. Donald Davie. OxBTC

Remembrance. Emily Brontë. BoLoP; BoWoP; EBEV; HAP; ILP (1975 ed.); NOBE; OBP; VLP; WPE
(Cold in the Earth.) PBWP

Remembrance. Sir Thomas Wyatt. See Lover Showeth How He Is Forsaken . . .

Remembrance Day. Vernon Scannell. HeHu

Remembrance Day. In school assemblies, talk. War. Thomas W. Shapcott. FPA

Remembrance of a Color inside a Forest, A. Ray A. Young Bear. CDW

Rememorised, Maurice Devane. Austin Clarke. Fr. Mnemosyne Lay in Dust. CMoP (1970 ed.)

Reminder, The. Thomas Hardy. CMoP (1970 ed.)

Reminiscence, A. Anne Brontë. WPE

Reminiscence, sel. Padraic Colum.
"I saw the wind to-day, " II. CaYB; ECBV

Reminiscence. Wallace Irwin. NOBL

Reminiscent Reflection. Ogden Nash. FaBoCo

Remnant Ghosts at Dawn. Oliver La Grone. FB

Remnants. Cathy Song. PHC

Remonstrance. Philodemos the Epicurean, tr. fr. Greek by Dudley Fitts. OLR

R-e-m-o-r-s-e. George Ade. OBAL

Remorse. Richmond Lattimore. PoA

Remorse for Time, The. Howard Nemerov. NCSH

Remorse is memory awake. Emily Dickinson. NOBA; Psy

Remote and ineffectual don. Lines to a Don. Hilaire Belloc. FaBoCo; OBSV

Remote Country. Sydney Tremayne. MS

Remote from our sordid world. Purity. Hayim Lenski, tr. by Pearl Grodensky. VWA

Remote House. Hans Magnus Enzensberger. LP

Remote sky, prolonged to the sea's brim, A. For "Ruggiero and Angelica" by Ingres. Dante Gabriel Rossetti. VLP

Remote, unfriended, melancholy, slow. The Traveller. Goldsmith. BIrV; LAuP

Removal, The. W. S. Merwin. TCP

Removal from Terry Street, A. Douglas Dunn. LP; POL

Removal: Last Part. Carroll Arnett. VoR

Remove away that blackning church. An Ancient Proverb. Blake. *Fr.* Several Questions Answered. MBPR

Removed from Europe's feuds, a hateful scene. A Warning to America. Philip Freneau. TAP

Renaming the Evening. Eric Pankey. AMV-81

Rendezvous, The. Steven Graves. PPoD

Rendezvous. Edna St. Vincent Millay. RiTi

Rendezvous. Alan Seeger. *See* I Have a Rendezvous with Death.

Rendez-vous Manqué dans la Rue Racine. J. M. Synge. BIrV

Renegade Wants Words, The. James Welch. CDW; SA

Renew the old stories, it is said almost every day. The Old Stories. Gene Frumkin. AMV-80

Renewal. Lord Russell Brain. PMW

Renewal, A. James Merrill. CoPAm

Renewal, The. Theodore Roethke. VGW

Renewal by Her Element. Denis Devlin. CIP

Renewal of the cycle. The Mikveh. Blu Greenberg. AMV-80

Reno, 2 A.M. Sam Hamill. TAT

Renoir's Confidences. J. Michael Pilz. AMV-81

Renouncement. Alice Meynell. BoLoP; NOBE; WPE

Renouncing of Love, A. Sir Thomas Wyatt. GBL ("Farewell, love, and all thy laws for ever.") AAS; OAEL-1; SoSe

Rent. Jane Cooper. TAP

Rent man knocked, The. Madam and the Rent Man. Langston Hughes. UsP

Renunciation—is a piercing virtue. Emily Dickinson. PiAm

Repartée. Charles Follen Adams. OBAL

Repeated Shapes, The. Donald Hall. CoPAm

Repentant Judas. Joseph Kalar. SPT

Repetition. Wyatt Prunty. AMV-81

Repetition of Words and Weather. Ruth Stone. BoWoP

Reply, The. Philip Levine. PoA

Reply. Victoria McCabe. POL

Reply, A. *Unknown.* FaBoCo
(Answer.) PoPle
(Limerick: "Dear Sir, your astonishment's odd.") NOBL

Reply of the Free Woman. Sharlot Hall. WPW

Reply to Dipsychus. Arthur Hugh Clough. FaBoCo

Reply to Marriage Proposal. Irihapeti Rangi te Apakura, *tr. fr. Maori by* Roger Oppenheim *and* Allen Curnow. PBWP

Re-plyed, extorted, oft transposed, and fleeting. Sea Voyage. William Empson. CMoP (1970 ed.)

Report from a Forest Logged by the Weyerhaeuser Company. David Wagoner. CNW

Report from the Correspondent They Fired. David McElroy. AmPA

Report of Health. John Updike. PBMP

Report on a Memorial Service: A Letter to Mark Van Doren. William Claire. PoUp

Report on Experience. Edmund Blunden. FaBoTw (1975 ed.); NOBE

Report Song in a Dream, A. Nicholas Breton. GBL
(Wooing in a Dream.) NOBE

Report to Crazy Horse. William Stafford. MPA

Reporting Back. William Stafford. CoPAm

Reporting on my friend after his fall. Don't Call. Edward Lowbury. PMW

Reportless subjects, to the quick. Emily Dickinson. NOBA

Repose. Alfred Lichtenstein, *tr. fr. German by* Mary Zilzer. VWA

Repose of Rivers. Hart Crane. CMoP (1970 ed.); ExPo (1973 ed.); ILP (1975 ed.); NoAM; NOBA; UsP

Repose they know in storefronts, The. The Village of the Presents. James McMichael. AmPA

Repression of War Experience. Siegfried Sassoon. CMoP (1970 ed.); NoAM

Reprise of One of A.G.'s Best Poems! Amiri Baraka. PCho

Reproach to Julia. Robert Graves. FaBoEE

Reproaches. William Price Turner. SLP

Reptilian green the wrinkled throat. Sir Gawaine and the Green Knight. Yvor Winters. NoAM; PAIC; PoIA; UsP; VGW

Republic, The. Longfellow. *Fr.* The Building of the Ship. BTTM

Republic 1939, The. James Liddy. CIP

Republic of the West. On a Rhine Steamer. James Kenneth Stephen. NOBL

Republican Genius of Europe, The. Philip Freneau. VoPo

Repulse, The. Thomas Stanley. MetP

Request. Stephen Shrader. PHC

Requiem: A Surrealist Graveyard. Chuck Miller. AcAn

Requiem: "Farewell my friend." Martin T. O'Connor. AMV-80

Requiem: "I watch the roses float." Stephen Vincent. NeAC

Requiem: "In the sudden white silence, where are you?" Jean Garrigue. UsP

Requiem: "No, not far beneath some foreign sky then." "Anna Akhmatova," *tr. fr. Russian by* Robin Kemble. NAWM-2 (Requiem 1935–1940, *tr. by* Richard McKane.) BoWoP

Requiem: "Pour out your light, O stars." Ivor Gurney. FaBoEE; FaBoTw (1975 ed.)

Requiem: "Under the wide and starry sky." Robert Louis Stevenson. DL; FaPoR; ILP (1975 ed.); NOBE; PCOP; PIM; RhR

Requiem: "Will they stop." Kenneth Fearing. CMoP (1970 ed.)

Requiem after Seventeen Years. Dahlia Ravikovitch, *tr. fr. Hebrew by* Chana Bloch. VWA

Requiem for a Personal Friend. Eavan Boland. PFIr

Requiem for a River. Kim Williams. RFM

Requiem for Innocence, A. William R. Mitchell. AATT

Requiem for Sonora. Richard Shelton. MPA

Requiem for the Croppies. Seamus Heaney. BIrV; CIP

Requiem for the Plantagenet Kings. Geoffrey Hill. NoAM

Requiem for the '30's. William Pillin. SPT

Requiem 1935–1940. "Anna Akhmatova." *See* Requiem: "No, not far beneath some foreign sky then."

Requiem of a War-Baby. Joan Watton. PFIr

Requiescat. Matthew Arnold. HeIP; ILP (1975 ed.); NOBE; PBMP; PPM

Rescue, The. Robert Creeley. CAPP

Rescue, The. Ian Serraillier. FPB

Rescue, The. Hal Summers. PoTa

Rescue the Dead. David Ignatow. ConAP; VGW

Resemblance. *Tr. fr. Hawaiian by* N. B. Emerson. WTO

Resembles life what once was deem'd of light. What Is Life? Samuel Taylor Coleridge. MBPR

Reservation Special. Lew Blockcolski. VoR

Reservoir, The. Edward Field. GP

Resident Stranger, The. Harley Elliott. HeS

Residue of Song. Marvin Bell. AmPA

Resign the rhapsody, the dream. To the Muse. Robert Louis Stevenson. EBEV

Resignation. Matthew Arnold. VLP

Resignation Day. Richard Friedman. FiCh

Resignation—To Faustus. Arthur Hugh Clough. VLP

Resisting Each Other. Anne Waldman. RiTi

Resisting poetry I am becoming a poem. Moon. Derek Walcott. NoAM

Resolute Courtier, The. Thomas Shipman. GBL

Resolution. Ted Berrigan. OFD

Resolution and Independence. Wordsworth. CABA (1972 ed.); EBEV; HAP; InPS; LFH; MAT; MBPR; NOBE; OAEL-2; PPP; SoSe

"I was a traveller then upon the moor," sel. SpRo

Resolution in Four Sonnets, of a Poetical Question Put to Me by a Friend, Concerning Four Rural Sisters. Charles Cotton. Prf Two Rural Sisters, sel. BoLoP

Resolution of Dependence. George Barker. FaBoTw (1975 ed.)

Resolv'd to love, unworthie to obtaine. Henry Constable. Fr. Diana. ESo

Resolve, The. Mary Lee, Lady Chudleigh. WPE

Resolve, The. Denise Levertov. RFM

Resolving Doubts. William Dickey. CoPAm

Resound my voyse, ye wodes that here me plain. Sir Thomas Wyatt. AAS

Resounding. Katherine Soniat. AMV-81

Respect the dreams of old men, said the cricket. Song for September. Robert Fitzgerald. VGW

Respectabilities. Jon Silkin. NoAM

Respectable Burgher, The. Thomas Hardy. CMoP (1970 ed.); NoAM; VLP

Respectable Folks, The. Henry David Thoreau. AmVN

Respectable People. Austin Clarke. CMoP (1970 ed.)

Respondez! Walt Whitman. NoAM

Responding Voice. Francisco A. de Icaza, tr. fr. Spanish by Samuel Beckett. PBMP

Response. Mary Ursula Bethell. ATNZ

Responses. Robert Hershon. POL

Responsively. To Redound. William Harmon. CSP

Responsory, 1948, A. Thomas Merton. VGW

Rest. Mathilde Blind. SBG

Rest, The. Ezra Pound. Fr. Lustra. NoAM; NOBA ("O helpless few in my country.") PoA

Rest. Christina Rossetti. NOBE; OAEL-2

Rest. Jacob Isaac Segal, tr. fr. Yiddish by Seymour Mayne. VWA

Rest lightly O Earth upon this wretched Nearchos. Epitaph of Nearchos. Ammianus, tr. by Dudley Fitts. WeW

Rest Only in the Grave. James Clarence Mangan. BIrV

Rested near Nefertete. Carol Bergé. MMD

Resting Figure. Denise Levertov. AnMo

Resting Place. Jon Silkin. VWA

Restless forms of living light. Address to Certain Gold Fishes. Hartley Coleridge. VLP

Restless he rolls about from whore to whore. Earl of Rochester. Fr. A Satire on Charles II. OBSV

Restless needle, where my beads. Bead Work. Hazel Hall. WPW

Restless water of sound, The. War Requiem. Del Marie Rogers. NPW

Restoration of Enheduanna to Her Former Station, The. Enheduanna, tr. fr. Sumerian; ad. by Aliki and Willis Barnstone. BoWoP

Result of Our Investigation, The. Charles S. Bouslog. PHC

Results of a Scientific Survey. Bruce Cutler. AMV-80

Results of the Polo Game. Grace Butcher. RiTi

Résumé. Dorothy Parker. DL; InPK; OBAL; SS

Resurgence. Robert Louis Stevenson. PPM

Resurrection. R. P. Blackmur. PoA

Resurrection, The. Jonathan Brooks. AmNP (1974 ed.)

Resurrection. Margiad Evans. OBW

Resurrection. Kenneth Fearing. CMoP (1970 ed.)

Resurrection. Frank Horne. OFD; PoBA

Resurrection, The. William Edward Taylor. AMV-80

Resurrection, The. Nathaniel Wanley. SCP-2

Resurrection, The, sel. W. B. Yeats.
Two Songs from a Play. CABA (1972 ed.); CMoP (1970 ed.); ExPo (1973 ed.); HAP; ILP (1975 ed.); NIL; NOBE; OAEL-2; OBP; PPoe; PPP

"I saw a staring virgin stand," I. FaBoTw (1975 ed.)

Resurrection and Immortality. Henry Vaughan. SCP-1

Resurrection of the Dead. Aliza Shenhar, tr. fr. Hebrew by Linda Zisquit. VWA

Resurrection Possible and Probable, The. Robert Herrick. ILP (1975 ed.)

Resurrection Quatrain. Kelly Cherry. BCr

Resurrection Song. Thomas Lovell Beddoes. FaBoEE; InPK; PMW

Resuscitation. John Stone. CSP

Retaliation. Goldsmith. ESaP
Sels.
"Here Reynolds is laid and, to tell you my mind." FaBoEE
On Edmund Burke. PMW
("Here lies our good Edmund, whose genius was such.") FaBoEE

Retired Boxer, The. Lucilius, tr. fr. Greek by Tom Dodge. LiSp

Retired Cat, The. William Cowper. PCat

Retired gardener of solitudes. N.Y. to L.A. by Jet Plane. Sonya Dorman. GOA

Retired School-Teacher. Heather McHugh. PCho

Retired this hour from wondering crowds. Walter Savage Landor. GBL

Retirement, sel. William Cowper.
Statesman in Retirement, The. PPoD

Retirement of the Elephant, The. Russell Edson. AmPA

Retreat. Amy Bushnell. AMV-80

Retreat. Martha Collins. AMV-80

Retreat[e], The. Henry Vaughan. CABA (1972 ed.); FF; HAP; HeIP; InPS; MetP; NIL; NOBE; OAEL-1; OBP; OBW; PIM; PoIA; PoPle; PPP; SCP-1

Retreat of Ita Cagney, The. Michael Hartnett. CIP

Retreat to Vermont was orderly at first, The. Safe Places. Constance Urdang. GP

Retribution often is. Alison Wyrley Birch. PPM

Retrospect. Ina Coolbrith. WPW

Retrospect. Lonnie L. Landrum. DNGG

Retrospect, A. Coventry Patmore. VLP

Return. Michael Anania. HeS

Return, The. Arna Bontemps. PoBA; WIF

Return, The. Bruce Bennett Brown. TAT

Return, The. Alistair Campbell. ATNZ

Return. C. P. Cavafy, tr. fr. Modern Greek by Rae Dalven. LoAs

Return. Jane Cooper. UsP

Return. Seamus Deane. BIrV; IPM

Return. Daniel Halpern. PCho

Return, The. Edna St. Vincent Millay. NoAM; PPM

Return, The. Shmuel Moreh, tr. fr. Arabic by Yoffee Berkovitz. VWA

Return, The. Stanley Moss. POL

Return, The ("The doors flapped open in Ulysses' house"). Edwin Muir. CMoP (1970 ed.)

Return, The ("The veteran Greeks came home"). Edwin Muir. CMoP (1970 ed.)

Return, The. Leonard Nathan. EC

Return, The. Ezra Pound. CMoP (1970 ed.); ExPo (1973 ed.); HAP; NoAM; NOBA; PPoe; PSN; VGW; WeW

Return. Earl of Rochester. *See* Song, A: "Absent from thee, I languish still."

Return, The. Theodore Roethke. PoA

Return, The. Dennis Saleh. NeAC

Return. Theodore Spencer. PoA

Return. M. L. Sussman. AMV-81

Return, The. Edward Taylor. *Fr.* Preparatory Meditations, First Series. EAP

Return. Wordsworth. *Fr.* The River Duddon. HAP

Return again, my forces late dismayed. Amoretti, XIV. Spenser. SoSe

Return from Luluabourg. Michael Jackson. ATNZ

Return Journey. Paul Henderson. ATNZ

Return, light of wing. The Cage. Avner Treinin, *tr. by* A. C. Jacobs. VWA

Return of Astraea, The. Ben Jonson. NOBE

Return of Robinson Jeffers, The. Robert Hass. AmPA

Return of the Dead, The, *sel.* Samar Attar. "And you came back." PBWP

Return of the Goddess Artemis. Robert Graves. PoA

Return of the Native. Amiri Baraka. BPo

Return of the Sire de Nesle A. D. 16—, The. Herman Melville. NOBA

Return often and take me. Return. C. P. Cavafy, *tr. by* Rae Dalven. LoAs

Return to Astolat. Gail White. AMV-81

Return to Dachau. B. Z. Niditch. AMV-81

Return to Hinton. Charles Tomlinson. CMoP (1970 ed.)

Return to Prinsengracht. Janice Blue-Swartz. AMV-81

Return to the Valley. Elfreida Read. AMV-80

Return to Work, The. William Carlos Williams. CTBA

Return we to the dangers of the night. Juvenal, *tr. by* Dryden. *Fr.* Satires, III. OAEL-1

Returne Thee, Hairt. Alexander Scott. SLP

Returned from college R——gets a wife. The Discontented Student. St. George Tucker. OBAL

Returned from the opera, as lately I sat. A Bon Mot. *Unknown.* POL

Returned to Frisco, 1946. W. D. Snodgrass. ILP (1975 ed.)

Returned to life. Lazarus. Stuart Dybek. TC

Returned to Say. William Stafford. ConAP

Returning after dark, I thought. Traditional Red. Robert Huff. CoPAm; HoPM (1975 ed.)

Returning at Night. Jim Harrison. VGW

Returning from its daily quest, my spirit. Sonnet: Guido Cavalcanti to Dante. Guido Cavalcanti, *tr. by* Shelley. OBVE

Returning from the Funeral. Patricia Henley. NPW

Returning, I find her just the same. Passing Visit to Helen. D. H. Lawrence. CMoP (1970 ed.)

Returning to Goleufryn ("Returning to my grandfather's house, after this exile"). Vernon Watkins. OBW

Returning to Roots of First Feeling. Robert Duncan. PoA

Returning, We Hear the Larks. Isaac Rosenberg. OAEL-2; VWA

Reuben and Rachel, *with music.* Harry Birch. PSoN

Reuben Bright. E. A. Robinson. IPWM; NQBA; PoIA; PPM; STS; TAP

Reuben, I have long been thinking. Reuben and Rachel. Harry Birch. PSoN

Reuben Ranzo. *Unknown.* AmFP; FSW

Reuben, Reuben. *Unknown.* FSW

Reuben's Cabin. Robert Morgan. TAT

Reunion. Heather Cadsby. AMV-81

Reunion. Carolyn Forché. PCho

Reunion. Judith Herzberg, *tr. fr. Dutch by* Shirley Kaufman. BoWoP

Reunion. E. A. Robinson. NoAM; NOBA

Reve was a slendre colerik man, The. The Reeve. Chaucer. *Fr.* The Canterbury Tales: Prologue. OxBM

Revealed and yet dwelling hidden in the cave. *Tr. fr. Sanskrit by* Raimundo Panikkar. *Fr.* Upanishads. ILwL

Reveille. A. E. Housman. CMoP (1970 ed.); PPM; SoSe; STS

Reveille. Ted Hughes. PPP

Reveille. Lola Ridge. WPE

Revel, A. Donagh MacDonagh. PFIr

Revelation. Jerald Bullis. AMV-81

Revelation. Dryden. *Fr.* The Hind and the Panther, I. BoReV (Confessio Fidei.) NOBE

Revelation. Robert Frost. PPM

Revelation. Peter Meinke. AATT

Revelation, The. Coventry Patmore. *Fr.* The Angel in the House, I, viii. GBL; HAP

Revelation. William Soutar. MS

Revelation. Robert Penn Warren. NoAM

Revelation came on Jane, A. Jump-to-Glory Jane. George Meredith. VLP

Revelation of the Bare Ass. Doug Blazek. CPA

Revenant, The. Margaret Atwood. Psy

Revenant, The. Peter Cooley. HeS

Revenant, The. Walter de la Mare. GBL

*Revenge, The.* Tennyson. BTTM; FaPo (Ballad of the Fleet, A.) FaPoR

Revenge of Rain-in-the-Face, The. Longfellow. BPAW

Revenge of the Hunted. R. A. D. Ford. LiSp

Revenger's Tragedy, The, *sel.* Cyril Tourneur. "Age and bare bone/ Are e'er allied in action," *fr.* III, iv. OBP "And now methinks I could e'en chide myself." SCP-2

Revenue Man Blues. *Unknown.* BluL

Reverend Butler came by. Madam and the Minister. Langston Hughes. NOBA

Reverend Henry Ward Beecher, The. An Eggstravagance. Oliver Wendell Holmes. FaBoNo

Rev. Homer Wilbur's "Festina Lente." James Russell Lowell. *Fr.* The Biglow Papers, 2d Series. OBAL

Reverend Mother Prioress. Betty Ruth Bird. AATT

Reverend William Winterborne, The. Bishop Winterbourne. Walter de la Mare. FaBoNo

Reverie. Victor Hugo, *tr. fr. French by* Mary Ann Caws. NAWM-2

Reverie of Poor Susan, The. Wordsworth. MBPR

Reversionary. Stevie Smith. FaBoEE

Review from Staten Island. Gloria C. Oden. PoBA; PPP

Reviewing me without undue elation. A Choice of Weapons. Stanley Kunitz. VGW

Revisit, A. Elizabeth Shinoda. PHC

Revisiting the Field. Walter Pavlich. AMV-81

Revival. George Garrett. CSP

Revival, The. Henry Vaughan. BoReV; PoPle (Unfold! Unfold!) ILP (1975 ed.)

Revival. David Wagoner. CNW

Revive Us Again. William Paton Mackay. BLSH, *with music*; FSW

Revolt. Rachel, *tr. fr. Hebrew by* Robert Friend. VWA

Revolt of Islam, The, *sels.* Shelley. MBPR "For, before Cythna loved it, had my song," *fr.* II "I sate beside the steersman then, and gazing, " VIII.

Revolution. Susan Griffin. RiTi

Revolution. A. E. Housman. ILP (1975 ed.)

Revolution in the Revolution in the Revolution. Gary Snyder. PiAm

Revolution is the pod. Emily Dickinson. WIF
Revolutionaries, The. R. P. Lister. NOBL
Revolutionary. James P. Friel. AMV-81
Revolutionary, The/ element remained. Mrs. Hamer. Jane Stembridge. NMM
Revolutionary Dreams. Nikki Giovanni. CNA; GP
Revolutionary Letter # 1. Diane DiPrima. RiTi
Revolutionary Letter # 4. Diane DiPrima. GP; RiTi
Revolutionary Letter # 16. Diane DiPrima. VoA
Revolutionary Letter # 19. Diane DiPrima. IHMS
Revolutionary Letter # 21. Diane DiPrima. RiTi
Revolutionary Letter # 29. Diana DiPrima. GP
Revolutionary Letter # 36. Diane DiPrima. GP; VoA
Revolutionary Letter # 40. Diane DiPrima. GP
Revolutionary Screw, The. Don L. Lee. GP
Reward of Service. *Unknown, tr. fr. German by* F. C. Nicholson. LoAs
Rewards of Farming, The. *Unknown. See* Farmer's Life, A.
Rex regum, for whom praise flows freely. Poem on His Death-Bed. Meilyr Brydydd, *tr. by* Joseph P. Clancy. OBW
Reynard. Gwen Dunn. DuDr
Reynard the Fox, *sels.* John Masefield.
  "From the Gallows Hill to the Tineton Copse." OBP
  "Meet was at 'The Cock and Pye,' The." OxBTC
  "Ock Gurney and old Pete were there." CMoP (1970 ed.)
Rhapsody. William Stanley Braithwaite. AmNP (1974 ed.)
Rhapsody. Frank O'Hara. NoAM; NYP
Rhapsody on a Windy Night. T. S. Eliot. CMoP (1970 ed.); ExPo (1973 ed.); HeIP
Rhetoric. Michael Berryhill. AAN
Rhetoric of Langston Hughes, The. Margaret Danner. FB
Rhine is running deep and red, The. The Island of the Scots. William Edmondstoune Aytoun. VLP
Rhino is a homely beast, The. The Rhinoceros. Ogdon Nash. OBAL
Rhinoceros. William Hart-Smith. BoAnP
Rhinoceros, The. Ogden Nash. OBAL
Rhinoceros. Adrien Stoutenburg. BoAnP
Rhoda Pitkin. Edgar Lee Masters. *Fr.* The New Spoon River. NoAM
Rhododendron Plant, The. Allen Katzman. WeW
Rhododendrons. Tess Gallagher. AAN
Rhodora, The. Emerson. HeIP; ILP (1975 ed.); LFH; NOBA; PiAm; PPM; TAP
Rhomboidal Dirge, *sel.* George Wither.
  "But why,/ O fatal Time." SCP-2
Rhydcymerau. D. Gwenallt Jones, *tr. fr. Welsh by* Anthony Conran. OBW
Rhyme. Louise Bogan. LoAs
Rhyme for a Chemical Baby. Joseph Cook. QQQ; SpRo
Rhyme for a Geological Baby. Joseph Cook. QQQ; SpRo
Rhyme for Astronomical Baby. Joseph Cook. QQQ; SpRo
Rhyme for Botanical Baby. Joseph Cook. QQQ; SpRo
Rhyme for Night. Joan Aiken. DuDa
Rhyme for the Child as a Wet Dog. Judith Johnson Sherwin. TAP
Rhyme of the Dead Self. A. R. D. Fairburn. ATNZ
Rhyme of the Fishermen's Children. *Unknown.* GBP
Rhyme of the poet, The. Merlin, II. Emerson. AmVN; NOBA; PiAm
Rhymes (?). Henry S. Leigh. NOBL
Rhymes and rhymers pass away. Walt Whitman. *Fr.* By Blue Ontario's Shore, XIII. InPS
Rhymes on the Road, *sel.* Thomas Moore.
  "And is there then no earthly place." OBSV

Rhyming a Friend's Poem. Yü Hsüan-chi, *tr. fr. Chinese by* Geoffrey Waters. BoWoP
Rhyming Prophecy for a New Year. Leonard Cooper. FaBoCo
Rhyming with a Friend. Yü Hsüan-chi, *tr. fr. Chinese by* Geoffrey Waters. BoWoP
Rhythm, The. Robert Creeley. UsP
Rhythm. Ruth Stone. FoP
Rhythm and blues. The Blues Today. Mae Jackson. PoBA
Rhythm it is we. Spirits Unchained. Keorapetse Kgositsile. PoBA
Rib Sandwich. William J. Harris. CNA
Ribald Romeos Less and Less Berattle. Horace, *tr. fr. Latin by* John Frederick Nims. Odes, I, 25. MAT
  ("Young bloods come round less often now, The," *tr. by* James Michie.) BoLoP
Ribbe ne rele ne spinne ich ne may. A Servant-Girl's Holiday. *Unknown.* OxBM
Ribh Considers Christian Love Insufficient. W. B. Yeats. BoReV
Ribs and Terrors, The. Herman Melville. *See* Father Mapple's Hymn.
Rice. Carol Muske. AmPA
Rice and Mats, *sel.* Dolores Kendrick.
  Late Morning: Oahu. PoUp
Rice and Mice. Edward Lear. TDH
Rich and Poor; or, Saint and Sinner. Thomas Love Peacock. FaBoCo; NOBE; NOBL; OBSV
Rich blood disturbed my thought. Arrival. John Wain. EBEV
Rich Days. W. H. Davies. FSFS
Rich fools there be, whose base and filthy heart. Astrophel and Stella, XXIV Sir Philip Sidney. Epi
Rich Irish Lady, A. *Unknown.* AmFP, 2 *versions;* FSW
Rich is the peace o' the elements the nicht owre the Land/ o' Joy. The Path of the Old Spells. Donald Sinclair, *tr. fr. Gaelic.* MS
Rich Lady over the Sea, The. *Unknown.* AIW
Rich Man, The. Franklin P. Adams. OBAL; SoSe
Rich Man and the Poor Man, The. *Unknown.* FSW
Rich Man, Trust Now. Thomas Nashe. TT
Rich Morning. Robert Farren. PFIr
Rich Old Miser, A. *Unknown.* AmFP
Rich Widow, The. *Unknown.* AmFP
Richard II. Shakespeare. *See* King Richard II.
Richard III. Shakespeare. *See* King Richard III.
Richard Cory. E. A. Robinson. AmVN; BBGO; CMoP (1970 ed.); DL; FF; HAP; ILP (1975 ed.); InPK; IP; IPWM; MiP; NIL; NOBA; PAIC; PoTa; SFF; SoSe; STS; TAP; TH; UsP; WIF
Richard Cory. Paul Simon. InPK; UsP; WIF
Richard Hofstadter and Michael Wallace, a Documentary History of American Violence. Jim Rosenberg. Epi
Richard Hunt's Arachne. Robert Hayden. FB
"Richard, may I ask a question? What is an episteme?" Richard Howard. *Fr.* Compulsive Qualifications. PoA
Richard Pigott, the Forger, *sel.* William McGonagall.
  "For by forged letters he tried to accuse Parnell." PeD
Richard Roe and John Doe. Robert Graves. CMoP (1970 ed.)
Richard Tolman's Universe. Leonard Bacon. PAIC
"Richard, what will it be like when you ask the questions?" Richard Howard. *Fr.* Compulsive Qualifications. PoA
Riches I hold in light esteem. The Old Stoic. Emily Brontë. FaPoR; NOBE
Riches we find inside will be in rich light, The. Approaching the Castle. Richard Hugo. SoSe (1977 ed.)
Richest realm of all the earth, The. The Poet's Confidence. Coventry Patmore. *Fr.* The Angel in the House. VLP

Richness. Arthur J. Bull. HeHu

Rickety steam engine clatters, The. Cutting Wood: After a Family Photograph. Norbert Krapf. BrS

Rick's Bag of Tricks. Rick Cannon. PoUp

Riddle: "From Belsen a crate of gold teeth." William Heyen. GP

Riddle: "He went to the wood and caught it." *Unknown.* GBP

Riddle: "I saw five birds all in a cage." *Unknown.* GBP

Riddle, A: "I walk on two legs." Cynthia Ozick. VWA

Riddle: "Stiff standing on the bed." *Unknown.* POL

Riddle: "Their tongues are knives, their forks are hands and feet." Adrian Mitchell. FaBoEE; GBL

Riddle, A: "There is one that has a head without an eye." Christina Rossetti. OxBChV

Riddle, The: "What it is, the literal size." Robert Creeley. PiAm

Riddle, The: "White men's children spread over the earth." Georgia Douglas Johnson. PoBA

Riddle, A: "Why is a pump like V-sc--nt C-stl-r--gh?" Thomas Moore. *See* What's My Thought Like?

Riddle, A (for Ponge), sel. George MacBeth. "It is always handled." TSWA

Riddle of Night. Jiri Mordecai Langer, *tr. fr. Hebrew by* Gabriel Preil *and* Howard Schwartz. VWA

Riddle Song, The. *Unknown. See* I Gave My Love a Cherry.

Riddles and Lies. Christine Zawadiwsky. AMV-80

Riddles of government he solves. Blind Spot. Alison Wyrley Birch. PPM

Riddles Wisely Expounded. *Unknown.* FaBoBa; GBP; ILP (1975 ed.); PeBB

Riddling Knight, The. *Unknown.* AIW; PBMP

"Riddling world, A!" one cried. The Two Questions. Alice Meynell. WPE

Ride. Josephine Miles. RiTi

Ride a cock-horse to Banbury Cross. Mother Goose. GSB, *with music;* MG

Ride-by-Nights, The. Walter de la Mare. DuDa

Ride her up and down in your little brass wagon. Little Brass Wagon. *Unknown.* FSW

Ride 'Im Cowboy. A. L. Freebairn. PH; SPo

Ride in the swing. Tune: Crimson Lips Adorned. Li Ching-chao, *tr. by* C. H. Kwôck *and* Vincent McHugh. PBWP

Ride me around in your big blue car. Success Story. Alfred Hayes. SPT

Ride the High Country. David R. Slavitt. PPoD

Rider, The. Ann Stanford. WPE

Rider Victory, The. Edwin Muir. CMoP (1970 ed.)

Riders, The. Robert Friend. GP

Riders. Linda Peavy. PH

Riders Held Back, The. Louis Simpson. ConAP

Riders of the Stars. Henry Herbert Knibbs. BPAW

Ridge, The, sel. John Cowper Powys. "Aye! What a thing is the passing of Cronos, the angular-minded." OBW

Ridge in Wind. Peggy Simson Curry. WPW

Ridin'. Charles Badger Clark, Jr. BPAW

Riding. William Allingham. OxBChV

Riding. Florence Grossman. PH

Riding a One-eyed Horse. Henry Taylor. PH

Riding across John Lee's Finger. Stanley Crouch. PoBA

Riding adown the country lanes. Robert Bridges. VLP

Riding by there every day. Dog Hospital. Peter Wild. AmPA; GP; MPA

Riding Double. Peter Wild. AmPA

Riding down the old hillroad in his red pickup. Old Toby. Keith Wilson. MPA

Riding in the Rain. Maxine W. Kumin. RFM

Riding Lesson. Henry Taylor. PH

Riding Stable in Winter, The. John Tagliabue. PH

Riding the blue sapphire mountains. Mahadevi, *tr. fr. Kannada by* A. K. Ramanujan. BoWoP; PBWP

Riding the Elevator into the Sky. Anne Sexton. NYP

Riding to it feels like being in the bedroom in Rimini. University of Illinois at Chicago Circle Lecture Series. Paul Carroll. FiCh

Riding Together. William Morris. NOBE; OAEL-2

Riding Westward. Harvey Shapiro. GP; NYP; VWA

Riding with Some North Vietnamese Students in a Polish Elevator, 1966. Roger Mitchell. PAIC

Riding wooden horses from the hot Christmas Caves. The Bronze Rider, Wellington. Robin Hyde. ATNZ

Rifled honeycomb, The. John Montague. *Fr.* The Cave of Night. CIP

Riflemen's Song at Bennington. *Unknown.* BTTM (Riflemen at Bennington, The.) FSW

Rift Tide. Ruth M. Walsh. QQQ

Rigged poker-stiff on her back. All the Dead Dears. Sylvia Plath. AnMo; CAPP; CoPAm; IHMS

Right after her birth, they crowded in. Anaesthesia. Jean Valentine. TAP

Right after our Thanksgiving feast. The Skeleton Walks. X. J. Kennedy. IWK

Right art thou who wouldst rather be. Platonic Love. Coventry Patmore. *Fr.* The Angel in the House. VLP

Right down the shocked street with a siren-blast. A Fire-Truck. Richard Wilbur. NCSH

Right mistakes—that rich movement, The. Accepting Surprise. William Stafford. EC

Right On: White America. Sonia Sanchez. PoBA

Right Thinking Man. Marge Piercy. RiTi

Right to Life, The. John N. Morris. AMV-80

Right True End, The. *Gond Oral Tradition, tr. by* V. Elwin *and* S. Hivale. WTO

Right well I wote, most mighty Soveraine. The Faerie Queene, II, *induction.* Spenser. OAEL-1; PAIC

Righteous Man, The. Samuel Butler. OBSV

Rigid Body Sings. James Clerk Maxwell. FaBoCo; SpRo

Rigoletto. Newman Levy. OBAL

Rigorists. Marianne Moore. NU; SBG

Rigs o' Barley, The. Burns. LoAs (Corn Riggs.) SLP (Corn Rigs Are Bonie.) OBP (Song: "It was upon a Lammas night.") BoLoP

Riley. Charles Causley. SO

Rilke, my river, I know your locked look of a poet. Visions. Kathleen Spivack. AmPA

Rim of the desert is the Yucca land, The. In the Yucca Land. Madge Morris. BPAW

Rimbaud and Verlaine, precious pair of poets. Conrad Aiken. Preludes for Memnon, LVI. NoAM

Rimbaud in Abyssinia. Ellen McEvilley Griffin. NPW

Rimbaud's Farewell to Europe. Anthony Glavin. IPM

Rime Intrinsica, Fontmell Magna, Sturminster Newton and Melbury Bubb. Dorset. John Betjeman. MPo

Rime of the Ancient Mariner, The. Samuel Taylor Coleridge. CABA (1972 ed.); EBEV; Epi; HAP; HoPM (1975 ed.); ILP (1975 ed.); InPS; MBPR; NOBE; OAEL-2; PPoD; RhR *Sels.*
"He prayeth best, who loveth best," *fr.* VII. CTV
Icebergs, *fr.* I. EcS
"Sun now rose upon the right, The," II. OBP
Water-Snakes, *fr.* IV. EcS

Rime of the Ancient Mariner, The. Bruce Haley. PPoD

Rime, the rack of finest wits. A Fit of Rime against Rime. Ben Jonson. MAT; OAEL-1; PAIC

Rimrock, Where It Is. Hayden Carruth. NNaP

Rin and rout, rin and rout. The Deevil's Waltz. Sydney Goodsir Smith. FaBoTw (1975 ed.)

Ring, The. Diane Wakoski. PoA

Ring-a-ring-a-roses. *Unknown.* MG
(Ring-a-ring o' roses.) GSB, *with music;* SpRo

Ring-a-ring o' neutrons. Paul Dehn. *Fr.* A Leaden Treasury of English Verse. QQQ; SpRo

Ring-a-ring o' roses. *See* Ring-a-ring-a-roses.

Ring around a rosey. Squat Down, Josey. *Unknown.* AmFP

Ring Of, The. Charles Olson. NOBA; VGW

Ring of fear, A. My Daughter's Ring. Barbara Eve. TV

Ring Out, Wild Bells. In Memoriam A. H. H., CVI. Tennyson. FaPoR; OFD
(New Year, The.) PIM

Ring out your bells, let mourning shows be spread. A Litany. Sir Philip Sidney. CABA (1972 ed.); GBL; UnPo (1976 ed.)

Ring Presented to Julia, A. Robert Herrick. BBL

Ring, ring the lily-bell! Lily-Bell. Roger Wescott. PCOP

Ring, sing! ring, sing! pleasant Sabbath bells! The Green Gnome. Robert Buchanan. PoTa

Ring so worn as you behold, The. A Marriage Ring [*or* His Late Wife's Wedding-Ring]. George Crabbe. BoLoP; NOBE

Ring the bell! *Unknown.* MG

Ring the bells backward; I am all on fire. John Cleveland. *Fr.* The Rebel Scot. PeD

Ring—ting! I wish I were a primrose. Wishing. William Allingham. OxBChV

Ringers, The. John Peck. AmPA

Ringing the Bells. Anne Sexton. BiP; CAPP; FF; ILP (1975 ed.); TAP; VGW

Ringing tire iron, A. Some Good Things to Be Said for the Iron Age. Gary Snyder. CoPAm; HoPM (1975 ed.); WeW

Ringless. Diane Wakoski. Prf

Ringleted Youth of My Love. *Unknown, tr. fr. Modern Irish by* Douglas Hyde. PFIr; WTO

Ringsend. Oliver St. John Gogarty. OxBTC

Rino's Song. Lynne Lawner. IHMS

Rintrah roars and shakes his fires in the burdened air. The Marriage of Heaven and Hell. Blake. LAuP; MBPR; OAEL-2

Rio Grande. *Unknown.* FSW

Río Grande de Loíza. Julia de Burgos, *tr. fr. Spanish by* Grace Schulman. InW

Riot. Gwendolyn Brooks. BPo; CAPP; FiCh; PoBA; Psy; TAP
"John Cabot, out of Wilma, once a Wycliffe," *sel.* TT

Riot Rythmes U.S.A., *sel.* Raymond R. Patterson.
"We are the same in our despair." GP

Riot, tumult, anticipated disturbances. Matthew Mead. *Fr.* The Administration of Things. TwMBP

Rioting the roadsides, the fall colors. Fall Colors. Jerome Mazzaro. AMV-81

Riots and Rituals. Richard W. Thomas. PoBA

Ripe and Bearded Barley, The. *Unknown.* GBP

Ripe, Being Plunged into Fire. Friedrich Hölderlin, *tr. fr. German by* James Blair Leishman. OBVE

Ripeness. Ruth Whitman. TSWA

Ripeness Is All. J. V. Cunningham. PiAm

Ripeness is all; her in her cooling planet. To an Old Lady. William Empson. FaBoTw (1975 ed.); Moon; NoAM; NOBE

Ripley or not. A Street in Kaufman-ville. James Cunningham. JB

Rip-off # 1: Hippie Capitalism. Geof Hewitt. NeAC

Ripper Collins' Legacy. Don Johnson. LiSp

Riprap. Gary Snyder. NOBA; PPoD

Riptide. Marge Piercy. MMD

Rise and Fall, The. Philip Dacey. AAN

Rise and Fall of Creede, The. Cy Warman. BPAW

Rise and Fall of the Swagger Stick, The. William Jay Smith. WasP

Rise and Shine. *Unknown.* FSW

Rise! arise! arise! The Sunrise Call. *Tr. by* N. Barnes. WTO

Rise at 7:15. Good Morning Love! Paul Blackburn. NoAM

Rise, heart! thy Lord is risen. Sing His praise. Easter. George Herbert. SCP-1

Rise, heir[e] of fresh eternity. Easter Day. Richard Crashaw. MetP; SCP-1

"Rise, man the wall, our clarion's blast." Hymn of the Alamo. Reuben M. Potter. BPAW

Rise not till noon, if life be but a dream. Epigram. Matthew Prior. NIL

Rise of capitalism parallels the advance of romanticism, The. Definition of Blue. John Ashbery. Epi

Rise, rise from sluggishness, fly fast my dear. The Verses of the Talkative Knight. Mary Sidney Wroth, Countess of Montgomery. *Fr.* Urania. WPE

Rise then, ere ruin swift surprize. John Trumbull. *Fr.* M'Fingal. GOA

Rise to the surface, O my hidden strength! Six Poems, 1. Joseph Freeman. SPT

Rise, underground sleepers, rise from the grave. Ode against St. Cecilia's Day. George Barker. PoA

Rise Up, O Men of God, *with music.* William Pierson Merrill. AH

"Rise up, rise up, my seven brave sons." Earl Brand (The Douglas Tragedy). *Unknown.* FaBoBa

"Rise up, rise up, now, Lord Douglas," she says. The Douglas Tragedy. *Unknown.* IPWM; PeBB

Rise up, rise up, you seven sleepers. Earl Brand. *Unknown.* FSW

Rise Up, Shepherd, and Follow. *Unknown.* FSW

Rise up, thou monstrous ant-hill on the plain. Wordsworth. *Fr.* The Prelude, VII. HAP

Rise, Ye Children, *with music.* Justus Falckner, *tr. fr. German by* Emma Frances Bevan. AH

Rise You Up, My True Love. *Unknown.* AmFP

Risen is the sleeper from the vaulted past. War. Georg Heym, *tr. by* Peter Viereck. AMV-80

Rises at five, just when a late moon. The Insomniac Sleeps Well for Once and. Hayden Carruth. NNaP

Rising, The/ Let me proceed by this way. Canoe-hauling Chant. *Tr. by* Apirana Ngata. WTO

Rising at dawn to pee, I thought I saw you. In Memory of My Cat Domino: 1951-1966. Roy Fuller. PSN

Rising Five. Norman Nicholson. MPo

Rising fondly before me. The Beloved's Image. *Tr. by* M. W. Beckwith. WTO

Rising from bed. Poem before Birth. George MacBeth. SLP

Rising from the pale valley, the rivers unseen from here. Oxford Commination. Paris Leary. AMV-81

Rising Glory of America, The, *sel.* Philip Freneau.
"Now shall the adventurous muse attempt a theme." AmVN

Rising High Water Blues. *Unknown.* BluL

Rising in lamplight dying at dawn. Voices Answering Back: The Vampires. Lawrence Raab. AmPA

Rising in the Morning. Hugh Rhodes. OxBChV

Rising of the Buffalo Men. *Unknown, tr. fr. American Indian.* SFF
("I rise, I rise/ I who makes the earth to tremble.") ANTL

Rising of the Moon, The. *Unknown.* FSW; RDB, *with music*

Rising sun complies with our weak sight, The. Edmund Waller. *Fr.* To the King, upon His Majesty's Happy Return. SCP-2

Rising through sky. Planet Dream. T. Alan Broughton. FAF

Rising tide of shade in the thin gullies, The. Evening. Andrew Taylor. FPA

Risk, The. Anne Sexton. BoWoP

Risselty-Rosselty. *Unknown.* FSW

Rissem. Sandra M. Gilbert. AMV-81

Rita Rio. Richard Williams. AAN

Rite, The. Dudley Randall. HoPM (1975 ed.)

Rites for Cousin Vit, The. Gwendolyn Brooks. *Fr.* The Womanhood. BPo; HAP; WPE

Rites of Passage. Audre Lorde. CNA; PoBA

Ritual, The. Paul David Ashley. DNGG

Ritual, The. Joy Gwillim. AMV-80

Ritual, The. Marge Piercy. MMD

Ritual, The. E. J. Pratt. NoAM

Ritual for extracting pain. On the Run. William Sprunt. AAN

Ritual Mouse, A. William Meredith. PBMP

Ritual of Departure. Thomas Kinsella. CIP; CMoP (1970 ed.)

Ritual Three. David Ignatow. ConAP

Ritual to Read to Each Other, A. William Stafford. SoS

Rituals. Lori Shpunt. PoUp

Rivage. Hunter Brown. AAN

Rival Curates, The. W. S. Gilbert. BBL; VLP

Rivalry. Alden Nowlan. POL

Rivals, The. James Stephens. NoAM; PCOP; RAE

Riven Quarry, The. Gloria C. Oden. PoBA

River, The. Robert Adamson. GAS

River, The. Sam Cornish. PoBA

River, The. Hart Crane. *Fr.* The Bridge: Powhatan's Daughter. CMoP (1970 ed.); GOA; NoAM; NOBA; PiAm

River, The. Richard Kell. IPM

River, The. Edwin Muir. MS

River, A. A. K. Ramanujan. MPo

River, The. James Stephens. ECBV

River, The. Phyllis Hoge Thompson. PHC

River, The. Leo Vroman. VWA

River and Light. Siv Cedering Fox. RiTi

River at its brim, The. Landscape 4. Robert Gray. CAAP

River brought down, The. How We Heard the Name. Alan Dugan. NoAM

River Compared to an Oratorical Sentence, The. Luis de Góngora, *tr. fr. Spanish by* Edward Meryon Wilson. *Fr.* The First Solitude. OBVE

River Crossing, The. Denis Glover. ATNZ

River Dart, The. *Unknown.* GBP

River does not move, The. Quai de l'Horloge. Peter Nelson. PHC

River Don, The. *Unknown.* GBP

River Duddon, The, *sels.* Wordsworth.
  After-Thought, XXXIV. MBPR
  (Valediction to the River Duddon.) NOBE
  "Child of the clouds! remote from every taint," II. MBPR
  "Not envying Latian shades—if yet they throw," I. MBPR Return. HAP

River flows between me and the dead, A. Neighbours. Patrick King. IPM

River God, The. Stevie Smith. FaBoNo; FaBoTw (1975 ed.); PBWP

River is a thought that pours slowly, The. Landscape. R. A. Simpson. GAS

River is deep and the river is wide. Kansas City Blues. *Unknown.* FSW

River Kleeg, The. Greg Kuzma. BrS

River-march-drowse. Lorine Niedecker. RiTi

River-Mates. Padraic Colum. LoAs; PFIr

River-Merchant's Wife, The: A Letter. Li Po, *tr. tr. Chinese by* Ezra Pound. BoLoP; CABA (1972 ed.); HAP; InPK; InPS; IPWM; LoAs; NIL; NoAM; NOBA; NOBE; OBVE; PAIC; PPoe; PPP; SoS; TAP; TPo; UnPo (1976 ed.)

River of Bees, The. W. S. Merwin. HeIP

River of Dart, O river of Dart. The Dart. *Unknown.* GBP

River of Rivers in Connecticut, The. Wallace Stevens. HAP; NOBA; VGW

River plunges to the spillway floor, The. The Good Life. Robert Francis. PoIA

River rattles its money, A. Sleeping Out in Vermont. Conrad Hilberry. PPoD

River Rhyme. William Carlos Williams. PoA

River-Rhythm Town. Quincy Troupe. SES

River Road. Stanley Kunitz. NoAM

River Road. Mary Shumway. NVAP

River Roads. Carl Sandburg. VGW

River Roses. D. H. Lawrence. CMoP (1970 ed.); GBL; OAEL-2

Riversong. Michael Anania. HeS

River Song. Weldon Kees. NoAM; PPP

River Swelleth More and More, The. Henry David Thoreau. NOBA

River That Is East, The. Galway Kinnell. NYP

River that must turn full after I stop dying. "A 11." Louis Zukofsky. *Fr.* "A." VGW

River, that rollest by the ancient walls. Stanzas to the Po. Byron. OAEL-2

River this November afternoon, The. The Double Vision. C. Day Lewis. NoAM

River turns, The. The Pike. Theodore Roethke. STS

River was announcing, The. The River Crossing. Denis Glover. ATNZ

River waters ran luke-cold about, The. Virginia Woolf. Gerald Locklin. PoW

Riverbed. David Wagoner. CNW

Riverdale Lion. John Robert Colombo. LP

Riverfront, St. Louis. John Knoepfle. TAT

Rivers. J. C. Squire. PES

Rivers and Mountains. John Ashbery. NoAM; NOBA

Rivers Arise; Whether Thou Be the Son. Milton. InPK

River's blue where it reflects the sky, The. Absence of Noise Presence of Sound. Olga Broumas. PCho

Riverside Drive, November Fifth. Katha Pollitt. AMV-81

Rivets. N. S. Olds. RhR

Rizpah. Tennyson. PAIC; VLP

Roach, The. John Raven. BPo; HoPM (1975 ed.)

Roaches. Edward Field. NYP

Road, The. Helene Johnson. AmNP (1974 ed.)

Road, The. Edwin Muir. CMoP (1970 ed.)

Road Again, The. Tom Matthews. IPM

Road along the Thumb and Forefinger, The ("The road all the way up along the coast"). Mark Hickey. AMV-81

Road at My Door, The. W. B. Yeats. Meditations in Time of Civil War, V. BIrV; NOBE

Road at the top of the rise, The. The Middleness of the Road. Robert Frost. NOBA

Road beneath the giant original trees, The. Sanctuary. Judith Wright. WPE

Road can't be as sad as a shoe is sad, A. Shoe. John Perreault. EAS

Road climbs, villages, The. Going. Peter Everwine. NNaP

Road dark, the country wild, the pair, The. Two Companions and the Bear. David Slavitt. BCr

Road deepening in the North, A. The Stone Harp. John Haines. CNW

Road ends with the hills, The. Black Tarn. V. Sackville-West. SBG

Road from Adonoi to I Don't Know. The Three Towns. Howard Nemerov. AMV-81

Road goes ever on and on, The. The Old Walking Song. J. R. R. Tolkien. RFM

Road in Kentucky, A. Robert Hayden. NCSH

Road is a crayon line, A. One bus. Child's Drawing. Allan Block. FAF

Road Is Wider than Long, The, *sel.* Roland Penrose. "They breathe with the night." EAS

Road Not Taken, The. Robert Frost. CMoP (1970 ed.); HAP; HeIP; ILP (1975 ed.); LFH; NoAM; PoIA; RFM; SoSe; STS; TAP; VoPo

Road of Birds, The. Harry Humes. AMV-80

Road outside the window was "our" road, The. Thomas McGrath. *Fr.* Letter to an Imaginary Friend. GP

Road runs straight with no turning, the circle, The. Black People: This Is Our Destiny. Amiri Baraka. CAPP; CNA

Road Show. Geoff Page. FPA

Road the Crows Own, The. Susan Astor. AMV-81

Road to Pengya, The. Tu Fu, *tr. fr. Chinese by* Rewi Alley *and* Edward Field. Prf

Road to School, The. Joy M. Lane. AMV-81

Road to Texas, The. Berta Hart Nance. BPAW

Road to Utterly. H. H. Lewis. SPT

Road to your house leads past the motley plane trees, The. I Am Moved by a Necessity from Within. Daisy Aldan. RiTi

Road to Zoagli, The. Max Beerbohm. FaBoNo

Road turned out to be a cul-de-sac, The. Brothers and Sisters. Judith Wright. GAS

Road twisted through tongues of rock, The. The Vowels of Another Language. Tom Disch. PoA

Road was one she saw each day, The. The Sacrament. Robert P. Tristram Coffin. TH

Road winds down through autumn hills, The. Tour 5. Robert Hayden. PPP

Roadmenders' Song, The. *Gond Oral Tradition, tr. by* V. Elwin *and* S. Hivale. WTO

Road Runner. Sharlot M. Hall. BPAW

Road-Runner, The. Philip Whalen. VoA

Roadrunner and Coyote. Sharon Leiter. AAN

Road-runner dodged through the chaparral, A. A California Idyl. Ernest McGaffey. BPAW

Roads, The. Stephen Stepanchev. SA

Roads Also, The. Wilfred Owen. EBEV

Roads are very dirty, my boots are very thin, The. *Unknown.* CC

Road's End. Rolf Jacobsen, *tr. fr. Norwegian by* Robert Bly. NU

Road's End, The. John Montague. TwMBP

Roads go on, ending only, The. The Runner. Jerah Chadwick. AMV-81

Roads have come to their end now, The. Road's End. Rolf Jacobsen, *tr. by* Robert Bly. NU

Roads were jammed, The. Snow in the City. Danny Siegel. VWA

Roaring alongside he takes for granted, The. Sandpiper. Elizabeth Bishop. HeIP; ILP (1975 ed.); PiAm

Roaring company that festive night, A. The Dark and the Fair. Stanley Kunitz. LoAs

Roaring Frost, The. Alice Meynell. WPE

Rob me and maim me! Why, man, take such pains. To One Who Quotes and Detracts. Walter Savage Landor. FaBoEE

Robbed of our rights, and by such water-rats? In Defiance to the Dutch. *Unknown.* APAS

Robber, The. "Hugh MacDiarmid," *after the Cretan.* OBVE

Robbers. *Unknown.* ECBV

Robbers came to our house, The. *Unknown.* GBP

Robbing and Stealing Blues. *Unknown.* BluL

Robbing the Tree Hive. Ernest G. Moll. PoTa

Robene and Makyne ("Robene sat on gud grene hill"). Robert Henryson. BoLoP

Robens' Promised Land. George Purdom. WTO

Robert. Lucille Clifton. CAAP

Robert Bruce's March to Bannockburn. Burns. *See* Scots Wha Hae.

Robert Frost. Robert Lowell. NoAM

Robert Fulton. Ann Stanford. GP

Robert Lowell. Richard O'Connell. AMV-81

Robert of Lincoln. Bryant. EAP

Robert Whitmore. Frank Marshall Davis. BPo; PoBA

Roberta. *Unknown.* BluL

Robertin Tush. *Unknown.* GBP

Robert's Farm. *Unknown.* FSW

Robin, A. Walter de la Mare. CMoP (1970 ed.); PB

Robin, The. Thomas Hardy. RAE

Robin and Gandelein. *Unknown.* OxBM

Robin and Richard were two pretty men. Mother Goose. BBL; MG

Robin and the wren, The. Robin, Wren, Martin, Swallow. *Unknown.* GBP

Robin Goodfellow, *sel. Unknown.* Lily, Germander, and Sops-in-Wine, *fr.* Pt. II. ECBV

Robin Hood. Gray Burr. NCSH

Robin Hood. Keats. MBPR

Robin Hood. Phyllis McGinley. *Fr.* Speaking of Television. OBSV

Robin Hood. *Unknown.* OSF

Robin Hood and Allen a Dale. *Unknown.* GBP; PeBB

Robin Hood and Little John. *Unknown.* AmFP

Robin Hood and the Bishop of Hereford. *Unknown.* PeBB

Robin Hood and the Monk. *Unknown.* FaBoBa

Robin Hood and the Sheriff. *Unknown.* PeBB

Robin Hood's Death. *Unknown.* FaBoBa

Robin Hood's gone to Nottinghame gane. Robin Hood and the Sheriff. *Unknown.* PeBB

Robin in Winter, The, *sel.* William Cowper. "No noise is here, or none that hinders thought." BoAnP

Robin, I've been reading Faust. Reading Faust. Judah Goldin. AMV-81

Robin on a leafless bough. Robin Redbreast. W. H. Davies. PB

Robin Redbreast. William Allingham. OxBChV

Robin Redbreast. W. H. Davies. PB

Robin Redbreast. Stanley Kunitz. Prf

Robin Redbreast in a Cage, A, *abr.* Blake. *Fr.* Auguries of Innocence. AKE
(Three Things to Remember, 6 *ll.*) ECBV

Robin Redbreast's Testament. *Unknown.* GBP

Robin sings of willow-buds, The. Bird Song. Laura E. Richards. PCOP

Robin, Wren, Martin, Swallow. *Unknown.* GBP

Robin's Poem, A. Nikki Giovanni. AmNP (1974 ed.)

Robin's Song, The. *Unknown, at. to* Richard Honeywood. ECBV; RAE

Robinson. Weldon Kees. AnMo; NoAM

Robinson at cards at the Algonquin; a thin. Aspects of Robinson. Weldon Kees. AnMo; NYP

Robinson at Home. Weldon Kees. AnMo

Robinson Crusoe. Robert Creeley. *Fr.* An Illness. UsP

Robinson Crusoe's Story. Charles Edward Carryl. *Fr.* Davy and the Goblin, *ch.* 11. ECBV

Robyn, A/ Joly Robyn. Sir Thomas Wyatt. AAS

Roc, The. Richard Eberhart. CMoP (1970 ed.)

Rock, The, *sel.* T. S. Eliot.
   "O Light Invisible, we praise Thee!" *fr.* Chorus X. ILwL

Rock, The. Mary Fabilli. AMV-81

Rock, The. W. S. Merwin. NYP

Rock, The. *Unknown, tr. fr. Welsh by* Geoffrey Grigson. GBL

Rock, a leaf, mud, even the grass, A. The Concealment: Ishi, the Last Wild Indian. William Stafford. TCP

Rock About My Saro Jane. *Unknown.* FSW

Rock and Hawk. Robinson Jeffers. IPWM; NoAM; NOBA

Rock and precipice. Landscape. Octavio Paz, *tr. by* Charles Tomlinson. OBVE

Rock Climbing. Jane Cooper. NMM

Rock drops in a bucket, A. Waters. Donald Hall. UsP

Rock Island Line, The. *Unknown.* AmFP; FSW

Rock-like mud unfroze a little and rills, The. The Manor Farm. Edward Thomas. ExPo (1973 ed.)

Rock 'n' Row Me Over. *Unknown.* FSW

Rock-O-La plays Country and Western, The. Writing on Napkins at the Sunshine Club, Macon, Georgia 1971. David Bottoms. TAT

Rock of Ages. Augustus Montague Toplady. BLSH, *with music;* BLSo, *with music;* FaPoR; FSW

Rock Painting. Carroll Arnett. VoR

Rock Pilgrim. Herbert Palmer. OxBTC

Rock Pool, The. Alfred Noyes. EcS

Rock Pool, The. Edward Shanks. EcS

Rock swallows the snake, The. Kindred. Douglas Stewart. MAuV

Rock-a My Soul. *Unknown.* FSW

Rock-a-by Lady, The. Eugene Field. PCOP

Rock-a-Bye Baby, *with music.* Effie I. Canning. FSN

Rock-a-bye baby, on [*or* in] the tree top. Mother Goose. FSW; GSB, *with music*

Rock-a-bye, baby, thy cradle is green. Mother Goose. MG

Rock'd in the Cradle of the Deep, *with music.* Emma Hart Willard. PSoN

Rocking. A. R. Ammons. GP

Rocking Hymn, A. George Wither. OxBChV

Rockland. Julia Randall. CSP; WPE

Rocks. Richard Packer. FPA

Rocks and Gravel. Alan Lomax *and* W. B. Richardson. FSW

Rocks have been my pillow, baby. Homeless Blues. *Unknown.* BluL

Rocky Acres. Robert Graves. NoAM; UnPo (1976 ed.)
   "This is a wild land, country of my choice," *sel.* IP

Rocky Island, The. *Unknown.* AmFP

Rocky Mountains, The. *Unknown.* AmFP

Rocky Road to Dublin, The. *Unknown.* FaBoBa

Rod was but a harmless wand, The. The Virtues of Sid Hamet, the Magician's Rod. Swift. APAS

Roddy M'Corley. *Unknown.* FSW

Rodeo. Edward Lueders. MPA; SPo

Rodin to Rilke. Emily Grosholz. AMV-80

Roe (and my joy to name), thou art now to go. To William Roe. Ben Jonson. OAEL-1

Roethke Plain. John Malcolm Brinnin. NoAM; TAP

Rogation Sunday. William Carlos Williams. TT

Roger and Me. Anne Le Dressay. AMV-81

Roger the Dog. Ted Hughes. FPB

Rokeby, *sels.* Sir Walter Scott.
   Allen-a-Dale, *fr.* III. PoTa

Brignall Banks, *fr.* IIJ. ILP (1975 ed.)
   Rover's Farewell, The, *fr.* III. NOBE

Rokeby Venus, The. Robert Conquest. NoAM

Roll, *Alabama,* Roll. *Unknown.* AIW

Roll Call: A Land of Old Folk and Children. Isaac J. Black. CNA

Roll forth, my song, like the rushing river. The Nameless One. James Clarence Mangan. BIrV

Roll in My Sweet Baby's Arms. *Unknown.* FSW

Roll, Jordan, Roll. *Unknown.* AH, *with music;* FSW

Roll on, sad world! not Mercury or Mars. Sonnet. Frederick Goddard Tuckerman. *Fr.* Sonnets. PiAm

Roll on the Ground. *Unknown.* AmFP; FSW

Roll on, thou ball, roll on! To the Terrestrial Globe. W. S. Gilbert. FaBoNo

Roll on, thou deep and dark blue Ocean—roll! Byron's Address to the Ocean. Byron. *Fr.* Childe Harold's Pilgrimage, IV. EcS; RhR

Roll Over. *Unknown.* FSW

Roll the Cotton Down. *Unknown.* AmFP

Roll the Union On. Claude Williams *and* Lee Hays. FSW

Rolled over on Europe: the sharp dew frozen to stars. Stephen Spender. CMoP (1970 ed.)

Rolleth the seventh wave. Gavin Bantock. *Fr.* Christ. TwMBP

Rolling along through Ohio. Ohio. John Updike. AMV-80

Rolling and tossing out sparkles like roses. Night Landscape. Joan Aiken. DuDa

Rolling away from Chicago. Derricks. R. R. Cuscaden. ANTL

Rolling clouds of greasy smoke. The Forest Fire. Arthur W. Monroe. BPAW

Rolling English Road, The. G. K. Chesterton. NOBE; NOBL; OxBTC; PPoD

Rolling from St. Patrick's, The. Burial of An Irish President. Austin Clarke. BIrV

Rolling Home. Charles Mackay. FSW

Rolling Log Blues. *Unknown.* BluL

Rolling off the freeway, the football crowd. Saturday Afternoon. Larry Rubin. CSP

Rolling wheel that runneth often round, The. Amoretti, XVIII. Spenser. Epi

Rolly Trudum. *Unknown.* AmFP
   (Lolly-Too-Dum.) FSW

Roman Candle. Neil Weiss. LoAs

Roman Earl, The. *Unknown, tr. fr. Irish by* Douglas Hyde. OBVE

Roman Fountain. Louise Bogan. SBG

Roman, A, had an/ artist, a freedman. Marianne Moore. *Fr.* The Jerboa. CMoP (1970 ed.)

Roman Kamin grunted through art class. In Imago Dei: Fiat Lux. Roderick Hartigh Jellema. AATT

Roman Officer Writes, A. C. M. Doughty. *Fr.* The Dawn in Britain. FaBoTw (1975 ed.)

Roman Road, The. Thomas Hardy. NOBE

Roman Roman, A. Crescenzo del Monte, *tr. fr. Judeo-Romanesque by* Barbara Garvin. VWA

Roman ruins below. Under the Cellar. Ralph Salisbury. MPA

Roman soldiers come riding in full speed. "Sin-Killer" Griffin. *Fr.* The Man of Calvary. AmFP

Roman threw us a road, a road, The. History. G. K. Chesterton. *Fr.* Songs of Education. OBSV

Roman Virgil, thou that singest. To Virgil. Tennyson. OAEL-2

Romance, A. Chester Kallman. PoA

Romance. Poe. *See* Introduction: "Romance, who loves to nod and sing."

Romance. Walter James Turner. NOBE

Romance of the precise is not the elision, The. Adult Epigram. Wallace Stevens. NIL

Romance of the Rose, The, *sel.* Guillaume de Lorris *and* Jean de Meun, *tr. fr.* French by F. S. Ellis. "Short space my feet had traversed ere." OAEL-1

Romance, who loves to nod and sing. Introduction [*or* Romance]. Poe. ILP (1975 ed.); NOBA

Romanies in Town, The. Anne Beresford. LP; MPo

Romans Angry about the Inner World. Robert Bly. NoAM; NOBA; PPoe

Romans, rheumatic, gouty, came. La Condition Botanique. Anthony Hecht. NoAM

Romantic, The. Colin Ellis. POL

Romantic. George Garrett. CoPAm; HoPM (1975 ed.)

Romantic Age, The. Ogden Nash. SFF

Romantic Poem. Anne Waldman. RiTi

Romantics. Maurice Lindsay. MS

Rome. J. V. Cunningham, *after the Latin of* Janus Vitalis Panormitanus. OBVE

Rome. Thomas Hardy. VLP

Rome, Conquerer, Conquered. Joshua Sylvester. FaBoEE

Rome Ryme. Joseph Hall. *Fr.* Virgidemiarum, Bk. IV, Satire VII. TVS

Romeo and Juliet, *sels.* Shakespeare.
"Alas, that love whose view is muffled still," *fr.* I, i. LFH
"But, soft! What light through yonder window breaks?" *fr.* II, ii. Moon
(Juliet.) PCOP
"Gallop apace, you fiery-footed steeds," *fr.* III, ii. GBL
"How oft when men are at the point of death," *fr.* V, iii. DL
"If I profane with my unworthiest hand," *fr.* I, v. BiP; IP; SoSe
"Lady, by yonder blessed moon I swear," *fr.* II, ii. Moon
"O, then I see Queen Mab hath been with you," *fr.* I, iv. STS
"Wilt thou be gone? it is not yet near day," *fr.* III, v. PAIC

Romp. Dave Etter. WeW

Romping. John Ciardi. CTBA; NCSH

Ron talked continuously/ to a complete stranger. A Great Talker. William Lindsay. PMW

Rondeau: "By two black eyes my heart was won." *Unknown.* FaBoCo

Rondeau: "Help me to seek, for I lost it there." Sir Thomas Wyatt. *See* Help Me to Seek.

Rondeau: "Jenny kissed me when we met." Leigh Hunt. *See* Jenny Kiss'd Me.

Rondeau: "Of Eden lost, in ancient days." George Ellis. PAIC

Rondel: Autumn. Matt Field. AMV-80

Rondel: "Beside the idle summer sea." W. E. Henley. NIL

Rondel: "Kissing her hair I sat against her feet." Swinburne. PAIC

Rondel: "Now that I am fifty-six." Muriel Rukeyser. FF

Rondel of Love [*or* Luve], A. Alexander Scott. BoLoP; SLP

Rondel; the Wanderer. Austin Dobson. PAIC

Rondelay, A: "Chloe found Amyntas lying." Dryden. PAIC

Roof Garden, The. Howard Moss. MAT; NYP

Roof is shattered, the bone house splintered, The. In Memory of G. K., for 50 Years the College Carpenter. Robert A. Martin. AATT

Roof of the World, The. Michael Dennis Browne. AmPA

Roofers roof from the bottom up, The. Technique. Philip Pierson. AMV-80

Roofs are lit with rain, The. Vincent Buckley. *Fr.* Stroke. MAuV

Roofs over the shops, The. Christmas Eve. Patricia Beer. HeHu

Roof's peak is eye. Sitting Here. Robert Creeley. RRA

Rooftop Winter. Dwayne Thorpe. AMV-80

Roofwalker, The. Adrienne Rich. PiAm; PPP; Psy

Rook he sells feathers, yet he still doth cry. Upon Rook: Epigram. Robert Herrick. CaPo

Rooks, The. Jane Euphemia Browne. OxBChV

Rooks, The. *Unknown.* GBP

Rooks above the convent walls, The. The Convent. "Seumas O'Sullivan." PFIr; POL

Rooks are building on the trees, The. The Rooks. Jane Euphemia Browne. OxBChV

Rook's nest do rock on the tree-top, The. Lullaby. William Barnes. VLP

Room, The. Conrad Aiken. ILP (1975 ed.); NOBA

Room, The. Duncan Glen. MIS

Room, The. De Leon Harrison. PoBA

Room. Shirley Kaufman. NMM

Room. Glenn John Kim. PHC

Room, The. W. S. Merwin. NOBA

Room, The. William Soutar. EBEV

Room. Ruth Stone. BoWoP

Room, The. Mark Strand. UsP

Room above the Square, The. Stephen Spender. NOBE

Room after room. Love in a Life. Robert Browning. NOBE

Room Conditioner. A. R. Ammons. PCho

Room is four walls, A. Walls. Alice Corbin. WPW

Room must be warmer than, The. How the Invalids Make Love. Susan Feldman. AmPA

Room of Her Own, A. Rita Garitano. FoP

Room of Return ("Room over the Hudson"). Galway Kinnell. NYP

Room Poems. Eli Bachar, *tr. fr.* Hebrew by Jeremy Garber. VWA

Room, room, make room for the bouncing belly. Pleasure Reconciled to Virtue. Ben Jonson. OAEL-1

Room! room to turn around in, to breathe and be free. Kit Carson's Ride. Joaquin Miller. BPAW

Room the size of a warehouse, A. Cairo Hotel. J. R. Rowland. MAuV

Room was a, The/ red glow. We Dance like Ella Riffs. Carolyn M. Rodgers. CNA; PoBA

Room was divided by a curtain, The. The Tailor's Wedding. Louis Simpson. NNaP

Room was suddenly rich and the great bay-window was, The. Snow. Louis MacNeice. BiP; CIP; CMoP (1970 ed.); ExPo (1973 ed.); NoAM; NOBE; OxBTC

Room where someone, A. Avenue Y. Anita Barrows. VWA

Room with Revolutionists. Edwin Rolfe. SPT

Rooming House. Ted Kooser. POL

Rooms. Charlotte Mew. PBWP

Roosevelt, Renaissance, Gem, Alhambra, The. Movies. Langston Hughes. ILP (1975 ed.)

Rooster Be? or a Crow? *Unknown. See* To Be or Not to Be.

Roosters. Elizabeth Bishop. CoPAm

Roosters. Elizabeth J. Coatsworth. SO

Roosters Will Crow, The. Cecília Meireles, *tr. fr.* Portuguese by John Nist *and* Yolanda Leite. PBWP

Root. Miklós Radnóti, *tr. fr.* Hungarian by Steven Polgar *and* Stephen Berg *and* S. J. Marks. VWA

Root Cellar. Theodore Roethke. HeIP; PiAm; PoIA; PPP

Root-Crops. Derek Bowman. MIS

Root Eater, The. Ai. CAAP

Root Hog or Die. *Unknown.* AmFP; FSW

Roots. Lorraine Sutton. NW

Roots and Branches. Robert Duncan. VGW

Roots are filament-thin in this grave air. Lava Tubes. John Unterecker. PHC

Roots around your soul and eyes, The. Sweating It Out on Winding Stair Mountain. Jim Barnes. CDW

Roots of fern, The. In Split: Diocletian's Palace. Stephen Stepanchev. SA

Roots of mankind are tangled in my hair, The. Epitaph. Wendy Rose. CDW

Roots of Revolution in the Vegetable Kingdom, The. Constance Urdang. GP

Roped bear's friendly enough there, The. Muse. M. Deiter Keyishian. BCr

Ropewalk, The. Longfellow. PiAm

Rorate coeli desuper. Unto Us a Child Is Born. William Dunbar. BoReV

Rory and Liam are dead and gone. In Memoriam. Padraig de Brun. WTO

Rosalie. Danny L. Rendleman. TC

Rosalie, the Prairie Flower, *with music.* George Frederick Root. BLSo

Rosalynde; or, Euphues' Golden Legacy, *sel.* Thomas Lodge. Rosalind's Madrigal. NOBE

Rosary, The, *with music.* Robert Cameron Rogers. BLSH; BLSo; FSN

Rosciad, The ("Roscius deceas'd, each high aspiring play'r"). Charles Churchill. EPC

Rose, The. Thomas Howell. FSFS

Rose. Kathleen Raine. WPE

Rose, The. Theodore Roethke. BiP; InPS; NOBA; PiAm; PPoe

Rose, The. Christina Rossetti. PF

Rose, The. William Carlos Williams. NOBA

Rose, The/ was not searching for the sunrise. Casida of the Rose. Federico García Lorca, *tr. by* Robert Bly. NU

Rose and grape, pear and bean. *Unknown, tr. fr. Spanish by* Willis Barnstone. BoWoP

Rose-apple is in fruit, The. Show Me the Way. *Unknown, tr. by* U Win Pe. PBWP

Rose Aylmer. Walter Savage Landor. BoLoP; CABA (1972 ed.); HAP; HeIP; HoPM (1975 ed.); ILP (1975 ed.); NIL; NOBE; UnPo (1976 ed.)

Rose Bay Willow Herb. Judy Ray. AMV-81

Rose-cheeked [*or* cheekt] Laura, Come. Thomas Campion. ExPo (1973 ed.); InPK; InPS; OAEL-1; PAIC (Laura.) NOBE ("Rose-cheekt Lawra, come.") AAS

Rose Connoley. *Unknown.* AmFP

Rose fades, The. Poem. William Carlos Williams. NIL

Rose Family, The. Robert Frost. NIL; OBAL; SoSe

Rose, harsh rose. Sea Rose. Hilda Doolittle ("H. D."). NoAM

Rose in October, A. James Whitcomb Riley. OBAL

Rose in the Garden. *Unknown.* AmFP

Rose is a rose, The. The Rose Family. Robert Frost. NIL; OBAL; SoSe

Rose Is Dying, The. E. E. Cummings. NIL

Rose kissed me today. A Kiss. Austin Dobson. *Fr.* Rose-Leaves. PPoD

Rose-Leaves, *sels.* Austin Dobson.
   Kiss, A. PPoD
   Urceus Exit. PAIC
   (Triolet.) PoPle

Rose of all the world is not for me, The. The Little White Rose. Compton Mackenzie. MS

Rose of Solitude, The. William Everson. PiAm

Rose of the World, The. W. B. Yeats. CMoP (1970 ed.); NIL

Rose of Tralee, The. C. Mordaunt Spencer. BLSH, *with music;* FSW

Rose, on this terrace fifty years ago. The Roses on the Terrace. Tennyson. VLP

Rose Red's hair is brown as fur. An Embroidery. Denise Levertov. BCr; NMM; NU; RiTi

Rose That Bore Jesu, The. *Unknown.* OxBM

Rose, the Lily, the Sun and the Dove, The. Heine, *tr. fr. German by* P. G. L. Webb. NAWM-2

Rose Tree, The. W. B. Yeats. CMoP (1970 ed.)

Rose upon the wall, The. The Canticle of the Rose. Edith Sitwell. NoAM

Rose was sick and, smiling, died, The. The Funeral Rites of the Rose. Robert Herrick. CABA (1972 ed.); CaPo; NIL

Roseberry to his lady says. Supper Is Na Ready. *Unknown.* GBP

Rosebud. Jon Anderson. CAAP

Rosebud Morales, my friend. Pentecost. Ai. PCho

Rosemary Freeth. Rosemary's Teeth. Michael Dugan. FPB

Rosemary, Rosemary, let down your hair. A Nonsense Song. Stephen Vincent Benét. OBAL

Rosemary's Teeth. Michael Dugan. FPB

Roses. Geoffrey Lehmann. CAAP

Roses. *Unknown.* OxBM

Roses and Revolutions. Dudley Randall. BPo; CNA; ConAP; NoAM; PoBA; TAP

Roses are red,/ Violets blue;/ Pinks are sweet. *Unknown.* PCOP

Roses are red, diddle diddle, lavender's blue. The Lady's Song in Leap Year. *Unknown.* GBP

Roses at first were white. How Roses Came Red. Robert Herrick. CaPo

Roses Gone Wild. John Taylor. AMV-80

Roses of Queens, The. Claire Nicholas White. NYP

Roses of Sa'adi, The. Marceline Desbordes-Valmore, *tr. fr. French by* Barbara Howes. BoWoP

Roses on the Terrace, The. Tennyson. VLP

Roses, Revisited, in a Paradoxical Autumn. J. W. Cullum. AMV-81

Roses, their sharp spines being gone. A Bridal Song. *At. to* Shakespeare. *Fr.* The Two Noble Kinsmen, I, i. NOBE

Roses, too, need pruning, The. The Parting Chores. Danny L. Rendleman. TC

Roses with the scent bred out. In Lieu. Louis MacNeice. CMoP (1970 ed.)

Rosewood Casket. *Unknown.* FSW

Rosh Pina. Dovid Knut, *tr. fr. Russian by* Daniel Weissbort. VWA

Rosie Bakungan. Edward Smith. EC

Rosy Apple, Lemon or Pear. *Unknown.* POL

Rosy shield upon its back, A. The Dead Crab. Andrew Young. FaBoTw (1975 ed.)

Rotation. Julian Bond. FF; NIL

Rothesay, O. *Unknown.* FSW

Rothko. James Moore. AMV-81

Roubaix Cemetery. Franklin Brainard. HeS

Rou-cou spoke the dove. Song of Fixed Accord. Wallace Stevens. InPS

Rouen. May Wedderburn Cannan. OxBTC

Rough. Stephen Spender. *See* My Parents Kept Me.

Rough fir, hauled from the hills. The Making of the Cross. William Everson. VGW

Rough wind, that moanest loud. A Dirge. Shelley. CABA (1972 ed.); GrRo; ILP (1975 ed.); InPK; NOBE; TPo; UsP; VoPo

Rough winds do shake/ do shake/ the darling buds of May. Song: "Rough Winds Do Shake the Darling Buds of May." Louis Simpson. SFF

Roughly estimated ones, who do not sort well, The. The Monuments of Hiroshima. D. J. Enright. HeHu

Roughly figured, this man of moderate habits. Life Cycle of Common Man. Howard Nemerov. MPo; NIL; TPo

Roulette. Brewster Ghiselin. WasP

Round. Rachel Boimwall, *tr. fr. Yiddish by* Gabriel Preil *and* Howard Schwartz. VWA

Round, The. Philip Booth. NCSH

Round. Weldon Kees. NoAM

Round a cleft in the cliffs to come upon. Venus of the Salty Shell. Denis Devlin. BIrV

Round about, round about. Counting Out Rhyme. *Unknown.* SpRo

Round and round. Private Transport. Adrian Mitchell. FaBoEE

Round and round and round I spin. Discovery. Myra Cohn Livingston. LCL

Round and Round Hitler's Grave. *Unknown.* FSW

Round, calm faces rosy with the cold, The. Japanese Children. James Kirkup. RAE

Round dance of day has gone. Sitting Alone in Tulsa Three A.M. Lance Henson. VoR

Round-head round-eyed Sebastian. Photograph of a Baby. Charles Brasch. ATNZ

Round Her Neck She Wore a Yellow Ribbon. *Unknown.* FSW

Round-hoof'd, short-jointed, fetlocks shag and long. A Horse. Shakespeare. *Fr.* Venus and Adonis. ExPo (1973 ed.)

Round Miss Bell's pond the grasses and weeds. Reynard. Gwen Dunn. DuDr

'Round my Indiana homestead wave the cornfields. On the Banks of the Wabash, Far Away. Paul Dresser. BLSo; FSN; FSW

Round Song, A. Rhyll McMaster. FPA

Round Table, The. Peggy Susberry Kenner. JB

Round the Bay of Mexico. *Unknown.* FSW

Round the cape of a sudden came the sea. Parting at Morning. Robert Browning. FF; HeIP; ILP (1975 ed.); LoAs; NOBE; PAIC; SoSe; STS; UnPo (1976 ed.); VLP

Round Things. William Barnes. VLP

Round Trip to Chicago. Martha Shelley. WBN

Rounded world is fair to see, The. Nature. Emerson. ILP (1975 ed.)

Roundel: "Now welcome, somer, with thy sunne softe." Chaucer. *See* Now Welcom[e], Summer.

Roundhouse Voices, The. Dave Smith. AMV-80; LiSp

Roundup Cook, The. Robert V. Carr. BPAW

Rouse for Stevens, A. Theodore Roethke. OBAL

Route 40—Ohio, U.S.A. Milton Kessler. CoPAm

Route 95 North: New Jersey. P. C. Bowman. AMV-80

Route of evanescence, A. Emily Dickinson. AmVN; TT

Route Six. Stanley Kunitz. AMV-80

Route 29. Catharine Savage Brosman. AMV-81

Routes. Peter Everwine. FiCP; NNaP

Rover killed the goat. Brave Rover. Max Beerbohm. GDP

Rover, with the good brown head. Matthew Arnold. *Fr.* Matthias. PCat

Rovers, The, *sel.* George Canning.
Song by Rogero. FaBoNo

Rover's Farewell, The. Sir Walter Scott. *Fr.* Rokeby, III. NOBE

Roving breezes come and go, The. The Traveling Post Office. Andrew Barton Paterson. PoTa

Roving Gambler Blues. *Unknown.* FSW

Roving Shanty Boy, The. *Unknown.* AmFP

Row after row with strict impunity. Ode to the Confederate Dead. Allen Tate. CABA (1972 ed.); HeIP; ILP (1975 ed.); LFH; NoAM; NOBA; TAP; UnPo (1976 ed.)

Row between the Cages, The. Thomas Armstrong. VLP

Row of Houses. John Robert Quinn. AMV-80

Row of pearls, A. Seeds. James Reeves. ECBV

Row, Row, Row Your Boat. *Unknown.* FSW

Row us out from Desenzano, to your Sirmione row! "Frater Ave atque Vale." Tennyson. HAP; InPS

Rowan County Crew, The. James William Day. AmFP

Rowboat, The. Philip Dacey. AAN

Rower pulls the lake along his oar, A. O Rare! W. Dale Nelson. PoUp

Rowing. Anne Sexton. BoWoP

Rowing between Pond and Western Islands. "A Loon Call." Richard Eberhart. AMV-80

Rowing in Turns. David Swanger. PCho

Rows of cells are unroofed, The. The Old Prison. Judith Wright. MAuV

Rows of Cold Trees, The. Yvor Winters. NoAM; NOBA

Rows of stones are fenced, The. A Graveyard in Oberammergau, 1960. Peter Nelson. PHC

Roy Bean. *Unknown.* BPAW; OBAL

Royal Angler, The, *sel. Unknown.*
"Methinks I see our mighty monarch stand." OBSV

Royal Education. Winthrop Mackworth Praed. OBSV

Royal Fisherman, The. *Unknown.* GBP; PeBB

*Royal George,* The. William Cowper. *See* On the Loss of the *Royal George.*

Royal Iguanas, The. Mura Dehn. TVo

Royal Palm. Hart Crane. CMoP (1970 ed.); NoAM

Royal Slave, The, *sel.* William Cartwright.
"Come, my sweet, whiles every strain." SCP-2

Royalties. D. J. Enright. NOBL

Royalty. Luci Shaw. AATT

R-P-O-P-H-E-S-S-A-G-R. E. E. Cummings. ILP (1975 ed.); InPK; PiAm; PPP; TPo

Ruaumoko—the Earthquake God. Mohi Turei, *tr. fr. Maori by* A. Armstrong. WTO

Rub, A. John Banister Tabb. OBAL

Rub a dub dub,/ Three men in a tub. Mother Goose. MG; NOBL

Rubáiyát of Omar Khayyám of Naishápúr, The. Omar Khayyám, *tr. fr. Persian by* Edward Fitzgerald. BiP, *much abr.;* FaPoR, *abr.;* HAP, *abr.;* HeIP; VLP; WeW, *much abr.*
*Sels.*
"Ah, with the Grape my fading Life provide." EBEV
"Awake! for Morning in the Bowl of Night." ILP (1975 ed.)
"Book of verses underneath the bough, A." HoPM (1975 ed.); NOBE
"Iram indeed is gone with all his rose." OBVE
"Myself when young did eagerly frequent." ILwL
"They say the Lion and the Lizard keep." EBEV
"Wake! For the sun, who scattered into flight." FF; OBP

Rubber penis, the wig, false breasts, The. Poggio. Lawrence Durrell. OxBTC

Rubbing alcohol. The Smell of Life. Morty Sklar. AcAn

Rubin. Charles Cooper. PoBA

Ruddigore, *sels.* W. S. Gilbert.
Darned Mounseer, The. NOBL
Mad Margaret's Song. PCOP

Rudolph Reed was oaken. The Ballad of Rudolph Reed. Gwendolyn Brooks. TT

Rue. *Unknown.* FSW

Rueful Lamentation, A. Sir Thomas More. AAS

Rufus Mitchell's Confession. *Unknown.* AmFP

Rugby Chapel. Matthew Arnold. ILP (1975 ed.); VLP

Rugged forehead that with grave foresight, The. Spenser. The Faerie Queene, IV, *proem.* OAEL-1

Rugweaver kept his daughters at home, unmarried, The. A Turkish Story. Katha Pollitt. AAN

Ruin, The. Dafydd ap Gwilym, *tr. fr. Welsh by* Rolfe Humphries. OBW

Ruin, The. *Unknown, tr. fr. Anglo-Saxon by* Gavin Bone. EBEV

"Ruin seize thee, ruthless King." The Bard. Thomas Gray. LAuP; NOBE; OAEL-1

Ruined Cottage, The. Wordsworth. MBPR; OAEL-2; PoIA

Ruined Maid, The. Thomas Hardy. BoLoP; CABA (1972 ed.); CMoP (1970 ed.); HeIP; InPK; NOBL; OBP; OxBTC; PoIA; PPoD; PPoe; WeW; WIF

Ruined, time ruined, all these once good things. Rimrock, Where It Is. Hayden Carruth. NNaP

Ruins of an old house stand, The. House. Leonard Clark. FPB

Ruins of the City of Hay. Randolph Stow. GAS

Ruins under the Stars, *sel.* Galway Kinnell. "Sometimes I see them." RFM

Rule, Britannia. James Thomson. *Fr.* Alfred, a Masque, II, v (*by* Thomson *and* David Mallet). BLSH, *with music*; BTTM; FaPoR; VoPo

Rule of the road is a paradox quite, The. Mother Goose. MG

Rules/ Were made for novices and fools. Samuel Butler. *Fr.* Arts and Sciences. SCP-2

Rum Tum Tugger, The. T. S. Eliot. FaBoNo

Rumbling sound of man. Buzz. Jim Tollerud. VoR

Rumbling under blackened girders, Midland, bound for Cricklewood. Parliament Hill Fields. John Betjeman. FaBoTw (1975 ed.); NOBE

Rumination. Richard Eberhart. CoPAm

Rummaging through childhood. Snapshot. Colette Inez. AATT

Rumor You Called My Name. Susan North. FoP

Rumors open up. The Morning Star. Primus St. John. PoBA

Rumpled river, The. River Rhyme. William Carlos Williams. PoA

Rumpled sheet, A. The Term. William Carlos Williams. TSWA

Rumps of horses, The. On Rears. Mary Hedin. PH

Run. Merrill Leffler. PoUp

Run Come See. Blind Blake. FSW

Run it through backwards, so I can dissect it. Time Study. Philip Roberts. FPA

Run like rats from the plague in you. Saint Colman's Song for Flight. Padraic Fiacc. IPM

Run Little Dogies. *Unknown.* BPAW

Run, Nigger, Run! *Unknown.* BPo

Run on, run on, in a way causing shaking motion on the sidewalk. Autolycus' Song. Richard L. Greene. SpRo

Run out the boat, my broken comrades. Thalassa. Louis MacNeice. BIrV; NOBE

Run seaward, launch upon the air, and sound your desolate cry. Herring-Gull. John Hall Wheelock. EcS

Run, shepherds, run where Bethlehem blest appears. The Nativity. William Drummond of Hawthornden. SCP-2

Run the razor along your lip. The Distant Lover. Kraft Rompf. AAN

Runagate Runagate. Robert Hayden. BPo; CNA; PoBA

Runaway, The. Robert Frost. ECBV; PH; PPM; VGW

Runaway, The. Larry Rubin. CSP

Runaway Slave at Pilgrim's Point, The. Elizabeth Barrett Browning. SBG

Runes. Emmett Jarrett. VoA

Runilda's Chant. George Darley. *Fr.* Ethelstan. PFIr

Runnable Stag, A. John Davidson. FaPoR; HAP; OxBTC

Runner, The. Jerah Chadwick. AMV-81

Runner, The. Gary Gildner. TAP

Runner, The. Walt Whitman. InPS; LiSp; MiP; PPoD; SPo

Runner at Sauteurs, The. Derek Walcott. *Fr.* Another Life. OBP

Running. Richard Wilbur. NCSH

Running across to the lot. Lucille Clifton. CAAP

Running along a bank, a parapet. The Path. Edward Thomas. NoAM

Running Away from Home. Carolyn Kizer. CNW

Running Back. Dave Smith. LiSp

Running Blind. Nancy Jones. LiSp

Running from the shadow-coach. Entry. Edwin Rolfe. SPT

Running It Backward. John N. Morris. GP

Running the earth in those years of meadows. Return to the Valley. Elfreida Read. AMV-80

Running through Sleep. Kathleen Norris. IHMS

Running through the thick wiry grasses to the pond. Shore. Jean Garrigue. TAP

Running under Street Lights. Christy White. AMV-80

Running Water Music. Gary Snyder. ILP (1975 ed.); PiAm

Running your apartment. Getting into Focus. Miriam Palmer. RiTi

Runoff. A. R. Ammons. PPP

Runs falls rises stumbles on from darkness into darkness. Runagate Runagate. Robert Hayden. BPo; CNA; PoBA

Rupert Weber. Poem for Rupert Weber, 85 Years Too Late. Ed Lipman. CPA

Ruptured Melodies. Art Lange. FiCh

Rural Dance about the Maypole, The. *Unknown.* GBP "Come lasses and lads," *sel.* CC

Rural Life. George Crabbe. *Fr.* The Village. NOBE

Rural Route. R. T. Smith. AMV-81

Rural Scenery. John Scott of Amwell. PES

Rural Simplicity. H. J. Byron. NOBL

Rushes of Radnor Pond, The. Tony Friedson. PHC

Rushing. Ray A. Young Bear. CDW

Rushing along on a narrow reach. The Main-Sheet Song. Thomas Fleming Day. RhR

Rushing, the brushing, the wind in your face, The. Galloping. Cordelia Chitty. PH

Rushmore ("Rushing to Rushmore, speeding as we read"). Harold Witt. TAT

Russia. William Carlos Williams. VGW

Russian penicillin—that was the magic. Garlic. Marvin Bell. GP

Russian Poem II, The. Dan Gerber. TC

Russian Poem IV, The. Dan Gerber. TC

Russian sailed over the blue Black Sea, A. "Soldier, Rest!" Robert Jones Burdette. OBAL

Russians. Keith Douglas. OxBTC

Rust. Michael Hogan. DNGG

Rust, a little pile of western color, lies, The. We Continue. W. S. Merwin. CAPP

Rust destroys the wheat. The New Wife. *Gond Oral Tradition, tr. by* V. Elwin *and* S. Hivale. WTO

Rusted and without tires. 1937 Ford Convertible. Tom McKeown. NVAP

Rusted Chain, The. Yosef Damana ben Yeshaq, *tr. fr. Amharic by* Ephraim Isaac. VWA

Rustle among bones. Only wind, the bodiless angel. Emptiness. Ray. Otto Orban, *tr. by* Emery George. VWA

Rustling of Grass, The. Alfred Noyes. FSFS

Rustling of the silk is discontinued, The. Liu Ch'e. Ezra Pound. OBVE; VGW

Ruston, Louisiana: 1952. Cleopatra Mathis. AMV-80

Ruth, *sel.* Bible, *O.T.* "And Ruth said, Intreat me not to leave thee," I: 16–17. FF

Ruth. Laura Freedgood. SFF

Ruth. Thomas Hood. BoLoP; NOBE; PIM

Ruth. Pauli Murray. NMM

Ruth. Wordsworth. MBPR

Ruthless Rhyme. J. A. Lindon. OSF

Ruyter the while, that had our ocean curbed. Andrew Marvell. *Fr.* The Last Instructions to a Painter. SCP-1

Rye Whiskey. *Unknown.* FSW

Ryōkan. William Heyen. AMV-81

Rythm. Iain Crichton Smith. LP; MPo

# S

S F. Ernest Leverett. QQQ

SM. Stanley Moss. AMV-81; NYP

SOS. Amiri Baraka. BPo; CNA; PoBA

Sabbath. Jean Burden. AMV-81

Sabbath. Rivka Fried. VWA

Sabbath. Jakov de Haan, *tr. fr. Dutch by* David Soetendorp. VWA

Sabbath. John Harris. PoW

Sabbath. David Rosenmann-Taub, *tr. fr. Spanish by* Charles Guentheer. VWA

Sabbath. Alexander Scott. MS

Sabbath Day Was By, The, *with music.* Howard Chandler Robbins. AH

Sabbath i the Mearns. Douglas Young. MS

Sabbath, the pious carry no money. A Voice out of the Tabernacle. Louis Zukofsky. VWA

Sabbatical. Linda Zisquit. VWA

Sabidi, I love thee not, nor why I wot. Translated out of Martial. Martial, *tr. by* John Weever. PAIC

Sabinas Hidalgo. Diane Kruchkow. FAF

Sabine. John Batki. AcAn

Saboteur, The. Richard Di Grazia. PoW

Sabrina. Milton. *Fr.* Comus. NOBE
("Sabrina fair.") EBEV
(Song: "Sabrina fair.") EcS

Sacco-Vanzetti. Moishe Leib Halpern, *tr. fr. Yiddish by* David G. Roskies *and* Hillel Schwartz. VWA

Sacheverell the learned. To the Tune of "Ye Commons and Peers Pray Lend Me Your Ears." *Unknown.* APAS

Sacrament, The. Robert P. Tristram Coffin. TH

Sacramental Meditations. Edward Taylor. *See* Preparatory Meditations.

Sacramento. *Unknown.* FSW

Sacred Children, The. H. R. Hays. EAS

Sacred Emily. Gertrude Stein. OBAL

Sacred Heart of Jesus Bleeds for You, The. Elton Glaser. NVAP

Sacred Hearth, The. David Gascoyne. FaBoTw (1975 ed.)

Sacred muse that first made love divine, The. Gulling Sonnets, VI. Sir John Davies. PAIC

Sacred to the Memory of Maria (To Say Nothing of Jane and Martha) Sparks. "Max Adeler." FaBoCo

Sacrifice, The. Chana Bloch. VWA

Sacrifice, The, *much abr.* George Herbert. SCP-1

Sacrifice. Nana Issaia, *tr. fr. Modern Greek by* Helle Tzalopoulou Barnstone. BoWoP

Sacrifice, The. Moshe Yungman, *tr. fr. Yiddish by* Marcia Falk. VWA

Sacsahuamán, you know, where they drag out. Visit Peru: Of Stoned Incas' Land. Teresa A. McCarthy. NPW

Sad . . . and Glad. Brian Lee. FPB

Sad and mournful history, A. The Cabin Creek Flood. *Unknown.* AmFP

Sad Child's Song, The. Mark Van Doren. SO

Sad Day in Berlin. Sarah Kirsch, *tr. fr. German by* Gerda Mayer. PBWP

Sad-eyed Lady of the Lowlands. Bob Dylan. BiP

Sad for those without sweet Anglo-Saxon. The Change. David O'Bruadair, *tr. by* Austin Clarke. BIrV

Sad Indian, The ("Sad heart, the gymnast of inertia, does not count"). Hart Crane. PoA

Sad Is the Seagull. Larin Paraske, *tr. fr. Finnish by* Jaakko A. Ahokas. PBWP

Sad lagoons. Film Vermouth: Six o'Clock Show. Magda Portal, *tr. by* Allan Francovich *and* Kathleen Weaver. PBWP

Sad lot, to have no hope! Though lowly kneeling. The Visionary Hope. Samuel Taylor Coleridge. MBPR

Sad music from vermilion strings. Telling My Feelings. Yü Hsüan-chi, *tr. by* Geoffrey Waters. BoWoP

Sad, purple well! whose bubbling eye. Abel's Blood. Henry Vaughan. OBW

Sad Results of Thinking. *Unknown.* SFF
("Centipede was happy quite, A.") CTV

Sad seamstress, The. House Guest. Elizabeth Bishop. CoPAm; NCSH; TAP

Sad Shepherd, The, *sels.* Ben Jonson.
Death and Love, *fr.* I, v. NOBE
("Though I am young and cannot tell.") ILP (1975 ed.)
"Foul ill spirit hath possessed her, A," *fr.* II, ii. SCP-1
"Here she was wont to go, and here! and here!" I, i. ILP (1975 ed.)

Sad Song, The. John Fletcher. *See* Away, Delights.

Sad Song, This Time, A. Rolfe Humphries. PAIC

Sad Story, A. Pope. *Fr.* Moral Essays, Epistle III. BoReV

Sad Tale of Mr. Mears, The. *Unknown.* PoTa

Sad to see the leaves abandoning. Winterscape. Jess Perlman. AMV-80

Sadde all alone, not long I musing satte. Licia, I. Giles Fletcher the Elder. ESo

Saddest place that e'er I saw, The. Screaming Tarn. Robert Bridges. PoTa

Saddle. William Haskel Simpson. BPAW

Saddle and Cell. The Three Marias, *tr. fr. Portuguese by* Helen R. Lane. BoWoP

Sadie/ the cleaning lady. "Personals." Leatrice W. Emeruwa. RiTi

Sadie and Maud. Gwendolyn Brooks. CoPAm; NoAM; NOBA; TAP

Sadies's Playhouse. Margaret Danner. PoBA

Sadly the dead leaves rustle in the whistling wind. The Church of a Dream. Lionel Johnson. OAEL-2

Sadly They Perish. Herman Spector. SPT

Sadness. William Cartwright. SCP-2

Sadness. Tennyson. FaBoEE

Sadness in Spring. *Unknown, tr. fr. Welsh by* Gwyn Jones. OBW

Sadness in the human visage stares, The. At an Exhibition of Historical Paintings, Hobart. Vivian Smith. GAS; MAuV

Sadness, of course, and confusion. My Death. Mark Strand. CAAP

Sadness of our lives, The. Brooding. David Ignatow. PBMP; TCP

Sadness of the Moon, The. Baudelaire, *tr. fr. French by* F. P. Trumm. Moon

Sadness of Things for Sappho's Sickness, The. Robert Herrick. PoPle

Safari to Bwagamoyo. Bwagamoyo. Lebert Bethune. PoBA

Safari West. John A. Williams. InPS

Safe behind shady carports, sleeping under. Suburban. David Malouf. FPA

Safe Flights. Barbara Guest. RiTi

Safe in the magic of my woods. The Voice. Rupert Brooke. BuTh

Safe in their alabaster chambers. Emily Dickinson. NOBA; PiAm; WPE

Safe Places. Patricia Garfinkel. PoUp

Safe Places. Constance Urdang. GP

Safe Swimming. Beaumont *and* Fletcher. *Fr.* The Faithful Shepherdess. BBL

Safe upon the solid rock the ugly houses stand. Second Fig. Edna St. Vincent Millay. PoA; TH; TPo

Safe where I cannot lie yet. Christina Rossetti. BoReV

Safed. Dovid Knut, *tr. fr. Russian by* Daniel Weissbort. VWA

Safed and I. Molly Myerowitz Levine. VWA

Safely. David Ignatow. BrS

Safety at Forty; or, An Abecedarian Takes a Walk. L. E. Sissman. Prf

Safety of the king and's royal throne, The. The Tune to the Devonshire Cant. *Unknown.* APAS

Safety pin on the floor. Fox Court, Winter. Cathy Colman. NPW

Saftly, saftly, through the mirk. The Lanely Müne. William Soutar. MS

Saga of Gisli, The, *sels. Tr. fr. Icelandic by* George Johnston. "Goddess of threads gladly." OBVE
" 'Wife, land of the wave fire.' " OBVE

Sage, The. Denise Levertov. VoA

Sagebrush. Charles Erskine Scott Wood. BPAW

Sagesse, *sel.* Paul Verlaine, *tr. fr. French.* "My God, you have wounded me with love." ILwL

Sagest of women, even of widows, she. Byron. *Fr.* Don Juan, I. NOBL

Said ("Agatha Christie to"). George Starbuck. OBAL

Said ("J. Alfred Prufrock to"). George Starbuck. OBAL

Said/ a hip/ lip-ful. Leg-acy of a Blue Capricorn. James Cunningham. JB

Said a cat, as he playfully threw. Only Teasing. *Unknown.* TDH

Said a fellow from North Philadelphia. Church Bells. Berton Braley. TDH

Said a lachrymose Labrador seal. The Feminine Seal. Oliver Herford. TDH

Said a lady beyond Pompton Lakes. The Car's in the Hall. Morris Bishop. TDH

Said a lady who wore a swell cape. Nature and Art. Oliver Herford. TDH

Said a maid, "I will marry for lucre." Money Makes the Marriage. *Unknown.* TDH

Said a saucy young skunk to a gnu. The Skunk to the Gnu. Gerard Neyroud. TDH

Said a snake to a frog with a wrinkled skin. Hospitality. John Banister Tabb. ECBV

Said a sporty young person named Groat. A Sporty Young Person. *Unknown.* TDH

Said a woman and a dollar a bout the same. Out on Santa Fe— Blues. *Unknown.* BluL

Said Abner, "At last thou art come! Ere I tell, ere thou speak." Saul. Robert Browning. PFD; VLP

Said an asp to an adder named Rhea. Serpentine Verse. Joseph S. Newman. TDH

Said Hanrahan. P. J. Hartigan. MAuV

Said, I, Oh, give me simplicity. Rural Simplicity. H. J. Byron. NOBL

Said Jerome K. Jerome to Ford Madox Ford. Mutual Problem. William Cole. OBAL; POL

Said, Pull her up a bit will you, Mac, I want to unload there. Reason. Josephine Miles. InPK; NCSH; NoAM; PoIA; PPoD; SS; TAP

Said the bird in search of a cage. A Bird in Search of a Cage. Robert Pack. SFF

Said the birds of America. The Birds of America. James Broughton. BoAnP

Said the cat to the owl. A Witch Flies By. Elizabeth Hough Sechrist. IWK

Said the crab: "Tis not beauty or birth." The Oratorical Crab. Oliver Herford. TDH

Said the Duck to the Kangaroo. The Duck and the Kangaroo. Edward Lear. OxBChV

Said the Eagle. The Eagle's Song. Mary Austin. GOA

Said the elephant to the giraffe. The Elephant and the Giraffe. Charlotte Osgood Carter. TDH

Said the engineer, "Radio waves." Not Lost in the Stars. Bruce Bliven. QQQ

Said the Englishman: "W'at's all this bloomin' wow?" Foreigners at the Fair. Fred Emerson Brooks. OBAL

Said the first little chicken. The Chickens. *Unknown.* ECBV

Said the fur-coated dame to the hairless pup. Canine Amenities. *Unknown.* GDP

Said the grave dean of Westminster. A Refusal. Thomas Hardy. FaBoCo

Said the Lion: "On music I dote." The Musical Lion. Oliver Herford. TDH

Said the Lion to the Lioness—"When you are amber dust." Heart and Mind. Edith Sitwell. OxBTC

Said the little warbling vireo. Fable of the Talented Mockingbird. Scott Bates. BoAnP

Said the mole: "You would never suppose." The Mendacious Mole. Oliver Herford. TDH

Said the mouse with scholastical hat. The Scholastic Mouse. "A. B. P." TDH

Said the Poet to the Analyst. Anne Sexton. Psy

Said the robin to the sparrow. Overheard in an Orchard. Elizabeth Cheney. CTV

Said the shark to the flying fish over the phone. The Flattered Flying Fish. E. V. Rieu. SO

Said the spider, in tones of distress. The Eternal Feminine. Oliver Herford. TDH

Said the sun, "I'm about to sink and disappear." The Lamp. A. Buttigieg. RAE

Said the trout to the fluke. Johnshaven. *Unknown.* GBP

Said the very old man at the drum. Homesick Song. William Haskel Simpson. BPAW

Said the wife to her husband. Rift Tide. Ruth M. Walsh. QQQ

Said the Wind to the Moon, "I will blow you out." George MacDonald. *Fr.* The Wind and the Moon. CaYB; LCL

Said Zwingli to Muntzer. How to Start a War. Phyllis McGinley. OBSV

Saigon Tea. Perry Oldham. AAN

Sail at the mast head dips from side to side, The. *Tr. fr. Aborigine by* C. H. Berndt. WTO

Sail Away. Robert Adamson. CAAP

Sail Away Ladies. *Unknown.* FSW

Sail, Monarchs, rising and falling. Roots and Branches. Robert Duncan. VGW

Sail of Claustra, Aelis, Azalais. The Alchemist. Ezra Pound. CMoP (1970 ed.)

Sail on, sail on, O Ship of State! The Ship of State. Longfellow. RhR

Sailing. Susan Murray. NowV

Sailing from the United States. Stanley Moss. VGW

Sailing Home from Rapallo. Robert Lowell. NoAM; TAP

Sailing in Crosslight. Anita Skeen. IHMS

Sailing in the boat when the tide runs high. Rose in the Garden. *Unknown.* AmFP

Sailing or Drowning. Allen Curnow. ATNZ

Sailing, Sailing. Gray Burr. SPo

Sailing Sailing. Godfrey Marks. FSW

Sailing to an Island. Richard Murphy. MPo

Sailing to Byzantium. W. B. Yeats. AnMo; BiP; CABA (1972 ed.); CMoP (1970 ed.); ExPo (1973 ed.); FF; HAP; HeIP; HoPM (1975 ed.); ILP (1975 ed.); InPK; InPS; LFH; NIL; NoAM; NOBE; OAEL-2; OxBTC; PAIC; PPoD; PPoe: PPP; PSN; SoSe; STS; TT; UnPo (1976 ed.); UsP; WIF

Sailing to Jerusalem. Alan Dugan. ILP (1975 ed.)

Sailor. Langston Hughes. ECBV; PoA

Sailor and His Bride, The. *Unknown.* AmFP

Sailor at Midnight, A. E. N. Sargent. NMM; WBN

Sailor Boy, The. Tennyson. AIW

Sailor Man. H. Sewell Bailey. RhR

Sailor on Deep Blue Sea. *Unknown.* FSW

Sailor tells the children, The. Kingdoms. Oliver St. John Gogarty. RAE

Sailor to His Parrot, The. W. H. Davies. BoAnP; RhR

"Sailorman, I'll give to you." The Silver Penny. Walter de la Mare. CMoP (1970 ed.); WIF

Sailors' Alphabet, The. *Unknown.* AmFP

Sailors come/ To the drum/ Out of Babylon. Hornpipe. Edith Sitwell. OAEL-2

Sailor's Consolation, The. William Pitt, *wr. at. to* Charles Dibdin. FaBoCo; PoPle

Sailors on Leave. Owen Dodson. AmNP (1974 ed.)

Sailor's Song, A. Hazel Harper Harris. RhR

Sailors there are of gentlest breed. Commemorative of a Naval Victory. Herman Melville. HAP; UnPo (1976 ed.)

Sailor's trade is a weary life, A. The Rocky Island. *Unknown.* AmFP

Sailor's Yarn, A. James Jeffrey Roche. RhR

Sails flashing to the wind like weapons. Middle Passage. Robert Hayden. AmNP (1974 ed.); BPo; CoPAm; ILP (1975 ed.); NoAM; PAIC; PoBA; TC

Saint. Robert Graves. CMoP (1970 ed.)

Saint. Stéphane Mallarmé, *tr. fr. French by* Roger Fry. NAWM-2

St. Agnes' Eve. Tennyson. ILP (1975 ed.); PIM

St. Agnes' Eve—Ah, bitter chill it was! The Eve of St. Agnes. Keats. AnMo; CABA (1972 ed.); HAP; HoPM (1975 ed.); ILP (1975 ed.); LFH; MBPR; NIL; OAEL-2; PAIC; PoIA; STS

St. Asaph's. Kingsley Amis. OxBTC

St. Bartholomew Remembers Jesus Christ as an Athlete. Alan Wearne. GAS

Saint Bridget was. The Giveaway. Phyllis McGinley. PBMP

St. Ciaran and the Birds. Ciaran Carson. CIP; IPM

Saint Colman's Song for Flight. Padraic Fiacc. IPM

St. Crispin's Day. Shakespeare. *See* Henry V before Agincourt.

Saint Elène, I thee pray. Prayer to St. Helena. *Unknown.* OxBM

St. Francis of Assisi and the Miserable Jews. Jozef Wittlin, *tr. fr. Polish by* Isaac Komen. VWA

St. George. Charlie Walker. AmFP

St. Govan. Arthur Glyn Prys-Jones. OBW

Saint Harmony my patroness. Paul Goodman. VGW

St. Helena Lullaby, A. Kipling. EBEV

Saint-Henri Spring. Milton Acorn. NeAC

St. Ignatius Loyola, Founder of the Jesuits: His Autobiography. John L'Heureux. PAIC

St. Irvyne, *sel.* Shelley.
"And the storm-fiends wild rave." PeD

St. Isaac's Church, Petrograd. Claude McKay. AmNP (1974 ed.); PoBA

St. James Infirmary. *Unknown.* AmFP; FSW

St. John, *sels.* Bible, *N.T.*
"I am the resurrection, and the life," XI: 25-26. CTV
"I am the true vine, and my Father is the husbandman," XV: 1-18. OBVE

Saint John [the] Baptist. William Drummond of Hawthornden. NOBE; OBP; PIM

St. John was staring skyward. Wormwood. James E. Warren, Jr. AATT

St. John's Park. James McAuley. MAuV

Saint Jorge, our Lady knight. For the Night-Mare. *Unknown.* OxBM

Saint Joseph, let you send me a comrade true and kind. The Choice. Winifrid M. Letts. PFIr

Saint Joseph, Saint Peter, Saint Paul! Prayer for Fine Weather. Shane Leslie. PFIr; POL

Saint Judas. James Wright. ConAP; NOBA; TCP

St. Julien's Eve. James Cunningham. JB

St. Kevin. *Unknown.* WTO

St. Louis Blues. W. C. Handy. BLSo, *with music;* FF

St. Luke, *sels.* Bible, *N.T.*
"And it came to pass in those days, that there went out a decree from Caesar Augustus," II. NAWM-1
"And there were in the same country shepherds," II: 8-14. PChr
("There were some shepherds living in the same part of the country," II: 8-20, *Phillips version.*) CTV
"Feare not, litle flocke, for it is your fathers good pleasure to give you the kingdome, " XII: 32-40. OBVE
Magnificat, The, I: 46-56. BoWoP; ILwL
("And Marie said, My soule doth magnifie the Lord.") OBVE
"Then drew near unto him all the publicans and sinners," XV. NAWM-1

Saint Luke the Painter. Dante Gabriel Rossetti. The House of Life, LXXIV. VLP

St. Luke's Little Summer. Edward Lowbury. PMW

St. Malachy. Thomas Merton. VGW

Saint Malcolm. Jewel C. Latimore. BPo

St. Mark, *sels.* Bible, *N.T.*
"And as soon as it was morning the chief priests," XV: 1-39. DL
"And he said, So is the kingdome of God," IV: 26-32. OBVE

St. Mark. Christopher Smart. *Fr.* Hymns and Spiritual Songs. LAuP

Saint Mary Magdalene; or, The Weeper. Richard Crashaw. SCP-1
(Weeper, The, *abr.*) OAEL-1
"And now where're he strayes" *sel.* FaBoCo

St. Matthew, *sels.* Bible, *N.T.*
"And seeing the multitudes, he went up into a mountain," V. BiP; NAWM-1 (V-VII)
"Blessed are the poor in spirit," V: 3-10. CTV; OBVE (3-16)
("How happy are those who know their need for God," V: 3-12, *Phillips version.*) CTV
For Whosoever Will Save His Life Shall Lose It, XVI: 25-26. PBMP
"Lay not up for yourselves treasures upon earth," VI: 19-21 CTV
Lilies of the Field, The, VI: 28-30. PF
Lord's Prayer, The, VI: 9-13. CTV
"No man can serve two masters," VI: 24-29. OBVE
"Then one of the twelve, called Judas Iscariot," XXVI: 14–XXVIII. NAWM-1

St. Matthias. Christopher Smart. *Fr.* Hymns and Spiritual Songs. LAuP

Saint Nicholas. Marianne Moore. WPE

Saint Patrick's Day, 1973. Wendy Rose. CDW

St. Paul never saw a sight like this. United 555. Richard Eberhart. PoIA

Saint Peter sat by the celestial gate. The Vision of Judgment. Byron. ESaP; MBPR; OAEL-2; OBSV, *sts.* 1-23

St. Peter's Day was celebrated by St. Brendan at sea. The Fish at Mass. *Unknown, tr. by* J. F. Webb. BIrV

St. Peter's, that old angelic church. The Cross and the Weathercock. James Nolan. AATT

St. Roach. Muriel Rukeyser. GP

St. Simeon Stylites. Tennyson. OAEL-2

Saint Steven [*or* Seynt Stevene] was a clerk in King Herowdes halle. Saint Stephen and Herod. *Unknown.* OxBM; PeBB

St. Thomas. Ferdinand G. Christgau. TDH

St. Thomas Aquinas thought. Vulture. Kenneth Rexroth. *Fr.* A Bestiary. NNaP

St. Valentine. Marianne Moore. OFD

St. Valentine. William Carlos Williams. LoAs

St. Valentine is gone with his sweet arts. February Loves. Richmond Lattimore. LoAs

St. Valentine's Day. Wilfrid Scawen Blunt. The Love Sonnets of Proteus, LV. LoAs

Saint Vesta! Oh thou sanctifying saint. To Vesta. Thomas Middleton. Moon

St. Vincent's. W. S. Merwin. NYP

Sainted isle of old, The. The Shan Van Vocht. *Unknown.* BTTM

Saints are gathering at the real, The. The Confirmers. A. R. Ammons. TAP

Saint's Bridge. Lola Ridge. WPE

Saints in Glory, We Together, *with music.* Nehemiah Adams. AH

Saints look at dirt. *Unknown, tr. fr. Pashto by* Saduddin Shpoon. PBWP

Sair Fyel'd, Hinny. *Unknown.* GBP

Saith the poet of nonsense. Scraps of Lear. Edward Lear. FaBoNo

Sakiyeh, The. Mathilde Blind. SBG

Sal Got a Meatskin. *Unknown.* FSW

Salad La Raza. Janet Campbell Hall. VoR

Salamanca Doctor's Farewell, The. *Unknown.* APAS

Salami. Philip Levine. NNaP; NOBA; TAP

Salangadou. *Tr. fr. French Creole.* FSW

Salcombe Seaman's Flaunt to the Proud Pirate, The. *Unknown.* PeBB

Sale. Josephine Miles. POL; WPE

Sale. Miller Williams. WeW

Sale began—young girls were there, The. The Slave Auction. Frances E. W. Harper. BPo

Sale of Smoke, A. Roberta Spear. AmPA

Salem. Robert Lowell. CABA (1972 ed.)

Salesman, The. Mary Moore. NPW

Salesman. Ruth Roston. AMV-80

Salesman is an it that stinks Excuse, A. E. E. Cummings. NIL; NoAM

Sally Ann. *Unknown.* FSW

Sally Brown. Thomas Hood. *See* Faithless Sally Brown.

Sally Brown. *Unknown.* AmFP; FSW

Sally from Coventry, The. George Walter Thornbury. BTTM

Sally Goodin. *Unknown.* AmFP; FSW

Sally, having swallowed cheese. Cruel, Clever Cat. Geoffrey Taylor. FaBoEE

Sally in Our Alley. Henry Carey. BLSo, *with music*; BoLoP; FSW; NOBE; PCOP; PoPle

Sally is dead, and the children stand around. Death of a Dog. Peter Bland. ATNZ

Sally is gone that was so kindly. Ha'nacker Mill. Hilaire Belloc. FaPoR; OxBTC

Sally is the laundress, and every Saturday. The Dolls' Wash. Juliana Horatia Ewing. OxBChV

Sally My Dear. *Unknown.* FSW

Sally's Garden. *Unknown.* AmFP

Salmon, The. Christian Morgenstern, *tr. fr. German by* Geoffrey Grigson. FaBoNo

Salmon and red wine. Raisins and Nuts. Charles Reznikoff. VWA

Salmon Cycle. Avner Treinin, *tr. fr. Hebrew by* Robert Friend. VWA

Salmon remarked to his mate, A. Sliding Scale. Norman R. Jaffray. TDH

Salmon-trout drifts in the stream, The. Fish and the Shadow. Ezra Pound. ExPo (1973 ed.)

Salome. George Garrett. CoPAm; PPoD

Salome was a dancer. *Unknown.* WTO

Salomon. Pierre Morhange, *tr. fr. French by* Edouard Roditi. VWA

Saloon is gone up the creek, The. Hemmed-in Males. William Carlos Williams. *Fr.* A Folded Skyscraper. MAT

Salsa. Tony Moreno. NW

Salt. Lucille Clifton. GP

Salt. Nicholas Flocos. SA

Salt. Ruth Stone. NMM

Salt creek mouths unflushed by the sea. The South Coast. William Everson. PiAm

Salt flakes fleck my skin. Dead Neck. Sue Standing. AMV-81

Salt grass silent of hooves, the lake stinks. Vestiges. Basil Bunting. TwMBP

Salt Lesson, The. Carol Frost. AAN

Salt of the Earth. D. H. Lawrence. NoAM

Salt Pork, The. Robert Clayton Casto. HeIP

Salted chips, The. In the Morning. Paulette Dusdall Zachariou. NPW

Saltlick, A. Dimple. Coleman Barks. *Fr.* Body Poems. NVAP

Salty Dog Blues. *Unknown.* FSW

Salus Mundi. Mary Elizabeth Coleridge. *See* I Saw a Stable.

Salutation. Ezra Pound. HeIP; NOBA; PiAm; TAP; VGW

Salutation, The. Thomas Traherne. ILP (1975 ed.); MetP

Salutation the Second. Ezra Pound. NOBA

Salute! Lawrence Ferlinghetti. MIT

Salute. Oliver Pitcher. PoBA

Salute to Life. Dmitri Shostakovitch. FSW

Salute to the Elephant. Odeniyi Apolebieji, *tr. fr. Yoruba by* S. A. Babalola. WTO

Salute Your Partner. *Unknown.* AmFP

Salvador Dali. David Gascoyne. EAS; OxBTC

Salvador Dali almost foresaw it. Nuclear Land. Ellen Tifft. AMV-81

Salvaging Spikes. Robert Vas Dias. HeS

Salvation army band. Sunday Morning. Ettore Rella. SPT

Salvation Army lass, The. Lola Ridge. *Fr.* Ward X. WPE

Salvation to all that will is nigh. Annunciation. John Donne. SCP-1

Sam Bass. *Unknown.* AmFP; FSW

Sam Hall. *Unknown.* AmFP; FSW; PeBB; UnPo (1976 ed.) (Ballad of Sam Hall, The.) FSW; VLP

Sam Spritsail's a lad you'd delight in. The Mariners' Compass. *Unknown.* RhR

Sam Swipes. Frederick Marryat. RhR

Samantha the golden retriever. Me and Samantha. Pyke Johnson, Jr. GDP

Samarkand. Arthur J. Bull. HeHu

Same Dream, The. Shlomit Cohen, *tr. fr. Hebrew by* Myra Glazer Schotz. VWA

Same Gesture, The. John Montague. BIrV

Same Gesture, The. Basil Payne. IPM

Same in Blues. Langston Hughes. *Fr.* Lenox Avenue Mural. InPS; WIF

Same Lady, The. Jeanette Nichols. RiTi

Same leaves over and over again, The! In Hardwood Groves. Robert Frost. HAP

Same old souvenirs, The. Niagara Falls Nocturne. Len Gasparini. NeAC

Same Old Trick. William W. Pratt. QQQ

Same sequence as the night before, The. Shutting the Curtains. Bink Noll. GP

Same Side of the Canoe, The. Alda do Espírito Santo, *tr. fr. Portuguese by* Allan Francovich *and* Kathleen Weaver. PBWP

Samela. Robert Greene. *Fr.* Menaphon. GBL; NOBE

Sampler from Haworth. Frances Minturn Howard. WPE

Sampson Imitated. *Unknown, wr. at. to* Benjamin Franklin. *See* Quatrain: "Jack, eating rotten cheese, did say."

Sam's World ("Sam's mother has"). Sam Cornish. CC; CNA

Samson. Amir Gilboa, *tr. fr. Hebrew by* Stephen Mitchell. VWA

Samson Agonistes. Milton. OAEL-1
   *Sels.*
   "All is best, though we oft doubt." NOBE
   "But see here comes thy reverend Sire." EBEV
   "Feast and noon grew high, and Sacrifice, The." EBEV
   "Let me obtain forgiveness of thee, Samson." EBEV
   "Light the prime work of God to me is extinct." SCP-1
   "Oh how comely it is and how reviving." BoReV; NOBE; SCP-1
   "This, this is he; softly a while." UnPo (1976 ed.)
   Ways of God, The. BoReV
   "While their hearts were jocund and sublime." SCP-1
   "Wilt thou then serve the Philistines with that gift." EBEV

Samson Rends His Clothes. Anadad Eldan, *tr. fr. Hebrew by* Ruth Nevo. VWA

Samuel. Charles Reznikoff. *Fr.* Five Groups of Verse. SA

Samuel Allen. *Unknown.* AmFP

Samuel, Book I. Bible, *O.T. See* First Samuel.

Samuel, Book II. Bible, *O.T. See* Second Samuel.

Samuel Brown. Phoebe Cary. OBAL

Samuel Sewall. Anthony Hecht. ConAP

Samurai and Hustlers. Joe Johnson. CNA

San Diego Poem, A. Simon J. Ortiz. CDW

San Francisco. Mary Austin. BPAW

San Francisco. Ina Coolbrith. WPW

San Francisco Arising. Edwin Markham. BPAW

San Francisco Bay. Joaquin Miller. BPAW

San Francisco Company, The. *Unknown.* AmFP

San Francisco County Jail Cell B-6. Conyus. PoBA

San Francisco Falling. Edwin Markham. BPAW

San Francisco from the Sea. Bret Harte. BPAW

San Francisco Poem. John Logan. NNaP

San Joaquin. William Everson. CoPAm

San Quentin, sing sing, alcatraz. Bogey. Lee L. Berkson. AMV-81

San Quentin was brilliant. Within the halls. The Convicts' Ball. Ambrose Bierce. BPAW

Sanary. Katherine Mansfield. ATNZ

Sanct Christopher II ("Sanct Christopher's a muckle sanct and strang"). Robert Garioch, *after the Italian of* Giuseppe Belli. OBVE

Sancta Silvarum, *sel.* Lionel Johnson.
   "Moon labours through black cloud, The," II-IV. VLP

Sanctimonious Poets, The. Friedrich Hölderlin, *tr. fr. German by* Robert Bly. NU

Sanctimony. *Malay Oral Tradition, tr. by* R. J. Wilkinson. WTO

Sanctioned by eagles, this house. Here they'd met. National Shrine. X. J. Kennedy. CoPAm

Sanctity. Patrick Kavanagh. BIrV

Sanctuary. Clifford Dyment. PoA

Sanctuary, The. Ford Madox Ford. PoA

Sanctuary. Judith Wright. WPE

Sanctuary. Elinor Wylie. BoWoP; Psy

Sanctuary should exist on earth. To Any M. F. H. V. Sackville-West. SBG

Sand. Charles Higham. LP

Sand and Snow. Laurence Lieberman. ILP (1975 ed.)

Sand Creek. Charles G. Ballard. UnPo (1976 ed.); VoR

Sand Dunes. Robert Frost. RFM

Sand Hill Road. Morton Grosser. SoS

Sand Painters, The. Ben Belitt. GOA

Sand Paintings. Alice Corbin. BPAW

Sand: the crystalline children. Kneeling Here, I Feel Good. Marge Piercy. NeAC

Sand white as frost: the moon stayed hard and high. The Galloway Shore. Sydney Tremayne. MS

Sandhill Crane, The. Mary Austin. BPAW; ECBV; WPW

Sandhill People. Carl Sandburg. CMoP (1970 ed.)

Sandlot Days. M. P. Flynn. CTV

Sandpaper, Sandpiper, Sandpit. Warren Slesinger. AMV-80

Sandpile Town. Aileen Fisher. CTV

Sandpiper. Elizabeth Bishop. HeIP; ILP (1975 ed.); PiAm

Sandpiper, The. Witter Bynner. EcS

Sandpiper, The. Celia Thaxter. CTV; EcS; OxBChV; PCOP

Sand-pipings, *sel.* Leonora Speyer.
   Gulls. TH

Sandra and that boy that's going to get her in trouble. Cora Punctuated with Strawberries. George Starbuck. NCSH

Sands of Dee, The. Charles Kingsley. FaPoR; PoPle; VLP

Sandstone carriage, A. For Cal. James Cunningham. JB

Sandwich in Spain now, and the duke in love. The Third Advice to a Painter. Andrew Marvell. APAS

Sandwich Man, The. Ron Padgett. ConAP

Sandy Maranoa, The. *At. to* A. W. Davis. MAuV

Sandy shore and sea-weed. Sea Shore. John Kitching. FPB

Sandy shore: and why. Shiki, *tr. fr. Japanese.* WeW

Sane Revolution, A. D. H. Lawrence. SFF; TPo

Sanford Barney. *Unknown.* AmFP
   (State of Arkansas, The, *diff. version.*) FSW

Sang: "There's a reid lowe in yer cheek." Robert McLellan. MS; SLP

Sang on Absence, *sel. At. to* James I, King of Scotland.
   "Faithful messinger, which is the nicht, The." SLP

Sang Solomon to Sheba. Solomon to Sheba. W. B. Yeats. CMoP (1970 ed.)

Sank through easeful. The Diver. Robert Hayden. BPo; LiSp

Sanquhar, whom this earth could scarce contain. William Drummond of Hawthornden. FaBoEE

Sanskrit. Les A. Murray. *Fr.* Walking to the Cattle-Place. CAAP

Santa Ana came storming, as a storm might come. The Defence of the Alamo. Joaquin Miller. BPAW; BTTM

Santa Barbara Earthquake, The. *Unknown.* AmFP

Santa Caterina. Myra Glazer Schotz. VWA

Santa Claus. Walter de la Mare. PChr

Santa Claus. Christopher Hassall. OxBTC

Santa Claus. Dom Moraes. NoAM

Santa Claus. Howard Nemerov. HAP; NowV; TPo

Santa Claus and the Mouse. Emilie Poulsson. MN

Santa Fe Trail, The. Arthur Chapman. BPAW

Santa Lucia. Teodoro Cottrau, *tr. fr. Italian.* BLSH, *with music;* FSW

Santo Domingo Corn Dance. R. P. Dickey. TAT

Santorin. James Elroy Flecker. FaBoTw (1975 ed.)

Santy Ana. *Unknown.* AIW
(Santy Anno.) FSW

Sap rises from the sodden ditch. For Jane Myers. Louise Glück. CAAP

Sapho and Phao, *sel.* John Lyly.
"My shag-hair Cyclops, come, let's ply." EBEV

Sapling springs, the milkweed blooms, The: obsolete nature. Adrienne Rich. *Fr. Ghazals: Homage to Ghalib.* NIL

Saplings of the green-tipped birch, The. Never Tell. *Unknown, tr. by* Anthony Conran. OBW

Sappa Creek, The. Gary Snyder. NCSH

Sapphic Love! Sculptress of far more than stone. Alex. Lynn Strongin. *Fr. First Aspen.* RiTi

Sapphics. D. B. Wyndham Lewis. NOBL

Sapphics. Swinburne. LoAs; PAIC

Sapphire, The. W. S. Merwin. PoA

Sappho. Olga Cabral. WBN

Sappho/ Sister/Mother. Invocation to Sappho. Elsa Gidlow. IHMS

"Sappho, if you do not come out." Sappho, *tr. fr. Greek by* Willis Barnstone. BoWoP

Sara in Her Father's Arms. George Oppen. GP; NNaP

Saragossa. Henry Sambrooke Leigh. FaBoCo

Sarah. Edna Aphek, *tr. fr. Hebrew by* Yishai Tobin. VWA

Sarah. Delmore Schwartz. VWA

Sarah/ was a woman. Sarah. Edna Aphek, *tr. by* Yishai Tobin. VWA

Sarah Samantha. *Unknown.* TDH

Sarah's Song. Jane Flanders. PoUp

Sarai. Joseph Sherman. VWA

Sara's fingers will find the way. Cutting Out a Dress. Dennis Schmitz. PCho

Sarasvati. James Stephens. NoAM

Saratoga Ending. Weldon Kees. AnMo

Sarentino-South Tyrol. Philip Brantingham. AMV-80

Sargon. Arthur J. Bull. HeHu

Saris go by me from the embassies, The. The Woman at the Washington Zoo. Randall Jarrell. HAP; ILP (1975 ed.); PSN; TAP; UnPo (1976 ed.); UsP; WasP

Sasha and the Poet. Jean Valentine. VGW

Saskatchewan Dusk. C. M. Buckaway. AMV-80

Sassafras Tea. Mary Effie Lee Newsome. ECBV

Sat in the Center. Samuel Makidemewabe, *tr. fr. Cree Indian by* Howard Norman. TC

Sat in the sun. Virginia. Elouise Loftin. PoBA

Sat there/ In a folding chair. Jim. Barbara Howes. GP

Sat up all night and lugged at the moon. Critter. W. M. Ransom. CDW

Satan and Michael. Byron. *Fr. The Vision of Judgment.* UsP

Satan and the Fallen Angels. Milton. *Fr. Paradise Lost, I.* SCP-1

Satan as Rebel-Liberator. Milton. *Fr. Paradise Lost, I.* OBP
("Is this the region, this the soil, the clime.") FF

Satan Discovers Eden. Milton. *Fr. Paradise Lost, IV.* ExPo (1973 ed.)

Satan Flies to the Sun. Milton. *Fr. Paradise Lost, III.* SCP-1

Satan is following me. *Zulu Oral Tradition, tr. by* H. Tracey. WTO

Satan is on your tongue, sweet singer, with. Secular Elegies, III. George Barker. PAIC

Satan's Address to the Sun. Milton. *Fr. Paradise Lost, IV.* BiP

Satchmo. Melvin B. Tolson. BPo

Satie, at the End of Term. Simon Curtis. NOBL

Satire, A, *sel.* John Oldham.
"On Butler who can think without rage." OBSV

Satire: "Kind pity chokes my spleen; brave scorn forbids." John Donne. Satires, III. CABA (1972 ed.); OAEL-1; PAIC; SCP-1
("Kind pity chokes my spleen; brave scorn forbids.") EBEV

Satire III: "Long, Dodington, in debt, I long have sought." Edward Young. *Fr. Love of Fame, the Universal Passion.* LAuP

Satire: "Well, I may now receive, and die: my sin." John Donne. Satires, IV. OBSV; TVS

Satire: "Were I who to my cost already am." Earl of Rochester. *See* Satire against Mankind, A.

Satire Addressed to a Friend, A, *sel.* John Oldham.
"If you're so out of love with happiness." OBSV

Satire against Mankind, A. Earl of Rochester. OAEL-1; OBSV; PAIC
"Were I (who to my cost already am)," *sel.* SCP-2
(Homo Sapiens.) NOBE

Satire against Wit, A. Sir Richard Blackmore. APAS

Satire Entitled the Witch, A, *sel. Unknown.*
"She with whom troops of bustuary slaves." SCP-2

Satire on Charles II, A, *sel.* Earl of Rochester.
"Restless he rolls about from whore to whore." OBSV

Satire on Old Rowley. *Unknown.* APAS

Satire on Women, *sel.* Edward Young.
"Atheists are few; most nymph a godhead own." SoSe

Satire upon the French King, A. Thomas Brown. APAS

Satire upon the Heads. Thomas Gray. FaBoCo

Satire upon the Licentious Age of Charles II, *sel.* Samuel Butler.
"How silly were those sages heretofore." NOBL

Satires, *sels.* John Donne.
"Kind pity chokes my spleen; brave scorn forbids," III. CABA (1972 ed.); EBEV; OAEL-1; PAIC; SCP-1
"Seek true religion, O where? Mirreus," *fr.* III. OBSV
"Sir, though (I thank God for it) I do hate," *fr.* II. OBSV
"Thou shalt not laugh in this leaf, Muse, nor they," V. OBSV
"Well, I may now receive, and die: my sin," IV. OBSV; TVS

Satires, *sel.* Horace, *tr. fr. Latin.* TVS
"Some think my satyre's too too tart," II, 1, *tr. by* Thomas Drant.
("There are, to whom I seem excessive sour," *tr. by* Ben Jonson.)

Satires, *sels.* Juvenal, *tr. fr. Latin.*
"But of all the plagues, the greatest is untold," *fr.* VI, *tr. by* Dryden. OBSV
"Give store of days, good Jove, give length of years," *fr.* X, *tr. by* Henry Vaughan. OBSV
Hannibal ("Produce the urn that Hannibal contains"), *fr.* X, *tr. by* William Gifford. OBVE
Hannibal ("Put Hannibal i' th' scale"), *fr.* X, *tr. by* Henry Vaughan. OBVE
Hannibal ("Throw Hannibal on the scales, how many pounds"), *fr.* X, *tr. by* Robert Lowell. OBVE
"In Saturn's reign, at Nature's early birth," *fr.* VI, *tr. by* Dryden. OAEL-1; OBSV; OBVE
"Jove, grant me length of life, and years' good store," *fr.* X, *tr. by* Dryden. SCP-1
"'Life! length of life!' for this, with earnest cries," *fr.* X, *tr. by* William Gifford. OBVE
"Return we to the dangers of the night," *fr.* III, *tr. by* Dryden. OAEL-1
Sejanus ("How many men are killed by power, by power"), *fr.* X, *tr. by* Robert Lowell. OBVE

Sejanus ("Some ask for envy'd pow'r; which publick hate"), *fr.* X, *tr. by* Dryden.  OBVE

Sejanus ("What crowds by envied power, the wish of all"), *fr.* X, *tr. by* William Gifford.  OBVE

"When the last Flavius, drunk with fury, tore," *fr.* IV, *tr. by* William Gifford.  OBVE

Satires, *sel.*  John Oldham, *after the French of* Boileau.
"Of all the creatures, in the world, that be," *fr.* VIII.  OBVE

Satires, *sels.*  Persius, *tr. fr. Latin by* Dryden.  SCP-1
"Thus fares the drudge; but thou, whose life's a dream," *fr.* IV.
"Yawning youth, scarce half awake, essays, The," *fr.* III.

Satires, *sels.*  Sir Thomas Wyatt.
"My mother's maids [*or* maydes], when they did sew and spin [*or* sowe and spynne], II.  AAS; TVS
"Myne [*or* Mine] owne John Poyntz, sins [*or* since] ye delight to know," I.  AAS; OBSV; OBVE
"Spending hand that alway poureth out [*or* powreth owte], A," III.  AAS; TVS

Satires of Circumstance, *sel.*  Thomas Hardy.
By Her Aunt's Grave, III.  LFH; SFF

Satirical Elegy on the Death of a Late Famous General, A.  Swift.  CABA (1972 ed.); ESaP; FF; HoPM (1975 ed.); NIL; OBSV; PAIC; PBMP; SS
(Satyrical Elegy on the Death of a Late Famous General.) ExPo (1973 ed.)

Satirical Poem about Drink, A, *sel.*  Chimedin Jigmed, *Mongol Oral Tradition, tr. by* C. R. Bawden
"There is drink fermented."  WTO

Satirical Romance, A, *sels.*  Sister Juana Inés de la Cruz, *tr. fr. Spanish by* Judith Thurman.
"Critics: in your sight."  PBWP
"Ignorant men, who disclaim."  PBWP
"What humour can be so rare."  PBWP

Satisfaction.  A. R. Ammons.  GP

Satisfaction—is the agent.  Emily Dickinson.  NOBA

Satisfactions of the Mad Farmer, The.  Wendell Berry.  PiAm

Saturday Afternoon.  Larry Rubin.  CSP

Saturday Afternoon at the Movies.  John Logan.  NNaP

Saturday Afternoon, When Chores Are Done.  Harryette Mullen.  AMV-81

Saturday Blues.  *Unknown.*  BluL

Saturday in New York.  Anne Beresford.  MPo

Saturday Market.  Charlotte Mew.  WPE

Saturday morning. I rehearse.  David's Harp.  Gwen Harwood.  MAuV

Saturday Night.  Rubee Dreher Moxley.  NPW

Saturday Night in the Parthenon.  Kenneth Patchen.  EAS

Saturday Night in the Village.  Giacomo Leopardi, *tr. fr. Italian by* Robert Lowell.  OBVE

Saturday Night Out.  Jim Mulac.  AcAn

Saturday: The Small Pox.  Lady Mary Wortley Montagu.  WPE

Saturdays/ I am telling Anne.  What Is There?  Ruth Lisa Schechter.  RiTi

Saturday's Child.  Countee Cullen.  InPK; OFD; PoBA

Saturday's Child.  Edelin Coleman Fields.  PoUp

Satyr.  Charles Gullans.  PoA

Satyrical Elegy on the Death of a Late Famous General.  Swift.  *See* Satirical Elegy on the Death of a Late Famous General, A.

Satyrs' Catch, The.  Ben Jonson.  *See* Song of the Satyrs.

Satyrs used to fall for nymphs.  Love-Songs, at Once Tender and Informative.  Samuel Hoffenstein.  OBAL

Satyrus Peregrinans, *sel.*  William Rankins.
"By this time long-gowned Lumen walked abroad."  OBSV

Saucepan of shining copper, The.  How I Was Her Kitchen-Boy.  Gunter Grass, *tr. by* Betty Falkenberg.  AMV-81

Sauchs in the Reuch Heuch Hauch, The.  "Hugh MacDiarmid."  NoAM

Saul.  Robert Browning.  PFD; VLP

*Sels.*
"I believe it! 'tis Thou God, that givest, 'tis I who receive," XVIII.  ILwL
Psalm of David, A, *fr.* IX.  PIM

Saul.  Amir Gilboa, *tr. fr.* Hebrew *by* Shirley Kaufman.  VWA

Saul.  Else Lasker-Schüler, *tr. fr.* German *by* Joachim Neugroschel.  VWA

Saul.  Isaac Rosenberg.  VWA

Saul and the Witch of Endor and the Vision of Samuel.  Byron.  PIM

Saul, Afterward, Riding East.  John Malcolm Brinnin.  Prf

Saul did much care and diligence express.  Rowland Watkyns.  FaBoEE

Saul! Saul!  Saul.  Amir Gilboa, *tr. by* Shirley Kaufman.  VWA

Saul's Song of Love.  Shaul Tchernichovsky, *tr. fr.* Hebrew *by* Robert Friend.  VWA

Saunders Point.  Henry Combellick.  BrS

Sauntering in the orchard we bit the fruit.  The Struggle with the Angel.  Claude Vigée, *tr. by* Elizabeth Savage.  VWA

Sausage.  Edgar A. Guest.  OBAL

Sausage, The.  *Unknown.*  OSF

Savage lion in the zoo.  Supper for a Lion.  Dorothy Aldis.  CaYB

Savage's romance, The.  New York.  Marianne Moore.  NYP

Savannah Mama.  *Unknown.*  BluL

Savarin.  Richard Williams.  AAN

Save by the Old Road none attain the new.  Coventry Patmore.  FaBoEE

Save it all; you do not know.  1915: A Pre-Raphaelite Ending, London.  Richard Howard.  NoAM

Save on the rare occasion when the sun.  On a Sundial.  Hilaire Belloc.  POL

Save yourself. Run and leave me. I must go back.  C. S. Lewis.  Fr. Epigrams and Epitaphs, 6.  EBEV

Saved.  Maria Teresa Horta, *tr. fr.* Portuguese *by* Suzette Macedo.  PBWP

Saved by his foreign tongue, one king.  Messages for Herod.  Charles Doyle.  ATNZ

Saved. Yet not saved.  The Starface.  Madeline Gleason.  MIT

Saving Tallow.  Barbara Guest.  RiTi

Saving the Harvest.  Geoffrey Lehmann.  MAuV

Saviour, like a Shepherd Lead Us, *with music.*  Dorothy Ann Thrupp.  BLSH

Saviour, Sprinkle Many Nations, *with music.*  Arthur Cleveland Coxe.  AH

Saviour, Thy Dying Love, *with music.*  Sylvanus D. Phelps.  AH

Saviour, Who Thy Flock Art Feeding, *with music.*  William Augustus Mühlenberg.  AH

Saw a lamb being born.  Lamb.  Michael Dennis Browne.  NU

Saw the last of my Spanish shampoo.  Today.  Liz Lochhead.  MS; SLP

Saw ye owt o' ma' lad.  The Waggoner.  *Unknown.*  GBP

Saxons of Flint, The.  *Unknown, tr. fr.* Welsh *by* Mary C. Llewelyn.  OBW

Saxophone and subway.  The Rock.  W. S. Merwin.  NYP

Saxophone turned into a dolphin, The.  Albert Ayler: Eulogy for a Decomposed Saxophone Player.  Stanley Crouch.  PoBA

Say/ Did you see that magnificent blonde beast.  Ski Trail.  Samuel Allen.  FB

Say "Au Revoir," but Not "Good-bye," *with music.*  Harry Kennedy.  FSN

Say, Billie, when yer startin' off a-nuttin with yer sack.  Punkin Pie.  Harry Edward Mills.  PeD

Say, darkeys [*or* darkies] hab you seen de massa.  Kingdom Coming.  Henry Clay Work.  BLSo; PSoN

Say, dear Maria! is the modish life. A Familiar Epistle. Ann Murry. WPE

Say, dwarf, for it seems to me. *Tr. fr. Icelandic by* W. H. Auden *and* Paul B. Taylor. *Fr.* The Words of the All-Wise. OBVE

Say father, say mother. Dove's Song in Winter. *Zulu Oral Tradition, tr. by* B. W. Vilakazi. WTO

Say, friend, if all is well still with the bowers. Vidya, *tr. by* Daniel H. H. Ingalls. *Fr.* The Wanton. PBWP

Say, friends, have you heard it? Merry-go-round. Sean O'Meara. IPM

Say Goodbye to Big Daddy. Randall Jarrell. LiSp

Say it's an important event like this. Off to Patagonia. Theodore Weiss. TAP

Say, lad, have you things to do? A. E. Housman. VLP

Say, lay/ off the doll biz, Daedalus. The Priapupation of Queen Pasiphae. Jonathan Williams. CSP

Say, ma'am dear, did ye never hear. Molly Brannigan. *Unknown.* RDB

Say me, wight in the brom. Wight in the Broom. *Unknown.* OxBM

Say, my Orinda, why so sad? A Dialogue of Absence 'twixt Lucasia and Orinda. Katherine Philips. SCP-2

Say Not the Struggle Nought Availeth. Arthur Hugh Clough. CABA (1972 ed.); FaPoR; ILP (1975 ed.); NOBE; OAEL-2; PPM; VLP; VPC (Courage!) PCOP

Say of them/ They knew no Spanish. To the Veterans of the Abraham Lincoln Brigade. Genevieve Taggard. OFD

Say, sweetest, whether thou didst use me well. To Cynthia: On Her Being an Incendiary. Sir Francis Kynaston. HAP

Say that the men of the old black tower. The Black Tower. W. B. Yeats. BoReV; CMoP (1970 ed.); UsP

Say that it is a crude effect, black reds. Bouquet of Roses in Sunlight. Wallace Stevens. ILP (1975 ed.)

Say That We Saw Spain Die. Edna St. Vincent Millay. SBG

Say there were six, say there were a dozen. Depression. Rex Burwell. AMV-80

Say This of Horses. Minnie Hite Moody. PCOP

Say what slim youth, with moist perfumes. Horace, *tr. by* Christopher Smart. Odes, I, 5. OBVE

Say who is this with silvered hair. Robert Bridges. VLP

Say you talking 'bout your red ripe tomato. T-Bone Steak Blues. *Unknown.* BluL

Saying. A. R. Ammons. TSWA

Saying Goodbye. Suzanne Juhasz. IHMS

Saying One Thing. Robert Long. AMV-81

Sayings from the Northern Ice. William Stafford. BCr; NU

Sayre. Lynn Strongin. IHMS; RiTi

Says a Miser to a Mouse, "My dear Mr. Mouse." The Miser and the Mouse. Christopher Smart. MN. *See also* To a Mouse says a Miser. . .

Says His Grace to Will Green, whom he found in his stall. Death and the Cobbler. *Unknown.* APAS

Says I went to Lake Michigan. Lake Michigan Blues. *Unknown.* BluL

Says-so is in a woe of shuddered. Irritable Song. Russell Atkins. AmNP (1974 ed.)

Says the auld man/ To the oak tree. Many a Long Year. *Unknown.* PoPle

Says the Miner to the Mucker. *Unknown.* AmFP

Says the Pont to the Blyth. Pont and Blyth. *Unknown.* GBP

Says the window. Indoors. George Johnston. PoA

Says Tweed to Till. Tweed and Till. *Unknown.* GBP

Says William to Henry, "I cannot conceive." Henry's Secret. Dorothy Kilner. OxBChV

Scab, The. Ettore Rella. SPT

Scaffolding. Seamus Heaney. IPM; LP

Scalded cat. Night Letter. Marge Piercy. NMM

Scales, The. William Empson. CMoP (1970 ed.); LFH

Scales of the Eyes, The. Howard Nemerov. CMoP (1970 ed.) "In the water cave, below the root," *sel.* NoAM

Scaling small rocks, exhaling smog. Central Park. Robert Lowell. NYP

Scalp Dance Song. *Tr. fr. Tewa Indian by* H. J. Spinden. WTO

Scandal or two, A. Tattle. Godfrey Turner. NOBL

Scandalize My Name. *Unknown.* FSW

Scandalous man, A. Mr. Tom Narrow. James Reeves. SO

Scant and straggling her yellow hair. An Old Woman. D Gwenallt Jones, *tr. by* H. Idris Bell. OBW

Scapegoat. W. R. Rodgers. CIP

Scapular of birds hung fast, A. Eclipses. Nancy Sullivan. TAP

Scar. Coleman Barks. *Fr.* Body Poems. NVAP

Scarborough Fair. *Unknown.* BLSo, *with music;* FSW; GSB, *with music*

Scarce do I pass a day, but that I hear. Meditation 8. Philip Pain. NOBA; PiAm

Scarcely, I think; yet it indeed *may* by. For "An Allegorical Dance of Women" by Andrea Mantegna. Dante Gabriel Rossetti. VLP

Scare-Fire, The. Robert Herrick. HAP

Scarecrow, The. Walter de la Mare. OxBTC

Scarecrow. Ricardo da Silveira Lobo Sternberg. PoW

Scarecrow, The. Andrew Young. FaBoTw (1975 ed.)

Scarecrow Independence. James Kirkup. FPB

Scared?/ are responsible negros running. Concerning One Responsible Negro with Too Much Power. Nikki Giovanni. BPo

Scarlet Woman, The. Fenton Johnson. PoBA

Scarlet Woman, The. "Hugh MacDiarmid." SLP

Scarlett Rocks. Thomas Edward Brown. EcS

Scars take us back to places we have been, The. Memoranda. William Dickey. CoPAm

Scat! Scitten. David McCord. ECBV

Scattered Leaves. Lance Henson. VoR

Scaurus hates Greek, and is become. Epigram. *Unknown.* PiAm

Scazons. C. S. Lewis. EBEV

Scel Lem Duib. *Unknown, tr. fr. Irish by* Flann O'Brien. BIrV

Scenario. Barbara Eve. TV

Scenario VI. Amiri Baraka. Epi

Scene, The. Denis Glover. ATNZ

Scene from a Play, Acted at Oxford, Called "Matriculation." Thomas Moore. OBSV

Scene is set now, The: in a silent room. Transfusion. Merrill Moore. PoA

Scene on the Banks of the Hudson, A. Bryant. PiAm

Scenery. Ted Joans. PoBA

Scenes from the Fall of Troy. William Morris. PAIC

Scenes of my childhood, The, how oft I recall! My Infundibuliform Hat. Charles Follen Adams. OBAL

Scent of unseen jasmine on the warm night beach, The. Malaga. Pearse Hutchinson. BIrV

Scentless laurel a broad leaf displays, The. Walter Savage Landor. FaBoEE

Schedules ("Schedules come in different forms, all crushing"). John Dean. AMV-81

Schemmelfennig. Bret Harte. OBAL

Schizophrenia. Elizabeth Bartlett. PMW.

Schizophrenic, wrenched by two styles. Codicil. Derek Walcott. NoAM

Schloss, The. David Kirby. CSP

Schloss Voss, built between 1600 and 1650. Das Schloss. Lincoln Kirstein. NoAM

Scholar-Gipsy, The. Matthew Arnold. CABA (1972 ed.); EBEV; HAP; HeIP; ILP (1975 ed.); NOBE; OAEL-2; VLP
"Go, for they call you, shepherd, from the hill," *sel.* PoPle
Scholar II. Seamus Deane. CIP
Scholars. Walter de la Mare. NoAM
Scholars, The. W. B. Yeats. CMoP (1970 ed.); IP; OAEL-2; PoA; WIF
Scholar's Life, The. Samuel Johnson. *Fr.* The Vanity of Human Wishes. NOBE; OBSV
Scholar's Wife, The. Susan Mernit. VWA
Scholastic Mouse, The. "A. B. P." TDH
School Children. *See* Schoolchildren.
School Days. Will D. Cobb. BLSH, *with music*; FSW
School Is Over. Kate Greenaway. CTV
School is over. It is too hot. The Lonely Street. William Carlos Williams. PoA
School of Beauty's a tavern now, The. A Street in Bronzeville: Southeast Corner. Gwendolyn Brooks. VGW
School of Night, The. A. D. Hope. PoA
School that looks like an army barracks, A. Ecole St. Luc. Ray Fraser. NeAC
School Boy, The. Blake. *Fr.* Songs of Experience. MBPR
Schoolboy's Complaint, A. *Unknown.* OxBM
Schoolboys in Winter. John Clare. VLP
Schoolboy's Lot, A. *Unknown.* OxBM
Schoolboys still their morning rambles take, The. Schoolboys in Winter. John Clare. VLP
Schoolchildren. W. H. Auden. TT
School Children, The. Louise Glück. AmPA
Schoolma'am of much reputation, A. No Talking Shop. Minnie Leona Upton. TDH
Schoolmaster. George Rostrevor Hamilton. FaBoEE
Schoolmaster, The. *Unknown.* GBP
Schoolmaster Abroad with His Son, The. Charles Stuart Calverley. NOBL
Schoolmaster's Admonition, A. *Unknown.* OxBChV
Schoolmaster's Precepts, A. John Penkethman. OxBChV
Schoolmistress. Clive Sansom. LP; MPo
School-Mistress, The. William Shenstone. EPC; LAuP
School's Out. W. H. Davies. BBGO
Schoolyard in April. Kenneth Koch. PoA
Schooner *Fred Dunbar*, The. Amos Hanson. AmFP
Schreckhorn, The. Thomas Hardy. OAEL-2; OBP
Schubertiana. Tomas Tranströmer, *tr. fr. Swedish by* Robert Bly. NU
Schwiegermutterlieder. Tony Harrison. InPS
Science. Robinson Jeffers. MPA; NU; WIF
Science as Art. Hugh Seidman. AmPA
Science Fiction. Reed Whittemore. GP
Science finds out ingenious ways to kill. The Modern World. Colin Ellis. FaBoEE
Science for the Young. Wallace Irwin. QQQ
Science, that simple saint, cannot be bothered. Dr. Sigmund Freud Discovers the Sea Shell. Archibald MacLeish. BiP; SoSe
Science, the agile ape, may well. Coventry Patmore. FaBoEE
Science! true daughter of Old Time thou art! Sonnet—To Science. Poe. Al Aaraaf: Prologue. AmVN; ILP (1975 ed.); InPK; LFH; PAIC: PBMP; PiAm; PPoD; TAP; WIF
Scientific Proof. J. W. Foley. QQQ
Scientist, The. Janet Burroway. SoSe
Scientist has a test tube full of sheep, A. Counting Sheep. Russell Edson. FiCP
Scientists sit long of nights, The. Astronaut's Choice. M. M. Darcy. QQQ
Scintilla. William Stanley Braithwaite. AmNP (1974 ed.)

Scintillate, scintillate, globule orific. The Little Star. *Unknown.* SpRo
Scobble for whoredom whips his wife; and cries. Upon Scobble: Epigram. Robert Herrick. CaPo; FaBoEE
Scoffers, The. Blake. *See* Mock On, Mock On, Voltaire, Rousseau.
Scorflufus. Spike Milligan. OSF
Scorn Not the Sonnet. Wordsworth. BiP; Epi; HeIP; ILP (1975 ed.); LFH
("Scorn not the sonnet; critic, you have frowned.") EBEV; MBPR; OBP
"Scorn not the sonnet," though its strength be sapped. On a Magazine Sonnet. Russell Hillard Loines. OBAL
Scorpion, The. Hilaire Belloc. BoAnP
Scorpion, The. William Plomer. NoAM
Scorpion. Stevie Smith. EBEV
Scorpion is black as soot, The. The Scorpion. Hilaire Belloc. BoAnP
Scot, a Welsh and an Irish Man, A. *Unknown.* GBP
Scotland. Alexander Gray. MS
Scotland 1941. Edwin Muir. MS
Scotland the Wee. Tom Buchan. MS
Scotland's Burning. *Unknown.* FSW
Scotland's Winter. Edwin Muir. MS; OxBTC
Scots in Berwick (1296), The. *Unknown.* OxBM
Scots Wha Hae. Burns. FaPoR; ILP (1975 ed.); OAEL-1
(Bannockburn.) BTTM
(Bruce to His Men at Bannockburn.) FaPo
(Robert Bruce's March to Bannockburn.) NOBE
(Scots Wha Ha'e wi' Wallace Bled.) CABA (1972 ed.); FSW
Scott-Moncrieff's Beowulf. Charles Spear. ATNZ
Scottes out of Berwik and of Abirdene. Halidon Hill. Laurence Minot. OxBM
Scottish Grace, A. Burns. PIM
Scottsboro. *Unknown.* InPK
Scottsboro, Too, Is Worth Its Song. Countee Cullen. ILP (1975 ed.); PoBA
Scourge of Villainy, The, *sels.* John Marston. TVS
Cynic Satyre, A, VII.
"In serious jest and jesting seriousness," Proemium, Bk. III.
Inamorato Curio, VIII.
Scrapbooks. Nikki Giovanni. CNA
Scrape no more your hairless chins. Advice to the Old Beaux. Sir Charles Sedley. ILP (1975 ed.); SCP-2
Scraps. Susannah Fried, *tr. fr. Slovak by* Anthony Rudolf. VWA
Scraps of Lear. Edward Lear. FaBoNo
Scrawled in Pencil in a Sealed Railway Car. Dan Pagis, *tr. fr. Hebrew by* Anthony Rudolf. VWA
Scrawny yank of kid, A. The Evening Gown. Karen Swenson. WBN
Screamer Discusses Methods of Screaming, A. James Schevill. TAP
Screaming Tarn. Robert Bridges. PoTa
Screams that I screamed, despairing, aching. My White Book of Poems. Rachel, *tr. by* N. N. VWA
Screendoor whines, clacks, The. Night on Hatchet Cove. Denise Levertov. PiAm; Psy
Screw Spring. William M. Hoffman. FF
Scribblers, The. Walter Savage Landor. OBSV
("Why should scribblers discompose.") FaBoEE
Scribe. Paul Auster. VWA
Scribe, The. Walter de la Mare. CMoP (1970 ed.)
Scrievin. Alexander Scott. MS
Scrim of Twilight, dropping on Manhattan, A. A March with All Drums Muffled. Reuel Denney. NYP
Scripts I used to write for the young actor, The. Written, Directed by and Starring. James Simmons. IPM

Scriptural 1. Anselm Hollo. AcAn

Scroll. Stanley Moss. VWA

Scroppo's Dog. May Swenson. GDP

Scrubbed pink/ They look the most naked of animals. Pigs. John Cotton. BoAnP

Scrunched down in the seats. Winter. D. W. Donzella. FAF

Scrutiny [or Scrutinie], The. Richard Lovelace. BoLoP; CaPo; GBL; LoAs
  (Why Should You Swear?) ILP (1975 ed.)

Scunner. "Hugh MacDiarmid." FaBoTw (1975 ed.)

Scylla and Charybdis. Thomas Kinsella. OxBTC

Scylla Toothless. *Unknown.* SoSe (1977 ed.)

Scyros. Karl Shapiro. HoPM (1975 ed.); ILP (1975 ed.)

Scyther. Liam O'Mahony. IPM

Scything. Basil Dowling. ATNZ

Sea, The. W. H. Davies. FaBoTw (1975 ed.)

Sea. Conrad Hilberry. TC

Sea, The/ tore a rib from its side. Water without Sound. Malka Heifetz Tussman, *tr. by* Marcia Falk. VWA

Sea and the Hills, The. Kipling. OBP

Sea and the Mirror, The, *sel.* W. H. Auden.
  Song of the Master and Boatswain. BoLoP
    (Master and Boatswain.) FaBoTw (1975 ed.)

Sea and the Skylark, The. Gerard Manley Hopkins. LFH

Sea at evening moves across the sand, The. Soldiers Bathing. F. T. Prince. OxBTC

Sea awoke at midnight from its sleep, The. The Sound of the Sea. Longfellow. EcS

Sea Bells. Richard Eberhart. AMV–80

Sea-Birds. Elizabeth Akers Allen. EcS

Sea Birds, The. Van K. Brock. NVAP

Sea Boy on the Giddy Mast, A. John Clare. PPP

Sea breaks, The. Sea. Conrad Hilberry. TC

Sea Breathes Quietly, Menelaus, The. Frank Stewart. PHC

Sea Breeze. Stéphane Mallarmé, *tr. fr. French by* Roger Fry. NAWM–2

Sea Call. Margaret Widdemer. RhR

Sea called, The. Remembering Home. Susan Petrykewycz. AMV–80

Sea Calm. Langston Hughes. CaYB

Sea-Change. W. W. Gibson. EcS

Sea Change. John Masefield. FaBoTw (1975 ed.); PoTa

Sea cries with its meaningless voice, The. Pibroch. Ted Hughes. OAEL–2; TwMBP

Sea Dialogue, A. Oliver Wendell Holmes. OBAL

Sea Dirge, A. Shakespeare. *See* Full Fathom Five Thy Father Lies.

Sea Dreams, *sel.* Tennyson.
  What Does Little Birdie Say? PCOP
    (Cradle Song.) OxBChV

Sea-Elephant, The. William Carlos Williams. NU

Sea-Fairies, The. Tennyson. EcS

Sea-Fever. John Masefield. CTV; FaPoR; ILP (1975 ed.); IPWM; OxBTC; PPM; RhR; SFF

Sea-Games. Aliza Shenhar, *tr. fr. Hebrew by* Linda Zisquit. VWA

Sea gives her shells to the shingle, The. Dedication. Swinburne. VLP

Sea gleamed deep blue in the sunlight, The. Homage to Marcel Proust. Thomas MacGreevy. CIP

Sea go dark, dark with wind. Wild Iron. Allen Curnow. ATNZ

Sea Grapes. Derek Walcott. SoSe (1977 ed.)

Seagull, The. Dafydd ap Gwilym, *tr. fr. Welsh by* Glyn Jones. OBW

Seagull, The. Mary Howitt. OxBChV

Sea-Gull, The. Ogden Nash. SoSe; UsP

Seagull, The. Siôn Phylip, *tr. fr. Welsh by* Joseph P. Clancy. OBW

Sea-Gull, The. *Unknown.* GBP

Seagulls. Robert Francis. RFM

Seagulls inland, The. The Natural Order of Things. Harley Elliott. NeAC

Seagulls on the Serpentine. Alfred Noyes. EcS

Sea Gypsy, The. Richard Hovey. RhR

Sea has made a wall for its defence, The. Shoreline. Mary Barnard. PoA

Sea-Hawk. Richard Eberhart. BoAnP; EcS

Sea is calm tonight, The. Dover Beach. Matthew Arnold. AnMo; BiP; CABA (1972 ed.); Epi; ExPo (1973 ed.); FF; GrRo; HAP; HeIP; HoPM (1975 ed.); ILP (1975 ed.); InPK; InPS; IP; IPWM; LFH; MAT; NIL; NOBE; NU; OAEL–2; OBP; PAIC; PBMP; PES; PFD; PoIA; PoPle; PPoD; PPoe; PPP; Prf; RhR; SFF; SoSe; TPo; UnPo (1976 ed.); UsP; VLP; VoPo; WeW

Sea is enormous, but calm with evening, The. Whale at twilight. Elizabeth J. Coatsworth. BoAnP

Sea is obsidian, The. Fire Island. Rita Mae Brown. IHMS

Sea-King, The. L. Frank Tooker. RhR

Sea-King's Burial, The. Charles MacKay. RhR

Sea Known. John Sollid. PoW

Sea laments, The. Echoes. Walter de la Mare. EcS

Sea laying it down, the sea saying it, The. The Wheel. Rosalie Moore. RiTi

Sea Legs. Susan Feldman. AmPA

Sea-Limits, The. Dante Gabriel Rossetti. EcS; ILP (1975 ed.); OAEL–2; VLP

Sea Longing. Sara Teasdale. EcS

Sea Love. Charlotte Mew. OxBTC

Sea Lullaby. Elinor Wylie. PBMP

Sea-Mew, The. Elizabeth Barrett Browning. VLP

Sea-mew on a sea-king' wrist alighting, A. Dedication to "Songs of the Springtides." Swinburne. VLP

Sea-Monster. Gertrud Kolmar, *tr. fr. German by* Henry A. Smith. VWA

Sea, The! O the sea! *Tr. fr. Hawaiian.* WTO

Sea of Silence Exhales Secrets, The. Hayim Nachman Bialik, *tr. fr. Hebrew by* Gabriel Levin. VWA

Sea of stretch'd ground-swells. Walt Whitman. *Fr.* Song of Myself, XXII. GrRo

Sea Otter, Dream Poem to My Mother. Katherine Doak. NPW

Sea pearl, western star. On Leaving. Gertrudis Gomez de Avellaneda, *tr. by* Frederick Sweet. PBWP

Sea Poppies. Hilda Doolittle ("H. D."). PiAm

Sea-preserved, heaped with sea-spoils. Picture of a Nativity. Geoffrey Hill. NoAM

Sea-Ritual, The. George Darley. Syren Songs, V. BIrV; EcS

Sea Rose. Hilda Doolittle ("H. D."). NoAM

Sea runs back against itself, The. Winter Seascape. John Betjeman. SS

Sea Shanty. Clifford Dyment. POL

Sea Shell. Amy Lowell. LCL

Sea-Shell Murmurs. Eugene Lee-Hamilton. SoSe

Sea Shore. John Kitching. FPB

Sea-Song, A. Allan Cunningham. *See* Wet Sheet and a Flowing Sea, A.

Sea Song, A. D. M. Dolben. EcS

Sea-Sonnet. V. Sackville-West. EcS; SBG

Sea-Spell, A. Dante Gabriel Rossetti. VLP

Sea still plunges where as naked boys, The. The Grotto. Francis Scarfe. PoA

Sea Surface Full of clouds. Wallace Stevens. CMoP (1970 ed.); VGW

Sea Turtle. Liston Pope. AMV-80

Sea-Turtle and the Shark, The. Melvin B. Tolson. *Fr.* Harlem Gallery. Ip; PoBA; SoSe (1977 ed.)

Sea Variations. R. A. Simpson. CAAP

Sea Voyage. William Empson. CMoP (1970 ed.)

Sea-Voyage from Tenby to Bristol, A. Katherine Philips. SBG; WPE

Sea was as blue as the sky, The. The Real Thing. Ronald Wallace. AMV-81

Sea waves are green and wet. Sand Dunes. Robert Frost. RFM

Sea Wind, The. Harry Martinson, *tr. fr. Swedish by* Robert Bly. NU

Sea Wolf, The. Violet McDougal. EcS

Seafarer. Archibald MacLeish. NoAM

Seafarer, The. Earl of Surrey. *See* Complaint of the Absence of Her Lover. . .

Seafarer, The ("May I for my own self song's truth reckon"). *Unknown, tr. fr. Anglo-Saxon by* Ezra Pound. ExPo (1973 ed.); FaBoTw (1975 ed.); HeIP

Seafarer, The ("My purpose is to tell my own true tale"). *Unknown, tr. fr. Anglo-Saxon by* John Wain. EBEV

Seafarer, The ("The tale I frame shall be found to tally"). *Unknown, tr. fr. Anglo-Saxon by* Michael Alexander. OBVE

Seal. William Jay Smith. EcS; FPB; RFM

Seal at Stinson Beach. Roberta Hill. VoR

Seal in the Lowry Park Zoo, The. Richard Mathews. AATT

Seal of Fire. Mordecai Temkin, *tr. fr. Hebrew by* Jeremy Garber. VWA

Seal Rock. Sue Baugh. AMV-81

Sealchie Song. *Unknown.* PeBB

Sealess World, A. Joan Campbell. EcS

Seals, The. Dorothy Aldis. CTV

Seals. David R. Slavitt. CoPAm

Seals all flap, The. The Seals. Dorothy Aldis. CTV

Seals at High Island. Richard Murphy. CIP

Seaman's Life, The. *Unknown.* RhR

Seams. Hazel Hall. WPW

Sean the hunchback, sadly. Beyond the Liss. John Montague. TwMBP

Séance. Francis King. PoA

Seance. Edouard Roditi. EAS

Search. Claribel Alegria, *tr. fr. Spanish by* Aliki *and* Willis Barnstone. BoWoP

Search, The. Denis Glover. ATNZ

Search, The. Michael Hamburger. VWA

Search, The. John Logan. FoP

Search. Elisavietta Ritchie. AATT

Search all the Christian climes from pole to pole. Daniel Defoe. *Fr.* Reformation of Manners. OBSV

Search. Search. Seek. Seek. A Weary Song to a Slow Sad Tune. Li Ch'ing-chao, *tr. by* Kenneth Rexroth. BoWoP

Searcher of souls, you who in heaven abide. A Prayer. Samuel Butler. FaBoEE

Searching. Ralph Tabor Williams. PHC

Searching for souvenirs among some rubble. A Post-Mortem. Siegfried Sassoon. PBMP

Searching for the Desert Blues. *Unknown.* BluL

Searching my heart for its true sorrow. Exiled. Edna St. Vincent Millay. PPM; RhR

Searching was easy and memory ripens, The. Blood Donor. Robert Morgan. HeHu

Seas are quiet when the winds give o'er, The. Old Age. Edmund Waller. *Fr.* Of the Last Verses in the Book. NOBE

Seascape. Elizabeth Bishop. PPP

Seascape. Francis Brett Young. OxBTC

Seascape shift, The. Distinctions. Charles Tomlinson. CMoP (1970 ed.)

Seascape with Bookends. Charles Edward Eaton. AMV-80

Seaside, The. Charles Tennyson Turner. VPC

Seaside Golf. John Betjeman. LiSp; PPM; SPo

Season, ending, makes no sign, but the wind. Conserves. David Mus. *Fr.* The Joy of Cooking. PoA

Season late, day late, sun just down, and the sky. Birth of Love. Robert Penn Warren. UnPo (1976 ed.)

Season of Calypso. Home from Russia. Dan Gerber. TC

Season of mists and mellow fruitfulness. To Autumn. Keats. AnMo; BiP; CABA (1972 ed.); EBEV; Epi; ExPo (1973 ed.); FF; FSFS; HAP; ILP (1975 ed.); IP; IPWM; LFH; MBPR; NIL; NOBE; NU; OAEL-2; OBP; PBMP; PoIA; PoPle; PPoD; PPoe; PPP; Prf; SoSe; STS; TT; UnPo (1976 ed.); UsP; WIF

Season 'Tis, My Lovely Lambs, The. E. E. Cummings. NIL; UnPo (1976 ed.)

Seasonal Phenomenon. Richard Armour. BBGO

Seasons. Hayden Carruth. TVo

Seasons, The, *sels.* James Thomson.
Autumn.
Autumnal Moon, The. NOBE
Hymn on the Seasons, A. LAuP; PIM
Spring. LAuP
Spring Flowers. NOBE; PF
Summer.
" 'Tis raging noon; and, vertical, the sun." EBEV; OAEL-1
Winter.
"Keener tempests come, The: and, fuming dun." EBEV
"When from the pallid sky the sun descends." OAEL-1
Winter Night, A. NOBE

Seasons/ changes moods. A Common Poem. Carolyn M. Rodgers. CNA

Seat of the soul is where the inner world, The. Aphorism. "Novalis," *tr. by* Charles E. Passage. NU

Seat Was Up, The. Judith McCombs. WBN

Seated on a metal folding chair. Dtah Dtah. David Kherdian. SA

Seated on her bed legs spread open. Joyce Mansour, *tr. fr. French by* Willis Barnstone. BoWoP

Seated once by a brook, watching a child. The Brook. Edward Thomas. OAEL-2

Seated one day at the organ. A Lost Chord. Adelaide Anne Procter. VLP

Seated statue of himself he seems, A. Farm Boy after Summer. Robert Francis. NCSH

Seaward goes the sun, and homeward by the down. The Cliffside Path. Swinburne. A Midsummer Holiday, VI. VLP

Sea-ward, White Gleaming. Samuel Taylor Coleridge. BiP

Seaway. Grace Wilson. AMV-81

Sea-Weed. D. H. Lawrence. EcS

Seaweed. Longfellow. TAP
Equinox, The, *sel.* RhR
("When descends on the Atlantic.") EcS

Seaweed, seaweed, drifting, drifting. *Ad. by* Hannah Tatana, *tr. fr. Maori by* Barry Mitcalfe. WTO

Sea-weed sways and sways and swirls. Sea-Weed. D. H. Lawrence. EcS

Seaweeds. Sandra McPherson. AmPA

Second Advice to a Painter, The. Andrew Marvell. APAS

2nd Air Force. Randall Jarrell. CMoP (1970 ed.)

Second Anniversary, The. John Donne. *See* Of the Progress of the Soul.

Second Avenue Winter. Charles Simic. NYP

Second-best Bed, The. Howard Nemerov. NIL

Second Carolina Said-Song. A. R. Ammons. OBAL

Second class is the second grade, The. Primary Lesson: The Second Class Citizens. Sun-Ra. PoBA

Second Coming, The. Dannie Abse. NoAM

Second Coming, The. Carl Clark. JB

Second Coming, The. John William Corrington. HoPM (1975 ed.)

Second Coming, The. W. B. Yeats. AnMo; BIrV; CABA (1972 ed.); CMoP (1970 ed.); ExPo (1973 ed.); FF; GrRo; HAP; HeIP; HoPM (1975 ed.); ILP (1975 ed.); InPK; InPS; IPWM; MAT; NIL; NoAM; NOBE; OAEL-2; OBP; OxBTC; PBMP; PPoD; PPoe; PPP; PSN; STS; TCP; TT; UnPo (1976 ed.); VoPo; WeW; WIF, 2 versions

Second-fated, The. Robert Graves. NoAM

Second Fig. Edna St. Vincent Millay. PoA; TH; TPo

Second Generation, The. Menachem Z. Rosensaft. AMV-81

Second Glance at a Jaguar. Ted Hughes. NoAM

Second grade mornings. Dogskin Rug. Adrien Stoutenburg. GP

Second-hand sights, like crumpled. Newark, for Now (68). Carolyn M. Rodgers. PoBA

Second Heart, The. Ellen Wittlinger. TV

Second Honeymoon. *Unknown, tr. fr. Irish by* Augustus Young. BIrV

Second Hymn to Lenin. "Hugh MacDiarmid." OAEL-2, *abr.*; TwMBP

"Oh it's nonsense, nonsense," *sel.* MS

Second Hymn to the Night, The. "Novalis," *prose poem version tr. fr. German by* Robert Bly. *Fr.* Hymns to the Night. NU

Second man I love, The. Spring. Carole Gregory Clemmons. PoBA

Second Night, The. M. L. Hester, Jr. AMV-80

Second Night in N.Y.C. after 3 Years. Gregory Corso. BuTh

Second Part, The. David Hilton. AcAn

Second Poem the Night-Walker Wrote, The. Goethe, *tr. fr. German by* Robert Bly. NU

Second Psalm: The Signals. W. S. Merwin. CAAP

Second Rapture, The. Thomas Carew. CaPo

Second Reading. Richard Beyer. AMV-81

Second Samuel, *sel.* Bible, *O.T.*
  David's Lament, I: 19-27. FF
  ("Beauty of Israel is slaine upon thy high places, The: how are the mightie fallen!") OBVE

Second Sapphic Fragment/ Fainetai Moi. Sappho, *tr. fr. Greek by* Harvey Bialy. MIT

Second Satire of the First Book of Horace Imitated, The, *sel.* Pope.
  "With all a woman's virtues but the pox." OBSV

Second Sermon on the Warpland, The. Gwendolyn Brooks. BPo; NOBA; PoBA

Second Shadow. Theodore Roethke. PoA

Second Shaman Song. Gary Snyder. Myths and Texts: Burning, I. NOBA
  ("Squat in swamp meadows.") Epi

Second Skins—A Peyote Song. Joseph Bruchac. CDW

Second Violinist's Son, The. Debora Gregor. AMV-80

Second Wind. Ruth Stephan. FoP

Secondline for Susan. Jonetta Barras-Abney. PoUp

Secrecy. Samuel Daniel. *Fr.* Hymen's Triumph. OLR

Secrecy Protested. Thomas Carew. CaPo

Secret, The. John Clare. GBL

Secret, The. Robert P. Tristram Coffin. FSFS

Secret, The. Denise Levertov. AnMo; PBMP; Psy; SFF

Secret, A. Eve Merriam. CC

Secret, The ("Hark, Celia, hark!). *Unknown.* SCP-2

Secret, The ("We have a secret, just we three"). *Unknown.* CTV; ECBV; PCOP; *wr. at. to* Emily Dickinson

Secret cone will drop in Rothiemurcus, A. Forecast for a Quiet Night. Robin Fulton. MS

Secret in the Cat, The. May Swenson. GP

Secret Irish, The. Allen Hoey. AMV-81

Secret is a secret, any size, A. The Secret. Robert P. Tristram Coffin. FSFS

Secret Love. John Clare. *See* I Hid My Love.

Secret love or two, I must confesse, A. Thomas Campion. AAS

Secret of Seeds, The. Melvin Dixon. NW

Secret of the Sea, The. Longfellow. RhR

Secret of the Sea, The. Susan K. Phillips. RhR

Secret of these hills was stone, and cottages, The. The Pylons. Stephen Spender. LP; NoAM

Secret People, The. G. K. Chesterton. FaPoR; OxBTC

Secret Policeman. Vincent Buckley. GAS

Secret Sits, The. Robert Frost. InPK; TH; UsP

Secret they are, sealed, annealed, and brainless. Oystering. Richard Howard. NoAM

Secretaries drive by the factory, The. Night Shift at the Plating Division of Keeler Brass. James B. Allen. HeS

Secretary. Ted Hughes. InPK; NIL; SFF

Secretary, The. Matthew Prior. NIL

Secretary, The. Peter Redgrove. OxBTC

Secrets, *sels.* Jessie Orton Jones.
  "Did you ever have a chipmunk for a friend?" XII. CTV
  "Flowers always know what they should do," VI. CTV
  "How could God think of so many kinds of houses?" XXI. CTV
  "I am glad I'm who I am," VIII. CTV
  "I can climb our apple tree," IX. CTV
  "Sometimes I hear God's whisper in the night," V. CTV
  "We have tulips in our flower bed," VII. CTV

Secrets. Edward Lowbury. FPB

Secrets ("The secrets I keep"). Linda Pastan. AMV-80

Secrets of the Earth, The. Blake. NOBE

Secular Elegies, *sel.* George Barker.
  "Satan is on your tongue, sweet singer, with," III PIAC

Secular Games. Richard Howard. PoA

Secular Masque, The. Dryden. ExPo (1973 ed.); OBP; PAIC
*Sels.*
  All, All of a Piece. HAP; InPS
  "Cronos, Cronos, mend thy pace." SCP-1
  "With horns and with hounds I waken the day." NOBE

Seder, 1944. Friedrich Torberg, *tr. fr. German by* Erna Baber Rosenfeld. VWA

Sedge-Warbler, The. Ralph Hodgson. PB

Sedge-Warblers. Edward Thomas. PoPle

Sedna. Lyn Lifshin. MMD

Seduced Girl. Hedylos, *tr. fr. Greek by* Louis Untermeyer. BoLoP

Seduction. Nikki Giovanni. NMM; RiTi

Seduction, The. Suzanne Berger Rioff. NMM

Seduction of Hero, The. Christopher Marlowe. *Fr.* Hero and Leander, Second Sestiad. NIL

Seduction of Juan, The. Byron. *Fr.* Don Juan. OBP

See/ how they trace. Birds in Snow.' Hilda Doolittle ("H. D."). PoA

See/ it was like this when. Lawrence Ferlinghetti. *Fr.* A Coney Island of the Mind. CoPAm

See a pin and pick it up. *Unknown.* MG

See, a small space in the woods. The Man. Judith McCombs. BCr

See all the people getting off the bus. Mark Rahschulte. AMV-80

See, all the silver roads wind in, lead in. The Sufficient Place. Edwin Muir. MS

See an old unhappy bull. The Bull. Ralph Hodgson. OxBTC

See, and not see; and if thou chance t' espy. To the Generous Reader. Robert Herrick. CaPo

See columns rang'd in proud Palladian style! *Unknown.* FaBoEE

See commons, peers, and ministers of state. Edward Young. *Fr.* Love of Fame, the Universal Passion. OBSV

See! from the brake the whirring pheasant springs. The Shoot. Pope. *Fr.* Windsor Forest. PB

See her come bearing down, a tidy craft! A Note on Wyatt. Kingsley Amis. WeW

See here, nice Death, to please his palate. Epitaph. *At.* to Pope. FaBoEE

See here the diving beetle is split. Creatures. Maxine W. Kumin. BoAnP

"See, here's the workbox, little wife." The Workbox. Thomas Hardy. InPK; UnPo (1976 ed.)

See how easily our trap comes up. Crabbing. Marky Daniel. AMV-81

See how he dives. Seal. William Jay Smith. EcS; FPB; RFM

See how he loves me. Generations. Joseph Awad. AMV-81

See how like twilight slumber falls. Charles Cotton. SCP-2

See how the flowers as at parade. The Garden at Appleton House. Andrew Marvell. *Fr.* Upon Appleton House. PF; PoPle

See how she strips her lily for the sun. The Double Looking Glass. A. D. Hope. GAS

See how the brown kelp withers in air. Landed: A Valentine. Richard Howard. PoA

See how the orient dew. On a Drop of Dew. Andrew Marvell. AnMo; BoReV; HAP; ILP (1975 ed.); MetP; NIL; PAIC

See How the Rising Sun, *with music.* Elizabeth Scott. AH

See,—how the shining share. God Save the Plough. Lydia Huntley Sigourney. OBAL

See how the sun has somewhat not of light. El Greco. E. L. Mayo. HoPM (1975 ed.)

See how the willing earth gave way. The Fall. Edmund Waller. SCP-2

See! In the troubled glow of dawn. Environs of Vanholt II. Charles Spear. ATNZ

See Lucifer like lightning fall. Third Sunday in Lent. John Keble. *Fr.* The Christian Year. VLP

See, one physician, like a sculler, plies. Joseph Jekyll. FaBoEE

See, saw, Margery Daw,/ Johnny shall have a new master. Mother Goose. MG

See, saw, Margery Daw/ Sold her bed and lay upon straw. *Unknown.* MG

See-saw sacradown,/ which is the way to London town? Mother Goose. MG

Seesaw, sacradown, sacradown. To Boston Town. *Unknown.* ECBV

See, see the mighty hunter, fiercely bland. For the Opening of the Hunting Season. Morris Bishop. BoAnP; SPo

See that brave and trembling motorman. The Dying Mine Brakeman. Orville Jenks. AmFP

See that [*or* the] building which, when my mistress living. A Well-wishing to a Place of Pleasure. *Unknown.* GBL; SCP-2

See that señor so amorous and menacing. The Amorous Señor. Ogden Nash. TDH

See that wreck there in the gutter. The Outcast. Frank Elwood Sanford. PeD

See the chariot at hand here of Love. The Triumph of Charis [*or* Her Triumph]. Ben Jonson. *Fr.* A Celebration of Charis. CABA (1972 ed.); EBEV; ILP (1975 ed.); InPS; LoAs; NOBE; PoPle

See the fountain opened wide. Zion's Sons and Daughters. *Unknown.* AmFP

See the headlands yonder stand. Dirge Sung at Death. *Tr. fr. Maori by* John White. WTO

See the kitten on the wall. The Kitten and the Falling Leaves. Wordsworth. PCat; PCOP

See! The Mother Corn comes hither. An Indian Hymn of Thanks to Mother Corn. *Unknown, tr. fr. Pawnee Indian.* CC

See the pretty snowflakes. Falling Snow. *Unknown.* CTV

See the scaffold it is mounted. Life of the Mannings. *Unknown.* FaBoBa

See, the smell of my sone is as the smell of a feld. Bible, *O.T., tr. by* William Tyndale. Genesis, XXVII: 27–29. OBVE

See the smoking bowl before us! Burns. *Fr.* The Jolly Beggars. OBP

See, the visor's pulled off and the zealots are arming. The Western Rebel. *Unknown.* APAS

See the young man I've laid out. Funeral Lament (Kommos) from Epiros. *Tr. fr. Modern Greek by* Elene Kolb. BoWoP

See there the taper's dim and doleful light. Verses on the Snuff of a Candle, Made in Sickness. Anne Wharton. SCP-2

See, they return; ah, see the tentative. The Return. Ezra Pound. CMoP (1970 ed.); ExPo (1973 ed.); HAP; NoAM; NOBA; PPoe; PSN; VGW; WeW

See this air, how empty it is of angels. Five for the Grace of Man. Winfield Townley Scott. VGW

See this girl in the picture? Song for My Mother. Alan Chong Lau. NW

See those cherries, how they cover. The Cherries, a Parable. Thomas Moore. OBSV

See two passenger trains, Lawd. Dey Got Each and de Udder's Man. *Unknown.* WTO

See what a clouded majesty, and eyes. To My Worthy Friend Master Peter Lely. Richard Lovelace. CaPo

See what a lovely shell. The Shell. Tennyson. *Fr.* Maud, II. EcS

See what delights in sylvan scenes appear! Sylvan Delights. Pope. *Fr.* Pastorals: Summer. NOBE

See where black water. Strip Mining Pit. Dan Gillespie. TAT

See where Capella with her golden kids. Edna St. Vincent Millay. Epitaph for the Race of Man, VI. CMoP (1970 ed.)

See where 'tis fallen, among a ring of boys. The Boys and the Bubble. Samuel Wesley. SCP-2

See, whilst thou weep'st, fair Cloe, see. To Cloe Weeping. Matthew Prior. PAIC

See, whirling snow sprinkles the starvèd fields. The Palm Willow. Robert Bridges. VLP

See who comes over the red blossomed heather. The Bold Fenian Men. *Unknown.* FSW

See, Will, 'Ere's a Go. *Unknown.* FaBoNo

See with what constant motion. Gratiana Dancing and Singing. Richard Lovelace. CaPo

See with what simplicity. The Picture of Little T. C. in a Prospect of Flowers. Andrew Marvell. ExPo (1973 ed.); NOBE; OAEL-1; PPP

See! yonder hill the bitterns seek. Kisses. *Malay Oral Tradition, tr. by* R. J. Wilkinson *and* R. O. Winstedt. WTO

See you that beauteous queen, which no age tames? To Etesia Looking from Her Casement at the Full Moon. Henry Vaughan. Moon

See you the ferny ride that steals. Puck's Song. Kipling. *Fr.* Puck of Pook's Hill. OxBChV; PoPle

Seed Journey. Gregory Corso. VGW

Seed Leaves. Richard Wilbur. NCSH; PiAm

Seed of Nimrod, The. De Leon Harrison. PoBA

Seed of Reality, The. Max von Hartmann. AMV-80

Seed-potatoes, staring their eyes. Root-Crops. Derek Bowman. MIS

Seed Shop, The. Muriel Stuart. MS

Seeding. Mary Moore. NPW

Seedlings. Susan Weston. PHC

Seedlings in the Mail. Marge Piercy. MMD

Seeds. James Reeves. ECBV

Seeds in a dry pod, tick, tick, tick. Petit, the Poet. Edgar Lee Masters. *Fr.* Spoon River Anthology. CMoP (1970 ed.); InPK; NoAM; NOBA; TAP

Seeds of Lead. Amir Gilboa, *tr. fr. Hebrew by* Stephen Mitchell. VWA

Seeds of Love, The. *Unknown, at. to* Mrs. Fleetwood Habergham. AIW; GBP, *longer version*

Seed-Time. George Meredith. FSFS

Seedy Henry rose up shy in de world. John Berryman. *Fr.* Dream Songs. PiAm

Seeing and Doing. John Dean. AMV-81

Seeing Auden Off. Philip Booth. PoA

Seeing Eye, The. Ezra Pound. ExPo (1973 ed.)

Seeing good places/ for my hands. The Time We Climbed Snake Mountain. Leslie Silko. VoR

Seeing in flight along the lifting wind. Message. Dorothy M. Richardson. PoA

Seeing in the Dark. Matthew Brennan. AMV-81

Seeing its corners, it is square. Benediction for the Felt. *Mongol Oral Tradition, tr. by* C. R. Bawden. WTO

Seeing me weary. Back to Africa. Erica Jong. RiTi

Seeing Nellie Home (Aunt Dinah's Quilting Party). Francis Kyle. *See* When I Saw Sweet Nelly Home.

Seeing the coyote flash across the road. Watch for Fallen Rock. Madeline DeFrees. MPA

Seeing the Elephant. *Unknown.* AIW

Seeing the Plum Blossoms by the River. Lady Ise, *tr. fr. Japanese by* Etsuko Terasaki *and* Irma Brandeis. BoWoP

Seeing the Returning Geese. Lady Ise, *tr. fr. Japanese by* Etsuko Terasaki *and* Irma Brandeis. BoWoP

Seeing the snowman standing all alone. Boy at the Window. Richard Wilbur. IP; SoS; TH

Seeing them over and over each. Pickers. Peter Brett. AMV-81

Seeing thou art faire, I barre not thy false playing. Ovid, *tr. by* Christopher Marlowe. Amores, III, 13. OBVE

Seeing you/ in the laundromat. Thinking Twice in the Laundromat. Harley Elliott. NeAC

Seek love/ Without the light-low night. Love at Stress-Point. Ruthe T. Spinnanger. AATT

Seek not man to please, for that. Isabella Whitney. *Fr.* A Sweet Nosegay, or Pleasant Posy. WPE

Seek out reality, leave things that seem. W. B. Yeats. *Fr.* Vacillation. BoReV

Seek the Lord! Thomas Campion. BoReV

Seek True Religion! John Donne. *Fr.* Satires, III. BoReV; NOBE

("Seek true religion. O where? Mirreus.") OBSV

Seeker, The. Ahmos Zu-Bolton II. PoUp

Seekers of Lice, The. Arthur Rimbaud. *See* Lice-Hunters, The.

Seeking a Mooring. Wang Wei, *tr. fr. Chinese by* Kenneth Rexroth *and* Ling Chung. BoWoP

Seeking, earnestly seeking in the gloom. The Creation of Man. *Maori Oral Tradition, tr. by* John White. WTO

Seeking in squalor lean, elusive youth. Nightwood. William Jay Smith. PoA

Seeking necessity, he only found. Live Man's Epitaph. Francis Hope. BuTh

Seeking the words. Poem for Jan. Joseph Bruchac. CDW

Seems like a long time. The Partial Explanation. Charles Simic. FiCP

Seen at a Fashionable Night Spot. Katie Louchheim. PoUP

Seen from a great distance. My Father's House. Steven Orlen. AAN

Seen my lady home las' night. A Negro Love Song. Paul Laurence Dunbar. ILP (1975 ed.)

Seen through the Trees behind Which You're Walking. Brian Patten. BuTh

Seepage of time rots judgment, makes it slip. Darkened Windows. Ronald Bottrall. PoA

Seer foretold that I would love one day, A. Sonnet. Louise Labé, *tr. by* Joan Keefe *and* Richard Terdiman. PBWP

Seething over inwardly. His Confession. "The Archpoet," *tr. by* Helen Waddell. NAWM-1

Seferis. Lawrence Durrell. EBEV

Seismograph. Ephraim Auerbach, *tr. fr. Yiddish by* Howard Schwartz. VWA

Seized with a sudden fancy for fresh meat. *Unknown, tr. by* Shelley. *Fr.* Homer's Hymn to Mercury. OBVE

Seizure. James E. Warren, Jr. AMV-81

Sejanus ("How many men are killed by power, by power"). Juvenal, *tr. fr. Latin by* Robert Lowell. *Fr.* Satires, X. OBVE

Sejanus ("Some ask for envy'd pow'r; which publick hate"). Juvenal, *tr. fr. Latin by* Dryden. *Fr.* Satires, X. OBVE

Sejanus ("What crowds by envied power, the wish of all"). Juvenal, *tr. fr. Latin by* William Gifford. *Fr.* Satires, X. OBVE

Seldom "can't." Christina Rossetti. CTV

Seldom is the tent full, but tonight he expects the local radio. Faith Healer Come to Rabun County. David Bottoms. CSP; TAT

Seldom named. Gerda, My Husband's Wife. Eve Triem. GP

Select a small pumpkin that's solid and sound. Pumpkin Pie. Sharlot Hall. WPW

Selected Epigrams. *Unknown, tr. fr. Byzantine Greek by* Patrick Diehl. PBWP

Self. Norman Henry Pritchard II. PoBA

Self Accuser, A. John Donne. FaBoEE

Self-conscious Horse, The. David Rafael Wang. FoP

Self-Deceiver, The. Thomas Stanley, *after the Spanish of* Juan Perez de Montalvan. OBVE

Self-Dependence. Matthew Arnold. IPWM; PBMP; VLP

Self Dirge. Wendy Rose. CDW

Self-employed. David Ignatow. NNaP

Self-Hatred of Don L. Lee, The. Don L. Lee. BPo

Self-Interviews. Peter Mladinic. BrS

Self-Knowledge. Samuel Taylor Coleridge. MBPR

Self-Pity. D. H. Lawrence. BoAnP; OxBTC

Self-Portrait. Cedil Bodker, *tr. fr. Danish by* Nadia Christensen. BoWoP

Self-Portrait. Nina Cassian, *tr. fr. Rumanian by* Herbert Kuhner. VWA

Self-Portrait. Allen Curnow. ATNZ

Self-Portrait. A. K. Ramanujan. FoP

Self-Portrait. Orlando Romero. FoP

Self-Portrait, as a Bear. Donald Hall. SO

Self-Portrait as Still Life. Donald Justice. FoP

Self-Portrait: Microcosm, or, Song of Mixed-Blood. Robert J. Conley. FoP

Self-Portrait: Women with Children. Pamela Stewart. FoP

Self to Self. Charles Brasch. ATNZ

Self Unsatisfied Runs Everywhere, The. Delmore Schwartz. PoA

Self-unseeing, The. Thomas Hardy. EBEV; HAP; NOBE; VLP

Self's the Man. Philip Larkin. NOBL

Selfsame Song, The. Thomas Hardy. CMoP (1970 ed.)

Selfsame surface that billowed once with, The.  Skin Flick.  Fred Chappell.  PPoD

Selfsame toothless voice for death or bridal, The.  Bell Speech. Richard Wilbur.  CABA (1972 ed.)

Selichos.  Francis Landy.  VWA

Selling Ruined Peonies.  Yü Hsüan-chi, *tr. fr. Chinese by* Geoffrey Waters.  BoWoP

Selling the House.  Sandra McPherson.  CNW

Semblables, The.  William Carlos Williams.  ILP (1975 ed.); NOBA

Semele Recycled.  Carolyn Kizer.  WBN

Semele to Jupiter.  Congreve.  LoAs
   (Song: "With my frailty don't upbraid me.")  POL

Semen.  Coleman Barks.  *Fr. Body Poems.*  NVAP

Semen.  Martha Paley Francescato, *tr. fr. Spanish by* Willis Barnstone.  BoWoP

Semi-private Room.  Alden Nowlan.  NeAC

Semi-Revolution, A.  Robert Frost.  NIL; WIF

Seminar.  Erica Jong.  RiTi

Semphill, his hat stuck full of hooks.  Trout Fisher.  George Mackay Brown.  MS

Sempronius,/ Sends greeting, warden of this Roman shore.  A Roman Officer Writes.  C. M. Doughty.  *Fr. The Dawn in Britain.*  FaBoTw (1975 ed.)

Senator, A.  *Unknown.*  TDH

Senator Smoot (Republican, Ut.).  Invocation.  Ogden Nash. OBAL

Send but a song oversea for us.  To Walt Whitman in America. Swinburne.  VLP

Send cards send.  Notes on a Long Evening.  David Phillips. NeAC

Send down thy winged angel, God!  A Prayer in Sickness. "Barry Cornwall."  PIM

Send Forth, O God, Thy Light and Truth, *with music.*  John Quincy Adams.  AH

Send home my long-strayed eyes to me.  The Message.  John Donne.  PAIC

Send me no flowers, for they will die before they leave America. Junglegrave.  S. E. Anderson.  PoBA

Send-off, The.  Wilfred Owen.  InPS; OBW; OxBTC; PSN; SoSe

Send soldiers again to kill you, García.  Lines to García Lorca. Amiri Baraka.  TCP

Sending to the War.  William Morris.  *Fr. The Pilgrims of Hope.* VLP

Senile.  Pat Folk.  NowV

Senior Members.  Sean Lucy.  CIP

Senlin, a Biography, *sel.*  Conrad Aiken.
   "It is morning, Senlin says, and in the morning," II, ii.  NoAM
   (Morning Song.)  CMoP (1970 ed.); SoSe

Señor Torres.  Luís Omar Salinas.  SA

Senryu.  Les A. Murray.  GAS

Sensational Relatives.  Alexis Krasilovsky.  AMV-80

Sense of Coolness, A.  Quincy Troupe.  PoBA

Sense of Property, A.  Anthony Thwaite.  MPo

Sense of the Sleight-of-Hand Man, The.  Wallace Stevens. CABA (1972 ed.); HAP; ILP (1975 ed.); NOBA; PoA

Sense with keenest edge unusèd.  Pater Filio.  Robert Bridges. CMoP (1970 ed.)

Senseless school, where we must give, A.  A Young Man's Epigram on Existence.  Thomas Hardy.  NoAM

Senses' Festival, The.  John Cleveland.  *See* To the State of Love.

Sensibility.  Louis Simpson.  GP

Sensibility! O La!  Theodore Roethke.  UsP

Sensible Girl's Reply to Moore's, A.  Walter Savage Landor. FaBoEE

Sensible People.  James Stephens.  RAE

Sensitive Cat, The.  Alice Brown.  TDH

Sensitive Man, A.  Morris Bishop.  TDH

Sensitive Philanthropist, The.  D. J. Enright.  HeHu

Sensitive Plant, The.  Shelley.  MBPR
*Sels.*
   Garden, A, *fr.* I.  PCOP
   "Whether the sensitive plant, or that," *conclusion.*  OAEL-2

Sensualists, The.  Theodore Roethke.  CNW

Sensuous Latin poet, now I will go off with a thermos, A.  Lynn Strongin.  *Fr. First Aspen.*  IHMS; RiTi

Sent for this case, I found an executive.  Emergency Gastrectomy. Peter Dale.  PMW

Sent from the Capital to Her Elder Daughter.  Lady Otomo of Sakanone, *tr. fr. Japanese by* Geoffrey Bownas *and* Anthony Thwaite.  BoWoP

Sent to Wen T'ing-yün on a Winter Night.  Yü Hsüan-chi, *tr. fr. Chinese by* Geoffrey Waters.  BoWoP

Sentence.  Billy Collins.  AAN

Sentence for Konarak.  John Montague.  TwMBP

Sentences we studied are rungs upon the ladder Jacob saw, The. Luzzato.  Charles Reznikoff.  VWA

Sentences while Remembering Hiraethog.  T. Glynne Davies, *tr. fr. Welsh by* R. Gerallt Jones.  OBW

Sentience.  Sandra McPherson.  CNW; PoA

Sentimental Ode.  Tom Buchan.  MIS

Sentiments, The.  *Unknown.*  APAS

Sentinel's Song, A.  Rarawa Kerehoma, *tr. fr. Maori by* Barry Mitcalfe.  WTO

Sentries stood here when the river was called.  Hidden Falls. John Minczeski.  BrS

Sentry, The.  Alun Lewis.  PSN

Senzangakhona.  *Zulu Oral Tradition, tr. by* T. Cope.  WTO

Sepal, petal, and a thorn, A.  Emily Dickinson.  PiAm

Separate.  Eve Shelnutt.  TC

Separate place between the thought and felt, A.  The Corridor. Thom Gunn.  NowV; PPP

Separate Way, *sel.*  Charles Reznikoff.
   Kaddish: "Upon Israel and upon the rabbis."  SA

Separated Lovers.  *Unknown.*  OAEL-1; OxBM

Separation.  Samuel Taylor Coleridge.  MBPR

Separation.  W. S. Merwin.  HAP

Separation.  Duane Niatum.  VW

Separation.  Gary Sange.  NVAP

Separation demands that.  E. Ethelbert Miller.  PoUp

Separation on the River Kiang.  Ezra Pound.  UnPo (1976 ed.)

Sephestia's Song to Her Childe.  Robert Greene.  *Fr. Menaphon.* ILP (1975 ed.); OBP
   (Sephestia's Lullaby.)  NOBE

Sepoy servant, Nate, the natural son, A.  1864.  Richard Howard. CABA (1972 ed.)

September.  Mary Elizabeth Coleridge.  FSFS

September.  Marilyn Hacker.  NYP

September.  Ted Hughes.  BoLoP; OLR

September.  Aldous Huxley.  EBEV

September.  W. D. Snodgrass.  PSN

September Butterfly.  Mollie Boring.  AMV-80

September, 1819.  Wordsworth.  MBPR

September 1802.  Near Dover.  Wordsworth.  MBPR

September 1, 1802.  Wordsworth.  MBPR

September 1, 1939.  W. H. Auden.  CMoP (1970 ed.)

September Midnight.  Sara Teasdale.  PoA

September 1957 summoned by my vision-agent.  Vision of Rotterdam.  Gregory Corso.  NoAM

September 1913.  W. B. Yeats.  CMoP (1970 ed.); HAP; NoAM; PPoe

September rain falls on the house. Sestina. Elizabeth Bishop. WeW

September 2. Wendell Berry. PoA

September 7. Ellen Bass. NMM

Sept. 16, 1961, Poem. Jack Kerouac. VoA

September, the First Day of School. Howard Nemerov. PPoD

September. The gypsy and the nightingale. Autumn. Itzik Manger, *tr. by* Ruth Whitman. VWA

September: the noon hour: a thriving prince. Dilemma of a Dead Man about to Wake Up. Stanley Burnshaw. SPT

September 30. Dick Lourie. NeAC

September twenty-second, Sir: today. After the Surprising Conversions. Robert Lowell. CABA (1972 ed.); ConAP; HAP; ILP (1975 ed.); NoAM; PAIC; PPP; STS

September Valentine. Frank Sullivan. SPo

September was when it began. The Coming of the Plague. Weldon Kees. VGW

Sepulchre. George Herbert. SCP-1

Sequel, The. Theodore Roethke. MPA

Sequel to the Purple Cow. Gelett Burgess. FaBoCo (Cinq Ans Après.) OBAL (Confession.) FaBoNo

Sequence. George Barker. PoA

Sequence. James Harrison. CoPAm

Sequence for a Young Widow Passing. Deborah Munro. IHMS

Sequence of Generations, The. Hayim Be'er, *tr. fr. Hebrew by* Stephen Mitchell. VWA

Sequence of Women, A. James Harrison. CoPAm

Sequitor: A Love Poem. Cinda Kornblum. AcAn

Seravazza. Hoyt W. Fuller. PoBA

Serenade: "Stars of the summer night." Longfellow. *Fr.* The Spanish Student, I, iii. PAIC

Serenade: "Thou moon, like a white Christus hanging." Kenneth Slessor. POL

Serenade: "Tin-type tune the locusts make, The." Dorothy Donnelly. NCSH

Serenade for two Poplars, A. Esther Raab, *tr. fr. Hebrew by* Robert Friend *and* Shimon Sandbank. VWA

Serenade of a Loyal Martyr. George Darley. NOBE

Serenade of Angels. Rina Lasnier, *tr. fr. French by* Jan Pallister. AMV-81

Serenades. Seamus Heaney. HeHu

Serene Art. Lewis Warsh. MIT

Serene descent, as a red leaf's descending. Epitaph. Sara Teasdale. PoA

Serene, indifferent of Fate. San Francisco from the Sea. Bret Harte. BPAW

Serengeti Sunset. Andrew Oerke. POL

Serenity in Stones, The. Simon J. Ortiz. CDW

Sgt. stands so fluently in leather, The. On a Photo of Sgt. Ciardi a Year Later. John Ciardi. CoPAm

Sergeant's Weddin', The. Kipling. OxBTC

Sergei's a flower. Song. Ruth Herschberger. FF

Serial Monogamy. Michael C. Blumenthal. PoUp

Serials are all wound up now, The. Where Are You Now Superman? Brian Patten. FF

Series of white squares, each, A. Flight. Pamela Alexander. AAN

Serious Merriment of Women, The. Patricia Goedicke. TAP

Serious Omission. John Farrar. PCOP

Serious over my cereals I broke one breakfast my fast. Breakfast with Gerard Manley Hopkins. Anthony Brode. NOBL

Sermon on Swift, A. Austin Clarke. BIrV

Sermon on the Warpland, The. Gwendolyn Brooks. BPo; NOBA; PoBA

Sermonette. Ishmael Reed. PoBA

Sermons and epigrams have a like end. To the Reader. Robert Hayman. NIL

Serpent, The. Theodore Roethke. DuDr; ECBV

Serpent is shut out from paradise, The. To Edward Williams. Shelley. MBPR

Serpent Muses, The. Peggy Henderson. NMM

Serpentine Verse. Joseph S. Newman. TDH

Serronydion. Jack Hirschman. CPA

"Serva tibi minas!" The Judge with the Sore Rump. St. George Tucker. OBAL

Servant-Girl's Holiday, A. *Unknown.* OxBM

Servant Man, The. *Unknown.* AmFP

Servant to Servants, A. Robert Frost. CMoP (1970 ed.); Epi

Service is joy, to see or swing. Allow. Tennis. Margaret Avison. NoAM

Service Is No Heritage. *Unknown.* OxBM

Serving-Men's Song, A. John Lyly. *Fr.* Alexander and Campaspe, I, iii. NOBE

Sessions was held the other day, A. The Wits. Sir John Suckling. CaPo

Sestina: Altaforte. Ezra Pound. CABA (1970 ed.); FaBoTw (1975 ed.); NOBA

Sestina: "Farewell, Oh sun, Arcadia's clearest light." Sir Philip Sidney. *Fr.* Arcadia. PAIC ("Farewell, O sun, Arcadia's clearest light.") NIL

Sestina: "I saw my soul at rest upon a day." Swinburne. VLP

Sestina: "Is this the object." Judith Kroll. AmPA

Sestina: "September rain falls on the house." Elizabeth Bishop. WeW

Sestina from the Home Gardener. Diane Wakoski. CABA (1972 ed.); NoAM

Sestina in a Cantina. Malcolm Lowry. PAIC

Sestina in Time of Winter. Patrick Anderson. PoA

Sestina of the Lady Pietra degli Scrovigni. Dante, *tr. fr. Italian by* Dante Gabriel Rossetti. LoAs; OAEL-2; OBVE

Sestina of the Tramp-Royal. Kipling. PAIC

Set Down, Servant. *Unknown.* FSW

Set love in order, thou that lovest me. Cantica: Our Lord Christ: of Order. St. Francis of Assisi, *tr. by* Dante Gabriel Rossetti. OBVE

Set me as a seal on your heart. Bible, *O.T. Fr.* The Song of Solomon, *ad. by* Willis Barnstone. BoWoP

Set me whereas the sun doth parch the green. A Vow to Love Faithfully, Howsoever He Be Rewarded. Petrarch, *tr. by* the Earl of Surrey. Sonnets to Laura: To Laura in Life, CXIII. AAS; HAP; ILP (1975 ed.); PAIC

Set of phrases learnt by rote, A. The Furniture of a Woman's Mind. Swift. PPoe

Set out at any hour, from behind. L'Education Sentimentale. David Malouf. CAAP

Set the foot down with distrust upon the crust of the world—it is thin. Underground System. Edna St. Vincent Millay. SBG

Set the mousetrap, Put the bottles out. Suppose We Sleep. Comleth Ellis. IPM

Set where the upper streams of Simois flow. Palladium. Matthew Arnold. OAEL-2; PPP; VLP

Seth Compton died, and by that alone. Rhoda Pitkin. Edgar Lee Masters. *Fr.* The New Spoon River. NoAM

Seth Dismounts Thrice. Marnie Walsh. VW

Setters mark the turf and run. The Hunt. Daniel Halpern. LiSp

Setting. Eve Shelnutt. TC

Setting, The/ had no special theme. Slow Riff for Billy. James Cunningham. JB

Setting of the Moon, The. Giacomo Leopardi, *tr. fr. Italian by* John Heath-Stubbs. Moon

Setting/ Slow Drag. Carolyn M. Rodgers. JB

Settler. Stewart Lindh. PoA

Settlers, The. Judith Hemschemeyer. SO

Settling In. Mary Stroh. EC

Settling In. Floyd C. Stuart. TAT

Settling Some Old Football Scores. Morris Bishop. LiSp; SPo

Seumas Beg. James Stephens. OxBTC

Seven. Nicanor Parra, *tr. fr. Spanish by* Miller Williams. POL

Seven around the moon go up. The Pinwheel's Song. John Ciardi. SO

Seven Black Friars sitting back to back. Blackfriars. Eleanor Farjeon. OxBChV

Seven Blessings of Mary, The. *Unknown. See* Joys of Mary, The.

Seven bonnie sisters on an isle in the west. Counting-out Rhyme. Helen Adam. PoIA

Seven candles in silver sticks. Planter. Richard Murphy. *Fr.* The Battle of Aughrim. BIrV

Seven Cent Cotton and Forty Cent Meat. *Unknown.* FSW

Seven Days, The, *sel.* Reed Whittemore.
On First Knowing God, III. GP

Seven days a week. The Widows. Eve Shelnutt. TC

Seven dog-days we let pass. Queens. J. M. Synge. GBL

Seven Dreams. John Bayliss. EAS

Seven, frog-legged among the boys. Linda. John Stone. CoPAm

Seven Hells of Jigoku Zoshi, The, *sels.* Jerome Rothenberg.
Fifth Hell, The. NNaP
Sixth Hell, The. NNaP

700 pounds, no neck. Bear. D. C. Berry. BCr

700 years ago. Slim Man Canyon. Leslie Silko. VoR

Seven-League Boots, The. Ilarie Voronca, *tr. fr. Rumanian by* Willis Barnstone *and* Matei Calinescu. VWA

Seven Mexican Children. Tom Schmidt. NeAC

Seven Old Men, The. Baudelaire, *tr. fr. French by* Roy Campbell. OBVE

Seven Preludes to Silence. Richard Shelton. MPA

Seven Rainy Months. William Plomer. OxBTC

Seven Seals. D. H. Lawrence. LoAs

Seven Sharp Propeller Blades. John Ciardi. QQQ

Seven Sins, The. *Unknown.* OxBM

Seven Sister Blues. *Unknown.* BluL

Seven Songs for a Cool Man, *sel.* Robin Fulton.
"Don't touch the trees—their soft bark will suck your/ fingers dry." MS

Seven sweet singing birds up in a tree. The Dream of a Girl Who Lived at Sevenoaks. William Brighty Rands. OxBChV

Seven-Tenths of a Second. Clinton F. Larson. MPA

Seven Virgins, The. *Unknown.* GBP; PeBB

Seven wealthy towns contend for Homer dead. A Cure for Poetry. *Unknown, after* George Buchanan. FaBoEE

Seven Wonders of North Wales, The. *Unknown.* OBW

Seven Woodland Crows. Gerald Vizenor. VoR

Seven-Year Body Cycle, The: To My Cells Replacing Themselves for the Fourth Time. David Steingass. NVAP

Seven years I have kept him, dead. The Corpse-Keeper. *Unknown, tr. by* W. S. Merwin. BoWoP

Seven years I orbit around you. Sabbatical. Linda Zisquit. VWA

1780 a.d. in the street they flung foam about and a young. Poems (I-XI). Philip O'Connor. EAS

Seventeen, no great event. For Stephen. Christopher Brookhouse. AMV-80

Seventeen people/ Aligned in a crescent. A Family Circle. Beth Joselow. PoUp

1738. Pope. *See* Epilogue to the Satires.

Seventeen Warnings in Search of a Feminist Poem. Erica Jong. AmPA; WBN
(Sixteen Warnings in Search of a Feminist Poem.) NVAP

Seventeen years ago you said. A Quoi Bon Dire. Charlotte Mew. OxBTC

Seventh, The. Attila Jozsef, *tr. fr. Hungarian by* John Batki. EC

Seventh dragon turned to his wife, The. Where Two o'Clock Came From. Kenneth Patchen. SO

Seventh Eclogue. Miklós Radnóti, *tr. fr. Hungarian by* Emery George. VWA

Seventh Georgic. George Economou. POL

Seventh Olympic Hymn. Pindar, *tr. by* Robin Blaser. *Fr.* Odes. Epi

Seventh robin, The. Poem without a Metaphor. David Allan Evans. NVAP

Seventh Son. Ed Roberson. PoBA

Seventy. Margaret Reynolds. MIS

78 Miners in Mannington, West Virginia. Louis Phillips. TAT

74th Street. Myra Cohn Livingston. CTBA

Seventy-seven betrayers will stand by the road. To My Daughter. Hyam Plutzik. BiP

Seventy Six Trombones, *with music.* Meredith Willson. BLSo

Seventy thousand dead and gone. Bring 'Em Home. Barbara Dane *and others.* FSW

73,000 Days to Breakthrough. Julia Watson Barbour. PoUp

Several Questions Answered, *sels.* Blake.
Ancient Proverb, An. MBPR
Eternity ("He who binds [*or* bends] to himself a joy"). BoReV; EBEV; FaBoEE; LAuP; MBPR; NOBE; WIF
Question Answer'd, The. FaBoEE; GBL
("What is it men in women do require?") MBPR; NIL; OAEL-2

Several things announced the fact to us. New Territory. Eavan Boland. CIP

Sever'd from sweete content, my live's sole light. To His Absent Diana. Henry Constable. Diana, *introd.* ESo

Severed at the hip, Howard. He's Known His Lesson for Years. R. P. Kingston. NVAP

Severed Selves. Dante Gabriel Rossetti. The House of Life, XL. BoLoP; VPC

Severity. Arthur J. Bull. HeHu

Sevier County Runaway, The. Besmilr Brigham. Psy

Sex and the Over Forties. Peter Porter. CAAP

Sex, as they harshly call it. Two Songs. Adrienne Rich. CABA (1972 ed.); ILP (1975 ed.); NOBA; Psy; TAP

Sex fingers toes. Dear John, Dear Coltrane. Michael S. Harper. AmPA; NVAP

Sex floated like a moon. A Circle, a Square, a Triangle and a Ripple of Water. Jane Cooper. TAP

Sex Play in Four Acts. Doug Fetherling. NeAC

Sext. W. H. Auden. *Fr.* Horae Canonica. TCP

Sexton stood one Sabbath eve, A. Those Wedding Bells Shall Not Ring Out! Monroe H. Rosenfeld. FSN

Sexual Delinquent. U. A. Fanthorpe. PMW

Sexual intercourse began. Annus Mirabilis. Philip Larkin. OBAL

Sexual Soup. Erica Jong. GP

Seymour and Chantelle or Un Peu de Vice. Stevie Smith. SBG

Seynt Stevene was a clerk. *See* Saint Steven was a clerk. . .

Seynt Valentynes Day. Chaucer. *Fr.* The Parliament of Fowls. PB

Shabbat Morning. Bradley R. Strahan. AMV-81

Shabby man on a bench, A. New Youngfellow. Stanley Burnshaw. SPT

Shabbytown Fugue. Thomas W. Shapcott. FPA

Shack and a few trees, The. After Work. Gary Snyder. CoPAm; HoPM (1975 ed.); NNaP

Shack outside Boise, The. Vern Rutsala. PoW
Shacked Up at the Ritz. Doug Fetherling. NeAC
Shackley-Hay. *Unknown.* GBP
Shad-Blow Tree, The. Louise Glück. NVAP
Shade. Charles Lynch. CNA
Shade-Seller, The. Josephine Jacobsen. TAP
Shades of Callimachus, Coan ghosts of Philetas. Ezra Pound. *Fr.* Homage to Sextus Propertius. CMoP (1970 ed.); ExPo (1973 ed.); HAP; NoAM; NOBA; OBVE
Shades of night were falling fast, The. A. E. Housman. FaBoNo; SpRo
Shades of night were falling fast, The. Excelsior. Longfellow. FaPoR; SpRo
Shades that I alone can see. Ballad of the Two Grandfathers. Nicolás Guillén, *tr. by* D. J. Flakoll *and* Claribel Alegria. TVo
Shadow. Walter de la Mare. ILP (1975 ed.)
Shadow, The. Ben Jonson. *See* That Women Are but Men's Shadows.
Shadow/ flutters/ through/ the forest, A. Family Game. Morton Marcus. NVAP
Shadow, The/ ran before it lengthening. Up at La Serra. Charles Tomlinson. TwMBP
Shadow and Shade. Allen Tate. VGW
Shadow and Substance. *Unknown. See* I Heard a Noise and Wishèd for a Sight.
Shadow-Bride. J. R. R. Tolkien. SO
Shadow Dirge. R. P. Dexter. LiSp
Shadow is floating through the moonlight, A. The Bird of Night. Randall Jarrell. CoPAm; DuDa; NCSH; RFM; TSWA
Shadow Life. Robert F. Reid III. AMV-81
Shadow of a Branch, The. Edith Marcombe Shiffert. WPE
Shadow of Cain, The. Edith Sitwell. OxBTC
Shadow of the little fishing launch, The. The Parrot Fish. James Merrill. NOBA
Shadow of the Old City. Yehuda Amichai, *tr. fr. Hebrew by* Shirley Kaufman. VWA
Shadow of the plane, The. Looking Down on West Virginia. John Dickson. AMV-81
Shadow of the Venetian blind on the painted wall. Forties Flick. John Ashbery. CAAP
Shadow Show. Ruth Dallas. ATNZ
Shadow streamed into the wall, The. Shadow and Shade. Allen Tate. VGW
Shadowbox: In a Milltown. Norman Macleod. SPT
Shadowboxing. James Tate. CAAP
Shadowed by your dear hair, your dear kind eyes. The Sanctuary. Ford Madox Ford. PoA
Shadowless Man, The. Gordon Challis. ATNZ
Shadows. Samuel Daniel *Fr.* Tethys' Festival. NOBE ("Are they shadows that we see?") ExPo (1973 ed.)
Shadows. D. H. Lawrence. BoReV; ILP (1975 ed.); OxBTC
Shadows, The. Iain Crichton Smith. SLP
Shadows. *Tr. fr. Tewa Indian by* H. J. Spinden. WTO
Shadows fall like men. Nocturne for the U.S. Congress. Victor Contoski. GP
Shadows in the Water. Thomas Traherne. BoReV; HAP; ILP (1975 ed.); MetP; OAEL-1; SCP-2
Shadows of bars suggest perhaps. The Parakeet. Keith Sinclair. ATNZ
Shadows of night were a-comin' down swift, The. Higher. *Unknown.* SpRo
Shadows of the rooks fly up the hill, The. Arques. Arthur Symons. Amoris Exsul, XI. VLP
Shadows, shadows,/ Hug me round. Escape. Georgia Douglas Johnson. PoBA

Shadows slowly creeping. Prairie Lullaby. *Unknown.* BPAW
Shadow's Song, The. Yvor Winters. POL
Shadows where the Mewlips dwell, The. The Mewlips. J. R. R. Tolkien. SO
Shadowy daughter of Urthona stood before red Orc, The. America a Prophecy. Blake. MBPR; OAEL-2
Shadrach/ Shake the bed. *Unknown.* FaBoNo
Shadwell Anatomized. Dryden. *Fr.* MacFlecknoe. OBP
Shadwell and Settle are both fools to Bays. *At. to* Thomas Shadwell. *Fr.* The Tory Poets: A Satire. SCP-2
Shadwell Stair. Wilfred Owen. FaBoTw (1975 ed.)
Shady Grove. *Unknown.* FSW
Shag, The. Christopher Isherwood. *See* Common Cormorant, The.
Shaggy, and lean, and shrewd, with pointed ears. The Woodman's Dog. William Cowper. *Fr.* The Task, V. GDP
Shaggy Dog, A. *Unknown.* TDH
Shaka, *sel. Zulu Oral Tradition, tr. by* T. Cope. "Young viper grows as it sits, The." WTO
Shake hands with Hector the Dog. Hector the Dog. Kate Barnes. GDP
Shake, A, in time of/ the mind's kaleidoscope. On Galtymore. Joan Keefe. IPM
Shake Keane, Trumpet. John Smith. *Fr.* Jazz for Five. MPo
Shaken already, I know. Goodbye, Sally. James Simmons. BIrV
Shakespeare. Matthew Arnold. BiP; CABA (1972 ed.); LFH
Shakespeare Milton Keats are dead. Song of Allegiance. R. A. K. Mason. ATNZ
Shakespeare on the Sea. Shakespeare. *Fr.* Pericles, III, i. RhR
Shakespeare would have savored his coarse, irate. "How Long Hast Thou Been a Gravemaker?" David Perkins. NCSH
Shakespearean fish swam the sea, far away from land. Three Movements. W. B. Yeats. CMoP (1970 ed.); FaBoEE
"Shakin like the." On a Country Road. Harley Elliot. NeAC
Shaking in White streetlight in. Our Vegetable Love Shall Grow. Elaine Feinstein. POL
Shall hog with holy child converse? Hog at the Manger. Norma Farber. PChr
Shall I abide this jesting? *Unknown.* GBL
Shall I begin at the beginning. Yiddish. Abraham Sutskever, *tr. by* Seymour Levitan. VWA
Shall I connect for this world's eyes. The Dumb World. W. H. Davies. BoAnP
Shall I come, sweet love, to thee. A Lover's Plea. Thomas Campion. AAS; EBEV; GBL; HAP; LoAs; NOBE
Shall I compare thee to a summer's day? Sonnets, XVIII. Shakespeare. BoLoP; GBL; HAP; HeIP; ILP (1975 ed.); InPK; InPS; IP; IPWM; MAT; NIL; NOBE; OAEL-1; OLR; PAIC; PBMP; PPM; PPoe; STS; TPo
Shall I complain, or not? Or shall I mask. Ovid, *tr. by* Henry Vaughan. *Fr.* De Ponto, IV, 3a. OBVE
Shall I dwell in my shell? The Snail's Monologue. Christian Morgenstern, *tr. by* Max Knight. BoAnP
Shall I pull the curtains against the coming night? If You Will. Josephine Miles. GP
Shall I strew on thee rose or rue or laurel. Ave atque Vale. Swinburne. NOBE; OAEL-2; VLP
Shall I tell you who will come. Words from an Old Spanish Carol. Ruth Sawyer. PChr
Shall I then hope when faith is fled? Thomas Campion. AAS
Shall I then praise the heavens, the trees, the earth. Anne Bradstreet. *Fr.* Contemplations. PBWP
Shall I thus ever long, and be no whit the near. The Lady Prayeth the Return of Her Lover Abiding on the Seas. *Unknown.* GBL

Shall I wasting in despair. A Lover's Resolution. George Wither. *Fr.* Fair Virtue. BoLoP; NOBE; PAIC; PoPle; SS

Shall Man, O God of Light, *with music.* Timothy Dwight. AH

Shall pride a heap of sculptur'd marble raise. Epitaph on Laurence Sterne. David Garrick. FaBoEE

Shall royal praise be rhym'd by such a ribald. On the Candidates for the Laurel. Pope. FaBoEE

Shall we assault the pain? The Hour of the Parting. John Shaw Neilson. MAuV

Shall We Gather at the River? Robert Lowry. *See* Beautiful River.

Shall we go dance the hay? The hay? A Report Song in a Dream [*or* Wooing in a Dream]. Nicholas Breton. GBL; NOBE

Shall we have a family born. For Walter Lowenfels. Wendy Rose. CDW

Shall we sit here some more. August at the Lake. David Young. AmPA

Shallot, A. Richard Wilbur. GP

Shallows of the Ford, The. Henry Herbert Knibbs. BPAW

Shalom. Denise Levertov. NoAM

Shalom Chaverim. *Unknown, tr. fr. Hebrew.* FSW

Shaman. Will Inman. GP

Shaman. Esther M. Leiper. AMV-81

Shaman. Paul Nelson. PHC

Shaman Songs 12. Gene Fowler. MIT

Shame. Richard Wilbur. ConAP; PPoD; UsP

Shameful Death. William Morris. VLP

Shan Van Vocht, The. *Unknown.* BTTM; GBP (Shan Van Voght.) FSW

Shancoduff. Patrick Kavanagh. BIrV; CIP; FaBoTw (1975 ed.)

Shandon Bells, The. Francis Sylvester Mahony. PFIr

Shane O'Neill's Cairn. Robinson Jeffers. NoAM; NOBA

Shaneen and Maurya Prendergast. Patch-Shaneen. J. M. Synge. PFIr

Shanty Boys and the Pine, The. *Unknown.* AmFP

Shanty Man's Life, A. *Unknown.* AmFP

Shapcot [*or* Shapcott], to thee the fairy state. Oberon's Feast. Robert Herrick. CaPo; SCP-1

Shape of a rat, The? Theodore Roethke. *Fr.* The Lost Son. OSP

Shape of Death, The. May Swenson. LoAs; TAP

Shape of my second son's head, The. To WCW. Alice Notley. FiCh

Shape of the Fire, The. Theodore Roethke. CMoP (1970 ed.)

Shaper circles the wood, The. The Brown Bird. Dan Johnson. PoUp

Shapes and Signs. James Clarence Mangan. PFIr

Shapes, Vanishings. Henry Taylor. AMV-81

Shark, The. John Ciardi. MiP

Shark flopped on the porch, The. James Dickey. *Fr.* The Shark's Parlor. MiP

Sharks. Dick Lourie. NeAC

Sharks in Shallow Water. Fred Levinson. AmPA

Shark's Parlor, The. James Dickey. CSP
"Shark flopped on the porch, The," *sel.* MiP

Sharktooth Creek. Peter Nelson. PHC

Sharon Will Be No/ Where on Nobody's Best-Selling List. Sharon Scott. JB

Sharp is the night, but stars with frost alive. Winter Heavens. George Meredith. CABA (1972 ed.)

Sharp Ridge, The. Robert Graves. FaBoEE

Sharpening grandpa's scythe. David Martinson. *Fr.* Nineteen Sections from a Twenty Acre Poem. TAT

Shash, The. *Unknown.* APAS

Shasta. Witter Bynner. BPAW

"Shatnes" or Uncleanliness. Eliezer Steinbarg, *tr. fr. Yiddish by* Seth L. Wolitz. VWA

Shattered Sabbath. Roberta B. Goldstein. AMV-81

Shattered water made a misty din, The. Once by the Pacific. Robert Frost. BPAW; CMoP (1970 ed); HAP; HeIP; ILP (1975 ed.); NOBA; PiAm; RhR; VGW; WeW

Shattering of Love, The. *Gond Oral Tradition, tr. by* V. Elwin *and* S. Hivale. WTO

Shaving. Charles David Wright. AMV-81

Shawano Lake, Wisconsin. Robert Gillespie. NVAP

Shazam. R. P. Dickey. HeS

She. Vincente Huidobro, *tr. fr. Spanish by* Dudley Fitts. LoAs

She. Theodore Roethke. BoLoP

She. Richard Wilbur. AnMo; ConAP; NIL

She. Manfred Winkler, *tr. fr. Hebrew by* Mary Zilzer. VWA

She acquired an eye. My Mother's Breakfront. Janet Sternburg. TV

She always played Mother as a child. Child Bearing. Charles Ghigna. AMV-81

She appeared before me that night: the vanquished one. The Ancient Law. André Spire, *tr. by* Stanley Burnshaw. VWA

She as a veil down to the slender waist. Before the Fall. Milton. *Fr.* Paradise Lost, IV. NIL

She asked brown eyes, "Burn me loose." Seal at Stinson Beach. Roberta Hill. VoR

She asked me, aching-eyed. Emily Drowned. William Duncan. PMW

She asked me twice. Pity. William Mills. CoPAm; CSP

She: At His Funeral. Thomas Hardy. VLP

She Attempts to Refute the Praises That Truth, Which She Calls Passion, Inscribed on a Portrait of the Poet. Sister Juana Ines de la Cruz, *tr. fr. Spanish by* Willis Barnstone. BoWoP ("This coloured counterfeit that thou beholdest," *tr. by* Samuel Beckett.) PBWP

She Being Brand. E. E. Cummings. NOBA; SFF; TPo

She brings that breath, and music too. The Visitor. W. H. Davies. GBL; OBW

She by the river sate, and sitting there. Upon Julia Weeping. Robert Herrick. ExPo (1973 ed.)

She came from country closed. Decorating Problem. Sonya Dorman. RiTi

She cannot see. Nursing Home. Linda Parker. HeS

She carried the eggs in her straw hat. The Bee Woman. Jim Wayne Miller. CSP

She carries life in her body. Poem before Birth. Alexander Scott. MS

She clasps a jewel. Words. David Phillips. NeAC

She climbed the ladder looking over the wall at the party. Jim Harrison. *Fr.* Ghazals. InPS

She climbs the stairs. Quickview. Antar S. K. Mberi. SES

She coils her body around me. Love Poem. Howard Schwartz. HeS

She come in one morning. Boss's Dream. Herbert Scott. TC

She comes on at night. From St. Luke's Hospital. Madeleine L'Engle. CTBA

She comes up the walk toward her back door. Longing for the Persimmon Tree. Millen Brand. TAT

She Contrasts with Herself Hippolyta. Hilda Doolittle ("H. D."). SBG

She coulda been somethin. Ho. Al Young. GP

She crouched into my palm. Captive Bird. Alison Wyrley Birch. PPM

She danced, near nude, to tom-tom beat. Zalka Peetruza. Ray Garfield Dandridge. PoBA

She dealt her pretty words like blades. Emily Dickinson. HAP

She didn't know it yet. Poem. Diane Kruchkow. FAF

She didn't know she was beautiful.  On Getting a Natural.  Dudley Randall.  FB; PoBA

She didn't lie long, they said.  Not Dead but Sleeping.  Elizabeth Bartlett.  PMW

She died after the beautiful snow had melted.  In Memorial.  J. Gordon Coogler.  OBAL

She died in June, while yet the woodbine sprays.  Mary—A Reminiscence.  Charles Tennyson Turner.  VPC

She died turning aside from the sink.  Another Death.  D. E. Borrell.  FF

She does not know.  No Images.  Waring Cuney.  AmNP (1974 ed.); MAT

She does not talk.  Floor: Five.  Stephen Vincent.  *Fr.* Elevator Landscapes.  NeAC

She Doesn't Want to Bring the Tides in Any More.  Ruth Whitman.  RiTi

She doesn't wear/ costume jewelry.  Gwendolyn Brooks.  Don L. Lee.  NoAM

She Dreams Herself Titanic.  Barbara Drake.  TC

She dreams of swimming the Platte.  Calamity Jane Greets Her Dreams.  Kathleen Lignell.  AMV-80

She dreams of the desert again.  Magdalene, Afterward.  Karen Whitehill.  NPW

She drew back; he was calm.  The Subverted Flower.  Robert Frost.  CMoP (1970 ed.); HAP; NoAM; NOBA; WeW

She Dwelt among the Untrodden Ways.  Wordsworth.  *Fr.* Lucy. AnMo; BoLoP; CABA (1972 ed.); FF; HAP; HeIP; ILP (1975 ed.); IP; MBPR; OAEL-2; PBMP; PCOP; PoIA; PPP; SpRo; UnPo (1976 ed.); WIF, 2 *versions*

She Employed the Familiar "Tu" Form.  Doug Fetherling.  NeAC

She enters the bus demurely.  Puerto Ricans in New York, I.  Charles Reznikoff.  CTBA; VoA

She even thinks that up in heaven.  For a Lady I Know.  Countee Cullen.  HeIP; InPK; NIL; OBAL; TAP; WIF

She fears him, and will always ask.  Eros Turannos.  E. A. Robinson.  CMoP (1970 ed.); GBL; HAP; ILP (1975 ed.); IPWM; NoAM; NOBA; PiAm; PoA; PPoe; STS; TAP

She fell asleep on Christmas Eve.  My Sister's Sleep.  Dante Gabriel Rossetti.  VLP

She fell away in her first ages spring.  Spenser.  *Fr.* Daphnaida.  PoPle

She felt so good.  Cobbler.  Karren Alenier.  PoUp

She finds grief, her meat.  Hyena.  Carol Muske.  AmPA

She floats/ in a white shell.  Riddle of Night.  Jiri Mordecai Langer, *tr. by* Gabriel Preil *and* Howard Schwartz.  VWA

She flourished in the 'Twenties, "hectic" days of peace.  Mews Flat Mona.  William Plomer.  FaBoTw (1975 ed.)

She follows their races and climbings.  Crippled Child at the Window.  Melissa Cannon.  AMV-80

She found herself 7 no less.  Snow White.  Robert Gillespie.  NVAP

She glows against.  The Pro.  Karen Swenson.  AMV-81

She goes but softly, but she goeth sure.  Upon the Snail [*or a* Snail].  Bunyan.  OxBChV; SCP-2

She goes with her pot for water.  Who Can Tell?  *Gond Oral Tradition, tr. by* V. Elwin *and* S. Hivale.  WTO

She got off, according to the diary.  The Arrival of My Mother.  Keith Wilson.  GP

She grew from the crowd.  A Former Love.  Giles Gordon.  SLP

She grew ninety years through sombre winter.  Epitaph on a Fir-Tree.  Richard Murphy.  FaBoTw (1975 ed.)

She grew up in bedeviled southern wilderness.  The Ballad of Sue Ellen Westerfield.  Robert Hayden.  NoAM

She guessed there wasn't any time for tears.  The Stoic.  Gwendolen Haste.  WPW

She had a little time to think.  Leda Reconsidered.  Mona Van Duyn.  NMM

She had a name among the children.  A Cat.  Edward Thomas.  BoAnP

She had a way with comedy and men.  Marilyn Monroe.  Paul Ramsey.  PPoD

She had no business doin' it, but she come out o' the East.  The Peeler's Lament.  *Unknown.*  WTO

She had no choice.  On the Edge.  Alison Wyrley Birch.  PPM

She had thought the studio would keep itself.  Living in Sin.  Adrienne Rich.  FF; IHMS; RiTi; SoSe (1977 ed.); TAP; UnPo (1976 ed.)

She handles bones, dull gray or ivory hued.  On Hearing a Beautiful Young Woman Describe Her Class in Physical Anthropology.  A. J. Hovde.  AMV-81

She has a husband, he a wife.  Modern Love.  J. V. Cunningham.  POL

She has begun to see men invite themselves.  The Professional.  David Ignatow.  NNaP

She has dreams of wolves it bewilders.  Landscape without Touch.  Olga Broumas.  CNW

She has finished and sealed the letter.  Parting, without a Sequel.  John Crowe Ransom.  SoSe

She has given all her beauty to the water.  Island Rose.  Hamish MacLaren.  MS

She has lost her innocence.  The Return.  Leonard Nathan.  EC

She has not found herself a hard pillow.  To Clarissa Scott Delany.  Angelina Weld Grimké.  AmNP (1974 ed.)

She has only the memory and is cut loose.  Andromache Afterwards.  Linda Gregg.  AAN

She has refused injections to kill pain.  Woman in the Hospital for Incurables.  Daphne Gloag.  PMW

She has the immaculate look of the new.  Chinese Baby Asleep.  Dorothy Donnelly.  NCSH

She hears me strike the board and say.  Father and Child.  W. B. Yeats.  RRA; TCP

She held his head of close hard hair.  All One.  Millen Brand.  GP

She hissed in my ear.  Lilith.  Donald Finkel.  VWA

She hovered hooded, blue-eyed.  Catechism, 1958.  W. M. Ransom.  CDW

She Hugged Me and Kissed Me.  *Unknown.*  BPo

She hung away her years, her eyes grew young.  Waiting for the Bus.  D. J. Enright.  OxBTC

She hung her laundry in the morning.  Mennonite Farm Wife.  Janet Kauffman.  TC

She, in dowdy dress and dumpy.  Still Life: Lady with Birds.  Quandra Prettyman.  PoBA

She in whose lipservice.  The Goddess.  Denise Levertov.  NOBA

She is/ a multiplicate/ of falters.  Multiple I.  Richard Tipping.  FPA

She is a weak sister, that ocean.  Finding Roots.  Judith Minty.  HeS

She is all there.  For My Lover, Returning to His Wife.  Anne Sexton.  IHMS; NMM; RiTi; UnPo (1976 ed.); WPE

She is as in a field a silken tent.  The Silken Tent.  Robert Frost.  CABA (1972 ed.); ExPo (1973 ed.); ILP (1975 ed.); InPK; NOBA; PAIC; PiAm; PPoD; SoSe; TAP; WIF

She is dead.  Birthdays.  Hilde Domin, *tr. by* Tudor Morris.  BoWoP

She is dead; and all which die.  The Dissolution.  John Donne.  ILP (1975 ed.)

She Is Far from the Land.  Thomas Hood.  FaBoNo

She is first seen dancing which is a figure.  The Origin of Cities.  Robert Hass.  PCho

She is getting too big. They live in two rooms. Approaching the Canvas. Kathleen Spivack. PCho

She is in full color. The Girl/The Girlie Magazine. Pat Gray. AMV-81

She Is More to Be Pitied than Censured. William B. Gray. FSN, *with music;* FSW

She is most fair. The Unknown. Edward Thomas. GBL

She is named Melissa. Melissa. Carolyn D. Redl-Hlus. AMV-80

She is not fair to outward view. Song. Hartley Coleridge. PCOP

She Is Not for Me. *Gond Oral Tradition, tr. by* V. Elwin *and* S. Hivale. WTO

She is purposeless as a cyclone; she must move. Cubist Portrait. Marjorie Allen Seiffert. PoA

She is Queen Nofretete translated into. Nofretete. Felix Pollak. HeS

She is standing on my lids. Lady Love. Paul Eluard, *tr. by* Samuel Beckett. OBVE

She is still telling the tides where to begin. Despite All That. Ann Stanford. CPA

She is teck'wi. The Taboo Woman. *Tr. fr. Zuni Indian by* K. Kennedy. WTO

She is the dark sister. Iscah. Howard Schwartz. VWA

She is the knife-thrower's lady. On a Professional Couple in a Side-Show. Alan Dugan. GP

She is the night: all horror is of her. Christopher Brennan. *Fr.* Lilith. MAuV

She is the one you call sister. The Mirror in Which Two Are Seen as One. Adrienne Rich. NIL; NNaP; RiTi; WBN

She is the woman I follow. Why I Died. Erica Jong. RiTi

She is washed by white-water, white if she looked up. Fish. Daniel Halpern. AmPA

She kept an antique shop—or it kept her. My Grandmother. Elizabeth Jennings. LP; MPo

She kept her songs, they took so little space. Love Songs in Age. Philip Larkin. PPP; PSN

She knew. The wife's voice. Other Woman. Judith Moffett. AAN

She lay all naked in her bed. *Unknown.* BoLoP

She lay down beneath a thorn. Fine Flowers in the Valley. *Unknown.* RDB

She lay in her girlish sleep at ninety-six. Castoff Skin. Ruth Whitman. InPK

She leans across a golden table. For Amy Lowell. Countee Cullen. PoA

She left me at the silent time. Lines Written in the Bay of Lerici. Shelley. MBPR; OAEL-2

She lies ablow my body's lust and love. Continent o Venus. Alexander Scott. MS; SLP

She lies far inland, and no stick nor stone of her. Inland City. John Crowe Ransom. CMoP (1970 ed.)

She lies on her left side her flank golden. Landscape as a Nude. Archibald MacLeish. Frescoes for Mr. Rockefeller's City, I. CMoP (1970 ed.); UnPo (1976 ed.)

She lived in storm and strife. That the Night Come. W. B. Yeats. PoIA

She lives by Cherry Hill where the dirt road. The Chosen. Carl Dennis. AMV-81

She looked over his shoulder. The Shield of Achilles. W. H. Auden. AnMo; EBEV; ExPo (1973 ed.); HAP; ILP (1975 ed.); NOBE; PoA; PoIA; SoSe; TT; WeW

She looks out in the blue morning. The Window. Conrad Aiken. CMoP (1970 ed.)

She Lost Her Sheep. J. Moyr Smith. FaBoNo

She loves, and she confesses too. Honour. Abraham Cowley. BoLoP

She loves the wind. The Old One and the Wind. Clarice Short. IHMS; MPA

She made him a roof with her hands. Fourth Psalm: The Cerements. W. S. Merwin. CAAP

She married him because. Because. Paul Johnson. AMV-81

She may be old, ninety years. Bottle Up and Go. *Unknown.* FSW

She May Have Seen Better Days, *with music.* James Thornton. FSN

She might, so noble from head. A Thought from Propertius. W. B. Yeats. OAEL-2

She Moved through the Fair. Padraic Colum. AIW; BIrV

She moved through the garden in glory, because. Marigold. Richard Garnett. PCat

She never asked to lose innocence. God, Woman, Egg. Helena Minton. FAF

She, of whom the ancients seemed to prophesy. John Donne. *Fr.* An Anatomy of the World: The First Anniversary. SCP-1

She often lies with her hands behind her head. For My Daughter. Ronald Koertge. GP

She only lit the closet and the bathroom. The Disordering. Lynda Yates. AMV-81

She only said she wished there was a place. What She Wished. Marilyn Throne. AMV-81

She packs the flower beds with leaves. For Fran. Philip Levine. FF

She pauses in the act of dressing. Chamber Music. John Ditsky. AMV-81

She peered through the curtain, and courteous. Gawain and the Temptress. *Unknown, tr. by* Burton Raffel. *Fr.* Sir Gawain and the Green Knight. OBP

She planted each spruce, blue as the Blue Mountains. Spruce. Phillip William George. NW

She played me false, but that's not why. Our Photograph. Frederick Locker-Lampson. NOBL

She pops their flanks with a rawhide whip. Pony Girl. Jane P. Moreland. PH

She Proves the Inconsistency of the Desires and Criticism of Men Who Accuse Women of What They Themselves Cause. Sister Juana Ines de la Cruz, *tr. fr. Spanish by* Aliki *and* Willis Barnstone. BoWoP

She pulled her gown from her shoulders. Alcestis. Maura Stanton. PCho

She pulled me out the kitchen door. Monkshood. Marie Harris. MMD

She Rebukes Hippolyta. Hilda Doolittle ("H. D."). SBG

She remembers seasons. Poison. Nancy Mairs. NPW

She returned from the clinic. Unhappy Diary Days. Gerald Vizenor. VoR

She rose to his requirement—dropt. Emily Dickinson. CABA (1972 ed.)

She Said I Said He Lied. Michael Rosen. FPB

She said, if tomorrow my world were torn in two. The 5:32. Phyllis McGinley. *Fr.* I Know a Village. NMM; WPE

She sang beyond the genius of the sea. The Idea of Order at Key West. Wallace Stevens. AnMo; CMoP (1970 ed.); FF; HAP; HeIP; ILP (1975 ed.); NIL; NoAM; NOBA; PiAm; PPoD; PPP; TAP; TT

She sat across from me and her eyes. Parting. Gabriel Preil, *tr. by* Laya Firestone. VWA

She sat and sang alway. Song. Christina Rossetti. GBL

She sat down below a thorn. The Cruel Mother [*or* Fine Flowers in the Valley]. *Unknown.* FaBoBa; InPK; PeBB; UsP

She sat in a chair across the room, staring at him. Mark Strand. *Fr.* Inside the Story. UsP

She sat looking like. Geriatric. John Gonzalez. PMW

She says how/ is it when you. John Knoepfle. *Fr.* The Ten-Fifteen Community Poems. MAT

She says, "I am content when wakened birds." Wallace Stevens. *Fr.* Sunday Morning. TT

She shifts her pelvis to the tune of muted bells. The Pinball Queen of South Illinois St. Stephen Tietz. AMV-80

She should have died hereafter. Shakespeare. *Fr.* Macbeth, V, v. DL; IP; SoSe

She sights a bird, she chuckles. Emily Dickinson. SoSe (1977 ed.)

She sits beside him. Renoir's Confidences. J. Michael Pilz. AMV-81

She sits in her glass garden. The One Whose Reproach I Cannot Evade. George Hitchcock. EAS

She sits in the park. Her clothes are out of date. In the Park. Gwen Harwood. MAuV

She sits on the floor. Letters. Charles Bukowski. GP

She sits upon her Bulbul. Edward Lear. FaBoNo

She sits with one hand poised against her head. Dialogue. Adrienne Rich. TAP

She slid past. And She Was Bad. Marvin Wyche, Jr. AmNP (1974 ed.)

She Smiled like a Holy-Day. *Unknown.* BBL

She sought the Studios, beckoning to her side. Heiress and Architect. Thomas Hardy. VLP

She speaks always in her own voice. The Portrait. Robert Graves. CABA (1972 ed.); CMoP (1970 ed.); LoAs; PBMP

She Speaks the Morning's Filigree. Philip Lamantia. VGW

She spoke no English. Eureka. Ruth O. Maunders. AMV-80

She spoke to me gently with words of sweet meaning. Song. Patrick MacDonogh. PFIr

She springs from the ground-clinging thicket, her face. Veneris Venefica Agrestis. Charles Tomlinson, *after* Lucio Piccolo. OBVE

She staked her feathers—gained an arc. Emily Dickinson. PiAm

She stands/ In the quiet darkness. Troubled Woman. Langston Hughes. CTBA

She stands beside me, stands away. Like Rousseau. Amiri Baraka. PoA

She stepped two paces forward. She. Vincente Huidobro, *tr. by* Dudley Fitts. LoAs

She stole my pencil-case, red leather. The Thief. Josephine Jacobsen. WPE

She stood/ apart from the grazing herd. The Death of an Elephant. Gianfranco Pagnucci. NU

She stood breast high amid the corn. Ruth. Thomas Hood. BoLoP; NOBE; PIM

She stood hanging wash before sun. Ghetto Lovesong—Migration. Carole Gregory Clemmons. NMM; PoBA

She stood in her snood and arasaid. Love. *Unknown, tr. fr. Gaelic.* SLP

She Stoops to Conquer, *sel.* Goldsmith.
Song: "Let school-masters puzzle their brain," *fr.* I, ii. BIrV (Three Pigeons, The.) ILP (1975 ed.)

She stripped herself of all except pretense. On an Ecdysiast. John Ciardi. IP

She suffers like a red stone, small as a carat. Sisters. Sandra McPherson. AmPA

She swam smiling in the river. Waiting to Be Fed. Ray A. Young Bear. CDW

She talks not, plays not, visits not, in bed. *Unknown.* FaBoEE

She Tells Her Love while Half Asleep. Robert Graves. BoLoP; EBEV; FaBoTw (1975 ed.); GBL; NOBE; OxBTC

She tells me with claret she cannot agree. Drinking Song. *Unknown.* NOBL

She that but little patience knew. On a Political Prisoner. W. B. Yeats. OAEL-2

She that holds me under the laws of love. Sir Arthur Gorges. GBL

She, the sensual creature, the green singer. Slow Dancer That No One Hears but You. Duane Niatum. CDW

She thinks God wants a wife. At St. Mary's for the Aged. Eve Shelnutt. TC

She thus; when I had great desire to prove. Homer, *tr. by* George Chapman. *Fr.* The Odyssey, XI. OBVE

She Tied Up Her Few Things. John Clare. HAP

She, to Him. Thomas Hardy. OxBTC

She told how they used to form for the country dances. One We Knew. Thomas Hardy. VLP

She told me. A Hopi Woman Talking. Joy Harjo. SA

She told the story, and the whole world wept. Harriet Beecher Stowe. Paul Laurence Dunbar. AmVN; BPo; ILP (1975 ed.)

She told them when they came and found him there. The Reason. Gwendolen Haste. WPW

She took her name beneath according skies. The Ritual. E. J. Pratt. NoAM

She took the dappled partridge flecked with blood. Sonnet. Tennyson. CABA (1972 ed.)

She tosses and rumples alone on the double bed. Flying Fox. Thomas W. Shapcott. FPA

She tosses, one midnight so close. Midwest U. F. O. David Steingass. NVAP

She transplanted each spruce, blue as the. Spruce. Phillip William George. VoR

She truly needs good character. Women. *Yoruba Oral Tradition, tr. by* Ulli Beier. WTO

She turned in the high pew, until her sight. A Church Romance. Thomas Hardy. FaBoTw (1975 ed.); NOBE; OxBTC; VLP

She used to let her golden hair fly free. Petrarch, *tr. by* Morris Bishop. Sonnets to Laura: To Laura in Life, LXIX. NAWM-1

She Vowed Him This. William Box. BuTh

She Walked Unaware. Patrick MacDonogh. BoLoP; FaBoTw (1975 ed.); PFIr

She walks a beach assaulted by the sea. Thanksgiving 1963. Philip Booth. IPWM

She walks down the road. Girl with the Green Skirt. Dana Naone. CDW

She Walks in Beauty. Byron. BoLoP; CABA (1972 ed.); FF; HeIP; ILP (1975 ed.); InPS; IPWM; MBPR; NOBE; PBMP; PCOP; SLP; WIF

She walks she talks. Miss America. Anne Sadowski. SES

She walks—the lady of my delight. The Shepherdess. Alice Meynell. SBG; PCOP; PeD

She Wandered through the Garden Fence. Keith Reid. GrRo

She wanted rain. Dust. Kathleen Spivack. BoWoP

She wants to seduce a homosexual Jesuit. Carolyn Maisel. *Fr.* Pig Woman. FoP

She was a gently shaking chandelier. Denials 1. Jane Somerville. AMV-80

She was a maid of high degree. He Took Her. Tom Masson. OBAL

She Was a Phantom of Delight. Wordsworth. CTV; HeIP; ILP (1975 ed.); MBPR; OAEL-2; PBMP; UsP; VoPo

She was afraid of men. Chicken-Licken. Maya Angelou. FF

She was all around me. The Blue Wing. Donald Hall. ConAP

She Was Always Knitting, Weaving. Hugh Fox. TC

She Was Bred in Old Kentucky, *with music.* Harry Braisted. FSN

She was eager to be heard and nibbled on memories. One-Eleven Grape Street. Dan Masterson. CoPAm

She was in her orange Volks waiting. Hell Hath No Fury. Charles Bukowski. GP

She Was in love with the same danger. Triolet. Sandra McPherson. CNW

She was just a parson's daughter. It's the Syme the Whole World Over. *Unknown.* FSW

She was lyin face down in her face. Song. William Knott. MAT

She was my staff and I am blind. Jana Bai, *tr. fr. Marathi by* Willis Barnstone. BoWoP

She was never a dog that had much sense. Of an Ancient Spaniel in Her Fifteenth Year. Christopher Morley. GDP

She was newly betrothed, and. Cornelia's Window. Julie Kane. AMV-81

She was no armored cruiser of twice six thousand tons. The Warship of 1812. *Unknown.* BTTM

She Was Poor but She Was Honest. *Unknown.* FaBoCo; GBP; NOBL; PeBB

She was skilled in music and the dance. Alas! Poor Queen. Marion Angus. MS

She was so esthetic and culchud. The Cultured Girl Again. Ben King. OBAL

She was so small and pretty. Art's Variety. David McFadden. NeAC

She was still upset. Bubba Esther, 1888. Ruth Whitman. AMV-81

She was urgent to speak of the moon: she offered delight. An Old Woman Speaks of the Moon. Ruth Pitter. WPE

She wears her middle age like a cowled. From a Correct Address in a Suburb of a Major City. Helen Sorrells. WPE

She went away from us upon a snow-white. The Dwarf. Gerald Locklin. GP

She Went to Stay. Robert Creeley. OBAL

She went upstairs to make her bed. The Butcher's Boy. *Unknown.* FSW

She Wept, She Railed. Stanley Kunitz. VGW

She who has power to call her man. An Unsaid Word. Adrienne Rich. NMM

She who is always in my thoughts prefers. Bhartrihari, *tr. fr. Sanskrit by* John Brough. BoLoP

She-Who-Opens. Yvonne. AAN

She who was burned more than half her body. The Praises. Charles Olson. VGW

She wiped his face and brought away. The Sixth Station. Jean Marie Luecke. AATT

She wishes her eyes did not sting mornings. Fish. Sandra Witt. AMV-80

She with whom troops of bustuary slaves. *Unknown. Fr.* A Satire Entitled the Witch. SCP-2

She woke up under a loose quilt. The Evacuee. R. S. Thomas. MPo

She wore a new "terra-cotta" dress. A Thunderstorm in Town. Thomas Hardy. BoLoP; GBL

She wore lipstick and powder. My Mother Was Always Dressed. Abigail Luttinger. TV

She wouldn't like Agnes to be. Agnes. Kathleen Fraser. WBN

She yelled/ the horses are prancing thru introductions. The 97th Kentucky Derby. Geoff Young. PoW

Sheafe of Snakes used heretofore to be, A. To Mr. George Herbert. John Donne. OBVE

Shearing, The. *Unknown, tr. fr. Welsh by* Glyn Jones. OBW

Shearing, as the gardener. That's All? Anna Hajnal, *tr. by* Jascha Kessler. PBWP

Sheaves, The. E. A. Robinson. CMoP (1970 ed.); ExPo (1973 ed.); HAP; ILP (1975 ed.); NoAM; NOBA; PiAm; TAP

Shechem. David Shevin. VWA

Sheep. W. H. Davies. PoTa; RAE

Sheep, The. Ann *or* Jane Taylor. OxBChV

Sheep Beezness, The. S. Omar Barker. BPAW

Sheep-bell tolleth curfew time, The. Coventry Patmore. PPM

Sheep-boy whistled loud, and lo, The! Elegiac Verse. Wordsworth. MBPR

Sheep Child, The. James Dickey. CAPP; CoPAm; GP; NoAM; NOBA; Prf; TAP

Sheep Country. Peggy Pond Church. BPAW; WPW

Sheep Fair, A. Thomas Hardy. Prf

Sheep get up and make their many tracks, The. Sheep in Winter. John Clare. BoAnP

Sheep-Herder, The. Charles Badger Clark, Jr. BPAW

Sheep-Herder's Lament, The. Arthur Chapman. BPAW

Sheep Herding. Sharlot Hall. WPW

Sheep in Fog. Sylvia Plath. PSN

Sheep in the Rain. James Wright. AMV-80

Sheep in Winter. John Clare. BoAnP

Sheep is blind, The; a passing owl. The Blind Sheep. Randall Jarrell. OBAL

Sheep on these hills, The. Judith Serin. NPW

Sheep Ranching. Owen Wister. BPAW

Sheepdog Trials in Hyde Park. C. Day Lewis. NoAM; OxBTC; SoSe (1977 ed.)

Sheepman. Frank Ormsby. IPM

Sheep's in the meadow, The. Bonny at Morn. *Unknown.* GBP

Sheep-Skin and Beeswax. *Unknown.* RAE

Sheet-Monger, Blanket-Hoarder. Philip Legler. TC

Sheet of writing paper, The. The Alchemist. Richard Church. OxBTC

Sheets of night mist travel a long valley, The. Mist Forms. Carl Sandburg. CMoP (1970 ed.)

Sheets of water are washed out on the shore as. Shore. Alan Bold. MS

Sheets were frozen hard, and they cut the naked hand, The. Christmas at Sea. Robert Louis Stevenson. PoTa

Sheffield grinder's a terrible blade, The. The Grinders; or, The Saddle on the Right Horse. *Unknown.* GBP

Sheffield 'Prentice, The. *Unknown.* AmFP

Shekhina. Karl Wolfskehl, *tr. fr. German by* Erna Baber Rosenfeld. VWA

Shekhina and the Kiddushim. Edouard Roditi. VWA

Shell, The. George MacBeth. SLP; UsP

Shell, The. David McCord. LCL

Shell, The. James Stephens. CMoP (1970 ed.); EcS

Shell, The. Tennyson. *Fr.* Maud, II, ii. EcS

Shell, The. Vernon Watkins. EcS

Shell, The. Mary Webb. EcS

She'll Be Comin' 'round the Mountain. *Unknown.* BLSH, *with music;* BLSo, *with music;* FSW; GSB, *with music*

Shellbrook [Dorset]. William Barnes. VLP

Shellbrook [National English]. William Barnes. VLP

Shelley and jazz and lieder and love and hymn-tunes. Louis MacNeice. *Fr.* Autumn Journal. NOBL

Shelley's "Arethusa" Set to New Measures. Robert Duncan. CMoP (1970 ed.)

Shelley's Skylark. Thomas Hardy. VLP

Shells. Medb Mahony. AMV-80

Shelter this candle from the wind. To the Wife of a Sick Friend. Edna St. Vincent Millay. SBG

Shelter was possible. Instead. Elements of Night. Arthur Gregor. LoAs

Sheltered from the falling snow, inside the stable. Chekhov Comes to Mind at Harvard. William T. Freeman. AMV-81

Sheltered from the spring wind by/ A Silver screen. The Old Anguish. Chu Shu-chen, *tr. by* Kenneth Rexroth. BoWoP

Shelving slimy river Don, The. The River Don. *Unknown.* GBP

Shema. Primo Levi, *tr. fr. Italian by* Ruth Feldman *and* Brian Swann. VWA

Shenandoah. *Unknown.* BLSo, *with music;* FSW
(Across the Wide Missouri, *with music.*) BLSH

Shephard loveth thow me vell? Song. Jean Passerat, *tr by* William Drummond of Hawthornden. OBVE

Shepheard Paris bore the Spartan bride, The. *See* Shepherd Paris bore the Spartan bride, The.

Shepheard, what's Loue, I pray thee tell? The Shepherd's Description of Love. *At. to* Sir Walter Ralegh. LoAs

Shepheardes Calender, The, *sels.* Spenser.
April. ILP (1975 ed.)
   Lay to Eliza, The. NOBE
     Fair flower Delice, The. PF, 1 *st.*
August. PAIC
June. PAIC
November. Epi
October. OAEL-1

Shepherd, The. James K. Baxter. ECBV

Shepherd, The. Blake. *Fr.* Songs of Innocence. MBPR; PIM

Shepherd. William Stafford. PoA

Shepherd and Shepherdess. Thomas Hennell. FaBoTw (1975 ed.)

Shepherd Boy Sings in the Valley of Humiliation, The. Bunyan. *Fr.* The Pilgrim's Progress. NOBE
("He that is down needs fear no fall.") EBEV

Shepherd, Ned Vaughan, A. Ned Vaughan. Walter de la Mare. FaBoEE

Shepherd on his journey heard when nigh, The. The Fox. John Clare. BoAnP

Shepherd [*or* Shepheard] Paris bore the Spartan bride, The. Daphnis. Theocritus, *tr. by* Dryden. *Fr.* Idylls, XXVII. OBVE; SCP-1

Shepherd, Show Me How to Go, *with music.* Mary Baker Eddy. AH

Shepherd shrieves in Egyptian light, De. Pocomania. Derek Walcott. NoAM

Shepherd stands at one end of the arena, A. Sheepdog Trials in Hyde Park. C. Day Lewis. NoAM; OxBTC; SoSe (1977 ed.)

Shepherd! that with thin amorous, sylvan song. The Good Shepherd. Lope de Vega, *tr. by* Longfellow. PIM

Shepherd Who Stayed, The. Theodosia Garrison. PChr

Shepherdess. Norman Cameron. Three Love Poems, III. GBL; SLP

Shepherdess, The. Alice Meynell. PCOP; PeD; SBG

Shepherdess' Valentine, *sel.* Francis Andrewes.
"I bear, in sign of love." OFD

Shepherds all, and maidens fair. John Fletcher. *Fr.* The Faithful Shepherdess, II, i. SCP-2

Shepherd's Calendar, The, *sels.* John Clare.
February. NOBE
July.
"Loud is the summer's busy song." FSFS

Shepherd's daughter watching sheep, A. The Knight and the Shepherd's Daughter. *Unknown.* AmFP

Shepherd's Description of Love, The. *At. to* Sir Walter Ralegh. LoAs

Shepherd's Dochter, The. Douglas Young. MS; SLP

Shepherds Had an Angel, The. Christina Rossetti. PIM

Shepherd's House, The, *sel.* Alfred de Vigny, *tr. fr. French by* Robert Bly.
"Eva, I agree to love, among creation, all the creatures!" NU

Shepherd's Hut, The. Andrew Young. OxBTC

Shepherds' Hymn, The. Richard Crashaw. *Fr.* In the Holy Nativity of Our Lord God. NOBE
("Gloomy night embraced the place.") SCP-1

Shepherd's Sirena, The, *sels.* Michael Drayton. SCP-2
"Near to the silver Trent."
"Our mournful Philomel."
"Verdant meads are seen, The."
"When she looks out by night."

Shepherd's Song at Christmas. Langston Hughes. PChr

Shepherd's Tale, The. Raoul Ponchon, *tr. fr. French by* James Kirkup. PoTa

Shepherd's Week, The, *sels.* John Gay.
Friday; or, The Dirge. ILP (1975 ed.)
Wednesday; or, The Dumps. OAEL-1

Shepherd's Wife's Song, The. Robert Greene. *Fr.* Greene's Mourning Garment. HAP

Sheridan's Ride. Thomas Buchanan Read. BTTM

Sheriff's Report, The. Arthur Chapman. BPAW

Sherman Cyclone, The. *Unknown.* AmFP

She's a copperheaded waitress. Ella, in a Square Apron, along Highway 80. Judy Grahn. *Fr.* The Common Woman. NMM

She's All My Fancy Painted Him. "Lewis Carroll." FaBoNo

She's an enchanting little Israelite. Orientale. W. E. Henley. PeD

She's Gone Blues. *Unknown.* BluL

She's gone. She was my love, my moon or more. Complaint. James Wright. CoPAm; NOBA; TAP; VGW

She's learned to hold her gladness lightly. A Lesson in Detachment. Vassar Miller. CSP

She's Leaving Home. John Lennon *and* Paul McCartney. RRA; SoS

She's like the Swallow. *Unknown.* FSW

She's little and she's low she's right down on the ground. She's Mine. *Unknown.* BluL

She's My Love. Augustus Young, *tr. fr. Irish.* CIP

She's taen her petticoat by the band. Tam Lin. *Unknown.* AIW

She's taught me that I mustn't bark. Remarks from the Pup. Burges Johnson. GDP

She's the camera. Judy-One. Don L. Lee. TAP

Shetland Funeral. James Rankin. MIS

Shew! Fly, Don't Bother Me. *Unknown. See* Shoo Fly, Don't Bother Me.

Shield of Achilles, The. W. H. Auden. AnMo; EBEV; ExPo (1973 ed.); HAP; ILP (1975 ed.); NOBE; PoA; PoIA; SoSe; TT; WeW

Shield of War, The. Thomas Sackville. *Fr.* A Mirror for Magistrates. NOBE

Shift, here, in town, not meanest among squires. On Lieutenant Shift. Ben Jonson. OBSV

Shih Ching, *sels. Unknown, tr. fr. Chinese by* Arthur Waley.
"Very handsome gentleman, A." BoWoP
Widow's Lament. BoWoP

Shilling life will give you all the facts, A. Who's Who. W. H. Auden. BBGO; CABA (1972 ed.); NoAM

Shiloh; a Requiem. Herman Melville. AmVN; FF; ILP (1975 ed.); NOBA

Shine alone, shine nakedly, shine like bronze. Nuances of a Theme by Williams. Wallace Stevens. CMoP (1970 ed.)

Shine, O sun! tenderly on my skin. Love Dirge. *Tr. fr. Maori by* John White. WTO

Shine, "O world!" don't weary the gulping Pole. Frank O'Hara. *Fr.* Life on Earth. UnPo (1976 ed.)

Shine On, Harvest Moon, *with music.* Nora Bayes *and* Jack Norworth. BLSH

Shine on me, moon. A Sentinel's Song. Rarawa Kerehoma, *tr. by* Barry Mitcalfe. WTO

Shine Out, Fair Sun. *Unknown.* ILP (1975 ed.)

Shine, Perishing Republic. Robinson Jeffers. CMoP (1970 ed.);
ExPo (1973 ed.); FF; ILP (1975 ed.); IPWM; MAT; NoAM;
NOBA; PiAm; PPoD; TAP; UnPo (1976 ed.); VGW; VoPo;
WIF

Shine, Republic. Robinson Jeffers. GOA

Shining. Kathleen Spivack. AMV–81

Shining children in the fog. The Swimming Lesson. Robert
Hershon. NeAC

Shiny record aibums scattered over. As You Leave Me.
Etheridge Knight. ConAP; FF; NNaP

Ship, The. Richard Church. FPB

Ship, The. J. F. Hendry. MS; SLP

Ship and Her Makers, The. John Masefield. RhR

Ship goes sailing down the bay, The. Goodbye, My Lover,
Goodbye. Unknown. FSW

Ship I have got in the North Country, A. The Golden Vanity.
Unknown. PoPle

Ship, leaving or arriving, of my lover. After a Passage in
Baudelaire. Robert Duncan. CMoP (1970 ed.); ExPo (1973
ed.); PoA

Ship moves, The. 4th of July. William Carlos Williams. PoA

Ship of Death, The. D. H. Lawrence. CMoP (1970 ed.); ExPo
(1973 ed.); FaBoTw (1975 ed.); NoAM; OAEL-2

Ship of Rio, The. Walter de la Mare. PoPle

Ship of State, The. Longfellow. RhR

Ship That Never Returned, The. Henry Clay Work. FSW

Ship with shields before the sun, A. Near Avalon. William
Morris. OAEL-2

Ships. Douglas Dunn. MS

Ship's master:/ before him, in the waist and before it. David
Jones. Fr. The Anathemata. FaBoTw (1975 ed.)

Ships That Pass in the Night. Longfellow. RhR

Shipwreck. George Mackay Brown. LP

Shipwreck, The. E. Harriet Palmer. RhR

Shipyard cranes have come down again, The. Landscape with
One Figure. Douglas Dunn. MS

Shir Ma'alot/ A Song of Degrees. Richard Flantz. VWA

Shira. Howard Schwartz. VWA

Shires, The. Unknown. OxBM

Shirley 4 Years Later. Alta. MMD

Shirley McDaniel Ain't Dead. Lee Howard. PoUp

Shirley standing on the table. Stockton State Mental Hospital
1962. Alta. MMD

Shirley Temple. Cyril R. Michael. PeD

Shirt, The. Elizabeth Brunazzi. PoUp

Shirt, The. Hilda Morley. AMV–81

Shirt, The. Jon Silkin. NoAM

Shirt of a Lad, The. Unknown, tr. fr. Welsh by Anthony Conran.
OBW

Shirt races in the meadow, A. Storm. Agnes Nemes Nagy, tr. by
Laura Schiff. PBWP

Shiva. Robinson Jeffers. NoAM; NOBA

Shivering in fever, weak and parched to sand. Dream of Dying.
Thomas Lovell Beddoes. ILP (1975 ed.)

Shivers. Aileen Fisher. CaYB

Shlof Mayn Kind, Shlof Keseyder (Sleep My Child). Unknown,
tr. fr. Yiddish. FSW

Shlup, shlup, the dog. Denise Levertov. Fr. Six Variations.
HeIP; InPK

Shock. Billy Collins. AAN

Shocked that she missed the footbridge! The Suicide. V. R.
Laing. PoA

Shoe. John Perreault. EAS

Shoe-tying, The. Robert Herrick. CaPo

Shoes are made to fit the feet. Gond Oral Tradition, tr. by V.
Elwin and S. Hivale. WTO

Shoes fall on their feet. How Things Fall. Donald Finkel.
VWA

Shoes insted of slippers down the stairs. The Couple Upstairs.
Hugo Williams. POL

Sholto Peach Harrison you are no son of mine. Correspondence
between Mr. Harrison in Newcastle and Mr. Sholto Peach
Harrison in Hull. Stevie Smith. FaBoNO

Shon a Morgan. Unknown. GBP

Shoo! be far off! fly. A Charm against the Dumps. David
Malouf. GAS

Shoo Fly, Don't Bother Me. Unknown. FSW
(Shew! Fly, Don't Bother Me, longer version, with music, at. to
Billy Reeves and to T. Brigham Bishop.) PSon

Shoofly, The. Felix O'Hare. AmFP

Shoot, The. Pope. Fr. Windsor Forest. PB

Shootin' with Rasputin. Unknown. FSW

Shooting at the Moon. Kim Yo-sop, tr. by Ko Won. Moon

Shooting Gallery. Martin Galvin. AMV–80

Shooting Song, A. William Brighty Rands. OxBChV

Shop. Robert Browning. VLP

Shop teacher told you you'd end up, The. Self-Interviews. Peter
Mladinic. BrS

Shopkeepers. Mani Leib, tr. fr. Yiddish by Richard Fein.
AMV–81

Shoplifting Poetry. Martin Steingesser. AAN

Shopping. Jane Chance Nitzche. AMV–80

Shopping for Meat in Winter. Oscar Williams. MiP

Shore. Alan Bold. MS

Shore. Jean Garrigue. TAP

Shore Leave Lorry. Roy Fuller. NoAM

Shore looked wild, without a trace of man. Byron. Fr. Don
Juan, II. HAP

Shore of Life, The. Robert Fitzgerald. VGW

Shore wind is cold on my travel clothes, the. Abutsu the Nun, tr.
by Edwin O. Reischauer. The Diary of the Waning Moon.
PBWP

Shoreham: Twilight Time. Samuel Palmer. OAEL-2

Shoreline. Mary Barnard. PoA

Shoreline. Seamus Heaney. HeHu

Shores. Sorley MacLean, tr. fr. Gaelic by Iain Crichton Smith.
SLP

Shores are crown'd with people, The. Luis Vaz de Camoëns, tr.
by Sir Richard Fanshawe. Fr. The Lusiads. OBVE

Shores of anguish. Magda Portal, tr. fr. Spanish by Allan
Francovich and Kathleen Weaver. PBWP

Short cut, A. Bruce Holsapple. FAF

Short cut home lay through the cemetery, The. The Mistress.
Joan Barton. OxBTC

Short day has grown, A. The Place of V. Ray A. Young Bear.
VoR

Short Eulogy. Zali Gurevitch, tr. fr. Hebrew by Gabriel Levin.
VWA

Short grass and the hillside, a level road. Paths They Kept
Barren. John Garmon. AMV–81

Short Haired Woman. Unknown. BluL

Short History of the Teaching Profession, A. Sister Maura.
AMV–80

Short Lay of Sigurd, The. Unknown, tr. fr. Old Norse by William
Morris and Eiriks Magnusson. Fr. The Elder Edda. OBVE

Short Night, The. Buson, tr. fr. Japanese by Harold G.
Henderson. Moon

Short Order. Charles Bukowski. HoPM (1975 ed.)

Short Paean of Simon Forman the Astrologer, The: To Tronco,
His Wife. David Kirby. AAN

Short Pastoral. Leonard Nathan. MIT

Short Sermon. Louis Untermeyer, after the German. CTV

Short service, to be sure, A. Lament for a Leg. John Ormond. OBW

Short Song of Congratulation, A. Samuel Johnson. CABA (1972 ed.); EBEV; HAP; ILP (1975 ed.); InPK; InPS; LAuP; NOBE; OBSV
(One-and-Twenty.) PoPle
(To a Young Heir.) IP; UnPo (1976 ed.)

Short space my feet had traversed ere. Guillaume de Lorris *and* Jean de Meun, *tr. by* F. S. Ellis. *Fr.* The Romance of the Rose. OAEL-1

Short squat. The Stepmother. Cathy Ackerson. PoW

Short Story, A. Michael Cooper. BCr

Short Subjects. Carolyn Stoloff. RiTi

Short Walk Alone. Alan Stephens. FoP

Short Winter Tale, A. Natan Zach, *tr. fr. Hebrew by* Peter Everwine *and* Shula Starkman. VWA

Short'nin' Bread, *with music. Unknown.* BLSo

Shorty George. *Unknown.* FSW

Shot. Emma Lou Thayne. MPA

Shot at Random, A. D. B. Wyndham Lewis. FaBoCo

Shot, A: from crag to crag. Hunting Season. W. H. Auden. LiSp

Shot gold, maroon and violet, dazzling silver, emerald, fawn. A Prairie Sunset. Walt Whitman. PiAm

Shot? so quick, so clean an ending? A. E. Housman. STS

Shot with a Hot Rot Gun. Michael Goode. NowV

Should all the world so wide to atoms fall. Our Insufficiency to Praise God Suitably, for His Mercy. Edward Taylor. *Fr.* God's Determinations. PiAm

Should auld acquaintance be forgot. Auld Lang Syne. Burns. AKE; BiP; BLSH; BLSo; FSW; LAuP; NOBE

Should Dennis print how once you robb'd your brother. On Dennis. Pope. FaBoEE

Should hope and fear thy heart alternate tear. The Present Time. Congreve. NIL

Should I believe you, e'en my oaths are witty. *Unknown.* FaBoEE

Should I get married? Should I be good? Marriage. Gregory Corso. CABA (1972 ed.); CoPAm; InPS; NoAM; OBAL; PPoD; PPP; TAP

Should I say, my people? I turned stone. Maratea Porto: Saying Goodbye to the Vitolos. Richard Hugo. MAT

Should I speak unthinkingly. At First Sight. Alastair Reid. SLP

Should I with silver tooles delve through the hill. Edward Taylor. Preparatory Meditations: Second Series, LVI. EAP

Should I worry about choosing. Begging on North Main. Dabney Stuart. AMV-81

Should no man write, say you, but such as do excel? That No Man Should Write but Such as Do Excel. George Turberville. PPoD

Should some ill painter, in a wild design. Horace, *tr. by* John Oldham. *Fr.* The Art of Poetry. OBVE

Should the wide world roll away. Stephen Crane. The Black Riders, X. BiP

Should they not have the best of both worlds? Mules. Paul Muldoon. CIP

Should We Legalize Abortion? Frank O'Hara. NoAM

Should you ask me, whence these stories? The Song of Hiawatha: Introduction. Longfellow. NOBA; PiAm

Should you, my lord, while you pursue my song. Phillis Wheatley. *Fr.* To the Right Honorable William, Earl of Dartmouth. BPo

Should you revisit us. New Approach Needed. Kingsley Amis. OxBTC; TPo

Shoulder of rock, A. High Island. Richard Murphy. CIP

Shouldering shapes of the skies of Broceliande. Taliessin's Song of the Unicorn. Charles Williams. FaBoTw (1975 ed.)

Shout came from the loquacious ones, A. A Welsh Ballad. Edmwnd Prys, *tr. by* Gwyn Williams. OBW

Shout for Joy. *Unknown.* AmFP

Shout, Little Lulu. *Unknown.* AmFP

Shouting Song. *Unknown.* AmFP

Shovel Man, The. Carl Sandburg. HAP

Shoveling dung in Denver's Field. The Hanging Man. Karl Kopp. FoP

Shovelling Iron Ore. *Unknown.* GBP

Show, The. Wilfred Owen. NoAM; OBP; OBW; OxBTC

Show me, dear Christ, thy spouse, so bright and clear. Holy Sonnets, XVIII. John Donne. ExPo (1973 ed.); ILP (1975 ed.); SCP-1; TT

Show Me the Way. *Unknown, tr. fr. Burmese by* U Win Pe. PBWP

Show me thy feet: show me thy legs, thy thighs. To Dianeme. Robert Herrick. CaPo; POL

Show the runner coming through the shadows. The Runner. Gary Gildner. TAP

Showing a torn sleeve, with stiff and shaking fingers the old man. Charles Reznikoff. *Fr.* Five Groups of Verse. SA

Shredded Wheat. Louis Dudek. AKE

Shriek said the saw smile said the mice. To the Age's Insanities. Marie Ponsot. VGW

Shrieks in dark leaves. The rumpled owl. Hunger and Thirst. John Peale Bishop. PoA

Shrinking to enter, did. Your heart. Part of the Vigil. James Merrill. NoAM

Shropshire Lad, A. A. E. Housman. *Poems indexed separately by titles and first lines.*

Shroud keeps scratching my eyes my nuts my, The. Breathing, at Last, in the Wichita Art Museum. D. Clinton. HeS

Shrouded Stranger, The. Allen Ginsberg. CoPAm

Shrouding of the Duchess of Malfi. John Webster. *See* Hark, Now Everything Is Still.

Shrovetide's Countenance. Rabelais, *tr. fr. French by* Sir Thomas Urquhart. FaBoNo

Shrubbery, The. William Cowper. NOBE

Shtil Di Nacht (Silent Is the Night). Hirsh Glik, *tr. fr. Yiddish.* FSW

Shubble, The. Walter de la Mare. FaBoNo; TDH

Shuddering geography pulls the dead sentences, A. Pastoral. James Tipton. HeS

Shuddring the Spectre howls, his howlings terrify the night. Blake. *Fr.* Jerusalem. OAEL-2

Shuffle and reshuffle. Still the times will stack. Carmen Saeculare. John Taylor. NowV

Shuffle and shudder of Autumn, The. Autumn Imagined. Donald Davie. PoA

Shuffling along in her broken shoes from the slums. Douglas Stewart. *Fr.* Lady Feeding the Cats. BoAnP

Shulamit in Her Dreams. Marcia Falk. VWA

Shut not so soon; the dull-eyed [*or* dull-ey'd] night. To Daisies, Not to Shut So Soon. Robert Herrick. CaPo; GBL; ILP (1975 ed.); InPK

Shut Not Your Doors. Walt Whitman. NOBA

Shut off the radio. Putting the Croutons Back into the Jar. Diane Kruchkow. FAF

Shut Out. Christina Rossetti. VLP

Shut Out That Moon. Thomas Hardy. CMoP (1970 ed.); ILP (1975 ed.); NoAM; NOBE

Shut, shut the door, good John! Epistle to Dr. Arbuthnot [*or* An Epistle from Mr. Pope, to Dr. Arbuthnot]. Pope. CABA (1972 ed.); ESaP; HoPM (1975 ed.); InPS; OAEL-1; PAIC

Shut up. Shut up. There's nobody here. The Beast in the Space. W. S. Graham. FaBoTw (1975 ed.); PoA

Shutter of time darkening ceaselessly, The. August. Louis MacNeice. PoPle

Shutting the Curtains. Bink Noll. GP

Shutting the door. The Best Thing Going. George Mattingly. AcAn

Shy Geordie. Helen B. Cruikshank. MS

Shyly the silver-hatted mushrooms make. May. John Shaw Neilson. GAS; MAuV

Si Me Quieres Escribir (If You Want to Write Me). *Unknown, tr. fr. Spanish.* FSW

Si, señor, is halligators here, your guidebook say it. Sinalóa. Earle Birney. CABA (1972 ed.)

Siamese twins: one, maddened by. Twins. Robert Graves. FaBoEE

Siberia. James Clarence Mangan. BIrV

Sibilla's Dirge. Thomas Lovell Beddoes. *Fr. Death's Jest Book.* NOBE

Sibrandus Schafnaburgensis. Robert Browning. *Fr. Garden Fancies.* OBP

Sibyl of the Waters. Ruth Fainlight. VWA

Sic 'Em Dogs On. *Unknown.* BluL

Sic et Non. Sir Herbert Read. FaBoTw (1975 ed.)

Sic Transit Gloria Scotia. "Hugh MacDiarmid." CMoP (1970 ed.)

Sic Vita. Henry King. BBGO; ILP (1975 ed.); NIL; NOBE; WIF
("Like to the falling of a star.") FF

Sic Vita. Henry David Thoreau. *See* I Am a Parcel of Vain Strivings Tied.

Sicilian Muse, thy voice and subject raise. The Golden Age. *Unknown.* APAS

Sicilian Muses, sing we greater things. Virgil, *tr. by* Sir John Beaumont. Eclogues, IV. OBVE

Sicily and Naples; or, The Fatal Union: a Tragedy, *sel.* Samuel Harding.
"Noblest bodies are but gilded clay." SCP-2

Sick Child, A. Randall Jarrell. SO; VGW

Sick Love. Robert Graves. BoLoP; CMoP (1970 ed.); EBEV; ExPo (1973 ed.); HAP; NoAM; NOBE; OAEL-2

Sick of the piercing company of women. A Country Walk. Thomas Kinsella. CIP; CMoP (1970 ed.)

Sick Rose, The. Blake. *Fr.* Songs of Experience. BoLoP; CABA (1972 ed.); ExPo (1973 ed.); HAP; HeIP; ILP (1975 ed.); InPK; InPS; LAuP; LFH; MBPR; NIL; NOBE; OAEL-2; PAIC; PoIA; PPP; STS; WeW

Sick Shark, The. Morris Bishop. TDH

Sick stomach. Bix Beiderbecke. Night Is No More or Less Important than Bad Circles or "Ksing." Carol Frost. AAN

Sick unto Death of Love. *Malay Oral Tradition, tr. by* R. J. Wilkinson *and* R. O. Winstedt. WTO

Sickens my gut, Yellow Bittern. The Yellow Bittern. *Tr. fr. Irish by* Tom MacIntyre. CIP

Sickle Pears. Owen Dodson. AmNP (1974 ed.)

Sickness of Adam, The. Karl Shapiro. ILP (1975 ed.)

Sickness of desire, that in dark days, The. Melancholia. Robert Bridges. CMoP (1970 ed.)

Side by Side. Adrienne Rich. CoPAm

Side by side on the narrow bed. That Room. John Montague. CIP

Side by side, their faces blurred. An Arundel Tomb. Philip Larkin. HeIP; MPo; PPP

Sidewalk Restoration. Ron Ikan. NVAP

Sidewalks of New York, The. James W. Blake. BLSH, *with music;* BLSo; *with music;* FSN, *with music;* FSW

Sidewinder, The. Charles F. Lummis. BPAW

Siding near Chillicothe, A. Richmond Lattimore. ANTL

Siege and the assault being ceased at Troy, The. Sir Gawain and the Green Knight. *Unknown, tr. by* Brian Stone. OAEL-1

Siege of Rhodes, The, *sel.* Sir William Davenant.
"These are court-monsters, cormorants of the crown." SCP-2

Siege, The; or, Love's Convert, The, *sel.* William Cartwright.
"My most honoured father." SCP-2

Siena. Swinburne. VLP

Sierra. Alfonsina Storni, *tr. fr. Spanish by* Rachel Benson. PBWP

Sierra Kid, *sel.* Philip Levine.
He Faces the Second Winter. PoA

Siesta of a Hungarian Snake. Edwin Morgan. InPK

Sifting Stones at Capri. Susan Whiting. GAS

Sigh as It Ends. John Berryman. WeW

Sigh escapes, A—falls, really, like a corpse from a closet. The Why Bother Club. Barry Schechter. FiCh

Sigh, in the wind fall flowers, their petals dance. Selling Ruined Peonies. Yü Hsüan-chi, *tr. by* Geoffrey Waters. BoWoP

Sigh no more, ladies, sigh no more. Shakespeare. *Fr.* Much Ado about Nothing, II, iii. FF; SS; STS

Sighed a dear little shipboard divinity. Conrad Aiken. OBAL

Sight in Camp in the Daybreak Gray and Dim, A. Walt Whitman. BiP; ExPo (1973 ed.); ILP (1975 ed.); NoAM; OFD; TAP

Sight of the English is getting me down, The. Hiraeth in N.W.3. Wynford Vaughan-Thomas. NOBL

Sighted a black tornado of. Comments. Peggy Susberry Kenner. JB

Sighting down the silver barrel. The League of Selves. Alvin Toffler. AMV-80

Sightseeing. Desmond O'Grady. IPM

Sightseer Named Sue, A. *Unknown.* TDH

Sigil. Hilda Doolittle ("H. D."). VGW

Sigismundo. Linda Gregg. AmPA

Sigmund Freud. Howard Nemerov. PoA

Sign, The. Paul Blackburn. TAT

Sign. Marge Piercy. Psy

Sign first in the sky, then other tokens, A. From a Plague Year. David Malouf. FPA

Sign that I might, A. Prayer. Patrick King. IPM

"Sign there." I signed, but still uneasily. A Document. Judith Wright. MAuV

Signal, The. David Ignatow. NNaP

Signals. Jewel C. Latimore. PoBA

Signals. Keith Waldrop. AMV-81

Signature. Hannah Kahn. IHMS

Signature. Larry Mollin. NeAC

Signature. Carol Orlock. AMV-81

Signature, A. F. Eugene Warren. AATT

Signature for Tempo. Archibald MacLeish. VGW

Signature of All Things, The. Kenneth Rexroth. NNaP; NU

Signatures. Daniel Hoffman. VGW

Signboard, The. Robert Creeley. ConAP

Significance of a Veteran's Day, The. Simon J. Ortiz. GP

Signpost. Robinson Jeffers. TCP

Signs. Gjertrud Schnackenberg. PoA

Signs of the Seasons. *Unknown.* ECBV

Signs of wear. Monogram 29. Martina Werner, *tr. by* Rosemarie Waldrop. BoWoP

Signs of Winter. John Clare. Epi
"Cat runs races with her tail, The," *sel.* OAEL-2

Siilenboor. *Mongol Oral Tradition, tr. by* C. R. Bawden. WTO

Silence. Bella Akhmadulina, *tr. fr. Russian by* Daniel Halpern. BoWoP

Silence. E. E. Cummings. CMoP (1970 ed.)

Silence. Thomas Hood. EBEV; NOBE

Silence. Edward Lucie-Smith. LP

Silence. Marianne Moore. CMoP (1970 ed.); LFH; NOBA; PiAm; PSN; Psy; SBG ("My father used to say.") PPM

Silence. W. J. Turner. FSFS

Silence, The/ like a threat. Dancer. Geoff Page. FPA

Silence, and a starry night. Shtil Di Nacht (Silent Is the Night). Hirsh Glik, *tr. fr. Yiddish.* FSW

Silence, and stealth of days! 'Tis now. Since Thou Art Gone. Henry Vaughan. SCP-1

Silence, and the heat lights shimmer like a mist of sifted silver. Spring in the Desert. Sharlot Hall. WPW

Silence augmenteth grief, writing increaseth rage. An Epitaph upon the Right Honorable Sir Philip Sidney. Fulke Greville. Prf

Silence beside the Pacific. The Reach of Silence. Charles Black. AMV-81

Silence brought by the dark night: Eryri's. Nightfall. Walter Davies, *tr. by* Anthony Conran. OBW

Silence Concerning an Ancient Stone. Rosario Castellanos, *tr. fr. Spanish by* George D. Schade. PBWP

Silence hovers over the earth, A. A Late Spring Day in My Life. Robert Bly. NCSH

Silence in Court. "Lewis Carroll." *See* Evidence Read at the Trial of the Knave of Hearts.

Silence in Mallorca. Genevieve Taggard. SPT

Silence is first, The. Still water. Demolition. Philip Raisor. AMV-81

Silence of a city, how awful at midnight, The. Samuel Taylor Coleridge. MBPR

Silence of Bears, The. Richard Pflum. BCr

Silence of the year, The. Landscape of the Star. Adrienne Rich. TT

Silence: one would willingly consume it. Silence. Edward Lucie-Smith. LP

Silence rules in the home. The Convoy. Juan Antonio Corretjer, *tr. by* Julio Marzán. InW

Silence slipping around like death, A. A Winter Twilight. Angelina Weld Grimké. PoBA

Silence Spoke with Your Voice. Ryah Tumarkin Goodman. AAN

Silence will continue, The. Red Flowers. Tanya Felix. PHC

Silences. Arthur O'Shaughnessy. VLP

Silent, about-to-be-parted-from house. Invocation. Denise Levertov. PoA

Silent alone, where none or saw, or heard. Anne Bradstreet. *Fr.* Contemplations. PBWP

Silent at last, beneath the silent ground. On the Death of Echo. Hartley Coleridge. BoAnP; GDP

Silent girl at the spindle, The. The Spinning Girl. Nathan Alterman, *tr. by* Ruth Nevo. VWA

Silent is the house: all are laid asleep. The Visionary. Emily Brontë. BoReV; NOBE; PBWP

Silent Love, A. Sir Edward Dyer. BoLoP; NOBE (Lowest Trees Have Tops, The.) HAP; WeW ("Lowest trees have tops, the ant her gall, The.") EBEV

Silent Movies. Pedro Juan Pietri. InW

Silent Night! Holy Night! Joseph Mohr, *tr. fr. German.* BLSH, *with music;* FSW; GSB, *with music*

Silent Noon. Dante Gabriel Rossetti. The House of Life, XIX. HAP; ILP (1975 ed.); OBP; SoSe (1977 ed.); VLP

Silent nymph, with curious eye! Grongar Hill. John Dyer. EPC; LAuP; OBW; PAIC

Silent, O Moyle, be the roar of thy water. The Song of Fionnuala. Thomas Moore. BIrV

Silent Poem. Robert Francis. FiCP

Silent silent night. Blake. MBPR

Silent Slain, The. Archibald MacLeish. CABA (1972 ed.); CMoP (1970 ed.); NIL; POL

Silent Snake, The. *Unknown.* CaYB

Silent Spinney, The. Seamus Redmond. FPB

Silent stream flows on and in its glass, The. The River. Edwin Muir. MS

Silent Tower of Bottreau, The. Robert Stephen Hawker. VPC

Silent, you say, I'm grown of late. Walter Savage Landor. GBL

Silently grave as voyeurs in a powder room. At the Dancing School of the Sisters Schwartz. Judson Jerome. SFF

Silesian Weavers, The. Heine, *tr. fr. German by* Aaron Kramer. NAWM-2

Silhouette. Annette M'Baye, *tr. fr. French by* Kathleen Weaver. PBWP

Silhouettes, they lean against a ringed moon. Paiute Ponies. Jim Barnes. CDW

Silica Carbonate Rock. Fred Berry. NU

Silk Weaver's Daughter, The. *Unknown.* AmFP

Silked, or smoked from that field. Whether Firelocked. Mary Shumway. HeS

Silken Tent, The. Robert Frost. CABA (1972 ed.); ExPo (1973 ed.); ILP (1975 ed.); InPK; NOBA; PAIC; PiAm; PPoD; SoSe; TAP; WIF

Silkworms, The. Douglas Stewart. GAS; MAuV

Silly. All giggles and ringlets and never. Romping. John Ciardi. CTBA; NCSH

Silly boy 'tis full moon yet, thy night as day shines clearly. Thomas Campion. GBL

Silly Dog. Myra Cohn Livingston. GDP

Silly zebras don't know, The. Zoo Dream. David Barker. GP

Silver. A. R. Ammons. CSP

Silver. Walter de la Mare. CTV; ILP (1975 ed.); IPWM; PPM; SS

Silver. Peter Wild. FoP

Silver birch is a dainty lady, The. Child's Song in Spring. Edith Nesbitt. OxBChV

Silver Bullet, The. Constance Fowlkes. PoUp

Silver carpeting of sand, A. Pacific Dawn. Alison Wyrley Birch. PPM

Silver Dagger, The. *Unknown.* AmFP

Silver Dollar. Kathleen Wiegner. MMD

Silver dust. Pear Tree. Hilda Doolittle ("H. D."). BoWoP; CMoP (1970 ed.); NOBA; UnPo (1976 ed.)

Silver Jack's Religion. John P. Jones. BPAW

Silver Jubilee. Llewelyn Wyn Griffith. OBW

Silver Lucifer, A. Lunar Baedeker. Mina Loy. VGW

Silver Penny, The. Walter de la Mare. CMoP (1970 ed.); WIF

Silver Racer, The. Joseph Colin Murphey. AMV-80

Silver Screen. Leonard Clark. RAE

Silver spoons, The/ were warbling. Here Comes. Erica Jong. PPoD

Silver Swan, The. *Unknown.* HAP; HeIP; ILP (1975 ed.); InPK; NIL; PoPle (*At. to* Orlando Gibbons); SoSe (1977 ed.)

Silver Tassie, The. Burns. NOBE (My Bonnie Mary.) PoPle

Silver tetradrachm of King Antigonos, The. Coin from B.C. Nicholas Flocos. SA

Silver Threads among the Gold. Eben Eugene Rexford. BLSH, *with music;* BLSo, *with music;* FSW; PSoN, *with music*

Silver-vested monkey trips, A. Cortège. Paul Verlaine, *tr. by* Arthur Symons. OBVE

Silver watch you've worn for years, A. Some Slippery Afternoon. Daniela Gioseffi. AAN; WBN

Silver Wedding. Ralph Hodgson. OxBTC

Silvery Tide, The. *Unknown.* AmFP

Simile. N. Scott Momaday. CDW

Simile, A. Matthew Prior. ILP (1975 ed.)

Simile for Her Smile, A. Richard Wilbur. HoPM (1975 ed.); InPK; OLR; UsP; WIF

Similes for Two Political Characters of 1819. Shelley. InPS (To Sidmouth and Castlereagh.) MBPR

Simon and the Tarantula. James Wright. NNaP

Simon Gerty. Elinor Wylie. OBAL

Simon Lee. Wordsworth. MBPR

Simon Legree—a Negro Sermon. Vachel Lindsay. The Booker Washington Trilogy, I. TAP

Simon Peter is slaying the roosters. All-Hallows Children. Eve Shelnutt. TC

Simon Soggs' Thanksgiving. W. A. Croffut. PoTa

Simon the Cyrenian Speaks. Countee Cullen. AmNP (1974 ed.); BPo; HAP

Simple. Naomi Long Madgett. FB; PoBA

Simple and fresh and fair from winter's close emerging. The First Dandelion. Walt Whitman. PF

Simple Beast. Mark Van Doren. TH

Simple child, A. We Are Seven. Wordsworth. MBPR; OxBChV; SpRo

Simple flick of the switch, A. Running It Backward. John N. Morris. GP

Simple-minded interstates have it now, The. Western Ways. Richmond Lattimore. AMV–80

Simple Ode. Kendrick Smithyman. ATNZ

Simple Prayer, A. St. Francis of Assisi, *tr. fr. Italian.* CTV

Simple Purification, The. Kabir, *ad. fr. Hindi by* Robert Bly. NU

Simple nosegay, A! was that much to ask? The Troll's Nosegay. Robert Graves. SoSe

Simple Simon met a pieman. Mother Goose. MG

Simple-Song. Marge Piercy. CTBA; Psy; TSWA

Simple soul, who so early in the morning. Charles Reznikoff. *Fr.* Depression. CTBA

Simplex Munditiis. Ben Jonson, *tr. fr. the Latin of* Jean Bonnefons. *Fr.* Epicoene; or, The Silent Woman, I, i. HoPM (1975 ed.); NOBE; OBP; PBMP (Clerimont's Song.) InPS; OAEL–1; PPP ("Still to be neat, still to be dressed.") CABA (1972 ed.); FF; GBL; HAP; HeIP; ILP (1975 ed.); IP; NIL; PoPle

Simplicity ("Persicos odi"). Horace. *See* Fie on Eastern Luxury!

Simplicity. Carl Rakosi. *See* Americana XV: Simplicity.

Simplicity. Louis Simpson. ILP (1975 ed.); InPS; Prf

Simplicity Aims Circularly. Anna Walters. VoR

Simplicity assuages. Apology. J. V. Cunningham. PiAm

Simplicity so graven hurts the sense. So Graven. Josephine Miles. NoAM

Simplification, A. Richard Wilbur. CMoP (1970 ed.)

Simplify Me When I'm Dead. Keith Douglas. OxBTC

Simply by sailing in a new direction. Landfall in Unknown Seas. Allen Curnow. ATNZ

Simply to breathe. An Emblem of Two Foxes. Barry Spacks. CoPAm; HoPM (1975 ed.)

Simultaneously. David Ignatow. NCSH; POL; WeW

Simultaneously, as soundlessly. Prime. W. H. Auden. CMoP (1970 ed.)

Simultaneously, five thousand miles apart. Simultaneously. David Ignatow. NCSH; POL; WeW

Sin. George Herbert. Epi

Sin of Omission, The. Margaret Elizabeth Munson Sangster. SoSe

Sin of self-love possesseth all mine eye. Sonnets, LXII. Shakespeare. EBEV

Sinalóa. Earle Birney. CABA (1972 ed.)

Since. W. H. Auden. InPS

Since/ Malcolm died. Aardvark. Julia Fields. CNA; OFD

Since all that beat about in nature's range. Constancy to an Ideal Object. Samuel Taylor Coleridge. MBPR; OBP

Since all the riches of this world. Blake. OAEL–2

Since brass, nor stone, nor earth, nor boundless sea. Sonnets, LXV. Shakespeare. CABA (1972 ed.); Epi; FF; HAP; InPS; NOBE; PoIA; STS; UnPo (1976 ed.)

Since Brunswick's smile has authoris'd my muse. Edward Young. *Fr.* The Instalment. FaBoCo

Since by just flames the guilty piece is lost. Advice to the Painter. Matthew Prior. APAS

Since Christmas they have lived with us. Balloons. Sylvia Plath. MPo; NCSH

Since Easter was a month ago. Written on an Egg. Eduard Mörike, *tr. by* Doris Orgel. CC

Since Feeling Is First. E. E. Cummings. BiP; SFF; STS; TVo

Since I am coming to that holy room. Hymn to God My God, in My Sickness. John Donne. AnMo; CABA (1972 ed.); EBEV; HeIP; ILP (1975 ed.); MetP; NIL; OAEL–1; PPP; SCP–1; SoSe

Since I believe in God the Father Almighty. Johannes Milton, Senex. Robert Bridges. BoReV; CMoP (1970 ed.); OBP

Since I do trust Jehova still. Bible, *O.T.* Psalms, XI, *paraphrased by* Sir Philip Sidney. OBVE

Since I emerged that day from the labyrinth. The Labyrinth. Edwin Muir. CMoP (1970 ed.); NoAM

Since I entered the inner rooms. Written on a Leaf. *Unknown, tr. by* Geoffrey Waters. BoWoP

Since I have been so quickly done for. Epitaph on an Infant Eight Months Old. *Unknown.* SoSe

Since I have seen a bird one day. The Truth. W. H. Davies. FaBoTw (1975 ed.); UsP

Since I left you, mine eye is in my mind. Sonnets, CXIII. Shakespeare. WeW

Since I must love your north. To My Mountain. Kathleen Raine. SLP

Since I must needs into thy school [*or* schoole] return [*or* returne]. A Lady's [*or* Ladies] Prayer to Cupid. Thomas Carew, *after* Giovanni Battista Guarini. CaPo; OBVE

Since I noo mwore do zee your feace. The Wife a-Lost. William Barnes. BoLoP; HAP; VPC

Since I'm a girl. *Unknown, tr. fr. Spanish by* Willis Barnstone. BoWoP

Since in religion all men disagree. To Caelia. *Unknown.* FaBoEE

Since Jesus Came into My Heart, *with music.* R. H. McDaniel. BLSH

Since Juliet's on ice, and Joan. Carpe Diem. C. K. Stead. ATNZ

Since last the tutelary hearth. Christmas Family Reunion. Peter De Vries. NOBL

Since life is nothing in your philosophy. Nothing. Julia de Burgos, *tr. by* Aliki *and* Willis Barnstone. BoWoP

Since, Lord, to thee/ A narrow way and little gate. Holy Baptism. George Herbert. SCP–1

Since Man's a little world, to make it great. An Epigram on Woman. Philip Ayres. FaBoEE

Since me and Jesus got: married. Jesus Make Up My Dying Bed. *Unknown.* BluL

Since mine was never the heroic gesture. To Hugh MacDiarmid. G. S. Fraser. MS

Since morning you've been on the tennis court. The Fields of the Country. Jane Garland Katz. AAN

Since Most Poets Write Nonsense. Francis Coleman Rosenberger. PoUp

Since most sharks have no flotation bladders and must swim. Nurse Sharks. William Matthews. FiCP

"Since mountains sink to vales, and valleys die." The Bathos. Richard Porson. FaBoEE

Since my birth. Clockwork. Paul F. Fericano. CPA

Since my old friend is grown so great. A Dialogue. Pope. POL

Since naturally black is naturally beautiful. Naturally. Audre Lorde. CNA

Since Nature's Works Be Good. Sir Philip Sidney. *Fr.* Arcadia. ILP (1975 ed.)

Since now I dare not ask. The Sharp Ridge. Robert Graves. FaBoEE

Since of no creature living the last breath. Edna St. Vincent Millay. VGW

Since Reverend Doctors now declare. The Respectable Burgher. Thomas Hardy. CMoP (1970 ed.); NoAM; VLP

Since she must go, and I must mourn, come night. His Parting from Her. John Donne. Elegies, XII. EBEV

Since she whom I loved hath paid her last debt. Holy Sonnets, XVII. John Donne. SCP-1

Since Shylock's book has walk'd the circles here. To a Noisy Politician. Philip Freneau. TAP

Since that moment is lost, I hardly remember. Consent. Gregory Jerozal. PoUp

Since that night/ I cannot know myself. Izumi Shikibu, *tr. fr. Japanese by* Willis Barnstone. BoWoP

Since the instant exists I sing. Motive. Cecilia Meireles, *tr. by* Don Wilson. AMV-81

Since the night is dark. *Unknown, tr. fr. Spanish by* Willis Barnstone. BoWoP

Since the shell came and took you in its arms. The Shell. George MacBeth. SLP; UsP

Since the storm two nights ago. The Recognition. Denise Levertov. VGW

Since Then. Yehuda Amichai, *tr. fr. Hebrew by* Shlomo Vinner *and* Howard Schwartz. VWA

Since Then. D. J. Enright. OBSV

Since there's no help, come, let them kiss and part. The Limited. Robert Penn Warren. PoA

Since there's no help [*or* helpe], come let us kiss [*or* kisse] and part. Farewell to Love. Michael Drayton. *Fr.* Idea. AAS; BoLoP; CABA (1972 ed.); Epi; ExPo (1973 ed.); GBL; HAP; HeIP; ILP (1975 ed.); InPK; InPS; LoAs; NOBE; OAEL-1; PAIC; PBMP; PoIA; PoPle; PPoD; PPoe; SoSe; VoPo

Since this is the last night I keep you home. Seven Seals. D. H. Lawrence. LoAs

Since Thou Art Gone. Henry Vaughan. SCP-1

Since thou wouldst needs (bewitch'd with some ill charms!). To One Married to an Old Man. Edmund Waller. FaBoEE

Since Thursday last, the bare living-room. Bicycle. David Malouf. FPA

Since thy third curing of the French infection. Against an Old Lecher. Sir John Harington. FaBoEE

Since Time began, such alphabets begin. From a Cheerful Alphabet. John Updike. FaBoCo

Since to obtaine thee, nothing me will sted. His Remedie for Love. Michael Drayton. *Fr.* Idea. AAS

Since we agreed to let the road between us. No Road. Philip Larkin. EBEV; ILP (1975 ed.)

Since we are told it we believe it's true. Surprise. Anthony Cronin. CIP; IPM

Since we had always sky about. Can. Lit. Earle Birney. CABA (1972 ed.)

Since we had changed. Message. Allen Ginsberg. ConAP; VGW

Since We Loved. Robert Bridges. VLP

Since, when you die, delight. Modern Love Poems. *Somali Oral Tradition, tr. by* B. W. Andrzejewski *and* M. Laurence. WTO

Since without Thee We Do No Good. Elizabeth Barrett Browning. PIM

Since you ask, most days I cannot remember. Wanting to Die. Anne Sexton. ConAP; IHMS; NoAM; TAP

"Since you refuse to communicate by telephone." Survivors. Mordecai Marcus. AMV-81

Since you would claim the sources of my thought. Sonnet. Louise Bogan. FoP

Since you wrote a poem. What Color is Lonely. Carolyn M. Rodgers. BPo

Since You've Been Away. Attila Jozsef, *tr. fr. Hungarian by* John Batki. EC

Sincere Flattery of R. B. James Kenneth Stephen. NOBL

Sincere Flattery of W. W. (Americanus). James Kenneth Stephen. NOBL; SpRo

Sinful to Flirt. *Unknown.* AmFP

Sing a song of critics. Valentine. Ernest Hemingway. OBAL

Sing a Song of Honey. Barbara Euphan Todd. FSFS

Sing a Song of Juniper. Robert Francis. ECBV; NCSH

Sing a song of sixpence. Mother Goose. MG; SpRo

Sing, ballad-singer, raise a hearty tune. The Ballad-Singer. Thomas Hardy. At Castlebridge Fair, I. BoLoP; OLR; VLP

Sing care away, with sport and play. Heart's Ease. *Unknown. Fr.* Misogonus. WIF

Sing, cuccu, nu! Sing, cuccu! Sumer Is Ycumen In. *Unknown.* OAEL-1

Sing hey! Sing hey!/ For Christmas Day. *Unknown.* PChr

Sing his praises that doth keep. Hymn to Pan. John Fletcher. *Fr.* The Faithful Shepherdess, I, ii. NOBE

Sing ho! for a brave and a gallant ship. Ten Thousand Miles Away. *Unknown.* FSW

Sing it. Utter the phrase, the fine word. Bard. William Everson. PiAm

Sing jigmijole the pudding-bowl. Kissing of My Dame. *Unknown.* GBL

Sing lullaby, as women doe [*or* do]. The Lullabie [*or* Lullaby] of a Lover. George Gascoigne. AAS; EBEV; HAP

Sing Me a New Song. John Henrik Clarke. PoBA

Sing Me a Song. Robert Louis Stevenson. AIW; NOBE

Sing me at morn but only with your laugh. Song of Songs. Wilfred Owen. OBP

Sing me the men ere this. He Would Have His Lady Sing. Digby Mackworth Dolben. EBEV

"Sing me to sleep." The Snake and the Snake-Charmer. E. V. Rieu. ECBV

Sing, My Soul, *with music. Unknown.* AH

Sing out, pent souls, sing cheerfully! The Vintage to the Dungeon. Richard Lovelace. CaPo

Sing, Poet, 'tis a merry world. Glasgow. Alexander Smith. VPC

Sing praise/ Sing praise. Canto del Señor Segovia. David Sten Herrstrom. AATT

Sing, sing, what shall I sing? Mother Goose. MG

Sing softly, Muse, the Reverend Henry White. B Flat. Douglas Stewart. GAS; MAuV

Sing them over again to me. Wonderful Words of Life. Philip Paul Bliss. BLSH

Sing to the Lord Most High, *with music.* Timothy Dwight. AH

Sing to whom a hallelujah? Whom endorse? The Umbrella, the Cane, and the Broom. Eliezer Steinbarg, *tr. by* Curt Leviant. VWA

Sing We and Chant It. Thomas Morley. EBEV; WIF

Sing we for love and idleness. An Immorality. Ezra Pound. CMoP (1970 ed.); NOBA; OBAL; OLR; VoPo

Singe we alle and say we thus. My Purse. *Unknown.* EBEV; OxBM

Sing while you may, O bird upon the tree! Dark Wings. James Stephens. PoA

Singee a songee sick a pence. Nursery Song in Pidgin English. *Unknown.* SpRo

Singers are gone from the Cornmarket-place, The. After the Fair. Thomas Hardy. At Casterbridge Fair, VII. CMoP (1970 ed.); HAP; VLP

Singer's House, The. Seamus Heaney. CIP; EBEV

Singers to Come. Alice Meynell. WPE

Singing. Peter Shelton. AKE

Singing Aloud. Carolyn Kizer. IHMS

Singing at the Plough. Cotton Mather. *See* My Heart, How Very Hard It's Grown.

Singing Cat, The. Stevie Smith. OxBTC; PCat

Singing Lesson, The. David Wagoner. MPA

Singing of Niagara, and the Huron squaws. The Possibility of New Poetry. Robert Bly. ConAP

Singing robes fly onto your body, The. The Poem Rising by Its Own Weight. Denise Levertov. GP

Singing, today I married my white girl. Epithalamion. Dannie Abse. OBW

Single clover plank, A. Emily Dickinson. PiAm

Single flow'r he sent me, since we met, A. One Perfect Rose. Dorothy Parker. OBAL; OLR; PAIC; PoIA; PPM

Single Girl. *Unknown.* FSW

Singleman. Alfred Hayes. SPT

Single man stands like a bird-watcher, A. The Mouth of the Hudson. Robert Lowell. NYP; PSN; STS

Single naked wire at ground level, A. George Jonas. *Fr.* To Christian Montpelier. NeAC

Single Sonnet. Louise Bogan. NIL

Sings a Bird. John Nist. AMV-80

Sing-Song: A Nursery Rime Book. Christina Rossetti. *Poems indexed separately by titles and first lines.*

Singular Metamorphosis, A. Howard Nemerov. ConAP

Singular Self, The. Charles Bukowski. CoPAm

Singularly and in pairs the decade has been ripped by bullets. Lines. Herbert Martin. PoBA

Sinking of the *Titanic*. *Unknown.* PAIC

Sinner, Is Thy Heart at Rest? *with music.* Jared B. Waterbury. AH

Sinner Man. *Unknown.* FSW

Sinner man sat on the gates of hell, A. No Hiding Place Down There. *Unknown.* GBP

Sinners, Will You Scorn the Message? *with music.* Jonathan Allen. AH

Sins of Kalamazoo, The. Carl Sandburg. VGW

Sins we commit, in act or in thought, become birds, The. Flighty Poem. John Pauker. PoUp

Sioux, The. *Unknown.* TDH

Sioux Indians, The. *Unknown.* AmFP

Sipping Cider through a Straw. *Unknown. See* Sucking Cider through a Straw.

Sipping whiskey and gin. Analysands. Dudley Randall. BPo; CABA (1972 ed.)

Sipsop's Song. Blake. *Fr.* An Island in the Moon. FaBoNo

Sir,/ Ere you pass this threshold, stay. To the King, at His Entrance into Saxham: By Master John Crofts. Thomas Carew. CaPo

Sir/ I read of late. Four Questions Addressed to His Excellency, the Prime Minister. James Vaughn. AmNP (1974 ed.)

Sir-/ The Lord pardon the people of this town. Message to the Editor. Patrick Galvin. IPM

Sir Andrew Barton, 2 *versions. Unknown.* AmFP

Sir—awaiting you. Waiting for the Emperor Tenji. Princess Nukada, *tr. by* Cid Corman *and* Susumu Kamaike. PBWP

Sir Bedivere Bors. Frederick B. Opper. TDH

Sir Beelzebub. Edith Sitwell. BoWoP; HoPM (1975 ed.); OBP; OxBTC

Sir Brian had a battleaxe with great big knobs on. Bad Sir Brian Botany. A. A. Milne. BBL

Sir Christopher Wren. E. C. Bentley. *Fr.* Clerihews. FaBoCo; InPK

Sir Edward Michael Pakenham. Ballad of New Orleans. Charles G. Wilson. BTTM

Sir Edward, that was by este tho mid power gret ynow. Town against Gown at Oxford. Robert of Gloucester. *Fr.* Chronicle. OxBM

Sir Eglamour. Samuel Rowlands. ECBV; FaBoNo

Sir Eustace Grey, *sel.* George Crabbe. Frenzy. NOBE

Sir Francis Drake; or, Eighty-eight. *Unknown.* GBP

Sir Gawain and the Green Knight. *Unknown, tr. fr. Middle English by* Brian Stone. OAEL-1 *Sels.*
   Gawain and the Lady of the Castle, *orig. and mod. English prose.* OxBM
   ("Thus laykes this lorde by lynde-wodes eves.") EBEV, *orig. only*
   Gawain and the Temptress, *tr. by* Burton Raffel. OBP

Sir Gawaine and the Green Knight. Yvor Winters. NoAM; PAIC; PoIA; UsP; VGW

Sir George and Lady Cepheus of Upper Slaughter. Agony Column. A. D. Hope. SoSe

Sir Hudibras ("When civil fury first grew high"). Samuel Butler. *See* Presbyterian Knight.

Sir Hudibras, His Passing Worth. Samuel Butler. *Fr.* Hudibras, I. EBEV; FaBoCo; OAEL-1; SCP-2

Sir Hudson Lowe, Sir Hudson *Low.* To Sir Hudson Lowe. Thomas Moore. OBSV

Sir Hugh; or, The Jew's Daughter. *Unknown.* AmFP; FaBoBa

Sir Humphry Davy. E. C. Bentley. *Fr.* Clerihews. FaBoCo

Sir, I admit your general rule. Epigram. Pope. BBL; FaBoEE; NIL

Sir, I encountered Death. Incident in a Rose Garden. Donald Justice. NCSH

Sir John Barleycorn. *Unknown.* FaBoBa

Sir Joseph's Song. W. S. Gilbert. *Fr.* H.M.S. *Pinafore.* PPM; RhR

Sir Joshua Reynolds. Blake. FaBoCo
   ("When Sir Joshua Reynolds died.") FaBoEE

Sir Lionel. *Unknown.* AmFP

Sir Marmaduke. George Colman the Younger. PeBB

Sir Menenius Agrippa, the Friend of the People. Robert Brough. VLP

Sir, more than kisses letters mingle souls. To Sir Henry Wotton. John Donne. TVS

Sir, no man's enemy, forgiving all. Petition. W. H. Auden. CMoP (1970 ed.)

Sir, now unravelled is the Golden Fleece. To Dr. F. B. on His Book of Chess. Richard Lovelace. CaPo

Sir of the C Stream. Valerie Sinason. PMW

Sir Olf rode fast toward Thurston's walls. The Erl-King's Daughter. Johann Gottfried Herder, *tr. by* James Clarence Mangan. PoTa

Sir Orfeo. *Unknown.* OxBM

Sir Patrick Spens [*or* Spence]. *Unknown.* AIW; AmFP; BiP; CABA (1972 ed.); DuDr; EBEV; Epi, *with music;* ExPo (1973 ed.); FaBoBa; FaPoR; FF; HAP; HoPM (1975 ed.); ILP (1975 ed.); InPK; InPS; IP; NIL; NOBE; OAEL-1, *with music;* PAIC; PBMP; PeBB; PoIA; PPP; SoSe (1977 ed.); UnPo (1976 ed.); WeW

Sir Rider Haggard. W. H. Auden. FaBoCo

Sir, say no more. Trumbull Stickney. InPK

Sir Thomas Armstrong's Last Farewell to the World. *Unknown.* APAS

Sir Thomas Becket wore a gray sackcloth. Becket. Virginia Gilbert. NPW

Sir, though (I thank God for it) I do hate. John Donne. *Fr.* Satires, II. OBSV

Sir Walter Ralegh to the Queen. Sir Walter Ralegh. AAS Passions, *st.* 1. PoPle

Sir Walter Raleigh Sailing in the Low-lands ("Sir Walter Raleigh has built a ship"). *Unknown.* BBL

Sir William Dyer, Knight, *sels.* Lady Catherine Dyer.
"If a large heart joined with a noble mind." SCP-2
"My dearest dust, could not thy hasty day." SCP-2
(Epitaph on the Monument of Sir William Dyer at Colmworth, 1641.) BoLoP

Sir, you should notice me: I am the Man. Epitaph. Lascelles Abercrombie. BBGO

Sire. W. S. Merwin. VGW

Sired by old hearts. Colette, Poor Clare. Colette Inez. AATT

Siren Chorus. George Darley. *See* Mermaiden's Vesper-Hymn, The.

Siren sang, and Europe turned away, A. To the Western World. Louis Simpson. ConAP; CoPAm; GOA; NOBA; TAP

Siren Song. Margaret Atwood. *Fr.* Songs of the Transformed. HAP; PoA

Sirens' Song, The. William Browne. *Fr.* Inner Temple Masque. NOBE; PoPle
(Syrens' Song, The.) GBL

Sirens' Song, The. Homer, *tr. fr. Greek by* Robert Fitzgerald. *Fr.* The Odyssey, XII. GrRo

Sirius/ what mystery is this? Hilda Doolittle ("H. D."). *Fr.* The Walls Do Not Fall. PBWP

Sirius, a Dog Star. Peter Kostakis. FiCh

Sirmio, thou dearest dear of strands. Catullus, *tr. fr. Latin by* Thomas Hardy. OBVE

Siskins, The. Theodore Roethke. PB

Sisseton Indian Reservation, The. Richard Lyons. TAT

Sister. Gabriela Mistral, *tr. fr. Spanish by* Langston Hughes. BoWoP

Sister, Awake! *Unknown.* NOBE; PoPle

Sister Helen. Dante Gabriel Rossetti. VLP

Sister Lou. Sterling A. Brown. AmNP (1974 ed.); PoBA

Sister of love-lorn poets, Philomel! To the Nightingale. Samuel Taylor Coleridge. MBPR

Sister Pharaoh. Ruth Whitman. MAT

Sister Rose. Richard Martin. AMV-81

"Sister, sister, go to bed." Brother and Sister. "Lewis Carroll." FaBoNo

Sister was wedged beside the wicker basket. The Burned Bridge. Ruth Stone. WPE

Sister Zahava. Edith Bruck, *tr. fr. Italian by* Anita Barrows. VWA

Sisters, The. Roy Campbell. BoLoP; FaBoTw (1975 ed.)

Sisters, The. Amy Lowell. SBG

Sisters. Sandra McPherson. AmPA

Sisters. Adrienne Rich. IHMS

Sisters. Alberta Turner. HeS

Sisters,/ The Blue Nun has eloped with one. With a Bottle of Blue Nun to All My Friends. Madeline DeFrees. CNW; GP; MPA

Sisters are always drying their hair. Triolet against Sisters. Phyllis McGinley. MiP

Sisters, Daughters. Roderick Hartigh Jellema. PoUp

Sisters, listen to my story. The Kent State Massacre. Jack Warshaw *and* Barbara Dane. FSW

Sisters, sisters:/ with your large brown eyes. That Life, That Love, That Fine. Horace Coleman. SES

Sisyphus. Robert J. Burdette. PoTa

Sisyphus. Robert Garioch. MS

Sit down by the side of your mother, my boy. Mother's Advice. *Unknown.* AmFP

Sit down with me awhile beside the heath-corner. Erica. Mary Ursula Bethell. ATNZ

Sit on the bed. I'm blind, and three parts shell. A Terre. Wilfred Owen. OxBTC

Site. Harry Clifton. IPM

Site of Ambush, *sel.* Eilean Ni Chuilleanain.
"At alarming bell daybreak, before." CIP

Sith, in dark speech, Carvilios hymn unfolds. Hymn to the Sun. C. M. Doughty. *Fr.* The Dawn in Britain. FaBoTw (1975 ed.)

Sith that you both are like in life. To a Married Couple That Could Not Agree. Timothy Kendall. PAIC

Sith Venus had her mole, Helen her stain. Against Proud Poor Phryna. John Davies of Hereford. FaBoEE

Sits at the window, waits the threatened steel. Medusa. Vincent O'Sullivan. ATNZ

Sitteth alle stille and herkneth to me. The Song of Lewes. *Unknown.* OxBM

Sitting, The. Maxine Chernoff. FiCh

Sitting alone (as one forsook). The Vision. Robert Herrick. CaPo

Sitting Alone in Tulsa Three A.M. Lance Henson. VoR

Sitting at a window. Mother Tabbyskins. Elizabeth Anna Hart. OxBChV

Sitting at her table, she serves. Nani. A. A. Rios. GP

Sitting at table, or. Dialectique. Hugh Maxton. CIP

Sitting at the kitchen table. Going Home. Thomas Lux. NVAP

Sitting Bard, The. Sir Owen Seaman. NOBL

Sitting Bear Mountain. Barbara Lovell. BCr

Sitting between the sea and the buildings. The Painter. John Ashbery. NOBA

Sitting Bull's Will versus the Sioux Treaty of 1868 and Monty Hall. A. K. Redwing. VoR

Sitting by the roadside on a summer day. Goober Peas. *Unknown.* FSW; PSoN

Sitting by the streams that glide. Bible, *O.T.* Psalms, CXXXVII, *paraphrased by* Thomas Carew. OAEL-1

Sitting down near him in the shade. The Smoker. Robert Huff. CNW; GP; PoW

Sitting Here. Robert Creeley. RRA

Sitting here in my house. Suburban Madrigal. John Updike. SoS

Sitting in Bib Overalls, Workshirt, Boots on the Monument to Liberty in the Center of the Square, Jacksonville, Illinois. Louis Daniel Brodsky. AMV-81

Sitting in my car. The Caller. Jim Mulac. AcAn

Sitting in the shelter of this porch, I struggle. The Origins of Escape. Charles P. R. Tisdale. AMV-81

Sitting in the Woods: A Contemplation. W. R. Moses. NCSH

Sitting, legs crossed, copper-toned old man. My Song. King D. Kuka. VoR

Sitting on the toilet. 38 Main Street. Lyn Lifshin. TV

Sitting straightbacked, a modest Irish miss. A Lesson in Love. Philip Hobsbaum. OxBTC

Sitting under the mistletoe. Mistletoe. Walter de la Mare. SO

Sitting up all night with a dead bear. Drinking with a Dead Bear. D. C. Berry. BCr

Sitting upright in the 2 a.m. blackness, off-balance. Too Many Miles of Sunlight between Us. Jack Myers. AMV-80

Situation. Langston Hughes. OBAL

6:00 A.M. Richard W. Thomas. TC

Six Badgers, The. Robert Graves. RAE

Six beds in a square room: you give your name. Wait. Timothy Steele. PoA

Six Creatures on the Way. Stanley Noyes. PoW

Six Days. Tom Raworth. TwMBP

Six days and only buzzing/ in the ears. Attempts: 1964. Gray Jacobik. PoUp

Six days before election—not a poster up! Cross of Flame. Robert Gessner. SPT

Six Days of Creation, The. James McAuley. CAAP

Six days on snowshoes. Hunting Fragment. Gary Lawless. FAF

Six disorderly bears. Bad Example. Isabella Fey. BoAnP

Six Divine Circles. Gail Ghai. AMV-81

Six Dukes Went a-Fishing. *Unknown.* FaBoBa

Six Eagles. Thomas Peacock. VoR

Six Feet Under. Janet Campbell Hale. VoR

Six-foot nest of the sea-hawk, The. Sea-Hawk. Richard Eberhart. BoAnP; EcS

Six foot two in his moccasins. Alibi. Zoe A. Tilghman. BPAW

Six-forty-two Farm Commune Struggle Poem. Jay Leifer. MAT

Six-Horse Limited Mail, The. Ethel Romig Fuller. BPAW

Six hundred dark feet from the cliffs. "But Still in Israel's Paths They Shine." Carter Revard. VoR

Six Hundred Thousand Letters, The. Harvey Shapiro. VWA

Six kilos of cat! Fat Cat. John Ronan. AMV-81

Six Kisses. Nancy Sullivan. LoAs

Six lessons. Ode to a Violin. Luís Omar Salinas. SA

Six Movements on a Theme. David Ignatow. NNaP

Six o'Clock. Trumbull Stickney. PPoB

Six o'clock and/ the sun rises across the river. Love Poem. Miller Williams. MAT

Six of them climbed aboard. The Boys. Anthony Thwaite. LP

6 p.m./ middle of South Dakota. After the Funeral of Assam Hamady. Sam Hamod. SA

Six Periods of Creation, The. *Maori Oral Tradition, tr. by* Richard Taylor. WTO

Six Poems. Joseph Freeman. SPT
 "Between us lies the issue clear," 5.
 "Hordes that battle for the world's domain, The," 4.
 "I accept the universe, which ranges," 3.
 "I grant you, then, the variants," 6.
 "Our age has Caesars, though they wear silk hats," 2.
 "Rise to the surface, O my hidden strength," 1.

Six Poets in Search of a Lawyer. Donald Hall. SoSe

Six porwigles. Porwigles. Julie Holder. FPB

Six Religious Lyrics, *sel.* Karl Shapiro.
 "I sing the simplest flower," I. CMoP (1970 ed.)

Six Reveilles to Match My Self-Indulgence, *sel.* Wilder Bentley.
 "Up, up, old Benedict, the bard who would," IV. MIT

Six, seven years ago. He Makes a House Call. John Stone. CSP

Six Significant Landscapes, *sel.* Wallace Stevens.
 "Rationalists, wearing square hats," VI. PoIA

Six Small Songs for a Silver Flute. Barry Spacks. PCho

Six Statues in a Park. Floyd C. Stuart. FAF

6/10/75. Darlene Pearlstein. FiCh

Six Ten Sixty-nine. Conyus. PoBA

Six Variations. Denise Levertov. ConAP
 "Shlup, shlup, the dog," *sel.* HeIP; InPK

Six Week Old Blues. *Unknown.* BluL

Six Years Later. Joseph Brodsky, *tr. fr. Russian by* Richard Wilbur. AMV-80

Six years Victoria's been throned. Four Victorian Photographs. Roger McDonald. FPA

Sixes and Sevens. Roderick Hartigh Jellema. AATT

"Sixpence a week," says the girl to her lover. By Aunt's Grave. Thomas Hardy. Satires of Circumstance, III. LFH; SFF

16/53. Marge Piercy. NeAC

Sixteen Warnings in Search of a Feminist Poem. Erica Jong. *See* Seventeen Warnings in Search of a Feminist Poem.

Sixteen years old and beautiful. Girl. A. W. Purdy. NoAM

6th and Walnut Street. Rubee Dreher Moxley. NPW

Sixth Day, The. Betty Adcock. LiSp

Sixth Hell, The. Jerome Rothenberg. *Fr.* The Seven Hells of Jigoku Zoshi. NNaP

Sixth Station, The. Jane Marie Luecke. AATT

Sixth Winter, The. Edwin Rolfe. SPT

Sixties, The. Thomas Listmann. AMV-80

Sixties, I think, were not a total loss, The. January 15 as a National Holiday. Carter Revard. VoR

Skagway. John Haines. CNW

Skaters, The. John Williams. CoPAm; LiSp

Skaters, The. Wordsworth. *Fr.* The Prelude, I. LiSp; SPo ("And in the frosty season, when the sun.") FSFS

'Skeeter and Peter, The. Marie Bruckman MacDonald. TDH

'Skeeters are [*or* am] a-hummin' on the [*or* de] honeysuckle vine. Kentucky Babe. Richard Henry Buck. BLSH; FSN

Skein, The. Carolyn Kizer. LoAs; VGW

Skeleton. Coleman Barks. *Fr.* Body Poems. NVAP

Skeleton, The. G. K. Chesterton. FaBoTw (1975 ed.)

Skeleton in Armor, The. Longfellow. CTV

Skeleton is hiding in the closet as it should, The. Everything in Its Place. Arthur Guiterman. ECBV; OBAL

Skeleton Key. John Hollander. InPK

Skeleton of the Great Moa in the Canterbury Museum, Christchurch, The. Allen Curnow. ATNZ

Skeleton Once in Khartoum, A. *Unknown.* IWK

Skeleton Walks, The. X. J. Kennedy. IWK

Skerryvore. Robert Louis Stevenson. ILP (1975 ed.)

Skerryvore: The Parallel. Robert Louis Stevenson. ILP (1975 ed.)

Sketch for a Job Application Blank. Jim Harrison. AmPA; NoAM

Sketch 48b.11. Ezra Pound. BBGO

Sketch from Loss of Memory. Sonya Dorman. SoS

Sketch of His Own Character. Thomas Gray. LAuP

Sketch of Lord Byron's Life. Julia A. Moore. OBAL

Sketches of Harlem. David Henderson. CABA (1972 ed.); PAIC

Ski Trail. Samuel Allen. FB

Skialetheia, *sel.* Everard Guilpin.
 "Let me alone, I prithee, in this cell," Satire V. TVS

Skid Row Safari. Elisabeth Murawski. PoUp

Skier. Robert Francis. LiSp; NCSH; RFM

Skiers. Robert Penn Warren. *Fr.* In the Mountains. LiSp; SPo; TCP

Skies have sunk and hid the upper snow, The. Les Vaches. Arthur Hugh Clough. PeD

Skies they were ashen and sober, The. Ulalume—a Ballad. Poe. LFH; NOBA; PiAm; TAP

Skiing champs, The. Hunger. Lennart Bruce. MiP

Skilful Spearman, A! *Tr. fr. Hawaiian.* WTO

Skill, A/ inborn or learned. Altered Circumstances. Francis Coleman Rosenberger. PoUp

Skill in Killing, A. George Abbe. FAF

Skilled to pull wires, he baffles Nature's hope. The Boss. James Russell Lowell. OBAL

Skimbleshanks: The Railway Cat. T. S. Eliot. FaBoCo; NOBL

Skimmers. Paul Baker Newman. CSP; EcS

Skimming lightly, wheeling still. Shiloh; a Requiem. Herman Melville. AmVN; FF; ILP (1975 ed.); NOBA

Skin. Roland Flint. PoUp

Skin. Philip K. Jason. AMV-81

Skin-and-Bone Lady, The. *Unknown.* AmFP

Skin Divers, The. George Starbuck. SPo

Skin Diving in the Virgins. John Malcolm Brinnin. TAP

Skin Flick. Fred Chappell. PPoD

Skin Man. *Unknown.* BluL

Skin of/ elm ebony eucalyptus. Emma in My Third Eye. Renée Roper. NPW

Skin of the sea, The. In Sylvia Plath Country. Erica Jong. IHMS

Skin quickens to noises, The. One Eyed Black Man in Nebraska. Sam Cornish. PoBA

Skin ripples over my body like moon-wooed water, The. Prison Song. Alan Dugan. PoA

Skin Song. Laurence Lieberman. CoPAm

Skin that is a closed curtain. Poll. Ed Roberson. PoBA

Skin the Goat's Curse on Carey. *Unknown.* BIrV

Skinfull of bowls, he bowls them. Second Glance at a Jaguar. Ted Hughes. NoAM

Skinning a Rabbit. Norbert Krapf. HeS

Skinny Girl, The. Anne Hébert, *tr. fr. French by* Willis Barnstone. BoWoP

Skinny Mrs. Snipkin. Mrs. Snipkin and Mrs. Wobblechin. Laura E. Richards. OxBChV

Skinny Salvador went in first, a diamond. Intimations at the Lake, 1963. Helena Minton. FAF

Skinny waterfalls, footpaths, The. Lastness. Galway Kinnell. NNaP

Skins hang on fence-wires, purple, blue and green. Delivering Lambs. David Campbell. MAuV

Skip to My Lou. *Unknown.* AmFP; ECBV; FSW

Skipper Ireson's Ride. Whittier. NOBA; OBAL

Skipping Stones. Allan D. Farber. SoSe

Skirt Dance. Ishmael Reed. FF

Skirting the river road (my forenoon walk, my rest). The Dalliance of the Eagles. Walt Whitman. BiP; BoAnP; CABA (1972 ed.); HAP; HeIP; InPK; LoAs; PiAm; POL; PPoe; PPP; TAP

Skittery two-year-olds. Morgans in October. Suzanne Brabant. PH

Skreak and skritter of evening gone, The. Autumn Refrain. Wallace Stevens. WeW

Skull. Coleman Barks. *Fr.* Body Poems. NVAP

Skull, The. Ian Young. NeAC

Skull closes like a closet, The. The Closet. Dave Smith. HeS

Skull in the Desert, The. Alison A. Trimpi. AMV-81

Skulls as Drums. John Wheelwright. SPT

Skunk cabbage, bloodroot. The Round. Philip Booth. NCSH

Skunk Hour. Robert Lowell. BiP; CAPP; CMoP (1970 ed.); ConAP; HAP; HeIP; ILP (1975 ed.); InPK; LFH; NIL; NoAM; NOBA; PiAm; PPP; STS; TAP; TCP; WeW

Skunk to the Gnu, The. Gerard Neyroud. TDH

Skunks, *sel.* Robinson Jeffers.
"We have little animals here." BoAnP

Sky, The. Susan Griffin. RiTi

Sky a black sphere, The. Lighthouse in the Night. Alfonsini Storni, *tr. by* Aliki *and* Willis Barnstone. BoWoP

Sky, a dome of glaring brass, The. 112 at Presidio. Virginia Long. AMV-80

Sky a shock, the gingkos yellow fever, The. Riverside Drive, November Fifth. Katha Pollitt. AMV-81

Sky, be blue, and more than blue. Denouement. Kenneth Fearing. SPT

Sky can't get in, The. Room. Shirley Kaufman. NMM

Sky Clears, The. *Tr. fr. Chippewa Indian by* Frances Densmore. OBVE

Sky Diver. Adrien Stoutenburg. LiSp; SPo; TSWA

Sky Diving. Richmond Lattimore. LiSp; SPo

Sky droops like the lapel on a corpse, The. Mother and the Moon. Martha Yoak. NPW

Sky hangs heavy tonight, The. Negro Woman. Lewis Alexander. PoBA

Sky House. Ralph Storey. SES

Sky is a dead fish, The. The Plaque in the Reading Room for My Classmates Killed in Korea. F. D. Reeve. GOA

Sky Is Blue, The. David Ignatow. FF; NNaP

Sky is blue, or something, The. Anyway, it's there. Words, for E. Tom Leonard. SLP

Sky is haywire alive with fire, The. Weeding in January. Louis Daniel Brodsky. AMV-80

Sky is low, the clouds are mean, The. Emily Dickinson. FSFS; PBMP

Sky is overcast, The. A Night-Piece. Wordsworth. Moon

Sky, lazily disdaining to pursue, The. Georgia Dusk. Jean Toomer. AmNP (1974 ed.); BPo; ILP (1975 ed.); NoAM; PoBA

Sky, The—like a lunatic's dream. Landscape. Abrahm Sutskever, *tr. by* Ruth Whitman. VWA

Sky links cloud waves, links dawn fog. Li Ch'ing-chao, *tr. fr. Chinese by* Willis Barnstone *and* Sun Chu-chin. BoWoP

Sky lowers, the angry weight, The. The Immigrant's Stars. Jordan Smith. AAN

Sky Patterns. Jeannette Maino. AMV-80

Sky so pale, and the trees, such frail things, The. A la Promenade. Paul Verlaine, *tr. by* Arthur Symons. OBVE

Sky-splitting Pink Rubber Bistro, The. Rochelle Owens. RiTi

Sky unfolding its blankets to free, The. Morning Workout. Babette Deutsch. LiSp

Sky walks into the florist's shop, The. Buying Lilies. Stephen Stepanchev. SA

Sky Was Candy Luminous, The. E. E. Cummings. AKE

Sky was gray, boats outlined the shore, The. The Invasion of America. Celino *and* Steff. EC

Sky was the white soil you. Drop. George MacBeth. TwMBP

Sky was yellow, The. Halloween. Ivy O. Eastwick. IWK

Skye Boat Song, *with music.* Sir Harold Boulton. GSB

Skykomish River Running. Richard Hugo. PoA

Skylark and Nightingale. Christina Rossetti. PCOP

Skylarks. Ted Hughes. HAP

Skylights purse red roofs in shallow. A Landscape by Cezanne. Art Lange. FiCh

Skyline of New York does not excite me, The. Review from Staten Island. Gloria C. Oden. PoBA; PPP

Skymen coming down out of the clouds land. A Poem for Deep Thinkers. Amiri Baraka. EC

Sky's unresting cloudland, that with varying play, The. Robert Bridges. *Fr.* The Testament of Beauty, I. EBEV

Skyscrapers. Rachel Field. ECBV

Skyscrapers Stand Proud. Carl Sandburg. PiAm

Slabs of Her Eyes, The. Patricia Goedicke. Psy

"Slack your rope, hangs-a-man." The Maid Freed from the Gallows [*or* The Hangman's Tree]. *Unknown.* AIW; ExPo (1973 ed.)

Slade's Anatomy of the Horse. Leon Slade. FPA

Slain Lamb of God, *with music.* Nicolaus L. Zinzendorf, *tr. fr. German by* Sheema Z. Buehne. AH

Slamming down of a badge, The. Resignation Day. Richard Friedman. FiCh

Slant of sun on dull brown walls, A. War Is Kind, XIV. Stephen Crane. AmVN; PiAm

Slant sheen/ wrinkled silver. Letters to Walt Whitman, II. Ronald Johnson. VGW

Slanted World. Rhyll McMaster. FPA

Slashed clouds leak gold. Along the slurping wharf. Fishing Harbour towards Evening. Richard Kell. CIP; LP; MPo

Slaughter-House, The. Alfred Hayes. NowV

Slaughterhouse Boys, The. William Meissner. AMV-81

Slaughter-Room Picture, The. David Steingass. CoPAm

Slave, The. James Oppenheim. PPM

Slave, The. Jones Very. TAP

Slave and the Iron Lace, The. Margaret Danner. AmNP (1974 ed.); BPo

Slave Auction, The. Frances E. W. Harper. BPo

Slave Marriage Ceremony Supplement. *Unknown.* BPo; POL; TAP

Slave Quarters. James Dickey. CAPP

Slave Singing at Midnight, The. Longfellow. GOA

Slavery. Robert Herrick. PAIC

Slavery Chain Done Broke at Last. *Unknown.* FSW

Slave's Dream, The. Longfellow. FaPoR

Sleek as a lizard at round of a stone. Penetration and Trust. George Meredith. VLP

Sleep M. R. Doty. AMV-80

Sleep. Bravig Imbs. EAS

Sleep. William Knott. EAS

Sleep. Greg Kuzma. NVAP

Sleep. Rhyll McMaster. CAAP

Sleep. Dana Naone. CDW

Sleep. Kenneth Slessor. GAS

Sleep. Yvor Winters. POL

Sleep aches deeply in the eyes; taste of ashes. Night-Shift. Joseph Kalar. SPT

Sleep and Poetry. Keats. MBPR
    *Sels.*
    "O for ten years, that I may overwhelm." OAEL-2; TT
    "What is more gentle than a wind in summer?" FSFS

Sleep, Angry Beauty, Sleep. Thomas Campion. FF

Sleep at noon. Window blind. Hurricane. Archibald MacLeish. NCSH

Sleep, baby mine, Desire, nurse Beauty singeth. Sir Philip Sidney. NOBE

Sleep Close to Me. Gabriela Mistral, *tr. fr. Spanish by* D. M. Pettinella. PBWP

Sleep, Darling. Sappho, *tr. fr. Greek by* Mary Barnard. IPWM

Sleep evades me, there's no light. Verses Written during a Sleepness Night. Pushkin, *tr. by* Babette Deutsch. PPM

Sleep half sleep half silence and with reasons. Sonnet. Ted Berrigan. CAAP; Epi

Sleep in the Heat. Laura Jensen. AmPA

Sleep insures/ an added identity. 10/17/75. Darlene Pearlstein. FiCh

Sleep is a country of water. Country of Water. Bernice Ames. WPE

Sleep is the gift of many spiders. Drowsy. Carl Sandburg. OSP

Sleep late with your dream. Owen Dodson. *Fr.* Poems for My Brother Kenneth. PoBA

Sleep-Learning. Ruth Fainlight. NMM

Sleep, Leviathan, shouldering the Asian. Looking at Kapiti. Alistair Campbell. ATNZ

Sleep, McKade. Evening Song. Kenneth Fearing. EAS

Sleep, Mr. Speaker! it's surely fair. Stanzas to the Speaker Asleep. Winthrop Mackworth Praed. OBSV; VLP

Sleep, my child [*or* love], and peace attend thee. All through the Night. Harold Boulton, *also at. to* David Owen. BLSH; FSW; GSB

Sleep my child, sleep. Shlof Mayn Kind, Shlof Keseyder (Sleep My Child). *Unknown.* FSW

Sleep, my child—sleep, it is late! Lullaby for Miriam. Richard Beer-Hofmann, *tr. by* Jonathan Griffin. VWA

Sleep, my love, and peace attend thee. *See* Sleep, my child, and peace attend thee.

Sleep now. Lullaby. Shlomo Vinner, *tr. by* Laya Firestone. VWA

Sleep now, O sleep now. James Joyce. GBL

Sleep of the late afternoon, The. Resounding. Katherine Soniat. AMV-81

Sleep on, my love, in thy cold bed. Henry King. *Fr.* Exequy on His Wife. PoPle

Sleep on the Fraser. Patrick Lane. NeAC

Sleep only with strangers. George Jonas. NeAC

Sleep plays hide-and-seek with darkness. Night Blessing. Philip William George. VW

Sleep, sleep, poor youth! sleep, sleep in peace. Thomas Durfey. *Fr.* Don Quixote. SCP-2

Sleep softly. . .eagle forgotten. . .under the stone. The Eagle That Is Forgotten. Vachel Lindsay. CMoP (1970 ed.); NOBA; VoPo

Sleep sweetly in your humble graves. Ode. Henry Timrod. AH; AmVN; GOA; NOBA; TAP

Sleep was only a dream. Chicago: Near West-Side Renewal. Dennis Schmitz. AmPA

Sleep Watch. Lance Henson. VoR

Sleepdancers, The. Peter Viereck. BCr

Sleeper, The. Sydney Clouts. VWA

Sleeper, The. Edward Field. LiSp; SPo

Sleeper, The. Poe. NOBA; TAP

Sleeper, The. William Soutar. SLP

Sleeper Rise. *Gond Oral Tradition, tr. by* V. Elwin *and* S. Hivale. WTO

Sleeping/ under the longest root. In the Generation That Laughed at Me. Susan Hartman. AAN

Sleeping Alone. Kurt J. Fickert. AMV-80

Sleeping at Last. Christina Rossetti. HeIP

Sleeping at the Beach. Lucile Burt. AMV-81

Sleeping Beauty. Olga Broumas. CNW

Sleeping Beauty, The, *sel.* Edith Sitwell.
    "In the great gardens, after bright spring rain." OxBTC
    (Innocent Spring, The.) NOBE

Sleeping Beauty, The: Variation of the Prince. Randall Jarrell. PoA

Sleeping Fury, The. Louise Bogan. IHMS; RiTi

Sleeping Giant, The. Donald Hall. NCSH

Sleeping in a Cave. Naomi Shihab Hye. AMV-81

Sleeping in fever, I am unfit. For God while Sleeping. Anne Sexton. CABA (1972 ed.); CAPP; CoPAm

Sleeping in the Forest. Mary Oliver. NU

Sleeping in the Woods. David Wagoner. MPA

Sleeping Lord, The, *sel.* David Jones.
    "Tawny-black sky-scurries." OBW

Sleeping on the Sisters Land. William Stafford. CNW

Sleeping Out in Vermont. Conrad Hilberry. PPoD

Sleeping Out with My Father. Gibbons Ruark. CSP

Sleeping Pill. Diana O Hehir. AMV-81

Sleeping with Foxes. Roberta Hill. CDW

Sleeping with Women. Kenneth Koch. NoAM

Sleepless. Al-Khansa, *tr. fr. Arabic by* Willis Barnstone. BoWoP

Sleepless ghost perpetually striving, The. Eros Out of the Sea. Dilys Bennett Laing. PoA

Sleepless hours who watch me as I lie, The. Hymn of Apollo. Shelley. ILP (1975 ed.); MBPR; OAEL-2

Sleepless on a Summer Night. Umberto Saba, *tr. fr. Italian by* Keith Bosley. VWA

Sleeplessly circle the waves. Laurence Binyon. *Fr.* Look Not Too Deep. EcS

Sleeplessness of Our Time. R. A. D. Ford. AMV-81

Sleepmonger,/ deathmonger. The Addict. Anne Sexton. CTBA

Sleepwalker, The. Nelly Sachs, *tr. fr. German by* Michael Hamburger. BoWoP

Sleepwalkers. Bella Akhmadulina, *tr. fr. Russian by* Barbara Einzig. BoWoP

Sleepwalkers' Ballad. Federico García Lorca. *See* Somnambulistic Ballad.

Sleepy Betsy from her pillow. The Bedpost. Robert Graves. SO

Sleepy little village, The. Medora, N.D. Richard Lyons. HeS

Sleepy Man Blues. *Unknown.* BluL

Sleepy Song. Arthur Guiterman. ECBV

Sleet Storm on the Merritt Parkway. Robert Bly. ConAP; NOBA

Sleight-of-Hand. Bruce Dawe. CAAP

Slender Fingers ("Slender, delicate, soft jade"). Chao Luan-luan, *tr. fr. Chinese by* Kenneth Rexroth *and* Ling Chung. BoWoP

Slender Lad, The. *Unknown, tr. fr. Welsh by* Kenneth Jackson. OBW

Slender Maid. Joseph Eliyia, *tr. fr. Modern Greek by* Rae Dalven. VWA

Slender man in jogging duds. Running Blind. Nancy Jones. LiSp

Slice of Wedding Cake, A. Robert Graves. BoLoP; BuTh; NOBE; OxBTC

Sliced with shade and scarred with snow. Inverbeg. J. F. Hendry. MS

Slicing Button Mushrooms. Derek Bowman. MIS

Slide Night. Andrew Taylor. FPA

Sliding on Skates in Very Hard Frost. Nahum Tate. SCP-2

Sliding Scale. Norman R. Jaffray. TDH

Sliding step unlocks a hero's cure, A. Oedipus, Pentheus. David Bromwich. AMV-81

Sliding Trombone. Georges Ribemont-Dessaignes, *tr. fr. French by* David Gascoyne. EAS

Sliding Two Mirrors. Tom Raworth. TwMBP

Slight Confusion, A. James Reiss. AmPA

Slight of Hands, A. Karren L. Alenier. PoUp

Slight unpremeditated words are borne. Love's Witness. Aphra Behn. BoWoP

Slightly before the middle of Congressman Pudd. E. E. Cummings. FaBoEE; OBAL

Slim/ city. Tree. Mbembe. NW

Slim and singing copper girl, A. Early Copper. Carl Sandburg. HeIP; PiAm

Slim Cunning Hands. Walter de la Mare. FaBoEE; NIL

Slim dragonfly. Arthur Mitchell. Marianne Moore. PiAm

Slim in Hell ("Slim Greer went to heaven"). Sterling A. Brown. BPo; FB

Slim Man Canyon. Leslie Silko. VoR

Slimy obscene creatures, insane. The Nigga Section. Welton Smith. BPo

Slip of loveliness, slim, seemly. In Praise of a Girl. Huw Morus, *tr. by* Gwyn Williams. OBW

Slip off the husk of gravity to lie. The New Icarus. Vassar Miller. TPo

Slipping on snow. A Question of Balance. Fay Enos. PHC

Slipping Out of Intensive Care. Florence Trefethen. AMV-80

Slipping, she fell into the sitting-room. Girl with Coffee Tray. John Fuller. LP

Sloped-down shark nose. Regarding Wave, II. Gary Snyder. CAAP

Sloping at a 45° angle. Umbaji Park. David Kherdian. SA

Sloth, The. Isabella Gardner. BoAnP

Sloth, The. Theodore Roethke. OBAL; SS

Slouches over four-bit beers. The Linebacker at Forty. Jon Wallace. AMV-81

Slovenly Peter. Heinrich Hoffmann. *Poems indexed separately by titles and first lines.*

Slow Boone. Hildegarde Flanner. WPW

Slow, cold breathing, The. The Marsh, New Year's Day. Peter Everwine. NNaP

Slow Dance. David St. John. AmPA

Slow Dancer That No One Hears but You. Duane Niatum. CDW

Slow down,/ You move too fast. The 59th Street Bridge Song. Paul Simon. TCP

Slow Drag Dead. Alcide Pavageau. Miller Williams. TAT

Slow, heavy, deadly was my pace: the cold. Death. Keats. *Fr.* The Fall of Hyperion. OBP

Slow lines lay down the curve, curve. Mother in the 45¢ Bottle. Paul Blackburn. NYP

Slow Mama Slow. *Unknown.* BluL

Slow May. Spring in These Hills. Archibald MacLeish. NCSH

Slow Movement. William Carlos Williams. PoA

Slow moves the acid breath of noon. Field of Autumn. Laurie Lee. NCSH

Slow Oxen. Ilya Rubin, *tr. fr. Russian by* Linda Zisquit. VWA

Slow Pacific Swell, The. Yvor Winters. HeIP; NoAM; NOBA; PiAm

Slow pass the hours—ah, passing slow! Ballade Tragique à Double Refrain. Max Beerbohm. OBSV

Slow Rain. Gabriela Mistral, *tr. fr. Spanish by* Gunda Kaiser *and* James Tipton. PBWP

Slow Riff for Billy. James Cunningham. JB

Slow sail'd the weary mariners and saw. The Sea-Fairies. Tennyson. EcS

Slow sleepy curl of cigaret smoke and butts, The. Worker Uprooted. Joseph Kalar. SPT

Slow, slow, fresh fount, keep time with my salt tears. Echo's Lament of Narcissus. Ben Jonson. *Fr.* Cynthia's Revels. ExPo (1973 ed.); ILP (1975 ed.); InPK; NIL; OAEL-1; PoIA; SoSe

Slow Spring. Katharine Tynan. FSFS

Slow Starter, The. Louis MacNeice. MPo; PBMP

Slow Sun./ Deep Dew. Stubborn Ground. Patricia Elliott. EC

Slow the Kansas sun was setting o'er the wheat fields far away. Towser Shall Be Tied Tonight. *Unknown.* BoAnP

Slow to Come, Quick a-Gone. William Barnes. VLP

Slow toiling upward from the misty vale. Nearing the Snow-Line. Oliver Wendell Holmes. PiAm

Slowly. Mary Elizabeth Coleridge. SoSe (1977 ed.)

Slowly, by God's Hand Unfurled, *with music.* William Henry Furness. AH

Slowly he sways that head that cannot hear. Rattler, Alert. Brewster Ghiselin. HAP; WeW

Slowly, O so slowly, longing rose up. Christ Walking on the Water. W. R. Rodgers. NoAM

Slowly, silently, now the moon. Silver. Walter de la Mare. CTV; ILP (1975 ed.); IPWM; PPM; SS

Slowly, Slowly. *Unknown, tr. fr. Gabon Pygmy by* C. M. Bowra. WeW

Slowly, Slowly Wisdom Gathers. Mark Van Doren. PoA

Slowly the muddy pool becomes a river. Let the Dead Depart in Peace. *Yoruba Oral Tradition, tr. by* Ulli Beier. WTO

Slowly the night blooms, unfurling. Flowers of Darkness. Frank Marshall Davis. AmNP (1974 ed.); PoBA

Slowly the poison the whole blood stream fills.  Missing Dates.
William Empson.  CMoP (1970 ed.); HAP; ILP (1975 ed.);
NIL; NoAM; NOBE; OAEL-2; PAIC; PSN; UnPo (1976 ed.)

Slowly the ponderous doors of lead imponderous.  Sleep.  Bravig
Imbs.  EAS

Slowly the salt of the earth becomes salt of the sea.  Salt of the
Earth.  D. H. Lawrence.  NoAM

Slowly the sea is parted from the sky.  North of Berwick.
Sydney Tremayne.  MS

Slowly the women file to where he stands.  Faith Healing.  Philip
Larkin.  NoAM

Slowly, without sun, the day sinks.  Fairbanks under the Solstice.
John Haines.  CNW

Slowness ("Slowness, says Rodin, is beauty").  Gibbons Ruark.
SFF

Slug.  Gwen Head.  GP

Slug.  Theodore Roethke.  CABA (1972 ed.)

Sluggard, The.  Isaac Watts.  HAP; OxBChV; SpRo

Slugs.  John Kitching.  FPB

Slumber Did My Spirit Seal, A.  Wordsworth.  Fr. Lucy.
AnMo; BiP; CABA (1972 ed.); ExPo (1973 ed.); HAP; HeIP;
ILP (1975 ed.); InPK; InPS; IP; MBPR; NIL; NOBE;
OAEL-2; PAIC; PBMP; PoIA; PoPle; PPP; UnPo (1976 ed.)

Slumber Party.  Carson McCullers.  CTV

Slumbersong.  Rainer Maria Rilke, tr. fr. German by M. D. Herter
Norton.  LoAs

Slump.  Vassar Miller.  BoWoP

Slurped/ and waters moved.  Lee-ers of Hew.  James
Cunningham.  JB

Sly ducks, The.  The Rushes of Radnor Pond.  Tony Friedson.
PHC

Smack on his back in the snow.  Roger Pfingston.  Fr. Two
Stories about Cameras.  BCr

Small, The.  Theodore Roethke.  SO

Small, A/ bottle/ of blackish.  Death [or Dance].  Lynn
Sukenick.  CPA; RiTi

Small Aircraft.  Bella Akhmadulina, tr. fr. Russian by Daniel
Halpern.  BoWoP

Small as a fox and like.  Our Lucy (1956-1960).  Paul Goodman.
GDP

Small bird/ tracks.  Rain.  Lance Henson.  VoR

Small Bird's Nest Made of White Reed Fiber, A.  Robert Bly.
NNaP

Small birds play in the ivy.  A Spring Day on Campus.  Gilbert
Schedler.  AMV-80

Small birds swirl around, The.  The Small.  Theodore Roethke.
SO

Small black blobs on the beach are the heads, The.  The Class.
Josephine Jacobsen.  GP

Small blue flowers like points.  The Voice.  Philip Levine.
PCho

Small-boned/ quicksilver thing.  Quicksilver Thing.  Philip
Legler.  TC

Small Bones Ache.  Moshe Dor, tr. fr. Hebrew by Ruth Fainlight.
VWA

Small boy, four years, A.  Terminal.  D. J. Enright.  HeHu; LP

Small boys and girls can draw a house.  Drawing.  Roy Fuller.
MN

Small Brown Bear, The.  Michael Baldwin.  FPB

Small, busy flames play through the fresh laid coals.  To My
Brothers.  Keats.  MBPR; TT

Small Celandine, The.  Wordsworth.  MBPR

Small child of a wind, A.  Requiem for Sonora.  Richard Shelton.
MPA

Small children starved to death.  After Advertising Ended.  Ed
Ochester.  AAN

Small Comment.  Sonia Sanchez.  NIL

Small Country.  Claribel Alegría, tr. fr. Spanish by Aliki and Willis
Barnstone.  BoWoP

Small Discovery, A.  James A. Emanuel.  LCL

Small dogs look at the big dogs, The.  The Seeing Eye.  Ezra
Pound.  ExPo (1973 ed.)

Small Dragon, A.  Brian Patten.  DuDr; LP

Small Elegy, A.  Jiri Orten, tr. fr. Czech by Lyn Coffin.  AMV-81

Small eyes water on the branch.  Another Face.  Ray A. Young
Bear.  CDW

Small Farm, A.  Michael Hartnett.  CIP

Small Favors.  Dale Matthews.  AAN

Small finger curves outward, A.  Lemuel Johnson.  Fr. Hand on
the Navel.  AAN

Small Frogs Killed on the Highway.  James Wright.  NNaP

Small Hotel, The.  Michael Longley.  CIP

Small jeweled creatures.  Hummingbirds.  E. Margaret Clarkson.
AATT

Small lights pirouette.  Peterhead in May.  Burns Singer.  MS

Small man suffers the indignities of childhood, The.  Paul Klee.
Ruthven Todd.  EAS

Small metal box I was given.  The Charge.  Anselm Hollo.
TwMBP

Small nests/ On branches up high.  A Bird's Nest.  Erez Biton,
tr. by Judith Katz.  VWA

Small Poem about the Hounds and the Hares.  Lisel Mueller.
GP

Small Prayer.  Weldon Kees.  PoA; VGW

Small procession waddles single file, A.  Ducks.  Phoebe Hesketh.
BoAnP

Small Room with Large Windows, A.  Allen Curnow.  ATNZ

Small Score, A.  Delmore Schwartz.  PBMP

Small service is true service while it lasts.  Written in the Album
of a Child.  Wordsworth.  OxBChV

Small, significant bumps would appear on your skin.  If I Were in
Charge of Epiphanies.  Stephen Dunn.  NVAP

Small Song.  A. R. Ammons.  POL

Small space.  Two Tile Beaks.  Maria Amalia Fonte Boa, tr. by
Willis Barnstone and Nelson Cerqueira.  BoWoP

Small Talk.  Don Marquis.  PoTa

Small Town History.  John L. Sellers.  DNGG

Small Town: The Friendly.  Stephen Dunn.  POL

Small Tribute, A.  William Harrold.  HeS

Small type of great ones, that do hum.  A Fly Caught in a
Cobweb.  Richard Lovelace.  CaPo

Small vellum environment, A.  Page from the Koran.  James
Merrill.  PCho

Small War, A.  Leslie Norris.  HeHu

Small White House.  Robert Penn Warren.  Fr. Notes on a Life
to Be Lived.  NoAM

Small Woman on Swallow Street.  W. S. Merwin.  ConAP

Smaller role for peanut butter, A.  Being Adult.  Bill Zavatsky.
POL

Smaller than molehills their breasts.  A View toward Wife
Trading.  Robert Gillespie.  NVAP

Smallest breath.  Two Clouds.  Lawrence Raab.  AMV-80

Smart and stylish girl and you see, A.  Ta-Ra-Ra Boom-De-Ay!
Unknown.  FSN; VLP

Smart Little Bear, The.  Mark Fenderson.  TDH

Smart little gent with the shoebutton eyes, The.  Wiseguy Type.
Herman Spector.  SPT

Smart man was Bishop Colenso, A.  Colenso Rhymes for
Orthodox Children.  Bret Harte.  OBAL

Smear of blue peat smoke, The.  The Shepherd's Hut.  Andrew
Young.  OxBTC

Smell!  William Carlos Williams.  TAP; WeW

Smell of death is so powerful, The.   Marguerite de Navarre, *tr. fr. French by* Aline Allard.   PBWP

Smell of drought on every side.   Smell of Rain.   Sharlot Hall.   WPW

Smell of fresh wood or lumbermen carving, The.   Digging for Singapore.   David James.   TC

Smell of Life, The.   Morty Sklar.   AcAn

Smell of Rain.   Sharlot Hall.   WPW

Smell of sage, The.   Church Poem.   Joyce Carol Thomas.   CNA

Smell of Wood, The.   John Stevens Wade.   FAF

Smell of woodyards in the rain is strong, The.   Woodyards in the Rain.   Anne Marriott.   AKE

Smelling a Stone in the Middle of Winter.   Tom Hennen.   HeS

Smelling coffee.   The Salesman.   Mary Moore.   NPW

Smells.   Ronald Koertge.   PoW

Smile, The.   Joan Aiken.   TVo

Smile, The.   Blake.   MBPR

Smile.   D. M. Thomas.   AMV-81

Smile/ to see the lake.   Lorine Niedecker.   VGW

Smile at Me.   Musa Moris Farhi.   VWA

Smile at the Birdie.   Polly Mann.   NPW

Smile at us, pay us, pass us; but do not quiet forget.   The Secret People.   G. K. Chesterton.   FaPoR; OxBTC

Smile, Death.   Charlotte Mew.   WPE

Smile is already there, The.   Smile.   D. M. Thomas.   AMV-81

Smile of iceboxes annihilates me, The.   An Appearance.   Sylvia Plath.   CAPP

Smile Was, The.   Dannie Abse.   PMW

Smiling girls, rosy boys.   Mother Goose.   ECBV

Smiling morn, the breathing spring, The.   The Birks of Invermay.   David Mallet.   SLP

Smiling Mouth and Laughing Eyen Grey, The.   Charles d'Orléans.   HAP

Smith at the organ is like an anvil being.   The Sound of Afroamerican History Chapt II.   S. E. Anderson.   PoBA

Smith Brothers' Lumber Shed.   Hildegarde Flanner.   WPW

SMLE.   Les A. Murray.   CAAP

Smoke.   Jane Cooper.   UsP

Smoke.   Henry David Thoreau.   AmVN; IPWM (Light-winged Smoke, Icarian Bird.)   ILP (1975 ed.); NOBA; TAP

Smoke-color; haze thinly over the hills, low hanging.   August.   William Everson.   PiAm

Smoke contending with smoke which will be maddest.   Portrait of an Engine Driver.   Bobi Jones, *tr. by* Joseph P. Clancy.   OBW

Smoke from the train-gulf hid by hoardings blunders upward.   Birmingham.   Louis MacNeice.   CMoP (1970 ed.); ILP (1975 ed.)

Smoke of Birds, A.   Malcolm Cowley.   TSWA

Smoke, shadowy deep smoke.   Masks.   Brian Swann.   AMV-81

Smoke Shop Owner's Daughter, The.   Jean Garrigue.   UsP

Smoke when the sun fell and when it rose.   Peter Levi.   *Fr.* Life Is a Platform.   FaBoTw (1975 ed.)

Smoked Herring, The.   Charles Cros, *tr. fr. French by* A. L. Lloyd.   PoTa

Smoker, The.   Robert Huff.   CNW; GP; PoW

Smoker Parrot, The.   John Shaw Neilson.   MAuV

Smokestack Lightnin'.   *Unknown.*   BluL

Smokey the Bear Sutra.   *Unknown.*   MAT

Smokey's Gettin' Old.   Jessica Tarahata Hagedorn.   MMD

Smoking all that much has got her eyes.   He Records a Little Song for a Smoking Girl.   James Whitehead.   GP

Smoking Drugs wtih Strangers.   George Bowering.   NeAC

Smoking My Prayers.   Simon Ortiz.   VW

Smoky rain riddles the ocean plains, A.   My Father Paints the Summer.   Richard Wilbur.   NCSH; NOBA

Smoldering dry fern.   And What of Me?   Liz Sohappy Bahe.   CDW

Smooth lake, The.   Wilderness.   Ralph Mecklenburger.   SFF

Smooth smell of Manhattan taxis, The.   Dance of the Infidels.   Al Young.   PoBA

Smooth song/ the jukebox sang.   Rosie Bakungan.   Edward Smith.   EC

Smudging.   Diane Wakoski.   AmPA

Smugglers, The.   Owen Wister.   BPAW

Smuggler's Song, A.   Kipling.   *Fr.* Puck of Pook's Hill.   DuDr; OxBChV; PoPle; PoTa

Snail, The.   Vincent Bourne, *tr. fr. Latin by* William Cowper.   OBVE

Snail.   John Drinkwater.   LCL; RAE

Snail, The.   A. P. Herbert.   BoAnP

Snail, The.   Richard Lovelace.   CaPo; OAEL-1; SCP-2

Snail, The.   James Reeves.   ECBV

Snail ("The snail crawls over blackness").   Shinkichi Takahashi, *tr. fr. Japanese by* Lucien Stryk *and* Takashi Ikemoto.   NU

Snail is climbing up the window-sill, A.   For a Five-Year-Old.   Fleur Adcock.   ATNZ

Snail moves like a, The.   Hedgehog.   Paul Muldoon.   BIrV

Snail pushes through a green, The.   Considering the Snail.   Thom Gunn.   MPA; SoSe (1977 ed.)

Snail upon the wall.   Snail.   John Drinkwater.   LCL; RAE

Snail who had a way, it seems, A.   The Snail's Dream.   Oliver Herford.   CTV; PCOP

Snails.   *Aborigine Oral Tradition.*   WTO

Snail's Dream, The.   Oliver Herford.   CTV; PCOP

"Snails lead slow idyllic lives."   The Widow's Yard.   Isabella Gardner.   RiTi

Snail's Monologue, The.   Christian Morgenstern, *tr. fr. German by* Max Knight.   BoAnP

Snake.   D. H. Lawrence.   CMoP (1970 ed.); HeIP; HoPM (1975 ed.); ILP (1975 ed.); NoAM; NOBE; NU; OAEL-2; PPP

Snake.   David McCord.   CaYB

Snake, The.   Morton Marcus.   CPA

Snake.   Theodore Roethke.   AKE; ECBV; MPA; NOBA; RFM

Snake and the Snake-Charmer, The.   E. V. Rieu.   ECBV

Snake came to my water-trough, A.   Snake.   D. H. Lawrence.   CMoP (1970 ed.); HeIP; HoPM (1975 ed.); ILP (1975 ed.); NoAM; NOBE; NU; OAEL-2; PPP

Snake-Charmer, The.   Thomas Gordon Hake.   VLP

Snake-Charmer, The.   Sarojini Naidu.   PBWP

Snake climbs.   Snake Poem I.   Joy Harjo.   SA

Snake Dance.   Lyn Lifshin.   FAF; RiTi

Snake Doctor Blues.   *Unknown.*   BluL

Snake Eyes.   Amiri Baraka.   VGW

Snake Handling Religious Service.   Charles Wright.   *Fr.* Tattoos.   GP

Snake Hill.   Joseph Bruchac.   NW

Snake Hill.   Jay Parini.   AMV-81

Snake horse stops at bronx clouds.   Bronxomania.   Victor Hernández Cruz.   SA

Snake Hunt.   David Wagoner.   GP

Snake Poem I.   Joy Harjo.   SA

Snake Rock.   Christopher Middleton.   FoP

Snake Sermon.   Dave Smith.   CSP

Snake tooth pinches his own mail, The.   Remorse.   Richard Lattimore.   PoA

Snake Yarn, A.   W. T. Goodge.   ECBV

Snakehips, the bandleader, wore a gallant grin.   The Bombing of the Cafe de Paris 1941.   Vernon Scannell.   HeHu

Snakes.   Peter Wild.   AmPA; GP

Snakes, Mongooses, Snake-Charmers and the Like. Marianne Moore. CMoP (1970 ed.); ExPo (1973 ed.)

Snakes of September, The. Stanley Kunitz. AMV-81

Snapper, The. William Heyen. AmPA

Snaps for Dinner, Snaps for Breakfast, and Snaps for Supper. George Moses Horton. OBAL

Snapshot. Colette Inez. AATT

Snapshot for Miss Bricka Who Lost in the Semifinal Round of the Pennsylvania Lawn Tennis Tournament at Haverford, July, 1960, A. Robert Wallace. LiSp

Snapshot of a Pedant. George Garrett. WIF

Snapshots. Ron McCurdy. PHC

Snapshots of a Daughter-in-Law. Adrienne Rich. NIL; NMM
"You, once a belle in Shreveport," I. NCSH

Snapshots of the Cotton South. Frank Marshall Davis. PoBA

Snare, The. James Stephens. CMoP (1970 ed.); ECBV

Snaw, snaw, coom faster. Snow. Unknown. GBP

Snawdon Woods. Forbes Macgregor. MIS

Sneaked about here. By the Road. Geoffrey Grigson. OxBTC

Sneeze on a Monday, sneeze for danger. Mother Goose. MG

Snickles and podes. Mean Song. Eve Merriam. CaYB

Sniff of the real, that's, The. Autobiography. Thom Gunn. FoP

Sniffed, dilating my nostrils. Elvin's Blues. Michael S. Harper. BPo

Snoring Bedmate, The. Unknown, tr. fr. Irish by John V. Kelleher. BIrV

Snorting his pleasure in the dying sun. Landscape, Deer Season. Barbara Howes. LiSp; MiP; POL

Snow. Kenneth O. Hanson. MPA

Snow. Louis MacNeice. BiP; CIP; CMoP (1970 ed.); ExPo (1973 ed.); NoAM; NOBE; OxBTC

Snow. Edward Thomas. FaBoTw (1975 ed.)

Snow. Unknown. GBP

Snow. Hubert Witheford. ATNZ

Snow/ on insulated roofs. Reflections on Limitations. Albert Howard Carter. AATT

Snow Chant. T. Alan Broughton. FAF

Snow circles the barn, wanting to break in. Winter Lambing. James Tipton. TC

Snow Country. David Etter. SFF

Snow Country Weavers. James Welch. CDW; MPA

Snow dances and the frost flies, The. Plum Blossoms. Chu Shu-chên, tr. by Kenneth Rexroth and Ling Chung. PBWP

Snow dissolv'd no more is seen, The. Horace, tr. by Samuel Johnson. Odes, IV, 7. LAuP; OBVE

Snow drifts melt in the streets, pock-marked at the curb. What Train Will Come? William Jay Smith. PPoD

Snow falling and night falling fast, oh, fast. Desert Places. Robert Frost. BiP; CABA (1972 ed.); CMoP (1970 ed.); ILP (1975 ed.); IP; IPWM; LFH; NCSH; NoAM; NOBA; PiAm; PPoD; PPP; TAP; TT; UnPo (1976 ed.)

Snow falling outside, The. Written on a Paper Napkin. Len Gasparini. NeAC

Snow falls deep, The; the forest lies alone. Gipsies [or Gypsies]. John Clare. Epi; ILP (1975 ed.); OBP

Snow falls like wedding rice. Coming On to Winter. Doug Flaherty. HeS

Snow falls on the cars in Doctor's Row and hoods the headlights. Doctors' Row. Conrad Aiken. HAP; NYP

Snow falls, stops, starts again. A House by the Tracks. Dave Etter. TAT

Snow fell/ on the smiling of the sheep. Christmas Morning. Steven Lautermilch. AMV-80

Snow-Girl. Yunna Moritz, tr. fr. Russian by Elaine Feinstein. VWA

Snow-Gum, The. Douglas Stewart. GAS; MAuV

Snow had begun in the gloaming, The. The First Snowfall. James Russell Lowell. TAP

Snow has left the cottage top, The. February. John Clare. Fr. The Shepherd's Calendar. NOBE

Snow-hills all about. Ice-Skaters. Elder Olson. LiSp

Snow in Europe. David Gascoyne. LP; MPo

Snow in Jerusalem, A. Hayim Naggid, tr. fr. Hebrew by Shlomo Vinner and Howard Schwartz. VWA

Snow in Madrid. Joy Davidman. SPT

Snow in New York. May Swenson. NYP; UsP

Snow in Summer. Daisy Aldan. RiTi

Snow in the City. Rachel Field. ECBV

Snow in the City. Danny Siegel. VWA

Snow in the Suburbs. Thomas Hardy. CMoP (1970 ed.); ILP (1975 ed.); IPWM; OAEL-2; OxBTC; PPP

Snow Is for Tracking the Invisible Man. Shiela Heldenbrand. AcAn

Snow is lying on my roof. Lullabye. Kathryn Stripling. AMV-80

Snow is out of fashion. Snow in the City. Rachel Field. ECBV

Snow Lies Sprinkled on the Beach, The. Robert Bridges. EcS; NoAM

Snow Line. John Berryman. Fr. Dream Songs. PoA

Snow Man. See Snowman.

Snow on my brother's grave. Afternoon. George Scarbrough. CSP

Snow on Saddle Mountain, The. Kenji Miyazawa, tr. fr. Japanese by Gary Snyder. IPWM; NoAM; NOBA

Snow Party, The. Derek Mahon. CIP

Snow, Snow. Marge Piercy. AMV-81

Snow squall comes down, A. High Field—First Day of Winter. Gary Eddy. AMV-80

Snow-Stars. Frances Frost. CTV

Snow Storm. See Snowstorm.

Snow that never drifts, The. Emily Dickinson. SoSe

Snow went into the steaming radiators. Convoy. James Neugass. SPT

Snow White. Robert Gillespie. NVAP

Snow White. Ed Ochester. GP

Snow-white clouds did float on high, The. A Father Out, an' Mother Hwome. William Barnes. VPC

Snow wind-whipt to ice. Winter. Richard Hughes. OBW

Snow-Ball, The. Soame Jenyns, after the Latin of Petronius Afranius. OBVE

Snow-bound; a Winter Idyl. Whittier. AmVN, abr.; NOBA; PiAm; TAP
"Sun that brief December day, The," sel. FSFS

Snowbound City, The. John Haines. EAS

Snowdrop, The. Samuel Taylor Coleridge. PF

Snowdrop, The. Walter de la Mare. PF

Snowdrop, The. Tennyson. FSFS

Snowdrop in purest white arraie, The. A Church Calendar of English Flowers. Unknown. PF

Snowdrops. Margiad Evans. OBW

Snowfall, A. Richard Eberhart. FiCP

Snowfall, The. Gwerfyl Mechain, tr. fr. Welsh by Kenneth Jackson. OBW

Snowfall, The. Donald Justice. CoPAm; VGW

Snowfall. W. S. Merwin. NNaP

Snowfall in the Afternoon. Robert Bly. CAPP; EAS; NOBA

Snow-Flake, The. Walter de la Mare. FSFS; LCL; NCSH

Snowflake on asphodel, clear ice on rose. Conrad Aiken. CMoP (1970 ed.)

Snow-Flakes. Longfellow. FSFS; NOBA; TAP; UnPo (1976 ed.)

Snowfox, The. Arctic Vixen. Michael Baldwin. FPB

Snow Man, The. Wallace Stevens. CABA (1972 ed.); CMoP (1970 ed.); HAP; HeIP; InPK; MAT; NU; PiAm; STS; TT; UsP

Snowman in March, A. Paul Ramsey. CSP

Snowmobile, A. Manchild. Emma Lou Thayne. MPA

Snows are fled away, leaves on the shaws, The. Diffugere Nives. Horace, *tr. by* A. E. Housman. Odes, IV, 7. OBVE

Snows of yesteryear, The? Polar Expedition. George M. Young. FAF

Snowstorm, The. Pearl Riggs Crouch. BPAW

Snow-Storm, The. Emerson. AmVN; FSFS; ILP (1975 ed.); IPWM; NOBA; PiAm; PPoD; Prf; TAP; UnPo (1976 ed.); VoPo

Snow Storm, The. Edna St. Vincent Millay. PoA

Snowy Day, A. *Unknown, tr. fr. Welsh by* H. Idris Bell. OBW

Snowy, Flowy, Blowy. The Twelve Months. "Sir Gregory Gander." CTV

Snowy Night. John Haines. NCSH

Snub nose, the guts of twenty mules. New Farm Tractor. Carl Sandburg. AKE

Snuffboxes, The. *Unknown.* PoTa

Snug at the club two fathers sat. The Fathers. Siegfried Sassoon. NoAM

So? James P. Vaughn. AmNP (1974 ed.)

So./ I am becoming an elephant. Cool Morning Shower in Early Spring. Larry Levis. OSP

So Abram rose, and clave the wood, and went. The Parable of the Old Men [*or* Man] and the Young. Wilfred Owen. GrRo; OBP; WIF

So advised, did you laugh and forget. Before the Statue of a Laughing Man. William C. Bowie. AMV-81

So all day long the noise of battle roll'd. Morte d'Arthur. Tennyson. DL; ILP (1975 ed.); NIL; OAEL-2; PAIC; VLP

So an age ended, and its last deliverer died. Sonnets from China, X. W. H. Auden. CMoP (1970 ed.); ExPo (1973 ed.)

So as they travelled, the drouping night. Spenser. *Fr.* The Faerie Queene, IV, 5. OAEL-1

So be it. I am. Hayden Carruth. VGW

So Beautiful Is the Tree of Night. Pauline Hanson. TAP

So black great great grandmomma. Black Sheba. Jodi Braxton. WBN

So, bored with dragons, he lay down to sleep. Beowulf. Kingsley Amis. FaBoCo

So! breakers of broncos! With miles of jagged wire. Breakers of Broncos. Lew Sarett. BPAW

"So careful of the type?" but no. In Memoriam A. H. H., LVI. Tennyson. BoReV; ExPo (1973 ed.); FF; HAP

So Castlereagh had cut his throat! The worst. Epigrams on Castlereagh. Byron. ExPo (1973 ed.)

So Close Should Be Our Love. *Gond Oral Tradition, tr. by* V. Elwin *and* S. Hivale. WTO

So cold the wintry winds do blow. The Unquiet Grave. *Unknown.* AIW

So cool and so composed. Song of the Intruder. Maria Jacobs. AMV-81

So crewell prison, howe could betyde, alas. *See* So cruel prison. . .

So Crow found Proteus—steaming in the sun. Truth Kills Everybody. Ted Hughes. InPS

So cruel [*or* crewell] prison how could betide, alas. In Windsor Castle. Earl of Surrey. AAS; HAP; ILP (1975 ed.); NOBE

So Cynthia seems star chamber's president. Cynthia. Edward Benlowes. *Fr.* Theophila; or, Love's Sacrifice. Moon

So Davies wrote: "This leaves me in the pink." "In the Pink." Siegfried Sassoon. CMoP (1970 ed.)

So died John So. On John So. *Unknown.* FaBoEE

So different, this man. Marriage. William Carlos Williams. IPWM; PoA

So diligent the work of my parents. The Tremor. David McKain. AAN

So dream thy sails, O phantom bark. The Phantom Bark. Hart Crane. CMoP (1970 ed.)

So dry and clean. The Skull in the Desert. Alison A. Trimpi. AMV-81

So earth's inclined toward the one invisible. Winter Scene. Marguerite Young. NU; WPE

So fallen! so lost! the light withdrawn. Ichabod. Whittier. NOBA; PBMP; TAP; VoPo

So far as our story approaches the end. A Light Woman. Robert Browning. VLP

So fell behind his day. Trends and Conditions: Miscellaneous File. A. Wilber Stevens. MPA

So forth she comes, and to her coche does clyme. Spenser. *Fr.* The Faerie Queene, I, 4. OAEL-1

So, friend, your shop was all your house! Shop. Robert Browning. VLP

So from the years their gifts were showered: each. Sonnets from China, I. W. H. Auden. CMoP (1970 ed.)

So from this life, male in its first motion. Vittoria Colonna. Roy Marz. PoA

So Going around Cities. Ted Berrigan. FiCh

So good bye, Mrs. Brown. To-Day I Leave Mrs. Brown's Lodgings. Sir Walter Scott. FaBoEE

So Good Luck came, and on my roof did light. Good Luck [*or* The Coming of Good Luck]. Robert Herrick. ECBV; FaBoEE

So Graven. Josephine Miles. NoAM

So Handy, Me Boys, So Handy. *Unknown.* AmFP

So hard for women to believe each other. Apron Strings. Marge Piercy. TAP

So having ended, silence long ensewed. Nature's Reply to Mutability. Spenser. *Fr.* The Faerie Queene, VII, 7. NOBE

So He has cut his throat at last! He? Who? Epigrams on Castlereagh. Byron. ExPo (1973 ed.)

So he sits down. His host will play for him. Concert Scene. John Logan. CoPAm

So Hector spake; the Trojans roared applause. Homer, *tr. by* Tennyson. *Fr.* The Iliad, VIII. OBVE

So here we are again. Groundhog Day. Michael Hogan. DNGG

So humble things thou hast borne for us, O God. Veni Creator. Alice Meynell. ILwL; WPE

So I am your "darling girl!" Remonstrance. Philodemos the Epicurean, *tr. by* Dudley Fitts. OLR

So I cut my hair; so I'm shorn. Song of the Strange Young Duckling. Deborah Munro. IHMS

So, i finished another bottle of coke. The Death of Democracy. John Sjoberg. AcAn

So I Let Her Go, 2 *versions. Unknown.* AmFP

So I Said I Am Ezra. A. R. Ammons. NoAM; NOBA; PoIA

So I was in the city on this day. Apocalypse in Springtime. Lex Banning. GAS

So I would hear out those lungs. Buckdancer's Choice. James Dickey. NoAM; NOBA

So in Love, *with music.* Cole Porter. BLSo

So in Pieria, from the wedded bliss. In Memory of Bryan Lathrop. Edgar Lee Masters. PoA

So in the sinful streets, abstracted and alone. Easter Day II. Arthur Hugh Clough. PFD; VPC

So it comes to this, then. Winter Watch. Jeff Daniel Marion. AMV-80

So It Happens. Irving Feldman. GP

So it has come to this. In a Home Relief Bureau. Alfred Hayes. SPT

So it is, my dear. Even So. Dante Gabriel Rossetti. NOBE; VLP

So it's you? Fugue and Variations. George Hitchcock. FoP

So I've come south this time. Tracks. Brad Lee Shurmantine. AMV-81

So Jah Seh. Peter Kostakis. FiCh

So light no one noticed. The Song. Edward Dorn. VGW

So Little Wanted. Cid Corman. GP

So lonely am I. Ono no Komachi, *tr. fr. Japanese by* David Keene. BoWoP; PBWP

So Long. Jayne Cortez. BoWoP

So Long. William Stafford. Epi

So long,/ So far away. Afro-American Fragment. Langston Hughes. PBMP

So long as we speak the same language. Useless Words. Carl Sandburg. PBMP; PPoD

So long had life together been that now. Six Years Later. Joseph Brodsky, *tr. by* Richard Wilbur. AMV-80

So Long Solon. Jack Myers. AmPA

So Long? Stevens. John Berryman. HAP; NOBA

So looks Anthea when in bed she lies. To Anthea Lying in Bed. Robert Herrick. AnMo; SCP-1

So lucky I was in being born. Yankee Cradle. Robert P. Tristram Coffin. ECBV

So luminous around them lay the air. Oystercatchers. Christopher Middleton. FaBoTw (1975 ed.)

So Many Cenotaphs. Peter Bland. ATNZ

So many days, oh so many days. Love. Pablo Neruda, *tr. by* Alastair Reid. LP

So many new crimes since then! Since Then. D. J. Enright. OBSV

So many pigeons at Columbus. Poem. Arthur Gregor. VGW

So many stories written here. Written in a Copy of "The Earthly Paradise," Dec. 25, 1870. William Morris. *Fr.* The Earthly Paradise. VLP

So many thousands for a house! David Garrick. FaBoEE

So many times she'd called him in at dusk. Evening. Alison Wyrley Birch. PPM

So many wagons they have cut that good road down. Chock House Blues. *Unknown.* BluL

So many women, writing. Daughterly. Kathleen Spivack. TV

So Miss Myrtle is going to marry? The Charming Woman. Helen Selina Sheridan. WPE

So much behind the bald phrase. Being Here (or Anywhere). Charles Doyle. ATNZ

So much depends. The Red Wheelbarrow. William Carlos Williams. CMoP (1970 ed.); HAP; HoPM (1975 ed.); InPK; NIL; NoAM; NOBA; NowV; OSP; PiAm; SFF; SoSe (1977 ed.); TAP; TSWA; TT; UnPo (1976 ed.); UsP; WIF

So much have I [*or* I have] forgotten in ten years. Flame-Heart. Claude McKay. AmNP (1974 ed.); ILP (1975 ed.)

So much is parchment where I gloom. The Black Mesa. James Merrill. PoA

So much marble, and grass. The Capitol: Spring. Joan LaBombard. PoW

So much she caused she cannot now account for. Old Woman. Elizabeth Jennings. BuTh

So much that is weak has survived. The Weak. Greg Kuzma. HeS

So, my sweet thing, a little tighter yet. Scenes from the Fall of Troy. William Morris. PAIC

So Nigh Is Grandeur ("In an age of fops and toys"). Emerson. Voluntaries, III. PCOP

So nigh is grandeur to our dust. Emerson. *Fr.* Voluntaries, III. CTV

So now the very bones of you are gone. Doricha. Poseidippus, *tr. by* E. A. Robinson. FaBoEE; OBVE

So oft as I with state of present time. Spenser. *Fr.* The Faerie Queene, V, *proem.* OAEL-1

So on he fares, and to the border comes. Satan Discovers Eden. Milton. *Fr.* Paradise Lost, IV. ExPo (1973 ed.)

So, on the bloody sand, Sohrab lay dead. Sohrab Dead. Matthew Arnold. *Fr.* Sohrab and Rustum. NOBE

So once again, hearing the tired aunts. In the House of the Dying. Jane Cooper. CoPAm; NMM

So open was his mind, so wide. The Independent. Phyllis McGinley. FaBoEE

So Orpheus stared, on passing the dog of hell. The Young Chess Player. Keith Sinclair. ATNZ

So pleasing a light. The Moon. Robert Duncan. *Fr.* Passages. PiAm

So proud she was to die. Emily Dickinson. NOBA

So, pure and dutiful, she sought that place. *Unknown.* *Fr.* The Mahabharata. DL

So put your nightdress on. Bedtime. Ian Hamilton Finlay. MS

So quiet it was in that high, sun-steeped room. Nuremberg. Kenneth Slessor. MAuV

So Quietly. Leslie Pinckney Hill. PoBA

So saying, light-foot Iris passed away. Homer, *tr. by* Tennyson. *Fr.* The Iliad, XVIII. OBVE

So several factions from this first ferment. Achitophel: The Earl of Shaftsbury. Dryden. *Fr.* Absalom and Achitophel, Pt. I. NOBE

So she took up a number twelve crewel needle. Agatha. Nadine Major. POL

So she went into the garden. The Great Panjandrum. Samuel Foote. ECBV; FaBoCo

So, since your heart is set on those sweet fields. To Colman Returning. *At.* to Colman, *tr. by* Helen Waddell. BlrV

So small are the flowers of Seamu. Ezra Pound *and* Noel Stock, *fr. Egyptian hieroglyphics.* BoWoP; PBWP

So smell those odours that do rise. To the Most Fair and Lovely Mistress Anne Soame, Now Lady Abdie. Robert Herrick. CaPo; NOBE

So smooth, so sweet, so silv'ry is thy voice. Upon Julia's Voice. Robert Herrick. AnMo; CABA (1972 ed.); InPK; NIL; NOBE; SCP-1; SoSe

So, so, breake off this last lamenting kisse. The Expiration. John Donne. LoAs

So, So. It is an old man sleeping here. In the Forest. Pinhas Sadeh, *tr. by* Harris Lenowitz. VWA

So soft in the hemlock wood. Robert Hillyer. *Fr.* Pastorals. PAIC

So soft streams meet, so springs with gladder smiles. The Welcome to Sack. Robert Herrick. CaPo

So, some tempestuous morn in early June. Matthew Arnold. *Fr.* Thyrsis. FSFS; PoPle

So spake our mother Eve, and Adam heard. The Banishment. Milton. *Fr.* Paradise Lost, XII. NOBE

So squeezed, wince you I scream? I love you & hate. John Berryman. *Fr.* Homage to Mistress Bradstreet. FF

So summer comes in the end to these few stains. The Beginning. Wallace Stevens. VGW

So Sweet Love Seemed That April Morn. Robert Bridges. ILP (1975 ed.)

So swete a kis yestrene [*or* yistrene] fra thee I reft. To His Mistress [*or* Maistres]. Alexander Montgomerie. GBL; SLP

So take a happy view. A Happy View. C. Day Lewis. CMoP (1970 ed.)

So tall was a cowboy called Slouch. Tall. *Unknown.* TDH

So that soldierly legend is still on its journey. Kearney at Seven Pines. Edmund Clarence Stedman. BTTM

So that the vines burst from my fingers. Ezra Pound. Cantos, XVII. ExPo (1973 ed.)

So that's my role—the professional defendant. Ovid, tr. by Guy Lee. Amores, II, 7. NAWM-1

So the committee met again, and again. The Committee. C. Day Lewis. BiP; CMoP (1970 ed.)

So the distances are Galatea. The Distances. Charles Olson. PiAm

So the foemen have fired the gate, men of mine. The Knight's Leap. Charles Kingsley. PoTa

So the last day's come at last, the close of my fifteen year. The Old Place. B. E. Baughan. ATNZ

So the Seeds Are Growing. Joe South. PoRo

So the spring has come? Basho, tr. fr. Japanese. WeW

So the subject is death again today. For My Friend Michele. Linda Gregg. AAN

So the wedding guest, unknown. We Let Each Other Go. Coleman Barks. CSP

"So then you won't fight?" Dooley Is a Traitor. James Michie. OxBTC

So there stood Matthew Arnold and this girl. The Dover Bitch. Anthony Hecht. CABA (1972 ed.); ILP (1975 ed.); MAT; NOBA; NOBL; NowV; OBAL; PAIC; PPP; SFF; TPo; UnPo (1976 ed.); VGW

So they came. The Animals' Arrival. Elizabeth Jennings. PBWP

So they laid oars. Against the Sun. George MacBeth. TwMBP

So they rode/ Into a land of wells and gardens, where. Sir Edwin Arnold. Fr. The Light of Asia, I. VLP

So they went, leaving a picnic-litter of talk. The Party. W. R. Rodgers. BIrV

So This Is Earth. Morty Sklar. AcAn

So this is it. At the Western Wall. Barbara F. Lefcowitz. VWA

So this is, Jimmy, where we live. An Urgent Letter. Hugh Maxton. IPM

So This Is Nebraska. Ted Kooser. EC

So This Is Our Revolution. Sonia Sanchez. GP

So this is the dust that passes through porcelain. The Iron Lung. Stanley Plumly. AmPA

So through that unripe day you bore your head. Philip Larkin. NoAM

So through the sun-laced woods they went. The Sphere of Glass. John Lehmann. LoAs

So thus he sorrowed till it was day. King Pellam's Launde. David Jones. In Parenthesis, IV. NoAM

So Tired Are All My Thoughts. Thomas Campion. SCP-2

So, to the mind long brooding but on it. Frederick Goddard Tuckerman. Fr. Sonnets. AmVN

So Touch Our Hearts with Loveliness, with music. Gail Brook Burket. AH

So vile was poor Wat, such a miscreant slave. Burns. FaBoEE

So we are taking off our masks, are we, and keeping. Homosexuality. Frank O'Hara. CoPAm; NYP; PoA; TAP

"So we diverted the river," he said. Requiem for a River. Kim Williams. RFM

So we lay down and made our love. One-Day Diary. John Biguenet. CoPAm

So we meet as of old where the rosevine. Person to Person. Gwen Harwood. GAS

So we must say goodbye, my darling. Goodbye. Alun Lewis. BoLoP; MPo; OxBTC; PSN

So we reveal our status. Hilda Doolittle ("H. D."). Fr. The Walls Do Not Fall. NoAM

So We'll Go No More a-Roving. Byron. BoLoP; FF; HAP; HeIP; ILP (1975 ed.); LoAs; MBPR; NOBE; OAEL-2; OLR; PoPle; SLP; SoSe; WeW
(We'll Go No More a-Roving.) FaPoR; Moon

So well I love thee as without thee I. Verses Made the Night before He Died. Michael Drayton. GBL; NOBE

So, we're estranged again—how it goes on! Drought. David Holbrook. OxBTC

So We've Come at Last to Freud. Alice Walker. IHMS

So what said the others and the sun went down. Mrs. Alfred Uruguay. Wallace Stevens. InPS; PiAm

So when the shadows laid asleep. The Kingfisher. Andrew Marvell. Fr. Upon Appleton House. PB

So while the blear-eyed pimp beside me walked. Easter Day II, earlier version. Arthur Hugh Clough. VLP

So you came to hear the poetry in the park. July Noon in Dupont Circle. Ann Darr. PoUp

So you dance with me. Ellen Cooney. NPW

So you have swept me back. Eurydice. Hilda Doolittle ("H. D."). VGW

So you said you'd go home to work on your father's farm. To a Young Poet Who Died. John Logan. CAPP

So you're going away. Good Bye, My Lady Love. Joseph E. Howard. FSN

So zestfully canst thou sing? The Blinded Bird. Thomas Hardy. BiP; CMoP (1970 ed.); NoAM

So-and-so Reclining on Her Couch. Wallace Stevens. NOBA

Soap (II). Jerome Rothenberg. NNaP

Soapship went a-rocking, A. The Voyage of Jimmy Poo. James A. Emanuel. AmNP (1974 ed.)

Sober, he thinks of her; so he gets drunk. Man and Woman. Robert Conquest. OxBTC

Soccer. Andrei Voznesensky, tr. fr. Russian by Anselm Hollo. LiSp; SPo

"Social Science." Thomas Edward Brown. PeD

Social Studies. Mary Neville. POL

Society has quite forsaken all her wicked courses. Anglicized Utopia. W. S. Gilbert. OBSV

Society upon the Stanislaus, The. Bret Harte. BPAW; OBAL (Plain Language from Truthful James.) FaBoCo

Society's Child. Janis Ian. WIF

Sock left by the road, A. Judith Serin. NPW

Socrates and Alcibiades. Friedrich Hölderlin, tr. fr. German by Michael Hamburger. LoAs

Socratic. Hilda Doolittle ("H. D."). HoPM (1975 ed.)

Sodenly afraid, half waking, half sleeping. A Woman Sat Weeping. Unknown. OxBM

Sodger laddie's socht a hoose, A. Under the Greenwood Tree. "Hugh MacDiarmid," after the Cretan. OBVE

Sodom's Sister City. Yehuda Amichai, tr. fr. Hebrew by Shirley Kaufman. VWA

Sofa, The. William Cowper. Fr. The Task. LAuP

Soft/ The stars are melting. Sopranosound, Memory of John. Sharon Bourke. CNA

Soft answer turneth away wrath, A. Bible, O.T. Fr. Proverbs. BiP

Soft Answers. Robert Bagg. FF

Soft as the voice of an angel. Whispering Hope. Septimus Winner. PSoN

Soft as the wind your hair. Love Song. Joseph Macleod. SLP

Soft cheeks & all that jazz. Patience, No Speed. George Mattingly. AcAn

Soft light, low. Finding Words in Winter. John Judson. HeS

Soft lips of the heat register, The. Her Hair Is Wet. Allan Kornblum. AcAn

Soft morning. Sycamores. In this one some women pass. Lecture with Slides, Film Clips and Tape. Marilyn Krysl. NPW

Soft o'er the fountain. Juanita. Caroline Norton. BLSH; FSW

Soft rainbows, tumbling fleeces of grey cloud. In Aeternum. James McAuley. MAuV

Soft she was, young. Dead Girl. Anna Hajnal, *tr. by* Jascha Kessler. VWA

Soft Snow. Blake. FF; FSFS; SoSe; WeW

Soft sodden fields. The new lambs cry. In Northern Tasmania. James McAuley. MAuV

Soft songs, like birds, die in poison air. Apology for Apostasy? Etheridge Knight. NeAC

Soft thoughts ease on down. Like Fire Spreadin/ the Joylessness. Thulani Nkabinde. NW

Soft! what light through yonder window breaks? Juliet. Shakespeare. *Fr.* Romeo and Juliet, II, ii. PCOP

Soft White. Lee Harwood. EAS

Softened by time's consummate plush. Emily Dickinson. NOBA

Softly along the road of evening. Nod. Walter de la Mare. OxBTC

Softly and gently, dearly-ransom'd soul. Angel. Cardinal Newman. *Fr.* The Dream of Gerontius. PFD

Softly and humbly to the Gulf of Arabs. Beach Burial. Kenneth Slessor. GAS; MAuV

Softly and Tenderly Jesus Is Calling, *with music.* Will L. Thompson. BLSH

Softly croons the radiogram, loudly hoot the owls. Invasion Exercise on the Poultry Farm. John Betjeman. NOBL

Softly Fades the Twilight Ray, *with music.* Samuel Francis Smith. AH

Softly, in the dusk, a woman is singing to me. Piano. D. H. Lawrence. CMoP (1970 ed.); HAP; HeIP; ILP (1975 ed.); InPK; NIL; NoAM; NOBE; OAEL-2; PoPle; PPM; PPP; UnPo (1976 ed.); WeW

Softly Now the Light of Day, *with music.* George Washington Doane. AH

Softly she hunted. She could hear the others. Celia. J. S. Harry. FPA

Softly, so casual. Snow in Madrid. Joy Davidman. SPT

Softly the Capitol Hill Surveys Its Scene. Josephine Miles. WasP

Softly the crane's foot crumples a star. Recollection. Dorothy Donnelly. NCSH

Softly the dead stir, call, through the afternoon. A Cemetery in New Mexico. A. Alvarez. VWA

Softly, White and Pure. Dorothy R. Fulton. AMV-80

Soho. Joseph Brodsky, *tr. fr. Russian by* Alan Myers. VWA

Sohrab and Rustum. Matthew Arnold. VLP
     Sohrab Dead, *sel.* NOBE

Soil now gets a rumpling soft and damp, The. The Strong Are Saying Nothing. Robert Frost. AnMo; CMoP (1970 ed.)

Soil Searcher. J. Joyce. CTBA

Soil was deep and the field well-sited, The. A Failure C. Day Lewis. NOBE

Sojourn in the Whale. Marianne Moore. SBG

Sojourner Truth. Robert Hayden. *Fr.* Stars. CNA

Sojourners at Phoenix. Judith Rodriguez. FPA

Solace. Clarissa Scott Delany. AmNP (1974 ed.); PoBA

Solar Creation. Charles Madge. OxBTC

Solar Signals. L. Pearl Schuck. AMV-81

Sold. R. R. Cuscaden. ANTL

Soldier, The. Rupert Brooke. 1914, V. BTTM; FaPoR; FF; HeIP; NOBE; OxBTC; PAIC; PoA; VoPo ("If I should die, think only this of me.") PPM

Soldier, The. Robert Frost. ILP (1975 ed.); OFD; WeW

Soldier ants, the red-eyed starlings, The. In the Jungle. D. J. Enright. HeHu

Soldier Boy for Me. *Unknown.* AmFP

Soldier from the wars returning. A. E. Housman. STS

Soldier [*or* Souldier] Going to the Field, The. Sir William Davenant. MetP; NOBE

Soldier is, The/ all alone. Glove Glue. Ken Belford. NeAc

Soldier, oh soldier, a-coming from the plain. The Bold Soldier. *Unknown.* FSW

Soldier passed me in the freshly fallen snow, A. To a Conscript of 1940. Sir Herbert Read. ExPo (1973 ed.)

"Soldier, Rest!" Robert Jones Burdette. OBAL

Soldier, Rest! Sir Walter Scott. *Fr.* The Lady of the Lake, I. NOBE

Soldier, Won't You Marry Me? *Unknown.* AIW; AmFP; OLR (Soldier, Soldier, Won't You Marry Me?) DuDr; FSW

Soldiers. *Unknown.* FaBoEE; GBP

Soldiers are citizens of death's grey land. Dreamers. Siegfried Sassoon. NoAM

Soldiers are marching over the pontoon bridge. Nike. Adam Wazyk, *tr. by* Isaac Komem. VWA

Soldiers Bathing. F. T. Prince. OxBTC

Soldier's Dream, The. Thomas Campbell. FaPoR

Soldier's Dream. Wilfred Owen. ILwL

Soldiers from town to the foot of the hill, The. The Ballad of Bunker Hill. *Unknown.* BTTM

Soldiers never do die well. Champs d'Honneur. Ernest Hemingway. PoA

Soldier's Plea for the Y.M.C.A., A. Joseph Samuel Reed. PeD

Soldiers Plundering a Village. Anthony Thwaite. HeHu

Soldier's Song, The. *Unknown.* NIL

Soldiers who wish to be a hero. Soldiers. *Unknown.* FaBoEE; GBP

Soldier's Wooing, The, 2 *versions. Unknown.* AmFP

Sole-hungering Camel. Oliver Herford. TDH

Sole positive of night. Ne Plus Ultra. Samuel Taylor Coleridge. MBPR; OAEL-2

Sole true something—This! In Limbo's den, The. Limbo. Samuel Taylor Coleridge. MBPR; OAEL-2; OBP

Sole watchman of the flying stars, guard me. Eleven Addresses to the Lord, III. John Berryman. PiAm; UnPo (1976 ed.)

Solemn Farewell to the World, A. Nicholas Breton. TVS

Solemn pastors. The MJQ. Joyce Carol Thomas. CNA

Solemn plain-faced child stands gazing there, A. A Portrait. Walter de la Mare. NoAM

Solemnly swearing, to swear as an oath to you. Vera from My Childhood. Judy Grahn. The Common Woman, VII. GP

Solid and dull, my primary school. Contacts with the Past. R. A. Simpson. FPA

Solid houses in the mist, The. New Year's. Charles Reznikoff. VGW

Solid Mountain. George Bowering. NeAC

Solidarity Forever. Ralph Chaplin. FSW

Soliloquies. Denis Glover. ATNZ

Soliloquies, The. Edward Weismiller. PAIC

Soliloquy. Francis Ledwidge. HoPM (1975 ed.)

Soliloquy in an Air-Raid. Roy Fuller. PoA

Soliloquy of a Turkey. Paul Laurence Dunbar. BPo

Soliloquy of the Spanish Cloister. Robert Browning. AnMo; CABA (1972 ed.); Epi; FaBoCo; ILP (1975 ed.); InPK; IP; NIL; NOBL; OAEL-2; OBP; PAIC; PoIA; STS

Solitaire. George Garrett. CSP

Solitary, The. Shelley. MBPR

Solitary, The. Sara Teasdale. IPWM; PPM

Solitary Confinement. Phyllis Webb. *Fr.* The Kropotkin Poems. MMD

Solitary invalid in a fuchsia garden, A. The Philosopher and the Birds. Richard Murphy. CIP

Solitary prospector, A. Sunstrike. Douglas Livingstone. MPo

Solitary Reaper, The. Wordsworth. AnMo; CABA (1972 ed.); ExPo (1973 ed.); FaPoR; HAP; ILP (1975 ed.); InPS; MBPR; NOBE; OAEL-2; PoPle; PPP; SoSe; UnPo (1976 ed.); WeW

Solitary Song. *Unknown, tr. fr.* Eskimo. WTO

Solitary Visions of a Kaufmanoid.  James Cunningham.  JB

Solitude.  Walter de la Mare.  CMoP (1970 ed.)

Solitude.  A. R. D. Fairburn.  ATNZ

Solitude.  A. A. Milne.  LCL

Solitude.  Charles Simic.  GP

Solitude.  Wordsworth.  *See* Lucy Gray; or, Solitude.

Solitude, an Ode, *sel.*  James Grainger.
"O Solitude, romantic maid."  LFH

Solitude, an Ode.  Pope.  *See* Ode on Solitude.

Solitude Late at Night in the Woods.  Robert Bly.  BiP; IPWM;
SFF; VGW

Solitude that unmakes me one of men.  Compensation.
Robinson Jeffers.  PAIC

Solo for Clarinet.  Raymond Ward.  ATNZ

Solo Late Show over Easter Break.  R. T. Smith.  AAN

Solomon and Morolph, Their Last Encounter.  Oscar Levertin, *tr.
fr. Swedish by* Richard Burns *and* Göran Printz-Pahlson.
VWA

Solomon and the Witch.  W. B. Yeats.  NoAM

Solomon Grundy.  Mother Goose.  BBL; MG

Solomon Grundy.  Frederick Winsor.  *Fr.* The Space Child's
Mother Goose.  QQQ

"Solomon? Since I've talked with him I've thought."  Homestead
in Idaho.  Clinton F. Larson.  MPA

Solomon to Sheba.  W. B. Yeats.  CMoP (1970 ed.)

Soluble Noughts and Crosses; or, California, Here I Come.
Roger Roughton.  EAS

Solution.  Emerson.  OBAL

Solution, The.  Brian Merriman, *tr. fr. Modern Irish by* Arland
Ussher.  *Fr.* The Midnight Court.  BIrV

Solutions.  David Barton.  AMV-81

Solvitur Acris Hiems.  Horace, *tr. by* Louis MacNeice.  Odes, I,
4.  Epi

"Sombra?"  The Shade-Seller.  Josephine Jacobsen.  TAP

Sombre and rich, the skies.  By the Statue of King Charles at
Charing Cross.  Lionel Johnson.  NOBE; VLP

Sombre the night is.  Returning, We Hear the Larks.  Isaac
Rosenberg.  OAEL-2; VWA

Some after a night of sex, some hungover.  Fall Practice.
Dabney Stuart.  CoPAm

Some are bewildered in the maze of schools.  Pope.  *Fr.* An
Essay on Criticism.  OBSV

Some Are Born.  Stevie Smith.  FaBoCo

Some are in prison; some are dead.  The Chumbs.  Theodore
Roethke.  NoAM

Some are teethed on a silver spoon.  Saturday's Child.  Countee
Cullen.  InPK; OFD; PoBA

Some ask for envy'd pow'r; which publick hate.  Sejanus.
Juvenal, *tr. by* Dryden.  *Fr.* Satires, X.  OBVE

Some autumn leaves a painter took.  The Sumach Leaves.  Jones
Very.  NOBA

Some awful.  Sounds.  Robert Creeley.  GP

Some beauties yet no precepts can declare.  Pope.  *Fr.* An Essay
on Criticism.  HAP

Some Boys.  John Penkethman.  OxBChV

Some by their friends, more by themselves thought wise.  Dryden.
*Fr.* Absalom and Achitophel, Pt. I.  OBSV

Some can gaze and not be sick.  A. E. Housman.  FaBoEE;
OBSV

Some can leave the truth unspoken.  Truth.  Eileen Duggan.
ATNZ

Some candle clear burns somewhere I come by.  The Candle
Indoors.  Gerard Manley Hopkins.  ILP (1975 ed.)

Some Chicks Just Can't Tell a Cézanne from a Sears.  Gordon
Kirkwood Yates.  CPA

Some clouds are rainclouds.  On the Pole.  Uri Zvi Greenberg, *tr.
by* Robert Mezey *and* Ben Zion Gold.  VWA

Some cowpoke named her Nevada.  Nevada.  Stanley Noyes.
PH

Some cry up Haydn, some Mozart.  Free Thoughts on Several
Eminent Composers.  Charles Lamb.  FaBoCo

Some curse that traitor Judas life and limb.  Francis Quarles.
FaBoEE

Some Day.  *See also* Someday.

Some Day.  Shel Silverstein.  PH

Some Day.  James Steele.  SES

Some day/ I may.  What Someone Said When He Was Spanked.
John Ciardi.  FPB

Some day I will go to Aarhus.  The Tollund Man.  Seamus
Heaney.  BIrV; EBEV; HeHu

Some day, when I lose you.  Slumbersong.  Rainer Maria Rilke,
*tr. by* M. D. Herter Norton.  LoAs

Some day, when trees have shed their leaves.  After the Winter.
Claude McKay.  PoBA

Some Days/ Out Walking Above.  De Leon Harrison.  PoBA

Some days a road streams back, a road you took.  Other Lives.
Patricia Hooper.  AMV-81

Some days, I'm sorely tempted to throw out the baby.
Lamentations of an Au Pair Girl.  Susan Feldman.  AmPA

Some Days the Blood Is Warm and Certain.  Gene Frumkin.
CoPAm

Some die too late and some too soon.  The Lost Occasion.
Whittier.  NOBA

Some dogs are brats.  For a Good Dog.  Arthur Guiterman.
GDP

Some Dreams They Forgot.  Elizabeth Bishop.  NoAM

Some dreams we have are nothing else but dreams.  The Haunted
House.  Thomas Hood.  EBEV

Some dust,/ such as it is.  Mothsong.  William Harmon.  CSP

Some Eyes Condemn.  Edward Thomas.  NoAM

Some farms have graveyards tucked upon a knoll.  Horse
Graveyard.  Fred Lape.  PH

Some Feelings.  Michael Benedikt.  ConAP

Some few yards from the hut the standing beeches.  Poem in the
Matukituki Valley.  James K. Baxter.  ATNZ

Some Fishy Nonsense.  Laura E. Richards.  CTV

Some 5-Day Drunk Poems.  Simon J. Ortiz.  NW

Some flowers there are that rear their heads on high.  Lily of the
Valley.  Hartley Coleridge.  PF

Some folks jump up and down all night and d-a-n-c-e.  It's G-L-
O-R-Y to Know I'm S-A-V-E-D.  *Unknown.*  FSW

Some food, some sun.  Human Needs.  *Unknown.*  POL

Some for a little while do love, and some for long.  Sonnet.
Countee Cullen.  SoS

Some Foreign Letters.  Anne Sexton.  ILP (1975 ed.)

Some Frenchmen.  John Updike.  FaBoCo

Some girls wear short dresses.  Nehi Blues.  *Unknown.*  BluL

Some Good Things Left after the War with the Sioux.  John
Calvin Rezmerski.  HeS

Some Good Things to Be Said for the Iron Age.  Gary Snyder.
CoPAm; HoPM (1975 ed.); WeW

Some hae meat, and canna eat.  A Scottish Grace.  Burns.  PIM

Some Harvard men, stalwart and hairy.  Edward Gorey.  OBAL

Some hearts there are of deeper sort.  Lyon.  Herman Melville.
PeD

Some in the Godspeed, the Susan C.  Enough.  Marianne Moore.
NOBA

Some in their harts their mistris colours bears.  Chloris, XXIX.
William Smith.  AAS

Some keep the Sabbath going to church.  Emily Dickinson.
IPWM; PBMP; PiAm

Some Kind of Giant. Sheila Pritchard. BoAnP

Some Kind of Toughguy. Gene Frumkin. CoPAm

Some Kisses from "The Kama Sutra." Hugo Williams. BoLoP

Some Knots. Edwin Honig. NoAM

Some know how/ to row. The Art of Rowing. John Elsberg. PoUp

Some Last Questions. W. S. Merwin. CAPP

Some leagues into that land I too have fared. Animae Superstiti. Charles Spear. ATNZ

Some lines after the Razing of the Sioux City Armour's Plant. David Allan Evans. HeS

Some little mice sat in a barn to spin. Mother Goose. MG

Some look at nature for the surface: eye. Nature Lover. John Frederick Nims. CoPAm

Some Me of Beauty. Carolyn M. Rodgers. CNA

Some men break your heart in two. Experience. Dorothy Parker. PPM

Some men marriage do commend. De Se. John Weever. FaBoEE

Some men sayen that I am blac. The Dark Lady. Unknown. OxBM

Some men, some men. Chant for Dark Hours. Dorothy Parker. SBG

Some men, 'tis said, prefer a woman fat. Nathaniel Parker Willis. Fr. The Lady Jane: A Humorous Novel in Rhyme. OBAL

Some months she hath been dead (but, being dead). John Donne. Fr. An Anatomy of the World: The First Anniversary. SCP-1

Some morning, while you and I are dozing. Intruder. Susan Feldman. AmPA

Some ne'er advance a judgment of their own. Pope. Fr. An Essay on Criticism. OBSV

Some Newly-discovered Prophecies of Nostradamus. David Lake. FPA

Some nights when you're off. The Avenues. David St. John. AMV-80

Some nine years gone, as we dwelt together. Dedication. Swinburne. VLP

Some of my best friends are white boys. Friends [or Broadminded]. Ray Durem. PoBA; SoSe (1977 ed.)

Some of the grandest have chosen marble. Gravestones. Floyd C. Stuart. AMV-80

Some of the time, going home, I go. Looking for the Buckhead Boys. James Dickey. LiSp

Some of their chiefs were princes of the land. Dryden. Fr. Absalom and Achitophel, Pt. I. EBEV

Some of us/ these days. Resurrection. Frank Horne. OFD; PoBA

Some "old Robin Down" they call me. Ibby Damsel. Unknown. AmFP

Some Oral Stanzas. Thomas Lux. NVAP

Some part of us lives. The Fourth Dimension. Leonard Nathan. AMV-81

Some people,/ no matter what you give them. Adam's Complaint. Denise Levertov. BoWoP; NNaP

Some people admire the work of a fool. Blake. OAEL-2

Some people are born. For Kenneth Patchen. Wayne Miller. MIT

Some people are young and nothing. Footnote upon the Construction of the Masses. Charles Bukowski. CoPAm

Some people cannot endure. Going the Rounds: A Sort of Love Poem. Anthony Hecht. BoLoP

Some people hang portraits up. A Likeness. Robert Browning. InPS; VLP

Some people know how to love. Poem of Explanations. Dahlia Ravikovitch, tr. by Chana Bloch. BoWoP

Some people long to have plenty money. Ease It to Me Blues. Unknown. BluL

Some people make fun. Roots. Lorraine Sutton. NW

Some people stop hunting because they get tired. On Dressing to Go Hunting. Unknown. PH

Some people tell me God takes care of old folks and fools. Fool's Blues. Unknown. BluL

Some pimps wear summer hats. What? Langston Hughes. OBAL

Some pretty face remembered in our youth. Fragment. John Clare. VLP

Some prowl sea-beds, some hurtle to a star. X Ray. Dannie Abse. PMW

Some questions they won't answer. Secrets. Edward Lowbury. FPB

Some Ruse. Hastings Wyman, Jr. PoUp

Some San Francisco Poems. George Oppen. NNaP

Some say/ it was a pear. Pears. Linda Pastan. VWA

Some say cavalry and others claim. Sappho, tr. fr. Greek by Willis Barnstone. BoWoP

Some say, compar'd to Bononcini. Epigram on Handel and Bononcini. John Byrom. FaBoEE; NOBL

Some say my love has proved unfaithful. The Weeping Willow. Unknown. AmFP

Some say that ever 'gainst that season comes. Shakespeare. Fr. Hamlet, I, i. OFD; PChr

Some say the world will end in fire. Fire and Ice. Robert Frost. AnMo; BiP; CABA (1972 ed.); CMoP (1970 ed.); FaBoEE; FaPo; FF; HeIP; HoPM (1975 ed.); ILP (1975 ed.); InPK; LoAs; MiP; NoAM; NOBA; PoIA; PPP; SoSe; STS; TAP; TT

Some Scribbles for a Lumpfish. Thomas Johnson. AMV-80

Some shapes cannot be seen in a glass. Holding the Mirror Up to Nature. Howard Nemerov. PoA

Some silent movie star. The Flicker. Lew Blockcolski. VoR

Some sit pale and scared, not touching the comics. Immunisation Day. Elizabeth Bartlett. PMW

Some Slippery Afternoon. Daniela Gioseffi. AAN; WBN

Some sort of fire leaped out of the dirty and poor and merciless city. Hymn. Otto Orban, tr. by Emery George. VWA

Some steerage. In a Dream Ship's Hold. Suzanne Bernhardt. VWA

Some Syrian rainmaker. Assumption. Padraic Fallon. BIrV

Some talk of Alexander, and some of Hercules. The British Grenadiers. Unknown. BTTM; FSW

Some that have deeper digged love's mine than I. Love's Alchemy. John Donne. AnMo; CABA (1972 ed.); NIL; OAEL-1

Some that reporte great Alexanders life. Thomas Watson. Fr. Hekatompathia. AAS

Some there are who are present at such occasions. On the Suicide of a Friend. Reed Whittemore. ConAP

Some they will talk of bold Robin Hood. Robin Hood and the Bishop of Hereford. Unknown. PeBB

Some thing is lost in me. Man Thinking about Woman. Don L. Lee. CNA; IPWM; NoAM

Some things are blessedly alyrical. Give Us This Day Our Daily Day. Robert J. Levy. AMV-81

Some things are very dear to me. Sonnet. Gwendolyn B. Bennett. AmNP (1974 ed.); PoBA

Some things go to sleep in such a funny way. How They Sleep. Unknown. CTV

Some things will never change although. Far Trek. June Brady. QQQ

Some think my satyre's too too tart. Satires, II, 1. Horace, tr. by Thomas Drant. TVS

Some think that in the Christian scheme. Consideration for Others. Christopher Smart. OxBChV

Some thirty inches from my nose. W. H. Auden. FaBoEE

Some thought it mounted to the Lunar sphere. The Lock. Pope. *Fr.* The Rape of the Lock. Moon

Some Thoughts. Gary Simmons. SFF

Some time. *See also* Sometime.

Some time in the dark hours. Snowfall. W. S. Merwin. NNaP

Some time now past in the autumnal tide. Contemplations. Anne Bradstreet. EAP; WPE, *abr.*

Some time when the river is ice ask me. Ask Me. William Stafford. FiCP

Some Trees. John Ashbery. CAPP; ConAP

Some twenty years of marital agreement. J. V. Cunningham. POL

Some twitch of the pajamas. Bad Dreams. Billy Collins. AAN

Some tyme I fled the fyre that me brent. Sir Thomas Wyatt. AAS

Some Verses upon the Burning of Our House July 10th, 1666. Anne Bradstreet. *See* Upon the Burning of Our House, July 10th, 1666.

Some were for setting up a king. Samuel Butler. *Fr.* Hudibras, III, 2. EBEV

Some Western Haikus, *sels.* Jack Kerouac. VoA
  "And the quiet cat."
  "In my medicine cabinet."
  "Nodding against."
  "Rain has filled, The."
  "Straining at the padlock."
  "Those birds sitting."

Some with sharp swords, to tell O most accursed! Margaret Cavendish, Duchess of Newcastle. *Fr.* The Fort or Castle of Hope. SCP-2

Some women marry houses. Housewife. Anne Sexton. NMM; Psy

Some Words. Judith Wright. CAAP; GAS

Some would dive in the lagoon. Alfred Noyes. *Fr.* The Enchanted Island. EcS

Some years of late, in 'Eighty-eight, as I do well remember-a. Sir Francis Drake; or, Eighty-eight. *Unknown.* GBP

Somebody. Tennyson. NOBL
  ("Somebody being a nobody.") FaBoEE

Somebody/ Cut his hair. Young Poet. Myron O'Higgins. PoBA

Somebody and Somebody Else and You. Edwin Rolfe. SPT

Somebody being a nobody. Somebody. Tennyson. FaBoEE; NOBL

Somebody Call. Carolyn M. Rodgers. JB

Somebody has given my. Proust's Madeleine. Kenneth Rexroth. NoAM

Somebody just keep on calling me. Stocking Feet Blues. *Unknown.* BluL

Somebody knocked. Who's There? Frances Frost. ECBV

Somebody loses whenever somebody wins. Crapshooters. Carl Sandburg. VGW

Somebody rang the bell. A Secret. Eve Merriam. CC

Somebody said that it couldn't be done. It Couldn't Be Done. Edgar A. Guest. PPM

Somebody told me I wouldn't know how to choose. Song: Paper. Keith Waldrop. MAT

Somebody under my window. Leaf out of a Rhyming Diary. Hugh McCrae. MAuV

Somebody who should have been born. The Abortion. Anne Sexton. CAPP; IHMS; MAT; NMM; Psy

Somebody's/ house is on fire. Fire. Anita Barrows. RiTi

Somebody's Darling. Marie Ravenel de la Coste. UnPo (1976 ed.)

Somebody's Gone. Charles Henri Ford. EAS

Somebody's hiding. Cheek. Coleman Barks. *Fr.* Body Poems. NVAP

Somebody's knockin' at th' door. The Collier's Wife. D. H. Lawrence. OxBTC

Somebody's Sweetheart I Want to Be, *with music.* Will D. Cobb. FSN

Someday. *See also* Some Day.

Someday Baby. *Unknown.* BluL

Someday Snoopy will be dead. Peanuts. Gerald Locklin. CPA

Someday Song for Sophia, A. Rochelle Ratner. PCho

Somedays now/ I can squash a cockroach. Wendy G. Rickert. NMM

Somehow/ I cannot think of god. Hypnopompic Poem. William Cole. POL

Somehow/ I had come to the desert. Abraham in Egypt. Howard Schwartz. VWA

Somehow, I keep thinking it is too late. Suburbia: Impossibilities of Change. Adrianne Marcus. CPA

Somehow it should have been. Masks. Elizabeth Fenton. NMM

Somemore cigarettes, some buckhorn, some calligraphy. Fantastic Collections of Stamps. John Sjoberg. AcAn

Some One. Walter de la Mare. LCL

Someone. Sam Reavin. CaYB

Someone approaches to say his life is ruined. The Dream. David Ignatow. MAT; NNaP

Some one came knocking. Some One. Walter de la Mare. LCL

Someone else/ looked at the sky. Izumi Shikibu, *tr. fr. Japanese by* Willis Barnstone. BoWoP

Someone else, I see. Man Missing. Charles Brasch. ATNZ

Someone fits a flute to his lips, and. Deception. Alfred Corn. PoA

Someone Gone Away Downstairs. Jeanette Nichols. RiTi

Someone had been walking in and out. The Origin of Baseball. Kenneth Patchen. IPWM; LiSp; TPo

Someone has built a dirigible in my parlor. Zeppelin. Andrew Glaze. CSP; WeW

Someone has just. Where Are You Now? Mary Britton Miller. ECBV

Someone has shut the shining eyes, straightened and folded. Beside the Bed. Charlotte Mew. WPE

Someone I know—and he's very near. Get Up or You'll Be Late for School, Silly. John Ciardi. ECBV

Someone, I tell you,/ will remember us. Sappho, *tr. fr. Greek by* Willis Barnstone. BoWoP

Someone in a prayer-shawl is walking over your ramparts. Vilna. Moishe Kulbak, *tr. by* Joachim Neugroschel. VWA

Someone in the next apartment. Room. Ruth Stone. BoWoP

Someone Is Beating a Woman. Andrei Voznesensky, *tr. fr. Russian by* Jean Garrigue *and* Max Hayward. BuTh

Someone is breathing in the room. Waking. Hugh Maxton. BIrV; CIP; IPM

Someone is Dead. Lament. Anne Sexton. ConAP; UsP; WPE

Someone is locking out the stars and the yellow flowers. Old Man in a Moon Loft. T. Glynne Davies. OBW

Someone is playing a trombone. The Nocturne in the Corner Phonebox. Andrew Taylor. FPA; GAS

Someone is smoking in the darkness. First Star. Dave Smith. AMV-81

Someone Knocks. Peter Everwine. NNaP

Someone lives in a cave. The Fury of Abandonment. Anne Sexton. UsP

Someone must make out the cards. What Was Her Name? John Ciardi. MiP

Someone next door is moving things about. Thin Partition. Gordon Challis. ATNZ

Someone passes.  Lady Murasaki Shikibu, *tr. fr. Japanese by* Kenneth Rexroth.  BoWoP; OLR

Someone recently asked my kid.  Son of Toad.  Gerald Locklin. BrS

Someone Sits at the Harp.  Jon Lang.  AMV-81

Someone stole a winter from my life.  The Groundhog Foreshadowed.  Steven Sher.  AMV-80

Someone told me long ago.  Have You Ever Seen the Rain? J. C. Fogerty.  PoRo

Someone walks my father's way.  On the Way.  Mordechai Husid, *tr. by* Seymour Mayne *and* Rivka Augenfeld.  VWA

Someone who well knew how she'd toss her chin.  Loose Woman. X. J. Kennedy.  WeW

Someplace Else.  Marge Piercy.  NeAC

*Somethin' Else* and/ *Kind of Blue*.  Cannon Arrested.  Michael S. Harper.  CNA

Something.  Jared Smith.  AMV-81

Something about It, *sel.*  John Hollander. Its Lunch.  GP

Something about your smile is more than you.  Becoming Is Perfection.  Tom Johnson.  AMV-81

Something always remains a mystery.  A Classical Idyll. Avraham Huss, *tr. by* Mark Elliott Shapiro.  VWA

Something broke the dream.  Poem.  John Gill.  NeAC

Something broken Something.  Nightbreak.  Adrienne Rich. IHMS; PiAm

Something continues and I don't know what to call it.  To Dana for Her Birthday.  W. S. Merwin.  PCho

Something disturbs your big pale limbs among.  For Delphine. James Simmons.  POL

Something Else They Say.  Mbembe.  NW

Something for My Russian Friends.  Edmund Wilson.  OBAL

Something for Supper.  Carroll Arnett.  VoR

Something for the Touts, the Nuns, the Grocery Clerks and You. Charles Bukowski.  CPA

Something forgotten twenty years: though my fathers.  A Map of the Western Part of the County of Essex in England.  Denise Levertov.  ConAP

Something hangs in back of me.  The Wings.  Denise Levertov. CAPP

Something happened the other day that never happened before. Shovelling Iron Ore.  *Unknown.*  GBP

Something has ceased to come along with me.  Death of a Son. Jon Silkin.  BBGO; FF; IPWM; NoAM; OxBTC; PPoD; VWA

Something has snapped.  A Cold Snap.  Robert Tait.  SLP

Something I saw or thought I saw.  On the Heart's Beginning to Cloud the Mind.  Robert Frost.  CMoP (1970 ed.)

Something I want to communicate to you.  With the Door Open. David Ignatow.  CTBA

Something immense and lonely.  Foreboding.  John Haines. ConAP

Something Inside Focuses My Attention.  Richard W. Thomas. TC

Something inspires the only cow of late.  The Cow in Apple Time. Robert Frost.  CABA (1972 ed.); PSN

Something is dead.  Prologue to "Rhymes and Rhythms."  W. E. Henley.  VLP

Something Is Dying Here.  Thomas McGrath.  TAT

Something is happening.  Last Will and Testament.  Alvin Aubert.  CoPAm

Something is tearing, tearing a hole.  Good Friday.  Arlene De Bevoise.  AMV-81

Something kept the photograph wet.  I've Got Connections at the Circus.  Beth Joselow.  PoUP

Something like an Apple.  James Reiss.  CAAP

Something massively large has slept.  Something.  Jared Smith. AMV-81

Something Missing on the Left.  Elizabeth Albrecht.  PoUp

Something of how the homing bee at dusk.  Southern Gothic. Donald Justice.  NIL

Something old and tyrannical burning there.  A Coal Fire in Winter.  Thomas McGrath.  NU

Something Passionate for Cinda.  Allan Kornblum.  AcAn

Something red my father wears now.  Song of a Youth Whose Father Was Killed in the War.  *Unknown, tr. by* Mary Austin. WPW

Something startles me where I thought I was safest.  This Compost.  Walt Whitman.  CABA (1972 ed.)

Something, the sandwich and the coffee.  Young Woman in Apathy.  Christopher Middleton.  TwMBP

Something there is that doesn't love a wall.  Mending Wall. Robert Frost.  CMoP (1970 ed.); ExPo (1973 ed.); HAP; HoPM (1975 ed.); ILP (1975 ed.); InPS; IP; IPWM; LFH; NoAM; NOBA; NowV; PiAm; PoIA; PPoD; SoSe (1977 ed.); STS; TAP; VGW

Something there is, whose veiled creation was.  Lao Tzu, *tr. by* Raymond B. Blakney.  *Fr.* Tao Teh King.  ILwL

Something to lose; it came in the equipment.  Going Back to Oxford.  Eiléan Ní Chuilleanáin.  IPM

Something Told the Wild Geese.  Rachel Field.  CTV

Something was whispered.  Accusation.  Utahania, *tr. fr. Eskimo.* WTO

Something went crabwise.  The Presence.  Maxine W. Kumin. RFM; TSWA; WPE

Something you said—I found it written down.  A Postcard to Send to Sumer.  William Bronk.  VGW

Sometime.  *See also* Some time.

Sometime during eternity.  Lawrence Ferlinghetti.  *Fr.* A Coney Island of the Mind.  CAPP; NoAM; TPo

Sometime I Loved.  *Unknown.*  OxBM

Sometime in Fraunce dwelled a plowman.  How the Ploughman Learned His Paternoster.  *Unknown.*  OxBM

Sometime [*or* Somtyme] this world was so steadfast [*or* stedfast] and stable.  Lack of Steadfastness [*or* Stedfastnesse]. Chaucer.  ILP (1975 ed.); PBMP

Sometimes.  Hermann Hesse, *tr. fr. German by* Robert Bly.  NU

Sometimes/ I cool out.  Spacin.  Ronda Davis.  JB

Sometimes/ Sometimes there is a.  Patchwork.  Lindiwe Mabuza. SES

Sometimes/ the poems.  Sharon Scott.  JB

Sometimes, / when the bars close.  Leaves and Ashes.  Michael Waters.  AAN

Sometimes a child is washed from that warm room.  Verse for Vestigials.  Elizabeth Allen.  AMV-80

Sometimes a huge wave of thought.  Song for a Day.  Francisco Arriví, *tr. by* Julio Marzán.  InW

Sometimes a lantern moves along the night.  The Lantern out of Doors.  Gerard Manley Hopkins.  AnMo;CMoP (1970 ed.); VLP

Sometimes a rain comes.  A Rain of Rites.  Jayanta Mahapatra. PoA

Sometimes a wild thing.  Yours Truly.  Leonard Nathan.  AMV-80

Sometimes after the break of a bone.  Painlessly out of Ourselves. William Page.  AMV-81

Sometimes, as a child.  Olga Broumas.  CNW

Sometimes at night when the wind blows hard.  The Loch Ness Monster.  Tom Buchan.  SLP

Sometimes before great events a person will try.  Things That Happen.  William Stafford.  NNaP

Sometimes, childishly watching a beetle, thrush or trout.  Clarence Mangan.  Thomas Kinsella.  CIP

Sometimes goldfinches one by one will drop.  Yellow Flutterings. Keats.  PCOP

Sometimes he brays.  Donkey.  Vasko Popa, *tr. by* Anne Pennington.  TSWA

Sometimes he walked to occupy.  Generation 2.  Sam Cornish. NVAP

Sometimes he was cool like an eternal.  Lester Young.  Ted Joans.  AmNP (1974 ed.)

Sometimes I.  Song of the Thunders.  *Tr. by* Frances Densmore. OBVE

Sometimes I am a young child.  World within a World.  Debra Woolard Bender.  AMV–80

Sometimes I can believe.  Valediction.  Lawrence Raab.  AMV–81

Sometimes I catch a glimpse of it.  The Presence.  Dana Naone. CDW

Sometimes I envy those.  The Mole.  John Haines.  NCSH

Sometimes I Feel like a Motherless Child.  *Unknown.*  BLSo, *with music*; FSW; WIF

Sometimes I feel like I will never stop.  To Satch [*or* American Gothic].  Samuel Allen.  AmNP (1974 ed.); BuTh; CTBA; LiSp; NIL; PoBA; SoSe; SPo; TPo; TVo

Sometimes I get the feeling that I have been here before. Reincarnation.  Mae Jackson.  PoBA

Sometimes I Go to Camarillo and Sit in the Lounge.  K. Curtis Lyle.  PoBA

Sometimes I hear God's whisper in the night.  Secrets, V.  Jessie Orton Jones.  CTV

Sometimes I picture you—as now, among.  Images.  Andrew Whittaker.  IPM

Sometimes I say things.  Poems for My Father.  Michael Delp. TC

Sometimes I see them.  Galway Kinnell.  *Fr.* Ruins under the Stars.  RFM

Sometimes I see them coming.  Benediction.  Myra Sklarew. VWA

Sometimes I sit with both eyes closed.  Parrot.  Alan Brownjohn. BBL

Sometimes I stare into an awning of spirit.  Sometimes I Go to Camarillo and Sit in the Lounge.  K. Curtis Lyle.  PoBA

Sometimes I Think of Maryland.  Jodi Braxton.  CNA

Sometimes I think of those whose lives touch mine.  I Think of Those.  Paul Henderson.  ATNZ

Sometimes I think that my body is a vase.  A Chinese Vase. Edward Hirsch.  AMV–80

Sometimes I think the hills.  The Hills.  Rachel Field.  LCL

Sometimes I walk where the deep water dips.  Frederick Goddard Tuckerman.  *Fr.* Sonnets.  NOBA; PiAm

Sometimes I Want to Go Up.  Rachel Korn, *tr. fr. Yiddish by* Ruth Whitman.  VWA

Sometimes if you look close enough.  Trolls.  Cash Terrell. DNGG

Sometimes I'm happy.  MANICdepressant.  Kim Dammers. POL

Sometimes I'm happy; la la la la la la la.  Joy Sonnet in a Random Universe.  Helen Chasin.  NIL

Sometimes I'm their first.  The First Time.  James L. White. BrS

Sometimes in the over-heated house, but not for long.  Fame. Charlotte Mew.  PBWP; SBG

Sometimes, in the palpitating chrysalis of night.  Listening-Post. Martin C. Rosner.  AMV–80

Sometimes in weariness I stop.  Years.  Jon Anderson.  AmPA; FoP

Sometimes in winter you see one.  Porcupines.  Robley Wilson, Jr.  AMV–81

Sometimes it happens.  The Porch.  Gary Gildner.  AMV-80

Sometimes it is inconceivable that I should be the age I am.  The Child.  W. S. Merwin.  NoAM

Sometimes it seems.  The Children.  Susan MacDonald.  IHMS

Sometimes just being alone seems the bad thing.  The Bad Thing. John Wain.  BuTh

Sometimes late at night dozing over a book.  Flying.  Henry Carlile.  AMV–80

Sometimes Life Is Not a Literary Experience, *sel.*  Eugene Lesser. "Tonight I sat on my back porch."  OSP

Sometimes my mind is like a house where no one lives.  The Visit. Jim Gauer.  AMV–81

Sometimes, riding in a car, in Wisconsin.  Three Kinds of Pleasures.  Robert Bly.  ANTL

Sometimes the flautist's hands.  Awkward Song for My Sisters. Allan Kornblum.  AcAN; EC

Sometimes the night echoes to prideless wailing.  Sonnet.  John Berryman.  NoAM

Sometimes the sea lays.  Dragging in Winter.  David McElroy. AmPA

Sometimes the wind is all I need.  Fickle in the Arms of Spring. Susie Fry.  AMV–81

Sometimes they smear the evening on the air.  Bat Angels.  Larry Levis.  AmPA

Sometimes this quiet settles in like a stone.  A Letter from a Friend.  Carolyn Maisel.  IHMS

Sometimes thou seemest not as thyself alone.  Heart's Compass. Dante Gabriel Rossetti.  The House of Life, XXVII.  PAIC

Sometimes walking late at night.  Butcher Shop.  Charles Simic. AmPA; NNaP; NVAP; PCho

Sometimes we meet like old lovers.  Dede's return to New Mexico.  Summer Brenner.  RiTi

Sometimes, when a bird cries out.  Sometimes.  Hermann Hesse, *tr. by* Robert Bly.  NU

Sometimes when a man is old.  Passages.  David Walker. AMV–80

Sometimes when clouds float.  At the Edge of Town.  William Stafford.  NNaP

Sometimes when I look in the mirror over the breakfast table. The Fable of the Airplanes.  Richard Williams.  AAN

Sometimes when my eyes are red.  My Sad Self.  Allen Ginsberg. ILP (1975 ed.); IPWM; NoAM; UnPo (1976 ed.)

Sometimes When Night.  V. Sackville-West.  SBG; WPE

Sometimes when the boy was troubled he would go.  The Cave. Glenn W. Dresbach.  RFM; SoS

Sometimes, when winding slow by brook and bower.  Frederick Goddard Tuckerman.  *Fr.* Sonnets.  AmVN

Sometimes when you watch the fire.  Long Distance.  William Stafford.  CoPAm; SO

Sometimes, when you're called a bastard.  When Something Happens.  James A. Randall, Jr.  BPo

Sometimes with One I Love.  Walt Whitman.  GBL

Sometimes you almost get a punch in.  Shadowboxing.  James Tate.  CAAP

Sometimes you feel/ alone within your ribs.  What Is Needed. Marcos Rodríguez Frese, *tr. by* Julio Marzán.  InW

Sometimes you hear, fifth-hand.  Poetry of Departures.  Philip Larkin.  CMoP (1970 ed.); FF; HeIP; ILP (1975 ed.); LP; NowV; SS; UsP

Sometimes your medulla.  Living in the Present.  Clarinda Harriss Lott.  AMV–81

Somewhere.  Robert Creeley.  NoAM

Somewhere.  James E. Warren, Jr.  AATT

Somewhere/ a niche.  Wish.  Lance Henson.  CDW

Somewhere a forest, every.  These Leaves.  William Stafford. NNaP

Somewhere afield here something lies.  Shelley's Skylark. Thomas Hardy.  VLP

Somewhere beneath that piano's superb sleek black. The Piano. D. H. Lawrence. WeW

Somewhere between our nervousness and. "Portrait de Femme." Irving Feldman. NoAM

Somewhere cities burn. April 68. Sam Cornish. CNA

Somewhere Farm. Guy Rotella. AMV–81

Somewhere, farther even than the Sahara. Clove as Egg. Daniel Halpern. CAAP

Somewhere Friendly. Bruce Dawe. CAAP

Somewhere I Have Never Travelled, Gladly Beyond. E. E. Cummings. BoLoP; ILP (1975 ed.); InPS; LoAs; SoS; STS; VGW

Somewhere I read how, long since oh very. Parable of Two Talents. Kendrick Smithyman. ATNZ

Somewhere, I think in Dakota. A Sound from the Earth. William Stafford. NNaP; RFM

Somewhere in all this mess. Pettigrew Museum. John Calvin Rezmerski. HeS

Somewhere in California miners rise. Fitz Hugh Lane Goes to the Masthead. Wesley McNair. FAF

Somewhere in Chelsea, early summer. Relating to Robinson. Weldon Kees. AnMo; NYP

Somewhere in his body a blood-clot is moving. Little Death. Gwyn Thomas, tr. by Joseph P. Clancy. OBW

Somewhere in Kansas, a friend found. A Place in Kansas. Ted Kooser. HeS

Somewhere in the field. The Field. Douglas Lawder. PH

Somewhere in the quiet lakes. A Dream of Lakes. Laurence Lieberman. HeS

Somewhere in the world. Shekhina. Karl Wolfskehl, tr. by Erna Baber Rosenfeld. VWA

Somewhere inside me. Coming Back Home. Ray A. Young Bear. CDW

Somewhere inside something is walking about. The Compound. Evan Jones. GAS

Somewhere Is Such a Kingdom. John Crowe Ransom. CMoP (1970 ed.)

Somewhere near here a new-loosed creek sloughs down. A Walk in March. Tim Reynolds. MAT

Somewhere now she takes off the dress I am putting. Palindrome. Lisel Mueller. IHMS

Somewhere nowhere in Utah, a boy by the roadside. Utah. Anne Stevenson. NCSH

Somewhere on his travels the strange child. Santa Claus. Howard Nemerov. HAP; NowV; TPo

Somewhere on these bare rocks in some bare hall. For a College Yearbook. J. V. Cunningham. NoAM

Somewhere or Other. Christina Rossetti. NOBE

Somewhere out past the high walls. The Edge of Town. William Clamurro. AMV–81

Somewhere outside, sky and sea. The Last Boat of the Season. Robin Fulton. MS

Somewhere outside your window. A Sense of Coolness. Quincy Troupe. PoBA

Somewhere, sometime, in an April twilight. Dedicatory. Willa Cather. WPE

Somewhere the lines were down. Power Failure. Dabney Stuart. NVAP

Somewhere the sun is shining. Beautiful Isle of Somewhere. Jessie B. Pounds. FSN

Somewhere, then—the bottom. There. William Harmon. AMV–80

Somewhere there is a coil of glass within. A Coil of Glass (I). Stanley Burnshaw. SPT

Somewhere we should sit down and rest. Just a While. Frantisek Gottlieb, tr. by Ewald Osers. VWA

Somewhere You Exist. Manfred Winkler, tr. fr. Hebrew by Mary Zilzer. VWA

Somewhere you have been. To His Love in Middle-Age. Edwin Brock. AMV–80

Somnambulist. J. R. Hervey. ATNZ

Somnambulist Blue, The. Keith Althaus. AAN

Somnambulistic Ballad. Federico García Lorca, tr. fr. Spanish by Roy and Mary Campbell. TCP
(Ballad of the Sleepwalker, The, tr. by Langston Hughes.) Epi
(Sleepwalkers' Ballad, tr. by John Frederick Nims.) WeW

Son, A. Kipling. Fr. Epitaphs of the War. FaBoEE

"Son,"/ my father used to say. Father and I in the Woods. David McCord. SO

Son, Condemned, The. Larry Rubin. GP

Son Davie. Unknown. LFH

Son, my son! Lament of a Man for His Son. Unknown, tr. by Mary Austin. BPAW; DL

Son o' ol' Miz McAuliffe, the widder o' Box-Car Jack. Pool-Shootin' Roy. Damon Runyon. SPo

Son of a Gun. Padraic Fiacc. IPM

Son of Enops, Thestor next he smote, The. Homer, tr. by William Cowper. Fr. The Iliad, XVI. OBVE

Son, of great fortune have I none. Christine to Her Son. Christine de Pisan, tr. by Barbara Howes. BoWoP

Son of the King of the Moy, The. Unknown, tr. fr. Irish by John Montague. BIrV

Son of the old moon-mountains African! To the Nile. Keats. MBPR

Son of Toad. Gerald Locklin. BrS

"Son," said my mother. The Ballad of the Harp-Weaver. Edna St. Vincent Millay. PBMP; PoTa

Son, upon whose shoulders hung the world one dark Friday. The Vinedresser Yearns over His Vineyard. Irene Dayton. AATT

Son, you have two more months. D-Day Minus. Edwin Brock. BBGO

Sonet: "Fra bank to bank, fra wood to wood I rin." Mark Alexander Boyd. See Fra Bank to Bank, . . .

Sonet Written in Prayse of the Browne Beautie, A. George Gascoigne. AAS

Song, A: "Absent from thee, I languish still." Earl of Rochester. BoLoP; GBL
(Return.) NOBE

Song: "Adieu, farewell earths blisse." Thomas Nashe. See Adieu, Farewell Earth's Bliss.

Song: "Ae fond kiss, and then we sever." Burns. See Ae Fond Kiss.

Song: "Afternoon cooking in the fall sun." Robert Hass. AmPA

Song: "Ah false Amyntas, can that hour." Aphra Behn. Fr. The Dutch Lover. WPE

Song: "All in green went my love riding." E. E. Cummings. See All in Green Went My Love Riding.

Song: "All joy to mortals, joy and mirth." Aphra Behn. Fr. Emperor of the Moon. WPE

Song: "As I walked out one evening." W. H. Auden. See As I Walked Out One Evening.

Song, A: "Ask me no more where Jove bestows." Thomas Carew. CABA (1972 ed.); CaPo; GBL; HeIP; HoPM (1975 ed.); ILP (1975 ed.); InPS; NOBE; OBP; PoPle; PPP
(Ask Me No More.) HAP; SCP-2

Song: "Boat is chafing at our long delay, The." John Davidson. PoPle

Song: "Chloris, forbear a while." Henry Bold. GBL

Song: "Choose now among this fairest number." William Browne. GBL

Song: "Circumstance has estranged my friend."   Carl Rakosi. BrS

Song: "Come live with me and be my love."   C. Day Lewis. *See* Come, Live with Me and Be My Love.

Song: "Come, melt thy soul in mine, that when unite."   Sir William Davenant. *Fr.* The Temple of Love.   SCP-2

Song: "Curse upon that faithless maid, A."   Aphra Behn. *Fr.* Emperor of the Moon.   WPE

Song: "Deftly, admiral, cast your fly."   W. H. Auden.   PSN

Song: "Dressed up in my melancholy."   M. Carl Holman. AmNP (1974 ed.)

Song: "False though she be to me and love."   Congreve.   POL ("False though she be to me and love.")   BoLoP; NOBE

Song: "Feathers of the willow, The."   Richard Watson Dixon. NOBE

Song: "Fire, fire."   Henry Bold.   GBL

Song: "Flowers that in thy garden rise, The."   Sir Henry Newbolt. FaBoTw (1975 ed.)

Song: "Follow thy fair sun, unhappy shadow!"   Thomas Campion. *See* Follow Thy Fair Sun.

Song: "Fresh from the dewy hill, the merry year."   Blake. MBPR

Song: "From whence cometh song?"   Theodore Roethke.   NCSH

Song: "Gather kittens while you may."   Oliver Herford.   AKE; SpRo

Song: "Give me leave to rail at you."   Earl of Rochester.   LoAs

Song: "Go and catch a falling star."   John Donne.   AnMo; CABA (1972 ed.); EBEV; HAP; HeIP; ILP (1975 ed.); InPK; InPS; NIL; NOBE; PBMP; PoIA; PoPle; PPoD; PPoe; SoSe; UsP; VoPo
(Go and Catch a Falling Star.)   BiP; IP
(Song: "Goe, and catche a falling starre.")   BuTh; HoPM (1975 ed.); OBP

Song: "Go lovely rose."   Edmund Waller.   *See* Go, Lovely Rose.

Song: "Goe, and catche a falling starre."   John Donne.   *See* Song: "Go and catch a falling star."

Song: Good Counsel to a Young Maid.   Thomas Carew.   CaPo

Song: "Hair/ like heather, father would boast."   Marie Harris. MMD

Song: "Hark, hark!/ Bow-wow."   Shakespeare.   *Fr.* The Tempest, I, ii.   SoSe

Song: "Help me now."   Emmett Jarrett.   NeAC

Song: "Hence burgundy, claret, and port."   Keats.   MBPR

Song: How Can I Care?   Robert Graves.   GBL

Song: "How sweet I roamed [*or* roam'd] from field to field."   Blake.   CABA (1972 ed.); LoAs; MBPR; OAEL-2; OLR; STS
(Prince of Love, The.)   NOBE

Song: "Hush, hush! tread softly! hush, hush, my dear!"   Keats. MBPR

Song: "I almost went to bed."   Leonard Cohen.   SoS

Song: "I have loved flowers that fade."   Robert Bridges.   VLP

Song: "I hid my love when young while I."   John Clare.   *See* I Hid My Love.

Song: "I lately vow'd, but 'twas in haste."   John Oldmixon.   POL

Song: "I love my lady's eyes."   Robert Bridges.   VLP

Song: "I love the jocund dance."   Blake.   MBPR

Song: "I peeled bits of straw and I got switches too."   John Clare. VLP

Song: "I would not feign a single sigh."   John Clare.   GBL

Song: "I'd much rather sit there in the sun."   Ruth Krauss.   SO

Song: "It was upon a Lammas night."   Burns.   *See* Rigs o' Barley, The.

Song: "Know then, my brethren, heaven is clear."   *Unknown. Fr.* The Song of Anarchus.   FaBoCo

Song: "Lark now leaves his wat'ry nest, The."   Sir William Davenant.   *See* Aubade: "Lark now leaves . . ."

Song: "Let it be forgotten, as a flower is forgotten."   Sara Teasdale.   PoA

Song: "Let school-masters puzzle their brain."   Goldsmith.   *Fr.* She Stoops to Conquer.   BIrV
(Three Pigeons, The.)   ILP (1975 ed.)

Song: "Linnet in the rocky dells, The."   Emily Brontë.   HAP ("Linnet in the rocky dells, The.")   VLP

Song: "Little onion lay by the fireplace, A."   Nicholas Moore. EAS

Song, A: "Lord, when the sense of thy sweet grace."   Richard Crashaw.   IPWM

Song: "Love a woman? You're an ass!"   Earl of Rochester. GBL; NOBL

Song: "Love and harmony combine."   Blake.   MBPR

Song: "Love in fantastic triumph sate."   Aphra Behn.   *Fr.* Abdelazer.   NOBE; WPE
(Love Arm'd)   SBG

Song: "Love still has something of the sea."   Sir Charles Sedley. GBL; NOBE

Song: "Lovers in ladies' magazines."   Thomas McGrath.   VGW

Song: "Lying is an occupation."   Laetitia Pilkington.   WPE

Song: "Master, the swabber, the boatswain, and I, The." Shakespeare.   *Fr.* The Tempest, II, ii.   NOBL; RhR ("Master, the swabber, the boatswain and I, The.")   FF; OBP; PoPle

Song: Mediocrity in Love Rejected.   Thomas Carew.   CaPo; GBL

Song: "Memory, hither come."   Blake.   MBPR; STS

Song: "Merchant, to secure his treasure, The."   Matthew Prior. *See* Ode, An: "Merchant, to secure his treasure, The."

Song: "Misty and dim, a bush in the wilds of Kapa'a."   Kaiama, *tr. fr. Hawaiian by* N. B. Emerson.   WTO

Song: "Morning opened/ Like a rose."   Donald Justice.   NCSH

Song: "Mother Mother shave me."   *Tr. fr. Nyasa by* Ulli Beier. BoWoP

Song: "My cabinets are oyster-shells."   Margaret Cavendish, Duchess of Newcastle.   *Fr.* The Convent of Pleasure.   WPE ("My cabinets are oyster-shells.")   SCP-2
(Song by Lady Happy, as a Sea Goddess.)   EcS

Song, A: "My name is sweet Jenny, my age is sixteen."   *Unknown.* POL

Song: "My silks and fine array."   Blake.   LAuP; MBPR (My Silks and Fine Array.)   GBL; UnPo (1976 ed.)

Song: "My straying thoughts, reduced stay."   Anne Collins. WPE

Song: "Nay but you, who do not love her."   Robert Browning. VoPo

Song: "Never seek to tell thy love."   Blake.   *See* Love's Secret.

Song: "Never take her away."   Vinícius de Moraes, *tr. fr. Portuguese by* Richard Wilbur.   RRA

Song: "No, no, fair heretic, it needs must be."   Sir John Suckling. *Fr.* Aglaura, IV, i.   CABA (1972 ed.); CaPo

Song: "Now and then there will arise."   *Tr. fr. Chippewa Indian by* Frances Densmore.   OBVE

Song: "Now in golden glory goes."   Lionel Johnson.   VLP

Song: "Now sleeps the crimson petal, now the white."   Tennyson. *See* Now Sleeps the Crimson Petal.

Song: "Nymphs and shepherds dance no more."   Milton.   *Fr.* Arcades.   LoAs

Song: "Oh, bid my tongue be still."   Richard Watson Dixon. VLP

Song: "O blush not so! O blush not so!"   Keats.   MBPR

Song, A: "Oh do not wanton with those eyes."   Ben Jonson. LoAs

Song: "O Joie."   Paul Mariah.   BrS

Song, The: "O! Lady dear, fair is thy noon."   James Hogg.   *Fr.* The Queen's Wake.   SLP

Song: "Oh! Love, that stronger art than wine." Aphra Behn. *Fr.* The Lucky Chance. WPE

Song: "O ruddier than the cherry." John Gay. *Fr.* Acis and Galatea. NOBE

Song: "O Where Are You Going?" W. H. Auden. *See* O Where Are You Going?

Song: "O whistle, and I'll come to ye, my lad." Burns. *See* O Whistle, and I'll Come to You, My Lad.

Song: "Oh, with the hunger of the sea, forever born anew." John Hall Wheelock. LoAS

Song: "Old Adam, the carrion crow." Thomas Lovell Beddoes. *Fr.* Death's Jest Book, V, iv. EBEV; ILP (1975 ed.); OAEL-2; OBP

Song: Old Rowley the King. *Unknown.* APAS

Song: "On the side of the road." Edmond Jabès, *tr. fr. French by* Anthony Rudolf. VWA

Song: "Once my heart was a summer rose." Edith Sitwell. UsP

Song: Organic Years, The. Marvin Bell. NVAP

Song: "Out upon it, I have lov'd." Sir John Suckling. *See* Constant Lover, The.

Song: "Owl is abroad, The." Ben Johnson. *See* Witches' Charm, The.

Song: Paper. Keith Waldrop. MAT

Song: Persuasions to Enjoy. Thomas Carew. *See* Persuasions to Enjoy.

Song: "Pious Selinda goes to prayers." William Congreve. BoLoP; FaBoCo; SoSe (1977 ed.)
(Pious Selinda.) NOBE

Song: "Rarely, rarely, comest thou." Shelley. MBPR

Song: "Rough Winds Do Shake the Darling Buds of May." Louis Simpson. SFF

Song: "Sabrina fair." Milton. *See* Sabrina.

Song: "Sergei's a flower." Ruth Herschberger. FF

Song: "She is not fair to outward view." Hartley Coleridge. PCOP

Song: "She sat and sang alway." Christina Rossetti. GBL

Song: "She spoke to me gently with words of sweet meaning." Patrick MacDonogh. PFIr

Song: "She was lyin face down in her face." William Knott. MAT

Song: "Shephard loveth thow me vell?" Jean Passerat, *tr. fr. French by* William Drummond of Hawthornden. OBVE

Song, The: "So light no one noticed." Edward Dorn. VGW

Song, A: "Song, A/ That seemed so brief at first." Howard Schwartz. VWA

Song: "Song tells us of our old way of living, The." John Ashbery. UsP

Song, The: "Song, The! the song! song!" Hemda Roth, *tr. fr. Hebrew by* Mariana Potasman. VWA

Song: "Spirit haunts the year's last hours, A." Tennyson. HeIP; ILP (1975 ed.); PoPle

Song: "Stay, Phoebus, stay!" Edmund Waller. ILP (1975 ed.)

Song: "Stranger lighted from his steed, The." Keats. SS

Song: "Stranger, you who hide my love." Stephen Spender. FaBoTw (1975 ed.)

Song: "Sweet beast, I have gone prowling." W. D. Snodgrass. SoSe

Song: "Sweetest love, I do not go." John Donne. BoLoP; HeIP; NOBE; OAEL-1
(Sweetest Love, I Do Not Go.) BiP; VoPo

Song: "Sylvia the fair, in the bloom of fifteen." Dryden. EBEV; LoAs

Song: "Tell me not, sweet, I am unkind." Richard Lovelace. *See* To Lucasta, Going to the Wars.

Song, The: "That day, in the slipping of torsos and straining flanks." Lola Ridge. WPE

Song, A: "There is a blue sky." Edward Dorn. ConAP

Song: "There was a jolly miller once." *At. to* Isaac Bickerstaffe. *See* Miller of the Dee ("There was a jolly miller once").

Song: "There's a barrel of porter at Tammany Hall." Fitz-Greene Halleck. OBAL

Song: "Those rivers run from that land." Robert Creeley. VGW

Song, A: "Thou art the soul of a summer's day." Paul Laurence Dunbar. AmNP (1974 ed.)

Song: To Amarantha, That She Would Dishevel Her Hair. Richard Lovelace. *See* To Amarantha, That She Would Dishevel Her Hair.

Song: To Celia ("Come, my Celia, let us prove"). Ben Jonson. *See* Come, My Celia.

Song: To Celia ("Drink to me, only, with thine eyes"). Ben Jonson. *See* To Celia ("Drink to me only . . .").

Song: To Cynthia. Ben Jonson. *See* Hymn to Diana.

Song: To My Inconstant Mistress. Thomas Carew. *See* To My Inconstant Mistress.

Song: "We raise de wheat." *Unknown.* BPo
(We Raise de Wheat.) TAP

Song: "What do you/ want, love. To be." Robert Creeley. TCP

Song: "What I took in my hand." Robert Creeley. PoA

Song: "What think you of this age now." *Unknown.* APAS

Song: "Whaur yon broken brig hings owre." William Soutar. MS

Song: "When early morn walks forth in sober grey." Blake. MBPR

Song: "When I am dead, my dearest." Christina Rossetti. AKE; BiP; BoLoP; DL; EBEV; FF; GBL; ILP (1975 ed.); NOBE; OAEL-2; UsP; VLP; WPE
(When I Am Dead, My Dearest.) PBMP; PPM

Song: "When lovely woman stoops to folly." Goldsmith. *Fr.* The Vicar of Wakefield, *ch.* 24. BoLoP; ILP (1975 ed.); LAuP; NOBE
(Stanzas on Woman.) ExPo (1973 ed.)
(When Lovely Woman Stoops to Folly.) HAP; HeIP; PoIA; UnPo (1976 ed.)

Song: "When maidens are young, and in their spring." Aphra Behn. *Fr.* The Emperor of the Moon. FF

Song, A: "When the white man." Lindiwe Mabuza. SES

Song: "When working blackguards come to blows." Ebenezer Elliott. EBEV

Song: "Where I walk out." Yvor Winters. BoAnP; POL

Song: "Where in blind files." Eavan Boland. CIP; IPM

Song: "Whilst Alexis lay pressed." Dryden. *Fr.* Marriage à la Mode, IV, ii. BoLoP
("Whilst Alexis lay prest.") FF; LoAs

Song: "Whipped by sorrow now." Miklós Radnóti, *tr. fr. Hungarian by* Steven Polgar *and* Stephen Berg *and* S. J. Marks. VWA

Song: "Who can say." Tennyson. BBGO

Song: "Why do bells for Christmas ring?" Eugene Field. CTV

Song: "Why should a foolish marriage vow." Dryden. *See* Why Should a Foolish Marriage Vow.

Song: "Why should your face so please me." Edwin Muir. SLP

Song: "Why so pale and wan, fond lover?" Sir John Suckling. *See* Why So Pale and Wan?

Song: "Widow bird sate mourning for her love, A." Shelley. NOBE; PoPle; UsP

Song: Willing Prisoner to His Mistress, The. Thomas Carew. CaPo

Song: "With my frailty don't upbraid me." Congreve. *See* Semele to Jupiter.

Song: "Year's at the spring, The." Robert Browning *See* Year's at the Spring, The.

Song: "Young flowers were whispering in melody." Poe. *Fr.* Al Aaraaf. NOBA

Song: "You're wondering if I'm lonely." Adrienne Rich. PBWP

Song, A/ That seemed so brief at first. A Song. Howard Schwartz. VWA

Song about Major Eatherly, A. John Wain. NowV; OxBTC

Song about Mary. Adrian Mitchell. PeBB

Song about Myself. Keats. MBPR; TT, *st.* 1
   (Naughty Boy, The, *st.* 4.) CTV; PCOP
   (No Difference, *st.* 4.) ECBV
   (There Was a Naughty Boy.) FaBoCo, *st.* 4; OxBChV, *sts.* 1 *and* 4
   (Verses from a Letter.) EBEV

Song against Grocers, The. G. K. Chesterton. FaBoCo

Song and Poetry. *Unknown, tr. fr. Welsh by* Gwyn Jones. OBW

Song at Morning, A. Edith Sitwell. CMoP (1970 ed.)

Song at Night. Norman Nicholson. FaBoTw (1975 ed.)

Song at San Carlos Bay. Brewster Ghiselin. MPA

Song at the Beginning of Autumn. Elizabeth Jennings. OxBTC

Song at the Feast of Brougham Castle. Wordsworth. MBPR

Song at the Skirts of Heaven. Uri Zvi Greenberg, *tr. fr. Hebrew by* Zvi Jagendorf. VWA

Song at the Well, The. George Peele. *Fr.* The Old Wives' Tale. ExPo (1973 ed.)
   ("Gently dip, but not too deep.") InPS

Song Ballet (I Was Sixteen Years of Age). *Unknown.* AmFP

Song Be Delicate. John Shaw Neilson. GAS; MAuV

Song Bewailing the Time of Christmas, A. *Unknown.* SCP-2

Song by Lady Happy, as a Sea-Goddess. Margaret Cavendish, Duchess of Newcastle. *See* Song: "My cabinets are oystershells."

Song by Mr. Cypress. Thomas Love Peacock. *Fr.* Nightmare Abbey. OAEL-2

Song by Rogero. George Canning. *Fr.* The Rovers. FaBoNo

Song by the Wavering Nymph. Aphra Behn. SBG

Song Called "His Hide Is Covered with Hair," The. Hilaire Belloc. FaBoNo

Song for a Birth or a Death. Elizabeth Jennings. EBEV

Song for a Dance. Abraham Sutskever, *tr. fr. Yiddish by* Ruth Whitman. VWA

Song for a Dancer. Kenneth Rexroth. TAP

Song for a Dark Girl. Langston Hughes. PoBA

Song for a Day, *sel.* Francisco Arriví, *tr. fr. Spanish by* Julio Marzán.
   "Sometimes a huge wave of thought." InW

Song for a Girl on Her First Menstruation. *Tr. fr. Papuan by* Joe Prentuo. BoWoP

Song for a Little House. Christopher Morley. CTV

Song for a Lost Art. Virginia Brasier. AMV-81

Song for a Marriage. Vassar Miller. PAIC

Song for a New Generation. Gertrude May Lutz. AMV-80

Song for a Transformation, *sel.* Francisco Arriví, *tr. fr. Spanish by* Julio Marzán.
   "This tree/ growing out of me." InW

Song for Afterwards. Francisco Lopez Merino, *tr. fr. Spanish by* Richard O'Connell. LoAs

Song for an Able Bastard, A. Eric Linklater. SLP

Song for Autumn. Andrew Young. GBL

Song for "Buvez les Vins du Postillon"—Advt. Jean Garrigue. TAP

Song for Dov Shamir. Dannie Abse. VWA
   (Song of a Hebrew.) WTO

Song for Everybody. Robert Paul Smith. ECBV

Song for Healing. Roberta Hill. CDW

Song for Ishtar. Denise Levertov. AnMo; NMM; NoAM; PiAm; Psy

Song for Meeting a Friend. Rafael Jesús González. BrS

Song for My Father. Jessica Tarahata Hagedorn. NW

Song for My Mother. Alan Chong Lau. NW

Song for St. Cecilia's Day. W. H. Auden. FaBoTw (1975 ed.)

Song for Saint Cecilia's Day, 1687, A. Dryden. AnMo; BiP; CABA (1972 ed.); HAP; ILP (1975 ed.); InPS; LFH; NIL; OAEL-1; PPP; SCP-1
   "Trumpet's loud clangour, The," *sel.* RAE

Song for September. Robert Fitzgerald. VGW

Song for Seven Parts of the Body, *sels.* Maxine W. Kumin. POL
   "I have a life of my own," III.
   "These nubbins/ these hangers-on," VII.
   "They have eyes that see not," V.

Song for Sigmund Freud, A. Kelly Cherry. PPoD

Song for Simeon, A. T. S. Eliot. BuTh

Song for Solomon Heine, A. Kraft Rompf. AAN

Song for Sunsets. Earle Birney. MPA

Song for the Elephant Hunt, *sel. Unknown, tr. fr. Gabon Pygmy by* C. M. Bowra.
   "In the frightened forest the tree sleeps, the leaves are dead." WeW

Song for the Last Act. Louise Bogan. LoAs; UnPo (1976 ed.); WPE

Song for the Luddites. Byron. MBPR

Song for the Lute. Thomas Campion. *See* Thrice Toss These Oaken Ashes in the Air.

Song for the Middle of the Night, A. James Wright. ILP (1975 ed.); WeW

Song for the Newborn. *Unknown, tr. fr. Grande Pueblo Indian by* Mary Austin. OFD; WPE

Song for the Nkazi or the Final Ironies. Thulani Nkabinde. NW

Song for the Passing of a Beautiful Woman. *Unknown, tr. fr. Paiute Indian by* Mary Austin. WPW

Song for the Ragged Schools of London, A. Elizabeth Barrett Browning. SBG

Song for the Skull of Black Bear. David Wagoner. BCr

Song for the Soul Going Away. David Wagoner. CNW

Song for the Soul Returning. David Wagoner. CNW

Song for the unsung heroes who rose in the country's need, A. The Unsung Heroes. Paul Laurence Dunbar. BPo

Song for the Woman Singing at the Café Trieste. Bart Schneider. AAN

Song Form. Amiri Baraka. CTBA

Song from a Country Fair. Leonie Adams. PoIA

Song from Aella. Thomas Chatterton. *See* Minstrel's Song, The.

Song from Shakespear's Cymbelyne, A. William Collins. LAuP
   (Dirge in "Cymbeline.") NOBE

Song from the Unfinished Man. Paul David Ashley. DNGG

Song from the Waters. Thomas Lovell Beddoes. *Fr.* Death's Jest Book. NOBE

Song in Autumn. Robert D. Fitzgerald. MAuV

Song in Passing, A. Yvor Winters. VGW

Song in the Cold Season. Samuel French Morse. PoA

Song in the Front Yard, A. Gwendolyn Brooks. IPWM; NoAM; NOBA; PoBA

Song in the valley of Nemea, A. Nemea. Lawrence Durrell. FaBoTw (1975 ed.)

Song in Time of Order 1852, A. Swinburne. VLP

Song in Time of Revolution 1860, A. Swinburne. VLP

Song in White. Anne Le Dressay. AMV-80

Song Mt. Tamalpais Sings, The. Lew Welch. MIT

Song My. Susan Griffin. NMM

Song My Paddle Sings, The. Pauline Johnson. BPAW

Song of a Child's Spirit. *Unknown, tr. fr. Pueblo Indian.* AKE

Song of a Common Lover. Flavien Ranaivo, *tr. fr. French by* Alan Ryder. BuTh

Song of a Hebrew. Dannie Abse. *See* Song for Dov Shamir.

Song of a Man about to Die in a Strange Land. *Unknown, tr. fr. Chippewa Indian by* Mary Austin. DL; WPW

Song of a Man Who Has Come Through, The. D. H. Lawrence. CMoP (1970 ed.); InPS; NoAM; OxBTC

Song of a Passionate Lover. *Unknown. See* Come Not Near My Songs.

Song of a Rat. Ted Hughes. CMoP (1970 ed.)

Song of a Second April. Edna St. Vincent Millay. CMoP (1970 ed.)

(Song of Second April.) PPM

Song of a Sick Child. *Malay Oral Tradition, tr. by* R. J. Wilkinson *and* R. O. Winstedt. WTO

Song of a Woman Abandoned by the Tribe. *Unknown, tr. fr. Shoshone Indian by* Mary Austin. BPAW; WPE; WPW

Song of a Young Lady to Her Ancient Lover, A. Earl of Rochester. BoLoP; EBEV; GBL

Song of a Youth Whose Father Was Killed in the War. *Unknown, tr. fr. Sioux Indian by* Mary Austin. WPW

Song of Abuse. *Yoruba Oral Tradition, tr. by* Ulli Beier *and* B. Gbadamosi. WTO

Song of Allegiance. R. A. K. Mason. ATNZ

Song of Amergin. *Unknown. See* Alphabet Calendar of Amergin.

Song of Anarchus, The, *sel. Unknown.*

Song: "Know then, my brethren, heaven is clear." FaBoCo

Song of Autumn I. Baudelaire, *tr. fr. French by* C. F. McIntyre. NAWM-2

Song of Basket-weaving. Constance Lindsay Skinner. BPAW

Song of Bekotsidi, The. *Tr. fr. Navajo Indian by* Washington Matthews. OBVE

Song of Bliss. Spenser. *Fr.* The Faerie Queene, II, 12. FF

("Whiles some one did chaunt this lovely lay, The.") OBVE

Song of Callicles, The. Matthew Arnold. *Fr.* Empedocles on Etna, II. NOBE; OAEL-2

Song of Caribou, Musk Oxen, Women, and Men Who Would Be Manly. *Tr. fr. Eskimo.* WTO

"Glorious it is/ to see long-haired winter caribou," *sel.* RFM

Song of Ceres. Katherine Doak. NPW

Song of Cove Creek Dam, The. *Unknown.* AmFP

Song of Creation, The. *Tr. fr. Sanskrit by* Raimundo Panikkar. *Fr.* Vedic Hymns. ILwL

Song of Crede, The. *Unknown, tr. fr. Irish by* Alfred Perceval Graves. BIrV

Song of David, The, *sel.* Christopher Smart.

David before Saul. PIM

Song of Deborah, The. Bible, *O.T.* Judges, V: 1-31. BoWoP; PBWP

Song of Degrees. Paul Auster. VWA

Song of Despair. Rangiaho, *tr. fr. Maori by* Barry Mitcalfe. WTO

Song of Duke William. Hilaire Belloc. FaBoNo

Song of Expectancy. George Hitchcock. EAS; MIT

Song of Finis, The. Walter de la Mare. ILP (1975 ed.)

Song of Fionnuala, The. Thomas Moore. BIrV

Song of Fixed Accord. Wallace Stevens. InPS

Song of Hate for Eels. Arthur Guiterman. OBAL

Song of Hiawatha, The, *sels.* Longfellow.

"From his wanderings far to eastward," *fr.* XXI. GOA

Hiawatha and Mudjekeewis, IV. AKE

Introduction: "Should you ask me, whence these stories?" NOBA; PiAm

Old Nokomis Sings, *fr.* III. ECBV

("By the shores of Gitche Gumee.") CTV; SpRo

Song of Joy. Uvavnuk, *tr. fr. Eskimo.* WTO

Song of Lewes, The. *Unknown.* OxBM

Song of Liberty, A. Blake. MBPR

Song of Longing. *Gond Oral Tradition, tr. by* V. Elwin *and* S. Hivale. WTO

Song of Longing. *Tr. fr. Maori by* John White. WTO

Song of Marion's Men. Bryant. BTTM

Song of Mr. Toad, The. Kenneth Grahame. *Fr.* The Wind in the Willows. NOBL

Song of Moses and the Lamb, The. *Unknown. See* O Lord, Almighty God.

Song of Myself. Walt Whitman. AmVN; NOBA; PiAm; TAP; VoPo, *much abr.*

*Sels.*

Animals, *fr.* XXXII. POL

("I think I could turn and live awhile with the animals.") HAP; NU; TPo

Battle of the *Bonhomme Richard* and the *Serapis,* XXXV-XXXVI. UnPo (1976 ed.)

"Big doors of the country barn stood open and ready, The," IX. RAE

Grass, *fr.* VI. UsP

"Houses and rooms are full of perfumes," *fr.* II. UnPo (1976 ed.)

"I am he that walks with the tender and growing night," *fr.* XXI. ExPo (1973 ed.)

"I am the poet of the Body and I am the poet of the Soul," XXI. BiP; WeW

"I am the teacher of athletes," XLVII. AnMo

"I believe a leaf of grass is no less than the journey-work of the stars," *fr.* XXXI. InPS

"I believe in the flesh and the appetites," *fr.* XXIV. Prf

"I believe in you my soul," V. BiP; Prf

"I celebrate myself and sing myself," I. AnMo; BiP

"I know I have the best of time and space," XLVI. BiP

"I resist anything better than my own diversity." *fr.* XVI-XVII. UsP

"I understand the large heart of heroes," *fr.* XXXIII. InPS

"My lovers suffocate me," *fr.* XLV. LoAs

"My signs are a rain-proof coat, good shoes, a staff cut from the woods," *fr.* XLVI. Prf

"Now I will do nothing but listen," XXVI. HoPM (1975 ed.); LFH

"Past and present wilt, The," LI. AnMo

"Sea of stretch'd ground-swells," *fr.* XXII. GrRo

"Spotted hawk swoops by and accuses me, The," LII. AnMo; BiP

Stallion, The, *fr.* XXXII. PCOP; PH

"These are really the thoughts of all men in all ages and lands," XVIII. BiP

"Trippers and askers surround me," *fr.* IV. InPS; UnPo (1976 ed.)

"Twenty-eight young men bathe by the shore," XI. ExPo (1973 ed.); HAP; LoAs

"Walt Whitman, a kosmos, of Manhattan the son," XXIV. AnMo

("Walt Whitman, an American, one of the roughs, a kosmos," 11 *ll.*) GrRo

Song of Nezahualcoyotl. *Unknown, tr. fr. Aztec.* DL

Song of Occident. Claude Vigée, *tr. fr. French by* Anthony Rudolf. VWA

Song of Poverty. *Gond Oral Tradition, tr. by* V. Elwin *and* S. Hivale. WTO

Song of Praise, A. Countee Cullen. BiP

Song of Praise for an Ox. Abraham Sutskever, *tr. fr. Yiddish by* Ruth Whitman. VWA

Song of Quoodle, The. G. K. Chesterton. DuDr

Song of Roland, The, *abr. Unknown, tr. fr. Old French by* Dorothy L. Sayers. NAWM-1

Song of Saul before His Last Battle. Byron. PIM

Song of Second April. Edna St. Vincent Millay. *See* Song of a Second April.

Song of Seyd Nimetollah of Kuhistan. Emerson. NOBA

Song of Shadows, The. Walter de la Mare. ILP (1975 ed.)
(Song of the Shadows, The.) CMoP (1970 ed.)

Song of Sickness, A. Hine Tangikuku, *tr. fr. Maori* by Barry Mitcalfe. WTO

Song of Sitting Bull. *Unknown.* GOA

Song of Snow-white Heads. Cho Wen-chün, *tr. fr. Chinese* by Authur Waley. BoWoP

Song of Solomon, The, *sels.* Bible, *O.T.*
"Behold, thou art fair," IV. BiP
"For, lo, the winter is past," II: 11-12. CTV
"How beautiful are thy feet in sandals, O prince's daughter!" VII: 1-9. OBP
"I am come into my garden, my sister, my spouse," V. OBVE
"I am my lover's and he desires me," *ad. by* Willis Barnstone. BoWoP
"I am the rose of Sharon, and the lily of the valleys," II. BiP; BoLoP; FF; GBL; OBVE
(Song of Songs.) OLR
"I sleep but my heart is awake," *ad. by* Willis Barnstone. BoWoP
"In my bed at night," *ad. by* Willis Barnstone. BoWoP
"My love has gone down to his garden," *ad. by* Willis Barnstone. BoWoP
"My love is white and ruddy," *ad. by* Willis Barnstone. BoWoP
"Set me as a seal on your heart," *ad. by* Willis Barnstone. BoWoP
"Song of songs, which is Solomon's, The," I. OBVE
"Turning to him, who meets me with desire," VII: 10-13, *tr. by* Marcia Falk. PBWP
"Under the quince tree," VIII: 5, *tr. by* Marcia Falk. PBWP
"Voice of my beloved, The," II: 8-17. PBMP
("Voice of my darling, The," *ad. by* Willis Barnstone.) BoWoP
"Yes, I am black! and radiant," I: 5-6, *tr. by* Marcia Falk. PBWP

Song of Songs, The. Bible, *O.T. See* Song of Solomon, The.

Song of Songs. Wilfred Owen. OBP

Song of Sukkaartik, the Assistant Spirit. Ajukutooq, *tr. fr. Eskimo.* WTO

Song of the Banana Man. Evan Jones. MPo

Song of the Banjo, The. Kipling. VLP

Song of the Banner at Daybreak, *sel.* Walt Whitman.
"Father what is that in the sky beckoning to me with long finger?" CC

Song of the Battery Hen. Edwin Brock. LP; MPo

Song of the Black Bear. *Unknown, tr. fr. Navajo Indian.* BCr

Song of the Blue-Corn Dance. *Tr. fr. Hopi Indian* by Natalie Curtis. WTO

Song of the Border. Gordon W. Norris. BPAW

Song of the Bowmen of Shu. Ezra Pound, *after the Chinese.* OBVE

Song of the Bride. Susan Mernit. VWA

Song of the Brook, The. Tennyson. *See* Brook, The.

Song of the Camp, The. Bayard Taylor. BTTM

Song of the Cape of Good Hope. Christian Schubart, *tr. fr. German* by Alfred Baskerville, *ad. by* Robert Bly. NU

Song of the Cauld Lad of Hylton. *Unknown.* GBP

Song of the Closing Service. Aliza Shenhar, *tr. fr. Hebrew* by Linda Zisquit. VWA

Song of the Darkness. John Bricuth. CSP

Song of the Death of Mr. Thewlis, The, *abr. Unknown.* SCP-2

Song of the Degrees, A, *sel.* Ezra Pound.
"Wind moves above the wheat, The." AKE

Song of the Desert. Eliza R. Snow. WPW

Song of the Dying Gunner A.A.1. Charles Causley. AIW

Song of the Fallen Deer. *Tr. fr. Piman Indian* by Frank Russell. OBVE

Song of the Farmworker. T. R. Jahns. AMV-80

Song of the Flume, The. *At. to* Anna M. Fitch. BPAW

Song of the Freedman. *Unknown.* PBMP

Song of the Fucked Duck. Marge Piercy. BoWoP; NMM

Song of the Galley-Slaves. Kipling. HAP; OBP

Song of the GPO, A. Gerry Hamill. NOBL

Song of the Gulf Stream. Francis Alan Ford. RhR

Song of the Hanged. Eléni Vakaló, *tr. fr. Modern Greek* by James Damaskos. PBWP

Song of the Happy Shepherd, The. W. B. Yeats. NoAM; VLP

Song of the Ill-Married. *Unknown, tr. fr. French* by Patricia Terry. BoWoP

Song of the Indian Maid, The. Keats. *Fr.* Endymion. NOBE

Song of the Intruder. Maria Jacobs. AMV-81

Song of the Jellicles, The. T. S. Eliot. FaBoNo; LCL; OxBChV; PCat; PoPle

Song of the Last Jewish Child. Edmond Jabès, *tr. fr. French* by Anthony Rudolf. VWA

Song of the Lioness for Her Cub. *Tr. fr. Hottentot* by Thomas Hahn. BoWoP

Song of the Lotos-Eaters. Tennyson. *Fr.* The Lotos-Eaters. NOBE
("There is sweet music here that softer falls.") HeIP

Song of the Lower Classes, The. Ernest Charles Jones. VLP

Song of the Mad Prince, The. Walter de la Mare. EBEV; NoAM; NOBE; OxBChV; UsP

Song of the Master and Boatswain. W. H. Auden. *Fr.* The Sea and the Mirror. BoLoP
(Master and Boatswain.) FaBoTw (1975 ed.)

Song of the Mean Mary Jean Machine, The. James Baker Hall. FiCP; TAT

Song of the Militant Romance, The. Percy Wyndham Lewis. FaBoTw (1975 ed.); OxBTC

Song of the Murdered Child. *Unknown.* GBP

Song of the Old Mother, The. W. B. Yeats. IPWM; PFIr

Song of the Old Woman. *Tr. fr. Eskimo* by Paul Emile Victor, *ad. by* Armand Schwerner. BoWoP

Song of the Open Road. Ogden Nash. AKE; FaBoCo; ILP (1975 ed.); OBAL; TPo

Song of the Open Road. Walt Whitman. NOBA; PPM
"Afoot and light-hearted I take to the open road," *sel.* RFM

Song of the Reed Sparrow, The. *Unknown.* OxBChV

Song of the Reim-Kennar, The. Sir Walter Scott. OAEL-2

Song of the Sabbath. Kadia Molodowsky, *tr. fr. Yiddish* by Jean Valentine. PBWP

Song of the Satyrs. Ben Jonson. *Fr.* Oberon, the Fairy Prince. PoPle
(Elves' Song.) BBL
(Satyrs' Catch, The.) FaBoNo

Song of the Sea. Richard Burton. RhR

Song of the Shadows, The. Walter de la Mare. *See* Song of Shadows, The.

Song of the Shirt, The. Thomas Hood. FaPoR; VLP
"Work—work—work," *sel.* VoPo

Song of the Sky Loom. *Unknown, tr. fr. Tewa Indian* by Herbert J. Spinden. TSWA; WTO

Song of the Smoke, The. W. E. B. DuBois. PoBA; UnPo (1976 ed.)

Song of the Son. Jean Toomer. AmNP (1974 ed.); ILP (1975 ed.); NIL; PoBA

Song of the Strange Young Duckling. Deborah Munro. IHMS

Song of the Stygian Naiades. Thomas Lovell Beddoes. OAEL-2

Song of the Three Holy Children, The. Bible, Apocrypha. ILwL

Song of the Three Hundred Thousand Drunkards in the United States, *sel.* William B. Tappan.
"We come! we come! to fill our graves." PeD

Song of the Thunders. *Tr. fr. Chippewa Indian* by Frances Densmore. OBVE

Song of the Trees. *Tr. fr. Chippewa Indian by* Frances Densmore. OBVE

Song of the Trees of the Black Forest. Edmond Jabès, *tr. fr. French by* Anthony Rudolf. VWA

Song of the Trout Fisher, The. Ikinilik, *tr. fr. Eskimo.* WTO

Song of the Tusk. Anselm Hollo. AcAn

Song of the Western Men, The. Robert Stephen Hawker. BTTM

Song of the Zambra Dance. Dryden. *Fr.* The Conquest of Granada. ILP (1975 ed.)

Song of This House, The. Stephen Vincent. NeAC

Song of Three Smiles. W. S. Merwin. NOBA; VGW

Song of Wandering Aengus, The. W. B. Yeats. AKE; CABA (1972 ed.); CMoP (1970 ed.); ILP (1975 ed.); MAT; OBP; PBMP; VLP; WIF

Song of Western Man, The. Robert Stephen Hawker. FaPoR

Song of Winter, A. Emily Jane Davis Pfeiffer. OBW

Song of Winter, A. *Unknown, tr. fr. Old Irish by* Kuno Meyer. PFIr

Song on May Morning. Milton. FSFS

Song on New Year's Day before the King, A. Thomas Flatman. SCP-2

Song (Prelude). Cosmo Pieterse. SES

Song tells us of our old way of living, The. Song. John Ashbery. UsP

Song that she sang was all written, The. The Moon of Mobile. Thomas Holley Chivers. OBAL

Song the Body Dreamed in the Spirit's Mad Behest, The. William Everson. PiAm

Song—the Owl. Tennyson. *See* Owl, The.

Song (The Wren). Henry Kanabus. FiCh

Song Three—A Search for Taiping Ghosts. Alan Chong Lau. NW

Song-Throe, The. Dante Gabriel Rossetti. The House of Life, LXI. VLP

Song thumbed down a cruiser for a ride, A. James Cunningham. *Fr.* The Narrator's Trance. JB

Song to a Fair Young Lady Going out of Town in the Spring. Dryden. CABA (1972 ed.); ILP (1975 ed.)

Song to a Lover. *Tr. fr. Amharic (Ethiopia) by* Willis Barnstone. BoWoP

Song to a Lute, A. Sir John Suckling. CaPo

Song to Accompany the Bearer of Bad News. David Wagoner. PPoD

Song to Be Attached. Hollis Summers. CoPAm

Song to Be Sung by the Father of Infant Female Children. Ogden Nash. PPM

Song to David, A. Christopher Smart. BoReV, *abr.*; EPC; LAuP; NOBE, *abr.*; OAEL-1; OBW, *much abr.*
  *Sels.*
  Adoremus. OBP
  "Beauteous the fleet before the gale." PIM
  Fruits of the Earth. OBP
  Gloria. OBP
  (Glory of Christ, The.) PIM
  Man of Prayer, The. PIM
  "O Thou, that sit'st upon a throne." EBEV
  "Strong is the lion—like a coal." HAP

Song to Mithras, A. Kipling. BTTM

Song to Promote Growth. *Tr. fr. Navajo Indian by* Washington Matthews. OBVE

Song to the Men of England. Shelley. ExPo (1973 ed.); ILP (1975 ed.); InPS; MBPR; PBMP; SFF

Song to the Ninth Grade. Pamela Crawford Holahan. AIW

Song to the Runaway Slave. *Unknown.* BPo

Song Tournament: New Style. Louis Untermeyer. OBAL

Song Turning Back into Itself, The. Al Young. CAAP
  "Ocean Springs Missippy," 3. CNA

Song will deceive you, the scent will incite you to sing, The. You Cannot Go Down to the Spring. John Shaw Neilson. MAuV

Song Written at Sea in the First Dutch War. Charles Sackville. NOBE

Songbook of Sebastian Arrurruz, The, *sel.* Geoffrey Hill. "Love, oh my love, it will come." PSN

Song-ily. *Unknown.* ECBV

Songs, The. Martin Bell. FF

Songs. Denis Glover. ATNZ
  "If everywhere in the street," II.
  "These songs will not stand," I.

Songs. David Steingass. HeS

Songs, The. *Tr. fr. Zuni Indian by* K. Kennedy. WTO

Songs are sung in my mind. Pearl Seed. Charles Kingsley. PCOP

Songs for the Cisco Kid; or, Singing for the Face. K. Curtis Lyle. PoBA

Songs for the Cisco Kid; or, Singing: Song # 2. K. Curtis Lyle. PoBA

Songs for the Four Parts of the Night. Owl Woman (Juana Manwell), *tr. fr. Papago by* Frances Densmore. PBWP

Songs from the Maker of Totems. Duane Niatum. VW

Songs in the Turtle Dance at Santa Clara. *Tr. fr. Tewa Indian by* H. J. Spinden. WTO

Songs My Mother Taught Me, *with music. Unknown, tr. fr. German by* Natalia Macfarren. BLSH

Songs of Education, *sels.* G. K. Chesterton.
  For the Crèche. FaBoCo
  Geography. OBSV
  History. OBSV

Songs of Experience, *sels.* Blake.
  Ah! Sun-flower. CABA (1972 ed.); ExPo (1973 ed.); HAP; LAuP; MBPR; NIL; OAEL-2; PF; PoPle; PPP; STS; TT; UnPo (1976 ed.); WeW
    ("Ah Sun-flower! weary of time.") EBEV; PoIA
  Angel, The. LAuP; MBPR
  Chimney Sweeper, The ("A little black thing among the snow"). CABA (1972 ed.); LAuP; MBPR; OAEL-2; PPoe; PPP; STS; TT
  Clod and the Pebble, The. AnMo; CABA (1972 ed.); ILP (1975 ed.); InPS; LAuP; LoAs; MBPR; NOBE; PoIA; SS; STS
  Earth's Answer. InPS; LAuP; MBPR; OAEL-2; STS; TT
  Fly, The. LAuP; MBPR; OBP; PBMP; PCoP
  Garden of Love, The. CABA (1972 ed.); ExPo (1973 ed.); GBL; HAP; ILP (1975 ed.); IPWM; LAuP; LoAs; MAT; MBPR; NIL; OBP; PoIA; PPoe; SoSe (1977 ed.); SS; STS; TPo; WIF
  Hear the Voice of the Bard, *Introd.* EBEV; NOBE; NU; OBP (Introduction: "Hear the voice of the bard!") CABA (1972 ed.); HAP; InPS; LAuP; MBPR; OAEL-2; STS; TT
  Holy Thursday ("Is this a holy thing to see"). FF; ILP (1975 ed.); InPS; LAuP; MBPR; OAEL-2; STS
  Human Abstract, The. BiP; ExPo (1973 ed.); LAuP; MBPR; OAEL-2; PoIA; PPP; STS
  Infant Sorrow. InPS; LAuP; MBPR; PoIA; PoPle; STS
  Little Boy Lost, A ("Nought loves another as itself"). ILP (1975 ed.); MBPR; OBP; STS
  Little Girl Found, The. MBPR; RRA
  Little Girl Lost, A ("Children of the future age"). MBPR; RRA
  Little Girl Lost, The ("In futurity/ I prophetic see"). MBPR; RRA
  Little Vagabond, The. MBPR; OBSV
  Lilly, The. MBPR
  London ("I wander thro' each charter'd street"). AnMo;

CABA (1972 ed.); ExPo (1973 ed.); FF; GrRo; HAP; HeIP;
ILP (1975 ed.); InPK; InPS; IP; LAuP; LFH; MAT; MBPR;
NIL; NOBE; OAEL-2; OBP; PAIC; PoIA; STS; TPo; TT;
UnPo (1976 ed.); UsP; VoPo; WIF
My Pretty Rose Tree. BoLoP; LAuP; MBPR
Nurse's Song ("When the voice of children are heard on the
green/ And whisprings are in the dale"). CABA (1972 ed.);
FF; LAuP; MBPR; STS
Poison Tree, A. AnMo; CABA (1972 ed.); HAP; HoPM (1975
ed.); ILP (1975 ed.); IP; IPWM; LAuP; LFH; MBPR;
PBMP; PoIA; PPoD; PPoe; PPP; SFF; SoSe (1977 ed.); STS;
WIF
School Boy, The. MBPR
Sick Rose, The. BoLoP; CABA (1972 ed.); ExPo (1973 ed.);
HAP; HeIP; ILP (1975 ed.); InPK: InPS; LAuP; LFH;
MBPR; NIL; NOBE; OAEL-2; PAIC; PoIA; PPP; STS;
WeW
Tiger, The. FaPoR; ILwL; InPS; IP; NIL; NOBE; PBMP;
PCOP; PoPle; SoSe; SpRo; UnPo (1976 ed.); WIF, 3 *versions*
(Tyger, The.) BiP; BoReV; CABA (1972 ed.); ExPo (1973
ed.); FF; HAP; HeIP; HoPM (1975 ed.); ILP (1975 ed.);
InPK; IPWM; LAuP; LFH; MBPR; OAEL-2; OBP; PoIA;
PPoD; PPoe; PPP; STS; TT; WeW
To Tirzah. BoReV; MBPR; NOBE; OAEL-2; STS
Voice of the Ancient Bard, The. MBPR
Songs of Innocence, *sels.* Blake.
Blossom, The. MBPR; PB
Chimney Sweeper, The ("When my mother died I was very
young"). AnMo; FF; HeIP; ILP (1975 ed.); InPK; LAuP;
MBPR; OAEL-2; OxBChV; PPoe; PPP; SoSe; STS; UsP
Cradle Song, A: "Sweet dreams form a shade." LAuP; MBPR;
PCOP; STS
Divine Image, The ("To mercy pity peace and love"). BoReV;
ILP (1975 ed.); LAuP; MBPR; NOBE; OAEL-2; PoIA; PPP;
STS; TT
Dream, A. LAuP; MBPR; PoPle
Echoing [or Ecchoing] Green, The. CABA (1972 ed.); FSFS;
LAuP; MBPR; UnPo (1976 ed.)
Holy Thursday (" 'Twas on a Holy Thursday, their innocent
faces clean"). BoReV; ILP (1975 ed.); InPS; LAuP; MBPR;
NOBE; OAEL-2; OFD; STS; TT
Infant Joy. LAuP; MBPR
Lamb, The. CABA (1972 ed.); ExPo (1973 ed.); HeIP; ILP
(1975 ed.); InPS; LAuP; LCL; LFH; MBPR; NIL; OAEL-2;
OxBChV; PAIC; PCOP; PIM; PoIA; RAE; SoSe; STS; TT;
UnPo (1976 ed.)
Laughing Song. LAuP; MBPR; OxBChV
(Laughter.) ECBV
Little Black Boy, The. AnMo; BiP; CABA (1972 ed.); HeIP;
ILP (1975 ed.); InPK; LAuP; LFH; MBPR; OAEL-2; OBP;
OxBChV; SoSe (1977 ed.); STS
Little Boy Found, The. LAuP; MBPR
Little Boy Lost, The ("Father, father, where are you going?").
LAuP; MBPR
Night. MBPR; OxBChV
Nurse's Song ("When the voices of children are heard on the
green/ And laughing"). LAuP; MBPR; OxBChV; STS
On Anothers Sorrow. MBPR
Piping Down the Valleys Wild. HeIP; NIL; NOBE; PoPle
(Introduction: "Piping down the valleys wild.") CABA (1972
ed.); ILP (1975 ed.); InPS; LAuP; MBPR; OAEL-2; STS;
TPo; TT
(Piper, The.) LCL; OxBChV
(Piper's Song, The.) PCOP
Shepherd, The. MBPR; PIM
Spring. FSFS; LCL; MBPR
Songs of Maximus, The. Charles Olson. CoPAm
*Sels.*
"All/ wrong," II. NoAM
"Colored pictures," I. NoAM
"This morning of the small snow," III. PPP

Songs of Selma, The, *sel.* James Macpherson.
"Colma—It is night." SLP
Songs of tears. To the Spirit of Carlos Gardel. Victor
Hernández Cruz. SA
Songs of the Priestess. Malka Heifetz Tussman, *tr. fr. Yiddish by*
Marcia Falk. VWA
Songs of the Transformed, *sel.* Margaret Atwood.
Siren Song. HAP; PoA
Songs of Waking. William Pitt Root. FoP
Songs that erupt, The. Chorus. Jack Kerouac. *Fr.* Mexico City
Blues. PiAm
Songs to a Lady Moonwalker. Abraham Sutskever, *tr. fr. Yiddish
by* Ruth Whitman. VWA
Songs to Survive the Summer. Robert Hass. AmPA
Sonic Boom. John Updike. QQQ; SoS
"Sonja Henie," the young girl. Preface. Theodore Weiss. VGW
Sonne hath twyse brought forthe the tender grene, The. Earl of
Surrey. AAS
Sonne his journey ending in the west, The. Henry Constable.
*Fr. Diana.* ESo
Sonnet XVI: "After an age when thunderbolts and hail." Louise
Labé, *tr. fr.* French by Willis Barnstone. BoWoP
Sonnet XIX: "After having slain very many beasts." Louise
Labé, *tr. fr.* French by Willis Barnstone. BoWoP
Sonnet: "Alas, 'tis true I have gone here and there." Shakespeare.
*See* Sonnets, CX.
Sonnet XIV: "Although I cry and though my eyes still shed."
Louise Labé, *tr. fr.* French by Willis Barnstone. BoWoP
(Sonnet: "As long as I continue weeping," *tr. by* Joan Keefe
*and* Richard Terdiman.) PBWP
Sonnet, A: "Amazing thing happened to me, An." Daniil
Kharms, *tr. fr. Russian by* George Gibian. FaBoNo
Sonnet: "And change with hurried hand has swept these scenes."
Frederick Goddard Tuckerman. *Fr.* Sonnets, II, xviii.
HAP; NOBA; PiAm; TAP
Sonnet: "And so one sees all living matter perish." Louise Labé,
*tr. fr.* French by Frederic Prokosch. LoAs
(Sonnet VII: "We see each living thing finally die," *tr. by*
Willis Barnstone.) BoWoP
Sonnet: "As a decrepit father takes delight." Shakespeare.
*See* Sonnets, XXXVII.
Sonnet: "As an unperfect actor on the stage." Shakespeare. *See*
Sonnets, XXIII.
Sonnet: "As fast as thou shalt wane, so fast thou grow'st."
Shakespeare. *See* Sonnets, XI.
Sonnet: "As long as I continue weeping." Louise Labé. *See*
Sonnet XIV: "Although I cry and though my eyes still shed."
Sonnet IX: "As soon as I lie down in my soft bed." Louise Labé,
*tr. fr.* French by Willis Barnstone. BoWoP
Sonnet: "Avenge, O Lord, thy slaughtered saints, whose bones."
Milton. *See* On the Late Massacre in Piedmont.
Sonnet: "Azured vault, the crystal circles bright, The." James I,
King of England. Moon
Sonnet: "Banging around in a cigarette she isn't 'in love.' " Ted
Berrigan. CAAP
Sonnet: "Batter my heart, three-personed God; for you." John
Donne. *See* Holy Sonnets.
Sonnet: "Being your slave, what should I do but tend."
Shakespeare. *See* Sonnets, LVII.
Sonnet: "Beware of Benjamin Franklin, he is totally lacking in
grace." Ted Berrigan. CAAP
Sonnet: " 'Broken heart,' A . . . but can a heart break, now?"
John Berryman. Epi
Sonnet: "But man finds means, grant him but place and room."
Frederick Goddard Tuckerman. *Fr.* Sonnets, V, iv. PiAm
Sonnet: "Captain or colonel, or knight in arms." Milton.
OAEL-1; PAIC

Sonnet VI: "Coming of that limpid star is twice, The." Louise Labé, *tr. fr.* French by Willis Barnstone. BoWoP

Sonnet: "Crumbled rock of London is dripping under, The." Roy Fuller. PoA

Sonnet: "Cry, crow." Hayden Carruth. NNaP

Sonnet: Dante Alighieri to Guido Cavalcanti. Dante, *tr. fr.* Italian by Shelley. OBVE

Sonnet: "Dear Ron: hello. Your name is now a household name." Ted Berrigan. CAAP

Sonnet: "Devouring Time, blunt thou the lion's paws." Shakespeare. *See* Sonnets, XIX.

Sonnet XXIV: "Don't blame me, ladies, if I've loved. No sneers." Louise Labé, *tr. fr.* French by Willis Barnstone. BoWoP
(Sonnet: "Don't scold me, ladies, if I have loved," *tr. by* Carol Cosman.) PBWP

Sonnet I: "Dost see how unregarded now." Sir John Suckling. CaPo

Sonnet: England in 1819. Shelley. *See* England in 1819.

Sonnet: "Eternal Lord! eased of a cumbrous load." Michelangelo, *tr. fr.* Italian by Wordsworth. PIM

Sonnet: "Expense of spirit in a waste of shame, The." Shakespeare. *See* Sonnets, CXXIX.

Sonnet: "Fair is my love, and cruel as she is fair." Samuel Daniel. *Fr.* To Delia. HoPM (1975 ed.)
("Fair[e] is my love, and cruel as she's fair.") AAS; ILP (1975 ed.); NOBE

Sonnet: "Farewell! thou art too dear for my possessing." Shakespeare. *See* Sonnets, LXXXVII.

Sonnet: "Five A.M. on East Fourteenth I'm out to eat." Tom Clark. Epi

Sonnet: "For Nature daily through her grand design." Frederick Goddard Tuckerman. *Fr.* Sonnets, I, xxvi. PiAm

Sonnet: "Fra banc to banc, fra wod to wod, I rin." Mark Alexander Boyd. *See* Fra Bank to Bank, . . .

Sonnet: "Francis Marion nudges himself gently into the big blue sky." Ted Berrigan. CAAP

Sonnet: "From fairest creatures we desire increase." Shakespeare. *See* Sonnets, I.

Sonnet IV: "From that first flash when awful Love took flame." Louise Labé, *tr. fr.* French by Willis Barnstone. BoWoP

Sonnet: "From you have I been absent in the spring." Shakespeare. *See* Sonnets, XCVIII.

Sonnet: "Full many a glorious morning have I seen." Shakespeare. *See* Sonnets, XXXIII.

Sonnet: "Gray his head goes his feet green." Ted Berrigan. CAAP

Sonnet: Guido Cavalcanti to Dante. Guido Cavalcanti, *tr. fr.* Italian by Shelley. OBVE

Sonnet: "Harum-scarum haze on the Pollock streets." Ted Berrigan. CAAP

Sonnet: "He came in silvern armor, trimmed with black." Gwendolyn B. Bennett. AmNP (1974 ed.); PoBA

Sonnet, A: "His golden locks time hath to silver turned." George Peele. *See* His Golden Locks . . .

Sonnet: "How do I love thee? Let me count the ways." Elizabeth Barrett Browning. *See* Sonnets from the Portuguese: "How do I love thee. . ."

Sonnet: "How like a winter hath my absence been." Shakespeare. *See* Sonnets, XCVII.

Sonnet: "How oft when thou, my music, music play'st." Shakespeare. *See* Sonnets, CXXVIII.

Sonnet: "How soon hath time, the subtle thief of youth." Milton. *See* How Soon Hath Time, the Subtle Thief of Youth.

Sonnet: "How strange to be gone in a minute." Ted Berrigan. CAAP

Sonnet: "How strange to be gone in a minute! A man." Ted Berrigan. CAAP

Sonnet: "I am closing my window. Tear silence the wind." Ted Berrigan. Epi

Sonnet XVII: "I flee the city, temples, and each place." Louise Labé, *tr. fr.* French by Willis Barnstone. BoWoP

Sonnet: "I had no thought of violets of late." Alice Dunbar Nelson. PoBA

Sonnet: "I lift—lift you five States away your glass." John Berryman. Epi

Sonnet: "I like to beat people up." Ted Berrigan. CAAP

Sonnet VIII: "I live, I die, I burn myself and drown." Louise Labé, *tr. fr.* French by Willis Barnstone. BoWoP

Sonnet: "I must not grieve my love, whose eyes would read." Samuel Daniel. *Fr.* To Delia. LoAs

Sonnet: "I never saw that you did painting need." Shakespeare. *See* Sonnets, LXXXIII.

Sonnet: "I on my horse, and Love on me, doth try." Sir Philip Sidney. *See* Astrophel and Stella, XLIX.

Sonnet: "I said I splendidly loved you; it's not true." Rupert Brooke. BuTh

Sonnet: "I saw magic on a green country road." Michael Hartnett. BIrV

Sonnet: "I wake up back aching from soft bed Pat." Ted Berrigan. CAAP

Sonnet XX: "I was foretold that on a certain day." Louise Labé, *tr. fr.* French by Willis Barnstone. BoWoP
(Sonnet: "Seer foretold that I would love one day, A," *tr. by* Joan Keefe *and* Richard Terdiman.) PBWP

Sonnet XIII: "If I could linger on his lovely chest." Louise Labé, *tr. fr.* French by Aliki *and* Willis Barnstone. BoWoP

Sonnet: "If thou survive my well-contented day." Shakespeare. *See* Sonnets, XXXII.

Sonnet: "If thy soul check thee that I come so near." Shakespeare. *See* Sonnets, CXXXVI.

Sonnet: "Ile give thee leave my love, in beauties field." Earl of Stirling. *Fr.* Aurora. SLP

Sonnet: "Imprimis: I forgot all day your face." Conrad Aiken. LoAs

Sonnet: "In every dream thy lovely features rise." William Barnes. BoLoP

Sonnet: "In Joe Brainard's collage its white arrows." Ted Berrigan. Epi

Sonnet: "In my paintings for they are present." Ted Berrigan. CAAP

Sonnet: "Is it for fear to wet a widow's eye." Shakespeare. *See* Sonnets, IX.

Sonnet: "Is there a great green commonwealth of Thought." John Masefield. ILP (1975 ed.)

Sonnet: "It is a human universe: and I." Ted Berrigan. Epi

Sonnet: "It is night. You are asleep. And beautiful tears." Ted Berrigan. CAAP

Sonnet: "It's 8:54 a.m. Brooklyn it's the 28th of July and." Ted Berrigan. CAAP

Sonnet: "Joyful ants nest on the roof of my tree." Ted Berrigan. CAAP

Sonnet XVIII: "Kiss me again, rekiss me, kiss me more." Louise Labé. *See* Sonnet: "O kiss me yet again, O kiss me over."

Sonnet: "Lackying my loue I go from place to place." Spenser. *See* Amoretti, LXXVIII.

Sonnet: "Let me not to the marriage of true minds." Shakespeare. *See* Sonnets, CXVI.

Sonnet: "Lift not the painted veil which those who live." Shelley. MBPR

Sonnet: "Like as the waves make towards the pebbled shore." Shakespeare. *See* Sonnets, LX.

Sonnet: "Like as, to make our appetites more keen." Shakespeare. *See* Sonnets, CXVIII.

Sonnet: "Lo, as a careful housewife runs to catch."  Shakespeare. *See* Sonnets, CXLIII.

Sonnet: "Look in thy glass and tell the face thou viewest." Shakespeare. *See* Sonnets, III.

Sonnet: "Love is too young to know what conscience is." Shakespeare. *See* Sonnets, CLI.

Sonnet XII: "Lute, companion of my calamity."  Louise Labé, *tr. fr. French by* Aliki *and* Willis Barnstone.  BoWoP

Sonnet: "Methought I saw my late espoused saint."  Milton.  *See* On His Deceased Wife.

Sonnet: "Most glorious Lord of Life, that on this day."  Spenser. *See* Amoretti, LXVIII.

Sonnet: "My dream a drink with Lonnie Johnson."  Ted Berrigan. CAAP; NoAM

Sonnet: "My God, where is that ancient heat towards thee." George Herbert.  *See* To His Mother.

Sonnet: "My love, I have betrayed you seventy times."  Conrad Aiken.  LoAs

Sonnet: "My love is as a fever, longing still."  Shakespeare. *See* Sonnets, CXLVII.

Sonnet: "My mistress' eyes are nothing like the sun." Shakespeare.  *See* Sonnets, CXXX.

Sonnet: "No longer mourn for me when I am dead." Shakespeare.  *See* Sonnets, LXXI.

Sonnet: "No more be grieved at that which thou hast done." Shakespeare.  *See* Sonnets, XXXV.

Sonnet: "No worst, there is none. Pitched past pitch of grief." Gerard Manley Hopkins.  *See* No Worst, There Is None.

Sonnet: "Not marble, nor the gilded monuments."  Shakespeare. *See* Sonnets, LV.

Sonnet: "Not mine own fears nor the prophetic soul." Shakespeare.  *See* Sonnets, CVII.

Sonnet: "Not the round natural world, not the deep mind." Frederick Goddard Tuckerman.  *Fr.* Sonnets; I, xxviii. PiAm

Sonnet I: "Not Ulysses, no, nor any other man."  Louise Labé, *tr. fr. Italian by* Willis Barnstone.  BoWoP

Sonnet: "Now the bat circles on the breeze of eve."  Anne Radcliffe.  WPE

Sonnet I: "Now there is a love of which Dante does not speak unkindly."  Robert Duncan.  GP

Sonnet XXII: "O blazing Sun, how happy you are there."  Louise Labé, *tr. fr. French by* Willis Barnstone.  BoWoP

Sonnet XI: "O eyes clear with beauty, O tender gaze."  Louise Labé, *tr. fr. French by* Willis Barnstone.  BoWoP

Sonnet: "Oh for a poet—for a beacon bright."  E. A. Robinson. ILP (1975 ed.)

Sonnet: "Oh for some honest lover's ghost."  Sir John Suckling. *See* Doubt of Martyrdom, A.

Sonnet II: "O handsome chestnut eyes, evasive gaze."  Louise Labé, *tr. fr. French by* Willis Barnstone.  BoWoP

Sonnet: "O, how much more doth beauty beauteous seem." Shakespeare.  *See* Sonnets, LIV.

Sonnet III: "O interminable desires, O futile hope."  Louise Labé, *tr. fr. French by* Willis Barnstone.  BoWoP

Sonnet: "O kiss me yet again, O kiss me over."  Louise Labé, *tr. fr. French by* Frederic Prokosch.  LoAs
(Sonnet XVIII: "Kiss me again, rekiss me, kiss me more," *tr. by* Willis Barnstone.)  BoWoP

Sonnet, A: "O lovely O most charming pug."  Marjory Fleming. FaBoCo

Sonnet: "O! Never say that I was false of heart."  Shakespeare. *See* Sonnets, CIX

Sonnet: "O nightingale, that on yon bloomy spray."  Milton. *See* O Nightingale, That on Yon Bloomy Spray.

Sonnet II: "Of thee, kind boy, I ask no red and white."  Sir John Suckling.  CaPo

Sonnet: "On the 15th day of November in the year of the motorcar."  Ted Berrigan.  VW

Sonnet: On the Late Massacre in Piedmont.  Milton.  *See* On the Late Massacre in Piedmont.

Sonnet: "One day I wrote her name upon the strand."  Spenser. *See* Amoretti, LXXV.

Sonnet: "One still dark night I sat alone and wrote."  Frederick Goddard Tuckerman.  *Fr.* Sonnets, II, xxxiii.  PiAm

Sonnet: "Orgasm completely, The."  Tom Clark.  PPoD

Sonnet: "Our Sunday morning when dawn-priests were applying." John Berryman.  Epi
("Our Sunday morning when dawn-priests were applying.") BoLoP

Sonnet: Political Greatness.  Shelley.  OBP
(Political Greatness.)  NIL

Sonnet: "Poor soul, the center of my sinful earth."  Shakespeare. *See* Sonnets, CXLVI.

Sonnet: Rapture Concerning His Lady, A.  Guido Cavalcanti, *tr. fr. Italian by* Dante Gabriel Rossetti.  LoAs
(Sonnet VII: "Who is she that comes, makyng turn every man's eye," *tr. by* Ezra Pound.)  OBVE

Sonnet: "Roll on, sad world! not Mercury or Mars."  Frederick Goddard Tuckerman.  *Fr.* Sonnets, II, xvii.  PiAm

Sonnet: "Seer foretold that I would love one day, A."  Louise Labé.  *See* Sonnet XX: "I was foretold that on a certain day."

Sonnet: "Shall I compare thee to a summer's day?"  Shakespeare. *See* Sonnets, XVIII.

Sonnet: "She took the dappled partridge flecked with blood." Tennyson.  CABA (1972 ed.)

Sonnet: "Sin of self-love possesseth all mine eye."  Shakespeare. *See* Sonnets, LXII.

Sonnet: "Since brass, nor stone, nor earth, nor boundless sea." Shakespeare.  *See* Sonnets, LXV.

Sonnet: "Since I left you, mine eye is in my mind."  Shakespeare. *See* Sonnets, CXIII.

Sonnet: "Since you would claim the sources of my thought." Louise Bogan.  FoP

Sonnet: "Sleep half sleep half silence and with reasons."  Ted Berrigan.  CAAP; Epi

Sonnet: "Some for a little while do love, and some for long." Countee Cullen.  SoS

Sonnet: "Some things are very dear to me."  Gwendolyn B. Bennett.  AmNP (1974 ed.); PoBA

Sonnet: "Sometimes I walk where the deep water dips." Frederick Goddard Tuckerman.  *Fr.* Sonnets; III, x.  PiAm

Sonnet: "Sometimes the night echoes to prideless wailing."  John Berryman.  NoAM

Sonnet, A: "Sonnet is a moment's monument, A."  Dante Gabriel Rossetti.  The House of Life, *introd.*  HeIP; ILP (1975 ed.); NIL: PAIC; SoSe; VLP

Sonnet, The: "Sonnet, she told the crowd of bearded, The." Daniel Hoffman.  GP

Sonnet: "Summer so histrionic, marvelous dirty days."  Ted Berrigan.  CAAP; Epi

Sonnet: "That time of year thou mayst in me behold." Shakespeare.  *See* Sonnets, LXXIII.

Sonnet: "Then hate me when thou wilt; if ever, now." Shakespeare.  *See* Sonnets, XC.

Sonnet: "There, on the darkened deathbed, dies the brain."  John Masefield.  EBEV
(There, on the Darkened Deathbed.)  DL

Sonnet: "They basted his caption on top of the fat sheriff, 'The Pig.'"  Ted Berrigan.  CAAP

Sonnet: "They that have power to hurt and will do none." Shakespeare.  *See* Sonnets, XCIV.

Sonnet: "This virgin, beautiful and lively day."  Stéphane Mallarmé, *tr. fr. French by* Roger Fry.  NAWM-2

Sonnet: "Those hours that with gentle work did frame." Shakespeare. *See* Sonnets, V.

Sonnet: "Thou blind fool, Love, what dost thou to mine eyes." Shakespeare. *See* Sonnets, CXXXVII

Sonnet: "Three silences made him a single word." R. P. Blackmur. PoA

Sonnet: "Thy bosom is endearèd with all hearts." Shakespeare. *See* Sonnets, XXXI.

Sonnet: "Tired with all these, for restful death I cry." Shakespeare. *See* Sonnets, LXVI.

Sonnet: "'Tis better to be vile than vile esteemed." Shakespeare. *See* Sonnets, CXXI

Sonnet XV: "To honor the return of sparkling sun." Louise Labé, *tr. fr. French by* Willis Barnstone. BoWoP

Sonnet: "To me, fair friend, you never can be old." Shakespeare. *See* Sonnets, CIV.

Sonnet: To Science. Poe. *See* Sonnet—to Science.

Sonnet: "Today as I passed through the market-place." Robert Hillyer. *Fr.* A Sonnet Sequence. TH

Sonnet: "Too many fucking mosquitoes under the blazing sun." Ted Berrigan. CAAP

Sonnet: "Two loves I have of comfort and despair." Shakespeare. *See* Sonnets, CXLIV.

Sonnet, A: "Two voices are there: one is of the deep." James Kenneth Stephen. FaBoCo; NOBL; PPoD; SpRo

Sonnet: "Under the mountain, as when first I knew." Frederick Goddard Tuckerman. *Fr.* Sonnets, II, xvi. HAP; PiAm; TAP

Sonnet: "Unthrifty loveliness, why dost thou spend." Shakespeare. *See* Sonnets, IV.

Sonnet: "Upon a day, came sorrow in to me." Dante, *tr. fr. Italian by* Dante Gabriel Rossetti. LoAs

Sonnet: "Wan as pale thighs making apple belly strides." Ted Berrigan. CAAP

Sonnet: "Was it the proud full sail of his great verse." Shakespeare. *See* Sonnets, LXXXVI.

Sonnet VII: "We see each living thing finally die." Louise Labé. *See* Sonnet: "And so one sees all living matter perish."

Sonnet: "Weary with toil, I haste me to my bed." Shakespeare. *See* Sonnets, XXVII.

Sonnet: "Weary year his race now having run, The." Spenser. *See* Amoretti, LXII.

Sonnet XXIII: "What good is it to me if long ago." Louise Labé, *tr. fr. French by* Willis Barnstone. BoWoP

Sonnet XXI: "What grandeur makes a man seem venerable?" Louise Labé, *tr. fr. French by* Willis Barnstone. BoWoP

Sonnet: "What is your substance, whereof are you made." Shakespeare. *See* Sonnets, LIII.

Sonnet: "What thwarts this fear I love." Ted Berrigan. CAAP

Sonnet: "What was ashore, then?. . .Cargoed with forget." John Berryman. Epi

Sonnet XV: "When dead the winter snows in crystals shine." Richard Eberhart. UsP

Sonnet: "When forty winters shall besiege thy brow." Shakespeare. *See* Sonnets, II.

Sonnet: "When I catch sight of your fair head." Louise Labé. *See* Sonnet X: "When I perceive your blond and graceful head."

Sonnet: "When I consider how my light is spent." Milton. *See* On His Blindness.

Sonnet: "When I do count the clock that tells the time." Shakespeare. *See* Sonnets, XII.

Sonnet: "When I have seen by Time's fell hand defaced." Shakespeare. *See* Sonnets, LXIV.

Sonnet X: "When I perceive your blond and graceful head." Louise Labé, *tr. fr. French by* Willis Barnstone. BoWoP (Sonnet: "When I catch sight of your fair head," *tr. by* Joan Keefe *and* Richard Terdiman.) PBWP

Sonnet: "When in disgrace with fortune and men's eyes." Shakespeare. *See* Sonnets, XXIX.

Sonnet: "When in the chronicle of wasted time." Shakespeare. *See* Sonnets, CVI.

Sonnet: "When my love swears that she is made of truth." Shakespeare. *See* Sonnets, CXXXVIII.

Sonnet: "When to the sessions of sweet silent thought." Shakespeare. *See* Sonnets, XXX.

Sonnet: "Where are we to go when this is done?" Alfred A. Duckett. AmNP (1974 ed.); PoBA

Sonnet V: "White Venus limpid wandering in the sky." Louise Labé, *tr. fr. French by* Aliki *and* Willis Barnstone. BoWoP

Sonnet VII: "Who is she that comes, makyng turn every man's eye." Guido Cavalcanti. *See* Sonnet: Rapture Concerning His Lady, A.

Sonnet: "Who will believe my verse in time to come." Shakespeare. *See* Sonnets, XVII.

Sonnet: "Whoever hath her wish, thou hast thy Will." Shakespeare. *See* Sonnets, CXXXV.

Sonnet: "Why is my verse so barren of new pride." Shakespeare. *See* Sonnets, LXXVI.

Sonnet: "Wind has blown the rain away and blown, A." E. E. Cummings. PAIC

Sonnet: "With how sad steps, Oh Moon." Sir Philip Sidney. *See* Astrophel and Stella, XXXI.

Sonnet: "Withered leaves fly higher than dolls can see, The." Ted Berrigan. CAAP

Sonnet: "Woman is singing the song and summer." Ted Berrigan. CAAP

Sonnet: "Woman's face with nature's own hand painted, A." Shakespeare. *See* Sonnets, XX.

Sonnet: "Women have loved before as I love now." Edna St. Vincent Millay. PoA

Sonnet-Ballad, The. Gwendolyn Brooks. SoS; TT; WeW

Sonnet for a Loved One. Dorothy Joslin. AMV-80

Sonnet for a Picture. Swinburne. *Fr.* Heptalogia. FaBoNo; OAEL-2

Sonnet for All Greeks Living Now. Darrell Gray. AcAn

Sonnet for Salvador; or; One Could Do Worse than Be a Celery King. Gary Miranda. AAN

Sonnet Found in a Deserted Mad-House. *Unknown.* FaBoCo; FaBoNo

Sonnet in Allusion to Various Recent Histories and Notices of the French Revolution. Wordsworth. MBPR

Sonnet in Search of an Author. William Carlos Williams. Epi

Sonnet is a moment's monument, A. A Sonnet. Dante Gabriel Rossetti. The House of Life, *introd.* HeIP; ILP (1975 ed.); NIL; PAIC; SoSe; VLP

Sonnet is a sleek iambic beast, The. Sonnet Sonnet. John D. Engle, Jr. AMV-81

Sonnet of Black Beauty. Lord Herbert of Cherbury. PAIC

Sonnet of Brotherhood. R. A. K. Mason. ATNZ

Sonnet of the Moon, A. Charles Best. SoSe (Of the Moon.) Moon

Sonnet on a Still Night. J. V. Cunningham. PoA

Sonnet on Chillon. Byron. *Fr.* The Prisoner of Chillon. ExPo (1973 ed.); ILP (1975 ed.); LFN; PAIC; PBMP

Sonnet on Hearing the Dies Irae Sung in the Sistine Chapel. Oscar Wilde. PIM

Sonnet on Launching Some Bottles Filled with Knowledge into the Bristol Channel. Shelley. MBPR

Sonnet on the Death of a Friend. Keats. PIM ("As from the darkening gloom a silver dove.") MBPR

Sonnet on the Death of [Mr.] Richard West. Thomas Gray. LAuP; PAIC (On the Death of Richard West.) NOBE

Sonnet on the Projected Kendal and Windermere Railway. Wordsworth. MBPR
(On the Projected Kendal and Windermere Railway.) VLP

Sonnet Reversed. Rupert Brooke. NOBL

Sonnet Sequence, A, sel. Robert Hillyer.
"Today as I passed through the market-place," VIII. TH

Sonnet, she told the crowd of bearded, The. The Sonnet. Daniel Hoffman. GP

Sonnet—Silence. Poe. NOBA; PiAm

Sonnet Sonnet. John D. Engle, Jr. AMV-81

Sonnet to a Clam. John Godfrey Saxe. BoAnP

Sonnet to a Negro in Harlem. Helene Johnson. AmNP (1974 ed.); NIL

Sonnet to a Tyrant. Mary Anne Ellis. AMV-80

Sonnet to Britain. William Edmonstoune Aytoun. FaBoCo

Sonnet to Byron. Shelley. MBPR

Sonnet to Gath. Edna St. Vincent Millay. BoWoP; CMoP (1970 ed.)

Sonnet to Harriet on Her Birthday. Shelley. MBPR

Sonnet to My Mother. George Barker. LoAs; PAIC; SoS
(To My Mother.) FF; IP; LP; NCSH; OxBTC

Sonnet to Negro Soldiers. Joseph Seamon Cotter, Jr. PoBA

Sonnet—to Science. Poe. Al Aaraaf: Prologue. AmVN; InPK; PAIC; PBMP; PiAm; PPoD; TAP; WIF
(Sonnet: To Science.) ILP (1975 ed.)
(To Science.) LFH

Sonnet to Seabrook. David Ray. AMV-80

Sonnet to Sleep. Keats. See To Sleep.

Sonnet to the Prince Regent. Byron. MBPR

Sonnet to the River Otter. Samuel Taylor Coleridge. MBPR; OAEL-2

Sonnet to William Wilberforce, Esq. William Cowper. ILP (1975 ed.)

Sonnet 21. Paul Goodman. VGW

Sonnet with a Different Letter at the End of Every Line. George Starbuck. OBAL

Sonnet Written in the Church-Yard at Middleton, in Sussex. Charlotte Smith. See Press'd by the Moon, Mute Arbitress of Tides.

Sonnet Written in the Cottage Where Burns Was Born. Keats. MBPR

Sonnet Written upon Ben Nevis. Keats. MBPR

Sonnets, sels. Shakespeare.
I. "From fairest creatures we desire increase." STS
II. "When forty winters shall besiege thy brow." FF
III. "Look in thy glass, and tell the face thou viewest." CABA (1972 ed.)
IV. "Unthrifty loveliness, why dost thou spend." GrRo
V. "Those hours that with gentle work did frame." STS
IX. "Is it for fear to wet a widow's eye." STS
XI. "As fast as thou shalt wane, so fast thou grow'st." STS
XII. "When I do count the clock that tells the time." InPS; NIL; OAEL-1; STS; VoPo
XVII. "Who will believe my verse in time to come." STS
XVIII. "Shall I compare thee to a summer's day?" BoLoP; GBL; HAP; HeIP; ILP (1975 ed.); InPS; InPK; IP; IPWM; MAT; NIL: NOBE; OAEL-1; OLR; PAIC; PBMP; PPM; PPoe; STS; TPo
XIX. "Devouring Time, blunt thou the lion's paws." EBEV; Epi; MAT; OAEL-1
XX. "Woman's face with nature's own hand painted, A." OAEL-1
XXIII. "As an unperfect actor on the stage." BiP; OBP
XXVII. "Weary with toil, I haste me to my bed." ILP (1975 ed.); STS
XXIX. "When, in disgrace with fortune and men's eyes." EBEV; Epi; GBL; HAP; HeIP; ILP (1975 ed.); LFH; NIL;

NOBE; OAEL-1; OBP; PAIC; PoIA; PPM; PPoe; PPP; Prf; STS; TPo
XXX. "When to the sessions of sweet silent thought." BiP; CABA (1972 ed.); EBEV; Epi; ExPo (1973 ed.); FF; GBL; HAP; ILP (1975 ed.); InPS; NOBE; OAEL-1; PAIC; PoIA; PoPle; PPM; PPP; STS; TPo; VoPo; WIF
XXXI. "Thy bosom is endeared with all hearts." NOBE
XXXII. "If thou survive my well-contented day." ILP (1975 ed.); STS
XXXIII. "Full many a glorious morning have I seen." EBEV; HAP; ILP (1975 ed.); OAEL-1; PPP
XXXV. "No more be grieved at that which thou hast done." CABA (1972 ed.); UnPo (1976 ed.)
XXXVII. "As a decrepit father takes delight." STS
LIII. "What is your substance, whereof are you made." EBEV; OAEL-1
LIV. "O, how much more doth beauty beauteous seem." STS
LV. "Not marble, nor the gilded monuments." CABA (1972 ed.); Epi; FF; HeIP; ILP (1975 ed.); InPK; NIL; NOBE; OAEL-1; PAIC; PPoe; STS; WIF
LVII. "Being your slave, what should I do but tend." HAP; LoAs; STS
LX. "Like as the waves make towards the pebbled shore." EBEV; Epi; ILP (1975 ed.); NIL; NOBE; UnPo (1976 ed.)
LXII. "Sin of self-love possesseth all mine eye." EBEV
LXIV. "When I have seen by Time's fell hand defaced." CABA (1972 ed.); HAP; HeIP; ILP (1975 ed.); NOBE; OAEL-1; PAIC; PPoe; STS
LXV. "Since brass, nor stone, nor earth, nor boundless sea." CABA (1972 ed.); Epi; FF; HAP; InPS; NOBE; PoIA; STS; UnPo (1976 ed.)
LXVI. "Tired with all these, for restful death I cry." EBEV; HAP; InPS; NOBE; OAEL-1; WeW
LXXI. "No longer mourn for me when I am dead." EBEV; Epi; GBL; HAP; ILP (1975 ed.); PPoe; SoSe; STS
LXXIII. "That time of year thou may'st in me behold." BiP; BoLoP; CABA (1972 ed.); EBEV; Epi; ExPo (1973 ed.); FF; FSFS; GBL; HAP; HeIP; HoPM (1975 ed.); ILP (1975 ed.); InPK; InPS; IPWM; LFH; LoAs; NIL; NOBE; OAEL-1; OBP; PBMP; PoIA; PoPle; PPoD; PPP; SoSe; STS; UnPo (1976 ed.); UsP
LXXVI. "Why is my verse so barren of new pride." EBEV; TPo
LXXXIII. "I never saw that you did painting need." STS
LXXXVI. "Was it the proud full sail of his great verse." OAEL-1
LXXXVII. "Farewell! thou art too dear for my possessing." EBEV; InPS; LoAs; NOBE; OAEL-1; PPoD
XC. "Then hate me when thou wilt; if ever, now." EBEV; NOBE
XCIV. "They that have power to hurt, and will do none." CABA (1972 ed.); Epi; ExPo (1973 ed.); InPS; IP; LoAs; NOBE; OAEL-1; PPoe; PPP
XCVII. "How like a winter hath my absence been." CABA (1972 ed.); ILP (1975 ed.); NOBE; OAEL-1; PoIA
XCVIII. "From you have I been absent in the spring." EBEV; FSFS; ILP (1975 ed.); NOBE; PoPle
CIV. "To me, fair friend, you never can be old." GBL; HeIP; LoAs; Prf
CVI. "When in the chronicle of wasted time." NOBE; OAEL-1; PPoe; STS
CVII. "Not mine own fears nor the prophetic soul." CABA (1972 ed.); EBEV; HAP; OAEL-1; PPoe
CIX. "O! Never say that I was false of heart." ILP (1975 ed.); NOBE; STS
CX. "Alas, 'tis true I have gone here and there." EBEV
CXIII. "Since I left you, mine eye is in my mind." WeW
CXVI. "Let me not to the marriage of true minds." CABA (1972 ed.); Epi; ExPo (1973 ed.); GBL; HAP; HeIP; ILP (1975 ed.); InPK; InPS; IPWM; LFH; NIL; NOBE; OAEL-1; OBP; PBMP; PoIA; PPoe; PPP; SoSe; STS; UnPo (1976 ed.); VoPo

CXVIII. "Like as, to make our appetites more keen."   CABA (1972 ed.)

CXXI. " 'Tis better to be vile than vile esteemed."   OAEL-1

CXXVIII. "How oft when thou, my music, music play'st."   Epi; ILP (1975 ed.)

CXXIX. "Expense of spirit in a waste of shame, The."   BiP; CABA (1972 ed.); EBEV; Epi; ExPo (1973 ed.); GBL; HAP; HeIP; ILP (1975 ed.); InPS; LFH; LoAs; NIL; NOBE; OAEL-1; OBP; PoIA; PPoe; PPoD; PPP; UnPo (1976 ed.); WeW

CXXX. "My mistress' eyes are nothing like the sun."   BiP; BoLoP; CABA (1972 ed.); EBEV; Epi; FF; HAP; HoPM (1975 ed.); ILP (1975 ed.); InPK; InPS; IP; IPWM; LFH; NIL; OAEL-1; PBMP; PoIA; PoPle; PPoD; PPP; SoSe; STS; VoPo; WeW; WIF

CXXXV. "Whoever hath her wish, thou hast thy Will."   Epi; OAEL-1

CXXXVI. "If thy soul check thee that I come so near."   Epi

CXXXVII. "Thou blind fool, Love, what dost thou to mine eyes."   WeW

CXXXVIII. "When my love swears that she is made of truth."   BiP; CABA (1972 ed.); EBEV; Epi; ILP (1975 ed.); LoAs; OAEL-1; OBP; PoIA; PPoD; PPP; SoSe

CXLIII. "Lo, as a careful housewife runs to catch."   BiP; ILP (1975 ed.); InPK

CXLIV. "Two loves I have of comfort and despair."   CABA (1972 ed.); EBEV; Epi; NIL; OAEL-1

CXLVI. "Poor soul, the centre of my sinful earth."   BiP; CABA (1972 ed.); Epi; ExPo (1973 ed.); HAP; InPK; NIL; NOBE; OAEL-1; OBP; PoIA; PPoe; PPP

CXLVII. "My love is as a fever, longing still."   EBEV; HoPM (1975 ed.)

CLI. "Love is too young to know what conscience is."   BiP; EBEV; HeIP

Sonnets, *sels.*   Frederick Goddard Tuckerman.
"All men,—the preacher saith,—whate'er or whence," I, xvii. AmVN
"And borne with theirs, my proudest thoughts do seem," I, iii. AmVN
"And change with hurried hand has swept these scenes," II, xviii. HAP; NOBA; PiAm; TAP
"And she—her beauty never made her cold," I, xv. AmVN
"And so the day drops by; the horizon draws," I, v. AmVN
"As when, down some broad river dropping, we," I, viii. AmVN
"But man finds means, grant him but place and room," V, iv. PiAm
"By this low fire I often sit to woo," I, xxv. AmVN
"For Nature daily through her grand design," I, xxvi. AmVN; PiAm
"Gertrude and Gulielma, sister-twins," II, xv. HAP
"Hast thou seen reversed the prophet's miracle," IV, x. NOBA
"Here, where the red man swept the leaves away," IV, ix. NOBA; TAP
"Nor looks that backward life so bare to me," I, iv. AmVN
"Not proud of station, nor in worldly pelf," I, xiv. AmVN
"Not the round natural world, not the deep mind," I, xxviii. AmVN; PiAm; PPoD
"O Father, God! to whom, in happier days," I, xxi. AmVN
"One still dark night I sat alone and wrote," II, xxxiii. PiAm
"Roll on, sad world! not Mercury or Mars," II, xvii. PiAm
"So, to the mind long brooding but on it," I, xxvii. AmVN
"Sometimes I walk where the deep water dips," III, x. NOBA; PiAm
"Sometimes, when winding slow by brook and bower," I, i. AmVN
"Still craves the spirit: never Nature solves," I, xx. AmVN
"Still pressing through these weeping solitudes," II, xi. NOBA
"Thin little leaves of wood fern, ribbed and toothed," III, iv. TAP

"Under the mountain, as when first I knew," II, xvi. HAP; PiAm; TAP
"Upper chamber in a darkened house, An," I, x. AmVN; NOBA; PiAm; TAP
"What profits it to me, though here allowed," I, xi. AmVN
"Wherefore, with this belief, held like a blade," I, ii. AmVN
"Yes: though the brine may from the desert deep," II, iii. HAP
"Yet Nature, where the thunder leaves its trace," I, xvi. AmVN
"Yet wear we on; the deep light disallowed," I, ix. AmVN

Sonnets—Actualities, *sel.*   E. E. Cummings.
I Like My Body When It Is with Your Body.   AnMo; BoLoP; SFF; TT; VGW

Sonnets at Christmas (I-II).   Allen Tate.   HAP; NoAM; NOBA; PAIC; VGW
"Ah, Christ, I love you rings to the wild sky," II.   LFH

Sonnets Attempted in the Manner of Contemporary Writers, *sels.* Samuel Taylor Coleridge.
On a Ruined House in a Romantic Country.   Epi
(House That Jack Built, The.)   AKE
To Simplicity.   Epi

Sonnets for Pictures: "Our Lady of the Rocks."   Dante Gabriel Rossetti.   *See* For "Our Lady of the Rocks" by Leonardo da Vinci.

Sonnets frae Siberia, *sel.*   Donald Campbell.
Aiberdeen.   MIS
Minding.   MIS

Sonnets from China, *sels.*   W. H. Auden.
"Chilled by the present, its gloom and its noise," XVIII.   PPP
"Far from a cultural centre he was used," XIII.   CMoP (1970 ed.)
"He stayed, and was imprisoned in possession," IV.   CMoP (1970 ed.)
'He was their servant (some way he was blind)," VII.   CMoP (1970 ed.)
"He watched the stars and noted birds in flight," VI.   CMoP (1970 ed.)
"His care-free swagger was a fine invention," V.   CMoP (1970 ed.)
"So an age ended, and its last deliverer died," X.   CMoP (1970 ed.)
(So an Age Ended.)   ExPo (1973 ed.)
"So from the years their gifts were showered: each," I.   CMoP (1970 ed.)
"They wondered why the fruit had been forbidden," II.   CMoP (1970 ed.)

Sonnets from the Portuguese, *sels.*   Elizabeth Barrett Browning.
"Beloved, my beloved, when I think," XX.   VPC; WPE
"Beloved, thou hast brought me many flowers," XLIV.   ILP (1975 ed.); WPE
"Face of all the world is changed, I think, The," VII.   VLP
"First time he kissed me, he but only kissed," XXXVIII.   LoAs
"First time that the sun rose on thine oath, The," XXXII.   WPE
"Heavy heart, Belovèd, have I borne, A," XXV.   ILP (1975 ed.)
"How do I love thee? Let me count the ways," XLIII.   BoLoP; FF; HeIP; HoPM (1975 ed.); ILP (1975 ed.); InPS; IPWM; LFH; LoAs; NIL; OLR; PAIC; PPM; SFF; VPC; UnPo (1976 ed.); WPE
"I never gave a lock of hair away," XVIII.   HAP; VPC
"I thought once how Theocritus had sung," I.   GBL; NOBE; PAIC; VPC; WPE
"If thou must love me, let it be for nought," XIV.   HeIP; LoAs; NOBE; PBMP; TPo; UnPo (1976 ed.); WPE
"Let the world's sharpness like a clasping knife," XXIV.   VLP
"My letters! all dead paper, mute and white!" XXVIII.   HAP
"My poet, thou canst touch on all the notes," XVII.   VLP
"When our two souls stand up erect and strong," XXII.   BoWoP; NOBE; SBG; VLP; WPE
"Yet, love, mere love, is beautiful indeed," X.   VLP

Sonnets in Quaker Language, *sels.*    Hildegarde Flanner.
"Hearing a sound that may be thy return," VI.   WPE
"Thee sets a bell to swinging in my soul," II.   WPE
Sonnets of the Blood, *sels.*   Allen Tate.   PoA
"Fire I praise was once perduring flame, The" VII.
"Near to me as my flesh, my flesh and blood," II.
"Not power nor the storied hand of God," IX.
"Times have changed, there is not left to us, The" IV.
"What is this flesh and blood compounded of," I.
Sonnets of the Triple-headed Manichee, *sel.*   George Barker.
"Keelhauled across the star-wrecked death of God," II.   PoA
Sonnets on Eminent Characters, *sels.*   Samuel Taylor Coleridge.
Burke.   MBPR
La Fayette.   MBPR
Priestley.   MBPR
Sonnets on the Divina Commedia.   Longfellow.   *See* Divina
Commedia (*poems introductory to* Longfellow's *tr. of the
Divine Comedy*).
Sonnets on the Seasons, *sel.*   Hartley Coleridge.
November.   FSFS
Sonnets on the War, *sel.*   Sydney Dobell
"I saw the human millions as the sand."   VLP
Sonnets—Realities, *sel.*   E. E. Cummings.
Cambridge Ladies Who Live in Furnished Souls, The.   Epi;
HeIP; InPK; NoAM; NOBA; OBAL; TAP; TT; WIF
Sonnets to Be Written from Prison.   Robert Adamson.   CAAP;
GAS
Sonnets to Delia.   Samuel Daniel.   *See* To Delia.
Sonnets to His Mystresse Diana, *sel.*   J. Soowthern.
"Thou find'st not heere, neither the furious alarmes."   ESo
Sonnets to Idea.   Michael Drayton.   *See* Idea.
Sonnets to Laura, *sels.*   Petrarch, *tr. fr. Italian.*
To Laura in Death.
"Eyes that drew from me such fervent praise, The," XXIV, *tr.
by* Edwin Morgan.   NAWM-1
"Go, grieving rimes of mine, to that hard stone," LX, *tr. by*
Morris Bishop.   NAWM-1
"Great is my envy of you, earth, in your greed," XXXII, *tr. by*
Edwin Morgan.   NAWM-1
"My flowery and green age was passing away," XLVII, *prose
tr. by* J. M. Synge.
(He Understands the Great Cruelty of Death.)   BIrV
"When my heart was the amorous worms' meat," XXXVI, *tr.
by* Anna Maria Armi.
(Amorous Worms' Meat, The.)   LoAs
To Laura in Life.
"Blest be the day, and blest the month and year," XLVII, *tr.
by* Joseph Auslander.   NAWM-1
"Father of heaven, after squandered days," XLVIII, *tr. by*
R. G. Barnes.   Epi
("Father in heaven, after each lost day," *tr. by* Bernard
Bergonzi.)   NAWM-1
"I find [*or* fynde] no peace and all my war[r] is done," CIV, *tr.
by* Sir Thomas Wyatt.   AAS; ILP (1975 ed.); OAEL-1
OBVE; PPoe
(Description of the Contrarious Passions in a Lover.)   FF;
PAIC
"It was the morning of that blessed day," III, *tr. by* Joseph
Auslander.   NAWM-1
"Long[e] love that in my thought doth harbour, The," CIX, *tr.
by* Sir Thomas Wyatt.   CABA (1972 ed.); Epi; ILP (1975
ed.); NIL; OAEL-1; OBVE
(Lover for Shamefastnesse Hideth His Desire within His
Faithfull Hart, The.)   AAS, 2 *versions*
"Love that liveth and reigneth in my thought," CIX, *tr. by* the
Earl of Surrey.   Epi
("Love that doth raine and live within my thought.")
AAS; OBVE
(Love That Doth Reign and Live within My Thought.)
HeIP; ILP (1975 ed.); NIL; OAEL-1

(Complaint of a Lover Rebuked.)   CABA (1972 ed.)
"My galley [*or* galy] charged with forgetfulness," CLVI, *tr. by*
Sir Thomas Wyatt.   AAS; BiP; CABA (1972 ed.); Epi;
HAP; ILP (1975 ed.); LFH; OAEL-1; OBVE; PPP; WeW
(Lover Compareth His State to a Ship in Perilous Storm
Tossed on the Sea, The.)   GBL; HeIP; PAIC
"Set me wheras the sun doth parch the green [*or* sonne dothe
perche the grene]," CXIII, *tr. by* the Earl of Surrey.   AAS;
HAP; ILP (1975 ed.)
(Vow to Love Faithfully, Howsoever He Be Rewarded, A.)
PAIC
"She used to let her golden hair fly free," LXIX, *tr. by* Morris
Bishop.   NAWM-1
"White doe appeared to me over green, A," CLVII, *tr. by*
R. G. Barnes.   Epi
Sonnets to Orpheus, *sels.*   Rainer Maria Rilke, *tr. fr. German.*
"This is the creature there has never been," Pt. II, IV, *tr. by*
James Blair Leishman.   OBVE
"Torn apart by us ever and again,"   ILwL
"Where, in what ever-blissfully watered gardens," Pt. II, XVII,
*tr. by* James Blair Leishman.   OBVE
Sonnets—Unrealities, *sel.*   E. E. Cummings.
"It may not always be so; and I say."   BoLoP; TT
Sonnets upon the Punishment of Death, *sels.*   Wordsworth.
Apology.   VLP
"Ye brood of Conscience—Spectres! that frequent."   PeD
Sons, *sel.*   Kathleen Lubeck.
"Through the noonday sun."   NPW
Sons.   Don Polson.   AMV-81
Sons, my sons.   Black Star Line.   Henry Dumas.   PoBA
Sons of freedom, listen to me, and ye daughters, too, give ear.
James Bird.   *Unknown.*   AmFP
Sons of Levi, The.   *Unknown.*   AmFP
Sons of Liberty, The.   *Unknown.*   AIW
Sons of the prophet are hardy and bold, The.   Abdul, the Bulbul
Amir.   *Unknown.*   FSW
Sons of War sometimes are known, The.   Evan Lloyd.   *Fr.* The
Methodist.   OBSV
Sons, seek not me among these polished stones.   Charles
Cavendish to His Posterity.   Ben Jonson.   SCP-1
Sonsito.   Victor Hernandez Cruz.   MIT
Soo Line, Reading, Pacific Fruit.   The Other Side.   Thomas
Reiter.   AMV-80
Soon as/ you stop.   Cleavage.   A. R. Ammons.   OBAL
Soon as Glumdalclitch mist her pleasing care.   The Lamentation
of Glumdalclitch.   Pope.   Epi
Soon as the dismal news came down.   Oxford Barber's Verses on
the Queen's Death.   *Unknown.*   APAS
Soon as the father saw the rosy morn.   Ovid, *tr. by* Joseph
Addison.   *Fr.* Metamorphoses.   OBVE
Soon as the sun forsook the eastern main.   An Hymn to the
Evening.   Phillis Wheatley.   WPE
Soon ripe, soon rot. Young saint, old divell.   First Satan's Assault
against Those That First Came Up to Mercy's Terms.
Edward Taylor.   *Fr.* God's Determinations.   EAP
Soon, summer's drum will shake the earth no longer.   Fall of
Leaves.   D. S. Savage.   PoA
Soon the advertisements.   The Table.   Jennifer Maiden.   CAAP
Soon we shall plunge into the chilly fogs.   Song of Autumn I.
Baudelaire, *tr. by* C. F. McIntyre.   NAWM-2
Sooner or Later.   Sam Cornish.   CNA
Sooner or Later.   John Digby.   EAS
Sooner or later I will forget.   No Difference.   Beverly Lawn.
AMV-81
Sooner tears than sleep this midnight.   The Wind's Lament.
John Morris-Jones. *tr. by* Anthony Conran.   OBW
Soonest Mended.   John Ashbery.   CAAP; Prf

Soote Season, The.  Earl of Surrey, *after* Petrarch.  AAS; HeIP; NIL
  (Description of Spring.)  ILP (1975 ed.)
  ("Soote season, that bud and blome furth bringes, The.")  OBVE
  (Spring.)  NOBE

Soothing sigh of the night wind, the whine of a coyote's call, The.  Ranch at Twilight.  *Unknown.*  BPAW

Soothsayer.  Mary Ursula Bethell.  ATNZ

Sophistication.  Vassar Miller.  NCSH

Soprano sings, A. The poem.  Cat Poem.  Henry Graham.  UsP

Sopranosound, Memory of John.  Sharon Bourke.  CNA

Soraidh Slan Don Oidhche Areir.  Niall Mor MacMuireadach, *tr. fr. Irish by* Maire Cruise O'Brien.  BIrV

Sorcery.  Jessica Tarahata Hagedorn.  NW

Sorrow.  Chu Shu-chen, *tr. fr. Chinese by* Kenneth Rexroth.  BoWoP

Sorrow.  D. H. Lawrence.  CMoP (1970 ed.); PSN

Sorrow how high it is.  Dark Song.  A. R. Ammons.  MAT

Sorrow is my own yard.  The Widow's Lament in Springtime.  William Carlos Williams.  CMoP (1970 ed.); HAP; IPWM; NoAM; NOBA; PSN; TAP

Sorrow Is the Only Faithful One.  Owen Dodson.  AmNP (1974 ed.); PoBA

Sorrow of Love, The ("The brawling of a sparrow in the eaves").  W. B. Yeats.  OAEL-2; OBP; PoIA

Sorrow of Love, The ("The quarrel of the sparrows in the eaves").  W. B. Yeats.  NoAM; OAEL-2; PoIA; VLP

Sorrowing nymph, oh why display.  On a Statue of Sir Arthur Sullivan.  G. Rostrevor Hamilton.  FaBoCo

Sorrows of Werther, The.  Thackeray.  FaBoCo; NOBL; PoPle; VLP

Sorry.  R. S. Thomas.  LP

Sort of a Song, A.  William Carlos Williams.  BiP; HoPM (1975 ed.); PoIA; TAP

Sorting out letters and piles of my old.  Mementos, 1.  W. D. Snodgrass.  CABA (1972 ed.); CoPAm; FF; HeIP; ILP (1975 ed.); PiAm; PPP; TPo; UnPo (1976 ed.)

Sorting, Wrapping, Packing, Stuffing.  James Schuyler.  NoAM

So-shu dreamed.  Ancient Wisdom, Rather Cosmic.  Ezra Pound.  NOBA

Sot-Weed Factor, The.  Ebenezer Cook.  EAP

Soul.  D. L. Graham.  PoBA

Soul, A.  Randall Jarrell.  CMoP (1970 ed.)

Soul and race.  Here Where Coltrane Is.  Michael S. Harper.  CNA; PoBA

Soul and the Body, The.  Sir John Davies.  *Fr.* Nosce Teipsum.  NOBE

Soul-Drift.  Mathilde Blind.  SBG

Soul has bandaged moments, The.  Emily Dickinson.  PiAm

Soul has many motions, body one, The.  The Motion.  Theodore Roethke.  MPA

Soul is a region without definite boundaries, The.  Terrain.  A. R. Ammons.  ConAP

Soul is lonely, The.  La Selva.  Cid Corman.  VGW

Soul Longs to Return Whence It Came, The.  Richard Eberhart.  CMoP (1970 ed.)

Soul of a coconut can't live, The.  Coconut.  Mario Satz, *tr. by* Willis Barnstone.  VWA

Soul of my child, Princess Splendid!  Invocation before the Rice Harvest.  *Malay Oral Tradition, tr. by* R. O. Winstedt.  WTO

Soul of my soul! it cannot be.  The Sympathy.  Owen Felltham.  SCP-2

Soul selects her own society, The.  Emily Dickinson.  AmVN; BoWoP; CABA (1972 ed.); CMoP (1970 ed.); InPK; InPS; IP; NoAM; NOBA; PAIC; Psy; SBG; TAP; TT; UnPo (1976 ed.); WPE

Souldier Going to the Field, The.  Sir William Davenant.  *See* Soldier Going to the Field, The.

Soul's Beauty.  Dante Gabriel Rossetti.  The House of Life, LXXVII.  VLP

Soul's Expression, The.  Elizabeth Barrett Browning.  VLP

Souls from Purgatory they come.  Negrun.  Lucille F. Travis.  AATT

Soul's Garment, The.  Margaret Cavendish, Duchess of Newcastle.  WPE

Soul's Liberty.  Anna Wickham.  PPM

Souls of men! why will ye scatter.  Come to Jesus.  Frederick William Faber.  VLP

Souls of poets dead and gone.  Lines of the Mermaid Tavern.  Keats.  ILP (1975 ed.); MBPR; TT

Souls of the Slain, The.  Thomas Hardy.  CMoP (1970 ed.); PPM

Souls of Women at Night, The.  Wallace Stevens.  CMoP (1970 ed.)

Soul's shining place, The.  About the Heavenly Life.  Luis de León, *tr. fr. Spanish.*  ILwL

Soul's Travelling, the, *sel.*  Elizabeth Barrett Browning.  "God, God!/ With a child's voice I cry."  ILwL

Sound.  Jim Harrison.  VGW

Sound, The/ then a soft halo around it.  Ruptured Melodies.  Art Lange.  FiCh

Sound and Sense.  Pope.  *Fr.* An Essay on Criticism, Pt. II.  SoSe; UnPo (1976 ed.)
  ("True ease in writing comes from art, not chance").  HAP

Sound and sweet in the big gray barrels.  Apples to Keep.  Frances Frost.  ECBV

Sound from the Earth, A.  William Stafford.  NNaP; RFM

Sound like I can hear this morning.  Death Bells.  *Unknown.*  BluL

Sound not the depths for anchorage, but ways.  Seaway.  Grace Wilson.  AMV-81

Sound of Afroamerican History Chapt I, The.  S. E. Anderson.  PoBA

Sound of Afroamerican History Chapt II, The.  S. E. Anderson.  PoBA

Sound of faint thunder, The.  At the Drive-In: "John Wayne vs. God."  A. A. Dewey.  HeS

Sound of happy laughter leap with shadows on the walls.  Taos Winter.  Patty L. Harjo.  VoR

Sound of Night, The.  Maxine W. Kumin.  WPE

Sound of Rain, The.  Bella Akhmadulina, *tr. fr. Russian by* Daniel Halpern *and* Albert Todd.  BoWoP

Sound of Silence, The.  Paul Simon.  PBMP; WIF

Sound of snails—crying.  Snails.  *Aborigine Oral Tradition.*  WTO

Sound of the Sea, The.  Longfellow.  EcS

Sound of the Wind That Is Blowing, The, *sel.*  J. Kitchener Davies, *tr. fr. Welsh by* Joseph P. Clancy.  "Today,/ there came a breeze thin as the needle of a syringe."  OBW

Sound of Trees, The.  Robert Frost.  NoAM

Sound of water running, The.  Civilization.  Tom Schmidt.  NeAC

Sound of your lips beating, The.  Thoughts for My Grandmother.  Laya Firestone.  VWA

Sound, Sound the Clarion.  Thomas Osbert Mordaunt, *formerly at. to* Sir Walter Scott.  *Fr.* Verses Written during the War, 1756-1763.  FaBoEE; FaPoR; NOBE; PCOP

Sound the flute!  Spring.  Blake.  *Fr.* Songs of Innocence.  FSFS; LCL; MBPR

Sound variegated through beneath lit.  Gyre's Galax.  Norman Henry Pritchard II.  PoBA

Sounding.  Jenne Andrews.  HeS

Sounding the horn.  The Blacksmith 1970.  Sean Clarkin.  IPM

Soundless, The/ light drifts over. The Light of the World. B. Alquit, *tr. by* Howard Schwartz. VWA

Soundlessly, a tide at the ear. Awakening. John Haines. EAS

Sounds. Paul David Ashley. DNGG

Sounds. Robert Creeley. GP

Sounds are heard too high for ears. Watching Television. Robert Bly. BiP

Sounds East European, doesn't it? Yet. Richard Hoffman. UsP

Sounds in the Evening, The. Eleanor Farjeon. FPB

Sounds like big. Waking from a Nap on the Beach. May Swenson. RFM

Sounds of Ireland, The. Windharp. John Montague. CIP

Sounds of us, The. Our Sobbing Must Be Heard. Grace Cavalieri. AATT

Soup. Carl Sandburg. AKE; NOBE; TH

Soup Jar, The. Dabney Stuart. CoPAm; CSP

Soup of Venus, The. James Tate. AmPA

Soup on a Cold Day. Nellie Hill. AMV-81

Soup Song. Maurice Sugar. FSW

Sour daylight cracks through my sleep-caked lids, The. The Distant Winter. Philip Levine. VGW

Source immaterial of material naught. The Rejected "National Hymns." "Orpheus C. Kerr." OBAL

Sources of Good Counsel. Peter Idley. OxBChV

Sourdough french bread and pinot chardonnay. Maps. Robert Hass. CAAP

Sourdough mountain called a fire in. The Text. Gary Snyder. *Fr.* Myths and Texts: Burning. Epi

Soursobs. Richard Tipping. CAAP

Sourwood Mountain. *Unknown.* AmFP; FSW; GBP

Souster. Ray Fraser. NeAC

South African Bloodstone. Quincy Troupe. CNA

South American Sway. Margaretta Byers. ECBV

South Atlantic clouds rode low, The. Safari West. John A. Williams. InPS

South Australia. *Unknown.* FSW

South Carolina Baptismal Procession. David Childers. AAN

South Coast, The. William Everson. PiAm

South Country, The. Hilaire Belloc. PES

South Country. Kenneth Slessor. GAS; MAuV

South End. Conrad Aiken. CMoP (1970 ed.); HoPM (1975 ed.)

South-Folk in Cold Country. Ezra Pound, *after the Chinese.* OBVE

South of My Days. Judith Wright. GAS; WPE

South of the Border. Virginia Real Nicholas. AMV-80

South of the border and north of the sea. Song of the Border. Gordon W. Norris. BPAW

South of the bridge on Seventeenth. Fifteen. William Stafford. SoS

South of the Great Sea. *Unknown, tr. fr. Chinese by* Arthur Waley. OLR

South Shore Line. John Schlesinger. AMV-80

South Wind. Mary Logue. NPW

South Wind. Nathan Yonathan, *tr. fr. Hebrew by* Richard Flantz. VWA

South-wind brings, The. Threnody. Emerson. PAIC

South-wind strengthens to a gale, The. Low Barometer. Robert Bridges. CMoP (1970 ed.); NoAM

Southbound. Betty Adcock. CSP

Southbound on the Freeway. May Swenson. BBGO; SoS

Southeast, and storm, and every weathervane. Hatteras Calling. Conrad Aiken. NoAM; NOBA; TAP

Southeast Ramparts of the Seine, The. Judit Tóth, *tr. fr. Hungarian by* Emery George. VWA

Souther, wind, souther! Rhyme of the Fishermen's Children. *Unknown.* GBP

Southern Blues. *Unknown.* BluL

Southern Cop. Sterling A. Brown. SoSe (1977 ed.); WIF

Southern Exposures. G. E. Murray. AMV-81

Southern Gothic. Donald Justice. NIL

Southern Mansion. Arna Bontemps. AmNP (1974 ed.); CNA; FB; FF; PoBA; SoSe; UsP

Southern Pines. John Peale Bishop. GOA

Southern Road. Sterling A. Brown. BPo; FB; PoBA

Southern Road, The. Dudley Randall. CNA; PAIC; PoBA

Southern Season. Alice Moser Claudel. TAT

Southern trees bear a strange fruit. Strange Fruit. Lewis Allan. PoIA

Southrons, hear your country call you! Dixie. Albert Pike. BTTM

Southward through Eden went a river large. Adam and Eve in Paradise. Milton. *Fr.* Paradise Lost, IV. SCP-1

Southwest Passage. Dudley Fitts. PoA

South-west wind, how pleasant in the face, The. Beans in Blossom. John Clare. VLP

Souvenir. E. A. Robinson. NoAM

Souvenir from Sicily on the shelf, A. Worm Within. Anthony Thwaite. HeHu

Souvenirs. Melvin Dixon. NW

Souvenirs. Dudley Randall. BPo

Sovereign and Transforming Grace, *with music.* Frederic Henry Hedge. AH

Sovereign beauty which I do admire, The. Amoretti, III. Spenser. PAIC

Sow. Sylvia Plath. AnMo; CoPAm

Sow Came In, The. *Unknown.* NOBL

Sow Took the Measles, The. *Unknown.* FSW

Sower, The. Mathilde Blind. SBG; WPE

Sower a Singer, The. Cotton Mather. *See* When the Seed of Thy Word Is Cast.

Sowing in the morning, sowing seeds of kindness. Bringing in the Sheaves. Knowles Shaw. BLSH; FSW

Sowing on the Mountain. *Unknown.* FSW

Sowing Season. Evening. Victor Hugo, *tr. fr. French by* Mary Ann Caws. NAWM-2

Sow's Ear, A. Theodore Weiss. NoAM

Soyer is gone! Then be it said. On the Death of the Great Chef Alexis Soyer. *Unknown.* FaBoEE

Space. William Hart-Smith. GAS

Space. X. J. Kennedy. Moon

Space Being (Don't Forget to Remember) Curved. E. E. Cummings. Epi; NoAM
(Space Being Curved.) STS

Space Child's Mother Goose, The, *sels.* Frederick Winsor.
"Hydrogen Dog and the Cobalt Cat, The." QQQ
"Little Bo-Beep." QQQ
"Probable-Possible, my black hen." QQQ
"Solomon Grundy." QQQ
"This little pig built a spaceship." QQQ

Space Eater Camps at Fifth Lake, The. Reg Saner. GP

Space is too full. Did nothing happen here? American Farm, 1934. Genevieve Taggard. VGW; WPW

Space-Wanderer's Homecoming. Peter Viereck. AMV-80

Spacin. Ronda Davis. JB

Spacious Firmament on High, The. Joseph Addison. FaPoR; NIL; PIM (*At. to* Andrew Marvell)
(Ode: "Spacious firmament on high, The.") BoReV; HeIP; ILwL; IPWM

Spade-bearded Grandfather, squat Lenin. Summer Pogrom. Fay Zwicky. GAS

Spade Is Just a Spade, A. Walter Everette Hawkins. PoBA

Spades take up leaves. Gathering Leaves. Robert Frost. VGW

Spaghetti. Shel Silverstein. OSF

Spain is located somewhere between Polk Street and Laguna Beach. Cante Jondo for Soul Brother Jack Spicer. Steve Jonas. EC

Span of Life, The. Robert Frost. GDP; HoPM (1975 ed.); IP; SoSe

Spanish Curate, The, *sel.* Beaumont *and* Fletcher.
Jacobean Merrymaking, *fr.* III, ii. BBL

Spanish Descent, The. Daniel Defoe. APAS

Spanish expression *Cuando yo era muchacho*, The. Habla Usted Español? James Reiss. AmPA

Spanish Friar, The, *sels.* Dryden.
Farewell, Ungrateful Traitor, *fr.* V, i. BoLoP; HAP; ILP (1975 ed.); NOBE; PoPle
" 'Twere well your judgments but in plays did range," *fr.* prologue. OBSV

Spanish Gipsy, The, *sel.* Thomas Middleton.
"Trip it gipsies, trip it fine." ILP (1975 ed.)

Spanish heavens spread their brilliant starlight. Freiheit (Freedom). Karl Ernst *and* Peter Daniel, *tr. fr. German.* FSW

Spanish Is the Loving Tongue. *Unknown.* FSW; RDB, *with music.*

Spanish is the tongue of lovers. Mi Corazón. Gordon W. Norris. BPAW

Spanish Johnny. Willa Cather. BPAW

Spanish Lady in Dublin City, The, *with music. Unknown.* RDB

Spanish noon is a blaze of azure fire, and the dusty pilgrims, The. The Exodus (August 3, 1492). Emma Lazarus. *Fr.* By the Waters of Babylon. WPE

Spanish Student, The, *sel.* Longfellow.
Serenade: "Stars of the summer night," *fr.* I, iii. PAIC

Spanish War, The. "Hugh MacDiarmid." CMoP (1970 ed.)

Sparafucile fought his peasant war. Dead Fly. Eilean Ni Chuilleanain. CIP

Spare Professor, grave and bald, The. At a Reading. Thomas Bailey Aldrich. OBAL

Spare Quilt, The. John Peale Bishop. GOA

Spare then the person, and expose the vice. Pope. *Fr.* Epilogue to the Satires. OBSV

Spare Us, O Lord, Aloud We Pray, *with music.* Isaac Watts. AH

"Spare us of dying beauty," cries out Youth. Of Dying Beauty. Louis Zukofsky. PoA

Spark of Laurel, A. Stanley Kunitz. NoAM

Sparkles from the Wheel. Walt Whitman. AmVN; BiP

Sparkling Water. Richard Schaaf. TAT

Spark's Farewell to Its Clay, The. R. A. K. Mason. ATNZ

Sparrow, The. William Carlos Williams. InPS; PiAm; VGW

Sparrow dips in his wheel-rut bath, The. The Five Students. Thomas Hardy. CMoP (1970 ed.); ExPo (1973 ed.)

Sparrow-hawk proud did hold in wicked jail, A. *Unknown.* EBEV

Sparrow-Hawk's Complaint, The. *Unknown.* OxBM
(Timor Mortis.) FF

Sparrow in the Dust, A. Ruth Domino, *tr. fr. Italian by* Daniel Hoffman *and* Jerre Mangione. BoWoP

Sparrow in the Zoo, The. Howard Nemerov. NoAM
(Epigram: Political Reflexion.) NIL

Sparrow in Winter. Shinkichi Takahashi, *tr. fr. Japanese by* Lucien Stryk *and* Takashi Ikemoto. NU

Sparrows drift over the mess hall. Christmas Poem. Michael Hogan. DNGG

Sparrows in College Ivy. Edgar Wolfe. AMV-81

Sparrow's Nest, The. Wordsworth. MBPR

Spartan Wrestler, The. Damagetus, *tr. fr. Greek by* Tom Dodge. LiSp

Spassky at Reykjavik. David Fisher. AMV-81

Spastic Child on a Pony, A. Judith Smallshaw. PMW

Spatial depths of being survive. The Lost Dancer. Jean Toomer. PoBA

Spawn of fantasies. Love Songs. Mina Loy. VGW; WPE

Spawn of Slums, The. James W. Thompson. BPo

Spawning in Northern Minnesota. David McElroy. AmPA

Speak. Bea Opengart. AMV-80

Speak. James Wright. HAP; TAP; WeW

Speak for us, great sea. Great Sea. Charles Brasch. ATNZ

Speak Gently. David Bates. SpRo

Speak gently, Spring, and make no sudden sound. Four Little Foxes. Lew Sarett. RFM

Speak like Rain. Jerred Metz. VWA

Speak not ill of womankind. Against Blame of Woman. Gerald, Earl of Desmond, *tr. by* the Earl of Longford. BIrV

"Speak not of niceness, when there's chance of wreck." Sir Walter Scott. *Fr.* Peveril of the Peak. FaBoEE

Speak roughly to your little boy. The Duchess's Lullaby. "Lewis Carroll." *Fr.* Alice's Adventures in Wonderland. FaBoCo; FaBoNo; SpRo

Speak, Satire, for there's none can tell like thee. The True-born Englishman. Daniel Defoe. APAS

"Speak! speak! thou fearful guest!" The Skeleton in Armor. Longfellow. CTV

Speak to me. Take my hand. What are you now? Effort at Speech between Two People. Muriel Rukeyser. PoIA; UsP; VoPo; WeW

Speak to us who. Tiresias. George Garrett. CoPAm

Speake gentle heart, where is thy dwelling place? Thomas Watson. *Fr.* Hekatompathia. AAS

Speaker, The. Charles G. Ballard. VoR

Speaker opens his mouth, The. Persistent Narrative. Ken Smith. TwMBP

Speakin' in general, I'ave tried 'em all. Sestina of the Tramp-Royal. Kipling. PAIC

Speaking. Michael Ryan. AmPA

Speaking as a woman who has thought. Cosmetic. Gretchen Herbkersman. AMV-80

Speaking for Them. Hayden Carruth. GP

Speaking like wind. Swimmer. Gladys Cardiff. CDW

Speaking of marvels, I am alive. Alive Together. Lisel Mueller. IHMS

Speaking of Poetry. John Peale Bishop. NIL

Speaking of Television, *sels.* Phyllis McGinley.
Almost Any Evening. TH
Reflections Dental. TH
Robin Hood. OBSV

Speaking: The Hero. Felix Pollak. CTBA

Speaking Tree, The. Muriel Rukeyser. VGW

Spearmen heard the bugle sound, The. Beth-Gêlert. William Robert Spencer. GDP

Special Bulletin. Langston Hughes. PoBA

Special Delivery. John Montague. CIP

Special Jurymen of England! who admire your country's laws. Damages, Two Hundred Pounds. Thackeray. OBSV

Special Rider Blues. *Unknown.* AmFP

Specimen of an Induction to a Poem. Keats. MBPR

Speck of protoplasm in a finch's egg, The. Birdsong. James Burns Singer. FaBoTw (1975 ed.)

Speck of Sand, A. Paul Celan, *tr. fr. German by* Joachim Neugroschel. VWA

Speck that would have been beneath my sight, A. A Considerable Speck. Robert Frost. OBAL; PBMP; PPP; STS

Speckled cat and a tame hare, A. Two Songs of a Fool. W. B. Yeats. CMoP (1970 ed.)

Speckled horse is bucking, The. *Mongol Oral Tradition, tr. by* C. R. Bawden. WTO

Speckled with glints of star and moonshine. Samuel Hoffenstein. *Fr.* Mr. Walter de la Mare Makes the Little Ones Dizzy. SpRo

Spectacle of Truth, The. John Hewitt. CIP

Spectacular Blossom. Allen Curnow. ATNZ

Spectator ab Extra. Arthur Hugh Clough. FaBoCo
"Come along, 'tis the time, ten or more minutes past," *sel.* OBSV

Spectator's Guide to Contemporary Art, *sels.* Phyllis McGinley. On the Farther Wall, Marc Chagall. OBSV
Squeeze Play. FaBoEE; OBSV

Spectators only on this bustling stage. Charles Churchill. *Fr.* Night; an Epistle to Robert Lloyd. OBSV

Spectra, *sel.* Witter Bynner.
"If I were only dafter," Opus 6. InPK

Spectral Attitudes, The. André Breton, *tr. fr. French by* David Gascoyne. EAS

Spectral Lovers. John Crowe Ransom. GBL; HeIP; LoAs; PiAm

Spectre is haunting America—the spectre of hoodooism, A. Black Power Poem. Ishmael Reed. BPo

Spectrum. William Dickey. SoSe

Spectrum. Mari Evans. BPo

Speculation. Howard Nemerov. TAP

Speculators, The. Thackeray. OBSV

Speech. Henry Taylor. CSP; MAT

Speech after long silence; it is right. After Long Silence. W. B. Yeats. BoLoP; CMoP (1970 ed.); HeIP; HoPM (1975 ed.); NIL; OAEL-2; PPP; PSN; UnPo (1976 ed.); WIF

Speech for an Abdication. Harry Stessel. AAN

Speech for the Repeal of the McCarran Act. Richard Wilbur. CMoP (1970 ed.); GOA

Speechless: Upon the Marriage of Two Deaf and Dumb Persons. Philip Bourke Marston. VLP

"Speed, bonnie boat, like a bird on the wing." Skye Boat Song. Sir Harold Boulton. GSB

Speed of Darkness, The. Muriel Rukeyser. WBN

Speeding. Arlie "Franko" Durham. DNGG

Spell, The. Amiri Baraka. PiAm

Spell. Robert Francis. GP

Spell, The. Robert Herrick. CaPo

Spell against Sorrow. Kathleen Raine. PBWP

Spell It. *Unknown.* TDH

Spellbound. Emily Brontë. *See* Night Is Darkening round Me.

Spelling Bee at Angels, The. Bret Harte. PoTa

Spelling reformer indicted, A. Ambrose Bierce. *Fr.* The Devil's Dictionary. OBAL

Spelt from Sibyl's Leaves. Gerard Manley Hopkins. CMoP (1970 ed.); OAEL-1

Spend the years of learning squandering. Gnome. Samuel Beckett. BIrV

Spending hand that alway poureth out [*or* powreth owte], A. Sir Thomas Wyatt. Satires, III. AAS; TVS

Spenser! a jealous honourer of thine. Keats. MBPR

Spenser's Ireland. Marianne Moore. NoOM; NOBA; PAIC; TAP

Spent purpose of a perfectly marvellous, The. In Favor of One's Time. Frank O'Hara. PoA

Sphere of Glass, The. John Lehmann. LoAs

Sphere of pure chance, free agent of no cause. Calvin in the Casino. Turner Cassity. NIL

Sphinx, The. Emerson. NOBA

Spicer's Instant Poetry. James Reeves. MPo

Spider. Thomas Cole. PoA

Spider, The. Richard Eberhart. PoA

Spider. Norma Farber. PChr

Spider, The. Kenneth Mackenzie. BoAnP

Spider and the Clock, The. Sol Funaroff. SPT

Spider and the Fly, The. Mary Howitt. ECBV; OxBChV

Spider and the Ghost of the Fly, The. Vachel Lindsay. VGW

Spider as an artist, The. Emily Dickinson. PiAm

Spider bite the size of a dinner plate, A. Into the Dark. Paul Monette. AmPA

Spider expects the cold of winter, The. The Spider. Richard Eberhart. PoA

Spider holds a silver ball, The. Emily Dickinson. NIL; PiAm

Spider in the bath, A. The image noted. The Image. Roy Fuller. OxBTC

Spider in the Grapes. Thomas James. HeS

Spider sewed at night, A. Emily Dickinson. PiAm

Spider spreads her webs, whether she be. Letter to Maria Gisborne. Shelley. MBPR

Spider, Unsurprised, The. Peter Klappert. AAN

Spider's web, The. Special Delivery. John Montague. CIP

Spike Driver Blues. *Unknown.* BluL

Spike Island: Convicted Labour. Joan Keefe. IPM

Spikes of new smell driven up nostrils. Gary Snyder. *Fr.* Myths and Texts: Burning, XIII. FoP

Spilled from a mildewed box. Grandfather. John Leax. AATT

Spilled Milk. John Haines. GP

Spin the ball! I reel, I burn. Song of Seyd Nimetollah of Kuhistan. Emerson. NOBA

Spindrift. Galway Kinnell. IPWM

Spinning Earth, The. Aileen Fisher. FPB

Spinning Girl, The. Nathan Alterman, *tr. fr. Hebrew by* Ruth Nevo. VWA

Spinning Song. Edith Sitwell. DuDr

Spinning Wheel, The. John Francis Waller. PFIr; PoTa

Spinoza/ Collected curiosa. Clerihew. *Unknown.* NOBL

Spinster. Sylvia Plath. CoPAm

Spinster's Lullaby. Vassar Miller. BoWoP; CSP; NMM; RiTi

Spire cranes, The. Its statue is an aviary. Dylan Thomas. PoA

Spires, firm on their monster feet rose light and thin, The. Denis Devlin. *Fr.* The Heavenly Foreigner. CIP

Spirit. Mei Berssenbrugge. SA

Spirit, The. Doug Turner. AMV-81

Spirit breathes upon the word, The. The Light and the Glory of the Word. William Cowper. PIM

Spirit Craft, The. Charles G. Ballard. VoR

Spirit Epiloguizes, The. Milton. *Fr.* Comus. NOBE

Spirit haunts the year's last hours, A. Song. Tennyson. HeIP; ILP (1975 ed.); PoPle

Spirit in Our Hearts, The, *with music.* Henry Ustic Onderdonk. AH

Spirit Lake, Iowa, this January morning is ten below. Tea. Ann Struthers. AMV-80

Spirit Land, The. Jones Very. HAP

Spirit-like before Light. Arthur Gregor. VWA

Spirit of Freedom, Thou Dost Love the Sea. Henry Nehemiah Dodge. RhR

Spirit of Life, in This New Dawn, *with music.* Earl B. Marlatt. AH

Spirit of Plato. *Unknown, tr. fr. Greek by* Shelley. OBVE

Spirit of 34th Street, The. Peggy Shriver. AMV-80

Spirit of Wrath, The. William Heyen. AmPA

Spirit seems to pass, A. Lausanne. Thomas Hardy. FaBoTw (1975 ed.)

Spirit Song. *Tr. fr. Eskimo.* WTO

Spirit who sweepest the wild harp of time. Ode to the Departing Year. Samuel Taylor Coleridge. MBPR

Spirits. Victor Hernandez Cruz. PoBA

Spirits and illusions have died. Life from the Lifeless. Robinson Jeffers. CMoP (1970 ed.)

Spirits, Dancing. Arthur Gregor. VGW

Spirit's Epochs, The. Coventry Patmore. *Fr.* The Angel in the House, I, viii. EBEV; GBL

Spirit's Odyssey, The. M. Krishnamurti. PeD

Spirits of well-shot woodcock, partridge, snipe. Death of King George V. John Betjeman. NOBE

Spirits/ Someone. Karoniaktatie. NW

Spirit's Song. Louise Bogan. LoAs

Spirits Unchained. Keorapetse Kgositsile. PoBA

Spirits were in neutral space, before, The. Satan and Michael. Byron. *Fr.* The Vision of Judgment. UsP

Spiritual, A. Paul Laurence Dunbar. BPo

Spiritual. Michael S. Harper. NW

Spiritualist, The. Leon Slade. FPA

Spiritus Sanctus. Betty Ruth Bird. AATT

Spit. Charles Kenneth Williams. FoP; VWA

Spitballer. Fred Chappell. LiSp; PPoD

Spits of glitter in lowgrade ore. Conserving the Magnitude of Uselessness. A. R. Ammons. NoAM

Spittal wiver are no' very nice. The Wives of Spittal. *Unknown.* GBP

Spitting/ on this platform. Underground Poetry. Pedro Pietri. NYP

Spitting on Ira Rosenblatt. Robert Hershon. NeAC

Spleen. Sydney Goodsir Smith. MS

Spleen LXXV ("Old Pluvius, month of rains, in peevish mood"). Baudelaire, *tr. fr. French by* Kenneth O. Hanson. NAWM–2

Spleen LXXVI ("I have more memories than if I had lived a thousand years"). Baudelaire, *tr. fr. French by* Anthony Hecht. NAWM–2

Spleen LXXVII ("I'm like the king of a rain-country, rich"). Baudelaire, *tr. fr. French by* Robert Lowell. NAWM–2

Spleen LXXVIII ("When the low heavy sky weighs like a lid"). Baudelaire, *tr. fr. French by* Sir John Squire. NAWM–2

Splendid paper palace, The. The Mask and the Poem. Alejandra Pizarnik, *tr. by* Alina Rivero. VWA

Splendid Shilling, The. John Philips. EPC; OAEL–1, *abr.*; PAIC

Splendid Thing Growing, A. Primus St. John. MPA

Splendid Village, The, *sel.* Ebenezer Elliott.
"Village! thy butcher's son, the steward now." OBSV

Splendidis Longum Valedico Nugis. Sir Philip Sidney. *See* Leave Me, O Love.

Spendor. Shin Shalom, *tr. fr. Hebrew by* Abraham Birman. VWA

Splendor Falls on Castle Walls, The. Tennyson. *Fr.* The Princess, Pt. III. CTV; HeIP; ILP (1975 ed.); InPK; OAEL–2; PoIA
(Blow, Bugle, Blow.) NOBE; UnPo (1976 ed.)
(Bugle, The.) PoPle

Splendour recurrent/ in cherry-wood. Fraternitas. Ezra Pound, *after the Chinese.* OBVE

Splinter. Carl Sandburg. PCOP; SoSe; UsP

Split-cedar, The/ smoked salmon. The Way West, Underground. Gary Snyder. CNW

Split the lark—and you'll find the music. Emily Dickinson. ILP (1975 ed.)

Spoiling daylight inched along the bar-top, The. The Mill. Richard Wilbur. SoSe (1977 ed.)

Spoils. Robert Graves. HAP; UsP; WeW

Spoilt. D. J. Enright. HeHu

Spokane Falls 1874. Phillip William George. NW; VoR

Spoken by Venus on Seeing Her Statue Done by Praxiteles. *Tr. fr. Greek.* FaBoEE

Sponge out nostrils—ugh!—and eyes. More to It than Riding. J. A. Lindon. PH

Spontaneous Me. Walt Whitman. UsP

Spontaneous Requiem for the American Indian. Gregory Corso. MAT

Spook Sheep. Gérard de Nerval, *tr. fr. French by* Andrew Hoyem. Epi

Spool, The. Ben Belitt. PPoD

Spoon, The. Charles Simic. NNaP

Spoon River Anthology, *sels.* Edgar Lee Masters.
Amanda Barker. NoAM
Anne Rutledge. CMoP (1970 ed.); HAP; NoAM; NoBA; OFD
Arlo Will. PBMP
Butch Weldy. PSN
Carl Hamblin. CMoP (1970 ed.); OBSV
Cassius Hueffer. NoAM
Circuit Judge, The. FaBoEE
Cooney Potter. CTBA
Daisy Fraser. CMoP (1970 ed.); HAP
Dora Williams. HAP
Editor Whedon. CMoP (1970 ed.); FaboEE; NoAM; NOBA; OBSV
Elsa Wertman. NoAM
Fiddler Jones. CMoP (1970 ed.); NoAM; TAP
Frank Drummer. NoAM
Hamilton Greene. NoAM
Hill, The. CMoP (1970 ed.); NoAM; NOBA; TAP
Jonathan Swift Somers. OBAL
Judge Somers. FaBoEE; OBSV
Lucinda Matlock. CMoP (1970 ed.); FF; HAP; IPWM; NoAM; NOBA; PBMP; PPM; UsP; VoPo
Petit, the Poet. CMoP (1970 ed.); InPK; NoAM; NOBA; TAP
Spooniad, The. OBAL
Village Atheist, The. PPM
Willie Metcalf. IPWM

Spooniad, The. Edgar Lee Masters. *Fr.* Spoon River Anthology. OBAL

Spooning in gravy. The Diner. Gloria Bussel Koster. NPW

Spoonmeat at Bill Porter's in the Hall. After Tennyson. Edward Lear. FaBoNo

Sporting Acquaintances. Siegfried Sassoon. OxBTC

Sporting Life Blues. *Unknown.* FSW

Sports and gallantries, the stage, the arts, the antics of dancers. Boats in a Fog. Robinson Jeffers. LFH; RhR

Sportsfield. A. D. Hope. MAuV

Sports Field. Judith Wright. LiSp; MAuV

Sportsman, The. David McCord. LiSp; SPo

Sporty Young Person, A. *Unknown.* TDH

Sporus. Pope. *Fr.* Epistle to Dr. Arbuthnot. NOBE; OBSV

Spot of my youth! whose hoary branches sigh. Lines Written beneath an Elm in the Churchyard of Harrow. Byron. MBPR

Spotlights had you covered, The. A Poem about Poems about Vietnam. Jon Stallworthy. NoAM

Spots on black skin. Blind Old Woman. Clarence Major. PoBA

Spotted hawk swoops by and accuses me, The. Song of Myself, LII. Walt Whitman. AnMo; BiP

Spouting Horn, The. Nelson Bentley. LoAs

Sprawled/ on our faces in the spring. The Hen Flower. Galway Kinnell. CAAP; NNaP

Sprawled on the crates [*or* bags] and sacks [*or* crates] in the rear of the truck. Green, Green Is El Aghir. Norman Cameron. FaBoTw; OxBTC

Spray. D. H. Lawrence. EcS

Spraying the Potatoes. Patrick Kavanagh. BIrV

Spread back across the air, wings wide. Gulls Land and Cease to Be. John Ciardi. TPo

Spread on the roadway. The Cyclists. Amy Lowell. WPE

Spreading and low, unwatered, concentrate. The California Oaks. Yvor Winters. GOA; MPA

Spring. Blake. *Fr.* Songs of Innocence. FSFS; LCL; MBPR

Spring, The. Thomas Carew. CaPo; ILP (1975 ed.); OBP; PPoe

Spring. Carole Gregory Clemmons. PoBA

Spring, The. Abraham Cowley. *Fr.* The Mistress. HAP; MetP

Spring. John Donne. *See* Love's Growth.

Spring. Frederick Feirstein. AMV–81

Spring. Michael Hogan. TAT

Spring. Gerard Manley Hopkins. FSFS; HAP; ILP (1975 ed.); NoAM; NOBE; OAEL–2; OBP; SoSe; VLP

Spring. Moishe Kulbak, *tr. fr. Yiddish by* Ruth Whitman. VWA

Spring. Linda McCarriston. AMV–81

Spring. Edna St. Vincent Millay. BoWoP; BuTh

Spring. Thomas Nashe. *Fr.* Summer's Last Will and Testament. NOBE; RAE
(Spring, the Sweet Spring.) HeIP; NIL

Spring. Lola Ridge. WPE

Spring. Shakespeare. *Fr.* Love's Labour's Lost, V, ii. FSFS; HAP; ILP (1975 ed.); IPWM; NIL; OAEL–1; SoSe; UnPo (1976 ed.)
(Cuckoo Sings, The.) PoPle
("When daisies pied and violets blue.") BiP; FF; HeIP; InPK; NOBE; OBP

Spring. Princess Shikishi, *tr. fr. Japanese by* Hiroaki Sato. PBWP

Spring. Earl of Surrey. *See* Soote Season, The.

Spring. James Thomson. *Fr.* The Seasons. LAuP

Spring ("Lenten is come with love to towne"). *Unknown. See* Lenten Ys Come with Love to Toune.

Spring. Ruth Whitman. IHMS

Spring again. Out of Mourning. Anthony S. Abbott. AMV–81

Spring, and a new pair of moccasins! Sunflower Moccasins. Phillip William George. NW; VoR

Spring and All ("By the road to the contagious hospital"). William Carlos Williams. CABA (1972 ed.); CMoP (1970 ed.); ExPo (1973 ed.); HAP; NoAM; NOBA; PiAm; PPoe; TAP; TCP; UsP
("By the road to the contagious hospital.") PSN
(Poem.) UnPo (1976 ed.)

Spring and Fall. Gerard Manley Hopkins. AnMo; BiP; CMoP (1970 ed.); EBEV; FF; HAP; HeIP; HoPM (1975 ed.); ILP (1975 ed.); InPK; InPS; IP; MAT; NIL; NOBE; PAIC; PoPle; PPoe; PPP; VLP; VoPo; WeW; WIF

Spring, and the Blind Children. Alfred Noyes. OxBTC

Spring at Fort Okanogan. Ramona Wilson. VoR

Spring at her height on a morn at prime. Ballade of Youth and Age. W. E. Henley. VLP

Spring at Nant Dywelan. Bobi Jones, *tr. fr. Welsh by* Joseph P. Clancy. OBW

Spring before a War ("Spring came early that year"). Dudley Randall. TC

Spring Cleaning. Sheryl Dare. PHC

Spring Cleaning. Phillip William George. VoR

Spring comes in with all her hues and smells, The. A Spring Morning. John Clare. GBL

Spring Coming. A. R. Ammons. InPK

Spring Day. John Ashbery. NOBA

Spring Day on Campus, A. Gilbert Schedler. AMV–80

Spring Death. Russell Marano. AMV–81

Spring Festival on the River, The. John Peck. AmPA

Spring Flowers. James Thomson. *Fr.* The Seasons: Spring. NOBE; PF

Spring flowers and autumn moon enter poems. For Hidden Mist Pavilion. Yü Hsüan-chi, *tr. by* Geoffrey Waters. BoWoP

Spring for All Seasons. James Welch. SA

Spring Garland. Shakespeare. *Fr.* The Winter's Tale, IV, iii. PF

Spring-gazing Song. Hsüeh T'ao, *tr. fr. Chinese by* Carolyn Kizer. BoWoP

Spring Goeth All in White. Robert Bridges. FSFS

Spring has come to the pass. Two Springs. Li Ch'ing-chao, *tr. by* Kenneth Rexroth. BoWoP

Spring Has Come to Town with Love. *Unknown. See* Lenten Ys Come with Love to Toune.

Spring has darkened with activity, The. Time and the Garden. Yvor Winters. NoAM; VGW

Spring hath her own bright days of calm and peace. Robert Bridges. The Growth of Love, XXIV. VLP

Spring Hawks. Jim Thomas. AMV–81

Spring-heeled Jack. James K. Baxter. ECBV

Spring I remember wild canaries. Saint-Henri Spring. Milton Acorn. NeAC

Spring Images. James Wright. TH

Spring in his death abounds among the lily islands. Elegy on My Father. Allen Curnow. ATNZ

Spring in Iowa comes in three days. March Rite: Getting It Up. A. G. Sobin. HeS

Spring in New Hampshire. Claude McKay. BPo

Spring in New York. *Unknown.* IP

Spring in the Desert. Sharlot Hall. WPW

Spring in the Desert. Arthur Truman Merrill. BPAW

Spring in These Hills. Archibald MacLeish. NCSH

Spring in Virginia. Ramona Wilson. VoR

Spring in Washington. James Den Boer. TAT

Spring is a shock to winter's placid senses. A Time: A Season. Patricia Ramsey. AATT

Spring is coming by a many signs, The. Young Lambs. John Clare. DuDr

Spring is coming, spring is coming. May Day. *Unknown.* CTV

Spring Is like a Perhaps Hand. E. E. Cummings. IPWM; PiAm; TAP; VGW

Spring is passing and. Empress Jito, *tr. fr. Japanese by* Cid Corman *and* Susumu Kamaike. PBWP

Spring is past and over these many days. September. Aldous Huxley. EBEV

Spring is short. Yosano Akiko, *tr. fr. Japanese by* Geoffrey Bownas *and* Anthony Thwaite. BoWoP; PBWP

Spring is showery, flowery, bowery. Mother Goose. CTV; ECBV

Spring is the period. Emily Dickinson. TAP

Spring Memorandum, A. Robert Duncan. PoA

Spring Morning, A. John Clare. GBL

Spring Morning. D. H. Lawrence. CMoP (1970 ed.)

Spring Morning—Santa Fe. Lynn Riggs. BPAW

Spring Morning: Waking. Emily Seelbinder. AMV–81

Spring Mountain Climb. Richard Eberhart. LiSp

Spring Night. Su Tung-p'o, *tr. fr. Chinese by* Burton Watson. Prf

Spring Night in Shokoku-ji, A. Gary Snyder. VGW

Spring night—one hour worth a thousand gold coins. Spring Night. Su Tung-p'o, *tr. by* Burton Watson. Prf

Spring 1942. Roy Fuller. OxBTC

Spring of the Thief. John Logan. BiP; CAPP; NNaP

Spring Offensive of the Snail, The. Marge Piercy. TAP; WBN

Spring over the City. Anne Hébert, *tr. fr. French by* Kathleen Weaver. PBWP

Spring Poem. Bin Ramke. AMV–81

Spring Pools. Robert Frost. NoAM; NOBA; PiAm; TCP

Spring Quiet. Christina Rossetti. FSFS; VoPo; WPE

Spring Rain. Issa, *tr. fr. Japanese by* Harold G. Henderson. NIL

Spring Rain. Ettore Rella. SPT

Spring rain. Haiku. Kaga no Chiyo, *tr. by* R. H. Blyth. PBWP

Spring Revue. Charlotte Mortimer. NowV

Spring Rites. Martin Robbins. AMV–81

Spring Sequence. Judith Minty. AMV–80

Spring Song. Robert Browning. *See* Year's at the Spring, The.

Spring Song. *Tr. fr. Chippewa Indian by* Frances Densmore. OBVE

Spring Stops Me Suddenly. Valentin Iremonger. PFIr

Spring Street in '58. Derek Walcott. NYP

Spring sun bends down between the branches, The. Stephen's Green Revisited. Richard Weber. PFIr

Spring, the sweet spring, is the year's pleasant king. Spring. Thomas Nashe. *Fr.* Summer's Last Will and Testament. HeIP; NIL; NOBE; RAE

Spring Thoughts. Huang-fu Jan, *tr. fr. Chinese by* Witter Bynner. OFD

Spring Thoughts Sent to Tzu-an. Yü Hsüan-chi, *tr. fr. Chinese by* Geoffrey Waters. BoWoP

Spring Thunder. Mark Van Doren. TH

Spring Vacation: The Smithsonian. Elisavietta Ritchie. PoUp

Spring was a month late, autumn a month early. Robin Fulton. *Fr.* The Voice of the Surbahar, IV. MIS

Spring Waters, *sels.* "Ping Hsin," *tr. fr. Chinese by* Kai-yu Hsu. "Falling star, The." PBWP "In shaping the snow into blossoms." BoWoP

Spring wind on the Bowery, A. Spring. Lola Ridge. WPE

Springboard, The. Louis MacNeice. PoA

Springer Mountain. James Dickey. CAPP

Springfield Mountain. *Unknown.* AIW; AmFP; BLSO, *with music;* FSW

Springs, The. Wendell Berry. GP

Springtime. Drummond Hadley. FoP

Springtime, The. Denise Levertov. ConAP

Springtime of the earth has come, The. Isaiah Shembe, *tr. fr. Zulu by* B. G. M. Sundkler. WTO

Springtime, Summer and Fall: days to behold a world. In Due Season. W. H. Auden. Prf

Sprinkle Me, Just. Patricia Goedicke. Psy

Spruce. Phillip William George. NW; VoR

Spruce Is Standing Lonely, A. Heine, *tr. fr. German by* Max Knight *and* Joseph Fabry. NAWM–2

Spruce Macaronis, and pretty to see. The Maryland Battalion. John Williamson Palmer. BTTM

Spur, The. W. B. Yeats. SoSe

Spurgeon would daub designs on flowerpots. John Beecher. *Fr.* To Live and Die in Dixie. GP

Sputin. Ishmael Reed. CPA

Squabbling Blues. *Unknown.* BluL

Squad of soldiers lies beside a river, A. An Old Photo in an Old Life. Daniel Hoffman. SoSe

Squalid, empty-headed hen, A. Hen under Bay-Tree. Ruth Pitter. OxBTC

Squall. John Moore. NCSH

Square at Dawn, The. James Tate. NoAM

Square-heeled boat sets off for the Statue, The. To the Statue. May Swenson. GOA; NYP

Square of the hypotenuse of the right triangle, The. Pythagorean Razzle-Dazzle. Sid Gary. QQQ

Square sheets—they saw the marble into. Island Quarry. Hart Crane. PPP; PSN

Square, squat room, A (a cellar on promotion). Waiting. W. E. Henley. In Hospital, II. ILP (1975 ed.); VLP

Squares. Michael Hamburger. FF

Squashes. Charles Edward Eaton. CSP

Squat Down, Josey. *Unknown.* AmFP

Squat, granular skinned. Toad. John Cotton. BoAnP

Squat in swamp shadows. Second Shaman Song. Gary Snyder. *Fr.* Myths and Texts: Burning. Epi; NOBA

Squatting under the weight. 527 Cathedral Parkway. Rika Lesser. NYP

Squeal. Louis Simpson. UnPo (1976 ed.)

Squeeze Play. Phyllis McGinley. *Fr.* Spectator's Guide to Contemporary Art. FaBoEE; OBSV

Squid-jiggin' Ground, The. *Unknown.* FSW

Squint. Edward Lowbury. PMW

Squinting against neon signs. Eclipse. Anita Endrezze Probst. CDW

Squire and Mildmaid; or, Blackberry Fold. *Unknown.* InPK

Squire he had whose name was Ralph, A. Independent Squire. Samuel Butler. *Fr.* Hudibras, I, 1. NOBE

Squirrel, The. ("Squirrel he's a funny little thing"). *Unknown.* FSW

Squirrel, The ("Whisky Frisky"). *Unknown.* CTV; PCOP

Squirrel in Sunshine. William Cowper. BoAnP

Squirrel near Library. Genevieve Taggard. WPE

Squirrel Stand. Jim Wayne Miller. CSP

Squirrels. Al Young. NVAP

Squirrels in Wind Pine. David Kherdian. FAF

Squyer of Lowe Degre, The, *sel. Unknown.* Diversions for an Unhappy Princess. OxBM

Sri Rama's Raiment. *Malay Oral Tradition, tr. by* R. O. Winstedt. WTO

Stabilities. Anne Stevenson. NCSH

Stability before Departure. Alan Dugan. NowV

Stable, The. Jill Hoffman. PH

Stable Cat, The. Leslie Norris. PChr

Stable-lamp is lighted, A. A Christmas Hymn. Richard Wilbur. MPo; OFD; PChr

Stack o' Dollars. *Unknown.* BluL

Stacked up the sky with strata of rose shale. Theoria in Early Morning. William R. Mitchell. AATT

Stacking Up. Rita Rosenfeld. AMV–81

Stacks, like blunt impassive temples, rise, The. Cambridgeshire. Frances Cornford. PES

Stadium, The. William Heyen. LiSp

Staff is now greased, The. The Hag. Robert Herrick. CaPo

Stag-Hunt. *Unknown.* OxBM

Stage is set in darkness, The. A table, small, oval. The Chandelier as Protagonist. William Virgil Davis. AMV–80

Stage Love. Swinburne. NIL

Stage-road runs on the sunrise plain, The. Laguna Perdida. Maynard Dixon. BPAW

Stagehand. Phyllis Speros. PoW

Stages on a Journey Westward. James Wright. CABA (1972 ed.)

Stagolee. *Unknown.* FSW; MAT

Staid schizophrenic named Struther, A. Limerick. *Unknown.* NIL

Stained Glass. Willis Barnstone. AMV–81

Stained Glass Man, The. Cynthia Macdonald. FiCP

Stained Glass Woman, The. Cynthia MacDonald. AAN

Stained with blood from a hare. Fleadh. Michael Longley. CIP

Staircase, The. Samuel Allen. PoBa

Staircase with a Hundred Steps, The. Benjamin Péret, *tr. fr. French by* David Gascoyne. EAS

Stairs mount to his eternity, The. The Staircase. Samuel Allen. PoBa

Stairway is not, The. The Jacob's Ladder. Denise Levertov. AnMo; CoPAm; IPWM; PPP

Stalemate at Attica. Horace Coleman. SES

Stalks of Wild Hay. H. L. Davis. PoA

Stall so tight he can't raise heels or knees, The. Bronco Busting, Event #1. May Swenson. LiSp; PH

Stallion, The. Tudur Aled, *tr. fr. Welsh by* Joseph P. Clancy. OBW

Stallion, The. Boynton Merrill, Jr. PH

Stallion, The. Alan Porter. PH

Stallion, The. Walt Whitman. *Fr.* Song of Myself, XXXII. PCOP; PH

Stalls were empty in the shed, The. Afterward. Mark Van Doren. TH

Stammerers, The. Margaret Kent. AMV-80

Stamp Blues. *Unknown.* BluL

Stampede, The. Arthur I. Caldwell. BPAW

Stampede, The. Freeman E. Miller. BPAW

Stand close around, ye Stygian set. Dirce. Walter Savage Landor. *Fr.* Pericles and Aspasia. EBEV; FaBoEE; GBL; HAP; ILP (1975 ed.); NOBE; OAEL-2; PoPle; VLP; WeW

Stand close to me. The Promise. Phyllis Hoge Thompson. PHC

Stand Navy down the field. Anchors Aweigh. Alfred H. Miles. BLSH

Stand on the highest pavement of the stair. La Figlia Che Piange. T. S. Eliot. AnMo; BuTh; FaBoTw (1975 ed.); GBL; HeIP; MAT; OxBTC; PiAm; PoA; PSN; UnPo (1976 ed.); VGW

Stand out, maids, and look on the land of Cynddylan. *Unknown, tr. fr. Welsh. Fr.* The Elegy on Cynddylan. OBW

Stand still, and I will read to thee. A Lecture upon the Shadow. John Donne. CABA (1972 ed.); Epi; InPK; UnPo (1976 ed.)

Stand still. The trees ahead and bushes beside you. Lost. David Wagoner. GP; PoA

Stand still, true poet that you are! Popularity. Robert Browning. OAEL-2

Stand still, you floods, do not deface. On Sight of a Gentlewoman's Face in the Water. Thomas Carew. CaPo

Stand! the ground's your own, my braves! Warren's Address at Bunker Hill. John Pierpont. BTTM; GOA

Stand this way—near the window. My Picture. Adelaide Anne Procter. PeD

Stand-to: Good Friday Morning. Siegfried Sassoon. FaBoTw (1975 ed.)

Stand Up! D. H. Lawrence. OxBTC

Stand up and rejoice! a great day is here! Hallelujah, I'm a-Travelin'. Harry Raymond. FSW

Stand up, but not for Jesus. Stand Up! D. H. Lawrence. OxBTC

Stand Up! Stand Up for Jesus, *with music.* George Duffield, Jr. AH; BLSH

"Stand up, stand up, thou May Janet." May Janet. Swinburne. VLP

Stand wel, moder, under roode. At the Crucifixion. *Unknown.* OxBM

Stand with thy nose against. Of One That Had A Great Nose. George Turberville. FaBoEE

Standards of the king go forth, The. Venantius Fortunatus, *tr. fr. Latin by* Helen Waddell. NAWM-1

Standing aloof in giant ignorance. To Homer. Keats. CABA (1972 ed.); EBEV; MBPR

Standing at the edge of the warped dock. The Crane's Ascent. Nick Bozanic. AMV-81

Standing at the station. Depot Blues. *Unknown.* BluL

Standing corn is green, the wild in flower, The. Nunc Viridant Segetes. Sedulius Scottus, *tr. by* Helen Waddell. BIrV; NAWM-1

Standing guests, a grotesque glade, The. The Party. Margaret Avison. PoA

Standing here in the pulpit primly. The Preacher Considers His Sermon. Elmer F. Suderman. AATT

Standing high on the shoulders of all things, all things. The Place at Albert Bay. Muriel Rukeyser. PoA

Standing in the 14th st snack place. Poem to My New Jacket. Fran Winant. MMD

Standing on a string of grey rocks. Andrew Talks to Gulls. George Roberts. BrS

Standing on my head makes. Ingestion. Barry McDonald. POL

Standing on 127th the. Langston. Mari Evans. CNA

Standing on the Corner. Philip Levine. NNaP

Standing there they began to grow skins. Pilgrims. Jean Valentine. TAP

Standing under the shower. A Dream of Washed Hair. Rhyll McMaster. CAAP

Standing up on lifted, folded rock. By Frazier Creek Falls. Gary Snyder. CNW; GOA

Standing uptight in books against the wall. Stained Glass. Willis Barnstone. AMV-81

Standing where the city and the forest. Leaves and Ashes. John Haines. MPA

Standing with raised arms before. Edwardian Hat. Betty Parvin. POL

Stane-chack! Malison of the Stone-chat. *Unknown.* GBP

Stanley Matthews. Alan Ross. LiSp; OxBTC

Stanza Put on Westminster Hall Gate, A. *Unknown.* APAS

Stanzas: "How smooth that lake expands its ample breast!" Anne Radcliffe. WPE

Stanzas: "I heard thy fate without a tear." Byron. PBMP

Stanzas: "I thought I woke: the midnight sun." Paul Goodman. PoA

Stanzas: "I'll not weep that thou art going to leave me." Emily Brontë. IPWM; WPE

Stanzas: "In a drear-nighted December." Keats. MBPR; NOBE

Stanzas: "Often rebuked, yet always back returning." Emily Brontë. OAEL-2; PBWP

Stanzas: "Princes and kings decay and die." Philip Freneau. GOA

Stanzas: "You say you love; but with a voice." Keats. MBPR

Stanzas—April, 1814. Shelley. MBPR

Stanzas, for Music ("There be none of Beauty's daughters"). Byron. ILP (1975 ed.); OAEL–2 (For Music.) PoPle

Stanzas for Music ("There's not a joy the world can give . . ."). Byron. HAP

Stanzas for My Daughter. Horace Gregory. RRA

Stanzas from the Grande Chartreuse. Matthew Arnold. OAEL-2; VLP

Stanzas in Meditation. Gertrude Stein. PoA "How I wish I were able to say what I think," *sel.* PBWP

Stanzas in Memory of the Author of "Obermann." Matthew Arnold. VLP

Stanzas of the Graves, The, *sel. Unknown, tr. fr. Welsh by* Gwyn Jones. "Graves the rain makes wet and sleek, The." OBW

Stanzas on the Emigration to America, and Peopling the Western Country. Philip Freneau. *See* On the Emigration to America.

Stanzas on Woman. Goldsmith. *See* Song: "When lovely woman stoops to conquer."

Stanzas to ——: "Well, some may hate, and some may scorn." Emily Brontë. WPE

Stanzas to a Lady, on Leaving England. Byron. MBPR

Stanzas to Augusta. Byron. ILP (1975 ed.)

Stanzas to the Po. Byron. OAEL-2

Stanzas to the Speaker Asleep. Winthrop Mackworth Praed. OBSV; VLP

Stanzas, Written in Dejection, near Naples. Shelley. CABA (1972 ed.); ILP (1975 ed.); MBPR; PBMP

Stanzas Written in My Pocket-Copy of Thomson's "Castle of Indolence." Wordsworth. MBPR

Stanzas Written on the Road between Florence and Pisa. Byron. ILP (1975 ed.)

Star, The. Jane Taylor. CTV; ECBV; OxBChV; SpRo

Star. Joanie Whitebird. GP

Star,/ If you are. A Christmas Tree. William Burford. SoSe

Star Blanket. Ray A. Young Bear. CDW

Star crashes in a small plaza and a bird loses its eyes, A. The Things I Say Are True. Blanca Varela, tr. by Donald Yates. BoWoP

Star Dust, with music. Mitchell Parish. BLSo

Star-face Lightfoot, sired by the Fox. Monologue of the Rating Morgan in Rutherford County. C. F. MacIntyre. PH

Star-gazing, U.S.A. Skaidrite Stelzer. TC

Star in the Hills, The. William Stafford. SFF

Star Journey. Naomi Long Madgett. BPo

Star light, star bright. First Star. Unknown. ECBV

Star-nosed Mole, The. Robert Wallace. BoAnP

Star of Empire poets say, The. Ho! Westward Ho! Ossian E. Dodge. BLSo

Star of the Evening. James M. Sayles. SpRo

Star of the Western Skies. Unknown. BPAW

Star Quality. Chris Wallace-Crabbe. CAAP

Star Quilt. Roberta Hill. CDW

Star Ride. H. H. Lewis. SPT

Star Song, The: A Carol to the King. Robert Herrick. SCP-1

Star-spangled Banner, The. Francis Scott Key. BLSH, with music; BLSo, with music; BTTM; CTV; FaPo; FaPoR; FSW; NIL; TAP

Star-Splitter, The. Robert Frost. PAIC

Star-Talk. Robert Graves. FSFS; OxBTC

Star that bids the shepherd fold, The. Comus Speaks. Milton. Fr. Comus. NOBE; PPoe

Stared, astonied all. È, the Feasting Florentines. Daniel Hoffman. VGW

Starer, The. Rhyll McMaster. CAAP

Stare's Nest by My Window, The. W. B. Yeats. Meditations in Time of Civil War, VI BIrV; NOBE

Starface, The. Madeline Gleason. MIT

Stargazer, The. Unknown. OxBChV

Stark Boughs on the Family Tree. Mary Oliver. SoS

Starlight Night, The. Gerard Manley Hopkins. ExPo (1973 ed.); ILP (1975 ed.); InPS; PoPle; PPP; VLP

Starling, The. John Heath-Stubbs. MPo

Starlings. Laura Jensen. AMV-81

Starlings. Norman MacCaig. BoAnP

Starlings and History. Charles Doyle. ATNZ

Starlings descend at nightfall. A Smoke of Birds. Malcolm Cowley. TSWA

Starred Coverlet, The. Robert Graves. BuTh; LoAs

Starring Role. Ron McCurdy. PHC

Starry Night, The. Anne Sexton. ExPo (1973 ed.); NoAM

Starry Sky. Charles Simic. POL

Stars, sel. Robert Hayden.
 Sojourner Truth. CNA

Stars. Alden Nowlan. POL

Stars/ stars/ and grass deepening. Songs of Waking. William Pitt Root. FoP

Stars and Flowers. Christina Rossetti. PCOP

Stars are circles of children. Everything Is Round. Gabriela Mistral, tr. by D. M. Pettinella. PBWP

Stars are dropping thick as stones into the twiggy. Stars over the Dordogne. Sylvia Plath. PoA

Stars are everywhere tonight, The. Daisies. Andrew Young. PF

Stars are forth, the moon above the tops, The. Byron. Fr. Manfred: A Dramatic Poem, III, iv. OAEL-2

Stars are growing, The. Star-gazing, U.S.A. Skaidrite Stelzer. TC

Stars are pinned against the sky, The. It Is the Stars That Govern Us. Michael Magee. PoA

Stars are thundering in the sky, The. Gond Oral Tradition, tr. by V. Elwin and S. Hivale. WTO

Stars at their zenith, more tranquil than you, The. The Stars on Shabbat. Avraham Shlonsky, tr. by Francis Landy. VWA

Stars Climb Girders of Light. Bert Meyers. MAT

Stars have given me a hard fate, The. Gaspara Stampa, tr. fr. Italian by Lynne Lawner. PBWP

Stars have not dealt me the worst they could do, The. A. E. Housman. EBEV

Stars, I have seen them fall. A. E. Housman. SoSe; VoPo

Stars in the sky are as big as coins. Turkish Love Songs, tr. by Reza Baraheni and Zahra-Soltan Shokoohtaezeh. BoWoP

Stars in your face, The. In Missing. Ray A. Young Bear. CDW

Stars, larger than sun, are pores vibrating. Late Advisory for Intergalactic Travellers Such as Poets. Will Inman. FoP

Stars of the summer night. Serenade. Longfellow. Fr. The Spanish Student. PAIC

Stars on Shabbat, The. Avraham Shlonsky, tr. fr. Hebrew by Francis Landy. VWA

Stars over snow. Night. Sara Teasdale. FSFS

Stars over the Dordogne. Sylvia Plath. PoA

Stars shine down, the. Rosh Pina. Dovid Knut, tr. by Daniel Weissbort. VWA

Stars Shine So Faithfully. Jane Flanders. AMV-80

Stars Stand Up in the Air, The. Unknown, tr. fr. Irish by Thomas MacDonagh. BIrV

Stars, the stars everlasting are fugitives also, The. Emerson. POL

Stars walk downhill. Concert. Robert Sward. VGW

Stars Wheel in Purple. Hilda Doolittle ("H. D."). NOBA; TAP

Starship. David McAleavey. AMV-81

Start and Goal. Christina Rossetti. VoPo

Start not—or deem my spirit fled. Lines Inscribed upon a Cup Formed from a Skull. Byron. InPK; MBPR

Start with a simple room. Plucking Out a Rhythm. Lawson Fusao Inada. AmPA

Starting again. A Dark Country. Derek Mahon. BIrV

Starting at Dawn. Sun Yün-feng, tr. fr. Chinese by Kenneth Rexroth and Ling Chung. PBWP

Starting Early from the Ch'u-ch'êng Inn. Po Chü-i, tr. fr. Chinese by Arthur Waley. OBVE

Starting from Central Station. David Campbell. MAuV

Starting from Paumanok, sel. Walt Whitman.
 "Dead poets, philosophs, priests." InPS

Starting from San Francisco. Lawrence Ferlinghetti. BiP; CAPP; PiAm

Starting Over. Shirley Kaufman. VWA

Startling to observe on the face of a Dorset yeoman. The "Dorset Nose." Clive Sansom. MPo

Starved old gelding, blind and lamed, A. An Irish Marriage Night. Brian Merriman, tr. by Frank O'Connor. Fr. The Midnight Court. BIrV

Starving of Bangladesh, The. Encounter with Hunger. Brian Vanderlip. AMV-81

Starving to Death on a Government Claim. Unknown. AmFP; BPAW; FSW; OBAL

Stasis in darkness. Ariel. Sylvia Plath. AnMo; CABA (1972 ed.); CMoP (1970 ed.); ExPo (1973 ed.); HeIP; InPK; NoAM; NOBA; PBWP; PiAm; Psy

State, a state, oh! dungeon state indeed, A. Edward Taylor. Preparatory Meditations: Second Series, LXXVII. EAP

State Fair Pigs. Roger Pfingston. TAT

State in Indian Language Was Called "Running Water," The. Besmilr Brigham. Psy

State Message: A Midwestern Small Town. Robert Flanagan. HeS

State of Arkansas, The. *Unknown. See* Sanford Barney.

State set its whole official will, The. To the Carp, and Those Who Hunt Her. James Hazard. AMV-80

State Street is lonely today. Aunt Jane Allen has driven her chariot to heaven. Aunt Jane Allen. Fenton Johnson. PoBA

State Street's cold mingling. Chicago/ 3 Hours. Victor Hernandez Cruz. ANTL

Stately homes of England, The. The Homes of England. Felicia Dorothea Hemans. FaPoR; SBG; WPE

Stately, kindly, lordly friend. To a Cat. Swinburne. PCat

Stately mirror's all-enamelled case, A. Joseph Beaumont. *Fr.* Psyche; or, Love's Mystery Displaying the Intercourse betwixt Christ and the Soul. SCP-2

*Stately Southerner,* The. *Unknown. See* Yankee Man-of-War, The.

Stately Structure of This Earth, The, *with music.* Martha Brewster. AH

Statement and Vision, Two Signs of History. James Whitehead. CoPAm

Statement on Our Higher Education. W. M. Ransom. CDW

States when they black out and lie there rolling, The. Falling. James Dickey. CAAP

Statesboro Blues. *Unknown.* BluL

Stateside. R. P. Kingston. NVAP

Statesman, The. Hilaire Belloc. NOBE

Statesman in Retirement, The. William Cowper. *Fr.* Retirement. PPoD

Statesman is an easy man, A. The Old Stone Cross. W. B. Yeats. PBMP

Statesman's Holiday, The. W. B. Yeats. CMoP (1970 ed.); OxBTC

Static. Barton Sutter. AMV-81

Static Autumn. Yvor Winters. PoA

Stationmaster is garrulous in, The. Daphne Stillorgan. Denis Devlin. CIP

Stations. Ted Hughes. NoAM

Statue, The. Kenneth Allott. EAS

Statue, The. Hilaire Belloc. NIL; POL

Statue, The. John Berryman. NYP

Statue, The. Roy Fuller. NOBE

Statue and the Bust, The. Robert Browning. TT

Statue of Liberty, The. Edward Field. TAT

Statue, tolerant through years of weather, The. The Statue. John Berryman. NYP

Statues, The. W. B. Yeats. NoAM; OAEL-2; WeW

Statues in the Public Gardens, The. Howard Nemerov. ConAP

Staunin noo aside his braw bress-haunled coffin. My Faither. Duncan Glen. MIS; MS

Stavro's dead. A truant vine. Epitaph. Lawrence Durrell. FaBoCo

Stay All Night, Stay a Little Longer. *Unknown.* AmFP

Stay beautiful/ but dont stay down underground too long. For Poets. Al Young. CNA; PoBA; RFM

Stay here, fond youth, and ask no more, be wise. Against Fruition. Sir John Suckling. CaPo

Stay near me—do not take thy flight! To a Butterfly. Wordsworth. MBPR

Stay near me. Speak my name. Oh, do not wander. Mid Century Love Letter. Phyllis McGinley. PPM

Stay, O sweet, and do not rise. Aubade. *Unknown.* BoLoP; NOBE

Stay, Phoebus, stay. Song. Edmund Waller. ILP (1975 ed.)

Stay silent/ keep away from sharks. Anticipation of Sharks. Diane Wakoski. MAT

Stay, Spring. Andrew Young. FaBoTw (1975 ed.)

Stay yet, pale flower, though coming storms will tear thee. On a Rose in December. Ebenezer Elliott. FaBoEE

Stay your rude steps, or e'er your feet invade. John Hookham Frere. *Fr.* The Loves of the Triangles. FaBoNo

Staying Ahead. Malcolm Glass. AMV-81

Staying Alive. David Wagoner. CABA (1972 ed.); CoPAm; IPWM; MiP; RFM; TSWA

Staying in the Mountains in Summer. Yü Hsüan-chi, *tr. fr. Chinese by* Geoffrey Waters. BoWoP

Staying Married. Dick Allen. FAF

Staying Up on Jack's Fork near Eminence, Missouri. Albert Salsich. AMV-80

Steadfast Cross. *Unknown.* OxBM

Steadfastness. Sir Thomas Wyatt. *See* Forget Not Yet.

Steady hand, a scalpel's fluent stroke, A. The Knife. Judith Smallshaw. PMW

Steady heart, which in its steadiness, The. Angina Pectoris. W. R. Moses. NCSH

Steady Rain. Lynn Merrill. AMV-80

Steakbones. Peter Wild. MPA

Steal Away to Jesus. *Unknown.* BLSH, *with music*; BPo; FSW

Stealin', Stealin'. *Unknown.* FSW

Stealing white from the withered moon. Halloween. Myra Cohn Livingston. OFD

Stealthily parting the small-hours silence. A Child Half-asleep. Tony Connor. BuTh; UsP

Steam, *sel.* Ebenezer Elliott. "No; there he moves, the thoughtful engineer," VII *and* VIII. VLP

Steam had mustered since we'd heard. Local Destruction. Perry Oldham. AAN

Steam in Sacrifice. Robert Herrick. CaPo

Steam Shovel. Charles Malam. DuDr

Steam Song. Gwendolyn Brooks. GP

Steam Threshing-Machine, The. Charles Tennyson Turner. VLP; VPC

Steamboat Bill. *Unknown.* FSW

Steamboats, Viaducts, and Railways. Wordsworth. VLP

Steamer on the Seedbed. Janet Kauffman. *Fr.* Tobacco. TC

Steamfitter had no notion of buying an opal, The. Opal. Josephine Miles. PAIC

Steddefast cross, inmong alle other. Steadfast Cross. *Unknown.* OxBM

Steed bit his master, The. On a Clergyman's Horse Biting Him. *Unknown.* FaBoCo; FaBoEE; SoSe

Steekit, consecrat, fou o fire but fuel. Douglas Young, *after the French of* Paul Valéry. *Fr.* The Kirkyaird by the Sea. OBVE

Steel? Derick Thomson, *tr. fr. Gaelic by author.* MS

Steel-bright blades drove into his neck and thin wrist. Death of the Astronomer. Philip Roberts. FPA

Steel Glass [*or* Steele Glas], The. George Gascoigne. AAS "And who desires, at large to know my name," *sel.* TVS

Steel Mill Reversal. Norman Macleod. SPT

Steel Mills. Rachel Albright. ANTL

Steel on Stane. Alexander Scott. MS

Steel print, A: two stags with antlers locked.  New Kelso.
Roderick Watson.  MIS

Steel snaps and stabs.  Strawberry-bright.  Jennifer Maiden.
CAAP

Steel worker on the girder, The.  The Building of the Skyscraper.
George Oppen.  GOA

Steely train in the stupid green, The.  Train: Abstraction.
Genevieve Taggard.  WPE

Steep.  Robert Morgan.  CSP

Steeple-Jack, The.  Marianne Moore.  Fr. Part of a Novel, Part of
a Poem, Part of a Play.  BoWoP; CMoP (1970 ed.); HAP;
ILP (1975 ed.); NoAM; NOBA; PBWP; SBG; WPE

Steer hither, steer, your winged pines.  The Sirens' Song.  William
Browne.  Fr. Inner Temple Masque.  GBL; NOBE; PoPle

Steer on, courageous sailor!  Columbus.  Schiller, tr. by Erika
Gathmann Koessler.  OFD

Steir bogle, squat bogle.  Spleen.  Sydney Goodsir Smith.  MS

Stella at Wood-Park.  Swift.  BIrV

Stella since thou so right a princess art.  Astrophel and Stella,
CVII.  Sir Philip Sidney.  OBP

Stella this day is thirty-four.  On Stella's Birthday.  Swift.
InPK; NIL; OAEL-1; SoSe

Stella's Birthday ("This day, whate'er the fates decree").  Swift.
OAEL-1

Stenka Razin.  Unknown, tr. fr. Russian.  FSW

Step aside, you ornery tenderfeet.  I'm an Old Cowhand.  Johnny
Mercer.  OBAL

Step Away from Them, A.  Frank O'Hara.  ConAP; NYP; VGW

Step in, young man, I know your face.  The Gaol Song.
Unknown.  GBP

Step is taken, and all the world's before me, A.  The River.
Robert Adamson.  GAS

Step It Up and Go.  Unknown.  FSW

Step on His Head.  James Laughlin.  VGW

Step on the path, A.  Ireland Lake.  Robert Hershon.  NeAC

Step Out onto the Planet.  Lew Welch.  VoA

Stepfather Blues.  Unknown.  BluL

"Stephen Smith, University of Iowa sophomore, burned what he
said was his draft card."  Of Late.  George Starbuck.
NowV; VGW

Stephen's Green Revisited.  Richard Weber.  PFIr

Stepmother, The.  Cathy Ackerson.  PoW

Stepping out of the bath.  Discovering Parts of a Body.  Rhyll
McMaster.  CAAP; GAS

Stepping Outside.  Tess Gallagher.  AmPA

Stepping-Stones, The.  Wordsworth.  PoIA

Stepping Westward.  Denise Levertov.  CAPP; NMM; Psy;
VGW; WBN

Stepping Westward.  Wordsworth.  ILP (1975 ed.); MBPR

Steps.  Roberta Hill.  VoR

Steps.  Frank O'Hara.  CAPP; ConAP

Steps are saucered in the trodden parts, The.  The Old Provincial
Council Buildings, Christchurch.  Allen Curnow.  ATNZ

Steps out/ from a lily.  Woman.  Carl Rakosi.  TAP

Stereo.  Don L. Lee.  AmNP (1974 ed.); POL

Stern daughter of the voice of God!  Ode to Duty.  Wordsworth.
BiP; MBPR; OAEL-2

Stern eagle of the far north-west.  The Song of the Reim-Kennar.
Sir Walter Scott.  OAEL-2

Stern mouth, lid eyes, green body.  Lizard.  Paul Mills.  MIS

Stethoscope, The.  Dannie Abse.  PMW

Stethoscope tells what everyone fears, The.  Academic.  Theodore
Roethke.  FaBoEE; OBAL

Stevedore.  Leslie M. Collins.  AmNP (1974 ed.)

Stew Meat Blues.  Unknown.  BluL

Stewball.  Unknown.  FSW

Stick of Incense, A.  W. B. Yeats.  AnMo

Stick the finger inside.  Black Mail.  Alice Walker.  AmPA

Stick was almost a staff, The.  Hebrew Letters in the Trees.  J.
Rutherford Willems.  VWA

Stick your patent name on a signboard.  The River.  Hart Crane.
Fr. The Bridge: Powhatan's Daughter.  CMoP (1970 ed.);
GOA; NoAM; NOBA; PiAm

Sticks and Stones.  Paulette Dusdall Zachariou.  NPW

Sticks and stones are hard on bones.  A Choice of Weapons.
Phyllis McGinley.  SS

Sticks-in-a-drowse droop over sugary loam.  Cuttings.  Theodore
Roethke.  AnMo; NoAM; NOBA; PiAm; TAP; UnPo (1976
ed.)

Stiff as the icicles in their beards, the Ice Kings.  The Labors of
Thor.  David Wagoner.  GP; MPA

Stiff in a white coat.  A Child's Visit to the Biology Lab.
Kathleen Spivack.  AmPA

Stiff Shirts.  Derek Bowman.  MIS

Stiff spokes of this wheel, The.  July in Washington.  Robert
Lowell.  Prf; WasP

Stiff standing on the bed.  Unknown.  GBL; POL

Stigmata.  Virginia R. Terris.  AAN

Still.  A. R. Ammons.  TT; UsP

Still.  Lucille Clifton.  CAAP; InPS

Still.  Aila Meriluoto, tr. fr. Finnish by Jaakko A. Ahokas.  PBWP

Still,/ I would leap too.  Small Frogs Killed on the Highway.
James Wright.  NNaP

Still/ our breath our sun.  Joanne Kyger.  MIT

Still a bit dazed.  Saul, Afterward, Riding East.  John Malcolm
Brinnin.  Prf

Still accelerating,/ my right foot useless, the needle passes.  In a
Dream, the Automobile.  Adrian Marcus.  SFF

Still, after all, the kelp remain.  At the Western Shore.  Sarah
Youngblood.  IHMS

Still Birth.  Catherine Rutan.  AMV-81

Still Branches.  Jack Simcock  BuTh

Still, Citizen Sparrow.  Richard Wilbur.  AnMo; CMoP (1970
ed.); CoPAm; HoPM (1975 ed.); ILP (1975 ed.); NoAM

Still craves the spirit: never Nature solves.  Frederick Goddard
Tuckerman.  Fr. Sonnets.  AmVN

Still creeping, still degenerous soul.  A Dithyramb.  John Hall.
SCP-2

Still day here, A.  Children Killed in War.  D. J. Enright.  HeHu

"Still Do I Keep My Look, My Identity . . ."  Gwendolyn Brooks.
PoA

Still Falls the Rain.  Edith Sitwell.  BoReV; BoWoP; NoAM;
NOBE; OBP

Still Growing.  Unknown.  FaBoBa; InPK, with music

Still Gyte, Man?  George Campbell Hay.  MS

Still Here.  Langston Hughes.  BPo; BuTh

Still I'm for upper.  Satisfaction.  A. R. Ammons.  GP

Still in October, the woodcock.  On the Mountain.  Ruth Stone.
BoWoP

Still, it is dear defiance now to carry.  Flags.  Gwendolyn Brooks.
AmNP (1974 ed.)

"Still, let my tyrants know, I am not doomed to wear."  The
Prisoner.  Emily Brontë.  BoReV; NOBE

Still Life.  Regina M. Austin.  AMV-80

Still-Life.  Elizabeth Daryush.  WPE

Still Life.  Claudia Dobkins.  NPW

Still Life.  Rosemary Dobson.  MAuV

Still Life.  Henry Kanabus.  FiCh

Still Life.  Ralph Mecklenburger.  SFF

Still Life.  Vivian Smith.  AMV-80; AMV-81

Still Life.  Reed Whittemore.  ConAP; PoUp

Still life and movement, thunder and repose. After the Riot. William Pillin. SPT

Still Life: Lady with Birds. Quandra Prettyman. PoBA

Still must I hear?—shall hoarse Fitzgerald bawl. English Bards, and Scotch Reviewers. Byron. MBPR

Still night. The old clock ticks. Last Night in Calcutta. Allen Ginsberg. NoAM

Still, passed through the spokes of an old wheel. Reincarnation (I). James Dickey. CoPAm; HoPM (1975 ed.)

Still playing. In the Cabinet. Shlomo Vinner, tr. by Laya Firestone and Howard Schwartz. VWA

Still pressing through these weeping solitudes. Frederick Goddard Tuckerman. Fr. Sonnets. NOBA

Still round the world triumphant discord flies. A Picture of the Times. Philip Freneau. EAP; PiAm

Still scene scintillates, The. Glass World. Dorothy Donnelly. NCSH

Still silver in their polished myth. Crack of Doom. Albert Howard Carter. AATT

Still sits the school-house by the road. In School Days. Whittier. OxBChV

Still, still my eye will gaze long fixed on thee. The Columbine. Jones Very. NOBA; PiAm

Still, Still with Thee, with music. Harriet Beecher Stowe. AH

Still the mighty mountains stand. Epilogue to Alun Mabon. John Ceiriog Hughes, tr. by H. Idris Bell. OBW

Still the Mind Smiles. Robinson Jeffers. CMoP (1970 ed.)

Still to be neat, still to be dressed [or drest]. Simplex Munditiis [or Clerimont's Song]. Ben Jonson. Fr. Epicoene; or, The Silent Woman, I, i. CABA (1972 ed.); FF; GBL; HAP; HeIP; HoPM (1975 ed.); ILP (1975 ed.); InPs; IP; NIL; NOBE; OAEL-1; OBP; PBMP; PoPle; PPP

Still Voice of Harlem, The. Conrad Kent Rivers. CNA; PoBA

Still Wrestling. Phil Boiarski. AMV-81

Still young, our faces may deceive. Four Poems, 3. Joseph Freeman. SPT

Stillborn Silence. Richard Flecknoe. SCP-2

Stilled is the quarrel over his bones. At Dante's Grave. Ezra Zussman, tr. by D. Shnayorson. VWA

Stillness, The/ of the wood. The Figures. Robert Creeley. UnPo (1976 ed.)

Stillness and moonlight, with. Loneliness. Hayden Carruth. FiCP

Stillness in the grove, not a rustling sound. Moscow Nights. M. Matusovskii and V. Solovyov-Sedoi, tr. fr. Russian. FSW

Stillness of the rose, The. The Rose. William Carlos Williams. NOBA

Stingier your suppers, The. Karl Marx. Al Lee. AmPA

Stinging Nettle. Gwen Head. GP

Stingo! to thy bar-room skip. Anacreontic to Flip. Royall Tyler. OBAL

Stink of Burning Egg, The. Virginia R. Terris. AAN

Stir not the sand too much, for there lies Stuyvesant. Epitaph for Peter Stuyvesant. Henricus Selyns. NYP

Stir the Wallaby Stew. Unknown. FaBoBa

Stirling's Hotel. Unknown. AmFP

Stitches. Hazel Hall. WPW

Stockdoves, The. Andrew Young. BoAnP

Stocking and Shirt. James Reeves. ECBV

Stocking Feet Blues. Unknown. BluL

Stockton State Mental Hospital 1962. Alta. MMD.

Stocky, cocky little man, A. Instamatic. Edwin Morgan. FF

Stocky woman at the door, The. The Last Day and the First. Theodore Weiss. LoAs; VGW

Stockyard, The. J. C. Squire. OxBTC

Stoic, The. Gwendolen Haste. WPW

Stoic, The: For Laura von Courten. Edgar Bowers. PiAm

Stolen base, metaphor. Grand Slammer. R. R. Knudson. SPo

Stolen Child, The. W. B. Yeats. CMoP (1970 ed.); TT

Stolen Peonies, The. William Carlos Williams. TT

Stomach. Kathleen Norris. OBAL

Stomach in my throat. Coasting toward Midnight at the Southeastern Fair. David Bottoms. AMV-81

Stomach of goat, crushed. Salami. Philip Levine. NNaP; NOBA; TAP

Stond who so list upon the slipper toppe. Seneca, tr. by Sir Thomas Wyatt. Fr. Thyestes. AAS; OBVE

Stone, The. Paul Blackburn. NYP

Stone. Juliet Chayat. AMV-80

Stone. Charles Simic. NU

Stone, The. Thomas Vaughan. OBW

Stone/ cold/ daylight. Poem for Etheridge. Sonia Sanchez. BPo

Stone, The/ would like to be. Evolution. May Swenson. TCP

Stone Age. Floyd C. Stuart. FAF

Stone and the Blade of Grass in the Warsaw Ghetto, The. David Scheinert, tr. fr. French by Edouard Roditi. VWA

Stone and the Obliging Pond. Felix Pollak. POL

Stone-cutters fighting time with marble, you foredefeated. To the Stone-Cutters. Robinson Jeffers. ILP (1975 ed.); LFH; MPA; NIL; NOBA; PiAm

Stone found me in bright sunlight, The. The Stone. Paul Blackburn. NYP

Stone from which I carved you. A Speck of Sand. Paul Celan, tr. by Joachim Neugroschel. VWA

Stone Giant. Joseph Bruchac. CDW

Stone goes straight, The. Washington Monument by Night. Carl Sandburg. CMoP (1970 ed.); OFD

Stone Gullets. May Swenson. InPK

Stone Harp, The. John Haines. CNW

Stone Mountain Face. Peter Blue Cloud. NW

Stone Poems, The. Ken Smith. TwMBP

Stone Troll, The. J. R. R. Tolkien. SO

Stone Words for Robert Lowell. Richard Eberhart. AMV-80

Stone zombies. Junkies Is. Horace Coleman. SES

Stones, The. Wendell Berry. GP

Stones. Michael C. Blumenthal. PoUp

Stones. William Jeffrey. MS

Stones, The. Ralph J. Mills, Jr. BrS

Stones, The. Sylvia Plath. CAPP; SBG

Stones (a miracle to mortal view), The. Ovid, tr. by Dryden. Fr. Metamorphoses, I. OBVE

Stones: Avesbury. Daisy Aldan. PoA

Stones in Jordan's stream, The. Stones. William Jeffrey. MS

Stones in My Passway. Unknown. BluL

Stones of the desert town, The. The Lodging. George Mackay Brown. MS

Stones rattle on the hillside, The. My Cow. Howard McCord. GP

Stones surpass the silence. Another Stone Poem. Philip Dacey. AMV-81

Stonetalk. Jacques Hamelin, tr. fr. French by Ria Leigh-Louhuizen. AMV-80

Stonewall Jackson's Way. John Williamson Palmer. BTTM

Stoneyard, The. Peter Trias. AAN

Stony Brook Tavern. J. D. Reed. NeAC

Stony Grey Soil. Patrick Kavanagh. CIP

Stony Lonesome. Langston Hughes. NOBA; PiAm

Stood straight/ holding the choker high. Gary Snyder. Myths and Texts: Logging, III. NOBA

Stood-up. Bruce Byfield. AMV-80

Stoop on the log-house is brown with sweet rain-rot, The. Joan Finnigan. *Fr.* May Day Rounds: Renfrew County. IPWM; WPE

Stop! Lee Blair. TDH

Stop, Christian passer-by!—Stop, child of God. Epitaph. Samuel Taylor Coleridge. MBPR; OAEL-2

Stop! Don't touch me. *Unknown, tr. fr. Spanish by* Willis Barnstone. BoWoP

Stop! for thy tread is on an empire's dust! The Field of Waterloo. Byron. *Fr.* Childe Harold's Pilgrimage. BTTM; ILP (1975 ed.); InPS

Stop: if you're racing at night. Happy at 40. Peter Meinke. GP

Stop Kicking My Dog Around. *Unknown.* GDP

Stop, let me have the truth of that! Dîs Aliter Visum; or, Le Byron de Nos Jours. Robert Browning. VLP

Stop look listen. Crossing. Philip Booth. GOA

Stop playing, poet! May a brother speak? "Transcendentalism: A Poem in Twelve Books." Robert Browning. VLP

Stop playing with your melancholy. Goethe, *tr. by* Walter Kaufmann. *Fr.* Faust. DL

Stop, stop and listen for the bough top. The Blackbird of Derrycairn. *Unknown, tr. by* Austin Clarke. BIrV

Stop the Alabama bus I don't wanna ride. Alabama Bus. *Unknown.* BluL

Stop there, old one, within your haven. Lament for Apirana Ngata. Arnold Reedy, *tr. by* Barry Mitcalfe. WTO

Stoplight. William Pitt Root. SFF

Stopped in Memphis. Steven Bauer. AMV-80

Stopping by Woods on a Snowy Evening. Robert Frost. BiP, CABA (1972 ed.); CMoP (1970 ed.); ECBV; FF; FSFS; HAP; HeIP; HoPM (1975 ed.); ILP (1975 ed.); InPK; InPS; IPWM; LFH; NIL; NoAM; NOBA; PiAm; PoIA; PPM; PPoD; PSN; SoSe; STS; TAP; TT; UnPo (1976 ed.)

Stopping near Highway 80. David Ray. HeS; TAT

Stops. Lucille Clifton. CAAP

Store in Havana, The. José Kozer, *tr. fr. Spanish by* David Unger. VWA

Stories. Jon Anderson. HeS

Stories from Kansas. William Stafford. RFM

Stories in Kinsman's Park. Margaret Atwood. Psy

Stories of Snow. P. K. Page. PoA

Stories of the Street. Leonard Cohen. GrRo

Storks like elbows had a fit of falling, The. There's No Place to Sleep in This Bed, Tanguy. Charles Henri Ford. EAS

Storm, The. Walter de la Mare. EcS

Storm, The, *sel.* John Donne.
"But when I waked, I saw that I saw not." PoPle (Storm at Sea, A.) NOBE

Storm, The. John Hay. AMV-81

Storm. Agnes Nemes Nagy, *tr. fr. Hungarian by* Laura Schiff. PBWP

Storm, The. Theodore Roethke. NCSH

Storm. Judith Wright. WPE

Storm and Quiet. Richard Eberhart. AMV-81

Storm at Sea, A. John Donne. *Fr.* The Storm. NOBE ("But when I waked, I saw that I saw not.") PoPle

Storm at Sea. *Malay Oral Tradition, tr. by* R. O. Winstedt. WTO

Storm broke, and it rained, The. Frogs. Louis Simpson. BoAnP; InPS; TH

Storm-Cock's Song, The. "Hugh MacDiarmid." OxBTC

Storm Cone, The. Kipling. OxBTC

Storm-dances of gulls, the barking game of seals, The. Divinely Superfluous Beauty. Robinson Jeffers. HeIP; PiAm

Storm End. Jonathan Griffin. TSWA

Storm Fear. Robert Frost. CMoP (1970 ed.); IPWM; PPM; UsP

Storm has come again today, The. Beyond the Storm. James Bertolino. HeS

Storm House, The. Elizabeth Jennings. WPE

Storm in Summer, A. Wilfrid Scawen Blunt. FaBoTw (1975 ed.)

Storm in the Desert. Radcliffe Squires. MPA

Storm is over, lady, The. Fiddler's Song. George Mackay Brown. MS; SLP

Storm lifts from Wales. The Hanged Man. Kenneth Rexroth. MPA

Storm moves, A. Flood Disaster in Gallup, New Mexico. Linda Parker. TC

Storm not, brave friend, that thou hadst never yet. To Scilla. Sir Charles Sedley. FaBoEE

Storm on the Island. Seamus Heaney. NCSH

Storm that needed a mountain, A. Found in a Storm. William Stafford. RFM

Storm Tide on Mejit. *Unknown, tr. fr. Micronesian by* Augustin Krämer *and* Willard Trask. RFM

Storm Warning. Alice Bardsley. AMV-80

Storm Warnings. Adrienne Rich. NIL

Storm was coming, that was why it was dark, A. Sudden Things. Donald Hall. EAS

Storm-Wind, The. William Barnes. NOBE

Storm Windows. Howard Nemerov. ConAP

Storm winds carry snow. Deer Song. Leslie Silko. VoR

Stormalong. *Unknown.* AIW

Storms Are on the Ocean, The. *Unknown.* FSW

Storm's End. Leonora Speyer. TH

Storms lend you wings, destroyer of the lands. Inanna and Enlil. Enheduanna, *tr. fr. Sumerian.* BoWoP

Stormy Day, A. *Unknown, tr. fr. Hawaiian.* WTO

Stormy Hebrides, The. William Collins. *Fr.* An Ode on the Popular Superstitions. NOBE

Stormy Night in Autumn. Chu Shu-chen, *tr. fr. Chinese by* Kenneth Rexroth. BoWoP

Stormy Petrel, The. "Barry Cornwall." EcS

Stormy Scenes of Winter, The, 2 *versions. Unknown.* AmFP

Stormy the night and the waves roll high. Asleep in the Deep. Arthur J. Lamb. FSN

Story. Dennis Saleh. NeAC

Story, The. Charles Simic. NNaP

Story, A. William Stafford. NNaP; PoTa; RFM

Story, A. Eric Torgersen. TC

Story, A, a story! Rowing. Anne Sexton. BoWoP

Story, a story, a story anon, A. The Bishop of Canterbury. *Unknown.* AmFP

Story about Chicken Soup, A. Louis Simpson. NNaP; NoAM; TAP

Story about Indians, A. The Climate of Paradise. Louis Simpson. NOBA

Story for a Child, A. Cynthia MacDonald. AAN

Story from Another World. Paul Petrie. AMV-81

Story haunts this tribe that cannot wipe from its eyes, The. Isaac. Stanley Burnshaw. VWA

Story I shall tell today, The. The Nightingale. Marie de France, *tr. by* Patricia Terry. BoWoP

Story of a Hotel Room. Rosemary Tonks. OxBTC

Story of a Well-made Shield, The. N. Scott Momaday. CDW

Story of Abraham and Hagar, The. Edna Aphek, *tr. fr. Hebrew by* Yishai Tobin. VWA

Story of Augustus Who Would Not Have Any Soup, The. Heinrich Hoffmann, *tr. fr. German.* OxBChV; SpRo

Story of Fidgety Philip, The. Heinrich Hoffmann, *tr. fr. German.* OxBChV

Story of Flying Robert, The.   Heinrich Hoffmann, *tr. fr. German.* SpRo

Story of Good, The.   Phyllis Janik.   IHMS

Story of Isaac.   Leonard Cohen.   GrRo; VWA; WIF

Story of Johnny Head-in-Air, The.   Heinrich Hoffmann, *tr. fr. German.*   OxBChV

Story of Little Suck-a-Thumb, The.   Heinrich Hoffmann, *tr. fr. German.*   SpRo

Story of My Life, The.   Carroll Arnett.   VoR

Story of My Life, The.   Hollis Summers.   TPo

Story of Prince Agib, The.   W. S. Gilbert.   FaBoCo

Story of Samuel Jackson, The.   Charles Godfrey Leland.   PoTa

Story of the Gadsbys, The, *sel.* Kipling.
    Winners, The.   FaPoR

Story of the Pot and the Kettle, The.   Charles Montagu.   APAS

Story of the Rose, The, *with music.* "Alice."   FSN

Story of the Zeros, The.   Victor Hernandez Cruz.   PoBA

Story-Teller, The.   Mark Van Doren.   CTBA; ECBV; TH

Story was always the same, The.   The Migrations of People.
    Dorothy Leiser.   AMV-80

Story Which Should Have Happened.   Peter Porter.   CAAP

Stout poet tiptoes, The.   A Poet's Household.   Carolyn Kizer.
    POL

Stove.   Ken Belford.   NeAC

Stowaway in a fold.   The Witnesses.   X. J. Kennedy.   PChr

Stowed away in a Montreal lumber room.   O God! O Montreal!
    [*or* A Psalm of Montreal].   Samuel Butler.   FaBoCo; OBSV

Strahan, Tonson, Lintot of the times.   To Mr. Murray.   Byron.
    FaBoCo; PAIC

Straight-backed as a Windsor chair.   Schoolmistress.   Clive
    Sansom.   LP; MPo

Straight-jacketing sprang to every lock.   Austin Clarke.   *Fr.*
    Mnemosyne Lay in Dust.   CMoP (1970 ed.)

Straight, the swift, the debonair, The.   Magnets.   Countee Cullen.
    PBMP

Straightening the Warp.   Douglas Blazek.   EC

Straining against a winter's day.   Uprooted.   Maurice Lindsay.
    MS

Straining at the padlock.   Jack Kerouac.   *Fr.* Some Western
    Haikus.   VoA

Strains of Sight.   Robert Duncan.   CMoP (1970 ed.); ExPo (1973
    ed.)

Straits, The.   Valerie Gillies.   SLP

Strampin' the bent, like the Angel o' Daith.   Molecatcher.   Albert
    D. Mackie.   MS

Strand on the Green.   *Unknown.*   GBP

Strange,/ strange.   Alone in the Grange.   Gregory Harrison.
    FPB

Strange,/ That in this nigger place.   Esthete in Harlem.
    Langston Hughes.   BPo; SS

Strange—as I sat brooding here.   Lucy.   Walter de la Mare.
    CMoP (1970 ed.)

Strange atoms unto ourselves.   Lovelight.   Georgia Douglas
    Johnson.   AmNP (1974 ed.)

Strange beauty, eight-limbed and eight-handed.   Octopus.   A. C.
    Hilton.   FaBoCo

Strange bed, whose recurrent dream we are, The.   Hotel de
    l'Univers et Portugal.   James Merrill.   PoA

Strange bird.   Youth.   James Wright.   ILP (1975 ed.)

Strange but true is the story.   The Sea-Turtle and the Shark.
    Melvin B. Tolson.   *Fr.* Harlem Gallery.   IP; PoBA; SoSe
    (1977 ed.)

Strange creeper.   The Creeper.   Tom Schmidt.   NeAC

Strange, dear, but true, dear.   So in Love.   Cole Porter.   BLSo

Strange Encounter.   Anselm Hollo.   AcAn

Strange Fits of Passion Have I Known.   Wordsworth.   *Fr.* Lucy.
    AnMo; EBEV; Epi; GBL; ILP (1975 ed.); LoAs; MBPR;
    NOBE; OAEL-2; PPP; SoSe

Strange Fruit.   Lewis Allan.   PoIA

Strange Funeral in Braddock, A.   Michael Gold.   SPT

Strange Guest, The.   Itzik Manger, *tr. fr. Yiddish by* Stephen
    Garrin.   VWA

Strange Hells.   Ivor Gurney.   OxBTC

Strange how our failures shine in memory.   The Old Upright I
    Did Not Learn to Play.   Nicholas Flocos.   SA

Strange Kind (II).   J. D. Reed.   Moon

Strange Legacies.   Sterling A. Brown.   CNA; PoBA

Strange Meeting.   Wilfred Owen.   CMoP (1970 ed.); Expo (1973
    ed.); HeIP; HoPM (1975 ed.); ILP (1975 ed.); NoAM;
    NOBE; OAEL-2; OBP

Strange Meetings, *sel.* Harold Monro.
    Birth.   PoA

Strange Monsters.   Rowland Watkyns.   FaBoEE

Strange now to think of you, gone without corsets & eyes.
    Kaddish.   Allen Ginsberg.   ExPo (1973 ed.); NOBA; VWA

Strange tears without.   Genealogy of a Generation.   Tina Foriyes.
    PoW

Strange that I did not know him then.   An Old Story.   E. A.
    Robinson.   TH

Strange, that such horror and such grace.   To a Fair Lady Playing
    with a Snake.   Edmund Waller.   EBEV; HoPM (1975 ed.)

Strange that we should sit here like this.   Baseball Pitcher.
    Mabel M. Kuykendall.   LiSp

Strange the formation of the eely race.   William Diaper, *after the
    Greek of* Oppian.   *Fr.* Halieutica.   OBVE

Strange to step straight into the beautiful dawn.   Miraculous
    Dawn.   R. Williams Parry, *tr. by* Joseph P. Clancy.   OBW

Strange Visitor, The.   *Unknown.*   GBP

Strangely/ my mother's sad eyes.   X-Ray.   David Ray.   IPWM

Strangely assorted, the shape of song and the bloody man.   The
    Military Harpist.   Ruth Pitter.   FaBoTw (1975 ed.)

Stranger, The.   Walter de la Mare.   OxBTC

Stranger, The.   William Everson.   CoPAm; FF

Stranger, The.   Jean Garrigue.   NOBA

Stranger, The.   Juan Gelman, *tr. fr. Spanish by* Yishai Tobin.
    VWA

Stranger, A.   Lionel Johnson.   VLP

Stranger, The.   Adrienne Rich.   NNaP

Stranger! Approach this spot with gravity!   A Dentist.   *Unknown.*
    FaBoCo; FaBoEE

Stranger came to the door at eve, A.   Love and a Question.
    Robert Frost.   LoAs

Stranger has come, A.   Love in the Asylum.   Dylan Thomas.
    LoAs

Stranger, if thou hast learned a truth which needs.   Inscription for
    the Entrance to a Wood.   Bryant.   AmVN; BiP; EAP; ILP
    (1975 ed.); PiAm; PPoD; TAP

Stranger, if you passing meet me and desire to speak to me.   To
    You.   Walt Whitman.   BiP

Stranger in the Pumpkin, The.   John Ciardi.   IWK

Stranger in Your Town, A.   Michael McMahon.   FAF

Stranger lighted from his steed, The.   Song.   Keats.   SS

Stranger Not Ourselves, The.   William Stafford.   NNaP

Stranger, pause and drop a tear.   Sacred to the Memory of Maria
    (To Say Nothing of Jane and Martha) Sparks.   Max Adeler.
    FaBoCo

Stranger! Tell the people of Spoon River two things.   Unknown
    Soldiers.   Edgar Lee Masters.   *Fr.* The New Spoon River.
    NoAM; TAP

Stranger than the Worst.   Babette Deutsch.   WPE

Stranger, the bark you see before you says.   The Yacht.   Catullus,
    *tr. by* John Hookham Frere.   OBVE

Stranger walks into the dark room, The. Seance. Edouard Roditi. EAS

Stranger, when you come to/ Lakedaimon. Simonides, *tr. fr. Greek by* Kenneth Rexroth. OBVE

Stranger, wond'ring, stalks, and stares upon, The. Rome, Conqueror, Conquered. Joshua Sylvester. FaBoEE

Stranger, you who hide my love. Song. Stephen Spender. FaBoTw (1975 ed.)

Strangers, The. Robert Morgan. HeHu

Strangers. William Stafford. NNaP

"Strangers are we and pilgrims here!" At a Friends' Meeting. Mary Elizabeth Coleridge. WPE

Strangers ask. The Tower. Philip Booth. PAIC

Strangers' eyes don't see. Memorial Poem. Jacob Glatstein, *tr. by* Ruth Whitman. VWA

Strangers have vanished, The. The Strangers. Robert Morgan. HeHu

Strangers on a train. Travels with the Band-Aid Army. Lance Henson. VoR

Strangest of adventures, The. Lord Arnaldos. James Elroy Flecker. PoTa

Strangled child, forty years old, old, The. Madonna and Daughter. Carol Bergé. MMD

Strapped down. Notes from the Delivery Room. Linda Pastan. RiTi

Strapped to my seat, I turn. Above It All. Philip Levine. NOBA

Strapped to the roof rack of her. The Song of the Mean Mary Jean Machine. James Baker Hall. FiCP; TAT

Strategies. Welton Smith. PoBA

Straunge Passion of a Lover, A. George Gascoigne. AAS

Straus Park. Gerald Stern. NYP

Straw, The. Robert Graves. OxBTC

Straw bonnet, The. Southern Season. Alice Moser Claudel. TAT

Strawberries. Dorothy Hughes. AMV-81

Strawberries. Edwin Morgan. BoLoP

Strawberries in Mexico. Ron Padgett. EAS

Strawberries that in gardens grow. Wild Strawberries. Robert Graves. FSFS

Strawberry-bright. Jennifer Maiden. CAAP

Strawberry Fields Forever. John Lennon *and* Paul McCartney. GrRo

Strawberry Roan, The. Curley W. Fletcher. BPAW; FSW

Strawberry Shrub, The. Edna St. Vincent Millay. CMoP (1970 ed.)

Straws like tame lightnings lie about the grass. Summer Farm. Norman MacCaig. OxBTC

Stray Animals. James Tate. NoAM

Stray Dog, near Ecully. Margaret Avison. PoA

Stray Things. Dan Johnson. PPoD

Strayed Reveller, The. Matthew Arnold. OAEL-2; VLP

Straying Student, The. Austin Clarke. BIrV; CIP

Streak of car paint, A. Uptown. Paul Zweig. NYP

Stream flowing steadily over a stone does not wet its core, A. An Elder's Reproof to His Wife. Abdillaahi Muuse, *tr. by* B. W. Andrezejewski *and* I. M. Lewis. WTO

Stream has taken its shred of sound, The. Winter Night, Cold Spell. Howard Nelson. AMV-81

Streams of Bunclody, The. *Unknown.* BIrV

Streams of Lovely Nancy, The. *Unknown.* FaBoBa

Street. George Oppen. GP

Street, The. Octavio Paz, *tr. fr. Spanish by* Willis Knapp Jones. FF

Street, The. Ken Smith. TwMBP

Street Car Blues. *Unknown.* BluL

Streetcorner. Bill Knott. PCho

Street Corner College. Kenneth Patchen. SPT

Street Demonstration. Margaret Walker. BPo; CNA

Street Fight. Harold Monro. FaBoTw (1975 ed.)

Street Fire. Daniel Halpern. AmPA; NYP

Street Iconoclasts. Pancho Aguila. NW

Street in Bronzeville, A: Southeast Corner. Gwendolyn Brooks. VGW

Street in Kaufman-ville, A. James Cunningham. JB

Street is very long and filled with silence, The. The Street. Octavio Paz, *tr. by* Willis Knapp Jones. FF

Street Scene. Peter Suffolk. PoTa

Street Scenes from All Over. Elisavietta Ritchie. AATT

Street Song. Thom Gunn. HeIP

Street Song. Edith Sitwell. CMoP (1970 ed.)

Street Sounds to the Soldiers' Tread, The. A. E. Housman. PPP

Street Where I Live, The. Virginia Floyd. AATT

Street Window. Carl Sandburg. SFF

Streetlights blink Dont Walk Walk, The. Downtown Roanoke. R. H. W. Dillard. PPoD

Streets. D. J. Enright. HeHu

Streets. Amy Lowell. RiTi; SBG

Streets also have eyes, The. The Messiah. Moshe Yungman, *tr. by* David G. Roskies *and* Hillel Schwartz. VWA

Streets are a bit confused, The. Drunken Streets. Malka Locker, *tr. by* Jeremy Garber. VWA

Streets are full of the scent of us—odors of onions drifting from. We of the Streets. Richard Wright. SPT

Streets of Air, The. Malcolm Cowley. *Fr.* Blue Juniata. PoA

Streets of Cairo; or, The Poor Little Country Maid, *with music.* James Thornton. FSN

Streets of Glory. *Unknown.* FSW

Streets of Laredo, The. Louis MacNeice. AIW; MPo; PeBB

Streets of Laredo, The. *Unknown. See* Cowboy's Lament.

Streets of New York, The, *with music.* Henry Blossom. FSN

Streets of the roaring town. On a Soldier Fallen in the Philippines. William Vaughn Moody. AmVN; LFH; NOBA

Streets outside have ice on them, The. My Grandfather Always Promised Us. Liam Rector. AMV-80

Streetsinger is sick, The. Three. Gregory Corso. SA

Strength. Richard Wright. SPT

Strength and dignity are her clothing. Bible, *O.T.* Proverbs, XXXI: 25-29. CTV

"Strength of That Food, The." Jane Marie Luecke. AATT

Strength through Joy. Kenneth Rexroth. VGW

Strengthened to live, strengthened to die for. In Distrust of Merits. Marianne Moore. NIL; VoPo

Stretch forth! stretch forth! from the south to the north! The Anglo-Saxon Race: A Rhyme for Englishmen. Martin Tupper. PeD

Stretched out on the grass. Engaged. Octavio Paz, *tr. by* Muriel Rukeyser. PBMP

Stretching her head toward the stars. Pliny Jane. Mildred Luton. PH

Strew on her roses, roses. Requiescat. Matthew Arnold. HeIP; ILP (1975 ed.); NOBE; PBMP; PPM

Strict hairshirt of circumstance tears the flesh. The Veterans. Donagh MacDonagh. CIP

Strictly for Posterity. Charles Simic. NNaP

Strictly mathematic God, A. Quatrain. Arthur J. Bull. HeHu

Strictures on the Economy of Nature. George Outram. FaBoCo

Strife is grown between Virtue and Love, A. Astrophel and Stella, LII. Sir Philip Sidney. NIL

Strike a match. Within Us, Too. R. H. Grenville. AMV-80

Strike among the Poets, A. *Unknown.* FaBoCo

Strike, churl; hurl, cheerless wind, then; heltering hail. Fragment. Gerard Manley Hopkins. OBP

Strike the concertina's melancholy string! The Story of Prince Agib. W. S. Gilbert. FaBoCo

Strike the tent! the sun has risen; not a vapor streaks the dawn. The Bison Track. Bayard Taylor. AmVN

Strike ye our land. Buffalo Dance. Alice Corbin, *after Chippewa Indian*. BPAW

Striking a Pose. Kevin Ireland. ATNZ

Striking like a hammer. Bird Cry. Martha Webb. PHC

String-chewing bass players. Mingus. Bob Kaufman. PoBA

String of acronyms, A. Casi-Gato Aka Carnedechivo nee Ricardo Sánchez (Sometimes!). Ricardo Sánchez. FoP

String of pearls, A. The Woman. Edwin Morgan. MS

Stringer, The. James Brasfield. AMV-81

Strings lay all about. The Disconnection. Rita Mae Brown. IHMS

Strip Mining Pit. Dan Gillespie. TAT

Strip off your clothes and give them to a man. The Visiting Hour. David Wagoner. HoPM (1975 ed.)

Strip to the waist and have a seat. The doctor. Words. Miller Williams. AMV-81

Striped blouse in a clearing by Bazille, A. Ceremony. Richard Wilbur. NoAM

Striped pebbles somersault, The. Sifting Stones at Capri. Susan Whiting. GAS

Striped philistine with quick, A. Requiem for a Personal Friend. Eavan Boland. PFIr

Striped Shell, A. Ruth Dallas. ATNZ

Stripped/ you're beginning to float free. November 1968. Adrienne Rich. NMM

Stripper, The. Anita Endrezze Probst. CDW

Stripping off another yard of line. Casting at Night. Allen Hoey. AMV-80

Stripping the green tissue from the flowers. Bridesmaid. Robley Wilson, Jr. AMV-80

Strive not, vain lover, to be fine. Richard Lovelace. SCP-2

Striving brothers, students in the community colleges of the world. The Voice of the Future. Michele Wallace. WBN

Stroke, *sels.* Vincent Buckley.
"At the merest handshake I feel his blood," VII. MAuV
"In the faint blue light," I. MAuV
"Roofs are lit with rain, The," VI. MAuV

Stroke. Susan Irene Rea. EC

Strokes. William Stafford. ConAP

Strong am I among mortals, not without a name. Hippolytus. Euripides, *tr. by* Rex Warner. NAWM-1

Strong and slippery, built for the midnight grass-party confronted by four cats. Peter. Marianne Moore. CMoP (1970 ed.)

Strong ankled, sun burned, almost naked. Vitamins and Roughage. Kenneth Rexroth. NoAM

Strong Are Saying Nothing, The. Robert Frost. AnMo; CMoP (1970 ed.)

Strong Black women. Woman. Margo Bohanon. SES

Strong Bond, The. Juana de Ibarbourou, *tr. fr. Spanish by* Linda Scheer. PBWP

Strong Feeling for Poultry, A. Roy Blount, Jr. TDH

Strong gongs groaning as the guns boom far. G. K. Chesterton. *Fr.* Lepanto. IP

Strong imagination from my youth has been combined, A. The Caulker. M. A. Lewis. PoTa

Strong is the horse upon his speed. The Man of Prayer. Christopher Smart. *Fr.* A Song to David. PIM

Strong is the lion—like a coal. Christopher Smart. *Fr.* A Song to David. HAP

Strong Men. Sterling A. Brown. BPo; CNA; FB; PoBA

Strong men keep coming on, The. Upstream. Carl Sandburg. MiP; PiAm

Strong Men, Riding Horses. Gwendolyn Brooks. PoBA

Strong-minded Lady, A. Morris Bishop. TDH

Strong Son of God, immortal Love. In Memoriam A. H. H., Proem. Tennyson. BoReV; HAP; ILP (1975 ed.); OAEL-2; PFD; PIM; VLP

Strong song tows, A. Coda. Basil Bunting. *Fr.* Briggflatts. OAEL-2; TwMBP

Strong sun across the sod can make. Song for the Passing of a Beautiful Woman. *Unknown, tr. by* Mary Austin. WPW

Strong Wind, A. Austin Clarke. PFIr

Strong wings in the stormy weather. Gulls. Leonora Speyer. *Fr.* Sand-pipings. TH

Stronger than alcohol, more great than song. Ted Berrigan. EAS

Strongest creature for his size, The. Weary Will. A. B. Paterson. BoAnP

Strongly it bears us along in swelling and limitless billows. The Homeric Hexameter Described and Exemplified. Schiller, *tr. by* Samuel Taylor Coleridge. MBPR

Struck dumb at arm's length. A Child's Nativity. John N. Morris. GP

Structure. Alberta Turner. HeS

Struggle, The. Sully-Prudhomme, *tr. fr. French by* Arthur O'Shaughnessy. PPM

Struggle for the Roads. Bruce Severy. VW

Struggle with the Angel, The. Claude Vigée, *tr. fr. French by* Elizabeth Savage. VWA

Struggling rill insensibly is grown, The. The Stepping-Stones. Wordsworth. PoIA

Strumming your melodic hair. Mouth of the Amazon. R. P. Gira. AMV-80

Strung Out with Elgar on a Hill, *sel.* Jonathan Williams. "All you ask is." GP

Strut for Roethke, A. John Berryman. NOBA

Stuart's gallantry . . . I recall how once. Wild Honey. Alistair Campbell. ATNZ

Stubborn Ground. Patricia Elliott. EC

Stubborn Spring pushed through the cold twigs. The Boarder. Frederick Feirstein. NYP

Studded with flies. State Fair Pigs. Roger Pfingston. TAT

Student. Cheng Min, *tr. fr. Chinese by* Kenneth Rexroth *and* Ling Chung. PBWP

Student, The. Frederick Eckman. IPWM

Student, The. Marianne Moore. NowV

Student, The. Dabney Stuart. NowV

Student Courting, A. *Unknown.* OxBM

Student, do the simple purification. The Simple Purification. Kabir, *ad. by* Robert Bly. NU

Students groan, The. Etudes. Laurence W. Thomas. AMV-80

Study in Aesthetics, The. Ezra Pound. CMoP (1970 ed.); ExPo (1973 ed.); InPS; NOBA; UsP

Study in Punctuation. Arthur J. Bull. HeHu

Study of a Spider, The. Lord De Tabley. VLP

Study of Reading Habits, A. Philip Larkin. NOBL; PPP; SoSe

Study of Two Pears. Wallace Stevens. InPK; InPS; NU

Study Peace. Amiri Baraka. PoBA

Study War No More. *Unknown.* FSW

Stuff. H. B. Johnson. AMV-80

Stuff of the moon. Nocturne in a Deserted Brickyard. Carl Sandburg. ILP (1975 ed.)

Stuffed birds in a/ cage. Lyn Lifshin. *Fr.* Walking thru Audley End Mansion Late Afternoon. RiTi

Stuffed owls drum in my heart. Fear. Thomas Peacock. VoR

Stuffy chill of clouded Summer, crowdsmell, booksmell. Supervising Examinations. Sean Lucy. CIP

Stumbling. Dick Lourie. NeAC

Stump, The. Donald Hall. MiP

Stump Farming. James Tipton. TC

Stump Is Not the Tombstone, The. Ralph W. Seager. AMV-81

Stumpfoot on 42nd Street. Louis Simpson. NNaP; NYP; TCP; UnPo (1976 ed.); VGW

Stumptown Attends the Picture Show. David Bottoms. GP

Stun. James Schuyler. MAT

Stunned cabin boy, A. Miscarriage. Michael Longley. POL

Stunned in that first estrangement. What We Said. W. D. Snodgrass. GP

Stunt Flier, The. John Updike. BBGO

Stupendious love! All saints astonishment! Edward Taylor. Preparatory Meditations: First Series, X. EAP

Stupendous God! how shrinks our bounded sense. Robert Montgomery. *Fr.* The Omnipresence of the Deity. VLP

Stupidity Street. Ralph Hodgson. OxBTC; PCOP; UsP

Sturdie plowman lustie, strong and bold, The. Foote-Ball. Sebastian Brant. SPo

Sturdiest of forest trees, The. The Holly. Walter de la Mare. CMoP (1970 ed.)

Sturdy ploughman doth the soldier see, The. Joseph Hall. *Fr.* Virgidemiarum. OBSV

Sturdy tutsan strikes out, The. Tutsan. Charles Senior. MIS

Stutterer. Alan Dugan. CAPP

Style. Charles Bukowski. HoPM (1975 ed.)

Style. Howard Nemerov. NoAM

Style 5. William Wantling. CPA

Style is the answer to everything. Style. Charles Bukowski. HoPM (1975 ed.)

Suave and paltry man, my enemy, A. In the Tail of the Scorpion. Genevieve Taggard. VGW

Subalterns, The. Thomas Hardy. CMoP (1970 ed.); NoAM; OAEL-2; PPP; VLP

Subaltern's Love-Song, A. John Betjeman. BoLoP; HAP; LiSp; NOBL; OxBTC; PPoD

Subject. Marie Ponsot. VGW

Submarine Voyage, The: A Pindaric Poem in Four Parts, *sels.* Thomas Heyrick.
"Hence curiosity me led." SCP-2
"Neptune sat in his chariot high." SCP-2
"There two that struggling into the deep." SCP-2

Submerged city, The. Cologne. Hilde Domin, *tr. by* Tudor Morris. VWA

Sub-Prefix. 1. Under, Beneath, Below: As In. Joanne de Longchamps. PoW

Substance of leaves, The. Leaves. Ross Shideler. PoW

Substantiations, *sel.* Vidya, *tr. fr. Sanskrit by* Daniel H. H. Ingalls.
"One born to hardship in his place and station." PBWP

Subterranean Homesick Blues. Bob Dylan. InPK

Subtle chain of countless rings, A. Nature. Emerson. ILP (1975 ed.)

Suburb, The. Anne Stevenson. NMM

Suburban. David Malouf. FPA

Suburban Dream. Edwin Muir. OxBTC

Suburban Dusk. Bert Meyers. EAS

Suburban Madrigal. John Updike. SoS

Suburbia: Impossibilities of Change. Adrianne Marcus. CPA

Suburbs are known only to dogs and children. We Told You So. Nancy Keesing. MAuV

Subversive Sublime. Tom Buchan. MIS

Subverted Flower, The. Robert Frost. CMoP (1970 ed.); HAP; NoAM; NOBA; WeW

Subway, The. Allen Tate. ILP (1975 ed.); NoAM; NOBA; NYP; PiAm

Subway from New Britain to the Bronx, The. Randall Jarrell. NYP

Subway messes me up, The. Tubes. Larry Mollin. NeAC

Subway Witnesses, The. Lorenzo Thomas. PoBA

Success. Rupert Brooke. OxBTC

Success, The. Kermit Coad. PHC

Success. William Empson. OxBTC

Success. Emma Lazarus. SBG

Success. *Unknown.* CTV

Success in Malaria Research. Sir Ronald Ross. PMW

Success is counted sweetest. Emily Dickinson. AmVN; AnMo; CABA (1972 ed.); CMoP (1970 ed.); InPS; LFH; NOBA; PPM; PPoD; SBG; SPo; TAP; TPo; WPE

Success is like some horrible disaster. After Publication of Under the Volcano. Malcolm Lowry. FaBoTw (1975 ed.)

Success is speaking words of praise. Success. *Unknown.* CTV

Success Story. Patricia Goedicke. AAN

Success Story. Alfred Hayes. SPT

Success to the Newport Railway. The Newport Railway. William McGonagall. PeD

Successful Scot. Joseph Gordon Macleod ("Adam Drinan"). MS

Succubi. John Newlove. NeAC

Succubus, The. Robert Graves. OAEL-2

Such a calmness. Rest. Jacob Isaac Segal, *tr. by* Seymour Mayne. VWA

Such a dismal lot to see. Road to Utterly. H. H. Lewis. SPT

Such a merry suburb! Dachau. John Malcolm Brinnin. GP

Such a prelate, I trow. John Skelton. *Fr.* Why Come Ye Not to Court. OBSV

Such a sad celebration. A Grain of Moonlight. Asya, *tr. by* Gabriel Preil *and* Howard Schwartz. VWA

Such as in God the Lord Do Trust, *with music.* William Kethe. AH

Such as to himself eternity's changed him. The Tomb of Edgar Poe. Stéphane Mallarmé, *tr. by* Roger Fry. NAWM-2

Such as unto himself at last Eternity changes him. The Tomb of Edgar Poe. Stéphane Mallarmé, *tr. by* author. NAWM-2

Such brazen slatterns. Dandelions. Gerda Mayer. POL

Such easy, easy hours. Moon as Medusa. Vinnie-Marie D'Ambrosio. IHMS

Such Foolish Old Dames. Sam S. Stinson. TDH

Such glorious faith as fills your limpid eyes. Verse for a Certain Dog. Dorothy Parker. GDP

Such Is Holland! Petrus Augustus de Genestet, *tr. fr. Dutch by* Adriaan Barnouw. POL

Such is the way of the world. "St.-John Perse," *tr. by* T. S. Eliot. *Fr.* Anabasis, IV. OBVE

Such moving sounds from such a careless touch. Of My Lady Isabella Playing on the Lute. Edmund Waller. HAP

Such poor folk as to law do go. Isabella Whitney. *Fr.* A Sweet Nosegay, or Pleasant Posy. WPE

Such shameless bards we have; and yet 'tis true. Pope. *Fr.* An Essay on Criticism. OBSV

Such should this day be, so the sun should hide. On the Marriage of T. K. and C. C., the Morning Stormy. Thomas Carew. BoLoP

Such Stuff as Dreams. Franklin P. Adams. SpRo

Such subtile filigranity and nobless of construccion. "Wellcome, to the Caves of Artá!" Robert Graves. NOBL

Such time as from her mother's tender lap. The Discontented Satyre. Thomas Lodge. TVS

Such Tophet was; so looked the grinning fiend. Thomas Gray. FaBoEE

Such walls, like honey, and the old are happy. Luss Village. Iain Crichton Smith. MS

Such was God's poem, this world's new essay. Music. Abraham Cowley. *Fr.* Davideis, I. SCP-2

Suche waywarde wais hath love, that moste parte in discorde. Earl of Surrey. AAS

Such wonder seized, though after Heaven seen. Satan Flies to the Sun. Milton. *Fr.* Paradise Lost, III. SCP-1

Sucking Cider through a Straw. *Unknown.* GBP (Sipping Cider through a Straw.) FSW

Sucking soup out of a spoon. On a Wednesday. Jody Aliesan. AMV-80

Suction's Anthem. Blake. *Fr.* An Island in the Moon. FaBoNo

Sudden and from horizon to horizon driven steady. Storm End. Jonathan Griffin. TSWA

Sudden Assertion. Kenneth Leslie. BoAnP; GDP; POL

Sudden blow, A: the great wings beating still. Leda and the Swan. W. B. Yeats. AnMo; CABA (1972 ed.); CMoP (1970 ed.); EBEV; Epi; ExPo (1973 ed.); FF; HAP; HeIP; ILP (1975 ed.); InPK; LFH; NIL; NoAM; NOBE; NowV; OAEL-2; OBP; PAIC; PoIA; PPoD; PPoe; PPP; PSN; SoSe; STS; TCP; WeW

Sudden Gale in Spring. Martha Banning Thomas. ECBV

Sudden Light. Dante Gabriel Rossetti. BoLoP; NOBE; OAEL-2; VLP; VPC

Sudden Obscurity. Kermit Coad. PHC

Sudden Shower. John Clare. Epi

Sudden Thaw. Andrew Young. MS

Sudden Things. Donald Hall. EAS

Sudden upriseth from her stately place. Spenser. *Fr.* The Faerie Queene, I, iv. PPP

Sudden wakin', a sudden weepin', A. Man's Days. Eden Phillpotts. OxBTC

Suddenly, after the quarrel, while we waited. The Quarrel. Conrad Aiken. LoAs

Suddenly all the fountains in the park. The Fountains. W. R. Rodgers. PFIr; POL

Suddenly everything stops. Slump. Vassar Miller. BoWoP

Suddenly half in jest. Album Leaf. Stéphane Mallarmé, *tr. by* Keith Bosley. OBVE

Suddenly her breast has never been larger. Impotence. Marvin Bell. AmPA

Suddenly his mouth filled with sand. Death of a Poet. Charles Causley. OxBTC

Suddenly his poor body. Stations. Ted Hughes. NoAM

Suddenly I heard squeals. Integration. Richard Kell. IPM

Suddenly I saw the cold and rook-delighting heaven. The Cold Heaven. W. B. Yeats. HAP; NoAM; OAEL-2; WeW

Suddenly, in my world of you. You Went Away. Norman MacCaig. SLP

Suddenly in October the morning air. What I Have. Susan North. AMV-81

Suddenly it was quiet as a Sunday. The Wave. Daryl Hine. Prf

"Suddenly she slapped me, hard across the face." Elizabeth in Italy. Richard Weber. BoLoP

Suddenly the old fancy has me! Battery Park, High Noon. Ben Belitt. NYP

Suddenly there were cakes and everything. Roberto Vargas. CPA

Suddenly there were forms there. Horses. Gwyn Thomas, *tr. by* Joseph P. Clancy. OBW

Suddenly they are there as I. The Windows. Ron Loewinsohn. GP

Suddenly they came flying, like a long scarf of smoke. The Thing. Theodore Roethke. CMoP (1970 ed.)

Sue works in a shop. John's driving a bus. Our Family. Leonard Clark. RAE

Sueños. James Reiss. FiCP

Suez Crisis, The. *Somali Oral Tradition, tr. by* B. W. Andrzejewski. WTO

Suffenus whom you know, the witty. Catullus, *tr. fr. Latin by* Matthew Prior. OBVE

Suffer the Children. Audre Lorde. PoBA

Sufferance of her race is shown, The. "Formerly a Slave." Herman Melville. TAP

Suffering has settled like a sly disguise. A Korean Woman Seated by a Wall. William Meredith. PHC

Sufficient Place, The. Edwin Muir. MS

Suffolk Miracle, The, 2 *versions. Unknown.* AmFP

Sugar-Candy Bird, A. Ian Young. NeAC

Sugar-cane is just a cubit high, The. Love Songs (Dadaria.) *Gond Oral Tradition, tr. by* V. Elwin *and* S. Hivale. WTO

Sugar dripping into your vein, The. Firstborn. Charles Wright. BrS; GP

Sugar in the Cane. Tennessee Williams. OBAL

Sugar-Plum Tree, The. Eugene Field. CTV; OxBChV; PCOP

Sugarfields. Barbara Mahone. CNA; PoBA

Suggested by a Picture of the Bird of Paradise. Wordsworth. VLP

Suggestion Made by the Posters of the *Globe,* A. J. E. Thorold Rogers. FaBoEE

Suicide, The. Joanne Casullo. NPW

Suicide. Bob Kaufman. CPA

Suicide, A. Tom Kryss. NeAC

Suicide, The. V. R. Laing. PoA

Suicide, The. Edward Lowbury. PMW

Suicide. Alice Walker. FF

Suicide before Coffee in a Furnished Room. Herman Spector. SPT

Suicide off Egg Rock. Sylvia Plath. PPP

Suicide Pond. Kathy McLaughlin. PoA

Suicides, The. George MacBeth. NoAM

Suicide's Grave, The. W. S. Gilbert. *Fr.* The Mikado. VLP

Suit, The. Leonard Cohen. BBGO

Suite for Marriage, A. David Ignatow. NNaP

Suite: Judy Blue Eyes. Stephen Stills. WIF

Suite to Fathers. Jim Harrison. AmPA

Suitor, The. Jane Kenyon. TC

Sukey, you shall be my wife. The Proposal of Marriage. *Unknown.* BBL

Sukkot. Sol Lachman. VWA

Sulkily the sticks burn, and though they crackle. Under the Pot. Robert Graves. FaBoEE

Sulky Sue. *Unknown.* BBL

Sullenly a gale. Red Cloud. John G. Neihardt. BPAW

Sultan, The. *Unknown.* TDH

Sumach Leaves, The. Jones Very. NOBA

Sumer is comen and winter gon. An Easter Song. *Unknown.* OxBM

Sumer Is Icumen In. *Unknown. See* Cuckoo Song.

Summa is i-cumen in. Baccalaureate. David McCord. OBAL; SpRo

Summary. Sonia Sanchez. BPo

Summer. Conrad Aiken. NoAM

Summer. Moishe Kulbak, *tr. fr. Yiddish by* Ruth Whitman. VWA

Summer. Josephine Miles. WPE

Summer. Christina Rossetti. FSFS; PBMP; PoPle (Summer Days.) CTV

Summer. Ernesto Trejo. CPA

Summer. Diane Wakoski. IPWM; VGW

Summer. Ramona Wilson. VoR

Summer/ Is on the hill. Miracle. William Soutar. MS

Summer!/ the painting is organized. The Corn Harvest. William Carlos Williams. *Fr.* Pictures from Brueghel. PPP

Summer and autumn had been so wet, The. Bishop Hatto. Robert Southey. PoTa

Summer, and noon, and a splendour of silence, felt. A Nympholept. Swinburne. VLP

Summer, betray this tree again! Misericordia. Margaret Mead. PoA

Summer Celestial. Stanley Plumly. PCho

Summer Cloud, A. Waldo Williams, *tr. fr. Welsh by* Joseph P. Clancy. OBW

Summer comes/ The ziczac hovers. Magalu. Helene Johnson. PoBA

Summer Countries, The. Henry Rago. VGW

Summer Dawn. William Morris. NOBE; OAEL-2

Summer Days. Christina Rossetti. *See* Summer.

Summer days were sandlot days. Sandlot Days. M. P. Flynn. CTV

Summer Ending, The. Glenway Wescott. PoA

Summer ends now; now, barbarous in beauty, the stooks arise. Hurrahing in Harvest. Gerard Manley Hopkins. AnMo; BiP; CMoP (1970 ed.); ILP (1975 ed.); OBP; VLP

Summer Evening. John Clare. PCOP

Summer Evening Churchyard, Lechdale, Gloucestershire, A, *abr.* Shelley. PIM

Summer Farm. Norman MacCaig. OxBTC

Summer Garden. "Anna Akhmatova", *tr. fr. Russian by* Stephen Stepanchev. BoWoP

Summer Harvest Spreads the Fields, The, *with music.* Nathan Strong. AH

Summer holds me here, The. The Aspen's Song. Yvor Winters. POL

Summer holds, The: upon its glittering lake. Chorus. W. H. Auden. *Fr.* The Dog beneath the Skin. OxBTC

Summer Holiday. Robinson Jeffers. MiP

Summer in England, 1914. Alice Meynell. SBG; WPE

Summer in Fairbanks. Leon Stokesbury. NVAP

Summer is all a green air. Summer Music. May Sarton. NCSH

Summer is come, and evening spreads its gold. Return. Theodore Spencer. PoA

Summer is fading. Afternoons. Philip Larkin. PSN

Summer Is Gone. *Unknown, tr. fr. Early Irish by* Sean O'Faolain. PFIr

Summer is gone with all its roses. Bitter for Sweet. Christina Rossetti. GBL

Summer Is Icumen [*or* a-Coming] In. *Unknown. See* Cuckoo Song.

Summer is over, the old cow said. Moo! Robert Hillyer. OBAL; TH

Summer journeys. Manhattan. Lorenz Hart. OBAL

Summer Malison, The. Gerard Manley Hopkins. CMoP (1970 ed.); NoAM

Summer morning—five o'clock. In the Courtyard. Miriam Ulinover, *tr. by* Seth L. Wolitz. VWA

Summer Music. May Sarton. NCSH

Summer near the River. Carolyn Kizer. VGW

Summer nests uncovered by autumn wind, The. Birds' Nests. Edward Thomas. HeIP

Summer Night, A. W. H. Auden. PSN

Summer Night. Hayim Nachman Bialik, *tr. fr. Hebrew by* Robert Friend. VWA

Summer Night. Leonard Cohen. TCP

Summer Night, A. Ben Maddow. SPT

Summer night, a woman rests. Window. Anne Cherner. AMV-80

Summer, 1970. Daniel Halpern. AmPA

Summer 1970. Lindiwe Mabuza. SES

Summer, 1960, Minnesota. Robert Bly. InPS

Summer of nineteen eighteen, The. The Bad Old Days. Kenneth Rexroth. NNaP; NoAM

Summer of 'sixty-three, sir, and Conrad was gone away. Kentucky Belle. Constance Fenimore Woolson. PH; PoTa

Summer on the Great American Desert. Rufus B. Sage. BPAW

Summer Oracle. Audre Lorde. PoBA

Summer Pogrom. Fay Zwicky. GAS

Summer Rain. Hartley Coleridge. VLP

Summer so histrionic, marvelous dirty days. Sonnet. Ted Berrigan. CAAP; Epi

Summer Solstice. Alan Garner. BuTh

Summer Solstice. Marilyn Krysl. NPW

Summer Song. John Ciardi. ECBV

Summer Song, A. George Peele. *Fr.* The Old Wife's Tale. NOBE
("When as the rye reach to the chin.") GBL

Summer Song. W. W. Watt. QQQ

Summer Song for Me and My Aunts. Patricia Beer. HeHu

Summer Stars. Carl Sandburg. RFM

Summer Storm. Richard B. Kent. AMV-80

Summer Storm. Louis Simpson. WeW

Summer Street. Ana Ilce, *tr. fr. Spanish by* Steven White. AMV-81

Summer that I was ten, The. The Centaur. May Swenson. NMM; PH; PoIA; SO

Summer Visitors. Stephen Clark. AMV-81

Summer was dry, dry the garden. On the Debt My Mother Owed to Sears Roebuck. Edward Dorn. ConAP

Summer: West Side. John Updike. SoS

Summer will come with its warm, clear light. Out on the Hillside. Mary Gilmore. MAuV

Summer Words of a Sistuh Addict. Sonia Sanchez. BPo; TV
(Summer Words for a Sister Addict.) UnPo (1976 ed.)

Summer's Darkness. Elizabeth Hanson. NPW

Summer's Last Will and Testament, *sels.* Thomas Nashe.
Adieu, Farewell Earth's Bliss. EBEV; HAP; HeIP; PPoe; WeW
(In a Time of Pestilence.) HoPM (1975 ed.)
(In Plague Time.) FaPoR
(In Time of Pestilence.) NOBE; PoPle; UsP
(Litany in Time of Plague, A.) CABA (1972 ed.); DL; NIL; OAEL-1; PPoD; PPP
(Song: "Adieu, farewell earths blisse.") OBP
Autumn. OAEL-1
"Fair Summer droops, droop men and beast therefore." SCP-2
Spring, the Sweet Spring. HeIP; NIL; NOBE; RAE
"This is the last stroke my tongue's clock must strike." SCP-2

Summer's residue, The. Lines with a Gift of Herbs. Janet Lewis. WPW

Summer's sun is warm and bright. Pleasant Changes. Jane Euphemia Browne. OxBChV

"Summertime and the Living." Robert Hayden. BPo; NCSH; PoBA; PPP; UsP

Summing-up, The. Stanley Kunitz. OBAL

Summing Up, A. Gabriel Preil, *tr. fr. Hebrew by* Jeremy Garber. VWA

Summing Up, The. James Simmons. POL

Summing Up in Italy. Elizabeth Barrett Browning. VLP

Summit. Michael McPherson. PHC

Summit Lake. Mark Thalman. AMV-81

Summon now the kings of the forest. Mmenson. Edward Brathwaite. MPo

Summoned by Bells, *sel.* John Betjeman.
"My dear deaf father, how I loved him then." OxBTC

Summons, The. James Dickey. LiSp

Summons in Indiana, The. William Stafford. AnMo

Sun. James Dickey. CAPP

Sun, The. John Drinkwater. LCL

Sun. Marianne Moore. PiAm

Sun, The. Andrew Oerke. PoA

Sun, The. Anne Sexton. PBWP

Sun, The, *sel.* Vidya, *tr. fr. Sanskrit by* Daniel H. H. Ingalls. "I praise the disk of the rising sun." PBWP

Sun. Diane Wakoski. VoA

Sun/ proud Bessemer peltwarmer beauty. War Winters. Earle Birney. MPA

Sun and I. Ken Mammone. AMV-81

Sun and I, The. Monument in Bone. Phillip William George. UsP

Sun and moon at the same time. On Certain Days of the Year. Nancy Simpson. AMV-81

Sun and Moon So High and Bright, The, *with music. Unknown.* AH

Sun and softness. Sun Song. Langston Hughes. CNA

Sun and the Moon and Fear of Loneliness, The. *Tr. fr. Eskimo.* WTO

Sun appearing, The: a pendant. Plainview: 3. N. Scott Momaday. CDW

Sun became a small round moon, The. Climbing in Glencoe. Andrew Young. LiSp

Sun begins on the harp of trees, on snow. Two Women at JFK Gravesite. Margaret Gibson. WasP

Sun breaks over the eucalyptus. Marin-An. Gary Snyder. PoIA; TAT; WeW

Sun, bright lemon from the blinds, The. Morning Light. Louis Dudek. AMV-80

Sun burns out, The. The Last Fire. Moishe Steingart, *tr. by* Gabriel Preil. VWA

Sun Came, The. Etheridge Knight. NeAC; PoBA

Sun came up, The. Rain Rain on the Splintered Girl. Ishmael Reed. PoBA

Sun cheers us for a pin-point, flicks, then westers. Mating Answer. Ronald Bottrall. PoA

Sun Children. Leslie Silko. VoR

Sun descending in the west, The. Night. Blake. *Fr.* Songs of Innocence. MBPR; OxBChV

Sun does arise, The. The Ec[c]hoing Green. Blake. *Fr.* Songs of Innocence. CABA (1972 ed.); FSFS; LAuP; MBPR; UnPo (1976 ed.)

Sun drops below the elms. Routes. Peter Everwine. FiCP; NNaP

Sun Drops Red, The. Nellie Burget Miller. WPW

Sun eyed fire-macaw sits in a white tree, The. A Dream in Cold. Besmilr Brigham. Psy

Sun fails, The/ to rise, so I. Twilight at Noon. George Weiner. PoUp

Sun hangs, The/ medals. Robert Wallace. *Fr.* First Dandelions. OSP

Sun has gone down, The. Sad . . . and Glad. Brian Lee. FPB

Sun has left the middle of the sky, The. Family. Eve Shelnutt. TC

Sun has long been set, The. Wordsworth. MPBR

Sun Has Set, The. Emily Brontë. UnPo (1976 ed.) ("Sun has set, and the long grass now, The.") VLP

Sun Heals, A. Jewel C. Latimore. JB

Sun in Capricorn, The. Joyce Mansour, *tr. fr. French by* Carol Cosman. PBWP

Sun, in clownish yellow, but not a clown, The. Wallace Stevens. *Fr.* Esthétique du Mal. NOBA

Sun, The, is a gold coin slipping into/ an envelope of sea. Mediterranean. Ruth Whitman. VWA

Sun is a huntress young, The. An Indian Summer Day on the Prairie. Vachel Lindsay. BPAW; RFM

Sun is a rose window. To a Butterfly. L. Pearl Schuck. AMV-80

Sun is always in the sky, The. Breakfast Time. James Stephens. ECBV

Sun is blue and scarlet on my page, The. Falling Asleep over the Aeneid. Robert Lowell. NIL; NoAM

Sun is eclipsed, The; and one by one. Poetry Today. John Heath-Stubbs. POL

Sun is folding, cars stall and rise, The. The New World. Amiri Baraka. NoAM

Sun is gone down, The. Things We Can Depend On. George MacDonald. CTV

Sun is like an open furnace door, The. Last Look Round St. Martin's Fair. Thomas Hardy. OBP

Sun is lord and god, sublime, serene, The. The Lake of Gaube. Swinburne. OAEL-2; VLP; VPC

Sun is low, to say the least, The. The Sunset. Gelett Burgess. FaBoNo

Sun is more free than blood today, The. How Can I Say It Any Other Way. Cynthia Nibbelink. TC

Sun is rising, The. Healing Song. *Tr. by* Frances Densmore. OBVE

Sun is set, The; the swallows are asleep. Evening: Ponte a Mare, Pisa. Shelley. MBPR

Sun is shining in my backdoor, The. Myself When I Am Real. Al Young. CNA; PoBA

Sun is the blind eyes of statues gilded, The. The Sun. Andrew Oerke. PoA

Sun is warm, the sky is clear, The. Stanzas, Written in Dejection, near Naples. Shelley. CABA (1972 ed.); ILP (1975 ed.); MBPR; PBMP

Sun makes music as of old, The. The Chorus of the Archangels. Goethe, *tr. by* Shelley. *Fr.* Faust. OBVE

Sun marks the sea with a sign, The. The Last Covenant. Naomi Lazard. AAN

Sun [*or* Sunne] may set and rise, The. Sir Walter Ralegh, *after the Latin of* Catullus. FaBoEE; OBVE

Sun, my relative. A Prayer. *Unknown.* AKE

Sun Now Risen, The, *with music.* Johann Conrad Beissel. AH

Sun now rose upon the right, The. Samuel Taylor Coleridge. *Fr.* The Rime of the Ancient Mariner. OBP

Sun of Grace, The. *Unknown.* OxBM

Sun of July beats down on the small white house, The. Small White House. Robert Penn Warren. *Fr.* Notes on a Life to Be Lived. NoAM

Sun of My Perfection Is a Glass, The. Attar, *tr. fr. Persian.* ILwL

Sun of the Sleepless! Byron. Moon

Sun, of whose terrain we creatures are, The. Solar Creation. Charles Madge. OxBTC

Sun on hillsides, wind on seas. Desolation. *Unknown, tr. by* Aneirin Talfan Davies. OBW

Sun rests in itself, The. The Equator at Quito; or, The Will to Die. Rainer Schulte. SES

Sun rides higher, The. February. John Updike. CC

Sun rises, The. In Fields of Summer. Galway Kinnell. RFM; VGW

Sun rises in the south east corner of things, The. A Ballad of the Mulberry Road. Ezra Pound. UsP

Sun [*or* Sunne] Rising, The. John Donne. AnMo; BiP; BoLoP; CABA (1972 ed.); ExPo (1973 ed.); FF; GBL; HAP; HeIP; ILP (1975 ed.); InPS; IPWM; MetP; NIL; NOBE; OAEL-1; PoPle; PPP; SCP-1; SoSe; TT

Sun rose over a mound of corpses, The. I Hear a Voice. H. Leivick, *tr. by* David G. Roskies. VWA

Sun rushed up the sky, The; the taxi flew. Parting as Descent. John Berryman. CoPAm

Sun Set, and Up Rose the Yellow Moon, The. Byron. *Fr. Don Juan*, I. Moon

Sun sets, The. The wind moans. Ts'ai Yen, *tr. by* Kenneth Rexroth *and* Ling Chung. *Fr.* 18 Verses Sung to a Tatar Reed Whistle. BoWoP

Sun shines bright in the [*or* on my] old Kentucky home, The. My Old Kentucky Home. Stephen Collins Foster. BLSH; BLSo; FSW; PSoN

Sun Shines over the Mountain, The. *Unknown.* AmFP

Sun shines through you, The. Triptych. Luci Shaw. AATT

Sun sinks softly to his ev'ning post, The. The Rejected "National Hymns." "Orpheus C. Kerr." OBAL

Sun Song. Langston Hughes. CNA

Sun sounds, according to ancient custom, The. The Chorus of the Archangels. Goethe, *tr. by* Shelley. *Fr.* Faust. OBVE

Sun streaked the coffee urn. The Deaths of Paragon. John Woods. IPWM

Sun struts over the asphalt world, The. Noon of the Sunbather. Marge Piercy. NMM

Sun-tanned men and women, toiling there together. Reapers. Mathilde Blind. SBG; WPE

Sun, that brave man, The. The Brave Man. Wallace Stevens. PBMP

Sun that brief December day, The. Snow-bound; a Winter Idyl. Whittier. AmVN; FSFS; NOBA; PiAm; TAP

Sun that in Breadalbane's lake doth fall, The. The Botanist's Vision. Sydney Dobell. VLP

Sun, the moon, the stars, the seas, the hills and the plains, The. The Higher Pantheism. Tennyson. PAIC; SpRo; VLP

Sun, the Worker, The. Isidor Schneider. SPT

Sun, they say, is dying, The. Vermilion Cliffs. Radcliffe Squires. MPA

Sun-treader, life and light be thine for ever! Robert Browning. *Fr.* Pauline. VLP

Sun upon the Weirdlaw Hill, The. The Dreary Change. Sir Walter Scott. OAEL-2

Sun Used to Shine, The. Edward Thomas. FaBoTw (1975 ed.)

Sun was shining on the sea, The. The Walrus and the Carpenter. "Lewis Carroll." *Fr.* Through the Looking-Glass. AKE; FaBoCo; FaBoNo; NOBL; OxBChV; RhR

Sun went down beyond yon hill, The. To Be a Farmer's Boy. *Unknown.* GSB

Sun, when it shines on traffic, has a look. Noon on Alameda Street. Hilegarde Flanner. WPW

Sun Wields Mercy, The. Charles Bukowski. MAT

Sun woke me this morning loud, The. A True Account of Talking to the Sun at Fire Island. Frank O'Hara. NNaP

Sunbeams in the east are spread, The. Epithalamion Made at Lincoln's Inn. John Donne. PAIC

Sunday. Laura Beausoleil. NPW

Sunday. D. J. Enright. HeHu

Sunday. Cinda Kornblum. AcAn

Sunday. Josephine Miles. PoA

Sunday. Lawrence R. Rungren. AMV-80

Sunday Afternoon. Denise Levertov. ConAP; IHMS; SoS

Sunday afternoon/ and couples walk the breakwater. Veracruz. Robert Hayden. AmNP (1974 ed.)

Sunday afternoon and the water. Fording the River. Seamus Deane. CIP

Sunday Afternoon in St. Enodoc Church, Cornwall, *sel.* John Betjeman.
"Where deep cliffs loom enormous, where cascade." PES

Sunday Afternoons. Anthony Thwaite. OxBTC

Sunday and sunlight ashen on the Square. The Self Unsatisfied Runs Everywhere. Delmore Schwartz. PoA

Sunday Dreamer's Guide to Yarrow, Missouri, A. Jim Barnes. HeS

Sunday Evening with Elizabeth, Age 5. Martha Yoak. NPW

Sunday Evenings. John Hollander. NYP

Sunday, Guadalajara. Anthony Ostroff. MIT

Sunday in Glastonbury. Robert Bly. ConAP

Sunday in Inwood Park. Picnic. Adrienne Rich. CoPAm

Sunday in South Carolina. Robert Parham. AMV-80

Sunday lamb cracks its fat, The. Mary's Song. Sylvia Plath. CAAP

Sunday Morning. Louis MacNeice. HeIP; NIL

Sunday Morning. Wayne Moreland. PoBA

Sunday Morning. Ettore Rella. SPT

Sunday Morning. Wallace Stevens. BiP; CABA (1972 ed.); CMoP (1970 ed.) ExPo (1973 ed.); HAP; HeIP; LFH; NIL; NOBA; PiAm; PoA, *early version;* PoIA; PPoD; PPoe; PSN; TAP; WeW
"She says, 'I am content when wakened birds,'" *sel.* TT

Sunday morning and her mother's hands. Birmingham 1963. Raymond R. Patterson. CNA; GP; PoBA

Sunday morning: here we live jostling and tricky. Newtown. Ted Berrigan. FiCh

Sunday morning just at nine. Down Went McGinty. Joseph Flynn. FSN

Sunday morning restlessness. Second Reading. Richard Beyer. AMV-81

Sunday Night. Alan Ziegler. AAN

Sunday Service. Dana Naone. PHC

Sunday shuts down on this twentieth-century evening. Boy with His Hair Cut Short. Muriel Rukeyser. InPK; SPT; VGW; WPE

Sunday strollers along a sewage-choked Schuylkill. To Some Millions Who Survive Joseph E. Mander, Sr. Sarah E. Wright. PoBA

Sunday the only day we don't work. A Walk. Gary Snyder. NoAM; NOBA; UsP

Sundays. Marieve Rugo. AMV-81

Sundays too my father got up early. Those Winter Sundays. Robert Hayden. CNA; CoPAm; CTBA; FF; GP; HAP; IPWM; NoAM; PoBA; PPP; SoSe (1977 ed.); UnPo (1976 ed.)

Sundays when the wind blows. Sunday. Lawrence R. Rungren. AMV-80

Sundered from this beauty is its fond lover. Elegy in the Orongorongo Valley. Hubert Witheford. ATNZ

Sundew, The. Swinburne. VLP

Sundial spins beneath her eyes, A. In June. Darrell Gray. AcAn

Sundown at Darlington 1878. Lance Henson. VoR

Sunflower. Charles Bukowski. VoA

Sun-Flower, The. Dora Greenwell. WPE

Sunflower. Rolf Jacobsen, *tr. fr. Norwegian by* Robert Bly. NU

Sunflower Moccasins. Phillip William George. NW; VoR

Sunflower Rock. Paul Blackburn. NoAM

Sunflower Sutra. Allen Ginsberg. MAT; NOBA; PiAm

Sunflowers, The. Douglas Stewart. POL

Sunglare and sea pale as tears. Blackfish Poem. Milton Acorn. NeAC

Sunglasses, *sel.* Tom Clark.
"Air is interesting, The." OSP

Sunjuice. Erica Jong. MMD

Sunk Lyonesse. Walter de la Mare. EcS

Sunlight. Joseph Bruchac. AMV-80

Sunlight folds back pages of quiet shadows. At Hans Christian Andersen's Birthplace, Odense, Denmark. Maurice Lindsay. MS

Sunlight inches down. The White Piano. Ralph J. Mills, Jr. HeS

Sunlight lies along my table. The Weather of Six Mornings. Jane Cooper. IHMS

Sunlight, moonlight. Dream-Song. Walter de la Mare. PoPle

Sunlight on the Garden, The. Louis MacNeice. BiP; CMoP (1970 ed.); EBEV; HAP; NoAM; NOBE; OxBTC; PPoe; UsP

Sunlight on the water, The. Riversong. Michael Anania. HeS

Sunlight passes through the mountain as if the stone. Sunlight. Joseph Bruchac. AMV-80

Sunlight seems fragile, The. After the Dark Months. Ronald Mann. PMW

Sunlight speaks, and its voice is a bird, The. The Humming Bird. Harry Kemp. PCOP

Sunlight there is crisped to stone. Autumn—for My Son. Christine Churches. GAS

Sunlight upon Judaea's hills! The Crucifixion. Whittier. PIM

Sunne may set and rise, The. *See* Sun may set and rise, The.

Sunne Rising, The. John Donne. *See* Sun Rising, The.

Sunned in the South, and here to-day. To Flowers from Italy in Winter. Thomas Hardy. PF

Sunning. James S. Tippett. ECBV; GDP

Sunning during Session Break at Camp Lake Hubert for Girls, Brainerd, Minnesota. Mary Walker. PoUp

Sunny Bank. *Unknown.* GBP

Sunny Prestatyn. Philip Larkin. CABA (1972 ed.); NoAM

Sunrise. Sidney Lanier. PiAm

Sunrise. Jim Tollerud. VoR

Sunrise at Sea. Swinburne. RhR

Sunrise Call, The. *Tr. fr. Pueblo Indian by* N. Barnes. WTO

Sun's heat collects in leaf crystals. Topsoil. Robert Morgan. CSP

Sun's perpendicular rays, The. William Lort Mansel. FaBoEE

Sun's rays, The. The Eagle Sings. *Unknown.* AKE

Sun Set. Umberto Aridjis, *tr. fr. Spanish by* Eliot Weinberger. AMV-81

Sunset, The. Gelett Burgess. FaBoNo

Sunset. Ron Weber. PoUp

Sunset/ molten bronze. Tune: Endless Union. Li Ching-chao, *tr. by* C. H. Kwôck *and* Vincent McHugh. PBWP

Sunset after Rain. W. S. Merwin. PoA

Sunset and evening star. Crossing the Bar. Tennyson. BiP; CABA (1972 ed.); DL; FaPoR; FF; HeIP; ILP (1975 ed.); InPK; NOBE; OAEL-2; PBMP; PFD; PIM; PPM; RhR; SoSe (1977 ed.); VLP; VoPo

Sunset Horn. Myron O'Higgins. AmNP (1974 ed.)

Sunset in the Sea. Tom Hood. FaBoNo

Sunset of the City, A. Gwendolyn Brooks. PBWP

Sunset Song. *Tr. fr. Pueblo Indian by* N. Barnes. WTO

Sunshade, The. Thomas Hardy. OxBTC

Sunshine of Paradise Alley, The, *with music.* Walter H. Ford. FSN

Sunshine on paddocks backvards. August Fugue. Thomas Shapcott. CAAP

Sunshiny shower, A. *Unknown.* MG

Sunstrike. Douglas Livingstone. MPo

Sunt Leones. Stevie Smith. SBG

Sunup (Variation on a Theme by Baudelaire). Naomi Clark. CPA

Super-cool/ ultrablack. But He Was Cool; or, He Even Stopped for Green Lights. Don L. Lee. AmNP (1976 ed.); BPo; NoAM; PoBA

Super Flumina Babylonis. Swinburne. VLP

Super-suburbia of the Southern Seas. Farewell to New Zealand. Wynford Vaughan-Thomas. NOBL

Superballs. Tom Clark. EAS

Superman. John Updike. BBGO; LiSp; LP

Supermarket. Felice Holman. QQQ

Supermarket in California, A. Allen Ginsberg. ConAP; CoPAm; HAP; HeIP; ILP (1975 ed.); NIL; NOBA; PBMP; PiAm; PPoD; TAP; TCP; TPo; UnPo (1976 ed.); VoA

Superscription, A. Dante Gabriel Rossetti. The House of Life, XCVII. NOBE; OAEL-2; VLP; VPC

Superstitious Ghost, The. Arthur Guiterman. IWK

Supervising Examinations. Sean Lucy. CIP

Supper after the Last, The. Galway Kinnell. NOBA

Supper for a Lion. Dorothy Aldis. CaYB

Supper Is Na Ready. *Unknown.* GBP

Suppliant, The. Georgia Douglas Johnson. PoBA

Support Your Local Police Dog. Carter Revard. VoR

Suppose. Lewis Horne. AMV-81

Suppose—/ Ah well, suppose. Above the Wall. Susannah P. Malarkey. AMV-80

Suppose he had been tabled at thy teats. Luke XI: Blessed Be the Paps Which Thou Hast Sucked. Richard Crashaw. CABA (1972 ed.); PeD; SCP-1

Suppose it is true. She-Who-Opens. Yvonne. AAN

Suppose me dead; and then suppose. Swift. *Fr.* Verses on the Death of Doctor Swift. NOBE

Suppose that every soldier. Consider This. Bruce Cutler. BCr

Suppose the ceiling went outside. The Ceiling. Theodore Roethke. ECBV; LCL

Suppose the dead could crown their wit. A Responsory, 1948. Thomas Merton. VGW

Suppose the little cowslip. Deeds of Kindness. *Unknown.* CTV

Suppose the ruler used to mark our days. Suppose. Lewis Horne. AMV-81

Suppose they had cheated me out of my. Remember Times for Sandy. Carolyn M. Rodgers. JB

Suppose those/ who made/ wars. Nigerian Unity/ or Little Niggers Killing Little Niggers. Don L. Lee. NeAC

Suppose we are standing together a minute. April. Jean Valentine. TAP

Suppose We Sleep. Conleth Ellis. IPM

Suppose you could not turn away. Portholes. Conrad Hilberry. TC

Suppose You Met a Witch, *sel.* Ian Serraillier.
"Suppose you met a witch." CC

Suppose you screeve? or go cheap-jack? Villon's Straight Tip to All Cross Coves. W. E. Henley. FaBoCo

Suppose you stood facing. Pierrot le Fou. Adrienne Rich. PiAm

Suppose you were dreaming about your family. Benign Neglect/ Mississippi, 1970. Primus St. John. PoBA

Supposed Confessions of a Second-rate Sensitive Mind. Tennyson. VLP

Suppositions. Margherita Faulkner. AMV-80

Suppressed. *Unknown.* TDH

Supremacy. E. A. Robinson. NoAM

Supreme Fortune Falls Soonest. Robert Herrick. CaPo

Sur le Pont d'Avignon (On the Bridge at Avignon). *Tr. fr. French.* FSW

Surcease. Patrick Lane. NeAC

Sure a Poor Man. *Tr. fr. Hawaiian by* M. K. Pukui *and* A. L. Korn. WTO

Sure an' twas a/ fine st. patrick's day. Saint Patrick's Day, 1973. Wendy Rose. CDW

Sure are sorry to/ see ya go not really. You Got Parole. Dana "The Mouse" Merkel. DNGG

Sure as hell. Blueline. Ken Belford. NeAC

Sure as Hell, the Devil. Another One for the Devil. David C. Childers. AMV-80

Sure it was so. Man in those early days. Corruption. Henry Vaughan. OAEL-1; Prf; SCP-1

Sure the night was smooth. The Night Was Smooth. James Bertolino. POL

Surely A-flat may be forgiven. Lois in Concert. Charles Moorman. AMV-81

Surely among a rich man's flowering lawns. Ancestral Houses. W. B. Yeats. Meditations in Time of Civil War, I. OAEL-2

Surely I know that. Phoning My Son Long Distance. Ted Kooser. HeS

Surely in my eyes that light is now lost. The Photograph of Myself. Jon Anderson. AmPA

Surely it is death to come here. Tlanusi' yi, the Leech Place. Gladys Cardiff. CDW

Surely most signs pass me by unnoticed. Driving North from Savannah on My Birthday. Paul Zimmer. AMV-81

Surely that moan is not the thing. Fog-Horn. W. S. Merwin. TCP; TSWA

Surely the day will come. Guns. John Woods. GP

Surely You Remember. Dahlia Ravikovitch, *tr. fr. Hebrew by* Chana Bloch. VWA

Surf-Casting. W. S. Merwin. NOBA

Surfaces. David Madden. AMV-80

Surfaces. Jane Mayhall. NYP

Surfer, The. Judith Wright. WPE

Surfer and Others. Sonya Dorman. SPo

Surfers at Santa Cruz. Paul Goodman. FF; LiSp; SPo

Surfers beautiful as men, The. Middle Aged Midwesterner at Waikiki Again. John Logan. PHC

Surgeon and the Ape, The ("The surgeon once owned a big ape"). *Unknown.* TDH

Surgeons must be very careful. Emily Dickinson. ILP (1975 ed.); TAP

Surgical Ward. W. H. Auden. SoS

Surprise. Anthony Cronin. CIP; IPM

Surprise ("Surprise, surprise, they're flying in today"). Harold Witt. AMV-81

Surprised by Evening. Robert Bly. CAPP; VGW

Surprised by Joy—Impatient as the Wind. Wordsworth. BoLoP; HAP; ILP (1975 ed.); LoAs; MBPR; NOBE; OAEL-2; OBP; PoIA; PoPle; RRA

Surprising my dupe by his egg of Oedipus. Dirge for Three Trumpets. *Unknown.* EAS

Surreal morning grey. The Change. Michael Dransfield. CAAP; FPA

Surrender, The. Henry King. BoLoP; EBEV; SCP-2

Surrounded by tigers. The Life of the Wolf. Gary Gildner. AmPA

Survey. Paul Lawson. GP

Survey of Literature. John Crowe Ransom. OBAL; TAP; UsP; VGW

Survival. Albert Goldbarth. NVAP

Survival. Barbara Greenberg. RiTi

Survival. William Stafford. PoW

Survival This Way. Simon J. Ortiz. CDW

Surviving. James Welch. CDW; SA

Surviving the Wreck. Betty Adcock. CSP

Survivor, The. Robert Graves. CMoP (1970 ed.)

Survivor. Archibald MacLeish. NCSH

Survivor. Judy Dothard Simmons. CNA

Survivor, The. R. S. Thomas. FaBoTw (1975 ed.)

Survivors. Elaine Feinstein. VWA

Survivors, The. Judith Hemschemeyer. TV

Survivors. Mordecai Marcus. AMV-81

Survivors, The. Miriam Waddington. VWA

Susan. Robin Magowan. EAS

Susan, we meet in late fall. The Meeting. Kathleen Spivack. NMM

Susan would meet with Richard and with Ned. Like Mistress, Like Maid. Samuel Rowlands. SCP-2

Susanna and the Elders. Adelaide Crapsey. PAIC; WPE

Susannah and the Elders. *Unknown.* OLR

Susannah Prout. Walter de la Mare. FaBoEE

Susannah the fair. Susannah and the Elders. *Unknown.* OLR

Susie Asado. Gertrude Stein. RiTi; TAP

Suspended over her/ grey wool skirt and sweater. My Father's House. Peter Nicoletta. PoW

Sussex. Kipling. BTTM; PES

Sutter's Fort, Sacramento. Lucius Harwood Foote. BPAW

Suzanne Takes You Down. Leonard Cohen. BiP; GrRo; InPK; NIL; SFF; TCP; UsP; WIF

Suzie's New Dog. John Ciardi. GDP

Swaggering prince. Python. *Yoruba Oral Tradition tr. by* Ulli Beier. WTO

Swagman, The. C. J. Dennis. ECBV

Swain, give o'er your fond pretension. Hildebrand Jacob. FaBoEE

Swallow, The. Lucy Aikin. OxBChV

Swallow, The. John Clare. ILP (1975 ed.)

Swallow, The. Abraham Cowley, *after the Greek of* Anacreon. EBEV

Swallow, The. Christina Rossetti. PCOP

Swallow flew in the curves of an eight, The. Overlooking the River Stour. Thomas Hardy. PES

Swallow leaves her nest, The. Song from the Waters. Thomas Lovell Beddoes. *Fr.* Death's Jest Book. NOBE

Swallow sings "Dawn," The. Ezra Pound *and* Noel Stock, *fr.* Egyptian hieroglyphics. BoWoP

Swallow, that on rapid wing. The Swallow. Lucy Aikin. OxBChV

Swallow the Lake. Clarence Major. PoBA

Swallowing. Harold Bond. AMV-81

Swallows, The. Elizabeth J. Coatsworth. LCL

Swallows. Thomas Hornsby Ferril. MPA; RFM

Swallows flap in waves against the house, The. Late Spring: A Heaving, a Turning. John Gill. NeAC

Swallows hide, The. From Life. Lazer Eichenrand, *tr. by* Gabriel Preil *and* Howard Schwartz. VWA

Swallow's Nest, The. Sir Edwin Arnold. PCOP

Swam too far out: the swell took him. Elegy for a School-Friend. Augustus Young. BIrV

Swamp. Roberta Hill. VoR

Swamp reeds murmur the song, The. Marsh Leaf. David Wagoner. PoA

Swampstrife and spatterdock. The Marsh. W. D. Snodgrass. PiAm

Swan. D. H. Lawrence. CMoP (1970 ed.)

Swan, The. W. R. Rodgers. NoAM

Swan, The. Theodore Roethke. VGW

Swan and Shadow. John Hollander. PoA; WeW

Swan Bathing, The. Ruth Pitter. BoAnP

Swan Lake. John Unterecker. PHC

Swannanoa Tunnel. *Unknown.* FSW

Swans, The. Clifford Dyment. BoAnP

Swans. Morley Jamieson. SLP

Swans, The. Edith Sitwell. CMoP (1970 ed.); WPE

Swan's Feet, The. E. J. Scovell. OxBTC

Swans in their grey and silver park. An Effect of Light. Vivian Smith. MAuV

Swans rise up with their wings in day, The. The Boys and the Geese. Padraic Fiacc. PFIr

Swans Sing before They Die. Samuel Taylor Coleridge. FaBoCo (Epigram: "Swans sing before they die.") AKE (On a Bad Singer.) FaBoEE

Swansong. Carol Muske. AmPA

Swapping Song, *with music. Unknown.* RDB

Swarm off the cool water. The Lake Flies of Winnebago. Doug Flaherty. HeS

Swarming Bees, The. James Laughlin. VGW

Swart-smeked Smithes. *Unknown. See* Blacksmiths, The.

Swarthy bee is a buccaneer, The. A More Ancient Mariner. Bliss Carmen. OBAL

Swathe of violet at break of day, A. Joachim of Flora. Charles Spear. ATNZ

Sway song. Eye of God. Jim Tollerud. VoR

Swear by what the sages spoke. Under Ben Bulben. W. B. Yeats. CMoP (1970 ed.); HAP; NoAM; OxBTC

Sweat like drops of blood run down, The. Dark Was the Night. *Unknown.* AmFP

Sweat Song. Peter Blue Cloud. VoR

Sweating It Out on Winding Stair Mountain. Jim Barnes. CDW

Swedenborg's Skull. Vernon Watkins. FaBoTw (1975 ed.)

Swedes. Edward Thomas. OAEL-2

Sweeney. Henry Lawson. MAuV

Sweeney Agonistes, *sels.* T. S. Eliot.
"Under the bamboo." UnPo (1976 ed.)
"You'll be my little seven stone missionary!" UnPo (1976 ed.)

Sweeney among the Nightingales. T. S. Eliot. CABA (1972 ed.); CMoP (1970 ed.); HAP; HeIP; InPK; NIL; NoAM; NOBA; NOBE; PAIC; PPP; TT

Sweeney Erect. T. S. Eliot. AnMo; OxBTC; STS; VGW

Sweep thy faint strings, Musician. The Song of [the] Shadows. Walter de la Mare. CMoP (1970 ed.); ILP (1975 ed.)

Sweeping she comes, as she would brush the ground. Thomas Nashe. *Fr.* The Choice of Valentines; or, The Merry Ballad of Nashe His Dildo. SCP-2

Sweet, The. Ai. GP

Sweet, acidulous, down-reaching thrill, A. Ode on a Jar of Pickles. Bayard Taylor. SpRo

Sweet Adeline. Richard H. Gerard. BLSH, *with music;* FSN, *with music;* FSW

Sweet Afton. Burns. *See* Afton Water.

Sweet Amarillis, by a spring's. Upon Mistress Elizabeth Wheeler under the Name of Amarillis. Robert Herrick. CaPo

Sweet and Low. Tennyson. *Fr.* The Princess, Pt. II. BiP; BLSH, *with music;* CTV; FSW; ILP (1975 ed.); OxBChV

Sweet-and Twenty. Shakespeare. *See* Feste's Song.

Sweet antidote to sorrow, toil and strife. To a Segar. Samuel Low. OBAL

Sweet Apple. James Stephens. CMoP (1970 ed.)

Sweet are the pleasures that to verse belong. To George Felton Mathew. Keats. MBPR

Sweet are the thoughts that savor of content. Maesia's Song [*or* A Mind Content]. Robert Greene. *Fr.* Farewell to Folly. ILP (1975 ed.); PCOP; PPM; UnPo (1976 ed.)

Sweet Armida took this charge on hand, The. Tasso, *tr. by* Edward Fairfax. *Fr.* Godfrey of Bulloigne; or, The Recoverie of Jerusalem, IV. OBVE

Sweet Auburn, loveliest village of the plain. The Deserted Village. Goldsmith. ILP (1975 ed.); LAuP; NOBE; OAEL-1

Sweet Auburn! parent of the blissful hour. Goldsmith. *Fr.* The Deserted Village. EBEV

Sweet baby, sleep: what ails my dear? A Rocking Hymn. George Wither. OxBChV

Sweet baked apple dappled cinnamon speckled sin of mine. Love Child—a Black Aesthetic. Everett Hoagland. BPo

Sweet, be not proud of those two eyes. To Dianeme. Robert Herrick. CaPo; NOBE; PoPle; SCP-1

Sweet beast, I have gone prowling. Song. W. D. Snodgrass. SoSe

Sweet beats of jazz impaled on slivers of wind. Walking Parker Home. Bob Kaufman. PoBA

Sweet Benedict, whilst thou art young. To His Little Son Benedict from the Tower of London. John Hoskyns. OxBChV

Sweet Betsy from Pike. *Unknown.* AmFP, *with music;* BLSo, *with music;* BPAW; FaBoBa; FSW; OBAL; PeBB, *with music*

Sweet bird, that shunn'st the noise of folly. Milton. *Fr.* Il Penseroso. SCP-1

Sweet By and By. Sanford Filmore Bennett. *See* In the Sweet Bye-and-Bye.

Sweet Caroline. *Unknown.* PoPle

Sweet Chestnuts. John Walsh. DuDr

Sweet chimes! that in the loneliness of night. Chimes. Longfellow. PiAm

Sweet cyder is a great thing. Great Things. Thomas Hardy. NOBE; PPM

Sweet Dancer. W. B. Yeats. AnMo

Sweet day, so cool, so calm, so bright. Virtue. George Herbert. CABA (1972 ed.); ExPo (1973 ed.); HAP; HeIP; ILP (1975 ed.); NIL; NOBE; OAEL-1; PoPle; PPP; SCP-1; SoSe; UsP

Sweet, deep sense of mystery filled the wood, A. In Cool, Green Haunts. Mahlon Leonard Fisher. WeW

Sweet Diane. George Barlow. CNA

Sweet disorder in the dress, A. Delight in Disorder. Robert Herrick. AnMo; BiP; CABA (1972 ed.); CaPo; EBEV; FF; HAP; HeIP; ILP (1975 ed.); InPK; InPS; IP; NIL; NOBE; OAEL-1; PBMP; PoIA; PoPle; PPoe; PPP; UsP

Sweet dreams form a shade. A Cradle Song. Blake. *Fr.* Songs of Innocence. LAuP; MBPR; PCOP; STS

Sweet earth, he ran and changed his shoes to go. Arrangements with Earth for Three Dead Friends. James Wright. NIL

Sweet Echo, sweetest nymph, that liv'st unseen. The Lady Sings. Milton. *Fr.* Comus. NOBE

Sweet empty sky of June without a stain. Epochs. Emma Lazarus. SBG

Sweet Evelina. *Unknown.* FSW

Sweet flower! belike one day to have. To the Daisy. Wordsworth. MBPR

Sweet Genevieve. George Cooper. BLSH, *with music;* BLSo, *with music;* FSW; PSoN, *with music*

Sweet girl graduate, lean as a fawn, A. Nancy Hanks, Mother of Abraham Lincoln. Vachel Lindsay. CMoP (1970 ed.)

Sweet heart,/ A morning, climbing in its brass. Letter from an Island. John Malcolm Brinnin. TAP

Sweet Highland girl, a very shower. To a Highland Girl. Wordsworth. MBPR

Sweet Hour of Prayer, *with music.* William W. Walford. BLSH

Sweet in her green cell the flower of beauty slumbers. Serenade of a Loyal Martyr. George Darley. NOBE

Sweet Is the Budding Spring of Love, *with music.* John Hippisley. BLSo

Sweet is the rose, but growes upon a brere. Amoretti, XXVI. Spenser. ILP (1975 ed.)

Sweet Jane. *Unknown.* AmFP

Sweet Jesu. *Unknown.* OxBM

Sweet, Let Me Go. *Unknown.* BuTh

Sweet little bird in russet coat. The Autumn Robin. John Clare. DuDr

Sweet Louise. Gladstone Yearwood. SES

Sweet marmalade of kisses newly gathered. Margaret Cavendish, Duchess of Newcastle. *Fr.* Nature's Dessert. SCP-2

Sweet Mary the first time she ever was there. Mary. Blake. MBPR

Sweet Meat Has Sour Sauce; or, The Slave-Trader in the Dumps. William Cowper. OBSV

Sweet mermaid of the incomparable eyes. The Mermaid. Ben King. OBAL

Sweet Muse, Descend. Isaac Watts. BoReV; NOBE

Sweet Music's Power. John Fletcher. King Henry VIII, *fr.* III, i. NOBE

Sweet, my sweet. Leonora Speyer. *Fr.* Cantares. TH

Sweet Nosegay, A, or Pleasant Posy, *sels.*     Isabella Whitney. WPE
  "Do not account that for thine own."
  "Gold savours well, though it be got."
  "In loving, each one hath free choice."
  "Little gold in law will make, A."
  "Present day we cannot spend, The."
  "Seek not man to please, for that."
  "Such poor folk as to law do go."

Sweet notes in dimensionless clusters. The X of the Unknown. Tom Clark. LiSp

Sweet one I love you. Reasons. Tom McGrath. SLP

Sweet orange grove, the fairest of the isle. The Beauties of Santa Cruz. Philip Freneau. EAP

Sweet Patuni. *Unknown.* BluL

Sweet Peace, where dost thou dwell? I humbly crave. Peace. George Herbert. SoSe (1977 ed.)

Sweet Rivers of Redeeming Love, *with music.* John A. Granade. AH

Sweet Rosie O'Grady, *with music.* Maude Nugent. FSN

Sweet Sally took a cardboard box. The Ballad of the Light-eyed Little Girl. Gwendolyn Brooks. SoS

Sweet semi-circled Cynthia played at maw. Mockado, Fustian, and Motley. John Taylor. FaBoNo

Sweet sensibility, that dwells enshrin'd. George Canning *and* John Hookham Frere. *Fr.* New Morality. ESaP

Sweet she was, as kind a love. She Smiled like a Holy-Day. *Unknown.* BBL

Sweet Slug-a-Bed. *Unknown.* FaBoCo

Sweet smell of earth and easy rain. Sleeping Out with My Father. Gibbons Ruark. CSP

Sweet Soledad. Alejandro Murguia. CPA

Sweet Song. Vernon Scannell. FPB

Sweet sounds, oh, beautiful music, do not cease! On Hearing a Symphony of Beethoven. Edna St. Vincent Millay. VoPo

Sweet spirit! Sister of that orphan one. Epipsychidion. Shelley. MBPR

"Sweet spring is your." E. E. Cummings. NCSH; PiAm

Sweet Suffolk owl, so trimly dight. *Unknown.* EBEV

Sweet summer breeze, whispering trees. Kiss Me Again. Henry Blossom. BLSo

Sweet, sweet Caroline. Sweet Caroline. *Unknown.* PoPle

Sweet, sweet is the greeting of eyes. Keats. MBPR

Sweet, sweet, sweet, let me go. *Unknown.* GBL

Sweet sweet sweet sweet sweet tea. Susie Asado. Gertrude Stein. RiTi; TAP

Sweet Thing. *Unknown.* FSW

"Sweet, thou art pale." The Three Enemies. Christina Rossetti. VLP

Sweet trees who shade this mould. *Unknown, tr. fr. Spanish by* James Mabbe. GBL

Sweet Trinity, The. *Unknown.* AmFP

Sweet Tuxedo girl you see, A. Ta-ra-ra Boom-der-é. Henry J. Sayers. BLSo; FSW

Sweet Was the Song. Walter Savage Landor. PPM

Sweet Western Wind, whose luck it is. To the Western Winds. Robert Herrick. CaPo

Sweet William he married a wife. The Wife Wrapt in Wether's Skin. *Unknown.* AIW; AmFP

Sweet William rode up to the old man's gate. Earl Brand. *Unknown.* AmFP

Sweet William's Farewell to Black-eyed Susan. John Gay. BoLoP
  (All in the Downs, *folk version.*) AmFP
  (Black-eyed Susan.) RhR

Sweet William's Ghost, A *version. Unknown.* AIW

Sweet Woodley! oh! how fresh an' gay. Woodley. William Barnes. VPC

Sweete hand, the sweet but cruell bowe thou art. Henry Constable. *Fr.* Diana. ESo

Sweetening of the Year, The. John Shaw Neilson. MAuV

Sweeter Our Fruits, The. H. H. Lewis. SPT

Sweeter than sour apples flesh to boys. Ted Berrigan. EAS

Sweetest li'l' feller, ev'rybody knows. Mighty Lak' a Rose. Frank L. Stanton. BLSo; FSN

Sweetest Love, I Do Not Go. John Donne. *See* Song: "Sweetest love, I do not go."

Sweetest Saviour, if my soul. Dialogue. George Herbert. BoReV

Sweetest Story Ever Told, The, *with music.* R. M. Stults. BLSo; FSN

Sweetness. *Unknown, tr. fr. Irish by* John Montague. BIrV

Sweit rois of vertew and of gentilnes. To a Lady [*or* Ladye]. William Dunbar. EBEV; GBL; SLP

Swell guy, you got to die. To an American Workman Dying of Starvation. Genevieve Taggard. SPT

Swell the Anthem, Raise the Song, *with music.* Nathan Strong. AH

Swell'd with our late successes on the foe. Dryden. *Fr.* Annus Mirabilis. EBEV

Swerve, The. William Stafford. GP

Swerving east, from rich industrial shadows. Here. Philip Larkin. CMoP (1970 ed.)

Swete were the sauce would please ech kind of tast. Walter Rawely of the Middle Temple, in Commendation of the Steele Glasse. Sir Walter Ralegh. AAS

Swift, *sel.* Thomas Caulfield Irwin.
  "It was a dim October day." BIrV

Swift. Delmore Schwartz. PoA

Swift as a spirit hastening to his task. The Triumph of Life. Shelley. MBPR; OAEL-2

Swift boomerang, come get! December 18th. Anne Sexton. *Fr.* Eighteen Days without You. CAPP

Swift cries answering back. Evening Ride. Jill Hoffman. PH

Swift fleet the billowy clouds along the sky. Charlotte Smith. *Fr.* Montalbert. BoWoP; WPE

Swift goes the sooty swallow o'er the heath. The Swallow. John Clare. ILP (1975 ed.)

Swift had pains in his head. War Poet. Roy Fuller. HoPM (1975 ed.)

Swift had sailed into his rest. Swift's Epitaph. W. B. Yeats. CMoP (1970 ed.); OBVE

Swift Love, Sweet Motor. Hildegarde Flanner. WPE; WPW

Swift red flesh, a winter king, The. The Dance. Hart Crane. *Fr.* The Bridge: Powhatan's Daughter. PiAm

Swift to the western bounds of this wide land. On the Completion of the Pacific Telegraph. Jones Very. ILP (1975 ed.); TAP

Swift wild birds on wind and water. A Chapter from Geography. William Pillin. SPT

Swifter than hail. Tanka. Akiko No Yosano, *tr. by* Kenneth Rexroth. PAIC

Swiftly walk over the western wave. To Night. Shelley. ILP (1975 ed.); MBPR; OAEL-2

Swift's Epitaph. W. B. Yeats. CMoP (1970 ed.); OBVE

Swim in Ohuira Bay, A. Robert Peterson. NeAC

Swim on your back. Avalanche. Janet Emig. SPo

Swimmer. Gladys Cardiff. CDW

Swimmer. Robert Francis. LiSp

Swimmer in the Rain. Robert Wallace. FiCP; LiSp

Swimmers, The. Allen Tate. InPS; NOBA

Swimmer's Dream, A, *sel.* Swinburne.
   "Dream, a dream is it all—the season, A." EcS

Swimming by Night. James Merrill. VGW

Swimming Chenango Lake. Charles Tomlinson. NoAM

Swimming down to us. Moon Man. Jean Valentine. Moon

Swimming in the Pacific. Robert Penn Warren. AMV-80

Swimming in the Town. Ian Serraillier. FPB

Swimming is a gift. Let Go: Once. Gerald Fleming. AMV-81

Swimming Lesson, The. Robert Hershon. NeAC

Swimming Pool, The. Sandra Hochman. RiTi

Swimming Pool. Maria Teresa Horta, *tr. fr. Portuguese by* Suzette Macedo. PBWP

Swimming pool is closed, The. Swimming in the Town. Ian Serraillier. FPB

Swine com jingling doun Pelton lonin, The. Pigs o' Pelton. *Unknown.* GBP

Swineherd. Eilean Ni Chuilleanain. BIrV; CIP; PFIr

Swing, The. Robert Louis Stevenson. CTV; LCL

Swing dat hammer—hunh. Southern Road. Sterling A. Brown. BPo; FB; PoBA

Swing in the Willow Swung Out, The. Hugh Fox. TC

Swing Low, Sweet Chariot ("I ain't never been to heaven"). *Unknown.* GBP

Swing Low, Sweet Chariot ("I looked over Jordan and what did I see"). *Unknown.* BLSH, *with music;* BLSo, *with music;* FSW; UnPo (1976 ed.); WIF

Swing One, Swing All. George Bradley. AMV-80

Swing Song, A ("Swing, swing"). William Allingham. CTV

Swing Swong. *Unknown.* ECBV

Swinging Chick. Ern Alpaugh *and* Dewey G. Pell. InPK

Swinging mill bell changed its rate, The. Lone Striker. Robert Frost. PPM

Swinging out over the hinterland. Night Duty. Jill Thomas. PMW

Swinging the Baby. *Unknown.* ECBV

Swinging trouble light sweeps through black, A. Taking Down. Janet Kauffman. *Fr.* Tobacco. TC

Swirl sleeping in the waterfall! Chomei at Toyama. Basil Bunting. OxBTC; TwMBP

Switchback. Edith Sitwell. PBWP

Switzerland, *sels.* Matthew Arnold.
   Farewell, A: "My horse's feet beside the lake," III. VLP
   Isolation: To Marguerite, IV. VLP
   Meeting, I. VLP
   Parting, II. VLP
   Terrace at Berne, The, VII. VLP
   To Marguerite—Continued, V. BoLoP; EBEV; ILP (1975 ed.); NOBE; OAEL-2; PFD; PPP; SoSe (1977 ed.); VLP

Switzerland. Anthony Thwaite. HeHu

Swoon of noon, a trance of tide, A. In a Bye-Canal. Herman Melville. AmVN

Swooning swim to less and less. Buddha. Herman Melville. HeIP; PiAm

Sword in his right hand, a stone in his left hand, A. The Bronze David of Donatello. Randall Jarrell. WIF

Sword in length a reaping-hook amain. King Harald's Trance. George Meredith. VLP

Sword of Bunker Hill, The. William Ross Wallace. BTTM

Sword of light is unsheathed from the cloud, A. Parting. Shlomo Vinner, *tr. by* Laya Firestone *and* Howard Schwartz. VWA

Sword or stealth, strength or ancient blood. Matthew Mead. *Fr.* The Administration of Things. TwMBP

Sword sang on the barren heath, The. Blake. FaBoEE

Sworded man whose trade is blood, A. Separation. Samuel Taylor Coleridge. MBPR

Swung in the hollows of the deep. Cradle-Song of the Fisherman's Wife. Ella Higginson. WPW

Sybil of months, and worshipper of winds. November. John Clare. FSFS

Sycamore Tree, The. *Unknown.* AmFP

Sycophantic Fox and the Gullible Raven, The. Guy Wetmore Carryl. PBMP

Sydney Cove, 1788. Peter Porter. GAS

Sydney? It's a building site now, says Kevin. Telling the Cousins. Les A. Murray. AMV-81

Syllabus, The. Manfred Jurgensen. FPA

Sylvan Delights. Pope. *Fr.* Pastorals: Summer. NOBE

Sylvan slopes with corn-clad fields, The. September, 1819. Wordsworth. MBPR

Sylvester's Dying Bed. Langston Hughes. NoAM; UnPo (1976 ed.)

Sylvia. Shakespeare. *See* Who Is Sylvia?

Sylvia the fair, in the bloom of fifteen. Song. Dryden. EBEV; LoAs

Sylvia's Death. Anne Sexton. WBN

Sylvie and Bruno, *sel.* "Lewis Carroll."
   Mad Gardener's Song, The. BBL, 5 *sts.;* FaBoCo; FaBoNo; OxBChV; PBMP

Sylvie and Bruno Concluded, *sels.* "Lewis Carroll."
   King-Fisher Song, The. FaBoNo
   Pig Tale, The, *abr.* RAE

Sylvius, your hands near my mouth are heady flowers. Marguerite Burnat-Provins, *tr. fr. French by* Cassia Berman. BoWoP

Symbol inside this poem is my father's feet, The. The Pawnbroker. Maxine W. Kumin. NVAP

Symbol of war, a war, The. All That Is Perfect in Woman. William Carlos Williams. BiP

Symbolism. Karen Swenson. TVo

Symbols. John Drinkwater. WIF

Symbols. Christina Rossetti. VLP

Symbols. Steve Toth. AcAn

Symon's Lesson of Wisdom for All Manner of Children. *Unknown.* OxBChV

Sympathy. Paul Laurence Dunbar. AmNP (1974 ed.); ILP (1975 ed.); PoBA

Sympathy, The. Owen Felltham. SCP-2

Symphony. Alfred Dorn. AMV-80

Symphony. Frank Horne. AmNP (1974 ed.)

Symphony No. 3, in D Minor. Jonathan Williams. *Fr.* Mahler. VGW

Symposium, The, *sel.* Leah Goldberg, *tr. fr. Hebrew by* Robert Alter.
   "Outside the cats are wailing." PBWP

Symptom Recital. Dorothy Parker. SBG

Symptoms of Love. Robert Graves. BoLoP

Syren Songs, *sels.* George Darley.
   Mermaidens' Vesper-Hymn, The, VI. GBL (Siren Chorus.) BIrV
   Sea-Ritual, The, V. BIrV; EcS

Syrens' Song, The. William Browne. *See* Sirens' Song, The.

Syria. Keith Douglas. PSN

## T

T.B. Blues. Leadbelly (Huddie Ledbetter). BluL

T-Bone Steak Blues. *Unknown.* BluL

T. C. (Terry Callier; True Christian). Walter Bradford. FiCh; HeS

TKO. Richard Peck. SPo

T of the pole is someone, The. In Pursuit of the Family. Jenne Andrews. HeS

T. R. Donald Hall. PoA

T. S. Eliot. W. H. Auden. OBAL

T. S. Eliot. Robert Lowell. NoAM; NOBA

T.V. Commercial No. 073. Jesús Papoleto Mélendez. NW

T was a tidy young tapir. A Tidy Young Tapir. Carolyn Wells. TDH

Tabernacle of Peace. Hayim Be'er, *tr. fr. Hebrew by* Stephen Mitchell. VWA

Table, The. Michael Heffernan. PoA

Table, The. Jennifer Maiden. CAAP

Table Manners (I-II). Gelett Burgess. CTV

Table Manners. James Montgomery Flagg. TDH

Table Rules for Little Folks. *Unknown.* OxBChV

Table was filled with many objects, The. The "Utopia." Lee Harwood. EAS

Tableau. Countee Cullen. PoBA

Tablerock. Darryl Wally. AMV-81

Tables. Naomi Clark. AMV-80

Tables Turned, The. Wordsworth. IPWM; MBPR; OAEL-2

Taboo Woman, The. *Tr. fr. Zuni Indian by* K. Kennedy. WTO

Tact. Oliver Herford. TDH

Tact. Paul Pascal. WeW

Tact. E. A. Robinson. NoAM

Tadhg sat up on his hills. Senior Members. Sean Lucy. CIP

Tadlow. Abel Evans. FaBoCo

Taffy was a Welshman, Taffy was a thief. Mother Goose. GBP; MG

Tag, I.D. John S. Harris. MPA

Tagus, fare well, that westward with thy stremes. Sir Thomas Wyatt. AAS

Tail. Dennis Saleh. CPA

Tail behind, a trunk in front, A. The Elephant, or the Force of Habit. A. E. Housman. NOBL

Tailor. Eleanor Farjeon. OxBChV

Tailor, The. Patricia Garfinkel. AMV-80

Tailor Called Sorrow, A. Betti Alver, *tr. fr. Estonian by* Willis Barnstone *and* Felix Oinas. BoWoP

Tailor's Wedding, The. Louis Simpson. NNaP

Tain't Nobody's Business. *Unknown.* BluL

Taisigh Agat Fein Do Phog. *Unknown, tr. fr. Irish by* Maire Cruise O'Brien. BIrV

Tak for Sidst. Babette Deutsch. PoA

Take a Drink on Me. *Unknown.* FSW

Take a golden comb. This Earthen Body. *Gond Oral Tradition, tr. by* V. Elwin *and* S. Hivale. WTO

Take a look, i/ sd. For Kelley. Ken Belford. NeAC

Take a pound of butter made in May. Recipe for Toothache. *Unknown.* SCP-2

Take a statement: the same as yesterday's dictation. Vowel Movements. Daryl Hine. PoA

Take a trip with me in nineteen thirteen. The 1913 Massacre. Woody Guthrie. FSW

Take a Walk around the Corner. *Unknown.* BluL

Take a Whiff on Me. Leadbelly (Huddie Ledbetter). FSW

Take a Whiff on Me. *Unknown.* NOBA

Take Back Your Gold, *with music.* Louis W. Pritzkow. FSN

Take, for instance, a woman at a desk in a white room. Absence. Kathy Mangan. AMV-81

Take fortune as it falls, as one adviseth. The Author, of His Own Fortune. Sir John Harington. FaBoEE

Take four hundred years of exploitation. Racist Delicious. Lonnie L. Landrum. DNGG

Take, gentle marble, to thy trust. An Elegy upon His Tomb in Herndon-Hill Church, Erected by His Wife, Who Speaks. James Howell. OBW

Take heart, the journey's ended. In the Town. *Unknown, tr. by* Eleanor Farjeon. PChr

Take heed of loving me. John Donne. GBL

Take Him away, he's dead as they die. Obituary. Kenneth Fearing. VGW

Take in prospering hand a shining cup. Seventh Olympic Hymn. Pindar, *tr. by* Robin Blaser. *Fr.* Odes. Epi

Take it from me kiddo. Poem, or Beauty Hurts Mr. Vinal. E. E. Cummings. InPS; NIL; OBAL; PAIC; PiAm; PPoe

Take me as I drive alone. White Blossoms. Robert Mezey. VWA

Take me back to Arizona as it was in early days. Back to Arizona. Earl Alonzo Brininstool. BPAW

Take Me Out to the Ball Game. Jack Norworth. BLSH, *with music*; OBAL

Take my hand. There are two of us in this cave. The Blind Leading the Blind. Lisel Mueller. IHMS; PCho

Take My Life and Let It Be, *with music.* Frances Ridley Havergal. BLSH

Take my share of Soul Food. High on the Hog. Julia Fields. CNA

Take note, passers-by, of the sharp erosions. The Circuit Judge. Edgar Lee Masters. *Fr.* Spoon River Anthology. FaBoEE

Take, O take the cream away. Breakfast Song in Time of Diet. Stoddard King. OBAL

Take, O! take those lips away. At the Moated Grange. Shakespeare. *Fr.* Measure for Measure, IV, i. BiP; EBEV; GBL; HeIP; ILP (1975 ed.); InPS; NOBE; OAEL-1; STS

Take of me what is not my own. Envoi. Kathleen Raine. NOBE

Take off your hat. *Zulu Oral Tradition, tr. by* H. Tracey. WTO

Take One:/ They are next to each other. Two Pennies Found on the Gravel. David Kherdian. FAF

Take one chicken from three to five pounds. Savarin. Richard Williams. AAN

Take One Home for the Kiddies. Philip Larkin. OxBTC

Take Something like a Star. Robert Frost. STS

Take the Name of Jesus with You, *with music.* Lydia Baxter. BLSH

Take, then, this image for what it is worth. The Cage. George Garrett. SS

Take this blessing. Benediction. William Freedman. VWA

Take this flyswatter and exterminate the angels. Adolph Hitler Meditates on the Jewish Problem. Oscar Hahn, *tr. by* James Hoggard. AMV-81

Take This Hammer. *Unknown.* FSW

Take this hammer and carry it to my captain. Spike Driver Blues. *Unknown.* BluL

Take this kiss upon the brow! A Dream within a Dream. Poe. AmVN; GBL; ILP (1975 ed.); NOBA; PiAm; TAP

Take this solemn tip. Octopus. Sam Reavin. CaYB

Take this stabbing or that rape. Monologue through Bars. Nelson Hubbell. AMV-81

Take Thou Our Minds, Dear Lord, *with music.* William H. Foulkes. AH

Take thy hat, my little Laura. Edward Newman. *Fr.* The Insect Hunters. PPoD

Take time, my dear, ere Time takes wing. Fading Beauty. *Unknown.* FaBoEE

Take to the highway. Country Road. James Taylor. PoRo

Take up the pen and write a text. *Malay Oral Tradition, tr. by* R. J. Wilkinson *and* R. O. Winstedt. WTO

Take up the White Man's burden.   The White Man's Burden. Kipling.   BTTM

Take what is at hand.   Ode on a Decision to Settle for Less. William Pillen.   VWA

Take Your Accusation Back!   Kittaararter, *tr. fr. Eskimo.*   WTO

Take Your Fingers Off It.   *Unknown.*   FSW

Take your time kind mama I'm gonna do it just as slow as I can. Slow Mama Slow.   *Unknown.*   BluL

Taken from the.   The Primitive.   Don L. Lee.   BPo

Taken Town, The.   Constance Carrier.   FAF

Takes All Kinds.   R. P. Dickey.   POL

Taking a shell he had never seen.   Outposts.   J. S. Harry. CAAP

Taking a Walk with You.   Kenneth Koch.   CABA (1972 ed.); CAPP

Taking and Losing.   Martha Webb.   PHC

Taking between them/ A specially straight willow tree.   Eulogy to the Bow and Arrow.   *Mongol Oral Tradition, tr. by* C. R. Bawden.   WTO

Taking Down.   Janet Kauffman.   *Fr.* Tobacco.   TC

Taking, giving back their lives.   The Field Hospital.   Paul Muldoon.   CIP

Taking Leave of the Old.   Clarice Short.   PPoD

Taking Off.   Ronald Rogers.   VW

Taking Off.   *Unknown.*   CTV

Taking Off My Clothes.   Carolyn Forché.   AmPA

Taking Out Jim.   John Walsh.   RAE

Taking pity on this scrag-end of the city.   One Kingfisher and One Yellow Rose.   Eileen Brennan.   PFIr

Taking this painting at an appropriate distance.   Art Market: Leopoldville.   Michael Jackson.   ATNZ

Taking us by and large, we're a queer lot.   The Sisters.   Amy Lowell.   SBG

Tale, The.   Patricia Beer.   HeHu

Tale.   W. S. Merwin.   TH

Tale, The.   Charles Simic.   CAAP

Tale half told and hardly understood, A.   Exodus for Oregon. Joaquin Miller.   BPAW

Tale I frame shall be found to tally, The.   The Seafarer. *Unknown, tr. by* Michael Alexander.   OBVE

Tale is told of a doomed planet whose, The.   Easier.   James Harrison.   AMV-80

Tale of Drury Lane, A.   Horace Smith.   FaBoCo

Tale of Genji, The, *sel.*   Murasaki Shikibu, *tr. fr. Japanese by* Kenneth Rexroth *and* Ikuko Atsumi.   "Lady Murasaki says."   BoWoP

Tale of Genji.   Hugh Seidman.   AmPA

Tale of Last Stands, A.   Fred Red Cloud.   VW

Tale of Lord Lovell, The.   *Unknown.   See* Lord Lovel.

Tale of the Mice, The.   "Lewis Carroll."   MN

Tale the Hermit Told, The.   Alastair Reid.   PoTa

Tale was always simple—once, The.   The Tale.   Patricia Beer. HeHu

Talented Man, The.   Winthrop Mackworth Praed.   NOBL

Tales of a Wayside Inn, *sel.*   Longfellow.
Paul Revere's Ride (The Landlord's Tale), *fr.* Pt. I.   BTTM; CTV; FaPo; FaPoR; OBAL

Tales of Brave Ulysses.   Eric Clapton *and* Martin Sharp.   GrRo

Tales of Shatz.   Dannie Abse.   VWA

Tales of the Islands.   Derek Walcott.   OxBTC

Tales of witches warned me.   Blemishes.   James Hart.   AMV-81

Taliessin's Song of the Unicorn.   Charles Williams.   FaBoTw (1975 ed.)

Talisman, A.   Marianne Moore.   NCSH

Talisman for the New Year, A.   Deena Metzger.   RiTi

Talk about killing.   In a life.   A Sow's Ear.   Theodore Weiss. NoAM

Talk about the shade of the sheltering palms.   Under the Anheuser Bush.   Andrew B. Sterling.   OBAL

Talk about your harbor girls around the corner, Sally.   Haul Away, My Rosy.   *Unknown.*   AmFP

Talk like a jellyfish can ruin a party.   At the Chairman's Housewarming.   William Stafford.   AnMo

Talk not of wasted affection.   Longfellow.   *Fr.* Evangeline.   CTV

Talk to me.   Tic.   Coleman Barks.   *Fr.* Body Poems.   NVAP

Talk to Me, Baby.   Michael Dennis Browne.   BrS

Talk to Me, Talk to Me.   Hedva Harkavi, *tr. fr. Hebrew by* Tova Weizman.   VWA

Talk was of too much, too, The.   Zürich, zum Storchen.   Paul Celan, *tr. by* Joachim Neugroschel.   VWA

Talker, The.   Mona Van Duyn.   POL

Talking across Kansas.   Paula Kwon.   AMV-80

Talking after Christmas Blues.   Adrian Henri.   *See* Adrian Henri's Talking after Christmas Blues.

Talking along in this not quite prose way.   Near.   William Stafford.   ConAP; UsP

Talking Back.   David Wagoner.   MPA

Talking Blues.   *Unknown.*   FSW

Talking Designs.   Liz Sohappy Bahe.   CDW

Talking Fish, The.   Ruth Stone.   BoWoP

Talking in Bed.   Philip Larkin.   BoLoP

Talking Nothin'.   *Unknown.*   FSW

Talking of Ezra Pound and long-dead pantos.   Robert Nichols. *Fr.* Fisbo.   OBSV

Talking to God.   Garry Cleveland Myers.   CTV

Talking to her, he knew it was the end.   Hector.   Valentin Iremonger.   CIP

Talking to Myself.   *Unknown.*   BluL

Talking to the Forest.   David Wagoner.   CNW

Talking to the Mule.   Laura Jensen.   AmPA

Talking to the Townsfolk in Ideal, Georgia.   Isaac J. Black. CNA

Talking Union.   Lee Hays, Millard Lampell, *and* Pete Seeger. FSW

Talks with Himself.   Bruce Severy.   HeS

Tall.   *Unknown.*   TDH

Tall among the corn stalks.   Ruth.   Laura Freedgood.   SFF

Tall and fair.   Death of a Fair Girl.   Alpheus Butler.   PeD

Tall and freckled and sandy.   Middleton's Rouseabout.   Henry Lawson.   MAuV

Tall and singularly dark you pass among the breakers.   Louis Zukofsky.   NoAM

Tall buildings darken the sidewalks like a blight.   Promised Land. Mary Engel.   AMV-80

Tall camels of the spirit, The.   "A World without Objects Is a Sensible Emptiness."   Richard Wilbur.   ConAP; NoAM; NOBA; PiAm; PoA

Tall candles' tapered waxes scent the air.   Guyana.   Fern Pankratz Ruth.   AMV-80

Tall chestnuts keep away the sun and moon.   Concordance.   Paul Violi.   AMV-81

Tall ears.   What Is It?   Marie Louise Allen.   CTV

Tall Figures of Giacometti, The.   May Swenson.   WIF

Tall glass, round loaf and tumbled cloth.   Still Life.   Rosemary Dobson.   MAuV

Tall Men Riding.   S. Omar Barker.   BPAW

Tall, narrow girl, with second year belt.   Nurse.   May Ivimy. PMW

Tall Nettles.   Edward Thomas.   FaBoTw (1975 ed.)

Tall pines pine, The.   The Cow Slips Away.   Ben King.   ECBV

Tall poles leaned like dust-bowl fences. Absence. Jeannette Barnes. AMV-80

Tall snake without strut or buttress. Snake Rock. Christopher Middleton. FoP

Tall timber stood here once. Improved Farm Land. Carl Sandburg. RFM

Tall trees. Song (Prelude). Cosmo Pieterse. SES

Tall Wind, The. K. O. Arvidson. ATNZ

Taller than the stair of Qtub Minar. Howrah Bridge. James K. Baxter. ATNZ

Taller to-day, we remember similar evenings. W. H. Auden. CMoP (1970 ed.)

Tallest poet for his height. Arroyo. Tom Weatherly. PoBA

Tally. Josephine Miles. NoAM

Tallyho-Hum. Ogden Nash. PH

Tallyho! Tallyho!/ Echo faints far astray. The Hunt. Walter de la Mare. BoAnP

Talmudist. Stanley Burnshaw. VWA

Talysarn. Brenda Chamberlain. OBW

Tam i' the Kirk. Violet Jacob. GBL; MS; SLP

Tam Lin. *Unknown.* AIW, 2 *versions*; Epi; FaBoBa; NOBE; PeBB

Tam o' Shanter. Burns. OAEL-1

Tam Pierce. *Unknown.* FSW

Tamales. "O. Henry." BPAW

Tamaracks swing light away. Swamp. Roberta Hill. VoR

Tambour. István Vas, *tr. fr. Hungarian by* Jascha Kessler. VWA

Tambourine. James Cunningham. JB

Tamburlaine the Great, *sels.* Christopher Marlowe.
  "Ah, fair Zenocrate, divine Zenocrate!" *fr.* Pt. I, Act V. EBEV
  Overreacher, The, *fr.* Part I, Act I. NIL

Tame Cat. Ezra Pound. OBAL

Tamed by island, breakwater, inlet. The House on the Barge. Beth Bentley. CNW

Tamed by Miltown, we lie on Mother's bed. Man and Wife. Robert Lowell. BoLoP; ConAP; PSN

Tamer and Hawk. Thom Gunn. FaBoTw (1975 ed.)

Tammuz. Nathan Alterman, *tr. fr. Hebrew by* Robert Friend. VWA

Tammy Messer. *Unknown.* FaBoEE

Tamping Ties ("Tamp 'em up solid"). *Unknown.* AmFP

Tanagra! think not I forget. Corinna, to Tanagra, from Athens. Walter Savage Landor. *Fr.* Pericles and Aspasia. NOBE

Tangled [*or* Tanglid] I was in love's snare. Sir Thomas Wyatt. AAS; ILP (1975 ed.)

Tangled in a web of white. Wedding. Lucille Day. PoW

Tangled web indeed we weave, A. Women's Degrees. A. D. Godley. NOBL

Tanglid I was yn loves snare. *See* Tangled I was in love's snare.

Tango. Elena Jordana, *tr. by* Kathrine Jason. AMV-80

Tanka: "In the evening/ Quiet of the country town." Noin Hoshi, *tr. fr. Japanese by* Nobuyuki Yuasa. PAIC

Tanka: "Once, far over the breakers." Akiko no Yosano, *tr. fr. Japanese by* Kenneth Rexroth. PAIC

Tanka: "Swifter than hail." Akiko No Yosano, *tr. fr. Japanese by* Kenneth Rexroth. PAIC

Tanks. Rhyll McMaster. FPA

Tannen-/ baum/ whose secret, A. Fable of the Transcendent Tannenbaum. Scott Bates. PoTa

Tannhauser. Newman Levy. OBAL

Tantalos. Paulus Silentiarius, *tr. fr. Greek by* Dudley Fitts. LoAs

Tantanoola Tiger, The. Max Harris. GAS

Tanya. Jay Parini. AMV-80

Tao in the Yankee Stadium Bleachers. John Updike. LiSp; SPo

Tao Teh King, *sel.* Lao Tzu, *tr. fr. Chinese by* Raymond B. Blakney.
  "Something there is, whose veiled creation was." ILwL

Taos Drums. William Haskel Simpson. BPAW

Taos Winter. Patty L. Harjo. VoR

Taped to the wall of my cell are 47 pictures: 47 black. The Idea of Ancestry. Etheridge Knight. BPo; ConAP; CNA; CSP; NNaP; PoBA; PPoe; UsP

Taper wastes within yon window-pane, The. The Drunkard's Last Market. Charles Tennyson Turner. VPC

Tapestry, The. Howard Nemerov. PCho; Prf

Tapestry. Charles Simic. NVAP

Tappster, fill another ale. Drinking Song. *Unknown.* OxBM

Tapu. A. R. D. Fairburn. ATNZ

Tara Is Grass. *Unknown, tr. fr. Irish by* Padraic Pearse. POL

Tarantella. Hilaire Belloc. SpRo

Tarantula rattling at the lily's foot, The. O Carib Isle! Hart Crane. NoAM; PoA; VGW

Ta-ra-ra Boom-der-é, *with music.* Henry J. Sayers. BLSo; FSW (Ta-Ra-Ra Boom-De-Ay!, *diff. version.*) FSN; VLP (*At. to* Richard Morton)

Target. R. P. Lister. SoS; SoSe

Target shudders in the layered heat, The. Technique on the Firing Line. Turner Cassity. PoA

Tarquin and Tullia. Arthur Mainwaring. APAS

Tarred Gull. Elisavietta Ritchie. AATT

Tarrier's Song. *Unknown.* AIW
  (Drill, Ye Tarriers, Drill!) FSW (*At. to* Thomas F. Casey); RDB, *with music*

Tarry Buccaneer, The. John Masefield. PoTa; RhR

Tarry with Me, O My Saviour, *with music.* Caroline Sprague Smith. AH

"Tartar eyes, The." To Comrade Lenin. Isidor Schneider. SPT

Tartary. Walter de la Mare. OxBChV

Tartuffe; or, The Impostor. Molière, *tr. fr. French by* Richard Wilbur. NAWM-2

Tarzan, *sel.* Ronald Koertge.
  "What did Tarzan know." OSP

Tarzan, Old. Allan Block. FAF

Tashkent Breaks into Bloom. "Anna Akhmatova," *tr. fr. Russian by* Richard McKane. BoWoP

Task, The. John Ashbery. CAAP

Task, The, *sels.* William Cowper.
  City Corruption, *fr.* IV. NIL
  Flowers in Winter, *fr.* VI. PF
  Green-House, The, *fr.* III. PF
  "Lord of all, himself through all diffused, The," *fr.* VI. OAEL-1
  Sofa, The, I. LAuP
  Winter Morning Walk, The, V. LAuP
  Woodman's Dog, The, *fr.* V. GDP

Taste. John Updike. AMV-81

"Taste of Honey, A." King D. Kuka. VW

Tastes. Arthur J. Bull. HeHu

Tattle. Godfrey Turner. NOBL

Tattooed Lady, The. Bonnie Gordon. PoUp

Tattoos, *sels.* Charles Wright.
  Janitor, The; Kindergarten, Corinth. GP
  Snake Handling Religious Service. GP

Taught early that his mother's skin was the sign of error. Mr. Z. M. Carl Holman. SoSe

Taught Me Purple. Evelyn Tooley Hunt. SoS

Taught to Be Polite. Virginia Brady Young. AMV-81

Tauhid. Askia Muhammad Touré. PoBA

Taunt. *Malay Oral Tradition, tr. by* R. J. Wilkinson *and* R. O. Winstedt. WTO

Tavern in the Town. *Unknown. See* There Is a Tavern in the Town.

Tawny-black sky-scurries. David Jones. *Fr.* The Sleeping Lord. OBW

Taxi, The. Amy Lowell. BoWoP; PBWP

Taxicab Blues. Ahmos Zu-Bolton II. PoUp

Taxi-cab whore out at Iver, A. Limerick. Victor Gray. NOBL

Taxi Crab. Shel Silverstein. OSF

Taxis, The. Louis MacNeice. OxBTC

Tay Bridge Disaster, The. William McGonagall. PeD; PPoD, *abr.*

Te Deum. Gertrud von Le Fort, *tr. fr. German.* ILwL

Te Deum. Charles Reznikoff. VWA

Te Whetu Plains. Edward Tregear. ATNZ

Tea. Wallace Stevens. CABA (1972 ed.)

Tea. Ann Struthers. AMV-80

Tea at the Palaz of Hoon. Wallace Stevens. PoA

Tea by the Sea. Edward Lear. TDH

Tea for Two, *with music.* Irving Caesar. BLSo

Tea in a Space-Ship. James Kirkup. MPo

Tea Party. Harry Behn. LCL

Tea Party. Mary R. Hurley. CTV

Tea-rose tea-gown, etc., The. Ezra Pound. *Fr.* Hugh Selwyn Mauberley. NOBE

Tea-Shop, A. Ruth Dallas. ATNZ

Tea Shop, The. Ezra Pound. BBGO; HeIP

Teach me, Father, how to go. A Prayer. Edwin Markham. CTV

Teach me the secret of thy loveliness. To a Wind-Flower. Madison Cawein. PCOP

Teach the Rover. *Unknown.* PeBB

Teacher, The. Erica Jong. TPo

Teacher, A. Bruce McGregor. AKE

Teacher, A. Reed Whittemore. NCSH; TPo

Teacher Bruin said, "Cub, bear in mind." The Smart Little Bear. Mark Fenderson. TDH

Teacher of Poetry, The. William Packard. PPoD

Teacher stands before the class, The. The Teacher. Erica Jong. TPo

Teacher Taught Me, A. Anna Walters. VoR

Teacher to Heloise, The (After Waddell). Daniel Burke. AMV-81

Teacher's got a temper, A. A Teacher. Bruce McGregor. AKE

Teaching. Al Young. NW

Teaching Penguins to Fly. Barry Spacks. GP

Teaching Swift to Young Ladies. William Dickey. PoA

Teaching the Ape to Write Poems. James Tate. GP

Teahouse. Nicholas Rinaldi. AMV-81

Tears. Elizabeth Barrett Browning. WPE

Tears. Lizette Woodworth Reese. PPM

Tears. Edith Sitwell. CMoP (1970 ed.)

Tears. Edward Thomas. PoPle

Tears. *Unknown. See* Weep You No More, Sad Fountains.

Tears, Idle Tears. Tennyson. *Fr.* The Princess, Pt. IV. FaPoR; HAP; InPK; InPS; NIL; NOBE; OAEL-2; PoIA; PPoe; PPP; UnPo (1976 ed.); VoPo; WeW

Tears of Rage. Bob Dylan. RRA

Tears of St. Francis. Robert Duncan. CAAP

Tears, the firebursts and the vows, The. Cracked Looking Glass. Jean Garrigue. LoAs

Teasers, The. William Empson. OxBTC

Teasing; or, I Was Only, Only Teasing You, *with music.* Cecil Mack. FSN

Teasing Song. Princess Magogo, *tr. fr. Zulu by* D. K. Rycroft. WTO

Teasing the Nuns. Karl Shapiro. MPA

Technical Supplement, A. *sel.* Thomas Kinsella. "It is hard to beat a good meal." CIP

Technically they were all the same. The Art of Love. Richard Grossman. AMV-81

Technique. Philip Pierson. AMV-80

Technique on the Firing Line. Turner Cassity. PoA

Ted Speaking. Lynn Steele. BCr

Teechur. Dick Higgins. MiP

Te-ell me milkcow. Milkcow's Calf Blues. *Unknown.* BluL

Teeth bare to the wind. Bicycle Rider. Eugene McCarthy. SPo

Teeth Mother Naked at Last, The. Robert Bly. CAAP; NNaP "Excellent Roman knives slip along the ribs," *sel.* GP

Teeth of flowers, hairnet of dew. I Am Going to Sleep (Suicide Poem). Alfonsina Storni, *tr. by* Aliki *and* Willis Barnstone. BoWoP

Teevee. Eve Merriam. QQQ

Tee-Vee Enigma. Selma Raskin. QQQ

Tefillin: phylacteries. The Journey with Hands and Arms. Benjamin Saltman. VWA

Telegram. Dick Lourie. NeAC

Telegram arrived, The. Nobody's Business. James Tate. PCho

Telemachus and the Bow. Randall Colaizzi. AMV-81

Telemann. Helen Chasin. TV

Telephone, The. Robert Frost. LoAs; SO

Telephone. Robin Shectman. AMV-81

Telephone Arguin' Blues. *Unknown.* BluL

Telephone Connection. Gabrielle Edgcomb. PoUp

Telephone Conversation. Wole Soyinka. SFF; SoSe; TPo

Telephone Directory. Harry Crosby. EAS

Telephone line goes cold, A. The Farm on the Great Plains. William Stafford. HAP; VGW

Telephone Lineman. Ernest Kroll. AMV-81

Telephone Operator, The. Pat-Therese Francis. AMV-80

Telephone Poles. John Updike. UsP

Telephone poles, The. Crossing Kansas by Train. Donald Justice. ANTL; OSP

Telephones, Muzak. Vincent Buckley. *Fr.* Golden Builders. CAAP

Telephoning God. Gary Soto. AAN; CPA

Telephonist. Janet Frame. WPE

Telescope at Siding Springs, The. Geoffrey Lehmann. GAS

Tele/ vision. Amiri Baraka. UsP

Television/ radio sunday benevolent sunday. They Are Killing All the Young Men. David Henderson. PoBA

Television aerials, Chinese characters. On Roofs of Terry Street. Douglas Dunn. OxBTC

Tell a wise person, or else keep silent. The Holy Longing. Geothe, *tr. by* Robert Bly. NU

Tell all my mourners. Wake. Langston Hughes. OBAL

Tell all the truth but tell it slant. Emily Dickinson. HeIP; ILP (1975 ed.); NoAM; NOBA; PiAm; PPP; Psy; TAP; UnPo (1976 ed.)

Tell her I love. Stanzas for My Daughter. Horace Gregory. RRA

Tell, if thou canst, and truly, whence doth come. Upon Julia's Unlacing Herself. Robert Herrick. SCP-1

Tell It like It Is. Dudley Randall. TC

Tell me,/ Was Venus more beautiful. Venus Transiens. Amy Lowell. PoA

Tell me about yourself they. A Word in Edgeways. Charles Tomlinson. NOBL

Tell Me Again. Nigâr Hanim, *tr. fr. Turkish by* Tâlat S. Halman. PBWP

Tell me, daughter, my pretty daughter. Cossante. Pero Meogo, *tr. by* Yvor Winters. AIW

Tell me good Hobbinoll, what garres thee greete? Aprill. Spenser. *Fr.* The Shepheardes Calender. ILP (1975 ed.)

Tell Me Man Blues. *Unknown.* BluL

Tell me, men with wisdom gifted. Hiraeth. *Unknown, tr. by* Aneirin Talfan Davies. OBW

Tell me, my friend, do you think that the grain would sprout in the furrow. Arthur Hugh Clough. *Fr.* Amours de Voyage, III, ii. OBP

Tell me, my love, since Hymen tied. An Hymeneal Dialogue. Thomas Carew. SCP-2

Tell me no more of constancy. Against Constancy. Earl of Rochester. GBL

Tell me no more of minds embracing minds. No Platonic Love. William Cartwright. CABA (1972 ed.); GBL; ILP (1975 ed.); OAEL-1; SCP-2

Tell me not here, it needs not saying. A. E. Housman. NOBE; OAEL-2; OxBTC; PoPle; PSN

Tell me not in joyous numbers. Stephen Crane. AmVN; OBAL

Tell me not, in mournful numbers. A Psalm of Life. Longfellow. AH; AmVN; CABA (1972 ed.); CTV; PiAm; TAP

Tell me not of joy; there's none. The Dead Sparrow. William Cartwright. BoAnP

Tell me not, Sweet, I am unkind. Lines Where Beauty Lingers. Franklin P. Adams. OBAL

Tell me not, sweet, I am unkind. To Lucasta, Going to the Wars. Richard Lovelace. BuTh; CABA (1972 ed.); CaPo; ExPo (1973 ed.); FF; GBL; HAP; HeIP; HoPM (1975 ed.); ILP (1975 ed.); InPK; InPS; IP; NIL; NOBE; OAEL-1; OBP; PBMP; PoIA; SoSe; VoPo; WIF

Tell me now in what hidden way is. The Ballad of Dead Ladies. Villon, *tr. by* Dante Gabriel Rossetti. OBVE; PAIC

Tell me, O Octopus, I begs. The Octopus. Ogden Nash. CTV; ILP (1975 ed.)

Tell me, O tell, what kind of thing is wit. Ode: Of Wit. Abraham Cowley. OAEL-1; PAIC

Tell Me Pretty Maiden; or, English Girls and Clerks, *with music.* Owen Hall. FSN

Tell me, Pyrrha, what fine youth. Horace, *tr. by* William Browne. Odes, I, 5. OAEL-1

Tell Me, Tell Me. Marianne Moore. Psy

"Tell me, tell me,/ Unknown stranger." The Galliass. Walter de la Mare. FaBoTw (1975 ed.)

Tell me, tell me, gentle robin. The Cat and the Bird. George Canning. ECBV

Tell me, tell me, Sean O'Farrell, tell me why you hurry so? The Rising of the Moon. *Unknown.* RDB

Tell me, tell me, smiling child. Emily Brontë. VLP

Tell me the tales that to me were so dear. Long, Long Ago. Thomas Haynes Bayly. BLSH; BLSo; FSW; PSoN

Tell me though safest end of all our woe. On Death. Anne Killigrew. BoWoP

Tell me was a glorie ever seen. Loch Leven. Sydney Goodsir Smith. MS

Tell me, water. Hadaka De Hanasu. Jody Manabe. PHC

Tell Me What Month Was My Jesus Born In. *Unknown.* FSW

Tell me what time do the trains come through your town. Black Horse Blues. *Unknown.* BluL

"Tell me what you're doing over here, John Gorham." John Gorham. E. A. Robinson. NoAM; SoSe (1977 ed.)

Tell me whaur, in whit countrie. Ballat o the Leddies o Langsyne. Villon, *tr. by* Tom Scott. OBVE

Tell Me Where Is Fancy Bred. Shakespeare. *Fr.* The Merchant of Venice, III, ii. OAEL-1; STS

Tell Old Bill. *Unknown.* FSW

Tell Our Daughters. Besmilr Brigham. IHMS

Tell tale, tit! Mother Goose. MG

Tell the random pilgrims. Eve's Advice to the Children of Israel. Joachim Neugroschel. VWA

Tell Them I'm Struggling to Sing with Angels. David Meltzer. VWA

Tell them in Lakedaimon, passer-by. Simonides, *tr. fr. Greek.* FaBoEE

Tell us, old man. Old Man. David E. Stern. AMV-81

"Tell us, streaming lady." History. James Liddy, *tr. fr. Irish.* CIP

Tell us, thou clear and heavenly tongue. The Star Song: A Carol to the King. Robert Herrick. SCP-1

Tell Us, Ye Servants of the Lord, *with music.* William Staughton. AH

Tell you? ha! who. Maximus, to Gloucester, Letter 2. Charles Olson. NoAM

Tell you I chyll. The Tunnyng of Elynour Rummyng. John Skelton. AAS

Telling It. Nancy Sullivan. TAP

Telling lies to the young is wrong. Lies. Yevgeny Yevtushenko, *tr. by* Robin Milner-Gulland *and* Peter Levi. LP

Telling My Feelings. Yü Hsüan-chi, *tr. fr. Chinese by* Geoffrey Waters. BoWoP

Telling the Bees. Whittier. NOBA; TAP

Telling the Cousins. Les A. Murray. AMV-81

Tèma con Variazioni. "Lewis Carroll." FaBoNo; SpRo

Temper. Rose Fyleman. OxBChV

Temperaments, The. Ezra Pound. BoLoP; NoAM; NOBA

Temperance Billiards Rooms, The. P. J. Kavanagh. OxBTC

Temperature Variations. Elisavietta Ritchie. PoUp

Tempest, The ("How should I praise thee, Lord!"). George Herbert. BoReV

Tempest, The. Shakespeare. OAEL-1, *with music Sels.*
  Ariel's Song: "Come unto these yellow sands," *fr.* I, ii. NOBE ("Come unto these yellow sands.") HeIP; PoPle; SpRo
  Ariel's Song: "Full fathom five thy father lies," *fr.* I, ii. AKE; NOBE
  (Full Fathom [*or* Fadom] Five Thy Father Lies.) BiP; EBEV; EcS; ExPo (1973 ed.); HAP; HeIP; HoPM (1975 ed.); ILP (1975 ed.); InPK; InPS; OBP; PoIA; PoPle; PPoe; STS; WIF
  (Sea Dirge, A.) RhR
  Ariel's Song: "Where the bee sucks, there suck I," *fr.* V, i. NOBE; SoSe
  ("Where the bee sucks, there suck I.") CABA (1972 ed.); HeIP; ILP (1975 ed.); LCL; PCOP; PoIA
  "Honour, riches, marriage—blessing," *fr.* IV, i. PoPle
  "Master, the swabber, the boatswain and I, The," *fr.* II, ii. FF; OBP; PoPle
  (Song: "Master, the swabber, the boatswain and I, The.") NOBL; RhR
  Postscript ("Our revels now are ended"), *fr.* IV, i. TPo
  Song: "Hark, hark!/ Bow-wow," *fr.* I, ii. SoSe
  "Ye elves of hills, brooks, standing lakes, and groves," *fr.* V, i. EBEV

Tempest, The. Henry Vaughan. SCP-1

Tempest, The ("Cease rude Boreas blust'ring railers"). *Unknown.* AmFP

Temple, The. Robert Herrick. CaPo

Temple, The. Gustave Kahn, *tr. fr. French by* Edouard Roditi. VWA

Temple, A. Kenneth Patchen. EAS

Temple, The. C. H. Sisson. OxBTC

Temple is full of blood, The. Salvador Villanueva, *tr. fr. Spanish by* Julio Marzán. InW

Temple of Love, The, *sel.* Sir William Davenant.
  Song: "Come, melt thy soul in mine, that when unite." SCP-2

Temple of the Animals, The. Robert Duncan. NOBA

Tempora Mutantur. James Russell Lowell. HAP

"Temporary Escape." Leonard Keller. CPA

Temporary Problems. Larry Rubin. AMV-80

Tempt me no more; for I. C. Day Lewis. *Fr.* The Magnetic Mountain. PoA

Temptation. William Cowper. PIM

Temptation, The. Iain Crichton Smith. MS

Temptation of the Magic Banquet. Milton. *Fr.* Paradise Regained, II. SCP-1

Temptations still nest in it like basilisks. Dead Hand. W. S. Merwin. CAPP; InPK

Tempted and tried, we're oft made to wonder. Farther Along. *Unknown.* FSW

Ten bloody years with this quill lying. Invocation. Valentin Iremonger. BIrV

Ten Commandments, The ("Have thou no other gods but me"). *Unknown.* OxBChV

Ten Commandments, Seven Deadly Sins, and Five Wits. *Unknown.* FaBoEE

Ten dancers glide. Ballad of the Ten Casino Dancers. Cecilia Meireles, *tr. by* James Merrill. BoWoP

Ten Days Leave. W. D. Snodgrass. UnPo (1976 ed.)

Ten Definitions of Poetry. Carl Sandburg. WIF

Ten-Fifteen Community Poems, The, *sel.* John Knoepfle. "She says how/ is it when you." MAT

Ten Little Injuns. Septimus Winner. OBAL

Ten months after Florimel happen'd to wed. Another True Maid. Matthew Prior. FaBoEE

Ten, nine, eight. Let's Send a Rocket. Kit Patrickson. FPB

Ten o'Clock News. Simon Ortiz. VW

Ten o'clock train to New York, The. Winter. Ruth Stone. BoWoP

Ten of the night is Talavera tolling. The Field of Talavera. Thomas Hardy. *Fr.* The Dynasts. CMoP (1970 ed.)

10/17/75. Darlene Pearlstein. FiCh

Ten Sonnets for Today. Phil Stanway. AMV-80

Ten Thousand Cattle. Owen Wister. BPAW

Ten thousand flakes about my windows blow. Walter Savage Landor. FaBoEE

Ten Thousand Miles. *Unknown.* AmFP

Ten Thousand Miles Away. *Unknown.* FSW

Ten thousand times ten thousand. Henry Alford. VLP

Ten years/ and will you be/ a footnote. Return to Hinton. Charles Tomlinson. CMoP (1970 ed.)

Ten years ago it seemed impossible. In Progress. Christina Rossetti. BoWoP; WPE

Ten years ago this minute, he possibly sat. The Days. Donald Hall. CoPAm

Ten years!—and to my waking eye. The Terrace at Berne. Matthew Arnold. Switzerland, VII. VLP

Ten years together without yet a cloud. Firelight. E. A. Robinson. NoAM

Tenancy, The. Mary Gilmore. MAuV

Tenant. Danny L. Rendleman. TC

Tenant Farmer. Robert Ward. AMV-81

Tenantry. George Scarbrough. CSP; TAT

Tender Buttons, *sel.* Gertrude Stein.
Blue Coat, A. PBWP; RiTi
Celery. RiTi
Cooking. RiTi
More. PBWP
Nothing Elegant. PBWP
Pastry. RiTi
Petticoat, A. RiTi
Piano, A. PBWP
Water Raining. PBWP; RiTi

Tender each to the other, gentle. Imperialists in Retirement. Edward Lucie-Smith. MPo

Tender fingers ran up my ankle. "Can I Tempt You to a Pond Walk?" James Schuyler. PoA

Tenderfoot, The. *Unknown.* FSW

Tenderness, ache on me, and lay your neck. James Dickey. *Fr.* The Zodiac. TAP

Tenderness and resolution! Reliquary. Hart Crane. PoA

Tenderness of dignity of souls, The. Peter Viereck. *Fr.* Crass Times Redeemed by Dignity of Souls. HoPM (1975 ed.)

Tending. Paula Rankin. AMV-81

Tenebrae. Paul Celan, *tr. fr. German by* Joachim Neugroschel. VWA

Tenebrae. Austin Clarke. BIrV; CIP

Tenebrae. Denise Levertov. CABA (1972 ed.)

Tenebris. Angelina Weld Grimké. PoBA

Tennessee. *Unknown.* AmFP

Tennis. Margaret Avison. NoAM

Tennis. Nina Nyhart. AMV-81

Tennis. Robert Pinsky. PCho

Tennis Court Oath, The. John Ashbery. NoAM; TAP

Tennis Pro. Lawrence Jay Dessner. AMV-81

Tentacled for food. In the Sea of Tears. Naomi Replansky. GP

Tentacles, Leaves. Lyn Lifshin. RiTi

Tenth Pastoral, The; or, Gallus. Virgil, *tr. fr. Latin by* Dryden. Epi

Tenth Symphony. John Ashbery. NOBA

Tenting on the Old Camp Ground. Walter Kittredge. FSW; PSoN, *with music.*
(Tenting Tonight.) BLSo, *with music.*

Tenuous and Precarious. Stevie Smith. FaBoNo; OxBTC; UsP

Tenzone. Ezra Pound. *Fr.* Contemporania. PoA

Terce. James McMichael. PoA

Terence, This Is Stupid Stuff. A. E. Housman. BiP; CABA (1972 ed.); CMoP (1970 ed.); HeIP; ILP (1975 ed.); InPK; NIL; NoAM; SoSe; STS; VLP

Term, The. William Carlos Williams. TSWA

Terminal. D. J. Enright. HeHu; LP

Teminal Days at Beverly Farms. Robert Lowell. PSN

Terminus. Emerson. ILP (1975 ed.); NOBA; PAIC; PiAm; TAP

Terms of all kinds mellow with time, growing. Their Speech, Compared with Wisdom and Poetry. Robert Pinsky. *Fr.* Essay on Psychiatrists. PoA

Ternarie of Littles, upon a Pipkin of Jelly Sent to a Lady, A. Robert Herrick. ECBV

Ternissa. Walter Savage Landor. *Fr.* The Hellenics. NOBE

Terpsichore looks kindly on me. Korinna, *tr. fr. Greek by* John Dillon. PBWP

Terra Australis. Douglas Stewart. GAS; MAuV

Terra Australis. Chris Wallace-Crabbe. MAuV

Terra Cotta. K. Curtis Lyle. CNA

Terra-cotta house in the moonlight, The. Birth of a Country. Agnes Gergely, *tr. by* Emery George. VWA

Terra Incognita. D. H. Lawrence. OBP

Terrace at Berne, The. Matthew Arnold. Switzerland, VII. VLP

Terraces rise and fall, The. Going to Sleep in the Country. Howard Moss. PPoD

Terrain. A. R. Ammons. ConAP

Terraplane Blues. *Unknown.* BluL

"Terre des Hommes." Ruth Lisa Schechter. RiTi

Terrible/ a horse at night. Lawrence Ferlinghetti. CoPAm; HoPM (1975 ed.)

Terrible childbed hast thou had, my dear, A. Shakespeare. *Fr.* Pericles, III, i. EBEV

Terrible Dactyl, Son of Rodan. Edward Proffitt. PoIA

Terrible Door, The. Harold Monro. BoLoP; FaBoTw (1975 ed.)

Terrible is my plight this night. Wolves for Company. *Unknown.* BIrV

Terrible lodgings. In the frightful lodgings. Lodgers. Julian Tuwin, *tr. by* Isaac Komem. VWA

Terrible oldness, The. The Fisherman. Sam G. Harrison. AMV-80

Terrible People, The. Ogden Nash. TAP

Terrifying are the attent sleek thrushes on the lawn. Thrushes. Ted Hughes. TwMBP

Territory. Susan Wood-Thompson. AMV-81

Territory of the diamond, The. Hogs in the Sky. Charles Bukowski. EC

Terror. Robert Penn Warren. PoA

Terror by Night, The. Giacomo Leopardi, *tr. fr. Italian by* John Heath-Stubbs. Moon

Terry is sitting in the kafeneion writing letters to all his friends. Human Relations. Emmett Jarrett. NeAC

Terror strikes lightly your stillness. Spider. Thomas Cole. PoA

Terror swoops down on his heart like a vulture. Ezekiel. A. N. Stencl, *tr. by* Joseph Leftwich. VWA

Tess's Lament. Thomas Hardy. FaBoTw (1975 ed.)

Test, The. Emerson. OBAL

Test, The. Robert Friend. GP

Test. Jonathan Price. CoPAm

Testament, The, *abr.* Villon, *tr. fr. French by* Galway Kinnell. NAWM-1

Testament of Beauty, The, *sels.* Robert Bridges.
  Ethick, *fr.* IV. OxBTC
  "Sky's unresting cloudland, that with varying play, The," *fr.* I. EBEV

Testament of Cresseid, The, *sels.* Robert Henryson.
  "I mend the fyre and beikit me about." EBEV
  "Wha wait if all that Chauceir wrait was trew?" SLP

Testament of Perpetual Change, The. William Carlos Williams. GOA

Testimonial. Langston Hughes. ILP (1975 ed.)

Testimonies. Weldon Kees. NYP

Testimonies for a School Prayer. Serge Gavronsky. NowV

Testimony. Carolyn M. Rodgers. BPo

Testimony Concerning a Sickness. Doug Blazek. CPA

Testing Ground. Karla M. Hammond. AMV-81

Testing-Tree, The. Stanley Kunitz. MAT; UnPo (1976 ed.)

Testubicles spill blood across the page. Crossedroads. Martin Staples Shockley. FF

Tête-à-Tête. Edwin Honig. NoAM

Tethys' Festival, *sel.* Samuel Daniel.
  Shadows. NOBE
  ("Are they shadows that we see?") ExPo (1973 ed.)

Tewa Song of War. *Unknown, tr. fr. Mayan by* Daniel G. Brinton. PBMP

Texas. Amy Lowell. BPAW

Texas Cowboy, The ("Oh, I am a Texas Cowboy"). *Unknown.* AmFP

Texas cowboy on a barroom floor, A. The Hell-bound Train. *Unknown.* BPAW

Texas Ranger, The. Margie B. Boswell. BPAW

Texas Rangers, The, *diff. versions. Unknown.* BPAW; FSW

Texas, you swagger in our veins. Driving North from Kingsville, Texas. Naomi Shihab. TAT

Text. Aaron Zeitlin, *tr. fr. Yiddish by* Ruth Whitman. VWA

Text, The. Gary Snyder. Myths and Texts: Burning, XVII. Epi

Textures. Carol Bergé. MMD

Thack church and a wooden steeple, A. Legsby, Lincolnshire. *Unknown.* GBP

Thalassa. Louis MacNeice. BIrV; NOBE

Thalassa, Thalassa. James Neugass. SPT

Thalassius. Swinburne. VLP

Thames nocturne of blue and gold, The. Impression du Matin. Oscar Wilde. CABA (1972 ed.); VLP

Thamuris Marching. Robert Browning. OAEL-2

Than (By Yon Sunset's Wintry Glow). E. E. Cummings. VGW

Thanatopsis. Bryant. AmVN; DL; EAP; ILP (1975 ed.); NOBA; PiAm; TAP; VoPo
  "To him who in the love of Nature holds," *sel.* CTV

Thank God, bless God, all ye who suffer not. Tears. Elizabeth Barrett Browning. WPE

Thank God, thank God, we do believe. A Christmas Carol. Christina Rossetti. PChr

Thank Heaven! the crisis. For Annie. Poe. NOBA; PiAm; VoPo

Thank You, *sel. Unknown, tr. fr. Seneca Indian by* Richard Johnny John.
  "Now so many people that are in this place," Part I. IPWM

Thank you for asking this question. What Is Salt? John Vernon. PPoD

Thank you for letting us. The No Need for, the Computer Concern Error Letter. Lyn Lifshin. EC

Thank You for the Valentine. Diane Wakoski. CoPAm; HoPM (1975 ed.)

Thank you for your recent letter. Dear Mother. Emmett Jarrett. NeAC

Thank You, Jesus, for this day. Marie C. Turk. CTV

Thank you, my children, my students. As I Grow Older and Fatten on Myself. Joseph Carson. AMV-80

Thank You Poem for the Andersons, The. Phillip Hey. NVAP

Thank you, pretty cow, that made. The Cow. Ann *or* Jane Taylor. OxBChV

Thank you, thank you, lovely plant. Have You Thanked a Green Plant Today. Don Anderson. QQQ

Thanks. *Unknown.* CTV

Thanks, Robert Frost. David Ray. PCho

Thanks to Industrial Essex. Donald Davie. OxBTC

Thanksgiving. Sharon Barba. RiTi

Thanksgiving. Louis Driscoll. CTV

Thanksgiving. Robert Herrick. OFD

Thanksgiving. Kenneth Koch. VGW

Thanksgiving. John N. Morris. OFD

Thanksgiving after Communion. *Tr. from Gaelic by* Douglas Hyde. WTO

Thanksgiving Day. Lydia Maria Child. CTV; ECBV

Thanksgiving for a former, doth invite. Thanksgiving. Robert Herrick. OFD

Thanksgiving Hymn. *Unknown. See* Prayer of Thanksgiving.

Thanksgiving in Boston Harbor, The. Hezekiah Butterworth. BTTM

Thanksgiving 1963. Philip Booth. IPWM

Thanksgiving. They have/ taken a sample. 78 Miners in Mannington, West Virginia. Louis Philips. TAT

Thanksgiving to God, for His House, A. Robert Herrick. HAP; OFD

Thar's More in the Man than Thar Is in the Land. Sidney Lanier. NOBA

Thar's no respect fer youth er age. Californy Stage. *Unknown.* BPAW

Thassyrrans king, in peas with fowle desyre. Earl of Surrey. AAS

That a force surged, pressed to her sides. This Time a Tree Turns into a Woman. Beth Bentley. CNW

That Bad Music. Robert Harris. CAAP

That beauty I ador'd before. Westminster Drollery, 1671. Aphra Behn. SBG

That bird that bears our branchy future flies. Anzac Ceremony. Kendrick Smithyman. ATNZ

That blacksnake across the furrows. The Motorcyclist's Song. DeWitt Bell. MiP

That Black Snake Moan. *Unknown.* BluL

That boat has killed three people. Unlucky Boat. George Mackay Brown. MS

That Bright Chimeric Beast. Countee Cullen. AmNP (1974 ed.)

That Brings Us to the Woodstove in the Wilds, at Night. Walter Hall. AMV–81

That broken star. David McCord. *Fr.* A Christmas Package. PChr

That bull-necked blotch-faced farmer from Drumlore. Ghosts' Stories. Alastair Reid. MS

That came through our town. I Never Saw the Train. Jean Roberts. AMV–80

That child will never lie in me, and you The Unknown Child. Elizabeth Jennings. PBWP

That Chinese restaurant was a joke. The Will to Change. Adrienne Rich. NMM

That civilisation may not sink. Long-legged Fly. W. B. Yeats. AnMo; CMoP (1970 ed.); FaBoTw (1975 ed.); InPK; InPS; NoAM; NOBE; PPoe; PSN; TT

That conversation we were always on the edge. Adrienne Rich. *Fr.* Twenty-one Love Poems. BoWoP

"That cop was powerful mean." The Idiot. Dudley Randall. BPo

That "Craning of the Neck." Isabella Gardner. WPE

That Crawling Baby Blues. *Unknown.* BluL

That crazed girl improvising her music. The Crazed Girl. W. B. Yeats. InPS

That Crazy War. *Unknown.* FSW

That dandy/ 82 years old. In the Convalescent Hospital. Jean Pumphrey. TPo

That dandy black-and-white gentleman doodling notes. Magpie and Pines. Louis Johnson. ATNZ

That Dark Other Mountain. Robert Francis. CC; LiSp; NCSH; SoS

That Day. John Leax. AATT

That Day. Anne Sexton. BoWoP; ConAP

That day, in the slipping of torsos and straining flanks. The Song. Lola Ridge. WPE

That Day of Wrath, That Direful Day, *with music.* Thomas of Celano, *tr. fr. Latin.* AH

That day the/ words/ formed. That Day. John Leax. AATT

That day we brought our Beautiful One to lie. Two Days. W. E. Henley. VLP

That day when oats were reaped, and wheat was ripe. When Oats Were Reaped. Thomas Hardy. OxBTC

That death may not be casual. Epilogue. James Singer Burns. FaBoTw (1975 ed.)

That Death should thus from hence our Butler catch. In Obitum Promi. Henry Parrot. FaBoCo

That dog was always a dizzy blond. Dame. Susan Astor. AMV–80

That dog with daisies for eyes. The Dog of Art. Denise Levertov. NoAM

That enraged and frightened woman of Goya. La Pesadilla. Gerde Penfold. GP

That Familiar way the Bowmans have always had. Members of the Family. Derek Bowman. MIS

That flattering glass whose smooth face wears. A Looking-Glass. Thomas Carew. CaPo

That flower unseen, that gem of purest ray. In a Churchyard. Richard Wilbur. HeIP; PiAm

That for seven lustres I did never come. To the Reverend Shade of His Religious Father. Robert Herrick. CaPo

That force is lost. Snake Eyes. Amiri Baraka. VGW

That frantic error I adore. The Apostasy of One and But One Lady. Richard Lovelace. CaPo

That girl has borne too much. The Girl Who Had Borne Too Much. John Woods. GP

That God of ours, the Great Geometer. Grace to Be Said at the Supermarket. Howard Nemerov. AnMo; MPo

That goose died in opaque dream. Again, Kapowsin. Richard Hugo. CNW

That great ox, built just right! The Frog Who Would Be an Ox. La Fontaine, *tr. by* Marianne Moore. NAWM–2

That grey morning I left you asleep. Mysterious Britain. Amy Clampitt. AMV–81

That Harp You Play So Well. Marianne Moore. PoA

That hatless chewed woman sending me messages. In the Smoking Car. Ruth Whitman. RiTi

That he was born it cannot be denied. On a Certain Alderman. John Cunningham, *after* Simonides. FaBoEE

That her serene influence should spread. Two Loves. Richard Eberhart. CMoP (1970 ed.); LoAs

That hobnailed goblin, the bobtailed Hob. Country Dance. Edith Sitwell. NoAM

That hoùr-glass, which there ye see. The Hour-Glass. Robert Herrick. CaPo

That house you took me to. Number 14. Keith Bosley. LP

That hump of a man bunching chrysanthemums. Old Florist. Theodore Roethke. CTBA; NCSH; PiAm

That Hypocrite. *Unknown.* BPo

That I do bring myself to death. I Look at an Old Photo of Myself with Love. May Swenson. FoP

That I went to warm my self in Lady Betty's chamber, because I was cold. To Their Excellencies the Lords Justices of Ireland, the Humble Petition of Frances Harris. Swift. Epi; ILP (1975 ed.)

That is no country for old men. Sailing to Byzantium. W. B. Yeats. AnMo; BiP; CABA (1972 ed.); CMoP (1970 ed.); ExPo (1973 ed.); FF; HAP; HeIP; HoPM (1975 ed.) ILP (1975 ed.); InPK; InPS; LFH; NIL; NoAM; NOBE; OAEL–2; OxBTC; PAIC; PPoD; PPoe: PPP; PSN; SoSe; STS; TT; UnPo (1976 ed.); UsP; WIF

That Is Not Indifference. Howard G. Hanson. AMV–81

That it should end in an Albert Pick hotel. At the End of the Affair. Maxine W. Kumin. CoPAm; TAP

That it will never come again. Emily Dickinson. NOBA

That Justice is a blind goddess. Justice. Langston Hughes. BPo

That kid's my buddy. Buddy. Langston Hughes. ILP (1975 ed.)

That king spent fifty years or more. Citadels. Richard Kell. PFIr

That kiss meant to sear my heart forever. Time Lapse with Tulips. Tess Gallagher. AAN

That labor/ a face to remember in wonder. Sappho, *tr. fr. Greek by* Guy Davenport. OBVE

That Life, on Film. Lynn Sukenick. RiTi

That Life, That Love, That Fine. Horace Coleman. SES

That lifted blade transformed our jangling clans. James Russell Lowell. *Fr.* Under the Old Elm. GOA

That 'lil girl that Daddy loved. Ted Kooser. *Fr.* Themes for Country-Western Singers. POL

That Little Black Cat. D'Arcy Wentworth Thompson. OxBChV

That Little Hatchet. C. Butler-Andrews. PeD

That Little Lump of Coal. *Unknown.* AmFP

That loaf of bread you baked. Ice-Storm, April, 1974. Skaidrite Stelzer. TC

That Lonesome Train Took My Baby Away. *Unknown.* BluL

That longing you have to be invisible. Blue Window. Katha Pollitt. AAN

That love is all there is. Emily Dickinson. NOBA

That love which once was nearest to my heart. Vetus Flamma. Robert Mezey. PoA

That lovely spot which thou dost see. Upon a Mole in Celia's Bosom. Thomas Carew. CaPo; SCP-2

That lover of a night. Crazy Jane on God. W. B. Yeats. CMoP (1970 ed.); EBEV; Epi; OxBTC

That man entered through my eyes. Dream of the Forgotten Lover. Lucia Fox, *tr. by* R. Maghan. BoWoP

That Man in Manhattan. Shannon Keith Kelley. AMV-80

That mare stood in the field. All through the Rains. Gary Snyder. ConAP; VoA

That matter of the murder is hushed up. The Cenci. Shelley. MBPR

That me alone you lov'd, you once did say. Catullus, *tr. fr. Latin by* Richard Lovelace. OBVE

That mirror/ Which makes of men a transparency. Moments of Vision. Thomas Hardy. OAEL-2

That Moment. Ted Hughes. FF

That moment now embalmed in decrepitude. The Resurrection. William Edward Taylor. AMV-80

That Morn Which Saw Me Made a Bride. Robert Herrick. *See* Upon a Maid That Dyed the Day She Was Marryed.

That motion which doth from the mouth proceed. What Makes Echo. Margaret Cavendish, Duchess of Newcastle. SCP-2

That Mountain Far Away. *Unknown, tr. fr. Tewa Indian by* Herbert Joseph Spinden. PBMP

That mountain there. Pilgrimage Song. *Unknown, tr. by* Mary Austin. WPE

That Nature Is a Heraclitean Fire and of the Comfort of the Resurrection. Gerard Manley Hopkins. AnMo; BiP; CABA (1972 ed.); Epi; OAEL-2; VLP

That night she felt those searching hands. Mary, Mother of Christ. Countee Cullen. PChr

That night the dog let night in. Mad Dog. Robert Siegel. FAF

That night the moon drifted over the pond. The Prediction. Mark Strand. EAS; NVAP

That Night When Joy Began. W. H. Auden. OxBTC; PPoD; SoSe

That night when October played. Concert. Michael Arvey. AMV-81

That night your great guns, unawares. Channel Firing. Thomas Hardy. BiP; CABA (1972 ed.); CMoP (1970 ed.); EBEV; ExPo (1973 ed.); HAP; HeIP; ILP (1975 ed.); InPK; IP; NIL; NoAM; OAEL-2; OBP; OxBTC; PPM; PPoD; SoSe (1977 ed.); UnPo (1976 ed.); VoPo

That no fair woman will, wonder not why. Catullus, *tr. fr. Latin by* Richard Lovelace. OBVE

That No Man Should Write but Such as Do Excel. George Turberville. PPoD

That none beguiled be by time's quick flowing. Love's Clock. Sir John Suckling. CaPo

That nose is out of drawing. With a gasp. Sonnet for a Picture. Swinburne. *Fr.* Heptalogia. FaBoNo; OAEL-2

That Nova was a moderate star like our good sun. Nova. Robinson Jeffers. CMoP (1970 ed.); HAP

That old 'Frisco train left a mile a minute. 'Frisco Town. *Unknown.* BluL

That "old last act"! Two Songs, 2. Adrienne Rich. CABA (1972 ed.)

That old lonely lovely way of living. For the Old Highlands. Douglas Young. MS

That old nineteenth-century hold. Salvaging Spikes. Robert Vas Dias. HeS

That old oak in the orchard. Alive at the End of the Journey. James Tipton. TC

That Old-Time Religion. *Unknown.* BLSH, *with music* (Give Me That Old Time Religion.) FSW

That on her lap she casts her humble eye. On the Blessed Virgin's Bashfulness. Richard Crashaw. HAP; ILP (1975 ed.)

That once which pained to think of. The Forgiven Past. Laura Riding. NoAM; PBWP

That one small boy with a face like pallid cheese. Incendiary. Vernon Scannell. HeHu

That orbéd maiden with white fire laden. Orbed Maiden. Shelley. *Fr.* The Cloud. Moon

That Orpheus Calliops sonne who stayde the running brooke. Seneca, *tr. by* John Studley. *Fr.* Medea, III. OBVE

That our earth mother may wrap herself. Our Earth Mother. *Tr. fr. Zuni Indian by* R. Bunzel. WTO

That Poem. Juan Sáez Burgos, *tr. fr. Spanish by* Julio Marzán. InW

That practising bird is sharpening his call. Before Dawn. Ann Darr. MiP

That promising morning. The Lesson. David Wagoner. MPA

That raft we rigged up, under the water. A Distance from the Sea. Weldon Kees. NoAM

That ragged/ leaking raft held. Ireland. Richard Ryan. CIP

"That red fox." The Trap. William Beyer. PoTa

That Room. John Montague. CIP

That sail in cloudless light. Sea Grapes. Derek Walcott. SoSe (1977 ed.)

That same look. Leslie. Marvin Wyche, Jr. AmNP (1974 ed.)

That sculptor we know, the passionate-eyed son of a quarryman. An Artist. Robinson Jeffers. VGW

That season when the leaf deserts the bole. October 1. Karl Shapiro. PoA

That seat of science, Athens. Free America. *At. to* Joseph Warren. BTTM

That sensualist Rodin, who used his mouth. Rodin to Rilke. Emily Grosholz. AMV-80

That she adored me as the most. Elegy on Any Lady by George Moore. Max Beerbohm. FaBoEE

That Sharp Knife. Thomas Wolfe. NCSH

That she must change so soon her curving city. Peter's Little Daughter Dies. Kenneth Patchen. RRA

That shore, with its seagulls. Lake Michigan. David Kherdian. FAF

That Silence. Andrew Taylor. FPA

That single whitethroat, he that lives nearby. Dissonance. Cedric Whitman. AMV-80

That smoke/ would remain. If It All Went Up in Smoke. George Oppen. VWA

That soldier with a machinegun bolted. Two Summers in Moravia. Roger McDonald. CAAP; GAS

That somebody, my own special one. Shadows. *Tr. fr. Tewa Indian by* H. J. Spinden. WTO

That song it sing the sweetness. Steam Song. Gwendolyn Brooks. GP

That song there I borrow. Take Your Accusation Back! Kittaararter, *tr. fr. Eskimo.* WTO

That sound like the scratch. One, The Other, And. Wendy Wieber. NMM

That spot of blood on the drawingroom wall. The Conversation in the Drawingroom. Weldon Kees. EAS

That sturdy little son of mine. Physical Fitness. Alison Wyrley Birch. PPM

That Summer. Sam Ragan. CSP

That summer nothing would do. Herbert Scott. POL

That Sunday at the zoo I understood the child. The Family Group. Madeline DeFrees. *Fr.* Figures for a Carrousel. MPA

That Sunday, on my oath, the rain was a heavy overcoat. Mary Hines. Padraic Fallon, *after* Anthony Raftery. SoSe

That teacher gave me a new name . . . again. Name Giveaway. Phillip William George. NW; VoR

That the glass would melt in heat. The Glass of Water. Wallace Stevens. CABA (1972 ed.); STS; TAP

That the Night Come. W. B. Yeats. PoIA

That the poet "does not number the streaks of the tulip." To Hugh MacDiarmid. Edwin Morgan. FaBoTw (1975 ed.)

That the war would be over before they got to you. When You Have Forgotten Sunday: The Love Story. Gwendolyn Brooks. VoPo

That thou mayst injure no man, dove-like be. Prudent Simplicity. William Cowper. FaBoEE

That time/ in the sun. When Sun Came to Riverwoman. Leslie Silko. NW; VoR

That time/ we all heard it. Paul Robeson. Gwendolyn Brooks. CNA; PoBA

That time coming out from under. Polar Bear. Ramon Guthrie. ExPo (1973 ed.)

That time of evening, weightless and disparate. Blackwater Mountain. Charles Wright. CSP

That time of year thou mayst in me behold. Sonnets, LXXIII. Shakespeare. BiP; BoLoP; CABA (1972 ed.); EBEV; Epi; ExPo (1973 ed.); FF; GBL; HAP; HeIP; HoPM (1975 ed.); ILP (1975 ed.); InPK; InPS; IPWM; LFH; LoAs; NIL; NOBE; OAEL-1; OBP; PBMP; PoIA; PoPle; PPoD; PPP; SoSe; STS; UnPo (1976 ed.); UsP

That time of year you may in me behold. The Winter Twilight, Glowing Black and Gold. Delmore Schwartz. NoAM

That towering place, gabled and huge. Introductory. *Unknown, tr. by* Burton Raffel. *Fr.* Beowulf. OBP

That trumpet tongue which taught a nation. The Demagogue. Phyllis McGinley. FaBoEE

"That turn'll get her," I said. Toujours la Politesse. Ezra Pound, *after the Chinese.* OBVE

That was a year of suddenness. Initial Response. Katherine Soniat. AMV-80

"That was great weather last week." Funeral of Paddy Haugh. Jerome Kiely. IPM

That was the proverb. Let my mistress be. Long and Lazy. Robert Herrick. FaBoEE

That was the year. A Poem to Delight My Friends Who Laugh at Science-Fiction. Edwin Rolfe. TPo

That Was Then. Isabella Gardner. EC; GP

That way the moonflower and the sunflower this. Morning Dialogue. Conrad Aiken. NoAM

That We Head Towards. Stephany Fuller. BPo

That which brings death upon you. Amen. Alvaro Mutis, *tr. by* James Normington. AMV-81

That which her slender waist confined. On a Girdle. Edmund Waller. CABA (1972 ed.); FF; HeIP; InPK; SoSe

That which pushes upward. Consulting I Ching Smoking Pot Listening to the Fugs Sing Blake. Allen Ginsberg. TT

That Which We Call a Rose. Michael Dransfield. FPA

That which we dare invoke to bless. In Memoriam A. H. H., CXXIV. Tennyson. BoReV

That Which You Call "Love Me." Luis Rosales, *tr. from Spanish by* Lynn C. Jacox. AMV-81

That white coconut, the sun. Cloud Shadows. John Updike. VoPo

That Whitsun, I was late getting away. The Whitsun Weddings. Philip Larkin. NoAM; OxBTC; PSN

That winter, dark came early. Carpenter. Arthur Smith. BrS

That winter love spoke and we raised no objection. Jig. C. Day Lewis. PFIr

That within me. Anomie. Patricia Ramsey. AATT

"That woman there is almost dead." The Rat. W. H. Davies. OBW; OxBTC

That woman, vacuum in her mouth. The Great Nebula in Andromeda. Hugh Seidman. AmPA

That Women Are but Men's Shadows. Ben Jonson. InPS (Shadow, The.) NOBE

That year/ we seemed to harden. The Broken Year. Ron Talney. PoW

That year of the cloud, when my marriage failed. River Road. Stanley Kunitz. NoAM

That year there were many communications. Steel Mill Reversal. Norman Macleod. SPT

That you, the reader. This Is to Signify. Dave Morice. AcAn

That you worked. Poems to My Father. Rae Desmond Jones. CAAP

That your honour's petitioners (dealers in rhymes). To the Right Hon. Henry Pelham. Edward Moore. OBSV

That your little finger. The Wishbone. Rae Desmond Jones. CAAP

Thatched roof rings like heaven where mice, The. Byre. Norman MacCaig. BoAnP; MS

Thatcher. Seamus Heaney. HeHu

Thatcher, The. Brendan Kennelly. CIP

That's All? Anna Hajnal, *tr. fr. Hungrian by* Jascha Kessler. PBWP

That's Ethan Allen on the monument. Green Mountain Boy. Florida Watts Smyth. ECBV

That's Jack. Jack. Charles Henry Ross. OxBChV

That's Life? Alan Bold. FF

That's my grandpa behind the meatcase. The Age of the Butcher. Stuart Friebert. AMV-80

That's my last Duchess painted on the wall. My Last Duchess. Robert Browning. BiP; CABA (1972 ed.); ExPo (1973 ed.); FF; HAP; HoPM (1975 ed.); ILP (1975 ed.); InPS; IPWM; LFH; MAT; NIL; NOBE; OAEL-2 PAIC; PBMP; PoIA; PoPle; PPoD; PPP; SoSe; SS; STS; TT; VLP; WeW; WIF

That's No Way to Get Along. *Unknown.* BluL

That's not any old six-foot rabbit. Nearly Everybody Loves Harvey Martin. William D. Barney. LiSp

That's Our Lot. Moishe Leib Halpern, *tr. fr. Yiddish by* Kathryn Hellerstein. VWA

"That's the end of that." The Man in Overalls. Edward Lueders. MPA

That's the way Tod Johnson signed. X. R. P. Dickey. HeS

Thaw. T. Alan Broughton. AMV-81

Thaw. Lyn Lifshin. FAF

Thaw. Edward Thomas. EBEV; FaBoTw (1975 ed.); OxBTC

Thaw in the City. Lou Lipsitz. MAT; NCSH

Theater Hat, The. Carolyn Wells. TDH

Thee entirely I have loved. George Wither. *Fr.* Philarete to His Mistress. PeD

Thee, Father, first they sung Omnipotent. Milton. *Fr.* Paradise Lost, III. ILwL

Thee finds me in the garden, Hannah, —come in! The Quaker Widow. Bayard Taylor. AmVN

Thee for my recitative. To a Locomotive in Winter. Walt Whitman. ILP (1975 ed.); InPK; LFH; NoAM; TAP; WIF

Thee, God, I come from, to thee go. Gerard Manley Hopkins. VLP

Thee, ocean, once again do I behold. The Beauty of the Ocean. Thomas M. Walker. RhR

Thee Pompey thy past deeds by turns infest. Lucan, *tr. by* Nicholas Rowe. *Fr.* Pharsalia, I. OBVE

Thee sets a bell to swinging in my soul. Hildegarde Flanner. *Fr.* Sonnets in Quaker Language. WPE

Thee, the son of God most high. Delphic Hymn to Apollo. Swinburne. VLP

Thee, Thee, Only Thee. Thomas Moore. GBL

Theh Thet Hi Can Wittes Fule-Wis. *Unknown.* HAP

Their ardour kindless all the Grecian pow'rs. Homer, *tr. by* Pope. *Fr.* The Iliad, XII. OBVE

Their attendant nuns spare the tourists well. Bathing the Aged. Paul Monette. AmPA

Their Attitudes Differ. Margaret Atwood. Psy

Their auburn or black hair, curly hair. Just This. István Vas, *tr. by* Jascha Kessler. VWA

Their barbarism did not assuage the grief. The Retreat of Ita Cagney. Michael Hartnett. CIP

Their black truck rattled up the dusty hill. The Diviners. Mary Oliver. WPE

Their boughs curve upward in praise. White Pines. Barry Silesky. AMV–80

Their calendars are based on rice. Rice. Carol Muske. AmPA

Their cone-like Cabins. Charles G. Ballard. VoR

Their dresses were splashed on the green. Picnic on the Lawn. Vernon Scannell. HeHu

Their feet on London, their heads in the grey clouds. Whit Monday. Louis MacNeice. OAEL–2

Their ground they stil made good. Homer, *tr. by* George Chapman. *Fr.* The Iliad, V. OBVE

Their idiom, their dimension. Intimations of Immortality, Cuttingsville, Vermont, 1880. Constance Carrier. FAF

Their intuition/ Was as elegant as the stars above the mesa. Los Alamos: Manhattan. David Rowbotham. CAAP

Their laughter like a sprinkling of salt. The Herring-Girls. Derick Thomson. MS

Their lips upon each other's lips are laid. Speechless: Upon the Marriage of Two Deaf and Dumb Persons. Philip Bourke Marston. VLP

Their minds are so frail the least squeak upsets them. Dismissing Progress and Its Progenitors. George Reavey. EAS

Their Mouths Full. David Ignatow. GP

Their pink mouths opened wide. After the Deformed Woman Is Made Correct. Robert Lietz. AMV–80

Their rugs are sodden, their heads are down. Gun Teams. Gilbert Frankau. OxBTC

Their sense is with their senses all mixed in. Modern Love, XLVIII. George Meredith. LoAs; OAEL–2

Their smooth dark flames flicker at time's own root. The Cycads. Judith Wright. MAuV

Their spare, fanatic sentry comes. Ants and Others. Adrien Stoutenburg. BoAnP

Their Speech, Compared with Wisdom and Poetry. Robert Pinsky. *Fr.* Essay on Psychiatrists. PoA

Their Strange Evaluation. Deirdra Baldwin. PoUp

Their time past, pulled down. Burning the Christmas Greens. William Carlos Williams. NoAM; NOBA; PiAm; TT

Their tongues are knives, their forks are hands and feet. Riddle. Adrian Mitchell. FaBoEE; GBL

Their voices heard, I stumble suddenly. One More New Botched Beginning. Stephen Spender. CMoP (1970 ed.); NoAM

Their wings beat the floor. Angels in the House. Jerred Metz. VWA

Them, Crying. James Dickey. NowV

Them that's got shall have. God Bless the Child. Arthur Herzog, Jr. *and* Billie Holiday. WIF

Them wuz the days. Cumberland Gap Drifter. Big John Birkbeck. EC

Theme and Variations. Edna St. Vincent Millay. SBG

Theme for English B. Langston Hughes. ILP (1975 ed.); NoAM; NOBA; PoIA

Theme in Yellow. Carl Sandburg. LCL

Theme no poet gladly sung. Prudence. Emerson. OBAL

Theme One: The Variations. August Wilson. PoBA

Themes. Denis Glover. ATNZ

Themes for Country-Western Singers, *sel.* Ted Kooser. "That 'lil girl that Daddy loved." POL

Then. Walter de la Mare. RAE

Then. Gary Gildner. FiCP

Then. John Morgan. AMV–81

Then. Edwin Muir. CMoP (1970 ed.); MS; PoA

Then Achilles/ Before all the Danaans. The Funeral Games for Patroclus: Wrestling to a Draw. Homer, *tr. by* Ennis Rees. *Fr.* The Iliad, XXIII. LiSp

Then all became silent. White Bird. Matti Megged, *tr. by* Howard Schwartz. VWA

Then Almitra spoke again and said, "And what of Marriage, Master?" Kahlil Gibran. *Fr.* The Prophet. PPM

Then Almitra spoke, saying, We would ask now of Death. Kahlil Gibran. *Fr.* The Prophet. DL

Then and Now. Paul Laurence Dunbar. PBMP

Then and Now. Kath Walker. IHMS

Then call me traitor if you must. To Certain Critics. Countee Cullen. BPo

Then came one with two bulldogs at his tail. Cock Lorell's Boat. *Unknown.* TVS

Then cease fond satyres, quipping epigrammatists. A Prophecy of This Present Year 1600. John Weever. TVS

Then darkness Europe's face did overspread. Sir John Denham. *Fr.* The Progress of Learning. SCP–2

Then did he friendly leave. The Song of the Death of Mr. Thewlis. *Unknown.* SCP–2

Then drew near unto him all the publicans and sinners. Bible, *N.T.* St. Luke, XV. NAWM–1

Then find me some World Peace! In Answer to a Request to Write a Poem on World Peace. Elisavietta Ritchie. AATT

Then first he form'd th' immense and solid shield. Homer, *tr. by* Pope. *Fr.* The Iliad, XVIII. OBVE

Then fled, O brethren, the wicked juba. The Ballad of Nat Turner. Robert Hayden. BPo; VGW

Then fold up without pause. Mill Town. Genevieve Taggard. SPT

Then has a man less might than a beste. The Newly Born. *Unknown. Fr.* The Pricke of Conscience. OxBM

Then hate me when thou wilt; if ever, now. Sonnets, XC. Shakespeare. EBEV; NOBE

Then I came to the house of wood. The Incurable Home. John Haines. CNW

Then I said to the elegant ladies. Sappho, *tr. fr. Greek by* Willis Barnstone. BoWoP

Then is our charter, Pollexfen, quite lost? The Great Despair of the London Whigs. *Unknown.* APAS

Then it was dusk in Illinois, the small boy. First Song. Galway Kinnell. BiP; CTBA; NCSH

Then lay I lax. Circe. William Gibson. PoA

Then leave old regret. A Moral Poem. J. V. Cunningham. VGW

Then Lelex rose, an old experienc'd man. Ovid, *tr. by* Dryden. *Fr.* Metamorphoses, VIII. OBVE

Then let us boast of ancestors no more. Daniel Defoe. *Fr.* The True-born Englishman. OBSV

Then Margery Milk-Duck. John Skelton. *Fr.* The Tunning of Elinor Rumming. EBEV; OAEL–1

Then Milton rose up from the heavens of Albion ardorous! Blake. *Fr.* Milton. OAEL–2

Then of the antique flame the greater horn. Ulysses. Dante, *tr.*
   *by* Longfellow. *Fr.* Divina Commedia: Inferno. Epi

Then one of the twelve, called Judas Iscariot. Bible, *N.T.* St.
   Matthew, XXVI: 14–XXVIII. NAWM–1

Then out at Shellbrook, roun' by stile an' tree. Shellbrook
   [Dorset]. William Barnes. VLP

Then ran ther a route of ratones, as it were. Belling the Cat.
   William Langland. *Fr.* The Vision of Piers Plowman.
   OxBM

Then rising in his rage above the shores. Homer, *tr. by* Pope.
   *Fr.* The Iliad, XXI. OBVE

Then 'round the Bay of Mexico. Round the Bay of Mexico.
   *Unknown.* FSW

Then said that royall Pere in sober wise. Spenser. *Fr.* The
   Faerie Queene, I, 12. OAEL–1

Then sang Deborah and Barak. The Song of Deborah. Bible,
   *O.T. Fr.* Judges. BoWoP; PBWP

Then saw they how there hove a dusky bare. The Death of
   Arthur. Tennyson. *Fr.* Idylls of the King. PIM

Then saw they that the mighty Quest was won! Robert Stephen
   Hawker. *Fr.* The Quest of the Sangraal. VLP

Then see it! in distressing. The Last Turn. William Carlos
   Williams. NYP

Then sent the King Constantine. The Pound of Flesh.
   *Unknown. Fr.* Cursor Mundi. OxBM

Then sprang up first the golden age, which of itself maintained.
   Ovid, *tr. by* Arthur Golding. *Fr.* Metamorphoses, I.
   OAEL–1

Then Strip Lads, and to It. Sir Walter Scott. SPo

Then the air was perfect. And his descent. The Parachutist. Jon
   Anderson. AmPA; LiSp

Then the band of Geats, young and brave. To the Sea.
   *Unknown, tr. by* Burton Raffel. *Fr.* Beowulf. OBP

Then the Ermine. Marianne Moore. PoA

Then the knee of the wave. Reclining Figure. Donald Hall.
   ConAP

Then the long sunlight lying on the sea. The Insusceptibles.
   Adrienne Rich. ConAP; HeIP; InPK

Then the Lord answered Job out of the whirlewind, and sayd.
   Bible, *O.T.* Job, XXXVIII. OBVE

Then the Lord answered Job out of the whirlwind. The War
   Horse. Bible, *O.T. Fr.* Job, XXXIX. PH

Then the Skins Fall Apart. Dara Wier. TV

Then there is this civilising love of death, by which. Ignorance of
   Death. William Empson. CMoP (1970 ed.); NoAM

Then there was the guy. Free Enterprise. Charles Stetler. GP

Then they paraded Pompey's urn. Jenny Mastoraki, *tr. fr. Modern
   Greek by* Nikos Germanakos. BoWoP; PBWP

Then they took whole stones according to the law. Bible,
   Apocrypha. *Fr.* First Maccabees. OFD

Then this poor woman's blind. Oh Oh Blues. *Unknown.* BluL

Then let's go together. Thomas Otway. *Fr.* The Orphan;
   or, The Unhappy Marriage, IV, ii. SCP–2

Then up I rose, and make no more delay. Elizabeth Melvill, Lady
   Culross. *Fr.* A Godly Dream. WPE

Then was I cast from out my state. Frenzy. George Crabbe.
   *Fr.* Sir Eustace Grey. NOBE

Then we descended, as into a labyrinth. Fear. Aldo Camerino,
   *tr. by* Anita Barrows. VWA

Then what is the answer?—Not to be deluded by dreams. The
   Answer. Robinson Jeffers. CMoP (1970 ed.)

Thence forward by that painfull wa they pas. Spenser. *Fr.* The
   Faerie Queene, I, 10. OAEL–1

Theocritus. Oscar Wilde. NOBE

Theodore Roethke. Morton Paley. AMV–81

Theologia Germanica. David Malouf. CAAP

Theological Limerick. T. Lindsay. FaBoCo

Theology. Ted Hughes. NoAM

"Theon to his father Theon greetings. Another." To Theon from
   His Son Theon. C. A. Trypanis. NCSH

Theophila; or, Love's Sacrifice, *sels.*      Edward Benlowes.
   "Angels by one sin fell: so, man; how then," *fr.* Canto II.
   SCP–2

Cynthia. Moon
   "Might souls converse with souls by angel-way," *fr.* Canto I.
   SCP–2
   "Muse! twang the powerful harp and brush each string," *fr.*
   Canto III. SCP–2

Theophilus Thistledown. *Unknown.* CTV
   (Tongue-Twister.) BBL

Theoretikos. Oscar Wilde. VLP

Theoria in Early Morning. William R. Mitchell. AATT

Theory. Dorothy Parker. SBG

Theory of flight. Muriel Rukeyser. STP

Ther is no rose of swich vertu. The Rose That Bore Jesu.
   *Unknown.* OxBM

Ther mighte men the royal egle finde. Seynt Valentynes Day.
   Chaucer. *Fr.* The Parliament of Fowls. PB

Ther was also a Nonne, a Prioresse. *See* There was also a nun, a
   Prioress.

Therapeutist, The. Beth Bentley. AMV–80

Therapy. Patricia Ball. PMW

Therapy. Ken Poyner. AMV–81

There. Mary Elizabeth Coleridge. BoReV

There. William Harmon. AMV–80

There. Robert Mezey. TSWA

There/ is someone I can bear. W. S. Landor. Marianne Moore.
   OBAL; Psy

There ain't but three men who really can spend my dough. Three
   Men. *Unknown.* BluL

There Ain't No Bugs on Me. *Unknown.* FSW

There ain't no more cane on this Brazos. Ain't No More Cane on
   this Brazos. *Unknown.* FSW

There ain't nothing special about me. The Country Singer. Carl
   Rakosi. HeS

There all the golden codgers lay. News for the Delphic Oracle.
   W. B. Yeats. CMoP (1970 ed.); NoAM

There are/ two methods. In the Case of Lobsters. Petra von
   Morstein, *tr. by* Rosemarie Waldrop. BoWoP

There are a very few moments when you. Psalm. Avraham Ben-
   Yitzhak, *tr. by* A. C. Jacobs. VWA

There are aisles. The Lost Aisles. Herbert Scott. TC

There are also the dark exciting days of. The Dark Exciting
   Days. Karl Shapiro. CoPAm

There Are Bad Times Just around the Corner. Noel Coward.
   NOBL

There are blows in life so violent—I can't answer! The Black
   Riders. Cesar Vallejo, *tr. by* Robert Bly. EC

There are caverns/ under our feet. Shirley Kaufman. BoWoP

There are cemeteries that are lonely. Nothing but Death. Pablo
   Neruda, *tr. by* Robert Bly. EAS

There are days to which God. The Days. Paul Blocklyn.
   AMV–80

There are days when I think the future sets. The Mountains.
   W. S. Merwin. UsP

There are dealers in pictures named Agnew. Dante Gabriel
   Rossetti. FaBoEE

There Are Delicacies. Earle Birney. MPA

There are depths in a household. The Whale in the Blue Washing
   Machine. John Haines. CNW

There are different ways of dying without. After the Revolution.
   Marilyn Hacker. AmPA

"There are dreams that need rest." Okay. Sharon Scott. JB

There are 86,400 seconds in every 24 hours.  A Desperate Measure.  Nigel Dennis.  WIF

There are fairies at the bottom of our garden!  Fairies.  Rose Fyleman.  OxBChV

There are fish that we never quite catch swimming.  The Final Solstice.  Robert Adamson.  CAAP

There are flowers of Zait in the garden.  Ezra Pound *and* Noel Stock, *fr. Egyptian hieroglyphics.*  BoWoP; PBWP

There are four men mowing down by the Isar.  A Youth Mowing.  D. H. Lawrence.  NoAM

There are four verses to put down.  Ap Huw's Testament.  R. S. Thomas.  BuTh

There are half-naked men who stand.  The Glass Eaters.  George Jonas.  NeAC

There are (I scarce can think it, but am told.)  The First Satire of the Second Book of Horace.  Pope.  OAEL-1; OBSV; PPP

There are in our existence spots of time.  Wordsworth.  *Fr.* The Prelude, XII.  PoIA

There are in paradise.  The Shepherd Who Stayed.  Theodosia Garrison.  PChr

There Are in Such Moments.  David I. Silverstein.  AMV-80

There Are Lime Trees in Leaf on the Promenade.  Tom Raworth.  TwMBP

There are limits to how long we live.  All That Glitters.  Allan Kornblum.  AcAn

There are long days and short ones to be told.  About Long Days.  Anthony Ostroff.  MPA

There are lots of places to go.  White Collar Ballad.  Weldon Kees.  AnMo

There are many cumbersone ways to kill a man.  Five Ways to Kill a Man.  Edwin Brock.  DL; IPWM; SFF; TPo; TSWA

There are many dead in the brutish desert, who lie uneasy.  First Elegy, End of a Campaign.  Hamish Henderson.  *Fr.* Elegies for the Dead in Cyrenaica.  MS

There are many diseases.  Scorflufus.  Spike Milligan.  OSF

There are many like him here, without epitaph, without a mound.  The Grave.  Shaul Tchernichovsky, *tr. by* Robet Mezey *and* Shula Starkman.  VWA

There are many monsters that a glassen surface.  The Octopus.  James Merrill.  GP

There Are Many Things That Please Me.  Thomas Lux.  AAN

There are many Washingtons.  Which Washington?  Eve Merriam.  CC

There are many ways to die.  History among the Rocks.  Robert Penn Warren.  GOA

There are many who think of Quintia in terms of beauty.  Catullus, *tr. fr. Latin by* Horace Gregory.  NAWM-1

There are men in the village of Erith.  Erith, on the Thames.  *Unknown.*  GBP

There are more stars than people.  The Astrologer Argues Your Death.  Charles deGravelles.  AMV-81

There are no angels yet.  Gabriel.  Adrienne Rich.  Psy; VGW

There are no comrade roses at my window.  Listening Back.  Ina Coolbrith.  WPW

There are no cracks in the wall.  Charlie 12.  Michael Small.  DNGG

There are no crosses.  A Death in the Desert.  Charles Tomlinson.  FF; TwMBP

There are no dry bones.  The Bones of My Father.  Etheridge Knight.  UsP

There are no nightmares now. Only when memory settles.  Seravezza.  Hoyt W. Fuller.  PoBA

There are no nymphs on deserts.  A Tour of the Southwest.  Edward Lueders.  MPA

There are no roads but the frost.  Old Age Compensation.  James Wright.  NNaP

There are no rules for so much sadness.  "Woman with Tongue in Cheek."  Daniela Gioseffi.  RiTi

There are no stars to-night.  My Grandmother's Love Letters.  Hart Crane.  CMoP (1970 ed.); NoAM; NOBA; PSN; UsP

There are no trees under the earth.  Eurydice.  Phyllis Thompson.  PCho

There are only two things now.  New Year's Eve.  D. H. Lawrence.  BoLoP

There are people go to Carmel.  At Carmel.  Mary Austin.  WPW

There are people, I know, to be found.  Drinking Song.  James Kenneth Stephen.  NOBL

There are, perhaps, whom passion gives a grace.  The Aged Lover Discourses in the Flat Style.  J. V. Cunningham.  NoAM; PPoD

There are pines that are tall enough.  An Elegy Is Preparing Itself.  Donald Justice.  HoPM (1975 ed.)

There are places I'll remember all my life.  In My Life.  John Lennon *and* Paul McCartney.  GrRo

There are portraits and still-lifes.  Paring the Apple.  Charles Tomlinson.  CMoP (1970 ed.); OxBTC; TwMBP

There Are Roughly Zones.  Robert Frost.  CMoP (1970 ed.); PPP

There are seeds within the tide.  City.  Joseph Bruchac.  CDW

There are several attitudes towards Christmas.  The Cultivation of Christmas Trees.  T. S. Eliot.  OFD

There are so many lies in nature.  Degas.  Paul Monette.  AmPA

There are so many roots to the tree of anger.  Who Said It Was Simple.  Audre Lorde.  WBN

There are some/ secrets.  July 31.  Norman Jordan.  PoBA

There are some birds in these valleys.  The Decoys.  W. H. Auden.  CMoP (1970 ed.)

There are some heights in Wessex, shaped as if by a kindly hand.  Wessex Heights.  Thomas Hardy.  CMoP (1970 ed.); IPWM; OAEL-2

There are some people i know.  Sorcery.  Jessica Tarahata Hagedorn.  NW

There are some people who are very resourceful.  Hearts of Gold.  Ogden Nash.  AKE

There are some qualities—some incorporate things.  Sonnet—Silence.  Poe.  NOBA; PiAm

There are some things in life.  *Unknown.*  SFF

There are some things which, left unsaid, are true.  Paradox.  Benjamin K. Bennett.  POL

There are songs too wide for sound. There are quiet.  Answerers.  William Stafford.  PCho

There are stone breakers in straw hats.  About Infinity: A Self-Portrait.  Norman Dubie.  FoP

There are strange hells within the minds war made.  Strange Hells.  Ivor Gurney.  OxBTC

There are the Alps. What is there to say about them?  On the Fly-Leaf of Pound's Cantos.  Basil Bunting.  FaBoTw (1975 ed.); NoAM; OxBTC

There are these small cliffs.  The Singular Self.  Charles Bukowski.  CoPAm

There are things/ you could have said.  The Final Fall.  Alexandre L. Amprimoz.  AMV-81

There are things to be said. No doubt.  Cid Corman.  VGW

There are those.  I've Heard Them Talk: For My Main Man.  Ralph Storey.  SES

There are those to whom place is unimportant.  The Rose.  Theodore Roethke.  BiP; InPS; NOBA; PiAm; PPoe

There are three names.  National Security.  Archibald MacLeish.  GOA

There are three valleys where the warm sun lingers.  The Long Harbour.  Mary Ursula Bethell.  ATNZ

There are three Cezannes. Three Cezannes. George Whipple. AMV-80

There are times when. May Sarton. *Fr.* The Invocation to Kali. RiTi

There are, to whom I seem excessive sour. Satire, II, 1. Horace, *tr. by* Ben Jonson. TVS

There are too many waterfalls here. Questions of Travel. Elizabeth Bishop. NOBA

There are truths you Americans need to be told. American Literature. James Russell Lowell. *Fr.* A Fable for Critics. AmVN; OBSV

There are twelve months in all the year. How Robin Hood Rescued the Widow's Sons. *Unknown.* PoTa

There are two bends in the road, and an unexpected dip. Pont y Caniedydd. Alun Llywelyn-Williams, *tr. by* Joseph P. Clancy. OBW

There are two different kinds, I believe, of human attraction. Arthur Hugh Clough. *Fr.* Amours de Voyage, II, xi. OBP

There are two kinds of rat. The Migratory Rats. Heine, *tr. by* Ernst Feise. NAWM-2

There are two facing peacocks. Chenille. James Dickey. NoAM

There are two landscapes. A July Storm: Johnson, Nemaha County, Nebraska. Steve Hahn. AMV-81

There are two Mays. Emily Dickinson. NOBA

There are two miseries in human life. Walter Savage Landor. FaBoEE

There are vast realms of consciousness still undreamed of. Terra Incognita. D. H. Lawrence. OBP

There are voices of pain. Lost in a Norther. Hamlin Garland. BPAW

There are voices, voices. Light's dying. Birds have quit. John Berryman. *Fr.* Dream Songs. CAPP

There are wolves in the next room waiting. The Wolves. Allen Tate. ILP (1975 ed.); NoAM; NOBA; PiAm; PoA

There are women of many descriptions. The Rebel Girl. Joe Hill. FSW

There are words like freedom. Refugee in America [*or* Words like Freedom]. Langston Hughes. BPo; CC; GOA

There are words that can only be said on paper. Words. Robert Finch. PoA

There arent. Untitled Requiem for Tomorrow. Conyus. PoBA

There at the top of the world. Harlem in January. Julia Fields. CNA

There be four things which are little upon the earth. Bible, *O.T.* Proverbs, XXX: 24-25. CTV

There be none of Beauty's daughters. Stanzas for Music. Byron. ILP (1975 ed.); OAEL-2; PoPle

There be three badgers on a mossy stone. The Three Badgers. "Lewis Carroll." FaBoNo

There beyond Hay Creek turn at. Finding Sky Ranch. William Stafford. CNW

There blows a cold wind today, today. To Keep the Cold Wind Away. *Unknown.* OxBM

There cam' seven Egyptians on a day. The Gypsy Countess. *Unknown.* PoPle

There came a day at summer's full. Emily Dickinson. LoAs; NoAM; NOBA; PiAm; TT

There came a ghost to Margret's door. Sweet Williams's Ghost. *Unknown.* AIW

There came a wind like a bugle. Emily Dickinson. CMoP (1970 ed.); ILP (1975 ed.); NoAM; NOBA

There came an image in Life's retinue. Death-in-Love. Dante Gabriel Rossetti. The House of Life, XLVIII. VLP

There came from Normandy an old. The Two Lovers. Marie de France, *tr. by* Patricia Terry. BoWoP

There came three men from out of the west. Sir John Barleycorn. *Unknown.* FaBoBa

There came two gentlemen. The Cock. Ewa Lipska, *tr. by* Peter Jay *and* Geri Lipschultz. VWA

There came unto me yesterday. A Bob-tailed Flush. John R. Painter. BPAW

There came you wishing me. José Garcia Villa, *tr. fr. Spanish by* Ben F. Carruthers. LoAs

There can be no end where. Dog Dream. Ron Welburn. NW

There can be no explanation. His Side/ Her Side. Jeffrey Skinner. AMV-81

There can be no power in a square. Lines. Brian Swann. AMV-81

There can be no songs for dead children. Kindertotenlieder. Michael Longley. CIP

There chanced to be a pedlar bold. The Bold Pedlar and Robin Hood. *Unknown.* AIW

There Charon stands, who rules the dreary coast. Virgil, *tr. by* Dryden. *Fr.* The Aeneid, VI. OBVE

There comes a time when everything is laced. The Imagination of Necessity. Andrei Codrescu. EAS

There comes Emerson first, whose rich words, every one. Emerson. James Russell Lowell. *Fr.* A Fable for Critics. AmVN; NOBA; PAIC; TAP

There comes Poe, with his raven, like Barnaby Rudge. Poe and Longfellow [*or* Poe]. James Russell Lowell. *Fr.* A Fable for Critics. AmVN; NOBA; TAP

There died a myriad. Ezra Pound. *Fr.* Hugh Selwyn Mauberley. FF; IP; NIL; NOBE; PiAm; TCP

There dwelt a man in fair Westmoreland. Johnie Armstrong. *Unknown.* BiP; FaBoBa; HoPM (1975 ed.)

There dwelt a miller hale and bold. The Miller of Dee. *Unknown.* GBP

There dwelt in a cave, and winding I thought lower. Following. William Stafford. BCr

There exists no proof as. E. C. Bentley. *Fr.* Clerihews. NOBL

There Exists the Eternal Fact of Conflict. Stephen Crane. TT

There Goes a Girl Walking. Dodie Meeks. AMV-81

There Gowans Are Gay. *Unknown.* GBP

There grew two olives, closest of the grove. Homer, *tr. by* Pope. *Fr.* The Odyssey, V. OBVE

There grows no rootless flower. The First Reader. Winfield Townley Scott. PoA

There had been portents. The Black Death. Philip Dacey. GP

There had been years of passion—scorching, cold. "And There Was a Great Calm." Thomas Hardy. CMoP (1970 ed.); OAEL-2

There has been. To W. C. W. M. D. Alfred Kreymborg. PoA

There has been a light snow. In a Train. Robert Bly. CAPP; POL

There has been no change. Autumn. Princess Shikishi, *tr. by* Hiroaki Sato. PBWP

There Has to Be a Jail for Ladies. Thomas Merton. VGW

There have been days. Wedding Poem. Michael Waters. AAN

There have been times when I well might have passed and the ending have come. Thomas Hardy. In Tenebris, III. OAEL-2

There he is crawling stomach and elbows. The Mad Farmer Stands Up in Kentucky for What He Thinks Is Right. James Baker Hall. TAT

"There he is," yells Father. Yellow Cat. Gregory Harrison. FPB

There he moved, cropping the grass at the purple canyon's lip. The Horse Thief. William Rose Benét. BPAW

There he stands. see? Two Jazz Poems. Carl Wendell Hines, Jr. AmNP (1974 ed.)

There he was—having spent. "Yes, But. . ." Theodore Weiss. TAP

There I could never be a boy. Poem. Frank O'Hara. NNaP

There, in that other world, what waits for me? There. Mary Elizabeth Coleridge. BoReV

There in the bracken was the ominous spoor mark. The Tantanoola Tiger. Max Harris. GAS

There, in the corner, staring at his drink. Docker. Seamus Heaney. HeHu; NoAM

There in the flower garden. *Unknown, tr. fr. Spanish by* Willis Barnstone. BoWoP

There in the hard light. An Irish Lake. W. R. Rodgers. BIrV

There, in the market, with Mrs. Peters. Journal of the Storm. Greg Kuzma. AmPA

There Is. Louis Simpson. ConAP

There is/ A welcome at the door to which no one comes? Angel Surrounded by Paysans. Wallace Stevens. PPP; TT

There is a bale of hay. Beside the Road. Ken Belford. NeAC

There is a balm in Gilead, to make the wounded whole. Balm in Gilead. *Unknown.* FSW

There is a big artist named Val. Dante Gabriel Rossetti. FaBoEE

There is a bird in the poplars! Metric Figure. William Carlos Williams. AKE

There is a bird that hangs head-down and cries. Thirst. Genevieve Taggard. WPW

There is a bird who, by his coat. The Jackdaw. William Cowper. PB

There is a black bird with eyes. Two Gardens. Henry Graham. UsP

There is a blue sky. A Song. Edward Dorn. ConAP

There is a blue star, Janet. Baby Toes. Carl Sandburg. LCL

There Is a Box. Uri Zvi Greenberg, *tr. fr. Hebrew by* Robert Mezey *and* Ben Zion Gold. VWA

There is a careful look. Existence. Sheila Moon. AMV-80

There is a change—and I am poor. A Complaint. Wordsworth. NOBE

There is a charm I can't explain. The Big Sunflower. Bobby Newcomb. BLSo

There is a charm in footing slow across a silent plain. Lines Written in the Highlands after a Visit to Burns's Country. Keats. MBPR

There is a cheater by profession. Cheating Droone. "T. M." *Fr.* Micro-Cynicon. TVS

There is a child unborn. The Child Unborn. Humbert Wolfe. BuTh

There is a conflict of jurisdictions here. Intersection. Florence Dolgorukov. AMV-80

There is a cool river. Detroit. Donald Hall. ANTL

There is a cop who is both prowler and father. Rape. Adrienne Rich. GP; TT

There is a creator named God. On the Painter Val Prinsep. Dante Gabriel Rossetti. FaBoEE

There is a crying in the world. End of the World. Else Lasker-Schüler, *tr. by* Willis Barnstone *and* Michael Gillespie. BoWoP

There is a dale in Ida, lovelier. *See* There lies a vale in Ida, lovelier.

There is a dark planet striking against us. Invisible. The Dark Planet. John Heath-Stubbs. OAEL-2

There is a door. The Door. Lewis Turco. CoPAm

There is a door in these hands that has been. Ode. James Tipton. TC

There is a dream of eternal warmth. Overcoats. Larry Kramer. AMV-80

There is a drear and lonely tract of hell. Supremacy. E. A. Robinson. NoAM

There is a fever of the spirit. Song by Mr. Cypress. Thomas Love Peacock. *Fr.* Nightmare Abbey. OAEL-2

There is a fine stuffed chavender. A False Gallop of Analogies. Warham St. Leger. FaBoCo

There is a fish so large. Night Fishing. Michael Waters. AAN

There is a flower blossoming out of season. Flower Ensnarer of Psalms. Rossana Ombres, *tr. by* I. L. Salomon. BoWoP

There is a flower, the lesser celandine. The Small Celandine. Wordsworth. MBPR

There is a flower the stiffening vein blood retreats. Elegy for Michael Dransfield. Rodney Hall. FPA

There is a flower within my heart. Daisy Bell; or, A Bicycle Built for Two. Harry Dacre. BLSo; FSN; FSW

There is a flowr sprung of a tree. The Fairest Flower. John Audelay. OxBM

There is a fountain fill'd with blood. Praise for the Fountain Opened. William Cowper. PIM

There is a frame around my. Judith Johnson Sherwin. *Fr.* The Frame. OSP

There Is a Garden in Her Face. Thomas Campion. AAS; BiP; CABA (1972 ed.); HeIP; ILP (1975 ed.); InPK; NIL; OAEL-1, *with music*
(Cherry-ripe.) BoLoP; NOBE; PPoe

There is a girl you like so you tell her. Courtship. Mark Strand. GP

There is a great amount of poetry in unconscious/ fastidiousness. Critics and Connoisseurs. Marianne Moore. CMoP (1970 ed.); NoAM; NOBA; PSN

There is a great river this side of Stygia. The River of Rivers in Connecticut. Wallace Stevens. HAP; NOBA; VGW

There Is a Green Hill. Cecil Frances Alexander. OxBChV

There is a green spell stolen from Birmingham. A Death at Winson Green. Francis Webb. GAS; MAuV

There is a halo around the moon. Debt. *Gond Oral Tradition, tr. by* V. Elwin *and* S. Hivale. WTO

There is a hawk that is picking the birds out of our sky. Shiva. Robinson Jeffers. NoAM; NOBA

There is a heigh-ho in these glowing coals. Heigh-ho on a Winter Afternoon. Donald Davie. OxBTC

There Is a High Place, *with music*. Edwin Markham. AH

There is a house in New Orleans. The House of the Rising Sun. *Unknown.* FSW

There is a Hungarian/ word for everything. Poem in Hungarian. Beth Joselow. PoUp

There is a joyful night in which we lose. When the Dumb Speak. Robert Bly. CAPP; NoAM; NOBA

There is a kind of lace laid over the city, a lightness. The Serious Merriment of Women. Patricia Goedicke. TAP

There is a knocking in the skull. Listen. Ogden Nash. ILP (1975 ed.)

There Is a Lady Sweet and Kind. *Unknown, at. to* Thomas Ford. EBEV; GBL; HeIP; LoAs, *abr.*
(Lady Sweet and Kind, A.) PCOP
(Passing By, *abr.*) NOBE

There Is a Land Mine Eye Hath Seen, *with music*. Gurdon Robins. AH

There is a land of pure delight. The Heavenly Canaan. Isaac Watts. BoReV; PIM

There is a languor of the life. Emily Dickinson. BoWoP

There is a light in the snow. The Revenant. Peter Cooley. HeS

There is a litany. Compline. Debora Greger. AMV-81

There is a little gentleman. The Bee. *Unknown.* ECBV

There is a little hollow. Moon of the Springing Grass. Nellie Burget Miller. WPW

There Is a Little House. Sheila Heldenbrand. AcAn

There is a little lightning in his eyes. Of Robert Frost. Gwendolyn Brooks. NoAM; NOBA

There is a little lonely grave. The Unknown Grave. Letitia Elizabeth Landon. VLP

There is a loud night and the collective forces. The Collective Forces. Deirdra Baldwin. PoUp

There is a magic melting pot. The Melting Pot. Dudley Randall. BPo

There is a man walking. The People. Joy Harjo. SA

There is a meadow. Last Light. Robert Kelly. VGW

There is a memory stays upon old ships. Old Ships. David Morton. CTV

There is a middleaged man, Tim Flanagan. The Middleaged Man. Louis Simpson. NNaP

There is a myth, a tale men tell. The Pearl. Hans Christian Andersen, *tr. by* Charles Wharton Stork. LoAs

There is a pain—so utter. Emily Dickinson. BoWoP; NOBA

There is a panther caged within my breast. The Black Panther. John Hall Wheelock. FF

There is a party tonight. The Party at the Contessa's House. Brian Robertson. AMV-80

There is a place I know. I Hope I Never Go There. Cash Terrell. DNGG

There is a place in Montana where the grass stands up two feet. Rosebud. Jon Anderson. CAAP

There is a place where contrarieties are equally true. The Vision of Beulah. Blake. *Fr.* Milton, II. OAEL-2

There is a place where love begins and a place. Explanations of Love. Carl Sandburg. SFF

There is a pleasure in the pathless woods. Byron. *Fr.* Childe Harold's Pilgrimage, IV. LFH

There is a poor sneak called Rossetti. On Himself. Dante Gabriel Rossetti. FaBoEE

There is a quality of pain. A Quality of Pain. Barbara D. Holender. TVo

There is a river clear and fair. Fragment in Imitation of Wordsworth. Catherine Fanshawe. FaBoNo

There is a road that turning always. The Road. Edwin Muir. CMoP (1970 ed.)

There is a secret room. The Same Gesture. John Montague. BIrV; IPM

There is a selfhood in my nothingness. Al-Hallaj, *tr. fr. Persian.* ILwL

There is a silence where hath been no sound. Silence. Thomas Hood. EBEV; NOBE

There is a singer everyone has heard. The Oven Bird. Robert Frost. HeIP; NoAM; NOBA; PiAm; PoIA; PPP; TAP; TT; VoPo

There is a smile of love. The Smile. Blake. MBPR

There is a soldier on the battlefield. *Unknown, tr. fr. Chinese by* Geoffrey Waters. BoWoP

There is a song to be sung at night. The Middle of the Night. Karla Kuskin. IWK

There is a space for winter here. Heron's Bay. Martin Galvin. AMV-81

There is a spell, for instance. Hilda Doolittle ("H. D."). *Fr.* The Walls Do Not Fall. NoAM

There is a spot, 'mid barren hills. Emily Brontë. *Fr.* A Little While. PES

There is a story in my book. Witchcraft. Siddie Joe Johnson. ECBV

There is a stream, I name not its name. Arthur Hugh Clough. *Fr.* The Bothie of Tober-na-Vuolich. VLP

There is a stream which rises. Joseph Bruchac. CDW

There is a supreme God in the ethnological section. Homage to the British Museum. William Empson. CMoP (1970 ed.)

There is a tall long-sided dame. Samuel Butler. *Fr.* Hudibras, II, 1. OBSV

There Is a Tavern in the Town. *Unknown, at. to* William H. Hills. BLSH, *with music;* BLSo, *with music;* FSW; PSoN, *with music,* (Tavern in the Town.) GSB, *with music*

There is a thorn; it looks so old. The Thorn. Wordsworth. MBPR

There is a through-otherness about Armagh. Armagh. W. R. Rodgers. NoAM; PFIr

There Is a Tide. Sydney Goodsir Smith. SLP

There is a time of notation. Lines on the Back of a Leary Bailfund Card. Mary Norbert Körte. MIT

There is a tiny wind in our room. Loving. Shirley Kaufman. VWA

There is a tree, by day. Tenebris. Angelina Weld Grimké. PoBA

There is a tree native in Turkestan. Note on Local Flora. William Empson. PSN

There is a vanishing act performed in certain sorts of writing. Disappearances. Sean Lucy. IPM

There is a void, outside of existence, which if entered into. Blake. *Fr.* Jerusalem. MBPR

There is a wailing baby under every stone. Poem. Norman MacCaig. EAS

There is a war going on. Tony Connor. Twelve Secret Poems, 3. UsP

There is a white mare that my love keeps. Alex Comfort. LoAs

There is a wind where the rose was. Autumn. Walter de la Mare. OxBTC

There is a window stuffed with hay. The Hay Hotel. Oliver St. John Gogarty. BIrV

There is a wolf in me . . . fangs pointed for tearing gashes. Wilderness. Carl Sandburg. PiAm

There is a woman climbing a glass hill. Two Women. Naomi Replansky. NMM

There is a woman in a white or blue. An American Gothic. Dick Allen. FAF

There is a woman in our town. William Carlos Williams. *Fr.* Paterson. CMoP (1970 ed.)

There is a woman running. The Joining. Gerda Norvig. VWA

There is a word at heart for the next of death. Written in Exile. Kathleen Raine. WPE

There is a world of pain beyond the heart. Sonnet for a Loved One. Dorothy Joslin. AMV-80

There is a yew tree, pride of Lorton Vale. Yew Trees. Wordsworth. CABA (1972 ed.); UnPo (1976 ed.)

There is a young lady, whose nose. Edward Lear. OxBChV

There is a young Muslim Chinese. Taunt. *Malay Oral Tradition, tr. by* R. J. Wilkinson *and* R. O. Windstedt. WTO

There is always a journey. Water. Judith McPheron. AMV-81

There is an evening coming in. Going. Philip Larkin. CMoP (1970 ed.); NowV; PSN

There Is an Hour of Peaceful Rest, *with music.* William B. Tappan. AH

There is an old cook house not far away. Old Soldiers Never Die. *Unknown.* FSW

There is an old he-wolf named Gambart. Dante Gabriel Rossetti. FaBoEE

There is another kind of sleep. Hematite Lake. James Galvin. AMV-80

There is another world above this one. Gary Snyder. *Fr.* Through the Smoke Hole. PoA

There is Bryant, as quiet, as cool, and as dignified. Bryant. James Russell Lowell. *Fr.* A Fable for Critics. AmVN; NOBA; TAP

There is death enough in Europe without these. Dead Ponies. Brenda Chamberlain. OBW; WPE

There is delight in singing, though none hear. To Robert Browning. Walter Savage Landor. ILP (1975 ed.)

There is drink fermented. Chimedin Jigmed, *tr. by* C. R. Bawden. *Fr.* A Satirical Poem about Drink. WTO

There is fear in/ Turning the mind away. The Sun and the Moon and Fear of Loneliness. *Tr. fr.* Eskimo. WTO

There is, finally, a design of sorts. Room. Glenn John Kim. PHC

There is fire in the lower hold. Fire Down Below. *Unknown.* FSW

There Is Good News. Josephine Jacobsen. AMV-80

There Is Gray in My Eyebrows. Karl Shapiro. CoPAm

There is grey in your hair. The Aged Woman to Her Sons. Babette Deutsch. AMV-81

There is grey in your hair. Broken Dreams. W. B. Yeats. PSN

There is Hawthorne, with genius so shrinking and rare. Hawthorne. James Russell Lowell. *Fr.* A Fable for Critics. NOBA; TAP

There is health in thy gray wing. To a Marsh Hawk in Spring. Henry David Thoreau. PB

There is joy in/ Feeling the warmth. Eskimo Chant. *Unknown, tr. by* Knud Rasmussen. RFM

There is little in afternoon tea. On Drawing-Room Amenities. Gelett Burgess. FaBoNo

There is Lowell, who's striving Parnassus to climb. Lowell. James Russell Lowell. *Fr.* A Fable for Critics. AmVN; NOBA; TAP

There is more than one rain. Rain. Peter Sears. AMV-80

There is more to this meadow under the mountains. Meadow Grass. Michael Mott. AMV-80

There is much to be said. An Education in Tongues. Brian Swann. AAN

There is much work to be done before we leave. Moving Out. Joyce Carol Oates. AMV-81

There is naught for thee by thy haste to gain. The Created. Jones Very. AmVN; PiAm

There is no answer. We do here what we will. The Unsurpers. Edwin Muir. CMoP (1970 ed.)

There is no chance, no destiny, no fate. Will. Ella Wheeler Wilcox. PPM

There is no form but shape! Rant Block. Michael McClure. EAS

There is no frigate like a book. Emily Dickinson. ECBV; SoSe; TAP; WIF

There is no God, as I was taught in youth. John Masefield. CMoP (1970 ed.)

"There is no God," the foolish saith. The Cry of the Human. Elizabeth Barrett Browning. PIM

"There is no God," the wicked saith. Arthur Hugh Clough. *Fr.* Dipsychus, Pt. I, sc. v. NOBE; VPC

There is no happy life. Love's Matrimony. William Cavendish, Duke of Newcastle. SCP-2

There is no harmony in victory. Cromwell. Paul Mills. MIS

There is no language of the natural. Twin Sister. Jim Long. PHC

There Is No Light. Lindiwe Mabuza. SES

There is no limit to the number of times. From Father to Son. Emyr Humphreys. OBW

There is no loveliness in death. The Layer-out. S. L. Henderson Smith. PMW

There is no more good water. No More Good Water. *Unknown.* BluL

There Is No Name So Sweet on Earth, *with music.* George Washington Bethune. AH

There is no need of any spring to come. No Spring. Alice Corbin. WPW

There is no one here. Matisse: "The Red Studio." W. D. Snodgrass. WIF

There Is No Place. Aleksander Wat, *tr. fr. Polish by* Isaac Komem. VWA

"There is no place to turn," she said. The Sensualists. Theodore Roethke. CNW

There is no rest for her, and sleep has left her bed. *Gond Oral Tradition, tr. by* V. Elwin *and* S. Hivale. WTO

There is no Silence in the Earth—so silent. Emily Dickinson. FaBoEE

There is no sky today. Echoes of birds. Counterparts. Stephen Dobyns. PoA

There is no sound under the frost. Frost round the House. Anne B. Murray. MS

There is no surrealist blood. The Blood Supply in New York City Is Low. Terry Stokes. NYP

There Is No Time. Elaine H. Jennings. NPW

There is no time. XXth Century. Robert Hillyer. TH

There is no weapon like a woman's weeping. The Death of Sappho. Nell Altizer. PHC

There is not in my mind one sullen fate. Richard Lovelace. *Fr.* On Sannazar's Being Honoured. SCP-2

There is not much about the hamster. The Hamster. Ogden Nash. ILP (1975 ed.)

There Is Nothin' like a Dame. Oscar Hammerstein II. OBAL

There is nothing at all pretty about death. Esthetique du Machiavel. George Starbuck. PAIC

There Is Nothing New in New York. Miguel Piñero. NYP

There is nothing new in what is said. Late Sewing. Hazel Hall. WPW

There is nothing now. To learn. The Fortress. Louise Glück. NVAP

There is nothing to complain of now. Christmas Poem. David Hilton. AcAn

There is now not a single. Winter Scene. A. R. Ammons. WeW

There is one animal of merit. The Ferret. Lord Alfred Douglas. BBL

There is one grief worse than any other. Daughter. Ellen Bryant Voigt. AMV-80

There is one, never seen, behind that window. Michael Smith. IPM

There is one story and one story only. To Juan at the Winter Solstice. Robert Graves. CMoP (1970 ed.); EBEV; NoAM; OAEL-2; OBP

There is one sure way. The Fourth Option. Henry Rasof. AMV-80

There is one that has a head without an eye. A Riddle. Christina Rossetti. OxBChV

There is one who sits in his room. The Ancestors. Anita Barrows. VWA

There Is Only One of Everything. Margaret Atwood. MMD

There is pleasure in the wet, wet clay. The Lie. Kipling. NOBL

There Is Power. Joe Hill. FSW

There is red/ on the clown-lady's lips. Toulouse Lautrec. Astrid Tollefsen, *tr. by* Nadia Christensen. PBWP

There is so much good in the worst of us. Good and Bad. Edward Wallis Hoch. CTV

There is so much potential. Wheels. Vicki Viidikas. CAAP

There is some beauty in sorrow. Placing a $2 Bet for a Man Who Will Never Go to the Horse Races Any More. Diane Wakoski. UnPo (1976 ed.)

There is some demon turning me into an old man. The Banjo. Robert Winner. FF

There is some great sensitivity I want to rip. Nightmares: Part Three. Lynn Moskowitz. AMV-81

There is some that like the city. Ridin'. Charles Badger Clark, Jr. BPAW

There Is Something. Deborah Pope. AMV-81

There is something about a Martini. A Drink with Something in It. Ogden Nash. PPM

There is something between us. Breasts. Donald Hall. OBAL

There is something of every good-bye in this. There Is Something. Deborah Pope. AMV-81

There is something suspicious about the spring. The Green Beginning. Warren Slesinger. HeS

There is sorrow enough in the natural way. The Power of the Dog. Kipling. BoAnP; GDP

There is speed and stress and richness here for the eye. Richness. Arthur J. Bull. HeHu

There is sweet music here that softer falls. Song of the Lotos-Eaters. Tennyson. Fr. The Lotos-Eaters. HeIP; NOBE

There is the moon, there is the sun. The Universe. Mary Britton Miller. CTV

There is the prayer of the father. The Prayers. Howard Schwartz. VWA

There is the star bloom of the moss. Forest. Jean Garrigue. NOBA

There is this cave. The Jewel. James Wright. CAPP; FoP; ILP (1975 ed.); OSP

There is unknown dust that is near us. Surprised by Evening. Robert Bly. CAPP; VGW

There is Whittier, whose swelling and vehement heart. Whittier. James Russell Lowell. Fr. A Fable for Critics. AmVN; NOBA

There is your brain. The Resident Stranger. Harley Elliott. HeS

There isn't much a man can do. The Jellyfish. William Pitt Root. BoAnP; NVAP

There it was, word for word. The Poem That Took the Place of a Mountain. Wallace Stevens. PiAm

There lies a somnolent lake. In the Past. Trumbull Stickney. NOBA

There lies a vale [or There is a dale] in Ida, lovelier. Oenone. Tennyson. VLP

There livd a man in yonder glen. Get Up and Bar the Door. Unknown. PAIC

There liv'd, as authors tell, in days of yore. The Nun's Priest's Tale. Chaucer, mod. version by Dryden. Fr. The Canterbury Tales. OBVE

There lived a fat old lady, in London she did dwell. The Old Lady of London. Unknown. AmFP

There Lived a King. W. S. Gilbert. Fr. The Gondoliers. PoPle; PoTa

There lived a lady, a lady gay. The Wife of Usher's Well. Unknown. AIW

There lived a Puddy in a well. The Puddy and the Mouse. Unknown. GBP

There lived a sage in days of yore. A Tragic Story. Adelbert von Chamisso, tr. by Thackeray. CTV; ECBV; PCOP

There lived a small hermaphrodite beside the silver Brent. The Waif. Walter de la Mare. FaBoNo

There lived a wife at Usher's well. The Wife of Usher's Well. Unknown. AIW; EBEV; Epi; FaBoBa; ILP (1975 ed.); NOBE; OAEL-1; PeBB; SoSe

There Lived among the Untrodden Ways. Hartley Coleridge. SpRo

There lived an old lord by the northern sea. The Two Sisters. Unknown. AIW

There lived an old man in the kingdom of Tess. The New Vestments. Edward Lear. RAE

There lived an old woman at Lynn. Unknown. OxBChV

There may be a basement to the Atlantic. Somebody's Gone. Charles Henri Ford. EAS

There may be a moment, just before the face. Living/Dying. Peter Steele. GAS

There may be some way back. A Girl at the Center of Her Life. Joyce Carol Oates. CoPAm

There must be something that links them all. The Obsession. Rosy Liggett. AMV-80

There,—my blessing with you! Shakespeare. Fr. Hamlet, I, iii. PPM

There, my lad, lie the Articles. Scene from a Play, Acted at Oxford, Called "Matriculation." Thomas Moore. OBSV

There never yet was honest man. Loving and Beloved. Sir John Suckling. CaPo

There never yet was woman made. Woman's Constancy. Sir John Suckling. CaPo

There now, where the first crumb. Solitude. Charles Simic. GP

There, on the Darkened Deathbed. John Masefield. See Sonnet: "There, on the darkened deathbed, dies the brain."

There on the sea sails wandered. The Names of Georgian Women. Bella Akhmadulina, tr. by Stanley Noyes and Olga Carlisle. BoWoP

There on the top of the down. June Bracken and Heather. Tennyson. PPoe

There once was a bright young physician. Limerick. Unknown. NIL

There once was a cow with a double udder. The Cow. Theodore Roethke. OBAL

There once was a day when. Shot with a Hot Rot Gun. Michael Goode. NowV

There once was a fastidious yak. The Fastidious Yak. Oliver Herford. TDH

There once was a frog. A Legend of Lake Okeefinokee. Laura E. Richards. ECBV

There once was a girl named Myrtle. Myrtle. Theodore Roethke. OSP; RAE

There once was a happy hyena. The Happy Hyena. Carolyn Wells. TDH

There once was a kind armadillo. The Kind Armadillo. Oliver Herford. TDH

There once was a man from Nantucket. Unknown. IP

There once was a man named Michael Finnigin. Michael Finnigin. Unknown. GSB

There once was a man who said, "Damn!" Limerick. M. E. Hare. NOBL

There once was a man who said, "God." Limerick [or Idealism]. Ronald Arbuthnott Knox. FaBoCo; NOBL; PoPle

There once was a man who said, "Oh." The Disobliging Bear. Carolyn Wells. TDH

There once was a Master of Arts. Master of Arts. Cosmo Monkhouse. TDH

There once was a peach on a tree. The Peach. Abbie Farwell Brown. TDH

There once was [or was once] a pious young priest. Limerick [or The Pious Young Priest]. Unknown. BBL; NIL; TDH

There Once Was a Puffin. Florence Page Jaques. CTV

There once was a sensitive cat. The Sensitive Cat. Alice Brown. TDH

There once was a spinster of Ealing. Limerick. Unknown. NIL

There once was a Union maid. Union Maid. Woody Guthrie. FSW

There once was a wicked young minister. Conrad Aiken. OBAL

There once was a Willow, and he was very old. The Willow-Man. Juliana Horatia Ewing. OxBChV

There once was a witch. Mixed Brews. Clive Sansom. FPB

There once was a wonderful wizard. Limerick. Conrad Aiken. FaBoNo

There once was an Ichtyosaurus. The Ichthyosaurus. Unknown. CTV

There once were some people called Sioux. The American Indian. *Unknown.* FaBoCo

There once were three brothers from merry Scotland. Sir Andrew Barton. *Unknown.* AmFP

There ought to be capital punishment for cars. Thoughts on Capital Punishment. Rod McKuen. InPK

There rolls the deep where grew the tree. In Memoriam A. H. H., CXXIII. Tennyson. BoReV; HAP; NOBE

There sat down, once, a thing on Henry's heart. John Berryman. *Fr.* Dream Songs. CAPP; ExPo (1973 ed.); HAP; PiAm; PPoD; PSN

There sate the seniors of the Trojan Race. Homer, *tr.* by Pope. *Fr.* The Iliad, III. OBVE

There seems to be a large gap. Ugly Neck. D. J. Enright. HeHu

There shall be no more songs. Black Power. Alvin Saxon. PoBA

There she is, out in the rain. Silly Dog. Myra Cohn Livingston. GDP

There she sits a'-smokin'. Motorcycle Irene. Skip Spence. MAT

There She Stands a Lovely Creature. *Unknown.* AmFP; OLR

There should always be something casual. The Operation. S. L. Henderson Smith. PMW

There should have been the Old Manse under creeper. Story Which Should Have Happened. Peter Porter. CAAP

There shouldn't be a North. The Carolinas. David Ray. TAT

There sits a fair couple courting. The Jealous Brothers. *Unknown.* AmFP

There, spring lambs jam the sheepfold. Watercolor of Grantchester. Sylvia Plath. SBG

There stand three mills on Manor Water. Manor Water. *Unknown.* GBP

There still is coal in many houses. The Sixth Winter. Edwin Rolfe. SPT

There the black river, boundary to hell. The Southern Road. Dudley Randall. CNA; PAIC; PoBA

There the blue-green gums are a fringe of remote disorder. Envoi for a Book of Poems. James McAuley. GAS

There the companions of his fall, o'erwhelmed. Immortal Hate. Milton. *Fr.* Paradise Lost, I. NOBE

There the most daintie Paradise on ground. The Bower of Bliss [or Guyon's Temptation]. Spenser. *Fr.* The Faerie Queene, II, 12. EBEV; NIL; OBP

There, there is no mountain within miles. Nebraska. Jon Swan. RFM

There they are/ Thirty at the corner. The Blackstone Rangers. Gwendolyn Brooks. ExPo (1973 ed.); NoAM; NowV; PoBA

There they are in the billard room of the faculty club. The Modern Chinese History Professor Plays Pool Every Tuesday and Thursday. James Baker Hall. TAT

There they are, my fifty men and women. One Word More. Robert Browning. VLP

There they are now. Three Sentences for a Dead Swan. James Wright. NoAM; NOBA

There they go. Seed Journey. Gregory Corso. VGW

There they were. A Day at the Races. Louis Phillips. PH

There they were, as if our memory hatched them. Triptych. Seamus Heaney. CIP

There they were many, O God, so many. They. Mani Leib, *tr.* by David G. Roskies *and* Hillel Schwartz. VWA

There two that struggling into the deep. Thomas Heyrick. *Fr.* The Submarine Voyage: A Pindaric Poem in Four Parts. SCP-2

There wanders many a lighted star. The North Star. John Morris-Jones, *tr.* by Anthony Conran. OBW

There was a bad poet named Clough. On Arthur Hugh Clough. Swinburne. FaBoEE

There was a battle in the north. Geordie. *Unknown.* FaBoBa

There Was a Boy. Wordsworth. *Fr.* The Prelude, V. SoSe (1977 ed.)

There was a boy bedded in bracken. Carol. John Short. FaBoTw (1975 ed.); MPo

There was a boy whose name was Jim. Jim, Who Ran Away from His Nurse, and Was Eaten by a Lion. Hilaire Belloc. BBL; OxBChV

There was a brave knight of Lorraine. A Brave Knight. Mary Mapes Dodge. TDH

There was a bridge that Rozinante would not cross. The Bridge of Heraclitus. George Reavey. BIrV

There was a bright fellow named Peter. The 'Skeeter and Peter. Marie Bruckman MacDonald. TDH

There was a brightness in the branches. The Leaves. Ron Loewinsohn. GP

There Was a Child Went Forth. Walt Whitman. BiP; CTV; InPS; PBMP; SoSe; TAP; TPo

"There was a child went forth every day," *sel.* RFM

There was a clever skipper, in Akron he did dwell. The Clever Skipper. *Unknown.* AmFP

There was a clock in Grandad's house. Two Clocks. John Daniel. LP

There was a composer named Bong. Hit Tune. *Unknown.* TDH

There Was a Crimson Clash of War. Stephen Crane. UnPo (1976 ed.)

There was a crooked man, and he went a crooked mile. Mother Goose. MG

There was a dark and awful wood. Wood. Thomas Hornsby Ferril. MPA

There was a darkness in this man. Lincoln. John Gould Fletcher. *Fr.* Lincoln. OFD

There was a desperado from the wild and woolly West. The Desperado. *Unknown.* FSW

There was a fair maiden who lived on the shore. The Fair Maid by the Shore. *Unknown.* AmFP

There was a fair young creature who lived by the seaside. The Silvery Tide. *Unknown.* AmFP

There was a faith-healer of Deal. Mind and Matter. *Unknown.* BBL; FaBoCo

There was a farmer had a dog. Bingo. *Unknown.* FSW

There was a farmer's son kept sheep upon a hill. The Lady's Policy [or Blow Away the Morning Dew]. *Unknown.* FSW; RDB

There was a frank lady of Dedham. A Limerick of Frankness. "X. Y. Z." TDH

There was a Friar, a wanton one and merry. Chaucer, *mod. version by* Nevill Coghill. *Fr.* The Canterbury Tales: Prologue. BiP

There was a gallant lady all in her tender youth. Canada-I-O. *Unknown.* AmFP

There was a gallant ship, a gallant ship was she. The *Golden Vanity.* *Unknown.* PBMP

There was a giant by the Orchard Wall. In the Orchard. James Stephens. SO

There was a graven image of desire. A Cameo. Swinburne. LoAs

There was a gray rat looked at me. Rat Riddles. Carl Sandburg. SO

There was a great battle Saturday morning. The Battle of Argoed Llwyfain. Taliesin, *tr.* by Anthony Conran. OBW

There was a great white wall—bare, bare, bare. The Smoked Herring. Charles Cros, *tr.* by A. L. Lloyd. PoTa

There was a green branch hung with many a bell.　The Dedication to a Book of Stories Selected from the Irish Novelists.　W. B. Yeats.　OBP

There was a hag who kept two chambermaids.　The Hag and the Slavies.　La Fontaine, *tr. by* Edward Marsh.　OBVE

There was a jolly fat frog that did in the river swim O.　The Frog and the Crow.　*Unknown.*　GBP

There was a jolly miller once.　The Miller of the Dee.　*Unknown.*　BBL; GSB; PFIr

There was a kind Lady called Gregory.　James Joyce.　FaBoEE

There was a king, and a very great king.　Lady Diamond. *Unknown.*　PeBB

There was a knicht riding frae the east.　Riddles Wisely Expounded.　*Unknown.*　FaBoBa; GBP; ILP (1975 ed.); PeBB

There was a Knight, a most distinguished man.　Persons of the Prologue.　Chaucer, *mod. version by* Nevill Coghill.　*Fr.* The Canterbury Tales.　BiP; OBP

There was a knight and a lady bright.　The Broomfield Hill. *Unknown.*　PeBB

There was a knight, and he was young.　The Baffled Knight. *Unknown.*　SLP

There was a lady all skin and bone.　The Skin-and-Bone Lady. *Unknown.*　AmFP

There was a lady in the north.　The Dowie Dens of Yarrow. *Unknown.*　FSW

There was a lady lived in a hall.　Two Red Roses across the Moon.　William Morris.　VLP

There was a lady lived in York.　The Cruel Mother.　*Unknown.* AmFP; FSW

There was a Lady Loved a Swine.　*Unknown.*　*See* Lady Who Loved a Swine, The

There was a lady of beauty rare.　The Wife of Usher's Well. *Unknown.*　AmFP

There was a lady who loved a swine.　The Lady Who Loved a Swine.　*Unknown.*　RDB

There was a little boy and a little girl.　Mother Goose.　MG

There Was a Little Girl, 1 *st.　At. to* Longfellow.　OxBChV; PCOP

There was a little guinea-pig.　A Guinea-Pig Song [*or* The Precise Guinea-Pig].　*Unknown.*　ECBV; OxBChV

There was a little man/ And he had a little gun.　Mother Goose. ECBV; MG, *longer version*

There was a little man and he had a little can.　No More Booze. *Unknown.*　OBAL

There was a little mouse who lived on a hill.　The Mouse's Courting Song.　*Unknown.*　AIW

There was a little rill of water, near the den.　The Coyote.　Carter Revard.　VoR

There was a little ship in South Amerikee.　The Sweet Trinity. *Unknown.*　AmFP

There was a little turtle.　The Little Turtle.　Vachel Lindsay. CTV; LCL; OBAL; PCOP; RAE

There was a lizard kept me company.　Gecko.　Noel Lloyd. RAE

There was a lofty ship, and she put out to sea.　The Golden Vanity.　*Unknown.*　FSW

There was a Lord in London town.　Lady Isabel and the Elf Knight.　*Unknown.*　FSW

There was a lord of worthy fame.　The Lady Isabella's Tragedy. *Unknown.*　GBP

There Was a Maid Went to the Mill.　*Unknown.*　GBP

There was a man a-coming from the south.　Trooper and Maid. *Unknown.*　AmFP

There Was a Man and He Was Mad.　*Unknown.*　GBP

There was a man, and his name was Dob.　Whose Dog? Whose Cat?　*Unknown.*　ECBV

There was a man in Arkansaw.　Tuscaloosa Sam.　"Orpheus C. Kerr."　OBAL

There was a man in olden times.　Dives and Lazarus.　*Unknown.* AmFP

There was a man in the land of Uz whose name was Job.　Bible, *O.T.* Job.　NAWM-1

There was a man lived in the moon.　Aiken Drum.　*Unknown.* FaBoNo

There was a man lived quite near us.　The Man with the Wooden Leg.　Katherine Mansfield.　ATNZ

There was a man made a thing.　*Unknown.*　GBP

There was a man named Johnny Sands, who married Betty Hague. Johnny Sands.　*Unknown.*　AmFP

There was a man named Mingram Mo.　Mingram Mo.　David McCord.　ECBV

There was a man, now please take note.　Bill Groggin's Goat. *Unknown.*　FSW

There Was a Man of Double Deed.　*Unknown.*　GBP; InPK; WeW

There was a man of Thessaly.　The Man of Thessaly.　*Unknown.* FaBoCo; FaBoNo; MG

There was a man that lived in England.　Lord Bateman. *Unknown.*　FSW

There was a man who dwelt alone.　Shadow-Bride.　J. R. R. Tolkien.　SO

There was a man who had a clock.　The Sad Tale of Mr. Mears. *Unknown.*　PoTa

There was a man who married a maid. She laughed as he led her home.　I Love My Love.　Helen Adam.　NMM

There was a man with tongue of wood.　War Is Kind, XVI. Stephen Crane.　PiAm

There Was a Monkey.　*Unknown.*　ECBV; RAE

There was a most odious yak.　The Yak.　Theodore Roethke. ECBV; LCL

There Was a Naughty Boy.　Keats.　*See* Song about Myself.

There was a noted hero, Jack Dolan was his name.　The Wild Colonial Boy.　*Unknown.*　AIW

There was a Pig, that sat alone.　The Pig Tale.　"Lewis Carroll." *Fr.* Sylvie and Bruno Concluded.　RAE

There was a Presbyterian cat.　The Auld Seceder Cat.　*Unknown.* FaBoCo

There was a professor called Chesterton.　A Professor Called Chesterton.　W. S. Gilbert.　TDH

There was a professor of Beaulieu.　Materialism.　C. E. M. Joad. FaBoCo

There was a queer fellow named Woodin.　A Queer Fellow Named Woodin.　Edward Bradley.　TDH

There was a rich lady, from London she came.　A Rich Irish Lady.　*Unknown.*　AmFP

There was a rich lady lived over the sea.　The Rich Lady over the Sea.　*Unknown.*　AIW

There was a rich man and he lived in Jerusalem.　The Rich Man and the Poor Man.　*Unknown.*　FSW

There was a rich merchant in London did dwell.　Dinah and Villikens.　*Unknown.*　RDB

There was a river that rose.　The River.　James Stephens.　ECBV

There was a river under First and Main.　Prairie Town.　William Stafford.　PPoD

There was a road ran past our house.　The Unexplorer.　Edna St. Vincent Millay.　PoA

There was a roaring in the wind all night.　Resolution and Independence.　Wordsworth.　CABA (1972 ed.); EBEV; HAP; InPS; LFH; MAT; MBPR; NOBE; OAEL-2; PPP; SoSe

There Was a Sang.　Helen B. Cruickshank.　SLP

There was a seed.　When Roots Get Too Deep.　Michael Small. DNGG

There was a serpent who had to sing. The Serpent. Theodore Roethke. DuDr; ECBV

There was a shepherd's son. Blow the Winds, I-Ho. *Unknown.* GBP; PeBB

There was a ship a-sailing off North America. The Green Willow Tree. *Unknown.* AIW

There was a ship of Rio. The Ship of Rio. Walter de la Mare. PoPle

There was a ship that sailed upon the lowland sea. The *Golden Vanity. Unknown.* RDB

There was a sick man of Tobago. *Unknown.* OxBChV

There was a sightseer named Sue. A Sightseer Named Sue. *Unknown.* TDH

There was a slumbrous silence in the air. Richard Henry Horne. *Fr.* Orion. VLP

There was a small maiden named Maggie. A Shaggy Dog. *Unknown.* TDH

There was a snake that dwelt in Skye. The Fastidious Serpent. Henry Johnstone. ECBV

There was a sound of revelry by night. Waterloo [*or* The Eve of Waterloo]. Byron. *Fr.* Childe Harold's Pilgrimage, III. EBEV; LFH; NOBE; PPoD

There was a stunted handpost just on the crest. Near Lanivet, 1872. Thomas Hardy. CMoP (1970 ed.); ILP (1975 ed.); NoAM

There was a sunlit absence. Mossbawn: Two Poems in Dedication. Seamus Heaney. BIrV; CIP

There was a taed wha thocht sae lang. The Philosophic Taed. William Soutar. MS

There was a time for discoveries. Voyage West. Archibald MacLeish. VGW

There was a time I yet remember well. Adbaston. C. B. Ash. PES

There was a time, methought it was but lately departed. Arthur Hugh Clough. *Fr.* Amours de Voyage, V, 5. OBP

There was a time, O Lesbia, when you said Catullus was the only man. Catullus, *tr. fr. Latin by* Horace Gregory. NAWM-1

There was a time (such songs begin this way). Inflation. Charles O. Hartman. PoA

There was a time when death was terror. New Fashions. George Moses Horton. OBAL

There was a time when I could fly, I swear it. I, Icarus. Alden Nowlan. NCSH

There was a time when I would magnify. Elegy for an Unknown Soldier. James K. Baxter. ATNZ

There was a time when meadow, grove, and stream. Ode: Intimations of Immortality from Recollections of Early Childhood. Wordsworth. BiP; CABA (1972 ed.); HAP; HeIP; ILP (1975 ed.); LFH; MBPR; NOBE; OAEL-2; OBP; PAIC; PBMP; PoIA; PPoD; PPoe; PPP; TPo

There was a time when we all were dancers. Gerrye Payne. NPW

There was a tree stood in the ground. The Green Grass Growing All Around. *Unknown.* ECBV

There was a wealthy merchant. The Wars of Santa Fe. *Unknown.* AmFP

There was a weasel lived in the sun. The Gallows. Edward Thomas. ILP (1975 ed.); InPS; NoAM; SFF; SoSe (1977 ed.); UnPo (1976 ed.)

There Was a Wee Bit Mousikie. *Unknown.* MN

There was a wee cooper who lived in Fife. The Wee Cooper of Fife. *Unknown.* FSW

There was a whispering in my hearth. Miners. Wilfred Owen. NOBE; OBW

There was a witch/ The witch had an itch. Two Witches. Alexander Resnikoff. IWK

There was a witch who met an owl. Hitchhiker. David McCord. IWK

There was a wood, a witches' wood. The Witches' Wood. Mary Elizabeth Coleridge. PBWP

There was a young boy [*or* man] of Quebec. The Boy of Quebec. *At. to* Kipling. FaBoCo; FaBoNo

There was a young curate of Kidderminster. A Young Curate of Kidderminster. *Unknown.* TDH

There was a young curate of Salisbury. *Unknown.* FaBoCo

There was a young doctor, from London he came. The Fair Damsel from London. *Unknown.* AmFP

There was a young fellow called Crouch. Limerick. Victor Gray. NOBL

There was a young fellow from Boise. A Young Fellow from Boise. John Straley. TDH

There was a young fellow named Hall/ Who fell in a spring, clothes and all. A Fellow Named Hall. J. F. Wilson. TDH

There was a young fellow named Hall/ Who fell in the spring in the fall. A Happy Time. *Unknown.* IP

There was a young fellow named Shear. A Young Fellow Named Shear. John Ciardi. TDH

There was a young fellow named West. Suppressed. *Unknown.* TDH

There was a young Fellow of Caius. Limerick. *Unknown.* NOBL

There was a young Fellow of King's. Limerick. *Unknown.* NOBL

There was a young Fellow of Wadham. Limerick. *Unknown.* NOBL

There was a young fir-tree of Bosnia. The Fir-Tree of Bosnia. Dante Gabriel Rossetti. FaBoNo

There was a young girl of Asturias. A Young Girl of Asturias. *Unknown.* TDH

There was a young hopeful named Sam. Jammy. Elizabeth Ripley. TDH

There was a young lady from Cork. A Young Lady from Cork. Ogden Nash. TDH

There was a young lady from Del. A Young Lady from Delaware. *Unknown.* TDH

There was a young lady named Bright. Relativity [*or* Faster than Light.]. Arthur Buller. FaBoCo; NOBL; PoIA; QQQ

There was a young lady named Min. Min. *Unknown.* ECBV

There was a young lady named Sue. A Young Lady Named Sue. *Unknown.* TDH

There was a young lady of Corsica. Limerick. Edward Lear. FaBoNo

There was a young lady of Crete. A Young Lady of Crete. *Unknown.* TDH

There was a young lady of Ealing. A Young Lady of Ealing. *Unknown.* TDH

There was a young lady of Lynn/ Who was so uncommonly thin. Limerick. *Unknown.* CTV; SoSe

There was a young lady of Munich. A Young Lady of Munich. *Unknown.* TDH

There was a young lady of Niger. Lady and Tiger. *Unknown.* DuDr; ECBV; SoSe

There was a young lady of Norway. Edward Lear. EBEV

There was a young lady of Oakham. A Young Lady of Oakham. *Unknown.* TDH

There was a young lady of Rheims. Moonshine. Walter de la Mare. TDH

There was a young lady of Riga. Limerick. *Unknown.* CTV; FaBoCo

There Was a Young Lady of Rome. Ogden Nash. QQQ

There was a young lady of Ryde. *Unknown.* BBL

There was a young lady of Spain. *Unknown.* FaBoCo

There was a young lady of station. "Lewis Carroll." FaBoNo

There was a young lady of Sweden. Edward Lear. EBEV

There was a young lady of Trent. Limerick. *Unknown.* NIL

There was a young lady of Tyre. The Young Lady of Tyre. Edward Lear. TDH

There was a young lady of Wilts. A Young Lady of Wilts. *Unknown.* TDH

There was a young lady whose bonnet. Edward Lear. EBEV

There was a young lady whose dream. Food for a Cat. David Starr Jordan. TDH

There was a young lady whose eyes. Edward Lear. EBEV

There was a young lady whose nose. Edward Lear. EBEV

There was a young maid who said "Why." Limerick. *Unknown.* SoSe

There was a young man from Elnora. Lenora. *Unknown.* TDH

There was a young man from Trinity. *Unknown.* SFF

There was a young man of Japan. *Unknown.* FaBoCo

There was a young man of Mauritius. Theological Limerick. T. Lindsay. FaBoCo

There was a young man of Montrose. Arnold Bennett. FaBoNo

There was a young man of Quebec. *See* There was a young boy of Quebec.

There was a young man of St. Bees. *Unknown, at. to* W. S. Gilbert. FaBoCo

There was a young man on a plain. A Young Man Who Loved Rain. William Jay Smith. TDH

There was a young man so benighted. The Guest. *Unknown.* ECBV

There was a young man who said, "Damn!" Determinism [*or* Predestination]. *Unknown.* FaBoCo; PoPle

There was a young man with a beard. Beatnik Limernik. Norman R. Jaffray. TDH

There was a young person named Crockett. Crockett. William Jay Smith. TDH

There was a young person of Crete. Limerick. Edward Lear. FaBoNo

There was a young puppy called Howard. The Young Puppy [*or* Howard]. A. A. Milne. GDP; TDH

There was a young soldier called Edser. Edser. Spike Milligan. TDH

There was a young waitress named Myrtle. A Mock Miracle. Oliver Herford. TDH

There was a young woman called Starkie. Mendelian Theory [*or* Limerick]. *Unknown.* FaBoCo; NOBL

There was a young woman from Aenos. The Young Woman from Aenos. *Unknown.* OBAL

There was a young woman named Plunnery. Edward Gorey. OBAL

There was a youth[e], and a well belovd youth[e]. The Bailiff's Daughter of Islington. *Unknown.* AIW; FaBoBa; FSW; PBMP; RDB

There was airy music and sport at the fair. The Fair at Windgap. Austin Clarke. OxBTC

There [*or* Ther] was also a nun [*or* Nonne], a Prioress. The Prioress [*or* Madam Eglantine]. Chaucer. *Fr.* The Canterbury Tales: Prologue. NOBE; OxBM; UsP

There was always the river or the train. Grandmother Watching at Her Window. W. S. Merwin. VGW

There was an ancient carver that carved of a saint. The Figurehead. Crosbie Garstin. PoTa

There was an ancient spring inside the glacier. Found. Carol Muske. AmPA

There was an Archbishop named Tait. Archbishop Tait. *Unknown.* FaBoNo

There was an earthquake. The Earthquake. *Tr. fr. Zuni Indian by* K. Kennedy. WTO

There was an exclusive old oyster. The Exclusive Old Oyster. Laura A. Steel. TDH

There was an Indian, who had known no change. The Discovery. J. C. Squire. OFD

There was an island in the sea. Atlantis. Conrad Aiken. Priapus and the Pool, XV. EcS

There was an old cat named Macduff. The Genial Grimalkin. J. G. Francis. TDH

There was an old farmer in Sussex did dwell. The Farmer's Curst Wife. *Unknown.* AIW

There was an old grocer of Goring. Green. Walter de la Mare. FaBoNo

There was an old lady of Chertsey. Edward Lear. OxBChV

There was an old lady of Dover. The Old Lady from Dover. Carolyn Wells. TDH

There was an old lady of France. Edward Lear. LCL

There was an old lady of Harrow. An Old Lady of Harrow. *Unknown.* TDH

There was an old looney of Rhyme. An Old Looney. *Unknown.* TDH

There Was an Old Man. James Kirkup. FPB

There was an old man/ And he had a calf. *Unknown.* ECBV

There was an old man and for begging he was bound. The Beggarman. *Unknown.* RDB

There was an old man at the foot of the hill. The Farmer's Curst Wife. *Unknown.* AmFP

There was an old man by Salt Lake. An Old Man by Salt Lake. William Jay Smith. TDH

There was an old man from Peru/ Who dreamed he was eating his shoe. *See* There was an old man of Peru/ Who dreamt he was eating his shoe.

There was an old man in a Barge. Edward Lear. EBEV

There was an old man in a boat. Limerick. Edward Lear. EBEV; FaBoNo

There was an old man in a tree. Limerick. Edward Lear. FaBoNo; OxBChV

There was an old man in a trunk. Ultimate Reality. Ogden Nash. FaBoCo

There was an old man lived over the hill. The Devil and The Farmer's Wife. *Unknown.* FSW

There was an old man lived out in the wood. Green Broom. *Unknown.* PoTa

There was an old man named Michael Finnigan. Michael Finnigan. *Unknown.* FSW

There was an old man of Boulogne. *Unknown.* FaBoCo

There was an old man of Cape Horn. Edward Lear. EBEV

There was an old man of Cape Race. *Unknown.* FaBoCo

There was an old man of Dumbree. Edward Lear. OxBChV

There was an old man of Dunblane. Edward Lear. EBEV

There was an old man of Dundee. Limerick. Edward Lear. FaBoNo

There Was an Old Man of Dunoon. *Unknown.* IP

There was an old man of El Hums. Limerick. Edward Lear. FaBoNo

There was an old man of Girgenti. Limerick. Edward Lear. FaBoNo

There was an old man of Hawaii. An Old Man of Hawaii. *Unknown.* TDH

There was an old man of high feather. A What-Is-It. Ruth McEnery Stuart *and* Albert Bigelow Paine. TDH

There was an old man of Hong Kong. Limerick. Edward Lear. FaBoCo

There was an old man of Ibreem. Edward Lear. EBEV

There was an old man of Kamschatka. Limerick. Edward Lear. NOBL

There was an old man of Khartoum. Limerick. W. R. Inge. NOBL

There was an old man of Madras. Limerick. Edward Lear. FaBoNo

There was an old man of [*or* from] Peru/ Who dreamt he was eating his shoe. Limerick. *Unknown.* SoSe; TDH

There was an old man of Peru/ Who never knew what he should do. Edward Lear. EBEV

There was an old man of Peru/ Who watched his wife making a stew. A Fatal Mistake. Edward Lear. EBEV; TDH

There was an old man of Spithead. Limerick. Edward Lear. FaBoNo

There was an old man of the Dee. Limerick. Edward Lear. FaBoNo

There was an old man of the East. Edward Lear. EBEV

There was an old man of the Hague. The Old Man of the Hague. Edward Lear. TDH

There was an old man of the Nile. An Old Man of the Nile. Edward Lear. TDH; VLP

There was an old man of the West. Edward Lear. EBEV

There was an old man of Thermopylae. Limerick. Edward Lear. EBEV; FaBoNo; NOBL

There was an old man of Three Bridges. Limerick. Edward Lear. FaBoNo

There was an old man of Toulon. An Old Man of Toulon. William Jay Smith. TDH

There was an old man of Vesuvius. Limerick. Edward Lear. FaBoNo

There was an old man of West Dumpet. Edward Lear. EBEV

There was an old man of Whitehaven. Edward Lear. EBEV; VLP

There was an old man on the Border. Edward Lear. EBEV; LCL

There was an old man said, "I fear." The Shubble. Walter de la Mare. FaBoNo; TDH

There was an old man that lived in a wood. *See* There was an old man who lived in the wood.

There was an old man who liv'd in Middle Row. The Five Hens. *Unknown.* GBP

There was an old man who [*or* that] lived in the [*or* a] wood. Father Grumble [*or* Old Man in the Wood]. *Unknown.* AmFP; FSW

There was an old man who made his will. The Dishonest Miller. *Unknown.* AmFP

There was an old man who said, "How." Edward Lear. OxBChV

There was an old man who said, "Hush!" Limerick. Edward Lear. FaBoCo: NOBL; OxBChV

There was an old man who screamed out. Edward Lear. EBEV

There was an old man whose despair. Limerick. Edward Lear. FaBoNo; VLP

There was an old man with a beard,/ Who said, "It is just as I feared!" Limerick [*or* Nesting]. Edward Lear. CTV; ECBV; FaBoCo; FaBoNo; NOBL; OxBChV

There was an old man with a gong. The Old Man with a Gong. Edward Lear. TDH

There was an old man with a gun. Miss Pheasant. Walter de la Mare. FaBoNo

There was an old man with a ribbon. Limerick. Edward Lear. FaBoNo

There was an old miller and he lived all alone. The Miller. *Unknown.* FSW

There was an old miser at Reading. *Unknown.* OxBChV

There was an old party of Lyme. *Unknown.* FaBoCo; FF

There was an old person of Anerley. Limerick. Edward Lear. FaBoCo

There was an old person of Bar. Limerick. Edward Lear. FaBoNo

There was an old person of Basing. Edward Lear. EBEV

There was an old person of Blythe. Edward Lear. EBEV

There was an old person of Bow. Edward Lear. EBEV; VLP

There was an old person of Brussels. Limerick. Edward Lear. FaBoNo

There was an old person of Burton. Edward Lear. EBEV

There was an old person of Cassel. Edward Lear. EBEV

There was an old person of Cromer. An Old Person of Cromer. Edward Lear. TDH

There was an old person of Crowle. Limerick. Edward Lear. FaBoNo

There was an old person of Dover. Limerick. Edward Lear. FaBoNo

There was an old person of Dutton. Edward Lear. EBEV

There was an old person of Ewell. Rice and Mice. Edward Lear. TDH

There was an old person of Grange. Limerick. Edward Lear. FaBoNo

There was an old person of Gretna. Edward Lear. OxBChV; VLP

There was an old person of Harrow. Limerick. Edward Lear. FaBoNo

There was an old person of Hove. Limerick. Edward Lear. FaBoNo

There was an old person of Philae. Limerick. Edward Lear. FaBoNo

There was an old person of Prague. Edward Lear. EBEV

There was an old person of Putney. Tea by the Sea. Edward Lear. TDH

There was an old person of Rhodes. Edward Lear. EBEV

There was an old person of Sparta. Edward Lear. DuDr

There was an old person of Tring. An Old Person of Tring. *Unknown.* TDH

There was an old person of Twickenham. Limerick. Edward Lear. FaBoNo

There was an old person of Ware. Edward Lear. LCL

There was an old person of Wick. Limerick. Edward Lear. FaBoNo

There was an old person who said. The Oil Lamp. William Jay Smith. TDH

There was an old person whose habits. Limerick [*or* Hurtful Habits]. Edward Lear. FaBoNo; TDH

There was an old skinflint of Hitching. Buttons. Walter de la Mare. FaBoNo

There Was an Old Soldier. *Unknown.* FSW

There was an old soldier of Bicester. *Unknown.* FaBoNo; OxBChV

There was an old stupid who wrote. A Person of Note. Walter Parke. TDH

There was an old vicar of Sinder. J. J. Walter de la Mare. FaBoNo

There was an old villain. Oh, How He Lied. *Unknown.* FSW

There was an old wife and she lived all alone. The Old Wife and the Ghost. James Reeves. ECBV; IWK; RAE

There was an old woman/ Lived under a hill. Mother Goose. MG; MN

There was an old woman, and what do you think? Mother Goose. MG

There was an old woman, as I've heard tell. Mother Goose. ECBV; MG; PoTa

There was an old woman as ugly as sin. An Old Woman. Charles Henry Ross. OxBChV

There was an old woman called Nothing-at-all. Mother Goose. MG

There was an old woman in our town. Eggs and Marrowbone. *Unknown.* FSW; RDB

There was an old woman in Surrey. *Unknown.* OxBChV

There was an old woman lived on the seashore. The Two Sisters. *Unknown.* AmFP; FSW

There was an old woman named Towl. Mistress Towl. *Unknown.* FaBoNo; OxBChV

There was an old woman of Croydon. *Unknown.* BBL

There was an old woman of Harrow. Old Woman of Harrow. *Unknown.* FaBoNo

There was an old woman tossed up in a basket. Mother Goose. ECBV; MG

There was an old woman who lived in a shoe. Mother Goose. MG

There was an old woman who rode on a broom. Old Woman on a Broom. *Unknown.* ECBV

There was an old woman who sowed a corn seed. The Magic Seeds. James Reeves. ECBV

There was an owd yowe wi' only one horn. The One-horned Ewe. *Unknown.* GBP

There was an ox, there was a flea. Partners. Jaime Castiello. ECBV

There was ance a may, and she lo'ed na men. Werena My Heart Licht. Lady Grizel Baillie. SLP

There was, before me. The Black Riders, XXI. Stephen Crane. PiAm

There was blood on the saddle. Blood on the Saddle. *Unknown.* FSW

There was Dai Puw. He was no good. On the Farm. R. S. Thomas. OxBTC

There was great beauty by the Tree. Eve. Arthur J. Bull. UnPo (1976 ed.)

There was, in the village of Patton. Good Thinking. *Unknown.* TDH

There was little mignonette in life. War Poem. Ilya Ehrenburg, *tr. by* Leonard Opalov. AMV-81

There was movement at the station. The Man from Snowy River. Andrew Barton Paterson. MAuV; PH

There was Nadja's glove flickering somewhere. Requiem: A Surrealist Graveyard. Chuck Miller. AcAn

There was never a leaf on bush or tree. James Russell Lowell. The Vision of Sir Launfal, Pt. II. PIM

There was never a sound beside the wood but one. Mowing. Robert Frost. CMoP (1970 ed.); HoPM (1975 ed.); LFH; NOBA; PPP; VGW

There was never nothing more me pained [*or* payned]. Sir Thomas Wyatt. AAS; GBL

There was no change in the summer wind. In the Flowering Season. Michael Roberts. FaBoTw (1975 ed.)

There was no stir among the trees. An Aboriginal Simile. Mary Gilmore. GAS

There was once a dear little gnome. Gnome Matter. Carolyn Wells. TDH

There was once a high wall, a bare wall. The Red Herring. George MacBeth. SO

There was once a hog theater where hogs performed. A Performance at Hog Theater. Russell Edson. AmPA

There was once a man of Bengal. *Unknown.* BBL

There was once a pious young priest. *See* There once was a pious young priest.

There was once a young man of Oporta. "Lewis Carroll." FaBoNo

There was once an old tailor of Hickery Mo. The Old Tailor. Walter de la Mare. ECBV

There was one among us who rose. Death of a Friend. Pauli Murray. PoBA

There Was One I Met upon the Road. Stephen Crane. The Black Riders, XXXIII. TT

There was one in the room, thinking of the sherry. The Visitors. Elizabeth Bartlett. PMW

There was really no disturbance. Death in the Family. Alison Wyrley Birch. PPM

There was scurrying and scrimmage. When the Animals Left the Ark. *Unknown.* RAE

There was six jovial tradesmen, they all sat down to drinking. When Jones's Ale Was New. *Unknown.* AmFP

There Was Something White Sticking Out of the Sand. Hugh Fox. TC

There was sparkling water, too small. The Cwm above Penrhiwceiber. Robert Morgan. HeHu

There was such speed in her little body. Bells for John Whiteside's Daughter. John Crowe Ransom. AnMo; CMoP (1970 ed.); FF; HAP; HeIP; HoPM (1975 ed.); ILP (1975 ed.); InPK; InPS; IP; NIL; NoAM; NOBA; PAIC; PiAm; PolA; PPoD; PPP; PSN; RRA; SoS; SoSe; TAP; UnPo (1976 ed.); VGW; VoPo; WeW; WIF

There was that horse. The White Stallion. Pete Morgan. SLP

There was the buffalo blowing. Composition. Peter Blue Cloud. VoR

There was this road. The Legs. Robert Graves. NoAM

There was this time in Boston. The Wedding Night. Anne Sexton. PoA

There was three kings into the east. John Barleycorn. Burns. AIW; Epi

There was three ladies playd at the ba. The Cruel Brother. *Unknown.* PeBB

There was, 'tis said, and I believe, a time. The Parish Register. George Crabbe. *Fr.* Burials, III. OAEL-1

There was twa sisters in a bow'r. The Twa Sisters. *Unknown.* FaBoBa; ILP (1975 ed.)

There we crossed Trent and on the other side. Richard Corbet. *Fr.* Iter Boreale. SCP-2

There were always five. Sisters. Alberta Turner. HeS

There Were an Old and Wealthy Man. *Unknown.* AmFP

There were black railings. Black Railings. Robert Morgan. HeHu

There were blood spots on the skirt. James Cunningham. *Fr.* The Narrator's Trance. JB

There were cities here in the hills. Louis Johnson. *Fr.* Four Poems from the Strontium Age. ATNZ

There were days I could see. The Man Who Knew the Colt Boy. Gene Keller. TVo

There Were Fierce Animals in Africa. Alvin Aubert. CSP; GP

There were fifteen men in green. Men in Green. David Campbell. GAS

There were five of us within the room. I Come to Bury Caesar. Sydney Justin Harris. PoA

There were four of us about the bed. Shameful Death. William Morris. VLP

There were ghosts that returned to earth to hear his phrases. Large Red Man Reading. Wallace Stevens. HAP

There were great birds circling. The Homecoming. Norman Kreitman. PMW

There were many of us at the time. Gavin Bantock. *Fr.* Hiroshima TwMBP

There were miners from Bisbee. Tramp Miner's Song. *Unknown.* AmFP

There were never strawberries. Strawberries. Edwin Morgan. BoLoP

There were ninety and nine that safely lay. The Ninety and Nine. Elizabeth Cecilia Clephane. BLSH; FSW; VLP

There were no antelope on the balcony. Midnight Special. Kenneth Patchen. VGW

There were no drawings on the page. Water Poems. Sandra McPherson. CAAP

There were no men and women then at all. Then. Edwin Muir. CMoP (1970 ed.); MS; PoA

There were no undesirables or girls in my set. Commander Lowell. Robert Lowell. VGW

There were only Adam and Eve. From the Dust. Elaine Dallman. VWA

There were six and six nobles. Glenlogie. *Unknown.* Epi

There were some shepherds living in the same part of the country. Bible, *N.T.* St. Luke, II: 8–20. CTV

There were ten in the bed. Roll Over. *Unknown.* FSW

There were the roses, in the rain. The Act. William Carlos Williams. VGW

There were the starlings hunched against the sky. Rooftop Winter. Dwayne Thorpe. AMV–80

There were thirty million English who talked of England's might. The Last of the Light Brigade. Kipling. BTTM

There were three brothers in merry Scotland. Henry Martin. *Unknown.* FSW

There were three cherry trees once. The Three Cherry Trees. Walter de la Mare. CMoP (1970 ed.)

There were three crows sat on a tree. *See* There were three ravens sat on a tree.

There were three crows sat on a tree/ Oh, Billy Magee Magaw. Billy Magee Magaw. *Unknown.* FSW

There Were Three Ghostesses. *Unknown.* CTV

There were three gipsies a-come to my door. The Wraggle Taggle Gipsies. *Unknown.* DuDr; FSW

There were three in the meadow by the brook. The Code. Robert Frost. InPS; PoA; UnPo (1976 ed.)

There Were Three Jovial Welshman. *Unknown.* GBP

There were three kings cam frae the East. Heine in Scots. Alexander Gray. MS

There were three ladies [*or* maids] lived in a bower [*or* barn]. Babylon; or, The Bonnie Banks o' Fordie. *Unknown.* AmFP; PAIC

There were three men of Gotham. The Three Wise Men of Gotham. *Unknown.* FaBoNo

There were three ravens [*or* crows] sat on a tree. The Three Ravens. *Unknown.* AIW; AmFP; CABA (1972 ed.); Epi; ExPo (1973 ed.); FaBoBa; FSW; GBP; HeIP; InPK; IP; LFH; OAEL-1;PeBB; RDB; UnPo (1976 ed.)

There were three sailors of Bristol city. Little Billee. Thackeray. BBL; ECBV; FaBoCo; NOBL; PoPle

There were three sisters fair and bright. The Riddling Knight. *Unknown.* AIW; PBMP

There were times. Alma Villanueva. NW

There were twa brethren in the North. The Twin [*or* Twa] Brothers. *Unknown.* EBEV; PBMP

There were twa sisters sat in a bour. Binnorie. *Unknown.* AIW; PoPle

There were two great trees. Laly, Laly. Mark Van Doren. SO

There were two lofty ships from old England came. High Barbaree. *Unknown.* FSW

There where the course is. At Galway Races. W. B. Yeats. LiSp

There where the deepe did show his sandy flore. Bible, *O.T.* Psalms, LXXVIII, *paraphrased by* Countess of Pembroke. OBVE

There, where the sun shines first. The Azalea. Coventry Patmore. *Fr.* The Unknown Eros. GBL

There will be a homecoming. There will. Homecoming. Lewis Packer. FPA; GAS

There will be a rusty gun on the wall, sweetheart. A. E. F. Carl Sandburg. CMoP (1970 ed.)

There will be a talking of lovely things. Michael Hartnett. IPM

There will be butterflies. Butterflies. Haniel Long. PCOP

There will be no examination in Long Term Suffering. Long Term Suffering. Richard Eberhart. GP

There will be no Holyman crying out this year. Jitterbugging in the Streets. Calvin C. Hernton. PoBA

There will be no more cats. Mort aux Chats. Peter Porter. CAAP

There will be no slogans, no mottoes. President Langton. Daniel J. Langton. TPo

There will be no speech from. No Speech from the Scaffold. Thom Gunn. OxBTC

There will be rose and rhododendron. Elegy before Death. Edna St. Vincent Millay. CMoP (1970 ed.)

There will be the cough before the silence, then. Dictum: For a Masque of Deluge. W. S. Merwin. NoAM

There will come a day when you will remember history all too well. The Last Page but One. Charles Edward Eaton. WasP

There will greet you at the end, Vasco. Wine from the Cape. Turner Cassity. AMV–81

There ye gang, ye draft. The Grace of God and the Meth-Drinker. Sydney Goodsir Smith. MS

There you go, a four-year-old. Good-by, Steer. Robert V. Carr. BPAW

There you may see the eyelids of the morn. Henry More. *Fr.* Psychozoia; or, The First Part of the Song of the Soul, Canto I. SCP-2

There'd ha'e to be nae warnin'. Times ha'e changed. Prayer for a Second Flood. "Hugh MacDiarmid.". EBEV

Therefore above the rest Ambition sat. Giles Fletcher the Younger. *Fr.* Christ's Victory and Triumph. SCP-2

Therefore all seasons shall be sweet to thee. Samuel Taylor Coleridge. *Fr.* Frost at Midnight. FSFS

Therefore he no more troubled the pool of silence. The Poet. George Mackay Brown. MS

Therefore I Must Tell the Truth. Torlino, *tr. fr. Navajo Indian by* Washington Matthews. ExPo (1973 ed.)

Therefore let pass, as they are transitory. Milton. *Fr.* Paradise Regained, IV. OAEL-1

There'll Be a Hot Time. Joe Hayden. *See* Hot Time in the Old Town.

There's a band of men who roam this land. Ballad of Badmen. Owen Dodson. FB

There's a barrel of porter at Tammany Hall. Song. Fitz-Greene Halleck. OBAL

There's a barrel-organ carolling across a golden street. The Barrel-Organ. Alfred Noyes. SoSe

There's a big hollow tree down the road here from me. Mountain Dew. *Unknown.* FSW

There's a big ship sailing on the il-li-al-lay oh. A Big Ship Sailing. *Unknown.* FSW

There's a bird perched on my shoulder. Bird. Agnes Nemes Nagy, *tr. by* Bruce Berlind. BoWoP

There's a bower of roses by Bendemeer's stream. Bendemeer's Stream. Thomas Moore. FSW

There's a breathless hush in the Close tonight. Vitaï Lampada. Sir Henry Newbolt. BTTM; FaPoR

There's a breathless hush on the freeway tonight. Wild Dreams of a New Beginning. Lawrence Ferlinghetti. GP

There's a brief spring in all of us and when it finishes. To S. T. C. on His 179th Birthday, October 12th, 1951. Maurice Carpenter. FaBoTw (1975 ed.)

There's a brown 'cross town and she's. Deceitful Brownskin Blues. *Unknown.* BluL

There's a certain slant of light. Emily Dickinson. AmVN; BoWoP; CABA (1972 ed.); CMoP (1970 ed.); ExPo (1973 ed.); FSFS; HAP; HeIP; ILP (1975 ed.); NoAM; NOBA; PiAm; PoIA; PPP; SBG; TT; VoPo; WPE

There's a charming Irish lady with a roguish winning way. Bedelia. William Jerome. FSN

There's a church in the valley by the wildwood. The Little Brown Church in the Vale. William S. Pitts. BLSH

There's combative artist named Whistler. Dante Gabriel Rossetti. FaBoEE

There's a danger zone, not a stranger zone. On the Amazon. C. Gray *and* G. Newman. UsP

There's a day we feel gay. On a Sunday Afternoon. Andrew B. Sterling. FSN

There's a dusky, husky maiden in the Arctic. When the Iceworms Nest Again. Robert W. Service. FSW

There's a faerie at the bottom of my garden. My Garden. Janice Appleby Succorsa. HoPM (1975 ed.)

There's a fairmer up in Cairnie. Drumdelgie. *Unknown.* GBP

There's a farmer tilling. Quickview #2. Antar S. K. Mberi. SES

There's a Feeling. Marcia Bullwinkle. AMV-80

There's a feeling comes a stealing. You're a Grand Old Flag. George M. Cohan. FSN

There's a feeling gathering inside me. There's a Feeling. Marcia Bullwinkle. AMV-80

There's a Footprint of Love & Disorder Karoniaktatie. NW

There's a fortune to be made in just about everything. My Great Great etc. Uncle Patrick Henry. James Tate. GP; OBAL

There's a Friend for little children. Albert Midlane. *Fr.* Above the Bright Blue Sky. OxBChV

There's a glen in Aghadoe, Aghadoe, Aghadoe. Aghadoe. John Todhunter. PFIr

There's a good time coming, boys. The Good Time Coming. Charles Mackay. VLP

There's a graveyard in our street. Carbreakers. Marian Lines. FPB

There's a great mystery. Diddie Wa Diddie. *Unknown.* BluL

There's a grey wind wails on the clover. Numerous Celts. J. C. Squire. SpRo

There's a Hole in My Bucket, *with music. Unknown.* GSB

There's a house in Baltimore. Goodbye 'Liza Jane. *Unknown.* FSW

There's a knack in living with you. Living with You. Angela Langfield. FF

There's a Lady in Washington Heights. Morris Bishop. QQQ

There's a Land That Is Fairer than Day. Sanford Fillmore Bennett. *See* In the Sweet Bye-and-bye.

There's a little black train a-coming. Little Black Train. *Unknown.* AmFP

There's a little rosewood casket. Little Rosewood Casket. *Unknown.* FSW

There's a little side street such as often you meet. The Sunshine of Paradise Alley. Walter H. Ford. FSN

There's a long funny shiver. All Kinds of Shivers. Lilian Moore. CaYB

There's a low green valley on the old Kentucky shore. Darling Nelly Gray. Benjamin Russel Hanby. BLSo; FSW; PSoN

There's a magpie keeps jolting me awake at dawn. Trend Spotter. William Price Turner. MS

There's a Man Goin' 'Round Takin' Names. *Unknown.* FSW (Angel of Death, The.) AmFP

There's a man, I really believe, compares with. Sappho, *tr. fr. Greek by* J. F. Nims. WeW

There's a man who's been out sailing. Cactus Tree. Joni Mitchell. GrRo

There's a man with a nose. Ambrose Bierce. *Fr.* The Devil's Dictionary. OBAL

There's a mean black snake been suckin' my rider's tongue. Black Snake. *Unknown.* BluL

There's a new grave up on Boot Hill, where we've planted Rowdy Pete. Pete's Error. Arthur Chapman. BPAW

There's a mouse house. I Wouldn't. John Ciardi. ECBV

There's a notable family named Stein. Limerick. *Unknown.* NOBL

There's a palace in Florence, the world knows well. The Statue and the Bust. Robert Browning. TT

There's a patch of old snow in a corner. A Patch of Old Snow. Robert Frost. CMoP (1970 ed.)

There's a place I've dreamed about far away. Adventure. Harry Behn. CTV

There's a plump little chap in a speckled coat. Bob White. George Cooper. PCOP

There's a pretty fuss and bother both in country and in town. A New Song on the Birth of the Prince of Wales. *Unknown.* FaBoBa; VLP

There's a pretty spot in Ireland I always claim for my land. Where the River Shannon Flows. James I. Russell. FSN

There's a Red Brick Wall. Nancy Chambers. FPB

There's a reid lowe in yer cheek. Sang. Robert McLellan. MS; SLP

There's a saucy, wild packet and a packet of fame. The *Dreadnought. Unknown.* AmFP

There's a sensitive man in Toms River. A Sensitive Man. Morris Bishop. TDH

There's a small café off the Avenue. Wardour Street. Humbert Wolfe. OxBTC

There's a star in the East on Christmas morn. Rise Up, Shepherd, and Follow. *Unknown.* FSW

There's a story told about Bogong Jack. Bogong Jack and the Trooper. John Manifold. FPA

There's a street in Trieste where I see my reflection. Three Streets. Umberto Saba, *tr. by* Anita Barrows. VWA

There's a taste of salt in the falling rain. Night Visitor. Alison Wyrley Birch. PPM

There's a thrush that sings in a shadowy wood. City Bird. Theda Kenyon. ECBV

There's a time in each year that we always hold dear. In the Good Old Summertime. Ren Shields. BLSo; FSN; FSW

"There's a tree in father's garden, lovelye William," says she. Lovelye William. *Unknown.* AmFP

There's a valley in Spain called Jarama. Jarama Valley. *Unknown.* FSW

There's a vaporish maiden in Harrison. A Vaporish Maiden. Morris Bishop. TDH

There's a vile old man. Limeraiku. Ted Pauker. NOBL

There's a whisper down the line at 11:39. Skimbleshanks: The Railway Cat. T. S. Eliot. FaBoCo; NOBL

There's a white cow standing upon the hill. The Cow. Knute Skinner. PCho

There's a woman like a dew-drop, she's so purer than the purest. Earl Mertoun's Song. Robert Browning. PoPle

There's a yellow rose of Texas that I am going to see. The Yellow Rose of Texas. *Unknown.* BLSo; FSW; PSoN

There's a yel-;low sponge. Never in This World You Will Drop a Yellow Sponge. Rochelle Owens. WBN

There's all sorts of fowl and fish. An Invitation to Lubberland. *Unknown.* FaBoNo; GBP

There's beauty in the deep. The Deep. John G. C. Brainard. RhR

There's been a death in the opposite house. Emily Dickinson. AmVN; InPS; SoSe (1977 ed.)

"There's been an accident," they said. Mr. Jones. Harry Graham. FaBoCo

There's big waves and little waves. Waves. Eleanor Farjeon. EcS

There's comfort in black February firs. February Thaw. Arthur J. Bull. HeHu

There's definitely been a mistake. An Unraveled Thought. Shlomit Cohen, *tr. by* Myra Glazer Schotz. VWA

There's four square miles of timber, mostly oak. Wild Pigs. Ted Kooser. TAT

There's good cooks and there's bad ones. The Roundup Cook. Robert V. Carr. BPAW

There's heaven above, and night by night. Johannes Agricola in Meditation. Robert Browning. OAEL-2

There's Holmes, who is matchless among you for wit. Holmes. James Russell Lowell. Fr. A Fable for Critics. NOBA

There's in my mind a woman. In Mind. Denise Levertov. Epi; InPS; NMM; RiTi

There's little in taking or giving. Coda. Dorothy Parker. SBG

There's little joy in life for me. On the Death of Anne Brontë. Charlotte Brontë. WPE

There's little personal grief in a quiet old death. The Death of My Grandmother. G. S. Fraser. MS

There's lots of funny goings-on the public don't suspect. Montgomery. H. A. C. Evans. GDP

"There's machinery in the butterfly." The Horrid Voice of Science. Vachel Lindsay. PoA

There's more in words than I can teach. Loving and Liking. Dorothy Wordsworth. OxBChV

There's More Pretty Girls than One. Unknown. AmFP

There's much afoot in heaven and earth this year. The Rainy Summer. Alice Meynell. OxBTC; SBG

There's Music in the Air, with music. Fanny Crosby. BLSo

There's my old man. The Famous Hot Pepper Eating Contest. Sam Hamod. SA

There's naught but care on every hand. See There's nought but care on ev'ry han'.

There's nawbody comes near my hoose ony mair. Herberie. Forbes Macgregor. MIS

There's no Avenging Angel. The Tree of Life Is Also a Tree of Fire. Gerda Norvig. VWA

There's no better dog nor Hardcastle's Rake. Rake. Dorothy Una Ratcliffe. BoAnP; GDP

There's no end to wisdom, no mask for folly. To the Elephants. Nathan Alterman, tr. by Ruth Nevo. VWA

There's no hiding here in the glare of the desert. Desert Song. Glenn Ward Dresbach. BPAW

There's no hiding place down here. No Hiding Place. Unknown. FSW

There's no horse this time. To the Coast. Denis Glover. ATNZ

There's no more to be done, or feared, or hoped. After the Last Breath. Thomas Hardy. VLP

There's No Place to Sleep in This Bed, Tanguy. Charles Henri Ford. EAS

There's no smoke in the chimney. The Deserted House. Mary Elizabeth Coleridge. RAE

There's no such thing as a student. Teaching. Al Young. NW

There's no way out. In the Suburbs. Louis Simpson. CoPAm; MAT; SFF; TH

There's not a hill in all the view. John Clare. PES

There's not a joy the world can give like that it takes away. Stanzas for Music. Byron. HAP

There's not a tint that paints the rose. God Is Everywhere. Unknown. CTV

There's not on earth a thing more vile and base. A Prayer for Faith. Michelangelo Buonarroti, tr. by John Addington Symonds. ILwL

There's nothing grieves me, but that age should haste. Michael Drayton. Fr. Idea. AAS; OAEL-1

"There's nothing mysterious about the skull." The Scientist. Janet Burroway. SoSe

There's nothing you can say to a man who drinks. The Drunken Man. Steven Orlen. AAN

There's nought [or naught] but care on ev'ry han'. Green Grow the Rashes [or Rushes], O. Burns. FSW; LAuP; PBMP; PPP

There's old Molly Hogan who cooks from a book. Stirling's Hotel. Unknown. AmFP

There's one in every city. Passing Stockyards Where They Killed the Buffalo. Harley Elliott. HeS

There's one leaf in the birchwoods that's shining. The Insistence. Gerard Malanga. AAN

There's one rides very sagely on the road. Upon the Horse and His Rider. Bunyan. OxBChV

There's one thing I like about that gal of mine. One Way Gal. Unknown. BluL

There's snow in every street. Winter. J. M. Synge. OxBTC; POL

"There's someone at the door," said gold candlestick. Green Candles. Humbert Wolfe. SO

There's something happenin' here. For What It's Worth. Stephen Stills. PoRo; WIF

There's something in a flying horse. Peter Bell. Wordsworth. MBPR

There's something in a stupid ass. Epilogue. Byron. PAIC

There's something to think about. The Smell of Wood. John Stevens Wade. FAF

There's teuch sauchs growin' i' the Reuch Heuch Hauch. The Sauchs in the Reuch Heuch Hauch. "Hugh MacDiarmid." NoAM

There's that mirk room I ken. The Room. Duncan Glen. MIS

There's the story of me sitting in the grass in the dark. In the Dead of the Night. Norman Dubie. AmPA

There's the tree, shaded and stolid as death. Seven-Tenths of a Second. Clinton F. Larson. MPA

There's the wonderful love of a beautiful maid. Love. Unknown. SFF; SoSe

There's thik wold hag, Moll Brown, look zee, jus' past! A Witch. William Barnes. VLP

There's this to remember about the gnu. The Gnu. Theodore Roethke. ECBV

There's three fair maids went to play at ball. The Cruel Brother. Unknown. AmFP

There's two white horses in a line. Two White Horses in a Line. Unknown. BluL

Theresa. John Pass. AMV-81

Therese. Alden Nowlan. NeAC

Theresienstadt Poem. Robert Mezey. VWA

Thermometer is not to be believed, The. Facts of Winter. Marie Harris. MMD

Thermopylae. Simonides. See On the Spartan Dead at Thermopylae.

Thermostatic Man, The. Gordon Challis. ATNZ

Therwith, when he was ware and gan beholde. Troilus Laments Criseyde's Absence. Chaucer. Fr. Troilus and Criseyde, V. OxBM

These. William Carlos Williams. NoAM; NOBA; PBMP; TCP; UsP

These acres, always again lost. Lost Acres. Robert Graves. NoAM

These acts are the real guts of everyday. Safe Places. Patricia Garfinkel. PoUp

These all their care expend on outward show. Edward Young. Fr. Love of Fame, the Universal Passion. OBSV

These animals, it was said, were not ordinary animals. Sirius, a Dog Star. Peter Kostakis. FiCh

These apartment acres, good only. Instructions for a Park. Brad Walker. AMV-80; AMV-81

These are also/ The war victims. "O.D." Zack Gilbert. CNA

These are amazing: each. Some Trees. John Ashbery. CAPP; ConAP

These are court-monsters, cormorants of the crown. Sir William Davenant. Fr. The Siege of Rhodes. SCP-2

These are men! the gaunt, unforesold, the vocal. Ol' Bunk's Band. William Carlos Williams. NOBA

These are my legs. I don't have to tell them, legs. Walter Jenks' Bath. William Meredith. CoPAm; HoPM (1975 ed.)

These are my murmur-laden shells that keep. On Some Shells Found Inland. Trumbull Stickney. EcS

These are my people. The Country Alphabet. Linda Parker. TC

These are not my sentiments. Louis Zukofsky. *Fr.* Light. NoAM

These are not ordinary children. A Music Lesson. Ann Ward. PMW

These are notes to lightning in my bedroom. Star Quilt. Roberta Hill. CDW

These are our immortals. Looking at Models in the Sears Catalogue. Philip Dacey. HeS

These are really the thoughts of all men in all ages and lands. Walt Whitman. Song of Myself, XVIII. BiP

These are the arrows that murder sleep. The Song of Crede. *Unknown, tr. by* Alfred Perceval Graves. BIrV

These are the days when birds come back. Emily Dickinson. FF; FSFS; PBMP; PiAm

These are the dog days. Songs to Survive the Summer. Robert Hass. AmPA

These are the dream machines. The Nightmare Factory. Maxine W. Kumin. NVAP

These are the gardens of the desert, these. The Prairies. Bryant. AmVN; EAP; NOBA; PiAm; TAP

These are the kinds of injury that. Horn, Mouth, Pit, Fire. William Dickey. AMV-81

These are the last crumbs of winter. Winter Flowers. Wade Hall. AATT

These are the men who. The Nuclear Physicists. Peggy Pond Church. WPW

These are the nights when the geese. A Gaggle of Geese, a Pride of Lions. John Moore. DuDa

These are the small hours when. Epithalamion. Michael Longley. CIP

These are the stone paths. Breakfast. Robin Shectman. AMV-80

These are the well-to-do, the managers of the nation. In a Hotel Lobby. Isidor Schneider. SPT

These are the words that leap. Words. Jean Burden. AMV-81

These are their shambles: night falling. The Bears in the Land-Fill. Lewis Turco. BCr

These, as they change, Almighty Father, these. A Hymn on the Seasons. James Thomson. *Fr.* The Seasons LAuP; PIM

These attempts to drink coffee. The New Formalists. Marvin Bell. AMV-81

These be/ Three silent things. Triad. Adelaide Crapsey. PAIC; WPE

These birds were born singing for joy. Another Song of the Same Woman, to Some Partridges, Sent to Her Alive. Florencia del Pinar, *tr. by* Julie Allen. BoWoP

These Bones. Thomas Herbert Parry-Williams, *tr. fr. Welsh by* H. Idris Bell. OBW

These bright colors of red. Ode to a Homemade Coffee Cup. Marine Robert Warden. AMV-81

These chairs they have no words to utter. Wordsworth. MBPR

These children—with their careless hair. The Collector. Richard Behm. AMV-81

These Damned Trees Crouch. Jim Barnes. CDW

These Days. Robert Jones. AMV-81

These Days. Charles Olson. TSWA

These Days. William Stafford. NNaP

These days I get up with the birches. Days in White. Ingeborg Bachmann, *tr. by* Daniel Huws. BoWoP

These days in prison seem a decayed time where. Decayed Time. Jean Wahl, *tr. by* Charles Guenther. VWA

These Days the Papers in the Street. Charles Reznikoff. VGW

These days the river. These Days. Robert Jones. AMV-81

These dead astronauts cannot decay. The Everlasting Astronauts. Tom Buchan. MS

These dice in my hand. The Dice Player. Dale Matthews. AAN

These dirt mounds make the dead seem fat. Indian Graves at Jocko. Richard Hugo. MPA

These Dreamings Mine. James O. Taylor. BuTh

These dried-out paint brushes which fell from my lips. Sestina from the Home Gardener. Diane Wakoski. CABA (1972 ed.); NoAM

These errors loved no less than the saint loves arrows. Elegy. George Barker. FaBoTw (1975 ed.)

These evenings,/ out where the Lackawanna boxcars. Winter Twilight. Jeff Schiff. AMV-81

These exquisite rags carry. A Box for Tom. James Tate. FiCP

These eyes of timid cherubim. Primula Scotica. Charles Senior. MIS

These February days, though few. Lent Tending. J. Barrie Shepherd. AMV-80

These Feet for Rosa Parks. Margo Bohanon. SES

These fell miasmic rings of mist, with ghoulish menace bound. Prejudice. Georgia Douglas Johnson. AmNP (1974 ed.); PoBA

These flowers are I, poor Fanny Hurd. Voices from Things Growing in a Churchyard. Thomas Hardy. OxBTC

These fought in any case. Ezra Pound. *Fr.* Hugh Selwyn Mauberley. FF; HeIP; NIL; NOBE; PiAm; PPoe; VGW

These fresh beauties, we can prove. Why Flowers Change Color. Robert Herrick. HAP

These germs are medusan: a touch. Isolation Ward. Robert L. Koenig. AMV-81

These grand and fatal movements toward death. Rearmament. Robinson Jeffers. PSN

These hands that caress the flower. Bloom. Greg Hannan. PoUp

These hearts were woven of human joys and cares. The Dead. Rupert Brooke. 1914, IV. PoA

These Horses Came. Ray A. Young Bear. CDW

These, in the day when heaven was falling. Epitaph on an Army of Mercenaries. A. E. Housman. BTTM; CMoP (1970 ed.); NIL; NoAM; NOBE; OBP; OxBTC; PPP; PSN; UnPo (1976 ed.)

These Indians explain away their hair. A Night at the Napi in Browning. Richard Hugo. TAT

These Indians once imitated life. The Only Bar in Dixon. James Welch. AmPA; FF

These islands gathering images. Matsushima. Harry Guest. TwMBP

These labouring wits, like paviours, mend our ways. Edward Young. *Fr.* Epistles to Mr. Pope. OBSV

These Lacustrine Cities. John Ashbery. CAPP; NIL; UnPo (1976 ed.)

These Leaves. William Stafford. NNaP

These little limbs [*or* limmes]. The Salutation. Thomas Traherne. ILP (1975 ed.); MetP

These locusts by day, these crickets by night. Wallace Stevens. PoA

These lovely groves of fountain-trees that shake. Golden Bough. Elinor Wylie. PBWP

These lover's inklings which our loves enmesh. Counsel to Unreason. Léonie Adams. PoA

These Magicians. Sarah Provost. AMV-81

These market-dames, mid-aged, with lips thin-drawn. Former Beauties. Thomas Hardy. At Casterbridge Fair, II. NoAM

These massacres of the superior peoples. John Berryman. *Fr.* Dream Songs. CAPP

These men were kings, albeit they were black. Black Majesty. Countee Cullen. PoBA; VGW

These mountains have heard God. The Tillamook Burn. William Stafford. CNW

These new night. Ivory Masks in Orbit. Keorapetse Kgositsile. PoBA

These nubbins/ these hangers-on. Maxine W. Kumin. *Fr.* Song for Seven Parts of the Body. POL

These nymphs I would perpetuate. The Afternoon of a Faun: Eclogue. Stéphane Mallarmé, *tr. by* Roger Fry. NAWM-2

These Obituaries of Rattlesnakes Being Eaten by the Hogs. Roger Weingarten. AmPA

These only wait. In the Columbia River Gorge, after a Death. Sandra McPherson. CNW

These plaintive verse, the postes of my desire. Samuel Daniel. *Fr.* To Delia AAS

These poems/ they are things that I do. June Jordan. FoP

These poems are too much tangled with the error. To the Reader. Edgar Bowers. PiAm

These pools that, though in forests, still reflect. Spring Pools. Robert Frost. NoAM; NOBA; PiAm; TCP

These Purists. William Carlos Williams. OBAL

These riotoures three, of which I telle. Three Revellers Search for Death. Chaucer. *Fr.* The Canterbury Tales: The Pardoner's Tale. OxBM

These royall kinges, that reare up to the skye. Thomas Sackevyll in Commendation of the Worke to the Reader. Thomas Sackville. AAS

These seven houses have learned to face one another. On a Painting by Patient B of the Independence State Hospital for the Insane. Donald Justice. ConAP

These songs/ may be known. Two Clouds. Dan Gerber. TC

These songs will not stand. Songs, I. Denis Glover. ATNZ

These spectres resting on plastic stools. Cafe in Warsaw. Allen Ginsberg. HAP; TT

These sticks I am holding. This Preparation. Simon Ortiz. VW

These suggestions by Asians are not taken seriously. Asian Peace Offers Rejected without Publication. Robert Bly. CAPP; NoAM

These the dread days which the seers have foretold. The Death of Justice. Walter Everette Hawkins. PoBA

These things bear the brain's fruit. High Are the Winter Rivers. Dave Smith. HeS

These to His Memory—since he held them dear. Dedication. Tennyson. *Fr.* Idylls of the King. CABA (1972 ed.); VLP

These to me are beautiful people. Preference. Elinor Wylie. Psy

"These tourists, heaven preserve us! needs must live." The Brothers. Wordsworth. MBPR

These tracings from a world that's dead. To Violet. Basil Bunting. PoA

These Trees Are. Susan Strayer Deal. AMV-81

These Trees Stand. W. D. Snodgrass. NoAM; PoIA; PPP

These Two. Howard Schwartz. VWA

These two great men battling like lovers. All-In Wrestlers. James Kirkup. SPo

These umbered cliffs and gnarls of masonry. Rome. Thomas Hardy. VLP

These walls, so full of monument and bust. The Abbey Church at Bath. Henry Harington. FaBoEE

These were the sounds that dinned upon his ear Dream of Winter. George Mackay Brown. FaBoTw (1975 ed.)

These wet rocks where the tide has been. Low-Tide. Edna St. Vincent Millay. RhR

These Women All. —— Heath. FaBoCo

These women have no language and so they chatter. Lines for Those to Whom Tragedy Is Denied. Joyce Carol Oates. CoPAm; IHMS

These women love hard. Pretzels. E. Ethelbert Miller. PoUp

These woods are one of my great lies. The Owl. W. S. Merwin. PPP

These words are all of me. Love Poem. Lewis Turco. NowV

These words we have swallowed. Your Eyes, Your Name. William Matthews. NVAP

Theseus: A Trilogy. Yvor Winters. NOBA

Theseus and Ariadne. Robert Graves. HAP

Thesis. William Walter De Bolt. AMV-80

Thesis. Edward Dorn. NOBA

Thesis, Antithesis, and Nostalgia. Alan Dugan. NowV

Thespian in Jerusalem. Myra Glazer Schotz. VWA

Thessalian. Winifred Bryher. PoA

Thetis is the moon-goddess. Hilda Doolittle ("H. D."). *Fr.* Helen in Egypt. Moon

They. Donald Finkel. CoPAm; GP

They. Mani Leib, *tr. fr. Yiddish by* David G. Roskies *and* Hillel Schwartz. VWA

"They." Siegfried Sassoon. CMoP (1970 ed.); OBSV

They. R. S. Thomas. OxBTC

They/ say/ you/ went/ abroad. Incidental Pieces to a Walk. James Cunningham. JB

They, after the slow building of the house. Asmodeus. Geoffrey Hill. FaBoTw (1975 ed.)

They aint no use a-telling, boy, what's for you to do. Dan Ellis's Boys. *Unknown.* AmFP

They all arrived, and then with generous show. The Wedding Feast. Luis de Góngora, *tr. by* Edward Meryon Wilson. *Fr.* The First Solitude. OBVE

They all see the same movies. Powwow. W. D. Snodgrass. SoS

They All Want to Play Hamlet. Carl Sandburg. NOBA

They alone are left me; they alone still faithful. My Dead. Rachel, *tr. by* Robert Mezey. VWA

They amputated/ Your thighs off my hips. A Pity; We Were Such a Good Invention. Yehuda Amichai, *tr. by* Assia Gutmann. BoLoP; LoAs

They are able, with science, to measure the millionth of a millionth of an electron-volt. C Stands for Civilization. Kenneth Fearing. SPT

They are aging in attic. Advice to the Lovelorn. Linda Parker. HeS; TC

They are all dead: our reaching hands half a century long. A Fresco for A. MacLeish. Alfred Hayes. SPT

They are all dying. Death as History. Jay Wright. PoBA

They Are All Gone. Henry Vaughan. *See* They Are All Gone into the World of Light.

They are all gone away. The House on the Hill. E. A. Robinson. AmVN; TH; UsP; VoPo

They Are All Gone into the World of Light. Henry Vaughan. HeIP; ILP (1975 ed.); InPS; MetP; NOBE; OAEL-1; SCP-1
(Departed Friends.) PIM
(Friends Departed.) BoReV
(World of Light, The.) PMW

They are always living. The Animal's Christmas. Philip Dacey. GP; HeS; NVAP

They are and suffer; that is all they do. Surgical Ward. W. H. Auden. SoS

They are coming through the bright fields. Falling in Love with Tygers. Thomas Bush. NVAP

They are cutting down the great plane-trees at the end of the gardens. The Trees Are Down. Charlotte Mew. WPE

They are digging everywhere. From street to street. Vincent Buckley. Golden Builders, IV. CAAP; GAS

They are disturbed even by my hair. My Strawlike Hair. Asya, *tr. by* Gabriel Preil *and* Howard Schwartz. VWA

They are eternal as angels and demons. Photographing the Facade—San Miguel de Allende. Betsy Colquitt. AMV-80

They are gathered, astounded and disturbed. The Last Supper. Rainer Maria Rilke, *tr. by* M. D. Herter Norton. OFD

They are here, Svetlana, as they were there. Sojourners at Phoenix. Judith Rodriguez. FPA

They Are Killing All the Young Men. David Henderson. PoBA

They are lang deid, folk that I used to ken. Elegy. Robert Garioch. MS

They are moving inwards; the circle is closing. Man Meeting Himself. Howard Sergeant. EAS

They are no substitutes for gas masks. Newspaper Hats. Jim Howard. AMV-81

They are not extinct. The Dodos. Cash Terrell. DNGG

They are not here. And we, we are the Others. The Absent. Edwin Muir. NoAM

They are not long, the weeping and the laughter. Vitae Summa Brevis Spem Nos Vetat Incohare Longam. Ernest Dowson. HAP; NOBE; VLP

They are not silent like workhorses. Donkeys. Edward Field. BoAnP

They are out-of-date. Normal Lives. Dick Allen. FAF

They are preparing to begin again. The Task. John Ashbery. CAAP

They are pulling down that London hotel. Reproaches. William Price Turner. SLP

They are rattling breakfast plates in basement kitchens. Morning at the Window. T. S. Eliot. CABA (1972 ed.); PiAm; PoA; PSN; TT

They are rebuilding/ the old bridge, the Nagara. Lady Ise, *tr. fr. Japanese by* Etsuko Terasaki *and* Irma Brandeis. BoWoP

They are restless. Dickens Characters. Robert Morgan. HeHu

They are taking all my letters, and they. The Dishonest Mailmen. Robert Creeley. PiAm

They are the clean boys from the midwest. Seminar. Erica Jong. RiTi

They are the last romantics, these candles. Candles. Sylvia Plath. NMM; PSN

They are the oldest living captive race. Ginkgoes in Fall. Howard Nemerov. GP

They are the slums of great cities, with narrow streets. In the Ghetto. Hugo Sonnenschein, *tr. by* Edouard Roditi. VWA

They are there on the other side of the hill. The Stammerers. Margaret Kent. AMV-80

They are with us always, but they have the wit. The Distances They Keep. Howard Nemerov. BoAnP

They asked for bread. For Our Soldiers Who Fell in Russia. Franco Fortini, *tr. by* Ruth Feldman. VWA

They basted his caption on top of the fat sheriff, "The Pig." Sonnet. Ted Berrigan. CAAP

They bear him to his resting-place. She: At His Funeral. Thomas Hardy. VLP

They beat the tom-tom, they plucked the guitar. Fandango. "Stanley Vestal." BPAW

They began to build a church, stone and brick. Study in Punctuation. Arthur J. Bull. HeHu

They began to sway to the. When These Old Barns Lost Their Inhabitants. David Kherdian. FAF; TAT

They bide their time off serpentine. Ancient Monuments. John Ormond. OBW

They breathe with the night. Roland Penrose. *Fr.* The Road Is Wider than Long. EAS

They brought him in on a stretcher from the world. Grandfather. Derek Mahon. LP

They brought it along and they slipped it in. Heart Burial. Geoffrey Grigson. POL

They built the front, upon my word. On the Building of a New Church. *Unknown.* FaBoEE

They call all experience of the senses mystic when the experience is considered. Mystic. D. H. Lawrence. WeW

They call it regional, this relevance. Lake Chelan. William Stafford. BiP; ILP (1975 ed.)

They call me and I go. Complaint. William Carlos Williams. TCP

They call me Hanging Johnny. Hanging Johnny. *Unknown.* GBP

They call, "The Prince has come." Miss Hewett's Shenanigans. Dorothy Hewett. GAS

They call this "Black North." Names. G. C. Dawe. IPM

They call your name in vain. St. Francis of Assisi and the Miserable Jews. Josef Whittlin, *tr. by* Isaac Komem. VWA

"They called it Annandale—and I was there." How Annandale Went Out. E. A. Robinson. ILP (1975 ed.); NoAM; NOBA; PAIC; PoIA; PPoD

They called it sin. The Label. Ruthe T. Spinnanger. AATT

They called them shadblow or service bush. Those Trees That Line the Northway. Ellen Perreault. AMV-81

They came down the road. The Dancing Bear. Greg Kuzma. BCr

They came for you, fumbling through fog. The Fourth of July Drowning. Judith Minty. TC

They came hurrying across the mountain highway. Monkeys on Mt. Hiei. Edith Marcombe Shiffert. WPE

They came in to the little town. We Are Going. Kath Walker. GAS

They came out of the sun undetected. The Raid. William Everson. NoAM; PiAm; TCP

They came running over the perilous sands. 1945. Sir Herbert Read. OxBTC

The can call you/ to the morgue. The Chance You Take. Harrison Fisher. PoUp

They Can't Do That. *Unknown.* WTO

They cared for nothing but the days and hours. The Disinherited. Charles Spear. ATNZ

"They carry on." Floodtide. Askia Muhammad Touré. PoBA

They cast lots on the day of Azazel. Lament for Azazel. Francis Landy. VWA

They Cast Their Nets in Galilee, *with music.* William A. Percy. AH

They clear the left side for him. Oscar Robertson: Peripheral Vision. William Matthews. PPoD

They climbed the upward path, through absolute silence. Orpheus and Eurydice. Ovid, *tr. by* Rolfe Humphries. *Fr.* Metamorphoses. GrRo

They come in search of front porch. Tourism. Lillie D. Chaffin. TAT

They come into. Feeding the Lions. Norman Jordan. CTBA; PoBA

They come not within the tall woods. To One Elect. S. I. Hayakawa. PoA

They come to me talking about your safety. To My Daughter, 1936. Genevieve Taggard. SPT

They cross the frontier as their names cross your pages. The New Emigration. Kay Boyle. WPE

They crossed her face with blood. A Hope for Those Separated by War. Sidney Keyes. BuTh

They crucified my Lord, an' He never said a mumbalin' word. Crucifixion. *Unknown.* BPo; TAP

They cruise by. On Watching Pimps. Quincy Troup. SES

"They cut it in squares." Socratic. Hilda Doolittle ("H. D."). HoPM (1975 ed.)

They depart from what they have failed. The Migrants. Wendell Berry. CSP

They did it George. They did it. Conversation with Washington. Myra Cohn Livingston. OFD

They didn't get me. Alma Villanueva. NW

They didn't have much trouble. Teaching the Ape to Write Poems. James Tate. GP

They didn't hire him. Gary Snyder. *Fr.* Hitch Haiku. InPK

They dither softly at her bedroom door. Cover Her Face. Thomas Kinsella. CIP

They do not come with furred caps. Barbarians. John Fowles. POL

They do not live in the world. The Animals. Edwin Muir. CMoP (1970 ed.); EBEV; HeIP; PoIA

They do not paint a still-life. The Art Lesson. Robert Morgan. HeHu

They do not speak but into their empty mood. Two Old Men Look at the Sea. J. R. Hervey. ATNZ

They done took Cordelia. Stony Lonesome. Langston Hughes. NOBA; PiAm

They don't get anywhere. The Couple Overheard. William Meredith. CoPAm; HoPM (1975 ed.); NoAM

They don't have gibbons in Nebraska. Nebraskan Childhood. Daniel Halpern. CAAP

They don't hold grudges. First Monday Scottsboro Alabama. Tom Weatherly. PoBA

They don't move much. Mostly. Old Men in a Home. May Ivimy. PMW

They Don't Speak English in Paris. Ogden Nash. OBAL

They dragged you from homeland. Strong Men. Sterling A. Brown. BPo; CNA; FB; PoBA

They Dream Only of America. John Ashbery. CAPP; EAS

They dressed us up in black. The Funeral. Walter de la Mare. CMoP (1970 ed.)

They droop like sad fuchsias from our bodies. The Grief of Our Genitals. Henry Carlile. GP

They drove to the market with ringing pockets. Hamnavoe Market. George Mackay Brown. MS

They dunno how it is. Rythm. Ian Crichton Smith. LP; MPo

They eat beans mostly, this old yellow pair. The Bean Eaters. Gwendolyn Brooks. CAPP; CoPAm; HAP; HeIP; IPWM; MAT; PoBA; TAP; TT

They Eat Out. Margaret Atwood. Psy ("In restaurants we argue.") NeAC

They End It. Dave Morice. AcAn

They erect gallows in the prison yard. The Condemned. Edmond Jabès, *tr.* by Jack Hirschman. VWA

They Feed They Lion. Philip Levine. MAT; NNaP; NoAM; NOBA; Prf

They feel the calm delight, and thus proceed. Walking by the Sea. George Crabbe. PMW

They feigned maturity, natural defence. Classroom. James Aitchison. MS

They Flee from Me That Sometime Did Me Seek [*or* Seke]. Sir Thomas Wyatt. *See* Lover Showeth How He Is Forsaken...

They formed the ritual circle. A Local Man Remembers [*or* Goes to] the Killing Ground. James Whitehead. CoPAm; CSP

They gave me the wrong name, in the first place. Her Story. Naomi Long Madgett. IHMS; PoBA; TPo

They gave my father a television. Death. Howard Byatt. FF

They go in different ways. No One Talks about This. Carl Rakosi. GP

They grew in beauty side by side. The Graves of a Household. Felicia Dorothea Hemans. FaPoR; VLP; WPE

They had been there a month; the water had begun to tear them apart. A Negro Soldier's Viet Nam Diary. Herbert Martin. PoBA

They had never had one in the house before. Bronzeville Woman in a Red Hat. Gwendolyn Brooks. TT

They had pulled her out of the river. Along the River. D. J. Enright. HeHu

They had secured their beauty to the dock. The Crowd. John Masefield. OxBTC

They had supposed their formula was fixed. The White Troops Had Their Orders, but the Negroes Looked like Men. Gwendolyn Brooks. PBMP

They had told me. The January of 75. Alan Chong Lau. NW

They hanged him on a clement morning, swung. Epitaph. Dennis Scott. SFF

They hanged Jeff Buckner from a sycamore tree. Jeff Buckner. Frank Beddo. WTO

They hanged the King of Ai at eventide. The King of Ai. Hyam Plutzik. VWA

They haul away our nights in manure trucks. Another Load. William Harrold. HeS

They have a king and officers of sorts. Honey-Bees. Shakespeare. King Henry V, *fr.* I, ii. PCOP

They have all gone across. Cold Feet. Brian Lee. FPB

They have been with us a long time. Telephone Poles. John Updike. UsP

They have brought you here. The Shack outside Boise. Vern Rutsala. PoW

They have carried the mahogany chair and the cane rocker. Mourning Picture. Adrienne Rich. UsP

They had chiseled on my stone the words. Cassius Hueffer. Edgar Lee Masters. *Fr.* Spoon River Anthology. NoAM

They have come by carloads. Surfers at Santa Cruz. Paul Goodman. FF; LiSp; SPo

They have connived at those jewelled fascinations. Auspice of Jewels. Laura Riding. NoAM

They have dreamed as young men dream. Old Black Men. Georgia Douglas Johnson. PoBA

They have eyes that see not. Maxine W. Kumin. *Fr.* Song for Seven Parts of the Body. POL

They have fenced in the dirt road. Burial. Alice Walker. AmPA; CSP; WBN

They have forgotten that wolves. The Villages. R. E. Sebenthall. HeS

They have launched the little ship. The Ship. Richard Church. FPB

They have [*or* They've *or* Th'have] left thee naked, Lord. O that they had! On Our Crucified Lord, Naked and Bloody. Richard Crashaw. CABA (1972 ed.) HoPM (1975 ed.); ILP (1975 ed.); OAEL-1; SCP-1

They have left us, all the summer's mornings. Classical Autumn. Robert Clayton Casto. AMV-81

They have loved the shadows. The Seal in the Lowry Park Zoo. Richard Mathews. AATT

They have minute faces like walrussed grandpas. The Brineshrimp. Rhyll McMaster. FPA

They have sed. Hospital/Poem. Sonia Sanchez. BPo; PoBA

They have spilled no blood there. The Western Myth. John Boland. IPM

They have stood long in the sun. Greens. Greg Kuzma. HeS

They have taken the gable from the roof of clay. Swedes. Edward Thomas. OAEL-2

They have turned, and say that I am dying. That. I Substitute for the Dead Lecturer. Amiri Baraka. NOBA

They Have Turned the Church Where I Ate God. Gary Gildner. GP

They have won out at last and laid us bare. The Invaders. Yvor Winters. PiAm

They haven't got no noses. The Song of Quoodle. G. K. Chesterton. DuDr

They hire you for the silk to line their budgets. Advice from Euterpe. Carter Revard. VoR

They hold their hands over their mouths. The Poets Agree to Be Quiet by the Swamp. David Wagoner. CoPAm; VGW

They hurt no one. They rove the North. In Fur. William Stafford. RFM

They keep coming at me. Stops. Lucille Clifton. CAAP

They killed you and didn't tell us where they. Epitaph for the Tomb of Adolfo Baez Bone. Ernesto Cardenal, *tr. by* Janet Brof. POL

They knew the conjugations of the flesh. Emeritus, n. Henri Coulette. FF

They know no more than I would how to stand. The Visitors. Peter Dale. PMW

They lean against the cooling car, backs pressed. The Discovery of the Pacific. Thom Gunn. HeIP; MIT

They lean over the path. Orchids. Theodore Roethke. AnMo; CMoP (1970 ed.); ExPo (1973 ed.); PF; PiAm; PPoe

They leaned a good stout rail against the tree. Robbing the Tree Hive. Ernest G. Moll. PoTa

They leave their love-lorn haunts. Wedded. Isaac Rosenberg. PoPle

They leave us so to the way we took. In Neglect. Robert Frost. VGW

They left him behind. Mission Uncontrolled. Richard Peck. MiP

They left the primrose glistening in its dew. Spring, and the Blind Children. Alfred Noyes. OxBTC

They left their Babylon bare. The Destruction of Jerusalem by the Babylonian Hordes. Isaac Rosenberg. VWA

They let the children out of school. To the Woodville Depot. D. C. Berry. AAN

They libbit William Wallace. On a North British Devolutionary. Douglas Young. MS

They lie unwatched, in waste and vacant places. The Dwellings of Our Dead. Arthur H. Adams. ATNZ

They lied about. Strange Kind (II). J. D. Reed. Moon

They live alone. Neighbors. David Allan Evans. HeS

They live by the Lakes, an appropriate quarter. On the Lake Poets. Charles Townsend. FaBoEE

They live in Parallel Worlds. William J. Harris. CNA

They looked so good. The Young Fenians. Padraic Fallon. BIrV

They looked soft floating down. Invasion North. Richard Hugo. GP

They meet but with unwholesome springs. Against Them Who Lay Unchastity to the Sex of Women. William Habington. MetP

They mouth love's language. A Memory of the Players in a Mirror at Midnight. James Joyce. NoAM

They moved like rivers in their mended stockings. The Grandmothers. Mary Oliver. UsP; WPE

They mowed the meadow down below. The Island. Dorothy Aldis. ECBV

They must be shown as about to taste of the tree. Adam and Eve. C. H. Sisson. FaBoTw (1975 ed.)

They must to keep their certainty accuse. The Leaders of the Crowd. W. B. Yeats. EBEV; SFF

They named it Aultgraat—Ugly Burn. The Black Rock of Kiltearn. Andrew Young. FaBoTw (1975 ed.)

They named the huge one Grendel. Grendel. *Unknown, tr. by* Burton Raffel. *Fr.* Beowulf. NU; OBP

They never even slow/ their steady, cud-chewing plod. Camels. Jean Nordhaus. PoUp

They paddle with staccato feet. Pigeons. Richard Kell. BoAnP

They pass too fast. Ships, and there's time for sighing. Earth Has Shrunk in the Wash. William Empson. CMoP (1970 ed.)

They pointed me out on the highway, and they said. The Traveller. John Berryman. PoA; UsP; VGW

They Pray the Best Who Pray and Watch, *with music.* Edward Hopper. AH

They put him here because God came at night. Dementia Praecox. Morris Bishop. PoA

They rest: the cat curls next the sleeping wife. Night Thoughts. Richard Bastian. AATT

They Return. Jay MacPherson. *Fr.* The Way Down. PoA

They rode north. Blackie Thinks of His Brothers. Stanley Crouch. PoBA

They rose up in a twinkling cloud. The Stockdoves. Andrew Young. BoAnP

They roused him with muffins—they roused him with ice. The Baker's Tale. "Lewis Carroll." *Fr.* The Hunting of the Snark. EBEV

They said the furnaces were cold. The Factory. Olga Cabral. GP

They said, "Wait." Well, I waited. Alabama Centennial. Naomi Long Madgett. BPo

They said, "You are no longer a lad." Battle Won Is Lost. Phillip William George. VW

They sat. They stood about. Of Commerce and Society. Geoffrey Hill. PPoe

The sate to meat, and Satyrane his chaunce. Spenser. *Fr.* The Faerie Queene, III, 9. OAEL-1

They say a church once stood in this Anglian field. Archaeology. Richard Church. PES

They say a tropic river threads the seas. The Gulf Stream. Henry Bellamann. RhR

They say, God wot! On the Death of the Giraffe. Thomas Hood. FaBoEE

They say, his strange, large eyes. Father. Margit Kaffka, *tr. by* Laura Schiff. PWP

They say I do not realize. Me Again. Kenneth Rexroth. VoA

They say ideal beauty cannot enter. Hiram Powers' "Greek Slave." Elizabeth Barrett Browning. SBG; VLP

They say I'm crazy got no sense. I Don't Care. Jean Lenox. FSN

They say its's better to be poor. Rain Has Fallen on the History Books. David Rosenberg. VWA

They say it's just a pumpkin. How Come? Sara Asheron. CaYB

They Say My Verse Is Sad: No Wonder. A. E. Housman. NoAM

They say one good shot deserves another. Fools. Glenn Hardin. AMV-81

They say Revis found a flatrock. Mountain Bride. Robert Morgan. GP

They say "Son." Old Black Men Say. James A. Emanuel. PoBA

They say that blood is salt. Gifts. Leon Stokesbury. GP

They say that every idle word. Idle Words. Walter Savage Landor. OBSV

They say that freedom is a constant struggle. Freedom Is a Constant Struggle. *Unknown.* FSW

They say that plants don't talk, nor do. Rosalia de Castro, *tr. fr. Spanish by* Aliki *and* Willis Barnstone. BoWoP

They say that Richard Cory owns. Richard Cory. Paul Simon. InPK; UsP; WIF

They say that trees scream. High Frequency. Marge Piercy. MMD

They say that when they burned young Shelley's corpse. The Fishes and the Poet's Hands. Frank Yerby. AmNP (1974 ed.)

They say the Lion and the Lizard keep. Omar Khayyám, *tr. by* Edward Fitzgerald. *Fr.* The Rubáiyát of Omar Khayyám. EBEV

They say the men are. The Men Are Coming Back! Barry Cole. OxBTC

They say the Phoenix is dying, some say dead. News of the Phoenix. A. J. M. Smith. ExPo (1973 ed.)

They say the sea is cold, but the sea contains. Whales Weep Not! D. H. Lawrence. CMoP (1970 ed.); ExPo (1973 ed.); NU; OBP; PPoe

They say the sirens called a man. The Goose Fish. William Logan. AAN

They say the white bear huge and thick. Albino Bear. Douglas Lawder. BCr

They say there is a land. Idaho. *Unknown.* BPAW; GBP

They say there is a sweeter air. A Carriage from Sweden. Marianne Moore. HAP; SoSe; WeW

They say 'tis sinful to flirt. Sinful to Flirt. *Unknown.* AmFP

They say you lurk here still, perhaps. Prayer to the Mothers. Diane DiPrima. RiTi

They sent him back to her. The letter came. Not to Keep. Robert Frost. CMoP (1970 ed.)

They served tea in the sandpile, together with. The Party. Reed Whittemore. BBGO; ConAP; LP; NCSH

They set the fish upon the table. Pesci Misti. Leonard Aaronson. FaBoTw (1975 ed.)

They set the slave free, striking off his chains. The Slave. James Oppenheim. PPM

They shall go down unto life's borderland. Sonnet to Negro Soldiers. Joseph Seamon Cotter, Jr. PoBA

They shook the green leaves down. Magic Fox. James Welch. CDW

They should be held in the open. Classes. Keith Wilson. NowV

They shoved me into the hole. The Artist Underground. Ann Stanford. MPA

They shut me up in prose. Emily Dickinson. InPS; NOBA; SBG

They shut the road through the woods. The Way through the Woods. Kipling. ILP (1975 ed.); NOBE; OxBChV; OxBTC; PoPle; RFM; VLP

They signed to play the leading man. Curtain Call. Alan Ziegler. AAN

They sing their dearest songs. During Wind and Rain. Thomas Hardy. CMoP (1970 ed.); ExPo (1973 ed.); HAP; ILP (1975 ed.); InPK; NIL; OAEL-2; OxBTC; PoPle; PPP

They sit among music of waterfall leaves. Six Statues in a Park. Floyd C. Stuart. FAF

They sit and smoke on the esplanade. At a Watering Place. Thomas Hardy. CMoP (1970 ed.)

They Slept while Jesus Prayed. Henry Tim Chambers. AATT

They slew by night. The Pentecost Castle. Geoffrey Hill. HAP

They slip on to the bus, hair piled up high. The Young Ones. Elizabeth Jennings. OxBTC

They Sometimes Call Me. Wendy Rose. CDW

They spent my life plotting against me. Possessions. Ken Smith. EAS

They splay at a bend of the road, rifles slung, the. The Spool. Ben Belitt. PPoD

They spoke/ of the queen at night growing. Short Eulogy. Zali Gurevitch, *tr. by* Gabriel Levin. VWA

They stand in a row like chimneys. Poplars. Henry Grynberg, *tr. by* Isaac Komem. VWA

They started with his best guitar. The Day They Ate the Baritone. Samuel Hazo. PPoD

They step from the high plane and begin to tumble. Sky Diving. Richmond Lattimore. LiSp; SPo

They stood—rain pelting at window, shrouded sea. In the Local Museum. Walter de la Mare. HAP

They strolled down the lane together. A Farmer's Boy. *Unknown.* PoPle

They talk of short-lived pleasure—be it so. Mutation. Bryant. EAP

They tell me (but I really can't). My Aunt's Spectre. Mortimer Collins. PoTa

They tell me I have to exercise to lose weight. Amen. Jaime Sabines, *tr. by* Steve Kowit. AMV-81

They tell me she's crazy. Going Home. Renée Roper. NPW

They tell of a hunter named Shephard. A Hunter Named Shephard. *Unknown.* TDH

They tell us: We are the barren who give. On Christ's Birth (To Sisters). Jane Marie Luecke. AATT

They that go down to the sea in ships. Bible, *O.T.* Psalms, CVII: 23-31. CTV; RhR

They that have power to hurt, and will do none. Sonnets, XCIV. Shakespeare. CABA (1972 ed.); Epi; ExPo (1973 ed.); InPS; IP; LoAs; NOBE; OAEL-1; PPoe; PPP

They that in play can do the thing they would. The Growth of Love, I. Robert Bridges. NoAM

They think I gonna smuggle. The Poem Is Mightier than the Switchblade. Richard W. Thomas. TC

They think I like it here, I guess. Comanche. Gary Gildner. PH

They throw in Drummer Hodge, to rest. Drummer Hodge. Thomas Hardy. EBEV; HAP; ILP (1975 ed.); InPS; NoAM; VLP

They told me. Witch. Jean Tepperman. NMM

They told me, Heraclitus, they told me you were dead. Heraclitus. William Johnson Cory, *after* Callimachus. FaBoEE; FaPoR; InPK; NOBE; VLP

They told me you had been to her. Evidence Read at the Trial of the Knave of Hearts. "Lewis Carroll." *Fr.* Alice's Adventures in Wonderland. FaBoCo; FaBoNo; PBMP; SS

They took me from the white sun and they. A Little Boy Lost. Jerome Rothenberg. VoA

They took me out. Ku Klux. Langston Hughes. BPo

They took the blue from the skies. The Air Force Blue. Scott *and* Textor. BLSH

They took the whole Cherokee nation. The Lament of the Cherokee Reservation Indian. John D. Loudermilk. PoRo

They trace their ancestry. The Legend of Paper Plates. John Haines. GP; PPoD

They understood each other well. The Maze. Norman Kreitman. PMW

They unfold before the sky. Doors. Therese Plantier, *tr. by* Willis Barnstone *and* Elene Kolb. BoWoP

They uprooted an ancient cave. Archaeologists. Real Faucher. AMV-80

They used to tell me I was building a dream. Brother, Can You Spare a Dime? E. Y. Harburg. AIW

They wade through beer cans. Cowboys: Three. Rod McKuen. MiP

They wait like darkness not becoming stars. The New Pietà: For the Mothers and Children of Detroit. June Jordan. PoBA

They walk dangerously. The Home. Susan Axelrod. NMM

They walk on the edge of the world. Vanguardia. Sandra Maria Esteves. NW

They walked in straitened ways. The Old Ladies. Colin Ellis. OxBTC

They watch each other. Interface. Pamela Alexander. AAN

They Watch Me with Radar. Lee Lally. PoUp

They watch the big vats bubbling over. Octobers. Christopher Middleton. TwMBP

They weave a slow andante as in sleep. The Andante of Snakes. Arthur Symons. VLP

They Went Home. Maya Angelou. IHMS

They went off on the buckboard in the rain. Ranchers. Maurice Lesemann. BPAW

They went to sea in a Sieve, they did. The Jumblies. Edward Lear. BBL; CTV; EBEV; FaBoNo; OxBChV; SS

They went with axe and rifle, when the trail was still to blaze. Western Wagons. Rosemary *and* Stephen Vincent Benét. BPAW

They were alone once more; for them to be. Byron. *Fr.* Don Juan, IV. EBEV

They were at play, she and her cat. Femme et Chatte. Paul Verlaine, *tr. by* Arthur Symons. OBVE

They were both still. Lamentations. Louis Glück. BoWoP; PCho

They were dancing as if. Glass. Takake Uchino Lento. BoWoP

They were dark/ parachutes opening. Black Silk Skirts. Elizabeth Brunazzi. PoUp

They were human, they suffered. Founding Fathers, Nineteenth-Century Style. Robert Penn Warren. *Fr.* Promises. NoAM

They were landing and the great thrust. The Choice. Robert Morgan. HeHu

They were like fish meal. Lead. Jayne Cortez. PoBA

They were printed daily in the newspapers. Epithets of War—III: Casualties. Vernon Scannell. HeHu

They were singing Old MacDonald in the schoolbus. Chorus. John Ciardi. SS

They were so mean they could not between them. As in Their Time. Louis MacNeice. POL

They were the Thompsons. I Wasn't No Mary Ellen. Linda King. GP

They were women then. Women. Alice Walker. GOA

They who in folly or mere greed. Where Are the War Poets? C. Day Lewis. OxBTC

They Who Possess the Sea. Marguerite Janvrin Adams. RhR

They will bury that fair body and cover you. Epitaph on a Young Child. Ivor Gurney. FaBoEE

They will catch me. On Hearing the Airlines Will Use a Psychological Profile to Catch Potential Skyjackers. Stephen Dunn. AmPA; SoSe (1977 ed.)

They will come for you in morning. Whispers. Roberta Hill. CDW

They will never die on that battlefield. Uccello. Gregory Corso. FF

They will never get to Moscow. Three Sisters. Erica Jong. UsP

They will not leave me, the lives of other people. The Hunched. Douglas Dunn. LP

They will soon be down. For the Last Wolverine. James Dickey. LiSp

They wondered why the fruit had been forbidden. Sonnets from China, II. W. H. Auden. CMoP (1970 ed.)

They wore light dresses and their arms were bare. A Pride of Ladies. Anne Halley. NMM

They work in an iron mill. Irondale. Stephen Stepanchev. SA

"They'd come to pick me up in their Chargers." Central Maryland, 1963. Gray Jacobik. PoUp

They'd learn more playing stickball in the street. Ghetto Summer School. Douglas Worth. FF

They'll come again to the apple tree. The Building of the Nest. Margaret Sangster. PCOP

They'll None of 'Em Be Missed. W. S. Gilbert. *Fr.* The Mikado. VLP

They're altogether otherworldly now. Grandparents. Robert Lowell. PiAm

They're beautiful, really, three. To My Sister, from the Twenty-seventh Floor. Michael Knoll. AMV-81

They're changing guard at Buckingham Palace. Buckingham Palace. A. A. Milne. OxBChV

They're dancing. two step. Club 82: Lisa. Cynthia Kraman Genser. NYP

They're dying off, the kerchiefed. Elegy for Bella, Sarah, Rosie, and All the Others. Sonya Dorman. GOA

They're Moving Father's Grave. *Unknown.* FSW

They're out of sorts in Sunderland. There Are Bad Times Just around the Corner. Noel Coward. NOBL

They're out of the dark's ragbag, these two. Blue Moles. Sylvia Plath. BiP

They're putting Man-Fix on my hair. Wanting Out. Gavin Ewart. EAS

They're selling postcards of the hanging. Desolation Row. Bob Dylan. InPS; WIF

They're taking down a tree at the front door. Learning by Doing. Howard Nemerov. HAP; NowV

They're Tearing Down a Town. Jud Strunk. QQQ

They've/ given us/ this day. 5/30/75. Darlene Pearlstein. FiCh

They've Come. Alfonsina Storni, *tr. fr. Spanish by* Aliki *and* Willis Barnstone. BoWoP

They've killed you. Martyrdom. Richard W. Thomas. PoBA

They've left Thee naked, Lord; O that they had. *See* They have left thee naked . . .

They've opened up a road in the jungle and found. 2976. Julia Uceda, *tr. by* Willis Barnstone. BoWoP

They've paid the last respects in sad tobacco. Padraic O'Conaire, Gaelic Storyteller. F. R. Higgins. PFIr

Th'have left thee naked, Lord, O that they had! *See* They have left thee naked . . .

Thick crust, coarse-grained as limestone rough-cast, A. Churning Day. Seamus Heaney. HeHu

Thick lay the dust, uncomfortably white. Summer Rain. Hartley Coleridge. VLP

Thick lids of night closed upon me, The. The Souls of the Slain. Thomas Hardy. CMoP (1970 ed.); PPM

Thick snow, the path, an evergreen. First Story. Steven Orlen. AAN

Thick water laps. The Fisherman. Dabney Stuart. LiSp; NVAP; SPo

Thief, The. Josephine Jacobsen. WPE

Thief, The. Stanley Kunitz. VGW

Thief in me is running a, The. Zapata and the Landlord. A. B. Spellman. PoBA

Thief is dying in the moonlit night, The. Dying Thief. Itzik Manger, *tr. by* Stephen Garrin. VWA

Thief Jones. Robert P. Tristram Coffin. MiP

Thieves, The. Robert Graves. BoLoP; CMoP (1970 ed.); ExPo (1973 ed.); OAEL-2; WeW

Thieves gave more to blue. Detroit City. Jill Witherspoon Boyer. CNA

Thieving hands poke around where. Mother. Aldo Camerino, *tr. by* Anita Barrows. VWA

Thin and graceful. The Tightrope Walker. Rochelle Ratner. WBN

Thin feet are caught. The Wanderer. Claude Vigée, *tr. by* Anthony Rudolf. VWA

Thin filaments of/ seasons bind us. On Linden Street. Shelley Ehrlich. AMV-80

Thin ill-natured ghost that haunts the king, A. The Nine. John Sheffield, Duke of Buckingham and Normanby. APAS

Thin in beard, and thick in purse. On Tom-o-Combe. *Unknown.* FaBoEE

Thin Jake. Michael Dugan. FPB

Thin lip, it is said, A. The Trumpet Shall Sound. John V. Hicks. AMV-81

Thin little leaves of wood fern, ribbed and toothed. Frederick Goddard Tuckerman. Sonnets, III, iv. TAP

Thin long bird. The Road-Runner. Philip Whalen. VoA

Thin mask of my sleep, The. Lament for the European Exile. A. L. Strauss, *tr. by* A. C. Jacobs. VWA

Thin Partition. Gordon Challis. ATNZ

Thin wickedly intricate, the. The Dark Area. Russell Atkins. FB

Thine Am I. Burns. VoPo

Thine eye the glasse where I behold my hart. Henry Constable. *Fr.* Diana. ESo

Thine eyes shall see the light of distant skies. To Cole, the Painter, Departing for Europe. Bryant. EAP; PiAm; TAP

Thine Eyes Still Shined. Emerson. NOBA

Thing, The. Theodore Roethke. CMoP (1970 ed.)

Thing, The/ To do/ Is organize. Poem. Kenneth Koch. CAPP

Thing about a shark is—teeth, The. About the Teeth of Sharks. John Ciardi. CaYB

Thing could barely stand, The. Yet taken. The Bull Calf. Irving Layton. InPK

Thing itself was rough and crudely done, The. The Knight in the Wood. Lord De Tabley. VLP

Thing of beauty is a joy for ever, A. Endymion, a Poetic Romance, I. Keats. CTV; ILP (1975 ed.); MBPR; NIL; PMW; PPM; STS; VoPo

Thing Poem. Petra von Morstein, *tr. fr. German by* Rosemarie Waldrop. BoWoP

Thing Remembered, A. Kendrick Smithyman. ATNZ

Thing to do is try for that sweet skin, The. Catch What You Can. Jean Garrigue. VGW

Thing which fades, A. Ono no Komachi, *tr. fr. Japanese by* Arthur Waley. BoWoP; PBWP

Things, The. Conrad Aiken. HAP

Things. Walter de la Mare. PoA

Things. W. S. Merwin. HAP

Things. Louis Simpson. TCP

Things/ do not know their collective name. Workaday Morning. Astrid Tollefsen, *tr. by* Nadia Christensen. PBWP

Things About Comin' My Way. *Unknown.* FSW

Things Are as They Are. Chuck Miller. *See* Things as They Are.

Things are born out of ideas. Symbols. Steve Toth. AcAn

Things are the mind's mute looking-glass. Things. Walter de la Mare. PoA

Things as They Are. Chuck Miller. EC (Things Are as They Are.) AcAn

Things concentrate at the edges; the pond-surface. Marginalia. Richard Wilbur. CMoP (1970 ed.); PoA

Things I do not understand. Knowledge. Harold M. Grutzmacher. AMV-81

Things I have and. Drifting The. Lyn Lifshin. MMD

Things I Say Are True, The. Blanca Varela, *tr. fr. Spanish by* Donald Yates. BoWoP

Things I'm told, I could raise your hair, The. The Old Man's Tale. Brian Merriman, *tr. by* David Marcus. *Fr.* The Midnight Court. BIrV

Things inside things endure. Good Souls, to Survive. Brendan Kennelly. IPM

Things Made by Iron. D. H. Lawrence. BBGO

Things Men Have Made. D. H. Lawrence. NoAM

Things might not be so bad. The Historian. Christopher Middleton. TwMBP

Things never get lost. Like Children of the Summertime Playing at Cards. Julie Herrick White. AMV-80

Things of Late. David Phillips. NeAC

Things start to happen. This is not. To Sherrie. Joseph Matuzak. AMV-81

Things That Happen. William Stafford. NNaP

Things that make a life to please, The. A Happy Life. Martial, *tr. by* Sir Richard Fanshawe. OBVE

Things That Make a Soldier Great, The. Edgar A. Guest. NIL

Things that make the happier life, are these, The. Martial, *tr. fr. Latin by* Ben Jonson. FaBoEE; OBVE

Things That Matter, The. Edith Nesbit. OxBTC

Things That Might Have Been. Jorge Luis Borges, *tr. fr. Spanish by* Alastair Reid. AMV-80

Things to Do around a Lookout. Gary Snyder. CAPP; TAP

Things to Do around a Ship at Sea. Gary Snyder. CAPP

Things to Do in New York (City). Ted Berrigan. NoAM

Things to Do in Providence. Ted Berrigan. EC; UsP

Things to draw with compasses, The. Circles. Harry Behn. CTV; LCL

Things to Work For. Jim Mulac. AcAn

Things We Can Depend On. George MacDonald. CTV

Things we, sinking. En Route. Theodore Weiss. PCho

Things we'll donate to the world. Poem H. Vincente Rodríguez Nietzche, *tr. by* Julio Marzán. InW

"Think as I Think." Stephen Crane. The Black Riders, XLVII. WeW

Think back now to that cleft. The Power Station. James Merrill. ConAP

Think further on thyself, my soul, and think. John Donne. *Fr.* Of the Progress of the Soul: The Second Anniversary. SCP-1

Think how many men have bluntly died. De Gustibus. James Worley. NIL

Think how we touch each other when we sight land. Bay of Resolve. Richard Hugo. CNW

Think Lang. Marion Angus. MS

Think me not unkind and rude. The Apology. Emerson. AmVN

Think no more, lad; laugh, be jolly. A. E. Housman. CABA (1972 ed.); CMoP (1970 ed.); STS

Think not by rigorous judgment seized. Three Epitaphs on John Hewet and Sarah Drew, I. Pope. NIL

Think not 'cause men flattering say. To A. L.: Persuasions to Love. Thomas Carew. CaPo

Think not, nor for a moment let your mind. Edna St. Vincent Millay. VGW

Think Not When You Gather to Zion, *with music.* Eliza R. Snow. AH

Think, O my soul. Phaedra. Hilda Doolittle ("H. D."). SBG

Think of a tree-lined city street. Parade: Liberation Day. Kevin Ireland. ATNZ

Think of friends. Morning Smallfire in Lukachukai Mountains. Simon J. Ortiz. FoP

Think of gentleness, as when. Motherhood. Susan Ludvigson. AMV-81

Think of it little, a fib. The Lie. Al Lee. AmPA

Think of the storm roaming the sky uneasily. Little Exercise. Elizabeth Bishop. NCSH; UnPo (1976 ed.)

Think on Yesterday. *Unknown.* OxBM

Think Tank. Eve Merriam. QQQ

Think that this world against the wind of time. Signature for Tempo. Archibald MacLeish. VGW

Think then, my soul, that death is but a groom.   John Donne.
  *Fr.* Of the Progress of the Soul: The Second Anniversary.
  BoReV

Think thinktank THINK.   Think Tank.   Eve Merriam.   QQQ

Think well of those whose fortune fell.   Anonymous.   Anne
  Hazlewood Brady.   WBN

Think you I am not fiend and savage too?   To the White Fiends.
  Claude McKay.   PoBA

Thinker, The.   William Carlos Williams.   TT

Thinking about Carnevale's Wife.   Wesley McNair.   FAF

Thinking about the Past.   Donald Justice.   PCho

Thinking Back Seven Years and Being Here Now.   David Curry.
  HeS

Thinking for Berky.   William Stafford.   PPoD; RRA

Thinking hard, hunting rhymes, humming by my lamp.   Sent to
  Wen T'ing-yün on a Winter Night.   Yü Hsüan-chi, *tr. by*
  Geoffrey Waters.   BoWoP

Thinking is not a smile.   For Mattie and Eternity.   Sterling D.
  Plumpp.   CNA

Thinking myself in a warm country.   Six Movements on a Theme.
  David Ignatow.   NNaP

Thinking of a Relation between the Images of Metaphors.
  Wallace Stevens.   UsP

Thinking of Bookshops.   James Liddy.   CIP

Thinking of her had saddened me at first.   Celandine.   Edward
  Thomas.   OxBTC; PF

Thinking of rain clouds that rose over the city.   St. Vincent's.
  W. S. Merwin.   NYP

Thinking of Tents.   Reed Whittemore.   TAP

Thinking of "The Autumn Fields."   Robert Bly.   NNaP

Thinking of the Lost World.   Randall Jarrell.   NoAM; NOBA

Thinking of You.   Dick Lourie.   NeAC

Thinking of you.   Love Poem 3.   Laughton Johnston.   SLP

Thinking on my life under.   It Says.   Jon Silkin.   VWA

Thinking the unthinkable.   19??.   Dan Georgakas.   NowV

Thinking to take on the power.   The Wives of Mafiosi.   Erica
  Jong.   AmPA

Thinking Twice in the Laundromat.   Harley Elliott.   NeAC

Thinking we were safe—insanity!   Story of a Hotel Room.
  Rosemary Tonks.   OxBTC

Think'st thou I saw thy beauteous eyes.   To Caroline.   Byron.
  MBPR

Think'st Thou to Seduce Me Then.   Thomas Campion.   BiP

Thinner now/ we are together.   Air Is.   John Michael Brennan.
  MAT

Thir riveris and thir watteris kepit war.   Virgil, *tr. by* Gavin
  Douglas.   *Fr.* The Aeneid, VI.   OBVE

Third Advice to a Painter, The.   Andrew Marvell.   APAS

Third Alley Blues.   *Unknown.*   BluL

Third Avenue in Sunlight.   Anthony Hecht.   CoPAm; NYP; PPP

Third Century, The, *sel.*   Thomas Traherne.
  News.   NOBE; PoPle
  (On News.)   BoReV; MetP

Third Child.   Peter Meinke.   AATT

Third Day in a Strange City.   Carol Bergé.   MMD

Third Degree.   Langston Hughes.   BPo; BuTh

Third Dimension, The.   Denise Levertov.   NoAM

Third Elegy, Leaving the City.   Hamish Henderson.   *Fr.* Elegies
  for the Dead in Cyrenaica.   MS

Third Sermon on the Warpland, The.   Gwendolyn Brooks.   BPo
  "Fire./ That is their way of lighting candles in the darkness,"
  *sel.* TT

Third Sunday in Lent.   John Keble.   *Fr.* The Christian Year.
  VLP

Third Thing, The.   D. H. Lawrence.   AKE

Third Voice, The.   "Lewis Carroll."   *Fr.* The Three Voices.   VLP

Third World, The.   Lawrence Ferlinghetti.   TCP

Thirst.   Musa Moris Farhi.   VWA

Thirst.   Genevieve Taggard.   WPW

Thirsty earth soaks up the rain, The.   Drinking.   Abraham
  Cowley, *after* Anacreon.   CABA (1972 ed.); FF; HeIP;
  NOBE; OBP; OBVE; PAIC; PMW; PoPle; WeW

Thirsty Island.   Jim Tollerud.   VoR

13:IV:72.   David Kherdian.   BCr

Thirteen o'Clock.   Kenneth Fearing.   ExPo (1973 ed.)

Thirteen Preludes for Pioneer Square.   John Logan.   CAAP

Thirteen Ways of Looking at a Blackbird.   Wallace Stevens.
  CABA (1972 ed.); CMoP (1970 ed.); InPK; IPWM; NoAM;
  NOBA; PoIA; TAP; TSWA; VoPo

Thirteen will attend.   Another Meeting.   Lawrence A. Lucas.
  AMV–80

Thirteen's no age at all.   Portrait of a Girl with Comic Book.
  Phyllis McGinley.   CTBA; IPWM; SoS; SoSe (1977 ed.)

30th Birthday.   Alice Notley.   FiCh

Thirty Bob a Week.   John Davidson.   EBEV; FaBoTw (1975
  ed.); InPS; NoAM; NOBE; OAEL–2; OBP; OxBTC; VLP

Thirty candles and one.   The Birthday.   Philip Dacey.   AmPA

Thirty Childbirths.   Millen Brand.   AMV–80

Thirty days hath September.   Mother Goose.   CTV; MG

Thirty days hath September.   *Unknown.*   CTV

Thirty days in jail with my back turned to the wall.   Jailhouse
  Blues.   *Unknown.*   BluL

.38, The.   Ted Joans.   WeW

Thirty-eight.   Charlotte Smith.   SBG

38 Main Street.   Lyn Lifshin.   TV

Thirty eighth year, The.   Lucille Clifton.   AmPA; CAAP; FoP

34 Blues.   *Unknown.*   BluL

Thirty generations have stood and listened.   The Font.   Clive
  Sansom.   BuTh

Thirty miles or so south of L. A.   View from an Institution.
  Franz Wright.   AMV–81

Thirty-nine thousand.   Dennis Trudell.   NVAP

Thirty-one Camels, The.   Rachel Korn, *tr. fr. Yiddish by* Howard
  Schwartz.   VWA

36 just men.   The Lamed-Vov.   Rose Ausländer, *tr. by* Ewald
  Osers.   VWA

"Thirty," the doctor said, "three grains, each one."   Felo de Se.
  Thomas Blackburn.   OxBTC

Thirty-three Triads.   *Unknown. See* Triads.

This act reminds me, ge'men, under favour.   Four Epigrams on
  the Naturalization Bill.   John Byrom.   NOBL

This advantage to be seized; and here, an escape prepared against
  an evil day.   Dividends.   Kenneth Fearing.   SPT

This ae nighte [*or* ean night], this ae nighte.   The Lyke-Wake
  Dirge.   *Unknown.*   GBP; HAP; HoPM (1975 ed.); NOBE

This Afternoon.   Juan Sáez Burgos, *tr. fr. Spanish by* Julio
  Marzán.   InW

This afternoon as I sat.   Elegy for Jack Bowman.   Joseph
  Bruchac.   CDW

This afternoon, darling, when you were here.   Letter from a Death
  Bed.   John Ciardi.   NCSH

This afternoon, discomfortable dead.   The Possessed.   John
  Berryman.   UsP

This afternoon, my love, speaking to you.   In Which She Satisfies
  a Fear with the Rhetoric of Tears.   Sister Juana Inés de la
  Cruz, *tr. by* Aliki *and* Willis Barnstone.   BoWoP

This ain't Torquemada.   Dialect Quatrain.   Marcus B. Christian.
  AmNP (1974 ed.)

This almost bare tree is racing.   November through a Giant
  Copper Beech.   Edwin Honig.   NoAM

This anchorage will do.   A Diary of the Sailors of the North.
  David Shulman.   VWA

This and That. Arthur J. Bull. HeHu

This antique dome the insatiate tooth of time. The Deserted Farm-House. Philip Freneau. EAP; NIL

This be the meed, that thy song creates a thousand-fold echo! Ad Vilmum Axiologum. Samuel Taylor Coleridge. MBPR

This beast that rends me in the sight of all. Edna St. Vincent Millay. VGW

This beauty made me dream there was a time. Sedge-Warblers. Edward Thomas. PoPle

This beauty that I see. Poem. James Schuyler. PoA

This being a fair and peaceful day. Benediction for the Tent. *Mongol Oral Tradition, tr. by* C. R. Bawden. WTO

This Blatant Beast was finally overcome. Saint. Robert Graves. CMoP (1970 ed.)

This blue-washed, old, thatched summerhouse. The Old Summerhouse. Walter de la Mare. CMoP (1970 ed.)

This body offers to carry us for nothing. Finding the Father. Robert Bly. BrS

This bond of the prelates I pray you revoke. Now God Stand Up for Bastards. Brian Merriman, *tr. by* Arland Ussher. *Fr.* The Midnight Court. BIrV

This book was written in order to change the world. Foreword to New Numbers. Christopher Logue. OxBTC

This boy went out in a snow blizzard. Sat in the Center. Samuel Makidemewabe. TC

This Bread I Break Was Once the Oat. Dylan Thomas. FaBoTw (1975 ed.)

This bread is rock, not wheat. The Bread of Our Affliction. Martin Grossman. VWA

This bridal day with gold I will enchain. Bridal Day. Compton Mackenzie. SLP

This broken bottle. Haiku. Elisavietta Ritchie. AATT

This brown woman's voice. Nina Simone. Lance Jeffers. CNA

This burly son of a bitch. Not Just Yet. Carter Revard. VoR

This burning in the eyes, as we open doors. In Danger from the Outer World. Robert Bly. CAPP

This Business of Dying. John Skoyles. AAN

This busy, vast, inquiring soul. Insatiableness. Thomas Traherne. ILP (1975 ed.)

This cargo of confessions, messages. The Postman. Gordon Challis. ATNZ

This Cat. Faye Kicknosway. TC

This celestial seascape, with white herons got up as angels. Seascape. Elizabeth Bishop. PPP

This city is haunted by young men without ambition. A Cloud of Ghosts. Russell Grant. PMW

This cluck of water in the tangles. The Voices of Nature. Thomas Edward Brown. PeD

This Cold Nothing Else. Dara Wier. CSP

This coloured counterfeit that thou beholdest. Sister Juana Inés de la Cruz, *tr. fr. Spanish by* Samuel Beckett. PBWP

This Compost. Walt Whitman. CABA (1972 ed.)

This country girl. Peter Whigham. *Fr.* Love Poems of the VIth Dalai Lama. TwMBP

This country might have. Right On: White America. Sonia Sanchez. PoBA

This country needs a few. Dragon Lesson. James Hearst. AMV-80

This couple like two asphalt flowers. The Living. Raymond Ward. ATNZ

This cross section, here incorrectly titled. Robert Fulton. Ann Stanford. GP

This Cross-Tree Here. Robert Herrick. NIL; OFD; PAIC

This cup has touched. The Wine Cup. Meleager, *tr. by* Dudley Fitts. OLR

This darkness has a quality. Composition for Words and Paint. Fleur Adcock. ATNZ

This darksome burn, horseback brown. Inversnaid. Gerard Manley Hopkins. CABA (1972 ed.); CMoP (1970 ed.); InPK; NoAM; OAEL-2; UnPo (1976 ed.)

This Day. Hildegarde Flanner. WPE

This day is called the feast of Crispian. Henry V before Agincourt [*or* St. Crispin's Day]. Shakespeare. King Henry V, *fr.* IV, iii. FaPoR; FF

This day of all our days has done. Byron. FaBoEE

This day relenting God. Success in Malaria Research. Sir Ronald Ross. PMW

This day the children of Speakthunder. In My Lifetime. James Welch. CDW

This day, whate'er the fates decree. Stella's Birthday. Swift. OAEL-1

This day when I lay my hope aside. This Day. Hildegarde Flanner. WPE

This day will be remembered by America's noble sons. The Battle of Bull Run. *Unknown.* AmFP

This day writhes with what? The Ultimate Poem Is Abstract. Wallace Stevens. PoA

This Decoration. Hayden Carruth. NNaP

This definition poetry doth fit. Thomas Randolph. FaBoEE

This desert still remembers Eden. Indian. Jeanne Doriot. AMV-81

This dog barking at me now. Dog, Midwinter. Raymond Souster. GDP

This dog will eat anything. Greedy Dog. James Hurley. FPB

This dragon had two furious wings. The Dragon of Wantley. *Unknown.* DuDr

This dread is like a calm. Winter Holding off the Coast of North America. N. Scott Momaday. CDW

This dreadful, dark and dismal day. Frankie Silvers. Frances Silvers. AmFP

This dream the world is having about itself. Vocation. William Stafford. CNW

This dry and lusty wind has stirred all night. Dream Vision. J. V. Cunningham. PiAm

This dry night nothing unusual. The War Horse. Eavan Boland. BIrV; CIP; IPM

This dumbell bee must be working. How the Laws of Physics Love Chocolate. Reg Saner. GP

This ean night, this ean night. *See* This ae nighte, this ae nighte.

This Earthen Body. *Gond Oral Tradition, tr. by* V. Elwin *and* S. Hivale. WTO

This Easter, Arthur Winslow, less than dead. In Memory of Arthur Winslow. Robert Lowell. PAIC; STS; UsP

This egle, of which I have you told. Jove's Eagle Carries Chaucer into Space. Chaucer. *Fr.* The House of Fame. OxBM

This endris night. Lullay, By-by, Lullay. *Unknown.* EBEV; OxBM

This England ("This royal throne of kings, this sceptered isle"). Shakespeare. King Richard II, *fr.* II, i. VoPo (England.) BTTM (John of Gaunt Speaks.) FaPoR

This Englishwoman is so refined. Stevie Smith. FaBoEE

This evening holds her breath. Winter Night. C. Day Lewis. PoA

This evening I prepared Wardance Soup. Wardance Soup. Phillip William George. VoR

This evening, my love, even as I spoke vainly. Sister Juana Inés de la Cruz, *tr. fr. Spanish by* Judith Thurman. PBWP

This Evening, without Blinking. Pattiann Rogers. AMV-80

This Excellent Machine. John Lehmann. OxBTC

This face had no use for light, took none of it. Made Shine. Josephine Miles. NoAM

This face you got. Phizzog. Carl Sandburg. UsP

This Fall ("This fall the japanese maple turned coral red"). Jody Aliesan. AMV-81

This far you have slid. My Childhood's Bedroom. Charles Tisdale. AMV-80

This feast-day of the sun, his altar there. The Hill Summit. Dante Gabriel Rossetti. The House of Life, LXX. VLP

This February in Berkeley. Outside Every Window Is a Flowering Thing. Anita Skeen. AMV-81

This February morning, walking early to work. A February Morning. Leslie Norris. HeHu

This finde I write in Poesie. Ceix and Alceone. John Gower. *Fr.* Confessio Amantis, IV. OxBM

This first Sunday in June, this green. Decoration Day. Bennie Lee Sinclair. TAT

This flattering glass, whose smooth face wears. On His Mistress Looking in a Glass. Thomas Carew. CaPo

This Flock So Small, *with music.* Anna Nitschmann, *tr. fr. German by* Sheema Z. Buehne. AH

This Form of Life Needs Sex. Allen Ginsberg. NNaP

This gang who protect me. Wulf and Eadwacer. Richard Ryan. CIP

This garden needs you. Between its walls. The Deserted Garden. Ann Stanford. AMV-81

This gentleman the charming duck. A Trueblue Gentleman. Kenneth Patchen. RAE; SO

This girl/ Waits at the corner. Girl, Boy, Flower, Bicycle. M. K. Joseph. ATNZ; MiP

This "good plan, fleshed in childhood"; these fruits. Jerusalem. Jon Silkin. VWA

This grandson of fishes holds inside him. Evolution from the Fish. Robert Bly. NoAM; NOBA

This graveyard with its umbrella pines. An Island Cemetery. W. H. Auden. TT

This green-and-red, yellow-naped Amazon parrot, Pythagoras. Talking Back. David Wagoner. MPA

This ground once was consecrated. Cry for a Disused Synagogue in Booysens. Mannie Hirsch. VWA

This guy on t.v. The Electric Cop. Victor Hernandez Cruz. PoBA

This Hand. Elinor Wylie. Psy

This handless clock stares blindly from its tower. A Clock in the Square. Adrienne Rich. HeIP; NIL

This harpie with dry red curls. Red Dust. Philip Levine. NNaP

This here white cab driver. Taxicab Blues. Ahmos Zu-Bolton II. PoUp

This here's a tale of a sho-nuff man. Big John Henry. Margaret Walker. WIF

This holy night in open forum. Office Party. Phyllis McGinley. OBSV

This holy season fit to fast and pray. Amoretti, XXII. Spenser. ILP (1975 ed.)

This Houre Her Vigill. Valentin Iremonger. CIP; OxBTC; PFIr

This House. Ray A. Young Bear. CDW

This house has been far out at sea all night. Wind. Ted Hughes. LP; MPo; SoSe

This house is floored with water. The Water Below. Fleur Adcock. ATNZ

This house rises into a metallic sky. Homestead. Horace Gregory. SPT

This Humanist whom no beliefs constrained. Epigram. J. V. Cunningham. VGW

This I beheld, or dreamed it in a dream. Opportunity. Edward Rowland Sill. PCOP

This ignorance upon my tongue. On Reading Aloud My Early Poems. John Williams. WeW

This immaculate steel door is a structured ocean. Muse Elektrique. Paul Mariah. CPA

This Indian weed, that once did grow. Tobacco. Philip Freneau. TAP

This institution,/ perhaps one should say enterprise. Marriage. Marianne Moore. NOBA; RiTi

This instrument. Telephone. Robin Shectman. AMV-81

This involves more than just the water standing. Country Landscape. Sherod Santos. AMV-80

This is a corner of heaven here. In Carpenter's Woods. Gerald Stern. PCho

This is a damned inhuman sort of war. Unseen Fire. R. N. Currey. MPo; OxBTC

This is a day wondrous as the five newborn. Celebration. Menke Katz. MN

This is a decade of insomnia. Sleeplessness of Our Time. R. A. D. Ford. AMV-81

This is a dream I needed. Old Man. Philip Booth. AMV-80

This is a legend from Siskiyou Bar. Coyote and the Star. Arthur Guiterman. BPAW

This is a lie. Adam and Eve at the Garden Gate. Marsha Pomerantz. VWA

This is a morning of/ white parakeets. Morning Poem. Jennivien-Diana Beenen. AMV-81

This is a morning to say something. A Morning to Remember; or, E Pluribus Unum. Edward Dorn. NoAM

This is a new sort of poem. Buy One Now. D. J. Enright. NOBL

This is a place of ease. Pastoral. Marion Strobel. PoA

This Is a Poem. Hilary-Anne Farley. AKE

This Is a Poem for Patrick Casey, *sel.* Jack Anderson. "Patrick Casey is sitting on the beach." OSP

This Is a Poem for the Dead. Michael Ryan. AmPA

This Is a Poem for the Fathers and for Michael Ryan. Thomas Lux. AmPA

This Is a Poem to My Son Peter. Peter Meinke. GP

This is a room no different from the rest. The Emergency Room. S. L. Henderson Smith. PMW

This is a room with a death. The Death Watchers. Alice Ryerson. AMV-80

This is a schoolyard. Children's Games. William Carlos Williams. NIL

This is a silence. Arabesque. Fred Johnson. PoBA

This is a slice of the oldest. Tree. Daniel Hoffman. IPWM

This is a Spring I am already/ troubled with. Dear James Wright. Ann Darr. PoUp

This is a story declining, as landscape. Stories. Jon Anderson. HeS

This is a stray donkey wearing. Driving Home. Jonathan London. AMV-81

This is a tale of the body, its inert. Case. Phyllis Janowitz. AMV-81

This is a troubled time in Alabama. Examples of Worker Correspondence. Michael Gold. SPT

This is a white. Imperial Thumbprint. Tom Weatherly. PoBA

This is a wild land, country of my choice. Rocky Acres. Robert Graves. IP; NoAM; UnPo (1976 ed.)

This is about the summer and the wheels of sleep. The Salt Pork. Robert Clayton Casto. HeIP

This is about the women of that country. The Women in Vietnam. Grace Paley. NMM

This is all flummery, a feast of sham. The Rasslers. William D. Barney. LiSp

This is an/ ignominious tale about the naming. My Mother Takes My Wife's Side. David Kherdian. SA

This Is an African Worm. Margaret Danner. BPo

This is an easy poem to make.  An Easy Poem.  Terry Kennedy.
AMV–80
This is before electricity.  Game after Supper.  Margaret Atwood.
Psy
This is Campidojo, whaur Titus ran.  Campidoglio.  Robert
Garioch, *after* Guiseppe Belli.  OBVE
This is Cherry running for her life.  12 Photographs of
Yellowstone.  Ronald Koertge.  GP
This is dying, to cut off a part of yourself.  Attis.  George
Stanley.  MIT
This is earthquake.  Today.  Langston Hughes.  VGW
This is enchanted country, lies under a spell.  Bonac.  John Hall
Wheelock.  PPoD
This is everyone's marriage.  Nesting.  Dennis Saleh.  NeAC
This is for the tear spilled on my blue silk dress.  Being Admired.
Grace Cavalieri.  PoUp
This is 46th street.  Salsa.  Tony Moreno.  NW
This Is Halloween.  Dorothy Brown Thompson.  IWK
This is her picture as she was.  The Portrait.  Dante Gabriel
Rossetti.  VLP
This is how forever is.  Lineage.  Reba Terry.  AMV–81
This is how to come in.  Welcome.  Harvey Feinberg.  POL
This Is Just to Say.  William Carlos Williams.  Epi; FF; HoPM
(1975 ed.); InPK; InPS; NOBA; OSP; PBMP; PiAm; SoSe;
SpRo; SS; TAP; TPo; VoA
This is like a place.  Snowy Night.  John Haines.  NCSH
This is Morgan's country: now steady, Bill.  Morgan's Country.
Francis Webb.  GAS
This is my body.  Starring Role.  Ron McCurdy.  PHC
This is my coliseum.  The Womb Is Ruins.  Helena Minton.
FAF
This is my country, all this golden plain.  The Greater Country.
Grace V. Watkins.  AMV–80
This is my curse.  Pompous, I pray.  J. V. Cunningham.  HAP
This Is My Father's World.  Maltbie Davenport Babcock.  AH,
*with music;* CTV
This is my last cry.  For Stephen Dixon.  Zack Gilbert.  PoBA
This is my letter to the world.  Emily Dickinson.  AmVN;
NoAM; NOBA; PAIC; SoSe (1977 ed.); TAP; WPE
This Is My Own, My Native Land.  Sir Walter Scott.  *Fr.* The
Lay of the Last Minstrel, VI.  BTTM
("Breathes there the man, with soul so dead.")  SoSe
(Innominatus.)  PBMP
(Native Land.)  SFF
(Patriot, The.)  FaPoR
(Patriotism.)  CTV; NOBE
This is my play's last scene, here heavens appoint.  Holy Sonnets,
VI.  John Donne.  EBEV; NIL
This is my wolf.  He sits.  The Appointment.  Maxine W. Kumin.
NMM
This is no country for hedonists.  The Mirrors of Jerusalem.
Barbara F. Lefcowitz.  AMV–80; VWA
This is no green bird, but gray with bright red.  The Gossip.
Daniel Halpern.  SO
This is no poet's heaven.  Colophon for Lan-t'ing Hsiu-Hsi.
John Peck.  AmPA
This Is Not a Poem.  Luís Omar Salinas.  SA
This is not real: this is the shape of a dream spun.  Grant Wood's
American Landscape.  Winfield Townley Scott.  GOA
This is not sorrow, this is work: I build.  The Tomb of Lieutenant
John Learmonth, A.I.F.  J. S. Manifold.  GAS; MAuV
This is not the man that women choose.  Act of Love.  Vernon
Scannell.  SFF
This is not the way I am.  Biography in the First Person.
Stephen Dunn.  FoP; NVAP
This is one of those letters I meant to write.  Unwritten Letters.
Steven Orlen.  BrS

This is our lot if we live so long and labour unto the end.  The
Old Men.  Kipling.  OBSV
This is the age.  Time of the Mad Atom.  Virginia Braiser.
QQQ
This is the Arsenal.  From floor to ceiling.  The Arsenal at
Springfield.  Longfellow.  ILP (1975 ed.)
This is the autumn and our harvest.  Charles Reznikoff.  *Fr.* New
Year's.  OFD
This is the beauty of being alone.  Stray Animals.  James Tate.
NoAM
This is the black day when.  The Dark Morning.  Thomas
Merton.  PoA
This is the black sea-brute bulling through wave-wrack.
Leviathan.  W. S. Merwin.  ConAP; NoAM; NOBA; TCP
This is the bricklayer; hear the thud.  Sanctuary.  Elinor Wylie.
BoWoP; Psy
This is the chapel of the holy.  Jindrichuv Hradec.  Christopher
Middleton.  TwMBP
This is the church of giraffes.  Survival.  Albert Goldbarth.
NVAP
This is the city where men are mended.  The Stones.  Sylvia
Plath.  CAPP; SBG
This is the country of the Norman tower.  A Warning to
Conquerors.  Donagh MacDonagh.  CIP
This is the creature there has never been.  Rainer Maria Rilke, *tr.*
*by* James Blair Leishman.  Sonnets to Orpheus, Pt. II, iv.
OBVE
This is the day His hour of life draws near.  Sonnets at Christmas,
I.  Allen Tate.  HAP; NoAM; NOBA; PAIC; VGW
This is the debt I pay.  The Debt.  Paul Laurence Dunbar.
AmNP (1974 ed.); CABA (1972 ed.); SS
This is the desk I sit at.  That Day.  Anne Sexton.  BoWoP;
ConAP
This is the dragon's country, and these his own streams.  Dragon
Country: To Jacob Boehme.  Robert Penn Warren.  PPP
This is the easy time, there is nothing doing.  Wintering.  Sylvia
Plath.  NMM
This is the factory.  The Old Maid Factory.  Constance Urdang.
GP
This is the field where the battle did not happen.  At the Un-
National Monument along the Canadian Border.  William
Stafford.  HAP; HeIP; SoSe
This is the football hero's moment of fame.  Settling Some Old
Football Scores.  Morris Bishop.  LiSp; SPo
This is the forest primeval.  The murmuring pines and the
hemlocks.  Longfellow.  *Fr.* Evangeline: Prologue.  SpRo
This is the gay cliff of the nineteenth century.  Brooklyn Heights.
John Wain.  NYP; OxBTC
This is the grave of Mike O'Day.  On Mike O'Day.  *Unknown.*
FaBoEE; IP
This Is the Hand.  Michael Rosen.  FPB
This is the horror that, night after night.  Gerald Gould.  OxBTC
This is the hour that we must mourn.  Tenebrae.  Austin Clarke.
BIrV; CIP
This is the house of Bedlam.  Visits to St. Elizabeths.  Elizabeth
Bishop.  VGW
This is the house of Circe, queen of charms.  Circe.  Lord De
Tabley.  VLP
This is the house that Jack built.  Mother Goose.  AKE, *abr.*;
MG; SpRo
This Is the Key of the Kingdom.  *Unknown.*  ECBV; Prf
(Key of the Kingdom, The.)  BBL
This is the key to it.  The Breast.  Anne Sexton.  CABA (1972
ed.)
This is the kind/ of marriage they live in.  The Way Sun Keeps
Falling Away from Every Window.  Lyn Lifshin.  NeAC

This is the lair of the landlady. The Landlady. Margaret Atwood. Psy

This is the Landlords' Circle, built by me. Inferno: A New Circle. Frank Ormsby. CIP

This is the last place, there is nowhere else to go. The Song Mt. Tamalpais Sings. Lew Welch. MIT

This is the last stroke my tongue's clock must strike. Thomas Nashe. *Fr.* Summer's Last Will and Testament. SCP-2

This Is the Life. Louis MacNeice. NoAM

This is the light of the mind, cold and planetary. The Moon and the Yew Tree. Sylvia Plath. Moon; MPo; PPP; VGW; WPE

This is the light we dream in. Negatives. Charles Wright. PoA

This is the meadow of the mind. A Way of Keeping. Nancy Willard. IHMS

This is the metre Columbian. The soft-flowing trochees and dactyls. The Metre Columbian. *Unknown.* SpRo

This is the Mexican. Tamales. "O. Henry." BPAW

This is the midnight—let no star. The Storm Cone. Kipling. OxBTC

This is the moment. Wind-Chimes in a Temple Ruin. Earle Birney. MPA

This is the month, and this the happy morn. On the Morning of Christ's Nativity. Milton. BoReV; Epi; ILP (1975 ed.); SCP-1

This is the morning. The Charge. Jay Wright. FB

This is the most ridiculous womb! Womb Song. Susan Fromberg Schaeffer. IHMS

This is the moth that came inside. The Moth. Prentice Baker. AATT

This is the night mail crossing the border. Night Mail. W. H. Auden. OxBTC

This Is the Non-existent Beast. Cid Corman. GP

This is the nunnery. Nunnery. Katherine Doak. NPW

This is the one song everyone. Siren Song. Margaret Atwood. *Fr.* Songs of the Transformed. HAP; PoA

This is the only thing that clarifies my life. Days of 1978. Gerald Stern. AMV-81

This is the only way it can be. Twilight. Tenant Farmer. Robert Ward. AMV-81

This is the Pentagon building. Pentagonia. G. E. Bates. SpRo

This is the place: be still for a while, my high-pressure steamboat! Nauvoo. Bayard Taylor. OBAL

This is the place where I was born. Alfred Allen. *Fr.* Clashenure Skyline. IPM

This is the plaza of Paradise. Marigold. John Haines. POL

This is the plum season, the nights. Late August. Margaret Atwood. MMD

This is the possum's tree. The Possum Tree. Irene Gough. ECBV

This is the prettiest motiön. To a Lady That Desired Me I Would Bear My Part with Her in a Song. Richard Lovelace. CaPo

This is the projectionist's nightmare. The Projectionist's Nightmare. Brian Patten. LP

This is the rain on Mozart's grave. Lives of the Saints. Jon Anderson. FiCP

This is the ring my father gave me. The Alexandrite Ring. Margaret Ryan. AMV-81

This is the room. Those windows. Poem Written after Contemplating the Adverb "Primarily." Christopher Middleton. TwMBP

This is the sea. In these uneven walls. The Rock Pool. Edward Shanks. EcS

This is the seed of scorn; prolific swine. The Acorn. Arthur J. Bull. HeHu

This is the shape of the leaf, and this of the flower. Conrad Aiken. Priapus and the Pool, IV. CMoP (1970 ed.); NOBA

This is the ship of pearl, which, poets feign. The Chambered Nautilus. Oliver Wendell Holmes. *Fr.* The Autocrat of the Breakfast-Table. AmVN; EcS; HoPM (1975 ed.); ILP (1975 ed.); NOBA; PiAm; VoPo

This is the sin against the Holy Ghost. The Unpardonable Sin. Vachel Lindsay. BiP; CMoP (1970 ed.)

This is the song that the night birds sing. Tall Men Riding. S. Omar Barker. BPAW

This is the southeast section of town now. The Southeast Ramparts of the Seine. Judit Tóth, *tr. by* Emery George. VWA

This is the stagnant hour. Drunken Lover. Owen Dodson. AmNP (1974 ed.)

This is the story of/ The brawny Brady riflemen. Brady's Bend. Martha Keller. PoTa

This is the story of Timid Tim. The Witch in the Wintry Wood. Aileen Fisher. IWK

This is the sum of it. On My 18th Birthday. John William Corrington. CoPAm

This is the surest death. Mortality. Naomi Long Madgett. PoBA

This is the sweet song. Sweet Song. Vernon Scannell. FPB

This is the tale of Ephraim. Ephraim the Grizzly. Arthur Guiterman. BPAW

This is the tale of how Tim one. Aileen Fisher. *Fr.* The Witch in the Wintry Wood. CaYB

This is the tale that was told to me. A Sailor's Yarn. James Jeffrey Roche. RhR

This is the terminal: the light. At the San Francisco Airport. Yvor Winters. HeIP; InPK; MPA; NIL; NOBA; RRA

This is the time of the crit, the creeple, and the makeiteer. Five Men against the Theme "My Name Is Red Hot. Yo Name Ain Doodley Squat." Gwendolyn Brooks. CNA

This is the time of year. The Armadillo. Elizabeth Bishop. NoAM; NOBA; PiAm; TAP; VGW

This is the time, when most divine to hear. Religious Musings. Samuel Taylor Coleridge. MBPR

This is the toll of the desert. The Toll of the Desert. Arthur W. Monroe. BPAW

This is the truth what I now tell you. The Miramichi Fire. *Unknown.* AmFP

This is the urgency: Live! The Second Sermon on the Warpland. Gwendolyn Brooks. BPo; NOBA; PoBA

This is the village where we grew. Our Town. Ann Stanford. CPA

This is the way in. The words. June 1967 at Buchenwald. Alan Bold. UsP

This is the way it was at Uncle Rob's. History Lesson for My Son. Ted Kooser. POL

This is the way the ladies ride:/ Tri, tre, tre, tree. Mother Goose. MG

This is the way we come. Riding in the Rain. Maxine W. Kumin. RFM

This is the weather the cuckoo likes. Weathers. Thomas Hardy. PoPle; PPM

This is the week when Christmas comes. In the Week When Christmas Comes. Eleanor Farjeon. LCL; PChr

This is the Wheel of Dreams. Carriers of the Dream Wheel. N. Scott Momaday. CDW

This is winter, this is night, small love. By Candlelight. Sylvia Plath. SBG

This is the world we wanted. Gretel in Darkness. Louise Glück. AmPA; GP; NVAP

This is thy hour O Soul, thy free flight into the wordless. A Clear Midnight. Walt Whitman. HAP

This is to say, my dear Augusta. King William's Dispatch to Queen Augusta. Coventry Patmore. FaBoEE

This Is to Signify. Dave Morice. AcAn

This Is Today.   David W. Martinez.   VW

This is what I want to happen.   Offering.   *Unknown, ad. by* Robert Bly.   NU

This is where/ the light sleeps.   Lullaby.   Sue Owen.   AMV-80

This is where the serpent lives, the bodiless.   The Auroras of Autumn.   Wallace Stevens.   CMoP (1970 ed.)

This is where we're at the gate.   Photograph at the Cloisters: April 1972.   Helen Chasin.   NMM

This island, garlanded with wild woods.   Archilochus, *tr. fr. Latin by* Guy Davenport.   OBVE

This Italian square.   Dancers at the Moy.   Paul Muldoon.   BIrV

This jar of roses and carnations on the window-sill.   Decoration.   Mary Ursula Bethell.   ATNZ

This Journey.   Ingrid Jonker, *tr. fr. Afrikaans by* Jack Cope *and* William Plomer.   BoWoP

This Kansas boy who never saw the sea.   Kansas Boy.   Ruth Lechlitner.   ANTL

This knot I knit.   To Know Whom One Shall Marry.   *Unknown.* GBP

This lady has a special.   The Beardsley Flesh.   Henry Kanabus.   FiCh

This lady, ripe and calm and fresh.   Sir William Davenant.   *Fr.* The Just Italian.   SCP-2

This Lady She Wears a Dark Green Shawl.   *Unknown.*   AmFP

This lake was clean (we used to swim in it once).   The Moorhen Pond.   Tom Earley.   BoAnP

This Land.   Ian Mudie.   BuTh

This land is your land.   Is This Land Your Land?   *Unknown.* FSW

This land was ours before we were the land's.   The Gift Outright.   Robert Frost.   IPWM

This land won't lie down.   Driving to Sauk City.   Warren Woessner.   TAT

This Landscape, These People.   Zulfikar Ghose.   MPo

This Last Pain.   William Empson.   CMoP (1970 ed.); EBEV; ExPo (1973 ed.); ILP (1975 ed.); NoAM; OAEL-2

This lay, a favorite of mine.   Honeysuckle (Chevrefoil).   Marie de France, *tr. by* Patricia Terry.   BoWoP

This lean commuter busies.   Pendulum.   John Updike.   BBGO

This legend is told of me.   Actaeon.   Rayner Heppenstall.   FaBoTw (1975 ed.)

This legendary house, this dear enchanted tomb.   Monticello.   May Sarton.   GOA

This let me further add, that nature knows.   Of the Pythagorean Philosophy.   Ovid, *tr. by* Dryden.   *Fr.* Metamorphoses, XV.   OBVE

This level reach of blue is not my sea.   Fair Weather.   Dorothy Parker.   SBG

This Life.   Rita Dove.   AmPA

This Life a Theater.   Palladas, *tr. fr. Greek by* Robert Bland.   NIL

This life is not a circus where.   Lawrence Ferlinghetti.   *Fr.* A Coney Island of the Mind.   PPP

This life like no other.   Poem.   Gregory Orr.   AmPA

This life passes as fast as you drink it.   The I.R.A. Man Revisits His Hideout.   Catherine O'Neill.   PoUp

This life which seems so fair.   Madrigal.   William Drummond of Hawthornden.   OAEL-1; SCP-2

This lilac loses its leaves.   Vertigos or Contemplation of Something That Is Over.   Alejandra Pizarnik, *tr. by* Yishai Tobin.   VWA

This Lime-Tree Bower My Prison.   Samuel Taylor Coleridge.   HeIP; ILP (1975 ed.); MBPR; NIL; PAIC

This little bride and groom are.   E. E. Cummings.   PiAm

This little house is sugar.   Winter Sweetness.   Langston Hughes.   ECBV

This Little Light of Mine.   *Unknown.*   FSW

This little pig built a spaceship.   Frederick Winsor.   *Fr.* The Space Child's Mother Goose.   QQQ

This little pig went to market.   Mother Goose.   MG

This little vault, this narrow room.   Epitaph on the Lady Mary Villiers.   Thomas Carew.   CaPo; NIL

This Living Hand, Now Warm and Capable.   Keats.   BoLoP; CABA (1972 ed.) HAP; ILP (1975 ed.); InPK; InPS; MBPR; OAEL-2
   (Lines Supposed to Have Been Addressed to Fanny Brawne.) LoAs
   (To Fanny Brawne.)   NOBE

This lonely figure of not much fun.   Absent-minded Professor.   Howard Nemerov.   NowV

This long straight line of elegant limousines highly polished.   A Burial in the Country.   Paul Clause.   AATT

This, Lord, was an anxious brother and.   Funeral Oration for a Mouse.   Alan Dugan.   HAP; ILP (1975 ed.); NoAM; PPP

This lonely following in the old town.   Lines for a Young Wanderer in Mexico.   John Logan.   PoA

This loud morning.   The Third World.   Lawrence Ferlinghetti.   TCP

This love is a rich cry over.   A Black Wedding Song.   Gwendolyn Brooks.   CNA

This lovely flower fell to seed.   For My Grandmother.   Countee Cullen.   Four Epitaphs, 1.   AmNP (1974 ed.); ILP (1975 ed.); PoBA; VGW

This Lunar Beauty.   W. H. Auden.   OxBTC

"This making of bastards great."   Song: Old Rowley the King.   *Unknown.*   APAS

This man contrived (but yet no glory won).   Epigram on the Unknown Inventor of Scissors.   L. E. Jones.   POL

This man escaped the dirty fates.   Flyer's Fall.   Wallace Stevens..   CABA (1972 ed.)

This man, this ape with laughter in his mouth.   For the Revolution.   Joy Davidman.   SPT

This man, this poet, said.   A Spark of Laurel.   Stanley Kunitz.   NoAM

This man, this stranger in my arms.   Indian Summer.   Barbara Howes.   IHMS

This man though he had played the fool.   In Memoriam Brendan Behan.   Paul Durcan.   IPM

This man who seems to be my husband.   Orange Tree Dream.   Judith Serin.   NPW

This massive, carved medieval harp of Irish oak.   The Library.   John Logan.   AMV-80

This mast, new-shaved, through whom I rive the ropes.   Choosing a Mast.   Roy Campbell.   FaBoTw (1975 ed.); RhR

This matted and glossy photo of Yesenin.   Jim Harrison.   *Fr.* Letters to Yesenin.   TC

This meeting has gone on with small interruptions.   The Organizer's Bogeymen.   Marge Piercy.   Psy

This might be nature—twenty stories high.   The Picture [*or* New York 1962: Fragment].   Robert Lowell.   NoAM; NYP

This might have been a place for sleep.   Thistledown.   Harold Monro.   OxBTC

This mighty empire hath but feet of clay.   Theoretikos.   Oscar Wilde.   VLP

This Monument Will Outlast.   Horace, *tr. by* Ezra Pound.   Odes, III, 30.   Epi

This morn my friend Al mentioned his wife had taken a job.   The Day of the Pancreas.   David McFadden.   NeAC

This Morning.   Lucille Clifton.   OSP

This Morning.   Javier Gálvez.   FF

This Morning.   Muriel Rukeyser.   BoWoP; IPWM; NMM

This morning/ a gun held at a man's ear.   "He Killed Many of My Men."   John Bennett.   BuTh

This morning/ my child dances naked. Variations on a Theme. Mark Vinz. HeS

This morning/ on entering the cold chapel. Introit. Paul Murray. IPM

This morning/ with a class of girls outdoors, I saw. In a Spring Still Not Written of. Robert Wallace. CoPAm; WIF

This morning Amanda. Amanda Dreams She Has Died and Gone to the Elysian Fields. Maxine W. Kumin. GP

This morning, because the snow swirled deep. Oatmeal Deluxe. Stephen Dobyns. AMV–81

This morning came down. Four Fawns. Barbara Howes. AMV–80

This morning, father. A Christmas Gift. David Mura. BrS

This morning, flew up the lane. Lady Lost. John Crowe Ransom. UnPo (1976 ed.)

This morning he studied the dead wasps. Holding On. Richard Jackson. AMV–80

This morning I do not despair. The Vestal in the Forum. James Wright. AMV–81

This morning I found a hare gaoled alive in a gin. The Trapped Hare. Basil Dowling. ATNZ

This morning I held Harriet in my head. True Love. Joe Johnson. CNA

This morning I threw the windows. Jay Wright. PAIC

This morning I woke/ to an impatient scratching on the window. Apricot Tree. Magda Isanos, tr. by Willis Barnstone and Matei Calinescu. BoWoP

This morning I wrote a poem. Akriel's Consolation. William Pillin. AMV–80

This morning more rats come. Fists. Joseph Hansen. PoW

This morning my paper arrived. Dear Editor. Faye Kicknosway. TC

This morning of my birthday, rain is starting to fall. Bar Mitzvah. Steve Orlen. GP

This morning of the small snow. The Songs of Maximus, III. Charles Olson. PPP

This morning on the beach where the last wash of spray. The Wedding. Sandra Kohler. AMV–80

This morning, timely rapt with holy fire. On Lucy, Countess of Bedford. Ben Jonson. ILP (1975 ed.)

This morning trimming ivy in. Not Blindly in the Dark. Robert M. Stanley. AMV–81

This morning we shall spend a few minutes. Money. Howard Nemerov. WeW

This morning, when he looked at me. Black All Day. Raymond R. Patterson. PoBA

This morning when I awoke,/ I found the enemy had invaded. Bella Ciao. Unknown, tr. fr. Italian. FSW

This mortal body of a thousand days. Sonnet Written in the Cottage Where Burns Was Born. Keats. MBPR

This mossy bank they press'd. A Pastoral Dialogue. Thomas Carew. CaPo; GBL; SCP-2

This moth caught in the room tonight. Lying Awake. W. D. Snodgrass. HoPM (1975 ed.); ILP (1975 ed.)

This my heart, so flowing and so simple. Poem of the Intimate Agony. Julia de Burgos, tr. by Julio Marzán. InW

This Narrow Stage. Theodore Weiss. NoAM

This new Daks suit, greeny-brown. Metamorphosis. Peter Porter. OxBTC

This New Day, with music. Vail Read AH

This Night. Nathan Alterman, tr. fr. Hebrew by Ruth Nevo. VWA

This Night. Osip Mandelstam, tr. fr. Russian by Daniel Weissbort. VWA

This night of no moon. Ono no Komachi, tr. fr. Japanese by Donald Keene. PBWP

This night presents a play, which publick rage. Prologue to Hugh Kelly's "A Word to the Wise." Samuel Johnson. EBEV; FaPoR

This Night Sees Ireland Desolate. Aindrais MacMarcuis, tr. fr. Irish by Robin Flower. BIrV

"This night shall thy soul be required of thee." Scorpion. Stevie Smith. EBEV

This night's calm water. Whatever Is, Is Right. Frank Gaik. AMV–81

This nine-pound hammer is a little too heavy. Nine-Pound Hammer. Unknown. FSW

This, O my stomach, is a painting. American Heritage. Robert Sward. OBAL

This old hen, she laid an egg. The Lost Egg. Percy Illot. ECBV

This Old Man. Unknown. FSW

This old soul, you know, time she left Chicago. The Panama Limited. Unknown. BluL

This Olympian pug you see now, Sir, once possessed. Boxer Loses Face and Fortune. Lucilius, tr. by Tom Dodge. LiSp

This one is entering her teens. The Romantic Age. Ogden Nash. SFF

This one was put in a jacket. Counting the Mad. Donald Justice. ConAP; FF; LP; NIL; UnPo (1976 ed.); UsP

This only grant me, that my means may lie. Of Myself. Abraham Cowley. ILP (1975 ed.)

This other speaks of bones, blood wet. Fair/ Boy Christian Takes a Break. Jim Harrison. NoAM

This page I send you, sir, your Newgate fate. A Poem upon the Imprisonment of Mr. Calamy in Newgate. Robert Wild. APAS

This Pain. John Hall Wheelock. UsP

This painful love dissect to the last shred. The Lovers. Conrad Aiken. LoAs

This piston's infinite recurrence is. La Marche des Machines. A. S. J. Tessimond. MPo

This pit is Hell where through thou now must go. Elizabeth Melvill, Lady Culross. Fr. A Godly Dream. WPE

This place is cold. Three Poems for the Indian Steelworkers. Joseph Bruchac. CDW

This place moves from me. Poem before Departure. Jean Burden. UsP; WPE

This place (quoth she) they say's enchanted. Samuel Butler. Fr. Hudibras, II, 1. NOBL

This Place Rumord to Have Been Sodom. Robert Duncan. NOBA; PPP

This pleasant tale is like a little copse. Keats. MBPR

This plot of ground. Dedication for a Plot of Ground. William Carlos Williams. TT

This poem I write to teach the reader. Writing in England Now. Philip O'Connor. OxBTC

This poem is an erection. Erotic Suite. José Luis Vega, tr. by Julio Marzán. InW

This Poem Is for Bear. Gary Snyder. Myths and Texts: Hunting, VI. BCr; CNW; NOBA; NU

This Poem Is for Deer. Gary Snyder. Myths and Texts: Hunting, VIII. CAPP; NOBA

This poetry gets bored of being alone. Living Poetry. Hugo Margenat, tr. by Julio Marzán. InW

This pool in a pure frame. Reason and Nature. J. V. Cunningham. PiAm

This Poor Man. W. J. Gruffydd, tr. fr. Welsh by Gwyn Jones. OBW

This porthole overlooks a sea. Bendix. John Updike. SoS

This Preparation. Simon Ortiz. VW

This pretty bird, oh, how she flies and sings! Upon the Swallow. Bunyan. OxBChV

This Pretty Woman. *Unknown.* OxBM

This queen of prey (now prey to you). A Lady with a Falcon on Her Fist. Richard Lovelace. CaPo

This quiet dust was gentlemen and ladies. Emily Dickinson. CMoP (1970 ed.); DL

This quiet morning light. To Mark Anthony in Heaven. William Carlos Williams. NOBA

This quiet mound beneath. Corporal Pym. Walter de la Mare. FaBoEE

This, quoth the Eskimo master. Latter-Day Geography Lesson. R. A. K. Mason. ATNZ

This racer of the watry plain. Catullus, *tr. fr. Latin.* OBVE

This rain that has come from far away, like breath. Lifelines. T. R. Hummer. AMV–80

This random blood affronts my pensive day. Critic Undefiled. A. Wilber Stevens. MPA

This ration card, once shocking pink. The Ration Card. Liz Sohappy Bahe. CDW

This river ground to quiet in Sylvana. At the Stilli's Mouth. Richard Hugo. MPA

This road is so fuzzy. Cinéma Vérité. Dorothy Walters. IHMS

This root of bog-oak the sea dug up she found. Trouvaille. Richard Murphy. CIP

This rose tree is not made to bear. Envy. Charles *and* Mary Lamb. OxBChV

This royal throne of kings, this sceptered isle. This England [*or* John of Gaunt Speaks]. Shakespeare. *Fr.* King Richard II. BTTM; FaPoR; VoPo

This sacred lake/ is the soul/ of the world. Chad. Edward Brathwaite. MPo

This sadness stains me. Afterimage. James Beall. PoUp

This said, he reacht to take his sonne. Homer, *tr. by* George Chapman. *Fr.* The Iliad, VI. OBVE

This saying good-by on the edge of the dark. Good-by and Keep Cold. Robert Frost. CMoP (1970 ed.)

This sea will never die, neither will it ever grow old. Middle of the World. D. H. Lawrence. HAP

This second night. The Second Night. M. L. Hester, Jr. AMV–80

This seems, in a world where love must take its chances. Mona Van Duyn. Footnotes to "The Autobiography of Bertrand Russell," II. HAP

This sentence have I left behind. A Nameless Epitaph. Matthew Arnold. FaBoEE

This Shell. Mark Van Doren. SPo

This Ship in the Dock. Michael Rosen. OSF

This ship is the ship of butchery and increase. Songs for the Cisco Kid: or Singing: Song #2. K. Curtis Lyle. PoBA

This Shirt. Arturo Trías, *tr. fr. Spanish by* Julio Marzán. InW

This silken wreath, which circles in mine arm. Upon a Ribband. Thomas Carew. CaPo; OAEL–1

This Site Is Occupied. Nashira N'tosha. NW

This sky, for instance. Deschutes River. Raymond Carver. NVAP

This sky is to be opened. Hermetic Bird. Philip Lamantia. VGW

This small cry of keys. Found with Chain. Robin Johnson. PoW

"This small lodge is now." Old Man, the Sweat Lodge. Phillip William George. VW

This small town bus station has its own drunk. Waiting for the Bus. Alan Ziegler. AAN

This Solitude of Cataracts. Wallace Stevens. PiAm

This song of journeys into sorrow. A Woman's Message. *Unknown, tr. by* Burton Raffel. OBP

This soup is cold. The Soup of Venus. James Tate. AmPA

This sparrow/ who comes to sit at my window. The Sparrow. William Carlos Williams. InPS; PiAm; VGW

This speech all Troyans did applaud. Homer, *tr. by* George Chapman. *Fr.* The Iliad, VIII. OBVE

This spoke, a huge wave tooke him by the head. Homer, *tr. by* George Chapman. *Fr.* The Odyssey, V. OBVE

This spoonful of chocolate tapioca. Thinking of the Lost World. Randall Jarrell. NoAM; NOBA

This spring as it comes bursts up in bonfires green. The Enkindled Spring. D. H. Lawrence. NoAM

This still life is still life after all. Still Life. Vivian Smith. AMV–80; AMV–81

This still life of cups mocking the table. Still Life. Claudia Dobkins. NPW

This story goes on a long time. My Children's Book. John N. Morris. AMV–80

This strange thing must have crept. Fork. Charles Simic. AmPA; GP

This straw horse and this crabshell. Spirit. Mei Berssenbrugge. SA

This Subway Station. Charles Reznikoff. LP

This Summer and Last. Thomas Hardy. OxBTC

This Sun Is Hot. *Unknown.* BPo

This sunlight shames November where he grieves. Autumn Idleness. Dante Gabriel Rossetti. *Fr.* The House of Life. GBL; ILP (1975 ed.); OAEL–2

This sycamore, oft musical with bees. Inscription for a Fountain on a Heath. Samuel Taylor Coleridge. MBPR

This, That and the Other. Howard Nemerov. AnMo

This that I give you now. Bread. Stanley Burnshaw. SPT

This that is washed with weed and pebblestone. The Figurehead. Léonie Adams. WPE

This, the last ornament among the peers. Hilaire Belloc. OBSV

This, the twentieth day of March. A Letter to Three Irish Poets. Michael Longley. BIrV

This they know well: the Goddess yet abides. In Her Praise. Robert Graves. BIrV

This, this is he; softly a while. Milton. *Fr.* Samson Agonistes. UnPo (1976 ed.)

This Time a Tree Turns into a Woman. Beth Bentley. CNW

This time I recognize your limp. You Again. Beth Bentley. CNW

This to the crown, and blessing of my life. A Letter to Dafnis. Countess of Winchilsea. SBG

This Tokyo. Gary Snyder. CAPP

This town is haunted by some good deed. Aunt Mabel. William Stafford. AnMo

This Train ("This train is bound for glory, this train"). *Unknown.* FSW

(This Train Don't Carry No Gamblers.) AmFP

This tree/ growing out of me. Song for a Transformation. Francisco Arriví, *tr. by* Julio Marzán. InW

This Troilus, with blisse of that supprysed. Chaucer. *Fr.* Troilus and Criseyde, III. EBEV

This truly wonderful steed. Title of a Swift Horse. *Mongol Oral Tradition, tr. by* C. R. Bawden. WTO

This unheated star is not the kind to take in pious babble. Computer. Otto Orban, *tr. by* Emery George. VWA

This Unimportant Morning. Lawrence Durrell. BoLoP; OxBTC

This urge, wrestle, resurrection of dry sticks. Cuttings. Theodore Roethke. AnMo; NoAM; NOBA; PiAm; PPoe; TAP; UnPo (1976 ed.)

This vale of teargas. Unlawful Assembly. D. J. Enright. OxBTC

This valley after the storms can be beautiful. San Joaquin. William Everson. CoPAm

This valley is not ours, nor these mountains.    Red Earth.    Alice Corbin.    WPW

This vanishing old road.    The New Direction.    Emerson Blackhorse Mitchell.    VW

This very day, a little while ago, you lived.    Dead on the War Path.    *Tr. fr. Tewa Indian by* H. J. Spinden.    WTO

This virgin, beautiful and lively day.    Sonnet.    Stéphane Mallarmé, *tr. by* Roger Fry.    NAWM-2

This wall-paper has lines that rise.    Missing My Daughter. Stephen Spender.    RRA

This was a poet—it is that.    Emily Dickinson.    NOBA

This was a rich morning.    Rich Morning.    Robert Farren.    PFIr

This was childhood.    The Worms.    Carolyn Kizer.    IPWM

"This was Mr. Bleaney's room. He stayed."    Mr. Bleaney.    Philip Larkin.    BuTh; HoPM (1975 ed.); InPS; PPoe

This was my dream: I saw a forest.    Robert Browning.    Bad Dreams, III.    OAEL-2; TT; VLP

This was our heritage.    An Ode on the Despoilers of Learning in an American University.    Yvor Winters.    ExPo (1973 ed.)

This was our valley, yes.    The Dam.    Patric Dickinson.    PoTa

This was the crucifixion on the mountain.    Altarwise by Owl-Light, VIII.    Dylan Thomas.    CMoP (1970 ed.); Epi; NoAM

This was the hawk's way. This way the hawk.    Hawk's Way.    Ted Olson.    HoPM (1975 ed.)

This was the peaceable kingdom: the river flows.    Edward Hicks: "The Peaceable Kingdom."    Ann Stanford.    PPoD

This was the woman: what now of the man?    Modern Love, III. George Meredith.    PAIC

This water, sad and fearful.    Slow Rain.    Gabriela Mistral, *tr. by* Gunda Kaiser *and* James Tipton.    PBWP

This way from the north.    Corn-grinding Song.    *Tr. fr. Tewa Indian.*    WPW; WTO

This way, oh turn your bows.    The Sirens' Song.    Homer, *tr. by* Robert Fitzgerald.    *Fr.* The Odyssey.    GrRo

This what it was.    The Meat Epitaph.    Michael Benedikt.    FiCP

This which I write now.    Inheritance.    George Bruce.    MS

This white explosion of water plunges down.    The Falls of Falloch.    Sydney Tremayne.    MS

This wight all mercenary projects tries.    Sir Samuel Garth.    *Fr.* The Dispensary.    OBSV

This will be a chocolate cake.    Cooking.    Myra Cohn Livingston.    ECBV

This will really try you.    Mamma!    Frank Horne.    BPo

This Wind.    Tom Kryss.    NeAC

This wind from Fife has cruel fingers, scooping.    Double Life. Norman MacCaig.    MS

This wine-press is call'd war on earth.    Blake.    *Fr.* Milton, I.    EBEV

This winter in a rosy railroad car.    Dreamed-up for Winter. Arthur Rimbaud, *tr. by* William Mead.    LoAs

This Woman Will Not Bear Children.    Toi Derricotte.    NPW

This woman vomiten her.    Present.    Sonia Sanchez.    CNA

This Wonderful World.    Mary Britton Miller.    ECBV

This world/ is amazingly flat.    Natalya Gorbanyevskaya, *tr. fr. Russian by* Barbara Einzig.    BoWoP

This world a hunting is.    William Drummond of Hawthornden.    SCP-2

This World Fares as a Fantasy.    *Unknown.*    OxBM

This world is gradually becoming a place.    John Berryman.    *Fr.* Dream Songs.    NoAM; NOBA

This world is not conclusion.    Emily Dickinson.    IPWM

This world is not my home, I'm just a-passing through.    I Can't Feel at Home in This World Anymore.    *Unknown.*    FSW

This world is very odd we see.    Reply to Dipsychus.    Arthur Hugh Clough.    FaBoCo

This world of ours thus runneth upon wheels.    Michael Drayton.    *Fr.* To My Noble Friend Master William Browne: Of the Evil Time.    SCP-2

This world of strange creations, so prodigal in wastefulness of life.    Of Curious Questions.    Martin Farquhar Tupper.    VLP

This Year.    Joseph Hutchison.    AMV-81

This year I intended children    Margaret Atwood.    NeAC

"This year she has changed greatly"—meaning you.    Change. Robert Graves.    OxBTC

This year we are making/ nothing but elegies.    Dufferin, Simcoe, Grey.    Margaret Atwood.    AMV-81

Thise olde gentil Britons in hir dayes.    The Franklin's Prologue. Chaucer.    *Fr.* The Canterbury Tales.    OAEL-1

Thistle and darnel and dock grew there.    Nicholas Nye.    Walter de la Mare.    DuDr

Thistle whips spitefully across brown thigh.    Judean Summer. Fay Lipshitz.    VWA

Thistledown.    Denis Glover.    ATNZ

Thistledown.    James Merrill.    UnPo (1976 ed.)

Thistledown.    Harold Monro.    OxBTC

Thistledown blows over the poisoned fields.    The Martyred Earth. Ewart Milne.    BIrV

Thistle down's flying, though the winds are all still, The.    Autumn. John Clare.    HAP; NU; OBP

Thistles.    Ted Hughes.    MPo; NoAM; OxBTC; PSN

Tho'.    *See also* Though.

Tho' grief and fondness in my breast rebel.    London.    Samuel Johnson.    LAuP

Tho I die on a distant strand.    The Cool, Grey City of Love. George Sterling.    BPAW

Tho' I'm no Catholic.    The Catholic Bells.    William Carlos Williams.    CMoP (1970 ed.); InPS; NOBA

Tho We All Speak.    Daniel Ort.    AMV-80

Tho when as chearelesse night ycovered had.    Spenser.    *Fr.* The Fairie Queene, III, 12.    OAEL-1

Thocht, The.    William Soutar.    MS

Thomas and Charlie.    Peter Wild.    AmPA

Thomas Hardy.    Walter de la Mare.    NoAM

Thomas Iron-Eyes.    Marnie Walsh.    VW

Thomas Logge.    Walter de la Mare.    FaBoEE

Thomas Rymer.    *Unknown. See* Thomas the Rhymer.

Thomas Sackevyll in Commendation of the Worke to the Reader. Thomas Sackville.    AAS

Thomas the Rhymer.    *Unknown.*    InPS; NOBE; OAEL-1, *with music*; Prf
   (Thomas Rymer.)    AIW; FaBoBa; HAP; NIL; PeBB
   (Thomas the Rimer.)    InPK
   (True Thomas.)    PoTa

Thorn, The.    Wordsworth.    MBPR

Thorn Forever in the Breast, A.    Countee Cullen.    BiP

Thorn tree, pale and sharp, The.    The Tree of Hatred.    Shmuel Moreh.    VWA

Thorns have whitened along the way, The.    Do Not Accompany Me.    Shimon Halkin, *tr. by* Ruth Nevo.    VWA

Thornton Beach.    Michael McClure.    RhR

Thoroughbred Horse, The.    Oliver Herford.    TDH

Those awful words "Till death do part."    Early Thoughts of Marriage.    Nathaniel Cotton.    OxBChV

Those Being Eaten by America.    Robert Bly.    PPoD

Those Betrayed at Dawn.    Stanislaw Wygodski, *tr. fr. Polish by* Isaac Komem.    VWA

Those birds sitting.    Jack Kerouac.    *Fr.* Some Western Haikus.    VoA

Those black planes, whose speed makes silent air.    A March on Washington.    Radcliffe Squires.    WasP

Those Boys That Ran Together.    Lucille Clifton.    CNA; PoBA

Those buffalo, white, that gather in the bean field. Winter in Elwell. James Tipton. HeS; TC

Those calm swamp-green eyes. Pisces Child. Sandra McPherson. NMM

Those Cambridge generations, Russell's, Keynes'. On Bertrand Russell's "Portraits from Memory." Donald Davie. FaBoTw (1975 ed.)

Those Chu Lai priests who raised me as a boy. A Viet Cong Sapper Dies. Stephen Sossaman. AMV–81

Those, Cynthia, that do taste the honey-dew. To Cynthia, on Sugar and Her Sweetness. Sir Francis Kynaston. SCP-2

Those days, the angry persons were the old. Angry Old Men. Basil Payne. PFIr

Those days when it was all right. Letter to E. Franklin Frazier. Amiri Baraka. BPo; PoBA

Those Denver evenings I'd drag myself. Going to Press. Judith Moffett. AMV–80

Those dreams that on the silent night intrude. On Dreams. Swift. BIrV

Those—dying then. Emily Dickinson. CABA (1972 ed.)

Those envied places which do know her well. A Day of Love. Dante Gabriel Rossetti. The House of Life, XVI. VLP

Those evening clouds, that setting ray. On the Setting Sun. Sir Walter Scott. PIM

Those eyes (dear Lord) once brandons of desire. On Mary Magdalene. William Drummond of Hawthornden. OAEL–1

Those eyes still shine which promised that behind. Pygmalion. Hans Brockerhoff. AMV–80

Those famous men of old, the Ogres. Ogres and Pygmies. Robert Graves. CABA (1972 ed.); CMoP (1970 ed.); NoAM

"Those fantastic forms, fang-sharp." City without Walls. W. H. Auden. NYP

Those five or six young guys. Blues. Derek Walcott. OBP

Those Flapjacks of Brown's. Bert Leston Taylor. OBAL

Those four black girls blown up. American History. Michael S. Harper. BPo

Those gathered by heartache in alien lands. Beyond Memory. Monny de Boully, *tr. by* Aleksander Nejgebauer. VWA

Those good citizens the clouds. A Passing Illness. Peter Wild. MPA

Those great rough ranters, Branns. A Simplification. Richard Wilbur. CMoP (1970 ed.)

Those greetings! those goodbyes! Kennedy Airport. Aaron Kramer. AMV–80

Those groans men use. The Mutes. Denise Levertov. AnMo; IHMS; NOBA; Psy; RiTi

Those hands which you so clapt, go now and wring. Upon the Lines and Life of the Famous Scenic Poet, Master William Shakespeare. Hugh Holland. OBW

Those hours that with gentle work did frame. Sonnets, V. Shakespeare. STS

Those I Love. Victor Contoski. GP

Those Images. W. B. Yeats. CMoP (1970 ed.)

Those in the vegetable rain retain. Stories of Snow. P. K. Page. PoA

Those Last, Late Hours of Christmas Eve. Lou Ann Welte. PChr

Those legs you left here still stick. Leavings. Barbara A. Holland. WBN

Those long uneven lines. MCMXIV. Philip Larkin. EBEV

Those lumbering horses in the steady plough. Horses. Edwin Muir. CMoP (1970 ed.); OAEL–2; PoPle

Those lustrous eyes but tell me this. Fred Emerson Brooks. *Fr.* Kissing. PeD

Those men who love the *crwth* and harp. Song and Poetry. *Unknown, tr. by* Gwyn Jones. OBW

Those moments, tasted once and never done. Cornish Cliffs. John Betjeman. MPo; PAIC

Those mornings in green mountains. Virginia Beach. Stanley Plumly. AMV–81

Those mothers down there off the hill. Seventh Son. Ed Roberson. PoBA

Those my friendships most obtain. Contentment. Nathaniel Cotton. OxBChV

Those old Jews in their shadowy habits. Long and Shadowy Habits. Gene Frumkin. PoW

Those Old Zen Blues. James Broughton. GP

Those paths on the mountainside. Circumambulation of Mt. Tamalpais. Andrew Hoyem. PoA

Those quaint old worn-out words! Antiques. Walter de la Mare. PoA

Those red men you offended were my brothers. In My First Hard Springtime. James Welch. AmPA; CDW; MPA

Those rivers in that lost country. Rivers. J. C. Squire. PES

Those rivers run from that land. Song. Robert Creeley. VGW

Those roman stones. Dan, the Dust of Masada Is Still in My Nostrils. Ruth Whitman. VWA

Those scraps of paper. Scraps. Susannah Fried, *tr. by* Anthony Rudolf. VWA

Those streets in my youth. Going North. Luís Omar Salinas. CPA

Those that can give, open their hands this day. A New Year's Sacrifice: To Lucinda. Thomas Carew. CaPo

Those things which make life truly blest. The Happy Life. Martial, *tr. by* Sir Edward Sherburne. PAIC

Those trackless deeps, where many a weary sail. The Trackless Deeps. Shelley. RhR

Those Trees That Line the Northway. Ellen Perreault. AMV–81

Those upon whom Almighty doth intend. The Frowardness of the Elect in the Work of Conversion. Edward Taylor. *Fr.* God's Determinations. EAP

Those vitreous vivariums. Ode of Odium on Aquariums. Arthur Guiterman. BoAnP

Those Wedding Bells Shall Not Ring Out! *with music.* Monroe H. Rosenfeld. FSN

Those Were the Days. *Zulu Oral Tradition, tr. by* H. Tracey. WTO

Those who cannot love the heavens or the earth. The Chaff. W. S. Merwin. PPP

Those who have laid the harp aside. To Wordsworth. Walter Savage Landor. OAEL–2

Those who love cats which do not even purr. Cats. Francis Scarfe. BoAnP; PCat

Those who loved me. Memento Vivendi. Eva Brudne. VWA

Those who split wood know. To a Young Poet. Paula Bennett. AMV–81

Those Winter Sundays. Robert Hayden. CNA; CoPAm; CTBA; FF; GP; HAP; IPWM; NoAM; PoBA; PPP; SoSe (1977 ed.); UnPo (1976 ed.)

Those Zionists. Crescenzo del Monte, *tr. fr. Judeo-Romanesque by* Barbara Garvin. VWA

Thou are not, Penshurst, built to envious show. *See* Thou art not, Penshurst . . .

Thou art a lady;/ If only to go warm were gorgeous. Shakespeare. *Fr.* King Lear, II, iv. OBP

Thou Art Indeed Just, Lord, If I Contend. Gerard Manley Hopkins. CABA (1972 ed.); CMoP (1970 ed.); HAP; HoPM (1975 ed.); ILP (1975 ed.); IP; NoAM; NOBE; OAEL–2; PoIA; UnPo (1976 ed.); VLP; WIF (Justus Quidem Tu Es, Domine.) EBEV

Thou art not faire, for all thy red and white. Thomas Campion. AAS

Thou art [*or* are] not, Penshurst, built to envious show. To Penshurst. Ben Jonson. CABA (1972 ed.); NIL; OAEL-1; PAIC; PPP; SCP-1; TVS

Thou Art, O God. Thomas Moore. PIM

Thou Art, O God, the God of Might, *with music.* Emily Swan Perkins. AH

Thou art reprieved old year, thou shalt not die. Epithalamion. John Donne. SCP-1

Thou art so fair, and young withal. Youth and Beauty. Aurelian Townsend. GBL

Thou art the soul of a summer's day. A Song. Paul Laurence Dunbar. AmNP (1974 ed.)

Thou art the source that causes our river to flow. Jalal al-Din Rumi, *tr. fr. Persian.* ILwL

Thou Art the Tree of Life, *with music.* Edward Taylor. AH

Thou Art the Way, *with music.* George Washington Doane. AH

Thou art to all lost love the best. To the Willow Tree. Robert Herrick. CaPo

Thou blind fool, Love, what dost thou to mine eyes. Sonnets, CXXXVII. Shakespeare. WeW

Thou Blind Man's Mark. Sir Philip Sidney. *Sometimes considered Sonnet CIX of* Astrophel and Stella. CABA (1972 ed.); Epi; HeIP; PPP (Desire.) NOBE

Thou blossom bright with autumn dew. To the Fringed Gentian. Bryant. FSFS; PCOP; PiAm; TAP

Thou, born to sip the lake or spring. On a Honey Bee. Philip Freneau. TAP

Thou brown, bare-breasted, voiceless mystery. To the Colorado Desert. Madge Morris. BPAW

Thou cursed cock, with thy perpetual noise. On a Cock at Rochester. Sir Charles Sedley. FaBoEE; POL

Thou damn'd antipodes to common sense. To Mr. Edward Howard, on His Plays. Charles Sackville. ESaP

Thou fair-hair'd angel of the evening. To the Evening Star. Blake. ILP (1975 ed.); LAuP; MBPR; OAEL-2; PPP; STS

Thou find'st not heere, neither the furious alarmes. J. Soowthern. *Fr.* Sonnets to His Mystresse Diana. ESo

Thou foolish bird, of feathers proud. On a Peacock. Thomas Heyrick. PB

Thou foul-mouthed wretch! Why dost thou choose. The Sailor to His Parrot. W. H. Davies. BoAnP; RhR

Thou genius of connubial love, attend. Happy Marriage. Thomas Blacklock. SLP

Thou God of this great vast, rebuke these surges. Shakespeare on the Sea. Shakespeare. *Fr.* Pericles, III, i. RhR

Thou Grace Divine, Encircling All, *with music.* Eliza Scudder. AH

Thou grimmest far o grusome tykes. To a Hedgehog. Samuel Thompson. BIrV

Thou hast made me, and shall thy work decay? Holy Sonnets, I. John Donne. BoReV; EBEV; ILP (1975 ed.); NOBE

Thou hast made me endless, such is thy pleasure. Rabindranath Tagore. *Fr.* Gitanjali. ILwL

Thou hast not left the rough-barked tree to grow. I Was Sick and in Prison. Jones Very. NOBA

Thou hast not rais'd, Ianthe, such desire. Walter Savage Landor. *Fr.* Ianthe. GBL

Thou hearest the nightingale begin the song of spring. The Vision of Beulah [*or* The Birds]. Blake. *Fr.* Milton, II. NOBE; PB

Thou heaven-threatening rock, gentler than she! Echo to a Rock. Lord Herbert of Cherbury. PAIC

Thou ill-formed offspring of my feeble brain. The Author to Her Book. Anne Bradstreet. EAP; ILP (1975 ed.); InPK; NOBA; PiAm; TAP

Thou in Whose Swordgreat Story Shine the Deeds. E. E. Cummings. Epi

Thou know'st, my Julia, that it is thy turn. To Julia, the Flaminica Dialis, or Queen-Priest. Robert Herrick. CaPo

Thou large-brained woman and large-hearted man. To George Sand: I. A Desire. Elizabeth Barrett Browning. BoWoP

Thou leanest to the shell of night. James Joyce. EBEV

Thou Long Disowned, Reviled, Oppressed, *with music.* Eliza Scudder. AH

Thou, Lord, Hast Been Our Sure Defense, *with music.* John Hopkins. AH

Thou Lord of Hosts, Whose Guiding Hand, *with music.* Octavius Brooks Frothingham. AH

Thou mastering me. The Wreck of the *Deutschland.* Gerard Manley Hopkins. BoReV; CMoP (1970 ed.); NoAM; NOBE; PFD; VLP

Thou mercenary renagade, thou slave. To Mr. Bays. Charles Sackville. APAS

Thou miserable city! where the gloom. On Leaving London for Wales. Shelley. MBPR

Thou moon, like a white Christus hanging. Serenade. Kenneth Slessor. POL

Thou more than most sweet glove. Ben Jonson. *Fr.* Cynthia's Revels. GBL

Thou Mother with Thy Equal Brood, *sel.* Walt Whitman. "Thou wonder world yet undefined, unform'd." PeD

Thou must be true to thyself. Be True. Horatius Bonar. CTV

Thou One in All, Thou All in One, *with music.* Seth Curtis Beach. AH

Thou, Our Elder Brother. Whittier. ILwL

Thou, paw-paw-paw; thou, glurd; thou, spotted. Adam's Task. John Hollander. PPP

Thou percievest the flowers put forth their precious odours. The Odours of Flowers. Blake. *Fr.* Milton, II. PF

Thou saidst that I alone thy heart cou'd move. Catullus, *tr. fr. Latin by* William Walsh. OBVE

Thou saist Love's dart. To Oenone. Robert Herrick. CaPo

Thou saist my lines are hard. To My Ill Reader. Robert Herrick. CaPo

Thou seest me, Lucia, this year droop. Crutches. Robert Herrick. CaPo

Thou seest the hills candied with snow. To Thaliarchus. Horace, *tr. by* Sir Richard Fanshawe. Odes, I, 9. OBVE

Thou sent'st to me a heart was crowned. The Crowned Heart. *Unknown.* PoPle

Thou shalt have one God only; who. The Latest Decalogue. Arthur Hugh Clough. BiP; BoReV; CABA (1972 ed.); EBEV; ExPo (1973 ed.); FaBoCo; FaBoEE; FF; HAP; HoPM (1975 ed.); ILP (1975 ed.); NIL; NOBE; OAEL-2; OBSV; PBMP; PPP; SoSe; SS; VLP; VPC

Thou Shalt Not. Malka Heifetz Tussman, *tr. fr. Yiddish by* Marcia Falk. VWA

Thou shalt not laugh in this leaf, Muse, nor they. Satires, V. John Donne. OBSV

Thou shalt say to the eye of the strange woman: Be the water. In Egypt. Paul Celan, *tr. by* Joachim Neugroschel. VWA

Thou snowy farm with thy five tenements! Elinda's [*or* Ellinda's] Glove. Richard Lovelace. CaPo; SCP-2

Thou sorrow, venom elfe. Upon a Spider Catching a Fly. Edward Taylor. EAP; NIL; NOBE

Thou speckled little trout so fair. The Trout of the Well. *Unknown, tr. by* G. R. D. McLean. SLP

Thou still unravished bride of quietness. Ode on a Grecian Urn. Keats. AnMo; BiP; CABA (1972 ed.); EBEV; ExPo (1973 ed.); FF; HAP; HeIP; HoPM (1975 ed.); ILP (1975 ed.); InPK; InPS; IP; LFH; MBPR; NIL; NOBE; OAEL-2; OBP; PAIC; PBMP; PPoD; PPoe; PPP; SoSe; STS; TT; UnPo (1976 ed.); WIF

Thou stranger, which for Rome in Rome here seekest. Joachim du Bellay, *tr. by* Spenser. *Fr.* Antiquitez de Rome. OBVE

Thou supreme Goddess! by whose power divine. Oedipus Tyrannus; or Swellfoot the Tyrant. Shelley. MBPR

Thou swear'st thou'lt drink no more; kind Heaven send. To Julius. Martial, *tr. by* Sir Charles Sedley. FaBoEE

Thou that sellest the word of God. Against the Friars. *Unknown.* OxBM

Thou thinkst 'tis much that this contentious storm. Shakespeare. *Fr.* King Lear, III, iv. OBP

Thou, to whom the world unknown. Ode to Fear. William Collins. ILP (1975 ed.); LAuP; PAIC

Thou, too, sail on, O Ship of State! The Republic. Longfellow. *Fr.* The Building of the Ship. BTTM

Thou tool of faction, mercenary scribe. Upon the Anonymous Author of Legion's Humble Address to the Lords. Thomas Brown. APAS

Thou two-faced year, Mother of Change and Fate. 1492. Emma Lazarus. WPE

Thou wast that all to me, love. To One in Paradise. Poe. BoLoP; PiAm; TAP

Thou wert the morning star among the living. To Stella. Plato, *tr. by* Shelley. FaBoEE; OBVE

Thou who didst hang upon a barren tree. Long Barren. Christina Rossetti. PBWP; VLP

Thou who hast slept all night upon the storm. To the Man-of-War Bird. Walt Whitman. BoAnP; EcS

Thou who stealest fire. Ode to Memory. Tennyson. VLP

Thou who, when fears attack. Ode to Tobacco. Charles Stuart Calverley. FaBoCo

Thou who wilt not love, do this. Upon Some Women. Robert Herrick. CaPo

Thou who wouldst see the lovely and the wild. Monument Mountain. Bryant. EAP

Thou, who wouldst wear the name. The Poet. Bryant. EAP; TAP

Thou whose birth on earth. The Peace-Giver. Swinburne. *Fr.* Christmas Antiphones. PIM

Thou, whose diviner soul hath caus'd thee now. To Mr. Tilman after He Had Taken Orders. John Donne. EBEV

Thou whose spell can raise the dead. Saul and the Witch of Endor and the Vision of Samuel. Byron. PIM

Thou wilt remember. Thou art not more dear. Robert Browning. *Fr.* Pauline. OAEL-2

Thou woman bute fere. An Orison to the Blessed Virgin. William Herebert. BoReV

Thou wonder world yet undefined, unform'd. Walt Whitman. *Fr.* Thou Mother with Thy Equal Brood. PeD

Thou youngest virgin-daughter of the skies. To the Pious Memory of the Accomplished Young Lady Mrs. Anne Killigrew. Dryden. ILP (1975 ed.); OAEL-1; SCP-1

Though. *See also* Tho'.

Though a Fool. Robert Francis. GP

Though All the Fates Should Prove Unkind. Henry David Thoreau. HAP
(Lines.) ILP (1975 ed.)

Though Amaryllis Dance in Green. *Unknown.* NIL

Though authors are a dreadful clan. I Missed His Book, but I Read His Name. John Updike. OBAL

Though come down in the world to. Camel. Jon Stallworthy. BoAnP

Though conscience void of all offence. Praise. Christopher Smart. OxBChV

Though countless as the grains of sand. Boethius, *tr. by* Samuel Johnson. The Consolation of Philosophy, II, 2. OBVE

Though dusty wits dare scorn astrology. Astrophel and Stella, XXVI. Sir Philip Sidney. OAEL-1

Though earthworms are so cunningly contrived. Wet Morning. Janet Frame. ATNZ

Though Fatherland Be Vast, *with music.* Allen Eastman Cross. AH

Though good things answer many good intents. Crosses. Robert Herrick. CaPo

Though her mother told her/ Not to go a-bathing. Leda and the Swan. Oliver St. John Gogarty. HAP

Though here it is already hot. Blackberry Winter. Peter Huggins. AMV-81

Though he's turned forty, they call him Idiot Boy. Idiot Boy. Rowland M. Hill. AMV-81

Though I am dark. *Unknown, tr. fr. Spanish by* Willis Barnstone. BoWoP

Though I am Laila of the Persian romance. Princess Zeb-un-Nissa, *tr. fr. Persian by* Willis Barnstone. BoWoP

Though I am young, and cannot tell. Death and Love. Ben Jonson. *Fr.* The Sad Shepherd, I, v. ILP (1975 ed.); NOBE

Though I look like you. Hand Me Down Blues. Calvin Forbes. PHC

Though I must live here, and by force. To My Mistress in Absence. Thomas Carew. CaPo

Though I regarded not. Earl of Surrey. AAS

Though I Should Seek, *with music.* Henry Ustic Onderdonk. AH

Though I Speak with the Tongues of Men and Angels. Bible, *N.T. Fr.* First Corinthians. BiP; OAEL-1; PBMP

Though I Thy Mithridates Were. James Joyce. NoAM

Though it is only February, turned. Letter from Germany. Emily Grosholz. AMV-81

Though it seemed, to childish wonder. Star Ride. H. H. Lewis. SPT

Though it's true we were young girls when we met. For Jan, in Bar Maria. Carolyn Kizer. RiTi; VGW

Though I've a Clever Head. *Unknown.* HAP

Though joy is better than sorrow, joy is not great. Joy. Robinson Jeffers. CMoP (1970 ed.)

Though knowledge must be got with pain. For Scholars and Pupils. George Wither. OxBChV

Though leaves are many, the root is one. The Coming of Wisdom with Time. W. B. Yeats. FaBoEE; POL; SoSe

Though loath to grieve. Ode Inscribed to W. H. Channing. Emerson. HAP; ILP (1975 ed.); NOBA; PAIC; PiAm; TAP

"Though logic-choppers rule the town." Tom O'Roughley. W. B. Yeats. CMoP (1970 ed.)

Though marriage by some folks. My Three Wives. *Unknown, after* Etienne Pasquier. FaBoEE

Though much a little map unfolds, more still. The River Compared to an Oratorical Sentence. Luis de Góngora, *tr. by* Edward Meryon Wilson. *Fr.* The First Solitude. OBVE

Though My Thoughts, *with music.* Francis Daniel Pastorius, *tr. fr. German by* Sheema Z. Buehne. AH

Though naughty flesh will multiply. No Mean City. Patrick MacDonogh. BIrV

Though no kin to those fine glistening. Christening-Day Wishes for My God-Child. Robert P. Tristram Coffin. OFD

Though pleasures still can touch my soul. How Singular. Tom Hood. FaBoNo

Though regions far divided. The Constant Lover. Aurelian Townsend. BBL

Though riders be thrown in black disgrace. *Unknown, tr. fr. Irish by* Douglas Hyde. BIrV

Though rous'd by that dark Vizir Riot rude. Priestley. Samuel Taylor Coleridge. *Fr.* Sonnets on Eminent Characters. MBPR

Though somewhat large, exuberant, and truculent. Byron. *Fr.* Don Juan, IX. OAEL-2

Though spacious lands and oceans and far skies. Through a Glass, Darkly. Basil Dowling. ATNZ

Though supposedly Spring. Journal Entry: April 5, 1974. Dan Gerber. TC

Though the barn is so warm. The Palomino Stallion. Alden Nowlan. BoAnP; PH; POL

Though the Clerk of the Weather insist. Pebbles. Herman Melville. AmVN

Though the crocuses poke up their heads in the usual places. Vernal Sentiment. Theodore Roethke. VoPo

Though the day of my destiny's over. Stanzas to Augusta. Byron. ILP (1975 ed.)

Though the great song return no more. The Nineteenth Century and After. W. B. Yeats. FaBoEE

Though the Muse be gone away. Persistency of Poetry. Matthew Arnold. VLP

Though the world has slipped and gone. Lullaby. Edith Sitwell. CMoP (1970 ed.)

Though there are distances between us. Desert Warfare. Michael Longley. CIP

Though three men dwell on Flannan Isle. Flannan Isle. W. W. Gibson. PoTa

Though to good breeding she made no pretence. On a Gentleman Marrying His Cook. Colin Ellis. FaBoEE

Though to strangers' approach. Paired Lives. W. R. Rodgers. CIP

Though trembling waves of roadside heat. Transcontinental. Richard Wright. SPT

Though truth and falsehood be. Seek True Religion! John Donne. *Fr.* Satires, III. BoReV; NOBE

Though we have put. Song in Autumn. Robert D. Fitzgerald. MAuV

Though we lived in the same lane. Answering Li Ying Who Showed Me His Poems about Summer Fishing. Yü Hsüan-chi, *tr. by* Geoffrey Waters. BoWoP

Though you may be absent here, I needs must say. The Spring. Abraham Cowley. *Fr.* The Mistress. HAP; MetP

Though you be faire and beautiful withall. William Smith. Chloris, XXVI. ESo

Though you should build a bark of dead men's bones. Cancelled Stanza of the Ode on Melancholy. Keats. MBPR

Though your strangenesse frets my hart. Thomas Campion. AAS

Thought, A. Robert Louis Stevenson. CTV

Thought-Fox, The. Ted Hughes. HeIP; NCSH; NoAM

Thought from Propertius, A. W. B. Yeats. OAEL-2

Thought I heard the wind. Spring at Fort Okanogan. Ramona Wilson. VoR

Thought in the Center of a Memory, A. J. Charles Green. DNGG

Thought is deeper than all speech. Enosis. Christopher Pearse Cranch. ILP (1975 ed.)

Thought looking out on thought. Opening of Eyes. Laura Riding. NoAM

Thought of a Briton on the Subjugation of Switzerland. Wordsworth. MBPR; PBMP; SpRo

Thought of what America would be like, The. Cantico del Sole. Ezra Pound. OBAL

Thought of writing came to me today, The. W. H. Auden. *Fr.* Letter to Lord Byron. NOBL

Thought rattles along the empty railings. Respectable People. Austin Clarke. CMoP (1970 ed.)

Thoughtful little Willie Frazer. Science for the Young. Wallace Irwin. QQQ

Thoughts. Michael Benedikt. ConAP

Thoughts. John Sjoberg. AcAn

Thoughts. Quincy Troupe. SES

Thoughts about My Daughter before Sleep. Sandra Hochman. TV

Thoughts about the Person from Porlock. Stevie Smith. FaBoCo

Thoughts for My Grandmother. Laya Firestone. VWA

Thoughts for You (When She Came Back from the Mountains). Ranice Henderson Crosby. NMM

Thoughts from a Bottle. Carl Clark. JB

Thoughts from the Pacific. Lindiwe Mabuza. SES

Thoughts from the Wall. Damon Bordenave. PoW

Thoughts in Exile. Su Tung P'o, *tr. fr. Chinese by* Kenneth Rexroth. IPWM

Thoughts of a Young Girl. John Ashbery. ConAP; RRA; TAP; VGW

Thoughts of Chairman Mao. David Young. AmPA; CAAP

Thoughts of God. *Tr. frcm Gaelic by* Douglas Hyde. WTO

Thoughts of Phena. Thomas Hardy. OxBTC

Thoughts on Capital Punishment. Rod McKuen. InPK

Thoughts on Looking into a Thicket. John Ciardi. PoIA

Thoughts on One's Head. William Meredith. HAP

Thoughts on Pain. Sallie Chesham. AATT

Thoughts while Driving Home. John Updike. SoS

Thou'lt fight, if any man call Thebe whore. To Sergius. Sir Charles Sedley. FaBoEE

Thou'rt more inconstant than the wind or sea. The Hypocrite. John Caryll. APAS

Thou's welcome, wean! Mishanter fa' me. A Poet's Welcome to His Love-begotten Daughter. Burns. RRA

Thousand and One Nights, The, *sel.* Al-Khansa, *tr. fr. Arabic by* E. Powys Mathers.
For Her Brother. PBWP

Thousand burdened burrows filled, A. The Rise and Fall of Creede. Cy Warman. BPAW

Thousand deaths a day, A. Resurrection of the Dead. Aliza Shenhar, *tr. by* Linda Zisquit. VWA

Thousand dollars now (cash), A. The Blue Tattoo. Emma Lou Thayne. MPA

Thousand doors ago, A. Young. Anne Sexton. MPo; NCSH

Thousand gloomy walks the bower contains, A. Aphra Behn. *Fr.* A Voyage to the Island of Love. SCP-2

Thousand Martyrs I Have Made, A. Aphra Behn. SBG

Thousand miles beyond this sun-steeped wall, A. Sea Longing. Sara Teasdale. EcS

Thousand miles from land are we, A. The Stormy Petrel. "Barry Cornwall." EcS

Thousand Things, The. Christopher Middleton. TwMBP

Thousand times have I herd men telle, A. Old Books. Chaucer. *Fr.* The Legend of Good Women: Prologue. OxBM

Thousand years from now, A. The Extermination of the Jews. Marvin Bell. VWA

Thousand years, you said, A. Parting. Lady Heguri, *tr. by* Geoffrey Bownas *and* Anthony Thwaite. BoLoP; OLR

Thousands/ of weird little figurines. Semen. Coleman Barks. *Fr.* Body Poems. NVAP

Thousands/ upon thousands of innocent lives. If U Are a Poet. Gladstone Yearwood. SES

Thracian Filly, The. Anacreon, *tr. fr. Greek by* Tom Dodge. LiSp

Thracian Wonder, The, *sels. Unknown, at. to* John Webster *and* William Rowley. GBL
"Love is a law, a discord of such force," *fr.* I, i.
Love Pursued, *fr.* I, i.
"Whither shall I go," *fr.* II, i.

Thraso. William Walsh. NIL

Thraw oot your shaddaws. Moonlight among the Pines. "Hugh MacDiarmid." OAEL-2

Thrawn water? Aye, owre thrawn to be aye thrawn! By Wauchopeside. "Hugh MacDiarmid." EBEV

Thread. Catherine Lucy Czerkawska. SLP

Thread, A/ of meaning. Meaning light. The Dead Lady Canonized. Amiri Baraka. CAPP

Thread/ without cloth. Poverty. Margaret Reynolds. MIS

Thread of Life, The, *sel.* Christina Rossetti. "Irresponsive silence of the land, The." NOBE (Aloof.) UsP

Thread Suns. Paul Celan, *tr. fr. German by* Michael Hamburger. OBVE

Thread the nerves through the right holes. Resurrection Song. Thomas Lovell Beddoes. FaBoEE; InPK; PMW

Threading the palm, a web of tiny lines. Signs. Gjertrud Schnackenberg. PoA

Threads to Be Woven Later. Linda Pastan. PoUp

Three. Gregory Corso. SA

Three. John N. Morris. GP

3 A.M. Mbembe. NW

Three a.m.—a far bell. December. Gary Snyder. InPS

3 a.m. in New York. Jean Valentine. NYP

Three anti-depressants and one diuretic a day. Bruce Beaver. *Fr.* Letters to Live Poets, XII. MAuV

Three Badgers, The. "Lewis Carroll." FaBoNo

Three black boys. Panther. Sam Cornish. PoBA

Three blind mice. Mother Goose. FaBoNo; FSW; MG; MN

Three boys, American, in dungarees. February 22. John Updike. GOA

Three Brown Girls Singing. M. Carl Holman. NIL

Three Bushes, The, *sel.* W. B. Yeats. Lady's Third Song. FaBoTw (1975 ed.)

Three Cezannes. George Whipple. AMV-80

Three Cheers for the Black, White and Blue. Ruth Pitter. BoAnP

Three Cherry Trees, The. Walter de la Mare. CMoP (1970 ed.)

Three Children. *Unknown.* NOBL

Three Colts Exercising in a Six-Acre. Joseph Campbell. BoAnP; PFIr

Three Concrete Poems. Mark Axelrod. AAN

Three countries blacken and vanish. L'Aurore Grelottante. Peter Levi. UsP

3 Days after Father's Day. Allan Kornblum. AcAn

Three days and still the slow fogged rain. Kumara God. Peter Bland. ATNZ

Three days of ocean riding. Incident at Mossel Bay. Mary Balzs. AMV-81

Three days of rest. The Sun in Capricorn. Joyce Mansour, *tr. by* Carol Cosman. PBWP

Three days rain and. Short Pastoral. Leonard E. Nathan. MIT

Three days we had. First Thanksgiving. Myra Cohn Livingston. CC

Three decades of my life had passed. Hebrew Lesson. Max Brod, *tr. fr. German.* AMV-80

Three Enemies, The. Christina Rossetti. VLP

Three Epitaphs on John Hewet and Sarah Drew. Pope. NIL "Here lie two poor lovers, who had the mishap," III. FaBoEE

Three excellent qualities in narration. Triads [*or* Thirty-three Triads]. *Unknown, tr. by* Thomas Kinsella. BIrV; PFIr

Three-faced, The. Robert Graves. FaBoEE

Three faces.../mirrored in the muddy streams of living. For Andy Goodman—Michael Schwerner—and James Chaney. Margaret Walker. BPo

Three Fates, The. Rosemary Dobson. BoWoP

Three Fishers, The. Charles Kingsley. FaPoR

Three Fitts. Stewart Parker. CIP

Three flutes, two oboes, English horn, violins. Guide to the Symphony. Weldon Kees. VGW

Three Found Poems. George Hitchcock. OBAL

Three Foxes, The. A. A. Milne. OxBChV

Three Friends. *Tr. fr. Yoruba by* Ulli Beier. BoWoP

Three Friends of Mine. Jimmy Santiago Baca. DNGG

Three from the Market. Sandra McPherson. RiTi

Three Ghostesses. *Unknown.* IWK

Three gooses: geese. Goose, Moose, and Spruce. David McCord. ECBV

Three Greeks. Richard Packer. FPA

Three grey boys tracked us to an old house. In One Battle. Amiri Baraka. BPo

Three Grey Geese. *Unknown.* SoSe

Three halves of you are elsewhere. How to Reach the Moon. Marsha Pomerantz. VWA

Three hand-spike raps on the forward hatch. Reefing Topsails. Walter Mitchell. RhR

Three hands rest. Setting. Eve Shelnutt. TC

Three Hermits, The. W. B. Yeats. CMoP (1970 ed.)

Three Holy Kings from Morgenland. Heine, *tr. fr. German by* Herman Eichenthal. PChr

Three hours ago he blundered up the trench. A Working Party. Siegfried Sassoon. CMoP (1970 ed.)

Three hugest dinosaurs do not outweigh. The Blue Whale. Robert Watson. MAT

Three hundred fillings high. New Block. Patric Dickinson. LP

Three hundred from one village. 1867: Last Sounds. Gerry O'Egan. POL

300,000,000. What Happened Here Before. Gary Snyder. NNaP

Three Hundred Thousand More. James Sloan Gibbons. BTTM

"Three in heaven I hope" said old Jane to Henry. John Berryman. *Fr.* Dream Songs. RRA

Three jolly farmers. Off the Ground. Walter de la Mare. PoTa

Three jolly gentlemen. The Huntsmen. Walter de la Mare. BBL; DuDa; PH

Three Kinds of Pleasures. Robert Bly. ANTL

Three Kingdoms Of Nature, The. Gotthold Lessing, *tr. fr. German by* Alfred Baskerville, *ad. by* Robert Bly. NU

Three Kings, The. Rubén Darío, *tr. fr. Spanish by* Lysander Kemp. PChr

Three Kings, The. Longfellow. PIM

Three Knights from Spain. *Unknown. See* We Are Three Brethren Come from Spain.

Three Lectures on the Skeleton. George M. Young, Jr. FAF

Three little fellows sing to the wind. Tohub. Jakov van Hoddis, *tr. by* Charles Guenther. VWA

Three little ghostesses. Three Ghostesses. *Unknown.* IWK

Three Little Kittens, The. *Unknown, at. to* Eliza Lee Follen *and to* Eliza Cook. BBL ("Three little kittens they lost their mittens.") MG

Three little lads were seated one day. Her Eyes Don't Shine like Diamonds. David Marion. FSN

Three little mice ran up the stairs. *Unknown.* MN

Three little mice sat down to spin. Mother Goose. MN

Three little ones splash in the shallows along the beach. The Hot Day and Human Nature. Gordon Johnston. AMV-81

Three Little Pigs, The. Sir Alfred Scott Gatty. DuDr; OxBChV

Three little ponies who didn't like their hay. Three Ponies. Arthur Guiterman. ECBV

Three little words we often use. The Nine Parts of Speech. *Unknown.* ECBV

Three Love Poems. Norman Cameron. FaBoTw (1975 ed.) From a Woman to a Greedy Lover, I. FaBoEE In the Queen's Room, II. OxBTC Shepherdess, III. GBL; SLP

Three Love Poems, *sel.* Sandra Hochman. "Crows, pheasants, cuckoos, toucans," 1. UsP

Three Love Poems for My Wife. George Bruce. SLP

Three lovely sisters working were. The Parcae; or, Three Dainty Destinies: The Armillet. Robert Herrick. CaPo

Three matches in a folder, you and me. Epigram: Night-Piece. J. V. Cunningham. PiAm

Three measures of breadth I take. Measures. Joseph Gordon Macleod ("Adam Drinan"). MS

Three Men. *Unknown.* BluL

Three men coming down the winter hill, The. Winter Landscape. John Berryman. CoPAm; NIL; UsP; WIF

Three Mirrors, The. Edwin Muir. NoAM

3 Models of the Universe. May Swenson. Psy

Three Modes of History and Culture. Amirii Baraka. NoAM

Three mounted buglers laced in gold. A Battle Picture. Herman Melville. PiAm

Three Movements, The. Donald Hall. NowV

Three Movements. W. B. Yeats. CMoP (1970 ed.); FaBoEE

Three Moves. John Logan. CAPP

Three Musicians, The. Aubrey Beardsley. VLP

Three o'clock. The bus lurches. Good Friday. Edwin Morgan. MS

Three of us/ in the bar. Jazz. Carolyn M. Rodgers. JB

Three of us went to the top of the city. Poem from the Empire State. June Jordan. BPo

3 of Washingtons heads. George Washington Goes to a Girlie Movie. Aram Boyajian. NeAC

Three Old Brothers. Frank O'Connor. PFIr

Three old hermits took the air. The Three Hermits. W. B. Yeats. CMoP (1970 ed.)

Three Pigeons, The. Goldsmith. *See* Song: "Let school-masters puzzle their brain."

Three Poems, *sel.* "Ping Hsin," *tr. fr. Chinese by* Julia C. Lin. "Fishing boats have returned, The!" PBWP

Three Poems about Children. Austin Clarke. CIP

Three Poems for the Indian Steelworkers. Joseph Bruchac. CDW

Three poets, in three distant ages born. Lines Printed under the Engraved Portrait of Milton. Dryden. HeIP; InPK; OAEL-1

Three Ponies. Arthur Guiterman. ECBV

Three Portraits. George Hitchcock. VGW

Three Power Dances, *sel.* Judith Johnson Sherwin. First Dance: God Who Walks like a Bear. BCr

Three Problems. Katharine Edgar Cobey. PoUp

Three Ravens, The ("There were three ravens [*or* crows] sat on a tree"). *Unknown.* AIW; AmFP; CABA (1972 ed.); Epi, *with music*; ExPo (1973 ed.); FaBoBa; FSW; GBP; HeIP; InPK; IP; LFH; OAEL-1, *with music;* PeBB; RDB, *with music;* UnPo (1976 ed.)

Three Revellers Search for Death. Chaucer. *Fr.* The Canterbury Tales: The Pardoner's Tale. OxBM

Three Riddles. Brian Swann. TSWA

Three roads were shadowy and the sky over. Vanessa Vanessa. Ewart Milne. BIrV

Three sang of love together. A Triad. Christina Rossetti. PBWP; VLP

Three Sayings from Highlands, North Carolina. Jonathan Williams. OBAL

Three Seasons. Christina Rossetti. ILP (1975 ed.)

Three Sentences for a Dead Swan. James Wright. NoAM; NOBA

Three silences made him a single word. Sonnet. R. P. Blackmur. PoA

Three Sisters. Walter de la Mare. FaBoEE

Three Sisters. Erica Jong. UsP

3:16 and One Half. Charles Bukowski. GP

Three Songs, The. Bayard Taylor. PoTa

Three Songs from the Haida. Constance Lindsay Skinner. BPAW

Three Songs of Mary, *sel.* Madeleine L'Engle. O Simplicitas. PChr

Three spirits came to me. April. Ezra Pound. CMoP (1970 ed.)

Three square miles clear-cut. Report from a Forest Logged by the Weyerhaeuser Company. David Wagoner. CNW

3 Stanzas about a Tree. Marvin Bell. Prf

3 Stones. Roderick Watson. MIS

Three strange men came to the Inn. A Lady Comes to an Inn. Elizabeth J. Coatsworth. PoTa; SO

Three Streets. Umberto Saba, *tr. fr. Italian by* Anita Barrows. VWA

Three strings, a neck of almond, and the heart. Balalaika. Norman Dubie. AmPA

Three summers since I chose a maid. The Farmer's Bride. Charlotte Mew. BoLoP; OxBTC; PoIA; SBG; WPE

Three Sunrises from Amtrak. Florence Dolgorukov. AMV-81

Three Things. May Sarton. AMV-80

Three things must epigrams, like bees, have all. *Unknown, tr. fr. Latin.* NIL

Three things remind me of you. Meditation. Carl Rakosi. VWA

Three things seek my death. Devil, Maggot and Son. *Unknown.* SoSe

Three things there are more beautiful. The Beautiful. W. H. Davies. BBGO

Three things there be that prosper all apace. To His Son. Sir Walter Ralegh. InPS; PPoe

Three Things to Remember. Blake. *See* Robin Redbreast in a Cage, A.

Three times last night/ I woke up certain. How to End the Summer Alone. Lori Shpunt. PoUp

Three times the Carline grain'd and rifted. Lucky Spence's Last Advice. Allan Ramsay. EPC

Three X Three. Sonia Sanchez. WBN

Three-toed tree toad, The. Nocturne. Arthur Guiterman. ECBV

Three Towns, The. Howard Nemerov. AMV-81

Three trees there are, and good are they. Trystan and Esyllt. *Unknown, tr. by* Gwyn Jones. OBW

Three Troopers, The. George Walter Thornbury. BTTM

Three Valentines to the Wide World, *sel.* Mona Van Duyn. "When, in the middle of my life, the earth stalks me." RiTi

Three virgins at the break of day. The Golden Net. Blake. MBPR; UsP

Three Voices, The, *sel.* "Lewis Carroll." Third Voice, The. VLP

Three weeks, and now I hear! My Olson Elegy. Irving Feldman. Prf

Three weeks gone and the combatants gone. Vergissmeinicht. Keith Douglas. InPS; OxBTC; SoSe

Three Weeks in the State of Loneliness. Marge Piercy. MMD

Three Wise Men of Gotham, The ("There were three men of Gotham"). *Unknown.* FaBoNo

Three wise men of Gotham. Mother Goose. FaBoNo; MG

Three Wise Old Women. Elizabeth T. Corbett. OxBChV

Three Women. Liz Lochhead. MIS

Three Women, *sel.* Sylvia Plath. "I see her in my sleep, my red, terrible girl." TV

Three Women Blues. *Unknown.* BluL

Three Years She Grew in Sun and Shower. Wordsworth. *Fr.* Lucy. AnMo; HAP; ILP (1975 ed.); MBPR; NOBE; OAEL-2

Three Young Rats ("Three young rats with black felt hats"). *Unknown.* ECBV; FaBoNo; PoPle (Rats, Ducks, Dogs, Cats, Pigs.) GBP

Threefold terror of love, The; a fallen flare.   The Mother of God.
W. B. Yeats.   ExPo (1973 ed.)

Threes.   Carl Sandburg.   CMoP (1970 ed.)

Threnody: "Let happy throats be mute."   Donald Jeffrey Hayes.
AmNP (1974 ed.)

Threnody: "Only quiet death."   Waring Cuney.   AmNP (1974
ed.)

Threnody: "South-wind brings, The."   Emerson.   PAIC

Threnody: "Truth is a golden sunset far away."   I. O. Scherzo.
HoPM (1975 ed.)

Threshed corn lay piled like grit of ivory.   The Barn.   Seamus
Heaney.   HAP; HeHu

Threshing-Machine, The.   Alice Meynell.   WPE

Threw a woman's shoe.   My Atlas Poet.   George Bowering.
NeAC

Thrice, and above, blest, my soul's half, art thou.   A Country
Life: To His Brother, Master Thomas Herrick.   Robert
Herrick.   CaPo

Thrice Blest the Man, *with music.*   John Barnard.   AH

Thrice happy flowers!   *Unknown.   Fr.* The Masque of Flowers.
SCP-2

Thrice he came.   Malacoda.   Samuel Beckett.   CIP

Thrice the brinded cat hath mew'd.   Shakespeare.   *Fr.* Macbeth,
IV, i.   OFD

Thrice Toss These Oaken Ashes in the Air.   Thomas Campion.
EBEV; HAP; MAT; OAEL-1
(Love-Charms.)   NOBE
(Song for the Lute.)   PoPle

Thrice Welcome First and Best of Days, *with music.*   Isaac
Chanler.   AH

Thrice welcome to the Norther.   Ode to the Norther.   William
Lawrence Chittenden.   BPAW

Thriftles thred which pampred beauty spinnes, The.   A Sonet
Written in Prayse of the Browne Beautie.   George Gascoigne.
AAS

Thrifty Soprano, A.   Ogden Nash.   TDH

Thrifty Young Fellow, A.   *Unknown.*   TDH

Thrippsy pillivinx.   A Letter to Evelyn Baring.   Edward Lear.
FaBoNo

Thro elm and maple and syringa branches.   Commencement.
Constance Carrier.   WPE

Throbbing—all I can hear!   Drums.   Martha Chosa.   VW

Throng of eyes.   Covenant.   Paul Auster.   VWA

Through a blue-buoyant lake of air wavers.   Dream of Ascent.
James Applewhite.   NVAP

Through a Glass, Darkly.   Basil Dowling.   ATNZ

Through a Glass Eye, Lightly.   Carolyn Kizer.   BoWoP

Through a mist of tears I watch the years.   The Covered Wagon.
Lena Whittaker Blakeney.   BPAW

Through a square sealed-off with.   A Word about Freedom and
Identity in Tel Aviv.   Jon Silkin.   VWA

Through a wild midnight all my mountainous past.   The Monster.
Henry Rago.   PoA

Through all my youth/ I followed my lusts.   It's Just the Same to
Me.   Hermann Hesse.   ILwL

Through all the employments of life.   John Gay.   *Fr.* The
Beggar's Opera, I, i.   ILP (1975 ed.)

Through All Your Abstract Reasoning.   Brian Patten.   FaBoTw
(1975 ed.)

Through alpine meadows soft-suffused.   Stanzas from the Grande
Chartreuse.   Matthew Arnold.   OAEL-2; VLP

Through an ascending emptiness.   Maya.   E. A. Robinson.
PiAm

Through and through the inspired leaves.   The Book-Worms.
Burns.   FaBoEE

Through autumn evening, water whirls thin blue.   The Castle of
Thorns.   Yvor Winters.   NoAM

Through Binoculars.   Charles Tomlinson.   OAEL-2

Through clock,/ To tell how night draws hence, I've none.   His
Grange, or Private Wealth.   Robert Herrick.   CaPo

Through course of time.   Wheel.   Ciaran Carson.   IPM

Through dangly woods the aimless Doze.   The Doze.   James
Reeves.   CTV

Through every age, eternal God.   Isaac Watts.   AmFP

Through every night we hate.   Mothers, Daughters.   Shirley
Kaufman.   BoWoP; GP; NMM; RiTi; TPo; TV

Through frost and snow locked from mine eyes.   To Saxham.
Thomas Carew.   CaPo

Through hesitations, fits-and-starts.   Disco Fever.   Barry
Schechter.   EC

Through it,/ over young women's abdomens tense.   The
Stethoscope.   Dannie Abse.   PMW

Through lane or black archway.   The Young Woman of Beare.
Austin Clarke.   NoAM

Through lenses the world opens.   Microscope.   Gwyn Thomas.
OBW

Through life's dull road, so dim and dirty.   On My Thirty-third
Birthday.   Byron.   BBGO; FaBoEE

Through Old Farmhouse Windows.   Allan Block.   FAF

Through our laced and latticed windows.   Shacked Up at the Ritz.
Doug Fetherling.   NeAC

Through Ruddy Orchards.   Mary Oliver.   WPE

Through swamps and alligators I wend my weary way.   On the
Lakes of Ponchartrain.   *Unknown.*   AmFP

Through that pure virgin shrine.   The Night.   Henry Vaughan.
BoReV; EBEV; MetP; NOBE; OAEL-1; OBW; SCP-1

Through that window—all else being extinct.   The Room.
Conrad Aiken.   ILP (1975 ed.); NOBA

Through the ample open door of the peaceful country barn.   A
Farm Picture.   Walt Whitman.   InPS; PPoe

Through the Appalachian valleys, with his kit a buckskin bag.
Ballad of Johnny Appleseed.   Helmer O. Oleson.   CTV

Through the black pockets.   Train to Reflection.   Lawrence T.
O'Neill.   AMV-80

Through the black, rushing smoke-bursts.   The Song of Callicles.
Mattew Arnold.   *Fr.* Empedocles on Etna, II.   NOBE;
OAEL-2

Through the bound cable strands, the arching path.   Atlantis.
Hart Crane.   *Fr.* The Bridge.   NYP

Through the car window goes Kingsley Martin.   On Throwing a
Copy of the New Statesman into the Coorong.   Max Harris.
GAS

Through the Dark the Dreamers Came, *with music.*   Earl B.
Marlatt.   AH

Through the Eye of the Needle.   Daniela Gioseffi.   AAN

Through the garden of shadow-/ flowers.   The Boy and the
Lantern.   Evaristo Ribera Chevremont, *tr. by* Julio Marzán.
InW

Through the gate.   The Colt.   Raymond Knister.   AKE

Through the great sinful streets of Naples as I past.   Easter Day,
Naples, 1849.   Arthur Hugh Clough.   PFD; VLP; VPC

Through the hanging turkey's mouth.   A Skill in Killing.   George
Abbe.   FAF

Through the house what busy joy.   The First Tooth.   Charles *and*
Mary Lamb.   OxBChV

Through the long death of the moon.   The Death of the Moon.
David Wagoner.   PoA

Through the Looking-Glass, *sels.*   "Lewis Carroll."
Humpty Dumpty's Song, *fr. ch.* 6.   OxBChV
(Humpty Dumpty's Recitation.)   FaBoCo; FaBoNo
("In winter, when the fields are white.")   EBEV
Jabberwocky, *fr. ch.* 1.   AnMo; BiP; CABA (1972 ed.); CTV;
DuDr; EBEV; FaBoCo; FaBoNo; FF; HeIP; HoPM (1975
ed.); ILP (1975 ed.); InPK; InPS; NIL; NOBE; NOBL;

OAEL-2; OBP; OxBChV; PCOP; PoIA; PPoe; PPM; PPP; SpRo; TPo; UsP; VLP; WIF

Walrus and the Carpenter, The, *fr. ch.* 4. AKE; FaBoCo; FaBoNo; NOBL; OxBChV; RhR
("'Time has come, The,' the Walrus said," 1 *st.*) CTV

White Knight's Song, The, *fr. ch.* 8. FaBoCo; ILP (1975 ed.); InPS; NOBE; NOBL; OAEL-2; OBP
(Aged Aged Man, The.) OxBChV; SpRo
(Ways and Means.) ECBV
(White Knight's Ballad, The.) FaBoNo; HAP; VLP

Through the Metidja to Abd-el-Kadr. Robert Browning. PeD

Through the Night of Doubt and Sorrow. Sabine Baring-Gould. FaPoR

Through the night on fire with my blood. She Speaks the Morning's Filigree. Philip Lamantia. VGW

Through the noonday sun. Kathleen Lubeck. *Fr.* Sons. NPW

Through the open French window the warm sun. Still-Life. Elizabeth Daryush. WPE

Through the revolving door. Alligator on the Escalator. Eve Merriam. SO

Through the salt mouth of the river. Riverbed. David Wagoner. CNW

Through the shadow/ which turns. Michael S. Howden. PHC

Through the Smoke Hole, *sel.* Gary Snyder.
"There is another world above this one." PoA

Through the soft pulp. Hand Saw. Erica Funkhouser. AMV-81

Through the trees outside small. Departure. George Hitchcock. GP

Through the vague mornng, the heart preoccupied. Bombers. C. Day Lewis. CMoP (1970 ed.)

Through the white winter palace. At Kilbryde Castle. Lorn M. MacIntyre. SLP

Through the Whole Long Night. H. Leivick, *tr. fr. Yiddish by* Ruth Whitman. VWA

Through this indifferent winter's gaze. Beggar and Poet. Robert A. Martin. AATT

Through thy battlements, Newstead, the hollow winds whistle. On Leaving Newstead Abbey. Byron. MBPR

Through time their sharp features. The Indians on Alcatraz. Paul Muldoon. CIP

Through Two layers of Glass. Anselm Hollo. AcAn

Through Warmth and Light of Summer Skies, *with music.* Austin Faricy. AH

Through weeds and thorns, and matted underwood. The Picture; or, The Lover's Resolution. Samuel Taylor Coleridge. MBPR

Through what long heaviness, assayed in what strange fire. Carthusians. Ernest Dowson. VLP

Through Willing Heart and Helping Hand, *with music.* Frederick Lucian Hosmer. AH

Through winter streets to steer your course aright. Trivia; or, The Art of Walking the Streets of London. John Gay. EPC

Through woods, Mme Une Telle, a trifle ill. Autumn Chapter in a Novel. Thom Gunn. OxBTC

Through You. Edwin Honig. TAP

Throughout Australian history no tongue or pen can tell. The Death of Morgan. *Unknown.* FaBoBa

Throughout the day we are able to ban the voices. Henriëtte Roland-Holst, *tr. fr. Dutch by* Manfred Wolf. PBWP

Throughout the field I find no grain. Winter in Durnover Field. Thomas Hardy. PoIA

Throughout the World If It Were Sought. Sir Thomas Wyatt. MAT

Throw Away the Flowers. Elizabeth Daryush. PBWP

Throw away thy rod. Discipline. George Herbert. BoReV; ExPo (1973 ed.); NOBE; PAIC; SCP-1

Throw Hannibal on the scales, how many pounds. Hannibal. Juvenal, *tr. by* Robert Lowell. *Fr.* Satires, X. OBVE

Throw Him Down M'Closkey; or, M'Closkey's Great Fight, *with music.* John W. Kelly. FSN

Throwing a bomb is bad. Ethics for Everyman. Roger Woddis. NOBL

Throwing stone perhaps its surface carved, A. 3 Stones. Roderick Watson. MIS

Thrown Away. Kipling. *See* Horses.

Thrown backwards first, head over heels in the wind. To My Friend Whose Parachute Did Not Open. David Wagoner. SFF

Thrown suddenly into a corner of the world. Exodus 1940. Alfred Wolfenstein, *tr. by* Erna Baber Rosenfeld. VWA

Thru Blue Eyes. Ahmos Zu-Bolton II. AAN

Thrush before Dawn, A. Alice Meynell. WPE

Thrush, linnet, stare, and wren. In Glencullen. J. M. Synge. PFIr; RAE

Thrushes. Ted Hughes. TwMBP

Thrushes sing as the sun is going, The. Proud Songsters. Thomas Hardy. NoAM; PB; UsP

Thrush's Nest, The. John Clare. BoAnP; PB

Thrush's Nest, The. Richard Ryan. PFIr

Thrust of the dragon's tight bone, The. The Dream Feast (Three Poems). Anita Endrezze Probst. VoR

Thrust of your body, The. Love Poem. Mark Wangberg. TC

Thud of apples. November Morning. Mary Ann Larkin. PoUp

Thule, the Period of Cosmography. *Unknown.* HAP

Thumb. Philip Dacey. POL

Thumb, The. Dennis Saleh. MAT; NeAC

Thumb, for a summer's promise, The. The Sand Painters. Ben Belitt. GOA

Thumb, loose tooth of a horse. Bestiary for the Fingers of My Right Hand. Charles Simic. AmPA

Thumbing Old Magazines. Gerald Vizenor. VoR

Thumbing through someone else's book. Thinking Back Seven Years and Being Here Now. David Curry. HeS

Thumping old tunes give a voice to its whereabouts. Fairground. W. H. Auden. LP

Thunder in a Moment of Calm. Joseph Kalar. SPT

Thunder in the Garden. William Morris. VLP

Thunder of waves out of the dying west. Oreti Beach. Charles Brasch. ATNZ

Thunder Song. *Unknown, tr. fr. Omaha Indian.* TVo

Thunderstorm in South Dakota. Kay Boyle. WPE

Thunderstorm in Town, A. Thomas Hardy. BoLoP; GBL

Thurn, A. John Berryman. NOBA

Thursday. Edna St. Vincent Millay. PoA

Thursday night at Slug's. McCoy Tyner at Slugs. Quincy Troupe. SES

Thursday was baking day in our house. Baking Day. Rosemary Joseph. MPo

Thus at the panting dove a falcon flies. Homer, *tr. by* Pope. *Fr.* The Illiad, XXII. OBVE

Thus being entred, they behold around. Spenser. *Fr.* The Faerie Queene, II, 12. OAEL-1

Thus by himself compelled to live each day. Peter Grimes; the Outcast. George Crabbe. *Fr.* The Borough, Letter XXII. NOBE

Thus charg'd he; nor Argicides denied. Homer, *tr. by* George Chapman. *Fr.* The Odyssey, V. OBVE

Thus Crosslegged on Round Pillow Sat in Space. Allen Ginsberg. NNaP

Thus did my days pass on, and now at length. Wordsworth. *Fr.* The Prelude, II. BoReV

Thus down a lone valley with cedars o'er spread. Columbia. *Unknown.* AmFP

Thus fares the drudge; but thou, whose life's a dream. Persius, *tr. fr. Latin by* Dryden. *Fr. Satires, IV.* SCP-1

Thus fell the King, who yet surviv'd the state. Virgil, *tr. by* Sir John Denham. *Fr. The Aeneid, II.* OBVE

Thus have I shunned the fire for fear of burning. Shakespeare. *Fr. The Two Gentlemen of Verona, I, iii.* GBL

Thus I awakede, wot God, when I wonede in Cornehille. Long Will in London. William Langland. *Fr. The Vision of Piers Plowman.* OxBM

Thus it befell upon a night. Medea's Magic. John Gower. *Fr. Confessio Amantis, V.* OxBM

Thus laykes this lorde by lynde-wodes [or lunde-wodes] eves. Gawain and the Lady of the Castle. *Unknown. Fr.* Sir Gawain and the Green Knight. EBEV; OxBM

Thus piteously Love closed what he begat. Modern Love, L. George Meredith. EBEV; HAP; ILP (1975 ed.); NOBE; OAEL-2; PAIC; PFD; VPC

Thus queth Alfred. Wealth and Wisdom. *At. to* Alfred, King of England. *Fr. The Proverbs of Alfred.* OxBM

Thus saith my Chloris bright. Giovanni Battista Guarini, *tr. fr. Italian.* GBL

Thus saying, from her side the fatal key. Milton. *Fr. Paradise Lost, II.* EBEV

Thus should have been our travels. Over 2000 Illustrations and a Complete Concordance. Elizabeth Bishop. NoAM

Thus Spake the Saviour, *with music.* Jeremy Belknap. AH

Thus spoke the Lord to Israel. Amalek. Friedrich Torberg, *tr. by* Erna Baber Rosenfeld. VWA

Thus spoke the senator from Arizona. Birds and Man. Lindiwe Mabuza. SES

Thus sung Orpheus to his strings. *Unknown.* GBL

Thus talking hand in hand alone they pass'd. Milton. *Fr. Paradise Lost, IV.* EBEV

Thus the old men lamented. Pogroms. André Spire, *tr. by* Stanley Burnshaw. VWA

Thus the poet is a beached gypsy. Jim Harrison. *Fr. Letters to Yesenin.* TC

Thus they in heav'n, above the starry sphear. Milton. *Fr. Paradise Lost, III.* EBEV

Thus to Glaucus spoke/ Divine Sarpedon. Homer, *tr. by* Sir John Denham. *Fr. The Iliad, XII.* OBVE

Thus will despair/ In ecstasy of nightmare. The Succubus. Robert Graves. OAEL-2

Thus with imagin'd wing our swift scene flies. Shakespeare. King Henry V, *fr. III, Prologue.* EBEV

Thwick-a-thwack. Thomas Dekker. *Fr. London's Tempe.* SCP-2

Thy azure robe I did behold. Julia's Petticoat. Robert Herrick. CaPo; SCP-1

Thy bosom is endearèd with all hearts. Sonnets, XXXI. Shakespeare. NOBE

Thy Brother's Blood. Jones Very. AmVN; NOBA; TAP

Thy byrth, thy beautie, nor thy brave attyre. Farewell with a Mischeife. George Gascoigne. AAS

Thy country, Wilberforce, with just disdain. Sonnet to William Wilberforce, Esq. William Cowper. ILP (1975 ed.)

Thy country's curse is on thee, darkest crest. To the Lord Chancellor. Shelley. MBPR

Thy eyes and eyebrows I could spare. *Unknown.* FaBoEE

Thy fingers make early flowers of. E. E. Cummings. LoAs

Thy flattering picture, Phryne, is like thee. Phryne. John Donne. FaBoEE

Thy [or Your] friendship oft has made my heart to ache [or ake]. To William Hayley [or To Hayley]. Blake. FaBoCo; FaBoEE; FF

Thy functions are ethereal. On the Power of Sound. Wordsworth. VLP

Thy grace, dear Lord's my golden wrack, I finde. Edward Taylor. Preparatory Meditations: First Series, XXXII. EAP

Thy humane frame, my glorious Lord, I spy. Edward Taylor. Preparatory Meditations: First Series, VII. PiAm

Thy Kingdom Come. Elmer F. Suderman. AATT

Thy look of love has power to calm. To Harriett. Shelley. MBPR

Thy Loving Kindness, Lord, I Sing, *with music.* George Barrell Cheever. AH

Thy Mercies, Lord, To Heaven Reach, *with music.* William Kethe. AH

Thy nags (the leanest things alive). Epigram. Matthew Prior. FaBoEE

Thy Praise, O God, in Zion Waits, *with music.* Jacob Kimball. AH

Thy praise or dispraise is to me alike. To Fool, or Knave. Ben Jonson. FaBoEE; SoSe

Thy Rising Is Beautiful. Akhnaton (Amenhotep IV), *tr. fr. Egyptian.* ILwL

Thy sacred succour, Arethusa, bring. The Tenth Pastoral; or, Gallus. Virgil, *tr. by* Dryden. Epi

Thy satin vesture richer than looms. Copa de Oro. Ina Coolbrith. WPW

Thy sooty godhead I desire. To Vulcan. Robert Herrick. CaPo

Thy soul/ Grown delicate with satieties. O Atthis. Ezra Pound. PoA

Thy summer voice, Musketaquit. Two Rivers. Emerson. NOBA

Thy trivial harp will never please. Merlin, I. Emerson. AmVN; NOBA; PiAm

Thy voice slow rising like a spirit, lingers. To Constantia Singing. Shelley. MBPR

Thy wisdom speak in me, and bids me dare. Shelley. *Fr. Epipsychidion.* OAEL-2

Thyestes, *sels.* Seneca, *tr. fr. Latin.*
"O yee, whome lorde of lande and waters wyde," *fr. III, tr. by* Jasper Heywood. OBVE
"Stond who so lyst upon the slipper toppe," *fr. II, tr. by* Sir Thomas Wyatt. AAS; OBVE
("Climb at court for me that will," *tr. by* Andrew Marvell.) OBVE
("Let him that will, ascend the tottering seat," *tr. by* Sir Matthew Hale.) OBVE
("Let who so lyst with might mace to raygne," *tr. by* Jasper Heywood.) OBVE
("Upon the slippery tops of humane state," *tr. by* Abraham Cowley.) OBVE

Thyme. *Unknown.* AmFP

Thyrsis. Matthew Arnold. Epi; NOBE; VLP
*Sels.*
Hill-Side Flowers, *st.* 12. PF
"How changed is here each spot man makes or fills!" *sts.* 1–3. PES
"So, some tempestuous morn in early June," *sts.* 6–7. FSFS; PoPle

Thyrsis and Milla, arm in arm together *Unknown.* GBL

Thyrsis, the music of that murmuring spring. Winter. Pope. *Fr. Pastorals.* PAIC

Tic. Coleman Barks. *Fr. Body Poems.* NVAP

Tichborne's Elegy. Chidiock Tichborne. *See* Elegy: "My prime of youth is but a frost of cares."

Tick Picking in the Quetico. Don Johnson. PHC

Tick-a-lock rock-a-bye. Child's Game. Judson Jerome. DuDa

Ticket, The, said: to SFO. Man of Letters. Warren Knox. QQQ

Tickled,/ my thoughts wander. Celebration for My Mother. Wendy Rose. CDW

Tidal Pool. Sara Henderson Hay. EcS

Tiddle-de-dumpty, tiddle-de-dee. Coquetry. Eugene Field. ECBV

Tide. George Mattingly. AcAn

Tide be runnin' the great world over. Sea Love. Charlotte Mew. OxBTC

Tide Pools. Dave Smith. AMV-81

Tide Rises, the Tide Falls, The. Longfellow. AmVN; ILP (1975 ed.); LFH; NOBA; PBMP; PiAm; RAE; RhR; TAP; VoPo

Tide River, the. Charles Kingsley. *Fr.* The Water Babies. OxBChV

Tides. Will H. Blackwell. AMV-80

Tides, The. Bryant. TAP

Tides, The. Longfellow. EcS

Tides. Fred Ostrander. MIT

Tides. A. G. Prys-Jones. RhR

Tides, The. Quiet Days in Sutherland. Robin Fulton. MIS

Tides of dreadful creation rocked lonely Henry. John Berryman. *Fr.* Dream Songs. ILP (1975 ed.)

Tides Run up the Wairau, The. Eileen Duggan. ATNZ

Tides shape the sides of the agate mountain. On Visiting My Son, Port Angeles, Washington. Duane Niatum. CDW

Tidy Young Tapir, A. Carolyn Wells. TDH

Tidying Up. Nancy Weber. AMV-80

Tie your own noose if you want to be. The Advice of an Efficiency Expert. Augustus Young. CIP

Tie Your Tongue, Sir? Robert Paul Smith. ECBV

Tied under My Heart. Judith Smallshaw. PMW

Ties. Dabney Stuart. CoPAm; LiSp; SPo

Tiger, The. Blake. *Fr.* Songs of Experience. FaPoR; ILwL; InPS; IP; NIL; NOBE; PBMP; PCOP; SoSe; SpRo; UnPo (1976 ed.); WIF, *3 versions*
(Tyger, The.) BIP; BoReV; CABA (1972 ed.); ExPo (1973 ed.); FF; HAP; HeIP; HoPM (1975 ed.); ILP (1975 ed.); InPK; IPWM; LAuP; LFH; MBPR; OAEL-2; OBP; PoIA; PoPle; PPoD; PPoe; PPP; STS; TT; WeW

Tiger, The. Robert Creeley. GP

Tiger. Claude McKay. BPo

Tiger. *Yoruba Oral Tradition, tr. by* B. King. WTO

Tiger at Play. Joanna Baillie. PCat

Tiger Christ unsheathed his sword. For the One Who Would Take Man's Life in His Hands. Delmore Schwartz. ILP (1975 ed.); NoAM; VGW

Tiger in the tiger-pit, The. Lines for an Old Man. T. S. Eliot. FaBoTw (1975 ed.)

Tiger! Tiger! [*or* Tyger! Tyger!] burning bright. The Tiger [*or* Tyger]. Blake. *Fr.* Songs of Experience. BiP; BoReV; CABA (1972 ed.); ExPo (1973 ed.); FaPoR; FF; HAP; HeIP; HoPM (1975 ed.); ILP (1975 ed.); ILwL; InPK; InPS; IP; IPWM; LAuP; LFH; MBPR; NIL; NOBE; OAEL-2; OBP; PBMP; PCOP; PoIA; PoPle; PPoD; PPoe; PPP; SoSe; SpRo; STS; TT; UnPo (1976 ed.); WeW; WIF

Tight,—proof, unavailable. Falling Out. Helen Chasin. IHMS

Tightly-folded bud. Born Yesterday. Philip Larkin. RRA

Tight Rope. Amiri Baraka. CNA

Tightrope Walker, The. Rochelle Ratner. WBN

Tightrope Walker. Vernon Scannell. NCSH

Tihuitkli. Luís Omar Salinas. SA

Tiki. Forrest Anderson. AATT

Tilda Tidbury. *Unknown.* RAE

Till Death Do Us Part. Leila Miccolis, *tr. fr. Portuguese by* Willis Barnstone *and* Nelson Cerqueira. BoWoP

Till I shall come again, let this suffice. A Panegyric to Sir Lewis Pemberton. Robert Herrick. CaPo

Till now your indiscretion sets us free. Eves Apologie. Emilia Lanier. BoWoP

Till the Sea Runs Dry. *Malay Oral Tradition, tr. by* R. J. Wilkinson. WTO

Till the slow daylight pale. The Sun-Flower. Dora Greenwell. WPE

Till thinking had worn out my enterprise. Spring Mountain Climb. Richard Eberhart. LiSp

Till you've earned. Mahádéviyakka, *tr. fr. Kannada by* A. K. Ramanujan. PBWP

Tillamook Burn, The. William Stafford. CNW

Tilth. Robert Graves. FaBoEE; OBSV

Tim, an Irish Terrier. Winifrid M. Letts. GDP

Tim Evans was a prisoner. Go Down You Murderers. Ewan MacColl. FSW

Tim Finnegan liv'd in Walkin Street. Finnegan's Wake. *Unknown.* FaBoBa; FSW

Timber (Jerry the Mule). *Unknown.* FSW

Timbuctu. Edward Brathwaite. MPo

Time. Allen Curnow. ATNZ

Time. Avraham Huss, *tr. fr. Hebrew by* Mark Elliott Shapiro. VWA

Time. John Huddlestone Wynne. OxBChV

Time, A: A Season. Patricia Ramsey. AATT

Time admires ruin. The wonders of collapse. Colossi. Albert De Pietro. AATT

Time and again/ the world heals itself. Cathedrals. W. S. Doxey. AMV-80

Time and again I've longed for adventure. All the Things You Are. Oscar Hammerstein II. BLSo

Time and the Garden. Yvor Winters. NoAM; VGW

Time and the weather wear away. Poem. Donald Justice. PoA

Time bagged you at last. Poem for Vladimir. G. Ripley. AMV-81

Time began in time begotten—this night. His Coming. Irene Dayton. AATT

Time came, The. For John Berryman. Virginia Gilbert. NPW

Time changeth still, and we are changed with time. Time's Metamorphosis. Richard Middleton. TVS

Time does not bring relief; you all have lied. Edna St. Vincent Millay. PPM

Time draws near the birth of Christ, The. In Memoriam A. H. H., XXVIII. Tennyson. LFH; PChr; SoSe

Time drops in decay. The Moods. W. B. Yeats. VLP

Time Exposures. Muriel Rukeyser. PoA

Time feels so vast that were it not. Emily Dickinson. PiAm

Time has an end, they say. Hilda Doolittle ("H. D."). *Fr.* Good Frend. NOBA; VGW

Time has been that these wild solitudes, The. A Winter Piece. Bryant. EAP

Time has come for us to part, The. I'm Through with You. *Unknown.* WTO

"Time has come, The," the Walrus said. The Walrus and the Carpenter, 1 st. "Lewis Carroll.". *Fr.* Through the Looking-Glass. CTV

Time Hath Been, The. Joseph Skipsey. VIP

Time heals not: it extends a sorrow's scope. Epigram. J. V. Cunningham. VGW

Time I dropped your almost body down, The. The Lost Baby Poem. Lucille Clifton. InPK; RiTi; WPE

Time I went to church I sat, The. Mr. Rockefeller's Hat. Helen Bevington. OBAL

Time in the Rock; or, Preludes to Definition, *sels.* Conrad Aiken.
"Bird flying past my head said previous previous, The," LXII. VGW
"But no, the familiar symbol, as that the," XCII. VGW
"Mysticism, but let us have no words," XI. VGW

"What face she put on it, we will not discuss," LXXXIV. VGW

"Where we were walking in the day's light, seeing," XXXVII. VGW

Time is divided into. Time Is the Mercy of Eternity. Kenneth Rexroth. VGW

Time is not remote when I, The. Swift. *Fr.* Verses on the Death of Doctor Swift. EBEV; NOBE; NOBL

Time is not, when I remember you, my grandmothers. After Looking into a Genealogy. Peggy Pond Church. WPW

Time is of the essence. This is a highly skilled. Polo Grounds. Rolfe Humphries. HoPM (1975 ed.); LiSp

Time Is Open, The. Joanne Kyger. RiTi

Time is Swiftly Rolling On, The. Berryman Hicks. AH, *with music*
　(Dying Father's Farewell, The, *diff. version.*) AmFP

Time Is the Mercy of Eternity. Kenneth Rexroth. VGW

Time it took he could have, The. The Invention of the Telephone. Peter Klappert. AmPA

Time I've Lost in Wooing, The. Thomas Moore. HoPM (1975 ed.); PFIr; VoPo

Time Lapse with Tulips. Tess Gallagher. AAN

Time of Change, A. Egan O'Rahilly, *tr. fr. Irish by* Eavan Boland. BIrV

Time of Creation Has Come, The. *Yoruba Oral Tradition, tr. by* Ulli Beier. WTO

Time of Day. Selden Rodman. PoA

Time of Fish Dying. Gabriela Melinescu, *tr. fr. Rumanian by* Stavros Deligiorgis. BoWoP

Time of grease beginneth at Midsummer day. Julians Barnes. *Fr.* Book of Hunting. WPE

Time of the Mad Atom. Virginia Braiser. QQQ

Time of Waiting in Amsterdam. Ingrid Jonker, *tr. fr. Afrikaans by* Jack Cope *and* William Plomer. BoWoP

Time of year has grown indifferent. The Man Whose Pharynx Was Bad. Wallace Stevens. PiAm

Time Out. Donald Finkel. HoPM (1975 ed.)

Time Out. Patricia Henley. NPW

Time Out. John Montague. BoAnP; PFIr

Time Passing, Beloved. Donald Davie. BoLoP

Time present and time past. Burnt Norton. T. S. Eliot. *Fr.* Four Quartets. CMoP (1970 ed.); HeIP; ILP (1975 ed.)

Time quietly compiling us like sheaves. Seferis. Lawrence Durrell. EBEV

Time, Real and Imaginary. Samuel Taylor Coleridge. MBPR; NOBE; PBMP

Time Recover'd. Thomas Stanley, *after the Italian of* Girolamo Casone. OBVE

Time Reminded Me. Julia Uceda, *tr. fr. Spanish by* Willis Barnstone. BoWoP

Time Study. Philip Roberts. FPA

Time, sweeping, desolates. To Be Absent without Leave. Kendrick Smithyman. ATNZ

Time that is moved by little fidget wheels. Five Bells. Kenneth Slessor. GAS; MAuV

Time they misdirected themselves to a wake, The. The Continuance. William Bronk. GP

Time ticks away the centre of my pride. The Empty Glen. R. Crombie Saunders. MS

Time to Die. Ray Garfield Dandridge. PoBA

Time to Get Up. Robert Louis Stevenson. *See* Time to Rise.

Time to Kill. Edward Lowbury. PMW

Time to put off the world and go somewhere. Beggar to Beggar Cried. W. B. Yeats. CMoP (1970 ed.); NoAM

Time to Rise. Robert Louis Stevenson. CTV; OxBChV; PCOP
　(Time to Get Up.) DuDr

Time to Talk, A. Robert Frost. NCSH

Time to tell you things are well, A. Snow Country Weavers. James Welch. CDW; MPA

Time-Travel. Sharon Olds. AMV–80

Time Upon a Once. Robert Paul Smith. ECBV

Time was, and that was termed the time of Gold. Joseph Hall. *Fr. Virgidemiarum.* OBSV

Time was the apple Adam ate. Original Sequence. Philip Booth. SFF

Time Was the Trail Went Deep. Charles G. Ballard. VW

Time was when his half million drew. Bewick Finzer. E. A. Robinson. CMoP (1970 ed.); PPP; STS

Time We Climbed Snake Mountain, The. Leslie Silko. VoR

Time will assuage. To the Reader. J. V. Cunningham. NoAM

Time will say nothing but I told you so. If I Could Tell You. W. H. Auden. PSN

Time Will Surely Come, The, *with music.* Robert T. Daniel. AH

Time you won your town the race, The. To an Athlete Dying Young. A. E. Housman. BiP; BTTM; CABA (1972 ed.); CMoP (1970 ed.); DL; ExPo (1973 ed.); HAP; HeIP; ILP (1975 ed.); InPK; IP; IPWM; LiSp; MiP; NIL; NoAM; PBMP; PPoD; PPoe; SoSe; SPo; STS; TT; UnPo (1976 ed.); VLP; WIF

Timeclock. Herman Spector. SPT

Timepiece, A. James Merrill. HoPM (1975 ed.); NoAM; UsP

Times, The, *sel.* Charles Churchill.
　"Is a son born into this world of woe?" OBSV

Times ain't now nothing like they used to be, The. James Alley. *Unknown.* BluL

Time's an hand's-breadth; 'tis a tale. Time. John Huddlestone Wynne. OxBChV

Times Are Getting Hard. *Unknown.* FSW

Times are swiftly drawing nigh. When You and I Must Part. *Unknown.* AmFP

Time's Dedication. Delmore Schwartz. VGW

Time's Fool. Ruth Pitter. OxBTC; WPE

Times have changed. Anything Goes. Cole Porter. OBAL

Times have changed, there is not left to us, The. Allen Tate. *Fr.* Sonnets of the Blood. PoA

Time's Metamorphosis. Richard Middleton. TVS

Time's Offerings. Richard Eberhart. FoP

Time's sea hath been five years at its slow ebb. To——. Keats. MBPR

Times Square Parade. Robert Watson. NYP

Time's Winged Chariot (poets say). To His Not-So-Coy Mistress. Wynford Vaughan-Thomas. NOBL

Timid and hot-tempered. Vincent Buckley. *Fr.* Golden Builders. CAAP

*Timmini yimre.* Lemuel Johnson. *Fr.* Hand on the Navel. AAN

Timmy Pimmy. *Unknown.* ECBV

Timon of Athens, *sel.* Shakespeare.
　"Warr'st thou 'gainst Athens?" *fr.* IV, iii. EBEV

Timon of Athens, the Man-Hater, *sel.* Thomas Shadwell.
　"Well, babbling philosophical rascal." SCP–2

Timor Mortis. *Unknown. See* Sparrow-Hawk's Complaint, The.

Timor Mortis Conturbat Me. William Dunbar. NOBE, *abr.*
　(I That in Heill Wes and Glaidness.) HAP
　(Lament for the Makaris.) EBEV
　(Lament for the Makers.) OAEL–1
　(Lament for the Poets, *tr. fr. Middle English by* Andrew Glaze *and* Selden Rodman.) OBP

Timothy. Thomas James. HeS

Timothy Grady. Leroy F. Jackson. OSF

Timothy Tiggs and Tomothy Toggs. Some Fishy Nonsense. Laura E. Richards. CTV

Timothy Winters. Charles Causley. MPo

Tin Can, The. William Jay Smith. CoPAm

Tin Cup Blues. *Unknown.* BluL

Tin-Ore. *Malay Oral Tradition, tr. by* W. W. Skeat. WTO

Tin Roof Blues. Sterling A. Brown. PoUp

Tin shack, where my baby sleeps on his back. Everything: Eloy, Arizona, 1956. Ai. AmPA; FF

Tinder, The. Thomas Carew. CaPo

Tinker's Wife. Patrick Kavanagh. CIP; NoAM

Tinkle, Tinkle! The Waterfall. Frank Dempster Sherman. CTV

Tintadgel bells ring o'er the tide. The Silent Tower of Bottreau. Robert Stephen Hawker. VPC

Tintern Abbey. Edward Davies. *Fr.* Chepstow: A Poem. OBW

Tintern Abbey. Wordsworth. *See* Lines Composed a Few Miles above Tintern Abbey.

Tintock. *Unknown.* GBP

Tin-type tune the locusts make, The. Serenade. Dorothy Donnelly. NCSH

Tiny ant at night you would be seeking, The. The Disdainful Mistress. *Malay Oral Tradition, tr. by* R. J. Wilkinson *and* R. O. Winstedt. WTO

Tiny Baby Lizard, The. Besmilr Brigham. RiTi

Tiny baby, you're ugly. King D. Kuka. VoR

Tiny fish enjoy themselves, The. Little Fish. D. H. Lawrence. AKE; OxBTC

Tiny green birds skate over the surface of the room. Saturday Night in the Parthenon. Kenneth Patchen. EAS

Tiny island, A. Ladybug. François Dodat, *tr. by* Bert *and* Odette Meyers. BoAnP

Tiny monkey looks at me, The. Haiku. José Juan Tablada, *tr. by* Samuel Beckett. PBMP

Tiny new emotions, The. Poem. Tom Clark. ConAP

Tiny nut, a bit of tasteless betel, A. Carved on an Areca Nut. Ho Xuan Huong, *tr. by* Nguyen Ngoc Bich. PBWP

Tiny scratch upon your, A. Alligator Bites. Janet Campbell Hale. NW

Tiny snow of the stunningly cold black day. In the Snowfall. Gwerfyl Mechain, *tr. by* Willis Barnstone. BoWoP

Tiny spill of bird-things in a swirl, A. The Finches. Thomas W. Shapcott. BoAnP

Tiny, turreted occurrence, The. Profile of a Day. Ruthe T. Spinnanger. AATT

Tip-burning wings. Vita-Sheet. Ruth Weiss. MIT

Tip-of-the-Single-Feather. Velema, *tr. fr. Fijian by* B. H. Quain. WTO

Tirade. Honor Moore. WBN

Tir'd nature's sweet restorer, balmy sleep! Edward Young. Night Thoughts: Night the First. EPC; LAuP

Tired. Fenton Johnson. PoBA

Tired and bloodshot. Abraham Sutskever. Seymour Mayne. VWA

Tired and dejected hair dripping. Diane. Stewart McIntosh. SLP

Tired as I Can Be. *Unknown.* BluL

Tired cattle stumbled on the dusty trail. Babies of the Pioneers. Eunice W. Luckey. BPAW

Tired Lizi Tired. Lindiwe Mabuza. SES

Tired of lips and gums. The Palace for Teeth. Abigail Luttinger. AMV–80

Tired of the bitter repose where my idleness hurts. Stéphane Mallarmé, *tr. fr. French by* Roger Fry. NAWM–2

Tired of this urbanity. 4/20/75. Darlene Pearlstein. FiCh

Tired Tim. Walter de la Mare. LCL

Tired with all these, for restful death I cry. Sonnets, LXVI. Shakespeare. EBEV; HAP; InPS; NOBE; OAEL–1; WeW

Tired Worker, The. Claude McKay. BPo

Tires revolve, blurring, The. Night Driving. Sharyn November. AMV–80

Tiresias, *sel.* Austin Clarke.
"My mother wept loudly." CIP

Tiresias. George Garrett. CoPAm

Tiresias. Tennyson. VLP

Tiriel, *sel.* Blake.
"And aged Tiriel stood and said: 'Where does the thunder sleep?' " Epi

Tirocinium; or, A Review of Schools, *sels.* William Cowper.
"Father, who designs his babe a priest, The." OBSV
"To you, then, tenants of life's middle state." OBSV
"Would you your son should be a sot or dunce." OBSV

" 'Tis a hundred years," said the bosun bold. The Whale. *Unknown.* RhR

'Tis a new life;—thoughts move not as they did. The New Birth. Jones Very. AmVN; NOBA; PiAm

'Tis a world of silences. I gave a cry. Silences. Arthur O'Shaughnessy. VLP

'Tis advertised in Boston, New York and Buffalo. Blow Ye Winds in the Morning. *Unknown.* AmFP; FSW

'Tis affection but dissembled. Sidney Godolphin. SCP–2

'Tis all the way to Toe-town. Foot-Soldiers. John Banister Tabb. OBAL

'Tis bad enough in man or woman. On Inclosures [*or* Enclosures]. *Unknown.* FaBoCo; FaBoEE

'Tis better to be vile than vile esteemed. Sonnets, CXXI. Shakespeare. OAEL–1

'Tis Christmas weather, and a country house. Modern Love, XXIII. George Meredith. PAIC

'Tis Curiosity's Benefit Night. Her Fancy Ball. Thomas Hood. *Fr.* Miss Kilmansegg and Her Precious Leg. VLP

'Tis done—and shivering in the gale. Stanzas to a Lady, on Leaving England. Byron. MBPR

'Tis done—but yesterday a king. Ode to Napoleon Buonaparte. Byron. MBPR

'Tis eight o'clock,—a clear March night. The Idiot Boy. Wordsworth. MBPR

'Tis evening: the black snail has got on his track. Evening. John Clare. VLP

'Tis fine to see the Old World, and travel up and down. America for Me. Henry van Dyke. SoSe

'Tis gone, that bright and orbèd blaze. Evening Hymn. John Keble. PFD; VLP

'Tis goodbye then to last night. Soraidh Slan Don Oidhche Areir. Niall Mor MacMuireadach, *tr. by* Maire Cruise O'Brien. BIrV

'Tis grown almost a danger to speak true. Ben Jonson. *Fr.* Epistle to Katherine, Lady Aubigny. SCP–1

'Tis hard to say, if greater want of skill. An Essay on Criticism. Pope. CABA (1972 ed.); HAP; OAEL–1

'Tis known, at least it should be, that throughout. Beppo: A Venetian Story. Byron. MBPR; NOBL; OBSV

'Tis liberty to serve one lord. Slavery. Robert Herrick. PAIC

'Tis love's commission—justly it may call. Love's Commission. William Cavendish, Duke of Newcastle. SCP–2

'Tis Midnight and on Olive's Brow, *with music.* William B. Tappan. AH

'Tis midnight o'er the dim mere's lonely bosom. Midnight. Tennyson. VLP

'Tis mirth that fills the veins with blood. Mirth. Francis Beaumont. *Fr.* The Knight of the Burning Pestle. PPM

'Tis morning; and the sun with ruddy orb. The Winter Morning Walk. William Cowper. *Fr.* The Task. LAuP

'Tis mute, the word they went to hear on high Dodona mountain. The Oracles. A. E. Housman. BTTM; HAP

'Tis my sole plague to be alone. Robert Burton. *Fr.* The Anatomy of Melancholy: The Author's Abstract of Melancholy. SCP–2

'Tis near the morning watch: the dim lamp burns. The Morning Watch. Jones Very. PiAm

'Tis never or but seldom known. Power and Peace. Robert Herrick. CaPo

" 'Tis no sin for a man to labour in his vocation." The Ballad of Villon and Fat Madge. Villon, *tr. by* Swinburne. LoAs; OBVE

'Tis not enough for one that is a wife. Lady Elizabeth Carey. *Fr.* Mariam, III. WPE

'Tis not for her to plough the deep. What Is, and What Is Not for Woman. Eliza R. Snow. WPW

'Tis not for the unfeeling, the falsely refined. The Farmer of Tilsbury Vale. Wordsworth. EBEV

'Tis not that Dying hurts us so. Emily Dickinson. BoWoP

'Tis not that I am weary grown. Upon His Leaving His Mistress. Earl of Rochester. GBL; OBP

'Tis not that love is less or sorrow more. Fear Has Cast Out Love. Wilfrid Scawen Blunt. The Love Sonnets of Proteus, XXXVI. VLP

'Tis not the world nor what can please. *Unknown.* SCP-2

'Tis now since I began to dy. Upon Absence. Katherine Philips. PBWP

'Tis now since I sat down before. Love's Siege. Sir John Suckling. CaPo

'Tis of a blind beggar who a long time was blind. The Blind Beggar. *Unknown.* AmFP

'Tis of a brave young highwayman. Brennan on the Moor. *Unknown.* FSW

'Tis of a gallant Yankee ship that flew the stripes and stars. The Yankee Man-of-War. *Unknown.* BTTM

'Tis of a handsome female as you may understand. The Handsome Cabin Boy. *Unknown.* FSW

'Tis of a jolly soldier that lately came from war. The Jolly Soldier. *Unknown.* AmFP

'Tis of a lady both fair and handsome. The Servant Man. *Unknown.* AmFP

'Tis of a pedlar, a pedlar trim. The Bold Pedlar and Robin Hood. *Unknown.* AmFP

'Tis [*or* Oh! 'tis] of a rich merchant who in London did dwell. Villikins [*or* Vilikins] and His Dinah. *At. to* Edward Laman Blanchard; *also at. to* Sam Cowell. FSW; PoTa; VLP

'Tis of a sad and dismal story that happened off the fatal rock. The Loss of the *New Columbia. Unknown.* AmFP

'Tis of a wild Colonial boy, Jack Doolan [*or* Dulan] was his name. The Wild Colonial Boy. *Unknown.* FaBoBa; FSW; PeBB

'Tis of my country that I would endite. Ezra Pound. *Fr.* L'Homme Moyen Sensuel. OBSV

'Tis of the Father Hilary. World's Worth. Dante Gabriel Rossetti. VLP

'Tis raging noon; and vertical, the sun. James Thomson. *Fr.* The Seasons: Summer. EBEV; OAEL-1

'Tis sad to see the sons of learning. He That Never Read a Line. *Unknown, tr. by* Robin Flower. PFIr

'Tis said, that some have died for love. Wordsworth. MBPR

'Tis spring; come out to ramble. The Lent Lily. A. E. Housman. FSFS

'Tis spring, warm glows the south. Birds' Nests. John Clare. OAEL-2; VLP

'Tis still observ'd, that Fame ne'er sings. Fame. Robert Herrick. FaBoEE

'Tis Strange. Eugene Field. TDH

'Tis strange! I saw the skies. Dreams. Thomas Traherne. SCP-2

'Tis strange, the miser should his cares employ. To Richard Boyle, Earl of Burlington: Of the Use of Riches. Pope. Moral Essays, Epistle IV. OAEL-1; PPP

'Tis summer time on Bredon. Hugh Kingsmill. FaBoCo; NOBL

'Tis Sweet to Rest in Lively Hope. *Unknown.* AmFP

'Tis the Gift to Be Simple, *with music. Unknown.* AH

'Tis the last rose of Summer, left blooming alone. The Last Rose of Summer. Thomas Moore. FSW

'Tis the middle of night by the castle clock. Christabel. Samuel Taylor Coleridge. MBPR; OAEL-2; OBP

'Tis the voice of the Lobster: I heard him declare. Alice's Recitation [*or* The Lobster]. "Lewis Carroll." *Fr.* Alice's Adventures in Wonderland, *ch.* 10. FaBoCo; FaBoNo; NOBL; OxBChV; SpRo

'Tis the voice of the sluggard: I heard him complain. The Sluggard. Isaac Watts. HAP; OxBChV; SpRo

'Tis "the witching time of night." Keats. MBPR

'Tis the year's [*or* yeares] midnight, and it is the day's [*or* dayes]. A Nocturnal[l] upon Saint Lucy's [*or* S. Lucies] Day, Being the Shortest Day. John Donne. AnMo; EBEV; GBL; MetP; NOBE; OAEL-1; OBP; PoPle; PPP; SCP-1

'Tis time, I think, by Wenlock town. A. E. Housman. PES; PoPle

'Tis time this heart should be unmoved. On This Day I Complete My Thirty-sixth Year. Byron. CABA (1972 ed.); ILP (1975 ed.); MBPR; NIL; OAEL-2

'Tis to yourself I speak; you cannot know. Yourself. Jones Very. AmVN; ILP (1975 ed.); NOBA

'Tis true, dear Ben, thy just chastising hand. To Ben Jonson. Thomas Carew. CaPo

'Tis true I write and tell me by what rule. The Appology. Countess of Winchilsea. SBG

'Tis true—they shut me in the cold. Emily Dickinson. SBG

'Tis true, 'tis day, what though it be? Break of Day. John Donne. CABA (1972 ed.); PAIC; PoIA; SoSe (1977 ed.)

'Tis Winter Now, *with music.* Samuel Longfellow. AH

Tit for Tat: A Tale. John Aikin. OxBChV

Tit-tat-toe. *Unknown.* MG

Titan! to whose immortal eyes. Prometheus. Byron. InPS; MBPR; NOBE; OAEL-2

*Titanic,* The. *Unknown.* AmFP; FSW

*Titanic* Blues. *Unknown.* BluL

Titanic Litany. John Wheelwright. SPT

Titans, The. Betti Alver, *tr. fr. Estonian by* Willis Barnstone *and* Felix Oinas. BoWoP

Tithe, The: To the Bride. Robert Herrick. CaPo

Tithes. Luci Shaw. AATT

Tithonus. Tennyson. CABA (1972 ed.); HAP; ILP (1975 ed.); NOBE; OAEL-2; OBP; PoPle; PPP; VLP

Title divine—is mine! Emily Dickinson. NOBA; PAIC; PiAm

Title of a Swift Horse. *Mongol Oral Tradition, tr. by* C. R. Bawden. WTO

Titmouse, The. Emerson. PiAm

Tittery-Irie-Aye. *Unknown.* AmFP

Titus Groan, *sel.* Mervyn Peake. Frivolous Cake, The. BBL

Titus reads neither prose nor rhyme. The Writer. Hildebrand Jacob. FaBoCo

"Titus, Son of Rembrandt: 1665." Richard J. Lyons. AMV-81

Tlanusi' yi, the Leech Place. Gladys Cardiff. CDW

To ("A child (a boy) bouncing"). William Carlos Williams. OBAL

To——: "Cold earth slept below, The." Shelley. MBPR

To——: "Had I a man's fair form, then might my sighs." Keats. MBPR

To——: "Hadst thou liv'd in days of old." Keats. MBPR

To——: "Half in the dim light from the hall." William Stanley Braithwaite. PoBA

To——: "Music, when soft voices die." Shelley. ExPo (1973 ed.); HeIP; ILP (1975 ed.); MBPR

("Music, when soft voices die.") NOBE

To——: "Oh! There are spirits of the air." Shelley. MBPR

To——: "One word is too often profaned." Shelley. BoLoP; ILP (1975 ed.); MBPR; NOBE; PPP

To——: "Time's sea hath been five years at its slow ebb." Keats. MBPR

To——: "What can I do to drive away." Keats. MBPR; OAEL–2

To——: "When passions's trance is overpast." Shelley. MBPR

To——: With the Following Poem. Tennyson. *Introd. poem to* The Palace of Art. VLP

To a Baseball. *Unknown.* LiSp; SPo

To a Bed of Tulips. Robert Herrick. CaPo

To a Blossoming Pear Tree. James Wright. HAP

To a Butterfly. L. Pearl Schuck. AMV–80

To a Butterfly ("I've watched you now a full half-hour"). Wordsworth. MBPR; PCOP

To a Butterfly ("Stay near me—do not take thy flight!"). Wordsworth. MBPR

To a Cactus Seller. Anwar Shaul, *tr. fr. Arabic by* Yoffee Berkovitz. VWA

To a Calvinist in Bali. Edna St. Vincent Millay. NoAM

To a Captain in Sinai. Ada Aharoni. AMV–81

To a Captious Critic. Paul Laurence Dunbar. BPo

To a Cat. Keats. PCat
  (To Mrs. Reynold's Cat.) MBPR

To a Cat. Swinburne. PCat

To a Caty-did. Philip Freneau. EAP; TAP

To a Certain Most Certainly Certain Critic. David McCord. OBAL

To a Child at the Piano. Alastair Reid. MS

To a Child Born in Time of Small War. Helen Sorrells. WPE

To a Child Dancing in the Wind. W. B. Yeats. BBGO; ILP (1975 ed.); PFIr

To a Child Five Years Old. Nathaniel Cotton. OxBChV
  (To a Child of Five Years Old.) PMW

To a Child of Quality [Five Years Old]. Matthew Prior. NIL; NOBE; RRA

To a Child Running with Outstretched Arms in the Canyon de Chelly. N. Scott Momaday. CDW

To a Child Trapped in a Barber Shop. Philip Levine. InPK; NoAM; NOBA; TAP; VGW

To a Comrade in Arms. Alun Lewis. FaBoTw (1975 ed.)

To a Conscript of 1940. Sir Herbert Read. ExPo (1973 ed.)

To a Courtesan a Thousand Years Dead. Paul Eldridge. PoA

To a Covetous Churl. Edward May. FaBoEE

To A. D. W. E. Henley. Echoes, XVIII. HoPM (1975 ed.); LoAs
  (Blackbird, The.) PCOP

To a Dark Girl. Gwendolyn B. Bennett. PoBA

To a Deaf and Dumb Little Girl. Hartley Coleridge. VLP

To a Dictatorial Sultan. *Somali Oral Tradition, tr. by* B. W. Andrzejewski. WTO

To a Dog Injured in the Street. William Carlos Williams. LFH

To a Dying Girl. Clinton F. Larson. MPA

To a Fair Lady Playing with a Snake. Edmund Waller. EBEV; HoPM (1975 ed.)

To a Faithless Friend. Salaan Arrabey, *tr. fr. Somali by* M. Laurence. WTO

To a Family Man in His Family Room. Rosemary Daniell. WBN

To a Fat Lady Seen from the Train. Frances Cornford. SpRo; WeW

To a Fighter Killed in the Ring. Lou Lipsitz. LiSp; SPo

To a Fish. Leigh Hunt. *Fr.* The Fish, the Man, and the Spirit. NOBL
  (To Fish.) EcS

To a Foreign Friend. Leonard Nathan. GP

To a 14 Year Old Girl in Labor and Delivery. John Stone. CoPAm

To a Friend. Matthew Arnold. PAIC

To a Friend. William Carlos Williams. LoAs

To a Friend Concerning Several Ladies. William Carlos Williams. VGW

To a Friend Going on a Journey. Mahammed Abdille Hassan, *tr. fr. Somali by* M. Laurence. WTO

To a Friend, on Her Examination for the Doctorate in English. J. V. Cunningham. VGW

To a Friend, Who Recommended a Wife to Him. *Unknown.* PiAm

To a Friend Who Sent Me Some Roses. Keats. MBPR
  (Musk Rose, The.) PF

To a Friend Whose Work Has Come to Nothing. W. B. Yeats. BiP; IP; OAEL–2; PoA; PoIA; SoSe (1977 ed.)

To a Friend Whose Work Has Come to Triumph. Anne Sexton. PoIA; SoSe (1977 ed.); TPo

To a Friend's Child. Aliki Barnstone. BoWoP

To a Fugitive. James Wright. TH

To a Gentlewoman Objecting to Him His Grey Hairs. Robert Herrick. CaPo; SCP–1

To a Girl Who Lives in a Tree. Audre Lorde. WBN

To a God Unknown. David Eller. VWA

To a good man of most dear memory. Written after the Death of Charles Lamb. Wordsworth. MBPR

To a Goose. Robert Southey. NOBL

To a Ground-Lark. David Campbell. *Fr.* Cocky's Calendar. MAuV

To a Hedgehog. Samuel Thompson. BIrV

To a high hill where never yet stood tree. Thomas Otway. *Fr.* The Poet's Complaint of His Muse. SCP–2

To a Highland Girl. Wordsworth. MBPR

To a Horse. Jill Hoffman. PH

To a Husband. Maya Angelou. IHMS

To a Jack Rabbit. S. Omar Barker. BPAW

To a Jilt. Martin Armstrong. FaBoEE

To A. L.: Persuasions to Love. Thomas Carew. CaPo

To a Lady [*or* Ladye]. William Dunbar. EBEV; GBL; SLP

To a Lady. J. B. Morton. POL

To a Lady: Of the Characters of Women. Pope. *See* Moral Essays.

To a Lady on Her Marriage. William Bell. PAIC

To a Lady on the Death of Her Husband. Phillis Wheatley. TAP

To a Lady That Desired I Would Love Her. Thomas Carew. CaPo

To a Lady That Desired Me I Would Bear My Part with Her in a Song. Richard Lovelace. CaPo

To a Lady That Forbade to Love before Company. Sir John Suckling. CaPo; SCP–2

To a Late Poplar. Patrick Kavanagh. PFIr

To a Little Boy Learning to Fish. Robert D. Hoeft. AMV–81

To a Little Girl. Gustav Kobbé. PCOP

To a Locomotive in Winter. Walt Whitman. ILP (1975 ed.); InPK; LFH; NoAM; TAP; WIF

To a Lost Sweetheart. Don Marquis. POL

To a Louse. Burns. ILP (1975 ed.); PBMP

To a Magnificent Spinner, Murdered. Genevieve Taggard. WPW

To a Married Couple That Could Not Agree. Timothy Kendall. PAIC

To a Marsh Hawk in Spring. Henry David Thoreau. PB

To a Mosquito. Bryant. EAP

To a Mouse [on Turning Her Up in Her Nest, with the Plough, November 1785]. Burns. BiP; FF; HAP; HeIP; ILP (1975 ed.); InPS; IP; LAuP; MN; OAEL–1; PAIC; PoIA; PPP

To a Mouse says a Miser, "My dear Mr. Mouse." The Miser and the Mouse. Christopher Smart. RAE. *See also* Says a Miser to a Mouse. . .

To a Nightingale. Keats. *See* Ode to a Nightingale.

To a Noisy Politician. Philip Freneau. TAP

To a Nun. John Ormond, *after the Welsh.* EBEV; FaBoTw (1975 ed.)

To a Passer-by. Baudelaire, *tr. fr. French by* C. F. McIntyre. NAWM–2

To a Persistent Phantom. Frank Horne. AmNP (1974 ed.)

To a Poet I Knew. Jewel C. Latimore. PoBA

To a Poet, Who Would Have Me Praise Certain Bad Poets, Imitators of His and Mine. W. B. Yeats. FaBoEE; PFIr

To a Poor Old Woman. William Carlos Williams. OBAL; PoIA; TAP; TVo

To a Portrait of Lermontov. Margarita Aliger, *tr. fr. Russian by* Elaine Feinstein. VWA

To a Portuguese Man-o-War. Four Homages. Allan Block. FAF

To a President. Witter Bynner. OBAL

To a Proud Old Woman Watching the Tearing Down of the Hurricane Shed. Kay Boyle. MIT

To a Race Horse at Ascot. Jennie M. Palen. PH

To a Red-headed Do-good Waitress. Alan Dugan. CAPP; NowV

To a Red-Wheat Field. Charles Tennyson Turner. VPC

To a Republican Friend: Continued. Matthew Arnold. VLP

To a Republican Friend, 1848. Matthew Arnold. PAIC; VLP

To a Reviewer Who Admired My Book. John Ciardi. OBAL

To a Romantic. Allen Tate. PiAm

To a Scarecrow; or, Malkin, Left Long after Harvest. Charles Tennyson Turner. VPC

To a Seaman Dead on Land. Kay Boyle. PoA

To a Seamew. Swinburne. VLP

To a Segar. Samuel Low. OBAL

To a Single Shadow without Pity. Sam Cornish. PoBA

To a Skylark. Shelley. BoAnP, *abr.*; HAP; InPS; MBPR; OAEL–2; PB; PBMP; PCOP; VoPo
(Ode to a Skylark.) NOBE

To a Skylark. Wordsworth. MBPR
(To the Skylark.) PCOP, 6 *ll.*

To a Snail. Marianne Moore. CMoP (1970 ed.); PiAm; UsP

To a Snow-Flake. Francis Thompson. FSFS

To a Solitary Disciple. William Carlos Williams. VGW

To a Squirrel at Kyle-Na-No. W. B. Yeats. LCL
(To a Squirrel.) PCOP

To a Steam Roller. Marianne Moore. BoWoP; CMoP (1970 ed.); ILP (1975 ed.); LFH; Psy; VGW

To a Stranger. Walt Whitman. NoAM; NOBA

To a Student Poet, Hospitalized, Having "Broken with Reality." Roderick Hartigh Jellema. AATT

To a Swallow. John Peale Bishop, *after the Greek of* Euenus. OBVE

To a "Tenting" Boy. Charles Tennyson Turner. VPC

To a Traveler. Su Tung P'o, *tr. fr. Chinese by* Kenneth Rexroth. HoPM (1975 ed.)

To a Troubled Friend. James Wright. PCho

To a Tyrant. Joseph Brodsky, *tr. fr. Russian by* Alan Myers. VWA

To a Very Beautiful Lady. Ruthven Todd. SLP

To a Visiting Poet in a College Dormitory. Carolyn Kizer. PoA

To a Wall of Flame in a Steel Mill, Syracuse, New York, 1969. Larry Levis. AMV–81

To a Waterfowl. Bryant. AmVN; EAP; HoPM (1975 ed.); IPWM; NOBA; PB; PCOP; PiAm; PIM; SoSe; TAP

To a Waterfowl. Donald Hall. OBAL

To a Wind-Flower. Madison Cawein. PCOP

To a Woman Half a World Away. Dick Allen. CoPAm

To a woman that I knew. Her Eyes. John Crowe Ransom. OBAL

To a Woman Who Wants Darkness and Time. Gerald W. Barrax. PoBA

To a Young Ass. Samuel Taylor Coleridge. MBPR

To a Young Beauty. W. B. Yeats. CMoP (1970 ed.)

To a Young Brother. Maria Jane Jewsbury. OxBChV

To a Young Girl. David Rosenmann-Taub, *tr. fr. Spanish by* Charles Guenther. VWA

To a Young Girl. W. B. Yeats. EBEV; OLR; PSN; SoSe

To a Young Heir. Samuel Johnson. *See* Short Song of Congratulation, A.

To a Young Lady. Wordsworth. MBPR

To a Young Lady with a Poem on the French Revolution. Samuel Taylor Coleridge. MBPR

To a Young Poet. Paula Bennett. AMV–81

To a Young Poet Who Fled. John Logan. CAPP

To a Young Wretch. Robert Frost. OFD

To Adam, His Scribe. Chaucer. OAEL–1; OxBM

To Age. Walter Savage Landor. SoSe

To Ailsa Rock. Keats. MBPR

To Alexander Meiklejohn, *sel.* John Beecher.
"I read your testimony and I thought." GOA

To Alfred Tennyson. Walter Savage Landor. POL

To All Brothers. Sonia Sanchez. BPo

To All Sisters. Sonia Sanchez. PoBA

To all who carve their love on a picnic table. Open Letter from a Constant Reader. Mona Van Duyn. GP; PoA

To all you ladies now at Bath. Farewell to Bath. Lady Mary Wortley Montagu. WPE

To all you ladies now at land. Song, Written at Sea in the First Dutch War. Charles Sackville. NOBE

To Allegra Florence in Heaven, *sel.* Thomas Holley Chivers.
"As an egg, when broken, never." PeD

To Alpha Dryden Eberhart November 26, 1977, on Being Seventy-five. Richard Eberhart. PCho

To Althea, from Prison. Richard Lovelace. BiP; CABA (1972 ed.); CaPo; GBL; HAP; HeIP; ILP (1975 ed.); InPS; MetP; NOBE; PoPle

To Amarantha, That She Would Dishevel Her Hair. Richard Lovelace. HoPM (1975 ed.); SCP–2
(Song: To Amarantha, That She Would Dishevel Her Hair.) CaPo

To Amy. J. Gordon Coogler. OBAL

To an Aging Charioteer. Leontius Scholasticus, *tr. fr. Greek by* Tom Dodge. LiSp

To an American Poet Just Dead. Richard Wilbur. IP

To an American Workman Dying of Starvation. Genevieve Taggard. SPT

To an Artist. Burns. PBMP

To an Athlete Dying Young. A. E. Housman. BiP; BTTM; CABA (1972 ed.); CMoP (1970 ed.); DL; ExPo (1973 ed.); HAP; HeIP; ILP (1975 ed.); InPK; IP; IPWM; LiSp; MiP; NIL; NoAM; PBMP; PPoD; PPoe; SoSe; SPo; STS; TT; UnPo (1976 ed.); VLP; WIF, 3 *versions*

To an Athlete Turned Poet. Peter Meinke. LiSp; SPo

To an Author. Philip Freneau. AmVN; EAP; NOBA

To an Elder Poet. William Carlos Williams. PoA

To an Estranged Wife. Gary Young. AMV–81

To an Imaginary Father. Wendy Rose. CDW

To an Indian Poet. Patty L. Harjo. VoR

To an Old Friend.  Margaret R. Litchfield.  PoUp

To an Old Lady.  William Empson.  FaBoTw (1975 ed.); Moon; NoAM; NOBE

To an Old Lady Dead.  Siegfried Sassoon.  PoPle

To an Old Philosopher in Rome.  Wallace Stevens.  NoAM; NOBA; TT

To an Oriole.  Edgar Fawcett.  PCOP

To Antenor.  Katherine Philips.  SBG

To Anthea.  Robert Herrick.  CaPo; SCP-1

To Anthea Lying in Bed.  Robert Herrick.  AnMo; SCP-1

To Anthea, Who May Command Him Anything.  Robert Herrick. CaPo; ILP (1975 ed.); NOBE; OAEL-1

To Any M. F. H.  V. Sackville-West.  SBG

To Any Member of My Generation.  George Barker.  PAIC

To Anybody at All.  Margaret Tait.  SLP

To Apis the boxer.  On Apis the Prizefighter.  Lucilius, *tr. by* Dudley Fitts.  WeW

To Apollo and Diana.  Horace, *tr. fr. Latin by* Branwell Brontë. Odes, I, 21.  OBVE

To Aristius Fuscus.  Horace, *tr. fr. Latin by* Samuel Johnson. Odes, I, 22.  OBVE

To Art.  Dante Gabriel Rossetti.  POL

To Arthur's court, when men began.  A Scot, a Welsh and an Irish Man.  *Unknown.*  GBP

To Asra.  Samuel Taylor Coleridge.  MBPR

To assassinate the Chase Manhattan Bank.  The Plot to Assassinate the Chase Manhattan Bank.  Carl Larsen.  FF; TPo

To Aunt Rose.  Allen Ginsberg.  CABA (1972 ed.); VGW

To Autumn.  Blake.  FSFS; MBPR

To Autumn.  Keats.  AnMo; BiP; EBEV; Epi; FF; FSFS; HAP; ILP (1975 ed.); IP; IPWM; LFH; MBPR; NIL; NOBE; NU; OAEL-2; OBP; PBMP; PoIA; PoPle; PPoD; PPoe; PPP; Prf; SoSe; STS; TT; UnPo (1976 ed.); UsP; WIF (Ode to Autumn.)  CABA (1972 ed.); ExPo (1973 ed.)

To B. C.  Sir John Suckling.  CaPo

To B. R. Haydon.  Keats.  MBPR

To B. R. Haydon.  Wordsworth.  MBPR

To Barba.  Edward May.  FaBoEE

To Bary Jade.  Charles Follen Adams.  OBAL

To Be a Farmer's Boy, *with music.  Unknown.*  GSB

To Be a Master in Your House.  Natan Zach, *tr. fr. Hebrew by* Peter Everwine *and* Shula Starkman.  VWA

To be a mistress.  Kiyoko Tsuda, *tr. fr. Japanese by* Edith Marcombe Shiffert *and* Yuki Sawa.  BoWoP

To Be a Pilgrim.  Bunyan.  *See* Pilgrim, The.

To be a poet and not know the trade.  Sanctity.  Patrick Kavanagh.  BIrV

To be a successful and competent vet.  The Vet.  Guy Boas. BoAnP

To be a whore, despite of grace.  Madrigal.  Charles Cotton. FaBoEE

To be able/ and not to do it.  To an Elder Poet.  William Carlos Williams.  PoA

To be able to see every side of every question.  Editor Whedon. Edgar Lee Masters.  *Fr.* Spoon River Anthology.  CMoP (1970 ed.); FaBoEE; NoAM; NOBA; OBSV

To Be Absent without Leave.  Kendrick Smithyman.  ATNZ

To be alive—is power.  Emily Dickinson.  PiAm

To be an orphan.  The Orphan.  *Unknown, tr. by* Arthur Waley. PoA

To be blithe, clear-headed.  The Cang.  Harry Clifton.  IPM

To Be Carved on a Stone at Thoor Ballylee.  W. B. Yeats. FaBoEE; NoAM

To be homeless is a pride.  A Jealous Man.  Robert Graves. CMoP (1970 ed.)

To Be in Love.  Gwendolyn Brooks.  IHMS; OLR; SoS; TPo

To be in love is like going out.  The Business.  Robert Creeley. CAPP

To be married.  The Relationship.  Stephen Vincent.  NeAC

To be moved comes of want, though want be complete. 1892–1941.  Louis Zukofsky.  PoA

To be my own Messiah to the.  The Rows of Cold Trees.  Yvor Winters.  NoAM; NOBA

To be near/ Yet not to wake.  Spell.  Robert Francis.  GP

To Be or Not to Be.  *Unknown.*  FaBoCo (Rooster Be? Or a Crow?)  ECBV

To be, or not to be—that is the question.  Shakespeare.  *Fr.* Hamlet, III, i.  BiP; FF; HoPM (1975 ed.); STS

To be played upon/ you must be empty.  All Day Satori.  Brian Lynch.  IPM

To be put on the train and kissed and given my ticket. Observation Car.  A. D. Hope.  NoAM

To Be Quicker.  Don L. Lee.  JB

To Be Recited to Flossie on Her Birthday.  William Carlos Williams.  VGW

To be sad in the morning.  Poem.  William Pillen.  VWA

To Be Sung on the Water.  Louise Bogan.  VGW

To be ten and skinny.  Exodus.  Anita Endrezze Probst.  CDW

To be the father of the fatherless.  Sonnet to the Prince Regent. Byron.  MBPR

To Beatrice Stuart Wortley: Aetat 2.  Alfred Austin.  PeD

To Bed.  Diane Wakoski.  CAAP

To bed, to bed, kind turtles, now, and write.  Robert Herrick. *Fr.* A Nuptiall Song, or Epithalamie, on Sir Clipseby Crew and His Lady.  OBP

To begin with he was a beautiful object.  Louis MacNeice.  *Fr.* The Death of a Cat.  PCat

To Ben Jonson.  Thomas Carew.  CaPo

To Bert Campaneris.  Tom Clark.  LiSp

To biographers, in rebuttal.  Lives of the Poet.  Ron Miles. AMV–81

To Blok/ words that had stuck together.  Blok: Let Me Learn the Poem.  Aram Boyajian.  NeAC

To Blossoms.  Robert Herrick.  CaPo; PF

To Bobby Seale.  Lucille Clifton.  CNA; PoBA

To Boris Pasternak.  Aleksander Kushner, *tr. fr. Russian by* Dimitry Pospielovsky *and* Keith Bosley.  VWA

To Boston Town.  *Unknown.*  ECBV

To brave and to know the unknown.  The Unknown.  John Davidson.  PAIC

To Brooklyn Bridge.  Hart Crane.  *Fr.* The Bridge.  CABA (1972 ed.); ILP (1975 ed.); InPS; NOBA; NYP (Proem: To Brooklyn Bridge.)  CMoP (1970 ed.); ExPo (1973 ed.); HeIP; NoAM; PAIC; PiAm; TAP

To Caelia.  *Unknown.*  FaBoEE

To call a bird a bird, a tree a tree.  The Naturalist.  Margaret Reynolds.  MIS

To Calliope.  Robert Graves.  CMoP (1970 ed.)

To Cara, after an Interval of Absence.  Thomas Moore.  PeD

To Caroline ("Oh! when shall the grave hide for ever my sorrow"). Byron.  MBPR

To Caroline ("Think'st thou I saw thy beauteous eyes").  Byron. MBPR

To Carry the Child.  Stevie Smith.  NoAM

To Castara ("Why should we fear to melt away in death"). William Habington.  SCP-2

To Castara: Of True Delight.  William Habington.  SCP-2

To Castara: Of What We Were before Our Creation.  William Habington.  SCP-2

To Castara: The Reward of Innocent Love.  William Habington. SCP-2

To Cattraeth's vale in glitt'ring row. Aneirin, *tr. by* Thomas Gray. *Fr.* The Gododdin. OBVE

To cause accord or to aggre. Sir Thomas Wyatt. AAS

To celebrate this season I must find. Forsythia Is the Color I Remember. Joseph Cherwinski. AMV–80

To Celia ("Drink to me only with thine eyes"). Ben Jonson. AKE; BoLoP; InPK; NOBE; OBVE
  (Drink to Me Only with Thine Eyes.) BiP; BLSH, *with music*; BLSo, *with music*; FSW
  (Song: To Celia.) CABA (1972 ed.); GBL; HeIP; ILP (1975 ed.); IP; OAEL–1

To Celia. Sir Charles Sedley. NOBE

To Certain Critics. Countee Cullen. BPo

To Charles Cowden Clarke. Keats. MBPR

To Chatterton. Keats. MBPR

To Cheer Our Minds. William Ronksley. OxBChV

To "Chick." Frank Horne. *Fr.* Letters Found near a Suicide. BPo

To Children. Lawrence McGaugh. PoBA

To Chloe ("Vitas hinnuleo"). Horace, *tr. fr. Latin.* Odes, I, 23. LoAs, *tr. by* Austin Dobson; OBVE, *tr. by* Branwell Brontë

To Chloe Who Wish'd Her Self Young Enough for Me. William Cartwright. MetP

To Christ on the Cross. Robert Herrick. PIM

To Christ Our Lord. Galway Kinnell. InPK; MiP; NIL; RFM

To Christian Montpelier, *sel.* George Jonas.
  "Single naked wire at ground level, A." NeAC

To Christopher North. Tennyson. FaBoEE

To Chuck. Sonia Sanchez. UsP

To Clarissa Scott Delany. Angelina Weld Grimké. AmNP (1974 ed.)

To Cloe Weeping. Matthew Prior. PAIC

To Cloris ("Cloris, I cannot say your eyes"). Sir Charles Sedley. BoLoP

To Cole, the Painter, Departing for Europe. Bryant. EAP; PiAm; TAP

To Colman Returning. *At. to* Colman, *tr. fr. Medieval Latin by* Helen Waddell. BIrV

To come back from the sweet South, to the North. Italia, Io Ti Saluto. Christina Rossetti. WPE

To come to the river. The Resolve. Denise Levertov. RFM

To come up behind you. Agitprop. Marge Piercy. MMD

To Comrade Lenin. Isidor Schneider. SPT

To Constantia Singing. Shelley. MBPR

To Corinth. Walter Savage Landor. ILP (1975 ed.)

To covet and resist for years. The Gash. William Everson. GP

To Critics. Robert Herrick. CaPo

To Crown It. Robert Herrick. CaPo

To cut a shape out in form of a man. What Is She Trying to Do, to Pattern Love. Besmilr Brigham. RiTi

To Cynthia: Learn'd Lapidaries. Sir Francis Kynaston. SCP-2

To Cynthia: On Concealment of Her Beauty. Sir Francis Kynaston. NOBE

To Cynthia: On Her Being an Incendiary. Sir Francis Kynaston. HAP

To Cynthia: On Her Embraces. Sir Francis Kynaston. GBL

To Cynthia, on Her Looking-Glass. Sir Francis Kynaston. SCP-2

To Cynthia, on Sugar and Her Sweetness. Sir Francis Kynaston. SCP-2

To D——, Dead by Her Own Hand. Howard Nemerov. PoA

To Daffodils [*or* Daffadills]. Robert Herrick. AKE; CaPo; ExPo (1973 ed.); FSFS; InPS; NOBE; PAIC; PCOP; PPP; SCP-1; SoSe (1977 ed.); UnPo (1976 ed.); WIF

To Daisies, Not To Shut So Soon. Robert Herrick. CaPo; GBL; ILP (1975 ed.); InPK

To Dana for Her Birthday. W. S. Merwin. PCho

To David, about His Education. Howard Nemerov. NowV; SFF

To deal with death, ignore it. La Vie En Rose. Peter Schjeldahl. CAAP

To Dean Bourn, a Rude River in Devon, by Which Sometimes He Lived. Robert Herrick. CaPo

To Death. Oliver St. John Gogarty. FaBoEE

To Death. Shelley. MBPR

To Delia. Samuel Daniel. ESo
*Sels.*
  "Beauty, sweet love, is like the morning dew." NOBE; PAIC
  "Care-charmer sleep [*or* sleepe], son [*or* sonne] of the sable night." AAS; Epi; ILP (1975 ed.); InPS; IPWM; NIL; NOBE; OAEL–1; PAIC
  "Fair [*or* Faire] is my love, and cruel [*or* cruell] as she's fair." AAS; ILP (1975 ed.); NOBE
  (Sonnet: "Fair is my love, and cruel as she is fair.") HoPM (1975 ed.)
  "I Must not grieve my love, whose eyes would read." PoPle
  "I once may see when yeares shall wreck my wrong." AAS
  "If so it hap, this of-spring of my care." AAS
  "If this be love, to draw [*or* drawe] a weary [*or* wearie] breath." AAS; GBL
  "Let others sing of knights and paladins [*or* palladines]." AAS; NIL; NOBE
  "Look, Delia, how we esteem the half-blown rose." HeIP; ILP (1975 ed.)
  "None other fame mine unambitious muse." AAS
  Sonnet: "I must not grieve my love, whose eyes would read." LoAs
  "These plaintive verse, the postes of my desire." AAS
  "When men shall find thy flower, thy glory, pass." NOBE

To Delmore Schwartz. Robert Lowell. NoAM

To demolish it. All Splendor on Earth. Karin Kiwus, *tr. by* Almut McAuley. BoWoP

To Desi as Joe as Smoky the Lover of 115th Street. Audre Lorde. CNA

To destroy or deride Creation's task. Kashrut. Edouard Roditi. VWA

To Dianeme ("Dear, though to part it be hell"). Robert Herrick. CaPo

To Dianeme ("Give me one kiss"). Robert Herrick. CaPo; SoSe

To Dianeme ("Show me thy feet; show me thy legs, thy thighs"). Robert Herrick. CaPo; POL

To Dianeme ("Sweet, be not proud of those two eyes"). Robert Herrick. CaPo; NOBE; PoPle; SCP-1

To die be given us, or attain! Resignation. Matthew Arnold. VLP

To die old. Ancient of Days. Anthony Rudolf. VWA

To die—takes just a little while. Emily Dickinson. PBMP

To die with a forlorn hope, but soon to be raised. The Survivor. Robert Graves. CMoP (1970 ed.)

To Dinah Washington. Etheridge Knight. PoBA

To Diotima. Friedrich Hölderlin, *tr. fr. German by* Michael Hamburger. LoAs

To Disraeli. Shirley Brooks. NOBL

To Dives. Hilaire Belloc. OBSV

To Doctor Bale. Barnabe Googe. PAIC

To Doctor Empiric. Ben Jonson. FaBoEE

To Dr. F. B. on His Book of Chess. Richard Lovelace. CaPo

To Dr. Kipling. Richard Porson. FaBoCo

To draw no envy, Shakespeare, on thy name. To the Memory of My Beloved, the Author, Mr. William Shakespeare, and What He Hath Left Us. Ben Jonson. CABA (1972 ed.); HAP; HeIP; ILP (1975 ed.); OAEL–1; OBP

To dream of love, and, waking, to remember you. Dreams. Arthur Symons. PoA

To dream the impossible dream. The Impossible Dream. Joe Darion. BLSo

To Drift Down. Janet Carncross Chandler. AMV–81

To drift with every passion till my soul. Hélas! Oscar Wilde. VLP

To Drink. Gabriela Mistral, *tr. fr. Spanish by* Gunda Kaiser. NU

To drum-beat and heart-beat a soldier marches by. Nathan Hale. Francis Miles Finch. BTTM

To Earth. James Applewhite. PoA

To Earthward. Robert Frost. BiP; CABA (1972 ed.); LoAs; NoAM; NOBA; PPoe; TAP

"To eat a green fig, my dear." Green Figs at Table. James K. Baxter. ATNZ

To Edward Fitzgerald. Robert Browning. ExPo (1973 ed.)

To Edward Williams. Shelley. MBPR

To Electra ("I dare not ask a kiss"). Robert Herrick. CaPo; HoPM (1975 ed.)

To Electra ("I'll come to thee in all those shapes"). Robert Herrick. CaPo

To Eliza, with a Tulip-fashioned Watch. Robert Baron. SCP-2

To Elsie. William Carlos Williams. CABA (1972 ed.); CMoP (1970 ed.); InPS; NOBA

To Emily. Arthur Gregor. AMV–80

To Emily Dickinson. Hart Crane. CMoP (1970 ed.); NoAM; NOBA; TAP

To Emily Dickinson. Yvor Winters. PiAm

To end it all, the people elected a thumb. The Thumb. Dennis Saleh. MAT; NeAC

To enrich the earth I have sowed clover and grass. Enriching the Earth. Wendell Berry. PiAm

To escape from internal dragons. Modern Architecture. Norman Nathan. AMV–81

To Etesia Looking from Her Casement at the Full Moon. Henry Vaughan. Moon

To every action, they say. Newton's Third. Jake T. W. Hubbard. AMV–80

To every animal who eats or shoots his own kind. Salute. Lawrence Ferlinghetti. MIT

To every man. The Treehouse. James A. Emanuel. AmNP (1974 ed.); BPo; PoBA

To everything. Turn! Turn! Turn! Pete Seeger. WIF

To Everything There Is a Season. Bible, *O. T. Fr.* Ecclesiastes. FF; NAWM–1; OBVE; PBMP

To explain the nature of fishes in craft of verse. The Whale. *Unknown, tr. by* Gavin Bone. EBEV

To fair Fidele's grassy tomb. A Song from Shakespear's Cymbelyne. William Collins. LAuP; NOBE

To fall, like an apple, no mind. In the Emptied Rest Home. Bella Akhmadulina, *tr. by* Jean Valentine *and* Olga Carlisle. BoWoP

To Fanny. Keats. EBEV; LoAs
  (I Cry Your Mercy.) BoLoP; LoAs; MBPR; PPP

To Fanny Brawne. Keats. *See* This Living Hand, Now Warm and Capable.

To feed the baby's quite a chore. High Chair and Low Spirits. Richard Armour. BBGO

To feel and speak the astonishing beauty of things. The Beauty of Things. Robinson Jeffers. PoA

To feel this, a/ conversion to form. The Transformation. Don Eulert. CPA

To Fez Cobra. Ted Joans. GP

To fight aloud is very brave. Emily Dickinson. WPE

To find, he'd like to say, the god. Star Quality. Chris Wallace-Crabbe. CAAP

To find the western path. Morning. Blake. OAEL–2; STS

To Fine Lady Would-be. Ben Jonson. FaBoEE

To Fish. Leigh Hunt. *See* To a Fish.

To Flaxman. Blake. FaBoEE

To flee from memory. Emily Dickinson. FaBoEE

To fleece the Fleece from golden sheep. The Scales of the Eyes. Howard Nemerov. CMoP (1970 ed.)

To fling my arms wide. Dream Variation. Langston Hughes. AmNP (1974 ed.); HAP; MiP; NOBA; PiAm; PoBA; WeW

To Flood Stage Again. James Wright. NOBA; Prf

To Flossie. William Carlos Williams. TH

To Flowers from Italy in Winter. Thomas Hardy. PF

To Fool, or Knave. Ben Jonson. FaBoEE; SoSe

To Ford Madox Ford in Heaven. William Carlos Williams. NoAM; NOBA

To Forget Self and All. Allen Curnow. ATNZ

To forgive enemies Hayley does pretend. Blake. FaBoEE

To Fortune on Buying a Ticket in the Irish Lottery. Samuel Taylor Coleridge. MBPR

To free me from domestic strife. At Hadleigh, Suffolk. *Unknown.* FaBoCo

To freight cars in the air. The Descent of Winter (Section 10/30). William Carlos Williams. InPK

To Frighten a Storm. Gladys Cardiff. CDW

To G. A. W. Keats. MBPR

To gallop horses (or eat buns). Poem about a Poem about a Poem. Robert Conquest. WIF

To gather flowers Sappha went. The Apron of Flowers. Robert Herrick. CaPo

To gather the wood with a hard eye. Wood Walk. A. Wilber Stevens. MPA

To George Felton Mathew. Keats. MBPR

To George Sand: I. A Desire. Elizabeth Barrett Browning. BoWoP

To George Sand: II. A Recognition. Elizabeth Barrett Browning. BoWoP; SBG

To get betimes in Boston town I rose this morning early. A Boston Ballad. Walt Whitman. OBAL

To give—and forgive. Short Sermon. Louis Untermeyer. CTV

To give up everything. Huck Finn at Ninety, Dying in a Chicago Boarding House Room. James Schevill. TAP

To go in the dark with a light is to know the light. To Know the Dark. Wendell Berry. GP

To God. Blake. OAEL–2

To God Our Strength Shout Joyfully, *with music.* Henry Ainsworth. AH

To God: to illuminate all men. Beginning with Skid Road. Psalm III. Allen Ginsberg. CAPP

To grass, or leaf, or fruit, or wall. The Snail. Vincent Bourne, *tr. by* William Cowper. OBVE

To Greet a Letter-Carrier. William Carlos Williams. OBAL

To Groves. Robert Herrick. CaPo

To H. Blake. *See* To William Hayley.

To H. C. Wordsworth. MBPR

To Harriet ("Harriet! thy kiss to my soul is dear"). Shelley. MBPR

To Harriett ("Thy look of love has power to calm"). Shelley. MBPR

To have ears like Ted Williams' eyes. Hearing. William Claire. PoUp

To have found at last that noble, candid speech. William Butler Yeats. A. D. Hope. MAuV

To have gold in your back yard and not know it. Tom O' Bedlam among the Sunflowers. Thomas James. HeS

To have stepped lightly among European marbles. Hark Back. Richard Eberhart. TH

To Hayley. Blake. *See* To William Hayley.

To heal you Hieronymus I had brought you. Bear's Blood. Ileana Malancioiu, *tr. by* Stavros Deligiorgis. BoWoP

To hear a dripping water tap in a house. Betweens. Norman MacCaig. EAS

To hear an oriole sing. Emily Dickinson. PB

To Heaven. Ben Jonson. ExPo (1973 ed.); HAP; ILP (1975 ed.); ILwL; PPoe; UnPo (1976 ed.)

To Helen ("Helen, thy beauty is to me"). Poe. AmVN; BoLoP; CABA (1972 ed.); ExPo (1973 ed.); FaPo; GBL; HAP; HeIP; HoPM (1975 ed.); ILP (1975 ed.); InPS; LFH; NIL; NOBA; PAIC; PBMP; PiAm; TAP; WIF

To Helen in a Huff. Nathaniel Parker Willis. OBAL

To Helen (of Troy, N.Y.). Peter Viereck. CoPAm (Lyricism of the Weak, The.) WeW

To Hell with Commonsense. Patrick Kavanagh. CIP; FaBoTw (1975 ed.)

To Hell with Your Fertility Cult. Gary Snyder. PPoD

To Henrietta, on Her Departure for Calais. Thomas Hood. OxBChV

To Her Dead Mate: Montana, 1966. Elizabeth Libbey. AmPA

To Her in Absence: A Ship. Thomas Carew. CaPo

To Her Love. Edward May. FaBoEE

To hide her ordure, claws the cat. A Quarrelsome Bishop. Walter Savage Landor. FaBoEE; OBSV

To him who in the love of Nature holds. Thanatopsis. Bryant. AmVN; CTV; DL; EAP; ILP (1975 ed.); NOBA; PiAm; TAP; VoPo

To His Absent Diana. Henry Constable. Diana, *introd.* ESo

To His Book ("Go thou forth, my book, though late"). Robert Herrick. CaPo

To His Book ("Have I not blessed thee? Then go forth; nor fear"). Robert Herrick. CaPo

To his book's end this last line he'd have placed. Robert Herrick. CaPo

To His Child. William Bullokar. OxBChV

To His Coy Love. Michael Drayton. LoAs

To His Coy Mistress. Andrew Marvell. AnMo; BIP; BoLoP; CABA (1972 ed.); EBEV; Epi; ExPo (1973 ed.) FF; GBL; HAP; HeIP; HoPM (1975 ed.); ILP (1975 ed.); InPK; InPS; IP; IPWM; LFH; LoAs; MAT; MetP; NIL; NOBE; OAEL-1; OBP; PAIC; PBMP; PoIA; PoPle; PPoD; PPoe; PPP; SCP-1; SoSe; TT; UnPo (1976 ed.); UsP; VoPo; WEW; WIF

To His Dead Body. Siegfried Sassoon. NoAM

To His Dying Brother, Master William Herrick. Robert Herrick. CaPo; PoPle

To His Excellency George Washington. Phillis Wheatley. OFD; SBG; WPE

To His Friend, Master R. L., in Praise of Music and Poetry. Richard Barnfield. ILP (1975 ed.)
("If musique and sweet poetrie agree.") AAS

To His Friend, on the Untunable Times. Robert Herrick. CaPo

To His Honoured and Most Ingenious Friend, Master Charles Cotton. Robert Herrick. CaPo

To His Kinsman, Master Thomas Herrick, Who Desired to Be in His Book. Robert Herrick. CaPo

To His Kinswoman, Mistress Penelope Wheeler. Robert Herrick. CaPo

To His Lady. Henry VIII, King of England. EBEV

To His Little Son Benedict from the Tower of London. John Hoskyns. OxBChV

To His Love. *Unknown.* GBL

To His Love in Middle-Age. Edwin Brock. AMV-80

To His Lovely Mistresses. Robert Herrick. CaPo; ILP (1975 ed.)

To His Lute. Sir Thomas Wyatt. *See* Lover Complaineth the Unkindness . . .

To His Mistress. Asclepiades, *tr. fr. Greek by* Dudley Fitts. NIL

To His Mistress. James Graham, Marquess of Montrose. *See* I'll Never Love Thee More.

To His Mistress [*or* Maistres]. Alexander Montgomerie. GBL; SLP

To His Mistress ("Your husband will be with us at the treat"). Ovid, *tr. fr. Latin by* Dryden. Amores, I, 4. BoLoP
("Your husband? Going to the same dinner as us?" *tr. by* Guy Lee.) NAWM-1

To His Mistress. Earl of Rochester. LoAs

To His Mistress Desiring to Travel with Him as His Page. John Donne. *See* On His Mistress.

To His Mistress Going to Bed. John Donne. *See* Going to Bed.

To His Mistresse. Robert Herrick. OFD

To His Mistresses ("Help me! Help me! now I call"). Robert Herrick. CaPo; LoAs

To His Mistresses ("Put on your silks, and piece by piece"). Robert Herrick. CaPo

To His Mistris Going to Bed. John Donne. *See* Going to Bed.

To His Mother. George Herbert. ILP (1975 ed.)
(Sonnet: "My God, where is that ancient heat towards thee.") OAEL-1

To His Not-So-Coy Mistress. Wynford Vaughan-Thomas. NOBL

To His Son. Sir Walter Ralegh. InPS; PPoe

To His Son Bennet. John Hoskyns. FaBoEE

To His Son, Vincent Corbet. Richard Corbet. OxBChV

To His Watch When He Could Not Sleep. Lord Herbert of Cherbury. NOBE

To hold my own hand in some secret place. Knee Deep. Ted Joans. GP

To Homer. Keats. CABA (1972 ed.); EBEV; MBPR

To honor the return of sparkling sun. Sonnet XV. Louise Labé, *tr. by* Willis Barnstone. BoWoP

To Hope. Keats. MBPR

To Horace. David Lake. FPA

To Houston at Gonzales town, ride, Ranger, for your life. The Men of the Alamo. James Jeffrey Roche. BPAW

To Hugh MacDiarmid. G. S. Fraser. MS

To Hugh MacDiarmid. Edwin Morgan. FaBoTw (1975 ed.)

To hurt the Negro and avoid the Jew. University. Karl Shapiro. NowV

To I. Lavrentevaya. Natalya Gorbanyevskaya, *tr. fr. Russian by* Daniel Weissbort. BoWoP

To Ianthe ("Past ruined Ilion Helen lives"). Walter Savage Landor. *See* Past Ruined Ilion . . .

To Imagination. Emily Brontë. ILP (1975 ed.); VLP

To Inez Milholland. Edna St. Vincent Millay. WPE

To Insure Survival. Simon J. Ortiz. CDW

To interpret the wood you first must fall. The Fables. David Malouf. CAAP

To Ireland in the Coming Times. W. B. Yeats. NoAM

To J.F.K. 14 Years After. Roger Weaver. AMV-80

To J. H. Reynolds, Esq. Keats. MBPR
"O that our dreamings all, of sleep or wake," *sel.* OAEL-2

To James. Frank Horne. *Fr.* Letters Found Near a Suicide. BPo; PAIC

To James Smith. Burns. HoPM (1975 ed.)

To Jane: The Invitation. Shelley. MBPR

To Jane: The Recollection. Shelley. MBPR

To Jesus on His Birthday. Edna St. Vincent Millay. VoPo

To Jesus Villanueva, with Love. Alma Villanueva. NW

To Joanna. Wordsworth. MBPR

To John I ow'd great obligation. Epigram. Matthew Prior. FaBoCo; FaBoEE; OBVE

To Juan at the Winter Solstice. Robert Graves. CMoP (1970 ed.); EBEV; NoAM; OAEL-2; OBP

To Julia ("Her eyes the glow-worm lend thee"). Robert Herrick See Night-Piece, to Julia, The.

To Julia ("How rich and pleasing thou, my Julia, art"). Robert Herrick. CaPo

To Julia ("Julia, when thy Herrick dies"). Robert Herrick. CaPo

To Julia de Burgos. Julia de Burgos, tr. fr. Spanish by Grace Schulman. BoWoP; PBWP

To Julia, the Flaminica Dialis, or Queen-Priest. Robert Herrick. CaPo

To Julius. Martial, tr. fr. Latin by Sir Charles Sedley. FaBoEE

To justify the quiver in my quill. Poet's Prayer. M. L. Sussman. AMV-80

To Kalòn. Ezra Pound. PoA

To Kate, Skating Better than Her Date. David Daiches. CTBA; SPo

To Keep a True Lent. Robert Herrick. BoReV (True Lent, A.) OFD

To Keep the Cold Wind Away. Unknown. OxBM

To keep your marriage brimming. A Word to Husbands. Ogden Nash. POL

To kill a bat is easy. Easy as a Bat. Gond Oral Tradition, tr. by V. Elwin and S. Hivale. WTO

To kill its enemies and cheat its friends. International Conference. Colin Ellis. FaBoEE

To Know the Dark. Wendell Berry. GP

To know there are rhododendrons on the slopes of the Himalayas. Nearer. Judith Herzberg, tr. by Shirley Kaufman. BoWoP; VWA

To Know Whom One Shall Marry. Unknown. GBP

To Kosciusko. Keats. MBPR

To Krishna Haunting the Hills. Andal, tr. fr. Tamil by Willis Barnstone. BoWoP

To L. Julianne Perry. PoBA

To L. B. C. L. M. Robert Bridges. PPM ("I love all beauteous things.") CMoP (1970 ed.); EBEV

To L. H. B. Katherine Mansfield. ATNZ

To Lake Aghmoogenegamook. The American Traveller. "Orpheus C. Kerr." FaBoCo; OBAL

To Lar. Robert Herrick. CaPo

To Laura Phelan: 1880-1906. Leon Stokesbury. NVAP

To Laurels. Robert Herrick. CaPo

To leave the earth was my wish, and no will stayed my rising. A Temple. Kenneth Patchen. EAS

To Leonard and Kerstin, with a Gift of Books. Alberta Turner. HeS

To Li Po from Tu Fu. Carolyn Kizer. GP

To lie at the edge of the forest. In Memory of Francois Rabelais. Yunna Moritz, tr. by Elaine Feinstein. VWA

To Lindsay. Allen Ginsberg. ConAP

To Live and Die in Dixie. John Beecher. CSP
Sels.
"Confederate veterans came to town." GP
"Old Maggie's sweat would drip and sizzle." GP
"Spurgeon would daub designs on flowerpots." GP

To live illusionless, in the abandoned mine. Double Monologue. Adrienne Rich. NIL; Psy

To live in/ myself. Drifting. Kathleen Spivack. IHMS

To live in hell, and heaven to behold. Henry Constable. Fr. Diana. AAS; ILP (1975 ed.)

To live in Wales is to be conscious. Welsh Landscape. R. S. Thomas. LP; MPo

To Live Merrily, and to Trust to Good Verses. Robert Herrick. CaPo

To live's a gift, to dye's a debt that we. The Porch. Philip Pain. PiAm

To London once my stepps I bent. London Lickpenny. Unknown. OxBM

To Look at Any Thing. John Moffitt. RFM; SFF; TPo

To loosen with all ten fingers held wide and limber. Moss-gathering. Theodore Roethke. ILP (1975 ed.); PiAm; RFM; VGW

To Lord Byron. Keats. MBPR

To lordings proud I tune my lay. Duke upon Duke. Pope. Epi

To lose it all at once. Marina Tsvetayeva, tr. by Paul Schmidt. Fr. The Daughter of Jairus. BoWoP

To love November, a turned joy. Late in Fall. Ramona Wilson. VoR

To love someone/ Who does not return that love. Lady Kasa, tr. fr. Japanese by Harold P. Wright. PBWP

To Lucasta ("Ah, Lucasta, why so bright"). Richard Lovelace. CaPo

To Lucasta, from Prison. Richard Lovelace. CaPo

To Lucasta, Going beyond the Seas. Richard Lovelace. CaPo; ILP (1975 ed.); PoPle

To Lucasta, [on] Going to the Wars. Richard Lovelace. BuTh; CABA (1972 ed.); CaPo; ExPo (1973 ed.); FF; GBL; HAP; HeIP; HoPM (1975 ed.); ILP (1975 ed.); InPK; InPS; IP; NIL; NOBE; OBP; PBMP; PoIA; SoSe; WIF (Going to the Wars.) VoPo
(Song: "Tell me not, sweet, I am unkind.") OAEL-1

To Lucasta: Her Reserved Looks. Richard Lovelace. CaPo

To Luve Unluvit. Alexander Scott. SLP

To Lydia. Horace, tr. fr. Latin by Philip Francis. Odes, I, 25. OBVE

To "Lydia Languish." Austin Dobson. VLP

To Madame A. V. Pletneff. Karolina Pavlova, tr. fr. French by Paul Schmidt. PBWP

To Maecenas. Horace, tr. fr. Latin by Thomas Flatman. OBVE

To mak a ballant. Recipe: To Mak a Ballant. Alexander Scott. MS

To make a final conquest of all me. The Fair Singer. Andrew Marvell. LoAs; NOBE; PoPle

To make a juju of my own. A Juju of My Own. Lebert Bethune. InPS; PoBA

To Make a Play. May Swenson. Psy

To make a prairie it takes a clover and one bee. Emily Dickinson. ANTL; BoWoP; HeIP; PCOP; PPM

To make a start. Preface. William Carlos Williams. Fr. Paterson. CMoP (1970 ed.); ILP (1975 ed.); NoAM; NOBA

To make do, making a living. Eaton's Boatyard. Philip Booth. PCho

To Make It Real. Peter Porter. UsP

To make me do the thing I will, I won't. The Human Animal. Jane Mayhall. TAP

To make quick way I'll leap o'er heavy blocks. Dryden. Fr. Absalom and Achitophel, Pt. II. OBSV

To make reparation for love so blindly rejected. No Reparation. Charles Brasch. ATNZ

To make the big time you must learn. Mastering the Craft. Vernon Scannell. HeHu

To make this scene I climb miles. The Space Eater Camps at Fifth Lake. Reg Saner. GP

To Margaret. Gerard Manley Hopkins. BBGO

To Margot Heinemann. John Cornford. See Huesca.

To Marguerite ("Yes! in the sea of life enisled"). Matthew Arnold. Fr. Switzerland. ILP (1975 ed.); NOBE; SoSe (1977 ed.)
(To Marguerite—Continued.) BoLoP; EBEV; OAEL-2; PFD; PPP; VLP

To Maria Gisborne in England, from Italy. Shelley. Fr. Letter to Maria Gisborne. NOBE

To Mark Anthony in Heaven. William Carlos Williams. NOBA

To market, to market. The Cost-of-Living Mother Goose. Dow Richardson. QQQ

To market, to market/ To buy a plum cake. Mother Goose. MG

To market, to market, to buy a fat pig. Mother Goose. MG

To Mary. William Cowper. LAuP; PAIC

To Mary: I Sleep with Thee, and Wake with Thee. John Clare. GBL

To Mary: It Is the Evening Hour. John Clare. BoLoP; GBL

To Mary Wollstonecraft Godwin. Shelley. MBPR

To Master Davenant for Absence. Sir John Suckling. CaPo

To Master George Sandys, Treasurer for the English Colony in Virginia, *sel.* Michael Drayton.
    "As if to symptoms we may credit give." SCP-2

To Master Henry Lawes, the Excellent Composer of Lyrics. Robert Herrick. CaPo

To Maystres Isabell Pennell. John Skelton. *See* To Mistress Isabel Pennell.

To Maystres Jane Blenner-Haiset. John Skelton. *Fr.* The Garlande of Laurell. AAS

To Maystres Margaret Hussey. John Skelton. *See* To Mistress Margaret Hussey.

To me, fair friend, you never can be old. Sonnets, CIV. Shakespeare. GBL; HeIP; LoAs; Prf

To me he seems like a god. Sappho, *tr. fr. Greek by* Willis Barnstone. BoWoP

To me, one silly task is like another. Cassandra. Louise Bogan. HAP; PBWP; RiTi; SBG; VGW

To Meadows. Robert Herrick. CaPo; NOBE

To meake up rhymes, my mind wer zoo a-vire. The Young Rhymer Snubbed. William Barnes. VLP

To Meath of the pastures. A Drover. Padraic Colum. PFIr

To meditate the marvel of mixed media. Mixed Media. James Schevill. AMV-81

To Meet Mr. Lincoln. Eve Merriam. CC

To Melancholy. Countess of Winchilsea. WPE

To Mercy, Pity, Peace, and Love. The Divine Image. Blake. *Fr.* Songs of Innocence. BoReV; ILP (1975 ed.); LAuP; MBPR; NOBE; OAEL-2; PoIA; PPP; STS; TT

To Midnight. *Unknown.* BPAW

To Minerva. Thomas Hood. FaBoCo; FaBoNo; NOBL

To Minnie. Robert Louis Stevenson. SLP

To Mirikitani. Geraldine Kudaka. NW

To Miss ——: On Her Playing upon the Harpsichord. Samuel Johnson. CABA (1972 ed.)

To Miss Laetitia Van Lewen. Constantia Grierson. WPE

To Mr. Bays. Charles Sackville. APAS

To Mr. Cyriac Skinner upon His Blindness. Milton. ILP (1975 ed.); SCP-1

To Mr. Edward Howard, on His Plays. Charles Sackville. ESaP

To Mr. George Herbert. John Donne. OBVE

To Mr. Henry Lawes. Katherine Philips. SBG; WPE

To Mr. Murray. Byron. FaBoCo

To Mr. Rowland Woodward. John Donne. PAIC

To Mr. Tilman after He Had Taken Orders. John Donne. EBEV

To Mistress [or Maystres] Isabel[l] Pennell. John Skelton. *Fr.* The Garlande of Laurell. AAS; NOBE; RRA

To Mistress Katherine Bradshaw the Lovely, That Crowned Him with Laurel. Robert Herrick. CaPo

To Mrs. Magdalen Herbert, *sel.* John Donne.
    "Mad paper, stay! and grudge not here to burn." SCP-1

To Mistress [or Maystres] Margaret Hussey. John Skelton. *Fr.* The Garlande of Laurell. AAS; EBEV; HeIP; HoPM (1975 ed.); LoAs; NOBE; OAEL-1; PAIC; PPoe; PPP

To Mistress Margery Wentworth. John Skelton. *Fr.* The Garlande of Laurell. EBEV; NOBE

To Mrs. Reynolds's Cat. Keats. *See* To a Cat.

To Mrs. Thrale on Her Thirty-fifth Birthday. Samuel Johnson. FaBoEE

To Morfydd. Lionel Johnson. OAEL-2

To Mother. Frank Horne. *Fr.* Letters Found near a Suicide. BPo

To Mother and Steve. Mari Evans. BPo; PoBA; Psy

To move over shifting borders. Eeva-Liisa Manner, *tr. by* Jaakko A. Ahokas. *Fr.* Cambrian. PBWP

To Music ("Begin to charm, and as thou strok'st mine ears"). Robert Herrick. CaPo

To Music: A Song. Robert Herrick. CaPo

To Music, to Becalm a Sweet-sick Youth. Robert Herrick. CaPo; SCP-1

To Music, to Becalm His Fever. Robert Herrick. CaPo

To musicke bent is my retyred minde. Thomas Campion. AAS

To My Admired and Soul-loved Friend, Master of All Essentials and True Knowledge, Mr. Harriots, *sel.* George Chapman.
    "To you, whose depth of soul measures the height." SCP-2

To My Body. Nancy Sullivan. TAP

To My Brother George ("Full many a dreary hour have I past"). Keats. MBPR

To My Brother George ("Many the wonders I this day have seen"). Keats. MBPR

To My Brother Miguel: In Memoriam. César Vallejo, *tr. fr. Spanish by* John Knoepfle *and* James Wright. MiP

To My Brothers. Keats. MBPR; TT

To My Cat. Rosamund Marriott Watson. PCat

To My Child. Abraham Sutskever, *tr. fr. Yiddish by* David G. Roskies *and* Hillel Schwartz. VWA

To My Contemporaries. Edwin Rolfe. SPT

To My Country. "Rahel," *tr. fr. Hebrew by* Diane Mintz. PBWP

To My Cousin Mary, for Mending My Tobacco Pouch. Francis Scott Key. OBAL

To My Daughter. Walter Savage Landor. RRA

To My Daughter. Hyam Plutzik. BiP

To My Daughter. Stephen Spender. RRA

To My Daughter, 1936. Genevieve Taggard. SPT

To My Daughter the Junkie on a Train. Audre Lorde. CNA

To My Dear and Loving Husband. Anne Bradstreet. BoWoP; EAP; FF; HAP; HeIP; ILP (1975 ed.); NOBA; PiAm; SBG; TAP; VoPo; WPE

To My Dear Friend Mr. Congreve, on His Comedy Called "The Double-Dealer." Dryden. EBEV; OAEL-1

To my dear wife. A Last Will and Testament. John Winstanley. OBSV

To My Excellent Lucasia, on Our Friendship. Katherine Philips. SBG; SCP-2; WPE

To My Father. Tony Curtis. AMV-81

To My Father. Susannah Fried, *tr. fr. Slovak by* Anthony Rudolf. VWA

To My Father. W. S. Graham. FaBoTw (1975 ed.)

To My Father. John Haines. CNW

To My Father. Charles Waterman. BrS

To My Father on Pearl Harbor Day. D. W. Donzella. FAF

To my firstborn land, in the south. The Firstborn Land. Ingeborg Bachmann, *tr. by* Daniel Huws. BoWoP

To My Former Student on the Occasion of Birth. Madeline Bass. WBN

To My Four-Year-Old Daughter. Gail Todd. TV

To My Friend. Wilfred Owen. OBP

To My Friend. Francis Thompson. PoA

To My Friend G. N., from Wrest. Thomas Carew. CaPo

To My Friend Whose Parachute Did Not Open.   David Wagoner.
SFF

To My Gingerbread Mistress, *sel.*   Samuel Wesley.
"Dear miss, not with a lie to cheat ye."   SCP-2

To My God in His Sickness.   Philip Levine.   NNaP

To My Honour'd Kinsman, John Driden, of Chesterton, *sel.*
Dryden.
"No porter guards the passage of your door."   EBEV

To My Ill Reader.   Robert Herrick.   CaPo

To My Inconstant Mistris[s].   Thomas Carew.   MetP; NOBE
(Song: To My Inconstant Mistress.)   CaPo; GBL

To My Infant Daughter ("Alas, that I should be").   Yvor Winters.
VGW

To My Ingenious and Worthy Friend William Lowndes, Esq.
John Gay.   OBSV

To My Mistress in Absence.   Thomas Carew.   CaPo

To My Mistress Sitting by a River's Side: An Eddy.   Thomas
Carew.   CaPo

To My Most Dearly Loved Henry Reynolds, *sel.*   Michael
Drayton.
First Steps up Parnassus.   NOBE

To My Mother.   George Barker.   *See* Sonnet to My Mother.

To My Mountain.   Kathleen Raine.   SLP

To My Ninth Decade.   Walter Savage Landor.   PAIC

To My Noble Friend Master William Browne: Of the Evil Time,
*sels.*   Michael Drayton.   SCP-2
"As men oft laugh at little babes when they."
"Dear friend, be silent and with patience see."
"Into the clouds the devil lately got."
"This world of ours thus runneth upon wheels."

To My Noble Kinsman, Thomas Stanley, Esquire, on His Lyric
Poems Composed by Master John Gamble.   Richard
Lovelace.   CaPo

To My Old Schoolmaster.   Whittier.   NOBA

To my parents I am/ a thick layer of innovation.   Houses, Past
and Present.   Eli Bachar, *tr. by* Jeremy Garber.   VWA

To my people it's as though he gave them a sacrifice.   Eadwacer.
*Unknown.*   WPE

To my prowd foe thus, sister, humblie saye.   Virgil, *tr. by* Earl of
Surrey.   *Fr.* The Aeneid, II.   OBVE

To my revenge and to her desperate fears.   The Bubble: A Song.
Robert Herrick.   CaPo

To My Sister.   Olga Berggolts, *tr. fr. Russian by* Daniel Weissbort.
BoWoP

To My Sister.   David Kherdian.   SA

To My Sister.   Wordsworth.   LoAs; OAEL-2
(Lines Written at a Small Distance from My House.)   MBPR
"It is the first mild day of March," *sel.*   FSFS

To My Sister, from the Twenty-seventh Floor.   Michael Knoll.
AMV-81

To My Son.   Margaret Johnston Griffin.   SoSe

To My Son, Not Yet Born.   William Virgil Davis.   AMV-81

To My Son Parker, Asleep in the Next Room.   Bob Kaufman.
PoBA; VGW

To My Soul in Its Blindness.   Phineas Fletcher.   SCP-2

To my true king I offered free from stain.   A Jacobite's Epitaph
[*or* Epitaph on a Jacobite].   Macaulay.   EBEV; FaPoR;
NOBE;

To My Truly Valiant, Learned Friend, Who in His Book Resolved
the Art Gladiatory into the Mathematics.   Richard Lovelace.
CaPo

To my twin who lives in a cruel country.   The Dual Site.
Michael Hamburger.   AIW; NowV

To My Valentine.   *Unknown.*   CTV; ECBV

To My Wife.   Edwin Brock.   BuTh

To My Wife.   J. V. Cunningham.   PiAm

To My Wife.   Jack Simcock.   BuTh

To My Wife Asleep.   Edward Tick.   AMV-80

To My Worthy Friend Master George Sandys, on His Translation
of the Psalms.   Thomas Carew.   CaPo

To My Worthy Friend Master Peter Lely.   Richard Lovelace.
CaPo

To My Young Lady Lucy Sidney.   Edmund Waller.   ILP (1975
ed.)

To My Youngest Kinsman, R. L.   Abraham Chear.   OxBChV

To Myself.   Art Lange.   FiCh

To Myself, Late, in a Myrtle Grove.   Robert Peterson.   NeAC

To Nature.   Samuel Taylor Coleridge.   MBPR; OAEL-2

To Nature, in her shop on day, at work compounding simples.
Filling an Order.   John Townsend Trowbridge.   OBAL

To Ned.   Herman Melville.   NOBA

To Night.   Shelley.   ILP (1975 ed.); MBPR; OAEL-2

To Night.   *Unknown.*   Moon

To Night.   Joseph Blanco White.   EBEV; PPM; SoSe

To no longer taste like the taste of whiskey.   Safe Flights.
Barbara Guest.   RiTi

To no one Muse does she her glance confine.   On a Squinting
Poetess.   Thomas Moore.   FaBoCo

To Nobodaddy.   Blake.   MBPR; OAEL-2

To Noel.   Gabriela Mistral, *tr. fr. Spanish by* Doris Dana.   PChr

To Nowhere.   David Ignatow.   NCSH

To Nysus.   Sir Charles Sedley.   FaBoEE; OBSV

To O. E. A.   Claude McKay.   BPo

To Oenone.   Robert Herrick.   CaPo

To Oliver Cromwell.   Milton.   *See* To the Lord General
Cromwell.

To One Elect.   S. I. Hayakawa.   PoA

To One Far Away, Dancing.   C. Stephen Finley.   AMV-81

To one fixed star my spirit clings.   One Fixed Star.   Ardoin
Casgrain.   PPM

To One in Bedlam.   Ernest Dowson.   VLP

To One in Paradise.   Poe.   BoLoP; PiAm; TAP

To One Married to an Old Man.   Edmund Waller.   FaBoEE

To One Who Has Been Long in City Pent.   Keats.   ILP (1975
ed.); MBPR; NIL; PMW; TT;VoPo
(To One Who Has Been Long.)   STS

To One Who Quotes and Detracts.   Walter Savage Landor.
FaBoEE

To One Who Would Make a Confession.   Wilfrid Scawen Blunt.
PPM

To onpreise womene it were a shame.   A Woman Is a Worthy
Thing.   *Unknown.*   FaBoCo

To Otto Bauer.   Alfred Hayes.   SPT

To Our House-Dog Captain.   Walter Savage Landor.   OBP

To our ruined vineyard come.   Love Song for the Future.   Vassar
Miller.   NCSH

To our theme—The man who has stood on the Acropolis.   Byron.
*Fr.* Don Juan, XI.   InPS; OBSV

To overcome the haunting of a ghost.   The Spiritualist.   Leon
Slade.   FPA

To Paris that was once her owne though now it be not so.   Ovid,
*tr. by* George Turberville.   *Fr.* Heroides.   OBVE

To Patriotic America.   Herb Middleton.   CPA

To Paul Eluard.   Jorie Graham.   AMV-80

To Penshurst.   Ben Jonson.   CABA (1972 ed.); NIL; OAEL-1;
PAIC; PPP; SCP-1, *abr.*; TVS

To Perilla.   Robert Herrick.   CaPo; ILP (1975 ed.)

To Persuade a Lady.   Michael Benedikt.   CAAP

To Pete Atkin: A Letter from Paris, *sel.*   Clive James.
"Weather's cleared, The. We're filming at Versailles."   OBSV

To Phillis [*or* Phyllis], to Love and Live with Him.   Robert
Herrick.   CaPo; LoAs

To Philocles [*or* Phylocles], Inviting Him to Friendship. "Ephelia." SCP-2; WPE

To Phoebe. W. S. Gilbert. OLR; WIF

To Phyllis. Edmund Waller. ILP (1975 ed.)

To Ping-ku, Asleep. Lawrence Durrell. RRA

To place one's little boy—just so. Archery. Walter de la Mare. FaBoNo

To Poem. Lyn Lifshin. NeAC; Psy

To Poesy. Tennyson. VLP

To Poets. Walter Savage Landor. FaBoEE

To prinke me up and make me higher plaste. George Gascoigne. AAS

To print, or not to print—that is the question. Hamlet's Soliloquy Imitated. Richard Jago. FaBoCo

To print our poems the propulsive cause. Fame Makes Us Forward. Robert Herrick. CaPo

To prove himself no plagiary, Moore. On J. M. S. Gent. Pope. FaBoEE

To Pyrrha ("Quis multa gracilis"). Horace, *tr. fr. Latin by* Milton. Odes, I, 5. LoAs
("What slender youth bedewed with liquid odours.") EBEV; OBVE; SCP-1

To R——before Leaving to Fight in Unknown Terrain. Nina Serrano. MIT

To R. B. Gerard Manley Hopkins. CMoP (1970 ed.); OAEL-2; PoIA; VLP

To R. K. James Kenneth Stephen. FaBoCo; FaBoEE; NOBL; VLP

To rack and torture thy unmeaning brain. On the Supposed Author of a Late Poem "In Defense of Satire." Earl of Rochester. APAS

To Rail or Jest, Ye Know I Use It Not. Sir Thomas Wyatt. Epi

To read my booke the virgin shie. Martial, *tr. fr. Latin by* Robert Herrick. OBVE

To Redistort a Weltanschauung. Matthew Mead. TwMBP

To Redound. William Harmon. CSP

To Redouté. John Ashbery. PoA

To Remain. C. P. Cavafy, *tr. fr. Modern Greek by* Nikos Stangos *and* Stephen Spender. BoLoP

To remember is not always to go back to what was. Time Reminded Me. Julia Uceda, *tr. by* Willis Barnstone. BoWoP

To Richard Boyle, Earl of Burlington: Of the Use of Riches. Pope. Moral Essays, Epistle IV. OAEL-1; PPP

To Richard Wright. Conrad Kent Rivers. AmNP (1974 ed.); CABA (1972 ed.); PoBA

To robbers furious, and to lovers tame. Samuel Johnson, *after the Latin of* Joachim du Bellay. FaBoEE

To Robert Browning. Walter Savage Landor. ILP (1975 ed.)

To Robert Lowell and Osip Mandelstam. Frederick Seidel. AMV-81

To Rosemond. Chaucer. CABA (1972 ed.).
(To Rosemounde.) ILP (1975 ed.); OAEL-1

To Roses in the Bosom of Castara. William Habington. NIL; SCP-2

To run a thousand miles from a thousand men. Open the Heart. Charles Brasch. ATNZ

To S. R. Crockett. Robert Louis Stevenson. NOBE

To S. T. C. on His 179th Birthday, October 12, 1951. Maurice Carpenter. FaBoTw (1975 ed.)

To safeguard man from wrongs, there nothing must. Distrust. Robert Herrick. CaPo

To Sally. John Quincy Adams. OBAL

To Satch. Samuel Allen. AmNP (1974 ed.); CTBA; LiSp; NIL; PoBA; SoSe; SPo; TVo
(American Gothic.) BuTh; TPo

To save your world, you asked this man to die. Epitaph for the Unknown Soldier. W. H. Auden. FaBoCo

To Saxham. Thomas Carew. CaPo

To say it once held daisies and bluebells. The Broken Bowl. James Merrill. PoA

To School! Stevie Smith. FaBoEE

To Science. Poe. *See* Sonnet—to Science.

To Scilla. Sir Charles Sedley. FaBoEE

To Scotland came the tall American. Black Tomintoul. Ian Hamilton Finlay. MS; SLP

To scratch with a/ Nail in a bare/ Patch. Cryptology. Ernest Kroll. PoUp

To see a strange outlandish fowl. Henry Farley. FaBoEE

To see a world in a grain of sand. Auguries of Innocence. Blake. BiP; CABA (1972 ed.); EBEV; FaPoR; InPK; LAuP; MBPR; OAEL-2; OBP; PCOP; PPoe; VoPo

To see both blended in one flood. Upon the Infant Martyrs. Richard Crashaw. OAEL-1; PAIC

To See Him Again. Gabriela Mistral, *tr. fr. Spanish by* Doris Dana. OLR

To see such dainty ghosts as you appear. On Meeting a Gentlewoman in the Dark. *Unknown.* FaBoEE

To see them coming headstrong. In Love with the Bears. Greg Kuzma. BCr

To Sergius. Sir Charles Sedley. FaBoEE

To Sextus. Martial, *tr. fr. Latin by* Sir Charles Sedley. FaBoEE

To Shadow. Charles O. Hartman. AAN

To Sherrie. Joseph Matuzak. AMV-81

To shoot a man against the National Library wall! Warm Protest. D. J. Enright. HeHu

To shoot, to shoot, would be my delight. A Shooting Song. William Brighty Rands. OxBChV

To Show How Humble, *with music. Unknown.* AH

To shred them: a narrow labor, and simply toss. Destruction of Letters. Babette Deutsch. WPE

To Sidmouth and Castlereagh. Shelley. *See* Similes for Two Political Characters of 1819.

To sign for a single passport. Practicing. Sonia Gernes. AMV-80

To Silvestre Revueltas of Mexico, in His Death. Pablo Neruda, *tr. fr. Spanish by* Harry Thomas. AMV-81

To Simplicity. Samuel Taylor Coleridge. *Fr.* Sonnets Attempted in the Manner of Contemporary Writers. Epi

To sing of wars, of captains [*or* captaines], and of kings. The Prologue. Anne Bradstreet. BoWoP; EAP; NOBA; SBG; TAP; WPE

To Sing the People. Lucille F. Travis. AATT

To sin's a vice in nature, and we find. Daniel Defoe. *Fr.* More Reformation. OBSV

To Sir Charles Sherrington. Lord Russell Brain. PMW

To Sir Henry Wotton ("Here's no more news than virtue"). John Donne. PAIC

To Sir Henry Wotton ("Sir, more than kisses letters mingle souls"). John Donne. TVS

To Sir Hudson Lowe. Thomas Moore. OBSV

To Sir Robert Wroth. Ben Jonson. TVS
"How bless'd art thou canst love the country, Wroth," *sel.* SCP-1

To Sir Toby. Philip Freneau. ILP (1975 ed.); TAP

To sit composing like a sunlit ghost. The Table. Michael Heffernan. PoA

To Sleep. Barbara Fialkowski. AMV-81

To Sleep. Keats. MBPR; NIL; OBP; PMW; STS
(Sonnet to Sleep.) PPM

To Sleep. Sir Philip Sidney. *See* Astrophel and Stella, Sonnets, XXXIX.

To Sleep. Charlotte Smith. WPE

To Sleep. Wordsworth. MPBR

To sleep easy at night. Mother Goose. CTV

To smash the simple atom. Atomic Courtesy. Ethel Jacobson. QQQ

To Soar in Freedom and in Fullness of Power. Walt Whitman. RFM

To So-kin of Rakuyo, ancient friend, Chancellor of Gen. Exile's Letter. Li Po, *tr. by* Ezra Pound. TCP

To Some Ladies. Keats. MBPR

To Some Millions Who Survive Joseph E. Mander, Sr. Sarah E. Wright. PoBA

To Song. Olga Berggolts, *tr. fr. Russian by* Daniel Weissbort. BoWoP

To speak in a flat voice. Speak. James Wright. HAP; TAP; WeW

To speak in summer in a lecture hall. Lecture Hall. Patrick Kavanagh. FaBoTw (1975 ed.); NoAM

To speak of death is to deny it, is. Consolatio Nova: For Alan Swallow. J. V. Cunningham. MPA; PiAm

To speak of my influences. Jean Garrigue. LoAs

"To Speak of Woe That Is in Marriage." Robert Lowell. CAPP; NoAM

To speak out clean. Telling It. Nancy Sullivan. TAP

To speke of an unkinde man. Adrian and Bardus. John Gower. *Fr.* Confessio Amantis, V. OxBM

To spend uncounted years of [*or* in] pain. Why Think? By Thinking You Grow Old. Arthur Hugh Clough. PoIA; WeW

To Spring. Blake. LAuP; MBPR; OAEL-2; PPP

To Spring. Charlotte Smith. WPE

To Stand Up Straight. A. E. Housman. OAEL-2

To Stanislaw Wyspianski. Katherine Mansfield. ATNZ

To start the world of old. It Is Almost the Year Two Thousand. Robert Frost. TH

To Start With. J. S. Harry. CAAP

To stave off disaster, or bring the devil to heel. Tapu. A. R. D. Fairburn. ATNZ

To steal from those that steal from you. Raffaele Minichiello. Sandra McPherson. CAAP

To Stella. Plato, *tr. fr. Greek by* Shelley. FaBoEE; OBVE

To stop time, a twig spinning. A Juggle of Myrtle Twigs. Edward Codish. VWA

To struggle against a falling mountain of opposition. Life. James Steele. SES

To stub an oar on a rock where none should be. Basking Shark. Norman MacCaig. BoAnP

To Summer. Blake. LAuP; MBPR

To Summer. Alan Nadel. AMV-80

To sup with thee thou didst me home invite. The Invitation. Robert Herrick. CaPo

To Switzerland, right up the Rhine. The Salmon. Christian Morgenstern, *tr. by* Geoffrey Grigson. FaBoNo

To Sycamores. Robert Herrick. CaPo

To Sylvia. An Imitation of Anacreon. *Unknown.* PiAm

To T. H., a Lady Resembling My Mistress. Thomas Carew. CaPo

To T. S. Eliot. Emanuel Litvinoff. VWA

To take the big gamble, leave the church. La Divina Commedia. David Malouf. CAAP

To tell the truth, I really am. The All-Night Waitress. Maura Stanton. AmPA

To tell you from the start, I have lost him. He Whose Hand and Eye Are Gentle. *Unknown, tr. by* Kenneth Jackson. OBW

To Teresa. Iván Silén, *tr. fr. Spanish by* Julio Marzán. InW

To Thaliarchus. Horace, *tr. fr. Latin by* Sir Richard Fanshawe. Odes, I, 9. OBVE

To That Most Senseless Scoundrel, the Author of Legion's Humble Address to the Lords. Thomas Brown. APAS

To the Accuser Who Is the God of This World. Blake. *See* Gates of Paradise, The.

To the Age's Insanities. Marie Ponsot. VGW

To the Anxious Mother. Valente Malangatana, *tr. fr. Portuguese by* Dorothy Guedes *and* Philippa Rumsey. BBGO

To the Archbishop of Tuam. *Unknown.* FaBoEE

To the Author of "To My Brother Miguel." Tony Quagliano. PHC

To the Authoress of "Aurora Leigh." Sydney Dobell. PeD

To the Bat. *Unknown.* BBL

To the Body. Coventry Patmore. OAEL-2; VLP

To the Cambro-Britons and Their Harp, His Ballad of Agincourt. Michael Drayton. *See* Ballad of Agincourt, The.

To the Carp, and Those Who Hunt Her. James Hazard. AMV-80

To the Children at the Family Album. William Stafford. PoW

To the City of London. William Dunbar. EBEV

To the Coast. Denis Glover. ATNZ

To the Colorado Desert. Madge Morris. BPAW

To the Countess of Bedford ("Reason is our soul's left hand"). John Donne. PAIC
    "Honour is so sublime perfection," *sel.* SCP-1

To the Countess of Salisbury, *sel.* John Donne.
    "Fair, great, and good: since seeing you we see." SCP-1

To the Cuckoo. F. H. Townsend. FaBoNo

To the Cuckoo. Wordsworth. MBPR; PB

To the Daisy ("Sweet flower! belike one day to have"). Wordsworth. MBPR

To the Dandelion. James Russell Lowell. PF

To the Dead Ladies. David Bristol. PoUp

To the Dead of the International Brigade. Sol Funaroff. SPT

To the Detractor. Robert Herrick. SCP-1

To the dim light and the large circle of shade. Sestina of the Lady Pietra degli Scrovigni. Dante, *tr. by* Dante Gabriel Rossetti. LoAs; OAEL-2; OBVE

To the Divine Neighbor. Judah Leib Teller, *tr. fr. Yiddish by* Gabriel Preil *and* Howard Schwartz. VWA

To the Earl of Dorset. Ambrose Philips. EPC

To the Earl of Oxford, Late Lord Treasurer. Swift, *after the Latin of* Horace. OBVE

To the edge of Europe, the eighteenth edge. John Berryman. *Fr.* Dream Songs. RRA

To the Elephants. Nathan Alterman, *tr. fr. Hebrew by* Ruth Nevo. VWA

To the Evening Star. Blake. ILP (1975 ed.); LAuP; MBPR; OAEL-2; PPP; STS

To the Fair Clarinda, Who Made Love to Me, Imagin'd More than Woman. Aphra Behn. SBG

To the Field Mice. Richard Eberhart. BoAnP

To the Film Industry in Crisis. Frank O'Hara. CAPP; NoAM; NOBA; OBAL

To the Four Courts, Please. James Stephens. BIrV; PFIr; UnPo (1976 ed.)

To the Fringed Gentian. Bryant. FSFS; PCOP; PiAm; TAP

To the Garden the World. Walt Whitman. AmVN; GrRo

To the Gardener at Nuneham. Horace Walpole. FaBoEE

To the Generous Reader. Robert Herrick. CaPo

To the Gentlewoman of Llanarth Hall. Evan Thomas, *tr. fr. Welsh by* Gwyn Jones. OBW

To the Ghost of Martial. Ben Jonson. PAIC

To the God of Love. E. V. Knox. NOBL

To the Good Thief. Saunders Lewis, *tr. fr. Welsh by* Gwyn Thomas. OBW

To the Governor & Legislature of Massachusetts. Howard Nemerov. PPoD

To the Grasshopper and the Cricket. Leigh Hunt. ILP (1975 ed.)
(Grasshopper and the Cricket, The.) PCOP

To the Greek Anthologists. George Rostrevor Hamilton, *after the Greek of* Satyros. FaBoEE

To the Hand. W. S. Merwin. EAS

To the Harbormaster. Frank O'Hara. RhR

To the hard-working miner whose dangers are great. The Hard-working Miner. *Unknown.* AmFP

To the Heart. Tadeusz Rozewicz, *tr. fr. Polish by* Victor Contoski. POL

To the Holy Spirit. Yvor Winters. PiAm; VGW

To the Humpback Whales. Harold J. Morowitz. RhR

To the Immortal Memory and Friendship of That Noble Pair, Sir Lucius Cary and Sir Henry Morison. Ben Jonson. NOBE; OAEL-1; PAIC
Noble Nature, The, *sel.* VoPo
("It is not growing like a tree.") CABA (1972 ed.); HeIP; SoSe
(Lily of a Day, A.) PCOP

To the Jews. Blake. *Fr.* Jerusalem MBPR

To the Jews in Poland. Jozef Wittlin, *tr. fr. Polish by* Isaac Komem. VWA

To the King, at His Entrance into Saxham: By Master John Crofts. Thomas Carew. CaPo

To the King, upon His Coming with His Army into the West. Robert Herrick. CaPo

To the King, upon His Majesty's Happy Return, *sel.* Edmund Waller.
"Rising sun complies with our weak sight, The." SCP-2

To the King's Most Excellent Majesty. Phillis Wheatley. TAP

To the Ladies. Mary Lee, Lady Chudleigh. WPE

To the Ladies Who Saw Me Crown'd. Keats. MBPR

To the Lady-Bird. Caroline Anne Bowles. PPM

To the Lady in the Chemisette with Black Buttons. Nathaniel Parker Willis. OBAL

To the Lady May. Aurelian Townsend. GBL

To the Lady Portrayed by Margaret Dumont. John Hollander. OBAL
(For the Passing of Groucho's Pursuer.) PoA

To the Lady Radegunde, with Violets. Venantius Fortunatus, *tr. fr. Latin by* Helen Waddell. NAWM-1

To the Lairds o' Convention 'twas Claverhouse spoke. *See* To the Lords o' Convention...

To the Lawyer from His Only Lately Neglected Tort. Carol Stager. PoW

To the legion of the lost ones, to the cohort of the damned. Gentlemen-Rankers. Kipling. BTTM

To the Lord Chancellor. Shelley. MBPR

To the Lord General Cromwell, May 1652. Milton. CABA (1972 ed.); Epi
(To Oliver Cromwell.) GBP

To the Lords [*or* Lairds] o' Convention 'twas Claverhouse [who] spoke. Bonnie Dundee. Sir Walter Scott. *Fr.* The Doom of Devergoil. BTTM; RDB

To the Man after the Harrow. Patrick Kavanagh. CIP

To the Man I Live With. Ann Menebroker. IHMS

To the Man-of-War Bird. Walt Whitman. BoAnP; EcS

To the Man Who Sidled Up to Me and Asked: "How Long You in fer, Buddy?" Etheridge Knight. NeAC

To the Marquis of Graham on His Marriage. *Unknown.* OBSV

To the Memory of Lord Halifax, *sel.* Ambrose Philips.
"Weeping o'er the sacred urn." FaBoCo

To the Memory of Mr. Oldham. Dryden. CABA (1972 ed.); EBEV; HAP; HeIP; InPK; InPS; NIL; NOBE; OAEL-1; PAIC; PPoe; PPP; Prf

To the Memory of My Beloved, the Author, Mr. William Shakespeare, and What He Hath Left Us. Ben Jonson. CABA (1972 ed.); HAP; HeIP; ILP (1975 ed.); OAEL-1; OBP
"I, therefore, will begin. Soul of the age!" *sel.* NOBE

To the Memory of the Brave Americans. Philip Freneau. EAP; ILP (1975 ed.)
(Eutaw Springs.) BTTM

To the Men of Kent. October, 1803. Wordsworth. MBPR

To the Men Who Hold the Line. W. F. Barron. SPo

To the Mercy Killers. Dudley Randall. DL

To the Minister Liu. Yü Hsüan-chi, *tr. fr. Chinese by* Geoffrey Waters. BoWoP

To the Mocking Bird. Richard Henry Wilde. BoAnP

To the Moon. George Darley. Moon

To the Moon. Babette Deutsch. Moon

To the Moon. Goethe, *tr. fr. German by* John Frederick Nims. Moon

To the Moon. Shelley. MBPR; Moon; PBMP; PPP

To the Moon. Charlotte Smith. Moon

To the Moon. Yvor Winters. HeIP; MPA

To the Moon and Back. William Plomer. Moon

To the Most Excellent and Learned Shepheard Collin Cloute. William Smith. Chloris: Dedication. AAS

To the Most Fair and Lovely Mistress Anne Soame, Now Lady Abdie [*or* Abdy]. Robert Herrick. CaPo; NOBE

To the Most Virtuous Mistress Pot, Who Many Times Entertained Him. Robert Herrick. CaPo

To the Mother from Scarsdale Who Asked about Publishing Her Daughter's Poems. Madeline Bass. WBN

To the much-tossed Ulysses, never done. Ulysses. Robert Graves. CMoP (1970 ed.); FaBoTw (1975 ed.); NoAM

To the Muse. Robert Louis Stevenson. EBEV

To the Muse. James Wright. NNaP

To the Muses. Blake. HAP; HeIP; LAuP; MBPR; NOBE; OAEL-2; STS

To the Museums. Isidor Schneider. SPT

To the New Annex to the Detroit County Jail. Richard W. Thomas. PoBA

To the New Year. Thomas Carew. CaPo

To the Nightingale. Samuel Taylor Coleridge. MBPR

To the Nightingale. Countess of Winchilsea. PAIC; SBG; WPE

To the Nile. Keats. MBPR

To the Noble Sir Francis Drake. Thomas Beedome. SCP-2

To the Noblest and Best of Ladies [*or* Ladyes], the Countess of Denbigh. Richard Crashaw. MetP
(Letter to the Countess of Denbigh against Irresolution and Delay in Matters of Religion, A.) BoReV
"Astonished nymphs their flood's strange fate deplore, The." *sel.* OBP

To the north-east/ is the park of Mousseaux. Found Poem with Grafts 1866. Christopher Middleton. TwMBP

To the ocean now I fly. The Spirit Epiloguizes. Milton. *Fr.* Comus. NOBE

To the One God. *Tr. fr. Sanskrit by* Raimundo Panikkar. *Fr.* Vedic Hymns. ILwL

To the Other Side. T. Alan Broughton. FAF

To the Pay Toilet. Marge Piercy. GP

To the pines, to the pines. *Unknown.* WTO

To the Pious Memory of the Accomplished Young Lady Mrs. Anne Killigrew. Dryden. ILP (1975 ed.); OAEL-1; SCP-1

To the Postmaster General. Peter Redgrove. AMV-81

To the President Crossing the Potomac. Grace Cavalieri. WasP

To the Queen ("O loyal to the royal in thyself"). Tennyson. Idylls of the King: Dedication. VLP

To the Queen of Hearts goes the Ace of Sorrow. The Queen of Hearts. *Unknown.* FSW

To the Reader. Baudelaire, *tr. fr. French by* Roy Campbell. GrRo

To the Reader. Edgar Bowers. PiAm

To the Reader. J. V. Cunningham. NoAM

To the Reader. Robert Hayman. NIL

To the Reader. Denise Levertov. VGW

To the Reader of Master William Davenant's Play, The Wits. Thomas Carew. CaPo

To the Reader of These Sonnets. Michael Drayton. Idea, *introd.* AAS; ESo

To the Republicans of North America. Shelley. MBPR

To the Respective Judges. *Unknown.* APAS

To the Rev. F. D. Maurice. Tennyson. VLP

To the Rev. Mr. Powell. Christopher Smart. OBW

To the Reverend Shade of His Religious Father. Robert Herrick. CaPo

To the Rev. W. L. Bowles, 2 *versions.* Samuel Taylor Coleridge. MBPR

To the Right Hon. Henry Pelham. Edward Moore. OBSV

To the Rt. Hon. the Lady C. Tufton. Countess of Winchilsea. SBG

To the Right Honourable the Lord High Treasurer. Ben Jonson. SCP-1

To the Right Honourable William, Earl of Dartmouth. Phillis Wheatley. SBG
  "Should you, my lord, while you pursue my song," *sel.* BPo

To the River Duddon. Norman Nicholson. PES

To the River Itchin, near Winton. William Lisle Bowles. OAEL-2

To the Rose. Robert Herrick. IP

To the Rose upon the Rood of Time. W. B. Yeats. ILP (1975 ed.); NoAM; VLP

To the Sad Moon. Sir Philip Sidney. *See* Astrophel and Stella, Sonnets, XXXI.

To the Same. Ben Jonson. OAEL-1
  ("Kiss me, sweet; the wary lover.") BiP; OBVE

To the Same Flower. Wordsworth. MBPR

To the Sea. *Unknown, tr. fr. Anglo-Saxon by* Burton Raffel. *Fr.* Beowulf. OBP

To the Skylark. Wordsworth. *See* To a Skylark.

To the Small Celandine. Wordsworth. MBPR; PCOP

To the Snake. Denise Levertov. NMM; PoA; Psy; SFF

To the Snipe. John Clare. Epi

To the Sour Reader. Robert Herrick. ILP (1975 ed.)

To the Spirit of Carlos Gardel. Victor Hernández Cruz. SA

To the State of Love; or, The Senses' Festival. John Cleveland. PeD; SCP-2

To the Statue. May Swenson. GOA; NYP

To the Stolen Children. Robert Hahn. AAN

To the Stone-Cutters. Robinson Jeffers. ILP (1975 ed.); LFH; MPA; NIL; NOBA; PiAm

To the suburban house you return again. Portrait of a Marriage. Dannie Abse. NoAM

To the Sun. Ramon Fernandez, *tr. fr. Spanish by* Darrell Gray. EC

To the Swallow. William Cowper, *after the Greek of* Euenus. OBVE

To the Terrestrial Globe. W. S. Gilbert. FaBoNo

To the Thoughtful Reader. William Meredith. NoAM

To the Trade. James Neugass. SPT

To the Tune of the Coventry Carol. Stevie Smith. FaBoTw (1975 ed.)

To the Tune of "Ye Commons and Peers Pray Lend Me Your Ears." *Unknown.* APAS

To the Tune "Red Embroidered Shoes." Huang O, *tr. fr. Chinese by* Kenneth Rexroth *and* Ling Chung. PBWP

To the Tune "Soaring Clouds." Huang O, *tr. fr. Chinese by* Kenneth Rexroth *and* Ling Chung. PBWP
  ("You held my lotus blossom.") BoWoP

To the Tune "The River Is Red." Ch'iu Chin, *tr. fr. Chinese by* Kenneth Rexroth *and* Ling Chung. PBWP
  ("How many wise men and heroes.") BoWoP

To the University of Cambridge, in New-England. Phillis Wheatley. SBG; TAP

To the Unknown God. Friedrich Nietzsche, *tr. fr. German.* ILwL

To the Upright. Stephen Dunn. NVAP

To the Veterans of the Abraham Lincoln Brigade. Genevieve Taggard. OFD

To the Victor. William Ellery Leonard. PPM

To the Virginian Voyage. Michael Drayton. Epi; HAP; ILP (1975 ed.); NOBE

To the Virgins, to Make Much of Time. Robert Herrick. AnMo; BoLoP; CABA (1972 ed.); CaPo; FF; GBL; HAP; HeIP; ILP (1975 ed.); InPK; InPS; IPWM; LFH; NIL; NOBE; OAEL-1; OLR; PAIC; PBMP; PPoe; SFF; SoSe; SpRo
  (Counsel to Girls, *st.* 1) AKE

To the Water Nymphs, Drinking at the Fountain. Robert Herrick. CaPo; ILP (1975 ed.)

To the Western Wind. Robert Herrick. CaPo

To the Western World. Louis Simpson. ConAP; CoPAm; GOA; NOBA; TAP

To the White Critics. Carolyn M. Rodgers. SA

To the White Fiends. Claude McKay. PoBA

To the Wife of a Sick Friend. Edna St. Vincent Millay. SBG

To the Willow Tree. Robert Herrick. CaPo

To the Woodville Depot. D. C. Berry. AAN

To the Work, *with music.* Fanny Crosby. BLSH

To the young man I would say. I'm Older than You, Please Listen. A. R. D. Fairburn. ATNZ

To the Young Poets, Except Children, Who Haven't Earned the Title. James Humphrey. FoP

To Thee, Eternal Soul, Be Praise, *with music.* Richard W. Gilder. AH

To thee, fair freedom! I retire. Written at an Inn at Henley. William Shenstone. NOBE

To Thee, O God, *with music.* Abiel Holmes. AH

To Thee, O God, the Shepherd Kings, *with music.* John G. C. Brainard. AH

To thee obeyeth all the East as far as Ganges goes. Ovid, *tr. by* Arthur Golding. *Fr.* Metamorphoses, IV. OBVE

To Thee the Tuneful Anthem Soars, *with music.* Mather Byles. AH

To Thee, Then, Let All Beings Bend, *with music.* Nathaniel Evans. AH

To Their Excellencies the Lords Justices of Ireland, the Humble Petition of Frances Harris. Swift. ILP (1975 ed.)
  (Humble Petition of Frances Harris, The.) Epi

To them who crossed the flood. Inscription for Marye's Heights, Fredericksburg. Herman Melville. UnPo (1976 ed.)

To Theodora. *Unknown.* OxBChV

To Theon from His Son Theon. C. A. Trypanis. NCSH

To these whom death again did wed. An Epitaph upon Husband and Wife Who Died and Were Buried Together. Richard Crashaw. EBEV; FaBoEE; ILP (1975 ed.); NIL; NOBE

To Thine Eternal Arms, O God, *with music.* Thomas Wentworth Higginson. AH

To think to know the country and not know. A Hillside Thaw. Robert Frost. CMoP (1970 ed.); ExPo (1973 ed.)

To those who know the Lord I speak. Hymn. William Cowper. PAIC

To Those Who Sing America. Frank Marshall Davis. FB

To throw away the key and walk away. The Walking Tour. W. H. Auden. CMoP (1970 ed.)

To Tirzah. Blake. *Fr.* Songs of Experience. BoReV; MBPR; NOBE; OAEL-2; STS

To Toussaint L'Ouverture. Wordsworth. InPK; MBPR; NOBE; OBP; PBMP; PPP

To true roses uplifted on the bilious tide of evening. To Redouté. John Ashbery. PoA

To Trust. Antonia Pozzi, *tr. fr. Italian by* Lynne Lawner. PBWP

To Turn Back. John Haines. ConAP

To Tzu-an. Yü Hsüan-chi, *tr. fr. Chinese by* Geoffrey Waters. BoWoP

To Understand/ each other: anything. Their Attitudes Differ. Margaret Atwood. Psy

To V. S. Christopher Brennan. MAuV

To Venus. Horace, *tr. fr. Latin by* Ben Jonson. Odes, IV, 1. OBVE

To Vesta. Thomas Middleton. Moon

To Vietnam. Charlie Cobb. PoBA

To Vineyarders in cold Korea. Pinkletinks. Grace Elisabeth Allen. ECBV

To Violet. Basil Bunting. PoA

To Violets. Robert Herrick. CaPo

To Virgil. Tennyson. OAEL-2

To Virgins. Robert Herrick. CaPo

To Vulcan. Robert Herrick. CaPo

To WCW. Alice Notley. FiCh

To W. C. W. M. D. Alfred Kreymborg. PoA

To W. R. W. E. Henley. *See* Madam Life's a Piece in Bloom.

To W. T. Scott. John Ciardi. NowV

To wade the Jordan, and not to believe! In Jerusalem. Elisavietta Ritchie. AATT

To Waken an Old Lady. William Carlos Williams. HAP; InPK; PSN

To walk abroad is, not with eyes. Walking. Thomas Traherne. EBEV

To Walk on Hills. Robert Graves. UsP

To Walt Whitman in America. Swinburne. VLP

To watch the tipsy cripples on the beach. After Tennyson. Edward Lear. FaBoNo

To western woods, and lonely plains. On the Emigration to America. Philip Freneau. GOA; PiAm; TAP

To what a cumbersome unwieldiness. Love's Diet. John Donne. ILP (1975 ed.)

To what intent or purpose was Man made. As Concerning Man. Alexander Radcliffe. OBSV

To what purpose, April, do you return again? Spring. Edna St. Vincent Millay. BoWoP; BuTh

To What Strangers, What Welcome. J. V. Cunningham. NoAM Sels.
   "Half hour for coffee, and at night, A," X. PiAm
   "Identity, that spectator," XV. PiAm
   "Innocent to innocent," IX. PiAm
   "Night is still, The. The unfailing surf," VIII. PiAm
   (Miramar Beach.) PoA

To Whistler, American. Ezra Pound. PoA

To whom I owe the leaping delight. A Dedication to My Wife. T. S. Eliot. BoLoP; FF

To Whom It May Concern. Anne Sadowski. SES

To whom none ever said scat. Epitaph for Bathsheba. Whittier. PCat

To whom now, Pyrrha, art thou kind? Catullus, *tr. by* Abraham Cowley. Odes, I, 5. OBVE

To William Hayley. Blake. FaBoCo
   (To H.) FF
   (To Hayley.) FaBoEE

To William Roe. Ben Jonson. OAEL-1

To William (Whom We Have Missed.) P. G. Wodehouse. NOBL

To William Wordsworth. Samuel Taylor Coleridge. MBPR; OAEL-2

To William Wordsworth from Virginia. Julia Randall. CSP; NMM; WPE

To Wilt Chamberlain. Tom Meschery. SPo

To win our fight and our demands. The Picket Line Song. *Unknown.* FSW

To win the love of women one should first discover. Kenneth Koch. The Art of Love, Pt. I. NNaP

To Winter. Blake. MBPR

To Women, as Far as I'm Concerned. D. H. Lawrence. InPS; WeW

To Wordsworth. John Clare. OAEL-2

To Wordsworth. Walter Savage Landor. OAEL-2

To Wordsworth. Shelley. MBPR

To write in verse has been my pleasing choice. To the Rt. Hon. the Lady C. Tufton. Countess of Winchilsea. SBG

To X. Tom Scott. SLP

To Xanadu, Which Is Beth Shaul. Arye Sivan, *tr. fr. Hebrew by* Anthony Rudolf *and* Natan Zach. VWA

To You. Frank Horne. *Fr.* Letters Found near a Suicide. BPo

To You. Kenneth Koch. CAPP

To You. Walt Whitman. BiP

To You Building the New House. Nelly Sachs, *tr. fr. German by* Keith Bosley. VWA

To you I'll sing a good old song. Ye Ancient Yuba Miner of the Days of '49. Samuel C. Upham. AIW

To you, morning and evening. Prayers to Liberty. Anwar Shaul, *tr. by* Yoffee Berkovitz. VWA

To you [*or* yow], my purse [*or* purs], and to none [*or* noon] other wight. The Complaint of Chaucer to His Purse. Chaucer. CABA (1972 ed.); ILP (1975 ed.); InPK; OAEL-1; OxBM; PAIC; PPoD

To You on the Broken Iceberg. Tess Gallagher. GP

To you, then, tenants of life's middle state. William Cowper. *Fr.* Tirocinium; or, A Review of Schools. OBSV

To you this little village is dear as the moon. Dear as the Moon. *Gond Oral Tradition, tr. by* V. Elwin *and* S. Hivale. WTO

To you, whose depth of soul measures the height. George Chapman. *Fr.* To My Admired and Soul-loved Friend, Master of All Essentials and True Knowledge, Mr. Harriots. SCP-2

To your left is the Gettysburg Address engraved on a medalion. Lecture before a Lecture on Pushkin. George M. Young, Jr. FAF

To Your Question. Duane Niatum. CDW

To youths, who hurry thus away. On a Painted Woman. Shelley. FaBoCo

Toad. John Cotton. BoAnP

Toad, The. Gerald Locklin. GP

Toad and the Frog, The. *Unknown.* PCOP

Toad-Eater, The. Burns. POL

Toad School. Merle Meeter. AATT

Toad Suck Ferry. H. R. Stoneback. TAT

Toad the power mower caught, A. The Death of a Toad. Richard Wilbur. AnMo; BiP; CABA (1972 ed.); CMoP (1970 ed.); NoAM; PoA; PoIA

Toads. Philip Larkin. CMoP (1970 ed.); ExPo (1973 ed.); NoAM; NOBL; OxBTC; SoSe (1977 ed.)

Toads Revisited. Philip Larkin. CMoP (1970 ed.); NOBL; SoSe (1977 ed.)

Toadstool comes up in a night, A. A Lesson. Christina Rossetti. PCOP

Toadstool Wood, The. James Reeves. DuDa

Toast, A. Charles Stetler. GP

Tobacco. Philip Freneau. TAP

Tobacco. Robert Harris. CAAP; GAS

Tobacco, sels. Janet Kauffman.
  Cultivating. TC
  Preface: Topping. TC
  Steamer on the Seedbed. TC
  Taking Down. TC

Tobacco is a filthy weed. Unknown. FaBoEE

Tobacco Men. James Applewhite. CSP

Tobacconist of Eighth Street, The. Richard Eberhart. NYP

Toccata of Galuppi's, A. Robert Browning. HAP; LFH; NOBE; OAEL-2; PAIC; TT

To-Day. Mary Frances Butts. CTV

Today. Langston Hughes. VGW

Today. Liz Lochhead. MS; SLP

Today. Richard Shelton. MPA

Today. Jones Very. TAP

Today. Margaret Walker. FB

Today! Ella Wheeler Wilcox. SoSe

Today/ 5000 miles across the waters. Exhortation. Rafael Jesús González. CPA

Today/ I am one-thousand, nine-hundred and seventy-five years old. Happy Birthday America. Pancho Aguila. NW

Today/ I am 24. January 3, 1970. Mae Jackson. PoBA

Today/ I lost my temper. For Witches. Susan Sutheim. NMM

Today/ the clocks strike. Lever de Rideau. Mary Ursula Bethell. ATNZ

Today,/ there came a breeze thin as the needle of a syringe. J. Kitchener Davies, tr. by Joseph P. Clancy. Fr. The Sound of the Wind That Is Blowing. OBW

Today, a bush is a bush to me. The Immigrant. David Hilton. AcAn

Today, a candle in a glass. Poem for My Grandfather. A. C. Jacobs. VWA

Today a silver coffin guards St. Agnes'. Catacombs. István Vas, tr. by Jascha Kessler. VWA

To-day, all day, I rode upon the Down. St. Valentine's Day. Wilfrid Scawen Blunt. Fr. The Love Sonnets of Proteus. LoAS

Today as I passed through the market-place. A Sonnet Sequence, VIII. Robert Hillyer. TH

Today as well there seems to be something unfilled. A Transparent Autumn. Sadamu Fujiwara, tr. by Ichiro Kono and Rikutaro Fukuda. IPWM

Today at the Gateway. Butter. Tom Schmidt. NeAC

Today, autumn. The Fire of Despair Has Been Our Saviour. Robert Bly. CoPAm

Today beneath Benignant Skies, with music. Denis Wortman. AH

Today between skirmishes. For Alan Blanchard. John Oliver Simon. NeAC

Today Blackness. For Muh' Dear. Carolyn M. Rodgers. CNA

To-day, Cheng, I touched your face. The Prisoner. Keith Douglas. PSN

Today, Day of the Dead, procession of shadows. Pentachromatic. Julia de Burgos, tr. by Julio Marzán. InW

Today for the first time. A New Dress. Rachel Korn, tr. by Ruth Whitman. VWA

Today has it all, sunshine. Gwyn Williams. Fr. Aspects of Now. OBW

Today I am walking alone in a bare place. Late November in a Field. James Wright. CAPP; NNaP

Today I get this letter from you and the sun. You (III). Tom Clark. EAS

Today I have seen all I wish. At the Water Zoo. E. V. Knox. BoAnP

To-Day I Leave Mrs. Brown's Lodgings. Sir Walter Scott. FaBoEE

Today I lost my temper. Unknown. CTV

Today I love you so much I mistrust you. Fish and Swimmers and Lonely Birds Sweep Past Us. Mei Berssenbrugge. NW; SA

Today I rejoice; I even treat myself kindly. Uncovering. Cynthia MacDonald. UsP

Today I saw a picture of the cancer cells. The Cancer Cells. Richard Eberhart. HAP

Today I saw a place no one has seen. Iron Heaven. Betti Alver, tr. by Willis Barnstone and Felix Oinas. BoWoP

Today I saw a woman plowing a furrow. Sister. Gabriela Mistral, tr. by Langston Hughes. BoWoP

Today I saw a woman wrapped in rags. At the Slackening of the Tide. James Wright. CABA (1972 ed.); UnPo (1976 ed.); VGW

To-day I think. Digging. Edward Thomas. FSFS; OxBTC

Today I trade my last unwise. How It Goes On. Maxine W. Kumin. FiCP

Today I want/ everything. The Greed Song. Albert Goldbarth. AMV-80

Today I was awakened by the moon. Remembering Lutsky. Rayzel Zychlinska, tr. by Marc Kaminsky. VWA

Today I was pleased by the image. Tune. Carl Rakosi. GP

Today I'll draw/ A line in the dust. Adam's Death. Gabriel Levin. VWA

Today I'll remember forever and ever. Counting. Harry Behn. ECBV

Today in Peru, this first day of summer. Pastoral. Lawrence Raab. AmPA

Today Is a Day of Great Joy Victor Hernandez Cruz. TPo; WIF

Today is forest green. Forest Green. Thulani Nkabinde. NW

Today is our 16th anniversary. Chicken Unlimited. Peter Meinke. AAN

Today is the third day. July 12. Simon J. Ortiz. NW

To-day my hands have been flattered. Lingerie. Hazel Hall. WPW

Today my mother and sisters. They've Come. Alfonsina Storni, tr. by Aliki and Willis Barnstone. BoWoP

Today my mother's letter said. Not to March. Kris Hackleman. AMV-80

Today on the folly-made desert. Now What Good That Do? H. H. Lewis. SPT

Today on the lip of a bowl in the backyard. The Caterpillar. Miller Williams. CoPAm

Today out of the window. The Trembling of the Veil. Allen Ginsberg. TT

Today she parades her shape like swellings of song. Portrait of a Pregnant Woman. Bobi Jones, tr. by Joseph P. Clancy. OBW

Today, spading out thistles. Things to Work For. Jim Mulac. AcAn

Today, the angels are all writing postcards. Saying One Thing. Robert Long. AMV-81

Today the birds are singing and. Pray in May. James J. Metcalfe. SoSe

Today, the first dead leaf in the hall. A Dead Leaf. Howard Moss. NYP

Today the jailbird maple in the yard. For My Son on the Highways of His Mind. Maxine W. Kumin. CoPAm; MAT

Today the leaves cry, hanging on branches swept by wind. The Course of a Particular. Wallace Stevens. PPoe

To-day the lot caved in upon me. Page from a Diary. Desmond O'Grady. NoAM

To-day the woods are trembling through and through. Corn. Sidney Lanier. AmVN

Today the world unwrapped itself again. Summer. Moishe Kulbak, *tr. by* Ruth Whitman. VWA

Today there are holes in/ the air. Parole Denial. J. Charles Green. DNGG

Today They Are Roasting Rocky Norse. Gary Gildner. PCho

Today they cut down the oak. The Stump. Donald Hall. MiP

To-day we have naming of parts. Yesterday. Naming of Parts. Henry Reed. Lessons of the War, I. ExPo (1973 ed.); FF; HeIP; HoPM (1975 ed.); ILP (1975 ed.); InPK; InPS; MPo; NOBE; OxBTC; PoIA; PPoD; SoS; SoSe; UnPo (1976 ed.); UsP; VoPo; WIF

Today we saw a tiger. The Tiger. Robert Creeley. GP

Today We've Moved. Jim Harrison. HeS

Todd. Stewart Conn. MS

Tod's Hole, The. *Unknown.* GBP

Toe upon [*or* after] toe, a snowing flesh. Nude Descending a Staircase. X. J. Kennedy. ConAP; HeIP; HoPM (1975 ed.); NIL; PoA; POL; PPoD; WIF

Toe'osh: A Laguna Coyote Story. Leslie Silko. CDW; NW; VoR

Toffee-Slab. Brian Lee. FPB

Together. Maxine W. Kumin. BoWoP; NMM; WBN

Together we look. Finding a Dead Mole with My Sons. Joseph Bruchac. EC

Tohub. Jakov van Hoddis, *tr. fr. German by* Charles Guenther. VWA

Toilet, The. Pope. *Fr.* The Rape of the Lock, I. NOBE (Belinda's Morning.) ExPo (1973 ed.)

Token, A. Robert Creeley. VGW

Token, The. F. T. Prince. FaBoTw (1975 ed.); OxBTC

Token of Attachment, A. J. Adair Strawson. TDH

Tokens. William Barnes. VLP

Tokens of Love, The ("I had four brothers over the sea"). *Unknown.* GBP

Tokens of Love, The ("I have a yong suster"). *Unknown. See* I Have a Young Sister.

Tokyo West. Alfred Corn. NYP

Told me and told me. Where It's At. Carol Bergé. MMD

Tolerance of Crows, The. Charles Donnelly. CIP

Toll for the brave. On the Loss of the *Royal George.* William Cowper. EBEV; FaPoR; NOBE

Toll no bell for me, dear Father, dear Mother. The Changeling. Charlotte Mew. SoSe

Toll of the Desert, The. Arthur W. Monroe. BPAW

Tollund Man, The. Seamus Heaney. BIrV; EBEV; HeHu

Tolusa. Luís Omar Salinas. CPA

Tom Ball's Barn. Ted Kooser. GP

Tom Brown. *Unknown.* FSW

Tom done buck and Bill won't pull. Whoa Back, Buck. Leadbelly (Huddie Ledbetter). FSW

Tom Dooley. *Unknown.* AmFP; BLSo, *with music;* FSW; GSB, *with music*

Tom—garlanded with squat and surly steel. Tom's Garland: Upon the Unemployed. Gerard Manley Hopkins. VLP

Tom, He Was a Piper's Son. *Unknown.* GBP; MG

Tom Jones's Plum Tree. *Unknown.* AmFP

Tom Long. *Unknown.* EBEV

Tom Matte. Ogden Nash. SPo

Tom Mooney Walks at Midnight. Michael Gold. SPT

Tom o'Bedlam ("From the hag and hungry goblin"). *Unknown. See* Tom o' Bedlam's Song.

Tom o' Bedlam ("The moon's my constant mistress"). *Unknown.* PoPle

Tom o' Bedlam among the Sunflowers. Thomas James. HeS

Tom o' Bedlam's Song. *Unknown.* Moon; OBP
(Loving Mad Tom.) HAP; NOBE; WeW
(Tom o'Bedlam.) EBEV; OAEL-1

Tom on the Beach. George Bruce. MS

Tom O'Roughley. W. B. Yeats. CMoP (1970 ed.)

"Tom Pearse [*or* Pearce], Tom Pearse, lend me your gray mare." Widdecombe [*or* Widdicombe] Fair. *Unknown.* DuDr; GSB; PH

Tom Sucklebat, in dressing-gown, without his teeth. An Administrator. Geoffrey Grigson. FaBoEE

Tom Thumb's Epitaph. *Unknown.* DuDr

Tom Tiler; or, The Nurse. *Unknown.* APAS

Tom told his dog called Tim to beg. Tom's Little Dog. Walter de la Mare. GDP

Tom-tom, c'est moi. The blue guitar. Wallace Stevens. The Man with the Blue Guitar, XII. CMoP (1970 ed.)

Tom, Tom, the piper's son. Mother Goose. MG

Tom Wedgewood Tells. Brian W. Aldiss. NOBL

Tomb. David Semah, *tr. fr.* Arabic by Yoffee Berkovitz. VWA

Tomb of an Ancestor. Allen Curnow. ATNZ

Tomb of Edgar Poe, The. Stéphane Mallarmé, *tr. fr. French.* NAWM-2, 2 *versions, tr. by* Roger Fry *and by the author*

Tomb of Heracles, The. James McAuley. *Fr.* The Hero and the Hydra. MAuV

Tomb of Lieutenant John Learmonth, A. I. F., The. J. S. Manifold. GAS; MAuV

Tomb of the Kings, The. Anne Hébert, *tr. fr. French.* BoWoP, *tr. by* Aliki *and* Willis Barnstone; PBWP, *tr. by* Kathleen Weaver

Tomb of Time, The. Albert Howard Carter. AATT

Tombs of the Covenanters nod together. The Cemetery near Burns' Cottage. Iain Crichton Smith. MS

Tombstone told when she died, The. Dylan Thomas. OxBTC

Tombstone with Cherubim. Horace Gregory. TPo

Tom-Cat, The. Don Marquis. BoAnP; SS

Tom Cat Blues. *Unknown.* FSW

Tommy. Kipling. BTTM; CABA (1972 ed.); EBEV; FaPoR; OxBTC

Tommy's Gone to Hilo. *Unknown.* FSW

To-morowe ye shall on hunting fare. Diversions for an Unhappy Princess. *Unknown. Fr.* The Squyer of Lowe Degre. OxBM

Tomorrow. Kenneth Fearing. CMoP (1970 ed.)

To-Morrow. Lope de Vega, *tr. fr. Spanish by* Longfellow. PIM

Tomorrow afternoon. The Tragedy of Action. Dan Gerber. HeS

Tomorrow, and Tomorrow, and Tomorrow. Shakespeare. *Fr.* Macbeth, V, v. FF; TPo

Tomorrow, at Daybreak. Victor Hugo, *tr. fr. French by* Mary Ann Caws. NAWM-2

Tomorrow dawn that gathers up the night. The Tramp. Rayne Mackinnon. MIS

Tomorrow Is Saint Valentine's Day. Shakespeare. *Fr.* Hamlet, IV, v. CC; CTV; LCL; OFD; WIF

Tomorrow, Julia, I betimes must rise. The Perfume. Robert Herrick. CaPo

Tomorrow let loveless, let lover tomorrow make love. The Vigil of Venus. *Unknown, tr. by* Allen Tate. GBL

"Tomorrow morn I'll be sixteen, and Billy Grimes the rover." Billy Grimes. *Unknown.* AmFP

Tomorrow morning, some poet will wake up. Modern Poetry. Anita Skeen. IHMS

Tomorrow the Heroes. A. B. Spellman. CNA; PoBA

To-morrow you will live, you always cry. Martial, *tr. fr. Latin by* Abraham Cowley. FaBoEE; NIL; OBVE

Tomorrows. James Merrill. OBAL

To-Morrow's the Fair. *Unknown.* CC; GBP

Tom's Angel. Walter de la Mare. AIW

Tom's Garland: Upon the Unemployed. Gerard Manley Hopkins. VLP

Tom's Little Dog. Walter de la Mare. GDP

Tom's sickness did his morals mend. Epigram. Matthew Prior. FaBoEE

Tongue, never cease to sing Fidessae's praise. Bartholomew Griffin. Fidessa, More Chaste than Kind, XXXI. ESo

Tongue-Twister. *Unknown. See* Theophilus Thistledown.

Tongues. Sharon Berg. AMV-80

Tongues of Fire. Jorge Plescoff, *tr. fr. Spanish by* Yishai Tobin. VWA

Tonight. Iain Crichton Smith. SLP

To-Night. Edward Thomas. PoPle

Tonight,/ a cricket sings in the dark grass. 9/3/76. Laban Chang. PHC

Tonight/ the moon shines like a new ax. Everything Must Go. Tom Crawford. NVAP

Tonight a blackout. Twenty years ago. Christmas Eve under Hooker's Statue. Robert Lowell. CAPP; ConAP; FF; LFH; PiAm

Tonight, at Least, My Sinner. *Gond Oral Tradition, tr. by* V. Elwin *and* S. Hivale. WTO

Tonight at Noon. Adrian Henri. MPo

Tonight Everyone in the World Is Dreaming the Same Dream. Susan Litwack. VWA

Tonight, grave sir, both my poor house and I. Inviting a Friend to Supper. Ben Jonson, *after* Martial. BiP; ILP (1975 ed.); NIL; NOBE; OAEL-1; PPP; TVS

Tonight I am one of a number. Before the Frost. Harley Elliott. HeS

Tonight I can write the saddest line. Pablo Neruda, *tr. fr. Spanish by* W. S. Merwin. BoLoP; OLR

Tonight I could die as easily as the grass. In the Soul Hour. Robert Mezey. AmPA

Tonight I find the/ Calendar with its days. Angel. Gary Soto. AMV-80

Tonight I have a date. A Serenade for Two Poplars. Esther Raab, *tr. by* Robert Friend *and* Shimon Sandbank. VWA

Tonight I have taken all that I was. Rhyme of the Dead Self. A. R. D. Fairburn. ATNZ

Tonight I looked at the pale northern sky. Back. Robert Mezey. AmPA

Tonight I sat on my back porch. Eugene Lesser. *Fr.* Sometimes Life Is Not a Literary Experience. OSP

Tonight I saw so many windows. Little Political Poem. Edward Hirsch. AMV-81

Tonight I walk straight into it. The Killing. Arthur Smith. AAN

Tonight I watch my father's fair. Two Postures beside a Fire. James Wright. BrS; GP

Tonight I'll meet you: yes, tonight. I know. A Letter. Burns Singer. MS; SLP

Tonight in dark cabins and silver yards. Power of Women. Barbara Sobol. PoUp

Tonight in Fort Morgan. Anthropology in Fort Morgan, Colorado. Sam Hamod. TAT

Tonight in the pub I talked with Ernie Jones. Battlefields. Vernon Scannell. HeHu

Tonight is the night. Hallowe'en. Harry Behn. CC; IWK

Tonight I've watched. Sappho, *tr. fr. Greek by* Mary Barnard. Moon

Tonight, like every night, you see me here. In a Coffee Pot. Alfred Hayes. SPT

Tonight my children hunch. "It Out-Herods Herod. Pray You, Avoid It." Anthony Hecht. CoPAm; NCSH; NoAM; NOBA

Tonight Sally and I are making stuffed grapeleaves. Leaves. Sam Hamod. SA

Tonight, the barn is sitting under the rain. Exit, Pursued by a Bear. James Tipton. HeS; TC

Tonight the brittle trees. Cold. Glyn Hughes. LP

Tonight the City. R. L. Cook. AMV-81

Tonight the Famous Psychiatrist. Louis Simpson. SFF

Tonight the moon is high, to summon all. Elegy. William Bell. FaBoTw (1975 ed.)

Tonight the moths. Tyranny of Moths. Gerald Vizenor. VoR

Tonight the Sabbath dreams stalk. Sabbath. Rivka Fried. VWA

Tonight the spirit of an elder. Havdolah. Susan Litwack. VWA

To-night the winds began to rise. In Memoriam A. H. H., XV. Tennyson. BiP; FSFS; NOBE

To-night, to-night,/ The pillow fight. End of Term. *Unknown.* PoPle

Tonight we drive back late from talk and supper. Called For. Anthony Thwaite. HeHu

Tonight we sat,/ telly dead. Old Man. Alan J. Carr. AMV-80

Tonight When You Leave. Gayle Elen Harvey. AMV-81

Tonight you are a hundred miles away. Tonight. Iain Crichton Smith. SLP

Tonight you broke into my dreams. For Anne, Who Doesn't Know. Gail Fox. IHMS

Tonite, thriller was. Beware: Do Not Read This Poem. Ishmael Reed. BPo; CNA; Epi; IPWM; NCSH; PoBA; WeW

Tonopah Bill was a desert rat who had traveled the gold. The Ballad of Tonopah Bill. *Unknown.* BPAW

Tonsilectomy. James W. Rivers. AMV-81

Tonto. Ronald Koertge. GP

Tony Get the Boys. D. L. Graham. PoBA

Tony O. Colin Francis. FaBoCo

Tony shot his Delia. Delia's Gone. Blind Blake (Blake Alphonso Higgs). FSW

Tony the Turtle. E. V. Rieu. ECBV; SO

Too Blue. Langston Hughes. SFF

Too Dark. Mark McCloskey. PoA

Too dense to have a door. The Haystack. Andrew Young. POL

Too elementary. Reply. Victoria McCabe. POL

Too green the springing April grass. Spring in New Hampshire. Claude McKay. BPo

Too green. Too green. Marijuana Patch on the State Hospital's Former Grounds. Nathan Whiting. HeS

Too happy time dissolves itself. Emily Dickinson. NOBA

Too Late. Rachel Korn, *tr. fr. Yiddish by* Seymour Mayne *and* Rivka Augenfeld. VWA

Too late for love, too late for joy. Bride Song. Christina Rossetti. *Fr.* The Prince's Progress. WPE

Too little/ has been said. The Door. Charles Tomlinson. PoA

Too long outside your door I have shivered. The Terrible Door. Harold Monro. BoLoP; FaBoTw (1975 ed.)

Too many fucking mosquitoes under the blazing sun. Sonnet. Ted Berrigan. CAAP

Too Many Miles of Sunlight between Us. Jack Myers. AMV-80

Too many of the dead, some I knew well. In the Backs. Frances Cornford. PES

Too many people scribbling on each others' tongues. Peace Prospect. Daniela Gioseffi. RiTi

Too Much. *Unknown.* TDH

Too much thought. Day-Dreamer. Louis Untermeyer, *after the German.* CTV

Too poor for a bribe, and too proud to importune. Sketch of His Own Character. Thomas Gray. LAuP

Too proud you are. Gladioli for My Mother. Harriet Bernstein. AMV-81

Too sad is the grief in my heart! Elegy for His Daughter Ellen. Goronwy Owen, *tr. by* Kenneth Jackson. OBW

"Too tame, too pretty," you said. At Staufen. Michael Hamburger. VWA

Too tight, it is running over. Fence Wire. James Dickey. VGW

Too tired and too fastidious for lies. Protestant Courts Catholic. James Simmons. IPM

Tooten Out Blues. *Unknown.* BluL

Toothless Satires. Joseph Hall. *See* Virgidemiarum.

Top people, The. Means Test. D. J. Enright. HeHu

Tops of the spruces here have always done, The. Jefferson Valley. John Hollander. PPP

Topsoil. Robert Morgan. CSP

Topsy-Turvy World. William Brighty Rands. ECBV; OxBChV

Torch of love dispels the gloom, The. Walter Savage Landor. GBL

Torn apart by us ever and again. Rainer Maria Rilke. *Fr.* Sonnets to Orpheus. ILwL

Torn between griefs, which grief shall I lament. Sophocles, *tr. by* Ezra Pound. *Fr.* Women of Trachis. OBVE

Torn into light, you woke wriggling. How Much Earth. Philip Levine. NNaP

Tornado. William Stafford. AnMo

Tornado Soup. A. K. Redwing. VoR

Tornado Warning. Karl Shapiro. MPA

Tornado Watch. Paul Shuttleworth. AMV-80

Toroi Bandi. *Mongol Oral Tradition, tr. by* C. R. Bawden. WTO

Torrent, A/ of cobalt bullets. Lacrimas or There Is a Need to Scream. K. Curtis Lyle. PoBA

Torso, The: Passages 18. Robert Duncan. GP

Tortoise, The. Cid Corman. InPK; VGW

Tortoise. Joanne de Longchamps. BoAnP

Tortoise Gallantry. D. H. Lawrence. CMoP (1970 ed.); NoAM

Tortoise Shout. D. H. Lawrence. NoAM

Tortoise-Shell. D. H. Lawrence. CMoP (1970 ed.); ExPo (1973 ed.); OAEL-2

Tortoiseshell Cat, The. Patrick Reginald Chalmers. BoAnP; PCat

Tory Pledges. Thomas Moore. FaBoCo; OBSV

Tory Poets, The: A Satire, *sel. At. to* Thomas Shadwell. "Shadwell and Settle are both fools to Bays." SCP-2

Toss me a kiss, and take your leave with laughter. No Madam Butterfly. Louise Hajek. AMV-80

Tossed in a troubled sea of griefs, I float. To Her in Absence: A Ship. Thomas Carew. CaPo

Tossing loneliness of many nights, The. Legende. Hart Crane. PSN

Total loss/ by physical severance. Injury to Insured. John Daniel. TwMBP

Total Revolution, A. Oscar Williams. WIF

Totem. Nissim Ezekiel. VWA

Totem. Léopold Sédar Senghor, *tr. fr. French by* Gerald Moore *and* Ulli Beier. BuTh

T'other eb'ning eb'ryting was still, Oh! babe. Mister Johnson. Ben Harney. OBAL

Tottel's Miscellany, *sel.* Richard Tottel. "Twixt nature and Pygmalion there might appear great strife." OAEL-1

Touch. Thom Gunn. CMoP (1970 ed.); LoAs; MPo; TPo

Touch. Erica Jong. RiTi

Touch. Octavio Paz, *tr. fr. Spanish by* Charles Tomlinson. BoLoP

Touch/ is what the eyes do, sometimes. From a Brother Dreaming in the Rye. James Cunningham. JB

Touch but thy lyre, my Harry, and I hear. To Master Henry Lawes, the Excellent Composer of Lyrics. Robert Herrick. CaPo

Touch it: it won't shrink like an eyeball. A Life. Sylvia Plath. NOBA; UsP

Touch my hand as though it were an old coin. Sailing in Crosslight. Anita Skeen. IHMS

Touch of cold in the autumn night, A. Autumn. T. E. Hulme. Moon; PAIC

Touch of Moonlight, The. Keith Wilson. FoP

Touch Tenderly. Helen Berryhill. TPo

Touch Thou Mine Eyes, *with music.* Marion Franklin Ham. AH

Touches me. Katherine. Paul F. Fericano. CPA

Touching. Katie Savage. PoUp

Touching books. For Gabriel. Laya Firestone. VWA

Touching me, you touch. The Wind. Charles Simic. NVAP

Touching the well-springs. Therapy. Patricia Ball. PMW

Touching, you said, is the last best thing. Eschatology. Heather Banks. PoUp

Touchstone. James Worley. AMV-80

Tough./ Precise./ You/ move/ like/ a cougar. Movement. Gary Lawless. FAF

Tough guy. Star of David. The Cabdriver's Smile. Denise Levertov. NYP

Tough Ones, The. Errol Miller. AMV-80

Toughest gal I ever did see. Kissie Lee. Margaret Walker. NMM

Toujours la Politesse. Ezra Pound, *after the Chinese.* OBVE

Toulouse Lautrec. Astrid Tollefsen, *tr. fr. Norwegian by* Nadia Christensen. PBWP

Tour, The. Katharine Edgar Cobey. PoUp

Tour 5. Robert Hayden. PPP

Tour of the Southwest, A. Edward Lueders. MPA

Touring the Hawkeye State. Gary Gildner. HeS

Touris', white man, wipin' his face. Song of the Banana Man. Evan Jones. MPo

Tourism. Lillie D. Chaffin. TAT

Tourist, The. Garret Keizer. AMV-81

Tourist came in from Orbitville, A. Southbound on the Freeway. May Swenson. BBGO; SoS

Tourist from Syracuse, The. Donald Justice. CoPAm

Tourist Guide: How You Can Tell for Sure When You're in South Dakota. Jim Heynen. GP; PoW

Tourist, spare the avid glance. The Attic Landscape. Herman Melville. NOBA; OBAL

Touristicism. John Batki. AcAn

Tourists arrive, swarming, The. Spring in Washington. James Den Boer. TAT

Tours. Stephen Shu Ning Liu. AMV-80

Toussaint, the most unhappy man of men! To Toussaint L'Ouverture. Wordsworth. InPK; MBPR; NOBE; OBP; PBMP; PPP

Toward. Ricardo Sanchez. NW

Toward Light. Maurice Lindsay. MS

Toward Myself. Leah Goldberg, *tr. fr. Hebrew by* Robert Friend. VWA

Toward the last in the morning she could not. Old Dog. William Stafford. BoAnP; GDP

Toward the sea turning my troubled eye. The Huge Leviathan. Spenser. *Fr.* Visions of the World's Vanity. EcS

Toward, toward, ever toward. Toward. Ricardo Sanchez. NW

Toward world's end, through the bare. The Magi. Louise Glück. PoA

Towards a City That Sings. June Jordan. NYP

Towards nightfall when the wind. Winter Mask. Allen Tate. Prf

Towards the evening of her splendid day. The Fragment. Hilaire Belloc. POL

Towards the Noel that morte saison. Villonaud for This Yule. Ezra Pound. PAIC

Towards the poem/ as towards. Projections for an Eagle Escaped in This City, March 1965. Nathaniel Tarn. TwMBP

Towards the Source, *sel.* Christopher Brennan.
"Yellow gas is fired from street to street, The." MAuV

T'owd pig's got mezzles an' she's deead, poor thing. The Dead Pig. *Unknown.* FaBoNo

Tower, The. Philip Booth. PAIC

Tower, The. Dan Pagis, *tr. fr. Hebrew by* Stephen Mitchell. VWA

Tower, The. W. B. Yeats. CMoP (1970 ed.); NoAM
"It is time that I wrote my will," III. STS

Tower of Babel, The. Nathaniel Crouch. OxBChV

Towery city and branchy between towers. Duns Scotus's Oxford. Gerard Manley Hopkins. EBEV; Epi; NoAM; OBP; PES; VLP

Town. Gary Soto. CPA; NW

Town against Gown at Oxford. Robert of Gloucester. *Fr.* Chronicle. OxBM

Town Betrayed, The. Edwin Muir. CMoP (1970 ed.)

Town Boy Yearning. Roger McDonald. FPA

Town Clerk's Views, The. John Betjeman. CMoP (1970 ed.)

Town Clinics. Margaret Gillies. PMW

Town does not exist, The. The Starry Night. Anne Sexton. ExPo (1973 ed.); NoAM

Town Dump, The. Howard Nemerov. BiP; CMoP (1970 ed.); ILP (1975 ed.); MAT; NIL

Town grew, as with the lime-pits, The. A History of the Father. Charles Buckmaster. CAAP

Town has tinged the country, The. And the stain. City Corruption. William Cowper. *Fr.* The Task, IV. NIL

Town I Left. Helen Sorrells. IHMS; PoW

Town I Was Born In, The. Yehuda Amichai, *tr. fr. Hebrew by* A. C. Jacobs. VWA

Town is tilted toward the stream, The. A Sunday Dreamer's Guide to Yarrow, Missouri. Jim Barnes. HeS

Town of Bricked Pathways, The. Roger McDonald. CAAP

Town of Hill, The. Donald Hall. FiCP; TAP

Town Owl. Laurie Lee. PB

Town Rat and the Country Rat, The. La Fontaine, *tr. fr. French by* Marianne Moore. NAWM-2
(City Rat and the Country Rat, The, *tr. by* Elizur Wright.) OBVE

Town remembers no such plenty, The. Lancashire Winter. Tony Connor. OxBTC

Town, the churchyard, and the setting sun, The. On Visiting the Tomb of Burns. Keats. MBPR; NIL

Towser Shall Be Tied Tonight, *parody. Unknown.* BoAnP

Toy, The. Cid Corman. GP

Toyland, *with music.* Glen MacDonough. BLSo; FSN

Toys, The. Coventry Patmore. *Fr.* The Unknown Eros, I, x. BoReV; EBEV; ILP (1975 ed.); PAIC; PIM; SoSe; VPC

Toys. Abraham Sutskever, *tr. fr. Yiddish by* Seymour Levitan. VWA

Traces. David Lehman. UsP

Tracing Back. Jane Mayhall. WBN

Track. Tomas Tranströmer, *tr. fr. Swedish by* Robert Bly. EAS

Track-lining Song. *Unknown.* AmFP

Track of a broad rattler, dragged over dust at dawn, The. The Catch. Brewster Ghiselin. HAP; MPA; PoW

Tracking. Virginia R. Terris. AAN

Tracking Rabbits: Night. Jim Barnes. CDW

Tracking the Sled, Christmas 1951. Jeanne Murray Walker. AMV-81

Trackless Deeps, The. Shelley. RhR

Tracks. Mei Berssenbrugge. NW

Tracks. Peter Cooley. HeS

Tracks. Brad Lee Shurmantine. AMV-81

Tracks in the snow. Photograph of the Back of My House. Del Marie Rogers. NPW

Tracks reached. Ode: Infinity. Ralph Storey. SES

Tract. William Carlos Williams. BiP; DL; FF; MiP; NIL; NoAM; NOBA; PPoD; TAP; TCP; VGW

Traded by my father in a drunken rage. Poem to a Mule, Dead Twenty Years. Guy Owen. BoAnP; POL

Trader. Jim Harrison. NoAM

Trader I am to the African shore, A. Sweet Meat Has Sour Sauce; or, The Slave-Trader in the Dumps. William Cowper. OBSV

Traders, parsons, and stoolpigeons. Value Neuter. Kenneth Rexroth. MPA

Trading Chicago. Charles O. Hartman. AMV-80

Tradition. Stephen Crane. NIL

Tradition. David James. TC

Tradition, thou art for suckling children. Tradition. Stephen Crane. NIL

Traditional Funeral Songs. *Tr. fr. Modern Greek by* Willis Barnstone *and* Elene Kolb. BoWoP

Traditional Grammarian as Poet, The. Ted Hipple. POL

Traditional Red. Robert Huff. CoPAm; HoPM (1975 ed.)

Traditions. Seamus Heaney. IPM

Traffic. William Hart-Smith. GAS

Traffic glitters towards dull junction, The. Vincent Buckley. *Fr.* Golden Builders. CAAP

Traffic Lights. Lina Kasdaglis, *tr. fr. Modern Greek by* Edmund *and* Mary Keeley. BoWoP

Traffic up and down the coast all day. Traffic. William Hart-Smith. GAS

Tragedy, A. Théophile Marzials. PeD; PPoD

Tragedy, A. Tom Masson. OBAL

Tragedy of Action, The. Dan Gerber. HeS

Tragedy of the Leaves, The. Charles Bukowski. CoPAm; CPA; HoPM (1975 ed.)

Tragedy of Valentinian, The, *sels.* John Fletcher.
Care-charming Sleep, *fr.* V, ii. ILP (1975 ed.)
Hear, Ye Ladies, *fr.* II, v. NOBE
Love's Emblems, *fr.* II, iv. BoLoP; NOBE
(Now the Lusty Spring.) FF

Tragic Story, A. Adelbert von Chamisso, *tr. fr. German by* Thackeray. CTV; ECBV; PCOP

Tragical History of Doctor Faustus. Christopher Marlowe. *See* Doctor Faustus.

Tragi-Comedy of Titus Oates, The. *Unknown.* APAS

Tragicomic Conceit. Miguel González-Gerth. FoP

Trahison des Clercs; against the Perversion of Language. Ezra Pound. PAIC

Trail All Your Pikes. Countess of Winchilsea. ExPo (1973 ed.); WPE

Trail beside the River Platte, The. William Heyen. GOA

Trail climbing/ you have to watch your footing.  Finding a Poem.  Eve Merriam.  RFM

Trail climbs in zig-zags, The.  The Trail up Wu Gorge.  Sun Yün-feng, *tr. by* Kenneth Rexroth *and* Ling Chung.  BoWoP; PBWP

Trail Herd, The,  *Unknown.*  BPAW

Trail Horse, The.  David Wagoner.  PH

Trail into Kansas, The.  W. S. Merwin.  GOA

Trail to Mexico, The.  *Unknown.*  AmFP; BPAW; FSW, *diff. version*

Trail up Wu Gorge, The.  Sun Yün-feng, *tr. fr. Chinese by* Kenneth Rexroth *and* Ling Chung.  BoWoP; PBWP

Trailing her father, bearing his hand axe.  Goose.  Richard Emil Braun.  NoAM

Trailing My Balloon.  Stephen Stepanchev.  SA

Train, The.  Alan Brownjohn.  OxBTC

Train.  Ken Smith.  EAS

Train/ run off/ nine mile, The.  Chain Gang Trouble.  *Unknown.*  BluL

Train, The.  A hot July.  On either hand.  Travelling Home.  Frances Cornford.  PES

Train: Abstraction.  Genevieve Taggard.  WPE

Train Dogs, The.  Pauline Johnson.  GDP

Train has stopped running, The.  South Shore Line.  John Schlesinger.  AMV-80

Train Is Off the Track, The.  *Unknown.*  AmFP

Train Journey.  Judith Wright.  GAS; PBWP

Train moves, The.  Landscape with Minute Wildflowers.  Hugh Maxton.  CIP

Train of Religion, The,  *sel.*  Martin Farquhar Tupper.  "How beautiful their feet."  FaBoCo

Train Ride.  John Wheelwright.  VGW

Train Runs Late to Harlem, The.  Conrad Kent Rivers.  PoBA

Train shot through the dark, The.  Return.  Seamus Deane.  BIrV; IPM

Train Stops at Healy Fork, The.  John Haines.  TAT

Train through the night of the town, The.  In the Train.  Arthur Symons.  City Nights, I.  VLP

Train to Reflection.  Lawrence T. O'Neill.  AMV-80

Train Tune.  Louise Bogan.  ECBV

Train will come tomorrow year, The.  The Train.  Alan Brownjohn.  OxBTC

Train Window.  Frank Stewart.  PHC

Training.  D. J. Enright.  HeHu

Training on the Shore.  Shlomo Vinner, *tr. fr. Hebrew by* Laya Firestone *and* Howard Schwartz.  VWA

Train's french horn sighs, sheds a few tears, The.  To I. Lavrentevaya.  Natalya Gorbanyevskaya, *tr. by* Daniel Weissbort.  BoWoP

Trains Made of Stone.  Ray A. Young Bear.  CDW

Traits: Inner Portrait.  Jeremy Ingalls.  FoP

"Tra la la la—See me dance the polka."  Neptune—Polka.  Edith Sitwell.  NOBE

Tra-La-Larceny.  Oliver Herford.  TDH

Trala Trala Trala La-le-la.  William Carlos Williams.  OFD

Tramp, The.  Joe Hill.  FSW

Tramp, The.  Rayne Mackinnon.  MIS

Tramp Miner's Song.  *Unknown.*  AmFP

Tramp! Tramp! Tramp! or, The Prisoner's Hope.  George Frederick Root.  BLSo, *with music;* FSW; PSoN, *with music*

Trampwoman's Tragedy, A.  Thomas Hardy.  VLP

Tramway climbs from Merthyr to Dowlais, The.  The Deluge 1939.  Saunders Lewis, *tr. by* Gwyn Thomas.  OBW

Trance.  Mary Ursula Bethell.  ATNZ

Tranquillity! thou better name.  Ode to Tranquillity.  Samuel Taylor Coleridge.  MBPR

Transaction.  A. R. Ammons.  PoA

Transandean Railway, The.  Thomas Kretz.  AMV-80

"Transcendentalism: A Poem in Twelve Books."  Robert Browning.  VLP

Transcontinent.  Donald Hall.  MiP

Transcontinental.  Richard Wright.  SPT

Transferring my ashes from the urn.  The Burial.  Mark Thalman.  AMV-80

Transfiguration.  Djuna Barnes.  EAS

Transfiguration, The.  Robert Herrick.  CaPo

Transfigured Life.  Dante Gabriel Rossetti.  The House of Life, LX.  VLP

Transformation, The.  Don Eulert.  CPA

Transformation.  Quincy Troupe.  CNA

Transformations.  Thomas Hardy.  NoAM; PPP

Transfusion.  Merrill Moore.  PoA

Transit.  Richard Wilbur.  PCho

Translated into language it is something like this.  The Voice.  Judith Herzberg, *tr. by* Shirley Kaufman.  VWA

Translated out of Martial.  Martial, *tr. fr. Latin by* John Weever.  PAIC

Translating.  Ruth Whitman.  VWA

Translation.  Roy Fuller.  NOBE; OxBTC

Translation.  Rika Lesser.  PoA

Translation From, A.  Fred Levinson.  AmPA

Translation from Original.  Joanne Casullo.  NPW

Translation of a Chinese Tribute to Jade.  Alice Notley.  FiCh

Translation of an Unwritten Spanish Poem.  Steven Goldsberry.  PHC

Translation of Lines by Benserade.  Samuel Johnson, *after the French of* Isaac Benserade.  CABA (1972 ed.)  ("In bed we laugh, in bed we cry.")  FaBoEE

Translations from the English.  George Starbuck.  VGW

Translator, The.  Patrick L. Clary.  PoUp

Translator attempted to bare things unsaid, The.  A Lesson in Translation.  Gabriel Preil, *tr. by* Howard Schwartz.  VWA

Translator to Translated.  Ezra Pound.  FaBoEE

Translucent green on the wall, a dance of leaves.  The Green Afternoon.  Henry Rago.  VGW

Transparent Autumn, A.  Sadamu Fujiwara, *tr. fr. Japanese by* Ichiro Kono *and* Rikutaro Fukuda.  IPWM

Transparent Closet, The.  Martha Shelley.  WBN

Transplanting.  Theodore Roethke.  PiAm

Transplantitis.  Lester A. Sobel.  QQQ

Trap, The.  William Beyer.  PoTa

Trap doors take a Sunday afternoon drive.  The Law of Falling and Catching Up.  Cathleen Quirk.  MMD

Trapped Hare, The.  Basil Dowling.  ATNZ

Trapper, The.  Peter Klappert.  AAN

Trapping Bear.  John Minczeski.  BCr

Trapping fairies in West Virginia.  Gelett Burgess.  FaBoNo

Travel.  Edna St. Vincent Millay.  PPM

Travel.  Robert Louis Stevenson.  CTV

Traveller, The.  John Berryman.  PoA; UsP; VGW

Traveler, The.  David Bottoms.  AMV-80

Traveller, The.  Goldsmith.  LAuP  "Remote, unfriended, melancholy, slow,"  *sel.*  BIrV

Traveller, The.  *Unknown.*  AmFP

Traveller approaching.  Goat Songs.  Ray Drew.  VoA

Traveller Has Regrets, The.  G. S. Fraser.  MS

Traveler take heed for journeys undertaken in the dark of the year.  October Journey.  Margaret Walker.  AmNP (1974 ed.); PoBA

Traveller who walks a temperate zone, A.  Against Romanticism.  Richard Wilbur.  NoAM

Travelers, The. Patricia Hubbell. CTV

Travelers, The. James Reeves. POL

Traveller's Curse after Misdirection. Robert Graves. CMoP (1970 ed.); ExPo (1973 ed.); HoPM (1975 ed.); NCSH

Travelin' Blues. *Unknown.* BluL

Traveling. Anne Waldman. RiTi

Travelling/ where darkness hauls the world. Tanks. Rhyll McMaster. FPA

Travelling, a man met a tiger, so. Good Taste. Christopher Logue. RAE

Travelling Bear, The. Amy Lowell. BCr

Traveling Boy. William Meredith. NoAM

Traveling for days to reach you. Journey. Diane Wakoski. IHMS

Travelling Home. Frances Cornford. PES

Traveling in Europe. Keith Althaus. AAN

Traveling North. John Woods. POL

Traveling Out, The. Lucile Adler. IHMS

Traveling Post Office, The. Andrew Barton Paterson. PoTa

Traveling Riverside Blues. *Unknown.* BluL

Traveling sky goes landward, the blind mass, The. Headland. Brewster Ghiselin. PoA

Travelling south, leaves overflow the farms. The Puritan on His Honeymoon. Robert Bly. FF

Traveling through the Dark. William Stafford. BiP; BoAnP; CABA (1972 ed.); CNW; ConAP; HAP; ILP (1975 ed.); InPK; NCSH; PoTa; SFF; SoS; TSWA; UsP; WeW

Travelling to My Second Marriage on the Day of the First Moonshot. Robert Nye. SLP

Traveling up the lonesome trail. Doney-gal. *Unknown.* BPAW

Travels with the Band-Aid Army. Lance Henson. VoR

Traverse City Zoo. Jim Harrison. BoAnP

Travis, the Kid Was All Heart. Terry Stokes. AmPA

Tread back—and back, the lewd and lay! Horace, *tr. by* Gerard Manley Hopkins. Odes, III, 1. OBVE

Tread lightly here, for here, 'tis said. An Epitaph on a Robin-Redbreast. Samuel Rogers. FaBoEE

Tread softly; bid a solemn music sound. Epitaph. J. B. Morton. FaBoEE

Treason doth never prosper; what's the reason? Of Treason [*or* Treason]. Sir John Harington. ExPo (1973 ed.); FaBoCo; FaBoEE; FF; InPK; NIL

Treason of Sand. Hemda Roth, *tr. fr. Hebrew by* Mariana Potasman. VWA

Treasure in Heaven. John Godfrey Saxe. PIM

Treat the woman tenderly, tenderly. *Unknown.* POL

Treating of songs. The Knight of the Sad Face. Rafael Jesús González. MIT

Treaty-Trip from Shulus Reservation. Patrick Lane. NeAC

Trebetherick. John Betjeman. CMoP (1970 ed.)

Treblinka Gas Chamber. Phyllis Webb. MMD

Tree. Florence Barbera. PoUp

Tree, The. E. R. Cole. AATT

Tree. Daniel Hoffman. IPWM

Tree, The. Anna Madge Hopewell. RAE

Tree. Mbembe. NW

Tree, The. Ezra Pound. CMoP (1970 ed.); PBMP; PiAm

Tree. Burns Singer. MS

Tree, The. Joel Sloman. VGW

Tree. A. J. M. Smith. IPWM

Tree, A. *Unknown.* PCOP

Tree, The. Pat Wilson. ATNZ

Tree Animals. Laurence Lieberman. CoPAm

Tree at My Window. Robert Frost. InPK; NoAM; PSN; TAP; USP

Tree beside the synagogue atones, A. Yom Kippur. Linda Pastan. VWA

Tree enters and says with a bow, A. The Lesson. Miroslav Holub, *tr. by* Ian Millner *and* George Theiner. LP

Tree I know where a love-bird's lighted, A. Open the Door. *Malay Oral Tradition, tr. by* R. J. Wilkinson *and* R. O. Winstedt. WTO

Tree in the Wood, The. *Unknown.* AmFP

Tree Is Father to the Man, The. Lou Lipsitz. NCSH

Tree-leaves labour up and down. Nobody Comes. Thomas Hardy. BiP

Tree Man. Rennie McQuilkin. AMV-81

Tree of Death, The. Claude Vigée, *tr. fr. French by* J. R. Le Master *and* Kenneth L. Beaudoin. VWA

Tree of Diana, The. Alejandra Pizarnik, *tr. fr. Spanish by* Yishai Tobin. VWA

Tree of Hatred, The. Shmuel Moreh, *tr. fr. Arabic by author.* VWA

Tree of intense, The. Ode to the Watermelon. Pablo Neruda, *tr. by* Robert Bly. EAS; NU

Tree of Knowledge. Edward Lowbury. VWA

Tree of Life Is Also a Tree of Fire, The. Gerda Norvig. VWA

Tree of Rivelin, The. Ebenezer Elliott. VLP

Tree outside the window. The Tree. Anna Madge Hopewell. RAE

Tree, paddock, river: plan. Inheritance. Kendrick Smithyman. ATNZ

Tree Party. Louis MacNeice. OxBTC

Tree, the Bird, The. Theodore Roethke. PiAm

Tree to Flute. Anna Hajnal, *tr. fr. Hungarian by* Jascha Kessler. VWA

Tree, too, wants to bend over, The. 3 Stanzas about a Tree. Marvin Bell. Prf

Tree. Tree. Do you want to become a man? Tree. Burns Singer. MS

Tree will not ask for relief, The. From a Distance. Marvin Bell. HeS

Treehouse, The. James A. Emanuel. AmNP (1974 ed.); BPo; PoBA

Trees. Sara Coleridge. OxBChV

Trees, *abr.* Joyce Kilmer. AKE

Trees. W. S. Merwin. GP

Trees, The. Adrienne Rich. ILP (1975 ed.); NOBA; PiAm; TT; WPE

Trees, The. William Carlos Williams. TCP

Trees, The: A Convict Monologue. Thomas W. Shapcott. FPA; GAS

Trees and Evening Sky. N. Scott Momaday. CDW

Trees are afraid to put forth buds, The. A Backward Spring. Thomas Hardy. PPP

Trees Are Down, The. Charlotte Mew. WPE

Trees are full of holes. Holes of Green. Aileen Fisher. FPB

Trees are growing, The. The Princess Who Fled to the Castle. Francis Landy. VWA

Trees are in their autumn beauty, The. The Wild Swans at Coole. W. B. Yeats. AnMo; BoAnP; CABA (1972 ed.); CMoP (1970 ed.); FSFS; HeIP; ILP (1975 ed.); IP; IPWM; NoAM; PB; PPP; PSN; STS; TCP; TT; UnPo (1976 ed.); VoPo

Trees are tall, but the moon is small, The. Hide and Seek. Robert Graves. FPB

Trees ask me, The. Who Am I? Felice Holman. RFM

Trees—being trees, The. The Trees. William Carlos Williams. TCP

Trees file along curbs. Shrub-faces. Bell Weather. Lewis Turco. AMV-80

Trees have been born. In Memoriam Paul Celan. Gad Hollander. VWA

Trees in the Garden. D. H. Lawrence. CMoP (1970 ed.)

Trees in the garden rained flowers, The. War Is Kind, XXVI. Stephen Crane. SFF

Trees in the old days used to stand. Carentan O Carentan. Louis Simpson. MPo; NOBA

Trees inside are moving out into the forest, The. The Trees. Adrienne Rich. ILP (1975 ed.); NOBA; PiAm; TT; WPE

Tree's leaves may be ever so good, A. Leaves Compared with Flowers. Robert Frost. NOBA

Trees Lose Parts of Themselves inside a Circle of Fog. Francis Ponge, tr. fr. French by Robert Bly. NU

Trees of Life, The. Jones Very. NOBA

Trees Once Walked and Stood. Joshua Tan Pai, tr. fr. Hebrew by Yishai Tobin. VWA

Trees, sway high. Winter: The Abandoned Nest. Ron Baxter. WeW

Trees they are tall and the leaves they are green, The. Daily Growing. Unknown. FSW

Trees they do grow high, The. Still Growing. Unknown. FaBoBa; InPK

Trees turn, The. Leaflight. Dorothy Donnelly. NCSH

Treetalk and windsong are. Sugarfields. Barbara Mahone. CNA; PoBA

Treetops. Marvin Bell. AmPA

Trellie. Lance Jeffers. CNA; FB

Trembling. Aliza Shenhar, tr. fr. Hebrew by Linda Zisquit. VWA

Trembling before Thine Awful Throne, with music. Augustus L. Hillhouse. AH

Trembling of the Veil, The. Allen Ginsberg. TT

Trembling, sand-dollar. Grunion. Wendy Rose. CDW

Trembling train clings to the leaning wall, The. Moonrise in the Rockies. Ella Higginson. WPW

Tremor, The. David McKain. AAN

Trend Spotter. William Price Turner. MS

Trends and Conditions: Miscellaneous File. A. Wilber Stevens. MPA

Trestle Bridge, The. Carolyne Wright. AMV–80

Tretis of the Tua Mariit Wemen and the Wedo, The, sel. William Dunbar.
　"Bot of ane bowrd in to bed I sall yow breif yit." EBEV

Triad. Adelaide Crapsey. PAIC; WPE

Triad. Donald Foster. AMV–80

Triad, A. Christina Rossetti. PBWP; VLP

Triads. Swinburne. PBMP

Triads. Unknown, tr. fr. Irish by Thomas Kinsella. BIrV (Thirty-three Triads.) PFIr

Trial, A. Alan Dugan. NoAM

Trial. Rachel Hadas. AAN

Trial, The. Gershom Scholem, tr. fr. German by Jonathan Griffin. VWA

Trial and Error. Phyllis McGinley. BBL

Trials of a Tourist. Anne Tibble. FaBoCo

Triangle Ladies, The. Carol Artman Montgomery. AMV–80

Tribal Cemetery. Janet Campbell Hale. NW; VW

Tribal Memories. Robert Duncan. Fr. Passages. NOBA; PiAm

Tribal Stumps ("Tribal mixed bloods"). Gerald Vizenor. VoR

Tribe Searching, A. Shlomo Reich, tr. fr. French by Mira Reich. VWA

Tribute. Alice Notley. FiCh

Tribute, The. Coventry Patmore. Fr. The Angel in the House, I, iv. EBEV

Tribute. Al Young. NVAP; SA

Tribute to Henry Ford. Richard Kostelanetz. NIL; TAP

Tribute to Kafka for Someone Taken. Alan Dugan. CAPP; CoPAm; NoAM; WeW

Tribute to the Angels, sels. Hilda Doolittle ("H. D.").
　"Invisible, indivisible Spirit." BoWoP
　"Not in our time, O Lord." NOBA
　"We have seen her/ the world over." RiTi; VGW

Trick, The/ without anyone. Geography of the Near East. Al Young. NW

Trick for Tyburn, or a Prison Rant, A. Unknown. APAS

Trick Is Consciousness, The. Paula Gunn Allen. FoP

Trick or Treat. David McCord. IWK

Trick that everyone abhors, A. Rebecca, Who Slammed Doors for Fun and Perished Miserably. Hilaire Belloc. NOBL; SO

Trickle Drops. Walt Whitman. PeD

Trickle of water from, A. Hard Way to Learn. James Hearst. AMV–80

Tricks. Sharon Olds. TV

Tricks of the weather. Reeving. Michael Anania. HeS

Trico's Song: "What bird so sings, yet so does wail?" John Lyly. Fr. Alexander and Campaspe, V, i. OBP (Welcome to Spring.) NOBE

Trifle. Georgia Douglas Johnson. AmNP (1974 ed.)

Trifle for Trafalgar Day, A. Ted Pauker. NOBL

Trifles. William Everson. CoPAm

Trifling Women. Unknown. AmFP

Trilce: "In that corner, where we slept together." César Vallejo, tr. fr. Spanish by James Wright. LoAs

Trilobite, grapholite, nautilus pie. Rhyme for a Geological Baby. Joseph Cook. QQQ; SpRo

Trilogy for X, sel. Louis MacNeice.
　"And love hung still as crystal over the bed." CIP; GBL

Trilogy of the Night. Quincy Troupe. SES

Trimming the Sails. Vassar Miller. NMM

Trinity, The. William Langland. Fr. The Vision of Piers Plowman. OxBM

Trinity Churchyard. Muriel Rukeyser. NYP

Trinity Place. Carl Sandburg. NYP

Trinity Sunday. George Herbert. PAIC

Trinket. Marvin Bell. FoP

Trio. Edwin Morgan. MPo

Trio for Two Cats and a Trombone. Edith Sitwell. PBWP

Triolet: "Child is father to the man, The." Gerard Manley Hopkins. See "Child Is Father to the Man, The."

Triolet: "I intended an ode." Austin Dobson. See Urceus Exit.

Triolet: "I wish I were a jelly fish." G. K. Chesterton. LCL

Triolet: "She was in love with the same danger." Sandra McPherson. CNW

Triolet against Sisters. Phyllis McGinley. MiP

Trip, The. Emmett Jarrett. NeAC

Trip it gipsies, trip it fine. Thomas Middleton. Fr. The Spanish Gipsy. ILP (1975 ed.)

Trip on the Staten Island Ferry, A. Audre Lorde. CNA

Trip to Four or Five Towns, A. John Logan. ConAP; NNaP

Trip to the Grand Banks, A. Amos Hanson. AmFP

Trip trap in a gap. Unknown. GBP

Trip upon Trenchers. Unknown. NOBL

Triphammer Bridge. A. R. Ammons. NOBA

Triple Feature. Denise Levertov. FF

Triple Fool, The. John Donne. GBL; ILP (1975 ed.)

Triple Mirror, The. Gloria C. Oden. IHMS

Trippers and askers surround me. Walt Whitman. Fr. Song of Myself, IV. InPS; UnPo (1976 ed.)

Tripping on sutures used to sew the wounds. Low...the Violence Begins Low. Ann Darr. WBN

Triptych. Greg Hannan. PoUp

Triptych. Seamus Heaney. CIP

Triptych. Luci Shaw. AATT

Tristium, *sels.* Ovid, *tr. fr. Latin by* Henry Vaughan.
  "And here I wish my soul died with my breath," *fr.* III, 3a.
  OBVE
  "And on this day, which poets unto thee," *fr.* V, 3. OBVE
Trite usages in tamest style. Thomas Hardy. *Fr.* A Jog-Trot
  Pair. PeD
Triumph of Charis, The. Ben Jonson. *Fr.* A Celebration of
  Charis. CABA (1972 ed.); ILP (1975 ed.); InPS; NOBE;
  PoPle
  (Her Triumph.) EBEV; LoAs
Triumph of Dullness, The. Pope. *Fr.* The Dunciad. NOBE
  ("In vain, in vain—the all-composing hour.") EBEV
Triumph of Infidelity, The, *sel.* Timothy Dwight.
  Gathering, The. EAP
Triumph of Life, The. Shelley. MBPR; OAEL-2
Triumph of Time, The. Swinburne. VLP; VPC
  "I will go back to the great sweet mother," *sel.* SoSe
Triumph of Vice, The. Pope. *Fr.* Epilogue to the Satires.
  NOBE
  ("Virtue may choose the high or low degree.") NIL; OBSV
Triumphant Demons stand, and Angels start. The Heart's
  Abysses. Walter Savage Landor. FaBoEE; OBSV
Triumphs of the Prince D'Amour, The, *sel.* Sir William
  Davenant.
  "Unarm! unarm! No more your fights." SCP-2
Trivia; or, The Art of Walking the Streets of London. John Gay.
  EPC
  *Sels.*
  "Experienced men, inured to city ways," *fr.* II. OAEL-1
  "Let due civilities be strictly paid," *fr.* II. OAEL-1
  "Where the mob gathers, swiftly shoot along," *fr.* III. OAEL-1
  "Who can the various city frauds recite," *fr.* III. OAEL-1
Troades, *sel.* Seneca, *tr. fr. Latin by* Earl of Rochester.
  "After death nothing is, and nothing death," *fr.* II. EBEV;
  OBVE
Trochee trips from long to short. Metrical Feet. Samuel Taylor
  Coleridge. NIL; OxBChV
Troika, The. Louis Simpson. NoAM; NOBA
Troilus and Cressida, *sel.* Shakespeare.
  On Degree, *fr.* I, iii. ExPo (1973 ed.)
  (Order and Degree.) NIL
Troilus and Criseyde, *sels.* Chaucer.
  Complaint of Troilus, The, *fr.* V. NOBE
  Criseyde Sees Troilus Return from Battle, *fr.* II. OxBM
  Go, Little Book ("Go, litel book, go litel myn tragedy"), *fr.* V.
  OAEL-1; OxBM
  ("Go little book, go, my little tragedy," *mod. by* Seldon
  Rodman.) OBP
  "If no love is, O God, what fele I so," *fr.* I. FF; LoAs;
  OAEL-1
  "O cruel day, accusour of the joie," *fr.* III. PAIC
  O Yonge Freshe Folkes, *fr.* V. ExPo (1973 ed.); OxBM
  (Love Unfeigned.) BoReV; NOBE
  "Owt of thise blake wawes for to saylle," *fr.* II. ILP (1975 ed.)
  "This Troilus, with blisse of that supprysed," *fr.* III. EBEV
  Troilus Laments Criseyde's Absence, *fr.* V. OxBM
Troll, The. Jack Prelutsky. IWK
Troll sat alone on his seat of stone. The Stone Troll. J. R. R.
  Tolkien. SO
Troll Songs. Karoniaktatie. NW
Troll Trick. B. J. Lee. IWK
Trolley has stopped long since, The. The Dump. Donald Hall.
  TCP
Trolls. Cash Terrell. DNGG
Troll's Nosegay, The. Robert Graves. SoSe
Troop home to silent grots and caves! The Mermaidens' Vesper-
  Hymn [*or* Siren Chorus]. George Darley. Syren Songs, VI.
  BIrV; GBL

Trooper and Maid. *Unknown.* AmFP, 2 *versions*
  (Trooper and the Maid, The.) FSW
Troops, The. Siegfried Sassoon. CMoP (1970 ed.)
Troops exulting sate in order round, The. Homer, *tr. by* Pope.
  *Fr.* The Iliad, VIII. OBVE
Tropic tonight, burning, filled with fast trains. At the Band
  Concert. John Malcolm Brinnin. PoA
Tropics, The. Holly Prado. NPW
Tropics. Ellen Bryant Voigt. AAN
Tropics in New York, The. Claude McKay. AmNP (1974 ed.);
  ILP (1975 ed.); NIL; NoAM; PBMP; PoBA
Tropisms on John Berryman. Gerald Vizenor. VoR
Trot Along, Pony. Marion Edey *and* Dorothy Grider. CTV
Trotting Around. Benjamin Saltman. PoW
Troubador. J. Edgar Simmons. TAT
Trouble. James Wright. FF; InPK
Trouble, not of clouds, or weeping rain, A. On the Departure of
  Sir Walter Scott from Abbotsford, for Naples. Wordsworth.
  EBEV
Trouble-shooting. William Stafford. AMV-80
Trouble was too much, The. Indian Love Song. Lew
  Blockcolski. VoR
Trouble with you is, The. Love in a Warm Room in Winter.
  James Wright. OBAL
Troubled was a house in Ealing. The Widow's Plot; or, She Got
  What Was Coming to Her. William Plomer. NoAM
Troubled Woman. Langston Hughes. CTBA
Troupial, A. Milton Bracker. TDH
Trousers first of ancient fabric. Sri Rama's Raiment. *Malay
  Oral Tradition, tr. by* R. O. Winstedt. WTO
Trout. Seamus Heaney. CIP
Trout, The. John Montague. BoAnP; PFIr; SFF
Trout Fisher. George Mackay Brown. MS
Trout Fishing in Virginia. Michael Beirne McMahon. AMV-80
Trout of the Well, The. *Unknown, tr. fr. Gaelic by* G. R. D.
  McLean SLP
Trouvaille. Richard Murphy. CIP
Troy. Edwin Muir. CMoP (1970 ed.)
Truant, The. E. J. Pratt. NoAM
Truck bodies rest, The. Art on the Swing-Shift, Truck Assembly.
  Eric Johnson. PoW
Truckdriver. Gary Sange. NVAP
Truck Drivers. Terri Haag. CTBA
Trucker Drives through His Lost Youth, A. David Bottoms.
  CSP
Trucker feels how calloused, The. Lives. Lawrence Russ. TC
Truckers, The. Allan Kornblum. AcAn
True. Phillip William George. NW
True Account of Talking to the Sun at Fire Island, A. Frank
  O'Hara. NNaP
True and Joyful News. *Unknown.* APAS
Trueblue Gentleman, A. Kenneth Patchen. RAE; SO
True-blue the salmon—from his sally. No Place like Home.
  Llawdden. OBW
True-born Englishman, The. Daniel Defoe. APAS
  *Sels.*
  "Breed's described, The: Now, Satire, if you can,"*fr.* II. OBSV
  "In their religion they are so unev'n," *fr.* II. OBSV
  "Labouring poor, in spite of double pay," *fr.* II. NOBL
  "Then let us boast of ancestors no more," *conclusion.* OBSV
  "Wherever God erects a house of prayer," *fr.* I. NOBL; OBSV
True Cat, A. Anna Seward. PCat
True Child ("True Child of God, stand innocently awed").
  Marion Hodge. AMV-81
True Confession, A. Jon Stallworthy. NoAM

True Confessions of George Barker, The, *sel.* George Barker. "I sent a letter to my love." FaBoTw (1975 ed.)

True daughters of Lilith, night demons. Summer Night. Hayim Nachman Bialik, *tr. by* Robert Friend. VWA

True ease in writing comes from art, not chance. Sound and Sense. Pope. *Fr.* An Essay on Criticism. HAP; SoSe; UnPo (1976 ed.)

True Englishmen, drink a good health to the miter. A New Catch in Praise of the Reverend Bishops. *Unknown.* APAS

True Facts of the Case, The. Anthony Euwer. OBAL

True genius, but true woman! dost deny. To George Sand: II. A Recognition. Elizabeth Barrett Browning. BoWoP; SBG

True, I have always been happy that all the things that are inside the body. To Persuade a Lady. Michael Benedikt. CAAP

True Import of Present Dialogue, Black vs. Negro, The. Nikki Giovanni. BPo; PoBA

True Is True. Mark Van Doren. LoAs

True Knight, The. Ella Wheeler Wilcox. PeD

True Lent, A. Robert Herrick. *See* To Keep a True Lent.

True Love. Joe Johnson. CNA

Truelove. Mark Van Doren. AIW

True Love at Last. D. H. Lawrence. TPo

True love is sweet and true love is pleasant. William Hall. *Unknown.* AmFP

True love, true love, don't lie to me. In the Pines (Where Did You Sleep Last Night?) Leadbelly (Huddie Ledbetter). FSW

True love, true love, what have I done. In the Pines. *Unknown.* AmFP

True Lover, The. A. E. Housman. LoAs

True Lovers Bold, The. *Unknown.* AmFP

True Maid, A. Matthew Prior. FaBoCo; FaBoEE; NIL

True: nor love or loving is ultimate. "A Taste of Honey." King D. Kuka. VW

True Picture Restored, A. Vernon Watkins. NoAM

True poesy is not in words. Pastoral Poesy. John Clare. OAEL-2

True Religion. Forrest Anderson. AATT

True Son of God, Eternal Light, *with music.* P. J. Cormican. AH

True Song, The. John Montague. IPM

True Story of Snow White, The. Bruce Bennett. AAN

True, the time, to one who does not love farce. A Little Scraping. Robinson Jeffers. NoAM

True Thomas lay o'er yond grassy [*or* on Huntlie] bank. Thomas the Rhymer [*or* Thomas Rymer *or* True Thomas]. *Unknown.* AIW; FaBoBa; HAP; InPK; InPS; NIL; NOBE; OAEL-1; PeBB; PoTa; Prf

True to your might winds on dusky shores. On the Death of William Edward Burghardt Du Bois by African Moonlight and Forgotten Shores. Conrad Kent Rivers. PoBA

True, we are the children. The Second Generation. Menachem Z. Rosensaft. AMV-81

True, we must tame our rebel will. Courage. Matthew Arnold. OAEL-2

True wit is nature to advantage dressed. Pope. *Fr.* An Essay on Criticism. HAP; UsP

Truisms, The. Louis MacNeice. NOBE; OBSV

Truly honoured lady, the Lady Venetia Digby, The. Ben Jonson. *Fr.* Eupheme. SCP-1

Truly in the east/ The white bean. Song to Promote Growth. *Tr. by* Washington Matthews. OBVE

Truly, my Satan, thou art but a dunce. To the Accuser Who Is the God of This World. Blake. *Fr.* The Gates of Paradise. CABA (1972 ed.); HAP; OAEL-2; OBP

"Truly We Can Only Allow Our Paintings to Speak." Jean Pumphrey. TPo

Trumpet, The, *sel.* Robinson Jeffers. Grass on the Cliff, V. PoA

Trumpet Shall Sound, The. John V. Hicks. AMV-81

Trumpeter swan's neck was curved, The. At The Smithsonian. Vanessa Haley. AMV-81

Trumpets blow, The. The Indians. Peter Wild. MPA

Trumpet's loud clangour, The. Dryden. *Fr.* A Song for St. Cecilia's Day. RAE

Trumpets sound and steeples ring. A Trick for Tyburn, or a Prison Rant. *Unknown.* APAS

Trumpet's voice, loud and authoritative, The. Reasons for Attendance. Philip Larkin. BiP; NowV; OBP

Trundled from/ the strangeness of the sea. The Sea-Elephant. William Carlos Williams. NU

Trunk won't budge, The; I open it. Calvin in the Attic Cleans. Craig Weeden. AMV-81

Tru's god Lizi. Tired Lizi Tired. Lindiwe Mabuza. SES

Trust. Art Lange. FiCH

Trust and Obey, *with music.* J. H. Sammis. BLSH

Trust in Me, *with music.* Unknown. AH

Trusty, dusky, vivid, true. My Wife. Robert Louis Stevenson. DL

Truth. Gwendolyn Brooks. *Fr.* The Womanhood. TH

Truth. Chaucer. BoReV; OAEL-1; OxBM

Truth, The. W. H. Davies. FaBoTw (1975 ed.); UsP

Truth. Eileen Duggan. ATNZ

Truth. James Hearst. TPo

Truth. Claude McKay. BPo

Truth. Howard Nemerov. CoPAm; HoPM (1975 ed.); ILP 1975 ed.)

Truth. Susan Fromberg Schaeffer. IHMS

Truth, The. Phyllis Hoge Thompson. PHC

Truth. *Unknown.* OxBM

Truth about My Sister and Me, The. Anita Endrezze Probst. CDW

Truth Brought to Light, or Murder Will Out. Stephen College. APAS

Truth I do not stretch or shove, The. The Dog. Ogden Nash. GDP

Truth I pursued, as Fancy sketch'd the way. Samuel Taylor Coleridge. FaBoEE

Truth is a golden sunset far away. Threnody. I. O. Scherzo. HoPM (1975 ed.)

"Truth Is Blind, The." David Gascoyne. EAS

Truth is not the secret of a few. Lawrence Ferlinghetti. WIF

Truth Kills Everybody. Ted Hughes. InPS

Truth, like a mysterious, silken cat. Open Your Hand. Dorothy R. Fulton. AMV-81

Truth like the Belly of a Woman Turning, The. Gary Snyder. NNaP

Truth-loving Persians do not dwell upon. The Persian Version. Robert Graves. CMoP (1970 ed.); ExPo (1973 ed.); FaBoCo; NIL; NoAM; NOBL; WeW

Truth the Best. Elizabeth Turner. OxBChV

Truth the Dead Know, The. Anne Sexton. CoPAm; NoAM; PBWP; Psy; TAP

Truth, the whole truth always, The. A True Confession. Jon Stallworthy. NoAM

Truthful man, that's me, A. Guantanamera. Jose Marti, *ad. by* Pete Seeger *and* Hector Angulo. FSW

Truth's Complaint over England. Thomas Lodge. TVS

Try Brillo on the Slimy Stove. Phyllis Gotlieb. BBGO

Try new words for pig and feel what happens. How to Become a Poet. Mark McCloskey. PoW

Try on your wings; I ken vera weel. An Apprentice Angel. "Hugh MacDiarmid." MS

Trying to Change the Subject. Susan Bartels Ludvigson. BCr

Trying to chop mother down is like. She Went to Stay. Robert Creeley. OBAL

Trying to Forget. John Wieners. MIT

Trying to get the whiskey to do it and after that. The Apparition. Michael Heffernan. HeS

Trying to open locked doors with a sword, threading. Sojourn in the Whale. Marianne Moore. SBG

Trying to Shovel Out. Philip Legler. TC

Trying to Talk with a Man. Adrienne Rich. NIL; RiTi; WBN

Tryptych for Jan Bockelson, A. John Oliver Simon. NeAC

Tryst, The. Walter de la Mare. AIW

Tryst. Eve Merriam. NMM

Tryst, The. William Soutar. EBEV; MS; SLP (Trysting Place, The.) BoLoP

Tryst, The. John Banister Tabb. OBAL

Tryst, The. *Unknown, tr. fr. Welsh by* Joseph P. Clancy. OBW

Tryst after Death, The. *Unknown, tr. fr. Old Irish by* Kuno Meyer. Epi

Trystan and Esyllt. *Unknown, tr. fr. Welsh by* Gwyn Jones. OBW

Trysting Bush, The. Joanna Baillie. WPE

Trysting Place, The. William Soutar. *See* Tryst, The.

Tu Du,/ Skies blue. Thomas Holley Chivers. *Fr.* Chinese Serenade for the Ut-Kam and Tong-Koo. PeD

Tu Non Se' in Terra, Si Come Tu Credi. Kathleen Raine. WPE

Tubes. Larry Mollin. NeAC

Tudor indeed is gone and every rose. Ezra Pound. *Fr.* Canto LXXX. FaBoTw (1975 ed.)

Tuesday. Zishe Landau, *tr. fr. Yiddish by* Ruth Whitman. VWA

Tuesday, 5 March (Morning) 1963. Pier Paolo Pasolini, *tr. fr. Italian by* Nigel Thompson. AMV-81

Tuft of Flowers, The. Robert Frost. IPWM; LFH

Tuft of Kelp, The. Herman Melville. FaBoEE; SoSe

Tulips. Sylvia Plath. HAP; ILP (1975 ed.); IPWM; OSP, 4 *ll.*; PPP; PSN; Psy; WPE

Tumbalalaika. *Tr. fr. Yiddish.* FSW

Tumbled out of heaven. The Blue Day Journey. Gwyn Jones. OBW

Tumbleweed. Ramona Carden. VW

Tumbling. *Unknown.* DuDr; OxBChV

Tumbling-Hair. E. E. Cummings. BBGO

Tumbling, pausing, leaping, knocking together. Metaphysic of Snow. Donald Finkel. PoA

Tumultuous Plenty in the Heavens. Sorley Maclean, *tr. fr. Gaelic; English version by* Iain Crichton Smith. MS

Tuna turn. A Fishy Square Dance. Eve Merriam. ECBV

Tunbridge Wells. Earl of Rochester. OBSV

Tundra, The. John Haines. ConAP

Tune. Carl Rakosi. GP

Tune, A. Arthur Symons. BoLoP

Tune beyond us as we are, A. Wallace Stevens. The Man with the Blue Guitar, VI. CMoP (1970 ed.)

Tune: Butterfly Woos the Blossoms, The. Li Ching-chao, *tr. fr. Chinese by* C. H. Kwôck *and* Vincent McHugh. PBWP

Tune: Crimson Lips Adorned. Li Ching-chao, *tr. fr. Chinese by* C. H. Kwôck *and* Vincent McHugh. PBWP ("After kicking on the swing," *tr. by* Kenneth Rexroth *and* Ling Chung.) BoWoP

Tune: Endless Union. Li Ching-chao, *tr. fr. Chinese by* C. H. Kwôck *and* Vincent McHugh. PBWP

Tune in to a raga. Assassination Raga. Lawrence Ferlinghetti. CAPP

Tune is cowboy, The; the words, sentimental crap. D-Y Bar. James Welch. CDW

Tune: Magnolia Blossom. Li Ching-chao, *tr. fr. Chinese by* C. H. Kwôck *and* Vincent McHugh. PBWP

Tune thy musicke to thy hart. Thomas Campion. AAS

Tune to the Devonshire Cant, The. *Unknown.* APAS

Tuneful Hipponax rests him here. Epitaph of Hipponax. Theocritus, *tr. by* Charles Stuart Calverley. FaBoEE

Tuneful poet, Britain's glory. The Mutual Congratulations of the Poets Anna Seward and Hayley. Richard Porson. FaBoEE; OBSV

Tunes fainter on winds waywarder than others. Graves Are Made to Waltz On. Peter Viereck. PoA

Tuning myself by morning coffee. May Morn. Michael McClure. EAS

Tunnel, The. Hart Crane. *Fr.* The Bridge. CMoP (1970 ed.); MAT; NYP

Tunnel, The. Mark Strand. HeIP; WeW

Tunnel Blaster on Bear and Brotherhood. John Knoepfle. BCr

Tunnyng [*or* Tunning] of Elynour [*or* Elinor] Rummyng [*or* Rumming], The. John Skelton. AAS "Then Margery Milkduck," *sel.* EBEV; OAEL-1

Tupelo Destruction, The. *Unknown.* AmFP

Turkey in the Straw. *Unknown.* BLSH, *with music, ad. by* James Morehead; BLSo, *with music;* FSW; GBP

Turkish Bakery, The. *Unknown, tr. fr. Korean by* Peter H. Lee. PBWP

*Turkish Revery, The, with music. Unknown.* RDB

Turkish Story, A. Katha Pollitt. AAN

Turkish Trench Dog, The. Geoffrey Dearmer. GDP

Turn Again. *Unknown.* OxBM

Turn again, turn again, turn once again. Carrousel Tune. Tennessee Williams. OBAL

Turn Back, O Man. Louis Bourgeois *and* Clifford Bax. PoRo

Turn Blind. Paul Celan, *tr. fr. German by* Joachim Neugroschel. VWA

Turn of October, The. Norman Macleod. SPT

Turn of the Road, The. James Stevens. SO

Turn on the Footlights: The Perils of Pedagogy. John Marshall Carter. AMV-80

Turn on Your Side and Bear the Day to Me. George Barker. OxBTC

Turn Right Next Corner. Wichita Vortex Sutra. Allen Ginsberg. CAPP

Turn the Glasses Over. *Unknown.* FSW

Turn the Key Deftly. Edwin Brock. POL

Turn the page of stone and there. Eeva-Liisa Manner, *tr. by* Jaakko A. Ahokas. *Fr.* Cambrian. PBWP

Turn! Turn! Turn! Pete Seeger. WIF

Turn, Turn, Unhappy Souls, Return, *with music.* Henry Alline. AH

Turner's Camp on the Chippewa. *Unknown.* AmFP

Turning. Bonnie Gordon. PoUp

Turning, The. Philip Levine. VGW

Turning, The. Lawrence Russ. TC

Turning a corner, taking a hill. Shoreline. Seamus Heaney. HeHu

Turning and re-turning. Ixion. Lex Banning. GAS

Turning and turning in the widening gyre. The Second Coming. W. B. Yeats. AnMo; BIrV; CABA (1972 ed.); CMoP (1970 ed.); ExPo (1973 ed.); FF; GrRo; HAP; HeIP; HoPM (1975 ed.); ILP (1975 ed.); InPK; InPS; IPWM; MAT; NIL; NoAM; NOBE; OAEL-2; OBP; OxBTC; PBMP; PPoD; PPoe; PPP; PSN; STS; TCP; TT; UnPo (1976 ed.); VoPo; WeW; WIF

Turning, following the arrows through. The House of Madam Juju. Kanai Mieko, *tr. by* Christopher Drake. BoWoP

Turning Forty-five, after Drinks and Dirty Jokes and Talk of Women. Philip Legler. TC

Turning Into. Robert Duncan. EAS

Turning it over, considering, like a madman. John Berryman. *Fr.* Dream Songs. NoAM; PiAm

Turning, orange and black, dream. Coyotes Fighting. Keith Wilson. MPA

Turning Point. Margaret Gillies. PMW

Turning Point. W. L. Holshouser. AMV-81

Turning, returning on world winds that know. Angel Eye of Memory. John Malcolm Brinnin. PoA

Turning the nuts one at a time. Changing a Tire by the Missouri River. Harley Elliott. HeS

Turning Thirty. W. D. Ehrhart. AMV-81

Turning to him, who meets me with desire. Bible, *O.T.* The Song of Solomon, VII: 10-13. PBWP

Turnip Crier, The. Samuel Johnson. *See* Burlesque of Lope de Vega.

Turquoise and scarlet. Japan. Gavin Bantock. TwMBP

Turquoise Mechanic's Son, The. Steve Toth. AcAn

Turtle, The. Ogden Nash. OBAL; SoSe; TAP

Turtle, The. Diane Wakoski. *Fr.* Greed. NoAM

Turtle, clam and crab as well, The. Covering the Subject. Richard Armour. CTV

Turtle Dove, The. Geoffrey Hill. FaBoTw (1975 ed.)

Turtle Dove. *Unknown.* FSW

Turtle lives 'twixt plated decks, The. The Turtle. Ogden Nash. OBAL; SoSe; TAP

Turtle Soup. "Lewis Carroll." *Fr.* Alice's Adventures in Wonderland, *ch.* 10. FaBoNo; SpRo (Beautiful Soup.) BBL

Turtle swims slowly, The. The Turtle. Diane Wakoski. *Fr.* Greed. NoAM

Turtle with eyes, The. Four Poems. Ray A. Young Bear. Epi

Turtle's Belly, The. Ellen Pearce. IHMS

Turtle's Song, The. *Unknown.* BPo

Tuscaloosa Sam. "Orpheus C. Kerr." OBAL

Tusked octopi the sign of. A Certain World. Ruth Herschberger. WBN

Tusks that clashed in mighty brawls, The. On the Vanity of Earthly Greatness. Arthur Guiterman. HoPM (1975 ed.); InPK; NIL

Tussock burned to fine gold, and the sheep bore golden fleeces. Evening Walk in Winter. Mary Ursula Bethell. ATNZ

Tutivillus, the devil of hell. Chatterers in Church. *Unknown.* EBEV; OxBM

Tutor who tooted the flute, A. Limerick. Carolyn Wells. CTV; SoSe

Tutsan. Charles Senior. MIS

Twa bodachs, I mind, had a threep ae day. Mercy o' Gode. Pittendrigh MacGillivray. MS

Twa Brothers, The. *Unknown.* *See* Twin Brothers, The.

Twa Corbies, The. *Unknown.* AIW; CABA (1972 ed.); Epi; ExPo (1973 ed.); FaBoBa; HAP; ILP (1975 ed.); InPK; LFH; PAIC; PBMP; PoPle; PPP; SoSe; UnPo (1976 ed.)

Twa Magicians, The. *Unknown.* GBP; PeBB (Two Magicians, The.) OAEL-1

Twa Sisters, The. *Unknown.* *See* Two Sisters, The.

'Twas a calm, still night. Lilly Dale. H. S. Thompson. BLSo

'Twas a long parting—but the time. Emily Dickinson. LoAs

'Twas a new feeling—something more. Did Not. Thomas Moore. BoLoP

'Twas a sunny day in June. Dear Old Girl. Richard Henry Buck. FSN

'Twas a tough task, believe it, thus to tame. Upon Dr. Davies's British Grammar. James Howell. OBW

'Twas at the Cimarron Crossing. Oliver Wiggins. "Stanley Vestal." BPAW

'Twas at the royal feast, for Persia won. Alexander's Feast; or, The Power of Music. Dryden. FaPo; FaPoR; ILP (1975 ed.); NOBE; OAEL-1

'Twas autumn and 'round me the leaves were descending. The Banks of Champlain. *Unknown.* AmFP

'Twas Bedford Special Assize, one daft Mid-summer's Day. Ned Bratts. Robert Browning. VLP

'Twas brillig, and the slithy toves. Jabberwocky. "Lewis Carroll." *Fr.* Through the Looking-Glass. AnMo; BiP; CABA (1972 ed.); CTV; DuDr; EBEV; FaBoCo; FaBoNo; FF; HeIP; HoPM (1975 ed.); ILP (1975 ed.); InPK; InPS; NOBE; NOBL; OAEL-2; OBP; OxBChV; PCOP; PoIA; PPM; PPoe; PPP; SpRo; TPo; UsP; VLP; WIF

'Twas Brillo, and the G.E. Stoves. Jabber-Whacky. Isabelle Di Caprio. QQQ

'Twas Christmas Eve, the month was May. A Tragedy. Tom Masson. OBAL

'Twas down at Aunty Jackson's. Walking for That Cake. Ed Harrigan. BLSo

'Twas down at Dan McDevitt's at the corner of this street. Throw Him Down M'Closkey; or, M'Closkey's Great Fight. John W. Kelly. FSN

'Twas down by Brannigan's Corner, one morning I did stray. Johnson's Motor Car. *Unknown.* FSW

'Twas down by the glenside. The Bold Fenian Men. *Unknown.* RDB

'Twas early one morning a fair maid arose. A Kiss in the Morning Early. *Unknown.* GBP

'Twas early one morning in the month of May. The Green Bushes. *Unknown.* AIW

'Twas earlye, earlye in the spring. Earlye, Earlye, in the Spring. *Unknown.* AmFP

'Twas Euclid, and the theorem pi. Plane Geometry. Emma Rounds. QQQ; SpRo

'Twas Ever Thus. Henry Sambrooke Leigh. FaBoCo; SpRo

'Twas ever thus from childhood's hour! Disaster. Charles Stuart Calverley. SpRo

Twas Friday morn when we set sail. The Mermaid. *Unknown.* FSW

'Twas going to snow—'twas snowing! Curse his luck! The Drove-Road. W. W. Gibson. OxBTC

'Twas in eighteen hundred and fifty three. Greenland Fisheries. *Unknown.* FSW

'Twas in Koolau I met with the rain. The Rain. *Tr. by* N. B. Emerson. WTO

'Twas in Rosemary Lane, sirs. Neddy Nibble'm and Biddy Finn. *Unknown.* GBP

'Twas in the merry month of May. Barb'ry Allen. *Unknown.* BLSH

'Twas in the middle of the night. Mary's Ghost. Thomas Hood. PoTa

'Twas in the time when oranges surrender. The Man Who Prayed. John Shaw Neilson. MAuV

'Twas in the year '92, in the merry month of June. The Girl on the Greenbriar Shore. *Unknown.* FSW

'Twas in the year of 1898, and on the 21st of June. The Albion Battleship Calamity. William McGonagall. PeD

'Twas in the year of forty-nine. The Greenland Whale. *Unknown.* GBP; PeBB

'Twas in the year two thousand and one. The Last Man. Thomas Hood. VLP

'Twas just behind the woodshed. My First Cigar. Robert J. Burdette. PoTa

'Twas late, and the gay company was gone. The Declaration. Nathaniel Parker Willis. OBAL

'Twas like a maelstrom, with a notch. Emily Dickinson. CABA (1972 ed.); CMoP (1970 ed.); ExPo (1973 ed.)

'Twas mercy brought me from my pagan land. On Being Brought from Africa to America. Phillis Wheatley. FF; GOA; HeIP; IPWM; NOBA; PiAm; SBG; TAP; WPE

'Twas midnight—Donna Julia was in bed. Byron. *Fr.* Don Juan, I. BiP

'Twas midnight—through the lattice, wreath'd. Jasmine. Thomas Moore. *Fr.* Lalla Rookh: The Light of the Haram. PF

'Twas moonlight in the ripe barley. The Walking of the Moon-Woman. John Shaw Neilson. MAuV

'Twas more than a million years ago. Annabel Lee. Stanley Huntley. SpRo

'Twas my Belovèd spake. Canticle. John Norris. SCP-2

'Twas my last waking thought, how it could be. The Two Founts. Samuel Taylor Coleridge. MBPR

'Twas not for some calm blessing to receive. Her Muff. Richard Lovelace. SCP-2

'Twas of a brisk young sailor, as I have heard it said. Johnny German. *Unknown.* AmFP

'Twas of a nobleman's daughter. Caroline and Her Young Sailor Bold. *Unknown.* AmFP

'Twas on a Holy Thursday, their innocent faces clean. Holy Thursday. Blake. *Fr.* Songs of Innocence. BoReV; ILP (1975 ed.); InPS; LAuP; MBPR; NOBE; OAEL-2; OFD; STS; TT

'Twas on a lofty vase's side. Ode on the Death of a Favourite Cat, Drowned in a Tub of Gold Fishes. Thomas Gray. EBEV; Epi; FaBoCo; HoPM (1975 ed.); ILP (1975 ed.); LAuP; NOBE; NOBL; OAEL-1; PBMP; PCat; PoPle; PPP

'Twas on a Monday morning, just at the break of day. *Maggie Mac. Unknown.* AmFP

'Twas on a Monday morning, right early in the year. Charlie Is My Darling. Lady Caroline Nairne. RDB

'Twas on a summer's day—the sixth of June. Byron. *Fr.* Don Juan, I. PPP

'Twas on the eighth of January, just at the dawn of day. The Battle of New Orleans. *Unknown.* AmFP

'Twas on the field of Antietam where many's the soldier fell. The Battle of Antietam Creek. *Unknown.* AmFP

'Twas on the shores that round our coast. The Yarn of the *Nancy Bell.* W. S. Gilbert. BBL; FaBoCo; HoPM (1975 ed.); NOBL; PeBB; VLP

'Twas one of those dark, cloudy days. Emily Brontë. VLP

'Twas out in California in the days of Forty-Nine. How Bill Went East. George S. Bryan. PoTa

'Twas silent below on the desert. Death Valley. Jack H. Lee. BPAW

'Twas summer and the sun was mounted high. The Ruined Cottage. Wordsworth. MBPR; OAEL-2; PoIA

'Twas sung of old in hut and hall. Birthday Verses Written in a Child's Album. James Russell Lowell. OxBChV

'Twas the gray of early morning when the dreadful cry of "Fire!" The Milwaukee Fire. *Unknown.* AmFP

'Twas the lean coyote told me, baring his slavish soul. The Desert. Henry Herbert Knibbs. BPAW

'Twas the night before Christmas, when all through the house. A Visit from St. Nicholas. Clement Clarke Moore. CTV; FaPo; NIL; OBAL; OxBChV; PChr; PCOP

'Twas warm—at first—like us. Emily Dickinson. CMoP (1970 ed.); SoSe (1977 ed.)

'Twas When the Seas Were Roaring. John Gay. HAP

'Twas when the spousal time of May. Coventry Patmore. *Fr.* The Angel in the House, II, vii. GBL

'Twas yesterday He made me and tomorrow I shall die. Song of the Gulf Stream. Francis Alan Ford. RhR

Tweed and Till. *Unknown.* GBP

Tweedle-dum and Tweedle-dee. Mother Goose. MG; NOBL

Tweedside. Lord Yester. SLP

Twelfth Morning; or, What You Will. Elizabeth Bishop. PSN

Twelfth Night. John Peale Bishop. NIL

Twelfth Night, *sels.* Shakespeare.
  "Come away, come away death," *fr.* II, iv. AIW; GBL; ILP (1975 ed.); NOBE; PoPle; STS
    (Dirge: "Come away, come away, death.") UsP
  "O mistress mine, where are you roaming?" *fr.* II, iii. BiP; GBL; HAP; HeIP; ILP (1975 ed.); InPS; NIL; NOBE; OAEL-1; OLR
    (Feste's Song.) BoLoP
    (Sweet-and-Twenty.) GrRo
  "When that I was and a little tiny boy," *fr.* V, i. EBEV; HeIP; NOBE; OAEL-1; OBP; PPoe; WIF

Twelve and ugly. Dresses. Kathleen Fraser. NMM

Twelve Days of Christmas, The. *Unknown.* AmFP; BBL; BLSH, *with music;* FSW; PChr

Twelve elements in slow orbit, The. Upon Looking at a Book of Astrology. David McFadden. NeAC

Twelve Gates to the City. Nikki Giovanni. IHMS; PoBA

Twelve Gates to the City. *Unknown.* FSW

Twelve Hotels, The. George MacBeth. TwMBP

Twelve Huntsmen with Horns. *Unknown.* RAE

Twelve Lines about the Burning Bush. Melech Ravitch, *tr. fr. Yiddish by* Ruth Whitman. VWA

Twelve Months, The. "Sir Gregory Gander." CTV

Twelve o'clock./ Along the reaches of the street. Rhapsody on a Windy Night. T. S. Eliot. CMoP (1970 ed.); ExPo (1973 ed.); HeIP

Twelve o'clock—a misty night. The Highwayman's Ghost. Richard Garnett. PoTa

12 o'Clock Freight. Hildegarde Flanner. WPW

12 o'Clock News. Elizabeth Bishop. GP; WeW

12 October. Myra Cohn Livingston. CC

12 Photographs of Yellowstone. Ronald Koertge. GP

Twelve Secret Poems, *sels.* Tony Connor.
  "Dull headaches on dark afternoons," 3. UsP
  "There is a war going on," 6. UsP

Twelve snails went walking after night. The Haughty Snail-King. Vachel Lindsay. SO

Twelve years ago I was twelve. From. Richard Terrill. AMV-81

XXth Century. Robert Hillyer. TH

Twentieth-Century Americanism. Joy Davidman. SPT

Twentieth-Century Blues. Kenneth Fearing. CMoP (1970 ed.)

Twentieth year is well nigh past, The. To Mary. William Cowper. LAuP; PAIC

Twenty abreast down the Golden Street ten thousand riders marched. Riders of the Stars. Henry Herbert Knibbs. BPAW

Twenty below. It is too cold. Prayer for Fish. Ronald Wallace. AMV-80

Twenty bracelets and a cackle later. Janis Joplin and the Folding Company. Bayla Winters. AMV-80

Twenty degrees below the normal for May. On Lake Michigan—1972. John Matthias. HeS

28 VIII 69. Laura Chester. IHMS

Twenty-eight turquoise glass trading beads. Portrait of a Woman I Won't Know. Carol Orlock. PoW

Twenty-eight young men bathe by the shore. Song of Myself, XI. Walt Whitman. ExPo (1973 ed.); HAP; LoAs

Twenty-first Century, The. Kevin Hart. GAS

25 Spontaneous Lines Greeting the World. Jim Tyack. AMV-80

Twenty five years of the endless war. Thomas Parkinson. *Fr.* The New Antigone. MIT

Twenty, forty, sixty, eighty. Then. Walter de la Mare. RAE

24 December. John Judson. HeS

Twenty-four Hours. Myra Sklarew. PoUp

Twenty-four kilometers to the camp. Atlas' Daughter. Polly Mann. NPW

Twenty-four Years. Dylan Thomas. CMoP (1970 ed.); MAT; NoAM

Twenty men stand watching the muckers. Muckers. Carl Sandburg. CTBA

Twenty new sparrows. Deep in Winter. Ted Kooser. HeS

Twenty nine years of stale cake and flat ale. The Gorilla at Twenty Nine Years. J. D. Reed. NeAC

Twenty-one Love Poems, *sels.* Adrienne Rich.
"I come home from you through the early light of spring," IV. BoWoP
"That conversation we were always on the edge," XX. BoWoP

21.10.17/ left billet. Excerpts from a Diary of a War (3). John Daniel. TwMBP

Twenty-one Years. *Unknown.* AmFP

Twenty-seven Bums Give a Prostitute the Once. E. E. Cummings. OBAL

Twenty-seventh of March, The. Bryant. EAP

Twenty-third Flight. Earle Birney. HeIP

Twenty-third Psalm, The. Alan Simpson. SFF

23rd Street Runs into Heaven. Kenneth Patchen. SPT

Twenty Words/ Twenty Days. Gael Turnbull. TwMBP

Twenty Year Marriage. Ai. BoWoP; CAAP; GP

Twenty years ago it seemed the same. Time's Offerings. Richard Eberhart. FoP

Twenty years, forty years, it's nothing. The Cold Spring. Denise Levertov. CAAP; Psy

Twenty years hence my eyes may grow. Walter Savage Landor. GBL

'Twer when the busy birds did vlee. Milken Time. William Barnes. VPC

'Twer where the zun did warm the lewth. The Bean Vield. William Barnes. VLP

'Twere folly if ever/ The Whigs should endeavor. A New Ballad. *Unknown.* APAS

'Twere well your judgments but in plays did range. Dryden. *Fr.* The Spanish Friar, *prologue.* OBSV

Twice. Christina Rossetti. BoReV; GBL; NOBE; UsP; VLP

Twice a Week the Winter Thorough. A. E. Housman. LiSp

Twice during dinner. To a Family Man in His Family Room. Rosemary Danielle. WBN

Twice I have written you that I am unhappy. A Letter to Her Father. Inib-sarri, *tr. by* Willis Barnstone. BoWoP

Twice I waked in the night. Penelope. Mary Gilmore. MAuV

Twice of the Same Fever. Robert Graves. LoAs

Twice or thrice had I loved thee. Air[e] and Angels. John Donne. LoAs; MetP; OAEL-1; Prf; SCP-1

Twice Shy. Seamus Heaney. NCSH

Twice Times Then Is Now. Ibn Hazm Al-Andalusi, *tr. fr.* Persian by Omar Pound. OBVE

Twice upon a time. Duality. Dannie Abse. NoAM

Twicknam [*or* Twickenham] Garden. John Donne. EBEV; SCP-1

Twilight. John Masefield. OxBTC

Twilight at Noon. George Weiner. PoUp

Twilight at the Zoo. Alex Rodger. NCSH

Twilight. By now the genial sea of dusk. Half Past Four, October. Anna Hajnal, *tr. by* Daniel Hoffman. BoWoP

Twilight Comes. Hayden Carruth. NNaP

Twilight glitters on the fragmented glass. Judeebug's Country. Joe Johnson. PoBA

Twilight in California. Philip Dow. AmPA

Twilight in Middle March, A. Francis Ledwidge. BIrV

Twilight is here, soft breezes bow the grass. In Exile. Emma Lazarus. SBG

Twilight it is, and the far woods are dim, and the rooks cry. Twilight. John Masefield. OxBTC

Twilight Man, A. Harry Guest. TwMBP

Twilight of Disquietude, The, *sel.* Christopher Brennan. "What do I know? myself alone." MAuV

Twilight of Freedom. Osip Mandelstam, *tr. fr. Russian by* Andrew Glaze. VWA

Twilight Shadows round Me Fall, The, *with music.* Ernest Edwin Ryden. AH

Twilight Thoughts in Israel. Melech Ravitch, *tr. fr. Yiddish by* Seymour Levitan. VWA

Twilighted reek in a blood-rugged hall. Stood-up. Bruce Byfield. AMV-80

Twilight's Last Gleaming. Arthur W. Monks. OFD

Twin Brothers, The. *Unknown.* PBMP
(Twa Brothers, The.) EBEV

Twin Lakes Hunter. A. B. Guthrie, Jr. PoTa

Twin Sister. Jim Long. PHC

Twin streaks twice higher than cumulus. Vapor Trails. Gary Snyder. CAPP

Twined together and, as is customary. Never Such Love. Robert Graves. BoLoP

Twinings Orange Pekoe. Judith Moffett. PoA

Twinkle of twilight. Rapture. Randolph Carlson. AMV-80

Twinkle, twinkle, little bat. The Mad Hatter's Song. "Lewis Carroll." *Fr.* Alice's Adventures in Wonderland. CTV; FaBoNo; NOBL; SpRo

Twinkle, twinkle, little star. Paul Dehn. SpRo

Twinkle, twinkle, little star. The Star. Jane Taylor. CTV; ECBV; OxBChV; SpRo

Twins, The. Berton Braley. TDH

Twins. Robert Graves. FaBoEE

Twins, The. Henry S. Leigh. CTV

Twins, The. Mona Van Duyn. GP

Twirling your blue skirts, travelling the sward. Blue Girls. John Crowe Ransom. CMoP (1970 ed.); GBL; LFH; NoAM; SS; TAP; VGW; VoPo; WeW

Twiss is a tidy bundle, chirped joyous Henry, The. John Berryman. *Fr.* Dream Songs. RRA

Twist me a crown of windflowers. A Crown of Windflowers. Christina Rossetti. OxBChV

Twist-Rime on Spring. Arthur Guiterman. ECBV

Twist thou and twine! in light and gloom. Featherstone's Doom. Robert Stephen Hawker. VPC

Twitched strings, the clang of metal, beaten drums. Javanese Dancers. Arthur Symons. VLP

Twitching in the cactus. Deathwatch. Michael S. Harper. AmPA; PoBA

Twittingpan seized my arm, though I'd have gone. The Encounter. Edgell Rickword. OxBTC

'Twixt handkerchief and nose. A Rub. John Banister Tabb. OBAL

'Twixt kings and tyrants there's this difference known. Kings and Tyrants. Robert Herrick. ILP (1975 ed.)

'Twixt nature and Pygmalion there might appear great strife. Richard Tottel. *Fr.* Tottel's Miscellany. OAEL-1

'Twixt optimist and pessimist. The Difference. *Unknown.* CTV

'Twixt the coastline and the border lay the town of Grog-an'-Grumble. Grog-an'-Grumble Steeplechase. Henry Lawson. PH

'Twixt the seas and the deserts. Just California. John S. McGroarty. BPAW

Two. Margarita Aliger, *tr. fr. Russian by* Elaine Feinstein. VWA

Two. Robert Canzoneri. HoPM (1975 ed.)

Two, The. Irving Feldman. UsP

Two. Moishe Kulbak, *tr. fr. Yiddish by* Ruth Whitman. VWA

Two. Dana Naone. PHC

2 AM: moonlight. The train has stopped. Track. Tomas Tranströmer, *tr. by* Robert Bly. EAS

Two aldermen, three lawyers, five physicians. Of a Zealous Lady. Sir John Harington, *after* Martial. FaBoEE

Two Alternatives to One Moment's Experience. Jim Farrar. DNGG

Two and the Sea. Jacqueline M. Fitzgerald. PPM

Two angels among the throng of angels. A Vision. Denise Levertov. PiAm

Two Appeals to John Harralson, Agent, Nitre and Mining Bureau, C.S.A. *Unknown.* OBAL

Two April Mornings, The. Wordsworth. EBEV; MBPR

Two Are Together. Geoffrey Grigson. GBL

Two Armies. Stephen Spender. OxBTC

Two at Showtime. Suzanne Brabant. PH

Two athletes/ dancing in the cathedral. Spring Images. James Wright. TH

Two Bad Things in Infant School. D. J. Enright. HeHu

Two baths in one day! Man and Woman. Don L. Lee. NeAC

Two Beers in Argyle, Wisconsin. Dave Etter. ANTL

Two Birds. Kathleen Linnell. AMV-81

Two birds, flying East, hit the night. A Happening. Denise Levertov. UsP

Two Bits. Sharlot M. Hall. BPAW

Two black heifers and a red. Drinking Time. D. J. O'Sullivan. PFIr

Two blue glasses of neat. Living in the Moment. Marilyn Hacker. NYP

Two books a prayer shawl and one glass eye. Formations. William Freedman. VWA

Two boys from 4C who appeared, The. Two Sec. Mods. Zulfikar Ghose. LP

Two boys uncoached are tossing a poem together. Catch. Robert Francis. InPK; LiSp; NCSH; WIF

Two boys, whose birth beyond all questions springs. Charles Churchill. *Fr.* The Prophecy of Famine. OBSV

Two bronzes, but they were passing bronze before. Two Wrestlers. Robert Francis. LiSp; SPo

Two Brothers, The. *Unknown.* AmFP

Two Burdens, The. Philip Bourke Marston. VLP

Two burning fires of love. Turning Point. Margaret Gillies. PMW

Two Byzantine Pieces. Rodney Hall. FPA

Two campers (King Lear and his clown?). Outward Bound. James Simmons. IPM

Two Captains, The. William Johnson Cory. *See* Ballad for a Boy, A.

Two cats/ One up a tree. Diamond Cut Diamond. Ewart Milne. ECBV; PCat

Two-Cent Coal. *Unknown.* AmFP

Two centuries ago Linnaeus said "nose frightful, tears pitiful" of you. The Sloth. Isabella Gardner. BoAnP

Two Christs were at Golgotha. Early Lynching. Carl Sandburg. UsP

Two Clocks. John Daniel. LP

Two Clouds. Dan Gerber. TC

Two Clouds. Lawrence Raab. AMV-80

Two coffees in the Español, the last. Conrad Aiken. Preludes for Memnon, II. NoAM

Two college sophs of Cambridge growth. Cassinus and Peter. Swift. OAEL-1; PPP

Two Communist Poets. Irving Layton. AMV-81

Two Companions and the Bear. David Slavitt. BCr

Two Days. W. E. Henley. VLP

Two days ago the sky was. Autumn Rain. Kenneth Rexroth. NU

Two days ago they were playing the piano. Malvolio in San Francisco. Jack Gilbert. NowV

Two Deaths. Elizabeth Jennings. LP

Two Decisions. Vernon Watkins. OxBTC

Two Dedications, *sels.* Gwendolyn Brooks.
Chicago Picasso, The. BPo; ILP (1975 ed.); Psy
Wall, The. ILP (1975 ed.); PoBA

Two Dogs Have I. Ogden Nash. GDP

Two Drinking Songs. T'ao Yuan-ming, *tr. fr. Chinese by* Marjorie Sinclair, *ad. by* Robert Bly. NU

Two drummers sat at dinner, in a grand hotel one day. Mother Was a Lady; or, If Jack Were Only Here. Edward B. Marks. FSN

Two Eskimo Songs. Ted Hughes. ExPo (1973 ed.)

Two evils, monstrous either one apart. Winter Remembered. John Crowe Ransom. HAP; NOBA; UnPo (1976 ed.); VGW

Two eyes, two hands. Gemini. Robert Creeley. PiAm

Two-faced Too. *Unknown, tr. fr. Welsh by* Glyn Jones. OBW

Two Faces. Anthony Thwaite. HeHu

Two Figures. Molly Peacock. AMV-81

Two Figures from the Movies. William Meredith. PPoD

Two Fishermen. Stanley Moss. VWA

Two for the Hampton Institute. David Young. CAAP

Two Founts, The. Samuel Taylor Coleridge. MBPR

Two Friends. David Ignatow. PBMP

Two Gardens. Arlene De Bevoise. AMV-80

Two Gardens. Henry Graham. UsP

Two Gentlemen of Verona, The, *sels.* Shakespeare.
"Thus have I shunned the fire for fear of burning," *fr.* I, iii. GBL
"Who is Silvia? what is she," *fr.* IV, ii. ILP (1975 ed.); STS (Sylvia.) PCOP
(Who Is Sylvia?) OAEL-1

Two ghosts I know once traded heads. Whose Boo Is Whose? X. J. Kennedy. IWK

Two Gifts. *Unknown, tr. fr. Catalan by* Willis Barnstone. BoWoP

Two Girls. Howard Nemerov. AnMo

Two girls discover. The Secret. Denise Levertov. AnMo; PBMP; Psy; SFF

Two Girls Singing. Iain Crichton Smith. MS

2 gods. Good Stuff Cookies. Anselm Hollo. AcAn

Two Graces. Robert Herrick. *See* Grace for a Child *and* Grace for Children, A.

Two gray-winged farmers of the sea, they ride. Maine Sea Gulls. Russell Hoban. BoAnP

Two Hangovers. James Wright. ILP (1975 ed.)

Two have frozen; one—a misfortune. The Mouse. Sandra McPherson. CNW

"Two Hearts Divided." R. Williams Parry, *tr. fr. Welsh by* Joseph P. Clancy. OBW

Two hearts: two blades of grass I braid together. Weaving Love-Knots 2. Hsüeh T'ao, *tr. by* Carolyn Kizer. BoWoP

Two Hoboes. *Unknown.* WTO

Two Hookers. A. K. Redwing. VoR

Two horses in yellow light. August. Adrienne Rich. NNaP; PBWP

Two hours after I saw her. Shawn Wong. *Fr.* Kicking Lego Blocks. NW

225 days under grass. For Jane. Charles Bukowski. CoPAm; CPA; HoPM (1975 ed.)

Two hundred wagons, rolling out to Oregon. The Oregon Trail. Arthur Guiterman. BPAW

Two in August. John Crowe Ransom. PPP

Two in Bed. A. B. Ross. CTV

Two in the Campagna. Robert Browning. EBEV; ExPo (1973 ed.); LoAs; NOBE; OAEL-2; VLP

Two infants vis-à-vis. Bleecker Street. Jean Garrigue. NYP; TAP

Two Invocations of Death. Kathleen Raine. OxBTC

Two Jays at St. Louis. Ferdinand G. Christgau. TDH

Two Jazz Poems. Carl Wendell Hines, Jr.. AmNP (1974 ed.)

Two Jerusalems rise up. Jerusalem. Ruben Kanalenstein, tr. by Yishai Tobin. VWA

Two Kitchen Songs. Edith Sitwell. CMoP (1970 ed.)

Two ladies with high social aims. Such Foolish Old Dames. Sam S. Stinson. TDH

Two Lean Cats. Myron O'Higgins. PoBA

Two leaps the water from its race. A Mill. William Allingham. FaBoEE; POL

Two legs sat upon three legs. Unknown. MG

Two Letters from Chang-kan. Li Po, tr. fr. Chinese by Shigeyoshi Obata. OLR

Two liddle niggers all dressed in white. Raise a "Rucus" To-Night. Unknown. BPo; TAP

Two Lines from the Brothers Grimm. Gregory Orr. AmPA

Two Lips. Thomas Hardy. BoLoP

Two little arabs adult and arabesque. Hans Arp, tr. fr. French by Harriet Watts. FaBoNo

Two little children one morning. You Tell Me Your Dream, I'll Tell You Mine. Seymour Rice and Albert H. Brown. FSN

Two little creatures. Monkeys. Padraic Colum. OxBTC

Two little eyes to look to God. Unknown. CTV

Two little girls, one fair, one dark. The Lost Children. Randall Jarrell. PBMP; RRA; TAP

Two Little Kittens. Unknown. OxBChV

Two Little Miss Lloyds, The. Elizabeth Turner. OxBChV

Two little ships were sailing by. Upon a Christmas Morning. Unknown. AmFP

2 little whos. E. E. Cummings. OLR

Two Lives. William Pillin. SPT

Two lofty ships of Eng-e-land set sail. The Wild Barbaree. Unknown. AmFP

Two: Long After. Alfons Korn. PHC

Two Look at Two. Robert Frost. ILP (1975 ed.); NU

Two Lovers, The. Marie de France, tr. fr. French by Patricia Terry. BoWoP

Two Loves. Richard Eberhart. CMoP (1970 ed.); LoAs

Two loves I have of comfort and despair. Sonnets, CXLIV. Shakespeare. CABA (1972 ed.); EBEV; Epi; NIL; OAEL-1

Two Magicians, The. Unknown. See Twa Magicians, The.

Two magpies under the cypresses, The. What Birds Were There. William Everson. NoAM

Two Maidens [or Maids] Went Milking [or a-Milking] One Day. Unknown. FSW; RDB, with music

Two main diseases. A Trial. Alan Dugan. NoAM

Two Memories. "Hugh MacDiarmid." MS

Two Memories. Cleopatra Mathis. AAN

Two Memories of a Rented House in a Southern State. Dave Smith. CSP

Two men look out through the same bars. Pessimist and Optimist. Frederick Langbridge. SoSe (1977 ed.)

Two Mice, The. Robert Henryson. OxBM

Two Minds. Sara Teasdale. TPo

Two Mornings. Lawrence McGaugh. PoBA

Two Mornings and Two Evenings. Elizabeth Bishop. PoA

Two murders this month. October. Greg Pape. AmPA

Two negro slaves. The Sevier County Runaway. Besmilr Brigham. Psy

Two nights in Manchester: nothing much to do. Mr. Cooper. Anthony Thwaite. OxBTC

Two Noble Kinsmen, The, sel. At. to Shakespeare. Bridal Song, A: "Roses, their sharp spines being gone," fr. I, i. NOBE

209 Canal. Richard Howard. NYP; TAP

Two, of course there are two. Death and Co. Sylvia Plath. CMoP (1970 ed.); ConAP; FF

Two of Cups, The. Emmett Jarrett. NeAC

Two of us roof my house, The. Ed Shreckongost. Ed Ochester. TAT

Two Old Crows. Vachel Lindsay. FaBoNo; OBAL

Two Old Ladies. Siegfried Sassoon. OxBTC

Two Old Men. David McAleavey. PoUp

Two Old Men. Lorine Niedecker. TVo

Two Old Men Look at the Sea. J. R. Hervey. ATNZ

Two on a Journey. Basil Payne. IPM

Two or Three: A Recipe [or Receipt] to Make a Cuckold. Pope. AnMo; BoLoP; FaBoEE

Two pairs of hands go round. Korf's Clock. Christian Morgenstern, tr. by Geoffrey Grigson. FaBoNo

Two Parents, The. "Hugh MacDiarmid." FaBoTW (1975 ed.); OxBTC

Two parts lye, and one part quicklime. Mr. Cherry. Paul Baker Newman. AMV-81

Two Pennies Found on the Gravel. David Kherdian. FAF

Two People. E. V. Rieu. ECBV

Two people are in the room. Remember. Steve Toth. AcAn

Two people in a room, speaking harshly. Novella. Adrienne Rich. PPP

Two people live in Rosamund. Two People. E. V. Rieu. ECBV

Two people live side by side. Two. Moishe Kulbak, tr. by Ruth Whitman. VWA

Two Pieces after Suetonius. Robert Penn Warren. NOBA

Two pilgrims, broiling in the sun. Beware of Dogmas. Ebenezer Elliott. FaBoEE

Two Poems. Don L. Lee. UsP
"I ain't seen no poems stop a .38."
"Last week/ my mother died."

Two Poems about President Harding. James Wright. NoAM

Two Poems (after A. E. Housman). Hugh Kingsmill. NOBL

Two Poems Based on Fact. Frank J. Lepkowski. AMV-81

2 Poems for Black Relocation Centers. Etheridge Knight. NNaP; NoAM

2 Poems Written on Turning Around Too Quickly while Hiking. Morton Marcus. NVAP

Two-pointer by New York! Boryla leaps! N.B.A. Prelim, Boston Garden. Thomas Whitbread. PPoD

Two policemen laughed, The. Policemen Laughing. Ray Fraser. NeAC

Two Postures beside a Fire. James Wright. BrS; GP

Two Presentations. Robert Duncan. InPS

Two Pursuits. Christina Rossetti. WPE

Two-quart virgin in my lap, A. The Aged Wino's Counsel to a Young Man on the Brink of Marriage. X. J. Kennedy. FF

Two Questions, The. Alice Meynell. WPE

Two Rain Songs. Unknown, tr. fr. Papago Indian. AKE

Two Rats, The. Unknown. ECBV; PoPle
(What Became of Them?) OxBChV

Two Red Roses across the Moon. William Morris. VLP

Two Refugees. Mordecai Marcus. VWA

Two Rivers. Emerson. NOBA

Two roads diverged in a yellow wood. The Road Not Taken. Robert Frost. CMoP (1970 ed.); HAP; HeIP; ILP (1975 ed.); LFH; NoAM; PoIA; RFM; SoSe; STS; TAP; VoPo

Two Roads, Etc. Dorothy Walters. IHMS

Two Rural Sisters. Charles Cotton. *Fr.* Resolution in Four Sonnets, of a Poetical Question, Concerning Four Rural Sisters. BoLoP

Two Salesmen in Search of a Country. Robert Gessner. SPT

Two sculptors. Four Translations from the English of Robert Hershon. Robert Hershon. NeAC

Two Sec. Mods. Zulfikar Ghose. LP

Two Selves, The. Margaret Avison. NoAM

Two separate divided silences. Severed Selves. Dante Gabriel Rossetti. The House of Life, XL. BoLoP; VPC

Two Shapes. Arthur Gregor. TAP

Two shots down and I'm exalted. Alan Dugan. GP

Two Sisters, The. *Unknown.* AIW; AmFP; FSW; MAT (Binnorie.) AIW; PoPle
(Twa Sisters, The.) FaBoBa; ILP (1975 ed.)

Two Sleepers, The. Robin Skelton. MPA

Two Songs. C. Day Lewis. HAP; NoAM
Come, Live with Me and Be My Love, II. BoLoP; ILP (1975 ed.)
(Song: "Come live with me and be my love.") NIL

Two Songs. Adrienne Rich. CABA (1972 ed.); ILP (1975 ed.); NOBA; Psy; TAP

Two Songs from a Play. W. B. Yeats. *Fr.* The Resurrection. CABA (1972 ed.); CMoP (1970 ed.); ExPo (1973 ed.); FaBoTw (1975 ed.); HAP; ILP (1975 ed.); NIL; NOBE; OAEL-2; OBP; PPoe; PPP

Two Songs of a Fool. W. B. Yeats. CMoP (1970 ed.)

Two Sonnets. John Ashbery.
Dido. CAPP; VGW
Idiot, The. VGW

Two Spirits, The: an Allegory. Shelley. MBPR; OAEL-2; Prf

Two spoons of sherry. The Witch's Work Song. T. H. White. FaBoNo

Two spotted cows spread out on warm rocks. At the Confluence of the Soleduck, the Bogachiel and the Quillayute. Beth Bentley. CNW

Two Springs. Li Ch'ing-chao, *tr. fr. Chinese by* Kenneth Rexroth. BoWoP

Two statesmen met by moonlight. What the Moon Saw. Vachel Lindsay. FaBoEE

Two Stories about Cameras, *sel.* Roger Pfingston.
"Smack on his back in the snow." BCr

Two suicides, not in the one season. Waikato Railstop. Kendrick Smithyman. ATNZ

Two Summers in Moravia. Roger McDonald. CAAP; GAS

Two sweeter babes you nare did see. *Unknown.* FaBoEE

Two Takes from Love in Los Angeles. Al Young. CoPAm

Two that could not have lived their single lives. Two in August. John Crowe Ransom. PPP

2976. Julia Uceda, *tr. fr. Spanish by* Willis Barnstone. BoWoP

2001: The Tennyson/Hardy Poem. Gavin Ewart. FaBoCo

Two Tile Beaks. Maria Amalia Fonte Boa, *tr. fr. Portuguese by* Willis Barnstone *and* Nelson Cerqueira. BoWoP

Two Times Two is Four. H. Leivick, *tr. fr. Yiddish by* Ruth Whitman. VWA

Two Tramps in Mud Time. Robert Frost. CMoP (1970 ed.); NoAM; STS

Two Travellers, The. C. J. Boland. PFIr

Two Trees, The. W. B. Yeats. OAEL-2; VLP

Two Trinities. Kenneth Mackenzie. GAS

221-1424. Sonia Sanchez. NIL

Two Variations. Denise Levertov. PPoe
Enquiry, *sel.* RiTi

Two Vietnamese Women. Herbert Krohn. AAN

Two Views of a Cadaver Room. Sylvia Plath. AnMo; CMoP (1970 ed.)

Two Views of Two Ghost Towns. Charles Tomlinson. NoAM

Two virtues ride, by stallion, by nag. The Death of Myth-making. Sylvia Plath. PoA

Two voices are there: one is of the deep. A Sonnet. James Kenneth Stephen. FaBoCo; NOBL; PPoD; SpRo

Two voices are there; one is of the sea. Thought of a Briton on the Subjugation of Switzerland. Wordsworth. MBPR; PBMP; SpRo

Two Voices in a Meadow. Richard Wilbur. PBMP; SoS; UnPo (1976 ed.)

Two wedded hearts, if ere were such. Samuel Taylor Coleridge. MBPR

Two Weeks after an April Frost. Steven Helmling. AMV-80

Two Went Up into the Temple to Pray. Richard Crashaw. HAP

Two White Horses in a Line. *Unknown.* BluL

Two wild duck of the upland spaces. Duck. John Lyle Donaghy. BIrV

Two winding rails. The Transandean Railway. Thomas Kretz. AMV-80

Two Witches. Robert Frost. CMoP (1970 ed.)
Witch of Coös, The, *sel.* NoAM; NOBA; PAIC

Two Witches, The. Robert Graves. SO

Two Witches. Alexander Resnikoff. IWK

Two Women. Naomi Replansky. NMM

Two Women at JFK Gravesite. Margaret Gibson. WasP

Two Women with Mangoes. Steven Cramer. AMV-80

Two worlds there are. One you think. Cleaning the Well. Fred Chappell. CSP

Two Wrestlers. Robert Francis. LiSp; SPo

Two Years Later. W. B. Yeats. ILP (1975 ed.)

Two young maids in a beauty fair. *Malay Oral Tradition, tr. by* R. O. Winstedt. WTO

'Twould ring the bells of Heaven. The Bells of Heaven. Ralph Hodgson. ILP (1975 ed.); NOBE; PPoD

Ty Cobb Story, The. Tom Clark. LiSp

Tyger, The. Blake. *See* Tiger, The.

Tyger! Tyger! James Nolan. AATT

Tyger! Tyger! burning bright. *See* Tiger! Tiger! burning bright.

Tyin' a Knot in the Devil's Tail. Gail Gardner. FSW

Tyndarus attempting too kis a fayre lasse with a long nose. Of Tyndarus, That Frumped a Gentlewoman. *Unknown, tr. by* Richard Stanyhurst. BIrV

Type of the antique Rome! Rich reliquary. The Coliseum. Poe. NOBA

Tyrannic Love, *sel.* Dryden.
Ah, How Sweet It Is to Love! *fr.* IV, i. HoPM (1975 ed.)

Tyranny of Moths. Gerald Vizenor. VoR

Tyrant, why swel'st thou thus. Bible, *O.T.* Psalms, LII, *paraphrased by* Countess of Pembroke. OBVE

Tyrants are meeting, the bastards, The. The Briefing. David Kirby. CSP

Tyre, Pergamum, and Troy. The Defenses. Ben Maddow. SPT

Tyson's Corner. Primus St. John. PoBA

Tywater. Richard Wilbur. CMoP (1970 ed.); ConAP

Tzu Yeh Songs, *sels. Tr. fr. Chinese by* Arthur Waley. BoWoP
"All night I could not sleep."
"At the time when blossoms."
"I heard my love was going to Yang-chou."
"I will carry my coat and not put on my belt."

# U

UA Flight to Chicago. Duane Ackerson. PoW

U bet u wer. To a Poet I Knew. Jewel C. Latimore. PoBA

"U.C. China Expert." Headlines. Foster Robertson. CPA

U feel that way sometimes. Mixed Sketches. Don L. Lee. BPo; TAP

U Name This One. Carolyn M. Rodgers. NMM; PoBA

U. S. A., The. Grantland Rice. SPo

U.S. Coast and Geodetic Survey Ship *Pioneer*, The. Robert Hershon. NeAC

U. S. 1946 King's X. Robert Frost. NIL

U.S. Sailor with the Japanese Skull, The. Winfield Townley Scott. ExPo (1973 ed.)

Ubi Iam Sunt? Richard L. Greene. PAIC

Ubi Sunt Qui ante Nos Fuerunt? *Unknown.* HAP; ILP (1975 ed.); PAIC; WeW, 3 sts.
  (Ubi Sunt, *longer version.*) OxBM
  (Where Are the Ones Who Lived Before? *mod. English.*) HAP
  ("Where beeth they biforen us weren.") EBEV

Uccello. Gregory Corso. FF

Ugliest little boy. The Life of Lincoln West. Gwendolyn Brooks. FB; FiCh

Ugly Child, The. Elizabeth Jennings. RAE

Ugly Neck. D. J. Enright. HeHu

Ugly old man, An. No Great Matter. David Lawson. VGW

Uhuru. Mari Evans. CNA

Ulalume—a Ballad. Poe. NOBA; PiAm; TAP
  "Skies they were ashen and sober, The," *sel.* LFH, 1 *st.*

Ulezalka, Ulezalka. The Tailor. Patricia Garfinkel. AMV-80

Ulivfak's Song of the Caribou. *Unknown, tr. fr. Caribou Eskimo.* AKE

Ulster. Hans Adler. AMV–81

Ultima Ratio Regum. Stephen Spender. CMoP (1970 ed.); LP; MPo; OAEL-2; SFF; SoS

Ultima Thule. Longfellow. AmVN

Ultimate Anthology. Martin Bell. POL

Ultimate Antientropy, The. Theodore Weiss. NoAM

Ultimate in a serrate sky. Among Mountains. Reuben Tam. PHC

Ultimate Poem Is Abstract, The. Wallace Stevens. PoA

Ultimate Problems. William Stafford. NU

Ultimate Reality. Ogden Nash. FaBoCo

Ulysses. Dante, *tr. fr. Italian by* Longfellow. *Fr. Divina Commedia: Inferno.* Epi

Ulysses. Robert Graves. CMoP (1970 ed.); FaBoTw (1975 ed.); NoAM

Ulysses, *sel.* James Joyce.
  Yes. FF

Ulysses. Tennyson. AnMo; CABA (1972 ed.); EBEV; Epi; FaPoR; FF; HAP; HeIP; HoPM (1975 ed.); ILP (1975 ed.); InPK; InPS; IP; IPWM; LFH; NIL; NOBE; OAEL-2; PAIC; PoIA; PoPle; PPoe; PPP; SoSe; UnPo (1976 ed.); UsP; VLP

Ulysses and the Siren. Samuel Daniel. CABA (1972 ed.); HAP; NOBE; PAIC

Ulysses' Library. David Daiches. PoA

Umbaji Park. David Kherdian. SA

Umber dowagers of Henry Street, The. September. Marilyn Hacker. NYP

Umber was painting of a lion fierce. Upon Umber: Epigram. Robert Herrick. CaPo

Umbilical. Eve Merriam. CTBA

Umbra is the thing itself, The. The Result of Our Investigation. Charles S. Bouslog. PHC

Umbrella, the Cane, and the Broom, The. Eliezer Steinbarg, *tr. fr. Yiddish by* Curt Leviant. VWA

Umh——uhumh! Umh——uhumh/ Get a breath of that country air. Country Air. Mike Love *and* Brian Wilson. PoRo

Ummmmh oh ain't got no mama now. That Black Snake Moan. *Unknown.* BluL

Un Canadien Errant (An Exiled Canadien). *Tr. fr. French.* FSW

Una Anciana Mexicana. Alice Corbin. WPW

Unaccustomed ripeness in the wood, An. Elizabeth. Robert Lowell. *Fr. Harriet.* CAPP; LoAs

Un-American Investigators. Langston Hughes. BPo

Unarm! unarm! No more your fights. Sir William Davenant. *Fr. The Triumphs of the Prince D'Amour.* SCP-2

Unbeliever, The. Elizabeth Bishop. NoAM

Unborn, The. Thomas Hardy. CMoP (1970 ed.)

Unbounded is thy range; with varied style. The Stormy Hebrides. William Collins. *Fr. An Ode on the Popular Superstitions.* NOBE

Unbridling Our Horses. Barney Bush. BrS

Uncertain What to Wear. William Jay Smith. TDH

Uncertainty. Wordsworth. *Fr. Ecclesiastical Sonnets.* MBPR

Uncessant minutes, whilst you move you tell. To His Watch When He Could Not Sleep. Lord Herbert of Cherbury. NOBE

Uncivill sickness, hast thou no regard. Henry Constable. *Fr. Diana.* ESo

Unclaimed. Florida Watts Smyth. PH

Uncle. Philip Levine. NNaP

Uncle Bull-boy. June Jordan. PoBA

Uncle Charlie lived alone. All Up and Down the Lines. Robert Cooperman. AMV-80

Uncle Death. Walter Clark. NCSH

Uncle Dog: The Poet at 9. Robert Sward. VGW

Uncle Edward's Affliction ("Uncle Edward was colour-blind"). Vernon Scannell. HeHu

Uncle Henry. W.H. Auden. NOBL

Uncle Iv Surveys His Domain from His Rocker. Jonathan Williams. OBAL

Uncle James. Margaret Mahy. FPB

Uncle Joe. *Unknown.* FSW

Uncle Reuben. *Unknown.* FSW

Uncle Roderick. Norman MacCaig. MPo

Uncle sent for O. T. told him we have to fight. O. T.'s Blues. Waring Cuney. MAT

Uncle Umbert. Shel Silverstein. OSF

Unclench Yourself. Marge Piercy. NeAC

Uncles. Harold Norse. PoW

Uncomly in cloistre I cowre ful of care. Choristers Training. *Unknown.* OxBM

Unconscious Woman. Jill Thomas. PMW

Unconsumable material is everywhere. The Square at Dawn. James Tate. NoAM

Uncovering. Cynthia MacDonald. UsP

Undead, The. Richard Wilbur. CAPP; ConAP

Undefined Tenderness, An. Joel Oppenheimer. VGW

Under. George Bowering. NeAC

Under. J. C. Squire. FaBoTw (1975 ed.)

Under a bent when the night was deep. William Morris. *Fr. The Earthly Paradise.* PChr

Under a lawn, than skies more clear. Upon Roses. Robert Herrick. SCP-1

Under a red face, black velvet shyness. Chicago Morning. Ted Berrigan. FiCh

Under a sky studded with asterisks. On the Night in Question. Patricia Goedicke. TAP

Under a splintered mast. A Talisman. Marianne Moore. NCSH

Under a spreading chestnut-tree. The Village Blacksmith. Longfellow. AmVN; CTV; FaPoR; OBAL; PCOP; PPM

Under a swaying. El Dorado. Richard Ryan. BIrV

Under a toadstool/ Crept a wee Elf. The Elf and the Dormouse. Oliver Herford. PCOP

Under Ben Bulben. W. B. Yeats. CMoP (1970 ed.); HAP; NoAM; OxBTC
*Sels.*
"Cast a cold eye." FaBoEE
"Under bare Ben Bulben's head." WeW

Under cracking pieces of the moon, eelpout. Spawning in Northern Minnesota. David McElroy. AmPA

Under 500 kings three kingdoms groan. The Parliament Dissolved at Oxford. *Unknown.* APAS

Under God's violent unsleeping eye. Difference. T. H. Jones. OBW

Under great yellow flags and banners of the ancient cold. The Shadow of Cain. Edith Sitwell. OxBTC

Under hawk-watch. Fisherman. Philip Booth. LiSp; SPo

Under her deep plush roof. "Vierge Ouvrante." Miriam Palmer. NMM; RiTi

Under his careful crown he keeps. King Midas Has Asses' Ears. Donald Finkel. CoPAm

Under Milk Wood, *sel.* Dylan Thomas.
"Johnnie Crack and Flossie Snail." LCL; RAE

Under my eaves untiring all the spring day. A Natural Grace. C. K. Stead. ATNZ

Under my elbow. In my elbow. Sun. Diane Wakoski. VoA

Under my thoughts may I God-thoughts find. Thoughts of God. *Tr. from Gaelic by* Douglas Hyde. WTO

Under my window. Letter in Winter. Raymond R. Patterson. PoBA

Under my window-ledge the waters race. Coole Park and Ballylee, 1931. W. B. Yeats. CMoP (1970 ed.); NoAM; PPP; PSN

Under our stillness fled the same low hooves. The Racetrack. Jane Cooper. LoAs

Under pressure only wood keeps its grain, spike and screw. Elective Affinities. David Malouf. CAAP

Under Restless Clouds. Hanny Michaelis, *tr. fr. Dutch by* Marjolijn de Jager. VWA

Under Seconal/ my apartment diminishes. Day Sleeper. James L. White. HeS

Under Sorrow's Sign. Gofraidh Fionn O'Dalaigh, *tr. fr. Irish by* John Montague. BIrV

Under Stone. Elaine Feinstein. VWA

Under the Anheuser Bush. Andrew B. Sterling. OBAL

Under the Arc de Triomphe: October 17. Marilyn Hacker. PoA

Under the arch of life, where love and death. Soul's Beauty. Dante Gabriel Rossetti. The House of Life, LXXVII. VLP

Under the bamboo. T. S. Eliot. *Fr.* Sweeney Agonistes. UnPo (1976 ed.)

Under the Bamboo Tree, *with music.* Bob Cole. BLSo; FSN

Under the bed they searched, and there they found. Byron. *Fr.* Don Juan, I. PoIA

Under the big 500-watted lamps, in the huge sawdusted. The Slaughter-House. Alfred Hayes. NowV

Under the bronze crown. A Baroque Wall-Fountain in the Villa Sciarra. Richard Wilbur. BiP; CAPP; SoSe

Under the bronze-lipped Jesus bell. Bell at Midnight. May Miller. PPoD

Under the Catalpa Trees. Gary Young. AMV-81

Under the Cellar. Ralph Salisbury. MPA

Under the concrete benches. Weed Puller. Theodore Roethke. AnMo; PiAm; STS

Under the dawn I wake my two-wheel friend. Yevgeny Yevtushenko, *tr. by* Robin Milner-Gulland *and* Peter Levi. *Fr.* On a Bicycle. SPo

Under the dusty print of hobnailed boot. Country Press. Rosemary Dobson. GAS; MAuV

Under the dying sun. The Reaper. L. H. Allen. MAuV

Under the Earth. Abraham Sutskever, *tr. fr. Yiddish by* Ruth Whitman. VWA

Under the Eildon Tree, *sel.* Sydney Goodsir Smith.
Elegy XIII: "I got her in the Black Bull." MS

Under the El on Sunday afternoon. Aside. Alan Dugan. PoA

Under the forest, where the day is dark. The Manzanita. Yvor Winters. VGW

Under the Greenwood Tree ("A sodger laddie's socht a hoose"). "Hugh MacDiarmid," *after the Cretan.* OBVE

Under the Greenwood Tree. Shakespeare. *Fr.* As You Like It, II, v. CTV; ECBV; HeIP; HoPM (1975 ed.); ILP (1975 ed.); InPS; OAEL-1; UnPo (1976 ed.)

Under the Greenwood Tree ("In summer time when leaves grow green"). *Unknown.* GBP

Under the Hill. Richard Eberhart. PoA

Under the hive-like dome the stooping haunted readers. The British Museum Reading Room. Louis MacNeice. NOBE

Under the house, between the road the sea-cliff. Grass on the Cliff. Robinson Jeffers. *Fr.* The Trumpet. PoA

Under the Ladder to Heaven. Elizabeth Fenton. NMM

Under the Lime Tree. Walther von der Vogelweide, *tr. fr. German by* Thomas Lovell Beddoes. GBL
("Under the lime-tree, on the daisied ground.") OBVE

Under the lintel at midnight. Under the Sign of the Fisher. Bertram Higgins. MAuV

Under the Locust Blossoms. Frederick Goddard Tuckerman. NOBA

Under the long dark boughs, like jewels red. Cherry Robbers. D. H. Lawrence. OBP; PoIA

Under the low dark sky and the sodden leaves. Wet Summer: Botanic Gardens. Nan McDonald. MAuV

Under the Maud Moon. Galway Kinnell. CAAP; NNaP

Under the Mirabeau Bridge the Seine/ Flows and our love. The Mirabeau Bridge. Guillaume Apollinaire, *tr. by* W. S. Merwin. OBVE

Under the Mirabeau bridge the Seine/ Flows with our loves. The Mirabeau Bridge. Guillaume Apollinaire, *tr. by* Quentin Stevenson. BoLoP

Under the Mistletoe. Countee Cullen. PChr

Under the Moon. George Bruce. MS

Under the most ideal remedy. A Poem on Inter-uterine Device. A. Rasheed Ghazi. PeD

Under the mountain, as when first I knew. Sonnet. Frederick Goddard Tuckerman. *Fr.* Sonnets. HAP; PiAm; TAP

Under the oak tree, oak tree. *Unknown, tr. fr. Spanish by* Willis Barnstone. BoWoP

Under the Old Elm, *sels.* James Russell Lowell. GOA
"Never to see a nation born," *fr.* VII.
"That lifted blade transformed our jangling clans," *fr.* VII.

Under the olive trees, from the ground. The Coward. Stephen Spender. NoAM

Under the opening fingers of the dawn. Homer, *tr. by* Robert Fitzgerald. The Odyssey, VIII–XI. NAWM-1

Under the orchid, blooming as it bloomed. The Subway from New Britain to the Bronx. Randall Jarrell. NYP

Under the parabola of a ball. How to Kill. Keith Douglas. NOBE

Under the plum-blossoms are nightingales. Desolation. Amy Lowell. PoA

Under the pond, among rocks. The Dragonfly. Howard Nemerov. PoA

Under the Pot. Robert Graves. FaBoEE

Under the quince tree. Bible, *O.T.* The Song of Solomon, VIII:5. PBWP

Under the roof and the roof's shadow turns. The Merry-go-round. Rainer Maria Rilke, *tr. by* C. F. MacIntyre. WeW

Under the Ruins of Poland. Itzik Manger, *tr. fr. Yiddish by* Mirriam Waddington. VWA

Under the rusting elms his separate path. The Student. Dabney Stuart. NowV

Under the shadow of a stately pile. At Florence. Wordsworth. VLP

Under the Shawl. Rose Drachler. VWA

Under the Sign of Moth. David Wagoner. AMV-81; PCho

Under the Sign of the Fisher. Bertram Higgins. MAuV

Under the sky's/ armpit. The Golden-eyed Crossbow. Claude Pélieu. MIT

Under the Stone I Saw Them Flow. Horace Gregory. SPT

Under the thick beams of that swirly smoking light. The Examination. W. D. Snodgrass. CABA (1972 ed.); CAPP; ConAP

Under the too white marmorial Lincoln Memorial. The March. Robert Lowell. NowV

Under the trees. Running Water Music. Gary Snyder. ILP (1975 ed.); PiAm

Under the trees the leaves go down. Rondel: Autumn. Matt Field. AMV-80

Under the waning moon. Starting at Dawn. Sun Yün-feng, *tr. by* Kenneth Rexroth *and* Ling Chung. PBWP

Under the Waterfall. Thomas Hardy. BoLoP

Under the whip of wanting. Sub-Prefix. 1. Under, Beneath, Below: As In. Joanne de Longchamps. PoW

Under the wide and starry sky. Requiem. Robert Louis Stevenson. DL; FaPoR; ILP (1975 ed.); NOBE; PCOP; PIM; RhR

Under the Williamsburg Bridge. Galway Kinnell. NYP

Under the Willow-Shades. Sir William Davenant. BoLoP; ILP (1975 ed.)

Under the willow the willow. Recruiting Drive. Charles Causley. OxBTC

Under the willow whose roots are shallow. May-Fly. John Heath-Stubbs. SoSe

Under the Wood. *Unknown.* *See* Me Rueth, Mary.

Under these historic skies. From Jerusalem: A First Poem. Gabriel Preil, *tr. by* Robert Friend. VWA

Under this marble, or under this sill. Epitaph on Himself. Pope. FaBoEE

Under this sod lies a great bucking hoss. To Midnight. *Unknown.* BPAW

Under this stone/ Lies a Reverend Drone. An Epitaph upon That Profound and Learned Casuist, the Late Ordinary of Newgate. Thomas Brown. OBSV

Under this stone, reader, survey. On Sir John Vanbrugh, Architect. Abel Evans. FaBoCo; FaBoEE

Under Way. Bruce Dawe. CAAP

Under Which Lyre, a Reactionary Tract for the Times. W.H. Auden. NOBL

Under yonder beech-tree single [*or* standing] on the green-sward. Love in the Valley. George Meredith. NOBE; OAEL-2; VLP; VPC

Under your Milky Way. Return of the Goddess Artemis. Robert Graves. PoA

Under Your Voice, among Legends. Phyllis Beauvais. NMM

Underdeveloped Country, An. D. J. Enright. NOBL

Underground grower, blind and a common brown, An. Potato. Richard Wilbur. CAPP

Underground Parking, The. Gary Soto. AAN; CPA

Underground Poetry. Pedro Pietri. NYP

Underground space, like water, is running out. Apartments on First Avenue. Cynthia Macdonald. NYP

Underground Stream, The. James Dickey. NOBA

Underground System. Edna St. Vincent Millay. SBG

Underneath a cypress shade, the Queen of Love sat mourning. *Unknown.* GBL

Underneath my belt. When I Was Lost. Dorothy Aldis. CaYB

Underneath my lids another eye has opened. From the Prison House. Adrienne Rich. NNaP

Underneath the growing grass. The Bourne. Christina Rossetti. ILP (1975 ed.)

Underneath the House. Rhyll McMaster. FPA; GAS

Underneath this marble stone/ Lie two beauties join'd in one. Epitaph of Pyramus and Thisbe. Abraham Cowley. FaBoEE

Underneath this sable [*or* marble] hearse [*or* herse]. On the Countess Dowager of Pembroke. William Browne. CABA (1972 ed.); FaBoEE; HAP; ILP (1975 ed.); NIL; NOBE; OAEL-1; OBP; PoPle; SCP-2; WeW

Underneath this wooden cross there lies. Epitaph. Karl Shapiro. *Fr.* Elegy for a Dead Soldier. OFD

Underneath were the everlasting arms. I Looked over Jordan. Lane Dunlop. NowV

Undertaker asks for clothes, The. Grave Clothes. Karen Swenson. AMV-80

Undertakers' Club, The. *Unknown.* GBP

Undertaker's Horse, The. Kipling. FaBoNo

Undertaking, The. John Donne. NOBE

Undertaking, The. Louis Glück. NVAP

Undertow, The: Hatteras Island. Gary Stein. PoUp

Underwater. Michael Schmidt. SoSe

Underwater eyes, an eel's. An Otter. Ted Hughes. CMoP; (1970 ed.); NoAM

Underwater, this is the cathedral. Underwater. Michael Schmidt. SoSe

Underwear. Lawrence Ferlinghetti. OBAL; TPo

Underworld. George Garrett. SS

Undo! *Unknown.* BoReV; OxBM

Undone, undone the lawyers are. The Downfall of Charing Cross. *Unknown.* FaBoCo

Undreamed, The. Elaine V. Emans. AMV-81

Undressing her hair. The Voyeur. Deanna Louise Pickard. AMV-80

Undulating golden waves of ripened. High Plains Harvest. Bruce Morton. AMV-81

Unduly elected body of our elders, An. Elegy for Yards, Pounds, and Gallons. David Wagoner. PoA; SoSe (1977 ed.)

Unearthing. Betsy Rosenberg. VWA

Uneasiness of the night surrounds me, The. In a Night. Ann Marie Savage. AMV-81

Unemployed: 2 A.M. Sol Funaroff. SPT

Unemployment. William Mills. HoPM (1975 ed.)

Unemployment in our bones, The. Derry. Seamus Deane. CIP

Unexpected, The. Ai. CAAP

Unexpected Pleasure, An. *Unknown.* FaBoCo

Unexpected Visit. Fleur Adcock. ATNZ

Unexplorer, The. Edna St. Vincent Millay. PoA

Unexpressible Love, The. William Cavendish, Duke of Newcastle. SCP-2

Unfair to Men. *Unknown, tr. fr. Welsh by* Gwyn Jones. OBW

Unfair to Women. *Unknown, tr. fr. Welsh by* Gwyn Jones. OBW

Unfaith and Faith. Robert Browning. *Fr.* Bishop Blougram's Apology. BoReV

Unfaithful Married Woman, The. Federico García Lorca, *tr. fr. Spanish by* Rolfe Humphries. LoAs

Unfathomable Sea! Shelley. RhR

Unfelt, unheard, unseen. Lines. Keats. MBPR

Unfinished History. Archibald MacLeish. VGW

Unfold! Unfold! Theodore Roethke. STS

Unfold, unfold! take in His light.   The Revival.   Henry Vaughan.
    BoReV: ILP (1975 ed.); PoPle

Unforgetting, afflicted heart.   Black Poppies.   Wayne Miller.
    CPA

Unforgiven, The.   E. A. Robinson.   CMoP (1970 ed.)

Unfortunate Coincidence.   Dorothy Parker.   PoIA; SBG

Unfortunate Lover, The.   Andrew Marvell.   TT

Unfortunate Lover, An.   *Unknown.*   OxBM

Unfortunate Lovers, The, *sel.*   Sir William Davenant.
    "You fiends and furies, come along!"   SCP-2

Unfortunate Miller, The.   A. E. Coppard.   FaBoTw (1975 ed.);
    PoTa

Unfortunate Miss Bailey.   George Colman the Younger.   FSW;
    GBP; PeBB
    (Miss Bailey's Ghost.)   FaBoBa

Unfriendly friendly universe.   The Child Dying.   Edwin Muir.
    FaBoTw (1975 ed.)

Unfurls in rain.   The Newest Banana Plant Leaf.   Ingrid Wendt.
    NMM

Ungratefulness.   George Herbert.   ILP (1975 ed.)

Unhappy Diary Days.   Gerald Vizenor.   VoR

Unhappy dreamer, who outwinged in flight.   On the Death of a
    Metaphysician.   George Santayana.   PAIC

Unhappy people in a happy world, An.   Wallace Stevens.   *Fr.*
    The Auroras of Autumn.   CMoP (1970 ed.)

Unhappy Schoolboy, The.   *Unknown.*   OxBChV

Unhappy summer you.   This Summer and Last.   Thomas Hardy.
    OxBTC

Unhappy verse, the witness of my unhappy state.   Iambicum
    Trimetrum.   Spenser.   BoLoP; EBEV

Unhatch you April butterflies.   'Ode to a Fat Cat.   Annabel
    Farjeon.   PCat

Unhistoric Story, The.   Allen Curnow.   ATNZ

Unholy Missions.   Bob Kaufman.   CNA

Unholy Roller   H. H. Lewis.   SPT

Unhumans walk around.   But, Still, He.   Henry N. Lucas.
    AMV-81

Unhurt, There Is No Help.   Allen Curnow.   ATNZ

Unicorn.   Nicholas Stuart Gray.   ECBV

Unicorn.   William Jay Smith.   SO

Unicorn, The.   Ella Young.   PCOP

Unicorn with the long white horn, The.   Unicorn.   William Jay
    Smith.   SO

Unidentified Flying Object.   Robert Hayden.   NCSH

Unifying Principle, The.   A. R. Ammons.   NOBA

Union Barge on Staten Island, The.   Louis Simpson.   NYP

Union Maid.   Woody Guthrie.   FSW

Union Man.   Albert Morgan.   AmFP

·Union Pier Michigan. We called it Shapiro.   That Was Then.
    Isabella Gardner.   EC; GP

Union Train.   Lee Hays, Millard Lampell, *and* Pete Seeger.   FSW

Unique among Girls.   *Malay Oral Tradition, tr. by* R. J. Wilkinson
    *and* R. O. Winstedt.   WTO

Unique planets break.   The Place.   Kenneth Rexroth.   MPA

Unison, A.   William Carlos Williams.   Epi; NOBA

Unite, unite, let us all unite.   The Padstow Night Song.
    *Unknown.*   GBP

United 555.   Richard Eberhart.   PoIA

United Front.   Bertolt Brecht *and* Hans Eisler.   FSW

United States, The.   William Carlos Williams.   LoAs

United States Prepare for the Permanent Revolution, The.
    George Hitchcock.   EAS

United States Tony.   David Kherdian.   SA

Unity.   Jakov de Haan, *tr. fr. Dutch by* David Soetendorp.   VWA

Univac to Univac.   Louis B. Salomon.   FF; QQQ

Universal Explicator, The.   Erica Jong.   NVAP

Universal Passion, The.   Edward Young.   *See* Love of Fame, the
    Universal Passion.

Universal Prayer, The.   Pope.   ILP (1975 ed.); ILwL; PIM

Universality of things, The.   The Eyeglasses.   William Carlos
    Williams.   NoAM

Universe, The.   Mary Britton Miller.   CTV

Universe, The.   May Swenson.   Psy

Universe expands and contracts like a great heart, The.   The
    Great Explosion.   Robinson Jeffers.   IPWM

University.   Karl Shapiro.   NowV

University Curriculum.   William Price Turner.   POL

University Examinations in Egypt.   D. J. Enright.   NowV;
    OxBTC

University of Illinois at Chicago Circle Lecture Series.   Paul
    Carroll.   FiCh

Unknown, The.   John Davidson.   PAIC

Unknown, The.   Edward Thomas.   GBL

Unknown Child, The.   Elizabeth Jennings.   PBWP

Unknown Citizen, The.   W. H. Auden.   BiP; BuTh; CABA (1972
    ed.); FF; HeIP; InPK; IPWM; LP; NIL; NOBL; OBSV;
    PAIC; PoIA; PPoD; SFF; SoS; SoSe; UnPo (1976 ed.); WIF

Unknown Color, The.   Countee Cullen.   ECBV

Unknown Dead, The.   Henry Timrod.   AmVN

Unknown Eros, The.   Coventry Patmore.   *Poems indexed
    separately by titles and first lines.*

Unknown faces in the street.   The Turning.   Philip Levine.
    VGW

Unknown Girl in the Maternity Ward.   Anne Sexton.   NoAM

Unknown Grave, The.   Letitia Elizabeth Landon.   VLP

Unknown love/ Is as bitter a thing.   Lady Otomo of Sakanoe, *tr.
    fr. Japanese by* Arthur Waley.   PBWP
    ("Unknown love/ is bitter," *tr. by* Willis Barnstone.)   BoWoP

Unknown Shores.   D. M. Thomas, *after the French of* Théophile
    Gautier.   MPo

Unknown Smoke.   Archie Washburn.   VW

Unknown Soldiers.   Edgar Lee Masters.   *Fr.* The New Spoon
    River.   NoAM; TAP

Unlawful Assembly.   D. J. Enright.   OxBTC

Unless We Guard Them Well.   Jane Merchant.   QQQ

Unless you remind me.   Pavlov.   Naomi Long Madgett.   BPo

Unlike my subject now shall be my song.   Earl of Chesterfield.
    FaBoEE

Unlikely angels, although by and large well met.   Pacelli and the
    Ethiop.   Turner Cassity.   GP

Unloading Rails.   *Unknown.*   AmFP

Unloved, The.   Robert Canzoneri.   CoPAm

Unlucky Boat.   George Mackay Brown.   MS

Unmade girl on my bed, The.   Easter Sunday: Not the Artist.
    Ralph Adamo.   CoPAm

Unmasked, our friend confesses. Drained of hope.   Murder
    Mystery.   Timothy Steele.   AMV-81

Unnatural Powers.   Robinson Jeffers.   PBMP

Unnoticed—/ The shriveled old woman in faded-flower print.
    Paso por Aqui.   Wade Hall.   AATT

Unnoticed Woman from Whose Kind Large Flesh.   E. E.
    Cummings.   Epi

Unnumbered suppliants crowd preferment's gate.   Samuel
    Johnson.   *Fr.* The Vanity of Human Wishes.   OBSV

Unpacking our summer house, I found.   An Untitled Poem, about
    an Uncompleted Sonnet.   Sanford Pinsker.   AMV-81

Unpardonable Sin, The.   Vachel Lindsay.   BiP; CMoP (1970 ed.)

Unplanned Design.   Neal Bowers.   AMV-80

Unpredicted, The.   John Heath-Stubbs.   BoLoP

Unprofitableness.   Henry Vaughan.   ILP (1975 ed.)

Unpurged images of day recede, The.   Byzantium.   W. B. Yeats.
    CABA (1972 ed.); CMoP (1970 ed.); EBEV; HAP; ILP (1975

ed.); InPS; NIL; NoAM; NOBE; OAEL-2; OxBTC; PPP; STS; UsP

Unquiet Grave, The. *Unknown.* AIW; AmFP, *shorter version;* Epi, *shorter version, with music;* ExPo (1973 ed.); FaBoBa; FSW; GBP; HAP; HeIP; ILP (1975 ed.); InPK; OAEL-1, *with music;* PeBB; PoPle; SLP; WeW; WIF

Unquiet thought, whom at the first I bred. Amoretti, II. Spenser. PAIC

Unraveled Thought, An. Shlomit Cohen, *tr. fr. Hebrew by* Myra Glazer Schotz. VWA

Unreal tall as a myth. The Bear on the Delhi Road. Earle Birney. BCr; BoAnP; HeIP; MPA

Unreal the Buffalo Is Standing. *Unknown.* GOA

Unreturning Native, The. Basil Dowling. ATNZ

Unripe Peach, An. Rebecca Fein. OSP

Unsaid. A. R. Ammons. CSP; NOBA

Unsaid Word, An. Adrienne Rich. NMM

Unsatisfied Yearning. Richard Kendall Munkittrick. GDP

Unseemly as a marvellous and astral renegade. Queen Anne's Lace. June Jordan. TAP

Unseen Fire, An. Michael G. Cooke. AMV-81

Unseen Fire. R. N. Currey. MPo
   "This is a damned inhuman sort of war," *sel.* OxBTC

Unseen Flight. Markos Georgeou. AMV-80

Unseen Horses. Joan Byers Grayston. PH

Unseen she comes again. Despair. James F. Mersmann. BCr

Unseen, snow slides from over-laden boughs. Fire-Queen. Ruth Fainlight. PoA

Unsettled Motorcyclist's Vision of His Death, The. Thom Gunn. PoA

Unsleeping City. Federico García Lorca, *tr. fr. Spanish by* Ben Belitt. NYP

Unstable dreame, accordyng to the place. The Lover Having Dreamed Enjoying of His Love, Complaineth That the Dreame Is Not either Longer or Truer. Sir Thomas Wyatt. AAS

Unsucked drugs asway. Tenant. Danny L. Rendleman. TC

Unsung Heroes, The. Paul Laurence Dunbar. BPo

Unter der Linde. George Ellenbogen. AMV-81

Unthrifty loveliness, why dost thou spend. Sonnets, IV. Shakespeare. GrRo

Until fall, a grasshopper/ Chose to chirr. The Grasshopper and the Ant. La Fontaine, *tr. by* Marianne Moore. NAWM-2

Until Tatum passed. Standing on the Corner. Philip Levine. NNaP

Until that sun, which keeps. Trains Made of Stone. Ray A. Young Bear. CDW

Until the age of five/ my hair was blond. In My Brother's House. Mick Fedullo. BrS

Until the Cows Come Home. Michael McMahon. FAF

Until the desert knows. Emily Dickinson. NOBA

Until They Have Stopped. Sarah E. Wright. PoBA

Untitled. Daryl Hine. NoAM

Untitled. James A. Randall, Jr. BPo

Untitled. Michele Wallace. WBN

Untitled I. Ishmael Reed. CNA

Untitled Poem, about an Uncompleted Sonnet, An. Sanford Pinsker. AMV-81

Untitled Requiem for Tomorrow. Conyus. PoBA

Untitled X. Sandra Maria Esteves. NW

Unto Jehovah Sing Will I, *with music.* Henry Ainsworth. AH

Unto no body my woman saith she had rather a wife be. Catullus, *tr. fr. Latin by* Sir Philip Sidney. OBVE

Unto Our God Most High We Sing, *with music.* John Vance Cheney. AH

Unto the boundles ocean of thy beautie. To Delia. Samuel Daniel. ESo

Unto this place when as the Elfin Knight. The Hill of the Graces. Spenser. *Fr.* The Faerie Queene, VI, 10. NOBE

Unto Us a Child Is Born. William Dunbar. BoReV

Untouched grandeur in the hinterlands. Life in the Boondocks. A. R. Ammons. HAP

Unusual thing called a Troupial, An. A Troupial. Milton Bracker. TDH

Unveiling, The. Suzanne Bernhardt. VWA

Unwanted. Edward Field. SS

Unwanted, The. Mary Gordon. IHMS

Unwatch'd, the garden bough shall sway. Tennyson. In Memoriam A. H. H., CI. PoPle

Unweary'd watch their list'ning leaders keep, Th'. Homer, *tr. by* Pope. *Fr.* The Iliad, X. OBVE

Unwelcome. Mary Elizabeth Coleridge. PoPle; SS; WPE

Unwelcome. Irma Dovey. AMV-80

Unwinding the spool of the morning. Invocation. Vassar Miller. NCSH

Unwritten Letters. Steven Orlen. BrS

Unyielding in the pride of his defiance. The Flying Dutchman. E. A. Robinson. PiAM

Up a hill, short. Boulder. Ted Berrigan. FiCh

Up and down the beach. The Skin Divers. George Starbuck. SPo

Up against the Wall. Cleve Phillips. AMV-81

Up against the wall. David Gitin. MIT

Up against the wall. To Fez Cobra. Ted Joans. GP

Up all night. The Wakening. Sam Hamill. AMV-80

Up aloft amid the rigging. Rolling Home. Charles Mackay. FSW

Up and betimes across the asphalt water. Pepys Bar, West Forty-eighth Street, 8 a.m. L. E. Sissman. NYP

Up and down the City Road. Pop Goes the Weasel! *At. to* W. R. Mardale. FaBoNo; PoPle

Up and up soars the Evening Star, hanging there in the sky. The Evening Star. *Aborigine Oral Tradition, tr. by* R. M. Berndt. *Fr.* The Moon-Bone Cycle. WTO

Up at a Villa—Down in the City. Robert Browning. ILP (1975 ed.); NOBE; PPP; STS

Up at Huw's farm nature. Huw's Farm. Robert Morgan. HeHu

Up at La Serra. Charles Tomlinson. TwMBP

Up from Down Under. David McCord. ECBV

Up from the bottom. Flag. Reg Saner. GP

Up from the bronze, I saw. Roman Fountain. Louise Bogan. SBG

Up from the desert desolate and bleak. The Organ Cactus. Dorothy Scarborough. BPAW

Up from the Egg: The Confessions of a Nuthatch Avoider. Ogden Nash. BoAnP

Up from the log cabin to the capitol. Edwin Markham. *Fr.* Lincoln, the Man of the People. OFD

Up from the meadows rich with corn. Barbara Frietchie. Whittier. BTTM; FaPo; FaPoR; NOBA; OBAL; PPM

Up from the mud among the fiddlers. Washington on the Constitutional Journey: 1791. Paul Baker Newman. CSP

Up from the south at break of day. Sheridan's Ride. Thomas Buchanan Read. BTTM

Up from West 86 St., banging, against all hope. The Fabulous Teamsters. Judith Johnson Sherwin. NYP

Up-front ones are marvelous, The. My Teeth. Ed Ochester. GP

Up go the children, up the rungs. The Playground. Michael Bedard. BBGO

Up-Hill. *See* Uphill.

Up I Arose in Verno Tempore. *Unknown.* GBP

Up in the Air. James S. Tippett. ECBV

Up in the attic on row on row. Stark Boughs on the Family Tree. Mary Oliver. SoS

Up in the elevator went the nuns. Teasing the Nuns. Karl Shapiro. MPA

Up in the heavenly saloon. Arizona Nature Myth. James Michie. NOBL

Up in the mountains, it's lonesome all the time. The Mountain Whippoorwill. Stephen Vincent Benét. PoTa

Up in the North, a long way off. Out Goes She. *Unknown.* PoPle

Up in this quiet room here, reading your letter. Fidelities. Jean Valentine. NYP

Up into the Silence the Green. E. E. Cummings. STS

Up on his pedestal. Lines to the South. John William Corrington. CSP

Up on the Downs. John Masefield. NOBE

Up on the mountain my Lord spoke. Every Time I Feel the Spirit. *Unknown.* FSW

Up on their brooms the witches stream. The Ride-by-Nights. Walter de la Mare. DuDa

Up out of the African. Ted Joans. GP

Up Rising. Robert Duncan. *Fr.* Passages. NNaP

Up, sun and mery wether! Sometime I Loved. *Unknown.* OxBM

Up Tailes All. Robert Herrick. LoAs

Up the airy mountain. The Fairies. William Allingham. ECBV; LCL; NOBE; OxBChV; PCOP; PoPle

Up the ash tree climbs the ivy. Upper Lambourne. John Betjeman. FaBoTw (1975 ed.)

Up the dirt road. Viejo. Joseph Somoza. TVo

Up the hill/ Hurry me not. *Unknown.* PH

Up the Noran Water. Shy Geordie. Helen B. Cruikshank. MS

Up the reputable walks of old established trees. The Campus on the Hill. W. D. Snodgrass. ILP (1975 ed.); NIL; NoAM; NowV; TAP; WIF

Up the river, where it thins out. Leaving Here. Stephen Philbrick. AMV-81

Up There. W. H. Auden. OxBTC

Up There. Margo Bohanon. SES

Up through five green. And This Is My Father. Marcus J. Grapes. AMV-80

Up to Date. "Hugh MacDiarmid." FaBoCo

Up to his shoulders. The Bird Fancier. James Kirkup. ECBV

Up to the bed by the window, where I be lyin'. Old Shepherd's Prayer. Charlotte Mew. OxBTC; WPE

Up to the throne of God is borne. The Labourer's Noon-Day Hymn. Wordsworth. PIM

Up! Up! my friend, and quit your books. The Tables Turned. Wordsworth. IPWM; MBPR; OAEL-2

Up, up, old Benedict, the bard who would. Wilder Bentley. *Fr.* Six Reveilles to Match My Self-Indulgence. MIT

Up! Up! You brothers, now be strong. Song of the Cape of Good Hope. Christian Schubart, *ad. by* Robert Bly. NU

Up where the white bluffs fringe the plain. Prairie Wolves. Robert V. Carr. BPAW

Up where the world grows cold. A North Pole Story. Menella Bute Smedley. OxBChV

Upanishads, *sels. Tr. fr. Sanskrit by* Raimundo Panikkar. ILwL
"He said to Patancala Kapya and to the students."
"One alone is God; there cannot be a second."
"Revealed and yet dwelling hidden in the cave."

Upasara, the heifer after first mating. Sanskrit. Les A. Murray. *Fr.* Walking to the Cattle-Place. CAAP

Upended, it crouches on broken limbs. Poem. Charles Tomlinson. CMoP (1970 ed.)

Up-Hill [*or* Uphill]. Christina Rossetti. ECBV; HAP; IPWM; NOBE; OAEL-2; PPP; SS; VLP; VPC; WPE

Upland. A. R. Ammons. NOBA

Upland farmers have all gone, The. Above Penmaenmawr. Tony Connor. MPo

Uplift a thousand voices full and sweet. Ode Sung at the Opening of the International Exhibition. Tennyson. VLP

Upon a Black Twist, Rounding the Arm of the Countess of Carlisle. Robert Herrick. CaPo

Upon a Child ("Here a pretty baby lies"). Robert Herrick. SCP-1

Upon a Child That Died ("Here she lies, a pretty bud"). Robert Herrick. CaPo; InPK; SCP-1

Upon a Christmas Morning. *Unknown.* AmFP

Upon a day, came sorrow in to me. Sonnet. Dante, *tr. by* Dante Gabriel Rossetti. LoAs

Upon a Dead Man's Head. John Skelton. HAP
(Uppon a Deedmans Hed.) AAS

Upon a Delaying Lady. Robert Herrick. PoPle

Upon a Dying Lady. W. B. Yeats. UnPo (1976 ed.)

Upon a Fool. John Hoskyns. FaBoEE

Upon a Gloomy Night. St. John of the Cross. *See* Dark Night, The.

Upon a great black horse-ily. Song-ily. *Unknown.* ECBV

Upon a House Shaken by the Land Agitation. W. B. Yeats. CMoP (1970 ed.)

Upon a Maid ("Gone she is a long, long way"). Robert Herrick. CaPo

Upon a Maid ("Here she lies in bed of spice"). Robert Herrick. CaPo; FaBoEE

Upon a Maid That Dyed the Day She Was Marryed. Robert Herrick, *after the Greek of* Meleager. OBVE
(That Morn Which Saw Me Made a Bride.) NIL

Upon a Mole in Celia's Bosom. Thomas Carew. CaPo; SCP-2

Upon a mountain's height, far from the sea. The Wanderer. Eugene Field. BPAW

Upon a Notorious Shrew. *Unknown.* FaBoEE

Upon a Ribband. Thomas Carew. CaPo; OAEL-1

Upon a Rich Country Gentleman. *Unknown.* FaBoEE

Upon a Sabbath-day it fell. The Eve of St. Mark. Keats. MBPR

Upon a simmer Sunday morn. The Holy Fair. Burns. LAuP; OBSV

Upon a Snail. Bunyan. *See* Upon the Snail.

Upon a Spider Catching a Fly. Edward Taylor. EAP; NIL; NOBA; TAP

Upon a stairway built of brick. The Fearful Finale of the Irascible Mouse. Guy Wetmore Carryl. ECBV

Upon a sudden, as I gazing stood. Rachel Speght. *Fr.* A Dream. WPE

Upon a time before the faery broods. Lamia. Keats. MBPR

Upon a time the jaguars came. In Puerto Vallarta. Anthony Ostroff. MPA; PoW

Upon a Wasp Child with Cold. Edward Taylor. EAP; NOBA; PiAm; SCP-2

Upon a Young Mother of Many Children. Robert Herrick. CaPo

Upon Absence. Katherine Philips. PBWP

Upon an Image from Dante, *sel.* Sacheverell Sitwell.
"All there was of men was the smoke above their houses." PES

Upon an obscure night. St. John of the Cross, *tr. fr. Spanish by* Arthur Symons. ILwL

Upon Appleton House. Andrew Marvell. SCP-1
*Sels.*
"And now to the abyss I pass." OAEL-1
Garden at Appleton House, The ("See how the flowers as at parade"). PoPle

(Garden, A.) PF

Garden of Appleton House, The ("When in the east the morning ray"). NOBE

Kingfisher, The. PB

Upon Batt. Robert Herrick. FaBoEE

Upon Ben Jonson. Robert Herrick. CaPo

Upon Boys Diverting Themselves in the River. Thomas Foxton. OxBChV

Upon Bunce: Epigram. Robert Herrick. CaPo

Upon Christ's Nativity, or Christmas. Rowland Watkyns. OBW; SCP-2

Upon Dr. Davies's British Grammar. James Howell. OBW

Upon Easter Day. Richard Crashaw. See Easter Day.

Upon Groins: Epigrams. Robert Herrick. CaPo

Upon Hearing His High Sweet Tenor Again. Joseph Langland. AMV–81

Upon Her Feet. Robert Herrick. CaPo

Upon Her Soothing Breast. Emily Brontë. BoWoP

Upon Her Voice. Robert Herrick. CaPo

Upon His Julia. Robert Herrick. SpRo

Upon His Leaving His Mistress. Earl of Rochester. GBL (Upon Leaving His Mistress.) OBP

Upon His Majesty's Being Made Free of the City. Andrew Marvell. See On the Lord Mayor and Court of Aldermen, Presenting the Late King and Duke of York Each with a Copy of Their Freedoms.

Upon His Picture. Thomas Randolph. NOBE

Upon His Sister-in-Law, Mistress Elizabeth Herrick. Robert Herrick. CaPo

Upon Israel and upon the rabbis. Kaddish. Charles Reznikoff. Fr. Separate Way. SA

Upon Jack and Jill: Epigram. Robert Herrick. CaPo

Upon Julia Washing Herself in the River. Robert Herrick. CaPo

Upon Julia Weeping. Robert Herrick. Expo (1973 ed.)

Upon Julia's Arctics. Bert Leston Taylor. OBAL

Upon Julia's Breasts. Robert Herrick. CaPo; SCP-1

Upon Julia's Clothes. Robert Herrick. AnMo; CABA (1972 ed.); CaPo; ExPo (1973 ed.); FF; GBL; HAP; HeIP; HoPM (1975 ed.); ILP (1975 ed.); InPS; IPWM; LFH; NIL; NOBE; OAEL-1; PAIC; PoIA; PoPle; PPP; SCP-1; SpRo; SS; WeW; WIF
("Whenas in silks my Julia goes.") EBEV

Upon Julia's Ribband. Robert Herrick. CaPo

Upon Julia's Unlacing Herself. Robert Herrick. SCP-1

Upon Julia's Voice. Robert Herrick. AnMo; CABA (1972 ed.); InPK; NIL; NOBE; SCP-1; SoSe

Upon Leaving His Mistress. Earl of Rochester. See Upon His Leaving His Mistress.

Upon Leaving the Parole Board Hearing. Conyus. PoBA

Upon Looking at a Book of Astrology. David McFadden. NeAC

Upon Love, by Way of Question and Answer. Robert Herrick. CaPo

Upon Love Fondly Refused for Conscience's Sake. Thomas Randolph. OAEL-1

Upon Lucia Dabbled in the Dew. Robert Herrick. SCP-1

Upon Lulls. Robert Herrick. CaPo

Upon Master Ben Jonson: Epigram. Robert Herrick. See Upon Mr. Ben Jonson: Epigram.

Upon Master Edmund Spenser. Francis Beaumont. FaBoEE

Upon Master Walter Montagu's Return from Travel. Thomas Carew. CaPo

Upon Mr. Ben Jonson: Epigram. Robert Herrick. SCP-1 (Upon Master Ben Jonson: Epigram.) CaPo

Upon Mistress Elizabeth Wheeler under the Name of Amarillis. Robert Herrick. CaPo

Upon Moon. Robert Herrick. Moon

Upon My Dear and Loving Husband His Going into England Jan. 16, 1661. Anne Bradstreet. EAP (O Thou Most High Who Rulest All, with music.) AH

Upon My Lady Carlisle's Walking in Hampton-Court Garden. Sir John Suckling. CaPo

Upon My Lord Brohall's Wedding. Sir John Suckling. CaPo

Upon My Lord Chief Justice's Election of My Lady Anne Wentworth for His Mistress. Thomas Carew. CaPo

Upon my right side I me lay. Prayer for Good Dreams. Unknown. OxBM

Upon my word and honour. Mother Goose. MG

Upon Nothing. Earl of Rochester. OBSV; SCP-2

Upon One of the Maids of Honour to Queen Elizabeth. John Hoskyns. FaBoEE

Upon Our Saviour's Tomb wherein Never Man Was Laid. Richard Crashaw. OAEL-1

Upon Pagget. Robert Herrick. CaPo

Upon Prew His Maid. Robert Herrick. CaPo; InPK

Upon Rook: Epigram. Robert Herrick. CaPo

Upon Roses. Robert Herrick. SCP-1

Upon Scobble: Epigram. Robert Herrick. CaPo; FaBoEE

Upon Showbread: Epigram. Robert Herrick. CaPo

Upon Sir John Lawrence's Bringing Water over the Hills to My Lord Middlesex's House at Wiston. Sir John Suckling. CaPo

Upon Some Alterations in My Mistress, after My Departure into France. Thomas Carew. CaPo

Upon Some Women. Robert Herrick. CaPo

Upon Sybilla. Robert Herrick. CaPo

Upon the Anonymous Author of Legion's Humble Address to the Lords. Thomas Brown. APAS

Upon the Author of the "Satire against Wit." Sir Charles Sedley. APAS

Upon the beach are thousands of crabs; they are. Crustaceans. Roy Fuller. NoAM

Upon the Body of Our Blessèd Lord, Naked and Bloody. Richard Crashaw. See On Our Crucified Lord, Naked and Bloody.

Upon the Book and Picture of the Seraphical Saint Teresa. Richard Crashaw. See Flaming Heart, The.

Upon the Burning of Our House, July 10th, 1666. Anne Bradstreet. EAP; WPE
(Here Follows Some Verses upon the Burning of Our House.) BoWoP
(Some Verses upon the Burning of Our House July 10th, 1666.) NOBA; TAP
(Verses upon the Burning of Our House.) PiAm; SBG

Upon the Curtain of Lucasta's Picture It Was Thus Wrought. Richard Lovelace. CaPo

Upon the Death of a Gentleman. Richard Crashaw. MetP

Upon the Death of George Santayana. Anthony Hecht. CoPAm

Upon the Death of Mr. King Drowned in the Irish Seas. John Cleveland. See On the Memory of Mr. Edward King. . .

Upon the Death of Sir Albert Morton's Wife. Sir Henry Wotton. BoLoP; FaBoEE; PoPle; PPM; WeW

Upon the Death of the Lord Hastings, sel. Dryden. "Blisters with pride swelled." PeD

Upon the Decease of My Infant Lady. Clement Barksdale. SCP-2

Upon the Double Murther of King Charles I. Katherine Philips. SBG

Upon the eyes, the lips, the feet. Extreme Unction. Ernest Dowson. BoReV; OAEL-2; VLP

Upon the fifth day of November. On Mr. Pricke. Unknown. FaBoEE

Upon the First Sight of New England. Thomas Tillam. *See* Uppon the First Sight of New England, June 29, 1638.

Upon the flowery forefront of the year. Thalassius. Swinburne. VLP

Upon the Heavenly Scarp. A. M. Klein. PoA

Upon the hill my lover stands. The House o' the Mirror. Helen Adam. MAT; NMM

Upon the hills new grass is seen. Twist-Rime on Spring. Arthur Guiterman. ECBV

Upon the Holy Sepulchre. Richard Crashaw. FaBoEE

Upon the Horse and His Rider. Bunyan. OxBChV

Upon the Image of Death. Robert Southwell. BoReV; NOBE

Upon the Infant Martyrs. Richard Crashaw. OAEL-1; PAIC

Upon the Intimations of Love's Mortality. Jean Garrigue. LoAs

Upon the King's Return from Flanders. Henry Hall. APAS

Upon the King's Voyage to Chatham to Make Bulwarks against the Dutch. *Unknown.* APAS

Upon the Lake. Hayim Lenski, *tr. fr. Hebrew by* Robert Friend. VWA

Upon the Lines and Life of the Famous Scenic Poet, Master William Shakespeare. Hugh Holland. OBW

Upon the Loss of His Mistresses. Robert Herrick. CaPo

Upon the man who's buried here. J. E. Thorold Rogers. FaBoEE

Upon the Nipples of Julia's Breasts. Robert Herrick. CaPo; SCP-1

Upon the poop the captain stands. The Shipwreck. E. Harriet Palmer. RhR

Upon the rivers of Babylon, there we sat and wept. Bible, *O.T. (Douay-Rheims Version).* Psalms, CXXXVII. OAEL-1

Upon the Same [Detractor] ("I asked thee oft what poets thou hast read"). Robert Herrick. CaPo

Upon the Saying That My Verses Were Made by Another. Anne Killigrew. WPE

Upon the slippery tops of humane state. Seneca, *tr. by* Abraham Cowley. *Fr.* Thyestes, II. OBVE

Upon the Snail. Bunyan. SCP-2 (Upon a Snail.) OxBChV

Upon the street they lie. The Children. William Soutar. MS

Upon the Sudden Restraint of the Earl of Somerset, Then Falling from [*or* out of] Favour. Sir Henry Wotton. NOBE; SCP-2

Upon the Swallow. Bunyan. OxBChV

Upon the Troublesome Times. Robert Herrick. CaPo

Upon the wall, drawn by a child's hand. Hidden Things. Ann Stanford. MPA

Upon the Weathercock. Bunyan. OxBChV

Upon this greying page you wrote. On Looking at a Copy of Alice Meynell's Poems. Amy Lowell. SBG

Upon this marble bust that is not I. To Inez Milholland. Edna St. Vincent Millay. WPE

Upon this place the great Gustavus died. On Gustavus Adolphus, King of Sweden. Sir Thomas Roe. FaBoEE

Upon this primrose hill. The Primrose, Being at Montgomery Castle. John Donne. GBL

Upon This Rock. Ruthven Todd. PoA

Upon Umber: Epigram. Robert Herrick. CaPo

Upon Visiting His Lady by Moonlight. "A. W." Moon

Upon Wedlock, and Death of Children. Edward Taylor. EAP

Upon Westminster Bridge Sept. 3, 1802. Wordsworth. *See* Composed upon Westminster Bridge.

Upon Your Leaving. Etheridge Knight. NeAC; NNaP

Upper chamber in a darkened house, An. Frederick Goddard Tuckerman. *Fr.* Sonnets. AmVN; NOBA; PiAm; TAP

Upper Family. Maxwell Bodenheim. OBAL

Upper Lambourne. John Betjeman. FaBoTw (1975 ed.)

Upper Meadows, The. Yvor Winters. PiAm

Upper skies are palest blue, The. Robert Bridges. VLP

Upper slopes are busy with the cricket, The. Elegy on the Dust. Thom Gunn. NoAM

Uppon a Deedmans Hed. John Skelton. *See* Upon a Dead Man's Head.

Uppon the First Sight of New England, June 29, 1638. Thomas Tillam. GOA (Hail, Holy Land, *with music.*) AH

Uprooted. Sol Funaroff. SPT

Uprooted. Maurice Lindsay. MS

Uprose the King of Men with speed. The Descent of Odin; an Ode from the Norse Tongue. Thomas Gray. LAuP

Uprose, uprose, the stony fields uprose. The Tree, the Bird. Theodore Roethke. PiAm

Upsouth. Adesanya Alakoye. PoUp

Upstairs Downstairs. Hervey Allen. PoA

Upstairs on the third floor. Bottled: New York. Helene Johnson. PoBA

Upstairs the sanders. The Furniture Factory. Vern Rutsala. BrS

Upstate New York. The House You Looked For. William Pitt Root. NVAP

Upstream. Carl Sandburg. MiP; PiAm

Upsurge. Robert Gessner. SPT

Uptown. Allen Ginsberg. FF; TT

Uptown. Paul Zweig. NYP

Uptown on Lenox Avenue. Prime. Langston Hughes. PoBA

Upturning with a band. Authentic Tidings. Wordsworth. *Fr.* The Prelude, VI. BoReV

Urania, *sels.* Mary Sidney Wroth, Countess of Montgomery. WPE
 Duke's Song, The.
 Lindamira's Complaint.
 Morea's Sonnet.
 Pamphilia to Amphilanthus.
 Pamphilia's Sonnet.
 Verses of the Talkative Knight, The ·

Urban Convalescence, An. James Merrill. NOBA; NowV; NYP

Urban day has got her blue straw hat on, The. Ode to an Urban Day. Raymond Ward. ATNZ

Urban Experience, The: Part One. Lew Blockcolski. VoR

Urban Experience, The: Part Two. Lew Blockcolski. VoR

Urban Pollution. John Armstrong. PMW

Urbanite Delapidate. Herman Spector. SPT

Urceus Exit. Austin Dobson. *Fr.* Rose-Leaves. PAIC (Triolet: "I intended an ode.") PoPle

Urge to stroke the dead, The. Rabbits. Dennis Schmitz. FiCP

Urgency. Betsy Sholl. AMV-80

Urgent Letter, An. Hugh Maxton. IPM

Uriel. Emerson. AmVN; NOBA; PiAm

Urizen. Blake. *See* Book of Urizen.

Urn Burial. Ted Hughes. EBEV

Uru-tu-sendo's Song. *Tr. fr. Tewa Indian by* H. J. Spinden. WTO

Ursula. David Ray. VGW

Ursula, in a garden, found. Cy Est Pourtraicte, Madame Ste. Ursule, et les Unze Mille Vierges. Wallace Stevens. LoAs

Us. Julius Lester. PoBA

Us. Anne Sexton. CAPP

Us Idle Wenches. *Unknown.* PoPle

Us Two. A. A. Milne. OxBChV

Us two was pals, the Kid and me. The Kid's Last Fight. *Unknown.* SPo

Use maketh maistry, this hath been said alway. Of Use. John Heywood. FaBoEE

Use, then, my lust for whisky and for thee. The Light of Life. "Hugh MacDiarmid." CMoP (1970 ed.)

Used to have a gal, she was little and low. Step It Up and Go. *Unknown.* FSW

Used years. In Passing. J. Barrie Shepherd. AMV-81

Useful these bowls may be. China Shop Vigil. Christopher Middleton. TwMBP

Useless./ Our shouts bounce off him. The Old Dog. Alasdair MacLean. LP

Useless to ask what this was. Bark. Don Welch. GP

Useless Words. Carl Sandburg. PBMP; PPoD

Uses of Poetry. Winfield Townley Scott. PoA

Usk. T. S. Eliot. Landscapes, III. BiP

Usual exquisite boredom of patrols, The. Hugh Popham. OxBTC

Usually they/ go, women like that. Women like That. Lyn Lifshin. Psy

Usurpers, The. Edwin Muir. CMoP (1970 ed.)

Ut, re, mi, fa, sol, la. *Unknown.* FaBoNo

Utah. Anne Stevenson. NCSH

Utah Carroll. *Unknown.* FSW

Utah Iron Horse, The. *Unknown.* AmFP

Utilitarian View of the *Monitor's* Fight, A. Herman Melville. UnPo (1976 ed.)

Utility. T. R. Jahns. AAN

"Utopia," The. Lee Harwood. EAS

Utopia. Jewel C. Latimore. BPo

Utrillo on the wall. A nun is climbing. In a Mental Hospital Sitting Room. Elizabeth Jennings. LP


# V


V. B. Nimble, V. B. Quick ("V. B. Wigglesworth wakes at noon"). John Updike. CTBA

V.D. Clinic. Adrien Stoutenburg. GP

V. Innocentia Veritas Viat Fides Circumdederunt Me Inimici Mei. Sir Thomas Wyatt. AAS

V-Letter. Karl Shapiro. NoAM

Vacancy. Daniela Gioseffi. WBN

Vacant Chair, The. Henry Washburn *and* George Frederick Root. FSW

Vacant Lot, The. Gwendolyn Brooks. NoAM; NOBA

Vacation. William Stafford. POL; SFF

Vacation Trip. William Stafford. CTBA

Vachel, the stars are out. To Lindsay. Allen Ginsberg. ConAP

Vacillation. W. B. Yeats. NoAM
*Sels.*
"Although the summer sunlight gild." BoReV
"Must we part, Von Hügel, though much alike, for we." BoReV
"My fiftieth year had come and gone." BoReV; IP
"Seek out reality, leave things that seem." BoReV

Vacuum. Josephine Miles. Moon

Vacuum cleaner held over my head, A. In a Dream. David Ignatow. PoA

Vagrant, A. Erik Axel Karlfeldt, *tr. fr. Swedish by* Charles Wharton Stork. PPM

"Vagrant visitor erstwhile, The." Out into Essex. John Betjeman. PES

Vague Lyric by G. M. Max Beerbohm. FaBoEE

Vain Gratuities. E. A. Robinson. SS

Vain Learning. Fulke Greville. *Fr.* Caelica. BoReV

Vain Virtues. Dante Gabriel Rossetti. The House of Life, LXXXV. VLP

Vain World Adieu. *Unknown.* AmFP

Vain worldly yearnings in my breast. At Parting. Heine, *tr. by* Dwight Durling. NAWM-2

Vala, Night the Ninth Being the Last Judgment. Blake. *Fr.* The Four Zoas. MBPR
(Night the Ninth Being the Last Judgment.) OAEL-2

Vala; or, The Four Zoas. Blake. *See* Four Zoas, The.

*Vale* from Carthage. Peter Viereck. CoPAm; SS

Vale of twilight filled with silver-gray, The. Experience. Hugo von Hofmannsthal, *tr. by* John N. Miller. AMV-81

Valediction, A: Forbidding Mourning. John Donne. AnMo; CABA (1972 ed.); ExPo (1973 ed.); FF; HAP; HeIP; HoPM (1975 ed.); ILP (1975 ed.); InPK; InPS; MetP; NIL; NOBE; OAEL-1; PoIA; PoPle; PPoD; PPoe; PPP; SCP-1; SoSe; TT; UnPo (1976 ed.); VoPo; WIF

Valediction, A: "If we must part." Ernest Dowson. BoLoP

Valediction, A: Of Weeping. John Donne. CABA (1972 ed.); HAP; HeIP; ILP (1975 ed.); MetP; OAEL-1; SCP-1; TT

Valediction: "Sometimes I can believe." Lawrence Raab. AMV-81

Valediction, A: "We're bound for the blue water where the great winds blow." John Masefield. RhR

Valediction Forbidding Mourning, A. Adrienne Rich. NIL; NoAM; PoIA; TT

Valediction to the River Duddon. Wordsworth. *See* After-Thought.

Valentine. Len Gasparini. NeAC

Valentine. Ernest Hemingway. OBAL

Valentine for a Lady, A. Lucilius, *tr. fr. Greek by* Dudley Fitts. OFD

Valentine for Earth. Frances Frost. QQQ

Valentine for Marianne Moore, A. Elder Olson. PAIC

Valentines. Henry Dumas. CC

Valentines to My Mother, 1880. Christina Rossetti. OFD

Valiant hot eastern bull. Poet's Prayer para Yukio Mishima. Pancho Aguila. NW

Valiant Seaman's Happy Return to His Love, The. *Unknown.* GBP; PeBB

Valley. Robert Morgan. HeHu

Valley floors. A Collage for Richard Davis—Two Short Forms. De Leon Harrison. PoBA

Valley of Men, The. Uri Zvi Greenberg, *tr. fr. Hebrew by* Robert Mezey *and* Ben Zion Gold. VWA

Valley of the Elwy, The. Gerard Manley Hopkins. LoAs

Valley Where I Don't Belong, A. Marge Piercy. IHMS

Valleys crack and burn, the exhausted plains, The. The Mahratta Ghats. Alun Lewis. OBW

Valse Oubliée. John Heath-Stubbs. OxBTC

Valuable. Stevie Smith. OxBTC

Value Neuter. Kenneth Rexroth. MPA

Vampire's Aubade. W. D. Snodgrass. PAIC

Vandals, The. Jenny Mastoraki, *tr. fr. Modern Greek by* Nikos Germanakos. BoWoP

Vandergast and the Girl. Louis Simpson. CoPAm

Van Diemen's Land. *Unknown.* FaBoBa; FSW

Vanessa Vanessa. Ewart Milne. BIrV

Van Gogh. Lynn Strongin. RiTi

Vanguard of liberty, ye men of Kent. To the Men of Kent. October, 1803. Wordsworth. MBPR

Vanguardia. Sandra Maria Esteves. NW

Vanish. John Oliver Simon. MIT

Vanished. Steve Eng. AMV-81

Vanished house that for an hour I knew, A. Souvenir. E. A. Robinson. NoAM

Vanishing Point.  Peter Cooley.  AmPA

Vanishing Point: Urban Indian.  Wendy Rose.  NW

Vanitas Vanitatum.  John Webster.  *Fr*. The Devil's Law Case.
NOBE; OBP
  (All the Flowers of the Spring.)  ILP (1975 ed.)

Vanity.  Anna Wickham.  FaBoTw (1975 ed.)

Vanity of All Worldly Things, The.  Anne Bradstreet.  EAP

Vanity of Existence, The.  Philip Freneau.  EAP

Vanity of Human Wishes, The.  John Leax.  MiP

Vanity of Human Wishes, The: The Tenth Satire of Juvenal
Imitated.  Samuel Johnson.  CABA (1972 ed.); EBEV;
ESaP; HeIP; LAuP; OAEL-1
*Sels.*
  Charles XII of Sweden.  NOBE
  "Let Observation, with extensive view."  PoIA
  Power of Prayer, The.  NOBE
    (Prayer: "Where then shall Hope and Fear their objects
    find?")  BoReV
  "Unnumbered suppliants crowd preferment's gate."  OBSV
  "When first the college rolls receive his name."  OBSV
  (Scholar's Life, The.)  NOBE

Vanity of the World, The.  Siôn Cent, *tr. fr. Welsh by* Joseph P.
Clancy.  OBW

Vanity of Vanities.  Bible, *O.T.  Fr.* Ecclesiastes.  NAWM-1
(I:2-11); PBMP (I:2-II:26)

Vanity, saith the preacher, vanity!  The Bishop Orders His Tomb
at Saint Praxed's Church.  Robert Browning.  AnMo; CABA
(1972 ed.); Epi; GrRo; HAP; HeIP; ILP (1975 ed.); IPWM;
LFH; OAEL-2; PPoe; PPP; STS

Vanity, vanity, all is vanity.  Ha! Original Sin.  Ogden Nash.
FaBoCo

Vantage.  Brewster Ghiselin.  MPA; PPoD

Van Winkle.  Hart Crane.  *Fr.* The Bridge: Powhatan's Daughter.
PiAm

Vapor Trail Reflected in the Frog Pond.  Galway Kinnell.  SoS;
VGW

Vapor Trails.  Gary Snyder.  CAPP

Vaporish Maiden, A.  Morris Bishop.  TDH

Vaquero.  Edward Dorn.  VoA

Vaquero.  Joaquin Miller.  BPAW

Variables of Green.  Robert Graves.  FaBoEE

Variation.  Peter Wild.  GP

Variation on Heraclitus.  Louis MacNeice.  NoAM

Variation on the Gothic Spiral.  W. S. Merwin.  PoA

Variations.  Randall Jarrell.  VGW

Variations Done for Gerald van de Wiele.  Charles Olson.
NoAM; NOBA

Variations: #21.  James Stephens.  WIF

Variations on a Baedecker.  Stanley Burnshaw.  SPT

Variations on a Theme.  Mark Vinz.  HeS

Variations on a theme by morning.  Cocoa Morning.  Bob
Kaufman.  AmNP (1974 ed.)

Variations on a Theme by William Carlos Williams.  Kenneth
Koch.  CAPP; FF; SpRo

Variations on a Time Theme, *sels.*  Edwin Muir.  NoAM
  "Child in Adam's field I dreamed away, A."
  "Now at the road's quick turn."
  "Ransomed from darkness and released in Time."

Variations on an Air Composed on Having to Appear in a Pageant
as Old King Cole.  G. K. Chesterton.  NOBL

Varick Street.  Elizabeth Bishop.  NYP

Variety.  *Yoruba Oral Tradition, tr. by* E. Lasebikan.  WTO

Variety is bewildering in its sameness, The.  Letter from the
North Atlantic.  John Williams.  CoPAm

Various members of the hierarchy move, The.  A Morning Letter.
Robert Duncan.  PoA

Various the Roads of Life.  Walter Savage Landor.  NIL
  ("Various the roads of life; in one.")  FaBoEE

Varuna.  *Tr. fr. Sanskrit by* Raimundo Panikkar.  *Fr.* Vedic
Hymns.  ILwL

Varus, whom I chanced to meet.  Catullus, *tr. fr. Latin by* John
Hookham Frere.  OBVE

Vase of Flowers, A.  John Ashbery.  ConAP

Vases of Wombs, The.  Daniela Gioseffi.  RiTi

Vassar, class of.  Portrait of a Woman.  Kathryn Ruby.  WBN

Vast Light.  Richard Eberhart.  CMoP (1970 ed.)

Vast oceanic movements, the flux and reflux of immeasurable.
Currents.  Emma Lazarus.  *Fr.* By the Waters of Babylon.
WPE

Vast stone trunk of mountain lifts above, The.  Anchorage in
Time (II).  Stanley Burnshaw.  SPT

Vastness.  Tennyson.  VLP

Vaticide.  Myron O'Higgins.  PoBA

Vaudeville.  Lincoln Kirstein.  NoAM

Vaunting Oak.  John Crowe Ransom.  VGW

Vedic Hymns, *sels.  Tr. fr. Sanskrit by* Raimundo Panikkar.
ILwL
  Forgive, Lord, Have Mercy!
  Song of Creation, The.
  To the One God.
  Varuna.

Vegetable Destiny.  Nina Cassian, *tr. fr. Rumanian by* Michael
Impey *and* Brian Swann.  PBWP

Vegetable, I Will Not Be, A.  Donna Whitewing.  ANTL; VW

Vegetables/ and jewelry, right displayed.  For Instance.  Robert
McAlmon.  PoA

Vegetarian Sings, A.  Audrey Conard.  AMV-81

Vehicle gives a lurch but seems, The.  Foetal Song.  Joyce Carol
Oates.  IHMS

Veiled in that light amazing.  The Dispraise of Absalom.
*Unknown, tr. by* Robin Flower.  BIrV

Veld Eclogue, A: The Pioneers.  Roy Campbell.  OBSV

Velocity with which they write, The.  Movie Actors Scribbling
Letters Very Fast in Crucial Scenes.  Jean Garrigue.  TAP

Velvet Shoes.  Elinor Wylie.  FSFS; IP; PPM

Vending myself.  Investment.  Norman Nathan.  MiP

Venerable mother toothache.  A Charm against the Toothache.
John Heath-Stubbs.  InPK

Veneris Venefica Agrestis.  Charles Tomlinson, *after the Italian of
Lucio Piccolo.*  OBVE

Venezuela.  *Unknown.*  FSW

Veni Creator.  Alice Meynell.  ILwL; WPE

Veni, Creator Spiritus.  *Unknown, paraphrased from Latin by*
Dryden.  BoReV; FaPoR; ILwL; PIM

Venice.  James Wright.  AMV-81

Venice and Sunset.  Byron.  *Fr.* Childe Harold's Pilgrimage, IV.
PAIC

Venice, 182-.  John Berryman.  CoPAm

Venom.  James Dickey.  PoA

Ventriloquist, The.  Robert Huff.  GP

Venus againe thou mov'st a warre.  To Venus.  Horace, *tr. by*
Ben Jonson.  Odes, IV, 1.  OBVE

Venus and Adonis, *sels.*  Shakespeare.
  "At this Adonis smiles as in disdain."  EBEV
  Courser and Jennet.  NOBE
    ("But lo, from forth a copse that neighbours by.")  PoPle;
    PH
  " 'Fondling,' she saith, 'since I have hemmed thee here.' "
  OAEL-1
  Horse, A.  ExPo (1973 ed.)
  "Imperiously he leaps, he neighs, he bounds."  BoAnP

Venus and Cupid.  Mark Alexander Boyd.  *See* Fra Bank to
Bank, Fra Wood to Wood I Rin.

Venus and the Lute Player. Paul Engle. WIF

Venus, and yong Adonis sitting by her. *See* Venus, with young Adonis sitting by her.

Venus Fly Trap, The. Readymade. John Perreault. EAS

Venus glows in the east. Work to Do toward Town. Gary Snyder. VGW

Venus has lit her silver lamp. The Lamp in the West. Ella Higginson. WPW

Venus of the Louvre. Emma Lazarus. SBG

Venus of the Salty Shell. Denis Devlin. BIrV

Venus Pudica stands bent. The Lady of the Castle. John Hollander. GP

Venus' Return to the Sea. Gene Fowler. CPA

Venus, take my votive glass. The Lady Who Offers Her Looking-Glass to Venus. Matthew Prior, *after* Plato. FaBoEE

Venus Transiens. Amy Lowell. PoA

Venus Vigils. *Unknown. See* Vigil of Venus, The.

Venus, with young Adonis sitting by her. Bartholomew Griffin. *Fr.* The Passionate Pilgrim, XI. LoAs ("Venus, and yong Adonis sitting by her," *sl. diff. version in* Fidessa, More Chaste than Kind.) ESo

Vera, from My Childhood. Judy Grahn. The Common Woman, VII. GP

Veracruz. Robert Hayden. AmNP (1974 ed.)

Verb/ of what's warm in an itch. Homage to Hans Hofmann. Art Lange. FiCh

Verdant meads are seen, The. Michael Drayton. *Fr.* The Shepherd's Sirena. SCP-2

Vergier. *Unknown, tr. fr. Provençal by* Ezra Pound. GBL

Vergissmeinicht. Keith Douglas. InPS; SoSe (Vergissmeinnicht.) OxBTC

Verifying the Dead. James Welch. CDW

Verigin, Moving in Alone. John Newlove. NeAC

Verigin 3. John Newlove. NeAC

Verily/ The sky clears. The Sky Clears. *Tr. by* Frances Densmore. OBVE

Vermilion Cliffs. Radcliffe Squires. MPA

Vermont Conversation. Patricia Hubbell. CTBA

Vernal Ague, The. Philip Freneau. EAP

Vernal Sentiment. Theodore Roethke. VoPo

Verona. James Wright. NNaP

Verona by the poet's pencil drawn. Sir William Davenant. Gondibert, II, 1. SCP-2

Veronica's lost in the garden. In the Sly Gardens. Sonya Dorman. RiTi

Vers de Société. Philip Larkin. PSN

Versatile Historian, The. James Welch. SA

Verse ("What should we know"). Oliver St. John Gogarty. WIF

Verse, a breeze mid blossoms straying. Youth and Age. Samuel Taylor Coleridge. MBPR

Verse for a Certain Dog. Dorothy Parker. GDP

Verse for Vestigials. Elizabeth Allen. AMV-80

Verse in Praise of Lord Henry Howard, Earl of Surrey. George Turberville. PAIC

Verse? Writing verse? Dear man, are you insane? A Hat in the Ring. J. S. Manifold. GAS

Verses ("Poor fellow, what is it to you"). Sir Charles Hanbury Williams. OBW

Verses Composed on the Eve of His Execution. James Graham, Marquis of Montrose. *See* On Himself, upon Hearing What Was His Sentence.

Verses Found in His Bible. Sir Walter Ralegh. *See* Epitaph: "Even such is Time, which takes in trust."

Verses from a Letter. Keats. *See* Song about Myself.

Verses Intended to Be Written below a Noble Earl's Picture. Burns. HoPM (1975 ed.)

Verses Made the Night before He Died. Michael Drayton. NOBE ("So well I love thee, as without thee I.") GBL

Verses Made the Night before He Dyed. Sir Walter Ralegh. *See* Epitaph: "Even such is Time, which takes in trust."

Verses Occasioned by the Sudden Drying Up of St. Patrick's Well, *sel.* Swift. "Wretched Ierne! with what grief I see." OBSV

Verses of the Talkative Knight, The. Mary Sidney Wroth, Countess of Montgomery. *Fr.* Urania. WPE

Verses on a Rose Street Muse. Charles Senior. MIS

Verses on Accepting the World. Joseph Brodsky, *tr. fr. Russian by* Dimitry Pospielovsky *and* Keith Bosley. VWA

Verses on the Death of Doctor Swift, *sels.* Swift. "Doctors tender of their fame, The." NOBL "My female friends, whose tender hearts." NOBL "Perhaps I may allow, the Dean." NOBE "Suppose me dead; and then suppose." NOBE "Time is not remote when I, The." EBEV; NOBE; NOBL

Verses on the Prospect of Planting Arts and Learning in America. George Berkeley. *See* On the Prospect of Planting . . .

Verses on the Snuff of a Candle, Made in Sickness. Anne Wharton. SCP-2

Verses Said to Be Written on the Union. Swift. APAS

Verses upon the Burning of Our House. Anne Bradstreet. *See* Upon the Burning of Our House, July 10th, 1666.

Verses Written during a Sleepless Night. Pushkin, *tr. fr. Russian by* Babette Deutsch. PPM

Verses Written during the War, 1756–1763, *sel.* Thomas Osbert Mordaunt, *formerly at. to* Sir Walter Scott. Sound, Sound the Clarion. FaPoR; NOBE ("Sound, sound the clarion, fill the fife!") FaBoEE; PCOP

Verses Written in a Lady's Sherlock upon Death. Earl of Chesterfield. EBEV

Verses Written on Sand. Melech Ravitch, *tr. fr. Yiddish by* Seymour Mayne *and* Rivka Augenfeld. VWA

Versions of Sunlight. James Applewhite. NVAP

Vertical Is Our New Sight. Daisy Aldan. AATT

Vertigos or Contemplation of Something That Is Over. Alejandra Pizarnik, *tr. fr. Spanish by* Yishai Tobin. VWA

Vertue. George Herbert. *See* Virtue.

Very dead of night: no noise, The. Ditty. Roger Hecht. NowV

Very earth will disown you, The. God Wills It. Gabriela Mistral, *tr. by* K. G. C. LoAs

Very first blessing that Mary had, The. The Seven Blessings of Mary. *Unknown.* FSW

Very first joy that Mary had, The. The Joys of Mary. *Unknown.* AmFP

Very gently struck/ The quay night bell. W. S. Graham. The Nightfishing, I. MS

Very handsome gentleman, A. *Tr. fr. Chinese by* Arthur Waley. *Fr.* Shih Ching. BoWoP

Very happy. It was a matter of totally differe. A Short Story. Michael Cooper. BCr

Very Heroical Epistle in Answer to Ephelia, A. Earl of Rochester. APAS

Very like a Whale. Ogden Nash. HAP; InPK; PoIA; UsP; WeW

Very Odd Fish, A. D'Arcy Wentworth Thompson. OxBChV

Very Old, The. Thomas Galloway. AMV-80

Very old are the woods. All That's Past. Walter de la Mare. NOBE; OAEL-2; OxBTC

Very Old Woman, A. Clayton Eshleman. MAT

Very personal truth is very hard to discuss, A. The Main Problem in Portraiture. Elisavietta Ritchie. AATT

Very Polite Man, A. *Unknown.* TDH

Very portly crow, A. A Note on Master Crow. Jean Garrigue. BoAnP

Very small children in patched clothing, The. The Study in Aesthetics. Ezra Pound. CMoP (1970 ed.); ExPo (1973 ed.); InPS; NOBA; UsP

Very thin/ and opaque. Snake. David McCord. CaYB

Very true, the linnets sing. Autumnal Song. Walter Savage Landor. OAEL-2

Vesica Piscis. Coventry Patmore. VLP

Vespers. A. A. Milne. OxBChV; SpRo

Vessels. Howard Schwartz. VWA

Vessels of heavenly medicine! may the breeze. Sonnet on Launching Some Bottles Filled with Knowledge into the Bristol Channel. Shelley. MBPR

Vestal in the Forum, The. James Wright. AMV-81

Vestal Lady on Brattle, The. Gregory Corso. NoAM

Vestiges. Basil Bunting. TwMBP

Vesture of the Soul, The." Æ." PFIr

Vet, The. Guy Boas. BoAnP

Veteran. Lola Ridge. WPE

Veteran Greeks came home, The. The Return. Edwin Muir. CMoP (1970 ed.)

Veteran Sirens. E. A. Robinson. NoAM; NOBA; PiAm

Veterans, The. Donagh MacDonagh. CIP

Vet's Rehabilitation. Ray Durem. PoBA

Vetus Flamma. Robert Mezey. PoA

Viable. A. R. Ammons. TAP

Vicar, The. George Crabbe. Fr. The Borough, Letter III. OBSV

Vicar of Bray, The. Unknown. AIW; ESaP; FSW; GBP; NOBE; NOBL; OBSV; RDB, with music

Vicar of Wakefield, The, sels. Goldsmith.
  Elegy on the Death of a Mad Dog, An, fr. ch. 17. AIW; FaBoCo; GDP; ILP (1975 ed.); LAuP; PCOP; PoPle; SS; TPo
  Song: "When lovely woman stoops to folly," fr. ch. 24. BoLoP; ILP (1975 ed.); LAuP; NOBE
  (Stanzas on Woman.) ExPo (1973 ed.)
  (When Lovely Woman Stoops to Folly.) HAP; HeIP; PoIA; UnPo (1976 ed.)

Vice. Anthony Hecht. OBAL

Vice ("Vice is a monster of so frightful mien"). Pope. Fr. Essay on Man, Epistle II. PPM

Vice most obscene and unsavoury, A. Limerick. Unknown. NOBL

Vicious Winter finally yields, The. Heart's Needle, X. W. D. Snodgrass. PSN

Viciousness in the kitchen! Lesbos. Sylvia Plath. RiTi

Vicissitudes of the world, O Olaad, are like the clouds of the seasons, The. To a Dictatorial Sultan. Somali Oral Tradition, tr. by B. W. Andrzejewski. WTO

Vickie. Marnie Walsh. VW

Victim, The. Michael Burkard. AAN

Victim not of an accident. A Proposal for Recycling Wastes. Marge Piercy. GP

Victim of Aulis, The. Dannie Abse. NoAM

Victor Was a Little Baby. W. H. Auden. PeBB

Victories of Love, The, sel. Coventry Patmore.
  "Your love lacks joy, your letter says," II, v. GBL

Victory. Eileen Duggan. ATNZ

Victory. Eleanor Ross Taylor. CSP

Victory comes late. Emily Dickinson. InPK

Victory in Defeat. Edwin Markham. PPM

Viejo. Joseph Somoza. TVo

"Vierge Ouvrante." Miriam Palmer. NMM; RiTi

Viet Cong Sapper Dies, A. Stephen Sossaman. AMV-81

Vietnam. Clarence Major. PoBA

Vietnam #4. Clarence Major. FF; PoBA

View. Christian J. Van Geel, tr. fr. Dutch by Emilie Peech and W. S. Di Piero. AMV-81

View from an Attic Window, The. Howard Nemerov. ConAP

View from an Institution. Franz Wright. AMV-81

View from Here, The. William Stafford. RFM

View from the Planetarium. David Barker. GP

View from the Window. Jane McCoy. AMV-80

View it, by day, from the back. Movie House. John Updike. PPoD

View of a Pig. Ted Hughes. BoAnP; CABA (1972 ed.); OxBTC; SoSe

View of Christ's Kingdom, A, sel. William Williams, tr. fr. Welsh by Saunders Lewis and Gwyn Jones.
  Marriage in Eden, The. OBW

View of Louisiana. Cleopatra Mathis. TAT

View of the Capitol from the Library of Congress. Elizabeth Bishop. WasP

View of the Earth from Space, A. Ron Weber. PoUp

View of the Organ Mountains North of Las Cruces, New Mexico, A. Gene Frumkin. FoP

View of Vienna from Schonbrunn. Peggy Ruse. NPW

View toward Wife Trading, A. Robert Gillespie. NVAP

Viewpoint. George Scarbrough. AMV-81

Views. Harriet Susskind. AMV-80

Views from the High Camp. W. S. Merwin. ConAP

Views of Our Sphere. Ernest Sandeen. Moon

Vigil. David J. Feela. BrS

Vigil, The. Shlomo Reich, tr. fr. French by Mira Reich. VWA

Vigil of Venus, The. Unknown, tr. fr. Latin by Allen Tate. GBL
  Sels.
  "Goddesse bade the nymphs remove, The," tr. by Thomas Stanley. OBVE
  "Love he to morrow, who lov'd never," tr. by Thomas Stanley. OBVE

Vigil Strange I Kept on the Field One Night. Walt Whitman. AmVN; NOBA; TAP

Vigils. Siegfried Sassoon. CMoP (1970 ed.)

Vigndig A Fremd Kind (Babysitter's Song). Unknown, tr. fr. Yiddish. FSW

Vignette: 1922. Lawrence P. Spingarn. AMV-81

Vigorous matron of Baxter, A. Hog-calling. Roy Blount, Jr. TDH

Viking Terror, The. Unknown, tr. fr. Old Irish by Kuno Meyer. PFIr
  (Vikings, The, tr. by John Montague.) BIrV

Vile Stanhope, demons blush to tell. On Lord Chesterfield and His Son. Unknown. FaBoCo

Vilikins and His Dinah. At. to Edward Laman Blanchard. See Villikins and His Dinah.

Villa Thermidor. George Hitchcock. GP

Village, The. George Crabbe. LAuP
  Sels.
  Oncoming Industrial Revolution, The, fr. I. OBP
  Rural Life, fr. I. NOBE
  "Village life, and every care that reigns, The," fr. I. ILP (1975 ed.); OAEL-1

Village. Juan Ramón Jiménez. See Lamb Was Bleating Softly, The.

Village, The. Meridel Le Sueur. GP

Village Atheist, The. Edgar Lee Masters. Fr. Spoon River Anthology. PPM

Village Blacksmith, The. Longfellow. AmVN; CTV; FaPoR; OBAL; PCOP; PPM

Village Doctor, The. Margaret Gillies. PMW

Village has always lain in the path of the conqueror, The. The Village. Meridel Le Sueur. GP

Village life, and every care that reigns, The. The Village. George Crabbe. ILP (1975 ed.); LAuP; OAEL-1

Village of Balmaquhapple, The. James Hogg. FaBoCo

Village of the Presents, The. James McMichael. AmPA

Village pedagogue announced one day, A. The Snuffboxes. *Unknown.* PoTa

Village Tale, A. May Sarton. BoAnP; GDP

Village! thy butcher's son, the steward now. Ebenezer Elliott. *Fr.* The Splendid Village. OBSV

Village Tudda, The. Kenneth Patchen. VGW

Villagers all, this frosty tide. Kenneth Grahame. *Fr.* The Wind in the Willows. PChr

Villagers and Death, The. Robert Graves. HeIP

Villages, The. R. E. Sebenthall. HeS

Villain, The. W. H. Davies. OxBTC; SoSe

Villanelle: "Every day our bodies separate." Marilyn Hacker. AmPA

Villanelle: "It is the pain, it is the pain, endures." William Empson. CMoP (1970 ed.); ILP (1975 ed.); LoAs; NoAM; OAEL-2

Villanelle: "It's all a trick, quite easy when you know it." W. W. Skeat. FaBoCo

Villanelle: "Like twilight bleeding on a winter day." John Nist. AMV-81

Villanelle, The: "Regard the motion of the Villanelle." Donald Harington. AMV-81

Villanelle: The Psychological Hour. Ezra Pound. ExPo (1973 ed.)

Villanelle of Acheron. Ernest Dowson. VLP

Villanelle of the Poet's Road. Ernest Dowson. PAIC; UnPo (1976 ed.)

Villanelle with a Line by Yeats. Bruce Bennett. AMV-80

Villikins [or Vilikins] and His Dinah. *At. to* Edward Laman Blanchard; *also at. to* Sam Cowell. FSW; PoTa; VLP

Villonaud for This Yule. Ezra Pound. PAIC

Villon's Straight Tip to All Cross Coves. W. E. Henley, *after* Villon. FaBoCo

Vilna. Moishe Kulbak, *tr. fr. Yiddish by* Joachim Neugroschel. VWA

Vilna Puzzle, A. Sasha Chorny, *tr. fr. Russian by* Daniel Weissbort. VWA

Vincent van Gogh. "Truly We Can Only Allow Our Paintings to Speak." Jean Pumphrey. TPo

Vindication. Daniil Kharms, *tr. fr. Russian by* George Gibian. FaBoNo

Vine, The. Robert Herrick. CaPo

Vine and Fig Tree. Shalom Altman. FSW

Vinedresser Yearns over His Vineyard, The. Irene Dayton. AATT

Vinegaroon. Witter Bynner. BPAW

Vines tougher than wrists. Forcing House. Theodore Roethke. PiAm

Vineyard, The. W. S. Merwin. NNaP

Vintage to the Dungeon, The. Richard Lovelace. CaPo

Violence on Television. Louis Jenkins. NU

Violence swaddles all (love-) acts before and after. Peter Whigham. *Fr.* Astapovo, or What Are We to Do. TwMBP

Violent bear it away, The. Question. Lucille F. Travis. AATT

Violent Space, The. Etheridge Knight. BPo

Violet, The. Jane Taylor. PCOP

Violet and the Rose, The ("The violet in the wood, that's sweet to-day"). Augusta Webster. PCOP

Violin Tree, The. Joel Rosenberg. VWA

Violinist's shadow vanishes, The. Cadenza. Ted Hughes. CMoP (1970 ed.)

Violins in Repose. Jorge Plescoff, *tr. fr. Spanish by* Yishai Tobin. VWA

Viper, The. Hilaire Belloc. FaBoNo

Viper, The. Ruth Pitter. FaBoTw (1975 ed.)

Virgidemiarum, *sels.* Joseph Hall.
  "Great is the folly of a feeble brain," Bk. I, Satire VII. EBEV; TVS
  "I first adventure, with foolhardy might," Prologue, Bk.I. TVS
  "I wot not how the world's degenerate," Bk. IV, Satire VI. TVS
  "In the heavens' universal alphabet," Bk. II, Satire VII. TVS
  Rome Ryme, Bk. IV, Satire VII. TVS
  "Sturdy ploughman doth the soldier see, The," Bk. IV, *fr.* Satire VI. OBSV
  "Time was, and that was termed the time of Gold," Bk. III, Satire I. OBSV
  "When Gullion died (who knows not Gullion?)," Bk. III, Satire VI. TVS
  "Who doubts? The laws fell down from heaven's height," Bk. II, Satire III. OBSV
  "With some pot-fury, ravished from their wit," Bk. I, Satire III. NIL

Virgil's Farewell to Dante. Dante, *tr. fr. Italian by* Laurence Binyon. *Fr.* Divina Commedia: Purgatorio, XXVII. FaBoTw (1975 ed.)

Virgin, The. *Unknown.* GBP

Virgin is thinking of a child, The. Leonardo's Secret. Robert Bly. NNaP

Virgin Jewess, Rising with a Cry, The. Prentice Baker. AATT

Virgin Mary, The. Edgar Bowers. PiAm

Virgin Mary, The. Robert Herrick. SCP-1

Virgin Mary, The. *Unknown, tr. fr. Welsh by* Joseph P. Clancy. OBW

Virgin Mary Had One Son. *Unknown.* FSW

Virgin Mary to Christ on the Cross, The. Robert Southwell. PIM

Virgin Pictured in Profile. Rosanna Warren. AMV-81

Virgin Sturgeon, The. *Unknown.* FSW

Virginal, A. Ezra Pound. CMoP; (1970 ed.); ILP (1975 ed.); NIL; NoAM; NOBA; TAP

Virginia. T. S. Eliot. Landscapes, II. BiP

Virginia. Elouise Loftin. PoBA

Virginia Beach. Stanley Plumly. AMV-81

Virginia Woolf. Gerald Locklin. PoW

Virginia's Bloody Soil. *Unknown.* AmFP

Virgins promis'd when I died. An Epitaph upon a Child. Robert Herrick. FaBoEE

Virgins, sing the virgin huntress. To Apollo and Diana. Horace, *tr. by* Branwell Brontë. Odes, I, 21. OBVE

Virgin's Song, The. *Unknown.* BoReV; NOBE; OxBM

Virtue. George Herbert. CABA (1972 ed.); ExPo (1973 ed.); HAP; HeIP; ILP (1975 ed.); NIL; NOBE; OAEL-1; PPP; SCP-1; SoSe; UsP
  (Vertue.) PoPle

Virtue conceal'd within our breast. Swift, *after the Latin of* Horace. OBVE

Virtue, dear friend, needs no defence. Horace, *tr. by* Earl of Roscommon. Odes, I, 22. OBVE

Virtue may choose the high or low degree. The Triumph of Vice. Pope. *Fr.* Epilogue to the Satires. NIL; NOBE; OBSV

Virtue of Shape, A. Thom Swiss. AMV-80

"Virtue of Uncreatedness, The." Alice Notley. FiCh

Virtues of Carnation Milk, The. David Ogilvy. OBAL

Virtues of Sid Hamet, the Magician's Rod, The. Swift. APAS

Virtuous, witty, proud and gay. The Romantic. Colin Ellis. POL

Virtus Vera Nobilitas. Mildmay Fane, Earl of Westmorland. SCP-2

Visibility stretches for miles, bringing the sea. Soup on a Cold Day. Nellie Hill. AMV-81

Visible, invisible. A Jellyfish. Marianne Moore. TPo

Visible tallow of the hurricane night. Saving Tallow. Barbara Guest. RiTi

Vision, A. John Clare. OAEL-2; PPP

Vision. Harry Crosby. EAS

Vision, The. Daniel Defoe. APAS

Vision, The ("Methought I saw as I did dream in bed"). Robert Herrick. CaPo

Vision, The ("Sitting alone as one forsook"). Robert Herrick. CaPo

Vision, A. Denise Levertov. PiAm

Vision. Edward Lowbury. PMW

Vision. W. S. Merwin. GP

Vision, The. Thomas Traherne. ILwL

Vision by Sweetwater. John Crowe Ransom. CMoP (1970 ed.); NOBA; UsP

Vision Concerning Piers Plowman, The. *See* Vision of Piers Plowman, The.

Vision doesn't mean anything real. American Poets. Marvin Bell. NVAP

Vision of a Queen of Fairyland, A. Tadhg Dall O'Huiginn, *tr. by* the Earl of Longford. *Fr.* The First Vision. BIrV

Vision of Belshazzar, The. Byron. FaPo; PIM

Vision of Beulah, The. Blake. *Fr.* Milton, II. NOBE; OAEL-2 (Birds, The.) PB

Vision of Felicity, The. William Everson. PiAm

Vision of God, The. Dante, *tr. fr. Italian by* Laurence Binyon. *Fr.* Divina Commedia: Paradiso, XXXIII. ExPo (1973 ed.)

Vision of Judgment, The. Byron. ESaP; MBPR; OAEL-2
Sels.
"At length with jostling, elbowing, and the aid." OBSV
"Saint Peter sat by the celestial gate." OBSV
Satan and Michael. UsP

Vision of MacConglinne, The, *sel.* MacConglinne, *tr. fr. Middle Irish.*
"Vision that appeared to me, A," *tr. by* Kuno Meyer. FaBoNo; PFIr
("Vision that appeared, The," *tr. by* John Montague, *after* Kuno·Meyer.) BIrV; OBVE

Vision of Montezuma Preserve, N.Y. Ron Welburn. NW

Vision of Piers Plowman, The, *sels.* William Langland.
Belling the Cat (C *text*). OxBM
Et Incarnatus Est, *fr.* Passus II (C *text*). BoReV; NOBE
Glutton in the Tavern (C *text*). OxBM
Jousting of Jesus, The, *fr.* Passus XVIII *and* XXI (B *and* C *texts*). BoReV
Long Will in London (C *text*). OxBM
Our Needy Neighbours (C *text*). OxBM
Poet, Rebuked, Responds, The, *fr.* Passus XII, *mod. by* Selden Rodman. OBP
Prologue: "In a summer season, when soft was the sun." OAEL-1, *mod. by* J. B. Trapp (B *text*); OBP, *mod. by* Selden Rodman
(Field Full of Folk, The, A *text*.) OxBM
("In a somer seson, whan softe was the sonne.") EBEV
Trinity, The (C *text*). OxBM
"What for feere of this ferly and of the false Jewes," *fr.* Passus XVIII. EBEV
"What this mountain means, and the murky dale," Passus I (B *text*), *mod. by* J. B. Trapp. OAEL-1
"Yet I courbed on my knees and cried hire of grace," *fr.* Passus II. EBEV

Vision of Poets, A, *sel.* Elizabeth Barrett Browning.
"Fiery throb in every star, A." PeD

Vision of Rotterdam. Gregory Corso. NoAM

Vision of Sin, The. Tennyson. OAEL-2; VLP

Vision of Sir Launfal, The, *sels.* James Russell Lowell.
"And what is so rare as a day in June?" *fr.* Prelude to Pt. 1. CTV; FSFS
"There was never a leaf on bush or tree," *fr.* Pt. II. PIM

Vision of the Future; the Flood. Milton. *Fr.* Paradise Lost, XI. SCP-1

Vision of the Mermaids, The, *sel.* Gerard Manley Hopkins.
"Mermaids six or seven." EcS

Vision of the Night, The. Philip Freneau. *Fr.* The House of Night. EAP

Vision of Truth, A. J. C. Squire. NOBL

Vision that appeared, The. MacConglinne, *tr. by* John Montague, *after* Kuno Meyer. *Fr.* The Vision of MacConglinne. BIrV; OBVE

Vision that appeared to me, A. MacConglinne, *tr. by* Kuno Meyer. *Fr.* The Vision of MacConglinne. FaBoNo; PFIr

Vision to Electra, The. Robert Herrick. LoAs

"Vision," we said, hearing how things turned out. Vision. Edward Lowbury. PMW

Visionary, The. Emily Brontë. BoReV; NOBE; PBWP

Visionary Hope, The. Samuel Taylor Coleridge. MBPR

Visions. Kathleen Spivack. AmPA

Visions of the Daughters of Albion. Blake. MBPR; OAEL-2

Visions of the World's Vanity, *sel.* Spenser.
Huge Leviathan, The. EcS

Visions of You. Tim Burke. PHC

Visions you never saw, The. Grandfather. Lance Henson. CDW

Visit. A. R. Ammons. VoA

Visit, A. Sherwood Anderson. PoA

Visit, The. Emerson. NOBA

Visit, The. Jim Gauer. AMV–81

Visit, The. Phillip William George. VoR

Visit, The. William J. Rewak. AMV–80

Visit. Eve Shelnutt. TC

Visit. James Welch. AmPA

Visit from St. Nicholas, A. Clement Clarke Moore. CTV; FaPo; NIL; OBAL; OxBChV; PChr; PCOP

Visit Home, A. Joseph Glazer. VWA

Visit of the Gods, The. Schiller, *tr. fr. German by* Samuel Taylor Coleridge. OBVE

Visit Peru: Of Stoned Incas' Land. Teresa A. McCarthy. NPW

Visit to Bridge House, A. Richard Weber. BIrV

Visit to My Father-in-Law on Memorial Day, A. Peggy Ruse. NPW

Visit to the Asylum, A. Edna St. Vincent Millay. SO

Visit to the Museum. R. A. Simpson. GAS

Visit to the Zoo for the First Kidney Transplant Mothers and Their Children, A. Daphne Gloag. PMW

Visitant, The. Theodore Roethke. CMoP (1970 ed.); PPoe; UnPo (1976 ed.)

Visitant to our dumbly human home. The Great Moth. Robert Gittings. OxBTC

Visitation. Elisavietta Ritchie. AATT

Visitations. Jennifer Crewe. AMV–80

Visitations from a Wartime Childhood, *sel.* George Bruce.
"Of the five waiters, white, stiff-shirt fronted." MS

Visiting home to tell my people. A Long Overdue Thankyou Note to the Girl Who Taught Me Loving. Tom Schmidt. NeAC

Visiting Hour. Stewart Conn. MS

Visiting Hour. Norman MacCaig. LP; MS

Visiting Hour, The.  David Wagoner.  HoPM (1975 ed.)

Visiting Poet.  John Frederick Nims.  InPK

Visting the Dead.  Ciaran Carson.  CIP

Visiting the Oracle.  Lawrence Raab.  AmPA

Visiting you, we slept in the arms of.  Pennsylvania Academy of Fine Arts.  Ernest Kroll.  AMV-80

Visitor, A.  "Lewis Carroll."  FaBoNo

Visitor, The.  W. H. Davies.  GBL; OBW

Visitor, The.  Duane Niatum.  UsP

Visitor to warsaw.  Portrait of a Jew Old Country Style.  Jerome Rothenberg.  NNaP

Visitors, The.  Elizabeth Bartlett.  PMW

Visitors, The.  Peter Dale.  PMW

Visitors.  Marie Harris.  MMD

Visitors.  Tu Fu, tr. fr. Chinese by Kenneth Rexroth.  IPWM

Visits to St. Elizabeths.  Elizabeth Bishop.  VGW

Vita Nuova.  Stanley Kunitz.  VGW

Vita-Sheet.  Ruth Weiss.  MIT

Vita Silenziosa.  Brian Swann.  AAN

Vitae Summa Brevis Spem Nos Vetat Incohare Longam.  Ernest Dowson.  HAP; NOBE; VLP

Vitaï Lampada.  Sir Henry Newbolt.  BTTM; FaPoR

Vital spark of heavenly flame!  Ode: The Dying Christian to His Soul.  Pope.  ILP (1975 ed.)

Vitality.  Maria Amália Fonte Boa, tr. fr. Portuguese by Willis Barnstone and Nelson Cerqueira.  BoWoP

Vitamins and Roughage.  Kenneth Rexroth.  NoAM

Virtrines of pearly gowns, bright porcelains.  Fifth Avenue Parade.  Anthony Hecht.  NYP

Vittoria Colonna.  Roy Marz.  PoA

Vivaldi.  Stuart Dybek.  TC

Vivamus, Mea Lesbia, atque Amemus.  Thomas Campion, after Catullus.  See My Sweetest Lesbia, Let Us Live and Love.

Vive la Canadienne.  Tr. fr. French.  FSW

Vive la Compagnie.  Unknown.  FSW; PSoN, with music

Vive Noir!  Mari Evans.  IHMS; PoBA; Psy

Vivid hardened ocean, A.  New Mexican Desert.  Witter Bynner.  BPAW

Vivien's Song.  Tennyson.  Fr. Idylls of the King.  OAEL-2

Vivisection.  Gene Fowler.  CPA

Vixen, The.  John Clare.  BoAnP

Vixi Puellis Nuper Idoneus.  Sir Thomas Wyatt.  See Lover Showeth How He Is Forsaken . . .

Vobiscum Est Iope.  Thomas Campion.  See Among the Shades.

Vocation.  William Stafford.  CNW

Voice, The.  Rupert Brooke.  BuTh

Voice, The.  George Chambers.  HeS

Voice.  Claudia Dobkins.  NPW

Voice, The.  Thomas Hardy.  BoLoP; CMoP (1970 ed.); GBL; HAP; NoAM; OAEL-2; PoPle; PSN

Voice, The.  Judith Herzberg, tr. fr. Dutch by Shirley Kaufman.  VWA

Voice, The.  Philip Levine.  PCho

Voice.  W. S. Merwin.  NNaP

Voice.  Stanley Moss.  AMV-80

Voice, The.  Theodore Roethke.  NowV; VGW

Voice from Danang.  Thomas Dillon Redshaw.  MAT

Voice from Out of the Night, A.  Lisel Mueller.  GP

Voice from the Roses, A.  Maxine W. Kumin.  NMM

Voice from the Well, The.  George Peele.  Fr. The Old Wife's Tale.  NOBE

Voice from under the Table, A.  Richard Wilbur.  HAP; NOBA

Voice in the Crowd.  Ted Joans.  AmNP (1974 ed.)

Voice in the Dark.  A. L. Strauss, tr. fr. Hebrew by Robert Friend.  VWA

Voice in your chest speaks the language, The.  Harold.  Stephen Tudor.  HeS

Voice of a Dissipated Woman inside a Tomb.  Sor Violante do Céu, tr. fr. Portuguese by Willis Barnstone.  BoWoP

Voice of America, 1961, The.  James Liddy.  CIP

Voice of Caesar, The.  W. H. Auden.  Fr. For the Time Being.  AnMo

Voice of God Is Calling, The, with music.  John Haynes Holmes.  AH

Voice of King Solomon's nightingale, The.  A Snow in Jerusalem.  Hayim Naggid, tr. by Shlomo Vinner and Howard Schwartz.  VWA

Voice of my beloved, The!  Bible, O.T.  Fr. The Song of Solomon.  PBMP

Voice of my darling, The.  Bible, O.T.  Fr. The Song of Solomon, ad. by Willis Barnstone.  BoWoP

Voice of the Ancient Bard, The.  Blake.  Fr. Songs Of Experience.  MBPR

Voice of the city is sleepless, The.  Salute to Life.  Dmitri Shostakovitch.  FSW

Voice of the Crocus.  Mildred N. Hoyer.  AMV-80

Voice of the Devil, The.  Blake.  Fr. The Marriage of Heaven and Hell.  NU

Voice of the Future, The.  Michele Wallace.  WBN

Voice of the glutton I heard with disdain, The.  The Glutton.  John Oakman.  OxBChV

Voice of the last cricket, The.  Splinter.  Carl Sandburg.  PCOP; SoSe; UsP

Voice of the Power of This World, The.  Gregory Hall.  NU

Voice of the Studio Announcer.  Archibald MacLeish.  Fr. The Fall of the City.  HoPM (1975 ed.)

Voice of the Surbahar, sels.  Robin Fulton.  MIS
  "It seems a frail mathematics, and ancient."
  "Spring was a month late, autumn a month early."

Voice on the Other End of the Line, The.  Leonard Randolph.  PoUp

Voice on the winds, A.  To Morfydd.  Lionel Johnson.  OAEL-2

Voice out of the Tabernacle, A.  Louis Zukofsky.  VWA

Voice Over.  Anthony Glavin.  IPM

Voice peals in this end of night, A.  A Thrush before Dawn.  Alice Meynell.  WPE

Voice, A, said, "Follow, follow": and I rose.  Two Pursuits.  Christina Rossetti.  WPE

Voice, The, said, "Hurl her down!"  The Lovely Shall Be Choosers.  Robert Frost.  NOBA

Voice, A, said, Look me in the stars.  A Question.  Robert Frost.  TH

Voice that breathed o'er Eden, The.  Holy Matrimony.  John Keble.  VLP

Voices.  Walter de la Mare.  UnPo (1976 ed.)

Voices, The.  Rainer Maria Rilke, tr. fr. German by Robert Bly.  EC

Voices Answering Back: The Vampires.  Lawrence Raab.  AmPA

Voices at the Window.  Sir Philip Sidney.  See Astrophel and Stella: Eleventh Song.

Voices from the Other World.  James Merrill.  GP

Voices from Things Growing in a Churchyard.  Thomas Hardy.  OxBTC

Voices in the air and in the earth.  When the Earth Is Cold.  Sol Funaroff.  SPT

Voices Inescapable, The.  Ann Stanford.  IHMS

Voices lifted high in singing.  Music.  Malay Oral Tradition, tr. by R. O. Winstedt.  WTO

Voices move, The. they are walking. it is time.  Not under Holly or Green Boughs.  Tom Raworth.  TwMBP

Voices moving about in the quiet house.  Falling Asleep.  Siegfried Sassoon.  FSFS; OxBTC

Voices of birds are. Is Is Like Is. Adrien Stoutenburg. TSWA

Voices of Heroes. Horace Gregory. OFD

Voices of Nature, The. Thomas Edward Brown. PeD

Voices of the Night, *sel.* Longfellow.
Prelude: "Pleasant it was, when woods were green." FSFS

Void only. "Ping Hsin," *tr. by* Kenneth Rexroth *and* Ling Chung. *Fr.* Multitudinous Stars. PBWP

Volatile Kerryman, The. Owen Roe O'Sullivan, *tr. fr. Irish by* Sean O'Riada. BIrV

Volcanic Venus. D. H. Lawrence. InPS; POL

Volcanoes. Bella Akhmadulina, *tr. fr. Russian by* W. H. Auden. PBWP

Volpone, *sels.* Ben Jonson.
"Come, my Celia, let us prove," *fr.* III, vii. HeIP; ILP (1975 ed.); OBVE
(Come, My Celia.) CABA (1972 ed.); FF; IPWM; NIL
(Song: To Celia.) BiP; OAEL-1, *with music.*
"Death of mine honor, with the city's fool!" *fr.* II, iii. SCP-1

Voltaire at Ferney. W. H. Auden. PoA

Voluntaries, *sel.* Emerson.
So Nigh Is Grandeur, III. PCOP
("So nigh is grandeur to our dust," *last* 4 *ll.*) CTV

Volunteer, The. Herbert Asquith. OxBTC

Volunteers, The. Janet Kauffman. TC

Voodoo on the Un-Assing of Janis Joplin. Carolyn M. Rodgers. JB

Vorthy cit, von Vitsunday, A. Mr. and Mrs. Vite's Journey. *Unknown.* NOBL

Votaries know. A Poem for Integration. Alvin Saxon. PoBA

Vote, The. Ralph Knevet. SCP-2

Voting Machine. Norman Nathan. AMV–80

Vow, The. Anthony Hecht. ConAP; CoPAm; ILP (1975 ed.); Prf

Vow to Love Faithfully, Howsoever He Be Rewarded, A. Petrarch, *tr. fr. Italian by* the Earl of Surrey. Sonnets to Laura: To Laura in Life, CXIII. PAIC
("Set me wheras the sonne dothe perche the grene.") AAS
("Set me whereas the sun doth parch the green.") HAP; ILP (1975 ed.)

Vowel Movements. Daryl Hine. PoA

Vowels. Peter West. AKE

Vowels of Another Language, The. Tom Disch. PoA

Vox Clero. *Unknown.* APAS

Vox Humana. Thom Gunn. ILP (1975 ed.)

Vox Populi. Dryden. *Fr.* The Medal. NOBE; UsP

"Voy wawm" said the dustman. Hymn to the Sun. Michael Roberts. OxBTC

Voyage. Donald G. H. Schramm. AMV–81

Voyage. Stephen Stepanchev. SA

Voyage. Stanislaw Wygodski, *tr. fr. Polish by* Isaac Komen. VWA

Voyage Itself, The. Ben Jonson. TVS

Voyage of Jimmy Poo, The. James A. Emanuel. AmNP (1974 ed.)

Voyage on the Thames, The. Pope. *Fr.* The Rape of the Lock, II. NOBE
("Not with more glories, in th' ethereal plain.") EBEV

Voyage to the Island of Love, A, *sels.* Aphra Behn.
Dream, The. PBWP
"Thousand gloomy walks the bower contains, A." SCP-2

Voyage to the Moon. William Dickey. CoPAm; Moon

Voyage to the Moon. Archibald MacLeish. Moon; PBMP

Voyage West. Archibald MacLeish. VGW

Voyages (I-VI). Hart Crane. CMoP (1970 ed.); NoAM; NOBA; TAP
*Sels.*

---

"Above the fresh ruffles of the surf," I. CABA (1972 ed.); PSN; VGW

"And yet this great wink of eternity," II. ExPo (1973 ed.); HAP; ILP (1975 ed.); PAIC; PiAm; PPoe; PPP; UnPo (1976 ed.); VGW

"Infinite consanguinity it bears," III. LoAs

"Meticulous, past midnight in clear rime," V. PSN

"Where icy and bright dungeons lift," VI. CABA (1972 ed.); ExPo (1973 ed.); HAP; UnPo (1976 ed.)

"Whose counted smile of hours and days," IV. ILP (1975 ed.)

Voyeur, The. Deanna Louise Pickard. AMV–80

Vulgar Error, A. J. E. Thorold Rogers. FaBoEE

Vulture, The. Hilaire Belloc. FPB; OxBChV

Vulture. Robinson Jeffers. BoAnP; NOBA; PiAm

Vulture. Kenneth Rexroth. *Fr.* A Bestiary. NNaP

Vulture and the Husbandman, The. A. C. Hilton. FaBoCo

Vulture eats between his meals, The. The Vulture. Hilaire Belloc. FPB; OxBChV

Vulture of the Plains, The. Hamlin Garland. BPAW

Vultures are being spring-cleaned, The. Building Society Blues. Roger Roughton. EAS

Vulture's very like a sack, The. Ecology. X. J. Kennedy. BoAnP

Vultures waft circles. Remnant Ghosts at Dawn. Oliver La Grone. FB

# W

W. C. W. David Ray. POL

W. H. *Eheu!* Samuel Taylor Coleridge. FaBoEE

W. S. Landor. Marianne Moore. OBAL; Psy

W. W. Amiri Baraka. HeIP; NOBA; PiAm; PoBA

W was a wild worm. A Wild Worm. Carolyn Wells. TDH

Waäit till our Sally cooms in, fur thou mun a' sights to tell. The Northern Cobbler. Tennyson. EBEV

Wabash Cannonball, *Unknown.* BLSo, *with music;* FSW

Waddles after/ her mistress. Old Dog. Raymond Souster. GDP

Wade/ through black jade. The Fish. Marianne Moore. NoAM; PBMP; PiAm; UsP

Wade in the Water. *Unknown.* FSW

Wading upstream we bump his carcass. Raccoon Skeleton at Long Plain Creek. Helena Minton. FAF

Wae's Me for Prince Charlie. William Glen. BTTM

Wae's me, wae's me. Song of the Cauld Lad of Hylton. *Unknown.* GBP

Waggon-Maker, The. John Masefield. EBEV

Waggoner, The. *Unknown.* GBP

Wagner. Rupert Brooke. FaBoTw (1975 ed.); NOBL

Wagon Train, The. Sam L. Simpson. BPAW

Wagon Wheels. S. E. LaMoure. AMV–81

Wagoner's Lad, The. *Unknown.* AmFP; FSW

Wagons loom like blue caravans in the dusk, The. Harvest Home. Sir Herbert Read. RAE

Wagtail's Nest, The. Kenneth Mackenzie. MAuV

Waif, The. Walter de la Mare. FaBoNo

Waikato Railstop. Kendrick Smithyman. ATNZ

Wail, wail, ah for Adonis! He is lost to us, lovely Adonis. Lament for Adonis. Bion, *tr. by* John Addington Symonds. Epi

Wailing, wailing, wailing, the wind over land and sea. Rizpah. Tennyson. PAIC; VLP

Wailings of a maiden I recite, The. Wednesday; or, The Dumps. John Gay. *Fr.* The Shepherd's Week. OAEL-1

Waillie. *Unknown.* *See* Waly, Waly ("When cockle shells turn silver bells").

Waily, Waily. *Unknown.* *See* Waly, Waly ("When cockle shells turn silver bells").

Waist up, I know. Mermaid. Helena Minton. FAF

Wait. P. D. Cummins. BuTh

Wait, The. Phyllis Janowitz. AMV-80

Wait. Timothy Steele. PoA

Wait a Little! *Unknown.* BoReV; OxBM

Wait for Me. Robert Creeley. NOBA; PPP

Wait for the Wagon. *Unknown, at. to* R. Bishop Buckley. BLSo, *with music;* FSW; PSoN, *with music*

Wait, Kate! You skate at such a rate. To Kate, Skating Better than Her Date. David Daiches. CTBA; SPo

Wait; the great horned owls. Owls. W. D. Snodgrass. BoAnP

Wait 'till the Sun Shines, Nellie. Andrew B. Sterling. BLSH, *chorus only, with music;* BLSo, *with music;* FSN, *with music;* FSW

Wait till Then. Mark Van Doren. SO

Waiter waited, the cook ate, The. What Happened? What Do You Expect? Alan Dugan. NowV

Waiting. Jane Cooper. TAP

Waiting. Ed Cox. PoUp

Waiting. Robert Creeley. VGW

Waiting. Fay Enos. PHC

Waiting. W. E. Henley. In Hospital, II. ILP (1975 ed.); VLP

Waiting. Philip Levine. CPA

Waiting. Liz Stout. AMV-81

Waiting,/ for their moment to die. Up There. Margo Bohanon. SES

Waiting at the Church; or, My Wife Won't Let Me, *with music.* Fred W. Leigh. FSN

Waiting by the window. The Last Gangster. Gregory Corso. CoPAm; SA

Waiting Carefully. Nancy P. Kamm. AMV-80

Waiting Child, The. Mel Takahara. PHC

Waiting for breakfast, while she brushed her hair. Philip Larkin. NoAM

Waiting for Her. Alden Nowlan. NeAC

Waiting for Icarus. Muriel Rukeyser. NNaP

Waiting for It. May Swenson. BoAnP

Waiting for Lilith. Jascha Kessler. VWA

Waiting for the Bus. D. J. Enright. OxBTC

Waiting for the Bus. Alan Ziegler. AAN

Waiting for the corpse. Shetland Funeral. James Rankin. MIS

Waiting for the Doctor. Colette Inez. IHMS

Waiting for the Emperor Tenji. Princess Nukada, *tr. fr. Japanese by* Cid Corman *and* Susumu Kamaike. PBWP

Waiting for the end, boys, waiting for the end. Just a Smack at Auden. William Empson. FaBoCo; UnPo (1976 ed.)

Waiting for the Transformation. Judith Minty. TV

Waiting for when the sun an hour or less. In Santa Maria del Popolo. Thom Gunn. CMoP (1970 ed.); ExPo (1973 ed.); MPA

Waiting for You to Come By. Simon J. Ortiz. CDW

Waiting in Faith. Michelangelo Buonarroti, *tr. fr. Italian.* ILwL

Waiting in Front of the Columnar High School. Karl Shapiro. HAP

Waiting in the Cafe. Stan Rice. MIT

Waiting is the poem of waiting. On Arrival. Richard Howard. TAP

Waiting-Room, The. Robin Fulton. PoA

Waiting Rooms. Howard Nemerov. PoA

Waiting rooms are full of "characters," The. Pretending Not to Sleep. Ian Hamilton. NoAM

Waiting, the Hallways under Her Skin Thick with Dreamchildren. Lyn Lifshin. FAF; NeAC

Waiting to Be Fed. Ray A. Young Bear. CDW

Wake, The. Madeline DeFrees. RiTi

Wake, The. Robert Herrick. PAIC

Wake. Langston Hughes. OBAL

Wake, The. Wyatt Prunty. AMV-80

Wake. Elizabeth Spires. AMV-80

Wake All the Dead. Sir William Davenant. *Fr.* The Law against Lovers. HAP; ILP (1975 ed.); OBP; SCP-2

Wake. And my eyes stun. I Wake, My Friend, I. Faye Kicknosway. IHMS

Wake as you will, but wake in me. To Song. Olga Berggolts, *tr. by* Daniel Weissbort. BoWoP

Wake at the Well, The. *Unknown.* GBP

Wake, child with the flute. Mirabai, *tr. fr. Hindi by* Willis Barnstone *and* Usha Nilsson. BoWoP

Wake! For the sun, who scattered into flight. Omar Khayyám, *tr. fr. Persian by* Edward Fitzgerald. *Fr.* The Rubáiyát of Omar Khayyám of Naishápúr. BiP; FF; OBP; VLP

Wake, friend, from forth thy lethargy! the drum. Ben Jonson. *Fr.* An Epistle to a Friend (Mr. Colby) to Persuade Him to the Wars. SCP-1

Wake, Isles of the South, *with music.* William B. Tappan. AH

Wake me up at five-thirty please. Hotel. Adam Wazyk, *tr. by* Isaac Komem. VWA

Wake Nicodemus. Henry Clay Work. FSW

Wake Not for the World-heard Thunder. A. E. Housman. CMoP (1970 ed.); NoAM

Wake, now my love, awake; for it is time. Spenser. *Fr.* Epithalamion. GBL

Wake, shake, day's a-breakin'. Green Corn. *Unknown.* FSW

Wake: the silver dusk returning. Reveille. A. E. Housman. CMoP (1970 ed.); PPM; SoSe; STS

Wake the Song of Jubilee, *with music.* Leonard Bacon. AH

Wake up high up. Things to Do in New York (City). Ted Berrigan. NoAM

Wake Up, Jacob. *Unknown.* FSW

Wake up mama turn your lamp down lo-ow. Statesboro Blues. *Unknown.* BluL

Wake-up Niggers. Don L. Lee. PoBA

Wake up, wake up, darlin' Cory [*or* Corey]. Darling Cory [*or* Darlin' Corey]. *Unknown.* AmFP; FSW

Waked by the Gospel's Powerful Sound, *with music.* Samson Occom. AH

Wakefield Second Shepherd's Play, The. *Unknown.* OAEL-1, *mod. English*

Wakeful, vagrant, restless thing. Ode to Fancy. Philip Freneau. EAP

Wakening, The. Sam Hamill. AMV-80

Wakening pang had grown a sullen ache, The. Quem Queritis. Albert Howard Carter. AATT

Wakes, bluejean morning, sound of. Geography. Michael Dransfield. CAAP

Waking. Hugh Maxton. BIrV; CIP; IPM

Waking, The ("I strolled across/ An open field"). Theodore Roethke. CNW; RFM

Waking, The ("I wake to sleep, and take my waking slow"). Theodore Roethke. BiP; CNW; HAP; HeIP; InPS; NoAM; NOBA; PiAm; PPP; SoSe; STS; TAP; TCP; VoPo (Waking Just before Sleeping, The.) PPM

Waking alone in a multitude of loves when morning's light. On the Marriage of a Virgin. Dylan Thomas. STS

Waking at Night. Morton Marcus. MIT

Waking beside you I watch this night. Alba for Mélusine. Ramon Guthrie. LoAs

Waking Bird Refutes, The. Allen Curnow. ATNZ

Waking, child, while you slept, your mother took. Ethel Anderson. *Fr.* Bucolic Eclogues. WPE

Waking close to the trees. In the Mountain Cabin. Del Marie Rogers. NPW

Waking Early. R. L. Barth. AMV-81

Waking Early Sunday Morning. Robert Lowell. NOBA

Waking from a Nap on the Beach. May Swenson. RFM

Waking from Sleep. Robert Bly. CAPP; EAS; InPS; NoAM; NOBA

Waking, I always waked you awake. Jean Garrigue. LoAs

Waking in New York, *sel.* Allen Ginsberg. "On the roof cloudy sky fading sun rays," II. NYP

Waking in Nice. Patricia Traxler. AMV-81

Waking in the Blue. Robert Lowell. CoPAm; PiAm; PPP; PSN; UnPo (1976 ed.)

Waking Just before Sleeping, The. Theodore Roethke. *See* Waking, The ("I wake to sleep, and take my waking slow").

Waking one morning, he was alarmed to find. He Smelt the Smell of Death within the Marrow. Louis Johnson. ATNZ

Waking thickened by crow's light. Continuum. Adreinne Rich. TT

Waking this morning. This Morning. Muriel Rukeyser. BoWoP; IPWM; NMM

Waking to Leopards. Nancy Mairs. NPW

Waking to Snowfall. Roderick Hartigh Jellema. AATT

Waking Up. J. Charles Green. DNGG

Waking Up. Edward Lense. AMV-80

Waking Up. Tom Schmidt. GP

Waking up late this morning, in full sunlight. 9:00. Patricia Hooper. AMV-81

Wakonda! Talako! deathonic turkey gobbling. Spontaneous Requiem for the American Indian. Gregory Corso. MAT

Walam Olum; or, Red Score, *sel. Tr. fr. Delaware Indian by* Daniel G. Brinton. "After the Seizer there were ten chiefs, and there was much warfare south and east." OBVE

Waldeinsamkeit. Emerson. NOBA

Walden Pond/ All those noxious gases rising from it. Jack Spicer. *Fr.* "Graphemics." VGW

Waldheim Cemetery. Robert Sward. ANTL

Wale whyt as whalles bon, A. The White Beauty. *Unknown.* OxBM

Wales. Norman Nicholson. PES

Wales England Wed. Ernest Rhys. OBW

Wales Visitation. Allen Ginsberg. CAPP; NNaP; NOBA; Prf

Walk, The. Thomas Hardy. CMoP (1970 ed.); PSN

Walk. Frank Horne. BPo

Walk. Brian Merriman, *tr. fr. Modern Irish by* Brendan Behan. *Fr.* The Midnight Court. BIrV

Walk, A. Gary Snyder. NoAM; NOBA; UsP

Walk about the Subway Station. Charles Reznikoff. NYP

Walk among the seas. Juan Gómez-Quiñones. CPA

Walk east. Dawn polishes the sky. Direction. Roberta Hill. CDW

Walk Home, The. Reed Whittemore. ConAP

Walk in Jerusalem, Just like John. *Unknown.* FSW

Walk in Late Summer, A. Theodore Roethke. MPA

Walk in March, A. Tim Reynolds. MAT

Walk in the light! So shalt thou know. Walking in the Light. Bernard Barton. VLP

Walk on your heels. Achilles Tendon. Coleman Barks. *Fr.* Body Poems. NVAP

Walk out into your country. Who Shall Die. James A. Randall, Jr. BPo

Walk proud, walk straight, let your thoughts race. Musings. Patty Harjo. VW

Walk this mile in silence. Pastourelle. Donald Jeffrey Hayes. AmNP (1974 ed.)

Walk thru the house. Spirits/ Someone. Karoniaktatie. NW

Walk Together Children. *Unknown.* BPo

Walk with de Mayor of Harlem. David Henderson. PoBA Mayor of Harlem, De, *sel.* UsP

Walk with My Cat, A. Virginia R. Terris. AAN

Walk with the sun. Dream Song. Lewis Alexander. PoBA

Walked in the front. Today. Richard Shelton. MPA

Walking. Frank O'Hara. TAT

Walking. Thomas Traherne. EBEV

Walking alone on a strange street. Paths. Vern Rutsala. MPA

Walking along the Sea of Galilee. Dovid Knut, *tr. fr. Russian by* John Glad. VWA

Walking among sceptre-headed. Walking-Sticks and Paperweights and Watermarks. Marianne Moore. PoA

Walking Around. David Galler. AMV-81

Walking Around. Pablo Neruda, *tr. fr. Spanish by* Robert Bly. EAS

Walking around in the park. Toads Revisited. Philip Larkin. CMoP (1970 ed.); NOBL; SoSe (1977 ed.)

Walking at evening along the edge of the loma. Elegy for Another Day. Peggy Pond Church. WPW

Walking at last by the tame little edge of the sea. Evening before Rain. L. A. G. Strong. OxBTC

Walking at night along the meadow way. *Unknown, tr. fr. Czech.* FSW

Walking at night on asphalt campus. Death News. Allen Ginsberg. NoAM

Walking Blues. *Unknown.* BluL

Walking by map, I chose unwonted ground. On the Hall at Stowey. Charles Tomlinson. CMoP (1970 ed.); NoAM

Walking by the Sea. George Crabbe. PMW

Walking down the alley. Alley-Walker. Joan Smith. AMV-80

Walking eight hundred. Removal: Last Part. Carroll Arnett. VoR

Walking for That Cake, *with music.* Ed Harrigan. BLSo

Walking from the killing place. Death and the Arkansas River. Frank Stanford. FiCP

Walking Home at Night. Daniel Weissbort. VWA

Walking. I begin to notice. Lost Country. Warren Woessner. HeS

Walking, I heard the water dripping, running in the gutter. Partly to My Cat. Ellen Bass. NMM

Walking in a meadow green. *Unknown.* BoLoP

Walking in a Swamp. David Wagoner. HAP

Walking in the Light. Bernard Barton. VLP

Walking into a hall full of nurses. A Poem for Richard Speck. Michael McMahon. FAF

Walking into Love, *sel.* Marge Piercy. Meditation in My Favorite Position. RiTi

Walking Late. John Montague. CIP

Walking Milwaukee. Harold Witt. TAT

Walking north toward the point, I come on a dead seal. The Dead Seal near McClure's Beach. Robert Bly. NNaP; NU

Walking of the Moon-Woman, The. John Shaw Neilson. MAuV

Walking on Sunday. Richard Murphy. IPM

Walking on the Green Grass. *Unknown.* AmFP

Walking on the step of the shingle, here. Wales. Norman Nicholson. PES

Walking Out. Betty Adcock. CSP

Walking out, I flushed some meadowlarks. The Duck Pond at Mini's Pasture, a Dozen Years Later. Philip Dow. AmPA

Walking out of the "big E." Before the Stuff Comes Down. Gary Snyder. HeIP; PiAm

Walking Parker Home. Bob Kaufman. PoBA

Walking Past Paul Blackburn's Apt. on 7th St.   Diane Wakoski.
  TAP

Walking Song.   William E. Hickson.   OxBChV

Walking-Sticks and Paperweights and Watermarks.   Marianne
  Moore.   PoA

Walking the Beach.   Sarah Youngblood.   IHMS

Walking the small oval of Gibbs Pond.   I Move to Random
  Consolations.   William Heyen.   AmPA

Walking the suburbs in the afternoon.   Suburban Dreams.
  Edwin Muir.   OxBTC

Walking through the Country.   Dennis Provisor.   PoRo

Walking through the Upper East Side.   Erica Jong.   NYP

Walking through twisted hollow pathways.   Peter Blue Cloud.
  VoR

Walking thru Audley End Mansion Late Afternoon, *sels.*   Lyn
  Lifshin.   RiTi
  "Down the hall a bookcase."
  "In some places the color."
  "Stuffed birds in a/ cage."
  "Why her bedroom is a/ trip."

Walking, to see.   Getting Home.   Judith Rodriguez.   FPA

Walking to the Cattle-Place, *sels.*   Les A. Murray.   CAAP
  Artery, The.
  Birds in Their Title Work Freeholds of Straw.
  Death Words.
  Names of the Humble, The.
  Sanskrit.

Walking to the Mail.   Tennyson.   VLP

Walking to your house.   The Death of Neruda.   Danny L.
  Rendleman.   TC

Walking to-day by a cottage I shed tears.   Scazons.   C. S. Lewis.
  EBEV

Walking Tour, The.   W. H. Auden.   CMoP (1970 ed.)

Walking towards the house, the terraces.   Sestina in Time of
  Winter.   Patrick Anderson.   PoA

Walking up sands, offal is gaped from a tunnel seaward.
  Reclaimed Area.   Jon Silkin.   NoAM

Walking with God.   William Cowper.   BoReV; ILP (1975 ed.);
  PIM

Walking with the baby through the garden.   Seedlings.   Susan
  Weston.   PHC

Walking with you.   Friend.   Gwendolyn Brooks.   CNA

Walking with you and another lady.   A Dream of Jealousy.
  Seamus Heaney.   CIP

Walking without Snowshoes.   Elizabeth Hanson.   NPW

Walking Wounded.   Vernon Scannell.   HeHu

Walks up to a lady.   Paffer Jocker.   John Sjoberg.   AcAn

Wall, The.   Ludvik Askenazy, *tr. fr. Czech.*   VWA

Wall, The.   Gwendolyn Brooks.   *Fr.* Two Dedications.   ILP
  (1975 ed.); PoBA

Wall, The.   Raymond Carver.   NVAP

Wall, The.   David Jones.   PoA; TwMBP

Wall continues, The.   Before the Actual Cold.   Ray A. Young
  Bear.   VoR

Wall Test, The.   Louis Simpson.   GP

Wallabout Martyrs, The.   Walt Whitman.   GOA

Wallace Stevens Gives a Reading.   Harriet Zinnes.   AMV-81

Wallace Stevens, what's he done?   The Rouse for Stevens.
  Theodore Roethke.   OBAL

Walloping Window-Blind, The.   Charles E. Carryl.   *See* Capital
  Ship, A.

Wallowing in this bloody sty.   The Drunken Fisherman.   Robert
  Lowell.   AnMo; CMoP (1970 ed.); CoPAm; NOBA; STS;
  VGW

Walls.   Alice Corbin.   WPW

Walls divide us from water and from light, The.   Charles Brasch.
  *Fr.* Nineteen Thirty-nine.   ATNZ

Walls Do Not Fall, The, *sels.*   Hilda Doolittle ("H. D.").
  "In me (the worm) clearly."   NoAM
  "Incident here and there, An."   NoAM
  "Sirius/ what mystery is this?"   PBWP
  "So we reveal our status."   NoAM
  "There is a spell, for instance."   NoAM
  "We have seen how the most amiable."   BoWoP; PBWP
  "When in the company of the gods."   NoAM

Walls . . . iridescent with eyes.   The Fifth-Floor Window.   Lola
  Ridge.   WPE

Walls of the maelstrom are painted with trees, The.   Poem.
  Charles Madge.   EAS

Walls, wire, fields, and a crumbly road.   Cape Cornwall.   Paul
  Mills.   MIS

Walnut bark, walnut sap.   Dogget Gap.   *Unknown.*   AmFP

Walnut-Leaf Scent.   Laurence Binyon.   BBGO

Walrus and the Carpenter, The.   "Lewis Carroll."   *Fr.* Through
  the Looking-Glass, *ch.* 4.   AKE; FaBoCo; FaBoNo; NOBL;
  OxBChV; RhR
  " 'Time has come, The,' the Walrus said," 1 *st.*   CTV

Walrus Hunting.   Aua, *tr. fr. Eskimo.*   WTO

Walsingham.   *Unknown, sometimes at. to* Sir Walter Ralegh.
  BoLoP; NOBE; PPP
  ("As you came from the holy land.")   AAS; GBL; LoAs
  (As You [*or* Ye] Came from the Holy Land of Walsingham.)
   HAP; InPS; PoPle
  (Ballad: "As you came...")   PAIC

Walt Whitman.   Emanuel Carnevali.   PoA

Walt Whitman.   Edwin Honig.   PAIC; TAP

Walt Whitman, a kosmos, of Manhattan the son.   Song of Myself,
  XXIV.   Walt Whitman.   AnMo

Walt Whitman, an American, one of the roughs, a kosmos.   Walt
  Whitman.   *Fr.* Song of Myself, XXIV.   GrRo

Walt Whitman at Bear Mountain.   Louis Simpson.   ConAP; ILP
  (1975 ed.)

Walt Whitman loafed under the trees.   Ode to Walt Whitman.
  Michael Gold.   SPT

Walter Jenks' Bath.   William Meredith.   CoPAm; HoPM (1975
  ed.)

Walter Llywarch.   R. S. Thomas.   PSN

Walter Mitty.   Leonard Bird.   FoP

Walter Rawely of the Middle Temple, in Commendation of the
  Steele Glasse.   Sir Walter Ralegh.   AAS

Walter Spaggot.   Peter Wesley-Smith.   RAE

Waltz, The, *sel.*   Byron.
  "Muse of the many-twinkling feet! whose charms."   OBSV

Waltz.   Heather Tosteson Reich.   AMV-80

Waltz against the Mountains.   Thomas Hornsby Ferril.   VGW

Waltz in, waltz in, ye little kids, and gather round my knee.   The
  Spelling Bee at Angels.   Bret Harte.   PoTa

Waltz Me Around Again Willie; or, 'Round, 'Round, 'Round, *with
  music.*   Will D. Cobb.   FSN

Waltzing Matilda.   Andrew Barton Paterson.   FSW; GBP; PeBB;
  PoTa; RDB, *with music*

Waly, Waly ("O Waly, Waly up the bank").   *Unknown.*   HAP;
  SLP
  (Lament of Barbara Douglas.)   PoPle
  (O Waly, Waly up the Bank.)   AIW; FaBoBa; GBP

Waly, Waly ("When cockle shells turn silver bells").   *Unknown.*
  AmFP
  (Cockleshells, *with music.*)   RDB
  (Jamie Douglas.)   AIW
  (Waillie.)   FSW
  (Waily, Waily.)   AIW

Wan/ Swan.   The Bereaved Swan.   Stevie Smith.   FaBoNo;
  FaBoTw (1975 ed.)

Wan as pale thighs making apple belly strides.   Sonnet.   Ted
  Berrigan.   CAAP

Wand of that fisherman witching the waves, The. Marlin. Brewster Ghiselin. MPA; PPoD

Wanderer, The. W. H. Auden. CMoP (1975 ed.); ILP (1975 ed.); NoAM; WeW

Wanderer, The, Christopher Brennan. GAS
"Land I came thro' last was dumb with night, The," *sel.* MAuV

Wanderer, The. Eugene Field. BPAW

Wanderer, The. Seamus Heaney. CIP

Wanderer. Jessica Powers. AMV-80

Wanderer, The. *Unknown, tr. fr. Old English.* Epi, *tr. by* Andrew Hoyem; OAEL-1, *tr. by* Charles W. Kennedy

Wanderer, The. Claude Vigée, *tr. fr. French by* Anthony Rudolf. VWA

Wanderer, The: A Rococo Study, *sel.* William Carlos Williams. Paterson—The Strike. Epi

Wanderers, The. William Morris. *Fr.* The Earthly Paradise. VPC

Wanderer's Grave, The. Rufus B. Sage. BPAW

Wanderer's Night Song. Goethe, *tr. fr. German by* Longfellow. PPM

Wanderer's Song, A. John Masefield. RhR

Wandering. *Unknown.* FSW

Wandering above a sea of glass. Down on My Luck. A. R. D. Fairburn. ATNZ

Wandering by the heave of the town park, wondering. On the Closing of Millom Ironworks. Norman Nicholson. FaBoTw (1975 ed.)

Wandering Chorus. B. Alquit, *tr. fr. Yiddish by* Howard Schwartz. VWA

Wandering Jew, The. Benjamin Fondane, *tr. fr. French by* Edouard Roditi. VWA

Wandering Jew, The. Robert Mezey. VWA

Wandering Jews. Nancy Keesing. VWA

Wandering minstrel I, A. W. S. Gilbert. *Fr.* The Mikado. AIW

Wandering oversea dreamer. Prayer after World War. Carl Sandburg. VGW

Wandering through cold streets tangled like old string. Brussels in Winter. W. H. Auden. OxBTC

Wanderlust. Alison Wyrley Birch. PPM

Wand'ring in this place as a wilderness. *Unknown.* GBL

Wandsworth Common. David Bromwich. PoA

Wang Chieh made the first printed book in China in 848. Midrash. David Meltzer. CPA

Waning Moon, The. Shelley. Moon; PoPle

Waning moon looks upward, this grey night, The. Nostalgia. D. H. Lawrence. PoA

Want quickens wit: Want's pupils needs must work. The Fishermen. Theocritus, *tr. by* Charles Stuart Calverley. OBVE

Wanted/ to give away pride. A Defeat. Denise Levertov. PBWP

Wanted, Wanted: Dolores Haze. Vladimir Nabokov. RRA

Wanting a Mummy. Sandra McPherson. AmPA

Wanting Out. Gavin Ewart. EAS

Wanting to be myself, alone. Cock Crow. Rosemary Dobson. MAuV

Wanting to Die. Anne Sexton. ConAP; IHMS; NoAM; TAP

Wanton, *sel.* Silabhattarika, *tr. fr. Sanskrit*
"My husband is the same who took my maidenhead," *tr. by* Daniel H. H. Ingalls. PBWP
("My husband is the same man who first pierced me," *tr. by* Willis Barnstone.) BoWoP

Wanton, The, *sel.* Vidya, *tr. fr. Sanskrit by* Daniel H. H. Ingalls.
"Say, friend, if all is still well with the bowers." PBWP

Wanton herd of rakes protest, The. To Lydia. Horace, *tr. by* Philip Francis. Odes, I, 25. OBVE

Wanton Merry Friar, A. Chaucer. *Fr.* The Canterbury Tales: Prologue. BoReV
("Frere ther was, a wantowne and a merye, A.") BiP

Wanton troopers riding by, The. The Nymph Complaining for the Death of Her Fawn [*or* Faun]. Andrew Marvell. Epi; HeIP; OAEL-1; PAIC; SCP-1

Wanton with long delay the gay spring leaping cometh. April 1885. Robert Bridges. OxBTC

Wants. Philip Larkin. PoIA

Wants of Man, The, *abr.* John Quincy Adams. OBAL

Wants to be admired. The Horse in the Drugstore. Tess Gallagher. AmPA

Wantword. Charles Brasch. ATNZ

Waolani Stream, 1955/1975. Eric Chock. PHC

War. Dryden. *Fr.* Annus Mirabilis. SCP-1

War ("The aged in the villages"). Miguel Hernández, *tr. fr. Spanish by* Edwin Honig. IPWM

War ("All the mothers in the world"). Miguel Hernández, *tr. fr. Spanish by* James Wright. EC; Epi

War. Georg Heym, *tr. fr. German by* Peter Viereck. AMV-80

War. Joseph Langland. FF; IPWM

War. Patricia Ramsey. AATT

War. Thomas W. Shapcott. FPA

War against the Trees, The. Stanley Kunitz. HAP; NoAM

War and Silence. Robert Bly. CAPP

War Bride. Douglas Worth. FF

War canoes were ready. Thirsty Island. Jim Tollerud. VoR

War has begun, The. The Root Eater. Ai. CAAP

War Horse, The. Bible, *O.T.* Job, XXXIX: 19–25. PH

War Horse, The. Eavan Boland. BIrV; CIP; IPM

War Horses. William Cole. PH

War in Heaven. Milton. *Fr.* Paradise Lost, VI. OBP

War Is Kind, *sels.* Stephen Crane.
"Fast rode the knight," VIII. PiAm
I Explain the Silvered Passing of a Ship at Night, VI. TT
I Have Heard the Sunset Song of the Birches, VII. TT
"Impact of a dollar upon the heart, The," XX. PiAm
Little Ink More or Less, A, IV. VoPo
"Man said to the universe, A," XXI. AmVN; FaBoEE; FF; NIL; OBAL; OBSV; PiAm; PoIA; SFF; TAP; TT; WeW
Newspaper Is a Collection of Half-Injustices, A, XII. TT
On the Desert, XI. TT
"Slant of sun on dull brown walls, A," XIV. AmVN; PiAm
"There was a man with tongue of wood," XVI. PiAm
"Trees in the garden rained flowers, The," XXVI. SFF
War Is Kind, I (title poem). PAIC; PiAm; TAP; VoPo; WIF (Do Not Weep, Maiden, for War Is Kind.) BiP; NOBA
"Wayfarer, The," XIII. PiAm

War is no longer declared. Every Day. Ingeborg Bachmann, *tr. by* Michael Hamburger. PBWP

War is not declared any more. Every Day. Ingeborg Bachmann, *tr. by* Christopher Middleton. BoWoP

War Is the Statesman's Game. Shelley. *Fr.* Queen Mab, IV. FF

War Poem. Ilya Ehrenburg, *tr. fr. Russian by* Leonard Opalov. AMV-81

War Poem. Jim Mulac. AcAn

War Poet. Roy Fuller. HoPM (1975 ed.)

War Poet. Sidney Keyes. BuTh

War Requiem. Del Marie Rogers. NPW

War Song. *Zulu Oral Tradition, tr. by* D. K. Rycroft. WTO

War Song of Dinas Vawr, The. Thomas Love Peacock. *Fr.* The Misfortunes of Elphin. CABA (1972 ed.); ExPo (1973 ed.); FaPoR; HAP; OAEL-2; PoPle; PoTa

War Summer. James Applewhite. NVAP

War Walking Near. Ray A. Young Bear. CDW

War War. Michael Goode. NowV

War Winters. Earle Birney. MPA

Ward, and still in bonds, one day, A. Regeneration. Henry Vaughan. CABA (1972 ed.); SCP-1

Ward has no heart, they say; but I deny it. Samuel Rogers. FaBoEE

Ward X, sel. Lola Ridge. "Salvation Army lass, The." WPE

Wardance. Phillip William George. NW; VoR

Wardance Soup. Phillip William George. VoR

Warden Said to Me the Other Day, The. Etheridge Knight. FF

Wardour Street. Humbert Wolfe. OxBTC

Waring. Robert Browning. VLP

Waring of Sonora-Town. Henry Herbert Knibbs. BPAW

Warm and savory sleep of sated desire, The. Nightlines. Paul Clause. AATT

Warm Day in Winter. David McAleavey. PoUp

Warm Protest. D. J. Enright. HeHu

Warm rain, sunny wind start to break the chill. Li Ch'ing-chao, tr. fr. Chinese by Willis Barnstone and Sua Chu-chin. BoWoP

Warm sun is failing, the bleak wind is wailing, The. Autumn; a Dirge. Shelley. FSFS

Warm walnut seats crisscross braces. Powwow remnants. Lew Blockcolski. VoR

Warming a set of new bones. Ruth Dallas. Fr. Letter to a Chinese Poet. ATNZ

Warned, warned for years. Love Poem. Susan Irene Rea. AMV-80

Warning, The. Adelaide Crapsey. OSP; WPE (Cinquain: A Warning.) WeW

Warning, The. Robert Creeley. CoPAm; TAP; VGW

Warning. Langston Hughes. BPo

Warning. Jenny Joseph. LP; MPo; OxBTC; TVo

Warning, The. Longfellow. PiAm

Warning ("My mother said"). Unknown. ECBV

Warning, A. Mary A. Webber. TDH

Warning and Reply. Emily Brontë. WPE

Warning of Winter. Mary Ursula Bethell. ATNZ

Warning to America, A. Philip Freneau. TAP

Warning to Beware, A. Unknown. OxBM

Warning to Children. Robert Graves. OAEL-2; SO

Warning to Conquerors, A. Donagh MacDonagh. CIP

Warning wind finds out my resting-place, A. The March Bee. Edmund Blunden. PoPle

Warrant Is Out for the Arrest of Henry Miller, A. Anselm Hollo. AcAn

Warren Pryor. Alden Nowlan. BBGO

Warren's Address [at Bunker Hill]. John Pierpont. BTTM; GOA

Warrior, A/ I have been. Song of Sitting Bull. Unknown. GOA

Warrior Dreams. Ray A. Young Bear. VW

Warrior Nation Trilogy. Lance Henson. VoR

Warriors and chiefs! should the shaft or the sword. Song of Saul before His Last Battle. Byron. PIM

Warrior's Song. Mary Austin. BPAW

Warr'st thou 'gainst Athens? Shakespeare. Fr. Timon of Athens, IV, iii. EBEV

Warrumbungles loomed like derelict whales, The. The Telescope at Siding Springs. Geoffrey Lehmann. GAS

Wars of Santa Fe, The. Unknown. AmFP

Wars of the Roses, The. Unknown. GBP

Warship of 1812, The. Unknown. BTTM

Wartime Blues. Unknown. BluL

Wary of time O it seizes the soul tonight. Easter Eve. Muriel Rukeyser. VGW

Was a Man. Philip Booth. NCSH; VGW

Was born obedient. Robert. Lucille Clifton. CAAP

Was broken./ He bade a warrior abandon his horse. The Battle of Maldon. Unknown, tr. by Charles W. Kennedy. OAEL-1

Was he a mining on the flat. He Done His Level Best. "Mark Twain." BPAW

Was He Married? Stevie Smith. NoAM

Was I clever enough? Was I charming? Thoughts while Driving Home. John Updike. SoS

Was I moving through the invisible glass. The Glass Door. Robert Watson. GP

Was I summoned. Eve's Birth. Kim Chernin. VWA

Was I surprised! Uncle Death. Walter Clark. NCSH

Was I too glib about eternal things. The Sequel. Theodore Roethke. MPA

Was it a dream, or did I see it plain? Amoretti, LXXVII. Spenser. NIL

Was it a dream? We sailed, I thought we sailed. A Dream. Matthew Arnold. GBL

Was It All Worth While? Zulu Oral Tradition, tr. by H. Tracey. WTO

Was it for this I uttered prayers. Grown-up. Edna St. Vincent Millay. NoAM; TH

Was it indolence,/ this sitting around. The Origin of Species. Myra Sklarew. PoUp

Was It Not Curious? Stevie Smith. NoAM

Was it not the goddess of the moon. Moon. Elizabeth Brewster. MMD

Was it really you all the time? Dream Sequence, Part 9. Naomi Long Madgett. BPo

Was it the proud full sail of his great verse. Sonnets, LXXXVI. Shakespeare. OAEL-1

Was my bones. What She Wanted. Ronald Koertge. GP

Was said around home nobody. Dark Corner. Robert Morgan. CSP

Was she so chaste? She Rebukes Hippolyta. Hilda Doolittle ("H. D."). SBG

Was that a crystal butterfly's wing. Mistakable Identity. Elaine V. Emans. AMV-80

Was there ere sic a parish, a parish, a parish. Little Dunkeld. Unknown. GBP

Was this the daughter you bargained for. The Mutant. Anita Barrows. RiTi

Was this the face that launched a thousand ships? Helen of Troy. Christopher Marlowe. Fr. Doctor Faustus. EBEV; FF; GBL; HeIP; NIL

Was this world built for happiness, that man. Sydney Dobell. Fr. Balder. PeD

Was two sisters loved one man. The Two Sisters. Unknown. MAT

Was Worm. May Swenson. BoAnP

Was ye not sadly frighten'd, honest Harry. A Dialogue between Sir John Jobson and Harry Homespun. John Byrom. EPC

Was you ever in Quebec? Hieland Laddie. Unknown. FSW

Wash. Eilean Ni Chuilleanain. BIrV; IPM

Wash. John Updike. TSWA

Wash Day. Larry Mollin. NeAC

Wash-Day Wonder. Dorothy Faubion. QQQ

Wash man out of the earth, shear off. Wash. Eilean Ni Chuilleanain. BIrV; IPM

Wash Well the Fresh Fish. Unknown. PoPle

Washed by the rain, dust and grime are laid. Starting Early from the Ch'u-ch'êng Inn. Po Chü-i, tr. by Arthur Waley. OBVE

Washed in Silver. James Stephens. Moon

Washed in Water. Rayne Mackinnon. MIS

Washer-Windows, The. Paul Clause. AATT

Washing Kai in the sauna. The Bath. Gary Snyder. GP; NNaP; TAP

Washing My Son.  Jonathan Holden.  AMV-81

Washing Windows.  Barry Spacks.  NCSH

Washing Your Feet.  John Ciardi.  FoP

Washington.  Nancy Byrd Turner.  CTV; ECBV

Washington.  *Unknown.*  OFD
  (George Washington.)  CTV

Washington caldwell jones could spit.  City Summer.  Martin
  Galvin.  PoUp

Washington Cathedral.  Karl Shapiro.  WasP

Washington, D.C.  Ernest Kroll.  WasP

Washington Interregnum.  Reed Whittemore.  WasP

Washington Migrants.  Roderick Jellema.  WasP

Washington Monument by Night.  Carl Sandburg.  CMoP (1970
  ed.); OFD
  "Wind bit hard at Valley Forge one Christmas, The," *sel.*  CC

Washington on the Constitutional Journey: 1791.  Paul Baker
  Newman.  CSP

Washington, the brave, the wise, the good.  Washington [*or*
  George Washington].  *Unknown.*  CTV; OFD

Washingtonian, The.  May Miller.  WasP

Washington's Monument, February 1885.  Walt Whitman.  OFD

Washrags.  Vern Rutsala.  GP

Washwater blond said that no self-respecting, The.  Folding the
  Panties.  Ronald Koertge.  AAN

Washyuma Motor Hotel.  Simon J. Ortiz.  GP

Wasn't I stupid to assume.  Lines to Nefertiti.  Peter Kostakis.
  FiCh

Wasn't it just that.  In More's Hotel.  Robert Nye.  SLP

Wasn't popular in high school for.  Harelip Mary.  Ronald
  Koertge.  GP

Wasn't That a Mighty Storm?  *Unknown.*  AmFP

Wasn't this the site, asked the historian.  House and Land.  Allen
  Curnow.  ATNZ

Wasn't your mother a woman?  Hennamma, *tr. fr. Kannada by*
  Willis Barnstone.  BoWoP

Wasp, The.  H. A. C. Evans.  OSF

Wasp.  Alden Nowlan.  BoAnP

Wasp, climbing the window pane.  Epigrams, I-IX.  Howard
  Nemerov.  OBAL

Waspish.  Robert Frost.  BoAnP

Wasps' Nest, The.  George MacBeth.  OxBTC

Wasps or hornets rattle on the sills.  Her Sleep.  Jill Hoffman.
  TV

Wasp's Song, The.  "Lewis Carroll."  FaBoNo

Wassail Song ("Here we come a-wassailing").  *Unknown.*  FSW
  (Here We Come A-Wassailing.)  PChr

Wassail Song ("We have been a walking").  *Unknown.*  GBP

Wassail the trees, that they may bear.  Robert Herrick.  *Fr.*
  Ceremonies for Christmas.  PChr

Waste.  Harry Graham.  FaBoCo

Waste Land, The.  T. S. Eliot.  CABA (1972 ed.); CMoP (1970
  ed.); HAP; NoAM; NOBA; NOBE; OAEL-2; OxBTC;
  PiAm; PPoe; TAP; UnPo (1976 ed.)
  *Sels.*
  "If there were the sound of water only," *fr.* V.  IP
  "Phlebas the Phoenician, a fortnight dead," *fr.* IV.  IP
  (Death by Water.)  OBVE

Waste not, want not, is a maxim I would teach.  Rowland
  Howard.  CTV

Waste Places.  James Stephens.  PPM

Watch, The.  Frances Cornford.  InPK; OxBTC

Watch.  John Daniel.  TwMBP

Watch, The.  May Swenson.  HAP; PoTa; SoSe (1977 ed.)

Watch a caterpillar.  Biology Lesson.  John D. Engle, Jr.  AMV-
  80

Watch any day his nonchalant pauses, see.  A Free One.  W. H.
  Auden.  CMoP (1970 ed.)

Watch for Fallen Rock.  Madeline DeFrees.  MPA

Watch it. That's the body: what goes on.  The Body.  William
  Bronk.  VGW

Watch long enough, and you will see the leaf.  Conrad Aiken.
  Preludes for Memnon, XIX.  CMoP (1970 ed.)

Watch me/ I am moving through the cages of the animals.
  Animal Poems.  Gwendolyn MacEwen.  MMD

Watch me bruise the air with my hawk winged flutterings.
  Miracle Worker.  Claudia Dobkins.  NPW

Watch, now.  Shadow Show.  Ruth Dallas.  ATNZ

Watch out for the bus.  Mercado.  Greg Pape.  AmPA

Watch out for the Egyptian.  Susan Sonde.  *Fr.* Bedtime Stories.
  PoUp

Watch out, my dear.  Praxilla, *tr. fr. Greek by* John Dillon.
  PBWP

Watch that net drift. Grey tides.  How to Catch Tiddlers.  Brian
  Jones.  LP

Watch the Lights Fade.  Robinson Jeffers.  CMoP (1970 ed.);
  NoAM; NOBA

Watch upon my wrist, The.  Parable.  W. H. Auden.  FaBoCo

Watch who you fuck with.  Hygiene.  Perry Oldham.  AAN

Watchdog.  Richard Armour.  ECBV

Watched clock never moves, they said, A.  The Slow Starter.
  Louis MacNeice.  MPo; PBMP

Watcher, The.  John Peck.  AmPA

Watcher of reedy places and cries.  Theodore Roethke.  Morton
  Paley.  AMV-81

Watchers, The.  Paul Blackburn.  PAIC

Watching Gymnasts.  Robert Francis.  LiSp; SPo

Watching hands transplanting.  Transplanting.  Theodore
  Roethke.  PiAm

Watching Jim Shoulders.  Leo Connellan.  TAT

Watching My Daughter Sew.  Katharine Privett.  AMV-81

Watching my paralytic friend.  The Figurehead.  Karl Shapiro.
  MPA

Watching Post.  C. Day Lewis.  MPo

Watching Rushcutters' bright bayful of masts and coloured keels.
  Angels' Weather.  Bruce Beaver.  GAS

Watching Salmon Jump.  Simon J. Ortiz.  CDW

Watching Snow.  Raymond Ward.  ATNZ

Watching Television.  Robert Bly.  BiP

Watching the Astronauts.  Retrospect.  Lonnie L. Landrum.
  DNGG

Watching the Dance.  James Merrill.  NIL

Watching the iris.  Amy Lowell.  TH

Watching the Jets Lose to Buffalo at Shea.  May Swenson.  LiSp

Watching the light.  Morality Play.  Pat Lowther.  MMD

Watching the lightning.  Bondage.  Hubert Witheford.  ATNZ

Watching the shied core.  As Bad as a Mile.  Philip Larkin.
  InPK

Watching the Sun Rise over Mount Zion.  Ruth Whitman.  VWA

Watching the White Image, electric moon.  In a Moonlit Hermit's
  Cabin.  Allen Ginsberg.  Moon

Watching this dawn's mnemonic of old dawning.  Sestina in a
  Cantina.  Malcolm Lowry.  PAIC

Watching You Draw.  Carol Cox.  MMD

Watching you in the mirror I wonder.  The Mirror.  Louise
  Glück.  GP

Watching You Walk.  Ruthven Todd.  SLP

Watching Your Gray Eyes.  Morton Marcus.  GP

Watchman, Tell Me, *with music.*  *Unknown.*  AH

Water.  Wendell Berry.  CSP

Water.  Edmond Jabes, *tr. fr. French by* Anthony Rudolf.  VWA

Water. Robert Lowell. CMoP (1970 ed.); ExPo (1973 ed.); HeIP; NOBA; PiAm

Water. Judith McPheron. AMV-81

Water. Leslie Norris. HeHu; OBW

Water a Thousand Feet Deep. Judith Rodriguez. GAS

Water and Light, Light and Water. Mark Perlberg. HeS

Water and Worship: An Open-Air Service on the Gatineau River. Margaret Avison. HAP

Water astonishing and difficult altogether. Water Raining. Gertrude Stein. *Fr.* Tender Buttons. PBWP; RiTi

Water Babies, The, *sels.* Charles Kingsley.
   Lost Doll, The. ECBV
   (Little Doll, The.) OxBChV
   Tide River, The. OxBChV
   Young and Old. EBEV; FaPoR; OxBChV; PCOP; TPo

Water Below, The. Fleur Adcock. ATNZ

Water bug is drawing the shadows, The. *Tr. fr. Yuman Indian by* Frances Densmore. OBVE

Water clock of melting snow, The. For My Grandfather in Greenfield Center. Joseph Bruchac. FAF

Water closing, The. Together. Maxine W. Kumin. BoWoP; NMM; WBN

Water Crowvoot, The. William Barnes. VPC

Water does not lie heavy and deep, The. Kinneret. Judith Herzberg, *tr. by* Shirley Kaufman. VWA

Water-Drinker, The. Edward Johnson. PeD

Water, for anguish of the solstice:—nay. For "A Venetian Pastoral" by Giorgione. Dante Gabriel Rossetti. VLP

Water-Girl. *Gond Oral Tradition, tr. by* V. Elwin *and* S. Hivale. WTO

Water-Hen, The. Violet Jacob. MS

Water-Hole, The. Charles Erskine Scott Wood. BPAW

Water is H$_2$O, hydrogen two parts, oxygen one. The Third Thing. D. H. Lawrence. AKE

Water is heavy silver over stone. What Any Lover Learns. Archibald MacLeish. PiAm

Water Is Wide, The. *Unknown.* FSW

Water Island. Howard Moss. Prf

Water like quartz, with the same kinds of strata, The. Nights Passed on Ward's Island, Toronto Harbour. Doug Fetherling. NeAC

Waterlilies. Marjorie Sinclair. PHC

Water of Kane, The. *Tr. fr. Hawaiian by* N. B. Emerson. WTO

Water on the Highway. Nancy Simpson. AMV-80

Water-Party, A. Robert Bridges. PoPle

Water Poems. Sandra McPherson. CAAP

Water Raining. Gertrude Stein. *Fr.* Tender Buttons. PBWP; RiTi

Water rubs against itself, The. At the Mouth of the Ardyne. Maurice Lindsay. MS

Water-Snakes. Samuel Taylor Coleridge. *Fr.* The Rime of the Ancient Mariner. EcS

Water Tank at Dusk, The. Sharlot Hall. WPW

Water Tower, The. James Paul. AMV-81

Water tower enclosures. Beyond Belief. Tom Luhrmann. AMV-81

Water-truck, The. Patrick Lane. NeAC

Water turns, The. You Are Happy. Margaret Atwood. MMD

Water under the Earth. Robert Bly. NNaP

Water was usually clean. Dead Man Creek. Van K. Brock. NVAP

Water, water I desire. The Scare-Fire. Robert Herrick. HAP

Water without Sound. Malka Heifetz Tussman, *tr. fr. Yiddish by* Marcia Falk. VWA

Waterchew! Gregory Corso. VGW

Watercolor of Grantchester Meadows. Sylvia Plath. SBG

Watercress. Janet Kauffman. TC

Watercress Seller, The. Thomas Miller. OxBChV

Waterfall. Seamus Heaney. NoAM

Waterfall, The. Frank Dempster Sherman. CTV

Waterfall, The. Henry Vaughan. BoReV; ILP (1975 ed.); LFH; NOBE; OBW

Waterfalls. Vernon Watkins. NoAM

Watergate Elegy, The. Robert Dana. WasP

Watergaw, The. "Hugh MacDiarmid." MS

Watering the Horse. Robert Bly. NCSH

Waterloo. Byron. *Fr.* Childe Harold's Pilgrimage. PPoD
   (Eve of Waterloo, The.) NOBE
   ("There was a sound of revelry by night.") EBEV; LFH

Watermelon. Ted Joans. GP

Watermelons. Charles Simic. OBAL; OSP

Waters. Donald Hall. UsP

Waters I'm going to go walking beside, The. The New Mystic. Al Young. NW

Waters, Indeed, Are to the Palate, Bitter, The. Hubert Witheford. ATNZ

Waters of earth come and go, The. Here and Now. Philip Levine. PoA; VWA

Waters of the well of life, The. The Well of Life. Sir Herbert Read. NoAM

Waters of Tyne, The. *Unknown.* GBP

Watershed, The. W. H. Auden. OAEL-2

Watershed, The. Alice Meynell. SBG

Watershed. Robert Penn Warren. PoA

Waterwall Blues. Howard Moss. UsP

Watts. Shirley Kaufman. NMM

Watts. Conrad Kent Rivers. PoBA

Watts. Alvin Saxon. PoBA

Wauken by nicht, and bydand on some boon. Portrait of Mary Stuart, Holyrood. Lewis Spence. MS

Wave, The. Daryl Hine. Prf

Wave, The. David Phillips. NeAC

Wave approaching and the wave returning, The. Sequence. George Barker. PoA

Wave Symphony, The. Arthur Davison Ficke. *Fr.* Four Japanese Paintings. PoA

Wave withdrawing, the. "Dover Beach"—a Note to That Poem. Archibald MacLeish. FF

Wavering planet most unstable, The. *Unknown.* Moon

Waves. Eleanor Farjeon. EcS

Waves surge higher still, The. Elegy: Ise Lamenting the Death of Empress Onshi. Lady Ise, *tr. by* Etsuko Terasaki *and* Irma Brandeis. BoWoP

Waves that are white far out. Marine. Rolfe Humphries. EcS

Waves that danced about the rock have gone, The. Grandmother and Child. Ruth Dallas. ATNZ

Waving good-bye to mum. At the Airport. Evan Jones. MAuV

Waxwings. Robert Francis. NU

Way, The. Robert Creeley. BoLoP; PPP

Way a crow, The. Dust of Snow. Robert Frost. CMoP (1970 ed.); FSFS; IPWM; SoSe; SS; TAP; TSWA; UnPo (1976 ed.); WeW

Way and the Way Things Are, The. Nila NorthSun. GP

Way at night these piping peepers, The. The Peepers in Our Meadow. Archibald MacLeish. NCSH

Way Down, The. Philip Levine. NOBA

Way Down, The, *sel.* Jay MacPherson.
   They Return. PoA

Way down in Columbus, Georgia. Columbus Stockade Blues. Woody Guthrie. FSW

Way down in the bottom. Poor Little Johnny. *Unknown.* AmFP

Way down in the meadow where the lily first blows. Sweet Evelina. *Unknown.* FSW

Way down in yonders low valley, in some lonesome place. Pretty Saro. *Unknown.* AmFP

Way down south in Dixie. Song for a Dark Girl. Langston Hughes. PoBA

Way down south where bananas grow. The Grasshopper and the Elephant. *Unknown.* CTV

Way down South where I was born. A Long Time Ago. *Unknown.* AmFP

Way down upon the Swanee River [*or* de Swannee ribber]. The Old Folks at Home. Stephen Collins Foster. BLSH; BLSo; FSW: PSoN

Way down upon the Wabash, such land was never known. Elanoy. *Unknown.* FSW

Way down yonder in the middle of the field. Let Me Fly. *Unknown.* FSW

Way enchased with glass and beads, A. The Temple. Robert Herrick. CaPo

Way goes snaking upward through the heat, The. Remote Country. Sydney Tremayne. MS

Way high up in the Syree peaks. Tyin' a Knot in the Devil's Tail. Gail Gardner. FSW

'Way high up the Mogollons. The Glory Trail. Badger Clark. BPAW; PH; PoTa

Way I gained my titles, The. Champagne Charlie. *At. to* George Leybourne. BLSo

Way I read a letter's—this, The. Emily Dickinson. InPS; LoAs; TT; WPE

Way I walked that Sunday night, I was one of them, The. Let's All Meet and Have a Party Sometime. John Birkby. BuTh

Way in which blackness appeals, The: it beckons, calls. Black. Nicholas Rinaldi. AMV-80

Way It Happens to You, The. Harold Bond. NVAP

Way It Is, The. Gloria C. Oden. CNA; IHMS

Way It Is, The. Mark Strand. CAAP

Way It Is, The. Richard Williams. AAN

Way It Really Happened, The. Lori Shpunt. PoUp

Way It Was, The. Lucille Clifton. WPE

Way of Keeping, A. Nancy Willard. IHMS

Way of Pain, The. Wendell Berry. AMV-80

Way out in California. The Santa Barbara Earthquake. *Unknown.* AmFP

Way Out in Idaho. *Unknown.* AmFP; BPAW; FSW

'Way out in Western Texas, where the Clear Fork's waters flow. The Cowboys' Christmas Ball. William Lawrence Chittenden. BPAW

Way Out West. Amiri Baraka. ExPo (1973 ed.); PoBA

Way Sun Keeps Falling Away from Every Window, The. Lyn Lifshin. NeAC

Way the ball, The. The Jump Shooter. Dennis Trudell. LiSp

Way the Bird Sat, The. Ray A. Young Bear. CDW; VoR

Way the buildings curve (as if a thought), The. Central Park South. Donald Revell. NYP

Way the cooked shoes sizzle, The. Amanda Is Shod. Maxine W. Kumin. PH

Way the hell-bent years consume my pleasure, The. Elegy. Pushkin, *tr. by* Robley Wilson, Jr. AMV-80

Way Through, The. Denise Levertov. CoPAm

Way through the Woods, The. Kipling. ILP (1975 ed.); NOBE; OxBChV; OxBTC; PoPle; RFM; VLP

Way to call up quick wishes. On Seeing a Torn Out Coin Telephone. Martin Robbins. MAT

Way to Hump a Cow Is Not, The. E. E. Cummings. NoAM; NOBA; TT

Way to Live, The. *Unknown.* VLP

Way to Make a Living, A. James Wright. NNaP

Way up in my tree I'm sitting by my fire. Gypsy Eyes. Jimi Hendrix. GrRo

Way up yonder in the sky. Buckeye Jim. *Unknown.* FSW

Way We Live Now, The. Robert Dana. AMV-80

Way We Wonder, The. Robert Pack. WIF

Way West, Underground, The. Gary Snyder. CNW

Wayfarer, The. War Is Kind, XIII. Stephen Crane. PiAm

Wayfarers in the Wilderness, *with music.* Alexander R. Thompson. AH

Wayfaring man though a fool, The. Though a Fool. Robert Francis. GP

Wayfaring Stranger. *Unknown. See* I Am a Poor Wayfaring Stranger.

Ways and Means. "Lewis Carroll." *See* White Knight's Song.

Ways and the Peoples, The. Randall Jarrell. PoA

Ways of Day. Robert Penn Warren. *Fr.* Notes on a Life to Be Lived. NoAM

Ways of God, The. Milton. *Fr.* Samson Agonistes. BoReV

Ways of Loving. Theodore Weiss. GP

Wayside Station, The. Edwin Muir. FaBoTw (1975 ed.); PSN

Wayzgoose, The, *sel.* Roy Campbell.
    "Attend my fable if your ears be clean." OBSV

Waz, adverse to thinking. No Bargains Today. Peggy Susberry Kenner. JB

We all—/ stones, people, little shards of glass in the sun. Text. Aaron Zeitlin, *tr. by* Ruth Whitman. VWA

We all have/ A bench in the park to reach. George Jonas. NeAC

We all have/ A new arm. The New Arm. Tom Hennen. HeS

We all have our faults. Mine is trying to write poems. Singing Aloud. Carolyn Kizer. IHMS

We all knew you/ you played at the Cotton Club. A Half Note for the Duke. Karl Carter. PoUp

We all must work with what we have. A Vegetarian Sings. Audrey Conard. AMV-81

We all scream, most of us inside. A Screamer Discusses Methods of Screaming. James Schevill. TAP

We all went to town one day. Bessie Dreaming Bear. Marnie Walsh. VW

We all were watching the quiz on television. A Singular Metamorphosis. Howard Nemerov. ConAP

We always ran out when we heard it come. The Six-Horse Limited Mail. Ethel Romig Fuller. BPAW

We Are. Maxine W. Kumin. WBN

We are/ at peace. April 29, 1975. David Hilton. AcAn

We are/ sorry to have to. You Understand the Requirements. Lyn Lifshin. NeAC; RiTi

We are a band of brothers, and native to the soil. The Bonnie Blue Flag. Harry Macarthy. BLSo; BTTM; PSoN

We are a meadow where the bees hum. Bedtime. Denise Levertov. AnMo; IHMS

We are a People. Lance Henson. VoR

We Are Acrobats. Jozef Habib Gerez, *tr. fr.* Turkish by Musa Moris Farhi *and* Anthony Rudolf. VWA

We Are All a Little Mad. John Gonzalez. PMW

We are all keen to take a look at him. Sexual Delinquent. U. A. Fanthorpe. PMW

We are all rushing nowhere. Who of Those Coming After. Darcy Gottlieb. AMV-81

We are already on the moon. Vacuum. Josephine Miles. Moon

We are approaching sleep: the chestnut blossoms in the mind. Awakening. Robert Bly. ConAP; UsP

We are as clouds that veil the midnight moon. Mutability. Shelley. MBPR

We are asleep under mirrors. What do I. Before the War. Marilyn Hacker. AmPA

We are at the hauling then hoping for it. W. S. Graham. *Fr.* The Nightfishing, III. MS

We are being born again. For My Wife. Steven Lautermilch. AMV-80

We Are Building a Strong Union. *Unknown.* FSW

We are burning/ in our heads. A Poet Recognizing the Echo of the Voice. Diane Wakoski. NIL; Psy

We are captives now, prisoners of this. Like the Poets of Ancient China. Vern Rutsala. MPA

We are children grown strange. The Russian Poem II. Dan Gerber. TC

We are climbing Jacob's ladder. Jacob's Ladder. *Unknown.* FSW

We are coming, Father Abraham, three hundred thousand more. Three Hundred Thousand More. James Sloan Gibbons. BTTM

We are coming from the cotton fields. Song of the Freeman. *Unknown.* PBMP

We are croaking as does the frog. We Object. *Tr. fr. Maori by* A. Armstrong. WTO

We are diagnosing the dream. Getting to the End. Cynthia MacDonald. AAN

We are driving through South Dakota. Primer Lesson. Mark Vinz. TAT

We are drowning now. Alienation (To My Son). Lucille F. Travis. AATT

We are eating up the planet, the New York Times. Revolutionary Letter #16. Diana DiPrima. VoA

We are enfolded, encased. Thornton Beach. Michael McClure. RhR

We are festive weepers, etching names on every stone. In the Old City. Yehuda Amichai, *tr. by* Laya Firestone *and* Howard Schwartz. VWA

We Are Going. Kath Walker. GAS

We are going down a long slide. Shirley Kaufman. BoWoP

We are going to see the rabbit. The Rabbit. Alan Brownjohn. MPo

We are hypnotized by the flash of sun. Sleeping at the Beach. Lucile Burt. AMV-81

We are in Chicago's Waldheim cemetery. Waldheim Cemetery. Robert Sward. ANTL

We are keeping an eye on the girls, so that the kvass. Marina Tsvetayeva, *tr. fr. Russian by* Elaine Feinstein *and* Angela Livingstone. PBWP

We are landless dream farmers. Dream Farmer. Jill Witherspoon Boyer. CNA

We Are Leaning Away. Gayle Elen Harvey. AMV-80

We are little airy creatures. The Five. Swift. ECBV

We are lovers/ after our fashion. The Dancer from the Dance. Suzanne Juhasz. IHMS

We are making a map: as two lovers. Case Notes. Kenyon Alexander. PMW

We are mistaken to call it dancing. Swan Lake. John Unterecker. PHC

We are near, Lord. Tenebrae. Paul Celan, *tr. by* Joachim Neugroschel. VWA

We are never free of the voices. The Voices Inescapable. Ann Stanford. IHMS

We are not come to wage a strife. The Day-Breakers. Arna Bontemps. AmNP (1974 ed.); PoBA

We are not conceited. Coupling. Cynthia Macdonald. WBN

We are not going to steal the water tower. Stopping Near Highway 80. David Ray. HeS; TAT

We are not in God's hands. The Truth. Phyllis Hoge Thompson. PHC

We are not lovers. Man and Wife. Anne Sexton. CAPP

We are not the first. Shakespeare. *Fr.* King Lear, V, iii. PoPle

We are not the ones who are afraid of science. Something Passionate for Cinda. Allan Kornblum. AcAn

We are nude beneath our costumes. The Metaphysical Paintings. John Perreault. EAS

We are old friends. Hunger. Charles Simic. NNaP

We Are on Our Journey Home, *with music. Unknown.* AH

We are our poems, their summation. Pushed to the Scroll. Winifred Hamrick Farrar. AMV-80

We are ourselves but carriers. Life. Epigram: For a Woman with Child. J. V. Cunningham. PiAm

We are prepared: we build our houses squat. Storm on the Island. Seamus Heaney. NCSH

We Are Seven. Wordsworth. MBPR; OxBChV; SpRo

We are singing for the face of cisco. Songs for the Cisco Kid; or, Singing for the Face. K. Curtis Lyle. PoBA

We are so tired; my heart and I. Rest. Mathilde Blind. SBG

We are sorry to inform you. In Answer to Your Query. Naomi Lazard. AAN; GP

We are sorry we cannot use the enclosed. Form Rejection Letter. Philip Dacey. AAN; AmPA; PCho

We are squared off in the snow. Brothers Together in Winter. Harley Elliott. NeAC

We are standing facing each other. Margaret Atwood. NeAC

We are stretched upon a field. In a New Year. John McNally. PoUp

We are talking in bed. You show me snapshots. A Family Man. Maxine W. Kumin. CoPAm; IHMS; TAP

We are the Akhail. Our youth persists. Laila Boasting. Laila Akhyaliyya, *tr. by* Willis Barnstone. BoWoP

We are the birds always charmed by you. Postman Cheval. André Breton, *tr. by* David Gascoyne. EAS

We are the children born. The Children. Vincent O'Sullivan. ATNZ

We are the frogs who will not turn to princes. Rebels from Fairy Tales. Hyacinthe Hill. SO

We are the hollow men. The Hollow Men. T. S. Eliot. AnMo; BiP; InPS; OAEL-2; PBMP; STS; TCP; TT

We are the music-makers. Ode. Arthur O'Shaughnessy. FaPoR; PFIr; PPM; VLP; WIF

We are the same in our despair. Raymond R. Patterson. *Fr.* Riot Rhymes U.S.A. GP

We are the weavers. Macramé. Michael D. Riley. AMV-81

We are things of dry hours and the involuntary plan. Kitchenette Building. Gwendolyn Brooks. BPo; FF; UnPo (1976 ed.)

We Are Three Brethren Come from Spain. *Unknown.* GBP (Three Knights from Spain.) PoPle

We are three, clearly three. Beckoned in Dream to the Unconscious. David Kherdian. FAF

We are three women eating out. Crepes Flambeau. Tess Gallagher. AMV-81

We are tired of your tiresome imitations of Mayakovsky. Answer to Voznesensky and Evtushenko. Frank O'Hara. NNaP

We Are Transmitters. D. H. Lawrence. OxBTC

We are two countries girded for the war. Foreign Affairs. Stanley Kunitz. WasP

We are unfair. We Own the Night. Amiri Baraka. PoBA

We are waltzing now into the moonlit morning. Waltz against the Mountains. Thomas Hornsby Ferril. VGW

We are watching our old aunts. Indian Summer, 1927. Anne Hussey. AMV-81

We Are Watching, We Are Waiting, *with music.* William O. Cushing. AH

We are with one another. No Smiles. Frank Lamont Phillips. AmNP (1974 ed.)

We are women of different origins. For Mariella, in Antrona. Tobey A. Simpson. AMV-80

We arrive like sunlight in winter: tentative. Pine Needles. Warren Slesinger. HeS

We artists have strange nerves! In a Hotel Writing-Room. John Cowper Powys. OxBTC

We Assume: On the Death of Our Son, Reuben Masai Harper. Michael S. Harper. AmPA

We ate our breakfast lying on our backs. Breakfast. W. W. Gibson. OxBTC

We Be Soldiers Three. *Unknown.* GBP

We Become New. Marge Piercy. TAP; WBN

We began this conversation in the spring. Becoming Real. Barry Goldensohn. AMV–81

We begin on all fours. Wrestlers. S. Lewandowski. BrS

We believe books and music. Words from the Window of a Railway Car. Anatoly Steiger, *tr. by* John Glad. VWA

We boogied when I was eight. Autobiography Part Two: Rock and Roll. Jessica Tarahata Hagedorn. MMD

We bought him at auction, tranquillized to a drooping halt. Clancy. David Wagoner. PH

We bought him for a watchdog. Watchdog. Richard Armour. ECBV

We bought it. The Rhododendron Plant. Allen Katzman. WeW

We Bring No Glittering Treasures, *with music.* Harriet C. Phillips. AH

We brought them. Finally. Bruce Severy. HeS

We brush the other, invisible moon. Sleep. William Knott. EAS

We brushed our hair back and our. The Last Refuge. Augustus Young. BIrV

We built a hut, my brother and I. The Hut. Hilda Van Stockum. CTV

We bump against each other heavily. City/Market. Charlotte A. Raines. PoUp

We Bumped Off Your Friend the Poet. Harold Norse. CPA

We but begin to hope to know, having known. Subject. Marie Ponsot. VGW

We came to the edge. A Pretty Woman. Simon J. Ortiz. CDW; PoW

We came to the outer light down a ramp in the dark. Westland Row. Thomas Kinsella. NoAM

We came when there were no more horses. Marie Harris. *Fr.* Interstate. AAN

We Can Be Together. Paul Kantner. GrRo

We can begin now. X. Roland Tharp. PHC

We can endure the eyes. At the Jewish Museum. Linda Pastan. VWA

We can sclim up by words. Words. Duncan Glen. MIS

We cannot go to the country. Raleigh Was Right. William Carlos Williams. NoAM

We cannot walk like Byron among Ayasoluk's ruined. The Pleasure of Ruins. J. D. McClatchy. PoA

We canoe a creek. Girl Friends. Rosemary Daniell. WBN

We can't grumble about accommodation. Song of the Battery Hen. Edwin Brock. LP; MPo

We carried you in our arms. Tears of Rage. Bob Dylan. RRA

We Carry Eggshells. Hanny Michaelis, *tr. fr. Dutch by* Marjolijn de Jager. VWA

We caught the tread of dancing feet. The Harlot's House. Oscar Wilde. InPK; PPoD

We chanced in passing by that afternoon. The Black Cottage. Robert Frost. ILP (1975 ed.); VGW

We climb the flat stones. Summit. Michael McPherson. PHC

We climbed to the very top that August day. Castle Rock. Frederick Morgan. AMV–81

We Climb Upwards. Quincy Troupe. SES

We come!/ We come! Ben Jonson. *Fr.* The Golden Age Restored. SCP-1

We come on the sloop *John B. John B.* Sails. *Unknown.* FSW

We come! we come! to fill our graves. William B. Tappan. *Fr.* Song of the Three Hundred Thousand Drunkards in the United States. PeD

We Continue. W. S. Merwin. CAPP

We could have crossed the road but hesitated. The Interrogation. Edwin Muir. CMoP (1970 ed.)

We could not ignore the sky in those days. Before the War. James Pendergast. AMV–81

We couldn't even keep the furnace lit! To Delmore Schwartz. Robert Lowell. NoAM

We crave your condescension. The Mulligan Guard. Ned Harrigan. BLSo

We crossed by ferry to the bare island. By Ferry to the Island. Iain Crichton Smith. MPo

We curl into your eyes. The Female God. Isaac Rosenberg. FaBoTw (1975 ed.)

We Dance like Ella Riffs. Carolyn M. Rodgers. CNA; PoBA

We dance round in a ring and suppose. The Secret Sits. Robert Frost. InPK; TH; UsP

We dance without passion but the movement. Waltz. Heather Tosteson Reich. AMV–80

We descended the first night from Europe. Coming Back to America. James Dickey. NYP

We deserved that earth-shot from the. Views of Our Sphere. Ernest Sandeen. Moon

We Did It. Yehuda Amichai, *tr. fr. Hebrew by* Harold Schimmel. BoLoP

We did surgeries together. I warned her. Farewell, Gibson Square. Elizabeth Bartlett. PMW

We didn't think/ nuthin. Poems about Playmates. Ronda Davis. JB

We died in Zortman on a Sunday. The Renegade Wants Words. James Welch. CDW; SA

We do lie beneath the grass. Sibilla's Dirge. Thomas Lovell Beddoes. *Fr.* Death's Jest Book. NOBE

We do not wish anything to happen. Chorus. T. S. Eliot. *Fr.* Murder in the Cathedral. OxBTC

We don't know the ins and outs. The Wall. David Jones. PoA; TwMBP

We Don't Know What to Plan or Say or Do. Lee Lally. PoUp

We don't lack people here on the Northern coast. Amusing Our Daughters. Carolyn Kizer. CNW; VGW

We dream—it is good we are dreaming. Emily Dickinson. BoWoP

We drove as far east as we could. Bar Harbor. Marita Garin. AMV–81

We drove south from Burwash Landing. At White River. John Haines. FiCP

We edge the boat in tight among stumps. The Limits of Departure. Bruce Weigl. AMV–81

We enter the darkened hall. The Physical Imperfections of Old Films. Paul Ramsey. PPoD

We fashion spears. Hunt. David Childers. AAN

We feel more than we see of the winter. An Unseen Fire. Michael G. Cooke. AMV–81

We few, we happy few, we band of brothers. Shakespeare. King Henry V, *fr.* IV, iii. UnPo (1976 ed.)

We finished clearing the last. Above Pate Valley. Gary Snyder. ConAP; ILP (1975 ed.)

We followed her unto the chamber-door. The Palace of Pleasant Regard. Lady of the Assembly. *Fr.* The Assembly of Ladies. WPE

We Fooled Ourselves. Jozef Habib Gerez, *tr. fr. Turkish by* Musa Moris Farhi *and* Anthony Rudolf. VWA

We found a mouse in the chalk quarry today. Anne and the Field-Mouse. Ian Serraillier. MN; RAE

We found among the trees a flock of crows. Dread of Darkness. George Keithley. PoW

We found him there on the desert. Bones in the Desert. Ned White. BPAW

We found the deer. The Lost Deer. Joseph Bruchac. FAF

We from childhood play'd together. Comrades. Felix McGlennon. FSN

We gather together to ask the Lord's blessing. Prayer of Thanksgiving [or Thanksgiving Hymn]. *Unknown, tr. by* Theodore Baker. BLSo; CTV

We Go. Karl Wolfskehl, *tr. fr. German by* Harry Zohn. VWA

We go back. Proclamation/ From Sleep, Arise. Carolyn M. Rodgers. JB

We go no more to Calverly's. Calverly's. E. A. Robinson. NoAM

We go out in the stony midnight. Thomas McGrath. Letter to an Imaginary Friend, Part One, VIII, 4. NNaP

We go out into the night. Gerard Malanga. BCr

We got into the carriage. It was hot. Travelling to My Second Marriage on the Day of the First Moonshot. Robert Nye. SLP

We got sunlight on the sand. There Is Nothin' like a Dame. Oscar Hammerstein II. OBAL

We got this idea. Our Hands in the Garden. Anne Hébert, *tr. by* A. Poulin, Jr. BoWoP

We Greet Each Other in the Side, *abr. Unknown.* PeD

We grew up in a time. What Lies on Us. Bruce Dawe. CAAP

We grind horns. A Talisman for the New Year. Deena Metzger. RiTi

We had a city also. Hand in hand. Decline and Fall. John Frederick Nims. CoPAm

We had a female passenger who came. September 1, 1802. Wordsworth. MBPR

We had better conserve our water. Inadequate Aqua Extremis. Ruth M. Walsh. QQQ

We had known from the beginning this could happen. Robert Dana. *Fr.* Natural Odes/ American Elegies. HeS

We had more than/ we could use. Words. Vern Rutsala. GP

We had red earth once to smear on our cheeks. Arrowy Dreams. Witter Bynner. GOA

We had the notion it was dawn. Five. Weldon Kees. PPP

We had to make catalogues. Patience. Bartola Cattafi, *tr. by* Rina Ferrarelli. AMV-81

We had to take the world as it was given. Ideal Landscape. Adrienne Rich. NIL; NoAM; PoIA

We have a dear old daddy. Father's Whiskers. *Unknown.* FSW

We have a secret, just we three. The Secret. *Unknown.* CTV; ECBV; PCOP

We have all been in rooms. Adultery. James Dickey. CAPP; CSP; PPoD; TAP; WeW

We have bathed, where none have seen us. Bridal Song. Thomas Lovell Beddoes. *Fr.* Death's Jest Book. GBL

We have been a walking. Wassail Song. *Unknown.* GBP

We Have Been Believers. Margaret Walker. PoBA

We have been on trial for our life for so many years. On the Jewish Day of Judgment in the Year 1942 (5703). Jozef Wittlin, *tr. by* Isaac Komem. VWA

We have been sailing in a certain small fountain. About This Course. David Shapiro. PoA

We have been shown. Six Variations. Denise Levertov. ConAP

We have climbed the mountain. Here in Katmandu. Donald Justice. ConAP; HeIP; LiSp; NIL; RFM; UsP

We have come home here. Eyes of the Garden. Laura Chester. RiTi

We have come to a quiet valley in the hills. Lois Johnson. *Fr.* Four Poems from the Strontium Age. ATNZ

We have come to love this coastline. Premonition of Winter. Hugh Maxton. IPM

We have cried in our despair. When Helen Lived. W. B. Yeats. CMoP (1970 ed.); NIL

We have developed a woman. Seen at a Fashionable Night Spot. Katie Louchheim. PoUP

We have done with dogma and divinity. After Trinity. John Meade Falkner. OxBTC

We have everything and we have nothing. Something for the Touts, the Nuns, the Grocery Clerks and You. Charles Bukowski. CPA

We have forgot, who safe in cities dwell. Sea-Sonnet. V. Sackville-West. EcS; SBG

We have found our peace, and move with a turning globe. Epithalamium. A. R. D. Fairburn. NAV

We have gone out in boats upon the sea at night. Passage over Water. Robert Duncan. NoAM; NOBA

We have little animals here. Robinson Jeffers. *Fr.* Skunks. BoAnP

We have loiter'd and laugh'd in the flowery croft. A Garden Lyric. Frederick Locker-Lampson. PeD

We have loved each other in this time twenty years. Unfinished History. Archibald MacLeish. VGW

We have made hawks. Shaman Songs 12. Gene Fowler. MIT

We have met late—it is too late to meet. A Denial. Elizabeth Barrett Browning. GBL

We have moving over us, over head and spire. Sunday. Josephine Miles. PoA

We have no heart for the fishing, we have no hand for the oar. The Dykes. Kipling. VLP

We have no idea what his fantastic head. Archaic Torso of Apollo. Rainer Maria Rilke, *tr. by* Robert Bly. NU

We have no prairies. Bogland. Seamus Heaney. HeHu

We have not been happy, my Lord, we have not been too happy. Chorus. T. S. Eliot. *Fr.* Murder in the Cathedral. OxBTC

We have reached the end of pastime, for always. End of Play. Robert Graves. EBEV

We have returned too. Lemuel Johnson. *Fr.* Hand on the Navel. AAN

We have seen her/ the world over. Hilda Doolittle ("H. D."). *Fr.* Tribute to the Angels. RiTi; VGW

We have seen how the most amiable. Hilda Doolittle ("H. D."). *Fr.* The Walls Do Not Fall. BoWoP; PBWP

We have seen thee, queen of cheese. Queen of Cheese. James McIntyre. PeD

We have states of things you never. The Undreamed. Elaine V. Emans. AMV-81

We have struck the regions wherein we are keel or reef. Zone. Louise Bogan. WPE

We have tangled together. Growing Together. Joyce Carol Oates. IHMS

We have the statue for it—Liberty. Address to the Refugees. John Malcolm Brinnin. GOA

We have the sweet noise of the sea at our back. Near Catalonia. Joy Davidman. SPT

We have these drums. Percussions. Ron Welburn. CNA

We have tulips in our flower bed. Jessie Orton Jones. Secrets, VII. CTV

We have turned together. Soundings. Jenne Andrews. HeS

We have watched again. Among Hawks. Lance Henson. VoR

We hear it still, hey mister. Comrade—Mister. Isidor Schneider. SPT

We heard the thrushes by the shore and sea. In Kerry. J. M. Synge. GBL

We heard thunder. Nothing great—on high.  Mouse Night: One of Our Games.  William Stafford.  MN; NCSH

We hunted and we halloed.  Cape Ann.  *Unknown.*  BLSo; FSW

We in the Fields.  William Everson.  PiAm

We Irish pride ourselves as patriots.  Ireland.  John Hewitt.  CIP

We is gathahed hyeah, my brothahs.  An Ante-Bellum Sermon.  Paul Laurence Dunbar.  BPo

We jeer/ and we sneer.  Tee-Vee Enigma.  Selma Raskin.  QQQ

We jest went out to git him, and we did.  The Sheriff's Report.  Arthur Chapman.  BPAW

We keep going, we keep going.  Parting.  Michael Hogan.  GP

We killed a bat last night.  A Bat in the Monastery.  John L'Heureux.  SFF

We kissed at the barrier; and passing through.  On the Departure Platform.  Thomas Hardy.  NOBE; OxBTC

We knew the certain place of heaven above the loft.  Death Insurance.  Wade Hall.  AATT

We knock red yellow blue.  Croquet in Childhood.  Helena Minton.  FAF

We know he liked chockbeer and watermelon.  A Choctaw Chief Helps Plan a Festival.  Jim Barnes.  TAT

We know that skin is the border of life.  Skin.  Philip K. Jason.  AMV–81

We ladies sense it is the cuckoo builds no nest.  Liberation.  Ruth Stone.  BoWoP

We lay, the air-conditioner on.  Then.  John Morgan.  AMV–81

We learned that you don't shoot.  Statement on Our Higher Education.  W. M. Ransom.  CDW

We leave layers of ourselves.  Marie Harris.  *Fr.* Interstate.  AAN

We left the city when the summer day.  Indolence.  Robert Bridges.  VLP

We left the dusty.  Taking Out Jim.  John Walsh.  RAE

We Let Each Other Go.  Coleman Barks.  CSP

We Let It Go That He Was a Perfect Man.  Nicanor Parra, *tr. fr. Spanish by* Miller Williams.  POL

We lie back to back.  The Suitor.  Jane Kenyon.  TC

We lie side by side.  The Royal Iguanas.  Mura Dehn.  TVo

We, like shades that were first conjured up.  And through the Caribbean Sea.  Margaret Danner.  BPo

We listen to Debussy with the lights turned off.  Music in a Dark Room.  Elizabeth Bartlett.  PMW

We live here to eat.  Biological Light.  Primus St. John.  MPA

We Live in a Cage.  William J. Harris.  PoBA

We live in dread of something.  Stones.  Michael C. Blumenthal.  PoUp

We live in fragments.  Tight Rope.  Amiri Baraka.  CNA

We live with our mistakes.  Marie Harris.  *Fr.* Interstate.  AAN

We lived beneath the mat.  The Tale of the Mice.  "Lewis Carroll."  MN

We lived in language all our black selves.  When the Wine Was Gone.  Alvin Aubert.  CNA

We lived one and twenty year.  Upon a Notorious Shrew.  *Unknown.*  FaBoEE

We look out at them on clear nights, thrilled.  Examples of Created Systems.  William Meredith.  PCho

We Love the Venerable House, *with music.*  Emerson.  AH

We love thee, Ann Maria Smith.  The Editor's Wooing.  "Orpheus C. Kerr."  OBAL

We Love You the Way You Are.  David McFadden.  NeAC

We loved them, so we only crushed the skulls.  Cinco de Mayo, 1862.  A. A. Rios.  GP

We Lying by Seasand.  Dylan Thomas.  BiP; PoA

We made castles of grass, green halls, enormous stem-lined rooms.  The Riders.  Ann Stanford.  WPE

We made our little girl.  The Gingerbread House.  John Ower.  AMV–80

We make a home so as not to stay at home.  Customs.  Juan Gelman, *tr. by* Yishai Tobin.  VWA

We make our meek adjustments.  Chaplinesque.  Hart Crane.  CMoP (1970 ed.); NoAM; NOBA; VGW

We make ourselves a place apart.  Revelation.  Robert Frost.  PPM

We Manage Most When We Manage Small.  Linda Gregg.  AmPA

We marched, and saw a company of Canadians.  Canadians.  Ivor Gurney.  FaBoTw (1975 ed.)

We marry our grandfathers.  Extensions of Linear Mobility.  Jeanine Hathaway.  IHMS

We meet. And meeting repairs attention.  Casual Meeting.  Sam Bradley.  AMV–81

We Meet in the Lives of Animals.  Peter Everwine.  NNaP

We meet not as we parted.  Lines.  Shelley.  MBPR

We meet today in Freedom's cause.  Hold the Fort.  *Unknown.*  FSW

We meet tonight to pass the point of blame.  The Reckoning.  Alice Friman.  AMV–81

We met for supper in your flat-bottomed boat.  Dream Barker.  Jean Valentine.  VGW

We mind not now the merits of our kind.  Marriage and Money.  Sir Charles Sedley.  *Fr.* The Happy Pair.  OBSV

We move by means of our mud bumps.  The Tall Figures of Giacometti.  May Swenson.  WIF

We move from one.  The River.  Sam Cornish.  PoBA

We move in white heat morning.  The Geometry of Motion— Crossing the Golden Gate Bridge.  Kaye McDonough.  CPA

We move very fast and smoothly.  Good Times and No Bread.  Reginald Lockett.  CNA

We moved like fingers.  San Francisco Poem.  John Logan.  NNaP

We Must Be Free or Die.  Wordsworth.  FaPoR ("It is not to be thought of that the flood.")  MBPR; NOBE

We Must Be Polite, *sel.*  Carl Sandburg.  "If we meet a gorilla."  CaYB

We must burn up.  Vicente Rodríguez Nietzche, *tr. by* Julio Marzán.  *Fr.* Mural.  InW

We must kill our gods before they kill us.  Black Trumpeter.  Henry Dumas.  PoBA

We must not look for myths.  Poetry and Revolution.  William Pitt Root.  NVAP

We must sit down.  Councils.  Marge Piercy.  NeAC; RiTi; TSWA

We name a thing and then we know it.  Poem for My Eighth Year in Prison.  Michael Hogan.  DNGG

We named you.  Rachel.  Linda Pastan.  TV

We need a place much more than time.  Sentimental Ode.  Tom Buchan.  MIS

We Need a Whole Lot More of Jesus.  *Unknown.*  FSW

We need no runners here. Booze is law.  Harlem, Montana: Just Off the Reservation.  James Welch.  CDW; GP; SA; VW

We never know what to expect.  Our Annual Return to the Lake.  Robert D. Hoeft.  AMV–81

We Never Said Farewell.  Mary Elizabeth Coleridge.  IPWM; WPE

We never spent time in the mountains.  Interlude.  Welton Smith.  PoBA

We Object.  *Tr. fr. Maori by* A. Armstrong.  WTO

We observe ane anither cannily owre.  At a Pairty.  Donald Campbell.  MS

We of the Streets.  Richard Wright.  SPT

We outgrow love, like other things.  Emily Dickinson.  NOBA

We owe the ancients something. You have read. Fitz-Greene Halleck. *Fr. Fanny.* OBAL

We Own the Night. Amiri Baraka. PoBA

We park and stare. A full sky of the stars. The Death of the Sheriff. Robert Lowell. STS

We pass a stranger. He glances. The Stranger Not Ourselves. William Stafford. NNaP

We Passed by Green Closes. John Clare. VLP

We passed their graves. Peace. Langston Hughes. BPo

We Pity Our Bosses Five. *Unknown.* FSW

We plough and sow—we're so very, very low. The Song of the Lower Classes. Ernest Charles Jones. VLP

We Plough the Fields. Jane M. Campbell. FaPoR

We Praise Thee, God, for Harvests Earned, *with music.* John Coleman Adams. AH

We Praise Thee, If One Rescued Soul, *with music.* Lydia H. Sigourney. AH

We praise Thee O God! Revive Us Again. William Paton Mackay. BLSH; FSW

We pray to life's source, Mary. The Virgin Mary. *Unknown, tr. by* Joseph P. Clancy. OBW

We preside, brothers, over the twilight of freedom. Twilight of Freedom. Osip Mandelstam, *tr. by* Andrew Glaze. VWA

We pressed our faces. The Train Stops at Healy Fork. John Haines. TAT

We pulled for you when the wind was against us and the sails were low. Song of the Galley-Slaves. Kipling. HAP; OBP

We put Blake to sleep between us. Homosexual Sonnets. Kenneth Pitchford. GP

We put more coal on the big red fire. Father's Story. Elizabeth Madox Roberts. CC

We put out our hands on the window—cold. In Time of Need. William Stafford. UnPo (1976 ed.)

We put the urn aboard ship. Sappho, *tr. fr. Greek by* Mary Barnard. PBWP

We Rainclouds. Marvin Wyche, Jr. AmNP (1974 ed.)

We Raise de Wheat. *Unknown. See* Song: "We raise de wheat."

We ran across the meadow scabbed with cow-dung. Geoffrey Hill. Mercian Hymns, XXII. HAP

We reach for destinies beyond. Beyond What. Alice Walker. WBN

We Read of a People, *with music. Unknown.* AH

We Real Cool. Gwendolyn Brooks. BuTh; CAPP; CoPAm; FF; HAP; HeIP; HoPM (1975 ed.); ILP (1975 ed.); InPK; PoA; PoBA; PoIA; PPoD; Psy; SoSe; SS; TAP; TCP; WeW

We reden ofte and finde y-write. Sir Orfeo. *Unknown.* OxBM

We remember you/ calling America. Poetry Concert. Michael S. Harper. TAP

We remove fifty brass screws. Bonded. Anne Hazlewood. Brady. WBN

We ride down the coast hwy through the rain. The Great Santa Barbara Oil Disaster OR. Conyus. AmPA

We ripple aspen the way we move out. At the Cabin. Richard Hugo. CNW

We rise to comb the fine mist from our hair. A Wish for Water. Laura Chester. RiTi

We rode updrafts to Bolivia. Canibolos de la Montana. Renée Roper. NPW

We run the dangercourse. We Walk the Way of the New World. Don L. Lee. BPo; FiCh; NeAC; PoBA

We sail out of season into an oyster-gray wind. Crossing the Atlantic. Anne Sexton. NoAM

We sailed into the harbor. Island of Giglio. Harold Norse. GP

We sat across the table. The Friend. Marge Piercy. IPWM; NMM; RiTi

We sat in the Cambridge orchard drinking tea. In the Orchard. Robert Friend. GP

We sat together at one summer's end. Adam's Curse. W. B. Yeats. BIrV; CMoP (1970 ed.); ExPo (1973 ed.); LoAs; NoAM; OAEL-2; PFIr; PoIA; SoSe (1977 ed.); TT; VLP; WIF

We sat, two children, warm against the wall. The Gate. Edwin Muir. CMoP (1970 ed.)

We sat within the farm-house old. The Fire of Drift Wood. Longfellow. NOBA; PiAm; TAP; VoPo

We save fish heads we don't know why. The Politician. Michael McMahon. FAF

We saw a bloody sunset over Courtland. Remembering Nat Turner. Sterling A. Brown. PoBA

We saw a town by the track in Colorado. Holding the Sky. William Stafford. RFM

We saw anchored worlds in a shallow stream. Lying on a Bridge. Van K. Brock. NVAP

We saw and wooed each others' eyes. To Castara: The Reward of Innocent Love. William Habington. SCP-2

We saw, but surely, in the motley crowd. Cave of Staffa, I. Wordsworth. VLP

We saw it all. We saw the souvenir shops, and sitting. Niagara Falls. Alan Dugan. PoA

"We saw reindeer." Rigorists. Marianne Moore. NU; SBG

We saw the swallows gathering in the sky. Modern Love, XLVII. George Meredith. NOBE; OAEL-2

We say the sea is lonely; better say. The Open Sea. William Meredith. CoPAm; TAP; UnPo (1976 ed.)

We searched the wood again. The Writer Indulges a Hobby. Julia Randall. PPoD

We see each living thing finally die. Sonnet VII. Louise Labé, *tr. by* Willis Barnstone. BoWoP

We send you word of the Mother. Two Presentations. Robert Duncan. InPS

We Separate the Days. Henrik Nordbrandt, *tr. fr Danish by* Nadia Christensen. AMV-81

We shall be called harsh names by men unborn. Contemporary. Hortense Flexner. PoA

We shall come to-morrow morning, who were not to have her love. Emily Hardcastle, Spinster. John Crowe Ransom. CMoP (1970 ed.)

We shall find the cube of the rainbow. Emily Dickinson. ILP (1975 ed.)

We shall have everything we want. Ode to Joy. Frank O'Hara. PPP

We shall have to force ourselves. "Terre des Hommes." Ruth Lisa Schechter. RiTi

We shall meet but we shall miss him. The Vacant Chair. Henry Washburn *and* George Frederick Root. FSW

We Shall Never Want. Sydney Goodsir Smith. SLP

We shall not always plant while others reap. From the Dark Tower. Countee Cullen. BPo; PoBA

We Shall Not Be Moved. *Unknown.* FSW

We Shall Not Escape Hell. Marina Tsvetayeva, *tr. fr. Russian by* Elaine Feinstein. BoWoP

We shall not ever meet them bearded in heaven. On the Death of Friends in Childhood. Donald Justice. ConAP; NCSH

We Shall Overcome. *Unknown.* AH, *with music;* BLSo, *with music;* FSW; PBMP

We shall see her no more. The Rejected Member's Wife. Thomas Hardy. VLP

We Shall Walk through the Valley. *Unknown.* FSW

We shared not one idea in thirty years. A Reformer to His Father. James Simmons. BIrV

We sharpen our eye-teeth/ on air. Duelists. Anne Becker. PoUp

We should not worship suffering. What Wild-eyed Murderer. Peter Meinke. AATT

We shouldered like pigs along the rail to try.  Returned to Frisco, 1946.  W. D. Snodgrass.  ILP (1975 ed.)

We sigh above historic pages.  The True Knight.  Ella Wheeler Wilcox.  PeD

We sit indoors and talk of the cold outside.  There Are Roughly Zones.  Robert Frost.  CMoP (1970 ed.); PPP

We sit late, watching the dark slowly unfold.  September.  Ted Hughes.  BoLoP; OLR

We sit nebulous in steam.  Laundrette.  Liz Lochhead.  MIS

We sit outside.  Death of Dr. King.  Sam Cornish.  CNA; OFD; PoBA

We sit, staring at books.  Cut off from.  Perspective.  Adrianne Marcus.  MIT

We sit watching the afternoon summer smell ripely.  James Powell on Imagination.  Larry Neal.  BPo

We six pile in, the engine churning ink.  Nigger Song: An Odyssey.  Rita Dove.  AmPA

We soaped our hands.  Preface: Topping.  Janet Kauffaman.  *Fr.* Tobacco.  TC

We spar on the grass.  Moshudi.  Mark Wangberg.  TC

We spoke like public saints.  Call to Arms.  James Welch.  MPA; SA

We spoke tonight/ of the departure from Egypt.  The Departure.  Jeremy Robson.  VWA

We spray the fields and scatter.  Harvest Hymn.  John Betjeman.  PAIC

We spurred our parents to the kiss.  Children of Darkness.  Robert Graves.  NoAM

We stand here.  Matthew Mead.  *Fr.* Identities.  TwMBP

We stand naked behind the line.  On the Death of Sylvia Plath.  Judith Herzberg, *tr. by* Shirley Kaufman.  VWA

We stand on the edge of the wounds, hugging canned meat.  Dream of Rebirth.  Roberta Hill.  CDW

We stand sometimes.  Of Time.  Lindiwe Mabuza.  SES

We stayed the night in the pathless gorge.  Oh, Lovely Rock.  Robinson Jeffers.  NoAM; NU

We Still Must Follow.  E. L. Mayo.  AMV–81

We stood at first before the mast.  Gastric.  "C. T."  PeD

We stood by a pond that winter day.  Neutral Tones.  Thomas Hardy.  CABA (1972 ed.); CMoP (1970 ed.); HAP; HeIP; ILP (1975 ed.); InPK; LoAs; NoAM; OAEL–2; PPP; SS; UnPo (1976 ed.); VLP

We stood up before day.  In the Dordogne.  John Peale Bishop.  VGW

We stood upon the grass beside the road.  The Bluebells.  John Masefield.  PF

We stopped at her hut.  The Ballad of Ballymote.  Tess Gallagher.  GP

We swam by where she dangled.  Drowning Girl.  Beth Bentley.  CNW

We take it with us, the cry.  Departure.  Carolyn Forché.  AMV–80

We take place in what we believe.  Elephant Rock.  Primus St. John.  PoBA

We take the children to the park.  Stories in Kinsman's Park.  Margaret Atwood.  Psy

We Talked.  Americo Casiano.  NW

We talked about tobacco and the difficulties of getting it.  Black Stockman.  William Hart-Smith.  GAS

We talked with open heart, and tongue.  The Fountain.  Wordsworth.  MBPR

We Thank Thee, Lord, *with music.*  Calvin W. Laufer.  AH

We, the boys of Sanpete County, in obedience to the cause.  The Boys of Sanpete County.  *Unknown.*  AmFP

We, the captives of a thousand skies.  Farewell to Europe.  William Pillen.  VWA

We the People.  The Question, Is It?  Alfred G. Bailey.  AMV–81

We, the rescued.  Chorus of the Rescued.  Nelly Sachs, *tr. by* Harry Zohn.  VWA

We thought the grass.  Photographs: A Vision of Massacre.  Michael S. Harper.  PoBA

We Three.  Lilian Moore.  CC; IWK

We Three Kings of Orient Are.  John Henry Hopkins, Jr.  AH, *with music*; BLSH, *with music*; PChr

We thumbwrestle and I.  All Thumbs.  David Giber.  AMV–81

We Told You So.  Nancy Keesing.  MAuV

We tolerate closed doors by watching the sun.  Father and Daughter.  Joanne Casullo.  NPW

We too, we too, descending once again.  The Silent Slain.  Archibald MacLeish.  CABA (1972 ed.); CMoP (1970 ed.); NIL; POL

We too were created from clay.  Vessels.  Howard Schwartz.  VWA

We took our turn at the guard that night, just Sourdough Charlie and I.  The Stampede.  Freeman E. Miller.  BPAW

We took the mouse alive.  Poor Mouse.  Mei Berssenbrugge.  NW

We tore the green tree down.  Verifying the Dead.  James Welch.  CDW

We Try Not to Touch So Close.  John Sjoberg.  AcAn

We turn out the light to undress by.  Turn the Key Deftly.  Edwin Brock.  POL

We two are last in hell: what may we fear.  Barley-Break: or, Last in Hell.  Robert Herrick.  CaPo

We two stood simply friend-like side by side.  Inapprehensiveness.  Robert Browning.  VLP

We understand.  O Light.  Allen Kornblum.  AcAn

We used to gather at the high window.  When Mahalia Sings.  Quandra Prettyman.  MiP; PoBA

We used to picnic where the thrift.  Trebetherick.  John Betjeman.  CMoP (1970 ed.)

We used to spend the spring together.  The Most Beautiful Girl in the World.  Lorenz Hart.  OBAL

We wait for the.  A Charm against Pregnancy.  Harry Stessel.  AAN

We waited for an omnibus.  Walking Song.  William E. Hickson.  OxBChV

We waited in the desert encircled.  Sukkot.  Sol Lachman.  VWA

We wake entangled.  Occasion.  Roger Pfingston.  SFF

We wake to economical.  Reconcilable Differences.  Roger Sauls.  AMV–81

We walk alone on our roots.  Prayer for Kafka and Ourselves.  Anthony Rudolf.  VWA

We walk, as all around walks on creation.  In the Shadow of the Valley of Death.  Abu al-Qasim al-Shabbi.  DL

We walk past the Han stallion.  Museum with Chinese Landscapes.  Walter Cybulski.  AMV–81

We Walk the Way of the New World.  Don L. Lee.  BPo; FiCh; NeAC; PoBA

We walk together, breathing different air.  Chilled by Different Winds.  Alice Mackenzie Swaim.  AMV–80

We walk tonight.  The People Cannot Speak.  T. Alan Broughton.  FAF

We walked a mile from the road and with every step.  Daisies.  Alden Nowlan.  NeAC

We walked along, while bright and red.  The Two April Mornings.  Wordsworth.  EBEV; MBPR

We wanted Li Wing.  Lapsus Linguae.  Keith Preston.  OBAL

We wanted to feel at home somewhere.  The Prairie.  William Pillin.  SPT

We watched/ a red rooster. William Carlos Williams. *Fr.* Calypsos. TH

We watched her breathing through the night. The Death-Bed. Thomas Hood. NOBE; PIM

We watched her go the way she came. Gravely. James Welch. MPA

We watched our love burn with the lumberyard. The Lumberyard. Ruth Herschberger. WPE

We Wear the Mask. Paul Laurence Dunbar. AmNP (1974 ed.); CABA (1972 ed.); FF; IPWM; PBMP; PoBA; PPoD; UnPo (1976 ed.)

We went north/ to escape winter. Indian Song: Survival. Leslie Silko. CDW; VoR

We went off to the wake of the "whelpish youngster." Harvest of the Sea. Máire Mhac an tSaoi. PBWP

We went out, early one morning. Out Fishing. Barbara Howes. LiSp; PPoD; WPE

We went there on the train. Protocols. Randall Jarrell. VGW

We went there to confer. Detroit Conference of Unity and Art. Nikki Giovanni. HoPM (1975 ed.)

We went to look for stragglers on a ridge. Mushrooms. Basil Dowling. ATNZ

We went to see the old church yard little left. Foveran Sands. Roderick Watson. MIS

We were a multitude, until the hunters. Angels. Richard Burns. VWA

We were a people taut for war; the hills. Welsh History. R. S. Thomas. OBW

We were a tribe, a family, a people. Scotland 1941. Edwin Muir. MS

We were all under God. God. Boris Slutsky, *tr. by* Dimitry Pospielovsky *and* Keith Bosley. VWA

We were alone and did your life. To Children. Lawrence McGaugh. PoBA

We were alone on the prairies and mountains. The Turn of October. Norman Macleod. SPT

We were apart; yet, day by day. Isolation: To Marguerite. Matthew Arnold. Switzerland, IV. VLP

We were as tough as our glasses. Tyson's Corner. Primus St. John. PoBA

We were broke. The Dance Marathon. Lee Lally. PoUp

We were camped on the plains [*or* bend]. The Zebra Dun. *Unknown.* FSW; PH; PoTa

We were crowded in the cabin. Ballad of the Tempest. James T. Fields. RhR

We were forty miles from Albany. Erie. *Unknown.* FSW

We were going single file. A Bummer. Michael Casey. TSWA

We were gone from each other. Farewell. Iain Crichton Smith. SLP

We were just sitting there. The Day the Old Man Joined the Church (Xmas '66). Richard W. Thomas. TC

We were not superstitious; this medium. A Kind of Palmistry. Paul Murray. IPM

We Were of Them. William Pillin. SPT

We were out gathering full ripe. Many Voices. Samuel Makidemewabe. TC

We were out in Arizona, on the Painted Desert ground. Arizona. *Unknown.* AmFP

We were parked on a hill. Don 1958. Alta. MMD

We were sure to interrupt the traveller's siesta. Nausicaa with Some Attendants. Tom Lowenstein. VWA

We were up before anyone. Liard Hot Springs. Gordon Massman. CTBA

We were very tired, we were very merry. Recuerdo. Edna St. Vincent Millay. CTBA; NoAM; PoA; PPM; TAP

We were warned about frost, yet all day the summer. Early Frost. Leslie Norris. HeHu

We were young, we were merry, we were very very wise. Unwelcome. Mary Elizabeth Coleridge. PoPle; SS; WPE

We who also linger near the border of insanities. Near the Border of Insanities. Dannie Abse. PoA

We who are left, how shall we look again. Lament. W. W. Gibson. OxBTC

We who devour our unclean dead are now arisen. Letter to Robert. Mary Fabilli. IHMS

We who must act as handmaidens. A Muse of Water. Carolyn Kizer. NMM

We who strangely went astray. Richard Crashaw. *Fr.* In the Glorious Epiphany of Our Lord God. SCP-1

We who with songs beguile your pilgrimage. Prologue. James Elroy Flecker. *Fr.* The Golden Journey to Samarkand. FaPoR; OxBTC

We will deal in apples, plums and pears. The Way to Live. *Unknown.* VLP

"We will kill." After the Killing. Dudley Randall. CNA

We Will Not Fear, *with music.* David Diamond. AH

We will not withdraw from the game. Roulette. Brewster Ghiselin. WasP

We will pull, we will haul, hearty, healthy, and gay. Blow the Man Down. *Unknown.* AmFP

We will remember, surely, how we stood. Last Rite. John V. Hicks. AMV–81

We will return to life. Comanche Ghost Dance: An Impression. Lance Henson. VoR

We will watch the Northern Lights. *Unknown, tr. fr. Abanaki.* RFM

We Wish You a Merry Christmas. *Unknown.* FSW (Merry Christmas, A.) GSB, *with music*

We woke early. Names in Monterchi: To Rachel. James Wright. NNaP

We Won't Go Home till Morning, *with music. Unknown.* PSoN

We worked in the kitchen. The Function Room. Patrice Phillips. MAT

We would climb the highest dune. With Kit, Age 7, at the Beach. William Stafford. RFM

We Would See Jesus, *with music.* Anna B. Warner. AH

We zealots, made up of stiff clay. Let Us All Be Unhappy on Sunday. Lord Neaves. FaBoCo

Weak, The. Greg Kuzma. HeS

Weak Monk, The. Stevie Smith. BoWoP; FaBoTw (1975 ed.)

Weak-winged is song. Ode Recited at the Harvard Commemoration. James Russell Lowell. NOBA; PiAm

Wealth. Tony Moreno. NW

Wealth and Wisdom. *At. to* Alfred, King of England. *Fr.* The Proverbs of Alfred. OxBM

Wealth unto every man, I see. Worldly Wealth. Rowland Watkyns. FaBoEE

Weapons Training. Bruce Dawe. CAAP

Wear a dress. An Answer to a Man's Question, "What Can I Do about Women's Liberation?" Susan Griffin. MMD

Wear gold bracelets. The Ladies. Karen Bunting. PoW

Wearin' o' the Green, The. *Unknown. See* Wearing of the Green, The.

Wearing Breasts. Daniela Gioseffi. RiTi

Wearing my familiar worry wrapped. In the Penile Colony. Erica Jong. MMD

Wearing of the Green, The. *Unknown, add. words by* Dion Boucicault. BLSH, *with music;* BTTM; FaPoR; FSW; GBP; WTO
(Wearin' o' the Green, The.) AIW

Wearing the familiar Yankee pinstripes. And You Are There. Tom Clark. LiSp

Wearing White. Sandra McPherson. MPA

Wearing worry about money like a hair shirt. Worry about Money. Kathleen Raine. FaBoTw (1975 ed.)

Weary already, weary miles to-night. A Match with the Moon. Dante Gabriel Rossetti. VLP

Weary Blues, The. Langston Hughes. InPK; NoAM; NOBA

Weary, I open wide the antique pane. Poetry and the Poet. H. C. Bunner. OBAL

Weary I was, and thought to sit at rest. Elizabeth Melvill, Lady Culross. *Fr.* A Godly Dream. WPE

Weary lot is thine, fair maid, A. The Rover's Farewell. Sir Walter Scott. *Fr.* Rokeby, III. NOBE

Weary men, what reap ye? The Famine Year. Lady Wilde. PFIr

Weary of myself, and sick of asking. Self-Dependence. Matthew Arnold. IPWM; PBMP; VLP

Weary on ye, sad waves! On an Island. "Ethna Carbery." WPE

Weary Song to a Slow Sad Tune, A. Li Ch'ing-chao, *tr. fr. Chinese by* Kenneth Rexroth. BoWoP

Weary was when coming on a stream. Aswelay. Norman Henry Pritchard II. PoBA

Weary Will. A. B. Paterson. BoAnP

Weary with toil, I haste to my bed. Sonnets, XXVII. Shakespeare. ILP (1975 ed.); STS

Weary year his race now having run, The. Amoretti, LXII. Spenser. FSFS

Weasel, The. Lord Alfred Douglas. BBL

Weasel. Sylvia Read. RAE

Weasel-face:/ you've got me swimming the Tiber. Person to Person. Elisabeth Murawski. PoUp

Weasel (or a stoat), A. The Aesthete Weasel. Christian Morgenstern, *tr. by* Geoffrey Grigson. FaBoNo

Weather, The. Gavin Ewart. BBL

Weather Ear. Norman Nicholson. MPo

Weather Gallery, The. Liam Rector. PoUp

Weather here is raw, The. At Torrey Pines State Park. Jerome Mazzaro. FiCP

Weather of Olympus, The. Robert Graves. FaBoEE

Weather of Six Mornings, The. Jane Cooper. IHMS

Weather of this winter night, The, my mistress. Childlessness. James Merrill. ConAP

Weather Report. Elaine H. Jennings. NPW

Weather was fine, The. They took away his teeth. John Berryman. *Fr.* Dream Songs. CAPP

Weathering the Depths. Al Lee. AmPA

Weatherman has shown us everything, The. The Letters of Summer. Christopher Buckely. AMV–80

Weatherman of Sorrows. Emery E. George. AAN

Weathers. Thomas Hardy. PoPle; PPM

Weather's cleared, The. We're filming at Versailles. Clive James. *Fr.* To Pete Atkin: A Letter from Paris. OBSV

Weave Room Blues. *Unknown.* FSW

Weaver, The. John Haines. MPA

Weaver, The. Lisel Mueller. AMV–81

Weaver's Life. *Unknown.* FSW

Weaving Love-Knots. Hsüeh T'ao, *tr. fr. Chinese by* Carolyn Kizer. BoWoP

Weaving Love-Knots 2. Hsüeh T'ao, *tr. fr. Chinese by* Carolyn Kizer. BoWoP

Web, The. Gregory O'Donoghue. BIrV

Web, The. Theodore Weiss. NoAM

Webs. Carl Sandburg. TH

Webster was much possessed by death. Whispers of Immortality. T. S. Eliot. CMoP (1970 ed.); ExPo (1973 ed.); NoAM; NOBA

We'd have to love the nape of the neck more than the thigh. Conditions. José Luis Vega, *tr. by* Julio Marzán. InW

Wedded. Isaac Rosenberg. PoPle

Wedded Memories. Philip Bourke Marston. VLP

Wedding, The. Conrad Aiken. CMoP (1970 ed.); TAP

Wedding. George Mackay Brown. MS; SLP

Wedding. Lucille Day. PoW

Wedding, The. Roland Gant. BuTh

Wedding, The. Sandra Kohler. AMV–80

Wedding. Ewa Lipska, *tr. fr. Polish by* Peter Jay *and* Geri Lipshultz. VWA

Wedding, The. Coventry Patmore. *Fr.* The Angel in the House, II, xi. VLP

Wedding and Funeral. *Unknown.* GBP

Wedding cortège, A. Wedding. Ewa Lipska, *tr. by* Peter Jay *and* Geri Lipshultz. VWA

Wedding Feast, The. Luis de Góngora, *tr. fr. Spanish by* Edward Meryon Wilson. *Fr.* The First Solitude. OBVE

Wedding Night, The. Anne Sexton. PoA

Wedding Poem, The, *sel.* Lawrence Russ. "Night before you left, as you lay, The." AMV–80

Wedding Poem. Michael Waters. AAN

Wedding-Wind. Philip Larkin. BuTh; LoAs; MAT

Wedged into a hard huddle. The Edge. Ann Chandonnet. AMV–81

Wedges/ slide/ into cracks. Rail Splitting. Gary Lawless. FAF

Wedlock. Bink Noll. GP

Wednesbury Cocking, The. *Unknown.* FaBoBa; PeBB

Wednesday morning at five o'clock as the day begins. She's Leaving Home. John Lennon *and* Paul McCartney. RRA; SoS

Wednesday Night Prayer Meeting. Jay Wright. PoBA

Wednesday; or, The Dumps. John Gay. *Fr.* The Shepherd's Week. OAEL–1

Wednesdays at the bone orchard deliveries. Memo. Charles Lynch. PoBA

Wee bird cam' to our ha' door, A. Wae's Me for Prince Charlie. William Glen. BTTM

Wee Cooper of Fife, The. *Unknown.* FSW

Wee Davie Daylicht. Robert Tennant. OxBChV

Wee leave Creete Country; and our sayls unwrapped uphoysing. Virgil, *tr. by* Richard Stanyhurst. *Fr.* The Aeneid, III. OBVE

Wee man o' leather. *Unknown.* GBP

Wee, sleeket [*or* sleekit], cow'rin' [*or* cowran], tim'rous beastie. To a Mouse. Burns. BiP; FF; HAP; HeIP; ILP (1975 ed.); InPS; IP; LAuP; MN; OAEL–1; PAIC; PoIA; PPP

Wee Wee Man, The. *Unknown.* AIW; EBEV; GBP; OAEL–1, *with music;* PeBB (Little Wee Man, The, *version at. to* Ian Serraillier.) FPB

Wee Willie Gray. Burns. OxBChV

Wee Willie Winkie rins [*or* runs] through the town. Willie Winkie. William Miller. MG; NIL; OxBChV

Weed and herb and foxy flower. Song for a Lost Art. Virginia Brasier. AMV–81

Weed from Catholic Europe, it took root, A. Macao. W. H. Auden. TT

Weed Puller. Theodore Roethke. AnMo; PiAm; STS

Weeding in January. Louis Daniel Brodsky. AMV–80

Weeds. Ann Stanford. MPA

Weeds grow shamelessly/ on my tongue. Self-Portrait. Cecil Bodker, *tr. by* Nadia Christensen. BoWoP

Weedy light through the uncurtained glass, The. Hiatus. Margaret Avison. HAP

Week at Whinwood next to Christmas week, The. January: Cover Shooting. Wilfrid Scawen Blunt. *Fr.* An Idler's Calendar. VLP

Week in Paradise, A. John Ridland. NowV

Week of Che Guevara, hunted, hurt. October and November. Robert Lowell. MAT

Week on the Concord and Merrimack Rivers, A, *sels.* Henry David Thoreau.
  Conscience Is Instinct Bred in the House. HeIP; PiAm
  Haze. HeIP; PiAm
    (Woof of the Sun, Ethereal Gauze.) ILP (1975 ed.); TAP

Week-Seek. Jim Tollerud. VoR

Week-End Indian, The. Anita Endrezze Probst. VoR

Week-End Naturalist, The. Tom Buchan. MIS; MS

Weekly at the start. The Face. Lucien Stryk. GP

Weeksville Women. Elouise Loftin. PoBA

Weep, and weep long, but do not weep for me. To a Troubled Friend. James Wright. PCho

Weep for the dead, for they have lost this light. On Himself. Robert Herrick. FaBoEE

Weep not for me, Loved Woman. Warrior's Song. Mary Austin. BPAW

Weep [*or* Weepe] not, my wanton, smile upon my knee. Sephestia's Song to Her Childe. Robert Greene. *Fr.* Menaphon. ILP (1975 ed.); NOBE; OBP

Weep not, nor backward turn your beams. A Lover, upon an Accident Necessitating His Departure, Consults with Reason. Thomas Carew. CaPo

Weep not, weep not. Go Down Death. James Weldon Johnson. AmNP (1974 ed.); DL; PoBA

Weep! Weep! Weep! For Her Brother. Al-Khansa, *tr. by* E. Powys Mathers. *Fr.* The Thousand and One Nights. PBWP

Weep with me, all you that read. Epitaph on S. P., a Child of Queen Elizabeth's Chapel. Ben Jonson. CABA (1972 ed.); HeIP; HoPM (1975 ed.); NOBE; OAEL-1; PoPle; PPP; UnPo (1976 ed.)

Weep You No More, Sad Fountains. *Unknown.* EBEV; GBL; HAP; PoPle; SCP-2
  (Tears.) NOBE

Weepe not my wanton! smile upon my knee! *See* Weep not, my wanton, . . .

Weeper, The. David Bristol. PoUp

Weeper, The. Richard Crashaw. *See* Saint Mary Magdalene.

*Weepers Tower* in Amsterdam, The. Paul Goodman. VGW

Weeping o'er the sacred urn. Ambrose Philips. *Fr.* To the Memory of Lord Halifax. FaBoCo

Weeping rose in her dark night of leaves, The. A Song at Morning. Edith Sitwell. CMoP (1970 ed.)

Weeping Sad and Lonely. Charles C. Sawyer. *See* When This Cruel War Is Over.

Weeping Saviour, The. Elizabeth Barrett Browning. PIM

Weeping Sinner, Dry Your Tears, *with music.* Oliver Holden. AH

Weeping tree, A. What Am I? Abo Stoltzenberg, *tr. by* Gabriel Preil *and* Howard Schwartz. VWA

Weeping Willow, The. *Unknown.* AmFP

Weevily Wheat. *Unknown.* AmFP; FSW

Weighing the steadfastness and state. Man. Henry Vaughan. ILP (1975 ed.); MetP; NOBE; PMW; SCP-1

Weightless in water, swift as wind. This Shell. Mark Van Doren. SPo

Weights, The. Lawrence Russ. TC

Weighty volumes look important, The. The Library. Henry Shore. PMW

Weir Bridge. Padraic Fallon. CIP

Weird sister. In Salem. Lucille Clifton. AmPA

Weland from wounds underwent hardship. Deor. *Unknown, tr. by* Kemp Malone. PAIC

Weland knew fully affliction and woe. Deor's Lament. *Unknown, tr. by* Charles W. Kennedy. OAEL-1

Welcome, The. Abraham Cowley. *Fr.* The Mistress. BoLoP

Welcome. U. A. Fanthorpe. PMW

Welcome. Harvey Feinberg. POL

Wel/come back, brother. Huey. Etheridge Knight. NNaP

Welcome! but yet no entrance, till we bless. The Entertainment, or Porch-Verse, at the Marriage of Master Henry Northleigh and the Most Witty Mistress Lettice Yard. Robert Herrick. CaPo

Welcome for Etheridge, A. James Cunningham. JB

Welcome, good friend; as you have served your term. "Black Bart, PO8." Ambrose Bierce. BPAW

Welcome, grinned Henry, welcome fifty-one! John Berryman. *Fr.* Dream Songs. TAP

Welcome Home. Charles M. Purcell. EC

Welcome home, driving downhill. Lament City. Thomas Lux. AmPA

Welcome home from the exhausting voyage. Sea Legs. Susan Feldman. AmPA

Welcome joy, and welcome sorrow. Fragment. Keats. MBPR

Welcome, kind Death: my long tired spirit bear. Algernon Sidney's Farewell. *Unknown.* APAS

Welcome, Maids of Honour. To Violets. Robert Herrick. CaPo

Welcome me, if you will. For James Dean. Frank O'Hara. NNaP

Welcome, most welcome, to our vows and us. To the King, upon His Coming with His Army into the West. Robert Herrick. CaPo

Welcome, O Great Mary. Alice O'Gallagher, *tr. fr. Gaelic by* Douglas Hyde. WTO

Welcome, old friend! These many years. To Age. Walter Savage Landor. SoSe

Welcome, precious stone of the night. Welcome to the Moon. *Unknown, tr. fr. Gaelic.* Moon

Welcome, sulphur dioxide. Air. James Rado *and* Gerome Ragni. PoRo

Welcome, Sweet Rest, *with music.* Michael Wigglesworth. AH

Welcome the Wrath. Stanley Kunitz. VGW

Welcome thou of high estate. Welcome, O Great Mary. Alice O'Gallagher, *tr. by* Douglas Hyde. WTO

Welcome, thrice welcome to thy native place! Mary Gulliver to Captain Lemuel Gulliver. John Gay *and* Alexander Pope. OAEL-1

Welcome to Freedom's birth-place—and a den! Ode to the Cameleopard. Thomas Hood. FaBoNo

Welcome to Sack, The. Robert Herrick. CaPo

Welcome to Spring. John Lyly. *See* Trico's Song: "What bird so sings,..."

Welcome to the Moon. *Unknown, tr. fr. Gaelic.* Moon

Welcome to This House. Faye George. AMV-80

Welcome to this my college, and thought late. To His Kinsman, Master Thomas Herrick, Who Desired to Be in His Book. Robert Herrick. CaPo

Welcome to you rich autumn days. Rich Days. W. H. Davies. FSFS

Welcome, wild North-easter. Ode to the North-east Wind. Charles Kingsley. FaPoR

Welcome, Ye Hopeful Heirs of Heaven, *with music.* Phoebe Hinsdale Brown. AH

Welcomed to islands over the long water. Islanders, Inlanders. Michael Mott. PoA

Welfare Store. *Unknown.* BluL

Welkin's wind, way unhindered.   The Wind.   Dafydd ap Gwilym, *tr. by* Joseph P. Clancy.   OBW

Well, The.   Luis Pales Matos, *tr. fr. Spanish by* Donald Walsh.   InW

Well/ black mama, what's the/ matter with you today.   My Black Mama.   *Unknown.*   BluL

Well/ If I had my way.   If I Had My Way.   *Unknown.*   BluL

Well/ I'm gonna run, I'm gonna run.   I'm Gonna Run to the City of Refuge.   *Unknown.*   BluL

Well,/ When should she kill the child.   The Abortion.   Lucille Iverson.   WBN

Well-aimed Stare, The.   Hugo Margenat, *tr. fr. Spanish by* Julio Marzán.   InW

"We'll all be rooned," said Hanrahan.   Said Hanrahan.   P. J. Hartigan.   MAuV

Well all you ladies gather 'round.   Candy Man Blues.   *Unknown.*   BluL; FSW

Well, aye, last evenen, as I shook.   Zummer Thoughts in Winter Time.   William Barnes.   VLP

Well, babbling philosophical rascal.   Thomas Shadwell.   *Fr.* Timon of Athens, the Man-Hater.   SCP-2

We'll begin with a box, and the plural is boxes.   Why English Is So Hard!   *Unknown.*   CTV

Well boss I met.   Cheerio My Deario.   Don Marquis.   *Fr.* Archy and Mehitabel.   FaBoCo

Well clay its strange at last we've come to it.   The Spark's Farewell to Its Clay.   R. A. K. Mason.   ATNZ

Well, come along boys and listen to my tale.   The Old Chisholm Trail.   *Unknown.*   FSW

Well, Did You Evah?   Cole Porter.   OBAL

Well Dressed Man with a Beard, The.   Wallace Stevens.   BiP

Well formed is the child, well formed now.   The Dawn of Day.   Keaulumoko, *tr. by* M. W. Beckwith.   *Fr.* The Kumulipo: A Creation Chant.   WTO

Well, Froggie went a-courting and he did ride.   Froggie Went a-Courting.   *Unknown.*   AmFP

Well, gentlemen,/ You flag wavers.   To Those Who Sing America.   Frank Marshall Davis.   FB

We'll Go No More a-Roving.   Byron.   *See* So We'll Go No More . . .

We'll Go to Sea No More.   *Unknown.*   GBP

Well, Heaven be thank'd my first-love fail'd.   The County Ball.   Coventry Patmore.   *Fr.* The Angel in the House.   VPC

Well, here I am and.   Proteus.   Kathleen Wiegner.   MMD

Well, here we are; well, here we are!   Yale Boola!   A. M. Hirsh.   FSN

Well, Honest John.   John Clare.   Epi

Well House, The.   Robert Penn Warren.   PiAm

Well I ain't got no use for your red apple juice.   Red Apple Juice.   *Unknown.*   FSW

Well, I am a rambling, gambling man.   Rambling, Gambling Man.   Gil Houston.   FSW

Well, I don't care if it rains or freezes.   Plastic Jesus.   *Unknown.*   FSW

Well, I dreamed a dream the other night.   Prospecting Dream.   *Unknown.*   FSW

Well I got up this morning.   The Jinx Blues.   *Unknown.*   BluL

Well, I had an old dog and his name was Blue.   *See* I had a dog and his name was Blue.

Well, I had an old hen and she had a wooden leg.   Turkey in the Straw.   *Unknown.*   BLSH; FSW

Well, I may now receive, and die: my sin.   Satires, IV.   John Donne.   OBSV; TVS

Well I poisoned my man.   Blood Hound Blues.   *Unknown.*   BluL

Well I remember how you smiled.   Your Name upon the Sand.   Walter Savage Landor.   *Fr.* Ianthe.   BuTh; HAP

Well I say I work in the Conoco station.   Hottest Brand Goin'.   *Unknown.*   BluL

Well I think it's fine building jumbo planes.   Where Do the Children Play?   Cat Stevens.   PoRo; UsP

Well I want all you women folks to fall in line.   The Dirty Dozens.   *Unknown.*   BluL

Well, I was camped out on the draw at the head of Cimarron.   The Zebra Dun.   *Unknown.*   AmFP

Well, I went to California in the year of Seventy-six.   Root Hog or Die.   *Unknown.*   AmFP

Well I woke up this mornin'/ Half past four.   Stamp Blues.   *Unknown.*   BluL

Well, I woke up this morning/ I was feeling mighty bad.   Evil-hearted Man.   *Unknown.*   FSW

Well I woke up this mornin' it was Christmas Day.   Adrian Henri's Talking after Christmas Blues.   Adrian Henri.   BuTh; LP; MPo

Well, if a King's a lion, at the least.   Pope.   *Fr.* The First Epistle of the First Book of Horace Imitated.   OBSV

Well! If the Bard was weather-wise, who made.   Dejection: An Ode.   Samuel Taylor Coleridge.   CABA (1972 ed.); Epi; ILP (1975 ed.); MBPR; NOBE; OAEL-2; PPP

Well, if you must know all the facts.   A Visitor.   "Lewis Carroll."   FaBoNo

Well! I'm goin' home.   Special Rider Blues.   *Unknown.*   AmFP

Well I'm going to Memphis, come to stop at Cincinnat'.   On the Wall.   *Unknown.*   BluL

Well, I'm in love with a feller, a feller you have seen.   Common Bill.   *Unknown.*   AmFP

Well-informed Wight, A.   Oliver Herford.   TDH

Well it rained five days and the sky was dark as night.   Back Water Blues.   *Unknown.*   FSW

Well, it's partly the shape of the thing.   Limerick.   *Unknown.*   SoSe

Well, Jesus died to save me in all of my sin.   The Rock Island Line.   *Unknown.*   AmFP

Well last Monday morning.   The Gray Goose.   *Unknown.*   FSW

Well, Lizzie Anderson! seventeen men—and.   To a Friend.   William Carlos Williams.   LoAs

Well look a-here, honey.   Depot Blues.   *Unknown.*   AmFP

Well may I weene, faire ladies, all this while.   Spenser.   The Faerie Queene, III, 6.   OAEL-1

Well may that kisse be sweet that's giv'n t' a sleek.   Giovanni Battista Guarini, *tr. by* Sir Richard Fanshawe.   *Fr.* Il Pastor Fido.   OBVE

Well-meaning readers, you that come as friends.   Richard Crashaw.   *Fr.* The Flaming Heart.   OAEL-1

Well met, well met, my own true love.   The House Carpenter.   *Unknown.*   AmFP; FSW; RDB; WIF

We'll Never Be the Same (Until Later).   Grace Cavalieri.   AATT

We'll notice first they've quit turning their ears.   Talking to the Forest.   David Wagoner.   CNW

Well now, who does not know Katy Cline.   Katy Cline.   *Unknown.*   FSW

Well now you know my mama told me.   Six Week Old Blues.   *Unknown.*   BluL

Well of Life, The.   Sir Herbert Read.   NoAM

Well, Old Flame, the fire's out.   Static.   Barton Sutter.   AMV-81

Well, old spy.   Award.   Ray Durem.   BPo; CABA (1972 ed.); NIL; PoBA

Well pleasing 'tis to me.   Goat's-Leaf.   Marie de France, *tr. by* Aline Allard.   PBWP

Well Rising, The.   William Stafford.   ILP (1975 ed.)

Well-shadowed landscape, fare ye well!   Farewell to Love.   Sir John Suckling.   CaPo; SCP-2

Well, since you're from the other side of town.   Public-House Confidence.   Norman Cameron.   BBGO

Well, sir, 'tis granted I said Dryden's rhymes. An Allusion to Horace. Earl of Rochester. APAS

Well, so that is that. Now we must dismantle the tree. W. H. Auden. *Fr.* For the Time Being. OAEL-2

Well, so you've gone and overdone it again. Herrick Hospital, Fifth Floor. Al Young. CPA

Well, some may hate, and some may scorn. Stanzas to ——. Emily Brontë. WPE

Well, son, I'll tell you. Mother to Son. Langston Hughes. AmNP (1974 ed.); CABA (1972 ed.); CC; CTBA; IPWM; SO; SoS

Well, standing on the corner with a dollar in my hand. Hesitation Blues. *Unknown.* FSW

We'll stock up books. Striking a Pose. Kevin Ireland. ATNZ

"We'll talk all night until we swoon away," you promised. Eden Revisited. Vassar Miller. GP

Well the baby crying on up to his mama's knee. That Crawling Baby Blues. *Unknown.* BluL

Well, the night was dark and drizzly. There Ain't No Bugs on Me. *Unknown.* FSW

Well, the other night when I came home. The Intoxicated Rat. *Unknown.* FSW

Well the ugliest little thing. Killer Diller. *Unknown.* BluL

Well, then, I hate Thee, unrighteous picture. The Black Riders, XII. Stephen Crane. AmVN

Well then! I now do plainly see. The Wish. Abraham Cowley. *Fr.* The Mistress. ILP (1975 ed.); NOBE

Well then, the promis'd hour is come at last. To My Dear Friend Mr. Congreve on His Comedy Called "The Double-Dealer." Dryden. EBEV; OAEL-1

Well then, tomorrow! the wood exalts under the mild. Finally. Vittoria Aganoor Pompili, *tr. by* Brenda Webster. PBWP

Well, they are gone, and here must I remain. This Lime-Tree Bower My Prison. Samuel Taylor Coleridge. HeIP; ILP (1975 ed.); MBPR; NIL; PAIC

Well, they gave him his orders at Monroe, Virginia. The Wreck of the Old 97. *Unknown.* FSW

Well they'd made up their minds to be everywhere because why not. The Last One. W. S. Merwin. CoPAm; NoAM; VGW

Well, this bird comes, and under his wing is a crutch. The Bird. Moishe Leib Halpern, *tr. by* John Hollander. PPP

Well, to begin. What I Want in a Husband Besides a Mustache. Diane Wakoski. PPoD

We'll to the Woods No More. A. E. Housman. OAEL-2

Well, to-day Jeane is my set time vor to goo. Come an' Meet Me wi' the Children on the Road. William Barnes. VLP

Well tonight the damnfool sunset pitched. What Maisie Know She Don't Want No. Judith Johnson Sherwin. NoAM

Well-Travelled Roadway, The. John Newlove. NeAC

Well, The: Two Songs. *Gond Oral Tradition, tr. by* V. Elwin *and* S. Hivale. WTO

Well, Wanton Eye. Charles d'Orleans. HAP

Well Water. Randall Jarrell. NOBA; PPoD; VGW

Well we done told you. Jesus Is Coming Soon. *Unknown.* BluL

"Well," we say, "time to go." So then we pack. After Vacation. Katherine Hanley. AMV-81

Well, we will drive our beasts down early. Late Fair. Sean Lucy. IPM

Well well well. Motherless Children. *Unknown.* BluL

Well when you can't see the forest. Orange Juice Song. David Phillips. NeAC

Well, whilst we here, sonny, having fun. Kentucky Blues. *Unknown.* BluL

Well-wishing to a Place of Pleasure, A. *Unknown.* GBL; SCP-2

Well, world, you have kept faith with me. He Never Expected Much. Thomas Hardy. NoAM; OxBTC

Well yonder stands little Maggie. Little Maggie. *Unknown.* FSW

Well, you go back then to the central question. On the Last Page of the Last Yellow Pad. Miller Williams. AMV-80

Well, you know the sun is going down. Lowdown Dirty Blues. *Unknown.* AmFP

Well you wake up in the mornng. Midnight Special. Leadbelly (Huddie Ledbetter). FSW

Well-a come along boys and listen to my tale. The Old Chisholm Trail. *Unknown.* BLSH

"Wellcome, to the Caves of Artá!" Robert Graves. NOBL

Wellington again slaps the face with wind. Return Journey. Paul Henderson. ATNZ

Welsh Ballad, A. Edmwnd Prys, *tr. fr. Welsh by* Gwyn Williams. OBW

Welsh History. R. S. Thomas. OBW

Welsh Incident. Robert Graves. CMoP (1970 ed.); NOBE; OxBTC

Welsh Landscape. R. S. Thomas. LP; MPo

Welsh Marches, The. A. E. Housman. FaBoTw (1975 ed.)

Welshman in Exile Speaks, The. T. H. Jones. OBW

Welthistorische Perspektiven. Roderick Watson. MIS

Weltschmerz. Frank Yerby. AmNP (1974 ed.)

Wendigo, The. Ogden Nash. ECBV

Wendover. Art Cuelho. PoW

Wenes King Edward with his longe shankes. The Scots in Berwick (1296). *Unknown.* OxBM

Wenest thou, usher, with thyn cointise. A Schoolboy's Lot. *Unknown.* OxBM

Wenne, wenne, wenchichenne. Charm against Wens. *Unknown.* OxBM

Went down on Johnson Street. Bob McKinney. *Unknown.* BluL

Went into a shoestore to buy a pair of shoes. Sale. Josephine Miles. POL; WPE

Went into the world like a shining knife. A Signature. F. Eugene Warren. AATT

Went out to plant some tomatoes. Humidity. R. P. Dickey. HeS

Went up a year this evening. Emily Dickinson. HAP

Went up on the hill, 'bout 12 o'clock. Fishing Blues. *Unknown.* BluL

Went up on the mountain. Bile Them Cabbage Down. *Unknown.* FSW

Went walking/ in woods. The Boy. J. D. Whitney. BCr

We're All Dry. *Unknown.* NOBL

We're All in the Dumps. *Unknown. See* In the Dumps.

We're all met here together. We Won't Go Home till Morning. *Unknown.* PSoN

We're all met together here, to sit and to crack. The Work of the Weavers. *Unknown.* FSW

Were all our sins so empty of enjoyment. The Muted Screen of Graham Greene. Phyllis McGinley. FaBoEE

We're alone, Doney Gal, in the rain and hail. Doney Gal. *Unknown.* FSW

We're an Africanpeople. Don L. Lee. *Fr.* African Poems. CNA

Were [*or* Where] beth [*or* beeth] they [that] biforen us weren. Ubi Sunt Qui ante Nos Fuerent? *Unknown.* EBEV; HAP; ILP (1975 ed.); OxBM; PAIC; WeW

We're bound for blue water where the great winds blow. A Valediction. John Masefield. RhR

We're coming, we're coming, our brave little band. Away with Rum. *Unknown.* FSW

We're connecting. Poems for the New. Kathleen Fraser. IHMS; NMM; RiTi

We're 'er Majesty's bold troubleshooter; wherever they send us we goes. Bold Troubleshooters. Peter Veale. NOBL

We're foot—slog—slog—slog—sloggin' over Africa. Boots. Kipling. FaPoR

We're going to the fair at Holstenwall. Holstenwall. Sidney Keyes. FaBoTw (1975 ed.)

We're Gonna Move When the Spirit Says Move! *Unknown.* FSW

We're gonna roll, we're gonna roll. Roll the Union On. Claude Williams *and* Lee Hays. FSW

We're here to say goodbye. Beyond Silence (1). Andrew Taylor. CAAP

We're hoping to be arrested. Street Demonstration. Margaret Walker. BPo; CNA

Were I a king, I could command content. Epigram. Edward de Vere, Earl of Oxford. FaBoEE

Were I laid on Greenland's coast. Over the Hills and Far Away. John Gay. *Fr.* The Beggar's Opera. BLSo; ILP (1975 ed.); NOBE

Were I (who to my cost already am). A Satire against Mankind. Earl of Rochester. NOBE; OAEL-1; OBSV; PAIC; SCP-2

We're in the bookstore stealing poems. Shoplifting Poetry. Martin Steingesser. AAN

Were it undo that is y-do. He Is Far. *Unknown.* OAEL-1; OxBM

We're marching 'round the levee. Marching 'round the Levee. *Unknown.* AmFP

We're Marching to Zion, *with music.* Isaac Watts. BLSH

Were my hart as some mens are, thy errours would not move me. Thomas Campion. AAS

We're not going to die. For My Daughter in Reply to a Question. David Ignatow. RRA

We're older today. 6:00 A.M. Richard W. Thomas. TC

We're sailing down the river from Liverpool. Santy Anno. *Unknown.* FSW

Were Shakespeare born a twin, his lunar twin. To the Authoress of "Aurora Leigh." Sydney Dobell. PeD

We're tenting tonight on the old camp ground. Tenting on the Old Camp Ground. Walter Kittredge. BLSo; FSW; PSoN

We're the D-Day Dodgers, out [*or* way off] in Italy. Ballad of the D-Day Dodgers. *Unknown.* FSW; WTO

We're the hardrock men. Dynamite Song. *Unknown.* AmFP

Were ther outher in this town. His Sweetheart Slain. *Unknown.* OxBM

Were they ever there, whether you. Displacement. Horace Hamilton. AMV-80

We're up in a balloon. Survey. Paul Lawson. GP

Were you born of lioness in the Libyan Mountains. Catullus, *tr. fr. Latin by* Horace Gregory. NAWM-1

Were you ever in Quebec. Donkey Riding. *Unknown.* RAE

Were You There When They Crucified My Lord? *Unknown.* AH, *with music;* BPo; FSW

Werena My Heart Licht. Lady Grizel Baillie. SLP

Werther had a love for Charlotte. The Sorrows of Werther. Thackeray. FaBoCo; NOBL; PoPle; VLP

Wessex Heights. Thomas Hardy. CMoP (1970 ed.); IPWM; OAEL-2

West and away the wheels of darkness roll. Revolution. A. E. Housman. ILP (1975 ed.)

West drifts, a cathedral of air, The. Going. Richard Ryan. IPM

West End Blues. John Hollander. NYP

West Forties, The: Morning, Noon and Night. L. E. Sissman. NYP

West Helena Blues. *Unknown.* BluL

West, in Drag, The. Barbara Berman. PoUp

West London. Matthew Arnold. FF

West of Chicago. John Dimoff. RFM

West of the Sierras where. The California Phrasebook. Dennis Schmitz. AmPA

West of Your City. William Stafford. ILP (1975 ed.)

West of your door, Blue Mountain dreams of melting. Blue Mountain. Roberta Hill. VoR

West Palm Beach Storm, The. *Unknown.* AmFP

West Ridge Is Menthol-cool, The. D. L. Graham. PoBA

West-running Brook. Robert Frost. NOBA; PAIC; PiAm; SoSe; TT

West, so they say, is the home of the jay, The. Forty-five Minutes from Broadway. George M. Cohan. FSN

West Wind, The. John Masefield. PES; PPM

West Wind ("West wind tae the bairn"). *Unknown.* PoPle

West wind, blow from your prairie nest. The Song My Paddle Sings. Pauline Johnson. BPAW

Western Approach, The. Howard Nemerov. TAP

Western Movies. Jeffry Jensen. AMV-80

Western Myth, The. John Boland. IPM

Western Rebel, The. *Unknown.* APAS

Western Star, *sel.* Stephen Vincent Benét.
    "Oh, have you heard the gallant news." AIW

Western sun withdraws the shortened day, The. The Autumnal Moon. James Thomson. *Fr.* The Seasons: Autumn. NOBE

Western Wagons. Rosemary *and* Stephen Vincent Benét. BPAW

Western Ways. Richmond Lattimore. AMV-80

Western Wind. *Unknown.* BiP; CABA (1972 ed.); FF; GBP; HAP; HeIP; InPK; IPWM; MAT; NIL; NOBE; OAEL-1; PoIA; PPoD; PPP; UnPo (1976 ed.); WeW
    (Lover in Winter Plaineth for the Spring, The.) SpRo
    (O Western Wind.) HoPM (1975 ed.); PoPle; SLP; SpRo; UsP
    (O Westron Wind, When Will Thou Blow.) ExPo (1973 ed.)
    ("Western wind, when will [*or* wilt] thou blow.") BoLoP; EBEV; OLR
    (Western Winde.) LoAs
    (Westron Winde, When Will Thou Blow.) PPoe
    ("Westron wynd, when will thou blow.") GBL
    (Westryn Wynde, *with music.*) RDB

Western wind has blown but a few days, The. The Cranes. Po Chü-i, *tr. by* Arthur Waley. ECBV; OBVE

Western Wind, When Will Thou Blow. *Unknown. See* Western Wind.

Westland Row. Thomas Kinsella. NoAM

Westminster Drollery, 1671. Aphra Behn. SBG

Westphalian Song. *Unknown, tr. fr. German by* Samuel Taylor Coleridge. OBVE

Westron Winde, When Will Thou Blow. *Unknown. See* Western Wind.

Westward, hit a low note, for a roarer lost. A Strut for Roethke. John Berryman. NOBA

Westward the field of the cloth of gold. A Visit. Sherwood Anderson. PoA

Wet August, A. Thomas Hardy. PPP

Wet dawn inks are doing their blue dissolve, The. Winter Trees. Sylvia Plath. NMM; SBG

Wet Day. James McAuley. MAuV

Wet gray day—rain falling slowly, mist over the valley, A. Morels. William Jay Smith. MAT; PPoD; RFM

Wet Hair: If Now His Mother Should Come. Robert Penn Warren. *Fr.* Penological Study: Southern Exposure. NoAM

Wet mirrors covering soft peat. At Rushy Lagoon. James McAuley. MAuV

Wet Morning. Janet Frame. ATNZ

Wet Night, A. Richard Ryan. CIP

Wet Sheet and a Flowing Sea, A. Allan Cunningham. BTTM; RhR

    (Sea-Song, A.) FaPoR

Wet Snow. Norman MacCaig. MS

Wet streets. It has rained drops big as silver coins. Eighteen. Maria Banus, *tr. by* Willis Barnstone *and* Matei Calinescu. BoWoP; VWA

Wet Summer: Botanic Gardens. Nan McDonald. MAuV

Wet Time, A. Wendell Berry. PiAm

Wet Weather. Patricia Low. VGW

Wet Weather at Cannes. Edward Lear. FaBoNo

We've been here a week. Clydesdale New Town Walk. Duncan Glen. MIS

We've formed our band and are well manned. The Californian. *Unknown.* AmFP

We've fought with many men acrost the seas. Fuzzy-Wuzzy. Kipling. BTTM

We've found this Scott Fitzgerald chap. Effervescence and Evanescence. Keith Preston. OBAL

We've foxgloves in our garden. Foolish Flowers. Rupert Sargent Holland. CTV

We've made a great mess of love. The Mess of Love. D. H. Lawrence. OAEL-2

"We've no heard frae God this while." In Absentia. Alastair Mackie. MS

We've reached the land of desert sweet. *See* I've reached the land of desert sweet.

We've seen some trees when they are seized by storms. Less than Love. Aileen Campbell Nye. SLP

We've tabled it all. Tables. Naomi Clark. AMV-80

We've taken our burlap sacks and entered. The Killigrew Wood. Norman Dubie. AmPA

Wexford Girl, The. *Unknown.* AmFP

Wha kens on whatna Bethlehems. The Innumerable Christ. "Hugh MacDiarmid." EBEV

Wha lies here? Johnny Dow [*or* Doo]. *Unknown.* FaBoCo; FaBoEE

Wha wad na be in love. Maggie Lauder. *At. to* Francis Sempill of Beltrees. SLP

Wha wait if all that Chauceir wrait was trew? Robert Henryson. *Fr.* The Testament of Cresseid. SLP

"Wha you been, Lord Randal, my son?" Lord Randal. *Unknown.* AIW

Whack Fol the Diddle. Peadar Kearney. PFIr

Whale. William Rose Benét. EcS

Whale, The. John Donne. *Fr.* The Progresse of the Soule. EcS; OBP

Whale, The ("Cethegrande is a fis"). *Unknown.* OxBM

Whale, The (" 'Tis a hundred years,' said the bosun bold"). *Unknown.* RhR

Whale, The ("To explain the nature of fishes in craft of verse"). *Unknown, tr. fr. Anglo-Saxon by* Gavin Bone. EBEV

Whale at Twilight. Elizabeth J. Coatsworth. BoAnP

Whale butting through scraps of moving marble, The. Explorations. Louis MacNeice. ILP (1975 ed.)

Whale in the Blue Washing Machine, The. John Haines. CNW

Whale is killed as follows, A. Killing a Whale. David Gill. BoAnP

Whale Song. Francis Maguire. BoAnP; POL

Whales. Scott Bates. BoAnP

Whales, The. Marguerite Young. WPE

Whales have a tendency to move heavily. Whales. Scott Bates. BoAnP

Whales Weep Not! D. H. Lawrence. CMoP (1970 ed); ExPo (1973 ed.); NU; OBP; PPoe

Whaling for continents coveted deep in the south. The Unhistoric Story. Allen Curnow. ATNZ

Wham!/ Comes the wrecking ball. Construction. Virginia Schonborg. QQQ

Whan that April[l] with his shoures soote. Chaucer. The Canterbury Tales: Prologue. DuDr; ILP (1975 ed.); InPS; LFH; NIL; OAEL-1; PPP

Whan that Aprille with hise shoures soote. Aprilly. Bert Leston Taylor. OBAL

Whan that the knight had thus his tale ytold. The Miller's Prologue. Chaucer. *Fr.* The Canterbury Tales. OAEL-1

What? Langston Hughes. OBAL

What? Brian Lee. FPB

What/ has happened. Here. Robert Creeley. NOBA

What/ is it about. The Universe. May Swenson. Psy

What a beautiful day for a wedding in May! For Me and My Gal. Edgar Leslie *and* E. Ray Goetz. BLSo

What a beautiful thought I'm thinking. The Great Speckled Bird. *Unknown.* FSW

What a Coincidence? *Unknown.* AKE

What a cruel way to learn. For an Old Friend. Norbert Krapf. AMV-81

What a day, oh what a day. Shel Silverstein. OSF

What a fellowship, what a joy divine. Leaning on the Everlasting Arms. Elisha Hoffman. BLSH

What a fine tower the little boy is building with his blocks. Time. Avraham Huss, *tr. by* Mark Elliott Shapiro. VWA

What a Friend We Have in Cheeses! William Cole. OBAL

What a Friend We Have in Jesus. Joseph Scriven. BLSH, *with music;* FSW

What a Friend We Have in Mother. Charles E. Roat. FSW

What a funny thing for her to do! Nude Climbing a Flagpole. Tom McKeown. TC

What a girl called "the dailiness of life." Well Water. Randall Jarrell. NOBA; PPoD; VGW

What a Grand and Glorious Feeling. Bill Wolff. FSW

What a host you are, Mancinus. Martial, *tr. fr. Latin by* Peter Porter. OBVE

What a lovely, lovely moon. Young Politician. Alan Jackson. MS

What a malicious sense of humour. The Comedian. Irving Layton. AMV-81

What a moment of strange dreaming! Mind Flying Afar. Edgar Lee Masters. PoA

What a morning! We haven't had a day. Good Weather. Giuseppe Gioachino Belli, *tr. by* Miller Williams. AMV-81

What a Proud Dreamhorse. E. E. Cummings. VGW

What a relief, to find it in the *language.* Lapsus Linguae. Richard Howard. NoAM

What a thrill. Cut. Sylvia Plath. CABA (1972 ed.); CAPP; InPK; PiAm; TAP

What a View He Has. John Montague. IPM

What a Way to Lose the War. Luis Omar Salinas. SA

What a wonderful bird the frog are. The Frog. *Unknown.* ECBV

What a wonderful change in my life has been wrought. Since Jesus Came into My Heart. R. H. McDaniel. BLSH

What about that bad short you saw last week. Black People! Amiri Baraka. BPo

What after all do we know of this terrible "matter." Diamond Body. "Hugh MacDiarmid." TwMBP

What Ails My Fern? James Schuyler. UsP

What! alive and so bold, o earth? Lines Written on Hearing the News of the Death of Napoleon. Shelley. MBPR

What Am I? Abo Stoltzenberg, *tr. fr. Yiddish by* Gabriel Preil *and* Howard Schwartz. VWA

What am I? how produced? and for what end? Know Yourself. John Arbuthnot. PMW

What am I in the place of nourishment. A Curse on Uruk. Enheduanna, *tr. fr. Sumerian.* BoWoP

What am I? Nosing here, turning leaves over. Wodwo. Ted Hughes. NoAM; TwMBP

What Any Lover Learns. Archibald MacLeish. PiAm

What are days for? Days. Philip Larkin. EBEV; LP; PSN; UsP

What Are Heavy? Christina Rossetti. OxBChV ("What are heavy? sea-sand and sorrow.") FaBoEE

What are little boys made of, made of. Mother Goose. BBL; MG

"What are ruins to us." At Lindos. May Sarton. WPE

"What are the bugles blowin' for?" said Files-on-Parade. Danny Deever. Kipling. AIW; BTTM; Epi; FaBoBa; FaPoR; ILP (1975 ed.); InPS; NOBE; OxBTC; PBMP; PeBB; SFF; UnPo (1976 ed.); VLP

What are the five dreams of the elders? The Five Dreams. John Woods. FiCP; TC

What are they waiting for? Aren't they going to call me? Call Out My Number. Julia de Burgos, *tr. by* Julio Marzán. InW

What are we first? First, animals; and next. Modern Love, XXX. George Meredith. GBL; HAP; VPC

What are we gonna do with the baby-o? Prettiest Little Baby in the County-O. *Unknown.* FSW

What Are We Playing At? Andrée Chedid, *tr. fr. French by* Samuel Hazo *and* Mirene Ghossem. BoWoP

What Are Years? Marianne Moore. CMoP (1970 ed.); IP; NoAM; NOBA; PiAm

What are you able to build with your blocks? Block City. Robert Louis Stevenson. CTV

What are you doing? "Plus Ca Change." Philip Whalen. WeW

What are you doing here in this strange world that goes on and off. Traffic Lights. Lina Kasdaglis, *tr. by* Edmund Keeley *and* Mary Keeley. BoWoP

What are you, Lady?—naught is here. Every-Day Characters: Portrait of a Lady. Winthrop Mackworth Praed. NOBL

What are you, then, my love, my friend, my father. The Quarry. Vassar Miller. WPE

What asks the Bard? He prays for naught. After Horace. A. D. Godley. NOBL

What authors lose, their booksellers have won. On Authors and Booksellers. Pope. FaBoEE

What beasts and angels practice I ignore. Little Ode. Paul Goodman. PoA

What Became of Them? *Unknown. See* Two Rats, The.

What beckoning ghost, along the moonlight shade. Elegy to the Memory of an Unfortunate Lady. Pope. NOBE; OAEL-1; PAIC

What bird so sings, yet so does wail? Trico's Song [*or* Welcome to Spring]. John Lyly. *Fr.* Alexander and Campaspe. NOBE; OBP

What Birds Were There. William Everson. NoAM

"What bluid's that on thy coat lap." Son Davie. *Unknown.* LFH

What bring you, sailor, home from the sea? Luck. W. W. Gibson. ECBV; RAE

What business, or what hope brings thee to town. To Sextus. Martial, *tr. by* Sir Charles Sedley. FaBoEE

What can a man do that a beast cannot. In Shame and Humiliation. James Wright. CAPP

What can be wrong. Housewife. Susan Fromberg Schaeffer. IHMS; WBN

What can he want. The Panda. Harley Elliott. *Fr.* Animals That Stand in Dreams. NeAC

What can I do to drive away. To ——. Keats. MBPR; OAEL-2

What can I give Him. Christina Rossetti. *Fr.* A Christmas Carol: "In the bleak mid-winter." CC; CTV; LCL; PChr

What can I say? walking here, aware. The Chinese Graves in Beechworth Cemetery. Philip Mead. AMV-81

What can I send you under the earth. Traditional Funeral Songs. *Tr. fr. Modern Greek by* Willis Barnstone *and* Elene Kolb. BoWoP

What Can I Tell My Bones? Theodore Roethke. NOBA

What Can Lambkins Do? Christina Rossetti. PCOP

What can little T.O. do? On Tom Onslow, Earl of Onslow. *Unknown.* FaBoEE

What can melt a traveler's grief? Rhyming a Friend's Poem. Yü Hsüan-chi, *tr. by* Geoffrey Waters. BoWoP

What can the spirit believe? The Young Girl. Theodore Roethke. AnMo; LoAs; NoAM

What can Tommy Onslow do? On Thomas, Second Earl of Onslow. *Unknown.* FaBoCo

What can you do. Why Write Poetry? Pamela Oberon Davis. AMV-80

What can you do with a woman under thirty? Green Apples. Dudley Randall. FB; TC

What cannot be committed to memory, this can save. Photograph. Quandra Prettyman. PoBA

What care I if good God be. Egocentric. Stevie Smith. FaBoNo

What ceremony else? Shakespeare. *Fr.* Hamlet, V, i. EBEV

What cheerful bastard. Horace, Odes, 1, 5: Surfer's Paradise. J. M. Couper. GAS

What Child Is This? William Chatterton Dix. BLSH, *with music;* FSW

What college kids we've grown up. For Randie. Geof Hewitt. NeAC

What Color Is Lonely. Carolyn M. Rodgers. BPo

What Could Be. John Gill. NeAC

What Could It Be? William Cole. BoAnP

What could she say to the fantastic foolybear. Lawrence Ferlinghetti. *Fr.* A Coney Island of the Mind. CAPP

What could we do, he and I. Opposites. Carolyn Stoloff. RiTi

What Counsel Has the Hooded Moon. James Joyce. Chamber Music, XII. Moon

What crowds by envied power, the wish of all. Sejanus. Juvenal, *tr. by* William Gifford. *Fr.* Satires, X. OBVE

What cry was that. Encounter. Geraldine Hammond. IHMS

What danger is the pilgrim in. Bunyan. *Fr.* The Pilgrim's Progress. EBEV

What dawn is it? Aubade. Karl Shapiro. GP; VGW

What Day Is. Robert Penn Warren. PiAm

What day was it she slid. Birth of Venus. Constance Urdang. PoA

What demented malice, my silly Ravidus. Catullus, *tr. fr. Latin by* Celia *and* Louis Zukofsky. OBVE

What demons moved thee, what malicious fiends. To That Most Senseless Scoundrel, the Author of Legion's Humble Address to the Lords. Thomas Brown. APAS

What desperate nightmare rapts me to this land. Legacy: My South. Dudley Randall. PoBA

What Did I Dream? I Do Not Know. Robert Graves. DuDa

What did I find. A Is for Abracadabra. Eleanor Farjeon. ECBV

What did I study in your School of Night? The School Of Night. A. D. Hope. PoA

What did Tarzan know. Ronald Koertge. *Fr.* Tarzan. OSP

What did we say to each other. Simile. N. Scott Momaday. CDW

What did you think when first. The Triple Mirror. Gloria C. Oden. IHMS

What dire offense from amorous [ *or* am'rous] causes springs. The Rape of the Lock. Pope. AnMo; BiP; CABA (1972 ed.); HAP; ILP (1975 ed.); OAEL-1

What do a few crimes. Adultery. Alan Dugan. CAPP

What do hens say. Near and Far. Harry Behn. LCL

"What Do I Care." Sara Teasdale. VGW

What do I care. Pursuit. Hilda Doolittle ("H. D."). WPE

What do I know? myself alone. Christopher Brennan. *Fr.* The Twilight of Disquietude. MAuV

What do I stare at—not the colt. The White Horse. W. H. Davies. OxBTC

What do the people say, and what does the government do? Amours de Voyage, Canto II. Arthur Hugh Clough. OBSV; VPC

What do these old stories prove? Alfred Allen. *Fr.* Clashenure Skyline. IPM

What Do They Say. Gary Snyder. NNaP

What do we know of what is behind us? History. Arthur Gregor. TAP

What Do We Plant? Henry Abbey. CTV

What do we share with the past? Again for Hephaistos, the Last Time. Richard Howard. GP

What do you/ want, love. To be. Song. Robert Creeley. TCP

What do you call it, bobsled champion. Twentieth-Century Blues. Kenneth Fearing. CMoP (1970 ed.)

What do you do among the tomato plants? For the Poet's Father, on His Taking Up Gardening Late in Life. Philip Dacey. BrS

What Do You Do When It's Spring? John Woods. ConAP

What do you say to the voice. For My Brother Henry T. Sutton Jr. Lorraine Sutton. NW

What do you say to your mother on. Poem for My Mother. Lowell Jaeger. AMV-80

What Do You Say When a Man Tells You, You Have the Softest Skin. Mary Mackey. FF

What do you think. What Someone Told Me about Bobby Link. John Ciardi. CaYB

What, do you think, is the gypsy bible? The Gypsy Bible. Julian Tuwim, *tr. by* Isaac Komen. VWA

What do you think of the country? A Night in Nevada with a Friend from Italy. Luciano Mezzatta. PoW

What do you think of us in fuzzy endeavor. A Catch of Shy Fish. Gwendolyn Brooks. CAPP

What does It mean. Barriers I. Gerald Barrax. CSP

What Does It Mean? This Harmonica. Virginia Gilbert. NVAP

What does it mean to be born? The Point of Love. Alan Bold. SLP

What Does Little Birdie Say? Tennyson. *Fr.* Sea Dreams. PCOP
(Cradle Song.) OxBChV

What does love look like? The Shape of Death. May Swenson. LoAs; TAP

What does not change / is the will to change. The Kingfishers. Charles Olson. CMoP (1970 ed.); ILP (1975 ed.); NOBA; PiAm

What does she put four whistles beside heated rugs for? Random Generation of English Sentences; or, The Revenge of the Poets. William Jay Smith. OBAL

What Does the Bee Do? Christina Rossetti. OxBChV

What does the cracker. Self. Norman Henry Pritchard II. PoBA

What does the forest do monday through friday? Clerk's Song II. Norman H. Russell. VW

What does the hangman think about. The Hangman at Home. Carl Sandburg. AKE

What does the sea want, my clothes, my keys, my face? In Horse Latitudes. Katha Pollitt. AAN

What does the storm say? The Ways and the Peoples. Randall Jarrell. PoA

What does this sky mean to you? New Mexico Sky. Bill Pearlman. FoP

What doth he get who ere prefers. Virtus Vera Nobilitas. Mildmay Fane, Earl of Westmorland. SCP-2

What else can we do. What Are We Playing At? Andrée Chedid, *tr. by* Samuel Hazo *and* Mirene Ghossem. BoWoP

What else could we do, for the doors were guarded. Curfew. Paul Eluard, *tr. by* Quentin Stevenson. BoLoP

What face, in the water. Lament. William Carlos Williams. VGW

What face she put on it, we will not discuss. Conrad Aiken. *Fr.* Time in the Rock, LXXXIV. VGW

What Faire Pompe. Thomas Campion. Prf
("What fair pomp have I spied of glittering ladies.") GBL

What fall amounts to is really a cold infusion. The End of Fall. Francis Ponge, *tr. by* Robert Bly. NU

What falls before us like snow. Moth. Lance Henson. VoR

What favourite flowers are mine, I cannot say. Flowers. W. H. Davies. PF

What flowers come again. In Praise of Fascists. Joy Davidman. SPT

What for feere of this ferly and of the false Jewes. William Langland. *Fr.* The Vision of Piers the Plowman. EBEV

What form or shape to describe? Kabir, *tr. fr. Hindi by* Shukako Singh *and* Linda Hess. ILwL

What Form the World Has. William Bronk. AMV-80

What gall had he in him, so to begin Book VII. John Berryman. *Fr.* Dream Songs. RRA

What glories would we? Motions of the soul? The Renewal. Theodore Roethke. VGW

What Glorious Vision, *with music. At. to* Thomas Cradock. AH

What glory's this, my Lord? Should one small point. Edward Taylor. Preparatory Meditations: First Series, XXI. EAP

What God gives, and what we take. A Grace for Children [*or* An English Grace]. Robert Herrick. OxBChV; PIM; PoPle

What goes on. Poem for Mother's Day. Stanley Kiesel. HeS

What good are children anyhow? Children. Carolyn Kizer. CNW

What Good Is a Poet? L. X. Lanners. CPA

What good is it to me if long ago. Sonnet XXIII. Louise Labé, *tr. by* Willis Barnstone. BoWoP

What good is the sunshine. To Patriotic America. Herb Middleton. CPA

What grandeur makes a man seem venerable? Sonnet XXI. Louise Labé, *tr. by* Willis Barnstone. BoWoP

What great genius invented the waiting room? Waiting Rooms. Howard Nemerov. PoA

What great relief to stand here in the street. Walking Around. David Galler. AMV-81

What great yoked brutes with briskets low. Crossing the Plains. Joaquin Miller. AmVN; BPAW

What had become very clear to him. Abraham. Stephen Mitchell. VWA

What had you been thinking about. The Tennis Court Oath. John Ashbery. NoAM; TAP

What hand, what skill can form the artful piece. Advice to a Painter. *Unknown.* APAS

What Happened. Dorothy Aldis. ECBV

What Happened Here Before. Gary Snyder. NNaP

What happened there, it was not much. The Well House. Robert Penn Warren. PiAm

What happened to Cassandra? Burn Down the Icons. Grace Schulman. GP

What happened to Joey on our block. Of Kings and Things. Lillian Morrison. NCSH

What happened to the iceman after all? The Iceman. Gordon Challis. ATNZ

What happened to the ten lost tribes. Exile. Chana Bloch. GP

What Happened? What Do You Expect? Alan Dugan. NowV

What Happens. June Jordan. BPo

What happens to a dream deferred? Harlem [or Dream Deferred]. Langston Hughes. Fr. Lenox Avenue Mural. AmNP (1974 ed.); BiP; CABA (1972 ed.); CoPAm; FF; HeIP; HoPM (1975 ed.); ILP (1975 ed.); InPK; InPS; IP; NIL; PBMP; PoBA; PoIA; PPP; SoSe; WIF

What happens when the dog sits on a tiger. What Happens. June Jordan. BPo

What happens when the juice of the sun. Sunjuice. Erica Jong. MMD

What Happiness Can Equal Mine, with music. John David. AH

What happiness you gave to me. The Yew-Tree. Unknown, tr. by Geoffrey Grigson. GBL

What Hart Crane Meant. Thomas Head. PoW

What has aged you so. Yehuda Amichai. Seymour Mayne. VWA

What has become of our astonishment. The Way We Wonder. Robert Pack. WIF

What has bent you. The Pine at Timber-Line. Harriet Monroe. PoA

What Has Happened. Charles Angoff. AMV-81

What has happened in the world? Volcanic Venus. D. H. Lawrence. InPS; POL

What Has Happened to Lulu? Charles Causley. DuDr

What has risen in the dark and is? Voice in the Dark. A. L. Strauss, tr. by Robert Friend. VWA

What has the sea swept up? The Shell. Mary Webb. EcS

What has this bugbear death to frighten man. Against the Fear of Death. Lucretius, tr. by Dryden. Fr. De Rerum Natura. OAEL-1; OBVE

What has want to give. Envoi. Kathleen Raine. WPE

What hath man done that man shall not undo. He Was Made Man. Giles Fletcher the Younger. Fr. Christ's Victory and Triumph, I. BoReV

"What have I earned for all that work," I said. The People. W. B. Yeats. CMoP (1970 ed.)

What have I gilt, allace! or what deservit. Lancelot's Soliloquy in Prison. Unknown. Fr. Lancelot of the Laik. SLP

What have I made. The Children. Constance Urdang. IHMS

What, have I thus betrayed my liberty? Astrophel and Stella, XLVII. Sir Philip Sidney. GBL; LoAs; NIL

What Have They Done to the Rain. Malvina Reynolds. FSW; PoRo

What have we done? What cruel passion moved thee. Dialogue after Enjoyment. Abraham Cowley. BoLoP

"What have you there?" the great Panjandrum said. The Truant. E. J. Pratt. NoAM

What! Hayes acquitted! Armstrong's magazine! True and Joyful News. Unknown. APAS

What He Says. Robert Wallace. CoPAm

What heart could have thought you? To a Snow-Flake. Francis Thompson. FSFS

What heartache—ne'er a hill! From the Flats. Sidney Lanier. NOBA

What heav'n-intreated [or heaven-besieged] heart is this. To the Noblest and Best of Ladyes [or A Letter to the Countess of Denbigh]. Richard Crashaw. BoReV; MetP

What helps it if of love I sing. Hadewijch, tr. fr. Dutch by Frans van Rosevelt. PBWP

What Her Girl-Friend[s] Said to Her. Okkur Macatti, tr. fr. Tamil by A. K. Ramanujan. BoWoP; PBWP

What Holds the Universe Together. James Broughton. MIT

What hope is that? Alexander Smith. Fr. A Life-Drama. VLP

What Horace says is. Eheu Fugaces. "Thomas Ingoldsby." FaBoEE

What horrid sin condemned the teeming Earth. On Tobacco. Charles Cotton. OBSV

What hours I spent of precious time. Poetical Economy. Harry Graham. FaBoCo

What huge wooden grasshopper is crawling the hill? The Flow of Them All. Vicki Viidikas. FPA

What humour can be so rare. Sister Juana Inés de la Cruz, tr. by Judith Thurman. Fr. A Satirical Romance. PBWP

What hurrying human tides, or day or night! Broadway. Walt Whitman. NYP

What I am fashioning. After the Engraving. David Bromige. MIT

What I Did Last Summer. Ron Ikan. AMV-80

What I Expected. Stephen Spender. IPWM; NoAM; NOBE

What I fancy, I approve. No Loathsomeness in Love. Robert Herrick. BBL; GBL; PBMP

What I got out of women. The Stolen Peonies. William Carlos Williams. TT

What I Have. Susan North. AMV-81

What I have been is somewhere in this room. A Chiffonier with Glass Flowers. Reuel Denney. PHC

What I Know. Morton Marcus. SFF

What I like about Clive. Lord Clive. E. C. Bentley. Fr. Clerihews. NOBL; PoPle

What I like most is when. Crimes of Passion: The Slasher. Terry Stokes. AmPA

What I remember. Memory of a Porch. Donald Justice. NCSH

What I remember about that day. The 1st. Lucille Clifton. CAAP; InPS; TSWA

What I remember is fire, orange fire. The Janitor; Kindergarten, Corinth. Charles Wright. Fr. Tattoos. GP

What I Saw. Robert Duncan. NoAM; NOBA

What I shall leave thee none can tell. To His Son, Vincent Corbet. Richard Corbet. OxBChV

What I Tell Him. Simon J. Ortiz. CDW

What I Think of Hiawatha. J. W. Morris. SpRo

What I thought was love. The Liar. Amiri Baraka. NOBA; WIF

What I took in my hand. Song. Robert Creeley. PoA

What I walked down to the highway. Another Sunday Morning. Carter Revard. VoR

What I Want. Wing Tek Lum. PHC

What I Want in a Husband Besides a Mustache. Diane Wakoski. PPoD

What I wanted. In Weather. Robert Hass. AmPA

What I was would not work. Encounter in the Cage Country. James Dickey. BiP; CAPP

What I would be doing if I were out. Dreaming about Freedom. Jimmy Santiago Baca. AMV-80

What If. Myra Cohn Livingston. CC

What if a day, or a month, or a yeare. Thomas Campion. AAS; BiP; EBEV; ILP (1975 ed.)

What If a Much of a Which of a Wind. E. E. Cummings. NOBA; PoA; PPM; PPP; SoSe

What if before cars and transistors. Bettystown. Sydney Bernard Smith. IPM

What if he came back astounded. Hero. William Stafford. WasP

What if I bade you leave. Those Images. W. B. Yeats. CMoP (1970 ed.)

What if I know, Liebknecht, who shot you dead. January 1919. Christopher Middleton. TwMBP

What if I own more paper clips than I'll ever use. Jim Harrison. *Fr.* Letters to Yesenin. TC

What if it *was* a. For Tinkers Who Travel on Foot. Margaret Avison. NoAM

What if jealousy is just a bad dream? Miriam Palmer. NMM

What if Orpheus,/ confident in the hard. Orpheus in Greenwich Village. Jack Gilbert. POL

What if some little pain the passage have. Spenser. *Fr.* The Faerie Queene, I, ix. PoPle

What If the Saint Must Die, *with music.* John Peck. AH

What if these long races go on repeating themselves. Written in Dejection near Rome. Robert Bly. CoPAm

What if this present were the world's last night? Holy Sonnets, XIII. John Donne. BoReV; EBEV; ExPo (1973 ed.); HeIP; ILP (1975 ed.); InPS; PIM

What in our lives is burnt. August 1914. Isaac Rosenberg. EBEV; NOBE; OxBTC

What, in the Register of Doom, is writ. Bishop Orders His Tomb in St. Praxed's. Morris Bishop. OBAL

What in the World. Eve Merriam. ECBV

What! Irving? thrice welcome, warm heart, and fine brain. Irving. James Russell Lowell. *Fr.* A Fable for Critics. TAP

What is/ eternity? Home Alone These Last Hours of the Afternoon, Dusk Now, the Sabbath Setting In, I Sit Back, and These Words Start Welling Up in Me. Stephen Levy. VWA

What is a Communist? One who has yearnings. On Communists. Ebenezer Elliott. NOBL

What is a first love worth except to prepare for a second? John Milton Hay. FaBoEE

What Is a Jewish Poem? Myra Sklarew. VWA

What is a kiss? Why this, as some approve. A Kiss. Robert Herrick. CaPo

What is a modern Poet's fate? Thomas Hood. FaBoEE

What Is a Sonnet? Edward Watkins. AMV-80

What is a woman that you forsake her. Harp Song of the Dane Women. Kipling. *Fr.* Puck of Pook's Hill. HAP

What is Africa to me. Heritage. Countee Cullen. AmNP (1974 ed.); BPo; NoAM; PoBA; WIF

What is an epigram? a dwarfish whole. Samuel Taylor Coleridge. FaBoEE; NIL

What Is, and What Is Not for Woman. Eliza R. Snow. WPW

What Is Being Forgotten. Eloise Klein Healy. GP

What is black. Canto 4: Gullfish. Tom Weatherly. PoBA

What is bright or rare here, is called oriental. Two Figures. Molly Peacock. AMV-81

What is green in me. Stepping Westward. Denise Levertov. CAPP; NMM; Psy; VGW; WBN

What is happening to me now that loved faces. Childhood in Jacksonville, Florida. Jane Cooper. TAP

What Is He? D. H. Lawrence. SFF

What is he buzzing in my ears? Confessions. Robert Browning. NOBE; PoPle; UsP

What is he, this lordling, that cometh from the fight. Who Is This That Cometh from Edom? William Herebert. BoReV; OxBM

What Is It? Marie Louise Allen. CTV

What-Is-It, A. Ruth McEnery Stuart *and* Albert Bigelow Paine. TDH

What is it about a Great Northern boxcar. Great Northern. Dave Etter. CoPAm

What is it, children, sons of the ancient house of Cadmus? Oedipus Tyrannus. Sophocles, *tr. by* Luci Berkowitz *and* Theodore F. Brunner. NAWM-1

What is it, inside them and undeniable. The King's Men. William Heyen. PoA

What is it like to have just one shirt. The Likeness. Leonard Nathan. GP

What Is It Makes the Stranger? Robin Hyde. ATNZ

What is it men in women do require? The Question Answer'd. Blake. *Fr.* Several Questions Answered. FaBoEE; GBL; MBPR; NIL; OAEL-2

What is it more eyes doth wear. *Unknown.* GBP

What is it now with me. Fear of Death. John Ashbery. TAP

What is it to grow old? Growing Old. Matthew Arnold. OAEL-2; VLP; VoPo

"What is it you're mumbling, old Father, my Dad?" By the Exeter River. Donald Hall. AIW; MPo

What Is Left? Assata Shakur. AMV-80

What Is Left? István Vas, *tr. fr. Hungarian by* Emery George. VWA

What is Life? Samuel Taylor Coleridge. MBPR

What Is Lived. Carmen Valle, *tr. fr. Spanish by* Julio Marzán. InW

What is Man's Body? *Gond Oral Tradition, tr. by* V. Elwin *and* S. Hivale. WTO

What is more gentle than a wind in summer? Sleep and Poetry. Keats. FSFS; MBPR

What is more lovely than a day of sunshine. O Sole Mio. Eduardo di Capua. BLSH

What Is Needed. Marcos Rodríguez Frese, *tr. fr. Spanish by* Julio Marzán. InW

What Is Once Loved. Elizabeth J. Coatsworth. OSP

What is our innocence. What Are Years? Marianne Moore. CMoP (1970 ed.); IP; NoAM; NOBA; PiAm

What Is Our Life? A Play of Passion. Sir Walter Ralegh. EBEV; FaBoEE; ILP (1975 ed.); InPK; NIL; PPoD (All the World's a Stage.) NOBE (On the Life of Man.) AAS; OAEL-1

What is—"Paradise." Emily Dickinson. CMoP (1970 ed.)

What Is Pink? Christina Rossetti. OxBChV

What Is Red? Mary O'Neill. FPB

What Is Salt? John Vernon. PPoD

What Is She Trying to Do, to Pattern Love. Besmilr Brigham. RiTi

What is showed was always the same. The Night Mirror. John Hollander. Prf

What is so strange about a tree alone in an open field? Hunting Pheasants in a Cornfield. Robert Bly. ConAP

What is Stonehenge? It is the roofless past. Siegfried Sassoon. *Fr.* The Heart's Journey. PES

What is that growling! Screeching! Barking! Spring Cleaning. Phillip William George. VoR

What is the beginning? Love. Start and Goal. Christina Rossetti. VoPo

What is the boy now, who has lost his ball. The Ball Poem. John Berryman. FF; LiSP; NoAM; NOBA; SoSe; SPo

What Is the Case in Point? Abraham Reisen, *tr. fr. Yiddish by* Richard J. Fein. VWA

What is the head. Some Last Questions. W. S. Merwin. CAPP

What is the metre of the dictionary? Altarwise by Owl-Light, IV. Dylan Thomas. CMoP (1970 ed.)

What is the moral? Who rides may read. The Winner. Kipling. *Fr.* The Story of the Gadsbys. FaPoR

What is the name of King Ringang's daughter? Beauty Rohtraut. Eduard Möricke, *tr. by* George Meredith. OBVE

What is the silly radish doing. Martha Baird. *Fr.* Purpose for Radishes. OSP

What is the sorriest thing that enters Hell? Vain Virtues. Dante Gabriel Rossetti. The House of Life, LXXXV. VLP

What is the use of the rule insane. The Solution. Brian Merriman, *tr. by* Arland Ussher. *Fr.* The Midnight Court. BIrV

"What is the world, o soldiers?" Napoleon. Walter de la Mare. FaBoTw (1975 ed.); NOBE

What is the world? tell, Worldling (if thou know it). Mundus Qualis. Joshua Sylvester. FaBoEE

What is the Ziz? The Ziz. John Hollander. VWA

What Is There. Marvin Bell. GP

What Is There? Ruth Lisa Schechter. RiTi

What is there for us. Song of the Bride. Susan Mernit. VWA

What is there in the universal earth. To the Ladies Who Saw Me Crowned. Keats. MBPR

What is there left to be said? A Farewell. A. R. D. Fairburn. ATNZ

What is there they will not do to you? The First Test. Susan Fromberg Schaeffer. IHMS

What is there to recollect? Run. Merrill Leffler. PoUp

What is this flesh and blood compounded of. Allen Tate. *Fr.* Sonnets of the Blood. PoA

What is this huge box painted red and buff. Ballade of the Old-Time Engine. Eda H. Vines. QQQ

What is this life if, full of care. Leisure. W. H. Davies. CTV; ECBV; NOBE; PPM; WIF

What is this recompense you'd have from me? From a Woman to a Greedy Lover. Norman Cameron. Three Love Poems, I. FaBoEE; FaBoTw (1975 ed.)

What is this that I can see. Oh! Death. *Unknown.* AmFP

What is this that roareth thus? Motor Bus. Alfred Denis Godley. FaBoCo; FaBoNo; NOBL

What Is This Why? *Unknown.* OxBM

What is this wonderful thing? Brown and everywhere! Looking at a Dry Canadian Thistle Brought In from the Snow. Robert Bly. NNaP

What is to be done. Virginia Scott. NPW

What Is Truth? James Wright. OSP

What is unseen. Vision. W. S. Merwin. GP

What is weaker than a god? It groans hungry. Rosario Castellanos, *tr. fr. Spanish by* Willis Barnstone. BoWoP

What is your feeling about the revolutionary spirit. Firebrand. Harry Crosby. EAS

What is your substance, whereof are you made. Sonnets, LIII. Shakespeare. EBEV; OAEL-1

What it is/ gold eyelids. Kayumangi. Jessica Tarahata Hagedorn. MMD

What it is, the literal size. The Riddle. Robert Creeley. PiAm

What It Means, Living in the City. William Dickey. POL

What it would look like if really there were only. A Small Room with Large Windows. Allen Curnow. ATNZ

What jailhouse bars are more black. The Coweta County Courthouse. James Miller Robinson. AMV-80

What Jenner Said on Hearing in Elysium That Complaints Had Been Made of His Having a Statue. Shirley Brooks. FaBoEE

What joys attend [*or* joy attends] the fisher's life! The Fisher's Life. *Unknown.* GBP; RhR

What jungles he swung out of into the imagination! Gorilla Gorilla. Bruce Dawe. CAAP

What just streamed outward from that midsummer center, not periphery? Snow in Summer. Daisy Aldan. RiTi

What! kill a partridge in the month of May. Epitaph for Mr. Partridge. *Unknown.* AKE

What Kind of Mistress He Would Have. Robert Herrick. CaPo

What Kind of War? Larry Rottman. POL

What lack you, sir? What seek you? What will you buy? Thomas Newbery. *Fr.* The Great Merchant, Dives Pragmaticus, Cries His Wares. OxBChV

What laid, I said. Rhyme. Louise Bogan. LoAs

What large, dark hands are these at the window. Love on the Farm. D. H. Lawrence. CMoP (1970 ed.); FF; OBP

What Larkin bawled to hungry crowds. Inscription for a Headstone. Austin Clarke. BIrV; CIP

What lewd, naked, and revolting shape is this? Shopping for Meat in Winter. Oscar Williams. MiP

What Lies on Us. Bruce Dawe. CAAP

What Lips My Lips Have Kissed, and Where, and Why. Edna St. Vincent Millay. BoLoP; HoPM (1975 ed.); TAP

What little throat. The Blackbird by Belfast Lough. *Unknown, tr. by* Frank O'Connor. ECBV

What lively lad most pleasured me. A Last Confession. W. B. Yeats. BoLoP; CMoP (1970 ed.); HAP; OAEL-2; STS; WeW

What love did. The beast sleeps. Brief Explanation. Claudia Dobkins. NPW

What love is this of thine, that cannot bee. Edward Taylor. *Fr.* Preparatory Meditations: First Series, I. PiAm

What lovely things/ Thy hand hath made. The Scribe. Walter de la Mare. CMoP (1970 ed.)

What Maisie Know She Don't Want No. Judith Johnson Sherwin. NoAM

What makes a knave a child of God. Samuel Butler. *Fr.* Hudibras, III, i. NOBL; OBSV

What makes all subjects discontent. Samuel Butler. FaBoEE

What Makes Echo. Margaret Cavendish, Duchess of Newcastle. SCP-2

What makes that blood on the point of your knife? Edward. *Unknown.* FSW

What makes thee, fool, so fat? Fool, thee so bare? Epigram. Francis Quarles. *Fr.* Emblems. SCP-2

What makes you look so black, so glum, so cross? Eclogue. Edward Lear. FaBoNo

What makes you write at this odd rate? Epigram on Miltonicks. Samuel Wesley. POL

What man dost thou dig it for? Shakespeare. *Fr.* Hamlet, V, i. DL

What Matter? *Gond Oral Tradition, tr. by* V. Elwin *and* S. Hivale. WTO

What may the woman labor to confess? Modern Love, XXII. George Meredith. ILP (1975 ed.)

What may words say, or what may words not say. Astrophel and Stella, XXXV. Sir Philip Sidney. CABA (1972 ed.)

What mean these dreams, and hideous forms that rise. George the Third's Soliloquy. Philip Freneau. EAP; NOBA

What meaneth this? When I lie alone. Sir Thomas Wyatt. GBL

What Means This Glory round Our Feet? James Russell Lowell. PIM

What means this stately tablature. To My Noble Kinsman, Thomas Stanley, Esquire, on His Lyric Poems Composed by Master John Gamble. Richard Lovelace. CaPo

What means this watery canop' 'bout thy bed. On King Richard the Third, Who Lies Buried under Leicester Bridge. Sir John Suckling. CaPo

What Might Pass a Man as a Survivor. J. S. Harry. CAAP

What mischief Alexander Bell sowed wide. Dear Mr. Bell. Katie Louchheim. PoUp

What mist hath dimmed that glorious face? The Virgin Mary to Christ on the Cross. Robert Southwell. PIM

What more is there to love than I have loved? Montrachet-le-Jardin. Wallace Stevens. UsP

What My Child Learns of the Sea. Audre Lorde. PoBA; TV

What mystery pervades a well! Emily Dickinson. AmVN; SoSe (1977 ed.)

What nedeth these thretning wordes and wasted wynde? Sir Thomas Wyatt, *after the Italian of* Serafino. OBVE

What need you, being come to sense. September 1913. W. B. Yeats. CMoP (1970 ed.); HAP; NoAM; PPoe

What needs complaints. Comfort to a Youth That Had Lost His Love. Robert Herrick. NOBE

What needs my Shakespeare for his honored bones.  On Shakespeare.  Milton.  FaBoEE; ILP (1975 ed.)

What never filled?  Be thy lips screwed so fast.  Francis Quarles.  *Fr.* Emblems.  SCP-2

What News.  Walter Savage Landor.  BoLoP

What news for man in a broken house, old trees.  Autumn, Thurlby Domain.  Charles Brasch.  ATNZ

What Night Would It Be?  John Ciardi.  IWK

What! no more favours?  Not a ribband [*or* ribbon] more.  To a Lady That Forbade to Love before Company.  Sir John Suckling.  CaPo; SCP-2

What no, perdy, ye may be sure!  Sir Thomas Wyatt.  AAS

What not one poem yet.  Ah.  Greg Kuzma.  NVAP

What now.  Another Poem for Me.  Etheridge Knight.  NNaP

What now spirit.  All We Wanted.  Paul David Ashley.  DNGG

What nudity is beautiful as this.  Portrait of a Machine.  Louis Untermeyer.  MiP

What of earls with whom you have supped.  The Toad-Eater.  Burns.  POL

What of her glass without her?  The blank grey.  Without Her.  Dante Gabriel Rossetti.  *Fr.* The House of Life.  GBL; VLP

What of these verses that I write.  Narcissus: To Himself.  David Galler.  PoA

What on earth!  I fear and tremble.  Darkened in the Soul.  Napa, *tr. fr. Eskimo.*  WTO

What opposite discoveries we have seen!  Modern Discoveries.  Byron.  *Fr.* Don Juan, I.  OBP

What our Dame bids us do.  Ben Jonson.  *Fr.* The Masque of Queens.  OFD

What passing-bells for these who die as cattle?  Anthem for Doomed Youth.  Wilfred Owen.  BiP; BuTh; CMoP (1970 ed.); EBEV; HAP; HeIP; HoPM (1975 ed.); NoAM; NOBE; OAEL-2; OxBTC; PPoD; PPP; PSN; SoSe; WeW; WIF

What pleasure have great princes.  The Herdmen.  *Unknown.*  NOBE

What pleasures shall he ever find?  Nil Pejus Est Caelibe Vita.  Samuel Taylor Coleridge.  MBPR

What portents, from what distant region, ride.  On the Ice Islands Seen Floating in the German Ocean.  William Cowper.  OAEL-1

What profits it to me, though here allowed.  Frederick Goddard Tuckerman.  *Fr.* Sonnets.  AmVN

What rage is this?  what furour of what kynd?  Sir Thomas Wyatt.  AAS

What remains of summer.  The Cold.  Lance Henson.  CDW

What Riddle Asked the Sphinx.  Archibald MacLeish.  HoPM (1975 ed.)

What Rider Spurs Him from the Darkening East.  Edna St. Vincent Millay.  WPE

What Robin Told.  George Cooper.  CTV

What ruse of vision.  The Bear.  N. Scott Momaday.  CDW; VW

What savage beast would willfully consent to ride jammed haunch to haunch.  Bus Ride.  Lenore Kandel.  NMM

What says my brother?/ Death is a fearful thing.  Shakespeare.  *Fr.* Measure for Measure, III, i.  LFH

What Schoolmasters Say.  Martin Seymour-Smith.  OxBTC

What seas did you see.  A Conversation.  Dylan Thomas.  RFM

What seas what shores what grey rocks and what islands.  Marina.  T. S. Eliot.  BoReV; CMoP (1970 ed.); HeIP; NOBE; PiAm; PSN; RRA; TCP; UsP

What Secret Desires of the Blood.  Nelly Sachs, *tr. fr. German by* Keith Bosley.  VWA

What seems to us for us is true.  Perspective.  Coventry Patmore.  *Fr.* The Angel in the House.  FaBoEE; GBL

What Semiramis Said.  Vachel Lindsay.  Moon

What shakes the eye but the invisible?  The Decision.  Theodore Roethke.  MPA; VGW

What shall a mote up to a monarch rise?  Edward Taylor.  Preparatory Meditations: Second Series, XCV.  EAP

What shall avail me.  The Border.  Edwin Muir.  BoReV

What Shall He Tell That Son?  Carl Sandburg.  SoS

What shall I do with this absurdity.  The Tower.  W. B. Yeats.  CMoP (1970 ed.); NoAM

What shall I do with this old hunk of a man.  Old Man of the Sea.  Donal Murphy.  IPM

What Shall I Give?  Edward Thomas.  OxBChV

What Shall I Give My Children?  Gwendolyn Brooks.  BPo

What Shall I Pray for Today? *with music.*  Albert Morehead *and* James Morehead.  BLSH

What shall I say, because talk I must?  The Yellow Flower.  William Carlos Williams.  HAP; PiAm

What shall I say, my deare deare Lord? most deare.  Edward Taylor.  Preparatory Meditations: Second Series, CXLII.  EAP

What shall I say, my Lord?  With what begin?  Edward Taylor.  Preparatory Meditations: Second Series, XXIX.  HAP

What shall Presto do for pretty prattle.  Swift.  Delmore Schwartz.  PoA

What! shall that sudden blade.  Custer.  Edmund Clarence Stedman.  BPAW

What shall the world do with its children?  Romans Angry about the Inner World.  Robert Bly.  NoAM; NOBA; PPoe

What shall we be, sweet, you and I.  These Bones.  Thomas Herbert Parry-Williams, *tr. by* H. Idris Bell.  OBW

What shall we do.  Songs of the Priestess.  Malka Heifetz Tussman, *tr. by* Marcia Falk.  VWA

What shall we do for timber?  Kilcash.  *Unknown, tr. by* Frank O'Connor.  BIrV; PFIr

What Shall We Do with a Drunken Sailor?  *Unknown.*  FSW (Drunken Sailor, The, *with music.*)  GSB

What shall we sing? sings Harry.  Themes.  Denis Glover.  ATNZ

What shall we think!  Can people give away.  Dryden.  *Fr.* Absalom and Achitophel, Pt. I.  ILP (1975 ed.)

What She Said.  Maturai Eruttalan Centamputan, *tr. fr. Tamil by* A. K. Ramanujan.  BoLoP

What She Said to Her Girl-Friend.  Venmanipputi, *tr. fr. Tamil by* A. K. Ramanujan.  PBWP

What She Wanted.  Ronald Koertge.  GP

What She Wished.  Marilyn Throne.  AMV-81

What Ship Is This?  *Unknown.  See* Old Ship of Zion.

What sholde I saye? but, at the monthes ende.  The Wife's Fifth Husband.  Chaucer.  *Fr.* The Canterbury Tales: The Wife of Bath's Prologue.  OxBM

What should I say.  Farewell.  Sir Thomas Wyatt.  GBL; LoAs; NOBE

What should I speak in praise of Surrey's skill.  Verse in Praise of Lord Henry Howard, Earl of Surrey.  George Turberville.  PAIC

What should one.  The Picture of J. T. in a Prospect of Stone.  Charles Tomlinson.  PPP

What should we be without the sexual myth.  Men Made out of Words.  Wallace Stevens.  NOBA; TAP; VGW

What should we have taken.  Provisions.  Margaret Atwood.  IHMS

What should we know.  Verse.  Oliver St. John Gogarty.  WIF

What since August, when the sound.  Natural History.  Richard Howard.  TAP

What siren zooming is sounding our coming.  The Exiles.  W. H. Auden.  OxBTC

What slender youth, bedew'd with liquid odors. To Pyrrha. Horace, *tr. by* Milton. Odes, I, 5. EBEV; LoAs; OBVE; SCP-1

What smouldering senses in death's sick delay. The Kiss. Dante Gabriel Rossetti. The House of Life, VI. VLP

What so beyond all madness is the elf. Cupid Far Gone. Richard Lovelace. CaPo

What? So Soon! Langston Hughes. ILP (1975 ed.)

What soft, cherubic creatures. Emily Dickinson. AmVN; CABA (1972 ed.); HAP; WIF; WPE

What solemn sound the ear invades. Mount Vernon. *Unknown.* AmFP; OFD

What Someone Said When He Was Spanked. John Ciardi. FPB

What Someone Told Me about Bobby Link. John Ciardi. CaYB

What sort of man could inspire fear. Working for Dr. No. Valery Nash. PPoD

What soul would bargain for a cure that brings. Modern Love, XIV. George Meredith. PAIC

What sound awoke me? Dragon Skate. Gladys Cardiff. CDW

What sower walked over earth. Sunflower. Rolf Jacobsen, *tr. by* Robert Bly. NU

What spirit touched the faded lambrequin. The Ilex Tree. Agnes Lee. PoA

What Splendid Rays, *with music.* Christian Gregor, *tr. fr. German.* AH

What sticks with me is the pit. Moonwalk. John Engels. MAT

What, Still Alive at Twenty-two. Hugh Kingsmill. FaBoCo; InPK; NOBL; SpRo

What strange pleasure do they get who'd. Lew Welch. VoA

What stripling now thee discomposes. Horace, *tr. by* Sir Richard Fanshaw. Odes, I, 5. OBVE

What sugred termes, what all-perswading arte. Diella, IV. Richard Lynche. AAS; NIL

What sweeter music[k] can we bring. A Christmas Carol Sung to the King at Whitehall. Robert Herrick. PChr; PIM

What tag or term long to remain. True Religion. Forrest Anderson. AATT

What the Birds Said. Whittier. NOBA

What the Bones Do. David Bissonette. PoW

What the Bullet Sang. Bret Harte. PeD

What the Chairman Told Tom. Basil Bunting. OxBTC; TwMBP

What the child wants longs the man for. Ice Cream in Paradise. Robert Hollander. AMV-80

What the Devil Said. James Stephens. CMoP (1970 ed.)

What the Engines Said. Bret Harte. BPAW

What the eye sees is a dream of sight. To the Hand. W. S. Merwin. EAS

What the Moon Saw. Vachel Lindsay. FaBoEE

What the people learn out of lifting and hauling. Carl Sandburg. The People, Yes, Sec. 32. OBAL

What the Sonnet Is. Eugene Lee-Hamilton. HoPM (1975 ed.)

What the sun gives us. Cows Grazing at Sunrise. William Matthews. AMV-81

What the Thrush Said. Keats. EBEV; NIL; OBP

What the Thunder Said: A Fire Sermon. Sol Funaroff. SPT

What the Violins Sing in Their Baconfat Bed. Jean Arp, *tr. fr. French by* John Frederick Nims. WeW

What the wind harried, the fire worried. Deadfall. Martha Keller. ECBV

What Then? W. B. Yeats. CMoP (1970 ed.)

What then is poetry. Poetry. Claude Vigée, *tr. by* Anthony Rudolf. VWA

What thing/ should I sing. Dove. Norma Farber. PChr

What thing did I love that walks the street. The Contemporary Muse. Edgell Rickword. OBSV

What Thing Is Love? George Peele. *Fr.* The Hunting of Cupid. LoAs; NOBE

What things are steadfast? Not the birds. We Manage Most When We Manage Small. Linda Gregg. AmPA

What think you of this age now. Song. *Unknown.* APAS

What this mountain means, and the murky dale. William Langland, *mod. by* J. B. Trapp. *Fr.* The Vision of Piers Plowman, Passus I. OAEL-1

What thou lovest well remains. Ezra Pound. *Fr.* Cantos, LXXXI. CMoP (1970 ed.); FaBoTw (1975 ed.); InPS; NOBE

What Thou Lovest Well, Remains American. Richard Hugo. GP

What though, for showing truth to flatter'd state. Written on the Day That Mr. Leigh Hunt Left Prison. Keats. MBPR

What though my penne wax faynt. To Maystres Jane Blenner-Haiset. John Skelton. *Fr.* The Garlande of Laurell. AAS

What though while the wonders of nature exploring. To Some Ladies. Keats. MBPR

What thoughts I have of you tonight, Walt Whitman. A Supermarket in California. Allen Ginsberg. ConAP; CoPAm; HAP; HeIP; ILP (1975 ed.); NIL; NOBA; PBMP; PiAm; PPoD; TAP; TCP; TPo; UnPo (1976 ed.); VoA

What thwarts this fear I love. Sonnet. Ted Berrigan. CAAP

What Tidings? John Audelay. OxBM

What time the poet hath hymned. Oh, Hollow! Hollow! Hollow! W. S. Gilbert. FaBoNo

What Tomas Said in a Pub. James Stephens. CMoP (1970 ed.); NoAM

What Train Will Come? William Jay Smith. PPoD

What trifling coil do we poor mortals keep. Human Life. Matthew Prior. FaBoEE

What truly is will have no end. For an Amulet. A. R. D. Fairburn. ATNZ

What unknown affinity. The Search. Denis Glover. ATNZ

What vaileth trouth? or by it to take payn? Sir Thomas Wyatt. AAS

What vision or blindness lives. East Kentucky, 1967. Wendell Berry. CSP

What was ashore, then? . . . Cargoed with forget. Sonnet. John Berryman. Epi

What was he doing, the great god Pan. A Musical Instrument. Elizabeth Barrett Browning. ILP (1975 ed.); OAEL-2; OBP; VPC; WPE

What was he like, my God, what was he like? Fleeting Return. Juan Ramon Jimenez, *ad. by* William Moritz. AMV-80

What was her beauty in our first estate. She. Richard Wilbur. AnMo; ConAP; NIL

What Was Her Name? John Ciardi. MiP

What was it/ that caught in our throats that day. The Greek Room. James W. Thompson. BPo

What was it called. Custer Lives in Humbolt County. Janet Campbell Hale. UsP; VoR

What, was it Eden's apple. Fungi. David Lake. FPA

What was it like, that country house? Country Villa. Jean Garrigue. TAP

What was it the engines said. What the Engines Said. Bret Harte. BPAW

What was it? What was it? Woman as Market. Muriel Rukeyser. WBN

What was it you remember—the summer mornings. To Any Member of My Generation. George Barker. PAIC

What was most striking about them. Concerning the Dead Women: The Munitions Plant Explosion: June, 1918. Elizabeth Libbey. AmPA

What was that sound we heard. Why Must You Know? John Wheelwright. VGW

What was the name you called me? Evening Waterfall. Carl Sandburg. UsP

What was your war record, Prytherch? For the Record. R. S. Thomas. LP; MPo

What way does the Wind come? What way does he go? Address to a Child during a Boisterous Winter Evening. Dorothy Wordsworth. OxBChV

What We Can. Ray A. Young Bear. VoR

What We Have. Elizabeth Shinoda. PHC

What we have here is animal magick: the fox. The Joke and the Stars. Ted Berrigan. FiCh

What We Move Thru. Stephen Shrader. PHC

What We Said. W. D. Snodgrass. GP

What weight of ancient witness can prevail. Revelation [or Confessio Fidei]. Dryden. *Fr.* The Hind and the Panther, I. BoReV; NOBE

What Were They Like? Denise Levertov. HeIP; NIL; PPoD; TCP; VGW; WPE

What were we playing? Was it prisoner's base? Running. Richard Wilbur. NCSH

What Wild Dawns There Were. Denise Levertov. NOBA

What Wild-eyed Murderer. Peter Meinke. AATT

What will become of Hawaii? The Leper. Ka-'ehu, *tr. by* M. K. Pukui *and* A. L. Korn. WTO

What will i do next? My Star Spangled-Red Striped Socks. Abelardo Delgado. FoP

What will I do with seven billion cubic feet of clouds. Ghazal. Jim Harrison. WeW

What will it be like, the day death comes? The Day Death Comes. Faiz Ahmed Faiz, *tr. by* Naomi Lazard. AMV-81

What Will Remain after Me? Mendel Naigreshel, *tr. fr. Yiddish by* Joachim Neugroschel. VWA

What Will We Do for Linen? *Unknown.* GBP ("Och! what shall we do for linen?") WTO

"What will you have for your birthday?" Birthday Gifts. Herbert Asquith. OFD

What wonder strikes the curious, while he views. The Ants. John Clare. BoAnP

What wondrous life is this I lead! Andrew Marvell. *Fr.* The Garden. FSFS

What Wondrous Love Is This. *Unknown. See* Wondrous Love.

What wondrous pretty things I've seen. Young Master's Account of a Puppet Show. John Marchant. OxBChV

What word have you, interpreters, of men. Of Heaven Considered as a Tomb. Wallace Stevens. PoA

What words are these have fallen from me. Tennyson. In Memoriam A. H. H., XVI. EBEV

What words can you. The Death of a Symbol. Ralph Storey. SES

What worked/ for Donne. O My America. D. M. Thomas. TwMBP

What worth to me the seven treasures. An Elegy on the Death of Furuhi. Yamanoue Okura. DL

What Would I Do White? June Jordan. NMM

What would I do without this world faceless incurious. Samuel Beckett. NoAM

What would it mean to lose this life. Now It Can Be Told. Philip Levine. VWA

What would this man? Now upward will he soar. Pope. *Fr.* An Essay on Man, Epistle I. HeIP

What would we do without them. The Dead of the World. Jeanne Finley. AMV-81

What wourde is that that chaungeth not. Sir Thomas Wyatt. AAS

What Yo' Gwine to Do When Yo' Lamp Burn Down? *Unknown.* BPo

"What, you are stepping westward?" Stepping Westward. Wordsworth. ILP (1975 ed.); MBPR

What You Goin' to Do When the Rent Comes 'Round? Andrew B. Sterling. OBAL

What you gonna do. Wartime Blues. *Unknown.* BluL

What you gonna do when the liquor gives out. Sweet Thing. *Unknown.* FSW

What, you have never seen a lifeless thing flower. Not Men Alone. Edwin Rolfe. SPT

What You Need. Kathleen Fraser. AmPA

What you see here is a colorful illusion. She Attempts to Refute the Praises That Truth, Which She Calls Passion, Inscribed on a Portrait of the Poet. Sister Juana Ines de la Cruz, *tr. by* Willis Barnstone. BoWoP

What You Should Do Each Morning. Brian Patten. BuTh

What You Should Know to Be a Poet. Gary Snyder. NNaP

What You Waited For. Marge Piercy. MMD

What You Will: A Comedy, *sel.* John Marston. "Now is Albano's marriage-bed new hung." SCP-2

What'd you get, black boy. Mr. Roosevelt Regrets. Pauli Murray. PoBA

Whate'er I be, old England is my dam! The Old Chartist. George Meredith. VPC

Whate'er is born of mortal birth. To Tirzah. Blake. *Fr.* Songs of Experience. BoReV; MBPR; NOBE; OAEL-2; STS

Whate'er thy countrymen have done. Written in the Beginning of Mezeray's History of France. Matthew Prior. NOBE

Whate'er we leave to God, God does. Inspiration. Henry David Thoreau. NOBA

Whate'er you dream with doubt possessed. All Is Well. Arthur Hugh Clough. ILP (1975 ed.)

Whatever constitutes. The Act of Love. Robert Creeley. GP; HAP

Whatever damn thing goes wrong. The Engine: A Manual. Michael Dobberstein. AMV-81

"Whatever is here, it is." Confessions of the Life Artist. Thom Gunn. CMoP (1970 ed.)

Whatever is inside that sheet. A-Ha! Dorothy Aldis. IWK

Whatever Is, Is Right. Frank Gaik. AMV-81

Whatever it is, it must have. American Poetry. Louis Simpson. CoPAm; NoAM; NOBA; TAP; TH

Whatever it is, it's a passion. Love in America. Marianne Moore. GOA

Whatever it may be whoever it may be. Patna-Benares Express. Allen Ginsberg. TT

Whatever it was that went wrong—the stove aflame. A Word to a Father, Dead. John Alexander Allen. PPoD

Whatever law of yours, O God Varuna. Varuna. *Tr. fr. Sanskrit by* Raimundo Panikkar. *Fr.* Vedic Hymns. ILwL

Whatever lies panting on its side. Field with Figurations. Warren Slesinger. HeS

Whatever our faults, we can always engage. The Crocodile. Hilaire Belloc. BBL

Whatever sleeping in the world awakes. Creation of Anguish. Howard Nemerov. AnMo

Whatever story of their cruelty. On the Saviour's Wounds. Richard Crashaw. PAIC

Whatever we do, whether we light. Dilemma. David Ignatow. VGW

Whatever you call it. Elegy 3. Seamus Deane. CIP; IPM

Whatever you have to say, leave. These Days. Charles Olson. TSWA

Whatever You Say, Say Nothing. Seamus Heaney. IPM

Whatever your eye alights on this morning is yours. Years of Indiscretion. John Ashbery. NOBA

Whatever's good or bad or both. Nonsense Rhyme. Elinor Wylie. PBMP; Psy

Whatfor to 3 Who Stole My Shovel. Phyllis Gotlieb. BBGO

What'll We Do with the Baby-O. *Unknown.* FSW

What's a poem? A flat piece of paper. A Poem—Good or Bad—a Thing—with One Attribute—Flat. Melech Ravitch, *tr. by* Ruth Whitman. VWA

What's become of Waring. Waring. Robert Browning. VLP

What's filling up the mirror? O, it is not I. The Fat Man in the Mirror. Robert Lowell. AnMo; PoA

What's going to be the end for both of us—God? Twelve Lines about the Burning Bush. Melech Ravitch, *tr. by* Ruth Whitman. VWA

What's in a Word? Carol Shine. NowV

What's in the Cupboard. *Unknown.* GBP

What's in the room I have never entered. What? Brian Lee. FPB

What's in There? *Unknown.* RAE

What's it like to be homeless. The Child's Umbrella. Raymond Souster. AKE

What's left of the sunset's watered blood. Working on Wall Street. May Swenson. NowV

What's life but full of care and doubt. Domestic Didactics by an Old Servant. Thomas Hood. VLP

What's Living? Linda Hogan. AMV-81

What's love that's always strong? For Anybody's Martyr's Song. Jean Garrigue. LoAs

Whats My Name if Not Everyone Elses. Luís Omar Salinas. SA

What's My Thought Like? Thomas Moore. FaBoEE
(Riddle, A: "Why is a pump like V-sc--nt C-stl-r--gh?") FaBoCo

What's on this May morning in the hills? Ascension Thursday. Saunders Lewis, *tr. by* Gwyn Thomas. OBW

What's sweeter than at the end of a summer's day. Thanksgiving. Kenneth Koch. VGW

What's that?/ An Egg. Whoroscope. Samuel Beckett. NoAM

What's that rustling behind me? The Silent Spinney. Seamus Redmond. FPB

What's that we see from far? the spring of day. A Nuptial Song, or Epithalamy, on Sir Clipesby Crew and His Lady. Robert Herrick. CaPo; SCP-1

What's the balm. Poem. Alan Dugan. CAPP

What's the Railroad to Me. Henry David Thoreau. TAP

What's the weather on about? The Weather. Gavin Ewart. BBL

What's there to say about life. Testimony Concerning a Sickness. Doug Blazek. CPA

What's this? A dish for fat lips. The Shape of the Fire. Theodore Roethke. CMoP (1970 ed.)

What's up, today, with our lovers? The Lovers Go Fly a Kite. W. D. Snodgrass. NowV

What's worse than this past century? "Anna Akhmatova," *tr. fr. Russian by* Barbara Einzig. BoWoP

What's your name?/ Pudden Tame. *Unknown.* FaBoNo

Whatsover Hath Been Made, God Made. Dadu, *tr. fr. Sanskrit.* ILwL

Whaur are ye gaun. John Hielandman. *Unknown.* GBP

Whaur yon broken brig hings owre. Song. William Soutar. MS

Wheat District, The. Ted Enslin. FAF

Wheatfields of chiffon. Best of Show. Barbara Howes. GDP

Wheel. Ciaran Carson. IPM

Wheel, The. Robert Hayden. BPo

Wheel, The. Rosalie Moore. RiTi

Wheel, The. Edwin Muir. NoAM

Wheel of Fortune. *Unknown.* FSW

Wheel, oh wheel. Zekiel Saw the Wheel. *Unknown.* WIF

Wheel Revolves, The. Kenneth Rexroth. NoAM; RRA

Wheelchair Butterfly, The. James Tate. NoAM

Wheels. Heather McHugh. AAN

Wheels. Vicki Viidikas. CAAP

Wheels hurry onward, onward, The. A Cartload of Shoes. Abraham Sutskever, *tr. by* David G. Roskies. VWA

Wheels keep pulling, The. Driving Home. Madeline DeFrees. MPA

Wheer 'asta beän saw long and meä liggin' 'ere aloän? Northern Farmer: Old Style. Tennyson. VLP

Wheesht, Wheesht. "Hugh MacDiarmid." HAP; InPK; SLP

When. Dorothy Aldis. ECBV

When-/ a nation of. And All Call Him Uncle. Antar S. K. Mberi. SES

When—/ Sir/ Beelzebub. Sir Beelzebub. Edith Sitwell. BoWoP; HoPM (1975 ed.); OBP; OxBTC

When a Beau Goes In. Gavin Ewart. OxBTC

When a Body. Gene Dawson. AMV-80

When a daffodil I see. Divination by a Daffodil. Robert Herrick. CaPo

When a daughter tries suicide. The Risk. Anne Sexton. BoWoP

When a fellow loves a maiden. La Cucaracha. *Unknown.* BLSH

When a felon's not engaged in his employment. The Policeman's Lot. W. S. Gilbert. *Fr.* The Pirates of Penzance. NOBL

When a friend calls to me from the road. A Time to Talk. Robert Frost. NCSH

When a great wave disturbs the ocean cold. The Cataclysm. Edward Shanks. EcS

When a lad, I stood one day by a cottage far away. She Was Bred in Old Kentucky. Harry Braisted. FSN

"When a little baby dies." Praying to the Stars. Patrocinio Barela. PoW

When a man gets troubled in mind. Sleepy Man Blues. *Unknown.* BluL

When a Man Has Married a Wife. Blake. FaBoEE; FF; OAEL-2

When a Man Hath No Freedom to Fight for at Home. Byron. FaBoEE; PPoe; SS

When a man like Silvestre Revueltas. To Silvestre Revueltas of Mexico, in His Death. Pablo Neruda, *tr. by* Harry Thomas. AMV-81

When a man sweats. The Dog in Us. John Barnie. AMV-81

When a millionaire gyps a millionaire. The Scab. Ettore Rella. SPT

When a missile goes over the moon. Same Old Trick. William W. Pratt. QQQ

When a mounting skylark sings. Skylark and Nightingale. Christina Rossetti. PCOP

When a player gets to thinking. Everlasting Teamwork in Basketball. H. Victory. SPo

When a ship passes at night on the Clyde. Ships. Douglas Dunn. MS

When a statue turns its real gaze. After Plotinus. William Stafford. PoA

When a Twister, a-twisting, will twist him a twist. John Wallis. FaBoNo

When a woman cannot open her heart. Inscape. Susan Litwack. VWA

"When a woman take the blues." Heartblow. Michael S. Harper. NW

When a woman you scarcely know. Chance I. Alan Austin. PoUp

When a youngster. The Honeymooners. Cinda Kornblum. AcAn

When Abraham Lincoln was shoveled into the tombs. Cool Tombs. Carl Sandburg. CMoP (1970 ed.); HAP; HeIP; NoAM; NOBA; PAIC; PiAm; TAP

When Adam dalf and Eve span, go spire—if thou may spede. With I and E. *Unknown.* OxBM

When Adam day by day. Occasional Poem. A. E. Housman. NOBL

When Adam thus to Eve: "Fair consort, the hour." Milton. *Fr.* Paradise Lost, IV. UsP

When after dinner you smoke, gentlemen, remember. Ballad of Tampa. Joseph Freeman. SPT

When, after such a length of rolling years. Virgil, *tr. fr. Latin by* Dryden. *Fr.* Georgics, III. SCP-1

When age hath made me what I am not now. Upon His Picture. Thomas Randolph. NOBE

When Albert Einstein appeared. Hour of Concern. Lindley Williams Hubbell. TPo

When Alexander Pope strolled in the city. Mr. Pope. Allen Tate. CABA (1972 ed.); NIL; NoAM; NOBA; PAIC; VGW

When all/ My waterfall. Her Time. Theodore Roethke. MPA

When all birds else do of their music fail. Money Makes the Mirth. Robert Herrick. CaPo

When all has passed. Genesis. Lotte Kramer. VWA

When all is over and you march for home. Spoils. Robert Graves. HAP; UsP; WeW

When all my dust lies strewn. In Faith of Rising. X. J. Kennedy. UsP

When All My Five and Country Senses See. Dylan Thomas. ILP (1975 ed.);NoAM; PAIC; PoA; STS

When all of us wore smaller shoes. Ancient Lights. Austin Clarke. BIrV; CMoP (1970 ed.)

When all the rubble of our fears was piled. Apocalypse in Black and White. Robert Pack. CoPAm

When all the world is young, lad. Young and Old. Charles Kingsley. *Fr.* The Water Babies. EBEV; FaPoR; OxBChV; PCOP; TPo

When all the world was sore depressed. Shirley Temple. Cyril R. Michael. PeD

When all this All doth pass from age to age. Fulke Greville. *Fr.* Caelica. EBEV

"When all this is over," said the swineherd. Swineherd. Eilean Ni Chuilleanain. BIrV; CIP; PFIr

When All Thy Mercies, O My God! Joseph Addison. PIM

When an all-American gd. An All-American Guard. *Unknown.* TDH

When any mortal(even the most odd). E. E. Cummings. FaBoEE

When are we gonna get married. Buffalo Boy. *Unknown.* FSW

When as her lute is tuned to her voyce. Giles Fletcher the Elder. Licia, XXXI. ESo

When as I do record. *Unknown.* EBEV

When as in silks my Julia goes. *See* Whenas in silks my Julia goes.

When as man's life, the light of human lust. *See* Whenas man's life, . . .

When as the rye reach to the chin. A Summer Song. George Peele. *Fr.* The Old Wife's Tale. GBL; NOBE

When as we sat all sad and desolate. Bible, *O.T., paraphrased by* Francis Bacon. Psalms, CXXXVII. OAEL-1

When at last after long despair, our hopes ring true again. Catullus, *tr. fr. Latin by* Horace Gregory. NAWM-1

When at Night. Mark Perlberg. AMV-80

When Aunt Emily died, her husband would not look at her. New England Protestant. Richard Eberhart. *Fr.* Attitudes. TH

When Aunt Insomnia came back from the planet Mars. An Evening of Home Movies. Constance Urdang. UsP

When awful darkness and silence reign. The Dong with a Luminous Nose. Edward Lear. BBL; FaBoCo; FaBoNo; VLP

When baby's cries grew hard to bear. L'Enfant Glacé. Harry Graham. FaBoCo

When beechen buds begin to swell. The Yellow Violet. Bryant. EAP; PF; TAP

When before those eyes, my life and light. Gaspara Stampa, *tr. fr. Italian by* J. Vitiello. BoWoP

When bells stop ringing—church—begins. Emily Dickinson. PiAm

When Bibo thought fit from the world to retreat. Epigram. Matthew Prior. FaBoEE

When Bill gives me a book, I know. The Christmas Exchange. Arthur Guiterman. CTV

When Billy the Kid Rides Again. S. Omar Barker. BPAW

When birds break open the sky, a smell of snow. Winter Burn. Roberta Hill. VoR

When Black People Are. A. B. Spellman. BPo; CNA; PoBA

When bold Leander sought his distant fair. On Leander's Swimming over the Hellespont to Hero. Thomas Warton the Younger, *after* Martial. FaBoEE

When breezes are soft and skies are fair. Green River. Bryant. NOBA

When Britain first at Heaven's command. Rule, Britannia! James Thomson. *Fr.* Alfred, a Masque (*by* Thomson *and* David Mallett). BLSH; BTTM; FaPoR; VoPo

When Brother Jessen showed the tawny spot. Revival. David Wagoner. CNW

When brothers build a city. Malcolm, a Thousandth Poem. Conrad Kent Rivers. CNA

When Brothers Forget. Jill Witherspoon. Boyer. CNA

When Bunyan swung his whopping axe. Folk Tune. Richard Wilbur. AIW

When Burnet perceived that the beautiful dames. An Excellent New Ballad, Called the Brawny Bishop's Complaint. Arthur Mainwaring. APAS

When by mistake you miss. Your Own Image. Michael Ryan. HeS

When by my solitary hearth I sit. To Hope. Keats. MBPR

When by thy scorn, O murd'ress, I am dead. The Apparition. John Donne. CABA (1972 ed.); ExPo (1973 ed.); GBL; HeIP; NOBE; OAEL-1; PAIC; SCP-1

When by Zeus relenting the mandate was revoked. Phoebus with Admetus. George Meredith. NOBE

When Caesar Augustus had raised a taxation. No Room at the Inn. *Unknown.* FSW

When Caesar decided to measure the world. Nathaniel Tarn. *Fr.* The Beautiful Contradictions. TwMBP

When cats run home and light is come. The Owl. Tennyson. ECBV; PB; PoPle

When chapman billies leave the street. Tom o' Shanter. Burns. OAEL-1

When Charlie Bowdre married Manuela, we carried them. Michael Ondaatje. POL

When children are born in Victoria. Life-Cycle. Bruce Dawe. MAuV

When civil fury [*or* dudgeon] first grew high. Presbyterian Knight. Samuel Butler. *Fr.* Hudibras, I, 1. EBEV; NIL; NOBE; OAEL-1; PAIC; SCP-2

When clerks and navvies fondle. For X. Louis MacNeice. BoLoP

When cockle shells turn silver bells. Waly, Waly [*or* Cockleshells]. *Unknown.* AIW; AmFP; FSW; RDB

When cold, I huddle up, foetal, cross. Christmas Eve. A. R. Ammons. TT

When Coldness Wraps This Suffering Clay. Byron. ILP (1975 ed.)

When Cotton Haymes Walks Down the Street. Besmilr Brigham. RiTi

When cripples throw their crutches into the air.  Cripples.  Nina Cassian, *tr. by* Herbert Kuhner.  VWA

When curdling mists disturb the sight's.  Midnight.  Weldon Kees.  NoAM

When Dad Felt Bad.  Charles Causley.  FPB

When Daddy Died.  Duane Ackerson.  POL

When daffodils begin to peer.  Autolycus' Song.  Shakespeare.  *Fr.* The Winter's Tale, IV, ii.  AIW; BBL; NOBE; OAEL-1; OBP; PoPle

When daisies pied and violets blue.  Spring.  Shakespeare.  *Fr.* Love's Labour's Lost, V, ii.  BiP; FF; FSFS; HAP; HeIP; ILP (1975 ed.); InPK; IPWM; NIL; NOBE; OAEL-1; OBP; PoPle; SoSe; UnPo (1976 ed.)

When Daniel Boone goes by, at night.  Daniel Boone.  Stephen Vincent Benét.  GOA

When darkness crept and grew.  Under the Hill.  Richard Eberhart.  PoA

When day dawned with unusual light.  Sudden Thaw.  Andrew Young.  MS

When de Co'n Pone's Hot.  Paul Laurence Dunbar.  AmVN

When de night walks in, as black as a sheep.  Pop Goes de Weasel.  *Unknown.*  PSoN

When de Saints Go Ma'chin' Home.  Sterling A. Brown.  AmNP (1974 ed.)

When dead the winter snows in crystals shine.  Sonnet XV.  Richard Eberhart.  UsP

When death dances in.  Last Rites.  David Citino.  AMV-80

When descends on the Atlantic.  Seaweed.  Longfellow.  EcS; RhR; TAP

When despair for the world grows in me.  The Peace of Wild Things.  Wendell Berry.  CSP; HeIP; IPWM; NU; PiAm; VGW

When Dey 'Listed Colored Soldiers.  Paul Laurence Dunbar.  BPo

When did my manhood wake to its dying!  Watching Jim Shoulders.  Leo Connellan.  TAT

When did you begin your quest?  Absences.  James Tate.  CAAP

When did you start your tricks.  The Mosquito.  D. H. Lawrence.  BoAnP; PoPle

When Dido found Aeneas would not come.  A Note on the Latin Gerunds.  Richard Porson.  FaBoCo; FaBoEE

When do I see thee most, beloved one?  Lovesight.  Dante Gabriel Rossetti.  The House of Life, IV.  VLP

When Doris Danced.  Richard Eberhart.  CMoP (1970 ed.)

When early morn walks forth in sober grey.  Song.  Blake.  MBPR

When Earth's Last Picture Is Painted.  Kipling.  VLP (L'Envoi.)  ILP (1975 ed.)

When Eastern lovers feed the fun'ral fire.  Pope.  Three Epitaphs on John Hewet and Sarah Drew, II.  NIL

When England's multitudes observed with frowns.  Bungaloid Growth.  Colin Ellis.  FaBoEE

When Eve did with the snake dispute.  The Woman's Wish.  Matthew Prior.  FaBoEE

When Eve upon the first of Men.  A Reflection.  Thomas Hood.  FaBoEE

When evening is come.  Father Is Home.  *Unknown.*  ECBV

When every one to pleasing pastime hies.  Pamphilia to Amphilanthus.  Mary Sidney Wroth, Countess of Montgomery.  *Fr.* Urania.  WPE

When every pencil meant a sacrifice.  Warren Pryor.  Alden Nowlan.  BBGO

When Faces Called Flowers Float out of the Ground.  E. E. Cummings.  ILP (1975 ed.)

When fame brought the news of Great Britain's success.  Newcastle Beer.  John Cunningham.  EPC

When far-spent night persuades each mortal eye.  Astrophel and Stella, XCIX.  Sir Philip Sidney.  CABA (1972 ed.)

When father climbed the tabooed tree and shook.  The Holy Eye Is Blind.  Stephen Stepanchev.  SA

When Father Slept.  James Anderson.  AMV-80

When First.  Edward Thomas.  NoAM

When first/ the sun smiled.  For Yvonne, My Daughter.  Tony Moreno.  NW

When first, descending from the moorlands.  Extempore Effusion upon the Death of James Hogg.  Wordsworth.  EBEV; MBPR; NOBE; OAEL-2

When first Diana leaves her bed.  The Progress of Beauty.  Swift.  AnMo; CABA (1972 ed.)

When first, fair mistress, I did see your face.  To B. C.  Sir John Suckling.  CaPo

When first I came here I had hope.  When First.  Edward Thomas.  NoAM

When first I came to Louisville, some pleasure for to find.  The Lily of the West.  *Unknown.*  AmFP; FSW

When first I knew this forest.  The Forest.  Judith Wright.  MAuV

When first I saw the love-light in your eye.  When You Were Sweet Sixteen.  James Thornton.  FSN; FSW

When first my beloved came to my bed.  Epithalamium.  John Peale Bishop.  PAIC

When first my lines of heavenly joys made mention.  Jordan.  George Herbert.  OAEL-1; OBW; PPP

When First My Way to Fair I Took.  A. E. Housman.  POL; SoSe (1977 ed.)

When first our eyes engaged the startled Bird.  Recollection.  Marilyn R. Mumford.  AMV-80

When first the college rolls receive his name.  The Scholar's Life.  Samuel Johnson.  *Fr.* The Vanity of Human Wishes.  NOBE; OBSV

When first the peasant, long inclin'd to roam.  The Young Author.  Samuel Johnson.  LAuP

When first thou didst entice to thee my heart.  Affliction.  George Herbert.  BoReV; CABA (1972 ed.); MetP; NOBE; SCP-1

When first Thou on me, Lord, wrought'st Thy sweet print.  The Ebb and Flow.  Edward Taylor.  ILP (1975 ed.)

When first thy sweet and gracious eye.  The Glance.  George Herbert.  SCP-1

When First unto This Country.  *Unknown.*  FSW

When fishes flew and forests walked.  The Donkey.  G. K. Chesterton.  FaPoR

When Flora had ourfret the firth.  May Poem.  *Unknown.*  SLP

When, for days, heavy air.  Summer Storm.  Richard B. Kent.  AMV-80

When for eternal worlds we steer.  Vain World Adieu.  *Unknown.*  AmFP

When for the thorns with which I long, too long.  The Coronet.  Andrew Marvell.  BoReV; MetP; PoPle

When fortune's blind goddess had shied my abode.  Dick Turpin and Black Bess [*or* Bonnie Black Bess].  *Unknown.*  AmFP; BPAW

When forty winters shall besiege thy brow.  Sonnets, II.  Shakespeare.  FF

When Francus comes to solace with his whore.  In Francum.  Sir John Davies.  FaBoEE

When Freedom from her mountain height.  The American Flag.  Joseph Rodman Drake.  BTTM

When from the blossoms of the noiseful day.  To My Friend.  Francis Thompson.  PoA

When from the pallid sky the sun descends.  James Thomson.  *Fr.* The Seasons: Winter.  OAEL-1

When gardens shone with flowery pride.  On a Little Boy's Endeavouring to Catch a Snake.  Thomas Foxton.  OxBChV

When Gauguin was visiting Fiji. Limerick. Victor Gray. NOBL

When geometric diagrams and digits. "Novalis," *tr. by* Robert Bly. NU

When George the Third was reigning a hundred years ago. A Ballad for a Boy [*or* The Two Captains]. William Cory. FaPoR; OxBChV

When getting my nose in a book. A Study of Reading Habits. Philip Larkin. NOBL; PPP; SoSe

When God at first made man. The Pulley. George Herbert. HAP; HeIP; ILP (1975 ed.); InPK; InPS; IP; MetP; NOBE; OAEL-1; PPP

When God Descends with Men To Dwell, *with music.* Hosea Ballou I. AH

When God First Said. Natan Zach, *tr. fr. Hebrew by* Peter Everwine *and* Shula Starkman. VWA

When God in the Bible wants to promise. As Sand. Natan Zach, *tr. by* Jon Silkin. VWA

When God Lets My Body Be. E. E. Cummings. NOBA; STS

When God makes a great Man he intends all others to crush him. Arthur Hugh Clough. *Fr.* Amours de Voyage. OBSV

When God's holy law is read out. Unity. Jakov de Haan, *tr. by* David Soetendorp. VWA

When God's parachute failed. Religion Back Home. William Stafford. OBAL

When gold was first discovered at Coloma, near the hill. The National Miner. *Unknown.* AmFP

When good King Arthur ruled this land. Mother Goose. FaBoNo; MG

When good St. David, as old writs record. In Honour of St. David's Day. *Unknown.* OBW

When green buds hang in the elm like dust. A. E. Housman. SoSe (1977 ed.)

When Greenberg Speaks, Can a Poem Be Far Behind? Larry Zirlin. AAN

When Gullion died (who knows not Gullion?) Joseph Hall. *Fr.* Virgidemiarum. TVS

When Gwen heard at last. In Memoriam. W. J. Gruffydd, *tr. by* R. Gerallt Jones. OBW

When have I last looked on. Lines Written in Dejection. W. B. Yeats. STS

When he brings home a whale. Naughty Boy. Robert Creeley. NoAM; NOBA; VoA

When he came home. Poem. Sonia Sanchez. WBN

When he came out, into the world. Born Tying Knots. Samuel Makidemewabe. TC

When he cross'd O'Connell St. For James Joyce. Michael C. Ford. PoW

When he died I threw him over the wall. Cosimo. Andrew Taylor. GAS

When he gave up mountains he became. Climbing. Daniel Mark Epstein. AMV–80

When he has tired of playing big. A Handful of Small Secret Stones. Chris Bursk. AMV–81

When he killed the Mudjokivis. *See* He killed the noble Mudjokivis.

When he said/ the erection of poetry. What Hart Crane Meant. Thomas Head. PoW

When he sailed into the harbor. Korinna, *tr. fr. Greek by* Willis Barnstone. BoWoP

When he was a young man, an invalid. Success Story. Patricia Goedicke. AAN

When he was nine years old he went. Horror Film. Vernon Scannell. HeHu

When he was young, he broke horses. The Passion Drinker. Anita Endrezze Probst. VoR

When He Who Adores Thee. Thomas Moore. HoPM (1975 ed.)

When he, who is the unforgiven. The Unforgiven. E. A. Robinson. CMoP (1970 ed.)

When He Would Have His Verses Read. Robert Herrick. CaPo; NOBE

When hearing tales of Bubba Smith. Bubba Smith. Ogden Nash. SPo

When Helen Lived. W. B. Yeats. CMoP (1970 ed.); NIL

When her large, fair, reluctant eyelids fell. Living Marble. Arthur O'Shaughnessy. VLP

When He's at His Most Brawling. Patricia Goedicke. Psy

When Hip Was King. Walter Bradford. FiCh

When his match, when his match kept missing. Shaving. Charles David Wright. AMV–81

When I/ die/ I'm sure. The Rebel. Mari Evans. AmNP (1974 ed.); IHMS; PoBA; SoS; TPo

When I/ see you. Pressure. Anne Waldman. CAAP

When I/ took my. The Watch. May Swenson. HAP; PoTa; SoSe (1977 ed.)

When I a verse shall make. His Prayer to Ben Jonson. Robert Herrick. CaPo; ILP (1975 ed.)

When I Admire the Greatness, *with music.* Jacob Steendam, *tr. fr. Dutch.* AH

When I am aching with a pain or ills. Couplets for WCW. Martha Christina. AMV–80

When I am almost awake in the morning. Curtain World. Heather Morse. CaYB

When I am alone. The Fisherman's Wife. Amy Lowell. BoWoP

"When I am alone"—the words tripped off his tongue. Alone. Siegfried Sassoon. PPM

When I am an old woman I shall wear purple. Warning. Jenny Joseph. LP; MPo; OxBTC; TVo

When I am asleep. I Can Forget. Michael Small. DNGG

When I Am Dead. George MacBeth. OxBTC

When I am dead and over me bright April. I Shall Not Care. Sara Teasdale. TPo; UnPo (1976 ed.)

When I am dead, I hope it may be said. On His Books. Hilaire Belloc. FaBoCo; FaBoEE; PoIA; WeW

When I Am Dead, My Dearest. Christina Rossetti. *See* Song: "When I am dead, my dearest."

When I am grown to man's estate. Looking Forward. Robert Louis Stevenson. OxBChV

When I am in a great city, I know that I despair. City Life. D. H. Lawrence. ILP (1975 ed.); SoSe; UsP

When I am living in the midlands. The South Country. Hilaire Belloc. PES

When I am most afraid, then I begin. The Fear. Margaret Reynolds. MIS

When I Am Not with You. Sara Teasdale. TPo

When I am old and long turned gray. 2001: The Tennyson/ Hardy Poem. Ewart Gavin. FaBoCo

When I am sad and weary. Celia Celia. Adrian Mitchell. FaBoEE

When I am very earnestly digging. Pause. Mary Ursula Bethell. ATNZ

When I asked the very old man. Quotations. George Oppen. NNaP

When I awake and look at my feet. My Feet. Louis Jenkins. GP

When I Awoke. Raymond R. Patterson. PoBA

When I awoke this morning. The Blue Animals. Jon Anderson. AmPA

When I awoke with cold. Coffee. J. V. Cunningham. VGW

When I Began This Funny Journey. Chuck Miller. AcAn

When I beheld the Poet blind, yet bold. On Mr. Milton's Paradise Lost. Andrew Marvell. TT

When I behold the heavens as in their prime. Anne Bradstreet. *Fr.* Contemplations. PBWP

When I behold Thee, almost slain. To Christ on the Cross. Robert Herrick. PIM

When I bethink me on that speech whilere. Spenser. *Fr.* The Faerie Queene, VII, 8. LFH; OAEL-1

When I call to the dead to speak, the graves. Is There Life across the Street? Robert Watson. GP

When I came back, he was gone. My Father's Leaving. Ira Sadoff. AmPA

When I Came Back to Dancing Misery ("When I came back to the stuffed dragonfly"). George Hitchcock. PCho

When I Came from Colchis. W. S. Merwin. VGW

When I came on from Santa Fe. Desert Song. John Galsworthy. BPAW

When I Came to Israel. Bert Meyers. AMV–80; VWA

When I Came to London. Rachael Castelete, *tr. fr. Judezmo by* Stephen Levy. VWA

When I came to show you my summer cottage. Summer. Josephine Miles. WPE

When I can count the numbers far. Numbers. Elizabeth Madox Roberts. LCL

When I can hold a stone within my hand. Rumination. Richard Eberhart. CoPAm

When I can read my title clear. Ninety-fifth. Isaac Watts. AmFP

When I carefully consider the curious habits of dogs. Meditatio. Ezra Pound. PBMP; OBAL; OSP

When I catch sight of your fair head. Sonnet. Louise Labé, *tr. by* Joan Keefe *and* Richard Terdiman. PBWP

When I chanced to look over the wall in the glade. Bah! Walter de la Mare. BoAnP

When I conceived the child with star-green eyes. Sea-Monster. Gertrud Kolmar, *tr. by* Henry A. Smith. VWA

When I Consider. Margaret Griffith. AMV–80

When I consider how my life is spent. Reminiscent Reflection. Ogden Nash. FaBoCo

When I Consider How My Light Is Spent. Milton. *See* On His Blindness.

When I consider Life and its few years. Tears. Lizette Woodworth Reese. PPM

When I consider wearing white. When I Consider. Margaret Griffith. AMV–80

When I cry in the silent tears. A Cycle of Tears. Jim Kraus. PHC

When I declared. Separation. Gary Sange. NVAP

When I die choose a star. For My Daughter. David Ignatow. RRA

When I die, I'll sleep. Resurrection Quatrain. Kelly Cherry. BCr

When I do count the clock that tells the time. Sonnets, XII. Shakespeare. InPS; NIL; OAEL-1; STS; VoPo

When I do it, I remember how it was with us. Making Love to Myself. James L. White. BrS

When I face north a lost Cree. Returned to Say. William Stafford. ConAP

When I faced the bowling of Hirst. George Hirst. E. C. Bentley. *Fr.* Clerihews. PoPle

When I faded back to pass. Ties. Dabney Stuart. CoPAm; LiSp; SPo

When I fall asleep. Hands. Siv Cedering Fox. NVAP; OSP

When I fall asleep, and even during sleep. Baudelaire. Delmore Schwartz. VGW

When I feel a northwest town may trigger a poem. Assumptions. Richard Hugo. CNW

When I finally read Genesis to the children. Genesis. Harold Witt. SFF

When I First Came to This Land. Oscar Brand. FSW

When I first came to town, they called me a roving jewel. Katy Cruel. *Unknown.* FSW

When I found myself faced directly. To Emily. Arthur Gregor. AMV–80

"When I found where we had crashed, in the snow." He Said. Jean Valentine. TAP

When I gaze at the sun. A Moment Please. Samuel Allen. AmNP (1974 ed.); PoBA; SS

When I gaze upon the sky. Reflection from Sea and Sky. Walter Savage Landor. FaBoEE

When I get to be a composer. Daybreak in Alabama. Langston Hughes. CNA

When I get to heaven. Happy Day (or Independence Day). James Cunningham. JB

When I go. After Grave Deliberation. Elizabeth Flynn. AMV–80

When I go away from you. The Taxi. Amy Lowell. BoWoP; PBWP

When I go back to earth. The Answer. Sara Teasdale. PoA

When I go I will give you surely. Courtship. Alice Corbin. BPAW

When I go musing all alone. Robert Burton. *Fr.* The Anatomy of Melancholy. SCP-2

When I go out to sow the wheat. To a Ground-Lark. David Campbell. *Fr.* Cocky's Calendar. MAuV

When I got to the field they were burning my biplane. Dreams of the Wars. David Young. CAAP

When I grind glass. History as Diabolical Maternalism. Michael S. Harper. NW

When I grow up. Exigencies. Michael William Gilbert. AMV–80

When I had firmly answered "No." The Last Ride Together. James Kenneth Stephen. FaBoCo; UnPo (1976 ed.)

When I had learned enough to fail every test. My Flute. Herbert Krohn. AAN

When I had spread it all on linen cloth. The Wife's Tale. Seamus Heaney. HeHu; SoSe (1977 ed.)

When I had wings, my brother. To a Seamew. Swinburne. VLP

When I hang up my blue-and-white scarf. Jerusalem. Rose Ausländer, *tr. by* Ewald Osers. VWA

When I have been dead for several years. Poet's Wish. Valery Larbaud, *tr. by* William Jay Smith. LoAs

When I have borne in memory what has tamed. Wordsworth. MBPR

When I have ceased to break my wings. Wisdom. Sara Teasdale. TPo

When I Have Fears That I May Cease to Be. Keats. BiP; CABA (1972 ed.); EBEV; HAP; HeIP; HoPM (1975 ed.); ILP (1975 ed.); InPK; IPWM; LFH; MBR; NIL; OAEL-2; OBP; PAIC; PBMP; PoIA; PPoe; STS; TT; UnPo (1976 ed.); VoPo

When I have seen by Time's fell hand defaced. Sonnets, LXIV. Shakespeare. CABA (1972 ed.); HAP; HeIP; ILP (1975 ed.); NOBE; OAEL-1; PAIC; PPoe; STS

When I have settled down in bed. The Attack. Leonard Clark. RAE

When I have talked for an hour I feel lousy. The Dancers Inherit the Party. Ian Hamilton Finlay. FF

When I Hear Your Name. Gloria Fuertes, *tr. fr. Spanish by* Ada Long *and* Philip Levine. AMV–81

When I Heard at the Close of the Day. Walt Whitman. GBL

When I Heard Dat White Man Say. Zack Gilbert. PoBA

When I heard of Neruda. Regard to Neruda. Pat Lowther. MMD

When I Heard the Learn'd Astronomer. Walt Whitman. CABA (1972 ed.); FF; HAP; HeIP; IP; IPWM; PBMP; PPoD; SFF; SoSe (1977 ed.); TAP; VoPo; WIF

When I Held You to My Chest, You Fit.  Jack Myers.  AmPA

When I hit her on the head, it was good.  Herbert White.  Frank Bidart.  AmPA

When I kiss Eve.  Eden.  D. M. Thomas.  NCSH

When I last wrote.  Letter to a Young Father in Exile.  John Logan.  CAPP

When I lay back in my chair last night.  Eat 'Em Up Smith Tells All in South Africa.  Judith Johnson Sherwin.  NoAM

When I lay down to sleep dream the Wishing Well it rings.  I Am a Victim of the Telephone.  Allen Ginsberg.  GP; NYP; TT

When I lay in my mother's womb.  Before.  Ann Stanford.  GP

When I lay me down to sleep.  Insomnia the Gem of the Ocean.  John Updike.  QQQ

When I Learned to Whistle.  Gordon Lea.  AKE

When I leave this place.  For the Far Edge.  Mark Vinz.  HeS

When I left the States for gold.  Seeing the Elephant.  *Unknown.*  AIW

When I lie where shades of darkness.  Fare Well.  Walter de la Mare.  NOBE

When I look forth at dawning, pool.  Nature's Questioning.  Thomas Hardy.  IPWM; PBMP; VLP

When I looked at my poverty.  Poverty.  Charles Simic.  MAT

When I meet the morning beam.  The Immortal Part.  A. E. Housman.  SoSe (1977 ed.); TT; UnPo (1976 ed.); VLP

When I met Vivaldi it was dark.  Vivaldi.  Stuart Dybek.  TC

When i offer the sack.  The Gifts.  Charles Levendosky.  TAT

When I perceive your blond and graceful head.  Sonnet X.  Louise Labé, *tr. by* Willis Barnstone.  BoWoP

When I play on my fiddle in Dooney.  The Fiddler of Dooney.  W. B. Yeats.  PoPle

When I, poor Lais, with my crown.  Lais to Aphrodite.  E. A. Robinson, *after* Plato.  FaBoEE

When I put her out, once, by the garbage pail.  The Geranium.  Theodore Roethke.  MPo; UnPo (1976 ed.); WeW

When I reached his place.  It Was All Very Tidy.  Robert Graves.  OxBTC

When I Read Shakespeare.  D. H. Lawrence.  NoAM

When I recall your form and face.  Recollection of First Love.  William Soutar.  SLP

When I returned at last from Paris hoofbeats pounded.  Hobbes, 1651.  John Hollander.  NoAM

When I rolled three 7's.  Situation.  Langston Hughes.  OBAL

When I Roved a Young Highlander.  Byron.  SLP

When I ruled the world at six and would go to school in three weeks.  Pigeons.  James Mecklenburger.  SFF

When I said farewell.  Return.  M. L. Sussman.  AMV–81

When I said "You have grown thin."  Meeting after Separation.  Marula, *tr. by* Tambimuttu *and* G. V. Vaidya.  BoWoP

When I Saw Sweet Nelly Home.  Francis Kyle.  PSoN, *with music.*
(Aunt Dinah's Quilting Party.)  BLSH, *with music*
(Seeing Nellie Home.)  FSW

When I saw that clumsy crow.  Night Crow.  Theodore Roethke.  CoPAm; HoPM (1975 ed.); InPK; NCSH; STS; VGW

When I saw the dark clouds, I wept.  The Clouds.  Mirabai.  NU

When I say my name, I am telling you.  Conversation with God.  Jeanine Hathaway.  AMV–80

When I saw your head bow, I knew I had beaten you.  The Last Word.  Peter Davison.  InPK

When I say transparency, I don't mean seeing through.  The Apparent.  Linda Gregg.  AAN

When I see a couple of kids.  High Windows.  Philip Larkin.  PoIA

When I see a prairie schooner.  The Prairie Schooner.  Edward Everett Dale.  BPAW

When I see birches bend to left and right.  Birches.  Robert Frost.  BiP; CMoP (1970 ed.); ILP (1975 ed.); IPWM; LFH; NoAM; STS; TAP

When I see hir forrow me.  *Unknown, at. to* John Barbour.  *Fr.* The Buik of Alexander.  SLP

When I see how high it is.  So Beautiful Is the Tree of Night.  Pauline Hanson.  TAP

When I see milk spilled on the table.  Spilled Milk.  John Haines.  GP

When I see the earth ornate and lovely.  Veronica Gambara, *tr. fr. Italian by* Brenda Webster.  PBWP

When I see the little Buddhist scouts.  Reflections on a Small Parade.  Bob Kaufman.  VoA

When I see thee, wilt thou hock.  An Epistle to Celia.  D. C. Berry.  AAN

When I see you, who were so wise and cool.  Jealousy.  Rupert Brooke.  TPo

When I see your picture in its frame.  As If You Had Never Been.  Richard Eberhart.  UsP

When I Set Out for Lyonnesse.  Thomas Hardy.  InPS; VLP

When I Shall Be without Regret.  J. V. Cunningham.  NIL (Epitaph: "When I shall be without regret.")  InPK

When I started on my life's work.  The Chemist's Dream.  Patricia Beer.  HeHu

When I strip,/ stop walking/ and drop into sleep.  Anne-Marie Kegels, *tr. fr. French by* Willis Barnstone.  BoWoP

When I survey the bright.  Nox Nocti Indicat Scientiam.  William Habington.  NOBE

When I Survey the Wondrous Cross.  Isaac Watts.  AmFP; BLSH, *with music*; BoReV; FaPoR

When I think back to grammar school.  P.S. 42.  Gregory Corso.  SA

When I think of death.  Bop Lyrics.  Allen Ginsberg.  OBAL

When I think of the last great round-up.  The Great Round-up.  *Unknown.*  BPAW

When I think of the liberation of Palestine.  Israel.  Karl Shapiro.  MPA

When I through all my many poems look.  To the Most Virtuous Mistress Pot, Who Many Times Entertained Him.  Robert Herrick.  CaPo

When I took a job teaching in Massachusetts.  To the Governor & Legislature of Massachusetts.  Howard Nemerov.  PPoD

When I veined that quick syrup.  Glucose.  Dabney Stuart.  CoPAm

When I visit Europe and America's zoos.  Zoo You Too!  Ted Joans.  GP

When I visited Fort Robinson.  Fort Robinson.  Ted Kooser.  GP

When I wake and stir, he thumps his tail.  Wedlock.  Bink Noll.  GP

When I wake up.  Remote House.  Hans Magnus Enzensberger.  LP

When I walk home from school.  Oh, Joyous House.  Richard Janzen.  AKE

When I Want to Speak.  Rav Abraham Isaac Kook, *tr. fr. Hebrew by* Ben Zion Bokser.  VWA

When I was/ thirteen I.  Spring.  Ruth Whitman.  IHMS

When I was a bachelor bold and young.  Bachelor Bold and Young.  *Unknown.*  AmFP

When I was a bachelor [or batchelor] I lived all alone [or early and young].  The Foggy, Foggy Dew.  *Unknown.*  BLSH; FSW; GBP; GSB; PeBB; RDB

When I was a bachelor, I lived by myself.  Mother Goose.  MG

When I was a bachelor, I lived by myself.  Swapping Song.  *Unknown.*  RDB

When I was a batchelor early and young.  *See* When I was a bachelor I lived all alone.

When I was a beggarly boy. Aladdin. James Russell Lowell. PCOP

When I was a blonde I. First Corinthians at the Crossroads. Bruce Dawe. GAS

When I was a boy. The Piper's Progress. Francis Sylvester Mahony. PFIr

When I was a boy, a relative. A Way to Make a Living. James Wright. NNaP

When I was a boy desiring the title of man. George. Dudley Randall. BPo; ConAP; NoAM; TC

When I was a boy, I used to go to bed. The Remorse for Time. Howard Nemerov. NCSH

When I was a boy, the Milky Way. The Milky Way. Jon Anderson. BrS

When I was a boy we always did it this way. Hunting with My Father. Tom Absher. AMV-80

When I was a child. My People. Margery Himel. IHMS

When I was a child. Moon, Son of Heaven. Miyazawa Kenji, tr. by Gary Snyder. Moon

When I was a child. Sophistication. Vassar Miller. NCSH

When I was a child. Autobiographia Literaria. Frank O'Hara. NNaP; NOBA; OSP

When I was a child. The Truth about My Sister and Me. Anita Endrezze Probst. CDW

When I was a child. Why Do You Write about Russia? Louis Simpson. AMV-81

When I was a child and thought as a child, I put. The Wandering Jew. Robert Mezey. VWA

When I was a child I knew red miners. Childhood. Margaret Walker. IHMS; PBWP; PoBA

When I was a child I liked being with people. Song for a New Generation. Gertrude May Lutz. AMV-80

When I was a child in Germany. Stiff Shirts. Derek Bowman. MIS

When I was a child of five winters. Poor Wolf Speaks. Poor Wolf. NU

When I was a chile we used to play. Children's Rhymes. Langston Hughes. ILP (1975 ed.); InPS

When I was a girl. Two Gifts. Unknown, tr. by Willis Barnstone. BoWoP

When I was a good and quick little girl. Tr. fr. Pampa Indian by W. S. Merwin. BoWoP

When I was a kid. The External Element. David McFadden. NeAC

When I was a kid I loved Shredded Wheat. Shredded Wheat. Louis Dudek. AKE

When I was a lad I served a term. Sir Joseph's Song. W. S. Gilbert. Fr. H. M. S. Pinafore. PPM; RhR

When I was a lad of twenty. I Was a Bustlemaker Once, Girls. Patrick Barrington. PoPle

When I was a learner, I sought both night and day. Go Tell It on the Mountain. Unknown. FSW

When I was a little boy. Lack Wit. Unknown. BBL

When I Was a Little Girl. Alice Milligan. PFIr

When I was a little lad. Haul Away Joe. Unknown. FSW

When I was a single girl, I went dressed very fine. Oh, I Wish I Were Single Again. Unknown. AmFP

When I was a small boy. Waolani Stream, 1955/1975. Eric Chock. PHC

When I was a wee thing. The Kirk of the Birds, Beasts and Fishes. Unknown. GBP

When I was a windy boy and a bit. Lament. Dylan Thomas. PPP; TT

"When I was a young girl, I used to seek pleasure." One Morning in May; or, The Young Girl Cut Down in Her Prime. Unknown. AmFP

When I Was a Young Maid. Unknown. AmFP

When I was apprenticed in London. Blow the Candles Out. Unknown. FSW; RDB

When I was as high as that. A Memory. L. A. G. Strong. FaBoCo; NOBL; PFIr

When I was born. The Day's Ration. Emerson. PiAm

When I was born in a world of sin. G. K. Chesterton on His Birth. A. E. Housman. FaBoNo

When I was born in the great house on the bank of the sea. Poem of Distant Childhood. Noémia da Sousa, tr. by Allan Francovich and Kathleen Weaver. PBWP

When I was born on Amman hill. The Collier. Vernon Watkins. FaBoTw (1975 ed.); MPo; OBW

When I was bound apprentice. The Lincolnshire Poacher. Unknown. FSW; GBP

When I was but thirteen or so. Romance. Walter James Turner. NOBE

When I was christened. Perambulator Poem. David McCord. CC; OFD

When I was down beside the sea. At the Seaside. Robert Louis Stevenson. CTV; LCL; OxBChV

When I was fair and young and favour graced me. Elizabeth I, Queen of England. BoLoP; NIL

When I Was Growing Up. David Vogel, tr. fr. Hebrew by A. C. Jacobs. VWA

When I Was Home Last Christmas. Randall Jarrell. AIW

When I was in Missouri, would not let me be. I Will Turn Your Money Green. Unknown. BluL

"When I was just as far as I could walk." The Telephone. Robert Frost. LoAs; SO

When I was led again to the Akedah. The Akedah. Matti Megged, tr. by Howard Schwartz. VWA

When I was less self-conscious. More Self-conscious. Steve Toth. AcAn

When I was little more than six. The Radio Men. Elizabeth Jennings. FPB

When I Was Lost. Dorothy Aldis. CaYB

When I was lying in jail with my back turned to the wall. The Jailhouse Blues. Unknown. BluL

When I was on Night Line. Ego. Philip Booth. SoS

When I was once in Baltimore. Sheep. W. H. Davies. PoTa; RAE

When I Was One-and-Twenty. A. E. Housman. BiP; BoLoP; CMoP (1970 ed.); CTV; HeIP; ILP (1975 ed.); LoAs; MiP; NoAM; PBMP; PoPle, PPM; STS; TT

When I was seventeen, a man in the Dakar Station. Objets d'Art. Cynthia Macdonald. NMM; WBN

When I was sick and lay abed. The Land of Counterpane. Robert Louis Stevenson. CTV; EBEV; ECBV; ILP (1975 ed.); OxBChV

When I Was Single. Unknown. FSW

When I was single. I Wish I Was Single. Unknown. AmFP

When I was six years old. The Chinese Checker Players. Richard Brautigan. TVo

When I was skiing. Vigil. David J. Feela. BrS

When I was small, this continent was mine. Four Spacious Skies. Susan Astor. AMV-80

When I Was Soft as Ferns. Colette Inez. AATT

When I was ten, my mother, having sold. The Year of the Foxes. David Malouf. GAS

When I was the sissy of the block who nobody wanted on their team. The Sleeper. Edward Field. LiSp; SPo

When I was 12. Nora. Fran Winant. WBN

When I was twelve I was kidnapped and sold as a slave. A Psalm of Onan for Harp, Flute and Tambourine. Alden Nowlan. NeAC

When I was twelve in that far land. Only for Me. Mark Van Doren. NCSH

When I was very very. Mama Knows. Sharon Scott. JB

When I was visiting a nephew of 10. Acrophobe and Lapidary. James Bonk. HeS

When I was wed. The Golden Witch. Alan Dienstag. MIT

When I was yong, indewd'd with nature's graces. Barnabe Barnes. Parthenophil and Parthenophe, LIV. ESo

When I Was Young. Alun Llywelyn-Williams, *tr. fr. Welsh by* Gwyn Williams. OBW

When I was young. Due Date. Seymour Cain. AMV–80

When I was young. "Chew Mail Pouch." D. L. Klauck. AMV–81

When I was young/ I used to dream. Some Ruse. Hastings Wyman, Jr. PoUp

When I was young and in my prime,/ I flourished like a vine. Thyme. *Unknown.* AmFP

When I was young and in my prime,/ I thought I never could marry. Devilish Mary. *Unknown.* AmFP

When I was young and in my prime, my age twenty-two. The Lightning Flash. *Unknown.* AmFP

When I was young, and ower young. The Deil o'Bogie. Alexander Gray. MS

When I was young and wanted to see the sights. On His Queerness. Christopher Isherwood. OxBTC

When I was young and we were poor. Modifications. Ron Koertge. MiP

When I was young I believed in intellectual conversation. In the Men's Room(s). Marge Piercy. MMD

When I was young I had a care. Soliloquy. Francis Ledwidge. HoPM (1975 ed.)

When I Was Young I Tried to Sing. Donald Finkel. GP

When I was young I us'd to wait on Massa and hand him de plate. Jim Crack Corn [*or* The Blue-tail Fly]. *Unknown.* BLSH; BLSo; FSW; GBP; PSoN

When I was young, I went to school. The One Furrow. R. S. Thomas. HoPM (1975 ed.)

When I was young I woke gladly in the morning. Hoelderlin's Old Age. Stephen Spender. NoAM

When I was young my adult peers. Hickory Stick Hierarchy. Len G. Selle. AMV–80

When I was young, my ringlets waved. The Wasp's Song. "Lewis Carroll." FaBoNo

"When I was young," said Aunt to me. Other Fabrics, Other Mores! Anna Maria Lenngren, *tr. by* Nadia Christensen *and* Mariann Tiblin. PBWP

When I was younger. Pastoral. William Carlos Williams. SoS; TVo

When I Watch the Living Meet. A. E. Housman. CMoP (1970 ed.); STS; VLP; VoPo

When I watch you. Miss Rosie. Lucille Clifton. AmPA; CAAP; CNA; NMM; PoBA; RiTi

When I went/ to Gaza and met. Samson Rends His Clothes. Anadad Eldan, *tr. by* Ruth Nevo. VWA

When I went down to the river, poor boy. Poor Boy. *Unknown.* FSW

When I went into my garden, I found. Sister Bertken, *tr. fr. Dutch by* Willis Barnstone. BoWoP

When I went into my room, at mid-morning. Man and Bat. D. H. Lawrence. BoAnP

When I Went Off to Prospect. *Unknown.* AmFP

When I went out to kill myself, I caught. Saint Judas. James Wright. ConAP; NOBA; TCP

When I Went to the Circus. D. H. Lawrence. CMoP (1970 ed.); NoAM

When I went to the station. The Kalorama Triangle. Terence Winch. PoUp

When I would squat by holes and piles of dirt. The Unloved. Robert Canzoneri. CoPAm

When I wrote of the women in their dances and wildness, it was a mask. The Poem as Mask. Muriel Rukeyser. RiTi

When icicles by silver eaves. Winter Fairyland in Vermont. Francis P. Osgood. WeW

When icicles hang by the wall. Winter. Shakespeare. *Fr.* Love's Labour's Lost, V, ii. AKE; BiP; FF; FSFS; HAP; HeIP; ILP (1975 ed.); InPK; InPS; IPWM; NIL; NOBE; OAEL–1; OBP; SoSe; UnPo (1976 ed.); UsP; WeW

When idle in a poor Welsh mining valley. Rebel's Progress. Tom Earley. OBW

When I'm Alone. Richard W. Thomas. TC

"When I'm alone"—the words tripped off his tongue. Siegfried Sassoon. OxBTC

When I'm dead and buried. Don't You Weep after Me. *Unknown.* FSW

"When I'm discharged in Liverpool 'n' draws my bit o' pay." Hell's Pavement. John Masefield. PoTa; RhR

When in disgrace with fortune and men's eyes. Sonnets, XXIX. Shakespeare. EBEV; Epi; GBL; HAP; HeIP; ILP (1975 ed.); LFH; NIL; NOBE; OAEL–1; OBP; PAIC; PoIA; PPM; PPoe; PPP; Prf; STS; TPo

When, in her sad belly. Sunup (Variation on a Theme by Baudelaire). Naomi Clark. CPA

When, in my effervescent youth. Who'd Be a Hero (Fictional)? Morris Bishop. OBAL

When in my youth I travelled. The Migration of the Grey Squirrels. William Howitt. OxBChV

When in nineteen-thirty-seven, Etta Moten, sweetheart. The Convert. Margaret Danner. BPo

When in Rome. Mari Evans. AmNP (1974 ed.); NIL; SoSe

When in that gold. Listening to Foxhounds. James Dickey. InPS; LiSp; PPoD

When in the chronicle of wasted time. Sonnets, CVI. Shakespeare. NOBE; OAEL–1; PPoe; STS

When in the company of the gods. Hilda Doolittle ("H. D."). *Fr.* The Walls Do Not Fall. NoAM

When in the east the morning ray. The Garden of Appleton House. Andrew Marvell. *Fr.* Upon Appleton House. NOBE

When in the mask of night there shone that cut. Landing on the Moon. May Swenson. TAP

When, in the middle of my life, the earth stalks me. Mona Van Duyn. *Fr.* Three Valentines to the Wide World. RiTi

When in your middle years. The Lights in the Sky Are Stars. Kenneth Rexroth. RRA

When Israel against Philistia. David and Goliath. Nathaniel Crouch. OxBChV

When Israel came from Egypt's coast. Bible, *O.T., paraphrased by* Christopher Smart. Psalms, CXIV. OBVE

When Israel, of the Lord beloved. Rebecca's Hymn. Sir Walter Scott. *Fr.* Ivanhoe. PIM

When Israel Was in Egypt's Land. *Unknown. See* Go Down, Moses.

When Israel's daughters mourn'd their past offences. Epigram in a Maid of Honour's Prayer-Book. Pope. FaBoEE

When it burns before the harps and freezes behind the easels. Hans Arp, *tr. fr. French by* Harriet Watts. FaBoNo

When it comes to sex with other men. Homosexual Sonnets. Kenneth Pitchford. GP

When it is all over. Lost Moment. Hoyt W. Fuller. PoBA

When it is finally ours, this freedom. Frederick Douglass. Robert Hayden. AmNP (1974 ed.); BiP; CNA; CoPAm; GOA; GP; PBMP; PoBA

When it is not yet day. Looking for Mushrooms at Sunrise. W. S. Merwin. NOBA

When it is plucking time for my young son. Daisies. John Stevens Wade. FAF

When it rained five days and the skies turned dark as night. Back Water Blues. *Unknown.* BluL

When It Rains. H. A. Maxson. AMV–80

When it stood, my town was small. A Beginning. David Steingass. CoPAm

When it was first placed in my care. The National Animal. Barry Schechter. FiCh

When it was late/ the Baal Shem Tov. Wonders. Shirley Kaufman. VWA

When it was spring in Wisconsin, and the roosting crows. The Crows. John Engels. AMV–81

When it's dull, or if the sun is gleaming. Going Fishing. Lexie Griffiths. RAE

When I've been warm. Realities. Shirley Kaufman. MIT

When I've outlived three plastic hearts, or four. D.O.M., A.D. 2167. John Frederick Nims. CoPAm

When James, our great monarch, so wise and discreet. Upon the King's Voyage to Chatham to Make Bulwarks against the Dutch. *Unknown.* APAS

When Januar wind was blawin cauld. The Lass That Made the Bed to Me. Burns. OBP

When Jesus' friend had ceased to be. The Weeping Saviour. Elizabeth Barrett Browning. PIM

When Jesus Walked upon the Earth. Marion Brown Shelton. CTV

When Jill complains to Jack for want of meat. Upon Jack and Jill: Epigram. Robert Herrick. CaPo

When John Henry was a little babe [or fellow]. John Henry. *Unknown.* AmFP; BPo; FSW

When Johnny Comes Marching Home. Patrick Sarsfield Gilmore. BLSo, *with music*; FSW; PSoN, *with music*

When Jones's Ale Was New. *Unknown.* AmFP

When Jordan Hushed His Waters Still. Thomas Campbell. PIM

When Joseph was an old man. The Cherry-Tree Carol. *Unknown.* AmFP; FSW

When Kai is born. Not Leaving the House. Gary Snyder. IPWM; NIL

When kids are dying, lilacs. Blue with Blue. Benjamin Saltman. PoW

When Klopstock England defied. Blake. MBPR; OAEL–2

When lads have done with labor. Humbert Wolfe. SpRo

When lads were home from labour. Fancy's Knell. A. E. Housman. PoPle

When last mine eyes dislodged from thy beautie. *Unknown. Fr.* Zepheria. ESo

When Last Seen. Hortense Flexner. QQQ

When late I attempted your pity to move. An Expostulation. Isaac Bickerstaffe. FaBoCo; NIL; PFIr

When lately King James, whom our sovereign we call. The Clerical Cabal. *Unknown.* APAS

When lean Tom Paine blew on his thumbs. Citizen Paine. James Daugherty. ECBV

When learning's triumph o'er her barb'rous foes. Prologue Spoken [by Mr. Garrick] at the Opening of the Theatre in Drury-Lane, 1747. Samuel Johnson. EBEV; LAuP

When leaving the primrose, bayberry dunes, seaward. The Constant. A. R. Ammons. HAP

When liberty is headlong girl. Liberty. Archibald MacLeish. GOA

When, like a Running Grave. Dylan Thomas. OAEL–2

When Lilacs Last in the Dooryard Bloom'd. Walt Whitman. BiP; CABA (1972 ed.); Epi; ExPo (1973 ed.); HAP; ILP (1975 ed.); IPWM; NIL; NOBA; PAIC; PiAm; PPoe; PPP; TAP; VoPo.
*Sels.*
Carol of Death, The. DL

"In the swamp in secluded recesses." RFM
"When lilacs last in the dooryard bloom'd," 24 *ll.* OFD

When little people go abroad, wherever they may roam. To Henrietta, on Her Departure for Calais. Thomas Hood. OxBChV

When, long sequester'd from his throne. William Cowper. *Fr.* On the Queen's Visit to London, the Night of the Seventeenth of March, 1789. PeD

When longer yet dank death had wormed. Thomas Hardy. *Fr.* The Abbey Mason. PeD

When, loosened from winter's bonds. Princess Nukada, *tr. fr. Japanese.* PBWP

When Louis came home to the flat. Meet Me in St. Louis, Louis. Andrew B. Sterling. FSN; FSW; OBAL

When Love Meets Love. Thomas Edward Brown. PeD; UnPo (1976 ed.)

When love on time and measure makes his ground. *Unknown.* EBEV

When love with unconfined wings. To Althea, from Prison. Richard Lovelace. BiP; CABA (1972 ed.); CaPo; GBL; HAP; HeIP; ILP (1975 ed.); InPS; MetP; NOBE; PoPle

When Lovely Woman Stoops to Folly. Goldsmith. *See* Song: "When lovely woman stoops to folly."

When lusty diet and the frolic cup. Francis Quarles. *Fr.* The History of Samson. SCP–2

When lyart leaves bestrow the yird. The Jolly Beggars. Burns. LAuP

When Ma Rainey/ Comes to town. Ma Rainey. Sterling A. Brown. PoUp

When Maggie and I were acquaint. Tweedside. Lord Yester. SLP

When Magritte died. Homage to René Magritte. George Melly. EAS

When Mahalia Sings. Quandra Prettyman. MiP; PoBA

When maidens are young, and in their spring. Song. Aphra Behn. *Fr.* The Emperor of the Moon. FF

When Malindy Sings. Paul Laurence Dunbar. ILP (1975 ed.); PoBA

When Mama lay dying. Earth Changes. Kent Shire. AMV–80

When man and maiden meet, I like to see a drooping eye. The Modest Couple. W. S. Gilbert. PoTa

When man has conquered space. Earth's Bondman. Betty Page Dabney. ECBV

When many years we'd been apart. Reminiscence. Wallace Irwin. NOBL

When Mary pulled the sorrel's reins from Stephen. Hoppy. Edwin S. Godsey. PPoD

When maukin bucks, at early fucks. Ode to Spring. Burns. OBP

When May bedecks the naked trees. The Maryland Yellow-Throat. Henry Van Dyke. PCOP

When memory's fabled daughter. Notes for a History of Poetry. David Daiches. PoA

When men a dangerous disease did 'scape. To Doctor Empiric. Ben Jonson. FaBoEE

When men beeth meriest at her mele. Think on Yesterday. *Unknown.* OxBM

When men discovered freedom first. The Ash and the Oak. Louis Simpson. ConAP

When men shall find thy flower, thy glory, pass. Samuel Daniel. *Fr.* To Delia. NOBE

When men turn mob. Music and Drum. Archibald MacLeish. TH

When men were all asleep the snow came flying. London Snow. Robert Bridges. CMoP (1970 ed.); EBEV; FSFS; ILP (1975 ed.); NoAM; NOBE; OAEL–2; OxBTC; VLP

When midnight comes a host of dogs and men. Badger. John Clare. ExPo (1973 ed.); HAP; LiSp; NU; OAEL-2; PoIA; SoSe (1977 ed.); VLP

When mine eynen misteth. All Too Late. *Unknown.* OAEL-1

When Mr. Apollinax visited the United States. Mr. Apollinax. T. S. Eliot. PoA

When Mrs. Gorm (Aunt Eloise). Opportunity. Harry Graham. FaBoCo

When moiling seems at cease. "According to the Mighty Working." Thomas Hardy. CMoP (1970 ed.)

When Monmouth the chaste read those impudent lines. An Excellent New Ballad Giving a True Account of the Birth and Conception of a Late Famous Poem Called the Female Nine. Charles Sackville. APAS

When morning came. The Brother. Peter Everwine. NNaP

When mortals are at rest. *Unknown. Fr.* The Fairy Queen. DuDr

When Moses was as old as God. Moses and Joshua. Else Lasker-Schüler, *tr. by* Joachim Neugroschel. VWA

When mother keeled over into the meatloaf. When Greenberg Speaks, Can a Poem Be Far Behind? Larry Zirlin. AAN

When Mother Reads Aloud. *Unknown.* CTV

When mountain rocks and leafy trees. Nature's Lineaments. Robert Graves. FaBoTw (1975 ed.)

When music, heav'nly maid, was young. The Passions, an Ode to Music. William Collins. LAuP

When my Beloved appears. Ibn al-Arabi, *tr. fr. Arabic.* ILwL

When my blood flows calm as a purling river. Communism. Ella Wheeler Wilcox. PeD

When my body leaves me. Gone Away. Denise Levertov. SoS

When my brother Tommy. Two in Bed. A. B. Ross. CTV

When my devotions could not pierce. Denial. George Herbert. BoReV; ILP (1975 ed.); NOBE; OAEL-1

When my father had been dead a week. White Apples. Donald Hall. TAP

When my father spoke in his natural voice. Before the Breaking. Lee Pennington. AMV-81

When my grandmother left the faces with Mr. Hughes. Deaths and Pretty Cousins. David Campbell. CAAP

When my grave is broke up again. The Relic [*or* The Relique]. John Donne. CABA (1972 ed.); GBL; HAP; ILP (1975 ed.); MetP; NIL; NOBE; OAEL-1; PoPle; PPP; SCP-1; TT

When my heart was the amorous worms' meat. The Amorous Worms' Meat. Petrarch, *tr. by* Anna Maria Armi. *Fr.* Sonnets to Laura: To Laura in Death. LoAs

When my life was thrifty, thrifty. The Shearing. *Unknown, tr. by* Glyn Jones. OBW

When my little brother chanted. William Stafford. *Fr.* Religion Back Home. CC

When my love becomes/ All-powerful. Ono no Komachi, *tr. fr. Japanese by* Geoffrey Bownas *and* Anthony Thwaite. PBWP

When my love swears that she is made of truth. Sonnets, CXXXVIII. Shakespeare. BiP; CABA (1972 ed.); EBEV; Epi; ILP (1975 ed.); LoAs; OAEL-1; OBP; PoIA; PPoD; PPP; SoSe

When my mother died I was very young. The Chimney Sweeper. Blake. *Fr.* Songs of Innocence. AnMo; FF; HeIP; ILP (1975 ed.); InPK; LAuP; MBPR; OAEL-2; OxBChV; PPoe; PPP; SoSe; STS; UsP

When My Uncle Willie Saw. Carole Freeman. NMM

When my young brother was killed. War. Joseph Langland. FF; IPWM

When Narcissus died the pool of his pleasure changed. The Disciple. Oscar Wilde. OAEL-2

When Nature dreamt of making bores. Epigram: On Sir Roger Phillimore. *Unknown.* FaBoCo

When Nature made her chief work, Stella's eyes. Astrophel and Stella, VII. Sir Philip Sidney. CABA (1972 ed.); NIL

When nature's God for our offenses died. A Stanza Put on Westminster Hall Gate. *Unknown.* APAS

When Newton saw an apple fall, he found. Moon Shot. Byron. *Fr.* Don Juan, X. OBP

When next appeared a dam—so call the place. George Crabbe. PES

When night shadows slipped across the plain, I saw a man. A Nation Wrapped in Stone. Roberta Hill. BoWoP; CDW

When night stirred at sea. The Planter's Daughter. Austin Clarke. CIP; OxBTC; PFIr

When night-time bars me in. Snowdrops. Margiad Evans. OBW

When Noah, perceiving 'twas time to embark. The Dog's Cold Nose. Arthur Guiterman. ECBV; GDP; PoTa

When nothing is happening. How Everything Happens. May Swenson. HAP; Psy; RFM

When Oats Were Reaped. Thomas Hardy. OxBTC

When ocean-clouds over inland hills. Misgivings. Herman Melville. ILP (1975 ed.); NOBA; PiAm

When October gets too chilly. In the Yellow Light of Brooklyn. Al Lee. NYP

When Ogden his prosaic verse. On Dr. Samuel Ogden. R. P. Arden. FaBoCo

When Oisin came back to Ireland. Paul Muldoon. *Fr.* Armageddon, Armageddon. CIP

When old birds strangely-hearted strive to sing. The Sweetening of the Year. John Shaw Neilson. MAuV

When old corruption first begun. Quid the Cynic's Song. Blake. *Fr.* An Island in the Moon. FaBoNo

When old philosophers wrote the world's birth. A Panegyric on the Author of "Absalom and Achitophel." *Unknown.* APAS

When, on a yellowing hill, a tree. Patterns. Ruth Setterberg. AMV-81

When on Euphrates' banks we sate. Bible, *O.T., paraphrased by* Sir John Denham. Psalms, CXXXVII. OAEL-1

When on the coral-red steps of old brownstones. Summer: West Side. John Updike. SoS

When on thy lip my soul I breathe. The Killing Kiss. Thomas Stanley. SCP-2

When once the scourging prophet, with his cry. The Disused Table. Norman Cameron. OxBTC

When once the sun sinks in the west. Evening Primrose. John Clare. PF

When one billion insurance. Going Home. Tim Reynolds. NowV

When other fair ones [*or* ladies] to the shades [*or* groves] go down. On Certain Ladies. Pope. FaBoCo; FaBoEE

When others run to windows or out of doors. Part for the Whole. Robert Francis. PoA

When our brother Fire was having his dog's day. Brother Fire. Louis MacNeice. NoAM; NOBE

When our dean took a pious young spinster. Limerick. Victor Gray. NOBL

When our earth mother is replete with living waters. Prayer for Rain. *Unknown.* AKE

When Our Earthly Sun Is Setting, *with music.* Edwin H. Nevin. AH

When our two souls stand up erect and strong. Sonnets from the Portuguese, XXII. Elizabeth Barrett Browning. BoWoP; NOBE; SBG; VLP; WPE

When out a Shellbrook, round by stile and tree. Shellbrook [National English]. William Barnes. VLP

When over the flowery, sharp pasture's. Flowers by the Sea. William Carlos Williams. CMoP (1970 ed.); ExPo (1973 ed.); NoAM; TAP

When pails empty the last brightness. O You among Women. F. R. Higgins. BIrV

When paper bags wallow like demons. Deliver Me, O Lord, from My Daily Bread. Jeanne Murray Walker. AMV-80

When paper snaps in machines. The Boss Machine-Tender after Losing a Son. Paul Corrigan. AMV-81

When passion makes me discontent. Organ Solo. Knute Skinner. GP

When passion's trance is overpast. To ——. Shelley. MBPR

When Pat came o'er the hills his colleen for to see. The Whistling Thief. *Unknown.* PoTa

When pavements were blown up, exposing nerves. Epilogue to a Human Drama. Stephen Spender. CMoP (1970 ed.)

When Pelion wondering saw that rain, which fell. To Castara: Of What We Were before Our Creation. William Habington. SCP-2

When people come with big muddy feet. Go Throw Them Out. Moishe Leib Halpern, *tr. by* Ruth Whitman. VWA

When people's ill they come to I. On Dr. Isaac Letsome. *Unknown.* FaBoCo

When periwigs came first in wear. The Bald Cavalier. *Unknown.* OxBChV

When Piecrust first began to reign. A Fancy. *Unknown.* FaBoNo

When pleasing heat, and fragrant blooms inspire. Oppian, *tr. by* William Diaper. *Fr.* Halieuticks. PeD

When poets print their works, the scribbling crew. To My Ingenious and Worthy Friend William Lowndes, Esq. John Gay. OBSV

When politicos of the old life have departed. Washington Interregnum. Reed Whittemore. WasP

When quacks with pills political would dope us. Canopus. Bert Leston Taylor. NOBL

When raging [*or* ragyng] love with extreme pain [*or* payne]. Consolation. Earl of Surrey. AAS; EBEV; NOBE

When Reason's ray shines over all. On the Triumph of Rationalism. Alfred Ainger. FaBoCo

When resentments seem to have. A Lot of Hearts Are Pounding in the Universe. Allan Kornblum. AcAn

When Reuben Pantier ran away and threw me. Dora Williams. Edgar Lee Masters. *Fr.* Spoon River Anthology. HAP

When rising from the bed of death. Joseph Addison. BoReV

When rites and melodies begin. The Proof. W. H. Auden. OAEL-2

When roaring gloom surged inward and you cried. To His Dead Body. Siegfried Sassoon. NoAM

When Robin Hood and Little John. Robin Hood's Death. *Unknown.* FaBoBa

When Robin Hood was about eighteen years old. Robin Hood and Little John. *Unknown.* AmFP

When Roots Get Too Deep. Michael Smith. DNGG

When Running Felt Right. Linda McCloud. PoUp

When Ruth was left half desolate. Ruth. Wordsworth. MBPR

When Sarah Pierrepont let her spirit rage. Address to the Scholars of New England. John Crowe Ransom. GOA

When Serpents Bargain for the Right to Squirm. E. E. Cummings. InPK; SoSe; STS; TT

When Shakespeare, Jonson, Fletcher ruled the stage. In Defense of Satire. Sir Carr Scroope. APAS

When shall I see the half-moon sink again. End of Another Home Holiday. D. H. Lawrence. EBEV

When Shall My Pilgrimage, Jesus My Saviour, Be Ended? *with music. At. to* Andrew Rudman, *tr. fr. Swedish by* Ernest Edwin Ryden. AH

When Shall We All Meet Again? *with music. Unknown.* AH

When she asked. Educating the Body. Kevin Ireland. ATNZ

When she came on, straight. Black Is Beautiful. Philip Appleman. SFF

When she carries food to the table and stoops down. Part of Plenty. Bernard Spencer. GBL

When she looks out by night. Michael Drayton. *Fr.* The Shepherd's Sirena. SCP-2

When she put her hand on me. The First Time. John Newlove. NeAC

When she rises in the morning. Gloire de Dijon. D. H. Lawrence. CMoP (1970 ed.); GBL; ILP (1975 ed.); IPWM; LoAs; NoAM; TPo

When she said, "No." The Fisherman's Wife. David Wagoner. CNW

When she still used words, my mother told. My Mother's Childhood. Barry Spacks. GP

When she was found. Visiting the Dead. Ciaran Carson. CIP

When she was little. Poem for Aretha. Nikki Giovanni. PoBA

When Sir Joshua Reynolds died. Sir Joshua Reynolds. Blake. FaBoCo; FaBoEE

When skies wer peale wi' twinklen stars. Lydlinch Bells. William Barnes. VPC

When Skylab fell. How the Sky Begins to Fall. Joan Colby. AMV-81

When sly Jemmy Twitcher had smugged up his face. The Candidate. Thomas Gray. PPP

When Smoke Stood Up from Ludlow. A. E. Housman. SoSe

When Snow Falls. Katherine Hoskins. TCP

When snow like sheep lay in the fold. In Memory of Jane Fraser. Geoffrey Hill. NoAM; OxBTC

When snow melts, green mountains slope. Summit Lake. Mark Thalman. AMV-81

When Sol did cast no light. The Valiant Seaman's Happy Return to His Love. *Unknown.* GBP; PeBB

When some beloveds, 'neath whose eyelids lay. Bereavement. Elizabeth Barrett Browning. WPE

When some proud son of man returns to earth. Epitaph to a Dog [*or* Inscription on the Monument of a Newfoundland Dog]. Byron. GDP; MBPR

When someone/ pulls down a blind. Blindfold. Luci Shaw. AATT

When someone hangs up, having said. The Business Life. David Ignatow. NNaP

When Something Happens. James A. Randall, Jr. BPo

When sommer toke in hand the winter to assail. Earl of Surrey. AAS

When Spoon River became a ganglion. Marx the Sign Painter. Edgar Lee Masters. *Fr.* The New Spoon River. NoAM; TAP

When Spring came. *Unknown, tr. fr. Tlinglit Indian.* RFM

When spring comes. How We Must Teach the Children. Richard W. Thomas. TC

When Statesmen gravely say "We must be realistic." W. H. Auden. FaBoCo

When Stella strikes the tuneful string. To Miss ——: On Her Playing upon the Harpsichord. Samuel Johnson. CABA (1972 ed.)

When stubble lands were greening you came among the stooks. The Green Autumn Stubble. *Unknown.* WTO

When Sue Wears Red. Langston Hughes. CNA

When summer was approaching. First Love. *Unknown, tr. by* George F. Whicher. OLR

When Sun Came to Riverwoman. Leslie Silko. NW; VoR

When Sun Doth Rise, *with music.* Roger Williams. AH

When supper time is almost come. Milking Time. Elizabeth Madox Roberts. RAE

When Susanna Jones wears red. When Sue Wears Red. Langston Hughes. CNA

When Susan's work was done, she'd sit. Old Susan. Walter de la Mare. CMoP (1970 ed.)

When sycamore leaves wer a-spreaden. Woak Hill. William Barnes. VPC

When Tadlow walks the streets the paviours cry. Tadlow. Abel Evans. FaBoCo

When, Tender and Mild. Derick Thomson, *tr. fr. Gaelic by* Iain Crichton Smith. MS

When that happens. Resisting Each Other. Anne Waldman. RiTi

When that I was and a little tiny boy. Shakespeare. *Fr.* Twelfth Night, V, i. EBEV; HeIP; NOBE; OAEL-1; OBP; PPoe; WIF

When the/ sun. August 2. Norman Jordan. PoBA

When the African Arts. At Home in Dakar. Margaret Danner. FB

When the *Alabama's* keel was laid. Roll, *Alabama*, Roll. *Unknown.* AIW

When the alcoholic passed the crucial point. Point of No Return. Robert Graves. BIrV

When the Angels Are Exhausted. Yona Wallach, *tr. fr. Hebrew by* Leonore Gordon. VWA

When the Animals Left the Ark. *Unknown.* RAE

When the badger glimmered away. The Badgers. Seamus Heaney. CIP

When the Birds Go North Again. Ella Higginson. WPW

When the birds sang. *Unknown, tr. fr. Spanish by* Willis Barnstone. BoWoP

When the black herds of the rain were grazing. The Lost Heifer. Austin Clarke. BIrV

When the blackbird in the spring. *See* As the blackbird in the spring.

When the blind suppliant in the way. "Receive Thy Sight." Bryant. PIM

When the bones walk out of me. Never. George Reavey. BIrV

When the book is closed. The Book Ends, Immortality Begins. Adrianne Marcus. NPW

When the boughs of the garden hang heavy with rain. Thunder in the Garden. William Morris. VLP

When the boy undressed. The Skull. Ian Young. NeAC

When the breeze of a joyful dawn blew free. Recollections of the Arabian Nights. Tennyson. VLP

When the British warrior queen. Boadicea. William Cowper. FaPo; FaPoR

When the buffalo are all slaughtered. Poem after a Speech by Chief Seattle, 1855. Charles Brasher. AMV-81

When the children had ferried across the river. Children Visit the Island. Diane Wakoski. CAAP

When the child's forehead, full of red torments. The Seekers of Lice. Arthur Rimbaud, *tr. by* Wallace Fowlie. NAWM-2

When the clatter of reckless thought. Woman in an Abandoned House. Michael Bily-Hurd. AMV-81

When the clouds' swoln bosoms echo back the shouts. In Tenebris, II. Thomas Hardy. CMoP (1970 ed.); NoAM; OxBTC; VLP

When the cold comes. Where? When? Which? Langston Hughes. BPo

When the completely charming. Bernard. Raymond Souster. POL

When the Cows Come Home. Christina Rossetti. DuDr

When the crowd has cheered the hostile teams. Ballad of the Pigskin. Horace Spencer Fiske. SPo

When the crows fly away. My Love. Richard Shelton. MPA

When the dawn flames in the sky. At Dawning. Nelle Richmond Eberhart. BLSo

When the Day. Thomas Sessler, *tr. fr. German by* Herbert Kuhner. VWA

When the Days Grow Long. Hayim Nachman Bialik, *tr. fr. Hebrew by* A. C. Jacobs. VWA

When the drums come to your door. The Lost, Dancing. Edward Field. GP

When the Druzes come together. Diaspora Jews. Rachel Boimwell, *tr. by* Gabriel Preil *and* Howard Schwartz. VWA

When the Dumb Speak. Robert Bly. CAPP; NoAM; NOBA

When the eager squadrons of day are faint and disbanded. The Cult of the Celtic. Anthony C. Deane. NOBL

When the eagle soared clear through a dawn distilling of emerald. Crow and the Birds. Ted Hughes. OBP

When the Earth Is Cold. Sol Funaroff. SPT

When the earth is turned in spring. The Worm. Ralph Bergengren. CaYB

When the elephant's-ear in the park. Tea. Wallace Stevens. CABA (1972 ed.)

When the exhibition opens, it's. R.S.V.P. Peter Klappert. AAN

When the exposed spirit, busy in daytime. Time Exposures. Muriel Rukeyser. PoA

When the Eye of Day Is Shut. A. E. Housman. OAEL-2

When the Fairies. Edward Dorn. TAT

When the fang/ Of its white/ Incisor. Cuttlefish. Ernest Kroll. PoUp

When the far south glittered. Pilgrimage. Austin Clarke. CIP

When the farmer comes to town. The Farmer Is the Man. *Unknown.* FSW

When the farmers burned the furze away. Celibates. Eiléan Ní Chuilleanáin. IPM

When the fat Prince french-kissed Sleeping Beauty. Pantomime Diseases. Dannie Abse. PMW

When the fat woman's two brats. Beef. Leon Stokesbury. GP

When the feet of the rain tread a dance on the roofs. Gipsy-Night. Richard Hughes. OBW

When the fierce North-wind with his airy forces. The Day of Judgement [*or* Judgment]. Isaac Watts. EPC; HAP; ILP (1975 ed.); NOBE; PAIC

When the fifth month comes. Lady Ise, *tr. fr. Japanese by* Etsuko Terasaki *and* Irma Brandeis. BoWoP

When the fire-Mass over London was being said. Fire-Mass. Russell Grant. PMW

When the first bad news came, my mother. News of the World. Philip Levine. AMV-81

When the first drumtaps sound and trumpets buzz. Skulls as Drums. John Wheelwright. SPT

When the five o'clock whistle blows. Repentant Judas. Joseph Kalar. SPT

When the Five Prominent Poets. Josephine Jacobsen. TAP

When the flowers turn to husks. Cells Breathe in the Emptiness. Galway Kinnell. VGW

When the Flyin' Scot. Uncle Henry. W. H. Auden. NOBL

When the foreman whistled. Field Poem. Gary Soto. NW

When the forests have been destroyed their darkness remains. The Asians Dying. W. S. Merwin. CAPP; NOBA

When the Frost is on the Punkin. James Whitcomb Riley. AmVN; OBAL

When the game began between them for a jest. Stage Love. Swinburne. NIL

When the giraffes left their silos in Iowa. Giraffes: The American Version. Stephen Dunn. HeS

When the gnats dance at evening. Gnat-Psalm. Ted Hughes. NoAM

When the god, needing something, decided to become a swan. Leda. Rainer Maria Rilke, *tr. by* Robert Bly. NU

When the God Returns. Russell Edson. GP

When the gold fever raged I was doing very well. The Miner's Lament. *Unknown.* AmFP

When the grass was closely mown. The Dumb Soldier. Robert Louis Stevenson. OxBChV

When the grass, wet and matted. What Is There. Marvin Bell. GP

When the Greek sea. Sometimes, as a Child. Olga Broumas. CNW

When the green grass rose in the spring. On the Bright Side. Carter Revard. VoR

When the green woods laugh with the voice of joy. Laughing Song [or Laughter]. Blake. *Fr.* Songs of Innocence. ECBV; LAuP; MBPR; OxBChV

When the grey nets of winter skies hang. Spring Rites. Martin Robbins. AMV–81

When the gulls are dead. Gulls. Dolores Kendrick. PoUp

When the heart coughed. Resuscitation. John Stone. CSP

When the heat of the summer. A Dragonfly. Eleanor Farjeon. FPB

When the horses were no longer found in dreams. Second Avenue Winter. Charles Simic. NYP

When the hounds of spring are on winter's traces. Chorus. Swinburne. *Fr.* Atalanta in Calydon. ExPo (1973 ed.); HAP; HeIP; ILP (1975 ed.); NIL; NOBE; OAEL–2; PoPle; SoSe (1977 ed.); VPC

When the ice starts to shiver. On Edges. Adrienne Rich. Psy

When the Iceworms Nest Again. Robert W. Service. FSW

When the jet sprang into the sky. Geography Lesson. Zulfikar Ghose. LP; MPo

When the kid's forehead is full of red torments. Lice-Hunters. Arthur Rimbaud, *tr. by* Ezra Pound. NAWM–2

When the lad for longing sighs. A. E. Housman. OLR

When the Lamp Is Shattered. Shelley. PPP
(Lines: "When the lamp is shattered.") FF; ILP (1975 ed.); MBPR

When the last bus leaves, moths stream toward lights. Depot in Rapid City. Roberta Hill. BoWoP; UsP

When the last child left. October. Judith Goren. AMV–81

When the last Flavius, drunk with fury, tore. Juvenal, *tr. by* William Gifford. *Fr.* Satires, IV. OBVE

When the Last Riders. Natan Zach, *tr. fr. Hebrew by* Peter Everwine *and* Shula Starkman. VWA

When the last sea is sailed and the last shallow charted. D'Avalos' Prayer. John Masefield. EcS

When the little blue-bird. Let's Do It. Cole Porter. OBAL

When the Lord was a man of war and sailed out. The Life and Death of the Cantata System. Alan Dugan. ILP (1975 ed.)

When the low heavy sky weighs like a lid. Spleen LXXVIII. Baudelaire, *tr. by* Sir John Squire. NAWM–2

When the mare shows you. Mare. Judith Thurman. FPB; PH

When the master lived a king and I a starving hutted slave beneath the lash, and. On Listening to the Spirituals. Lance Jeffers. PoBA

When the Mississippi Flowed in Indiana. Vachel Lindsay. CMoP (1970 ed.); ILP (1975 ed.)

When the moon/ rides high. Autumn Ghost Sounds. *Unknown.* IWK

When the moon/ stays into morning. Hunting Song. Gene Fowler. BCr; CPA

When the moon shines o'er the corn. The Field Mouse. William Sharp. PCOP; MN

When the morning hymn. The Wonder-Teacher. Cynthia Ozick. VWA

When the morning star bleeds and silver-cry the Pleiades. Dream. Joseph Eliyia, *tr. by* Rae Dalven. VWA

When the morning was waking over the war. Among Those Killed in the Dawn Raid Was a Man Aged a Hundred. Dylan Thomas. LFH; STS

When the new alphabet soup of the earth. Red Movie. John Tranter. CAAP

When the night falls silently, the night falls silently. Glow Worm. Lila Cayley Robinson. BLSo

When the Nightingale Sings. *Unknown.* OxBM

When the nightingale to his mate. Alba. Ezra Pound. OBVE; PoIA; VGW; WeW

When the norse. Greenland, 850 A.D. Lyn Lifshin. MMD

When the old bitch barks at the bottom of my iron backstairs. The Second Part. David Hilton. AcAn

When the old Cove Creek Dam first was started. The Song of Cove Creek Dam. *Unknown.* AmFP

When the old flaming prophet climbed the sky. On a Virtuous Young Gentlewoman That Died Suddenly. William Cartwright. HAP

When the orchard that clings to the terrace. Love in Particular. John Malcolm Brinnin. NYP

When the other children go. The Invisible Playmate. Margaret Widdemer. CTV

When the ox-horn sounds in the buried hills. Second Psalm: The Signals. W. S. Merwin. CAAP

When the photographer comes in. Henry Miller: A Writer. Carol Lem. AMV–80

When the pine tosses its cones. Woodnotes, I. Emerson. NOBA

When the pistol muzzle oozing blue vapour. That Moment. Ted Hughes. FF

When the planners breached at last. Pine Tree. Geoff Page. FPA

When the pods went pop on the broom, green broom. A Runnable Stag. John Davidson. FaPoR; HAP; OxBTC

When the poles have gone under the gauzes of our fog. Light. Brewster Ghiselin. MPA

When the present has latched its postern behind my tremulous stay. Afterwards. Thomas Hardy. CMoP (1970 ed.); EBEV; OAEL–2; InPS; NOBE; OBP; PoPle; SoSe; TPo

When the proficient poison of sure sleep. E. E. Cummings. LoAs

"When the Pulitzers showered on some dope." Words for Hart Crane. Robert Lowell. CABA (1972 ed.); CMoP (1970 ed.)

When the pumpkin yellows. Winter Soon Is Coming. Elizabeth J. Coatsworth. ECBV

When the rain comes tumbling down. The Story of Flying Robert. Heinrich Hoffmann, *tr. fr. German.* SpRo

When the rain drums loud on the leaf. Resemblance. *Tr. fr. Hawaiian by* N. B. Emerson. WTO

When the Rain Raineth. *Unknown.* GBP

When the Revolution Really. Peter Michelson. HeS

When the ring gleamed white and your chair hugged the edge of it. Change of Address. Kathleen Fraser. WBN

When the Ripe Fruit Falls. D. H. Lawrence. CMoP (1970 ed.); ILP (1975 ed.); TPo

When the Roll Is Called Up Yonder, *with music.* James M. Black. BLSH

When the rooster jumps up on the windowsill. Cuba, 1962. Ai. AmPA

When the ropes droop and loosen, and the gust. For My Grandfather. Francis Webb. GAS

When the rose is slowing. Two Alternatives to One Moment's Experience. Jim Farrar. DNGG

When the Saints Come Marching In, *with music.* Edward C. Redding. BLSo

When the Saints Go Marching In. *Unknown.* FSW

When the sea comes in at Horsey Gap. Horsey Gap. *Unknown.* GBP

When the sea is as grey as her eyes. Soft White. Lee Harwood. EAS

When the Seed of Thy Word Is Cast, *with music.* Cotton Mather. AH

When the sheep are in the fauld, and the kye at hame. Ault Robin Gray. Lady Anne Lindsay. WPE

When the snow falls softly. Sandra Maria Esteves. NW

When the snow starts melting. The French Mood. Abo Stoltzenberg, tr. by Gabriel Preil and Howard Schwartz. VWA

When the speckled hen laid a white egg and. Racialism. John Blight. CAAP

When the spent sun throws up its rays on cloud. Acceptance. Robert Frost. CMoP (1970 ed.); UsP

When the spider dropped down from the ceiling. The Grandmother Came Down to Visit Us. Joseph Bruchac. CDW

When the storm/ gave me its dark clouds. For Michael. Karen L. Mitchell. AMV–80

When the streetcar stalled on Joy Road. On the Birth of Good and Evil during the Long Winter of '28. Philip Levine. PoW

When the summer fields are mown. Aftermath. Longfellow. NOBA; PiAm; TAP

When the sun/ falls behind the sumac. Loss. A. R. Ammons. ConAP

When the Sun Came. Josephine Miles. MPA ("When the sun came, the rooster expanded to meet it.") CoPAm

When the Sun Shines More Years than Fear. Janet Frame. ATNZ

When the sun shouts and people abound. Summer Holiday. Robinson Jeffers. MiP

When the sun whipped our skins. Cortes. A. A. Rios. GP

When the sun's perpendicular rays. Beginning of an Undergraduate Poem. Unknown. FaBoCo

When the swans turned my sister into a swan. The Black Swan. Randall Jarrell. CMoP (1970 ed.); ExPo (1973 ed.)

When the swift-rolling brook, swollen deep. The Storm-Wind. William Barnes. NOBE

When the sword of sixty comes nigh his head. Firdosi, tr. fr. Persian by Basil Bunting. OBVE

When the tea is brought at five o'clock. Milk for the Cat. Harold Monro. PCat

When the time has arrived. Trala Trala Trala Le-le-la. William Carlos Williams. OFD

When the tree limb falls down. About Yes and No. Steve Toth. AcAn

When the trial's in Belzoni. High Sheriff Blues. Unknown. BluL

When the troubled sea swells and surrounds. Vittoria da Colonna, tr. fr. Italian by Brenda Webster. PBWP

When the trumpet of the Lord shall sound. When the Roll Is Called Up Yonder. James M. Black. BLSH

When the tv has been turned off. The Gift. J. D. Whitney. NVAP

When the union's inspiration through the workers' blood shall run. Solidarity Forever. Ralph Chaplin. FSW

When the voices of children are heard on the green/ And laughing is heard on the hill. Nurse's Song. Blake. Fr. Songs of Innocence. LAuP; MBPR; OxBChV; STS

When the voices of children are heard on the green/ And whisprings are in the dale. Nurse's Song. Blake. Fr. Songs of Experience. CABA (1972 ed.); FF; LAuP; MBPR; STS

When the war-cry of Liberty rang through the land. The Death of Warren. Epes Sargent. BTTM

When the War Is Over. W. S. Merwin. PPoD

When the ways are heavy with mire and rut. The Ballade of Prose and Rhyme. Austin Dobson. PAIC

When the white feet of the baby beat across the grass. Baby-Movements. D. H. Lawrence. RRA

When the white flame in us is gone. Dust. Rupert Brooke. OxBTC

When the white fog burns off. The Depths. Denise Levertov. NU

When the white man. A Song. Lindiwe Mabuza. SES

When the wind blows loud and fearful. The Beggar Boy. Cecil Frances Alexander. OxBChV

When the wind is in the east. Unknown. MG

When the wind is in the thrift. By the Saltings. Ted Walker. EcS

When the wind works against us in the dark. Storm Fear. Robert Frost. CMoP (1970 ed.); IPWM; PPM; UsP

When the Wine Was Gone. Alvin Aubert. CNA

When the Work's All Done This Fall. Unknown. BPAW; FSW

When the world has lost. Containment. Howard Schwartz. HeS

When the World Is Burning. Ebenezer Jones. PoPle; VLP

When the world is white with snow. Bear. Kenneth Rexroth. BCr

When the world takes over for us. Lear. William Carlos Williams. NOBA; PoA

When the world turns completely upside down. Wild Peaches. Elinor Wylie. RiTi; SBG; WPE

When the world's folk, one day of freedom. The Labourer. Iolo Goch, tr. by Gwyn Williams. OBW

When there are so many we shall have to mourn. In Memory of Sigmund Freud. W. H. Auden. HAP; OAEL–2

When these inland gulls. Desert Gulls. Dan Gillespie. TAT

When These Old Barns Lost Their Inhabitants. David Kherdian. FAF; TAT

When they ask your name. Children. Russell Edson. AmPA

When they came/ breathing jasmine and raspberry. The Aunts. Jean Nordhaus. PoUp

When they confess that they have lost the penial bone. God Bless America. John Fuller. OBSV

When they escaped. Exodus. Harvey Shapiro. VWA

When they had won the war. The Inner Part. Louis Simpson. ILP (1975 ed.); InPS; PBMP; SFF

When they go out walking the Sioux. The Sioux. Unknown. TDH

When they in throngs a safe retirement seek. William Diaper, after the Greek of Oppian. Fr. Halieutica. OBVE

When they said Carrickfergus I could hear. The Singer's House. Seamus Heaney. CIP; EBEV

When they saw off Dai Evan's da. Fforestfawr. Kingsley Amis. Fr. The Evans Country. NOBL

When they say "To the wall." The Wall Test. Louis Simpson. GP

When they shot Malcolm Little down. At That Moment. Raymond R. Patterson. CABA (1972 ed.); PoBA

When they shot the bear out of his tree. The Marauder. Robley Wilson, Jr. BCr

When they stop poems. Today Is a Day of Great Joy. Victor Hernandez Cruz. TPo; WIF

When they take us into our. Interrogation. Robert Hahn. AAN

When they woke me. Coming Back. Joseph Bruchac. CDW

When Thickly Beat the Storms of Life, with music. Gurdon Robins. AH

When thin-strewn memory I look through. Miss Loo. Walter de la Mare. CMoP (1970 ed.); OxBTC

When Things Go Wrong with You. Unknown. FSW

When things in Washington get thick. The Rise and Fall of the Swagger Stick. William Jay Smith. WasP

When This Cruel War Is Over. Charles C. Sawyer. AmFP (Weeping Sad and Lonely.) FSW

When this fly lived, she used to play. A Fly That Flew into My Mistress's Eye. Thomas Carew. CaPo

When this troubled life is over, hide Thou me. Hide Thou Me. *Unknown.* AmFP

When this yokel comes maundering. The Plot against the Giant. Wallace Stevens. CMoP (1970 ed.); FF

When those renouned noble peers of Greece. Amoretti, XLIV. Spenser. CABA (1972 ed.)

When thou and I are dead, my dear. Inseparable. Philip Bourke Marston. BoLoP

When thou hast spent the lingring day in pleasure and delight. Gascoygnes Good Night. George Gascoigne. AAS

When thou must home to shades of underground. Among the Shades. Thomas Campion, *after* Propertius. AAS; BoLoP; CABA (1972 ed.); EBEV; GBL; HAP; ILP (1975 ed.); LoAs; NOBE; OBVE; PoPle

When thou, poor excommunicate. To My Inconstant Mistress [*or* Song]. Thomas Carew. CaPo; GBL; MetP; NOBE

When thou to my true love com'st. Westphalian Song. *Unknown, tr. by* Samuel Taylor Coleridge. OBVE

When Thy Heart with Joy O'erflowing, *with music.* Theodore Chickering Williams. AH

When Thy King Is a Boy, *sel.* Ed Roberson. "You black out the sun." PoBA

When to Her Lute Corinna [*or* Corrina] Sings. Thomas Campion. AAS; CABA (1972 ed.); ILP (1975 ed.); OAEL-1

When to the sessions of sweet silent thought. Sonnets, XXX. Shakespeare. BiP; CABA (1972 ed.); EBEV; Epi; ExPo (1973 ed.); FF; GBL; HAP; ILP (1975 ed.); InPS; NOBE; OAEL-1; PAIC; PoIA; PoPle; PPM; PPP; STS; TPo; VoPo; WIF

When Tom and Elizabeth took the farm. The Magpies. Denis Glover. ATNZ

When Toroi Bandi was alive. Toroi Bandi. *Mongol Oral Tradition, tr. by* C. R. Bawden. WTO

When trout swim down Great Ormond Street. Priapus and the Pool, III. Conrad Aiken. NoAM; NOBA

When tunes jigged nimbler than the blood. Song from a Country Fair. Leonie Adams. PoIA

When twilight comes to Prairie Street. The Winning of the TV West. John T. Alexander. CTV

When twins came, their father, Dan Dunn. The Twins. Berton Braley. TDH

When two/ bodies meet. Radiant Heat. Rochelle Owens. WBN

When two men meet for the first time in all. Law in the Country of the Cats. Ted Hughes. NowV

When Two Suns Do Appear. Sir Philip Sidney. *Fr.* Arcadia. Moon

When Uncle Devereux died. Dunbarton. Robert Lowell. MPo

When up aloft. The Robin. Thomas Hardy. RAE

When vain desire at last and vain regret. The One Hope. Dante Gabriel Rossetti. The House of Life, CI. OAEL-2; VLP

When Venus her Adonis found. The Death of Adonis. Philip Ayres, *after the Greek of* Theocritus. OBVE

When walking, they waddle, a little bit. The Nice Old Couple. Dorothy Aldis. TVo

When wars and ruined men shall cease. Prayer against Indifference. Joy Davidman. SPT

When warships anchored, spent in the Sound. Between Two Wars. R. P. Kingston. NVAP

When was it first they called each other mine? Unhurt, There Is No Help. Allen Curnow. ATNZ

When was it that the particles became. Wallace Stevens. PoA

When we are at last in that far heaven. The Birthday. Morley Jamieson. SLP

When we are dead, some hunting-boy will pass. The Statue. Hilaire Belloc. NIL; POL

When we are going toward someone we say. Simple Song. Marge Piercy. CTBA; Psy; TSWA

When we are in love, we love the grass. Love Poem. Robert Bly. BiP; InPS; OSP

When we are old and these rejoicing veins. Edna St. Vincent Millay. VGW

When we are two drunk suns. Yvonne Caroutch, *tr. fr. French by* Willis Barnstone *and* Elene Kolb. BoWoP

When we arrive there. The Twenty-first Century. Kevin Hart. GAS

When we came home from school one day. Goat. Siddie Joe Johnson. ECBV

When we came up from water, our eyes. Lying Down with Men and Women. John Woods. GP; TC

When we fell apart in the Badlands and lay still. In the Badlands. David Wagoner. UnPo (1976 ed.)

When we finally. There Is No Time. Elaine H. Jennings. NPW

When we first met we did not guess. Robert Bridges. POL

When we first rade down Ettrick. Ettrick. Lady John Scott. SLP; WPE

When we for age could neither read nor write. Of the Last Verses in the Book. Edmund Waller. EBEV; HAP; MetP; PAIC; SCP-2

When we fought the Yankees and annihilation was near. Jubilation T. Cornpone. Johnny Mercer. OBAL

When we get a good day here. Young Couples Strolling By. Carl Rakosi. InPS

When We Go Over to My Grandad's. Michael Rosen. FPB

When we got home, there was our Old Man. Pa. Leo Dangel. AMV-81

When we have come this long way. Anniversary Poem for the Cheyennes Who Fell at Sand Creek. Lance Henson. VoR

When We Hear the Eye Open. Bob Kaufman. CNA

When we heard it announced. The Ambassadors. Paul Lawson. GP; PPoD

When we in kind embracements had agre'd. *Unknown. Fr.* Zepheria. AAS

When we lay where Budmouth Beach is. Budmouth Dears. Thomas Hardy. *Fr.* The Dynasts. PoPle

When we learn. It Is the Season. Josephine Jacobsen. TAP

When we loved. Loving. Jane Stembridge. NMM

When we married. For Fear of Waking the Alarm Clock. Liam Murphy. IPM

When we moved here, pulled. An Oregon Message. William Stafford. Moon

When we, our weary limbs to rest. Bible, *O.T., paraphrased by* Nahum Tate *and* Nicholas Brady. Psalms, CXXXVII. OAEL-1

When we reached the island. The Island. Derick Thomson. MS

When we rolled up the three armored vehicles. One Morning We Brought Them Order. Al Lee. FF; WIF

When we see/ the houses again. The Removal. W. S. Merwin. TCP

When we shall finally be. The Fathers. John N. Morris. GP

When we shuddered and took into ourselves. The Whole Story. William Stafford. NNaP

When we sleep we arrive home. The House We Leave. Fredric Matteson. PoW

When we slept. Signature. Larry Mollin. NeAC

When we spurt off. Moving. William Matthews. POL

When we start breaking up in the wet darkness. Consolations of Philosophy. Derek Mahon. BIrV; CIP

When We Two Parted. Byron. BoLoP; HoPM (1975 ed.); ILP (1975 ed.); LFH; NOBE; OLR; PBMP; VoPo

When we wake. After a Journey. Ken Smith. TwMBP

When we walk with the Lord. Trust and Obey. J. H. Sammis. BLSH

When we walked outside at sunset. Abortion. Mei Berssenbrugge. SA

When we went to the zoo. Our Visit to the Zoo. Jessie Pope. PoPle

When we were a soft amoeba. Ere You Were Queen of Sheba. Sir Arthur Shipley. FaBoCo

When we were building Skua Light. The Dancing Seal. W. W. Gibson. EcS

When we were children. The Key of the Kingdom. Ed Reed. BBGO

When we were children, clasping hands. But You, My Darling, Should Have Married the Prince. Kathleen Spivack. AmPA; NMM

When we were children old Nurse used to say. The Quiet House. Charlotte Mew. EBEV; SBG

When we were farm-boys, years ago. Recollections of "Lalla Rookh." John Townsend Trowbridge. OBAL

When we were married eight years. Tryst. Eve Merriam. NMM

When we woke up at 7:30, it snowed. The Paradise Rug. Laurance Wieder. AAN

When weary with the long day's care. To Imagination. Emily Brontë. ILP (1975 ed.); VLP

When we'd make the rounds. Shazam. R. P. Dickey. HeS

When were you last at my house—or I at yours? Portrait of a Younger Twin. Thomas W. Shapcott. FPA

When wert thou born, Desire? Of the Birth and Bringing Up of Desire. Edward de Vere, Earl of Oxford. FaBoEE

When Westwell Downs I 'gan to tread. On Westwell Downs. William Strode. SCP-2

When what has helped us has helped us enough. The Place of Backs. W. S. Merwin. HoPM (1975 ed.)

)when what hugs stopping earth than silent is. E. E. Cummings. PoA

When, when and whenever death closes our eyelids. Ezra Pound. Fr. Homage to Sextus Propertius. NoAM; PoA

When whispering strains do softly steal [or with creeping wind]. In Commendation of Music. William Strode. ILP (1975 ed.); SCP-2

When Whistler's Mother's picture frame. To a Lost Sweetheart. Don Marquis. POL

When white people speak of being uptight. The Dancer. Al Young. PiAm; PoBA; SA

When Wild Confusion Wrecks the Air, with music. Mather Byles. AH

When will she come again. White Goddess. Hubert Witheford. ATNZ

When will that war end? My whole house is still. On Seeing Films of the War. Louis Coxe. PPoD

When will the stream be aweary of flowing. Nothing Will Die. Tennyson. PBMP

When Wilt Thou Teach the People? D. H. Lawrence. OBSV

When Windesor walles sustain'd my wearied arme. Earl of Surrey. AAS

When window-lamps had dwindled, then I rose. The Wanderer. Christopher Brennan. GAS

When Winds Are Raging, with music. Harriet Beecher Stowe. AH

When winds that move not its calm surface sweep. Moschus, tr. fr. Greek by Shelley. OBVE

When wine runs low, it is not worth the sparing. Joshua Sylvester, after the French of Pierre Mathieu. FaBoEE

When winter nites get long and the weather starts to chill. The Mice Celebrate Christmas. Alf Prøysen. MN

When with a serious musing I behold. The Marigold. George Wither. PF

When with much pains this boasted learning's got. Charles Churchill. Fr. The Author. OBSV

When with staid mothers' milk and sunshine warmed. Alfred Austin. Fr. The Human Tragedy. FaBoCo

When with the virgin morning thou dost rise. Matins, or Morning Prayer. Robert Herrick. CaPo

When working blackguards come to blows. Song. Ebenezer Elliott. EBEV

When world is water and all is flood, God said. Noah's Ark. Marguerite Young. WPE

When ye hunt at the roe, then shall ye see there. Julians Barnes. Fr. Book of Hunting. WPE

When Yon Full Moon. W. H. Davies. Moon

When you and I go down. Midnight Lamentation. Harold Monro. OxBTC

When You and I Grow Up. Kate Greenaway. CTV

When You and I Must Part. Unknown. AmFP

When you and I on the Palos Verdes cliff. Shane O'Neill's Cairn. Robinson Jeffers. NoAM; NOBA

When You and I Were Young, Maggie. George W. Johnson. BLSH, with music; BLSo, with music; FSW; PSoN, with music

When you and my true lover meet. The Lady's Third Song. W. B. Yeats. Fr. The Three Bushes. FaBoTw (1975 ed.)

When You Are Gone. Nance Van Winckel. AMV-81

When You Are Old. W. B. Yeats. BoLoP; CMoP (1970 ed.); GBL; HeIP; IPWM; LFH; NoAM; OxBTC; PPM; SFF; STS; TPo; TVo; UsP

When you are old and gray and full of sleep. Villanelle with a Line by Yeats. Bruce Bennett. AMV–80

When you arrange a still life, prune the parts. Something Missing on the Left. Elizabeth Albrecht. PoUp

When you awake. The Sleeper. Sydney Clouts. VWA

When you begin, begin at the beginning. The Grass. Helen Wolfert. RiTi

When You Blow on Dog. Lorraine Flanders. PHC

When you broke from me. Izumi Shikibu, tr. fr. Japanese by Willis Barnstone. BoWoP

When you call, your cheerfulness thick as armadillo hide. Best Friends. Judith Hemschemeyer. AMV-81

When you came to the other side. The Other. Peter Cooley. AMV–80

When you come, as you soon must, to the streets of our city. Advice to a Prophet. Richard Wilbur. CAPP; ExPo (1973 ed.); ILP (1975 ed.); MAT; NIL; PiAm; PPoD; PPP

When you come to the end of a perfect day. A Perfect Day. Carrie Jacobs Bond. BLSo

When you consider the radiance, that it does not withhold. The City Limits. A. R. Ammons. NoAM; NOBA; NYP; PoIA

When you drive on the freeway, cars follow you. Paranoia. Michael Dennis Browne. AmPA; SoSe (1977 ed.)

When you feel like saying something. The Most Vital Thing in Life. Granville Kleiser. SoSe (1977 ed.)

When you find yourself alone on the river island. Quechua Song. Unknown, tr. by Ruth Stephan. RRA

When you first feel the ground under your feet. Walking in a Swamp. David Wagoner. HAP

When you get out there. Catching a Horse. Barbara Winder. PH

When you go through. Poem for a Goodbye. Norman MacCaig. SLP

When you ground the lenses and the moons swam free. The Emancipators. Randall Jarrell. PoA

When you grow up you learn better. Before You're a Stranger. Raymond Fraser. AKE

When You Have Forgotten Sunday: The Love Story. Gwendolyn Brooks. BPo; FF; TT; VoPo

When you have wearied of the valiant spires of this country town. Oxford Canal. James Elroy Flecker. OxBTC

When you hear me walking. Nappy Head Blues. *Unknown.* BluL

When you left I made. Octobering. Margaret Gibson. AAN

When you look down from the airplane you see lines. Field and Forest. Randall Jarrell. VGW

When you look on my grave. *Unknown.* FaBoEE

When you look past. Song for the Woman Singing at the Café Trieste. Bart Schneider. AAN

When you looked back. Town. Gary Soto. CPA; NW

When you lose your money please don't lose your mind. Married Man Blues. *Unknown.* BluL

When you lost touch with lovers' bare skin. John Donne. James Simmons. CIP

When you love, or speak of it. Aphra Behn. BoWoP

When You Plant Cats in the Ground. Faye Kicknosway. TC

When you put on the feet be sure. Dr. Potatohead Talks to Mothers. Judith Johnson Sherwin. NoAM

When you put up your walls afresh. To You Building the New House. Nelly Sachs, *tr. by* Keith Bosley. VWA

When you ran through the sand all the miles. Moving Inland. Gregory Jerozal. PoUp

When you reach to touch the markings. Indian Rock, Bainbridge Island, Washington. Duane Niatum. CDW

When you realize you have come/ to prefer sleep. Night Fishing. Gary Stein. PoUp

When you see a guy reach for stars in the sky. Guys and Dolls. Frank Loesser. OBAL

When you see a pretty maiden who has just turn'd seventeen. You're Not the Only Pebble on the Beach. Harry Braisted. FSN

When you see me the last time. To the Sun. Ramon Fernandez. EC

When you send out invitations, don't ask me. Palladas, *tr. fr. Greek by* Tony Harrison. OBVE

When you shall see me in the toils of time. She, to Him. Thomas Hardy. OxBTC

When you show me. Colors for Mama. Barbara Mahone. CNA; PoBA

When you stand it in the dark. The Pouch. Thom Swiss. AAN

When you start for San Francisco. Humbug Steamship Companies. *Unknown.* BPAW

When you stop looking at the garden. Not Singing. Linda Gregg. AAN

When you swim in the surf off Seal Rocks, and your family. Family. Josephine Miles. GP

When you take your pill. The Pill versus the Springhill Mine Disaster. Richard Brautigan. NowV

When you the sunburnt pilgrim see. Good Counsel to a Young Maid. Thomas Carew. CaPo

When you think of the distances. The Distances. W. S. Merwin. NOBA

When you turn down your glass it's a sign. Table Manners. James Montgomery Flagg. TDH

When You Walk. James Stephens. ECBV

When you walked down the stairs. In Praise of Beverly. Steve Orlen. GP

When you wardance, sometimes you must. Wardance. Phillip William George. NW; VoR

When you was down sick down on your bed. She's Gone Blues. *Unknown.* BluL

When you were. For Angela. Zack Gilbert. PoBA

When you were/ a girl, you pricked. Woman. Umberto Saba, *tr. by* Christopher Millis. AMV-81

When you were here in wonderful Detroit. Goodbye David Tamunoemi West. Margaret Danner. BPo

When you were in high school, in the old red brick. To Alpha Dryden Eberhart November 26, 1977, on Being Seventy-five. Richard Eberhart. PCho

When you were lying on the white sand. Incident. Fleur Adcock. ATNZ

When You Were Sweet Sixteen. James Thornton. BLSH, *with music*; FSN, *with music*; FSW

When you were young you probably played. Alabama. Margo Bohanon. SES

When you whom Jules de Goncourt's prose. O Matre Pulchra. Charles Spear. ATNZ

When you withdrew the dagger of your grin. Sonnet to a Tyrant. Mary Anne Ellis. AMV-80

When you woke up among them. After Grief. Stanley Plumly. AmPA

When You Write Again. Ingrid Jonker, *tr. fr. Afrikaans by* Jack Cope *and* William Plomer. PBWP

When you wrote your letter it was April. Response. Mary Ursula Bethell. ATNZ

When young I scribbled, boasting, on my wall. The Summing-up. Stanley Kunitz. OBAL

When Young Ladies Get Married. *Unknown.* AmFP

When your birthday brings the world under your window. April Birthday. Ted Hughes. DuDr

When Your Cheap Divorce Is Granted. "Orpheus C. Kerr." OBAL

When your eyes gaze seaward. Golden Moonrise. William Stanley Braithwaite. PoBA

When your eyes shall be closing, your mouth be opening. *Tr. from Gaelic by* Douglas Hyde. WTO

When your hour was rung at last. Rendez-vous Manqué dans la Rue Racine. J. M. Synge. BIrV

When your oldest son reaches. Child Collecting. David James. TC

When Your Parents Grow Old. Joanne Hart. AMV-80

When your perfections to my thoughts appeare. Henry Constable. *Fr.* Diana. ESo

When your sperm enters me, it is altered. Adrienne Rich. *Fr.* Ghazals. CABA (1972 ed.); NIL

When You're Away. Samuel Hoffenstein. POL

When you're daydreaming. I Haven't Forgotten T. S. Eliot. David Kirby. AAN

When you're lying awake with a dismal headache. Nightmare. W. S. Gilbert. *Fr.* Iolanthe. FaBoNo; NOBL; PBMP

When you're out in smart society. Well, Did You Evah? Cole Porter. OBAL

When you're sailing in strange harbors, Cutty Sark, Cutty Sark. The Clipper *Dunbar* to the Clipper *Cutty Sark*. Ethel Anderson. PoTa

"When you've got a good hat." Between a Good Hat and Good Boots. Kell Robertson. TAT

When you've grown up, my dears, and are as old as I. Toyland. Glen MacDonough. BLSo; FSN

When you've just been jugged by an upright judge. They Can't Do That. *Unknown.* WTO

Whenas galoshed my Julia goes. Upon Julia's Arctics. Bert Leston Taylor. OBAL

Whenas in perfume Julia went. Herrick's Julia. Helen Bevington. SpRo

Whenas in silks my Julia goes. Upon Julia's Clothes. Robert Herrick. AnMo; CABA (1972 ed.); CaPo; EBEV; ExPo (1973 ed.); FF; GBL; HAP; HeIP; HoPM (1975 ed.); ILP (1975 ed.); InPS; IPWM; LFH; NIL; NOBE; OAEL-1; PAIC; PoIA; PoPle; PPP; SCP-1; SpRo; SS; WeW; WIF

Whenas [*or* When as] man's life, the light of human lust. Memento Mori. Fulke Greville. *Fr.* Caelica. BoReV; SCP-2

Whenas Queen Anne of great renown. A New Ballad. Arthur Mainwaring. APAS

Whenas the mildest month. The Rose. Thomas Howell. FSFS

Whenas the nightingale chanted her vespers. Mark Antony. John Cleveland. OAEL-1; SCP-2

Whenas we sat in Babylon. Bible, *O.T., paraphrased by* Thomas Sternhold *and* John Hopkins. Psalms, CXXXVII. OAEL-1

"Whence are you, learning's son?" The End of Clonmacnois. Frank O'Connor, *tr. fr. Irish.* CIP

Whence art thou, thirsty wind. O Thirsty Wind. *Tr. fr. Hawaiian by* N. B. Emerson. WTO

Whence comes Solace?—Not from seeing. On a Fine Morning. Thomas Hardy. VLP

Whence did all that fury come? A Stick of Incense. W. B. Yeats. AnMo

Whence Had They Come? W. B. Yeats. BoLoP

Whence, hardworn, drum. Tambour. István Vas, *tr. by* Jascha Kessler. VWA

Whence hast thou then, thou witless puss. Tiger at Play. Joanna Baillie. PCat

Whence let us go to. "The Nicest Phantasies Are Shared." Brian Coffey. CIP

Whene'er I come where ladies are. Love at Large. Coventry Patmore. *Fr.* The Angel in the House. VPC

Whene'er I see soft hazel eyes. The Lapful of Nuts. Sir Samuel Ferguson. VLP

Whene'er with haggard eyes I view. Song by Rogero. George Canning. *Fr.* The Rovers. FaBoNo

Whenever a fellow called Rex. Limerick. *Unknown.* NOBL

Whenever I move. 2 Poems Written on Turning Around Too Quickly while Hiking. Morton Marcus. NVAP

Whenever I pause. The Noise of the Village. *Tr. by* Frances Densmore. OBVE

Whenever I plunge my arm, like this. Under the Waterfall. Thomas Hardy. BoLoP

Whenever I Say "America." Nancy Byrd Turner. CTV

Whenever it rains. Telephones, Muzak. Vincent Buckley. *Fr.* Golden Builders. CAAP

Whenever Richard Cory went down town. Richard Cory. E. A. Robinson. AmVN; BBGO; CMoP (1972 ed.); DL; FF; HAP; ILP (1975 ed.); InPK; IP; IPWM; MiP; NIL;NOBA; ' PAIC; PoTa; SFF; SoSe; STS; TAP; TH; UsP; WIF

Whenever the dark cloud horses galloped. And Jesus Don't Have Much Use for His Old Suitcase Anymore. Tom Kryss. NeAC

Whenever the days are cool and clear. The Sandhill Crane. Mary Austin. BPAW; ECBV; WPW

Whenever the moon and stars are set. Windy Nights. Robert Louis Stevenson. ECBV; FPB; OxBChV; PH

Whenever the president of some country speaks. Hanging Clothes. Rolly Kent. AAN

Whenever the sheets are out. The Horse. Peter Wild. MPA

Whenever the Snakes Come. Hedva Harkavi, *tr. fr. Hebrew by* Tova Weizman. VWA

Whenever the summer-singed plains. Caller of the Buffalo. Mary Austin. BPAW

Whenever you drink all night you make. Martial, *tr. fr. Latin by* James Michie. FaBoEE

Whenever you want to leave the clay, the deep. Southern Exposures. G. E. Murray. AMV-81

Whenne ich see on roode. On the Passion. *Unknown.* OxBM

Whenne mine eynen misteth. All Too Late. *Unknown.* EBEV; OxBM

Wher is Paris and Heleine. Where Is Paris and Helene? Thomas of Hales. OxBM

Where a Roman judged a foreign people. Notre Dame. Osip Mandelstam, *tr. by* James Greene. OBVE

Where a safe hearth glows warm. Art and Civilization. Robert Conquest. NoAM

Where am I now? And what. A Song in Passing. Yvor Winters. VGW

Where am I? Sure I wander 'midst enchantment. Thomas Otway. *Fr.* The Orphan; or, The Unhappy Marriage. SCP-2

Where are all thy beauties now, all hearts enchaining? Thomas Campion. GBL

Where are Elmer, Herman, Bert, Tom and Charley. The Hill. Edgar Lee Masters. *Fr.* Spoon River Anthology. CMoP (1970 ed.); NoAM; NOBA; TAP

Where are the hands and feet. Give Me My Infant Now. Te-whaka-io-roa, *tr. by* John White. WTO

Where Are the Hebrew Children? *with music. At. to* Peter Cartwright. AH

Where are the heroes of yesteryear? Where, O Where? Milton Bracker. LiSp

Where Are the Ones Who Lived Before? *Unknown. See* Ubi Sunt Qui ante Nos Fuerunt?

Where are the passions they essayed. Ballade of Dead Actors. W. E. Henley. PPoD

Where are the people. Question. Norma Craig. POL

Where are the swains, who, daily labour done. The Oncoming Industrial Revolution. George Crabbe. *Fr.* The Village. OBP

Where Are the War Poets? C. Day Lewis. OxBTC

Where are they that barred the way. At Masada. Ernest Neufeld. AMV-81

Where are we going? We Were of Them. William Pillin. SPT

Where are we to go when this is done? Sonnet. Alfred A. Duckett. AmNP (1974 ed.); PoBA

Where are you. Words for Neruda. Paul Carroll. FiCh

Where are you going? asked Manny the Mayor. Jig Tune: Not for Love. Thomas McGrath. VGW

Where Are You Going, My Good Old Man? *Unknown.* FSW

"Where are you going, my little pig?" Little Piggy. Thomas Hood. ECBV

"Where are you going?" said the knight in the road. The False Knight upon the Road. *Unknown.* AmFP

"Where are you going to, my pretty maid?" The Milkmaid. *Unknown.* BBL; MG

"Where are you going tonight, tonight." John Evereldown. E. A. Robinson. CMoP (1970 ed.)

Where Are You Now? Mary Britton Miller. ECBV

Where Are You Now Superman? Brian Patten. FF

Where are your heroes, my little black ones. Poem for Black Boys. Nikki Giovanni. BPo

Where art thou? Flathead and Nez Perce Sin-ka-ha. William S. Lewis. BPAW

Where art thou, God? or where is he. The Inquisition. Thomas Beedome. SCP-2

Where art thou, my beloved son. The Affliction of Margaret. Wordsworth. MBPR

Where Babylon Ends. Nathaniel Tarn. VWA

Where be ye going, you Devon maid? Keats. MBPR

Where beeth they biforen us weren. *See* Were beth they biforen us weren.

Where can a man buy a cap for his knee? Foolish Questions. *Unknown, ad. by* William Cole. OSF

Where can we go today. Love (Dialogue) Poem. Michael Dransfield. FPA

Where cider ends there ale begins to reign. The Cambrian Swain. Edward Davies. *Fr.* Chepstow: A Poem. OBW

Where Claribel low-lieth. Claribel. Tennyson. PeD

Where clear air blew off the land. York Harbor Morning. George Garrett. CSP

Where cows did slowly seek the brink. The Bwoat. William Barnes. VLP

Where Cross the Crowded Ways of Life, *with music.* Frank Mason North. AH; BLSH

Where deep cliffs loom enormous, where casade. John Betjeman. *Fr.* Sunday Afternoon in St. Enodoc Church, Cornwall. PES

Where Did He Run To? Mark Van Doren. SO

"Where did I come from, Mother, and why?" Christmas Lullaby for a New-born Child. Yvonne Gregory. AmNP (1974 ed.)

Where did I dwell? I dwelt in the shadow of death. Wanderer. Jessica Powers. AMV-80

Where did it roll in from, that sea of light. In Two Fields. Waldo Williams, *tr. by* Gwyn Jones. OBW

Where did the voice come from? I hunted through the rooms. Bedtime Story for My Son. Peter Redgrove. BuTh

Where Did You Come From, Baby Dear? George MacDonald. OxBChV

Where Did You Get That Hat? *with music.* Joseph J. Sullivan. FSN

Where dips the rocky highland. The Stolen Child. W. B. Yeats. CMoP (1970 ed.); TT

Where do all the failed fathers. Failed Fathers. Lewis Turco. AMV-81

Where do shadows live? Lectures on the Biology of the Shadow. George M. Young, Jr. FAF

Where Do the Children Play? Cat Stevens. PoRo; UsP

"Where do the waters go that go." ¿Quien Sabe? Madge Morris. BPAW

Where do you go with your fury. Fury's Field. Cecil Bodker, *tr. by* Nadia Christensen. PBWP

Where does it hurt? Deed. Elisabeth Murawski. PoUp

Where dost thou careless lie. An Ode to Himself. Ben Jonson. Epi; ExPo (1973 ed.); HAP; ILP (1975 ed.); NOBE; PAIC; SCP-1

Where ends our chancel in a vaulted space. The Vicar. George Crabbe. *Fr.* The Borough. OBSV

Where five old graves lay circled on a hill. The Graveyard. Jane Cooper. CoPAm

Where Forlorn Sunsets. W. E. Henley. ILP (1975 ed.)

Where from the watch towers. Bay Poem. Lance Henson. VoR

Where go the birds when the rain. Jane Heap. PoA

Where Go the Boats? Robert Louis Stevenson. CTV; LCL; OxBChV

Where had I heard this wind before. Bereft. Robert Frost. SoSe (1977 ed.)

Where has tenderness gone, he asked the mirror. Delirium in Vera Cruz. Malcolm Lowry. FaBoTw (1975 ed.); OxBTC; UsP

Where has ti been, maw canny hinny? Captain Bover. *Unknown.* GBP

Where hast 'te been, ma' canny hinny? Ma Canny Hinny. *Unknown.* GBP

Where hast thou been since I saw thee. Ilkley Moor Baht 'At. *Unknown.* FSW

Where Have All the Flowers Gone? Pete Seeger. PoRo; SoS; WeW

"Where have you been all day, Rendal my son?" Lord Rendal. *Unknown.* RDB

Where have you been all the day, Billy Boy, Billy Boy. Billy Boy. *Unknown.* GSB

"Where have you been this while away." The Widow's Party. Kipling. PeBB; VLP

Where Have You Gone. Mari Evans. BPo; MiP; TPo

Where Have You Gone, Little Boy. Patty L. Harjo. VoR

Where He Leads Me I Will Follow, *with music.* E. W. Blandy. BLSH

Where he really hung, there. One More Time. James Welch. VW

Where he rows the dark. The Bear Who Came to Dinner. Adrien Stoutenburg. SO

Where he stood and where. Jew. James A. Randall, Jr. BPo

Where hills are hard and bare. Abraham's Knife. George Garrett. CSP

Where I Am Now. Harvey Shapiro. GP

Where I lived the river. Eclogues. Dennis Schmitz. NVAP

Where I wait, huge sea rhythms roll. Domesticating Two Landscapes. Madeline DeFrees. CNW

Where I Walk in Nebraska. Nancy G. Westerfield. AMV-80

Where I walk out. Song. Yvor Winters. BoAnP; POL

Where icy and bright dungeons lift. Voyages, VI. Hart Crane. CABA (1972 ed.); ExPo (1973 ed.); HAP; UnPo (1976 ed.)

Where I'm Staying Now. William Meredith. FoP

Where in blind files. Song. Eavan Boland. CIP; IPM

Where, in what ever-blissfully watered gardens. Rainer Maria Rilke, *tr. by* James Blair Leishman. *Fr.* Sonnets to Orpheus, Pt. II, XVII. OBVE

Where in what strange Elysium is now the *Literary Digest.* Ubi Iam Sunt? Richard L. Greene. PAIC

Where innocent bright-eyed daisies are. Daisies. Christina Rossetti. PCOP

Where is his mind, the old Greek farmer at the bar? His Good Time. Roland Flint. PoUp

Where Is Justice? Eliezer Steinbarg, *tr. fr. Yiddish by* Seth L. Wolitz. VWA

Where is my Chief, my master, this bleak night, mavrone! Ode to the Maguire. Eochaidh O'Hussey. BIrV

Where is my roof that kept out the rain? Roses Gone Wild. John Taylor. AMV-80

Where Is My Wandering Boy Tonight. Robert Lowry. FSW

Where Is Our Holy Church? *with music.* Edwin H. Wilson. AH

Where Is Paris and Helene? Thomas of Hales. OxBM

Where is that sugar, Hammond. Early Evening Quarrel. Langston Hughes. UnPo (1976 ed.); UsP

Where Is the Black Community? Joyce Carol Thomas. CNA

Where is the duke my father with his power? Shakespeare. King Richard II, *fr.* III, ii. PoPle

Where is the grave of Sir Arthur O'Kellyn? The Knight's Tomb. Samuel Taylor Coleridge. MBPR

Where is the Jim Crow section. Merry-go-round. Langston Hughes. CTBA

Where Is the Sea? Felicia Dorothea Hemans. RhR

Where is the star of Bethlehem? Christmas 1959 et Cetera. Gerald William Barrax. OFD; PChr

Where is the tree on which i stand. Sandra Maria Esteves. NW

Where is the white horse? The White Horse. Ann Stanford. MPA

Where is the world? not about. Merchant Marine. Josephine Miles. TAP; VGW

Where is the world we roved, Ned Bunn? To Ned. Herman Melville. NOBA

Where is this stupendous stranger? The Nativity of Our Lord and Saviour Jesus Christ. Christopher Smart. *Fr.* Hymns and Spiritual Songs. BoReV; EBEV; HAP; LAuP; NOBE; OBP; WeW

Where It Appears. Robert Duncan. *Fr.* Passages. PiAm

Where it is. Robert Creeley. PiAm

Where it says snow. Errata. Charles Simic. NNaP; NVAP

Where It's At. Carol Bergé. MMD

Where Knock Is Open Wide. Theodore Roethke. HAP; VGW "He watered the roses," *sel.* OSP

Where laurel hedges hide the coal and coke. Crematorium. John Betjeman. PoA

Where Lies the Land? Arthur Hugh Clough. BBGO; ILP (1975 ed.); NOBE; RhR

Where lies the land to which yon ship must go? Wordsworth. ILP (1975 ed.); MBPR

Where light is. To a Woman Who Wants Darkness and Time. Gerald W. Barrax. PoBA

Where, like a pillow on a bed. The Ecstasy [or Extasie]. John Donne. BoLoP; CABA (1972 ed.); ExPo (1973 ed.); HAP; ILP (1975 ed.); InPS; LoAs; MetP; NOBE; OAEL-1; OBP; PPoe; SCP-1

Where Liver Eatin' Johnson lies. Old Trail Town, Cody Wyoming. John Garmon. TAT

Where London's column, pointing at the skies. A Sad Story. Pope. *Fr.* Moral Essays, Epistle III. BoReV

Where long the shadows of the wind had rolled. The Sheaves. E. A. Robinson. CMoP (1970 ed.); ExPo (1973 ed.); HAP; ILP (1975 ed.); NoAM; NOBA; PiAm; TAP

Where marble stood and fell. Reflection in a Green Arena. Gregory Corso. VGW

Where metalled road invades light thinning air. Sándor Weöres, *tr. by* Edwin Morgan. *Fr.* The Lost Parasol. OBVE

Where might there be a refuge for me. Tell Me, Tell Me. Marianne Moore. Psy

Where Mission Creek Runs Hard for Joy. Richard Hugo. CNW

Where Mountain Lion Lay Down with Deer. Leslie Silko. VoR

Where my grandmother lived. Number Four. Doughtry Long. CNA; PoBA; SO

Where Nothing Dwelt but Beasts of Prey, *with music.* Isaac Watts. AH

Where Now Are the Hebrew Children? *with music. Unknown.* AH

Where now the high-rise-village highways. Out of the Past. Robert Wallace. POL

Where, O Where? Milton Bracker. LiSp

Where oh where is little Susie? Paw-Paw Patch. *Unknown.* FSW

Where once proud scarecrows stood. The Profligate. John T. Zaremba. DNGG

Where once we danced, where once we sang. An Ancient to Ancients. Thomas Hardy. CMoP (1970 ed.); OxBTC

Where once you stood alert, alive. Ode to a Vanished Operator in an Automatized Elevator. Loyd Rosenfeld. QQQ

Where others love and praise my verses, still. To The Detractor. Robert Herrick. SCP-1

Where peace goes whispering by. The Farm. Vassar Miller. NCSH

Where pollen crusts the pine bough. David Martinson. *Fr.* Nineteen Sections from a Twenty Acre Poem. TAT

Where rivers tumble. The Shepherd. James K. Baxter. ECBV

Where shall the eyes a darkness find. Huw Menai. *Fr.* Back in the Return. OBW

Where shall we go? August Afternoon. Marion Edey. FPB

Where shall we go? Where shall we go? June Fugue. Thomas Shapcott. CAAP; GAS

Where She Told Her Love. John Clare. VLP

Where She Was Not Born. Yvonne. CNA

Where sunless rivers weep. Dream Land. Christina Rossetti. VLP

Where sways the bronze of heavy wheat. Bread. William Pillin. SPT

Where the acorn tumbles down. The Fieldmouse. Cecil Frances Alexander. OxBChV

Where the ball ran into the bushes. 1939. Alan Brownjohn. LP

Where the bee sucks, there suck I. Ariel's Song. Shakespeare. *Fr.* The Tempest. CABA (1972 ed.); HeIP; ILP (1975 ed.); LCL; NOBE; PCOP; PoIA; SoSe

Where the bomb fell. Renewal. Lord Russell Brain. PMW

Where the camshaft weeps. Resting Place. Jon Silkin. VWA

Where the cedar leaf divides the sky. Passage. Hart Crane. CMoP (1970 ed.); ExPo (1973 ed.); NoAM; NOBA

Where the cities end. Transcontinent. Donald Hall. MiP

Where the city's ceaseless crowd moves on the livelong day. Sparkles from the Wheel. Walt Whitman. AmVN; BiP

Where the enemy has gone. Green Tanks and Other Hidden Vehicles of Destruction. Alex Kuo. NW

Where the Fight Was. Alice Corbin, *after Chippewa Indian.* BPAW

Where the Great Northern plunged in. The Wreck of the Great Northern. Robert Hedin. AMV-81

Where the Hayfields Were. Archibald MacLeish. DuDa

Where the lizard ran to its little prey. The Range in the Desert. Randall Jarrell. NOBA

Where the Mind Meets the Moon in Revolt. Helen Wolfert. *Fr.* Woman against the Moon. RiTi

Where the mob gathers, swiftly shoot along. John Gay. *Fr.* Trivia; or, The Art of Walking the Streets of London. OAEL-1

Where the Moosatockmaguntic. The Ballad of Hiram Hover. Bayard Taylor. FaBoCo; OBAL

Where the owl. Hunters. Sonya Dorman. RiTi

Where the pheasant roosts at night. The Vernal Ague. Philip Freneau. EAP

Where the Picnic Was. Thomas Hardy. OxBTC

Where the pools are bright and deep. A Boy's Song. James Hogg. BBL; CTV; FaPoR; OxBChV; PoPle

Where the printing-works buttress a church. The Coldness. Jon Silkin. CABA (1972 ed.); VWA

Where the quiet-coloured end of evening smiles. Love among the Ruins. Robert Browning. HAP; NOBE; OAEL-2; STS; VLP

Where the Red Lion flaring o'er the way. A Description of an Author's Bedchamber. Goldsmith. BIrV

Where the remote Bermudas ride. Bermudas. Andrew Marvell. AnMo; BoReV; CABA (1972 ed.); ExPo (1973 ed.); ILP (1975 ed.); MetP; NIL; NOBE

Where the River Shannon Flows, *with music.* James I. Russell. FSN

Where the seas are open moor. The Harpooning. Ted Walker. EcS

Where the shimmering sands of the desert beat. Two Bits. Sharlot M. Hall. BPAW

Where the Slow Fig's Purple Sloth. Robert Penn Warren. PiAm

Where the waters gently flow. The Song of the Reed Sparrow. *Unknown.* OxBChV

Where the wind. Footprints on the Glacier. W. S. Merwin. NoAM

Where then shall hope and fear their objects find? The Power of Prayer [or Prayer]. Samuel Johnson. *Fr.* The Vanity of Human Wishes. BoReV; NOBE

Where there is personal liking we go. The Hero. Marianne Moore. *Fr.* Part of a Novel, Part of a Poem, Part of a Play. CMoP (1970 ed.); NIL; NOBA; PoA

Where there's law, no woman gets justice. For Every Sister in the White Man's Jail. Rita Mae Brown. WBN

Where they came from once. The Cattle Ghosts. David Allan Evans. NVAP

Where this interior lies the bass are not/ biting. Working the Wood. Susan Sonde. PoUp

Where, thy true treasure? Gold Says, "Not in me." Edward
  Young. *Fr.* The Complaint; or, Night Thoughts, VI.
  OAEL-1

Where to hide a leaf, he said. The Place. Robert Wallace.
  CoPAm

Where to, Lady? Where do you want to go? Experiential
  Religion. Travis Du Priest. AMV-80

Where true love burns desire is love's pure flame. Desire.
  Samuel Taylor Coleridge. MBPR

Where Two o'Clock Came From. Kenneth Patchen. SO

Where two or three were heaped together, or fifty. The March.
  Robert Lowell. NowV

Where was I at the hour of sowing. Questions. Dagmar
  Hilarova, *tr. by* Ewald Osers. VWA

Where was the boundary between the bitter water. Salmon Cycle.
  Avner Treinin, *tr. by* Robert Friend. VWA

Where was the fault? You do not know nor can. The Garden.
  Stuart Silverman. CoPAm

Where was you last winter, boys. The Horse Trader's Song.
  *Unknown.* AmFP

Where We Are Going. Patricia Goedicke. AAN

Where we live, the teakettle whistles out. Now. William
  Stafford. NNaP

Where we made the fire. Where the Picnic Was. Thomas Hardy.
  OxBTC

Where We Must Look for Help. Robert Bly. ConAP

Where we went in the boat was a long bay. The Mediterranean.
  Allen Tate. GOA; HAP; VGW; WeW

Where we were walking in the day's light, seeing. Time in the
  Rock, XXXVII. Conrad Aiken. VGW

Where were the greenhouses going. Big Wind. Theodore
  Roethke. AnMo; CMoP (1970 ed.); NCSH; PiAm; PPoe;
  UsP; VGW

Where Were You? Lonnie L. Landrum. DNGG

Where? When? Which? Langston Hughes. BPo

Where, where are now the great reports. Fuimus Fumus. Joshua
  Sylvester. FaBoEE

Where, where but here have Pride and Truth. On Hearing That
  the Students of Our New University Have Joined the
  Agitation against Immoral Literature. W. B. Yeats. NoAM

Where you see the undersides of their wings. Skimmers. Paul
  Baker Newman. CSP; EcS

Where you traveled the body couldn't go. The Traveler. David
  Bottoms. AMV-80

Wherefore peep'st thou, envious day? *Unknown.* GBL

Wherefore, unlaurelled boy. George Darley. NOBE

Wherefore, with this belief, held like a blade. Frederick Goddard
  Tuckerman. *Fr.* Sonnets. AmVN

Wherein Consists the High Estate, *with music.* Ebenezer Dayton.
  AH

Wherelings Whenlings. E. E. Cummings. HAP; WeW

Where's Babe Ruth, the King of Swat? The Ballad of Dead
  Yankees. Donald Petersen. HeIP; LiSp

Where's master?/ At's prayers, sir, he. Ben Jonson. *Fr.* The
  Alchemist. LFH

Where's the meeting place for. Shir Ma'alot/ A Song of Degrees.
  Richard Flantz. VWA

Where's the poet? show him! show him. Fragment. Keats.
  MBPR

Where's the winning without chocolate. The Chocolate Soldiers.
  Calvin Forbes. MAT

Wheresoe'er I turn my view. Lines [Written] in Ridicule of
  Certain Poems Published in 1777. Samuel Johnson.
  FaBoCo; FaBoEE; PAIC; PPoD

Wheresoever ye fare by frith or by fell. Julians Barnes. *Fr.* Book
  of Hunting. WPE

Whereto should I express/ My inward heaviness? To His Lady.
  Henry VIII, King of England. EBEV

Wherever God erects a house of prayer. Daniel Defoe. *Fr.* The
  True-born Englishman, I. NOBL; OBSV

Wherever I am, there's always Pooh. Us Two. A. A. Milne.
  OxBChV

Wherever I go to find. Pigeons. Bert Meyers. EAS

Wherever I may be. The Absent One. Mary Queen of Scots, *tr.
  by* Antonia Fraser. SLP

Wherever I walked I went green among young growing. Trinity
  Churchyard. Muriel Rukeyser. NYP

Wherever shadow falls wherever the drowning. Contra Mortem.
  Hayden Carruth. PCho; PoA

Wherever we are in this country. Shawn Wong. *Fr.* Kicking
  Lego Blocks. NW

Wherever your voice moves. Love Song. Kosrof Chantikian.
  AMV-81

Whet all your wits and antidote your eyes. The Tragi-Comedy of
  Titus Oates. *Unknown.* APAS

Whet up your axe and whistle up your dog. Groundhog.
  *Unknown.* FSW

Whether dinner was pleasant, with the windows lit by gunfire.
  No Credit. Kenneth Fearing. CMoP (1970 ed.); SPT

Whether Firelocked. Mary Shumway. HeS

Whether on Ida's shady brow. To the Muses. Blake. HAP;
  HeIP; LAuP; MBPR; NOBE; OAEL-2; STS

Whether one paints five Helens. The Ultimate Antientropy.
  Theodore Weiss. NoAM

Whether or not I find the missing thing. But Not Forgotten.
  Luci Shaw. AATT

Whether or not I watch. The Egg of Nothing. John Taylor.
  AMV-81

Whether the bees have thoughts, we cannot say. The Long
  Waters. Theodore Roethke. CNW

Whether the graver did by this intend. On the Late
  Metamorphosis of an Old Picture of Oliver Cromwell's.
  *Unknown.* APAS

Whether the greater or the little death. Apology for Liberals.
  Joy Davidman. SPT

Whether the sensitive plant, or that. Shelley. *Fr.* The Sensitive
  Plant. OAEL-2

Whether the Turkish new-moon minded be. Astrophel and Stella,
  XXX. Sir Philip Sidney. Epi

Whether these lines do find you out. An Epistle. Sir John
  Suckling. PAIC

Whether what we sense of this world. William Bronk. VGW

Whether you strode from court to court. The Man, My Father.
  Marcia Lee Masters. HeS

Whetstone, The. Clarice Short. MPA

Which I wish to remark. The Heathen Chinee [*or* Plain Language
  from Truthful James]. Bret Harte. AmVN; BPAW;
  FaBoCo; NOBL; OBAL

Which I wish to remark. The Heathern Pass-ee. A. C. Hilton.
  FaBoCo; NOBL

Which is man who wot, and what. This World Fares as a
  Fantasy. *Unknown.* OxBM

Which Is My Little Boy. Tennessee Williams. SS

Which is real. The Indigo Glass in the Grass. Wallace Stevens.
  PoA

Which is the best to hit your taste. Epigram on Two Ladies.
  Sophia Burrell. POL

Which Is the Bow? *Unknown.* GBP

Which Is the Way to Somewhere Town? Kate Greenaway. CTV

Which Side Are You On? Florence Reese. FSW

Which Washington? Eve Merriam. CC

Which Wing the Angel Chooses. Vincent O'Sullivan. ATNZ

Which-a-way/ which-a-way. Bye Bye Baby Blues. *Unknown.* BluL

Whigs' Lamentation for the Death of Their Dear Brother College, The. *Unknown.* APAS

Whig's first letter of his odious name. An Acrostic on Wharton. *Unknown.* OBSV

While Adam slept, from him his Eve arose. *See* Whilst Adam slept, Eve from his side arose.

While an intrinsic ardor prompts to write. To the University of Cambridge in New England. Phillis Wheatley. SBG; TAP

While Beast instructs his fair and innocent wife. On Sir Voluptuous Beast. Ben Jonson. SCP-1

While back, my father got some letters, A. The Violin Tree. Joel Rosenberg. VWA

While breaking the big rock. Stone Giant. Joseph Bruchac. CDW

While Cecil Snores: Mom Drinks Cold Milk. James Cunningham. JB

While drinking, all at once I saw. The Three Kingdoms of Nature. Gotthold Lessing, *tr.* by Alfred Baskerville, *ad.* by Robert Bly. NU

While duns were knocking at my door. The Ramble: An Anti-heroic Poem. Alexander Radcliffe. SCP-2

While everyone else is laughing and drinking. Catullus, *tr. fr. Latin* by Peter Whigham. TwMBP

While going the road to sweet Athy. Johnny, I Hardly Knew Ye! *Unknown.* BIrV; FaBoBa; GBP; InPK; OBP; PeBB

While he slept, I poured salt in his ears. Judith Recalls Holofernes. Maura Stanton. AmPA

While he talked the wireless man listened. The Refugee. Dabney Stuart. GP

While I am on the dark bus and the spin of the wheels. A Grammar of the Soul. Margaret Gibson. AAN

While I Am Young, *with music.* Silas Ballou. AH

"While I sit at the door." Eve. Christina Rossetti. NIL

While I stood here, in the open, lost in myself. Milkweed. James Wright. NOBA; NU

While I was building neat. It Is Dangerous to Read Newspapers. Margaret Atwood. HeIP; Psy

While I watch the Christmas blaze. The Reminder. Thomas Hardy. CMoP (1970 ed.)

While I'm standin' guard the nicht I see. Bizerta. George Campbell Hay, *tr. fr. Gaelic* . MS

While in the mask of night there shone that cut. Landing on the Moon. May Swenson. Moon

While in this cavernous place employed. A Civil Servant. Robert Graves. InPK

While joy gave clouds the light of stars. The Villain. W. H. Davies. OxBTC; SoSe

While ladling butter from alternate tubs. On the Historians Freeman and Stubbs. J. E. Thorold Rogers. FaBoEE

While leanest beasts in pastures feed. Supreme Fortune Falls Soonest. Robert Herrick. CaPo

While, Lydia, I was lov'd of thee. A Dialogue between Horace and Lydia. Horace, *tr. by* Robert Herrick. Odes, III, 9. OBVE

While many a noble name, to virtue dear. Epistle to Peter Pindar. William Gifford. ESaP

While Mom and Dad. No Respect for Authority. Marisha Chamberlain. AAN

While my father walked through mud. 1905. David Ignatow. VWA

While my hair was still cut straight across my forehead. The River-Merchant's Wife: A Letter. Li Po, *tr. by* Ezra Pound. BoLoP; CABA (1972 ed.); HAP; InPK; InPS; IPWM; LoAs; NIL; NoAM; NOBA; NOBE; OBVE; PAIC; PPoe; PPP; SoS; TAP; TPo; UnPo (1976 ed.)

While Northward the hot sun was sinking o'er the trees. The Psalm. Robert Bridges. FaBoTw (1975 ed.)

While o'er Our Guilty Land, O Lord, *with music.* Samuel Davies. AH

While o'er the Deep Thy Servants Sail, *with music.* George Burgess. AH

While others slept I rose, and looked upon the garden. Trance. Mary Ursula Bethell. ATNZ

While rain, with eve in partnership. Beyond the Last Lamp. Thomas Hardy. NOBE

While she proclaims the beauty. For Josephina. Wayne Miller. CPA

While Shepherds Watched. Nahum Tate. GSB, *with music* ("While shepherds watched their flocks by night.") AmFP

While some go dancing reels and some. Three Old Brothers. Frank O'Connor. PFIr

While some on rights and some on wrongs. Fair and Free Elections. *Unknown.* FSW

While some "rap" over this turmoil. The Rhetoric of Langston Hughes. Margaret Danner. FB

While sorrows encompass me round. Death-Bed Song. *Unknown.* AmFP

While strolling along with the city's vast throng. She May Have Seen Better Days. James Thornton. FSN

While strolling down the street one eve upon mere pleasure bent. Just Tell Them That You Saw Me. Paul Dresser. FSN

While strolling through the hills one day. Tannhauser. Newman Levy. OBAL

While Strolling through the Park One Day. Ed Haley. BLSo, *with music;* FSW (Fountain in the Park, The.) FSN

While that my soul repairs to her devotion. Church Monuments. George Herbert. CABA (1972 ed.); HAP; ILP (1975 ed.); OAEL-1; SCP-1

While that the sun with his beams hot. Philon the Shepherd. *Unknown.* NOBE

While the blue noon above us arches. Annihilation. Conrad Aiken. GBL

While the cock with lively din. Milton. *Fr.* L'Allegro. SCP-1

While the Garden Grows. Cinda Kornblum. AcAn

While the heel rears up in petty arrogance. Oration on the Toes. Edward Brynes. AMV-81

While the leaves of the bamboo rustle. *Unknown, tr. fr. Japanese* by Geoffrey Bownas *and* Anthony Thwaite. BoLoP

While the milder Fates consent. A Lyric to Mirth. Robert Herrick. CaPo

While the other kids on the block. Jane. David Kresh. PoUp

While the Schools and the Teachers Are Teaching. Walt Whitman. AnMo

While the shot and shell were screaming upon the battlefield. Break the News to Mother. Charles Kassel Harris. FSN

While the storm clouds gather far across the sea. God Bless America. Irving Berlin. BLSo

While the sun is finishing. From Garvey's Farm: Seneca, Wisconsin. Ed Hoeppner. AMV-80

While the TV Is Shut Off. Diane Kruchkow. FAF

While the water-wagon's ringing showers. In the Isle of Dogs. John Davidson. PES; VLP

While their hearts were jocund and sublime. Milton. *Fr.* Samson Agonistes. SCP-1

While this America settles in the mould of its vulgarity, heavily thickening to empire. Shine, Perishing Republic. Robinson Jeffers. CMoP (1970 ed.); ExPo (1973 ed.); FF; ILP (1975 ed.); IPWM; MAT; NoAM; NOBA; PiAm; PPoD; TAP; UnPo (1976 ed.); VGW; VoPo; WIF

While Thracians shal with arrowes war, Iazyges with bowe. Ovid, *tr. by* Thomas Underdowne. *Fr.* Invective against Ibis. OBVE

While thus he thought, a monst'rous wave up-bore. Homer, *tr. by* Pope. *Fr.* The Odyssey, V. OBVE

While Titian was grinding rose madder. Limerick. *Unknown.* NOBL

While upon the journey of life. The Mask. Patty L. Harjo. VoR

While visiting Arundel Castle. Limerick. Victor Gray. NOBL

While walking at dusk in a strange city. Elegy. Pinhas Sadeh, *tr. by* Gabriel Preil *and* Howard Schwartz. VWA

While we are at peace. Albatross. Lele-io-Hoku, *tr. by* S. H. Elbert *and* N. Mahoe. WTO

While We Lowly Bow before Thee, *with music.* Daniel C. Colesworthy. AH

While we were fearing it, it came. Emily Dickinson. PPP; Psy

While we were visiting David's grave. Despair. Denise Levertov. NNaP; RiTi

While we were walking under the top. Poem. John Ashbery. EAS

While with a strong and yet a gentle hand. Edmund Waller. *Fr.* A Panegyric to My Lord Protector. SCP-2

While with labor assid'ous due pleasure I mix. The Secretary. Matthew Prior. NIL

While yet the Morning Star. The Unicorn. Ella Young. PCOP

While you read. The Cat. William Matthews. AmPA

Whiles I this standing lake. Sadness. William Cartwright. SCP-2

Whiles it can happen. Aince, I mind. Aiberdeen. Donald Campell. *Fr.* Sonnets frae Siberia. MIS

Whiles someone did chant this lovely lay, The. Song of Bliss. Spenser. *Fr.* The Faerie Queene, II. FF; OBVE

Whilom [*or* Whylom] ther was dwellynge at Oxenford. The Carpenter's Young Wife. Chaucer. *Fr.* The Canterbury Tales: The Miller's Tale. ExPo (1973 ed.); OAEL-1

Whilom ther was dwellynge in my contree. The Friar's Tale. Chaucer. *Fr.* The Canterbury Tales. PAIC

Whilst [*or* While] Adam slept, Eve from his side [*or* from him his Eve] arose. Adam and Eve. *Unknown.* FaBoEE; PoPle

Whilst Alexis lay pressed [*or* prest]. Song. Dryden. *Fr.* Marriage a-la-Mode. BoLoP; FF; LoAs

Whilst eccho cryes, what shall become of mee. Henry Constable. *Fr.* Diana. AAS

Whilst I beheld the neck o' the dove. Hymn. Patrick Carey. SCP-2

Whilst in This World I Stay, *with music.* Philip Pain. AH

Whil'st on Septimius panting brest. Ode: Acme and Septimius. Catullus, *tr. by* Abraham Cowley. OBVE

Whilst pale anxiety, corrosive care. On the Prospect of Establishing a Pantisocracy in America. Samuel Taylor Coleridge. MBPR

Whilst some the Troiane warres in verse recount. Parthenophil and Parthenophe, LX. Barnabe Barnes. ESo

Whilst thirst of praise and vain desire of fame. The Lady's Resolve. Lady Mary Wortley Montagu. BoWoP

Whilst thus my pen strives to eternize thee. Michael Drayton. *Fr.* Idea. AAS; PAIC

Whilst what I write I do not see. Written in Juice of Lemon. Abraham Cowley. *Fr.* The Mistress. CABA (1972 ed.)

Whil'st with hot scent, the Popish Tory crew. A Hue and Cry after Blood and Murder. *Unknown.* APAS

Whilst yet to prove. Farewell to Love. John Donne. OAEL-1

Whinlands. Seamus Heaney. HeHu; PF

Whip, The. Robert Creeley. NoAM

Whipped by sorrow now. Song. Miklós Radnóti, *tr. by* Steven Polgar *and* Stephen Berg *and* S. J. Marks. VWA

Whippet. Prudence Andrew. GDP

Whipping, The. Robert Hayden. GP; MiP; NCSH; PoBA; SFF

Whipping Cheare. *Unknown.* FaBoBa

Whirl up, sea. Oread. Hilda Doolittle ("H. D."). CMoP (1970 ed.); ExPo (1973 ed.); LFH; NoAM; NOBA; PiAm; RiTi; SBG; TAP; UsP; WeW

Whirl'd off at last, for speech I sought. Coventry Patmore. *Fr.* The Angel in the House, II, xi. GBL

Whirlwinds of Danger. *Unknown.* FSW

Whirr, The/ of the sewing machine. The Red Dress. James Bertolino. HeS

Whisker dripping bear grin. The Ainu Men. Gary Lawless. FAF

Whiskey Bill—a Fragment. *Unknown.* BPAW

Whiskey in the Jar. *Unknown.* FSW

Whiskey Johnny ("Whiskey is the life of man"). *Unknown.* FSW

Whiskey on your breath, The. My Papa's Waltz. Theodore Roethke. AnMo; CMoP (1970 ed.); CTBA; FF; HAP; HeIP; HoPM (1975 ed.); ILP (1975 ed.); InPK; InPS; IP; NCSH; NIL; NoAM; NOBA; NowV; PBMP; PoIA; PPoe; PPP; PSN; SoS; STS; TAP; VGW; WeW

Whisky, frisky. The Squirrel. *Unknown.* CTV; PCOP

Whisky Johnny. *Unknown.* AmFP

Whisky whipping g-string Jaguar megaton. Five Psalms of Common Man. Christopher Middleton. TwMBP

Whisper of the wind in, The. Idylls, I. Theocritus, *tr. by* William Carlos Williams. Epi

Whisper of yellow globes. Her Lips Are Copper Wire. Jean Toomer. NoAM

Whispering Clouds. Mariquita Platov. AMV-80

Whispering ghosts of the west. *Tr. fr. Maori by* John White. WTO

Whispering Hope, *with music.* Septimus Winner. PSoN

Whispers. Roberta Hill. CDW

Whispers. Myra Cohn Livingston. LCL

Whispers of Heavenly Death. Walt Whitman. NoAM

Whispers of Immortality. T. S. Eliot. CMoP (1970 ed.); ExPo (1973 ed.); NoAM; NOBA

Whistle, The/ of the bright. Belfast Lough. *Unknown, tr. by* John Montague. BIrV

Whistle, Daughter, Whistle. *Unknown.* AmFP; FSW

Whistle o'er the Lave o't. *Unknown.* GBP

Whistler's Father. Margaret Ryan. NPW

Whistles. Dorothy Aldis. CTV

Whistles like light in leaves, O light. The Heart Flies Up, Erratic as a Kite. Delmore Schwartz. PoA

Whistling geese that, The/ cover the sky. China Lake. John McNally. PoUp

Whistling past this cemetery in the dark. In Memoriam: Gertrud Kolmar, 1943. A. D. Hope. CAAP; GAS

Whistling Thief, The. *Unknown.* PoTa

Whistling Willie. Kaye Starbird. QQQ

Whit Monday. Louis MacNeice. OAEL-2

Whit was His nakede brest. White Was His Naked Breast. *Unknown.* OxBM

White. Marguerite Bouvard. AMV-81

White. Karl Krolow, *tr. fr. German by* Paul Morris. AMV-81

White an' Blue. William Barnes. GBL

White and blue, an outspread fan. Environs of Vanholt I. Charles Spear. ATNZ

White and blue my breathing lady leans. Venice, 182–. John Berryman. CoPAm

White Apples. Donald Hall. TAP

White as her hand fair Julia threw. The Snow-Ball. Soame Jenyns, *after the Latin of* Petronius Afranius. OBVE

White as paper a-sail in the air. *Malay Oral Tradition, tr. by* R. O. Winstedt. WTO

White as snow and snow it isn't. *Unknown.* GBP

White Bear, The. Paula Goff. BCr

White Bear. Susan Griffin. GP

White Beauty, The, *orig. and mod. English prose. Unknown.* OxBM

White Bird. Matti Megged, *tr. fr. Hebrew by* Howard Schwartz. VWA

White bird, A. Shira. Howard Schwartz. VWA

White bird featherless/ Flew from Paradise. *Unknown.* GBP

White bird featherless floats down through the air, A. *Unknown.* GBP

White Blossoms. Robert Mezey. VWA

White buck come in. Anadarko John. Carroll Arnett. VoR

White Butterflies. Swinburne. *See* Envoi: "Fly, white butterflies, out to sea."

White Cat of Trenarren, The. A. L. Rowse. OxBTC; PCat

White chocolate jar full of petals, The Chez Jane. Frank O'Hara. NoAM; NOBA; PoA

White Christmas. W. R. Rodgers. PFIr

White City, The. Claude McKay. BPo; NoAM; TAP

White cloud passed over the land, The. The Final Painting. Lee Harwood. EAS

White cock's tail, The. Ploughing on Sunday. Wallace Stevens. NCSH; RAE

White Collar Ballad. Weldon Kees. AnMo

White Crescents at the Bottoms of Fingernails. Coleman Barks. *Fr.* Body Poems. NVAP

White cups white. *Turkish Love Songs, tr. by* Reza Baraheni *and* Zahra-Soltan Shokoohtaezeh. BoWoP

White curtains of infinite fatigue. And the Seventh Dream Is the Dream of Isis. David Gascoyne. EAS

White day, black river. The Predicter of Famine. William Carlos Williams. VGW

White Devil, The, *sels.* John Webster.
    Call for the Robin Redbreast and the Wren, *fr.* V, iv. EBEV; HAP; HeIP; ILP (1975 ed.)
    (Cornelia's Song.) InPS
    (Dirge, A: "Call for the robin-redbreast and the wren.") NOBE; OBP
    "Do you hear, sir?" SCP-2

White doe appeared to me over green, A. Sonnets to Laura: To Laura in Life, CLVII. Petrarch, *tr. by* R. G. Barnes. Epi

White Doe of Rylstone, The: or, The Fate of the Nortons. Wordsworth. MPBR

White dusk moved ahead of them. Image of City. Lance Henson. VoR

White Fields. James Stephens. ECBV

White flour, earth-flesh, a cold fleece on the mountain. The Snowfall. Gwerfyl Mechain, *tr. by* Kenneth Jackson. OBW

White fog lifting and falling on mountain-brow. Wales Visitation. Allen Ginsberg. CAPP; NNaP; NOBA; Prf

White founts falling on the courts of the sun. Lepanto. G. K. Chesterton. BTTM; FaPo; FaPoR

White Goddess, The. Robert Graves. OAEL-2; OBP

White Goddess. Hubert Witheford. ATNZ

White-gowned woman making offering, A. Virgin Pictured in Profile. Rosanna Warren. AMV-81

White gulls that sit and float. The Echoing Cliff. Andrew Young. EcS; MS

White-haired Lover, *sel.* Karl Shapiro.
    "I swore to stab the sonnet with my pen." PoA

White hard rock. Silica Carbonate Rock. Fred Berry. NU

White Hare, The. Lilian Bowes-Lyon. OxBTC; PoPle

White Heliotrope. Arthur Symons. BoLoP; EBEV; InPS

White Horse, The. W. H. Davies. OxBTC

White Horse, The. D. H. Lawrence. PSN

White Horse, The. Ann Stanford. MPA

White horse came to our farm once, A. The White Stallion. Guy Owen. InPK

White Horse of Westbury, The. Charles Tennyson Turner. EBEV; VLP

White Horses. Eleanor Farjeon. PH

White horses galloping on the sand. The Black Cliffs, Ballybunion. Brendan Kennelly. PFIr

White horses, tails high, rise from the cedar. E Uni Que A The Hi A Tho, Father. Roberta Hill. VoR

White-hot midday in the Snake Park, A. In the Snake Park. William Plomer. NoAM; OxBTC

White House, The. Claude McKay. AmNP (1974 ed.); NIL; PoBA

White House Blues. *Unknown.* FSW

White in the Moon the Long Road Lies. A. E. Housman. CMoP (1970 ed.); TT

White is right. Argument. Langston Hughes. ILP (1975 ed.)

White Island, The; or, The Place of the Blest. Robert Herrick. BoReV; OAEL-1; SCP-1

White Isle of Leuce, The. Sir Herbert Read. FaBoTw (1975 ed.)

White Knight's Song, The. "Lewis Carroll." *Fr.* Through the Looking-Glass, *ch.* 8. FaBoCo; ILP (1975 ed.); InPS; NOBE; NOBL; OAEL-2; OBP
    (Aged Aged Man, The.) OxBChV; SpRo
    (Ways and Means.) ECBV
    (White Knight's Ballad, The.) FaBoNo; HAP; VLP

White knights strain to restore, The. Stalemate at Attica. Horace Coleman. SES

White Lady has asked me to dance, The. Fourth Dance Poem. Gerald W. Barrax. PoBA

White man is, The. 12 Gates to the City. Nikki Giovanni. IHMS; PoBA

White man is a tiger at my throat, The. Tiger. Claude McKay. BPo

White Man Pressed the Locks, The. James C. Kilgore. InPK

White Man's Burden, The. Kipling. BTTM

White marble squats among the mosquitos, The. A Memorial for Mr. Jefferson. Francis Coleman Rosenberger. WasP

White mares lashed to the sulky carriages. In Ohio. James Wright. NNaP

White mares of the moon rush along the sky, The. Night Clouds. Amy Lowell. TH

White men's children spread over the earth. The Riddle. Georgia Douglas Johnson. PoBA

White mist drifts across the shrouds, A. Impressions: II. La Mer. Oscar Wilde. VLP

White Monster, The. W. H. Davies. PPM

White moon, The, gleams through scudding/ Clouds. Sorrow. Chu Shu-chen, *tr. by* Kenneth Rexroth. BoWoP

White, orphaned camel kid, The. *Mongol Oral Tradition, tr. by* C. R. Bawden. WTO

White Pass Ski Patrol. John Logan. BiP; CAPP

White Paternoster, The. *Unknown.* GBP
    ("Matthew, Mark, Luke, and John.") MG

White peacock roosting, The. What I Saw. Robert Duncan. NoAM; NOBA

White People. David Henderson. PoBA

"White phosphorous, white phosphorous." Overheard over S. E. Asia. Denise Levertov. BoWoP

White Piano, The. Ralph J. Mills, Jr. HeS

White pine, yellow pine. Southern Pines. John Peale Bishop. GOA

White Pines. Barry Silesky. AMV-80

White Princess, The, *sel.* William Brighty Rands.
    Cat of Cats, The. DuDr; OxBChV
    (Kitten Speaks, The). PCOP

White-robed against the threefold white. At Glan-y-wern. Arthur Symons. Intermezzo: Pastoral, IV. VLP

White Room, The. Peter Cooley. NVAP

White Ropes.  Franklin Brainard.  HeS

White Rose, A.  John Boyle O'Reilly.  SoSe

White Rose is a quiet horse.  The Four Horses.  James Reeves. PH

White Roses.  John Ashbery.  TAP

White sagebrush desert, The.  Noon.  O Pioneers!  John Peale Bishop.  VGW

White Seal's Lullaby, The.  Kipling.  EcS

White seed tossed on glass.  Snow Chant.  T. Alan Broughton. FAF

White Serpent.  Nelly Sachs, *tr. fr. German by* Michael Hamburger.  BoWoP

White Shark, The: Notes for a History.  Kirtland Snyder.  AAN

White sheep, white sheep, on a blue hill.  *Unknown.*  GBP

White sheer tieback curtains.  Karen L. Kent.  NPW

White sheet on the tail-gate of a truck, A.  Elegy for a Dead Soldier.  Karl Shapiro.  HAP

White Ship, The.  Dante Gabriel Rossetti.  VLP

White sky, over the hemlocks bowed with snow.  The Buck in the Snow.  Edna St. Vincent Millay.  BoAnP

White Spider.  Marita Garin.  AMV-80

White Stallion, The.  Pete Morgan.  SLP

White Stallion, The.  Guy Owen.  InPK

White Steed of the Prairies, The.  J. Barber.  BPAW

White sunshine on sweating skulls.  May Mobilization.  Allen Ginsberg.  MIT

White Swan.  A. Glanz-Leyeles, *tr. fr. Yiddish by* Keith Bosley. VWA

White though ye be, yet, lilies, know.  How Lilies Came White. Robert Herrick.  CaPo

White tree on black tree.  Wet Snow.  Norman MacCaig.  MS

White Troops Had Their Orders, but the Negroes Looked like Men, The.  Gwendolyn Brooks.  PBMP

White velvet covers the town.  Jerusalem in the Snow.  Anath Bental, *tr. by* Howard Schwartz.  VWA

White Venus limpid wandering in the sky.  Sonnet V.  Louise Labé, *tr. by* Aliki *and* Willis Barnstone.  BoWoP

White walls of the Institution, The.  Now and Then.  Ian Hamilton.  NoAM

White Was His Naked Breast.  *Unknown.*  BoReV; OxBM

White woman have you heard.  Montgomery.  Sam Cornish. CNA; PoBA

White Worlds.  Jane Marie Luecke.  AATT

Whiteness.  Yunna Moritz, *tr. fr. Russian by* Elaine Feinstein. VWA

Whiter/ than the crust.  The Wind Sleepers.  Hilda Doolittle ("H. D.").  WPE

Whither dost thou hide from the magic of my flute-call?  The Snake-Charmer.  Sarojini Naidu.  PBWP

Whither, indeed, midst falling dew.  Poem Beginning with a Line Memorized at School.  Roderick Hartigh Jellema.  AATT

Whither, midst falling dew.  To a Waterfowl.  Bryant.  AmVN; EAP; HoPM (1975 ed.); IPWM; NOBA; PB; PCOP; PiAm; PIM; SoSe; TAP

Whither, O splendid ship, thy white sails crowding.  A Passer-by. Robert Bridges.  CMoP (1970 ed.); OAEL-2; OxBTC; PoPle

Whither, O whither wander I forlorn?  Oceana and Britannia. John Ayloffe.  APAS

Whither, say whither shall I fly.  The Frozen Zone: or, Julia Disdainful.  Robert Herrick.  CaPo; SCP-1

Whither shall I go.  *Unknown, at. to* John Webster *and* William Rowley.  *Fr.* The Thracian Wonder.  GBL

"Whither thus hastes my little book so fast?"  The Writer to His Book.  Thomas Campion.  ILP (1975 ed.)

Whither wilt thou lead me?  I'll go no further.  Shakespeare.  *Fr.* Hamlet, I, v.  ExPo (1973 ed.)

Whit'll ye dae when the wee Malkies come.  The Coming of the Wee Malkies.  Stephen Mulrine.  MS

Whitsun Weddings, The.  Philip Larkin.  NoAM; OxBTC; PSN

Whitsuntide an' Club Walken.  William Barnes.  VLP

Whittier.  James Russell Lowell.  *Fr.* A Fable for Critics. AmVN; NOBA

Whittingham Fair.  *Unknown.*  AIW; GBP

Who?  Jane Catermull.  FPB

Who.  Edwin Honig.  TAP

Who Am I?  Felice Holman.  RFM

Who am I?  I am a lady faithful to the ways.  Lady of the Ferry Inn.  Gwerfyl Mechain, *tr. by* Willis Barnstone.  BoWoP

Who am I worthless that You spent such pains.  A Prayer for the Self.  John Berryman.  *Fr.* Eleven Addresses to the Lord. PiAm; PPP

Who are these from the strange, ineffable places.  Arabia.  John Meade Falkner.  OxBTC

Who are these people at the bridge to meet me?  The Bee Meeting.  Sylvia Plath.  InPS; PPP; WPE

Who are these phantoms of men.  Phantoms.  Nashira N'tosha. NW

Who are these?  Why sit they here in twilight?  Mental Cases. Wilfred Owen.  BiP; CMoP (1970 ed.); NoAM

Who are they talking to in the big temple?  The Temple.  C. H. Sisson.  OxBTC

Who are they to be in their skin.  The Subway Witnesses. Lorenzo Thomas.  PoBA

Who are we to love.  A Footnote to a Gray Bird's Pause.  James Cunningham.  JB

"Who are we waiting for?"  "Soup burnt?"  The Feckless Dinner Party.  Walter de la Mare.  FaBoTw (1975 ed.); PoTa

Who are you.  To Desi as Joe as Smoky the Lover of 115th Street. Audre Lorde.  CNA

Who are you and whence do you come?  A Vagrant.  Erick Axel Karlfeldt, *tr. by* Charles Wharton Stork.  PPM

Who are you, listening to me, who are you.  Poem for Half White College Students.  Amiri Baraka.  BPo; CAPP; TAP; UnPo (1976 ed.)

Who are you, little I.  E. E. Cummings.  LCL

"Who are you, Sea Lady."  Santorin.  James Elroy Flecker. FaBoTw (1975 ed.)

"Who are you, slim hipped tussler?"  The Wrestling.  Abbie Huston Evans.  GP

Who are you there that from your icy tower.  The Astronomers of Mont Blanc.  Edgar Bowers.  PoA

Who are you?  Who am I?  Growing.  Kenneth Rexroth.  MPA

Who Be Kind To.  Allen Ginsberg.  NNaP

Who beckons the green ivy up.  The Miracle.  Walter de la Mare. UnPo (1976 ed.)

Who believes/ he is dead?  Under Stone.  Elaine Feinstein. VWA

Who borrows all your ready cash.  A Friend.  Marguerite Power. FaBoCo

Who but the Lord?  Langston Hughes.  BPo

"Who called?"  I said, and the words.  Echo.  Walter de la Mare. AKE

Who Calls?  Frances Clarke.  LCL

Who calls her two-faced?  Faces, she has three.  The Three-faced. Robert Graves.  FaBoEE

Who came to our door.  Footprints in the Night.  Elizabeth J. Coatsworth.  CaYB

Who Can Be Born Black.  Mari Evans.  CNA

Who can believe with common sense.  Epigram on Fasting. Swift.  OBVE

Who can forbear, and tamely silent sit.  A Satire against Wit.  Sir Richard Blackmore.  APAS

Who can grasp the gray hearts of shopkeepers? Shopkeepers. Mani Leib, *tr. by* Richard J. Fein. AMV-81

Who can retell the things that befell us. Mi Y'Malel (Who Can Retell?). *Tr. fr. Hebrew.* FSW

Who can say. Song. Tennyson. BBGO

Who can say. In the Heartland. Mark Vinz. GP

Who can say now. The Old Codger's Lament. Carl Rakosi. HeS

Who Can Tell? *Gond Oral Tradition, tr. by* V. Elwin *and* S. Hivale. WTO

Who can the various city frauds recite. John Gay. *Fr.* Trivia; or, The Art of Walking the Streets of London, III. OAEL-1

Who cared enough for the town to take these pictures. The Taken Town. Constance Carrier. FAF

Who comes from far away, what old gray man. The Horse. A. E. Coppard. BoAnP

Who comes here? The Grenadier. *Unknown.* BBL; GBP

Who comes to us in our dark. Isaac and Esau. Rose Drachler. VWA

Who could believe an ant in theory? Credibility. John Ciardi. InPK; WIF

Who could devise. The Shell. Vernon Watkins. EcS

Who could hate you? Your patched-together face. Apology to My Lady. Edward Falco. AMV-80

Who could have thought, but for eight days in space. Space. X. J. Kennedy. Moon

Who dares to drop the pin destruction of our silence. Can You Change a Shilling? Toni Del Renzio. EAS

Who dat a-knockin' at the door below. What You Goin' to Do When the Rent Comes 'Round? Andrew B. Sterling. OBAL

Who Did Swallow Jonah? *Unknown.* FSW

Who does not love the juniper tree? Juniper. Eileen Duggan. PChr

Who does not love the spring deserves no lovers. Georgian Spring. Roy Campbell. OBSV

Who Doth Not See the Measure of the Moon? Sir John Davies. Moon

Who doubts? The laws fell down from heaven's height. Joseph Hall. *Fr.* Virgidemiarum. OBSV

Who Drags the Fiery Artist Down? Clarence Day. FaBoCo

Who dreamed that beauty passes like a dream? The Rose of the World. W. B. Yeats. CMoP (1970 ed.); NIL

Who drives the horses of the sun. The Happiest Heart. John Vance Cheney. PCOP

Who drowns an ocean. Proverbs. Morton Marcus. NVAP

Who e'er. *See* Whoe'er.

Who even dead, yet hath his mind entire! Cantos, XLVII. Ezra Pound. CMoP (1970 ed.); PiAm; VGW

Who ever. *See* Whoever.

Who fed me from her gentle breast. My Mother. Ann Taylor. OxBChV

Who Goes Round My Pinfold Wall. *Unknown.* GBP

Who Goes with Fergus? W. B. Yeats. CABA (1972 ed.); CMoP (1970 ed.); InPK; NoAM; NOBE

Who has ever stopped to think of the divinity of Lamont Cranston? In Memory of Radio. Amiri Baraka. NIL

Who has not walked upon the shore. Robert Bridges. CMoP (1970 ed.)

Who Has Our Redeemer Heard, *with music.* Stephen C. Foster. AH

Who has seen the old baritone of my childhood? Another Poem on the Tearing Down of the Metropolitan Opera House. A. Wilber Stevens. MPA

Who Has Seen the Wind. Christina Rossetti. CTV; ECBV; LCL; PCOP
(Wind, The.) OxBChV

Who has sung the Dnieper? Heard at Dnieperstroi. Robert Gessner. SPT

Who hath desired the sea?—the sight of salt water unbounded. The Sea and the Hills. Kipling. OBP

Who hath given man speech? or what hath set therein. Chorus. Swinburne. *Fr.* Atalanta in Calydon. OAEL-2

Who hath herd of suche crueltye before? Sir Thomas Wyatt. AAS

Who have we here? Behold him and be mute. Samuel Rowlands. *Fr.* The Letting of Humour's Blood in the Head-Vein. TVS

Who having confused me with her mother. Beverly Fragments. Morgan Sanders. WBN

Who hears the humming. Breath. Philip Levine. FoP; MPA

Who Here Can Cast His Eyes Abroad, *with music.* Abiel Holmes. AH

Who Hurt You So? Edna St. Vincent Millay. TPo

Who I am. Song from the Unfinished Man. Paul David Ashley. DNGG

Who in his right mind. The President Is Not Funny. Sheila Heldenbrand. AcAn

Who in his thirties. For My Pop. Cash Terrell. DNGG

Who, in the dark, has cast the harbor-chain? Putting to Sea. Louise Bogan. PoA

Who, in the garden-pony carrying skeps. Horses. Dorothy Wellesley. OxBTC

Who in the world would ever have guessed. Easter Eggs. Harry Behn. CC

Who is it calling by the darkened river. Voices. Walter de la Mare. UnPo (1976 ed.)

Who is it that this dark night. Voices at the Window. Sir Philip Sidney. Astrophel and Stella: Eleventh Song. NOBE; PoPle

Who is my father is this world, in this house. The Irish Cliffs of Moher. Wallace Stevens. NOBA; VGW

Who is not a stranger still. Stephany Fuller. BPo

Who Is Sad? Elizabeth J. Coatsworth. ECBV

Who is she coming, whom all gaze upon. Sonnet: A Rapture Concerning His Lady. Guido Cavalcanti, *tr. by* Dante Gabriel Rossetti. LoAs

Who is she that comes, makyng turn every man's eye. Sonnet VII. Guido Cavalcanti, *tr. by* Ezra Pound. OBVE

Who Is Sylvia? Shakespeare. *Fr.* The Two Gentlemen of Verona, IV, ii. OAEL-1
(Sylvia.) PCOP
("Who is Silvia? what is she.") ILP (1975 ed.); STS

Who is the happy warrior? Who is he. Character of the Happy Warrior. Wordsworth. MBPR

Who is the noblest beast you can name? The Horse. Shel Silverstein. PH

Who is the ugly one slump-slopping down the street? Robert Penn Warren. *Fr.* Homage to Theodore Dreiser on the Centennial of His Birth. GP

Who is the we, who is. Revolutionary Letter #36. Diane DiPrima. GP; VoA

Who is this I hear?—Lo, this is I, thine heart. The Dispute of the Heart and Body of François Villon. Villon, *tr. by* Swinburne. OBVE

Who Is This That Cometh from Edom? William Herebert. BoReV; OxBM

Who is this whose feet. The Swan's Feet. E. J. Scovell. OxBTC

Who killed Cock Robin? Mother Goose. MG; OBP; RDB

Who killed John Keats? John Keats. Byron. FaBoEE; MBPR

Who kill'd Kildare? Who dar'd Kildare to kill? On the Earl of Kildare. *Unknown.* FaBoEE

Who killed Lawless Lean? Stevie Smith. BBGO

Who Killed Poor Robin? *Unknown.* AmFP

Who knew her. On the Fifth Anniversary of Bluma Sach's Death. Vinnie-Marie D'Ambrosio. IHMS

Who knocks at the door? Pope. *Fr.* The Art of Sinking in Poetry. AnMo

"Who knocks?" "I, who was beautiful." The Ghost. Walter de la Mare. CMoP (1970 ed.); NOBE; OAEL-2; OxBTC

Who Knows if the Moon's. E. E. Cummings. Moon; SO; UsP

Who knows the mighty secret. The Secret of the Sea. Susan K. Phillips. RhR

Who knows whether the sea heals or corrodes? Plague of Dead Sharks. Alan Dugan. NoAM

Who list the Romane greatnes forth to figure. Joachim du Bellay, *tr. by* Spenser. *Fr.* Antiquitez de Rome. OBVE

Who locked me. A Night in the Royal Ontario Museum. Margaret Atwood. PBWP

Who loves a garden loves a green-house too. The Green-House. William Cowper. *Fr.* The Task, III. PF

Who loves to peer up at the morning sun. On "The Story of Rimini." Keats. MBPR

Who lyst his welthe and eas Retayne. V. Innocentia Veritas Viat Fides Circumdederunt Me Inimici Mei. Sir Thomas Wyatt. AAS

Who made the sky? Who? Jane Catermull. FPB

Who, minter of medallions. Reading a Medal. Terence Tiller. FaBoTw (1975 ed.)

Who now does follow the foule Blatant Beast. Spenser. *Fr.* The Faerie Queene, VI, 10. OAEL-1

Who, now, seeing Her so. Et in Arcadia Ego. W. H. Auden. CMoP (1970 ed.)

Who of Those Coming After. Darcy Gottlieb. AMV-81

Who on your breast pillows his head now. A Lost Jewel. Robert Graves. LoAs

Who or why, or which or what. The Akond of Swat. Edward Lear. FaBoCo; FaBoNo

Who plays the hand that plays the instrument? Bard. Theodore Black. AMV-81

Who Points the Swallow. David Campbell. MAuV

Who prop, thou askest, in these bad days, my mind? To a Friend. Matthew Arnold. PAIC

Who rides at night, who rides so late? The Invisible King. Goethe, *tr. by* Robert Bly. NU

Who rideth through the driving rain. The King's Son. Thomas Boyd. AIW

Who Said It Was Simple. Audre Lorde. WBN

Who said "Peacock Pie?" The Song of the Mad Prince. Walter de la Mare. EBEV; NoAM; NOBE; OxBChV; UsP

Who (said the Moon). Edith Sitwell Assumes the Role of Luna. Robert Francis. Moon

Who Says. Musa Moris Farhi. VWA

Who says/ That it's by my desire. People Hide Their Love. Wu-ti, *tr. by* Arthur Waley. OLR

Who says/ the old man/ stayed his hand? Psalm of the Jealous God. Henry Abramovitch. VWA

Who says [*or* sayes] that fictions only and false hair. Jordan. George Herbert. CABA (1972 ed.); HAP; ILP (1975 ed.); NIL; OAEL-1; OBP; PAIC; PoPle; PPP

Who says that Giles and Joan at discord be? On Giles and Joan. Ben Jonson. NOBL

Who says these Romish pageants been too high. Rome Ryme. Joseph Hall. *Fr.* Virgidemiarum. TVS

Who Shall Deliver Me? Christina Rossetti. BoReV; PFD

Who Shall Die? James A. Randall, Jr. BPo

Who Shall Doubt. George Oppen. CAAP

Who shall have my faire lady? *Unknown.* LoAs

Who shall tell the lady's grief. On the Death of a Cat. Christina Rossetti. PCat

Who shall thy gay buffoonery describe? To the Mocking Bird. Richard Henry Wilde. BoAnP

Who Shined Shoes in Times Square. Lance Jeffers. CNA

Who showed me. To Flossie. William Carlos Williams. TH

Who smoke-snorts toasts o' My Lady Nicotine. After Robert Browning. G. K. Chesterton. NOBL

Who so list to hunt, I know where is an hind. *See* Whoso list to hunt...

Who stands, the crux left of the watershed. The Watershed. W. H. Auden. OAEL-2

"Who stuffed that white owl?" No one spoke in the shop. The Owl-Critic. James Thomas Fields. ECBV; OBAL; PoTa

Who-Tapped-the-Frogs-In. Samuel Makidemewabe, *tr. fr. Cree Indian by* Howard Norman. TC

Who Taught Caddies to Count? or, A Burnt Golfer Fears the Child. Ogden Nash. LiSp

Who Taught Them? *Unknown.* CTV

"Who Then Is Crazy?" Barry Spacks. GP

Who Threw the Overalls in Mistress Murphey's Chowder? *with music.* George L. Geifer. FSN

Who was he. Psalmen Gezangen. Irene Dayton. AATT

Who was it that took away my voice. Silence. Bella Akhmadulina, *tr. by* Daniel Halpern. BoWoP

Who was responsible for the very first arms deal. Peace. Michael Longley. CIP

Who was this girl. Looking at Pictures to Be Put Away. Gary Snyder. CoPAm; FF; InPS; NNaP

Who wd. cope in this Quick. The Web. Gregory O'Donoghue. BIrV

Who were the builders? Question not the silence. The Nameless Doon. William Larminie. BIrV

Who, who will be the next man to entrust his girl to a friend? Ezra Pound. *Fr.* Homage to Sextus Propertius. NoAM

Who will believe my verse in time to come. Sonnets, XVII. Shakespeare. STS

Who will endure. No Change of Place. W. H. Auden. OxBTC

Who will find this when I am lost indeed. Inscription in a Book. Gilean Douglas. AMV-81

Who Will Give Cover? Anadad Eldan, *tr. fr. Hebrew by* Ruth Nevo. VWA

Who will go drive with Fergus now. Who Goes with Fergus? W. B. Yeats. CABA (1972 ed.); CMoP (1970 ed.); InPK; NoAM; NOBE

Who will in fairest book of Nature know. Astrophel and Stella, LXXI. Sir Philip Sidney. CABA (1972 ed.); Epi; OAEL-1

"Who will pay for the milk I gave you?" Let Me Go. *Gond Oral Tradition, tr. by* V. Elwin *and* S. Hivale. WTO

Who will shoe my pretty little foot? The Lass of Roch Royal. *Unknown.* FSW

Who Will Stop His Hand from Giving Warmth. Alejandra Pizarnik, *tr. fr. Spanish by* Alina Rivero. VWA

Who will take away. Spell against Sorrow. Kathleen Raine. PBWP

Who wins his love shall lose her. Lost Love. Andrew Lang. SLP

Who Wot Nowe That Ys Here. *Unknown.* InPS

Who would/ who could. Now Ain't That Love? Carolyn M. Rodgers. BPo

Who would be/ A mermaid fair. Tennyson. *Fr.* The Mermaid. EcS; LCL

Who would be/ A merman bold. The Merman. Tennyson. EcS

Who would have thought that face of thine. Thomas Howell. *Fr.* The Lover Deceived Writes to His Lady. POL

Who would live in others' breath? Epitaph: Iohannis Sande. Thomas Bastard. FaBoEE

Who would suspect, or even know. A Vegetable, I Will Not Be. Donna Whitewing. ANTL; VW

Who would true valour see. The Pilgrim. Bunyan. *Fr.* The Pilgrim's Progress. CTV; EBEV

Who would want silver on the table?  Silver.  Peter Wild.  FoP

Who wrote *Who wrote Icon Basilike?*  On Christopher Wordsworth, Master of Trinity.  Benjamin Hall Kennedy.  FaBoCo; FaBoEE

Whoa Back, Buck.  Leadbelly (Huddie Ledbetter).  FSW

Who'd Be a Hero (Fictional)?  Morris Bishop.  OBAL

Who'd believe me if.  The Third Dimension.  Denise Levertov.  NoAM

Who'd ever think that Utah would stir the world so much?  Marching to Utah.  *Unknown.*  AmFP

Whoe'er has gone thro' London Street.  A Butcher.  Thomas Hood.  BBL

Whoe'er [*or* Who e'er] she be.  Wishes to His Supposed Mistress.  Richard Crashaw.  BoLoP; EBEV; SCP-1

Whoever comes to shroud me, do not harm.  The Funeral.  John Donne.  BiP; BoLoP; CABA (1972 ed.); EBEV; HeIP; OAEL-1; PoPle: TT

Whoever despises the clitoris despises the penis.  The Speed of Darkness.  Muriel Rukeyser.  WBN

Whoever guesses, thinks, or dreams he knows.  The Curse.  John Donne.  ILP (1975 ed.)

Whoever has a yod in his name.  Bella and the Golem.  Rossana Ombres, *tr. by* Edgar Pauk.  VWA

"Whoever has courage/ And fighting spirit in his heart."  The Funeral Games for Anchises; Entellus.  Virgil, *tr. by* Rolfe Humphries.  *Fr.* The Aeneid, V.  LiSp

Whoever has heard of St. Gingo.  The New Cecilia.  Thomas Lovell Beddoes.  OAEL-2

Whoever hath her wish, thou hast thy Will.  Sonnets, CXXXV.  Shakespeare.  Epi; OAEL-1

Whoever I am.  When I Was Young I Tried to Sing.  Donald Finkel.  GP

Whoever loves, if he do not propose.  Love's Progress.  John Donne.  Elegies, XVIII.  OAEL-1; SCP-1

Whoever swings an ax.  Ax.  Charles Simic.  GP

Whoever to finding fault inclines.  The Cynic.  St. George Tucker.  OBAL

Who ever will find such fortune.  Count Arnaldos.  *Unknown, tr. by* W. S. Merwin.  Epi

Whoever You Are.  Virginia R. Terris.  AAN

Whoever you are.  Little Sis.  David Kherdian.  AMV-80

Whole day have I followed in the rocks, The.  Fergus and the Druid.  W. B. Yeats.  VLP

Whole day long, under the walking sun, The.  The Sleeping Giant.  Donald Hall.  NCSH

Whole Duty of Children.  Robert Louis Stevenson.  CTV; OxBChV; PCOP

Whole field of poppies billowed, my beloved, The.  A Farewell Ballad of Poppies.  Eva Brudne.  VWA

Whole heap of nickles and a whole heap of dimes, A.  Shout, Little Lulu.  *Unknown.*  AmFP

Whole Relentless Process, The.  E. R. Cole.  AATT

Whole Story, The.  William Stafford.  NNaP

Whole towns shut down.  The Late Snow and Lumber Strike of the Summer of Fifty-Four.  Gary Snyder.  CNW; MPA

Whole week, A.  Hurting.  Vi Gale.  GP

Whole world disappeared on the first night, The.  The Raft of *The Medusa.*  T. E. Porter.  AAN

Whole World Is Coming, The.  *Unknown, tr. fr. American Indian.*  IPWM

Whole world now is but the minister, The.  Robert Bridges.  The Growth of Love, III.  VLP

Wholehearted he can't move.  The Eye Is More or Less Satisfied with Seeing.  Allen Curnow.  ATNZ

Wholesome.  William Meredith.  TAP

Who'll be the lover of that woman on the bench?  No Thank You.  John Skoyles.  AAN

Who'll take the coal from the mine?  Don't Look Now.  J. C. Fogerty.  PoRo

Whoopee Blues.  *Unknown.*  BluL

Whoopee-Ti-Yi-Yo!  *Unknown, ad. by* James Morehead.  *See* Git Along Little Dogies.

Whore.  Linda King.  GP

Whores are afraid to cross the street, The.  Eclogue.  David Bergman.  AMV-80

Whores of Naples, The.  Letter from Olga, Declaiming.  Danny L. Rendleman.  TC

Whores of Times Square troop to their stations, The.  Times Square Parade.  Robert Watson.  NYP

Whoroscope.  Samuel Beckett.  NoAM

Who's Gonna Shoe Your Pretty Little Foot?  *Unknown.*  FSW

Who's In?  Elizabeth Fleming.  DuDr

Who's in the Next Room.  Thomas Hardy.  PoPle

Who's killed the leaves?  Leaves.  Ted Hughes.  BBL

Who's Most Afraid of Death?  E. E. Cummings.  CMoP (1970 ed.); ExPo (1973 ed.); ILP (1975 ed.); VGW

Who's Next?  *Unknown.*  TDH

Who's that?  Going through the Old Photos.  Michael Rosen.  FPB

Who's that knocking on the window.  Innocent's Song.  Charles Causley.  MPo

Who's that ringing at our door-bell?  That Little Black Cat.  D'Arcy Wentworth Thompson.  OxBChV

Who's the Dover-based day tripper.  A Trifle for Trafalgar Day.  Ted Pauker.  NOBL

Who's the most important man this country ever knew?  Barney Google.  Billy Rose.  OBAL

Who's There?  Frances Frost.  ECBV

Who's there?  Nay, answer me: stand, and unfold yourself.  Shakespeare.  *Fr.* Hamlet, I, i.  ExPo (1973 ed.)

Who's Who.  W. H. Auden.  BBGO; CABA (1972 ed.); NoAM

Who's Who in America.  Mbembe.  NW

Whose anger was it.  Girl to Woman.  Nixeon Civille Handy.  AMV-80

Whose Boo Is Whose?  X. J. Kennedy.  IWK

Whose broken window is a cry of art.  Boy Breaking Glass.  Gwendolyn Brooks.  NoAM; NowV

Whose Dog? Whose Cat?  *Unknown.*  ECBV

Whose gold you carry, camel.  Timbuctu.  Edward Brathwaite.  MPo

Whose is that face?  Three Riddles.  Brian Swann.  TSWA

Whose is that noble dauntless brow?  Verses Intended to Be Written below a Noble Earl's Picture.  Burns.  HoPM (1975 ed.)

Whose is this horrifying face.  Ecce Homo.  David Gascoyne.  BoReV

Whose Little Pigs?  *Unknown.*  BBL

Whose love is given over-well.  Partial Comfort.  Dorothy Parker.  FaBoCo; OBAL

Whose Scene?  Ruth Stone.  BoWoP

Whose woods these are I think I know.  Stopping by Woods on a Snowy Evening.  Robert Frost.  BiP; CABA (1972 ed.); CMoP (1970 ed.); ECBV; FF; FSFS; HAP; HeIP; HoPM (1975 ed.); ILP (1975 ed.); InPK; InPS; IPWM; LFH; NIL; NoAM; NOBA; PiAm; PoIA; PPM; PPoD; PSN; SoSe; STS; TAP; TT; UnPo (1976 ed.);

Whoso in harvest mindeth to reap.  To His Child.  William Bullokar.  OxBChV

Whoso list to hunt, I know where is an hind.  Sir Thomas Wyatt, *after the Italian of* Petrarch.  AAS; BoLoP; CABA (1972 ed.); EBEV; Epi; GBL; HAP; ILP (1975 ed.); InPK; OAEL-1; OBVE

Whoso thou art that passest by this place.  An Epitaph of Maister Win Drowned in the Sea.  George Turberville.  FaBoEE

Whoso Would See This Song of Heavenly Choice, *with music.* John Wilson. AH

Whsst, and away, and over the green. Nothing. Walter de la Mare. ECBV

"Whu's aw thae fflag-poles ffur in Princess Street?" Heard in the Cougate. Robert Garioch. OxBTC

Why. Sonia Sanchez. WBN

Why/ so many eyes eye you. Coquette at Mission Control. Martin Galvin. PoUp

Why always in the morning? How in the Morning. Chuck Miller. EC

Why are our ancestors. Ancestors. Dudley Randall. BPo; CNA

Why are the faces here so lined? Public Bar. D. J. Enright. LP

Why are the public buildings so high? W. H. Auden. FaBoCo

Why are the stamps adorned with kings. Power to the People. Howard Nemerov. POL

Why are we by all creatures waited on? Holy Sonnets, XII. John Donne. CABA (1972 ed.)

Why are women so energetic? Energetic Women. D. H. Lawrence. InPS

"Why are your eyes as big as saucers—big as saucers?" Man in the Street. Robert Penn Warren. OBAL

Why art thou silent and invisible. To Nobodaddy. Blake. MBPR; OAEL-2

Why art thou silent! Is thy love a plant. Wordsworth. LoAs

Why boast we, Glaucus! our extended reign. Homer, *tr. by* Pope. *Fr.* The Iliad, XII. OBVE

Why Bother Club, The. Barry Schechter. FiCh

Why call an anti-missile. For, Behold the Day Cometh. Rochelle Owens. Psy

Why call the miser miserable? Byron. *Fr.* Don Juan, XII. UnPo (1976 ed.)

Why came I so untimely forth. To My Young Lady Lucy Sidney. Edmund Waller. ILP (1975 ed.)

Why cannot we eat enough for a week. Envying the Pelican. Richard Weber. CIP

Why canst thou not, as others do. The Appeal. Samuel Daniel. OLR

Why Can't I Leave You? Ai. AmPA; GP

"Why, Colin, since thou found'st such grace." Spenser. *Fr.* Colin Clout's Come Home Again. TVS

Why come ye hither, Redcoats, your mind what madness fills? Riflemen's Song at Bennington. *Unknown.* BTTM; FSW

Why Come Ye Not to Court, *sel.* John Skelton. "Such a prelate, I trow." OBSV

Why did all manly gifts in Webster fail? Emerson. GOA

Why did george washington. An Answer. John Sjoberg. AcAn

Why Did I Laugh Tonight? Keats. ILP (1975 ed.) ("Why did I laugh to-night? No voice will tell.") MBPR; OBP

Why did [*or do, wr.*] I write? what sin to me unknown. Pope. *Fr.* Epistle to Dr. Arbuthnot. EBEV; NIL

Why did man leave the trees? How Man Learned to Walk—and Run. Louis Dudek. AKE

Why did the Children Put Beans in Their Ears? Carl Sandburg. The People, Yes, Sec. 41. OBAL; PBMP

Why did the Lord give us agility. Common Sense. Ogden Nash. SFF

Why did the woman want to kill one dog? A Village Tale. May Sarton. BoAnP; GDP

Why did we not guess? The Suicide. Edward Lowbury. PMW

Why did you give no hint that night. The Going. Thomas Hardy. EBEV; NOBE; UnPo (1976 ed.)

Why Did You Go. E. E. Cummings. VGW

"Why did you melt your waxen man." Sister Helen. Dante Gabriel Rossetti. VLP

"Why do/ You thus devise." Susanna and the Elders. Adelaide Crapsey. PAIC; WPE

Why do bells for Christmas ring? Song. Eugene Field. CTV

Why do I batten down my doors. Storm Warning. Alice Bardsley. AMV-80

Why do I hate that lone green dell? Emily Brontë. VLP

Why do I imagine the death of Mandelstam. Preparing for Exile. Derek Walcott. OBP

Why do I post my love letters. Why Don't You Talk to Me? Alistair Campbell. ATNZ

Why do I see my house as a second body? House Poem. Jane Cooper. AMV-81

Why do some men want to create women? Pygmalion. Kathryn Ruby. WBN

Why do the Gentiles tumult. Bible, *O.T., paraphrased by* Milton. Psalms, II. OBVE

Why Do the Graces. Walter Savage Landor. SoSe ("Why do the Graces now desert the Muse?") FaBoEE

Why do the lilies goggle their tongues at me. Grotesque. Amy Lowell. BoWoP

Why do they whistle so loud, when they walk past the graveyard late at night? Thirteen o'Clock. Kenneth Fearing. ExPo (1973 ed.)

Why do we grumble because a tree is bent. Variety. *Yoruba Oral Tradition, tr. by* E. Lasebikan. WTO

Why do we labor at the poem. Reasons for Music. Archibald MacLeish. PiAm

Why Do We Mourn Departing Friends? *with music.* Isaac Watts. AH

Why do you hold the flag so high. Changing of the Guard. Charles G. Ballard. VW

Why do you love her? Questions [1]. Donald Hall. FF

Why do you play such dreary music. Radio. Frank O'Hara. PoA

Why do you rush through the field in trains. The Fat White Woman Speaks. G. K. Chesterton. SpRo

Why do you sell your poems. Yevtushenko! Paul Foreman. CPA

"Why do you stand in the dripping rye." The Woman in the Rye. Thomas Hardy. ILP (1975 ed.)

Why do you talk so much. For Robert Frost. Galway Kinnell. NOBA; VGW

"Why do you wear your hair like a man?" After Dilettante Concetti. Henry Duff Traill. FaBoCo

Why Do You Write about Russia? Louis Simpson. AMV-81

Why do your warships sail on my waters? I've Got to Know. Woody Guthrie. FSW; SoS

Why does it tear so. Hopi Lament. Charles Beghtol. BPAW

Why does the Raven cry aloud and no eye pities her? Enion's Lament. Blake. *Fr.* The Four Zoas. UsP

Why does the sea burn? Why do the hills cry? Zaydee. Philip Levine. NNaP; VWA

Why does the sea moan evermore? By the Sea. Christina Rossetti. EcS

Why does the thin grey strand. Sorrow. D. H. Lawrence. CMoP (1970 ed.); PSN

Why does this pretty boy from Kong-po. Peter Whigham. *Fr.* Love Poems of the VIth Dalai Lama. TwMBP

"Why does [*or dois*] your brand sae [*or so*] drop wi' blude [*or drap wi bluid*]." Edward, Edward. *Unknown.* AIW; BiP; CABA (1972 ed.); EBEV; ExPo (1973 ed.); FaBoBa; FaPoR; HAP; HoPM (1975 ed.); ILP (1975 ed.); InPK; InPS; IP; IPWM; LFH; NOBE; PeBB; PoIA; PPoe; SoSe

Why Don't They Go Back to Transylvania? Robert Peters. CPA

Why don't we rock the casket here in the moonlight. The Pale Blue Casket. Oliver Pitcher. PoBA

Why don't you/ catch me a pony. The Pony Blues. *Unknown.* BluL

Why don't you go down Old Hannah. Ol' Hannah. *Unknown.* BluL

Why Don't You Talk to Me? Alistair Campbell. ATNZ

Why don't you work like other men do? Hallelujah, I'm a Bum. *Unknown.* FSW

Why Dost Thou Shade Thy Lovely Face? Francis Quarles. Emblems, III, 7. BoReV

Why dost thou shade thy lovely face? O why. To His Mistress. Earl of Rochester. LoAs

"Why dost thou so explore." Homer, *tr. by* George Chapman. *Fr.* The Iliad, VI. OBVE

Why doth the ear so tempt the voice. To Castara: Of True Delight. William Habington. SCP-2

Why English Is So Hard! *Unknown.* CTV

Why Fires Are Lit December 21st. Michael McMahon. FAF

Why first, you don't believe, you don't and can't. Unfaith and Faith. Robert Browning. *Fr.* Bishop Blougram's Apology. BoReV

Why Flowers Change Color. Robert Herrick. HAP

Why from this her and him. E. E. Cummings. NoAM

Why from this window am I watching leaves? The Location of Things. Barbara Guest. NYP

Why God Permits Evil: For Answers to This Question of Interest to Many Write Bible Answers Dept. E-7. Miller Williams. CSP

Why, Grubbinol, dost thou so wistful seem? Friday; or, The Dirge. John Gay. *Fr.* The Shepherd's Week. ILP (1975 ed.)

Why Has This Ache. Gevorg Emin, *tr. fr.* Armenian by Diana Der Hovanessian. AMV–81

Why hast thou nothing in thy face? Eros. Robert Bridges. CMoP (1970 ed.); ExPo (1973 ed.); ILP (1975 ed.); NOBE

Why have such scores of lovely, gifted girls. A Slice of Wedding Cake. Robert Graves. BoLoP; BuTh; NOBE; OxBTC

Why have you risen, to stand with naked feet. With the Dawn. Thomas Caulfield Irwin. BIrV

Why, having won her, do I woo? The Married Lover. Coventry Patmore. *Fr.* The Angel in the House. VLP

Why He Was There. E. A. Robinson. CMoP (1970 ed.); NOBA

Why her bedroom is a/ trip. Lyn Lifshin. *Fr.* Walking thru Audley End Mansion Late Afternoon. RiTi

Why I Am Not a Painter. Frank O'Hara. ConAP; CoPAm; NoAM; NOBA; PoIA; VoA

Why I Am Offended by Miracles. David Bergman. AMV–80

Why I Can't Write a Poem about Lares. Iván Silén, *tr. fr. Spanish by* Julio Marzán. InW

Why I Can't Write My Autobiography. Rodger Kamenetz. VWA

Why I Didn't Go to Delphi. James Welch. CDW; MPA

Why I Died. Erica Jong. RiTi

Why I Drink. Henry Aldrich. NIL

Why I Sing the Blues. B. B. King. MAT

Why I would bring a wagon into battle. Willie B (2). Lucille Clifton. InPS

Why is a pump like Viscount Castlereagh? What's My Thought Like? [or A Riddle]. Thomas Moore. FaBoCo; FaBoEE

Why is everything I do in my life like a boomerang? Boomerang. John Perreault. EAS

Why is it said thou canst not live. Love. Shelley. MBPR

Why is my verse so barren of new pride. Sonnets, LXXVI. Shakespeare. EBEV; TPo

Why is the child so pale. Louise. Stevie Smith. SBG

Why Linger Yet upon the Strand? *with music.* Louis F. Benson. AH

Why Log Truck Drivers Rise Earlier than Students of Zen. Gary Snyder. NNaP

Why, Lord? *with music.* Mark Van Doren. AH

Why make so much of fragmentary blue. Fragmentary Blue. Robert Frost. NIL

Why Mira Can't Go Back to Her Old House. Mirabai, *tr. fr. Medieval Hindi; English version by* Robert Bly. NU

Why Most of Us Are Limping Away from Life. Eugene Ruggles. CPA

Why must i string my hate. Why. Sonia Sanchez. WBN

Why Must You Know? John Wheelwright. VGW

Why not despair of this world. The Radiance of Extinct Stars. Allan Kolski Horvitz. VWA

Why not mark out the land. Hard Questions. Margaret Tsuda. RFM

Why not someday. Bon Voyage. James Steele. SES

Why not? The mouths of the ginger blooms slide open. Chinoiserie. Charles Wright. AmPA

Why now so melancholy, Ben? Leviathan, or a Hymn to Poor Brother Ben. *Unknown.* APAS

Why now the word "Kalahari." Kalahari. Luis Palés Matos, *tr. by* Rachel Benson. InW

Why, O why. Grumblers. Leonard Clark. FPB

"Why of the sheep do you not learn peace?" An Answer to the Parson. Blake. FaBoEE

Why quails my heart? God riding with. Saul. Isaac Rosenberg. VWA

Why rejoice in beauty? What. Reflections. Antoinette Deshoulières, *tr. by* Yvor Winters. PBWP

Why repeat? I heard you the first time. Carl Sandburg. *Fr.* The People, Yes, Sec. 42. OBAL

Why say the idiot is not. The Locus. Cid Corman. VGW

Why seraphim like lutanists arranged. Evening without Angels. Wallace Stevens. TT; VGW

Why Should a Foolish Marriage Vow. Dryden. *Fr.* Marriage à la Mode, I, i. HeIP; ILP (1975 ed.); NIL (Song: "Why should a foolish marriage vow.") BuTh; LoAs

Why should a man think because the heart is vulnerable. Empirical History. Charles Doyle. ATNZ

Why should I be eaten by love. Untitled. James A. Randall, Jr. BPo

Why should I blame her that she filled my days. No Second Troy. W. B. Yeats. CABA (1972 ed.); CMoP (1970 ed.); NoAM; NOBE; OAEL-2; OxBTC; PPP; TT; WeW

Why should I care for the men of Thames. Blake. MBPR

Why should I have returned? Noah's Raven. W. S. Merwin. ILP (1975 ed.); NIL

Why should I keep holiday. Compensation. Emerson. TAP

Why should I let the toad work. Toads. Philip Larkin. CMoP (1970 ed.); ExPo (1973 ed.); NoAM; NOBL; OxBTC; SoSe (1977 ed.)

Why should I seek for love or study it? Ribh Considers Christian Love Insufficient. W. B. Yeats. BoReV

Why should I wish to tell you who I am? A Woman Combing. William E. Taylor. CSP

Why Should Not Old Men Be Mad? W. B. Yeats. ILP (1975 ed.)

Why should [the] scribblers discompose. The Scribblers. Walter Savage Landor. FaBoEE; OBSV

Why should this flower delay so long. The Last Chrysanthemum. Thomas Hardy. CMoP (1970 ed.)

Why Should Vain Mortals Tremble. Nathaniel Niles. *See* Bunker Hill.

Why should we fear to melt away in death. To Castara. William Habington. SCP-2

Why should you believe in magic. Consumed. James Tate. MAT

Why should you swear I am forsworn. The Scrutiny [*or* Scrutinie]. Richard Lovelace. BoLoP; CaPo; GBL; ILP (1975 ed.); LoAs

Why should your face so please me. Song. Edwin Muir. SLP

Why sleeps the future, as a snake enrolled. Ecclesiastical Sonnets: Conclusion. Wordsworth. MBPR

Why so drawn, so worn. Vampire's Aubade. W. D. Snodgrass. PAIC

Why So Pale and Wan? Sir John Suckling. *Fr.* Aglaura, IV, ii. BuTh; HoPM (1975 ed.); IP; NOBE; UnPo (1976 ed.) (Encouragement to a Lover.) PBMP (Song: "Why so pale and wan, fond lover?") BiP; BoLoP; CABA (1972 ed.); CaPo; HeIP; ILP (1975 ed.); InPS (Why So Pale and Wan, Fond Lover?) HAP

Why, Some of My Best Friends Are Women. Phyllis McGinley. NMM

Why speak of memory and death. Two Views of Two Ghost Towns. Charles Tomlinson. NoAM

Why speak of the use. Hayden Carruth. VGW

Why that alarming sigh? Dialogue. Agathias Scholasticus, *tr. by* Dudley Fitts. OLR

Why the Resurrection Was Revealed to Women. Catharina Regina von Greiffenberg, *tr. fr. German by* Michael Hamburger. PBWP

Why the Soup Tastes like the Daily News. Marge Piercy. MAT

Why then did he make, at such cost, crazy sounds? John Berryman. *Fr.* Dream Songs. RRA

Why Think? By Thinking You Grow Old. Arthur Hugh Clough. PoIA ("To spend uncounted years of pain.") WeW

Why this girl has no fear. Carmen. Victor Hernandez Cruz. PoBA

Why Tomas Cam Was Grumpy. James Stephens. CMoP (1970 ed.)

Why was a radio sinful? Lord knows. But it was. The Radio under the Bed. Reed Whittemore. PoUp

Why we should hesitate is not quite clear. Temporary Problems. Larry Rubin. AMV-80

"Why weep ye by the tide, ladie?" Jock of Hazeldean. Sir Walter Scott. ILP (1975 ed.)

Why were you born when the snow was falling. A Dirge. Christina Rossetti. SBG; VLP; VPC

Why, when Sunday closes the lid on this world. Sunday in South Carolina. Robert Parham. AMV-80

Why, whenever she can spy me. To Chloe. Horace, *tr. by* Branwell Brontë. Odes, I, 23. OBVE

Why, who makes much of a miracle? Miracles. Walt Whitman. PBMP; UsP

Why, why, what is this why. What Is This Why? *Unknown.* OxBM

Why will Delia thus retire. Receipt for the Vapours. Lady Mary Wortley Montagu. PBWP

Why will they never speak. The Grandfathers. Donald Justice. NCSH; PPoD

"Why William, on that old grey stone." Expostulation and Reply. Wordsworth. ILP (1975 ed.); MBPR; OAEL-2

Why without cease do I think of a bold youth. The Haunting. Irving Layton. NeAC

Why Would I Have Survived? Edith Bruck, *tr. by* Anita Barrows. VWA

Why Would I Want. William J. Harris. PoBA

Why Write Poetry? Pamela Oberon Davis. AMV-80

Whyles in the presence. Verses on a Rose Street Muse. Charles Senior. MIS

Whylom ther was dwellinge at Oxenford. *See* Whilom ther was dwellynge at Oxenford.

Why'n't you bring me. To Greet a Letter-Carrier. William Carlos Williams. OBAL

Wichita Vortex Sutra. Allen Ginsberg. CAPP

Wicked Lady of Gough Street. Todd S. J. Lawson. CPA

Wicked Tongues. *Unknown.* OxBM

Wicked Witch's Kitchen. X. J. Kennedy. IWK

Wicker Basket, A. Robert Creeley. CAPP; HAP; NoAM

Widdecombe [*or* Widdicombe] Fair. *Unknown.* DuDr; GSB, *with music;* PH

Widdreme, The. Sorley Maclean, *tr. fr. Gaelic; Scots version by* Sydney Goodsir Smith. MS

Widdy-widdy-wurkey. The Family. Rose Fyleman. DuDr

Wide as this night, old as this night is old and young as it is young. Lullaby. Kenneth Fearing. CMoP (1970 ed.)

Wide, ho? Ezra Pound, *after the Chinese.* OBVE

Wide Open Are Thy Hands, *with music.* Bernard of Clairvaux, *tr. fr. Latin by* Charles P. Krauth. AH

Wide tie, wing collars, vest, and derby hats. Laurel and Hardy. John Bricuth. CSP

Widely we are scattered. An Endless Chain. Abraham Reisen, *tr. by* Keith Bosley. VWA

Widest prairies have electric fences, The. Wires. Philip Larkin. MiP; SFF

Widow, The. Mariana B. Davenport. AMV-80

Widow, The. W. S. Merwin. UnPo (1976 ed.); VGW

Widow, The/ met a big blk. Making Out. Leatrice W. Emeruwa. RiTi

Widow bird sate mourning for her love, A. Song. Shelley. NOBE; PoPle; UsP

Widow in Wintertime, A. Carolyn Kizer. CNW; NIL

Widow of a Man Who Is Still Breathing, The. Michael Small. DNGG

Widow of Drynam, The. Patrick MacDonogh. PFIr

Widow of Glencoe, The, *sel.* William Edmonstoune Aytoun. "Do not lift him from the bracken." SLP

Widow, Sapphics, The. Robert Southey. ESaP

Widower, The. Royall Tyler. OBAL

Widows, The. Eve Shelnutt. TC

Widow's Lament. *Tr. fr. Chinese by* Arthur Waley. *Fr.* Shih Ching. BoWoP

Widow's Lament in Springtime, The. William Carlos Williams. CMoP (1970 ed.); HAP; IPWM; NoAM; NOBA; PSN; TAP

Widow's Old Broom, The. *Unknown.* AmFP

Widow's Party, The. Kipling. PeBB; VLP

Widow's Plot, The; or, She Got What Was Coming to Her. William Plomer. NoAM

Widow's Yard, The. Isabella Gardner. RiTi

Wife. Jenne Andrews. HeS

Wife, The. Robert Creeley. VGW

Wife a-Lost, The. William Barnes. BoLoP; HAP; VPC

Wife and Mother. Jonathan Sisson. AAN

Wife and servant are the same. To the Ladies. Mary Lee, Lady Chudleigh. WPE

Wife Killer. Vernon Scannell. HeHu

"Wife, land of the wave fire." *Tr. fr. Icelandic by* George Johnston. *Fr.* The Saga of Gisli. OBVE

Wife of Bath, The. Chaucer. *Fr.* The Canterbury Tales: Prologue. OxBM ("Good Wif was ther of biside Bathe, A.") BiP; EBEV; InPS; PPoe

Wife of Bath's Prologue, The. Chaucer. *Fr.* The Canterbury Tales. OAEL-1

*Sels.* "If there were no authority on earth," *mod. by* Nevill Coghill. OBP

Wife's Fifth Husband, The. OxBM

Wife of Bath's Tale, The. Chaucer. *Fr.* The Canterbury Tales. ILP (1975 ed.); OAEL-1

Wife of Kohelet. Shlomit Cohen, *tr. fr. Hebrew by* Yishai Tobin. VWA

Wife of Llew, The. Francis Ledwidge. PFIr

Wife of the Moon Man Who Never Came Back. Grace Butcher. RiTi

Wife of Usher's Well, The. *Unknown.* AIW, 2 *versions;* AmFP; EBEV; Epi; FaBoBa; ILP (1975 ed.); NOBE; OAEL-1, *with music;* PeBB; SoSe

Wife to Husband. Fleur Adcock. ATNZ

Wife was sitting at her reel ae night, A. The Strange Visitor. *Unknown.* GBP

Wife Who Would a Wanton Be, The. *Unknown.* FaBoCo

Wife-Woman, The. Anne Spencer. NoAM

Wife Wrapt in Wether's Skin, The. *Unknown.* AIW; AmFP

Wife's Complaint, The. *Unknown. See* Wife's Lament, The.

Wife's Fifth Husband, The. Chaucer. *Fr.* The Canterbury Tales: The Wife of Bath's Prologue. OxBM

Wife's Lament, The. *Unknown, tr. fr. Anglo-Saxon.* BoWoP, *tr. by* Willis Barnstone *and* Elene Kolb; IPWM; PBWP, *tr. by* Kemp Malone; WPE
(Wife's Complaint, The, *tr. by* Michael Alexander.) BoLoP

Wife's Tale, The. Seamus Heaney. HeHu; SoSe (1977 ed.)

Wiggley-Woggley Men, The. Spike Milligan. OSF

Wiggling head-first from the egg. The Tiny Baby Lizard. Besmilr Brigham. RiTi

Wight in the Broom. *Unknown.* OxBM

Wigs and Beards. Robert Graves. NOBL

Wild, The. Wendell Berry. VGW

Wild air, world-mothering air. The Blessed Virgin Compared to the Air We Breathe. Gerard Manley Hopkins. PoIA; VLP

Wild Barbaree, The. *Unknown.* AmFP
(High Barbaree.) FSW

Wild, bare, rock-fanged hills that all day long, The. The Water Tank at Dusk. Sharlot Hall. WPW

Wild beauty of an eagle, once born to virgin sky, The. The Folding Fan. Grey Cohoe. VW

Wild Bees. James K. Baxter. ATNZ

Wild Bill Jones. *Unknown.* AmFP

Wild bird singer, sing on. Sand Creek. Charles G. Ballard. UnPo (1976 ed.); VoR

Wild Boarder, The. Kenyon Cox. TDH

Wild Colonial [*or* Colloina] Boy, The *(diff. versions). Unknown.* AIW; AmFP; FaBoBa; FSW; PEBB

Wild Crab. Mary Ellen Solt. BoWoP; UsP

Wild Dog Rose, The. John Montague. BIrV; CIP

Wild Dreams of a New Beginning. Lawrence Ferlinghetti. GP

Wild Dreams of Summer What Is Your Grief. George Barker. OxBTC

Wild ducks/ float with the north wind. Sun Children. Leslie Silko. VoR

Wild Flowers. Shakespeare. *Fr.* A Midsummer Night's Dream, II, i. PF
("I know a bank where the wild thyme blows.") PoPle

Wild Geese   William Hart-Smith. BoAnP

Wild Geese, The. John Masefield. NoAM

Wild Honey. Alistair Campbell. ATNZ

Wild Honey. Aaron Schneider. BCr

Wild Honey Suckle, The. Philip Freneau. AmVN; EAP; ILP (1975 ed.); NOBA; PiAm; TAP

Wild horses graze under a full moon. The Problem of Wild Horses. Barbara Winder. PH

Wild Iron. Allen Curnow. ATNZ

Wild Lumberjack, The. *Unknown.* AIW

Wild Mustard River, The. *Unknown.* AmFP

Wild Negro Bill. *Unknown.* BPo

Wild nights!—Wild nights! Emily Dickinson. AmVN; LoAs; NOBA; OLR; PBWP; PiAm; SBG; TAP; TT; WeW; WPE

Wild Oats. Philip Larkin. InPS

Wild Oats. Norman MacCaig. OxBTC

Wild Old Wicked Man, The. W. B. Yeats. CMoP (1970 ed.); UsP

Wild Orphan. Allen Ginsberg. TCP

Wild Peaches. Elinor Wylie. RiTi; SBG; WPE
"Down to the Puritan marrow of my bones." IV. BoWoP; VoPo
(Puritan Sonnet.) PAIC; SoSe (1977 ed.)

Wild Pigs. Ted Kooser. TAT

Wild Rippling Water, The. *Unknown.* FaBoBa

Wild roved the Indians once. Grand Rapids. Julia A. Moore. OBAL

Wild Rover. *Unknown.* FSW

Wild Sports of the West. John Montague. CIP

Wild Strawberries. Robert Graves. FSFS

Wild Swans. Edna St. Vincent Millay. CMoP (1970 ed.); ILP (1975 ed.); PBWP; UnPo (1976 ed.)

Wild Swans at Coole, The. W. B. Yeats. AnMo; BoAnP; CABA (1972 ed.); CMoP (1970 ed.); FSFS; HeIP; ILP (1975 ed.); IP; IPWM; NoAM; PB; PPP; PSN; STS; TCP; TT; UnPo (1976 ed.); VoPo

Wild winds weep, The. Mad Song. Blake. ILP (1975 ed.); MBPR; OAEL-2; STS

Wild Woman's Resentment of Fakery. Rochelle Owens. RiTi

Wild Worm, A. Carolyn Wells. TDH

Wildcats Walking in the Dark. James Steele. SES

Wilderness. Ralph Mecklenburger. SFF

Wilderness, The. Kathleen Raine. BoWoP; WPE

Wilderness. Carl Sandburg. PiAm

Wilderness, The: but otherwise. Esther K. Comes to America: 1931. Jerome Rothenberg. NNaP

Wildernesse and the solitarie place shall be glad for them, The. Bible, *O.T.* Isaiah, XXXV. OBVE

Wildfire. Judit Tóth, *tr. fr. Hungarian by* Emery George. VWA

Wildflowers, Smoke. Lyn Lifshin. MMD

Wildness in the grass has closed, A. Invocation from a Lawn Chair. Mary Jane Irion. AMV-80

Wildwood Flower. *Unknown.* BLSo, *with music;* FSW

Wilhelmj. Robert J. Burdette. TDH

Wilkes Booth came to Washington, an actor great was he. Booth Killed Lincoln. *Unknown.* AmFP; OFD

Will, The. John Donne. EBEV

Will. Ella Wheeler Wilcox. PPM

Will and Testament. James Neugass. SPT

Will come for me, old man—I can feel him. Death, Putative Father. Sydney Bernard Smith. IPM

Will dissolves, the heart becomes excited, The. Soliloquy in an Air-Raid. Roy Fuller. PoA

Will God, always cold, have a temperature? Moral Ode. David Rosenmann-Taub, *tr. by* Charles Guenther. VWA

Will God forever cast us off. Jesse Mercer. AmFP

Will he always love me? Lady Horikawa, *tr. fr. Japanese by* Kenneth Rexroth. BoWoP; OLR

"Will I die?" you ask. For Andrew. Fleur Adcock. ATNZ

Will people accept them? Tenzone. Ezra Pound. *Fr.* Contemporania. PoA

Will sprawl, now that the heat of day is best. Caliban upon Setebos; or, Natural Theology in the Island. Robert Browning. EBEV; OAEL-2; VLP

Will the man who gets clean love his neighbor? Soap (II). Jerome Rothenberg. NNaP

Will the Weaver. *Unknown.* AmFP

Will There Be Any Stars in My Crown? *with music.*　E. E. Hewitt. BLSH

Will there never come a season.　To R. K.　James Kenneth Stephen.　FaBoCo; FaBoEE; NOBL; VLP

Will they never fade or pass!　The Farmer Remembers the Somme.　Vance Palmer.　GAS

Will they stop.　Requiem.　Kenneth Fearing.　CMoP (1970 ed.)

Will to be tickled wants; has got the itch.　*Unknown.*　FaBoEE

Will to Change, The.　Adrienne Rich.　NMM

Will to Live, The.　Mekeel McBride.　PCho

Will Waterproof's Lyrical Monologue.　Tennyson.　VLP

Will ye heare, what I can say.　Upon His Julia.　Robert Herrick. SpRo

Will you come a boating, my gay old hag.　The Gay Old Hag. *Unknown.*　BIrV

Will you come with me, my Phyllis dear.　Wait for the Wagon. *Unknown, at. to* R. Bishop Buckley.　BLSo; FSW; PSoN

Will you glimmer on the sea?　Moonrise.　Hilda Doolittle ("H. D.").　PoA

Will You Go, Lassie, Go?　*Unknown.*　FSW

Will you have me?　A Popular Romance.　Kevin Ireland. ATNZ

Will you hear of a bloody Battle.　Teach the Rover.　*Unknown.* PeBB

Will You Love Me in December as You Do in May? *with music.* James J. Walker.　FSN

Will you perhaps consent to be.　Delmore Schwartz.　LoAs

Will you sleep forever?　Korinna, *tr. fr. Greek by* John Dillon. PBWP

Will you sleep forever,/ Korinna?　Korinna, *tr. fr. Greek by* Willis Barnstone.　BoWoP

Will you, sometime, who have sought so long, and seek.　The Finder Found.　Edwin Muir.　PoA

"Will you walk a little faster?" said a whiting to a snail.　The Lobster Quadrille [*or* The Mock Turtle's Song].　"Lewis Carroll."　*Fr.* Alice's Adventures in Wonderland, *ch.* 10. FaBoNo; OxBChV; PoPle; VLP

"Will you walk into my parlor?" said the Spider to the Fly.　The Spider and the Fly.　Mary Howitt.　ECBV; OxBChV

"Will you wear white, my dear, oh my dear."　Jinnie Jinkins. *Unknown.*　AmFP

Will You, Won't You.　Mark Van Doren.　NCSH

Willa.　John Haines.　CNW

Willets, The.　May Swenson.　WPE

Willful waste brings woeful want.　Mother Goose.　CTV

William and Mary.　*Unknown.*　AmFP

Wm. Brazier.　Robert Graves.　NOBL

William Brown.　Joaquin Miller.　BPAW

William Butler Yeats.　A. D. Hope.　MAuV

William Dewy, Tranter Reuben, Farmer Ledlow late at plough. Friends Beyond.　Thomas Hardy.　VLP

William Hall.　*Unknown.*　AmFP

William, my teacher, my friend! dear William and dear Dorothea! Hexameters.　Samuel Taylor Coleridge.　MBPR

William Shakespeare to Mrs. Anne, Regular Servant to the Rev. Mr. Precentor of York.　Thomas Gray.　ILP (1975 ed.)

William, the wild round plums are falling.　The Dressing Stations. Norman Dubie.　AmPA

William Was a Royal Lover.　*Unknown.*　AmFP

William Wordsworth.　Sidney Keyes.　OxBTC

Williams Avenue Zionist Church, The.　Russia.　William Carlos Williams.　VGW

Williamsburg, *sel.*　Linda Pastan.　　Governor's Palace, The.　RiTi

Willie.　*Unknown.*　AmFP

Willie and Lady Margerie.　*Unknown.*　PeBB

Willie B (2).　Lucille Clifton.　InPS

Willie Bobo Was a Baaaa/aad Dude.　Jesús Papoleto Meléndez. NW

Willie Brew'd a Peck o' Maut.　Burns.　ILP (1975 ed.)

Willie Fitzgibbons who used to sell ribbons.　Waltz Me Around Again Willie; or, 'Round, 'Round, 'Round.　Will D. Cobb. FSN

Willie had a purple monkey climbing on a yellow stick.　In Memoriam.　Max Adeler.　FaBoCo

Willie Leonard; or, The Lake of Cold Finn.　*Unknown.*　AmFP

Willie Mays.　Paul Ramsey.　PPoD

Willie Metcalf.　Edgar Lee Masters.　*Fr.* Spoon River Anthology. IPWM

Willie o [*or of*] Winsbury.　*Unknown.*　AmFP; PeBB

Willie, take your little drum.　Patapan.　Bernard de la Monnoye, *tr. fr. French.*　PChr

Willie Taylor, *with music.*　*Unknown.*　RDB

Willie the Weeper.　*Unknown.*　*See* Willy the Weeper.

Willie was a widow's son.　Willie and Lady Margerie. *Unknown.*　PeBB

Willie Winkie.　William Miller.　OxBChV 　("Wee Willie Winkie runs through the town.")　MG; NIL

Willing Mistriss, The.　Aphra Behn.　*Fr.* The Dutch Lover.　SBG

Willow herb, the, The.　Rose Bay Willow Herb.　Judy Ray. AMV-81

Willow leaves dancing.　Eveningsong.　Ramona Wilson.　VoR

Willow-Man, The.　Juliana Horatia Ewing.　OxBChV

Willow Poem.　William Carlos Williams.　NCSH

Willow shining, The.　The Knowledge of Light.　Henry Rago. VGW

Willow-tassels grow in tremors of the spring wind.　Lines to Do with Youth.　Witter Bynner.　PoA

Willows.　Laura Schreiber.　AMV-81

Willows are willows everywhere.　Willows in Alma-Ata. Aleksander Wat, *tr. by* Isaac Komem.　VWA

Willows by the Water Side, The.　*Tr. fr. Tewa Indian by* H. J. Spinden.　WTO

Willows carried a slow sound, The.　Repose of Rivers.　Hart Crane.　CMoP (1970 ed.); ExPo (1973 ed.); ILP (1975 ed.); NoAM; NOBA; UsP

Willows in Alma-Ata.　Aleksander Wat, *tr. fr. Polish by* Isaac Komem.　VWA

Willowwood.　Dante Gabriel Rossetti.　The House of Life, XLIX-LII.　OAEL-2; VLP

Will's Love, The.　Besmilr Brigham.　IHMS

Willy ("Willy, enormous Saskatchewan grizzly").　Richard Moore. MAT

Willy Lyons.　William Stafford.　NNaP

Willy [*or* Willie] the Weeper.　*Unknown.*　FSW; GBP; OBAL; PeBB

Willy to Jinny.　Joseph Skipsey.　VLP

Willy Wet-Leg.　D. H. Lawrence.　CMoP (1970 ed.)

Willy's rare, and Willy's fair.　Rare Willie Drowned in Yarrow. *Unknown.*　AIW; GBP; PeBB

Wil't please your grace to go along with us?　A Quotation from Shakespeare with Slight Improvements.　"Lewis Carroll." FaBoNo

Wilt thou be gone? it is not yet near day.　Shakespeare.　*Fr.* Romeo and Juliet, III, v.　PAIC

Wilt thou forgive that sin where I begun.　A Hymn to God the Father.　John Donne.　BiP; BoReV; EBEV; HAP; ILP (1975 ed.); InPK; IP; MetP; NOBE; OAEL-1; PAIC; PPoe; TT; WIF

Wilt thou go with me, sweet maid.　An Invite to Eternity.　John Clare.　OAEL-2

Wilt Thou Not Visit Me?　Jones Very.　*See* Prayer, The: "Wilt thou not visit me?"

Wilt thou then serve the Philistines with that gift. Milton. *Fr.* Samson Agonistes. EBEV

Wiltshire Downs. Andrew Young. OxBTC

Wily Fox, The. Edward Davies. *Fr.* Chepstow: A Poem. OBW

"Wimmin's bizness, it's to cook." Man-sized Job. Sharlot Hall. WPW

Wind, The. Arthur J. Bull. HeHu

Wind, The. Alice Corbin, *after Chippewa Indian.* BPAW

Wind, The. Dafydd ap Gwilym, *tr. fr. Welsh by* Joseph P. Clancy. OBW

Wind. Sydney Dobell. PeD

Wind. Eugen Gomringer. WeW

Wind. Ted Hughes. LP; MPo; SoSe

Wind. *Malay Oral Tradition, tr. by* R. O. Winstedt. WTO

Wind, The. James Reeves. ECBV; FPB

Wind, The. Christina Rossetti. *See* Who Has Seen the Wind.

Wind, The. Charles Simic. NVAP

Wind, The. Ruth Stephan. FoP

Wind, The. James Stephens. CaYB; CTV; InPK; NoAM; PFIr

Wind, The. Robert Louis Stevenson. CTV

Wind, The. Song of the Trees. *Tr. by* Frances Densmore. OBVE

Wind and pines. Listening. Nancy Passy. AMV-81

Wind and Silver. Amy Lowell. BoWoP; IPWM; Moon; RiTi; SoSe

Wind and the Moon, The, *sels.* George MacDonald.
"Said the Wind to the Wind to the Moon, 'I will blow you out.' " CaYB; LCL

Wind and the rain are beating down, The. In My Dreams I Searched for You. *Gond Oral Tradition, tr. by* V. Elwin *and* S. Hivale. WTO

Wind as elder brother, The. Flight on Naked Wings. Melvin Dixon. NW

Wind at the Door, The. William Barnes. GBL

Wind begun to rock [*or* knead] the grass, The. Emily Dickinson. ECBV; HAP, *sl. diff.*

Wind billowing out the seat of my britches, The. Child on Top of a Greenhouse. Theodore Roethke. BuTh; DuDr; NCSH; PiAm; VGW

Wind, bird, and tree. The Words. David Wagoner. PoA; TSWA

Wind bit hard at Valley Forge one Christmas, The. Carl Sandburg. *Fr.* Washington Monument by Night. CC

Wind blew all my wedding-day, The. Wedding-Wind. Philip Larkin. BuTh; LoAs; MAT

Win blew strongly like the voice of fate, The. Christoph. Charles Spear. ATNZ

Wind blows a piece of paper to my feet, The. Streetcorner. Bill Knott. PCho

Wind blows out of the gates of the day, The. W. B. Yeats. *Fr.* The Land of Heart's Desire. PPM

Wind blows up the tent like a balloon, The. Crimson Tent. John Dos Passos. PoA

Wind-Chimes in a Temple Ruin. Earle Birney. MPA

Wind closes the door behind us, The. A Walk with My Cat. Virginia R. Terris. AAN

Wind comes from opposite poles, The. The Marriage. Mark Strand. EAS; NoAM

Wind comes like the chief mourner. Funeral. Joanna Thompson. AMV-81

"Wind doth blow today, my love, The." The Unquiet Grave. *Unknown.* ExPo (1973 ed.); GBP; HAP; HeIP; InPK; OAEL-1; PeBB; PoPle; SLP; WeW

Wind dust yellow cloud swirls. Black Mesa Mine No. 1. Gary Snyder. PoW

Wind flapped loose, the wind was still, The. The Woodspurge. Dante Gabriel Rossetti. EBEV; HAP; HeIP; InPK; NOBE; OAEL-2; PBMP; PF; UnPo (1976 ed.); VLP; VPC; WeW

Wind-flicked and ruddy her young body glowed. Sea-Change. W. W. Gibson. EcS

Windharp. John Montague. CIP

Wind has blown the rain away and blown, A. Sonnet. E. E. Cummings. PAIC

Wind has died, no motion now, The. The Estuary. A. R. D. Fairburn. ATNZ

Wind has no language to be chipped. Solar Signals. L. Pearl Schuck. AMV-81

Wind has no voice, really, The. Day Time Sequence/ November. Dalene Stowe. NPW

Wind has scattered my city to the sheep, The. Ruins of the City of Hay. Randolph Stow. GAS

Wind has swept from the wide atmosphere, The. A Summer Evening Churchyard, Lechlade, Gloucestershire. Shelley. PIM

Wind, heavy from the land, irons the surf, The. Offshore Breeze. Milton Acorn. NeAC

Wind in a Frolic, The. William Howitt. OxBChV

Wind in the Willows, The, *sels.* Kenneth Grahame.
Ducks' Ditty. OxBChV; PoPle
Song of Mr. Toad, The. NOBL
"Villagers all, this frosty tide." PChr

Wind Increases, The. William Carlos Williams. TT

Wind, Intrudes, Lifting Day. Wild Crab. Mary Ellen Solt. BoWoP; UsP

Wind is always blowing, A. Proverbial. John Seller Anson. AMV-80

Wind is blowing in the scent of formaldehyde, The. The Black Spring Becomes Anonymous. Sotère Torregian. MIT

Wind is blowing, A. The book being written. The Novel. Denise Levertov. ILP (1975 ed.); NoAM

Wind is carrying me round the sky, The. The Wind. Alice Corbin, *after Chippewa Indian.* BPAW

Wind is cold, The. Winter. Princess Shikishi, *tr. by* Hiroaki Sato. PBWP

Wind is desolate in the fields, The. The Deserted Homestead. Loren C. Eiseley. PoA

Wind is east but the hot weather continues, The. American Letter: For Gerald Murphy. Archibald MacLeish. ILP (1975 ed.)

Wind is enough to stack the snow, The. November Snow. E. J. Carson. AMV-81

Wind is loud, The. The Rescue. Ian Serraillier. FPB

Wind is 95, The. It still pours from the east. Bear Paw. Richard Hugo. MPA

Wind is not nigh. Zone of Death. William Everson. VGW

Wind is ruffling the tawny pelt, A. A Far Cry from Africa. Derek Walcott. NoAM; UnPo (1976 ed.)

Wind is shaking this house, The. The Storm House. Elizabeth Jennings. WPE

Wind is thin. *Tr. fr. Latin by* Willis Barnstone. *Fr.* Cambridge Songs. BoWoP

Wind is walking the tallest trees, The. Sudden Gale in Spring. Martha Banning Thomas. ECBV

Wind it blew from east to west, The. Get Up and Bar the Door. *Unknown.* AmFP

Wind licks hairs on shiny heads. Settling In. Floyd C. Stuart. TAT

Wind moves above the wheat, The. Ezra Pound. *Fr.* A Song of the Degrees. AKE

Wind of dawning riffles the young furze, The. Drafts for a Quatrain. Edmund Wilson. OBAL

Wind of the prairie, sweeping adown from the hills.   Wind Song.
Zoe A. Tilghman.   BPAW

Wind on the Corn.   Charles Tennyson Turner.   VPC

Wind one morning sprung up from sleep, The.   The Wind in a
Frolic.   William Howitt.   OxBChV

Wind outside this beach house, The.   The Beach House.   James
K. Baxter.   ATNZ

Wind picks at the clapboard.   Noah in New England.   Tom
Lowenstein.   VWA

Wind piercing, hill bare, hard to find shelter.   *Unknown, tr. by*
Joseph P. Clancy.   *Fr.* Winter.   OBW

Wind rifles itself up, The.   Words to the Wind.   Pier Giorgio Di
Cicco.   AMV-80

Wind rocks the car.   Like This Together.   Adrienne Rich.
PiAm; VGW

Wind runs free across our plains, The.   For Adolf Eichmann.
Primo Levi, *tr. by* Ruth Feldman *and* Brian Swann.   VWA

Wind scratches, The.   The Saboteur.   Richard Di Grazia.   PoW

Wind searching as a sieve of brass.   Storm at Sea.   *Malay Oral
Tradition, tr. by* R. O. Winstedt.   WTO

Wind Secrets.   Diane Wakoski.   AmPA

Wind Sleepers, The.   Hilda Doolittle ("H. D.").   WPE

Wind Song.   Zoe A. Tilghman.   BPAW

Wind Sou'west, The.   *Unknown.*   AmFP

Wind stood up, and gave a shout, The.   The Wind.   James
Stephens.   CaYB; CTV; InPK; NoAM; PFIr

Wind sucks downward like a gong, The.   Sudden Obscurity.
Kermit Coad.   PHC

Wind sways the pines, A.   Dirge in Woods.   George Meredith.
FF; VLP

Wind through the box-elder trees, The.   Poem against the British.
Robert Bly.   ConAP; InPS

Wind through the olive trees.   Long, Long Ago.   *Unknown.*
RAE

Wind Was on the Withered Heath, The.   J. R. R. Tolkien.   DuDr

Wind Was There, The.   Bravig Imbs.   EAS

Wind wheels over Manhattan like an enemy, The.   A Summer
Night.   Ben Maddow.   SPT

Wind whines and whines the shingle.   On the Beach at Fontana.
James Joyce.   PoA; SoSe

Wind, wind I hear you walking by, I hear.   Red Butte in Autumn.
Peggy Simson Curry.   WPW

Wind would tear a dead man's shroud.   Wind.   *Malay Oral
Tradition, tr. by* R. O. Winstedt.   WTO

Windfall.   Joel Arsenault.   AMV-81

Windham Thaw, The.   Arthur Guiterman.   ECBV

Windhover, The.   Gerard Manley Hopkins.   AnMo; BiP;
BoReV; CABA (1972 ed.); CMoP (1970 ed.); Epi; HAP; ILP
(1975 ed.); InPK; InPS; NIL; NoAM; NOBE; OAEL-2;
PAIC; PoPle; PPoD; PPoe; PPP; UnPo (1976 ed.); VLP;
VoPo; WeW

Windless city built on decaying granite, loose ends.   Thomas
McGrath.   Letter to an Imaginary Friend, Part Two, II, 2–5.
NNaP

Windmill, The.   Arthur J. Bull.   HeHu

Windmill in March.   Katharine Privett.   AMV-80

Windmill of Evening, The.   Shlomo Reich, *tr. fr. French by* Mira
Reich.   VWA

Window, The.   Conrad Aiken.   CMoP (1970 ed.)

Window.   Anne Cherner.   AMV-80

Window, The.   Robert Creeley.   CAPP; CoPAm; NoAM;
NOBA; TAP; VGW

Window.   Carl Sandburg.   OSP

Window Dressing.   William Peskett.   IPM

Window in the Breast.   *Unknown, tr. fr. Greek by* Walter
Headlam.   ECBV

Window insulates me from the street, The.   Maternity Gown.
David Holbrook.   OxBTC

Window is broken, A.   The Night Has Twenty-four Hours.
Pedro Juan Pietri.   InW

Window is nailed and boarded, The.   Hallaig.   Sorley Maclean.
MS

Window Ledge in the Atom Age.   E. B. White.   OBAL

Window pales, and by its paltry light, The.   Aubade: Donna
Anna to Juan, Still Asleep.   Richard Howard.   PoA

Window to the East.   Virginia Moran Evans.   AMV-80

Window was made of ice with bears lumbering across it.   Bad
Dream.   Louis MacNeice.   NoAM

Window was open all night long, The.   All Night Long.   Nina
Cassian, *tr. by* Herbert Kuhner.   VWA

Windows, The.   George Herbert.   AnMo; CABA (1972 ed.); ILP
(1975 ed.); NIL; SCP-1

Windows.   Mordechai Husid, *tr. fr. Yiddish by* Seymor Mayne *and*
Rivka Augenfeld.   VWA

Windows, The.   Ron Loewinsohn.   GP

Windows, The.   W. S. Merwin.   PHC

Windows, The/ look back into themselves.   The Way We Live
Now.   Robert Dana.   AMV-80

Windows are deep blue, The.   The Blue Church.   Peter Balakian.
AMV-80

Windows in Providence.   Aliki Barnstone.   BoWoP

Window's length beyond the Pleiades, A.   First Snow on an
Airfield.   John Ciardi.   PoA

Windows vanish, The: we cannot afford to buy.   A House All
Pictures.   Emery George.   AMV-81

Wind's bride seized me, The.   In the Open Fields.   Hugo
Sonnenschein, *tr. by* Edouard Roditi.   VWA

Winds had hushed at last as by command, The.   The Sower.
Mathilde Blind.   SBG; WPE

Wind's in the heart of me, a fire's in my heels, A.   A Wanderer's
Song.   John Masefield.   RhR

Wind's Lament, The.   John Morris-Jones, *tr. fr. Welsh by* Anthony
Conran.   OBW

Winds of Change, The.   Charles G. Ballard.   VoR

Winds of doctrine blow both ways at once, The.   Conrad Aiken.
*Fr.* A Letter from Li Po.   VGW

Winds of the World, give answer!   The English Flag.   Kipling.
BTTM

Wind's overbearing voices, The.   The Storm.   John Hay.
AMV-81

Winds snatch at the troll-tooth rocks.   Lighthouse.   Merle
Meeter.   AATT

Wind's spine is broken, The.   Storm Tide on Mejit.   *Unknown,
tr. by* Augustin Kramer *and* Willard Trask.   RFM

Winds through the olive trees.   Long, Long Ago.   *Unknown.*
CTV; PChr

Wind's word, the Hebrew Hallelujah.   Hallelujah: A Sestina.
Robert Francis.   PPoD

Windsor Forest, *sels.*   Pope.
"Groves of Eden, vanished now so long, The."   OAEL-1
Hunt, The.   NIL
Shoot, The.   PB

Windy Boy in a Windswept Tree.   Geoffrey Summerfield.   LP

Windy Gap.   David Campbell.   GAS

Windy Nights.   David Campbell.   MAuV

Windy Nights.   Robert Louis Stevenson.   ECBV; FPB; OxBChV;
PH

Wine and Water.   G. K. Chesterton.   FaBoCo

Wine and woman and song.   Villanelle of the Poet's Road.
Ernest Dowson.   PAIC; UnPo (1976 ed.)

Wine comes in at the mouth.   A Drinking Song.   W. B. Yeats.
BoLoP; LoAS; OAEL-2; POL

Wine Cup, The.   Meleager, *tr. fr. Greek by* Dudley Fitts.   OLR

Wine from the Cape. Turner Cassity. AMV–81

Wine-maiden. Midnight Dancer. Langston Hughes. FF

Wine Menagerie, The. Hart Crane. NoAM; NOBA; VGW

Wing Factory, The. Dona Stein. AMV–80

Winged bull trundles to the wired perimeter, The. C. Day Lewis. *Fr.* Flight to Italy. OxBTC

Winged in Gold. Euros Bowen. OBW

Winging It. Jack Myers. PCho

Wings, The. Denise Levertov. CAPP

Wings of a bird, The. Totem. Nissim Ezekiel. VWA

Wings of Time are black and white, The. Compensation. Emerson. NOBA

Wings outstretched, a horned owl. Signatures. Daniel Hoffman. VGW

Wingwalking in Oregon. Robert Peterson. MIT; NeAC

Winifred Waters. William Brighty Rands. OxBChV

Winked too much and were afraid of snakes. The Monkeys. Marianne Moore. CMoP (1970 ed.); NoAM; NOBA; UsP

Winners, The. Kipling. *Fr.* The Story of the Gadsbys. FaPoR

Winnie. Antar S. K. Mberi. SES

Winning of the TV West, The. John T. Alexander. CTV

Winning way, a pleasant smile, A. Little Annie Rooney. Michael Nolan. FSN

Winnsboro Cotton Mill Blues. *Unknown.* FSW

Wino. Ted Hughes. NoAM

Wino was eating soup, The. Tornado Soup. A. K. Redwing. VoR

Wino Will. Eve Merriam. *Fr.* The Inner-City Mother Goose. IPWM

Winter. Bella Akhmadulina, *tr. fr. Russian by* Barbara Einzig. BoWoP

Winter. Walter de la Mare. OAEL–2

Winter. John Lyle Donaghy. BIrV

Winter. D. W. Donzella. FAF

Winter. Richard Hughes. OBW

Winter. Mani Leib, *tr. fr. Yiddish by* Keith Bosley. VWA

Winter. Larry Levis. NVAP

Winter. Coventry Patmore. NOBE

Winter. Pope. *Fr.* Pastorals. PAIC

Winter. Shakespeare. *Fr.* Love's Labour's Lost, V, ii. AKE; FSFS; HAP; ILP (1975 ed.); IPWM; NIL; OAEL–1; SoSe; UnPo (1976 ed.); UsP; WeW
   (When Icicles Hang by the Wall.) BiP; FF; HeIP; InPK; InPS; NOBE; OBP

Winter. Princess Shikishi, *tr. fr. Japanese by* Hiroaki Sato. PBWP

Winter. Ruth Stone. BoWoP

Winter. J. M. Synge. OxBTC; POL

Winter. Tennyson. FSFS

Winter. Katharine Tynan. FSFS

Winter. William Carlos Williams. NCSH

Winter, *sel. Unknown, tr. fr. Welsh by* Joseph P. Clancy. "Wind piercing, hill bare, hard to find shelter." OBW

Winter, a Dirge. Burns. LAuP

Winter again and it is snowing. W. D. Snodgrass. Heart's Needle,V. ILP (1975 ed.)

Winter begins. Poem on the End of Sensation. Ken Stange. AMV–80

Winter Bouquet. W. D. Snodgrass. NowV

Winter breaks dissolving concrete. It Is Good to Know You. Jim Farrar. DNGG

Winter Burn. Roberta Hill. VoR

Winter clenched its fist, The. The Redwing. Patric Dickinson. BoAnP

Winter Coming On. Martin Bell, *after the French of* Jules Laforgue. OBVE; OxBTC

Winter Dance, San Domingo. Wendell B. Anderson. PoW

Winter Day. Susannah Fried, *tr. fr. Slovak by* Anthony Rudolf. VWA

Winter deepening, the hay all in, The. Richard Wilbur. PPM

Winter Drive. James McAuley. PoA

Winter: East Anglia. Edmund Blunden. LiSp; OxBTC

Winter Evening. Harry Behn. CaYB

Winter evening settles down, The. Preludes. T. S. Eliot. ExPo (1973 ed.); HeIP; ILP (1975 ed.); InPS; IP; PoIA; PPoD; PPP; PSN; UnPo (1976 ed.); VGW; WeW

Winter Exercise. Howard Nemerov. NowV

Winter Fairyland in Vermont. Francis P. Osgood. WeW

Winter fells. Deathward. John Lyle Donaghy. BIrV

Winter Flowers. Wade Hall. AATT

Winter: For an Untenable Situation. Alan Dugan. NIL; NowV

Winter Garden. Janet Lewis. WPW

Winter has broken against the bones. The Stoneyard. Peter Trias. AAN

Winter Heavens. George Meredith. CABA (1972 ed.)

Winter: hoarse, oracular. Daphne. Phyllis Hoge Thompson. PHC

Winter Holding off the Coast of North America. N. Scott Momaday. CDW

Winter in Another Country. Ai. AMV–81

Winter in Durnover Field. Thomas Hardy. PoIA

Winter in Elwell. James Tipton. HeS; TC

Winter in the Sierras. Mary Austin. BPAW

Winter Insomnia. Raymond Carver. NVAP

Winter is a far more fit. Hens in Winter. Robert P. Tristram Coffin. TH

Winter Is Another Country. Archibald MacLeish. NCSH

Winter is cold-hearted. Summer. Christina Rossetti. CTV; FSFS; PBMP; PoPle

Winter is gone, and spring is over. Alfred Austin. FaBoCo

Winter Is Here. "Katri Vala," *tr. fr. Finnish by* Jaakko A. Ahokas. PBWP

Winter is icummen in. Ancient Music. Ezra Pound. FaBoCo; FF; HeIP; ILP (1975 ed.); OBAL; PBMP; PoIA; SpRo

Winter is long in this climate. March. William Carlos Williams. NCSH

Winter is the king of showmen. Winter Morning. Ogden Nash. FPB

Winter Journey. Stanislaw Wygodski, *tr. fr. Polish by* Isaac Komem. VWA

Winter Lambing. James Tipton. TC

Winter Landscape. John Berryman. CoPAm; NIL; UsP; WIF

Winter Love. Elizabeth Jennings. BoLoP

Winter Mask. Allen Tate. Prf

Winter Memories. Henry David Thoreau. AmVN; VoPo (Within the Circuit of This Plodding Life.) NOBA; PiAm

Winter Moon. Langston Hughes. DuDa; PAIC

Winter Moon. Maria Luisa Spaziani, *tr. fr. Italian by* Lynne Lawner. PBWP

Winter Morning. Ogden Nash. FPB

Winter Morning. William Jay Smith. HeS; NCSH

Winter Morning Walk, The. William Cowper. The Task, V. LAuP

Winter Mornings. Nancy Mairs. NPW

Winter mornings. Back Road. Bruce Guernsey. AMV–81

Winter Mouse. Aileen Fisher. MN

Winter must be here, The. What We Can. Ray A. Young Bear. VoR

Winter, New Hampshire. David Kherdian. TAT

Winter Night, A. William Barnes. NOBE

Winter Night. C. Day Lewis. PoA

Winter Night. A. R. D. Fairburn. ATNZ

Winter Night, A. James Thomson. *Fr.* The Seasons: Winter. NOBE

Winter Night, Cold Spell. Howard Nelson. AMV–81

Winter Nightfall. J. C. Squire. OxBTC

Winter Nights. Thomas Campion. NOBE

Winter Nights. Lora Dunetz. AMV–80

Winter 1970, Fox River, Illinois. Ralph Salisbury. MPA

Winter Ocean. John Updike. InPK; OSP; SoSe

Winter of my infancy being over-past, The. Another Song. Ann Collins. SCP-2

Winter owl banked just in time to pass, The. Questioning Faces. Robert Frost. NCSH

Winter Piece, A. Bryant. EAP

Winter-Piece to a Friend Away, A. John Berryman. NOBA

Winter Ploughing. William Everson. NU

Winter Poem. Nikki Giovanni. OSP

Winter Pond. Mary Logue. NPW

Winter Remembered. John Crowe Ransom. HAP; NOBA; UnPo (1976 ed.); VGW

Winter Report. Ben Howard. PoA

Winter Scene. A. R. Ammons. WeW

Winter Scene, A. Reed Whittemore. NCSH

Winter Scene. Marguerite Young. NU; WPE

Winter Seascape. John Betjeman. SS

Winter Ship, A. Sylvia Plath. PSN

Winter Shore, The. Thomas Wade. OAEL-2

Winter Sketches. Charles Reznikoff. PoA

Winter-sky began to frown, The. Stella at Wood-Park. Swift. BIrV

Winter sled, A. Signs of the Seasons. *Unknown.* ECBV

Winter Sonnet. Anne Waldman. CAAP

Winter Soon Is Coming. Elizabeth J. Coatsworth. ECBV

Winter Storms, The. Sir William Davenant. SCP-2

Winter Sweetness. Langston Hughes. ECBV

Winter Talent, A. Donald Davie. OAEL-2

Winter: The Abandoned Nest. Ron Baxter. WeW

Winter to spring; the west wind melts the frozen rancour. Solvitur Acris Hiems. Horace, *tr. by* Louis MacNeice. Odes, I, 4. Epi

Winter Trees. Conrad Diekmann. LiSp

Winter Trees. Sylvia Plath. NMM; SBG

Winter Trout. James Dickey. LiSp

Winter Tuesday, the city pouring fire, A. Coming Home, Detroit, 1968. Philip Levine. TAT

Winter Twilight, A. Angelina Weld Grimké. PoBA

Winter Twilight. Jeff Schiff. AMV–81

Winter Twilight, Glowing Black and Gold, The. Delmore Schwartz. NoAM

Winter Verse for His Sister. William Meredith. TAP

Winter Wait, A. Charlotte A. Raines. PoUp

Winter Wakeneth All My Care. *Unknown.* HAP
(Winter Wakens All My Care.) HAP, *mod. English:* OxBM

Winter Warfare. Edgell Rickword. OxBTC

Winter Watch. Jeff Daniel Marion. AMV–80

Winter will bar the swimmer soon. Swimming Chenango Lake. Charles Tomlinson. NoAM

Winter Winds Cold and Blea. John Clare. GBL

Winter with the Gulf Stream. Gerard Manley Hopkins. CMoP (1970 ed.); ExPo (1973 ed.); NoAM; VLP

Winterfall. *Unknown.* OxBM
(Mirie It Is while Sumer Ilast.) HAP

Wintering. Sylvia Plath. NMM

Winterkill. Clarice Short. MPA

Winters close, Springs open, no child stirs, The. John Berryman. *Fr.* Homage to Mistress Bradstreet. NoAM

Winter's Onset from an Alienated Point of View. Alan Dugan. FF

Winter's Tale, The, *sels.* Shakespeare.
Autolycus as Peddler ("Lawn as white as driven snow"), *fr.* IV, iii. OAEL-1
Autolycus' Song ("Jog on, jog on the footpath way"), *fr.* IV, ii. SpRo
"Here's flowers for you," *fr.* IV, iii. GBL
"I would I had some flowers o' th' spring that might," *fr.* IV, iii. PoPle
Spring Garland, *fr.* IV, iii. PF
"When daffodils begin to peer," *fr.* IV, ii. AIW; OBP; PoPle
(Autolycus Sings.) NOBE
(Autolycus' Song.) OAEL-1
(Pedlar's Song, The.) BBL

Winter's Tale, A. Dylan Thomas. CMoP (1970 ed.)

Winterscape. Jess Perlman. AMV–80

Winter Time. Robert Louis Stevenson. OxBChV

Winter time is coming. Cold Wave Blues. *Unknown.* BluL

Wintertime nighs. In Tenebris. Thomas Hardy. IP; NOBE; OAEL-2

Wintry Manifesto, A. Chris Wallace-Crabbe. GAS

Wintry west extends his blast, The. Winter, a Dirge. Burns. LAuP

Winwick, Lancashire. *Unknown.* GBP

Wires. Philip Larkin. MiP; SFF

Wisconsin Farm Auction. David Steingass. NVAP

Wisdom. Linda Peavy. PH

Wisdom. Hy Sobiloff. VGW

Wisdom. Sara Teasdale. TPo

Wisdom. Frank Yerby. AmNP (1974 ed.)

Wisdom and Spirit of the universe! Wordsworth. *Fr.* The Prelude, I. NOBE

Wisdom has nothing to do with age. Wisdom. Hy Sobiloff. VGW

Wisdom is the finest beauty of a person. *Yoruba Oral Tradition, tr. by* Ulli Beier. WTO

Wise emblem of our politic world. The Snail. Richard Lovelace. CaPo; OAEL-1; SCP-2

Wise Empty Landscape with a Death in the Foreground. N. Scott Momaday. CDW

Wise fish digs his silver in, The. Night Catch. Heather McHugh. AmPA

Wise Guy. William Cole. OSF

Wiseguy Type. Herman Spector. SPT

Wise guys, The. Kid Stuff. Frank Horne. AmNP (1974 ed.); PChr; PoBA

Wise Johnny. Edwina Fallis. CTV

Wise may bring their learning, The. A Child's Offering. *Unknown.* CTV

Wise Men and Shepherds. Sidney Godolphin. *See* Hymn: "Lord, when the wise men came from far."

Wise men come here to shit. From a Lavatory Wall. *Unknown.* FaBoEE

Wise Men of Gotham, The. Thomas Love Peacock. FaBoNo

Wise Old Owl, A. Edward Hersey Richards. CTV
(More Wisdom.) BBL

Wise Rochefoucault a maxim writ. Swift. *Fr.* The life and Genuine Character of Dean Swift. NOBL

Wisely and well was it said of him. Addition to Kipling's "The Dead King (Edward VII), 1910." Max Beerbohm. FaBoEE

Wiser far than human seer. The Humble Bee. Emerson. CTV

Wisest scholar of the wight most wise, The. Astrophel and Stella, XXV. Sir Philip Sidney. OAEL-1

Wisga. Lew Blockcolski. VoR

Wish, The. Abraham Cowley. *Fr.* The Mistress. ILP (1975 ed.); NOBE

Wish, A. Eleanor Farjeon. CC

Wish. Lance Henson. CDW

Wish, A. Fanny Kemble. WPE

Wish, A. Laurence Lerner. FF; OxBTC

Wish, A. Samuel Rogers. FaPoR; NOBE

Wish, A. J. M. Synge. FaBoEE

Wish. Dorothy Brown Thompson. CTV

Wish for a Young Wife. Theodore Roethke. AnMo; LoAs; NoAM; STS; TAP

Wish for Water, A. Laura Chester. RiTi

Wish for Waving Goodbye, A. Roberta Hill. AMV-80

Wish I was in Bowling Green sittin' in a chair. Bowling Green. *Unknown.* FSW

Wish I was in London. Handsome Molly. *Unknown.* FSW

Wish I was in Tennessee. Tennessee. *Unknown.* AmFP

Wish, that of the living whole, The. In Memoriam A. H. H., LV. Tennyson. BoReV; ExPo (1973 ed.); HAP; PoIA

"Wish to Be Believed, The." Mona Van Duyn. PoA

Wishbone, The. Fred Bornhauser. PPoD

Wishbone, The. Rae Desmond Jones. CAAP

Wished to have been milk. Story. Dennis Saleh. NeAC

Wishes. Patty L. Harjo. VoR

Wishes for Her. Denis Devlin. CIP

Wishes of an Elderly Man, The. Sir Walter Alexander Raleigh. FaBoCo; FaBoEE; NOBL

Wishes to His (Supposed) Mistress. Richard Crashaw. BoLoP; EBEV; SCP-1

Wishing. William Allingham. OxBChV

Wishing for roses, I walk through the garden. Summer Garden. "Anna Akhmatova," *tr. by* Stephen Stepanchev. BoWoP

Wispy cuttings lie in rows, The. July in Indiana. Robert Fitzgerald. ANTL

Wistful,/ they speak of. The People. Robert Creeley. VGW

Wistful Butch Poem. Rochelle Owens. WBN

Wistful camera caught this four-year-old, The. Self-Portrait. Allen Curnow. ATNZ

Wistfulness covers the windows, like drapes. The Dead Letter Office. Maxine Chernoff. FiCh

Wit Wonders. *Unknown. See* God and Yet a Man, A?

Witch, A. William Barnes. VLP

Witch. Patricia Beer. HeHu

Witch, The. Mary Elizabeth Coleridge. WPE

Witch? Sam Reavin. CaYB

Witch. Jean Tepperman. NMM

Witch Doctor. Robert Hayden. AmNP (1974 ed.); MAT; NoAM

Witch Flies By, A. Elizabeth Hough Sechrist. IWK

Witch Going Down to Egypt, A. Raquel Chalfi, *tr. fr. Hebrew by* Alexandra Meiri *and* Myra Glazer Schotz. VWA

Witch in the Wintry Wood, The. Aileen Fisher. IWK

"This is the tale of how Tim one," *sel.* CaYB

Witch of Atlas, The. Shelley. MBPR

Witch of Coös, The. Robert Frost. *Fr.* Two Witches. ExPo (1973 ed.); NoAM; NOBA; PAIC

Witch of East Seventy-second Street, The. Morris Bishop. NYP

Witch that came, The (the withered hag). Provide, Provide. Robert Frost. CABA (1972 ed.); CMoP (1970 ed.); HAP; InPK; IPWM; NIL; NoAM; NOBA; PPP; SS; STS; TAP; UnPo (1976 ed.)

Witch, The! The Witch! Eleanor Farjeon. IWK

Witchcraft. Siddie Joe Johnson. ECBV

Witches, The. Iain Crichton Smith. MS

Witches and poets co-embrace like fate. Fatales Poetae. Henry Parrot. FaBoEE

Witches' Charm, The. Ben Jonson. *Fr.* The Masque of Queens. NOBE; UsP

("Owl is abroad, the bat and the toad, The.") SCP-1

(Song: "Owl is abroad, The," 6 *ll.*) PoPle

Witches flying past on broomsticks. Halloween. Mary Jane Carr. IWK

Witches' Menu. Sonja Nikolay. IWK

Witches' Wood, The. Mary Elizabeth Coleridge. PBWP

Witch's Ballad, The. William Bell Scott. VLP

Witch's Broom Notes. David McCord. IWK

Witch's Broomstick Spell. *Unknown.* GBP

Witch's Cat, The. Ian Serraillier. SO

Witch's House, The. Beate Goldman. PoUp

Witch's Milking Charm. *Unknown.* GBP

Witch's Work Song, The. T. H. White. FaBoNo

With. Carol Bergé. MMD

With a Book at Twilight. Jakov Steinberg, *tr. fr. Hebrew by* Mark Elliott Shapiro. VWA

With a Bottle of Blue Nun to All My Friends. Madeline DeFrees. CNW; GP; MPA

With a cry of fear. Hidden Bow. Mordecai Temkin, *tr. by* Jeremy Garber. VWA

With a garland of thornes kene. The Seven Sins. *Unknown.* OxBM

With a Gift of Rings. Robert Graves. GBL

With a great working of elbows. Wedding. George Mackay Brown. MS; SLP

With a Guitar, to Jane. Shelley. MBPR; OAEL-2

With a handful of weeds I weep in the slanting sun. Boudoir Lament. Yü Hsüan-chi, *tr. by* Geoffrey Waters. BoWoP

With a lantern that wouldn't burn. The Draft Horse. Robert Frost. CMoP (1970 ed.); HeIP; HoPM (1975 ed.); ILP (1975 ed.); PiAm

With a long stirrup under fern. Craswall. Roland Mathias. OBW

With a love a madness for Shelley. I Am 25. Gregory Corso. CoPAm

With a pert moustache and a ready candid smile. The Mixer. Louis MacNeice. FaBoTw (1975 ed.)

With a quick/ jump. Hello. Robert Creeley. TPo

With a spoon. The King of Harlem. Federico García Lorca, *tr. by* Ben Belitt. NYP

With a whirl of thought oppressed. The Day of Judgement. Swift. BIrV; ESaP; ILP (1975 ed.); NOBE; OAEL-1; OBSV; PPP

With a Wreath of Laurel. Ina Coolbrith. WPW

With all a woman's virtues but the pox. Pope. *Fr.* The Second Satire of the First Book of Horace Imitated. OBSV

With All Deliberate Speed. Don L. Lee. JB

With all its sinful doings, I must say. Italy and [*or* Versus] England. Byron. *Fr.* Beppo. NOBE; PAIC

With All My Heart, Jehovah, I'll Confess, *with music.* Henry Ainsworth. AH

With all my will, but much against my heart. A Farewell. Coventry Patmore. *Fr.* The Unknown Eros. BoLoP; NOBE

With all the heart in my body. Now Jentil Belly Down. *Unknown.* GBP

With all these loads of injuries opprest. Dryden. *Fr.* Absalom and Achitophel, Pt. I. EBEV

With an Antique Crystal Cup and Ring. John Sobieski Stuart. SLP

With an eye in the heart. Jean Charlot. Stefan Baciu. PHC

With Annie gone. For Anne. Leonard Cohen. FF; SoS; TCP

With banners furled, and clarions mute. The Night-March. Herman Melville. PiAm

With bent back, world's curve on it. Tom on the Beach. George Bruce. MS

With blackest moss the flower-plots [-pots, *wr.*]. Mariana. Tennyson. BiP; InPS; NOBE; OAEL-2; PoIA; PoPle; UnPo (1976 ed.); VLP

With blameless carriage I lived here. An Epitaph upon a Sober Matron. Robert Herrick. CaPo

With bodies bowed, with breath drawn in. The Cry of the High Hurdlers. Horace Spencer Fiske. SPo

With camel's hair I clothed my skin. Dream. Richard Watson Dixon. EBEV; VLP

With candour I confess my love. Ezra Pound *and* Noel Stock, *fr. Egyptian hieroglyphics.* BoWoP

With Child. Genevieve Taggard. LoAs; PPM; WPW

With Christ and All His Shining Train, *with music.* Thomas Prince. AH

With death doomed to grapple. Epitaph for William Pitt. Byron. FaBoEE; MBPR

With deathlace tickling my throat. Death-Lace. David Ray. MAT

With deep affection. The Shandon Bells. Francis Sylvester Mahony. PFIr

With delicate, mad hands, behind his sordid bars. To One in Bedlam. Ernest Dowson. VLP

With dirty collar and shoes unpolished. Anarchist. Anthony Cronin. CIP

With Donne, whose muse on dromedary trots. On Donne's Poetry. Samuel Taylor Coleridge. CABA (1972 ed.); MBPR; OAEL-2; PAIC; PPoD

With Due Deference to Thomas Wolfe. Joanne Townsend. AMV-81

With every blow of the wind. My Soul Hovers over Me. Joshua Tan Pai, *tr. by* Yishai Tobin. VWA

With every note/ of the mountain temple. *Unknown, tr. fr. Japanese by* Willis Barnstone. BoWoP

With every rising of the sun. Today! Ella Wheeler Wilcox. SoSe

With every soft gush of my feet. After Picking Rosehips. Harley Elliott. NeAC

With fairest flowers,/ Whilst summer lasts. Shakespeare. *Fr. Cymbeline, IV, ii.* EBEV

With faith I trust in Christ the Lord. Mrs. Saunder's Experience. *Unknown.* AmFP

With favoring winds, o'er sunlit seas. Ultima Thule. Longfellow. AmVN

With favour and fortune fastidiously blest. Swift. FaBoEE

With Fifteen-ninety or Sixteen-sixteen. On an Anniversary. J. M. Synge. FaBoEE; POL

With fingers weary and worn. The Song of the Shirt. Thomas Hood. FaPoR; VLP

With fires and lights we ward the winter off. Autumn Poem. Anthony Cronin. CIP

With flintlocked guns and polished stocks. In Hardin County, 1809. Lul E. Thompson. PoTa

With focus sharp as Flemish-painted face. The Dome of Sunday. Karl Shapiro. CMoP (1970 ed.); NoAM

With Francis Furini. Robert Browning. *Fr.* Parleyings with Certain People of Importance in Their Day. VLP

With Garments Flowing. John Clare. GBL

With gentleness/ his eyes filmed. Monument. Milton Acorn. NeAC

With gnarled hands folded on her idle hoe. The Woman in the Field. Nellie Burget Miller. WPW

With God and His Mercy, *with music.* Carl Olof Rosenius. AH

With great difficulty I managed to get out of my skin. Nanos Valaoritis. *Fr.* Birds of Hazard and Prey. MIT

With grenades of sumac fruit. Dinoland. Thomas Rieter. PPoD

With Happiness Stretchd across the Hills. Blake. STS

With hay, with how, with hoy! My Twelve Oxen. *Unknown.* OxBM

With hearts revived in conceit, new land and trees they eye. *At. to* Edward Johnson. *Fr.* Good News from New England. GOA

With her Betty Grable legs. Ode to a Young Dog. Vicki Viidikas. FPA

With her eyes closed. Sabbath. David Rosenmann-Taub, *tr. by* Charles Guenther. VWA

With high-jeweled hair. Empress in the Mirror. Colette Inez. WBN

With him ther was his sone, a yong Squyer. Chaucer. *Fr.* The Canterbury Tales: Prologue. DuDr

With his penis swollen for the girl on the next farm. Lugete O Veneres. R. A. K. Mason. ATNZ

With his tusk-like fierce moustaches and double-pointed beard. A Bully. *Malay Oral Tradition, tr. by* R. J. Wilkinson. WTO

With his work, as with a glove, a man feels the universe. Open and Closed Space. Tomas Tranströmer, *tr. by* Robert Bly. EAS

With honeysuckle, over-sweet, festoon'd. Arbor Vitae. Coventry Patmore. VLP

With horns and with hounds I waken the day. Dryden. *Fr.* The Secular Masque. NOBE

With how! fox, how! With hay! fox, hay! The False Fox. *Unknown.* OxBM

With How Sad Steps, O Moon, Thou Climb'st the Skies. Sir Philip Sidney. Astrophel and Stella, XXXI. BoLoP; Epi; GBL; HAP; HeIP; ILP (1975 ed.); InPK; InPS; IPWM; LoAs; MAT; Moon; NIL; OBP; PAIC; PBMP; PPoe; PPP; WeW
(To the Sad Moon.) NOBE

"With How Sad Steps, O Moon, Thou Climb'st the sky." Wordsworth. ILP (1975 ed.)

With huntis up, with huntis up. *Unknown.* TVS

With hym ther rood a gentil Pardoner. Chaucer. *Fr.* The Canterbury Tales: Prologue. BiP

With I and E, *orig. and mod. English prose. Unknown.* OxBM

With infinitely confident little variations of his finger-ends. Buzzard. Leslie Norris. HeHu

With innocent wide penguin eyes, three. Bird-witted. Marianne Moore. CMoP (1970 ed.); ILP (1975 ed.)

With it, Plato thought poets might rule the world. Rhetoric. Michael Berryhill. AAN

With its baby rivers and little towns. England. Marianne Moore. Psy

With its cloud of skirmishers in advance. An Army Corps on the March. Walt Whitman. InPS; PiAm; PPoe

With joy all relics of the past I hail. Old Ruralities. Charles Tennyson Turner. VPC

With joy Britannia sees her fav'rite goose. To the Marquis of Graham on His Marriage. *Unknown.* OBSV

With Kit, Age 7, at the Beach. William Stafford. RFM

With languages dispersed, men were not able. Four Epigrams on the Naturalization Bill. John Byrom. NOBL

With leering looks, bullfac'd, and freckled fair. On Jacob Tonson, His Publisher. Dryden. FaBoEE; OBSV

With longing I am lad. A Maid Mars Me. *Unknown.* OxBM

With love exceeding a simple love of the things. Melampus. George Meredith. VLP

With love so like fire they dared not. Parlour Piece. Ted Hughes. BuTh

With low thunder, with red bushes smooth. Red Rock Ceremonies. Anita Endrezze Probst. CDW

With lullay, lullay, like a child [*or* lyke a chylde]. My Darling Dear, My Daisy Flower. John Skelton. AAS; HAP; LoAs

With many a scowl. Troll Trick. B. J. Lee. IWK

With marjoram [or margerain] gentle. To Mistress Margery Wentworth. John Skelton. Fr. The Garlande of Laurell. EBEV; NOBE; OAEL-1

With Mercy for the Greedy. Anne Sexton. CAPP

With Monmouth cap and cutlass by my side. A Long Prologue to a Short Play. Sir Henry Sheers. APAS

With morning coffee. A.B.S. News. Ruth Lechlitner. WasP

With much ado you fail to tell. A Critic. Walter Savage Landor. FaBoEE

With my cousin/ I practiced motherhood. Still Birth. Catherine Rutan. AMV-81

With My Crowbar Key. William Stafford. ConAP

With my eyelids still squeezed. Waking to Leopards. Nancy Mairs. NPW

With my frailty don't upbraid me. Semele to Jupiter [or Song]. Congreve. LoAs; POL

With My God, the Smith. Uri Zvi Greenberg, tr. fr. Hebrew by Robert Mezey and Ben Zion Gold. VWA

With My Grandfather. Zelda, tr. fr. Hebrew by Marcia Falk. VWA

With my hat on backwards. One More Time. Richard Shelton. GP

With nets and kitchen sieves they raid the pond. The Pond. Anthony Thwaite. LP; MAT

With nought to hide or to betray. L'Amitié et l'Amour. John Swanwick Drennan. BIrV

With one black shadow at its feet. Mariana in the South. Tennyson. VLP

With one consuming roar along the shingle. Felixstowe, or The Last of Her Order. John Betjeman. OxBTC

With one dear friend we go up the highest mountain. Mountain Day. W. S. Merwin. PHC

With one letter of your many names. Love the Ruins. Malka Heifetz Tussman, tr. by Marcia Falk. VWA

With one who safeguards Gwynedd. The Stallion. Tudur Aled, tr. by Joseph P. Clancy. OBW

With our banners and our smiles. Christopher St. Liberation Day, June 28, 1970. Fran Winant. MMD

With paste of almonds Syb her hands doth scour. Upon Sybilla. Robert Herrick. CaPo

With people conformed. Dear Girl. Gregory Corso. NoAM

With Pipe and Flute. Austin Dobson. VLP

With Poems Already Begun. Rachel Korn, tr. fr. Yiddish by Seymour Mayne and Rivka Augenfeld. VWA

With porcupine locks. The Katzenjammer Kids. James Reaney. AKE

With proud thanksgiving, a mother for her children. For the Fallen. Laurence Binyon. NOBE; OxBTC

With rhythmic thud. The Green Corn Dance. Alice Corbin. BPAW

With rope, knife, gun, brass knucks, and bloody laws. Simple Beast. Mark Van Doren. TH

With Rue My Heart Is Laden. A. E. Housman. CMoP (1970 ed.); HAP; HeIP; HoPM (1975 ed.); InPK; NoAM; UnPo (1976 ed.); VoPo

With Rue My Heart Is Laden, parody. Samuel Hoffenstein. UnPo (1976 ed.)

"With sacrifice before the rising morn." Laodamia. Wordsworth. MBPR

With Serving Still. Sir Thomas Wyatt. InPK

With shoes on. Going Barefoot. Judith Thurman. FPB

With some pot-fury, ravished from their wit. Joseph Hall. Fr. Virgidemiarum, Bk. I, Satire III. NIL

With songs and honors sounding loud. Isaac Watts. AmFP

With spectacles set firmly upon the nose. The Wordy People. Jacqueline M. Fitzgerald. PPM

With splendour of a silver day. Night of Frost in May. George Meredith. VLP

With spray-can paint. SM. Stanley Moss. AMV-81; NYP

With stammering lips and insufficient sound. The Soul's Expression. Elizabeth Barrett Browning. VLP

With that delight the royal captive's brought. The Lady A. L., My Asylum in a Great Extremity. Richard Lovelace. CaPo

With that he stripped him to the ivory skin. Amorous Neptune. Christopher Marlowe. Fr. Hero and Leander. NOBE

With the Bait of Bread. Helene Pilbosian. AMV-81

With the Dawn. Thomas Caulfield Irwin. BIrV

With the Door Open. David Ignatow. CTBA

With the exact length and place of his father's stride. For a Father. Anthony Cronin. FaBoTw (1975 ed.)

With the Face. Laura Riding. NoAM

With the fierce rage of winter deep suffused. A Winter Night. James Thomson. Fr. The Seasons: Winter. NOBE

With the forks of flowers I eat the meat of morning. Lyric by Nine. Unknown. EAS

With the gaunt resolution. For George Oppen. Darrell Gray. AcAn

With the heavy steps of slow oxen. Slow Oxen. Ilya Rubin, tr. by Linda Zisquit. VWA

With the Herring Fishers. "Hugh MacDiarmid." MS

With the last whippoorwill call of evening. Birmingham. Margaret Walker. PoBA

With the motion of angels, out of. Skiers. Robert Penn Warren. Fr. In the Mountains. LiSp; SPo; TCP

With the Nuns at Cape May Point. David Earle Anderson. AMV-81

With the old kindness, the old distinguished grace. Upon a Dying Lady. W. B. Yeats. UnPo (1976 ed.)

With the one and the two and the three. A Beginning and an End. Edouard Roditi. VWA

With the slightest sound. My Son. Rex Veeder. HeS

With the spring rains, small spiders. Vincent Buckley. Fr. Golden Builders. CAAP

With the stars. For the Coming Year. Peter Everwine. OFD

With the sun. Patricia Parker. MIT

With the surgical hands. Diagnostic Center. Kenneth "Spider" Nicholson. DNGG

With the thinking of winter. The Cook. Ray A. Young Bear. CDW

With the Woodnymphs. Michael Smith. IPM

With the years my woes increased. The Paths of Prayer. Edouard Roditi. VWA

With Thee a moment! Then what dreams have play! Desire. "Æ." ILwL

With thee conversing I forget all time. Eve Speaks to Adam. Milton. Fr. Paradise Lost. GBL

With thee, in the desert. Emily Dickinson. LoAs

With their harsh leaves old rhododendrons fill. The Mountain Cemetery. Edgar Bowers. ConAP; CSP

With their lithe, long, strong legs. Bullfrog. Ted Hughes. RFM; TSWA

With these missing pieces. A Tribe Searching. Shlomo Reich, tr. by Mira Reich. VWA

With this ambiguous earth. Christ in the Universe. Alice Meynell. BoReV; NOBE

With this stone his foes honor Apis the fighter. Monument to a Boxer. Lucilius, tr. by Tom Dodge. LiSp

With torches I have wandered the dark poppy world. The Double Axe. Anne Hazlewood-Brady. IHMS

With troubled heart and trembling hand I write. In Memory of My Dear Grandchild Anne Bradstreet. Anne Bradstreet. BoWoP

With twilight I gather you here. Conjuration. Agnes Gergely, *tr.* by Emery George. VWA

With two hairs plucked from the chest of a baby squirrel. Persian Miniature. Jane Shore. PCho

With two 60's stuck on the scoreboard. Foul Shot. Edwin A. Hoey. SPo

With two white roses on her breasts. A Brown Girl Dead. Countee Cullen. TAP

With Usura. Cantos, XLV. Ezra Pound. CMoP (1970 ed.); NOBA; PiAm

With what a glory comes and goes the year! Autumn. Longfellow. FSFS

With what attentive courtesy he bent. The Guitarist Tunes Up. Frances Cornford. SoSe; UsP

With what deep murmurs through time's silent stealth. The Waterfall. Henry Vaughan. BoReV; ILP (1975 ed.); LFN; NOBE; OBW

With what, O Codrus! is thy fancy smit? Edward Young. *Fr.* Love of Fame, the Univeral Passion. OBSV

With whiskers bent. The Brown Bears of Boston. Roland Pease. BCr

With wine and words of love and every vow. Seduced Girl. Hedylos, *tr.* by Louis Untermeyer. BoLoP

With yellow pears leans over. Half of Life. Friedrich Hölderlin, *tr.* by James Blair Leishman. OBVE

With you for mast and sail and flag. The Narrow Sea. Robert Graves. FaBoEE

With you here at Mertu. Ezra Pound *and* Noel Stock, *fr. Egyptian hieroglyphics.* PBWP

With your/ foldedvoice. For Our Rising (Warrenssong). Angela Jackson. FiCh

With your guns and drums and drums and guns. Johnny I Hardly Knew You. *Unknown.* FSW

With your mercury mouth in the missionary times. Sad-eyed Lady of the Lowlands. Bob Dylan. BiP

With your permission, gentlemen. Trial. Rachel Hadas. AAN

With Zeus let our song begin! Praise of Zeus. Aratus of Soli, *tr. fr. Greek.* ILwL

Withal a meagre man was Aaron Stark. Aaron Stark. E. A. Robinson. AmVN; STS

Withered leaves fly higher than dolls can see, The. Sonnet. Ted Berrigan. CAAP

Within a delicate grey ruin. The Vestal Lady on Brattle. Gregory Corso. NoAM

Within a 'dobe wall. In Old Tuscon. Charles Beghtol. BPAW

Within a greenwood sweet of myrtle savour. *Unknown, tr. fr. Italian.* GBL

Within a thick and spreading hawthorn bush. The Thrush's Nest. John Clare. BoAnP; PB

Within my garden, rides a bird. Emily Dickinson. TT

Within our happy castle there dwelt one. Stanzas Written in My Pocket-Copy of Thomson's "Castle of Indolence." Wordsworth. MBPR

Within that porch, across the way. The Cat. W. H. Davies. NOBE; PCat

Within the cave, it is dark. safe. Gimel. Stuart Z. Perkoff. VWA

Within the Circuit of This Plodding Life. Henry David Thoreau. *See* Winter Memories.

Within the covert of a shady grove. Love Sleeping. Plato, *tr. by* Thomas Stanley. FaBoEE

Within the curved edge of quarter moon. The Path I Must Travel. Emerson Blackhorse Mitchell. VW

Within the deep and luminous subsistence of the High Light. Dante, *tr. fr. Italian. Fr.* Divina Commedia: Paradiso. ILwL

Within the Dream You Said. Philip Larkin. InPS

Within the gentle heart love shelters him. Canzone: Of the Gentle Heart. Guido Guinicelli, *tr. by* Dante Gabriel Rossetti. OBVE

Within the Gorges there is no lack of men. Invitation to Hsiao Ch'u-shih. Po Chü-i, *tr. by* Arthur Waley. OBVE

Within the mind strong fancies work. The Pass of Kirkstone. Wordsworth. MBPR

Within the oak a throb of pigeon wings. A Twilight in Middle March. Francis Ledwidge. BIrV

Within the purple graph of the Hokonuis, the dark. The Foxes. Janet Frame. WPE

Within the Shelter of Our Walls, *with music.* Elinor Lennen. AH

Within These Doors Assembled Now, *with music.* Oliver Holden. AH

Within this black hive to-night. Beehive. Jean Toomer. PoBA

Within this mindless vault. Epigram. J. V. Cunningham. VGW

Within this sober frame expect. Upon Appleton House. Andrew Marvell. SCP-1

Within Us, Too. R. H. Grenville. AMV-80

Without a door, through the smooth wall. At Night. Rachel Boimwell, *tr. by* Gabriel Preil *and* Howard Schwartz. VWA

Without a winter coat. Raising the Flag. Gerald Vizenor. VoR

Without Benefit of Declaration. Langston Hughes. AmNP (1974 ed.); IP

Without Ceremony. Vassar Miller. CoPAm

Without expectation. Summer Oracle. Audre Lorde. PoBA

Without dressmakers to connect. Because of Clothes. Laura Riding. NoAM

Without flocks or cattle or the curved horns. A Time of Change. Egan O'Rahilly, *tr. by* Eavan Boland. BIrV

Without Her. Dante Gabriel Rossetti. The House of Life, LIII. GBL; VLP

Without it, nothing exists. The Invention of Zero. Constance Urdang. VWA

Without Me You Won't be Able to See Yourself. Chaim Grade, *tr. fr. Yiddish by* Ruth Whitman. VWA

Without Name. Pauli Murray. AmNP (1974 ed.); PoBA

Without oars. On Looking into the Spilled Ink on the Porcelain. Wayne Andrews. PHC

Without singing, without the binding of midnight. Song for the Soul Returning. David Wagoner. CNW

Without so much/ as trying to look. You. Carroll Arnett. VoR

Without tears. Words at Farewell. Vahan Derian, *tr. by* Diana Der Hovanessian. AMV-81

Without that once clear aim, the path of flight. Stephen Spender. CMoP (1970 ed.)

Without the hall, and close upon the gate. The Gardens of Alcinous. Homer, *tr. by* George Chapman. *Fr.* The Odyssey, VII. OAEL-1; OBVE

Without the slightest basis/ for hypochondriasis. How Jack Found That Beans May Go Back on a Chap. Guy Wetmore Carryl. HoPM (1975 ed.)

Without this/ what is/ worth doing. Land. Carroll Arnett. VoR

Without warning their nest. A Call to Action. Ch'iu Chin, *tr. by* Kenneth Rexroth *and* Ling Chung. PBWP

Without You. Cid Corman. GP

Without your knowledge they are turning your wounds into words. A Latter Purification. Haim Guri, *tr. by* Mark Elliott Shapiro. VWA

Withouten you. Little Elegy. Elinor Wylie. LoAs; UsP

Witlesse gallant, a young wench that woo'd, A. Michael Drayton. *Fr.* Idea. AAS

Witness. Josephine Miles. GP; PoW

Witness to Death. Richmond Lattimore. VGW

Witnesses, The. X. J. Kennedy. PChr

Witnesses, The. Longfellow. GOA

Witnesses, The, *sel.* Clive Sansom.
"It was a night in winter." PChr

Wits, The. Sir John Suckling. CaPo

Witty as Horatius Flaccus. On Seeing Francis Jeffrey Riding on a Donkey. *At. to* Sydney Smith. FaBoEE

Witty scribbles of the clematis, The. Welcome. U. A. Fanthorpe. PMW

Wives in the Sere. Thomas Hardy. NOBE; VLP

Wives of Mafiosi, The. Erica Jong. AmPA

Wives of Spittal, The. *Unknown.* GBP

Wizard's Funeral, The. Richard Watson Dixon. VLP

Woak Hill. William Barnes. VPC

Wo'd I see Lawn, clear as the Heaven, and thin? The Lawn. Robert Herrick. LoAs

Wodwo. Ted Hughes. NoAM; TwMBP

Woe is me! Woe is me! The Ghost's Song. *Unknown.* RAE

Woe is me, my soul says, how bitter is my fate. Rahel Morpurgo, *tr. fr. Hebrew by* Robert Alter. PBWV

Woefully Arrayed. *Unknown, at. to* John Skelton. BoReV; CABA (1972 ed.)

Woke—the old King of Cumberland. The Old King. Walter de la Mare. AIW

Woke up, it was a Chelsea morning. Chelsea Morning. Joni Mitchell. GrRo; PoRo; WIF

Woke up this morning. That Lonesome Train Took My Baby Away. *Unknown.* BluL

Woke up this morning, gal 'twixt mid night and day. Barbecue Blues. *Unknown.* BluL

Woke Up This Morning with My Mind on Freedom. *Unknown.* FSW

Woken, I lay in the arms of my own warmth and listened. First Things First. W. H. Auden. UsP

Wolde God that it were so. Love Undeclared. *Unknown.* OxBM

Wolf. Peter Blue Cloud. VoR

Wolf. Kenneth Rexroth. *Fr.* A Bestiary. NNaP

Wolf and the Dog, The. La Fontaine, *tr. fr. French by* Elizur Wright. OBVE

Wolf and the Lamb, The. La Fontaine, *tr. fr. French by* Marianne Moore. NAWM-2

Wolf and the Stork, The. La Fontaine, *tr. fr. French by* Marianne Moore. OBVE

Wolf Dream. Edward Lense. AMV-81

Wolfman, The. Greg Kuzma. GP

Wolfram's Dirge. Thomas Lovell Beddoes. *Fr.* Death's Jest Book. NOBE

Wolf's cousin, The. Night Patrol. Josephine Jacobsen. WasP

Wolf's profile hangs, The. From the Window of the Beverly Wilshire Hotel. Michael McClure. EAS

Wolsey, or possibly my John of Gaunt. Santa Claus. Christopher Hassall. OxBTC

Wolves. John Haines. BoAnP

Wolves. Louis MacNeice. NoAM; OxBTC

Wolves, The. Allen Tate. ILP (1975 ed.); NoAM; NOBA; PiAm; PoA

Wolves can outeat anyone. The Wolf and the Stork. La Fontaine, *tr. by* Marianne Moore. OBVE

Wolves for Company. *Unknown, tr. fr. Irish.* BIrV

Wolves say to the dogs, The. J. Michael Yates. *Fr.* The Great Bear Lake Meditations. HoPM (1975 ed.)

Woman. Ai. GP

Woman. Margo Bohanon. SES

Woman. Jane Chambers. IHMS

Woman. Randall Jarrell. NoAM; NOBA

Woman. Elouise Loftin. PoBA

Woman, The. Edwin Morgan. MS

Woman. Carl Rakosi. TAP

Woman. Umberto Saba, *tr. fr. Italian by* Christopher Millis. AMV-81

Woman, A/ sleeps next to me on the earth. Night in the Forest. Galway Kinnell. CoPAm; TAP

Woman, A/ who loves a woman. Rapunzel. Anne Sexton. RiTi

Woman against the Moon, *sels.* Helen Wolfert. RiTi
Preparation of the Body, The.
Where the Mind Meets the Moon in Revolt.

Woman as Artist. Eleanor Ross Taylor. CSP

Woman as Market. Muriel Rukeyser. WBN

Woman at the Washington Zoo, The. Randall Jarrell. HAP; ILP (1975 ed.); PSN; TAP; UnPo (1976 ed.); UsP; WasP

Woman came to me, A. Michael Silverton. POL

Woman Combing, A. William E. Taylor. CSP

Woman comes, A. Fisherman. William Pitt Root. NVAP

Woman coming down the snowy road, A. Grey Woman. Gladys Cardiff. CDW

Woman Crossing the Road. Rhyll McMaster. CAAP

Woman, Don't Be Troublesome. Augustus Young, *tr. fr. Irish.* CIP

Woman dressed in half brown shoes, The. Mistaken Identity. Joanne Casullo. NPW

Woman Driving the Country Squire, The. David Dayton. AMV-81

Woman fears for man, he goes. Abel's Bride. Denise Levertov. VGW; WBN

"Woman for whom great gods might strive, A!" The Chosen. Thomas Hardy. LoAs

Woman from the Book of Genesis, A. Dovid Knut, *tr. fr. Russian by* John Glad. VWA

Woman gave me butter now, A. A Present of Butter. Tadhg Dall O'Huiginn, *tr. by* the Earl of Longford. BIrV

Woman Gets Restless, The. Barbara Drake. TC

Woman gives birth, A. The Future of the Fishbowl. Paul Hoover. FiCh

Woman grows old secretly, A. For Jeanette Piccard Ordained at 79. Renny Golden. AMV-80

Woman Grows Soon Old, A. Larin Paraske, *tr. fr. Finnish by* Jaakko A. Ahokas. PBWP

Woman-Hater, The, *sel.* Beaumont *and* Fletcher.
Come, Sleep, *fr.* III, i. ILP (1975 ed.)

Woman I have never seen before, A. Transit. Richard Wilbur. PCho

Woman, I may be a stone from. Bel Woman. Roman Adrian. DNGG

Woman I want, The. No More than Five. Fred Levinson. AmPA

*Woman*: If you weren't you who would you rather be? Flood. Roger McGough. FF

Woman in an Abandoned House. Michael Bily-Hurd. AMV-81

Woman in childbirth, fainting with cruel pain, A. To a Faithless Friend. Salaan Arrabey, *tr. by* M. Laurence. WTO

Woman in her room is standing at the mirror, The. The Importance of Mirrors. Helga Sandburg. IHMS

Woman in his belly stirs, The. When He's at His Most Brawling. Patricia Goedicke. Psy

Woman in Sunshine, The. Wallace Stevens. BiP

Woman in the, The. Marge Piercy. NMM

Woman in the Field, The. Nellie Burget Miller. WPW

Woman in the Hospital for Incurables. Daphne Gloag. PMW

Woman in the Rye, The. Thomas Hardy. ILP (1975 ed.)

Woman in the shape of a monster, A. Planetarium. Adrienne Rich. NIL; NoAM; NOBA; RiTi

Woman in the Window. Dennis M. Gaughan. PoUp

Woman Is a Worthy Thing, A. *Unknown.* FaBoCo; GBP; OxBM

Woman is by aptitude. *Unknown, tr. by* Gwyn Williams. *Fr.* Against Women. OBW

Woman is perfected, The. The Edge. Sylvia Plath. ILP (1975 ed.); PSN; RiTi; TAP; UsP

Woman is planting asters on the south wind side, A. And the Silver Turns into Night. Nathan Yonathan, *tr. by* Richard Flantz. VWA

Woman is singing the song and summer. Sonnet. Ted Berrigan. CAAP

Woman Is Talking to Death, A, *sels.* Judy Grahn. WBN
Death and Disfiguration.
Dressed as I Am, a Young Man Once Called Me Names in Spanish.
Mock Interrogation, A.

Woman let her hand trail, The. A Virtue of Shape. Thom Swiss. AMV-80

Woman Mourned by Daughters, A. Adrienne Rich. IHMS; NCSH; Psy; TV

Woman much missed, how you call to me, call to me. The Voice. Thomas Hardy. BoLoP; CMoP (1970 ed.); GBL; HAP; NoAM; OAEL-2; PoPle; PSN

Woman named Tomorrow, The. Four Preludes on Playthings of the Wind. Carl Sandburg. CMoP (1970 ed.); NOBA; PAIC; PiAm

Woman Needed Some Milk, A. Sheila Heldenbrand. AcAn

Woman neither young or old, she moves, A. My Mother's Life. William Meredith. AMV-81

Woman never knows what a good man she's got, A. Silver Dollar. Kathleen Wiegner. MMD

Woman of the House, The. Richard Murphy. IPM

Woman of Three Cows, The. *Unknown, tr. fr. Irish by* James Clarence Mangan. PFIr

Woman of West 705th Street, who was forgotten. A Revisit. Elizabeth Shinoda. PHC

Woman Poem. Nikki Giovanni. NMM; NoAM; Psy

Woman Poet, The. Gertrud Kolmar, *tr. fr. German by* Henry A. Smith. VWA

Woman Sat Weeping, A. *Unknown.* OxBM

Woman Shopping, A. Denis Glover. ATNZ

Woman Sings of Her Love, A. *Somali Oral Tradition, tr. by* B. W. Andrzejewski *and* I. M. Lewis. WTO

Woman, sitting and sewing in south window light, A. Morning Assignment. Mark Van Doren. OSP

Woman Skating. Margaret Atwood. IHMS

Woman speaks, A. The Hour of Feeling. Louis Simpson. FiCP

Woman Talking Man into Child. Elizabeth Albrecht. PoUp

Woman Thing, The. Audre Lorde. NMM

Woman through the Window. Marcia Falk. VWA

Woman to Child. Judith Wright. PBWP; WPE

Woman to Man. Ai. GP

Woman to Man. Judith Wright. GAS; MAuV; WPE

Woman to man, they lie. In Bloemfontein. Alan Ross. BoLoP

Woman Waits for Me, A. Walt Whitman. NOBA

Woman! when I behold thee flippant, vain. Keats. MBPR

Woman who has grown old, The. The Crows. Louise Bogan. SBG

Woman who lived, A. The Moon. Donald Hall. NCSH

Woman Who Loved to Cook, The. Erica Jong. TAP; WBN

Woman Who Loved Worms, The. Colette Inez. AATT; NMM; RiTi; WBN

Woman Who Raised Goats, The. Tess Gallagher. AAN

Woman who talks to death, A. Dressed as I Am, a Young Man Once Called Me Names in Spanish. Judy Grahn. *Fr. A Woman Is Talking to Death.* WBN

Woman who writes feels too much, A. The Black Art. Anne Sexton. PoA; Psy

Woman with a fine ironic face, A. Hypothesis. Jennifer Maiden. CAAP

Woman with Finger. Tom McKeown. NVAP

Woman with Flower. Naomi Long Madgett. AmNP (1974 ed.); FB

Woman with Girdle. Anne Sexton. NCSH; NoAM; SFF

Woman with no face walked into the light, A. Homage to Hieronymus Bosch. Thomas MacGreevy. BIrV; EAS

Woman with the caught fox. Plea for a Captive. W. S. Merwin. NoAM

Woman, women/ 1. An adult female person. The Dictionary Is an *His*torian: A Found Political Poem. Judith McCombs. IHMS

Woman, you are afraid of the forest. Maria Wine, *tr. fr. Swedish by* Nadia Christensen. PBWP

Woman, you'll never credit what. The Shepherd's Tale. Raoul Ponchon, *tr. by* James Kirkup. PoTa

Womanhod, wanton, ye want. *See* Womanhood, wanton . . .

Womanhood, The, *sels.* Gwendolyn Brooks.
Children of the Poor, The, I. PoA; WPE
"Exhaust the little moment. Soon it dies," X. TH
Old Laughter, V. TH
"One wants a Teller in a time like this," XI. WPE
Rites for Cousin Vit, The, VI. BPo; HAP; WPE
Truth, IX. TH

Womanhood [*or* Womanhod], wanton, ye want. John Skelton. AAS; LoAs

Womanisers. John Press. BoLoP

Woman's breasts, A. St. Valentine. William Carlos Williams. LoAs

Woman's Complaint. Stephen Mulrine. MS

Woman's Constancy. Sir John Suckling. CaPo

Woman's face with nature's own hand painted, A. Sonnets, XX. Shakespeare. OAEL-1

Woman's Faith. Sir Walter Scott. SLP

Woman's Liberation. Sister Maura. AMV-81

Woman's Message, A. *Unknown, tr. fr. Anglo-Saxon by* Burton Raffel. OBP

Woman's pink body could be preserved, A. Little Yellow Leaf. James Tate. NoAM

Woman's Reason, A. Gelett Burgess. FaBoNo

Woman's Sorrow, A, *sel.* Ho Nansorhon, *tr. fr. Korean by* Peter H. Lee.
"Yesterday I fancied I was young." PBWP

Woman's Wish, The. Matthew Prior. FaBoEE

Womb Is Ruins, The. Helena Minton. FAF

Womb Song. Susan Fromberg Schaeffer. IHMS

Women. Louise Bogan. PPM; SBG; VGW; WPE

Women. Adrienne Rich. NMM; Psy

Women. May Swenson. BoWoP; NMM; Prf; Riti

Women. Alice Walker. GOA

Women ("I like lemon on my salmon"). *Unknown.* IP

Women ("She truly needs good character"). *Yoruba Oral Tradition, tr. by* Ulli Beier. WTO

Women All Tell Me, The, *with music. Unknown.* BLSo

Women and Men. Hassan Sheikh Mumin, *tr. fr. Somali.* WTO

Women are dark and seem, The. Old Photographs. David Harsent. POL

Women are larger than I, The. Little League Women. Deena Metzger. RiTi

Women are ranged on one side of the loft, The. A Bad Dream in the Commune. Robert Hahn. AAN

Women at the Market. Angela Figueroa Aymerich, *tr. fr. Spanish by* Hardie St. Martin. PBWP

Women before were strangers. Dispatch Number Nine. Doug Fetherling. NeAC

Women Beware Women: A Tragedy, *sel.* Thomas Middleton. "Prithee forgive me,/ I did but chide in jest." SCP-2

Women Called Bossy Cowboys. Beth Jankola. AMV-80

Women don't travel in clubcars. George Jonas. NeAC

Women dream of, The. Mountains. Besmilr Brigham. RiTi

Women have loved before as I love now. Sonnet. Edna St. Vincent Millay. PoA

Women have no share in the encampments of this world. Women and Men. Hassan Sheikh Mumin, *tr. fr. Somali.* WTO

Women have no wilderness in them. Women. Louise Bogan. PPM; SBG; VGW; WPE

Women Hoping for Rain. David Tillinghast. AMV-81

Women hurry by. Manchild. Margo Bohanon. SES

Women in black picked up their violins. The Call. Jules Supervielle, *tr. by* Geoffrey Gardner. NU

Women in Brooklyn. Paul Zweig. NowV

Women in uniform. Omen of Victory. Mina Loy. InPK

Women in Vietnam, The. Grace Paley. NMM

Women know how to wait here. Lines for Marking Time. Robert Hill. BoWoP; CDW

Women like That. Lyn Lifshin. Psy

Women loving each other. Bad Girl Blues. *Unknown.* BluL

Women of Trachis, *sel.* Sophocles, *tr. fr. Greek by* Ezra Pound. "Torn between griefs, which grief shall I lament." OBVE

Women sit on a street in Brooklyn. Women in Brooklyn. Paul Zweig. NowV

Women whisk their skirts to the fiddle, The. A Song for Solomon Heine. Kraft Rompf. AAN

"Women with Tongue in Cheek." Daniela Gioseffi. RiTi

Women Who Are Hard Inside. Phyllis Gotlieb. BBGO

Women, whoever wishes to know my lord. Gaspara Stampa, *tr. fr. Italian by* J. Vitiello. BoWoP

Women with hats like the rear ends of pink ducks. To a Waterfowl. Donald Hall. OBAL

Women women women women. A Fixture. May Swenson. RiTi

Women's Degrees. A. D. Godley. NOBL

Womens ward. C44. Karen L. Kent. NPW

Won' you ring, old hammer? Hammer, Ring. *Unknown.* AmFP

Wonder. Langston Hughes. ILP (1975 ed.)

Wonder. Bernard Raymund. GDP

Wonder. Thomas Traherne. BoReV; HAP; PPoe; SCP-2

Wonder it is, and pitie ist, that shee. Henry Constable. *Fr.* Diana. ESo

Wonder not if I stay not here. To Master Davenant for Absence. Sir John Suckling. CaPo

Wonder-Teacher, The. Cynthia Ozick. VWA

Wonder where they come from? Clouds. Aileen Fisher. FPB

Wonderful bears that walked my room all night. Bears. Adrienne Rich. BCr; NCSH

Wonderful bird is the pelican, A. *Unknown.* FaBoCo

Wonderful day. 4/22/75. Darlene Pearlstein. FiCh

Wonderful Occupation, A. Piuvkaq, *tr. fr. Eskimo.* AKE (Joy of a Singer, The.) WTO

Wonderful One-Hoss Shay, The. Oliver Wendell Holmes. *See* Deacon's Masterpiece, The.

Wonderful time, A—the War. Green Memory. Langston Hughes. ILP (1975 ed.)

Wonderful Words of Life, *with music.* Philip Paul Bliss. BLSH

Wonderful workings of the world, The: wonderful. Cut the Grass. A. R. Ammons. HAP; PPP; TAP

Wonderful World, The. William Brighty Rands. CTV (World, The.) OxBChV

Wonders. Shirley Kaufman. VWA

Wonders are many and none is more wonderful than man. Glengormley. Derek Mahon. CIP

Wonders of "The Iliad." Paul Goodman. NIL

"Wondrous life!" cried Marvell at Appleton House. Round. Weldon Kees. NoAM

Wondrous Love. *Unknown, at. to* Alex Means. AmFP; BLSo, *with music;* FSW
(What Wondrous Love Is This, 2 *versions, with music.*) AH

Won't be rushed; will take. Old Men Working Concrete. Phillip Hey. FiCP

Won't Go to School. James Rankin. MIS

Won't you be my chauffeur. Me and My Chauffeur Blues. *Unknown.* BluL

Won't you come home Bill Bailey. Bill Bailey. Hughie Cannon. FSW

Won't you go down, old Hannah? Old Hannah. *Unknown.* FSW

Wood. Thomas Hornsby Ferril. MPA

Wood Butcher. Norman Hindley. AMV-81

Wood-doves are singing along the Perkiomen, The. Thinking of a Relation between the Images of Metaphors. Wallace Stevens. UsP

Wood-Dove's Note, The. Emily Huntington Miller. PCOP

Wood Fever. Jean Nordhaus. PoUp

Wood Floor Dreams. Lance Henson. VoR

Wood is bare, The: a river-mist is steeping. Elegy. Robert Bridges. ILP (1975 ed.); PoPle

Wood is full of shining eyes, The. The Magic Wood. Henry Treece. DuDa; EAS

Wood Walk. A. Wilber Stevens. MPA

Wood was rather old and dark, The. The Little Boy Lost. Stevie Smith. FaBoTw (1975 ed.); UsP

Wood Weasel, The. Marianne Moore. PiAm

Woodchuck Who Lives on Top of Mt. Ritter. John Oliver Simon. NeAC

Woodchuck who'd chucked lots of wood, A. Double Entendre. J. F. Wilson. TDH

Woodchucks. Maxine W. Kumin. HoPM (1975 ed.)

Woodcock rises, The. Ornithology. Siv Cedering Fox. NVAP

Wooden Horse then said, The. Jenny Mastoraki, *tr. fr. Modern Greek by* Nikos Germanakos. BoWoP; PBWP

Wooden Matches. Robert D. Hoeft. PoW

Wooden Ships. David Crosby, Paul Kantner, *and* Stephen Stills. GrRo

Wooden shoes resounded and died down. The European Night. Stanislav Vinaver, *tr. by* Vasa D. Mihailovich. VWA

Woodland Mass, The. Dafydd ap Gwilym, *tr. fr. Welsh by* Gwyn Williams. OBW

Woodley. William Barnes. VPC

Woodman Spare That Tree. George Pope Morris. BLSo, *with music;* CTV; FSW; PSoN, *with music*

Woodman's Dog, The. William Cowper. *Fr.* The Task, V. GDP

Woodnotes I ("When the pine tosses its cones"). Emerson. NOBA

"In unplowed Maine he sought the lumberers' gang," *sel.* TAP

Woodnotes II ("As sunbeams stream through liberal space"). Emerson. NOBA

Woodpeckers here are redheaded, The. Ornithology in Florida. Arthur Guiterman. BoAnP

Wood-Pile, The. Robert Frost. AnMo; CABA (1972 ed.); ILP (1975 ed.); iP; NoAM; STS; VGW

Woods are overhead over everywhere, The. James Cunningham. *Fr.* The Narrator's Trance. JB

Woods at Night, The. May Swenson. DuDa

Woods decay, the woods decay and fall, The.   Tithonus.
  Tennyson.  CABA (1972 ed.); HAP; ILP (1975 ed.); NOBE;
  OAEL-2; OBP; PoPle; PPP; VLP

Woods Gets Religion.   John Woods.  GP

Woods have a way of slanting light, The.   The Enlightenment.
  Patricia Sheppard.  AMV-81

Woods Night.   Tom Hennen.  GP

Woods of Arcady are dead, The.   The Song of the Happy
  Shepherd.  W. B. Yeats.  NoAM; VLP

Woods of the horizon, The.   Men in the City.  Alfonsina Storni,
  tr. by Rachel Benson.  PBWP

Woodsmoke, sheer grapebloom, smears.   The Clearing.  Stewart
  Conn.  MS

Woodspurge, The.   Dante Gabriel Rossetti.  EBEV; HAP; HeIP;
  InPK; NOBE; OAEL-2; PBMP; PF; UnPo (1976 ed.); VLP;
  VPC; WeW

Woodstock.   Joni Mitchell.  GrRo; IPWM; NIL

Woody says, "Let's make our soap."   Social Studies.  Mary
  Neville.  POL

Woodyards in the Rain.   Anne Marriott.  AKE

Woof of the Sun, Ethereal Gauze.   Henry David Thoreau.  See
  Haze.

Wooing Frog, The.   James Reeves.  SO

Wooing in a Dream.   Nicholas Breton.  See Report Song in a
  Dream, A.

Wooing of Etain, The.   Unknown, tr. fr. Irish by John Montague.
  BIrV

Woolward and wet-shod went I forth after.   The Jousting of Jesus.
  William Langland.  Fr. The Vision of Piers Plowman.
  BoReV

Woolworth's.   Donald Hall.  WeW

Word, The.   Basil Bunting.  PoA

Word, The.   Gustave Kahn, tr. fr. French by Edouard Roditi.
  VWA

Word about Freedom and Identity in Tel Aviv, A.   Jon Silkin.
  VWA

Word by Night.   Charles Brasch.  ATNZ

Word Can Become the Way It Sounds, A.   Helen Arana.  PoW

Word Drunk.   Jim Harrison.  IPWM

Word forms, The/ on the left.   A B C s.  Charles Olson.  NIL

Word goes round Repins, the murmur goes round Lorenzinis, The.
  An Absolutely Ordinary Rainbow.  Les A. Murray.  GAS

Word has come and Martha the ticket girl.   Stumptown Attends
  the Picture Show.  David Bottoms.  GP

Word has come from the kitchen.   Mary Hamilton.  Unknown.
  AmFP

Word has reached us here.   The Magdalena Silver Mine.  Gene
  Frumkin.  CoPAm

Word in Edgeways, A.   Charles Tomlinson.  NOBL

Word Is Deed, The.   John Wheelwright.  SPT

Word made flesh is seldom, A.   Emily Dickinson.  PiAm

Word Man, The.   Larry Moffi.  AMV-80

"Word" of a Watch-Dog, The.   Sandag, tr. by C. R. Bawden.
  WTO

"Word" of a Wolf Encircled by the Hunt, The.   Sandag, tr. by C.
  R. Bawden.  WTO

Word of advice about matters and things, A.   Written at the
  White Sulphur Springs.  Francis Scott Key.  OBAL

"Word" of an Antelope Caught in a Trap, The.   Sandag, tr. by C.
  R. Bawden.  WTO

Word of Encouragement, A.   J. R. Pope.  NOBL

Word of God, across the Ages, with music.  Ferdinand Q.
  Blanchard.  AH

Word of the sun to the sky, The.   Triads.  Swinburne.  PBMP

Word of Water, The.   E. L. Mayo.  PoA

Word over all, beautiful as the sky.   Reconciliation.  Walt
  Whitman.  HAP

Word "Plum," The.   Helen Chasin.  NIL

Word Poem.   Nikki Giovanni.  PoBA

Word, smash the four walls of my cage.   The Four Walls of My
  Cage.  George Reavey.  FoP

Word that in the beginning was the Word, The.   History of the
  Word.  Robert Graves.  UsP

Word to a Father, Dead, A.   John Alexander Allen.  PPoD

Word to Husbands, A.   Ogden Nash.  POL

Word went forth, The.   St. Thomas Aquinas, tr. fr. Latin by Helen
  Waddell.  NAWM-1

Words.   Jean Burden.  AMV-81

Words.   Robert Finch.  PoA

Words.   Duncan Glen.  MIS

Words.   Ulálume González De Leon, tr. fr. Spanish by Sara
  Nelson.  AMV-81

Words, The.   Lee Harwood.  EAS

Words.   Philip Levine.  VWA

Words.   David Phillips.  NeAC

Words.   Sylvia Plath.  AnMo; ConAP

Words.   Vern Rutsala.  GP

Words.   Rainer Schulte.  SES

Words, The.   David Wagoner.  PoA; TSWA

Words.   Miller Williams.  AMV-81

Words and Music, sel.   Samuel Beckett.
  "Age is when to a man."  BIrV

Words are ciphers.   Tree.  A. J. M. Smith.  IPWM

Words are flying out like endless rain into a paper cup.   Across
  the Universe.  John Lennon and Paul McCartney.  PoRo

Words are sardines packed.   Bell Too Heavy to Ring.  Tom
  Kryss.  NeAC

Words are written/ on the Wailing Wall.   Identity.  Robert
  Friend.  GP; VWA

Words at Farewell.   Vahan Derian, tr. fr. Armenian by Diana Der
  Hovanessian.  AMV-81

Words do not grow on the landscape.   Jean Malley.  PoA

Words for a design.   Grapefruit at Lights Out.  Judith Rodriguez.
  FPA

Words, for E.   Tom Leonard.  SLP

Words for Hart Crane.   Robert Lowell.  CABA (1972 ed.);
  CMoP (1970 ed.)

Words for his ugly mug his.   Ludwig's Death Mask.  Ted
  Hughes.  NoAM

Words for Neruda.   Paul Carroll.  FiCh

Words for the Wind.   Theodore Roethke.  LoAs; NoAM;
  NOBA; STS

Words from an Old Spanish Carol.   Ruth Sawyer.  PChr

Words from Storms and Geese in the Morning.   Jenne Andrews.
  HeS

Words from the Housewife.   Robert Hahn.  AAN

Words from the Window of a Railway Car.   Anatoly Steiger, tr.
  fr. Russian by John Glad.  VWA

Word's gane to the kitchen.   Mary Hamilton.  Unknown.  AIW;
  FaBoBa; PAIC; PeBB

Words have all fled the country, The, they are not expected back.
  Emigration.  Anita Barrows.  NMM

Words in the Mourning Time, sel.   Robert Hayden.
  "For King, for Robert Kennedy."  CNA

Words like Freedom.   Langston Hughes.  See Refugee in
  America.

Words never matter, The.   Reflections.  Lary H. Gibson.  PoW

Words of Oblivion and Peace.   Gabriel Preil, tr. fr. Hebrew by
  Robert Friend.  VWA

Words of our day, The.   The Same Side of the Canoe.  Alda do
  Espírito Santo, tr. by Allan Francovich and Kathleen Weaver.
  PBWP

Words of the All-Wise, The, *sel. Tr. fr. Icelandic by* W. H. Auden *and* Paul B. Taylor.
"Say, dwarf, for it seems to me." OBVE

Words scored upon a bone. Meditation on a Bone. A. D. Hope. MAuV

Words Spoken by Pasternak during a Bombing. Bella Akhmadulina, *tr. fr. Russian by* Jean Valentine *and* Olga Carlisle. BoWoP

Words That Speak of Death. Anadad Eldan, *tr. fr. Hebrew by* Anthony Rudolf *and* Natan Zach. VWA

Words, the Words, the Words, The. William Carlos Williams. BiP

Words to a Song. Agnes Nemes Nagy, *tr. fr. Hungarian by* Bruce Berlind. BoWoP

Words to My Mother. Alfonsina Storni, *tr. fr. Spanish by* Marion Hodapp *and* Mary Crow. AMV–80

Words to Remind Me of Grandmother. Andrés Castro Ríos, *tr. fr. Spanish by* Julio Marzán. InW

Words to the Wind. Pier Giorgio Di Cicco. AMV–80

Words Words Words. Marilyn Krysl. AMV–80

Wordsworth I love, his books are like the fields. To Wordsworth. John Clare. OAEL–2

Wordsworth, thou form almost divine, cried Henry. John Berryman. *Fr.* Dream Songs. CAPP

Wordsworth Unvisited. Hartley Coleridge. *See* He Lived amidst the' Untrodden Ways.

Wordsworth upon Helvellyn! Let the cloud. On a Portrait of Wordsworth by B. R. Haydon. Elizabeth Barrett Browning. HeIP

Wordsworth's Grave, *abr.* Sir William Watson. VLP

Wordy People, The. Jacqueline M. Fitzgerald. PPM

Work. Andrei Codrescu. EAS

Work?/ I don't have to work. Necessity. Langston Hughes. NOBA

Work all week for the man. Saturday's Child. Edelin Coleman Fields. PoUp

Work, for the Night Is Coming, *with music.* Anna Louise Walker. BLSH

Work in a mine and become a mine. Mine. Andrew Hudgins. AMV–80

Work is done, The. Young men and maidens, set. On Himself. Robert Herrick. CaPo

Work of Art. Clarice Short. MPA

Work of Artifice, A. Marge Piercy. IHMS

Work of the Weavers, The. *Unknown.* FSW

Work on the railroad. Roll on the Ground. *Unknown.* AmFP

Work Song. Raymond Mazisi Kunene, *tr. fr. Zulu by* D. K. Rycroft. WTO

Work-table, litter, books and standing lamp. Night Sweat. Robert Lowell. TAP; VGW

Work to Do toward Town. Gary Snyder. VGW

Work without Hope. Samuel Taylor Coleridge. AnMo; BiP; ILP (1975 ed.); IPWM; MBPR; NOBE

Work—work—work. Thomas Hood. *Fr.* The Song of the Shirt. VoPo

Workaday Morning. Astrid Tollefsen, *tr. fr. Norwegian by* Nadia Christensen. PBWP

Workbox, The. Thomas Hardy. InPK; UnPo (1976 ed.)

Worker, The. Richard W. Thomas. PoBA; TC

Worker Uprooted. Joseph Kalar. SPT

Workers' flag is deepest red, The. *See* People's flag is deepest red, The.

Workers on the S.P. Line to strike sent out a call, The. Casey Jones (Union). Joe Hill. FSW

Workers Rose on May Day or Postscript to Karl Marx, The. Audre Lorde. GP

Workhouse Boy, The. *Unknown.* GBP; PeBB; VLP

Working/ in a stupor. Bruce Holsapple. FAF

Working against Time. David Wagoner. MAT

Working for Dr. No. Valery Nash. PPoD

Working in a weave-room, fighting for my life. Weave Room Blues. *Unknown.* FSW

Working in the Mines. *Unknown.* AIW

Working is another way of praying. Song for Dov Shamir [*or* Song of a Hebrew]. Dannie Abse. VWA; WTO

Working Man, The. Gregory Donovan. AMV–81

Working Man Blues. *Unknown.* BluL

Working on Wall Street. May Swenson. NowV

Working Party, A. Siegfried Sassoon. CMoP (1970 ed.)

Working the Skeet House. Jon Eastman. AMV–80

Working the Wood. Susan Sonde. PoUp

Working with Tools. A. R. Ammons. NoAM

Workman with a spade in half a day, A. New Excavations. Leonora Speyer. *Fr.* Pompeii. TH

Work-out, The. Geoffrey Movius. MAT

Works and Days. V. H. Adair. PoW

Works and Days, *sel.* David Campbell. Lambing. MAuV

World, The. Francis Bacon. *See* World's a Bubble, The.

World, The. Robert Creeley. NoAM

World, The. Kathleen Raine. OxBTC

World, The. William Brighty Rands. *See* Wonderful World, The.

World, The. Christina Rossetti. BoWoP; VLP

World, The. Henry Vaughan. BoReV; CABA (1972 ed.); EBEV; HAP; HeIP; ILP (1975 ed.); ILwL; LFH; MetP; NOBE; OAEL–1; OBP; PPoe; PPP; SCP–1

World/ world you are wonderful. A Round Song. Rhyll McMaster. FPA

World a Hunt, The. William Drummond of Hawthornden. NOBE

World and the Child, The. James Merrill. CoPAm; PAIC

World as Meditation, The. Wallace Stevens. CABA (1972 ed.); HeIP; IPWM; NIL; PiAm; PPP

World below the Brine, The. Walt Whitman. BiP; EcS; InPS; MAT; PBMP

World cheats those who cannot read, The. A Mad Poem Addressed to My Nephews and Nieces. Po Chu-i, *tr. by* Arthur Waley. BBGO; BuTh

World Enough. Jeanine Hathaway. AMV–80

World has gone inside itself, The. Inside the Vision of Peace. Tom McKeown. TC

World has held great heros, The. The Song of Mr. Toad. Kenneth Grahame. *Fr.* The Wind in the Willows. NOBL

World Has Many Places Many Ways, The. Norman H. Russell. VW

World hath conquered, The. Tara Is Grass. *Unknown, tr. by* Padraic Pearse. POL

World, Hold Me Close. Virginia Floyd. AATT

World I did not wish to enter, A. A Necessitarian's Epitaph. Thomas Hardy. FaBoEE

World is, The/ not with us enough. O Taste and See. Denise Levertov. PBWP; PiAm; PPP; TAP

World Is a Beautiful Place, The. Lawrence Ferlinghetti. BBGO; CAPP; MiP

World is a bundle of hay, The. Epigram on John Bull. Byron. FaBoCo; FF

World Is a Mighty Ogre, The. Fenton Johnson. AmNP (1974 ed.)

World Is a Stubbed Toe, The. Mbembe. NW

World is a wind, The. Frames on Bright Faces. Bruce Severy. HeS

World is charged with the grandeur of God, The. God's Grandeur. Gerard Manley Hopkins. AnMo; BiP; BoReV; CABA (1972 ed.); CMoP (1970 ed.); Epi; ExPo (1973 ed.); FF; HAP; ILP (1975 ed.); ILwL; InPK; IP; IPWM; LFH; NoAM; NOBE; OAEL–2; OBP; PAIC; PoIA; PPP; SoSe; UnPo (1976 ed); VLP; VoPo

World is composed, The. The Grass Is a Reasonable Colour. John Newlove. NeAC

World Is Day-breaking, The. Sekiya Miyoshi. DuDr

World is fast bound in the snares of Varuna, The. "Hugh MacDiarmid." Fr. In Memoriam James Joyce. TwMBP

World is full of care, much like unto a bubble, The. Epigram. Nathaniel Ward. POL

World is full of gladness, The. Lemon Pie. Edgar A. Guest. OBAL

World is full of mostly invisible things, The. To David, about His Education. Howard Nemerov. NowV; SFF

World Is Full of Remarkable Things, The. Amiri Baraka. NIL

World is made of days and nights, The. Aren't You Glad. Charlotte Zolotow. CTV

World Is Not a Fenced-off Garden, The. Jakov Steinberg, tr. fr. Hebrew by Mark Elliott Shapiro. VWA

World Is Really a Sugarplum House in the Forest, The. Aram Boyajian. NeAC

World is several billion years of age, The. Winter Report. Ben Howard. PoA

World is so full of a number of things, The. Happy Thought. Robert Louis Stevenson. CTV; OxBChV; PCOP

"World is such a funny place, The." Relatively. Kathleen Millay. QQQ

World is the color of pumpkins, The. Butterflies on an Illinois Road. Helena Minton. FAF

World Is Too Much with Us, The. Wordsworth. BBGO; BiP; CABA (1972 ed.); Epi; ExPo (1973 ed.); FaPoR; HAP; HeIP; HoPM (1975 ed.); ILP (1975 ed.); InPK; IP; IPWM; LFH; MAT; MBPR; NOBE; OAEL–2; OBP; PAIC; PBMP; PoIA; PPoD; PPoe; PPP; SoSe (1977 ed.); TPo; VoPo; WIF

World of Bacteria. Sakutaro Hagiwara, tr. fr. Japanese by Graeme McD. Wilson. AMV–80

World of Darkness. Robert Chatain. PoA

World of Light, The. Henry Vaughan. See They Are All Gone into the World of Light.

World Outside, The. Denise Levertov. ConAP

World says No, The. No. E. M. Schorb. AMV–80

World So Wide, The. Unknown. OxBM

World swelters in the hollow of a stone, The. Lost Will. Roger McDonald. FPA

World, that all contains, is ever moving, The. Fulke Greville. Fr. Caelica. NIL

World, The—the clust'ring spheres he made. Fruits of the Earth. Christopher Smart. Fr. A Song to David. OBP

World, the Devil, and Tom Paine, The, with music. Unknown. AH

World turns mild, The; democracy, they say. Tempora Mutantur. James Russell Lowell. HAP

World War Two amputees, The. News from the V. A. A. D. Winans. PoW

World was first a private park, The. The Fisherman. Jay MacPherson. CABA (1972 ed.)

World Was Never Real to Me, The. George Randall Griffin. AMV–81

World within a World. Debra Woolard Bender. AMV–80

World within World. Peter Meinke. AATT

"World without Objects Is a Sensible Emptiness, A." Richard Wilbur. ConAP; NoAM; NOBA; PiAm; PoA

World world world world. Enueg II. Samuel Beckett. NoAM

World would fall to pieces any moment now, The. The Thermostatic Man. Gordon Challis. ATNZ

World Youth Song. Unknown. FSW

Worlde So wide, th'air so remuable, The. The World So Wide. Unknown. OxBM

Worldly Wealth. Rowland Watkyns. FaBoEE

World's a Bubble, The. Francis Bacon. SCP-2 (World, The.) PPoD

World's a stage, The. The trifling entrance fee. Hilaire Belloc. OxBTC

World's an inn, The; and I her guest. On the World. Francis Quarles. HAP

Worlds are breaking in my head, The. Yves Tanguy. David Gascoyne. EAS

World's as the world is, The; the nations rearm and prepare to. Night without Sleep. Robinson Jeffers. PiAm

World's Bliss, Have Good Day! Unknown. OxBM

World's End, The. William Empson. ILP (1975 ed.)

World's Fare. Charles Stetler. GP

World's great age begins anew, The. Shelley. Fr. Hellas. EBEV; HAP; HeIP; ILP (1975 ed.); NIL; NOBE; OAEL–2

World's great soul knows by protopathy, The. Psychathanasia; or, The Second Part of the Song of the Soul, Bk. III. Henry More. SCP-2

World's Last Unnamed Poem, The. A. K. Redwing. VoR

Worlds on worlds are rolling ever. Shelley. Fr. Hellas. HeIP

World's Worth. Dante Gabriel Rossetti. VLP

Worm, The. Willis Barnstone. VWA

Worm, The. Ralph Bergengren. CaYB

Worm artist, The. The Earth Worm. Denise Levertov. NOBA

Worm Fed on the Heart of Corinth, A. Isaac Rosenberg. OAEL–2

Worm Within. Anthony Thwaite. HeHu

Worms, The. Carolyn Kizer. IPWM

Worms and the Wind. Carl Sandburg. RAE

Wormwood. Thomas Kinsella. CIP; IPM

Wormwood. James E. Warren, Jr. AATT

Wormy apples at the grocery. Eco Right. Walt Gavenda. QQQ

Worn and torn by many fingers. A Family Album. Alter Brody. VWA

Worried Life Blues. Unknown. AmFP

Worried Man Blues. Unknown. FSW

Worry about Money. Kathleen Raine. FaBoTw (1975 ed.)

Worsening Situation. John Ashbery. NOBA

Worship. Elmer F. Suderman. AATT

Worst side of it all, The. White Roses. John Ashbery. TAP

Worstest Beast, The. Alan Jackson. MS

Worthy art Thou,/ O Lord, of praise. Deliverance from a Fit of Fainting. Anne Bradstreet. TAP

Worthy woman from beside Bath city, A. Chaucer, mod. version by Nevill Coghill. Fr. The Canterbury Tales: Prologue. BiP

Wotton, my little Bere dwells on a hill. Ad Henricum Wottonem. Thomas Bastard. FaBoEE

Would a circling surface vulture. Mahadevi, tr. fr. Kannada by A. K. Ramanujan. BoWoP

Would God I in that Golden City were. Edward Taylor. Fr. Preparatory Meditations: First Series, XXIII. EAP; PiAm

Would God that I and my darling. Tr. fr. Gaelic by Frank O'Connor. Fr. A Beggarman's Song. WTO

Would I could cast a sail on the water. The Collar-Bone of a Hare. W. B. Yeats. OxBTC

Would I might lie like this, without the pain. In Hospital. James Elroy Flecker. OxBTC

Would I were air that thou with heat opprest. Thomas Stanley. FaBoEE

Would I were chang'd into that golden shower. Sir Arthur Gorges. GBL

"Would it had been the man of our wish!" In the Room of the Bride-Elect. Thomas Hardy. BuTh

Would it please you if I strung my tears. The Race Question. Naomi Long Madgett. BPo

Would that I/ had known Aunt Cumi. The Ancient of Days. Jonathan Williams. CSP

Would that the structure brave, the manifold music I build. Abt Vogler. Robert Browning. BoReV; OAEL-2; TT; VLP

Would the world know how Godfrey lost his breath? Truth Brought to Light, or Murder Will Out. Stephen College. APAS

Would write a letter with/ my scissors mouth. Young Woman's neo-aramaic jewish persian Blues. Jerome Rothenberg, *after Persian folk poem.* BoWoP

Would you be famous and renowned in story. The Advice. *Unknown.* APAS

Would you be preserved from ruin? The Impartial Inspection. *Unknown.* APAS

Would you believe some-/ one who said he. Dance and Eye Me (Wicked)ly My Breath a Fixed Sphere. Rochelle Owens. NMM

Would you come back if I said the earth. Nadia Tueni, *tr. fr. French by* Willis Barnstone. BoWoP

Would you have freedom from wage slavery? There Is Power. Joe Hill. FSW

Would you have me brand it, scars. The Secret Irish. Allen Hoey. AMV-81

Would you hear of an old-time sea-fight? Battle of the *Bonhomme Richard* and the *Serapis.* Walt Whitman. Song of Myself, XXXV-XXXVI. UnPo (1976 ed.)

Would you, my friend, in little room express. Martial, *tr. fr. Latin by* Elijah Fenton. OBVE

Would you your son should be a sot or dunce. William Cowper. *Fr.* Tirocinium; or, A Review of Schools. OBSV

Wouldn't drive and wouldn't be led. February. Fred Chappell. CSP

Wouldnt think/t look at m. ˙Panther Man. James A. Emanuel. BPo

Wouldn't you like to know. Elementary. Jim Tollerud. VoR

Would'st be happy, little child. To Theodora. *Unknown.* OxBChV

Wouldst thou hear what man can say. Epitaph on Elizabeth, L. H. Ben Jonson. BiP; CABA (1972 ed.); FaBoEE; HAP; HeIP; NIL; SCP-1

Wound, The. Thom Gunn. PSN

Wound-Dresser, The. Walt Whitman. NOBA; TAP

Wounded Cupid, The. Robert Herrick, *after the Greek of* Anacreon. OBVE; OFD

Wounded deer—leaps highest, A. Emily Dickinson. TAP

Wounded hare looks out, The. Hare in Winter. Marge Piercy. NeAC

Wounded Hawk, The. Herbert Palmer. FaBoTw (1975 ed.)

Wounded Wilderness of Morris Graves, The. Lawrence Ferlinghetti. A Coney Island of the Mind, 11. WIF

Wounds. Michael Longley. IPM

Woyi, The. Lew Blockcolski. VoR

Wraggle Taggle Gipsies, The. *Unknown.* DuDr; FSW

Wrangler Kid, The. *Unknown.* BPAW

Wrap Me in Blankets of Momentary Winds. Harold Littlebird. VoR

Wrap up in a blanket in cold weather and just read. Things to Do around a Lookout. Gary Snyder. CAPP; TAP

Wrath of Peleus son, O muse, resound, The. Homer, *tr. by* Dryden. *Fr.* The Iliad, Invocation. OBVE

Wrathfull winter prochinge [*or* 'proaching] on a pace, The. The Induction to "A Mirror for Magistrates." Thomas Sackville. AAS; PAIC

Wreath, The. Robert Graves. BoLoP

Wreath, A. George Herbert. OAEL-1; SoSe (1977 ed.)

Wreath for Our Murdered Comrade Kobayashi, A. Michael Gold. SPT

Wreath of flowers as cold as snow, A. The Birth. Rosemary Dobson. MAuV

Wreathèd garland of deserved praise, A. A Wreath. George Herbert. OAEL-1; SoSe (1977 ed.)

Wreaths. Geoffrey Hill. PoA

Wreck. Noel Polk. AMV-81

Wreck of the *Deutschland*, The. Gerard Manley Hopkins. BoReV; CMoP (1970 ed.); NoAM; NOBE; PFD; VLP

Wreck of the Great Northern, The. Robert Hedin. AMV-81

Wreck of the *Hesperus*, The. Longfellow. CTV; FaPoR; RhR

Wreck of the *Julie Plante*, The. William Henry Drummond. PoTa

Wreck of the Old 97, The. *Unknown.* FSW

Wreck of the Royal Palm, The. *Unknown.* AmFP

Wreck of the *Thresher*, The. William Meredith. CoPAm

Wreckers/ Drilling and breaking rock. Constructions: Upper East Side. Sandra Hochman. NowV

Wrecks dissolve above us, The; their dust drops down from afar. The Deep-Sea Cables. Kipling. VLP

Wren, The. *Unknown.* OxBChV

Wren: Three Mirrors. Michael Burkard. AAN

Wrens and robins in the hedge. Christina Rossetti. PCOP

Wrestlers. S. Lewandowski. BrS

Wrestling, The. Abbie Huston Evans. GP

Wrestling Jacob. Charles Wesley. BoReV; NOBE

Wretched Flavia on her couch reclined, The. Saturday: The Small Pox. Lady Mary Wortley Montagu. WPE

Wretched Ierne! with what grief I see. Swift. *Fr.* Verses Occasioned by the Sudden Drying Up of St. Patrick's Well. OBSV

Wretched lost rejected lover, The. For the Moment. Richard Weber. PFIr

Wring the Swan's Neck. Enrique Gonzáles Martínez, *tr. fr. Spanish by* Samuel Beckett. Epi

Wrists. Alberta Turner. HeS

Writ on the Eve of My 32nd Birthday. Gregory Corso. SA

"Write a letter to Grandpa," my mother said, but he smelled old. A Memory. Mona Van Duyn. *Fr.* Recovery. RiTi

Write as you will. Young Poets. Nicanor Parra, *tr. by* Miller Williams. POL

Write it in gold—a spirit of the sun. Lines Written in a Blank Leaf of the Prometheus Unbound. Thomas Lovell Beddoes. OAEL-2

Write Me a Verse. David McCord. MN

Write-off, The. Charlotte Alexander. AAN

Write only/ to young boys. The Art of Poetry. Darrell Gray. AcAn

Write! write! help! help, sweet Muse! and never cease! Parthenophil and Parthenophe, XVIII. Barnabe Barnes. Epi

Writer, The. Hildebrand Jacob. FaBoCo

Writer, The. Richard Wilbur. UsP

Writer Indulges a Hobby, The Julia Randall. PPoD

Writer to His Book, The. Thomas Campion. ILP (1975 ed.)

Writer's Conference. E. Ethelbert Miller. PoUp

Writer's House, The. Dick Allen. FAF

Writing. Anthony Cronin. IPM

Writing a letter he said. Buffalo—Isle of Wight Power Cable. Anselm Hollo. TwMBP

Writing, I crushed an insect with my nail. Interlude. Karl Shapiro. PBMP

Writing in England Now. Philip O'Connor. OxBTC

Writing on Napkins at the Sunshine Club, Macon, Georgia 1971. David Bottoms. TAT

Writing you this, I can feel a dewclaw. Growing Wild. Jim Wayne Miller. GP

Written. Mary Ruelfe. AMV–81

Written after Swimming from Sestos to Abydos. Byron. LiSp; MBPR

Written after the Death of Charles Lamb. Wordsworth. MBPR

Written at an Inn at Henley. William Shenstone. NOBE

Written at the White Sulphur Springs. Francis Scott Key. OBAL

Written, Directed by and Starring. James Simmons. IPM

Written Forty Miles South of a Spreading City. Robert Bly. NNaP

Written in a Copy of Swift's Poems, for Wayne Burns. James Wright. NOBA

Written in a Copy of "The Earthly Paradise," Dec. 25, 1870. William Morris. *Fr.* The Earthly Paradise. VLP

Written in a Lady's Prayer Book. Earl of Rochester. BoLoP

Written in a Thunder Storm July 15th 1841. John Clare. VLP

Written in an open field. February Letter to Jack Spicer. Helen Luster. CPA

Written in an Ovid. Matthew Prior. FaBoEE

Written in Butler's Sermons. Matthew Arnold. VLP

Written in Dejection near Rome. Robert Bly. CoPAm

Written in Disgust of Vulgar Superstition. Keats. MBPR

Written in Early Spring. Wordsworth. *See* Lines Written in Early Spring.

Written in Emerson's Essays. Matthew Arnold. ILP (1975 ed.)

Written in Exile. Kathleen Raine. WPE

Written in Her French Psalter. Elizabeth I, Queen of England. PBWP; WPE

Written in Juice of Lemon. Abraham Cowley. *Fr.* The Mistress. CABA (1972 ed.)

Written in London, September, 1802. Wordsworth. *See* O Friend! I Know Not Which Way I Must Look.

Written in March. Wordsworth. CTV; MBPR; PBMP; UnPo (1976 ed.)

Written in Northampton County Asylum. John Clare. *See* I Am.

Written in Prison. John Clare. Epi; OAEL–2

Written in the Album of a Child. Wordsworth. OxBChV

Written in the Beginning of Mezeray's History of France. Matthew Prior. NOBE

Written in Unbridled Repugnance near Sioux Falls, Alabama— April 30, 1974. A. K. Redwing. VoR

Written on a Blank Page in Shakespeare's Poems. Keats. *See* Bright Star! Would I Were Steadfast as Thou Art.

Written on a Girl's Table-Napkin at Wiesbaden. Ronald Duncan. WeW

Written on a Leaf. *Unknown, tr. fr. Chinese by* Geoffrey Waters. BoWoP

Written on a Looking-Glass. *Unknown.* FaBoEE

Written on a Paper Napkin. Len Gasparini. NeAC

Written on a Wall at Woodstock. Elizabeth I, Queen of England. PBWP; WPE

Written on an Egg. Eduard Mörike, *tr. fr. German by* Doris Orgel. CC

Written on Seeing the Flowers, and Remembering My Daughter. Kao Ch'i, *tr. fr. Chinese.* DL

Written on the Day That Mr. Leigh Hunt Left Prison. Keats. MBPR

Written on the Stub of the First Paycheck. William Stafford. *Fr.* The Move to California. AnMo; InPK

Written on the Wall at Chang's Hermitage. Tu Fu, *tr. fr. Chinese by* Kenneth Rexroth. HoPM (1975 ed.)

Written over a Gate. John Sheffield. NIL

Written the Night before His Execution. Chidiock Tichbourne. *See* Elegy: "My prime of youth is but a frost of cares."

Written with a Diamond on Her Window at Woodstock. Elizabeth I, Queen of England. PBWP; WPE

Wrong Kind of Insurance, The. John Ashbery. NYP

Wrong Kind of Love. Ray A. Young Bear. VW

Wrote the clergy: "Our Dear Madame Prynne." A Hawthorne Garland. Richard Harter Fogle. OBAL

W's a well-informed wight. A Well-informed Wight. Oliver Herford. TDH

Wuid-reek. Sydney Goodsir Smith. SLP

Wulf and Eadwacer. Richard Ryan. CIP

Wulf and Eadwacer. *Unknown. See* Eadwacer.

Wyatt [*or* Wyat] resteth here, that quick[e] could[e] never rest. Earl of Surrey. AAS; ILP (1975 ed.)

Wykehamist's Address to Learning, A. P. N. Shuttleworth. FaBoCo

Wynken, Blynken, and Nod. Eugene Field. ECBV; Moon; OBAL; OxBChV; PCOP

Wynken De Worde. Frederick Von Ende. POL

Wyse men alwaye. A Mery Gest How a Sergeaunt Wolde Lerne to Be A Frere. Sir Thomas More. AAS

# X

X. R. P. Dickey. HeS

X. Roland Tharp. PHC

X marks the spot. Mark. Steve Toth. AcAn

X of the Unknown, The. Tom Clark. LiSp

X Ray. Dannie Abse. PMW

X-Ray. Elizabeth Bartlett. PMW

X-Ray. David Ray. IPWM

X2s and 42s (Into Northeast Washington). Ken Forde. PoUp

Xenophanes. Emerson. NOBA

Xerox. Ben Belitt. NYP

Xmas for the Boys. Gavin Ewart. OBSV

Xylographer started to cross the sea, A. The Zealless Xylographer. Mary Mapes Dodge. OBAL

# Y

Y digamos que, pensamos que, like. Foreign Policy Commitments; or, You Get into the Catamaran First, Old Buddy. Paul Blackburn. NowV

Y M & V Blues. *Unknown.* BluL

YWCA. Heather McHugh. AAN

Yacht, The. Catullus, *tr. fr. Latin by* John Hookham Frere. OBVE

("This racer of the watry plain," *tr. unknown.*) OBVE

Yachting in Arkansas. Craig Weeden. AMV–80

Yachts, The. William Carlos Williams. BiP; CMoP (1970 ed.); HeIP; ILP (1975 ed.); LiSp; NoAM; NOBA; PiAm; PPP; SoS; SPo

Yahrzeit. Dan Jaffe. VWA

Yahrzeit. Susan Fromberg Schaeffer. VWA

Yahrzeit Candle. Jean Nordhaus. AMV–81

Yahweh is my shepherd. Bible, *O.T.* Psalms, XXIII. SFF

Yai—yai—yai. Musk Oxen. Igjugarjuk, *tr. fr. Eskimo.* WTO

Yak, The. Hilaire Belloc. NOBL; OxBChV

Yak, The. Theodore Roethke. ECBV; LCL

Yaks come from far-off Tibet. Mary Ann Hoberman. OSF

Yale Boola!, *3 versions, with music.* H. S. Durand *and others.* FSN

Yall/ out there. A Chant for Young/Brothas and Sistuhs. Sonia Sanchez. BPo

Yamaha yamaha. Mysterious East. William Cole. OBAL

Yankee Cradle. Robert P. Tristram Coffin. ECBV

Yankee Doodle. *Unknown, at. to* Richard Schuckburg. AIW; AmFP; BLSH, *with music;* BLSo, *with music;* BTTM; CC; FSW; GBP; OBAL; PCOP

Yankee Doodle Boy, The, *with music.* George M. Cohan. BLSo; FSN

Yankee Man-of-War, The. *Unknown.* BTTM
(*Stately Southerner,* The.) AmFP

Yankee Poet. Robley Wilson, Jr. AMV–81

Yankee ship and a Yankee crew, A. The *Constitution's* Last Fight. James Jeffrey Roche. BTTM

"Yap-yap, yap-yap!" the little dog barked at the moon. The Dog. A. Buttigieg. RAE

Yaqui Women: Three Generations. Rick Casillas. GP

Yardbird's Skull. Owen Dodson. AmNP (1974 ed.); CNA; PoBA; TCP; VGW

Yarn of the *Loch Achray.* John Masefield. PoTa

Yarn of the *Nancy Bell,* The. W. S. Gilbert. BBL; FaBoCo; HoPM (1975 ed.); NOBL; PeBB; VLP

Yarrow Revisited. Wordsworth. VLP

Yarrow Unvisited. Wordsworth. MBPR

Yarrow Visited. Wordsworth. MBPR

Yawn, The. Paul Blackburn. CTBA; VoA

Yawning youth, scarce half awake, essays, The. Persius, *tr. fr. Latin by* Dryden. *Fr.* Satires, III. SCP–1

Ybor City. Duane Locke. CSP

Ye Alps audacious, thro' the heavens that rise. The Hasty-Pudding, I. Joel Barlow. EAP; NOBA; OBAL; PiAm; TAP

Ye angells bright, pluck from your wings a quill. Edward Taylor. *Fr.* Preparatory Meditations: Second Series, LX. PiAm

Ye are the temples of the Lord. The Exhortation of a Father to His Children. Robert Smith. OxBChV

Ye ayres and windes, ye elves of hilles. Ovid, *tr. by* Arthur Golding. *Fr.* Metamorphoses, VII. OBVE

Ye Banks and Braes. Burns. *See* Banks o' Doon, The.

Ye blushing virgins happy are. To Roses in the Bosom of Castara. William Habington. NIL; SCP–2

Ye brave bold men of 'Cotia. Robens' Promised Land. George Purdom. WTO

Ye brood of Conscience—Spectres! that frequent. Wordsworth. *Fr.* Sonnets upon the Punishment of Death. PeD

Ye cats that at midnight spit love at each other. An Appeal to Cats in the Business of Love. Thomas Flatman. GBL; HAP; PCat; SCP–2

Ye clouds! that far above me float and pause. France: An Ode. Samuel Taylor Coleridge. LFH; MBPR

Ye Commons and Peers. Jack Frenchman's Defeat. Congreve. APAS

Ye coop us up, and tax our bread. Caged Rats. Ebenezer Elliott. EBEV; VLP

Ye dayntye nymphs, that in this blessed brooke. The Lay to Eliza. Spenser. *Fr.* The Shepheardes Calender: April. NOBE

Ye distant spires, ye antique towers. Ode on a Distant Prospect of Eton College. Thomas Gray. CABA (1972 ed.); HeIP; ILP (1975 ed.); LAuP; NOBE; OAEL–1; PAIC; PES

Ye dreary plains, that round me lie. Summer on the Great American Desert. Rufus B. Sage. BPAW

Ye elms that wave on Malvern Hill. Malvern Hill. Herman Melville. AmVN; TAP

Ye elves of hills, brooks, standing lakes, and groves. Shakespeare. *Fr.* The Tempest, V, i. EBEV

Ye flippering soule. Let by Rain. Edward Taylor. NOBA

Ye flowery banks o' bonie Doon [*or* Ye banks and braes o' bonie Doon]. The Banks o' Doon [*or* Bonie Doon]. Burns. BoLoP; HeIP; NOBE; PoIA; SLP; UnPo (1976 ed.)

Ye fog that creeps there in the uplands. Invocation for a Storm. *Tr. fr. Hawaiian.* WTO

Ye gallants of Newgate, whose fingers are nice. Newgate's Garland. John Gay. FaBoBa

Ye gentlemen and ladies fair who grace this famous city. The Hunters of Kentucky. Samuel Woodworth. BLSo; BTTM; FSW

Ye goat-herd gods that love the grassy mountains. Sir Philip Sidney. *Fr.* Arcadia. HAP; NOBE; OAEL–1

Ye green-rob'd Dryads, oft' at dusky eve. The Enthusiast; or, The Lover of Nature. Joseph Warton. LAuP

Ye groves (the statesman at his desk exclaims.) The Statesman in Retirement. William Cowper. *Fr.* Retirement. PPoD

Ye happy floods! that now must pass. Lucasta Taking the Waters at Tunbridge: Ode. Richard Lovelace. SCP–2

Ye Hasten to the Grave! Shelley. GrRo

Ye have been fresh and green. To Meadows. Robert Herrick. CaPo; NOBE

"Ye have robbed," said he, "ye have slaughtered and made an end." He Fell among Thieves. Sir Henry Newbolt. FaPoR; OxBTC

Ye Highlands [*or* Hielands] and ye Lawlands. The Bonny Earl of Murray. *Unknown.* AIW; FaBoBa; FSW; PoPle; RDB

Ye ice-falls! ye that from the mountain's brow. Samuel Taylor Coleridge. *Fr.* Hymn before Sunrise, in the Valley of Chamouni. PIM

Ye learned sisters which have oftentimes. Epithalamion. Spenser. AAS; BoLoP; CABA (1972 ed.); Epi; ILP (1975 ed.); InPS; LoAs; NOBE; OAEL–1; PAIC

Ye lie, friend Pindar! and friend Thales! On a Quaker's Tankard. Walter Savage Landor. FaBoEE

Ye living lamps, by whose dear light. The Mower to the Glow-Worms. Andrew Marvell. AnMo; ILP (1975 ed.); NOBE; OAEL–1; PoPle; PPP

Ye loyal Britons, I pray draw near. The Battle of Shiloh. *Unknown.* AmFP

Ye maggots, feed on Willie's brains. Burns. FaBoEE

Ye Mariners of England. Thomas Campbell. BTTM; FaPoR; NOBE

Ye members of Parliament all. The Shash. *Unknown.* APAS

Ye mitered fathers of the land. The Sentiments. *Unknown.* APAS

Ye Nuns and Capuchins, begin the song. John Courtenay. *Fr.* A Poetical and Philosophical Essay on the French Revolution.... ESaP

Ye nymphs! if e'er your eyes were red. On the Lamented Death of Mrs. Throckmorton's Bullfinch. William Cowper. LAuP; PPP

Ye old mule, that thinck your self so fayre. Sir Thomas Wyatt. AAS

Ye Parliament of England. *Unknown.* AmFP; BTTM

Ye paultry underlings of state. On the Irish Club. Swift. OBSV

Ye people who delight in sin. The Hanging of Sam Archer. *Unknown.* AmFP

Ye powers above and heavenly poles. On Button the Grave-Maker. *Unknown.* FaBoEE

Ye Protestants of Ulster, I pray you join with me. Lisnagade. *Unknown.* WTO

Ye Realms below the Skies, *with music.* Hosea Ballou II. AH

Ye saints who dwell on Europe's shore. The Handcart Song. *Unknown.* AmFP

Ye saw't floueran in my breist. The Mandrake Hairt. Sydney Goodsir Smith. SLP

Ye say, they all have passed away. Indian Names. Lydia Huntley Sigourney. GOA

Ye Scattered Nations, *with music. Unknown, tr. fr. Latin by* Thomas Cradock. AH

Ye shadowy beings, that have rights and claims. Cave of Staffa, II. Wordsworth. VLP

Ye silent shades, whose each tree here. To Groves. Robert Herrick. CaPo

Ye sons of Columbia, your attention I do crave. Fuller and Warren. *At. to* Moses Whitecotton. AmFP

Ye sorrowing people! who from bondage fly. The Fugitive Slaves. Jones Very. TAP

Ye storm-winds of Autumn! Parting. Matthew Arnold. Switzerland, II. VLP

Ye tender-hearted people, I pray you lend an ear. Samuel Allen. *Unknown.* AmFP

Ye traced me on the desert wide. Apache Kid. Ned White. BPAW

Ye tradefull merchants, that with weary toyle. Amoretti, XV. Spenser. HeIP; ILP (1975 ed.); NIL; OAEL-1

Ye true lovers bold, come listen unto me. The True Lovers Bold. *Unknown.* AmFP

Ye valleys low where the milde whispers use. Flowers for a Funeral. Milton. *Fr.* Lycidas. PF

Ye vig'rous swains! while youth ferments your blood. The Hunt. Pope. *Fr.* Windsor Forest. NIL

Ye weary, heavy laden souls. The Lonesome Dove. *Unknown.* AmFP

Ye Were the Dawn. Sorley Maclean, *tr. fr. Gaelic; Scots version by* Douglas Young. MS

Ye who amid this feverish world would wear. Urban Pollution. John Armstrong. PMW

Ye who intelligent the third heaven move. The First Canzone of the Convito. Dante, *tr. by* Shelley. OBVE

Ye worthy patriots go on. An Encomium upon a Parliament. Daniel DeFoe. APAS

Ye young debaters over the doctrine. The Village Atheist. Edgar Lee Masters. *Fr.* Spoon River Anthology. PPM

Yea, but uncertain hopes are anchors feeble. Parthenophil and Parthenophe, XXI. Barnabe Barnes. Epi

Yea, the coneys are scared by the thud of hoofs. Chorus of the Years. Thomas Hardy. *Fr.* The Dynasts. CMoP (1970 ed.)

Yeah./they hang you up. To All Brothers. Sonia Sanchez. BPo

Yeah./ you can really. Rebolushinary X-mas. Carolyn M. Rodgers. JB

Yeah here am I. Two Jazz Poems. Carl Wendell Hines, Jr. AmNP (1974 ed.)

Yeah, I Is Uh Shootin Off at the Mouth. Carolyn M. Rodgers. SA

"Yeah" she said "my man's gone too." Conversation. Nikki Giovanni. CTBA

Yeah, you know Katie May's a good girl. Katie May. *Unknown.* BluL

Yeah, you remember the ghetto. The For Real Ghetto. Lonnie L. Landrum. DNGG

Year about to end, The. The Last Day of the Year. Su Tung P'o, *tr. by* Kenneth Rexroth. CC

Year after year I have watched. Li Ch'ing-chao, *tr. fr. Chinese by* Kenneth Rexroth. BoWoP

Year after year the princess lies asleep. Parabola. A. D. Hope. PoA

Year ago I fell in love with the functional ward, A. The Hospital. Patrick Kavanagh. BIrV; CIP

Year ago, on what was probably, A. Leaving the Flag Out All Night. Napoleon St. Cyr. FAF

Year ago you came, A. Pietà. James McAuley. MAuV

Year at its turn, The. The Last Day of the Year (New Year's Eve). Annette von Droste-Hülshoff, *tr. by* Willis Barnstone. BoWoP

Year dies fiercely, The: out of the north the beating storms. Year's End. William Everson. NoAM

Year 1812, The. Donald Davie, *after the Polish of* Adam Mickiewicz. OBVE

Year has come to us as though out of hiding, A. Early January. W. S. Merwin. VGW

Year has run thin through the tuning room of my mind, The. A Spring Memorandum. Robert Duncan. PoA

Year I made more money than my father, The. Making Money. John Woods. TC

Year lies fallen and faded, The. Autumn in Cornwall. Swinburne. PES

Year of Our Lord two thousand one hundred and seven, The. John Heath-Stubbs. *Fr.* An Ecclesiastical Chronicle. NOBL

Year of the Bird. Brian Swann. AmPA

Year of the Foxes, The. David Malouf. GAS

Year Passes, A. Amy Lowell. Moon

Year well remembered! Happy who beheld thee! The Year 1812. Donald Davie, *after* Adam Mickiewicz. OBVE

Yearner for silence, believing in the quiet mind, The. Between the Electric Rhythm and the Melodic Mind. James Schevill. MIT

Years. Jon Anderson. AmPA; FoP

Years. Anna Margolin, *tr. fr. Yiddish by* Ruth Whitman. VWA

Years ago,/ he began dialing your number. The Obscene Caller. Philip Dacey. AmPA

Years ago, at a private school. An Ever-fixed Mark. Kingsley Amis. NoAM

Years ago he drove a different route. A Trucker Drives through His Lost Youth. David Bottoms. CSP

Years and years we met in silence after my Bible class. Am I Not Your Son? Rudolph von Abele. PoUp

Year's at the Spring, The. Robert Browning. *Fr.* Pippa Passes, sc. i. CTV; InPK; PCOP; PIM; PPM (Pippa's Song.) LCL; UnPo (1976 ed.) (Song: "Year's at the Spring, The.") GrRo (Spring Song.) DuDr

Year's Awakening, The. Thomas Hardy. CMoP (1970 ed.); ILP (1975 ed.); OxBTC

Year's Burden [1870], A. Swinburne. VLP

Years creep slowly by, Lorena, The. Lorena. Henry De Lafayette Webster. FSW; PSoN

Year's End. Jim Barnes. HeS

Year's End. William Everson. NoAM

Year's End. Richard Wilbur. CAPP; HeIP

Years have concocted. Homecoming. Sean Clarkin. IPM

Years have gone, The. It is spring. Andrée Rexroth. Kenneth Rexroth. VGW

Years have made up my face, The. Toward Myself. Leah Goldberg, *tr. by* Robert Friend. VWA

Years I have stood. Scarecrow. Ricardo da Silveira Lobo Sternberg. PoW

Years Later. Ruth Stone. BoWoP

Years later I tried to clean out. Cleaning Stables. William Peskett. IPM

Years later my eyes clear up. Years Later. Ruth Stone. BoWoP

Years of Indiscretion. John Ashbery. NOBA

Years of love in a parked car, The. Sidewalk Restoration. Ron Ikan. NVAP

Years of the world's distance. My Grandmother Sifting. Jeff Daniel Marion. CSP

Years seem to tumble, The. Planting. Gary Snyder. BrS

Years they mistook me for you. Dodo. Henry Carlile. GP

Years—years ago—ere yet my dreams. The Belle of the Ball Room. Winthrop Mackworth Praed. FaBoCo

Years, years she came to me to dress. The Hairdresser. David Hopes. AMV–81

Yeats belongs to the nations, nay, to mankind. For the Centenary. James Simmons. IPM

Yeats could not walk in the disarming field without. The Empty Valley. J. R. Hervey. ATNZ

Ye'd wonder foo the seasons rin. The Neep-Fields by the Sea. Violet Jacob. MS

Yee wastefull woods beare witnes of my woe. William Smith. Chloris, XX. ESo

Yeerd she hadde, enclosed al aboute, A. Chauntecleer. Chaucer. Fr. The Canterbury Tales: The Nun's Priest's Tale. PB

Yeh./ billie. if someone. For Our Lady. Sonia Sanchez. IHMS

Yehuda Amichai. Seymour Mayne. VWA

Yei-ie's Child. Charles C. Long. VW

Yell for Yellow, A. Eve Merriam. ECBV

Yellow. Dan Gerber. TC

Yellow. De Leon Harrison. PoBA

Yellow. Josephine Jacobsen. GP

Yellow. Charles Wright. AmPA

Yellow becomes alive. Yellow. Josephine Jacobsen. GP

Yellow Bird, The. James W. Thompson. PoBA

Yellow Bittern, The. Cathal Buidhe MacGiolla Gunna, tr. fr. Irish. BIrV, tr. by Thomas MacDonagh; CIP, tr. by Tom MacIntyre

Yellow blood on the dunes. Before the Pacific. Blanca Varela, tr. by Willis Barnstone. BoWoP

Yellow Butter. Mary Ann Hoberman. OSF

Yellow butterflies. Koianimptiwa, tr. fr. Hopi Indian by Natalie Curtis. WTO

Yellow Cat. Gregory Harrison. FPB

Yellow chrysanthemums, The. Sequence for a Young Widow Passing. Deborah Munro. IHMS

Yellow cloud rising up from that fighting. Aborigine Oral Tradition. WTO

Yellow dot on her forehead, A. Love Medicine. Eda Lou Walton. BPAW

Yellow dusk: messenger fails to appear. Tr. fr. Chinese by Arthur Waley. OBVE

Yellow Flower, The. William Carlos Williams. HAP; PiAm

Yellow Flutterings. Keats. PCOP

Yellow gas is fired from street to street, The. Christopher Brennan. Fr. Towards the Source. MAuV

Yellow-haired Laddie, The. Unknown. GBP

Yellow-headed, gold-hammered, sunflower-lanterned, A. The Mounting Summer, Brilliant and Ominous. Delmore Schwartz. TPo

Yellow is for regret, the distal, the second hand. Yellow. Charles Wright. AmPA

Yellow leaf, from the darkness, A. Brooding Grief. D. H. Lawrence. CMoP (1970 ed.); ILP (1975 ed.)

Yellow-lit Budweiser signs over oaken bars. Uptown. Allen Ginsberg. FF; TT

Yellow november/comes swaying. Rushing. Ray A. Young Bear. CDW

Yellow platform shoes, purple bell-bottoms, orange silk shirt. Saturday Night. Rubee Dreher Moxley. NPW

Yellow Rose of Texas, The. Unknown. BLSo, with music; FSW; PSoN, with music

Yellow Submarine. John Lennon and Paul McCartney. PPoe

Yellow sun yellow. The Ballad of Red Fox. Melvin Walker LaFollette. BoAnP

Yellow the bracken. Autumn. Florence Hoatson. DuDr

Yellow Violet, The. Bryant. EAP; PF; TAP

Yellow Witch of Caribou, The. Clyde Robertson. BPAW

Yellow without Poetry. J. S. Harry. FPA

Yellow, yellow, hello, yellow. A Yell for Yellow. Eve Merriam. ECBV

Yellowjacket breaks its throat, The. Circling. Carole Oles. NPW

Yen's sorry. A Magpie Rhyme, Northumberland. Unknown. GBP

Yentel. Emily Leider. PoW

Yes. James Joyce. Fr. Ulysses. FF

Yes,/ And in that month when Proserpine comes back. That Sharp Knife. Thomas Wolfe. NCSH

Yes/ We drift. Embracing Exile. Lindiwe Mabuza. SES

Yes,/ You must crucify the worm. To a Little Boy Learning to Fish. Robert D. Hoeft. AMV–81

Yes and you know. The Brittle Eye. Henry Kanabus. FiCh

Yes as alike as entirely. To My Father. W. S. Graham. FaBoTw (1975 ed.)

Yes, as I live, I'll do't.—Nay stay. The Oath. Joseph Beaumont. SCP–2

Yes, Atticus, take it from me. Ovid, tr. by Guy Lee. Amores, I, 9. NAWM–1

Yes, brother your word had come. Hearing James Brown at the Café des Nattes. Richard A. Long. AmNP (1974 ed.)

Yes brothers you invented jazz. Tribute. Al Young. NVAP; SA

"Yes, But . . ." Theodore Weiss. TAP

Yes, contumelious fair, you scorn. The Author Apologizes to a Lady for His Being a Little Man. Christopher Smart. BoLoP

Yes, do you remember an inn. Lament for Lost Lodgings. Phyllis McGinley. SpRo

Yes, every poet is a fool. Epigram. Matthew Prior. FaBoCo; FaBoEE

Yes, faith is a goodly anchor. After the Burial. James Russell Lowell. UnPo (1976 ed.)

Yes, fickle Cambridge, Perkin's found this true. On the University of Cambridge's Burning the Duke of Monmouth's Picture. George Stepney. APAS

Yes, he's got her now. Blues. John Fuller. NOBL

Yes, he said, darling, yes, of course you tried. The Appointment. L. A. G. Strong. OxBTC

Yes! hope may with my strong desire keep pace. Michelangelo, tr. fr. Latin by Wordsworth. OBVE

Yes, I am black! and radiant. Bible, O.T. The Song of Solomon, I:5–6. PBWP

Yes, I am happy for you. Happy? Robert T. Kasold. DNGG

Yes, I remember Adlestrop. Adlestrop. Edward Thomas. DuDr; HAP; NOBE; OxBTC; PES

Yes I rolled and I tumbled. Dough Roller Blues. Unknown. BluL

Yes, I said, go out there. Answers to the Snails. Arthur Solway. AMV–81

Yes, I still have. Memories. Tony Moreno. NW

"Yes, I was only sidesman here when last." Bristol and Clifton. John Betjeman. CMoP (1970 ed.)

Yes, I wish all these animals. At the City Park Zoo. R. P. Dickey. BCr

Yes; I Write Verses. Walter Savage Landor. SoSe

Yes, I'm in love, I feel it now. The "Je Ne Sais Quoi." William Whitehead. SoSe

Yes! in the sea of life enisled. To Marguerite—Continued. Matthew Arnold. Fr. Switzerland. BoLoP; EBEV; ILP (1975 ed.); NOBE; OAEL–2; PFD; PPP; SoSe (1977 ed.); VLP

Yes, in the summer of 1773. Tom Wedgwood Tells. Brian W. Aldiss. NOBL

Yes, it is beautiful ever, let foolish men rail at it never. Arthur Hugh Clough. *Fr.* Dipsychus. VLP

Yes, it was the mountain echo. Wordsworth. MBPR

Yes, it's all right that the stars are like that. The Victim. Michael Burkard. AAN

Yes, lady, in the bright red suit. For the Woman Who Asked Me If I Believe in God and If I Pray. Kathleen Wiegner. MMD

Yes! let the rich deride, the proud disdain. Goldsmith. *Fr.* The Deserted Village. OBSV

Yes, look at me; I am the mask it wears. The Mask the Wearer of the Mask Wears. William Bronk. GP

Yes Miss/ Put up your pretty little mouth for a kiss. Admonition to the Muse. Geoffrey Taylor. FaBoEE

Yes, my friend/ hurry to the candle flame. Life Dance. Jim Farrar. DNGG

Yes! my Lesbia! let us prove. Catullus, *tr. fr. Latin by* Walter Savage Landor. OBVE

Yes, my soul takes pleasure in shattering its chains. God. Alphonse de Lamartine. ILwL

Yes, our faces are ten blanks. The Hands. Daniel David Moses. AMV-80

Yes solid mountain mingle in my brain. Solid Mountain. George Bowering. NeAC

Yes. Such were the eyes through which in rage and pain. Aunt Lucrezia. Alistair Campbell. ATNZ

Yes, the Agency Can Handle That. Kenneth Fearing. WeW

Yes, the candidate's a dodger. The Dodger. *Unknown.* AmFP; GBP

Yes, the Secret Mind Whispers. Al Young. PoBA

"Yes, the Town Clerk will see you." In I went. The Town Clerk's Views. John Betjeman. CMoP (1970 ed.)

Yes, theyll let you play. A Poem for Players. Al Young. GP

Yes, this is where I stood that day. Ballad of Hector in Hades. Edwin Muir. NoAM; NOBE

Yes, this was my husband, I. Four Years After. Patricia Beer. HeHu

Yes, thou art gone! and never more. A Reminiscence. Anne Brontë. WPE

Yes: though the brine may from the desert deep. Frederick Goddard Tuckerman. Sonnets, II, iii. HAP

Yes, we did a heap o'riggin'. Old Ship Riggers. H. A. Cody. RhR

Yes, we were happy that Sunday, walking. Lisel Mueller. GP

Yes, we were looking at each other. Looking at Each Other. Muriel Rukeyser. NNaP

Yes, we'll rally 'round the flag, boys, we'll rally once again. The Battle-Cry of Freedom. George Frederick Root. BTTM; PSoN

Yes; when the ways oppose. Ars Victrix. Austin Dobson. VLP

Yes, yes/it's time. My Spring Thing. Everett Hoagland. BPo

Yes, yes, I grant the sons of earth. The Question. James Beattie. FaBoCo

Yes you have said enough for the time being. The End Is near the Beginning. David Gascoyne. EAS

Yes you never miss your water water water. You Never Miss the Water. *Unknown.* BluL

Yes, yours, my love, is the right human face. The Confirmation. Edwin Muir. SLP

Yesterday. Fran Winant. MMD

Yesterday a shark was reported cruising. With the Nuns at Cape May Point. David Earle Anderson. AMV-81

Yesterday, at the Sessions held in Buckingham. A Case at Sessions. Walter Savage Landor. OBSV

Yesterday I bought a penny fiddle. The Penny Fiddle. Robert Graves. ECBV

Yesterday I fancied I was young. Ho Nansorhon, *tr. by* Peter H. Lee. *Fr.* A Woman's Sorrow. PBWP

Yesterday I found one left. The Survivor. R. S. Thomas. FaBoTw (1975 ed.)

Yesterday I knew no lullaby. Child of Our Time. Eavan Boland. CIP

Yesterday I stood on the balcony. Not Often. Ray Fraser. NeAC

Yesterday I wanted to. For Love. Robert Creeley. ConAP; NOBA; PiAm

Yesterday I was/ given flowers. Anthology Poem. Petra von Morstein, *tr. by* Rosemarie Waldrop. BoWoP

Yesterday I was told. Byron vs. DiMaggio. Peter Meinke. LiSp; SPo

Yesterday I went to pick up the sack. Sunday. Cinda Kornblum. AcAn

Yesterday in drizzling rain. A Tailor Called Sorrow. Betti Alver, *tr. by* Willis Barnstone *and* Felix Oinas. BoWoP

Yesterday Rebecca Mason. Truth the Best. Elizabeth Turner. OxBChV

Yesterday, sitting. Just. Judith Johnson Sherwin. TAP

Yesterday upon the stair. The Man Who Wasn't There. Brian Lee. FPB

Yesterday's December rain. White Ropes. Franklin Brainard. HeS

Yesterday's Illusion; or, Remembering the Thirties. Alun Llywelyn-Williams, *tr. fr. Welsh by* R. Gerallt Jones. OBW

Yet. Richard Hoffman. UsP

Yet another great truth I record in my verse. The Viper. Hilaire Belloc. FaBoNo

Yet Another Poem about a Dying Child. Janet Frame. ATNZ

"Yet Chloe [or Cloe] sure was formed without a spot." Chloe. Pope. *Fr.* Moral Essays. NOBE; OBSV

Yet Do I Marvel. Countee Cullen. AmNP (1974 ed.); BPo; FF; ILP (1975 ed.); IPWM; LFH; NoAM; PBMP; PoBA; SoS; SS; TAP

Yet Gentle Will the Griffin Be. Vachel Lindsay. ECBV; Moon

Yet I courbed on my knees and cried hire of grace. William Langland. *Fr.* The Vision of Piers Plowman, II. EBEV

Yet if His Majesty, our sovereign lord. Preparations. *Unknown.* NOBE; PoPle

Yet is God a curteis lord. A Warning to Beware. *Unknown.* OxBM

Yet it was plain she struggled, and that salt. Modern Love, VIII. George Meredith. LoAs

Yet, love, mere love, is beautiful indeed. Sonnets from the Portuguese, X. Elizabeth Barrett Browning. VLP

Yet Nature, where the thunder leaves its trace. Frederick Goddard Tuckerman. *Fr.* Sonnets. AmVN

Yet on the other side, faine would he start. Giovanni Battista Marino, *tr. by* Richard Crashaw. *Fr.* The Massacre of the Innocents. OBVE

Yet once more, O ye laurels, and once more. Lycidas. Milton. AnMo; BiP; CABA (1972 ed.); EBEV; Epi; ExPo (1973 ed.); HAP; ILP (1975 ed.); InPK; InPS; LFH; NIL; NOBE; OAEL-1; OBP; PAIC; PPoD; PPoe; PPP; SCP-1; UnPo (1976 ed.); WeW

Yet Ostia boasts of her regeneration. Daniel DeFoe. *Fr.* Reformation of Manners. OBSV

Yet shall my soule in silence still. Bible, *O.T.*, paraphrased by Countess of Pembroke. Psalms, LXII. PBWP

Yet there is no great problem in the world today. "Hugh MacDiarmid." *Fr.* Lament for the Great Music. OxBTC

Yet wear we on; the deep light disallowed. Frederick Goddard Tuckerman. *Fr.* Sonnets. AmVN

Yet what are all such gaieties to me. "Lewis Carroll." VLP

Yet, when I muse on what life is, I seem.  To a Republican Friend: Continued.  Matthew Arnold.  VLP

Yet, yet a moment, one dim ray of light.  Pope.  The Dunciad, IV.  OAEL-1

Yetzer ha Ra.  Edward Codish.  VWA

Yevtushenko!  Paul Foreman.  CPA

Yew-Tree, The.  *Unknown, tr. fr. Welsh by* Geoffrey Grigson.  GBL

Yew Trees.  Wordsworth.  CABA (1972 ed.); UnPo (1976 ed.)

Yew's black fingers wag, The.  Little Fugue.  Sylvia Plath.  ILP (1975 ed.)

Y'heave ho! my lads, the wind blows free.  Sailing Sailing.  Godfrey Marks.  FSW

Yiddish.  Judith Herzberg, *tr. fr. Dutch by* Shirley Kaufman.  VWA

Yiddish.  Abraham Sutskever, *tr. fr. Yiddish by* Seymour Levitan.  VWA

Yiddish Poet.  A. C. Jacobs.  VWA

Yiddish poet.  Move On, Yiddish Poet.  Jacob Glatstein, *tr. by* Ruth Whitman.  VWA

Yield.  Ronald Gross.  InPK

Yield Not to Temptation, *with music.*  Horatio R. Palmer.  BLSH

Yielding.  Shellie Keir Robbins.  AMV-80

Yillow, yillow, yillow.  Metamorphosis.  Wallace Stevens.  InPK; VGW

Yin and Yang.  Kenneth Rexroth.  MIT; MPA

Yin and yang, they say.  Night Fight.  Marge Piercy.  PCho

Yippee! she is shooting in the harbor! he is jumping.  Blocks.  Frank O'Hara.  EAS

Yiya wo!/ This land of the Baca.  Was It All Worth While?  *Zulu Oral Tradition, tr. by* H. Tracey.  WTO

Y'know/ even a cantaloupe has a cunt.  Composition.  Cathleen Quirk.  MMD

Yo/ smile.  Poem.  Sonia Sanchez.  WBN

Yogi, don't go away.  Mirabai, *tr. fr. Hindi by* Willis Barnstone *and* Usha Nilsson.  BoWoP

Yoke Soft and Dear, *with music.*  John C. Kunze.  AH

Yoke uneasy on the ox doth sit, The.  Philip Ayres.  FaBoEE

Yolanthe.  Dan Kenney.  MIT

Yom Kippur.  Chana Bloch.  VWA

Yom Kippur.  Eric Chaet.  VWA

Yom Kippur.  Lucille Day.  VWA

Yom Kippur.  Linda Pastan.  VWA

Yom Kippur: Fasting.  Ruth Whitman.  OFD

Yomi, Yomi.  *Tr. fr. Yiddish.*  FSW

Yon spark's a poet, by my troth!  The Difference.  Tadhg Dall O'Huiginn, *tr. by* Robin Flower.  BIrV

Yonder.  Richard Eberhart.  GOA

Yonder comes my baby all dressed in blue.  Cocaine Blues.  *Unknown.*  FSW

Yonder comes the dawn.  Uru-tu-sendo's Song.  *Tr. fr. Tewa Indian by* H. J. Spinden.  WTO

Yonder see the morning blink.  A. E. Housman.  CMoP (1970 ed.)

Yonder stands a pretty fair maiden.  No, Sir, No.  *Unknown.*  AmFP

Yonder they are coming.  It Is Mine, This Country Wide.  *Unknown.*  GOA

Yonder, yonder see the fair rainbow.  The Rainbow.  *Tr. fr. Hopi Indian by* Natalie Curtis.  WTO

York Harbor Morning.  George Garrett.  CSP

Yorunomado sat in.  The Black Hat.  Clayton Eshleman.  VGW

You.  Carroll Arnett.  VoR

You, *sels.*  Tom Clark.  EAS
  "Chords knotted together like insane nouns," IV
  "Door behind me was you, The," I.

"Today I get this letter from you and the sun," III.

"You are bright, tremendous, wow," II.

You.  Kenneth Rexroth.  *Fr.* A Bestiary.  HoPM (1975 ed.)

You.  John Tagliabue.  GP

You/ my bell-clapper.  Christmas Mass for a Little Atheist Jesus.  Claude Maillard, *tr. by* Maxine *and* Judith Kumin.  BoWoP

You/ Refuse to see.  Out.  Riots and Rituals.  Richard W. Thomas.  PoBA

You a man, man, man, who knows the other word.  Compozishun—to James Herndon and Others.  Ronald J. Goba.  NCSH

You Again.  Beth Bentley.  CNW

You again.  The ecstatic posture.  The victory symbol.  Memoir.  Roger Weingarten.  AMV-80

You agree/ With me.  A Question.  William Cole.  BoAnP

You ain't part Indian.  Wake-up Niggers.  Don L. Lee.  PoBA

You All Know the Story of the Other Woman.  Anne Sexton.  InPK

You Also, Gaius Valerius Catullus.  Archibald MacLeish.  NoAM; TAP

You also, our first great.  To Whistler, American.  Ezra Pound.  PoA

You always know what to expect.  The Country House.  Louis Simpson.  NOBA

You always read about it.  Cinderella.  Anne Sexton.  Psy

You and the woman under you.  Winging It.  Jack Myers.  PCho

You, Andrew Marvell.  Archibald MacLeish.  CMoP (1970 ed.); HAP; HeIP; HoPM (1975 ed.); NoAM; NOBA; PiAm; PoIA; PPP; SoSe; VoPo; WeW

You approach me carrying a book.  Superballs.  Tom Clark.  EAS

Your are/ Getting free.  Thoughts for You (When She Came back from the Mountains).  Ranice Henderson Crosby.  NMM

You are a beggar.  Bonner's Ferry Beggar.  Duane Clark.  AMV-81

You are a hard-boiled egg.  Me?  Lump.  Robert Phillips.  AMV-80

You are a landscape in the Tale of Terror.  For Cora Lightbody, R.N.  John Glassco.  PoA

You are a man, the artist gazing out at the mirror.  Pablo Anytime.  John Sjoberg.  AcAn

You Are a Part of Me.  Frank Yerby.  AmNP (1974 ed.)

You are a stool pigeon and.  Kenneth Rexroth, *after the Latin of* Martial.  NNaP

You are a tulip seen today.  A Meditation for His Mistress.  Robert Herrick.  CaPo; NOBE

You are all these people.  To a Single Shadow without Pity.  Sam Cornish.  PoBA

You Are Alms.  James W. Thompson.  PoBA

You are already/ asleep.  Touch.  Thomas Gunn.  CMoP (1970 ed.); LoAs; MPo; TPo

You are already flying away.  Business Trips.  Laurie Taylor.  AMV-80

You are barely able to walk.  But What I'm Trying to Say Mother Is.  Ai.  CAAP

You are beginning to look like a book.  To the Lawyer from His Only Lately Neglected Tort.  Carol Stager.  PoW

You are bright, tremendous, wow.  You, II.  Tom Clark.  EAS

You are carrying me, full consciousness, god that has desires.  Full Consciousness.  Juan Ramón Jiménez, *tr. by* Robert Bly.  NU

You are coming to me in the rain.  Rodney Hall.  *Fr.* The Owner of My Face.  CAAP

You are coming toward us.  Aunt Laura Moves toward the Open Grave of Her Father.  Joseph De Roche.  HeIP

You are coming very slowly, why do you delay. My Cobra Girl. *Gond Oral Tradition, tr. by* V. Elwin *and* S. Hivale. WTO

You are curious, you wish. Fishbowl. Margaret Atwood. MMD

You are disdainful and magnificent. Sonnet to a Negro in Harlem. Helene Johnson. AmNP (1974 ed.); NIL

You are falling asleep and I sit looking at you. After Dark. Adrienne Rich. VGW

You Are Growing into My Life. Louise Harris. AMV–81

You Are Happy. Margaret Atwood. MMD

You are here now. The Sleeping Fury. Louise Bogan. IHMS; RiTi

You are horizontal. Footpaths Cross in the Rice Field. "Lin Ling," *tr. by* Kenneth Rexroth *and* Ling Chung. PBWP

You are leaving. Cherbourg Airport. Katherine Edgar Cobey. PoUp

You are less than one-half. The Speaker. Charles Ballard. VoR

You are like a sun of the tropics. Luxury. Donald Justice. HeIP

You are like a whispering branch. Metaphors. Miklós Radnóti, *tr. by* Steven Polgar *and* Stephen Berg *and* S. J. Marks. VWA

You are looking now on old Tom Moore. The Days of 'Forty-nine. *Unknown.* BPAW

You are lying, O missionary! Raymond Mazisi Kunene, *tr. fr. Zulu by* D. K. Rycroft. WTO

You are made of a stone hard as its name is. Tiki. Forrest Anderson. AATT

You are made of almost nothing. The Dragonfly. Louise Bogan. HeIP; NIL

You are missing the straw hat. Skid Row Safari. Elisabeth Murawski. PoUp

You Are More than I Need. Rebbekka Kaplan. AMV–80

You are my friend. Lorine Niedecker. VGW

You are, my green island. Neither This nor That. Luis Palés Matos, *tr. by* Julio Marzán. InW

You are my shadow in the picture. Lines for Michael in the Picture. John Logan. CAPP

You are naked and have no clothes. Your Presence. Mordecai Temkin *tr. by* Jeremy Garber. VWA

You are not here! the quaint witch Memory sees. To Maria Gisborne in England, from Italy. Shelley. *Fr.* Letter to Maria Gisborne. NOBE

You are not looked for through the smog. To the Moon. Babette Deutsch. Moon

You are not merry, brother. Why not laugh. The Prodigal Son E. A. Robinson. LFH

You are not nearer God than we. Annunciation. Rainer Maria Rilke, *tr. by* James Blair Leishman. OBVE

You are not wanted. Periphery. Ruth Stone. GP

You are now/ In London, that great sea, whose ebb and flow. Shelley. *Fr.* Letter to Maria Gisborne. EBEV

"You are old, Father William," the young man cried. The Old Man's Comforts and How He Gained Them. Robert Southey. HoPM (1975 ed.); OxBChV; SpRo; UnPo (1976 ed.)

"You are old, Father William," the young man said. Father William. "Lewis Carroll." *Fr.* Alice's Adventure's in Wonderland. BiP; FaBoCo; FaBoNo; HoPM (1975 ed.); NOBL; OxBChV; SpRo; SS; TVo; UnPo (1976 ed.)

You are polishing me like old wood. Marriage Amulet. Nancy Willard. RiTi

You are right. In dreams I might well dance. Possession. Marie Ponsot. VGW

You are right. What we call Poetry is the boat. A New Poem. Robert Duncan. NNaP

You are rumpled like a sweater. Nothing More Will Happen [*or* Different Persuasions]. Marge Piercy. InPK; NeAC

You are small and intense. To a Child Running with Outstretched Arms in Canyon de Chelly. N. Scott Momaday. CDW

You are so beautifully thin and naive. Dear Patty, Dear Tania. Richard Mathews. GP

You are so small, I. Miss Cho Composes in the Cafeteria. James Tate. WeW

You are so witty, profligate, and thin. Epigram on Voltaire. Edward Young. FaBoCo

You Are the Brave. Raymond R. Patterson. NIL; PoBA

You are the cause of this destruction, Lesbia. Catullus, *tr. fr. Latin by* Horace Gregory. NAWM–1

You are the grain. I Think of Housman Who Said the Poem Is a Morbid Secretion, like a Pearl. Judith Kroll. UnPo (1976 ed.)

You are the mask I was given. Face. Richard Shelton. PCho

You are the problem I propose. The Metaphysical Amorist. J. V. Cunningham. VGW

You are the star. Afternoon at the Movies. Jim Mulac. AcAn

You are the town and we are the clock. Chorus. W. H. Auden. *Fr.* The Dog beneath the Skin. OxBTC

You are the woman. Jennifer. Howard McCord. FoP

You are tired. The Midnight Tennis Match. Thomas Lux. AmPA

You are what you eat and I. Cheerios. Peter Meinke. GP

"You are wise, Mr. Dodgson," the young child said. Lewis Carroll. Eleanor Farjeon. OxBChV

You are with me this evening, all my friends. Evening in the Walls. Jean Wahl, *tr. by* Charles Guenther. VWA

You are wrong about the crocus. Crocus. Joan Murray. AMV–80

You aren't a sun. To the Young Poets, Except Children, Who Haven't Earned the Title. James Humphrey. FoP

You arrive in Paradise feverish with anticipation, assuring. Home. Steve Kowit. AMV–81

You ask how old am I. Twice Times Then Is Now. Ibn Hazm Al-Andalusi, *tr. by* Omar Pound. OBVE

You ask me. To Madame A. V. Pletneff. Karolina Pavlova, *tr. by* Paul Schmidt. PBWP

You ask me for a song, folks. Cousin Jack Song. *At. to* Charley Tregonning. AmFP

You ask me, Lydia, "whether I." To "Lydia Languish." Austin Dobson. VLP

You ask me to sing, so I'll sing you a song. The Cranberry Song. Barney Reynolds. AmFP

You Ask Me, Why, though Ill at Ease. Tennyson. CABA (1972 ed.); ILP (1975 ed.); VLP

You ask what I have found, and far and wide I go. The Curse of Cromwell. W. B. Yeats. BIrV

You ask why gold and velvet bind. On a New Duke. *Unknown.* FaBoEE

You asked for green pepper. Coplas. *Tr. fr. Spanish.* FSW

You asked me. Wealth. Tony Moreno. NW

You asked me to enter the holy cloister. Banishment from Ur. Enheduanna, *tr. fr. Sumerian.* BoWoP

You asked what. The Hosts. W. S. Merwin. GP; PHC

You beat your pate, and fancy wit will come. Pope. FaBoEE; PoPle

You better come on in my kitchen. Come On in My Kitchen. *Unknown.* BluL

You better learn how to treat everybody. You Got to Go Down. *Unknown.* BluL

You better sure shall live, not evermore. Horace, *tr. fr. Latin by* Sir Philip Sidney. Odes, II, 10. OBVE

You black out the sun. Ed Roberson. *Fr.* When Thy King Is a Boy. PoBA

You black-maned, horse-haired, long-faced creature. To the Gentlewoman of Llanarth Hall. Evan Thomas, *tr. by* Gwyn Jones. OBW

You blame me that I do not write. Letter to a Friend. Jon Stallworthy. NoAM

You brave heroic minds. To the Virginian Voyage. Michael Drayton. Epi; HAP; ILP (1975 ed.); NOBE

You bring me good news from the clinic. Face Lift. Sylvia Plath. InPK; PPoD

You brought me bdellium and onyx, stones. Your Light. Ann Lee. AMV–80

You build it where you will be heard only by chance. The Cabin North of It All. James McMichael. AmPA

You built the new Court House, Spoon River. Benjamin Franklin Hazard. Edgar Lee Masters. *Fr.* The New Spoon River. GOA

You burst into the world with smiles wide as April. Sleeping with Foxes. Roberta Hill. CDW

You call collect from New York. Long Distance. Patrick L. Clary. PoUp

You call it fate? Comment against Lamp Post. Langston Hughes. ILP (1975 ed.)

You called yourself a dishwater blonde. What You Waited For. Marge Piercy. MMD

You came/ nourished by/ seaweed and moss. Dinosaur. Bonnie Hearn. AMV–80

You came. And you did well to come. Sappho, *tr fr. Greek by* Willis Barnstone. BoWoP

You came in out of the night. Francesca. Ezra Pound. PSN; UsP

You came out of pity for my empty mouth. Song for the Skull of Black Bear. David Wagoner. BCr

You came with your sorrows drifting through your eyes. July. W. Ralph Johnson. AMV–81

You Can Dig My Grave. *Unknown.* FSW

You can find them anywhere. The Hard Core. D. J. Enright. HeHu

You Can Get Despondent. Maurice Careme, *tr. fr. French by* Norma Farber. AMV–81

You can go back in a clap of blue metal. Southbound. Betty Adcock. CSP

You can go in the stall. Unclaimed. Florida Watts Smyth. PH

You can have daughters, sons. Inventing a Family. Dennis Saleh. *Fr.* A Guide to Familiar American Incest. NeAC

You Can Have It. Philip Levine. BrS

You can look into my face. Poem. Mike Todachine. CTBA

You can make a tidy leaf-pot out of sarai leaves. A Man's Need. *Gond Oral Tradition, tr. by* V. Elwin *and* S. Hivale. WTO

You can make castles of it, construct. Sand. Charles Higham. LP

You can, of course. The Rock. Mary Fabilli. AMV–81

You can only have a lot of power. To Summer. Alan Nadel. AMV–80

You can read it in the morning paper. We Need a Whole Lot More of Jesus. *Unknown.* FSW

You can read my letter now sure don't know my mind. Ham Hound Crave. *Unknown.* BluL

You can say anything. The Art of Poetry. Dennis Trudell. NowV

You can see the beach and the waves, you can see the sky. Eight Miles South of Grand Haven. Dave Kelly. AMV–80

You can see the derrick there. Hay Derrick. John S. Harris. MPA

You can send for my breakfast now, Governor. The Ballad of Jimmy Governor. Les A. Murray. GAS

You can take a tub with a rub and a scrub in a two-foot tank of tin. Pater's Bathe. Edward Abbott Parry. OxBChV

You can take away my mother. Umbilical. Eve Merriam. CTBA

"You can talk about yer sheep dorgs." Daley's Dorg Wattle. W. T Goodge. GDP

You can talk about your farms and your Chinaman's charms. The Cowboy's Life Is a Very Dreary Life. *Unknown.* AmFP

You can tear a grey hair out of your head. Sacco-Vanzetti. Moishe Leib Halpern, *tr. by* David G. Roskies *and* Hillel Schwartz. VWA

You cannot from the open window invade. The Crow. Rita Boumi-Pappás, *tr. by* Kimon Friar. PBWP

You Cannot Go Down to the Spring. John Shaw Neilson. MAuV

You cannot hope. Humbert Wolfe. FaBoEE; OxBTC

You cannot leave. Alma Villanueva. NW

You cannot picture the inspired love. Crimes They Got Away With. Harrison Fisher. PoUp

You cannot talk of violence. Revolutionary. James P. Friel. AMV–81

You can't breathe, the hard earth wriggles with worms. Concert at the Station. Osip Mandelstam, *tr. by* Andrew Glaze. AMV–81; VWA

You can't fight God. Advice. Horace Gregory. SPT

You can't keep it, I say. Civilizing the Child. Lisel Mueller. CTBA

You Can't Keep No Brown. *Unknown.* BluL

"You can't race me," said Johnny the Hare. The Hare and the Tortoise. Ian Serraillier. SO

You captains brave and bold, hear our cries, hear our cries. Captain [Robert] Kidd. *Unknown.* AmFP; PeBB

You come/ in ancestral wisdom. On the Naming Day. Jewel C Latimore. CNA

You come forth/ the color of a stone cliff. To Insure Survival. Simon J. Ortiz. CDW

You come from some other forest. Little Horse. W. S. Merwin. TH

You come home. Displacement. Alan Ziegler. AAN

You come to fetch me from my work tonight. Putting in the Seed. Robert Frost. NoAM

You could be sitting now in a carrel. A Late Aubade. Richard Wilbur. PAIC; SoSe

You could draw a straight line from the heels. Man Lying on a Wall. Michael Longley. CIP

You could not say, "What now?" you said, "Too late!" Letter to a Jealous Friend. James Simmons. CIP

You could not stop the snow the sky dumped down. Lines for a President. Robert Watson. PPoD

You could smell the river. For E. C. J. Emmett Jarrett. NeAC

You couldn't bear to grow old, but we grow old. John Berryman. *Fr.* Dream Songs. TAP

You couldn't pack a Broadwood half a mile. The Song of the Banjo. Kipling. VLP

You cut my passion back like a hedge, gardener. Tirade. Honor Moore. WBN

You dare not tell me. A Childless Witch. Raquel Chalfi, *tr. by* Alexandra Meiri *and* Myra Glazer Schotz. VWA

You darling girls of Bagaduce, who live along the shore. The Schooner *Fred Dunbar*. Amos Hanson. AmFP

You decant his blood out. Heart Surgery. E. Mitter. PMW

You deny me: and to what end? To His Mistress. Asclepiades, *tr. by* Dudley Fitts. NIL

You did late review my lays. To Christopher North. Tennyson. FaBoEE

You did not come. A Broken Appointment. Thomas Hardy. BiP; GBL; LoAs; NoAM

You did not see Him on the mountain of Transfiguration. To the Good Thief. Saunders Lewis, *tr by* Gwyn Thomas. OBW

You did not see wood made pliable by rot, or rust-devoured iron. To a Proud Old Woman Watching the Tearing Down of The Hurricane Shed. Kay Boyle. MIT

You did not suck at my mother's breasts. Lament. Yonathan Ratosh, *tr. by* Howard Schwartz. VWA

You did not walk with me. The Walk. Thomas Hardy. CMoP (1970 ed.); PSN

You died nine years ago today. February 11, 1977. Frederick Morgan. AMV-80

You do not do, you do not do. Daddy. Sylvia Plath. AnMo; BiP; BoWoP; CAPP; CMoP (1970 ed.); ExPo (1973 ed.); InPK; InPS; NMM; NoAM; NOBA; PiAm; Psy; RiTi; TPo; UnPo (1976 ed.)

You Do Not Have to Love Me. Leonard Cohen. NoAM

You do not know how beautiful you are. Ode to A Beautiful Woman. Carl Clark. JB

You do not move about, but try. Getting Lost in Nazi Germany. Marvin Bell. VWA

You do not want for words. Wantword. Chrles Brasch. ATNZ

You Do Not Write. Manfred Jurgensen. FPA

You, Doctor Martin. Anne Sexton. ILP (1975 ed.); Psy

You don't find him in crowds. The Man Who Closes Himself. Peter Cooley. NVAP

You don't know I pretend my dumb. Plea to Those Who Matter. James Welch. AmPA; SA

You drag by the knees before. Jogging. Gary Stein. AMV-81

You dreamed up a bottomless lake down South. Love is Loathing & Why. Dan Ford. AMV-81

You drive down Main Street. Tourist Guide: How You Can Tell for Sure When You're in South Dakota. Jim Heynen. GP; PoW

You drop a pearl, 'twill keep its hue. *Malay Oral Tradition, tr. by* R. J. Wilkinson *and* R. O. Winstedt. WTO

You drop apprehensively—the sun gone out. David Jones. *Fr.* In Parenthesis. TwMBP

You dynamiting the structure of our loves. Theory of Flight. Muriel Rukeyser. SPT

You earthly souls that court a wanton flame. La Belle Confidante. Thomas Stanley. SCP-2

You enter the areas beyond veiled light. Sleep Watch. Lance Henson. VoR

You enter the garden and do not recognize it. Eden. Lev Mak, *tr. by* Daniel Weissbort. VWA

You fall silent; I set my jaw. Black Hole in Space. Heddy Reid. PoUp

You, Farrell O'Reilly, I feared as a boy. Farrell O'Reilly. Oliver St. John Gogarty. OxBTC

You fawnes and silvans, when my Chloris brings. William Smith. Choris, V. ESo

You feel heavy and sad as though. Gregory Orr. *Fr.* Domestic Life. OSP

You fiends and furies, come along! Sir William Davenant. *Fr.* The Unfortunate Lovers. SCP-2

You fit into me. Margaret Atwood. POL

You flee their igloos. Husbands. Virginia R. Terris. AAN

You float up beneath my fingers. Darkroom. Gary Stein. PoUp

You follow, dress held high above. Fishing with My Daughter in Miller's Meadow. Lucien Stryk. GP

You fool yourself and live a crazy day. Voice of a Dissipated Woman inside a Tomb. Sor Violante do Céu, *tr. by* Willis Barnstonc. BoWoP

You gallop/ and the wind runs. Black Stallion. Michael Small. DNGG

You gaze at me teasingly through the window. Praxilla, *tr. fr. Greek by* Willis Barnstone. BoWoP

You, Genoese Mariner. W. S. Merwin. GOA

You gentleman and I up from the grime. December 24 and George McBride Is Dead. Richard Hugo. HoPM (1975 ed.)

You gentlemen of England far and near. The Wind Sou'west. *Unknown.* AmFP

You gentlemen of England who live at home at ease. The Bay of Biscay. *Unknown.* AmFP

You get a line and I'll get a pole, honey. Crawdad. *Unknown.* FSW

"You Get the Groceries, I'll Guard the Crib." Dennis Trudell. NVAP

You get to Gilead, let me know. Go Ahead; Goodbye; Good Luck; and Watch Out. William Bronk. GP

You Get Used to It. Adrian Mitchell. NowV

You girls who were seeking. Girls. Pablo Neruda, *tr. by* Donald D. Walsh. OLR

You glisten from the dreams. Train Window. Frank Stewart. PHC

You go away. Venus' Return to the Sea. Gene Fowler. CPA

You go outside. Sunday Night. Alan Ziegler. AAN

You go the barber. Machismo. Martin Steingesser. AAN

You Got Parole. Dana "The Mouse" Merkel. DNGG

You Got to Go Down. *Unknown.* BluL

You Got to Love Her with a Feeling. *Unknown.* BluL

You got to walk that lonesome valley. Lonesome Valley. *Unknown.* FSW

You Gotta Go Down (and Join the Union). *Unknown.* FSW

You Gotta Have Your Tips on Fire. Víctor Hernández Cruz. InW

You grinned/ "Come Mastah." Aah . . . You Ikenne Women. Mark Wangberg. TC

You grow up with music. The Second Violinist's Son. Debora Gregor. AMV-80

You had better hurry home. Hurry Home. Leonard Clark. FPB

You happen to get well. Elegy and Kaddish. David Rosenmann-Taub, *tr. by* Charles Guenther. VWA

You have a headache Rimbaud. Thoughts. John Sjoberg. AcAn

You have been good to me, I give you this. Idolatry. Arna Bontemps. AmNP (1974 ed.)

You have brought pearly beads. Pearly Beads. *Gond Oral Tradition, tr. by* V. Elwin *and* S. Hivale. WTO

You have come your way, I have come my way. Fronleichnam. D. H. Lawrence. GBL

You have consum'd my language, and my pen. Ovid, *tr. by* Henry Vaughan. De Ponto, Elegy III, 7. OBVE

You have gone through. Talks with Himself. Bruce Severy. HeS

You have granted me my full share of days. From the Crag. Mani Leib, *tr. by* David G. Roskies *and* Hillel Schwartz. VWA

You have heard, I suppose, of the man in the moon. The Coolie Chinee. Septimus Winner. OBAL

You have just come in the door. The Confession. Peter Cooley. AmPA

You have made a/ success. The Success. Kermit Coad. PHC

You have not heard my love's dark throat. A Song of Praise. Countee Cullen. BiP

You have only to wait, they will find you. Messengers. Louise Glück. CAAP

You have seen them. Above the freeways. Girls Who Wave at Cars from Bridges. Harold Bond. NVAP

You have so much to give they said. He Who Remains. Richard Shelton. MPA

You have spoken your holy command over the city. Inanna and the City of Uruk. Enheduanna, *tr. fr. Sumerian.* BoWoP

You have taken our love and turned it into coins of silver. A Poet's Wife. Amy Lowell. RiTi

You have the ingredients on hand. Recipe for an Ocean in the Absence of the Sea. Richard Howard. TAP

You have to be brainy, not drippy. Spell It. *Unknown.* TDH

You have to be depraved to go at all. At the Spa. James H. Bowden. AMV-81

You have to be quick to stamp out your own shadow. The Shadowless Man. Gordon Challis. ATNZ

You have your shadow. Your Shadow. Mark Strand. *Fr.* Elegy for My Father. Prf

You headlong hippogriff who match the gale. Life Is a Dream. Pedro Calderón de la Barca, *tr. by* Roy Campbell. NAWM-1

You held my lotus blossom. To the Tune "Soaring Clouds." Huang O, *tr. by* Kenneth Rexroth *and* Ling Chung. BoWoP; PBWP

You Held the Air. Stephen Tudor. HeS

You Hide ("You hide in the ostrich egg"). Edith Bruck, *tr. fr. Italian by* Ruth Feldman *and* Brian Swann. BoWoP

You, hiding there in your words. The Book. Adrienne Rich. RiTi

You hold me now completely in your hands. The Woman Poet. Gertrud Kolmar, *tr. by* Henry A. Smith. VWA

You hold up your photograph. Photographs. William Peskett. AMV-81

You hold your eager head. To a Romantic. Allen Tate. PiAm

You, husband, lying next to. Prowling the Ridge. Judith Minty. TC

You imagined the lover I will never be I am. Marie Harris. *Fr.* Interstate. AAN

You in Anger. James Reeves. OxBTC

"You inspire me," you said. Goat Dance. Ron Loewinsohn. GP

You intimidated me. I was thrown into hell without a trial. Denouement. Ruth Stone. BoWoP

You jam your arm into the white air. Poem. Mira Fish. FAF

You Jump First. Pedro Juan Pietri. InW

You keep eating and raising a family. A Suite for Marriage. David Ignatow. NNaP

You keep me waiting in a truck. Twenty Year Marriage. Ai. BoWoP; CAAP; GP

You kissed her, and I watched you for a moment. Metamorphoses. Vassar Miller. RiTi

You Know. Jean Garrigue. UnPo (1976 ed.)

You know. Eddie and Eve. Charles Bukowski. GP

You know, he didn't teach me any thing. Mark Van Doren. James Worley. AMV-81

You know her hustle. Asking for Ruthie. Judy Grahn. GP; NMM

You know him do you. Tunnel Blaster on Bear and Brotherhood. John Knoepfle. BCr

You know I said to Mark that I'm furious at you. The Quarrel. Diane DiPrima. NMM; RiTi

You know, I see, that four score years and ten. Exceptional. Thelma Lewis. AMV-80

You know it's April by the falling-off. B Negative. X. J. Kennedy. ConAP; WeW

You know me. Hypocrite. Ann M. Craig. PPoD

You know my secrets. Encounter. Dorothy Livesay. AMV-81

You know now mama. Alley Blues. *Unknown.* BluL

You know, or you don't know, that great Bacon saith. Byron. *Fr.* Don Juan. NOBL

"You know Orion always comes up sideways." The Star-Splitter. Robert Frost. PAIC

You know, she said, they made you. A Dress of Fire. Dahlia Ravikovitch, *tr. by* Chana Bloch. VWA

You know, sweetheart. A Letter. Rachel Korn, *tr. by* Ruth Whitman. VWA

You know the fellow. A Public Nuisance. Reginald Arkell. LiSp

You know the place: then. Sappho, *tr. fr. Greek by* Mary Barnard. PBWP

You know the records. They are there to read. Willie Mays. Paul Ramsey. PPoD

You know there is not much. To a Friend Concerning Several Ladies. William Carlos Williams. VGW

You know this dream. You move. The Owl. David Young. CAAP

You know those rose sherbets. You Know. Jean Garrigue. UnPo (1976 ed.)

You know those windless summer evenings, swollen to stasis. Cigales. Richard Wilbur. NoAM; NOBA

You know, we French stormed Ratisbon. Incident of the French Camp. Robert Browning. AKE; BTTM; FaPo; FaPoR; TT

You know what it is to be born alone. Baby Tortoise. D. H. Lawrence. BoAnP; CMoP (1970 ed.)

You landsmen and you seamen bold. The Loss of the *Due Dispatch. Unknown.* AmFP

You lay in wait. Sappho, *tr. fr. Greek by* Willis Barnstone. BoWoP

You let the door sway open on its hinges. A Figure of Plain Force. Michael Heffernan. HeS

You, Letting the Trees Stand as My Betrayer. Diane Wakoski. NoAM

You lie asleep on your back. Holy, Holy, Holy. Lawrence Russ. TC

You lie cooling and sleeping, the heat. Picture of Workers Resting. Patricia Beer. HeHu

You lie in my arms. Apocrypha. Stanley Moss. VWA

You lie in this Pittsburgh room. Pittsburgh. Peggy Ruse. NPW

You lie now in many coffins. For Malcolm: After Mecca. Gerald W. Barrax. CNA; PoBA

You lie there, with your line of stiff red griffins. Museum Piece No. 16228. Elaine Watson. AMV-81

You like those images of snow that ask emotion. Snow. Hubert Witheford. ATNZ

You live here because there's no other place. So Long Solon. Jack Myers. AmPA

You lived and moved among the best society. W. H. Auden. *Fr.* Letter to Lord Byron. OBSV

You look as though/ You know me. The Moon Ground. James Dickey. Moon

You look at yourself in the mirror, nothing. Primary Numbers. Edvard Kocbek, *tr. by* Herbert Kuhner *and* Peter Kersche. AMV-81

You look for her. Even. Marina Rivera. FoP

You looked at me today. For My Daughter's 20th Birthday. Walter Lowenfels. RRA

You lousy bitch. Wild Woman's Resentment of Fakery. Rochelle Owens. RiTi

You, love, and I. Counting the Beats. Robert Graves. GBL; HAP; OxBTC; UsP; WeW

You love? That's high as you shall go. The Attainment. Coventry Patmore. *Fr.* The Angel in the House. FaBoEE

You loved me because I brought you sugar cubes. Timothy. Thomas James. HeS

You loved me not at all, but let it go. Edna St. Vincent Millay. VGW

You made me feel so young again. Copper-Beech and Butter-Fingers. Pearse Hutchinson. CIP

You making small talk to hide reality. Conversation. K. Malley. AMV-80

You marched off southward with the fire of twenty. Danny. Malcolm Cowley. PoA

You may brag about your breakfast foods you eat at break of day. Sausage. Edgar A. Guest. OBAL

You may have heard (she said) about a girl. Atalanta. Ovid, *tr. by* Rolfe Humphries. *Fr.* Metamorphoses. LiSp

You may never see rain, unless you see. A Dance for Rain. Witter Bynner. BPAW

You may not believe it. The Pumpkin. Robert Graves. CaYB

You may rock us, you may shock us. Frisco's Defi. A. S. Hooper. BPAW

You may search/ the ocean. Searching for the Desert Blues. *Unknown.* BluL

You may talk about me just as much as you please. Hold the Wind. *Unknown.* GBP

You may talk o' gin and beer. Gunga Din. Kipling. BTTM; PPM; VLP

You may talk of Columbus's sailing. "Are Ye Right There, Michael?" (A Lay of the Wild West Clare.) Percy French. WTO

You meaner beauties of the night. On His Mistress, the Queen of Bohemia [*or* Elizabeth of Bohemia]. Sir Henry Wotton. BoLoP; GBL; HAP; MetP; NOBE; PoPle

You meet your friend, your face. Selected Epigrams. Kassia, *tr. by* Patrick Diehl. PBWP

You might at one time, when you were young perhaps. K. O. Arvidson. *Fr.* The Flame Tree. ATNZ

You might have died so many kinds of death. An Elegy. Maurice Lindsay. MS

You Move Forward. Thomas Sessler, *tr. fr. German by* Herbert Kuhner. VWA

"You must be very old, Sir Giles." Old Love. William Morris. PeD; VLP

You must do as they do at Hoo. Hoo, Suffolk. *Unknown.* GBP

You Must Have Been a Sensational Baby, *sel.* Harold Norse. "Pair of muscular calves, A." GP

You must have been still sleeping, your wife there. The Sacred Hearth. David Gascoyne. FaBoTw (1975 ed.)

You must live through the time when everything hurts. The Double Shame. Stephen Spender. LoAs

You must never take your eyes off it. Commanding a Telephone to Ring. Jack Anderson. AMV-81

You must remain very much alone. Presences. Zoé Karélli, *tr. by* Kimon Friar. PBWP

You must remember. Circuit Breaker. Sid Gary. QQQ

You must remember structures beyond cotton plains. If Blood Is Black Then Spirit Neglects My Unborn Son. Conrad Kent Rivers. PoBA

You must stand erect but at your ease, a posture. The Singing Lesson. David Wagoner. MPA

You must take the speckled stone, the dead-tired stone. Stonetalk. Jacques Hamelin, *tr. by* Ria Leigh-Louhuizen. AMV-80

You must wake and call me early, call me early, mother dear. Tennyson. *Fr.* The May Queen. CC

You, my branch, my lopped limb! Tree to Flute. Anna Hajnal, *tr. by* Jascha Kessler. VWA

You Naughty, Naughty Men, *with music.* T. Kennick. BLSo

You need lightning. To the Man Who Sidled Up to Me and Asked: "How Long You in fer, Buddy?" Etheridge Knight. NeAC

You need not see what someone is doing. Sext. W. H. Auden. *Fr.* Horae Canonica. TCP

You never asked to be a master. Quotations from Charwoman Me. Robin Morgan. WBN

You never frightened me. December 1970. John Tagliabue. GP

You never know who has your memory. You Gotta Have Your Tips on Fire. Victor Hernández Cruz. InW

You Never Miss the Water. *Unknown.* BluL

You never saw my rib cage. I would lie next to you. Farewell Poems. Sandra Hochman. RiTi

You never touch. Yosano Akiko, *tr. fr. Japanese by* Geoffrey Bownas *and* Anthony Thwaite. BoWoP; PBWP

You Northern Girl. Charles G. Ballard. VoR; VW

You now solicit a few enemy thrusts. D. B. Wyndham Lewis. *Fr.* If So the Man You Are. OBSV

You, once a belle in Shreveport. Snapshots of a Daughter-in-Law. Adrienne Rich. NCSH; NIL; NMM

You only love/ when you love in vain. Ode to Joy. Miroslav Holub, *tr. by* Ian Milner *and* George Theiner. BuTh

You open and close your eyes. What We Have. Elizabeth Shinoda. PHC

You open the front door with your good hand. Making Yourself at Home. David James. TC

"You ought to have seen what I saw on my way." Blueberries. Robert Frost. STS

You ought to see my blue-eyed Sally. Stay All Night, Stay a Little Longer. *Unknown.* AmFP

You ought to see my Cindy. Cindy. *Unknown.* BLSo; FSW

You over there, young man with the guide-book. "Home, Sweet Home," with Variations. H. C. Bunner. OBAL

You, passing along the path, if you see this tomb. Epitaph on a Dog. *Unknown, tr. by* Forrest Reid. ECBV

You play the flute. Longing. *Gond Oral Tradition, tr. by* V. Elwin *and* S. Hivale. WTO

You possess the sturdy elegance of a cannon. For Natalya Correia. Irving Layton. NeAC

You praise the firm restraint with which they write. On Some South African Novelists. Roy Campbell. FaBoCo; FaBoEE; InPK; NOBL; OxBTC

You prayer—, you blasphemy, you. Plashes the Fountain. Paul Celan, *tr. by* Michael Hamburger. OBVE

You probably could put their names to them. "As When Emotion Too Far Exceeds Its Cause." Gloria C. Oden. AmNP (1974 ed.)

You promise heavens free from strife. Mimnermus in Church. William Johnson Cory. NOBE; VLP

You promised to meet me down by the spring. Deep Water. *Unknown.* FSW

You promised to send me some violets. Did you forget? Letter from Town: The Almond Tree. D. H. Lawrence. PAIC

You raise the ax. The Anniversary. Ai. CAAP; GP

You read the New York Times. Alfred Corning Clark. Robert Lowell. NoAM

You really can't count on the bastard. Russell Banks. *Fr.* The Poem of the Year of the Bear. BCr

You recommend that the motive, in Chapter 8. Yes, the Agency Can Handle That. Kenneth Fearing. WeW

You refuse to own. Margaret Atwood. NeAC

You remember that whitefaced actor. Mime. Dick Allen. AMV-81

You remember the name was Jensen. What Thou Lovest Well, Remains American. Richard Hugo. GP

You replaced the Douglas firs. You, Letting the Trees Stand as My Betrayer. Diane Wakoski. NoAM

You return home. Homecoming. Dan Gerber. HeS; TC

You roar over the meadow and roar. Last Days. Richard Hugo. PoA

You said./ don't write me/ a love poem. Poem. Pearl Cleage Lomax. CNA

You said/ we will all. The Sky. Susan Griffin. RiTi

You said I stole your name when I married Steve. The Real Jane Flanders. Jane Flanders. PoUp

You said it was just sex, we had. After Swimming in the Pacific. Cathy Colman. NPW

You said it went all the way. Last Words, 1968. Lance Henson. CDW

You said that your people. To Richard Wright. Conrad Kent Rivers. AmNP (1974 ed.); CABA (1972 ed.); PoBA

You said to me:/ I would become your comrade. Nudities. André Spire, *tr. by* Stanley Burnshaw. VWA

You sang round-dance songs. Farewell. Liz Sohappy Bahe. CDW

You sat with a bottle of beer. After the Death of an Elder Klallam. Duane Niatum. CDW

You say, "Arāna." That sounds and is "arena" in German. A Word Can Become the Way It Sounds. Helen Arana. PoW

You say, as I have often given tongue. To a Poet, Who Would Have Me Praise Certain Bad Poets, Imitators of His and Mine. W. B. Yeats. FaBoEE; PFIr

You say, "I will come." Lady Otomo of Sakanoe, *tr. fr. Japanese by* Kenneth Rexroth. OLR

You say that I take a good deal upon myself. Monumentum Aere, Etc. Ezra Pound. NOBA

"You say that you believe in Democracy for everybody." Everybody but Me. Margaret Burroughs. FB

You say the king commands that I appear. Diptych. Velma West Sykes. IHMS

You say, to me-wards your affection's strong. Love Me Little, Love Me Long. Robert Herrick. CaPo; LoAs

You say you love; but with a voice. Stanzas. Keats. MBPR

You say you love me. A Letter Home. Kenneth "Spider" Nicholson. DNGG

You say you love me, nay, can swear it too. Robert Heath. POL

"You say you love me truly." True is True. Mark Van Doren. LoAs

You scream, waking from a nightmare. Little Sleep's-Head Sprouting Hair in the Moonlight. Galway Kinnell. RRA

You see me alone tonight. I Have Had to Learn to Live with My Face. Diane Wakoski. FoP

You see, my darling. Map Reading. David Citino. AMV–81

You see, my whole life. Woman Poem. Nikki Giovanni. NMM; NoAM; Psy

You see, the problem is. Blue like Death. James Welch. CDW

You see the ways the fisherman doth take. Neither Hook nor Line. Bunyan. LiSp

You see the worst of love, but not the best. Walter Savage Landor. GBL

You see them from train windows. Other Lives. Vern Rutsala. MPA

You See Them in the Alleys. Al Masarik. CPA

You see them vanish in their speeding cars. Fugue. Howard Nemerov. TAP

You see these little scars? Iambic Feet Considered as Honorable Scars. William Meredith. PoA

You see this Christmas tree all silver gold? Come Christmas. David McCord. PChr

You see this pebble-stone? The Cock and the Bull. Charles Stuart Calverley. FaBoCo; FaBoNo; VLP

You send me a photograph. Porno Love. Philip Dacey. NVAP

You send them back to me. Letters, Returned. Adrianne Marcus. NPW

You Serve the Best Wines Always, My Dear Sir. Martial *tr. fr. Latin by* J. V. Cunningham. InPK

You Shall. *Unknown.* BluL

You Shall above All Things Be Glad and Young. E. E. Cummings. NoAM; NOBA

You shall have no other gods before me. God Is Mr. Big, Real Big. Carl F. Burke. TPo

You shall not be overbold. The Titmouse. Emerson. PiAm

You should have, jean, stopped them. One More Time. Alvin Aubert. GP

You should see them now. Dear Vincent. Elizabeth Bartlett. PoW

You should see this one. Murphy. Patrick Williams. IPM

You should try to hear the name. The Name. Jalal ed-Din Rumi, *ad. by* Robert Bly. NU

You should understand that I use my body now. At Bickford's. Gerald Stern. NYP

You shouldn't be afraid of the dark. Lullaby for My Dead Child. Denise Jallais, *tr. by* Maxine *and* Judith Kumin. BoWoP

You shout to me. Views. Harriet Susskind. AMV–80

You shun me, Chloe, wild and shy. To Chloe. Horace, *tr. by* Austin Dobson. Odes, I, 23. LoAs

You sit for a moment, idling, remembering. The Lost Street. David Wagoner. MPA

You sit in the middle of the bed. To a Friend's Child. Aliki Barnstone. BoWoP

You sit on the porch steps. Possessions. Ai. CAAP

You sleeping child asleep, away. To Ping-ku, Asleep. Lawrence Durrell. RRA

You smiled, you spoke, and I believed. Walter Savage Landor. BoLoP; GBL; ILP (1975 ed.)

You smoke pot alone in your room. Solo Late Show over Easter Break. R. T. Smith. AAN

You speak with your. New Streets. F. A. Nettelbeck. EC

You speed by with your camera and your spear. Interview with a Tourist. Margaret Atwood. IHMS

You spent all summer in cool Kabul. *Unknown, tr. fr. Pashto by* Saduddin Shpoon. PBWP

You spoke me. The Long Word. Deirdre Ballantyne. AMV–80

You spot me in the rain journey. Rain Trip. Diane Wakoski. CABA (1972 ed.)

You spotted snakes with double tongue. Shakespeare. *Fr. A Midsummer Night's Dream,* II, ii. ECBV; NOBE

You stand behind the old black mare. Why Can't I Leave You? Ai. AmPA; GP

You stand near the window as lights wink. 23rd Street Runs into Heaven. Kenneth Patchen. SPT

You still sometimes sleep. Heron. Stanley Plumly. AmPA

You stood in our small boat. Friend with Spinning Rod. Napoleon St. Cyr. FAF

You stop shaving for a while and one morning. Bernard Welt. PoUp

You strange, astonished-looking, angle-faced. To a Fish. Leigh Hunt. The Fish, the Man, and the Spirit, I. EcS; HAP; NOBL

You, stranger, who only see us happy and free of care. Hunger. *Unknown, tr. by* Edward Field. IPWM

You strike everything down in battle. Inanna and Ishkur. Enheduanna, *tr. fr. Sumerian.* BoWoP

You strop my anger, especially. To the Pay Toilet. Marge Piercy. GP

You take my hand and. Margaret Atwood. HAP

You take the dollar. For One Moment. David Ignatow. NNAP; TCP; TVo

You Take the Pilgrims, Just Give Me the Progress. Loyd Rosenfield. QQQ

You take what it gives you, what a spinster. A Place by the River. William Keens. TAT

You talk about the Soo Locks. Going Up and Down. Jim Daniels. AMV–81

"You talk of snakes," said Jack the Rat. A Snake Yarn. W. T. Goodge. ECBV

You talk peaks and golden eagles. Llanberis Summer. Marianne Loyd. AMV–81

You tell me that silence. Gift. Mark Strand. NoAM

You Tell Me Your Dream, I'll Tell You Mine, *with music.* Seymour Rice *and* Albert H. Brown. FSN

You tell me you're promised a lover. A Letter of Advice. Winthrop Mackworth Praed. NOBL

You tender virgins, fairer than the snow with which you play. Edward May, *after the Latin of* John Parkhurst. FaBoEE

You that a stranger in mid-Rome seek Rome. Rome. J. V. Cunningham, *after the Latin of* Janus Vitalis Panormitanus. OBVE

You that are sprung of northern stock. To a Calvinist in Bali. Edna St. Vincent Millay. NoAM

You, that decipher out the fate. Mourning. Andrew Marvell. CABA (1972 ed.); SCP-1

You that do search for every purling spring. Astrophel and Stella, XV. Sir Philip Sidney. ILP (1975 ed.); OAEL-1

You That Have Been Often Invited, *with music. Unknown.* AH

You that have spent the silent night. Gascoignes Good Morrow. George Gascoigne. AAS

You that in love finde lucke and habundance. Sir Thomas Wyatt. AAS

You that know the way. Lemuel's Blessing. W. S. Merwin. CAPP; TCP

You that with allegory's curious frame. Astrophel and Stella, XXVIII. Sir Philip Sidney. ILP (1975 ed.); InPK; OAEL-1

You, the one woman that could have me all. To V. S. Christopher Brennan. MAuV

You, the woman; I, the man; this, the world. The Character of Love Seen as a Search for the Lost. Kenneth Patchen. VGW

You there, ain't your mamma never. Poem for Blackboys in Floppy Tie-Dye Hats. Jodi Braxton. WBN

You think it horrible that lust and rage. The Spur. W. B. Yeats. SoSe

You think they might come. Riding Double. Peter Wild. AmPA

You think you have always lived. Poem to a Potted Plant. Steve Toth. AcAn

You thought the leaden winter. Tales of Brave Ulysses. Eric Clapton *and* Martin Sharp. GrRo

You thought the sad and lonely little boy. The Celebrity. Edward Field. EC

You thunder at my side. The Snoring Bedmate. *Unknown, tr. by* John V. Kelleher. BIrV

You tickle the sophisticates. On Reading Mr. Ytche Bashes' Stories in Yiddish. Lester Ehrlichman. AMV-80

You tied Dick Randall to a tree. Bunny. Christopher Fahy. TAT

You to whom the earth's. Advice. E. di Pasquale. AMV-81

You told me, early last fall, you never had no man at all. Fare Thee Well Blues. *Unknown.* BluL

You told me: "I am not worthy of you." Marguerite Burnat-Provins, *tr. fr. French by* Cassia Berman. BoWoP

You told me it was/ because of me. Izumi Shikibu, *tr. fr. Japanese by* Willis Barnstone. BoWoP

You too if you work hard enough. Ponce de León: A Morning Walk. Al Young. HoPM (1975 ed.)

You Too? Me Too—Why Not? Soda Pop. Robert Hollander. NIL

You took the world and embraced. Pedro. Luis Omar Salinas. FF

You track for days. Hunting Dragons with Fire Tongues and Deep Smoky Throats. J. S. Harry. CAAP

You tramped around the town. Empty Raft. G. C. Dawe. IPM

You travel across the room. Distances. Linda Pastan. RiTi

You tried so hard to make me believe in this day. To My Father on Pearl Harbor Day. D. W. Donzella. FAF

You tug at words. Modern Kabbalist. Marcia Falk. UsP; VWA

You understand now/ what it means. On the Edge at Santorini. Michael C. Blumenthal. AMV-80

You Understand the Requirements. Lyn Lifshin. NeAC; RiTi

You unseen lightning flash, you darkly radiant light. On the Ineffable Inspiration of the Holy Spirit. Catharina Regina von Greiffenberg, *tr. by* Michael Hamburger. PBWP

You used to ask me once what was wrong. In Memoriam I. Franco Fortini, *tr. by* Ruth Feldman. VWA

You used to be my sugar, but. Tooten Out Blues. *Unknown.* BluL

You vilify me, but I rise above grief. Lament after Her Husband Bishr's Murder. Al-Khirniq, *tr. by* Willis Barnstone. BoWoP

You virgins that did late despair. Piping Peace. James Shirley. *Fr.* The Imposture. NOBE; SCP-2

You wake, shuddering, and as I kiss your back. The Contagiousness of Dreams. Diane Middlebrook. AMV-81

You wake up feeling. Ripeness. Ruth Whitman. TSWA

You walk down the road. Letting Go. Richard Shelton. AMV-81

You walk on. A Door. W. S. Merwin. EAS

You want coins? Roman? Greek? Nice vase? Head of god, goddess. Ali Ben Shufti. Anthony Thwaite. HeHu; OxBTC

You want the summer lightning, throw the knives. Ingeborg Bachmann, *tr. fr. German by* Daniel Huws. BoWoP

You want to go back. Margaret Atwood. NeAC

You want to integrate me into your anonymity. Black Narcissus. Gerald W. Barrax. PoBA

You want to know what's the matter with me, do yer? Reaping. Amy Lowell. SBG

You wanted the perfect setting. For Anna. Irving Layton. NeAC

You watched out for him or. Travis, the Kid Was All Heart. Terry Stokes. AmPA

You wear the face. Izumi Shikibu, *tr. fr. Japanese by* Willis Barnstone. BoWoP

You Went Away. Norman MacCaig. SLP

You were a girl of satin and gauze. The Wheel Revolves. Kenneth Rexroth. NoAM; RRA

You were at the door with the news. The Announcement. George Ellenbogen. AMV-80

You were being driven down to Prague. Polemical Elegy for Reinhardt Heydrich. Tom Buchan. MIS

You were brought up. Coming Up and Falling Down. Stephen Vincent. NeAC

You were lying on top of me. Night of Dreams. Laura Beausoleil. NPW

You were praised, my books. Salutation the Second. Ezra Pound. NOBA

You were standing at the window, silently. Watching Snow. Raymond Ward. ATNZ

You were the fence standing between our land and the descendants of Ali. Lament for a Dead Lover. Siraad Haad, *tr. by* B. W. Andrzejewski *and* I. M. Lewis. WTO

You were up early. Sunday. Laura Beausoleil. NPW

You Were Wearing. Kenneth Koch. CABA (1972 ed.); EAS; NIL; NNaP; NoAM; VoA

You Were Wearing Blue. Tom Raworth. TwMBP

You were wearing your Edgar Allan Poe printed cotton blouse. You Were Wearing. Kenneth Koch. CABA (1972 ed.); EAS; NIL; NNaP; NoAM; VoA

You were writing a long poem, yes. Residue of Song. Marvin Bell. AmPA

You were young—but that was scarcely to your credit. Gerald Gould. *Fr.* Monogamy. OxBTC

You were't even a. To L. Julianne Perry. PoBA

You, who/ Are more like/ A little girl. Serene Art. Lewis Warsh. MIT

You who desired so much—in vain to ask. To Emily Dickinson. Hart Crane. CMoP (1970 ed.); NoAM; NOBA; TAP

You who dump the beer cans in the lake. Malediction. Barry Spacks. InPK

You who give sustenance to your creatures, O God. Prayer for Rain. Sheikh Aqib Abdullahi Jama, *tr. by* B. W. Andrzejewski. WTO

You who go every Sunday to the Botanical Garden. Song for Afterwards. Francisco Lopez Merino, *tr. by* Richard O'Connell. LoAs

You who go out on schedule. Two Variations. Denise Levertov. PPoe; RiTi

You who have listened to the heart of the night. Nocturne II. Ruben Dario, *tr. by* Jan Pallister. AMV–81

You who hunger and thirst. Back to the Angels. William Walter De Bolt. AMV–81

You who live secure. Shema. Primo Levi, *tr. by* Ruth Feldman *and* Brian Swann. VWA

You who snore with your sleeping wife so near. Tristan Corbière, *tr. by* Christopher Pilling. *Fr.* Litany of Sleep. OBVE

You who were darkness warmed my flesh. Woman to Child. Judith Wright. PBWP; WPE

You who would sorrow even for a token. Reciprocity. Vassar Miller. IHMS

You, Whose Mother's Lover Was Grass. Gregory Corso. NoAM

You will ask how I came to be eavesdropping. Confession Overheard in a Subway. Kenneth Fearing. SoS

You will be aware of an absence, presently. For a Fatherless Son. Sylvia Plath. TSWA

You will be beautiful now. The Piercing. Pat Lowther. MMD

You will have the road gate open, the front door ajar. In Memory of My Mother. Patrick Kavanagh. BIrV

You Will Never Get Away No-O. Robert Abney. PoUp

You will probably have three children. Love Poem Investigation for A.T. Frank Frate. AMV–80

You will remember the kisses, real or imagined. Resurrection. Kenneth Fearing. CMoP (1970 ed.)

You will see him any day in Te Kuiti. The Gunfighter. Alistair Campbell. ATNZ

You Will See Your Lord a-Coming, *with music.* Unknown. AH

You worry me whoever you are. Badman of the Guest Professor. Ishmael Reed. BPo

You would extend the mind beyond the act. The Moralists. Yvor Winters. PiAm

You would have understood me, had you waited. Paul Verlaine, *tr. fr. French by* Ernest Dowson. BoLoP

You would not bend. For Kinte. Oliver La Grone. FB

You would not recognize me. The Tourist from Syracuse. Donald Justice. CoPAm

You would sleep with the moon. Alternatives. Peter Cooley. AmPA

You would take/everything. At Times. Kathleen Wiegner. MMD

You would think I'd be a specialist in contemporary. The Put-down Come On. A. R. Ammons. TT

You would think the fury of aerial bombardment. The Fury of Aerial Bombardment. Richard Eberhart. BiP; CMoP (1970 ed.); CoPAm; ExPo (1973 ed.); FF; HeIP; HoPM (1975 ed.);

ILP (1975 ed.); InPK; IP; IPWM; NIL; NoAM; PPoD; PSN; TAP; TCP; UnPo (1976 ed.); VGW; VoPo; WIF

You write with ease, to shew your breeding. Clio's Protest. Sheridan. FaBoEE

You'd Better Believe Him. Brian Patten. LP

You'd think that at 3:00 A.M. L'Elisir d'Amore. Dallas E. Wiebe. MAT

You'll ask, perhaps, wherefore I stay. An Excuse of Absence. Thomas Carew. CaPo

You'll be my little seven stone missionary! T. S. Eliot. *Fr.* Sweeney Agonistes. UnPo (1976 ed.)

You'll find me in the Laundromat. Laundromat. David McCord. QQQ

You'll find that I'm the sort. Abner Silver's "Pu-leeze! Mr. Hemingway!" Ring Lardner. OBAL

You'll find whenever the New Year comes. *Unknown.* CC

You'll go to the plaza. Camoes and the Debt. Sophia de Mello Breyner Andresen, *tr. by* Willis Barnstone *and* Nelson Cerqueira. BoWoP

You'll know it—as you know—tis noon. Emily Dickinson. PiAm

You'll Love Me Yet! Robert Browning. *Fr.* Pippa Passes, sc. iii. OLR

You'll never get me Banks, Hospitals. Poem to My Creditors. Thomas Lux. AAN

You'll Never Miss Your Jelly. *Unknown.* BluL

You'll wait a long, long time for anything much. On Looking Up by Chance at the Constellations. Robert Frost. CMoP (1970 ed.)

Young. Anne Sexton. MPo; NCSH

Young and Radiant, He Is Standing, *with music.* Allen Eastman Cross. AH

Young and Old. Charles Kingsley. *Fr.* The Water Babies. EBEV; FaPoR; OxBChV; PCOP; TPo

Young are quick of speech, The. On Teaching the Young. Yvor Winters. NoAM; NOBA

Young Author, The. Samuel Johnson. LAuP

"Young begin with generalizations, The." Carlo Parcelli. *Fr.* The Ontology of Accident. PoUp

Young Beichan (Lord Bateman). *Unknown.* FaBoBa

Young Ben he was a nice young man. Faithless Sally Brown. Thomas Hood. BBL; FaBoCo; NOBL

Young bloods come round less often now, The. Horace, *tr. by* James Michie. Odes, I, 25. BoLoP

Young boys forget about cars awhile, The. Results of the Polo Game. Grace Butcher. RiTi

Young but gloomy man, A. A Poem Is Not. Gary Catalano. GAS

Young Calidore is paddling o'er the lake. Calidore. Keats. MBPR

Young cat knew enough to lick her firstborn, but, The. Dill. Marie Harris. MMD

Young Charlottie; or, The Frozen Girl. *Unknown.* AmFP (Young Charlotte, *longer version.*) FSW

Young Chess Player, The. Keith Sinclair. ATNZ

Young Conquistador, The. Robert Peterson. GP

Young Conquistador, 15, The. Robert Peterson. GP

Young Corydon [*or* Coridon] and Phyllis [*or* Phillis]. On the Happy Corydon and Phyllis. Sir Charles Sedley. BoLoP; SCP-2; SFF

Young Couples Strolling By. Carl Rakosi. InPS

Young Curate of Kidderminster, A. *Unknown.* TDH

Young Dead Soldiers, The. Archibald MacLeish. OFD

Young Deer/Dust, A. Hemda Roth, *tr. fr. Hebrew by* Myra Glazer Schotz. VWA

Young Deputy, The. James Whitehead. CoPAm

Young Edward came to Emily his gold all for to show. Edwin in the Lowlands Low. *Unknown.* AmFP

Young Endymion sleeps Endymion's sleep, The. Keats. Longfellow. ILP (1975 ed.); TAP

Young engine-driver called Hunt, A. Limerick. Victor Gray. NOBL

Young Fellow from Boise, A. John Straley. TDH

Young Fellow Named Shear, A. John Ciardi. TDH

Young fellow walks about, The. Charles Reznikoff. CTBA

Young Fenians, The. Padraic Fallon. BIrV

Young fisherboys sing like the endless sea. That's Our Lot. Moishe Leib Halpern, *tr. by* Kathryn Hellerstein. VWA

Young flowers were whispering in melody. Song. Poe. *Fr.* Al Aaraaf. NOBA

Young flute player, The. Flute Player. *Gond Oral Tradition, tr. by* V. Elwin *and* S. Hivale. WTO

Young Girl. Menzies McKillop. SLP

Young Girl, The. Theodore Roethke. AnMo; LoAs; NoAM

Young Girl. Iain Crichton Smith. MS

Young Girl of Asturias, A. *Unknown.* TDH

Young girl stood beside me, The. The Orange Tree. John Shaw Neilson. GAS; MAuV

Young Girl's Song, The. Alvin J. Gordon. MiP

Young, groomed sullen men of boyless purpose. Highway 101, Seal Beach. Curtis Zahn. NowV

Young Heroes. Gwendolyn Brooks. BPo

Young heroes, the generous young men, The. Young Girl. Menzies McKillop. SLP

Young hound howls, A. Unemployment. William Mills. HoPM (1975 ed.)

Young Housewife, The. William Carlos Williams. HeIP; NoAM; PiAm; TAP

Young Hunting (" 'Get down, get down, lovin' Henry,' she cried"). *Unknown.* AmFP

Young Hunting ("Light you down, light you down, love Henry, she said"). *Unknown.* FaBoBa

Young Hunting ("O lady, rock never your young son young"). *Unknown.* PeBB

Young in Fall I said: the birds. Lorine Niedecker. VGW

Young Ionia, The. John Frederick Nims. PCho

Young Janie was a strappan lass. The Thocht. William Soutar. MS

Young Johnnie Steele has an Oldsmobile. In My Merry Oldsmobile. Vincent Bryan. FSN

Young Johnny sails the sea, young Johnny sails the shore. The Green Bed. *Unknown.* AmFP

Young Johnny the miller he courted of late. The Gray Mare. *Unknown.* AmFP

Young Johnstone. *Unknown.* PeBB

Young Juan wandered by the glassy brooks. The Seduction of Juan. Byron. *Fr. Don Juan,* I. OBP

Young kangaroo, Miss Hocket, A. Miss Hocket. *Unknown.* TDH

Young Lady from Cork, A. Ogden Nash. TDH

Young Lady from Delaware, A. *Unknown.* TDH

Young Lady Named Sue, A. *Unknown.* TDH

Young Lady of Crete. *Unknown.* TDH

Young Lady of Ealing, A. *Unknown.* TDH

Young Lady of Munich, A. *Unknown.* TDH

Young Lady of Oakham, A. *Unknown.* TDH

Young Lady of Tyre, The. Edward Lear. TDH

Young Lady of Wilts, A. *Unknown.* TDH

Young Lambs. John Clare. DuDr

Young Lochinvar came in from the West. At Cheyenne. Eugene Field. BPAW

Young lords o' the north country, The. Lady Maisery. *Unknown.* Epi

Young Love. Andrew Marvell. RRA; TT

Young Love lies sleeping. Dream-Love. Christina Rossetti. HAP

Young Lover, A. E. N. Sargent. WBN

Young man,/ Seize every minute. The Frost. Tzu Yeh. TVo

Young man and maid, pray lend attention. The Silver Dagger. *Unknown.* AmFP

Young man and the miller's lass they set out on the hill, The. The Miller's Daughter. *Unknown.* PeBB

Young man at the plate, bat bristling, The. A Post Card out of Panama. William D. Barney. LiSp

Young Man Cut Down in His Prime (St. James Hospital). *Unknown.* FSW

Young man in a carriage, driving like he's mad. Putting on the Style. *Unknown.* FSW

Young man is spaced out on the lawn, A. Maxims of a Park Vagrant. Nicholas Swift. AMV–80

Young Man Loves a Maiden, A. Heine, *tr. fr. German by* Ernest Feise. NAWM–2

Young man of twenty, A. Lost Picture. Ray Fraser. NeAC

Young Man on a Journey, A. *Unknown.* TDH

Young Man Thinks of Sons, The. R. A. K. Mason. ATNZ

Young man, wearing a loose jacket of light brown, A. Puerto Ricans in New York, II. Charles Reznikoff. CTBA; VoA

Young Man Who Loved Rain, A. William Jay Smith. TDH

Young Man Who Loved the Girl Who Took Care of Her Aging Father, The. Greg Kuzma. AmPA

Young Man Who Wouldn't Hoe Corn. *Unknown.* FSW

Young Man's Epigram on Existence, A. Thomas Hardy. NoAM

Young Man's Song, A. William Bell. FaBoTw (1975 ed.)

Young Master's Account of a Puppet Show. John Marchant. OxBChV

Young May Moon, The. Thomas Moore. Moon

Young Men Dancing. Thomas Stanley, *after the Greek of* Anacreon. OBVE

Young men on the roof watching the stars. Young Men You Are So Beautiful Up There. Patricia Goedicke. GP

Young men, they say, are bold and free. Beware, Oh, Take Care. *Unknown.* FSW

Young Men You Are So Beautiful Up There. Patricia Goedicke. GP

Young Mrs. Snooks was sick of sex. Nursery Rhyme. Kenneth Burke. OBAL

Young Molly Ban. *Unknown.* FaBoBa; ILP (1975 ed.); PeBB (Polly Vaughn.) AmFP

Young mouth laughs at a gift, A. Her Words. Theodore Roethke. LoAs

Young Negro Poet. Calvin C. Hernton. AmNP (1974 ed.)

Young niggers/ die old. Dedication to the Final Confrontation. Lloyd M. Corbin, Jr. PoBA

Young Ones, The. Elizabeth Jennings. OxBTC

Young Ones, Flip Side, The. James A. Emanuel. SS

Young Palmus was a ferryman. Shackley-Hay. *Unknown.* GBP

Young people all, attention give. Liverpool. *Unknown.* AmFP

Young people, all attention give. Mission. *Unknown.* AmFP

Young People Who Delight in Sin. *Unknown.* AmFP

Young Pilgrim Finds Refuge with the Goatherds, The. Luis de Góngora, *tr fr. Spanish by* Edward Meryon Wilson. *Fr.* The First Solitude. OBVE

Young Poet. Myron O'Higgins. PoBA

Young Poets. Nicanor Parra, *tr. fr. Spanish by* Miller Williams. POL

Young poets swim in schools like minnows. Poets Observed. F. C. Rosenberger. AMV–80

Young Politician. Alan Jackson. MS

Young Prince and the Young Princess, The. John Ashbery. ConAP

Young Puppy, The. A. A. Milne. GDP (Howard.) TDH

Young Revolutionist. Isidor Schneider. SPT

Young Reynard. George Meredith. HoPM (1975 ed.)

Young Rhymer Snubbed, The. William Barnes. VLP

Young School Mistress, A. *Unknown.* TDH

Young Soul. Amiri Baraka. BPo; CNA; TSWA

Young Stock. V. Sackville-West. OxBTC

Young Sycamore. William Carlos Williams. TAP

Young theologian named Fiddle, A. *Unknown.* CTV

Young things who frequent picture-palaces, The. Limerick. *Unknown.* NOBL

Young Training. Lawrence McGaugh. PoBA

Young Una, you were a rose in a garden. Tomas Costello, *tr. by* Frank O'Connor. *Fr.* A Lament for Una. WTO

Young unmarried man, with a good name, A. Byron. *Fr.* Don Juan. NOBL

Young viper grows as it sits, The. *Zulu Oral Tradition, tr. by* T. Cope. *Fr.* Shaka. WTO

Young Virgins Plucked Suddenly. Berl Pomerantz, *tr. fr. Hebrew by* Harold Schimmel. VMA

Young Widow. Patricia Beer. HeHu

Young Wife, A. D. H. Lawrence. PBMP; VoPo

Young wife stands at the kitchen, A. Not Speaking. Lawrence Russ. TC

Young woman, A. Portrait of My Mother on Her Wedding Day. Celia Gilbert. AMV–81

Young Woman from Aenos, The. *Unknown.* OBAL

Young Woman in Apathy. Christopher Middleton. TwMBP

Young Woman of Beare, The. Austin Clarke. NoAM

Young Woman's neo-aramaic jewish persian Blues. Jerome Rothenberg, *after Persian folk poem.* BoWoP

Young women are obsessed with beauty, The. The Clothes Pit. Douglas Dunn. OxBTC

Young Women with the Hair of Witches and No Modesty. Peter Redgrove. UsP

Younger Poet, A. Peter Schjeldahl. PoA

Youngest Schizophrene, The. Katherine Hoskins. TCP

Your Absence has gone through me. Separation. W. S. Merwin. HAP

Your Absence Has Not Taught Me. Doug Fetherling. NeAC

Your Air of My Air. Hugo Margenat, *tr. fr. Spanish by* Julio Marzán. InW

Your Animal. Gerald Stern. AMV–81

Your archival voice. The Music. Everett Hoagland. CNA

Your arms will clasp the gathered grain. The Island. Edwin Muir. OAEL–2

Your ashes will not stir, even on this high ground. In Carrowdore Churchyard. Derek Mahon. CIP

Your Attention Please. Peter Porter. LP; OxBTC

Your axe cuts high. The Clearing. David Gitin. PoW

Your back is rough all. Margaret Atwood. NeAC

Your bare white legs. The Beach at Veracruz. George Bowering. NeAC

Your beauty, ripe and calm, and fresh. The Philosopher and the Lover: To a Mistress Dying. Sir William Davenant. NOBE; Prf

Your Birds Build Sun-Castles with Song. Daniel Sloate. AMV–81

Your birthday comes to tell me this. E. E. Cummings. CC

Your Birthday in the California Mountains. Kenneth Rexroth. PoW

Your Black Bones Do Not Remember. Stacy Tuthill. PoUp

Your blonde beard crushes ice into. Departure. Elizabeth Hanson. NPW

Your blond hair and autumn sweater. Janna. King D. Kuka. VoR

Your blood does not flow, not even a little. A Poem for Diane Wakoski. Ray A. Young Bear. CDW

Your body derns. Scunner. "Hugh MacDiarmid." FaBoTw (1975 ed.)

Your body has moved to unstaunchable distance. N. Hugh Seidman. PoA

Your body is a pipeline. Air. Tomaz Salamun, *tr. by* Aleksandar Nejgebauer. VWA

Your body might have come from the loins of a prince. Moon of the Earth. *Gond Oral Tradition, tr. by* V. Elwin *and* S. Hivale. WTO

Your Body Is Stars. Stephen Spender. FaBoTw (1975 ed.)

Your bones left out all night. Beginning Again as Morning. Eugene Ruggles. MIT

Your bottoms are not purple. Horror Comic. Robert Conquest. OxBTC

Your Burnt-out Body. Peretz Markish, *tr. fr. Yiddish by* Keith Bosley. VWA

Your cauliflower served. New Uses for Old Utensils. Edward Proffitt. PoIA

Your celebrated hand. The Candidate. Allamae Ezell. AMV–80

Your center, the membrane of your center. Being on the Edge of Someone Else. Virginia R. Terris. AAN

Your cheekbones live. Cathy Colman. NPW

Your cheeks flat on the sand. Venus Khoury-Gata, *tr. fr. French by* Willis Barnstone. BoWoP

Your children are not your children. On Children. Kahlil Gibran. *Fr.* The Prophet. SFF

Your clear eye is the one absolutely beautiful thing. Child. Sylvia Plath. PBWP

Your closed eyes bulge like mushrooms. Letter to Kafka. Maura Stanton. AmPA

Your correspondent must be kidding when he says. Americana IX. Carl Rakosi. InPS

Your crops, old man, are in. Laying By. Randall Williams. AMV–80

Your desert land is. Navajo. William Haskel Simpson. BPAW

Your dog? What dog? You mean it?—that! Suzie's New Dog. John Ciardi. GDP

Your door is shut against my tightened face. The White House. Claude McKay. AmNP (1974 ed.); NIL; PoBA

Your elephant adolescence in sandlots Brooklyn. 16/53. Marge Piercy. NeAC

Your eyebrows are splotched on like market flies. The Prostitutes at Les Halles. Jane Mayhall. WBN

Your eyen [*or* yen] two will slay me suddenly. Merciless Beauty. Chaucer. BoLoP; EBEV; HAP; OxBM; PAIC

Your Eyes. Kosrof Chantikian. AMV–81

Your eyes are as black as twin pools at night. Little Papoose. Arthur Chapman. BPAW

Your eyes are just. Four-Word Lines. May Swenson. OSP; WPE

Your eyes are open. Carious Exposure. Gladys Cardiff. CDW

Your Eyes Have Their Silence. Gerald W. Barrax. CNA; PoBA

Your eyes I can see in the dark. The Beacon. Arthur Gregor. GP

Your Eyes, Your Name. William Matthews. NVAP

Your face/ half blue. Homage to Chagall. Kathleen Teague. MIT

Your face,/ so pale now it is blue. Poem. David St. John. AmPA

Your face/ stretched like a mask. Adrienne Rich. *Fr.* Leaflets. TT

Your face broods from my table, Suicide. John Berryman. *Fr.* Dream Songs. CAPP; TAP

Your face did not rot. The Lost Pilot. James Tate. UnPo (1976 ed.)

Your face has almost disappeared—a leaf. The End of a Meaningful Relationship. Kurt J. Fickert. AMV-81

Your face scrapes my sleep tonight. Letter to Be Disguised as a Gas Bill. Marge Piercy. MMD; WPE

Your faith is in what you hold. Chicago. Lola Ridge. PoA

Your father's farm was lovely that October. The black barn. Persimmon Trees, She Remembers, Not Far Away. David Baker. AMV-81

"Your father's gone," my bald headmaster said. The Lesson. Edward Lucie-Smith. BuTh; LP; MPo; NCSH; OxBTC

Your flesh is melted, I suppose. For Katherine, 1952-1961. Conrad Hilberry. TC

Your foe in war to overrate. Porson on His Majesty's Government. Richard Porson. FaBoCo

Your foundations are strong. Lewis. Derick Thomson. MS

Your Friend. Anselm Hollo. TwMBP

Your friends come fondly to your living room. Birthday Card for a Psychiatrist. Mona Van Duyn. IHMS

Your friendship oft has made my heart to ache. *See* Thy friendship . . .

Your ghost steps are already gone. Cycle. Frank Lonergan. AMV-81

Your ghost will walk, you lover of trees. "De Gustibus." Robert Browning. InPS

Your golden loins slake my lust for treasures. Prayer. Mike Newell. AMV-80

Your great-grandfather dreamed that his son. Letters to My Daughter, #3. Judith Minty. TV

Your hair all wrinkled and you full of sweat, your. I Can Tell by the Way You Smell. *Unknown.* BluL

Your Hand Full of Hours. Paul Celan, *tr. fr. German by* Michael Hamburger. OBVE

Your hand in your grandfather's. Michael's Room. Reginald Gibbons. AMV-81

Your hand trailed over the hammock's side. Ode to Joy. Daniel Hoffman. AMV-81

Your handkerchief should be blue. *Turkish Love Songs, tr. by* Reza Baraheni *and* Zahra-Soltan Shokoohtaezeh. BoWoP

Your Hands. Angelina Weld Grimké. PoBA

Your Hands. Joan Swift. PoW

Your hands lie open in the long fresh grass. Silent Noon. Dante Gabriel Rossetti. The House of Life, XIX. HAP; ILP (1975 ed.); OBP; SoSe (1977 ed.); VLP

Your hands, my dear, adorable. The Chilterns. Rupert Brooke. PPM

Your head is so fragrant tonight that only the sky is above it. Only the Sky. Pete Winslow. MIT

Your health, Master Willow. Contrive me a bat. Tree Party. Louis MacNeice. OxBTC

Your house seems built of wood. Poem for Valerie. Luke Breit. CPA

Your husband? Going to the same dinner as us? Ovid, *tr. by* Guy Lee. Amores, I, 4. NAWM-1

Your husband will be with us at the treat. To His Mistress. Ovid, *tr. by* Dryden. Amores, I, 4. BoLoP

Your innocence snuffed out. Candle. Jacob Isaac Segal, *tr. by* Seymour Mayne. VWA

Your kindness, sir, to me, is really kind. Horace, *tr. fr. Latin by* Francis Howes. OBVE

Your last name's the one I remember. Director. Lindeman. Mary Jane White. AMV-81

Your learning, James, in classics and romance. A Letter to a Teacher of English. Robert Hillyer. PAIC

Your least and lightest movement may be critical. The Man of Glass. Gordon Challis. ATNZ

Your leaves bound up compact and fair. To an Author. Philip Freneau. AmVN; EAP; NOBA

Your legs would be pretty, if you had legs. Portrait of a Nun. Bobi Jones, *tr. by* Joseph P. Clancy. OBW

Your letter came.—Glutted the earth and cold. A Winter-Piece to a Friend Away. John Berryman. NOBA

Your Light. Ann Lee. AMV-80

Your lips were so laughing. Langston Blues. Dudley Randall. CNA; FB

Your little voice. E. E. Cummings. OLR

Your love is dead, lady, your love is dead. Madrigal. R. S. Thomas. BoLoP

Your love lacks joy, your letter says. Coventry Patmore. *Fr.* The Victories of Love. GBL

Your love, love. The Lover to Himself. David Phillips. NeAC

Your love turned my body into water. Empress Nur Jahan, *tr. fr. Persian by* Willis Barnstone. BoWop

Your loveliness, I don't deny, needs lovers. Ovid, *tr. by* Guy Lee. Amores, III, 14. NAWM-1

Your lynx-eyes, Asia. "Anna Akhmatova," *tr. fr. Russian by* Stanley Kunitz *and* Max Hayward. BoWoP

Your midriff sags toward your knees. Woman with Girdle. Anne Sexton. NCSH; NoAM; SFF

Your milk was already poisoned. Childhood. Edith Bruck, *tr. by* Anita Barrows. VWA

Your mind and mine are such great lovers they. Two Minds. Sara Teasdale. TPo

Your mind and you are our Sargasso Sea. Portrait d'une Femme. Ezra Pound. CABA (1972 ed.); CMoP (1970 ed.); FF; ILP (1975 ed.); NoAM; NOBA; PPP; SoSe; TAP

Your mistress, that you follow whores, still taxeth you. A Self Accuser. John Donne. FaBoEE

"Your mom wear high-heeled sneakers!" Delia Dalya of the Sponged Stilts. Ron Welburn. NW

Your Mother. Sam Cornish. CNA

Your Musgraves, Clarges, Harleys, Foleys, Lowthers. On Squire Neale's Projects. *Unknown.* APAS

Your Name upon the Sand. Walter Savage Landor. *Fr.* Ianthe. BuTh
("Well I remember how you smiled.") HAP

Your nurse could only speak Italian. Sailing Home from Rapallo. Robert Lowell. NoAM; TAP

Your old hat hurts me, and those black. Dad. Elaine Feinstein. VWA

Your Own Image. Michael Ryan. HeS

Your parents don't like me. Farewell, Sweet Mary. *Unknown.* AmFP

Your Passing, Fleet Passing. Joseph Eliyia, *tr. fr. Modern Greek by* Rae Dalven. VWA

Your pinks, your tulips live an hour. To the Gardener at Nuneham. Horace Walpole. FaBoEE

Your Presence. Mordecai Temkin, *tr. fr. Hebrew by* Jeremy Garber. VWA

Your sculptured lips are sealed. To J.F.K. 14 Years After. Roger Weaver. AMV-80

Your Shadow. Mark Strand. *Fr.* Elegy for My Father. Prf

Your skin is coming loose. Divorce. Skaidrite Stelzer. TC

Your smiles are not, as other women's be. To the Lady May. Aurelian Townsend. GBL

Your smiling, or the hope, the thought of it. A Simile for Her Smile. Richard Wilbur. HoPM (1975 ed.); InPK; OLR; UsP; WIF

Your soul is a sealed garden. Clair de Lune. Paul Verlaine, *tr. by* Arthur Symons. Moon

Your spirit flows out over all the land between. Flow at Full Moon. R. A. K. Mason. ATNZ

Your steps are twisted. Friend at a Drug Clinic. John Gonzalez. PMW

Your subjects hope, dread Sire. To the King's Most Excellent Majesty. Phillis Wheatley. TAP

Your tears, Niobe. Hayden Carruth. VGW

Your thighs are appletrees. Portrait of a Lady. William Carlos Williams. CMoP (1970 ed.); NoAM; NOBA; PoIA; VoA

Your thorned back. Old Woman. Iain Crichton Smith. MS

Your turn. Grass of confusion. Journal for My Daughter. Stanley Kunitz. RRA

Your ugly token [*or* Youre ugly tokyn]. Upon a Deadman's Head. John Skelton. AAS; HAP

Your uncle, totem and curator bends. Christopher at Birth. Michael Longley. CIP

Your voice always whacked me right on the funny bone. Burying Blues for Janis. Marge Piercy. NeAC; WBN

Your voice at times a fist. To a Husband. Maya Angelou. IHMS

Your voice is the color of a robin's breast. To O.E.A. Claude McKay. BPo

Your voice on the telephone. Donald Hall. FF

Your voice sister. Mississippi Born. Pearl Cleage Lomax. CNA

Your voice speaks:/ Great God of my life, I will praise Thee. Te Deum. Gertrud von le Fort. ILwL

Your wand,/ the flowering stalk of the radish. The Magician. Diane Wakoski. Psy

Your Woods. Margaret Holley. AMV-80

Your words arrive. The Stones. Ralph J. Mills, Jr. BrS

Your words, my friend, right helpful caustics, blame. Astrophel and Stella, XXI. Sir Philip Sidney. CABA (1972 ed.)

Your World ("Your world is as big as you make it"). Georgia Douglas Johnson. AmNP (1974 ed.)

Your yen two wol slee me sodenly. *See* Your eyen two will slay me suddenly.

You're. Sylvia Plath. FaBoTw (1975 ed.); NCSH

You're a Grand Old Flag. George M. Cohan. CTV; FSN, *with music*

Your'e a mean mistreating mama. Mean Mistreater Mama. *Unknown.* BluL

"You're fired, Lane." The Water-Truck. Patrick Lane. NeAC

You're going into play? An instant more. To a Baseball. *Unknown.* LiSp; SPo

You're Going to Reap Just What You Sow. *Unknown.* AmFP

You're having a gay old time. Mommie. Sarah Kennedy. CPA

You're having a helluva good time. Girl with Car and Guitar. Ralph Mecklenburger. SFF

You're in the Army Now, *with music. Unknown.* BLSo

You're in the mood for freaky food? Wicked Witch's Kitchen. X. J. Kennedy. IWK

You're my friend/ I was the man the Duke spoke to. The Flight of the Duchess. Robert Browning. VLP

You're not alone when you are still alone. Give Me Myself. Michael Drayton. *Fr.* Idea. PPM

You're Not the Only Pebble on the Beach, *with music.* Harry Braisted. FSN

You're Nothing but a Spanish Colored Kid. Felipe Luciano. PoBA

You're probably wondering. Little Keats' Soliloquy. Leon Stokesbury. NVAP

You're ready to decide. Of Birthright. Eric Torgersen. TC

You're sickly pale—a crooked root. The Measuring. Jared Carter. AMV-80

You're still a young man. Heaven for Railroad Men. David Wojahn. BrS

You're sweating it out, no wonder you freeze. The Puritan Hacking Away at Oak. Todd Gitlin. AMV-80

You're the Flower of My Heart. Richard H. Gerard. *See* Sweet Adeline.

You're the Top. Cole Porter. OBAL; UnPo (1976 ed.)

You're through—now walking up and down. The Aging Athlete. Neil Weiss. LiSP

You're too late. The Blues: A Literary Eclogue. Byron. MBPR

Youre ugly tokyn. *See* Your ugly token.

"You're very normal for a poet." A Hard Night's Daze. Basil Payne. IPM

You're wondering if I'm lonely. Song. Adrienne Rich. PBWP

Yours is a benison. Pregnancy. Mira Fish. FAF

Yours Truly. Leonard Nathan. AMV-80

Yourself. Jones Very. AmVN; ILP (1975 ed.); NOBA

Youth. "Laurence Hope." WeW

Youth. James Wright. ILP (1975 ed.)

Youth and Age. Samuel Taylor Coleridge. MBPR

Youth and Age. W. B. Yeats. FaBoEE

Youth and Age on Beaulieu River, Hants. John Betjeman. FaBoTw (1975 ed.)

Youth and Art. Robert Browning. STS

Youth and Beauty. Aurelian Townsend. GBL

Youth and Beauty. William Carlos Williams. RRA

Youth and Love. John Gay. *Fr.* The Beggar's Opera, II, i. NOBE

Youth and Love. Robert Louis Stevenson. SLP

Youth and the Northwind, The. John Godfrey Saxe. PoTa

Youth gone, and beauty gone if ever there. Christina Rossetti. *Fr.* Monna Innominata. GBL

Youth in apparel that glittered, A. The Black Riders, XXVII. Stephen Crane. PiAm; TT

Youth Mowing, A. D. H. Lawrence. NoAM

Youth of delight come hither. The Voice of the Ancient Bard. Blake. *Fr.* Songs of Experience. MBPR

Youth one day in a garden fair, A. The Story of the Rose. "Alice." FSN

Youth rambles on life's arid mount. The Progress of Poesy. Matthew Arnold. VLP

Youth there was, Elpenor was he nam'd, A. Homer, *tr. by* Pope. *Fr.* The Odyssey, X. OBVE

Youth walks up to the white horse, to put its halter on, The. The White Horse. D. H. Lawrence. PSN

Youth with Red-gold Hair, The. Edith Sitwell. FaBoTw (1975 ed.)

Youth worries all night long about whether he can, A. Tumbalalaika. *Tr. fr.* Yiddish. FSW

Youthful passion seeps through my mind. Tomb. David Semah, *tr. by* Yoffee Berkovitz. VWA

Youth's Antiphony. Dante Gabriel Rossetti. The House of Life, XIII. VLP

Youth's Spring-Tribute. Dante Gabriel Rossetti. The House of Life, XIV. ILP (1975 ed.); VLP

Youth's the season made for joys. Youth and Love. John Gay. *Fr.* The Beggar's Opera, II, i. NOBE

You've already learned heels down. The Limits of Equitation. Barbara Winder. AMV-81

You've asked me what the lobster is weaving there. Enigmas. Pablo Neruda, *tr. by* Robert Bly. NU

You've Been A Good Old Wagon, but You've Done Broke Down. Ben Harney. OBAL

You've come into my life like frost heaves. Frost Heaves. Michael Dorris. AMV-80

You've got nice knees. Love Song. Gavin Ewart. OxBTC

You've got to cross that lonesome valley. The Lonesome Valley. *Unknown.* RDB

You've gotten in through the transom. To a Child Trapped in a Barber Shop. Philip Levine. InPK; NoAM; NOBA; TAP; VGW

You've had your problems. To Bert Campaneris. Tom Clark. LiSp

You've heard of the Gresford disaster. The Gresford Disaster. *Unknown.* AIW; GBP; PeBB

You've made yourself in clay. Poem for a Son. Heather Cadsby. AMV-80

You've not yet put on. Countin the Ol One Hundred. Shirley Williams. CPA

You've plucked a curlew, drawn a hen. On an Island. J. M. Synge. BIrV

You've seen a strawberry. Nevertheless. Marianne Moore. CMoP (1970 ed.)

You've seen coalminers coming up. Underworld. George Garrett. SS

You've started today on life's journey. Have Courage, My Boy, to Say No! L. M. Hilton. WTO

You've Told Me, Maro. Martial, *tr. fr. Latin by* F. Lewis. NIL

Ys yt possyble. *See* Is it possible.

Yucca clump, The/ is blooming. The Yucca Moth. A. R. Ammons. NOBA

Yucca in the Moonlight. Glen Ward Dresbach. BPAW

Yucca Is Yellowing. William Haskel Simpson. BPAW

Yucca Moth, The. A. R. Ammons. NOBA

Yugoslav Cemetery. Celeste Turner Wright. WPE

Yuh Lookin Good. Carolyn M. Rodgers. BPo

Yule Days, The. *Unknown.* GBP

Yule's Come, and Yule's Gane. *Unknown.* GBP

Yves Tanguy. David Gascoyne. EAS

# Z

Zachary Zed. James Reeves. QQQ

Zack Bumstead uster flosserfize. A Philosopher. Sam Walter Foss. OBAL

Zack's eyes can't. Washing My Son. Jonathan Holden. AMV-81

Zalka Peetruza. Ray Garfield Dandridge. PoBA

Zanzibar Pete and Zoom-along Dick. Nancy Chambers. FPB

Zapata and the Landlord. A. B. Spellman. PoBA

Zayde, I drove all night to get here. A Place to Live. Martin Grossman. AMV-80

Zaydee. Philip Levine. NNaP; VWA

Zealless Xylographer, The. Mary Mapes Dodge. OBAL

Zealot without a Face. Charles Dobzynski, *tr. fr. French by* Anita Barrows. VWA

Zealous locksmith died of late, A. *Unknown.* FaBoEE

Zebra. "Isak Dinesen." MiP; RFM

Zebra, born both black and white, The. The Miscegenous Zebra. Roland Young. BoAnP

Zebra Dun, The, *diff. versions.* *Unknown.* AmFP; FSW; PH; PoTa

Zebras, The. Roy Campbell. PoPle

Zeenty, peenty, heathery, mithery. *Unknown.* GBP

Zeimbekiko. Robin Magowan. EAS

Zekiel Saw the Wheel. *Unknown.* WIF

Zepheria, *sels. Unknown.*
 "And is it by immutable decree." ESo
 "From the revenew of thine eyes' exchequer." ESo

 "How often hath my pen, mine heart's solicitour." ESo
 "How shall I deck my love in love's habiliment." ESo
 "Illuminating lamps, ye orbs christallite." ESo
 "When last mine eyes dislodged from thy beautie." ESo
 "When we in kind embracements had agre'd." AAS

Zephyr. *Unknown.* TDH

Zeppelin. Andrew Glaze. CSP; WeW

Zero/ zero/ zero/ the museum of modern art. The Story of the Zeros. Victor Hernandez Cruz. PoBA

Zero night. Heart/Song for Christopher Raymond. Bill Pauly. BrS

Zero vicinity, The. Darkness at Noon. Richard Friedman. FiCh

Zeus lies in Ceres' bosom. Cantos, LXXXI. Ezra Pound. NoAM; NOBA; VGW

Zeus was once overheard to shout at Hera. The Weather of Olympus. Robert Graves. FaBoEE

Zeyde. Roberta Metz. AMV-81

Zimmer Drunk and Alone, Dreaming of Old Football Games. Paul Zimmer. MAT

Zimmer Envying Elephants. Paul Zimmer. GP

Zimmer in Grade School. Paul Zimmer. GP

Zimmer in Winter. Paul Zimmer. FoP

Zimmer's Hard Dream. Paul Zimmer. GP

Zimmer's Last Gig. Paul Zimmer. AMV-80

Zimri: The Duke of Buckingham. Dryden. *Fr. Absalom and Achitophel, Pt. I.* NOBE; OBSV

Zinnia. Mary Ellen Solt. UsP

Zion's noblest Sons are weeping! On the Death of the Dearly Beloved and Much Lamented Father. Eliza R. Snow. WPW

Zion's Sons and Daughters. *Unknown.* AmFP

Zip Coon, *with music. Unknown.* PSoN

Zippora Returns to Moses at Rephidim. Rose Drachler. VWA

Ziz, The. John Hollander. VWA

Zizi's Lament. Gregory Corso. Epi; VGW

Zlotchev, My Home. Moishe Leib Halpern, *tr. fr. Yiddish by* Richard J. Fein. VWA

Zodiac, The, *sel.* James Dickey.
 "Tenderness, ache on me, and lay your neck." TAP

Zodiac Rhyme, The. *Unknown.* GBP

Zog Nit Keynmol (Tell Us No More). *Unknown, tr. fr. Yiddish.* FSW

Zohara. Jack Hirschman. VWA

Zolgotz. *Unknown.* AmFP

Zone. A. R. Ammons. TT

Zone. Louise Bogan. WPE

Zone of Death. William Everson. VGW

Zong, A: "O Jenny, don't sobby! vor I shall be true." William Barnes. BoLoP

Zong Belegt Baatar. *Mongol Oral Tradition, tr. by* C. R. Bawden. WTO

Zoo, The. Anthony Ostroff. MPA

Zoo day, today. And How It Goes. Anselm Hollo. TwMBP

Zoo Dream. David Barker. GP

Zoo keepers, though they grow more doctoral. Rarity. Ralph Robin. PoUp

Zoo You Too! Ted Joans. GP

Zooming across the sky. Up in the Air. James S. Tippett. ECBV

Zorba. James Liddy. IPM

Zounds, gramercy, and rootity-toot! Robin Hood. Phyllis McGinley. *Fr. Speaking of Television.* OBSV

Zummer Thoughts in Winter Time. William Barnes. VLP

Zun a-Lighten Eyes a-Shut, The. William Barnes. VLP

Zürich, zum Storchem. Paul Celan, *tr. fr. German by* Joachim Neugroschel. VWA

# AUTHOR INDEX

"A.N." *See* "N.,A."

**Aal, Katharyn Machan**
Ants.
He says he wrote by moonlight.

**Aaron, Jonathan**
Death of the Sports-Car Driver, The.

**Aaronson, Leonard**
Pesci Misti.

**Abbe, George**
I Saw an Army.
Last Patch of Snow.
My Friend, the Doctor.
Passer, The.
Skill in Killing, A.

**Abbey, Henry**
What Do We Plant?

**Abbott, Anthony S.**
Out of Mourning.

**Abbott, Steve**
Reading Today's Newspaper.

**Abelard, Peter**
David's Lament for Jonathan.

**Abele, Rudolph von**
About That of Which One Cannot
  Speak, One Must Be Silent.
Am I Not Your Son?
Poet Counterpoet.

**Abercrombie, Lascelles**
All Last Night.
Epitaph: "Sir, you should notice me: I
  am the Man."

**Abhau, Elliot**
Indecision Means Flexibility.

**Abney, Robert**
You Will Never Get Away No-O.

**Abramovitch, Henry**
Psalm of the Jealous God.

**Abse, Dannie**
Angels.
Doctor, The.
Duality.
Epithalamion: "Singing, today I married
  my white girl."
French Master, The.
Letter to Alex Comfort.
Near the Border of Insanities.
Night Out, A.
Pantomime Diseases.
Pathology of Colours.
Portrait of a Marriage.
Second Coming, The.
Smile Was, The.
Song for Dov Shamir.
Stethoscope, The.
Tales of Shatz.
Victim of Aulis, The.
X Ray.

**Absher, Tom**
Hunting with My Father.

**Abu al-Qasim al-Shabbi**
In the Shadow of the Valley of Death.

**Abutsu the Nun**
Diary of the Waning Moon, The, *sel.*

**Acconci, Vito Hannibal**
Re.

**Ackerson, Cathy**
Stepmother, The.

**Ackerson, Duane**
UA Flight to Chicago.
When Daddy Died.

**Ackley, Randall**
For a Young Woman Lying Alone in
  Bed.

**Acorn, Milton**
Blackfish Poem.
Ghostly Story.
I'd Like to Mark Myself.
I've Gone and Stained with the Color of
  Love.
Lover That I Hope You Are.
Monument.
Offshore Breeze.
On Saint-Urbain Street.
Poem for a Singer.
Saint-Henri Spring.

**Adair, V. H.**
Works and Days.

**Adam, Helen**
Counting-out Rhyme.
House o' the Mirror, The.
I Love My Love.

**Adamo, Ralph**
Easter Sunday: Not the Artist.
Low along the River.

**Adams, Arthur H.**
Dwellings of Our Dead, The.

**Adams, Bob, Paul Schindler** and **David
  Lewis.** *See* **Lewis, David, Paul
  Schindler** and **Bob Adams**

**Adams, Charles Follen ("Yawcob Strauss")**
John Barley-Corn, My Foe.
Misplaced Sympathy.
My Infundibuliform Hat.
Repartée.
To Bary Jade.

**Adams, Elijah**
Ashland Tragedy, The, 2 *versions.*

**Adams, Franklin Pierce ("F. P. A.")**
Composed in the Composing Room.
Double Standard, The.
If.
Lines Where Beauty Lingers.
Rich Man, The.
Such Stuff as Dreams.

**Adams, Herbert R.**
He Don't Know the Inside Feel.

**Adams, James Barton**
At a Cowboy Dance.

**Adams, John Coleman**
We Praise Thee, God, for Harvests
  Earned, *with music.*

**Adams, John G.**
Heaven Is Here, *with music.*

**Adams, John Quincy**
Send Forth, O God, Thy Light and
  Truth, *with music.*
To Sally.
Wants of Man, The, *abr.*

**Adams, Léonie**
Caryatid.
Counsel to Unreason.

Figurehead, The.
Grapes Making.
Song from a Country Fair.

**Adams, Marguerite Janvrin**
They Who Possess the Sea.

**Adams, Nehemiah**
Saints in Glory, We Together, *with
  music.*

**Adams, Sarah Flower**
Nearer, My God, to Thee.

**Adamson, Margot Robert**
Edinburgh.

**Adamson, Robert**
Final Solstice, The.
River, The.
Sail Away.
Sonnets to Be Written from Prison.

**Adcock, Betty**
Poetry Workshop in a Reform School.
Sixth Day, The.
Southbound.
Surviving the Wreck.
Walking Out.

**Adcock, Fleur**
Composition for Words and Paint.
For a Five-Year-Old.
For Andrew.
Incident.
Night Piece, *sel.*
Note on Propertius 1.5.
Unexpected Visit.
Water Below, The.
Wife to Husband.

**Addiego, John**
Berkeley Pier, The.

**Addison, Joseph**
Play-House, The.
Spacious Firmament on High, The.
When All Thy Mercies, O My God!
When rising from the bed of death.

**Ade, George**
Il Janitoro.
Microbe's Serenade, The.
R-e-m-o-r-s-e.

**"Adeler, Max" (Charles Heber Clark)**
In Memoriam.
Mr. Slimmer's Funeral Verses for the
  *Morning Argus.*
Sacred to the Memory of Maria (To Say
  Nothing of Jane and Martha) Sparks.

**Adler, Felix**
Hail the Glorious Golden City, *with
  music.*

**Adler, Hans**
Protect Me.
Ulster.

**Adler, Lucile**
Near Ganado.
Traveling Out, The.

**Adler, Mortimer J.**
Fearless, The.

**Adrian, Roman**
Bel Woman.
My Grandfather.

**"AE" (George William Russell)**
Exiles.
Germinal.
Vesture of the Soul, The.
**Aeschylus**
Prometheus Bound.
**Aesop (6th century B.C.)**
Ass in the Lion's Skin, The.
**Agathias Scholasticus**
Dialogue.
**Agee, James**
Lyric: "From now on kill America out
of your mind."
**Agnew, Edith**
Let me tell to you the story.
**Aguila, Pancho**
Female Femininity.
Folsom, August 11th: A Question of
Races.
Happy Birthday America.
Poet's Prayer para Yukio Mishima.
Prison Bi-Centennial Address, A.
Street Iconoclasts.
**Agustini, Delmira**
Blindness.
From Far Away.
**Aharoni, Ada**
To a Captain in Sinai.
**Ai (Florence Anthony)**
Abortion.
Anniversary, The.
But What I'm Trying to Say Mother Is.
Child Beater.
Country Midwife, The: A Day.
Cuba, 1962.
Everything: Eloy, Arizona, 1956.
Hangman.
Pentecost.
Possessions.
Root Eater, The.
Sweet, The.
Twenty Year Marriage.
Unexpected, The.
Why Can't I Leave You?
Winter in Another Country.
Woman.
Woman to Man.
**Aiken, Conrad**
Accomplices, The.
And in the Hanging Gardens.
Annihilation.
At a Concert of Music.
Atlantis.
Bend as the bow bends, and let fly the
shaft.
Blind Date.
Bread and Music.
Crab, The.
Dear Uncle Stranger.
Discordants, sels.
Doctor's Row.
Hatteras Calling.
Herman Melville.
Letter from Li Po, A, sel.
Limerick: "Animula vagula blandula."
Limerick: "It's time to make love: douse
the glim."
Limerick: "On the deck of a ship called
the Masm."
Limerick: "There once was a wonderful
wizard."
Lovers, The.

Morning Dialogue.
Morning Song.
Multitudes Turn in Darkness.
North Infiinity Street.
Obituary in Bitcherel.
Preludes for Memnon, sels.
Priapus and the Pool, sels.
Quarrel, The.
Rimbaud and Verlaine, precious pair of
poets.
Room, The.
Senlin, a Biography, sel.
Sighed a dear little shipboard divinity.
Snowflake on asphodel, clear ice on rose.
Sonnet: "Imprimis: I forgot all day your
face."
Sonnet: "My love, I have betrayed you
seventy times."
South End.
Summer.
There once was a wicked young minister.
Things, The.
Time in the Rock; or, Preludes to
Definition, sels.
Wedding, The.
Window, The.
**Aiken, Joan**
Grandfather.
John's Song.
Night Landscape.
Rhyme for Night.
Smile, The.
**Aikin, John**
Tit for Tat: A Tale.
**Aikin, Lucy**
Beggar Man, The.
Swallow, The.
**Ainger, A. C.**
God Is Working His Purpose Out.
**Ainger, Alfred**
On the Triumph of Rationalism.
**Ainsworth, Henry**
Fire in My Meditation Burned, with
music.
Give Ear, O Heavens, to That Which I
Declare, with music.
How Long, Jehovah? with music.
I Minded God, with music.
I Spread Out unto Thee My Hands, with
music.
In the Distress upon Me, with music.
To God Our Strength Shout Joyfully,
with music.
Unto Jehovah Sing Will I, with music.
With All My Heart, Jehovah, I'll
Confess, with music.
**Aitchison, James**
Classroom.
Landscape with Lapwings.
Last Clean Bough, The.
**Ajukutooq**
Song of Sukkaartik, the Assistant Spirit.
**Akahito (Yamabe no Akahito)**
I passed by the beach.
I wish I were close.
Mists rise over, The.
**Akazome Emon**
I, who cut off my sorrows.
**Akesson, Sonja**
Autobiography.
**Akhmadulina, Bella**
At Night.

Autumn.
Bride, The.
Dream, A.
Fifteen Boys.
Goodbye.
In the Emptied Rest Home.
Names of Georgian Women, The.
Silence.
Sleepwalkers.
Small Aircraft.
Sound of Rain, The.
Volcanoes.
Winter.
**"Akhmatova, Anna" (Anna Andreyevna
Gorenko)**
Alone.
Each Day Is Anxious.
Grey-eyed King, The.
Guest, The.
Hands clenched under my shawl.
He loved three things in life.
How can you look at the Neva.
I taught myself to live simply and wisely.
I wrung my hands under my dark veil.
Lot's Wife.
Requiem: "No, not far beneath some
foreign sky then."
Summer Garden.
Tashkent Breaks into Bloom.
What's worse than this past century?
Your lynx-eyes, Asia.
**Akhnaton (Amenhotep IV)**
Thy Rising Is Beautiful.
**Akhyaliyya, Laila**
Laila Boasting.
Lamenting Tauba.
**Akiko, Yosano.** See **Yosano Akiko**
**Akin, Güflten**
Ellas and the Statues.
**Akjartoq**
Remembering.
**Alabaster, William**
Incarnatio Est Maximum Dei Donum.
**Alakoye, Adesanya**
Upsouth.
**Al-Arabi, Ibn**
My heart has become capable of every
form.
**Alba, Nanina**
Be Daedalus.
For Malcolm X.
**Albert, Richard E.**
Malfunction.
**Albiach, Anne-Marie**
État, sel.
He accepts the circle, speech and so.
**Albrecht, Elizabeth**
Something Missing on the Left.
Woman Talking Man into Child.
**Albright, Rachel**
LaSalle Street.
Steel Mills.
**Alcott, Louisa May**
Little Kingdom I Possess, A.
**Alcuin**
Lament for the Cuckoo.
**Aldan, Daisy**
Christmas.
Everywhere in constancy, He is intoning,
Look! Look!
Green at Colmar.

I Am Moved by a Necessity from Within.
No longer will I close an opaque door.
Snow in Summer.
Stones: Avesbury.
Vertical Is Our New Sight.

**Aldana, Francisco de**
Image of God, The.

**Alderson, A. F.**
Montezuma.

**Aldington, Richard**
Evening.
Images.

**Aldis, Dorothy**
A-Ha!
Blum.
Fourth of July Night.
Island, The.
Little.
Mouths.
Nice Old Couple, The.
No One Heard Him Call.
Seals, The.
Supper for a Lion.
What Happened.
When.
When I Was Lost.
Whistles.

**Aldiss, Brian W.**
Progression of the Species.
Tom Wedgwood Tells.

**Aldrich, Henry**
Five Reasons, The.
Why I Drink.

**Aldrich, Thomas Bailey**
At a Reading.
Fannie ("Fannie has the sweetest foot").
Memory.

**Alegria, Claribel**
Disillusionment.
Loneliness and July Ninth.
Search.
Small Country.

**Aleixandre, Vicente**
After Love.
Old Man and the Sun, The.

**Alenier, Karren L.**
Cobbler.
Energy Sources.
Slight of Hands, A.

**Aleqaajik**
Great grief came over me.

**Alexander, Bonnie L.**
Lapidary.

**Alexander, Cecil Frances**
All Things Bright and Beautiful.
Beggar Boy, The.
Fieldmouse, The.
Jesus Calls Us, with music.
Once in Royal David's City.
There Is a Green Hill.

**Alexander, Charlotte**
Write-off, The.

**Alexander, John T.**
Winning of the TV West, The.

**Alexander, Kenyon**
Case Notes.
Evocations.

**Alexander, Lewis**
Dream Song.
Enchantment.
Negro Woman.

Nocturne Varial.

**Alexander, Pamela**
Air.
Flight.
Interface.

**Alexander, Sir William.** *See* **Stirling, William Alexander, Earl of**

**Alford, Henry**
Come, ye thankful people, come.
Mendip Hills over Wells, The.
Ten thousand times ten thousand.

**Alfred, William**
Mary Lifted from the Dead, *with music.*

**Al-Hallaj**
Ecstasy, The.
There is a selfhood in my nothingness.

**Ali, Muhammed (Cassius Clay)**
Clay Comes Out to Meet Terrell.
I Dance and I Have a Fast Hook.

**"Alice"**
Story of the Rose, The, *with music.*

**Aliesan, Jody**
On a Wednesday.
This Fall ("This fall the japanese maple turned coral red").

**Aliger, Margarita**
House in Meudon.
To a Portrait of Lermontov.
Two.

**Alighieri, Dante.** *See* **Dante Alighieri**

**Al-Khansa**
Elegy for Her Brother Sakhr.
For Her Brother.
In Death's Field.
Night, The.
On Her Brother.
On Her Brother Sakhr.
Rain to the Tribe.
Sleepless.
Thousand and One Nights, The, *sel.*

**Al-Khirniq**
Lament after Her Husband Bishr's Murder.

**Allan, Lewis**
Strange Fruit.

**Allcock, John**
Death Is a Door.
Looking Up.

**Allen, Dick**
American Gothic, An.
Depression: My Father Speaks to My Mother.
Green Pastures.
Mime.
Normal Lives.
Podunk, 1941.
Present, The.
Staying Married.
To a Woman Half a World Away.
Writer's House, The.

**Allen, Edward**
Best Line Yet, The.

**Allen, Elizabeth**
Verse for Vestigials.

**Allen, Elizabeth Akers**
Sea-Birds.

**Allen, Grace Elisabeth**
Pinkletinks.

**Allen, Hervey**
Upstairs Downstairs.

**Allen, James B.**
Homecoming, The.

Night Shift at the Plating Division of Keeler Brass.

**Allen, John Alexander**
Word to a Father, Dead, A.

**Allen, Jonathan**
Sinners, Will You Scorn the Message? *with music.*

**Allen, Leslie Holdsworth**
Reaper, The.

**Allen, Marie Louise**
Angleworms.
What Is It?

**Allen, Paula Gunn**
Lament of My Father, Lakota.
Trick Is Consciousness, The.

**Allen, Samuel ("Paul Vesey")**
Dylan, Who Is Dead.
If the Stars Should Fall.
Moment Please, A.
My Friend.
Nat Turner.
Ski Trail.
Staircase, The.
To Satch.

**Alline, Henry**
Amazing Sight! The Saviour Stands, *with music.*
Hard Heart of Mine, *with music.*
Turn, Turn, Unhappy Souls, Return, *with music.*

**Allingham, William**
Dream, The [*or* A].
Eviction, The.
Fairies, The.
Laurence Bloomfield in Ireland, *sel.*
Memory, A.
Mill, A.
Riding.
Robin Redbreast.
Swing Song, A ("Swing, swing").
Wishing.

**Allison, Drummond**
Brass Horse, The.
Dedication: "Had there been peace there never had been riven."
No Remedy.

**Allott, Kenneth**
Lament for a Cricket Eleven.
Statue, The.

**Alma-Tadema, Laurence**
If No One Ever Marries Me.

**Alohikea, Alfred**
Glory of Hanalei is its heavy rain, The.

**Alpaugh, Ern** *and* **Dewey G. Pell**
Swinging Chick.

**Alquit, B. (Eliezer Blum**
Light of the World, The.
Wandering Chorus.

**Alta**
After Reading Sylvia Plath.
And Why Are All the Voices I Hear Divided into Colors?
Anybody Could Write This Poem. All You Have to Say Is Yes.
Art of Enforced Deprivation, The.
Bitter Herbs.
Car has pulled up outside, A.
Daily Courage Doesn't Count.
Don 1958.
Euch, are you having your period?
Euridice.
Fighting my dependency.

Firebird.
First Pregnancy.
He asked me what was I fantasizing.
How can people stand to be around me?
   I'm always babbling.
I Don't Have No Bunny Tail on My
   Behind.
I Never Saw a Man in a Negligee.
I promised I would but I can't.
I slept alone last nite but when you
   know you dont have to.
Penus envy, they call it.
Shirley 4 Years Later.
Stockton State Mental Hospital 1962.

**Alterman, Nathan**
Poem about Your Face.
Spinning Girl, The.
Tammuz.
This Night.
To the Elephants.

**Althaus, Keith**
In the Hammersmith Public Library.
Indian Summer Garden Party.
Middle River.
Poem: "Begin here; where I began."
Somnambulist Blue, The.
Traveling in Europe.

**Altizer, Nell**
Death of Sappho, The.
Haleiwa Churchyard.
Hunger.

**Altman, Shalom**
Vine and Fig Tree.

**Alvarez, Alfred**
Cemetery in New Mexico, A.
Dying.
Fortunate Fall, The.
Lost.
Mourning and Melancholia.

**Alver, Betti**
Iron Heaven.
Painter in the Lion Cage, The.
Tailor Called Sorrow, A.
Titans, The.

**Ama Ata Aidoo, Christine**
Prelude: "I am the bird of the wayside."

**Amen, Grover**
Cot, The.

**Ames, Bernice**
Country of Water.
Getting to Emily's.

**Ames, Jay**
On Corwen Road.

**Amichai, Yehuda**
Advice.
God Has Pity on Kindergarten Children.
I Am a Leaf.
I Am Sitting Here.
I Think of Oblivion.
In the Old City.
Jerusalem, Port City.
Lament: "Diameter of the bomb was
   thirty centimeters, The."
Lay Your Head on My Shoulder.
Not Like a Cypress.
Of Three or Four in a Room.
On the Day of Atonement.
On the Wide Stairs.
Pity, A; We Were Such a Good
   Invention.
Quick and Bitter.
Shadow of the Old City.

Since Then.
Sodom's Sister City.
Town I Was Born In, The.
We Did It.

**Amini, Johari.**   *See* **Latimore, Jewel C.**

**Amir, Aharon**
Cock.
Nothingness.

**Amis, Kingsley**
Aberdarcy: The Main Square.
After Goliath.
Against Romanticism.
Beowulf.
Bookshop Idyll, A.
Dream of Fair Women, A.
Evans Country, The, *sels.*
Ever-fixed Mark, An.
Helbatrawss, The.
Langwell.
Last War, The.
New Approach Needed.
Note on Wyatt, A.
Pendydd.
St. Asaph's.

**Amis, Lewis R.**
Jehovah, God, Who Dwelt of Old, *with
   music.*

**Ammons, Archie Randolph**
After Yesterday.
Apologia pro Vita Sua.
Arc Inside and Out, The.
Auto Mobile.
Ballad: "I want to know the unity in all
   things."
Cascadilla Falls.
Chaos Staggered up the Hill.
Chasm.
Christmas Eve.
City Limits, The.
Clarity.
Classic.
Cleavage.
Close-Up.
Confirmers, The.
Conserving the Magnitude of
   Uselessness
Constant, The.
Coon Song.
Corsons Inlet.
Coward.
Cut the Grass.
Dark Song.
Diner.
Eternal City, The.
First Carolina Said-Song.
Gravelly Run.
Guitar Recitativos.
Hardweed Path Going.
He Held Radical Light.
Hippie Hop.
Hymn: "I know if I find you I will have
   to leave the earth."
Identity.
Imperialist.
Laser.
Life in the Boondocks.
Loss.
Marble.
Mechanism.
Mirrorment.
Mountain Liar.
Needs.

Open.
Periphery.
Play.
Plunder.
Poetics.
Prospecting.
Put-down Come On, The.
Rocking.
Room Conditioner.
Runoff.
Satisfaction.
Saying.
Second Carolina Said-Song.
Silver.
Small Song.
So I Said I Am Ezra.
Spring Coming.
Still.
Terrain.
Transaction.
Triphammer Bridge.
Unifying Principle, The.
Unsaid.
Upland.
Viable.
Visit.
Winter Scene.
Working with Tools.
Yucca Moth, The.
Zone.

**Amorosi, Ray**
Nothing Inside and Nothing Out.

**Amprimoz, Alexandre L.**
Final Fall, The.

**Anacreon**
Thracian Filly, The.

**Anania, Michael**
Reeving.
Return.
Riversong.

**Andal**
Cuckoo, noisy among the Shenbaka
   flowers.
O people who live in the world.
To Krishna Haunting the Hills.

**Andersen, Astrid Hjertenaes**
Before the sun goes down.

**Andersen, Hans Christian**
Pearl, The.

**Anderson, Bill**
Letter from a Black Soldier.
Outbreak.

**Anderson, David Earle**
With the Nuns at Cape May Point.

**Anderson, Don**
Have You Thanked a Green Plant
   Today.

**Anderson, Eloise**
Mini Spooks, The.

**Anderson, Ethel**
Bucolic Eclogues, *sel.*
Clipper *Dunbar* to the clipper *Cutty
   Sark,* The.

**Anderson, Forrest**
Metropole.
Tiki.
True Religion.

**Anderson, Jack**
Aesthetics of the Moon.
Commanding a Telephone to Ring.
Garden of Situations, A.
Going to Norway.

Invention of New Jersey, The.
Ode to Pornography.
This Is a Poem for Patrick Casey, *sel.*
**Anderson, James**
When Father Slept.
**Anderson, Jon**
Blue Animals, The.
Campaign for Peace in Our Time, The.
Commitment, A.
In Autumn.
In Sepia.
John Clare.
Lives of the Saints.
Milky Way, The.
Mouths of the Poor, The.
Parachutist, The.
Photograph of Myself, The.
Rosebud.
Stories.
Years.
**Anderson, Kenneth L.**
Hope.
**Anderson, Patrick**
Sestina in Time of Winter.
**Anderson, S. E.**
Junglegrave.
Sound of Afroamerican History Chapt I,
The.
Sound of Afroamerican History Chapt
II, The.
**Anderson, Sherwood**
Evening Song.
Visit, A.
**Anderson, Wendell B.**
Winter Dance, San Domingo.
**Andresen, Sophia de Mello Breyner**
Camoes and the Debt.
Dead Men, The.
Dionysius.
Mirrors, The.
**Andrew, Prudence**
Whippet.
**Andrewes, Francis**
Shepherdess' Valentine, *sel.*
**Andrews, Colman**
Four Postcards from Italy.
**Andrews, Jenne**
Autumn Horses.
In Pursuit of the Family.
Reach of Winter, The.
Sounding.
Wife.
Words from Storms and Geese in the
Morning.
**Andrews, Wayne**
On Looking into the Spilled Ink on the
Porcelain.
**Angelou, Maya**
Chicken-Licken.
No Loser, No Weeper, *sel.*
They Went Home.
To a Husband.
**Anghelaki-Rooke, Katerina**
Before they ripen into diffused spririts.
Notes on My Father, *sel.*
**Angoff, Charles**
God Is Here Again.
What Has Happened.
**Angus, Marion**
Alas! Poor Queen.
Anemones.
Mary's Song.

Think Lang.
**Anson, John Seller**
Lighthouse, The.
Proverbial.
**Anthony, Edward ("A. C. Gate")**
Bloodhound, The.
Collies, The.
Dachshund, The.
**Anthony, Florence.** *See* **Ai**
**Anthony, George**
Autumn Evening.
**Antipater of Sidon**
Never again, Orpheus.
**Antoninus, Brother.** *See* **Everson, William**
**Anyte**
Alive, this man was Manes, a common
slave.
I, Hermes, have been set up.
I am Hermes. I stand in the crossroads
by a windy.
Lounge in the shade of the luxuriant
laurel's.
**Aphek, Edna**
Sarah.
Story of Abraham and Hagar, The.
**Apolebieji, Odeniyi**
Salute to the Elephant.
**Apollinaire, Guillaume**
Mirabeau Bridge, The.
Moonlight.
**Applegarth, George S.**
Charge of the Grid Brigade.
**Appleman, Philip**
Black Is Beautiful.
East Hampton: The Structure of Sound.
Memo to the 21st Century.
**Applewhite, James**
Bordering Manuscript.
Dream of Ascent.
My Grandfather's Funeral.
On the Homefront.
Ravine, The.
Red Wing Hawk.
To Earth.
Tobacco Men.
Versions of Sunlight.
War Summer.
**Aquinas, Saint Thomas.** *See* **Thomas
Aquinas, Saint**
**Araaya, Hailu**
Marital Journey, The.
**Arana, Helen**
Word Can Become the Way It Sounds,
A.
**Aratus of Soli**
Praise of Zeus.
**Arberg, H. W.** *and* **Edmund L. Gruber.**
*See* **Gruber, Edmund L.** *and* **H. W.
Arberg**
**Arbuthnot, John**
Epitaph on Colonel Francis Chartres.
Know Yourself.
**Archer, Nuala**
Flies Love Me.
**Archilochos**
Decks awash,/ Mast-top dipping.
Like Odysseus under the ram.
May he lose his way on the cold sea.
On the Daughter of Lykambes.
**Arden, Richard Pepper, Baron Alvanley**
On Dr. Samuel Ogden.
**Ardinger, Richard**

At 85.
**Aridjis, Umberto**
Sun Set.
**Ariosto, Ludovico**
Orlando Furioso, *sels.*
**Aristophanes**
Lysistrata.
**Arkell, Reginald**
Public Nuisance, A.
**Armand, Octavio**
Possible Love Poem to the Usurer.
**Armour, Richard**
Common Carrier.
Copy.
Covering the Subject.
Deus ex Machina.
Enticer.
Fish Story.
Good Sportsmanship.
Hiding Place.
High Chair and Low Spirits.
Library.
On His Marks.
Seasonal Phenomenon.
Watchdog.
**Armstrong, John**
Urban Pollution.
**Armstrong, Martin**
To a Jilt.
**Armstrong, Thomas**
Row between the Cages, The.
**"Armytage, R."** *See* **Watson, Rosamund
Marriot**
**Arnatkoak**
Personal Song.
**Arnett, Carroll**
Anadarko John.
Drunk.
Land.
Removal: Last Part.
Rock Painting.
Something for Supper.
Story of My Life, The.
You.
**Arnold, Sir Edwin**
Light of Asia, The, *sels.*
Swallow's Nest, The.
**Arnold, George**
Beer.
**Arnold, Gertrude Thomas**
Desert Bloom.
**Arnold, Lila**
Paisley Ceiling, The.
**Arnold, Matthew**
Bacchanalia; or, The New Age, *sel.*
Buried Life, The.
Courage.
Cruel, but composed and bland.
Dover Beach.
Dream, A.
Empedocles on Etna.
Epilogue to Lessing's Laocoön.
Farewell, A: "My horse's feet beside the
lake."
Forsaken Merman, The.
Growing Old.
Hill-Side Flowers.
In Harmony with Nature.
In Utrumque Paratus.
Last Word, The.
Lines Written in Kensington Gardens.
Matthias, *sels.*

Meeting.
Memorial Verses.
Memory-Picture, A.
Nameless Epitaph, A.
Palladium.
Parting.
Persistency of Poetry.
Philomela.
Progress of Poesy, The.
Requiescat.
Resignation.
Rugby Chapel.
Scholar-Gipsy, The.
Self-Dependence.
Shakespeare.
So, some tempestuous morn in early
 June.
Sohrab and Rustum.
Song of Callicles, The.
Stanzas from the Grande Chartreuse.
Stanzas in Memory of the Author of
 "Obermann."
Strayed Reveller, The.
Switzerland, sels.
Terrace at Berne, The.
Thyrsis.
To a Friend.
To a Republican Friend, 1848.
To a Republican Friend: Continued.
To Marguerite ("Yes! in the sea of life
 enisled").
West London.
Written in Butler's Sermons.
Written in Emerson's Essays.

**Arp, Hans**
Domestic Stones, The (fragment).
I Am a Horse.
Two little arabs adult and arabesque.
When it burns before the harps and
 freezes behind the easels.

**Arp, Jean**
What the Violins Sing in Their Baconfat
 Bed.

**Arrabey, Salaan**
To a Faithless Friend.

**Arriví, Francisco**
Song for a Day, sel.
Song for a Transformation, sel.

**Arsenault, Joel**
Windfall.

**Arundel, Anne Howard, Duchess of.** See
 **Howard, Anne, Duchess of Arundel**

**Arvey, Michael**
Concert.
Follower.

**Arvey, Verna**
All That I Am, with music.

**Arvidson, K. O.**
Fish and Chips on the Merry-go-round.
Tall Wind, The.

**Asbaje, Juana de.** See **Juana Inés de la
 Cruz, Sister**

**Ash, Charles Bowker**
Adbaston.

**Ashbery, John**
As One Put into the Packet-Boat.
Civilization and Its Discontents.
Definition of Blue.
Dido.
Farm Implements and Rutabagas in a
 Landscape.
Fear of Death.

Forties Flick.
Grand Abacus.
How much longer will I be able to
 inhabit the divine sepulcher.
Ice-Cream Wars, The.
Idiot, The
If the Birds Knew.
Instruction Manual, The.
Last Month.
Le Livre Est sur la Table.
Leaving the Atocha Station.
Man of Words, A.
Märchenbilder.
Mixed Feelings.
No Way of Knowing.
One Thing That Can Save America, The.
Our Youth.
Painter, The.
Picture of Little J. A. in a Prospect of
 Flowers, The.
Poem: "While we were walking under
 the top."
Rivers and Mountains.
Some Trees.
Song: "Song tells us of our old way of
 living, The."
Soonest Mended.
Spring Day.
Task, The.
Tennis Court Oath, The.
Tenth Symphony.
These Lacustrine Cities.
They Dream Only of America.
Thoughts of a Young Girl.
To Redouté.
Two Sonnets.
Vase of Flowers, A.
White Roses.
Worsening Situation.
Wrong Kind of Insurance, The.
Years of Indiscretion.
Young Prince and the Young Princess,
 The.

**Asheron, Sara**
Echo.
How Come?

**Ashley, Nova Trimble**
Humiliation Revisited.

**Ashley, Paul David**
All We Wanted.
Beauty.
Ending an Affair.
Ladies in Love.
Prison.
Ritual, The.
Song from the Unfinished Man.
Sounds.

**Ashmore, John**
Ex M. Antonio Flaminio, Ad Agellum
 Suum.

**Askenazy, Ludvik**
Wall, The.

**Askew, Anne**
Ballad Which Anne Askew Made and
 Sang When She Was in Newgate, The.

**Asquith, Herbert**
Birthday Gifts.
Hairy Dog, The.
Mare, The.
Volunteer, The.

**Astor, Susan**
Dame.

Four Spacious Skies.
Road the Crows Own, The.

**Asturias, Miguel Angel**
Indians Come Down from Mixco, The.

**Asya (Asya Gay)**
Celan.
Deer, The.
Grain of Moonlight, A.
My Strawlike Hair.
My True Memory.
Pause a Moment.

**Atchity, Kenneth John**
Delicate Impasse, A.

**Atkins, Russell**
At War.
"Dangerous Condition": Sign on Inner-
 City House.
Dark Area.
Inner-City Lullaby.
Irritable Song.
It's Here in The.
Narrative.
New Storefront.
Night and a Distant Church.
On the Fine Arts Garden, Cleveland.
Probability and Birds in the Yard.

**Attar**
Sun of My Perfection Is a Glass, The.

**Atwood, Margaret**
Accident Has Occurred, The.
After All You Are Quiet.
After the agony in the guest/ bedroom.
Against Still Life.
At first I was given centuries.
Carrying Food Home in Winter.
Daguerreotype Taken in Old Age.
Death of a Young Son by Drowning.
Dream 2: Brian the Still-Hunter.
Dream 3: Night Bear Which Frightened
 Cattle.
Dufferin, Simcoe, Grey.
Eden Is a Zoo.
Elegy for the Giant Tortoises.
Explorers, The.
First Element.
First Prayer.
Fishbowl.
Game after Supper.
Habitation.
I can change my-/ self more easily.
Interview with a Tourist.
It Is Dangerous to Read Newspapers.
Landlady, The.
Late August.
Lying here, everything in me.
Midwinter, Presolstice.
Night in the Royal Ontario Museum, A.
Provisions.
Revenant, The.
Siren Song.
Songs of the Transformed, sel.
Stories in Kinsman's Park.
Their Attitudes Differ.
There Is Only One of Everything.
They Eat Out.
This year I intended children
We are standing facing each other.
Woman Skating.
You Are Happy.
You fit into me.
You refuse to own.
You take my hand and.

You want to go back.
Your back is rough all.
**Aua**
Bear Hunting.
Morning Prayer.
Walrus Hunting.
**Aubert, Alvin**
Balls and Chain.
Bessie Smith's Funeral.
Blood to Blood.
Codicil.
Last Will and Testament.
Levitation.
Nat Turner in the Clearing.
One More Time.
There Were Fierce Animals in Africa.
When the Wine Was Gone.
**Aubert, Rosemary**
Love Poem: "I want/ to make a myth of you."
**Audelay, John**
Fairest Flower, The.
Love of God, The.
Passion of Christ Strengthen Me.
What Tidings?
**Auden, Wystan Hugh**
Aesthetic Point of View, The.
As I Walked Out One Evening.
At the Manger Mary Sings.
Average, The.
Brussels in Winter.
Carry Her over the Water.
Casino.
Chorus: "Summer holds, The: upon its glittering lake."
Chorus: "You are the town and we are the clock."
City without Walls.
Consider.
Cultural Presupposition, The.
Dear, though the night is gone.
Decoys, The.
Dog beneath the Skin, The, *sels.*
Doggerel by a Senior Citizen.
Epitaph for the Unknown Soldier.
Epitaph on a Tyrant.
Et in Arcadia Ego.
Exiles, The.
Fairground.
Fall of Rome, The.
First Things First.
Fish in the unruffled lakes.
Free One, A.
Gare du Midi.
Good-bye to the Mezzogiorno.
Hammerfest.
Henry Adams.
Horae Canonica, *sel.*
Hunting Season.
If I Could Tell You.
In Due Season.
In Memory of Sigmund Freud.
In Memory of W. B. Yeats.
In Praise of Limestone.
Island Cemetery, An.
James Watt.
Journey to Iceland.
Lady Weeping at the Crossroads.
Law like Love.
Letter, The.
Letter to Lord Byron, *sels.*
Lost on a fogbound spit of sand.

Love Feast, The.
Lullaby: "Lay your sleeping head, my love."
Macao.
Marginalia, *sel.*
May with its light behaving.
Miss Gee.
Missing.
Moon Landing.
More Loving One, The.
Musée des Beaux Arts.
New Year Letter, *sels.*
Night Mail.
No Change of Place.
Now the leaves are falling fast.
O What Is That Sound [Which So Thrills the Ear].
O Where Are You Going?
Ode to Terminus.
Ode to the Medieval Poets.
On the Circuit.
On This Island.
Orators, The, *sel.*
Our Bias.
Our Hunting Fathers.
Parable.
Paysage Moralisé.
Petition.
Poem: "He watched with all his organs of concern."
Poem: "O who can ever praise enough."
Prime.
Private faces in public places.
Prologue: "By landscape reminded once of his mother's figure."
Prologue: "O love, the interest itself in thoughtless heaven."
Proof, The.
Schoolchildren.
Sea and the Mirror, The, *sel.*
September 1, 1939.
Sext.
Shield of Achilles, The.
Since.
Sir Rider Haggard.
Some thirty inches from my nose.
Song: "Deftly, admiral, cast your fly."
Song for St. Cecilia's Day.
Song of the Master and Boatswain.
Sonnets from China, *sels.*
Summer Night, A.
Surgical Ward.
T. S. Eliot.
Taller to-day, we remember similar evenings.
That Night When Joy Began.
This Lunar Beauty.
Uncle Henry.
Under Which Lyre, a Reactionary Tract for the Times.
Unknown Citizen, The.
Up There.
Victor Was a Little Baby.
Voice of Caesar, The.
Voltaire at Ferney.
Walking Tour, The.
Wanderer, The.
Watershed, The.
When Statesmen gravely say "We must be realistic."
Who's Who.
Why are the public buildings so high?

**Audiberti, Jacques**
If I die let my widow go.
**Auerbach, Ephraim**
Seismograph.
**"Aunt Effie."** *See* **Browne, Jane Euphemia**
**"Aunt Mary."** *See* **Lathbury, Mary Artemisia**
**Ausländer, Rose**
Father.
Hasidic Jew from Sadagora.
In Chagall's Village.
Jerusalem.
Lamed-Vov, The.
My Nightingale.
Passover.
Phoenix.
**Ausonius, Decimus Magnus**
I am that Dido which thou here do'st see.
On the sicilian strand a hare well wrought.
**Auster, Paul**
Convenant.
Hieroglyph.
Scribe.
Song of Degrees.
**Austin, Alan**
Chance I.
Eating Ground Zero.
On Flying into Washington over the Pentagon.
**Austin, Alfred**
Human Tragedy, The, *sel.*
Is Life Worth Living?
To Beatrice Stuart Wortley: Aetat 2.
Winter is gone, and spring is over.
**Austin, Mary**
At Carmel.
Caller of the Buffalo.
Eagle's Song, The.
Elf Owl.
Grizzly Bear.
Heart's Friend, The.
Neither Spirit nor Bird.
Prairie-Dog Town.
Prayer to the Mountain Spirit.
San Francisco.
Sandhill Crane, The.
Warrior's Song.
Winter in the Sierras.
**Austin, Regina M.**
Still Life.
**Ava, Frau**
I am yours, you are mine.
**Avery, Richard K.**
And the Cock Begins to Crow, *with music.*
**Avison, Margaret**
For Tinkers Who Travel on Foot.
Hiatus.
Lament, A: "Gizzard and some ruby inner parts, A."
Nameless One, A.
Party, The.
Stray Dog, near Ecully.
Tennis.
Two Selves, The.
Water and Worship: An Open-Air Service on the Gatineau River.
**Awad, Joseph**
Generations.
In a World of Change.

**Axelrod, Mark**
Three Concrete Poems.
**Axelrod, Susan**
Home, The.
**Ayer, Frederick Fanning**
Indictment, The, *abr.*
**Ayloffe, John**
Britannia and Raleigh.
Marvell's Ghost.
Oceana and Britannia.
**Ayres, Philip**
Death of Adonis, The.
Epigram on Woman, An.
Fly, The.
Yoke uneasy on the ox doth sit, The.
**Ayton, Sir Robert**
Inconstancy Reproved.
**Aytoun, William Edmonstoune**
[*or*Edmondstoune]
Execution of Montrose, The.
Island of the Scots, The, *abr.*
Massacre of the Macpherson, The.
Old Scottish Cavalier, The.
Sonnet to Britain.
Widow of Glencoe, The, *sel.*
**Aytoun, William Edmonstoune** *and* Sir
Theodore Martin
Lay of the Lovelorn, The.


# B

**"B. V." ("Bysshe Vanolis").** *See*
Thomson, James (1834-1882)
**Babcock, Donald C.**
O God, in Whom the Flow of Days, *with
music.*
**Babcock, Maltbie Davenport**
Be Strong.
This Is My Father's World.
**Baca, Jimmy Santiago**
Another Love Poem.
Dreaming about Freedom.
Three Friends of Mine.
**Bachar, Eli**
Dawn of Jaffa Pigeons, A.
Houses, Past and Present.
Room Poems.
**Bachmann, Ingeborg**
Curriculum Vitae.
Days in White.
Every Day.
Firstborn Land, The.
Great Freight, The.
Out of the corpse-warm vestibule of
heaven steps the sun.
You want the summer lightning, throw
the knives.
**Baciu, Stefan**
Jean Charlot.
**Bacon, Barbara**
In Between the Curve.
**Bacon, Francis**
World's a Bubble, The.
**Bacon, Leonard (1802-81)**
Hail, Tranquil Hour of Closing Day,
*with music.*
O God, beneath Thy Guiding Hand,
*with music.*

Wake the Song of Jubilee, *with music.*
**Bacon, Leonard (b. 1887)**
Richard Tolman's Universe.
**Baer, William**
Books.
**Bagg, Robert**
Soft Answers.
**Bahe, Liz Sohappy**
And What of Me?
Farewell: "You sang round-dance
songs."
Grandmother Sleeps.
Once Again.
Parade, The.
Printed Words.
Ration Card, The.
Talking Designs.
**Bailey, Alfred G.**
Question, Is It, The?
**Bailey, Alice Morrey**
Defiant One, The.
**Bailey, H. Sewell**
Sailor Man.
**Bailey, Philip James**
Poem: "Poetry is itself a thing of God."
**Baillie, Joanna**
Tiger at Play.
Trysting Bush, The.
**Baird, Martha**
Confidence.
**Baker, Carlos**
Men of Sudbury, The.
**Baker, David**
Hermit.
Persimmon Trees, She Remembers, Not
Far Away.
**Baker, Donald W.**
Formal Application.
**Baker, Karle Wilson**
Courage.
**Baker, Prentice**
Moth, The.
Pine Assessor, The.
Virgin Jewess, Rising with a Cry, The.
**Baker, Verna Tomlinson**
Bird ecstatic with the spring, A.
Clarity of spring, The.
Night filled, A:/ Light pinning the dark.
**Balaban, John**
"Faith and Practice."
**Balakian, Peter**
Blue Church, The.
**Balazs, Mary**
Incident at Mossel Bay.
Pregnant Teenager on the Beach.
**Baldwin, Deirdra**
Blue Chairs.
Collective Forces, The.
Their Strange Evaluation.
**Baldwin, Michael**
Arctic Vixen.
Small Brown Bear, The.
**Baldwin, Neil**
Gaining, with Departure.
**Ball, Julie**
Recovery.
**Ball, Patricia**
Baby Giraffe.
Cavatina.
Therapy.
**Ballantyne, Deirdre**
Long Word, The.

**Ballard, Charles G.**
Changing of the Guard.
During the Pageant at Medicine Lodge.
Grandma Fire.
Man of Property, The.
Memo.
Navajo Girl of Many Farms.
Now the People Have the Light.
Sand Creek.
Speaker, The.
Spirit Craft, The.
Their cone-like Cabins.
Time Was the Trail Went Deep.
Winds of Change, The.
You Northern Girl.
**Ballard, Rae**
Father of the Victim.
**Ballou, Hosea, I**
Dear Lord, Behold Thy Servants, *with
music.*
In God's Eternity, *with music.*
When God Descends with Men To
Dwell, *with music.*
**Ballou, Hosea, II**
Ye Realms below the Skies, *with music.*
**Ballou, Silas**
Almighty God in Being Was, *with music.*
While I Am Young, *with music.*
**Bancroft, James Henry**
Brother, Though from Yonder Sky, *with
music.*
**Bangs, John Kendrick**
Little Elf, The.
**Banker, Iowna Elizabeth**
Lion Thoughts.
**Banks, Heather**
Eschatology.
Haying.
Pines.
**Banning, Lex**
Apocalypse in Springtime.
**Bantock, Gavin**
Bard.
Blame.
Christ, *sel.*
Dirge: "Body lies under the ground."
Hiroshima, *sel.*
Ichor, *sel.*
Ixion.
Japan.
Joy.
Person, *sel.*
**Banus, Maria**
Eighteen.
Gift Hour.
New Notebook, The.
**Baraka, Imamu Amiri (LeRoi Jones)**
Agony, An. As Now.
At the National Black Assembly.
Audubon, Drafted.
Babylon Revisited.
Balboa, the Entertainer.
Ballad of the Morning Streets.
Beautiful Black Women.
Biography.
Black Art.
Black Bourgeoisie.
Black People!
Black People: This Is Our Destiny.
Bumi.
Cold Term.
Dance, The.

Dead Lady Canonized, The.
Duncan Spoke of a Process.
Each Morning.
End of Man Is His Beauty, The.
Evil Nigger Waits for Lightnin'.
For Hettie.
Funeral Poem.
Guerrilla Handbook, A.
Horatio Alger Uses Scag.
Hymn for Lanie Poo, *sel.*
I Substitute for the Dead Lecturer.
In Memory of Radio
In One Battle.
Incident.
Invention of Comics, The.
Ka 'Ba.
Leadbelly Gives an Autograph.
Leroy.
Letter to E. Franklin Frazier.
Liar, The.
Like Rousseau.
Lines to Garcia Lorca.
New World, The.
Numbers, Letters.
Order of Service.
Part of the Doctrine.
People's Choice, The: The Dream Poems II.
Poem for Black Hearts, A.
Poem for Deep Thinkers, A.
Poem for Democrats, A.
Poem for Half White College Students.
Poem for Speculative Hipsters, A.
Poem for Willie Best, A.
Poem Some People Will Have to Understand, A.
Political Poem.
Politics of Rich Painters, The.
Preface to a Twenty Volume Suicide Note.
Pressures, The.
Reprise of One of A.G.'s Best Poems!
Return of the Native.
Scenario VI.
Snake Eyes.
Song Form.
SOS.
Spell, The.
Study Peace.
Tele/ vision.
Three Modes of History and Culture.
Tight Rope.
W. W.
Way Out West.
We Own the Night.
World Is Full of Remarkable Things, The.
Young Soul.
**Barba, Sharon**
Cycle of Women, A.
Dropping toward Stillness.
Letter Reaching Out to My Sister, 1600 Miles.
Thanksgiving.
**Barbauld, Anna Laetitia**
Mouse's Petition, The.
**Barber, J.**
White Steed of the Prairies, The.
**Barbera, Florence**
Birds, The.
Tree.
**Barbour, John**

Bruce, The, *sel.*
**Barbour, Julia Watson**
73,000 Days to Breakthrough.
**Bardsley, Alice**
Storm Warning.
**Barela, Patrocinio**
Praying to the Stars.
**Barham, Richard Harris.** *See* **"Ingoldsby, Thomas"**
**Baring-Gould, Sabine**
Now the Day Is Over.
Onward, Christian Soldiers.
Through the Night of Doubt and Sorrow.
**Barker, David**
Lispy Bails Out.
Matisse Tits.
Packard.
View from the Planetarium.
Zoo Dream.
**Barker, George**
Calamiterror, *sel.*
Elegy: "These errors loved no less than the saint loves arrows."
In Memory of a Friend.
Keelhauled across the star-wrecked death of God.
Memorial Couplets for the Dying Ego.
News of the World II ("In the first year of the last disgrace").
News of the World III ("Let her lie naked here, my hand resting").
Ode against St. Cecilia's Day.
On a Friend's Escape from Drowning off the Norfolk Coast.
Resolution of Dependence.
Secular Elegies, *sel.*
Sequence.
Sonnet to My Mother.
To Any Member of My Generation.
True Confessions of George Barker, The, *sel.*
Turn on Your Side and Bear the Day to Me.
Wild Dreams of Summer What Is Your Grief.
**Barker, Jane**
Coming from —— in a Dark Night.
Epitaph on the Secretary to the Muses.
In Commendation of the Female Sex.
Parting with——.
**Barker, Squire Omar**
Fine!
Jackrabbits.
Law West of the Pecos, The.
Sheep Beezness, The.
Tall Men Riding.
To a Jack Rabbit.
When Billy the Kid Rides Again.
**Barks, Coleman**
Achilles Tendon.
Adam's Apple.
Back Just below the Shoulder Blades.
Body Poems, *sels.*
Brain.
Bruises.
Cheek.
Dimple.
Downy Hair in the Shape of a Flame.
Genitals.
Hair on the Chest.
Liver.

Mule, The.
Scar.
Semen.
Skeleton.
Skull.
Tic.
We Let Each Other Go.
White Crescents at the Bottoms of Fingernails.
**Barksdale, Clement**
Upon the Decease of My Infant Lady.
**Barlow, George**
Mellowness and Flight.
Sweet Diane.
**Barlow, Joel**
Advice to a Raven in Russia.
Along the Banks, *with music.*
Columbiad, The, *sel.*
Hasty Pudding, The.
Judge Me, O God, *with music.*
O God of My Salvation, Hear, *with music.*
**Barnard, Lady Anne.** *See* **Lindsay, Lady Anne**
**Barnard, John**
Nations That Long in Darkness Walked, *with music.*
Thrice Blest the Man, *with music.*
**Barnard, Mary**
Shoreline.
**Barnes, Barnabe**
Blast of wind, a momentary breath, A.
Parthenophil and Parthenophe, *sels.*
**Barnes, Djuna**
Transfiguration.
**Barnes, Jim**
Accident at Three Mile Island.
Autobiography, Chapter XII: Hearing Montana.
Autobiography: Last Chapter.
Bone Yard.
Camping Out on Rainy Mountain.
Captive Stone, The.
Choctaw Chief Helps Plan a Festival, A.
Halcyon Days.
Last Look at La Plata, Missouri.
Lying in a Yuma Saloon.
Old Soldiers Home at Marshalltown, Iowa.
Paiute Ponies.
Sunday Dreamer's Guide to Yarrow, Missouri, A.
Sweating It Out on Winding Stair Mountain.
These Damned Trees Crouch.
Tracking Rabbits: Night.
Year's End.
**Barnes, Julians**
Book of Hunting, *sels.*
**Barnes, Kate**
Hector the Dog.
Mare, A.
**Barnes, William**
Air an' Light.
Bean Vield, The.
Black an' White.
Bwoat, The.
Child an' the Mowers, The.
Come an' Meet me wi' the Children on the Road.
Day's Work a-Done.
Dock-Leaves.

Easter Zunday.
Eclogue: The Common a-Took In.
Evenen in the Village.
Father Out, an' Mother Hwome, A.
Grammer's Shoes.
Green.
Hallowed Pleaces.
Heedless o' My Love.
In the Spring.
Jenny's Ribbons.
Leady-Day, an' Ridden House.
Lowshot Light.
Lydlinch Bells.
Milken Time.
Mother's Dream, The.
Musings.
My Love's Guardian Angel.
Naighbour Playmeates.
Round Things.
Shellbrook [Dorset].
Shellbrook [National English].
Slow to Come, Quick a-Gone.
Sonnet: "In every dream thy lovely
    features rise."
Storm-Wind, The.
Tokens.
Water Crowvoot, The.
White an' Blue.
Whitsuntide an' Club Walken.
Wife a-Lost, The.
Wind at the Door, The.
Winter Night, A.
Witch, A.
Woak Hill.
Woodley.
Young Rhymer Snubbed, The.
Zong, A: "O Jenny, don't sobby! vor I
    shall be true."
Zummer Thoughts in Winter Time.
Zun a-Lighten Eyes a-Shut, The.
**Barnett, Anthony**
Book of Mysteries, The.
Celan.
Cloisters.
Crossing.
Marriage, A.
**Barney, William D.**
Caught in the Pocket.
Nearly Everybody Loves Harvey Martin.
Post Card out of Panama, A.
Rasslers, The.
**Barnfield, Richard**
Philomel.
To His Friend, Master R. L., in Praise of
    Music and Poetry.
**Barnie, John**
Dog in Us, The.
**Barnstone, Aliki**
Mating the Goats.
To a Friend's Child.
Windows in Providence.
**Barnstone, Willis**
Borges.
Gas Lamp.
Good Beasts, The.
Grandfather.
I wish to paint my eyes.
Miklos Radnoti.
Paradise.
Stained Glass.
Worm, The.
**Baron, Robert**

To Eliza, with a Tulip-fashioned Watch.
**Barras-Abney, Jonetta**
Give Me a Forty Cent Token or a
    Gallon of Gas and an Hour to Get
    There.
Peace.
Secondline for Susan.
**Barrax, Gerald W.**
Barriers 1.
Barriers 2.
Black Narcissus.
Christmas 1959 et Cetera.
Efficiency Apartment.
For Malcolm: After Mecca.
Fourth Dance Poem.
If She Sang.
Moby Christ.
To a Woman Who Wants Darkness and
    Time.
Your Eyes Have Their Silence.
**Barreno, Maria Isabel** *and* **Maria Teresa
    Horta** *and* **Maria Velho da Costa.** *See*
    **Marias, The Three**
**Barrington, Patrick**
I Was a Bustlemaker Once, Girls.
**Barron, W. F.**
To the Men Who Hold the Line.
**Barrows, Anita**
Ancestors, The.
Avenue Y.
Emigration.
Fire.
Letter to a Friend in an Unknown Place.
Mutant, The.
Reflections.
**Barson, Alfred**
On the Death of Parents.
**Bart-Williams, Gaston**
God Bless Us.
**Barth, John**
Minstrel's Last Lay, The.
**Barth, R. L.**
Waking Early.
**Bartlett, Elizabeth**
Dear Vincent.
Farewell, Gibson Square.
Immunisation Day.
In Days of New.
Music in a Dark Room.
Not Dead but Sleeping.
Private Hurricane.
Schizophrenia.
Visitors, The.
X-Ray.
**Barton, Bernard**
Walking in the Light.
**Barton, David**
Solutions.
**Barton, Fred**
Death of the Sailor's Wife, The.
**Barton, Joan**
Mistress, The.
**Baruch, Dorothy**
Popcorn-Popper, The ("The popcorn
    man").
**Basho (Matsuo Basho)**
Haiku: "Lightning gleam, A."
Haiku: "New moon in the sky."
Lightning in the sky!
On a withered branch.
So the spring has come?
**Bass, Ellen**

Celia.
First Menstruation.
For My Mother.
I am the sorrow in the wheat fields.
In Celebration.
Partly to My Cat.
September 7.
**Bass, Madeline**
Continuing.
To My Former Student on the Occasion
    of Birth.
To the Mother from Scarsdale Who
    Asked about Publishing Her
    Daughter's Poems.
**Bass, Madeline Tiger**
It's Bear Air.
**Bastard, Thomas**
Ad Henricum Wottonem.
De Naevo in Facie Faustinae.
Epitaph: Iohannis Sande.
In Gaetam.
**Baster, Andrew**
Judas.
**Bastian, Richard**
Good Friday.
Night Thoughts.
Poem for One Who Bares a Pome, A.
**Bat-Miriam, Yocheved**
Distance Spills Itself.
**Bateman, Doris I.**
My Rocking Chair.
**Bates, David**
Speak Gently.
**Bates, G. E.**
Pentagonia.
**Bates, Katherine Lee**
America the Beautiful.
**Bates, Scott**
Fable of the Talented Mockingbird.
Fable of the Transcendent Tannenbaum.
Whales.
**Batki, John**
Down the Block.
Invention of the Gun, The.
Love Poem: "I am a traveler."
Mallarme on July 14, 1889 ("Mallarme
    liked his wine").
Night and Day.
Sabine.
Touristicism.
**Batt, Roy**
Emily Dickinson—in Appreciation.
**Baudelaire, Charles**
Abyss, The.
Beauty.
Correspondences.
Damned Women.
Former Life.
Giantess, The.
Heautontimoroumenos.
Her Hair.
I adore you as much as the vault of
    night.
Injured Moon, The.
Intimate Associations.
Invitation to the Voyage.
Inward Conversation.
Jewels, The.
Little Old Women, The.
Meditation.
Peace, Be at Peace, O Thou My
    Heaviness.

Sadness of the Moon, The.
Seven Old Men, The.
Song of Autumn I.
Spleen LXXV ("Old Pluvius, month of rains, in peevish mood").
Spleen LXXVI ("I have more memories than if I had lived a thousand years").
Spleen LXXVII ("I'm like the king of a rain-country, rich")
Spleen LXXVIII ("When the low heavy sky weighs like a lid").
To a Passer-by.
To the Reader.

**Bauer, Steven**
Stopped in Memphis.

**Baugh, Sue**
Seal Rock.

**Baughan, B. E.**
Old Place, The.

**Baxter, James Keir**
At Akitio.
At Taieri Mouth.
Ballad of Calvary Street.
Bay, The.
Beach House, The.
Crossing Cook Strait.
Election 1960.
Elegy for an Unknown Soldier.
Green Figs at Table.
High Country Weather.
Homecoming, The.
Howrah Bridge.
Lament for Barney Flanagan.
Lion Skin, The.
Morgue, The.
My Love Late Walking.
Old Man Jeremy.
On the Death of Her Body.
Perseus.
Pig Island Letters, *sel.*
Poem in the Matukituki Valley.
Shepherd, The.
Spring-heeled Jack.
Wild Bees.

**Baxter, Lydia**
Take the Name of Jesus with You, *with music.*

**Baxter, Ron**
Moon Mission.
Winter: The Abandoned Nest.

**Bayes, Nora** *and* Jack Norworth
Shine On, Harvest Moon, *with music.*

**Bayes, Ron H.**
Casketmaker, The.
Philadelphia Airport, The.

**Bayliss, John**
Apocalypse and Resurrection.
Seven Dreams.

**Bayly, Thomas Haynes**
Gaily the Troubadour, *with music.*
Long, Long Ago,.
Mistletoe Bough, The.

**Beach, Joseph Warren**
Horatian Ode.

**Beach, Seth Curtis**
Mysterious Presence! Source of All, *with music.*
Thou One in All, Thou All in One, *with music.*

**"Beachcomber."** *See* **Morton, John Bingham**

**Beall, James**

Afterimage.
Indiana State Highway Patrol.
Quiet Sun, The.

**Beard, Cathy**
Any April.

**Beardsley, Aubrey**
Three Musicians, The.

**Beattie, James**
Question, The.

**Beattie, James Hay**
On the Author of the *Treatise of Human Nature.*

**Beaumont, Francis**
Mirth.
Pining for Love.
Upon Master Edmund Spenser.

**Beaumont, Francis** *and* **John Fletcher**
Aspatia's Song.
Come, Sleep.
Safe Swimming.
Spanish Curate, The, *sel.*
Woman-Hater, The, *sel.*

**Beaumont, Sir John**
Of My Dear Son, Gervase Beaumont.
Relish of the Muse, The.

**Beaumont, Joseph**
Gnat, The.
Home ("Home's home, although it reachèd be").
Honour ("Ambitious sir, take heed!").
Jesus Inter Ubera Mariae.
Oath, The.
Psyche; or, Love's Mystery, *sels.*

**Beausoleil, Laura**
Night of Dreams.
On the Border of Impossibility.
Sunday.

**Beauvais, Phyllis (Phyllis Harris)**
Outside.
Under Your Voice, among Legends.

**Beaver, Bruce**
Angel's Weather.
Lauds and Plaints, *sels.*
Letters to Live Poets, *sels.*

**Becker, Anne**
Antietam Creek: In the North They Named the Battles after Bodies of Water.
Duelists.
From a Print by Maillol.

**Beckett, Samuel**
Age is when to a man.
Alba.
Enueg I.
Enueg II.
Gnome.
I would like my love to die.
Malacoda.
What would I do without this world faceless incurious.
Whoroscope.
Words and Music, *sel.*

**Bedard, Michael**
Playground, The.

**Beddo, Frank**
Jeff Buckner.

**Beddoes, Thomas Lovell**
Beautiful Night, A.
Bridal Song.
Death's Jest Book, *sels.*
Dream of Dying.
Dream-Pedlary.

Lines Written in a Blank Leaf of the Prometheus Unbound.
Love of Flowers, The.
New Cecilia, The.
Phantom Wooer, The.
Resurrection Song.
Sibilla's Dirge.
Song: "Old Adam, the carrion crow."
Song from the Waters.
Song of the Stygian Naiades.
Wolfram's Dirge.

**"Bede, Cuthbert" (Edward Bradley)**
Entrance Exams.
Queer Fellow Named Woodin, A.

**Beebe, Lucius**
Quid Restat, *abr.*

**Beecher, John**
Aztec Figurine.
Desert Holy Man.
Humble Petition to the President of Harvard, A.
To Alexander Meiklejohn, *sel.*
To Live and Die in Dixie.

**Beedome, Thomas**
Inquisition, The.
To the Noble Sir Francis Drake.

**Beeler, Janet**
Feeding Time.
Photographer's Wife, The.

**Beenen, Jennivien-Diana**
Morning Poem.

**Be'er, Hayim**
Love Song.
Sequence of Generations, The.
Tabernacle of Peace.

**Beer, Patricia**
Abbey Tomb.
After Death.
Armistice Day.
Arms.
Branch Line, The.
Chemist's Dream, The.
Christmas Eve.
Clock, The.
Concert at Long Melford Church.
Dream of Hanging, A.
Estuary, The.
Female, Extinct.
Four Years After.
Ghost.
Killing of the Sparrows, The.
Lion Hunts.
Love Song.
One Man One Vote.
Pardoner's Tale Blues.
Picture of Workers Resting.
Postilion Has Been Struck by Lightning, The.
Summer Song for Me and My Aunts.
Tale, The.
Witch.
Young Widow.

**Beer-Hofmann, Richard**
Lullaby for Miriam.

**Beerbohm, Max**
Addition to Kipling's "The Dead King (Edward VII), 1910."
Ballade Tragique à Double Refrain.
Brave Rover.
Elegy on Any Lady by George Moore.
Epitaph for G. B. Shaw.
Luncheon, A.

On the Imprint of the First English
   Edition of "The Works of Max
   Beerbohm."
   Police Station Ditties.
   Road to Zoagli, The.
   Vague Lyric by G. M.
**Beers, Ethel Lynn**
   All Quiet along the Potomac To-Night,
   *with music.*
**Beevers, John**
   Atameros.
**Beghtol, Charles**
   Hopi Lament.
   Hopi Prayer.
   In Old Tucson.
**Behan, Dominic**
   Patriot Game, The.
**Behm, Richard**
   Collector, The.
   Hunt of the Poem, The.
**Behn, Aphra**
   Abdelazer, *sel.*
   And Forgive Us Our Trespasses.
   Disappointment, The.
   Dream, The.
   Dutch Lover, The, *sels.*
   Love's Witness.
   Lucky Chance, The, *sel.*
   Not to sigh and to be tender.
   Ode to Love, An.
   On Her Loving Two Equally.
   Song: "Ah false Amyntas, can that
     hour."
   Song: "All joy to mortals, joy and
     mirth."
   Song: "Curse upon that faithless maid,
     A."
   Song: "Love in fantastic triumph sate."
   Song: "Oh! Love, that stronger art than
     wine."
   Song: "When maidens are young, and in
     their spring."
   Song by the Wavering Nymph.
   Thousand Martyrs I Have Made, A.
   To the Fair Clarinda, Who Made Love
     to Me, Imagin'd More than Woman.
   Voyage to the Island of Love, A, *sels.*
   Westminster Drollery, 1671.
   When you love, or speak of it.
   Willing Mistriss, The.
**Behn, Harry**
   Adventure ("There's a place I've
     dreamed about far away").
   Christmas Carol, A: "Angel told Mary,
     An."
   Christmas Morning.
   Circles.
   Counting.
   Easter Eggs.
   Gnome.
   Hallowe'en.
   Kite, The.
   Near and Far.
   New Little Boy, The.
   Tea Party.
   Winter Evening.
**Beidler, Martha**
   Mohammed Ibrahim Speaks.
**Beissel, Johann Conrad**
   Sun Now Risen, The, *with music.*
**Beker, Ruth**
   Don't Show Me.

**"Belasco, F."** *See* **Rosenfeld, Monroe F.**
**Belford, Ken**
   Beside the Road.
   Blueline.
   Branches Back Into.
   Dusk.
   For Kelley.
   Glove Glue.
   Hunchbacked and corrected.
   In spots/ it is warm enough.
   New Potatoes.
   Peanuts.
   Stove.
**Belisle, Eugene L.**
   At 21.
**Belitt, Ben**
   Battery Park, High Noon.
   Moon Walk.
   Sand Painters, The.
   Spool, The.
   Xerox.
**Belknap, Jeremy**
   Far from Our Friends, *with music.*
   Thus Spake the Saviour, *with music.*
**Bell, Charles G.**
   Approaching Washington.
**Bell, DeWitt**
   Motorcyclist's Song, The.
**Bell, Martin**
   Songs, The.
   Ultimate Anthology.
   Winter Coming On.
**Bell, Marvin**
   About That.
   Acceptance Speech.
   American Poets.
   Cabin in Minnesota, A.
   Delicate Bird Who Is Flying Up Our
     Asses, The.
   Extermination of the Jews, The.
   From a Distance.
   Garlic.
   Gemwood.
   Getting Lost in Nazi Germany.
   He Said To.
   Her Dream House.
   Here.
   Home Front, The.
   Impotence.
   In the Home.
   Israeli Navy, The.
   Memory, A.
   Music of the Spheres, The.
   New Formalists, The.
   On Returning to Teach.
   Perfection of Dentistry, The.
   Residue of Song.
   Song: Organic Years, The.
   3 Stanzas about a Tree.
   Treetops.
   Trinket.
   What Is There.
**Bell, William**
   Elegy: "Tonight the moon is high, to
     summon all."
   On a Dying Boy.
   To a Lady on Her Marriage.
   Young Man's Song, A.
**Bellamann, Henry**
   Gulf Stream, The.
**Bellamy, Francis**
   Pledge to the Flag, The, *with music.*

**Bellerby, Frances**
   Bereft Child's First Night.
   Inconclusive Evening, An.
**Belli, Giuseppe Gioachino**
   Death with a Coda.
   Good Weather.
**Belloc, Hilaire**
   Birds in their little nests agree.
   Bison, The.
   Camelopard, The.
   Chamois, The.
   Crocodile, The.
   Dedication on the Gift of a Book to a
     Child.
   Discovery.
   Early Morning, The.
   Epitaph on the Favourite Dog of a
     Politician.
   Epitaph on the Politician Himself.
   False Heart, The.
   Fatigue.
   First in his pride the orient sun's
     display.
   Fragment, The: "Towards the evening of
     her splendid day."
   Frog, The.
   Gnu, The.
   Godolphin Horne.
   Ha'nacker Mill.
   Henry King [Who Chewed Bits of
     String].
   Hippopotamus, The.
   I am a sundial, turned the wrong way
     round.
   I am a sundial. Ordinary words.
   Is There Any Reward?
   Jack and His Pony, Tom.
   Jim.
   Jim, Who Ran Away from His Nurse,
     and Was Eaten by a Lion.
   Juliet.
   Justice of the Peace, The.
   Lines for a Christmas Card.
   Lines to a Don.
   Llama, The.
   Lord Abbott.
   Lord Epsom.
   Lord Finchley.
   Lord Lundy.
   Matilda Who Told Lies, and Was
     Burned to Death.
   Moral Alphabet, A, *sel.*
   On a General Election.
   On a Puritan.
   On a Sundial ("I am a sundial, and I
     make a botch").
   On a Sundial ("Save on the rare
     occasion when the sun").
   On His Books.
   On Lady Poltagrue, a Public Peril.
   On Mundane Acquaintances.
   On Noman, a Guest.
   On Paunch, a Parasite.
   On Vital Statistics.
   Python, The.
   Rebecca, Who Slammed Doors for Fun
     and Perished Miserably.
   Scorpion, The.
   Song Called "His Hide Is Covered with
     Hair," The.
   Song of Duke William.
   South Country, The.

Statesman, The.
Statue, The.
Tarantella.
This, the last ornament among the peers.
To Dives.
Viper, The.
Vulture, The.
World's a stage, The. The trifling
  entrance fee.
Yak, The.
**Bellows, Isabel Frances**
Curious Charlie.
G Is for Gustave.
Ignorant Ida.
Naughty Young Nat.
Operatic Olivia.
**Beman, Nathan S. S.**
Jesus, I Come to Thee, *with music.*
**Ben Yeshaq, Yosef Damana**
Rusted Chain, The.
**Ben-Yitzhak, Avraham**
Blessed Are Those Who Sow and Do
  Not Reap.
I Didn't Know My Soul.
Psalm: "There are a very few moments
  when you."
**Benbow, Margaret**
Old Biograph Girl, The.
**Bender, Debra Woolard**
World within a World.
**Benedikt, Michael**
Clement Attlee.
Divine Love.
European Shoe, The.
Eye, The.
Fate in Incognito.
Fraudulent Days.
Going and Coming: Two Poems.
Grand Guignols of Love, The.
Let Me Out.
Meat Epitaph, The.
Some Feelings.
Thoughts.
To Persuade a Lady.
**Benét, Laura**
My Fairy Steed.
**Benét, Rosemary** *and* **Stephen Vincent**
**Benét**
Abraham Lincoln.
Lewis and Clark.
Nancy Hanks.
Western Wagons.
**Benét, Stephen Vincent**
American Names.
Daniel Boone.
Hymn in Columbus Circle.
Invocation: "American muse, whose
  strong and diverse heart."
John Brown's Body, *sels.*
Melora's Song.
Metropolitan Nightmare.
Mountain Whippoorwill, The.
Nightmare, with Angels.
Nonsense Song, A.
Western Star, *sel.*
**Benét, William Rose**
Horse Thief, The.
Jesse James.
Whale.
**Benjamin, Saul Hillel**
At Summer's End.
**Benlowes, Edward**

Cynthia.
Theophila; or, Love's Sacrifice, *sels.*
**Benn, Gottfried**
Beautiful Youth.
**Bennard, George**
Old Rugged Cross, The, *with music.*
**Bennett, Alan**
Place-Names of China.
**Bennett, Anna Elizabeth**
Hush Thee, Princeling, *with music.*
**Bennett, Arnold**
Love Affair, A.
There was a young man of Montrose.
**Bennett, Benjamin K.**
Paradox.
**Bennett, Bruce**
Poetry Is.
True Story of Snow White, The.
Villanelle with a Line by Yeats.
**Bennett, Gwendolyn B.**
Hatred.
Heritage.
Sonnet: "He came in silvern armor,
  trimmed with black."
Sonnet: "Some things are very dear to
  me."
To a Dark Girl.
**Bennett, Henry Holcomb**
Flag Goes By, The.
**Bennett, John**
"He Killed Many of My Men."
Little Boy, A.
**Bennett, Lerone, Jr.**
And Was Not Improved.
Blues and Bitterness.
**Bennett, Paula**
To a Young Poet.
**Bennett, Peggy**
Over the Green Sands.
**Bennett, Rowena Bastin**
Motor Cars.
**Bennett, Sanford Fillmore**
In the Sweet Bye-and-Bye.
**Benson, Arthur Christopher**
Land of Hope and Glory.
**Benson, Gerard**
Horse.
**Benson, Louis F.**
O Love That Lights the Eastern Sky,
  *with music.*
O Risen Lord upon the Throne, *with
  music.*
O Thou Whose Feet Have Climbed
  Life's Hill, *with music.*
Why Linger Yet upon the Strand? *with
  music.*
**Benson, Stella**
Frost.
Now I Have Nothing.
**Bental, Anath**
Angel Michael, The.
Jerusalem in the Snow.
**Bentley, Beth**
At the Confluence of the Soleduck, the
  Bogachiel and the Quillayute.
Birthing, The.
Drowning Girl.
Holding (After the Nez Perce).
House on the Barge, The.
Kennel.
Mothers.
Therapeutist, The.

This Time a Tree Turns into a Woman.
You Again.
**Bentley, Edmund Clerihew**
Adam Smith.
Art of Biography, The.
Ballade of Liquid Refreshment.
Clerihews, *sels.*
George the Third.
John Stuart Mill.
Lord Clive.
Professor James Dewar, F. R. S.
Sir Christopher Wren.
Sir Humphry Davy.
**Bentley, Nelson**
Spouting Horn, The.
**Bentley, Wilder**
Six Reveilles to Match My Self-
  Indulgence, *sel.*
**Benveniste, Asa**
Alchemical Cupboard, The.
**Beresford, Anne**
Romanies in Town, The.
Saturday in New York.
**Berg, Sharon**
Tongues.
**Berg, Stephen**
Desnos Reading the Palms of Men on
  Their Way to the Gas Chambers.
Don't Forget.
**Bergé, Carol**
Blues for a Cello Man.
Lying Down Hungry.
Madonna and Daughter.
Poem for Explorers.
Position.
Rested near Nefertete.
Textures.
Third Day in a Strange City.
Where It's At.
With.
**Bergengren, Ralph**
Worm, The.
**Berger, Art**
March on the Delta.
**Berger, Bruce**
False Cadence.
**Berger, Suzanne E.**
Mornings.
**Berggolts, Olga**
Infidelity.
To My Sister.
To Song.
**Bergman, David**
Eclogue: "Whores are afraid to cross the
  street, The."
Why I Am Offended by Miracles.
**Berkeley, George**
On the Prospect of Planting Arts and
  Learning in America.
**Berkson, Lee L.**
Bogey.
**Berlin, Irving**
God Bless America.
**Berman, Barbara**
Dupont Circle.
Not a Political Poem.
West, in Drag, The.
**Berman, Ruth**
Blessing, The.
**Bernard, Sidney**
Paraders for the Bomb.
**Bernard of Clairvaux, Saint**

Sigh as It Ends.
Snow Line.
So Long? Stevens.
Sonnet: " 'Broken heart,' A . . . but can a heart break, now?"
Sonnet: "I lift—lift you five States away your glass."
Sonnet: "Our Sunday morning when dawn-priests were applying."
Sonnet: "Sometimes the night echoes to prideless wailing."
Sonnet: "What was ashore, then?. . .Cargoed with forget."
Statue, The.
Strut for Roethke, A.
There are voices, voices. Light's dying. Birds have quit.
There sat down, once, a thing on Henry's heart.
These massacres of the superior peoples.
This world is gradually becoming a place.
"Three in heaven I hope" said old Jane to Henry.
Thurn, A.
Tides of dreadful creation rocked lonely Henry.
To the edge of Europe, the eighteenth edge.
Traveller, The.
Turning it over, considering, like a madman.
Twiss is a tidy bundle, chirped joyous Henry, The.
Venice, 182-.
Weather was fine, The. They took away his teeth.
Welcome, grinned Henry, welcome fifty-one!
What gall had he in him, so to begin Book VII.
Why then did he make, at such cost, crazy sounds?
Winter Landscape.
Winter-Piece to a Friend Away, A.
Winters close, Springs open, no child stirs, The.
Wordsworth, thou form almost divine, cried Henry.
You couldn't bear to grow old, but we grow old.
Your face broods from my table, Suicide.

**Berssenbrugge, Mei**
Abortion.
Book of the Dead, Prayer 14.
Chronicles: Number Three.
Chronicles: Numbers One and Two.
El Bosco.
Fish and Swimmers and Lonely Birds Sweep Past Us.
In Bhaudanath.
Old Man Let's Go Fishing in the Yellow Reeds of the Bay.
Poor Mouse.
Propeller Sleep.
Spirit.
Tracks.

**Bertken, Sister**
When I went into my garden, I found.

**Bertolino, James**
Beyond the Storm.

Employed.
Eve of July Fourth.
Marriage, The.
Night Was Smooth, The.
Red Dress, The.

**Best, Charles**
Sonnet of the Moon, A.

**Bethell, Mary Ursula**
Decoration.
Detail.
Erica.
Evening Walk in Winter.
Fall.
Lever de Rideau.
Long Harbour, The.
Midnight.
October Morning.
Pause.
Response.
Soothsayer.
Trance.
Warning of Winter.

**Bethune, George Washington**
Jesus, Shepherd of Thy Sheep, *with music.*
O for the Happy Hour, *with music.*
There Is No Name So Sweet on Earth, *with music.*

**Bethune, Lebert**
Blue Tanganyika.
Bwagamoyo.
Harlem Freeze Frame.
Juju of My Own, A.

**Betjeman, Sir John**
Arrest of Oscar Wilde at the Cadogan Hotel, The.
Beside the Seaside, *sels.*
Bristol and Clifton.
Christmas.
Cornish Cliffs.
Cottage Hospital, The.
Crematorium.
Death of King George V.
Diary of a Church Mouse.
Dorset.
Executive.
False Security.
Felixstowe; or, The Last of Her Order.
Harvest Hymn.
How to Get On in Society.
Hunter Trials.
Huxley Hall.
In Westminster Abbey.
Incident in the Early Life of Ebenezer Jones, Poet, 1828, An.
Inexpensive Progress.
Invasion Exercise on the Poultry Farm.
Ireland with Emily.
Late-flowering Lust.
Licorice Fields at Pontefract, The.
Longfellow's Visit to Venice.
Lord Cozens Hardy.
Meditation on the A30.
Metropolitan Railway, The.
Middlesex.
Myfanwy.
Norfolk.
On a Portrait of a Deaf Man.
Original Sin on the Sussex Coast.
Out into Essex.
Parliament Hill Fields.
Pot Pourri from a Surrey Garden.

Seaside Golf.
Subaltern's Love-Song, A.
Summoned by Bells, *sel.*
Sunday Afternoon in St. Enodoc Church, Cornwall, *sel.*
Town Clerk's Views, The.
Trebetherick.
Upper Lambourne.
Where deep cliffs loom enormous, where casade.
Winter Seascape.
Youth and Age on Beaulieu River, Hants.

**Bevington, Helen Smith**
Cataract at Lodore, The.
Herrick's Julia.
Mr. Rockefeller's Hat.
Mrs. Trollope in America.
Nature Study, after Dufy.
Oceans of Dr. Johnson, The.
Penguins in the Home ("A penguin hailed me at the door").

**Beyer, Richard**
Second Reading.

**Beyer, William**
Trap, The.

**Bhartrihari**
In former days we'd both agree.
She who is always in my thoughts prefers.

**Bialik, Hayim Nachman**
After My Death.
Footsteps of Spring.
I Didn't Find Light by Accident.
I Scattered My Sighs to the Wind.
My Song.
Place Me under Your Wing.
Sea of Silence Exhales Secrets, The.
Summer Night.
When the Days Grow Long.

**Biasotti, Raymond**
City.

**Bible, Apocrypha**
First Maccabees, *sel.*

**Bible, New Testament**
And as soon as it was morning the chief priests.
And he said, So soule doth magnifie the Lord.
And it came to pass in those days, that there went out a decree from Caesar Augustus.
And seeing the multitudes, he went up into a mountain.
And there were in the same country shepherds.
And why take ye thought for raiment?
Blessed are the poor[e] in spirit: for theirs is the kingdom[e] of heaven.
But some one will ask, "How are the dead raised?"
Lord's Prayer, The.
No man can serve two masters.
St. John, *sels.*
St. Luke, *sels.*
St. Mark, *sels.*
St. Matthew, *sels.*
Though I Speak with the Tongues of Men and Angels.

**Bible, Old Testament**
All things come alike to all.

And God saw that the wickedness of man was great.
And He Shall Judge among Nations.
And the Lord God planted a garden eastward in Eden.
And the whole earth was of one language, and of one speech.
And there came two angels to Sodom at even.
And there shall come forth a rod out of the stemme of Jesse.
Because the daughters of Zion are haughty.
Behold, my servant shall deal prudently.
Behold, thou art fair.
Blessed is the man that walketh not in the counsel of the ungodly.
Canst thou bind the cluster of the Pleiades.
Deuteronomy, *sel.*
Earth is the Lord's and the fulness thereof, The.
Exodus, *sel.*
Ffrom depth off sinn and from a diepe dispaire.
For everything there is a season.
For the Lordes parte is his folke.
For there is hope for a tree.
For thus saith the Lord to the men of Judah and Jerusalem.
Hannah's Thanksgiving.
Heavens declare the glory of God, The.
How beautiful are thy feet in sandals, O prince's daughter!
I returned, and saw under the sun.
I sleep but my heart is awake.
In the beginning God created the heaven and the earth.
Job, *abr.*
Jonah.
Judges, *sel.*
Let us now praise famous men.
Lord, thou hast been our dwelling place in all generations.
Lord Bless You and Keep You, The.
Lord is my shepherd, The; I shall not want.
O praise God in his holiness: praise him.
Out of the deep have I called unto thee, O Lord.
Proverbs, *sels.*
Psalms, *sels.*
Remember also thy Creator in the days of thy youth.
Second Samuel, *sel.*
Song of Solomon, The, *sels.*
Song of the Three Holy Children, The.
To Everything There Is a Season.
Vanity of Vanities.
War Horse, The.
**Bickerstaffe, Isaac**
Expostulation, An.
**Bickford, Gerald**
96 Vandam.
**Bidart, Frank**
Herbert White.
**Bienek, Horst**
Defeated Victor, The.
**Bierce, Ambrose**
Art.
"Black Bart, P08."
Convicts' Ball, The.

Devil's Dictionary, The, *sels.*
Don't Steal.
**Bierds, Linda**
Elegy for 41 Whales Beached in Florence, Ore., June, 1979.
Mid-Plains Tornado.
**Bigelow, J. S.**
Bat and the Scientist, The.
**Biguenet, John**
Everyone Begs for Mercy.
One-Day Diary.
**Billings, Robert**
Beast Enough.
**Billings, William**
David's Lamentation.
Heavenly Vision.
Let Tyrants Shake Their Iron Rod.
**Bily-Hurd, Michael**
Woman in an Abandoned House.
**Bingham, G. Clifton**
Love's Old Sweet Song, *with music.*
**Binyon, Laurence**
Burning of the Leaves, The.
For the Fallen.
Hunger.
Kennack Sands.
Little Dancers, The.
Look Not Too Deep, *sel.*
Walnut-Leaf Scent.
**Bion**
Lament for Adonis.
**Birch, Alison Wyrley**
Blind Spot.
Captive Bird.
Death Came Too Late.
Death in the Family.
Death of the Average Man.
Erudite of literature, The.
Evening.
History.
I cannot believe that there's any need.
In the city you had dirt and din.
It isn't government that rules.
Night Visitor.
On the Edge.
Pacific Dawn.
Physical Fitness.
Poetry.
Retribution often is.
Wanderlust.
**Birch, Harry**
Reuben and Rachel, *with music.*
**Bird, Betty Ruth**
Bambino.
Reverend Mother Prioress.
Spiritus Sanctus.
**Bird, Harold**   See **Littlebird, Harold**
**Bird, Leonard**
Walter Mitty.
**Birkbeck, Big John**
Cumberland Gap Drifter.
**Birkby, John**
Let's All Meet and Have a Party Sometime.
**Birney, Earle**
Anglosaxon Street.
Bear on the Delhi Road, The.
Biography.
Bushed.
Can. Lit.
El Greco: Espolio.

Ellesmereland I ("Explorers say that harebells rise").
Ellesmereland II ("And now in Ellesmereland there sits").
From the Hazel Bough.
Irapuato.
Letter to a Conceivable Great-Grandson.
Looking from Oregon.
Man Is a Snow.
Sinalóa.
Song for Sunsets.
There Are Delicacies.
Twenty-third Flight.
War Winters.
Wind-Chimes in a Temple Ruin.
**Bishop, Elissa**
At Nine o'Clock in the Spring.
**Bishop, Elizabeth**
Armadillo, The.
At the Fishhouses.
Brazil, January 1, 1502.
Casabianca.
Filling Station.
First Death in Nova Scotia.
Fish, The.
From the Country to the City.
From Trollope's Journal.
House Guest.
In the Waiting Room.
Insomnia.
Late Air.
Letter to N.Y.
Little Exercise.
Love Lies Sleeping.
Man-Moth, The.
Manners.
Map, The.
Monument, The.
One Art.
Over 2000 Illustrations and a Complete Concordance.
Prodigal, The.
Questions of Travel.
Roosters.
Sandpiper.
Seascape.
Sestina: "September rain falls on the house."
Some Dreams They Forgot.
Twelfth Morning; or, What You Will.
12 o'Clock News.
Two Mornings and Two Evenings.
Unbeliever, The.
Varick Street.
View of the Capitol from the Library of Congress.
Visits to St. Elizabeths.
**Bishop, John Peale**
Always, from My First Boyhood.
Ancestors, The.
Epithalamium: "When first my beloved came to my bed."
Fiametta.
Hunchback, The.
In the Dordogne.
O, Pioneers!
Recollection, A.
Southern Pines.
Spare Quilt, The.
Speaking of Poetry.
To a Swallow.
Twelfth Night.

**Bishop, Morris**
At a Modernist School.
Car's in the Hall, The.
Dementia Praecox.
Englishman with an Atlas, An; or,
America the Unpronounceable.
For the Opening of the Hunting Season.
Gas and Hot Air.
Hog-calling Competition.
How to Treat Elves.
I Hear America Griping.
Melody for Lute and Ocarina.
Opportunity's Knock.
Ozymandias Revisited.
Perforated Spirit, The.
Sensitive Man, A.
Settling Some Old Football Scores.
Sick Shark, The.
Strong-minded Lady, A.
There's a Lady in Washington Heights.
Vaporish Maiden, A.
Who'd Be a Hero (Fictional)?
Witch of East Seventy-second Street,
The.
**Bishop, Wendy**
Family History.
**Bissonette, David**
What the Bones Do.
**Biton, Erez**
Beginnings.
Bird's Nest, A.
Buying a Shop on Dizengoff.
**Bjornvig, Thorkild**
Owl, The.
**Black, Charles**
All Too Little on Pictures.
Reach of Silence, The.
**Black, D. M.**
Educators, The.
**Black, Isaac J.**
Roll Call: A Land of Old Folk and
Children.
Talking to the Townsfolk in Ideal,
Georgia.
**Black, James M.**
When the Roll Is Called Up Yonder,
*with music.*
**Black, Peter**
Man in the Bowler Hat, The.
**Black, Theodore**
Bard.
**Blackburn, Paul**
Assassination of President McKinley,
The.
Clickety-Clack.
Foreign Policy Commitments; or, You
Get into the Catamaran First, Old
Buddy.
Getting a Job.
Good Morning Love!
Hot Afternoons Have Been in West 15th
Street.
In Winter.
Invitation Standing.
Mosca.
Mother, in the 45¢ Bottle.
Obit Page.
Phone Call to Rutherford.
Plaza Reál with Palmtrees.
Sign, The.
Stone, The.
Sunflower Rock.

Watchers, The.
Yawn, The.
**Blackburn, Thomas**
Felo de Se.
Hospital for Defectives.
Oedipus.
**Blacker, Captain**
Battle of the Boyne, The.
**Blacklock, Thomas**
Happy Marriage.
**Blackmore, Sir Richard**
Satire against Wit, A.
**Blackmur, Richard P.**
Resurrection.
Sonnet: "Three silences made him a
single word."
**Blackwell, Will H.**
Tides.
**Blades, Leslie B.**
Out of Blindness.
**Blaikley, Howard**
From the Underworld.
**Blair, Eric.** *See* Orwell, George
**Blair, Lee**
Apple a Day, An.
Raisin Bread.
Stop!
**Blake, Howard**
Argent Solipsism.
**Blake, James W.**
Sidewalks of New York, The.
**Blake, William**
Abstinence sows sand all over.
Ah! Sun-Flower.
America a Prophecy.
Ancient Proverb, An.
And Did Those Feet in Ancient Time.
Angel, The.
Angel That Presided o'er My Birth, The.
Answer to the Parson, An.
Auguries of Innocence.
Blossom, The.
Book of Thel, The.
Book of Urizen, The.
Chimney Sweeper, The ("A little black
thing among the snow").
Chimney Sweeper, The ("When my
mother died I was very young").
Clod and the Pebble, The.
Cradle Song, A: "Sweet dreams form a
shade."
Crystal Cabinet, The.
Divine Image, A ("Cruelty has a human
heart").
Divine Image, The ("To mercy pity
peace and love").
Dream, A.
Earth's Answer.
Echoing [*or* Ecchoing] Green, The.
Eternity ("He who binds [*or* bends] to
himself a joy").
Fairy, The.
Fly, The.
Four Zoas, The, *sels.*
French Revolution, The.
Garden of Love, The.
Gates of Paradise, The, *sel.*
Give pensions to the Learned Pig.
Golden Net, The.
Grown old in love from seven till seven
times seven.

Hear the Voice of the Bard (*Introd. to
Songs of Experience*).
Hebrew nation did not write it, The.
Her Whole Life Is an Epigram.
Here lies John Trot, the friend of all
mankind.
Holy Thursday ("Is this a holy thing to
see").
Holy Thursday ("'Twas on a Holy
Thursday").
Human Abstract, The.
I asked a thief to steal me a peach.
I feared the fury of my wind.
I laid me down upon a bank.
I Saw a Chapel All of Gold.
I was buried near this dyke.
Infant Joy.
Infant Sorrow.
Island in the Moon, An, *sels.*
Lamb, The.
Laughing Song.
Laughter.
Let the Brothels of Paris Be Opened.
Lilly, The.
Little Black Boy, The.
Little Boy Found, The.
Little Boy Lost, A ("Nought loves
another as itself").
Little Boy Lost, The ("Father, father,
where are you going").
Little Girl Found, The.
Little Girl Lost, A ("Children of the
future age").
Little Girl Lost, The ("In futurity/ I
prophetic see").
Little Vagabond, The.
London ("I wander through each
chartered street").
Long John Brown and Little Mary Bell.
Love's Secret.
Mad Song.
Marriage of Heaven and Hell, The.
Mary.
Memorable Fancy, A ("An Angel came
to me and said").
Memorable Fancy, A ("As I was walking
among the fires of hell").
Mental Traveller, The.
Milton.
Mock On, Mock On, Voltaire, Rousseau.
Morning.
Motto to the Songs of Innocence and of
Experience.
Mr. Cromek to Mr. Stothard.
My Pretty Rose Tree.
My Spectre around Me Night and Day.
Nakedness of women, The.
Never pain to tell thy love.
Night.
Night passd and Enitharmon eer the
dawn returnd in bliss.
Nurse's Song ("When the voices of
children are heard on the green/ And
laughing is heard on the hill").
Nurse's Song ("When the voices of
children are heard on the green/ And
whisprings are in the dale").
O Lapwing, thou fliest around the heath.
O why was I born with a different face?
Odours of Flowers, The.
Of the sleep of Ulro! and of the passage
through.

On Anothers Sorrow.
On Cromek
Orator Prigg.
Piping Down the Valleys Wild (*Introd. to*
  Songs of Innocence).
Poison Tree, A.
Pretty sneaking knave I knew, A.
Pride of the peacock is the glory of God,
  The.
Question Answer'd, The.
Quid the Cynic's Song.
Robin Redbreast in a Cage, A, *abr.*
School Boy, The.
Secrets of the Earth, The.
Shepherd, The.
Sick Rose, The.
Silent silent night.
Since all the riches of this world.
Sipsop's Song.
Sir Joshua Reynolds.
Smile, The.
Soft Snow.
Some people admire the work of a fool.
Song: "Fresh from the dewy hill, the
  merry year."
Song: "How sweet I roamed [*or* roam'd]
  from field to field."
Song: "I love the jocund dance."
Song: "Love and harmony combine."
Song: "Memory, hither come."
Song: "My silks and fine array."
Song: "When early morn walks forth in
  sober grey."
Song of Liberty, A.
Songs of Experience, *sels.*
Songs of Innocence, *sels.*
Spring.
Suction's Anthem.
Sword sang on the barren heath, The.
Tiger, The.
Tiriel, *sel.*
To Autumn.
To Flaxman.
To forgive enemies Hayley does pretend.
To God.
To Nobodaddy.
To Spring.
To Summer.
To the Evening Star.
To the Jews.
To the Muses.
To Tirzah.
To William Hayley.
To Winter.
Vala, Night the Ninth Being the Last
  Judgment.
Vision of Beulah, The.
Visions of the Daughters of Albion.
Voice of the Ancient Bard, The.
Voice of the Devil, The.
When a Man Has Married a Wife.
When Klopstock England defied.
Why should I care for the men of
  Thames.
With Happiness Stretchd across the
  Hills.
**Blakely, Henry**
H. Rap Brown.
Morning Song.
**Blakeney, Lena Whittaker**
Covered Wagon, The.
**Blanchard, Ferdinand Q.**

O Child of Lowly Manger Birth, *with
  music.*
Word of God, across the Ages, *with
  music.*
**Blanchard, Laman**
Ode to the Human Heart.
**Bland, James A.**
Carry Me Back to Old Virginny, *with
  music.*
In the Evening by the Moonlight.
Oh, Dem Golden Slippers!
**Bland, Palladas**
This Life a Theater.
**Bland, Peter**
Death of a Dog.
Happy Army, The.
Kumara God.
Mother.
Past the Tin Butterflies and Plaster
  Gnomes.
Remembering England.
So Many Cenotaphs.
**Blandiana, Ana**
I need only fall asleep/ to return.
**Blandy, E. W.**
Where He Leads Me I Will Follow, *with
  music.*
**Blasing, Randy**
Horse.
**Blauner, Laurie**
Billiards.
**Blaustein, Rahel.**   See **Rachel**
**Blazek, Douglas**
Eichmann.
Human Firewood Piano, The.
Revelation of the Bare Ass.
Straightening the Warp.
Testimony Concerning a Sickness.
**Blessing, Richard**
Eagle, The.
**Blight, John**
Bone, The.
Doctor Black.
Gold Watch, The.
Home.
Larder.
Lowson.
Racialism.
**Blind, Mathilde**
Dead, The.
Lassitude.
Manchester by Night.
Mourning Women.
Reapers.
Rest.
Sakiyeh, The.
Soul-Drift.
Sower, The.
**Blind Blake (Blake Alphonso Higgs)**
Delia's Gone.
Run Come See.
**Blishen, Edward**
Abroad Thoughts.
**Bliss, Paul Southworth**
Lucas Park (Saint Louis).
**Bliss, Philip Paul**
Almost Persuaded, *with music.*
Hold the Fort.
Wonderful Words of Life, *with music.*
**Bliven, Bruce**
Not Lost in the Stars.
**Blixen, Karen.**   See **"Dinesen, Isak"**

**Bloch, Chana**
Converts, The.
Exile.
Furniture.
Noah.
Paradise.
Sacrifice, The.
Yom Kippur.
**Block, Allan**
Animal, The.
Causeway.
Child's Drawing.
46 and Recalling.
Four Homages.
High Tension Wires.
In Noah's Wake.
In the Glue Factory.
January Thaw.
Tarzan, Old.
Through Old Farmhouse Windows.
**Blockcolski, Lew**
After the First Frost.
Flicker, The.
Flint Hills, The.
49 Stomp, The.
Indian Love Song.
Langston Hughes.
My Dream.
Peyote Vision.
Playing Pocahontas.
Powwow Remnants.
Reservation Special.
Urban Experience, The: Part One.
Urban Experience, The: Part Two.
Wisga.
Woyi, The.
**Blocklyn, Paul**
Days, The.
**Blok, Aleksandr [*or* Alexander]
  Aeksandrovich**
Dances of Death, *sel.*
Little Catkins.
Red Glow in the Sky, A.
**Bloom, Barbara**
From the Ice Age.
**Bloom, Robert**
Achromatic Bear, The.
As If Trooth.
Hawk, The.
In the Evening as from a Cradle.
Regenerate.
**Blossom, Henry**
Because You're You, *with music.*
Kiss Me Again, *with music.*
Streets of New York, The, *with music.*
**Blount, Charles**
Dialogue between King William and the
  Late King James on the Banks of the
  Boyne, A.
**Blount, Roy, Jr.**
Against Broccoli.
For the Record.
Gryll's State ("Gryll/ Had his fill").
Hearty Cook, A.
Hog-calling.
Lady Track Star, A.
Strong Feeling for Poultry, A.
**Blue Cloud, Peter**
Composition.
Coyote's Song.
Crow.
Death Chant.

Hawk Nailed to a Barn Door.
Stone Mountain Face.
Sweat Song.
Walking through twisted hollow
    pathways.
Wolf.
**Blue-Swartz, Janice**
Return to Prinsengracht.
**Blum, Eliezer.** *See* **Alquit, B.**
**Blumenthal, Michael C.**
Flirtation, The.
Serial Monogamy.
Stones.
**Blumenthal-Weiss, Ilse**
Jewish Child Prays to Jesus, A.
**Blunden, Edmund**
Almswomen.
Forefathers.
Giant Puffball, The.
Lonely Love.
March Bee, The.
Midnight Skaters, The.
Report on Experience.
Winter: East Anglia.
**Blunt, Wilfrid Scawen**
And then fate strikes us. First our joys
    decay.
Farewell to Juliet.
Joy's Treachery.
Love Sonnets of Proteus, The,*sels.*
Old Squire, The.
St. Valentine's Day.
Storm in Summer, A.
To One Who Would Make a Confession.
**Bluwstein, Rachel** *See* **Rachel**
**Bly, Robert**
After Long Busyness.
After the Industrial Revolution, All
    Things Happen at Once.
Andrew Jackson's Speech.
Asian Peace Offers Rejected without
    Publication.
At a March against the Vietnam War.
Awakening.
Busy Man Speaks, A.
Christmas Eve Service at Midnight at St.
    Michael's.
Clear Air of October, The.
Come with Me.
Counting Small-boned Bodies.
Dead Seal near McClure's Beach, The.
Driving to Town Late to Mail a Letter.
Driving toward the Lac Qui Parle River.
Evolution from the Fish.
Extra Joyful Chorus for Those Who
    Have Read This Far, An.
Fallen Tree, The.
Finding the Father.
Fire of Despair Has Been Our Saviour,
    The.
For My Son Noah, Ten Years Old.
Great Society, The.
Hearing Men Shout at Night on
    Macdougal Street.
Hollow Tree, A.
Hunting Pheasants in a Cornfield.
Hurrying Away from the Earth.
In a Mountain Cabin in Norway.
In a Train.
In Danger from the Outer World.
Johnson's Cabinet Watched by Ants.
Late Spring Day in My Life, A.

Laziness and Silence.
Leonardo's Secret.
Looking at a Dead Wren in My Hand.
Looking at a Dry Canadian Thistle
    Brought In from the Snow.
Looking at Some Flowers.
Looking Backward.
Looking into a Face.
Looking into a Tide Pool.
Love Poem: "When we are in love, we
    love the grass."
November Day at McClure's.
Old Boards.
Origin of the Praise of God, The.
Pilgrim Fish Heads.
Poem against the British.
Poem against the Rich.
Poem in Three Parts.
Possibility of New Poetry, The.
Puritan on His Honeymoon, The.
Reading in Fall Rain.
Romans Angry about the Inner World.
Sleet Storm on the Merritt Parkway.
Small Bird's Nest Made of White Reed
    Fiber, A.
Snowfall in the Afternoon.
Solitude Late at Night in the Woods.
Summer, 1960, Minnesota.
Sunday in Glastonbury.
Surprised by Evening.
Teeth Mother Naked at Last, The.
Thinking of "The Autumn Fields."
Those Being Eaten by America.
Three Kinds of Pleasures.
Waking from Sleep.
War and Silence.
Watching Television.
Water under the Earth.
Watering the Horse.
When the Dumb Speak.
Where We Must Look for Help.
Written Forty Miles South of a
    Spreading City.
Written in Dejection near Rome.
**Boas, Guy**
Vet, The.
**Bobango, Gerald**
Educational Administration Professor's
    Prayer, The.
**Bock, Frederick**
Aubade: The Desert.
**Bode, Carl**
Pigeon Pie.
**Boden, Frederick**
Mining Places.
**Bodenheim, Maxwell**
Upper Family.
**Bodker, Cecil**
Calendar.
Fury's Field.
Self-Portrait.
**Boethius (Anicius Manlius Severinus
    Boethius)**
Consolation of Philosophy, The, *sels.*
**Bogan, Louise**
After the Persian.
Animal, Vegetable and Mineral.
Cassandra.
Crossed Apple, The.
Crows, The.
Dragonfly, The.
Dream, The.

Evening in the Sanitarium.
Frightened Man, The.
Henceforth, from the Mind.
Hypocrite Swift.
Knowledge.
Late.
Medusa.
Men Loved Wholly beyond Wisdom.
Night.
Old Countryside.
Putting to Sea.
Question in a Field.
Rhyme.
Roman Fountain.
Single Sonnet.
Sleeping Fury, The.
Song for the Last Act.
Sonnet: "Since you would claim the
    sources of my thought."
Spirit's Song.
To Be Sung on the Water.
Train Tune.
Women.
Zone.
**Bogardus, Edgar**
Eastward to Eden.
**Bogin, George**
Alone in the House.
**Bohanon, Margo**
Alabama.
Apartheid.
Blues Suite.
Dark Reflections.
Manchild.
These Feet for Rosa Parks.
Up There.
Woman.
**Boiarski, Phil**
Still Wrestling.
**Boimwall, Rachel**
At Night.
Diaspora Jews.
Lifelong.
Round.
**Boker, George Henry**
Dirge for a Solider.
**Boland, C. J.**
Two Travellers, The.
**Boland, Eavan**
Athene's Song.
Child of Our Time.
Famine Road, The.
From the Painting "Back from Market"
    by Chardin.
New Territory.
Prisoners.
Requiem for a Personal Friend.
Song: "Where in blind files."
War Horse, The.
**Boland, John**
Death of the Family, The.
Idyll: "Dogs behind, I'm running for the
    trees."
Western Myth, The.
**Bold, Alan**
I drink to forget, but whenever I think.
June 1967 at Buchenwald.
Point of Love, The.
Realm of Touching, The.
Shore.
That's Life?
**Bold, Henry**

Song: "Chloris, forbear a while."
Song: "Fire, fire."
**Bolles, Matthew**
Here, Lord, Retired, I Bow in Prayer, *with music.*
**Bolton, Edmund**
Canzone Pastoral in Honor of Her Majesty, A.
Palinode, A.
**Bolz, Jody**
On a Night like This.
**Bomze, Nahum**
City of Light.
Pshytik.
**Bonar, Horatius**
Be True.
Little While, A.
**Bond, Carrie Jacobs**
I Love You Truly, *with music.*
Perfect Day, A, *with music.*
**Bond, Harold**
Girls Who Wave at Cars from Bridges.
It Is Oregon, The Highway Looms.
Letter from Birmingham.
Swallowing.
Way It Happens to You, The.
**Bond, Julian**
Bishop of Atlanta, The: Ray Charles.
Rotation.
**Bone, Edith**
On Myself.
**Bonk, James**
Acrophobe and Lapidary.
Elegy for a Polish Grandaunt.
Painting an Old Apartment.
**Bontemps, Arna**
Black Man Talks of Reaping, A.
Close Your Eyes!
Dark Girl.
Day-Breakers, The.
God Give to Men ("God give the yellow man").
Golgotha Is a Mountain.
Idolatry.
Nocturne at Bethesda.
Nocturne of the Wharves.
Reconnaissance.
Return, The.
Southern Mansion.
**Booth, Philip**
Big Dog.
Cold Water Flat.
Crossing.
Deer Isle.
Dreamscape.
Eaton's Boatyard.
Ego.
Elegy for a Diver.
First Lesson.
Fisherman.
If It Comes.
Incredible Yachts, The.
Lines from an Orchard Once Surveyed by Thoreau.
Misery of Mechanics, The.
Oid Man.
One Man's Wife.
Original Sequence.
Round, The.
Seeing Auden Off.
Thanksgiving 1963.
Tower, The.

Was a Man.
**Boothroyd, Basil**
Best of Two Worlds.
**Borawski, Walta**
Normal as Two Ships in the Night.
**Bordenave, Damon**
Thoughts from the Wall.
**Borenstein, Emily**
Grandfather Yoneh.
Life of the Letters.
**Borges, Jorge Luis**
Ode Written in 1966.
Things That Might Have Been.
**Boring, Mollie**
September Butterfly.
**Bornhauser, Fred**
Wishbone, The.
**Borrell, D. E.**
Another Death.
**Borsa, Victor**
Demolition.
**Borson, Roo**
Now and Again.
**Bosley, Keith**
Number 14.
**Bossidy, John Collins**
Boston ("I come from the city of Boston").
**Bost, Marcia Inzer**
Mountain Born.
**Boswell, Margie B.**
Texas Ranger, The.
**Bosworth, Martha**
Angle of Vision.
**Bottoms, David**
Coasting toward Midnight at the Southeastern Fair.
Copperhead, The.
Faith Healer Come to Rabun County.
Stumptown Attends the Picture Show.
Traveler, The.
Trucker Drives through His Lost Youth, A.
Writing on Napkins at the Sunshine Club, Macon, Georgia 1971.
**Botton, Isaac de**
Desire.
**Bottrall, Ronald**
Darkened Windows.
Mating Answer.
**Boulton, Harold**
All through the Night.
Skye Boat Song, *with music.*
**Bourdillon, Francis William**
Night Has a Thousand Eyes, The.
**Bourke, Sharon**
Sopranosound, Memory of John.
**Bourne, Vincent**
Snail, The.
**Bouslog, Charles S.**
Biographical Sketch.
Result of Our Investigation, The.
**Bouvard, Marguerite**
White.
**Bowden, James H.**
At the Spa.
**Bowen, Donna**
Little Searcher, The.
**Bowen, Euros**
Blackthorn.
Nettles in May.
Winged in Gold.

**Bowen, James K.**
Edge, The.
**Bowering, George**
AW6 May 25, 1974.
Beach at Veracruz, The.
Egg, The.
Grass, Grass.
My Atlas Poet.
Smoking Drugs wtih Strangers.
Solid Mountain.
Under.
**Bowers, Edgar**
Adam's Song to Heaven.
Afternoon at the Beach, An.
Amor Vincit Omnia.
Astronomers of Mont Blanc, The.
Autumn Shade, *sels.*
Centaur Overheard, The.
Mountain Cemetery, The.
Prince, The.
Stoic, The: For Laura von Courten.
To the Reader.
Virgin Mary, The.
**Bowers, Neal**
Archetypes.
Unplanned Design.
**Bowes-Lyon, Lilian**
White Hare, The.
**Bowie, Walter Russell**
O Holy City Seen of John, *with music.*
**Bowie, William C.**
Before the Statue of a Laughing Man.
**Bowles, Caroline Anne (Mrs. Robert Southey)**
To the Lady-Bird.
**Bowles, Paul**
Extract.
**Bowles, William Lisle**
Avenue in Savernake Forest.
Bells, Ostend, The.
To the River Itchin, near Winton.
**Bowman, Derek**
Members of the Family.
Old Sinner.
Peeled Wand.
Root-Crops.
Slicing Button Mushrooms.
Stiff Shirts.
**Bowman, Jacquelyn**
Barbara's Poem.
**Bowman, P. C.**
Homing.
Route 95 North: New Jersey.
**Bowndheri, Ilmi**
As Camels Who Have Become Thirsty.
**Box, William**
She Vowed Him This.
**Boyajian, Aram**
American Commencement.
Blok: Let Me Learn the Poem.
Death of the Epileptic Poet Yesenin, The.
George Washington Goes to a Girlie Movie.
Hairs in My Nose, The.
Poetry is in the Darkness.
World Is Really a Sugarplum House in the Forest, The.
**Boyd, Mark Alexander**
Fra Bank to Bank, Fra Wood to Wood I Rin.

**"Boyd, Nancy."** *See* **Millay, Edna St. Vincent**

**Boyd, Thomas**
King's Son, The.

**Boye, Karin**
Dedication, A, *sel.*

**Boyer, Jill Witherspoon**
Detroit City.
Dream Farmer.
King Lives.
When Brother's Forget.

**Boyle, Kay**
American Citizen, *sel.*
For James Baldwin.
For Marianne Moore's Birthday.
Invitation in It, The.
Monody to the Sound of Zithers.
New Emigration, The.
October 1954.
Thunderstorm in South Dakota.
To a Proud Old Woman Watching the Tearing Down of the Hurricane Shed.
To a Seaman Dead on Land.

**Bozanic, Nick**
Crane's Ascent, The.

**Brabant, Suzanne**
Morgans in October.
Two at Showtime.

**Bracker, Milton**
Troupial, A.
Where, O Where?

**Bradford, Walter**
Chicago Centennial or: The Town Hall Meeting.
Eighty-third Street Chicago, 1969, Scene at the Salaam Restaurant.
Poem for Foster, A.
Poem with a Conclusion, A.
T. C. (Terry Callier; True Christian).
When Hip Was King.

**Bradford, William**
And Truly It Is a Most Glorious Thing, *with music.*

**Bradley, Edward.** *See* **"Bede, Cuthbert"**

**Bradley, George**
In Bed with a River.
Swing One, Swing All.

**Bradley, Katherine** *and* **Edith Cooper.** *See* **"Field, Michael"**

**Bradley, Mary E.**
Pansy.

**Bradley, Sam**
Casual Meeting.

**Bradstreet, Anne**
Another ("As loving hind that, hartless, wants her deer").
As Weary Pilgrim, Now at Rest.
Author to Her Book, The.
Before the Birth of One of Her Children.
Childhood.
Contemplations.
Deliverance from a Fit of Fainting.
Dialogue between Old England and New, A.
Flesh and the Spirit, The.
Here lies,/ A worthy matron of unspotted life.
In Honour of That High and Mighty Princess Queen Elizabeth of Happy Memory.
In Memory of My Dear Grandchild Anne Bradstreet.

In Memory of My Dear Grandchild Elizabeth Bradstreet.
In Reference to Her Children, 23 June, 1656.
Letter to Her Husband, Absent upon Public Employment, A ("As loving hind...").
Letter to Her Husband, Absent upon Publick Employment, A ("My head, my heart, mine eyes,...").
Meditation.
Of the Four Ages of Man.
On My Grandchild Simon Bradstreet.
Prologue, The: "To sing of wars, of captain[e]s, and of kings."
Silent alone, where none or saw, or heard.
To My Dear and Loving Husband.
Upon My Dear and Loving Husband His Going into England Jan. 16, 1661.
Upon the Burning of Our House, July 10th, 1666.
Vanity of All Worldly Things, The.

**Brady, Anne Hazlewood**
Anonymous.
Bonded.
Justice Has Become a Woman.

**Brady, June**
Far Trek.

**Bragg, Linda Brown**
Our Blackness Did Not Come to Us Whole.
Poem about Beauty, Blackness, Poetry, A.

**Brain, Lord Russell**
Hiroshima.
John Donne Speaks from His Grave.
Portrait of William Harvey.
Post Mortem.
Renewal.
To Sir Charles Sherrington.

**Brainard, Franklin**
Inland Sea.
Raingatherer.
Roubaix Cemetery.
White Ropes.

**Brainard, John Gardner Calkins**
Deep, The.
To Thee, O God, the Shepherd Kings, *with music.*

**Braiser, Virginia**
Time of the Mad Atom.

**Braisted, Harry**
She Was Bred in Old Kentucky, *with music.*
You're Not the Only Pebble on the Beach, *with music.*

**Braithwaite, William Stanley**
Golden Moonrise.
In a Grave-Yard.
Rhapsody.
Scintilla.
To——: "Half in the dim light from the hall."

**Braley, Berton**
Church Bells.
Twins, The.

**Brame, Terence**
Black Clouds.
No Meaning.

**Bramston, James**
Man of Taste, The, *sel.*

**Brand, Marian Frances**
Apple-Logia.
Ebony: Contemporary.
Homily: Contemporary.

**Brand, Millen**
All One.
Clausa Germanis Gallia.
Last Families in the Cabins, The.
Longing for the Persimmon Tree.
Thirty Childbirths.

**Brand, Oscar**
When I First Came to This Land.

**Brandi, John**
How to Get to New Mexico.

**Brant, LeRoy V.**
Green Plumes of Royal Palms, *with music.*
Oh, Day of Days, *with music.*

**Brant, Sebastian**
Foote-Ball.

**Brantingham, Philip**
Sarentino-South Tyrol.

**Brasch, Charles**
Ambulando.
Autumn, Thurlby Domain.
Cry Mercy.
Ergo Sum.
Great Sea.
Letter from Thurlby Domain.
Man Missing.
Nineteen Thirty-nine, *sel.*
No Reparation.
Open the Heart.
Oreti Beach.
Photograph of a Baby.
Physics of Love.
Self to Self.
Wantword.
Word by Night.

**Brasfield, James**
Stringer, The.

**Brasher, Charles**
Poem after a Speech by Chief Seattle, 1855.

**Brasier, Virginia**
Song for a Lost Art.

**Brathwaite, Edward**
Chad.
Mmenson.
Timbuctu.

**Brathwaite, Richard**
I Am Not as I Wish.
Nature's Embassy, *sel.*

**Braude, Michael**
Curtain Speech.

**Braun, Richard Emil**
Domestic Duties.
Goose.
Niagara.

**Brautigan, Richard**
All Watched Over by Machines of Loving Grace.
Chinese Checker Players, The.
Curiously Young like a Freshly-dug Grave.
Day They Busted the Grateful Dead, The.
Gee, You're So Beautiful That It's Starting to Rain.
Haiku Ambulance.
Have You Ever Had a Witch Bloom like a Highway.

It's Raining in Love.
Karma Repair Kit: Items 1-4.
November 3.
On Pure Sudden Days like Innocence.
Our Beautiful West Coast Thing.
Pill versus the Springhill Mine Disaster,
The.
**Braxton, Jodi**
Black Sheba.
Miss Maime.
Poem for Blackboys in Floppy Tie-Dye
Hats.
Sometimes I Think of Maryland.
**Brecht, Bertolt**
First Psalm, The.
**Brecht, Bertolt** *and* Hans Eisler
United Front.
**"Breitmann, Hans."** *See* **Leland, Charles
Godfrey**
**Breitt, Luke**
Night Atlas.
Poem for Valerie.
**Brennan, Christopher John**
Burden of Tyre, The, *sel.*
Epilogue: "O life, O radiance, love,
delight."
Lilith, *sel.*
Quest of Silence, The, *sel.*
To V. S.
Towards the Source, *sel.*
Twilight of Disquietude, The, *sel.*
Wanderer, The,
**Brennan, Eileen**
One Kingfisher and One Yellow Rose.
**Brennan, J. Keirn**
Let the Rest of the World Go By.
**Brennan, John Michael**
Air Is.
**Brennan, Joseph Payne**
Raccoon on the Road.
**Brennan, Matthew**
Noon Glare.
Seeing in the Dark.
**Brenner, Summer**
Dede's Return to New Mexico.
For Paige.
Mother, they say you looked Irish.
**Brereton, Jane**
On Mr. Nash's Picture at Full Length.
**Bress, Christine**
Mountaineers, The.
**Breton, André**
Always for the first time.
Dreams.
Freedom of Love.
Postman Cheval.
Spectral Attitudes, The.
**Breton, Nicholas**
Cradle Song, A: "Come, little babe,
come, silly soul."
Honourable Entertainment Given to the
Queen's Majesty in Progress at
Elvetham, The, 1591, *sel.*
Pastoral of Phillis and Coridon, A.
Ploughman's [*or* Plowman's] Song, The.
Rare News.
Report Song in a Dream, A.
Solemn Farewell to the World, A.
**Brett, Peter**
Night Teeth.
Pickers.
**Brewster, Elizabeth**

Disqualification.
For the Unknown Goddess.
Moon.
On Reading Another Poet.
Playing the Bones.
Princess Addresses the Frog Prince, The.
**Brewster, Martha**
Stately Structure of This Earth, The, *with
music.*
**Bricuth, John**
Laurel and Hardy.
Song of the Darkness.
**Bridges, Robert**
April 1885.
Awake, my heart, to be loved, awake,
awake!
Cliff-Top, The.
Elegy on a Lady Whom Grief for the
Death of Her Betrothed Killed.
Elegy: "Wood is bare, The: a river-mist
is steeping."
Eros.
Ethick.
Evening Darkens Over, The.
Garden in September, The.
Hill Pines Were Sighing, The.
I never shall love the snow again.
I will not let thee go.
Indolence.
Johannes Milton, Senex.
Laus Deo.
London Snow.
Low Barometer.
Melancholia.
My delight and thy delight.
Nightingales.
North Wind in October.
On a Dead Child.
Palm Willow, The.
Passer-by, A.
Pater Filio.
Philosopher to His Mistress, The.
Poor Poll.
Psalm, The: "While Northward the hot
sun was sinking o'er the trees."
Riding adown the country lanes.
Say who is this with silvered hair.
Screaming Tarn.
Since We Loved.
Snow Lies Sprinkled on the Beach, The.
So Sweet Love Seemed That April Morn.
Song: "I have loved flowers that fade."
Song: "I love my lady's eyes."
Spring Goeth All in White.
Testament of Beauty, The, *sels.*
To L. B. C. L. M.
Upper skies are palest blue, The.
Water-Party, A.
When we first met we did not guess.
Who has not walked upon the shore.
**Bridges-Adams, W.**
Fragment from the Elizabethans.
**Brigham, Besmilr**
Dream in Cold, A.
Heaved from the Earth.
Mountains.
Rain Sleets Flat.
Sevier County Runaway, The.
State in Indian Language Was Called
"Running Water," The.
Tell Our Daughters.
Tiny Baby Lizard, The.

What Is She Trying to Do, to Pattern
Love.
When Cotton Haymes Walks Down the
Street.
Will's Love, The.
**Brine, Mary Dow**
Hearts and Flowers, *with music.*
**Brininstool, Earl Alonzo**
Back to Arizona.
**Brinnin, John Malcolm**
Address to the Refugees.
American Plan.
Angel Eye of Memory.
At the Band Concert.
Bird Talk.
Dachau.
Hotel Paradiso e Commerciale.
John Without Heaven.
Letter from an Island.
Love in Particular.
New England Sampler, A.
Nuns at Eve.
Roethke Plain.
Saul, Afterward, Riding East.
Skin Diving in the Virgins.
**Brissenden, R. F.**
Death of Damiens or l'Apres-midi des
Lumieres, The.
**Bristol, David**
I Put My Two fingers, Pound and
Whitman, into a Wall Socket.
To the Dead Ladies.
Weeper, The.
**Broaddus, Andrew**
Help Thy Servant, *with music.*
**Brock, Edwin**
Clutter of Mothers, A.
D-Day Minus.
Evolution.
Five Ways to Kill a Man.
Life Style, The.
Song of the Battery Hen.
To His Love in Middle-Age.
To My Wife.
Turn the Key Deftly.
**Brock, Van K.**
Bellair.
Ceremonies, The.
Dead Man Creek.
Evidence, The.
Land of the Old Fields, The.
Lying on a Bridge.
Sea Birds, The.
**Brockerhoff, Hans**
Pygmalion.
**Brod, Max**
Hebrew Lesson.
**Brode, Anthony**
Breakfast with Gerard Manley Hopkins.
**Brodsky, Joseph**
Etude.
Jewish Cemetery near Leningrad, A.
Monument to Pushkin.
Pilgrims.
Six Years Later.
Soho.
To a Tyrant.
Verses on Accepting the World.
**Brodsky, Louis Daniel**
Ancestry.
Buffalo.
Death Comes to the Salesman.

My Flying Machine.
Sitting in Bib Overalls, Workshirt, Boots on the Monument to Liberty in the Center of the Square, Jacksonville, Illinois.
Weeding in January.

**Brody, Alter**
Family Album, A.
Ghetto Twilight.
Lamentations.

**Brome, Alexander**
Drinking Song.

**Bromige, David**
After the Engraving.

**Bromwich, David**
From the Righteous Man Even the Wild Beasts Run Away.
Oedipus, Pentheus.
Wandsworth Common.

**Bronk, William**
After the Spanish Chroniclers.
Aspects of the World Like Coral Reefs.
Body, The.
Continuance, The.
Feeling, The.
Go Ahead; Goodbye; Good Luck; and Watch Out.
Mask the Wearer of the Mask Wears, The.
Metonymy as an Approach to a Real World.
Postcard to Send to Sumer, A.
What Form the World Has.
Whether what we sense of this world.

**Bronson, Daniel Ross**
Cleaning Up, Clearing Out.

**Brontë, Anne ("Acton Bell")**
Reminiscence, A.

**Brontë, Charlotte ("Currer Bell")**
Mementos, *sel.*
On the Death of Anne Brontë.

**Brontë, Emily ("Ellis Bell")**
All hushed and still within the house.
At such a time, in such a spot.
Aye, there it is! It wakes to-night.
Day Dream, A.
Death.
Fall, Leaves, Fall.
How Still, How Happy.
I Am the Only Being Whose Doom.
I Gazed upon the Cloudless Moon.
I saw thee, child, one summer's day.
I'll come when thou art saddest.
Last Lines.
Last Words.
Little While, A, *sel.*
Love and Friendship.
Night Is Darkening round Me.
Night-Wind, The.
Old Stoic, The.
Prisoner, The.
Remembrance.
Song: "Linnet in the rocky dells, The."
Stanzas: "I'll not weep that thou art going to leave me."
Stanzas: "Often rebuked, yet always back returning."
Stanzas to ——: "Well, some may hate, and some may scorn."
Sun Has Set, The.
Tell me, tell me, smiling child.
To Imagination.

'Twas one of those dark, cloudy days.
Upon Her Soothing Breast.
Visionary, The.
Warning and Reply.
Why do I hate that lone green dell?

**Brooke, Fulke Greville, 1st Baron.** *See* **Greville, Fulke, 1st Baron Brooke**

**Brooke, Rupert**
Chilterns, The.
Clouds.
Dead, The ("These hearts were woven").
Dust.
Failure.
Great Lover, The.
Heaven.
Hill, The.
Jealousy.
1914, *sels.*
Old Vicarage, Grantchester, The.
Peace.
Soldier, The.
Sonnet: "I said I splendidly loved you; it's not true."
Sonnet Reversed.
Success.
Voice, The.
Wagner.

**Brookhouse, Christopher**
For Stephen.

**Brooks, Fred Emerson**
Barnyard Melodies.
Foreigners at the Fair.
Pat's Opinion of Flags.

**Brooks, Gwendolyn**
Aspect of Love, Alive in the Ice and Fire, An.
Ballad of Chocolate Mabbie, The.
Ballad of Rudolph Reed, The.
Ballad of the Light-eyed Little Girl, The.
Bean Eaters, The.
Beverly Hills, Chicago.
Big Bessie Throws Her Son into the Street.
Black Wedding Song. A.
Blackstone Rangers, The.
Boy Breaking Glass.
Boys. Black.
Bronzeville Man with a Belt in the Back.
Bronzeville Woman in a Red Hat.
Catch of Shy Fish, A.
Chicago *Defender* Sends a Man to Little Rock, The.
Chicago Picasso, The.
Children of the Poor, The.
Cynthia in the Snow.
Egg Boiler, The.
Empty Woman, The.
Estimable Mable.
First Fight. Then Fiddle. Ply the Slipping String.
Five Men against the Theme "My Name Is Red Hot. Yo Name Ain Doodley Squat."
Flags.
Friend.
Horses Graze.
Hunchback Girl: She Thinks of Heaven.
In Honor of David Anderson Brooks, My Father.
Jessie Mitchell's Mother.
Kitchenette Building.

Last Quatrain of the Ballad of Emmet Till, The.
Life of Lincoln West, The.
Lovely Love, A.
Lovers of the Poor, The.
Malcolm X.
Martin Luther King, Jr.
Medgar Evers.
Mother, The.
Negro Hero.
Now Mrs. Sallie.
Of De Witt Williams on His Way to Lincoln Cemetery.
Of Robert Frost.
Old Laughter.
Old-Marrieds, The.
Old Mary.
Old Tennis Player.
Otto.
Paul Robeson.
Penitent Considers Another Coming of Mary, A.
Pete at the Zoo.
Piano after War.
Preacher, The: Ruminates behind the Sermon.
Riot.
Rites for Cousin Vit, The.
Sadie and Maud.
Second Sermon on the Warpland, The.
Sermon on the Warpland, The.
Song in the Front Yard, A.
Sonnet-Ballad, The.
Steam Song.
"Still Do I Keep My Look, My Identity . . ."
Street in Bronzeville, A: Southeast Corner.
Strong Men, Riding Horses.
Sunset of the City, A.
Third Sermon on the Warpland, The.
To Be in Love.
Truth.
Two Dedications,*sels.*
Vacant Lot, The.
Wall, The.
We Real Cool.
What Shall I Give My Children?
When You Have Forgotten Sunday: The Love Story.
White Troops Had Their Orders, but the Negroes Looked like Men, The.
Womanhood, The, *sels.*
Young Heroes.

**Brooks, Jonathan**
Resurrection, The.

**Brooks, Phillips**
Christmas Everywhere.
O Little Town of Bethlehem.

**Brooks, Robert A.**
Angle of Repose.
Bicycliary.
Literature.

**Brooks, Shirley**
For A' That and A' That, *parody.*
New Proverb.
"Prize" Poem, A.
To Disraeli.
What Jenner Said on Hearing in Elysium That Complaints Had Been Made of His Having a Statue.

**Brosman, Catharine Savage**

Route 29.

**Brough, Robert**
My Lord Tomnoddy.
Sir Menenius Agrippa, the Friend of the People.

**Broughton, James Richard**
Afterword: Song of Song.
Birds of America, The.
It Was the Worm.
Those Old Zen Blues.
What Holds the Universe Together.

**Broughton, T. Alan**
Cave Where Night Sleeps, The.
Gift for Mary MacLane, A.
My Father Dragged by Horses.
People Cannot Speak, The.
Planet Dream.
Snow Chant.
Thaw.
To the Other Side.

**Broumas, Olga**
Absence of Noise Presence of Sound.
Cinderella.
Five Interior Landscapes.
Landscape with Leaves and Figure.
Landscape with Next of Kin.
Landscape with Poets.
Landscape without Touch.
Oregon Landscape with Lost Lover.
Sleeping Beauty.
Sometimes, as a child.

**Brown, Abbie Farwell**
Fisherman, The.
Friends.
Peach, The.

**Brown, Albert H.** *See* **Rice, Seymour** *and* **Albert H. Brown**

**Brown, Alice**
Sensitive Cat, The.

**Brown, Allan**
Girl in a Black Bikini.

**Brown, Bruce Bennett**
Return, The.

**Brown, Charles O.**
History of Arizona, The: How It Was Made and Who Made It.

**Brown, Christy**
Come Softly to My Wake.
End.

**Brown, George Mackay**
Country Girl.
Dream of Winter.
Fiddler's Song.
Haddock Fishermen.
Hamnavoe Market.
Lodging, The.
Lord of the Mirrors, *sel.*
Old Fisherman with Guitar.
Old Women, The.
Poet, The.
Shipwreck.
Trout Fisher.
Unlucky Boat.
Wedding.

**Brown, Hunter**
Rivage.

**Brown, Kate Louise**
Little Plant, The.

**Brown, Michael R.**
Brown Bug, The.

**Brown, Phoebe Hinsdale**

Welcome, Ye Hopeful Heirs of Heaven, *with music.*

**Brown, Rita Mae**
Aristophanes' Symposium.
Dancing the Shout to the True Gospel; or, The Song Movement Sisters Don't Want Me to Sing.
Disconnection, The.
Fire Island.
For Every Sister in the White Man's Jail.
Hymn to the 10,000 Who Die Each Year on the Abortionist's Table in Amerika.
New Lost Feminist, The.

**Brown, Rosalie Moore.** *See* **Moore, Rosalie**

**Brown, Sterling Allen**
After Winter.
Crispus Attucks McCoy.
Foreclosure.
Long Gone.
Ma Rainey.
Old Lem.
Old Woman Remembers, An.
Remembering Nat Turner.
Sister Lou.
Slim in Hell ("Slim Greer went to heaven").
Southern Cop.
Southern Road.
Strange Legacies.
Strong Men.
Tin Roof Blues.
When de Saints Go Ma'chin' Home.

**Brown, Sydney**
Maple Leaf Rag, *with music.*

**Brown, Thomas (Tom)**
Colonels here in solemn manner meet, The.
Doctor Fell.
Epitaph upon That Profound and Learned Casuist, The Late Ordinary of Newgate, An.
Our fathers took oaths as of old they took wives.
Reader, beneath this turf I lie.
Satire upon the French King, A.
To That Most Senseless Scoundrel, the Author of Legion's Humble Address to the Lords.
Upon the Anonymous Author of Legion's Humble Address to the Lords.

**Brown, Thomas Edward**
Between Our Folding Lips.
Conjergal Rights.
Disguises.
I Bended unto Me.
In the Coach. *sel.*
My Garden.
Pain, *sel.*
Scarlett Rocks.
"Social Science."
Voices of Nature, The.
When Love Meets Love.

**Browne, Jane Euphemia ("Aunt Effie")**
Great Brown Owl, The.
Little Raindrops.
Pleasant Changes.
Rooks, The.

**"Browne, Matthew."** *See* **Rands, William Brighty**

**Browne, Michael Dennis**

Hallowe'en 1971.
Iowa.
Iowa, June.
Lamb.
Man, The.
Paranoia.
Plants, The.
Power Failure.
Roof of the World, The.
Talk to Me, Baby.

**Browne, Sir Thomas**
In yellow meadows I take no delight.
O for a toe, such as the funeral pyre.

**Browne, William 1591-1643**
Britannia's Pastorals,*sels.*
Epigram: "King to Oxford sent a troop of horse, The."
Glide soft, ye silver floods.
In Obitum M. S. x Maij, 1614.
Inner Temple Masque, *sel.*
On the Countess Dowager of Pembroke.
Sirens' Song, The.
Song: "Choose now among this fairest number."

**Browne, William (twentieth century)**
Harlem Sounds: Hallelujah Corner.

**Browning, Elizabeth Barrett**
Adequacy.
Aurora Leigh, *sel.*
Bereavement.
Cry of the Children, The.
Cry of the Human, The.
Curse for a Nation, A.
Dead Pan, The.
Denial, A.
Grief.
Hiram Powers' "Greek Slave."
Hugh Stuart Boyd.
Lord Walter's Wife.
Mother and Poet.
Musical Instrument, A.
My Doves.
On a Portrait of Wordsworth by B. R. Haydon.
Poet, The.
Runaway Slave at Pilgrim's Point, The.
Sea-Mew, The.
Since without Thee We Do No Good.
Song for the Ragged Schools of London, A.
Sonnets from the Portuguese,*sels.*
Soul's Expression, The.
Summing Up in Italy.
Tears.
To George Sand: I. A Desire.
To George Sand: II. A Recognition.
Vision of Poets, A, *sel.*
Weeping Saviour, The.

**Browning, Robert**
Abt Vogler.
Andrea del Sarto.
Any Wife to Any Husband.
Apparent Failure.
Asolando, *sels.*
Bad Dreams, *sel.*
Bishop Blougram's Apology.
Bishop Orders His Tomb at Saint Praxed's Church, The.
By the Fire-Side.
Caliban upon Setebos; or, Natural Theology in the Island.
Cardinal and the Dog, The.

Cavalier Tunes.
"Childe Roland to the Dark Tower Came."
Cleon.
Confessional, The ("It is a lie—their Priests, their Pope").
Confessions ("What is he buzzing in my ears?").
Count Gismond.
"De Gustibus."
Development.
Dis Aliter Visum; or, Le Byron de Nos Jours.
Dramatis Personae, *sel.*
Earl Mertoun's Song.
Englishman in Italy, The.
Epilogue: "At the midnight in the silence of the sleep-time."
Epilogue: " 'Poets pour us wine, The.' "
Epistle, An, Containing the Strange Medical Experience of Karshish, the Arab Physician.
Face, A.
Flight of the Duchess, The.
Fra Lippo Lippi.
Garden Fancies.
Grammarian's Funeral, A.
Heretic's Tragedy, The.
Holy-Cross Day.
Home Thoughts, from the Sea.
Home Thoughts from Abroad.
How It Strikes a Contemporary.
How They Brought the Good News from Ghent to Aix.
In a Gondola, *sels.*
Inapprehensiveness.
Incident of the French Camp.
Instans Tyrannus.
Johannes Agricola in Meditation.
Laboratory, The: Ancien Régime.
Last Ride Together, The.
Light Woman, A.
Likeness, A.
Lost Leader, The.
Lost Mistress, The.
Love among the Ruins.
Love in a Life.
Magical Nature.
Master Hugues of Saxe-Gotha.
May and Death.
Meeting at Night.
Memorabilia.
Moth's kiss, first, The!
My Last Duchess.
My Star.
Natural Magic.
Ned Bratts.
Now.
Old Pictures in Florence.
One Word More.
Pan and Luna.
Parleyings with Certain People of Importance in Their Day, *sel.*
Parting at Morning.
Patriot, The.
Pauline, *sels.*
Phases of the Moon.
Pictor Ignotus.
Pied Piper of Hamelin, The.
Pippa Passes, *sels.*
Popularity.
Porphyria's Lover.

Prologue: " 'Poet's age is sad, The: for why?' "
Prospice.
Psalm of David, A.
Rabbi Ben Ezra.
Saul.
Shop.
Sibrandus Schafnaburgensis.
Soliloquy of the Spanish Cloister.
Song: "Nay but you, who do not love her."
Statue and the Bust, The.
Thamuris Marching.
Through the Metidja to Abd-el-Kadr.
To Edward Fitzgerald.
Toccata of Galuppi's, A.
"Transcendentalism: A Poem in Twelve Books."
Two in the Campagna.
Unfaith and Faith.
Up at a Villa—Down in the City.
Waring.
With Francis Furini.
Year's at the Spring, The.
You'll Love Me Yet!
Youth and Art.

**Brownjohn, Alan**
Class Incident from Graves.
Elephant.
Farmer's Point of View.
For My Son.
1939.
Parrot.
Rabbit, The.
Railings, The.
Train, The.

**Brownstein, Michael**
Children, It's Time.
Poem in Two Parts.

**Bruce, George**
Fisherman, The.
Gateway to the Sea, A (I).
Inheritance.
Kinnaird Head.
Laotian Peasant Shot.
Love in Age.
Three Love Poems for My Wife.
Tom on the Beach.
Under the Moon.
Visitations from a Wartime Childhood, *sel.*

**Bruce, John**
Pike, The.

**Bruce, Lennart**
Hunger.
Photo, The.
Poem: "I meet Mother on the street."

**Bruchac, Joseph**
Black Sweeper.
City.
Coming Back.
Cross Fox.
Deer in the Prison, The.
Drum Songs.
Elegy for Jack Bowman.
Finding a Dead Mole with My Sons.
For a Winnebago Brave.
For My Grandfather in Greenfield Center.
Frozen Hands.
Grandmother Came Down to Visit Us, The.

Hiking.
How I Cancelled My Life Insurance.
Leaving the Prison.
Lost Deer, The.
Migration.
Near the Old Slave Fort.
Path, The.
Poem for Jan.
Second Skins—A Peyote Song.
Snake Hill.
Stone Giant.
Sunlight.
There is a stream which rises.
Three Poems for the Indian Steelworkers.

**Bruck, Edith**
Birth.
Childhood.
Equality, Father!
Go, Then.
Let's Talk, Mother.
Sister Zahava.
Why Would I Have Survived?
You Hide ("You hide in the ostrich egg").

**Brucker, H. P.**
Praise Now Your God, *with music.*

**Brudne, Eva**
Farewell Ballad of Poppies, A.
Memento Vivendi.

**Brummels, J. V.**
Jeans.

**Brunazzi, Elizabeth**
Black Silk Skirts.
Faits-divers or News in Brief.
Shirt, The.

**Brush, Thomas**
Falling in Love with Tygers.
Gerard de Nerval.
Mailman, The.
Problem with Dreams, The.

**Bryan, George S.**
How Bill Went East.

**Bryan, Vincent**
In My Merry Oldsmobile, *with music.*

**Bryant, Helen**
Lost Companions.

**Bryant, Frederick J., Jr.**
Cathexis.
Patience of a People.

**Bryant, William Cullen**
Antiquity of Freedom, The.
As Shadows Cast by Cloud and Sun, *with music.*
Death of Lincoln, The.
Death of the Flowers, The.
Forest Hymn, A.
Future Life, The.
Green River.
Hunter of the Prairies, The.
Hymn of the City.
Hymn to Death.
I Cannot Forget with What Fervid Devotion.
Indian at the Burial-Place of His Fathers, An.
Inscription for the Entrance to a Wood.
Journey of Life, The.
Meditation on the Rhode Island Coal, A.
Mighty One, before Whose Face, *with music.*

Monument Mountain.
Mutation.
Oh, Fairest of the Rural Maids.
Oh Mother of a Mighty Race.
O Thou Whose Own Vast Temple
   Stands, *with music.*
Old Man's Counsel, The.
Painted Cup, The.
Path, The.
Poet, The.
Prairies, The.
"Receive Thy Sight."
Robert of Lincoln.
Scene on the Banks of the Hudson, A.
Song of Marion's Men.
Thanatopsis.
Tides, The.
To a Mosquito.
To a Waterfowl.
To Cole, the Painter, Departing for
   Europe.
To the Fringed Gentian.
Twenty-seventh of March, The.
Winter Piece, A.
Yellow Violet, The.
**Bryher, Winifred**
Blue Sleep.
Thessalian.
**Brynes, Edward**
Oration on the Toes.
**Buber, Martin**
Fiddler, The.
I Consider the Tree.
**Buchan, Tom**
Camas Tuath.
Everlasting Astronauts, The.
Fighting Talk.
Loch Ness Monster, The.
Low Road, The.
Polemical Elegy for Reinhardt Heydrich.
Scotland the Wee.
Sentimental Ode.
Subversive Sublime.
Week-End Naturalist, The.
**Buchanan, Robert Williams**
Green Gnome, The.
**Buck, Chief John**
Memorial Ode.
**Buck, Richard Henry**
Dear Old Girl, *with music.*
Kentucky Babe, *with music.*
**Buckaway, C. M.**
Saskatchewan Dusk.
**Buckham, John Wright**
Hills of God, Break Forth in Singing,
   *with music.*
O God, above the Drifting Years, *with
   music.*
**Buckley, Christopher**
Letters of Summer, The.
Light Rain.
**Buckley, Tim**
Goodbye and Hello.
**Buckley, Vincent**
Fitzroy, Carlton.
Golden Builders, *sels.*
No New Thing.
Puritan Poet Reel.
Secret Policeman.
Stroke,*sels.*
Telephones, Muzak.
**Buckmaster, Charles**

History of the Father, A.
**Budenz, Julia**
Crockery.
**Bukowski, Charles**
Another Academy.
Eddie and Eve.
Footnote upon the Construction of the
   Masses.
For Jane.
Hell Hath No Fury.
Hogs in the Sky.
I Met a Genius.
If We Take.
Letters.
Living, *sel.*
Loser, The.
Love Poem for All the Women I Have
   Known, A.
My Style.
Peace.
Priest and the Matador, The.
Short Order.
Singular Self, The.
Something for the Touts, the Nuns, the
   Grocery Clerks and You.
Style.
Sun Wields Mercy, The.
Sunflower.
3:16 and One Half.
Tragedy of the Leaves, The.
**Bulfinch, Stephen Greenleaf**
Hail to the Sabbath Day, *with music.*
**Bull, Arthur J.**
Acorn, The.
Bureaucrat, The.
Collector's Note.
Deinosaurs.
Enemies, The.
Eve.
February Thaw.
His Theology.
I Am Drawn Still to the Desert.
Jungle, The.
Modernismus; or, Prayer for Standstill.
Nature.
New Coventry Cathedral, The.
November.
On the Fen: A Stormy Day near
   Heckington.
Quatrain: "Strictly mathematic God, A."
Richness.
Samarkand.
Sargon.
Severity.
Study in Punctuation.
Tastes.
This and That.
Wind, The.
Windmill, The.
**Bullett, Gerald**
Church Mouse, The.
**Bullis, Jerald**
Revelation.
**Bullokar, William**
To His Child.
**Bullwinkle, Marcia**
There's a Feeling.
**Bulwer-Lytton, Edward Robert, 1st Earl of
   Lytton.** *See* **"Meredith, Owen"**
**Bunner, Freda Newton**
Country Cemetery.
**Bunner, Henry Cuyler**

Grandfather Watts's Private Fourth.
"Home Sweet Home," with Variations.
Mignonette.
Poetry and the Poet.
**Bunting, Basil**
Briggflatts,*sels.*
Chomei at Toyama.
Coda.
Darling of Gods and Men, beneath the
   gliding stars.
Fearful Symmetry.
Fishermen.
On the Fly-Leaf of Pound's Cantos.
Orotava Road, The.
Poet appointed dare not decline.
To Violet.
Vestiges.
What the Chairman Told Tom.
Word, The.
**Bunting, Karen**
Ladies, The.
**Bunyan, John**
Neither Hook nor Line.
Of the Boy and Butterfly.
Of the Child with the Bird on the Bush.
Pilgrim, The.
Pilgrim's Progress, The, *sels.*
Shepherd Boy Sings in the Valley of
   Humiliation, The.
Upon the Horse and His Rider.
Upon the Snail.
Upon the Swallow.
Upon the Weathercock.
**Burden, Jean**
Lost Word.
Poem before Departure.
Poem for Eric Barker.
Sabbath.
Words.
**Burdette, Robert Jones**
My First Cigar.
Orphan Born.
Sisyphus.
"Soldier, Rest!"
Wilhelmj.
**Burford, William**
Christmas Tree, A.
On the Apparition of Oneself.
**Burgess, Anthony**
Lines: Inspired by the Controversy on
   the Value or Otherwise of Old English
   Studies.
**Burgess, Gelett**
Ballad of the Hyde Street Grip.
On Drawing-Room Amenities.
Parisian Nectar.
Purple Cow, The.
Radical Creed, A.
Remarkable Art.
Sequel to the Purple Cow.
Sunset, The.
Table Manners (I-II).
Trapping fairies in West Virginia.
Woman's Reason, A.
**Burgess, George**
Harvest Dawn Is Near, The, *with music.*
While o'er the Deep Thy Servants Sail,
   *with music.*
**Burgin, Richard**
Concertmaster.
**Burgos, Julia de**
Call Out My Number.

Nothing.
Pentachromatic.
Poem of the Intimate Agony.
Poem to My Death.
Poem with the Final Tune.
Río Grande de Loíza.
To Julia de Burgos.

**Burkard, Michael**
Gaslight.
Victim, The.
Wren: Three Mirrors.

**Burke, Carl F.**
God Is Mr. Big, Real Big.

**Burke, Daniel**
Ash Wednesday.
Teacher to Heloise, The (After Waddell).

**Burke, Kenneth**
Civil Defense.
Conspirators, The.
Frigate Jones, the Pussyfooter.
Heavy, Heavy—What Hangs Over?
If All the Thermo-nuclear Warheads.
Know Thyself.
Nursery Rhyme.

**Burke, Tim**
Poem for the 10th Year.
Visions of You.

**Burket, Gail Brook**
From Countless Hearts, *with music.*
So Touch Our Hearts with Loveliness,
   *with music.*

**Burleigh, William Henry**
Abide Not in the Realm of Dreams, *with
   music.*
Lead Us, O Father, in the Paths of
   Peace, *with music.*

**Burnat-Provins, Marguerite**
Fruits you give me are more savory than
   others, The.
Sylvius, your hands near my mouth are
   heady flowers.
You told me: "I am not worthy of you."

**Burns, Carol**
Long-Distance.

**Burns, Jim**
End Bit, The.

**Burns, Richard**
Angels.
Mandelstam.

**Burns, Robert**
Address to the Deil.
Address to the Unco Guid, or the
   Rigidly Righteous.
Ae Fond Kiss.
Afton Water.
Auld Lang Syne.
Banks o' Doon, The.
Bonnie Lesley.
Book-Worms, The.
Cares o' Love, The.
Comin' thro' tne Rye.
Cotter's Saturday Night, The.
Elegy: "Mourn, little harebells owre the
   lea," *abr.*
Epistle to a Young Friend.
Epitaph for James Smith.
Epitaph on a Schoolmaster.
Epitaph on Holy Willie.
Epitaph on John Dove.
For A' That, and A' That.
Grace after Dinner.
Green Grow the Rashes [*or* Rushes], O.

Head pure, sinless quite of brain or soul,
   A.
Here cursing swearing Burton lies.
Hey for a Lass wi' a Tocher.
Holy Fair, The.
Holy Willie's Prayer.
How Can I Keep My Maidenhead.
I Hae a Wife o' My Ain.
I Love My Jean.
I murder hate by field or flood.
I'm Owre Young to Marry Yet.
It Is Na, Jean, Thy Bonie Face.
It Was A' for Our Rightfu' King.
John Anderson, My Jo ("John Anderson
   my jo, John,/ When we were first
   acquent").
John Barleycorn [a Ballad].
Jolly Beggars, The.
Lass That Made the Bed to Me, The.
Lo worms enjoy the seat of bliss.
Love and Liberty (The Jolly Beggars),
   *sel.*
Luath.
Mother's Lament for the Death of Her
   Son, A.
My Heart's in the Highlands.
No more of your titled acquaintances
   boast.
O, Were I on Parnassus Hill.
O, Wert Thou in the Cauld Blast.
O Were My Love Yon Lilac Fair.
O Whistle, and I'll Come to You, My
   Lad.
Ode to Spring.
On a Noisy Polemic.
On Elphinston's Translation of Martial.
On James Grieve, Laird of Boghead,
   Tarbolton.
On Lord Galloway.
On Mr. Pitt's Hair-Powder Tax.
Once Fondly Lov'd.
Paraphrase of the First Psalm.
Poet's Welcome to His Love-begotten
   Daughter, A.
Rantin Dog the Daddie o't, The.
Red, Red Rose, A.
Rigs o' Barley, The.
Scots Wha Hae.
Scottish Grace, A.
See the smoking bowl before us!
Silver Tassie, The.
So vile was poor Wat, such a miscreant
   slave.
Tam o' Shanter.
Thine Am I.
To a Louse.
To a Mouse [on Turning Her Up in Her
   Nest, with the Plough, November
   1785].
To an Artist.
To James Smith.
Toad-Eater, The.
Wee Willie Gray.
Willie Brew'd a Peck o' Maut.
Winter, a Dirge.
Ye maggots, feed on Willie's brains.

**Burns, William**
Nazi Headquarters: El Monte,
   California.

**Burnshaw, Stanley**
Anchorage in Time (I).
Anchorage in Time (II).

Bread.
Coil of Glass, A (I).
Coil of Glass, A (II).
Dilemma of a Dead Man about to Wake
   Up.
Eartha.
House in St. Petersburg.
I, Jim Rogers.
Isaac.
Mr. Tubbe's Morning Service.
New Youngfellow.
Talmudist.
Variations on a Baedecker.

**Burr, Gray**
Eye.
Indian Summer.
Robin Hood.
Sailing, Sailing.

**Burrell, Sophia**
Epigram on Two Ladies.

**Burroughs, Margaret**
Everybody but Me.

**Burroway, Janet**
Scientist, The.

**Burrowes, Elizabeth**
O God, Send Men, *with music.*

**Bursk, Chris**
Handful of Small Secret Stones, A.

**Burt, Bates G.**
O God of Youth, *with music.*

**Burt, Dan**
Poolhall, The.

**Burt, Lucile**
Sleeping at the Beach.

**Burton, Richard**
Old Santa Fe Trail, The.
Song of the Sea.

**Burton, Robert**
Anatomy of Melancholy, The, *sel.*

**Burwell, Rex**
Depression.

**Busch, Ernst**
Hans Beimler.

**Bush, Barney**
Unbridling Our Horses.

**Bushby, D. Maitland**
Drifting.

**Bushnell, Amy**
Retreat.

**Buson (Taniguchi Buson)**
As the Spring Rains Fall.
Haiku: "Halo of the moon, The."
Piercing Chill I Feel, The.
Short Night, The.

**Butcher, Grace**
Assignment.
On Driving behind a School Bus for
   Mentally Retarded Children.
Results of the Polo Game.
Wife of the Moon Man Who Never
   Came Back.

**Butler, Alpheus**
Death of a Fair Girl.

**Butler, Lynne**
Man in the Dream Is Death, The.

**Butler, Samuel (1612-80)**
Arts and Sciences, *sels.*
Ass will with his long ears fray, An.
Authority is a disease, and cure.
Convert's but a fly, that turns about, A.
Devil was more generous than Adam,
   The.

Elephant in the Moon, The: A Satire, *sel.*
Far greater numbers have been lost by hopes.
Great philosopher did choke, A.
Greatest saints and sinners have been made, The.
Hudibras, *sels.*
Hypocrisy will serve as well.
Independent Squire.
Inventions.
Married man comes nearest to the dead, A.
On William Prynne.
Presbyterian Knight.
Quoth Cibber to Pope, tho' in verse you foreclose.
Satire upon the Licentious Age of Charles II, *sel.*
Sir Hudibras, His Passing Worth.
What makes all subjects discontent.

**Butler, Samuel (1835-1902)**
O God! O Montreal!
Prayer, A: "Searcher of souls, you who in heaven abide."
Righteous Man, The.

**Butler, William Allen**
Nothing to Wear.

**Butler-Andrews, C.**
That Little Hatchet.

**Butterworth, Hezekiah**
Thanksgiving in Boston Harbor, The.

**Buttigieg, A.**
Cock, The.
Dog, The.
Lamp, The.

**Butts, Mary Frances**
To-Day.

**Buzea, Constanta**
I'm Not Here / Never Was.

**Byatt, Howard**
Death.

**Byers, Margaretta**
South American Sway.

**Byfield, Bruce**
Stood-up.

**Byles, Mather**
Great God, How Frail a Thing Is Man, *with music.*
Great God, Thy Works, *with music.*
To Thee the Tuneful Anthem Soars, *with music.*
When Wild Confusion Wrecks the Air, *with music.*

**Bynner, Witter ("Emanuel Morgan")**
Adobe House, An.
Arrowy Dreams.
Dance for Rain, A.
Grieve Not for Beauty ("Grieve not for the invisible, transported brow").
Lines to Do with Youth.
New Mexican Desert.
Sandpiper, The.
Shasta.
Spectra, *sel.*
To a President.
Vinegaroon.

**Byrd, Bobby**
Let Me for Once.

**Byrom, John**
Dialogue between Sir John Jobson and Harry Homespun.

Epigram on Handel and Bononcini.
Four Epigrams on the Naturalization Bill.
Hymn for Christmas Day, A.
Jacobite Toast, A.
My Spirit Longeth for Thee.
On Trinity Sunday, *sel.*
On Two Monopolists.

**Byron, George Gordon Noel Byron, 6th Baron**
And I Have Loved Thee, Ocean!
Beppo: A Venetian Story.
Blues, The: A Literary Eclogue.
Bright Be the Place of Thy Soul!
Bull Fight, The.
Byron's Address to the Ocean.
Childe Harold's Pilgrimage, *sels.*
Darkness.
Dedication: "Bob Southey! You're a poet—poet-laureate."
Destruction of Sennacherib, The.
Don Juan, *abr.*
Dream, The, *sel.*
Dying Gladiator, The.
English Bards, and Scotch Reviewers.
Epigram: "In digging up your bones, Tom Paine."
Epigram on John Bull.
Epigrams on Castlereagh.
Epilogue: "There's something in a stupid ass."
Epistle to Augusta.
Epitaph for Castlereagh, An.
Epitaph for William Pitt.
Epitaph to a Dog.
Fare Thee Well.
Farewell! If Ever Fondest Prayer.
Field of Waterloo, The.
First Kiss of Love, The.
Fragment: "I would to heaven that I were so much clay."
Giaour, The: A Fragment of a Turkish Tale.
Growing Old.
Isles of Greece, The.
Italy and England.
John Keats.
Lake Leman woos me with its crystal face.
Lara, *sel.*
Lines Addressed to a Young Lady.
Lines Inscribed upon a Cup Formed from a Skull.
Lines on Hearing That Lady Byron Was Ill.
Lines to Mr. Hodgson.
Lines Written beneath an Elm in the Churchyard of Harrow.
Love and Death.
Maid of Athens Ere We Part.
Manfred: A Dramatic Poem.
Modern Discoveries.
Moon Shot.
Nurse's Dole in the Medea, The.
Ode to Napoleon Buonaparte.
On Leaving Newstead Abbey.
On My Thirty-third Birthday.
On the Death of a Young Lady, Cousin to the Author.
On the Death of Mr. Fox.
On This Day I Complete My Thirty-sixth Year.

Prayer of Abel, The.
Prisoner of Chillon, The.
Prometheus.
Race.
Remember thee! remember thee!
Satan and Michael.
Saul and the Witch of Endor and the Vision of Samuel.
Seduction of Juan, The.
She Walks in Beauty.
So We'll Go No More a-Roving.
Song for the Luddites.
Song of Saul before His Last Battle.
Sonnet on Chillon.
Sonnet to the Prince Regent.
Stanzas: "I heard thy fate without a tear."
Stanzas for Music.
Stanzas to a Lady, on Leaving England.
Stanzas to Augusta.
Stanzas to the Po.
Stanzas Written on the Road between Florence and Pisa.
Sun of the Sleepless!
Sun Set, and Up Rose the Yellow Moon, The.
This day of all our days has done.
To Caroline ("Oh! when shall the grave hide for ever my sorrow").
To Caroline ("Think'st thou I saw thy beauteous eyes").
To Mr. Murray.
To our theme—The man who has stood on the Acropolis.
Venice and Sunset.
Vision of Belshazzar, The.
Vision of Judgment, The.
Waltz, The, *sel.*
Waterloo.
When a Man Hath No Freedom to Fight for at Home.
When Coldness Wraps This Suffering Clay.
When I Roved a Young Highlander.
When We Two Parted.
Written after Swimming from Sestos to Abydos.

**Byron, Henry James**
Rural Simplicity.

**C**

**Cabral, Olga**
Factory, The.
Life and Death among the Xerox People.
Lillian's Chair ("Lillian had just arisen from her chair").
Occupation: Spinster.
Sappho.

**Cader, Teresa D.**
On the Edge of a Safe Sleep.

**Cadsby, Heather**
Poem for a Son.
Reunion.

**Caedmon**
Caedmon's Hymn.

**Caeiro, Alberto (Fernando Pessoa)**
I don't bother with rhymes.

**Caesar, Irving**
Tea for Two, *with music.*
**Cain, Seymour**
Due Date.
My Son, My Son.
**Calderón de la Barca, Pedro**
Life Is a Dream.
**Caldwell, Arthur I.**
Stampede, The.
**Callimachus**
Elegy on Herakleitos.
One Who Runs Away, The.
**Calverley, Charles Stuart**
Ballad: "Auld wife sat at her ivied door,
The."
Beer.
Cock and the Bull, The.
Companions.
Disaster.
"Forever."
In the Gloaming.
Lines on Hearing the Organ.
Lovers, and a Reflection.
Ode to Tobacco.
Proverbial Philosophy: Of Reading.
Schoolmaster Abroad with His Son, The.
**Camerino, Aldo**
Calm.
Fear.
For a Voice That Is Singing.
Mother.
Night.
Recluse.
**Cameron, Norman**
Compassionate Fool, The.
Disused Temple, The.
Firm of Happiness, Limited, The.
Forgive Me, Sire.
From a Woman to a Greedy Lover.
Green, Green Is El Aghir.
In the Queen's Room.
Public-House Confidence.
Shepherdess.
Three Love Poems.
**Camoëns [ or Camoës], Luis de**
Dear gentle soul, who went so soon
away.
Lusiads, The, *sels.*
**Camp, James**
Bruckner.
**Campana, Dino**
Night Character.
**Campbell, Alastair**
Images.
**Campbell, Alistair**
At a Fishing Settlement.
Aunt Lucrezia.
Bitter Harvest.
Blue Rain.
Elegy: "Now he is dead, who talked."
Gathering Mushrooms.
Gunfighter, The.
Hut near Desolated Pines.
Looking at Kapiti.
My Mother.
O Catch Miss Daisy Pinks.
Purple Chaos.
Return, The.
Why Don't You Talk to Me?
Wild Honey.
**Campbell, David**
Australian Dream, The.

Cocky's Calendar, *sel.*
Dear Maurice.
Deaths and Pretty Cousins.
Delivering Lambs.
Lambing.
Men in Green.
Mothers and Daughters.
Night Sowing.
Starting from Central Station.
To a Ground-Lark.
Who Points the Swallow.
Windy Gap.
Windy Nights.
Works and Days, *sel.*
**Campbell, Donald**
Ablow the Mune.
Aiberdeen.
At a Pairty.
Betrayal in Morninside.
Cougait Revisited.
Laneliest Place in the Warld, The.
Minding.
Sonnets frae Siberia, *sel.*
**Campbell, Jane M.**
We Plough the Fields.
**Campbell, Joan**
Sealess World, A.
**Campbell, Joseph ("Seosamh
MacCathmhaoil")**
Ad Limina.
Antiquary, The.
Blanaid's Song ("Blanaid loves roses").
Butterfly in the Fields.
Darkness.
Gombeen, The.
Harvest Song.
I Will Go with My Father a-Ploughing.
Ideal and Reality.
Old Woman, The.
Three Colts Exercising in a Six-Acre.
**Campbell, Roy**
Autumn.
Choosing a Mast.
Fishing Boats in Martigues.
Georgiad, The, *sel.*
Georgian Spring.
Golden Shower, The, *sel.*
Good Resolution, A.
Heartbreak Camp.
Horses on the Camargue.
Luis de Camões.
On Some South African Novelists.
On the Same [Some South African
Novelists].
Sisters, The.
Veld Eclogue, A: The Pioneers.
Zebras, The.
**Campbell, Thomas**
Battle of the Baltic.
Gilderoy, *sel.*
Hohenlinden.
Lord Ullin's Daughter.
Parrot, The.
Soldier's Dream, The.
When Jordan Hushed His Waters Still.
Ye Mariners of England.
**Campion, Thomas**
Among the Shades.
Are you what your faire lookes expresse?
Author of light, revive my dying spright.
Be thou then my beauty named.
Beauty, Since You So Much Desire.

Beauty Is but a Painted Hell.
Blame not my cheeks, though pale with
love they be.
Breake now my heart and dye! Oh no,
she may relent.
Come, chearfull day, part of my life, to
mee.
De Profundis.
Devotion.
Elegye, An: "Constant to none, but ever
false to me."
Follow Thy Fair Sun [Unhappy
Shadow].
Give beauty all her right.
Harden now thy tyred hart with more
then flinty rage.
Hark, All You Ladies.
I care not for these ladies.
I must complain, yet doe enjoy my love.
In Praise of Neptune.
Integer Vitae.
It Fell on a Summer's Day.
Jack and Joan.
Jacke and Jone, they thinke no ill.
Kind[e] are her answers [or answeres].
Lover's Plea, A.
Mistress, Since You So Much Desire.
My Sweetest Lesbia [Let Us Live and
Love].
Never Love Unless[e] You Can.
Now Winter Nights Enlarge.
O Come Quickly!
Raving warre, begot.
Rose-cheeked [or cheekt] Laura, Come.
Secret love or two, I must confesse, A.
Seek the Lord!
Shall I then hope when faith is fled?
Silly boy 'tis full moon yet, thy night as
day shines clearly.
Sleep, Angry Beauty, Sleep.
So Tired Are All My Thoughts.
There Is a Garden in Her Face.
Think'st Thou to Seduce Me Then.
Thou art not faire, for all thy red and
white.
Though your strangenesse frets my hart.
Thrice Toss These Oaken Ashes in the
Air.
To musicke bent is my retyred minde.
Tune thy musicke to thy hart.
Were my hart as some mens are, thy
errours would not move me.
What Faire Pompe.
What if a day, or a month, or a yeare.
When to Her Lute Corinna [or Corrina]
Sings.
Where are all thy beauties now, all
hearts enchaining?
Winter Nights.
Writer to His Book, The.
**Campos, Haroldo de**
If.
**Canfield, Harry Clifford**
On the Loss of U.S. Submarine S4, *sel.*
**Cannan, May Wedderburn**
Rouen.
**Canning, Effie I.**
Baby Mine, *with music.*
Rock-a-Bye Baby, *with music.*
**Canning, George**
Ballynahinch.
Cat and the Bird, The.

Elderly Gentleman, The.
Ipecacuanha.
Political Despatch, A.
Progress of Man, The, *sel.*
Rovers, The, *sel.*
Song by Rogero.

**Canning, George** *and* John Hookham Frere
Friend of Humanity and the Knife-Grinder, The.
Inscription: "For one long term, or e'er her trial came."
New Morality, *sel.*

**Cannon, Hughie**
Bill Bailey Won't You Pleases Come Home.

**Cannon, Melissa**
Crippled Child at the Window.

**Cannon, Rick**
Babies.
Box of Air, The.
Rick's Bag of Tricks.

**Cantrell, Charles**
Aladdin's Lamp.
Amputee, The.

**Canzoneri, Robert**
One Lion, Once.
Two.
Unloved, The.

**Caparoso, Fred**
Private Places.

**Capua, Eduardo di**
O Sole Mio, *with music.*

**Carb, Alison B.**
Israeli Soldier's Nightmare, An.

**"Carbery, Ethna" (Anna Johnston MacManus)**
Brian Boy Magee.
King of Ireland's Cairn, The, *abr.*
Love-Talker, The.
On an Island, *abr.*

**Carden, Ramona**
Moccasins of an Old Man, The.
Tumbleweed.

**Cardenal, Ernesto**
Epitaph for the Tomb of Adolfo Baez Bone.

**Cardiff, Gladys**
Carious Exposure.
Combing.
Dragon Skate.
Grey Woman.
Leaves like Fish.
Long Person.
O nuclear wind, when wilt thou blow.
Swimmer.
Tlanusi' yi, the Leech Place.
To Frighten a Storm.

**Cardinali, Edward**
Freeway.

**Cardona-Hine, Alvaro**
Hearing My Son Play.
Menashtash.

**Carew, Thomas**
Another [Epitaph on the Lady Mary Villiers] ("Purest soul that e'er was sent, The").
Boldness in Love.
Celia Bleeding: to the Surgeon.
Celia Singing ("Hark, how my Celia, with the choice").
Deposition from Love, A.
Disdain Returned.

Elegy upon the Death of the Dean of St. Paul's, Dr. John Donne.
Epitaph on the Lady Mary Villiers ("The Lady Mary Villiers lies").
Epitaph on the Lady Mary Villiers ("This little vault, this narrow room").
Excuse of Absence, An.
Fly That Flew into My Mistress's Eye, A.
For a Picture Where a Queen Laments over the Tomb of a Slain Knight.
Good Counsel to a Young Maid.
Hymeneal Dialogue, An.
Hymeneal Song on the Nuptials of the Lady Anne Wentworth and the Lord Lovelace, An.
Ingrateful Beauty Threatened.
Lady's Prayer to Cupid, A.
Looking-Glass, A.
Lover, upon an Accident Necessitating His Departure, Consults with Reason, A.
Love's Force.
Maria Wentworth.
New Year's Sacrifice, A: To Lucinda.
On His Mistress Looking in a Glass.
On Sight of a Gentlewoman's Face in the Water.
On the Death of Donne.
On the Marriage of T. K. and C. C., the Morning Stormy.
Pastoral Dialogue, A.: Shepherd. Nymph. Chorus.
Persuasions to Enjoy.
Rapture, A.
Second Rapture, The.
Secrecy Protested.
Song, A: "Ask me no more where Jove bestows."
Song: Good Counsel to a Young Maid.
Song: Mediocrity in Love Rejected.
Song: Willing Prisoner to His Mistress, The.
Spring, The.
Tinder, The.
To A. L.: Persuasions to Love.
To a Lady That Desired I Would Love Her.
To Ben Jonson.
To Her in Absence: A Ship.
To My Friend G. N., from Wrest.
To My Inconstant Mistris[s].
To My Mistress in Absence.
To My Mistress Sitting by a River's Side: An Eddy.
To My Worthy Friend Master George Sandys, on His Translation of the Psalms.
To Saxham.
To T. H., a Lady Resembling My Mistress.
To the King, at His Entrance into Saxham: By Master John Crofts.
To the New Year.
To the Reader of Master William Davenant's Play, The Wits.
Upon a Mole in Celia's Bosom.
Upon a Ribband.
Upon Master Walter Montagu's Return from Travel.
Upon My Lord Chief Justice's Election

of My Lady Anne Wentworth for His Mistress.
Upon Some Alterations in My Mistress, after My Departure into France.

**Carey, Lady Elizabeth**
Mariam, *sels.*

**Carey, Henry**
Namby-Pamby.
Sally in Our Alley.

**Carey [or Cary], Patrick**
Crucifixus pro Nobis.
Hymn: "Whilst I beheld the neck o' the dove."
Nulla Fides.

**Carleton, Will M.**
Doctor's Story, The.
Johnny Rich, *sel.*

**Carlile, Henry**
Dodo.
Flying.
Grandmother.
Grief of Our Genitals, The.

**Carlson, Randolph**
Rapture.

**Carman, Bliss**
Lord of My Heart's Elation, *with music.*
Marigolds.
More Ancient Mariner, A.

**Carmi, T.**
Author's Apology, The.
Condition, The.

**Carnevali, Emanuel**
Queer Things.
Walt Whitman.

**Carney, Julia A. Fletcher**
Little Things.

**Carolan, Turlough**   *See* O'Carolan, Turlough

**Caroutch, Yvonne**
Child of silence and shadow.
I come to you with the vertigoes of the source.
Limb of forests rises up, The.
Night opens like an almond.
When we are two drunk suns.

**Carpenter, Maurice**
To S. T. C. on His 179th Birthday, October 12, 1951.

**Carr, Alan J.**
Old Man.

**Carr, Mary Jane**
Halloween.

**Carr, Robert V.**
Comin' to Town.
Cowboy and the Stork, The.
Enlightenment.
Good-by, Steer.
Home.
Old Cowboy's Lament, The.
Prairie Wolves.
Roundup Cook, The.

**Carrier, Constance**
At Tripolis.
Commencement.
Elegy: "Here where the elm trees were."
Intimations of Immortality, Cuttingsville, Vermont, 1880.
Pro Patria, *abr.*
Taken Town, The.

**Carroll, Jim**
Distances, The.

**"Carroll, Lewis" (Charles Lutwidge Dodgson)**
Acrostic.
Alice's Adventures in Wonderland, *sels.*
Alice's Recitation.
Baker's Tale, The.
Brother and Sister.
Duchess's Lullaby, The.
Evidence Read of the Trial of the Knave of Hearts.
Father William.
Hiawatha's Photographing.
His sister named Lucy O'Finner.
How Doth the Little Crocodile.
Humpty Dumpty's Song [*or* Recitation].
Hunting of the Snark, The.
Jabberwocky.
Kingfisher Song, The.
Lobster Quadrille, The.
Mad Hatter's Song.
My Fairy.
My Fancy.
Palace of humbug, The.
Pig Tale, The.
Quotation from Shakespeare with Slight Improvements, A.
Sylvie and Bruno, *sel.*
Sylvie and Bruno Concluded.
Tale of the Mice, The.
Tèma con Variazioni.
There was a young lady of station.
There was once a young man of Oporta.
Third Voice, The.
Three Badgers, The.
Three Voices, The, *sel.*
Through the Looking-Glass, *sels.*
Turtle Soup.
Walrus and the Carpenter, The.
Wasp's Song, The.
White Knight's Song, The.
Yet what are all such gaieties to me.
**Carroll, Paul**
Father.
Ode to Delmore Schwartz.
University of Illinois at Chicago Circle Lecture Series.
Words for Neruda.
**Carroll, Wallace**
Cried the Lip.
**Carruth, Hayden**
Ah, you beast of love.
Contra Mortem.
Emergency Haying.
Fear and Anger in the Mindless Universe.
Hard Journey, A. Yes.
Insomniac Sleeps Well for Once and, The.
Loneliness.
Once more by the brook the alder leaves.
Our Tense and Wintry Minds, *with music.*
Rimrock, Where It Is.
Seasons.
So be it. I am.
Sonnet: "Cry, crow."
Speaking for Them.
This Decoration.
Twilight Comes.
Why speak of the use.
Your tears, Niobe.
**Carryl, Charles Edward**

Alphabet of Questions, An.
Camel's Complaint, The.
Davy and the Goblin, *sels.*
My Recollectest Thoughts.
Robinson Crusoe's Story.
**Carryl, Guy Wetmore**
Domineering Eagle and the Inventive Bratling, The.
Embarrassing Episode of Little Miss Muffet, The.
Fearful Finale of the Irascible Mouse, The.
Harmonious Heedlessness of Little Boy Blue, The.
How a Girl Was Too Reckless of Grammar.
How Jack Found That Beans May Go Back on a Chap.
Sycophantic Fox and the Gullible Raven, The.
**Carson, Ciaran**
Bomb Disposal, The.
Car Cemetery, The.
Half-Moon Lake, The.
Insular Celts, The.
St. Ciaran and the Birds.
Visting the Dead.
Wheel.
**Carson, E. J.**
November Snow.
**Carson, Joseph**
As I Grow Older and Fatten on Myself.
**Carter, Albert Howard**
Christmas Needles.
Crack of Doom.
Critique for Our Times.
For the Spring Being.
In the Wilderness.
Peter.
Quem Queritis.
Reflections on Limitations.
Tomb of Time, The.
**Carter, Charlotte Osgood**
Elephant and the Giraffe, The.
**Carter, Hodding**
In the Jury Room.
**Carter, Jared**
For Jack Chatham.
Measuring, The.
**Carter, Jefferson**
How to Write a Poem about the Desert
**Carter, John Marshall**
Turn on the Footlights: The Perils of Pedagogy.
**Carter, Karl**
Half Note for the Duke, A.
**Carter, Laura Lee**
Madness.
**Carter, Sydney**
Friday Morning.
Lord of the Dance.
**Cartwright, William**
Bill of Fare, A, *sel.*
Dead Sparrow, The.
No Platonic Love.
On a Virtuous Young Gentlewoman That Died Suddenly.
On the Circumcision: For the King's Music.
Royal Slave, The, *sel.*
Sadness.
Siege, The; or, Love's Convert, The, *sel.*

To Chloe Who Wish'd Her Self Young Enough for Me.
**Carver, Raymond**
Deschutes River.
Drinking while Driving.
Hunter.
Luck.
Wall, The.
Winter Insomnia.
**Cary, Patrick** *See* Carey, Patrick
**Cary, Phoebe**
Day Is Done, The.
Don't Give Up.
Jacob.
Leak in the Dike, The.
Samuel Brown.
**Caryll, John**
Hypocrite, The.
Naboth's Vineyard.
**Case, Mose**
Arkansas Traveller, The, *with music.*
**Casewit, Curtis W.**
End of the Affair.
**Casey, Michael**
Bummer, A.
**Casey, Peter**
Merry Jovial Beggar, The.
**Casgrain, Ardoin**
I Believe.
One Fixed Star.
**Casiano, Americo**
Music Box Sang, The.
We Talked.
**Casillas, Rick**
Yaqui Women: Three Generations.
**Cassel, Irwin M.**
I Love Life, *with music.*
**Cassian, Nina**
All Night Long.
Blood.
Cripples.
Hills picking up the/ moonlight like.
Knowledge.
Like Gulliver.
Ordeal.
Self-Portrait.
Vegetable Destiny.
**Cassity, Turner**
Calvin in the Casino.
Carpenters.
Chronology.
Gardens of Proserpine, The.
L'Aigle A Deux Jambes.
New Dolores Leather Bar, The.
Pacelli and the Ethiop.
Technique on the Firing Line.
Wine from the Cape.
**Castelete, Rachael**
When I Came to London.
**Castellanos, Rosario**
Great fish's eyes never shut, The.
O cloud that wants to be the sky's arrow.
Silence Concerning an Ancient Stone.
What is weaker than a god? It groans hungry.
**Castiello, Jaime**
Partners.
**Castiglione, Jack**
Noisy Boys.
**Castillo, Otto Rene**
Apolitical Intellectuals.

**Casto, Robert Clayton**
Classical Autumn.
Salt Pork, The.
**Castro, Michael**
Grandfathers.
Percolating Highway.
**Castro, Rosalía de**
Crickets and locusts, cicadas.
How placidly shine/ The river, the
    spring, and the Sun.
In the sky, clearest blue.
Long May.
Now all that sound of laughter, sound of
    singing.
The say that plants don't talk, nor do.
**Castro Ríos, Andrés**
For Nothing.
Words to Remind Me of Grandmother.
**Casullo, Joanne**
Father and Daughter.
Mistaken Identity.
Suicide, The.
Translation from Original.
**Catacalos, Rosemary**
Homecoming Celebration.
**Catalano, Gary**
Poem Is Not, A.
**Cater, Catherine**
Here and Now.
**Catermull, Jane**
Who?
**Cather, Willa Sibert**
Dedicatory: "Somewhere, sometime, in
    an April twilight."
Grandmither, Think Not I Forget.
Spanish Johnny.
**Cato, Nancy**
Independence.
**Cattafi, Bartola**
Patience.
**Catullus, Caius [or Gaius] Valerius**
Break off/ fallen Catullus.
Caelius, my Lesbia, that one, that only
    Lesbia.
Come, Lesbia, let us live and love.
Come and let us live my deare.
Dianae Sumus in Fide.
Each moment of the long-liv'd day.
Egnatius has fine teeth, and those.
Fabullus I will treat you handsomely.
From the quarters of the compass.
Furius, Aurelius, bound to Catullus.
Her that I love, I hate!
I hate and love./ And if you ask me
    why.
I hate and love. Why? You may ask but.
I hate and love, wouldst thou the reason
    know?
I love and hate. Ah! never ask why so!
If a man can find rich consolation,
    remembering his good deeds.
Lesbia Forever on Me Rails.
Lesbia loads me night and day with her
    curses.
Lesbia speaks evil of me with her
    husband near.
Lesbia's sparrow.
Miserable Catullus, stop being foolish.
Miss her, Catullus? don't be so inept to
    rail.
My Lesbia let us love and live.

My life, my love, you say our love will
    last forever.
My mistress sayes she'll marry none but
    me.
My woman says that she would rather
    wear the wedding-veil for me.
No woman, if she is honest, can say that
    she's/ been blessed with greater love,
    my Lesbia.
None could ever say that she.
Now my mind's been brought to such
    extremes.
Ode: Acme and Septimius.
Phyllis Corydon clutched to him.
Poor damned Catullus, here's no time
    for nonsense.
Sirmio, thou dearest dear of strands.
Suffenus whom you know, the witty.
That me alone you lov'd, you once did
    say.
That no fair woman will, wonder not
    why.
There are many who think of Quintia in
    terms of beauty.
There was a time, O Lesbia, when you
    said Catullus was the only man.
This racer of the watry plain.
Thou saidst that I alone thy heart cou'd
    move.
Unto no body my woman saith she had
    rather a wife be.
Varus, whom I chanced to meet.
Were you born a lioness in the Libyan
    Mountains.
What demented malice, my silly
    Ravidus.
When at last after long despair, our
    hopes ring true again.
While everyone else is laughing and
    drinking.
Yacht, The.
Yes! my Lesbia! let us prove.
**"Caudwell, Christopher" (Christopher St.**
    **John Sprigg)**
Classic Encounter.
Progress of Poetry, The.
**Causley, Charles**
Ballad for Katharine of Aragon, A.
Ballad of the Bread Man.
Betjeman, 1984.
Chief Petty Officer.
Colonel Fazackerley.
Cowboy Song.
Death of a Poet.
Envoi: "I am the Prince."
Hawthorn White.
I Am the Great Sun.
I Saw a Jolly Hunter.
Innocent's Song.
Nursery Rhyme of Innocence and
    Experience.
Recruiting Drive.
Riley.
Song of the Dying Gunner A.A.1.
Timothy Winters.
What Has Happened to Lulu?
When Dad Felt Bad.
**Cavafy, Constantine P.**
On the Street.
Return.
To Remain.
**Cavalcanti, Guido**

Donna Me Prega.
Sonnet: Guido Cavalcanti to Dante.
Sonnet: Rapture Concerning His Lady,
    A.
**Cavalieri, Grace**
After the Fact.
Being Admired.
Black in Virginia.
Christmas.
Come to a Wedding.
Cry, The.
Novus Ordo Seclorum.
Offer of Friendship, The.
Orphanage, The.
Our Sobbing Must Be Heard.
To the President Crossing the Potomac.
We'll Never Be the Same (Until Later).
**Cavanass, J. M.**
By the Waters of Minnetonka, *with*
    *music.*
**Cavendish, Margaret, Duchess of**
    **Newcastle.** *See* **Newcastle, Margaret**
    **Cavendish, Duchess of**
**Cavendish, William, Duke of Newcastle.**
    *See* **Newcastle, William Cavendish,**
    **Duke of**
**Cawein, Madison**
To a Wind-Flower.
**Cedering, Siv.** *See* **Fox, Siv Cedering**
**Ceely, John**
Bear.
**"Ceiriog."** *See* **Hughes, John Ceiriog**
**Celan, Paul**
Ash-Glory.
Cello Entry.
Corona.
Etched Away From.
Fugue of Death.
Hut Window.
In Egypt.
In Prague.
Irish.
Jugs, The.
Just Think.
Leap-Centuries.
Over Three Nipple-Stones.
Plashes the Fountain.
Psalm: "No one kneads us again of earth
    and clay."
Speck of Sand, A.
Tenebrae.
Thread Suns.
Turn Blind.
Your Hand Full of Hours.
Zürich, zum Storchem.
**Centamputan, Maturai Eruttalan**
What She Said.
**Céu, Sor Violante do**
Voice of a Dissipated Woman inside a
    Tomb.
**Chadwick, Jerah**
Runner, The.
**Chaet, Eric**
Letter Catches Up with Me, A.
Yom Kippur.
**Chaffin, Lillie D.**
Haiku, for Cinnamon.
Tourism.
**Chalfi, Abraham**
My Father.
One Who Is Missing, The.
**Chalfi, Raquel**

Childless Witch, A.
Like a Field Waiting.
Witch Going Down to Egypt, A.
**Challis, Gordon**
Asbestos-suited Man in Hell, The.
Iceman, The.
Inflammable Man, The.
Man of Glass, The.
Oracle, The.
Postman, The.
Shadowless Man, The.
Thermostatic Man, The.
Thin Partition.
**Chalmers, Patrick Reginald**
Cuckoo, The.
Tortoiseshell Cat, The.
**Chalpin, Lila**
Curse of a Fisherman's Wife.
**Chamberlain, Brenda**
Dead Ponies.
Islandman.
Lament: "My man is a bone ringed with weed."
Talysarn.
**Chamberlain, Marisha**
No Respect for Authority.
**Chambers, George**
Life, The.
Voice, The.
**Chambers, Henry Tim**
Beforehand and Afterward ("Beforehand, liars studied how to lie").
God Walks among the Dust.
Prophet.
They Slept while Jesus Prayed.
**Chambers, Jane**
Woman.
**Chambers, Nancy**
It's Dark Outside.
There's a Red Brick Wall.
Zanzibar Pete and Zoom-along Dick.
**Chamisso, Adelbert von**
Tragic Story, A.
**Chandler, Janet Carncross**
Leave the Top Plums.
**Chandonnet, Ann**
Edge, The.
**Chang, Laban**
Driving Up to Kokee Park in the Summer.
9/3/76.
**Chanler, Isaac**
Awake My Soul, Betimes Awake, *with music*.
Thrice Welcome First and Best of Days, *with music*.
**Chantikian, Kosrof**
Love Song.
Your Eyes.
**Chao Li-hua**
Farewell: "My boat goes west, yours east."
**Chao Luan-luan**
Slender Fingers ("Slender, delicate, soft jade").
**Chapin, Carol Earle**
Highway Construction.
**Chapin, Edwin Hubbell**
Hark! Hark! with Harps of Gold, *with music*.
O Thou, Who Didst Ordain the Word.

Ocean Burial, The, *with music*.
**Chaplin, Ralph**
Commonwealth of Toil, The.
Mourn Not the Dead.
Solidarity Forever.
**Chapman, Arthur**
Blanket Injun, The.
Dead Prospector, The.
Last Drift.
Little Papoose.
Out Where the West Begins.
Pete's Error.
Santa Fe Trail, The.
Sheep-Herder's Lament, The.
Sheriff's Report, The.
**Chapman, George (1559?-1634)**
Bridal Song.
Conspiracy of Charles, Duke of Byron, The, *sel.*
Hoer and Leander, *sels.*
Ovid's Banquet of Sense, *sel.*
To My Admired and Soul-loved Friend, Master of All Essentials and True Knowledge, Mr. Harriots, *sel.*
**Chappell, Fred**
Cleaning the Well.
February.
My Grandmother Washes Her Feet.
Northwest Airlines (My Emergency Instructions Were in Chinese).
Skin Flick.
Spitballer.
**Char, René**
Basket-Weaver's Love, The.
**Charles I, King of England**
On a Quiet Conscience.
**Charles, Dorthi**
Concrete Cat.
**Charles, Ed**
Athlete's Prayer, An.
**Charles d'Orléans.** See **Orléans, Charles, Duc d'**
**Chartier, Alain**
I turn you out of doors.
**Chase-Riboud, Barbara**
Come with Me, *sel.*
**Chasin, Helen**
City Pigeons.
Falling Out.
Joy Sonnet in a Random Universe.
Looking Out.
Mythics.
Photograph at the Cloisters: April 1972.
Poetess Kō Ōgimi, The.
Recovery Room, The: Lying-in.
Telemann.
Word "Plum," The.
**Chatain, Robert**
World of Darkness.
**Chatterton, Thomas**
Aella, *sel.*
Elinoure and Juga.
Excelente Balade of Charitie, An.
Minstrel's Song, The.
On Resignation.
**Chaucer, Geoffrey**
Balade: "Hide, Absalon, thy gilte tresses clear."
Ballade against Woman Inconstant, A.
But, sires, o word forgat I in my tale.
Canterbury Tales, The, *sels.*
Clerk of Oxford, The.

Complaint of Chaucer to His Purse, The.
Complaint of Troilus, The.
Controlling the Tongue.
Criseyde Sees Troilus Return from Battle.
Eagle Converses with Chaucer, The.
Former Age, The.
Friar's Tale, The.
Gentilesse.
Go, Little Book ("Go, litel book, go, litel myn tragedy").
House of Fame, The, *sels.*
Jove's Eagle Carries Chaucer into Space.
Knight's Tale, The, *sel.*
Lak of Stedfastnesse.
Love Unfeigned.
Manciple's Tale, The, *sels.*
Merciless Beauty.
Mice before Milk.
Mill at Trumpington, The.
Miller's Prologue, The.
Miller's Tale, The.
Nun's Priest's Prologue, The.
Nun's Priest's Tale, The.
Old Books.
Pardoner's Prologue, The.
Pardoner's Tale, The.
Parliament of Fowls, The, *sels.*
Persons of the Prologue.
Poor Parson, A.
Prioress, The.
Reeve, The.
Seynt Valentynes Day.
Three Revellers Search for Death.
To Adam, His Scribe.
To Rosemond.
Troilus and Criseyde, *sels.*
Truth.
Wanton Merry Friar, A.
Wife of Bath's, The.
Wife of Bath's Prologue, The.
Wife of Bath's Tale, The.
Wife's Fifth Husband, The.
**Chayat, Juliet**
Stone.
**Chear, Abraham**
To My Youngest Kinsman, R. L.
**Chedid, Andrée**
What Are We Playing At?
**Cheever, George Barrell**
Blest Be the Wondrous Grace, *with music*.
Thy Loving Kindness, Lord, I Sing, *with music*.
**Cheney, Elizabeth**
Overheard in an Orchard.
**Cheney, John Vance**
Happiest Heart, The.
Unto Our God Most High We Sing, *with music*.
**Cheng Min**
Student.
**Chen Hsieh**
Number One Daughter of the Wang Family, The.
**Cherbury, Edward Herbert, 1st Baron.** See **Herbert of Cherbury**
**Cherkovski, Neeli**
Fresno Notebook.
Love Poem without Anyone in It.
**Cherner, Anne**
Everglade.

Window.
**Chernin, Kim**
Eve's Birth.
**Chernoff, Maxine**
Abridged Bestiary, An.
Dead Letter Office, The.
Fred Astaire.
Last Auroch, The.
Painting.
Sitting, The.
**Cherry, Kelly**
Resurrection Quatrain.
Song for Sigmund Freud, A.
**Cherwinski, Joseph**
Forsythia Is the Color I Remember.
**Chesham, Sallie**
Aside to Julie.
Into the Sky.
Mark This.
Thoughts on Pain.
**Chester, Laura**
Eyes of the Garden.
Hibernating in an Old Lost
    Neighbourhood.
House Guest, The.
Pavane for the Passing of a Child.
28 VIII 69.
Wish for Water, A.
**Chesterfield, Philip Dormer Stanhope, 4th
    Earl of**
On Miss Eleanor Ambrose, a Celebrated
    Beauty in Dublin.
Unlike my subject now shall be my song.
Verses Written in a Lady's Sherlock
    upon Death.
**Chesterton, Frances**
How Far Is It to Bethlehem?
**Chesterton, Gilbert Keith**
After Lord Tennyson.
After Robert Browning.
After Swinburne.
After Walt Whitman.
After W.B. Yeats.
Antichrist, or the Reunion of
    Christendom: An Ode.
Ballad of Abbreviations, A.
Ballade of Suicide, A.
Donkey, The.
Elegy in a Country Churchyard.
Fat White Woman Speaks, The.
For the Crèche.
Gold Leaves.
History.
Lepanto.
Old Song, The.
Oneness of the Philosopher with Nature,
    The.
On the Dangers Attending Altruism on
    the High Seas.
Rolling English Road, The.
Secret People, The.
Skeleton, The.
Song against Grocers, The.
Song of Quoodle, The.
Songs of Education, sels.
Triolet: "I wish I were a jelly fish."
Variations on an Air Composed on
    Having to Appear in a Pageant as Old
    King Cole.
Wine and Water.
**Chettle, Henry**
Diaphenia.

**Chevalier, Albert**
My Old Dutch: A Cockney Song.
**Chikamatsu Monzaemon**
Love Suicides at Sonezaki, The, sel.
**Child, Lydia Maria**
Thanksgiving Day.
**Childe, Rowland**
Haworth in May.
**Childers, David C.**
Another One for the Devil.
Hunt.
South Carolina Baptismal Procession.
**Childress, William**
Dreamer, The.
Metamorphosis of Aunt Jemima, The.
**Chilgren, Delia**
Big Sur Summer.
Letter to My Father.
Nightwalker.
**Chimako, Tada**
Mirror.
**Ching, Laureen**
Memorial Day.
**Chittenden, William Lawrence**
Cowboys' Christmas Ball, The.
Ode to the Norther.
**Chitty, Cordelia**
Galloping.
**Ch'iu Chin**
Call to Action, A.
To the Tune "The River Is Red."
**Chivers, Thomas Holley**
Chinese Serenade for the Ut-Kam and
    Tong-Koo, sel.
Lily Adair.
Moon of Mobile, The.
Railroad Song, sel.
To Allegra Florence in Heaven, sel.
**Chiyo**
Don't dress for it.
Hardly spring, with ice.
Once my parents were older.
**Chock, Eric**
Waolani Stream, 1955/1975.
**Chorny, Sasha**
Vilna Puzzle, A.
**Chosa, Martha**
Drums.
**Cho Wen-chün**
Song of Snow-white Heads.
**Christensen, Inger**
Men's Voices.
**Christgau, Ferdinand G.**
St. Thomas.
Two Jays at St. Louis.
**Christian, Marcus B.**
Dialect Quatrain.
McDonogh Day in New Orleans.
**Christina, Martha**
Couplets for WCW.
**Christine de Pisan.**   See **Pisan, Christine
de**
**Christoph, Rosemary**
Recognitions, The: Seedtime.
**Christopher, Nicholas**
Big City Glissando.
John Garfield.
**Chu Shu-chen**
Alone.
Lost.
Morning.
Old Anguish, The.

Plum Blossoms.
Sorrow.
Stormy Night in Autumn.
**Chudleigh, Mary Lee, Lady**
Offering, The: Part One.
Resolve, The.
To the Ladies.
Chuilleanáin, Eiléan Ní.   See **Ní
    Chuilleanáin, Eiléan**
**Chukovsky, Kornei**
Crocodile ("Once a haughty crocodile
    left his home upon the Nile").
Crocodile ("Once there was a
    crocodile").
**Church, Peggy Pond**
Abiquiu—Thursday in Holy Week.
After Looking into a Genealogy.
Elegy for Another Day.
For the Hippolytus of Euripides.
Nuclear Physicists, The.
Sheep Country.
**Church, Richard**
Alchemist, The.
Archaeology.
Be Frugal.
Cat, The.
Poppies, The.
Ship, The.
**Churches, Christine**
Autumn—for My Son.
**Churchill, Charles**
Apology Addressed to the Critical
    Reviewers, The.
Author, The.
Dedication, The: "Health to great
    Gloucester—from a man unknown."
Night; an Epistle to Robert Lloyd, sel.
Pains of Education, The.
Prophecy of Famine, The, sels.
Rosciad, The ("Roscius deceas'd, each
    high aspiring play'r").
Times, The, sel.
**Ciardi, John**
About the Teeth of Sharks.
Apology for a Lost Classicism, An.
Ballad of the Icondic.
Benefits of an Education, The.
Box Comes Home, A.
Boy.
Cat Heard the Cat-Bird, The.
Chorus: "They were singing Old
    MacDonald in the schoolbus."
Credibility.
Damn Her.
Dawn of the Space Age.
Death's the Classic Look.
Dollar Dog, The.
Dragons.
Epitaph: "Here, time concurring (and it
    does)."
Evil Eye, The.
Exit Line.
Faces.
Falling Asleep.
First Snow on an Airfield.
Get Up or You'll Be Late for School,
    Silly!
Gift, The.
Goodnight.
Gulls Land and Cease to Be.
Happy Family, The.
I Wouldn't.

In Place of a Curse.
Journal.
Letter from a Death Bed.
Magus, A.
Man from the Woods, The.
Man in the Onion Bed, The.
Margaret Nash Got Wet but I Don't
   Know How.
Most Like an Arch This Marriage.
No White Bird Sings.
Old Miser Named Quince, An.
On a Photo of Sgt. Ciardi a Year Later.
On an Ecdysiast.
On Evolution.
On Flunking a Nice Boy out of School.
Pinsheel's Song, The.
Polo Match.
Romping.
Seven Sharp Propeller Blades.
Shark, The.
Stranger in the Pumpkin, The.
Summer Song.
Suzie's New Dog.
To a Reviewer Who Admired My Book.
To W. T. Scott.
Thoughts on Looking into a Thicket.
Washing Your Feet.
What Night Would It Be?
What Someone Said When He Was
   Spanked.
What Someone Told Me about Bobby
   Link.
What Was Her Name?
Young Fellow Named Shear, A.
**Cibber, Colley**
Blind Boy, The.
**Citèkù Ndaaya**
Ndaaya's Kàsàlà, *sel.*
**Citino, David**
Last Rites.
Map Reading.
**Claire, William**
Dream of Southern Roads.
Hearing.
Report on a Memorial Service: A Letter
   to Mark Van Doren.
**Clampitt, Amy**
Mysterious Britain.
On the Disadvantages of Central
   Heating.
**Clamurro, William**
Edge of Town, The.
**Clancy, Joseph P.**
Boxer.
**Clapton, Eric** *and* Martin Sharp
Tales of Brave Ulysses.
**Clare, John**
Ants, The.
Autumn Change.
Autumn Robin, The.
Autumn ("The thistledown's flying . . .").
Ballad: "Blackbird has built in the
   pasture agen, The."
Beans in Blossom.
Birds' Nests.
Child Harold, *sels.*
Crow Sat on the Willow, The.
Dewdrops.
Eternity of Nature, The.
Evening.
Evening Primrose.
Faithless Shepherd, A.

Fear of Flowers, The.
February.
First Love.
Flight of Birds, The.
Fox, The.
Fragment: Language Has Not the
   Power.
Fragment: "Some pretty face
   remembered in our youth."
Gipsies ("The snow falls deep; the forest
   lies alone").
Hailstorm in June 1831, The.
Hen's Nest.
Hesperus.
I Am.
I Hid My Love.
Invite to Eternity, An.
John Clare.
Ladybird, The, *sel.*
Little Trotty Wagtail.
Love lives beyond.
Lover's Invitation, The.
Maid o' the West, The.
Milking Shed, The.
Missel-Thrush's Nest, The.
Mouse's Nest.
Nature's Hymn to the Deity.
November.
Pastoral Poesy.
Peasant Poet, The.
Poets Love Nature.
Red Robin, The.
Remember Dear Mary.
Schoolboys in Winter.
Sea Boy on the Giddy Mast, A.
Secret, The.
She Tied Up Her Few Things.
Sheep in Winter.
Shepherd's Calendar, The, *sels.*
Signs of Winter.
Song: "I peeled bits of straw and I got
   switches too."
Song: "I would not feign a single sigh."
Spring Morning, A.
Sudden Shower.
Summer Evening.
Swallow, The.
There's not a hill in all the view.
Thrush's Nest, The.
To Mary: I Sleep with Thee, and Wake
   with Thee.
To Mary: It Is the Evening Hour.
To the Snipe.
To Wordsworth.
Vision, A.
Vixen, The.
We Passed by Green Closes.
Well, Honest John.
Where She Told Her Love.
Winter Winds Cold and Blea.
With Garments Flowing.
Written in a Thunder Storm July 15th
   1841.
Written in Prison.
Young Lambs.
**Claremon, Neil**
Half-Year Birthday.
**Clark, Badger.** *See* **Clark, Charles Badger,
   Jr.**
**Clark, Carl**
Allegory in Black.
Conundrum.

No More.
Ode to a Beautiful Woman.
Second Coming, The.
Thoughts from a Bottle.
**Clark, Charles Badger, Jr. (Badger Clark)**
Glory Trail, The.
Legend of Boastful Bill, The.
Night Herder, The.
Ridin'.
Sheep-Herder, The.
**Clark, Charles Heber.** *See* **"Adeler, Max"**
**Clark, Duane**
Bonner's Ferry Beggar.
**Clark, Kevin**
Death Comes for the Old Cowboy.
**Clark, Leonard**
Attack, The.
Grumblers.
House.
Hurry Home.
Our Family.
Silver Screen.
**Clark, Melissa**
Deeper into Coleridge.
**Clark, Naomi**
Late Spring, Sur Coast.
Sunup (Variation on a Theme by
   Baudelaire).
Tables.
**Clark, Stephen**
Summer Visitors.
**Clark, Thomas**
And Our Gifts to the Seasons.
**Clark, Tom**
And You Are There.
Baseball.
Baseball and Classicism.
Daily News.
Doors.
Eyeglasses.
Going to School in France or America.
Greeks, The.
Like Musical Instruments.
Poem: "Tiny new emotions, The."
Sonnet: "Five A.M. on East Fourteenth
   I'm out to eat."
Sonnet: "Orgasm completely, The."
Sunglasses, *sel.*
Superballs.
To Bert Campaneris.
Ty Cobb Story, The.
X of the Unknown, The.
You, *sels.*
**Clark, Walter**
After Snow.
Free Will.
Morning After, The.
Uncle Death.
**Clarke, Austin**
Ancient Lights.
Burial of an Irish President.
Dirge: "He lies in state."
Envy of Poor Lovers, The.
Fair at Windgap, The.
Gracey Nugent.
Inscription for a Headstone.
Intercessors.
Irish-American Dignitary.
Jest, The.
Last Republicans, The.
Lost Heifer, The.
Marriage.

Martha Blake at Fifty-one.
Mnemosyne Lay in Dust, *sels.*
My mother wept loudly.
Night and Morning.
Penal Law.
Pilgrimage.
Planter's Daughter, The.
Respectable People.
Sermon on Swift, A.
Straying Student, The.
Strong Wind, A.
Tenebrae.
Three Poems about Children.
Tiresias, *sel.*
Young Woman of Beare, The.
**Clarke, Frances (Frances Clarke Sayers**
Who Calls?
**Clarke, Grant**
Rag Time Cowboy Joe.
**Clarke, James Freeman**
Brother, Hast Thou Wandered Far, *with music.*
Dear Friend, Whose Presence in the House, *with music.*
**Clarke, John Henrik**
Determination.
Sing Me a New Song.
**Clarkin, Sean**
Blacksmith 1970, The.
Homecoming.
**Clarkson, E. Margaret**
First Frost.
Hummingbird.
Pond Lily.
Prayer from a Stryker Frame.
**Clary, Patrick L.**
Jig for My Wake, A.
Long Distance.
Translator, The.
**Claudel, Alice Moser**
Southern Season.
**Claudian (Claudius Claudianus)**
Old Man of Verona, The.
**Clause, Paul**
Burial in the Country, A.
Loftiest spirit that ever flamed in flesh, The.
Nightlines.
Washer-Windows, The.
**Clay, Cassius.   See Ali, Muhammed**
**Cleanthes**
Hymn to Zeus.
**Cleavland, Benjamin**
O Could I Find from Day to Day, *with music.*
**Cleghorn, Sarah N.**
Golf Links Lie So Near the Mill, The.
**Clemens, Samuel Langhorne.   See "Twain, Mark"**
**Clementelli, Elena**
Etruscan Notebook, *sels.*
**Clemmons, Carole Gregory**
Ghetto Lovesong—Migration.
I'm Just a Stranger Here, Heaven Is My Home.
Love from My Father.
Spring.
**Clemo, Jack R.**
Burnt Bush, The.
Calvinist in Love, A.
**Clephane, Elizabeth Cecilia**
Ninety and Nine, The.

**Clerk, John**
Fane Wald I Luve.
**Clerk-Maxwell, James.   See Maxwell, James Clerk**
**Cleveland, John**
Antiplatonick, The.
Epitaph on the Earl of Strafford.
Fuscara; or, The Bee-Errant.
Mark Antony.
On the Memory of Mr. Edward King, Drowned in the Irish Seas.
Rebel Scot, The, *sels.*
To the State of Love; or, The Senses' Festival.
**Clewell, David**
After the Seance.
**Clifton, Harry**
Cang, The.
Site.
**Clifton, Lucille**
Admonitions.
Africa.
At Last We Killed the Roaches.
Breaklight.
Discoveries of Fire, The.
Driving through New England.
1st, The.
For de Lawd.
God Send Easter.
Good Times.
Her Love Poem.
I went to the valley.
If I Stand in My Window.
If Something Should Happen.
In Salem.
In the inner city.
July.
Lane Is the Pretty One.
Let There Be New Flowering.
Listen Children.
Lost Baby Poem, The.
Love Rejected.
Malcolm.
Miss Rosie.
My daddy's fingers move among the couplers.
My Mama Moved among the Days.
Poet, The.
Raising of Lazarus, The.
Robert.
Running across to the lot.
Salt.
Still.
Stops.
Thirty eighth year, The.
This Morning.
Those Boys That Ran Together.
To Bobby Seale.
Way It Was, The.
Willie B (2).
**Clinch, Timothy**
Politicians, 1972.
**Clinton, D.**
Breathing, at Last, in the Wichita Art Museum.
**Clockadale, Jill**
Change of Venue.
**Close, John**
In Respectful Memory of Mr. Yarker, *sel.*
**Clough, Arthur Hugh**
Actaeon.

All Is Well.
Amours de Voyage.
Bothie of Tober-na-Vuolich, The, *sels.*
Come Home, Come Home!
Dipsychus, *sels.*
Duty.
Easter Day, Naples, 1849.
Easter Day II.
Epi-Strauss-ium.
Grasses green of sweet content, The.
How Pleasant It Is to Have Money.
In the Great Metropolis.
Is it true, ye gods, who treat us.
It fortifies my soul to know.
It is not sweet content, be sure.
Latest Decalogue, The.
Les Vaches.
Look you, my simple friend, 'tis one of those.
My wind is turned to bitter north.
Natura Naturans.
Philip returned to his books, but returned to his Highlands after.
Put forth thy leaf, thou lofty plane.
Qua Cursum Ventus.
Qui Laborat, Orat.
Reply to Dipsychus.
Resignation—To Faustus.
Say Not the Struggle Nought Availeth.
Spectator ab Extra.
"There is no God," the wicked saith.
Where Lies the Land?
Why Think? By Thinking You Grow Old.
**Clouts, Sydney**
Firebowl.
Of Thomas Traherne and the Pebble Outside.
Portrait of Prince Henry, The.
Sleeper, The.
**Coad, Kermit**
Success, The.
Sudden Obscurity.
**Coady, Michael**
Provincial Obituary.
**Coatsworth, Elizabeth Jane**
All Goats.
Calling in the Cat.
Columbus and the Mermaids.
Daniel Webster's Horses.
Footprints in the Night.
Lady Comes to an Inn, A.
Mouse, The.
Open Door, The.
Rain Poem.
Roosters.
Swallows, The.
Whale at Twilight.
What Is Once Loved.
Who Is Sad?
Winter Soon Is Coming.
**Cobb, Charlie**
"Containing Communism."
For Sammy Younge.
Nation.
To Vietnam.
**Cobb, Thomas**
Bertram Declines.
**Cobb, Will D.**
School Days.
Somebody's Sweetheart I Want to Be, *with music.*

Waltz Me Around Again Willie; or,
  'Round, 'Round, 'Round, *with music.*
**Cobey, Katharine Edgar**
  Cherbourg Airport.
  Three Problems.
  Tour, The.
**Coblentz, Stanton A.**
  Land's End.
  Last Trail, The.
**Cochrane, Shirley G.**
  Invader.
  Leaving Home.
  Night Place.
  Old Women, The.
**Codish, Edward**
  Juggle of Myrtle Twigs, A.
  Yetzer ha Ra.
**Codrescu, Andrei**
  Early Fix.
  Grammar, A.
  Imagination of Necessity, The.
  Poetry Paper.
  Work.
**Cody, Hiram Alfred**
  Old Ship Riggers.
**Coffey, Brian**
  Advent, *sel.*
  Headrock.
  Missouri Sequence, *sel.*
  Muse, June, Related, *sel.*
  "Nicest Phantasies Are Shared, The."
  Odalisque.
**Coffin, Robert Peter Tristram**
  Christening-Day Wishes for My God-
    Child.
  Cows Are Coming Home in Maine.
  Crystal Moment.
  Hens in Winter.
  Hound on the Church Porch.
  Pheasant, The.
  Sacrament, The.
  Secret, The.
  Thief Jones.
  Yankee Cradle.
**Cohan, George M.**
  Forty-five Minutes from Broadway, *with*
    *music.*
  Give My Regards to Broadway, *with*
    *music.*
  Mary's a Grand Old Name, *with music.*
  Yankee Doodle Boy, The, *with music.*
  You're a Grand Old Flag.
**Cohen, Leonard**
  Bus, The.
  Elegy: "Do not look for him."
  For Anne.
  For E. J. P.
  Gift.
  Kite Is a Victim, A.
  Music Crept by Us, The.
  Only Tourist in Havana Turns His
    Thoughts Homeward, The.
  Queen Victoria and Me.
  Song: "I almost went to bed."
  Stories of the Street.
  Story of Isaac.
  Suit, The.
  Summer Night.
  Suzanne Takes You Down.
  You Do Not Have to Love Me.
**Cohen, Shlomit**
  Same Dream, The.

Unraveled Thought, An.
Wife of Kohelet.
**Cohoe, Grey**
  Folding Fan, The.
**Cokayne, Sir Aston**
  Epitaph on a Great Sleeper.
**Colaizzi, Randall**
  Telemachus and the Bow.
**Colby, Joan**
  How the Sky Begins to Fall.
  Old Nudists, The.
**Cole, Barry**
  Men Are Coming Back, The.
**Cole, Bob**
  Under the Bamboo Tree, *with music.*
**Cole, Eugene Roger**
  Apology for the Fall.
  Good Friday Explosives.
  Tree, The.
  Whole Relentless Process, The.
**Cole, G. D. H.**
  Civil Riot, *sel.*
**Cole, Katherine**
  Child, A.
**Cole, Thomas**
  Spider.
**Cole, William**
  Big Job.
  Have I Got Dogs!
  Hypnopompic Poem.
  Introduction: "Oh, such silliness!"
  It's such a shock, I almost screech.
  Just Dropped In.
  Lost Contact.
  Marriage Couplet.
  Mutual Problem.
  Mysterious East.
  Panteater, The.
  Poor Kid.
  Question, A.
  War Horses.
  What a Friend We Have in Cheeses!
  What Could It Be?
  Wise Guy.
**Coleman, Emily Holmes**
  Liberator, The.
**Coleman, Horace**
  Attica.
  Being Black.
  Dustoff: Med Evac.
  He Aint Risen, Baby, cause He Aint
    Gone Nowhere.
  In Ca Mau.
  In (What Few) Green (Barely) Parks.
  Junkies Is.
  Log: 19N 72E.
  Night Flare Drop, Tan Son Nhut.
  Stalemate at Attica.
  That Life, That Love, That Fine.
**Coleman, Mary Joan**
  Grandfather.
**Coleridge, Hartley**
  Address to Certain Gold Fishes.
  Dedicatory Sonnet to S. T. Coleridge.
  He Lived amidst th' Untrodden Ways.
  Lily of the Valley.
  November.
  On the Death of Echo.
  Song: "She is not fair to outward view."
  Sonnets on the Seasons, *sel.*
  Summer Rain.

There Lived among the Untrodden
  Ways.
To a Deaf and Dumb Little Girl.
**Coleridge, Mary Elizabeth**
  At a Friends' Meeting.
  Deserted House, The.
  Gifts.
  In Dispraise of the Moon.
  In London Town.
  Jealousy.
  "My True Love Hath My Heart and I
    Have His."
  Other Side of a Mirror, The.
  Our Lady.
  September.
  Slowly.
  There.
  Unwelcome.
  We Never Said Farewell.
  Witch, The.
  Witches' Wood, The.
**Coleridge, Samuel Taylor**
  Ad Vilmum Axiologum.
  Answer [*or* Answers] to a Child's
    Question.
  Apologia pro Vita Sua.
  Ballad of the Dark Ladie, The.
  Burke.
  Character, A.
  Christabel.
  Cologne.
  Constancy to an Ideal Object.
  Day-Dream, A.
  Day-Dream from an Emigrant to His
    Absent Wife, The.
  Dejection; an Ode.
  Desire.
  Destruction of the Bastille.
  Eolian Harp, The.
  Epitaph: "Stop, Christian passer-by!—
    Stop, child of God."
  Epitaph on an Infant.
  Epitaph on Himself.
  Fears in solitude.
  Foster-Mother's Tale, The.
  France: An Ode.
  Frost at Midnight.
  Hexameters.
  Human Life: On the Denial of
    Immortality.
  Hymn before Sunrise in the Vale [*or*
    Valley] of Chamouni.
  Inscription for a Fountain on a Heath.
  Knight's Tomb, The.
  Kubla Kahn; or, A Vision in a Dream.
  La Fayette.
  Lewti; or, The Circassian Love-Chaunt.
  Limbo.
  Lines Written in the Album at
    Elbingerode.
  Love.
  Love's Apparition and Evanishment.
  Mad Monk, The.
  Metrical Feet.
  Modern Critics.
  Monody on a Tea-Kettle.
  Monody on the Death of Chatterton.
  Ne Plus Ultra.
  New Moon, The.
  Nightingale, The.
  Nil Pejus Est Caelibe Vita.
  Ode to the Departing Year.

Ode to the Rain, An.
Ode to Tranquillity.
On a Lord.
On a Ruined House in a Romantic
  Country.
On Donne's Poetry.
On My Joyful Departure.
On the Prospect of Establishing a
  Pantisocracy in America.
Pains of Sleep, The.
Pantisocracy.
Phantom.
Phantom or Fact.
Picture, The; or, The Lover's Resolution.
Priestley.
Psyche.
Recantation Illustrated in the Story of
  the Mad Ox.
Reflections on Having Left a Place of
  Retirement.
Religious Musings.
Rime of the Ancient Mariner, The.
Sea-ward, White Gleaming.
Self-Knowledge.
Separation.
Silence of a city, how awful at midnight,
  The.
Snowdrop, The.
Sonnet to the River Otter.
Sonnets Attempted in the Manner of
  Contemporary Writers, *sels.*
Swans Sing before They Die.
Therefore all seasons shall be sweet to
  thee.
This Lime-Tree Bower My Prison.
Time, Real and Imaginary.
To a Young Ass.
To a Young Lady with a Poem on the
  French Revolution.
To Asra.
To Fortune on Buying a Ticket in the
  Irish Lottery.
To Nature.
To Simplicity.
To the Nightingale.
To the Rev. W. L. Bowles, 2 *versions.*
To William Wordsworth.
Truth I pursued, as Fancy sketch'd the
  way.
Two Founts, The.
Two wedded hearts, if ere were such.
Visionary Hope, The.
W. H. *Eheu!*
Water-Snakes.
What is an epigram? a dwarfish whole.
What is Life?
Work without Hope.
Youth and Age.
**Coleridge, Sara**
Around the Year.
Months, The.
Trees.
**Colesworthy, Daniel C.**
While We Lowly Bow before Thee, *with
  music.*
**College, Stephen**
Raree Show, A.
Truth Brought to Light, or Murder Will
  Out.
**Collins, Ann [*or* Anne]**
Another Song ("The winter of my
  infancy being over-past").

Song: "My straying thoughts, reduced
  stay."
**Collins, Billy**
Bad Dreams.
Library.
Sentence.
Shock.
**Collins, Judy**
Albatross.
My Father.
**Collins, Leslie M.**
Stevedore.
**Collins, Martha**
Retreat.
**Collins, Mortimer**
King Arthur Growing Very Tired
  Indeed.
My Aunt's Spectre.
**Collins, William**
How Sleep the Brave.
Lookout, The.
Ode Occasion'd by the Death of Mr.
  Thomson.
Ode on the Poetical Character.
Ode on the Popular Superstitions of the
  Highlands of Scotland, An.
Ode to Evening.
Ode to Fear.
Ode to Mercy.
Ode to Pity.
Ode to Simplicity.
Passions, The; an Ode to Music.
Song from Shakespear's Cymbelyne, A.
Stormy Hebrides, The.
**Colman, Benjamin**
God of My Life! *with music.*
**Colman, Cathy**
After Swimming in the Pacific.
Fox Court, Winter.
Your cheekbones live.
**Colman, George, the Younger**
On Sir Nathaniel Wraxall the Historian.
Sir Marmaduke.
Unfortunate Miss Bailey.
**Colombo, John Robert**
Riverdale Lion.
**Colonna, Vittoria da**
As When Some Hungry Fledgling Hears
  and Sees.
I live on this depraved and lonely cliff.
Like a hungry fledgeling that watches
  and hears.
O what transparent waves, what a
  tranquil sea.
When the troubled sea swells and
  surrounds.
**Colquitt, Betsy**
Photographing the Facade—San Miguel
  de Allende.
**Colum, Padraic**
Ballad Maker, A.
Book of Kells, The.
Drover, A.
I Saw the Wind Today.
Interior.
Monkeys.
Reminiscence, *sel.*
River-Mates.
She Moved through the Fair.
**Columcille [*or* Columba], Saint**
Clamour of the wind making music.
On some island I long to be.

**Combellick, Henry**
Saunders Point.
**Comfort, Alex**
Letter to an American Visitor.
Lovers, The.
There is a white mare that my love
  keeps.
**Conant-Bissell, Jane**
Milton's Wife on Her Twenty-third
  Birthday.
**Conard, Audrey**
Clinic: Examination.
Vegetarian Sings, A.
**Conder, Josiah**
Bread of heaven, on Thee we feed.
Day by day the manna fell.
**Congreve, William**
Jack Frenchman's Defeat.
Present Time, The.
Semele to Jupiter.
Song: "False though she be to me and
  love."
Song: "Pious Selinda goes to prayers."
**Conkling, Hilda**
Easter.
**Conley, Robert J.**
Self-Portrait: Microcosm, or, Song of
  Mixed-Blood.
**Conn, Stewart**
Arrivals.
Clearing, The.
Todd.
Visiting Hour.
**Connell, Jim**
Red Flag, The.
**Connellan, Leo**
Watching Jim Shoulders.
**Connor, Tony**
Above Penmaenmawr.
Apologue.
Child Half-asleep, A.
Elegy for Alfred Hubbard.
Fashionable Poet Reading.
Lancashire Winter.
Twelve Secret Poems, *sels.*
**Connor, Torrey**
Old Casa, The.
**Conquest, Robert**
Agents, The.
Art and Civilization.
By Rail through Istria.
Horror Comic.
Man and Woman.
Near the Death of Ovid.
Poem about a Poem about a Poem.
Rokeby Venus, The.
**Conrard, Harrison**
Dead on the Desert.
Hopi Prayer, A.
In Old Tucson.
**Constable, Henry**
Diana, *sels.*
My lady's presence makes the roses red.
**Contoski, Victor**
Bear's Blessing, The.
Broken Treaties, *sel.*
Dream 1971.
Kansa, The.
Mailman, The.
Money.
Moonlit Night in Kansas.
Nocturne for the U.S. Congress.

Those I Love.

**Conyus**
Great Santa Barbara Oil Disaster OR, The.
He's Doing Natural Life.
San Francisco County Jail Cell B-6.
Six Ten Sixty-nine.
Untitled Requiem for Tomorrow.
Upon Leaving the Parole Board Hearing.

**Coogler, J. Gordon**
Alas! Carolina!
Alas! for the South.
Byron.
In Memorial.
Mustacheless Bard, A.
Poor South! Her books get fewer and fewer.
Pretty Girl, A.
To Amy.

**Cook, Ebenezer**
Sot-Weed Factor, The.

**Cook, Eliza**
Mouse and the Cake, The.
Old Arm-Chair, The.

**Cook, Geoffrey**
Mount Tamalpais.

**Cook, Joseph**
Rhyme for a Chemical Baby.
Rhyme for a Geological Baby.
Rhyme for Astronomical Baby.
Rhyme for Botanical Baby.

**Cook, Mike**
Bootie Black and the Seven Giants.

**Cook, Paul H.**
Driving through the Pima Indian Reservation.

**Cook, R. L.**
Tonight the City.

**Cook, Russell Sturgis**
Just as Thou Art, *with music.*

**Cook, Stanley**
Chips.

**Cook, William W.**
Hudson Hornet.

**Cooke, Edmund Vance**
How Did You Die?
Perfect Gift, The.

**Cooke, Michael G.**
Unseen Fire, An.

**Coolbrith, Ina**
Copa de Oro.
Emblem, An.
From Russian Hill.
Listening Back.
Mariposa Lily, The.
Retrospect.
San Francisco.
With a Wreath of Laurel.

**Cooley, Peter**
Ah, Wilderness.
Alternatives.
Confession, The.
Floating Coathangers.
Man Who Closes Himself, The.
Other, The.
Packer City Poem.
Revenant, The.
Tracks.
Vanishing Point.
White Room, The.

**"Coolidge, Susan" (Sarah Chauncey Woolsey)**

Measles in the Ark

**Cooney, Ellen**
From four walls of/ ivory.
Monday Night in Winter.
So you dance with me.

**Cooper, Charles**
Dreams.
Honky.
Rubin.

**Cooper, Edith,** *and* **Katherine Bradley.** *See* "Field, Michael"

**Cooper, George**
Bob White.
Only One Mother.
Sweet Genevieve.
What Robin Told.

**Cooper, Jane**
Childhood in Jacksonville, Florida.
Circle, a Square, a Triangle and a Ripple of Water, A.
Faithful, The.
Graveyard, The.
House Poem.
Hunger Moon.
In the House of the Dying.
In the Last Few Moments Came the Old German Cleaning Woman.
Knowledge That Comes through Experience, The.
My Young Mother.
Praise.
Racetrack, The.
Rent.
Return.
Rock Climbing.
Smoke.
Waiting.
Weather of Six Mornings, The.

**Cooper, Leonard**
Rhyming Prophecy for a New Year.

**Cooper, Michael**
Poem for May Wilson, A.
Short Story, A.

**Cooperman, Robert**
All Up and Down the Lines.

**Cooperman, Stanley**
Redemption.

**Copeland, Benjamin**
Christ's Life Our Code, *with music.*
Our Fathers' God, *with music.*

**Copenhaver, Laura S.**
Heralds of Christ, *with music.*

**Coppard, Alfred Edgar**
Horse, The.
Unfortunate Miller, The.

**Corbet, Richard**
Fairies' Farewell, The.
Iter Boreale, *sel.*
Little lute, when I am gone.
Non Sequitor, A.
Nonsense.
To His Son, Vincent Corbet.

**Corbett, Elizabeth T.**
Three Wise Old Women.

**Corbière, Tristan (Edourd Joachim Corbière**
Litany of Sleep, *sel.*

**Corbin, Alice (Alice Corbin Henderson**
Blue Day.
Buffalo Dance.
Courtship.
Cundiyo.

From the Stone Age.
Green Corn Dance, The.
Indian Death.
Juan Quintana.
Listening.
No Spring.
On the Acequia Madre.
Parting.
Red Earth.
Sand Paintings.
Una Anciana Mexicana.
Walls.
Where the Fight Was.
Wind, The.

**Corbin, Lloyd M., Jr. (Djangatolum)**
Ali.
Dedication to the Final Confrontation.

**Corbin, Richard**
Of Bombs and Boys.

**Corcos, Francine**
I Suppose Her Mother Told Her.

**Corey, Del**
Books, lips, hands.   Hypodermic Release.
Hypodermic Release.

**Corinna.** *See* Korinna

**Corman, Cid**
Blessings Are.
Call it a louse—I'm.
Cincinnati.
Container, The.
Deceased.
Desk, The.
I have come far to have found nothing.
I'm a Baby.
It's Food.
La Selva.
Locus, The.
Old Pines, The.
So Little Wanted.
There are things to be said. No doubt.
This Is the Non-existent Beast.
Tortoise, The.
Toy, The.
Without You.

**Cormican, P. J.**
True Son of God, Eternal Light, *with music.*

**Corn, Alfred**
Deception.
Fifty-seventh Street and Fifth.
Tokyo West.

**Cornelius, Peter**
Christmas Tree, The.

**Cornford, Frances**
All Souls' Night.
Cambridgeshire.
Childhood.
Coast, The: Norfolk.
Country Bedroom, The, *sel.*
Dogs.
Guitarist Tunes Up, The.
Hills, The.
In the Backs.
Night Song.
On the Beach.
Parting in Wartime.
Princess and the Gypsies, The.
To a Fat Lady Seen from the Train.
Travelling Home.
Watch, The.

**Cornford, John**

**Cornish**
Huesca.

**Cornish, Sam**
April 68.
Black Man, A.
Death of Dr. King.
Dory Miller.
Forecast.
Frederick Douglass.
Generations 1.
Generations 2.
Home.
Lenox Christmas Eve 68.
Montgomery.
One Eyed Black Man in Nebraska.
Panther.
Ray Charles.
River, The.
Sam's World ("Sam's mother has").
Sooner or Later.
To a Single Shadow without Pity.
Your Mother.

**Cornish, William**
Knight and the Lady, The.

**"Cornwall, Barry" (Bryan Waller Procter)**
Babylon.
Belshazzar.
Prayer in Sickness, A.

**Corren, Marc Allen**
Do You Need the Gold Ring?

**Corretjer, Juan Antonio**
Convoy, The.
In Jail.

**Corrigan, Paul**
Boss Machine-Tender after Losing a
  Son, The.

**Corrington, John William**
For a Woodscolt Miscarried.
Grand Inquisitor Continues, The.
Guevara with Minutes to Go.
Lines to the South.
Mr. Clean.
On My 18th Birthday.
Pastoral: "In the fields."
Second Coming, The.

**Corso, Gregory**
Birthplace Revisited.
Body Fished from the Seine.
But I Do Not Need Kindness.
Dear Girl.
Dialogue—2 Dollmakers.
Difference of Zoos, A.
Dream of a Baseball Star.
Dreamed Realization, A.
Eastside Incidents.
God Is a Masturbator.
Hair.
I Am 25.
I Held a Shelley Manuscript.
In the Fleeting Hand of Time.
Italian Extravaganza.
Last Gangster, The.
Last Warmth of Arnold, The.
Mad Yak, The.
Marriage.
Paris.
Poets Hitchhiking on the Highway.
P.S. 42.
Reflection in a Green Arena.
Second Night in N.Y.C. after 3 Years.
Seed Journey.
Spontaneous Requiem for the American
  Indian.

Three.
Uccello.
Vestal Lady on Brattle, The.
Vision of Rotterdam.
Waterchew!
Writ on the Eve of My 32nd Birthday.
You, Whose Mother's Lover Was Grass.
Zizi's Lament.

**Cortés, Elías Hruska**
Mazeworks.

**Cortez, Jayne**
For Real.
I Am New York City.
Initiation.
Lead.
So Long.

**Corwin, Phillip**
Achilles.

**Cory, William Johnson**
Ballad for a Boy, A.
Heraclitus.
Mimnermus in Church.

**Cosier, Tony**
Not This Leaf Haunts Me.

**Coslett, Coslett**
Pole Star, The.

**Costanzo, Gerald**
Braille.
Man Who Invented Las Vegas, The.

**Costello, Tomas**
Lament for Una, A, *sel.*

**Cott, Jonathan**
He Spends Time in Southern California.

**Cotter, Joseph Seamon, Jr.**
And What Shall You Say?
Sonnet to Negro Soldiers.

**Cotton, Charles**
Burlesque upon the Great Frost, *sel.*
Epitaph on M. H., An.
Evening.
Litany, The: "From a ruler that's a
  curse."
Madrigal: "To be a whore, despite of
  grace."
On Tobacco.
Resolution in Four Sonnets, of a
  Poetical Question Put to Me by a
  Friend, Concerning Four Rural
  Sisters.
See how like twilight slumber falls.
Two Rural Sisters.

**Cotton, Elizabeth**
Oh, Babe, It Ain't No Lie.

**Cotton, John (b. 1925)**
Fragments.
Old Movies.
Pigs.
Toad.

**Cotton, Nathaniel**
Bee, the Ant, and the Sparrow, The.
Contentment.
Early Thoughts of Marriage.
To a Child Five Years Old.

**Cottrau, Teodoro**
Santa Lucia.

**Coulette, Henri**
Blue-eyed Precinct Worker, The.
Emeritus, n.
Family Goldschmitt, The.

**Councilman, Emily Sargent**
Between the Tides.

**Couper, J. M.**

Horace, Odes, 1, 5: Surfer's Paradise.

**Coursen, H. R.**
Fall Again.

**Courtenay, John**
Poetical and Philosophical Essay on the
  French Revolution . . . , A, *sel.*

**Cousins, James H.**
Corncrake, The.

**Coward, Noel**
Any Part of Piggy.
Boy Actor, The.
Mad Dogs and Englishmen.
There Are Bad Times Just around the
  Corner.

**Cowing, Sheila**
Hinge, The.

**Cowley, Abraham**
Answer to an Invitation to Cambridge,
  An.
Christ's Passion.
Country-Mouse, The.
Davideis, *sels.*
Dialogue after Enjoyment.
Drinking.
Ecstasy, The.
Epicure, The, *sel.*
Epitaph of Pyramus and Thisbe.
Hell.
Honour.
Love ("I'll sing of heroes, and of kings").
Mistress, The, *sels.*
Music.
Ode: Of Wit.
Of Myself.
On the Death of Mr. William Harvey [*or*
  Hervey].
Spring, The.
Swallow, The.
Welcome, The.
Wish, The.
Written in Juice of Lemon.

**Cowley, Abraham** *and* **Richard Crashaw**
On Hope by Way of Question and
  Answer between Abraham Cowley and
  Richard Crashaw.

**Cowley, Malcolm**
Blown Door, The.
Blue Juniata, *sel.*
Danny.
Long Voyage, The.
Nocturnal Landscape.
Smoke of Birds, A.
Streets of Air, The.

**Cowper, William**
Acquiescence of Pure Love, The.
Boadicea.
Castaway, The.
City Corruption.
Contrite Heart, The.
Diverting History of John Gilpin, The.
Epitaph: "Here Johnson lies—a sage by
  all allow'd."
Epitaph on a Hare.
Father, who designs his babe a priest,
  The.
Green-House, The.
Hymn: "To those who know the Lord I
  speak."
Jackdaw, The.
Jehovah-Jesus.
Light and Glory of the Word, The.
Light Shining Out of Darkness.

Lines Written during a Period of
    Insanity.
Lines Written on a Window Shutter at
    Weston.
Lovest Thou Me?
Narcissus.
Nightingale and the Glowworm, The.
On the Death of Mrs. Throckmorton's
    Bullfinch.
On the Ice Islands Seen Floating in the
    German Ocean.
On the Loss of the *Royal George*.
On the Queen's Visit to London, the
    Night of the Seventeenth of March,
    1789, *sel*.
Poplar-Field, The ("The poplars are
    felled, farewell to the shade").
Praise for the Fountain Opened.
Prudent Simplicity.
Retired Cat, The.
Retirement, *sel*.
Robin in Winter, The, *sel*.
Shrubbery, The.
Sofa, The.
Sonnet to William Wilberforce, Esq.
Squirrel in Sunshine.
Statesman in Retirement, The.
Sweet Meat Has Sour Sauce; or, The
    Slave-Trader in the Dumps.
Task, The, *sels*.
Temptation.
Tirocinium; or, A Review of Schools,
    *sels*.
To Mary.
To the Swallow.
Walking with God.
Winter Morning Walk, The.
Woodman's Dog, The.

**Cox, Carol**
All Three of Us.
From the Direction of the State Mental
    Institution.
He Left the Pine Ridge Reservation.
How the Indians Lost the Hot Springs.
Papa Doc Is Dead.
Watching You Draw.

**Cox, Ed**
After the Rent.
Harvard Graduate Speaking to His
    Troops.
Waiting.

**Cox, Kenyon**
Wild Boarder, The.

**Cox, Samuel K.**
Lord, Thou Hast Promised, *with music*.

**Coxe, Arthur Cleveland**
Father, Who Mak'st Thy Suff'ring Sons,
    *with music*.
Saviour, Sprinkle Many Nations, *with
    music*.

**Coxe, Louis**
On Seeing Films of the War.

**Crabbe, Chris Wallace-.** *See* **Wallace-
    Crabbe, Chris**

**Crabbe, George**
Borough, The, *sels*.
Frenzy.
Lady of the Manor, The.
Marriage Ring, A.
Oncoming Industrial Revolution, The.
Parish Register, The, *sels*.
Peter Grimes; the Outcast.

Phoebe Dawson, *sel*..
Rural Life.
Sir Eustace Grey, *sel*.
Vicar, The.
Village, The.
Walking by the Sea.
When next appeared a dam—so call the
    place.

**Craig, Ann M.**
Hypocrite.

**Craig, John**
O Hear My Prayer, Lord, *with music*.
O Lord, That Art My God and King,
    *with music*.

**Craig, Maurice James**
Ballad to a Traditional Refrain.
Poem: "High on a ridge of tiles."

**Craig, Norma**
Question.

**Cramer, Steven**
Two Women with Mangoes.

**Cranch, Christopher Pearse**
Enosis.
Pines and the Sea, The.

**Crane, Hart**
At Melville's Tomb.
Atlantis.
Ave Maria.
Black Tambourine.
Bridge, The,*sels*.
Broken Tower, The.
Cape Hatteras.
Carrier Letter.
Chaplinesque.
Dance, The.
Enrich My Resignation.
For the Marriage of Faustus and Helen.
Garden Abstract.
Harbor Dawn, The.
Hurricane, The.
In Shadow.
Indiana.
Island Quarry.
Key West.
Legend.
Legende.
My Grandmother's Love Letters.
Name for All, A.
National Winter Garden.
North Labrador.
O Carib Isle!
October-November.
Passage.
Pastorale: "No more violets."
Phantom Bark, The.
Praise for an Urn.
Reliquary.
Repose of Rivers.
River, The.
Royal Palm.
Sad Indian, The ("Sad heart, the
    gymnast of inertia, does not count").
To Brooklyn Bridge.
To Emily Dickinson.
Tunnel, The.
Van Winkle.
Voyages (I-VI).
Wine Menagerie, The.

**Crane, Stephen**
Behold, the Grave of a Wicked Man.
Black Riders Came from the Sea.
Black Riders, The, *sels*.

Blade of Grass, The.
Book of Wisdom, The.
God Came to a Man, A.
God in Wrath, A.
How, Then?
I Explain the Silvered Passing of a Ship
    at Night.
I Saw a Man [Pursuing the Horizon].
I Stood Musing in a Black World.
If I Should Cast Off This Tattered Coat.
In the Desert.
It Was Wrong to Do This Said the
    Angel.
Little Ink More or Less, A.
Man adrift on a slim spar, A.
Naked Woman and a Dead Dwarf, A.
Newspaper Is a Collection of Half-
    Injustices, A.
Ocean Said to Me Once, The.
On the Desert.
Once There Came a Man.
Tell me not in joyous numbers.
There Exists the Eternal Fact of
    Conflict.
There Was a Crimson Clash of War.
There Was One I Met upon the Road.
"Think as I Think."
Tradition.
War Is Kind, *sels*.

**Crane, Walter**
Crocus, The.

**Crapsey, Adelaide**
Guarded Wound, The.
November Night.
On Seeing Weather-beaten Trees.
Susanna and the Elders.
Triad.
Warning, The.

**Crashaw, Richard**
Charitas Nimia; or, The Dear Bargain.
Easter Day.
Epitaph upon Doctor Brook, An.
Epitaph upon Husband and Wife Who
    Died and Were Buried Together, An.
Flaming Heart, The, *sels*.
Hymn of the Nativity, Sung as by the
    Shepherds, An.
Hymn to the Name and Honour of the
    Admirable Saint Teresa, A.
In the Glorious Epiphany of Our Lord
    God, *sel*.
Luke VII: She Began to Wash His Feet
    with Tears.
Luke XI: Blessed Be the Paps Which
    Thou Hast Sucked.
Music's Duel.
On Marriage.
On Our Crucified Lord, Naked and
    Bloody.
On the Baptized Ethiopian.
On the Blessed Virgin's Bashfulness.
On the Saviour's Wounds.
Saint Mary Magdalene; or, The Weeper.
Shepherds' Hymn, The.
Song, A: "Lord, when the sense of thy
    sweet grace."
To the Noblest and Best of Ladies [*or*
    Ladyes], the Countess of Denbigh.
Two Went Up into the Temple to Pray.
Upon Our Saviour's Tomb wherein
    Never Man Was Laid.
Upon the Death of a Gentleman.

Upon the Holy Sepulchre.
Upon the Infant Martyrs.
Wishes to His (Supposed) Mistress.
**Crashaw, Richard** *and* **Abraham Cowley.**
*See* **Cowley, Abraham** *and* **Richard Crashaw**
**Crawford, Mrs. A. B.** *and* F. Nicholls Crouch
Kathleen Mavourneen.
**Crawford, John Wallace**
Broncho versus Bicycle.
**Crawford, Tom**
Enormous Sleep.
Everything Must Go.
Feeding Cycle of the Catfish, The.
Phone Call.
**Crawford, Vesta Pierce**
Pioneer Woman.
**Creeley, Robert**
Act of Love, The.
After Lorca.
Air: "Cat bird singing."
Air: "Love of a woman, The."
America.
Ballad of the Despairing Husband.
Business, The.
Counterpoint, A.
Cracks, The.
Crisis, The.
Death of Venus, The.
Dishonest Mailmen, The.
Door, The.
Fancy.
Figures, The.
Fire, The.
Flower, The.
For Fear.
For Love.
For No Clear Reason.
For Some Weeks.
Form of Women, A.
Friends, The.
Gemini.
Gift, The.
Hello.
Here.
Heroes.
Hill, The.
I Keep to Myself Such Measures.
I Know a Man.
If You.
Immoral Proposition, The.
In secret/ the out's in.
Innocence, The.
Invoice, The.
Joy.
Kore.
Language, The.
Lunch and After.
Man, The.
Memory, The.
Moon, The.
Name, The.
Naughty Boy.
Not Now.
Oh No.
Pattern, The.
People, The.
Please.
Quick-Step.
Rain, The.
Rescue, The.

Rhythm, The.
Riddle, The: "What it is, the literal size."
Robinson Crusoe.
She Went to Stay.
Signboard, The.
Sitting Here.
Somewhere.
Song: "Those rivers run from that land."
Song: "What do you/ want, love. To be."
Song: "What I took in my hand."
Sounds.
Tiger, The.
Token, A.
Wait for Me.
Waiting.
Warning, The.
Way, The.
Where it is.
Whip, The.
Wicker Basket, A.
Wife, The.
Window, The.
World, The.
**Crewe, Jennifer**
Visitations.
**Crews, Jacquelyne**
Auguries for Three Women.
**Croffut, William Augustus**
Simon Soggs' Thanksgiving.
**Cronin, Anthony**
Anarchist.
Apology.
Autumn Poem.
Baudelaire in Brussels.
Consolation.
Elephant to the Girl in Bertram Mills' Circus, The.
For a Father.
On the bog road the blackthorn flowers, the turf-stacks.
Poem: "Leaving aside then for all time the songs."
R.M.S. *Titanic, sel.*
Surprise.
Writing.
**Crooker, Barbara**
Moving.
**Cros, Charles**
Smoked Herring, The.
**Crosby, David**
Long Time Gone.
**Crosby, David, Paul Kantner,** *and* Stephen Stills
Wooden Ships.
**Crosby, Fanny (Frances Jane Crosby)**
All the Way My Saviour Leads Me.
Blessed Assurance, *with music.*
Jesus, Keep Me Near the Cross, *with music.*
Pass Me Not, O Gentle Saviour, *with music.*
There's Music in the Air, *with music.*
To the Work, *with music.*
**Crosby, Harry**
Firebrand.
Telephone Directory.
Vision.
**Crosby, Ranice Henderson**
Poem about a Seashell.

Thoughts for You (When She Came Back from the Mountains).
**Cross, Allen Eastman**
Gray Hills Taught Me Patience, The, *with music.*
Though Fatherland Be Vast, *with music.*
Young and Radiant, He Is Standing, *with music.*
**Crossman, Samuel**
My Song Is Love Unknown.
**Crosswell, William**
Lord! Lead the Way the Saviour Went, *with music.*
**Crouch, F. Nicholls** *and* **Mrs. A. B. Crawford.** *See* **Crawford, Mrs. A. B.** *and* **F. Nicholls Crouch**
**Crouch, Nathaniel**
David and Goliath.
Tower of Babel, The.
**Crouch, Pearl Riggs**
Snowstorm, The.
**Crouch, Stanley**
After the Rain.
Albert Ayler: Eulogy for a Decomposed Saxophone Player.
Blackie Thinks of His Brothers.
No New Music.
Riding across John Lee's Finger.
**Crow, Mary**
Foreign Streets.
Rain-in-the-Face.
**Crowe, Ronald**
Guns.
**Crowley, Finbarr**
Kilbarrack 1969.
**Cruceius, Annibal**
Fair Ursly, in a merry mood.
**Cruickshank, Helen B.**
Shy Geordie.
There Was a Sang.
**Cruz, Juana Inés de la.** *See* **Juana Inés de la Cruz**
**Cruz, Victor Hernández**
African Things.
Alone/ December/ Night.
Bronxomania.
California #2.
Carmen.
Chicago/ 3 Hours.
Electric Cop, The.
Energy.
Four Corners, The.
Going Uptown to Visit Miriam.
Group, The.
Los New Yorks.
Megalopolis.
Poem: "Greater cities are, The."
Sonsito.
Spirits.
Story of the Zeros, The.
To the Spirit of Carlos Gardel.
Today Is a Day of Great Joy
You Gotta Have Your Tips on Fire.
**Csoori, Sandor**
It Must Be Summer.
**Cudahy, Sheila**
Heroes of the Strip.
**Cuddihy, Michael**
My House.
**Cudmore, Daniel**
If could some Delius with divided hands.
**Cuelho, Art**

My Own Brand.
Wendover.

**Cullen, Countee**
Black Majesty.
Brown Boy to Brown Girl.
Brown Girl Dead, A.
For a Lady I Know.
For a Mouthy Woman.
For Amy Lowell.
For My Grandmother.
Four Epitaphs.
From the Dark Tower.
Heritage.
In Memory of Colonel Charles Young.
Incident.
Magnets.
Mary, Mother of Christ.
Only the Polished Skeleton.
Saturday's Child.
Scottsboro, Too, Is Worth Its Song.
Simon the Cyrenian Speaks.
Song of Praise, A.
Sonnet: "Some for a little while do love,
    and some for long."
Tableau.
That Bright Chimeric Beast.
Thorn Forever in the Breast, A.
To Certain Critics.
Under the Mistletoe.
Unknown Color, The.
Yet Do I Marvel.

**Cullen, Paula B.**
Cousins.

**Cullum, J. W.**
Roses, Revisited, in a Paradoxical
    Autumn.

**Cummings, Darcy**
Interphase.

**Cummings, Edward Estlin**
All Ignorance Toboggans into Know.
All in Green Went My Love Riding.
All Which Isn't Singing Is Mere Talking.
All worlds have halfsight, seeing either
    with.
Anyone Lived in a Pretty How Town.
As Freedom Is a Breakfastfood.
Being to timelessness as it's to time.
Buffalo Bill's.
But/ he" i/ staring.
Buy me an ounce and I'll sell you a
    pound.
Cambridge Ladies Who Live in
    Furnished Souls, The.
Chansons Innocentes, sels.
Come, Gaze with Me upon This Dome.
Dirty Colours of Her Kiss Have Just,
    The.
Dive for dreams.
Doll's boy's asleep.
Dying Is Fine)but Death.
First of All My Dreams Was of, The.
5.
Flotsam and Jetsam.
For Prodigal Read Generous.
Gee I Like to Think of Dead.
Goodby Betty, Don't Remember Me.
Greedy the People, The.
He as O, A.
Helves Surling Out of Eakspeasies Per
    (Reel) hapsingly.
Here Is Little Effie's Head.
Hist Whist.

How many moments must (amazing
    each.
I Am So Glad and Very.
I Carry Your Heart with Me (I Carry It
    In.
I Like My Body When It Is with Your
    Body.
I Sing of Olaf Glad and Big.
I Thank You God for Most This
    Amazing.
I was sitting in mcsorley's.
I Will Be.
If Everything Happens That Can't Be
    Done.
If I Have Made, My Lady, Intricate.
If I Should Sleep with a Lady Called
    Death.
If There Are Any Heavens.
If (touched by love's own secret) we, like
    homing.
If You Can't Eat You Got To.
(Im)C-A-T(mo).
Impressions, Number III.
IN) all those who got.
In Heavenly Realms of Hellas Dwelt.
In Just-/ Spring.
Is 5, sel.
It Is So Long Since My Heart Has Been
    with Yours.
It May Not Always Be So; and I Say.
It's Over a (See Just).
Jake Hates All the Girls.
Jimmie's Got a Goil.
L(a.
Ladies and Gentlemen This Little Girl.
Little joe gould has lost his teeth and
    doesn't know where.
Love is a place.
Love Is More Thicker than Forget.
Maggie and Milly and Molly and May.
Man Who Had Fallen among Thieves,
    A.
May I Feel Said He.
Me Up at Does.
Mr. U Will Not Be Missed.
My Father Moved through Dooms of
    Love.
My Love.
My Specialty Is Living Said.
My Sweet Old Etcetera.
Next to of Course God America I.
Nine Birds.
No Man, If Men Are Gods.
Nobody Loses All the Time.
Nothing False and Possible Is Love.
Notice the Convulsed Orange Inch of
    Moon.
Now air is air and thing is thing: no
    bliss.
Now I lay (with everywhere around).
Now (more near ourselves than we).
O It's Nice to Get Up in, the Slipshod
    Mucous Kiss.
O Sweet Spontaneous Earth.
O Thou to Whom the Musical White
    Spring.
Old Age.
Old Age Sticks.
One winter afternoon.
Peopleshaped Toomany-ness Far Too, A.
Pity This Busy Monster, Manunkind.
Plato Told Him.

Poem, or Beauty Hurts Mr. Vinal.
Politician, A.
Ponder, darling, these busted statues.
Pretty a Day, A.
Purer than Purest Pure, with music.
Q:dwo.
R-P-O-P-H-E-S-S-A-G-R.
Raise the Shade.
Rose Is Dying, The.
Salesman is an it that stinks Excuse, A.
Season 'Tis, My Lovely Lambs, The.
She Being Brand.
Silence.
Since Feeling Is First.
Sky Was Candy Luminous, The.
Slightly before the middle of
    Congressman Pudd.
Somewhere I Have Never Travelled,
    Gladly Beyond.
Sonnet: "Wind has blown the rain away
    and blown, A."
Sonnets—Actualities, sel.
Sonnets—Realities, sel.
Sonnets—Unrealities, sel.
Space Being (Don't Forget to
    Remember) Curved.
Spring Is like a Perhaps Hand.
"Sweet spring is your."
Than (By Yon Sunset's Wintry Glow).
This little bride and groom are.
Thou in Whose Swordgreat Story Shine
    the Deeds.
Thy fingers make early flowers of.
Tumbling-Hair.
Twenty-seven Bums Give a Prostitute
    the Once.
2 little whos.
Unnoticed Woman from Whose Kind
    Large Flesh.
Up into the Silence the Green.
Way to Hump a Cow Is Not, The.
What a Proud Dreamhorse.
What If a Much of a Which of a Wind.
When any mortal(even the most odd).
When Faces Called Flowers Float out of
    the Ground.
When God Lets My Body Be.
When Serpents Bargain for the Right to
    Squirm.
When the proficient poison of sure sleep.
)when what hugs stopping earth than
    silent is.
Wherelings Whenlings.
Who are you, little I.
Who Knows if the Moon's.
Who's Most Afraid of Death?
Why Did You Go.
Why from this her and him.
You Shall above All Things Be Glad and
    Young.
Your birthday comes to tell me this.
Your little voice.

**Cummins, P. D.**
Wait.

**Cuneo, Louis**
Haiku: "Clear light bulb smashed."
Haiku: "He tells us that."
Haiku: "Hey, laughing youths."
Haiku: "Once we talked."
Long Haiku No. 7.

**Cuney, Waring**
Finis.

Cunningham

No Images.
Threnody: "Only quiet death."
**Cunningham, Allan**
Wet Sheet and a Flowing Sea, A.
**Cunningham, James (Olumo)**
City Rises, The.
Covenant, The.
Footnote to a Gray Bird's Pause, A.
For Cal.
From a Brother Dreaming in the Rye.
Happy Day (or Independence Day).
High-cool/ 2.
Incidental Pieces to a Walk.
Lee-ers of Hew.
Leg-acy of a Blue Capricorn.
Narrator's Trance, The, *sels.*
Plea to My Sister, A.
Portrait of Rudy, A.
Rapping Along with Ronda Davis.
Slow Riff for Billy.
Solitary Visions of a Kaufmanoid.
St. Julien's Eve.
Street in Kaufman-ville, A.
Tambourine.
Welcome for Etheridge, A.
While Cecil Snores: Mom Drinks Cold
Milk.
**Cunningham, James Vincent**
Aged Lover Discourses in the Flat Style,
The.
Agnosco Veteris Vestigia Flammae.
All in Due Time.
And now you're ready who while she
was here.
Apology.
Bride loved old words, and found her
pleasure marred.
Chase, The.
Choice.
Coffee.
Consolatio Nova: For Alan Swallow.
Convalescence.
Dream Vision.
Elegy for a Cricket.
Envoi: "Hear me, whom I betrayed."
Epigram: "And what is love?
Misunderstanding, pain."
Epigram: "Dark thoughts are my
companions. I have wined."
Epigram: "Dear, if unsocial privacies
obsess me."
Epigram: For a Woman with Child.
Epigram: "Homer was poor. His
scholars live at ease."
Epigram: "How we desire desire! Joy of
surcease."
Epigram: "If wisdom, as it seems it is."
Epigram: "In whose will is our peace?
Thou happiness."
Epigram: "Life flows to death as rivers
to the sea."
Epigram: Night-Piece.
Epigram: "This Humanist whom no
beliefs constrained."
Epigram: "Time heals not: it extends a
sorrow's scope."
Epigram: "Within this mindless vault."
Epitaph for Someone or Other.
For a College Yearbook.
For My Contemporaries.
Friend, on this scaffold Thomas More
lies dead.

Here lies my wife. Eternal peace.
Here lies New Critic who would fox us.
History of Ideas.
In the thirtieth year of life.
Interview with Doctor Drink.
Lady, of anonymous flesh and face.
*Lip* was a man who used his head.
Meditation on Statistical Method.
Metaphysical Amorist, The.
Miramar Beach.
Modern Love.
Montana Fifty Years Ago.
Montana Pastoral.
Moral Poem, A.
Motto for a Sun Dial.
Neaera when I'm there is adamant.
On a cold night I came through the cold
rain.
Phoenix, The.
Pope from penance purgatorial, The.
Reason and Nature.
Ripeness Is All.
Rome.
Some twenty years of marital agreement.
Sonnet on a Still Night.
This is my curse. Pompous, I pray.
To a Friend, on Her Examination for
the Doctorate in English.
To My Wife.
To the Reader.
To What Strangers, What Welcome.
When I Shall Be without Regret.
**Cunningham, John**
Epigram: "Member of the modern great,
A."
Newcastle Beer.
On a Certain Alderman.
**Cunningham, Julia**
Hymn to Joy.
**Cunninghame-Graham, Robert.** *See*
**Graham, Robert**
**Curnow, Allen**
Eden Gate.
Elegy on My Father.
Eye Is More or Less Satisfied with
Seeing, The.
He Cracked a Word.
House and Land.
Jack-in-the-Boat.
Keep in a Cool Place.
Landfall in Unknown Seas.
Old Provincial Council Buildings,
Christchurch, The.
Out of Sleep.
Sailing or Drowning.
Self-Portrait.
Skeleton of the Great Moa in the
Canterbury Museum, Christchurch,
The.
Small Room with Large Windows, A.
Spectacular Blossom.
Time.
To Forget Self and All.
Tomb of an Ancestor.
Unhistoric Story, The.
Unhurt, There Is No Help.
Waking Bird Refutes, The.
Wild Iron.
**Curran, Edwin**
Painted Hills of Arizonas, The.
**Curran, John Philpot**
Let Us Be Merry.

**Curran, Mary Doyle**
No Fear.
**Currey, Ralph Nixon**
Jersey Cattle.
Unseen Fire.
**Curry, David**
I Am of These.
Thinking Back Seven Years and Being
Here Now.
**Curry, Peggy Simson**
Driving Down from the Big Horns.
Fishing at Sunrise.
Lupine Ridge.
Red Butte in Autumn.
Ridge in Wind.
**Curtis, Simon**
Satie, at the End of Term.
**Curtis, Tony**
To My Father.
**Cuscaden, R. R.**
Derricks.
Sold.
**Cushing, William O.**
We Are Watching, We Are Waiting, *with
music.*
**Cussrooee, Biddy**
My grief on the sea.
**Cutler, Bruce**
Consider This.
Results of a Scientific Survey.
**Cutting, Edith E.**
Against Gravity.
**Cutting, Sewall Sylvester**
God of the World, Thy Glories Shine,
*with music.*
Gracious Saviour, We Adore Thee, *with
music.*
**Cybulski, Walter**
Museum with Chinese Landscapes.
**Cynddelw Brydydd Mawr**
In Praise of Owain Gwynedd.
Petition for Reconciliation.
Poem on His Death-Bed.
**Czerkawska, Catherine Lucy**
Thread.

# D

"D., H." *See* **Doolittle, Hilda**
**Dabney, Betty Page**
Earth's Bondman.
**Dacey, Philip**
Amputee Soldier, The.
Animals' Christmas, The.
Anniversary.
Another Stone Poem.
Birthday, The.
Black Death, The.
Chain Letter.
For the Poet's Father, on His Taking Up
Gardening Late in Life.
Form Rejection Letter.
How I Escaped from the Labyrinth.
Looking at Models in the Sears
Catalogue.
Mystery Baseball.
Obscene Caller, The.
Perfectionist, The.

Porno Love.
Rise and Fall, The.
Rowboat, The.
Thumb.
**Dacre, Harry**
Daisy Bell; or, A Bicycle Built for Two, *with music.*
**Dadu**
Whatsover Hath Been Made, God Made.
**Dafydd ab Edmwnd**
Girl's Hair, A.
**Dafydd ap Gwilym**
Girls of Llanbadarn, The.
In Morfudd's Arms.
Ruin, The.
Seaguil, The.
Wind, The.
Woodland Mass, The.
**Dafydd Bach ap Madog Wladaidd**
Christmas Revel, A.
**Dafydd Benfras**
From Exile.
**Dafydd Nanmor**
Ode to Rhys ap Maredudd of Tywyn.
**Dahlberg, Edward**
Kansas City West Bottoms.
**Daiches, David**
Notes for a History of Poetry.
To Kate, Skating Better than Her Date.
Ulysses' Library.
**Daigon, Ruth**
Like an Ideal Tenant.
Night Flight.
**Dale, Edward Everett**
Prairie Schooner, The.
**Dale, Peter**
Emergency Gastrectomy.
Just Visiting.
Radium Therapy.
Visitors, The.
**Dali, Salvador**
Art of Picasso, The.
**Dallas, Ruth**
Among Old Houses.
Boy, The.
Deserted Beach.
Grandmother and Child.
Letter to a Chinese Poet, *sel.*
Shadow Show.
Striped Shell, A.
Tea-Shop, A.
Warming a set of new bones.
**Dallman, Elaine**
From the Dust.
**Daly, Thomas Augustine**
Day of the Circus Horse, The.
Pennsylvania Places.
**Damagetus**
Spartan Wrestler, The.
**D'Ambrosio, Vinnie-Marie**
Grace of Cynthia's Maidenhood, The.
Moon as Medusa.
On the Fifth Anniversary of Bluma Sach's Death.
**Dammers, Kim**
MANICdepressant.
**Dana, Mary Stanley Bunce**
O Sing to Me of Heaven, *with music.*
**Dana, Robert**
Horses.
Natural Odes/ American Elegies, *sels.*
Watergate Elegy, The.

Way We Live Now, The.
**Dandridge, Ray Garfield**
Time to Die.
Zalka Peetruza.
**Dane, Barbara** *and others*
Bring 'Em Home.
**Dangel, Leo**
Pa.
Plowing at Full Moon.
**Daniel, H. J.**
My Epitaph.
**Daniel, John**
Auto Icon.
Excerpts from a Diary of a War (1-3).
Injury to Insured.
My Wife Who Is American.
Of 91 Men Leaving an Underground Station.
Phrases for Everyday Use by the British in India.
Two Clocks.
Watch.
**Daniel, Marky**
Crabbing.
**Daniel, Robert T.**
Time Will Surely Come, The, *with music.*
**Daniel, Samuel**
Appeal, The.
Beauty, sweet love, is like the morning dew.
Care-Charmer Sleep.
First Flame.
Heavenly Eloquence.
Hymen's Triumph,*sels.*
Love Is a Sickness.
Musophilus, *sel.*
None other fame mine unambitious muse.
Secrecy.
Sonnet: "Fair is my love, and cruel as she is fair."
Sonnet: "I must not grieve my love, whose eyes would read."
Tethys' Festival, *sel.*
To Delia.
Ulysses and the Siren.
**Daniell, Rosemary**
Before the Fall.
Girl Friends.
I Want.
Of Jayne Mansfield, Flannery O'Connor, My Mother and Me.
To a Family Man in His Family Room.
**Daniels, Jim**
Going Up and Down.
**Danner, Margaret**
And through the Caribbean Sea.
At Home in Dakar.
Best Loved of Africa.
Convert, The.
Dance of the Abakweta, The.
Elevator Man Adheres to Form, The.
Far from Africa: Four Poems.
Garnishing the Aviary.
Goodbye David Tamunoemi West.
Grandson Is a Hoticeberg, A.
Painted Lady, The.
Rhetoric of Langston Hughes, The.
Sadies's Playhouse.
Slave and the Iron Lace, The.
This Is an African Worm.
**Dante Alighieri**

And now we walked along the solid mire.
Divina Commedia, *sels.*
First Canzone of the Convito, The.
Guido da Montefeltro.
Now hoisteth sail the pinnace of my wit.
Pier delle Vigne.
Sonnet: Dante Alighieri to Guido Cavalcanti.
Sonnet: "Upon a day, came sorrow in to me."
Ulysses.
Virgil's Farewell to Dante.
Vision of God, The.
**Darcy, Joseph P.**
Beyond the Window.
**Darcy, M. M.**
Astronaut's Choice.
**Dare, Sheryl**
For Tom (1945-1975).
Spring Cleaning.
**Dario, Ruben** (*originally* **Félix Rubén García Sarmiento**)
Nocturne II: "You who have listened to the heart of the night."
Three Kings, The.
**Darion, Joe**
Impossible Dream, The, *with music*
**Darley, George**
Ethelstan, *sel.*
Hundred-gated Thebes.
It Is Not Beauty I Demand.
Mermaidens' Vesper-Hymn, The.
Nepenthe, *sels.*
Phoenix, The.
Runilda's Chant.
Sea-Ritual, The.
Serenade of a Loyal Martyr.
Syren Songs,*sels.*
To the Moon.
Wherefore, unlaurelled boy.
**Darnley, Henry Stuart [*or* Stewart], Lord**
If Langour Makis Men Licht.
**Darr, Ann**
Before Dawn.
Dear James Wright.
Dear Oedipus.
For Great Grandmother and Her Settlement House.
Hangar Nine.
July Noon in Dupont Circle.
Love Is.
Low...the Violence Begins Low.
Oblique Birth Poem.
Pot-bellied Anachronism, The.
Relative Matter.
**Darwin, Erasmus**
Loves of the Plants, The, *sel.*
**Daryush, Elizabeth**
Armistice.
Look, The.
November Sun.
Still-Life.
**Das, Kamala**
House-Builders, The.
**Daugherty, James**
Citizen Paine.
**Daumal, Rene**
Four Cardinal Times of Day, The.
**Daunt, John**
Daybreak on a Pennsylvania Highway.
**Davenant [*or* D'Avenant], Sir William**

Aubade: "Lark now leaves his watery nest, The."
Endimion Porter and Olivia.
Gondibert, *sels.*
Just Italian, The, *sel.*
Law against Lovers, The, *sel.*
Luminalia, *sel.*
Night's Song.
Philosopher and the Lover, The: To a Mistress Dying.
Siege of Rhodes, The, *sel.*
Soldier [*or* Souldier] Going to the Field, The.
Song: "Come, melt thy soul in mine, that when unite."
Temple of Love, The, *sel.*
Triumphs of the Prince D'Amour, The, *sel.*
Under the Willow-Shades.
Unfortunate Lovers, The, *sel.*
Wake All the Dead.
Winter Storms, The.
**Davenport, Archilochus**
This island, garlanded with wild woods.
**Davenport, Guy**
Medusa, The.
**Davenport, Mariana B.**
Widow, The.
**David, John**
What Happiness Can Equal Mine, *with music.*
**Davidman, Joy**
Apology for Liberals.
For the Revolution.
In Praise of Fascists.
Near Catalonia.
Prayer against Indifference.
Snow in Madrid.
Twentieth-Century Americanism.
**Davidsohn, Hans.** *See* **Hoddis, Jakov van**
**Davidson, John**
Ballad of a Nun, A.
Ballad of Hell, A.
Cinque Port, A.
Frosty Morning, A.
In Romney Marsh.
In the Isle of Dogs.
London.
Runnable Stag, A.
Song: "Boat is chafing at our long delay, The."
Thirty Bob a Week.
Unknown, The.
**Davie, Donald**
Across the Bay.
Autumn Imagined.
Forests of Lithuania, The, *sel.*
Fountain, The.
Gardens No Emblems.
Having No Ear.
Heigh-ho on a Winter Afternoon.
July, 1964.
On Bertrand Russell's "Portraits from Memory."
Prose for Des Esseintes.
Remembering the 'Thirties.
Thanks to Industrial Essex.
Time Passing, Beloved.
Winter Talent, A.
Year 1812, The.
**Davies, Edward**

Cambrian Swain, The.
Chepstow: A Poem, *sels.*
**Davies, Gareth Alban**
Dance, The.
**Davies, Gloria Evans**
Her Name like the Hours.
**Davies, Hugh Sykes**
Music in an Empty House.
Poem: "In the stump of the old tree, where the heart has rotted out."
Poem: "It doesn't look like a finger it looks like a feather of broken glass."
**Davies, Idris**
Consider Famous Men, Dai Bach.
Do You Remember 1926?
High Summer on the Mountains.
Lay Preacher Ponders, The.
Mrs. Evans fach, you want butter again.
**Davies, Idris** *and* **Pete Seeger**
Bells of Rhymney.
**Davies, J. Kitchener**
Sound of the Wind That Is Blowing, The, *sel.*
**Davies, J. R. S.**
Cranes.
**Davis, John, of Hereford**
Against Gaudy-Bragging-Undoughty Daccus.
Against Proud Poor Phryna.
Author Loving These Homely Meats, Specially, viz.: Cream, Pancakes, Buttered Pippin-Pies, The.
Of Kate's Baldness.
**Davies, Sir John**
Affliction.
Gulling Sonnets.
Hymns of Astraea, *sel.*
In Francum.
In Fuscum.
In Librum.
Kate Being Pleased.
Nosce Teipsum, *sels.*
Of Astraea.
On the Deputy of Ireland's Child.
Orchestra; or, A Poeme of Dauncing, *sels.*
Praise of Dancing, The.
Soul and the Body, The.
Who Doth Not See the Measure of the Moon?
**Davies, Mary Carolyn**
Fishing Pole, The ("A fishing pole's a curious thing").
**Davies, Russell**
Book Reviews.
**Davies, Samuel**
Eternal Spirit, Source of Light, *with music.*
Lord, I Am Thine, *with music.*
While o'er Our Guilty Land, O Lord, *with music.*
**Davies, T. Glynne**
Caernarfon, 2 July 1969.
Old Man in a Moon Loft.
Sentences while Remembering Hiraethog.
**Davies, William Henry**
Beautiful, The.
Bright Day, A.
Cat, The.

Dog, The.
Dumb World, The.
Example, The.
Flowers.
Inquest, The.
Kingfisher, The.
Leisure.
Rabbit, The.
Rain, The.
Rat, The.
Rich Days.
Robin Redbreast.
Sailor to His Parrot, The.
School's Out.
Sea, The.
Sheep.
Truth, The.
Villain, The.
Visitor, The.
When Yon Full Moon.
White Horse, The.
White Monster, The.
**Davies, Walter**
Nightfall.
**Davis, Abijah**
Blest Is the Man Whose Tender Breast, *with music.*
**Davis, Frank Marshall**
Arthur Ridgewood, M.D.
Dancing Gal.
Flowers of Darkness.
Four Glimpses of Night.
Giles Johnson, Ph.D.
I Sing No New Songs.
"Onward Christian Soldiers!"
Robert Whitmore.
Snapshots of the Cotton South.
To Those Who Sing America.
**Davis, Gussie L.**
In the Baggage Coach Ahead, *with music.*
**Davis, Harold Lenoir**
Stalks of Wild Hay.
**Davis, Leasa**
Old woman sits, The.
**Davis, Lloyd**
Armstrong Spring Creek.
**Davis, Mary Evelyn Moore**
Battle-Flag, The.
**Davis, Ozora S.**
At Length There Dawns the Glorious Day, *with music.*
**Davis, Pamela Oberon**
Why Write Poetry?
**Davis, Paul**
Afternoon at Cannes.
**Davis, Ronda**
Invitation (To the Night and All Other Things Dark).
Parasitosis.
Personality Sketch, A: Bill.
Poems about Playmates.
Spacin.
**Davis, Thomas Osborne**
Geraldines, The.
Girl I left behind Me, The ("The dames of France are fond and free").
Lament for the Death of Eoghan Ruadh O'Neill.
**Davis, William Virgil**

Chandelier as Protagonist, The.
To My Son, Not Yet Born.

**Davison, Edward**
Owl, The.

**Davison, Peter**
Bed Time.
Firstling, The.
Last Word, The.

**Davison, Walter**
Ode: "At her fair hands how have I grace entreated."

**Dawe, Bruce**
Drifters.
First Corinthians at the Crossroads.
Frog Plague, The.
Gorilla Gorilla.
Homecoming.
Katrina.
Life-Cycle.
Not-so-good Earth, The.
Sleight-of-Hand.
Somewhere Friendly.
Under Way.
Weapons Training.
What Lies on Us.

**Dawe, G. C.**
Empty Raft.
Names.

**Dawe, Gerald**
Lives.

**Dawson, Gene**
When a Body.

**Dawson, William**
Lay of Oliver Gogarty, The.

**Day, Clarence**
Who Drags the Fiery Artist Down?

**Day, James William**
Rowan County Crew, The.

**Day, Lucille**
Labor.
Reject Jell-o.
Wedding.
Yom Kippur.

**Day, Thomas Fleming**
Main-Sheet Song, The.

**Day Lewis, Cecil**
Album, The.
Almost Human.
Bombers.
Circus Lion.
Come, Live with Me and Be My Love.
Committee, The.
Desire is a witch.
Do Not Expect Again.
Double Vision, The.
Failure, A.
Flight to Italy, sel.
Fox, The.
From Feathers to Iron, sel.
Gate, The.
Happy View, A.
Is It Far to Go?
Jig.
"Let Us Now Praise Famous Men."
Magnetic Mountain, The, sels.
My Mother's Sister.
Nearing Again the Legendary Isle.
Newsreel.
Now I have come to reason.
Now She Is like the White Tree-Rose.
Pegasus.
Reconciliation.

Sheepdog Trials in Hyde Park.
Two Songs.
Watching Post.
Where Are the War Poets?
Winter Night.

**Dayre, Sydney (Mrs. Cochran)**
Lesson for Mamma, A.
Morning Compliments.

**Dayton, David**
Woman Driving the Country Squire, The.

**Dayton, Ebenezer**
Wherein Consists the High Estate, *with music.*

**Dayton, Irene**
His Coming.
Psalmen Gezangen.
Vinedresser Yearns over His Vineyard, The.

**Deagon, Ann**
Basic Rescue.
Death of Phidias, The.
Going Under.
Jigsaw Puzzle.
Moving North.
Owl Pellet, The.

**Deal, Susan Strayer**
These Trees Are.

**Dean, John**
Schedules ("Schedules come in different forms, all crushing").
Seeing and Doing.

**Deane, Anthony C.**
Cult of the Celtic, The.
Ode, An: "I sing a song of sixpence, and of rye."

**Deane, Seamus**
After Derry, 30 January 1972.
Derry.
Elegy 3: "Whatever you call it."
Fording the River.
Northern Ireland: Two Comments.
Return.
Scholar II.

**Dearmer, Geoffrey**
Turkish Trench Dog, The.

**Dearmer, Percy**
Old Year Now Away Is Fled, The, *with music.*

**De Baca, Marc**
Lizards of La Brea, The.

**De Bevoise, Arlene**
Good Friday.
Two Gardens.

**De Bolt, William Walter**
Back to the Angels.
Thesis.

**De Boully, Monny**
Beyond Memory.

**DeBruhl, Melvin**
At Last.
Brown Circles.

**De Brun, Padraig**
In Memoriam.

**De Castro, Rosalía.** *See* Castro, Rosalía de

**Deems, Charles F.**
I Shall Not Want: In Deserts Wild, *with music.*

**Defoe, Daniel**
Encomium upon a Parliament, An.
More Reformation, *sel.*

Spanish Descent, The.
True-born Englishman, The.
Vision, The.

**DeFoe, Mark**
Euphoria, Euphoria.

**DeFrees, Madeline**
Barometer.
Beach Cliff Graffiti.
Catch of Summer, A, *sels.*
Domesticating Two Landscapes.
Driving Home.
Existing Light.
First-Class Relics: Letter to Dennis Finnell.
Grandmother Grant.
Hope Diamonds.
In the Hellgate Wind.
In the Scales: I.
In the Scales: II.
Indian Autobiographies.
Letter to an Absent Son.
"My Dream of Pure Invention."
Odd Woman, The.
Pendant Watch.
Peninsular.
Psalm for a New Nun.
Wake, The.
Watch for Fallen Rock.
With a Bottle of Blue Nun to All My Friends.

**De Gasztold, Carmen Bernos**
Prayer of the Donkey, The.
Prayer of the Mouse, The.
River Compared to an Oratorical Sentence, The.

**Degeyter, Pierre,** *and* **Eugene Potter** *See* **Potter, Eugene** *and* **Pierre Degeyter**

**DeGravelles, Charles**
Astrologer Argues Your Death, The.
Night Out, Tom Cat.

**Dehn, Mura**
Old Age.
Royal Iguanas, The.

**Dehn, Paul**
Armistice.
At the Dark Hour.
Come unto these yellow sands.
Game of Consequences, A.
Geiger, geiger, ticking slow.
I wandered angry as a cloud.
Leaden Treasury of English Verse, A, *sels.*
Ring-a-ring o' neutrons.
Twinkle, twinkle, little star.

**Dekker, Thomas**
Art thou poor, yet hast thou golden slumbers?
Cradle Song, A: "Golden slumbers kiss your eyes."
Death Terrible in Countenance.
Dekker His Dream, *sels.*
Extremities of Cold in Hell, The.
London's Tempe; or, The Field of Happiness, *sel.*
Noble Soldier, The, *sel.*
Pleasant Comedy of Patient Grissell, The, *sels.*
Thwick-a-thwack.

**De la Mare, Walter ("Walter Ramal")**
A-Apple Pie.
Alas, Alack!
All That's Past.

Antiques.
Archery.
At the Zoo.
Autumn.
Bah!
Bards, The.
Bishop Winterbourne.
Brueghel's Winter.
Bunches of Grapes.
Buttons.
Corporal Pym.
Dream-Song.
Dreamer, The.
Echo.
Echoes.
England.
False Dawn.
Fare Well.
Feckless Dinner Party, The.
Five Eyes.
Full Moon.
Funeral, The.
Galliass, The.
Ghost, The.
Green.
Hare, A.
Hi!
Holly, The.
Hunt, The.
Huntsmen, The.
Immanent.
In the Local Museum.
Iron.
It Might Be a Lump of Amber.
J. J.
Jim Jay.
John Mouldy.
Last Chapter, The.
Listeners, The.
Lucy.
March Hares.
Me.
Mermaids.
Miracle, The.
Miss Loo.
Miss Pheasant.
Miss T.
Mistletoe.
Moonshine.
Motley.
Napoleon.
Ned Vaughan.
Nicholas Nye.
Nod.
Nothing.
Off the Ground.
Old King, The.
Old Shellover.
Old Summerhouse, The.
Old Susan.
Old Tailor, The.
Peace.
Pooh!
Pool in the Rock, The.
Portrait, A.
Railway Junction, The.
Rainbow, The.
Rats.
Revenant, The.
Ride-by-Nights, The.
Robin, A.
Santa Claus.

Scarecrow, The.
Scholars.
Scribe, The.
Shadow.
Ship of Rio, The.
Shubble, The.
Silver.
Silver Penny, The.
Slim Cunning Hands.
Snow-Flake, The.
Snowdrop, The.
Solitude.
Some One.
Song of Finis, The.
Song of Shadows, The.
Song of the Mad Prince, The.
Storm, The.
Stranger, The.
Sunk Lyonesse.
Susannah Prout.
Tartary.
Then.
Things.
Thomas Hardy.
Thomas Logge.
Three Cherry Trees, The.
Three Sisters.
Tired Tim.
Tom's Angel.
Tom's Little Dog.
Tryst, The.
Voices.
Waif, The.
Winter.
**Delaney, John**
Golf Ball.
**Delany, Clarissa Scott**
Solace.
**De la Selva, Salomon**
Elegy: "My comrade is dead."
**Delgado, Abelardo**
My Star Spangled–Red Striped Socks.
**Del Monte, Crescenzo**
One Thing to Take, Another to Keep.
Roman Roman, A.
Those Zionists.
**De Longchamps, Joanne**
Tortoise.
**Delp, Michael**
Living with the Fat Man.
Love Poem: "Is the woman next door."
Poem for My Father.
**Del Renzio, Toni**
Can You Change a Shilling?
**De Melo e Castro, E. M.**
Monument.
**Demon, Andrew**
Reflections of a Trout Fisherman.
**De Morgan, Augustus**
Fleas, The.
**Dempster, Barry**
Mother.
**Dempster, Roland Tombekai**
Africa's Plea.
**DenBoer, James**
Casting a Vote.
Charming the Moon.
Spring in Washington.
**Denby, Edwin**
City without Smoke.
**Denham, Sir John**
Cooper's Hill, *sel.*

Had Cowley ne'er spoke, Killigrew ne'er
writ.
Progress of Learning, The, *sel.*
**Denney, Reuel**
Chiffonier with Glass Flowers, A.
Fixer of Midnight.
March with All Drums Muffled, A.
**Dennis, C. J.**
Swagman, The.
**Dennis, Carl**
Band, The.
Chosen, The.
**Dennis, Nigel**
Desperate Measure, A.
**Dennis, Zelma S.**
Irish Wind, An.
**De Pietro, Albert**
Colossi.
Dog Talk.
Meditations on Frost's "Stopping by
Woods."
Rejoinder.
**De Regnier, Beatrice Schenk**
I like winter, spring, summer, and fall.
Monsters Do Not Scare Me Much.
**Der Hovanessian, Diana**
Polar Bear.
**Derian, Vahan**
Words at Farewell.
**Derleth, August**
Planetary Arc-Light, The.
**De Roche, Joseph**
Aunt Laura Moves toward the Open
Grave of Her Father.
Blond.
**Derricotte, Toi**
Boxes.
Doll Poem ("Doll is sitting in a box").
Face as It Might Be of Love, The.
This Woman Will Not Bear Children.
**Derwood, Gene**
After Reading St. John the Divine.
**Desbordes-Valmore, Marceline**
Roses of Sa'adi, The.
**Deshoulières, Antoinette**
Reflections.
**Desmond, Gerald, Earl of**
Against Blame of Woman.
**Desnos, Robert**
Day It Was Night, The.
Poem to the Mysterious Woman.
**Desprez, Frank**
Lasca.
**Dessner, Lawrence Jay**
Tennis Pro.
**De Tabley, John Byrne Leicester Warren,
3d Baron**
Churchyard on the Sands, The.
Circe.
Knight in the Wood, The.
Power of Interval, The.
Study of a Spider, The.
**Deutsch, Babette**
Aged Woman to Her Sons, The.
Brother.
Barges on the Hudson.
Bull, A.
Destruction of Letters.
Fireworks.
Memory.
Morning Workout.
Mother, The.

Natural Law.
Poem, The: "Painter of Dante's awful ferry-ride, The."
Stranger than the Worst.
Tak for Sidst.
To the Moon.
**Deutsch, R. H.**
Afternoon of a Girl.
**De Vere, Aubrey Thomas**
In Ruin Reconciled.
Little Black Rose, The.
**De Vere, Edward, 17th Earl of Oxford**
Epigram: "Were I a king, I could command content."
If Women Could Be Fair.
**Devlin, Denis**
Ank'hor Vat.
Anteroom: Geneva.
Ascension.
Daphne Stillorgan.
Encounter.
Heavenly Foreigner, The, *sel.*
Lough Derg.
Renewal by Her Element.
Venus of the Salty Shell.
Wishes for Her.
**De Vries, Peter**
Bacchanal.
Beth Appleyard's Verses.
Christmas Family Reunion.
Loveliest of Pies.
Mirror.
Psychiatrist.
**De Vries, Rachel**
Jealousy.
**Dewey, A. A.**
At the Drive-In: "John Wayne vs. God."
Blizzard, The.
Coyote, The.
**Dexter, R. P.**
Shadow Dirge.
**Dey, Richard Morris**
Fog 9/76.
**De Young, Lily A.**
I Have a Place.
**Diack, Nar-Gad**
Day and night I scan the horizon.
**Diamond, David**
We Will Not Fear, *with music.*
**Diaper, William**
Brent: A Poem to Thomas Palmer Esq., *sels.*
**Dibdin, Charles**
Jolly Young Waterman, The.
Nothing like Grog.
**Dibdin, Thomas**
Child that has a cold we may suppose, A.
**Di Caprio, Isabelle**
Jabber-Whacky.
**Di Cicco, Pier Giorgio**
Friendship Game, The.
Words to the Wind.
**Dickens, Charles**
Cannibals' Grace before Meat, The.
Fine Old English Gentlemen, The; New Version.
**Dickey, James**
Adultery.
After the Night Hunt.
Bee, The.
Beholders, The.

Between Two Prisoners.
Birth, A.
Buckdancer's Choice.
Bums, on Waking.
Cancer Match, The.
Celebration, The.
Chenille.
Cherrylog Road.
Coming Back to America.
Deer among Cattle.
Dog Sleeping on My Feet, A.
Driver, The.
Encounter in the Cage Country.
Faces Seen Once.
Falling.
Fence Wire.
Fiend, The.
Firebombing, The.
For the Death of Vince Lombardi.
For the Last Wolverine.
For the Running of the New York City Marathon.
Gamecock.
Heaven of Animals, The.
Hospital Window, The.
Hunting Civil War Relics at Nimblewill Creek.
In the Mountain Tent.
In the Pocket.
In the Tree House at Night.
Inside the River.
Landfall, The.
Lifeguard, The.
Listening to Foxhounds.
Living There.
Looking for the Buckhead Boys.
Moon Ground, The.
Movement of Fish, The.
On Giving a Son to the Sea.
On the Hill below the Lighthouse.
Performance, The.
Pursuit from Under.
Reincarnation (I).
Reincarnation (II).
Shark's Parlor, The.
Sheep Child, The.
Slave Quarters.
Springer Mountain.
Summons, The.
Sun.
Them, Crying.
Underground Stream, The.
Venom.
Winter Trout.
Zodiac, The, *sel.*
**Dickey, R. P.**
Another View of the Beast.
At the City Park Zoo.
Early June.
Humidity.
Privacy.
Santo Domingo Corn Dance.
Shazam.
Takes All Kinds.
X.
**Dickey, William**
Another Given: The Last Day of the Year.
Exploration over the Rim.
For Every Last Batch When the Next One Comes Along.
Hope.

Horn, Mouth, Pit, Fire.
Lesson of the Master.
Memoranda.
Poet's Farewell to His Teeth, The.
Resolving Doubts.
Spectrum.
Teaching Swift to Young Ladies.
Voyage to the Moon.
What It Means, Living in the City.
**Dickinson, Emily**
After a hundred years.
After great pain, a formal feeling comes.
Ah, necromancy sweet!
Ah, Teneriffe!
Alter! When the hills do.
Altered look about the hills, An.
Apparently with no surprise.
"Arcturus" is his other name.
As imperceptibly as grief.
Beauty—be not caused—it is.
Because I could not stop for Death.
Bee his burnished carriage, A.
Bee! I'm expecting you!
Behind me—dips eternity.
Besides the autumn poets sing.
Bible is an antique volume, The.
Bird came down the walk, A.
Birthday of but a single pang.
Bone that has no marrow, The.
Brain—is wider than the sky, The.
Brain, within its groove, The.
Bustle in a house, The.
Circumference thou bride of awe.
Clock stopped, A.
Color—caste—denomination.
Come slowly—Eden!
Conscious am I in my chamber.
Crisis is a hair.
Crumbling is not an instant's act.
Dear March, come in.
Death is a dialogue between.
Death is the supple suitor.
Departed—to the judgment.
Did our best moment last.
Did the harebell loose her girdle.
Difference between despair, The.
Drama's vitallest expression is the common day.
Drowning is not so pitiful.
Drunkard cannot meet a cork, A.
Dying tiger, A—moaned for drink.
Elysium is as far as to.
Essential oils are wrung.
Everywhere of silver, An.
Experiment to me.
Exultation is the going.
"Faith" is a fine invention.
Fame is a fickle food.
Farther in summer than the birds.
Finding is the first act.
First day's night had come, The.
Forever—is composed of nows.
Further in summer than the birds.
Fuzzy fellow without feet, A.
God is a distant, stately lover.
God is indeed a jealous God.
He ate and drank the precious words.
He outstripped Time with but a bout.
He preached upon "breadth" till it argued him narrow.
He was weak, and I was strong—then.
Heart asks pleasure first, The.

Heart! We will forget him!
Heaven is so far of the mind.
"Heavenly Father"—take to thee.
Her face was in a bed of hair.
Her—"last poems."
His mansion in the pool.
Hope is a strange invention.
Hope is a subtle glutton.
"Hope" is the thing with feathers.
How brittle are the piers.
How many times these low feet
  staggered.
How the waters closed above him.
I am afraid to own a body.
I am alive—I guess.
I asked no other thing.
I breathed enough to take the trick.
I can wade grief.
I cannot live with you.
I could bring you jewels—had I a mind
  to.
I died for beauty—but was scarce.
I dreaded that first robin, so.
I dwell in Possibility.
I envy seas, whereon he rides.
I felt a cleaving in my mind.
I felt a funeral, in my brain.
I found the phrase to every thought.
I gave myself to him.
I got so I could hear [or take] his name.
I had been hungry, all the years.
I had not minded—walls.
I heard a fly buzz—when I died.
I know some lonely houses off the road.
I know that He exists.
I like a look of agony.
I like to see it lap the miles.
I lost a world the other day.
I meant to have but modest needs.
I never hear the word "escape."
I never lost as much but twice.
I never saw a moor.
I read my sentence—steadily.
I reason, earth is short.
I reckon—when I count at all.
I saw no way—the heavens were
  stitched.
I shall know why—when time is over.
I started early, took my dog.
I stepped from plank to plank.
I taste a liquor never brewed.
I watched the moon around the house.
I would not paint—a picture.
I years had been from home.
If I can stop one heart from breaking.
If you were coming in the fall.
I'll tell you how the sun rose.
I'm ceded—I've stopped being theirs.
I'm nobody! Who are you?
I'm "wife"—I've finished that.
In winter in my room.
It dropped so low—in my regard.
It is an honorable thought.
It sifts from leaden sieves.
It sounded as if the streets were running.
It struck me every day.
It was not death, for I stood up.
It will be Summer eventually.
It would have starved a gnat.
I've seen a dying eye.
Just lost, when I was saved!
Lad of Athens, faithful be.

Last night that she lived, The.
Light exists in spring, A.
Lightly stepped a yellow star.
Lightning is a yellow fork, The.
Like trains of cars on tracks of plush.
Little madness in the spring, A.
Me from myself—to banish.
Mine—by the right of the white election.
Mine enemy is growing old.
Moon was but a chin of gold, The.
Morns are meeker than they were, The.
Much madness is divinest sense.
My country need not change her gown.
My friend must be a bird.
My life closed twice before its close.
My life had stood—a loaded gun.
Name—of it—is "Autumn," The.
Narrow fellow in the grass, A.
Nature the gentlest mother is.
No crowd that has occurred.
Of all the souls that stand create.
Of bronze and blaze.
Of course—I prayed.
One dignity delays for all.
One need not be a chamber—to be
  haunted.
Our journey had advanced.
Our lives are Swiss.
Ourselves we do inter with sweet
  derision.
Over the fence.
Pain—expands the time.
Pain has an element of blank.
Papa above!
Pedigree of honey, The.
Perception of an object costs.
Poets light but lamps, The.
Precious, mouldering pleasure 'tis, A.
Presentiment—is that long shadow—on
  the lawn.
Prompt, executive bird is the jay, A.
Read, sweet, how others strove, *with
  music.*
Remorse is memory awake.
Renunciation—is a piercing virtue.
Reportless subjects, to the quick.
Revolution is the pod.
Route of evanescence, A.
Safe in their alabaster chambers.
Satisfaction—is the agent.
Sepal, petal, and a thorn, A.
She dealt her pretty words like blades.
She rose to his requirement—dropt.
She sights a bird, she chuckles.
She staked her feathers—gained an arc.
Single clover plank, A.
Sky is low, the clouds are mean, The.
Snow that never drifts, The.
So proud she was to die.
Softened by time's consummate plush.
Some keep the Sabbath going to church.
Soul has bandaged moments, The.
Soul selects her own society, The.
Spider as an artist, The.
Spider holds a silver ball, The.
Spider sewed at night, A.
Split the lark—and you'll find the music.
Spring is the period.
Success is counted sweetest.
Surgeons must be very careful.
Tell all the truth but tell it slant.
That it will never come again.

That love is all there is.
There are two Mays.
There came a day at summer's full.
There came a wind like a bugle.
There is a languor of the life.
There is a pain—so utter.
There is no frigate like a book.
There is no Silence in the Earth—so
  silent.
There's a certain slant of light.
There's been a death in the opposite
  house.
These are the days when birds come
  back.
They shut me up in prose.
This is my letter to the world.
This quiet dust was gentlemen and
  ladies.
This was a poet—it is that.
This world is not conclusion.
Those—dying then.
Time feels so vast that were it not.
'Tis not that Dying hurts us so.
'Tis true—they shut me in the cold.
Title divine—is mine!
To be alive—is power.
To die—takes just a little while.
To fight aloud is very brave.
To flee from memory.
To hear an oriole sing.
To make a prairie it takes a clover and
  one bee.
Too happy time dissolves itself.
'Twas a long parting—but the time.
'Twas like a maelstrom, with a notch.
'Twas warm—at first—like us.
Until the desert knows.
Victory comes late.
Way I read a letter's—this, The.
We dream—it is good we are dreaming.
We outgrow love, like other things.
We shall find the cube of the rainbow.
Went up a year this evening.
What is—"Paradise."
What mystery pervades a well!
What soft, cherubic creatures.
When bells stop ringing—church—
  begins.
While we were fearing it, it came.
Wild nights!—Wild nights!
Wind begun to rock [or knead] the grass,
  The.
With thee, in the desert.
Within my garden, rides a bird.
Word made flesh is seldom, A.
Wounded deer—leaps highest, A.
You'll know it—as you know—tis noon.
**Dickinson, John**
  Liberty Song, The, *with music.*
**Dickinson, Patric**
  Dam, The.
  New Block.
  Redwing, The.
**Dickson, John**
  Art Gallery.
  Looking Down on West Virginia.
**Die, Countess Beatritz de**
  I sing a song reluctantly.
  Lately I've felt a grave concern.
**Diekmann, Conrad**
  Winter Trees.
**Dienstag, Alan**

Golden Witch, The.
**Digby, John**
  One Night Away from Day.
  Sooner or Later.
**Di Grazia, Richard**
  Saboteur, The.
**Dillard, Annie**
  Arches and Shadows.
**Dillard, Richard H. W.**
  America Is Darken'd.
  Day I Stopped Dreaming about Barbara
    Steele, The.
  Downtown Roanoke.
  Hats.
  Kite.
  Looking for Asia.
  Meditation for a Pickle Suite.
**Dillon, George**
  Hard Lovers, The.
  One Beauty Still.
**Dillow, H. C.**
  Confrontations of March.
**Dilsaver, Paul**
  Corwin Psychiatric Ward, 1972.
**Di Michele, Mary**
  Piccante.
**Dimoff, John**
  West of Chicago.
**"Dinesen, Isak" (Karen Blixen)**
  Zebra.
**Diop, David**
  Africa.
**DiPasquale, Emanuel**
  Advice.
  Rain.
**Di Piero, W. S.**
  "Living, A."
  On Christmas Eve.
**DiPrima, Diane**
  Moon Mattress.
  Poem for the Subterranean Poor.
  Prayer to the Mothers.
  Quarrel, The.
  Revolutionary Letter # 1.
  Revolutionary Letter # 4.
  Revolutionary Letter # 16.
  Revolutionary Letter # 19.
  Revolutionary Letter # 21.
  Revolutionary Letter # 29.
  Revolutionary Letter # 36.
  Revolutionary Letter # 40.
**Disch, Tom**
  Homage to Carracci.
  Vowels of Another Language, The.
**Ditlevsen, Tove**
  Morning.
  Old Folk, The.
**Ditsky, John**
  Chamber Music.
  Mainline.
**Ditta, J. M.**
  In the Surgery.
**Divine, Jay**
  Coal Miner's Grace.
**Dix, William Chatterton**
  As with Gladness Men of Old.
  What Child Is This?
**Dixon, Alan**
  Chops.
**Dixon, Henry**
  Description of a Good Boy, The.
**Dixon, Maynard**

Laguna Perdida.
Navajo Song.
Plains, The.
**Dixon, Melvin**
  Flight on Naked Wings.
  Man Holding Boy in the Rain.
  Secret of Seeds, The.
  Souvenirs.
**Dixon, Richard Watson**
  Dream.
  Song: "Feathers of the willow, The."
  Song: "Oh, bid my tongue be still."
  Wizard's Funeral, The.
**Djalparmiwi**
  Blowflies Buzz, The.
**Djangatolum.** *See* **Corbin, Lloyd M., Jr.**
**Djanikian, Gregory**
  Michelangelo: "The Creation of Adam."
**Djurberaui**
  All You Others, Eat.
**Doak, Katherine**
  Fox Song.
  Nunnery.
  Sea Otter, Dream Poem to My Mother.
  Song of Ceres.
**Doane, George Washington**
  Fling Out the Banner! *with music.*
  Once More, O Lord, *with music.*
  Softly Now the Light of Day, *with music.*
  Thou Art the Way, *with music.*
**Doane, William Croswell**
  Ancient of Days, *with music.*
**Dobberstein, Michael**
  Engine, The: A Manual.
**Dobell, Sydney Thompson**
  Balder, *sel.*
  Botanist's Vision, The.
  Daft Jean.
  From a Calendar.
  German Legion, The.
  To the Authoress of "Aurora Leigh."
  Wind.
**Dobkins, Claudia**
  Brief Explanation.
  Miracle Worker.
  Still Life.
  Voice.
**Dobson, Austin**
  Ars Victrix.
  Ballade of Prose and Rhyme, The.
  Ballade of the Armada, A.
  Circe.
  Dora versus Rose.
  July.
  Kiss, A.
  Rondel; the Wanderer.
  Rose-Leaves,*sels.*
  To "Lydia Languish."
  Urceus Exit.
  With Pipe and Flute.
**Dobson, Rosemary**
  Birth, The.
  Bystander, The.
  Cock Crow.
  Country Morning.
  Country Press.
  Martyrdom of Saint Sebastian, The.
  Still Life.
  Three Fates, The.
**Dobyns, Stephen**
  Counterparts.
  Delicate, Plummeting Bodies, The.

Fear.
Oatmeal Deluxe.
**Dobzynski, Charles**
  Fable Merchant, The.
  Memory Air.
  Never Again, The.
  Zealot without a Face.
**"Doc Long."** *See* **Long, Doughtry, Jr.**
**Dock, Christopher**
  O Children, Would You Cherish? *with*
    *music.*
**Dodat, François**
  Dromedary.
  Ladybug.
**Dodd, Wayne**
  Night Poem.
**Doddridge, Philip**
  O God of Bethel.
  O Happy Day, *with music.*
**Dodge, Henry Nehemiah**
  Deep Calleth unto Deep.
  Spirit of Freedom, Thou Dost Love the
    Sea.
**Dodge, Mary Mapes**
  Brave Knight, A.
  Buttercup.
  Farmer in Bungleton, A.
  Little Miss Limberkin.
  Zealless Xylographer, The.
**Dodge, Ossian E.**
  Ho! Westward Ho! *with music.*
**Dodgson, Charles Lutwidge.** *See* **"Carroll,**
  **Lewis"**
**Dodson, Margery**
  Poem: "Entombed in my heart no blood
    flows to you."
**Dodson, Owen**
  Ballad of Badmen.
  Drunken Lover.
  For Edwin R. Embree.
  Hymn Written after Jeremiah Preached
    to Me in a Dream.
  I Break the Sky.
  Job's Ancient Lament.
  Mary Passed This Morning.
  Morning Duke Ellington Praised the
    Lord, The.
  Poems for My Brother Kenneth, *sel.*
  Sailors on Leave.
  Sickle Pears.
  Sorrow Is the Only Faithful One.
  Yardbird's Skull.
**Döhl, Reinhard**
  Pattern Poem with an Elusive Intruder.
**Dolben, Digby Mackworth**
  He Would Have His Lady Sing.
  Sea Song, A.
**Dolgorukov, Florence**
  Intersection.
  Three Sunrises from Amtrak.
**Domin, Hilde**
  Birthdays.
  Catalogue.
  Cologne.
  Dreamwater.
**Domino, Ruth**
  Sparrow in the Dust, A.
**Donaghy, John Lyle**
  Deathward.
  Duck.
  Portrait.
  Winter.

**Donne, John**
Air and Angels.
Anagram, The.
Anatomy of the World, An, *sel.*
Anniversary [*or* Anniversarie], The.
Annunciation.
Antiquary.
Apparition, The.
Autumnal, The.
Bait, The.
Blossom [*or* Blossome], The.
Break of Day.
Broken Heart, The.
Burnt Ship, A.
Canonization, The.
Change.
Curse, The.
Death, Be Not Proud.
Dissolution, The.
Dream, The ("Dear love, for nothing less than thee").
Ecstasy, The.
Elegies,*sels.*
Elegy: "Nature's lay idiot, I taught thee to love."
Elephant, The.
Epithalamion: "Thou art reprieved old year, thou shalt not die," *abr.*
Epithalamion, An; or, Marriage-Song on the Lady Elizabeth and Count Palatine Being Married on St. Valentine's Day, *abr.*
Epithalamion Made at Lincoln's Inn.
Expiration, The.
Farewell to Love.
Fever, A.
Flea, The.
Funeral, The.
God grant thee thine own wish, and grant thee mine.
Good Friday, 1613. Riding Westward.
Good Lord, Deliver Us!
Good-Morrow, The.
Holy Sonnets, *sels.*
Hymn to Christ, at the Author's Last Going into Germany, A.
Hymn to God My God, in My Sickness.
Hymn to God the Father, A.
I am a little world made cunningly.
In Eundem Macaronicon.
Indifferent, The.
Jealousy.
Lame Beggar, A.
Lecture upon the Shadow, A.
Letter to the Lady Carey and Mrs. Essex Rich, A, *sel.*
Litany, A, *sels.*
Lovers' Infiniteness.
Love's Alchemy.
Love's Deity [*or* Deitie].
Love's Diet.
Love's Growth; or, Spring.
Love's Progress.
Message, The.
Nativity.
New Philosophy, The.
Nocturnal[l] upon St Lucy's [*or* S. Lucies] Day, Being the Shortest Day, A.
Of the Progress of the Soul; the Second Anniversary, *sels.*

On His Mistress [*or* Mistris].
Phryne.
Poor soul, in this thy flesh what dost thou know?
Primrose, Being at Montgomery Castle, The.
Progresse of the Soule, The ("I sing the progress of a deathless soul"), *sels.*
Relic, The.
Satire: "Kind pity chokes my spleen; brave scorn forbids."
Satire: "Well, I may now receive, and die: my sin."
Satires, *sels.*
Seek True Religion!
Self Accuser, A.
Song: "Go and catch a falling star."
Song: "Sweetest love, I do not go."
Storm, The, *sel.*
Storm at Sea, A.
Sun [*or* Sunne] Rising, The.
Take heed of loving me.
To Mr. George Herbert.
To Mr. Rowland Woodward.
To Mrs. Magdalen Herbert, *sel.*
To Sir Henry Wotton ("Here's no more news than virtue").
To Sir Henry Wotton ("Sir, more than kisses letters mingle souls").
To the Countess of Bedford ("Reason is our soul's left hand").
To the Countess of Salisbury, *sel.*
Triple Fool, The.
Twicknam [*or* Twickenham] Garden.
Undertaking, The.
Valediction, A: Forbidding Mourning.
Valediction, A: Of Weeping.
Whale, The.
Will, The.
**Donnell, David**
Hotels.
**Donnelly, Charles**
Flowering Bars, The.
Heroic Heart.
Last Poem.
Tolerance of Crows, The.
**Donnelly, Dorothy**
Chinese Baby Asleep.
Glass World.
Leaflight.
Recollection.
Serenade: "Tin-type tune the locusts make, The."
**"Donovan."** *See* **Leitch, Donovan**
**Donovan, Gregory**
Working Man, The.
**Donovan, Rhoda**
No Signal for a Crossing.
**Donzella, D. W.**
Last Job I Held in Bridgeport, The.
To My Father on Pearl Harbor Day.
Winter.
**Dooley, Ebon**
Easter Bunny Blues Or All I Want for Xmas Is the Loop, The.
Prophet's Warning or Shoot to Kill, The.
Query.
**Doolittle, Hilda ("H. D.")**
Acon.
Along the Yellow Sand.

At Baia.
At Ithaca.
Birds in Snow.
Callypso Speaks.
Centaur Song.
Epigram: "Golden one is gone from the banquets, The."
Erige Cor Tuum ad Me in Caelum.
Eurydice.
Evadne.
Evening.
Flowering of the Rod, The, *sel.*
Fragment Thirty-six: "I know not what to do."
Fragment 113: "Not honey."
Garden, The, *sel.*
Good Frend, *sel.*
Heat.
Helen.
Helen in Egypt, *sels.*
Helmsman, The.
Hermes of the Ways.
Hippolytus Temporizes.
In Time of Gold.
Lethe.
Moon in Your Hands, The.
Moonrise.
Mysteries Remain, The.
Orchard.
Oread.
Pear Tree.
Phaedra.
Pool, The.
Pursuit.
Sea Poppies.
Sea Rose.
She Contrasts with Herself Hippolyta.
She Rebukes Hippolyta.
Sigil.
Stars Wheel in Purple.
Time has an end, they say.
Tribute to the Angels, *sels.*
Walls Do Not Fall, The, *sels.*
Wind Sleepers, The.
**Dor, Moshe**
Among the Pine Trees.
Dwelling, The.
Nightingales Are Not Singing.
Small Bones Ache.
**Doriot, Jeanne**
Indian.
**Dorman, Sonya**
Burglar, The.
Decorating Problem.
Elegy for Bella, Sarah, Rosie, and All the Others.
Hunters.
In the Sly Gardens.
N.Y. to L.A. by Jet Plane.
Sketch from Loss of Memory.
Surfer and Others.
**Dorn, Alfred**
Symphony.
**Dorn, Edward**
Biggest Killing, The.
Chronicle.
Comforted by Limestone.
Eugene Delacroix Says.
From Gloucester Out.
Gunslinger, *sels.*
Home on the Range, February 1962.

Idle Visitation, An.
Morning to Remember, A; or, E Pluribus Unum.
Mourning Letter, March 29 1963.
On the Debt My Mother Owed to Sears Roebuck.
Oxford, *sel.*
Song, A: "There is a blue sky."
Song, The: "So light no one noticed."
Thesis.
Vaquero.
When the Fairies.

**Dorris, Michael**
Frost Heaves.

**Dorset, Catherine Ann**
Peacock "At Home," The.

**Dorset, Charles Sackville, 6th Earl of.** *See* **Sackville, Charles, 6th Earl of Dorset**

**Dorset, Thomas Sackville, 1st Earl of.** *See* **Sackville, Thomas, 1st Earl of Dorset**

**Dos Passos, John**
Crimson Tent.

**Doty, M. R.**
Sleep

**Doughty, Charles Montague**
Dawn in Britain, The, *sels.*
Gauls Sacrifice, The.
Hymn to the Sun.
Roman Officer Writes, A.

**Douglas, Lord Alfred Bruce**
Ferret, The.
Lion, The.
Ostrich, The.
Weasel, The.

**Douglas, Ernest**
Out Where the West Begins: A Parody.

**Douglas, Gilean**
Inscription in a Book.

**Douglas, Keith**
Deceased, The.
Desert Flowers.
How to Kill.
John Anderson.
Knife, The.
Prisoner, The.
Russians.
Simplify Me When I'm Dead.
Syria.
Vergissmeinicht.

**Douglas, William** *and* **Lady John Scott**
Annie Laurie.

**Douglass, Suzanne**
No Holes Marred.
Progress.

**Doulis, Thomas**
Honored Dead, The.

**Dove, Rita**
Adolescence—II.
Nigger Song: An Odyssey.
This Life.

**Dovey, Irma**
Unwelcome.

**Dow, Philip**
Duck Pond at Mini's Pasture, a Dozen Years Later, The.
Life, The.
Playing.
Twilight in California.

**Dowling, Basil**
Halfwit.
Mushrooms.
Scything.

Through a Glass, Darkly.
Trapped Hare, The.
Unreturning Native, The.

**Dowson, Ernest Christopher**
Carthusians.
Exile.
Extreme Unction.
Jadis.
Last Word, A.
Non Sum Qualis Eram Bonae sub Regno Cynarae.
Princess of Dreams, The.
To One in Bedlam.
Valediction, A: "If we must part."
Villanelle of Acheron.
Villanelle of the Poet's Road.
Vitae Summa Brevis Spem Nos Vetat Incohare Longam.

**Doxey, W. S.**
Cathedrals.

**Doyle, Charles**
Being Here (or Anywhere).
Duel in the Camellias.
Empirical History.
Messages for Herod.
Starlings and History.

**Doyle, Sir Francis Hastings**
Private of the Buffs, The.

**Doyle, Susanne**
November Walk.

**Drachler, Rose**
As I Am My Father's.
Dark Scent of Prayer, The.
Isaac and Esau.
Letters of the Book, The.
Under the Shawl.
Zippora Returns to Moses at Rephidim.

**Drake, Barbara**
Ancestors, The.
Case History.
Good Friends and First Impressions.
Magic Children.
Old Folk Tale.
She Dreams Herself Titanic.
Woman Gets Restless, The.

**Drake, Joseph Rodman**
American Flag, The.
Culprit Fay, The, *sel.*

**Drake, Leah Bodine**
Mouse Heaven.

**Dransfield, Michael**
After a Birthday.
Change, The.
Geography.
Kathlyn.
Love (Dialogue) Poem.
Overdose.
Pas de Deux for Lovers.
That Which We Call a Rose.

**Drayton, Michael**
As love and I, late harbour'd in one inn.
Ballad of Agincourt, The.
Calling to mind since first my love begun.
Crier, The.
Dear, why should you command me to my rest.
Farewell to Love.
Fine Day, A.
First Steps up Parnassus.
Give Me Myself.
His Remedie for Love.

Idea.
Muses' Elizium, The, *sels.*
Shepherd's Sirena, The, *sels.*
To His Coy Love.
To Master George Sandys, Treasurer for the English Colony in Virginia, *sel.*
To My Most Dearly Loved Henry Reynolds, *sel.*
To My Noble Friend Master William Browne: Of the Evil Time, *sels.*
To the Reader of These Sonnets.
To the Virginian Voyage.
Verses Made the Night before He Died.

**Drennan, John Swanwick[***or***Swanick]**
Epigram: "Golden casket I designed, A."
Epigram: "Love signed the contract blithe and leal."
L'Amitié et l'Amour.
On the Telescopic Moon.

**Dresbach, Glenn Ward**
Cave, The.
Desert Song ("There's no hiding here in the glare of the desert").
Yucca in the Moonlight.

**Dresser, Paul**
Just Tell Them That You Saw Me, *with music.*
My Gal Sal, *with music.*
On the Banks of the Wabash, Far Away.

**Drew, Ray**
Goat Songs.

**"Drinan, Adam."** *See* **Macleod, Joseph Gordon**

**Drinkwater, John**
Birthright.
Invocation: "As pools beneath stone arches take."
Moonlit Apples.
Reciprocity.
Snail.
Sun, The.
Symbols.

**Driscoll, Jack**
Ice.

**Driscoll, Louis**
Thanksgiving.

**Dromgoole, Will Allen**
Building the Bridge.
Old Ladies.

**Dropkin, Celia**
Circus Dancer, A.

**Droste-Hulshoff, Annette von**
In the Grass.
Last Day of the Year, The (New Year's Eve)
On the Tower.

**Drouet, Minou**
Garden.

**Drummond, William, of Hawthorden**
Inexorable.
Ivory, Coral, Gold, The.
Madrigal: "Like the Idalian queen."
Madrigal: "This life which seems so fair."
Nativity, The.
Of Phyllis.
On Mary Magdalene.
Saint John [the] Baptist.
Sanquhar, whom this earth could scarce contain.
This world a hunting is.
World a Hunt, The.

**Drummond, William Henry**
Wreck of the *Julie Plante*, The.

**Dryden, John**
Absalom and Achitophel, Pt. I.
Achitophel: The Earl of Shaftesbury.
Ah, How Sweet It Is to Love!
Alexander's Feast: or, The Power of
  Music.
All, All of a Piece.
Amboyna; or, The Cruelties of the
  Dutch to the English Merchants, sel.
Amphitryon, sel.
Annus Mirabilis, sels.
Aureng-Zebe, sel.
Conquest of Granada, The, sel.
Crown Prince of Dullness, The.
Cymon and Iphigenia, sel.
Evening's Love, An, sel.
Farewell, Ungrateful Traitor.
Fire of London.
Hind and the Panther, The, sels.
Incantation to Oedipus.
Let him rail on, let his invective Muse.
Lines on a Paid Militia.
Lines on Seeing a Lock of Milton's Hair.
Lines Printed under the Engraved
  Portrait of Milton.
London after the Great Fire, 1666.
MacFlecknoe; or, A Satire upon the
  True-Blue Protestant Poet T. S.
Maiden Queen, The. sel.
Marriage à la Mode,sels.
Medal, The, sel.
Mercury's Song to Phaedra.
Ode, An: On the Death of Mr. Purcell.
Oedipus, sel.
Of these the false Achitophel was first.
On Jacob Tonson, His Publisher.
Portrait of "Og."
Prologue: "Our author by experience
  finds it true."
Prologue to His Royal Highness.
Reason and Religion.
Religio Laici, sel.
Revelation.
Rondelay, A: "Chloe found Amyntas
  lying."
Secular Masque, The.
Shadwell Anatomized.
Song: "Sylvia the fair, in the bloom of
  fifteen."
Song: "Whilst Alexis lay pressed."
Song for Saint Cecilia's Day, 1687, A.
Song of the Zambra Dance.
Song to a Fair Young Lady Going out
  of Town in the Spring.
Spanish Friar, The, sels.
To My Dear Friend Mr. Congreve, on
  His Comedy Called "The Double-
  Dealer."
To My Honour'd Kinsman, John
  Driden, of Chesterton, sel.
To the Memory of Mr. Oldham.
To the Pious Memory of the
  Accomplished Young Lady Mrs. Anne
  Killigrew.
Upon the Death of the Lord Hastings,
  sel.
Vox Populi.
War.
Why Should a Foolish Marriage Vow.
Zimri: The Duke of Buckingham.

**Dryden, John** *and* **Nahum Tate.**  *See* **Tate,
  Nahum** *and* **John Dryden**
**Du Bellay, Joachim**
Antiquitez de Rome, sels.
**Dubie, Norman**
About Infinity: A Self-Portrait.
Balalaika.
Dressing Stations, The.
In the Dead of the Night.
Killigrew Wood, The.
Monologue of Two Moons, Nudes with
  Crests. 1938.
Pastoral: "It all happened so fast. Fenya
  was in the straight chair."
Pennacesse Leper Colony for Women,
  The. Cape Cod. 1922.
**DuBois, William Edward Burghardt**
Song of the Smoke, The.
**Duché, Jacob**
Chilled by the Blasts of Adverse Fate,
  *with music.*
Great Lord of All, Whose Work of Love,
  *with music.*
**Duckett, Alfred A.**
Sonnet: "Where are we to go when this
  is done?"
**Dudek, Louis**
How Man Learned to Walk—and Run.
Morning Light.
Shredded Wheat.
**Dudley, William E.**
City, Lord, Where Thy Dear Life, The,
  *with music.*
**Duemer, Joseph**
Curses.
**Dufault, Peter Kane**
Evensong.
**Dufferin, Lady.**  *See* **Sheridan, Helen
  Selina**
**Duffield, George Jr.**
Stand Up! Stand Up for Jesus, *with
  music.*
**Dugan, Alan**
Actual Vision of Morning's Extrusion.
Adultery.
American against Solitude.
Aside.
Dedication for a Building.
Elegy for a Puritan Conscience.
Elegy: "I know but will not tell."
Fabrication of Ancestors.
For Masturbation.
From Heraclitus.
From Rome, for More Public Fountains
  in New York City.
Funeral Oration for a Mouse.
Holiday.
How We Heard the Name.
I never saw any point.
I've promised that I will not care about
  things.
Let Heroes Account to Love.
Letter to Eve.
Life and Death of the Cantata System,
  The.
Love Song: I and Thou.
Morning Song.
Niagara Falls.
On a Professional Couple in a Side-
  Show.
On a Seven-Day Diary.

On Alexander and Aristotle, on a Black-
  on-Red Greek Plate.
On Finding the Meaning of "Radiance."
On Hurricane Jackson.
On Rape Unattempted.
On Visiting Central Park Zoo.
On When McCarthy Was a Wolf
  amoung a Nation of Queer-Queers.
Plague of Dead Sharks.
Poem: "In the old days either the
  plaintiff or the defendant won or lost."
Poem: "Person who can do, The."
Poem: "What's the balm."
Prison Song.
Sailing to Jerusalem.
Stability before Departure.
Stutterer.
Thesis, Antithesis, and Nostalgia.
To a Red-headed Do-good Waitress.
Trial, A.
Tribute to Kafka for Someone Taken.
Two shots down and I'm exalted.
What Happened? What Do You Expect?
Winter: For an Untenable Situation.
Winter's Onset from an Alienated Point
  of View.
**Dugan, Michael**
Ella McStumping.
Herbaceous Plodd.
Rosemary's Teeth.
Thin Jake.
**Dugdale, Norman**
Anarchist.
**Duggan, Eileen**
Booty.
Bushfeller, The.
Have No Fear!
Juniper.
Pilgrimage.
Tides Run up the Wairau, The.
Truth.
Victory.
**Duguid, Sandra Ruth**
Bee, A/ Interestingly.
If it is a poem.
Maze of the Magi, A.
On Restoring Verticals.
Plato.
Rabbinic/ The cynic.
**Du Guillet, Pernette**
Chanson: "If they say my furred cloak."
**Duke, Richard**
After the fiercest pangs of hot desire.
Epithalamium upon the Marriage of
  Captain William Bedloe, An.
Panegyric upon Oates, A.
**Duke, William**
Hail Our Incarnate God! *with music.*
**Dumas, Edmund**
Our School Now Closes Out, *with music.*
**Dumas, Henry**
America.
Black Star Line.
Black Trumpeter.
Buffalo.
Knock on Wood.
Valentines.
**Dunann, Louella**
Hot Line.
**Dunbar, Paul Laurence**
Ante-Bellum Sermon, An.
Compensation.

Corn-Song, A.
Dawn.
Debt, The.
Frederick Douglass.
Harriet Beecher Stowe.
Haunted Oak, The.
In the Morning.
Life.
Misapprehension.
My Sort o' Man.
Negro Love Song, A.
Paradox, The.
Party, The.
Philosophy.
Poet, The.
Soliloquy of a Turkey.
Song, A: "Thou art the soul of a
   summer's day."
Spiritual, A.
Sympathy.
Then and Now.
To a Captious Critic.
Unsung Heroes, The.
We Wear the Mask.
When de Co'n Pone's Hot.
When Dey 'Listed Colored Soldiers.
When Malindy Sings.

**Dunbar, William**
Amendis to the Telyouris and Sowtaris
   for the Turnament Maid on Thame,
   The.
Ane Ballat of Our Lady, *sel.*
Lord Is Risen, The.
Of the Changes of Life.
Timor Mortis Conturbat Me.
To a Lady [*or* Ladye].
To the City of London.
Tretis of the Tua Mariit Wemen and the
   Wedo, The, *sel.*
Unto Us a Child Is Born.

**Duncan, Robert**
African Elegy, An.
After a Passage in Baudelaire.
Answering.
At Christmas.
At the Loom.
Ballad of Mrs. Noah, The.
Coming Out Of.
Dante Etudes, *sel.*
Envoy.
Etude from the Third Epistle.
Eyesight II.
Fire, The.
Fourth Song the Night Nurse Sang.
Homage and Lament for Ezra Pound in
   Captivity.
Interlude, An.
Law I Love Is Major Mover, The.
Moon, The.
Morning Letter, A.
My Mother Would Be a Falconress.
New Poem, A.
Night Scenes.
Often I Am Permitted to Return to a
   Meadow.
Orders.
Part-Sequence for Change, A.
Passage over Water.
Passages, *sels.*
Persephone.
Poem Beginning with a Line by Pindar,
   A.

Poetry, a Natural Thing.
Returning to Roots of First Feeling.
Roots and Branches.
Shelley's "Arethusa" Set to New
   Measures.
Sonnet I: "Now there is a love of which
   Dante does not speak unkindly."
Spring Memorandum, A.
Strains of Sight.
Tears of St. Francis.
Temple of the Animals, The.
This Place Rumord to Have Been
   Sodom.
Torso, The: Passages 18.
Tribal Memories.
Turning Into.
Two Presentations.
Up Rising.
What I Saw.
Where It Appears.

**Duncan, Ronald**
Written on a Girl's Table-Napkin at
   Wiesbaden.

**Duncan, William**
Emily Drowned.
Mother.

**Dunetz, Lora**
On the Night Express to Madrid.
Winter Nights.

**Dunkels, Marjorie**
Faith.

**Dunn, Douglas**
Clothes Pit, The.
From the Night-Window.
Hunched, The.
Landscape with One Figure.
Love Day, The.
New Girls, The.
On Roofs of Terry Street.
Removal from Terry Street, A.
Ships.

**Dunn, Gwen**
Reynard.

**Dunn, Stephen**
After He Said.
At Every Gas Station There Are
   Mechanics.
Biography in the First Person.
Building in Nova Scotia.
California, This Is Minnesota Speaking.
City Boy, The.
Cycle, The.
Day and Night Handball.
Dream, The.
For the Sleepless.
Giraffes: The American Version.
I Come Home Wanting to Touch
   Everywhere.
If I Were in Charge of Epiphanies.
Looking for a Rest Area.
Loss, The.
On Hearing the Airlines Will Use a
   Psychological Profile to Catch
   Potential Skyjackers.
Rapist, The.
Small Town: The Friendly.
To the Upright.

**Dunne, Carol**
Nursing the Hide.

**Dunsany, Edward John Moreton Drax
   Plunkett, 18th Baron**
Call to the Wild, A.

**Du Priest, Travis**
Experiential Religion.

**Durand, H. S.,** *and others*
Yale Boola!, *3 versions, with music.*

**Durcan, Paul**
Brighton Beach.
In Memoriam Brendan Behan.

**Durem, Ray**
Award.
Friends.
I Know I'm Not Sufficiently Obscure.
Problem in Social Geometry—The
   Inverted Square!
Vet's Rehabilitation.

**Durfey, Thomas**
Bee-hive, The.
Chloe's a Nymph.
Don Quixote, *sel.*
Early in the Dawning.
Gentle Breeze, A.
I'll Sail upon the Dog-Star.
Mountebank Song, The.
New Dialogue, Sung by a Boy and Girl
   at the Playhouse, A.
New Song Made in Honour of His
   Grace the Duke of Marlborough, A.

**Durham, Arlie "Franko"**
Prisoner, A.
Speeding.

**Durrell, Lawrence**
Ballad of the Oedipus Complex.
Bitter Lemons.
Coptic Poem.
Epitaph: "Stavro's dead. A truant vine."
Lesbos.
Mythology.
Nemea.
Poggio.
Seferis.
This Unimportant Morning.
To Ping-ku, Asleep.

**Durston, Georgia Roberts**
Hippopotamus, The.

**Duval, Quinton**
Morning Fog.

**DuVall, Jack**
Metroliner.

**Dwight, Timothy**
As Down a Lone Valley, *with music.*
Conquest of Canaan, The, *sel.*
Destruction of the Pequods, The.
Flourishing Village, The.
Gathering, The.
I Love Thy Kingdom, Lord, *with music.*
Prospect, The.
Shall Man, O God of Light, *with music.*
Sing to the Lord Most High, *with music.*
Triumph of Infidelity, The, *sel.*

**Dwyer, Frank**
On the Edge.

**Dybek, Stuart**
Flight.
In the Basement.
Lazarus.
Night of Voyeurs.
Poems of the Condemned Man, The.
Vivaldi.

**Dyer, Lady Catherine**
Epitaph on the Monument of Sir
   William Dyer At Colmworth, 1641.
If a large heart joined with a noble
   mind.

Sir William Dyer, Knight, *sels.*
**Dyer, Sir Edward**
　My Mind to Me a Kingdom Is.
　Silent Love, A.
**Dyer, John**
　Grongar Hill.
**Dylan, Bob**
　Dear Mister Congressman.
　Desolation Row.
　Father of Night.
　Hard Rain's a-Gonna Fall, A.
　Masters of War.
　Mister Tambourine Man.
　New Morning.
　One More Night.
　Sad-eyed Lady of the Lowlands.
　Subterranean Homesick Blues.
　Tears of Rage.
**Dyment, Clifford**
　As a boy with a richness of needs I
　　wandered.
　Man and Beast.
　Sanctuary.
　Sea Shanty.
　Swans, The.

**E**

**"Eagle, Solomon."** *See* **Squire, Sir John**
　**Collings**
**Earley, Tom**
　Jackdaw.
　Moorhen Pond, The.
　Rebel's Progress.
**"Eastaway, Edward."** *See* **Thomas, Edward**
**Eastburn, James Wallis**
　O Holy, Holy, Holy, Lord, *with music.*
**Eastman, Jon**
　Working the Skeet House.
**Eastwick, Ivy O.**
　Halloween.
**Eaton, Charles Edward**
　Cubistic Lovers, The.
　Last Page but One, The.
　Nude Poet, The.
　Seascape with Bookends.
　Squashes.
**Ebberts, Ruth N.**
　Kitchen Window.
**Eberhart, Nelle Richmond**
　At Dawning, *with music.*
**Eberhart, Richard**
　Analogue of Unity in Multeity.
　As If You Had Never Been.
　At Night.
　Attitudes, *sel.*
　Ball Game.
　Cancer Cells, The.
　Cold Fall.
　Cover me over, clover.
　Despair.
　Fear Death by Water.
　Flux.
　For a Lamb.
　Forms of the Human.
　Fury of Aerial Bombardment, The.
　Gods of Washington, D.C., The.
　Groundhog, The.

Hark Back.
Horse Chestnut Tree, The.
I walked over the grave of Henry James.
I Went to See Irving Babbitt.
If I Could Only Live at the Pitch That Is
　Near Madness.
In a Hard Intellectual Light.
Inability to Depict an Eagle.
Kaire.
Long Term Suffering.
"Loon Call, A."
"Mysticism Has Not the Patience to
　Wait for God's Revelation."
New England Bachelor, A.
New England Protestant.
On a Squirrel Crossing the Road in
　Autumn, in New England.
Plain Song Talk.
Reading Room, The New York Public
　Library.
Roc, The.
Rumination.
Sea Bells.
Sea-Hawk.
Snowfall, A.
Sonnet XV: "When dead the winter
　snows in crystals shine."
Soul Longs to Return Whence It Came,
　The.
Spider, The.
Spring Mountain Climb.
Stone Words for Robert Lowell.
Storm and Quiet.
Time's Offerings.
To Alpha Dryden Eberhart November
　26, 1977, on Being Seventy-five.
To the Field Mice.
Tobacconist of Eighth Street, The.
Two Loves.
Under the Hill.
United 555.
Vast Light.
When Doris Danced.
Yonder.
**Eberly, Ralph D.**
　Prodigal's Return.
**Eckman, Frederick**
　Old Man, Phantom Dog.
　Student, The.
**Economou, George**
　Seventh Georgic.
**Eddy, Gary**
　High Field—First Day of Winter.
**Eddy, Mary Baker**
　O'er Waiting Harp-Strings of the Mind,
　　*with music.*
　Shepherd, Show Me How to Go, *with*
　　*music.*
**Eddy, Zachary**
　Floods Swell around Me, Angry,
　　Appalling, *with music.*
　Jesus, Enthroned and Glorified, *with*
　　*music.*
**Edelman, Elaine**
　How Beautiful You Are: 3.
**Edey, Marion**
　August Afternoon.
　Trot Along, Pony.
**Edgcomb, Gabrielle**
　Columbus Day.
　Frog Prince.
　Telephone Connection.

**Edson, Russell**
　Childhood of an Equestrian, The.
　Children.
　Counting Sheep.
　In All the Days of My Childhood.
　Little Lady, The.
　Performance at Hog Theater, A.
　Pigeons.
　Prophylactic, The.
　Retirement of the Elephant, The.
　When the God Returns.
**Eggerth, Chuck**
　Much of Me.
**Ehrenburg, Ilya Grigoryevich**
　War Poem.
**Ehrhart, W. D.**
　Turning Thirty.
**Ehrlich, Shelley**
　On Linden Street.
**Ehrlichman, Lester**
　On Reading Mr. Ytche Bashes' Stories in
　　Yiddish.
**Eibel, Deborah**
　Freethinkers.
　Hagar to Ishmael.
　Kabbalist, The.
**Eichenrand, Lazer**
　From Life.
　Mute City, The.
　Prologue: "In your words."
**Eigner, Larry**
　All Intents.
　Closed System, The.
　Elysee.
　Fleche.
　Remember Sabbath Days.
**Eiseley, Loren C.**
　Deserted Homestead, The.
**Eisenberg, Susan**
　Grandpa Bear.
**Eisler, Hans and Bertolt Brecht.** *See*
　　**Brecht, Bertolt and Hans Eisler**
**Ela, David H.**
　Chosen Three, on Mountain Height,
　　The, *with music.*
**Eldan, Anadad**
　Samson Rends His Clothes.
　Who Will Give Cover?
　Words That Speak of Death.
**Eldridge, Paul**
　To a Courtesan a Thousand Years Dead.
**"Eliot, George" (Mary Ann [or Marian]**
　　**Evans Lewes Cross)**
　O May I join the Choir Invisible.
**Eliot, Thomas Stearns**
　Ash-Wednesday.
　Aunt Helen.
　*Boston Evening Transcript*, The.
　Burnt Norton.
　Cape Ann.
　Cat Morgan Introduces Himself.
　Chorus: "We do not wish anything to
　　happen."
　Chorus: "We have not been happy, my
　　Lord, we have not been too happy."
　Cousin Nancy.
　Cultivation of Christmas Trees, The.
　Dedication to My Wife, A.
　Dry Salvages, The.
　East Coker.
　Eyes that last I saw in tears.
　Four Quartets, *sels.*

Gerontion.
Growltiger's Last Stand.
Gus: The Theatre Cat.
Hippopotamus, The.
Hollow Men, The.
Journey of the Magi.
La Figlia Che Piange.
Lines for an Old Man.
Lines for Cuscuscaraway and Mirza
    Murad Ali Beg.
Lines to Ralph Hodgson, Esqre.
Little Gidding.
Love Song of J. Alfred Prufrock, The.
Macavity: The Mystery Cat.
Marina.
Morning at the Window.
Mr. Apollinax.
Murder in the Cathedral,*sels.*
Naming of Cats, The.
Portrait of a Lady.
Preludes (I–IV).
Rannoch, by Glencoe.
Rhapsody on a Windy Night.
Rock, The, *sel.*
Rum Tum Tugger, The.
Skimbleshanks: The Railway Cat.
Song for Simeon, A.
Song of the Jellicles, The.
Sweeney Agonistes, *sels.*
Sweeney among the Nightingales.
Sweeney Erect.
Virginia.
Waste Land, The.
Whispers of Immortality.
**Eliyia, Joseph**
Dream.
Epilogue: "I too was a little child once."
Rebecca.
Slender Maid.
Your Passing, Fleet Passing.
**Elizabeth I, Queen of England**
Doubt of Future Foes, The.
On Fortune.
On Monsieur's Departure.
When I was fair and young and favour
    graced me.
Written in Her French Psalter.
Written on a Wall at Woodstock.
Written with a Diamond on Her
    Window at Woodstock.
**Elizabeth of York, Queen**
My Heart Is Set upon a Lusty Pin.
**Ellenbogen, George**
Announcement, The.
Unter der Linde.
**Eller, David**
To a God Unknown.
**Ellerton, John**
Day Thou Gavest, Lord, Is Ended, The.
**Elliot, C. W.** *and* **J. R. Thomas**
Bonny Eloise.
**Elliot, Jane**
Flowers of the Forest, The; or, The
    Battle of Flodden.
Lament for Flodden, A.
**Elliott, Charlotte**
Just as I Am, *with music*
**Elliott, Ebenezer**
Beware of Dogmas.
Caged Rats.
Drone v. Worker.
Here lies the man who stripp'd Sin Bare.

How Different!
On a Rose in December.
On Communists.
Paddy, I have but stol'n your living.
Song: "When working blackguards come
    to blows."
Splendid Village, The, *sel.*
Steam, *sel.*
Tree of Rivelin, The.
**Elliott, George P.**
Her Dwarf.
**Elliott, Harley**
After Picking Rosehips.
Animals That Stand in Dreams, *sel.*
Before the Frost.
Blessed and Resting Uncle.
Brothers Together in Winter.
Changing a Tire by the Missouri River.
Crazy Horse Returns to South Dakota.
Natural Order of Things, The.
On a Country Road.
Outside Abilene.
Panda, The.
Passing Stockyards Where They Killed
    the Buffalo.
Planting, The.
Resident Stranger, The.
Thinking Twice in the Laundromat.
**Elliott, Patricia**
Stubborn Ground.
**Ellis, Colin**
Bungaloid Growth.
Epitaph, An: "He worshipped at the
    altar of Romance."
International Conference.
Modern World, The.
New Vicar of Bray, The.
Old Ladies, The.
On a Gentleman Marrying His Cook.
Romantic, The.
**Ellis, Conleth**
Flowers in Cellars.
Suppose We Sleep.
**Ellis, George**
Rondeau: "Of Eden lost, in ancient
    days."
**Ellis, Mary Anne**
Sonnet to a Tyrant.
**Ellis, Robert**
Hour of Sleep, The.
**Ellison, Joan Wyrick**
Mountain Heritage, A.
**Elsberg, John**
Art of Rowing, The.
**Elson, Virginia**
How Stars and Hearts Grow in Apples.
Not Being Wise.
**Elton, Charles**
Luriana, Lurilee.
**Eluard, Paul**
Curfew.
Lady Love.
One for All Time, The.
**Emans, Elaine V.**
Mistakable Identity.
Undreamed, The.
**Emanuel, James A.**
Church Burning: Mississippi.
Emmett Till.
For "Mr. Dudley," a Black Spy.
Get Up, Blues.
Negritude.

Negro, The.
Nightmare.
Old Black Men Say.
Panther Man.
Small Discovery, A.
Treehouse, The.
Voyage of Jimmy Poo, The.
Young Ones, Flip Side, The.
**Emerson, Ida** *and* **Joseph E. Howard.**   *See*
    **Howard Joseph E.** *and* **Ida Emerson**
**Emerson, Ralph Waldo**
Alphonso of Castile.
Apology, The.
Bacchus.
Blight.
Brahma.
Chickadee, The.
Compensation.
Concord Hymn.
Days.
Day's Ration, The.
Each and All.
Experience.
Fable: "Mountain and the squirrel,
    The."
Forbearance.
Give All to Love.
Good-bye.
Grace.
Guy.
Hamatreya.
Humble-Bee, The.
Mithridates.
Music.
Nature, ("The rounded world is fair to
    see").
Nature ("A subtle chain of countless
    rings").
Nemesis.
Ode Inscribed to W. H. Channing.
Pan.
Past, The.
Problem, The.
Prudence.
Rhodora, The.
Snow-Storm, The.
So Nigh Is Grandeur ("In an age of fops
    and toys").
Solution.
Song of Seyd Nimetollah of Kuhistan.
Sphinx, The.
Stars, the stars everlasting are fugitives
    also, The.
Terminus.
Test, The.
Thine Eyes Still Shined.
Threnody: "South-wind brings, The."
Titmouse, The.
Two Rivers.
Uriel.
Visit, The.
Voluntaries, *sel.*
Waldeinsamkeit.
We Love the Venerable House, *with
    music.*
Why did all manly gifts in Webster fail?
Woodnotes I ("When the pine tosses its
    cones").
Woodnotes II ("As sunbeams stream
    through liberal space").
Xenophanes.
**Emeruwa, Leatrice W.**

Making Out.
"Personals."
**Emig, Janet**
  Avalanche.
**Emin, Gevorg**
  Doesn't It Seem to You.
  Why Has This Ache.
**Emmett, Daniel Decatur**
  Boatman's Dance ("Boatman dance,
    boatman sing").
  Dixie ("I wish I was in the land of
    cotton"), *with music.*
  Old Dan Tucker.
**Emmons, Dick**
  Grass, Alas, The.
**Empson, William**
  Aubade: "Hours before dawn we were
    woken by the quake."
  Bacchus.
  Camping Out.
  Dissatisfaction with Metaphysics.
  Earth Has Shrunk in the Wash.
  Homage to the British Museum.
  Ignorance of Death.
  Invitation to Juno.
  Just a Smack at Auden.
  Legal Fiction.
  Let It Go.
  Missing Dates.
  Note on Local Flora.
  Reflection from Rochester.
  Scales, The.
  Sea Voyage.
  Success.
  Teasers, The.
  This Last Pain.
  To an Old Lady.
  Villanelle: "It is the pain, it is the pain,
    endures."
  World's End, The.
**Eng, Steve**
  Vanished.
**Engel, Mary**
  Promised Land.
**Engels, John**
  Crows, The.
  Moonwalk.
**Engle, John D., Jr.**
  Biology Lesson.
  Midway.
  Sonnet Sonnet.
**Engle, Paul**
  Dancer: Four Poems.
  In a Bar near Shibuya Station, Tokyo.
  Lord of Each Soul, *with music.*
  Moving In.
  Venus and the Lute Player.
**Engler, Robert Klein**
  Dichterliebe.
**English, Thomas Dunn**
  Ben Bolt; or, Ah! Don't You Remember.
**Enheduanna**
  Antiphonal Hymn in Praise of Inanna.
  Appeal to the Moongod Nanna-Suen to
    Throw Out Lugalanne.
  Condemning the Moongod Nanna.
  Crimes of Lugalanne.
  Curse on Uruk, A.
  Final Prayer.
  Inanna and An.
  Inanna and Ebih.
  Inanna and Enlil.

Inanna and Ishkur.
Inanna and the Anunna.
Inanna and the City of Uruk.
Inanna and the Divine Essences.
Restoration of Enheduanna to Her
  Former Station, The.
**Ennis, John**
  Deported.
**Enos, Fay**
  Question of Balance, A.
  Waiting.
**Enright, Dennis Joseph**
  Along the River.
  Always Learning.
  Am Steinplatz.
  And Two Good Things.
  Apocalypse.
  Buy One Now.
  Children Killed in War.
  Dreaming in the Shanghai Restaurant.
  Hard Core, The.
  In the Jungle.
  Insurance.
  Large Mercies.
  Means Test.
  Monuments of Hiroshima, The.
  Names.
  No Offence.
  Pitchfork Department.
  Public Bar
  Quagga, The.
  Royalties.
  Sensitive Philanthropist, The.
  Since Then.
  Spoilt.
  Streets.
  Sunday.
  Terminal.
  Training.
  Two Bad Things in Infant School.
  Ugly Neck.
  Underdeveloped Country, An.
  University Examinations in Egypt.
  Unlawful Assembly.
  Waiting for the Bus.
  Warm Protest.
**Enslin, Theodore (Ted)**
  District, The: Both Sides of Chandler
    River.
  On Such a Windy Afternoon.
  Wheat District, The.
**Enzensberger, Hans Magnus**
  Remote House.
**"Ephelia" (Joan Philips)**
  Maidenhead.
  To Philocles [*or* Phylocles], Inviting Him
    to Friendship.
**Epstein, Daniel Mark**
  Climbing.
  First Precinct Fourth Ward.
  Night Song from Backbone Mountain.
**Epstein, Elaine**
  Luck.
**Erickson, James**
  Fanny Brawne.
**Eristi-Aya**
  Letter to Her Mother, A.
**Erskine, Thomas Erskine, 1st Baron**
  James Alan Park/ Came naked stark.
  On Scott's "The Field of Waterloo."
  On Tom Moore's Translation of
    Anacreon.

**Eshleman, Clayton**
  Black Hat, The.
  Very Old Woman, A.
**Espírito Santo, Alda do**
  Same Side of the Canoe, The.
**Estes, Lawrence E.**
  Contentment.
**Esteves, Sandra Maria**
  Beginning, The/ is a circle.
  Cold place, A.
  Come into/ a quiet warm.
  For a sense of myself to sing.
  I am complexions of fire.
  I am the bird in transit for the winter.
  Untitled X.
  Vanguardia.
  When the snow falls softly.
  Where is the tree on which i stand.
**Etherege, Sir George**
  Ephelia to Bajazet.
**Etter, Dave**
  Autumn on the Wabash.
  Chicken.
  Fighter, The.
  Great Northern.
  House by the Tracks, A.
  Old Dubuque.
  Romp.
  Snow Country.
  Two Beers in Argyle, Wisconsin.
**Eugster, Carla**
  Raising Money.
**Eulert, Don**
  Transformation, The.
**Euripides**
  Greek Athlete, The.
  Hippolytus.
  Medea.
**Euwer, Anthony**
  Face, The.
  True Facts of the Case, The.
**Evans, Abbie Huston**
  In Space-Time Aware.
  Primary.
  Wrestling, The.
**Evans, Abel**
  Author's Epitaph, An. Written by
    Himself.
  Keep the commandments, Trapp, and go
    no further.
  On Sir John Vanbrugh, Architect.
  Tadlow.
**Evans, David Allan**
  Cattle Ghosts, The.
  Citizens' Complaint, The.
  Ford Pickup.
  Neighbors.
  Poem without a Metaphor.
  Pole Vaulter.
  Some lines after the Razing of the Sioux
    City Armour's Plant.
**Evans, Evan**
  Hall of Ifor Hael, The.
**Evans, Frances**
  Colours.
**Evans, H. A. C.**
  Egotist, The.
  Jimmy Jupp, Who Died of Over-eating.
  Liftman, The.
  Montgomery.
  Wasp, The.
**Evans, Margiad**

Rain.
Resurrection.
Snowdrops.
**Evans, Mari E.**
Alarm Clock, The.
And the Old Women Gathered.
Black Jam for Dr. Negro.
Emancipation of George-Hector (a
   Colored Turtle), The.
I Am a Black Woman.
If There Be Sorrow.
Into Blackness Softly.
Langston.
Marrow of My Bone.
Rebel, The.
Spectrum.
To Mother and Steve.
Uhuru.
Vive Noir!
When in Rome.
Where Have You Gone.
Who Can Be Born Black.
**Evans, Mary Ann [or Marian].** *See* **"Eliot,**
   **George"**
**Evans, Nathaniel**
To Thee, Then, Let All Beings Bend,
   *with music.*
**Evans, Virgina Moran**
Window to the East
**Eve, Barbara**
My Daughter's Ring.
Scenario.
**Everaerts, Jan Nicolai.** *See* **Johannes**
   **Secundus**
**Everhard, Jim**
Cute.
**Everson, William (Brother Antoninus)**
August.
Bard.
Canticle to the Waterbirds, A.
Dark Roots of the Rose, The.
First Winter Storm.
Flight in the Desert, The.
Gash, The.
In All These Acts.
Lava Bed.
Making of the Cross, The.
One Fragment for God.
Poet Is Dead, The.
Raid, The.
Rose of Solitude, The.
San Joaquin.
Song the Body Dreamed in the Spirit's
   Mad Behest, The.
South Coast, The.
Stranger, The.
Trifles.
Vision of Felicity, The.
We in the Fields.
What Birds Were There.
Winter Ploughing.
Year's End.
Zone of Death.
**Everwine, Peter**
Brother, The.
Burden of Decision, The.
Clearing, The.
Distance.
Drinking Cold Water.
For the Coming Year.
Going.
In the End.

Learning to Speak.
Marsh, New Year's Day, The.
Night.
Perhaps It's as You Say.
Routes.
Someone Knocks.
We Meet in the Lives of Animals.
**"Evoe."** *See* **Knox, Edmund George Valpy**
**Evtushenko, Evgeny.** *See* **Yevtushenko,**
   **Yevgeny.**
**Ewart, Gavin**
Lifelines.
Lines: "Other day I was loving a sweet
   little fruitpie-and-cream, The."
Love Song.
Miss Twye.
New Poet Arrives, A.
Officers' Mess.
2001: The Tennyson/Hardy Poem.
Wanting Out.
Weather, The.
When a Beau Goes In.
Xmas for the Boys.
**Ewer, W. N.**
How odd/ Of God.
**Ewing, Juliana Horatia**
Burial of the Linnet, The.
Dolls' Wash, The.
Friend in the Garden, A.
Garden Lore.
Willow-Man, The.
**Ezekiel, Nissim**
How My Father Died.
Lamentation: "My lips lack prophecy."
Totem.
**Ezell, Allamae**
Candidate, The.

**F**

**"F.P.A."** *See* **Adams, Franklin Pierce**
**Faber, Frederick William**
Come to Jesus.
Faith of Our Fathers, *with music.*
**Fabilli, Mary**
Letter to Robert.
Rock, The.
**Fabio, Sarah Webster**
Black Man's Feast.
Chromo.
Evil Is No Black Thing.
**Fagg, Martin**
Elegy on Thomas Hood.
**Fahy, Christopher**
Bunny.
Miss Ada.
**Fahy, Francis A.**
Queen of Connemara, The.
**Fainlight, Harry**
Bride, A.
Morning.
**Fainlight, Ruth**
Fire-Queen.
God's Language.
Hebrew Sibyl, The.
Lilith.
Sibyl of the Waters.
Sleep-Learning.

**Fairbairn, Nicholas**
Love in Edinburgh.
**Fairburn, Arthur Rex Dugard**
Back Street.
Cave, The.
Conversation in the Bush.
Down on My Luck.
Elements.
Epithalamium: "We have found our
   peace, and move with a turning
   globe."
Estuary, The.
Farewell, A: "What is there left to be
   said?"
For an Amulet.
Full Fathom Five.
I'm Older than You, Please Listen.
Imperial.
Rhyme of the Dead Self.
Solitude.
Tapu.
Winter Night.
**Fairchild, B. H.**
Late Game.
**Faiz, Faiz Ahmed**
Day Death Comes, The.
**Falckner, Justus**
Rise, Ye Children, *with music.*
**Falco, Edward**
Apology to My Lady.
**Falconer, Ross**
It Is Impossible.
**Falconer, William**
Description of a Ninety Gun Ship.
**Falk, Marcia**
Modern Kabbalist.
Shulamit in Her Dreams.
Woman through the Window.
**Falkner, John Meade**
After Trinity.
Arabia.
Christmas Day.
**Fallis, Edwina**
Wise Johnny.
**Fallon, Padraic**
Assumption.
For Paddy Mac.
Head, The.
Mary Hines.
Odysseus.
Pot Shot.
Weir Bridge.
Young Fenians, The.
**Fandel, John**
About My Students.
Out of Our Blue, sels.
**Fane, Mildmay, Earl of Westmorland.** *See*
   **Westmorland, Mildmay Fane, 2d Earl**
   **of**
**Fanshawe, Catherine**
Fragment in Imitation of Wordsworth.
**Fanshawe, Sir Richard**
Great Favorit Beheaded, A.
Ode, An, upon Occasion of His
   Majesty's Proclamation in the Year
   1630.
Of Beauty.
**Fanthorpe, U. A.**
Consultant's Holiday.
For Saint Peter.
In-Patients.
Job Description: Medical Records.

Patients.
Sexual Delinquent.
Welcome.

**Farber, Allan D.**
Skipping Stones.

**Farber, Norma**
Bow Down, Mountain, *with music.*
Crooked Carol.
Dove.
Hatch, The.
Hog at the Manger.
How They Brought the Good News by
    Sea.
Jubilate Herbis.
Judas, Joyous Little Son.
Ladybug's Christmas.
Nothing Gold Can Stay.
Spider.

**Farhi, Musa Moris**
God and Nature.
Paths to God.
Smile at Me.
Thirst.
Who Says.

**Faricy, Austin**
Through Warmth and Light of Summer
    Skies, *with music.*

**Farina, Richard**
Birmingham Sunday.

**Farjeon, Annabel**
Ode to a Fat Cat.

**Farjeon, Eleanor**
A Is for Abracadabra.
Alexander to His Horse.
Argus and Ulysses ("Argus was a
    puppy").
Blackfriars.
Cat.
Cats.
Children's Carol, The.
Dragonfly, A.
Holly and Mistletoe.
In the Week When Christmas Comes.
Jenny White and Johnny Black.
Kitten, A.
Lewis Carrol.
Mrs. Malone.
Neptune.
News! News!
Night Will Never Stay, The.
Quarrel, The.
Sounds in the Evening, The.
Tailor.
Waves.
White Horses.
Wish, A.
Witch, The! The Witch!

**Farjeon, Eleanor** *and* **Herbert Farjeon**
Henry VIII.

**Farley, Henry**
To see a strange outlandish fowl.

**Farley, Hilary-Anne**
This Is a Poem.

**Farley, Jean**
Night Riders.

**Farley, Susan**
How to Own Land.

**Farrar, Jim**
Bones Found in Chalk.
Hokusai.
Hurrying Home.
It Is Good to Know You.

Life Dance.
Two Alternatives to One Moment's
    Experience.

**Farrar, John**
Ambitious Mouse, The.
Chanticleer.
Serious Omission.

**Farrar, Winifred Hamrick**
Pushed to the Scroll.

**Farren, Robert Roibéard O'Faracháin**
Pets, The.
Rich Morning.

**Farrokhzad, Forugh**
Born Again.
I'm Sad.
In the land of dwarfs.
On Earth.
Once More.

**Faubion, Dorothy**
Wash-Day Wonder.

**Faucher, Real**
Archaeologists.

**Faulkner, Margherita**
Suppositions.

**Fauset, Jessie Redmond**
Oriflamme.

**Fawcett, Edgar**
To an Oriole.

**Fawcett, John**
Blest Be the Tie That Binds, *with music.*

**Fearing, Kenneth**
American Rhapsody (4).
Any Man's Advice to His Son.
C Stands for Civilization.
Confession Overheard in a Subway.
Cracked Record Blues.
Cultural Notes.
Dear Beatrice Fairfax.
Denouement.
Dirge: "1–2–3 was the number he played
    but today the number came 3–2–1."
Dividends.
Evening Song.
Green Light.
Love, 20¢ the First Quarter Mile.
Memo.
No Credit.
Obituary.
Pact.
Pay-off.
Requiem: "Will they stop."
Resurrection.
Thirteen o'Clock.
Tomorrow.
Twentieth-Century Blues.
Yes, the Agency Can Handle That.

**Federman, Raymond**
Lune Concrete.

**Fedo, David**
Camping at Thunder Bay.

**Fedullo, Mick**
In My Brother's House.

**Feela, David J.**
Cut.
Vigil.

**Fein, Rebecca**
Unripe Peach, An.

**Feinberg, Harvey**
Welcome.

**Feinstein, Elaine**
Against Winter.
Dad.

Our Vegetable Love Shall Grow.
Survivors.
Under Stone.

**Feirstein, Frederick**
Boarder, The.
"Grandfather" in Winter.
Spring.

**Feise, Heine**
Asra, The.

**Feldman, Alan**
Personals, The.

**Feldman, Irving**
Handball Players at Brighton Beach,
    The.
My Olson Elegy.
No-Night, The.
"Portrait de Femme."
Pripet Marshes, The.
So It Happens.
Two, The.

**Feldman, Ruth**
Lilith.
Nocturne: Homage to Whistler.

**Feldman, Susan**
How the Invalids Make Love.
Intruder.
Lamentations of an Au Pair Girl.
Sea Legs.

**Felix, Tanya**
Red Flowers.

**Felltham, Owen**
Sympathy, The.

**Fenderson, Mark**
Smart Little Bear, The.

**Fenton, Elizabeth**
Masks.
Under the Ladder to Heaven.

**Fenton, James** *and* **John Fuller**
Poem against Catholics.

**Ferguson, David**
Norman Morrison.

**Ferguson, James**
Auld Daddy Darkness.

**Ferguson, John**
Cock Crowing in a Poulterer's Shop, A.

**Ferguson, Robert**
Atlantis.

**Ferguson, Sir Samuel**
Fairy Thorn, The.
Lament for the Death of Thomas Davis.

**Fergusson, Robert**
Hallow-Fair.

**Fericano, Paul F.**
Clockwork.
Katherine.

**Ferlinghetti, Lawrence**
After the Cries of the Birds.
Assassination Raga.
Away above a Harborful.
Christ Climbed Down.
Coney Island of the Mind, A, *sels.*
Crazy/ to be alive in such a strange.
Dog.
Don't Let That Horse.
Fortune.
Frightened/ by the sound of my own
    voice.
General Song of Humanity, The.
I Am Waiting.
In Golden Gate Park That Day.
In Goya's Greatest Scenes.
In Woods Where Many Rivers Run.

Junkman's Obbligato.
Lost Parents.
One Thousand Fearful Words for Fidel
   Castro.
Oral Messages, *sel.*
Pennycandystore beyond the El, The.
Populist Manifesto.
Salute!
Starting from San Francisco.
Terrible/ a horse at night.
Third World, The.
This life is not a circus where.
Truth is not the secret of a few.
Underwear.
What could she say to the fantastic
   foolybear.
Wild Dreams of a New Beginning.
World Is a Beautiful Place, The.
Wounded Wilderness of Morris Graves,
   The.
**Fernandez, Carlos**
Cielito Lindo, *with music.*
**Fernandez, Ramon**
To the Sun.
**Ferre, Rosario**
I Hear You've Let Go.
**Ferril, Thomas Hornsby**
Always Begin Where You Are.
Lens for Plum Blossom.
Morning Star.
Noon.
Prairie Melts, The.
Swallows.
Waltz against the Mountains.
Wood.
**Ferriter, Pierce**
Lay Your Arms Aside.
**Ferry, David**
Johnson on Pope.
**Fertig, Nelle**
I Have Come to the Conclusion.
**Fetherling, Doug**
Bathing with Father.
Dialogue 4 1 Voice Only.
Diseases of the Moon.
Dispatch Number Nine.
Dispatch Number Sixteen.
Dispatch Number Sixty.
Genius Loci of the Morning.
Nights Passed on Ward's Island,
   Toronto Harbour.
Sex Play in Four Acts.
Shacked Up at the Ritz.
She Employed the Familiar "Tu" Form.
Your Absence Has Not Taught Me.
**Fethy, Sir John**
My Trewth Is Plicht.
**Fewell, Richard**
"Duke" and the "Count," The.
**Fey, Isabella**
Bad Example.
**Fiacc, Padraic**
Boy and the Geese, The.
Brendan Gone.
Deranged.
Gloss.
Haemorrhage.
Poet, The.
Saint Colman's Song for Flight.
Son of a Gun.
**Fialkowski, Barbara**
To Sleep.

**Fichman, Jakov**
Abishag.
Eve.
**Ficke, Arthur Davison**
Four Japanese Paintings, *sel.*
Perspective of Co-ordination.
**Fickert, Kurt J.**
End of a Meaningful Relationship, The.
Sleeping Alone.
**Fiedler, Leslie A.**
No Ghost Is True.
**Field, Charles K.**
Barriers Burned.
**Field, Edward**
Bill to My Father, A.
Bride of Frankenstein, The.
Celebrity, The.
Curse of the Cat Woman.
Donkeys.
Frankenstein.
Graffiti.
Icarus.
Lost, Dancing, The.
My Polish Grandma.
New York.
Ode to Fidel Castro.
Reservoir, The.
Roaches.
Sleeper, The.
Statue of Liberty, The.
Unwanted.
**Field, Eugene**
At Cheyenne.
Boy, The.
Coquetry.
Death of Robin Hood, The.
Duel, The.
Fly-away Horse, The.
Little Boy Blue.
Little Peach, The.
Pioneer, The.
Rock-a-by Lady, The.
Song: "Why do bells for Christmas
   ring?"
Sugar-Plum Tree, The.
'Tis Strange.
Wanderer, The.
Wynken, Blynken, and Nod.
**Field, Matt**
Farm Wife.
Rondel: Autumn.
**"Field, Michael" (Katherine Bradley *and*
   Edith Cooper)**
After Mass.
Macrinus against Trees.
**Field, Rachel Lyman (Mrs. Arthur
   Pederson)**
City Rain.
Fourth of July.
Green Fiddler, The.
Hills, The.
Merry-go-round.
Peabody Bird, The.
Skyscrapers.
Snow in the City.
Something Told the Wild Geese.
**Fielder, E. A.**
Of the Sea, a Song.
**Fields, Dorothy**
I Can't Give You Anything but Love,
   *with music.*
**Fields, Edelin Coleman**

Jazzman, The.
Saturday's Child.
**Fields, James Thomas**
Alarmed Skipper, The.
Ballad of the Tempest.
Jupiter and Ten.
Owl-Critic, The.
**Fields, Julia**
Aardvark.
Alabama.
Harlem in January.
High on the Hog.
Madness One Monday Evening.
No Time for Poetry.
Poem for Heroes, A.
Poems: Birmingham 1962–1964.
**Figueroa Aymerich, Angela**
Women at the Market.
**Finch, Anne (b.1908)**
Essay on Marriage, *sel.*
**Finch, Anne, Countess of Winchilsea.** *See*
   **Winchilsea, Anne Finch, Countess of**
**Finch, Francis Miles**
Blue and the Gray, The.
Nathan Hale.
**Finch, Robert**
Words.
**Finefrock, Margaret**
Demonstration.
**Fineran, Mary C.**
Night Train.
**Finkel, Donald**
Cain's Song.
Cross-eyed Lover, The.
Feeding the Fire.
Finders Keepers.
Genealogy.
Gesture.
Great Wave, The: Hokusai.
Hands.
How Things Fall.
Hunting Song.
It Makes No Difference.
King Midas Has Asses' Ears.
Lame Angel.
Lilith.
Metaphysic of Snow.
They.
Time Out.
When I Was Young I Tried to Sing.
**Finlay, Ian Hamilton**
Bedtime.
Black Tomintoul.
Dancers Inherit the Party, The.
Fisherman's Cross.
Green Waters.
Horizon of Holland, The.
It/ it is here.
**Finley, C. Stephen**
October Dusk.
To One Far Away, Dancing.
**Finley, Jeanne**
Dead of the World, The.
Divorce Dress, The.
**Finne, Diderik**
Apollo 113.
**Finnigan, Joan**
May Day Rounds: Renfrew County, *sel.*
Noon Hour.
**Firdausi [*or* Firdosi]**
When the sword of sixty comes nigh his
   head.

**Firestone, Laya**
Crow, Straight Flier, but Dark.
For Gabriel.
Listen to the Bird.
Thoughts for My Grandmother.
**Fischer, Otakar**
From the Depths.
**Fish, Mira**
Cape Cod Murders, 1968.
Oh, Say, Mr. Toffler.
Poem: "Four miles out the tide curls in."
Poem: "You jam your arm into the white air."
Pregnancy.
**Fishback, Margaret**
Babies: Just Babies.
**Fisher, Aileen**
Benjamin Jones Goes Swimming.
Birthday Cake.
Christmas Mouse.
Clouds.
Feather-Stitching.
Frog's Lament, The.
Halloween Concert.
Holes of Green.
Moles.
Sandpile Town.
Shivers.
Spinning Earth, The.
Winter Mouse.
**Fisher, David**
Spassky at Reykjavik.
**Fisher, Harrison**
Chance You Take, The.
Crimes They Got Away With.
Purity in What You Do.
**Fisher, Mahlon Leonard**
In Cool, Green Haunts.
**Fisher, Roy**
City.
**Fishman, Charles**
August 12, 1952.
**Fishman, Rachel**
Even If.
In the Beginning.
**Fiske, Horace Spencer**
Ballad of the Pigskin.
Cry of the High Hurdlers, The.
**Fitch, Eleazar Thompson**
By Vows of Love Together Bound, *with music.*
Lord, at This Closing Hour, *with music.*
**Fitton, Molly**
Linger longer, Olga.
**Fitts, Dudley**
Southwest Passage.
To His Mistress.
**Fitzgerald, F. Scott**
Football.
**Fitzgerald, Jacqueline M.**
Two and the Sea.
**Fitzgerald, Robert**
Cobb Would Have Caught It.
July in Indiana.
Metaphysical.
Metaphysician.
Midsummer.
Mise en Scène.
Park Avenue.
Patrum Propositum.
Shore of Life, The.
Song for September.

**Fitzgerald, Robert David**
Beginnings.
Face of the Waters, The.
Fifth Day.
Height.
Song in Autumn.
**Fitzpatrick, Susan**
More Than.
**Fixmer, Clyde**
Canal Street, Chicago.
**Flaccus, Aulus Persius.** *See* **Persius**
**Flaccus, Quintus Horatius.** *See* **Horace**
**Flagg, Hannah.** *See* **Gould, Hannah Flagg**
**Flagg, James Montgomery**
Table Manners.
**Flaherty, Doug**
Coming On to Winter.
For a Girl Whose Slow-Dying Called for My Blood.
Lake Flies of Winnebago, The.
Raspberries.
**Flanagan, Robert**
Atlas.
Heirloom.
State Message: A Midwestern Small Town.
**Flanders, Jane**
Cloisonne.
Real Jane Flanders, The.
Sarah's Song.
Stars Shine So Faithfully.
**Flanders, Lorraine**
When You Blow on Dog.
**Flanner, Hildegarde**
Dictionary.
Driving Clock.
Farewell, A: "My cat was a southerner and a lady."
Hawk Is a Woman.
Let Us Believe.
Moment.
Moon Song.
Noon on Alameda Street.
Prayer for This Day.
Slow Boone.
Smith Brothers' Lumber Shed.
Sonnets in Quaker Language, *sels.*
Swift Love, Sweet Motor.
This Day.
12 o'Clock Freight.
**Flantz, Richard**
Shir Ma'alot/ A Song of Degrees.
**Flatman, Thomas**
Appeal to Cats in the Business of Love, An.
Nudus Redibo.
On Marriage.
On Mrs. E. Montague's Blushing in the Cross-bath.
Song on New Year's Day before the King, A.
**Flax, Hjalmar**
Art.
Littoral.
**Flecker, James Elroy**
Epilogue: "Away, for we are ready to a man!"
Fragment, A: "I have heard a voice of broken seas."
Golden Journey to Samarkand, The, *sels.*
In Hospital.
Lord Arnaldos.

Old Ships, The.
Oxford Canal.
Parrot, The.
Prologue: "We who with songs beguile your pilgrimage."
Santorin.
**Flecknoe, Richard**
Stillborn Silence.
**Fleg, Edmond**
Dead Cities Speak to the Living Cities, The.
**Fleming, Elizabeth**
Who's In?
**Fleming, Gerald**
Let Go: Once.
**Fleming, Marjory**
Sonnet, A: "O lovely O most charming pug."
**Fletcher, Curley W.**
High-loping Cowboy, The.
Strawberry Roan, The.
**Fletcher, Giles, the Elder**
Licia, *sels.*
**Fletcher, Giles, the Younger**
Celestial City, The.
Christ's Victory and Triumph, *sels.*
He Was Made Man.
Palm Sunday: Good Friday.
**Fletcher, John**
Away, Delights.
Captain, The, *sel.*
Care-charming Sleep.
Chances, The, *sel.*
Faithful Shepherdess, The, *sels.*
Hear, Ye Ladies.
Hymn to Pan.
Love's Emblems.
Mad Lover, The, *sels.*
Melancholy ("Hence, all you vain delights").
Sweet Music's Power.
Tragedy of Valentinian, The, *sels.*
**Fletcher, John** and *See* **Beaumont, Francis** and **John Fletcher**
**Fletcher, John** and **William Rowley**
Maid in the Mill, The, *sel.*
**Fletcher, John** and others
Bloody Brother, The, *sel.*
Drink Today.
**Fletcher, John Gould**
Arizona Poems, *sels.*
Lincoln, *sel.*
Mexican Quarter.
Monadnock, The.
Rain in the Desert.
**Fletcher, Julia A.** *See* **Carney, Julia A. Fletcher**
**Fletcher, Phineas**
Divine Lover, The.
Divine Wooer, The, *sel.*
Drop, Drop, Slow Tears.
Locusts or Appolyonists, The, *sel.*
To My Soul in Its Blindness.
**Fletcher, Robert H.**
Ballad of Pug-nosed Lil, The.
**Flexner, Hortense**
Contemporary.
When Last Seen.
**Flint, Francis Stewart**
Eau-Forte.
**Flint, James**

In Pleasant Lands Have Fallen the
Lines, *with music.*
**Flint, Roland**
Follow.
His Good Time.
Skin.
**Flocos, Nicholas**
Allegiance to Aphrodite.
Bogart.
Coin from B.C.
Comfort from Arcadia.
Garden Blooms.
Gossip.
In the Gazebo.
Old Upright I Did Not Learn to Play,
The.
Salt.
**Florencia del Pinar**
Another Song of the Same Woman, to
Some Partridges, Sent to Her Alive.
**Flower, Robin**
Forest of Dean, The.
Passage at Night, The—The Blaskets.
**Flower, Sarah.** *See* **Adams, Sarah Flower**
**Floyd, Virginia**
Life, the Eternal Sacrament.
Street Where I Live, The.
World, Hold Me Close.
**Flynn, Elizabeth**
After Grave Deliberation.
**Flynn, Joseph**
Down Went McGinty, *with music.*
**Flynn, M. P.**
Decision.
Down in the Field.
Sandlot Days.
**Foerster, Richard**
Archne.
Nantucket's Widows.
**Fogel, Daniel Mark**
Metamorphic.
**Fogerty, John C.**
Bad Moon Rising.
Don't Look Now.
Have You Ever Seen the Rain?
**Fogle, Richard Harter**
Hawthorne Garland, A.
**Foley, James William**
Scientific Proof.
**Folger, Peleg**
Praise Ye the Lord. O Celebrate His
Fame, *with music.*
**Folk, Pat**
Empty Holds a Question.
Senile.
**Follen, Eliza Lee**
Lord, Deliver, Thou Canst Save, *with
music.*
O, Look at the Moon.
**Fondane, Benjamin**
By the Waters of Babylon.
Hertza.
Lullaby for an Emigrant.
Plain Song.
Wandering Jew, The.
**Fontaine, Jean de la.** *See* **La Fontaine,
Jean de**
**Fonte Boa, Maria Amalia**
Two Tile Beaks.
Vitality.
**Foot, Edward Edwin**

On the Inauguration of the Memorial
Statue, *sel.*
**Foote, Lucius Harwood**
Sutter's Fort, Sacramento.
**Foote, Samuel**
Great Panjandrum, The.
**Forbes, Calvin**
Chocolate Soldiers, The.
For You.
Gabriel's Blues.
Hand Me Down Blues.
Hours, The.
Lullaby for Ann-Lucian.
My Father's House.
Reading Walt Whitman.
**Forbes, John**
Ode to Tropical Skiing.
**Forché, Carolyn**
Burning the Tomato Worms.
Departure.
Kalaloch.
Reunion.
Taking Off My Clothes.
**Ford, Charles Henri**
Bad Habit, The.
January wraps up the wound of his arm.
Overturned Lake, The.
Plaint.
Somebody's Gone.
There's No Place to Sleep in This Bed,
Tanguy.
**Ford, Dan**
Love Is Loathing & Why.
**Ford, Ford Madox** (*formerly* **Ford Madox
Hueffer**)
Cat of the House, The.
Sanctuary, The.
**Ford, Francis Alan**
Song of the Gulf Stream.
**Ford, Gena**
Legacy.
Lines for a Hard Time.
Nude on the Bathroom Wall, The.
**Ford, John**
Broken Heart, The,*sels.*
Love's Martyrs.
**Ford, Michael C.**
For James Joyce.
**Ford, R. A. D.**
Revenge of the Hunted.
Sleeplessness of Our Time.
**Ford, Walter H.**
Sunshine of Paradise Alley, The, *with
music.*
**Forde, Ken**
X2s and 42s (Into Northeast
Washington).
**Foreman, Paul**
Yevtushenko!
**Forgotson, E. S.**
Elderly Nobody Erases Self in Central
Park.
**Foriyes, Tina**
Genealogy of a Generation.
**Forman, Nicole**
Labour of the Brain, Ballad of the Body.
**Fortini, Franco**
For Our Soldiers Who Fell in Russia.
Gutter, The.
In Memoriam I ("You used to ask me
once what was wrong").

In Memoriam II ("I do not
understand").
**Fortunatus.** *See* **Venantius Fortunatus,
Saint**
**Fosdick, Harry Emerson**
Prince of Peace His Banner Spreads,
The, *with music.*
**Fosdick, W. W.**
Aura Lea [*or* Lee], *with music.*
**Foss, Sam Walter**
Husband and Heathen.
Philosopher, A.
**Foster, Donald**
Triad.
**Foster, Stephen Collins**
Beautiful Dreamer.
Camptown Races, The [*or* De].
Jeanie with the Light Brown Hair.
My Old Kentucky Home.
Nelly Bly.
Oh! Susanna.
Old Black Joe, *with music.*
Old Dog Tray.
Old Folks at Home, The.
Who Has Our Redeemer Heard, *with
music.*
**Foulkes, William H.**
Take Thou Our Minds, Dear Lord, *with
music.*
**Fowler, Andrew**
Awake, My Soul! In Grateful Songs,
*with music.*
O Gracious Jesus, Blessed Lord! *with
music.*
**Fowler, Gene**
Flowering Cacti, The.
Her Majesty's Ship.
Hunting Song.
Indians, The.
Last Ancestor, The.
Shaman Songs 12.
Venus' Return to the Sea.
Vivisection.
**Fowler, Russell T.**
In Blanco County.
**Fowles, John**
Barbarians.
**Fowlkes, Constance**
Silver Bullet, The.
**Fox, Eldon Ray**
Bumper Sticker, The, on His Pickup
Said, "I'm a Lover, I'm a Fighter, I'm
a Wild Bull Rider."
**Fox, Gail**
For Anne, Who Doesn't Know.
**Fox, Hugh**
Apotheosis of Olde Towne, *sel.*
"Christ That Was a Real One," He Said.
His Reaction to Her Asking for a
Divorce.
She Was Always Knitting, Weaving.
Swing in the Willow Swung Out, The.
There Was Something White Sticking
Out of the Sand.
**Fox, Lucia**
Dream of the Forgotten Lover.
**Fox, Siv Cedering**
Cup of the Bear, The, *abr.*
Hands.
In the Taxidermist's Shop.
Ornithology.
Poem for My Mother.

Poem: "From what strange country do you come, then?"
River and Light.
**Fox-Smith, C.**
Mules.
**Foxton, Thomas**
On a Little Boy's Endeavouring to Catch a Snake.
Upon Boys Diverting Themselves in the River.
**Fraire, Isabel**
If night takes the form of a whale and.
**Frame, Janet**
At Evans Street.
Clown, The.
Footballer in the Small Room, The.
Foxes, The.
Rain on the Roof.
Telephonist.
Wet Morning.
When the Sun Shines More Years than Fear.
Yet Another Poem about a Dying Child.
**Frances, Harriette**
Holy Roller.
**Francis, Colin**
Tony O.
**Francis, Joseph G.**
Elephant Sat on Some Kegs, An.
Genial Grimalkin, The.
**Francis, Pat Therese**
Poem for a Neighbor.
Telephone Operator, The.
**Francis, Robert**
As Near to Eden.
Base Stealer, The.
Bouquets.
Burial.
By Night.
Catch.
Cold.
Cromwell.
Delicate the Toad.
Diver.
Edith Sitwell Assumes the Role of Luna.
Fair and Unfair.
Fall.
Farm Boy after Summer.
Fear, A.
Good Life, The.
Hallelujah: A Sestina.
High Diver.
Hound, The.
Juniper.
Like Ghosts of Eagles.
Night Train.
Part for the Whole.
Pitcher.
Play Ball!
Seagulls.
Silent Poem.
Sing a Song of Juniper.
Skier.
Spell.
Swimmer.
That Dark Other Mountain.
Though a Fool.
Two Wrestlers.
Watching Gymnasts.
Waxwings.
**Francis of Assisi, Saint**
Cantica: Our Lord Christ: of Order.

Simple Prayer, A.
**Francisco, Edward**
Lilith's Child.
**Franco, Veronica**
No more words! To the field, to arms.
**Frank, Peter**
On the Death of My Beard.
**Frankau, Gilbert**
Gun Teams.
**Franzen, John**
O God of Stars and Distant Space, *with music.*
**Fraser, Antonia**
My Mind to Me a Kingdom Is.
**Fraser, George S.**
Christmas Letter Home.
Death of My Grandmother, The.
Hometown Elegy.
Lean Street.
To Hugh MacDiarmid.
Traveller Has Regrets, The.
**Fraser, Kathleen**
Agnes.
Casa de Pollos.
Change of Address.
Dresses.
Flowers.
History of My Feeling, The.
How Tuesday Began.
Loving.
One of the Chapters.
Poem for a Hustler.
Poem in Which My Legs Are Accepted.
Poem Wondering If I'm Pregnant.
Poems for the New.
What You Need.
**Fraser, Ray**
Before You're a Stranger.
Cry of an Aged One, The.
Ecole St. Luc.
Flora.
Grotto, The.
In an Empty Window.
Lost Picture.
Not Often.
On Learning to Play the Guitar.
Policemen Laughing.
Souster.
**Frate, Frank**
Love Poem Investigation for A. T.
**Freebairn, A. L.**
Ride 'Im Cowboy.
**Freedgood, Laura**
Ruth.
**Freedman, William**
Benediction.
Formations.
**Freeman, Arthur**
Cat, Caged and Shrunken, The.
**Freeman, Carol [or Carole]**
Christmas Morning, I.
Do Not Think.
I Saw Them Lynch.
When My Uncle Willie Saw.
**Freeman, Enoch W.**
Hither We Come, Our Dearest Lord, *with music.*
**Freeman, James**
Lord of the Worlds Below! *with music.*
**Freeman, John**
Moon-Bathers.
**Freeman, Joseph**

Ballad of Tampa.
Prince Jernikidze.
Six Poems.
**Freeman, Mary E. Wilkins**
Ostrich Is a Silly Bird.
**Freeman, Robert**
Braving the Wilds All Unexplored, *with music.*
**Freeman, William T.**
Chekhov Comes to Mind at Harvard.
**Freke, John**
History of Insipids, The.
**Frémont, John Charles**
On Recrossing the Rocky Mountains after Many Years.
**French, Percy**
"Are Ye Right There, Michael?" (A Lay of the Wild West Clare.)
Come Back, Paddy Reilly.
Mountains of Mourne, The.
**Freneau, Philip**
American Soldier, The.
Beauties of Santa Cruz, The.
British Prison Ship, The, *sel.*
By Babel's Streams, *with music.*
Deserted Farm-House, The.
Dish of Tea, The.
Elegiac Lines on the Death of a Fiddler, Called Blind Jacob.
Fragment of Bion, A.
George the Third's Soliloquy.
Hessian Doctor, The.
Hurricane, The.
Indian Burying Ground, The.
Indian Convert, The.
Lines Addressed to Mr. Jefferson.
Literary Importation.
Ode: "God save the Rights of Man!"
Ode to Fancy.
On a Honey Bee.
On the Emigration to America.
On the Religion of Nature.
On the Uniformity and Perfection of Nature.
On the Universality and Other Attributes of the God of Nature.
Picture of the Times, A.
Prophecy of King Tammany, The.
Republican Genius of Europe, The.
Rising Glory of America, The, *sel.*
Stanzas: "Princes and kings decay and die."
To a Caty-did.
To a Noisy Politician.
To an Author.
To Sir Toby.
To the Memory of the Brave Americans.
Tobacco.
Vanity of Existence, The.
Vernal Ague, The.
Vision of the Night, The.
Warning to America, A.
Wild Honey Suckle, The.
**Frere, John Hookham**
Boy and the Parrot, The.
Fable, A: "Dingy donkey, formal and unchanged, A."
Fable of the Piece of Glass and the Piece of Ice, The.
Loves of the Triangles, The, *sel.*
**Frere, John Hookham** *and* **George**

Canning. *See* **Canning, George** *and*
  **John Hookham Frere**
**Fridley, Mandy Ann**
  Egg yolk feels, An.
**Friebert, Stuart**
  Age of the Butcher, The.
  Apron, The.
**Fried, Elliot**
  Charlton Heston.
  Daily I Fall in Love with Waitresses.
  I Can't Figure You Out.
  Mental Health.
**Fried, Rivka**
  Sabbath.
**Fried, Susannah**
  Scraps.
  To My Father.
  Winter Day.
**Friedlander, Ginny**
  Here Be Dragons.
**Friedman, Richard**
  Darkness at Noon.
  Resignation Day.
**Friedmann, Pavel**
  Butterfly, The.
**Friedson, Tony**
  Rushes of Radnor Pond, The.
**Friel, James P.**
  Revolutionary.
**Friend, Robert**
  Doll, The.
  Identity.
  In the Orchard.
  Practice of Absence, The.
  Riders, The.
  Test, The.
**Friman, Alice**
  Reckoning, The.
**Fringell, Dieter**
  Hopes, The.
**Fripp, Robert** *and* Peter Sinfield
  Pictures of a City.
**Frohlicher, John C.**
  Miners.
**Frost, Carol**
  Night Is No More or Less Important
    than Bad Circles or "Ksing."
  Salt Lesson, The.
**Frost, Frances Mary**
  Apples to Keep.
  Snow-Stars.
  Valentine for Earth.
  Who's There?
**Frost, Richard**
  Last Bite, The.
**Frost, Robert**
  Acceptance.
  Acquainted with the Night.
  After Apple-picking.
  Aim Was Song, The.
  All Revelation.
  Armful, The.
  At Woodward's Gardens.
  Away!
  Bear, The.
  Bearer of Evil Tidings, The.
  Birches.
  Birthplace, The.
  Black Cottage, The.
  Blue-Butterfly Day.
  Blueberries.
  Boeotian.

Brown's Descent.
Cabin in the Clearing, A.
Carpe Diem.
Christmas Trees (A Christmas Circular
  Letter).
Code, The.
Come In.
Considerable Speck, A.
Cow in Apple Time, The.
Death of the Hired Man, The.
Departmental.
Desert Places.
Design.
Directive.
Draft Horse, The.
Drumlin Woodchuck, A.
Dust of Snow.
Egg and the Machine, The.
Empty Threat, An.
Fire and Ice.
Flower-Boat, The.
For Allan, Who Wanted to See How I
  Wrote a Poem.
For Once, Then, Something.
For Travelers Going Sidereal.
Forgive, O Lord.
Fountain, a Bottle, a Donkey's Ears and
  Some Books, A.
Fragmentary Blue.
Freedom of the Moon, The.
Gathering Leaves.
Gift Outright, The.
Good-by and Keep Cold.
Good Hours.
Hardship of Accounting, The.
Hill Wife, The.
Hillside Thaw, A.
Home Burial.
House Fear.
Immigrants.
Importer, An.
Impulse, The.
In Dives' Dive.
In Hardwood Groves.
In Neglect.
In White.
In Winter in the Woods Alone.
Into My Own.
Investment, The.
It Is Almost the Year Two Thousand.
Kitchen Chimney, The.
Last Word of a Bluebird, The.
Leaf Treader, A.
Leaves Compared with Flowers.
Line-Storm Song, A.
Lockless Door, The.
Lone Striker.
Love and a Question.
Lovely Shall Be Choosers, The.
Mending Wall.
Middleness of the Road, The.
Minor Bird, A.
Moon Compasses.
Most of It, The.
Mowing.
Need of Being Versed in Country
  Things, The.
Neither Out Far nor In Deep.
Never Again Would Birds' Song Be the
  Same.
Not All There.
Not to Keep.

Nothing Gold Can Stay.
Old Man's Winter Night, An.
On Looking Up by Chance at the
  Constellations.
On the Heart's Beginning to Cloud the
  Mind.
Once by the Pacific.
Onset, The.
"Out, Out."
Oven Bird, The.
Pasture, The.
Patch of Old Snow, A.
Peck of Gold, A.
Prayer in Spring, A.
Pride of Ancestry.
Provide, Provide.
Putting in the Seed.
Question, A.
Questioning Faces.
Rabbit Hunter, The.
Range-finding.
Record Stride, A.
Reluctance.
Revelation.
Road Not Taken, The.
Rose Family, The.
Runaway, The.
Sand Dunes.
Secret Sits, The.
Semi-Revolution, A.
Servant to Servants, A.
Silken Tent, The.
Soldier, The.
Sound of Trees, The.
Span of Life, The.
Spring Pools.
Star-Splitter, The.
Stopping by Woods on a Snowy
  Evening.
Storm Fear.
Strong Are Saying Nothing, The.
Subverted Flower, The.
Take Something like a Star.
Telephone, The.
There Are Roughly Zones.
Time to Talk, A.
To a Young Wretch.
To Earthward.
Tree at My Window.
Tuft of Flowers, The.
Two Look at Two.
Two Tramps in Mud Time.
Two Witches.
U. S. 1946 King's X.
Waspish.
West-running Brook.
Witch of Coös, The.
Wood-Pile, The.
**Frothingham, Nathaniel L.**
  O God Whose Presence Glows in All,
    *with music.*
**Frothingham, Octavius Brooks**
  Thou Lord of Hosts, Whose Guiding
    Hand, *with music.*
**Frumkin, Gene**
  Long and Shadowy Habits.
  Magdalene Silver Mine, The.
  Meeting Anaïs Nin's Elena.
  Old Stories, The.
  On a Windy Day.
  Some Days the Blood Is Warm and
    Certain.

Some Kind of Toughguy.
View of the Organ Mountains North of
    Las Cruces, New Mexico, A.
**Fry, Susie**
Fickle in the Arms of Spring.
**Fuertes, Gloria**
Autobiography.
Climbing.
Human Geography.
Interior Landscape.
When I Hear Your Name.
**Fuest, Milan**
Moses' Account.
**Fujiwara, Sadamu**
Transparent Autumn, A.
**Fuller, Ethel Romig**
Six-Horse Limited Mail, The.
**Fuller, Hoyt W.**
Lost Moment.
Seravazza.
**Fuller, Jean Overton**
Not Marching Away to Be Killed.
**Fuller, John**
Blues.
Girl with Coffee Tray.
God Bless America.
Owls.
**Fuller, John** *and* **James Fenton.** *See*
    **Fenton, James** *and* **John Fuller**
**Fuller, Margaret**
Jesus a Child His Course Begun, *with*
    *music.*
**Fuller, Roy**
Autobiography of a Lungworm.
Barber, The.
Crustaceans.
Dark, The.
Day, The.
Death.
Drawing.
Faust's Servant.
Fifties, The.
Giraffes, The.
Image, The.
In Memory of My Cat Domino:
    1951–1966.
Leaving School.
Metamorphoses.
Nino, the Wonder Dog.
Pigeon.
Plate-glass doors form a dangerous duo.
Shore Leave Lorry.
Soliloquy in an Air-Raid.
Sonnet: "Crumbled rock of London is
    dripping under, The."
Spring 1942.
Statue, The.
Translation.
War Poet.
**Fuller, Stephany**
In the Silence.
Let Me Be Held When the Longing
    Comes.
My Love When This Is Past.
That We Head Towards.
Who is not a stranger still.
**Fullerton, Mary**
Emus.
**Fulton, Dorothy R.**
Open Your Hand.
Softly, White and Pure.
**Fulton, Robin**

Forecast for a Quiet Night.
Hung Red, *sel.*
Last Boat of the Season, The.
Northern Habitat, A.
Quiet Days in Sutherland.
Seven Songs for a Cool Man, *sel.*
Voice of the Surbahar, *sels.*
Waiting-Room, The.
**Funaroff, Sol**
Dusk of the Gods.
Last Superstition, The.
Spider and the Clock, The.
To the Dead of the International
    Brigade.
Unemployed: 2 A.M.
Uprooted.
What the Thunder Said: A Fire Sermon.
When the Earth Is Cold.
**Funge, Robert**
Arcady Revisited.
**Funkhouser, Erica**
Hammer.
Hand Saw.
**Furness, William Henry**
In the Morning I Will Pray, *with music.*
Slowly, by God's Hand Unfurled, *with*
    *music.*
**Fyleman, Rose**
Conversation.
Fairies.
Fairies Have Never a Penny to Spend,
    The.
Fairy Went a-Marketing, A.
Family, The.
I Don't Like Beetles.
Mice.
Mrs. Brown.
Temper.

**G**

**Gafford, Charlotte**
Poem Written in Winter.
Quills.
**Gaik, Frank**
Whatever Is, Is Right.
**Galbraith, Georgie Starbuck**
No Mixed Green Salad for Me, Thanks.
**Gale, Vi**
After Illness.
Bear.
Hurting.
**Gallagher, Joseph**
John J. Curtis.
**Gallagher, Tess**
Ballad of Ballymote, The.
Bird-Window-Flying.
Breasts.
Crepes Flambeau.
Horse in the Drugstore, The.
Keeping You Alive.
Kidnaper.
Poem in Translation, A.
Rhododendrons.
Stepping Outside.
Time Lapse with Tulips.
To You on the Broken Iceberg.
Woman Who Raised Goats, The.

**Gallaudet, Thomas H.**
Jesus, in Sickness and in Pain, *with*
    *music.*
**Galler, David**
Narcissus: To Himself.
Walking Around.
**Galloway, Thomas**
Very Old, The.
**Galsworthy, John**
Desert Song ("When I came on from
    Santa Fe").
**Gálvez, Javier**
This Morning.
**Galvin, Brendan**
Bear and Misterwriter.
Bear at the Academy of the Living Arts.
Old Trip by Dream Train, The.
**Galvin, James**
Hematite Lake.
**Galvin, Martin**
City Summer.
Coquette at Mission Control.
Heron's Bay.
Proverbial Man.
Shooting Gallery.
**Galvin, Patrick**
Aunt, The.
Ballad for My Mother
Cradle Song: "Listening/ To the dying
    voices."
Message to the Editor.
Miss Cecily Finch.
**Gambara, Veronica**
When I see the earth ornate and lovely.
**Gannett, William Channing**
From Heart to Heart, *with music.*
**Ganse, Hervey Doddridge**
Lord, I Know Thy Grace Is Nigh Me,
    *with music.*
**Gant, Roland**
Wedding, The.
**Garcia, Luis**
Passport, The.
**García Lorca, Federico**
Ballad of the Moon, Moon.
Blind Panorama of New York.
Casida of the Rose.
Faithless Wife, The.
Guitar.
Half Moon.
It Is True.
King of Harlem, The.
Lament for Ignacio Sánchez Mejías.
Landscape of the Vomiting Multitudes.
New York.
Poem of Solitude at Columbia
    University.
Somnambulistic Ballad.
Unfaithful Married Woman, The.
Unsleeping City.
**Gardner, Carl**
Dead Man Dragged from the Sea, The.
Reflections.
**Gardner, Gail**
Tyin' a Knot in the Devil's Tail.
**Gardner, Isabella**
At a Summer Hotel.
Cock-a-Hoop.
Fall in Massachusetts.
Gimboling.
Part of the Darkness.
Sloth, The.

That "Craning of the Neck."
That Was Then.
Widow's Yard, The.
**Gardner, Stephen**
Another Cross.
Carpenter's Real Anguish, The.
**Garfinkel, Patricia**
Dream while Wide Awake.
Incest in Orange.
Safe Places.
Tailor, The.
**Garin, Marita**
Bar Harbor.
White Spider.
**Garioch, Robert (Robert Sutherland)**
And They Were Richt.
Brither Worm.
Campidoglio.
Elegy: "They are lang deid, folk that I
    used to ken."
Heard in the Cougate.
I Was Fair Beat.
Judgment Day.
Nemo Canem Impune Lacessit.
Proem and Inscription for a Hermes.
Sanct Christopher II ("Sanct
    Christopher's a muckle sanct and
    strang").
Sisyphus.
**Garitano, Rita**
Room of Her Own, A.
**Garland, Hamlin**
Color in the Wheat.
Do you Fear the Wind?
Gift of Water, The.
Goin' Back T'morrer.
Horses Chawin' Hay.
Lost in a Norther.
Massasauga.
Passing of the Buffalo, The.
Vulture of the Plains, The.
**Garland, Jim**
I Don't Want Your Millions Mister.
**Garmon, John**
Light Morning Snow, We Wait for a
    Warmer Season.
Old Trail Town, Cody Wyoming.
Paths They Kept Barren.
**Garneau, Saint-Denys**
My House.
**Garner, Alan**
RIP.
Summer Solstice.
**Garnett, Jane**
Paris.
**Garnett, Richard**
Fair Circassian.
Highwayman's Ghost, The.
Marigold.
**Garrett, Caroline**
Guts.
**Garrett, George**
Abraham's Knife.
After Bad Dreams.
Cage, The.
For a Bitter Season.
Goodbye, Old Paint, I'm Leaving
    Cheyenne.
Revival.
Romantic.
Salome.
Snapshot of a Pedant.

Solitaire.
Tiresias.
Underworld.
York Harbor Morning.
**Garrick, David**
Epitaph on Laurence Sterne.
Friend Col and I, both full of whim.
On Oliver Goldsmith.
On Sir John Hill, M.D., Playwright.
So many thousands for a house!
**Garrigue, Jean**
Amsterdam.
Beside a fall there is a round wood pipe.
Bleecker Street.
Catch What You Can.
Country Villa.
Cracked Looking Glass.
Epitaph for My Cat.
For Anybody's Martyr's Song.
Forest.
From Venice Was That Afternoon.
Incantatory Poem.
Last Letter to the Scholar.
Movie Actors Scribbling Letters Very
    Fast in Crucial Scenes.
Note on Master Crow, A.
Now Snow Descends.
Old Haven.
Primer of Plato.
Remember That Country.
Requiem: "In the sudden white silence,
    where are you?"
Shore.
Smoke Shop Owner's Daughter, The.
Song for "Buvez les Vins du Postillon"—
    Advt.
Stranger, The.
To speak of my influences.
Upon the Intimations of Love's
    Mortality.
Waking, I always waked you awake.
You Know.
**Garrison, Theodosia Pickering (Mrs.
    Frederic J. Faulk)**
Shepherd Who Stayed, The.
**Garstin, Crosbie**
Figurehead, The.
**Garth, Sir Samuel**
Portrait of a Physician.
**Gary, Sid**
Circuit Breaker.
Pythagorean Razzle-Dazzle.
**Gascoigne, George**
Adventures of Master F. I., The, sel.
All were to little for the merchauntes
    hande.
And every yeare a worlde my will did
    deeme.
Arraignment of a Lover, The.
Before mine eye to feede my greedy will.
Councell Given to Master Bartholmew
    Withipoll.
Divorce of a Lover, The ("Divorce me
    nowe good death").
Farewell, A: "And if I did, what then?"
Farewell with a Mischeife.
For why? the gaines doth seldome quitte
    the charge.
Gascoignes Good Morrow.
Gascoignes Woodmanship.
Gascoygnes Good Night.
Memories, sel.

No haste but good, where wisdome
    makes the waye.
Sonet Written in Prayse of the Browne
    Beautie, A.
Steel Glas [or Steele Glas], The.
Straunge Passion of a Lover, A.
To prinke me up and make me higher
    plaste.
**Gascou, Rene**
After the Locust.
**Gascoyne, David**
And the Seventh Dream Is the Dream of
    Isis.
Cage, The.
Cubical Domes, The.
Ecce Homo.
Elegy, An: " Friend, whose unnatural
    early death."
End Is near the Beginning, The.
Orpheus in the Underworld.
Patmos.
Sacred Hearth, The.
Salvador Dali.
Snow in Europe.
"Truth Is Blind, The."
Yves Tanguy.
**Gaskin, Bob**
Letter to My Kinder.
**Gasparini, Len**
Accident, The.
Greasy Spoon Blues.
Kafka's Other Metamorphosis.
Niagara Falls Nocturne.
Valentine.
Written on a Paper Napkin.
**Gass, William H.**
On Being Photographed.
**"Gate, A.C."**  See **Anthony, Edward**
**Gatty, Sir Alfred Scott**
Three Little Pigs, The.
**Gatuira, Joseph**
Kariuki.
**Gauer, Jim**
Visit, The.
**Gaughan, Dennis M.**
Black Water Crossing.
Nighthawk, The.
Woman in the Window.
**Gauldin, Sara Saper**
Old Argonaut.
**Gavenda, Walt**
Eco Right.
**Gavronsky, Serge**
Testimonies for a School Prayer.
**Gay, Asya.**  See **Asya**
**Gay, John**
Acis and Galatea, sel.
All in the Downs.
Fables, sel.
Friday; or, The Dirge.
Mr. Pope's Welcome from Greece.
My Own Epitaph.
New Song of New Similies, A.
Newgate's Garland.
Over the Hills and Far Away.
Poet and the Rose, The.
Shepherd's Week, The, sels.
Song: "O ruddier than the cherry."
Sweet William's Farewell to Black-eyed
    Susan.
To My Ingenious and Worthy Friend
    William Lowndes, Esq.

Trivia; or, The Art of Walking the
Streets of London.
'Twas When the Seas Were Roaring.
Wednesday; or, The Dumps.
Youth and Love.
**Gay, John** and **Alexander Pope**
Mary Gulliver to Captain Lemuel
Gulliver, *abr.*
**Gaye, Marvin**
Mercy Mercy Me.
**Gegna, Suzanne**
Relics.
**Geifer, George L.**
Who Threw the Overalls in Mistress
Murphey's Chowder? *with music.*
**Gelman, Juan**
Customs.
Knife, The.
Stranger, The.
**Genestet, Petrus Augustus de**
Such Is Holland!
**Genser, Cynthia Kramer**
Club 82: Lisa.
**Geoghegan, J. B.**
Down in a Coal Mine.
**Georgakas, Dan**
Acrobat from Xanadu disdained all nets,
The.
19??.
**George, Emery E.**
Grief.
House All Pictures, A.
Projects.
Weatherman of Sorrows.
**George, Faye**
Welcome to This House.
**George, M. A.**
Morning.
**George, Phillip William**
America's Wounded Knee.
Ask the Mountains.
Battle Won Is Lost.
Eagle Feather [IV].
First Grade.
Monument in Bone.
Moon of Huckleberries.
Morning Vigil.
Name Giveaway.
Night Blessing.
Old Man, the Sweat Lodge.
Prelude to Memorial Song: 100 Years
Later.
Spokane Falls 1874.
Spring Cleaning.
Spruce.
Sunflower Moccasins.
True.
Visit, The.
Wardance.
Wardance Soup.
**George, Stefan**
Homecoming.
**Georgeou, Markos**
Unseen Flight.
**Gerard, Jim**
Angora, The.
**Gerard, Richard H.**
Sweet Adeline.
**"Geraud, Saint."** *See* **Knott, William (Bill)**
**Gerber, Dan**
Death and the Pineapple.
Fine Excess, A.

Home from Russia.
Homecoming.
Journal Entry: April 5, 1974.
Line, The.
Nocturnes I.
Russian Poem II, The.
Russian Poem IV, The.
Tragedy of Action, The.
Two Clouds.
Yellow.
**Gerez, Jozef Habib**
Call from the Afterworld.
We Are Acrobats.
We Fooled Ourselves.
**Gergely, Agnes**
Birth of a Country.
Conjuration.
Crazed Man in Concentration Camp.
Desert.
**Gernes, Sonia**
Practicing.
**Gershgoren, Sid**
Father.
Graham.
**Gershwin, Ira**
Blah, Blah, Blah.
Embraceable You, *with music.*
It Ain't Neccessarily So.
**Gessner, Robert**
Cross of Flame.
Declaration.
Exiles, The.
Heard at Dniperstroi.
Hymn for October.
Two Salesmen in Search of a Country.
Upsurge.
**Ghai, Gail**
Six Divine Circles.
**Ghazi, A. Rasheed**
Poem on Inter-uterine Device, A.
**Ghigna, Charles**
Child Bearing.
**Ghiselin, Brewster**
Catch, The.
Credo.
Dana Point.
Headland.
Light.
Love Letter.
Marlin.
Meridian.
Rattler, Alert.
Roulette.
Song at San Carlos Bay.
Vantage.
**Ghose, Zulfikar**
Crows, The.
Geography Lesson.
This Landscape, These People.
Two Sec. Mods.
**Giandi, Paul**
Midwestern Man.
**Gibbon, Monk**
Discovery, The.
I Tell Her She Is Lovely.
**Gibbons, James Sloan**
Three Hundred Thousand More.
**Gibbons, Reginald**
Michael's Room.
**Gibbs, Wolcott**
Declaration of Independence.
**Giber, David**

All Thumbs.
**Gibran, Kahlil**
Prophet, The, *sels.*
**Gibson, Barbara**
After the Quarrel.
**Gibson, Lary H.**
Reflections.
**Gibson, Margaret**
Apples.
Grammar of the Soul, A.
Long Walks in the Afternoon.
Lunes.
Octobering.
Two Women at JFK Gravesite.
**Gibson, Morgan**
Beyond the Presidency.
**Gibson, Walker**
Athletes.
Billiards.
In Memory of the Circus Ship *Euzkera*.
Killer Too, The.
**Gibson, Wilfrid Wilson**
All Being Well.
Breakfast.
Dancing Seal, The.
Drove-Road, The.
Flannan Isle.
Green Shag.
Henry Turnbull.
Ice, The.
Ice-Cart, The.
Lament: "We who are left, how shall we
look again."
Long Tom.
Luck.
Ponies, The.
Sea-Change.
Killer Too, The.
**Gibson, William**
Circe.
**Gidlow, Elsa**
Invocation to Sappho.
**Gifford, William**
Epistle to Peter Pindar.
**Gilbert, Celia**
Portrait of My Mother on Her Wedding
Day.
**Gilbert, Fred**
Man Who Broke the Bank at Monte
Carlo, The.
Midnight March, The.
**Gilbert, Jack**
Bay Bridge from Portrero Hill, The.
Malvolio in San Francisco.
Orpheus in Greenwich Village.
**Gilbert, Michael William**
Exigencies.
**Gilbert, Sandra M.**
Elegy "Pages of history open, The."
Fog Dream, The.
Getting Fired or "Not Being Retained."
Rissem.
**Gilbert, Virginia**
Becket.
Finding You.
For John Berryman.
Looking for a Place to Be Comfortable.
Pax Romana.
What Does It Mean? This Harmonica.
**Gilbert, Sir William Schwenck**
Anglicized Utopia.
Banquet Song.

Ben Allah Achmet; or, The Fatal Tum.
Bunthorne's Song: The Aesthete.
Darned Mounseer, The.
Englishman, The.
Etiquette.
Ferdinando and Elvira.
Flowers That Bloom in the Spring, The, *with music.*
Gentle Alice Brown.
Gondoliers, The, *sel.*
Iolanthe, *sel.*
Little Buttercup.
Mad Margaret's Song.
Merryman Sings, The.
Mikado, The, *sels.*
Modern Major-General, The.
Modest Couple, The.
Nightmare.
Oh, Hollow! Hollow! Hollow!
Patience, *sels.*
Perils of Invisibility, The.
Pirates of Penzance, The, *sels.*
Policeman's Lot, The.
Professor Called Chesterton, A.
Rival Curates, The.
Ruddigore, *sels.*
Sir Joseph's Song.
Story of Prince Agib, The.
Suicide's Grave, The.
There Lived a King.
They'll None of 'Em Be Missed.
To Phoebe.
To the Terrestrial Globe.
Yarn of the *Nancy Bell,* The.

**Gilbert, Zack**
For Angela.
For Stephen Dixon.
My Own Hallelujahs.
"O.D."
When I Heard Dat White Man Say.

**Gilboa, Amir**
Birth.
Isaac.
Joshua's Face.
Moses.
My Brother Was Silent.
Samson.
Saul.
Seeds of Lead.

**Gilburt, S. Gale**
Bequest.

**Gilder, Richard Watson**
To Thee, Eternal Soul, Be Praise, *with music.*

**Gildner, Gary**
After an All-Night Cackle with Sloth and Co. I Enter Mansion and Greet the Dawn.
Comanche.
Digging for Indians.
First Practice.
Geisha.
House on Buder Street, The.
Life of the Wolf, The.
Meeting the Reincarnation Analyst.
My Father after Work.
Nails.
Porch, The.
Runner, The.
Then.
They Have Turned the Church Where I Ate God.

Today They Are Roasting Rocky Norse.
Touring the Hawkeye State.

**Gilead, Zerubavel**
Absalom.
Flying Letters.
Pomegranate Tree in Jerusalem ("The pomegranate tree in my garden adorns itself").

**Gilkey, James G.**
O God, in Whose Great Purpose, *with music.*
Outside the Holy City, *with music.*

**Gill, Brendan**
Girls' Voices.

**Gill, David**
Killing a Whale.

**Gill, John**
As a Child Seeing a Cardinal.
Before the Thaw.
First Hymn.
"I Don't Hear Any Melody Breathing I Hear."
Late Spring: A Heaving, a Turning.
Poem: "Something broke the dream."
What Could Be.

**Gillespie, Dan**
Abandoned Copper Refinery.
Desert Gulls.
Strip Mining Pit.

**Gillespie, Robert**
Shawano Lake, Wisconsin.
Snow White.
View toward Wife Trading, A.

**Gillies, Margaret**
Library, The.
Night Sisters, The.
Town Clinics.
Turning Point.
Village Doctor, The.

**Gillies, Valerie**
Straits, The.

**Gilman, Samuel**
O God, Accept the Sacred Hour, *with music.*

**Gilmore, Joseph H.**
He Leadeth Me, *with music.*

**Gilmore, Mary**
Aboriginal Simile, An.
Nationality.
Nurse No Long Grief.
Out on the Hillside.
Penelope.
Tenancy, The.

**Gilmore, Patrick Sarsfield ("Louis Lambert")**
When Johnny Comes Marching Home.

**"Ginger." See Irwin, Wallace**

**Ginsberg, Allen**
America.
Asphodel, An.
Bayonne Turnpike to Tuscarora.
Bop Lyrics.
Cafe in Warsaw.
Cézanne's Ports.
Consulting I Ching Smoking Pot Listening to the Fugs Sing Blake.
Death News.
Death to Van Gogh's Ear!
Dream Record: June 8, 1955.
Ecologue.
End, The.

First Party at Ken Keseys with Hell's Angels.
Footnote to Howl.
Friday the Thirteenth.
Howl.
Hymmnn.
I Am a Victim of the Telephone.
In a Moonlit Hermit's Cabin.
In Back of the Real.
Kaddish.
Kral Majales.
Last Night in Calcutta.
Love Poem on Theme by Whitman.
Marijuana Notation.
May Mobilization.
Memory Gardens.
Message.
My Alba.
My Sad Self.
Night-Apple, The.
On Burroughs' Work.
Patna-Benares Express.
Poem Rocket.
Prophecy, A.
Psalm III: "To God: to illuminate all men. Beginning with Skid Row."
Shrouded Stranger, The.
Sunflower Sutra.
Supermarket in California, A.
This Form of Life Needs Sex.
Thus Crosslegged on Round Pillow Sat in Space.
To Aunt Rose.
To Lindsay.
Trembling of the Veil, The.
Uptown.
Waking in New York, *sel.*
Wales Visitation.
Who Be Kind To.
Wichita Vortex Sutra.
Wild Orphan.

**Ginsberg, Louis**
Hymn to Evil.
Morning in Spring.

**Gioseffi, Daniela**
After Drinking Water.
Eggs.
Paradise Is Not a Place.
Peace Prospect.
Some Slippery Afternoon.
Through the Eye of the Needle.
Vacancy.
Vases of Wombs, The.
Wearing Breasts.
"Women with Tongue in Cheek."

**Giovanni, Nikki**
Adulthood.
Beautiful Black Men.
Black Power.
Certain Peace, A.
Concerning One Responsible Negro with Too Much Power.
Conversation.
Detroit Conference of Unity and Art.
Dreams.
Ego Tripping.
For Saundra.
Funeral of Martin Luther King, Jr., The.
Kidnap Poem.
Knoxville, Tennessee.
Legacies.
Master Charge Blues.

Mothers.
My Poem.
Nikki-Rosa.
One ounce of truth benefits.
Poem for Aretha.
Poem for Black Boys.
Poem for Flora.
Poem for Unwed Mothers.
Poem of Angela Yvonne Davis.
Revolutionary Dreams.
Robin's Poem, A.
Scrapbooks.
Seduction.
True Import of Present Dialogue, Black vs. Negro, The.
Twelve Gates to the City.
Winter Poem.
Woman Poem.
Word Poem.

**Gira, R. P.**
Mouth of the Amazon.

**Gitin, David**
Clearing, The.
Up against the wall.

**Gitin, Maria**
Joy Farm.

**Gitlin, Todd**
Puritan Hacking Away at Oak, The.

**Gittings, Robert**
Great Moth, The.

**Gitzen, Julian**
Pheasant Hunter and the Arrowhead, The.

**Gladden, Washington**
O Lord of Life, *with music.*
O Master, Let Me Walk with Thee, *with music.*

**Gladish, David**
If Only.

**Glanz-Leyeles, A.**
Castles.
Madison Square.
White Swan.

**Glaser, Elton**
Asides and Memoranda.
Figure and Ground.
General's Wife, The.
Meal Piece.
Sacred Heart of Jesus Bleeds for You, The.

**Glaser, Michael S.**
Initials.

**Glass, Malcolm**
Staying Ahead.

**Glassco, John**
For Cora Lightbody, R.N.

**Glatstein, Jacob**
Evening Bread.
I'll Find My Self-Belief.
In a Ghetto.
Like Weary Trees.
Loyal Sins.
Memorial Poem.
Move On, Yiddish Poet.
Mozart.
Poet Lives, The.

**Glavin, Anthony**
Rimbaud's Farewell to Europe.
Voice Over.

**Glaze, Andrew**
Fantasy Street.
My South.

Zeppelin.
**Glazer, Joseph**
Visit Home, A.
**Gleason, Madeline**
Starface, The.
**Glen, Duncan**
Clydesdale New Town Walk.
Gullion, The.
My Faither.
Psychology.
Room, The.
Words.
**Glen, Emilie**
Apple Scoop.
Fun and Funerals ("Fun street/ Funeral street").
**Glen, William**
Wae's Me for Prince Charlie.
**Glickman, Susan**
Night Song for an Old Lover.
**Glik, Hirsh**
Shtil Di Nacht (Silent Is the Night).
**Gloag, Daphne**
Visit to the Zoo for the First Kidney Transplant Mothers and Their Children, A.
Woman in the Hospital for Incurables.
**Glover, Denis**
Camp Site.
Casual Man, The.
Crystallized Waves, The.
End, The.
Holiday Piece.
Magpies, The.
Once the Days.
Prayer, A: "Mother of God, in this brazen sun."
River Crossing, The.
Scene, The.
Search, The.
Soliloquies.
Songs.
Themes.
Thistledown.
To the Coast.
Woman Shopping, A.
**Glück, Louise**
All Hallows.
Fire, The.
Flowering Plum.
For Jane Myers.
For My Mother.
Fortress, The.
Garden, The.
Gift, The.
Gratitude.
Gretel in Darkness.
Lamentations.
Magi, The.
Messengers.
Mirror, The.
Phenomenal Survivals of Death in Nantucket.
Pond, The.
Racer's Widow, The.
School Children, The.
Shad-Blow Tree, The.
Undertaking, The.
**Goba, Ronald J.**
Compozishun—to James Herndon and Others.
**Goch, Iolo**

Labourer, The.
**Godin, Deborah**
January.
**Godley, Alfred Denis**
After Horace.
Motor Bus.
Women's Degrees.
**Godolphin, Sidney**
Hymn: "Lord, when the wise men came from far."
'Tis affection but dissembled.
**Godoy Alcayaga, Lucila.** *See* **Mistral, Gabriela**
**Godsey, Edwin S.**
Hoppy.
I Hope I Don't Have You Next Semester, But.
**Goedicke, Patricia**
After the Second Operation.
At Every Major Airport.
Circus Song.
Daily the Ocean between Us.
Dog Who Comes from Nowhere, The.
Escalator.
Great Depression, The.
In the Ocean.
Lost.
My Mother's/ My/ Death/ Birthday.
On the Night in Question.
One More Time.
Serious Merriment of Women, The.
Slabs of Her Eyes, The.
Sprinkle Me, Just.
Success Story.
When He's at His Most Brawling.
Where We Are Going.
Young Men You Are So Beautiful Up There.
**Goethe, Johann Wolfgang von**
Chorus of the Archangels, The.
Erl-King, The.
Holy Longing, The.
Mignon.
Pariah's Prayer, The.
Permanence in Change.
Prologue in Heaven.
Second Poem the Night-Walker Wrote, The.
To the Moon.
Wanderer's Night Song.
**Goetz, E. Ray** *and* **Edgar Leslie.** *See* **Leslie, Edgar** *and* **E. Ray Goetz**
**Goff, Paula**
White Bear, The.
**Goffin, Gerry** *and* Carole King
Child of Mine.
**Gogarty, Oliver St. John**
After Galen.
Back from the Country.
Farrell O'Reilly.
Hay Hotel, The.
Kingdoms.
Leda and the Swan.
O Boys! O Boys!
On the Use of Jayshus.
Ringsend.
To Death.
Verse ("What should we know").
**Gold, Edward**
Fish.
Heaven of Cowboys.
My Name.

**Gold, Jiri**
In the Cellars.
Inhabited Emptiness, An.

**Gold, Michael**
Examples of Worker Correspondence.
Ode to Walt Whitman.
Strange Funeral in Braddock, A.
Tom Mooney Walks at Midnight.
Wreath for Our Murdered Comrade
Kobayashi, A.

**Goldbarth, Albert**
Body Mechanics.
Dime Call.
From the Bridge.
Greed Song, The.
Letter Back to Oregon.
Note from an Exhibition.
On Sunday, the Beginning of the Week,
I Make a Religion.
Recipe.
Survival.

**Goldberg, Leah**
Answer.
God Once Commanded Us, A.
Heavenly Jerusalem, Jerusalem of the
Earth.
My Mother's House, *sel.*
Nameless Journey, *sel.*
Of Myself.
On the Hazards of Smoking.
Our Backs Are to the Cypress.
Symposium, The, *sel.*
Toward Myself.

**Goldemberg, Isaac**
Bar Mitzvah.
Jews in Hell, The.

**Golden, Renny**
For Jeanette Piccard Ordained at 79.

**Goldensohn, Barry**
Becoming Real.

**Goldensohn, Lorrie**
Ambulance Call.

**Goldin, Judah**
Reading Faust.

**Goldman, Beate**
Interpretations.
Witch's House, The.

**Goldman, Michael**
Orpheus.

**Goldsberry, Steven**
First Enemy, The.
I Have Two Hands.
Translation of an Unwritten Spanish
Poem.

**Goldsmith, Oliver**
Description of an Author's Bedchamber,
A.
Deserted Village, The.
Elegy on That Glory of Her Sex, Mrs.
Mary Blaize, An.
Elegy on the Death of a Mad Dog, An.
New Simile in the Manner of Swift, A.
O luxury! Thou curst by Heaven's
decree.
On Edmund Burke.
Parson, The.
Retaliation.
She Stoops to Conquer, *sel.*
Song: "Let school-masters puzzle their
brain."
Song: "When lovely woman stoops to
folly."

Traveller, The.
Vicar of Wakefield, The, *sels.*

**Goldstein, Jonas**
On Philosophy.

**Goldstein, Roberta B.**
Shattered Sabbath.

**Golffing, Francis C.**
Higher Empiricism, The.

**Goll, Yvan**
Clandestine Work.
Lilith.
Neïla.
Raziel.

**Gom, Leona**
Arrowheads.

**Gomez de Avellaneda, Gertrudis**
On Leaving.

**Gómez-Quiñones, Juan**
Walk among the seas.

**Gomringer, Eugen**
Wind.

**Góngora y Argote, Luis de**
Wedding Feast, The.
Young Pilgrim Finds Refuge with the
Goatherds, The.

**Gonick, Catherine**
Boys Brushed By, The.

**González, Angel**
I Look at My Hand.

**Gonzalez, John**
Friend at a Drug Clinic.
Geriatric.
We Are All a Little Mad.

**González, Rafael Jesús**
Exhortation.
Knight of the Sad Face, The.
Song for Meeting a Friend.

**González De Leon, Ulálume**
Words.

**González-Gerth, Miguel**
Tragicomic Conceit.

**Goodchild, Keighley**
Nautical Ballad.

**Goode, Michael**
Shot with a Hot Rot Gun.
War War.

**Goodell, Larry**
Poet's Appeal, The.

**Goodenough, J. B.**
Orchard Snow.

**Goodge, W. T.**
Daley's Dorg Wattle.
How We Drove the Trotter.
Snake Yarn, A.

**Goodman, Mitchell**
Coming and Going.
Man and Wife.

**Goodman, Paul**
April 1962.
Classical Quatrain, A.
Don Larsen's Perfect Game.
"Dreams Are the Royal Road to the
Unconscious."
Handball Players.
I planned to have a border of lavender.
Kent State, May 4, 1970.
Little Ode.
Long Lines.
Lordly Hudson, The.
My Daughter Very Ill.
Our Lucy (1956-1960).
Saint Harmony my patroness.

Sonnet 21.
Stanzas: " I thought I woke: the
midnight sun."
Surfers at Santa Cruz.
*Weepers Tower* in Amsterdam, The.
Wonders of "The Iliad."

**Goodman, Ryah Tumarkin**
Ancestors.
Business of Living, The.
Portrait.
Silence Spoke with Your Voice.

**Goodreau, William**
Longing, The.

**Googe, Barnabe**
Of Money.
Out of Sight, Out of Mind.
To Doctor Bale.

**Gorbanyevskaya, Natalya**
And there is nothing at all—neither fear.
Here, as in a painting, yellow noon
burns [or noon burns yellow].
In my own twentieth century.
Not because of you, not because of me,
just that.
This world/ is amazingly flat.
To I. Lavrentevaya.

**Gordett, Marea**
Marriage.

**Gordon, Adam Lindsay**
Question not, but live and labour.

**Gordon, Alvin J.**
Young Girl's Song, The.

**Gordon, Bonnie**
Tattooed Lady, The.
Turning.

**Gordon, Don**
Free Fall.

**Gordon, Giles**
Between Appointments.
Elegy: I. M. Orlando Tobias Gordon.
Former Love, A.

**Gordon, Mary**
Unwanted, The.

**Gordon, W. J. J.**
IBM Hired Her.

**Goren, Judith**
October.

**Gorenko, Anna Andreyevna.** *See*
"**Akhmatova, Anna**"

**Gorey, Edward**
Babe, with a cry brief and dismal, The.
From Number Nine, Penwiper Mews.
From the bathing machine came a din.
Lady who signs herself "Vexed," The.
Some Harvard men, stalwart and hairy.
There was a young woman named
Plunnery.

**Gorges, Sir Arthur**
Henceforth I will not set my love.
She that holds me under the laws of
love.
Would I were chang'd into that golden
shower.

**Gormley, Queen of Ireland**
Gormley's Laments, *sel.*

**Gotlieb, Phyllis**
First Person Demonstrative.
Morning Prayers of the Hasid, Rabbi
Levi Yitzhok, The.
Try Brillo on the Slimy Stove.
Whatfor to 3 Who Stole My Shovel.
Women Who Are Hard Inside.

**Gottheil, Gustav**
  Come, O Sabbath Day, *with music.*
**Gottlieb, Ann**
  Lady Luck.
**Gottlieb, Darcy**
  Who of Those Coming After.
**Gottlieb, Frantisek**
  Between Life and Death.
  Just a While.
**Gottlieb, Lynn**
  Eve's Song in the Garden.
**Gough, Irene**
  Lost—A Lizard.
  Possum Tree, The.
**Gould, Gerald**
  Monogamy, *sel.*
**Gould, Hannah Flagg**
  Day of God! Thou Blessed Day, *with music.*
**Gower, John**
  Adrian and Bardus.
  Confessio Amantis, *sels.*
  Medea's Magic.
**Grade, Chaim**
  Miracle, The.
  Refugees.
  Without Me You Won't be Able to See Yourself.
**Graham, Al**
  Casey's Daughter at the Bat.
  Interplanetary Limericks.
**Graham, D. L.**
  Soul.
  Tony Get the Boys.
  West Ridge Is Menthol-cool, The.
**Graham, Harry ("Col. D. Streamer")**
  Appreciation.
  Billy.
  L'Enfant Glacé.
  Lord Gorbals.
  Mr. Jones.
  Necessity.
  Opportunity.
  Poetical Economy.
  Waste.
**Graham, Henry**
  Cat Poem.
  Good Luck to You Kafka/ You'll Need It Boss.
  Two Gardens.
**Graham, James, Marques of Montrose**
  Epitaph on Charles I.
  I'll Never Love Thee More.
  On Himself, upon Hearing What Was His Sentence.
**Graham, Jorie**
  On Why I Would Betray You.
  To Paul Eluard.
**Graham, Robert (Robert Cunninghame-Graham)**
  O Tell Me How to Woo Thee.
**Graham, William Sydney**
  Beast in the Space, The.
  Children of Greenock, The.
  Constructed Space, The.
  I leave this at your ear for when you wake.
  Letter II.
  Letter V.
  Listen, Put on Morning.
  To My Father.
**Grahame, Kenneth**

Ducks' Ditty.
  Song of Mr. Toad, The.
  Wind in the Willows, The, *sels.*
**Grahn, Judy**
  Asking for Ruthie.
  Common Woman, The.
  Death and Disfiguration.
  Dressed As I Am, a Young Man Once Called Me Names in Spanish.
  Ella, in a Square Apron, along Highway 80.
  I have come to claim.
  Margaret, Seen through a Picture Window.
  Mock Interrogation, A.
  Vera, from My Childhood.
  Woman Is Talking to Death, A, *sels.*
**Granade, John A.**
  Come All Ye Mourning Pilgrims, *with music.*
  Sweet Rivers of Redeeming Love, *with music.*
**Grandsen, K. W.**
  Interview, An.
**Grant, Percy Stickney**
  Pacific, The.
**Grant, Richard E.**
  Broken Heart, Broken Machine.
**Grant, Russell**
  Cloud of Ghosts, A.
  Fire-Mass.
**Granville [or Grenville], George, Baron Lansdowne**
  Cloe ("Bright as the day, and like the morning fair").
  Cloe's the wonder of her sex.
  Love.
**Grapes, Marcus J.**
  And This Is My Father.
**Grass, Gunter**
  How I Was Her Kitchen-Boy.
**Grave, John**
  If Thou Wilt Hear, *with music.*
**Graves, Alfred Perceval**
  Father O'Flynn.
  Herring Is King.
**Graves, Benny**
  Boy, A.
**Graves, Robert**
  Acrobats.
  Apollo of the Physiologists.
  At First Sight.
  Bedpost, The.
  Blue-Fly, The.
  Broken Girth, The.
  Call It a Good Marriage
  Change.
  Children of Darkness.
  Civil Servant, A.
  Cool Web, The.
  Counting the Beats.
  Devil's Advice to Story-Tellers, The.
  Down, Wanton, Down!
  1805.
  End of Play.
  Escape.
  Eugenist, The.
  Face in the Mirror, The.
  Falcon Woman, The.
  Flying Crooked.
  Foreboding, The.
  From the Embassy.

Frosty Night, A.
  Full Moon.
  George II and the Chinese Emperor.
  Glutton, The.
  Grotesques.
  Hag-ridden.
  Hedges Freaked with Snow.
  Henry and Mary.
  Hide and Seek.
  History of the Word.
  In Broken Images.
  In Her Praise.
  In the Beginning Was a Word.
  In Time.
  It Was All Very Tidy.
  Jealous Man, A.
  Lament for Pasiphae.
  Laureate, The.
  Legs, The.
  Lost Acres.
  Lost Jewel, A.
  Lost Love.
  Love Story, A.
  Love without Hope.
  Lovers in Winter.
  Mark, The.
  My Name and I.
  Naked and the Nude, The.
  Narrow Sea, The.
  Nature's Lineaments.
  Never Such Love.
  Not to Sleep.
  Ogres and Pygmies.
  On Dwelling.
  Penny Fiddle, The.
  Persian Version, The.
  Philatelist Royal.
  Pier-Glass, The.
  Poet's Corner.
  Point of No Return.
  Portrait, The.
  Pumpkin, The.
  Queen Mother to New Queen.
  Quiet Glades of Eden, The.
  Recalling War.
  Reproach to Julia.
  Return of the Goddess Artemis.
  Richard Roe and John Doe.
  Rocky Acres.
  Saint.
  Second-fated, The.
  Sharp Ridge, The.
  She Tells Her Love while Half Asleep.
  Sick Love.
  Six Badgers, The.
  Slice of Wedding Cake, A.
  Song: How Can I Care?
  Spoils.
  Star-Talk.
  Starred Coverlet, The.
  Straw, The.
  Succubus, The.
  Survivor, The.
  Symptoms of Love.
  Theseus and Ariadne.
  Thieves, The.
  Three-faced, The.
  Tilth.
  To Calliope.
  To Juan at the Winter Solstice.
  To Walk on Hills.
  Traveller's Curse after Misdirection.

Troll's Nosegay, The.
Twice of the Same Fever.
Twins.
Two Witches, The.
Ulysses.
Under the Pot.
Variables of Green.
Villagers and Death, The.
Warning to Children.
Weather of Olympus, The.
"Wellcome, to the Caves of Artá!"
Welsh Incident.
What Did I Dream? I Do Not Know.
White Goddess, The.
Wigs and Beards.
Wild Strawberries.
Wm. Brazier.
With a Gift of Rings.
Wreath, The.

**Graves, Steven**
Rendezvous, The.

**Gray, Alexander**
Deil o' Bogie, The.
Fine Fechtin Mouse, The.
Heine in Scots.
On a Cat, Ageing.
Scotland.

**Gray, C.**
On the Amazon.

**Gray, Darrell**
Art of Poetry, The.
For George Oppen.
In June.
Musical Ape, The.
Ode to Jibberish.
Old Southern Critic Takes a Look at My
Poems, An.
Sonnet for All Greeks Living Now.

**Gray, John**
Les Demoiselles de Sauve.
Mishka.
Odiham.

**Gray, Nicholas Stuart**
Unicorn.

**Gray, Pat**
Girl, The/The Girlie Magazine.

**Gray, Patrick Worth**
Beyond the Firehouse.
Bread Loaf to Omaha, Twenty-eight
Hours.
Lines for My Father.

**Gray, Robert**
Greyhounds.
Landscape 4.
Meat Works, The.
North Coast Town.

**Gray, Thomas**
Bard, The.
Candidate, The.
Descent of Odin, The; an Ode from the
Norse Tongue.
Elegy Written in a Country Churchyard.
Epitaph on Dr. Keene.
Epitaph on Dr. Keene's Wife.
Fatal Sisters, The.
Ode on a Distant Prospect of Eton
College.
Ode on the Death of a Favourite Cat,
Drowned in a Tub of Gold Fishes.
Ode on the Pleasure Arising from
Vicissitude.
Ode on the Spring.

On Dr. Keene, Bishop of Chester.
On Lord Holland's Seat near Margate,
Kent.
Progress of Poesy, The.
Satire upon the Heads.
Sketch of His Own Character.
Sonnet on the Death of [Mr.] Richard
West.
Such Tophet was; so looked the grinning
fiend.
William Shakespeare to Mrs. Anne,
Regular Servant to the Rev. Mr.
Precentor of York.

**Gray, Victor**
Limerick: "Charlotte Brontë said, 'Wow,
sister! *What* a man!' "
Limerick: "Old East End worker called
Jock, An."
Limerick: "One morning old Wilfrid
Scawen Blunt."
Limerick: "Taxi-cab whore out at Iver,
A."
Limerick: "There was a young fellow
called Crouch."
Limerick: "When Gauguin was visiting
Fiji."
Limerick: "When our dean took a pious
young spinster."
Limerick: "While visiting Arundel
Castle."
Limerick: "Young engine-driver called
Hunt, A."

**Gray, William B.**
She Is More to Be Pitied than Censured.

**Grayston, Joan Byers**
Dexter.
Unseen Horses.

**Greasybear, Charley John**
Jesus Song.

**Greaves, John Woodcock**
John Peel.

**Green, F. Pratt**
Old Couple, The.

**Green, J. Charles**
Arioso, *sel.*
Day of Notes, A (That Fit into the
Puzzle of a Poem).
Freedom.
Inside the Wall of My Cell.
Isolation Cell Poem.
Parole Denial.
Thought in the Center of a Memory, A.
Waking Up.

**Green, Joseph**
Permit Us, Lord, to Consecrate, *with
music.*

**Green, Paul**
I am a piece of paper.

**Greenaway, Kate**
Little Wind.
School Is Over.
When You and I Grow Up.
Which Is the Way to Somewhere Town?

**Greenberg, Barbara L.**
Husband, The.
Judge Kroll.
Just after the Widow's Death.
Poem for Susan.
Survival.

**Greenberg, Blu**
Mikveh, The.

**Greenberg, Eliezer**

Dog and Tiger.

**Greenberg, Uri Zvi**
Almighty Lord, with One Accord, *with
music.*
Great Sad One, The.
Hour, The.
How It Is.
Like a Woman.
On the Pole.
Song at the Skirts of Heaven.
There Is a Box.
Valley of Men, The.
With My God, the Smith.

**Greene, Richard L.**
Autolycus' Song (In Basic English).
Ubi Iam Sunt?

**Greene, Robert**
Farewell to Folly, *sel.*
Greene's Mourning Garment, *sels.*
Hexametra Alexis in Laudem
Rosamundi.
Maesia's Song.
Menaphon, *sels.*
Samela.
Sephestia's Song to Her Childe.
Shepherd's Wife's Song, The.

**Greenwell, Dora**
Sun-Flower, The.

**Greenwood, Theresa**
Here I sit in my infested cubicle.

**Greger, Debora**
Compline.

**Gregg, Linda**
Andromache Afterwards.
Apparent, The.
Beckett Kit, The.
Defeated, The.
Figures near a Bridge.
For My Friend Michele.
Girl I Call Alma, The.
Gnostics on Trial.
Men like Salmon, The.
Not Singing.
Sigismundo.
We Manage Most When We Manage
Small.

**Gregor, Arthur**
Beacon, The.
Elements of Night.
Enough.
Guide, The
History.
Late Last Night.
Likeness, The.
Nameless Recognition, A.
Poem: "So many pigeons at Columbus."
Spirit-like before Light.
Spirits, Dancing.
To Emily.
Two Shapes.

**Gregor, Christian**
What Splendid Rays, *with music.*

**Gregor, Debora**
Second Violinist's Son, The.

**Gregory, Horace**
Advice.
And of Columbus.
Chinese Garden, The.
Chorus for Survival, *sel.*
Death and Empedocles 444 B.C.
Dempsey, Dempsey.
Hagen.

Hellbabies.
Homestead.
Longface Mahoney Discusses Heaven.
Meek Shall Disinherit the Earth, The.
Night-Walker, The.
O Metaphysical Head.
On a Celtic Mask by Henry Moore.
Passion of M'Phail, The, *sel.*
Prisoner's Song.
Rehearsal, The.
Stanzas for My Daughter.
Tombstone with Cherubim.
Under the Stone I Saw Them Flow.
Voices of Heroes.

**Gregory, Yvonne**
Christmas Lullaby for a New-born
  Child.

**Gregory the Great, Saint (c.540-604)**
Behold, the Shade of Night Is Now
  Receding, *with music.*

**Greiffenberg, Catharina Regina von**
On the Ineffable Inspiration of the Holy
  Spirit.
Why the Resurrection Was Revealed to
  Women.

**Greig, Andrew**
Marry the Lass?

**Grenfell, Julian**
Into Battle.

**Grenville, George.** See **Granville, George,**
  **Baron Lansdowne**

**Grenville, R. H.**
Within Us, Too.

**Greville, Fulke, 1st Baron Brooke**
Caelica, *sels.*
Chorus Sacerdotum.
Cynthia, because your horns look diverse
  ways.
Downe in the depth of mine iniquity.
Earth with thunder torne, with fire
  blasted, The.
Epitaph upon the Right Honorable Sir
  Philip Sidney, An.
I offer wrong to my beloved saint.
Love, the delight of all well-thinking
  minds.
Memento Mori.
Mustapha, *sels.*
Myra.
Vain Learning.

**Grew, Gwendolyn**
Burning the Letters.

**Grierson, Constantia**
To Miss Laetitia Van Lewen.

**Grieve, Christopher Murray.** *See*
  **"MacDiarmid, Hugh"**

**Griffin, Bartholomew**
Fidessa, More Chaste than Kind, *sels.*
Venus, with young Adonis sitting by her.

**Griffin, Ellen McEvilley**
Confession of a Young Hegelian.
Good Harbor Bay, Leland, Michigan.
If I Ask Whether the Islands.
Rimbaud in Abyssinia.

**Griffin, George Randall**
World Was Never Real to Me, The.

**Griffin, Jonathan**
Storm End.

**Griffin, Margaret Johnston**
To My Son.

**Griffin, "Sin-Killer"**
Man of Calvary, The, *sel.*

**Griffin, Susan**
Answer to a Man's Question, An, "What
  Can I Do about Women's
  Liberation?"
Grenadine.
I Like to Think of Harriet Tubman.
Love should grow up like a wild iris in
  the fields.
Revolution.
Sky, The.
Song My.
White Bear.

**Griffith, Llewelyn Wyn**
Silver Jubilee.

**Griffith, Margaret**
When I Consider.

**Griffiths, Lexie**
Going Fishing.

**Grigson, Geoffrey**
Administrator, An.
Before a Fall.
Bibliotheca Bodleiana.
Burials.
By the Road.
Critics and Poets.
End of the Affair.
Heart Burial.
May Trees in a Storm.
On a Lover of Books.
On the Relinquishment of a Title.
Professionals, The.
Two Are Together.

**Grimald, Nicholas**
Garden, The.
Garden, The.

**Grimké, Angelina Weld**
Black Finger, The.
Tenebris.
To Clarissa Scott Delany.
Winter Twilight, A.
Your Hands.

**Grindal, Edmund**
Give Peace in These Our Days, O Lord,
  *with music.*

**Griswold, Alexander V.**
Holy Father, Great Creator, *with music.*

**Grosholz, Emily**
Letter from Germany.
Rodin to Rilke.

**Gross, June**
Drivers of Boston, The.

**Gross, Ronald**
Barbie-Doll Goes to College.
Hero.
Hospital Care Authorization.
Yield.

**Grossbardt, Andrew**
At Pont-Aven, Gauguin's Last Home in
  France.
Jogging at Dusk.

**Grosser, Morton**
Sand Hill Road.

**Grossman, Allen**
By the Pool.
Lilith.

**Grossman, Florence**
Riding.

**Grossman, Martin**
Bread of Our Affliction, The.
Into the Book.
Place to Live, A.

**Grossman, Richard**

Art of Love, The.

**Gruber, Edmund L.**
Caissons Go Rolling Along, The.

**Gruber, Johanna A.**
Love That's Pure, Itself Disdaining, *with*
  *music.*

**Gruber, Edmund L.** *and* H. W. Arberg
Army Goes Rolling Along, The, *with*
  *music.*

**Gruffudd ab yr Ynad Coch**
Lament for Llywelyn ap Gruffudd.

**Gruffydd, Owen**
Men That Once Were, The, *sel.*

**Gruffydd, W. J.**
Gwladys Rhys.
In Memoriam.
This Poor Man.

**Grünewald, Alfred**
Lamp Now Flickers, The.

**Grutzmacher, Harold M.**
Knowledge.

**Grynberg, Henryk**
Anti-Nostalgia.
Dead Sea, The.
Listening to Confucius.
Poplars.

**Guarini, Giovanni Battista**
Faith, Hope, and Charity.
Golden Age, The.
Il Pastor Fido, *sels.*
Microcosm, The.
Thus saith my Chloris bright.

**Guernsey, Bruce**
Back Road.

**Guernsey, Wellington**
Alice, Where Art Thou?

**Guest, Barbara**
Direction.
Location of Things, The.
Safe Flights.
Saving Tallow.

**Guest, Edgar Albert**
Home.
It Couldn't Be Done.
Lemon Pie.
Sausage.

**Guest, Harry**
Matsushima.
Montage.
Twilight Man, A.

**Guevara, Miguel de**
Raise Me Up, Lord.

**Guidacci, Margherita**
All Saints' Day, *sel.*

**Guild, Marilla Merrimar**
Ocotillo in Bloom, The.

**Guillén, Jorge**
Metropolitan Night.

**Guillén, Nicolás**
Ballad of the Two Grandfathers.

**Guillet Pernette du** *See* **Du Guillet,**
  **Pernette**

**Guilpin, Everard**
Let me alone, I prithee, in this cell.
Skialetheia, *sel.*

**Guinicelli, Guido**
Canzone: Of the Gentle Heart.

**Guiterman, Arthur**
Ambiguous Dog, The.
Brief Essay on Man.
Christmas Exchange, The.
Coyote and the Star.

Dance of Gray Raccoon, The.
Daniel Boone.
Dog Parade, The.
Dog's Cold Nose, The.
Dorlan's Home Walk.
Eight Oars and a Coxswain.
Ephraim the Grizzly.
Everything in Its Place.
For a Good Dog.
Habits of the Hippopotamus.
Heredity.
Kag the Porcupine (The Misanthrope).
Little Lost Pup.
Mavrone.
Motto for a Dog House.
Nesting Time.
Nocturne: "Three-toed tree toad, The."
Ode of Odium on Aquariums.
Of Giving.
On the Vanity of Earthly Greatness.
Oregon Trail, The.
Ornithology in Florida.
Prairie Dog, The.
Quivira.
Sleepy Song.
Song of Hate for Eels.
Superstitious Ghost, The.
Three Ponies.
Twist-Rime on Spring.
Windham Thaw, The.

**Gullans, Charles**
Satyr.

**Gunderson, Keith**
Gypsy Motorcycle Club of South
  Minneapolis, The.
Naming the State Bird.

**Gunderson, Mary Alice**
Good Life, The.

**Gunn, Thom**
Annihilation of Nothing, The.
Autobiography.
Autumn Chapter in a Novel.
Black Jackets.
Byrnies, The.
Carnal Knowledge.
Confessions of the Life Artist.
Considering the Snail.
Corridor, The.
Discovery of the Pacific, The.
Elegy on the Dust.
Feel of Hands, The.
High Fidelity.
In Santa Maria del Popolo.
In the Tank.
Incident on a Journey.
Innocence.
Jesus and His Mother.
Messenger, The.
Modes of Pleasure.
Moly.
Monster, The.
My Sad Captains.
New York.
No Speech from the Scaffold.
On the Move.
Painkillers.
Street Song.
Tamer and Hawk.
Touch.
Unsettled Motorcyclist's Vision of His
  Death, The.
Vox Humana.

Wound, The.

**Gunning, Sara Ogan**
Girl of Constant Sorrow.

**Gurevitch, Zali**
Not Going with It.
Short Eulogy.

**Guri, Chaim**
Piyyut for Rosh Hashana.

**Guri, Haim**
Anath.
And on My Return.
Isaac.
Latter Purification, A.
My Samsons.
Nine Men out of a Minyan.
Rain.

**Gurney, Ivor**
Canadians.
Epitaph on a Young Child.
Requiem: "Pour out your light, O stars."
Strange Hells.

**Gustafson, Ingemar**
Locked In.

**Gustafson, Ralph**
Ramble on What in the World Why.

**Guthrie, A.B., Jr.**
Twin Lakes Hunter.

**Guthrie, Ramon**
Alba for Mélusine.
Polar Bear.

**Guthrie, Woody**
Columbus Stockade Blues.
Hard Traveling.
I've Got to Know.
Jesus Christ ("Jesus Christ was a man
  that travelled through the land").
Ludlow Massacre, The.
1913 Massacre, The.
Pastures of Plenty.
Plane Wreck at Los Gatos (Deportee).
Union Maid.

**Gutteridge, Bernard**
Man into a Churchyard.

**Gwenallt**   *See* **Jones, David Gwenallt**

**Gwerfyl Mechain**
Hostess of the Ferry Inn, The.
In the Snowfall.
Snowfall, The.

**Gwillim, Joy**
Ritual, The.

# H

**"H. D."**   *See* **Doolittle, Hilda**
**"H. H."**   *See* **Jackson, Helen Hunt**
**Haad, Siraad**
Lament for a Dead Lover.

**Haag, Terri**
Truck Drivers.

**Haan, Jakov de**
All Is God's.
God's Gifts.
Hanukah.
Sabbath.
Unity.

**Habercom, David**
Life Not Given, The.

**Habington, William**

Against Them Who Lay Unchastity to
  the Sex of Women.
Dialogue between Araphil and Castara,
  A.
Nox Nocti Indicat Scientiam.
Pretty Sport.
Quoniam Ego in Flagella Paratus Sum.
  David, *sel.*
To Castara ("Why should we fear to
  melt away in death").
To Castara: Of True Delight.
To Castara: Of What We Were before
  Our Creation.
To Castara: The Reward of Innocent
  Love.
To Roses in the Bosom of Castara.

**Hacker, Marilyn**
After the Revolution.
Alba: March.
Aube Provençale.
Before the War.
Elektra on Third Avenue.
La Fontaine de Vaucluse.
Living in the Moment.
Presentation Piece.
September.
Under the Arc de Triomphe: October
  17.
Villanelle: "Every day our bodies
  separate."

**Hackett, J. W.**
Haiku: "Bitter morning, A."

**Hackleman, Kris**
Not to March.

**Hadas, Rachel**
Trial.

**Hadewijch**
Ah yes, when love allows.
All Things Confine.
Had I been mindful of my high descent.
Love has seven names.
What helps it if of love I sing.

**Hadley, Drummond**
Springtime.

**Hadrian, Emperor (Publius Aelius
Hadrianus)**
Hadrian's Address to His Soul When
  Dying.

**Hafiz**
Lips of the one I love are my perpetual
  pleasure, The.
Love is where the glory falls.

**Hagedorn, Jessica Tarahata**
Autobiography Part Two: Rock and
  Roll.
Canto de Nada.
Christina.
Kayumangi.
Smokey's Gettin' Old.
Song for My Father.
Sorcery.

**Hagerup, Inger**
Emily Dickinson.

**Hagiwara, Sakutaro**
World of Bacteria.

**Hagthorpe, John**
Elegy upon the Death of the Most
  Illustrious Prince Henry, An, *sel.*

**Hahn, Oscar**
Adolph Hitler Meditates on the Jewish
  Problem.

**Hahn, Robert**

Bad Dream in the Commune, A.
Getting Through the Fifties: The
  Starkweather Case Revisited.
Interrogation.
To the Stolen Children.
Words from the Housewife.
**Hahn, Steve**
July Storm, A: Johnson, Nemaha
  County, Nebraska.
**Haines, John**
And When the Green Man Comes.
At White River.
Awakening.
Calendar, The.
Cauliflower, The.
Child in the Rug, The.
Choosing a Stone.
Cloud Factory, The.
Color, The.
Denali Road.
Deserted Cabin.
Dream of the Lynx.
Fairbanks under the Solstice.
Flight, The.
Foreboding.
Goshawk, The.
If the Owl Calls Again.
Incurable Home, The.
Invaders, The.
Leaves and Ashes.
Legend of Paper Plates, The.
Marigold.
Mirror, The.
Mole, The.
Poem like a Grenade, A.
Prayer to the Snowy Owl.
Skagway.
Snowbound City, The.
Snowy Night.
Spilled Milk.
Stone Harp, The.
To My Father.
To Turn Back.
Train Stops at Healy Fork, The.
Tundra, The.
Weaver, The.
Whale in the Blue Washing Machine,
  The.
Willa.
Wolves.
**Hajek, Louise**
No Madam Butterfly.
Toss me a kiss, and take your leave with
  laughter.  No Madam Butterfly.
**Hajime, Kamimura**
Firefly.
**Hajnal, Anna**
Dead Girl.
Fear.
Felled Plane Tree, The.
Half past Four, October.
That's All?
Tree to Flute.
**Hake, Thomas Gordon**
Snake-Charmer, The.
**Haldane, John Burdon Sanderson**
Cancer's a Funny Thing.
**Haldane, Sean**
I Meant to Tell You.
**Hale, Edward Everett**
Lend a Hand.
**Hale, Janet Campbell**

Aaron Nicholas, Almost Ten.
Alligator Bites.
Cinque.
Custer Lives in Humbolt County.
Desmet, Idaho, March 1969.
My Sisters the Summer of 53.
On a Catholic Childhood.
On Death and Love.
Red Eagle.
Salad La Raza.
Six Feet Under.
Tribal Cemetery.
**Hale, Robert Beverly**
Denise.
**Hale, Sarah Josepha Buell**
Mary's Lamb.
Our Father in Heaven, *with music.*
**Hales, Thomas.**  *See* **Thomas of Hales**
**Haley, Bruce**
Rime of the Ancient Mariner, The.
**Haley, Ed**
While Strolling through the Park One
  Day.
**Haley, Vanessa**
At the Smithsonian.
**Halkin, Shimon**
Do Not Accompany Me.
**Hall, Amanda Benjamin**
It Seems That God Bestowed Somehow,
  *with music.*
**Hall, Donald**
Airstrip in Essex, 1960, An.
Alligator Bride, The.
Blue Wing, The.
Body Politic, The.
Brain Cells, The.
Breasts.
By the Exeter River.
Child, The.
Christmas Eve in Whitneyville, 1955.
Cold Water.
Crew-cuts.
Days, The.
Detroit.
Dump, The.
Foundation of American Industry, The.
Gold.
In the Kitchen of the Old House.
Je Suis une Table.
Long River, The.
Man in the Dead Machine, The.
Moon, The.
My Son, My Executioner.
Names of Horses.
New Hampshire.
O Cheese.
Old Pilot's Death, The.
Ox Cart Man.
Photographs of China.
Poet at Twenty, A.
Professor Gratt.
Questions [1] ("Why do you love her").
Questions [2] ("How is it now").
Raisin, The.
Reclining Figure.
Repeated Shapes, The.
Self-Portrait, as a Bear.
Six Poets in Search of a Lawyer.
Sleeping Giant, The.
Stump, The.
Sudden Things.

T. R.
Three Movements, The.
To a Waterfowl.
Town of Hill, The.
Transcontinent.
Waters.
White Apples.
Woolworth's.
Your voice on the telephone.
**Hall, Gregory**
Voice of the Power of This World, The.
**Hall, Hazel**
Baby's Dress, A.
Bead Work.
Instruction.
Late Sewing.
Lingerie.
Listening Macaws, The.
Mending.
Seams.
Stitches.
**Hall, Henry**
Ballad on the Times, A.
On Sir John Fenwick.
Upon the King's Return from Flanders.
**Hall, James Baker**
Mad Farmer Stands Up in Kentucky for
  What He Thinks Is Right, The.
Modern Chinese History Professor Plays
  Pool Every Tuesday and Thursday,
  The.
Old Athens of the West Is Now a Blue
  Grass Tour, The.
Poet Finds an Ephemeral Home in a
  Truck Stop on the New Jersey
  Turnpike, ca. 1970, The.
Song of the Mean Mary Jean Machine,
  The.
**Hall, Joan Joffe**
Graffiti for Lovers.
Homeless, The.
**Hall, John (1627-56)**
Dithyramb, A.
On an Hour-Glass.
**Hall, Joseph**
Great is the folly of a feeble brain.
Prologue: "I first adventure, with
  foolhardy might."
Rome Ryme.
Virgidemiarum, *sels.*
**Hall, Katie V.**
Old, Filthy Beer Pail, The.
**Hall, Owen**
Tell Me Pretty Maiden; or, English Girl
  and Clerks, *with music.*
**Hall, R. W.**
Last Longhorn, The.
**Hall, Rodney**
Cruise for the Prosecution, A.
Domesticity.
Elegy for Michael Dransfield.
Lapse of Contract.
Medieval, The.
Out of the Earth We Come.
Owner of My Face, The, *sel.*
Two Byzantine Pieces.
Water Tank at Dusk, The.
**Hall, Sharlot Mabridth**
Away Out West.
Cash In.
In Old Tucson.
Man-sized Job.

Occultation of Venus, The.
Pumpkin Pie.
Reply of the Free Woman.
Road Runner.
Sheep Herding.
Smell of Rain.
Spring in the Desert.
Two Bits.

**Hall, Wade**
Dark Hope.
Death Insurance.
Eschatology.
Paso por Aqui.
Winter Flowers.

**Hall, Walter**
That Brings Us to the Woodstove in the Wilds, at Night.

**Halleck, Fitz-Greene**
Song: "There's a barrel of porter at Tammany Hall."

**Halley, Anne**
Against Dark's Harm.
Autograph Book/ Prophecy.
Dear God, the Day Is Grey.
Housewife's Letter: To Mary.
O Doctor Dear My Love.
Pride of Ladies, A.

**Halperin, Mark**
Franz Jagesttater's Epistemology.

**Halpern, Daniel**
Arriving.
Clove as Ego.
Endings.
Ethnic Life, The.
Fish.
Gossip, The.
Hermit, The.
Hunt, The.
Landing, The.
Late.
Nebraskan Childhood.
Return.
Street Fire.
Summer, 1970.

**Halpern, Leivick.** *See* **Leivick, H.**

**Halpern, Max**
Epigram: "In the neat parlor of their honeymoon."

**Halpern, Moishe Leib**
Bird, The.
Considering the Bleakness.
Go Throw Them Out.
Isaac Leybush Peretz.
Just Because.
Memento Mori.
Sacco-Vanzetti.
That's Our Lot.
Zlotchev, My Home.

**Ham, Marion Franklin**
As Tranquil Streams, *with music.*
O Thou Whose Gracious Presence Shone, *with music.*
Touch Thou Mine Eyes, *with music.*

**Hamblin, Robert W.**
On the Death of the Evansville University Basketball Team in a Plane Crash, December 13, 1977.

**Hamburger, Michael**
At Staufen.
Dual Site, The.
Lines on Brueghel's Icarus.

London Tom-Cat.
Memory.
Poet's Progress, A.
Search, The.
Squares.

**Hamelin, Jacques**
Stonetalk.

**Hamill, Gerry**
Song of the GPO, A.

**Hamill, Sam**
Gnostology.
Reno, 2 A.M.
Wakening, The.

**Hamilton, Bobb**
Poem to a Nigger Cop.

**Hamilton, Eugene Lee-.** *See* **Lee-Hamilton, Eugene**

**Hamilton, George Rostrevor ("George Rostrevor")**
Don's Holiday.
Exchange.
Exile.
No Occupation.
Old Ox, The.
On a Distant Prospect of an Absconding Bookmaker.
On a Statue of Sir Arthur Sullivan.
Schoolmaster.
To the Greek Anthologists.

**Hamilton, Horace**
Displacement.

**Hamilton, Ian**
Complaint.
Now and Then.
Pretending Not to Sleep.
Recruits, The.

**Hamm, Timothy**
Finding a Friend Home.

**Hammerstein, Oscar, II**
All the Things You Are, *with music.*
June Is Bustin' Out All Over, *with music.*
Kansas City.
Money Isn't Everything!
Ol' Man River, *with music.*
There Is Nothin' like a Dame.

**Hammond, Geraldine**
Encounter.

**Hammond, Jerry**
Feature Time.

**Hammond, Karla M.**
Expectancies: The Eleventh Hour.
Testing Ground.

**Hammond, Mac**
In Memory of V.R. Lang.

**Hamod, Sam**
After the Funeral of Assam Hamady.
Anthropology in Fort Morgan, Colorado.
Famous Hot Pepper Eating Contest, The.
Fight, The.
Leaves.
Lines to My Father.
Loss of Black Camels, The.
Mother's Day.

**Hampl, Patricia**
Blue Bottle.

**Hanaford, Phoebe A.**
Cast Thy Bread upon the Waters, *with music.*

**Hanby, Benjamin Russel**
Darling Nelly Gray.

**Handy, Nixeon Civille**
Girl to Woman.

**Handy, Will**
Didn't He Ramble.

**Handy, William Christopher**
St. Louis Blues.

**Hanes, Leigh**
Old Fence Post.

**Hanim, Leylâ**
Let's get going.

**Hanim, Nigâr**
Tell Me Again.

**Hankey, Katherine**
I Love to Tell the Story.

**Hankin, St. John Emile Clavering**
De Gustibus.

**Hanley, Katherine**
After Vacation.

**Hannan, Greg**
Bloom.
Chroma.
Triptych.

**Hannigan, Paul**
Carnation, The.

**Hans, Marcie**
Fueled.

**Hansen, Chadwick**
Creator of Infinities, *with music.*

**Hansen, Joseph**
Fists.

**Hanson, Amos**
Schooner *Fred Dunbar*, The.
Trip to the Grand Banks, A.

**Hanson, Elizabeth**
Departure.
Summer's Darkness.
Walking without Snowshoes.

**Hanson, Howard G.**
As Rocks Rooted.
That Is Not Indifference.

**Hanson, Joseph Mills**
Laramie Trail.

**Hanson, Kenneth O.**
Before the Storm.
Bouzouki.
Distance Anywhere, The.
Divide, The.
Elegiac.
First of All.
Montana.
Snow.

**Hanson, Pauline**
And I Am Old to Know.
From Creature to Ghost.
Love.
So Beautiful Is the Tree of Night.

**Hanzlicek, C. G.**
One Song, The.

**Harbaugh, Henry**
Jesus, I Live to Thee, *with music.*

**Harburg, E. Y.**
Brother, Can You Spare a Dime?

**Hardeman, Louise**
In Search of a Short Poem for My Grandmother.

**Hardenberg, Friedrich von.** *See* **"Novalis"**

**Hardin, Glenn**
Fools.

**Harding, Samuel**
Sicily and Naples; or, The Fatal Union: a Tragedy, *sel.*

**Hardison, O. B., Jr.**
A B C of Love, The.
King of the World.
Pro Musica Antiqua.
Pythagoras ("Pythagoras knew the world
  is symbols").
**Hardy, Thomas**
Abbey Mason, The, *sel.*
"According to the Mighty Working."
After a Journey.
After the Club-Dance.
After the Fair.
After the Last Breath.
After the Visit.
Afterwards.
Ah, Are You Digging on My Grave?
Ancient to Ancients, An.
Anniversary, An.
At a Hasty Wedding.
At a Watering Place.
At Casterbridge Fair, *sels.*
At Castle Boterel.
Backward Spring, A.
Bags of Meat.
Ballad-Singer, The.
Beauty, The, *sel.*
Beeny Cliff.
Bereft.
Beyond the Last Lamp.
Blinded Bird, The.
Broken Appointment, A.
Brother, The.
Budmouth Dears.
Bullfinches, The.
By Her Aunt's Grave.
Channel Firing.
Chorus of the Years.
Chosen, The.
Christmas: 1924.
Church Romance, A.
Comet at Yell'ham, The.
Commonplace Day, A.
Contretemps, The.
Convergence of the Twain, The.
Copying Architecture in an Old Minster.
Country Wedding, The (A Fiddler's
  Story).
Curtains Now Are Drawn, The.
Dark-eyed Gentleman, The.
Darkling Thrush, The.
Dream-Follower, The.
Drizzling Easter Morning, A.
Drummer Hodge.
During Wind and Rain.
Echo Elf Answers, The.
Epitaph for George Moore.
Epitaph on a Pessimist.
Fallow Deer at the Lonely House, The.
Farm-Woman's Winter, The.
First or Last.
Five Students, The.
For Life I Had Never Cared Greatly.
Former Beauties.
Friends Beyond.
Garden Seat, The.
God's Education.
Going, The.
Going and Staying.
Great Things.
Hap.
Haunter, The.
He Never Expected Much.

Heiress and Architect.
Heredity.
His Immortality.
Horses Aboard.
House of Hospitalities, The.
I Am the One.
I Found Her Out There.
I look into my glass.
I Need Not Go.
I never cared for Life: Life cared for me.
I Said to Love.
I watched a blackbird on a budding
  sycamore.
If It's Ever Spring Again.
If You Had Known.
In a Wood.
In Church.
In Tenebris.
In the Moonlight.
In the Room of the Bride-Elect.
In the Vaulted Way.
In Time of "The Breaking of Nations."
In Weatherbury Stocks.
Ivy-Wife, The.
Jog-Trot Pair, A *sel.*
Lacking Sense, The.
Last Chrysanthemum, The.
Last Look Round St. Martin's Fair.
Last Words to a Dumb Friend.
Lausanne.
Let Me Enjoy.
Levelled Churchyard, The.
Man He Killed, The.
Midnight on the Great Western.
Minute before Meeting, The.
Moments of Vision.
Mound, The.
Mute Opinion.
Nature's Questioning.
Near Lanivet, 1872.
Necessitarian's Epitaph, A.
Neutral Tones.
New Year's Eve.
Newcomer's Wife, The.
Night of the Dance, The.
1967.
Nobody Comes.
Old Furniture.
On a fine Morning.
On the Departure Platform.
On the Portrait of a Woman about to Be
  Hanged.
One We Knew.
Overlooking the River Stour.
Oxen, The.
Phantom Horsewoman, The.
Pity of It, The.
Poet, A.
Proud Songsters.
Rain on a Grave.
Refusal, A.
Regret Not Me.
Rejected Member's Wife, The.
Reminder, The.
Respectable Burgher, The.
Robin, The.
Roman Road, The.
Rome.
Ruined Maid, The.
Satires of Circumstance, *sel.*
Schreckhorn, The.
Self-unseeing, The.

Selfsame Song, The.
She: At His Funeral.
She, to Him.
Sheep Fair, A.
Shelley's Skylark.
Shut Out That Moon.
Snow in the Suburbs.
Souls of the Slain, The.
Subalterns, The.
Sunshade, The.
Tess's Lament.
This Summer and Last.
Thoughts of Phena.
Thunderstorm in Town, A.
To Flowers from Italy in Winter.
Trampwoman's Tragedy, A.
Transformations.
Two Lips.
Unborn, The.
Under the Waterfall.
Voice, The.
Voices from Things Growing in a
  Churchyard.
Walk, The.
Weathers.
Wessex Heights.
Wet August, A.
When I Set Out for Lyonnesse.
When Oats Were Reaped.
Where the Picnic Was.
Who's in the Next Room.
Winter in Durnover Field.
Wives in the Sere.
Woman in the Rye, The.
Workbox, The.
Year's Awakening, The.
Young Man's Epigram on Existence, A.
**Hare, Maurice Evan**
Byways in Biography.
Limerick: "There once was a man who
  said, 'Damn!' "
**Harford, David K.**
From the Batter's Box.
**Harington, Donald**
Villanelle, The: "Regard the motion of
  the Villanelle."
**Harington [or Harrington], Henry**
Abbey Church at Bath, The.
**Harington [or Harrington], Sir John (1561-
  1612)**
Against an Old Lecher.
Author, of His Own Fortune, The.
Author to His Wife, of a Woman's
  Eloquence, The.
Comparison of the Sonnet and the
  Epigram.
Of a Zealous Lady.
Of a Fair Shrew.
Of an Heroical Answer of a Great
  Roman Lady to Her Husband.
Of Treason.
**Harington, Lucy, Countess of Bedford**
Elegy: "Death be not proud, thy hand
  gave not this blow."
**Harjo, Joy**
Creek Mother Poem.
He Told Me His Name Was Sitting Bull.
Hopi Woman Talking, A.
Ignacio, Colorado, for You That Time.
Lame Deer.
Last Song, The.
Lost Weekend Bar, The.

People, The.
Snake Poem I.
**Harjo, Patty L. ("Ya-Ka-Nes")**
Death.
Mask, The.
Musings.
Taos Winter.
To an Indian Poet.
Where Have You Gone, Little Boy.
Wishes.
**Harkavi, Hedva**
It Was Gentle.
Talk to Me, Talk to Me.
Whenever the Snakes Come.
**Harmon, William**
Bureaucratic Limerick.
Dawn Horse, The.
Literacy: An Abandoned Ode.
Mothsong.
There.
To Redound.
**Harney, Ben**
Mister Johnson.
You've Been A Good Old Wagon, but
You've Done Broke Down.
**Harper, Frances E. W.**
Bury Me in a Free Land.
Slave Auction, The.
**Harper, Michael S.**
Afterword: A Film.
American History.
Barricades.
"Bird Lives": Charles Parker in St.
Louis.
Black Angel, The.
Blue Ruth: America.
Breaded Meat, Breaded Hands.
Cannon Arrested.
Come Back Blues.
Dark Way Home, The: Survivors.
Dear John, Dear Coltrane.
Deathwatch.
Effendi.
Elvin's Blues.
Grandfather.
Heartblow.
Heartblow: Messages.
Here Where Coltrane Is.
History as Diabolical Maternalism.
Ice-fishing House, The: Long Lake,
Minnesota.
Madimba: Gwendolyn Brooks.
Martin's Blues.
Meaning of Protest, The.
Mother Speaks, A: The Algiers Motel
Incident, Detroit.
Near the White House.
Newsletter from My Mother.
Nightmare Begins Responsibility.
Parable.
Photographs: A Vision of Massacre.
Poetry Concert.
Rat Fever: History as Hallucination.
Spiritual.
We Assume: On the Death of Our Son,
Reuben Masai Harper.
**Harrigan, Ned [or Ed]**
Mulligan Guard, The, *with music*.
Walking for That Cake, *with music*.
**Harrington, Edward**
Bushrangers, The.
**Harrington, Henry** See **Harington, Henry**

**Harrington, Sir John (1561–1612.)** *See*
**Harington, Sir John (1561–1612)**
**Harris, Charles Kassell**
After the Ball Is Over, *with music*.
Break the News to Mother, *with music*.
**Harris, Hazel Harper**
Sailor's Song, A.
**Harris, John**
Sabbath.
**Harris, John S.**
Hay Derrick
Tag, I.D.
**Harris, Louise**
You Are Growing into My Life.
**Harris, Marie**
Dill.
Facts of Winter.
I-93
Interstate, *sels*.
Learning.
Lemon Balm.
Luxury Apt.
Monkshood.
Song: "Hair/ like heather, father would
boast."
Visitors.
**Harris, Max**
On Throwing a Copy of the New
Statesman into the Coorong.
Tantanoola Tiger, The.
**Harris, Michael**
Ice Castle, The.
**Harris, Phyllis.** *See* **Beauvais, Phyllis**
**Harris, Robert**
That Bad Music.
Tobacco.
**Harris, Sydney Justin**
I Come to Bury Caesar.
**Harris, William J.**
For Bill Hawkins, a Black Militant.
Give Me Five.
Grandfather Poem, A.
Hey Fella Would You Mind Holding
This Piano a Moment.
Modern Romance.
Practical Concerns.
Rib Sandwich.
They live in Parallel Worlds.
We Live in a Cage.
Why Would I Want.
**Harrison, De Leon**
Collage for Richard Davis, A—Two
Short Forms.
Room, The.
Seed of Nimrod, The.
Some Days/ Out Walking Above.
Yellow.
**Harrison, Gregory**
Alone in the Grange.
Dustbin Men, The.
Yellow Cat.
**Harrison, James**
Bellevue.
Easier.
Eve's Version.
Moving.
Sequence.
Sequence of Women, A.
**Harrison, Janet E.**
Lament of a Last Letter.
**Harrison, Jim**
After Reading Takahashi.

After the Anonymous Swedish.
After the "invitation" by the preacher
she collapsed in the.
Fair/ Boy Christian Takes a Break.
Ghazals, *sels*.
Horse.
I Was Proud.
Jim—Age 38, 5'10", W.196, Strapping
Goggle-eyed Nordic Bankrupt.
Letters to Yesenin, *sels*.
Locations.
Poem: "Form is the woods: the beast."
Returning at Night.
Sketch for a Job Application Blank.
Sound.
Suite to Fathers.
Today We've Moved.
Trader.
Traverse City Zoo.
Word Drunk.
**Harrison, Sam G.**
Fisherman, The.
**Harrison, Tony**
Hands, The.
Schwiegermutterlieder.
**Harrold, William**
Another Load.
Flowers for the Grangerford Girl.
Small Tribute, A.
**Harry, J. S.**
Celia.
Hunting Dragons with Fire Tongues and
Deep Smoky Throats.
Hurry Hurry.
In the Park beside the Marina.
Little Grenade, The.
Outposts.
To Start With.
What Might Pass a Man as a Survivor.
Yellow without Poetry.
**Harsent, David**
Old Photographs.
Rag Doll to the Heedless Child, The.
**Hart, Elizabeth Anna**
Mother Tabbyskins.
**Hart, James**
Blemishes.
**Hart, Joanne**
When Your Parents Grow Old.
**Hart, John**
Confrontation.
**Hart, Joseph**
Come Ye Sinners, Poor and Needy, *with
music*.
**Hart, Kevin**
Twenty-first Century, The.
**Hart, Lorenz**
Blue Room, The.
Lady Is a Tramp, The.
Manhattan.
Most Beautiful Girl in the World, The.
Mountain Greenery.
My Heart Stood Still, *with music*.
**Hart-Smith, William**
Beach, The.
Black Stockman.
Otters.
Rhinoceros.
Space.
Traffic.
Wild Geese.
**Harte, Bret (Francis Bret Harte)**

Caldwell of Springfield.
Chiquita.
Colenso Rhymes for Orthodox Children.
Coyote.
Dickens in Camp.
Dow's Flat.
Further Language from Truthful James.
Grizzly.
Heathen Chinee, The.
Mission Bells of Monterey, The.
Mrs. Judge Jenkins (Being the Only
   Genuine Sequel to "Maud Muller").
San Francisco from the Sea.
Schemmelfennig.
Society upon the Stanislaus, The.
Spelling Bee at Angels, The.
What the Bullet Sang.
What the Engines Said.

**Harte, Walter**
Enchanted Region, The; or, Mistaken
   Pleasures.

**Hartford, John**
Poor Old Prurient Interest Blues, The.

**Hartigan, Patrick Joseph ("John O'Brien")**
Said Hanrahan.

**Hartman, Charles O.**
Before My Father before Me.
Inflation.
Mastodon.
Milkweed.
Prayer for Violets, A.
To Shadow.
Trading Chicago.

**Hartman, Susan**
After His Death.
In The Generation That Laughed at Me.

**Hartnett, Michael**
All That Is Left.
All the Death-Room Needs.
Death of an Irishwoman.
Domestic Scene.
Enamoured of the Miniscule.
For My Grandmother, Bridgid [or
   Bridget] Halpin.
I Have Exhausted the Delighted Range.
I Think Sometimes.
Prologue: "Pardon my omissions."
Retreat of Ita Cagney, The.
Small Farm, A.
Sonnet: "I saw magic on a green country
   road."
There will be a talking of lovely things.

**Hartsough, Lewis**
Come, Friends and Neighbors, Come,
   *with music.*
Let Me Go Where Saints Are Going,
   *with music.*

**Harvey, Frederick William**
November.

**Harvey, Gayle Elen**
Tonight When You Leave.
We Are Leaning Away.

**Harwood, Gwen**
All Souls'.
Barn Owl.
David's Harp.
Father and Child.
"I Am the Captain of My Soul."
In Brisbane.
In the Park.
Lion's Bride, The.
Night Thoughts.

Person to Person.

**Harwood, Lee**
Animal Days.
Blue Mosque, The.
Final Painting, The.
Plato Was Right Though.
Soft White.
"Utopia," The.
Words, The.

**"Hashimura Togo."**   *See* **Irwin, Wallace**

**Hashin**
Neither earth nor sky.

**Haskell, Jefferson**
My Latest Sun Is Sinking Fast, *with
   music.*

**Hass, Robert**
Against Botticelli.
Fall.
In Weather.
Maps.
Nineteenth Century as a Song, The.
Origin of Cities, The.
Politics of a Pornographer.
Pornographer, The.
Return of Robinson Jeffers, The.
Song: "Afternoon cooking in the fall
   sun."
Songs to Survive the Summer.

**Hassall, Christopher Vernon**
Santa Claus.

**Hassan, Mahammed Abdille**
Denunciation, A.
To a Friend Going on a Journey.

**Haste, Gwendolen**
Dorchester Plate.
Mocker, The.
Prairie Wolf.
Prayer of the Homesteader.
Ranch in the Coulee, The.
Reason, The.
Stoic, The.

**Hastings, Thomas**
Hail to the Brightness of Zion's Glad
   Morning, *with music.*
Now Be the Gospel Banner, *with music.*
Now from Labor and from Care, *with
   music.*

**Hatfield, Edwin Francis**
Hallelujah! Praise the Lord, *with music.*

**Hathaway, Jeanine**
Conversation with God.
Extensions of Linear Mobility.
In Random Fields of Impulse and
   Repose.
Reflections on a Womb Which Is Called
   "Vacant."
World Enough.

**Hathaway, William**
Coloring Margarine.

**Haug, James**
Long Season, The.

**Hauk, Barbara**
Getting Older Here.

**Hauroa, Matangi**
Lament: "I lie in darkness, as the dead
   shades gather."

**Hausman, Gerald**
Poem for Lorry.

**Havergal, Frances Ridley**
Take My Life and Let It Be, *with music.*

**Hawes, Stephen**
Pastime of Pleasure, The, *sel.*

**Hawker, Robert Stephen**
Burial Hour, The.
Doom-Well of St. Madron, The.
Fatal Ship, The.
Featherstone's Doom.
Legend of the Hive, A.
Poor Man and His Parish Church, The.
Quest of the Sangraal, The, *sel.*
Silent Tower of Bottreau, The.
Song of the Western Men, The.
Song of Western Man, The.

**Hawkins, Walter Everette**
Death of Justice, The.
Spade Is Just a Spade, A.

**Hawley, Richard A.**
January.

**"Hawthorne, Alice."**   *See* **Winner,
   Septimus**

**"Hay, Elijah."**   *See* **Seiffert, Marjorie
   Allen**

**Hay, George Campbell**
Auld Hunter, The.
Bizerta.
Old Fisherman, The.
Still Gyte, Man?

**Hay, John (b.1915)**
Music by the Waters.
Storm, The.

**Hay, John Milton (1838–1905)**
Defend Us, Lord, from Every Ill, *with
   music.*
Enchanted Shirt, The.
Good Luck and Bad ("Good luck is the
   gayest of all gay girls").
Pledge at Spunky Point, The.
What is a first love worth except to
   prepare for a second?

**Hay, Sara Henderson**
Curlew, The.
Tidal Pool.

**Hayakawa, S. I.**
To One Elect.

**Hayden, Joe**
Hot Time in the Old Town, A, *with
   music.*

**Hayden, Robert Earl**
Aunt Jemima of the Ocean Waves.
Baha'u'llah in the Garden of Ridwan.
Ballad for Sue Ellen Westerfield, The.
Ballad of Nat Turner, The.
Ballad of Remembrance, A.
Beginnings, *sel.*
Crispus Attucks.
Diver, The.
El-Hajj Malik El-Shabazz.
Frederick Douglass.
Full Moon.
Homage to the Empress of the Blues.
In the Mourning Time.
Kid.
Middle Passage.
Mourning Poem for the Queen of
   Sunday.
" 'Mystery Boy' Looks for Kin in
   Nashville."
Night, Death, Mississippi.
Night-blooming Cereus, The.
O Daedalus, Fly Away Home.
Peacock Room, The.
Richard Hunt's Arachne.
Road in Kentucky, A.
Runagate Runagate.

Sojourner Truth.
Stars, *sel.*
"Summertime and the Living."
Those Winter Sundays.
Tour 5.
Unidentified Flying Object.
Veracruz.
Wheel, The.
Whipping, The.
Witch Doctor.

**Hayes, Alfred**
Death of the Craneman, The.
Fresco for A. MacLeish, A.
I Always Come Home.
In a Coffee Pot.
In a Home Relief Bureau.
Joe Hill.
Port of New York, The.
Singleman.
Slaughter-House, The.
Success Story.
To Otto Bauer.

**Hayes, Donald Jeffrey**
Alien.
Appoggiatura.
Benediction.
Haven.
Poet.
Pastourelle.
Threnody: "Let happy throats be mute."

**Hayman, Robert**
Mad Answer of a Madman, A.
To the Reader.

**Hays, Hoffman Reynolds**
Age?
Case, The.
For One Who Died Young.
January.
Manhattan.
Sacred Children, The.

**Hays, Lee**
Talking Union.

**Hays, Lee, Millrd Lampell and Pete Seger**
*See* Seger, Pete ,Millard Lampell *and*
Lee Hays

**Hazard, James**
To the Carp, and Those Who Hunt Her.

**Hazlewood-Brady, Anne**
Double Axe, The.
Closer First to Earth.

**Hazo, Samuel**
Day They Ate the Baritone, The.
God and Man.
Maps for a Son Are Drawn as You Go.
Parachutist.

**Head, Gwen**
Slug.
Stinging Nettle.

**Head, Thomas**
What Hart Crane Meant.

**Healy, Eloise Klein**
Dark.
Los Angeles.
My Love Wants to Park.
What Is Being Forgotten.

**Heaney, Seamus**
Advancement of Learning, An.
Anahorish.
Badgers, The.
Barn, The.
Blackberry-picking.
Bog Queen.

Bogland.
Boy Driving His Father to Confession.
Churning Day.
Death of a Naturalist.
Digging.
Diviner, The.
Docker.
Dream of Jealousy, A.
Early Purges, The.
England's Difficulty.
Exposure.
Follower.
Forge, The.
Given Note, The.
Grauballe Man, The.
Gravities.
In Small Townlands.
Limbo.
Linen Town.
Mid-Term Break.
Mossbawn: Two Poems in Dedication.
Mother.
New Song, A.
Northern Hoard, A, *sel.*
Outlaw, The.
Personal Helicon.
Requiem for the Croppies.
Scaffolding.
Serenades.
Shoreline.
Singer's House, The.
Storm on the Island.
Thatcher.
Tollund Man, The.
Traditions.
Triptych.
Trout.
Twice Shy.
Wanderer, The.
Waterfall.
Whatever You Say, Say Nothing.
Whinlands.
Wife's Tale, The.

**Heap, Jane**
Where go the birds when the rain.

**Hearn, Bonita**
Before the Reincarnation.

**Hearn, Bonnie**
Dinosaur.

**Hearst, James**
Behind the Stove.
Dragon Lesson.
Hard Way to Learn.
New Calf, The.
Pause between Clock Ticks.
Truth.

**Heath, ——**
These Women All.

**Heath, Gertrude E.**
Merry Crocodile, The.

**Heath, Robert**
You say you love me, nay, can swear it
too.

**Heath, William**
Cold Feet in Columbus.
Haystack Calhoun.

**Heath-Stubbs, John**
Beggar's Serenade.
Charm against the Toothache, A.
Dark Planet, The.
Epitaph: "Mr. Heath-Stubbs as you
must understand."

History of the Flood, The.
May-Fly.
Mozart.
Poet in Need, A.
Poet of Bray, The.
Poetry Today.
Starling, The.
Unpredicted, The.
Valse Oubliée.

**Heber, Reginald**
From Greenland's Icy Mountains.
Holy, Holy, Holy!

**Hébert, Anne**
Alchemy of Day, The.
Bread Is Born.
Crown of Happiness.
Great Fountains, The.
Life in the Castle.
Offended, The.
Our Hands in the Garden.
Skinny Girl, The.
Spring over the City.
Tomb of the Kings, The.

**Hecht, Anthony**
Alceste in the Wilderness.
Birdwatchers of America.
Dover Bitch, The.
End of the Weekend, The.
Epitaph: "Here lies a poet, briefly
known as Hecht."
Epitaph: "Here lies fierce Strephon,
whose poetic rage."
Feast of Stephen, The.
Fifth Avenue Parade.
Firmness.
From the Grove Press.
Going the Rounds: A Sort of Love
Poem.
Improvisations on Aesop.
"It Out-Herods Herod. Pray You, Avoid
It."
Japan.
La Condition Botanique.
Letter, A.
Lizards and Snakes.
"More Light! More Light!"
Samuel Sewall.
Third Avenue in Sunlight.
Upon the Death of George Santayana.
Vice.
Vow, The.

**Hecht, Roger**
Ditty.

**Hedge, Frederic Henry**
Sovereign and Transforming Grace, *with
music.*

**Hedin, Mary**
On Rears.

**Hedin, Robert**
Wreck of the Great Northern, The.

**Hedley, Leslie Woolf**
Notes Scribbled on the Last Page of a
Novel.
On Seeing a Stamp from the Democratic
Republic of Vietnam.

**Hedylos**
Seduced Girl.

**Heffernan, Michael**
Apparition, The.
Daffodils.
Figure of Plain Force, A.
In Blessed Weather.

Kennedy.
Table, The.

**Heginbothom, Ottiwell**
Great God, let all my tuneful pow'rs.

**Heguri, Lady**
Parting.

**Heikel, Karin Alice** *See* **"Vala, Katri"**

**Heimler, Eugene**
After an Eclipse of the Sun.
Psalm: "Oh Lord, I have been staring
into a mirror."

**Heine, Cincinnatus** *See* **Miller, Joaquin**

**Heine, Heinrich**
At Parting.
Babylonian Sorrows.
Grave of Love, The.
How Slowly Time, the Loathsome Snail.
I crave an ampler, worthier sphere.
Lorelei, The.
Migratory Rats, The.
Morphine.
My Beauty, My Love, You Have Bound
Me.
My child, we were two children.
Rose, the Lily, the Sun and the Dove,
The.
Silesian Weavers, The.
Spruce Is Standing Lonely, A.
Three Holy Kings from Morgenland.
Young Man Loves a Maiden, A.

**Heldenbrand, Sheila**
Because the Savage.
Concentration.
Earl the Pearl.
God Said to the Angels.
President Is Not Funny, The.
Snow Is for Tracking the Invisible Man.
There Is a Little House.
Woman Needed Some Milk, A.

**Hellyer, Jill**
Calculating Female.

**Helmling, Steven**
Two Weeks after an April Frost.

**Hemans, Felicia Dorothea**
Casabianca.
Down a broad river of the western wilds.
Indian Woman's Death-Song.
Graves of a Household, The.
Homes of England, The.
Indian Woman's Death-Song.
Landing of the Pilgrim Fathers in New
England, The.
Memorial Pillar, The.
Orange Bough, The.
Properzia Rossi.
Where Is the Sea?

**Hemensley, Kris**
Melancholy Summer.
Mile from Poetry, A, *sel.*
Mr. Whitman to His Friends in the
Antipodes.
Poem of the Clear Eye, The, *sel.*

**Hemingway, Ernest**
Champs d'Honneur.
Chapter Heading.
Earnest Liberal's Lament, The.
Neo-Thomist Poem.
Valentine.

**Hemschemeyer, Judith**
Best Friends.
Dirty-billed Freeze Footy, The.
Petals of the Tulips, The.

Settlers, The.
Survivors, The.

**Henderson, Alice Corbin** *See* **Corbin,
Alice**

**Henderson, David**
Do Nothing till You Hear from Me.
Documentary on Airplane Glue, A.
Egyptian Book of the Dead
Keep on Pushing.
Louisiana Weekly # 4, The.
Sketches of Harlem.
They Are Killing All the Young Men.
Walk with de Mayor of Harlem.
White People.

**Henderson, Hamish**
Ding Dong Dollar.
Elegies for the Dead in Cyrenaica, *sels.*
First Elegy, End of a Campaign.
Third Elegy, Leaving the City.

**Henderson, Jock**
Martyr and the Army, The.

**Henderson, Paul**
Elegy: "Morning after death on the bar
was calm."
I Think of Those.
Object Lesson.
Return Journey.

**Henderson, Peggy**
Serpent Muses, The.

**Hendrix, Jimi**
Gypsy Eyes.

**Hendry, J. F.**
Constant North, The.
Inverbeg.
Ship, The.

**Henley, Patricia**
Days of Re-entry.
Near Caledonia.
Returning from the Funeral.
Time Out.

**Henley, William Ernest**
At Queensferry.
Ballade Made in Hot Weather.
Ballade of Dead Actors.
Ballade of Youth and Age.
Before.
Casualty.
I Send You Roses.
In Hospital.
Invictus.
London Voluntaries, *sels.*
Madam Life's a Piece in Bloom.
Margaritae Sorori.
Orientale.
Prologue to "Rhymes and Rhythms."
Rondel: "Beside the idle summer sea."
To A. D.
Two Days.
Villon's Straight Tip to All Cross Coves.
Waiting.
Where Forlorn Sunsets.

**Hennamma**
Wasn't your mother a woman?

**Hennell, Thomas**
Mermaiden, A.
Queen Anne's Musicians.
Shepherd and Shepherdess.

**Hennen, Tom**
Dirt Road.
Going into the Woods.
Job Hunting.
Minneapolis.

New Arm, The.
Old Folks Home.
Smelling a Stone in the Middle of
Winter.
Woods Night.

**Henri, Adrian**
Adrian Henri's Talking after Christmas
Blues.
Mrs. Albion You've Got a Lovely
Daughter.
Tonight at Noon.

**Henry VIII, King of England**
To His Lady.

**Henry, Francis**
Old Settler's Song, The.

**"Henry, O." (William Sidney Porter**
Tamales.

**Henryson, Robert**
Robene and Makyne ("Robene sat on
gud grene hill").
Testament of Cresseid, The, *sels.*
Two Mice, The.

**Henson, Lance**
Among Hawks.
Anniversary Poem for the Cheyennes
Who Fell at Sand Creek.
Bay Poem.
Between Rivers and Seas.
Cold, The.
Comanche Ghost Dance: An Impression.
Crazy Horse: The Last Morning.
Curtain.
Dawn in January.
Epitaph: Snake River.
Flock.
Grandfather.
Image of City.
Last Words, 1968.
Moon at Three A.M.
Moth.
Old Man Told Me.
Old Story.
Other.
Our Smoke Has Gone Four Ways.
Poem for Carroll, Descendant of Chiefs.
Rain.
Scattered Leaves.
Sitting Alone in Tulsa Three A.M.
Sleep Watch.
Sundown at Darlington 1878.
Travels with the Band-Aid Army.
Warrior Nation Trilogy.
We are a People.
Wish.
Wood Floor Dreams.

**Heppenstall, Rayner**
Actaeon.

**Herbert, Sir Alan Patrick**
Less Nonsense.
Lines for a Worthy Person Who Has
Drifted by Accident into a Chelsea
Revel.
Racing-Man, The.
Snail, The.

**Herbert, Edward** *See* **Herbert of
Cherbury, Edward Herbert, 1st Baron**

**Herbert, George**
Aaron.
Affliction ("Broken in pieces all
asunder").
Affliction ("When first thou didst entice
to thee my heart").

Agony, The.
Altar, The.
Ana(Mary-Army)gram.
Answer, The.
Artillery.
Bitter-sweet.
Bunch of Grapes, The.
Church Monuments.
Church Porch, The, *sel.*
Clasping of Hands.
Collar, The.
Content.
Courage.
Death.
Denial.
Dialogue.
Discipline.
Easter ("I got me flowers to straw thy way").
Easter ("Rise, heart! thy Lord is risen").
Easter Wings.
Flower, The.
Forerunners, The.
Glance, The.
Holdfast, The.
Holy Baptism ("Since, Lord, to thee/ A narrow way and little gate").
Holy Scriptures, The, I.
Hope.
Jordan ("When first my lines of heavenly joy made mention").
Jordan ("Who says that fictions only and false hair").
Life.
Love ("Immortal love, author of this great frame").
Love ("Love bade me welcome; yet my soul drew back").
Love-Joy.
Love Unknown.
Man.
Mortification.
Our Life Is Hid with Christ in God.
Paradise.
Peace.
Pearl, The.
Pilgrimage, The.
Posy, The.
Prayer: "Prayer the church's [*or* churches] banquet, angels' age."
Pulley, The.
Quip, The.
Redemption.
Sacrifice, The, *much abr.*
Sepulchre.
Sin.
Tempest, The ("How should I praise thee, Lord!").
To His Mother.
Trinity Sunday.
Ungratefulness.
Virtue.
Windows, The.
Wreath, A.

**Herbert, Mary, Countess of Pembroke**
*See* **Pembroke, Mary Sidney Herbert, Countess of**

**Herbert, Zbigniew**
Elegy of Fortinbras.
I Would Like to Describe.
Our Fear.

**Herbert of Cherbury, Edward Herbert, 1st Baron**
Echo to a Rock.
Elegy over a Tomb.
Idea, The. Made of Alnwick, in His Expedition to Scotland with the Army, 1639.
Ode upon a Question Moved, Whether Love Should Continue Forever?
Platonic Love.
Sonnet of Black Beauty.

**Herbkersman, Gretchen**
Cosmetic.

**Herder, Johann Gottfried von**
Erl-King's Daughter, The.

**Herea, Te Heuheu**
Mourning-Song for Rangiaho, A.

**Herebert, William**
My Folk, What Have I Done Thee?
Orison to the Blessed Virgin, An.
Who Is This That Cometh from Edom?

**Herford, Oliver**
Autograph Bore, The.
Conservative Owl, The.
Crocodile, The.
Earth.
Elf and the Dormouse, The.
Eternal Feminine, The.
Eve.
Fall of J. W. Beane, The.
Fastidious Yak, The.
Feminine Seal, The.
Grumbler Gruff, A.
Humorous Ant, The.
I Heard a Bird Sing.
Inquisitive Leopard, The.
Kind Armadillo, The.
King of Beasts.
Kitten's Thought, A.
Mendacious Mole, The.
Misapprehended Goose, The.
Mock Miracle, A.
Musical Lion, The.
Nature and Art.
Omnivorous Bookworm, The.
Oratorical Crab, The.
Ounce of Detention, The.
Quoter, A.
Snail's Dream, The.
Sole-hungering Camel.
Song: "Gather kittens while you may."
Tact.
Thoroughbred Horse, The.
Tra-La-Larceny.
Well-informed Wight, A.

**Herman, Reinhold W.**
Now I Set Me.

**Hernández, Miguel**
War ("All the mothers in the world").
War ("The aged in the villages").

**Hernton, Calvin C.**
D Blues.
Distant Drum, The.
Fall Down.
Jitterbugging in the Streets.
Madhouse.
Young Negro Poet.

**Herrick, Robert**
All Things Decay and Die.
Amber Bead, The.
Ambition.
Anacreontic ("Born I was to be old").

Anacreontic ("I must/ Not trust").
Anacreontic Verse.
Another on Her.
Apparition of His Mistress Calling Him to Elysium, The.
Apron of Flowers, The.
Argument of His Book, The.
Bad Season Makes the Poet Sad, The.
Bag of the Bee, The.
Barley-Break; or, Last in Hell.
Beggar to Mab, the Fairy Queen, The.
Bellman, The.
Body, The.
Bubble, The: A Song.
Canticle to Apollo, A.
Captived Bee, The: or, The Little Filcher.
Cat, A/ I keep, that plays about my.
Ceremonies for Candlemas Day, The.
Ceremonies for Candlemas Eve.
Ceremonies for Christmas, *sel.*
Cheat of Cupid, The; or, The Ungentle Guest.
Cherry-ripe.
Child's Present, A.
Christmas Carol Sung to the King [in the Presence] at Whitehall, A.
Clothes Do but Cheat and Cozen Us.
Comfort to a Youth That Had Lost His Love.
Conjuration, to Electra, A.
Corinna's Going a-Maying.
Country Life, A: To His Brother, Master Thomas Herrick.
Crosses.
Cruel Maid, The.
Crutches.
Curse, The: A Song.
Definition of Beauty, The.
Delight in Disorder.
Dew Sat on Julia's Hair.
Discontents in Devon.
Distrust.
Divination by a Daffodil.
Dream, The.
Dreams.
End of His Work, The.
Entertainment, or Porch-Verse, at the Marriage of Master Henry Northleigh and the Most Witty Mistress Lettice Yard, The.
Epitaph on Sir Edward Giles and His Wife.
Epitaph upon a Child, An ("Virgins promis'd when I died").
Epitaph upon a Sober Matron, An.
Epitaph upon a Virgin, An.
Epithalamy to Sir Thomas Southwell and His Lady, An.
Eye, The.
Fair Days; or, Dawns Deceitful.
Fame.
Fame Makes Us Forward.
Farewell Frost; or, Welcome the Spring.
Four Things Make Us Happy Here.
Frolic, A.
Frozen Zone, The; or Julia Disdainful.
Funeral Rites of the Rose, The.
God to Be First Served.
Good Luck.
Good-Night, or Blessing, The.
Grace for a Child.

Grace for Children, A.

Hag, The ("The hag is astride").

Hag, The ("The staff is now greased").

Her Leg [or Legs].

His Age, Dedicated to His Peculiar Friend, Master John Wickes, under the Name of Posthumus.

His Cavalier.

His Content in the Country.

His Creed.

His Desire.

His Farewell to Sack.

His Grange, or Private Wealth.

His Hope or Sheet-Anchor.

His Litany to the Holy Spirit.

His Own Epitaph.

His Poetry His Pillar.

His Prayer for Absolution.

His Prayer to Ben Jonson.

His Request to Julia.

His Return to London.

His Winding-Sheet.

Hock-Cart, or Harvest Home, The.

Hour-Glass, The.

How Lilies Came White.

How Roses Came Red.

How Violets Came Blue.

Ill Government.

Impossibilities to His Friend.

In the Dark None Dainty.

Invitation, The.

Julia's Petticoat.

Kings and Tyrants.

Kiss, A.

Kiss, The: A Dialogue.

Kisses Loathesome.

Kissing and Bussing.

Lawn, The.

Lips Tongueless.

Long and Lazy.

Love Me Little, Love Me Long.

Love What It Is.

Lovers How They Come and Part.

Lyric to Mirth, A.

Mad Maid's Song, The.

Man's Dying-Place Uncertain.

Matins, or Morning Prayer.

Meat without Mirth.

Meditation for His Mistress, A.

Mr. Robert Herrick, His Farewell unto Poetry.

Moderation.

Money Gets the Mastery.

Money Makes the Mirth.

Mount of the Muses, The.

Music.

My Daughter's Dowry.

New-Year's Gift Sent to Sir Simeon Steward, A.

Night-Piece, to Julia, The.

No Difference in the Dark.

No Loath[e]someness in Love.

No Lock against Lechery.

Not to Love.

Nothing New.

Nuptial Song, or Epithalamy, on Sir Clipesby Crew and His Lady, A.

Oberon's Feast.

Oberon's Palace.

Ode for Him, An.

Ode to Master Endymion Porter, upon His Brother's Death, An.

On Ben Jonson.

On Himself ("Born I was to meet with age").

On Himself ("Here down my wearied limbs I'll lay").

On Himself ("I fear no earthly powers").

On Himself ("I will no longer kiss").

On Himself ("I'll write no more of love, but now repent").

On Himself ("Let me not live, if I not love").

On Himself ("The work is done. Young men and maidens, set").

On Himself ("Weep for the dead, for they have lost this light").

Orpheus.

Panegyric to Sir Lewis Pemberton, A.

Parcae, The, or Three Dainty Destinies: The Armillet.

Perfume, The.

Peter-Penny, The.

Pillar of Fame, The.

Plaudite, or End of Life, The.

Poet Loves a Mistress, but Not to Marry, The.

Poetry Perpetuates the Poet.

Power and Peace.

Power in the People, The.

Primrose, The.

Resurrection Possible and Probable, The.

Ring Presented to Julia, A.

Sadness of Things for Sappho's Sickness, The.

Scare-Fire, The.

Shoe-tying, The.

Slavery.

Spell, The.

Star Song, The: A Carol to the King.

Steam in Sacrifice.

Supreme Fortune Falls Soonest.

Temple, The.

Ternarie of Littles, upon a Pipkin of Jelly Sent to a Lady, A.

Thanksgiving.

Thanksgiving to God, for His House, A.

This Cross-Tree Here.

Tithe, The: To the Bride.

To a Bed of Tulips.

To a Gentlewoman Objecting to Him His Grey Hairs.

To Anthea.

To Anthea, Who May Command Him Anything.

To Anthea Lying in Bed.

To Blossoms.

To Christ on the Cross.

To Critics.

To Crown It.

To Daffodils [or Daffadills].

To Daisies, Not To Shut So Soon.

To Dean Bourn, a Rude River in Devon, by Which Sometimes He Lived.

To Dianeme ("Dear, though to part it be hell").

To Dianeme ("Give me one kiss").

To Dianeme ("Show me thy feet; show me thy legs, thy thighs").

To Dianeme ("Sweet, be not proud of those two eyes").

To Electra ("I dare not ask a kiss").

To Electra ("I'll come to thee in all those shapes").

To Groves.

To His Book ("Go thou forth, my book, though late").

To His Book ("Have I not blessed thee? Then go forth; nor fear").

To his book's end this last line he'd have placed.

To His Dying Brother, Master William Herrick.

To His Friend, on the Untunable Times.

To His Honoured and Most Ingenious Friend, Master Charles Cotton.

To His Kinsman, Master Thomas Herrick, Who Desired to Be in His Book.

To His Kinswoman, Mistress Penelope Wheeler.

To His Lovely Mistresses.

To His Mistresse.

To His Mistresses ("Help me! Help me! now I call").

To His Mistresses ("Put on your silks, and piece by piece").

To Julia ("How rich and pleasing thou, my Julia, art").

To Julia ("Julia, when thy Herrick dies").

To Julia, the Flaminica Dialis, or Queen-Priest.

To Keep a True Lent.

To Lar.

To Laurels.

To Live Merrily, and to Trust to Good Verses.

To Master Henry Lawes, the Excellent Composer of Lyrics.

To Meadows.

To Mistress Katherine Bradshaw the Lovely, That Crowned Him with Laurel.

To Music ("Begin to charm, and as thou strok'st mine ears").

To Music: A Song.

To Music, to Becalm a Sweet-sick Youth.

To Music, to Becalm His Fever.

To My Ill Reader.

To Oenone.

To Perilla.

To Phillis [or Phyllis], to Love and Live with Him.

To Sycamores.

To the Detractor.

To the Generous Reader.

To the King, upon His Coming with His Army into the West.

To the Most Fair and Lovely Mistress Anne Soame, Now Lady Abdie [or Abdy].

To the Most Virtuous Mistress Pot, Who Many Times Entertained Him.

To the Reverend Shade of His Religious Father.

To the Rose.

To the Sour Reader.

To the Virgins, to Make Much of Time.

To the Water Nymphs, Drinking at the Fountain.

To the Western Wind.

To the Willow Tree.

To Violets.

To Virgins.

To Vulcan.
Transfiguration, The.
Up Tailes All.
Upon a Black Twist, Rounding the Arm of the Countess of Carlisle.
Upon a Child ("Here a pretty baby lies").
Upon a Child That Died ("Here she lies, a pretty bud").
Upon a Delaying Lady.
Upon a Maid ("Gone she is a long, long way").
Upon a Maid ("Here she lies in bed of spice").
Upon a Maid That Dyed the Day She Was Married.
Upon a Young Mother of Many Children.
Upon Batt.
Upon Ben Jonson.
Upon Bunce: Epigram.
Upon Groins: Epigrams.
Upon Her Feet.
Upon Her Voice.
Upon His Julia.
Upon His Sister-in-Law, Mistress Elizabeth Herrick.
Upon Jack and Jill: Epigram.
Upon Julia Washing Herself in the River.
Upon Julia Weeping.
Upon Julia's Breasts.
Upon Julia's Clothes.
Upon Julia's Ribband.
Upon Julia's Unlacing Herself.
Upon Julia's Voice.
Upon Love, by Way of Question and Answer.
Upon Lucia Dabbled in the Dew.
Upon Lulls.
Upon Mr. Ben Jonson: Epigram.
Upon Mistress Elizabeth Wheeler under the Name of Amarillis.
Upon Moon.
Upon Pagget.
Upon Prew His Maid.
Upon Rook: Epigram.
Upon Roses.
Upon Scobble: Epigram.
Upon Showbread: Epigram.
Upon Some Women.
Upon Sybilla.
Upon the Loss of His Mistresses.
Upon the Nipples of Julia's Breasts.
Upon the Same [Detractor] ("I asked thee oft what poets thou hast read").
Upon the Troublesome Times.
Upon Umber: Epigram.
Vine, The.
Virgin Mary, The.
Vision, The ("Methought I saw as I did dream in bed").
Vision, The ("Sitting alone as one forsook").
Vision to Electra, The.
Wake, The.
Welcome to Sack, The.
What Kind of Mistress He Would Have.
When He Would Have His Verses Read.
White Island, The; or, The Place of the Blest.
Why Flowers Change Color.

Wounded Cupid, The.
**Herron, Carol Olivia**
O Viajante.
**Herrstrom, David Sten**
Afternoon.
Canto del Señor Segovia.
**Herschberger, Ruth**
Certain World, A.
Displays of Skill: The Bat.
First Walk in the Park.
Huron, The.
In a Bar.
Lumberyard, The.
O Terry why is sex so quick.
Song: "Sergei's a flower."
**Hersey, Harold**
Lavender Cowboy, The.
**Hershon, Robert**
Boy Who Smells Like Cocoa, A.
Cooper & Bailey Great London Circus, The.
Four Translations from the English of Robert Hershon.
How to Walk in a Crowd.
Ireland Lake.
Kelly.
Responses.
Spitting on Ira Rosenblatt.
Swimming Lesson, The.
U.S. Coast and Geodetic Survey Ship *Pioneer*, The.
**Hervey, John Russell**
Children among the Tombstones.
Empty Valley, The.
Man on a Raft.
Somnambulist.
Two Old Men Look at the Sea.
**Herzberg, Judith**
Commentaries on the Song of Songs.
Kinneret.
Nearer.
On the Death of Sylvia Plath.
Reunion.
Voice, The.
Yiddish.
**Herzog, Arthur, Jr.,** *and* Billie Holiday
God Bless the Child.
**Hesketh, Phoebe**
Ducks.
**Hesse, Hermann**
Glorious World.
It's Just the Same to Me.
Sometimes.
**Hester, M. L., Jr.**
International Motherhood Assoc.
Second Night, The.
**Hewett, Dorothy**
In Moncur Street.
Miss Hewett's Shenanigans.
**Hewitt, E. E.**
Will There Be Any Stars in My Crown? *with music.*
**Hewitt, Geof**
Behind That Wall My Roommate Fucks His Girl.
Conversion.
Emergency at 8.
Explanation.
For Bill.
For Randie.
Letter.
Rip-off # 1: Hippie Capitalism.

**Hewitt, John**
Because I Paced My Thought.
From a Museum Man's Album.
Frontier, The.
In this Year of Grace.
Ireland.
Irishman in Coventry, An.
Minor Victorian Painter, A.
O Country People.
Once Alien Here.
Ram's Horn, The.
Spectacle of Truth, The.
**Hey, Phillip**
Epigrams.
Gunfighter.
Lines Written in Objection, or the Limpopo Express.
Old Men Working Concrete.
Thank You Poem for the Andersons, The.
**Heyen, William**
Bear, The.
Children, The.
Dog Sacrifice at Lake Ronkonkoma.
I Move to Random Consolations.
King's Men, The.
Redwings.
Riddle: "From Belsen a crate of gold teeth."
Ryókan.
Snapper, The.
Spirit of Wrath, The.
Stadium, The.
Trail beside the River Platte, The.
**Heym, Georg**
War.
**Heynen, Jim**
Morning Chores.
Tourist Guide: How You Can Tell for Sure When You're in South Dakota.
**Heyrick, Thomas**
On a Mandrake.
On a Peacock.
On an Indian Tomineios, the Least of Birds.
Submarine Voyage, The: A Pindaric Poem in Four Parts,*sels.*
**Heyward, Dubose**
Equinox, The.
**Heywood, John**
Jack and His Father.
Of Late and Never.
Of Loving a Dog.
Of Use.
On Botching.
**Heywood, Thomas**
Love's Good-Morrow.
Rape of Lucrece, The,*sels.*
**Hiatt, Ben**
David's Poem.
Folsom.
**Hickey, Mark**
Road along the Thumb and Forefinger, The ("The road all the way up along the coast").
**Hicks, Berryman**
Time is Swiftly Rolling On, The.
**Hicks, John V.**
Are You There, Mrs. Goose?
Last Rite.
Trumpet Shall Sound, The.
**Hickson, William E.**

Walking Song.

**Higgins, Bertram**
Under the Sign of the Fisher.

**Higgins, Brian**
Analogy.
Baedeker for Metaphysicians.
Corrupt Man in the French Pub, The.
Genesis.

**Higgins, Dick**
Teechur.

**Higgins, Frederick Robert**
At Flock Mass.
Chinese Winter.
Father and Son.
O You among Women.
Old Jockey, The.
Padraic O'Conaire, Gaelic Storyteller.

**Higginson, Ella**
Cradle-Song of the Fisherman's Wife.
In the Marsh.
Lamp in the West, The.
Moonrise in the Rockies.
October.
When the Birds Go North Again.

**Higginson, Mary Thacher**
In Shining Groups.

**Higginson, Nesta**    *See* **"O'Neill, Moira"**

**Higginson, Thomas Wentworth**
Past Is Dark with Sin and Shame, The,
   *with music.*
To Thine Eternal Arms, O God, *with*
   *music.*

**Higginson, William J.**
Loves and Lays of William J. Higginson,
   The.
On Reading Lao-tzu.

**Higgons, Bevil**
Mourners, The.

**Higgs, Blake Alphonso**    *See* **Blind Blake**

**Higgs, Ted**
From Mistra: A Prospect.

**Higham, Charles**
Kelly Show, The.
Sand.

**Hikmet, Nazim**
I Come and Stand at Every Door.

**Hilarova, Dagmar**
Questions

**Hilberry, Conrad**
Blind Girl on the Santa Fe.
For Katherine, 1952–1961.
Harry Houdini, The Hippodrome, New
   York, January 7, 1918.
Hunger.
Poet.
Portholes.
Sea.
Sleeping Out in Vermont.

**Hill, Donald L.**
Buzzing Doubt, The.

**Hill, Geoffrey**
Asmodeus.
Genesis
Imaginative Life, The.
In Memory of Jane Fraser.
Love, oh my love, it will come.
Mercian Hymns, *sels.*
Merlin.
Of Commerce and Society.
Offa's Laws.
Ovid in the Third Reich.
Pentecost Castle, The, *abr.*

Picture of a Nativity.
Requiem for the Plantagenet Kings.
Songbook of Sebastian Arrurruz, The,
   *sel.*
Turtle Dove, The.
Wreaths.

**Hill, Hyacinthe**
Rebels from Fairy Tales.

**Hill, Joe**
Casey Jones (Union).
Preacher and the Slave, The.
Rebel Girl, The.
Tramp, The.

**Hill, Leslie Pinckney**
So Quietly.

**Hill, Nellie**
Soup on a Cold Day.

**Hill, Roberta**
Beginning the Year at Rosebud, S.D.
Blue Mountain.
Depot in Rapid City.
Direction.
Dream of Rebirth.
E Uni Que A The Hi A Tho, Father.
Falling Moon.
In the Madison Zoo.
Lines for Marking Time.
Midnight on Front Street.
Nation Wrapped in Stone, A.
Night along the Mackinac Bridge.
Seal at Stinson Beach.
Sleeping with Foxes.
Song for Healing.
Star Quilt.
Steps.
Swamp.
Whispers.
Winter Burn.
Wish for Waving Goodbye, A.

**Hill, Rowland M.**
Idiot Boy.

**Hillhouse, Augustus L.**
Trembling before Thine Awful Throne,
   *with music.*

**Hillman, Brenda**
Ballet.

**Hillyer, Robert Silliman**
Assassination, The.
Letter to a Teacher of English, A.
Moo!
Pastorals, *sel.*
Sonnet Sequence, A, *sel.*
Sonnet: "Today as I passed through the
   market-place."
XXth Century.

**Hilton, Arthur Clement**
Heathen Pass-ee, The, *parody.*
Octopus.
Vulture and the Husbandman, The.

**Hilton, David**
April 29, 1975.
Cell Transplants.
Christmas Poem.
Immigrant, The.
In Praise of BIC Pens.
Last South Baltimore Poem.
Late November, Madison.
Man Upstairs, The.
Poem: "I want to be one of those
   poets."
Poet Tries to Turn In His Jock, The.
Second Part, The.

**Hilton, L. M.**
Have Courage, My Boy, to Say No!

**Himel, Margery**
My People.

**Hinde, Gertrude**
Donkey, The.

**Hindley, Norman**
Wood Butcher.

**Hine, Daryl**
August 13, 1966.
Bluebeard's Wife.
English Elegy, An.
Untitled.
Vowel Movements.
Wave, The.

**Hines, Carl Wendell, Jr.**
Two Jazz Poems.

**Hinkson, Katharine Tynan**    *See* **Tynan,**
   **Katharine**

**Hinshaw, Dawn**
Not-Knowing.

**Hippisley, John**
Sweet Is the Budding Spring of Love,
   *with music.*

**Hippius, Zinaida**
Grey Frock, A.
L'Imprévisibilité.

**Hipple, Ted**
Traditional Grammarian as Poet, The.

**Hirsch, Edward**
Chinese Vase, A.
Factories.
Little Political Poem.

**Hirsch, Mannie**
Cry for a Disused Synagogue in
   Booysens.

**Hirschfield, Theodore H.**
A. M.—P.M.

**Hirschman, Jack**
NHR.
Serronydion.
Zohara.

**Hitchcock, George**
Chauffeur of Lilacs, The.
Comedians, The.
Departure.
Figures in a Ruined Ballroom.
Fugue and Variations.
May All Earth Be Clothed in Light.
One Whose Reproach I Cannot Evade,
   The.
Song of Expectancy.
Three Found Poems.
Three Portraits.
United States Prepare for the Permanent
   Revolution, The.
Villa Thermidor.
When I Came Back to Dancing Misery
   ("When I came back to the stuffed
   dragonfly").

**Hitchner, John T.**
Remembering Apple Times.

**Hitomaro (Kakinomoto no Hitomaro)**
Gossip grows like weeds.

**Hoagland, Everett**
Anti-Semanticist, The.
It's a Terrible Thing!
Love Child—a Black Aesthetic.
Music, The.
My Spring Thing.

**Hoare, Prince**
*Arethusa*, The.

**Hoatson, Florence**
Autumn.
**Hoban, Russell**
Maine Sea Gulls.
**Hoben, Sandra**
Burns.
**Hoberman, Mary Ann**
I Was Riding to Poughkeepsie.
Mouse.
Yaks come from far-off Tibet.
Yellow Butter.
**Hobsbaum, Philip**
Astigmatic, The.
Lesson in Love, A.
Place's Fault, The.
**Hobson, Archie**
Base Chapel, Lejeune 4/79.
**Hobson, Rodney**
Man about the Kitchen, A.
**Hoccleve [or Occleve], Thomas**
Anxious Thought.
De Regimine Principum, sels.
Lament for Chaucer and Gower.
**Hoch, Edward Wallis**
Good and Bad.
**Hochman, Sandra**
Constructions: Upper East Side.
Couple, The.
Elephant, The.
Eyes of Flesh, The.
Farewell Poems.
Goldfish Wife, The.
Grief.
History of the Opera, A.
I Want to Tell You.
Postscript.
Swimming Pool, The.
Thoughts about My Daughter before
Sleep.
Three Love Poems, sel.
**Hoddis, Jakov van (Hans Davidsohn)**
End of the World.
Air Vision, The.
Tohub.
**Hodge, Arthur J.**
Five Were Foolish, with music.
**Hodge, Marion**
True Child ("True Child of God, stand
innocently awed").
**Hodges, Elizabeth**
Blue Ridge.
**Hodgson, Ralph**
And every sky was blue and rain.
Bells of Heaven, The.
Bull, The.
Eve.
Gently, years, gently!
Great Auk's Ghost, The.
Hammers, The.
House across the Way, The.
Hymn to Moloch.
Past comes back, The.
Sedge-Warbler, The.
Silver Wedding.
Stupidity Street.
**Hoeft, Robert D.**
Forty Pounds of Blackberries Equals
Thirteen Gallons of Wine.
If Things Grew Down.
Our Annual Return to the Lake.
To a Little Boy Learning to Fish.
Wooden Matches.

**Hoeppner, Ed**
From Garvey's Farm: Seneca,
Wisconsin.
**Hoey, Allen**
Casting at Night.
Secret Irish, The.
**Hoey, Edwin A.**
Foul Shot.
**Hoffenstein, Samuel**
I'd rather listen to a flute.
Love-Songs, at Once Tender and
Informative.
Mr. Walter de la Mare Makes the Little
Ones Dizzy, sel.
Poem Intended to Incite the Utmost
Depression, A.
When You're Away.
With Rue My Heart Is Laden, parody.
**Hoffman, Balthasar**
Be Glorified Eternally, with music.
**Hoffman, Daniel Gerard**
Ballad of No Proper Man.
Center of Attention, The.
City of Satisfactions, The.
È, the Feasting Florentines.
Himself.
Ode to Joy.
On the Industrial Highway.
Old Photo in an Old Life, An.
Signatures.
Tree.
**Hoffman, Elisha A.**
Leaning on the Everlasting Arms, with
music.
**Hoffman, Jill**
Evening Ride
Her Sleep.
Stable, The.
To a Horse.
**Hoffman, Richard**
Yet.
**Hoffman, William M.**
Screw Spring.
**Hoffmann, Heinrich**
Cruel Frederick.
Story of Augustus Who Would Not
Have Any Soup, The.
Story of Fidgety Philip, The.
Story of Flying Robert, The.
Story of Johnny Head-in-Air, The.
Story of Little Suck-a-Thumb, The.
**Hofmannsthal, Hugo von**
Experience.
**Hogan, Linda**
What's Living?
**Hogan, Michael**
Christmas Poem.
Fish.
Food Strike.
Groundhog Day.
Indulgences.
Letter from My Son.
One Summer in Charleston.
Parting.
Passing through Virginia.
Poem for My Eighth Year in Prison.
Prison Break.
Quiet Orderly Life, A.
Rust.
Spring.
**Hogg, James ("The Ettrick Shepherd")**
Boy's Song, A.

Love Is like a Dizziness.
Moon Was a-Waning, The.
Queen's Wake, The, sel.
Song, The: "O! Lady dear, fair is thy
noon."
Village of Balmaquhapple, The.
**Holahan, Pamela Crawford**
Song to the Ninth Grade.
**Holbrook, David**
Drought.
Maternity Gown.
**Holden, Jonathan**
Washing My Son.
**Holden, Molly**
Giant Decorative Dahlia.
Photograph of Haymaker, 1890.
**Holden, Oliver**
How Sweet Is the Language of Love,
with music.
Weeping Sinner, Dry Your Tears, with
music.
Within These Doors Assembled Now,
with music.
**Holder, Julie**
Centipede, A.
Porwigles.
**Hölderlin, Friedrich**
All the fruit is ripe, plunged in fire,
cooked.
Bread and Wine, sel.
Half of Life.
Ripe, Being Plunged into Fire.
Sanctimonious Poets, The.
Socrates and Alcibiades.
To Diotima.
**Holender, Barbara D.**
Quality of Pain, A.
**Holiday, Bille and Arthur Herzog, Jr.** See
**Herzog, Arthur, Jr., and Billie Holiday**
**Holland, Barbara A.**
Apples of Sodom and Gomorrah, The.
Leavings.
**Holland, Hugh**
Epitaph on Prince Henry.
Upon the Lines and Life of the Famous
Scenic Poet, Master William
Shakespeare.
**Holland, Robert**
Fisherman Casts His Line into the Sea,
The.
**Holland, Rupert Sargent**
Foolish Flowers.
**Hollander, Gad**
Argument against Metaphor.
Axioms.
Fugato (Coda.)
In Memoriam Paul Celan.
**Hollander, John**
Adam's Task.
Altarpiece Finished, The.
Appearance and Reality.
Breadth. Circle. Desert. Monarch.
Month. Wisdom.
Curse, The.
Great Bear, The.
Hall of Ocean Life.
Helicon.
Heliogabalus.
Historical Reflections.
Hobbes, 1651.
Jefferson Valley.
Lady of the Castle, The.

**Hollander**
Last Quarter.
Last Words.
Movie-going.
Night Mirror, The.
Ninth of July, The.
No Foundation.
Skeleton Key.
Sunday Evenings.
Swan and Shadow.
To the Lady Portrayed by Margaret
  Dumont.
West End Blues.
Ziz, The.

**Hollander, Robert**
Ice Cream in Paradise.
You Too? Me Too—Why Not? Soda
  Pop.

**Holley, Margaret**
Your Woods.

**Hollis, Jocelyn**
Meeting, The.

**Hollo, Anselm**
And How It Goes.
Awkward Spring.
Bison Flower Days.
Bouzouki Music.
Buffalo—Isle of Wight Power Cable.
Charge, The.
Discovery of LSD a True Story, The.
Elegy: "Laundry-basket is still there,
  The."
Empress Hotel Poems, The.
Good Stuff Cookies.
He She Because How.
Helsinki, 1940.
Instances.
Los Sedentarios.
On the Occasion of Becoming an Echo.
Scriptural 1.
Song of the Tusk.
Strange Encounter.
Through Two layers of Glass.
Warrant Is Out for the Arrest of Henry
  Miller, A.
Your Friend.

**Holloway, Geoffrey**
Deliverance.
Electroencephalogram.

**"Holm, Saxe."** See **Jackson, Helen Hunt**

**Holman, Felice**
5th of July, The.
Halloween Witches.
Supermarket.
Who Am I?

**Holman, Jesse L.**
Lord, in Thy Presence Here, *with music.*

**Holman, M. Carl**
And on This Shore.
Letter across Doubt and Distance.
Mr. Z.
Notes for a Movie Script.
Picnic: The Liberated.
Song: "Dressed up in my melancholy."
Three Brown Girls Singing.

**Holmes, Abiel**
To Thee, O God, *with music.*
Who Here Can Cast His Eyes Abroad,
  *with music.*

**Holmes, Elizabeth B.**
Pānini o ka Punahou.

**Holmes, John**
Herself.

Peace Is the Mind's Old Wilderness, *with
  music.*

**Holmes, John Haynes**
O'er Continent and Ocean, *with music.*
Voice of God Is Calling, The, *with music.*

**Holmes, Oliver Wendell**
Aestivation [an Unpublished Poem by
  My Late Latin Tutor].
Angel of Peace, Thou Hast Wandered
  Too Long, *with music.*
At the "Atlantic" Dinner.
Autocrat of the Breakfast-Table, The,
  *sels.*
Ballad of the Oysterman, The.
Broomstick Train, The, *sel.*
Chambered Nautilus, The.
Deacon's Masterpiece, The; or, The
  Wonderful "One-Hoss Shay."
Dorothy Q.
Eggstravagance, An.
Height of the Ridiculous, The.
Hymn of Trust.
Last Leaf, The.
Lord of All Being, Throned Afar, *with
  music.*
My Aunt.
Nearing the Snow-Line.
Ode for a Social Meeting.
Old Ironsides.
Our Father! While Our Hearts Unlearn,
  *with music.*
Sea Dialogue, A.

**Holmes, R. Ernest**
Black Lady in an Afro Hairdo Cheers
  for Cassius.

**Holmes, Reginald**
Little Girl's Heart.

**Holsapple, Bruce**
I polish, cook, or clean my nest.
I send these wild roses.
Quiet faces.
Short cut, A.
Working/ in a stupor.

**Holshouser, W. L.**
Turning Point.

**Holt, Ray**
My Morose Master-Sergeants.

**Holtz, Barry**
Isaac.

**Holub, Miroslav**
Dog in the Quarry, A, *sel.*
Door, The.
Five Minutes after the Air Raid.
History Lesson, A.
Lesson, The.
Napoleon.
Ode to Joy.

**Holyday, Barten**
Bogs, purgatory, wolves and ease, by
  fame.
Clay, sand, and rock, seem of a diff'rent
  birth.
Pride cannot see itself by mid-day light.

**Holz, Arno**
Phantasus, *sel.*

**Homer**
Ajax the swift swerv'd never from the
  side.
All grave old men, and souldiers they
  had bene, but for age.
And as in winter time when Jove his
  cold-sharpe javelines throwes.

And as when with the West-wind's
  flawes the sea thrusts up her waves.
And now Eurynome had bath'd the king.
And now his well-known bow the master
  bore.
And now man-slaughtering Pallas tooke
  in hand.
And now the Queene of women had
  intent.
And now was Paris come/ From his
  high towres.
And when they came together in one
  place.
Andromache's Lamentation.
As when an architect some palace wall.
As when devouring flames some forest
  seize.
As when of frequent bees.
At her departure his disdain return'd.
At this th' impatient hero sowrly smil'd.
Big with great purposes and proud, they
  sat.
But now, no longer deaf to honour's call.
Funeral Games for Patroclus, The:
  Wrestling to a Draw.
Gardens of Alcinous, The ("Close to the
  gates a spacious garden lies").
Gardens of Alcinous, The ("Without the
  hall and close upon the gate").
Helen's Lamentation.
Iliad, The, *much abr.*
Like leaves on trees the race of man is
  found.
Nestor.
New Coasts and Poseidon's Son.
Nor lingered Paris in the lofty house.
Nor long the trench or lofty walls
  oppose.
Now toils the heroe; trees on trees
  o'erthrown.
Odysseus and the Phaeacian Games.
Odyssey, The, *sels.*
Sirens' Song, The.
Youth there was, Elpenor was he nam'd,
  A.

**Ho Nansorhon**
Woman's Sorrow, A, *sel.*

**Hongo, Garrett Kaoru**
In Search of the Silent Zero.

**Honig, Edwin**
As a Great Prince.
Being Somebody.
November through a Giant Copper
  Beech.
Now, My Usefulness Over.
Some Knots.
Tête-à-Tête.
Through You.
Walt Whitman.
Who.

**Hood, Thomas**
As It Fell upon a Day.
Athol Brose.
Bridge of Sighs, The.
Butcher, A.
Carelesse Nurse Mayd, The.
Choosing Their Names.
Death-Bed, The.
Domestic Asides; or, Truth in
  Parentheses.
Domestic Didactics by an Old Servant.

Epicurean Reminiscences of a
  Sentimentalist.
Faithless Nellie [*or* Nelly] Gray.
Faithless Sally Brown.
Haunted House, The.
I Remember, I Remember.
Last Man, The.
Little Piggy.
Mary's Ghost.
Miss Kilmansegg and Her Precious Leg,
  *sel.*
No!
Nocturnal Sketch, A.
Ode: Autumn.
Ode to the Cameleopard.
On the Death of the Giraffe.
Our Village—by a Villager.
Poor dear dead have been laid out in
  vain, The.
Reflection, A.
Ruth.
She Is Far from the Land.
Silence.
Song of the Shirt, The.
To Henrietta, on Her Departure for
  Calais.
To Minerva.
What is a modern Poet's fate?
Work—work—work.
**Hood, Tom (Thomas Hood, Jr.)**
Cannibal Flea, The.
Confounded Nonsense.
Few Muddled Metaphors by a Moore-
  ose Melodist, A.
How Singular.
Quadrupedremian Song, A.
Sunset in the Sea.
**Hood-Adams, Rebecca**
Family Portrait.
**Hook, Theodore**
Cautionary Verses to Youth of Both
  Sexes.
**Hooper, H. S.**
Frisco's Defi.
**Hooper, Patricia**
9:00.
Other Lives.
**Hoover, Paul**
After the Unexpected Answer (Magritte).
Alarm Clock, The.
Barnabooth Enters Russia.
Civic Autobiography, A.
Depression Ode (11/23/75).
For Isidore Ducasse.
Future of the Fishbowl, The.
**Hope, Alec Derwent**
Advice to Young Ladies.
Agony Column.
Ascent into Hell.
Australia.
Bed, The.
Brides, The.
Circe.
Conquistador.
Coup de Grâce.
Death of the Bird, The.
Double Looking Glass, The.
Gateway, The.
Gauguin's Menhir, Tahiti ("Gauguin's
  Museum in Papeari bay").
Imperial Adam.
In Memoriam: Gertrud Kolmar, 1943.

Invaders, The.
Lingam and the Yoni, The.
Meditation on a Bone.
Moschus Moschiferus.
Observation Car.
Parabola.
School of Night, The.
Sportsfield.
William Butler Yeats.
**Hope, Francis**
Live Man's Epitaph.
**"Hope, Laurence" (Adela Florence Cory
  Nicolson)**
Youth.
**Hopes, David**
Hairdresser, The.
**Hopewell, Anna Madge**
Tree, The.
**Hopkins, Gerard Manley**
Alchemist in the City, The.
Andromeda.
As kingfishers catch fire, dragonflies
  draw flame.
Ashboughs.
At the Wedding March.
Beginning of the End, The.
Binsey Poplars.
Blessed Virgin Compared to the Air We
  Breathe, The.
Bugler's First Communion, The ("A
  bugler boy from barrack").
Caged Skylark, The.
Candle Indoors, The.
Carrion Comfort.
"Child Is Father to the Man, The."
Duns Scotus's Oxford.
Easter Communion.
Epithalamion: "Hark, hearer, hear what
  I do."
Felix Randal.
Fragment: "Strike, churl; hurl, cheerless
  wind, then; heltering hail."
God's Grandeur.
Habit of Perfection, The.
Heaven-haven.
Henry Purcell.
Hurrahing in Harvest.
I am like a slip of comet.
I Wake and Feel the Fell of Dark, Not
  Day.
In Honour of St. Alphonsus Rodriguez.
Inversnaid.
Lantern Out of Doors, The.
Leaden Echo and the Golden Echo, The.
Let me be to Thee as the circling bird.
May Magnificat, The.
Mrs. Hopley, on Seeing Her Children
  Say Goodnight to Their Father.
Moonrise.
My Own Heart Let Me More Have Pity
  On.
No Worst, There Is None.
Of vitures I most warmly bless.
Patience Hard Thing.
Pied Beauty.
Sea and the Skylark, The.
Spelt from Sibyl's Leaves.
Spring.
Spring and Fall.
Starlight Night, The.
Summer Malison, The.

That Nature Is a Heraclitean Fire and of
  the Comfort of the Resurrection.
Thee, God, I come from, to thee go.
Thou Art Indeed Just, Lord, If I
  Contend.
To Margaret.
To R. B.
Tom's Garland: Upon the Unemployed.
Valley of the Elwy, The.
Vision of the Mermaids, The, *sel.*
Windhover, The.
Winter with the Gulf Stream.
Wreck of the *Deutschland*, The.
**Hopkins, John (c.1520–1570)**
Thou, Lord, Hast Been Our Sure
  Defense, *with music.*
**Hopkins, John Henry, Jr. (1820–91)**
Alleluia! Christ Is Risen Today, *with
  music.*
We Three Kings of Orient Are.
**Hopkins, Josiah**
O Turn Ye, O Turn Ye, *with music.*
**Hopkins, Lee Bennett**
My Name.
**Hopkinson, Francis**
Arise and See the Glorious Sun, *with
  music.*
At Length the Busy Day Is Done, *with
  music.*
Battle of the Kegs, The.
Enraptured I Gaze, *with music.*
**Hopkinson, Joseph**
Hail, Columbia.
**Hoppe, Anna**
Precious Child, So Sweetly Sleeping, *with
  music.*
**Hopper, Edward**
Jesus, Saviour, Pilot Me, *with music.*
They Pray the Best Who Pray and
  Watch, *with music.*
**Hopper, Nora**
March.
**Hopper, Virginia Shearer**
In the Canadian Rockies.
**Horace (Quintus Horatius Flaccus)**
Art of Poetry, The, *sels.*
Dialogue between Horace and Lydia, A.
Diffugere Nives.
Fie on Eastern Luxury! ("Persicos odi").
Good bailiff of my farm, that snug
  domain.
Happy the Man.
If, O Maecenas, versed in lore antique.
If you can lie, Torquatus, when you
  take.
Lydia, in Heavens Name.
Odes, *sels.*
Philippus, for his pleadings famed afar.
Praise of Pindar, The.
Ribald Romeos Less and Less Berattle.
Satires, *sel.*
Solvitur Acris Hiems.
This Monument Will Outlast.
To Apollo and Diana.
To Aristius Fuscus.
To Chloe ("Vitas hinnuleo").
To Lydia.
To Maecenas.
To Pyrrha ("Quis multa gracilis").
To Thaliarchus.
To Venus.
Virtue, dear friend, needs no defence.

Your kindness, sir, to me, is really kind.
**Horan, Robert**
By Hallucination Visited.
**Horgan, Paul**
Now Evening Puts Amen to Day, *with music.*
**Horikawa, Lady**
Will he always love me?
**Horne, Frank**
Kid Stuff.
Letters [*or* Notes] Found near a Suicide.
Mamma!
On Seeing Two Brown Boys in a Catholic Church.
Patience.
Resurrection.
Symphony.
To a Persistent Phantom.
To "Chick."
To James.
To Mother.
To You.
Walk.
**Horne, Lewis**
Suppose.
**Horne, Richard Henry [*or* Hengist]**
Orion, *sels.*
**Horta, Maria Teresa**
Saved.
Swimming Pool.
**Horta, Maria Teresa *and* Maria Isabel Barreno *and* Maria Velho da Costa**
*See* **Marias, The Three**
**Horton, George Moses**
New Fashions.
Snaps for Dinner, Snaps for Breakfast, and Snaps for Supper.
**Horvitz, Allan Kolski**
King Saul.
Radiance of Extinct Stars, The.
**Hoskins, Ann**
High Wire Dancers.
**Hoskins, Katherine**
Baucis and Philemon.
When Snow Falls.
Youngest Schizophrene, The.
**Hoskyns, John**
Bellows Maker of Oxford, The.
Epitaph on Sir Walter Pye.
Epitaph on the Fart in the Parliament House.
Here lies the man that madly slain.
His Own Epitaph, When He Was Sick.
Of the Loss of Time.
On a Contentious Companion.
On a Whore.
On One That Lived Ingloriously.
To His Little Son Benedict from the Tower of London.
To His Son Bennet.
Upon a Fool.
Upon One of the Maids of Honour to Queen Elizabeth.
**Hosmer, Frederick Lucian**
From Age to Age They Gather, *with music.*
Hear, Hear, O Ye Nations, *with music.*
O Beautiful My Country, *with music.*
O Day of Light and Gladness, *with music.*
Through Willing Heart and Helping Hand, *with music.*

**Hoss, E. Embree**
O God, Great Father, Lord, and King, *with music.*
**Houck, James A.**
Children's Lenten Wisdom.
**Hough, Lindy**
Portrait of the Father.
**Houghton, Richard Monckton Milnes, 1st Baron** *See* **Milnes, Richard Monckton, 1st Baron Houghton**
**House, Tom**
Parable of the Sidewalk Tellers.
**Housman, Alfred Edward**
Along the Field as We Came By.
Amelia mixed the mustard.
As I Gird on for Fighting.
As into the Garden.
As through the wild green hills of Wyre.
Be still, my soul, be still: the arms you bear are brittle.
Because I liked you better.
Carpenter's Son, The.
Chestnut Casts His Flambeaux, The.
Could Man Be Drunk for Ever.
Crossing alone the nighted ferry.
Culprit, The.
Delight It Is in Youth and May.
Easter Hymn.
Eight o'Clock.
1887.
Elephant, The, or the Force of Habit.
Epitaph on an Army of Mercenaries
Fairies Break Their Dances, The.
Fancy's Knell.
Far in a western brookland.
Farewell to Barn and Stack and Tree.
First of May, The.
For My Funeral.
Fragment of a Greek Tragedy.
From Far, from Eve and Morning.
From the Wash the Laundress Sends.
G. K. Chesterton on His Birth.
Grenadier.
Hell Gate.
Her Strong Enchantments Failing.
Here Dead Lie We.
Ho, Everyone That Thirsteth.
I Did Not Lose My Heart.
I Hoed and Trenched and Weeded.
I Promise Nothing.
I to My Perils.
Immortal Part, The.
In my own shire, if I was sad.
In the Morning, in the Morning.
In Valleys Green and Still.
Infant Innocence.
Into My Heart an Air That Kills.
Is Football Playing?
Is My Team Ploughing?
Lads in their hundreds to Ludlow come in for the fair, The.
Laws of God, the Laws of Man, The.
Lent Lily, The.
Loitering with a Vacant Eye.
Loveliest of Trees [the Cherry Now].
Mill-stream, now that noises cease, The.
New Mistress, The.
New Year's Eve.
Night Is Freezing Fast, The.
Now Dreary Dawns the Eastern Light.
O Have You Caught the Tiger?
Occasional Poem.

Oh see how thick the goldcup flowers.
Oh stay at home, my lad, and plough.
Oh, When I Was in Love with You.
Oh Who Is That Young Sinner.
Olive, The.
On Forelands High in Heaven.
On moonlit heath and lonesome bank.
On the idle hill of summer.
On Wenlock Edge the wood's in trouble.
On your midnight pallet lying.
Oracles, The.
Others, I am not the first.
Parta Quies.
Profoundly True Reflections on the Sea.
Rain, it streams on stone and hillock, The.
Rainy Pleiads Wester, The.
Recruit, The.
Reveille.
Revolution.
Say, lad, have you things to do?
Shades of night were falling fast, The.
Shot? so quick, so clean an ending?
Soldier from the wars returning.
Some can gaze and not be sick.
Stars have not dealt me the worst they could do, The.
Street Sounds to the Soldiers' Tread, The.
Tell me not here, it needs not saying.
Terence, This Is Stupid Stuff.
They Say My Verse Is Sad: No Wonder.
Think no more, lad; laugh, be jolly.
'Tis time, I think, by Wenlock town.
To an Athlete Dying Young.
To Stand Up Straight.
True Lover, The.
Twice a Week the Winter Thorough.
Wake Not for the World-heard Thunder.
We'll to the Woods No More.
Welsh Marches, The.
When First My Way to Fair I Took.
When green buds hang in the elm like dust.
When I Was One-and-Twenty.
When I Watch the Living Meet.
When Smoke Stood Up from Ludlow.
When the lad for longing sighs.
When the Eye of Day Is Shut.
White in the Moon the Long Road Lies.
With Rue My Heart Is Laden.
Yonder see the morning blink.
**Houston, Gil**
Rambling, Gambling Man.
**Hovde, A. J.**
I Shall Never Go.
Of Mouse and Men.
On Hearing a Beautiful Young Woman Describe Her Class in Physical Anthropology.
**Hovey, Richard**
Barney McGee.
Eleazar Wheelock.
Sea Gypsy, The.
**Howard, Anne, Duchess of Arundel**
Elegy on the Death of Her Husband.
**Howard, Ben**
Winter Report.
**Howard, Frances Minturn**
Sampler from Haworth.
**Howard, Henry** *See* **Surrey, Henry Howard, Earl of**

**Howard, Jim**
Newspaper Hats.
**Howard, Joseph E.**
Good Bye, My Lady Love, *with music.*
Hello, Ma [*or* My] Baby.
**Howard, Lee**
Shirley McDaniel Ain't Dead.
**Howard, Quentin R.**
In the Corn Land.
**Howard, Richard**
Again for Hephaistos, the Last Time.
Aubade: Donna Anna to Juan, Still
   Asleep.
Compulsive Qualifications, *sels.*
1864.
Far Cry after a Close Call, A.
Giovanni da Fiesole on the Sublime; or,
   Fra Angelico's "Last Judgment."
Landed: A Valentine.
Lapsus Linguae.
Natural History.
1907, a Proposal from Paris.
1915: A Pre-Raphaelite Ending, London.
On Arrival.
Oystering.
Recipe for an Ocean in the Absence of
   the Sea.
Secular Games.
209 Canal.
**Howard, Rowland**
Waste not, want not, is a maxim I would
   teach.
**Howard-Jones, Stuart**
Hibernia.
**Howden, Michael S.**
Through the shadow/ which turns.
**Howe, Julia Ward**
Battle Hymn of the Republic, The.
**Howe, Solomon**
Our Kind Creator, *with music.*
**Howell, James**
Elegy upon His Tomb in Herndon-Hill
   Church, Erected by His Wife, Who
   Speaks, An.
Upon Dr. Davies's British Grammar.
**Howell, Thomas**
Lover Deceived Writes to His Lady,
   The, *sel.*
Of Misery.
Rose, The.
**Howes, Barbara**
At 79th and Park.
Best of Show.
Cat on Couch.
City Afternoon.
Conversation, A.
Danaë.
Death of a Vermont Farm Woman.
Early Supper.
Four Fawns.
Gulls.
In Autumn.
Indian Summer.
Jim.
Landscape, Deer Season.
Letter from the Caribbean, A.
Light and Dark.
Mercedes.
Monkey Difference.
New Leda, The.
Out Fishing.
Portrait of an Artist.

**Howitt, Mary**
Buttercups and Daisies.
Hummingbird, The.
Seagull, The.
Spider and the Fly, The.
**Howitt, William**
Migration of the Grey Squirrels, The.
Wind in a Frolic, The.
**Ho Xuan Hugong**
Buddhist Priest, A.
Carved on an Areca Nut.
Jackfruit, The.
**Hoy, Albert L.**
Hour of Prayer, The.
**Hoyem, Andrew**
Circumambulation of Mt. Tamalpais.
Filtres.
**Hoyer, Mildred N.**
Voice of the Crocus.
**Hoyt, Charles Hale**
Bowery, The, *with music.*
**Hricz, Lucy**
Modern American Nursing.
**Hroswitha**
In Praise of Virginity.
**Hsi-chün**
Lament of Hsi-chün.
**Hsüeh T'ao**
Spring-gazing Song.
Weaving Love-Knots.
Weaving Love-Knots 2.
**Hsü Pên**
Hermit, The.
**Huang-fu Jan**
Spring Thoughts.
**Huang O**
Every morning I get up/ Beautiful as the
   Goddess.
Farewell to a Southern Melody, A.
To the Tune "Red Embroidered Shoes."
To the Tune "Soaring Clouds."
**Hubbard, Jake T. W.**
Newton's Third.
**Hubbell, Lindley Williams**
Hour of Concern.
**Hubbell, Nelson**
Monologue through Bars.
**Hubbell, Patricia**
Lemons.
Mag.
Travelers, The.
Vermont Conversation.
**Huch, Ricarda**
Arrival in Hell.
Death Seed.
Music stirs me, for you.
**Huck, Ann Marie (Haralambie)**
Into Your Hands.
**Hudgins, Andrew**
Cats and Egypt.
Mine.
**Hudson, Frederick B.**
My Relatives for the Most Part.
**Hueffer, Ford Madox.** *See* **Ford, Ford
   Madox**
**Huff, Robert**
Codicil.
Dying Dentist, The.
Getting Drunk with Daughter.
Girl-watching at Grant's Pass.
Now.

Old High Walk, An.
On Hearing of the Death of Bernard
   Strempek.
On the Death of Theodore Roethke.
Porcupines.
Rainbow.
Smoker, The.
Traditional Red.
Ventriloquist, The.
**Huffstickler, Albert**
Prospectus.
**Huggins, Peter**
Blackberry Winter.
**Hughes, Barbara**
Hamden Provision Co.
How Clouds Move.
Mexico.
**Hughes, Dorothy**
Strawberries.
**Hughes, Glyn**
Cold.
Diggle Mill.
Epitaphs.
**Hughes, John Ceiriog ("Ceiriog")**
Epilogue to Alun Mabon.
Mountain Stream, The.
**Hughes, Langston**
Advice.
Afro-American Fragment.
American Heartbreak.
Angola Question Mark.
April Rain Song.
Argument.
Aunt Sue's Stories.
Backlash Blues, The.
Bad Morning.
Ballad of the Landlord.
Ballad of the Man Who's Gone.
Beale Street.
Be-Bop Boys.
Black Pierrot, A.
Blues at Dawn.
Brass Spittoons.
Buddy.
Carol of the Brown King.
Catch.
Children's Rhymes.
Christ in Alabama.
City.
College Formal: Renaissance Casino.
Comment against Lamp Post.
Cross.
Cultural Exchange.
Daybreak in Alabama.
Death in Yorkville.
Dinner Guest: Me.
Dive.
Down and Out.
Down in the Bass.
Dream Boogie.
Dream Variation [*or* Variations].
Dust Bowl.
Early Evening Quarrel.
Easy Boogie.
Ennui.
Epigram: "Oh, God of dust and
   rainbows."
Esthete in Harlem.
50-50.
Fire.
Florida Road Workers.
Frederick Douglass: 1817-1895.

Freedom.
Green Memory.
Harlem ("Here on the edge of hell").
Harlem ("What happens to a dream
  deferred").
Harlem Night Song.
Harlem Sweeties.
Havana Dreams.
Heaven.
Hope.
I Dream a World.
I, Too.
Impasse.
Island.
Jazzonia.
Juke Box Love Song.
Junior Addict.
Justice.
Ku Klux.
Late Last Night.
Lenox Avenue Mural.
Likewise.
Lincoln Monument: Washington.
Little Lyric (of Great Importance).
Live and Let Live.
Lord Has a Child, The, *with music.*
Lumumba's Grave.
Madam and the Minister.
Madam's Past History.
Mama and Daughter.
Mellow.
Merry-go-round.
Midnight Dancer.
Midnight Raffle.
Militant.
Morning After.
Mother to Son.
Motto.
Movies.
Mulatto.
Necessity.
Negro Servant.
Negro Speaks of Rivers, The.
Night Funeral in Harlem.
October 16: The Raid.
Old Walt.
Oppression.
Passing.
Passing Love.
Peace.
Pennsylvania Station.
Personal.
Preference.
Prime.
Question and Answer.
Refugee in America.
Sailor.
Same in Blues.
Sea Calm.
Shepherd's Song at Christmas.
Situation.
Song for a Dark Girl.
Special Bulletin.
Still Here.
Stony Lonesome.
Sun Song.
Sylvester's Dying Bed.
Testimonial.
Theme for English B.
Third Degree.
Today.
Too Blue.

Troubled Woman.
Un-American Investigators.
Wake.
Warning.
Weary Blues, The.
What?
What? So Soon!
When Sue Wears Red.
Where? When? Which?
Who but the Lord?
Winter Moon.
Winter Sweetness.
Without Benefit of Declaration.
Wonder.
**Hughes, Richard**
Gipsy-Night.
Winter.
**Hughes, Ted**
After Lorca.
April Birthday.
Bullfrog.
Cadenza.
Childish Prank, A.
Cleopatra to the Asp.
Crow and the Birds.
Crow Resting.
Crow's First Lesson.
Crow's Last Stand.
Crow's Theology.
Esther's Tomcat.
Fifth Bedtime Story.
Ghost Crabs.
Gnat-Psalm.
Hawk Roosting.
Horses, The.
Howling of Wolves, The.
In Laughter.
Jaguar, The.
Lake, The.
Law in the Country of the Cats.
Leaves.
Lovesong.
Ludwig's Death Mask.
Lupercalia.
My Brother Bert.
My Sister Jane.
New Year's Song.
November.
October Dawn.
Otter, An.
Out.
Parlour Piece.
Pennines in April.
Pibroch.
Pike.
Reveille.
Roger the Dog.
Second Glance at a Jaguar.
Secretary.
September.
Skylarks.
Song of a Rat.
Stations.
That Moment.
Theology.
Thistles.
Thought-Fox, The.
Thrushes.
Truth Kills Everybody.
Two Eskimo Songs.
Urn Burial.
View of a Pig.

Wind.
Wino.
Wodwo.
**Hughes, Thomas**
Dolgelley Hotel, The.
**Hugo, Richard**
Again, Kapowsin.
Approaching the Castle.
Assumptions.
At the Cabin.
At the Stilli's Mouth.
Bay of Resolve.
Bear Paw.
Church on Comiaken Hill, The.
December 24 and George McBride Is
  Dead.
Driving Montana.
Duwamish.
Glen Uig.
Graves at Elkhorn.
Graves in Queens.
Indian Graves at Jocko.
Invasion North.
Landscapes.
Last Days.
Letter to Bell from Missoula.
Letter to Garber from Skye.
Letter to Kathy from Wisdom.
Letter to Levertov from Butte.
Letter to Logan from Milltown.
Letter to Reed from Lolo.
Letter to Scanlon from Whitehall.
Letter to Wagoner from Port Townsend.
Letter to Welch from Browning.
Maratea Porto: Saying Goodbye to the
  Vitolos.
Mill at Romesdal.
Montana Ranch Abandoned.
Night at the Napi in Browning, A.
Ocean on Monday.
Places and Ways to Live.
Port Townsend, 1974.
Skykomish River Running.
What Thou Lovest Well, Remains
  American.
Where Mission Creek Runs Hard for
  Joy.
**Hugo, Victor**
Be like the bird, who.
Et Nox Facta Est.
Memory of the Night of the Fourth.
Reverie.
Sowing Season. Evening.
Tomorrow, at Daybreak.
**Huidobro, Vincente**
She.
**Hulme, Thomas Ernest**
Autumn.
Embankment, The.
Image.
**Humes, Harry**
Road of Birds, The.
**Hummer, T. R.**
Lifelines.
**Hummer, Terry**
Naming, The.
**Humphrey, J. Lee**
All Things Being Equal.
**Humphrey, James**
To the Young Poets, Except Children,
  Who Haven't Earned the Title.
**Humphreys, Emyr**

Apple Tree and a Pig, An.
From Father to Son.
**Humphries, Rolfe**
Around Thanksgiving.
Looking Up at Airplanes, Always.
Marine.
Polo Grounds.
Sad Song, This Time, A.
**Hunt, Evelyn Tooley**
Taught Me Purple.
**Hunt, Helen**    *See* **Jackson, Helen Hunt**
**Hunt, Leigh**
Abou Ben Adhem.
Fish, the Man, and the Spirit, The.
Jenny Kiss'd [*or* Kissed] Me.
Nile, The.
Nun, The.
To a Fish.
To the Grasshopper and the Cricket.
**Hunt, Roderick**
Flute Girl.
**Hunter, Robert**
Casey Jones ("Driving that train, high
on cocaine").
**Hunter, William**
Joyfully, Joyfully Onward I Move, *with
music.*
**Huntley, Stanley**
Annabel Lee, *parody.*
**Hurley, James**
Greedy Dog.
**Hurley, Mary R.**
Tea Party.
**Husid, Mordechai**
Cry of Generations, The.
On the Way.
Windows.
**Huss, Avraham**
Classic Idyll, A.
Green Refrain, A.
Nocturnal Thoughts.
Time.
**Hussey, Anne**
Indian Summer, 1927.
**Hutchinson, Abby**
Kind Words Can Never Die, *with music.*
**Hutchinson, Jesse**
Lincoln and Liberty.
**Hutchinson, Pearse**
Copper-Beech and Butter-Fingers.
Distortions.
Eight Frontiers Distant.
Gaeltacht.
Into Their True Gentleness.
Like Trees, Like Islands.
Malaga.
**Hutchinson, Robert**
Drifting, A.
My Brother's Braces.
**Hutchison, Joseph**
This Year.
**Huxley, Aldous**
September.
**Hwang Chin-i**
Blue hill is my desire, The.
I cut in two/ A long November night.
Mountains are steadfast but the
mountain streams.
**Hyde, Abby Bradley**
And Canst Thou, Sinner, Slight, *with
music.*

Dear Saviour, If These Lambs Should
Stray, *with music.*
**Hyde, Lewis**
Ants.
**"Hyde, Robin" (Iris Guiver Wilkinson)**
Beaches, The, *sel.*
Bronze Rider, Wellington, The.
Deserted Village, The.
Last Ones, The.
Pihsien Road.
What Is It Makes the Stranger?
**Hyde, William deWitt**
Creation's Lord, We Give Thee Thanks,
*with music.*
**Hye, Naomi Shihab**
Sleeping in a Cave.
**Hyett, Barbara Helfgott**
Last Flight of the Great Wallenda, The.
**Hywel ab Owain Gwynedd**
Exultation.
Poet's Loves, The.

# I

**Ian, Janis**
Society's Child.
**Ibarbourou, Juana de**
Assignation, The.
Strong Bond, The.
**Ibn al-Arabi**
He praises me, and I praise Him.
When my Beloved appears.
**Ibn Ezra, Abraham**
My Stars.
**Ibn Hazm Al-Andalusi**
Twice Times Then Is Now.
**Icaza, Francisco A. de**
Responding Voice.
**Idley, Peter**
Covetousness.
Sources of Good Counsel.
**Igjugarjuk**
Musk Oxen.
**Ignacio, Bruce**
Lost.
**Ignatow, David**
Against the Evidence.
All Quiet.
Allegory, An.
And the Same Words.
Bagel, The.
Bowery.
Brooding.
Business Life, The.
Dialogue, A.
Dilemma.
Dream, The.
Each Day.
East Bronx.
Elegy: "I must wait for a stranger to
knock on my door."
Europe and America.
Explorer, The.
For My Daughter.
For My Daughter in Reply to a
Question.
For One Moment.
Get the Gasworks.

He Puts Me to Rest.
Heart, The.
How Come?
I'm Here.
In a Dream.
In No Way.
Last Night.
My Own House.
Night at an Airport.
1905.
No Theory.
Notes for a Lecture.
Paper Cutter, The.
Professional, The.
Rescue the Dead.
Ritual Three.
Safely.
Self-employed.
Signal, The.
Simultaneously.
Six Movements on a Theme.
Sky Is Blue, The.
Suite for Marriage, A.
Their Mouths Full.
To Nowhere.
Two Friends.
With the Door Open.
**Ikan, Ron**
American Saturday Afternoon.
Babylon.
Sidewalk Restoration.
What I Did Last Summer.
**Ikhnaton**    *See* **Akhnaton**
**Ikinilik**
Song of the Trout Fisher, The.
**Ilce, Ana**
Summer Street.
**Illot, Percy**
Lost Egg, The.
**Iman, Yusef**
Love Your Enemy.
**Imbs, Bravig**
Sleep.
Wind Was There, The.
**Inada, Lawson Fusao**
Asian Brother, Asian Sister.
At the Stronghold.
Caption, Circa 1972.
From Our Album.
Making Miso.
Namely You.
Plucking Out a Rhythm.
**Inez, Colette**
Colette, Poor Clare.
Empress in the Mirror.
For Mama Streek.
Good news! Nilda Is Back.
Instructions for the Erection of a Statue
to Myself in Central Park.
Letters of a Name, The.
Mercedes, Her Aloneness.
Snapshot.
Waiting for the Doctor.
When I Was Soft as Ferns.
Woman Who Loved Worms, The.
**Ingalls, Jeremy**
Traits: Inner Portrait.
**Inge, Charles Cuthbert**
Certain Young Gourmet, A.
**Inge, William Ralph**
Limerick: "There was an old man of
Khartoum."

**Ingelow, Jean**
Divided.
Feathers and Moss.
One Morning, Oh, So Early!
**"Ingoldsby, Thomas" (Richard Harris Barham)**
Ingoldsby Legends, The, *sels.*
Jackdaw of Rheims, The.
Lay of St. Gengulphus A, *sel.*
Not a Sous Had He Got.
**Inib-sarri**
Letter to Her Father, A.
**Inman, Will**
Late Advisory for Intergalactic Travellers Such as Poets.
108 Tales of a Po'Buckra, *sel.*
Shaman.
**Ireland, Kevin**
Deposition.
Educating the Body.
Hidden Message, A.
Parade: Liberation Day.
Popular Romance, A.
Striking a Pose.
**Iremonger, Valentin**
Dog, The.
Hector.
Icarus.
Invocation: "Ten bloody years with this quill lying."
Spring Stops Me Suddenly.
This Houre Her Vigill.
**Irihapeti Rangi te Apakura**
Reply to Marriage Proposal.
**Irion, Mary Jane**
Invocation from a Lawn Chair.
**Irish, Jeff**
Boy Thirteen, A.
**Irwin, Thomas Caulfield**
Swift, *sel.*
With the Dawn.
**Irwin, Wallace ("Ginger"; "Hashimura Togo")**
Ballad of Hagensack, The.
Constant Cannibal Maiden, The.
Meditations of a Mariner.
Nautical Extravaganza, A.
Powerful Eyes o' Jeremy Tait, The.
Reminiscence.
Science for the Young.
**Isaacson, Jose**
Pre-Positions.
**Isanos, Magda**
Apricot Tree.
**Ise, Lady**
Because we suspected/ the pillow would say "I know."
Correspondence:/ when I have sad thoughts.
Elegy: Ise Lamenting the Death of Empress Onshi.
Even in my dreams/ I must no longer meet you.
Flower of waves, A.
Hanging from the branches of a green/ willow tree.
If it is you, there/ in the light boat on the pond.
Like a ravaged sea/ this bed.
Near a Waterfall at Ryumon.
News of the palace.
On Seeing the Field Being Singed.

Seeing the Plum Blossoms by the River.
Seeing the Returning Geese.
They are rebuilding/ the old bridge, the Nagara.
When the fifth month comes.
**Ise Tayu**
Clear water of the imperial pond, The.
**Isherwood, Christopher**
Common Cormorant, The.
On His Queerness.
**Issa (Kobayashi Issa)**
Buddha's Birthday: April 8, 1819.
Buddha's Death Day: February 15, 1815.
Crawl, laugh.
New Moon, The.
Oraga Haru, *sels.*
Spring Rain.
**Issaia, Nana**
Dream.
Sacrifice.
**Ivens, Michael**
First Day at School
**Iverson, Lucille**
Abortion, The.
Man, The.
Outrage.
**Ives, Rich**
Memory, a Small Brown Bird.
**Ivie, Kelly**
Gull Lake Reunion.
**Ivimy, May**
Ghosts of the Living.
Nurse.
Old Men in a Home.
On a Death in an Old People's Home.
**Iwa no Hime, Empress**
Longing for the Emperor.
**Izumi Shikibu**
As the rains of spring.
From darkness/ I go onto the road/ of darkness.
From darkness/ Into the path of darkness.
From that first night.
Here in this world/ I won't live.
I left my hills.
I wish you would come.
If you have no time.
If you love me.
Lying here alone.
Never could I think/ Our love a worldly commonplace.
On nights when hail/ falls noisily.
On this winter night.
Orange leaves are gone.
Recklessly/ I cast myself away.
Since that night/ I cannot know myself.
Someone else/ looked at the sky.
When you broke from me.
You told me it was/ because of me.
You wear the face.

**J**

**Jabès, Edmond**
Book Rises Out of the Fire, The.
Circular Cry, A.
Condemned, The.

Pulverized Screen, The.
Song: "On the side of the road."
Song of the Last Jewish Child.
Song of the Trees of the Black Forest.
Water.
**Jackson, Alan**
Person.
Worstest Beast, The.
Young Politician.
**Jackson, Angela**
Basementmusic: The Love Affair.
Blackmen: Who Make Morning.
For Our Rising (Warrenssong).
**Jackson, Helen Hunt ("H.H."; "Saxe Holm")**
Ballad of the Gold Country, A.
Cheyenne Mountain.
Poppies on the Wheat.
**Jackson, Leroy F.**
Fun.
Grandpa Dropped His Glasses.
Timothy Grady.
**Jackson, Mae**
Blues Today, The.
For Some Poets.
I Remember.
I Used to Wrap My White Doll Up in.
January 3, 1970.
Reincarnation.
**Jackson, Michael**
Art Market: Leopoldville.
Fille de Joie: Congo.
Return from Luluabourg.
**Jackson, Richard**
Holding On.
**Jackson, William (Haywood)**
Making an Impression.
**Jacob, Hildebrand**
Here Delia's buried at fourscore.
Swain, give o'er your fond pretension.
Writer, The.
**Jacob, Max**
It may be that a strange dream.
**Jacob, Violet**
Neep-Fields by the Sea, The.
Tam i' the Kirk.
Water-Hen, The.
**Jacobik, Gray**
Attempts: 1964.
Central Maryland, 1963.
5:30.
**Jacobs, A. C.**
Isaac.
Painting.
Poem for My Grandfather.
Yiddish Poet.
**Jacobs, Alex** *See* **Karoniaktatie**
**Jacobs, Catherine Haydon**
Autumn Orchard.
**Jacobs, Henry Eyster**
Lord Jesus Christ, We Humbly Pray, *with music.*
**Jacobs, Henry S.**
How Goodly Is Thy House, *with music.*
**Jacobs, Maria**
Embroidery.
Song of the Intruder.
**Jacobsen, Josephine**
Class, The.
Destinations.
49th and 5th, December 13.
Interrupted, The.

It is the Season.
Matadors, The.
Night Patrol.
Planet, The.
Rainy Night at the Writers' Colony.
Reason of Numbers, A.
Reindeer and Engine.
Shade-Seller, The.
There Is Good News.
Thief, The.
When the Five Prominent Poets.
Yellow.

**Jacobsen, Rolf**
Country Roads.
Old Age.
Road's End.
Sunflower.

**Jacobson, Ethel**
Atomic Courtesy.

**Jaeger, Lowell**
Poem for My Mother.

**Jaffe, Dan**
Owl in the Rabbi's Barn, The.
Yahrzeit.

**Jaffray, Norman R.**
Beatnik Limernik.
Sliding Scale.

**Jagger, Mick** and Keith Richard
Live with Me.

**Jago, Richard**
Hamlet's Soliloquy Imitated.

**Jahan, Nur, Empress**
Moon of Id came, The.
Your love turned my body into water.

**Jahns, T. R.**
Song of the Farmworker.
Utility.

**Jalal ed-Din Rumi** *See* **Rumi, Jalal ed-Din**

**Jallais, Denise**
Lullaby for My Dead Child.

**Jama, Sheikh Aqib Abdullahi**
Prayer for Rain.

**James I, King of England**
Ane Metaphoricall Invention of a
  Tragedie Called Phoenix, *sel.*
Constant Love in All Conditions.
For I complaine not of sic common cace.
Sonnet: "Azured vault, the crystal circles
  bright, The."

**James I, King of Scotland**
Kingis Quair, The,*sels.*
Nightingale's Song, The.

**James, Clive**
To Pete Atkin: A Letter from Paris, *sel.*

**James, David**
After Your Death.
Blind Man Who Sells Brushes, The.
Child Collecting.
Digging for Singapore.
Famous Outlaw Stops in for a Drink,
  The.
For Rent.
Making Yourself at Home.
Tradition.

**James, Thomas (1593–1635?)**
Lines on His Companions Who Died in
  the Northern Seas.

**James, Thomas (1946–74)**
Hunting for Blueberries.
Letter to a Mute.
Letters to a Stranger.
Mummy of a Lady Named

Jemutesonekh XXI Dynasty.
Reasons.
Spider in the Grapes.
Timothy.
Tom o' Bedlam among the Sunflowers.

**Jamieson, Morley**
Birthday, The.
Swans.

**Jammes, Francis**
Little Donkey, The.

**Jana Bai**
She was my staff and I am blind.

**Janik, Phyllis**
In the Field.
Story of Good, The.

**Jankola, Beth**
Women Called Bossy Cowboys.

**Janosco, Beatrice**
Garden Hose, The.

**Janowitz, Phyllis**
Case.
Wait, The.

**Janzen, Richard**
Oh, Joyous House.

**Jaques, Florence Page**
There Once Was a Puffin.

**Jarman, Mark**
Desire of Water, The.

**Jarrell, Randall**
Aging.
Bats.
Bird of Night, The.
Black Swan, The.
Blind Sheep, The.
Bronze David of Donatello, The.
Burning the Letters.
Camp in the Prussian Forest, A.
Chipmunk's Day, The.
Come to the Stone.
Death of the Ball Turret Gunner, The.
Eighth Air Force.
Elementary Scene, The.
Emancipators, The.
Field and Forest.
Forsaken Girl, The.
Front, A.
Game at Salzburg, A.
Girl in a Library, A.
Gunner.
House in the Wood, The.
In Montecito.
Islands, The.
Jamestown.
Jerome.
Jonah.
Knight, Death, and the Devil, The.
Lonely Man, The.
Losses.
Lost Children, The.
Märchen, The.
Mockingbird, The.
Next Day.
"Night before the Night before
  Christmas, The," *sel.*
90 North.
Old and the New Masters, The.
Orient Express, The.
Protocols.
Range in the Desert, The.
Say Goodbye to Big Daddy.
2nd Air Force.
Sick Child, A.

Sleeping Beauty, The: Variation of the
  Prince.
Soul, A.
Subway from New Britain to the Bronx,
  The.
Thinking of the Lost World.
Variations.
Ways and the Peoples, The.
Well Water.
When I Was Home Last Christmas.
Woman.
Woman at the Washington Zoo, The.

**Jarrett, Emmett**
Dear Mother
For E. C. J.
"Hamlet."
Human Relations.
Runes.
Song: "Help me now."
Trip, The.
Two of Cups, The.

**Jason, Philip K.**
Skin.

**Jastrun, Mieczyslaw**
Encirclement.
Jews, The.

**Jeffers, Lance**
Black Soul of the Land.
Breath in My Nostrils.
Grief Streams Down My Chest.
How High the Moon.
Love Pictures You as Black and Long-
  faced.
My Blackness Is the Beauty of This
  Land.
Nina Simone.
On Listening to the Spirituals.
Trellie.
Who Shined Shoes in Times Square.

**Jeffers, Robinson**
Animals.
Answer, The.
Antrim.
Apology for Bad Dreams.
Artist, An.
Ave Caesar.
Beaks of Eagles, The.
Beauty of Things, The.
Bed by the Window, The.
Birds.
Birds and Fishes.
Bloody Sire, The.
Boats in a Fog.
Broken Promise.
But I Am Growing Old and Indolent.
Carmel Point.
Cassandra.
Compensation.
Continent's End.
Credo.
Cruel Falcon, The.
Crumbs or the Loaf.
Deer Lay Down Their Bones, The.
Divinely Superfluous Beauty.
Evening Ebb.
Eye, The.
Fawn's Foster-Mother.
Fire on the Hills.
Flight of Swans.
Grass on the Cliff.
Gray Weather.
Great Explosion, The.

Hands.
House Dog's Grave, The.
Hurt Hawks.
Joy.
Life from the Lifeless.
Little Scraping, A.
Love the Wild Swan.
New Mexican Mountain.
Night.
Night without Sleep.
Nova.
Ocean.
Oh, Lovely Rock.
Original Sin.
Phenomena.
Post Mortem.
Purse-Seine, The.
Rearmament.
Rock and Hawk.
Science.
Shane O'Neill's Cairn.
Shine, Perishing Republic.
Shine, Republic.
Shiva.
Signpost.
Skunks, *sel.*
Still the Mind Smiles.
Summer Holiday.
To the Stone-Cutters.
Trumpet, The, *sel.*
Unnatural Powers.
Vulture.
Watch the Lights Fade.
We have little animals here.
**Jeffrey, Francis, Lord Jeffrey**
On Peter Robinson.
**Jeffrey, Mildred**
Death.
**Jeffrey, William**
Native Element.
Stones.
**Jeffries, Sir Charles**
Floral Tribute.
**Jekyll, Joseph**
See, one physician, like a sculler, plies.
**Jellema, Roderick Hartigh**
Because I Never Learned the Names of
  Flowers.
Four-square Gospel.
Fresh Fruit for Breakfast.
In Imago Dei: Fiat Lux.
On the Death of God.
Poem Beginning with a Line Memorized
  at School.
Sisters, Daughters.
Sixes and Sevens.
To a Student Poet, Hospitalized, Having
  "Broken with Reality."
Waking to Snowfall.
Washington Migrants.
**Jenkins, Brooks**
Loneliness.
**Jenkins, Louis**
Library.
Medicine.
My Feet.
Portage Poem.
Quiet Place, A.
Violence on Television.
**Jenks, Orville**
Dying Mine Brakeman, The.
**Jenner, Henry L.**
My Savior, Hear My Prayer.

**Jennett, Seán**
Barge Horse, The.
**Jennings, Elaine H.**
Each night/ just before dusk.
I am riding a lion.
There Is No Time.
Weather Report.
**Jennings, Elizabeth**
Animals' Arrival, The.
Answers.
Clothes.
Delay.
Doubts.
Fountain.
Friends.
In a Mental Hospital Sitting Room.
Interrogator, The.
My Grandmother.
Old Woman.
One Flesh.
Radio Men, The.
Song at the Beginning of Autumn.
Song for a Birth or a Death.
Storm House, The.
Two Deaths.
Ugly Child, The.
Unknown Child, The.
Winter Love.
Young Ones, The.
**Jennings, Humphrey**
Prose Poem.
**Jennings, Kate**
Divorce.
**Jennison, C. S.**
I'm Leery of Firms with Easy Terms.
**Jensen, Jeffry**
Portrait of a Reluctant Passenger.
Western Movies.
**Jensen, Laura**
After I Have Voted.
Household.
In the Hospital.
Indian.
Sleep in the Heat.
Starlings.
Talking to the Mule.
**Jenyns, Soame**
Doctor Johnson.
Modern Fine Gentleman, The.
Modern Fine Lady, The, *sel.*
Snow-Ball, The.
**Jerome, Judson**
At the Dancing School of the Sisters
  Schwarz.
Child's Game.
Deer Hunt.
Eve: Night Thoughts.
Plexus and Nexus.
Psychology Today.
**Jerome, William**
Bedelia, *with music.*
**Jerozal, Gregory**
Among Household Objects.
Consent.
Moving Inland.
**Jewett, Eleanore Myers**
Down among the Wharves.
**Jewsbury, Maria Jane**
Partings.
To a Young Brother.
**Jigmed, Chimedin**
For the Cultural Campaign.

Satirical Poem about Drink, A, *sel.*
**Jimason, Joanne**
Deep Sea Blues.
**Jiménez, Juan Ramón**
Deep Night.
Fleeting Return.
Full Consciousness.
Lamb Was Bleating Softly, The.
New Spring.
Nudes.
Oceans.
Poetry.
**Jito, Empress**
Spring is passing and.
**Jitrik, Noe**
Addio a la Mamma.
**Joad, C. E. M.**
Materialism.
**Joans, Ted**
Chickitten Gitten!
It Is Time.
Its Curtains.
Knee Deep.
Lester Young.
Love Tight.
Protective Grigri, The.
Scenery.
.38, The.
To Fez Cobra.
Up out of the African.
Voice in the Crowd.
Watermelon.
Zoo You Too!
**Johannes Secundus (Jan Nicoli Everaerts)**
Basia, *sel.*
**Johari Amini**  *See* Latimore, Jewel C.
**John of the Cross, Saint**
Dark Night, The.
Upon an obscure night.
**Johnson, Burges**
Contentment.
Remarks from the Pup.
**Johnson, Dan**
Brown Bird, The.
Crossing Over.
Madman ("A madman/ in a stream/
  provokes me").
Stray Things.
**Johnson, Denis**
Boarding, The.
**Johnson, Don**
Children's Hour, The.
Night Flight.
Ripper Collins' Legacy.
Tick Picking in the Quetico.
**Johnson, Donald**
Indian Summer Here, You in Honolulu.
**Johnson, Edward**
Water-Drinker, The.
**Johnson, Eric**
Art on the Swing-Shift, Truck Assembly.
**Johnson, Fenton**
Aunt Jane Allen.
Counting.
Daily Grind, The.
Negro Peddler's Song, A.
Old Repair Man, The.
Scarlet Woman, The.
Tired.
World Is a Mighty Ogre, The.
**Johnson, Fred**
Arabesque.

Coda.
Fire, Hair, Meat and Bone.
Noises.
**Johnson, George W.**
When You and I Were Young, Maggie.
**Johnson, Georgia Douglas**
Common Dust.
Conquest.
Credo.
Escape.
I Want to Die while You Love Me.
Lovelight.
Old Black Men.
Poet Speaks, The.
Prejudice.
Riddle, The: "White men's children
spread over the earth."
Suppliant, The.
Trifle.
Your World ("Your world is as big as
you make it").
**Johnson, H. B.**
Stuff.
**Johnson, Helen Armstead**
Affirmation.
Philodendron.
**Johnson, Helene**
Bottled: New York.
Invocation: "Let me be buried in the
rain."
Magalu.
Poem: "Little brown boy."
Road, The.
Sonnet to a Negro in Harlem.
**Johnson, James Weldon**
Creation, The.
Glory of the Day Was in Her Face, The.
Go Down Death.
Lift Every Voice and Sing.
Listen, Lord—a Prayer.
O Black and Unknown Bards.
**Johnson, Joe**
Anna.
If I Ride This Train.
Judeebug's Country.
Samurai and Hustlers.
True Love.
**Johnson, Lionel Pigot**
Bagley Wood.
By the Statue of King Charles at
Charing Cross.
Church of a Dream, The.
Dark Angel, The.
In Falmouth Harbour.
Magic.
Mystic and Cavalier.
Plato in London.
Precept of Silence, The.
Sancta Silvarum, sel.
Song: "Now in golden glory goes."
Stranger, A.
To Morfydd.
**Johnson, Loring**
In the mornings.
**Johnson, Louis**
Birthday, The.
Bread and a Pension.
He Smelt the Smell of Death within the
Marrow.
Here Together Met.
Magpie and Pines.
Matter of Urgency.

New Worlds for Old.
Perfect Symbol, The.
**Johnson, Michael L.**
Nancy, You Dance.
On the Dates of Poets.
**Johnson, Paul**
Because.
**Johnson, Pauline**
Lost Lagoon, The.
Song My Paddle Sings, The.
Train Dogs, The.
**Johnson, Pyke, Jr.**
Me and Samantha.
**Johnson, Rita**
Corner, The.
**Johnson, Robert**
Love in Vain.
**Johnson, Robin**
Found with Chain.
**Johnson, Ronald**
Letters to Walt Whitman, sels.
**Johnson, Samuel (1709–84)**
Ballad: "I put my hat upon my head."
Burlesque of Lope De Vega.
Charles XII of Sweden.
Comets and Princes.
Epitaph on William Hogarth.
Imitation of the Style of * * * *.
Lines Written in Ridicule of Certain
Poems Published in 1777.
London: A Poem in Imitation of the
Third Satire of Juvenal.
On Colley Cibber.
On the Death of Mr. [or Dr.] Robert
Levet, a Practiser in Physic.
Power of Prayer, The.
Prologue Spoken [by Mr. Garrick] at the
Opening of the Theatre in Drury-
Lane, 1747.
Prologue to "A Word to the Wise."
Scholar's Life, The.
Short Song of Congratulation, A.
To Miss ——: On Her Playing upon the
Harpsichord.
To Mrs. Thrale on Her Thirty-fifth
Birthday.
To robbers furious, and to lovers tame.
Translation of Lines by Benserade.
Vanity of Human Wishes, The: The
Tenth Satire of Juvenal Imitated.
Young Author, The.
**Johnson, Samuel (1822–82)**
City of God.
Father, in Thy Mysterious Presence
Kneeling, with music.
I Bless Thee, Lord, for Sorrows Sent,
with music.
Life of Ages, Richly Poured, with music.
**Johnson, Siddie Joe**
Goat.
I Did Not See a Mermaid?
Midnight in Bonnie's Stall.
Witchcraft.
**Johnson, Thomas**
Some Scribbles for a Lumpfish.
**Johnson, Tom**
Becoming Is Perfection.
**Johnson, W. Ralph**
July.
**Johnson, Willard**
Indian Song ("The fire on the hearth is
the woman's fire").

**Johnston, Anna.** See "Carbery, Ethna"
**Johnston, George**
Indoors.
**Johnston, Gordon**
Hot Day and Human Nature, The.
**Johnston, Laughton**
Love Poem 3.
**Johnstone, Henry, Lord Johnstone**
Fastidious Serpent, The.
**Jonas, George**
Eight Lines for a Script Girl.
Exit Lines.
Glass Eaters, The.
Let me put it this way.
Once More.
Peace.
Portrait: The Freedom Fighter.
Sleep only with strangers.
To Christian Montpelier, sel.
We all have/ A bench in the park to
reach.
Women don't travel in clubcars.
**Jonas, Gerald**
Day the T.V. Broke, The.
**Jonas, Steve**
Blackstone Park.
Cante Jondo for Soul Brother Jack
Spicer.
**Jones, Bobi**
Portrait of a Nun.
Portrait of a Pregnant Woman.
Portrait of an Engine Driver.
Spring at Nant Dywelan.
**Jones, Brian**
Death of a Cat.
How to Catch Tiddlers.
**Jones, David**
A, a, a, Domine Deus.
Anathemata, The, sels.
Angle-Land.
Five Unmistakable Marks, The.
In Parenthesis, sels.
King Pellam's Launde.
Redriff.
Sleeping Lord, The, sel.
Wall, The.
**Jones, David Gwenallt**
Cymru.
Earth, The.
Old Woman, An.
Rhydcymerau.
**Jones, Donald**
Old Man's Lark, An.
**Jones, Ebenezer**
When the World Is Burning.
**Jones, Ellis**
Eaves.
**Jones, Ernest Charles**
Song of the Lower Classes, The.
**Jones, Evan**
At the Airport.
Compound, The.
Falling Sickness, The.
Generations.
Lament of the Banana Man.
Language, Talk to Me.
Song of the Banana Man.
**Jones, Glyn**
Again.
Esyllt.
Profile of Rose.
**Jones, Gwilym R.**

Psalm to the Creatures.
**Jones, Gwyn**
Blue Day Journey, The.
**Jones, Jeanetta**
Involuntary flex.
**Jones, Jessie Orton**
Secrets, *sels.*
**Jones, John P.**
Silver Jack's Religion.
**Jones, L. E.**
Epigram on the Unknown Inventor of Scissors.
**Jones, LeRoi**    *See* **Baraka, Imamu Amiri**
**Jones, Nancy**
Running Blind.
**Jones, Patricia**
14th St/New York, *abr.*
**Jones, Paul**
Native African Revolutionaries.
**Jones, Rae Desmond**
Generator, The.
New Year 1974.
Poems to My Father.
Wishbone, The.
**Jones, Robert**
These Days.
**Jones, Sir William**
Epigram: "On parent knees, a naked new-born child."
**Jones, Thomas Gwynn**
Argoed.
**Jones, Thomas Harri**
Difference.
Welshman in Exile Speaks, The.
**Jong, Erica**
Aging.
Alcestis on the Poetry Circuit.
Back to Africa.
Becoming a Nun.
Bitter Pills for the Dark Ladies.
Climbing You.
Colder.
Dear Colette.
Dearest Man-in-the-Moon.
Divorce.
For a Marriage.
Fruit and Vegetables.
Here Comes.
Hook.
How You Get Born.
In Sylvia Plath Country.
In the Penile Colony.
Man under the Bed, The.
Mother.
Narcissus, Photographer.
Penis Envy.
Seminar.
Seventeen Warnings in Search of a Feminist Poem.
Sexual Soup.
Sunjuice.
Teacher, The.
Three Sisters.
Touch.
Universal Explicator, The.
Walking through the Upper East Side.
Why I Died.
Wives of Mafiosi, The.
Woman Who Loved to Cook, The.
**Jonker, Ingrid**
Dog.
I Am with Those.

Journey round the World.
Time of Waiting in Amsterdam.
When You Write Again.
**Jonson, Ben**
Ask Not to Know This Man.
Celebration of Charis, A, *sel.*
Charles Cavendish to His Posterity.
Come, My Celia.
Cynthia's Revels, *sels.*
Death and Love.
Dream, The.
Echo's Lament of Narcissus.
Elegy, An: "Let me be what I am, as Virgil cold," *abr.*
Epicoene; or, The Silent Woman, *sel.*
Epistle to a Friend (Mr. Colby) to Persuade Him to the Wars, An, *sel.*
Epistle to Katherine, Lady Aubigny, *sel.*
Epitaph on Elizabeth, L. H.
Epitaph on Master Philip Gray, An.
Epitaph on S. P. [Salomon *or* Salathiel Pavy], a Child of Queen Elizabeth's Chapel.
Eupheme, *sels.*
Fit of Rime against Rime, A.
Fortunate Isles, and Their Union, The, *sel.*
Golden Age Restored, The, *sel.*
Hermogenes's Song.
Hourglass, The.
Hymenaei, *sel.*
Hymn to Diana.
Hymn to God the Father, A.
In the Person of Woman Kind.
Inviting a Friend to Supper.
Masque of Queens, The,*sels.*
Noble Nature, The.
Oberon, the Fairy Prince, *sels.*
Ode, An: "High spirited friend."
Ode to Himself ("Come leave the loathèd stage").
Ode to Himself, An ("Where dost thou careless lie").
On Courtworm.
On Don Surly.
On Giles and Joan.
On Gut.
On Lieutenant Shift.
On Lucy, Countess of Bedford.
On My First Daughter.
On My First Son [*or* Sonne].
On Sir Voluptuous Beast.
On Something That Walks Somewhere.
On the Famous Voyage.
Pleasure Reconciled to Virtue (A Masque).
Return of Astraea, The.
Simplex Munditiis.
Song, A: "Oh do not wanton with those eyes."
Song of the Satyrs.
That Women Are but Men's Shadows.
To Celia ("Drink to me only with thine eyes").
To Doctor Empiric.
To Fine Lady Would-be.
To Fool, or Knave.
To Heaven.
To Penshurst.
To Sir Robert Wroth.
To the Ghost of Martial.

To the Immortal Memory and Friendship of That Noble Pair, Sir Lucius Cary and Sir Henry Morison.
To the Memory of My Beloved, the Author, Mr. William Shakespeare, and What He Hath Left Us.
To the Right Honourable the Lord High Treasurer.
To the Same.
To William Roe.
Triumph of Charis, The.
Volpone, *sels.*
Voyage Itself, The.
Witches' Charm, The.
**Jordan, David Starr**
Food for a Cat.
**Jordan, Dorothy** *and* **Annie McVicar**   *See* **McVicar, Annie** *and* **Dorothy Jordan**
**Jordan, June**
All the World Moved.
And Who Are You?
Cameo No. II.
For My Mother.
Getting Down to Get Over.
If You Saw a Negro Lady.
In Memoriam: Martin Luther King, Jr.
May 27, 1971: No Poem.
Maybe the Birds.
My Sadness Sits around Me.
Nobody Riding the Roads Today.
Okay "Negroes."
Poem for My Family.
Poem from the Empire State.
Poem: On Moral Leadership as a Political Dilemma.
Poem to My Sister, Ethel Ennis, Who Sang "The Star-spangled Banner" at the Second Inauguration of Richard Milhous Nixon.
Queen Anne's Lace.
Reception, The.
These poems/ they are things that I do.
Towards a City That Sings.
Uncle Bull-boy.
What Happens.
What Would I Do White?
**Jordan, Norman**
August 2.
Black Warrior.
Feeding the Lions.
July 31.
**Jordan, Thomas**
Let Us Drink and Be Merry.
**Jordana, Elena**
Tango.
**Joselow, Beth**
Family Circle, A.
Poem in Hungarian.
**Joseph, Jenny**
Warning.
**Joseph, Michael Kennedy**
Distilled Water.
Girl, Boy, Flower, Bicycle.
Mercury Bay Eclogue.
Nurse's Song.
Off Cape Leeuwen.
**Joseph, Rosemary**
Baking Day.
**Joslin, Dorothy**
Sonnet for a Loved One.
**Joyce, J.**
Soil Searcher.

**Joyce, James**
All Day I Hear the Noise of Waters.
Bahnhofstrasse.
Ballad of Persse O'Reilly, The.
Because your voice was at my side.
Ecce Puer.
Finnegans Wake, *sels.*
Flower Given to My Daughter, A.
Gentle lady, do not sing.
Holy Office, The.
I Hear an Army Charging upon the Land.
Lean out of the window.
Memory of the Players in a Mirror at Midnight, A.
Nightpiece.
O sweetheart, hear you.
On the Beach at Fontana.
Ondt and the Gracehoper, The.
Sleep now, O sleep now.
There was a kind Lady called Gregory.
Thou leanest to the shell of night.
Though I Thy Mithridates Were.
Ulysses, *sel.*
What Counsel Has the Hooded Moon.
Yes.

**Jozsef, Attila**
Seventh, The.
Since You've Been Away.

**Juana Inés de la Cruz, Sister** (*originally* Juana de Asbaje)
Crimson lute that comest in the dawn.
First Drean, *sel.*
I can't hold you and I can't leave you.
In Which She Satisfies a Fear with the Rhetoric of Tears.
Satirical Romance, A, *sels.*
She Attempts to Refute the Praises That Truth, Which She Calls Passion, Inscribed on a Portrait of the Poet.
She Proves the Inconsistency of the Desires and Criticism of Men Who Accuse Women of What They Themselves Cause.
This coloured counterfeit that thou beholdest.
This evening, my love, even as I spoke vainly.

**Judkins, Charles Otis**
Play, The.

**Judson, Adoniram**
Come Holy Spirit, Dove Divine, *with music.*
Our Father, God, *with music.*

**Judson, John**
Finding Words in Winter.
24 December.

**Judson, Sarah**
Proclaim the Lofty Praise, *with music.*

**Juergensen, Hans**
Anne Sexton.

**Juhász, Ferenc**
Birth of the Foal.

**Juhasz, Suzanne**
Dancer from the Dance, The.
Saying Goodbye.

**Jurgensen, Manfred**
Memory, A.
Mowing His Crew-cut.
Syllabus, The.
You Do Not Write.

**Justice, Donald**

About My Poems.
Anonymous Drawing.
Another Song ("Merry the green, the green hill shall be merry").
Assassination, The.
Beyond the Hunting Woods.
Bus Stop.
But That Is Another Story.
Counting the Mad.
Crossing Kansas by Train.
Elegy Is Preparing Itself, An.
First Death.
Grandfathers, The.
Here in Katmandu.
In Bertram's Garden.
Incident in a Rose Garden.
Local Storm, A.
Luxury.
Memory of a Porch.
Men at Forty.
On a Painting by Patient B of the Independence State Hospital for the Insane.
On the Death of Friends in Childhood.
Party.
Poem: "Time and the weather wear away."
Poem to Be Read at 3 A.M.
Self-Portrait as Still Life.
Snowfall, The.
Song: "Morning opened/ Like a rose."
Southern Gothic.
Thinking about the Past.
Tourist from Syracuse, The.

**Justus, May**
Good Neighbors.

**Juvenal (Decimus Junius Juvenalis)**
But of all the plagues, the greatest is untold.
Give store of days, good Jove, give length of years.
Hannibal.
Jove, grant me length of life, and years' good store.
Satires, *Sels.*
Sejanus ("How many men are killed by power, by power").
Sejanus ("Some ask for envy'd pow'r; which publick hate").
Sejanus ("What crowds by envied power, the wish of all").

**K**

**Kabir**
Clay Jug, The.
Friend, Hope for the Guest.
Simple Purification, The.
What form or shape to describe?

**Ka-'ehu**
Leper, The.

**Kaccipettu Nannakaiyar**
My lover capable of terrible lies.

**Kaffka, Margit**
Father.

**Kaga no Chiyo**
Haiku: "Autumn's bright moon."
Haiku: "Dew of the rouge-flower, The."

Haiku: "Spring rain."

**Kahn, Gustave**
Paris by Night.
Temple, The.
Word, The.

**Kahn, Hannah**
Signature.

**Kaiama**
Song: "Misty and dim, a bush in the wilds of Kapa'a."

**Kalar, Joseph**
After the Storm.
Bank.
Invocation to the Wind.
Night-Shift.
Nothing to Lose.
Now That Snow Is Falling.
Papermill.
Poolroom Faces.
Repentant Judas.
Thunder in a Moment of Calm.
Worker Uprooted.

**Kalidasa**
Is poetry always worthy when it's old.

**Kallman, Chester**
Dead Center.
Romance, A.

**Kamenetz, Rodger**
Biograph.
Christopher Magisto.
Pilpul.
Why I Can't Write My Autobiography.

**Kaminsky, Marc**
Erev Shabbos.

**Kamm, Nancy P.**
Waiting Carefully.

**Kammeyer, Virginia Maughan**
Compensation.

**Kanabus, Henry**
Beardsley Flesh, The.
Brittle Eye, The.
Centapod, The.
Day Birth Placard (for Amy), The.
Furnace Monkey.
Mandy as Night Bouquet.
Margie Silver.
Pleasant Evening, The.
Song (The Wren).
Still Life.

**Kanai Mieko**
House of Madam Juju, The.

**Kanalenstein, Ruben**
Jerusalem.

**Kandel, Lenore**
Blues for Sister Sally.
Bus Ride.
Circus, *sels.*
Freak Show and Finale.
Love in the Middle of the Air.

**Kane, Julie**
Cornelia's Window.

**Kanié, Anoma**
All That You Have Given Me, Africa.

**Kantner, Paul**
We Can Be Together.

**Kantner, Paul, David Crosby** *and* **Stephen Stills** *See* **Crosby, David, Paul Kantner** *and* **Stephen Stills**

**Kao Ch'i**
Written on Seeing the Flowers, and Remembering My Daughter.

**Kaplan, Allan**

Marvelous.

**Kaplan, Rebbekka**
You Are More than I Need.

**Karélli, Zoé**
Presences.

**Kariuki, Joseph**
Come Away, My Love.

**Karlfeldt, Erik Axel**
Vagrant, A.

**Karni, Yehuda**
Chambers of Jerusalem.
Four of Them, The.

**Karoniaktatie (Alex Jacobs)**
California Gold Rush.
1,000,001 Starlings.
Spirits/ Someone.
There's a Footprint of Love & Disorder
Troll Songs.

**Karp, Vickie**
Last Farmer in Queens, The.

**Kasa, Lady**
I dreamed I held/ a sword against my
  flesh.
I love and fear him.
To love someone/ Who does not return
  that love.

**Kasold, Robert T.**
Artistry.
Glass Flowers in a Glass Ball.
Happy?
Prison Dorm.

**Kass, Jerry**
Fidelity.

**Kassia**
Mary Magdalene.

**Katav, Shalom**
Pleading Voices.

**Kates, J.**
Life Story.

**Katz, Bobbi**
Recipe.

**Katz, Jane Garland**
Dressing for Our Spring Party.
Fields of the Country, The.
Photograph of the Hanging Pianos.

**Katz, Menke**
Celebration.
In the Year of Two Thousand.

**Katzin, Olga.** See **"Sagittarius"**

**Katzman, Allen**
Rhododendron Plant, The.

**Kauffman, Janet**
Cultivating.
Mennonite Farm Wife.
Preface: Topping.
Rally.
Steamer on the Seedbed.
Taking Down.
Tobacco, sels.
Volunteers, The.
Watercress.

**Kaufman, Bob**
African Dream.
Afterwards, They Shall Dance.
Battle Report.
Benediction.
Blues Note.
Cocoa Morning.
Come.
Falling.
Forget Me Not.
Heavy Water Blues.

I Have Folded My Sorrows.
Letter to the Chronicle.
Mingus.
Patriotic Ode on the Fourteenth
  Anniversary of the Persecution of
  Charlie Chaplin.
Reflections on a Small Parade.
Suicide.
To My Son Parker, Asleep in the Next
  Room.
Unholy Missions.
Walking Parker Home.
When We Hear the Eye Open.

**Kaufman, Shirley**
Always She Moves from Me.
Apples.
Beetle on the Shasta Daylight.
Burning of the Birds, The.
Dinosaur Tracks in Beit Zayit.
Her Going.
Hunger Artist, The.
I see bodies in the morning kneel.
Leah.
Looking for Maimonides: Tiberias.
Loving.
Mothers, Daughters.
Mountain, The.
New Graveyard: Jerusalem.
Next Year, in Jerusalem.
Realities.
Room.
Starting Over.
There are caverns/ under our feet.
Watts.
We are going down a long slide.
Wonders.

**Kavanagh, P. J.**
Temperance Billiards Rooms, The.

**Kavanagh, Patrick**
Canal Bank Walk.
Christmas Childhood, A, sel.
Come Dance with Kitty Stobling.
Dear Folks.
Epic.
Father Mat.
Great Hunger, The, sels.
Hospital, The.
I Had a Future.
If Ever You Go to Dublin Town.
In Memory of My Mother.
Inniskeen Road: July Evening.
Is.
Lecture Hall.
Lines Written on a Seat on the Grand
  Canal, Dublin.
October.
Pegasus.
Prelude: "Give us another poem, he
  said."
Sanctity.
Shancoduff.
Spraying the Potatoes.
Stony Grey Soil.
Tinker's Wife.
To a Late Poplar.
To the Man after the Harrow.

**Kay, Billy**
Furst Snaw.
Glencoe.

**Kay, W. Lowrie**
Lancaster County Tragedy.

**Kazan, Molly**

Kennedy.

**Keach, Benjamin**
How Glorious Are the Morning Stars,
  with music.

**Kearney, Lawrence**
Cuba.
Cyclist, The.
Kachinas.

**Kearney, Peadar**
Whack Fol the Diddle.

**Keating, Geoffrey**
Mourn for Yourself.

**Keats, John**
Acrostic of My Sister's Name.
Addressed to Haydon ("Great spirits
  now on earth are sojourning").
Addressed to Haydon
  ("Highmindedness, a jealousy for
  good").
After dark vapours have oppress'd our
  plains.
Ah! who can e'er forget so fair a being?
Answer to a Sonnet Ending Thus.
Are Then Regalities All Gilded Masks?
Asleep! O sleep a little while, white
  pearl!
Bright Star! Would I Were Steadfast as
  Thou Art.
Calidore.
Cancelled Stanza of the Ode on
  Melancholy.
Character of Charles Brown.
Dawlish Fair.
Day is gone, and all its sweets are gone,
  The!
Death.
Dedication to Leigh Hunt, Esq.
Dove.
Endymion [a Poetic Romance],sels.
Eve of St. Agnes, The.
Eve of Saint Mark, The.
Fall of Hyperion, The: A Dream.
Fancy.
Four seasons fill the measure of the year.
Fragment of an Ode to Maia.
Fragment: "Welcome joy, and welcome
  sorrow."
Fragment: "Where's the poet? show him!
  show him."
Gadfly, The.
Give me women, wine and snuff.
God of the Meridian.
Happy is England! I could be content.
How many bards gild the lapses of time!
Hymn to Apollo.
Hyperion; a Fragment.
Imitation of Spenser.
In a Drear-nighted December.
Isabella; or, The Pot of Basil.
Keen, fitful gusts are whisp'ring here and
  there.
King Stephen: A Fragment of a
  Tragedy.
La Belle Dame sans Merci.
Lamia.
Light feet, dark violet eyes, and parted
  hair.
Lines: "Unfelt, unheard, unseen."
Lines on Seeing a Lock of Milton's Hair.
Lines on the Mermaid Tavern.
Lines Rhymed in a Letter Received from
  Oxford.

Lines Written in the Highlands after a Visit to Burns's Country.
Meg Merrilies.
Modern Love.
O solitude! if I must with thee dwell.
Ode: "Bards of passion and of mirth."
Ode on a Grecian Urn.
Ode on Indolence.
Ode on Melancholy.
Ode to a Nightingale.
Ode to Apollo.
Ode to Fanny.
Ode to Psyche.
Oh, how I love, on a fair summer's eve.
On a Dream.
On a Leander Gem.
On a Summer's Day.
On Fame ("Fame, like a wayward girl, will still be coy").
On Fame ("How fever'd is the man, who cannot look").
On First Looking into Chapman's Homer.
On Peace.
On Receiving a Curious Shell, and a Copy of Verses.
On Receiving a Laurel Crown from Leigh Hunt.
On Seeing the Elgin Marbles [for the First Time].
On Sitting Down to Read King Lear Once Again.
On the Grasshopper and [the] Cricket.
On the Sea.
On the Sonnet.
On "The Story of Rimini."
On Visiting Staffa.
On Visiting the Tomb of Burns.
Pensive they sit, and roll their languid eyes.
Poet, The.
Robin Hood.
Sleep and Poetry.
Song about Myself.
Song: "Hence burgundy, claret, and port."
Song: "Hush, hush! tread softly! hush, hush, my dear!"
Song: "O blush not so! O blush not so!"
Song of the Indian Maid, The.
Song: "Stranger lighted from his steed, The."
Sonnet on the Death of a Friend.
Sonnet Written in the Cottage Where Burns Was Born.
Sonnet Written upon Ben Nevis.
Specimen of an Induction to a Poem.
Spenser! a jealous honourer of thine.
Stanzas: "In a drear-nighted December."
Stanzas: "You say you love; but with a voice."
Sweet, sweet is the greeting of eyes.
This Living Hand, Now Warm and Capable.
This pleasant tale is like a little copse.
'Tis "the witching time of night."
To——: "Had I a man's fair form, then might my sighs."
To——: "Hadst thou liv'd in days of old."
To——: "Time's sea hath been five years at its slow ebb."

To——: "What can I do to drive away."
To a Cat.
To a Friend Who Sent Me Some Roses.
To Ailsa Rock.
To Autumn.
To B. R. Haydon.
To Charles Cowden Clarke.
To Chatterton.
To Fanny.
To G. A. W.
To George Felton Mathew.
To Homer.
To Hope.
To J. H. Reynolds, Esq.
To Kosciusko.
To Lord Byron.
To My Brother George ("Full many a dreary hour have I past").
To My Brother George ("Many the wonders I this day have seen").
To My Brothers.
To One Who Has Been Long in City Pent.
To Sleep.
To Some Ladies.
To the Ladies Who Saw Me Crown'd.
To the Nile.
What the Thrush Said.
When I Have Fears That I May Cease to Be.
Where be ye going, you Devon maid?
Why Did I Laugh Tonight?
Woman! when I behold thee flippant, vain.
Written in Disgust of Vulgar Superstition.
Written on the Day That Mr. Leigh Hunt Left Prison.
Yellow Flutterings.

**Keaulumoku**
Birth of Sea and Land Life.
Crawlers, The.
Dawn of Day, The.
Dog Child, The.
Kumulipo, The: A Creation Chant, *sels.*

**Keble, John**
Christian Year, The, *sels.*
Eleventh Sunday after Trinity.
Evening Hymn.
Fill High the Bowl.
Holy Matrimony.
New Every Morning.
Third Sunday in Lent.

**Keefe, Joan**
Go Back.
On Galtymore.
Spike Island: Convicted Labour.

**Keeler, Charles**
Cleaning Ship.
Ocean Lullaby, An.

**Keenan, Terrance**
Phillips Mill.

**Keens, William**
Place by the River, A.

**Kees, Weldon**
Aspects of Robinson.
Beach in August, The.
Coming of the Plague, The.
Conversation in the Drawingroom, The.
Crack Is Moving Down the Wall, The.
Crime Club.
Distance from the Sea, A.

Five.
For My Daughter.
Guide to the Symphony.
Heat in the Room, The.
Henry James at Newport.
Hourglass, The, *sel.*
La Vita Nuova.
Midnight.
Obituary.
Patient Is Rallying, The.
Problems of a Journalist.
Relating to Robinson.
River Song.
Robinson.
Robinson at Home.
Round.
Saratoga Ending.
Small Prayer.
Testimonies.
White Collar Ballad.

**Keesing, Nancy**
Wandering Jews.
We Told You So.

**Kegels, Anne-Marie**
I write to make you suffer.
Nocturnal Heart.
When I strip,/ stop walking/ and drop into sleep.

**Keithley, George**
Dread of Darkness.

**Keizer, Garret**
Tourist, The.

**Kell, Richard**
Calypso.
Citadels.
Fishing Harbour towards Evening.
In the Beginning.
Integration.
Makers, The.
Pay Is Good, The.
Pigeons.
River, The.

**Keller, David**
In the Dream of the Body.

**Keller, Gene**
Man Who Knew the Colt Boy, The.

**Keller, Leonard**
"Temporary Escape."

**Keller, Martha**
Brady's Bend.
Deadfall.

**Kelley, Parham J.**
Heir to Several Yesterdays.

**Kelley, Shannon Keith**
That Man in Manhattan.

**Kellog, Arthur L.**
Hayseed, The.

**Kelly, Conor**
Nocturne: Lake Huron.

**Kelly, Dave**
And Then What.
Eight Miles South of Grand Haven.

**Kelly, John W.**
Throw Him Down M'Closkey; or, M'Closkey's Great Fight, *with music.*

**Kelly, M.**
Last Week I Took a Wife, *with music.*

**Kelly, Robert**
Last Light.
Moonshot.
Poem for Easter.

**Kelso, Peter**

Poems.

**Kemble, Fanny (Frances Anne)**
Wish, A.

**Kemp, Harry**
Humming Bird, The.

**Kempf, Elizabeth**
Before the Dive.

**Ken, Thomas**
All Praise to Thee, My God, This Night.

**Kendall, Timothy**
To a Married Couple That Could Not
Agree.

**Kendrick, Dolores**
Gulls.
Late Morning: Oahu.
Rice and Mats, *sel.*

**Kennedy, Benjamin Hall**
On Christopher Wordsworth, Master of
Trinity.

**Kennedy, Harry**
Say "Au Revoir," but Not "Good-bye,"
*with music.*

**Kennedy, Mary**
Newborn Colt, The.

**Kennedy, Sarah**
Mommie.

**Kennedy, Terry**
Easy Poem, An.

**Kennedy, X. J.**
Aged Wino's Counsel to a Young Man
on the Brink of Marriage, The.
Ars Poetica.
B. Negative.
Consumer's Report.
Creation Morning.
Cross Ties.
Down in Dallas.
Ecology.
Edgar's Story, *sel.*
Epitaph for a Postal Clerk.
First Confession.
In a Prominent Bar in Secaucus One
Day.
In Faith of Rising.
Japanese Beetles.
Last Lines.
Little Elegy.
Loose Woman.
Monstrous Mouse, A.
Mother's Nerves.
National Shrine.
Nature might chicken out, but "I love
you."
Nothing in Heaven Functions as It
Ought.
Nude Descending a Staircase.
Ode: "Old tumbril rolling with me till I
die."
Old Men Pitching Horseshoes.
On a Child Who Lived One Minute.
Skeleton Walks, The.
Space.
Whose Boo Is Whose?
Wicked Witch's Kitchen.
Witnesses, The.

**Kennelly, Brendan**
Black Cliffs, Ballybunion, The.
Certain Old Women.
Girl Next Door, The.
Good Souls, to Survive.
Grip, The.
Light Dying.

Limerick Train, The.
Moloney Remembers the Resurrection of
Kate Finucane.
My Dark Fathers.
Proof.
Thatcher, The.

**Kenner, Peggy Susberry**
Black Taffy.
Comments.
Image in the Mirror.
No Bargains Today.
Round Table, The.

**Kenney, Dan**
Yolanthe.

**Kennick, T.**
You Naughty, Naughty Men, *with music.*

**Kent, Karen L.**
Alan walks with his head upside down.
C44.
Mother your children give you.
White sheer tieback curtains.

**Kent, Louis**
Hunt, The.

**Kent, Margaret**
Stammerers, The.

**Kent, Richard B.**
Summer Storm.

**Kent, Rolly**
After the Stormy Night.
Hanging Clothes.
Old Wife, The.

**Kenyon, Jane**
At a Motel near O'Hare Airport.
Cages.
Circle on the Grass, The.
Suitor, The.

**Kenyon, Theda**
City Bird.

**Kerehoma, Rarawa**
Sentinel's Song, A.

**Kerouac, Jack (John Kerouac)**
Chorus: "Dharma law."
Chorus: "Praised be man, he is existing
in milk."
Chorus: "Songs that erupt, The."
Mexico City Blues,*sels.*
Pun for Al Gelpi, A.
Sept. 16, 1961, Poem.
Some Western Haikus, *sels.*

**Kerr, Alexander**
Mary and Her Dead Canary.

**"Kerr, Orpheus C." (Robert Henry Newell)**
American Traveller, The.
Columbia's Agony.
Neutral British Gentlemen, The.
O, Be Not Too Hasty, My Dearest.
Rejected "National Hymns," The.
Tuscaloosa Sam.
When Your Cheap Divorce Is Granted.

**Kessler, Edward**
Dodo, The.

**Kessler, Jascha**
Dying.
Waiting for Lilith.

**Kessler, Milton**
Beyond Anguish.
Lynching, The.
Route 40—Ohio, U.S.A.

**Kethe, William**
Old Hundredth.
Such as in God the Lord Do Trust, *with
music.*

Thy Mercies, Lord, To Heaven Reach,
*with music.*

**Key, Francis Scott**
Star-spangled Banner, The.
To My Cousin Mary, for Mending My
Tobacco Pouch.
Written at the White Sulphur Springs.

**Keyes, Sidney**
Death and the Plowman.
Grail, The.
Holstenwall.
Hope for Those Separated by War, A.
War Poet.
William Wordsworth.

**Keyishian, M. Deiter**
Muse.

**Keys, William**
Duo.

**Kgositsile, Keorapetse**
For Eusi, Ayi Kwei and Gwen Brooks.
Ivory Masks in Orbit.
My Name Is Afrika.
Origins.
Spirits Unchained.

**Kharms, Daniil**
Connection, The.
Sonnet, A: "Amazing thing happened to
me, An."
Vindication.

**Kherdian, David**
Above the Moving River.
Beckoned in Dream to the Unconscious.
Dtah Dtah.
For My Father: Two Poems.
Kato's Poem.
Lake Michigan.
Little Sis.
My Father.
My Mother and the Americans.
My Mother Takes My Wife's Side.
Squirrels in Wind Pine.
13:IV:72.
To My Sister.
Two Pennies Found on the Gravel.
Umbaji Park.
United States Tony.
When These Old Barns Lost Their
Inhabitants.
Winter, New Hampshire.

**Khoury-Gata, Venus**
Autumn made colors burn, The.
Your cheeks flat on the sand.

**Kickham, Charles J.**
My Ulick.

**Kicknosway, Faye**
Cat, The.
Cigarette Poem, The.
Crystal.
Dear Editor.
Gracie.
He Must Be Fat.
I Wake, My Friend, I.
Moon Travels Slow, The.
Oil Trucks. The Season of Despair, Your
Grass.
This Cat.
When You Plant Cats in the Ground.

**Kieffaber, Alan**
Easter Egg.

**Kiely, Jerome**
For a Young Cistercian Monk.
Funeral of Paddy Haugh.

**Kiesel, Stanley**
Don't Put Me.
Farewell, A: "Partner in the corner bar
is high, a grin."
Kindergarten Teacher.
Poem for Mother's Day.
**Kilgore, James C.**
White Man Pressed the Locks, The.
**Killens, Gail**
Boy from Tennessee.
**Killigrew, Anne**
Chloris' Charms Dissolved by Eudora
Farewel to Worldly Joyes, A ("Farewel
to unsubstantial joyes").
On Death.
On the Soft and Gentle Motions of
Eudora.
Upon the Saying That My Verses Were
Made by Another.
**Kilmer, Joyce**
Trees, *abr.*
**Kilner, Dorothy**
Henry's Secret.
**Kim, Glenn John**
Room.
**Kim Jung-ku**
Am I really old, as people say?
**Kim Kwang-wuk**
I like you, bamboo.
**Kim Nam-jo**
My Baby Has No Name Yet.
**Kim Yo-sop**
Shooting at the Moon.
**Kimball, Jacob**
Thy Praise, O God, in Zion Waits, *with
music.*
**King, B. B.**
Why I Sing the Blues.
**King, Ben (Benjamin Franklin King)**
But Then.
Cow Slips Away, The.
Cultured Girl Again, The.
Hair-Tonic Bottle, The.
If I Should Die.
Mermaid, The.
Pessimist, The.
**King, Carole** *and* **Gerry Goffin, Gerry** *and*
**Carole King**
**King, Francis**
Séance.
**King, Henry, Bishop of Chichester**
Contemplation upon Flowers, A.
Exequy, The.
Sic Vita.
Surrender, The.
**King, Linda**
Great Poet, The.
Hooked on the Magic Muscle.
I Wasn't No Mary Ellen.
Whore.
**King, Patrick**
Neighbours.
Prayer: "Sign that I might, A."
**King, Stoddard**
Breakfast Song in Time of Diet.
Difference, The.
Etude Géographique.
Hearth and Home.
**Kingsley, Charles**
Farewell, A: "My fairest child, I have no
song to give you."
Knight's Leap, The.

Lost Doll, The.
Ode to the North-east Wind.
Pearl Seed.
Sands of Dee, The.
Three Fishers, The.
Tide River, The.
Water Babies, The, *sels.*
Young and Old.
**Kingsmill, Hugh (Hugh Kingsmill Lunn)**
'Tis summer time on Bredon.
Two Poems (after A. E. Housman).
What, Still Alive at Twenty-two.
**Kingston, R. P.**
Between Two Wars.
He's Known His Lesson for Years.
Mystic Lake.
Stateside.
**Kinnell, Galway**
Avenue Bearing the Initial of Christ into
the New World, The, *sel.*
Bear, The.
Braemar.
Burning.
Call across the Valley of Not Knowing,
The, *sel.*
Cells Breathe in the Emptiness.
Correspondence School Instructor Says
Goodbye to His Poetry Students, The.
Dead Shall Be Raised Incorruptible,
The.
Duck-chasing.
First Song.
Flower Herding on Mount Monadnock.
For Robert Frost.
Garbage Disposal Truck, The.
Getting the Mail.
Hen Flower, The.
How Many Nights.
In Fields of Summer.
Little Sleep's-Head Sprouting Hair in the
Moonlight.
Middle of the Way.
Night in the Forest.
On Hardscrabble Mountain.
Path among the Stones, The.
Poems of Night.
Porcupine, The.
Promontory Moon.
River That Is East, The.
Room of Return ("Room over the
Hudson").
Ruins under the Stars, *sel.*
Spindrift.
Supper after the Last, The.
To Christ Our Lord.
Under the Maud Moon.
Under the Williamsburg Bridge.
Vapor Trail Reflected in the Frog Pond.
**Kinnick, B. Jo**
Fish Story.
**Kinsella, Thomas**
Ancestor.
Another September.
Baggot Street Deserta.
Ballydavid Pier.
Chrysalides.
Clarence Mangan.
Country Walk, A.
Cover Her Face.
Death Bed.
First Light.
Hen Woman.

In the Ringwood.
Je T'adore.
Mask of Love.
Mirror in February.
Nightwalker, *sel.*
Office for the Dead.
Ritual of Departure.
Scylla and Charybdis.
Technical Supplement, A. *sel.*
Westland Row.
Wormwood.
**Kipling, Rudyard**
Arithmetic on the Frontier.
Ballad of East and West, The.
Ballad of Minepit Shaw, The.
Beasts Are Very Wise, The.
Beginner, The.
Boots.
Bridegroom, The.
Chant-Pagan.
Cities and Thrones and Powers.
Code of Morals, A.
Cold Iron.
Common Form.
Coward, The.
Dane-Geld.
Danny Deever.
Dead Statesman, A.
Deep-Sea Cables, The.
Dykes, The.
'Eathen, The.
Eddi's Service.
Edgehill Fight.
English Flag, The.
Epitaphs of the War, 1914-18, *sels.*
Equality of Sacrifice.
For All We Have and Are.
Ford o' Kabul River.
Fuzzy-Wuzzy.
Gentlemen-Rankers.
Gethsemane.
Giffen's Debt.
Gods of the Copybook Headings, The.
Gunga Din.
Harp Song of the Dane Women.
Horses.
Hump, The.
Hyaenas, The.
If.
Jane Smith.
Jobson's Amen.
King, The.
Last Lap, The.
Last of the Light Brigade, The.
Lie, The.
Looking Glass, The.
McAndrew's Hymn.
Mandalay.
My Rival.
Old Men, The.
Power of the Dog, The.
Prelude to "Departmental Ditties."
Puck of Pook's Hill, *sels.*
Puck's Song ("See you the ferny ride
that steals").
Recessional.
Refined Man, The.
St. Helena Lullaby, A.
Sea and the Hills, The.
Sergeant's Weddin', The.
Sestina of the Tramp-Royal.
Smuggler's Song, A.

Son, A.
Song of the Banjo, The.
Song of the Galley-Slaves.
Song to Mithras, A.
Storm Cone, The.
Story of the Gadsbys, The, *sel.*
Sussex.
Tommy.
Undertaker's Horse, The.
Way through the Woods, The.
When Earth's Last Picture Is Painted.
White Man's Burden, The.
White Seal's Lullaby, The.
Widow's Party, The.
Winners, The.

**Kipp, Allan F.**
Cubist Blues in Poltergeist Major.

**Kirby, David**
Briefing, The.
I Haven't Forgotten T. S. Eliot.
Schloss, The.
Short Paean of Simon Forman the
   Astrologer, The: To Tronco, His Wife.

**Kirby, Jeannie**
I Wonder.

**Kircher, Pamela**
In the Small Boats of Their Hands.

**Kirkup, James**
All-In Wrestlers.
Bird Fancier, The.
Broken Toys, The.
Correct Compassion, A.
Cosy Cat Nap.
Dripping Tap, The.
Japanese Children.
Lonely Scarecrow, The.
Love in a Space-Suit.
Scarecrow Independence.
Tea in a Space-Ship.
There Was an Old Man.

**Kirsch, Sarah**
Sad Day in Berlin.

**Kirstein, Lincoln**
Bath.
Das Schloss.
Fall In.
Foresight.
Vaudeville.

**Kiss, Jozsef**
New Ahasuerus, The.

**Kissick, Gary**
Rain Quietude.

**Kistler, William**
He Wakes Again in Early Light.
Mask in Macy's.

**Kitching, John**
Can't Wait.
Lonely Boy.
Sea Shore.
Slugs.

**Kittaararter**
Take Your Accusation Back!

**Kittner, Alfred**
Blue Owl Song.
Old Jewish Cemetery in Worms.

**Kittredge, Walter**
Tenting on the Old Camp Ground.

**Kitzman, Darlene Button**
Doll House, The.

**Kivkarjuk**
I am but a little woman.

**Kiwus, Karin**

All Splendor on Earth.

**Kizer, Carolyn**
Amusing Our Daughters.
By the Riverside.
Children.
Columns and Caryatids.
Copulating Gods, The.
Dying Goddess, The.
For Jan, in Bar Maria.
Great Blue Heron, The.
Hera, Hung from the Sky.
Intruder, The.
Lines to Accompany Flowers for Eve.
Muse of Water, A.
One to Nothing.
Poet's Household, A.
Postcards from Rotterdam.
Pro Femina, *sels.*
Running Away from Home.
Semele Recycled.
Singing Aloud.
Skein, The.
Summer near the River.
Through a Glass Eye, Lightly.
To a Visiting Poet in a College
   Dormitory.
To Li Po from Tu Fu.
Widow in Wintertime, A.
Worms, The.

**Kizer, Gary**
For Laurence Jones.

**Klappert, Peter**
Estienne.
Gun, White Castle.
Invention of the Telephone, The.
J'Accuse.
Lord's Chameleons, The.
O'Connor the Bad Traveler.
Poem for L. C.
R.S.V.P.
Spider, Unsurprised, The.
Trapper, The.

**Klauber, Edgar**
On Buying a Dog.

**Klauck, D. L.**
"Chew Mail Pouch."

**Klein, Abraham Moses**
And in That Drowning Instant.
Commercial Bank.
Pastoral of the City Streets.
Upon the Heavenly Scarp.

**Klein, Binnie**
Next Time We Meet.

**Klein, Chris**
Bright Winter Morning.

**Kleiser, Granville**
Most Vital Thing in Life, The.

**Kloefkorn, William**
I Love Old Women.
Loony, *sels.*
My Love for All Things Warm and
   Breathing.
Otoe County in Nebraska.
Out-and-Down Pattern.

**Knapp, Shepherd**
Lord God of Hosts, *with music.*
Not Only Where God's Free Winds
   Blow, *with music.*

**Knell, Dane**
Reflections.

**Knevet, Ralph**
Deliverance, The.

Progress, The.
Vote, The.

**Knibbs, Henry Herbert**
Ballad of Billy the Kid, The.
Boomer Johnson.
Bosky Steer, The.
Desert, The.
Indigo Pete's J. B.
Long Road West, The.
Lost Range, The.
Oro Stage, The.
Riders of the Stars.
Shallows of the Ford, The.
Waring of Sonora-Town.

**Knies, Elizabeth**
Circles.

**Knight, Etheridge**
Another Poem for Me.
Apology for Apostasy?
As You Leave Me.
Bones of My Father, The.
Cell Song.
Feeling Fucked Up.
For Black Poets Who Think of Suicide.
For Dan Berrigan.
For Freckle-faced Gerald.
For Malcolm, a Year After.
Haiku: "Eastern guard tower."
Hard Rock Returns to Prison from the
   Hospital for the Criminal Insane.
He Sees through Stone.
Huey.
I Sing of Shine.
Idea of Ancestry, The.
It Was a Funky Deal.
My Life, the Quality of Which.
On Universalism.
On Watching Politicians Perform at
   Martin Luther King's Funeral.
Poem to Galway Kinnell, A.
Portrait of Malcolm X.
Sun Came, The.
To Dinah Washington.
To the Man Who Sidled Up to Me and
   Asked: "How Long You in fer,
   Buddy?"
2 Poems for Black Relocation Centers.
Upon Your Leaving.
Violent Space, The.
Warden Said to Me the Other Day, The.

**Knight, Henry Coggswell**
Lunar Stanzas.

**Knister, Raymond**
Colt, The.

**Knoepfle, John**
Riverfront, St. Louis.
Ten-Fifteen Community Poems, The, *sel.*
Tunnel Blaster on Bear and
   Brotherhood.

**Knoll, Michael**
To My Sister, from the Twenty-seventh
   Floor.

**Knott, William (Bill) ("Saint Geraud")**
Death.
(End) of Summer (1966).
Goodbye.
Hair Poem.
Poem: "At your light side trees shy."
(Poem) (Chicago) (The Were-Age).
Poem: "Only response, The."
Sleep.

Song: "She was lyin face down in her
   face."
Streetcorner.
**Knowles, James D.**
O God, though Countless Worlds of
   Light, *with music.*
**Knox, Edmund George Valpy ("Evoe")**
At the Water Zoo.
To the God of Love.
**Knox, Ronald Arbuthnott**
Absolute and Abitofhell.
Anglican curate in want, An.
Idealism.
**Knox, Warren**
Man of Letters.
**Knudson, R. R.**
Grand Slammer.
**Knut, Dovid**
Haifa.
Rosh Pina.
Safed.
Walking along the Sea of Galilee.
Woman from the Book of Genesis, A.
**Kobayashi Issa.**   *See* **Issa**
**Kobbé, Gustav**
To a Little Girl.
**Kocbek, Edvard**
Primary Numbers.
**Koch, Kenneth**
Down at the Docks.
Fresh Air.
Geography.
In Love with You.
Mending Sump.
Permanently.
Poem for My Twentieth Birthday.
Poem of the Forty-eight States, A.
Poem: "Thing, The/ To do/ Is
   organize."
Schoolyard in April.
Sleeping with Women.
Taking a Walk with You.
Thanksgiving.
To You.
Variations on a Theme by William
   Carlos Williams.
You Were Wearing.
**Koehler, Ted**
I've Got the World on a String, *with
   music.*
**Koenig, Alma Johanna**
Intimations.
**Koenig, Robert L.**
Isolation Ward.
**Koeppel, Frederic**
October.
**Koertge, Ronald**
Day Alvero Pineda Was Killed, The.
Dick Powell.
Folding the Panties.
For My Daughter.
Getting the License.
Harelip Mary.
Magic Words, The.
Modifications.
My Father.
Please.
Smells.
Tarzan, *sel.*
Tonto.
12 Photographs of Yellowstone.
What She Wanted.

**Koethe, John**
Mission Bay.
Picture of Little Letters.
**Kohler, Sandra**
Wedding, The.
**Koianimptiwa**
Yellow butterflies.
**Kolmar, Gertrud**
Jewish Woman, The.
Paris.
Sea-Monster.
Woman Poet, The.
**Konek, Carol**
Daring.
**Kook, Rav Abraham Isaac**
First One Drew Me, The.
Radiant Is the World Soul.
When I Want to Speak.
**Kooser, Ted**
Abandoned Farmhouse.
Blind Always Come as Such a Surprise,
   The.
Christmas Eve.
Country-Western Music.
Deep in Winter.
Fort Robinson.
Gates.
Goldfish Floats, The.
History Lesson for My Son.
I Put My Hand on His Head.
Late Lights in Minnesota.
Phil.
Phoning My Son Long Distance.
Place in Kansas, A.
Poem: "Get your tongue."
Rooming House.
So This Is Nebraska.
Themes for Country-Western Singers,
   *sel.*
Tom Ball's Barn.
Wild Pigs.
**Kopp, Karl**
Hanging Man, The.
Judge, The.
Manly Diversion.
**Korinna** [*or* **Corinna**]
Although I was her pupil,/ even I
   reproach Myrtis.
I blame Myrtis.
I Korinna am here to sing the courage.
Kithairon sang of cunning Kronos.
Terpsichore looks kindly on me.
When he sailed into the harbor.
Will you sleep forever,/ Korinna?
**Korn, Alfons**
Two: Long After.
**Korn, Rachel**
From Here to There.
I'm Soaked Through with You.
Keep Hidden from Me ("Keep from me
   all that I might comprehend!").
Letter, A.
Longing.
My Body.
New Dress, A.
Put Your Word to My Lips.
Sometimes I Want to Go Up.
Thirty-one Camels, The.
Too Late.
With Poems Already Begun.
**Kornblum, Allan**
All That Glitters.

Awkward Song for My Sisters.
Her Hair Is Wet.
Immediate Kindness.
Lot of Hearts Are Pounding in the
   Universe, A.
O Light.
Something Passionate for Cinda.
3 Days after Father's Day.
Truckers, The.
**Kornblum, Cinda**
A B C's.
Every Day I Go to Work.
Flowerpot Is an Ashtray, A.
Hey Animal—Eat This Popcorn.
Honeymooners, The.
Late Night at the Hamburg Inn.
Oil Spots in Every Parking Place.
Sequitor: A Love Poem.
Sunday.
While the Garden Grows.
**Körte, Mary Norbert**
Every Day Shaggy Man Mushroom.
Ghost Poem Five.
Letter 60.
Lines on the Back of a Leary Bailfund
   Card.
**Korzhavin, Naum**
Children of Auschwitz.
**Kostakis, Peter**
Black Swan, The.
Calypso for Committed Men.
Crayfish, The.
Galleries, The.
Lines to Nefertiti.
Sirius, a Dog Star.
So Jah Seh.
**Kostelanetz, Richard**
Concentric.
Tribute to Henry Ford.
**Koster, Gloria Bussel**
Diner, The.
Early Morning Song: The Snowstorm.
Interpretation.
**Kovner, Abba**
I Don't Know if Mount Zion.
Near.
Observation at Dawn.
**Kowit, Steve**
Home.
**Kozer, José**
Cleaning Day.
My Father, Who's Still Alive.
Store in Havana, The.
**Kramer, Aaron**
Kennedy Airport.
Now, before Shaving.
**Kramer, Larry**
Overcoats.
**Kramer, Lotte**
Genesis.
**Krapf, Norbert**
Cutting Wood: After a Family
   Photograph.
Darkness Comes to the Woods.
For an Old Friend.
Skinning a Rabbit.
**Krasilovsky, Alexis**
Sensational Relatives.
**Kraus, Jim**
Church with Long Steeple.
Cycle of Tears, A.
Incident, The.

**Krauss, Ruth**
Song: "I'd much rather sit there in the sun."
**Kreitman, Norman**
Homecoming, The.
Maze, The.
Poem in the Mirror.
**Kresh, David**
For Heidi, Caving.
Girl on the Run.
Jane.
**Kretz, Thomas**
Transandean Railway, The.
**Kreymborg, Alfred**
Indian Sky.
To W. C. W. M. D.
**Kriebel, Casper**
Now Sleep My Little Child So Dear, with music.
**Krishnamurti, M.**
Cloth of Gold, the, sel.
Spirit's Odyssey, The.
**Krohn, Herbert**
My Flute.
Two Vietnamese Women.
**Kroll, Ernest**
Cryptology.
Cuttlefish.
Mockingbird in Winter.
Pennsylvania Academy of Fine Arts.
Pounding It Out.
Telephone Lineman.
Washington, D.C.
**Kroll, Judith**
Dick and Jane.
I Think of Housman Who Said the Poem Is a Morbid Secretion, like the Pearl.
Not Thinking of America.
Sestina: "Is this the object."
**Krolow, Karl**
White.
**Kruchkow, Diane**
City Is Falling Apart, The.
Poem: "Camera records, The."
Poem: "For the 5th time."
Poem: "She didn't know it yet."
Putting the Croutons Back into the Jar.
Sabinas Hidalgo.
While the TV Is Shut Off.
**Krysl, Marilyn**
Dreams from War.
Lecture with Slides, Film Clips and Tape.
Summer Solstice.
Words Words Words.
**Kryss, T. L. Tom Krys s**
And Jesus Don't Have Much Use for His Old Suitcase Anymore.
Ballad of an Empty Table.
Bell Too Heavy to Ring.
Big Rocks, The.
Breaking Ground in Me.
Nothing Strange.
Red Eyes Lick the Night.
Suicide, A.
This Wind.
**Kshetrayya**
Dancing-Girl's Song.
**Kuapakaa**
Ocean Is like a Wreath, The.
**Kubo, Leonard**

Drumming Lightly.
**Kubo, Mari**
Green Apple.
Long Time Apart, A.
**Kücken, Friedrich Wilhelm**
How Can I Leave Thee? with music.
**Kudaka, Geraldine**
Crazy Soliloquy.
Okinawa Kanashii Monogatari.
To Mirikitani.
**Kuka, King D.**
Evening.
February Morning.
Gallery of My Heart.
Jackie.
Janna.
My Friend the Wind.
My Song.
"Taste of Honey, A."
Tiny baby, you're ugly.
**Kulbak, Moishe**
I Just Walk Around, Around, Around.
Spring.
Summer.
Two.
Vilna.
**Kumalo, Peter**
Play Song.
**Kumin, Maxine W.**
After Love.
Amanda Dreams She Has Died and Gone to the Elysian Fields.
Amanda Is Shod.
Appointment, The.
At the End of the Affair.
Body and Soul: A Meditation.
Creatures.
Envelope, The.
Family Man, A.
For a Shetland Pony Brood Mare Who Died in Her Barren Year.
For My Son on the Highways of His Mind.
400-Meter Freestyle.
Fräulein Reads Instructive Rhymes.
Halfway.
Hermit Picks Berries, The.
Hermit Wakes to Bird Sounds, The.
Horses, The.
How It Goes On.
Life's Work.
Lunar Probe, The.
Making the Jam without You.
Masochist, The.
May 10th.
Microscope, The.
Morning Swim.
Mother Rosarine.
My Horse, Amanda: The Summer of the Watergate Hearings.
Nightmare Factory, The.
Our Ground Time Here Will Be Brief.
Pawnbroker, The.
Presence, The.
Purgatory.
Riding in the Rain.
Sound of Night, The.
Together.
Voice from the Roses, A.
We Are.
Woodchucks.
**Kunene, Raymond Mazisi**

Work Song.
**Kunitz, Stanley Jasspon**
After the Last Dynasty.
Approach to Thebes, The.
Benediction.
Choice of Weapons, A.
Dark and the Fair, The.
End of Summer.
Father and Son.
Flight of Apollo, The.
For Proserpine.
For the Word Is Flesh.
Foreign Affairs.
Goose Pond.
He.
Hemorrhage, The.
Illumination, The.
Journal for My Daughter.
Knot, The.
Last Picnic, The.
Layers, The.
Mulch, The.
Old Cracked Tune, An.
Portrait, The.
Prophecy on Lethe.
River Road.
Robin Redbreast.
Route Six.
She Wept, She Railed.
Snakes of September, The.
Spark of Laurel, A.
Summing-up, The.
Testing-Tree, The.
Thief, The.
Vita Nuova.
War against the Trees, The.
Welcome the Wrath.
**Kunjufu, Johari M.** See **Latimore, Jewel C.**
**Kunze, John C.**
Yoke Soft and Dear, with music.
**Kuo, Alex**
Green Tanks and Other Hidden Vehicles of Destruction.
Loss.
Portrait of a Negative.
**Kürenberg, The Knight of**
Falcon, The.
**Kuroda, Saburoh**
Afternoon 3.
**Kushner, Aleksander**
To Boris Pasternak.
**Kuskin, Karla**
I Woke Up This Morning.
Middle of the Night, The.
Porcupine, The.
**Kuykendall, Mabel M.**
Baseball Pitcher.
**Kuzma, Greg**
After Sex.
Ah.
Among Friends.
Dancing Bear, The.
Dump, The.
First Camp.
Garden Report.
Greens.
Hose and Iron.
I Visit My Brother.
In Love with the Bears.
Journal of the Storm.
Melons.

Monster, The.
Peace, So That.
Pelican, The.
Poetry.
Poppies.
River Kleeg, The.
Sleep.
Weak, The.
Wolfman, The.
Young Man Who Loved the Girl Who
Took Care of Her Aging Father, The.

**Kwitko, Leib**
Esau.
My Fiddle.

**Kwon, Paula**
Talking across Kansas.

**Kyger, Joanne**
From this moment/ and hence
backwards.
In the high/ clear air.
Still/ our breath our sun.
Time Is Open, The.

**Kyle, Francis**
When I Saw Sweet Nelly Home.

**Kynaston, Sir Francis**
To Cynthia: Learn'd Lapidaries.
To Cynthia: On Concealment of Her
Beauty.
To Cynthia: On Her Being an
Incendiary.
To Cynthia: On Her Embraces.
To Cynthia, on Her Looking-Glass.
To Cynthia, on Sugar and Her
Sweetness.

# L

**Laarakker, Martin**
Indian.

**Labé, Louise**
Sonnet XVI: "After an age when
thunderbolts and hail."
Sonnet XIX: "After having slain very
many beasts."
Sonnet XIV: "Although I cry and
though my eyes still shed."
Sonnet: "And so one sees all living
matter perish."
Sonnet IX: "As soon as I lie down in my
soft bed."
Sonnet VI: "Coming of that limpid star
is twice, The."
Sonnet XXIV: "Don't blame me, ladies,
if I've loved. No sneers."
Sonnet IV: "From that first flash when
awful Love took flame."
Sonnet XVII: "I flee the city, temples,
and each place.'
Sonnet VIII: "I live, I die, I burn myself
and drown."
Sonnet XX: "I was foretold that on a
certain day."
Sonnet XIII: "If I could linger on his
lovely chest.
Sonnet XII: "Lute, companion of my
calamity."
Sonnet I: "Not Ulysses, no, nor any
other man."

Sonnet XXII: "O blazing Sun, how
happy you are there."
Sonnet XI: "O eyes clear with beauty, O
tender gaze."
Sonnet II: "O handsome chestnut eyes,
evasive gaze."
Sonnet III: "O interminable desires, O
futile hope."
Sonnet: "O kiss me yet again, O kiss me
over."
Sonnet XV: "To honor the return of
sparkling sun."
Sonnet XXIII: "What good is it to me if
long ago."
Sonnet XXI: "What grandeur makes a
man seem venerable?"
Sonnet X: "When I perceive your blond
and graceful head."
Sonnet V: "White Venus limpid
wandering in the sky."

**LaBombard, Joan**
Capitol, The: Spring.

**Lachman, Sol**
Sukkot.

**Lady of the Arbour**
Flower and the Leaf, The, *sel.*

**Lady of the Assembly**
Assembly of Ladies, The, *sel.*
Palace of Pleasant Regard, The.

**Laederach, Monique**
Penelope, *sels.*

**La Farge, Peter**
Ballad of Ira Hayes.

**La Follette, Melvin Walker**
All the Dead Birds.
Ballad of Red Fox, The.
Didactic Sonnet.

**La Fontaine, Jean de**
Cat into Lady.
Dairymaid and Her Milk-Pot, The.
Donkey and the Lapdog, The.
Eagle and the Beetle, The.
Fox and the Crow, The.
Fox and the Goat, The.
Frog Who Would Be an Ox, The.
Grasshopper and the Ant, The.
Hag and the Slavies, The.
Man and His Image, The.
Oak and the Reed, The.
Rat and the Elephant, The.
Town Rat and the Country Rat, The.
Wolf and the Dog, The.
Wolf and the Lamb, The,
Wolf and the Stork, The.

**Laforgue, Jules**
For the Book of Love.
Legend.

**Lagerkvist, Pär**
Purple Blemish, The.

**La Grone, Oliver**
Africland.
For Kinte.
Remnant Ghosts at Dawn.

**Lahpu**
Butterfly maidens.

**Laila, Akhyaliyya**
Camel.

**Laing, Dilys Bennett**
Dance of Burros.
Eros Out of the Sea.
Gentled Beast, The.

**Laing, Ronald David**

Finger Points to the Moon, A.
Jill.

**Laing, V. R.**
Suicide, The.

**Lake, David**
Fauna: March.
Fungi.
Some Newly-discovered Prophecies of
Nostradamus.
To Horace.

**Lake, Paul**
Old Folks Home, An.

**Lake, Richard**
Atavism.

**Lal Ded**
I drag a boat over the ocean.
Impermanence.

**Lallay, Michael**
My Life.

**Lally, Lee**
Dance Marathon, The.
They Watch Me with Radar.
We Don't Know What to Plan or Say or
Do.

**Lamantia, Philip**
Hermetic Bird.
She Speaks the Morning's Filigree.

**Lamar, Mirabeau Buonaparte**
Daughter of Mendoza, The.

**Lamartine, Alphonse Marie Louis de**
God.

**Lamb, Arthur J.**
Asleep in the Deep, *with music.*
Bird in a Gilded Cage, A.
Bird on Nellie's Hat, The, *with music.*

**Lamb, Charles**
Free Thoughts on Several Eminent
Composers.
Old Familiar Faces, The.

**Lamb, Charles** and Mary Lamb
Boy and the Snake, The.
Choosing a Name.
Cleanliness.
Envy.
Feigned Courage.
First Tooth, The.
Going into Breeches.

**"Lambert, Louis."** See **Gilmore, Patrick
Sarsfield**

**Lamdan, Yitzhak**
Massada, *sel.*

**LaMoure, S. E.**
Wagon Wheels.

**Lampell, Millard, Lee Hays** and **Pete
Seeger.** See **Seeger, Pete, Millard
Lampell** and **Lee Hays**

**Lampman, Archibald**
Midnight.

**Lamport, Felicia**
Capsule Philosophy.
Progress.

**Lancaster, Osbert**
Afternoons with Baedeker, *sels.*
Eireann.
Manhattan.

**Landau, Zishe**
I Have a Big Favour to Ask You,
Brothers.
Little Pig, The.
Of Course I Know.
Parts.
Tuesday.

**Landon, Letitia Elizabeth**
Child Screening a Dove from a Hawk, A.
Unknown Grave, The.

**Landor, Walter Savage**
Above all gifts we most should prize.
Age.
Alas! 'Tis Very Sad to Hear.
Alciphron and Leucippe.
Art thou afraid the adorer's prayer.
Autumnal Song.
Before a Saint's Picture.
Bourbons.
Called Proud.
Case at Sessions, A.
Clap, clap the double nightcap on!
Corinna, to Tanagra, from Athens.
Critic, A.
Defiance.
Dirce.
Distribution of Honours for Literature.
Duke of York's Statue, The.
Epigrams must be curt, nor seem.
Exhausted now her sighs, and dry her tears.
For an Epitaph at Fiesole.
Foreign Ruler, A.
Gebir, sel.
Georges, The.
God scatters beauty as he scatters flowers.
Had we two met, blythe-hearted Burns.
Have I, this moment, led thee from the beach.
Heart's Abysses, The.
Hellenics, The, sels.
Here lies Landor.
How often, when life's summer day.
Ianthe, sels.
Idle Words.
Ireland Never Was Contented.
Is it no dream that I am he.
Last Fruit off an Old Tree, The, sel.
Lately Our Poets.
Leaf after Leaf.
Love and Age.
Loves who many years held all my mind, The.
Memory.
Mother, I Cannot Mind My Wheel.
My hopes retire; my wishes as before.
Neither in idleness consume thy days.
No, thou hast never griev'd but I griev'd too.
No charm can stay, no medicine can assuage.
O fond, but fickle and untrue.
O friends! who have accompanied thus far.
O Friendship! Friendship! the shell of Aphrodite.
On a Quaker's Tankard.
On Death.
On Grey Cliffs.
On Himself.
On His Seventy-fifth Birthday.
On Seeing a Hair of Lucretia Borgia.
On the Heights.
On the Hellenics.
On the smooth brow and clustering hair.
Our youth was happy: why repine.
Parrot and Dove.

Past Ruined [or Ruin'd] Ilion Helen Lives.
Pericles and Aspasia, sels.
Poem: "I cannot tell, not I, why she."
Poet! I like not mealy fruit; give me.
Quarrelsome Bishop, A.
Reflection from Sea and Sky.
Remain, Ah Not in Youth Alone.
Retired this hour from wondering crowds.
Rose Aylmer.
Scentless laurel a broad leaf displays, The.
Scribblers, The.
Sensible Girl's Reply to Moore's, A.
Silent, you say, I'm grown of late.
Sweet Was the Song.
Ten thousand flakes about my windows blow.
Ternissa.
There are two miseries in human life.
To Age.
To Alfred Tennyson.
To Corinth.
To My Daughter.
To My Ninth Decade.
To One Who Quotes and Detracts.
To Our House-Dog Captain.
To Poets.
To Robert Browning.
To Wordsworth.
Torch of love dispels the gloom, The.
Twenty years hence my eyes may grow.
Various the Roads of Life.
What News.
Why Do the Graces.
Yes; I Write Verses.
You see the worst of love, but not the best.
You smiled, you spoke, and I believed.
Your Name upon the Sand.

**Landrum, Lonnie L.**
And Now Out of Sight.
Another Commercial.
Dissipation.
For Real Ghetto, The.
Racist Delicious.
Retrospect.
Where Were You?

**Landy, Francis**
Lament for Azazel.
Midrash on Hamlet.
Princess Who Fled to the Castle, The.
Selichos.

**Lane, Arthur**
Frankenstein Stagger, The.

**Lane, Joy M.**
Road to School, The.

**Lane, Patrick**
Beware the Months of Fire.
Elephants.
Gray Silk Twisting.
Love.
Loving She Stood Apart.
Mountain Oysters.
Sleep on the Fraser.
Surcease.
Treaty-Trip from Shulus Reservation.
Water-truck, The.

**Lang, Andrew**
Brahma.
Lost Love.

O Joy of Love's Renewing.
**Lang, Jon**
Someone Sits at the Harp.
**Langbridge, Frederick**
Pessimist and Optimist.
**Lange, Art**
Copenhagen.
For Pee Wee.
Homage to Hans Hofmann.
Landscape by Cezanne, A.
NYC.
Ruptured Melodies.
To Myself.
Trust.
**Langer, Jiri Mordecai**
On the Margins of a Poem.
Riddle of Night.
**Langfield, Angela**
Living with You.
**Langhorne, John**
Owen of Carron, sel.
**Langland, Joseph**
Hunters in the Snow: Brueghel.
Upon Hearing His High Sweet Tenor Again.
War.
**Langland, William**
Belling the Cat.
Et Incarnatus Est.
Glutton in the Tavern.
In a Somer Seson, Whan Softe Was the Sonne.
Jousting of Jesus, The.
Long Will in London.
Our Needy Neighbours.
Poet, Rebuked, Responds, The.
Trinity, The.
Vision of Piers Plowman, The, sels.
**Langley, Eve**
Native Born.
**Langton, Daniel J.**
Expecting.
Land's End.
President Langton.
**Lanier, Emilia**
Eves Apologie.
**Lanier, H. Glenn**
O Christ of Bethlehem, with music.
**Lanier, Sidney**
Corn.
Evening Song.
From the Flats.
Hound, The.
Into the Woods My Master Went, with music.
Marsh Song—At Sunset.
Marshes of Glynn, The.
My Springs.
Sunrise.
Thar's More in the Man than Thar Is in the Land.
**Lanners, L. X.**
What Good Is a Poet?
**Lao Tzu**
Tao Teh King, sel.
**LaPalma, Marina**
Disobedient Statue, The.
**Lape, Fred**
Going to Town.
Horse Graveyard.
Lambs Frolicking Home.
Laughing Faces of Pigs, The.

Old Grey.
Puppy.

**Lapidus, Jacqueline**
Coming Out.

**Larbaud, Valery**
Poet's Wish.

**Lardner, Ring**
Abner Silver's "Pu-leeze! Mr.
Hemingway!"
Hail to Thee, Blithe Owl.
Hardly a Man Is Now Alive.
Parodies of Cole Porter's "Night and
Day."
Quiescent, a Person Sits Heart and Soul.

**Larkin, Mary Ann**
November Morning.

**Larkin, Philip**
Afternoons.
Age.
Ambulances.
Annus Mirabilis.
Arundel Tomb, An.
As Bad as a Mile.
At Grass.
Born Yesterday.
Building, The.
Church Going.
Coming.
Days.
Dockery and Son (" 'Dockery was junior
to you' ").
Dry-Point.
Essential Beauty.
Explosion, The.
Faith Healing.
Fiction and the Reading Public.
First Sight.
Going.
Here.
High Windows.
Homage to a Government.
Home Is So Sad.
I Remember, I Remember.
If, My Darling.
Lines on a Young Lady's Photograph
Album.
Love Songs in Age.
Mr. Bleaney.
Myxomatosis.
Next, Please.
Night-Music.
MCMXIV.
No Road.
Nothing to Be Said.
Places, Loved Ones.
Poetry of Departures.
Reasons for Attendance.
Self's the Man.
So through that unripe day you bore
your head.
Study of Reading Habits, A.
Sunny Prestatyn.
Take One Home for the Kiddies.
Talking in Bed.
Toads.
Toads Revisited.
Vers de Société.
Waiting for breakfast, while she brushed
her hair.
Wants.
Wedding-Wind.
Whitsun Weddings, The.

Wild Oats.
Wires.
Within the Dream You Said.

**Larminie, William**
Nameless Doon, The.

**Larsen, Carl**
Plot to Assassinate the Chase Manhattan
Bank, The.

**Larson, Clinton F.**
Advent.
Cactus Stem.
Homestead in Idaho.
Seven-Tenths of a Second.
To a Dying Girl.

**Lasker-Schüler, Else**
Abel.
Abraham and Isaac.
Hagar and Ishmael.
Homesick.
Jacob.
Jacob and Esau.
Lord, Listen.
Love Song, A.
Moses and Joshua.
Pharaoh and Joseph ("Pharaoh rejects
his blossoming wives").
Reconciliation.
Saul.

**Lasnier, Rina**
Serenade of Angels.

**Lathbury, Mary Artemisia ("Aunt Mary")**
Break Thou the Bread of Life, *with
music.*
Day Is Dying in the West, *with music.*

**Lathum, William**
Prosopopoeia Corporis Animae
Valedicturi: Adios: Arrivederci.

**Latimer, Bette Darcie**
For William Edward Burghardt Du Bois
on His Eightieth Birthday.

**Latimore, Jewel C. (Johari Amini; Johari
M. Kunjufu)**
Before/ and After.
Brother.
Childhood.
On the Naming Day.
Positives.
Saint Malcolm.
Signals.
Sun Heals, A.
To a Poet I Knew.
Utopia.

**Lattimore, Richmond**
December Fragments.
Dolphin Seen Alone.
February Loves.
Game Resumed.
Lovely Swimmers, The.
Remorse.
Siding near Chillicothe, A.
Sky Diving.
Western Ways.
Witness to Death.

**Lau, Alan Chong**
Dream Songs of Haka Ancestors.
January of 75, The.
Song for My Mother.
Song Three—A  Search for Taiping
Ghosts.

**Laufer, Calvin W.**
We Thank Thee, Lord, *with music.*

**Laughlin, James**

Mountain Afterglow, The.
Step on His Head.
Swarming Bees, The.

**Laurance, Annabel**
My Brain.

**Laurino, Danny**
At the Gates.

**Laursen, Ross**
Death Penalty, The.

**Lautermilch, Steven**
Christmas Morning.
For My Wife.

**LaVoie, Kent**
Me and You and a Dog Named Boo.

**Lawder, Douglas**
Albino Bear.
Field, The.

**Lawless, Gary**
Ainu Men, The.
Confession, The.
Hunting Fragment.
Movement.
Rail Splitting.

**Lawlor, Joanne**
Gray Days.

**Lawn, Beverly**
No Difference.

**Lawner, Lynne**
Rino's Song.

**Lawrence, Blake**
Enion's Protest.

**Lawrence, David Herbert**
All I ask of a woman is that she.
American Eagle, The.
Andraitx—Pomegranate Flowers.
Baby-Movements.
Baby Tortoise.
Bavarian Gentians.
Beautiful Old Age.
Birds.
Bride, The.
Brooding Grief.
Cherry Robbers.
City Life.
Collier's Wife, The.
Death Is Not Evil, Evil is Mechanical.
Deepest Sensuality, The.
Desire is Dead.
Dog-tired.
Don Juan.
Don'ts.
Elephant Is Slow to Mate, The.
Elephants in the Circus.
End of Another Home Holiday.
Energetic Women.
Enkindled Spring, The.
Figs.
Flowers and Men.
Food of the North.
Fronleichnam.
Gazelle Calf, The.
Giorno dei Morti.
Gloire de Dijon.
Gods, The! The Gods!
Green.
"Gross, Coarse, Hideous" (Police
Description of My Pictures).
How Beastly the Bourgeois Is.
Hummingbird.
Hymn to Priapus.
Intimates.
It's No Good!

Kangaroo.
Kisses in the Train.
Letter from Town: The Almond Tree.
Lightning.
Little Fish.
Living, A.
Lizard.
Lord Tennyson and Lord Melchett.
Love on the Farm.
Man and Bat.
Medlars and Sorb-Apples.
Mess of Love, The.
Middle of the World.
Moonrise.
Mosquito, The.
Mosquito Knows, The.
Mountain Lion.
My Way Is Not Thy Way.
Mystic.
New Heaven and Earth.
New Houses, New Clothes.
New Year's Eve.
North Country, The.
Nostalgia.
Now It's Happened.
O! Start a Revolution.
On the Balcony
Passing Visit to Helen.
Pax.
Piano ("Softly, in the dusk, a woman is
    singing to me").
Piano, The ("Somewhere beneath the
    piano's superb sleek black").
Proper Pride.
Red-Herring.
Release.
River Roses.
Salt of the Earth.
Sane Revolution, A.
Sea-Weed.
Self-Pity.
Seven Seals.
Shadows.
Ship of Death, The.
Snake.
Song of a Man Who Has Come
    Through, The.
Sorrow.
Spray.
Spring Morning.
Stand Up!
Swan.
Terra Incognita.
Things Made by Iron.
Things Men Have Made.
Third Thing, The.
To Women, as Far as I'm Concerned.
Tortoise Gallantry.
Tortoise-Shell.
Tortoise Shout.
Trees in the Garden.
True Love at Last.
Volcanic Venus.
We Are Transmitters.
Whales Weep Not!
What Is He?
When I Read Shakespeare.
When I Went to the Circus.
When the Ripe Fruit Falls.
When Wilt Thou Teach the People?
White Horse, The.
Willy Wet-Leg.

Young Wife, A.
Youth Mowing, A.
**Lawrence, Terry**
    Harvester, The.
**Lawson, David**
    No Great Matter.
**Lawson, Henry**
    Grog-an'-Grumble Steeplechase.
    Middleton's Rouseabout.
    Sweeney.
**Lawson, Paul**
    Ambassadors, The.
    Survey.
**Lawson, Todd S. J.**
    Hamburger Mary's.
    Wicked Lady of Gough Street.
**Lawton, Jewell**
    I wonder.
**Layamon**
    Brut, The, *sel.*
    Death of Arthur, The.
**Layton, Irving**
    Aran Islands.
    Bull Calf, The.
    Comedian, The.
    For Anna.
    For Natalya Correia.
    From Colony to Nation.
    Golfers.
    Haunting, The.
    Icarus.
    Innocence.
    Jewish Main Street.
    Letter to a Librarian.
    Ohms.
    Osip Mandelshtam.
    Two Communist Poets.
**Lazar, David**
    Doctor Freud.
**Lazard, Naomi**
    In Answer to Your Query.
    Last Covenant, The.
    Ordinance on Failure.
    Ordinance on Winning.
**Lazarus, Emma**
    By the Waters of Babylon, *sels.*
    Currents.
    Echoes.
    Epochs.
    Exodus, The (August 3, 1492).
    1492.
    In Exile.
    In Memoriam: Rev. J. J. Lyons, *sel.*
    Magnetism.
    New Colossus, The.
    Success.
    Venus of the Louvre.
**Lea, Gordon**
    When I Learned to Whistle.
**Lea, Sydney**
    Accident.
**Leach, Christopher**
    Blackbird.
    Take a Whiff on Me.
    Whoa Back, Buck.
**Leadbelly (Huddie Ledbetter)**
    Bring Me a Little Water, Sylvie.
    Ha Ha This-a-Way.
    In the Pines (Where Did You Sleep Last
      Night?).
    It's Almost Day.
    Midnight Special.

Old Reilly (In Dem Long Hot Summer
    Days).
Poor Howard.
T.B. Blues.
**Leaf, Walter**
    Better Way, The.
**Lear, Edward**
    A Was Once an Apple Pie.
    After Tennyson.
    Akond of Swat, The.
    Alphabet ("A tumbled down, and hurt
      his Arm, against a bit of wood").
    C was papa's gray cat.
    Calico Pie.
    Children of the Owl and the Pussy-Cat,
      The.
    Cold Are the Crabs.
    Courtship of the Yonghy-Bonghy-Bo,
      The.
    Dingle Bank.
    Dong with a Luminous Nose, The.
    Duck and the Kangaroo, The.
    Eclogue: "What makes you look so
      black, so glum, so cross?"
    Fatal Mistake, A.
    How Pleasant to Know Mr. Lear.
    Incidents in the Life of My Uncle Arly.
    Jumblies, The.
    Lady and Tiger.
    Letter to Evelyn Baring, A.
    Limerick: "There was a young lady of
      Corsica."
    Limerick: "There was a young person of
      Crete."
    Limerick: "There was an old man in a
      boat."
    Limerick: "There was an old man in a
      tree."
    Limerick: "There was an old man of
      Dundee."
    Limerick: "There was an old man of El
      Hums."
    Limerick: "There was an old man of
      Girgenti."
    Limerick: "There was an old man of
      Hong Kong."
    Limerick: "There was an old man of
      Kamschatka."
    Limerick: "There was an old man of
      Madras."
    Limerick: "There was an old man of
      Spithead."
    Limerick: "There was an old man of the
      Dee."
    Limerick: "There was an old man of
      Thermopylae."
    Limerick: "There was an old man of
      Three Bridges."
    Limerick: "There was an old man of
      Vesuvius."
    Limerick: "There was an old man who
      said, 'Hush!'"
    Limerick: "There was an old man whose
      despair."
    Limerick: "There was an old man with a
      beard."
    Limerick: "There was an old man with a
      ribbon."
    Limerick: "There was an old person of
      Anerley."
    Limerick: "There was an old person of
      Bar."

Limerick: "There was an old person of Brussels."
Limerick: "There was an old person of Crowle."
Limerick: "There was an old person of Dover."
Limerick: "There was an old person of Grange."
Limerick: "There was an old person of Harrow."
Limerick: "There was an old person of Hove."
Limerick: "There was an old person of Philae."
Limerick: "There was an old person of Twickenham."
Limerick: "There was an old person of Wick."
Limerick: "There was an old person whose habits."
Love Song.
Menu.
Mr. and Mrs. Spikky Sparrow.
Mrs. Jaypher.
Mrs. Jaypher on Lemons.
New Vestments, The.
Nutcrackers and the Sugar-Tongs, The.
Old Man of the Hague, The.
Old Man of the Nile, An.
Old Person of Cromer, An.
Owl and the Pussy-Cat, The.
Pelican Chorus, The.
Pobble Who Has No Toes, The.
Quangle Wangle's Hat, The.
Rice and Mice.
Scraps of Lear.
She sits upon her Bulbul.
Tea by the Sea.
There is a young lady, whose nose.
There was a young lady of Norway.
There was a young lady of Sweden.
There was a young lady whose bonnet.
There was a young lady whose eyes.
There was a young lady whose nose.
There was an old lady of Chertsey.
There was an old lady of France.
There was an old man in a Barge.
There was an old man of Cape Horn.
There was an old man of Dumbree.
There was an old man of Dunblane.
There was an old man of Ibreem.
There was an old man of Peru/ Who never knew what he should do.
There was an old man of the East.
There was an old man of the West.
There was an old man of West Dumpet.
There was an old man of Whitehaven.
There was an old man on the Border.
There was an old man who said, "How."
There was an old man who screamed out.
There was an old person of Basing.
There was an old person of Blythe.
There was an old person of Bow.
There was an old person of Burton.
There was an old person of Cassel.
There was an old person of Dutton.
There was an old person of Gretna.
There was an old person of Prague.
There was an old person of Rhodes.
There was an old person of Sparta.
There was an old person of Ware.

Wet Weather at Cannes.
Young Lady of Tyre, The.
**Leary, Paris**
Oxford Commination.
**Leax, John**
Cycle, A.
Grandfather.
Grocery Shopping.
That Day.
Vanity of Human Wishes, The.
**Lebensboim, Razel.** *See* **Margolin, Anna**
**Lechlitner, Ruth**
A. B. S. News.
Aubade: "Long ago when I shouted in red letters."
Drawing by Ronnie C., Grade One.
Kansas Boy.
Lizard, The.
**Ledbetter, Huddie.** *See* **Leadbelly**
**Le Dressay, Anne**
Roger and Me.
Song in White.
**Ledwidge, Francis**
Had I a Golden Pound.
June.
Lament for Thomas MacDonagh.
Soliloquy.
Twilight in Middle March, A.
Wife of Llew, The.
**Lee, Agnes**
Ilex Tree, The.
**Lee, Al**
Among Sharks.
In the Yellow Light of Brooklyn.
Karl Marx.
Lie, The.
Maiden Lane.
One Morning We Brought Them Order.
Poem for the Year Twenty Twenty.
Weathering the Depths.
**Lee, Ann**
Your Light.
**Lee, B. J.**
Troll Trick.
**Lee, Brian**
Bones.
Cold Feet.
Man Who Wasn't There, The.
Sad . . . and Glad.
Toffee-Slab.
What?
**Lee, Dennis**
Billy Batter.
I Found a Silver Dollar.
**Lee, Don L. (Haki R. Madhubuti)**
Afterword, An: For Gwen Brooks.
Assassination.
Awareness.
Back Again, Home.
Big Momma.
Black Sketches.
But He Was Cool; or, He Even Stopped for Green Lights.
Change Is Not Always Progress.
Change-Up.
Communication in Whi-te.
Gwendolyn Brooks.
Judy-One.
Man and Woman.
Man Thinking about Woman.
Mixed Sketches.
Mwilu/ or Poem for the Living.

Nigerian Unity/ or Little Niggers Killing Little Niggers.
One Sided Shoot-out.
Poem for a Poet, A.
Poem to Complement Other Poems, A.
Positive Movement Will Be Difficult but Necessary.
Positives for Sterling Plumpp.
Primitive, The.
Re-act for Action ("Re-act to Animals").
Revolutionary Screw, The.
Self-Hatred of Don L. Lee, The.
Stereo.
To Be Quicker.
Two Poems.
Wake-up Niggers.
We Walk the Way of the New World.
With All Deliberate Speed.
**Lee, J. B.**
Clumsy.
**Lee, Jack H.**
Death Valley.
**Lee, Laurie**
April Rise.
Field of Autumn.
Long War, The.
Milkmaid.
Town Owl.
**Lee, Lawrence**
Dome, The.
**Lee, Mary.** *See* **Chudleigh, Mary Lee, Lady**
**Lee, Nathaniel**
Nathaniel Lee to Sir Roger L'Estrange.
**Lee, Rena**
Old Story, An.
**Lee, Richard E.**
Last Grizzly Bear in the State.
**Lee-Hamilton, Eugene**
Sea-Shell Murmurs.
What the Sonnet Is.
**Leeming, Owen**
End of Season.
Priests of Serrabonne, The.
**Lefcowitz, Barbara F.**
At the Grave of Albert Camus.
At the Western Wall.
Driftwood Dybbuk.
It Will Happen (1).
Matisse's Jazz Cut-Outs at the National Gallery.
Mirrors of Jerusalem, The.
**Le Fevre, Adam**
Metal Fatigue.
**Leffler, Merrill**
Dream Was of Rabbits, The.
Long Beach, 1975.
Run.
**Le Fort, Gertrud von**
Te Deum.
**Lefroy, Edward Cracroft**
Football-Player, A.
**Le Gallienne, Richard**
I Meant to Do My Work Today.
London Beautiful.
**Léger, Alexis Saint-Léger.** *See* **"Perse, St.-J"**
**Legg, Susan**
I'm a rabbit's foot.
**Legler, Philip**
Interview with a Tornado Victim on April 16, 1974, An.

Love and an Old Western at the Starlite
 Drive-In Theater.
Quicksilver Thing.
Sheet-Monger, Blanket-Hoarder.
Trying to Shovel Out.
Turning Forty-five, after Drinks and
 Dirty Jokes and Talk of Women.
**Le Guin, Ursula K.**
Mind Is Still, The.
**Lehman, David**
Blind Hopes.
For David Shapiro.
In Praise of Robert Penn Warren.
Journey into the Eye.
Ode: "People in the middle ages didn't
 think they were living."
Traces.
**Lehmann, Geoffrey**
For J. A. R. McKellar.
Out after Dark.
Roses.
Saving the Harvest.
Telescope at Siding Springs, The.
**Lehmann, John**
Sphere of Glass, The.
This Excellent Machine.
**Lehmann, R. C.**
Bath, The.
**Lehrer, Tom**
Pollution.
**Leib, Mani**
From the Crag.
In Little Hands.
Plum, A.
Psalmodist.
Pyre of My Indian Summer, The.
Shopkeepers.
They.
Winter.
**Leider, Emily**
Yentel.
**Leifer, Jay**
Six-forty-two Farm Commune Struggle
 Poem.
**Leigh, Fred W.**
Waiting at the Church; or, My Wife
 Won't Let Me, *with music.*
**Leigh, Henry Sambrooke**
Only Seven.
Rhymes (?).
Saragossa.
'Twas Ever Thus.
Twins, The.
**Leiper, Esther M.**
Black Bottom Bootlegger, The.
Shaman.
**Leiser, Dorothy**
Migrations of People, The.
**Leitch, Donovan ("Donovan")**
Observation, The.
**Leiter, Sharon**
Roadrunner and Coyote.
**Leivick, H. (Leivick Halpern)**
How Did He Get Here?
I Hear a Voice.
Through the Whole Long Night.
Two Times Two is Four.
**Leland, Charles Godfrey ("Hans
 Breitmann")**
Ballad by Hans Breitmann.
Breitmann in Politics, *sel.*
Hans Breitmann's Barty.

Story of Samuel Jackson, The.
**Leland, John**
Evening Shade.
Now Behold the Saviour Pleading, *with
 music.*
**Lele-io-Hoku**
Albatross.
**Lem, Carol**
Henry Miller: A Writer.
**L'Engle, Madeleine**
From St. Luke's Hospital.
O Simplicitas.
Three Songs of Mary, *sel.*
**Lennen, Elinor**
Within the Shelter of Our Walls, *with
 music.*
**Lenngren, Anna Maria**
Other Fabrics, Other Mores!
**Lennon, John** *and* Paul McCartney
Across the Universe.
Because.
Continuing Story of Bungalow Bill, The.
Day in the Life, A.
Eleanor Rigby.
Fool on the Hill, The.
For No One.
I Am the Walrus.
In My Life.
Norwegian Wood.
She's Leaving Home.
Strawberry Fields Forever.
Yellow Submarine.
**Le Noir, Phil**
Ol' Dynamite.
**Lenowitz, Harris**
Fringes, The.
Panegyric.
**Lenox, Jean**
I Don't Care, *with music.*
**Lense, Edward**
Waking Up.
Wolf Dream.
**Lenski, Hayim**
Language of Ancients.
Purity.
Upon the Lake.
**Lento, Takako Uchino**
Glass.
**León, Luis Ponce de**
About the Heavenly Life.
Life of the Blessed, The.
On Leaving Prison.
**Leonard, Eddie**
Ida, Sweet as Apple Cider, *with music.*
**Leonard, Tom**
Words, for E.
**Leonard, William Ellery**
To the Victor.
**Leontius Scholasticus**
To an Aging Charioteer.
**Leopardi, Giacomo**
Saturday Night in the Village.
Setting of the Moon, The.
Terror by Night, The.
**Lepkowski, Frank J.**
Two Poems Based on Fact.
**Lepore, Dominick J.**
Northward.
**Lerner, Arthur**
Raw Freedom.
**Lerner, Laurence**
Raspberries.

Wish, A.
**Lesemann, Maurice**
Cow-Ponies.
Ranchers.
**Leslie, Edgar** *and* E. Ray Goetz
For Me and My Gal.
**Leslie, Kenneth**
Knife and Sap.
Sudden Assertion.
**Leslie, Shane**
Muckish Mountain (The Pig's Back).
Prayer for Fine Weather.
**Lesser, Rika**
527 Cathedral Parkway.
Translation.
**Lessing, Gotthold Ephraim**
Three Kingdoms Of Nature, The.
**Lester, Julius**
In the Time of Revolution,*sels.*
On the Birth of My Son, Malcolm
 Coltrane.
Us.
**Le Sueur, Meridel**
Dead in Bloody Snow.
I Light Your Streets.
Village, The.
**Letts, Winifrid M. (Mrs. W.H. Foster
 Verschoyle)**
Bold Unbiddable Child, The.
Choice, The.
Fantasia.
Tim, an Irish Terrier.
**Levenberg, Diane**
After Selecting the Wedding Invitations.
Alchemy.
Dreaming of Conn-Eda.
Out of the Desert.
**Levendosky, Charles**
Gifts, The.
Heart Mountain Japanese Relocation
 Camp, The: 30 Years Later.
**Lever, Charles**
It's Little for Glory I Care.
Pope He Leads a Happy Life, The.
**Leverant, Robert**
Figures and Ground.
In His Poems Are El Greco's Hands.
**Leverett, Ernest**
S F.
**Levertin, Oscar**
At the Jewish Cemetery in Prague.
Solomon and Morolph, Their Last
 Encounter.
**Levertov, Denise**
Abel's Bride.
About Marriage.
Ache of Marriage, The.
Adam's Complaint.
Advent 1966.
Altars in the Street, The.
Art.
Bedtime.
Beyond the End.
Breathing, The.
By Rail through the Earthly Paradise,
 Perhaps Bedfordshire.
Cabdriver's Smile, The.
Cat as Cat, The.
City Psalm.
Claritas.
Cold Spring, The.
Come into Animal Presence.

Coming Fall, The, *sel.*
Day Begins, A.
Defeat, A.
Depths, The.
Despair.
Dog of Art, The.
During the Eichmann Trial, *sel.*
Earth Psalm.
Earth Worm, The.
"Else a Great Prince in Prison Lies."
Embroidery, An.
Enquiry.
Everything That Acts Is Actual.
February Evening in New York.
Garden Wall, The.
Goddess, The.
Gone Away.
Good Dream, The.
Grace-Note, The.
Ground-Mist, The.
Gulf, The.
Happening, A.
Hypocrite Women.
Illustration, The—A Footnote.
Illustrious Ancestors.
In Mind.
Invocation: "Silent, about-to-be-parted-
    from house."
Jacob's Ladder, The.
Lamentation, A: "Grief, have I denied
    thee?"
Libation.
Life at War.
Living.
Losing Track.
Mad Song.
Malice of Innocence, The.
Man, A.
Map of the Western Part of the County
    of Essex in England, A.
Matins.
Moon Tiger.
Mutes, The.
Night on Hatchet Cove.
90th Year, The.
Note to Olga (1966), A.
Novel, The.
O Taste and See.
Obsessions.
Old Adam, The.
Olga Poems.
One A.M.
Our Bodies.
Overheard over S.E. Asia.
Overland to the Islands.
Partial Resemblance.
Peachtree, The.
Pleasures.
Poem Rising by Its Own Weight, The.
Psalm Concerning the Castle.
Psalm Praising the Hair of Man's Body,
    A.
Quarry Pool, The.
Rainwalkers, The.
Recognition, The.
Relearning the Alphabet.
Resolve, The.
Resting Figure.
Sage, The.
Secret, The.
Shalom.
Shlup, shlup, the dog.

Six Variations.
Song for Ishtar.
Springtime, The.
Stepping Westward.
Sunday Afternoon.
Tenebrae.
Third Dimension, The.
To the Reader.
To the Snake.
Triple Feature.
Two Variations.
Vision, A.
Way Through, The.
What Were They Like?
What Wild Dawns There Were.
Wings, The.
World Outside, The.
**Levi, Peter**
In stone settlements when the moon is
    stone.
L'Aurore Grelottante.
**Levi, Primo**
For Adolf Eichmann.
Lilith.
Shema.
**Levin, Gabriel**
Adam's Death.
Etude for Voice and Hand.
Ishmael.
**Levin, Phillis**
Everything Has Its History.
**Levine, Ellen**
One Morning.
**Levine, Molly Myerowitz**
Safed and I.
**Levine, Philip**
Above It All.
After.
Animals Are Passing from Our Lives.
Another Life.
Any Night.
Ashes.
At the Fillmore.
Autumn.
Breath.
Clouds.
Coming Home, Detroit, 1968.
Detroit Grease Shop Poem.
Distant Winter, The.
Everything.
For Fran.
Gangrene.
Get Up.
Here and Now.
How Much Earth.
In the New Sun.
Lost Angel, The.
Midget, The.
My Angel.
My Life like Any Other.
My Son and I.
New Day, A.
New Season.
News of the World.
1933.
Now It Can Be Told.
On a Drawing by Flavio.
On the Birth of Good and Evil during
    the Long Winter of '28.
On the Edge.
Poem Circling Hamtramck, Michigan All
    Night in Search of You, The.

Red Dust.
Reply, The.
Salami.
Sierra Kid, *sel.*
Standing on the Corner.
They Feed They Lion.
To a Child Trapped in a Barber Shop.
To My God in His Sickness.
Turning, The.
Uncle.
Voice, The.
Waiting.
Way Down, The.
Words.
You Can Have It.
Zaydee.
**Levinson, Fred**
No More than Five.
Poem against Rats, A.
Poem: "Country, The/ was back in the
    hands of the patriots."
Sharks in Shallow Water.
Translation From, A.
**Levis, Larry**
Bat Angels.
Blue Stones.
Cool Morning Shower in Early Spring.
Fish.
For the Country.
Poem You Asked For, The.
To a Wall of Flame in a Steel Mill,
    Syracuse, New York, 1969.
Winter.
**Levy, Newman**
Midsummer Jingle, *sel.*
Rigoletto.
Tannhauser.
**Levy, Raphael.** *See* **Ryvel**
**Levy, Robert J.**
Give Us This Day Our Daily Day.
**Levy, Stephen**
Freely, from a Song Sung by Jewish
    Women of Yemen.
Friday Night after Bathing.
Home Alone These Last Hours of the
    Afternoon, Dusk Now, the Sabbath
    Setting In, I Sit Back, and These
    Words Start Welling Up in Me.
Judezmo Writer in Turkey Angry, A.
**Lewandowski, S.**
Wrestlers.
**Lewis, Alun**
All Day It Has Rained.
Dawn on the East Coast.
Goodbye.
In Hospital: Poona (I).
Jungle, The.
Mahratta Ghats, The.
Peasants, The.
Postscript: For Gweno.
Public Gardens, The.
Sentry, The.
To a Comrade in Arms.
**Lewis, Angelo**
America Bleeds.
Clear.
**Lewis, Cecil Day.** *See* **Day Lewis, Cecil**
**Lewis, Clive Staples**
Awake, My Lute!
Evolutionary Hymn.
On a Vulgar Error.
Scazons.

**Lewis, David, Paul Schindler** *and* Bob
   Adams
   Mother Pin a Rose on Me, *with music.*
**Lewis, Dominic Bevan Wyndham**
   **("Timothy Shy")**
   If So the Man You Are, *sels.*
   Sapphics.
   Shot at Random, A.
**Lewis, H. H.**
   Five Minutes, Oleo.
   Gone West.
   I'll Say!
   Just for Propaganda.
   Man from Moscow, The.
   Now What Good That Do?
   Road to Utterly.
   Star Ride.
   Sweeter Our Fruits, The.
   Unholy Roller
**Lewis, Howell Elvet**
   Life's Morning.
**Lewis, Janet**
   At Carmel Highlands.
   Country Burial.
   Girl Help.
   Hangar at Sunnydale, The: 1937.
   Lines with a Gift of Herbs.
   Remembered Morning.
   Winter Garden.
**Lewis, Michael Arthur**
   Caulker, The.
**Lewis, Percy Wyndham**
   Song of the Militant Romance, The.
**Lewis, Saunders**
   Ascension Thursday.
   Deluge 1939, The.
   Mary Magdalene.
   Pine, The.
   To the Good Thief.
**Lewis, Steven**
   Fort Wayne, Indiana 1964.
**Lewis, Thelma**
   Exceptional.
**Lewis, William S.**
   Blackfoot Sin-ka-ha.
   Flathead and Nez Perce Sin-ka-ha.
**Lewis Glyn Cothi**
   Lament for Siôn y Glyn.
**Leybourne, George**
   Man on the Flying Trapeze, The.
**L'Heureux, John**
   Bat in the Monastery, A.
   St. Ignatius Loyola, Founder of the
     Jesuits: His Autobiography.
**Liadan**
   Liadan Laments Cuirithir.
**Liasides, Pavlos**
   Fountain, The
**Libbey, Elizabeth**
   Before the Mountain.
   Concerning the Dead Women: The
     Munitions Plant Explosion: June,
     1918.
   Marceline, to Her Husband.
   To Her Dead Mate: Montana, 1966.
**Libera, Sharon Mayer**
   Mother.
   Patty, 1949–1961.
**Li Ch'ing-chao (Li Ching-Chao)**
   Clear Bright.
   How many evenings in the arbor by the
     river.

I let the incense grow cold.
Last night thin rain, gusty wind.
Light mist, then dense fog.
Melting in thin mist and heavy clouds.
Rattan bed, paper netting. I wake from
   morning sleep.
Red lotus incense fades on/ the jewelled
   curtain.
Sky links cloud waves, links dawn fog.
Tune: Butterfly Woos the Blossoms, The.
Tune: Crimson Lips Adorned.
Tune: Endless Union.
Tune: Magnolia Blossom.
Two Springs.
Warm rain, sunny wind start to break
   the chill.
Weary Song to a Slow Sad Tune, A.
Year after year I have watched.
**Li Chü**
   Harvesting Wheat for the Public Share.
**Lichtenstein, Alfred**
   Journey to the Insane Asylum, The.
   Repose.
**Liddy, James**
   History.
   Paean to Eve's Apple.
   Post Alcoholum Tristis.
   Prayer to Christ and Socrates.
   Republic 1939, The.
   Thinking of Bookshops.
   Voice of America, 1961, The.
   Zorba.
**Lieberman, Laurence**
   Crayon World, The.
   Dream of Lakes, A.
   God's Measurements.
   Homage to Austin Warren.
   Interview.
   My Father Dreams of Baseball.
   No One to Blame.
   Sand and Snow.
   Skin Song.
   Tree Animals.
**Lietz, Robert**
   After the Deformed Woman Is Made
     Correct.
**Lifshin, Lyn**
   Arizona Ruins.
   Beryl.
   Blue Bowl of Plums Invention, The.
   Ceremony.
   Developing Curious Survival Patterns
     against Winter Saltwinds The.
   Downstairs Two Old Lovers Meet.
   Drifting The.
   Even There.
   Family 8.
   For a Friend.
   Greenland, 850 A.D.
   In Spite of His Dangling Pronoun.
   Leaving Them, Letting the Farm
     Swallow.
   Monet's Les Nymphéas.
   My Mother and the Bed.
   Names.
   Nice.
   No Need for, the Computer Concern
     Error Letter, The.
   Not Quite Spring.
   On the New Road.
   Origin of Hot and Cold According to
     the Delawares, The.

Pulling Out.
Sedna.
Snake Dance.
Tentacles, Leaves.
Thaw.
38 Main Street.
To Poem.
Waiting, the Hallways under Her Skin
   Thick with Dreamchildren.
Walking thru Audley End Mansion Late
   Afternoon, *sels.*
Way Sun Keeps Falling Away from
   Every Window, The.
Wildflowers, Smoke.
Women like That.
You Understand the Requirements.
**Lifson, Martha**
   Quiet by Hillsides in the Afternoon.
**Liggett, Rosy**
   Obsession, The.
**Lightfoot, Gordon**
   Black Day in July.
**Lightman, Alan P.**
   Getting Under.
**Lignell, Kathleen**
   Calamity Jane Greets Her Dreams.
**Liliuokalani, Queen Lydia**
   Aloha Oe, *with music.*
**Lima, Frank**
   Primavera.
**Lima, Robert**
   Peripatetic.
**Lincoln, Abraham**
   I am not bound to win.
**Lindh, Stewart**
   Settler.
**Lindner, Carl**
   Mismatch.
**Lindon, J. A.**
   Learner.
   London Sparrow's If, A.
   More to It than Riding.
   My Garden, *parody.*
   Ruthless Rhyme.
**Lindop, Grevel**
   Perplexed by the Sunlight.
**Lindquist, Ray**
   On the Land.
**Lindsay, Lady Anne (Lady Anne Lindsay**
   **Barnard)**
   Auld Robin Gray.
**Lindsay, Sir David.**   *See* **Lyndsay, Sir**
   **David**
**Lindsay, John Vliet**
   Ode to the New York Mets.
**Lindsay, Maurice**
   At Hans Christian Andersen's
     Birthplace, Odense, Denmark.
   At the Mouth of the Ardyne.
   Ballad of Orpheus, A.
   Elegy, An: "You might have died so
     many kinds of death."
   Romantics.
   Toward Light.
   Uprooted.
**Lindsay, T.**
   Theological Limerick.
**Lindsay, Vachel**
   Abraham Lincoln Walks at Midnight.
   At Mass.
   Blacksmith's Serenade, The.
   Booker Washington Trilogy, The, *sel.*

Broncho That Would Not Be Broken, The.
Bryan, Bryan, Bryan, Bryan.
Congo, The.
Eagle That Is Forgotten, The.
Euclid.
Explanation of the Grasshopper, An.
Flower-fed Buffaloes, The.
Foreign Missions in Battle Array.
General William Booth Enters into Heaven.
Ghost of the Buffaloes, The.
Haughty Snail-King, The.
Horrid Voice of Science, The.
I Heard Immanuel Singing.
In Memory of a Child.
Indian Summer Day on the Prairie, An.
Leaden-eyed, The.
Little Turtle, The.
Moon's the North Wind's Cooky, The.
Mouse That Gnawed the Oak-Tree Down, The.
Nancy Hanks, Mother of Abraham Lincoln.
Rain.
Simon Legree—a Negro Sermon.
Spider and the Ghost of the Fly, The.
Two Old Crows.
Unpardonable Sin, The.
What Semiramis Said.
What the Moon Saw.
When the Mississippi Flowed in Indiana.
Yet Gentle Will the Griffin Be.

**Lindsay, William**
Extracts from a Police Surgeon's Notebook.
Feet Are Not Funny.
Great Talker, A.

**Lindskoog, Kathryn**
Light Showers of Light.

**Lines, Marian**
Building Site.
Carbreakers.

**Lingard, William Horace**
Captain Jinks.

**Linklater, Eric**
Memory, Now Distant, A.
Song for an Able Bastard, A.

**"Lin Ling" [or "Li Chi"] (Hu Yun-shang)**
Footpaths Cross in the Rice Field.

**Linnell, Kathleen**
Two Birds.

**Linthicum, John**
April.

**Lipkin, Jean**
Apocalypse.

**Lipman, Ed**
Poem for Rupert Weber, 85 Years Too Late.

**Li Po [or Li Tai Po or in Japanese Rihaku]**
Exile's Letter.
I Am a Peach Tree.
Invitation to Hsiao Ch'u-shih.
Jewel Stairs' Grievance, The ("The jewelled steps are already quite white with dew").
Lament of the Frontier Guard.
Lazy Man's Song.
Mad Poem Addressed to My Nephews and Nieces, A.
Poem by the Bridge at Ten-shin.
River-Merchant's Wife, The: A Letter.

Two Letters from Chang-kan.

**Lipshitz, Fay**
Aleph Bet, The.
Encounter in Jerusalem.
Judean Summer.

**Lipsitz, Lou**
Bedtime Story.
Conjugation of the Verb, "To Hope."
Pancho Villa.
Prospect Beach.
Radical in the Alligator Shirt, The.
Thaw in the City.
To a Fighter Killed in the Ring.
Tree Is Father to the Man, The.

**Lipska, Ewa**
Cock, The.
Flood, The.
If God Exists.
Wedding.

**Lisboa, Henriqueta**
Minor Elegy.

**Lisle, Rouget de.** See **Rouget de Lisle, Claude Joseph**

**Lisle, Thomas**
Power of Music, The.

**Lister, Richard Percival**
Cuckoo.
Lament of an Idle Demon.
Postscript to Die Schöne Müllerin.
Revolutionaries, The.
Target.

**Listmann, Thomas**
Sixties, The.

**Li Tai Po.** See **Li Po**

**Litchfield, Margaret R.**
Intermission.
To an Old Friend.

**Littlebird, Harold (Harold Bird)**
Alone Is the Hunter.
Coming Home in March.
Could I Say I Touched You.
Death in the Woods.
For Drum Hadley.
For the Girls 'cause They Know.
For Tom Numkena, Hopi/Spokane.
Gaa-a-Muna, a Mountain Flower.
Hummingbird.
If You Can Hear My Hooves.
In a Double Rainbow.
Mother/Deer/Lady.
Oh but It Was Good.
Old Moke.
Pennsylvania Winter Indian 1974.
Wrap Me in Blankets of Momentary Winds.

**Littlefield, Milton S.**
O Son of Man, Thou Madest Known, *with music.*

**Litvinoff, Emanuel**
If I Forget Thee.
To T. S. Eliot.

**Litwack, Susan**
Creation of the Child.
Havdolah.
Inscape.
Tonight Everyone in the World Is Dreaming the Same Dream.

**Liu, Stephen Shu Ning**
Tours.

**Livesay, Dorothy**
Encounter.
Pause.

**Livingston, Myra Cohn**
Conversation with Washington.
Cooking.
Discovery.
Father.
First Thanksgiving.
German Shepherd.
Grunion.
Haiku for Halloween.
Halloween.
Mill Valley.
Mourning Dove, The.
Old People.
On Reading: Four Limericks.
Only a Little Litter.
74th Street.
Silly Dog.
12 October.
What If.
Whispers.

**Livingstone, Douglas**
Conversation with a Giraffe at Dusk in the Zoo.
King, The.
Sunstrike.

**Llawdden**
No Place like Home.

**Lloréns Torres, Luis**
Love without Love.
Maceo.

**Lloyd, Arthur**
I'll Strike You with a Feather.

**Lloyd, Donald J.**
Bridal Couch.

**Lloyd, Evan**
Helen like the Rose.

**Lloyd, Noel**
Gecko.

**Lloyd-Evans, Paul L.**
Crowsfeet Splaying round His Eyes.

**Llwyd, Huw**
Fox's Counsel, The.

**Llywelyn ab y Moel**
Battle of Waun Gaseg, The.

**Llywelyn Goch ap Meurig Hen**
Lament for Lleucu Llwyd.

**Llywelyn-Williams, Alun**
In Berlin, August 1945: Lehrte Bahnhof.
Pont y Caniedydd.
When I Was Young.
Yesterday's Illusion; or, Remembering the Thirties.

**Lochhead, Liz**
Fourth of July Fireworks.
Her Place.
Laundrette.
Noises in the Dark.
Poem for My Sister.
Rainbow.
Three Women.
Today.

**Locke, Duane**
Bullfrog in a Pond Not Far from an Abandoned Farm, A.
Ybor City.

**Locker, Malka**
Clocks.
Drunken Streets.

**Locker-Lampson, Frederick**
Garden Lyric, A.
Our Photograph.

**Lockett, Reginald**

Good Times and No Bread.
**Locklin, Gerald**
Bobbie's Cat.
Don't Answer the Phone for Me the
  Same.
Dwarf, The.
Gunfighter.
Landladies.
Peanuts.
Pedagogy.
Son of Toad.
Toad, The.
Virginia Woolf.
**Loden, Rachel**
Poem: "If I come to you as some bitter
  herb."
**Lodge, Thomas**
Discontented Satyre, The.
Fig for Momus, A, *sel.*
In Commendation of a Solitary Life.
Phillis, *sels.*
Rosalynde; or, Euphues' Golden Legacy,
  *sel.*
Truth's Complaint over England.
**Loesser, Frank**
Guys and Dolls.
Once in Love with Amy, *with music.*
**Loewenthal, Tali**
Hebrew Script.
**Loewinsohn, Ron**
Goat Dance.
It Is an Outfielder.
Leaves, The.
Windows, The.
**Loftin, Elouise**
Pigeon.
Virginia.
Weeksville Women.
Woman.
**Logan, John (b. 1923)**
Abstract Love Poem.
Cape Elizabeth: A Photograph.
Century Piece for Poor Heine, A.
Concert Scene.
Dawn and a Woman.
Experiment That Failed, The.
Letter to a Young Father in Exile.
Library, The.
Lines for a Young Wanderer in Mexico.
Lines for Michael in the Picture.
Lines on His Birthday.
Lines to His Son on Reaching
  Adolescence.
Love Poem: "Last night you would not
  come."
Middle Aged Midwesterner at Waikiki
  Again.
On the Death of Keats.
Picnic, The.
Poem for My Brother.
San Francisco Poem.
Saturday Afternoon at the Movies.
Search, The.
Spring of the Thief.
Thirteen Preludes for Pioneer Square.
Three Moves.
To a Young Poet Who Fled.
Trip to Four or Five Towns, A.
White Pass Ski Patrol.
**Logan, Robert**
On a Prize Crucifix by a Student
  Sculptor.

**Logan, William**
Goose Fish, The.
My Father.
Protective Colors.
**Logue, Christopher**
Epitaph: "I am old."
Foreword to New Numbers.
Friday. Wet Dusk.
Good Taste.
Letters from an Irishman to a Rat.
**Logue, Mary**
Indian Warrior.
South Wind.
Winter Pond.
**Loines, Russell Hillard**
On a Magazine Sonnet.
**Lomax, Pearl Cleage**
Glimpse.
Jesus Drum.
Mississippi Born.
Poem: "You said./ don't write me/ a
  love poem."
**London, Jonathan**
Batches of New Leaves.
Driving Home.
**Lonergan, Frank**
Cycle.
**Long, Charles C.**
Yei-ie's Child.
**Long, Doughtry, Jr. ("Doc Long")**
Ginger Bread Mama.
Negro Dreams.
Number Four.
One Time Henry Dreamed the Number.
**Long, Haniel**
Butterflies.
**Long, Jim**
Twin Sister.
**Long, Peter**
Remember Thy Creator Now, *with
  music.*
**Long, Richard A.**
Hearing James Brown at Café des Nattes
  (Sidi-bou-Saïd, Tunisia).
Juan de Pareja: Painted by Velázquez.
**Long, Robert**
Saying One Thing.
**Long, Virginia**
Mares of Night.
112 at Presidio.
**Longchamps, Joanne de**
Sub-Prefix. 1. Under, Beneath, Below:
  As In.
**Longfellow, Henry Wadsworth**
Aftermath.
Arrow and the Song, The.
Arsenal at Springfield, The.
Autumn ("With what a glory comes and
  goes the year!").
Building of the Ship, The, *sel.*
Challenge, The.
Chaucer.
Children's Hour, The.
Chimes.
Cross of Snow, The.
Day Is Done, The.
Equinox, The.
Evangeline, *sels.*
Excelsior.
Fire of Drift-Wood, The.
God's Acre.
Hiawatha and Mudjekeewis.

Hymn to the Night.
I Heard the Bells on Christmas Day.
In the Churchyard at Cambridge.
Introduction: "Should you ask me,
  whence these stories?"
Jewish Cemetery at Newport, The.
Keats.
Killed at the Ford.
Luck of Edenhall, The.
Mezzo Cammin.
Milton.
Moonlight.
My Cathedral.
My Lost Youth.
Nature.
Norman Baron, The, *sel.*
Old Nokomis Sings.
Paul Revere's Ride.
Phantom Ship, The.
Prelude: "Pleasant it was, when woods
  were green."
Psalm of Life, A.
Rain in Summer.
Republic, The.
Revenge of Rain-in-the-Face, The.
Ropewalk, The.
Seaweed.
Secret of the Sea, The.
Serenade: "Stars of the summer night."
Ship of State, The.
Ships That Pass in the Night.
Skeleton in Armor, The.
Slave Singing at Midnight, The.
Slave's Dream, The.
Snow-Flakes.
Song of Hiawatha, The, *sels.*
Sound of the Sea, The.
Spanish Student, The, *sel.*
Tales of a Wayside Inn, *sel.*
Three Kings, The.
Tide Rises, the Tide Falls, The.
Tides, The.
Ultima Thule.
Village Blacksmith, The.
Warning, The.
Witnesses, The.
Wreck of the *Hesperus,* The.
**Longfellow, Samuel**
Again as Evening's Shadow Falls, *with
  music.*
Holy Spirit, Truth Divine, *with music.*
O Life That Maketh All Things New,
  *with music.*
'Tis Winter Now, *with music.*
**Longley, Michael**
Badger.
Camouflage.
Casualty.
Christopher at Birth.
Desert Warfare.
Emily Dickinson.
Epithalamion: "These are the small
  hours when."
Fleadh.
Irish Poetry.
Kindertotenlieder.
Letter to Three Irish Poets, A.
Man Lying on a Wall.
Miscarriage.
Peace.
Questionnaire for Walter Mitty, A.
Small Hotel, The.

Wounds.

**Longman, Doris**
Flight 382.

**Lope de Vega Carpio, Félix**
At Dawn The Virgin Is Born.
Good Shepherd, The.
Little Carol of the Virgin, A.
To-Morrow.

**Lopes, Michael**
Marriage.

**Lopez, Alonzo**
Direction.
I Am Crying from Thirst.
Lavender Kitten, The.

**López Velarde, Ramón**
Malefic Return, The.
My Cousin Agueda.

**Lorca, Federico García.** *See* **García Lorca, Federico**

**Lorde, Audre**
And What About the Children.
Birthday Memorial to Seventh Street, A.
Black Mother Woman.
Coal.
Eulogy for Alvin Frost.
Father, the Year Is Fallen.
Father Son and Holy Ghost.
For Each of You.
If You Come Softly.
Movement Song.
Naturally.
Now That I Am Forever with Child.
One Year to Life on the Grand Central
    Shuttle.
Oya.
Poem for a Poet, A.
Rites of Passage.
Suffer the Children.
Summer Oracle.
To a Girl Who Lives in a Tree.
To Desi as Joe as Smoky the Lover of
    115th Street.
To My Daughter the Junkie on a Train.
Trip on the Staten Island Ferry, A.
What My Child Learns of the Sea.
Who Said It Was Simple.
Woman Thing, The.
Workers Rose on May Day or Postscript
    to Karl Marx, The.

**Lott, Clarinda Harriss**
Living in the Present.

**Louchheim, Katie**
Dear Mr. Bell.
Grandfather.
Pride of Place.
Seen at a Fashionable Night Spot.

**Loudermilk, John D.**
Lament of the Cherokee Reservation
    Indian, The.

**Lourie, Dick**
Dream about Junior High School in
    America, The.
Getting a Poem in the Rain.
Gift, The.
Pearl Harbor Day 1970.
September 30.
Sharks.
Stumbling.
Telegram.
Thinking of You.

**Louthan, Robert**
Elegy for My Father.

**Love, Mike** *and* Brian Wilson
Country Air.

**Lovelace, Richard**
A la Bourbon.
Advice to My Best Brother, Colonel
    Francis Lovelace.
Anniversary on the Hymeneals of My
    Noble Kinsman, Thomas Stanley,
    Esquire, An.
Another [on the Snail.]
Ant, The.
Apostasy of One and But One Lady,
    The.
Black Patch on Lucasta's Face, A.
Calling Lucasta from Her Retirement.
Cupid Far Gone.
Elinda's Glove.
Falcon, The.
Fly about a Glass of Burnt Claret, A.
Fly Caught in a Cobweb, A.
Fool much bit by fleas put out the light,
    A.
Grasshopper, The.
Gratiana Dancing and Singing.
Her Muff.
In Allusion to the French Song.
La Bella Bona Roba.
Lady A. L., My Asylum in a Great
    Extremity, The.
Lady with a Falcon on Her Fist, A.
Loose Saraband, A.
Love Enthroned.
Love Made in the First Age: To Chloris.
Lucasta Taking the Waters at
    Tunbridge: Ode.
Lucasta's Fan, with a Looking-Glass in
    It.
Lucasta's World.
Mock Charon, A.
Mock Song, A.
Night.
On Sannazar's Being Honoured, *sel.*
Orpheus to Beasts.
Orpheus to Woods.
Painture.
Scrutiny [*or* Scrutinie], The.
Snail, The.
Strive not, vain lover, to be fine.
To a Lady That Desired Me I Would
    Bear My Part with Her in a Song.
To Althea, from Prison.
To Amarantha, That She Would
    Dishevel Her Hair.
To Dr. F. B. on His Book of Chess.
To Lucasta, from Prison.
To Lucasta, Going beyond the Seas.
To Lucasta, [on] Going to the Wars.
To Lucasta: Her Reserved Looks.
To Lucasta ("Ah, Lucasta, why so
    bright").
To My Noble Kinsman, Thomas
    Stanley, Esquire, on His Lyric Poems
    Composed by Master John Gamble.
To My Truly Valiant, Learned Friend,
    Who in His Book Resolved the Art
    Gladiatory into the Mathematics.
To My Worthy Friend Master Peter
    Lely.
Upon the Curtain of Lucasta's Picture It
    Was Thus Wrought.
Vintage to the Dungeon, The.

**Lovell, Barbara**

Sitting Bear Mountain.

**Loveman, Robert**
April Rain.

**Lover, Samuel**
Lanty Leary.
Paddy O'Rafther.

**Loving, Pierre**
Black Horse Rider, The.

**Low, Patricia**
First Day of the Hunting Moon, The.
Wet Weather.

**Low, Samuel**
To a Segar.

**Lowbury, Edward**
At Jesty's Tomb.
Discovering an Island.
Don't Call.
Elms in Winter.
Faster than Light.
In the Old Jewish Cemetery, Prague,
    1970.
Looking for Something?
Old Age of a Clown.
Phantom Limb, A.
Secrets.
Squint.
St. Luke's Little Summer.
Suicide, The.
Time to Kill.
Tree of Knowledge.
Vision.

**Lowell, Amy**
Carrefour.
Cyclists, The.
Desolation.
Dog-Days.
Epitaph on a Young Poet Who Died
    before Having Achieved Success.
Fisherman's Wife, The.
From One Who Stays.
Grotesque.
Katydids.
Last night it rained.
Lilacs.
Madonna of the Evening Flowers.
Meeting-House Hill.
Music.
Night Clouds.
Night lies beside me.
On Looking at a Copy of Alice
    Meynell's Poems.
Painted Ceiling, The.
Patterns.
Poet's Wife, A.
Proportion.
Reaping.
Sea Shell.
Sisters, The.
Streets.
Taxi, The.
Texas.
Travelling Bear, The.
Venus Transiens.
Watching the iris.
Wind and Silver.
Year Passes, A.

**Lowell, James Russell**
After the Burial.
Aladdin.
American Literature.
And what is so rare as a day in June?
Auspex.

Biglow Papers, The, *sels.*
Birthday Verses Written in a Child's Album.
Boss, The.
Bryant.
Cooper.
Courtin', The.
Emerson.
Fable for Critics, A, *sels.*
First Snowfall, The.
Freedom ("Men! whose boast it is that ye").
Hawthorne.
Holmes.
In an Album.
Irving.
Letter from a Candidate for the Presidency, A.
Lowell.
Misconception, A.
Ode Recited at the Harvard Commemoration.
Once to Every Man and Nation.
Pious Editor's Creed, The.
Poe and Longfellow.
Rev. Homer Wilbur's "Festina Lente."
Tempora Mutantur.
To the Dandelion.
Under the Old Elm, *sels.*
Vision of Sir Launfal, The, *sels.*
What Means This Glory round Our Feet?
Whittier.
**Lowell, Robert (1917-77)**
After the Surprising Conversions.
Alfred Corning Clark.
As a Plane Tree by the Water.
At a Bible House.
At the Altar.
At the Indian Killer's Grave.
Between the Porch and the Altar, *sels.*
Beyond the Alps.
Central Park.
Children of Light.
Christmas Eve under Hooker's Statue.
Cistercians in Germany.
Colloquy in Black Rock.
Commander Lowell.
Crucifix, The.
Dead in Europe, The.
Death from Cancer.
Death of the Sheriff, The.
Dolphin.
Drinker, The.
Drunken Fisherman, The.
Dunbarton.
Elizabeth.
Eye and Tooth.
Ezra Pound.
Fall 1961.
Falling Asleep over the Aeneid.
Fat Man in the Mirror, The.
For George Santayana.
For John Berryman, I.
For Sale.
For the Union Dead.
For Theodore Roethke.
Fourth of July in Maine.
Ghost, The.
Grandparents.
Harriet, *sel.*
History.

Holy Innocents, The.
Home after Three Months Away.
In Memory of Arthur Winslow.
In the Cage.
July in Washington.
Katherine's Dream.
Last Things, Black Pines at 4 a.m.
Lesson, The.
Long Summer, *sel.*
Man and Wife.
March, The ("Under the too white marmorial Lincoln Memorial").
March, The ("Where two or three were heaped together, or fifty").
Mary Winslow.
Memories of West Street and Lepke.
Mexico, *sel.*
Mouth of the Hudson, The.
Mr. Edwards and the Spider.
My Last Afternoon with Uncle Devereux Winslow.
Near the Ocean.
Neo-Classical Urn, The.
New Year's Day.
Night Sweat.
North Sea Undertaker's Complaint, The.
October and November.
Old Flame, The.
Opposite House, The.
Picture, The.
Public Garden, The.
Quaker Graveyard in Nantucket, The.
Reading Myself.
Robert Frost.
Sailing Home from Rapallo.
Salem.
Skunk Hour.
T. S. Eliot.
Teminal Days at Beverly Farms.
To Delmore Schwartz.
"To Speak of Woe That Is in Marriage."
Waking Early Sunday Morning.
Waking in the Blue.
Water.
Words for Hart Crane.
**Lowell, Robert Traill Spence (1816-91)**
Relief of Lucknow, The.
**Lowenfels, Walter**
For My Daughter's 20th Birthday.
**Lowenstein, Robert**
Peek-a-Boo.
**Lowenstein, Tom**
Horizon without Landscape.
Nausicaa with Some Attendants.
Noah in New England.
**Lowey, Mark**
On Living with Children for a Prolonged Time.
**Lowry, Betty**
Beasts of Boston, The.
**Lowry, Malcolm**
After Publication of Under the Volcano.
Delirium in Vera Cruz.
He Liked the Dead.
Sestina in a Cantina.
**Lowry, Robert**
Beautiful River, *with music.*
Where Is My Wandering Boy Tonight.
**Lowther, Pat**
Earth Sings Mi-fa-mi, The.
Morality Play.
Piercing, The.

Regard to Neruda.
Remembering How.
**Loy, Mina**
Love Songs.
Lunar Baedeker.
Omen of Victory
**Loyd, Marianne**
Llanberis Summer.
**Lubeck, Kathleen**
Sons, *sel.*
**Lucan (Marcus Annaeus Lucanus)**
Pharsalia, *sels.*
**Lucas, Henry N.**
But, Still, He.
**Luciano, Felipe**
You're Nothing but a Spanish Colored Kid.
**Lucie-Smith, Edward**
Dodo, The.
Giant Tortoise, The.
Imperialists in Retirement.
Ladybirds, The.
Lesson, The.
Lime-Tree, The.
Parrot, The.
Polar Bear, The.
Silence.
**Lucilius [*or* Lucillius]**
Boxer Loses Face and Fortune.
First in the Pentathlon.
Lean Gaius, who was thinner than a straw.
Monument to a Boxer.
On Apis the Prizefighter.
Retired Boxer, The.
Valentine for a Lady, A.
**Lucina, Sister Mary**
Rain.
**Luckey, Eunice W.**
Babies of the Pioneers.
**Lucus, Lawrence A.**
Another Meeting.
**Lucy, Sean**
Disappearances.
Game.
Late Fair.
Longshore Intellectual.
Senior Members.
Supervising Examinations.
**Ludvigson, Susan Bartels**
Child's Dream, The.
Motherhood.
Trying to Change the Subject.
**Luecke, Jane Marie**
On Christ's Birth (To Sisters).
Sixth Station, The.
"Strength of That Food, The."
White Worlds.
**Lueders, Edward**
Man in Overalls, The.
Rodeo.
Tour of the Southwest, A.
**Luhrmann, Tom**
Beyond Belief.
**Lum, Wing Tek**
Grateful Here.
What I Want.
**Lummis, Charles Fletcher**
Cannibalee: A Po'em of Passion.
Sidewinder, The.
**Lunn, Hugh Kingsmill** *See* **Kingsmill, Hugh**

**Luschei, Glenna**
Editor.
Prairie Schooner Poem.
**Luster, Helen**
Competitors, The.
February Letter to Jack Spicer.
**Luther, Martin**
Mighty Fortress, A, *with music.*
**Luton, Mildred**
Hossolalia.
Pliny Jane.
**Luttinger, Abigail**
My Mother Was Always Dressed.
Palace for Teeth, The.
**Luttrell, Henry**
O death, thy certainty is such.
On a Man Run Over by an Omnibus.
**Lutz, Gertrude May**
Cat of Many Years.
Song for a New Generation.
**Lux, Thomas**
Five Men I Know.
Going Home.
Graveyard by the Sea.
Green Prose.
History and Abstraction.
How to Cure Your Fever.
If You See This Man
Lament City.
Midnight Tennis Match, The.
My Grandmother's Funeral.
Poem to My Creditors.
Some Oral Stanzas.
There Are Many Things That Please Me.
This Is a Poem for the Fathers and for
    Michael Ryan.
**Lu Yu**
I Walk Out into the Country at Night.
**Lydgate, John**
Balade Simple.
Boy Serving at Table, The.
Fall of Princes, The, *sel.*
Froward Maymond ("Froward knave
    plainly to descrive, A").
Like a Midsummer Rose.
**Lyle, K. Curtis**
Lacrimas or There Is a Need to Scream.
Sometimes I Go to Camarillo and Sit in
    the Lounge.
Songs for the Cisco Kid; or, Singing for
    the Face.
Songs for the Cisco Kid; or, Singing:
    Song # 2.
Terra Cotta.
**Lyly, John**
Alexander and Campaspe, *sels.*
Cards and Kisses.
Pan's Syrinx ("Pan's Syrinx was a girl
    indeed").
Sapho and Phao, *sel.*
Serving-Men's Song, A.
Trico's Song: "What bird so sings, yet so
    does wail?"
**Lynch, Annette**
Bridgework.
Gratitude.
**Lynch, Brian**
All Day Satori.
Christmas Poem.
**Lynch, Charles**
If We Cannot Live as People.
Memo.

Shade.
**Lynch, Liam**
Aelred of Rievaulx.
**Lynch, Thomas Toke**
Lift up your heads, rejoice.
**Lyndsay [or Lindsay], Sir David**
Ane Satyre of the Thrie Estaitis, *sel.*
**Lynn, Ethel**    *See* **Beers, Ethel Lynn**
**Lyon, Lilian Bowes**    *See* **Bowes-Lyon,**
    **Lilian**
**Lyons, Richard**
Loyal Citizen.
Medora, N.D.
Sisseton Indian Reservation, The.
**Lyons, Richard J.**
"Titus, Son of Rembrandt: 1665."
**Lyte, Henry Francis**
Abide with Me.
**Lytle, William Haines**
Antony to Cleopatra.
**Lytton, Edward Robert Bulwer-Lytton, 1st**
    **Earl of**    *See* **"Meredith, Owen"**

# M

**"M., T."**
Cheating Droone.
Micro-Cynicon, *sel*
**Mabuza, Lindiwe**
Birds and Man.
Changeless Changes.
Embracing Exile.
Listening to Mbaqanga.
Of Time.
Patchwork.
Song, A: "When the white man."
Summer 1970.
There Is No Light.
Thoughts from the Pacific.
Tired Lizi Tired.
**Macadam, George**
Gentle Ambush, The.
**McAfee, Thomas**
If There Is a Perchance.
**McAleavey, David**
Can-Opener.
Casts from the Antique.
Driving; Driven.
Starship.
Two Old Men.
Warm Day in Winter.
**McAlmon, Robert**
For Instance.
**McAnally, Mary**
Our Mother's Body Is the Earth.
**Mac an Bhaird, Laoiseach**
**Man of Experience, A**
**Macarthy [or McCarthy], Harry**
Bonnie Blue Flag, The.
**Macaulay, Rose**
Devourers, The.
**Macaulay, Thomas Balungton Maccaulay,**
    **1st Barron**
Armada, The.
Battle of Naseby, The.
Horatius.
Ivry.
Jacobite's Epitaph, A.

Lays of Ancient Rome, *sel.*
Radical War Song, A.
**McAuley, James Phillip**
At Rushy Lagoon.
Because.
Envoi for a Book of Poems.
Hero and the Hydra, The, *sel.*
In Aeternum.
In Northern Tasmania.
In the Huon Valley.
Incarnation of Sirius, The.
Invocation: "Radiant Muse."
Mating Swans.
Merry-go-round.
Morning Voluntary.
Pietà.
Six Days of Creation, The.
St. John's Park.
Tomb of Heracles, The.
Wet Day.
Winter Drive.
**MacBeth *or* Macbeth, George**
Against the Sun.
At Hunegg.
Bats.
Bedtime Story.
Drop.
Early Warning.
Five-Minute Orlando MacBeth, The.
Marshall.
Miner's Helmet, The.
Orlando Commercial, The.
Owl.
Poem before Birth.
Political Orlando, The.
Red Herring, The.
Riddle, A (for Ponge), *sel.*
Shell, The.
Suicides, The.
Twelve Hotels, The.
Wasps' Nest, The.
When I Am Dead.
**Macbride, Hamish**
For Bonny Elspeth.
**McBride, Mekeel**
Will to Live, The.
**McCabe, Angela**
Back.
Blind Adolphus.
Bloom Street.
From Lois in London.
Inside History.
**McCabe, Victoria**
Reply.
**MacCaig, Norman**
Assisi.
Aunt Julia.
Basking Shark.
Beach Talk.
Betweens.
Boats.
Byre.
Celtic Cross.
Composers of Music.
Double Life.
Edinburgh Courtyard in July.
Family.
Fetching Cows.
Frogs.
Incident.
Message.
Milne's Bar.

Moorings.
Near Midnight.
November Night, Edinburgh.
Ordinary Day, An.
Poem for a Goodbye.
Poem: "There is a wailing baby under
  every stone."
Starlings.
Summer Farm.
Uncle Roderick.
Visiting Hour.
Wet Snow.
Wild Oats.
You Went Away.
**McCann, Michael Joseph**
O'Donnell Aboo.
**McCarriston, Linda**
Spring.
**McCarthy, Denis Florence**
Irish Wolf-Hound, The.
**McCarthy, Eugene**
Bicycle Rider.
Dogs of Santiago.
Dulles Airport.
Kilroy.
**McCarthy, Harry** *See* **Macarthy, Harry**
**McCarthy, Joanne**
Faint Praise on Your Fortieth Birthday.
**McCarthy, Teresa A.**
Anita, la Maldita.
Misericordia.
Visit Peru: Of Stoned Incas' Land.
**McCartney, Paul** *and* **John Lennon** *See*
  **Lennon, John** *and* **Paul McCartney**
**"MacCathmhaoil, Seosamh."** *See*
  **Campbell, Joseph**
**McClane, Kenneth A.**
Judge, The.
**McClatchy, J. D.**
Late Autumn Walk.
Pleasure of Ruins, The.
**McClintock, Charles W.**
Everybody Works but Father, *with
  music.*
**McCloskey, Mark**
Bear, The.
How to Become a Poet.
Lights Go On, The.
Only Leap That Matters, The.
Too Dark.
**McCloud, Linda**
When Running Felt Right.
**McClure, Michael**
Baja—Outside Mexicali.
From the Window of the Beverly
  Wilshire Hotel.
It is not youth that intrigues me but
  suppleness.
List, The.
May Morn.
Moiré.
Night Words: The Ravishing.
Ode to Joy.
Rant Block.
Thornton Beach.
**MacColl, Ewan**
Ballad of Ho Chi Minh.
First Time Ever I Saw Your Face, The.
Go Down You Murderers.
**MacColl, Ewan** *and* **Peggy Seeger**
Ballad of Springhill (The Springhill Mine
  Disaster).

**McCombs, Judith**
Dictionary Is an *Hi*storian, The: A
  Found Political Poem.
Hilda Lay in Hospital.
Hilda's Pelt.
Joe Was the Best of Them.
Man, The.
Seat Was Up, The.
**MacConglinne**
Vision of MacConglinne, The, *sel.*
**McCord, David**
Any Day Now.
Asleep and Awake.
Axolotl, The.
Baccalaureate.
Christmas Eve.
Christmas Package, A, *sels.*
Come Christmas.
Conversation.
Crows.
Easter Morning.
Epitaph on a Waiter.
Father and I in the Woods.
Gloss.
Glowworm.
Goose, Moose, and Spruce.
History of Education.
Hitchhiker.
Just Because.
Laundromat.
Mantis.
Mingram Mo.
Mr. Bidery's Spidery Garden.
Mr. Macklin's Jack-o'-Lantern.
Perambulator Poem.
Pickety Fence.
Queer.
Scat! Scitten.
Shell, The.
Snake.
Sportsman, The.
To a Certain Most Certainly Certain
  Critic.
Trick or Treat.
Up from Down Under.
Witch's Broom Notes.
Write Me a Verse.
**McCord, Howard**
Bear That Came to the Wedding, The.
In Iceland.
Jennifer.
My Cow.
**McCoy, Jane**
View from the Window.
**McCracken, Kathleen**
I Have Seen.
**McCrae, Hugh**
Fragment: "As if stone Caesar shook."
Leaf Out of a Rhyming Diary.
**McCrae, John**
In Flanders Fields.
**McCuaig, Ronald**
Au Tombeau de Mon Père.
Commercial Traveller's Wife, The.
Love Me and Never Leave Me.
**McCullers, Carson**
Slumber Party.
**McCullough, Ken**
For Galway.
**McCurdy, Harold**
August, at an Upstairs Window.
Petition.

**McCurdy, Ron**
Snapshots.
Starring Role.
**McDaniel, Judith**
For My Mother's Mother.
**McDaniel, R. H.**
Since Jesus Came into My Heart, *with
  music.*
**"MacDiarmid, Hugh" (Christopher Murray
  Grieve)**
Apprentice Angel, An.
Another Epitaph on an Army of
  Mercenaries.
At the Cenotaph.
Bagpipe Music.
Birth of a Genius among Men.
Bonnie Broukit Bairn, The.
British Leftish Poetry, 1930-40.
Cloudburst and Soaring Moon.
Cophetua.
Crystals like Blood.
Dead Liebknecht, The.
Diamond Body.
Empty Vessel.
Esplumeoir.
First Love.
Harry Semen.
I Heard Christ Sing.
In Memorium James Joyce, *sel.*
In the Pantry
Innumerable Christ, The.
Kind of Poetry I Want, The,*sels.*
Lament for the Great Music, *sel.*
Milk-Wort and Bog-Cotton.
Moonlight among the Pines.
My Love Is to the Light of Lights.
O Wha's the Bride?
Of My First Love.
Old Wife in High Spirits.
On the Ocean Floor.
Parley of Beasts.
Prayer for a Second Flood, A.
Reflections in a Slum.
Robber, The.
Sauchs in the Reuch Heuch Hauch, The.
Scarlet Woman, The.
Second Hymn to Lenin.
Storm-Cock's Song, The.
Two Parents, The.
Under the Greenwood Tree ("A sodger
  laddie's socht a hoose").
Up to Date.
Watergaw, The.
Wheesht, Wheesht.
With the Herring Fishers.
**MacDonagh, Donagh**
Charles Donnelly, *sel.*
Dublin Made Me.
Going to Mass Last Sunday.
Hungry Grass.
Just an Old Sweet Song.
Prothalamium.
Revel, A.
Veterans, The.
Warning to Conquerors, A.
**MacDonagh, Thomas**
John-John.
Man Upright, The.
Night Hunt, The.
**McDonald, Barry**
Ingestion.
**MacDonald, Cynthia**

Accomplishments.
Another Attempt at the Trick.
Apartments on First Avenue.
Coupling.
Getting to the End.
Insatiable Baby, The.
Instruction from Bly.
Objets d'Art.
Platform Builder, The.
Stained Glass Man, The.
Stained Glass Woman, The.
Story for a Child, A.
Uncovering.

**MacDonald, George**
Baby-Sermon, A.
Christmas Prayer, A.
Mammon-Marriage, A.
Things We Can Depend On.
Where Did You Come From, Baby
  Dear?
Wind and the Moon, The,*sels.*

**MacDonald, Marie Bruckman**
'Skeeter and Peter, The.

**McDonald, Nan**
Photograph of an Actress, c. 1860.
Wet Summer: Botanic Gardens.

**McDonald, Roger**
Consequence, The.
Flights.
Four Victorian Photographs.
Grasshopper.
Hollow Thesaurus, The.
Introspection.
Jack Hope.
Keepers.
Lost Will.
Town Boy Yearning.
Town of Bricked Pathways, The.
Two Summers in Moravia.

**MacDonald, Susan**
Children, The.
Cocktails.

**McDonald, Walter**
On Teaching David to Shoot.

**MacDonogh, Patrick**
Dodona's Oaks Were Still.
Escape to Love, *sel.*
No Mean City.
Now the Holy Lamp of Love.
She Walked Unaware.
Song: "She spoke to me gently with
  words of sweet meaning."
Widow of Drynam, The.

**MacDonough, Glen**
Toyland, *with music.*

**McDonough, Kaye**
For Kirke on his 34th Birthday.
Geometry of Motion, The—Crossing the
  Golden Gate Bridge.

**McDougal, Violet**
Sea Wolf, The.

**MacDuff, Edward**
Ed and Sid and Bernard.

**McElroy, David**
Dragging in Winter.
Making It Simple December 8, 1969.
Ode to a Dead Dodge.
Report from the Correspondent They
  Fired.
Spawning in Northern Minnesota.

**MacEwen, Gwendolyn**
Animal Poems.

**McFadden, David**
Art's Variety.
Day of the Pancreas, The.
External Element, The.
Fiddlehead, The.
It's a Different Story When You're
  Going into the Wind.
Kicking from Centre Field.
Pop.
Upon Looking at a Book of Astrology.
We Love You the Way You Are.

**McFarland, Ron**
Frost Warning.

**MacFayden, H. R.**
Lone Wild Fowl, The, *with music.*

**McFee, Michael**
Buster Keaton.
Easter Monday.

**McGaffey, Ernest**
California Idyl, A.
Geronimo.

**McGahey, Jeanne**
Lines for a Fifty-fifth Birthday.

**McGaugh, Lawrence**
To Children.
Two Mornings.
Young Training.

**McGhee, Brownie**
Betty and Dupree.

**MacGillivray, Pittendrigh**
Abasshyd.
Mercy o' Gode.

**McGinley, Phyllis**
About Children.
Adversary, The.
Almost Any Evening.
Angry Man, The.
Ballad of Befana, The.
Choice of Weapons, A.
Conquerors, The.
Country Club Sunday.
Customs of the Country, The.
Daniel at Breakfast.
Day after Sunday, The.
Death at Suppertime.
Demagogue, The.
Evening Musicale.
Female of the Species Is Hardier than
  the Male, The.
5:32, The.
Giveaway, The.
Homework for Annabelle.
How to Start a War
I Know a Village, *sels.*
Independent, The.
Lament for Lost Lodgings.
Last Year's Discussion: The Nobel
  Russian.
Launcelot with Bicycle.
Mid Century Love Letter.
Muted Screen of Graham Greene, The.
New England Pilgrimage, *sel.*
Occupation: Housewife.
Office Party.
Old Beauty, The.
On the Farther Wall, Marc Chagall.
Portrait of a Girl with Comic Book.
Publisher's Party.
Reflections at Dawn.
Reflections Dental.
Robin Hood.
Speaking of Television, *sels.*

Squeeze Play.
Trial and Error.
Triolet against Sisters.
Why, Some of My Best Friends Are
  Women.

**MacGiolla Gunna, Cathal Buidhe**
Yellow Bittern, The.

**McGlennon, Felix**
Comrades, *with music.*

**McGonagall, William**
Address to the New Tay Bridge, An.
Albion Battleship Calamity, The.
Newport Railway, The.
Railway Bridge of the Silvery Tay, The.
Richard Pigott, the Forger, *sel.*
Tay Bridge Disaster, The.

**McGough, Roger**
Fight of the Year, The.
Flood.
40-Love.
Goodbat Nightman.
If Life's a Lousy Picture, Why Not
  Leave before the End.
Let Me Die a Youngman's Death.
Mother the Wardrobe Is Full of
  Infantrymen.
My Busconductor.
My Cat and I.
Newly Pressed Suit, The.
P. C. Plod Versus the Dale St Dog
  Strangler.

**MacGowran, Hugh**
O'Rourke's Feast.

**McGrath, Thomas**
Blues for Jimmy.
Coal Fire in Winter, A.
Death for the Dark Stranger.
Jig Tune: Not for Love.
Letter for Marian, A.
Letter to an Imaginary Friend, Part One,
  *sels.*
Long Way outside Yellowstone, A.
Ode for the American Dead in Korea.
Something Is Dying Here.
Song: "Lovers in ladies' magazines."

**McGrath, Tom**
Paradox.
Reasons.

**MacGreevy, Thomas**
Aodh Ruadh O'Domhnaill.
De Civitate Hominum.
Homage to Hieronymus Bosch.
Homage to Marcel Proust.
Nocturne of the Self-evident Presence.
Recessional.

**McGregor, Bruce**
Teacher, A.

**Macgregor, Forbes**
Herberie.
Jezebel.
Lammermuir Lilt, The.
On Cementing Level the Stable Floor at
  the Old Manse.
Snawdon Woods.

**McGroarty, John S.**
Just California.
King's Highway, The.

**Machado, Antonio**
Lament of the Virtues and Verses on
  Account of the Death of Don Guido.
Rebirth.

**McHugh, Heather**

Corps d'Esprit.
Night Catch.
Note Delivered by a Female
  Impersonator.
Retired School-Teacher.
Wheels.
YWCA.
**McHugh, Vincent**
Mutabilities, The.
**McIntosh, Joan**
Are the Sick in Their Beds as They
  Should Be?
**McIntosh, Stewart**
Diane.
**MacIntyre, Carlyle Ferren**
Monologue of the Rating Morgan in
  Rutherford County.
**McIntyre, James**
Queen of Cheese.
**MacIntyre, Lorn M.**
At Kilbryde Castle.
**McIntyre, Philip, Jr.**
Rabbit, The.
**MacIntyre, Tom**
Child.
Corrs, The.
Father.
On Sweet Killen Hill.
**Mack, Cecil**
Teasing; or, I Was Only, Only Teasing
  You, *with music.*
**Mack, L. V.**
Biafra.
Death Songs.
**Mackail, John William**
Positivists ever talk in s-/ Uch an epic
  style as Dawkins.
**McKain, David**
Fireflies.
Late Show, The.
Moral Artistry.
Tremor, The.
**Mackay, Charles**
Rolling Home.
Sea-King's Burial, The.
**McKay, Claude**
After the Winter.
America.
Enslaved.
Flame-Heart.
Harlem Dancer, The.
I Know My Soul.
If We Must Die.
In Bondage.
Lynching, The.
Negro's Tragedy, The.
Outcast.
Pagan Isms, The.
Spring in New Hampshire.
St. Isaac's Church, Petrograd.
Tiger.
Tired Worker, The.
To O. E. A.
To the White Fiends.
Tropics in New York, The.
Truth.
White City, The.
White House, The.
**McKay, Lois Weakley**
Night.
**Mackay, Margaret Mackprang**
Dog Wanted.

**Mackay, William Paton**
Revive Us Again.
**MacKellar, Dorothea**
Once When She Thought Aloud.
**McKellar, John Alexander Ross**
Football Field: Evening.
Nominis Umbra.
**Mackellar, Thomas**
At the door of Mercy Sighing, *with
  music.*
**McKent, Robert J., Jr.**
Pre-History Repeats.
**Mackenzie, Compton**
Bridal Day.
Little White Rose, The.
**Mackenzie, Kenneth**
Moonlit Doorway, The.
Night Duty.
Old Inmate, An.
Spider, The.
Two Trinities.
Wagtail's Nest, The.
**McKeown, Tom**
Buffalo, Our Sacred Beast, The.
Desert World, The.
Early Morning of Another World.
Floating the Ghost River.
Graveyard Road, The.
Hair.
In the Winter of Tigers.
Inside the Vision of Peace.
Invitation of the Mirrors.
Lady in the Water Collection
  Department, The.
1937 Ford Convertible.
November on Lake Michigan.
Nude Climbing a Flagpole.
Woman with Finger.
**Mackey, Mary**
What Do You Say When a Man Tells
  You, You Have the Softest Skin.
**Mackey, Nate**
New and Old Gospel.
**Mackie, Alastair**
In Absentia.
Mongol Quine.
**Mackie, Albert D.**
Molecatcher.
Newsboy.
**McKillop, Menzies**
Young Girl.
**Mackinnon, Rayne**
Reilly.
Tramp, The.
Washed in Water.
**Mackintosh, E. A.**
Cha Till Maccruimein.
**Mackintosh, Newton**
Lucy Lake.
**Macklin, Elizabeth**
Leaving One of the State Parks after a
  Family Outing.
**McKuen, Rod**
Cowboys: One ("Brave/ they straddle
  the animals").
Cowboys: Three ("They wade through
  beer cans").
Cowboys: Two ("Huddled in the pits").
Plan.
Thoughts on Capital Punishment.
**MacLaren, Hamish**
Island Rose.

**McLaughlin, Kathy**
Suicide Pond.
**McLean, Alan**
Lizard.
**MacLean, Alasdair**
Hen Dying.
Old Dog, The.
**McLean, Albert, Jr.**
Petty Murder.
**MacLean, Sorley**
Autumn Day, An.
Dogs and Wolves.
Hallaig.
Hielant Woman.
My Een Are Nae on Calvary.
Shores.
Tumultuous Plenty in the Heavens.
Widdreme, The.
Ye Were the Dawn.
**MacLeish, Archibald**
American Letter: For Gerald Murphy.
Ars Poetica.
Black Humor.
Boy in the Roman Zoo.
Brave New World.
Burying Ground by the Ties.
Calypso's Island.
Conquistador, *sel.*
Corporate Entity.
Critical Observations.
Crossing.
"Dover Beach"—a Note to That Poem.
Dr. Sigmund Freud Discovers the Sea
  Shell.
Eleven.
End of the World, The.
Epistle to Be Left in the Earth.
Epistle to the Rapalloan.
Ezry.
Frescoes for Mr. Rockefeller's City.
Hebrides.
Hurricane.
Immortal Autumn.
L'An Trentiesme de Mon Eage [*or* Age].
Late Abed.
Liberty.
Lines for an Interment.
Memorial Rain.
Mother Goose's Garland.
Music and Drum.
National Security.
"Not Marble nor the Gilded
  Monuments."
Old Man to the Lizard, The.
Peepers in Our Meadow, The.
Poet Speaks from the Visitors' Gallery,
  A.
Prologue: "And the way goes on in the
  worn earth."
Reasons for Music.
Seafarer.
Signature for Tempo.
Silent Slain, The.
Spring in These Hills.
Survivor.
Unfinished History.
Voice of the Studio Announcer.
Voyage to the Moon.
Voyage West.
What Any Lover Learns.
What Riddle Asked the Sphinx.
Where the Hayfields Were.

Winter Is Another Country.
You Also, Gaius Valerius Catullus.
You, Andrew Marvell.
Young Dead Soldiers, The.
**McLellan, Robert**
Sang: "There's a reid lowe in yer cheek."
**"Macleod, Fiona."** *See* **Sharp, William**
**McLeod, Irene Rutherford (Mrs. Aubrey de Sélincourt)**
Lone Dog.
**Macleod, Joseph Gordon ("Adam Drinan")**
Love Song.
Measures.
Successful Scot.
**MacLeod, Mairi**
Complaint about Exile, A.
**Macleod, Norman**
After the Bombing of Barcelona.
Coal Strike.
Death in the City.
Design in Cotton Fabric.
Newsreel.
Not Steel Alone.
Passing of Joe Williams, The.
Proletarian Visit.
Red Dawn in the East, A.
Shadowbox: In a Milltown.
Steel Mill Reversal.
Turn of October, The.
**McMahon, Michael**
Birth of My Drinking Problem, The.
Dossier, The.
Maidenhead.
Poem for Richard Speck, A.
Politician, The.
Stranger in Your Town, A.
Until the Cows Come Home.
Why Fires Are Lit December 21st.
**McMahon, Michael Beirne**
Once upon a Nag.
Trout Fishing in Virginia.
**McMahon, Rhoda**
Loss! Loss!
Love! Love!
**MacManus, Ana Johnston** *See* **"Carbery, Ethna"**
**MacManus, Seumas**
Health to the Birds, A.
**MacMarcuis, Aindrais**
This Night Sees Ireland Desolate.
**McMaster, Guy Humphreys**
Carmen Bellicosum.
**McMaster, Rhyll**
Birds.
Brineshrimp, The.
Discovering Parts of a Body.
Dream of Washed Hair, A.
Here's Death.
Journey, The.
One for the Album.
Round Song, A.
Slanted World.
Sleep.
Starer, The.
Tanks.
Underneath the House.
Woman Crossing the Road.
**McMichael, James**
Cabin North of It All, The.
Great Garret, or 100 Wheels, The.
Inland Lighthouse, The.
Lutra, the Fisher.

Terce.
Village of the Presents, The.
**MacMuireadach, Niall Mor**
Soraidh Slan Don Oidhche Areir.
**McNair, Wesley**
Bald Spot, The.
Characters of Forgotten Dirty Jokes, The.
Fire in Enfield.
Fitz Hugh Lane Goes to the Masthead.
Leaving the Country House to the Landlord, Five Years Later.
Little Louey Comic, The.
Memory of Kuhre.
Thinking about Carnevale's Wife.
**McNally, John**
China Lake.
In a New Year.
March 26th, 1971.
**McNally, Leonard**
Lass of Richmond Hill, The, *with music.*
**MacNamee, Giolla Brighde**
Childless.
**MacNeice, Louis**
And love hung still as crystal over the bed.
As in Their Time.
Aubade: "Having bitten on life like a sharp apple."
August.
Autobiography.
Autumn Journal, *sels.*
Bad Dream.
Bagpipe Music.
Birmingham.
Bottleneck.
British Museum Reading Room, The.
Brother Fire.
Carrickfergus.
Charon.
Christina.
Death of a Cat, The, *sels.*
Death of an Actress.
Didymus.
Dublin.
Eclogue for Christmas, An.
Entirely.
Explorations.
Fanfare for the Makers, A, *abr.*
For X.
Glass Falling.
Grey Ones, The.
Horses.
Il Piccolo Rifiuto.
In Lieu.
Invocation: "Dolphin plunge, fountain play."
June Thunder ("Junes were free and full").
Leaving Barra.
Les Sylphides.
Libertine, The.
London Rain.
Mahabalipuram.
Mixer, The.
Museums.
Nature Morte.
Old Story, The.
Perdita.
Pet Shop.
Prayer before Birth.
Prayer in Mid-Passage.

Prognosis.
Slow Starter, The.
Snow.
Springboard, The.
Streets of Laredo, The.
Sunday Morning.
Sunlight on the Garden, The.
Taxis, The.
Thalassa.
This Is the Life.
Tree Party.
Trilogy for X, *sel.*
Truisms, The.
Variation on Heraclitus.
Whit Monday.
Wolves.
**McNeice, W. G.**
In Memory of Patrick Kavanagh.
Jack.
**McPeake, Francis**
Jug of Punch, The.
**McPheron, Judith**
Water.
**Macpherson, James ("Ossian")**
Oithona: A Poem.
Songs of Selma, The, *sel.*
**MacPherson, Jay**
Ark, The, *sel.*
Fisherman, The.
Natural Mother, The.
They Return.
Way Down, The, *sel.*
**McPherson, Michael**
Lightkeeper, The.
Summit.
**McPherson, Sandra**
Balm.
Bittern, The.
Coconut for Katerina, A.
Elegies for the Hot Season.
Gift of Trilliums, A.
His Body.
Holding Pattern.
In the Columbia River Gorge, after a death.
Lions.
Loneliness.
Marlow and Nancy.
Mouse, The.
1943.
Page.
Pisces Child.
Plant, The.
Pregnancy.
Preparation.
Raffaele Minichiello.
Seaweeds.
Selling the House.
Sentience.
Sisters.
Three from the Market.
Triolet: "She was in love with the same danger."
Wanting a Mummy.
Water Poems.
Wearing White.
**McQuilkin, Rennie**
New England Greenhouse.
Tree Man.
**McRoberts, Robert L.**
Photo of a Retired Farmer, Big Bend, Wisconsin.

Poem for My Students.
**MacSweeney, Barry**
If It Were Winter.
**McVicar, Annie** *and* Dorothy Jordan
Blue Bells of Scotland, The.
**Madden, David**
Surfaces.
**Maddow, Ben**
Acts of God.
City, The.
Defenses, The.
Green in the Halls.
Images of Poverty.
One Gardenia 50C.
Summer Night, A.
**Madge, Charles**
Birds of Tin, The.
Landscape I ("The character of a
landscape stands always in a
mysterious relation").
On One Condition.
Poem: "Walls of the maelstrom are
painted with trees, The."
Solar Creation.
**Madgett, Naomi Long (Naomi Long**
**Witherspoon)**
Alabama Centennial.
Black Woman.
Dream Sequence, Part 9.
Her Story.
Midway.
Mortality.
Offspring.
Pavlov.
Quest.
Race Question, The.
Simple.
Star Journey.
Woman with Flower.
**Madhubuti, Haki R.** *See* **Lee, Don L.**
**Magee, Michael**
It Is the Stars That Govern Us.
**Magid, Margo**
Night Watch.
**Maglow, T. O.**
Dylan Thomas.
**Magogo, Princess**
Teasing Song.
**Magorian, James**
Night Shift at the Poetry Factory, The.
**Magowan, Robin**
Days of 1956.
Paros.
Susan.
Zeimbekiko.
**Maguire, Francis**
Whale Song.
**Mahadevi (Mahadeviyakka)**
Like a silkworm weaving.
Like an elephant.
People,/ male and female.
Riding the blue sapphire mountains.
Till you've earned.
Would a circling surface vulture.
**Mahapatra, Jayanta**
Rain of Rites, A.
**Mahon, Derek**
Afterlives.
Consolations of Philosophy.
Dark Country, A.
Departure, A.
Disused Shed in County Wexford, A.

Ecclesiastes
Exit Molloy.
Girls in Their Seasons.
Glengormley.
Grandfather.
I Am Raftery. ("I am Raftery, hesitant
and confused").
Image from Beckett, An.
In Carrowdore Churchyard.
In the Aran Islands.
Matthew V. 29-30.
Prisoner, The.
Snow Party, The.
**Mahone, Barbara**
Colors for Mama.
Poem for Positive Thinkers, A.
Sugarfields.
**Mahony, Francis Sylvester ("Father**
**Prout")**
Piper's Progress, The.
Shandon Bells, The.
**Mahony, Medb**
Shells.
**Mahy, Margaret**
Pines, The.
Uncle James.
**Maiden, Jennifer**
Dew.
Hypothesis.
Over Coffee.
Strawberry-bright.
Table, The.
**Mailer, Norman**
Devils.
**Maillard, Claude**
Christmas Mass for a Little Atheist
Jesus.
**Maino, Jeannette**
Harvest.
Sky Patterns.
**Mainwaring, Arthur**
Excellent New Ballad, Called the
Brawny Bishop's Complaint, An.
Excellent New Song Called "Mat's
Peace," An.
New Ballad, A.
Queen's Speech, The.
Tarquin and Tullia.
**Mairs, Nancy**
Departure of the Women, The.
Poison.
Waking to Leopards.
Winter Mornings.
**Maisel, Carolyn**
Dream of Women, A.
Girl in the Willow Tree, The.
Letter from a Friend, A.
Pig Woman, *sel.*
She wants to seduce a homosexual
Jesuit.
**Major, Clarence**
Blind Old Woman.
Celebrated Return.
Design, The.
New Pietà, The: For the Mothers and
Children of Detroit.
Swallow the Lake.
Vietnam.
Vietnam #4.
**Major, Nadine**
Agatha.
**Mak, Lev**

Eden.
Flood, The.
**Makai, Emil**
Comet, The.
**Makere**
Lament for Taramoana.
**Makidemewabe, Samuel**
Born Tying Knots.
Dried Things Out.
Many Voices.
Rain Straight Down.
Sat in the Center.
Who-Tapped-the-Frogs-In.
**Malam, Charles**
Neighbors.
Steam Shovel.
**Malancioiu, Ileana**
Bear's Blood.
**Malanga, Gerard**
Insistence, The.
We go out into the night.
**Malangatana, Valente**
To the Anxious Mother.
**Malarkey, Susannah P.**
Above the Wall.
**Mallalieu, Herbert B.**
Empedocles on Etna.
Epilogue: "Phoenix on the hot sirocco's
breath."
**Mallarmé, Stéphane**
Afternoon of a Faun, The: Eclogue.
Album Leaf.
All the soul indrawn.
Fan for His Daughter, A.
Glazier, The.
Lace curtain stands effaced, A.
Saint.
Sea Breeze.
Tired of the bitter repose where my
idleness hurts.
Tomb of Edgar Poe, The.
**Mallet, David**
Birks of Invermay, The.
**Mallet, David** *and* **James Thomson** *See*
**Thomson, James** *and* **David Mallet**
**Malley, Jean**
Words do not grow on the landscape.
**Malley, K.**
Conversation.
**Mallory, Lee**
He insisted/ on being laid down/ in the
foothills.
**Mally, E. Louise**
Moon Rock.
**Maloney, Dennis**
Great Bear, The.
**Malouf, David**
Bicycle.
Carp, The.
Elective Affinities.
Elements of Geometry, The.
Fables, The.
From a Plague Year.
Gray's Anatomy.
Judas Touch, The.
La Divina Commedia.
L'Education Sentimentale.
Suburban.
Theologia Germanica.
Year of the Foxes, The.
**Mammone, Ken**
Sun and I.

**Manabe, Jody**
Hadaka De Hanasu.
**Mandel, Charlotte**
I'm Lucky.
**Mandelstam, Osip**
Ariosto.
Bitter Bread.
Concert at the Station
Like a Young Levite.
Not yet dead, not yet alone.
Notre Dame.
Phaedra.
Reed, A.
This Night.
Twilight of Freedom.
**Manfred, Freya**
For a Young South Dakota Man.
Moon Light.
**Mangan, James Clarence**
Irish Language, The.
Kathaleen Ny-Houlahan.
Nameless One, The.
Rest Only in the Grave.
Shapes and Signs.
Siberia.
**Mangan, Kathy**
Absence.
Cold Snap.
**Manger, Itzik**
Abishag Writes a Letter Home.
Abraham and Sarah.
Alone.
Autumn.
Dark Hand, A.
Dying Thief.
Evening.
Fairy Tales.
On the Road There Stands a Tree.
Rachel Goes to the Well for Water
("Rachel stands by the mirror and
plaits").
Strange Guest, The.
Under the Ruins of Poland.
**Manifold, John Streeter**
Bongong Jack and the Trooper.
Gatton Tragedy, The.
Griesly Wife, The.
Hat in the Ring, A.
Incognito.
Mankho's Philosophers.
Tomb of Lieutenant John Learmonth,
A. I. F., The.
**Mann, Polly**
Atlas' Daughter.
Museum Item 237.
Smile at the Birdie.
**Mann, Ronald**
After the Dark Months.
Blind Man, The.
Congers.
Four Things to See.
In Winter, Elms.
Limpet.
**Manner, Eeva-Liisa**
Cambrian, sels.
**Mannes, Marya**
Canticles to Men.
**Mannyng, Robert**
Dancers of Colbek, The.
Handlyng Synne, sel.
**Mansel, William Lort**
Sun's perpendicular rays, The.

**Mansfield, Katherine**
Man with the Wooden Leg, The.
Sanary.
To L. H. B.
To Stanislaw Wyspianski.
**Mansour, Joyce**
Auditory Hallucinations.
Embrace the Blade.
Last night I saw your corpse.
Seated on her bed legs spread open.
Sun in Capricorn, The.
**Manwell, Juana**   *See* **Owl Woman**
**Manzo, David P.**
Mind Alchemy.
**Mao Tse-tung**
Poem for Liu Ya-tzu.
**Marano, Russell**
Now I Am a Man.
Spring Death.
**Marchant, John**
Little Miss and Her Parrot.
Young Master's Account of a Puppet
Show.
**Marcus, Adrianne**
Beyond Logic.
Book Ends, Immortality Begins, The.
Divorce, The.
In a Dream, the Automobile.
Letters, Returned.
Lines Found on an Envelope.
Perspective.
Suburbia: Impossibilities of Change.
**Marcus, Mordecai**
Book of Verses, A.
Survivors.
Two Refugees.
**Marcus, Morton**
Family Game.
Hand.
Look Closely.
Mole, The.
Moonlit Rock, The.
Proverbs.
Snake, The.
2 Poems Written on Turning Around
Too Quickly while Hiking.
Waking at Night.
Watching Your Gray Eyes.
What I Know.
**Margenat, Hugo**
Living Poetry.
Well-aimed Stare, The.
Your Air of My Air.
**Margolin, Anna (Razel Lebensboim)**
Ancient Murderess Night.
Homecoming.
Mother Earth.
My Kin Talk.
Years.
**Margolis, Gary**
Keep It under Your Hat.
Rearrangement for the Brain.
**Marguerite de Navarre**
Autant en Emporte le Vent.
Smell of death is so powerful, The.
**Mariah, Paul**
Muse Elektrique.
Song: "O Joie."
**Marias, The Three (Maria Isabel Barreno**
*and* Maria Teresa Horta *and* Maria
Velho da Costa)
Conversation between the Chevalier de

Chamilly and Mariana Alcoforado in
the Manner of a Song of Regret.
Saddle and Cell.
**Marie de France**
Goat's-Leaf.
Nightingale, The.
Two Lovers, The.
**Marino, Giovanni Battista**
Lips and Eyes.
Madrigal: "Love now no fire hath left
him."
Massacre of the Innocents, The, *sel.*
**Marion, David**
Her Eyes Don't Shine like Diamonds,
*with music.*
**Marion, Jeff Daniel**
My Grandmother Sifting.
Winter Watch.
**"Mark Twain."**   *See* **"Twain, Mark"**
**Markham, Edwin**
Lincoln, the Man of the People, *sel.*
Lizard, The.
Man with the Hoe, The.
Prayer, A: "Teach me, Father, how to
go."
San Francisco Arising.
San Francisco Falling.
There Is a High Place, *with music.*
Victory in Defeat.
**Markish, Peretz**
In the Last Flicker of the Sinking Sun.
Your Burnt-out Body.
**Marks, Edward B.**
Mother Was a Lady; or, If Jack Were
Only Here, *with music.*
**Marks, Godfrey**
Sailing Sailing.
**Marks, Shirley**
Early Warning.
**Marlatt, Earl B.**
Spirit of Life, in This New Dawn, *with
music.*
Through the Dark the Dreamers Came,
*with music.*
**Marlowe, Christopher**
Amorous Neptune.
And now the sun that through the
horizon peeps.
Doctor Faustus, *sels.*
Edward the Second, *sel.*
Hero and Leander.
Hero Feels the Shaft of Love.
Love at First Sight.
Overreacher, The.
Passionate Shepherd to His Love,
The.
Seduction of Hero, The.
Tamburlaine the Great, *sels.*
**Marquis, Don (Donald Robert Marquis)**
Archy and Mehitabel, *sels.*
Archy at the Zoo.
Certain Maxims of Archy.
Cheerio My Deario.
Confession of a Glutton.
Freddy the Rat Perishes.
Honey Bee, The.
Old Trouper, The.
Pete at the Seashore.
Small Talk.
To a Lost Sweetheart.
Tom-Cat, The.

**Marriott, Anne**
Woodyards in the Rain.
**Marryat, Frederick**
Drinking Song.
Old Navy, The.
Sam Swipes.
**Marshak, Samuel**
Little House in Lithuania, The.
**Marshall, James**
Oregon Trail: 1851.
**Marston, John**
Antonio's Revenge, sel.
Cynic Satyre, A.
Inamorato Curio.
Metamorphosis of Pygmalion's Image,
The, sel.
What You Will: A Comedy, sel.
**Marston, Philip Bourke**
Inseparable.
Speechless: Upon the Marriage of Two
Deaf and Dumb Persons.
Two Burdens, The.
Wedded Memories.
**Martí, José**
Guantanamera.
**Martial (Marcus Valerius Martialis)**
Believe me, sir, I'd like to spend whole
days.
Dasius, chucker-out/ at the Turkish
Baths.
Epitaph for Erotion.
Garland of roses, whether you come.
Happy Life, The.
He unto whom thou art so partial.
Laid with papyrus to catch fire.
Lentinus! thou dost nought but fume,
and fret.
Lycoris darling, once I burned for you.
Near the Vipsanian columns where the
aqueduct.
Prithee die and set me free.
To-morrow you will live, you always cry.
To read my booke the virgin shie.
To Sextus.
Translated out of Martial.
You Serve the Best Wines Always, My
Dear Sir.
**Martin, Mrs. C. D.**
God Will Take Care of You, with music.
**Martin, Charles**
Leaving Buffalo.
**Martin, D. S.**
"O-U-G-H-"; or, The Cross Farmer.
**Martin, David**
I Am a Jew.
**Martin, Dorothy McGrath**
On the Merry, Merry-go-round.
**Martin, Herbert**
Antigone I.
Antigone VI.
Lines: "Singularly and in pairs the
decade has been ripped by bullets."
Negro Soldier's Viet Nam Diary, A.
**Martin, Richard**
Sister Rose.
**Martin, Robert A.**
At Poetry Workshop, Winter Semester.
Beggar and Poet.
In Memory of G. K., for 50 Years the
College Carpenter.
**Martin, Sarah Catherine**

Comic Adventures of Old Mother
Hubbard and Her Dog, The.
**Martin, Sir Theodor and William
Edmonstoune Aytoun** See Aytoun,
**William Edmonstoune and Sir
Theodore Martin**
**Martinez, David W.**
New Way, Old Way.
This Is Today.
**Martinez, Enrique Gonzales**
Last Journey.
Wring the Swan's Neck.
**Martinson, David**
Nineteen Sections from a Twenty Acre
Poem, sels.
**Martinson, Harry**
Sea Wind, The.
**Marula**
Meeting after Separation.
**Marvell, Andrew**
Bermudas.
Clorinda and Damon.
Coronet, The.
Damon the Mower.
Definition of Love, The.
Dialogue between the Resolved Soul and
Created Pleasure, A.
Dialogue between the Soul and Body, A.
Eyes and Tears.
Fair Singer, The.
Garden, The ("How vainly men
themselves amaze").
Garden of Appleton House, The.
Horatian Ode upon Cromwell's Return
from Ireland, An.
Last Instructions to a Painter, The.
Match, The.
Mourning.
Mower against Gardens, The.
Mower to the Glow-Worms, The.
Mower's Song, The.
Nostradamus's Prophecy.
Nymph Complaining for the Death of
Her Fawn, The.
On a Drop of Dew.
On Mr. Milton's Paradise Lost.
On the Lord Mayor and Court of
Aldermen, Presenting the Late King
and Duke of York Each with a Copy
of Their Freedoms.
Picture of Little T. C. in a Prospect of
Flowers, The.
Second Advice to a Painter, The.
Third Advice to a Painter, The.
To His Coy Mistress.
Unfortunate Lover, The.
Upon Appleton House.
Young Love.
**Mary Queen of Scots**
Absent One, The.
**Marz, Roy**
Vittoria Colonna.
**Marzán, Julio**
Epitaph: "Hours before my death."
Friday Evening.
Graduation Day, 1965.
**Marzials, Théophile Julius Henry**
Tragedy, A.
**Masahongva**
Now from the east.
**Masaoka Shiki**
Haiku: "All the hot night."

Sandy shore: and why
**Masarik, Al**
Cultural Exchange.
Poetry.
You See Them in the Alleys.
**Masefield, John**
All through the windless night the
clipper rolled.
Biography, sel.
Bluebells, The.
C. L. M.
Cape Horn Gospel—1 (" 'I was in a
hooker once,' said Karlssen").
Cardigan Bay.
Cargoes.
Consecration, A.
Crowd, The.
D'Avalos' Prayer.
Epilogue, An: "I have seen flowers come
in stony places."
Everlasting Mercy, The, sels.
From the Gallows Hill to the Tineton
Copse.
Hell's Pavement.
Laugh and Be Merry.
Lemmings, The.
Old Song Re-sung, A.
On Growing Old.
Partridges.
Reynard the Fox, sels.
Sea Change.
Sea-Fever.
Ship and Her Makers, The.
Sonnet: "Is there a great green
commonwealth of Thought."
Sonnet: "There, on the darkened
deathbed, dies the brain."
Tarry Buccaneer, The.
There is no God, as I was taught in
youth.
Twilight.
Up on the Downs.
Valediction, A: "We're bound for the
blue water where the great winds
blow."
Waggon-Maker, The.
Wanderer's Song, A.
West Wind, The.
Wild Geese, The.
Yarn of the Loch Achray.
**Mason, John**
General Song of Praise to Almighty
God, A.
**Mason, Ronald Allison Kells**
Body of John.
Ecce Homunculus.
Flow at Full Moon.
Footnote to John ii. 4.
If the Drink.
Judas Iscariot.
Latter-Day Geography Lesson.
Lugete O Veneres.
Nails and a Cross.
Oils and Ointments.
Old Memories of Earth.
On the Swag.
Our Love Was a Grim Citadel.
Song of Allegiance.
Sonnet of Brotherhood.
Spark's Farewell to Its Clay, The.
Young Man Thinks of Sons, The.
**Mason, Walt**

Football.
**Massman, Gordon**
  Liard Hot Springs.
**Masson, Tom (Thomas Lansing Masson)**
  Enough.
  He Took Her.
  My Poker Girl.
  Tragedy, A.
**Master, Thomas**
  Cat and the Lute, The.
**Masters, Edgar Lee**
  Amanda Barker.
  Anne Rutledge.
  Arlo Will.
  Benjamin Franklin Hazard.
  Butch Weldy.
  Carl Hamblin.
  Cassius Hueffer.
  Circuit Judge, The.
  Cooney Potter.
  Editor Whedon.
  Elsa Wertman.
  Fiddler Jones.
  Frank Drummer.
  Hamilton Greene.
  Hill, The.
  In Memory of Bryan Lathrop.
  Jonathan Swift Somers.
  Judge Somers.
  Keats to Fanny Brawne.
  Lost Orchard, The.
  Lucinda Matlock.
  Marx the Sign Painter.
  Meredith Phyfe.
  Mind Flying Afar.
  New Spoon River, The, *sels*.
  Petit, the Poet.
  Rhoda Pitkin.
  Spoon River Anthology,*sels*.
  Unknown Soldiers.
  Village Atheist, The.
  Willie Metcalf.
**Masters, Marcia Lee**
  At My Mother's Bedside.
  Figure.
  House in Chicago, The.
  Man, My Father, The.
**Masterson, Dan**
  Cook-out.
  One-Eleven Grape Street.
**Mastoraki, Jenny**
  Bridal bed, The. Above it.
  Crusaders knew the Holy Places, The.
  Death of a Warrior, The.
  Prometheus.
  Then they paraded Pompey's urn.
  Vandals, The.
  Wooden Horse then said, The.
**Mastrolia, Lilyan S.**
  Golden Gate: The Teacher.
**Matchett, William H.**
  Aunt Alice in April.
**Mathams, Walter J.**
  Jesus, Friend of Little Children.
**Mather, Cotton**
  Eternal God, How They're Increased,
    *with music*.
  I Lift My Eyes Up to the Hills, *with
    music*.
  My Heart, How Very Hard It's Grown,
    *with music*.

When the Seed of Thy Word Is Cast,
  *with music*.
**Matheson, George**
  O Love That Wilt Not Let Me Go, *with
    music*.
**Mathews, Richard**
  Blood and My Brother.
  Dear Patty, Dear Tania.
  Griffin.
  Oh, Do You Know the Muffin Man?
  Seal in the Lowry Park Zoo, The.
**Mathias, Roland**
  Craswall.
  Departure in Middle Age.
**Mathis, Cleopatra**
  Learning to Live with Friends.
  Man on the Bed, The.
  Pine Barrens: Letter Home.
  Rearranging My Body.
  Ruston, Louisiana: 1952.
  Two Memories.
  View of Louisiana.
**Matsuo Basho**   *See* **Basho**
**Matteson, Fredric**
  House We Leave, The.
**Matthews, Dale**
  Congress.
  Dice Player, The.
  Small Favors.
**Matthews, T. S.**
  Invisible Man, The.
**Matthews, Tom**
  Road Again, The.
**Matthews, William**
  Airline Breakfast, An.
  Blues for John Coltrane, Dead at 41.
  Cat, The.
  Cows Grazing at Sunrise.
  Directions.
  Invention of Astronomy, The.
  Late Movie, A.
  Moving.
  Nurse Sharks.
  Oh Yes.
  Oscar Robertson: Peripheral Vision.
  Praise.
  Your Eyes, Your Name.
**Matthias, John**
  In Columbus, Ohio.
  On Lake Michigan—1972.
**Mattingly, George**
  Best Thing Going, The.
  Cruising for Burgers.
  God's Words to the Last Ape.
  Goodbye Sonnet.
  History of Weather, The.
  Lives of the Poets, The, *sel*.
  Patience, No Speed.
  Tide.
**Matusovskii, M.** *and* **V. Solovyov-Sedoi**
  *See* **Solovyov-Sedoi, V.** *and* **M.
    Matusovskii**
**Matuzak, Joseph**
  To Sherrie.
**Maunders, Ruth O.**
  Eureka.
**Maura, Sister**
  Annunciation.
  Woman's Liberation.
**Mavimbela**
  My money! O, my money!
**Maxson, H. A.**

When It Rains.
**Maxton, Hugh**
  Cernunnos.
  Dialectique.
  Landscape with Minute Wildflowers.
  Mastrim: A Meditation, *sel*.
  Premonition of Winter.
  Urgent Letter, An.
  Waking.
**Maxwell, James Clerk**
  Rigid Body Sings.
**May, Edward**
  Five Things White.
  To a Covetous Churl.
  To Barba.
  To Her Love.
  You tender virgins, fairer than the snow
    with which you play.
**May, James Boyer**
  Psychological Dissertation.
**Mayakovsky, Vladimir**
  Brooklyn Bridge.
**Mayer, Gerda**
  Dandelions.
**Mayer, Hansjörg**
  Oil.
**Mayhall, Jane**
  City Sparrow.
  For the Market.
  Human Animal, The.
  Marshes, The.
  Prostitutes at Les Halles, The.
  Surfaces.
  Tracing Back.
**Mayne, Seymour**
  Abraham Sutskever.
  Afternoon's Angel.
  In the First Cave.
  Locusts of Silence.
  Yehuda Amichai.
**Mayo, Edward Leslie**
  El Greco.
  We Still Must Follow.
  Word of Water, The.
**Maze, Mack**
  If you see my mother, partner, tell her
    pray for me.
**Mazzaro, Jerome**
  At Torrey Pines State Park.
  Fall Colors.
**M'Baye, Annette**
  Silhouette.
**Mbembe (Milton Smith)**
  Blkness No. 2.
  Boy.
  High.
  Other Books by the Author?
  Poem: "One/ poem."
  Something Else They Say.
  3 A.M.
  Tree.
  Who's Who in America.
  World Is a Stubbed Toe, The.
**Mberi, Antar S. K.**
  And All Call Him Uncle.
  Juanito's Blues.
  Legacy for a Beboppin Gentle Giant:
    DuBois.
  New Quotas/ or Booker T. and Garvey
    Would Haved Loved South Africa.
  On the Inside Strong.
  Percussion Bittersweet.

Quickview.
Quickview #2.
Winnie.
**Mead, Margaret**
Misericordia.
**Mead, Matthew**
Administration of Things, The, *sels.*
Barbarians, The.
Identities,*sels.*
To Redistort a Weltanschauung.
**Mead, Philip**
Chinese Graves in Beechworth
   Cemetery, The.
**Mearns, Hughes**
Little Man Who Wasn't There, The.
**Mechtild of Magdeburg**
Flowering Light of the Godhead, The
**Mecklenburger, James**
No Matter How Her Thighs.
Pigeons.
**Mecklenburger, Ralph**
Girl with Car and Guitar.
Idolatry.
Poem at Semester's End.
Still Life.
Wilderness.
**Meeks, Dodie**
There Goes a Girl Walking.
**Meeter, Merle**
Birth Day.
Exigent Gymnastic, An.
Horseplay by Reverse Descartes.
Knell for Insularity.
Lighthouse.
Toad School.
**Megged, Matti**
Akedah, The.
Phoenix, The.
White Bird.
**Meidhre, Brian MacGiolla**   *See* **Merriman,
   Brian**
**Meilyr, Brydydd**
Poem on His Death-Bed.
**Meiners, Roger**
Marginal Music.
**Meinke, Peter**
Byron vs. DiMaggio.
Candles.
Cheerios.
Chicken Unlimited.
Everything We Do.
Happy at 40.
Necessary Bucket, A.
Preacher, Said the General.
Progress.
Revelation.
Third Child.
This Is a Poem to My Son Peter.
To an Athlete Turned Poet.
What Wild-eyed Murderer.
World within World.
**Meireles, Cecília**
Away from You.
Ballad of the Ten Casino Dancers.
Dead Horse, The.
Motive.
Pyrargyrite Metal, 9.
Roosters Will Crow, The.
**Meissner, William**
Coal Mine Disaster's Last Trapped Man
   Contemplates Salvation, The.
Slaughterhouse Boys, The.

**Mei Yao Ch'en**
Friend Advises Me to Stop Drinking, A
**Meleager**
Busy with love, the bumble bee.
Her Voice.
I'll Twine White Violets.
Lost Desire.
Love's night and a lamp.
Wine Cup, The.
**Mélendez, Jesús Papoleto**
And Doves Were Nowhere to Be Found.
Before the Bell Rings.
Open Poetry Reading.
T.V. Commercial No. 073.
Willie Bobo Was a Baaaa/aad Dude.
**Melinescu, Gabriela**
Birth.
Fall.
Time of Fish Dying.
**Mellichamp, Leslie**
Epitaph: "Here he lies moulding."
**Mello Breyner Andresen, Sophia de**   *See*
   **Andresen, Sophia de Mello Breyner**
**Melly, George**
Homage to René Magritte.
**Meltzer, David**
Back from London.
Eyes, the Blood, The.
Forte: For Tina.
His or her's.
Midrash.
Nature, *sel.*
Procedure is habit. I affirm it.
Tell Them I'm Struggling to Sing with
   Angels.
**Meltzer, Richard**
Poem moves down a page, A.
**Melvill, Elizabeth, Lady Culross**
Godly Dream, A, *sels.*
**Melville, Herman**
After the Pleasure Party.
Art.
Attic Landscape, The.
Battle Picture, A.
Bench of Boors, The.
Berg, The.
Billy Budd, Foretopman, *sel.*
Billy in the Darbies.
Blue-Bird, The.
Buddha.
Commemorative of a Naval Victory.
Conflict of Convictions, The.
Father Mapple's Hymn.
"Formerly a Slave."
Fragments of a Lost Gnostic Poem of
   the 12th Century.
House-Top, The.
In a Bye-Canal.
In a Garret.
In the Desert.
In the Prison Pen.
Inscription for Marye's Heights,
   Fredericksburg.
Lover and the Syringa-Bush, The.
Lyon.
Maldive Shark, The.
Malvern Hill.
March into Virginia, The.
Martyr, The.
Meditation, A.
Misgivings.
Moby Dick, *sel.*

New Ancient of Days, The.
Night-March, The.
Old Age in His Ailing.
Pebbles.
Pontoosuce.
Portent, The.
Ravaged Villa, The.
Return of the Sire de Nesle A. D. 16—,
   The.
Shiloh; a Requiem.
To Ned.
Tuft of Kelp, The.
Utilitarian View of the *Monitor's* Fight,
   A.
**Menai, Huw (Hugh Menai Williams)**
Back in the Return, *sel.*
**Mendelssohn, Asher**
Cordoba.
**Menebroker, Ann**
Catalysis.
Cognac and Farewell to My Sanity.
In the Half-Point Time of Night.
To the Man I Live With.
**Menzies, G. K.**
Poaching *in Excelsis.*
**Meogo, Pero**
Cossante.
**Mercer, Jesse**
Will God forever cast us off.
**Mercer, Johnny**
Glow-Worm, The.
I'm an Old Cowhand.
Jubilation T. Cornpone.
**Merchant, Jane**
Unless We Guard Them Well.
**Meredith, George**
Appeasement of Demeter, The.
Ballad of Past Meridian, A.
Child's Prayer, A.
Dirge in Woods.
Empedocles.
Juggling Jerry.
Jump-to-Glory Jane.
King Harald's Trance.
Love in the Valley.
Lucifer in Starlight.
Melampus.
Modern Love.
Night of Frost in May.
Ode to the Spirit of Earth in Autumn.
Old Chartist, The.
Penetration and Trust.
Phoebus with Admetus.
Promise in Disturbance, The.
Seed-Time.
Winter Heavens.
Young Reynard.
**Meredith, Joseph**
Midnight, Walking the Wakeful
   Daughter.
**"Meredith, Owen" (Edward Robert Bulwer-
   Lytton, 1st Earl of Lytton)**
Check to Song.
**Meredith, William**
At the Natural History Museum.
Bachelor.
Battle Problem.
Consequences.
Couple Overhead, The.
Earth Walk.
Effort at Speech.
Examples of Created Systems.

His Plans for Old Age.
Iambic Feet Considered as Honorable Scars.
Korean Woman Seated by a Wall, A.
Last Things.
Lines Written but Never Mailed from Hawaii.
Mild-spoken Citizen Finally Writes to the White House, A.
My Mother's Life.
Old Field Mowed for Appearances' Sake, An.
On Falling Asleep by Firelight.
Open Sea, The.
Preponderance, The.
Ritual Mouse, A.
Thoughts on One's Head.
To the Thoughtful Reader.
Traveling Boy.
Two Figures from the Movies.
Walter Jenks' Bath.
Where I'm Staying Now.
Wholesome.
Winter Verse for His Sister.
Wreck of the *Thresher*, The.

**Meriluoto, Aila**
Still.

**Merino, Francisco Lopez**
Song for Afterwards.

**Merkel, Dana "The Mouse"**
You Got Parole.

**Mernit, Susan**
Scholar's Wife, The.
Song of the Bride.

**Merriam, Eve**
Alligator on the Escalator.
Charm for Our Time, A.
Cheers.
Ding, Dong, Bell.
Fee, Fi, Fo, Fum.
Fertile Valley of the Nile, The.
Finding a Poem.
Fishy Square Dance, A.
Grandmother, Rocking.
Happy Birthday to Me.
How to Eat a Poem.
Ice-Creepers (for Cid Ricketts Sumner).
Inner-City Mother Goose, The, *sels.*
Jamboree for J, A.
Leaning on a Limerick, *sel.*
Martian.
Mean Song.
Neuteronomy.
Poets.
Secret, A.
Teevee.
Think Tank.
To Meet Mr. Lincoln.
Tryst.
Umbilical.
What in the World.
Which Washington?
Wino Will.
Yell for Yellow, A.

**Merrill, Arthur Truman**
Spring in the Desert.

**Merrill, Boynton, Jr.**
Stallion, The.

**Merrill, Carol**
Portrait.

**Merrill, James**
About the Phoenix.

After Greece.
Angel.
Black Mesa, The.
Broken Bowl, The.
Broken Home, The.
Childlessness.
Developers at Crystal River.
18 West 11th.
Foliage of Vision.
Furnished Room, The.
Grand Canyon, The.
Green Eye, The.
Hotel de l'Univers et Portugal.
Laboratory Poem.
Last Words.
Mad Scene, The.
Manos Karastefanis.
Matinees.
Octopus, The.
Page from the Koran.
Parrot Fish, The.
Part of the Vigil.
Power Station, The.
Preface to the Memoirs, A.
Renewal, A.
Swimming by Night.
Thistledown.
Timepiece, A.
Tomorrows.
Urban Convalescence, An.
Voices from the Other World.
Watching the Dance.
World and the Child, The.

**Merrill, Lynn**
Steady Rain.

**Merrill, William Pierson**
Not Alone for Mighty Empire, *with music.*
Rise Up, O Men of God, *with music.*

**Merriman, Brian [*or* Brian MacGiolla Meidhre]**
Country's Crisis, The.
Husband's Lament, The.
Irish Marriage Night, An.
Lament of the Unmarried Girl, The.
Maiden's Plight, The.
Midnight Court, The, *sels.*
Now God Stand Up for Bastards.
Old Man's Tale, The.
Solution, The.
Walk.

**Mersmann, James F.**
Despair.

**Mertins, Louis**
Rain Chant.

**Merton, Thomas**
Dark Morning, The.
Elegy for the Monastery Barn.
Lent in a Year of War.
Responsory, 1948, A.
St. Malachy.
There Has to Be a Jail for Ladies.

**Merwin, William Stanly**
Air: "Naturally it is night."
Another Year Come.
Approaches, The.
Asians Dying, The.
Assembly.
Avoiding News by the River.
Ballad of John Cable and Three Gentlemen.
Ballade of Sayings.

Birds Waking.
Black Plateau, The.
Bones, The.
Bread.
Caesar.
Carol of the Three Kings.
Chaff, The.
Child, The.
Cold before the Moonrise, The.
Dead Hand.
December Night.
Departure's Girl-Friend.
Dictum: For a Masque of Deluge.
Diggers, The.
Distances, The.
Divinities.
Door, A.
Drunk in the Furnace, The.
Early January.
Exercise.
February.
Finding a Teacher.
Fly.
Fog-Horn.
Footprints on the Glacier.
For a Coming Extinction.
For the Anniversary of My Death.
Fourth Psalm: The Cerements.
Full Moonlight in Spring.
Glass.
Grandfather in the Old Men's Home.
Grandmother Watching at Her Window.
Highway, The.
Home for Thanksgiving.
Horse, The.
Hosts, The.
I Live up Here.
In the Winter of My Thirty-eighth Year.
Initiate, The.
Judgment of Paris, The.
June Rain.
Last One, The.
Lemuel's Blessing.
Letter.
Leviathan.
Little Horse.
Looking for Mushrooms at Sunrise.
Low Fields and Light.
Moths, The.
Mountain, The.
Mountain Day.
Mountains, The.
Next Moon, The.
Noah's Raven.
Odysseus.
Old Boast, The.
One-Eye.
Owl, The.
Pens, The.
Place of Backs, The.
Plea for a Captive.
Removal, The.
River of Bees, The.
Rock, The.
Room, The.
St. Vincent's.
Sapphire.
Second Psalm: The Signals.
Separation.
Sire.
Small Woman on Swallow Street.
Snowfall.

Some Last Questions.
Song of Three Smiles.
Sunset after Rain.
Room, The.
Surf-Casting.
Tale.
Things.
To Dana for Her Birthday.
To the Hand.
Trail into Kansas, The.
Trees.
Variation on the Gothic Spiral.
Views from the High Camp.
Vineyard, The.
Vision.
Voice.
We Continue.
When I Came from Colchis.
When the War Is Over.
Widow, The.
Windows, The.
You, Genoese Mariner.

**Meschery, Tom**
As It Should Be.
Pro Basketball Players.
To Wilt Chamberlain.

**Mesens, E. L. T.**
Arid Husband, The.

**Messenger, Bill**
Carol Took Her Clothes Off.

**Metcalfe, James J.**
Pray in May.

**Metz, Jerred**
Angels in the House.
Divination.
Her True Body.
Speak like Rain.

**Metz, Roberta**
Zeyde.

**Metzger, Deena**
Little League Women.
Talisman for the New Year, A.

**Mew, Charlotte**
A Quoi Bon Dire.
Beside the Bed.
Cenotaph, The.
Changeling, The.
Domus Caedet Arborem.
Fame.
Farmer's Bride, The.
I So Liked Spring.
In the Fields.
Madeleine in Church.
Monsieur Qui Passe.
Narrow Door, The.
Old Shepherd's Prayer.
Quiet House, The.
Rooms.
Saturday Market.
Sea Love.
Smile, Death.
Trees Are Down, The.

**Meyer, Conny Hannes**
Beast That Rode the Unicorn, The.
Of the Beloved Caravan.

**Meyers, Bert**
Dark Birds, The.
Daybreak.
Garlic, The.
Landscapes.
Pigeons.
Stars Climb Girders of Light.

Suburban Dusk.
When I Come to Israel.

**Meynell, Alice**
Chimes.
Christ in the Universe.
Easter Night.
Father of Women, A.
General Communion, A.
In Manchester Square.
Launch, The.
Letter from a Girl to Her Own Old Age, A.
Maternity.
November Blue.
Parentage.
Poet of One Mood, A.
Rainy Summer, The.
Renouncement.
Roaring Frost, The.
Shepherdess, The.
Singers to Come.
Summer in England, 1914.
Threshing-Machine, The.
Thrush before Dawn, A.
Two Questions, The.
Veni Creator.
Watershed, The.

**Mezey, Robert**
Back.
Confession, A.
Couplets 20.
I Am Here.
In the Soul Hour.
New Year's Eve in Solitude.
Night on Clinton.
No Country You Remember.
There.
Theresienstadt Poem.
Vetus Flamma.
Wandering Jew, The.
White Blossoms.

**Mezquida, Anna Blake**
Chinatown.

**Mezzetta, Luciano**
Night in Nevada with a Friend from Italy, A.

**Mhac an tSaoi, Máire**
Harvest of the Sea.

**Mheic Cailein, Iseabal Ni**
Alas for Him Whose Sickness Is Love.

**Miccolis, Leila**
I wanted to see you,/ thighs showing.
Till Death Do Us Part.

**Michael, Cyril R.**
Shirley Temple.

**Michaelis, Hanny**
Listening.
Under Restless Clouds.
We Carry Eggshells.

**Michaelson, L. W.**
Godspeed to Such Harpoons.

**Michelangelo Buonarroti**
Prayer for Faith, A.
Sonnet: "Eternal Lord! eased of a cumbrous load."
Waiting in Faith.
Yes! hope may with my strong desire keep pace.

**Micheline, Jack**
On My Way to Boston Need Five Bucks.

**Michelson, Peter**
Parable for Our Time.

When the Revolution Really.

**Michie, James**
Arizona Nature Myth.
Dooley Is a Traitor.
Whenever you drink all night you make.

**Middlebrook, Diane**
Contagiousness of Dreams, The.
For You, Falling Asleep after a Quarrel.

**Middleton, Bill**
Cops and Robbers.

**Middleton, Christopher**
China Shop Vigil.
Disturbing the Tarantula.
Five Psalms of Common Man.
For a Junior School Poetry Book.
Found Poem with Grafts 1866.
Historian, The.
January 1919.
Jindrichuv Hradec.
Octobers.
Oystercatchers.
Poem Written after Contemplating the Adverb "Primarily."
Snake Rock.
Thousand Things, The.
Young Woman in Apathy.

**Middleton, Herb**
To Patriotic America.

**Middleton, Richard**
On a Dead Child.
Time's Metamorphosis.

**Middleton, Thomas**
Blurt, Master Constable, *sel.*
Night Sounds.
Spanish Gipsy, The, *sel.*
To Vesta.
Women Beware Women: A Tragedy, *sel.*

**Midlane, Albert**
Above the Bright Blue Sky, *sel.*

**Mihri Hatun**
At one glance/I loved you.

**Miklitsch, Robert**
As in the Land of Darkness.

**Milbauer, Joseph**
Interior.

**Miles, Alfred H.**
Anchors Aweigh, *with music.*

**Miles, C. Austin**
In the Garden, *with music.*

**Miles, Jeffrey**
Bear (Part Three).

**Miles, Josephine**
Apart from Branches.
As difference blends into identity.
Away.
Belief.
Bounty.
Campaign, The.
Civilian.
Conception.
Conservancies.
David.
Day the Winds, The.
Doctor Who Sits at the Bedside of a Rat, The.
Dream.
Entrepreneur chicken shed his tail feathers, surplus, The.
Family.
Find.
Forecast.
Gypsy.

Housewife.
I Telephoned a Friend.
If You Will.
In the Neighborhood.
In the town where every man is king.
I've been going around everywhere
　without any skin.
Made Shine.
Mailman Is Coming, The.
Maxim.
Merchant Marine.
Midweek.
None.
Oedipus.
On Inhabiting an Orange.
Opal.
Players.
Preliminary to Classroom Lecture.
Reason.
Ride.
Sale.
So Graven.
Softly the Capitol Hill Surveys Its Scene.
Summer.
Sunday.
Tally.
Vacuum.
When the Sun Came.
Witness.

**Miles, Ron**
Lives of the Poet.

**Miles, Sara**
Portrait in Available Light.

**Miles, Susan (Ursula Roberts)**
Microcosmos.

**Millard, Bob**
Bury Our Faces.

**Millard, Gertrude**
Nostalgia.

**Millay, Edna St. Vincent ("Nancy Boyd")**
Admetus, from my marrow's core I do.
Afternoon on a Hill.
And You as Well Must Die, Beloved
　Dust.
Apostrophe to Man.
Ballad of the Harp-Weaver, The.
Buck in the Snow, The.
Cameo, The.
Conscientious Objector.
Dirge without Music.
Eel Grass.
Elegy before Death.
Euclid Alone Has Looked on Beauty
　Bare.
Even in the moment of our earliest kiss.
Exiled.
First Fig.
Fitting, The.
From a Very Little Sphinx.
Gazing upon him now, severe and dead.
God's World.
Grown-up.
Hearing your words, and not a word
　among them.
Huntsman, What Quarry?
I, being a woman and distressed.
I Know I Am but Summer to Your
　Heart.
I Shall Forget You Presently, My Dear.
I Shall Go Back.
Intention to Escape from Him.
Justice Denied in Massachusetts.

Lament: "Listen, children:/ Your father
　is dead."
Love is not all; it is not meat nor drink.
Love is not blind. I see with single eye.
Low-Tide.
Memorial to D. C.,　*sel.*
My most distinguished guest and learnèd
　friend.
Never May the Fruit Be Plucked.
Night is my sister, and how deep in love.
Not in a silver casket cool with pearls.
O God, I Cried, No Dark Disguise, *with
　music.*
Oh, oh, you will be sorry for that word!
Oh, sleep forever in the Latmian cave.
On Hearing a Symphony of Beethoven.
On the Wide Heath.
Passer Mortuus Est.
Penitent, The.
Philosopher, The.
Pity Me Not because the Light of Day.
Plum Gatherer, The.
Portrait by a Neighbor.
Recuerdo.
Rendezvous.
Return, The.
Say That We Saw Spain Die.
Second Fig.
Since of no creature living the last
　breath.
Snow Storm, The.
Song of a Second April.
Sonnet to Gath.
Sonnet: "Women have loved before as I
　love now."
Spring.
Strawberry Shrub, The.
Theme and Variations.
Think not, nor for a moment let your
　mind.
This beast that rends me in the sight of
　all.
Thursday.
Time does not bring relief; you all have
　lied.
To a Calvinist in Bali.
To Inez Milholland.
To Jesus on His Birthday.
To the Wife of a Sick Friend.
Travel.
Underground System.
Unexplorer, The.
Visit to the Asylum, A.
What Lips My Lips Have Kissed, and
　Where, and Why.
What Rider Spurs Him from the
　Darkening East.
When we are old and these rejoicing
　veins.
Who Hurt You So?
Wild Swans.
You loved me not at all, but let it go.

**Millay, Kathleen**
Relativity.

**Miller, Adam David**
Crack in the Wall Holds Flowers.
Hungry Black Child, The.

**Miller, Carolyn**
Nocturnal Visitor.

**Miller, Chuck**
Duke of York (Courage), The.
For Judy.

How in the Morning.
I Write for Those Unknown.
Requiem: A Surrealist Graveyard.
Things as They Are.
When I Began This Funny Journey.

**Miller, E. Ethelbert**
Pretzels.
Separation demands that.
Writer's Conference.

**Miller, Emily Huntington**
Wood-Dove's Note, The.

**Miller, Errol**
Tough Ones, The.

**Miller, Freeman E.**
Stampede, The.

**Miller, Grace Maddock**
Poetic Tale.

**Miller, Harry S.**
Cat Came Back, The.

**Miller, Heather Ross**
Quail Walk.

**Miller, Jane**
May You Always Be the Darling of
　Fortune.

**Miller, Jim Wayne**
Bee Woman, The.
Growing Wild.
House of Readers, A.
Jim Worley Fries Trout on South
　Squalla.
Nostalgia for 70.
On the Wings of a Dove.
Squirrel Stand.

**Miller, Joaquin (Cincinnatus Heine [or
　Hiner] Miller)**
Columbus.
Crossing the Plains.
Cuba Libre.
Dead in the Sierras.
Defence of the Alamo, The.
Exodus for Oregon.
Kit Carson's Ride.
San Francisco Bay.
Vaquero.
William Brown.

**Miller, Mary Britton**
Cat.
Foal.
This Wonderful World.
Universe, The.
Where Are You Now?

**Miller, May**
Bell at Midnight.
Direction, The.
For a Young Friend Seeking "Identity."
History.
Park, The: U. S. A.
Washingtonian, The.

**Miller, Nellie Burget**
Italian Spring, 1945.
Ploughman, The.
Sun Drops Red, The.
Woman in the Field, The.

**Miller, Thomas**
Evening.
Watercress Seller, The.

**Miller, Vassar**
Accepting.
Adam's Footprint.
Beat Poem by an Academic Poet.
Bout with Burning.
Christmas Mourning.

Clash with Cliches, A.
Eden Revisited.
Encounter.
Farm, The.
Ghostly Beast, The.
Homecoming Blues.
Invocation: "Unwinding the spool of the morning."
Judas.
Lesson in Detachment, A.
Love Song for the Future.
Metamorphoses.
New Icarus, The.
On Approaching My Birthday.
One Morning.
Paradox.
Quarry, The.
Reciprocity.
Regret.
Slump.
Song for a Marriage.
Sophistication.
Spinster's Lullaby.
Trimming the Sails.
Without Ceremony.

**Miller, Wayne**
Black Poppies.
For Josephina.
For Kenneth Patchen.

**Miller, William**
Willie Winkie.

**Milligan, Alice**
When I Was a Little Girl.

**Milligan, Spike**
Edser.
Land of the Bumbley Boo, The.
Little tiny puppy dog.
My Sister Laura.
Scorflufus.
Wiggley-Woggley Men, The.

**Mills, Harry Edward**
Early Frogs, The.
Punkin Pie.

**Mills, Kerry**
At a Georgia Camp Meeting, with music.

**Mills, Paul**
Acorns.
Beinn Damph.
Cape Cornwall.
Cerne Giant, The.
Cromwell.
Fish, The.
Green Room, The.
Lizard.

**Mills, Ralph J., Jr.**
Door to the Sun.
For Years.
March Light.
Stones, The.
White Piano, The.

**Mills, William**
I Know a Spot Just over the Hill.
Pity.
Unemployment.

**Mills, William G.**
Arise, O Glorious Zion, with music.

**Millward, Pamela**
Just as the Small Waves Came Where No Waves Were.

**Milne, Alan Alexander**
Bad Sir Brian Botany.
Buckingham Palace.

Halfway Down.
King's Breakfast, The.
Lines Written by a Bear of Very Little Brain.
Mirror, The.
Missing.
Solitude.
Three Foxes, The.
Us Two.
Vespers.
Young Puppy, The.

**Milne, Ewart**
Diamond Cut Diamond.
Martyred Earth, The.
Vanessa Vanessa.

**Milnes, Richard Monckton, 1st Baron Houghton**
Good Night and Good Morning.
Lady Moon.

**Milosz, Czeslaw**
Poor Christian Looks at the Ghetto, A.

**Milton, John**
Adam and Eve in Paradise.
Adam Speaks ("Oh, why did God,/Creator wise").
Arcades, sel.
At a Solemn Music.
Banishment, The.
Before the Fall.
Beneath him with new wonder now he views.
But now lead on.
But see here comes they reverend Sire.
Conclusion: "High in front advanc'd/ The brandisht sword of God before them blaz'd."
Creation: The Fifth Day, Fishes and Birds.
Cyriack, Whose Grandsire on the Royal Bench.
Eve Contemplates Sharing Her Sin.
Eve Speaks to Adam ("With thee conversing I forget all time").
Evening in Eden.
He ended; and thus Adam last replied.
High on a throne of royal state, which far.
Holy Light.
How Soon Hath Time the Subtle Thief of Youth.
Hymn on the Morning of Christ's Nativity.
Il Penseroso.
Immortal Hate.
Invocation: "Of mans first disobedience, and the fruit."
Lady Sings, The.
L'Allegro.
Lawrence, of virtuous father virtuous son.
Light the prime work of God to me is extinct.
Lycidas.
Neptune.
O Nightingale, That on Yon Bloomy Spray.
On His Blindness.
On His Deceased Wife.
On Shakespeare.
On the Detraction Which Followed upon My Writing Certain Treatises ("A

book was writ of late called Tetrachordon").
On the Detraction Which Followed upon My Writing Certain Treatises ("I did but prompt the age to quit their clogs").
On the Late Massacre in Piedmont.
On the Morning of Christ's Nativity.
On the New Forcers of Conscience under the Long Parliament.
On the University Carrier ("Here lies old Hobson, Death hath broke his girt").
On Time.
Paradise Lost, sels.
Paradise Regained, sels.
Political Power.
Rivers Arise; Whether Thou Be the Son.
Sabrina.
Samson Agonistes.
Satan and the Fallen Angels.
Satan as Rebel-Liberator.
Satan Discovers Eden.
Satan Flies to the Sun.
Satan's Address to the Sun.
Song: "Nymphs and shepherds dance no more."
Song on May Morning.
Sonnet: "Captain or colonel, or knight in arms."
Spirit Epiloguizes, The.
Temptation of the Magic Banquet.
To Mr. Cyriac Skinner upon His Blindness.
To the Lord General Cromwell, May 1652.
Vision of the Future; the Flood.
War in Heaven.
Ways of God, The.

**Minard, Michael D.**
Musician Returning from a Cafe Audition, A.

**Minczeski, John**
Hidden Falls.
Old Ego Song ("Old ego climbing out of the trap door on the top of my head").
Trapping Bear.

**Miner, Virginia Scott**
Channel Water.
Elegy for Former Students.

**Minot, Laurence**
Halidon Hill.

**Minton, Helena**
Befriending the Weather.
Butterflies on an Illinois Road.
Croquet in Childhood.
Fireflies.
God, Woman, Egg.
Intimations at the Lake, 1963.
Mermaid.
Raccoon Skeleton at Long Plain Creek.
Womb Is Ruins, The.

**Minty, Judith**
Boundaries.
End of Summer, The.
Finding Roots.
Fourth of July Drowning, The.
Harbors.
Letters to My Daughters, 11.
Letters to My Daughters, 3.
Look to the Back of the Hand.
Palmistry for Blind Mariners.
Prowling the Ridge.

Spring Sequence.
Waiting for the Transformation.
**Mirabai**
At the Holi festival of color.
Clouds, The.
Friend, don't be angry.
Friend, how can I meet my lord?
Hari helps his people.
Hari, look at me a while.
I can't break with the Dark One.
I don't sleep. All night.
Keep me as your servant, O Girdhar.
Let me see you.
Mira is dancing with bells tied on her ankles.
My eyes are thirsty.
My love is in my house.
O King, I know you gave me poison.
Rana, I know you gave me poison.
Rana, why do you treat me as your enemy?
Wake, child with the flute.
Why Mira Can't Go Back to Her Old House.
Yogi, don't go away.
**Miranda, Gary**
Field Trip.
One That Got Away, The.
Sonnet for Salvador; or; One Could Do Worse than Be a Celery King.
**Mirikitani, Janice**
First Generation, The.
**Mistral, Gabriela** (*originally* **Lucila Godoy Alcayaga**)
Ballad: "He passed by with another."
Death Sonnet I.
Drops of Gall.
Dusk.
Everything Is Round.
God Wills It.
Midnight.
Sister.
Sleep Close to Me.
Slow Rain.
To Drink.
To Noel.
To See Him Again.
**Mitchell, Adrian**
Beggar, The.
Calypso's Song to Ulysses.
Celia Celia.
Child Is Singing, A.
Fifteen Million Plastic Bags.
Leaflets.
Norman Morrison.
Private Transport.
Quite Apart from the Holy Ghost.
Remember Suez?
Riddle: "Their tongues are knives, their forks are hands and feet."
Song about Mary.
You Get Used to It.
**Mitchell, Emerson Blackhorse**
Four Directions, The.
Miracle Hill.
New Direction, The.
Path I Must Travel, The.
**Mitchell, Joni**
Cactus Tree.
Chelsea Morning.
I Think I Understand.
Michael from Mountains.

Woodstock.
**Mitchell, Karen L.**
For Michael.
**Mitchell, Lucy Sprague**
House of the Mouse, The.
**Mitchell, Matthew**
Printing Jenny ("Printing Bibles is Jenny's daily chore").
**Mitchell, Nora**
Fisherman's Wife, The.
**Mitchell, Roger**
Riding with Some North Vietnamese Students in a Polish Elevator, 1966.
**Mitchell, Stephen**
Abraham.
Adam in Love.
Jacob and the Angel.
**Mitchell, Thomas**
Open Range.
**Mitchell, Walter**
Reefing Topsails.
**Mitchell, William R.**
Aboriginal Sin.
Benediction.
Benediction for Danny.
Christmas Prayer, A.
Epiphany on a Plot of Moonlight.
Had I but gone some forty days or more.
Requiem for Innocence, A.
Theoria in Early Morning.
**Mitsuhashi Takajo**
Hair ornament of the sun, The.
**Mitter, E.**
Heart Surgery.
Mood, A.
**Miyazawa, Kenji**
Moon, Son of Heaven.
Snow on Saddle Mountain, The.
**Miyoshi, Sekiya**
World Is Day-breaking, The.
**Mladinic, Peter**
Self-Interviews.
**Mocarski, Timothy P.**
City.
**Moffett, Judith**
Diehard.
Going to Press.
Other Woman.
Twinings Orange Pekoe.
**Moffi, Larry**
February.
Good Start, A.
Word Man, The.
**Moffitt, John**
To Look at Any Thing.
**Mohodahi**
On the holy day of your going out to war.
**Mohr, Joseph**
Silent Night! Holy Night!
**Mohr, William**
One Leg.
**Molière (Jean Baptiste Poquelin)**
Tartuffe; or, The Impostor.
**Moll, Ernest G.**
Eagles over the Lambing Paddock
Robbing the Tree Hive.
**Mollin, Larry**
As the World Turns.
Bunky Boy Bunky Boy Who's My Little Bunky Boy.

My Elbow Ancestry.
Signature.
Tubes.
Wash Day.
**Molodovsky [*or* Molodovski *or* Molodowsky], Kadya [*or* Kadia]**
And Yet.
In Life's Stable.
Jerusalem.
Night Visitors.
Song of the Sabbath.
**Molofsky, Merle**
Reflections.
**Momaday, N. Scott**
Angle of Geese.
Bear, The.
Blue.
But Then and There the Sun Bore Down.
Buteo Regalis.
Carriers of the Dream Wheel.
Colors of Night, The, *sel.*
Delight Song of Tsoai-Talee, The.
Eagle-feather Fan, The ("The Eagle is my power").
Earth and I Gave You Turquoise.
Forms of the Earth at Abiquiu.
Gourd Dancer, The.
Pit Viper.
Plainview: 3.
Rainy Mountain Cemetery.
Simile.
Story of a Well-made Shield, The.
To a Child Running with Outstretched Arms in the Canyon de Chelly.
Trees and Evening Sky.
Winter Holding off the Coast of North America.
Wise Empty Landscape with a Death in the Foreground.
**Mombert, Alfred**
Chimera, The.
**Monaghan, Pat**
Christmas at Vail: On Staying Indoors.
**Monette, Paul**
Bathing the Aged.
Degas.
Into the Dark.
**Monkhouse, Cosmo**
Master of Arts.
**Monks, Arthur W.**
Twilight's Last Gleaming.
**Monro, Harold**
Midnight Lamentation.
Milk for the Cat.
Overheard in a Saltmarsh.
Strange Meetings, *sel.*
Street Fight.
Terrible Door, The.
Thistledown.
**Monroe, Arthur W.**
Forest Fire, The.
Toll of the Desert, The.
**Monroe, Harriet**
Farewell, A: "Good-bye!—no, do not grieve that it is over."
In High Places.
Pine at Timber-Line, The.
**Montagu, Charles**
Story of the Pot and the Kettle, The.
**Montagu, Lady Mary Wortley**
Farewell to Bath.

**Montague** (continued)
Good Advice.
Lady's Resolve, The.
On the Death of Mrs. Bowes.
Receipt for the Vapours.
Saturday: The Small Pox.

**Montague, John**
All Legendary Obstacles.
Beginnings ("Beginnings of a language").
Beyond the Liss.
Cage, The.
Cave of Night, The, *sel.*
Chosen Light, The.
Country Fiddler, The.
Grafted Tongue, A.
Herbert Street Revisited.
Hymn to the New Omagh Road.
In Dedication.
Lament for the O'Neills.
Last Monster, The.
Like Dolmens round My Childhood, the
    Old People.
Murphy in Manchester.
New Siege, A: An Historical Meditation,
    *sel.*
Road's End, The.
Same Gesture, The.
Sentence for Konarak.
Special Delivery.
That Room.
Time Out.
Trout, The.
True Song, The.
Walking Late.
What a View He Has.
Wild Dog Rose, The.
Wild Sports of the West.
Windharp.

**Montale, Eugenio**
Eel, The.
Life's Evil.

**Montemayer, Carlos**
Heth.

**Montgomerie, Alexander**
Evin Dead Behold I Breathe, *sel.*
To His Mistress [*or* Maistres].

**Montgomerie, William**
Elegy for William Soutar.
Epitaph: "My brother is skull and
    skeleton now."

**Montgomery, Carol Artman**
Jimmy Bruder on Quincey Street.
Triangle Ladies, The.

**Montgomery, Countess of**   *See* **Wroth,**
    **Mary Sidney**

**Montgomery, Jack**
Addict.

**Montgomery, James**
At Home in Heaven.
Lift up your heads, ye gates of brass!

**Montgomery, Marion**
Aunt Emma, Uncle Al: A Short History
    of the South.

**Montgomery, Niall**
Eyewash.

**Montgomery, Whitney**
Death Rode a Pinto Pony.

**Montoya, José**
Forgive?

**Moody, Minnie Hite**
Say This of Horses.

**Moody, William Vaughn**
Gloucester Moors.

I Stood within the Heart of God, *with*
    *music.*
On a Soldier Fallen in the Philippines.

**Moon, Sheila**
Existence.

**Mooney, Stephen**
At the Airport in Dallas.

**Moore, Clement Clarke**
Lord of Life, All Praise Excelling, *with*
    *music.*
Visit from St. Nicholas, A.

**Moore, Daniel**
Diamond, The.

**Moore, Edward**
To the Right Hon. Henry Pelham.

**Moore, Honor**
Conversation in the Eighth Street
    Bookstore.
Mourning Pictures, *sel.*
My Mother's Moustache.
Tirade.

**Moore, James**
I Am the Man Who.
Rothko.

**Moore, Janice Townley**
Below Bald Mountain.
Out of Body.

**Moore, John**
Broken Gull, A.
Dingman's Marsh.
Gaggle of Geese, a Pride of Lions, A.
Squall.

**Moore, Julia A.**
And now, kind friends, what I have
    wrote.
Ashtabula Disaster.
Author's Early Life, The.
Grand Rapids.
Grand Rapids Cricket Club, *sel.*
Little Libbie.
Sketch of Lord Byron's Life.

**Moore, Lilian**
All Kinds of Shivers.
Do Ghouls?
I never saw/ a ghost on stilts.
I'm Skeleton.
No TV.
We Three.

**Moore, Marianne**
Arthur Mitchell.
Baseball and Writing.
Bear and the Garden-Lover, The.
Bird-witted.
Buffalo, The.
Carnegie Hall: Rescued.
Carriage from Sweden, A.
Critics and Connoisseurs.
Egyptian Pulled Glass Bottle in the
    Shape of a Fish, An.
England.
Enough.
Face, A.
Fish, The.
Frigate Pelican, The.
Granite and Steel.
Grave, A.
He "Digesteth Harde Yron."
Hero, The.
Hometown Piece for Messrs. Alston and
    Reese.
I May, I Might, I Must.
In Distrust of Merits.

In the Days of Prismatic Color.
In the Public Garden.
Jellyfish, A.
Like a Bulwark.
Love in America.
Marriage.
Melchior Vulpius.
Mind, Intractable Thing, The.
Mind Is an Enchanting Thing, The.
Monkeys, The.
Nevertheless.
New York.
No Swan So Fine.
Pangolin, The.
Paper Nautilus, The.
Part of a Novel, Part of a Poem, Part of
    a Play, *sels.*
Peter.
Pigeons.
Poetry.
Rigorists.
Saint Nicholas.
Silence.
Snakes, Mongooses, Snake-Charmers
    and the Like.
Sojourn in the Whale.
Spenser's Ireland.
St. Valentine.
Steeple-Jack, The.
Student, The.
Sun.
Talisman, A.
Tell Me, Tell Me.
That Harp You Play So Well.
Then the Ermine.
To a Snail.
To a Steam Roller.
W. S. Landor.
Walking-Sticks and Paperweights and
    Watermarks.
What Are Years?
Wood Weasel, The.

**Moore, Mary**
In the Cabin of Lost Fir Smells.
Li Po.
Salesman, The.
Seeding.

**Moore, Merrill**
How She Resolved to Act.
Transfusion.

**Moore, Nicholas**
Fivesucked the features of my girl by
    glory.
Island and the Cattle, The.
Patient, The.
Song: "Little onion lay by the fireplace,
    A."

**Moore, Richard**
Willy ("Willy, enormous Saskatchewan
    grizzly").

**Moore, Rosalie (Rosalie Moore Brown)**
After the Storm.
Imprecation for an Aesthetics Society
    with Newts, Warts, Waxes and Pins.
Letter to Belden.
Wheel, The.

**Moore, Thomas**
Argument, An.
At the Mid Hour of Night.
Believe Me, If All Those Endearing
    Young Charms.
Bendemeer's Stream.

Bird Let Loose, The.
Cherries, The, a Parable.
Child's Song.
Come, Ye Disconsolate.
Copy of an Intercepted Despatch from His Excellency Don Strepitoso Diabolo.
Did Not.
Epitaph on a Tuft-Hunter.
Epitaph on Robert Southey.
Fly to the desert, fly with me.
Fragment of a Character.
Fudge Family in Paris, The, *sel.*
Fum and Hum, the Two Birds of Royalty.
Harp That Once through Tara's Halls, The.
"I never nursed a dear gazelle."
I Saw from the Beach.
Irish Antiquities. ✓
Jasmine.
Joke Versified, A.
Last Rose of Summer, The.
Lying.
Minstrel Boy, The.
Nonsense.
O Thou Who Dry'st the Mourner's Tear.
Oft, in the Stilly Night.
On a Squinting Poetess.
Pastoral Ballad by John Bull, A.
Rhymes on the Road, *sel.*
Scene from a Play, Acted at Oxford, Called "Matriculation."
Song of Fionnuala, The.
Thee, Thee, Only Thee.
Thou Art, O God.
Time I've Lost in Wooing, The.
To Cara, after an Interval of Absence.
To Sir Hudson Lowe.
Tory Pledges.
What's My Thought Like?
When He Who Adores Thee.
Young May Moon, The.

**Moore, Thomas Sturge**
Daughter of Admetus, A.
On Harting Down.

**Moorman, Charles**
Lois in Concert.

**Moraes, Dom**
John Nobody.
Letter to My Mother.
Santa Claus.

**Moraff, Barbara**
Let us suppose the mind.

**Moran, Michael ("Zozimus")**
Pharao's Daughter.

**Mordaunt, Thomas Osbert**
Sound, Sound the Clarion.
Verses Written during the War, 1756–1763, *sel.*

**More, Henry**
Psychathanasia; or, The Second Part of the Song of the Soul, *sel.*
Psychozoia; or, The First Part of the Song of the Soul, *sels.*

**More, Sir Thomas (Saint Thomas More)**
Measure of Love, The.
Mery Gest How a Sergeaunt Wolde Lerne to Be a Frere, A.
Pageant Verses.
Prayer, A: "Grant, I thee pray, such heat into mine heart."

Rueful Lamentation, A.

**Moreh, Shmuel**
Melody.
Return, The.
Tree of Hatred, The.

**Morehead, Albert** *and* James Morehead
What Shall I Pray for Today? *with music.*

**Morejón, Nancy**
Central Park *Some People (3 P.M.).*

**Moreland, Jane P.**
Argument, The.
Pony Girl.

**Moreland, John Richard**
If I Could Grasp a Wave from the Great Sea.

**Moreland, Wayne**
Sunday Morning.

**Moreno, Tony**
For Yvonne, My Daughter.
Memories.
Miracle.
Salsa.
Wealth.

**Morgan, Albert**
Union Man.

**Morgan, Edwin**
Addition to the Family, An.
Canedolia.
Computer's First Christmas Card, The.
Death in Duke Street.
Fado.
Floating off to Timor.
French Persian Cats Having a Ball.
Good Friday.
In Glasgow.
In the Snack-Bar.
Instamatic.
King Billy.
Message Clear.
Oban Girl.
Opening the Cage: 14 Variations on 14 Words.
Pomander.
Siesta of a Hungarian Snake.
Strawberries.
To Hugh MacDiarmid.
Trio.
Woman, The.

**"Morgan, Emanuel."** *See* **Bynner, Witter**

**Morgan, Frederick**
Alexander.
Castle Rock.
Choice, The.
February 11, 1977.
From a Diary.
I Saw My Darling.
Legend.
Orpheus to Eurydice.

**Morgan, James Appleton**
Malum Opus.

**Morgan, Jean**
Misogynist, The.

**Morgan, Jenny**
Dyke, The.
Life-Style.

**Morgan, John**
Psychoanalysis of Fire, The.
Then.

**Morgan, Pete**
Big Hat or What, A?
White Stallion, The.

**Morgan, Robert**

Art Lesson, The.
Asylum for War Victims.
Birth of a Poet.
Black Railings.
Blood Donor.
Book of Stones.
Champion.
Choice, The.
Cwm above Penrhiwceiber, The.
Dark Corner.
Derelict Valley.
Dickens Characters.
Free Coal.
Hogpen.
Huw's Farm.
Men in Black.
Mirror Farming.
Mountain Bride.
Nightwatchman.
Reuben's Cabin.
Steep.
Strangers, The.
Topsoil.
Valley.

**Morgan, Robin**
Invisible Woman, The.
Lesbian Poem.
Matrilineal Descent.
News.
Quotations from Charwoman Me.

**Morgenstern, Christian**
Aesthete Weasel, The.
Funnels, The.
Knee on Its Own, The.
Korf's Clock.
Moonsheep, The.
On the Planet of Flies.
Philosophy Is Born.
Salmon, The.
Snail's Monologue, The.

**Morhange, Pierre**
Jew.
Lullaby in Auschwitz.

**Morice, Dave**
Apple.
Dread.
Eightball.
In the Middle of a Wind Tunnel.
In the Water.
Much Obliged.
My Brother.
On the Death of W. H. Auden.
They End It.
This Is to Signify.

**Möricke, Eduard**
Beauty Rohtraut.
Written on an Egg.

**Morison, Ted**
Avis.

**Moritake, Arakida**
Haiku: "Falling flower, The."

**Moritz, Yunna**
In Memory of Francois Rabelais.
Snow-Girl.
Whiteness.

**Morley, Christopher**
Animal Crackers.
Elegy Written in a Country Coal-Bin.
Forever Ambrosia.
Of an Ancient Spaniel in Her Fifteenth Year.
Old Swimmer, The.

Song for a Little House.
**Morley, Hilda**
Shirt, The.
**Morley, Jeff**
Dawn of Me, The.
**Morley, Thomas**
Sing We and Chant It.
**Moronelli da Fiorenza, Pier**
Canzonetta: A Bitter Song to His Lady.
**Morowitz, Harold J.**
To the Humpback Whales.
**Morpurgo, Rahel**
Woe is me, my soul says, how bitter is
  my fate.
**Morris, George Pope**
Woodman Spare That Tree.
**Morris, J. W.**
What I Think of Hiawatha.
**Morris, John N.**
Child's Nativity, A.
Fathers, The.
Hating Your Life.
In the Hamptons.
Letter from a Friend, A.
Mirror, The.
My Children's Book.
One Snowy Night in December.
Right to Life, The.
Running It Backward.
Thanksgiving.
Three.
**Morris, Lewis**
Poem of the Frost and Snow.
**Morris, Madge**
In the Yucca Land.
¿Quien Sabe?
To the Colorado Desert.
**Morris, William**
All for the Cause.
Apology, An.
August.
Blue Closet, The.
Day of Days, The.
Defence of Guenevere, The.
Earthly Paradise, The, *sels.*
Eve of Crecy, The.
February.
Garden by the Sea, A.
Haystack in the Floods, The.
Iceland First Seen.
June.
L'Envoi: "Here we are for the last time
  face to face."
Life and Death of Jason, The, *sel.*
Love Is Enough, *sel.*
March ("He ended; and midst those who
  heard were some").
Masters in This Hall.
May ("O love, this morn when the sweet
  nightingale").
Near Avalon.
October ("O love, turn from the
  unchanging sea, and gaze").
Old Love.
Outlanders, The.
Pilgrims of Hope, The, *sel.*
Riding Together.
Scenes from the Fall of Troy.
Sending to the War.
Shameful Death.
Summer Dawn.
Thunder in the Garden.

Two Red Roses across the Moon.
Wanderers, The.
Written in a Copy of "The Earthly
  Paradise," Dec. 25, 1870.
**Morris-Jones, John**
North Star, The.
Old Age.
Wind's Lament, The.
**Morrison, Lillian ("Lee Murchison")**
In the beginning was the/ Kickoff.
Of Kings and Things.
**Morse, Heather**
Curtain World.
**Morse, Samuel French**
Song in the Cold Season.
**Morstein, Petra von**
Anthology Poem.
For one who says he feels.
In the Case of Lobsters.
Justice.
. . .1968. . .
Thing Poem.
**Mortimer, Charlotte**
Pioneers, The.
Spring Revue.
**Morton, Bruce**
High Plains Harvest.
**Morton, David**
Mariners.
Old Ships.
**Morton, John Bingham ("Beachcomber")**
Dancing Cabman, The.
Epitaph: "Glassblower lies here at rest,
  A."
Epitaph: "Tread softly; bid a solemn
  music sound."
Health and Fitness.
Let poets praise the softer winds of
  spring.
Lovely Big Cow.
Now We Are Sick.
To a Lady.
**Morus, Huw**
In Praise of a Girl.
**Mosby, George, Jr.**
Birthday: Tara Regina.
**Moschus**
Cupid a Plowman.
Pan loved his neighbour Echo—but that
  child.
When winds that move not its calm
  surface sweep.
**Mosen, Julius**
Legend of the Crossbill, The.
**Moses, Daniel David**
Fall Song.
Hands, The.
**Moses, William Robert**
Angina Pectoris.
Impulse of October, The.
Little-League Baseball Fan.
Nature of Jungles, The.
Night Wind in Fall.
Sitting in the Woods: A Contemplation.
**Moskowitz, Lynn**
Nightmares: Part Three.
**Moss, Howard**
Adolescent's Song.
Burning Love Letters.
Cats and Dogs.
Dead Leaf, A.
Elegy for My Father.

Game of Chance, A.
Gift to Be Simple, The.
Going to Sleep in the Country.
Hand, The.
Horror Movie.
King Midas.
Long Island Night, The.
Long Island Springs.
Refrigerator, The.
Roof Garden, The.
Water Island.
Waterwall Blues.
**Moss, Stanley**
Apocrypha.
Clams.
Exchange of Hats, An.
God Poem.
Hangman's Love Song, The.
Prayer: "Give me a death like Buddha's,
  let me fall."
Return, The.
Sailing from the United States.
SM.
Scroll.
Two Fishermen.
Voice.
**Mossman, Bina**
I'm going to California.
**Mother Goose**
A Apple-pie.
A was an apple-pie.
All of a row.
As I was going to St. Ives.
As Tommy Snooks and Bessy Brooks.
Baa, baa, black sheep, have you any
  wool?
Baby, baby, naughty baby.
Barber, barber, shave a pig.
Birds of a feather flock together.
Bobby Shaftoe's gone to sea.
Bye, baby bunting./ Daddy's gone a-
  hunting.
Carrion crow sat on an oak, A.
Cat came fiddling out of a barn, A.
Cock-a-doodle-doo!
Cock doth crow, the wind doth blow,
  The.
Come, let's to bed.
Come when you're called.
Cross Patch/ Lift [*or* Draw] the latch.
Cry, baby, cry,/ Put your finger in your
  eye.
Curly locks! curly locks! wilt thou be
  mine?
Daffy-down-dilly [*or* Daffadowndilly] has
  come up to town.
Dance to your daddy.
Danty, baby, diddy.
Deedle, deedle, dumpling, my son John.
Dillar, a dollar, A,/ A ten o'clock
  scholar.
Ding, dong, bell/ Pussy's in the well!
Doctor Faustus was a good man.
Doctor Foster went to Glo'ster.
Elizabeth, Elspeth, Betsy, and Bess.
Fair maid who, [on] the first of May,
  The.
Farmer went riding [*or* trotting] upon his
  gray mare, A.
For want of a nail, the shoe was lost.
Four and twenty tailors went to kill a
  snail.

Frog he would a-wooing go, A.
Georgie Porgie, pudding and pie.
Girls and boys, come out to play.
Goosey, goosey, gander,/ Whither shall I wander?
Great A, little a.
Hark, hark, the dogs do bark.
Hector Protector was dressed all in green.
Here am I, little jumping Joan.
Here we go round the mulberry bush.
Hey [or High] diddle, diddle,/ The cat and the fiddle.
Hickety, Pickety,/ My black hen.
Hickory, dickory, dock.
Hot cross buns!
How many days has my baby to play?
How many miles to Babylon.
Humpty Dumpty sat on a wall.
Hush-a-bye, baby, on the tree top.
I had a little nut tree.
I had a little pony.
I love sixpence, pretty [or jolly] little sixpence.
I saw a ship a-sailing.
I saw three ships come sailing by.
If all the seas were one sea.
If all the world was apple-pie.
If I'd as much money as I could spend.
If wishes were horses.
I'll tell you a story.
Intry, mintry, cutry corn.
Jack and Jill went up the hill.
Jack be nimble.
Jack Sprat could eat no fat.
Johnny shall have a new bonnet.
Lady bird, lady bird, fly away home.
Lady-bug, lady-bug.
Lion and the unicorn, The.
Little Betty Blue.
Little Bo-Peep has lost her sheep.
Little Boy Blue, come, blow [up] your horn.
Little cock-sparrow sat on a green tree, A.
Little Dicky Dilver.
Little Jack Horner/ Sat in a corner.
Little Miss Muffett.
Little Nancy Etticoat.
Little Poll Parrot/ Sat in his garret.
Little Polly Flinders.
Little priest of Felton, The.
Little Robin Red-breast sat upon a tree.
Little Tom Tucker.
Long legs, crooked thighs.
Lucy Lockett lost her pocket.
Man in the wilderness asked [of] me, The [or A].
Mary, Mary, quite contrary.
Monday's child [or bairn] is fair of face.
Needles and pins, needles and pins.
North wind doth blow, The.
O, the grand old Duke of York.
Old King Cole.
Old Mother Goose, when.
"Old woman, old woman, shall we go shearing?"
Once I saw a little bird.
One misty, moisty morning.
One, two/ Buckle my shoe.
One, two, three, four.
Pat-a-cake, pat-a-cake, baker's man!

Pease-pudding hot.
Peter Piper picked a peck of pickled pepper.
Polly put the kettle on.
Poor old Robinson Crusoe!
Pussy-cat, pussy-cat, where have you been?
Queen of Hearts, The/ She made some tarts.
Ride a cock-horse to Banbury Cross.
Robin and Richard were two pretty men.
Rock-a-bye baby, on [or in] the tree top.
Rock-a-bye, baby, thy cradle is green.
Rub a dub dub,/ Three men in a tub.
Rule of the road is a paradox quite, The.
See, saw, Margery Daw,/ Johnny shall have a new master.
See-saw sacradown,/ which is the way to London town?
Simple Simon met a pieman.
Sing a song of sixpence.
Sing, sing, what shall I sing?
Smiling girls, rosy boys.
Sneeze on a Monday, sneeze for danger.
Solomon Grundy.
Some little mice sat in a barn to spin.
Spring is showery, flowery, bowery.
Taffy was a Welshman, Taffy was a thief.
Tell tale, tit!
There was a crooked man, and he went a crooked mile.
There was a little boy and a little girl.
There was a little man/ And he had a little gun.
There was an old woman/ Lived under a hill.
There was an old woman, and what do you think?
There was an old woman, as I've heard tell.
There was an old woman called Nothing-at-all.
There was an old woman tossed up in a basket.
There was an old woman who lived in a shoe.
Thirty days hath September.
This is the house that Jack built.
This is the way the ladies ride:/ Tri, tre, tre, tree.
This little pig went to market.
Three blind mice.
Three little mice sat down to spin.
To market, to market/ To buy a plum cake.
To market, to market, to buy a fat pig.
Tom, Tom, the piper's son.
Tweedle-dum and Tweedle-dee.
Upon my word and honour.
What are little boys made of, made of.
When good King Arthur ruled this land.
When I was a bachelor, I lived by myself.
Who killed Cock Robin?
Willful waste brings woeful want.
**Mott, Michael**
Islanders, Inlanders.
Meadow Grass.
**Moul, Keith**
Playing Catch.

**Mounsey, Messenger**
Here lie my old bones: my vexation now ends.
**Movius, Geoffrey**
Work-out, The.
**Moxley, Rubee Dreher**
Ol' Tim Legion.
Saturday Night.
6th and Walnut Street.
**Mozeen, Thomas**
Kilruddery Hunt, The.
**Mozeson, Isaac Elchanan**
Masada.
**Mririda n'Ait Attik**
God Hasn't Made Room.
Like Smoke.
**Mudie, Ian**
This Land.
**Mueller, Lisel**
Alive Together.
Civilizing the Child.
Farewell, a Welcome, A.
Gift of Fire, The.
Historical Museum, Manitoulin Island.
Life of a Queen.
Mermaid, The.
Night Song.
Nude by Edward Hopper, A.
Palindrome.
Small Poem about the Hounds and the Hares.
Voice from Out of the Night, A.
Weaver, The.
Yes, we were happy that Sunday, walking.
**Mühlenberg, William Augustus**
I Would Not Live Alway, *with music.*
Saviour, Who Thy Flock Art Feeding, *with music.*
**Muhringer, Doris**
Questions and Answers.
**Muir, Alexander**
Maple Leaf Forever, The, *with music.*
**Muir, E. A.**
Gulls.
**Muir, Edwin**
Absent, The.
Animals, The.
Annunciation, The.
Ballad of Hector in Hades.
Birthday, A.
Border, The.
Brothers, The.
Child Dying, The.
Childhood.
Combat, The.
Commemoration, The.
Confirmation, The.
Finder Found, The.
Gate, The.
Good Town, The.
Horses, The ("Barely a twelvemonth after").
Horses ("Those lumbering horses in the steady plough").
In Love for Long.
Interrogation, The.
Island, The.
Labyrinth, The.
Little General, The.
Love's Remorse.

Mary Stuart.
Merlin.
Myth, The.
Mythical Journey, The.
Oedipus.
One Foot in Eden.
Refugees, The.
Return, The ("The doors flapped open in Ulysses' house").
Return, The ("The veteran Greeks came home").
Rider Victory, The.
River, The.
Road, The.
Scotland 1941.
Scotland's Winter.
Song: "Why should your face so please me."
Suburban Dream.
Sufficient Place, The.
Three Mirrors, The.
Town Betrayed, The.
Troy.
Usurpers, The.
Wayside Station, The.
Wheel, The.

**Muir, John**
From garden to garden, ridge to ridge.

**Mukta Bai**
Although he has no form.
I live where darkness/ is not.

**Mulac, Jim**
Afternoon at the Movies.
Caller, The.
Cars.
Coffee Den, Cedar Rapids, The.
Elegy for Duke Ellington.
Feeling You Again.
Girl Clings to Coma.
Saturday Night Out.
Things to Work For.
War Poem.

**Muldoon, Paul**
Armageddon, Armageddon, sel.
Clonfeacle.
Dancers at the Moy.
Electric Orchard, The.
Elizabeth.
Field Hospital, The.
Hedgehog.
Indians on Alcatraz, The.
Lives of the Saints.
Macha.
Mules.

**Mullen, Harryette**
Saturday Afternoon, When Chores Are Done.

**Mulligan, J. B.**
Deja Vu.

**Mullins, Cecil J.**
Enemy, Enemy.

**Mulrine, Stephen**
Coming of the Wee Malkies, The.
Woman's Complaint.

**Mumford, Marilyn R.**
Recollection.

**Mumin, Hossan Sheikh**
Women and Men.

**Munday, Anthony**
Beauty Bathing.
I serve a mistress whiter than the snow.

Primaleon of Greece, sel.

**Munkittrick, Richard Kendall**
Bulb, A.
Unsatisfied Yearning.

**Munro, Bruce Weston**
Grandmother's Apple Pies.

**Munro, Deborah**
Sequence for a Young Widow Passing.
Song of the Strange Young Duckling.

**Mura, David**
Christmas Gift, A.

**Murano, Shiro**
Diving.

**Murasaki Shikibu, Lady**
Someone passes.
Tale of Genji, The, sel.

**Muratori, Fred**
Real Muse, The.

**Murawski, Elisabeth**
Deed.
Person to Person.
Skid Row Safari.

**"Murchison, Lee."** *See* **Morrison, Lillian**

**Murguia, Alejandro**
Dreams of Lost Atlantis.
Sweet Soledad.

**Murphey, Joseph Colin**
Silver Racer, The.

**Murphy, Donal**
Old Man of the Sea.

**Murphy, George E., Jr.**
Conestoga.

**Murphy, Liam**
For Fear of Waking the Alarm Clock.
Life to Let.

**Murphy, Richard**
Battle of Aughrim, The, sels.
Droit de Seigneur.
Enigma.
Epitaph on a Fir-Tree.
Girl at the Seaside.
High Island.
Little Hunger.
Pat Cloherty's Version of *The Maisie*.
Philosopher and the Birds, The.
Planter.
Poet on the Island, The.
Rapparees.
Reading Lesson, The.
Sailing to an Island.
Seals at High Island.
Trouvaille.
Walking on Sunday.
Woman of the House, The.

**Murray, Anne B.**
Frost round the House.

**Murray, G. E.**
Driving Wheels, The.
Pavement Artist, A.
Plant Rhythms, The.
Southern Exposures.

**Murray, Joan**
Crocus.

**Murray, John**
Hark! 'Tis the Saviour of Mankind, *with music*.

**Murray, Les A.**
Absolutely Ordinary Rainbow, An.
Artery, The.
Ballad of Jimmy Governor, The.
Birds in Their Title Work Freeholds of Straw.

Blood.
Buladelah-Taree Holiday Song Cycle, The.
Death Words.
Names of the Humble, The.
New England Farm, August 1914, A.
Princes' Land, The.
Sanskrit.
Senryu.
SMLE.
Telling the Cousins.
Walking to the Cattle-Place, sels.

**Murray, Paul**
Introit.
Kind of Palmistry, A.
Rain.

**Murray, Pauli**
Dark Testament.
Death of a Friend.
For Mack C. Parker.
Harlem Riot, 1943.
Mr. Roosevelt Regrets.
Ruth.
Without Name.

**Murray, Philip**
Heron, The.

**Murray, Robert Fuller**
Andrew M'Crie.
Every critic in the town.

**Murray, Susan**
Sailing.

**Murry, Ann**
Familiar Epistle, A.

**Mus, David**
Conserves.
Joy of Cooking, The, sel.

**Musella, Douglas**
Re-forming a Monument.

**Muske, Carol**
Child with Six Fingers.
Found.
Hyena.
Invention of Cuisine, The.
Rice.
Swansong.

**Mutis, Alvaro**
Amen.
Lied in Crete.

**Muuse, Abdillaahi**
Elder's Reproof to His Wife, An.

**Mycall, John**
Our States, O Lord, *with music*.

**Myers, Garry Cleveland**
Dear God,/ When someone tries to make me do.
Talking to God.

**Myers, Jack**
Apprentice Painter, The.
Day of Atonement.
Minyan, The.
Mirror for the Barnyard.
Mockingbird, Copy This.
So Long Solon.
Too Many Miles of Sunlight between Us.
When I Held You to My Chest, You Fit.
Winging It.

**Mylonas, Eva**
Holidays.

# N

**"N., A."**
Ascent of T.J. Jackson: A Soldier's Tale.
**Nabokov, Vladimir**
Literary Dinner, A.
Ode to a Model.
Wanted, Wanted: Dolores Haze.
**Nadel, Alan**
To Summer.
**Nagase Kiyoko**
Mother.
**Naggid, Hayim**
After the War.
Like a Pearl.
My Mother.
Snow in Jerusalem, A.
**Nagy, Agnes Nemes**
Bird.
I Carried Statues.
Storm.
Words to a Song.
**Naidu, Sarojini**
Snake-Charmer, The.
**Naigreshel, Mendel**
Nation.
What Will Remain after Me?
**Nairne, Carolina Oliphant, Baroness**
Charlie Is My Darling.
Laird o' Cockpen, The.
Land o' the Leal, The.
**Nakasuk**
Gull, it is said, The.
Invocation: "Land earth-root."
**Namanworth, Elaine**
Fishermen's Wives, The.
**Nance, Berta Hart**
Cattle.
Road to Texas, The.
**Naone, Dana**
Girl with the Green Skirt.
House of Light, The.
I make all the poetic pauses.
Long Distance.
Men Whose Tongues, The.
Old Photograph, The.
Presence, The.
Sleep.
Sunday Service.
Two.
**Napa**
Darkened in the Soul.
**Narihira (Ariwara no Narihira)**
I Have Always Known.
**Nash, Ogden**
Abominable Snowman, The.
Adventures of Isabel.
Amorous Señor, The.
Anatomy of Happiness, The.
Ant, The.
Boy Who Laughed at Santa Claus, The.
Bubba Smith.
Calling Spring VII–MMMC.
Co-ed protester named Lil, A.
Columbus.
Common Sense.
Confessions of a Born Spectator.
Consider the Auk.
Dick Szymanski.
Dog, The.

Dog's Best Friend Is His Illiteracy, A.
Drink with Something in It, A.
Duck, The.
First Families Move Over!
Genealogical Reflection.
Ha! Original Sin.
Hamster, The.
Handsome young rodent named Gratian, A.
Hearts of Gold.
Horrors, The.
Hunter, The.
Invocation: "Senator Smoot (Republican, Ut.)."
Kind of an Ode to Duty.
Kindly Unhitch That Star, Buddy.
Lama, The.
Lines to a World-famous Poet Who Failed to Complete a World-famous Poem; or, Come Clean, Mr. Guest!
Listen.
Love under the Republicans (or · Democrats).
Mel Allen, Mel Allen, Lend Me Your Cliché.
Mr. Artesian's Conscientiousness.
Morning Prayer.
New Nutcracker Suite, The, *sel.*
Octopus, The.
Old Men.
Panther, The.
Porcupine, The.
Portrait of the Artist as a Prematurely Old Man.
Poultries, The.
Private Dining Room, The.
Purist, The.
Reflection on a Wicked World.
Reflections on Ice-Breaking.
Reminiscent Reflection.
Rhinoceros, The.
Romantic Age, The.
Sea-Gull, The.
Song of the Open Road.
Song to Be Sung by the Father of Infant Female Children.
Tallyho-Hum.
Terrible People, The.
There Was a Young Lady of Rome.
They Don't Speak English in Paris.
Thrifty Soprano, A.
Tom Matte.
Turtle, The.
Two Dogs Have I.
Ultimate Reality.
Up from the Egg: The Confessions of a Nuthatch Avoider.
Very like a Whale.
Wendigo, The.
Who Taught Caddies to Count? or, A Burnt Golfer Fears the Child.
Winter Morning.
Word to Husbands, A.
Young Lady from Cork, A.
**Nash, Valery**
Working for Dr. No.
**Nashe [or Nash], Thomas**
Adieu, Farewell Earth's Bliss.
Autumn.
Rich Man, Trust Now.
Spring.
Summer's Last Will and Testament, *sels.*

**Nathan, Leonard**
Ellora.
Fourth Dimension, The.
Likeness, The.
Niño Leading an Old Man to Market.
One for the Fatherland.
Return, The.
Short Pastoral.
To a Foreign Friend.
Yours Truly.
**Nathan, Norman**
Investment.
Modern Architecture.
Voting Machine.
**Nathan, Robert**
Christian, Be Up, *with music.*
**Naylor, James Ball**
David and Solomon.
**Neagle, Dennis**
I Caught This Morning at Dawning.
**Neal, Larry**
Harlem Gallery: From the Inside.
James Powell on Imagination.
Malcolm X—An Autobiography.
**Neaves, Lord Charles**
Let Us All be Unhappy on Sunday.
**Negri, Ada**
Make Way!
**Neidus, Leib**
I Love the Woods.
I Often Want to Let My Lines Go.
In an Alien Place.
**Neihardt, John G.**
Death of Crazy Horse, The.
Red Cloud.
**Neilson, John Shaw**
Beauty Imposes.
Crane Is My Neighbour, The.
Hour of the Parting, The.
Little Militant, The.
Man Who Prayed, The.
May.
Native Companions Dancing.
Old Man in the Autumn, The.
Orange Tree, The.
Poor Can Feed the Birds, The.
Poor, Poor Country, The.
Smoker Parrot, The.
Song Be Delicate.
Sweetening of the Year, The.
Walking of the Moon-Woman, The.
You Cannot Go Down to the Spring.
**Nelson, Alice Dunbar**
Sonnet: "I had no thought of violets of late."
**Nelson, David**
My Days are Gliding Swiftly By
**Nelson, Howard**
Cows near the Graveyard, The.
Winter Night, Cold Spell.
**Nelson, Paul**
Average Night, The.
Shaman.
**Nelson, Peter**
Family Reunion.
Graveyard in Oberammergau, 1960, A.
Pin Ball Angel.
Quai de l'Horloge.
Sharktooth Creek.
**Nelson, Rodney**
Anabasis.
**Nelson, Sharon**

Pedlar.
**Nelson, Stanley**
Immigrants.
**Nelson, W. Dale**
O Rare!
**Nemerov, Howard**
Absent-minded Professor.
Blue Swallows, The.
Boom!
Brainstorm.
Brief Journey West, The.
Central Park.
Ceremony.
Creation of Anguish.
Dial Tone, The.
Distances They Keep, The.
Dragonfly, The.
Dream of Flying Comes of Age, The.
Elegy for a Nature Poet.
Epigrams, I-IX.
Fall Again, The.
First Day, The.
Flame of a Candle, The.
Fugue.
Ginkgoes in Fall.
Goldfish.
"Good-bye," said the river, "I'm going
   downstream."
Goose Fish, The.
Grace to Be Said at the Supermarket.
Great Society, Mark X, The.
History of a Literary Movement.
Holding the Mirror Up to Nature.
Human Condition, The.
I Only Am Escaped Alone to Tell Thee.
Icehouse in Summer, The.
Keeping Informed in D.C.
Learning by Doing.
Life, A.
Life Cycle of Common Man.
Lobsters.
Lot Later.
Make Love Not War.
May Day Dancing, The.
Moment.
Money.
Mousemeal.
Murder of William Remington, The.
Picture, A.
Power to the People.
Primer of the Daily Round, A.
Print-out, The.
Remorse for Time, The.
Santa Claus.
Scales of the Eyes, The.
Second-best Bed, The.
September, the First Day of School.
Sigmund Freud.
Singular Metamorphosis, A.
Sparrow in the Zoo, The.
Speculation.
Statues in the Public Gardens, The.
Storm Windows.
Style.
Tapestry, The.
This, That and the Other.
Three Towns, The.
To D——, Dead by Her Own Hand.
To the Governor & Legislature of
   Massachusetts.
Town Dump, The.
Truth.

Two Girls.
View from an Attic Window, The.
Waiting Rooms.
Western Approach, The.
Winter Exercise.
**Nerber, John**
Castaway.
**Neruda, Pablo (***originally* **Neftalí Ricardo
   Reyes Basualto)**
Always.
Body of a woman, white hills, white
   thigh.
Drunk as drunk on turpentine.
Enigmas.
Fable of the Mermaid and the Drunks.
Fear.
Fickle One, The.
Full October.
Girls.
I remember you as you were that final
   autumn.
Love.
Nothing but Death.
Ode to My Socks.
Ode to Salt.
Ode to the Watermelon.
Queen, The.
To Silvestre Revueltas of Mexico, in His
   Death.
Tonight I can write the saddest line.
Walking Around.
**Nerval, Gérard de (Gérard Labrunie)**
Delfica.
Golden.
Golden Lines.
Spook Sheep.
**Nesbit, Edith (Edith Nesbit Bland)**
Child's Song in Spring.
Mr. Ody met a body.
Things That Matter, The.
**Netser, Eli**
My Best Clothes.
**Nettelbeck, F. A.**
New Streets.
**Neufeld, Ernest**
At Masada.
**Neugass, James**
Before Battle: [The Lincolns at
   Villanueva de la Canada].
Convoy.
Give Us This Day.
Thalassa, Thalassa.
To the Trade.
Will and Testament.
**Neugroschel, Joachim**
Doves.
Eve's Advice to the Children of Israel.
**Neville, Mary**
Social Studies.
**Nevin, Edwin H.**
When Our Earthly Sun Is Setting, *with
   music.*
**Newbery, John**
Base-Ball.
**Newbery, Thomas**
Great Merchant, Dives Pragmaticus,
   Cries His Wares, The, *sel.*
**Newbolt, Sir Henry**
Admiral Death.
Admirals All.
Cities Drowned.
Commemoration.

Day's End.
Drake's Drum.
From Generation to Generation.
He Fell among Thieves.
Ireland, Ireland.
Master and Man.
Song: "Flowers that in thy garden rise,
   The."
Vitaï Lampada.
**Newcastle, Margaret Cavendish, Duchess of**
Bigness of Atoms, The.
Convent of Pleasure, The, *sel.*
Epigraph to the Theme of Love.
Fort or Castle of Hope, The, *sel.*
Hunting of the Hare, The, *sel.*
Mirth and Melancholy.
Nature's Cook, *sel.*
Nature's Dessert, *sel.*
Nature's Landskip, *sel.*
Nature's Prospect.
Of Loose Atoms.
On a Melting Beauty.
Song: "My cabinets are oyster-shells."
Soul's Garment, The.
Sweet marmalade of kisses newly
   gathered.
What Makes Echo.
**Newcastle, William Cavendish, Duke of**
Love's Flowers.
Love's Preparation.
Love's Vision.
Unexpressible Love, The.
**Newcomb, Bobby**
Big Sunflower, The, *with music.*
**Newcombe, Rosemarie**
At last I bless the hours.
**Newell, Mike**
Prayer: "Your golden loins slake my lust
   for treasures."
**Newell, Robert Henry.** *See* **"Kerr,
   Orpheus C."**
**Newlove, John**
First Time, The.
Grass Is a Reasonable Colour, The.
Of My Own Flesh.
Succubi.
Verigin, Moving in Alone.
Verigin 3.
Well-Travelled Roadway, The.
**Newman, Edward**
Insect Hunter, The, *sel.*
**Newman, John Henry, Cardinal**
Angel ("Softly and gently, dearly-
   ransomed soul").
Dream of Gerontius, The, *sels.*
Matins—Friday.
Matins—Sunday.
Pillar of [*or* and] the Cloud, The.
**Newman, Joseph S.**
Miss Tillie McLush.
Serpentine Verse.
**Newman, Michael**
Negative Passage.
**Newman, P. B.**
Great Bear, The.
**Newman, Paul Baker**
Mr. Cherry.
Skimmers.
Washington on the Constitutional
   Journey: 1791.
**Newsome, Mary Effie Lee**
Morning Light (The Dew-Drier).

Sassafras Tea.

**Newton, John**
Amazing Grace.
Mary to Her Savior's Tomb.
Name of Jesus, The.

**Neyroud, Gerard**
Skunk to the Gnu, The.

**Nezalhualcoyotl**
In vain was I born.

**Niatum, Duane**
After the Death of an Elder Klallam.
Ascending Red Cedar Moon.
Chief Leschi of the Nisqually.
Crow's Way.
Elegy for Chief Sealth.
Homage to Chagall.
Indian Rock, Bainbridge Island,
   Washington.
No One Remembers Abandoning the
   Village of White Fir.
Novelty Shop, The.
Old Woman Awaiting the Greyhound
   Bus.
On Hearing the Marsh Bird's Water Cry.
On Leaving Baltimore.
On Visiting My Son, Port Angeles,
   Washington.
Owl Seen in Rearview Mirror.
Separation.
Slow Dancer That No One Hears but
   You.
Songs from the Maker of Totems.
To Your Question.
Visitor, The.

**Nibbelink, Cynthia**
Black Lake.
Gypsies.
How Can I Say It Any Other Way.
Motive for Metaphor, The.
Out of the Gaping Distance.

**Nibbelink, Herman**
Meyer and I, we drove.

**Nicholas, Virginia Real**
South of the Border.

**Nichols, Jeanette**
Kind of Love, A.
Mostly People.
My Father Toured the South.
Same Lady, The.
Someone Gone Away Downstairs.

**Nichols, Robert**
Harlots' Catch.

**Nicholson, Kenneth "Spider"**
Diagnostic Center.
Letter.
Letter Home, A.

**Nicholson, Norman**
Caedmon.
Cleator Moor.
On the Closing of Millom Ironworks.
Rising Five.
Song at Night.
To the River Duddon.
Wales.
Weather Ear.

**Ní Chonaill , Eibhlín Dhubh.** *See*
   **O'Connell, Eibhlin Dubh**

**Ní Chuilleanáin, Eiléan**
Apparition, The.
Celibates.
Dead Fly.
Going Back to Oxford.

Lucina Schynning in Silence of the
   Night.
Old Roads.
Site of Ambush, *sel.*
Swineherd.
Wash.

**Nicoïdski, Clarisse**
Eyes.
Mouth.
Open Earth.
Remembering.

**Nicoletta, Peter**
My Father's House.

**Nicolson, Adela Florence Cory.** *See*
   **"Hope, Laurence"**

**Niditch, B. Z.**
Passover Dachau.
Return to Dachau.

**Niedecker, Lorine**
As praiseworthy/ the power of
   breathing.
For best work.
In the great snowfall before the bomb.
My mother saw the green tree toad.
Old man who seined.
Old Mother turns blue and from us.
Paean to Place.
River-march-drowse.
Smile/ to see the lake.
Two Old Men.
You are my friend.
Young in Fall I said: the birds.

**Nielson, Veneta**
Familiar.

**Nietzsche, Friedrich**
To the Unknown God.

**Nihoniho, Tuta**
Government!

**Nikolay, Sonja**
Witches' Menu.

**Niles, Nathaniel**
Bunker Hill, *with music.*

**Nims, John Frederick**
Clock without Hands.
Conclusion: "If what began (look far
   and wide) will end."
Decline and Fall.
D.O.M., A.D. 2167.
Girl Marcher.
Love and Death.
Love Poem: "My clumsiest dear, whose
   hands shipwreck vases."
Midwest.
Nature Lover.
Our Hero.
Parting: 1940.
Visiting Poet.
Young Ionia, The.

**Nist, John**
Made to See.
Sings a Bird.
Villanelle: "Like twilight bleeding on a
   winter day."

**Nitschmann, Anna**
This Flock So Small, *with music.*

**Nitzche, Jane Chance**
Shopping.

**Nkabinde, Thulani**
Accra 8/75.
Forest Green.
Like Fire Spreadin/ the Joylessness.
Missing MS.

Song for the Nkazi or the Final Ironies.

**Noailles, Anna de**
Image.

**No (hŏn-myŭng**
Cricket.
Deer.

**Noel, Henry**
Beauty's Excellency.

**Noel, Thomas**
Aconite, The.

**Noguere, Suzanne**
Pervigilium Veneris.

**Noin Hoshi**
Tanka: "In the evening/ Quiet of the
   country town."

**Nolan, James**
Cross and the Weathercock, The.
Locked in a Home for Les Enfants
   Dérangés en Dieu.
Tyger! Tyger!

**Nolan, Michael**
Little Annie Rooney, *with music.*

**Noll, Bink**
Divorce.
June.
Landscape with Pervert.
Picador Bit, The.
Quaker Hero, Burning.
Shutting the Curtains.
Wedlock.

**Nordan, Lewis**
He Fishes with His Father's Ghost.

**Nordbrandt, Henrik**
We Separate the Days.

**Nordhaus, Jean**
Aunts, The.
Camels.
Wood Fever.
Yahrzeit Candle.

**Norris, Gordon W.**
Mi Corazón.
Song of the Border.

**Norris, John**
Canticle.
Meditation, The.

**Norris, John W.**
Give Peace, O God, the Nations Cry,
   *with music.*

**Norris, Kathleen**
Evaporation Poems.
Focus.
Her Application to Elysium.
Memorandum/ The Accountant's
   Notebook.
Middle of the World, The.
Running through Sleep.
Stomach.

**Norris, Leslie**
Ballad of Billy Rose, The.
Barn Owl.
Buzzard.
Camels, the Kings' Camels, The.
Curlew.
Early Frost.
Elegy for David Beynon.
Elegy for Lyn James.
February Morning, A.
Girl's Song, A.
July the Seventh.
Last Leaves.
Man in Our Village, A.
Mice in the Hay.

Midwinter.
Nightingales.
October in the Lane.
One Leaf, The.
Owls.
Park at Evening, The.
Quiet-eyed Cattle, The.
Small War, A.
Stable Cat, The.
Water.
**Norse, Harold**
At the Trieste.
From All These, You.
In November.
Island of Giglio.
Uncles.
We Bumped Off Your Friend the Poet.
**North, Frank Mason**
Where Cross the Crowded Ways of Life,
*with music.*
**North, Susan**
Rumor You Called My Name.
What I Have.
**NorthSun, Nila**
Little Red Riding Hood.
Way and the Way Things Are, The.
**Norton, Caroline Elizabeth Sarah Sheridan**
Juanita.
**Norvig, Gerda**
Desert March.
Joining, The.
Tree of Life Is Also a Tree of Fire, The.
**Norworth, Jack**
Take Me Out to the Ball Game.
**Norworth, Jack and Nora Bayes.** *See*
**Bayes Nora and Jack Norworth**
**Notley, Alice**
For All the Songs I Sing.
In the Art Institute Library.
30th Birthday.
To WCW.
Translation of a Chinese Tribute to Jade.
Tribute.
"Virtue of Uncreatedness, The."
**Novak, Ladislav**
Gloria.
**"Novalis" (Friederich von Hardenberg)**
Aphorisms.
Second Hymn to the Night, The.
**November, Sharyn**
Night Driving.
**Novo, Salvador**
Departed Friend, The.
**Nowlan, Alden**
Baptism.
Beginning.
Bull Moose, The.
Daisies.
Golden Pyramids of the Sun, The.
Gypsies.
Hens.
I, Icarus.
Kyran's Christening.
Letter to a Young Friend.
Palomino Stallion, The.
Party at Bannon Brook.
Porch.
Psalm of Onan for Harp, Flute and
Tambourine, A.
Rivalry.
Semi-private Room.
Stars.

Therese.
Waiting for Her.
Warren Pryor.
Wasp.
**Noyes, Alfred**
Barrel-Organ, The, *abr.*
Rock Pool, The.
Rustling of Grass, The.
Seagulls on the Serpentine.
Spring, and the Blind Children.
**Noyes, Stanley**
Nevada.
Six Creatures on the Way.
**N'tosha, Nashira**
Phantoms.
This Site Is Occupied.
**Nugent, Maude**
Sweet Rosie O'Grady, *with music.*
**Nukada, Princess**
Waiting for the Emperor Tenji.
When, loosened from winter's bonds.
**Nuur, Faarah**
Limits of Submission, The.
Our Country Is Divided.
**Nye, Aileen Campbell**
Less than Love.
**Nye, Naomi Shihab**
New Skills.
**Nye, Robert**
In More's Hotel.
Proper Place, A.
Travelling to My Second Marriage on
the Day of the First Moonshot.
**Nyhart, Nina**
Tennis.
**Nyro, Laura**
And When I Die.

**O**

**Oakes, Philip**
Company.
**Oakman, John**
Glutton, The.
**Oates, Joyce Carol**
American City.
Foetal Song.
Girl at the Center of Her Life, A.
Growing Together.
Lines for Those to Whom Tragedy Is
Denied.
Moving Out.
Present Tense, The.
**Ober, Don**
Contemporary Fear.
**O'Bolger, T. D.**
Counsels of O'Riordan, the Rann
Maker, The.
**"O'Brien, John."** *See* **Hartigan, Patrick**
**Joseph**
**O'Bruadair, David**
Change, The.
Eire.
New Style, The.
O'Bruadair.
**Ocampo, Silvina**
Prisoner between the Panes of Glass.
**O'Carolan, Turlough**

Mabel Kelly.
Peggy Browne.
**Occleve, Thomas.** *See* **Hoccleve, Thomas**
**Occom, Samson**
Waked by the Gospel's Powerful Sound,
*with music.*
**Ochester, Ed**
After Advertising Ended.
Ed Shreckongost.
Farewell to the Moon, A.
For You.
Gift, The.
My Penis.
My Teeth.
Penn Central Station at Beacon, N.Y.,
The.
Snow White.
**Ochs, Phil**
Draft Dodger Rag.
Outside of a Small Circle of Friends.
**O'Connell, Eibhlin Dubh (Eibhlín Dhubh**
**Ní Chonaill**
Lament for Art O'Leary.
**O'Connell, Richard**
Etude.
Robert Lowell.
**O'Connor, Frank (***originally* **Michael**
**O'Donovan)**
Angry Poet, The.
End of Clonmacnois, The.
Hope.
Three Old Brothers.
**O'Connor, Martin T.**
Requiem: "Farewell my friend."
**O'Connor, Philip**
Fag-End.
Poems (I-XI).
Raspberry in the Pudding, The.
Writing in England Now.
**O'Connor, Tony**
Last of the Poet's Car.
**O'Críadáin, Seán**
Great-Aunts.
**O'Dalaigh, Gofraidh Fionn**
Under Sorrow's Sign.
**O'Dalaigh, Muireadach**
On the Death of His Wife.
**Odam, Joyce**
I Have Left You an Empty Room.
**Oden, Gloria C.**
"As When Emotion Too Far Exceeds Its
Cause."
Carousel, The.
Man White, Brown Girl and All That
Jazz.
Map, The.
Private Letter to Brazil, A.
Review from Staten Island.
Riven Quarry, The.
Triple Mirror, The.
Way It Is, The.
**O'Donoghue, Gregory**
Web, The.
**O'Donovan, Michael.** *See* **O'Connor,**
**Frank**
**O'Egan, Gerry**
1867: Last Sounds.
**Oerke, Andrew**
Serengeti Sunset.
Sun, The.
**O'Faracháin, Roibéard.** *See* **Farren,**
**Robert**

**O'Gallagher, Alice**
  Welcome, O Great Mary.
**Ogilvie, Will H.**
  Death of Ben Hall, The.
**Ogilvie-Laing, Galina V.**
  I Saw the Light Yesterday.
**Ogilvy, David**
  Virtues of Carnation Milk, The.
**Og MacWard, Fearghal**
  Flight of the Earls, The, 1607, *sel.*
**O'Grady, Desmond**
  Afternoon.
  Day Concludes Burning, The.
  Dying Gaul, The.
  Father, The.
  If I Went Away.
  Mad male-hearted woman in a prouder
    age, A.
  Page from a Diary.
  Pitch Piles Up in Part, The.
  Poet in Old Age Fishing at Evening,
    The.
  Poet Loves from Afar, The.
  Professor Kelleher and the Charles
    River.
  Sightseeing.
**O'Grady, Tom**
  Living in Another Man's House.
  Old Ladies, The.
**O'Hara, Frank**
  Abortion, An.
  Answer to Voznesensky and Evtushenko.
  As Planned.
  Autobiographia Literaria.
  Ave Maria.
  Biotherm (For Bill Berkson).
  Blocks.
  Chez Jane.
  Concert Champêtre.
  Day Lady Died, The.
  Easter.
  For James Dean.
  Homosexuality.
  Hunter, The.
  In Favor of One's Time.
  Les Etiquettes Jaunes.
  Les Luths.
  Meditations in an Emergency.
  Music.
  Ode: Salute to the French Negro Poets.
  Ode on Lust.
  Ode to Joy.
  Ode to Willem de Kooning.
  On Rachmaninoff's Birthday.
  Personal Poem.
  Poem: "At night Chinamen jump."
  Poem: "Eager note on my door said,
    'Call me,' The."
  Poem: "Lana Turner has collapsed!"
  Poem: "There I could never be a boy."
  Princess Elizabeth of Bohemia, as
    Perdita.
  Radio.
  Rhapsody.
  Should We Legalize Abortion?
  Step Away from Them, A.
  Steps.
  To the Film Industry in Crisis.
  To the Harbormaster.
  True Account of Talking to the Sun at
    Fire Island, A.
  Walking.

  Why I Am Not a Painter.
**O'Hare, Felix**
  Shoofly, The.
**O'Heffernan, Mahon**
  My Son, Forsake Your Art.
**O Hehir, Diana**
  Sleeping Pill.
  Lost Objects.
**"O. Henry."** *See* **"Henry, O."**
**O'Higgins, Myron**
  Sunset Horn.
  Two Lean Cats.
  Vaticide.
  Young Poet.
**O'Huiginn, Tadhg Dall**
  Difference, The.
  First Vision, The, *sel.*
  Present of Butter, A.
**O'Hussey, Eochaidh**
  Ode to the Maguire.
**Ojenke.** *See* **Saxon, Alvin**
**O'John, Calvin**
  Dancing Teepees.
**O'Keefe, John**
  Amo, Amas.
**O'Keeffe, Adelaide**
  Beasts and Birds.
  Kite, The.
**Okkur Macatti**
  Rains, already old, The.
  What Her Girl-Friend[s] Said to Her.
**Oku, Princess**
  How will you cross the autumn
    mountain alone?
**Olcott, Chauncey**
  My Wild Irish Rose.
**Oldham, John**
  Careless Good Fellow, The.
  Satire, A, *sel.*
  Satire Addressed to a Friend, A, *sel.*
  Satires, *sel.*
**Oldham, Perry**
  Hygiene.
  Local Destruction.
  Saigon Tea.
**Oldknow, Antony**
  Nude with Green Chair.
**Oldmixon, John**
  Song: "I lately vow'd, but 'twas in
    haste."
**Olds, N. S.**
  Rivets.
**Olds, Sharon**
  End of World War One, The.
  Fish Story.
  Time-Travel.
  Tricks.
**Oldys, William**
  Fly, The.
  On Himself.
**Oles, Carole**
  Brother at One Week.
  Circling.
  Francestown Suite.
  Poem for My Hands.
  Price of Breast in Las Vegas, The.
**Oleson, Helmer O.**
  Ballad of Johnny Appleseed.
**Oliphant, Carolina.** *See* **Nairne, Carolina**
  **Oliphant, Baroness**
**Oliphant, Thomas**
  Ash Grove, The, *with music.*

**Oliver, Mary**
  Diviners, The.
  Grandmothers, The.
  Mussels.
  Sleeping in the Forest.
  Stark Boughs on the Family Tree.
  Through Ruddy Orchards.
**Oliver, William Hosking**
  In the Fields of My Father's Youth.
**Oliver, William**
  I'll Have a Collier for My Sweetheart.
**Olsen, William**
  Addressing His Deaf Wife, Kansas,
    1916.
**Olson, Charles**
  A B C s.
  Distances, The.
  I, Maximus of Gloucester, to You.
  Kingfishers, The.
  La Chute.
  Letter 6.
  Maximus, to Gloucester, Letter 19.
  Maximus, to Gloucester, Letter 6.
  Maximus to Gloucester, Letter 27.
  Mazimus, to Gloucester, Letter 2.
  Maximus, to Himself.
  Moon Is the Number 18, The.
  Newly Discovered "Homeric" Hymn, A.
  Praises, The.
  Ring Of, The.
  Songs of Maximus, The.
  These Days.
  Variations Done for Gerald van de
    Wiele.
**Olson, Elder**
  Childe Roland, etc.
  Ice-Skaters.
  In Despair He Orders a New Typewriter.
  Valentine for Marianne Moore, A.
**Olson, Ernst W.**
  God of Peace, in Peace Preserve Us, *with*
    *music.*
**Olson, Ted**
  Hawk's Way.
**Olumo.** *See* **Cunningham, James**
**O'Mahony, Liam**
  Breaching Muse, The.
  Scyther.
**O'Malley, Emanuela**
  False Prophet.
**Omar Khayyám**
  Ah, with the Grape my fading Life
    provide.
  Book of verses underneath the bough, A.
  Rubáiyát of Omar Khayyám of
    Naishápúr, The.
**Ombres, Rossana**
  Bella and the Golem.
  Flower Ensnarer of Psalms.
**O'Meally, Bob**
  Make Music with Your Life.
**O'Meara, Sean**
  Astronaut.
  Merry-go-round.
**Ondaatje, Michael**
  When Charlie Bowdre married Manuela,
    we carried them.
**Onderdonk, Henry Ustic**
  On Zion and on Lebanon, *with music.*
  Spirit in Our Hearts, The, *with music.*
  Though I Should Seek, *with music.*
**Oneil, Henrietta**

Ode to the Poppy.
**O'Neill, Catherine**
Cowboy's Love Song.
I. R. A. Man Revisits His Hideout,
The.
Reluctant.
**O'Neill, Lawrence T.**
Train to Reflection.
**O'Neill, Mary**
What Is Red?
**"O'Neill, Moira" (Nesta Higginson Skrine)**
Her Sister.
Rachray Man, The.
**Ono no Komachi**
Color of the flowers, The,/ has faded.
Doesn't he realize/ that I am not/ like
the swaying kelp.
So lonely am I.
Thing which fades, A.
This night of no moon.
When my love becomes/ All-powerful.
**Opengart, Bea**
Speak.
**Oppen, George**
Book of Job and a Draft of a Poem to
Praise the Paths of the Living, The.
Building of the Skyscraper, The.
Exodus.
Forms of Love, The.
If It All Went Up in Smoke.
It Is Difficult Now to Speak of Poetry.
Latitude, Longitude.
Myth of the Blaze.
People, the People, The.
Population.
Psalm: "In the small beauty of the
forest."
Quotations.
Sara in Her Father's Arms.
Some San Francisco Poems.
Street.
Who Shall Doubt.
**Oppenheim, James**
Slave, The.
**Oppenheimer, Joel**
For John and Lucy.
Leave It to Me Blues.
Undefined Tenderness, An.
**Opper, Frederick B.**
Sir Bedivere Bors.
**O'Rahilly [or O'Reilly], Egan**
Brightest of the Bright, The.
Egan O Rahilly.
Inis Fal.
More Power.
Time of Change, A.
**Orban, Otto**
Computer.
Hymn: "Some sort of fire leaped out of
the dirty and poor and merciless city."
Ray.
**O'Reilly, Egan.** *See* **O'Rahilly, Egan**
**O'Reilly, John Boyle**
White Rose, A.
**Orfalea, Greg**
Kite Day at the Washington Monument.
**Orford, Horace Walpole, 4th Earl of.** *See*
**Walpole, Horace, 4th Earl of Oxford**
**"Orinda."** *See* **Philips, Katherine**
**Orleans, Charles, Duc d'**
Lost.
My Ghostly Father, I Me Confess.

Smiling Mouth and Laughing Eyen
Grey, The.
Well, Wanton Eye.
**Orlen, Steven**
Aga Khan, The.
Bar Mitzvah.
Drunken Man, The.
First Story.
In Praise of Beverly.
Jewish Family, The.
My Father's House.
My Grandmother and the Voice of
Tolstoy.
No Quarter.
Perfect One, The.
Unwritten Letters.
**Orlock, Carol**
Portrait of a Woman I Won't Know.
Signature.
**Ormond, John**
Ancient Monuments.
At His Father's Grave.
Lament for a Leg.
To a Nun.
**Ormsby, Frank**
Amelia Street.
Child, The.
Doorstep.
Inferno: A New Circle.
Interim.
Mrs. G. Watters.
On Devenish Island.
Ornaments.
Sheepman.
**O'Rourke, David**
For Your Inferiority Complex.
**Orpingalik**
My Breath.
**Orr, Gregory**
Dinner, The.
Doll, The.
Friday Lunchbreak.
Gathering the Bones Together.
Girl with 18 Nightgowns, The.
Like Any Other Man.
Love Poem: "Black biplane crashes into
the window, The."
Poem: "This life like no other."
Two Lines from the Brothers Grimm.
**Orred, Meta**
In the Gloaming.
**Ort, Daniel**
Tho We All Speak.
**Orten, Jiri**
Small Elegy, A.
**Ortiz, Simon J.**
Bony.
Creation, The: According to Coyote.
Crossing the Colorado River into Yuma.
Expectant Father, The.
Forming Child Poems.
Indian Guys at the Bar.
July 12.
Morning Smallfire in Lukachukai
Mountains.
My Mother and My Sisters.
Pretty Woman, A.
Relocation.
San Diego Poem, A.
Serenity in Stones, The.
Significance of a Veteran's Day, The.
Smoking Prayers.

Some 5-Day Drunk Poems.
Survival This Way.
Ten O'Clock News.
This Preparation.
To Insure Survival.
Waiting for You to Come By.
Washyuma Motor Hotel.
Watching Salmon Jump.
What I Tell Him.
**Orwell, George (Eric Blair)**
As One Non-Combatant to Another.
Dressed man and a naked man, A.
**Osgood, Francis P.**
Winter Fairyland in Vermont.
**O'Shaughnessy, Arthur William Edgar**
Living Marble.
Ode: "We are the music-makers."
Silences.
**"Ossian."** *See* **Macpherson, James**
**Ostrander, Fred**
Tides.
**Ostriker, Alicia**
Anxiety about Dying.
Old Men.
One, Annie and Me.
**Ostroff, Anthony**
About Long Days.
In Puerto Vallarta.
Looking Out to Sea.
On the Beach.
Sunday, Guadalajara.
Zoo, The.
**O'Sullivan, Daniel James**
Drinking Time.
**O'Sullivan, Owen Roe**
His Request.
Volatile Kerryman, The.
**"O'Sullivan, Seumas" (James Starkey)**
Blessing on the Cows, A.
Convent, The.
Cottage.
In North Great George's Street.
Lamplighter, The.
Piper, A.
Rain.
**O'Sullivan, Vincent**
Children, The.
Clown, and All the Sea behind Him.
Elegy for a Schoolmate.
Medusa.
Which Wing the Angel Chooses.
**Otomo of Sakanoe [or Sakanone], Lady**
My brother has on/ a thin robe.
My heart, thinking/ "How beautiful he
is.'
Sent from the Capital to Her Elder
Daughter.
Unknown love/ Is as bitter a thing.
You say, "I will come."
**Otto, Heinrich**
Lord, Dear God! to Thy Attending, *with
music.*
**Otway, Thomas**
Orphan, The; or, The Unhappy
Marriage, *sels.*
Poet's Complaint of His Muse, The, *sel.*
**OuMar Ba**
Drought.
**Outram, George**
Strictures on the Economy of Nature.
**Ovid (Publius Ovidius Naso)**
Amores, *sels.*

Atalanta
Baucis and Philemon.
Constant Penelope sends to thee,
  careless Ulysses.
Corinnae Concubitus.
Golden Age, The.
Heroides, *sel.*
I ask but right: let her that caught me
  late.
Medea Casts a Spell to Make Aeson
  Young Again.
Metamorphoses, *sels.*
Of the Pythagorean Philosophy.
Orpheus and Eurydice.
Pygmalion's Statue Comes to Life.
To His Mistress ("Your husband will be
  with us at the treat").
Tristium, *sels.*
Your loveliness, I don't deny, needs
  lovers.
**Owen, Goronwy**
Elegy for His Daughter Ellen.
Invitation, The.
**Owen, Guy**
Poem to a Mule, Dead Twenty Years.
White Stallion, The.
**Owen, Sue**
Owl, The.
**Owen, Wilfred**
A Terre.
Anthem for Doomed Youth.
Arms and the Boy.
Chances, The.
Disabled.
Dulce et Decorum Est.
Exposure.
Fragment: "I saw his round mouth's
  crimson deepen as it fell."
Futility.
Greater Love.
Insensibility.
Mental Cases.
Miners.
Parable of the Old Man [*or* Men] and
  the Young, The.
Roads Also, The.
Send-off, The.
Shadwell Stair.
Show, The.
Soldier's Dream.
Song of Songs.
Strange Meeting.
To My Friend.
**Owens, Grace W.**
Oh, Who Can Make a Flower?
**Owens, Rochelle**
All Owners of Meat Are Hospitable.
Dance and Eye Me (Wicked)ly My
  Breath a Fixed Sphere.
For, Behold the Day Cometh.
Let Us Honor Them.
Never in This World You Will Drop a
  Yellow Sponge.
Power of Love He Wants Shih
  (Everything), The.
Radiant Heat.
Sky-splitting Pink Rubber Bistro, The.
Wild Woman's Resentment of Fakery.
Wistful Butch Poem.
**Ower, John**
Cudworth's Undergraduate Ode to a
  Bare Behind.

Gingerbread House, The.
**Owl Woman (Juana Manwell)**
Songs for the Four Parts of the
  Night.
**Oxford, Earl of.** *See* **De Vere, Edward,
  17th Earl of Oxford**
**Ozerov, Lev**
Babi Yar.
**Ozick, Cynthia**
Riddle, A: "I walk on two legs."
Wonder-Teacher, The.

# P

**Pacernick, Gary**
Babel.
I Want to Write a Jewish Poem.
Labor Day.
**Pacheco, Henry L.**
Profetizador/ Old Prophet.
**Pacheco, Jose Emilio**
Fire.
**Pack, Robert**
Apocalypse in Black and White.
Bird in Search of a Cage, A.
Don't Sit under the Apple Tree with
  Anyone Else but Me.
Everything Is Possible.
Frog Prince, The: A Speculation on
  Grimm's Fairy Tale.
In a Field.
Kiss, The.
Love.
Mugger, The.
My Daughter.
Pack Rat, The.
Way We Wonder, The.
**Packard, William**
Teacher of Poetry, The.
**Packer, Lewis (Richard Packer)**
American Age, The.
Homecoming.
Name Me.
Pastoral with Visitor.
Rocks.
Three Greeks.
**Padgett, Ron**
After the Broken Arm.
December.
Sandwich Man, The.
Strawberries in Mexico.
**Paff, Eric W.**
On Sitting Up Late, Watching Kittens.
**Page, B. Sanford**
All Songs.
**Page, Edgar**
Beulah Land.
**Page, Geoff**
Cemetery, A/ is sideways moving.
Coloratura.
Dancer.
For William Carlos Williams.
Pine Tree.
Road Show.
**Page, Patricia K.**
Stories of Snow.
**Page, William**
Painlessly Out of Ourselves.

**Pagis, Dan**
Autobiography.
Brothers.
Draft of a Reparations Agreement.
Grand Duke of New York, The.
Hide and Seek.
Instructions for Crossing the Border.
Last Ones, The.
Scrawled in Pencil in a Sealed Railway
  Car.
Tower, The.
**Pagnucci, Gianfranco**
Death of an Elephant, The.
**Pain, Philip**
Meditation 10 ("Alas, what is the world?
  A sea of glass").
Meditation 62 ("How is it that I am so
  careless here").
Meditation 29 ("How mutable is every
  thing that here").
Meditation 9 ("Man's life is like a rose,
  that in the spring").
Meditation 8 ("Scarce do I pass a day
  but that I hear").
Porch, The.
Whilst in This World I Stay, *with music.*
**Paine, Thomas**
Liberty Tree.
**Painter, John R.**
Bob-tailed Flush, A.
**"Pai Wei" (Huang Su-ju)**
Madrid
**Palea**
Piano at Evening.
**Palen, Jennie M.**
To a Race Horse at Ascot.
**Palen, John**
Missouri Town.
**Palés Matos, Luis**
Doorway to Time in Three Voices.
Elegy for the Duke of Marmalade.
Kalahari.
Neither This nor That.
Well, The.
**Paley, Grace**
One day when I was a child, long ago.
Women in Vietnam, The.
**Paley Francescato, Martha**
Parody.
Semen.
**Palladas**
Grammar commences with a 5-line
  curse.
Loving the rituals that keep men close.
Naked I Came.
Poor devil that I am, being so attacked.
Racing, reckoning fingers flick.
When you send out invitations, don't ask
  me.
**Palmer, E. Harriet**
Parterre, The.
Shipwreck, The.
**Palmer, Herbert**
Aunt Zillah Speaks.
Call of the Fells, The.
Rock Pilgrim.
Wounded Hawk, The.
**Palmer, Horatio R.**
Yield Not to Temptation, *with music.*
**Palmer, John F.**
Band Played On, The, *with music.*
**Palmer, John Williamson**

Fight at San Jacinto, The.
Maryland Battalion, The.
Stonewall Jackson's Way.
**Palmer, Miriam**
Getting into Focus.
Raccoon Poem.
"Vierge Ouvrante."
What if jealousy is just a bad dream?
**Palmer, Ray**
Lord, My Weak Thought in Vain Would
Climb, *with music.*
My Faith Looks Up to Thee, *with music.*
**Palmer, Samuel**
Shoreham: Twilight Time.
**Palmer, Vance**
Farmer Remembers the Somme, The.
**Pan, Lady (Pan Chieh-yu)**
Present from the Emperor's New
Concubine, A.
**Panegoosho, M.**
Morning Mood.
**Pankey, Eric**
Renaming the Evening.
**Pantycelyn.** *See* **Williams, William**
**Pape, Greg**
For Rosa Yen, Who Lived Here.
La Llorona.
Mercado.
October.
**Papenhausen, Carol**
Album.
**Paraone, Tiwai**
Chant to Io.
**Paraske, Larin**
My Little Love Lies on the Ground.
Sad Is the Seagull.
Woman Grows Soon Old, A.
**Parcelli, Carlo**
Ontology of Accident, The, *sel.*
**Parham, Robert**
Sunday in South Carolina.
**Parini, Jay**
Snake Hill.
Tanya.
**Parish, Mitchell**
Star Dust, *with music.*
**Parke, Walter**
Person of Note, A.
**Parker, Dorothy**
Chant for Dark Hours.
Coda.
Comment.
Experience.
Fair Weather.
Flaw in Paganism, The.
Interior.
Love Song.
News Item.
Of a Woman, Dead Young.
One Perfect Rose.
Partial Comfort.
Portrait of the Artist.
Résumé.
Symptom Recital.
Theory.
Unfortunate Coincidence.
Verse for a Certain Dog.
**Parker, Edwin Pond**
Master, No Offering, *with music.*
**Parker, Linda**
Advice to the Lovelorn.
Brush Mask.

Country Alphabet, The.
Flood Disaster in Gallup, New Mexico.
Nursing Home.
**Parker, Patricia**
With the sun.
**Parker, Stewart**
Chicago Allegory.
Health.
Three Fitts.
**Parkhurst, John**
Of Alphus.
**Parkinson, Thomas**
New Antigone, The, *sel.*
**Parks, Lorine**
Person to Person.
**Parnell, Thomas**
Night-Piece on Death, A.
**Parnell, Thomas** *and* **Alexander Pope.** *See*
**Pope, Alexander** *and* **Thomas Parnell**
**Parra, Nicanor**
I Move the Meeting Be Adjourned.
Manifesto, *sels.*
Seven.
We Let It Go That He Was a Perfect
Man.
Young Poets.
**Parrish, Lydia A.**
Pay Me My Money Down.
**Parrot, Henry**
Fatales Poetae.
In Obitum Promi.
On a Poet.
**Parry, David Fisher**
Miniver Cheevy, Jr.
**Parry, Edward Abbott**
I Would Like You for a Comrade.
Jam Fish, The.
Pater's Bathe.
**Parry, R. Williams**
Branwen's Starling.
Fox, The.
Miraculous Dawn.
Old Boatman of Death's River, The.
On a Soldier Killed in the Great War.
"Two Hearts Divided."
**Parry-Williams, Sir Thomas Herbert**
Christmas Carol, A: "Close to a quarter
of a century since then."
Llyn y Gadair.
These Bones.
**Parsons, Clere**
Different.
Introduction: "I bespeak words."
**Parun, Vesna**
Mother of Man.
**Parvin, Betty**
Edwardian Hat.
**Pascal, Paul**
Tact.
**Pasolini, Pier Paolo**
Tuesday, 5 March (Morning) 1963.
**Pass, John**
Theresa.
**Passerat, Jean**
Song: "Shephard loveth thow me vell?"
**Passy, Nancy**
Listening.
**Pastan, Linda**
After Reading Nelly Sachs.
After X-Ray.
Air War.
At the Gynecologist's.

At the Jewish Museum.
Aubade: "In the early morning."
Bicentennial Winter.
City, The.
Distances.
Elsewhere.
Ethics.
Fresco.
Governor's Palace, The.
Notes from the Delivery Room.
Old Woman.
Pears.
Rachel.
Secrets ("The secrets I keep").
Threads to Be Woven Later.
Williamsburg, *sel.*
Yom Kippur.
**Pasternak, Boris Leonidovich**
Hops.
**Pastorius, Francis Daniel**
Great God, Preserver of All Things, *with
music.*
Though My Thoughts, *with music.*
**Patchen, Kenneth**
And with the Sorrows of This
Joyousness.
Animal I wanted, The.
Because He Liked to Be at Home.
Biography of Southern Rain.
Character of Love Seen as a Search for
the Lost, The.
Do the Dead Know What Time It Is?
Easy Decision, An.
Empty Dwelling Places.
Fox, The.
Gautama in the Deer Park at Benares
I'd Want Her Eyes to Fill with Wonder.
In Judgment of the Leaf.
In Order To.
In the footsteps of the walking air.
"It Is Big inside a Man."
Joe Hill Listens to the Praying.
"Let Us Have Madness Openly."
Letter on the Use of Machine Guns at
Weddings, A.
Letter to a Policeman in Kansas City, A.
Lions of fire, The.
Magical Mouse, The.
May I Ask You a Question.
Midnight Special.
Mirru.
Moon, Sun, Sleep, Birds, Live.
Naked Land, The.
O all down within the pretty meadow.
O Now the Drenched Land Wakes.
O terrible is the highest thing.
Orange Bears, The.
Origin of Baseball, The.
Peter's Little Daughter Dies.
Saturday Night in the Parthenon.
Street Corner College.
Temple, A.
Trueblue Gentleman, A.
23rd Street Runs into Heaven.
Village Tudda, The.
Where Two o'Clock Came From.
**Paterson, Andrew Barton**
Clancy of the Overflow.
Man from Snowy River, The.
Old Man Platypus.
Traveling Post Office, The.
Waltzing Matilda.

Weary Will.
**Paterson, Evangeline**
Armaments Race.
Parting from My Son.
**Patmore, Coventry Kersey Dighton**
Across the sky the daylight crept.
Angel in the House, The, *sels.*
Arbor Vitae.
Attainment, The.
Azalea, The.
Barren Shore, The.
Cathedral Close, The.
Constancy Rewarded.
County Ball, The.
Crocus, The.
Dean, The.
Departure.
1867.
Faint yet Pursuing.
Farewell, A: "With all my will, but
  much against my heart."
Flesh-Fly and the Bee, The.
From the small life that loves with tooth
  and nail.
How fair a flower is sown.
King William's Dispatch to Queen
  Augusta.
Kiss, The.
London Fete, A.
Love at Large.
Love's Reality.
Magna Est Veritas.
Married Lover, The.
Night and Sleep.
Perspective.
Platonic Love.
Poet's Confidence, The.
Retrospect, A.
Revelation, The.
Save by the Old Road none attain the
  new.
Science, the agile ape, may well.
Sheep-bell tolleth curfew time, The.
Spirit's Epochs, The.
To the Body.
Toys, The.
Vesica Piscis.
Victories of Love, The, *sel.*
Wedding, The.
Whirl'd off at last, for speech I sought.
Winter.
**Patrickson, Kit**
Let's Send a Rocket.
**Patten, Brian**
After Frost.
Interruption at the Opera House.
Little Johnny's Final Letter.
Little Johnny's Foolish Invention.
No Matter If You Remain Unaffected
  by.
Ode on Celestial Music.
Party Piece.
Portrait of a Young Girl Raped at a
  Suburban Party.
Projectionist's Nightmare, The.
Seen through the Trees behind Which
  You're Walking.
Small Dragon, A.
Through All Your Abstract Reasoning.
What You Should Do Each Morning.
Where Are You Now Superman?
You'd Better Believe Him.

**Patterson, Lindsay**
At Long Last.
**Patterson, Raymond R.**
At That Moment.
Birmingham 1963.
Black All Day.
I've Got a Home in That Rock.
Letter in Winter.
Night-Piece.
Performance.
Riot Rythmes U.S.A., *sel.*
When I Awoke.
You Are the Brave.
**Patton, G. W.**
Emigrant's Dying Child, The.
**Patton, Patti**
Birthday Party.
**Pau-Llosa, Ricardo**
Links.
**Pauker, John**
Braided Poem.
Flighty Poem.
Poet in Washington, The.
Property Settlement.
**Pauker, Ted**
Garland for a Propagandist.
Grouchy Good Night to the Academic
  Year, A.
Limeraiku.
Trifle for Trafalgar Day, A.
**Paul, James**
Water Tower, The.
**"Paul, John."** *See* **Webb, Charles Henry**
**Paul the Silentiary.** *See* **Paulus**
  **Silentiarius**
**Paulin, Tom**
Evening Harbour.
**Paulinaoq**
Dead Man's Song, Dreamed by One
  Who Is Alive.
**Paulus Silentiarius [or Paul the Silentiary]**
Epitaph, An: "My name—my country—
  what are they to thee?"
In Peterborough Churchyard.
Tantalos.
**Pauly, Bill**
Heart/ Song for Christopher Raymond.
**Pavlich, Walter**
Revisiting the Field.
**Pavlova, Karolina**
To Madame A. V. Pletneff.
**Paxton, Tom**
Bishop Cody's Last Request.
I Can't Help but Wonder Where I'm
  Bound.
Little Brand New Baby.
My Ramblin' Boy.
**Payne, Basil**
Angry Old Men.
Answer to Allegory, An.
Hard Night's Daze, A.
Same Gesture, The.
Two on a Journey.
**Payne, Gerrye**
Claritas.
For three days/ I've wanted to get
  married.
There was a time when we all were
  dancers.
**Payne, John Howard**
Clari, the Maid of Milan, *sel.*
Home, Sweet Home.

**Payne, Nina**
Conversation Hearts.
**Paz, Octavio**
Dawn.
Landscape.
Street, The.
Touch.
**Peace, Angela**
Indian Mounds.
**Peacock, Molly**
Two Figures.
**Peacock, Thomas**
Andonis, My Daughter.
Earth Song.
Fear.
For the Children.
In Respect of the Elderly.
Six Eagles.
**Peacock, Thomas Love**
Crotchet Castle, *sel.*
Friar of Rubygill, The.
Love and Age.
Maid Marian, *sel.*
Merry Jest of Robin Hood, A.
Misfortunes of Elphin, The, *sel.*
Newark Abbey.
Nightmare Abbey, *sel.*
Priest and the Mulberry Tree, The.
Rich and Poor; or, Saint and Sinner.
Song by Mr. Cypress.
War Song of Dinas Vawr, The.
Wise Men of Gotham, The.
**Peake, Mervyn Laurence**
Frivolous Cake, The.
Is There No Love Can Link Us?
Titus Groan, *sel.*
**Pearce, Ellen**
Orange Tree, The.
Turtle's Belly, The.
**Pearlman, Bill**
New Mexico Sky.
**Pearlstein, Darlene**
11/16/75.
11/22/75.
5/30/75.
5/2/75.
4/20/75.
4/22/75.
6/10/75.
10/17/75.
**Pearse, Padraic**
Last Lines—1916.
**Pease, Roland**
Brown Bears of Boston, The.
**Peavy, Linda**
Riders.
Wisdom.
**Peck, John**
Cider and Vesalius.
Colophon for Lan-t'ing Hsiu-Hsi.
Here Is a Song, *with music.*
Quarrel, A.
Ringers, The.
Spring Festival on the River, The.
Watcher, The.
What If the Saint Must Die, *with music.*
**Peck, Richard**
Geese, The.
Jump Shot.
Mission Uncontrolled.
TKO.
**Peck, Samuel Minturn**

Kiss in the Rain, A.
**Peele, George**
Arraignment of Paris, The, *sel.*
Bethsabe's Song.
David and Bethsabe, *sel.*
His Golden Locks Time Hath to Silver
Turned.
Hunting of Cupid, The, *sel.*
Oenone and Paris.
Old Wives' [*or* Wife's] Tale, The, *sels.*
Polyhymnia, *sel.*
Song at the Well, The.
Summer Song, A.
Voice from the Well, The.
What Thing Is Love?
**Pélieu, Claude**
Golden-eyed Crossbow, The.
**Pell, Dewey G. *and* Ern Alpaugh.** *See*
Alpaugh, Ern *and* Dewey G. Pell
**Pellicer, Carlos**
Etude.
**Pembroke, Mary Sidney Herbert, Countess
of**
If Ever Hapless Woman Had a Cause.
**Pence, Susan**
Night Harvest.
**Pendergast, James**
Before the War.
**Penfold, Gerda**
La Pesadilla.
Lust for Murder, The.
**Penkethman, John**
Schoolmaster's Precepts, A.
Some Boys.
**Pennington, Lee**
Before the Breaking.
**Penny, Rob**
And We Conquered.
Be Cool, Baby.
I Remember How She Sang.
Real People Loves One Another, The.
**Penrose, Roland**
Road Is Wider than Long, The, *sel.*
**Penstone, M. M.**
Praise to God for things we see.
**Percival, James Gates**
Coral Grove, The.
**Percy, William**
Coelia, *sels.*
**Percy, William A.**
They Cast Their Nets in Galilee, *with
music.*
**Pereira, Sam**
On the Eisenhower Stamp.
**Péret, Benjamin**
Making Feet and Hands.
Staircase with a Hundred Steps, The.
**Perez-Diotima, Leigh**
Lake Walk at New Year's.
**Perkins, David**
Blue Gift, The.
Doctor, I Dream of Sleep.
Falling in Love.
Growing Up.
"How Long Hast Thou Been a
Gravemaker?"
**Perkins, Emily Swan**
Thou Art, O God, the God of Might,
*with music.*
**Perkins, Michael**
Carpenter, The.
**Perkoff, Stuart Z.**

Aleph.
Gimel.
Hai.
**Perlberg, Mark**
In Praise of Lichen.
Water and Light, Light and Water.
When at Night.
**Perlin, Terry M.**
Clarity of Apples, The.
**Perlman, Anne S.**
Childbirth.
**Perlman, Jess**
Winterscape.
**Perreault, Ellen**
Those Trees That Line the Northway.
**Perreault, John**
Boomerang.
Metaphysical Paintings, The.
Mixture, The, *sel.*
Readymade.
Shoe.
**Perronet, Edward**
All Hail the Power of Jesus' Name.
Coronation, *with music.*
**Perry, Georgette**
Recognition.
**Perry, Julianne**
No Dawns.
To L.
**"Perse, St.-John" (Alexis Saint-Léger
Léger)**
Anabasis, *sel.*
**Persius (Aulus Persius Flaccus)**
Satires, *sels.*
Thus fares the drudge; but thou, whose
life's a dream.
Yawning youth, scarce half awake,
essays, The.
**Peseroff, Joyce**
Approaching Absolute Zero.
**Peskett, William**
Cleaning Stables.
Dreams.
Inheritors, The.
Photographs.
Window Dressing.
**Pessoa, Fernando.** *See* Caeiro, Alberto
**Peter, Robert**
O! Wherefore.
**Peters, Phillis Wheatley.** *See* Wheatley,
Phillis
**Peters, Robert**
Allen Ginsberg Blesses a Bride and
Groom: A Wedding Night Poem.
Arrival, New York Harbor.
Beach, The.
Claremont.
Night Regression Poem.
Parable of the Garden.
Parable of What You've Always Wanted
to Come True.
Why Don't They Go Back to
Transylvania?
**Petersen, Donald**
Ballad of Dead Yankees, The.
Going Back.
**Peterson, Elizabeth**
Lesson, The.
**Peterson, Mattie J.**
I Kissed Pa Twice after His Death.
**Peterson, Robert**
At Veronica's.

Dear America.
For the Minority.
Groom's Lament, The.
Hands folded like napkins in my lap.
Highway Patrol Stops Me, Going Too
Slow.
In the 2 A.M. Club, a working man's
bar.
Swim in Ohuira Bay, A.
To Myself, Late, in a Myrtle Grove.
Wingwalking in Oregon.
Young Conquistador, The.
Young Conquistador, 15, The.
**Peterson, Ruth De Long**
Midwest Town.
**Petrarch (ancesco Petrarca)**
Amorous Worms' Meat, The.
Bicause I have the still kept fro lyes and
blame.
Description of the Contrarious Passions
in a Lover.
Ever myn happe is slack and slo in
commyng.
He Understands the Great Cruelty of
Death.
Love That Doth Reign and Live within
My Thought.
Lover Compareth His State to a Ship in
Perilous Storm Tossed on the Sea,
The.
Lover for Shamefastnesse Hideth His
Desire within His Faithfull Hart, The.
Sonnets to Laura, *sels.*
Vow to Love Faithfully, Howsoever He
Be Rewarded, A.
**Petrie, Paul**
Dream, The.
From the Point.
Not Seeing Is Believing.
Old Pro's Lament, The.
Phases of Darkness, The.
Story from Another World.
**Petronius Arbiter (Caius Petronius Arbiter)**
Doing, a Filthy Pleasure Is, and Short.
Good God, what a night that was.
**Petroski, Henry**
From the Observation Deck, Austin.
Horse-Girl.
**Petrykewycz, Susan**
Home Again.
Remembering Home.
**Pettingell, Phoebe**
Ode on Zero.
**Pettit, Michael**
Poker Poem.
**Pevear, Richard**
Ovid.
**Pfeiffer, Emily Jane Davis**
Song of Winter, A.
**Pfingston, Roger**
Occasion.
State Fair Pigs.
**Pflum, Richard**
Home in Indianapolis.
Silence of Bears, The.
**Phair, George E.**
Old-fashioned Pitcher, The.
**Phelps, Sylvanus D.**
Saviour, Thy Dying Love, *with music.*
**Philbrick, Stephen**
Leaving Here.
**Philips, Ambrose**

To the Earl of Dorset.
To the Memory of Lord Halifax, *sel.*
**Phillips, Joan.** *See* **"Ephelia"**
**Philips, John**
Splendid Shilling, The.
**Philips, Katherine ("Orinda")**
Against Love.
Answer to Another Persuading a Lady
to Marriage, An.
Dialogue of Absence 'twixt Lucasia and
Orinda, A.
Friendship's Mystery, to My Dearest
Lucasia.
Orinda to Lucasia Parting, October
1661, at London.
Sea-Voyage from Tenby to Bristol, A.
To Antenor.
To Mr. Henry Lawes.
To My Excellent Lucasia, on Our
Friendship.
Upon Absence.
Upon the Double Murther of King
Charles I.
**Phillips, Cleve**
Up against the Wall.
**Phillips, David**
Fighting Her.
Lover to Himself, The.
Notes on a Long Evening.
Old Storm.
Orange Juice Song.
Things of Late.
Wave, The.
Words.
**Phillips, Frank Lamont**
Daybreak.
Genealogy.
Maryuma.
No Smiles.
**Phillips, Harriet C.**
We Bring No Glittering Treasures, *with
music.*
**Phillips, Homer**
Handyman.
**Phillips, Louis**
Day at the Races, A.
Elephant, The.
I Always Get Things Right.
On Nicknames.
78 Miners in Mannington, West
Virginia.
**Phillips, Patrice**
Function Room, The.
**Phillips, Robert**
Decks.
Letter to Auden, A.
Lump.
**Phillips, Rodney**
Out of You.
**Phillips, Susan K.**
Secret of the Sea, The.
**Phillpotts, Eden**
Houses, The.
Man's Days.
**Philodemos the Epicurean**
Remonstrance.
**Phocas, Nikos**
Diver, The.
**Phylip, William**
Farewell to Hendre Fechan.
**Picasso, Pablo**

Poem: "Hasten on your childhood to the
hour when white."
Poem: "In secret."
Poem: "In the corner a violet jug the
bells the folds of paper."
**Pichaske, David R.**
H. S. Beeney Auction Sales.
Reflections.
**Pickard, Deanna Louise**
Old Polish Lesson, An.
Voyeur, The.
**Pickard, Tom**
Rape.
**Pickering, John**
Farewell, Adieu, That Courtly Life.
**Picot, James**
For It Was Early Summer.
**Piercy, Marge**
Agitprop.
Apron Strings.
Burying Blues for Janis.
Cold and Married War, A.
Councils.
Death Dance, The.
Embryos.
Friend, The.
Gracious Goodness.
Hare in Winter.
High Frequency.
I Awoke with the Room Cold.
I Still Feel You.
In the Men's Room(s).
Kneeling Here, I Feel Good.
Learning Experience.
Letter to Be Disguised as a Gas Bill.
Meditation in My Favorite Position.
Morning Half-Life Blues, The.
My Mother's Novel.
Night Fight.
Night Letter.
Noon of the Sunbather.
Nothing More Will Happen.
Organizer's Bogeymen, The.
Peaceable Kingdom, The.
Proposal for Recycling Wastes, A.
Quiet Fog, The.
Right Thinking Man.
Riptide.
Ritual, The.
Seedlings in the Mail.
Sign.
Simple-Song.
16/53.
Snow, Snow.
Someplace Else.
Song of the Fucked Duck.
Spring Offensive of the Snail, The.
Three Weeks in the State of Loneliness.
To the Pay Toilet.
Unclench Yourself.
Valley Where I Don't Belong, A.
Walking into Love, *sel.*
We Become New.
What You Waited For.
Why the Soup Tastes like the Daily
News.
Woman in the, The.
Work of Artifice, A.
**Pierpont, James S.**
Jingle Bells.
**Pierpont, John**
Fourth of July, The.

Pilgrim Fathers, The.
Warren's Address [at Bunker Hill].
**Pierson, Philip**
Technique.
**Pieterse, Cosmo**
Song (Prelude).
**Pietri, Pedro Juan**
Night Has Twenty-four Hours, The.
Silent Movies.
Underground Poetry.
You Jump First.
**Pijewski, John**
Labor Camp, The.
**Pike, Albert**
Dixie ("Southrons, hear your country
call you!").
**Pilbosian, Helene**
With the Bait of Bread.
**Pilinszky, János**
Desert of Love, The.
Fable: "Once upon a time/ there was a
lonely wolf."
**Pilkington, Laetitia**
Song: "Lying is an occupation."
**Pillin [*or* Pillen], William**
After the Riot.
Akriel's Consolation.
Aviators, The.
Bread.
Chapter from Geography, A.
Farewell to Europe.
Grand Park, Chicago.
Housewife.
Night Poem in an Abandoned Music
Room.
O, Beautiful They Move.
Ode: "O battallions! O disaster!"
Ode on a Decision to Settle for Less.
Poem: "Moving thru the drifting mist."
Poem: "To be sad in the morning."
Poem for Anton Schmidt, A.
Prairie, The.
Requiem for the '30's.
Two Lives.
We Were of Them.
**Pilz, J. Michael**
Renoir's Confidences.
**Pincas, Israel**
Mediterranean.
**Pindar**
Seventh Olympic Hymn.
**"Pindar, Peter" (John Wolcot)**
Apple Dumplings and a King, The.
Poetical and Congratulatory Epistle to
James Boswell, Esq., A.
**Pinder, Mike**
Dawn Is a Feeling.
**Piñero, Miguel**
There Is Nothing New in New York.
**"Ping Hsin" (Hsieh Wang-ying)**
Multitudinous Stars, *sel.*
Orphan boat of my heart, The.
Spring waters, *sels.*
**Pinsker, Sanford**
For Allen Ginsberg, Who Cut Off His
Beard.
Untitled Poem, about an Uncompleted
Sonnet, An.
**Pinsky, Robert**
Dying.
Tennis.

Their Speech, Compared with Wisdom and Poetry.

**Pinto, Vivian de Sola.** *See* **Sola Pinto, Vivian de**

**Piron, Alexis**
Here lies Piron—a man of no position.

**Pisan, Christine de**
Alone am I, and alone I wish to be.
Christine to Her Son.
Epistle of Othea to Hector, The (A Lytil Bibell of Knyghthod), *sel.*
I am a widow, robed in black, alone.
I'll always dress in black and rave.

**Pise, Constantine**
Let the Deep Organ Swell, *with music.*

**Pitcher, Oliver**
Pale Blue Casket, The.
Raison d'Etre.
Salute.

**Pitchford, Kenneth**
Homosexual Sonnets.
Lobotomy.
Queen, The.

**Pitkin, Anne**
Homes, The.

**Pitt, William**
Sailor's Consolation, The.

**Pitter, Ruth**
But for Lust.
Eternal Image, The.
Hen under Bay-Tree.
Military Harpist, The.
O where is the dwelling I love the most.
Old Woman Speaks of the Moon, An.
Swan Bathing, The.
Three Cheers for the Black, White and Blue.
Time's Fool.
Viper, The.

**Pittis, William**
Battle Royal between Dr. Sherlock, Dr. South, and Dr. Burnet, The.

**Pitts, William S.**
Little Brown Church in the Vale, The, *with music.*

**Piuvkaq [or Pluvkaq]**
I wonder why.
It Is Hard to Catch Trout.
Joy of a Singer, The.
Mocking Song against Qaqortingneq.
Wonderful Occupation, A.

**Pizarnik, Alejandra**
Apart from Oneself.
Dawn.
Fear.
Mask and the Poem, The.
Privilege.
Tree of Diana, The.
Vertigos or Contemplation of Something That Is Over.
Who Will Stop His Hand from Giving Warmth.

**Planché, James Robinson**
Ching a Ring.
Love, You've Been a Villain.

**Plantenga, Bart**
Fire. 10/78.

**Plantier, Therese**
Doors.
Overdue Balance Sheet.

**Plath, Sylvia**
Aftermath.

All the Dead Dears.
Appearance, An.
Applicant, The.
Ariel.
Arrival of the Bee Box, The.
Balloons.
Bee Meeting, The.
Beekeeper's Daughter, The.
Black Rook in Rainy Weather.
Blackberrying.
Blue Moles.
By Candlelight.
Candles.
Child.
Colossus, The.
Cut.
Daddy.
Death and Co.
Death of Myth-making, The.
Disquieting Muses, The.
Edge.
Elm.
Event.
Face Lift.
Fever 103°.
For a Fatherless Son.
Gulliver.
Hanging Man, The.
Kindness.
Lady Lazarus.
Last Words.
Lesbos.
Life, A.
Little Fugue.
Love Letter.
Mary's Song.
Medallion.
Medusa.
Metamorphosis.
Metaphors.
Mirror.
Moon and the Yew Tree, The.
Morning Song.
Mushrooms.
Nick and the Candlestick.
Poppies in October.
Rabbit Catcher, The.
Sheep in Fog.
Sow.
Spinster.
Stars over the Dordogne.
Stones, The.
Suicide off Egg Rock.
Three Women, *sel.*
Tulips.
Two Views of a Cadaver Room.
Watercolor of Grantchester Meadows.
Winter Ship, A.
Winter Trees.
Wintering.
Words.
You're.

**Plato**
Kissing Helena.
Lais now old, that erst attempting lass.
Love Sleeping.
On a Seal.
Pan Piping.
To Stella.

**Platov, Mariquita**
Whispering Clouds.

**Plescoff, Jorge**

Ladder Has No Steps, The.
Ourobouros.
Tongues of Fire.
Violins in Repose.

**Plomer, William**
Father and Son: 1939.
Headline History.
In the Snake Park.
Mews Flat Mona.
Playboy of the Demi-World, The: 1938.
Positive, a Coxcomb.
Scorpion, The.
Seven Rainy Months.
To the Moon and Back.
Widow's Plot, The; or, She Got What Was Coming to Her.

**Plumly, Stanley**
After Grief.
End of the Indian Poems, The.
Fungo.
Giraffe.
Heron.
One Song.
Out-of-the-Body Travel.
Porches.
Pull of the Earth.
Summer Celestial.
Virginia Beach.

**Plumpp, Sterling**
Beyond the Nigger ("Beyond the outstretched hands").
For Mattie and Eternity.
Half Black, Half Blacker.
I Told Jesus.
Living Truth, The.

**Plunkett, Joseph Mary**
1867.

**Plutzik, Hyam**
Begetting of Cain, The.
Geese, The.
I Am Disquieted When I See Many Hills.
Jim Desterland.
King of Ai, The.
Of Objects Considered as Fortresses in a Baleful Place.
On the Photograph of a Man I Never Saw.
To My Daughter.

**Plymell, Charles**
Baltimore Eclipse.
For Cynara.

**Po Chü-i**
Cranes, The.
Eating Bamboo-Shoots.

**Poe, Edgar Allan**
Al Aaraaf, *sels.*
Alone.
Annabel Lee.
Bells, The.
City in the Sea, The.
Coliseum, The.
Conqueror Worm, The.
Dream-Land.
Dream within a Dream, A.
Dreams.
Eldorado.
Fall of the House of Usher, The, *sel.*
For Annie.
Haunted Palace, The.
Introduction: "Romance, who loves to nod and sing."

Israfel.
Lenore, 3 *versions.*
Ligeia, *prose tale, sel.*
Raven, The.
Sleeper, The.
Song: "Young flowers were whispering in melody."
Sonnet—Silence.
Sonnet—to Science.
To Helen ("Helen, thy beauty is to me").
To One in Paradise.
Ulalume—a Ballad.

**Polite, Frank**
Carmen Miranda.
Lantern.

**Polk, Noel**
Wreck.

**Pollak, Felix**
Historical Society Exhibit: Old Programme.
How I Got Myself Trapped.
Nofretete.
Speaking: The Hero.
Stone and the Obliging Pond.

**Pollard, Adelaide A.**
Have Thine Own Way, Lord! *with music.*

**Pollitt, Katha**
Blue Window.
In Horse Latitudes.
Riverside Drive, November Fifth.
Turkish Story, A.

**Polson, Don**
Sons.

**Pomerantz, Berl**
End of Summer.
Young Virgins Plucked Suddenly.

**Pomerantz, Marsha**
Adam and Eve at the Garden Gate.
How to Reach the Moon

**Pomeroy, Marnie**
News.

**Pomeroy, Ralph**
Corner.
English Train, Summer.
Looking at the Empire State Building.

**Pomfret, John**
Choice, The.

**Pompili, Vittoria Aganoor**
Fear.
Finally.

**Ponce de León, Luis.** *See* **León, Luis Ponce de**

**Ponchon, Raoul**
Shepherd's Tale, The.

**Pond, Margaret.** *See* **Church, Peggy Pond**

**Ponge, Francis**
Delights of the Door, The.
End of Fall, The.
Horse, The.
Oyster, The ("The oyster, about as large as a medium-sized stone").
Trees Lose Parts of Themselves inside a Circle of Fog.

**Ponsot, Marie**
Communion of Saints: The Poor Bastard under the Bridge.
Multipara: Gravida 5.
Possession.
Subject.
To the Age's Insanities.

**Poor Wolf**
Poor Wolf Speaks.

**Popa, Vasko**
Donkey.

**Pope, Alexander**
Apologia pro Vita Sua.
Art of Sinking in Poetry, The, *sel.*
Atticus.
Chloe.
Cibber! write all thy verses upon glasses.
Dialogue, A.
Duke of Buckingham, The.
Duke upon Duke.
Dunciad, The, *sels.*
Elegy to the Memory of an Unfortunate Lady.
Epigram in a Maid of Honour's Prayer-Book.
Epigram on One Who Made Long Epitaphs.
Epilogue to the Satires [*or* 1738].
Epistle to Dr. Arbuthnot.
Epistle to Miss [*or* Miss Teresa] Blount, on Her Leaving the Town after the Coronation.
Epitaph for One Who Would Not Be Buried in Westminster Abbey.
Epitaph on Himself.
Epitaph on James Moore Smythe.
Essay on Criticism, An.
Essay on Man, An,*sels.*
First Epistle of the First Book of Horace Imitated, The, *sel.*
First Satire of the Second Book of Horace, The.
For forms of government let fools contest.
Great Chain of Being, The.
Hunt, The.
In wit, as nature, what affects our hearts.
Know Thyself.
Lamentation of Glumdalclitch, The.
Lines on Swift's Ancestors.
Lines Written in Windsor Forest.
Little Learning, A.
Lock, The.
Lord Coningsby's Epitaph.
Moral Essays,*sels.*
Ode: Dying Christian to His Soul, The.
Ode on Solitude.
Ode on St. Cecilia's Day, *sel.*
Of all the causes which conspire to blind.
On a Certain Lady at Court
On Authors and Booksellers.
On Certain Ladies.
On Dennis.
On J. M. S. Gent.
On Poets.
On the Candidates for the Laurel.
On the Erection of Shakespeare's Statue in Westminster Abbey.
Pastorals, *sels.*
Power of Ridicule, The.
Rape of the Lock, The.
Sad Story, A.
Second Satire of the First Book of Horace Imitated, The, *sel.*
Sound and Sense.
Sporus.
Sylvan Delights.
Three Epitaphs on John Hewet and Sarah Drew.

To Richard Boyle, Earl of Burlington: Of the Use of Riches.
Toilet, The.
Triumph of Dullness, The.
Triumph of Vice, The.
Two or Three: A Recipe [*or* Receipt] to Make a Cuckold.
Universal Prayer, The.
Vice ("Vice is a monster of so frightful mien").
Voyage on the Thames, The.
What would this man? Now upward will he soar.
When Eastern lovers feed the fun'ral fire.
Who knocks at the door?
Winter.

**Pope, Alexander** *and* John Gay. *See* **Gay, John** *and* **Alexander Pope**

**Pope, Alexander** *and* Thomas Parnell
On Riding to See Dean Swift in the Mist of the Morning.

**Pope, Deborah**
There Is Something.

**Pope, J. R.**
Word of Encouragement, A.

**Pope, Jessie**
Our Visit to the Zoo.

**Pope, Liston**
Sea Turtle.

**Popham, Hugh**
Usual exquisite boredom of patrols, The.

**Porson, Richard**
Bathos, The.
Mutual Congratulations of the Poets Anna Seward and Hayley, The.
Note on the Latin Gerunds, A.
On a Doctor of Divinity.
Porson on German Scholarship.
Porson on His Majesty's Government.
Porson's Visit to the Continent.
To Dr. Kipling.

**Portal, Magda**
Film Vermouth: Six o'Clock Show.
Shores of anguish.

**Porter, Alan**
Stallion, The.

**Porter, Cole**
Anything Goes.
Brush Up Your Shakespeare.
Let's Do It.
My Heart Belongs to Daddy.
Night and Day, *with music.*
So in Love, *with music.*
Well, Did You Evah?

**Porter, Fairfield**
Island in the Evening, The.

**Porter, Peter**
Affair of the Heart.
Annotations of Auschwitz, *sel.*
Consumer's Report, A.
Exequy, An.
In the Giving Vein.
"In the New World Happiness Is Allowed."
Last of England, The.
London is full of chickens, on electric spits.
Metamorphosis.
Mort aux Chats.
Nine o'Clock Thoughts on the 73 Bus.
Non Piangere, Liù.
Notes to a Biographer.

Sex and the Over Forties.
Story Which Should Have Happened.
Sydney Cove, 1788.
To Make It Real.
Your Attention Please.
**Porter, T. E.**
Raft of *The Medusa*, The.
**Porter, William Sidney.**    *See* **"Henry, O."**
**Porumbacu, Veronica**
Of Autumn.
**Poseidippus**
Doricha.
**Posey, Alexander L.**
On the Capture and Imprisonment of
Crazy Snake, January, 1900.
**Potter, Eugene** *and* Pierre Degeyter
Internationale, The.
**Potter, Reuben M.**
Hymn of the Alamo.
**Potts, Charles**
March Wardrobe.
Para Olga.
**Potts, Paul**
For My Father.
Muse to an Unknown Poet, The.
**Poulsson, Emilie**
Santa Claus and the Mouse.
**Pound, Ezra**
Alba: "As cool as the pale wet leaves."
Alba: "When the nightingale to his
mate."
Alchemist, The.
Ancient Music.
Ancient Wisdom, Rather Cosmic.
And the Days Are Not Full Enough.
And Thus in Nineveh.
April.
Ballad of the Goodly Fere.
Ballad of the Mulberry Road, A.
Ballatetta.
Bathtub, The.
Beautiful Toilet, The.
Cantico del Sole.
Cantos, *sels.*
Cino.
Coda.
Coming of War, The: Actaeon.
Commission.
Contemporania, *sel.*
Dance Figure.
De Aegypto.
E. P. Ode pour l'Election de Son
Sepulchre.
Eleanor (she spoiled in a British
climate).
Elegy: "Me happy, night, night full of
brightness."
Envoi (1919).
Faun, The.
Fish and the Shadow.
For an officer/ in the old Capital, fox
fur.
For deep deer-copse beneath Mount
Han.
For E. McC.
Fragmenti.
Francesca.
Fraternitas.
"From the colour the nature."
Garden, The.
Garret, The.
Hang it all, Robert Browning.

Homage to Sextus Propertius, *sels.*
Hugh Selwyn Mauberley (Life and
Contacts).
I dreamt that I was God Himself.
Immorality, An.
In a Station of the Metro.
Itè.
Know then:/ Toward summer when the
sun is in Hyades.
Lake Isle, The.
L'Art, 1910.
L'Homme Moyen Sensuel, *sels.*
Liu Ch'e.
Marvoil.
Medallion.
Meditatio.
Mr. Housman's Message.
Monumentum Aere, Etc.
N.Y.
New Cake of Soap, The.
O Atthis.
Pact, A.
Paracelsus in Excelsis.
Pedlar.
Phyllidula.
Pick a fern, pick a fern, ferns are high.
Pine boat a-shift.
Portrait d'une Femme.
Reflection and Advice.
Rest, The.
Return, The.
Salutation.
Salutation the Second.
Seeing Eye, The.
Separation on the River Kiang.
Sestina: Altaforte.
Sketch 48b.11.
Song of the Bowmen of Shu.
Song of the Degrees, A, *sel.*
South-Folk in Cold Country.
Study in Aesthetics, The.
Tame Cat.
Tea Shop, The.
Temperaments, The.
Tenzone.
To Kalòn.
To Whistler, American.
Toujours la Politesse.
Trahison des Clercs; against the
Perversion of Language.
Translator to Translated.
Tree, The.
Villanelle: The Psychological Hour.
Villonaud for This Yule.
Virginal, A.
What thou lovest well remains.
When, when and whenever death closes
our eyelids.
Wide, ho?
**Pound, Ezra** *and* Noel Stock
I find my love fishing.
O flowers of Mekhemkh, give us peace!
Pomegranate speaks, The.
So small are the flowers of Seamu.
Swallow sings "Dawn," The.
There are flowers of Zait in the garden.
With candour I confess my love.
With you here at Mertu.
**Pounds, Jessie B.**
Beautiful Isle of Somewhere, *with music.*
**Powell, Amanda**
Leaving Home.

My Ice Man Begins to Move.
**Powell, Anthony**
Caledonia.
**Power, Marguerite (Countess of
Blessington)**
Friend, A.
**Powers, Jessica**
Cancer Patient.
Wanderer.
**Powys, John Cowper**
In a Hotel Writing-Room.
Ridge, The, *sel.*
**Poyner, Ken**
Therapy.
**Pozzi, Antonia**
To Trust.
**Prado, Holly**
Mouth That Is a Wound, The.
Night You Got Back from the
Mountains, The.
Tropics, The
**Prados, Emilio**
Dream.
**Praed, Winthrop Mackworth**
Arrivals at a Watering-Place.
Belle of the Ball Room, The.
Every-Day Characters: Portrait of a
Lady.
Good-Night to the Season.
Letter of Advice, A.
Ode to Popularity.
Royal Education.
Stanzas to the Speaker Asleep.
Talented Man, The.
**Prager, Marie-Francoise**
I'll act out a weird dream.
**Pratt, Agnes**
Death Takes Only a Minute.
Empathy.
**Pratt, Edwin John**
Prize Cat, The.
Ritual, The.
Truant, The.
**Pratt, William W.**
Same Old Trick.
**Praxilla**
Adonis, Dying.
Lovely girl, you look at me through the
window.
Most beautiful of things I leave is
sunlight.
Watch out, my dear.
You gaze at me teasingly through the
window.
**Preil, Gabriel**
Arriving.
Autumn Music.
Biographical Note.
Fishermen.
From Jerusalem: A First Poem.
Giving Up on the Shore.
Late Manuscript at the Schocken
Institute, A.
Lesson in Translation, A.
Letter Out of the Gray.
Like David.
Memory of Another Climate.
Parting.
Rains on the Island.
Summing Up, A.
Words of Oblivion and Peace.
**Prelutsky, Jack**

Troll, The.

**Prentiss, Elizabeth Payson**
More Love to Thee, O Christ, *with music.*

**Press, John**
Womanisers.

**Preston, Keith**
Effervescence and Evanescence.
Lapsus Linguae.

**Prettyman, Quandra**
Mood, The.
Photograph.
Still Life: Lady with Birds.
When Mahalia Sings.

**Prévert, Jacques**
Alicante.
Message, The.

**Price, E. Curmie**
Ballad of Bigger Thomas, The.

**Price, Jonathan**
Considered Reply to a Child, A.
Ezra Pound.
Glaze, The. You try to see.
Ice Cream.
Nine meshes of the net enclose.
Test.

**Price, Nancy**
Harbor.

**Pridmore, Jane**
In the Dark.

**Primrose, Lady Diana**
Chain of Pearl, A, *sel.*
Fourth Pearl, The: Temperance.

**Prince, Alison**
Dog howled and howled, The.

**Prince, Frank Templeton**
Question, The.
Soldiers Bathing.
Token, The.

**Prince, Thomas**
Give Ear, O God, to My Loud Cry, *with music.*
O Lord, Bow Down Thine Ear, *with music.*
With Christ and All His Shining Train, *with music.*

**Prior, Matthew**
Advice to the Painter.
Alma; or, The Progress of the Mind.
Another True Maid.
Answer to Chloe Jealous.
Chameleon, The.
Chaste Florimel.
Divine Blacksmith, The.
Dutch Proverb, A.
Epigram: "Rise not till noon, if life be but a dream."
Epigram: "Thy nags (the leanest things alive)."
Epigram: "To John I ow'd great obligation."
Epigram: "Tom's sickness did his morals mend."
Epigram: "When Bibo thought fit from the world to retreat."
Epigram: "Yes, every poet is a fool."
Epitaph, An: "Interr'd beneath this marble stone."
Epitaph: "Meek Francis lies here, friend, without stop or stay."
Fatal Love.
For My Own Monument.

Great Bacchus: From the Greek.
Human Life.
Jinny the Just.
Lady Who Offers Her Looking-Glass to Venus, The.
Letter to the Honourable Lady Miss Margaret Cavendish Holles-Harley, A.
Ode, An: "Merchant, to secure his treasure, The."
On Himself.
Phyllis's Age.
Quid Sit Futurum Cras Fuge Quaerere.
Reasonable Affliction, A.
Remedy, Worse than the Disease, The.
Secretary, The.
Simile, A.
To a Child of Quality [Five Years Old].
To Cloe Weeping.
True Maid, A.
Woman's Wish, The.
Written in an Ovid.
Written in the Beginning of Mezeray's History of France.

**Pritam, Amrita**
Daily Wages.

**Pritchard, Norman Henry, II**
Aswelay.
Gyre's Galax.
Self.

**Pritchard, Sheila**
Some Kind of Giant.

**Pritzkow, Louis W.**
Take Back Your Gold, *with music.*

**Privett, Katharine**
Watching My Daughter Sew.
Windmill in March.

**Probst, Anita Endrezze**
Canto Llano.
Dream Feast, The (Three Poems).
Eclipse.
Exodus.
In the Flight of the Blue Heron: To Montezuma.
Learning the Spells: A Diptych.
Manifest Destiny.
Notes from an Analyst's Couch.
Passion Drinker, The.
Raven/Moon.
Red Rock Ceremonies.
Stripper, The.
Truth about My Sister and Me, The.
Week-End Indian, The.

**Procter, Adelaide Anne**
Lost Chord, A.
My Picture.

**Procter, Bryan Waller.** *See* "Cornwall, Barry"

**Proffitt, Edward**
Melody.
New Uses for Old Utensils.
Our Decor.
Terrible Dactyl, Son of Rodan.

**Prokosch, Frederic**
Gothic Dusk, The.

**"Prout, Father."** *See* Mahony, Francis Sylvester

**Provisor, Dennis**
Walking through the Country.

**Provost, Sarah**
These Magicians.

**Prøysen, Alf**
Mice Celebrate Christmas, The.

**Pruitt, Bill**
Lilacs.

**Prunty, Wyatt**
Repetition.
Wake, The.

**Prys, Edmwnd**
Welsh Ballad, A.

**Prys, Thomas**
Poem to Show the Trouble That Befell Him When He Was at Sea, A.

**Prys-Jones, Arthur Glyn**
Day Which Endures Not, A.
St. Govan.
Tides.

**Pudney, John**
Aunts Watching Television.
Missing.

**Pumphrey, Jean**
In the Convalescent Hospital.
Poetry Liberation.
"Truly We Can Only Allow Our Paintings to Speak."

**Purcell, Charles M.**
Welcome Home.

**Purdom, George**
Robens' Promised Land.

**Purdy, Alfred Wellington**
Cariboo Horses, The.
Dead Seal.
Girl.
Nine Bean-Rows on the Moon.

**Pushkin, Aleksandr Sergeyevich**
Elegy: "Way the hell-bent years consume my pleasure, The."
Eugene Onegin, *sel.*
I loved you; even now I may confess.
Verses Written during a Sleepless Night.

# Q

**Qarshe, Cabdullaahi**
Colonialism ("The colonialist governments").

**Quagliano, Tony**
Cold Rain Obscures L. A. Tonight, A.
Hawk and Rock.
To the Author of "To My Brother Miguel."

**Quarles, Francis**
Are all such off'rings, as are crusht, and bruis'd.
Be Sad, My Heart.
Emblems,*sels.*
Epigram: "My Soul, sit thou a patient looker-on."
Epigram; "My soul, thy love is dear: 'twas thought a good."
Epigram: "What makes thee, fool, so fat? Fool, thee so bare?"
History of Samson, The, *sel.*
Hos Ego Versiculos.
My Beloved Is Mine and I Am His.
My soul, what's lighter than a feather? Wind.
On the Infancy of Our Saviour.
On the World.
On Those That Deserve It.
On Zacheus.

Our God and soldiers we alike adore.
Some curse that traitor Judas life and limb.
Why Dost Thou Shade Thy Lovely Face?

**Quasimodo, Salvatore**
Going Back.

**Quennell, Peter**
Divers, The.
Leviathan.

**Queremel, Angel Miguel**
Ballad of Love and Blood.

**Quevedo y Villegas, Francisco Gómez de**
I Saw the Ramparts of My Native Land.

**Quinn, John Robert**
At Times I Feel Like a Quince Tree.
Row of Houses.

**Quiñones, Juan Gómez.** *See* **Gómez-Quiñones, Juan**

**Quintana, Leroy V.**
Last Night There Was a Cricket in Our Closet.
Legacy II.
Nine Years after Viet Nam.

**Quirk, Cathleen**
Another Night on the Porch Swing.
Bird Calls.
Collaborations.
Composition.
"Hold Back the Edges of Your Gowns, Ladies, We Are Going through Hell."
Law of Falling and Catching Up, The.
Poem: "Crow flies between your phone and mine, The."

# R

**Raab, Esther**
Folk Tune.
Serenade for two Poplars, A.

**Raab, Lawrence**
Assassin's Fatal Error, The.
Attack of the Crab Monsters.
Pastoral: "Today in Peru, this first day of summer."
Two Clouds.
Valediction: "Sometimes I can believe."
Visiting the Oracle.
Voices Answering Back: The Vampires.

**Raba, Gyorgy**
Conversation.
Message.

**Rabelais, Francois**
Shrovetide's Countenance.

**Rabi'a the Mystic**
O my Lord, if I worship you from fear of Hell.
O my Lord, the stars glitter and eyes of men are closed.

**Raboff, Paul**
Jars.
Reb Hanina.

**Rachel** [*or* **Rahel**] (**Rachel Blunstein** *or* **Rahel Blaustein**)
My Dead.
My White Book of Poems.
Perhaps.
Rachel.

Revolt.
To My Country

**Racine, Jean**
Phaedra (Phèdre).

**Radcliffe, Alexander**
Ramble, The: An Anti-heroic Poem, *much abr.*

**Radcliffe, Anne**
Night.
Sonnet: "Now the bat circles on the breeze of eve."
Stanzas: "How smooth that lake expands its ample breast!"

**Radford, Dolly**
Buttercups.

**Radnóti, Miklós**
Forced March.
I Hid You.
In Your Arms.
Letter to My Wife.
Metaphors.
Picture Postcards.
Ragged Robin Opens, The.
Rain Falls. It Dries.
Root.
Seventh Eclogue.
Song: "Whipped by sorrow now."

**Rado, James** *and* **Gerome Ragni**
Air.

**Raffel, Burton**
Creation Myths.
Ecological Lecture.

**Raftery, Anthony**
County Mayo, The.
I Am Raftery. ("I am Raftery the poet").
Lass from Bally-na-Lee, The.

**Raftery, Gerald**
Apartment House.

**Ragan, Sam**
That Summer.

**Ragni, Gerome** *and* **James Rado.** *See* **Rado, James** *and* **Gerome Ragni**

**Rago, Henry**
Coming of Dusk upon a Village in Haiti, The.
Green Afternoon, The.
Knowledge of Light, The.
Monster, The.
Summer Countries, The.

**Rahschulte, Mark**
See all the people getting off the bus.

**Raine, Kathleen Jessie**
End of Love, The.
Envoi: "Take of me what is not my own."
Envoi: "What has want to give."
Eudaimon.
Human Form Divine, The.
In Time.
Instrument, The.
Message from Home.
Rose.
Spell against Sorrow.
To My Mountain.
Tu Non Se' in Terra, Si Come Tu Credi.
Two Invocations of Death.
Wilderness, The.
World, The.
Worry about Money.
Written in Exile.

**Raines, Charlotte A.**
City/Market.

Winter Wait, A.

**Raisor, Philip**
Demolition.

**Rakosi, Carl**
Americana IX: "Your correspondent must be kidding when he says."
Americana XIII: "Captain Patterson, the folks back home."
Americana XV: Simplicity.
Americana XVII: Reminder of William Carlos Williams, A.
Being Natural.
Country Singer, The.
Experiment with a Rat, The.
Florida.
In a Warm Bath.
Indomitable, The.
Meditation ("How long will you remain a boy?").
Meditation ("Lord, what is a man?").
Meditation ("Men are children of this world").
Meditation ("Three things remind me of you").
Medium IV, The: Sights.
Memoirs, The.
No One Talks about This.
Old Codger's Lament, The.
Poetry.
Song: "Circumstance has estranged my friend."
Tune.
Woman.
Young Couples Strolling By.

**Ralegh, Sir Walter**
Advice, The.
Description of Love, A.
Epitaph: "Even such is Time, which [*or* that] takes in trust."
Excuse, The.
Farewell to False Love, A.
Heaven's Queene.
Lie, The.
Methought I Saw the Grave Where Laura Lay.
Nymph's Reply to the Shepherd, The.
On the Snuff of a Candle.
Passionate Man's Pilgrimage, The.
Passions.
Poem of Sir Walter Rawleighs, A.
Sir Walter Ralegh to the Queen.
Sun [*or* Sunne] may set and rise, The.
To His Son.
Walter Rawely of the Middle Temple, in Commendation of the Steele Glasse.
What Is Our Life? A Play of Passion.

**Raleigh, Sir Walter Alexander (1861–1922)**
Wishes of an Elderly Man, The.

**"Ramal, Walter."** *See* **De la Mare, Walter**

**Ramanujan, A. K.**
River, A.
Self-Portrait.

**Ramanujan, Mahadevi**
Other men are thorn.

**Ramirez, Valentino**
Fishin' Blues.

**Ramke, Bin**
Spring Poem.

**Ramón Jiménez, Juan.** *See* **Jiménez, Juan Ramón**

**Ramsay, Allan**

Epigram: "Lasses, like nuts at bottom brown."
Generous Gentleman, The.
Lucky Spence's Last Advice.
Ode to Mr. F——.
Poet's Wish, The.
**Ramsey, Jarold**
Indian Painting, Probably Paiute, in a Cave Near Madras, Oregon.
**Ramsey, Patricia**
Anomie.
Creation, The.
Time, A: A Season.
War.
**Ramsey, Paul**
Advent Images, The.
Marilyn Monroe.
Physical Imperfections of Old Films, The.
Snowman in March, A.
Willie Mays.
**Ranaivo, Flavien**
Song of a Common Lover.
**Ranasinghe, Anne**
Auschwitz from Colombo.
Holocaust 1944.
**Randall, Dudley**
Abu.
After the Killing.
Analysands.
Ancestors.
Ballad of Birmingham.
Black Poet, White Critic.
Blackberry Sweet.
Booker T. and W. E. B.
Different Image, A.
Frederick Douglass and the Slave Breaker.
George.
Green Apples.
Hail, Dionysos.
Idiot, The.
Intellectuals, The.
Langston Blues.
Legacy: My South.
Melting Pot, The.
Memorial Wreath.
Old Witherington.
On Getting a Natural.
Pacific Epitaphs.
Perspectives.
Primitives.
Profile on the Pillow, The.
Rite, The.
Roses and Revolutions.
Southern Road, The.
Souvenirs.
Spring before a War ("Spring came early that year").
Tell It like It Is.
To the Mercy Killers.
**Randall, James A., Jr.**
Don't Ask Me Who I Am.
Execution.
Jew.
Untitled.
When Something Happens.
Who Shall Die?
**Randall, James Ryder**
Maryland, My Maryland!
**Randall, Julia**
Ballad of Eve, A.

For a Homecoming.
Rockland.
To William Wordsworth from Virginia.
Writer Indulges a Hobby, The
**Randolph, Innes**
Rebel, The.
**Randolph, Leonard**
Voice on the Other End of the Line, The.
**Randolph, Shawn**
Mad is like touching the devil.
**Randolph, Thomas**
Devout Lover, A.
Invocation: "Come from thy palace, beauteous Queen of Greece."
Milkmaid's Epithalamium, The.
On the Death of a Nightingale.
Phyllis.
Poet, The.
This definition poetry doth fit.
Upon His Picture.
Upon Love Fondly Refused for Conscience's Sake.
**Rands, William Brighty ("Mathew Browne")**
Cat of Cats, The.
Dream of a Boy Who Lived at Nine Elms, The.
Dream of a Girl Who Lived at Sevenoaks, The.
Pedlar's Caravan, The.
Reformation of Godfrey Gore, The.
Shooting Song, A.
Topsy-Turvy World.
White Princess, The, *sel.*
Winifred Waters.
Wonderful World, The.
**Rangiaho**
Song of Despair.
**Rankin, Carroll Watson**
Difficult Guest, A.
**Rankin, James**
Dustless Chalk.
Fair Isle Pattern.
Glasgow Botanic Gardens.
Grandpa.
Lamb.
Shetland Funeral.
Won't Go to School.
**Rankin, Jennifer J.**
Green Ash.
**Rankin, Jeremiah Eames**
God Be with You till We Meet Again, *with music.*
Laboring and Heavy Laden, *with music.*
**Rankin, Paula**
Love in Magnolia Cemetery.
Tending.
**Rankins, William**
By this time long-gowned Lumen walked abroad.
Satyrus Peregrinans, *sel.*
**Ransom, John Crowe**
Address to the Scholars of New England.
Amphibious Crocodile.
Blue Girls.
Captain Carpenter.
Dead Boy.
Dog.
Emily Hardcastle, Spinster.
Equilibrists, The.

Her Eyes.
Here Lies a Lady.
Inland City.
Janet Waking.
Judith of Bethulia.
Lady Lost.
Master's in the Garden Again.
Miss Euphemia.
Necrological.
Old Mansion.
Our Two Worthies.
Painted Head.
Parting at Dawn.
Parting, without a Sequel.
Persistent Explorer.
Philomela.
Piazza Piece.
Prelude to an Evening.
Somewhere Is Such a Kingdom.
Spectral Lovers.
Survey of Literature.
Two in August.
Vaunting Oak.
Vision by Sweetwater.
Winter Remembered.
**Ransom, W. M.**
Catachism, 1958.
Critter.
Grandpa's .45.
Indian Summer: Montana, 1956.
Message from Ohanapecosh Glacier.
On the Morning of the Third Night above Nisqually.
Statement on Our Higher Education.
**Raphael, Lennox**
Mike 65.
**Ras, Barbara**
At the Beginnings of the Andes.
**Raskin, Selma**
Tee-Vee Enigma.
**Rasof, Henry**
Fourth Option, The.
**Ratcliffe, Dorothy Una**
Rake.
**Ratcliffe, Stephen**
Postscript, on a Name.
**Ratner, Rochelle**
Captive, The.
Davening.
Poor Shammes of Berditchev, The.
Someday Song for Sophia, A.
Tightrope Walker, The.
**Ratosh, Yonathan**
Lament: "You did not suck at my mother's breast."
**Ratti, John**
Inside, Outside, and Beyond.
**Raven, John**
Assailant.
Inconvenience, An.
Roach, The.
**Ravenel, Beatrice**
Alligator, The.
**Ravenel de la Coste, Marie**
Somebody's Darling.
**Ravenscroft, Thomas**
Madrigal: "My mistress is as fair as fine."
**Ravikovich [or Ravikovitch], Dahlia**
Blue West, The.
Dress of Fire, A.
Everlasting Forests, The.

**Ravitch**
Poem of Explanations.
Requiem after Seventeen Years.
Surely You Remember.
**Ravitch, Melech (Zekharye Khone Bergner)**
Conscience.
Let Us Learn.
Poem, A—Good or Bad—a Thing—with
  One Attribute—Flat.
Twelve Lines about the Burning Bush.
Twilight Thoughts in Israel.
Verses Written on Sand.
**Rawlinson, Gloria**
Hare in the Snow, The.
Islands Where I Was Born, The.
Merry-go-round.
**Raworth, Tom**
Collapsible.
Empty Pain-Killer Bottles, The.
Here in Polynia.
Hot Day at the Races.
My Face Is My Own, I Thought.
North Africa Breakdown.
Not under Holly or Green Boughs.
Six Days.
Sliding Two Mirrors.
There Are Lime Trees in Leaf on the
  Promenade.
You Were Wearing Blue.
**Ray, David**
At Grand Canyon's Edge.
Blue Duck, The.
Card-Players, The.
Carolinas, The.
Death-Lace.
Dragging the Main.
Extreme Unction in PA.
Greens.
Landscape, The.
Orphans.
Ravenna.
Sonnet to Seabrook.
Stopping near Highway 80.
Thanks, Robert Frost.
Ursula.
W. C. W.
X-Ray.
**Ray, Judy**
Rose Bay Willow Herb.
**Rayford, Julian Lee**
Boom.
**Raymond, Harry**
Hallelujah, I'm a-Travelin'.
**Raymund, Bernard**
Wonder.
**Rea, Susan Irene**
Love Poem: "Warned, warned for
  years."
Poem for Dorothy Holt.
Stroke.
**Read, Elfreida**
Return to the Valley.
**Read, Sir Herbert**
Execution of Cornelius Vane, The.
Harvest Home.
Mutations of the Phoenix, sel.
1945.
Sic et Non.
To a Conscript of 1940.
Well of Life, The.
White Isle of Leuce, The.
**Read, Sylvia**
Monkey.

Weasel.
**Read, Thomas Buchanan**
Sheridan's Ride.
**Reaney, James**
Chough, The ("The chough, said a
  dictionary").
Crow, The.
Katzenjammer Kids, The.
**Reape, Lisa**
Leavetaking.
**Reavey, George**
Bridge of Heraclitus, The.
Dismissing Progress and Its Progenitors.
Four Walls of My Cage, The.
How many fires.
Never.
**Reavin, Sam**
Octopus.
Someone.
Witch?
**Reccardi, Joe**
Remembering Him.
**Rechter, Judith**
Fay Wray to the King.
**Rector, Liam**
Eventual Music, The ("Eventually
  someone knocks at your door
  eventually").
My Grandfather Always Promised Us.
Weather Gallery, The.
**Red Cloud, Fred**
Machu Picchu, Peru.
Tale of Last Stands, A.
**Redding, Edward C.**
When the Saints Come Marching In,
  with music.
**Redgrove, Peter**
Barbers, The, sels.
Bedtime Story for My Son.
Corposant.
Force, The.
Secretary, The.
To the Postmaster General.
Young Women with the Hair of Witches
  and No Modesty.
**Redi, Francesco**
Bacchus in Tuscany, sel.
**Redl-Hlus, Carolyn D.**
Melissa.
**Redmond, Eugene B.**
Definition of Nature.
Gods in Vietnam.
Love Necessitates.
Main Man Blues.
Midway in the Night: Blackman.
**Redmond, Seamus**
Silent Spinney, The.
**Redshaw, Thomas Dillon**
Voice from Danang.
**Redwing, A. K.**
Agent of Love.
Blue Jeaned Rock Queen in Search of
  Happiness on a Blind Thursday at 1/3
  Speed and Crying, A.
Chrome Babies Eating Chocolate
  Snowmen in the Moonlight.
Cosmic Eye.
Hoofer, The.
Lost Mohican Visits Hell's Kitchen, A.
Sitting Bull's Will versus the Sioux
  Treaty of 1868 and Monty Hall.
Tornado Soup.

Two Hookers.
World's Last Unnamed Poem, The.
Written in Unbridled Repugnance near
  Sioux Falls, Alabama—April 30, 1974.
**Reece, Byron Herbert**
Beetle in the Wood, The.
**Reed, Ed**
Key of the Kingdom, The.
**Reed, Henry**
Chard Whitlow.
Judging Distances.
Lessons of the War.
Morning.
Naming of Parts.
**Reed, Ishmael**
Al Capone in Alaska.
Badman of the Guest Professor.
Beware: Do Not Read This Poem.
Black Power Poem.
Feral Pioneers, The.
.05.
Gangster's Death, The.
I Am a Cowboy in the Boat of Ra.
Instructions to a Princess.
Rain Rain on the Splintered Girl.
Reactionary Poet, The.
Sermonette.
Skirt Dance.
Sputin.
Untitled I.
**Reed, J. D.**
Cripples.
Elders.
Ford Hospital.
Gorilla at Twenty Nine Years, The.
Organ Transplant.
Out from Lobster Cove.
Stony Brook Tavern.
Strange Kind (II).
**Reed, John**
Proud New York.
**Reed, Joseph Samuel**
Soldier's Plea for the Y.M.C.A., A.
**Reed, Langford**
Hail to the Town of Limerick.
Patriot, A.
**Reed, Thomas**
Indian, The.
**Reedy, Arnold**
Lament for Apirana Ngata.
**Rees, Grover, III**
Abelard at Cluny.
**Rees, John Machreth**
Merioneth.
**Reese, Florence**
Which Side Are You On?
**Reese, Lizette Woodworth**
Tears.
**Reeve, Franklin Dolier**
Botany Lesson.
Hope.
Plaque in the Reading Room for My
  Classmates Killed in Korea, The.
**Reeves, Goebel**
Hobo's Lullaby.
**Reeves, James**
Academic.
Bagatelle, A.
Beech Leaves.
Bobadil.
Bogus-Boo, The.
Castles and Candlelight.

Cows.
Doze, The.
Four Horses, The.
Gabble-Gabble.
Giant Thunder.
Grey Horse, The.
Horn, The.
If Pigs Could Fly.
Little Brother, The.
Little Fan.
Magic Seeds, The.
Mick.
Mr. Tom Narrow.
Mrs. Golightly.
Old Wife and the Ghost, The.
Seeds.
Snail, The.
Spicer's Instant Poetry.
Stocking and Shirt.
Toadstool Wood, The.
Travelers, The.
Wind, The.
Wooing Frog, The.
You in Anger.
Zachary Zed.
**Regelson, Abraham**
Moses on Mount Nebo.
**Reich, Heather Tosteson**
Waltz.
**Reich, Shlomo**
Golem, The.
Tribe Searching, A.
Vigil, The.
Windmill of Evening, The.
**Reid, Alastair**
At First Sight.
Curiosity.
Daedalus.
Day the Weather Broke, The.
Figures on the Frieze, The.
Ghosts' Stories.
Pigeons.
Propinquity.
Tale the Hermit Told, The.
To a Child at the Piano.
**Reid, Christopher**
Gladstone gave his name to the
   gladstone bag.
**Reid, Heddy**
Black Hole in Space.
**Reid, Keith**
She Wandered through the Garden
   Fence.
**Reid, Robert F., III**
Shadow Life.
**Reiner, Lois**
Father.
**Reingold, Paula**
And This Is Love.
**Reisen, Abraham**
Endless Chain, An.
Family of Eight, The.
Girls from Home.
Newcomers.
What Is the Case in Point?
**Reiss, James**
Approaching Washington Heights.
Breathers, The.
Brothers (I).
First Poem, The.
Green Tree, The.
Habla Usted Español?

Macy's Poem, The.
Morningside Heights: Fragment of a
   Film.
On Hot Days.
Slight Confusion, A.
Something like an Apple.
Sueños.
**Reiter, Thomas**
Dinoland.
Other Side, The.
**Rella, Ettore**
Bone and the Baby, The.
Ceasar and the Blind Men.
Cosmetic Survival.
Hieroglyphs.
Monkeys from Paradise.
Scab, The.
Spring Rain.
Sunday Morning.
**Remaly, Nancy**
August Afternoon.
**Rendall, Robert**
Angle of Vision.
**Rendleman, Danny L.**
Death of Neruda, The.
Drowned Darling, The.
Letter from Olga, Declaiming.
Midland.
Parting Chores, The.
Rosalie.
Tenant.
**Replansky, Naomi**
Brick not used in building, A.
Housing Shortage.
In the Sea of Tears.
Inheritance, An.
Mistress Addresses the Wife, The.
Two Women.
**Resnikoff, Alexander**
Bad and Good.
Big Game Hunter.
Longest Tale about the Longest Tail,
   The.
Two Witches.
**Revard, Carter**
Advice from Euterpe.
Another Sunday Morning.
"But Still in Israel's Paths They Shine."
Coming of Age in the County Jail.
Coyote, The.
Discovery of the New World.
Driving in Oklahoma.
ESP.
Getting Across.
Home Movies.
January 15 as a National Holiday.
North of Santa Monica.
Not Just Yet.
On the Bright Side.
Support Your Local Police Dog.
**Revell, Donald**
Central Park South.
**Revere, Jonathan**
Gull Skeleton.
**Rewak, William J.**
"Quick Now, Here, Now, Always."
Visit, The.
**Rewey, Marion Brimm**
Love Song for a Tyrant.
**Rexford, Eben Eugene**
Silver Threads among the Gold.
**Rexroth, Kenneth**

Andrée Rexroth.
Autumn Rain.
Bad Old Days, The.
Bear.
City of the Moon, The, sel.
Codicil.
Confusion.
Dialogue of Watching, A.
Discrimination.
Education.
Erotion rests here, in the/ Hastening
   shadows.
Fact.
Fifty.
Fish Peddler and Cobbler.
For a Masseuse and Prostitute.
For Mary.
Further Advantages of Learning.
GIC to HAR.
Great Canzon, The.
Growing.
Hanged Man, The.
Heart of Herakles, The.
Here is Klito's little shack.
Herring.
Horse.
I have sworn ten thousand times.
I Lais, once an arrow.
I used to tell you, "Frances, we grow
   old."
Inversely, as the Square of Their
   Distances Apart.
Letter to William Carlos Williams, A.
Lights in the Sky Are Stars, The.
Lion.
Lute Music.
Lyell's Hypothesis Again.
Lysidike dedicates.
Me Again.
Mirror in the Woods, The.
Naked out of the dark we came.
New Year, The.
Oh, who will shoe your pretty little foot.
Observations in a Cornish Teashop.
On the Eve of the Plebiscite.
Only Years.
Parity.
Place, The.
Proust's Madeleine.
Raccoon.
Signature of All Things, The.
Song for a Dancer.
Strength through Joy.
Time Is the Mercy of Eternity.
Value Neuter.
Vitamins and Roughage.
Vulture.
Wheel Revolves, The.
Wolf.
Yin and Yang.
You are a stool pigeon and.
Your Birthday in the California
   Mountains.
**Reyes Basualto, Neftalí Ricardo.**  *See*
   **Neruda, Pablo**
**Reynolds, Barney**
Cranberry Song, The.
**Reynolds, Malvina**
Little Boxes.
What Have They Done to the Rain.
**Reynolds, Margaret**
Acceptance.

Eruption.
Fear, The.
Naturalist, The.
Old Tiger and the God of the Water-Hole, The.
Poverty.
Seventy.
**Reynolds, Tim**
Going Home.
Walk in March, A.
**Rezmerski, John Calvin**
Driving at Night.
Pettigrew Museum.
Some Good Things Left after the War with the Sioux.
**Reznikoff, Charles**
About an Excavation.
After I Had Worked All Day.
Autobiography: Hollywood.
Body Is Like Roots Stretching, The.
Citizen, A.
Depression, *sel.*
Domestic Scenes, 2.
Five Groups of Verse, *sels.*
Fraser, I think, tells of a Roman.
Ghetto Funeral.
Going To and Fro and Walking Up and Down, *sels.*
Hebrew of Your Poets, Zion, The.
House-wreckers have left the door and a staircase, The.
How difficult for me is Hebrew.
How Shall We Mourn You Who Are Killed and Wasted.
I Will Go into the Ghetto.
I Will Write Songs against you.
Jacob.
Kaddish ("In her last sickness, my mother took my hand in hers").
Kaddish ("Upon Israel and upon the rabbis").
Lament of the Jewish Women for Tammuz.
Let Other People Come as Streams.
Letter, The.
Luzzato.
New Year's.
Out of the Strong, Sweetness.
Puerto Ricans in New York, (I & II).
Raisins and Nuts.
Samuel.
Separate Way, *sel.*
Showing a torn sleeve, with stiff and shaking fingers the old man.
Simple soul, who so early in the morning.
Te Deum.
These Days the Papers in the Street.
This Subway Station.
Walk about the Subway Station.
Winter Sketches.
Young fellow walks about, The
**Rhodes, Eugene Manlove**
Hired Man on Horseback, The.
**Rhodes, Hugh**
Rising in the Morning.
**Rhys, Ernest**
Wales England Wed.
**Ribemont-Dessaignes, Georges**
Sliding Trombone.
**Ribera Chevremont, Evaristo**
Boy and the Lantern, The, *abr.*

**Rice, Cale Young**
Nights on the Indian Ocean.
**Rice, Grantland**
Any Golf Championship.
Game Called.
U. S. A., The.
**Rice, Helen Steiner**
God, Are You There?
He Was One of Us.
It's Me Again, God.
Legend of the Raindrop, The.
Prayer for the Young and Lovely, A.
**Rice, Les**
Banks of Marble.
**Rice, Stan**
Waiting in the Cafe.
**Rice, Thomas D.**
Jim Crow.
Jump Jim Crow, *with music.*
**Rice, Seymour** and Albert H. Brown
You Tell Me Your Dream, I'll Tell You Mine, *with music.*
**Rich, Adrienne**
Abnegation.
After Dark.
Afterwake, The.
At a Bach Concert.
Attention.
August.
Aunt Jennifer's Tigers.
Autumn Sequence.
Bears.
Book, The.
Burning of Paper Instead of Children, The.
Burning Oneself In.
Clock in the Square, A.
Continuum.
Demon Lover, The.
Dialogue.
Diamond Cutters, The.
Did you think I was talking about my life?
Diving into the Wreck.
Double Monologue.
5:30 A.M.
Focus.
Friend I can trust is the one who will let me have my death, The.
From a Survivor.
From an Old House in America.
From here on, all of us will be living.
From the Prison House.
Gabriel.
Ghazals: Homage to Ghalib.
"I Am in Danger—Sir."
I Dream I'm the Death of Orpheus.
Ideal Landscape.
In the Woods.
Insusceptibles, The.
Knight, The.
Landscape of the Star.
Leaflets.
Like This Together.
Living in Sin.
Merced.
Mirror in Which Two Are Seen as One, The.
Mourning Picture.
Necessities of Life.
Night Watch.
Nightbreak.

Ninth Symphony of Beethoven Understood at Last as a Sexual Message.
Not like That.
Novella.
November 1968.
On Edges.
Orion.
Our Whole Life.
Peeling Onions.
Phantasia for Elvira Shatayev.
Picnic.
Pierrot le Fou.
Planetarium.
Power.
Primary Ground, A.
Prospective Immigrants Please Note.
Rape.
Readings of History.
Re-forming the Crystal.
Roofwalker, The.
Side by Side.
Sisters.
Snapshots of a Daughter-in-Law.
Song: "You're wondering if I'm lonely."
Storm Warnings.
Stranger, The.
Trees, The.
Trying to Talk with a Man.
Twenty-one Love Poems, *sels.*
Two Songs.
Unsaid Word, An.
Valediction Forbidding Mourning, A.
Will to Change, The.
Woman Mourned by Daughters, A.
Women.
**Richard, Keith** and **Mick Jagger.** *See* **Jagger, Mick** and **Keith Richard**
**Richards, Edward Hersey**
Wise Old Owl, A.
**Richards, George**
Almighty Spake, and Gabriel Sped, Th', *with music.*
Long as the Darkening Cloud Abode, *with music.*
**Richards, Laura Elizabeth**
Antonio.
Bird Song.
Bobbily Boo and Wollypotump.
Eletelephony.
Legend of Lake Okeefinokee, The.
Mrs. Snipkin and Mrs. Wobblechin.
Monkeys and the Crocodile, The.
My Uncle Jehoshaphat.
Poor Unfortunate Hottentot, The.
Queen of the Orkney Islands, The.
Some Fishy Nonsense.
**Richardson, Dorothy M.**
Message.
**Richardson, Dow**
Cost-of-Living Mother Goose, The.
**Richardson, James**
Dividing the House.
**Richardson, Justin**
Oocuck, The.
**Richmond, Steve**
Gagaku: "Pissed on her chest."
Gagaku: "Put my hand through TV screen."
**Richter, C. F.**
My Soul before Thee Prostrate Lies, *with music.*

**Rickert, Wendy G.**
Somedays now/ I can squash a cockroach.
**Rickword, Edgell**
Cascade, The.
Contemporary Muse, The.
Cosmogony.
Encounter, The.
Handmaid of Religion, The.
Winter Warfare.
**Riddell, Alan**
Circle, The.
**Riddell, Elizabeth**
Letter, The.
**Ridge, Lola**
Electrocution.
Fifth-Floor Window, The.
Reveille.
Saint's Bridge.
Song, The: "That day, in the slipping of torsos and straining flanks."
Spring.
Veteran.
Ward X, *sel.*
**Riding, Laura (Laura Riding Jackson)**
Auspice of Jewels.
Because of Clothes.
Forgiven Past, The.
Head Itself.
Map of Places, The.
Opening of Eyes.
With the Face.
**Ridland, John**
Assassination Poems.
Light Year, The.
Week in Paradise, A.
**Ridler, Anne**
Backgrounds to Italian Paintings: Fifteenth Century.
Choosing a Name.
Christmas and Common Birth.
For a Child Expected.
Nothing Is Lost.
Now Phillipa Is Gone.
On a Picture by Michele da Verona, of Arion as a Boy Riding upon a Dolphin.
**Ridley, George**
Cushie Butterfield.
**Rieu, Emile Victor**
Castaways, The.
Cat's Funeral.
Flattered Flying Fish, The.
Green Train, The.
Happy Hedgehog, The.
Paint Box, The.
Snake and the Snake-Charmer, The.
Tony the Turtle.
Two People.
**Riggs, Dionis Coffin**
Clamdigger, The.
**Riggs, Lynn**
Spring Morning—Santa Fe.
**Rigsbee, David**
Green Frogs.
**Rihaku.** *See* **Li Po**
**Riley, James Whitcomb**
Billy Could Ride.
Craqueodoom.
Diners in the Kitchen, The.
Extremes.
Little Hunchback, The.

Little Orphant Annie.
Old Man and Jim, The.
Raggedy Man, The.
Rose in October, A.
When the Frost is on the Punkin.
**Riley, Michael D.**
Macramé.
**Rilke, Rainer Maria**
Archaic Torso of Apollo.
Book of Pilgrimage, The.
Bridge of the Carousel.
Christ's Descent into Hell.
Do you know, I would quietly.
Foreboding.
Grief, The.
Kings of the world are growing old, The.
Knight, The.
Last Supper, The.
Leda.
Lovesong.
Man Watching, The.
Merry-go-round, The.
Moving Ahead.
Palm of the Hand.
Panther, The.
Pieta.
Slumbersong.
Sonnets to Orpheus, *sels.*
Voices, The.
**Rimbaud, Arthur**
Dark and Wrinkled.
Dreamed-up for Winter.
Drunken Boat, The.
Lice-Hunters, The.
**Rimmer, Christine**
How Night Falls in the Courtyard.
**Rimon, I. Z.**
I Am a King.
**Rin, Ishigaki**
Clams.
**Rinaldi, Nicholas**
Black.
Teahouse.
**Rioff, Suzanne Berger**
Cycles, Cycles.
Seduction, The.
**Rios, A. A.**
Cinco de Mayo, 1862.
Cortes.
Nani.
**Ripley, Elizabeth**
Jammy.
**Ripley, G.**
Poem for Vladimir.
**Ritchie, Elisavietta**
Curriculum Vitae: Incomplete.
Dachau, Now: "Roses Grow There, Fat with Blood."
Goals.
Haiku: "This broken bottle."
In Answer to a Request to Write a Poem on World Peace.
In Jerusalem.
Learning to Keep a Low Profile.
Main Problem in Portraiture, The.
Most Days.
Search.
Spring Vacation: The Smithsonian.
Street Scenes from All Over.
Tarred Gull.
Temperature Variations.
Visitation.

**Ritsos, Yannis**
After the Rain.
Motionless Swaying.
**Rivera, Etnairis**
I pull out of the depths of the earth.
**Rivera, Marina**
Even.
**Rivera-Avilés, Sotero**
Good Memory.
Rainy Morning.
**Rivero, Alina**
In the Fall.
**Rivers, Conrad Kent**
Death of a Negro Poet, The.
For All Things Black and Beautiful.
Four Sheets to the Wind and a One-Way Ticket to France [1933].
If Blood Is Black Then Spirit Neglects My Unborn Son.
In Defense of Black Poets.
Malcolm, a Thousandth Poem.
Mourning Letter from Paris, A.
On the Death of William Edward Burghardt Du Bois by African Moonlight and Forgotten Shores.
Prelude: "Night and the hood."
Still Voice of Harlem, The.
To Richard Wright.
Train Runs Late to Harlem, The.
Watts.
**Rivers, James W.**
Tonsilectomy.
**Roat, Charles E.**
What a Friend We Have in Mother.
**Robbins, Howard Chandler**
And Have the Bright Immensities, *with music.*
Put Forth, O God, Thy Spirit's Might, *with music.*
Sabbath Day Was By, The, *with music.*
**Robbins, Martin**
Cantor's Dream before the High Holy Days, A.
On Seeing a Torn Out Coin Telephone.
Spring Rites.
**Robbins, Richard**
For My Grandfather.
**Robbins, Shellie Keir**
Yielding.
**Roberson, Ed**
Blue Horses.
If the Black Frog Will Not Ring.
Mayday.
Othello Jones Dresses for Dinner.
Poll.
Seventh Son.
When Thy King Is a Boy, *sel.*
**Robert of Gloucester**
Chronicle, *sel.*
Town against Gown at Oxford.
**Roberts, Andrew**
How to Get a Garden.
**Roberts, Cecil**
Prayer for a Pilot.
**Roberts, Sir Charles G. D.**
Epitaph for a Sailor Buried Ashore.
**Roberts, Daniel C.**
God of Our Fathers, Whose Almighty Hand, *with music.*
**Roberts, David**
Beloved, The.
**Roberts, Elizabeth Madox**

Autumn.
Christmas Morning.
Circus, The.
Cold Fear.
Father's Story.
Firefly.
Hens, The.
Horse.
Little Bush.
Milking Time.
Numbers.
**Roberts, George**
Andrew Talks to Gulls.
**Roberts, Hortense Roberta**
Farmers.
**Roberts, Jean**
I Never Saw the Train.
**Roberts, Michael**
H.M.S. *Hero.*
Hymn to the Sun.
In the Flowering Season.
Langdale: Nightfall, January 4th.
**Roberts, Philip**
Breakthrough.
Death of the Astronomer.
Gertrude Stein.
Just Passing Through.
Time Study.
**Roberts, Sheila**
Poem for My Dead Husband.
**Roberts, Ursula.** *See* **Miles, Susan**
**Robertson, Brian**
Party at the Contessa's House, The.
**Robertson, Clyde**
Yellow Witch of Caribou, The.
**Robertson, Foster**
Headlines.
**Robertson, Kell**
Between a Good Hat and Good Boots.
Crossing West Texas (1966).
Julio.
Landscape, New Mexico.
**Robertson, Kirk**
Clorox Kid, The.
Giant Squid of Tsurai, The.
Postcard to a Foetus.
**Robertson, Robbie**
All La Glory.
**Robin, Ralph**
At School They Told Us.
Man Walked under a Plastic Decoration,
A.
Rarity.
**Robins, Gurdon**
There Is a Land Mine Eye Hath Seen,
*with music.*
When Thickly Beat the Storms of Life,
*with music.*
**Robinson, Anne**
Drummer, The.
**Robinson, Barbara B.**
Foreign Student.
**Robinson, David**
Awakening.
**Robinson, Edwin Arlington**
Aaron Stark.
As It Looked Then.
Bewick Finzer.
Calvary.
Calverly's.
Cassandra.
Charles Carville's Eyes.

Clerks, The.
Cliff Klingenhagen.
Companion, The.
Credo.
Dark Hills, The.
Eros Turannos.
Eutychides.
Firelight.
Flammonde.
Flying Dutchman, The.
For a Dead Lady.
George Crabbe.
Hillcrest.
House on the Hill, The.
How Annandale Went Out.
Inscription by the Sea, An.
John Evereldown.
John Gorham.
Karma.
Lais to Aphrodite.
Lost Anchors.
Luke Havergal.
Man against the Sky, The.
Many Are Called.
Maya.
Mighty Runner, A (Variation of a Greek
Theme.)
Mill, The.
Miniver Cheevy.
Mr. Flood's Party.
New England.
New Tenants, The.
Old Story, An.
Poor Relation, The.
Prodigal Son, The.
Raven, The.
Reuben Bright.
Reunion.
Richard Cory.
Sheaves, The.
Sonnet: "Oh for a poet—for a beacon
bright."
Souvenir.
Supremacy.
Tact.
Unforgiven, The.
Vain Gratuities.
Veteran Sirens.
Why He Was There.
**Robinson, James Miller**
Coweta County Courthouse, The.
**Robinson, Lila Cayley**
Glow Worm, *with music.*
**Robinson, Robert**
Come, Thou Fount of Every Blessing,
*with music.*
**Robinson, Roland**
I Had No Human Speech.
Myth and the Mountain, The.
**Robles, Al**
Rapping with One Million Carabaos in
the Dark.
**Robson, Jeremy**
Departure, The.
**Robson, Joseph Philip**
California.
**Roche, James Jeffrey**
*Constitution's* Last Fight, The.
Men of the Alamo, The.
Sailor's Yarn, A.
**Rochester, John Wilmot, 2d Earl of**
Against Constancy.

Allusion to Horace, An.
Commons' Petition to Charles II, The.
Disabled Debauchee, The.
Epistolary Essay from M.G. to O.B.
upon Their Mutual Poems, An.
Epitaph on Charles II.
Fall, The: A Song.
Homo Sapiens.
Imperfect Enjoyment, The.
Impromptu on Charles II.
Letter from Artemisia in the Town to
Cloe in the Country, A.
Love and Life.
Mistress, The.
On Poet Ninny.
On the supposed Author of a Late Poem
"In Defense of Satire."
Poet, whoe'er thou art, God damn thee.
Satire against Mankind, A.
Satire on Charles II, A, *sel.*
Song, A: "Absent from thee, I languish
still."
Song: "Give me leave to rail at you."
Song: "Love a woman? You're an ass!"
Song of a Young Lady to Her Ancient
Lover, A.
To His Mistress.
Tunbridge Wells.
Upon His Leaving His Mistress.
Upon Nothing.
Very Heroical Epistle in Answer to
Ephelia, A.
Written in a Lady's Prayer Book.
**Rockwell, Glen**
Keys.
**Rodger, Alex**
Twilight at the Zoo.
**Rodgers, Carolyn M.**
And When the Revolution Came.
And While We Are Waiting.
Breakthrough.
Common Poem, A.
For H. W. Fuller.
For Muh' Dear.
For Sapphires.
Greek Crazeology.
How I Got Ovah.
"In This House, There Shall Be No
Idols."
It Is Deep.
Jazz.
Jesus Was Crucified or: It Must Be
Deep.
Look at My Face, a Collage.
Mama's God.
Me, in Kulu Se and Karma.
Missing Beat.
Newark, for Now (68).
Non Poem about Vietnam, A.
Now Ain't That Love?
One.
Phoenix.
Poem/ Ditty-Bop.
Proclamation/ From Sleep, Arise.
Rebolushinary X-mas.
Remember Times for Sandy.
Setting/ Slow Drag.
Some Me of Beauty.
Somebody Call.
Testimony.
To the White Critics.
U Name This One.

Voodoo on the Un-Assing of Janis
  Joplin.
We Dance like Ella Riffs.
What Color Is Lonely.
Yeah, I Is Uh Shootin Off at the Mouth.
Yuh Lookin Good.
**Rodgers, William Robert**
Armagh.
Beagles.
Christ Walking on the Water.
Field Day.
Fountains, The.
Irish Lake, An.
Last Word, A.
Lovers, The.
Net, The.
Paired Lives.
Party, The.
Scapegoat.
Swan, The.
White Christmas.
**Roditi, Edouard**
Aurora Borealis.
Beginning and an End, A.
Habakkuk.
Hand.
Kashrut.
Paths of Prayer, The.
Seance.
Shekhina and the Kiddushim.
**Rodman, Frances**
Lost Dog.
**Rodman, Selden**
I Dreamed That Washington Lay
  Wreathed in Smoke.
Time of Day.
**Rodriguez, Judith**
Eskimo Occasion.
Getting Home.
Grapefruit at Lights Out.
Neither Up nor Down.
Nu-Plastik Fanfare Red.
Sojourners at Phoenix.
Water a Thousand Feet Deep.
**Rodríguez Frese, Marcos**
Beginning.
Leit.
What Is Needed.
**Rodríguez Nietzche, Vicente**
As Yet.
Mural, *sel.*
Poem H.
**Roe, Sir Thomas**
On Gustavus Adolphus, King of Sweden.
**Roecker, W. A.**
45th Parallel Sulks.
**Roethke, Theodore**
Academic.
Another woman: a change of tears.
Apparition, The.
Bat, The.
Beast, The.
Big Wind.
Bound.
Ceiling, The.
Chair, The.
Child on Top of a Greenhouse.
Chums, The.
Cow, The.
Cuttings ("Sticks-in-a-drowse droop over
  sugary loam").

Cuttings ("This urge, wrestle,
  resurrection of dry sticks").
Death Piece.
Decision.
Deep in their roots, all flowers keep the
  light.
Dinky.
Dolor.
Donkey, The.
Dream, The.
Dying Man, The.
Elegy for Jane.
Elegy: "Her face like a rain-beaten stone
  on the day she rolled off."
Epidermal Macabre.
Epigram: Mistake, The.
Epigram: Pipling.
Exorcism, The.
Far Field, The.
Field of Light, A.
First Meditation.
Flower Dump.
Forcing House.
Four for Sir John Davies.
Frau Bauman, Frau Schmidt, and Frau
  Schwartze.
Geranium The.
Give Way, Ye Gates.
Gnu, The.
Grandeurs of the crazy man alone, The.
Heard in a Violent Ward.
Her Longing.
Her Reticence.
Her Time.
Her Words.
Heron, The.
Hippo, The.
I rasp like a sick dog.
I would be with the wind.
I'm Here.
I'm lost in my name.
In a Dark Time.
In Evening Air.
Interlude.
Journey to the Interior.
Kitty-Cat Bird, The.
Lady and the Bear, The.
Lamb, The.
Light Listened.
Long Live the Weeds.
Long Waters, The.
Longing, The.
Lost Son, The.
Manifestation, The.
Meadow Mouse, The.
Meditation at Oyster River.
Meditations of an Old Woman,*sels.*
Minimal, The.
Moss-gathering.
Motion, The.
My Papa's Waltz.
Myrtle.
Night Crow.
Night Journey.
Old Florist.
Open House.
Orchids.
Pickle Belt.
Pike, The.
Prayer: "If I must of my senses lose."
Reckoning, The.
Renewal, The.

Return, The.
Root Cellar.
Rose, The.
Rouse for Stevens, A.
Second Shadow.
Sensibility! O La!
Sensualists, The.
Sequel, The.
Serpent, The.
Shape of the Fire, The.
She.
Siskins, The.
Sloth, The.
Slug.
Small, The.
Snake.
Song: "From whence cometh song?"
Storm, The.
Swan, The.
Thing, The.
Transplanting.
Tree, the Bird, The.
Unfold! Unfold!
Vernal Sentiment.
Visitant, The.
Voice, The.
Waking, The ("I strolled across/ An
  open field").
Waking, The ("I wake to sleep, and take
  my waking slow").
Walk in Late Summer, A.
Weed Puller.
What Can I Tell My Bones?
Where Knock Is Open Wide.
Wish for a Young Wife.
Words for the Wind.
Yak, The.
Young Girl, The.
**Rogers, Del Marie**
Desert.
In the Mountain Cabin.
Photograph of the Back of My House.
War Requiem.
**Rogers, George**
As Gentle Dews Distill, *with music.*
**Rogers, J.E. Thorold.** *See* **Thorold Rogers,
J.E.**
**Rogers, Pattiann**
This Evening, without Blinking.
**Rogers, Robert Cameron**
Rosary, The, *with music.*
**Rogers, Ronald**
Kindergarten.
Taking Off.
**Rogers, Samuel**
Epitaph on a Robin-Redbreast, An.
Ward has no heart, they say; but I deny
  it.
Wish, A.
**Rokeah, David**
Beginning.
I Am like a Book.
**Roland-Holst, Henriëtte**
Mother of Fisherman.
Throughout the day we are able to ban
  the voices.
**Rolfe, Edwin**
City of Anguish.
Definition.
Entry.
First Love.
Not Men Alone.

Poem to Delight My Friends Who
 Laugh at Science-Fiction, A.
Room with Revolutionists.
Sixth Winter, The.
Somebody and Somebody Else and You.
To My Contemporaries.

**Rolle of Hampole, Richard**
Ghostly Gladness.
Love Is Life, *orig. and mod. English*
 *prose.*

**Rolnik, Joseph**
At God's Command.
I'm Not Rich.
In Disguise.

**Romero, Orlando**
Self-Portrait.

**Rompf, Kraft**
Distant Lover, The.
Finger Spelling.
Islands for Seurat.
Song for Solomon Heine, A.

**Ronan, John**
Fat Cat.

**Ronksley, William**
To Cheer Our Minds.

**Ronsard, Pierre de**
Corinna in Vendome.
Nature withheld Cassandra in the skies.

**Root, George Frederick**
Battle-Cry of Freedom, The.
Just before the Battle, Mother.
Rosalie, the Prairie Flower, *with music.*
Tramp! Tramp! Tramp! or, The
 Prisoner's Hope.

**Root, Judith C.**
Gerbil Who Got Away, The.

**Root, William Pitt**
Fisherman.
House You Looked For, The.
Jellyfish, The.
Natural History of Dragons and
 Unicorns My Daughter and I Have
 Known, A.
Poetry and Revolution.
Songs of Waking.
Stoplight.

**Roper, Renée**
Canibolos de la Montana.
Emma in My Third Eye.
Going Home.

**Roripaugh, Robert**
For an Indian Bronc Rider Killed in a
 Highway Crash near Ethete,
 Wyoming.

**Rosales, Luis**
That Which You Call "Love Me."

**Roscoe, William**
Butterfly's Ball, The.

**Rose, Billy**
Barney Google.
Does the Spearmint Lose Its Flavor on
 the Bedpost Overnight?

**Rose, Sir George**
Chancery Suit, A.

**Rose, Sir George and James Smith.** *See*
 **Smith, James and Sir George Rose**

**Rose, Judith**
Bear, The.

**Rose, Wendy**
America.
Calling Home the Scientists.
Celebration for My Mother.

Epitaph: "Roots of mankind are tangled
 in my hair, The."
For My People.
For Ron Tanaka at Stanford.
For Steph.
For Walter Lowenfels.
Grunion.
Hupa Twined Pendant: A White Woman
 Speaks.
Loving.
Native American Studies, University of
 California at Berkeley 1975.
Oh Father.
Oh My People I Remember.
Poem to a Redskin.
Red/White Blues, The.
Saint Patrick's Day, 1973.
Self Dirge.
They Sometimes Call Me.
To an Imaginary Father.
Vanishing Point: Urban Indian.

**Rosemergy, Jim**
Human Dilemma.

**Rosen, Kenneth**
Abstinence.
Act, An.
Confab.
Girls.

**Rosen, Michael**
Father Says.
Giant Jojo.
Going through the Old Photos.
Hidebehind, The.
I Am the Youngest in Our House.
If You Don't Put Your Shoes On.
She Said I Said He Lied.
This Is the Hand.
This Ship in the Dock.
When We Go Over to My Grandad's.

**Rosenberg, Betsy**
Bird Song.
Unearthing.

**Rosenberg, David**
Maps to Nowhere.
Rain Has Fallen on the History Books.

**Rosenberg, Harold**
Epos.

**Rosenberg, Isaac**
August 1914.
Break of Day in the Trenches.
Chagrin.
Dead Man's Dump.
Destruction of Jerusalem by the
 Babylonian Hordes, The.
Female God, The.
God.
Immortals, The.
Jew, The.
Louse Hunting.
Midsummer Frost.
Returning, We Hear the Larks.
Saul.
Wedded.
Worm Fed on the Heart of Corinth, A.

**Rosenberg, Jim**
Richard Hofstadter and Michael
 Wallace, a Documentary History of
 American Violence.

**Rosenberg, Joel**
First Wedding in the World, The.
Violin Tree, The.

**Rosenberg, L. M.**

For Leningrad, and My Jewish
 Ancestors.

**Rosenberger, Francis Coleman**
Altered Circumstances.
Are You Just Back for a Visit or Are
 You Going to Stay?
Glass Snake, The.
Memorial for Mr. Jefferson, A.
Poets Observed.
Since Most Poets Write Nonsense.

**Rosenfeld, Marjorie Stamm**
David Homindae.

**Rosenfeld, Monroe H. ("F. Belasco")**
Johnny Get Your Gun, *with music.*
Those Wedding Bells Shall Not Ring
 Out! *with music.*

**Rosenfeld, Rita**
Stacking Up.

**Rosenfield, Loyd**
Ode to a Vanished Operator in an
 Automatized Elevator.
You Take the Pilgrims, Just Give Me the
 Progress.

**Rosenius, Carl Olof**
With God and His Mercy, *with music.*

**Rosenmann-Taub, David**
Elegy and Kaddish.
Moral Ode.
Prelude: "Afterwards, afterwards the
 wind between two mountains."
Sabbath.
To a Young Girl.

**Rosensaft, Menachem Z.**
Second Generation, The.

**Rosenthal, Abby**
June Song.

**Rosenthal, John**
Love's Fool.

**Rosenthal, Macha Louis**
Blue Boy on Skates (Twilight).
Jim Dandy.

**Roskolenko, Harry**
Nationalism.
Old World, New World.

**Rosner, Martin C.**
Listening-Post.

**Ross, A. B.**
Two in Bed.

**Ross, Alan**
In Bloemfontein.
Koala.
Radar.
Stanley Matthews.

**Ross, Charles Henry**
Jack.
John, Tom, and James ("John was a bad
 boy").
Old Woman, An.

**Ross, Sir Ronald**
Success in Malaria Research.

**Rossetti, Christina Georgina**
Advent.
After Death.
All the bells were ringing.
Aloof.
Apple Gathering, An.
Ash Wednesday.
Before the Paling of the Stars.
Better Resurrection, A.
Birthday, A.
Bitter for Sweet.
Bourne, The.

Bride Song.
By the Sea.
Caterpillar, The.
Catkin.
Christmas Carol, A: "In the bleak mid-winter."
Christmas Carol: "Thank God, thank God, we do believe."
Comparisons.
Crown of Windflowers, A.
Daisies.
Dirge, A: "Why were you born when the snow was falling?"
Dream Land.
Dream-Love.
Echo.
End, An.
Eve.
Ferry Me across the Water.
First Day, The.
Flint.
Frog and the Toad, The.
Frog's Fate, A.
From Sunset to Star Rise.
Fruits.
Goblin Market.
Golden Glories.
Good Friday.
Green Cornfield, A.
Half Moon Shows a Face of Plaintive Sweetness, The.
Hope and Joy.
Horses.
Hurt No Living Thing.
I do not look for love that is a dream.
I dug and dug amongst the snow.
If I Were a Queen.
In an Artist's Studio.
In Progress.
Incarnate Love.
Is the Moon Tired?
Italia, Io Ti Saluto.
Last Rites.
Lesson, A.
Long Barren.
Marvel of Marvels.
Maude Clare.
May.
Meeting.
Mirage.
Mix a pancake.
Monna Innominata.
My Dream.
None Other Lamb, None Other Name.
O Lady Moon.
Oh, Fair to See.
Old-World Thicket, An.
On the Death of a Cat.
On the Wing.
Passing Away.
Pause of Thought, A.
Pin Has a Head, A.
Poor Ghost, The.
Postman, The.
Prince's Progress, The, *sel.*
Rainbow, The.
Remember.
Rest.
Riddle, A: "There is one that has a head without an eye."
Rose, The.
Safe where I cannot lie yet.

Seldom "can't."
Shepherds Had an Angel, The.
Shut Out.
Skylark and Nightingale.
Sleeping at Last.
Somewhere or Other.
Song: "She sat and sang alway."
Song: "When I am dead, my dearest."
Spring Quiet.
Stars and Flowers.
Start and Goal.
Summer.
Swallow, The.
Symbols.
Thread of Life, The, *sel.*
Three Enemies, The.
Three Seasons.
Triad, A.
Twice.
Two Pursuits.
Up-Hill [*or* Uphill].
Valentines to My Mother, 1880.
What Are Heavy?
What Can Lambkins Do?
What Does the Bee Do?
What Is Pink?
When the Cows Come Home.
Who Has Seen the Wind.
Who Shall Deliver Me?
World, The.
Wrens and robins in the hedge.
Youth gone, and beauty gone if ever there.

**Rossetti, Dante Gabriel**
Alas, So Long!
Antwerp and Bruges.
Ardour and Memory.
Aspecta Medusa.
Autumn Idleness.
Autumn Song.
Barren Spring.
Blessed Damozel, The.
Body's Beauty.
Card-Dealer, The.
Dark Glass, The.
Day of Love, A.
Death-in-Love.
Even So.
Fir-Tree of Bosnia, The.
For "A Venetian Pastoral" by Giorgione.
For "An Allegorical Dance of Women" by Andrea Mantegna.
For "Our Lady of the Rocks" by Leonardo da Vinci.
For "Ruggiero and Angelica" by Ingres.
For "The Wine of Circe" by Edward Burne-Jones.
Heart's Compass.
Her Gifts.
Inclusiveness.
Jenny.
Kiss, The.
Life-in-Love.
Little While, A.
Lost on Both Sides.
Love's Last Gift.
Match with the Moon, A.
My Sister's Sleep.
Not as These.
Nuptial Sleep.
Old Song Ended, An.
On Himself.

On Refusal of Aid between Nations.
On Robert Buchanan, Who Attacked Him under the Pseudonym of "Thomas Maitland."
On the Painter Val Prinsep.
On the "Vita Nuova" of Dante.
One Hope, The.
Orchard-Pit, The.
Paris Railway-Station, The.
Penumbra.
Portrait, The ("O Lord of all compassionate control").
Portrait, The ("This is her picture as she was").
Saint Luke the Painter.
Sea-Limits, The.
Sea-Spell, A.
Severed Selves.
Silent Noon.
Sister Helen.
Song-Throe, The.
Sonnet, A: "Sonnet is a moment's monument, A."
Soul's Beauty.
Sudden Light.
Superscription, A.
There are dealers in pictures named Agnew.
There is a big artist named Val.
There is an old he-wolf named Gambart.
There's combative artist named Whistler.
To Art.
Transfigured Life.
Vain Virtues.
White Ship, The.
Willowwood.
Without Her.
Woodspurge, The.
World's Worth.
Youth's Antiphony.
Youth's Spring-Tribute.

**Rostand, Edmond**
Cyrano De Bergerac, *sel.*

**Rosten, Norman**
Aesthetic.
Nobody Dies like Humphrey Bogart.

**Roston, Ruth**
Salesman.

**"Rostrevor, George."**   See **Hamilton, George Rostrevor**

**Rotella, Guy**
High Summer.
Somewhere Farm.

**Roth, Hemda**
Song, The: "Song, The! the song!"
Treason of Sand.
Young Deer/Dust, A.

**Roth, Joseph**
Ahasuerus.

**Rothenberg, Jerome**
Alphabet Came to Me, The.
Beadle's Testimony, The.
Cokby, Part Two.
Esther K. Comes to America: 1931.
Letter to Paul Celan in Memory, A.
Little Boy Lost, A.
Poland/ 1931.
Portrait of a Jew Old Country Style.
Seven Hells of Jigoku Zoshi, The, *sels.*
Sixth Hell, The.
Soap (II).

Young Woman's neo-aramaic jewish persian Blues.
**Rottman, Larry**
What Kind of War?
**Rouget de Lisle, Claude Joseph**
Marseillaise, La.
**Roughton, Roger**
Building Society Blues.
Soluble Noughts and Crosses; or, California, Here I Come.
**Rounds, Emma**
Plane Geometry.
**Rous, Francis**
Help, Lord, because the Godly Man, *with music.*
Lord's My Shepherd, I'll Not Want, The, *with music.*
**Routhier, Adolphe**
O Canada!
**Rowbotham, Colin**
Relative Sadness.
**Rowbotham, David**
Cliff, The.
E = mc$^2$: Einstein at Princeton.
Los Alamos: Manhattan.
**Rowe, James**
Love Lifted Me, *with music.*
**Rowe, James Wilton**
Lake Chemo.
**Rowell, Charles H.**
Old Women Still Sing, The.
**Rowland, J. R.**
Cairo Hotel.
In Southeast Asia (Viet Nam).
**Rowlands, Samuel**
Letting of Humour's Blood in the Head-Vein, The, *sels.*
Like Mistress, Like Maid.
Sir Eglamour.
**Rowley, Francis H.**
I Will Sing the Wondrous Story, *with music.*
**Rowley William** *and* **John Fletcher.** *See* **Fletcher, John** *and* **William Rowley**
**Rowse, Alfred Leslie**
April Landscape.
White Cat of Trenarren, The.
**Royde-Smith, Naomi Gwladys**
Horse, The.
**Rozewicz, Tadeusz**
Leave Us Alone.
To the Heart.
**Ruark, Gibbons**
Blind Wish for Randall Jarrell, A.
Finding the Pistol.
Impromptu Immersion in Tom's Run. 1965.
Sleeping Out with My Father.
Slowness ("Slowness, says Rodin, is beauty").
**Rubin, Ilya**
Escape.
Handful of Ashes.
No Sense Grieving.
Poem from "The Revolution."
Slow Oxen.
**Rubin, Larry**
At the Birth of a Poet: Amherst, 1830.
Brother-in-Law, The.
Draft Dodger, The.
God Opens His Mail.
Manual, The.

Pact, The.
Runaway, The.
Saturday Afternoon.
Son, Condemned, The.
Temporary Problems.
**Ruby, Kathryn**
Banker's Daughter, The.
Portrait of a Woman.
Pygmalion.
**Rückert, Friedrich ("Freimund Raimar")**
And Then No More.
**Rudaki**
Came to me.
**Rudnik, Raphael**
Amsterdam Street Scene, 1972.
Penny Trumpet.
**Rudnitsky, Leah**
Birds Are Drowsing on the Branches.
**Rudolf, Anthony**
Ancient of Days.
Ashkelon.
Dubrovnik Poem (Emilio Tolentino).
Evening of the Rose.
Hands Up.
Prayer for Kafka and Ourselves.
**Ruebner, Tuvia**
Among Iron Fragments.
Document.
First Days.
I Left.
**Ruelfe, Mary**
Written.
**Ruffin, Paul**
Hotel Fire: New Orleans.
**Rufinus Domesticus**
Aut Neutrum . . . Vel Duos.
Complaint.
**Ruggles, Eugene**
Beginning Again as Morning.
God.
Why Most of Us Are Limping Away from Life.
**Ruggles, William B.**
Pioneer, The.
**Rugo, Marieve**
Borders.
In the Season of Wolves and Names.
Limbo.
Sundays.
**Rukeyser, Muriel**
Ajanta.
Akiba.
Along History.
Are You Born?—I.
Boy with His Hair Cut Short.
Boys of These Men Full Speed.
Church of Galilee, The.
City of Monuments.
Columbus.
Darkness Music.
Despisals.
Don Baty, the Draft Resister.
Easter Eve.
Effort at Speech between Two People.
Eyes of Night-Time.
Fields Where We Slept.
Gates, The, *sel.*
Gauley Bridge.
George Robinson: Blues.
Islands.
Käthe Kollwitz.

Little Stone in the Middle of the Road, in Florida, A.
Looking at Each Other.
Lynching of Jesus, The.
Mediterranean.
Mrs. Walpurga.
More Clues.
More of a Corpse than a Woman.
Motive.
Myth.
Night Feeding.
No one ever walking this our only earth.
Nuns in the Wind.
Place at Albert Bay, The.
Poem as Mask, The.
Poem (I Lived in the First Century).
Poem out of Childhood.
Question, The.
Reading Time: 1 Minute 26 Seconds.
Rondel: "Now that I am fifty-six."
St. Roach.
Speaking Tree, The.
Speed of Darkness, The.
Theory of flight.
This Morning.
Time Exposures.
Trinity Churchyard.
Waiting for Icarus.
Woman as Market.
**Rumi, Jalal ed-Din.** *or* **ud-Din**
Drunkards, The.
Happy the moment when we are seated in the Palace.
I am your mother, your mother's mother.
Lo, for I to myself am unknown.
Name, The.
Not in India, where fire rivers are.
Thou art the source that causes our river to flow.
**Rungren, Lawrence R.**
Sunday.
**Runyon, Damon (Alfred Damon Runyon)**
Babe Ruth.
Pool-Shootin' Roy.
**Ruse, Peggy**
Pittsburgh.
View of Vienna from Schonbrunn.
Visit to My Father-in-Law on Memorial Day, A.
**Russ, Lawrence**
Child, The.
Grandfather, *sel.*
Holy, Holy, Holy.
House-Trailer, The.
Lives.
Not Speaking.
Price of Paper, The.
Turning, The.
Weights, The.
**Russell, Ethel Green**
Gathering Gems.
Hunchback Pine.
Letter to Her Son's Commanding Officer.
Maple in November.
**Russell, George William.** *See* **æ**
**Russell, James I.**
Where the River Shannon Flows, *with music.*
**Russell, Norman H.**
Clerk's Song II.
Eyes of the Child Do Not See Me, The.

Great Way of the Man, The.
Indian School.
World Has Many Places Many Ways,
   The.
**Russell, Sanders**
Poem: "I keep feeling all space as my
   image."
**Rutan, Catherine**
Still Birth.
**Ruth, Fern Pankratz**
Guyana.
**Rutsala, Vern**
Eagle Squadron.
Fame.
Final Cut, The.
Furniture Factory, The.
In the Middle.
Journey Begins, The.
Less Is More.
Like the Poets of Ancient China.
Other Lives.
Paths.
Shack outside Boise, The.
Washrags.
Words.
**Ryan, Margaret**
Alexandrite Ring, The.
Dreams of Eurydice.
Whistler's Father.
**Ryan, Michael**
Barren Poem.
Hitting Fungoes.
Letter from an Institution: III.
Prothalamion.
Speaking.
This Is a Poem for the Dead.
Your Own Image.
**Ryan, Paddy**
Man That Waters the Workers' Beer,
   The.
**Ryan, Richard**
Deafness.
El Dorado.
From My Lai the Thunder Went West.
Going.
Ireland.
Knockmany.
Nightfall.
Thrush's Nest, The.
Wet Night, A.
Wulf and Eadwacer.
**Ryden, Ernest Edwin**
Twilight Shadows round Me Fall, The,
   *with music.*
**Ryerson, Alice**
Death Watchers, The.
**Ryojin Hisho**
May the man who gained my trust yet
   did not come.
**Ryvel (Raphael Levy)**
Pilgrimage to Testour, The.

# S

**Saba, Umberto**
Goat, The.
Sleepless on a Summer Night.
Three Streets.

Woman.
**Sabines, Jaime**
Amen.
**Sachs, Elizabeth Newton**
Celebration.
**Sachs, Nelly**
Above the rocking heads of the mothers.
Awakening—/ Voices of birds.
Burning Sand of Sinai.
But Perhaps.
Chorus of the Rescued.
Hasidim Dance.
In flight in escape.
In the blue distance.
Last one, The/ to die here.
Line Like.
O Night of the Crying Children.
O the Chimneys.
Oblivion! Skin.
One Chord.
Sleepwalker, The.
To You Building the New House.
What Secret Desires of the Blood.
White Serpent.
**Sackville, Charles, 6th Earl of Dorset**
À Madame, Madame B, Beauté
   Sexagenaire.
Dainty young heiress of Lincoln's Inn
   Fields, The.
Excellent New Ballad Giving a True
   Account of the Birth and Conception
   of a Late Famous Poem Called the
   Female Nine, An.
On Mr. Edward Howard, upon His
   British Princes.
On the Countess of Dorchester.
On the Young Statesmen.
Song Written at Sea in the First Dutch
   War.
To Mr. Bays.
To Mr. Edward Howard, on His Plays.
**Sackville, Thomas, 1st Earl of Dorset**
Shield of War, The.
Thomas Sackevyll in Commendation of
   the Worke to the Reader.
**Sackville-West, Victoria Mary (Mrs.
   Harold Nicolson)**
Aquarium, San Francisco, The.
Beechwoods at Knole.
Black Tarn.
Bull, The.
Craftsmen.
Greater Cats, The.
On the Lake.
Owl, The.
Persia.
Sea-Sonnet.
Sometimes When Night.
To Any M. F. H.
Young Stock.
**Sadeh, Pinhas**
Elegy: "While walking at dusk in a
   strange city."
In the Forest.
In the Garden of the Turkish Consulate.
Raya Brenner.
**Sadoff, Ira**
Concise History of the World, A.
Fifties, The.
My Father's Leaving.
Poem after Apollinaire.
**Sadowski, Anne**

Crucified.
Miss America.
Poem about Birth.
To Whom It May Concern.
**Sáez Burgos, Juan**
That Poem.
This Afternoon.
**Safka, Melanie**
I Don't Eat Animals (And They Don't
   Eat Me).
**Sagami, Lady**
In the gathering dew.
**Sage, Rufus B.**
Summer on the Great American Desert.
Wanderer's Grave, The.
**"Sagittarius" (Olga Katzin)**
Nerves.
**Sagstatter, Karen**
Among Mirrors in the Locker Room.
Half the Story.
Letter of Application Long Enough to
   Indicate Writing Ability.
**Sahl, Hans**
Greeting from a Distance.
Memo.
**St. Cyr, Napoleon**
All Men Are . . . Socrates Is.
Artery of the Sea.
Friend with Spinning Rod.
Leaving the Flag Out All Night.
Oriental.
**"Saint Geraud."**   *See* **Knott, William (Bill)**
**St. John, David**
Avenues, The.
For Lerida.
Poem: "Your face,/so pale now it is
   blue."
Slow Dance.
**St. John, Justin**
Hard Cheese.
**St. John, Primus**
All the Way Home.
Benign Neglect/ Mississippi, 1970.
Biological Light.
Carpenter, The.
Elephant Rock.
Lynching and Burning.
Morning Star, The.
Poem to My Notebook, A.
Splendid Thing Growing, A.
Tyson's Corner.
**St. Leger, Warham**
False Gallop of Analogies, A.
**St. Martin, Laura**
As I look out from the desk window.
Ocean is a strange, The.
**Sainte-Marie, Buffy**
My Country 'Tis of Thy People You're
   Dying.
Now That the Buffalo's Gone.
**Saiser, Marjorie**
Morning.
**Saito, Fumi**
Palm of the hand, The,/ is not aware of
   dying.
**Sakanoye [*or* Sakanoe *or* Sakanone], The
   Lady of [*or* Lady Otomo of] (Lady
   Otomo no Sakanoye).**  *See* **Otomo of
   Sakanoe, Lady**
**Salamun, Tomaz**
Air.
Eclipse.

**Salcman, Michael**
Open Heart.
**Saleh, Dennis**
Bed, The.
Furniture of the Poem, The.
Guide to Familiar American Incest, A,
   *sel.*
Inventing a Family.
Nesting.
Paul.
Return, The.
Story.
Tail.
Thumb, The.
**Salinas, Luís Omar**
Barefoot.
For the Waiter at Jhonny Pavlovs.
Going North.
Happiness Is a Charlie Chaplin Movie.
Ode to a Violin.
Ode to Mexican Experience.
Pedro.
Señor Torres.
This Is Not a Poem.
Tihuitkli.
Tolusa.
What a Way to Lose the War.
Whats My Name if Not Everyone Elses.
**Salisbury, Ralph**
Halo, A.
In the Children's Museum in Nashville.
Under the Cellar.
Winter 1970, Fox River, Illinois.
**Salmon, Arthur**
In the Dim City.
**Salomon, Louis B.**
Univac to Univac.
**Salsich, Albert**
Staying Up on Jack's Fork near
   Eminence, Missouri.
**Salter, Mary Jo**
England.
**Saltman, Benjamin**
Blue with Blues.
Fathers, The.
Journey with Hands and Arms, The.
Trotting Around.
**Sam, David A.**
On the Pavement.
**Sammis, J. H.**
Trust and Obey, *with music.*
**Sánchez, Ricardo**
Casi-Gato Aka Carnedechivo Nee
   Ricardo Sánchez (Sometimes!).
Drum.
Toward.
**Sanchez, Sonia**
Answer to Yo/ Question.
Black Magic.
Chant for Young/Brothas and Sistuhs,
   A.
Definition for Blk/ Children.
Don't Wanna Be.
For Our Lady.
Homecoming.
Hospital/ Poem.
Listenen to Big Black at S. F. State.
Nigger.
Now Poem. For Us.
Personal Letter No. 2.
Personal Letter No. 3.
Poem at Thirty.

Poem for Etheridge.
Poem for My Father, A.
Poem: "I've been a woman."
Poem: "Look at me 8th."
Poem: "When he came home."
Poem: "Yo/ smile."
Present.
Right On: White America.
Small Comment.
So This Is Our Revolution.
Summary.
Summer Words of a Sistuh Addict.
Three X Three.
To All Brothers.
To All Sisters.
To Chuck.
221–1424.
Why.
**Sandag**
"Word" of a Watch-Dog, The.
"Word" of a Wolf Encircled by the
   Hunt, The.
"Word" of an Antelope Caught in a
   Trap, The.
**Sandburg, Carl**
A. E. F.
Alice Corbin Is Gone.
Aprons of Silence.
Baby Toes.
Balloon Faces.
Bilbea.
Broken-Face Gargoyles.
Buffalo Dusk.
Caboose Thoughts.
Cheap Rent.
Cheer Leader, The.
Chicago.
Child of the Romans.
Clean Curtains.
Cool Tombs.
Crapshooters.
Cricket March.
Death Snips Proud Men.
Dinosaur Bones, The.
Doors.
Drowsy.
Early Copper.
Early Lynching.
Early Moon.
Elm Buds.
Evening Waterfall.
Explanations of Love.
Falltime.
Fence, A.
Finale.
Fog ("The fog comes/ on little cat
   feet").
Four Preludes on Playthings of the
   Wind.
Fourth of July Night.
Gargoyle.
Gone.
Good Morning America, *sel.*
Grass.
Grassroots.
Hangman at Home, The.
Happiness.
Harbor, The.
Hits and Runs.
I am the People, the Mob.
Illinois Farmer.
Improved Farm Land.

In Tall Grass.
Jazz Fantasia.
Laughing Child.
Lawyers Know Too Much, The.
Limited.
Little Girl Saw Her First Troop Parade,
   The.
Losers.
Lost.
Love in Labrador.
Mist Forms.
Muckers.
Mysterious Biography.
New Farm Tractor.
Nocturn Cabbage.
Nocturne in a Deserted Brickyard.
Old Timers.
On a Flimmering Floom You Shall Ride.
One Modern Poet.
Osawatomie.
Paper II.
People, Yes, The, *sels.*
Phizzog.
Potomac Town in February.
Prairie, *sel.*
Prayer after World War.
Prayers of Steel.
Primer Lesson.
Rat Riddles.
River Roads.
Sandhill People.
Shovel Man, The.
Sins of Kalamazoo, The.
Skyscrapers Stand Proud.
Soup.
Splinter.
Street Window.
Summer Stars.
Ten Definitions of Poetry.
Theme in Yellow.
They All Want to Play Hamlet.
Threes.
Trinity Place.
Upstream.
Useless Words.
Washington Monument by Night.
We Must Be Polite, *sel.*
Webs.
What Shall He Tell That Son?
Why Did the Children Put Beans in
   Their Ears?
Wilderness.
Window.
Worms and the Wind.
**Sandburg, Helga**
Importance of Mirrors, The.
**Sandeen, Ernest**
Mail from Home in the Sky.
Views of Our Sphere.
**Sanders, Morgan**
Beverly Fragments.
Looking for Lola.
"Many Brave Hearts Are Asleep in the
   Deep."
**Sanders, Thomas E.**
Machine Out of the God.
**Sanders, Velma**
Old House Place.
**Sandoval, Roberto**
Grandpa's Friend.
**Sandy, Stephen**
Ballad of Mary Baldwin, The.

Declension.
**Sandys, Edwin**
In Pilgrim Life Our Rest, *with music.*
**Sandys, George**
Bounty of Jehovah Praise, The, *with music.*
Judah in Exile Wanders, *with music.*
O Blest Estate, Blest from Above, *with music.*
**Saner, Reg**
Flag.
How the Laws of Physics Love Chocolate!
Orchestra.
Passing It On.
Space Eater Camps at Fifth Lake, The.
**Sanfedele, Ann**
Part of Fortune, The.
**Sanford, Frank Elwood**
Outcast, The.
**Sange, Gary**
Drive In Movie.
Lighthouse Keeper.
Separation.
Truckdriver.
**Sangster, Margaret Elizabeth (1894?– )**
In Gratitude for Friends.
**Sangster, Margaret Elizabeth Munson (1838–1912)**
Building of the Nest, The.
Sin of Omission, The.
**Sannazaro, Jacopo (Actius Sincerus Sannazarius)**
Like to these unmesurable montayns.
**Sansom, Clive**
Butterflies.
"Dorset Nose," The.
Font, The.
Mixed Brews.
Schoolmistress.
Witnesses, The, *sel.*
**Sant'Ana, Gloria de**
African Day.
**Santayana, George**
On the Death of a Metaphysician.
**Santos, Sherod**
Childhood.
Country Landscape.
**Sappho**
About the cool water.
All the while, believe me, I prayed.
Andromache's Wedding.
Andromeda/ forgot.
Come, holy tortoise shell.
Come out of Crete/ and find me here.
Dead shalt thou lie; and nought.
Don't ask me what to wear.
Glow and beauty of the stars, The.
He is more than a hero.
Here are fine gifts, children.
Hesperos, you bring home all the bright dawn disperses.
Honestly I wish I were dead!
I begin with words of air but delightful ones.
I could not hope/ to touch the sky.
I have no embroidered headband.
I hear that Andromeda.
If my nipples were to drip milk.
In gold sandals.
It would be wrong for us. It is not right.

Leave Krete and come to this holy temple.
Like a mountain whirlwind.
Like a sweet apple reddening on the high.
Love—bittersweet, irrepressible.
Marriage of Hector and Andromache, The.
Mother darling, I cannot work the loom.
My Atthis, although our dear Anaktoria.
My mother always said.
My muse, what ails this ardour?
Now in my/ heart I/ see clearly.
O dream from the blackness.
O Gongyla, my darling rose.
Ode to Anactoria.
On your dazzling throne, Aphrodite.
Peer of the gods is that man, who.
People do gossip.
"Sappho, if you do not come out."
Sleep, Darling.
Some say cavalry and others claim.
Someone, I tell you,/ will remember us.
That labor/ a face to remember in wonder.
Then I said to the elegant ladies.
There's a man, I really believe, compares with.
To me he seems like a god.
Tonight I've watched.
We put the urn aboard ship.
You know the place: then.
You lay in wait.
**Sarett, Lew**
Breakers of Broncos.
Four Little Foxes.
**Sargent, Elizabeth Nancy**
Sailor at Midnight, A.
Young Lover, A.
**Sargent, Epes**
Death of Warren, The.
Life on the Ocean Wave, A.
**Sargent, Robert**
Chronological Ordering of Art Cards, The.
Epistemologist, over a Brandy, Opining, The.
Now is Always the Miraculous Time.
Olaf and Sigurd ("Olaf the Viking, arriving by the eastern way").
**Saroyan, Aram**
Crickets.
**Sarton, May**
After All These Years.
At Lindos.
Baroque Image.
Bears and Waterfalls.
Burial.
Fruit of Loneliness.
Invocation to Kali, The, *sels.*
Kingdom of Kali, The.
Monticello.
Summer Music.
Three Things.
Village Tale, A.
**Sassoon, Siegfried**
Alone.
Arbor Vitae.
At Max Gate.
At the Grave of Henry Vaughan.
Attack.
Base Details.

Death-Bed, The.
December Stillness.
Does It Matter?
Dreamers.
Effect, The.
Everyone Sang ("Everyone suddenly burst out singing").
Faith Unfaithful.
Falling Asleep.
Fathers, The.
General, The.
Haunted.
In Barracks.
In the National Gallery.
"In the Pink."
Investiture, The.
Lamentations.
Middle Ages.
One-legged Man, The.
Picture-Show.
Post-Mortem, A.
Rear-Guard, The.
Repression of War Experience.
Sporting Acquaintances.
Stand-to: Good Friday Morning.
"They."
To an Old Lady Dead.
To His Dead Body.
Troops, The.
Two Old Ladies.
Vigils.
"When I'm alone"—the words tripped off his tongue.
Working Party, A.
**Satz, Mario**
Coconut.
Fish.
Lemon.
**Saul, George Brandon**
By Winter Seas.
**Sauls, Roger**
Reconcilable Differences.
**Saunders, Josephine**
Circle and the Question, The.
**Saunders, Mary Wright**
Remembering Day.
**Saunders, R. Crombie**
Empty Glen, The.
**Savage, Derek S.**
Fall of Leaves.
**Savage, Katie**
Touching.
**Savage, Richard**
Animalcule, a Tale, The.
Authors of the Town, The, *sel.*
Bastard, The.
Progress of a Divine, The, *sel.*
**Savant, John**
In the Time of the Rose.
**Savoie, Terry**
Far North, The.
**Sawyer, C. P.**
I Used to Love My Garden.
**Sawyer, Charles C.**
When This Cruel War Is Over.
**Sawyer, Ruth (Mrs. Albert C. Durand)**
Words from an Old Spanish Carol.
**Saxe, John Godfrey**
Blind Men and the Elephant, The.
Puzzled Census Taker, The.
Sonnet to a Clam.
Treasure in Heaven.

Youth and the Northwind, The.
**Saxon, Alvin (Ojenke)**
Black Power.
Poem for Integration, A.
Watts.
**Sayers, Frances Clarke.** *See* **Clarke, Frances**
**Sayers, Henry J.**
Ta-ra-ra Boom-der-é, *with music.*
**Sayles, James M.**
Star of the Evening.
**Saylor, Mark**
Hello, Sister.
**Scannell, Vernon**
Act of Love.
Ageing Schoolmaster, An.
Any Complaints?
Autobiographical Note.
Autumn.
Battlefields.
Bombing of the Cafe de Paris 1941, The.
Cat.
Death of a Snowman.
End of a Season.
Epithets of War—I: August 1914.
Epithets of War—III: Casualties.
Gunpowder Plot.
Here and Human.
Hide and Seek.
Horror Film.
Incendiary.
Jailbird.
Jealous Wife, The.
Legs.
Mastering the Craft.
Nettles.
Old Man's Song.
Picnic on the Lawn.
Poetry Reading.
Reformed Drunkard.
Remembrance Day.
Sweet Song.
Tightrope Walker.
Uncle Edward's Affliction ("Uncle Edward was colour-blind").
Walking Wounded.
Wife Killer.
**Scarborough, Dorothy**
Organ Cactus, The.
**Scarbrough, George**
Afternoon.
Tenantry.
Viewpoint.
**Scarfe, Francis**
Cats.
Cat's Eyes.
Grotto, The.
Kitchen Poem.
Merry Window, The.
Ode in Honour.
**Schaaf, Richard**
Sparkling Water.
**Schaechter-Gottesman, Beyle**
Meditation.
**Schaefer, Sister M. Cherubim**
Rejoice, Let Alleluias Ring, *with music.*
**Schaeffer, Susan Fromberg**
First Test, The.
Housewife.
Truth.
Womb Song.
Yahrzeit.

**Schaff, David**
Memoir.
**Schauffler, Robert Haven**
Divers.
**Schechter, Barry**
Disco Fever.
Little Hat, The.
National Animal, The.
Not a Clown.
On My 26th Birthday.
Practicing My Death.
Profile.
Why Bother Club, The.
**Schechter, Ruth Lisa**
And We Are Strangers to Each Other.
"Terre des Hommes."
What Is There?
**Schedler, Gilbert**
Spring Day on Campus, A.
**Scheinert, David**
Drunken Stones of Prague, The.
Stone and the Blade of Grass in the Warsaw Ghetto, The.
**Scherzo, I. O.**
Threnody: "Truth is a golden sunset far away."
**Schevill, James**
Between the Electric Rhythm and the Melodic Mind.
Freud: Dying in London, He Recalls the Smoke of His Cigar Beginning to Sing.
Green Frog at Roadstead, Wisconsin.
Huck Finn at Ninety, Dying in a Chicago Boarding House Room.
London Pavement Artist.
Looking at Wealth in Newport.
Mixed Media.
Screamer Discusses Methods of Screaming, A.
**Schiff, Harris**
In the Heart of the Empire.
**Schiff, Jeff**
Winter Twilight.
**Schiller, Johann Christoph Friedrich von**
Columbus.
Homeric Hexameter Described and Exemplified, The.
Ovidian Elegiac Metre Described and Exemplified, The.
Visit of the Gods, The.
**Schimmel, Harold**
Ancestors.
**Schindler, Paul, Bob Adams** *and* **David Lewis.** *See* **Lewis, David, Paul Schindler** *and* **Bob Adams**
**Schjeldahl, Peter**
Citizen.
Flower.
La Vie En Rose.
Younger Poet, A.
**Schlesinger, John**
South Shore Line.
**Schloss, David**
Poem, The: "I had never heard of the whiteness."
**Schmidt, Michael**
Underwater.
**Schmidt, Tom**
Black and White.
Broccoli.
Butcherboy.
Butter.

Civilization.
Creeper, The.
Drowning in Spanish.
In the Garden.
Long Overdue Thankyou Note to the Girl Who Taught Me Loving, A.
Seven Mexican Children.
Waking Up.
**Schmitz, Dennis**
California Phrasebook, The.
Chicago: Near West-Side Renewal.
Cutting Out a Dress.
Eclogues.
Goodwill, Inc.
If I Could Meet God.
Mole, The.
Name of Our Country, The.
Poke-Pole Fishing.
Rabbit Leaves, The.
Rabbits.
**Schnackenberg, Gjertrud**
Signs.
**Schneider, Aaron**
Wild Honey.
**Schneider, Bart**
Song for the Woman Singing at the Café Trieste.
**Schneider, Isidor**
Comrade—Mister.
Dollars.
In a Hotel Lobby.
Portrait of a False Revolutionist.
Reichstag Trial, The.
Sun, the Worker, The.
To Comrade Lenin.
To the Museums.
Young Revolutionist.
**Schneider, Pat**
In a Maple Wood.
**Scholem, Gershom**
Trial, The.
**Schonborg, Virginia**
Construction.
**Schorb, E. M.**
Hush, Hush, New House in Charlotte.
No.
**Schotz, Myra Glazer**
First Love Poem, The.
Santa Caterina.
Thespian in Jerusalem.
**Schramm, Donald G. H.**
Voyage.
**Schramm, Richard**
Penitence.
**Schreiber, Laura**
Delicate Balance, A.
Willows.
**Schubart, Christian**
Song of the Cape of Good Hope.
**Schubert, William H.**
Educational Music or Erosion.
**Schuck, L. Pearl**
Solar Signals.
To a Butterfly.
**Schulman, Grace**
Burial of a Fisherman in Hydra.
Burn Down the Icons.
Law, The.
**Schulte, Rainer**
Disorientation.
Equator at Quito, The; or, The Will to Die.

Harpsichord of Nerves, A.
Mexican Village.
Poetry.
Prayer: "In the beginning/ was Sunday."
Words.
**Schultz, Philip**
Apartment Hunter, The.
Mrs. Applebaum's Sunday Dance Class.
**Schuyler, James**
"Can I Tempt You to a Pond Walk?"
December.
Dining Out with Doug and Frank.
Greenwich Avenue.
Head, A.
Hudson Ferry.
In Earliest Morning.
Poem: "This beauty that I see."
Quick, Henry, the Flit!
Sorting, Wrapping, Packing, Stuffing.
Stun.
What Ails My Fern?
**Schwabsky, Barry**
Fragment of a Pastoral.
**Schwartz, Delmore**
Abraham.
America, America!
Baudelaire.
Beautiful American Word, Sure, The.
Dogs Are Shakespearean, Children Are
   Strangers.
Far Rockaway.
For the One Who Would Take Man's
   Life in His Hands.
Heart Flies Up, Erratic as a Kite, The.
Heavy Bear Who Goes with Me, The.
I Am a Book I neither Wrote nor Read.
In the Naked Bed, in Plato's Cave.
Jacob.
Journey of a Poem Compared to All the
   Sad Variety of Travel, The.
Mind Is an Ancient and Famous
   Capital, The.
Mounting Summer, Brilliant and
   Ominous, The.
Poem: "Old man in the crystal morning
   after snow."
Sarah.
Self Unsatisfied Runs Everywhere, The.
Small Score, A.
Swift.
Time's Dedication.
Will you perhaps consent to be.
Winter Twilight, Glowing Black and
   Gold, The.
**Schwartz, Hillel**
Bedtime.
**Schwartz, Howard**
Abraham in Egypt.
Adam's Dream.
Blessing of the Firstborn.
Containment.
Eve, The.
Gathering the Sparks
Iscah.
Love Poem: "She coils her body around
   me."
Maps.
New Year for Trees, The.
Our Angels.
Prayers, The.
Psalm: "Father/ You are the trunk."
Shira.

Song, A: "Song, A/ That seemed so
   brief at first."
These Two.
Vessels.
**Scott and Textor**
Air Force Blue, The, *with music.*
**Scott, Alexander (1520?–1590?)**
Lament of the Master of Erskine.
Returne Thee, Hairt.
Rondel of Love [*or* Luve], A.
To Luve Unluvit.
**Scott, Alexander (b. 1920)**
Ballade of Beauties.
Continent o Venus.
Cry.
Haar in Princes Street.
Poem before Birth.
Problems.
Recipe: To Mak a Ballant.
Sabbath.
Scrievin.
Steel on Stane.
**Scott, Clement**
Oh, Promise Me, *with music.*
**Scott, Dennis**
Epitaph: "They hanged him on a
   clement morning, swung."
**Scott, Duncan Campbell**
Forsaken, The.
**Scott, Elizabeth**
Now Let Our Hearts Their Glory Wake,
   *with music.*
See How the Rising Sun, *with music.*
**Scott, Francis Reginald**
MD Sewed Wrong Section of Colon.
**Scott, Geoffrey**
Frutta di Mare.
**Scott, Herbert**
Boss's Dream.
Butcher's Dream.
Butcher's Wife.
Checker.
Clerk's Dream, The.
Cracked Eggs.
Fear of Groceries, The.
Help Is on the Way.
Letter from a Working Girl.
Lost Aisles, The.
That summer nothing would do.
**Scott, John, of Amwell.**   *See* **Scott of**
   **Amwell, John**
**Scott, Lady John**
Ettrick.
**Scott, Lady John** *and* **William Douglass.**
   *See* **Douglass, William** *and* **Lady John**
   **Scott**
**Scott, Robert B. Y.**
O Day of God, Draw Nigh, *with music.*
**Scott, Sharon**
Between Me and Anyone Who Can
   Understand.
Come On Home.
Discovering.
Fisk is/ a/ negroid/ institution.
For Both of Us at Fisk.
Just Taking Note.
Little More About the Brothers and
   Sisters, A.
Mama Knows.
Oh---Yeah!
Okay.
On My Stand.

Our Lives.
Sharon Will Be No/ Where on Nobody's
   Best-Selling List.
Sometimes/ the poems.
**Scott, Tom**
Auld Sanct-Aundrians—Brand the
   Builder.
Daeth o Brand, The.
Real Muse, The.
To X.
**Scott, Virginia**
Elegy: "My mother in the witness box."
President says, The/eat fish.
What is to be done.
**Scott, Sir Walter**
Allen-a-Dale.
Bonnie Dundee.
Bride of Lammermoor, The, *sel.*
Brignall Banks.
Doom of Devergoil, The, *sel.*
Dreary Change, The.
From the French.
Harp of the North.
Heart of Midlothian, The, *sel.*
Hour with Thee, An.
Jock of Hazeldean.
Lady of the Lake, The, *sels.*
Lay of the Last Minstrel, The, *sel.*
Lochinvar.
Lord of the Isles, The, *sel.*
Lucy Ashton's song.
Lullaby of an Infant Chief.
Maid of Neidpath, The.
Marmion, *sel.*
Nora's Vow.
On a Thunder Storm.
On Having Piles.
On the Setting Sun.
Peveril of the Peak, *sel.*
Pibroch ("Pibroch of Donuil Dhu,
   pibroch of Donuil").
Proud Maisie.
Rebecca's Hymn.
Rokeby, *sels.*
Rover's Farewell, The.
Soldier, Rest!
Song of the Reim-Kennar, The.
Then Strip Lads, and to It.
This Is My Own, My Native Land.
To-Day I Leave Mrs. Brown's Lodgings.
Woman's Faith.
**Scott, William Bell**
Witch's Ballad, The.
**Scott, Winfield Townley**
First Reader, The.
Five for the Grace of Man.
Grant Wood's American Landscape.
May 1506 (Christopher Columbus
   Speaking).
Mr. Whittier.
O Lyric Love.
U.S. Sailor with the Japanese Skull, The.
Uses of Poetry.
**Scott-Gatty, Sir Alfred.**   *See* **Gatty, Sir**
   **Alfred Scott**
**Scott of Amwell, John**
I Hate That Drum's Discordant Sound.
Rural Scenery.
**Scovell, Edith Jay**
After Midsummer.
Alone.
Betrothal, A.

In a Wood.
Love's Immaturity.
Swan's Feet, The.
**Scriven, Joseph**
What a Friend We Have in Jesus.
**Scriven, R. C.**
Marrog, The.
**Scroope, Sir Carr**
Author's Reply, The.
In Defense of Satire.
**Scudder, Eliza**
Thou Grace Divine, Encircling All, *with music.*
Thou Long Disowned, Reviled, Oppressed, *with music.*
**Scully, James**
Chain Smoking.
Esperanza.
**Seager, Francis**
Prayer to Be Said When Thou Goest to Bed, A.
**Seager, Ralph W.**
Stump Is Not the Tombstone, The.
**Seagrave, Artis**
Let All Created Things, *with music.*
**Seaman, E. William**
Higgledy-piggledy/ Ludwig van Beethoven.
**Seaman, Sir Owen**
Birthday Ode to Mr. Alfred Austin, A.
Plea for Trigamy, A.
Sitting Bard, The.
**Sears, Edmund Hamilton**
Calm, on the Listening Ear of Night, *with music.*
It Came upon the [*or* a] Midnight Clear, *with music.*
**Sears, Peter**
Rain.
**Seay, James**
Grabbling in Yokna Bottom.
It All Comes Together outside the Restroom in Hogansville.
No Man's Good Bull.
**Sebenthall, R. E.**
Old Ones, The.
Villages, The.
**Sechrist, Elizabeth Hough**
Witch Flies By, A.
**Sedley, Sir Charles**
Advice to the Old Beaux.
Get You Gone.
Marriage and Money.
On a Cock at Rochester.
Out of French.
Phyllis Knotting.
Song: "Love still has something of the sea."
To Celia.
To Cloris ("Cloris, I cannot say your eyes").
To Nysus.
To Scilla.
To Sergius.
Upon the Author of the "Satire against Wit."
**Sedulius Scottus**
Apologia pro Vita Sua.
Easter Sunday.
**Seeger, Alan**
I Have a Rendezvous with Death.

**Seeger, Peggy** *and* **Ewan MacColl.** *See* MacColl, Ewan *and* Peggy Seeger
**Seeger, Pete**
Big Muddy, The.
Oleanna.
Turn! Turn! Turn!
Where Have All the Flowers Gone?
**Seeger, Pete** *and* **Idris Davies.** *See* Davies, Idris *and* Pete Seeger
**Seeger, Pete, Millard Lampell** *and* **Lee Hays**
Union Train.
**Seelbinder, Emily**
Spring Morning: Waking.
**Seferis, George**
Mythistorema.
**Segal, Jacob Isaac**
Candle.
Rest.
**Seib, Kenneth**
Fate of Birds, The.
**Seibert, T. Lawrence**
Casey Jones ("Come, all you rounders, if you want to hear").
**Seidel, Frederick**
To Robert Lowell and Osip Mandelstam.
**Seidman, Hugh**
Drop the Wires.
Great Nebula in Andromeda, The.
Making of Color, The.
Modes of Vallejo Street, San Diego, Los Angeles, The, *sels.*
N.
Science as Art.
Tale of Genji.
**Seifert, Jaroslav**
Dance-Song.
**Seiffert, Marjorie Allen ("Elijah Hay")**
Cubist Portrait.
**Sekula, Irene**
Mother Goose (Circa 2054).
**Sellar, Walter Carruthers** *and* **Robert Julian Yeatman.** *See* Yeatman, Robert
**Selle, Len G.**
Hickory Stick Hierarchy.
**Julian** *and* **Walter Carruthers Sellar**
**Sellers, Bettie M.**
Morning of the Red-tailed Hawk, The.
**Sellers, John L.**
Army Buddy Used to Say, An.
Historical Note, A (from George Washington to His Father.)
Marriage.
Reincarnation.
Small Town History.
**Seltzer, George R.**
Come, All Ye People, *with music.*
**Selyns, Henricus**
Epitaph for Peter Stuyvesant.
O Christmas Night, *with music.*
**Semah, David**
Prostration.
Tomb.
**Sen, Pradip**
Man on My Back, The.
**Seneca (Lucius Annaeus Seneca)**
Hercules Furens, *sel.*
Hercules Oetaetus, *sel.*
Medea, *sels.*
Thyestes, *sels.*
**Senghor, Léopold Sédar**

New York.
Totem.
**Seng-ts'an**
On Trust in the Heart.
**Senior, Charles**
Island Letter.
Poem: "Always loving or blithe."
Poem while Reading "The Naked Lunch" by William Burroughs.
Primula Scotica.
Tutsan.
Verses on a Rose Street Muse.
**Serchuk, Peter**
Bent Tree.
**Sergeant, Howard**
Inundation, The.
Man Meeting Himself.
**Serin, Judith**
Orange Tree Dream.
Sheep on these hills, The.
Sock left by the road, A.
**Serraillier, Ian**
After Ever Happily.
Andrew's Bedtime Story.
Anne and the Field-Mouse.
Death of the Cat.
Hare and the Tortoise, The.
Helicopter, The.
Mouse in the Wainscot, The.
Old Sussex Road, The.
Rescue, The.
Suppose You Met a Witch, *sel.*
Swimming in the Town.
Witch's Cat, The.
**Serrano, Nina**
To R——before Leaving to Fight in Unknown Terrain.
**Service, Robert W.**
Cremation of Sam McGee, The.
Inspiration.
Ordinary Man, The.
Reckoning, The.
When the Iceworms Nest Again.
**Sessler, Thomas**
Burnt Debris.
When the Day.
You Move Forward.
**Setterberg, Ruth**
Mirage, A.
Patterns.
**Settle, Elkanah**
Medal Reversed, The.
**Severy, Bruce**
Crossing into the Prairies.
Deserted Farms Poem.
Finally.
First and Last.
Frames on Bright Faces.
Opening Day.
Poems.
Struggle for the Roads.
Talks with Himself.
**Sewall, Samuel**
Once More, Our God, Vouchsafe to Shine! *with music.*
**Seward, Anna**
True Cat, A.
**Sexton, Anne**
Abortion, The.
Addict, The.
All My Pretty Ones.
Barefoot.

Belly Dancer's Daughter, The.
Black Art, The.
Breast, The.
Child Bearers, The.
Christmas Eve.
Cinderella.
Consorting with Angels.
Crossing the Atlantic.
December 18th.
Eighteen Days without You, *sel.*
Farmer's Wife, The.
For Eleanor Boylan Talking with God.
For God while Sleeping.
For My Lover, Returning to His Wife.
Fury of Abandonment, The.
Fury of Flowers and Worms, The.
Her Kind.
Housewife.
In Celebration of My Uterus.
In the Beach House.
In the Deep Museum.
Knee Song.
Lament: "Someone is dead."
Little Girl, My String Bean, My Lovely
    Woman.
Love Song.
Lullaby: "It is a summer evening."
Man and Wife.
Menstruation at Forty.
Mr. Mine.
Moon Song, Woman Song.
Moss of His Skin, The.
Mothers.
Nude Swim, The.
Pain for a Daughter.
Rapunzel.
Riding the Elevator into the Sky.
Ringing the Bells.
Risk, The.
Rowing.
Said the Poet to the Analyst.
Some Foreign Letters.
Starry Night, The.
Sun, The.
Sylvia's Death.
That Day.
To a Friend Whose Work Has Come to
    Triumph.
Truth the Dead Know, The.
Unknown Girl in the Maternity Ward.
Us.
Wanting to Die.
Wedding Night, The.
With Mercy for the Greedy.
Woman with Girdle.
You All Know the Story of the Other
    Woman.
You, Doctor Martin.
Young.
**Seymour, Alexander**
My Aim.
**Seymour-Smith, Martin**
He Came to Visit Me.
What Schoolmasters Say.
**Shackelford, Rudy**
Entreaties.
**Shadwell, Thomas**
Medal of John Bays, The: A Satire
    against Folly and Knavery.
Timon of Athens, the Man-Hater, *sel.*
**Shakespeare, William**

Alas! that love whose view is muffled
    still.
All the world's a stage.
All's Well That Ends Well, *sel.*
And my poor fool is hang'd! No, no, no
    life!
And nothing can we call our own but
    death.
Angels and ministers of grace defend us!
Antony and Cleopatra, *sels.*
Ariel's Song: "Come unto these yellow
    sands."
Ariel's Song: "Where the bee sucks,
    there suck I."
As You Like It, *sels.*
At the Moated Grange.
Autolycus' Song ("Jog on, jog on . . .").
Autolycus' Song ("When daffodils begin
    to peer").
Barge she sat in, like a burnished throne,
    The.
Birdsong.
Blow, Blow, Thou Winter Wind!
But, soft! What light through yonder
    window breaks.
Come Away, Come Away, Death.
Courser and Jennet.
Cowards die many times before their
    deaths.
Crabbed Age and Youth.
Cymbeline, *sels.*
Death of Kings, The.
Fear No More the Heat o' the Sun.
Feste's Song ("O mistress mine").
Full Fanthom Five Thy Father Lies.
Hamlet,*sels.*
Hark! hark! the lark at heaven's gate
    sings.
Honey-Bees.
Horse, A.
Horse, The.
I have done the deed.—Didst thou not
    hear a noise?
It Is the Cause, It Is the Cause, My
    Soul.
It Was a Lover, and His Lass.
Juliet.
Julius Caesar, *sels.*
King Henry IV, Pt. I, *sel.*
King Henry V, *sels.*
King Henry VIII, *sels.*
King Lear, *sels.*
King Richard II, *sels.*
King Richard III, *sel.*
Last Words of Cardinal Wolsey, The.
Let it be so; thy truth then be thy
    dower.
Lord, lord! methought what pain it was
    to drown.
Lovers and madmen have such seething
    brains.
Lover's eyes will gaze an eagle blind, A.
Love's Labour's Lost,*sels.*
Lunatic, the Lover, and the Poet, The.
Macbeth, *sels.*
Mark Antony Addresses the Mob.
Measure for Measure, *sels.*
Merchant of Venice, The, *sels.*
Midsummer Night's Dream, A, *sels.*
Much Ado about Nothing, *sel.*
Ophelia's Song.
Othello, *sels.*

Outcry upon Opportunity, An.
Pedlar's Song, The.
Pericles, *sels.*
Phoenix and [the] Turtle, The.
Postscript.
Puck's Night Song.
Quality of Mercy, The.
Queen, my lord, is dead, The.
Romeo and Juliet,*sels.*
She should have died hereafter.
Sigh no more, ladies, sigh no more.
Song: "Hark, hark!/ Bow-wow."
Song: "Master, the swabber, the
    boatswain, and I, The."
Sonnet: "As a decrepit father takes
    delight."
Sonnet: "As an unperfect actor on the
    stage."
Sonnet: "Being your slave, what should I
    do but tend."
Sonnet: "Devouring Time, blunt thou
    the lion's paws."
Sonnet: "Expense of spirit in a waste of
    shame, The."
Sonnet: "Farewell! thou art too dear for
    my possessing."
Sonnet: "From fairest creatures we
    desire increase."
Sonnet: "From you have I been absent
    in the spring."
Sonnet: "Full many a glorious morning
    have I seen."
Sonnet: "How like a winter hath my
    absence been."
Sonnet: "How oft when thou, my music,
    music play'st."
Sonnet: "I never saw that you did
    painting need."
Sonnet: "If thou survive my well-
    contented day."
Sonnet: "If thy soul check thee that I
    come so near."
Sonnet: "Is it for fear to wet a widow's
    eye."
Sonnet: "Let me not to the marriage of
    true minds."
Sonnet: "Like as the waves make
    towards the pebbled shore."
Sonnet: "Lo, as a careful housewife runs
    to catch."
Sonnet: "Love is too young to know
    what conscience is."
Sonnet: "My love is as a fever, longing
    still."
Sonnet: "My mistress' eyes are nothing
    like the sun."
Sonnet: "No longer mourn for me when
    I am dead."
Sonnet: "No more be grieved at that
    which thou hast done."
Sonnet: "Not marble, nor the gilded
    monuments."
Sonnet: "Not mine own fears nor the
    prophetic soul."
Sonnet: "O! Never say that I was false
    of heart."
Sonnet: "Poor soul, the center of my
    sinful earth."
Sonnet: "Shall I compare thee to a
    summer's day?"
Sonnet: "Since brass, nor stone, nor
    earth, nor boundless sea."

Sonnet: "That time of year thou mayst in me behold."
Sonnet: "Then hate me when thou wilt; if ever, now."
Sonnet: "They that have power to hurt and will do none."
Sonnet: "Thy bosom is endearèd with all hearts."
Sonnet: "Tired with all these, for restful death I cry."
Sonnet: "To me, fair friend, you never can be old."
Sonnet: "Two loves I have of comfort and despair."
Sonnet: "Unthrifty loveliness, why dost thou spend."
Sonnet: "When I do count the clock that tells the time."
Sonnet: "When I have seen by Time's fell hand defaced."
Sonnet: "When in disgrace with fortune and men's eyes."
Sonnet: "When in the chronicle of wasted time."
Sonnet: "When my love swears that she is made of truth."
Sonnet: "When to the sessions of sweet silent thought."
Sonnet: "Whoever hath her wish, thou hast thy Will."
Sonnets, *sels.*
Spring.
Spring Garland.
Tell Me Where Is Fancy Bred.
Tempest, The.
This England ("This royal throne of kings, this sceptered isle").
Thrice the brinded cat hath mew'd.
Thus have I shunned the fire for fear of burning.
Timon of Athens, *sel.*
To be, or not to be—that is the question.
Tomorrow, and Tomorrow, and Tomorrow.
Tomorrow Is Saint Valentine's Day.
Troilus and Cressida, *sel.*
Twelfth Night, *sels.*
Two Gentlemen of Verona, The, *sels.*
Under the Greenwood Tree.
When that I was and a little tiny boy.
Who Is Sylvia?
Wild Flowers.
Winter.
You spotted snakes with double tongue.
**Shakespeare, William** *and others*
Passionate Pilgrim, The, *sels.*
**Shakur, Assata**
What Is Left?
**Shalom, Shin**
Spendor.
**Shange, Ntozake**
Cross Oceans into My Heart.
Graduation Nite.
**Shanks, Edward**
Cataclysm, The.
Going In to Dinner.
On Holmbury Hill.
Rock Pool, The.
**Shannon, Monica**
Only My Opinion.
**Shapcott, Thomas William**
August Fugue.

Blue Paisley Shirt, The.
Ceremony for Cedar: 8.
Finches, The.
Flying Fox.
In Memory of Francis Webb.
June Fugue.
March Fugue.
Portrait of a Younger Twin.
Shabbytown Fugue.
Trees, The: A Convict Monologue.
War.
**Shapiro, David**
Falling Upwards.
**Shapiro, Harvey**
Blue Max.
Exodus.
Feast of the Ram's Horn.
Glory.
Heart, The.
Jerusalem Notebook, A.
Like a Beach.
Lines for the Ancient Scribes.
Mountain, Fire, Thornbush.
Musical Shuttle.
National Cold Storage Company.
Past Time.
Provincetown, Mass.
Riding Westward.
Six Hundred Thousand Letters, The.
Where I Am Now.
**Shapiro, Karl**
All Tropic Places Smell of Mold.
Alphabet, The.
Aubade: "What dawn is it?"
Auto Wreck.
Boy-Man.
Buick.
California Winter.
Conscientious Objector, The.
Cut Flower, A.
Dark Exciting Days, The.
Dirty Word, The.
Dome of Sunday, The.
Drug Store.
Elegy for a Dead Soldier.
Epitaph: "Underneath this wooden cross there lies."
Figurehead, The.
First Time, The.
Fly, The.
Girls Working in Banks.
Hospital.
In the Second-best Hotel in Tokyo.
Intellectual, The.
Interlude.
Israel.
Jew.
Jew at Christmas Eve, The.
Leg, The.
Lower the Standard: That's My Motto.
Manhole Covers.
Messias.
My Grandmother.
Necropolis.
Nostalgia.
October 1.
151st Psalm, The.
Phenomenon, The.
Poet.
Progress of Faust, The.
Quintana Lay in the Shallow Grave of Coral.

Scyros.
Sickness of Adam, The.
Six Religious Lyrics, *sel.*
Teasing the Nuns.
There Is Gray in My Eyebrows.
Tornado Warning.
University.
V-Letter.
Waiting in Front of the Columnar High School.
Washington Cathedral.
White-haired Lover, *sel.*
**Shapiro, Mark Elliott**
Dying under a Fall of Stars.
**Shargel, Zvi**
I Will Go Away.
Let Us Laugh.
Pictures on the Wall.
**Sharp, Martin** *and* **Eric Clapton.** *See* **Clapton, Eric** *and* **Martin Sharp**
**Sharp, Saundra**
Moon Poem.
**Sharp, William ("Fiona Macleod")**
Field Mouse, The.
Moon-Child, The.
**Sharpe, Peter**
Cold Front.
**Sharpe, Richard Scrafton**
Country Mouse and the City Mouse, The.
**Sharpless, Stanley J.**
"Go to the Ant."
**Shatford, Sarah Taylor**
Found.
**Shauger, Carol**
Preface: "Mother, don't read/ my poems."
**Shaul, Anwar**
Mother.
Prayers to Liberty.
To a Cactus Seller.
**Shaw, David T.**
Columbia, the Gem of the Ocean.
**Shaw, Dorothy Stott**
Caprice.
**Shaw, Knowles**
Bringing in the Sheaves.
**Shaw, Luci**
Blindfold.
But Not Forgotten.
Judas, Peter.
Of Consolation.
Royalty.
Tithes.
Triptych.
**Shaw, Robert B.**
Partial Draft.
**Sheaks, Barclay**
Friend's Passing, A.
**Sheck, Laurie**
Deer, The.
**Shectman, Robin**
Breakfast.
Telephone.
**Sheers, Sir Henry**
Long Prologue to a Short Play, A.
**Sheffield, John, Duke of Buckingham and Normanby**
Essay upon Satire, An.
Nine, The.
Written over a Gate.
**Shegonee, Loyal**

Loneliness.

**Shelley, Martha**
After Reading *The First Circle.*
Note to a New Lesbian.
Round Trip to Chicago.
Transparent Closet, The.

**Shelley, Percy Bysshe**
Adonais: An Elegy on the Death of John Keats.
Alastor; or, The Spirit of Solitude.
Arethusa.
Asia's Song.
Autumn; a Dirge.
Aziola, The.
Cenci, The.
Cloud, The.
Dirge, A: "Rough wind, that moanest loud."
Dirge for the Year.
England in 1819.
Epipsychidion.
Evening: Ponte a Mare, Pisa.
Evening: To Harriet
Exhortation, An.
Feelings of a Republican on the Fall of Bonaparte.
Fragment: To Byron.
Hate-Song, A.
Hell is a city much like London.
Hellas, *sels.*
Hymn of Apollo.
Hymn of Pan.
Hymn to Intellectual Beauty.
I met Murder on the way.
I will kneel at thine altar, will crown thee with bays.
Indian Serenade, The.
Julian and Maddalo.
Lament, A: "O world! O life! O time!"
Letter to Maria Gisborne.
Liberty.
Life Rounded with Sleep.
Lines to a Critic.
Lines: "We meet not as we parted."
Lines Written among the Euganean Hills.
Lines Written in the Bay of Lerici.
Lines Written on Hearing the News of the Death of Napoleon.
Love.
Love's Philosophy.
Mask of Anarchy, The.
Monarch's Funeral, The.
Mont Blanc.
Mourn Not for Adonais.
Mutability ("The flower that smiles to-day").
Mutability ("We are as clouds that veil the midnight moon").
Ode to Liberty.
Ode to Naples.
Ode to the West Wind.
Oedipus Tyrannus; or, Swellfoot the Tyrant.
On a Painted Woman.
On Keats.
On Leaving London for Wales.
Orbed Maiden.
Ozymandias.
Peter Bell the Third.
Prometheus Unbound.
Queen Mab, *sel.*

Question, The ("I dream'd that, as I wander'd by the way").
Rain.
St. Irvyne, *sel.*
Sensitive Plant, The.
Similes for Two Political Characters of 1819.
Solitary, The.
Song: "Rarely, rarely, comest thou."
Song: "Widow bird sate mourning for her love, A."
Song to the Men of England.
Sonnet: "Lift not the painted veil which those who live."
Sonnet on Launching Some Bottles Filled with Knowledge into the Bristol Channel.
Sonnet: Political Greatness.
Sonnet to Byron.
Sonnet to Harriet on Her Birthday.
Stanzas, Written in Dejection, near Naples.
Summer Evening Churchyard, Lechdale, Gloucestershire, A, *abr.*
To——: "Cold earth slept below, The."
To——: "Music, when soft voices die."
To——: "Oh! There are spirits of the air."
To——: "One word is too often profaned."
To——: "When passions's trance is overpast."
To a Skylark.
To Constantia Singing.
To Edward Williams.
To Harriet ("Harriet! thy kiss to my soul is dear").
To Harriett ("Thy look of love has power to calm").
To Jane: The Invitation.
To Jane: The Recollection.
To Maria Gisborne in England, from Italy.
To Night.
To the Lord Chancellor.
To the Moon.
To the Republicans of North America.
To Wordsworth.
Trackless Deeps, The.
Triumph of Life, The.
Two Spirits, The: an Allegory.
Unfathomable Sea!
Waning Moon, The.
War Is the Statesman's Game.
When the Lamp Is Shattered.
Witch of Atlas, The.
With a Guitar, to Jane.
World's great age begins anew, The.
Worlds on worlds are rolling ever.
Ye Hasten to the Grave!

**Shelnutt, Eve**
Advantages.
All-Hallows Children.
At St. Mary's for the Aged.
Family.
Family Getting Back to God.
Gift.
Grandfather.
Separate.
Setting.
Visit.
Widows, The.

**Shelton, Marion Brown**
When Jesus Walked upon the Earth.

**Shelton, Peter**
Singing.

**Shelton, Richard**
Children of Night.
Excerpts from the Notebook of the Poet of Santo Tomas.
Face.
He Who Remains.
How to Amuse a Stone.
Letter to a Dead Father.
Letting Go.
My Love.
Notes toward an Autobiography: The Poet at 41.
One More Time.
Requiem for Sonora.
Seven Preludes to Silence.
Today.

**Shembe, Isaiah**
Come In.
Dance Hymn.
I Am the Beginning.
Let Zulu Be Heard.
Springtime of the earth has come, The.

**Shenhar, Aliza**
Akedah, The.
Drunkenness of Pain, The.
Expectation.
Resurrection of the Dead.
Sea-Games.
Song of the Closing Service.
Trembling.

**Shenstone, William**
On the Clerk of a Country Parish.
School-Mistress, The.
Written at an Inn at Henley.

**Shepherd, Ambrosia**
Black Wonder, The.

**Shepherd, Sir Fleetwood**
Eptitaph on the Duke of Grafton.

**Shepherd, J. Barrie**
In Passing.
Lent Tending.

**Sheppard, Patricia**
Enlightenment, The.

**Sher, Steven**
Groundhog Foreshadowed, The.
Pilgrimage to Hennessey's.

**Sheridan, Caroline Elizabeth Sarah.** *See* **Norton, Caroline Elizabeth Sarah Sheridan**

**Sheridan, Helen Selina, Lady Dufferin**
Charming Woman, The.

**Sheridan, John D.**
Dan the Watchman.

**Sheridan, Michael**
Grace.

**Sheridan, Richard Brinsley**
Clio's Protest.
Geranium, The.
On Lady Anne Hamilton.

**Sherman, Frank Dempster**
Daisies.
Kite, A.
Waterfall, The.

**Sherman, Jane**
Night Storm.

**Sherman, Joseph**
Sarai.

**Sherwin, Judith Johnson**

Balance, The
Construction #13.
Dr. Potatohead Talks to Mothers.
Earth, The: To Marilyn.
Eat 'Em Up Smith Tells All in South
  Africa.
Fabulous Teamsters, The.
First Dance: God who Walks like a
  Bear.
Gentle Heart, A: Two.
Goddess.
Just.
Light Woman's Song, The.
Lights, Flowers.
Nightpiece.
Rhyme for the Child as a Wet Dog.
Three Power Dances, sel.
What Maisie Know She Don't Want No.
**Sherwin, Richard**
Jacob's Winning.
**Shevin, David**
Dawn.
Shechem.
**Shideler, Ross**
Leaves.
**Shields, Ren**
In the Good Old Summertime.
**Shiffert, Edith Marcombe**
Manners.
Monkeys on Mt. Hiei.
Shadow of a Branch, The.
**Shihab, Naomi**
Driving North from Kingsville, Texas.
Jefferson, Texas.
My Father and the Fig Tree.
Night Shift.
**Shiki.** See **Masaoka Shiki**
**Shikishi, Princess**
Autumn.
Blossoms have fallen, The.
Spring.
Winter.
**Shine, Carol**
What's in a Word?
**Shinoda, Elizabeth**
Revisit, A.
What We Have.
**Shipley, Sir Arthur**
Ere You Were Queen of Sheba.
**Shipley, Vivian**
First Holes Are Fresh.
**Shipman, Thomas**
Resolute Courtier, The.
**Shippen, William**
Character of a Certain Whig, The.
Pasquin to the Queen's Statue at St.
  Paul's.
**Shippey, Joseph**
Columbia College, 1796.
**Shiraishi Kazuko**
Phallus.
**Shire, Kent**
Earth Changes.
**Shirley, James**
Contention of Ajax and Ulysses, The,
  sel.
Cupid's Call.
Glories of Our Blood and State, The.
Imposture, The, sel.
On Her Dancing.
On the Duke of Buckingham.
Piping Peace.

**Shlonsky, Avraham**
Dress Me, Dear Mother.
New Genesis, A.
Pledge.
Prayer: "Forgive me, you whom they
  cast in a name."
Stars on Shabbat, The.
**Shockley, Martin Staples**
Crossedroads.
**Sholé, Mba**
Fish Does . . . Hip! The.
**Sholl, Betsy**
Urgency.
**Shorb, Michael**
First Ice of Winter.
**Shore, Henry**
Angel Collector, The.
Cave, The.
Child's Pulse, A.
Destroyers, The.
Eyes.
Library, The.
Obstetrician, The.
**Shore, Jane**
Astronomer's Journal, An.
Persian Miniature.
**Short, Clarice**
Encounter.
Imperfect Sympathies.
Old One and the Wind, The.
On the Shore of Crete.
Taking Leave of the Old.
Whetstone, The.
Winterkill.
Work of Art.
**Short, John**
Carol: "There was a boy bedded in
  bracken."
**Shostakovitch, Dmitri**
Salute to Life.
**Shpunt, Lori**
How to End the Summer Alone.
Rituals.
Way It Really Happened, The.
**Shrader, Stephen**
Easter.
Pantoum.
Public Utterance.
Request.
What We Move Thru.
**Shriver, Peggy**
Spirit of 34th Street, The.
**Shulman, David**
Diary of the Sailors of the North, A.
**Shulman, Max**
Honest Abe Lincoln.
**Shumway, Mary**
Before the Dark Is Down.
Cattails for Bennett.
Flight.
Gooseberry Wine.
Passage.
River Road.
Whether Firelocked.
**Shurmantine, Brad Lee**
Tracks.
**Shurtleff, Ernest W.**
Lead On, O King Eternal, with music.
**Shuttleworth, P. N.**
Wykehamist's Address to Learning, A.
**Shuttleworth, Paul**
Tornado Watch.

**"Shy, Timothy."** See **Lewis, Dominic
  Bevan Wyndham**
**Sidney, Mary, Countess of Pembroke.** See
  **Pembroke, Mary Sidney Herbert,
  Countess of**
**Sidney, Sir Philip**
Arcadia, sels.
Astrophel and Stella.
Desire.
Farewell, A: "Oft have I mused, but now
  at length I find."
Fourth Song: "Only joy, now here you
  are."
In martial sports I had my cunning tried.
In wonted walks, since wonted fancies
  change.
Lady My Treasure.
Leave Me, O Love.
Litany, A: "Ring out your bells, let
  mourning shows be spread."
My True Love Hath My Heart [And I
  Have His.]
Philomela.
Sestina: "Farewell, Oh sun, Arcadia's
  clearest light."
Since Nature's Works Be Good.
Sleep, baby mine, Desire, nurse Beauty
  singeth.
Thou Blind Man's Mark.
Voices at the Window.
When Two Suns Do Appear.
With How Sad Steps, O Moon, Thou
  Climb'st the Skies.
Ye goat-herd gods that love the grassy
  mountains.
**Siebert, Charles**
City Butterfly.
**Siegel, Danny**
Binni the Meshuggener.
Crippler, The.
Snow in the City.
**Siegel, Eli**
Fare Thee Well.
**Siegel, Robert**
Center of America, The.
Ego.
Mad Dog.
Nude.
Poet.
**Sigourney, Lydia Huntley**
Blessed Comforter Divine, with music.
God Save the Plough.
Indian Names.
Laborers of Christ! Arise, with music.
On the Death of Mrs. Felicia Hemans,
  sel.
Onward, Onward, Men of Heaven, with
  music.
We Praise Thee, If One Rescued Soul,
  with music.
**Sila (Silabhattarika)**
Wanton, sel.
**Silber, Irwin**
I Just Wanna Stay Home.
Put My Name Down.
**Silberschlag, Eisig**
Abraham.
Proust on Noah.
**Silbert, Layle**
Breathe In Breathe Out.
Good Morning.
Grand Hotel, Calcutta.

Relicts.

**Silén, Iván**
To Teresa.
Why I Can't Write a Poem about Lares.

**Silesky, Barry**
White Pines.

**Silk, Dennis**
Guide to Jerusalem.
Matronita.

**Silkin, Jon**
Coldness, The.
Death of a Bird.
Death of a Son.
Furnished Lives.
It Says.
Jerusalem.
Light.
Lilies of the Valley.
Reclaimed Area.
Respectabilities.
Resting Place.
Shirt, The.
Word about Freedom and Identity in
    Tel Aviv, A.

**Silko, Leslie**
Alaskan Mountain Poem #1.
Deer Song.
Four Mountain Wolves.
Hawk and Snake.
Horses at Valley Stores.
In Cold Storm Light.
Indian Song: Survival.
Love Poem: "Rain smell comes with the
    wind."
Poem for Ben Barney.
Poem for Myself and Mei: Abortion.
Prayer to the Pacific.
Preparations.
Slim Man Canyon.
Sun Children.
Time We Climbed Snake Mountain, The.
Toe'osh: A Laguna Coyote Story.
When Sun Came to Riverwoman.
Where Mountain Lion Lay Down with
    Deer.

**Sillitoe, Alan**
Picture of Loot.

**Silverman, Maxine**
Hair.

**Silverman, Stuart**
Game, The.
Garden, The.

**Silvers, Frances**
Frankie Silvers.

**Silverstein, David I.**
There Are in Such Moments.

**Silverstein, Shel**
Beware, My Child.
Boa Constrictor.
Enter This Deserted House.
For Sale.
Fourth, The.
Hector the Collector.
Horse, The.
Jimmy Jet and His TV Set.
My Invention.
Oh Have You Heard.
On Halloween.
Some Day.
Spaghetti.
Taxi Crab.
Uncle Umbert.

What a day, oh what a day.

**Silverton, Michael**
Adorable paratroopess alights, The.
Food drops off a fork, The.
I am yours and you are mine so.
Woman came to me, A.

**Simcock, Jack**
To My Wife.

**Simic, Charles**
Ax.
Bestiary for the Fingers of My Right
    Hand.
Bird, The.
Bones.
Breasts.
Brooms.
Butcher Shop.
Elementary Cosmogony.
Errata.
Fork.
Further Adventures of Charles Simic.
George Simic.
Hunger.
Nothing.
Partial Explanation, The.
Pastoral: "I came to a field."
Poem: "Every morning I forget how it
    is."
Poem without a Title.
Poverty.
Psalm: "Old ones to the side."
Second Avenue Winter.
Solitude.
Spoon, The.
Starry Sky.
Stone.
Story, The.
Strictly for Posterity.
Tale, The.
Tapestry.
Watermelons.
Wind, The.

**Simison, Greg**
My Family's under Contract to Cancer.

**Simmerman, Jim**
Cartoon.

**Simmons, Edgar**
At the Seed and Feed.

**Simmons, Gary**
Some Thoughts.

**Simmons, J. Edgar**
Father in Tennessee, A.
Troubador.

**Simmons, James**
Art and Reality.
Cavalier Lyric.
Experience.
Fear Test: Integrity of Heroes.
First Goodbye Letter, The.
For Delphine.
For the Centenary.
Goodbye, Sally.
John Donne.
Letter to a Jealous Friend.
Outward Bound.
Prodigal Thinks of His Mother, The.
Protestant Courts Catholic.
Reformer to His Father, A.
Summing Up, The.
Written, Directed by and Starring.

**Simmons, Judy Dothard**
Alabama.

Generations.
It's Comforting.
Survivor.

**Simon, John Oliver**
Don't Tell Bad Dreams Says Tita's
    Mother.
For Alan Blanchard.
In Swarthmore College Ethics Class.
Living in the Boneyard.
Tryptych for Jan Bockelson, A.
Vanish.
Woodchuck Who Lives on Top of Mt.
    Ritter.

**Simon, Paul**
Dangling Conversation.
59th Street Bridge Song, The.
Patterns.
Richard Cory.
Sound of Silence, The.

**Simone, Nina**
Four Women.

**Simonides (of Ceos)**
On the Spartan Dead at Thermopylae.

**Simpson, Alan**
Twenty-third Psalm, The.

**Simpson, Louis**
After Midnight.
American Dreams.
American Poetry.
As Birds Are Fitted to the Boughs.
Ash and the Oak, The.
Back in the States.
Big Dream, Little Dream.
Birch ("Birch tree, you remind me").
Carentan O Carentan.
Climate of Paradise, The.
Columbus.
Country House, The.
Custom of the World, The.
Doubting.
Dvonya.
Early in the Morning.
Friend of the Family, A.
Frogs.
Goodnight, The.
Green Shepherd, The.
Heroes, The.
Hot Night on Water Street.
Hour of Feeling, The.
In California.
In the Suburbs.
Inner Part, The.
Isidor.
Laurel Tree, The.
Lines Written near San Francisco.
Love and Poetry.
Man Who Married Magdalene, The.
Memories of a Lost War.
Middleaged Man, The.
Morning Light, The.
My Father in the Night Commanding
    No.
New Lines for Cuscuscaraway and Mirza
    Murad Ali Beg.
Night in Odessa, A.
On the Lawn at the Villa.
Port Jefferson.
Redwoods, The.
Riders Held Back, The.
Sensibility.
Simplicity.

Song: "Rough Winds Do Shake the
  Darling Buds of May."
Squeal.
Story about Chicken Soup, A.
Stumpfoot on 42nd Street.
Summer Storm.
Tailor's Wedding, The.
There Is.
Things.
To the Western World.
Tonight the Famous Psychiatrist.
Troika, The.
Union Barge on Staten Island, The.
Vandergast and the Girl.
Wall Test, The.
Walt Whitman at Bear Mountain.
Why Do You Write about Russia?
**Simpson, Nancy**
On Certain Days of the Year.
Water on the Highway.
**Simpson, Ronald Albert**
All Friends Together: A Survey of
  Present-Day Australian Poetry.
Contacts with the Past.
Gift, The.
Lake.
Landscape.
Midnight.
Modern Leader, A.
Sea Variations.
Visit to the Museum.
**Simpson, Sam L.**
Wagon Train, The.
**Simpson, Tobey A.**
For Mariella, in Antrona.
**Simpson, William Haskel**
Homesick Song.
Navajo.
Saddle.
Taos Drums.
Yucca Is Yellowing.
**Sinason, Valerie**
Sir of the C Stream.
**Sinclair, Bennie Lee**
Decoration Day.
Evangelist, The.
**Sinclair, Donald**
Path of the Old Spells, The.
**Sinclair, Keith**
Memorial to a Missionary.
Parakeet, The.
Young Chess Player, The.
**Sinclair, Marjorie**
Bombing of Kaho'olawe, The.
Waterlilies.
**Sinfield, Peter** and **Robert Fripp.**   **See**
  **Fripp, Robert** and **Peter Sinfield**
**Singer, Burns (James Burns Singer)**
Birdsong.
Epilogue: "That death might not be
  casual."
Home from Sea.
Letter, A.
Peterhead in May.
Tree.
**Singer, Sarah**
Family Plot.
**Siôn Cent**
Vanity of the World, The.
**Siôn Phylip**
Seagull, The.
**Sissman, Louis Edward**

Lüchow's and After.
New York Woman, The.
Nocturne, Central Park South.
Pepys Bar, West Forty-eighth Street, 8
  a.m.
Safety at Forty; or, An Abecedarian
  Takes a Walk.
West Forties, The: Morning, Noon and
  Night.
**Sisson, Charles Hubert**
Adam and Eve.
Carmen Saeculare.
Cranmer.
Human Relations.
Money.
Nature of Man, The.
Temple, The.
**Sisson, Jonathan**
Poem: "Horse in the grass, The."
Wife and Mother.
**Sitwell, Edith**
Anne Boleyn's Song.
Aubade: "Jane, Jane,/ Tall as a crane."
Canticle of the Rose, The.
Country Dance.
Dark Song.
Dirge for the New Sunrise.
Drum, The: The Narrative of the
  Demon of Tedworth.
Elegy for Dylan Thomas.
Evening.
Four in the Morning.
Heart and Mind.
Hornpipe.
Innocent Spring, The.
King of China's Daughter, The.
Madam Mouse Trots.
Most Lovely Shade.
Neptune—Polka.
Poet Laments the Coming of Old Age,
  The.
Shadow of Cain, The.
Sir Beelzebub.
Sleeping Beauty, The, *sel.*
Song: "Once my heart was a summer
  rose."
Song at Morning, A.
Spinning Song.
Still Falls the Rain.
Street Song.
Swans, The.
Switchback.
Tears.
Trio for Two Cats and a Trombone.
Two Kitchen Songs.
Youth with Red-gold Hair, The.
**Sitwell, Sir Osbert**
Maxixe.
Mrs. Busk.
**Sitwell, Sacheverell**
Cowslips.
Upon an Image from Dante, *sel.*
**Siv Cedering.**   **See Fox, Siv Cedering**
**Sivan, Arye**
Children's Song.
Forty Years Peace.
In Jerusalem Are Women.
To Xanadu, Which Is Beth Shaul.
**Sizemore, George**
Drill Man Blues.
**Sjoberg, John**
Answer, An.

Blue Tit.
Death of Democracy, The.
Fantastic Collection of Stamps.
Overalls.
Pablo Anytime.
Paffer Jocker.
Porch Window.
Thoughts.
We Try Not to Touch So Close.
**Sjolander, John P.**
Last Longhorn's Farewell, The.
Pine of Whiting Wood, The.
**Skeat, Walter William**
Villanelle: "It's all a trick, quite easy
  when you know it."
**Skeen, Anita**
Instructions.
Letter to My Mother.
Modern Poetry.
Outside Every Window Is a Flowering
  Thing.
Sailing in Crosslight.
**Skelton, John**
Anathema of Cats.
Auncient acquaintance, madam, betwen
  us twayn, The.
Ballade of the Scottyshe Kynge, A.
Bowge of Courte, The.
Colin Clout, *abr.*
Garlande of Laurell, The,*sels.*
Gup, Scot.
How the Doughty Duke of Albany like a
  Coward Knight Ran away Shamefully,
  *sel.*
Knolege, aquayntance, resort, favour
  with grace.
Manerly Margery Mylk and Ale.
My Darling Dear, My Daisy Flower.
Phyllyp Sparowe [*or* Philip Sparrow].
Prayer to the Father of Heaven, A.
To Maystres Jane Blenner-Haiset.
To Mistress Margery Wentworth.
To Mistress [*or* Maystres] Isabel[l]
  Pennell.
To Mistress [*or* Maystres] Margaret
  Hussey.
Tunnyng [*or* Tunning] of Elynour [*or*
  Elinor] Rummyng [*or* Rumming], The.
Upon a Dead Man's Head.
Why Come Ye Not to Court, *sel.*
Womanhood [*or* Womanhod], wanton, ye
  want.
**Skelton, Robin**
Gift, The.
History.
Letter V.
Two Sleepers, The.
**Skinner, Constance Lindsay**
Song of Basket-weaving.
Three Songs from the Haida.
**Skinner, Jeffrey**
His Side/ Her Side.
**Skinner, Knute**
Blackheads.
Cold Irish Earth, The.
Cow, The.
Imagine Grass.
Location.
Organ Solo.
**Skipsey, Joseph**
Get Up!
Golden Lot, A.

Mother Wept.
Time Hath Been, The.
Willy to Jinny.
**Skirrow, Desmond**
Ode on a Grecian Urn Summarized.
**Sklar, Morty**
Charlie Parker.
I Put the Telephone Back on Its
Receiver.
In Memory of My Being Late.
Jarashow.
Ma.
Mending ("The mending pillow is set
against the wall").
Modern Times.
Poem without the Word Love.
Red and Blue Noon.
Smell of Life, The.
So This Is Earth.
**Sklarew, Myra**
Benediction.
In Bed.
Instructions for the Messiah.
Origin of Species, The.
Poem of the Mother.
Twenty-four Hours.
What Is a Jewish Poem?
**Skoyles, John**
Evidence.
No Thank You.
This Business of Dying.
**Skrine, Nesta Higginson.** *See* **"O'Neill, Moira"**
**Skrzynecki, Peter**
Feliks Skrzynecki.
Kornelia Woloszczuk.
Migrant Hostel.
**Slade, Leon**
Alter Ego.
Hello Dolly.
Homage to a Homosexual.
Slade's Anatomy of the Horse.
Spiritualist, The.
**Slate, Ron**
Accomplice, The.
**Slavitt, David R.**
Day Sailing.
Epitaph for Goliath.
Jonah: A Report.
Ride the High Country.
Seals.
Two Companions and the Bear.
**Slesinger, Warren**
Field with Figurations.
Green Beginning, The.
Passage.
Pine Needles.
Sandpaper, Sandpiper, Sandpit.
**Slessor, Kenneth**
Beach Burial.
Captain Dobbin.
Cock-Crow.
Country Towns.
Five Bells.
Night-Ride, The.
Nuremberg.
Serenade: "Thou moon, like a white
Christus hanging."
Sleep.
South Country.
**Sloate, Daniel**
Your Birds Build Sun-Castles with Song.

**Sloman, Joel**
In a Remote Cloister Bordering the
Empyrean.
Tree, The.
**Slonimski, Antoni**
Conrad.
Conversation with a Countryman.
Elegy: "No more, no more Jewish
townships in Poland."
Jerusalem.
**Slowinsky, Stephanie**
It's True I'm No Miss America.
**Slutsky, Boris**
Burnt.
Dreams of Auschwitz.
God.
How They Killed My Grandmother.
**Small, Michael**
At Night.
At the Top.
Bed, The.
Black Stallion.
Charlie 12.
Dream, A.
I Can Forget.
Looking for Someone.
Narrow Street, A.
On Being Late.
Widow of a Man Who Is Still Breathing,
The.
**Smallshaw, Judith**
Birth.
Franco.
Knife, The.
Spastic Child on a Pony, A.
Tied under My Heart.
**Smart, Christopher**
Adoremus.
Author Apologizes to a Lady for His
Being a Little Man, The.
Consideration for Others.
David before Saul.
For Saturday.
Fruits of the Earth.
Gloria.
Gratitude.
Hymns and Spiritual Songs,*sels.*
Hymns for the Amusement of
Children,*sels.*
Jubilate Agno,*sels.*
Long-Suffering of God.
Man of Prayer, The.
Mirth.
Miser and the Mouse, The.
Morning Hymn, A.
Nativity of Our Lord and Saviour Jesus
Christ, The.
Praise.
St. Mark.
St. Matthias.
Song of David, The, *sel.*
Song to David, A.
To the Rev. Mr. Powell.
**Smedley, Menella Bute**
North Pole Story, A.
**Smith, Adrian Keith**
Rain.
**Smith, Alexander**
Glasgow.
**Smith, Arthur**
Breath.
Carpenter.

Dream of Fixing Things, The.
Killing, The.
**Smith, Arthur James Marshall**
News of the Phoenix.
Political Intelligence.
Tree.
**Smith, Barbara**
Next Door to Monica's Dance Studio.
Physical for My Son.
**Smith, Bertha Wilcox**
Mister Snow Man.
**Smith, Bessie**
Empty Bed Blues.
**Smith, Bruce**
Pelvic Meditation.
**Smith, Caroline Sprague**
Tarry with Me, O My Saviour, *with
music.*
**Smith, Charlotte**
Beachy Head, *sels.*
He May Be Envied, Who with Tranquil
Breast.
Invitation to the Bee.
Montalbert, *sel.*
Mute Is Thy Wild Harp, Now, O Bard
Sublime!
Press'd by the Moon, Mute Arbitress of
Tides.
Thirty-eight.
To Sleep.
To Spring.
To the Moon.
**Smith, Dave** [*or* **David**]
Blues for Benny Kid Paret.
Closet, The.
Cumberland Station.
Dome Poem.
Dying off Egg Island Bar.
First Star.
Gramercy Park Hotel.
Hard Times, but Carrying On.
How One Thing Leads to Another.
High Are the Winter Rivers.
Mean Rufus Throw-Down.
Night Fishing for Blues.
Perspective and Limits of Snapshots,
The.
Pietas: The Petrified Wood.
Pine Cones.
Roundhouse Voices, The.
Running Back.
Snake Sermon.
Tide Pools.
Two Memories of a Rented House in a
Southern State.
**Smith, Douglas**
Balcony Poems, The.
**Smith, Edward**
Rosie Bakungan.
**Smith, Edward Lucie-.** *See* **Lucie-Smith,
Edward**
**Smith, Eunice**
Dear Brethren, Are Your Harps in
Tune? *with music.*
Dear Happy Souls, *with music.*
**Smith, Florence Margaret.** *See* **Smith,
Stevie**
**Smith, Harry B.**
Gypsy Love Song, *with music.*
**Smith, Horace** [*or* **Horatio**]
Tale of Drury Lane, A.
**Smith, Iain Crichton**

By Ferry to the Island.
Cemetery near Burns' Cottage, The.
Farewell: "We were gone from each
  other."
Highland Portrait.
Luss Village.
Old Woman ("And she, being old, fed
  from a mashed plate").
Old Woman ("Your thorned back").
Rythm.
Shadows, The.
Temptation, The.
Tonight.
Two Girls Singing.
Witches, The.
Young Girl.

**Smith, J. Moyr**
Four and Twenty Merulae.
She Lost Her Sheep.

**Smith, James** *and* **Sir George Rose**
Conversation in Craven Street, Strand.

**Smith, Jared**
Something.

**Smith, Joan**
Alley-Walker.

**Smith, John (b. 1924)**
Colin Barnes, Drums.
First, Goodbye.
In a Curious Way.
Jazz for Five,*sels.*
Mud.
Shake Keane, Trumpet.

**Smith, Jordan**
Blue River Falls.
Immigrant's Stars, The.

**Smith, Ken**
After a Journey.
Amana Colonies, The.
Beyond Breath.
Facts.
Inventory/ Itinerary.
Old Mill, Newton St. Cyres.
Persistent Narrative.
Possessions.
Stone Poems, The.
Street, The.
Train.

**Smith, Margoret J.**
Cataract.

**Smith, Michael**
At the Appointed Hour They Came.
Blond Hair at the Edge of the Pavement.
Desolate Rhythm of Dying Recurs, The.
Finding no ghosts we must invent our
  own.
Geriatric Huts.
Here Is the Abattoir Where.
Public House Cinematics.
There is one, never seen, behind that
  window.
When Roots Get Too Deep.
With the Woodnymphs.

**Smith, Milton.** *See* **Mbembe**

**Smith, Naomi Gwladys Royde-.** *See*
  **Royde-Smith, Naomi Gwladys**

**Smith, Patrick**
In Flight.

**Smith, R. T.**
Angels We Have Heard on High.
Checking the Firing.
Poem for David Janssen.
Rural Route.

Solo Late Show over Easter Break.

**Smith, Robert (d. 1555)**
Exhortation of a Father to His Children,
  The.

**Smith, Robert Paul**
Song for Everybody.
Tie Your Tongue, Sir?
Time Upon a Once.

**Smith, S. L. Henderson**
Blood Transfusion.
Bones.
Emergency Room, The.
Layer-out, The.
Operation, The.
Physician, Heal Thyself.
Post-Mortem.

**Smith, Samuel Francis**
America.
As Flows the Rapid River, *with music.*
Morning Light Is Breaking, The, *with*
  *music.*
Softly Fades the Twilight Ray, *with*
  *music.*

**Smith, Samuel J.**
Arise, My Soul! With Rapture Rise! *with*
  *music.*

**Smith, Sidney Goodsir.** *See* **Smith,**
  **Sydney Goodsir**

**Smith, Stephen E.**
Death of Carmen Miranda, The.
Getting By on Honesty.

**Smith, Stevie (Florence Margaret Smith)**
Admire Cranmer! ("Admire the old man,
  admire him, admire him").
Avondale.
Away, Melancholy.
Celtic Fringe, The.
Cold as no love, and wild with all
  negation.
Conventionalist, The.
Correspondence between Mr. Harrison
  in Newcastle and Mr. Sholto Peach
  Harrison in Hull.
Dear Female Heart.
Dedicated Dancing Bull and the Water
  Maid, The, *sel.*
Edmonton, thy cemetery.
Egocentric.
Everything Is Swimming.
Exeat.
Fairy Story.
Frog Prince, The.
Heavenly City, The.
Here Lies. . .
I Love.
I Remember.
Jungle Husband, The.
Little Boy Lost, The.
Lord Barrenstock.
Louise.
Major Macroo.
Monsieur Pussy-Cat, Blackmailer.
Mother, among the Dustbins.
My Cats.
Not Waving but Drowning.
Occasional Yarrow, The.
Our Bog Is Dood.
Papa Love Baby.
Reversionary.
River God, The.
Scorpion.

Seymour and Chantelle or Un Peu de
  Vice.
Singing Cat, The.
Some Are Born.
Sunt Leones.
Tenuous and Precarious.
This Englishwoman is so refined.
Thoughts about the Person from
  Porlock.
To Carry the Child.
To School!
To the Tune of the Coventry Carol.
Valuable.
Was He Married?
Was It Not Curious?
Weak Monk, The.
Who Killed Lawless Lean?

**Smith, Sydney Bernard**
Bettystown.
Death, Putative Father.

**Smith, Sydney [or Sidney] Goodsir**
Cokkils.
Deevil's Waltz, The.
Elegy XIII: "I got her in the Black
  Bull."
Gangrel Rymour and the Pairdon of
  Sanct Anne, The, *sel.*
Grace of God and the Meth-Drinker,
  The.
Hamewith.
Largo.
Loch Leven.
Mandrake Hairt, The.
Spleen.
There Is a Tide.
We Shall Never Want.
Wuid-reek.

**Smith, Virginia E.**
Daysleep.

**Smith, Vivian**
At an Exhibition of Historical Paintings,
  Hobart.
Effect of Light, An.
Still Life.

**Smith, W. Atmar, II**
Piano Tuner, The.

**Smith, Welton**
Beast Section, The.
Interlude.
Malcolm.
Nigga Section, The.
Strategies.

**Smith, William**
Chloris, *sels.*
To the Most Excellent and Learned
  Shepheard Collin Cloute.

**Smith, William Hart-.** *See* **Hart-Smith,**
  **William**

**Smith, William Jay**
Abruptly All the Palm Trees.
American Primitive.
Beulah Louise.
Closing of the Rodeo, The.
Crockett.
Dachshunds ("The dachshund leads a
  quiet life").
Elegy: "I stood between two mirrors
  when you died."
Epitaph of a Stripper.
Massacre of the Innocents, The.
Miss Hartley.

Mr. Smith/ (With Nods to Mr. Lear and Mr. Eliot.)
Moon.
Morels.
Nightwood.
Oil Lamp, The.
Old Man by Salt Lake, An.
Old Man of Toulon, An.
Panda, The.
Pavane for the Nursery, A.
Random Generation of English Sentences; or, The Revenge of the Poets.
Rise and Fall of the Swagger Stick, The.
Seal.
Tin Can, The.
Uncertain What to Wear.
Unicorn.
What Train Will Come?
Winter Morning.
Young Man Who Loved Rain, A.

**Smithyman, Kendrick**
After.
Anzac Ceremony.
Blackleg.
Considerations, *sel.*
Die Bauernhochzeit.
Hint for the Incomplete Angler.
Inheritance.
Night-Piece.
Note on the Social Arts, A.
Parable of Two Talents.
Simple Ode.
Thing Remembered, A.
To Be Absent without Leave.
Waikato Railstop.

**Smyth, Florida Watts**
Green Mountain Boy.
Unclaimed.

**Smythe, Daniel**
Driftwood.

**Snively, Susan**
Afternoon with a Baby, An.

**Snodgrass, William DeWitt**
After experience taught me that all the ordinary.
April Inventory.
Campus on the Hill, The.
Examination, The.
Flat One, A.
Friend, A.
Heart's Needle.
Home Town
Leaving the Motel.
Lobsters in the Window.
Lovers Go Fly a Kite, The.
Lying Awake.
Marsh, The.
Matisse: "The Red Studio."
Mementos, 1 ("Sorting out letters and piles of my old").
Mementos, 2 ("I found them there today").
Men's Room in the College Chapel, The.
Monet: "Les Nymphéas."
No Use.
Operation, The.
Owls.
Partial Eclipse.
Planting a Magnolia.
Point Pelee in March.
Powwow.

Returned to Frisco, 1946.
September.
Song: "Sweet beast, I have gone prowling."
Ten Days Leave.
These Trees Stand.
Vampire's Aubade.
What We Said.
Winter Bouquet.

**Snow, Eliza R.**
Acrostic for Anna Geen.
Invocation, or the Eternal Father and Mother.
On the Death of the Dearly Beloved and Much Lamented Father.
Red Man of the South, The.
Red Man of the West, The.
Song of the Desert.
Think Not When You Gather to Zion, *with music.*
What Is, and What Is Not for Woman.

**Snyder, Gary**
Above Pate Valley.
After weeks of watching the roof leak.
After Work.
Again the ancient, meaningless.
All the Spirit Powers Went to Their Dancing Place.
All through the Rains.
August Was Foggy.
Autumn Morning in Shokoku-ji, An.
Avocado.
Bath, The.
Before the Stuff Comes Down.
Black Mesa Mine No. 1.
Burning the Small Dead.
By Frazier Creek Falls.
Dead by the Side of the Road, The.
December.
Dry Day just before the Rainy Season, A.
Elwha River, The.
First Shaman Song.
Floating World Picture: Spring in the Kitagami Mountains.
For John Chappell.
For Nothing.
Four Poems for Robin.
Foxtail Pine.
Great Mother, The.
Hay for the Horses.
Heifer Clambers Up, A.
Hitch Haiku, *sels.*
How rare to be born a human being!
I Went into the Maverick Bar.
It Pleases.
John Muir on Mt. Ritter.
Journeys.
Kyoto Born in Spring Song.
Kyoto: March.
Late Snow and Lumber Strike of the Summer of Fifty-Four, The.
Long Hair.
Looking at Pictures to Be Put Away.
Manichaeans, The.
Marin-An.
Meeting the Mountains.
Mid-August at Sourdough Mountain Lookout.
Milton by Firelight.
Mother Earth: Her Whales, *sel.*
Myths and Texts, *sels.*

Nansen.
Nooksack Valley.
Not Leaving the House.
Once Only.
Out West.
Pine Tree Tops.
Piute Creek.
Planting.
Prayer for the Great Family.
Regarding Wave, II.
Revolution in the Revolution in the Revolution.
Riprap.
Running Water Music.
Sappa Creek, The.
Second Shaman Song.
Some Good Things to Be Said for the Iron Age.
Spring Night in Shokoku-ji, A.
Text, The.
Things to Do around a Lookout.
Things to Do around a Ship at Sea.
This Poem Is for Bear.
This Poem Is for Deer.
This Tokyo.
To Hell with Your Fertility Cult.
Truth like the Belly of a Woman Turning, The.
Vapor Trails.
Walk, A.
Way West, Underground, The.
What Do They Say.
What Happened Here Before.
What You Should Know to Be a Poet.
Why Log Truck Drivers Rise Earlier than Students of Zen.
Work to Do toward Town.

**Snyder, Kirtland**
White Shark, The: Notes for a History.

**Sobel, Lester A.**
Transplantitis.

**Sobiloff, Hy**
Child's Sight, The.
Wisdom.

**Sobin, A. G.**
December Sky, The.
January Sky, The.
March Rite: Getting It Up.

**Sobol, Barbara**
Power of Women.

**Södergran, Edith**
Hope.
I saw a tree that was greater than all the others.
Pain.

**Sohappy, Liz.**   *See* **Bahe, Liz Sohappy**

**Sola Pinto, Vivian de**
In the Train.

**Sollid, John**
Sea Known.

**Solovyov-Sedoi, V. and M. Matusovskii**
Moscow Nights.

**Solt, Mary Ellen**
Forsythia.
Lilac.
Marriage.
Moonshot Sonnet.
Rain Down.
Wild Crab.
Zinnia.

**Solway, Arthur**
Answers to the Snails.

**Solway, David**
Powers of the Pawn, The.
**Somerville, Jane**
Denials 1.
**Somoza, Joseph**
Viejo.
**Sonde, Susan**
Bedtime Stories, *sel.*
Letter to Dr. C. from the Great Divide.
Working the Wood.
**Sondheim, Stephen**
Gee, Officer Krupke.
**Song, Cathy**
Remnants.
**Soniat, Katherine**
Initial Response.
Resounding.
**Sonnenschein, Hugo**
In the Ghetto.
In the Open Fields.
**Sophocles**
Antigone.
Colonus' Praise.
Oedipus at Colonus, *sel.*
Oedipus Tyrannus.
Women of Trachis, *sel.*
**Sorley, Charles Hamilton**
All the hills and vales along.
**Sorrells, Helen**
From a Correct Address in a Suburb of
a Major City.
Mountain Corral.
To a Child Born in Time of Small War.
Town I Left.
**Sorrentino, Gilbert**
Anatomy.
Handbook of Versification.
**Sossaman, Stephen**
Viet Cong Sapper Dies, A.
**Soto, Gary**
After Tonight.
Angel.
Field Poem.
History.
Hoeing.
Remember.
Telephoning God.
Town.
Underground Parking, The.
**Sousa, John Philip**
Feast of the Monkeys, The.
Have You Seen the Lady?
**Sousa, Noémia da**
Poem of Distant Childhood.
**Souster, Raymond**
Bernard.
Child's Umbrella, The.
Dog in the Fountain.
Dog, Midwinter.
Flight of the Roller Coaster.
Lift, The.
Man Who Finds That His Son Has
Become a Thief, The.
Old Dog.
**Soutar, William**
Children, The.
Gowk, The.
Lanely Müne, The.
Miracle.
Philosophic Taed, The.
Recollection of First Love.
Revelation.

Room, The.
Sleeper, The.
Song: "Whaur yon broken brig hings
owre."
Thocht, The.
Tryst, The.
**South, Joe**
So the Seeds Are Growing.
**Southey, Caroline Anne Bowles.** *See*
**Bowles, Caroline Anne**
**Southey, Robert**
Battle of Blenheim, The.
Bishop Hatto.
Cataract of Lodore, The.
Inchcape Rock, The.
March to Moscow, The.
Ode to a Pig while His Nose Was Being
Bored.
Old Man's Comforts and How He
Gained Them, The.
To a Goose.
Widow, Sapphics, The.
**Southey, Robert** *and* Samuel Taylor
Coleridge
Devil's Thoughts, The.
**Southgate, Margaret**
Pale faced, tight laced.
**Southwell, Robert**
Burning Babe, The.
Man to the Wound in Christ's Side.
Nativity of Christ, The.
New Heaven, New War.
New Prince, New Pomp.
Upon the Image of Death.
Virgin Mary to Christ on the Cross, The.
**Southwick, Marcia**
No Such Thing.
Owning a Dead Man.
**Soyinka, Wole**
Koko Oloro.
Telephone Conversation.
**Spacks, Barry**
Emblem of Two Foxes, An
Freshmen.
Last Fish, The.
Malediction.
Muse, The.
My Clothes.
My Mother's Childhood.
October.
Outrageously Blessed, The.
Six Small Songs for a Silver Flute.
Teaching Penguins to Fly.
Washing Windows.
"Who Then Is Crazy?"
**Spaziani, Maria Luisa**
Journey in the Orient.
Winter Moon.
**Spear, Charles**
Animae Superstiti.
At a Danse Macabre.
Balthasar.
Christoph.
Disinherited, The.
1894 in London.
Environs of Vanholt I.
Environs of Vanholt II.
Escape.
From a Book of Hours.
God Save the Stock.
Joachim of Flora.

Karl ("All day he stood at Weeping
Cross").
Karl ("Outside among the talking criss-
cross reeds").
Memoriter.
News from Paris.
O Matre Pulchra.
Prisoner, The.
Promised Land.
Scott-Moncrieff's Beowulf.
**Spear, Roberta**
August/ Fresno 1973.
Bat, The.
Bringing Flowers.
Sale of Smoke, A.
**Spector, Albert**
Eastside Chick with Drive.
**Spector, Herman**
Harlem River.
Night in New York.
Outcast.
Sadly They Perish.
Suicide before Coffee in a Furnished
Room.
Timeclock.
Urbanite Delapidate.
Wiseguy Type.
**Speer, Laurel**
Mirror Images.
**Speght, Rachel**
Dream, A, *sels.*
**Spellman, Alfred B.**
For My Unborn and Wretched Children.
In Orangeburg My Brothers Did.
John Coltrane: An Impartial Review.
Tomorrow the Heroes.
When Black People Are.
Zapata and the Landlord.
**Spence, Lewis**
Capernaum.
Portrait of Mary Stuart, Holyrood.
**Spence, Michael**
Fish Will Swim as Before, The.
Orchard, The.
**Spence, Skip**
Motorcycle Irene.
**Spencer, Anne**
At the Carnival.
For Jim, Easter Eve.
Lady, Lady.
Letter to My Sister.
Lines to a Nasturtium (A Lover Muses).
Wife-Woman, The.
**Spencer, Bernard**
Allotments: April.
Boat Poem.
Part of Plenty.
**Spencer, C. Mordaunt**
Rose of Tralee, The.
**Spencer, Lillian White**
Hopi Woman.
**Spencer, Theodore**
Escapist's Song.
Kind of Good-bye, A.
Return.
**Spencer, William Robert**
Beth-Gêlert.
**Spender, Stephen**
Acts passed beyond the boundary of
mere wishing.
Barn, The.
Beethoven's Death Mask.

Boy, Cat, Canary.
Chalk Blue Butterfly, The.
Coward, The.
Daybreak.
Double Shame, The.
Elementary School Classroom [or Class Room] in a Slum, An.
Express, The.
Funeral, The.
Hoelderlin's Old Age.
I Think Continually of Those Who Were Truly Great.
Icarus.
Judas Iscariot.
Landscape near an Aerodrome, The.
Living Values, The.
Marginal Field, The.
Marston.
Missing My Daughter.
Moving through the Silent Crowd.
My Parents Kept Me from Children Who Were Rough.
Not Palaces, an Era's Crown.
One More New Botched Beginning.
Perhaps.
Polar Exploration.
Pylons, The.
Rolled over on Europe: the sharp dew frozen to stars.
Room above the Square, The.
Song: "Stranger, you who hide my love."
To My Daughter.
Two Armies.
Ultima Ratio Regum.
What I Expected.
Without that once clear aim, the path of flight.
Your Body Is Stars.

**Spenser, Edmund**
Amoretti.
Aprill.
August.
Bower of Bliss, The ("Eftsoones they heard a most melodious sound").
Care in Heaven.
Cave of Despair, The.
Cease, Then, My Tongue!
Colin Clout's Come Home Again, sels.
Epithalamion: "Ye learned sisters which have oftentimes."
Faerie Queene, The, sels.
Garden of Adonis, The.
Hill of the Graces, The.
Huge Leviathan, The.
Iambicum Trimetrum.
June.
Lay to Eliza, The.
Masque of Cupid, The.
Mother Hubberd's Tale, sel.
Nature's Reply to Mutability.
Nought is on earth more sacred or divine.
November.
Prothalamion.
Song of Bliss.
Sonnet: "One day I wrote her name upon the strand."
Sonnet: "Weary year his race now having run, The."
Visions of the World's Vanity, sel.
**"Speranza."** See **Wilde, Lady Jane Francesca**

**Speros, Phyllis**
Stagehand.
**Speyer, Leonora**
Cantares, sels.
Gulls.
New Excavations.
Pompeii, sel.
Sand-pipings, sel.
Storm's End.
**Spicer, Jack**
"Graphemics," sels.
**Spilka, Arnold**
Boo Hoo.
Hippopotamuses.
**Spingarn, Lawrence P.**
Freeway Problems.
Ranch, The.
Vignette: 1922.
**Spinnanger, Ruthe T.**
Criteria.
Insight.
Label, The.
Last View, The.
Love at Stress-Point.
New York Skyline.
Profile of a Day.
Prophecy of the Grecian Urn.
**Spire, Andrè**
Ancient Law, The.
Hear, O Israel!
Nudities.
Poetics.
Pogroms.
**Spires, Elizabeth**
Wake.
**Spivack, Kathleen**
Approaching the Canvas.
But You, My Darling, Should Have Married the Prince.
Child's Visit to the Biology Lab, A.
Cripples.
Daughterly.
Dido: Swarming.
Drifting.
Dust.
Fugue.
Judgment, The.
Love u.s.a.
Meeting, The.
Mythmaking.
Private Pain in Time of Trouble.
Shining.
Visions.
**Sprigg, Christopher St. John.** See "**Caudwell, Christopher**"
**Sprunt, William**
Exercise in Solitude.
Mud.
On the Run.
**Squire, Sir John Collings ("Solomon Eagle")**
Discovery, The.
It Did Not Last.
Numerous Celts.
Rivers.
Stockyard, The.
Under.
Vision of Truth, A.
Winter Nightfall.
**Squires, Radcliffe**
Day in Salamanca, A.
March on Washington, A.

Storm in the Desert.
Vermilion Cliffs.
**Stafford, William**
Accepting Surprise.
Adults Only.
After Plotinus.
Among Strangers.
Animal That Drank Up Sound, The.
Answerers.
Ask Me.
At Cove on the Crooked River.
At Our House.
At the Bomb Testing Site.
At the Chairman's Housewarming.
At the Edge of Town.
At the Un-National Monument along the Canadian Border.
Aunt Mabel.
Behind the Falls.
Believing What I Know.
Bess.
Bridge Begins in the Trees, A.
Broken Home.
Concealment, The: Ishi, the Last Wild Indian.
Credentials.
Day You Are Reading This, The.
Deer Stolen.
Epitaph Ending in And, The.
Escape, The.
Existences.
Farm on the Great Plains, The.
Father, His Friend, and Another.
Father and Son.
Father's voice.
Fifteen.
Finding Sky Ranch.
Following.
Found in a Storm.
Freedom.
Help from History.
Hero.
Holding the Sky.
Humanities Lecture.
In Fur.
In Oregon.
In the Night Desert.
In the Oregon Country.
Lake Chelan.
Late at Night.
Late August at the Game Refuge.
Lifting Illegal Nets by Flashlight.
Listening.
Long Distance.
Moles.
Moment, The.
Mouse Night: One of Our Games.
Move to California, The, sel.
My father: October 1942.
My Party the Rain.
Near.
Now.
Old Dog.
One Home.
Oregon Message, An.
Our City Is Guarded by Automatic Rockets.
Our Kind.
Parentage.
Passing Remark.
People of the South Wind.
People Who Went By in Winter.

Prairie Town.
Priest Lake.
Quiet Town.
Religion Back Home.
Report to Crazy Horse.
Reporting Back.
Returned to Say.
Ritual to Read to Each Other, A.
Sayings from the Northern Ice.
Shepherd.
Sleeping on the Sisters Land.
So Long.
Sound from the Earth, A.
Star in the Hills, The.
Stories from Kansas.
Story, A.
Stranger Not Ourselves, The.
Strangers.
Strokes.
Summons in Indiana, The.
Survival.
Swerve, The.
These Days.
These Leaves.
Things That Happen.
Thinking for Berky.
Tillamook Burn, The.
To the Children at the Family Album.
Tornado.
Traveling through the Dark.
Trouble-shooting.
Ultimate Problems.
Vacation.
Vacation Trip.
View from Here, The.
Vocation.
Well Rising, The.
West of Your City.
Whole Story, The.
Willy Lyons.
With Kit, Age 7, at the Beach.
With My Crowbar Key.
Written on the Stub of the First
    Paycheck.

**Stager, Carol**
In Its Place.
To the Lawyer from His Only Lately
    Neglected Tort.

**Stallworthy, Jon**
Camel.
First Blood.
Here and There.
Letter from Berlin, A.
Letter to a Friend.
Poem about Poems about Vietnam, A.
True Confession, A.

**Stampa, Gaspara**
At dawn of the day the Creator.
Holy angels, in envy I cast no sigh.
If I could believe that death.
Love made me such that I live in fire.
Often I compare my lord to heaven.
Often when alone I liken my lord/ to the
    cosmos.
Stars have given me a hard fate, The.
When before those eyes, my life and
    light.
Women, whoever wishes to know my
    lord.

**Standing, Sue**
Dead Neck.

**Stanford, Ann**

Artist Underground, The.
Beating, The.
Before.
Blackberry Thicket, The.
Center of the Garden, The.
Deserted Garden. The.
Despite All That.
Double Mirror.
Edward Hicks: "The Peaceable
    Kingdom."
Gift, The.
Going Away.
Hidden Things.
Late Visitor, The.
Night of Souls.
Our Town.
Rider, The.
Robert Fulton.
Voices Inescapable, The.
Weeds.
White Horse, The.

**Stanford, Frank**
Death and the Arkansas River.

**Stange, Ken**
Poem on the End of Sensation.

**Stanhope, Philip Dormer.** *See*
    **Chesterfield, Philip Dormer Stanhope,**
    **4th Earl of**

**Stanhope, Rosamund**
At Eighty.

**Stanley, George**
Attis.

**Stanley, Robert M.**
Not Blindly in the Dark.

**Stanley, Thomas**
Beauty.
Grasshopper, The.
Killing Kiss, The.
La Belle Confidante.
Leaves Come Again, The.
Magnet, The.
Repulse, The.
Self-Deceaver, The.
Time Recover'd.
Would I were air that thou with heat
    opprest.
Young Men Dancing.

**Stanton, Frank Lebby**
Mighty Lak' a Rose, *with music.*

**Stanton, Maura**
Alcestis.
All-Night Waitress, The.
Extracts: From the Journal of Elisa
    Lynch.
Judith Recalls Holofernes.
Letter to Kafka.

**Stanway, Phil**
Ten Sonnets for Today.

**Starbird, Kaye**
Ann.
Minnie Morse.
Whistling Willie.

**Starbuck, George**
Chip.
Cora Punctuated with Strawberries.
Esthetique du Machiavel.
High Renaissance.
Margaret Are You Drug.
Monarch of the Sea.
Of Late.
Said ("Agatha Christie to").
Said ("J. Alfred Prufrock to").

Skin Divers, The.
Sonnet with a Different Letter at the
    End of Every Line.
Translations from the English.

**Stark, Irwin**
Poets of My Epoch.

**Stark, Lucien**
Away.

**Starkey, James.** *See* **"O'Sullivan,**
    **Seumas"**

**Staudt, David**
Circa 1814.

**Staughton, William**
Tell Us, Ye Servants of the Lord, *with*
    *music.*

**Stead, Christian Karlson**
Carpe Diem.
Natural Grace, A.
Pictures in a Gallery Undersea.

**Stedman, Edmund Clarence**
Aaron Burr's Wooing.
Ballad of Lager Bier, The.
Custer.
Kearney at Seven Pines.

**Steel, Laura A.**
Exclusive Old Oyster, The.

**Steele, James**
Bon Voyage.
Ecology.
Folk Poet.
For Mantee/ My Whole World Came
    Falling Down.
Life.
My Name Is a Name.
Other Side of Town Saturday Night,
    The.
Some Day.
Wildcats Walking in the Dark.

**Steele, Lynn**
Ted Speaking.

**Steele, Peter**
Living/Dying.

**Steele, Silas S.**
Kiss Me Quick and Go, *with music.*

**Steele, Timothy**
Epitaph: "Here lies Sir Tact, a
    diplomatic fellow."
Murder Mystery.
Wait.

**Steendam, Jacob**
Oh, Sing to God, *with music.*
When I Admire the Greatness, *with*
    *music.*

**Steiger, Anatoly**
Ancient Custom, An.
Words from the Window of a Railway
    Car.

**Stein, Dona**
Wing Factory, The.

**Stein, Gary**
Darkroom.
Jogging.
Night Fishing.
Undertow, The: Hatteras Island.

**Stein, Gertrude**
Afterwards, *sel.*
Blue Coat, A.
Celery.
Cézanne.
Cooking.
Four Saints in Three Acts, *sel.*
More.

Nothing Elegant.
Pastry.
Petticoat, A.
Piano, A.
Sacred Emily.
Stanzas in Meditation.
Susie Asado.
Tender Buttons, *sel.*
Water Raining.
**Steinbarg, Eliezer**
Bayonet and the Needle, The.
Horse and the Whip, The.
"Shatnes" or Uncleanliness.
Umbrella, the Cane, and the Broom,
  The.
Where Is Justice?
**Steinberg, David**
Mason Jar.
**Steinberg, Jakov**
Donkey Will Carry You, A.
With a Book at Twilight.
World Is Not a Fenced-off Garden, The.
**Steinbergh, Judith W.**
Bear ate the girl, The.
**Steingart, Moishe**
Generations.
Last Fire, The.
**Steingass, David**
Beginning, A.
Love Poem Beginning with I.
Midwest U. F. O.
Seven-Year Body Cycle, The: To My
  Cells Replacing Themselves for the
  Fourth Time.
Slaughter-Room Picture, The.
Songs.
Wisconsin Farm Auction.
**Steingesser, Martin**
Machismo.
Shoplifting Poetry.
**Stelzer, Skaidrite**
Divorce.
Dreaming the Ancestors.
Fish-Dream.
Ice-Storm, April, 1974.
"Pirushke" Lady Warns Me of Going
  Barefoot, The.
Progenitor.
Star-gazing, U.S.A.
**Stembridge, Jane**
City.
Loving.
Mrs. Hamer.
**Stencl, A. N.**
Ezekiel.
**Stennett, Samuel**
Promised Land, The.
**Stepanchev, Stephen**
Buying Lilies.
Holy Eye Is Blind, The.
In Split: Diocletian's Palace.
Irondale.
Roads, The.
Trailing My Balloon.
Voyage.
**Stephan, Ruth**
Second Wind.
Wind, The.
**Stephanou, Lydia**
"Case of Assault," A.
**Stephen, James Kenneth**

Ballade of the Incompetent Ballade-
  Monger, The.
Drinking Song.
Last Ride Together, The (From Her
  Point of View).
On a Parisian Boulevard.
On a Rhine Steamer.
Sincere Flattery of R. B.
Sincere Flattery of W. W. (Americanus).
Sonnet, A: "Two voices are there: one is
  of the deep."
To R. K.
**Stephens, Alan**
Short Walk Alone.
**Stephens, Harry**
Night-herding Song.
**Stephens, James**
Bessie Bobtail.
Breakfast Time.
Cage, The.
Centaurs, The.
Cow, The.
Dark Wings.
Deirdre.
Devil's Bag, The.
Glass of Beer, A.
Goat Paths, The.
Hate.
Hesperus, *sel.*
In the Orchard.
Little Things.
Main-Deep, The.
Market, The.
Nora Criona.
Paps of Dana, The.
Psychometrist.
Red Haired Man's Wife, The.
Rivals, The.
River, The.
Sarasvati.
Sensible People.
Seumas Beg.
Shell, The.
Snare, The.
Sweet Apple.
To the Four Courts, Please.
Variations: #21.
Washed in Silver.
Waste Places.
What the Devil Said.
What Tomas Said in a Pub.
When You Walk.
White Fields.
Why Tomas Cam Was Grumpy.
Wind, The.
**Stepney, George**
On the University of Cambridge's
  Burning the Duke of Monmouth's
  Picture.
**Sterling, Andrew B.**
Coax Me, *with music.*
Meet Me in St. Louis, Louis.
On a Sunday Afternoon, *with music.*
Under the Anheuser Bush.
Wait 'till the Sun Shines, Nellie.
What You Goin' to Do When the Rent
  Comes 'Round?
**Sterling, George**
Abalone Song, The.
Black Vulture, The.
City by the Sea, The.
Cool, Grey City of Love, The.

Father Coyote.
Pumas.
**Stern, David E.**
Old Man.
**Stern, Gerald**
At Bickford's.
Days of 1978.
Hungarian, The.
Immensity.
In Carpenter's Woods.
Modern Love.
One Foot in the River.
Power of Maples, The.
Straus Park.
Your Animal.
**Stern, Noah**
Grave at Cassino.
His Mother's Love.
**Sternberg, Ricardo da Silveira Lobo**
Scarecrow.
**Sternburg, Janet**
My Mother's Breakfront.
**Sternhold, Thomas**
Lord Descended from Above, The, *with*
  *music.*
My Shepherd Is the Living Lord, *with*
  *music.*
**Stessel, Harry**
Charm against Pregnancy, A.
Iowa.
Speech for an Abdication.
**Stetler, Charles**
Free Enterprise.
Graduate, The.
Jeep.
Policy of the House.
Toast, A.
World's Fare.
**Stevens, A. Wilber**
And One Other Thing.
Another Poem of the Tearing Down of
  the Metropolitan Opera House.
Critic Undefiled.
If You Should Die.
Trends and Conditions: Miscellaneous
  File.
Wood Walk.
**Stevens, Alex**
In Scorching Time.
**Stevens, Cat**
Where Do the Children Play?
**Stevens, James**
Turn of the Road, The.
**Stevens, Wallace**
Adult Epigram.
Anatomy of Monotony.
Anecdote of the Jar.
Angel Surrounded by Paysans.
Arrival at the Waldorf.
Auroras of Autumn, The, *sels.*
Autumn Refrain.
Bantams in Pine-Woods.
Beginning, The.
Bouquet of Roses in Sunlight.
Brave Man, The.
Connoisseur of Chaos.
Country Words.
Course of a Particular, The.
Curtains in the House of the
  Metaphysician, The.
Cy Est Pourtraicte, Madame Ste. Ursule,
  et les Unze Mille Vierges.

Dance of the Macabre Mice.
Death of a Soldier, The.
Depression before Spring.
Disillusionment of Ten o'Clock.
Domination of Black.
Dry Loaf.
Earthy Anecdote.
Emperor of Ice-Cream, The.
Evening without Angels.
Final Soliloquy of the Interior Paramour.
Flyer's Fall.
Glass of Water, The.
Hibiscus on the Sleeping Shores.
High poetry and low.
High-toned Old Christian Woman, A.
House Was Quiet and the World Was Calm, The.
I feel an apparition.
Idea of Order at Key West, The.
In the Carolinas.
Indigo Glass in the Grass, The.
Irish Cliffs of Moher, The.
It feels good as it is without the giant.
Large Red Man Reading.
Le Monocle de Mon Oncle.
Less and Less Human, O Savage Spirit.
Life Is Motion.
Lions in Sweden.
Lunar Paraphrase.
Man on the Dump, The.
Man Whose Pharynx Was Bad, The.
Martial Cadenza.
Men Made Out of Words.
Metamorphosis.
Mrs. Alfred Uruguay.
Montrachet-le-Jardin.
No Possum, No Sop, No Taters.
Not Ideas about the Thing but the Thing Itself.
Notes toward a Supreme Fiction, *sels.*
Of Hartford in a Purple Light.
Of Heaven Considered as a Tomb.
Of Modern Poetry.
Of the Manner of Addressing Clouds.
On the Road Home.
Our Stars Come from Ireland.
Peter Quince at the Clavier.
Plain Sense of Things, The.
Planet on the Table, The.
Pleasures of Merely Circulating, The.
Plot against the Giant, The.
Ploughing on Sunday.
Poem That Took the Place of a Mountain, The.
Postcard from the Volcano, A.
Primitive like an Orb, A.
Rabbit as [*wr.* Is] King of the Ghosts, A.
River of Rivers in Connecticut, The.
Sea Surface Full of clouds.
Sense of the Sleight-of-Hand Man, The.
Six Significant Landscapes, *sel.*
Snow Man, The.
So-and-so Reclining on Her Couch.
Song of Fixed Accord.
Souls of Women at Night, The.
Study of Two Pears.
Sunday Morning.
Tea.
Tea at the Palaz of Hoon.
These locusts by day, these crickets by night.

Thinking of a Relation between the Images of Metaphors.
Thirteen Ways of Looking at a Blackbird.
This Solitude of Cataracts.
To an Old Philosopher in Rome.
Ultimate Poem Is Abstract, The.
Well Dressed Man with a Beard, The.
When was it that the particles became.
Woman in Sunshine, The.
World as Meditation, The.

**Stevenson, Anne**
Indian Summer: Vermont.
Love.
Stabilities.
Suburb, The.
Utah.

**Stevenson, Robert Louis**
At the Seaside.
Bed in Summer.
Block City.
Careful Angler, The.
Celestial Surgeon, The.
Christmas at Sea.
Cow, The.
Dumb Soldier, The.
Escape at Bedtime.
From a Railway Carriage.
Good and Bad Children.
Happy Thought.
Hearts, like Doors.
Heather Ale.
House Beautiful, The.
How to Sing or Read.
I Will Make You Brooches.
Lamplighter, The.
Land of Counterpane, The.
Land of Nod, The.
Land of Story-Books, The.
Looking Forward.
My House.
My Shadow.
My Wife.
Not I.
Other Children.
Plain as the Glistering Planets Shine.
Rain.
Requiem: "Under the wide and starry sky."
Resurgence.
Sing Me a Song.
Skerryvore.
Skerryvore: The Parallel.
Swing, The.
Thought, A.
Time to Rise.
To Minnie.
To S. R. Crockett.
To the Muse.
Travel.
Where Go the Boats?
Whole Duty of Children.
Wind, The.
Windy Nights.
Winter Time.
Youth and Love.

**Steward, Joseph**
My Soul Would Fain Indulge a Hope, *with music.*

**Stewart, Douglas**
B Flat.
Gully, The.

Kindred.
Lady Feeding the Cats, *sel.*
Nesting Time.
Silkworms, The.
Snow-Gum, The.
Sunflowers, The.
Terra Australis.

**Stewart, Frank**
Another Color.
Consolation.
New England: Driving Back in Early April.
Orphee at Rest.
Sea Breathes Quietly, Menelaus, The.
Train Window.

**Stewart, George Craig**
As I Went Down to David's Town, *with music.*

**Stewart, Harold**
Flight of Wild Geese, A.

**Stewart, Pamela**
Central Park, 1916.
Self-Portrait: Women with Children.

**Stewart, Robert**
Plumber Arrives at Three Mile Island, The.

**Stickney, Trumbull**
In the Past.
Mnemosyne.
On Some Shells Found Inland.
Sir, say no more.
Six o'Clock.

**Still, Edward Rowland**
Opportunity.

**Stills, Stephen**
For What It's Worth.
Four and Twenty.
Suite: Judy Blue Eyes.

**Stills, Stephen, David Crosby** and **Paul Kantner.** *See* **Crosby, David, Paul Kantner** and **Stephen Stills**

**Stilwell, Joseph W.**
Lyric to Spring.

**Stineford, Raymond**
Breathe on the Glass.

**Stinson, Sam S.**
Such Foolish Old Dames.

**Stirling, William Alexander, Earl of**
Aurora, *sel.*
Sonnet: "Ile give thee leave my love, in beauties field."

**Stock, Noel** and **Ezra Pound.** *See* **Pound, Ezra** and **Noel Stock**

**Stocking, Jay T.**
O Master Workman of the Race, *with music.*

**Stockton, John H.**
Come, Every Soul, *with music.*

**Stockwell, Brenda S.**
Academic Affair.
Chances.
Easter Flood.

**Stokes, Terry**
All Morning.
Blood Supply in New York City Is Low, The.
Crimes of Passion: The Phone Caller.
Crimes of Passion: The Slasher.
Farmer, The.
Giving the Moon a New Chance.
Man All Grown Up Is Supposed To, A.
Travis, the Kid Was All Heart.

**Stokesbury, Leon**
Back Behind the Eyes.
Beef.
Gifts.
Graduate Assistant Tells about His Visit,
The.
Little Keats' Soliloquy.
Morning Song.
Summer in Fairbanks.
To Laura Phelan: 1880-1906.
**Stoloff, Carolyn**
Bearing It.
For the Suicide's Daughter.
Opposites.
Short Subjects.
**Stoltzenberg, Abo**
French Mood, The.
In Vistas of Stone.
What Am I?
**Stone, Arlene**
Germination.
**Stone, John**
Cadaver.
Death.
Double-Header.
Even Though.
He Makes a House Call.
How I'd Have It.
Linda.
Living with a Voodoo Doll.
Resuscitation.
To a 14 Year Old Girl in Labor and
Delivery.
**Stone, John A.**
Coming around the Horn.
**Stone, Ruth**
Advice.
Bargain.
Beginning to Live.
Burned Bridge, The.
Codicil.
Dark Conclusions.
Denouement.
I Have Three Daughters.
Liberation.
My Son.
On the Mountain.
Orchard.
Periphery.
Private Pantomime.
Repetition of Words and Weather.
Rhythm.
Room.
Salt.
Talking Fish, The.
Whose Scene?
Winter.
Years Later.
**Stone, Samuel John**
Church's One Foundation, The.
**Stoneback, H. R.**
Toad Suck Ferry.
**Storey, Ralph**
Caught Up in the Villa.
Death of a Symbol, The.
Home/Grown.
I've Heard Them Talk: For My Main
Man.
Ode: Infinity.
Portraits of 2 Lonely Women.
Sky House.
**Storni, Alfonsina**

Funeral Notices.
I Am Going to Sleep (Suicide Poem).
Lighthouse in the Night.
Men in the City.
My Sister.
Sierra.
They've Come.
Words to My Mother.
**Stout, Liz**
Waiting.
**Stoutenburg, Adrien**
Affinities.
Ants and Others.
Bear Who Came to Dinner, The.
Cicada.
Dogskin Rug.
Fashion Model at Home, The.
Is Is Like Is.
Ivory Paper Weight.
Model T.
Reel One.
Rhinoceros.
Sky Diver.
V.D. Clinic.
**Stow, Randolph**
As He Lay Dying.
Dust.
Ruins of the City of Hay.
**Stowe, Dalene**
Day Time Sequence/ November.
Muscle Building.
Poem to My Twin Possibility.
**Stowe, Harriet Beecher**
Abide in Me, O Lord, and I in Thee,
with music.
Still, Still with Thee, with music.
When Winds Are Raging, with music.
**Stowman, Annette Burr**
Fly, Ladybug.
**Strachey, Lytton**
Cat.
**Strahan, Bradley R.**
Shabbat Morning.
**Straley, John**
Young Fellow from Boise, A.
**Strand, Mark**
Black Maps.
Courtship.
Dead, The.
Door, The.
"Dreadful Has Already Happened, The."
Eating Poetry.
Elegy for My Father.
From a Litany.
He would look at the stars.
Inside the Story, sel.
Keeping Things Whole.
Letter.
Man in Black, The.
Man in the Tree, The.
Marriage, The.
My Death.
My Life.
My Life by Somebody Else.
New Year, The.
Night Piece.
Prediction, The.
Remains, The.
Room, The.
Tunnel, The.
Way It Is, The.
Your Shadow.

**Strauss, A. L.**
In Discreet Splendor.
Lament for the European Exile.
On the Path.
Voice in the Dark.
**Strauss, Avner**
Hollow Flute, The.
Portrait of a Widow.
**"Strauss, Yawcob."** See Adams, Charles
Follen
**Strawson, J. Adair**
Token of Attachment, A.
**"Streamer, Col. D."** See Graham, Harry
**Strebeck, George**
Joyful Sound It Is, A, with music.
**Streeter, Sebastian**
King Shall Reign in Righteousness, A,
with music.
Lo, What Enraptured Songs of Praise,
with music.
**Stricklin, Robert**
Hoot Owl Shift.
**Strobel, Marion**
Pastoral: "This is a place of ease."
**Stroblas, Laurie**
Circumstance.
Plot.
**Strode, William**
In Commendation of Music.
My love and I for kisses play'd.
Nightingale, The.
On a Great Hollow Tree.
On Chloris Walking in the Snow.
On the Bible.
On Westwell Downs.
**Stroh, Mary Swanson**
Excuses.
Farmer's Wife, The.
Liberation.
November Birthday.
Settling In.
**Strong, George A.**
Modern Hiawatha, The, parody.
**Strong, Leonard Alfred George**
Appointment, The.
Brewer's Man, The.
Coroner's Jury.
Evening before Rain.
Knowledgeable Child, The.
Mad-Woman, The.
Memory, A.
**Strong, Nathan**
Almighty Sovereign of the Skies! with
music.
Summer Harvest Spreads the Fields,
The, with music.
Swell the Anthem, Raise the Song, with
music.
**Strongin, Lynn**
Ascent.
Emily Dickinson Postage Stamp.
First Aspen, sels.
Miniatures IV.
Multiplication.
Our Bodies Young and Running in the
Sun.
Ready.
Sayre.
Van Gogh.
**Strunk, Jud**
They're Tearing Down a Town.
**Struthers, Ann**

Tea.
**Struthers, Eleanor**
Cat's Life, A.
**Stryk, Lucien**
Cherries.
Face, The.
Fishing with My Daughter in Miller's Meadow.
Friendship.
Liberator, The.
**Stuart, Dabney**
Ballad of the Volunteer, The.
Begging on North Main.
Exchange.
Fall Practice.
Fisherman, The.
Glucose.
His Third Decade.
Hunter, Prey.
Lesson in Oblivion, A.
Opposite Field, The.
Power Failure.
Refugee, The.
Soup Jar, The.
Student, The.
Ties.
**Stuart, Derek**
Aeroplane, The.
**Stuart, Floyd C.**
Balances.
Gravestones.
Hard Edge of Beauty.
Pilot.
Settling In.
Six Statues in a Park.
Stone Age.
**Stuart, John Sobieski**
With an Antique Crystal Cup and Ring.
**Stuart, Mary [or Marie].** *See* **Mary Queen of Scots**
**Stuart, Muriel**
In the Orchard.
Seed Shop, The.
**Stuart, Ruth McEnery**
What-Is-It, A.
**Stubbs, John Heath-.** *See* **Heath-Stubbs, John**
**Stubbs, Marcia**
In a Mirror.
**Stubbs, William**
Hymn on Froude and Kingsley, A.
**Stull, Richard**
Dedication: "In my dreams we are always together."
**Stults, Robert Morrison**
Sweetest Story Ever Told, The, *with music.*
**Stump, Roger**
Fear.
**Stupp, John**
First Cold Night of Autumn.
**Stutsman, Rebecca**
Honorable Mention.
**Style, Colin**
100 Year Old Woman at Christmas Dinner.
**Succorsa, Janice Appleby**
My Garden.
**Suckling, Sir John**
Against Absence.
Against Fruition.
Ballad upon a Wedding, A.

Barley-Break, A.
Constant Lover, The.
Doubt of Martyrdom, A.
Epistle An: "Whether these lines do find you out."
Farewell to Love.
Love's Clock.
Love's Offence.
Love's Siege.
Loving and Beloved.
Metamorphosis, The.
Miracle, The.
On King Richard the Third, Who Lies Buried under Leicester Bridge.
Pedlar of Small-Wares, A ("A pedlar I am, that take great care").
Song: "No, no, fair heretic, it needs must be."
Song to a Lute, A.
Sonnet I: "Dost see how unregarded now."
Sonnet II: "Of thee, kind boy, I ask no red and white."
To a Lady That Forbade to Love before Company.
To B. C.
To Master Davenant for Absence.
Upon My Lady Carlisle's Walking in Hampton-Court Garden.
Upon My Lord Brohall's Wedding.
Upon Sir John Lawrence's Bringing Water over the Hills to My Lord Middlesex's House at Wiston.
Why So Pale and Wan?
Wits, The.
Woman's Constancy.
**Suderman, Elmer F.**
Adam in the Garden.
On Listening to a Death-of-God Theologian Lecture in the Chapel.
Placid Pew, The.
Preacher Considers His Sermon, The.
Thy Kingdom Come.
Worship.
**Suffolk, Peter**
Street Scene.
**Sugar, Maurice**
Soup Song.
**Sukenick, Lynn**
Death.
Early Ella
Parting: A Game.
Poster, The.
That Life, on Film.
**Sullivan, Frank**
September Valentine.
**Sullivan, James**
As Sun, as Sea.
**Sullivan, Joseph J.**
Where Did You Get That Hat? *with music.*
**Sullivan, Nancy**
Eclipses.
His Necessary Darkness.
Number 1 by Jackson Pollock (1948).
Six Kisses.
Telling It.
To My Body.
**Sully-Prudhomme, René François Armand**
Struggle, The.
**Sulpicia**

At last love has come. I would be more ashamed.
Darling, I won't be your hot love.
Do you have a sweet thought, Cerinthus.
Have you heard? The troubles.
I'm grateful, really grateful.
It's nice that though you are casual about me.
Let your longing for me, my love.
**Summerfield, Geoffrey**
Windy'Boy in a Windswept Tree.
**Summers, Hal**
My Old Cat.
Rescue, The.
**Summers, Hollis**
At the Wax Museum.
Delivery, The.
Lost Pictures, The.
Peddler, The.
Song to Be Attached.
Story of My Life, The.
**Summers, Thomas O.**
Morning Bright, with Rosy Light, The, *with music.*
**Sund, Robert**
Afternoon,/ with just enough of a breeze for him to ride it.
Bunch Grass #37.
Dusty black beetle, A.
**Sun-Ra**
Nothing Is.
Plane, The: Earth.
Primary Lesson: The Second Class Citizens.
**Sun Yün-feng**
On the Road through Chang-te.
Starting at Dawn.
**Supervielle, Jules**
Call, The.
Full Sky.
Prophecy.
**Surrey, Henry Howard, Earl of**
Complaint by Night of the Lover Not Beloved, A.
Complaint of the Absence of Her Lover Being upon the Sea.
Consolation.
Dyvers thy death doo dyverslye bemone.
Exhortation to Learn by Others' Trouble.
Frailty and Hurtfulness of Beauty, The.
From Tuscan cam my ladies worthi race.
Geve place, ye lovers, here before.
Golden gift that nature did thee geve, The.
Great Macedon that out of Persy chased, The.
I never saw you, madam, lay apart.
In Cipres springes (wheras dame Venus dwelt).
In the rude age when scyence was not so rife.
In Windsor Castle.
In winters just returne, when Boreas gan his raigne.
Laid in My Quiet Bed.
London, hast thow accused me.
Norfolk sprang thee, Lambeth holds thee dead.
Sonne hath twyse brought forthe the tender grene, The.
Soote Season, The.

Suche waywarde wais hath love, that moste parte in discorde.

Thassyryans king, in peas with fowle desyre.

Though I regarded not.

Wyatt [*or* Wyat] resteth here, that quick[e] could[e] never rest.

**Susskind, Harriet**
Views.

**Sussman, M. L.**
Poet's Prayer.
Return.

**Sutheim, Susan**
For Witches.

**Sutherland, Robert.** *See* **Garioch, Robert**

**Sutskever, Abraham**
Banks of a River, The.
Cartload of Shoes, A.
How?
Landscape.
On My Wandering Flute.
Poetry.
Song for a Dance.
Song of Praise for an Ox.
Songs to a Lady Moonwalker.
To My Child.
Toys.
Under the Earth.
Yiddish.

**Sutter, Barton**
Static.

**Sutton, Lorraine**
For Leon.
For My Brother Henry T. Sutton Jr.
Ivan Silen P.R. Poet.
Roots.

**Su Tung P'o [*or* Tung-po]**
At the Washing of My Son.
Last Day of the Year, The.
On the Birth of His Son.
Spring Night.
Thoughts in Exile.
To a Traveler.

**Swaim, Alice Mackenzie**
Chilled by Different Winds.

**Swain, Leonard**
My Soul, Weigh Not Thy Life, *with music.*

**Swan, Jon**
Among Commuters.
Nebraska.

**Swanger, David**
Rowing in Turns.

**Swann, Brian**
Capricho.
Desert in the Sea.
Education in Tongues, An.
Lines.
Masks.
Paradigms of Fire.
Quiet.
Three Riddles.
Vita Silenziosa.
Year of the Bird.

**Swanton, John R.**
Bear Song.

**Sward, Robert**
American Heritage.
By the Swimming.
Concert.
How totally unpredictable we are to one another.

In Mexico.
1950's. The.
Uncle Dog: The Poet at 9.
Waldheim Cemetery.

**Sweeney, Barbara**
For We Are All Madwomen.

**Sweeney, Matthew**
Alone with the Dawn.

**Swenson, Karen**
Evening Gown, The.
Grave Clothes.
Lovers, The.
Pro, The.
Quilt, The.
Symbolism.

**Swenson, May**
After the Dentist.
All That Time.
Analysis of Baseball.
At Breakfast.
At the Museum of Modern Art.
Beginning to Squall.
Bronco Busting, Event #1.
Cardinal Ideograms.
Cat and the Weather.
Centaur, The.
Cloud-Mobile, The.
Couple, A.
Death Invited.
Even Sea, The.
Evolution.
Fable for When There's No Way Out.
Fashions in the 70's.
Feel like a Bird.
Feel Me.
Fire Island.
Five Horses.
Fixture, A.
Flying Home from Utah.
Four-Word Lines.
Frontispiece.
Green Red Brown and White.
How Everything Happens.
How to Be Old.
I Look at an Old Photo of Myself with Love.
July 4th.
Key to Everything, The.
Landing on the Moon.
Living Tenderly.
Lowering, The.
On Its Way.
Out of the Sea, Early.
Pair, A.
Question.
Scroppo's Dog.
Secret in the Cat, The.
Shape of Death, The.
Snow in New York.
Southbound on the Freeway.
Stone Gullets.
Tall Figures of Giacometti, The.
3 Models of the Universe.
To Make a Play.
To the Statue.
Universe, The.
Waiting for It.
Waking from a Nap on the Beach.
Was Worm.
Watch, The.
Watching the Jets Lose to Buffalo at Shea.

Willets, The.
Women.
Woods at Night, The.
Working on Wall Street.

**Swett, John**
In the Mines.

**Swift, Joan**
Line-up, The.
Your Hands.

**Swift, Jonathan**
Beautiful Young Nymph Going to Bed, A.
Cassinus and Peter.
Cat and the Rain, The.
Clever Tom Clinch Going to Be Hanged.
Daphne.
Day of Judgement [*or* Judgment], The.
Description of a City Shower, A.
Description of the Morning, A.
Epigram: "As Thomas was cudgeled one day by his wife."
Epigram on Fasting.
Epigram on Scolding.
Excellent New Song, Being the Intended Speech of a Famous Orator against Peace, An.
Fable of Midas, The.
Five, The.
Fool, to put up four crosses at your door.
Furniture of a Woman's Mind, The.
Gentle Echo on Woman, A.
Holyhead, Sept. 25th, 1727.
Lady's Dressing Room, The.
Legion Club, The, *sel.*
Life and Genuine Character of Dean Swift, The, *sel.*
Market Women's Cries.
On Dreams.
On Himself.
On His Own Deafness.
On Poetry: A Rhapsody.
On Stella's Birthday ("Stella this day is thirty-four").
On the Astrologer and Almanac Maker, John Partridge.
On the Collar of Mrs. Dingley's Lap-Dog.
On the Irish Club.
Onyons.
Phyllis; or, The Progress of Love.
Place of the Damned, The.
Power of Time, The.
Progress of Beauty, The.
Progress of Poetry, The.
Satirical Elegy on the Death of a Late Famous General, A.
Stella at Wood-Park.
Stella's Birthday ("This day, whate'er the fates decree").
Time is not remote when I, The.
To the Earl of Oxford, Late Lord Treasurer.
To Their Excellencies the Lords Justices of Ireland, the Humble Petition of Frances Harris.
Verses Occasioned by the Sudden Drying Up of St. Patrick's Well, *sel.*
Verses on the Death of Doctor Swift, *sels.*
Verses Said to Be Written on the Union.
Virtue conceal'd within our breast.

Virtues of Sid Hamet, the Magician's
   Rod, The.
With favour and fortune fastidiously
   blest.
**Swift, Nicholas**
Maxims of a Park Vagrant.
**Swilky, Jody**
Animation and Ego.
Nothing but Image.
**Swinburne, Algernon Charles**
Apologia.
At a Month's End.
At the Piano.
Atalanta in Calydon, *sels.*
Autumn in Cornwall.
Ave atque Vale.
Baby's feet, like sea-shells pink, A.
Ballad of Bath, A, *sel.*
Ballad of Dreamland, A.
Before Parting.
Before Sunset.
By the North Sea, *sels.*
Cameo, A.
Channel Passage, A.
Chorus: "When the hounds of spring are
   on winter's traces."
Chorus: "Who hath given man speech?
   or who hath set therein."
Christmas Antiphones, *sel.*
Cliffside Path, The.
Come into the orchard, Anne.
Cor Cordium.
Dead King, A.
Dead Love.
Dedication: "Sea gives her shells to the
   shingle, The."
Dedication: "Some nine years gone, as
   we dwelt together."
Dedication to "Songs of the
   Springtides."
Delphic Hymn to Apollo.
Dolores.
Envoi: "Fly, white butterflies, out to
   sea."
Flower Piece.
Forsaken Garden, A.
Garden of Proserpine, The.
God of Judgment, The.
Hawthorn Dyke.
Hendecasyllabics.
Heptalogia, The, *sels.*
Hermaphroditus.
Hertha.
Higher Pantheism in a Nutshell, The,
   *parody.*
Hymn of Man.
Hymn to Proserpine.
In Guernsey.
In Harbour.
In the Orchard.
Lake of Gaube, The.
Laus Veneris.
Leave-taking, A.
Leper, The.
Love and Sleep.
May Janet.
Midsummer Holiday, A, *sel.*
Nephelidia.
Nympholept, A.
Oblation, The.
On Arthur Hugh Clough.
On the Cliffs.

Peace-Giver, The.
Plus Ultra.
Poeta Loquitur.
Prelude to "Songs before Sunrise."
Rondel: "Kissing her hair I sat against
   her feet."
Sapphics.
Sestina: "I saw my soul at rest upon a
   day."
Siena.
Song in Time of Order 1852, A.
Song in Time of Revolution 1860, A.
Sonnet for a Picture.
Stage Love.
Sundew, The.
Sunrise at Sea.
Super Flumina Babylonis.
Thalassius.
To a Cat.
To a Seamew.
To Walt Whitman in America.
Triads.
Triumph of Time, The.
Year's Burden [1870], A.
**Swiss, Thomas (Thom)**
Letter from Des Moines.
Pouch, The.
Virtue of Shape, A.
**Swope, Mary**
Couple.
Gesture.
Loaded.
**Sykes, Velma West**
Diptych.
**Sylvester, Joshua**
Du Bartas His Divine Weeks and Works,
   *sels.*
1st Week 5th Day.
1st Week 6th Day.
Fuimus Fumus.
I hate these phrases: Of power absolute.
Mundus Qualis.
Omnia Somnia.
Rome, Conquerer, Conquered.
When wine runs low, it is not worth the
   sparing.
**Symons, Arthur**
Absinthe-Drinker, The.
Amends to Nature.
Amoris Exsul, *sel.*
At Dieppe, *sel.*
At Glan-y-Wern.
By Loe Pool.
By the Pool at the Third Rosses.
City Nights, *sel.*
Dreams.
Grey Wolf, The.
In Ireland, *sel.*
In the Train.
Intermezzo: Pastoral, *sel.*
Javanese Dancers.
Loom of Dreams, The.
Maquillage.
Nerves.
On the Beach.
Prologue to "London Nights."
Tune, A.
White Heliotrope.
**Symons, Julian**
Hart Crane.
**Synge, John Millington**

Curse, The.
Dread.
I curse my bearing, childhood, youth.
I read about the Blaskets and Dunquin.
In Glencullen.
In Kerry.
Is It a Month.
'Mergency Man, The.
On a Birthday.
On an Anniversary.
On an Island.
Passing of the Shee, The.
Patch-Shaneen.
Queens.
Question, A.
Rendez-vous Manqué dans la Rue
   Racine.
Winter.
Wish, A.
**Syrett, Lesley**
My Cat.
**Sze, Arthur**
Moon Is a Diamond, The.
**Szymborska, Wislawa**
Homecoming.
I am too near to be dreamt of by him.
In Praise of a Guilty Conscience.

# T

"T.M."  *See* "M., T."
**Tabb, John Banister**
Bicycles! Tricycles!
Close Quarters.
Clover.
Evolution.
Foot-Soldiers.
High and Low.
Hospitality.
Rub, A.
Tryst, The.
**Tablada, José Juan**
Haiku: "Although he never stirs from
   home."
Haiku: "Ants on inert cricket crawling."
Haiku: "Dragon-fly strives patiently,
   The."
Haiku: "Lumps of mud, the toads."
Haiku: "Red cold."
Haiku: "Tiny monkey looks at me, The."
**Tabley, Lord De.**  *See* **De Tabley, John
   Byrne Leicester Warren, 3d Baron**
**Tadema, Laurence Alma-.**  *See* **Alma-
   Tadema, Laurence**
**Taft, Margo**
I have been my arm.
**Taggard, Genevieve [Mrs. Kenneth Durant]**
American Farm, 1934.
Autumn Song for Anti-Fascists.
Enamel Girl, The.
Four Frescoes of the Future.
Geraniums, The.
In the Tail of the Scorpion.
Interior.
Life of the Mind, 1934.
Little Girl with Bands on Her Teeth,
   The.
Luau, The.

Middle-aged, Middle-Class Woman at Midnight, A.
Mill Town.
Silence in Mallorca.
Squirrel near Library.
Thirst.
To a Magnificent Spinner, Murdered.
To an American Workman Dying of Starvation.
To My Daughter, 1936.
To the Veterans of the Abraham Lincoln Brigade.
Train: Abstraction.
With Child.

**Taggart, George**
Moth and the Flame, The, *with music.*

**Tagliabue, John**
Assuming the Name of Any Next Child.
December 1970.
In the Palms of Ancient Bodhisattvas.
Riding Stable in Winter, The.
You.

**Tagore, Rabindranath**
Journey Nears the Road-End, The.
Paper Boats, *sel.*

**Tait, Margaret**
To Anybody at All.

**Tait, Robert**
Cold Snap, A.
No You.

**Takahara, Mel**
November's Lesson.
Waiting Child, The.

**Takahashi, Shinkichi**
Fish.
Snail ("The snail crawls over blackness").
Sparrow in Winter.

**Takamura, Kotaro**
My Poetry.

**Takvan, Marie**
Deepest Bow, The.

**Talarico, Ross**
Balancing, The.

**Taliesin**
Battle of Argoed Llwyfain, The.
Death Song for Owain ab Urien.

**Talney, Ron**
Broken Year, The.

**Tam, Reuben**
Among Mountains.
Falling.

**Tamura, Ryuichi**
Invisible Tree.

**Tan Pai, Joshua**
Life of Hard Times, The.
My Soul Hovers over Me.
Trees Once Walked and Stood.

**Tangikuku, Hine**
Song of Sickness, A.

**T'ao Yuan-ming [or T'ao Ch'ien]**
Two Drinking Songs.

**Tapp, Gary**
Insect Shuffle Method, The.

**Tappan, William B.**
Ransomed Spirit to Her Home, The, *with music.*
Song of the Three Hundred Thousand Drunkards in the United States, *sel.*
There Is an Hour of Peaceful Rest, *with music.*

'Tis Midnight and on Olive's Brow, *with music.*
Wake, Isles of the South, *with music.*

**Tarn, Nathaniel**
Beautiful Contradictions, The, *sels.*
Bring a Child Flowers.
Last of the Chiefs.
Nowhere for Vallejo, A, *sels.*
Projections for an Eagle Escaped in This City, March 1965.
Where Babylon Ends.

**Tasso, Torquato**
Aminta, *sel.*
Happiness of a Flea, The.
Pastoral, A: "Oh happy golden age."

**Tate, Allen**
Aeneas at Washington.
Buried Lake, The.
Emblems.
Fire I praise was once perduring flame, The.
Last Days of Alice.
Mediterranean, The.
Mr. Pope.
Mother and Son.
Oath, The.
Ode to Fear.
Ode to the Confederate Dead.
Paradigm, The.
Shadow and Shade.
Sonnets at Christmas (I-II).
Sonnets of the Blood, *sels.*
Subway, The.
Swimmers, The.
To a Romantic.
What is this flesh and blood compounded of.
Winter Mask.
Wolves, The.

**Tate, James**
Absences.
Blue Booby, The.
Book of Lies, The.
Box for Tom, A.
Coda.
Coming Down Cleveland Avenue.
Conjuring Roethke.
Consumed.
Dear Reader.
Distant Orgasm, The.
Flight.
It's Not the Heat So Much as the Humidity.
Little Yellow Leaf.
Lost Pilot, The.
Love Making.
Miss Cho Composes in the Cafeteria.
My Great Great etc. Uncle Patrick Henry.
Nobody's Business.
Pet Deer, The.
Pity Ascending with the Fog.
President Slumming, The.
Professor Waking, The.
Shadowboxing.
Soup of Venus, The.
Square at Dawn, The.
Stray Animals.
Teaching the Ape to Write Poems.
Wheelchair Butterfly, The.

**Tate, Nahum**
Now if thou hast one dram of grace.

Old England.
On Sight of Some Martyrs' Sepulchres.
Sliding on Skates in Very Hard Frost.
While Shepherds Watched.

**Tate, Nahum and John Dryden**
Absalom and Achitophel, Pt. II, *sels.*

**Taupin, Bernie**
King Must Die, The.

**Taylor, Alexander**
On the Knowledge of Things.

**Taylor, Andrew**
Beating, The ("Beating her sensible with a storm of tissues").
Cosimo.
Developing a Wife.
Evening.
Nocturne in the Corner Phonebox, The.
Old Colonist, The.
Slide Night.
That Silence.

**Taylor, Ann**
Baby's Dance, The.
Meddlesome Matty.
My Mother.
Notorious Glutton, The.
Pin, The.

**Taylor, Ann or Jane**
Cow, The.
Sheep, The.

**Taylor, Bayard**
Ballad of Hiram Hover, The.
Bison Track, The.
Camerados.
Nauvoo.
Night with a Wolf, A.
Ode on a Jar of Pickles.
On Leaving California.
Palabras Grandiosas.
Promissory Note, The.
Quaker Widow, The.
Song of the Camp, The.
Three Songs, The.

**Taylor, Bert Leston**
Aprilly.
Canopus.
Doxology.
Those Flapjacks of Brown's.
Upon Julia's Arctics.

**Taylor, Edward**
All dull, my Lord, my spirits flat, and dead.
Am I thy gold? Or purse, Lord, for thy wealth.
Angels Sung a Carol, The, *with music.*
Christ's Reply.
Did ever lord such noble house maintain.
Ebb and Flow, The.
God's Determinations,*sels.*
How sweet a Lord is mine? If any should.
Huswifery.
I kening through astronomy divine.
Joy of Church Fellowship Rightly Attended, The.
Let by Rain.
Lord, dub my tongue with a new tier of words.
My blessed Lord, art thou a lilly flower?
My dear, deare, Lord I do thee Saviour call.

**Taylor**

My gracious Lord, I would thee glory doe.
My shattred phancy stole away from mee.
Oh! Good, good, good, my Lord. What more love yet.
Oh Leaden heeld. Lord, give, forgive I pray.
Oh! What a thing is man? Lord, who am I?
Our Insufficiency to Praise God Suitably, for His Mercy.
Preface, The: "Infinity, when all things it beheld."
Preparatory Meditations, sels.
Prologue: "Lord, can a crumb of dust the earth outweigh."
Return, The.
Thou Art the Tree of Life, with music.
Thy grace, dear Lord's my golden wrack, I finde.
Thy humane frame, my glorious Lord, I spy.
Upon a Spider Catching a Fly.
Upon a Wasp Child with Cold.
Upon Wedlock, and Death of Children.
What love is this of thine, that cannot bee.
Would God I in that Golden City were.
Ye angells bright, pluck from your wings a quill.

**Taylor, Eleanor Ross**
In the Churchyard.
Victory.
Woman as Artist.

**Taylor, Geoffrey**
Admonition to the Muse.
Cruel, Clever Cat.
English Liberal.
Epitaph: "Nor practising virtue nor committing crime."
Gentlemen.

**Taylor, Henry**
Buildings and Grounds.
Campaign Promise.
Cool Women and Smart Horses Are the Pits.
Desperado, sels.
Flying Change, The.
Horse Show at Midnight, The.
Hughsville Scythe, The.
Remembering Kevan MacKenzie.
Riding a One-eyed Horse.
Riding Lesson.
Shapes, Vanishings.
Speech.

**Taylor, James**
Country Road.
Fire and Rain.

**Taylor, James O.**
Broken Promise.
These Dreamings Mine.

**Taylor, Jane**
Gleaner, The.
Greedy Richard.
Star, The.
Violet, The.

**Taylor, Jeffreys**
Lion and the Mouse, The.

**Taylor, John**
Carmen Saeculare.
Dick Swash.

Egg of Nothing, The.
Mockado, Fustian, and Motley.
Roses Gone Wild.

**Taylor, Laurie**
Business Trips.
Lake Harriet: Wind.

**Taylor, R. Dean**
Ain't It a Sad Thing?

**Taylor, Rod**
Dakota: October, 1822, Hunkpapa Warrior.
Death of Lester Brown, House Painter, The.

**Taylor, William E.**
I Must Come to Terms with Florida.
Woman Combing, A.

**Taylor, William Edward**
Resurrection, The.

**Tchernichovsky, Shaul**
Death of Tammuz, The.
Grave, The.
Man Is Nothing But.
Saul's Song of Love.

**Teague, Kathleen**
Homage to Chagall.

**Teasdale, Sara**
Answer, The.
Barter.
Beautiful Proud Sea.
Epitaph: "Serene descent, as a red leaf's descending."
"I Am Not Yours."
I Shall Not Care.
Long Hill, The.
Moonlight.
Moon's Ending.
Morning Song.
New Moon, The.
Night.
Sea Longing.
September Midnight.
Solitary, The.
Song: "Let it be forgotten, as a flower is forgotten."
Two Minds.
"What Do I Care."
When I Am Not with You.
Wisdom.

**Teitoku**
Both my child.

**Tekeyan, Vahan**
Future, The.

**Telesilla**
O Artemis and your virgin girls.

**Teller, Judah Leib**
Lines to a Tree.
Minor Key.
To the Divine Neighbor.

**Temkin, Mordecai**
Foul Water.
Hidden Bow.
Seal of Fire.
Your Presence.

**Tennant, Pamela.** *See* **Grey of Fallodon, Pamela Grey, Viscountess**

**Tennant, Robert**
Wee Davie Daylicht.

**Tennyson, Alfred Tennyson, 1st Baron**
Ancient Pistol, peacock Payne.
Aylmer's Field.
Becket, sels.
Blackbird, The.

Break, Break, Break.
Brook, The.
Charge of the Heavy Brigade, The.
Charge of the Light Brigade, The.
City Child, The.
Claribel.
Columbus, sel.
Come into the garden, Maud.
Come Not, When I Am Dead.
Crossing the Bar.
Demeter and Persephone.
Despair.
Duet.
Eagle, The.
Epic, The.
Fatima.
Flower in the Crannied Wall.
"Frater Ave atque Vale."
Goose, The.
Hendecasyllabics.
Hesperides, The.
Higher Pantheism, The.
Human Cry, The.
I ran upon life unknowing, without or science or art.
Idylls of the King, sels.
If these brief lays, of sorrow born.
In Love, if Love Be Love.
In Memoriam A. H. H.
In my youth the growls.
In the Garden at Swainston.
In the Valley of Cauteretz.
June Bracken and Heather.
Kraken, The.
Lady Clare.
Lady of Shalott, The.
Lilian.
Lines: "Here often, when a child I lay reclined."
Lo! in the middle of the wood.
Locksley Hall.
Locksley Hall, Sixty Years After.
Lotos-Eaters, The.
Lucretius.
Mariana.
Mariana in the South.
Marriage Morning.
Maud: A Monodrama.
May Queen, The, sel.
Mechanophilus, sel.
Merlin and the Gleam.
Mermaid, The.
Merman, The.
Midnight.
Miller's Daughter, The.
Milton.
Minnie and Winnie.
Mystic, The.
Northern Cobbler, The.
Northern Farmer: New Style.
Northern Farmer: Old Style.
Not only with no sense of shame.
Nothing Will Die.
Now Sleeps the Crimson Petal.
Oak, The.
Ode on the Death of the Duke of Wellington.
Ode Sung at the Opening of the International Exhibition.
Ode to Memory.
Oenone.
Of Old Sat Freedom on the Heights.

On the Jubilee of Queen Victoria, *abr.*
Owl, The.
Palace of Art, The.
Poet, The.
Poet's Song, The.
Popular ("Popular, popular, unpopular!").
Princess, The, *sels.*
Prologue: "Over! the sweet summer closes."
Recollections of the Arabian Nights.
*Revenge,* The.
Rizpah.
Roses on the Terrace, The.
Sadness.
Sailor Boy, The.
St. Agnes' Eve.
St. Simeon Stylites.
Sea Dreams, *sel.*
Sea-Fairies, The.
Shell, The.
Snowdrop, The.
Somebody.
Song of the Lotos-Eaters.
Song: "Spirit haunts the year's last hours, A."
Song: "Who can say."
Sonnet: "She took the dappled partridge flecked with blood."
Splendor Falls on Castle Walls, The.
Supposed Confessions of a Second-rate Sensitive Mind.
Sweet and Low.
Tears, Idle Tears.
Tiresias.
Tithonus.
To Christopher North.
To Poesy.
To the Queen ("O loyal to the royal in thyself").
To the Rev. F. D. Maurice.
To Virgil.
To——: With the Following Poem.
Ulysses.
Vastness.
Vision of Sin, The.
Vivien's Song.
Walking to the Mail.
What Does Little Birdie Say?
Will Waterproof's Lyrical Monologue.
Winter.
You Ask Me, Why, though Ill at Ease.

**Tennyson, Charles.** See **Turner, Charles Tennyson**

**Tepfer, Karen G.**
Nets on the Andrea Doria, The.

**Tepperman, Jean**
Going through Changes.
Witch.

**Teresa, Saint, of Avila.** See **Theresa, Saint, of Avila**

**Terrell, Cash**
Dodos, The.
For My Pop.
Hand of Ms. Fate, The.
I Hope I Never Go There.
Trolls.

**Terrill, Richard**
From.

**Terris, Virginia R.**
Being on the Edge of Someone Else.
Husbands.

Stigmata.
Stink of Burning Egg, The.
Tracking.
Walk with My Cat, A.
Whoever You Are.

**Terry, Lucy**
Bar's Fight, August 28, 1746.

**Terry, Reba**
Lineage.

**Teschemacher, Edward**
Because, *with music.*

**Tessimond, Arthur Seymour John**
Cats.
Epitaph on Any Man.
Jamaican Bus Ride.
La Marche des Machines.
Middle-aged Conversation.

**Te-whaka-io-roa**
Give Me My Infant Now.

**Textor** *and* **Scott.** See **Scott** *and* **Textor**

**Thackeray, William Makepeace**
At the Zoo.
Damages, Two Hundred Pounds.
Foreign Literature.
Georges, The (I-IV).
Jeames of Buckley Square.
Little Billee.
Sorrows of Werther, The.
Speculators, The.

**Thalman, Mark**
Burial, The.
Summit Lake.

**Tharp, Roland**
Colding Nights.
X.

**Thaxter, Celia (Laighton)**
August.
On Easter Day.
Sandpiper, The.

**Thayer, Ernest Lawrence**
Casey at the Bat.

**Thayne, Emma Lou**
Blue Tattoo, The.
Manchild.
Shot.

**Themes, R. S.**
Ngh.

**Theocritus**
Daphnis.
Enchantment, The.
Epitaph of Cleonicus.
Epitaph of Hipponax.
Eunica skornde me, when her I would have sweetly kist.
Fishermen, The.
Idylls, *sels.*
Ortho's Epitaph.

**Theresa [** *or* **Teresa], Saint, of Avila**
If, Lord, thy love for me is strong.
Let nothing disturb thee/ Nothing affright thee.
Poem: "Nothing move thee."

**Thomas, Donald Michael**
Dream.
Eden.
Elegy for an Android.
Missionary.
O My America.
Smile.
Unknown Shores.

**Thomas, Dylan**
After the Funeral.

Altarwise by Owl-Light, *sels.*
Among Those Killed in the Dawn Raid Was a Man Aged a Hundred.
And Death Shall Have No Dominion.
Ballad of the Long-legged Bait.
Before I Knocked and Flesh Let Enter.
Ceremony after a Fire Raid.
Conversation, A.
Conversation of Prayer, The.
Countryman's Return, The.
Do Not Go Gentle into That Good Night.
Ears in the Turrets Hear.
Especially When the October Wind.
Fern Hill.
Force That through the Green Fuse Drives the Flower, The.
Holy Spring.
Hunchback in the Park, The.
I Have Longed to Move Away.
I, in My Intricate Image.
I See the Boys of Summer.
If I were Tickled by the Rub of Love.
If My Head Hurt a Hair's Foot.
In Country Sleep.
In My Craft or Sullen Art.
Incarnate Devil.
It is the sinners' dust-tongued bell claps me to churches.
January 1939.
Johnnie Crack and Flossie Snail.
Lament: "When I was a windy boy and a bit."
Light Breaks Where No Sun Shines.
Love in the Asylum.
Not from this anger, anticlimax after.
O make me a mask and a well to shut from your spies.
On the Marriage of a Virgin.
Out of a War of Wits.
Over Sir John's Hill.
Poem in October.
Refusal to Mourn the Death, by Fire, of a Child in London, A.
Spire cranes, The. Its statue is an aviary.
This Bread I Break Was Once the Oat.
Tombstone told when she died, The.
Twenty-four Years.
Under Milk Wood, *sel.*
We Lying by Seasand.
When, like a Running Grave.
When All My Five and Country Senses See.
Winter's Tale, A.

**Thomas, Edward ("Edward Eastaway")**
Adlestrop.
After Rain.
And You, Helen.
As the Team's Head-Brass.
Aspens.
Birds' Nests.
Brook, The.
Cat, A.
Celandine.
Cherry trees bend over and are shedding, The.
Clouds That Are So Light, The.
Cock-Crow.
Digging.
February Afternoon.
Gallows, The.
Glory, The.

Green Roads, The.
Gypsy, The.
Haymaking.
Hollow Wood, The.
If I Should Ever by Chance.
In Memoriam (Easter, 1915).
It Rains.
Liberty.
Lights Out.
Like the Touch of Rain.
Manor Farm, The.
New House, The.
No One So Much as You.
October.
Old Man.
Out in the Dark.
Owl, The.
Path, The.
Rain.
Sedge-Warblers.
Snow.
Some Eyes Condemn.
Sun Used to Shine, The.
Swedes.
Tall Nettles.
Tears.
Thaw.
To-Night.
Unknown, The.
What Shall I Give?
When First.
**Thomas, Evan**
To the Gentlewoman of Llanarth Hall.
**Thomas, Gwyn**
Horses.
Little Death.
Microscope.
**Thomas, J. R. and C. W. Elliot.** *See*
**Elliot, C. W. and J. R. Thomas**
**Thomas, Jack**
At the Porno Factory.
**Thomas, Jill**
Night Duty.
Unconscious Woman.
**Thomas, Jim**
Getting Loaded.
Spring Hawks.
**Thomas, John**
Last Frontier, The.
**Thomas, Joyce Carol**
Church Poem.
I Know a Lady.
MJQ, The.
Poem for Otis Redding.
Where Is the Black Community?
**Thomas, Laurence W.**
Etudes.
**Thomas, Lorenzo**
Onion Bucket.
Subway Witnesses, The.
**Thomas, Martha Banning**
Sudden Gale in Spring.
**Thomas, Richard W.**
Amen.
Day the Old Man Joined the Church
(Xmas '66), The.
How We Must Teach the Children.
Life after Death.
Martyrdom.
Poem Is Mightier than the Switchblade,
The.
Riots and Rituals.

6:00 A.M.
Something Inside Focuses My Attention.
To the New Annex to the Detroit
County Jail.
When I'm Alone.
Worker, The.
**Thomas, Ronald Stuart**
Alpine.
Ap Huw's Testament.
Blackbird Singing, A.
Country Clergy, The.
Cynddylan on a Tractor.
Evacuee, The.
For the Record.
Here.
Hill Farmer Speaks, The.
Invasion on the Farm.
Madrigal: "Your love is dead, lady, your
love is dead."
Moor, The.
Mother and Son.
Musician, The.
On the Farm.
One Furrow, The.
Over.
Peasant, A.
Sorry.
Survivor, The.
They.
Walter Llywarch.
Welsh History.
Welsh Landscape.
**Thomas, Thomas Jacob**
Dic Siôn Dafydd.
**Thomas Aquinas, Saint**
Word went forth, The.
**Thomas More, Saint.** *See* **More, Sir**
**Thomas**
**Thomas of Celano**
Day of Judgment, The.
That Day of Wrath, That Direful Day,
*with music.*
**Thomas of Hales**
Where Is Paris and Helene?
**Thompson, Alexander R.**
Wayfarers in the Wilderness, *with music.*
**Thompson, Benjamin**
On a Fortification at Boston Begun by
Women.
**Thompson, D'Arcy Wentworth**
Crazy Arithmetic.
That Little Black Cat.
Very Odd Fish, A.
**Thompson, Dorothy Brown**
This Is Halloween.
Wish.
**Thompson, Francis**
At Lord's.
Ex Ore Infantium.
Hound of Heaven, The.
Kingdom of God, The.
To a Snow-Flake.
To My Friend.
**Thompson, H. S.**
Lilly Dale, *with music.*
**Thompson, James W.**
Constant Labor, A.
Greek Room, The.
Plight, The.
Spawn of Slums, The.
Yellow Bird, The.
You Are Alms.

**Thompson, Joanna**
Funeral.
Gone.
**Thompson, John**
Adultery at the Plaza.
Homecoming.
**Thompson, Larry**
Black Is Best.
**Thompson, Lulu E.**
In Hardin County, 1809.
**Thompson, Marilyn**
Phylogeny.
**Thompson, Paul**
Golden Stallion, The.
**Thompson, Phyllis Hoge**
Daphne.
Eurydice.
Promise, The.
River, The.
Truth, The.
**Thompson, Samuel**
April.
To a Hedgehog.
**Thompson, Will L.**
Softly and Tenderly Jesus Is Calling,
*with music.*
**Thomson, Barbara Earl**
Celebration for a Young Priest.
From Thursday.
Lesson from Jim Crane.
**Thomson, Derick**
Beyond Swordale.
Herring-Girls, The.
Island, The.
Lewis.
Lewis in Summer.
Steel?
When, Tender and Mild.
**Thomson, James (1700-1748)**
Autumnal Moon, The.
Castle of Indolence, The, *sel.*
Hymn on the Power of God, A.
Hymn on the Seasons, A.
Rule, Britannia.
Seasons, The, *sels.*
Spring.
Spring Flowers.
Winter Night, A.
**Thomson, James (1700-1748)** *and David*
Mallet
Alfred, a Masque, *sel.*
**Thomson, James (1834-1882; "B.V." or**
**"Bysshe Vanolis")**
City, The.
City of Dreadful Night, The.
City's Queen, The.
Once in a Saintly Passion.
**Thomson, Mary A.**
O Sion, Haste, Thy Mission High
Fulfilling, *with music.*
**Thoreau, Henry David**
Conscience Is Instinct Bred in the
House.
Epitaph on the World.
Great God! I Ask Thee for No Meaner
Pelf.
Haze.
I Am a Parcel of Vain Strivings Tied.
Inspiration.
Inward Morning, The.
My Boots.
My Love Must Be as Free.

Our Country.
Pray to What Earth Does This Sweet
    Cold Belong.
Respectable Folks, The.
River Swelleth More and More, The.
Smoke.
Though All the Fates Should Prove
    Unkind.
To a Marsh Hawk in Spring.
Week on the Concord and Merrimack
    Rivers, A,*sels.*
What's the Railroad to Me.
Winter Memories.
**Thorley, Wilfred**
Happy Sheep, The.
**Thornbury, George Walter**
Sally from Coventry, The.
Three Troopers, The.
**Thornton, James**
She May Have Seen Better Days, *with*
    *music.*
Streets of Cairo; or, The Poor Little
    Country Maid, *with music.*
When You Were Sweet Sixteen.
**Thorold Rogers, J. E.**
Here X. lies dead, but God's forgiving.
On a Distinguished Politician.
On the Historians Freeman and Stubbs.
Suggestion Made by the Posters of the
    *Globe,* A.
Upon the man who's buried here.
Vulgar Error, A.
**Thorp, N. Howard**
Billy the Kid or William H. Bonney.
Little Joe the Wrangler.
**Thorpe, Dwayne**
Gathering, The.
Rooftop Winter.
**Throne, Marilyn**
What She Wished.
**Thrupp, Dorothy Ann**
Saviour, like a Shepherd Lead Us, *with*
    *music.*
**Thurman, Judith**
Balloons!
Closet.
Flashlight.
Going Barefoot.
Mare.
**Thurston, Harry**
March Sound.
**Thwaite, Anthony**
Ali Ben Shufti.
Arabic Script.
At Asqefar.
At Dunkeswell Abbey.
At Dunwich.
Barrow, The.
Boys, The.
Called For.
Cleaning a Coin.
Disturbances.
Entry.
Inscriptions.
Lesson.
Mr. Cooper.
Monologue in the Valley of the Kings.
Pond, The.
Sense of Property, A.
Soldiers Plundering a Village.
Sunday Afternoons.
Switzerland.

Two Faces.
Worm Within.
**Tibble, Anne**
Trials of a Tourist.
**Tichborne [or Tichbourne], Chidiock**
Elegy: "My prime of youth is but a frost
    of cares."
**Tick, Edward**
To My Wife Asleep.
**Ticknor, Francis Orray**
Little Giffen.
**Tiempo, Cesar (Israel Zeitlin)**
Jewish Cemetery, The.
**Tietz, Stephen**
Pinball Queen of South Illinois St., The.
**Tifft, Ellen**
Nuclear Land.
**Tilden, Stephen**
O Heaven Indulge, *with music.*
**Tilghman, Zoe A.**
Alibi.
Wind Song.
**Tillam, Thomas**
Uppon the First Sight of New England,
    June 29, 1638.
**Tiller, Terence**
Reading a Medal.
**Tillinghast, David**
Women Hoping for Rain.
**Tillman, Charlie D.**
Lost after All.
**Timrod, Henry**
Charleston.
Ethnogenesis
Faint Falls the Gentle Voice, *with music.*
Most Men Know Love.
Ode: "Sleep sweetly in your humble
    graves."
Unknown Dead, The.
**Ting, Walasse**
Pepsi Generation.
**Tio, Elsa**
I am furious with myself.
**Tippett, James S.**
Park, The.
Sunning.
Up in the Air.
**Tipping, Richard**
Multiple I.
Soursobs.
**Tipton, James**
Alive at the End of the Journey.
America: The Elephant.
Dialogue.
Exit, Pursued by a Bear.
February I Turn Off the Porch Light and
    Go Outside.
Now Everyone Is Writing Poems about
    Indians.
Ode: "There is a door in these hands
    that has been."
Pastoral: "Shuddering geography pulls
    the dead sentences, A."
Stump Farming.
Winter in Elwell.
Winter Lambing.
**Tisdale, Charles P. R.**
My Childhood's Bedroom.
Origins of Escape, The.
**Todachine, Mike**
Poem: "You can look into my face."
**Todd, Barbara Euphan**

Sing a Song of Honey.
**Todd, Gail**
To My Four-Year-Old Daughter.
**Todd, Ruthven**
About Scotland, & C.
Broken Arrowheads at Chilmark,
    Martha's Vineyard.
It Was Easier.
Joan Miró ("After that war, when death
    had gone away").
Joan Miró ("Once there were peasant
    pots and a dry brown hare").
Paul Klee.
Personal History.
Poem: "I walk at dawn across the
    hollow hills."
To a Very Beautiful Lady.
Upon This Rock.
Watching You Walk.
**Todhunter, John**
Aghadoe.
**Toffler, Alvin**
League of Selves, The.
**"Togo, Hashimura."** *See* **irwin, Wallace**
**Tolkien, John Ronald Renel**
Cat.
Mewlips, The.
Old Walking Song, The.
Oliphaunt.
Shadow-Bride.
Stone Troll, The.
Wind Was on the Withered Heath, The.
**Tollefsen, Astrid**
Toulouse Lautrec.
Workaday Morning.
**Tollerud, Jim**
Bird of Power.
Buzz.
Earth.
Elementary.
Eye of God.
Rainier.
Sunrise.
Thirsty Island.
Week-Seek.
**Tolnay, Thomas**
Basement Watch, The.
**Tolson, Melvin B.**
African China.
Birth of John Henry, The.
Dark Symphony.
Harlem Gallery,*sels.*
Legend of Versailles, A.
Libretto for the Republic of Liberia, *sel.*
On the Founding of Liberia.
PSI.
Satchmo.
Sea-Turtle and the Shark, The.
**Tomlinson, Charles**
At Barstow.
Cavern, The.
Chances of Rhyme, The.
Chestnut Avenue at Alton House, The.
Death in the Desert, A.
Distinction.
Door, The.
Farewell to Van Gogh.
Fiascherino.
Idyll: "Door, A:/ Per L'Universo."
Las Trampas U.S.A.
Mr. Brodsky.
Observation of Facts.

On the Hall at Stowey.
Oxen: Ploughing at Fiesole.
Paring the Apple.
Picture of J. T. in a Prospect of Stone, The.
Poem: "Upended, it crouches on broken limbs."
Return to Hinton.
Swimming Chenango Lake.
Through Binoculars.
Two Views of Two Ghost Towns.
Up at La Serra.
Veneris Venefica Agrestis.
Word in Edgeways, A.

**Tomonori**
Cherry tree blossomed, The. Black was my hair.

**"Tomson, Graham R."** *See* **Watson, Rosamund Marriott**

**Tonks, Rosemary**
Farewell to Kurdistan.
Story of a Hotel Room.

**Tooker, L. Frank**
Sea-King, The.

**Toomer, Jean**
Beehive.
Brown River, Smile.
Cotton Song.
Evening Song.
Five Vignettes.
Georgia Dusk.
Her Lips Are Copper Wire.
Lost Dancer, The.
November Cotton Flower.
Reapers.
Song of the Son.

**Toplady, Augustus Montague**
Rock of Ages.

**Torberg, Friedrich**
Amalek.
Seder, 1944.

**Törel, Ali Sedat Hilmi**
My Indian Girl.
Nirvana.

**Torgersen, Eric**
I Have Come to Be One Who Cries.
In a Subdivision.
My Blindness.
Of Birthright.
One Year Later.
Poem for Russell Nowak, A.
Story, A.

**Torlino**
Therefore I Must Tell the Truth.

**Torneol, Nuño Fernández**
Lady's Farewell, The.

**Torregian, Sotère**
Black Spring Becomes Anonymous, The.

**Torres Bodet, Jaime**
Love.

**Torrington, Patricia**
Night Watch.

**Tóth, Judit**
Remembering.
Southeast Ramparts of the Seine, The.
Wildfire.

**Toth, Steve**
About Yes and No.
Fight Fire with Fire.
Golden Greats, The.
Hanged Man, The.
Magic Sam.

Mark.
More Self-conscious.
Poem to a Potted Plant.
Remember.
Symbols.
Turquoise Mechanic's Son, The.

**Tottel, Richard**
Tottel's Miscellany, *sel.*

**Touré, Askia Muhammad**
Floodtide.
JuJu.
Tauhid.

**Tourneur, Cyril**
Age and bare bone/ Are e'er allied in action.
And now methinks I could e'en chide myself.
Awake, oh Heaven, for (lo) the heavens conspire.
Revenger's Tragedy, The, *sel.*

**Towne, Charles Hanson**
Messed Damozel, The.

**Townsend [*or* Townshend], Aurelian**
Constant Lover, The.
Dialogue betwixt [*or* between] Time and a Pilgrim, A.
To the Lady May.
Youth and Beauty.

**Townsend, Charles**
On the Lake Poets.

**Townsend, F. H.**
To the Cuckoo.

**Townsend, Joanne**
With Due Deference to Thomas Wolfe.

**Townshend, Aurelian.** *See* **Townsend, Aurelian**

**Track, Soge**
Indian Love Letter.

**Traherne, Thomas**
Demonstration, The, *sel.*
Dreams.
Insatiableness.
News.
On Leaping over the Moon.
Poverty.
Preparative, The.
Salutation, The.
Shadows in the Water.
Third Century, The, *sel.*
Vision, The.
Walking.
Wonder.

**Traill, Henry Duff**
After Dilettante Concetti.

**Trakl, Georg**
At the Eastern Front.

**Tranströmer, Tomas**
Allegro: "After a black day, I play Haydn."
Guard Duty.
Man Awakened by a Song above His Roof, The.
Open and Closed Space.
Schubertiana.
Track.

**Tranter, John**
Alphabet Murders, The, *sel.*
Red Movie.

**Trapp, Joseph**
Epigram: "King George, observing with judicious eyes."

**Travis, Lucille F.**

Alienation (To My Son).
Bells, The.
Judas Before.
Negrun.
Question.
To Sing the People.

**Trawick, Leonard**
Feeling for Fish.

**Traxler, Patricia**
Contest of Nerves, The.
Waking in Nice.

**Treasone, Grace**
Life.

**Treece, Henry**
Conquerors.
Horror.
Magic Wood, The.

**Trefethen, Florence**
Slipping Out of Intensive Care.

**Tregear, Edward**
Te Whetu Plains.

**Tregonning, Charley**
Cousin Jack Song.

**Treinin, Avner**
Cage, The.
Deserted Shrine.
Salmon Cycle.

**Trejo, Ernesto**
Cloud Unfolding, The.
Summer.

**Tremayne, Sydney**
Falls of Falloch, The.
Galloway Shore, The.
Mixed Weather.
North of Berwick.
Remote Country.

**Tremblay, Bill**
Court We Live On, The.

**Tremblay, Gail**
Crow Voices.

**Trench, Herbert**
Jean Richepin's Song.

**Trevathan, Charles E.**
Bully Song, The, *with music.*

**Trevelyan, Robert Calverley**
Glamara.

**Trevisa, John**
Prologue to a Translation.

**Trías, Arturo**
Act of Faith.
Ars Poetica.
This Shirt.

**Trias, Peter**
Marriage of Here and There, The.
Movement in Provence.
Stoneyard, The.

**Triem, Eve**
Bordello, Revisited.
Gerda, My Husband's Wife.
Misdemeanor.
Reading, The.

**Triggs, Jeffery Alan**
Man on Move Despite Failures.

**Trimpi, Alison A.**
Skull in the Desert, The.

**Tropp, Stephen**
My Wife Is My Shirt.

**Troupe, Quincy**
Dirge: "It is the endless dance of the dead."
For Malcolm Who Walks in the Eyes of Our Children.

Franklin Avenue Blues People.
In Texas Grass.
McCoy Tyner at Slugs.
Old People Speak of Death, The.
On Watching Pimps.
Poem for Friends.
River-Rhythm Town.
Sense of Coolness, A.
South African Bloodstone.
Thoughts.
Transformation.
Trilogy of the Night.
We Climb Upwards.

**Trowbridge, John Townsend**
Darius Green and His Flying-Machine.
Filling an Order.
Recollections of "Lalla Rookh."

**Trudell, Dennis**
Art of Poetry, The.
Avenue.
Epilogue: "I have just joined a raggedy line."
Hotel in Paris.
I Was Driving across the Island.
Jump Shooter, The.
Locale, A.
Thirty-nine thousand.
"You Get the Groceries, I'll Guard the Crib."

**Trumbull, John**
M'Fingal, sel.

**Trusky, Tom**
Advising Anna Doolittle the White Antelope Allusion Will Escape Her Readers.

**Trypanis, Constantine A.**
To Theon from His Son Theon.

**Ts'ai Yen**
18 Verses Sung to a Tatar Reed Whistle, sels.

**Tsao, Wu**
On your slender body/ Your jade and coral girdle ornaments chime.

**Tsongas, George**
House Arrest.
Keep Your Face.

**Tsuda, Kiyoko**
To be a mistress.

**Tsuda, Margaret**
Commitment in a City.
Hard Questions.

**Ts'uei T'u**
On New Year's Eve.

**Tsvetayeva, Marina**
Ars.
I'd like to live with you.
Insomnia, sel.
Poem of the End, sels.
We are keeping an eye on the girls, so that the kvass.
We Shall Not Escape Hell.

**Tucker, F. Bland**
All Praise to Thee, with music.
Our Father, by Whose Name, with music.

**Tucker, St. George**
Cynic, The.
Discontented Student, The.
Judge with the Sore Rump, The.

**Tuckerman, Frederick Goddard**
All men,—the preacher saith,—whate'er or whence.

And borne with theirs, my proudest thoughts do seem.
And she—her beauty never made her cold.
And so the day drops by; the horizon draws.
As when, down some broad river dropping, we.
By this low fire I often sit to woo.
Cricket, The.
For Nature daily through her grand design.
Hast thou seen reversed the prophet's miracle.
Here, where the red man swept the leaves away.
Nor looks that backward life so bare to me.
November.
Sonnet: "And change with hurried hand has swept these scenes."
Sonnet: "But man finds means, grant him but place and room."
Sonnet: "For Nature daily through her grand design."
Sonnet: "Not the round natural world, not the deep mind."
Sonnet: "One still dark night I sat alone and wrote."
Sonnet: "Roll on, sad world! not Mercury or Mars."
Sonnet: "Sometimes I walk where the deep water dips."
Sonnet: "Under the mountain, as when first I knew."
Sonnets, sels.
Under the Locust Blossoms.
Upper chamber in a darkened house, An.
Yes: though the brine may from the desert deep.

**Tudor, Stephen**
Augur, The.
Harold.
Poem for Nancy.
You Held the Air.

**Tudur Aled**
Stallion, The.

**Tuéni, Nadia**
More distant than the dead sea.
Nothing but a man.
Would you come back if I said the earth.

**Tu Fu**
Night in the House by the River.
Road to Pengya, The.
Visitors.
Written on the Wall at Chang's Hermitage.

**Tu-kehu**
Oh, how my love/ With a whirling power.

**Tupper, Martin Farquhar**
Anglo-Saxon Race, The: A Rhyme for Englishmen.
Mercy to Animals: A Ballad of Humanity.
Of Curious Questions.
Train of Religion, The, sel.

**Tuquan, Fadwa**
After Twenty Years.

**Turberville, George**

Epitaph of Maister Win Drowned in the Sea, An.
Of One That Had a Great Nose.
That No Man Should Write but Such as Do Excel.
Verse in Praise of Lord Henry Howard, Earl of Surrey.

**Turbyfill, Mark**
Benediction.

**Turco, Lewis**
Bears in the Land-Fill, The.
Bell Weather.
Door, The.
Failed Fathers.
Forest beyond the Glass, The.
Love Poem: "These words are all of me."
Old Acquaintance, An.
Ordinary Evening in Cleveland, An.
Pilot, The.

**Turei, Mohi**
Ruaumoko—the Earthquake God.

**Turk, Marie C.**
Thank You, Jesus, for this day.

**Turnbull, Clive**
Lost Love.

**Turnbull, Gael**
Accident, An.
Learning to Breathe.
Twenty Words/ Twenty Days.

**Turner, Alberta**
Sisters.
Structure.
To Leonard and Kerstin, with a Gift of Books.
Wrists.

**Turner, Charles Tennyson**
After the School-Feast.
Country Dance, A.
Drunkard's Last Market, The.
Eustace and Edith.
Evening in Harvest Time, An.
Lion's Skeleton, The.
Mary—A Reminiscence.
Old Ruralities.
Old Stephen.
On Startling Some Pigeons.
On the Eclipse of the Moon of October 1865.
Quiet Tide near Ardrossan, The.
Seaside, The.
Steam Threshing-Machine, The.
To a Red-Wheat Field.
To a Scarecrow; or, Malkin, Left Long after Harvest.
To a "Tenting" Boy.
White Horse of Westbury, The.
Wind on the Corn.

**Turner, Doris**
Fragment Reflection I.
Reckoning A. M. Thursday.

**Turner, Doug**
Spirit, The.

**Turner, Elizabeth**
Canary, The.
How to Write a Letter.
Truth the Best.
Two Little Miss Lloyds, The.

**Turner, Godfrey**
Journal of Society, The.
Tattle.

**Turner, Gordon**

I Want to One Morning.
**Turner, Nancy Byrd**
Black and Gold.
God's Plan for Spring.
Washington.
Whenever I Say "America."
**Turner, Samuel S.**
November.
**Turner, Walter James**
Ecstasy, *abr.*
Life and Death.
Romance.
Silence.
**Turner, William Price**
Homely Accommodation, Suit Gent.
Personal Column.
Reproaches.
Trend Spotter.
University Curriculum.
**Tussman, Malka Heifetz**
At the Well.
I Say.
Love the Ruins.
Mount Gilboa.
Songs of the Priestess.
Thou Shalt Not.
Water without Sound.
**Tuthill, Stacy**
Your Black Bones Do Not Remember.
**Tuwhare, Hone**
Burial.
Girl in the Park, The.
Lament: "In that strident summer of
battle."
Muscle and Bone of Song.
Old Place, The.
Rain.
**Tuwim, Julian**
Gypsy Bible, The.
Jewboy.
Lodgers.
Mother.
**"Twain, Mark" (Samuel Langhorne
Clemens)**
Adventures of Huckleberry Finn, The,
*sel.*
Emmeline Grangerford's "Ode to
Stephen Dowling Bots, Dec'd."
**Tweedy, Henry Hallam**
Eternal God, Whose Power Upholds,
*with music.*
O Gracious Father of Mankind, *with
music.*
**Tyack, Jim**
25 Spontaneous Lines Greeting the
World.
**Tyler, Parker**
Anthology of Nouns.
Nijinsky.
**Tyler, Royall**
Anacreontic to Flip.
Gambling.
Hail to the Joyous Day, *with music.*
Love Song, A.
Original Epitaph on a Drunkard.
Widower, The.
**Tynan, Katharine (Katharine Tynan
Hinkson)**
August Weather.
Slow Spring.
Winter.
**Tyutchev, Fyodor Ivanovich**

Last Love.
**Tzara, Tristan**
Evening.
Mothers.
**Tzu Yeh**
Frost, The.

# U

**Uceda, Julia**
Time Reminded Me.
2976.
**Uchino, Takako.** *See* **Lento, Takako
Uchino**
**Ugaas, Raage**
Poet's Lament on the Death of His Wife.
**Ulinover, Miriam**
Havdolah Wine.
In the Courtyard.
**Ullman, Leslie**
Last Night They Heard the Woman
Upstairs.
**Unamuno, Miguel de**
Atheist's Prayer, The.
**Unger, Barbara**
Geological Faults.
**Unik, Pierre**
Manless Society, The.
**Unterecker, John**
August 22.
Falling.
Lava Tubes.
Portrait.
Swan Lake.
**Untermeyer, Louis**
Caliban in the Coal Mines.
Day-Dreamer.
Dog at Night.
Edgar A. Guest Considers "The Old
Woman Who Lived in a Shoe."
Edna St. Vincent Millay Exhorts Little
Boy Blue.
End of the Comedy.
Good Advice.
However they talk, whatever they say.
Portrait of a Machine.
Short Sermon.
Song Tournament: New Style.
**Updike, John**
Amish, The.
Bendix.
Cloud Shadows.
Ex-Basketball Player.
February.
February 22.
From a Cheerful Alphabet.
Golfers.
Hoeing.
I Missed His Book, but I Read His
Name.
Insomnia the Gem of the Ocean.
Minority Report.
Mosquito.
Movie House.
Ohio.
Pendulum.
Player Piano.
Recital.

Report of Health.
Some Frenchmen.
Sonic Boom.
Stunt Flier, The.
Suburban Madrigal.
Summer: West Side.
Superman.
Tao in the Yankee Stadium Bleachers.
Taste.
Telephone Poles.
Thoughts while Driving Home.
V. B. Nimble, V. B. Quick ("V. B.
Wigglesworth wakes at noon").
Wash.
Winter Ocean.
**Upham, Samuel C.**
Ancient Yuba Miner of the Days of '49,
Ye.
**Upton, Charles**
Moon, The.
**Upton, Minnie Leona**
No Talking Shop.
**Urdang, Constance**
Because the Three Moirai Have Become
the Three Maries.
Birth.
Birth of Venus.
Bread.
Change of Life.
Children, The.
Day the Houses Sank, The.
Evening of Home Movies, An.
Exercise for the Left Hand.
His Sleep.
Invention of Zero, The.
Leaving Mexico One More Time.
Old Maid Factory, The.
One-eyed Bridegroom, The.
Roots of Revolution in the Vegetable
Kingdom, The.
Safe Places.
**Uribe, Armando**
I love you and the rosebush.
**Usborne, Richard**
Casanova.
Epitaph on a Party Girl.
**Uvavnuk**
Song of Joy.
**Uvlunuaq**
I Should Be Ashamed.

# V

**"V., B."** *See* **Thomson, James (1834–1882**
**Vakaló, Eléni**
Genealogy.
My Father's Eye.
Song of the Hanged.
**"Vala, Katri" (Karin Alice Heikel)**
On the Meadow.
Winter Is Here.
**Valaoritis, Nanos**
Birds of Hazard and Prey, *sel.*
I Am.
**Valentine, Jean**
Anaesthesia.
April.
Dream Barker.

Fidelities.
He Said.
Moon Man.
Pilgrims.
Sasha and the Poet.
3 a.m. in New York.
**Valentino, Rita**
Good evening/ the time is now 5:55 pm.
**Valéry, Paul**
Footsteps, The.
Helen.
**Valian, Maxine Kent**
Blessing at Kellenberger Road.
**Valis, Noel Maureen**
Black Horse Running.
**Valle, Carmen**
Glen Miller's music is a trunk.
I'm going to break out.
What Is Lived.
**Vallejo, César**
And don't bother telling me anything.
Anger that breaks a man down into boys, The.
Black Riders, The.
Eternal Dice, The.
I have a terrible fear of being an animal.
Poem to Be Read and Sung.
To My Brother Miguel: In Memoriam.
Trilce: "In that corner, where we slept together."
**Vanada, Lillian Schulz**
Fuzzy wuzzy, creepy crawly.
**Van Arsdale, H.**
Lucky Louie Makes a Goal.
**Van Brunt, H. L.**
Lumiere.
**Vanderlip, Brian**
Encounter with Hunger.
**Vander Molen, Robert**
In the Bar.
**Van Doren, Mark**
Afterward.
Ancient Couple on Lu Mountain, The.
And Did the Animals?
Apple Hell.
Child at Winter Sunset, The.
Distant Runners, The.
Down Dip the Branches.
Dunce Song 6.
Envy the Old.
Family Prime.
First Snow of the Year, The.
Ghost Boy.
Good Morning.
I Had to Be Secret.
King Wind.
Laly, Laly.
Merry-go-round.
Morning Assignment.
Morning Worship.
Needles and Pins.
Old Ben Golliday.
Only for Me.
Praise Him Who Makes Us Happy, *with music.*
Rapunzel, Rapunzel.
Sad Child's Song, The.
Simple Beast.
Slowly, Slowly Wisdom Gathers.
Spring Thunder.
Story-Teller, The.
This Shell.

True Is True.
Truelove.
Wait till Then.
Where Did He Run To?
Why, Lord? *with music.*
Will You, Won't You.
**Van Duyn, Mona**
Billings and Cooings from "The Berkeley Barb."
Birthday Card for a Psychiatrist.
Death by Aesthetics.
Fear of Flying, The.
Gardener to His God, The.
Leda.
Leda Reconsidered.
Memory, A.
Open Letter from a Constant Reader.
Pieta, The, Rhenish, 14th C., The Cloisters.
Recovery, *sel.*
Relationships.
Talker, The.
Three Valentines to the Wide World, *sel.*
Twins, The.
"Wish to Be Believed, The."
**Van Dyke, Henry**
America for Me.
Four Things.
Jesus, Thou Divine Companion, *with music.*
Maryland Yellow-Throat, The.
O Lord Our God, Thy Mighty Hand, *with music.*
**Van Geel, Christian J.**
View.
End of the World.
**"Vanolis, Bysshe."** *See* **Thomson, James (1834–1882)**
**Van Rensselaer, James**
Note on Lizard's Feet, A.
**Van Spanckeren, Kathryn**
Muse Poem.
**Van Stockum, Hilda**
Hut, The.
**Van Walleghen, Michael**
Poem for My Great Grandfather.
**Van Winckel, Nance**
When You Are Gone.
**Varela, Blanca**
Before the Pacific.
Nobody will open the door for you.
Things I Say Are True, The.
**Vargas, Roberto**
Suddenly there were cakes and everything.
**Vas, István**
Catacombs.
Just This.
Tambour.
What Is Left?
**Vas Dias, Robert**
Impossibility, An.
Petoskey Stone.
Salvaging Spikes.
**Vaughan, Frances Downing**
New Calf, The.
**Vaughan, Henry**
Abel's Blood.
Awake! Glad Heart!
Bird, The.
Charnel-House, The.
Childhood.

Cock-crowing.
Corruption.
Dawning, The.
Easter Hymn.
Man.
Morning-Watch, The.
Night, The ("Through that pure virgin shrine").
Passion, The.
Peace.
Quickness.
Regeneration.
Relapse, The.
Religion.
Resurrection and Immortality.
Retreat[e], The.
Revival, The.
Since Thou Art Gone.
Tempest, The.
They Are All Gone into the World of Light.
To Etesia Looking from Her Casement at the Full Moon.
Unprofitableness.
Waterfall, The.
World, The.
**Vaughan, Thomas**
Stone, The.
**Vaughan-Thomas, Wynford**
Farewell to New Zealand.
Hiraeth in N.W.3.
To His Not-So-Coy Mistress.
**Vaughan Williams, Ursula**
Memorial Service.
**Vaughn, James P.**
Four Questions Addressed to His Excellency, the Prime Minister.
So?
**Vaux, Thomas, 2d Baron Vaux of Harrowden**
Aged Lover Renounceth Love, The.
**Vazakas, Byron**
Enigmatic Traveler, The.
**Veale, Peter**
Bold Troubleshooters.
**Veeder, Rex**
Magic.
My Son.
**Vega, José Luis**
Brotherhood.
Conditions.
Erotic Suite, *sels.*
**Vega Carpio, Lope de.** *See* **Lope de Vega Carpio, Felix**
**Velema**
Tip-of-the-Single-Feather.
**Velho da Costa, Maria** *and* **Maria Isabel Barreno** *and* **Maria Teresa Horta.** *See* **Marias, The Three**
**Venantius Fortunatus, Saint**
Standards of the king go forth, The.
To the Lady Radegunde, with Violets.
**Ventura, Michael**
After the Successful Psychotherapy.
**Vere, Edward de, 17th Earl of Oxford.** *See* **De Vere, Edward, 17th Earl of Oxford**
**Vergil.** *See* **Virgil**
**Verlaine, Paul**
A la Promenade.
Clair de Lune.
Cortège.
Femme et Chatte.

Sagesse, *sel.*
You would have understood me, had
  you waited.
**Vernon, John**
Not Having a History.
What Is Salt?
**Very, Jones**
Broken Bowl, The.
Clouded Morning, The.
Columbine, The.
Created, The.
Day of Denial, The.
Dead, The.
Eagles, The.
Enoch.
Fair Morning, The.
Fugitive Slaves, The.
Garden, The.
Grave-Yard, The.
Hand and Foot, The.
I Was Sick and in Prison.
Lament of the Flowers, The.
Lost, The.
New Birth, The.
New Man, The.
New World, The.
On the Completion of the Pacific
  Telegraph.
On Visiting the Graves of Hawthorne
  and Thoreau.
Prayer, The: "Wilt thou not visit me?"
Presence, The.
Slave, The.
Spirit Land, The.
Sumach Leaves, The.
Thy Brother's Blood.
Today.
Trees of Life, The.
Yourself.
**"Vesay, Paul."** *See* **Allen, Samuel**
**Victory, H.**
Everlasting Teamwork in Basketball.
**Vidya**
Friends,/ you are lucky you can talk.
Please keep an eye on my house for a
  few moments.
Substantiations, *sel.*
Sun, The, *sel.*
Wanton, The, *sel.*
**Viereck, Peter**
Graves Are Made to Waltz On.
Kilroy.
Mary, Mary.
1912-1952, Full Cycle.
Poet.
Sleepdancers, The.
Space-Wanderer's Homecoming.
To Helen (of Troy, N.Y.).
*Vale* from Carthage.
**Vigée, Claude**
Destiny of the Poet.
House of the Living.
Light of Judea.
Poetry.
Song of Occident.
Struggle with the Angel, The.
Tree of Death, The.
Wanderer, The.
**Vigny, Alfred de**
Shepherd's House, The, *sel.*

**Viidikas, Vicki**
Flow of Them All, The.
Hot Poem.
Keeping Watch on the Heart.
Loaded Hearts.
Ode to a Young Dog.
Wheels.
**Villa, José Garcia**
There came you wishing me.
**Villanueva, Alma**
There were times.
They didn't get me.
To Jesus Villanueva, with Love.
You cannot leave.
**Villanueva, Salvador**
I would go around biting my nails.
Maybe You Cannot Comprehend.
Temple is full of blood, The.
**Villon, François**
Ballad of Dead Ladies, The.
Ballad of Villon and Fat Madge,
  The.
Ballade to His Mistress.
Dispute of the Heart and Body of
  François Villon, The.
Old Lady's Lament for Her Youth,
  The.
Testament, The, *abr.*
**Vinaver, Stanislav**
Cathedral, A.
European Night, The.
Inscription, An: "Over the sheer rocks
  over the gorges."
**Vincent, Stephen**
Basketball.
Coming Up and Falling Down.
Elevator Landscapes,*sels.*
Floor: Five.
Floor: O.
Jealousy.
Mother.
Relationship, The.
Requiem: "I watch the roses float."
Song of This House, The.
**Vincent, W. G.**
Moonlight, *sel.*
**Vines, Eda H.**
Ballade of the Old-Time Engine.
**Vinner, Shlomo**
In the Cabinet.
Jerusalem.
Midnight and Ten Minutes.
Need to Love, The.
Parting.
Training on the Shore.
**Vinograd, Julia**
Investigation.
**Vinz, Mark**
Children, The.
For the Far Edge.
In the Heartland.
North Dakota Gothic.
Primer Lesson.
Variations on a Theme.
**Violi, Paul**
Concordance.
**Virgil [*or* Vergil] (Publius Vergilius Maro)**
Aeneid, The, *abr.*
And oft the owle with rufull song
  complaind.

Arms, and the man I sing, who forc'd by
  fate.
As when a fragment, from a mountain
  torn.
Funeral Games for Anchises, The:
  Entellus.
Georgics, *sel.*
Onto the hallowit steid bryng in, thai
  cry.
Tenth Pastoral, The; or, Gallus.
**Vizenor, Gerald**
Anishinabe Grandmothers.
Family Photograph.
February Park.
Haiku: "August heat."
Indians at the Guthrie.
North to Milwaukee.
Raising the Flag.
Seven Woodland Crows.
Thumbing Old Magazines.
Tribal Stumps ("Tribal mixed bloods").
Tropisms on John Berryman.
Tyranny of Moths.
Unhappy Diary Days.
**Vliet, R. G.**
Games, hard press and bruise of the
  flesh.
Girls on Saddleless Horses.
Love's own form.
**Vogel, David**
Black Flags Are Fluttering.
Days Were Great as Lakes.
How Can I See You, Love.
In Fine, Transparent Words.
Now I Have Forgotten All.
Our Childhood Spilled into Our Hearts.
Plain, Humble Letters.
When I Was Growing Up.
**Vogelweide, Walther von der.** *See* **Walther
  von der Vogelweide**
**Voigt, Ellen Bryant**
Claiming Kin.
Daughter.
Farm Wife.
Tropics.
**Volk, Joyce M.**
Places I Have Been.
**Von Ende, Frederick**
Wynken De Worde.
**von Hartmann, Max**
Seed of Reality, The.
**Vories, William M.**
Let There Be Light, *with music.*
**Voronca, Ilarie**
Quick and the Dead, The.
Seven-League Boots, The.
**Vorphal, Robert L.**
Perspective.
**Voznesensky, Andrei**
Antiworlds.
Darkmotherscream.
Dead Still.
Give Me Peace ("Give me quietness and
  peace").
I Am Goya.
New York Bird.
Soccer.
Someone Is Beating a Woman.
**Vroman, Leo**
Old Miniatures.
River, The.

# W

**"W., A."**
Upon Visiting His Lady by Moonlight.
**Waddington, Miriam**
Desert Stone.
Field of Night, The.
Survivors, The.
**Wade, John Stevens**
Clothesline, The.
Daisies.
Days like This.
May.
Smell of Wood, The.
**Wade, Thomas**
Winter Shore, The.
**Wagoner, David**
Burglar, The.
Clancy.
Death and Resurrection of the Birds,
   The.
Death of the Moon.
Elegy for a Forest Clear-cut by the
   Weyerhaeuser Company.
Elegy for Yards, Pounds, and Gallons.
Elegy while Pruning Roses.
Falling Asleep in a Garden.
Fisherman's Wife, The.
Guide to Dungeness Spit, A.
In the Badlands.
Labors of Thor, The.
Leaving Something Behind.
Lesson, The.
Looking for Mountain Beavers.
Lost.
Lost Street, The.
Making Up for a Soul.
Man Who Spilled Light, The.
Marsh Leaf.
Meeting a Bear.
Muse.
Ode to the Muse on Behalf of a Young
   Poet.
Osprey's Nest, The.
Poets Agree to Be Quiet by the Swamp,
   The.
Report from a Forest Logged by the
   Weyerhaeuser Company.
Revival.
Riverbed.
Singing Lesson, The.
Sleeping in the Woods.
Snake Hunt.
Song for the Skull of Black Bear.
Song for the Soul Going Away.
Song for the Soul Returning.
Song to Accompany the Bearer of Bad
   News.
Staying Alive.
Talking Back.
Talking to the Forest.
To My Friend Whose Parachute Did
   Not Open.
Trail Horse, The.
Under the Sign of Moth.
Visiting Hour, The.
Walking in a Swamp.
Words, The.
Working against Time.
**Wahl, Jean**

Evening in the Walls.
Lean Day in a Convict's Suit, A.
Prayer of a Little Hope.
**Wain, John**
Apology for Understatement.
Arrival.
Au Jardin des Plantes.
Bad Thing, The.
Brooklyn Heights.
Reason for Not Writing Orthodox
   Nature Poetry.
Song about Major Eatherly, A.
**Wakarpa**
Golden Sea-Otter, The.
**Wakefield, Samuel**
Music of His Steps, The, *with music.*
**Wakeman, John**
Love in Brooklyn.
**Wakoski, Diane**
Aging.
Anticipation of Sharks.
Apology, An.
Buddha Inherits 6 Cars on His Birthday,
   The.
Children Visit the Island.
Duchess Potatoes, The.
Father of My Country, The.
Fire Island Poem.
Greed, *sel.*
I Have Had to Learn to Live with My
   Face.
Ice Eagle, The.
In Gratitude to Beethoven.
In Place of a Phone Call to Arabia.
Inside Out, *sel.*
Journey.
Justice Is Reason Enough.
Love Letter Postmarked Van Beethoven
Love to My Electric Handmixer.
Magician, The.
Mechanic, The.
My Knees Go before the Firing Squad
   at Dawn.
My Mother Tries to Visit Me in the
   Dead of Night.
My Mother's Milkman.
Night a Sailor Came to Me in a Dream,
   The.
No More Soft Talk.
Ode to a Lebanese Crock of Olives.
Overweight Poem.
Patriotic Poem.
Placing a $2 Bet for a Man Who Will
   Never Go to the Horse Races Any
   More.
Poet Recognizing the Echo of the Voice,
   A.
Rain Trip.
Ring, The.
Ringless.
Sestina from the Home Gardener.
Smudging.
Summer.
Sun.
Thank You for the Valentine.
To Bed.
Turtle, The.
Walking Past Paul Blackburn's Apt. on
   7th St.
What I Want in a Husband Besides a
   Mustache.
Wind Secrets.

You, Letting the Trees Stand as My
   Betrayer.
**Walcott, Derek**
Another Life, *sel.*
Blues.
Bridge, The.
Chelsea, The.
Codicil.
Crusoe's Island.
Elegy: "Our hammock swung between
   Americas."
Far Cry from Africa, A.
Letter from Brooklyn, A.
Moon.
Nights in the Gardens of Port of Spain.
Piano Practice.
Pocomania.
Polish Rider, The.
Preparing for Exile.
Runner at Sauteurs, The.
Sea Grapes.
Spring Street in '58.
Tales of the Islands.
**Waldman, Anne**
Color of Honey.
Holy City.
How to Write.
Lines: "Lines which are the imitation of
   imagined veins."
Memorial Day: A Collaboration, *sel.*
Over Asia.
Pressure.
Resisting Each Other.
Romantic Poem.
Traveling.
Winter Sonnet.
**Waldrop, Keith**
Around the Block.
Before Bed.
Signals.
Song: Paper.
**Waldrop, Rosemarie**
Morning Has No House.
**Waley, Arthur**
Censorship.
**Walford, William W.**
Sweet Hour of Prayer, *with music.*
**Walker, Alice**
Beyond What.
Black Mail.
Burial.
Chic Freedom's Reflection.
Expect Nothing.
For My Sister Molly Who in the Fifties.
Green lawn/ a picket fence.
Hymn: "I well remember."
In These Dissenting Times.
Love, *sel.*
Medicine.
Mornings/ of an Impossible Love.
Old Warrior Terror, The.
Once, *sels.*
So We've Come at Last to Freud.
Suicide.
Women.
**Walker, Anna Louise**
Work, for the Night Is Coming, *with
   music.*
**Walker, Brad**
Instructions for a Park.
**Walker, Charlie**
St. George.

**Walker, David**
Passages.
**Walker, E. M.**
Anno Domini.
**Walker, James J.**
Will You Love Me in December as You
    Do in May? *with music.*
**Walker, Jeanne Murray**
Deliver Me, O Lord, from My Daily
    Bread.
Tracking the Sled, Christmas 1951.
**Walker, Kath**
Then and Now.
We Are Going.
**Walker, Margaret Abigail**
Ballad of the Hoppy-Toad.
Big John Henry.
Birmingham.
Childhood.
For Andy Goodman—Michael
    Schwerner—and James Chaney.
For Malcolm X.
For My People.
Girl Held without Bail.
Jackson, Mississippi.
Kissie Lee.
Lineage.
Molly Means.
October Journey.
Prophets for a New Day.
Street Demonstration.
Today.
We Have Been Believers.
**Walker, Mary**
Falls.
Sunning during Session Break at Camp
    Lake Hubert for Girls, Brainerd,
    Minnesota.
**Walker, Ted**
By the Saltings.
Harpooning, The.
**Walker, Thomas M.**
Beauty of the Ocean, The.
**Walker, William**
High o'er the Hills, *with music.*
**Wallace, Bronwen**
Generation Gap
Profile.
**Wallace, Jon**
Linebacker at Forty, The.
Puberty.
**Wallace, Michele**
Untitled.
Voice of the Future, The.
**Wallace, Robert**
After the Swimmer.
Aubade: N.Y.C.
Double Play, The.
Driving By.
First Dandelions, *sel.*
In a Spring Still Not Written of.
On the College Archery Range.
Out of the Past.
Place, The.
Snapshot for Miss Bricka Who Lost in
    the Semifinal Round of the
    Pennsylvania Lawn Tennis
    Tournament at Haverford, July, 1960,
    A.
Star-nosed Mole, The.
Swimmer in the Rain.
What He Says.

**Wallace, Ronald**
Father and Son.
One Hook.
Prayer for Fish.
Real Thing, The.
**Wallace, William Ross**
Sword of Bunker Hill, The.
**Wallace-Crabbe, Chris**
Allegiance, An.
Apparition, The.
Going to Cythera.
Introspection.
Old Men during a Fall of Government.
Star Quality.
Terra Australis.
Wintry Manifesto, A.
**Wallach, Yona**
Cradle Song: "Imagine lamenting our
    longing, no."
Death; She Was Always Here.
When the Angels Are Exhausted.
**Wallāda**
I wonder: is there no way for us to meet
    again.
If you were just in keeping our pact of
    love.
**Waller, Edmund**
At Penshurst ("Had Sacharissa lived
    when mortals made").
Dancer, The.
Fall, The.
Go, Lovely Rose.
Instructions to a Painter.
Long and Short Life.
Of English Verse.
Of My Lady Isabella Playing on the
    Lute.
Of the Last Verses in the Book.
Old Age.
On a Girdle.
On St. James's Park as Lately Improved
    by His Majesty.
Panegyric to My Lord Protector, A, *sel.*
Song: "Stay, Phoebus, stay!"
To a Fair Lady Playing with a Snake.
To My Young Lady Lucy Sidney.
To One Married to an Old Man.
To Phyllis.
To the King, upon His Majesty's Happy
    Return, *sel.*
**Waller, John Francis**
Spinning Wheel, The.
**Wallis, John**
When a Twister, a-twisting, will twist
    him a twist.
**Wally, Darryl**
Tablerock.
**Walpole, Horace, 4th Earl of Orford**
All praise your face, your verses none
    abuse.
Epitaphs on Two Piping-Bullfinches of
    Lady Ossory's.
Estate and an earldom at seventy-four,
    An!
On the Translation of Anacreon.
To the Gardener at Nuneham.
**Walsh, John**
Sweet Chestnuts.
Taking Out Jim.
**Walsh, Marnie**
Bessie Dreaming Bear.
Charlie Two-Head.

Emmet Kills-Warrior Turtle Mountain
    Reservation.
Seth Dismounts Thrice.
Thomas Iron-Eyes.
Vickie.
**Walsh, Ruth M.**
Inadequate Aqua Extremis.
Rift Tide.
**Walsh, William (1663-1708)**
Abigail's Lamentation for the Loss of
    Mr. Harley.
Despairing Lover, The.
Epigram, An: "Epigram should be, An—
    if right."
Love and Jealousy.
Lyce.
Thraso.
**Walter, Beatrice**
Photograph the Cat Licks, The.
**Walter, Howard Arnold**
I Would Be True.
**Walters, Anna**
Hartico.
I Am of the Earth.
My Brothers.
Simplicity Aims Circularly.
Teacher Taught Me, A.
**Walters, Dorothy**
Cinéma Vérité.
Flannery O'Connor.
Two Roads, Etc.
**Walters, Winifred Fields**
Navajo Signs.
**Walthall, Hugh**
"Breaking Up Is Hard to Do."
Halleluja Hardesty, Female Artist.
Occasional Apostrophe, An.
**Walther von der Vogelweide**
Under the Lime Tree.
**Walton, Eda Lou**
How Our Forefather Got His Wife.
Indian Death.
Love Medicine.
Marriage Dance, The.
**Walton, Izaak**
Angler's Song, The ("As inward love
    breeds outward talk").
**Walton, John**
God, the Port of Peace.
**Walton, Thelma**
God's Gifts to Me.
**Walworth, Clarence A.**
Holy God, We Praise Thy Name, *with
    music.*
**Wanek, Connie**
Bucket in the Well.
**Wang, David Rafael**
Self-conscious Horse, The.
**Wangberg, Mark**
Aah . . . You Ikenne Women.
Brother Simon Calls on Jesus Christ.
Ibo Woman.
It is Beautiful, It is Rain.
Life Is All Right.
Lizard and the Yellow Dandelion, The
    ("The lizard is wearing a dandelion").
Love Poem: "Thrust of your body, The."
Moshudi.
**Wang Ch'ing-hui**
Now the lotuses in the imperial lake.
**Wang Wei**
Seeking a Mooring.

**Waniek, Marilyn Nelson**
Herbs in the Attic.
Other Women's Children.
**Wanley, Nathaniel**
Felled at a Word?
Invitation, The.
Resurrection, The.
**Wantling, William**
Don't Shoot!
Style 5.
**Ward, Ann**
Music Lesson, A.
**Ward, Christopher**
Ballad of Benjamin Bones, The.
**Ward, Nathaniel**
Epigram: "World is full of care, much
like unto a bubble, The."
**Ward, Raymond**
For the Masked Ones.
Intimacy.
Living, The.
Ode to an Urban Day.
Solo for Clarinet.
Watching Snow.
**Ward, Robert**
Tenant Farmer.
**Wardell, W. S.**
Here/ where she dropped me.
No one is as acquainted with pain as I
am.
Our stars, ourselves.
**Warden, Marine Robert**
Ode to a Homemade Coffee Cup.
**Ware, Henry, Jr.**
Great God, the Followers of Thy Son,
with music.
**Warman, Cy**
Creede.
Rise and Fall of Creede, The.
**Warner, Anna B.**
Jesus Loves Me, This I Know, with
music.
One More Day's Work for Jesus, with
music.
We Would See Jesus, with music.
**Warner, Sylvia Townsend**
Dear Girl, The.
**Warren, F. Eugene**
Angry Sermon for Any Day in the
Week, An.
Bareback in Kansas.
Christographia 35.
Customarily Autumn.
Signature, A.
**Warren, James Edward, Jr.**
Alston Chapel.
Beneath Such Rains.
I Must Ask.
Perfect Poem Trumpets, The.
Seizure.
Somewhere.
Wormwood.
**Warren, John Byrne Leicester, Baron de
Tabley**   See DeTabley, John Byrne
Leicester Warren, Baron
**Warren, Robert Penn**
Ballad of Billie Potts, The.
Bearded Oaks.
Birth of Love.
Blow, West Wind.
Child Next Door, The.

Commuter's Entry in a Connecticut
Diary.
Debate: Question, Quarry, Dream.
Dragon Country: To Jacob Boehme.
Fall Comes in Back-Country Vermont.
Founding Fathers, Nineteenth-Century
Style.
Garden, The.
He Was Formidable.
History.
History among the Rocks.
Homage to Theodore Dreiser on the
Centennial of His Birth, sel.
Hunger and Thirst.
In Italian They Call the Bird Civetta.
In the Mountains, sel.
Internal Injuries.
Jet Must Be Hunting for Something,
The.
Lessons in History.
Limited, The.
Man in the Street.
Mango on the Mango Tree, The.
Mediterranean Beach, Day after Storm,
sel.
Mexico Is a Foreign Country: Four
Studies in Naturalism, sel.
Mortmain, sel.
Myth on Mediterranean Beach:
Aphrodite as Logos.
Natural History.
Nightmare of Mouse.
Notes on a Life to Be Lived, sels.
Original Sin: A Short Story.
Owl, The.
Patriotic Tour and Postulate of Joy.
Penological Study: Southern Exposure,
sel.
Promises, sel.
Pursuit.
Real Question Calling for Solution, A.
Red-Tail Hawk and Pyre of Youth.
Revelation.
Skiers.
Small White House.
Swimming in the Pacific.
Terror.
Two Pieces after Suetonius.
Watershed.
Ways of Day.
Well House, The.
Wet Hair: If Now His Mother Should
Come.
What Day Is.
Where the Slow Fig's Purple Sloth.
**Warren, Rosanna**
Omalos.
Virgin Pictured in Profile.
**Warren, William F.**
I Worship Thee, O Holy Ghost, with
music.
**Warsh, Lewis**
Serene Art.
**Warshawsky, Mark**
Oyfn Pripetshuk (On the Hearth).
**Warton, Joseph**
Enthusiast, The; or, The Lover of
Nature.
Ode to Fancy.
**Warton, Thomas the Younger**
Come, gentle sleep, death's image though
thou art.

Pleasures of Melancholy, The.
**Washburn, Archie**
Hogan.
Unknown Smoke.
**Washburn, Henry Stevenson**
Almighty God, Thy Constant Care, with
music.
Vacant Chair, The.
**Wat, Aleksander**
There Is No Place.
Willows in Alma-Ata.
**Waterbury, Jared B.**
I Have Fought the Good Fight, with
music.
Sinner, Is Thy Heart at Rest? with music.
**Waterman, Cary**
Death on the Farm
Love Poem: "Morning settles in."
Pig Poem.
**Waterman, Charles**
Neighbor.
New Cows, The.
To My Father.
**Waterman, Nixon**
Cheer for the Consumer.
If We Didn't Have to Eat.
**Waters, Michael**
Dead, The.
Leaves and Ashes.
Leaving America.
Night Fishing.
Wedding Poem.
**Watkins, Edward**
Acrobat.
Adam, Eve and the Big Apple.
What Is a Sonnet?
**Watkins, Grace V.**
Greater Country, The.
**Watkins, Vernon**
Ballad of the Three Coins.
Collier, The.
Cwmrhydyceirw Elegiacs.
Demands of the Muse.
Feather, The.
Foal.
For a Wine Festival.
Healing of the Leper, The.
Heron, The.
Indolence.
Mare, The.
Ode to Swansea.
Peace in the Welsh Hills.
Returning to Goleufryn ("Returning to
my grandfather's house, after this
exile").
Shell, The.
Swedenborg's Skull.
True Picture Restored, A.
Two Decisions.
Waterfalls.
**Watkyns, Rowland**
Antipathy.
Bad company is a disease.
Saul did much care and diligence
express.
Strange Monsters.
Upon Christ's Nativity, or Christmas.
Worldly Wealth.
**Watson, Elaine**
Museum Piece No. 16228.
**Watson, Robert**
Blue Whale, The.

Do You Love Me?
Glass Door, The.
Good Life, A.
Is There Life across the Street?
Lines for a President.
Times Square Parade.
**Watson, Roderick**
Black Forest.
Director of the Museum, The.
Foveran Sands.
New Kelso.
3 Stones.
Welthistorische Perspektiven.
**Watson, Rosamund Marriott ("Graham R. Tomson"; "R. Armytage")**
To My Cat.
**Watson, Thomas**
Hekatompathia; or, Passionate Century of Love, *sels.*
**Watson, Sir William**
Wordsworth's Grave, *abr.*
**Watt, W. W.**
Summer Song.
**Watterman, Catharine H.**
Come unto Me, When Shadows Darkly Gather, *with music.*
**Watton, Joan**
Requiem of a War-Baby.
**Watts, Alaric Alexander**
Austrian Army, An.
**Watts, Isaac**
Against Quarrelling and Fighting.
Broad Is the Road.
Cradle Hymn.
Day of Judgement [*or* Judgment], The.
Early, my God, without delay.
For the Lord's Day Evening.
Give to Our God Immortal Praise, *with music.*
Great God, attend while Zion sings.
Heavenly Canaan, The.
How Doth the Little Busy Bee.
How long, dear Savior, O how long.
Incomprehensible, The.
Joy to the World.
Ninety-fifth.
O God, Our Help in Ages Past.
Our God, Our Help in Ages Past.
Our Saviour's Golden Rule.
Sluggard, The.
Spare Us, O Lord, Aloud We Pray, *with music.*
Sweet Muse, Descend.
Through every age, eternal God.
We're Marching to Zion, *with music.*
When I Survey the Wondrous Cross.
Where Nothing Dwelt but Beasts of Prey, *with music.*
Why Do We Mourn Departing Friends? *with music.*
With songs and honors sounding loud.
**Wayman, Tom**
Poem Composed in Rogue River Park . . .
**Wazyk, Adam**
Ars Poetica.
Hotel.
Nike.
**Wearne, Alan**
Eating Out.
St. Bartholomew Remembers Jesus Christ as an Athlete.

**Weatherly, Frederick E.**
Nancy Lee, *with music.*
**Weatherly, Tom**
Arroyo.
Cantos, *sels.*
First Monday Scottsboro Alabama.
Imperial Thumbprint.
**Weaver, Roger**
To J.F.K. 14 Years After.
**Webb, Charles Henry ("John Paul")**
At the Ball!
Autumn Leaves.
**Webb, Francis**
Dawn Wind on the Islands.
Death at Winson Green, A.
Eyre All Alone.
Five Days Old.
For My Grandfather.
Harry.
Morgan's Country.
**Webb, Martha**
Any time,/ any time at all.
Bird Cry.
Cloud.
Looking Glass.
My Brother Hannu and the Poison Pool.
Taking and Losing.
**Webb, Mary**
Shell, The.
**Webb, Phyllis**
Antisong.
Ezra Pound.
For Fyodor.
Kropotkin Poems, The, *sel.*
Solitary Confinement.
Treblinka Gas Chamber.
**Webb, Thomas Harry Basil**
Ancient Prayer, An.
**Webber, Mary A.**
Warning, A.
**Weber, Bruce**
Nests.
**Weber, Nancy**
Tidying Up.
**Weber, Richard**
Elizabeth in Italy
Envying the Pelican.
For the Moment.
Head.
Lady and Gentleman.
Observation.
Poet's Day, The.
Primer for Schoolchildren, A.
Stephen's Green Revisited.
Visit to Bridge House, A.
**Weber, Ron**
Sunset.
View of the Earth from Space, A.
**Weber, Tom**
"I'm 92," Joe said.
**Webster, A. W.**
On the Wrong Side.
**Webster, Augusta**
Violet and the Rose, The ("The violet in the wood, that's sweet to-day").
**Webster, Diane**
Memory Movie.
**Webster, Henry De Lafayette**
Lorena.
**Webster, John**
Call for the Robin Redbreast and the Wren.

Devil's Law-Case, The, *sel.*
Duchess of Malfi, The, *sels.*
Hark, Now Everything Is Still.
I am come to make thy tomb.
Vanitas Vanitatum.
White Devil, The, *sels.*
**Weeden, Craig**
Calvin in the Attic Cleans.
Yachting in Arkansas.
**Weeks, Ramona**
Indian Graveyard, The.
**Weever, John**
De Se.
Prophecy of This Present Year 1600, A.
**Weever, Robert** *See* **Weaver, Robert**
**Weiant, Ted**
From a New and Wild Distance.
**Weigl, Bruce**
Limits of Departure, The.
**Weiman, Andrew**
Andy-Diana DNA Letter.
**Weiner, George**
Twilight at Noon.
**Weingarten, Roger**
Blue Bog Children.
Ethan Boldt.
Her Apron through the Trees.
Memoir.
These Obituaries of Rattlesnakes Being Eaten by the Hogs.
**Weirather, Larry**
Communion Portrait in Oil.
**Weismiller, Edward**
Boy, The.
Just Ask for a Demonstration.
Metamorphoses, The.
Poem: "I did nothing—/ Ended my hunger."
Soliloquies, The.
**Weiss, Neil**
Aging Athlete, The.
Roman Candle.
**Weiss, Ruth**
Vita-Sheet.
**Weiss, Theodore**
Art in America.
As You Like It.
Barracks Apt. 14.
Clothes Maketh the Man.
Dab of Color, A.
Egyptian Passage, An.
En Route.
Fire at Alexandria, The.
Last Day and the First, The.
Letter from the Pygmies, A.
Moral, The.
Off to Patagonia.
Preface: " 'Sonja Henie,' the young girl."
Sow's Ear, A.
This Narrow Stage.
Ultimate Antientropy, The.
Ways of Loving.
Web, The.
"Yes, But . . ."
**Weissbort, Daniel**
Aniversary.
Murder of a Community.
Walking Home at Night.
**Welburn, Ron**
Attica.
Avoidances.
Burgundy Phase.

Cecil County.
Delia Dalya of the Sponged Stilts.
Dog Dream.
Eulogy for Populations.
Hopes Are Full of Blisters ("Hopes of night places").
Percussions.
Vision of Montezuma Preserve, N.Y.

**Welch, Don**
Armless, The.
Bark.
Blue Heron

**Welch, James**
Across to the Peloponnese.
Arizona Highways.
Blackfeet, Blood and Piegan Hunters.
Blue Like Death.
Call to Arms.
Christmas Comes to Moccasin Flat.
D-Y Bar.
Directions to the Nomad.
Dreaming Winter.
Going to Remake This World.
Gravely.
Harlem, Montana: Just Off the Reservation.
In My First Hard Springtime.
In My Lifetime.
Lady in a Distant Face.
Magic Fox.
Man from Washington, The.
One More Time.
Only Bar in Dixon, The.
Plea to Those Who Matter.
Please Forward.
Renegade Wants Words, The.
Snow Country Weavers.
Spring for All Seasons.
Surviving.
Verifying the Dead.
Versatile Historian, The.
Visit.
Why I Didn't Go to Delphi.

**Welch, Lew**
Song Mt. Tamalpais Sings, The.
Step Out onto the Planet.
What strange pleasure do they get who'd.

**Welch, Marie De L.**
Ibis, The.
Mus Ridiculus Non.

**Welch, Noel**
Anne and the Peacock.

**Wellesley, Dorothy, Duchess of Wellington**
As Lambs into the Pen.
Horses.
Lighthouses.
Lost Lane.

**Wells, Carolyn**
Beggarly Bear, A.
Disobliging Bear, The.
Diversions of the Re-Echo Club.
Dragon, The.
Gnome Matter.
Happy Hyena, The.
How to Tell the Wild Animals.
Limerick: "Tutor who tooted the flute, A."
Old Lady from Dover, The.
Ossified Oyster, An.
Theater Hat, The.
Tidy Young Tapir, A.

Wild Worm, A.

**Wells, Marcus Morris**
Holy Spirit, Faithful Guide, *with music.*

**Wells, Will**
Fisherman, The.

**Welt, Bernard**
You stop shaving for a while and one morning.

**Welte, Lou Ann**
Those Last, Late Hours of Christmas Eve.

**Wendt, Ingrid**
Newest Banana Plant Leaf, The.
Personal Poem.

**Weöres, Sándor**
Lost Parasol, The, *sel.*

**Werner, Martina**
Monogram 4.
Monogram 29.
Monogram 23.

**Werth, Lloyd E.**
I'll Be Polite.

**Wescott, Glenway**
Poet at Night-Fall, The.
Summer Ending, The.

**Wescott, Roger**
Lily-Bell.
Mirror for Myself.

**Wesley, Charles**
Ah! Lovely Appearance of Death! *with music.*
Free Grace.
Gentle Jesus, Meek and Mild.
Hark, the Herald Angels Sing.
I Know That My Redeemer Lives, *with music.*
Jesus, Lover of My Soul.
Love Divine, *with music.*
Morning Hymn.
Wrestling Jacob.

**Wesley, John**
John Wesley's Rule.

**Wesley, Samuel (1662-1735)**
Boys and the Bubble, The.
Pindaric on the Grunting of a Hog, A.
To My Gingerbread Mistress, *sel.*

**Wesley, Samuel (1691-1739)**
Epigram on Miltonicks

**Wesley-Smith, Peter**
Walter Spaggot.

**West, John Foster**
Hill Hunger.

**West, Peter**
Vowels.

**West, Robert A.**
Come, Let Us Tune Our Loftiest Song, *with music.*

**Westendorf, Thomas P.**
I'll Take You Home Again, Kathleen.

**Westerfield, Nancy G.**
Carolers.
Where I Walk in Nebraska.

**Westmorland, Mildmay Fane, 2d Earl of**
Virtus Vera Nobilitas.

**Weston, Elizabeth**
Alphabet of Christmas Cheer.

**Weston, Mildred**
Central Park Tourney.
Query.

**Weston, Susan**
Seedlings.

**Westrup, J. M.**

Flying.

**Westwood, Thomas**
Mine Host of the "Golden Apple."

**Wever, Robert**
In Youth Is Pleasure.
Lusty Juventus, *sel.*

**Whalen, Philip**
For C.
Further Notice.
How Was Your Trip to L.A.?
Hymnus ad Patrem Sinensis.
"Plus Ça Change."
Road-Runner, The.

**Wharton, Anne**
Verses on the Snuff of a Candle, Made in Sickness.

**Wharton, Gordon**
Critic, The.
Plague, The.

**Wharton, Thomas Wharton, 1st Marquess of**
Lilliburlero (A New Song).

**Wheatley, Phillis**
Hymn to the Evening, An.
Hymn to the Morning, An.
Liberty and Peace.
On Being Brought from Africa to America.
On Virtue.
Should you, my lord, while you pursue my song.
To a Lady on the Death of Her Husband.
To His Excellency George Washington.
To the King's Most Excellent Majesty.
To the Right Honourable William, Earl of Dartmouth.
To the University of Cambridge, in New-England.

**Wheeler, Charles Enoch**
Adjuration.

**Wheelock, John Hall**
Afternoon: Amagansett Beach.
Ballad: "I dreamed I passed a doorway."
Beethoven.
Big I, The.
Black Panther, The.
Bonac.
Dear Men and Women.
Divine Insect, The.
Earth (" 'A planet doesn't explode' ").
Herring-Gull.
New York.
Song: "Oh, with the hunger of the sea, forever born anew."
This Pain.

**Wheelwright, John**
Bread-Word Giver.
Canal Street.
Father.
In Poets' Defence.
Skulls as Drums.
Titanic Litany.
Train Ride.
Why Must You Know?
Word Is Deed, The.

**Whigham, Peter**
Astapovo, or What Are We to Do, *sels.*
Erotion's Death.
Ingathering of Love, The, *sel.*
Love Poems of the VIth Dalai Lama,*sels.*

Orchard Is Not Cut Down, The ("The orchard is gone. A space").

**Whipple, George**
Three Cezannes.

**Whisler, Robert F.**
Collector, The.
Pigeons.

**Whitaker, Alexander**
Leaving the Dance.

**Whitbread, Thomas**
N. B. A. Prelim, Boston Garden.

**White, Christy**
Running under Street Lights.

**White, Claire Nicholas**
Roses of Queens, The.

**White, Elwyn Brooks**
Classic Waits for Me, A.
Commuters.
Dog around the Block.
Fashions in Dogs.
Marble-Top.
Window Ledge in the Atom Age.

**White, Gail**
Housecleaner, The.
Return to Astolat.

**White, Henry Kirke**
On the Death of Dermody, the Poet.

**White, James L.**
Anderson, Indiana.
Day Sleeper.
First Time, The.
Making Love to Myself.
Minneapolis White Castle, Winter '72.
Mover.

**White, Joan**
Afternoon Nap, The.

**White, Joseph Blanco**
Black Is a Soul.
To Night.

**White, Julie Herrick**
Like Children of the Summertime Playing at Cards.

**White, Mary Jane**
Lindeman.
Of All Plants, the Tree.

**White, Ned**
Apache Kid.
Bones in the Desert.

**White, Patrick**
Lyre.

**White, Terence Hanbury**
Witch's Work Song, The.

**Whitebird, Joanie**
Star.

**Whitehead, James**
About a Year after He Got Married He Would Sit Alone in an Abandoned Shack in a Cotton Field Enjoying Himself.
Delta Farmer in a Wet Summer.
First Lecture.
He Records a Little Song for a Smoking Girl.
Local Man Remembers Betty Fuller, A.
Local Man Remembers the Killing Ground, A.
Narrative Hooper and L.D.O. Sestina with a Long Last Line, The.
Statement and Vision, Two Signs of History.
Young Deputy, The.

**Whitehead, William**
Charge to the Poets, A, *sel.*
"Je Ne Sais Quoi," The.

**Whitehill, Karen**
Magdalene, Afterward.
Morning in Gainesville.
Penelope.

**Whitewing, Donna**
August 24, 1963—1:00 A.M.—Omaha.
Vegetable, I Will Not Be, A.

**Whitfield, James M.**
From America.

**Whiting, Nathan**
Good-by on an All Day Bean Planter.
Marijuana Patch on the State Hospital's Former Grounds.

**Whiting, Susan**
Sifting Stones at Capri.

**Whitman, Cedric**
Dissonance.

**Whitman, Ruth**
Almost Ninety.
Bubba Esther, 1888.
Castoff Skin.
Cutting the Jewish Bride's Hair.
Dan, the Dust of Masada Is Still in My Nostrils.
Flight.
Human Geography.
In the Smoking Car.
Marriage Wig, The.
Mediterranean.
Ripeness.
She Doesn't Want to Bring the Tides in Any More.
Sister Pharaoh.
Spring.
Translating.
Watching the Sun Rise over Mount Zion.
Yom Kippur: Fasting.

**Whitman, Walt**
Aboard at a Ship's Helm.
All the Past We Leave Behind, *with music.*
America.
Among the Multitude ("Among the men and women the multitude").
Are You the New Person Drawn toward Me?
Army Corps on the March, An.
As Adam Early in the Morning.
As I Ebb'd with the Ocean of Life.
As I Lay with My Head in Your Lap Camerado.
As If a Phantom Caress'd Me.
As Toilsome I Wandered Virginia's Woods.
Battle of the *Bonhomme Richard* and the *Serapis.*
Beat! Beat! Drums!
Beauty.
Bivouac on a Mountain Side.
Boston Ballad, A.
Broadway.
Broadway Pageant, A.
By Blue Ontario's Shore, *sels.*
By the Bivouac's Fitful Flame.
Carol of Death, The.
Cavalry Crossing a Ford.
City Dead-House, The.
City of Orgies.

Clear Midnight, A.
Come, Said My Soul.
Come Up from the Fields Father.
Crossing Brooklyn Ferry.
Dalliance of the Eagles, The.
Darest Thou Now O Soul.
Dismantled Ship, The.
Facing West from California's Shore.
Farm Picture, A.
First Dandelions, The.
From Montauk Point.
From Paumanok Starting I Fly like a Bird.
From Pent-up Aching Rivers.
Give Me the Splendid Silent Sun.
Glimpse, A.
Good-bye My Fancy!
Grass.
Had I the Choice.
I am the poet of the Body and I am the poet of the Soul.
I Hear America Singing.
I Hear It Was Charged against Me.
I Saw in Louisiana a Live-Oak Growing.
I Sit and Look Out.
I Think I Could Turn and Live with Animals.
In Paths Untrodden.
Joy, Shipmate, Joy.
Last Invocation, The.
Long, Too Long America.
Long I Thought That Knowledge Alone Would Suffice.
Look Down Fair Moon.
Mannahatta.
Me Imperturbe.
Miracles ("Why, who makes much of a miracle?").
Mocking-Bird, The.
My lovers suffocate me.
Night on the Prairies, *sel.*
Noiseless Patient Spider, A.
Now I will do nothing but listen.
O Captain! My Captain!
O Living Always, Always Dying.
Old War-Dreams.
On the Beach at Night.
On the Beach at Night Alone.
Once I Pass'd through a Populous City.
One's-Self I Sing.
Out of the Cradle Endlessly Rocking.
Out of the rolling ocean the crowd came a drop gently to me.
Passage to India, *sel.*
Poets to Come.
Prairie Sunset, A.
Reconciliation.
Respondez!
Runner, The.
Shut Not Your Doors.
Sight in Camp in the Daybreak Gray and Dim, A.
Sometimes with One I Love.
Song of Myself.
Song of the Banner at Daybreak, *sel.*
Song of the Open Road.
Sparkles from the Wheel.
Spontaneous Me.
Stallion, The.
Starting from Paumanok, *sel.*
There Was a Child Went Forth.
This Compost.

Thou Mother with Thy Equal Brood, *sel.*
To a Locomotive in Winter.
To a Stranger.
To Soar in Freedom and in Fullness of
   Power.
To the Garden the World.
To the Man-of-War Bird.
To You.
Trickle Drops.
Trippers and askers surround me.
Vigil Strange I Kept on the Field One
   Night.
Wallabout Martyrs, The.
Washington's Monument, February
   1885.
When I Heard at the Close of the Day.
When I Heard the Learn'd Astronomer.
When Lilacs Last in the Dooryard
   Bloom'd.
While the Schools and the Teachers Are
   Teaching.
Whispers of Heavenly Death.
Woman Waits for Me, A.
World below the Brine, The.
Wound-Dresser, The.

**Whitney, Isabella**
Sweet Nosegay, A, or Pleasant Posy,*sels.*

**Whitney, J. D.**
Bedtime.
Boy, The.
Gift,The.
Here.

**Whittaker, Andrew**
Images.

**Whittaker, Frederick**
Custer's Last Charge.

**Whittemore, Reed**
Clamming.
Day with the Foreign Legion, A.
Departure, The.
Fall of the House of Usher, The.
High School Band, The.
Ladders.
Ode to New York.
On the Suicide of a Friend.
Party, The.
Projection, A.
Radio under the Bed, The.
Science Fiction.
Seven Days, The, *sel.*
Still Life.
Teacher, A.
Thinking of Tents.
Walk Home, The.
Washington Interregnum.
Winter Scene, A.

**Whittier John Greenleaf**
Barbara Frietchie.
Barefoot Boy, The.
Cable Hymn, The.
Centennial Hymn.
Cities of the Plain, The.
Crucifixion, The.
Dear Lord and Father of Mankind, *with*
   *music.*
Drop Thy Still Dews.
Epitaph: "Bathsheba! to whom none
   ever said scat."
Eternal Goodness, The.
First-Day Thoughts.
Haschish, The.
Ichabod.

Immortal Love, Forever Full, *with music.*
In School Days.
Inscription: "Eagle, stooping from yon
   snow-blown peaks, The."
Lost Occasion, The.
Maud Muller.
Mother of Samson to Manoah, Her
   Husband, The.
My Playmate.
My Triumph.
O Thou! Whose Presence Went Before,
   *with music.*
Proem: "I love the old melodious lays."
Skipper Ireson's Ride.
Snow-bound; a Winter Idyl.
Telling the Bees.
Thou, Our Elder Brother.
To My Old Schoolmaster.
What the Birds Said.

**Whittingham, William**
Now Israel May Say, and That Truly,
   *with music.*

**Whur, Cornelius**
Female Friend, The.

**Wickham, Anna (Mrs. Patrick Hepburn)**
Conscience, The.
Dedication of the Cook.
Fired Pot, The.
Meditation at Kew.
Soul's Liberty.

**Widdemer, Margaret**
Invisible Playmate, The.
Sea Call.

**Widerberg, Siv**
Divorce.

**Wiebe, Dallas E.**
L'Elisir d'Amore.

**Wieber, Wendy**
One, The Other, And.

**Wieder, Laurance**
Letter to His Sister, A.
Paradise Rug, The.

**Wiegner, Kathleen**
At Times.
For the Woman Who Asked Me If I
   Believed in God and If I Pray.
Four Untitled Poems.
No Dice.
Proteus.
Silver Dollar.

**Wieners, John**
Le Chariot.
Moon Poems.
Trying to Forget.

**Wier, Dara**
Then the Skins Fall Apart.
This Cold Nothing Else.

**Wiggam, Lionel**
Grim Fairy Tale.

**Wigglesworth, Michael**
For Just Men Light Is Sown, *with music.*
God's Controversy with New-England.
Welcome, Sweet Rest, *with music.*

**Wilberforce, Samuel**
Impromptu.

**Wilbur, Richard**
Advice to a Prophet.
After the Last Bulletins.
All These Birds.
Altitudes.
April 5, 1974.

Baroque Wall-Fountain in the Villa
   Sciarra, A.
Beasts.
Beautiful Changes, The.
Bell Speech.
Black November Turkey, A.
Boy at the Window.
Ceremony.
Christmas Hymn, A.
Cigales.
Death of a Toad, The.
Digging for China.
Dubious Night, A.
Epistemology
Event, An.
Exeunt.
Eye, The.
Fire-Truck, A.
Folk Tune.
For Ellen.
Grasse: The Olive Trees.
Grasshopper, A.
He Was.
Hole in the Floor, A.
In a Churchyard.
In the Elegy Season.
In the Smoking Car.
Juggler.
Junk.
Lamarck Elaborated.
Late Aubade, A.
Looking into History.
Love Calls Us to the Things of This
   World.
Loves of the Puppets.
Marginalia.
Merlin Enthralled.
Mill, The.
Miltonic Sonnet for Mr. Johnson on His
   Refusal of Peter Hurd's Official
   Portrait, A.
Mind.
Museum Piece.
My Father Paints the Summer.
Objects.
On the Marginal Way.
Pangloss's Song.
Pardon, The.
Part of a Letter.
Piazza di Spagna, Early Morning.
Piccola Commedia.
Place Pigalle.
Playboy.
Potato.
Praise in Summer.
Running.
Seed Leaves.
Shallot, A.
Shame.
She.
Simile for Her Smile, A.
Simplification, A.
Speech for the Repeal of the McCarran
   Act.
Still, Citizen Sparrow.
To an American Poet Just Dead.
Transit.
Two Voices in a Meadow.
Tywater.
Undead, The.
Voice from under the Table, A.
Winter deepening, the hay all in, The.

"World without Objects Is a Sensible
    Emptiness, A."
Writer, The.
Year's End.
**Wilcox, Ella Wheeler**
Attraction.
Communism.
Today!
True Knight, The.
Will.
**Wild, Peter**
Dog Hospital.
For the El Paso Weather Bureau.
Gooseberries.
Horse, The.
Indians, The.
New Strip.
Passing Illness, A.
Riding Double.
Silver.
Snakes.
Steakbones.
Thomas and Charlie.
Variation.
**Wild, Robert**
Epitaph for a Godly Man's Tomb.
Iter Boreale.
Poem upon the Imprisonment of Mr.
    Calamy in Newgate, A.
**Wilde, Lady Jane Francesca ("Speranza")**
Famine Year, The.
**Wilde, Oscar**
Ballad of Reading Gaol, The, *abr.*
Disciple, The.
E. Tenebris.
Harlot's House, The.
Hélas!
Impression du Matin.
Impressions: II. La Mer.
Preface to the Picture of Dorian Gray.
Sonnet on Hearing the Dies Irae Sung in
    the Sistine Chapel.
Theocritus.
Theoretikos.
**Wilde, Richard Henry**
Oh! dearer by far than the land of our
    birth.
To the Mocking Bird.
**Wiljer, Robert**
Moose.
**Wilk, Melvin**
Blessing.
Learning to Speak.
**Wilkins, Mary E.** *See* **Freeman, Mary E.
    Wilkins**
**Wilkinson, Iris Guiver.** *See* **"Hyde,
    Robin"**
**Will, Frederic**
Long Lonely Lover of the Highway.
**Willard, Emma Hart**
Rock'd in the Cradle of the Deep, *with
    music.*
**Willard, Nancy**
Angels in Winter.
Clearing the Air.
For You, Who Didn't Know.
Foxfire.
Freak Show, The.
In the Hospital of the Holy Physician.
Marriage Amulet.
Poet's Wife Makes Him a Door So He
    Can Find the Way Home, The.

Way of Keeping, A.
**Willems, J. Rutherford**
Hebrew Letters in the Trees.
**Williams, Charles**
Mount Badon.
Taliessin's Song of the Unicorn.
**Williams, Sir Charles Hanbury**
Verses ("Poor fellow, what is it to
    you").
**Williams, Charles Kenneth**
Hood.
Spit.
**Williams, Claude** *and* **Lee Hays**
Roll the Union On.
**Williams, Edward**
Poet's Arbour in the Birchwood,
    The.
**Williams, Eliseus (Eifion Wyn)**
Heather Flowers.
**Williams, Emmett**
Like Attracts Like.
**Williams, Gwyn**
Aspects of Now, *sel.*
**Williams, Harry H.**
In the Shade of the Old Apple Tree, *with
    music.*
**Williams, Hugh Menai.** *See* **Menai, Huw**
**Williams, Hugo**
Butcher, The.
Couple Upstairs, The.
Some Kisses from "The Kama Sutra."
**Williams, John (b. 1922)**
Accessions to Autumn.
At the Theatre.
Cold Coffee.
Letter from the North Atlantic.
On Reading Aloud My Early Poems.
Passage.
Skaters, The.
**Williams, John A.**
Safari West.
**Williams, Jonathan**
Ancient Days, The.
Anthropophagites See a Sign on NC
    Highway 177 That Looks like Heaven,
    The.
Dealer's Choice and the Dealer Shuffles.
Hermit Cackleberry Brown, on Human
    Vanity, The.
Mahler, *sel.*
Mrs. Sadie Grindstaff, Weaver and
    Factotum.
News from Other Small Worlds.
Priapupation of Queen Pasiphaë, The.
Strung Out with Elgar on a Hill, *sel.*
Symphony No. 3, in D Minor.
Three Sayings from Highlands, North
    Carolina.
Uncle Iv Surveys His Domain from His
    Rocker.
**Williams, Kim**
Requiem for a River.
**Williams, Miller**
Alcide Pavageau.
Caterpillar, The.
Getting Experience.
Let Me Tell You.
Love Poem: "Six o'clock and/ the sun
    rises..."
Mardi Gras.
Neighbor, The.
Of Human Bondage.

On the Last Page of the Last Yellow Pad
    in Rome before Taking Off for Dacca
    on Air Bangladesh.
Plain.
Sale.
Why God Permits Evil: For Answers to
    This Question of Interest to Many
    Write Bible Answers Dept. E-7.
Words.
**Williams, Oscar**
Golden Fleece, The.
Shopping for Meat in Winter.
Total Revolution, A.
**Williams, Patrick**
Murphy.
**Williams, Ralph Tabor**
Searching.
**Williams, Randall**
Laying By.
**Williams, Rhydwen**
Baboon, The.
**Williams, Richard**
Fable of the Airplanes, The.
Rita Rio.
Savarin.
Way It Is, The.
**Williams, Roger**
Boast not proud English, of thy birth
    and blood.
How busie are the sonnes of men?
If Birds That Neither Sow nor Reap,
    *with music.*
When Sun Doth Rise, *with music.*
**Williams, Shirley**
Countin the Ol One Hundred.
If He Let Us Go Now.
Killing of the Birds, The.
**Williams, Tennessee**
Carrousel Tune.
Gold Tooth Blues.
Heavenly Grass.
Kitchen Door Blues.
My Love Was Light.
Paper Lantern, The.
Recuerdo, *sel.*
Sugar in the Cane.
Which Is My Little Boy.
**Williams, Theodore Chickering**
Hast Thou Heard It, O My Brother, *with
    music.*
My Country, to Thy Shore, *with music.*
When Thy Heart with Joy O'erflowing,
    *with music.*
**Williams, Sir Thomas Herbert Parry-.** *See*
    **Parry-Williams, Sir Thomas Herbert**
**Williams, Waldo**
Daffodil.
In Two Fields.
Summer Cloud, A.
**Williams, William (Pantycelyn)**
Guide Me, O Thou Great Jehovah.
I gaze across the distant hills.
Marriage in Eden, The.
View of Christ's Kingdom, A, *sel.*
**Williams, William Carlos**
Act, The.
All That Is Perfect in Woman.
Après le Bain.
Artist, The.
Asphodel, That Greeny Flower, *sels.*
At Kenneth Burke's Place.
At the Ball Game.

Ballad of Faith.
Between Walls.
Birdsong, The.
Bull, The.
Burning the Christmas Greens.
Calypsos, *sels.*
Catholic Bells, The.
Children, The.
Children's Games.
Clouds, The.
Coda.
Complaint.
Complete Destruction.
Corn Harvest, The.
Dance, The.
Danse Russe.
Dawn.
Death.
Dedication for a Plot of Ground.
Delineaments of the Giants, The.
Descent of Winter, The (Section 10/30).
Elegy for D. H. Lawrence, An.
Exercise No. 2.
Eyeglasses, The.
First Praise.
Fish.
Flowers by the Sea.
Folded Skyscraper, A, *sel.*
For Eleanor and Bill Monahan.
4th of July.
Gift, The.
Great Figure, The.
Hemmed-in Males.
History of Love, A.
Horse Show, The.
House, The.
Intelligent Sheepman and the New Cars, The.
Io Baccho!
Iris.
January Morning.
Jungle, The.
Lament: "What face, in the water."
Landscape with the Fall of Icarus.
Last Turn, The.
Le Médecin Malgré Lui.
Lear.
Lighthearted William.
Locust Tree in Flower, The.
Lonely Street, The.
Loving Dexterity, The.
March.
Marriage.
Mental Hospital Garden, The.
Metric Figure.
Nantucket.
Negro Woman, A.
Ol' Bunk's Band.
On Gay Wallpaper.
Orchestra, The.
Pastoral: "When I was younger."
Paterson, *sels.*
Paterson ("Before the grass is out the people are out").
Paterson—The Strike.
Pictures from Brueghel, *sels.*
Place (Any Place) to Transcend All Places.
Poem: "As the cat."
Poem: "On getting a card."
Poem: "Plastic surgeon who has, The."
Poem: "Rose fades, The."

Poor, The.
Portrait of a Lady.
Pot of Flowers, The.
Predicter of Famine, The.
Preface: "To make a start."
Proletarian Portrait.
Promenade, *sel.*
Queen-Ann's-Lace.
Raleigh Was Right.
Red Wheelbarrow, The.
Return to Work, The.
River Rhyme.
Rogation Sunday.
Rose, The.
Russia.
St. Valentine.
Sea-Elephant, The.
Semblables, The.
Slow Movement.
Smell!
Sonnet in Search of an Author.
Sort of a Song, A.
Sparrow, The.
Spring and All ("By the road to the contagious hospital").
Stolen Peonies, The.
Term, The.
Testament of Perpetual Change, The.
These.
These Purists.
Thinker, The.
This Is Just to Say.
To ("A child (a boy) bouncing").
To a Dog Injured in the Street.
To a Friend.
To a Friend Concerning Several Ladies.
To a Poor Old Woman.
To a Solitary Disciple.
To an Elder Poet.
To Be Recited to Flossie on Her Birthday.
To Elsie.
To Flossie.
To Ford Madox Ford in Heaven.
To Greet a Letter-Carrier.
To Mark Anthony in Heaven.
To Waken an Old Lady.
Tract.
Trala Trala Trala La-le-la.
Trees, The.
Unison, A.
United States, The.
Wanderer, The: A Rococo Study, *sel.*
Widow's Lament in Springtime, The.
Willow Poem.
Wind Increases, The.
Winter.
Words, the Words, the Words, The.
Yachts, The.
Yellow Flower, The.
Young Housewife, The.
Young Sycamore.
Youth and Beauty.
**Willis, Gary**
Assignment: Descriptive Essay.
**Willis, Love Maria**
Father, Hear the Prayer We Offer, *with music.*
**Willis, Nathaniel Parker**
Declaration, The.
Lady Jane, The: A Humorous Novel in Rhyme, *sels.*

To Helen in a Huff.
To the Lady in the Chemisette with Black Buttons.
**Willson, Dixie**
Mist and All, The.
**Willson, Meredith**
Seventy Six Trombones, *with music.*
**Wilmot, John, Earl of Rochester.** *See* **Rochester, John Wilmot, 2nd Earl of**
**Wilson, A. S.**
Hoddesdon.
**Wilson, August**
Theme One: The Variations.
**Wilson, Brian** *and* **Mike Love.** *See* **Love, Mike** *and* **Brian Wilson**
**Wilson, Charles G.**
Ballad of New Orleans.
**Wilson, Edmund**
Drafts for a Quatrain.
Not Here.
Something for My Russian Friends.
**Wilson, Edwin H.**
Where Is Our Holy Church? *with music.*
**Wilson, Fred**
How Do You Do, *Alabama*!
**Wilson, Gina**
Jim-Jam Pyjamas.
**Wilson, Grace**
Seaway.
**Wilson, J. F.**
Coloratura Named Luna, A.
Double Entendre.
Fellow Named Hall, A.
Let X Equal Half.
**Wilson, John (1588-1677)**
Armada, 1588, The.
**Wilson, John (1591-1667)**
Confess We All, before the Lord, *with music.*
For Lo! My Jonah How He Slumped, *with music.*
Whoso Would See This Song of Heavenly Choice, *with music.*
**Wilson, Keith**
Arrival of My Mother, The.
Celt in Me, The.
Classes.
Coyotes Fighting.
Day of the Wolf.
Lake above Santos, The.
Morning of the Wolf, The.
Old Toby.
On Drinking and a New Moon through the Window.
Rancher, The.
Touch of Moonlight, The.
**Wilson, Patrick Seymour**
Anchorage, The.
Cuvier Light.
Farewell, The: "And so, one day when the tide was away out."
Precious Pearl, The.
Tree, The.
**Wilson, Ramona**
Bags Packed and We Expected This.
Eveningsong.
Keeping Hair.
Late in Fall.
Meeting, The.
Overnight Guest.
Reading Indian Poetry.
Spring at Fort Okanogan.

**Wilson** *(continued)*
Spring in Virginia.
Summer.

**Wilson, Robert Noble Denison**
Elegy in a Presbyterian Burying-Ground.

**Wilson, Robley, Jr.**
At Night.
Bridesmaid.
Marauder, The.
Porcupines.
Yankee Poet.

**Winans, A. D.**
For Paddy O'Sullivan.
My Woman.
News from the V. A.
North Beach Poem.
Rebirth.

**Winant, Fran**
Christopher St. Liberation Day, June 28, 1970.
Nora.
Poem to My New Jacket.
Yesterday.

**Winch, Terence**
Excuses.
Kalorama Triangle, The.
Loss.

**Winchester, Caleb T.**
Lord Our God Alone Is Strong, The, *with music.*

**Winchester, Elhanan**
Behold with Joy, *with music.*

**Winchilsea, Anne Finch, Countess of**
Appology, The.
Clarinda's Indifference at Parting with Her Beauty.
Introduction, The: "Did I, my lines intend for publick view."
Letter to Dafnis, A.
Nocturnal Reverie, A.
On Myselfe.
Petition for an Absolute Retreat, The.
To Melancholy.
To the Nightingale.
To the Rt. Hon. the Lady C. Tufton.
Trail All Your Pikes.

**Winder, Barbara**
Catching a Horse.
Cuban Refugees on Key Biscayne.
February.
Limits of Equitation, The.
On the Farm.
Polar Bear at Crandon Park Zoo, Miami, The.
Problem of Wild Horses, The.

**Wine, Maria**
Love Me.
Woman, you are afraid of the forest.

**Wingate, Philip**
I Don't Want to Play in Your Yard, *with music.*

**Winkler, Manfred**
I Love What Is Not.
If My Hands Were Mute.
One Goes with Me along the Shore.
She.
Somewhere You Exist.

**Winner, Robert**
Banjo, The.
Miss Alderman.

**Winner, Septimus ("Alice Hawthorne")**
Coolie Chinee, The.
Der Deitcher's Dog, *with music.*

Lilliputian's Beer Song.
Listen to the Mocking Bird.
Ten Little Injuns.
Whispering Hope, *with music.*

**Winslow, Pete**
Only the Sky.

**Winsor, Frederick**
Little Bo-Peep.
Solomon Grundy.
Space Child's Mother Goose, The, *sels.*

**Winstanley, John**
Epigram on Florio.
Inventory of the Furniture of a Collegian's Chamber, An.
Last Will and Testament, A.
On a Certain Effeminate Peer.
On a Stingy Beau.

**Winters, Bayla**
Finisterra.
Janis Joplin and the Folding Company.

**Winters, Yvor**
Apollo and Daphne.
April.
Aspen's Song, The.
At the San Francisco Airport.
Before Disaster.
California Oaks, The.
Castle of Thorns, The.
Elegy, An: "Noon is beautiful, The: the perfect wheel."
Fable, The: "Beyond the steady rock the steady sea."
Fragment, A: "I cannot find my way to Nazareth."
Grave, The.
Hawk's Eyes.
Invaders, The.
John Day, Frontiersman.
John Sutter.
Manzanita, The.
Moralists, The.
Night of Battle.
Nocturne for October 31st, A.
Ode on the Despoilers of Learning in an American University, An.
On Teaching the Young.
Orpheus.
Precision, The.
"Quod Tegit Omnia."
Rows of Cold Trees, The.
Shadow's Song, The.
Sir Gawaine and the Green Knight.
Sleep.
Slow Pacific Swell, The.
Song in Passing, A.
Song: "Where I walk out."
Static Autumn.
Theseus: A Trilogy.
Time and the Garden.
To Emily Dickinson.
To My Infant Daughter ("Alas, that I should be").
To the Holy Spirit.
To the Moon.
Upper Meadows, The.

**Wise, Isaac M**
In Mercy, Lord, Incline Thine Ear, *with music.*

**Wise, Joseph**
Glory, *with music.*

**Wissinger, Kay**
In the Lake Country.

**Wister, Owen**
Pinto, The.
Sheep Ranching.
Smugglers, The.
Ten Thousand Cattle.

**Witheford, Hubert**
Arena, The.
At the Discharge of Cannon Rise the Drowned.
Barbarossa.
Bondage.
Cactuses, The.
Cloud Burst.
Displacement, The.
Elegy in the Orongorongo Valley.
King of Kings.
Snow.
Waters, Indeed, Are to the Palate, Bitter, The.
White Goddess.

**Wither, George**
Fair Virtue, *sel.*
For Scholars and Pupils.
I Loved a Lass.
Lord, Many Times Thou Pleased Art, *with music.*
Lover's Resolution, A.
Marigold, The.
Philarete to His Mistress, *sel.*
Rhomboidal Dirge, *sel.*
Rocking Hymn, A.

**Witherspoon, Naomi Long.** *See* **Madgett, Naomi Long**

**Witherup, William**
Crows.
Depression.

**Withington, Leonard**
O Saviour of a World Undone, *with music.*

**Witt, Harold**
Cheetah, The.
Conservative.
Dog Alive.
Ecology.
Genesis.
Her Birthday.
Mrs. Asquith Tries to Save the Jacarandas.
Rushmore ("Rushing to Rushmore, speeding as we read").
Surprise ("Surprise, surprise, they're flying in today").
Walking Milwaukee.

**Witt, Sandra**
Fish.

**Wittlin, Jozef**
Hymn about a Spoonful of Soup, A.
On the Jewish Day of Judgment in the Year 1942 (5703).
St. Francis of Assisi and the Miserable Jews.
To the Jews in Poland.

**Wittlinger, Ellen**
Second Heart, The.

**Woddis, Roger**
Ethics for Everyman.
Nothing Sacred.

**Wodehouse, Pelham Grenville**
Gourmet's Love-Song, The.
To William (Whom We Have Missed.)

**Woessner, Warren**
Airwaves.

Chippewa Lake Park.
Driving to Sauk City.
Flitcraft's Woods.
Looking at Power.
Lost Country.
Navajo Poem.

**Woiwode, Larry**
Deserted Barn, A.

**Wojahn, David**
Cold Glow: Icehouses.
Heaven for Railroad Men.

**Wolcot, John.** *See* **"Pindar, Peter"**

**Wolcott, Samuel**
Christ for the World! We Sing, *with music.*
Father! I Own Thy Voice, *with music.*

**Wolfe, Aaron R.**
Complete in Thee, No Work of Mine, *with music.*
Parting Hymn We Sing, A, *with music.*

**Wolfe, Charles**
Burial of Sir John Moore after [*or* at] Corunna, The.

**Wolfe, Edgar**
Sparrows in College Ivy.

**Wolfe, Humbert**
Autumn.
Blackbird, The.
Child Unborn, The.
D. H. Lawrence and James Joyce.
Dean Inge.
Gray Squirrel, The.
Green Candles.
Hilaire Belloc.
Wardour Street.
When lads have done with labor.
You cannot hope.

**Wolfe, Thomas**
Ben.
That Sharp Knife.

**Wolfenstein, Alfred**
Exodus 1940.

**Wolfert, Adrienne**
Golda.

**Wolfert, Helen**
Cat, The.
Grass, The.
Preparation of the Body, The.
Where the Mind Meets the Moon in Revolt.

**Wolff, Bill**
What a Grand and Glorious Feeling.

**Wolfskehl, Karl**
From Mount Nebo.
Shekhina.
We Go.

**Wong, Shawn**
Elegy for a Greenhouse.
Love among Friends.

**Wood, Charles Erskine Scott**
Sagebrush.
Water-Hole, The.

**Wood, John A.**
Morning from My Office Window.

**Wood, Marnie** *and* Harnie Wood
Corpulent Pig, A.

**Wood, Mary**
Flying Changes.

**Wood, Peggy**
My Aunt.

**Wood, Susan**
Learning to Live without You.

**Wood-Thompson, Susan**
Territory.

**Woodcock, George**
Green Grass and Sea.

**Woodford, Bruce P.**
Going Through.

**Woods, John**
Deaths of Paragon, The.
Everyone Born in 1926.
Five Dreams, The.
Girl Who Had Borne Too Much, The.
Guns.
Lie Closed, My Lately Loved.
Looking Both Ways before Crossing.
Lying Down with Men and Women.
Making Money.
Outburst from a Little Face.
Traveling North.
What Do You Do When It's Spring?
Woods Gets Religion.

**Woods, Nancy**
I Read a Tight-fisted Poem Once.

**Woodworth, Samuel**
Hunters of Kentucky, The.
Old Oaken Bucket, The.

**Woolsey, Sarah Chauncey.** *See* **"Coolidge, Susan"**

**Woolson, Constance Fenimore**
Kentucky Belle.

**Wooton, Sir Henry.** *See* **Wotton, Sir Henry**

**Wordsworth, Christopher**
All Saints' Day, Nov. 1.

**Wordsworth, Dorothy**
Address to a Child during a Boisterous Winter Evening.
Cottager to Her Infant, The.
Loving and Liking.

**Wordsworth, Elizabeth**
Good and Clever.

**Wordsworth, William**
Affliction of Margaret, The.
After-Thought.
Airey-Force Valley.
Alice Fell; or, Poverty.
Anecdote for Fathers.
Apology.
At Florence.
At the Grave of Burns, 1803.
Authentic Tidings.
Blest statesman he, whose mind's unselfish will.
Brothers, The.
Calais, August, 1802.
Calais, August 15, 1802.
Cave of Staffa, I ("We saw, but surely, in the motley crowd").
Cave of Staffa, II ("Ye shadowy beings, that have rights and claims").
Character of the Happy Warrior.
Characteristics of a Child Three Years Old.
Childhood and School-Time.
Complaint, A.
Complaint of a Forsaken Indian Woman, The.
Composed by the Sea-Side, near Calais, August 1802.
Composed by the Side of Grasmere Lake.
Composed in the Valley near Dover, on the Day of Landing.

Composed near Calais, on the Road Leading to Ardres.
Composed on a May Morning, 1838.
Composed upon an Evening of Extraordinary Splendour and Beauty.
Composed upon Westminster Bridge, September 3, 1802.
Convict, The.
Daffodils.
Dedication: "Memory of one particular hour, The."
Elegiac Verses.
Ellen Irwin; or, The Braes of Kirtle.
Even as a dragon's eye that feels the stress.
Evening Walk, An.
Expostulation and Reply.
Extempore Effusion upon the Death of James Hogg.
Farewell, A: "Farewell, thou little nook of mountain-ground."
Female Vagrant, The.
Flowers of January.
Fountain, The.
Glow-Worm, The.
Goody Blake, and Harry Gill.
Great men have been among us; hands that penned.
Guilt.
I grieved for Buonaparté, with a vain.
I have thoughts that are fed by the sun.
I Wandered Lonely as a Cloud.
Idiot Boy, The.
If thou indeed derive thy light from Heaven.
It Is a Beauteous Evening, Calm and Free.
Labourer's Noon-Day Hymn, The.
Laodamia.
Last of the Flock, The.
Leaves that rustled on this oak-crowned hill, The.
Liberty, *sel.*
Lines Composed a Few Miles above Tintern Abbey.
Lines Left upon a Seat in a Yew-Tree.
Lines Written in Early Spring.
London, 1802 ("Milton! thou shouldst be living...").
Longest Day, The.
Louisa.
Lucy, *complete, in 5 parts.*
Lucy Gray; or, Solitude.
Lyre! though such power do in thy magic live.
Mad Mother, The.
Matron of Jedborough and Her Husband, The, *sel.*
Matthew.
Michael: A Pastoral Poem.
Most sweet it is with unuplifted eyes.
Mutability.
My Heart Leaps Up When I Behold.
Night-Piece, A.
Nuns fret not at their convent's narrow room.
Nutting.
O Friend! I Know Not Which Way I Must Look.
Ode: Intimations of Immortality from Recollections of Early Childhood.

Ode on the Installation of His Royal Highness Prince Albert.
Ode to Duty.
Old Cumberland Beggar, The.
Old Man Travelling; Animal Tranquillity and Decay, a Sketch.
On the Departure of Sir Walter Scott from Abbotsford, for Naples.
On the Extinction of the Venetian Republic.
On the Power of Sound.
One Summer Evening.
Pass of Kirkstone, The.
Personal Talk.
Pet Lamb, The.
Peter Bell.
Place of Burial in the South of Scotland, A.
Poet, A!—He Hath Put His Heart to School.
Poet's Epitaph, A.
Power of armies is a visible thing, The.
Prelude, The [or, Growth of a Poet's Mind].
Prelude: "In desultory walk through orchard grounds."
Recluse, The; or, Home at Grasmere.
Resolution and Independence.
Return.
Reverie of Poor Susan, The.
Rise up, thou monstrous ant-hill on the plain.
River Duddon, The, *sels.*
Ruined Cottage, The.
Ruth.
Scorn Not the Sonnet.
September, 1819.
September 1802. Near Dover.
September 1, 1802.
She Dwelt among the Untrodden Ways.
She Was a Phantom of Delight.
Simon Lee.
Skaters, The.
Small Celandine, The.
Solitary Reaper, The.
Song at the Feast of Brougham Castle.
Sonnet in Allusion to Various Recent Histories and Notices of the French Revolution.
Sonnet on the Projected Kendal and Windermere Railway.
Sparrow's Nest, The.
Stanzas Written in My Pocket-Copy of Thomson's "Castle of Indolence."
Steamboats, Viaducts, and Railways.
Stepping-Stones, The.
Stepping Westward.
Strange Fits of Passion Have I Known.
Suggested by a Picture of the Bird of Paradise.
Sun has long been set, The.
Surprised by Joy—Impatient as the Wind.
Tables Turned, The.
There Was a Boy.
These chairs they have no words to utter.
Thorn, The.
Thought of a Briton on the Subjugation of Switzerland.
Three Years She Grew in Sun and Shower.

Thus did my days pass on, and now at length.
'Tis said, that some have died for love.
To a Butterfly ("I've watched you now a full half-hour").
To a Butterfly ("Stay near me—do not take thy flight!").
To a Highland Girl.
To a Skylark.
To a Young Lady.
To B. R. Haydon.
To H. C.
To Joanna.
To My Sister.
To Sleep.
To the Cuckoo.
To the Men of Kent. October, 1803.
To the Same Flower.
To the Small Celandine.
To Toussaint L'Ouverture.
Two April Mornings, The.
Uncertainty.
We Are Seven.
We Must Be Free or Die.
When I have borne in memory what has tamed.
Where lies the land to which yon ship must go?
White Doe of Rylstone, The: or, The Fate of the Nortons.
Why art thou silent! Is thy love a plant.
Wisdom and Spirit of the universe!
"With How Sad Steps, O Moon, Thou Climb'st the sky."
World Is Too Much with Us, The.
Written after the Death of Charles Lamb.
Written in March.
Written in the Album of a Child.
Yarrow Revisited.
Yarrow Unvisited.
Yarrow Visited.
Yes, it was the mountain echo.
Yew Trees.

**Work, Henry Clay**
Father, Dear Father, Come Home with Me Now.
Grandfather's Clock.
Kingdom Coming, *with music.*
Marching through Georgia.
Ship That Never Returned, The.
Wake Nicodemus.

**Worley, James**
De Gustibus.
Mark Van Doren.
Touchstone.

**Worsley, Alice F.**
Has Been.

**Worth, Douglas**
Ghetto Summer School.
War Bride.

**Worth, Kathryn**
Circus Elephants.

**Worth, Valerie**
Christmas Lights.
Christmas Ornaments.
Fireworks.
Haunted House.
Pumpkin.

**Wortman, Denis**
Today beneath Benignant Skies, *with music.*

**Wotton, Sir Henry**
Character of a Happy Life, The.
Hymn to My God in a Night of My Late Sickness, A.
On His Mistress, [*or* Mistris], the Queen of Bohemia.
Upon the Death of Sir Albert Morton's Wife.
Upon the Sudden Restraint of the Earl of Somerset, Then Falling from [*or* out of] Favour.

**Wratislaw, Theodore**
Eros D'Aute.
Orchids.

**Wray, Elizabeth**
As the Snow Falls, Another Breathes in an Adjoining Room.
Love Poem, I.

**Wrench, Margaret Stanley**
In the Radiotherapy Unit.

**Wright, Bruce McM.**
African Affair, The.

**Wright, Carolyne**
Early Fall: The Adirondacks.
Trestle Bridge, The.

**Wright, Celeste Turner**
Yugoslav Cemetery.

**Wright, Charles**
Blackwater Mountain.
Called Back.
Chinoiserie.
Death.
Delta Traveller.
Depression before the Solstice.
Dog Creek Mainline.
Fever Toy, The.
Firstborn.
Negatives.
New Poem, The.
Nightletter.
Northhanger Ridge.
Photographs.
Snake Handling Religious Service.
Tattoos, *sels.*
Yellow.

**Wright, Charles David**
Shaving.

**Wright, Constance**
I'm Bringing You Back.

**Wright, David**
Grasmere Sonnets.
Invocation to the Goddess, An.
Kleomedes.
Monologue of a Deaf Man.

**Wright, Franz**
View from an Institution.

**Wright, Fred W., Jr.**
Couch, The.

**Wright, Helen M.**
Golden Grain.

**Wright, James**
Arrangements with Earth for Three Dead Friends.
Ars Poetica: Some Recent Criticism.
As I Step over a Puddle at the End of Winter, I Think of an Ancient Chinese Governor.
At the Slackening of the Tide.
At Thomas Hardy's Birthplace, 1953.
Autumn Begins in Martins Ferry, Ohio.
Before the [*or* a] Cashier's Window in a Department Store.

Blessing, A.
Blue Teal's Mother.
Breath of Air, A.
Centenary Ode, A: Inscribed to Little Crow, Leader of the Sioux Rebellion.
Complaint.
Confession to J. Edgar Hoover.
Depressed by a Book of Bad Poetry, I Walk toward an Unused Pasture and Invite the Insects to Join Me.
Eisenhower's Visit to Franco, 1959.
Evening.
Gesture by a Lady with an Assumed Name, A.
I Try to Waken and Greet the World Once Again.
I Was Afraid of Dying.
In Ohio.
In Response to a Rumor That the Oldest Whorehouse in Wheeling, West Virginia, Has Been Condemned.
In Shame and Humiliation.
In Terror of Hospital Bills.
Jewel, The.
Late November in a Field.
Lights in the Hallway, The.
Living by the Red River.
Love in a Warm Room in Winter.
Lying in a Hammock at William Duffy's Farm.
Mad Fight Song for William S. Carpenter, 1966, A.
Mantova.
March.
Milkweed.
Miners.
Minneapolis Poem, The.
Mutterings over the Crib of a Deaf Child.
Names in Monterchi: To Rachel.
Northern Pike.
October Ghosts.
Ohio Valley Swains.
Old Age Compensation.
Old Dog in the Ruins of the Graves at Arles, The.
On Minding One's Own Business.
Outside Fargo, North Dakota.
Paul.
Poem about Breasts, A.
Prayer to the Lord Ramakrishna, A.
Presentation of Two Birds to My Son, A.
Redwings.
Saint Judas.
Sheep in the Rain.
Simon and the Tarantula.
Small Frogs Killed on the Highway.
Song for the Middle of the Night, A.
Speak.
Spring Images.
Stages on a Journey Westward.
Three Sentences for a Dead Swan.
To a Blossoming Pear Tree.
To a Fugitive.
To a Troubled Friend.
To Flood Stage Again.
To the Muse.
Trouble.
Two Hangovers.
Two Poems about President Harding.
Two Postures beside a Fire.
Venice.

Verona.
Vestal in the Forum, The.
Way to Make a Living, A.
What Is Truth?
Written in a Copy of Swift's Poems, for Wayne Burns.
Youth.
**Wright, Jay**
Altars and Sacrifice.
Charge, The.
Dead, The.
Death as History.
Homecoming Singer, The.
Invitation to Madison County, An.
This morning I threw the windows.
Wednesday Night Prayer Meeting.
**Wright, Judith**
Brother and Sisters.
Bull, The.
Bullocky.
Cycads, The.
Document, A.
Egrets.
Eve to Her Daughters.
Extinct Birds.
Forest, The.
Hawthorn Hedge, The.
Legend.
Lyrebirds.
Night Herons.
Old Prison, The.
Sanctuary.
Some Words.
South of My Days.
Sports Field.
Storm.
Surfer, The.
Train Journey.
Woman to Child.
Woman to Man.
**Wright, Richard**
Ah Feels It in Mah Bones.
Between the World and Me.
Child of the Dead and Forgotten Gods.
Four Haiku.
Hokku Poems.
I Am a Red Slogan.
I Have Seen Black Hands.
Strength.
Transcontinental.
We of the Streets.
**Wright, Sarah E.**
To Some Millions Who Survive Joseph E. Mander, Sr.
Until They Have Stopped.
**Wrigley, Robert**
Pain.
Rattlesnake, The.
**Wroth, Mary Sidney (Countess of Montgomery)**
Duke's Song, The.
Lindamira's Complaint.
Pamphilia to Amphilanthus.
Pamphilia's Sonnet.
Urania, sels.
Verses of the Talkative Knight, The.
**Wu Ti, Emperor**
People Hide Their Love.
**Wu Tsao**
Bitter rain in my courtyard.
**Wyatt, Andrea**
Founding Fathers, sel.

**Wyatt, Sir Thomas**
Alas, madam, for stealing of a kiss.
Appeal, An.
Behold, love, thy power how she despiseth!
Blame Not My Lute for He Must Sownde [or Sound].
Courtier's Life, The.
Divers [or Dyvers] doᵗh[e] use as I have heard and know.
Eche man me telleth I chaunge moost my devise.
Farewell, all my welfare.
Farewell: "What should I say."
Forget Not Yet.
He is not ded that somtyme hath a fall.
Help Me to Seek.
How oft have I, my dere and cruell foo.
I abide and abide and better abide.
If fansy would favor.
If waker care, if sodayne pale coulor.
In Eternum.
Is it possible [or Ys yt possyble].
It may be good, like it who list.
Lament my losse, my labor, and my payne.
Lover Complaineth the Unkindness of His Love, The.
Lover Having Dreamed Enjoying of His Love, Complaineth That the Dream Is Not either Longer or Truer, The.
Lover Showeth [or Sheweth] How He Is Forsaken of Such as He Sometime Enjoyed, The.
Luckes, my faire falcon, and your fellowes all.
Lyve thowe gladly, yff so thowe may.
Madame, withouten many wordes.
Marvaill no more all tho.
Me list no more to sing.
Mye love toke skorne my servise to retaine.
Myne [or Mine] owne John Poyntz, sins [or since] ye delight to know.
Now must I lerne to lyve at rest.
Once as methought Fortune me kissed.
Piller pearisht is whearto I lent, The.
Quondam was I in my leady's grace.
Renouncing of Love, A.
Resound my voyse, ye wodes that here me plain.
Robyn, A/ Joly Robyn.
Satires, sels.
Some tyme I fled the fyre that me brent.
Tagus, fare well, that westward with thy stremes.
Tangled [or Tanglid] I was in love's snare.
There was never nothing more me pained [or payned].
Throughout the World If It Were Sought.
To cause accord or to aggre.
To Rail or Jest, Ye Know I Use It Not.
V. Innocentia Veritas Viat Fides Circumdederunt Me Inimici Mei.
What meaneth this? When I lie alone.
What nedeth these thretning wordes and wasted wynde?
What no, perdy, ye may be sure!
What rage is this? what furour of what kynd?

What vaileth trouth? or by it to take
　payn?
What wourde is that that chaungeth not.
Who hath herd of suche crueltye before?
Whoso list to hunt, I know where is an
　hind.
With Serving Still.
Ye old mule, that thinck your self so
　fayre.
You that in love finde lucke and
　habundance.

**Wyche, Marvin, Jr.**
And She Was Bad.
Five Sense.
Leslie.
We Rainclouds.

**Wygodski, Stanislaw**
Going to the North.
Those Betrayed at Dawn.
Voyage.
Winter Journey.

**Wylie, Elinor**
Atavism.
Cold-blooded Creatures.
Confession of Faith.
Eagle and the Mole, The.
Epitaph: "For this she starred her eyes
　with salt."
Full Moon.
Golden Bough.
Hughie at the Inn.
Lament for Glasgerion.
Let No Charitable Hope.
Little Elegy.
Madman's Song.
Nebuchadnezzar.
Nonsense Rhyme.
Preference.
Prophecy.
Proud Lady, A.
Puritan Sonnet.
Sanctuary.
Sea Lullaby.
Simon Gerty.
This Hand.
Velvet Shoes.
Wild Peaches.

**Wyman, Hastings, Jr.**
Some Ruse.

**Wynand, Derk**
Observation.

**Wyndham, Harald**
Anarchist's Letter, An.

**Wynne, John Huddlestone**
Horse and the Mule, The.
Time.

**Wyse, Louis**
Did You See the *Times* Today?

# Y

**"Ya-Ka-Nes."**　*See* **Harjo, Patty L.**
**Yamamoue Okura**
Elegy on the Death of Furuhi, An.

**Yates, David C.**
Observer, The.

**Yates, Gordon Kirkwood**

Some Chicks Just Can't Tell a Cézanne
　from a Sears.

**Yates, J. Michael**
Great Bear Lake Meditations, The, *sels.*

**Yates, Lynda**
Disordering, The.

**Yearwood, Gladstone**
I Am the Soil.
If U Are a Poet.
Sweet Louise.

**Yeatman, Robert Julian**and **Walter
　Carruthers Sellar**
How I Brought the Good News from
　Aix to Ghent.

**Yeats, William Butler**
Acre of Grass, An.
Adam's Curse.
Aedh Thinks of Those Who Have
　Spoken Evil of His Beloved.
Aedh Wishes for the Cloths of Heaven.
After Long Silence.
All Things Can Tempt Me.
Among School Children.
Apparitions, The.
At Galway Races.
Ballad of Father Gilligan, The.
Ballad of Father O'Hart, The.
Ballad of Moll Magee, The.
Balloon of the Mind, The.
Beggar to Beggar Cried.
Black Tower, The.
Blood and the Moon.
Broken Dreams.
Brown Penny.
Byzantium.
Cap and Bells, The.
Cat and the Moon, The.
Chambermaid's First Song, The.
Chambermaid's Second Song, The.
Choice, The.
Chosen.
Church and State.
Circus Animals' Desertion, The.
Coat, A.
Cold Heaven, The.
Collar-Bone of a Hare, The.
Colonel Martin.
Coming of Wisdom with Time, The.
Coole Park and Ballylee, 1931.
Coole Park, 1929.
Cradle Song, A: "Angels are stooping,
　The."
Crazed Girl, The.
Crazed Moon, The ("Crazed through
　much child-bearing").
Crazy Jane and Jack the Journeyman.
Crazy Jane and the Bishop.
Crazy Jane Grown Old Looks at the
　Dancers.
Crazy Jane on God.
Crazy Jane on the Day of Judgment.
Crazy Jane on the Mountain.
Crazy Jane Reproved.
Crazy Jane Talks with the Bishop.
Curse of Cromwell, The.
Dawn, The.
Dedication to a Book of Stories Selected
　from the Irish Novelists, The.
Deep-sworn Vow, A.
Dialogue of Self and Soul, A.
Dolls, The.
Down by the Salley Gardens.

Dream of Death, A.
Drinking Song, A.
Easter 1916.
Ego Dominus Tuus.
Fallen Majesty.
Falling of the Leaves, The.
Fascination of What's Difficult, The.
Father and Child.
Fergus and the Druid.
Fiddler of Dooney, The.
Fisherman, The.
Folly of Being Comforted, The.
For Anne Gregory.
Four Ages of Man, The.
Fragment: "Locke sank into a swoon."
Friends.
Girl's Song.
Great Day, The.
Gyres, The.
Hawk, The.
He Hears the Cry of the Sedge.
Hosting of the Sidhe, The.
How shall I name you, immortal, mild,
　proud shadows?
"I Am of Ireland."
In Memory of Eva Gore-Booth and Con
　Markiewicz.
In Memory of Major Robert Gregory.
In the Seven Woods.
Indian Song, An.
Indian to His Love, The.
Indian upon God, The.
Irish Airman Foresees His Death, An.
John Kinsella's Lament for Mrs. Mary
　Moore.
Lady's First Song, The.
Lady's Third Song, The.
Lake Isle of Innisfree, The.
Lamentation of the Old Pensioner, The.
Lapis Lazuli.
Last Confession, A.
Leaders of the Crowd, The.
Leda and the Swan.
Lines Written in Dejection.
Living man is blind and drinks his drop,
　A.
Long-legged Fly.
Lover Mourns for the Loss of Love, The.
Lover Tells of the Rose in His Heart,
　The.
Lover's Song, The.
Lullaby: "Beloved, may your sleep be
　sound."
Magi, The.
Man Who Dreamed of Faeryland, The.
Meditations in Time of Civil War, *sels.*
Memory.
Mermaid, The ("The mermaid found a
　swimming lad").
Meru.
Michael Robartes and the Dancer.
Michael Robartes Bids His Beloved Be
　at Peace.
Model for the Laureate, A.
Mohini Chatterjee.
Mongan Laments the Change That Has
　Come upon Him and His Beloved.
Moods, The.
Mother of God, The.
Municipal Gallery Revisited, The.
Never Give All the Heart.
News for the Delphic Oracle.

Nineteen Hundred and Nineteen.
Nineteenth Century and After, The.
No Second Troy.
Old Men Admiring Themselves in the
    Water, The.
Old Stone Cross, The.
On a Political Prisoner.
On Being Asked for a War Poem
On Hearing That the Students of Our
    New University Have Joined the
    Agitation against Immoral Literature.
On Woman.
Parnell.
Parting.
Paudeen.
People, The.
Pity of Love, The.
Players Ask for a Blessing on the
    Psalteries and Themselves, The.
Politics.
Prayer for My Daughter, A.
Prayer for My Son, A.
Purgatory.
Ragged Wood, The.
Red Hanrahan's Song about Ireland.
Resurrection, The, *sel.*
Ribh Considers Christian Love
    Insufficient.
Road at My Door, The.
Rose of the World, The.
Rose Tree, The.
Scholars, The.
Second Coming, The.
September 1913.
Solomon and the Witch.
Solomon to Sheba.
Song of the Happy Shepherd, The.
Song of the Old Mother, The.
Song of Wandering Aengus, The.
Sorrow of Love, The ("The brawling of a
    sparrow in the eaves").
Sorrow of Love, The ("The quarrel of
    the sparrows in the eaves").
Spur, The.
Stare's Nest by My Window, The.
Statesman's Holiday, The.
Statues, The.
Stick of Incense, A.
Stolen Child, The.
Sweet Dancer.
Swift's Epitaph.
That the Night Come.
Those Images.
Thought from Propertius, A.
Three Bushes, The, *sel.*
Three Hermits, The.
Three Movements.
To a Child Dancing in the Wind.
To a Friend Whose Work Has Come to
    Nothing.
To a Poet, Who Would Have Me Praise
    Certain Bad Poets, Imitators of His
    and Mine.
To a Squirrel at Kyle-Na-No.
To a Young Beauty.
To a Young Girl.
To Be Carved on a Stone at Thoor
    Ballylee.
To Ireland in the Coming Times.
To the Rose upon the Rood of Time.
Tom O'Roughley.
Tower, The.

Two Songs from a Play.
Two Songs of a Fool.
Two Trees, The.
Two Years Later.
Under Ben Bulben.
Upon a Dying Lady.
Upon a House Shaken by the Land
    Agitation.
Vacillation.
What Then?
When Helen Lived.
When You Are Old.
Whence Had They Come?
Who Goes with Fergus?
Why Should Not Old Men Be Mad?
Wild Old Wicked Man, The.
Wild Swans at Coole, The.
Youth and Age.

**Yerby, Frank**
Calm after Storm.
Fishes and the Poet's Hands, The.
Weltschmerz.
Wisdom.
You Are a Part of Me.

**Yeshurun, Avot**
Poem on Our Mother, Our Mother
    Rachel, The.
Poem on the Guilt, The.
Poem on the Jews, The.

**Yester, Lord**
Tweedside.

**Yevtushenko, Yevgeny**
Lies.
People.

**Yoak, Martha**
Mother and I.
Mother and the Moon.
Sunday Evening with Elizabeth, Age 5.

**Yonathan, Nathan**
And the Silver Turns into Night.
Another Poem on Absalom
South Wind.

**York, Sarah E.**
I Am Weary of Straying, *with music.*

**Yosano Akiko**
No camellia.
Spring is short.
Tanka: "Once, far over the breakers."
Tanka: "Swifter than hail."
You never touch.

**Yoshihara, Sachiko**
Madness.

**Yots, Michael**
On a Friend's Suicide.

**Young, A!**
Birthday Poem.
Dance for Ma Rainey, A.
Dance for Militant Dilettantes, A.
Dance of the Infidels.
Dancer, The.
Dancing in the Street.
For Arl in Her Sixth Month.
For Kenneth and Miriam Patchen.
For Poets.
Geography of the Near East.
Groupie.
Herrick Hospital, Fifth Floor.
Ho.
In a Mist.
Kiss.
Lemons, Lemons.
Loneliness.

Lonesome in the Country.
Move Continuing, The.
Myself When I Am Real.
New Mystic, The.
Not Her, She Aint No Gypsy.
Pachuta, Mississippi/ A Memoir.
Paris.
Poem for Players, A.
Poem Found Emptying Out My Pockets.
Ponce de León: A Morning Walk.
Prestidigitator, The.
Song Turning Back into Itself, The.
Squirrels.
Teaching.
Tribute.
Two Takes from Love in Los Angeles.
Yes, the Secret Mind Whispers.

**Young, Andrew**
Beauty and Love.
Black Rock of Kiltearn, The.
Climbing in Glencoe.
Culbin Sands.
Daisies.
Dead Crab, The.
Echoing Cliff, The.
Falls of Glomach, The.
Haystack, The.
In December.
Last Snow.
Loch Brandy
Man and Cows.
Mountain, The.
Scarecrow, The.
Shepherd's Hut, The.
Song for Autumn.
Stay, Spring.
Stockdoves, The.
Sudden Thaw.
Wiltshire Downs.

**Young, Augustus**
Advice of an Efficiency Expert, The.
After Five Years.
Domestic Man.
Elegy for a School-Friend.
Heritage.
Last Refuge, The.
She's My Love.
Woman, Don't Be Troublesome.

**Young, David**
August at the Lake.
Boxcar Poem, The ("The boxcars drift
    by").
Death of the Novel, The.
Dreams of the Wars.
"It's a Whole World, the Body. A Whole
    World!"——Swami Satchidananda.
Man Who Swallowed a Bird, The.
Mandelstam.
Occupational Hazards.
Owl, The.
Thoughts of Chairman Mao.
Two for the Hampton Institute.

**Young, Douglas**
Caller rain frae abune.
Deid sall ye ligg, and ne'er a memorie.
For a Wife in Jizzen.
For the Old Highlands.
Kirkyaird by the Sea, The, *sel.*
Last Lauch.
Luve.
On a North British Devolutionary.
Sabbath i the Mearns.

Shepherd's Dochter, The.
**Young, E. R.**
Railroad Reverie.
**Young, Edward (1683-1765)**
Art of Happiness, The.
Epigram on Voltaire.
Instalment, The, *sel.*
Lavinia at Church.
Love of Fame, the Universal Passion, *sels.*
Night Thoughts [The Complaint], *sels.*
One to destroy, is murder by the law.
Satire III: "Long, Dodington, in debt, I long have sought."
Satire on Women, *sel.*
Tir'd nature's sweet restorer, balmy sleep!
**Young, Ella**
Unicorn, The.
**Young, Francis Brett**
Seascape.
**Young, Gary**
Doctor Rebuilds a Hand, The.
To an Estranged Wife.
Under the Catalpa Trees.
**Young, Geoff**
97th Kentucky Derby, The.
**Young, George M., Jr.**
Lecture before a Lecture on Pushkin.
Lecturer Seeks a Wife, The.
Lectures on the Biology of the Shadow.
Polar Expedition.
Three Lectures on the Skeleton.
**Young, Ian**
At Rochdale.
Double Exposure.
Elephants from the Sea.
It's no good/ being an actor.
Skull, The.
Sugar-Candy Bird, A.
**Young, Jackman**
Arkansas.
**Young, Marguerite**
Angels, The.
Noah's Ark.
Process, The.
Whales, The.
Winter Scene.
**Young, Neil**
Heart of Gold.
Here We Are in the Years.
**Young, Roland**
Goat, The.
Miscegenous Zebra, The.
**Young, Virginia Brady**
Taught to Be Polite.
**Young Bear, Ray A.**
Another Face.
Before the Actual Cold.
Black Dog.
Celebration.
Coming Back Home.
Cook, The.
Crow-Children Walk My Circles in the Snow, The.
Differences.
Empty Streams of Autumn
Four Poems.
In Dream: The Privacy of Sequence.
In Missing.
Listening Rock, The.
One Chip of Human Bone.

Place of O, The.
Place of V, The.
Poem for Diane Wakoski, A.
Remembrance of a Color inside a Forest, A.
Rushing.
Star Blanket.
These Horses Came.
This House.
Trains Made of Stone.
Waiting to Be Fed.
War Walking Near.
Warrior Dreams.
Way the Bird Sat, The.
What We Can.
Wrong Kind of Love.
**Youngblood, Sarah**
At the Western Shore.
Walking the Beach.
**Yradier, Sebastian**
Paloma, La, *with music.*
**Yü Hsüan-chi**
Answering Li Ying Who Showed Me His Poems about Summer Fishing.
At the End of Spring.
Boudoir Lament.
Elegy for the Wife of a Friend.
For Hidden Mist Pavilion.
For Kuo Hsiang.
Letting My Feelings Out.
On a Visit to Ch'ung Chen Taoist Temple.
Poem to the Tune "Riverbank Willows."
Regretful Thoughts.
Rhyming a Friend's Poem.
Rhyming with a Friend.
Selling Ruined Peonies.
Sent to Wen T'ing-yün on a Winter Night.
Spring Thoughts Sent to Tzu-an.
Staying in the Mountains in Summer.
Telling My Feelings.
To the Minister Liu.
To Tzu-an.
**Yungman, Moshe**
Don't Say.
Encounter in Safed.
Melons.
Messiah, The.
Sacrifice, The.
**Yvonne**
Deborah Lee.
1946.
Rachel and the Truth (c.1945).
Rachel at Thirteen.
Rachel at Twenty-three.
She-Who-Opens.
Where She Was Not Born.

# Z

**Z. Z.**
Here lies a poet—where's the great surprise!
**Zabel, Morton Dauwen**
Journal to Stella.
**Zach, Natan**
Against Parting.

As Sand.
Do Not Dream.
Foreign Country, A.
In This Deep Darkness ("In this deep heavy darkness").
Listening to Her.
No.
Peaceful Song, A.
Perhaps It's Only Music.
Quiet Light of Flies, The.
Short Winter Tale, A.
To Be a Master in Your House.
When God First Said.
When the Last Riders.
**Zachariou, Paulette Dusdall**
In the Embers at Midnight.
In the Morning.
Sticks and Stones.
**Zahn, Curtis**
Highway 101, Seal Beach.
**Zaid, Gabriel**
Late Again.
**Zaranka, William**
Junk.
**Zaremba, John T.**
Negotiations.
Profligate, The.
**Zaturenska, Marya Alexandrovna (Mrs. Horace Gregory)**
All Is Well with the Child.
Bird and the Muse.
Daisy, The.
Descent of the Vulture, The.
Girl's Song.
Hymn to Artemis, the Destroyer.
Intruder, The.
Lovers, The.
Lunar Tides, The.
Once in an Ancient Book.
Ophelia's Song.
**Zavatsky, Bill**
Being Adult.
**Zawadiwsky, Christine**
As Long as the Heart Beats.
Riddles and Lies.
**Zeb-un-Nissa, Princess**
Though I am Laila of the Persian romance.
**Zeiger, L. L.**
Fish, The.
**Zeitlin, Aaron**
Empty Apartment, The.
Ode to Freedom.
Text.
**Zeitlin, Israel.** *See* **Tiempo, Cesar**
**Zelda**
I Stood in Jerusalem.
In the Dry Riverbed.
Light a Candle.
Moon Is Teaching Bible, The.
With My Grandfather.
**Zelvin, Elizabeth**
Insomnia.
**Ziegler, Alan**
Curtain Call.
Displacement.
Guest, The
Sunday Night.
Waiting for the Bus.
**Zimmer, Paul**
Apple Blight.

Driving North from Savannah on My
  Birthday.
Lord Fluting Dreams of America on the
  Eve of His Departure from Liverpool.
One for the Ladies at the Troy Laundry
  Who Cooled Themselves for Zimmer.
Phineas Within and Without.
Poem Ending with an Old Cliché.
Zimmer Drunk and Alone, Dreaming of
  Old Football Games.
Zimmer Envying Elephants.
Zimmer in Grade School.
Zimmer in Winter.
Zimmer's Hard Dream.
Zimmer's Last Gig.

**Zimroth, Evan**
Lilly's Song.

**Zinnes, Harriet**
Wallace Stevens Gives a Reading.

**Zinzendorf, Nicolaus L.**
For Us No Night Can Be Happier, *with*
  *music.*
Slain Lamb of God, *with music.*

**Zirlin, Larry**
Dream Girl.
When Greenberg Speaks, Can a Poem
  Be Far Behind?

**Zisquit, Linda**
Circumcision, The.
Rachel's Lament.

Sabbatical.

**Zmuda, Bob**
Love Song.

**Zolotow, Charlotte**
Aren't You Glad.
Dog, A.
Little Old Man.
No One Would Believe.

**"Zozimus."** *See* **Moran, Michael**

**Zu-Bolton, Ahmos, II**
Answers for Ethelbert.
Beachhead Preachment.
Blackjack Moses ("Being a preacher").
Governor of Ollie Street, The.
Seeker, The.
Taxicab Blues.
Thru Blue Eyes.

**Zukofsky, Louis**
"A" (1–12), *sels.*
"A 11."
"A 4."
Ask of the sun.
Cars once steel and green, now old.
1892–1941.
Expounding the Torah.
For you I have emptied the meaning.
From the Head.
Green leaf that will outlast the winter,
  The.
I walk in the old street.

In Arizona/ (how many years in the
  mountains).
It's hard to see but think of a sea.
Light, *sels.*
Lines of this new song are nothing, The.
"Mantis."
Non Ti Fidar.
Of Dying Beauty.
On one of my long walks.
Reading and Talking.
Tall and singularly dark you pass among
  the breakers.
Voice out of the Tabernacle, A.

**Zussman, Ezra**
At Dante's Grave.
Last, The.

**Zweig, Paul**
Fly on the Water, A.
Uptown.
Women in Brooklyn.

**Zwicky, Fay**
Chosen, The—Kalgoorlie, 1894.
Summer Pogrom.

**Zychlinska, Rayzel**
Clothes, The.
My Mother's Shoes.
Remembering Lutsky.

**Zydek, Fredrick**
Dark Room.
Pond.

# SUBJECT INDEX

**Abelard, Peter**
Sic et Non.   Read
**Abilene, Texas**
Abilene.   *Unknown.*
**Abolitionists**
John Brown's Body.   *Unknown.*
Runagate Runagate.   Hayden.
Wake Nicodemas.   Work.
**Abominable Snowman**
Abominable Snowman, The.   Nash.
**Abortion**
Abortion.   Ai.
Abortion, The.   Iverson.
Abortion, An.   O'Hara.
Abortion, The.   Sexton.
Flowers.   Fraser.
Inquest, The.   Davies.
Lost Baby Poem, The.   Clifton.
Mother, The.   Brooks.
Should We Legalize Abortion?   O'Hara.
Unwanted, The.   Gordon.
Vow, The.   Hecht.
**Abraham**
Abraham.   Schwartz.
Abraham.   Silberschlag.
Abraham and Isaac.   Lasker-Schüler.
Abraham and Sarah.   Manger.
Abraham in Egypt.   Schwartz.
Hagar and Ishmael.   Lasker-Schüler.
Harlot's Catch.   Nichols.
Parable of the Old Man and the Young, The.   Owen.
Sacrifice, The.   Bloch.
Story of Abraham and Hagar, The.   Aphek.
**Absence**
How like a winter hath my absence been.   Sonnets, XCVII.
   Shakespeare.
Letter to Her Husband, Absent upon Public Employment, A.
   Bradstreet.
Like as the culver on the bared bough.   *Fr.* Amoretti.   Spenser.
Separation.   Merwin.
Somebody's Gone.   Ford.
Talking after Christmas Blues.   Henri.
Winter Remembered.   Ransom.
**Accidents**
Accident, The.   Gasparini.
At 79th and Park.   Howes.
Auto Wreck.   Shapiro.
Ballad of Springhill (The Springhill Mine Disaster).   MacColl
   *and* Seeger.
Blood Donor.   Morgan.
Blue-tail Fly, The.   *Unknown.*
Cut.   Plath.
Death of the Sports-Car Driver, The.   Aaron.
Down Went McGinty.   Flynn.
Dying Mine Brakeman, The.   Jenks.
George Allen.   *Unknown.*
Hay Derrick.   Harris.
Henry K. Sawyer.   *Unknown.*
It's Here in The.   Atkins.
Lady Track Star, A.   Blount.
Large Mercies.   Enright.
Out, Out.   Frost.
Poems about Playmates.   Davis.
Seven-Tenths of a Second.   Larson.
Tay Bridge Disaster, The.   McGonagall.
Worker, The.   Thomas.

Wreck of the Old 97, The.   *Unknown.*
Wreck of the Royal Palm, The.   *Unknown.*
**Achilles**
Achilles.   Corwin.
Shield of Achilles, The.   Auden.
**Acorns**
Acorn, The.   Bull.
Acorns.   Mills.
**Actaeon**
Actaeon.   Clough.
Actaeon.   Heppenstall.
**Acting and Actors**
Ballade of Dead Actors.   Henley.
Boy Actor, The.   Coward.
If I Were on the Stage.   Blossom
Movie Actors Scribbling Letters Very Fast in Crucial Scenes.
   Garrigue.
Old Trouper, The.   *Fr.* Archy and Mehitabel.   Marquis.
Rosciad, The.   Churchill.
Santa Claus.   Hassall.
Shirley Temple.   Michael.
They All Want to Play Hamlet.   Sandburg.
**Adam**
Adam and Eve.   Sisson.
Adam Driven from Eden.   *Unknown.*
Adam in Love.   Mitchell.
Adam in the Garden.   Suderman.
Adam in the Garden Pinning Leaves.   *Unknown.*
Adam Lay Y-bounden.   *Unknown.*
Adam's Task.   Hollander.
Banishment, The.   *Fr.* Paradise Lost.   Milton.
Discovery, The.   Gibbon.
First Wedding in the World, The.   Rosenberg.
Fortunate Fall, The.   Alvarez.
Garden, The.   Silverman.
God and Man.   Hazo.
Imperial Adam.   Hope.
Marriage in Eden, The.   Williams.
Occasional Poem.   Housman.
Original Sequence.   Booth.
Reveille.   Hughes.
Sickness of Adam, The.   Shapiro.
**Adams, Henry**
Henry Adams.   Auden.
**Adams, John Quincy**
Twilight's Last Gleaming.   Monks.
**Adderley, Julian ("Cannonball")**
Cannon Arrested.   Harper.
**Adlestrop, England**
Adlestrop.   Thomas.
**Adolescence**
Adolescence II.   Dove.
Classroom.   Aitchison.
Conventionalist, The.   Smith.
Fifteen.   Stafford.
Girl Friends.   Daniell.
Homework for Annabelle.   McGinley.
I Remember How She Sang.   Penny.
Impossibility, An.   Vas Dias.
Initial Response.   Soniat.
Lines to His Son on Reaching Adolescence.   Logan.
Little Girl, My String Bean, My Lovely Woman.   Sexton.
No Respect for Authority.   Chamberlain.
On the Edge.   Birch.
Overcoats.   Kramer.

Pennycandystore beyond the El, The. *Fr.* A Coney Island of the Mind. Ferlinghetti.
Portrait of Girl with Comic Book. McGinley.
Puberty. Wallace.
September 7. Bass.
16/53. Piercy.
Triolet against Sisters. McGinley.
Waiting in Front of the Columnar High School. Shapiro.
Young. Sexton.
Young Ones, The. Jennings.

**Adonis**
Death of Adonis, The. Ayres.
Venus, and yong Adonis sitting by her. *Fr.* Fidessa, More Chaste than Kind. Griffin.

**Adultery.** *See* **Infidelity.**

**Advent**
Advent. Larson.
Advent. *Unknown.*
Advent Images, The. Ramsey.

**Advertising**
After Advertising Ended. Ochester.
Double Standard, The. Adams.
Hymn in Columbus Circle. Benét.
Jabber-Whacky. Di Caprio.
Poem, or Beauty Hurts Mr. Vinal. Cummings.
Song of the Open Road. Nash.
Summer Song. Watt.
Virtues of Carnation Milk, The. *Unknown.*

**Aegean Sea**
Santorin. Flecker.

**Aeneas**
Aeneas at Washington. Tate.
Falling Asleep over the Aeneid. Lowell.

**Aesop**
Improvisations on Aesop. Hecht.

**Africa**
Africa. Diop.
African Affair, The. Wright.
African Dream. Kaufman.
African Elegy, An. Duncan.
African Things. Cruz.
Africa's Plea. Dempster.
Africland. La Grone.
All That You Have Given Me, Africa. Kanié.
Art Market: Leopoldville. Jackson.
Bedtime Story. MacBeth.
Blue Tanganyika. Bethune.
Bwagamoyo. Bethune.
Chad. Brathwaite.
Change Is Not Always Progress. Lee.
Colonialism. Qarshe.
Congo, The. Lindsay.
Coptic Poem. Durrell.
Driving through New England. Clifton.
Far Cry from Africa, A. Walcott.
Hearing James Brown at the Café des Nattes. Long.
Heritage. Bennett.
Heritage. Cullen.
Into the Dark. Monette.
Mmenson. Brathwaite.
Near the Old Slave Fort. Bruchac.
Old Laughter. Brooks.
Return from Luluabourg. Jackson.
Scorpion, The. Plomer.
Song of the Cape of Good Hope. Schubart.
There Were Fierce Animals in Africa. Aubert.
Timbuctu. Brathwaite.
Up Out of the African. Joans.

**Afton (river), Scotland**
Afton Water. Burns.

**Age.** *See* **Middle Age; Old Age.**

**Agincourt, Battle of**

Agincourt Carol, The. *Unknown.*
Ballad of Agincourt, The. Drayton.
King Henry the Fifth before Agincourt. *Fr.* King Henry V. Shakespeare.

**Aging**
Aging. Jarrell.
Aging. Jong.
Along the River. Enright.
Ambulando. Brasch.
At Bickford's. Stern.
But I Am Growing Old and Indolent. Jeffers.
Celebrity, The. Field.
Change of Life. Urdang.
Chard Whitlow. Reed.
Coming of Wisdom with Time, The. Yeats.
Descent, The. Williams.
Discovery. Belloc.
Due Date. Cain.
Eddie and Eve. Bukowski.
Fifty. Rexroth.
Frost, The. Tzu Yeh.
Game Resumed. Lattimore.
Grandmother, Rocking. Merriam.
Growing Old. Arnold.
Happy at 40. Meinke.
He Wakes Again in Early Light. Kistler.
His Plans for Old Age. Meredith.
I Look at an Old Photo of Myself with Love. Swenson.
In a Prominent Bar in Secaucus One Day. Kennedy.
Key of the Kingdom, The. Reed.
Lantern. Polite.
Let me ask You, Mind. *Unknown.*
Little Old Man. Zolotow.
Love in Age. Bruce.
Loveliest of Trees, the Cherry Now. Housman.
Man, A. Levertov.
Men at Forty. Justice.
Mornings. Berger.
My Father. Koertge.
Ode: Intimations of Immortality from Recollections of Early Childhood. Wordsworth.
Old Pro's Lament, The. Petrie.
Old Swimmer, The. Morley.
On Growing Old. Masefield.
Only Years. Rexroth.
Pastoral: "When I was younger." Williams.
Planting. Snyder.
Retired School-Teacher. McHugh.
Reunion. Forché.
Royal Iguanas, The. Dehn.
Terminus. Emerson.
That time of year thou mayst in me behold. Sonnets, LXXIII. Shakespeare.
3:16 and One Half. Bukowski.
To a Gentlewoman Objecting to Him His Grey Hairs. Herrick.
To Alpha Dryden Eberhart. Eberhart.
Tonight I've watched. Sappho.
Una Anciana Mexicana. Corbin.
Voice from Out of the Night, A. Mueller.
What I Expected. Spender.
What Lips My Lips Have Kissed, and Where, and Why. Millay.
When You Are Old. Yeats.
Will You Love Me in December as You Do in May? Walker.
Woman's Complaint. Mulrine.
You Can Have It. Levine.
Young and Old. *Fr.* The Water Babies. Kingsley.
*Timeless Voices* (TVo). Virginia Larrain, comp.

**Ailsa Craig, Scotland**
To Ailsa Rock. Keats.

**Air**
Air. Alexander.

Blessed Virgin Compared to the Air We Breathe, The.
   Hopkins.
I Hear America Griping. Bishop.
**Air Warfare**
   Americana XIII. Rakosi.
   Aviators, The. Pillin.
   Bombers. Day Lewis.
   Bombing of the Cafe de Paris 1914, The. Scannell.
   Brother Fire. MacNeice.
   Ceremony after a Fire Raid. Thomas.
   Children, The. Soutar.
   Crack of Doom. Carter.
   Dead in Europe, The. Lowell.
   Death of the Ball Turret Gunner, The. Jarrell.
   Firebombing, The. Dickey.
   Front, A. Jarrell.
   Fury of Aerial Bombardment, The. Eberhart.
   Gods in Vietnam. Redmond.
   Irish Airman Foresees His Death, An. Yeats.
   Journal. Ciardi.
   Losses. Jarrell.
   Man in the Dead Machine, The. Hall.
   Pilot, The. Turco.
   Preparation. McPherson.
   Raid, The. Everson.
   Revelation. Soutar.
   2nd Air Force. Jarrell.
   Soliloquy in an Air-Raid. Fuller.
   Still Falls the Rain. Sitwell.
   Usual exquisite boredom of patrols, The. Popham.
   When a Beau Goes In. Ewart.
   Words Spoken by Pasternak during a Bombing. Akhmadulina.
**Airline Stewardesses**
   Falling. Dickey.
**Airplane Crashes**
   On the Death of the Evansville University Basketball Team in a
      Plane Crash, December 13, 1977. Hamblin.
   Plane Wreck at Los Gatos. Guthrie.
**Airplanes.** *See* **Aviation and Aviators.**
**Airports**
   At a Motel near O'Hara Airport. Kenyon.
   At Every Major Airport. Goedicke.
   At the Airport. Jones.
   At the Airport in Dallas. Mooney.
   At the San Francisco Airport. Winters.
   Dulles Airport. McCarthy.
   Kennedy Airport. Kramer.
   Night at an Airport. Ignatow.
   Seeing Auden Off. Booth.
**Alabama (ship)**
   How Do You Do, *Alabama!* Wilson.
   Roll, *Alabama,* Roll. *Unknown.*
**Alabama (state)**
   Alabama. Simmons.
   Alabama Bound. *Unknown.*
   Daybreak in Alabama. Hughes.
**Alamo**
   Defence of the Alamo, The. Miller.
   Hymn of the Alamo. Potter.
   Last Fall of the Alamo. "O. Henry."
   Men of the Alamo, The. Roche.
**Alaska**
   Denali Road. Haines.
   Fairbanks under the Solstice. Haines.
   Invaders, The. Haines.
   Skagway. Haines.
   Summer in Fairbanks. Stokesbury.
   Train Stops at Healy Fork, The. Haines.
**Albert Hall (London)**
   Poem about Poems about Vietnam, A. Stallworthy.
**Alchemy and Alchemists**
   Alchemist, The. Pound.

Chemist's Dream, The. Beer.
Paracelsus in Excelsis. Pound.
**Alcoholism.** *See* **Drunkards.**
**Ale**
   Back and Side Go Bare. *Fr.* Gammer Gurton's Needle. *At. to*
      Stevenson.
   Bring Us in Good Ale. *Unknown.*
   Doll Thy Ale. *Unknown.*
   Johnson's Ale. *Unknown.*
   O mortal man, that lives by bread. *At. to* Ibbetson.
   On a Quaker's Tankard. Landor.
   When Jones's Ale Was New. *Unknown.*
**Alexander the Great**
   Alexander and Gymnosophists. *Unknown.*
   Alexander to His Horse. Farjeon.
   Alexander's Feast; or, The Power of Music. Dryden.
   On Alexander and Aristotle, on a Black-on-Red Greek Plate.
      Dugan.
   Santorin. Flecker.
   Speaking Tree, The. Rukeyser.
**Alfonso X, King of Castile and Leon**
   Alphonso of Castile. Emerson.
**Ali, Muhammed (Cassius Clay)**
   Ali. Corbin.
   Black Lady in an Afro Hairdo Cheers for Cassius. Holmes.
   Clay Comes Out to Meet Terrell. Ali.
   I Dance and I Have a Fast Hook. Ali.
**Alice in Wonderland**
   Last Days of Alice. Tate.
**Alienation**
   Alienation (To My Son). Travis.
   Alone/December/Night. Cruz.
   American Rhapsody (4). Fearing.
   Anomie. Ramsey.
   Average, The. Auden.
   Back Again, Home. Lee.
   Between Me and Anyone Who Can Understand. Scott.
   Blight. Emerson.
   Brooding. Ignatow.
   Chicken-Licken. Angelou.
   Chilled by Different Winds. Swaim.
   Dangling Conversation. Simon.
   Desolation Row. Dylan.
   Dirge: "1-2-3 was the number he played." Fearing.
   Effort at Speech between Two People. Rukeyser.
   Ergo Sum. Brasch.
   Howl. Ginsberg.
   I Am. Clare.
   In a Dark Time. Roethke.
   Invention of the Comics, The. Jones.
   It Is Oregon, the Highway Looms. Bond.
   Looking Up. Allcock.
   Love Song of J. Alfred Prufrock, The. Eliot.
   Man Missing. Brasch.
   Mr. Flood's Party. Robinson.
   No Bargains Today. Kenner.
   Not Waving but Drowning. Smith
   Old Maid Factory, The. Urdang.
   On the Apparition of Oneself. Burford.
   Outcast. McKay.
   Personality Sketch, A: Bill. Davis.
   Pressure. Waldman.
   Sound of Silence, The. Simon.
   Street Iconoclasts. Aguila.
   Unwanted. Field.
   Useless Words. Sandburg.
   Warren Pryor. Nowlan.
   Waste Land, The. Eliot.
   World Is Too Much with Us, The. Wordsworth.
   Writer's House, The. Allen.
**All Saints' Eve.** *See* **Halloween.**
**All Souls' Night**

All Souls' Night.   Cornford.

**Allen, Ethan**
Green Mountain Boy.   Smyth.

**Alligators**
Alligator, The.   Ravenel.
Alligator on the Escalator.   Merriam.

**Alphabet Poems**
A B C, An.   *Unknown.*
A B C Objects.   *Unknown.*
A B C of Love, The.   Hardison.
A Is for Abracadabra.   Farjeon.
A was an apple-pie.   Mother Goose.
A Was an Archer.   *Unknown.*
A Was Once an Apple Pie.   Lear.
Alphabet ("A tumbled down . . .").   Lear.
Alphabet of Christmas Cheer.   Weston.
Alphabet of Questions, An.   Carryl.
And with the Sorrows of This Joyousness.   Patchen.
Animal Alphabet, An.   *Unknown.*
Austrian Army, An.   Watts.
From a Cheerful Alphabet.   Updike.
Jamboree for J, A.   Merriam.
Lumberman's Alphabet, The.   *Unknown.*
Nursery Rhyme Alphabet, A.   *Unknown.*
Primer of the Daily Round, A.   Nemerov.
Sailors' Alphabet, The.   *Unknown.*

**Alphonsus Rodriguez, Saint**
In Honour of St. Alphonsus Rodriguez.   Hopkins.

**Alps**
Authentic Tidings.   *Fr.* The Prelude.   Wordsworth.
Hymn Before Sunrise in the Vale of Chamouni.   Coleridge.
Mont Blanc.   Shelley.
Nocturne of the Self-evident Presence.   MacGreevy.
On the Fly-Leaf of Pound's Cantos.   Bunting.
Sarentino-South Tyrol.   Brantingham.
Schreckhorn, The.   Hardy.

**Altgeld, John Peter**
Eagle That Is Forgotten, The.   Lindsay.

**Amana Colonies**
Amana Colonies, The.   Smith.

**America (United States of).**   *See* **United States.**

**American Revolution**
America Is Darken'd.   Dillard.
Ballad of Benjamin Bones, The.   Ward.
Ballad of Bunker Hill, The.   *Unknown.*
Battle of the Kegs, The.   Hopkinson.
Bombardment of Bristol, R.I., The.   *Unknown.*
Caldwell of Springfield.   Harte.
Capture of Major André, The.   *Unknown.*
Carmen Bellicosum.   McMaster.
Concord Hymn.   Emerson.
Cornwallis' Country Dance.   *Unknown.*
Death of Warren, The.   Sargent.
Dying Sergeant, The.   *Unknown.*
Farewell to Kingsbridge.   *Unknown.*
Maryland Battalion, The.   Palmer.
Nathan Hale.   Finch.
Nathan Hale.   *Unknown.*
Paul Revere's Ride.   *Fr.* Tales of a Wayside Inn.   Longfellow.
Picture of the Times, A.   Freneau.
Rich Lady over the Sea, The.   *Unknown.*
Riflemen's Song at Bennington.   *Unknown.*
Song of Marion's Men.   Bryant.
Sons of Liberty, The.   *Unknown.*
Sword of Bunker Hill, The.   Wallace.
To the Memory of the Brave Americans.   Freneau.
Warren's Address.   Pierpont.
Yankee Doodle.   *Unknown.*
Yankee Man-of-War, The.   *Unknown.*

**Americans**
Ave Caesar.   Jeffers.
Ballad of Abbreviations, A.   Chesterton.

Boy-Man.   Shapiro.
Byron vs. DiMaggio.   Meinke.
I Hear America Singing.   Whitman.
My Wife Who Is American.   Daniel.
On a Rhine Steamer.   Stephen.
On the Circuit.   Auden.
*See also* **United States.**

**Amish, The (Mennonite Christians)**
Amish, The.   Updike.
Winter Wait, A.   Raines.

**Amusement Parks**
Chippewa Lake Park.   Woessner.
Dinoland.   Rieter.

**Anatomy**
Cider and Vesalius.   Peck.

**Ancestors and Ancestry**
After Looking into a Genealogy.   Church.
Ancestors.   Goodman.
Ancestors.   Randall.
Ancestors.   Schimmel.
Black Star Line.   Dumas.
Country Alphabet, The.   Parker.
Cycle of Women, A.   Barba.
Dedication for a Plot of Ground.   Williams.
Dreaming the Ancestors.   Stelzer.
Fall of J. W. Beane, The.   Herford.
Forefathers.   Blunden.
Genealogy.   Phillips.
Generations.   Simmons.
Grandmother Grant.   DeFrees.
Heredity.   Guiterman.
Heritage.   Bennett.
Heritage.   Cullen.
Idea of Ancestry, The.   Knight.
Illustrious Ancestors.   Levertov.
Inheritance.   Bruce.
Lineage.   Walker.
Lost.   Ignacio.
Mothers.   Bentley.
Personal History.   Todd.
Pride of Ancestry.   Frost.
Stark Boughs on the Family Tree.   Oliver.
Then let us boast of ancestors no more.   *Fr.* The True-born Englishman.   Defoe.
3 Days after Father's Day.   Kornblum.
Tomb of an Ancestor.   Curnow.

**Andersen, Hans Christian**
At Hans Christian Andersen's Birthplace, Odense, Denmark.   Lindsay.

**André, John**
Capture of Major André, The.   *Unknown.*
Major André.   *Unknown.*

**Andromache**
Andromache Afterwards.   Gregg.

**Anemones**
Anemones.   Angus.

**Angels**
Air and Angels.   Donne.
Angel.   Merrill.
Angel Surrounded by Paysans.   Stevens.
Angels.   Abse.
Angels, The.   Young.
Angels in the House.   Metz.
Angels in Winter.   Willard.
Apprentice Angel, An.   "MacDiarmid."
Fall.   Melinescu.
God's Language.   Fainlight.
How Grand and How Bright.   *Unknown.*
Propeller Sleep.   Berssenbrugge.
Tom's Angel.   De la Mare.
Vision, A.   Levertov.

**Anger**

Achilles. Corwin.
Death Dance, The. Piercy.
Lot of Hearts Are Pounding in the Universe, A. Kornblum.
Lover Letter Postmarked Van Beethoven. Wakoski.
My Mother Takes My Wife's Side. Kherdian.
Poison Tree, A. *Fr.* Songs of Experience. Blake.
Temper. Fyleman.

**Angkor Wat**
Ank'hor Vat. Devlin.

**Animals**
Ad Limina. Campbell.
And Did the Animals? Van Doren.
Animals, The. Muir.
Animals. *Fr.* Song of Myself. Whitman.
Animals' Christmas, The. Dacey.
At the Zoo. Thackeray.
Barnyard, The. *Unknown.*
Barnyard Melodies. Brooks.
Beasts. Wilbur.
Beasts and Birds. O'Keeffe.
Bells of Heaven, The. Hodgson.
Bestiary, A. Rexroth.
Burial of the Linnet, The. Ewing.
Butterfly's Ball, The. Roscoe.
Byre. MacCaig.
Cage, The. Stephens.
Chenille. Dickey.
Come into Animal Presence. Levertov.
Creatures. Kumin.
Dog and Tiger. Greenberg.
Dumb World, The. Davies.
Eau-Forte. Flint.
Fiddle-I-Fee. *Unknown.*
Friendly Beasts, The. *Unknown.*
Froggie Went a-Courtin'. *Unknown.*
Gallows, The. Thomas.
Heaven of Animals, The. Dickey.
Horses Graze. Brooks.
Hymn to Joy. Cunningham.
Kindness to Animals. *Unknown.*
Lesson. Thwaite.
Mercy to Animals: A Ballad of Humanity. Tupper.
Mirror for the Barnyard. Myers.
Mrs. Malone. Farjeon.
Monkeys, The. Moore.
Mouse's Courting Song, The. *Unknown.*
My Father Kept a Horse. *Unknown.*
Neighbors. Malam.
Peacock "At Home," The. Dorset.
Pet Shop. MacNeice.
Psalm to the Creatures. Jones.
Raccoon's Got a Bushy Tail. *Unknown.*
Robin Redbreast in a Cage, A. *Fr.* Auguries of Innocence.
    Blake.
Self-Pity. Lawrence.
Snakes, Mongooses, Snake-Charmers and the Like. Moore.
Stockyard, The. Squire.
Take One Home for the Kiddies. Larkin.
Temple of the Animals, The. Duncan.
Tree in the Wood, The. *Unknown.*
When the Animals Left the Ark. *Unknown.*
Witnesses, The. Kennedy.
World of Darkness. Chatain.
Young Stock. Sackville-West.
Zoo, The. Ostroff.

**Animism**
Golden Lines. Nerval.
Intimate Associations. Baudelaire.
Sometimes. Hesse.

**Anne, Queen of England**
Golden Age, The. *Unknown.*
New Ballad, A. Mainwaring.

Pasquin to the Queen's Statue at St. Paul's. Shippen.
Queen's Speech, The. Mainwaring.

**Anteaters**
Pangolin, The. Moore.

**Antelopes**
Kob Antelope. *Unknown.*
"Word" of an Antelope Caught in a Trap, The. Sandag.

**Antietam Campaign**
Battle of Antietam Creek, The. *Unknown.*

**Antiques**
Ali Ben Shufti. Thwaite.

**Antony.** *See* **Marc Antony.**

**Ants**
Ant, The. Nash.
Ants. Aal.
Ants, The. Clare.
Ants. Hyde.
Ants and Others. Stoutenberg.
Country Roads. Jacobsen.
Departmental. Frost.
"Go to the Ant." Sharpless.
Grasshopper and the Ant, The. La Fontaine.
Immanent. De la Mare.
Ondt and the Gracehoper, The. *Fr.* Finnegans Wake. Joyce.
Solitude. Simic.

**Apartheid**
Apartheid. Bohanon.
New Quotas/ or Booker T. and Garvey Would Have Loved
    South Africa. Mberi.

**Apathy**
Leaden-eyed, The. Lindsay.
Pooh! De la Mare.
Written in a Thunder Storm July 15th 1841. Clare.

**Apes**
Best Loved of Africa. Danner.
Teaching the Ape to Write Poems. Tate.

**Aphrodite**
Blue Sleep. Bryher.
Ring of, The. Olson.
Sapphics. Swinburne.
*See also* **Venus.**

**Apollo**
Canticle to Apollo, A. Herrick.
Delphic Hymn to Apollo. Swinburne.
Hymn of Apollo. Shelley.
Many Are Called. Robinson.
Metric Figure. Williams.
Ode to Apollo. Keats.

**Apostles**
They Slept While Jesus Prayed. Chambers.

**Apple Trees**
Ballad of Johnny Appleseed. Oleson.
Kiss, The. Pack.
Mine Host of the "Golden Apple." Westwood.
Mother. Dempster.
Old Sinner. Bowman.
Saving the Harvest. Lehmann.

**Apples**
After Apple-picking. Frost.
Apple Hell. Van Doren.
Apple Scoop. Glen.
Apple-Logia. Brand.
Apples. Kaufman.
Apples to Keep. F. Frost.
Crossed Apple, The. Bogan.
Moonlit Apples. Drinkwater.
Mystic. Lawrence.
Paring the Apple. Tomlinson.
Sweet Apple. Stephens.
When It Rains. Maxson.

**"Appleseed, Johnny" (John Chapman)**
Ballad of Johnny Appleseed. Oleson.

**Apricots**
Apricot Tree. Isanos.
Vegetable Destiny. Cassian.
**April**
Allotments: April. Spencer.
April 1885. Bridges.
April Inventory. Snodgrass.
April Rise. Lee.
Aprilly. Taylor.
Forsythia Is the Color I Remember. Cherwinski.
Same Lady, The. Nichols.
Song of Second April. Millay.
Spring. Millay.
**April Fool's Day**
Oh Have You Heard. Silverstein.
**Aquariums**
At the Water Zoo. Knox.
Ode of Odium on Aquariums. Guiterman.
**Arabia**
Arabia. Falkner.
**Arabs**
Arabic Script. Thwaite.
**Arachne**
Wedding, The. Aiken.
**Aran Islands, Ireland**
Aran Islands. Layton.
**Arcadia**
Comfort from Arcadia. Flocos.
**Archaeology**
Archaeologists. Faucher.
Ashkelon. Rudolf.
Digging for Indians. Gildner.
Monologue in the Valley of the Kings. Thwaite.
**Archery**
On the College Archery Range. Wallace.
**Arethusa**
Arethusa. Shelley.
**Aristotle**
Humanities Lecture. Stafford.
**Arizona**
Arizona Poems, *sels.* Fletcher.
Back to Arizona. Brininstool.
Crossing the Colorado River into Yuma. Ortiz.
History of Arizona, The. Brown.
Painted Hills of Arizona, The. Curran.
**Arkansas**
Arkansas. Young.
Narrative Hooper and L.D.O. Sestina with a Long Last Line. Whitehead.
Sanford Barney. *Unknown.*
State of Arkansas, The. *Unknown.*
Toad Suck Ferry. Stoneback.
**Armada.** *See* **Spanish Armada.**
**Armagh, Ireland**
Armagh. Rodgers.
**Armenians**
For My Father: Two Poems. Kherdian.
**Armistice**
"And There Was a Great Calm." Hardy.
**Armstrong, Louis ("Satchmo")**
Satchmo. Tolson.
**Army Life**
Base Details. Sassoon.
By the Bivouac's Fitful Flame. Whitman.
Cavalry Crossing a Ford. Whitman.
Class Incident from Graves. Brownjohn.
Danny Deever. Kipling.
'Eathen, The. Kipling.
Execution of Cornelius Vane, The. Read.
Going in to Dinner. Shanks.
He Said To. Bell.
Lessons of the War. Reed.

Local Destruction. Oldham.
Officers' Mess. Ewart.
Spring 1942. Fuller.
Stand-to: Good Friday Morning. Sassoon.
Tenting on the Old Camp Ground. Kittredge.
Vaudeville. Kirstein.
Weapons Training. Dawe.
**Arnold, Matthew**
Dover Bitch, The. Hecht.
**Arrows**
Eulogy to the Bow and Arrow. *Unknown.*
**Art and Artists**
Against Botticelli. Hass.
Anecdote of the Jar. Stevens.
Anonymous Drawing. Justice.
Ars Victrix. Dobson.
Art. Flax.
Art. Levertov.
Art. Melville.
Art Lesson, The. Morgan.
Artist, An. Jeffers.
Artist, The. Williams.
Artist Underground, The. Stanford.
Chicago Picasso, The. Brooks.
Chronological Ordering of Art Cards, The. Sargent.
Dab of Color, A. Weiss.
Dog of Art, The. Levertov.
Egyptian Pulled Glass Bottle in the Shape of a Fish, An. Moore.
Epilogue to Lessing's Laocoön. Arnold.
Epitaph on an Unfortunate Artist. Graves.
Hallelujah Hardesty, Female Artist. Walthall.
Head. Weber.
I would not paint—a picture. Dickinson.
In the Jungle. Enright.
In the National Gallery. Sassoon.
Living Values, The. Spender.
London Pavement Artist. Schevill.
Martyrdom of Saint Sebastian, The. Dobson.
Miltonic Sonnet for Mr. Johnson on His Refusal of Peter Hurd's Official Portrait, A. Wilbur.
Musée des Beaux Arts. Auden.
Museum Piece. Wilbur.
My Mother and My Sisters. Ortiz.
Nature Morte. MacNeice.
Ode on a Grecian Urn. Keats.
Old and the New Masters, The. Jarrell.
Paring the Apple. Tomlinson.
Perfect Symbol, The. Johnson.
Preface to the Picture of Dorian Gray. Wilde.
Primitives. Randall.
That No Man Should Write but Such As Do Excel. Turberville.
To an Artist. Burns.
To B. R. Haydon. Wordsworth.
To My Son Parker, Asleep in the Next Room. Kaufman.
To the Stone-Cutters. Jeffers.
Upon Umber: Epigram. Herrick.
What Is Left? Vas.
Why I Am Not a Painter. O'Hara.
*See also* **Painting and Painters; Portraits; Sculpture and Sculptors; Statues.**
**Artemis**
Actaeon. Clough.
Hymn to Artemis, the Destroyer. Zaturenska.
Return of the Goddess Artemis. Graves.
There was a slumbrous silence in the air. *Fr.* Orion. Horne.
*See also* **Diana.**
**Arthurian Legend**
Death of Arthur, The. *Fr.* The Brut. Layamon.
Defence of Guenevere, The. Morris.
Doom-Well of St. Madron, The. Hawker.

Grail, The. Keyes.
Lady of Shalott, The. Tennyson.
Morte d'Arthur. *Fr.* Idylls of the King. Tennyson.
Near Avalon. Morris.
Percivale's Quest. *Fr.* Idylls of the King. Tennyson.
Sir Gawaine and the Green Knight. Winters.

**Ascension Day**
Ascension Thursday. Lewis.

**Ashes**
Ashes. Levine.
Burial, The. Thalman.
Children's Lenten Wisdom. Houck.

**Aspen Trees**
Aspens. Thomas.
Binsey Poplars. Hopkins.

**Asphodels**
Asphodel, That Greeny Flower. Williams.
Snowflake on asphodel, clear ice on rose. Aiken.

**Assassinations and Assassins**
Assassination, The. Justice.
Assassination. Lee.
Assassination Poems. Ridland.
Assassination Raga. Ferlinghetti.
Booth Killed Lincoln. *Unknown.*
Ceremony. Lifshin.
Charles Guiteau. *Unknown.*
Down in Dallas. Kennedy.
For Malcolm: After Mecca. Barrax.
League of Selves, The. Toffler.
Martyr, The. Melville.
Roulette. Ghiselin.
White House Blues. *Unknown.*
Zolgotz. *Unknown.*

**Asses.** *See* **Donkeys.**

**Assumption of the Virgin.** *See* **Mary, the Virgin.**

**Assyrians**
Destruction of Sennacherib, The. Byron.

**Astaire, Fred**
Fred Astaire. Chernoff.

**Astrology**
Upon Looking at a Book of Astrology. McFadden.
Zodiac Rhyme, The. *Unknown.*

**Astronauts**
Astronaut. O'Meara.
Astronaut's Choice. Darcy.
Everlasting Astronauts, The. Buchan.
Problems. Scott.
*See also* Space and Space Travel.

**Astronomers and Astronomy**
Astronomer's Journal, An. Shore.
Astronomers of Mont Blanc, The. Bowers.
Great Bear, The. Hollander.
Planetarium. Rich.
Stargazer, The. *Unknown.*
3 Models of the Universe. Swenson.
When I Heard the Learn'd Astronomer. Whitman.

**Atheism**
Atheist's Prayer, The. Unamuno.
There Is No God. *Fr.* Dipsychus. Clough.
There is no God, as I was taught in youth. Masefield.
Village Atheist, The. *Fr.* Spoon River Anthology. Masters.

**Athletes**
Aging Athlete, The. Weiss.
Athletes. Gibson.
Athlete's Prayer, An. Charles.
Boxer. Clancy.
Confessions of a Born Spectator. Nash.
Everlasting Teamwork in Basketball. Victory.
Ex-Basketball Player. Updike.
Greek Athlete, The. Euripides.
Kleomedes. Wright.
Old Pro's Lament, The. Petrie.

Pole-Vaulter, The. *Unknown.*
Pro Basketball Players. Meschery.
Runner, The. Whitman.
To an Aging Charioteer. Leontius Scholasticus.
To an Athlete Dying Young. Housman.
To an Athlete Turned Poet. Meinke.
To James. *Fr.* Letters Found Near a Suicide. Horne.

**Atlantis**
City in the Sea, The. Poe.
Dreams of Lost Atlantis. Murguia.
In some green island of the sea. *Fr.* Fragments. Masefield.

**Atomic Bomb**
Actual Vision of Morning's Extrusion. Dugan.
Any Day Now. McCord.
Atomic Courtesy. Jacobson.
Dirge for the New Sunrise. Sitwell.
Early Warning. Marks.
Hour of Concern. Hubbell.
If All the Thermo-Nuclear Warheads. Burke.
Little Johnny's Foolish Invention. Patten.
Pastoral: "In the fields." Corrington.
U. S. 1946 King's X. Frost.
*See also* **Hiroshima; Nuclear War.**

**Atoms**
Bigness of Atoms, The. Newcastle.
Our Insufficiency to Praise God Suitably, for His Mercy. *Fr.* God's Determinations. Taylor.
Third Thing, The. Lawrence.
Time of the Mad Atom. Brasier.
Walter Jenks' Bath. Meredith.

**Atterbury, Francis, Bishop of Rochester**
Epitaph: "Meek Francis lies here, friend, without stop or stay." Prior.

**Attica Prison, New York State**
Attica. Coleman.
Stalemate at Attica. Coleman.

**Attics**
Up There. Auden.

**Attis**
Attis. Stanley.

**Attucks, Crispus**
Crispus Attucks. Hayden.

**Auctions**
Homely Accommodation, Suit Gent. Turner.
Wisconsin Farm Auction. Steingass.

**Auden, Wystan Hugh**
Certain World, A. Herschberger.
Just a Smack at Auden. Empson.
On the Death of W. H. Auden. Morice.
Seeing Auden Off. Booth.

**August**
Angle of Vision. Bosworth.
August Afternoon. Edey.
August Weather. Tynan.
Late August at the Game Refuge. Stafford.
Mid-August at Sourdough Mountain Lookout. Snyder.
New England Farm, August 1914, A. Murray.

**Auschwitz, Poland**
Children of Auschwitz. Korzhavin.
Dreams of Auschwitz. Slutsky.
London is full of chickens on electric spits. *Fr.* Annotations of Auschwitz. Porter.

**Austin, Alfred**
Birthday Ode to Mr. Alfred Austin, A. Seaman.

**Australia**
Australia. Hope.
Death of Morgan, The. *Unknown.*
Eyre All Alone. Webb.
History of the Father, A. Buckmaster.
In Brisbane. Harwood.
Middleton's Rouseabout. Lawson.
South Country. Slessor.

Terra Australis. Stewart.
This Land. Mudie.
Waltzing Matilda. *Unknown.*
Wild Colonial Boy, The. *Unknown.*
*Contemporary American and Australian Poetry* (CAAP).
   Thomas Shapcott, ed.
*Golden Apples of the Sun, The* (GAS). Chris Wallace-Crabbe,
   ed.
*Map of Australian Verse, A* (MAuV). James McAuley, ed.

**Authors and Authorship**
Absolute and Abitofhell. Knox.
After Dilettante Concetti. Traill.
Author, The. Churchill.
Author to Her Book, The. Bradstreet.
Black Art, The. Sexton.
Country House, The. Simpson.
Dear Colette. Jong.
Form Rejection Letter. Dacey.
Great men have been among us; hands that penned.
   Wordsworth.
Hamlet's Soliloquy Imitated. Jago.
History of a Literary Movement. Nemerov.
In Praise of BIC Pens. Hilton.
In the Jungle. Enright.
Lake Isle, The. Pound.
Novel, The. Levertov.
On Some South African Novelists. Campbell.
On the Same. Campbell.
Relationships. Van Duyn.
This Monument Will Outlast. *Fr.* Odes. Horace.
To an Author. Freneau.
To Mr. Edward Howard, on His Plays. Sackville.
2001: Tennyson/Hardy Poem, The. Ewart.
Upon the Saying That My Verses Were Made by Another.
   Killigrew.
Young Author, The. Johnson.

**Autism**
Death of a Son. Silkin.

**Automation**
All Watched Over by Machines of Loving Grace. Brautigan.
Man About the Kitchen, A. Hobson.
Now I Set Me. Herman.
You Take the Pilgrims, Just Give Me the Progress. Rosenfield.

**Automobiles**
As a boy with a richness of needs I wandered. Dyment.
Auto Wreck. Shapiro.
Ballad of Faith. Williams.
Brides, The. Hope.
Buddha Inherits 6 Cars on His Birthday, The. Wakoski.
Buick. Shapiro.
Carbreakers. Lines.
Cars. Mulac.
Cherrylog Road. Dickey.
Fugue. Nemerov.
Gas and Hot Air. Bishop.
Heroes of the Strip. Cudahy.
In a Dream, the Automobile. Marcus.
In My Merry Oldsmobile. Bryan.
Johnson's Motor Car. *Unknown.*
Last of the Poet's Car. Connor.
Meditation on the A30. Betjeman.
Morning. Saiser.
Motor Cars. Bennett.
1937 Ford Convertible. McKeown.
Ode to a Dead Dodge. McElroy.
Packard. Barker.
Plastic Jesus. *Unknown.*
Seven-Tenths of a Second. Larson.
Southbound on the Freeway. Swenson.
Terraplane Blues. *Unknown.*
Tête-à-Tête. Honig.
Turquoise Mechanic's Son, The. Toth.

**Autumn**
Accessions to Autumn. Williams.
Autumn. Akhmadulina.
Autumn. Campbell.
Autumn. Clare.
Autumn. Hulme.
Autumn. Longfellow.
Autumn. *Fr.* Summer's Last Will and Testament. Nashe.
Autumn. Scannell.
Autumn. Wolfe.
Autumn; a Dirge. Shelley.
Autumn Change. Clare.
Autumn—For My Son. Churches.
Autumn Horses. Andrews.
Autumn Imagined. Davie.
Autumn In Cornwall. Swinburne.
Autumn Refrain. Stevens.
Autumn Song. D. G. Rossetti.
Before the Frost. Elliott.
Besides the autumn poets sing. Dickinson.
Burning of the Leaves, The. Binyon.
Clear Air of October, The. Bly.
Death of the Flowers, The. Bryant.
Digging. Thomas.
End of Fall, The. Ponge.
End of Summer, The. Minty.
Fall. Bethell.
Fall. Francis.
Fall of Leaves. Savage.
Falling Asleep. Sassoon.
Falltime. Sandburg.
Field of Autumn. Lee.
Fire of Despair Has Been Our Saviour, The. Bly.
Gold Leaves. Chesterton.
Immortal Autumn. MacLeish.
Indian Summer: Vermont. Stevenson.
Kicking the Leaves. Hall.
Late in Fall. Wilson.
Leaflight. Donnelly.
Morns are meeker than they were, The. Dickinson.
Name—of it—is "Autumn," The. Dickinson.
Night Wind in Fall. Moses.
North Wind in October. Bridges.
October. Koeppel.
October-November. Crane.
Ode: Autumn. Hood.
Ode to the Spirit of Earth in Autumn. Meredith.
Of Autumn. Porumbacu.
Red Butte in Autumn. Curry.
Rich Days. Davies.
Rondel: Autumn. Field.
Scattered Leaves. Henson.
Seed-Time. Meredith.
September. Snodgrass.
September Midnight. Teasdale.
Sign, The. Blackburn.
Song at the Beginning of Autumn. Jennings.
Song for Autumn. Young.
Song in Autumn. Fitzgerald.
Song of Autumn I. Baudelaire.
Survivor. MacLeish.
That time of year thou may'st in me behold. *Fr.* Sonnets,
   LXXIII. Shakespeare.
To Autumn. Blake.
To Autumn. Keats.
To the Fringed Gentian. Bryant.
Tonight the winds begin to rise. *Fr.* In Memoriam, A.H.H.
   Tennyson.
When the Frost Is on the Punkin. Riley.
Wild Swans at Coole, The. Yeats.
Winter Is Another Country. MacLeish.

**Aviation and Aviators**

Aeroplane, The. Stuart.
As a boy with a richness of needs I wandered. Dyment.
Darius Greene and His Flying-Machine. Trowbridge.
Dream of Flying Comes of Age, The. Nemerov.
Ego. Booth.
Flights. McDonald.
Flying. Carlile.
Flying Home from Utah. Swenson.
Hangar Nine. Darr.
In Flight. Smith.
Irish Airman Foresees His Death, An. Yeats.
Landscape near an Aerodrome, The. Spender.
My Flying Machine. Brodsky.
N.Y. to L.A. by Jet Plane. Dorman.
Old Pilot's Death, The. Hall.
Pilot. Stuart.
Pilot, The. Turco.
San Diego Poem, A. Ortiz.
Sonic Boom. Updike.
United 555. Eberhart.
Up in the Air. Tippett.
Vapor Trails. Snyder.
When a Beau Goes In. Ewart.
Winged bull trundles to the wired perimeter, The. *Fr.* Flight to Italy. Day Lewis.
*See also* **Air Warfare.**

# B

**Babel, Tower of**
From the four corners of the earth. *Fr.* The People, Yes. Sandburg.
Tower of Babel, The. Crouch.
**Babies**
Afternoon with a Baby, An. Snively.
Babies. Cannon.
Baby-Movements. Lawrence.
Baby's Dance, The. Taylor.
Baby's feet, like sea-shells pink, A. *Fr.* Étude Réaliste. Swinburne.
Breathers, The. Reiss.
Chinese Baby Asleep. Donnelly.
Copy. Armour.
Cradle Hymn. Watts.
Cradle Song, A: "Sweet dreams form a shade." *Fr.* Songs of Innocence. Blake.
Deathwatch. Harper.
Dolls, The. Yeats.
Ecce Puer. Joyce.
Elegy: I. M. Orlando Tobias Gordon. Gordon.
For Every Last Batch When the Next One Comes Along. Dickey.
High Chair and Low Spirits. Armour.
Infant Joy. *Fr.* Songs of Innocence. Blake.
Infant Sorrow. *Fr.* Songs of Experience. Blake.
Katrina. Dawe.
Little Brand New Baby. Paxton.
Make Love Not War. Nemerov.
Morning Song. Plath.
Night Feeding. Rukeyser.
Perambulator Poem. McCord.
Photograph of a Baby. Brasch.
Prettiest Little Baby in the County-O. *Unknown.*
Rock-a-bye Baby. Canning.
Sara in Her Father's Arms. Oppen.
Song for the Middle of the Night, A. Wright.
Song for the Newborn. *Unknown.*
Stunt Flier, The. Updike.

To the White Critics. Rodgers.
Unknown Girl in the Maternity Ward. Sexton.
We Assume: On the Death of Our Son, Reuben Masai Harper. Harper.
What'll We Do with the Baby-O? *Unknown.*
**Baboons**
At the Zoo. De la Mare.
Baboon. *Unknown.*
Baboon, The. Williams.
**Babylon**
Sargon. Bull.
**Bacchus**
Bacchus. Emerson.
Bacchus. Empson.
Bacchus's Opinion of Wine, and Other Beverages. *Fr.* Bacchus in Tuscany. Redi.
Great Bacchus: From the Greek. Prior.
**Bachelors**
After the Ball. Harris.
Bachelor's Life, A. *Unknown.*
I Don't Let the Girls Worry My Mind. *Unknown.*
New England Bachelor, A. Eberhart.
Nil Pejus Est Caelibe Vita. Coleridge.
**Bacteria**
World of Bacteria. Hagiwara.
**Badgers**
Badger, The. Clare.
Badger. Longley.
Catch, The. Ghiselin.
Six Badgers, The. Graves.
**Baldness**
Bald Cavalier, The. *Unknown.*
Of Kate's Baldness. Davies of Hereford.
**Baldwin, James**
For James Baldwin. Boyle.
**Bale, John**
To Doctor Bale. Googe.
**Ballads and Folk Songs**
*American Folk Poetry* (AmFP). Duncan Emrich, ed.
*As I Walked Out One Evening* (AIW). Helen Plotz, comp.
*Faber Book of Ballads, The* (FaBoBa). Matthew Hodgart, ed.
*Folksinger's Wordbook* (FSW). Irwin Silber *and* Fred Silber, eds.
*Penguin Book of Ballads, The* (PeBB). Geoffrey Grigson, ed.
*Richard Dyer-Bennet Folk Song Book, The* (RDB). Richard Dyer-Bennet, ed.
**Ballet**
For the Record. Blount.
Les Sylphides. MacNeice.
**Balloons**
Armadillo, The. Bishop.
Balloon Faces. Sandburg.
Balloons. Plath.
Balloons! Thurman.
Pop. McFadden.
**Baltimore, Maryland**
First Precinct Fourth Ward. Epstein.
**Bands**
Band, The. Dennis.
Band Played On, The. Palmer.
High School Band, The. Whittemore.
**Banjos**
Banjo, The. Winner.
Mama Don't 'Low. *Unknown.*
Song of the Banjo, The. Kipling.
**Banking and Bankers**
Bank. Kalar.
Bank of Marble. Rice.
Girls Working in Banks. Shapiro.
Plot to Assassinate the Chase Manhattan Bank, The. Larsen.
**Banners.** *See* **Flags.**
**Bannockburn, Battle of**

Robert Bruce's March to Bannockburn. Burns.

**Baptism**
Baptism. Nowlan.
Holy Baptism. Herbert.
Jesus, Master, O Discover. *Unknown.*
On the Baptized Ethiopian. Crashaw.

**Bar Mitzvahs**
Bar Mitzvah. Goldemberg.
Bar Mitzvah. Orlen.

**Barbers**
Barber, The. Fuller.
Barbers, The, *sels.* Redgrove.
Machismo. Steingesser.

**Bards**
Bard. Everson.
Bard, The. Gray.
Bard of Armagh, The. *Unknown.*
O Black and Unknown Bards. Johnson.
*See also* **Poetry and Poets.**

**Barley**
Ripe and Bearded Barley, The. *Unknown.*

**Barns**
Barn, The. Heaney.
Barn, The. Spender.
Byre. MacCaig.
Deserted Barn, A. Woiwode.
In Oregon. Stafford.
When These Old Barns Lost Their Inhabitants. Kherdian.

**Bars.** *See* **Taverns.**

**Baseball**
Analysis of Baseball. Swenson.
And You Are There. Clark.
At the Ball Game. Williams.
Athlete's Prayer, An. Charles.
Ball Game. Eberhart.
Ballad of Dead Yankees, The. Petersen.
Base Stealer, The. Francis.
Baseball. Clark.
Baseball and Classicism. Clark.
Baseball and Writing. Moore.
Baseball Pitcher. Kuykendall.
Casey at the Bat. Thayer.
Catch. Francis.
Cobb Would Have Caught It. Fitzgerald.
Cried the Lip. Carroll.
Don Larsen's Perfect Game. Goodman.
Dorlan's Home Walk. Guiterman.
Double Play, The. Wallace.
Double-Header. Stone.
From the Batter's Box. Harford.
Hero. Gross.
Hits and Runs. Sandburg.
Hometown Piece for Messrs. Alston and Reese. Moore.
It Is an Outfielder. Loewinsohn.
Jeep. Stetler.
Little-League Baseball Fan. Moses.
Mel Allen, Mel Allen, Lend Me Your Cliché. Nash.
My Father Dreams of Baseball. Lieberman.
Mystery Baseball. Dacey.
Nuns at Eve. Brinnin.
Ode to the New York Mets. Lindsay.
Of Kings and Things. Morrison.
Old-fashioned Pitcher, The. Phair.
Origin of Baseball, The. Patchen.
One to Nothing. Kizer.
Pitcher. Francis.
Polo Grounds. Humphries.
Post Card out of Panama, A. Barney.
Roundhouse Voices, The. Smith.
September Valentine. Sullivan.
Spitballer. Chappell.
Take Me Out to the Ball Game. Norworth.

Tao in the Yankee Stadium Bleachers. Updike.
To a Baseball. *Unknown.*
To Bert Campaneris. Clark.
To Satch (or American Gothic). Allen.
Ty Cobb Story, The. Clark.
Where, O Where? Bracker.
Willie Mays. Ramsey.

**Basketball**
As It Should Be. Meschery.
Basketball. Vincent.
Ex-Basketball Player. Updike.
Foul Shot. Hoey.
Jump Shooter, The. Trudell.
Jump Shot. Peck.
Lucky Louie Makes a Goal. Van Arsdale.
Mismatch. Lindner.
N.B.A. Prelim, Boston Garden. Whitbread.
Oscar Robertson: Peripheral Vision. Matthews.
Poet Tries to Turn In His Jock, The. Hilton.
To Wilt Chamberlain. Meschery.

**Basset Hounds**
Addition to the Family, An. Morgan.

**Baths and Bathing**
Bath. Kirstein.
Bath, The. Snyder.
Delicate Impasse, A. Atchity.
Friday Night after Bathing. Levy.
Gloire de Dijon. Lawrence.
In a Warm Bath. Rakosi.
Pater's Bathe. Parry.
Voyage of Jimmy Poo, The. Emanuel.
Washing Your Feet. Ciardi.

**Bats**
Bat. Lawrence.
Bat, The. Roethke.
Bat, The. Spear.
Bat and the Scientist, The. Bigelow.
Bat Angels. Levis.
Bat in the Monastery, A. L'Heureux.
Bats. Jarrell.
Bats. Macbeth.
Displays of Skill: The Bat. Herschberger.
Intruder, The. Kizer.
Mad Hatter's Song, The. *Fr.* Alice's Adventures in Wonderland. "Carroll."
Man and Bat. Lawrence.
Mind. Wilbur.
Seven Mexican Children. Schmidt.

**Baucis and Philemon**
Hosts, The. Merwin.
Then Lelex rose, an old experienc'd man. *Fr.* Metamorphoses. Ovid.

**Baudelaire, Charles**
After a Passage in Baudelaire. Duncan.
Ave atque Vale. Swinburne.
Baudelaire. Schwartz.
Baudelaire in Brussels. Cronin.

**Bazille, Frederic**
Ceremony. Wilbur.

**Beaches**
Afternoon: Amagansett Beach. Wheelock.
At the Slackening of the Tide. Wright.
Beach, The. Hart-Smith.
Beach, The. Peters.
Beach in August, The. Kees.
Beach Talk. MacCaig.
Brighton Beach. Durcan.
By the Swimming. Sward.
Deserted Beach. Dallas.
Eel Grass. Millay.
Fiascherino. Tomlinson.
German Shepherd. Livingston.

Littoral.  Flax.
Miramar Beach.  Cunningham.
On the Beach at Night Alone.  Whitman.
On the Marginal Way.  Wilbur.
Prospect Beach.  Lipsitz.
Shoreline.  Barnard.
Skin Divers, The.  Starbuck.
Snow Lies Sprinkled on the Beach, The.  Bridges.
Tidal Pool.  Hay.
Two and the Sea.  Fitzgerald.
With Kit, Age 7, at the Beach.  Stafford.
*See also*  **Shores**.

**Beagles**
Beagles.  Rodgers.
On the Death of Echo.  Coleridge.

**Bean, Judge Roy**
Fine!  Barker.
Law West of the Pecos, The.  Barker.
Roy Bean.  *Unknown.*

**Beans**
How Jack Found That Beans May Go Back on a Chap.  Carryl.

**Beards**
Father's Whiskers.  *Unknown.*

**Beardsley, Aubrey**
Beardsley Flesh, The.  Kanabus.

**Bears**
Achromatic Bear, The.  Bloom.
Albino Bear.  Lawder.
Bad Example.  Fey.
Bear, The.  Frost.
Bear, The.  Kinnell.
Bear, The.  Momaday.
Bear Hunting.  Aua.
Bear on the Delhi Road, The.  Birney.
Bear Who Came to Dinner, The.  Stoutenburg.
Bears.  Rich.
Bears and Waterfalls.  Sarton.
Black Bear sits alone, A.  *Fr.* Lastness.  Kinnell.
Embroidery, An.  Levertov.
Ephraim the Grizzly.  Guiterman.
Grizzly.  Harte.
Grizzly Bear.  Austin.
Grizzly Bear.  *Unknown.*
Lady and the Bear, The.  Roethke.
Lines Written by a Bear of Very Little Brain.  Milne.
Meeting a Bear.  Wagoner.
Moon of Huckleberries.  George.
Muse.  Keyishian.
Part of the Darkness.  Gardner.
Polar Bear, The.  Williams.
Self-Portrait, as a Bear.  Hall.
Small Brown Bear, The.  Baldwin.
This Poem Is for Bear.  *Fr.* Myths and Texts: Hunting.
  Snyder.
Travelling Bear, The.  Lowell.
Trying to Change the Subject.  Ludvigson.
Willy.  Moore.
*Bear Crossings* (BCr).  Anne Newman *and* Julie Suk, eds.

**Beaumont, Sir George**
Elegiac Stanzas.  Wordsworth.

**Beauty**
Alabama.  Fields.
Beautiful, The.  Davies.
Beautiful Changes, The.  Wilbur.
Beauty.  Ashley.
Beauty, The.  Hardy.
Beauty.  Whitman.
Beauty Imposes.  Neilson.
Beauty of Things, The.  Jeffers.
Beauty, sweet love, is like the morning dew.  *Fr.* To Delia.
  Daniel.
Beauty's Excellency.  Noel.

Blue Girls.  Ransom.
Clarinda's Indifference at Parting with Her Beauty.  Countess
  of Winchilsea.
Cold Term.  Jones.
Definition of Beauty, The.  Herrick.
Divinely Superfluous Beauty.  Jeffers.
Euclid Alone Has Looked on Beauty Bare.  Millay.
Frailty and Hurtfulness of Beauty, The.  Earl of Surrey.
Gee, You're So Beautiful That It's Starting to Rain.  Brautigan.
Gloire de Dijon.  Lawrence.
Glory, The.  Thomas.
Hymn to Intellectual Beauty.  Shelley.
I died for beauty—but was scarce.  Dickinson.
July 31.  Jordan.
Merciless Beauty.  Chaucer.
No Second Troy.  Yeats.
Ode on a Grecian Urn.  Keats.
Of Beauty.  Fanshawe.
Of Dying Beauty.  Zukofsky.
Old Lady's Lament for Her Youth, The.  Villon.
Peter Quince at the Clavier.  Stevens.
Pied Beauty.  Hopkins.
Question in a Field.  Bogan.
Saturday: The Small Pox.  Wortley.
She Walks in Beauty.  Byron.
Sorcery.  Hagedorn.
Study in Aesthetics, The.  Pound.
There are many who think of Quintia in terms of beauty.
  Catullus.
Thing of beauty is a joy forever, A.  *Fr.* Endymion.  Keats.
Tinder, The.  Carew.
To a Young Beauty.  Yeats.
To Cynthia: On Concealment of Her Beauty.  Kynaston.
To Dianeme ("Sweet, be not proud of those two eyes").
  Herrick.
To Helen.  Poe.
To me, fair friend, you never can be old.  *Fr.* Sonnets.
  Shakespeare.
Tremor, The.  McKain.
Upon Her Feet.  Herrick.
Upon the Nipples of Julia's Breast.  Herrick.
Valentine for a Lady, A.  Lucilius.

**Beauty Pageants**
Ballade of Beauties.  Scott.
Miss America.  Sadowski.

**Beavers**
Looking for Mountain Beavers.  Wagoner.

**Bedford, Countess of.**  *See* **Russell, Lucy, Countess of Bedford.**

**Beds**
Bed, The.  Hope.
Bed Time.  Davison.
Cot, The.  Amen.
In bed we laugh, in bed we cry.  Johnson.
Land of Counterpane, The.  Stevenson.

**Beech Trees**
November through a Giant Copper Beech.  Honig.

**Beer**
Ballad of Lager Bier, The.  Stedman.
Beer.  Arnold.
Beer.  Calverley.
Glass of Beer, A.  Stephens.
Man That Waters the Workers' Beer, The.  Ryan.
Newcastle Beer.  Cunningham.
Quartermaster Store, The.  *Unknown.*
Under the Anheuser Bush.  Sterling.

**Bees**
Animal, Vegetable and Mineral.  Bogan.
Arrival of the Bee Box, The.  Plath.
As I went owre the Hill o' Hoos.  *Unknown.*
Bee, The.  Dickey.
Bee, The.  *Unknown.*
Bee his burnished carriage, A.  Dickinson.

Bee, the Ant and the Sparrow, The. Cotton.
Beehive. Toomer.
Captived Bee, The: or, The Little Filcher. Herrick.
Couple, A. Swenson.
Dido: Swarming. Spivack.
Flesh-Fly and the Bee, The. Patmore.
Fuscara; or, The Bee-Errant. Cleveland.
Honey Bee, The. Marquis.
Honey-Bees. *Fr.* King Henry V. Shakespeare.
How Doth the Little Busy Bee. Watts.
Humble-Bee, The. Emerson.
Invitation to the Bee. Smith.
Legend of the Hive, A. Hawker.
Life of a Queen. Mueller.
Like trains of cars on tracks of plush. Dickinson.
Mantova. Wright.
March Bee, The. Blunden.
More Ancient Mariner, A. Carman.
On a Honey Bee. Freneau.
Single clover plank, A. Dickinson.
Some Kind of Giant. Pritchard.
Swarming Bees, The. Laughlin.
Telling the Bees. Whittier.
Wild Bees. Baxter.
**Beethoven, Ludwig van**
Beethoven. Wheelock.
Beethoven's Death Mask. Spender.
Dooms menace from tumults. Who's immune. Berryman.
In Gratitude to Beethoven. Wakoski.
Ludwig's Death Mask. Hughes.
**Beetles**
Dusty black beetle, A. Sund.
Eagle and the Beetle, The. La Fontaine.
Origin of Species, The. Sklarew.
Wee man o' leather. *Unknown.*
**Begging and Beggars**
Beggar and Poet. Martin.
Beggar Boy, The. Alexander.
Beggar Man, The. L. Aikin.
Beggarman, The. *Unknown.*
Blind Old Woman. Major.
Jolly Beggars, The. Burns.
Merry Jovial Beggar, The. Casey.
Old Cumberland Beggar, The. Wordsworth.
**Behan, Brendan**
In Memoriam Brendan Behan. Durcan.
**Beiderbecke, Bix**
In a Mist. Young.
**Belfast, Ireland**
Ballad to a Traditional Refrain. Craig.
**Bell, Alexander Graham**
Dear Mr. Bell. Louchheim.
**Belloc, Hilaire**
Hilaire Belloc. Wolfe.
**Bells**
Bell Speech. Wilbur.
Bells, The. Poe
Bells, The. Travis.
Bells of London, The. *Unknown.*
Bells, Ostend, The. Bowles.
Bredon Hill. Housman.
Broken Tower, The. Crane.
Catholic Bells, The. Williams.
Chimes. Meynell.
I Heard the Bells on Christmas Day. Longfellow.
Jingle Bells. Pierpont.
Mission Bells of Monterey. Harte.
Pilgrimage. Duggan.
Ringing the Bells. Sexton.
Sea Bells. Eberhart.
Shandon Bells, The. Mahony.
**Belshazzar**

Babylon. "Cornwall."
Vision of Belshazzar, The. Byron.
**Ben Bulben, Ireland**
Deserted Mountain, The. *Unknown.*
Under Ben Bulben. Yeats.
**Benbow, Admiral John**
Death of Admiral Benbow, The. *Unknown.*
**Bennington, Battle of**
Riflemen's Song at Bennington. *Unknown.*
**Beowulf**
Beowulf. Amis.
**Berkeley, George**
Fountain, The. Davie.
**Bermuda**
Bermudas. Marvell.
**Berrigan, Daniel**
For Dan Berrigan. Knight.
**Berryman, John**
For John Berryman. Gilbert.
For John Berryman, I. Lowell.
**Bertrand de Born**
Sestina: Altaforte. Pound.
**Bethlehem**
Christmas Morning. Roberts.
How Far Is It to Bethlehem? Chesterton.
Long, Long Ago. *Unknown.*
**Betjeman, Sir John**
Betjeman, 1984. Causley.
**Bible**
Bible is an antique volume, The. Dickinson.
Colenso Rhymes for Orthodox Children. Harte.
Genesis. Witt.
Holy Scriptures, The. Herbert.
Light and Glory of the Word, The. Cowper.
On the Bible. Strode.
Respectable Burgher, The. Hardy.
Word of God, across the Ages. Blanchard.
**Bicycles and Bicycling**
Bicycle. Malouf.
Bicycle Rider. McCarthy.
Bicycliary. Brooks.
Cyclists, The. Kearney.
Daisy Bell; or, A Bicycle Built for Two. Dacre.
Under the dawn I wake my two-wheel friend. *Fr.* On a Bicycle. Yevtushenko.
**Bigamy**
Moth and the Flame, The. Taggart.
There was an old party of Lyme. *Unknown.*
Those Wedding Bells Shall Not Ring Out! Rosenfeld.
**Billy the Kid (William H. Bonney)**
Ballad of Billy the Kid, The. Knibbs.
Billy the Kid ("Billy was a bad man"). *Unknown.*
Billy the Kid ("I'll sing you a true song of Billy the Kid"). *Unknown.*
Billy the Kid or William H. Bonney. Thorp.
Pizen Pete's Mistake. *At. to* Honey.
When Billy the Kid Rides Again. Barker.
**Bion**
Fragment of Bion, A. Freneau.
**Birch Trees**
Birch. Simpson.
Birches. Frost.
**Birds**
Aesthetic. Rosten.
After an All-Night Cackle with Sloth and Co. I Enter the Mansion and Greet the Dawn. Gildner.
After Death. Beer.
Air War. Pastan.
All These Birds. Wilbur.
"As When Emotion Too Far Exceeds Its Cause." Oden.
Beat Poem by an Academic Poet. Miller.
Belfast Lough. *Unknown.*

Bird came down the walk, A. Dickinson.
Bird Song. Richards.
Birds. Jeffers.
Birds. Lawrence.
Birds. McMaster.
Birds, The. *Unknown.*
Birds and Fishes. Jeffers.
Birds in the Garden. Rosen.
Birds of America, The. Broughton.
Birds Waking. Merwin.
Blinded Bird, The. Hardy.
Burning of the Birds, The. Kaufman.
Cage, The. Garrett.
Cape Ann. *Fr.* Landscapes. Eliot.
City Bird. Kenyon.
Clack your beaks you cormorants and kittiwakes. *Fr.* A
    Canticle to the Waterbirds. Everson.
Corncrake, The. Cousins.
Curlew. Norris.
Death and Resurrection of the Birds, The. Wagoner.
Death of a Bird. Silkin.
Death of the Bird, The. Hope.
Decoys, The. Auden.
Dissonance. Whitman.
Distances They Keep, The. Nemerov.
Dream in Cold, A. Brigham.
Echoing Cliff, The. Young.
Elizabeth. Muldoon.
Event, An. Wilbur.
Extinct Birds. Wright.
Fate of Birds, The. Seib.
Feel Like a Bird. Swenson.
Flight of Birds, The. Clare.
Flighty Poem. Pauker.
Garnishing the Aviary. Danner.
General Song of Humanity, The. Ferlinghetti.
Grumblers. Clark.
Health to the Birds, A. MacManus.
I Heard a Bird Sing. Herford.
Illustrious Ancestors. Levertov.
In Glencullen. Synge.
It Pleases. Synder.
Jackdaw of Rheims, The. "Ingoldsby."
Lady Lost. Ransom.
Minor Bird, A. Frost.
Mirrorment. Ammons.
Native Companions Dancing. Neilson.
Neighbor. Waterman.
Never Again Would Birds' Song Be the Same. Frost.
Nine Birds. Cummings.
No One to Blame. Lieberman.
No White Bird Sings. Ciardi.
Now (more near ourselves than we). Cummings.
Of the Child with the Bird on the Bush. Bunyan.
On an Indian Tomineios, the Least of Birds. Heyrick.
On the Death of Mrs. Throckmorton's Bullfinch. Cowper.
Ornithology. Fox.
Ornithology in Florida. Guiterman.
Oven Bird, The. Frost.
Oystercatchers. Middleton.
Philip Sparrow. Skelton.
"Plus Ça Change." Whalen.
Poem: "You jam your arm into the white air." Fish.
Presentation of Two Birds to My Son, A. Wright.
Prompt, executive bird is the jay, A. Dickinson.
Proud Songsters. Hardy.
Reincarnation (II). Dickey.
Rivals, The. Stephens.
Robin, Wren, Martin, Swallow. *Unknown.*
Rooks, The. *Unknown.*
Rose, The. Roethke.
Sea Birds, The. Brock.

Sea-Change. Masefield.
Selfsame Song, The. Hardy.
Serenades. Heaney.
She staked her feathers—gained an arc. Dickinson.
Skimmers. Newman.
Sky Patterns. Maino.
Somewhere Is Such a Kingdom. Ransom.
Spring in New York. *Unknown.*
Still Life: Lady with Birds. Prettyman.
Storm, The. De la Mare.
Storm-Cock's Song, The. "MacDiarmid."
Suggested by a Picture of the Bird of Paradise. Wordsworth.
Sympathy. Dunbar.
To a Ground-Lark. Campbell.
To a Waterfowl. Bryant.
To the Man-of-War Bird. Whitman.
Trouble-shooting. Stafford.
Truth, The. Davies.
Up from the Egg: The Confessions of a Nuthatch Avoider.
    Nash.
Wagtail's Nest, The. MacKenzie.
Washington Migrants. Jellema.
Waterfall, The. Vaughan.
What Birds Were There. Everson.
*Poetry of Birds, The* (PB). Samuel Carr, ed.
*See also* **names of birds (e.g., Canaries).**

**Birds' Nests**
Birds' Nests. Thomas.
Building of the Nest, The. Sangster.
Natural Grace, A. Stead.
Nesting Time. Guiterman.
Nesting Time. Stewart.

**Birds of Paradise**
In London Town. M. Coleridge.

**Bird-watching**
Up from the Egg: The Confessions of a Nuthatch Avoider.
    Nash.

**Birmingham, Alabama**
Ballad of Birmingham. Randall.
Birmingham 1963. Patterson.
Letters from Birmingham. Bond.

**Birth**
Before the Birth of One of Her Children. Bradstreet.
Birth. Bruck.
Birth. Smallshaw.
Birth Day. Meeter.
Birthdays. Domin.
Birthing, The. Bentley.
Childbirth. Perlman.
Christmas and Common Birth. Ridler.
Country Midwife, The: A Day. Ai.
Crooked Carol. Farber.
D-Day Minus. Brock.
Elegy: I. M. Orlando Tobias Gordon. Gordon.
Entry. Thwaite.
How You Get Born. Jong.
Infant Sorrow. *Fr.* Songs of Experience. Blake.
Interphase. Cummings.
July 12. Ortiz.
Lo! a Child Is Born. "MacDiarmid."
Mississippi Born. Lomax.
Night Was Smooth, The. Bertolino.
Notes from the Delivery Room. Pastan.
Our Sobbing Must Be Heard. Cavalieri.
Poem to Ease Birth. *Unknown.*
Prayer before Birth. MacNeice.
Queen Jane. *Unknown.*
Recovery Room, The: Lying-in. Chasin.
To a 14 Year Old Girl in Labor and Delivery. Stone.
To Insure Survival. Ortiz.
To the Anxious Mother. Malangatana.
**Birth Control.** *See* **Contraception.**

**Birthdays**
Birthday of but a single pang.  Dickinson.
Birthday Party.  Patton.
Can't Wait.  Kitching.
Happy Birthday to Me.  Merriam.
Her Birthday.  Witt.
Monday's child is fair of face.  Mother Goose.
On My Thirty-third Birthday.  Byron.
Poem for My Twentieth Birthday.  Koch.
Poem in October.  Thomas.
To Mrs. Thrale on Her Thirty-fifth Birthday.  Johnson.
Trala Trala Trala La-le-la.  Williams.
Twenty-seventh of March, The.  Bryant.
Writ on the Eve of My 32nd Birthday.  Corso.
Your birthday comes to tell me this.  Cummings.
**Bison.**  *See* **Buffaloes.**
**"Black Bart"**
Black Bart.  *Unknown.*
"Black Bart, P08."  Bierce.
**Black Hills (U.S.)**
Dreary Black Hills, The.  *Unknown.*
**Black Verse**
*American Negro Poetry* (AmNP 1974 ed.).  Arna Bontemps, ed.
*Black Poets, The* (BPo).  Dudley Randall, ed.
*Blues Line, The* (BluL).  Eric Sackheim, comp.
*Celebrations* (CNA).  Arnold Adoff, ed.
*Forerunners, The: Black Poets in America* (FB).  Woodie King, Jr., ed.
*Jump Bad: A New Chicago Anthology* (JB).  Gwendolyn Brooks, ed.
*Poetry of Black America, The* (PoBA).  Arnold Adoff, ed.
**Blackberries**
Blackberry-picking.  Heaney.
Blackberry Thicket, The.  Stanford.
Blackberrying.  Plath.
Forty Pounds of Blackberries Equals Thirteen Gallons of Wine.  Hoeft.
**Blackbirds**
Best of Two Worlds.  Boothroyd.
Blackbird.  Leach.
Blackbird, The.  Tennyson.
Blackbird, The.  Wolfe.
Blackbird by Belfast Lough, The.  *Unknown.*
Blackbird Singing, A.  Thomas.
Blackbird startles from the homestead hedge, The.  *Fr.* Child Harold.  Clare.
Blackbird's Song.  *Unknown.*
I watched a blackbird on a budding sycamore.  Hardy.
Redwing, The.  P. Dickinson.
Redwings.  Heyen.
Thirteen Ways of Looking at a Blackbird.  Stevens.
**Blackburn, Paul**
Walking Past Paul Blackburn's Apt. on 7th St.  Wakoski.
**Blackouts**
Power Failure.  Browne.
**Blacks**
Africa's Plea.  Dempster.
Allegory in Black.  Clark.
And Now Out of Sight.  Landrum.
At the National Black Assembly.  Baraka.
Being Black.  Coleman.
Big Momma.  Lee.
Black Art.  Baraka.
Black Jam for Dr. Negro.  Evans.
Black Majesty.  Cullen.
Black Mother Woman.  Lorde.
Black Tambourine.  Crane.
Blackberry Sweet.  Randall.
Blackjack Moses.  Zu-Bolton.
Blackstone Rangers.  Brooks.
Blue-eyed Precinct Worker, The.  Coulette.
But He Was Cool; or, He Even Stopped for Green Lights.  Lee.

Changeless Changes.  Mabuza.
Congo, The.  Lindsay.
Dab of Color, A.  Weiss.
Dance for Militant Dilettantes, A.  Young.
Dark Prophesy: I Sing of Shine.  Knight.
Dark Symphony.  Tolson.
Different Image, A.  Randall.
Dinner Guest: Me.  Hughes.
Dream Variation.  Hughes.
For a Lady I Know.  Cullen.
For Both of Us at Fisk.  Scott.
For de Lawd.  Clifton.
For My People.  Walker.
Good Morning.  Hughes.
Governor of Ollie Street, The.  Zu-Bolton.
Her Story.  Madgett.
Heritage.  Cullen.
Hot Poem.  Viidikas.
I Have Seen Black Hands.  Wright.
I, Too.  Hughes.
I was five.  Lee.
Image in the Mirror.  Kenner.
Incident.  Cullen.
Ka 'Ba.  Baraka.
Listening to Mbaqanga.  Mabuza.
Little Black Boy, The.  *Fr.* Songs of Innocence.  Blake.
Madimba: Gwendolyn Brooks.  Harper.
Main Man Blues.  Redmond.
Making Out.  Emeruwa.
Merry-go-round.  Hughes.
Metamorphosis of Aunt Jemima, The.  Childress.
Midway in the Night: Blackman.  Redmond.
Missing Beat.  Rogers.
Mr. Z.  Holman.
Mulatto.  Hughes.
Necessity.  Hughes.
Negro, The.  Emanuel.
Negro Servant.  Hughes.
Negro Speaks of Rivers, The.  Hughes.
Negro's Tragedy, The.  McKay.
Nikki-Rosa.  Giovanni.
O Black and Unknown Bards.  Johnson.
Of De Witt Williams on His Way to Lincoln Cemetery.  Brooks.
Old Black Joe.  Foster.
On Being Brought from Africa to America.  Wheatley.
On Universalism.  Knight.
Poem for Halfwhite College Students.  Baraka.
Poem for Players, A.  Young.
Poem to a Nigger Cop.  Hamilton.
Positive Movement Will Be Difficult but Necessary.  Lee.
Puzzled.  Hughes.
Quickview.  Mberi.
Refugee in America.  Hughes.
Remember Times for Sandy.  Rogers.
Robert.  Clifton.
September 1, 1802.  Wordsworth.
Sermon on the Warpland, The.  Brooks.
Sevier County Runaway, The.  Brigham.
Sonnet to a Negro in Harlem.  Johnson.
Southern Cop.  Brown.
Stereo.  Lee.
Telephone Conversation.  Soyinka.
That Life, That Love, That Fine.  Coleman.
Theme for English B.  Hughes.
There Is No Light.  Mabuza.
Tired Lizi Tired.  Mabuza.
2 Takes from Love in Los Angeles.  Young.
221-1424.  Sanchez.
Upstairs Downstairs.  Allen.
Vive Noir!  Evans.
Way It Is, The.  Oden.

Way It Was, The. Clifton.
We Climb Upwards. Troupe.
We Real Cool. Brooks.
We Walk the Way of the New World. Lee.
Where It's At. Bergé.
Where my grandmother lived. Long.
White Troops Had Their Orders but the Negroes Looked Like Men, The. Brooks.
Woman. Bohanon.
Woman Poem. Giovanni.
Women. Walker.
Yet Do I Marvel. Cullen.
Your Blacks Bones Do Not Remember. Tuthill.

**Blacksmiths**
Blacksmiths, The. *Unknown.*
Blacksmith's Song, The. *Unknown.*
Forge, The. Heaney.
Village Blacksmith, The. Longfellow.

**Blenheim, Battle of**
Battle of Blenheim, The. Southey.

**Blindness**
Blind Always Come as Such a Surprise, The. Kooser.
Blind Boy, The. Cibber.
Blind Fiddler, The. *Unknown.*
Blind Girl on the Santa Fe. Hilberry.
Blind Man, The. Mann.
Blindman, The. Swenson.
Blind Man Who Sells Brushes, The. James.
Blind Men and the Elephant, The. Saxe.
Discovering an Island. Lowbury.
Eggs and Marrowbone. *Unknown.*
Hugh Stuart Boyd. Browning.
On His Blindness. Milton.
Spring, and the Blind Children. Noyes.
To Mr. Cyriac Skinner upon His Blindness. Milton.
Who-Tapped-the-Frogs-In. Makidemewabe.

**Blood**
Little Death. Thomas.
Temple is full of blood, The. Villanueva.

**Bloodhounds**
Bloodhound, The. Anthony.

**Blue (color)**
Fragmentary Blue. Frost

**Bluebeard**
Bluebeard's Wife. Hine.

**Bluebells**
Bluebells, The. Masefield.

**Blueberries**
Blueberries. Frost.
Hermit Picks Blueberries, The. Kumin.
Secret, The. Coffin.

**Bluebirds**
Blue-Bird, The. Melville.
Last Word of a Bluebird, The. Frost.

**Bluefish**
Night Fishing for Blues. Smith.

**Blues (mood)**
Blues Suite. Bohanon.
Bound No'th Blues. Hughes.
Chromo. Fabio.
D Blues. Hernton.
Death Sting Me Blues. *Unknown.*
Get Up, Blues. Emanuel.
Good Mornin' Blues. *Unknown.*
St. Louis Blues. Handy.
Sporting Life Blues. *Unknown.*
Talking after Christmas Blues. Henri.
Too Blue. Hughes.
Weave Room Blues. *Unknown.*
Winnsboro Cotton Mill Blues. *Unknown.*

**Blues (music)**
Blues and Bitterness. Bennett.

Blues Note. Kaufman.
Blues Today, The. Jackson.
Coal Loadin' Blues. *Unknown.*
Depot Blues. *Unknown.*
East St. Louis Blues. *Unknown.*
Four O'Clock Flower Blues. *Unknown.*
Franklin Avenue Blues People. Troupe.
Gonna Lay My Head Down on Some Railroad Line. *Unknown.*
Homage to the Empress of the Blues. Hayden.
I Remember How She Sang. Penny.
I Rode Southern, I Rode L & N. *Unknown.*
Lowdown Dirty Blues. *Unknown.*
McCoy Tyner at Slugs. Troupe.
Mississippi Blues. *Unknown.*
Music, The. Hoagland.
Poem for Otis Redding. Thomas.
Ragged and Dirty. *Unknown.*
Railroad Blues, The. *Unknown.*
Ray Charles. Cornish.
Special Rider Blues. *Unknown.*
To Dinah Washington. Knight.
Train Is off the Track, The. *Unknown.*
Weary Blues, The. Hughes.
Why I Sing the Blues. B. B. King.
Worried Life Blues. *Unknown.*
Worried Man Blues. *Unknown.*
*Blues Line, The* (BluL). Eric Sackheim, comp.

**Boadicea**
Boadicea. Cowper.

**Boarding Houses**
Mr. Bleaney. Larkin.

**Boats**
Barges on the Hudson. Deutsch.
Beginning to Squall. Swenson.
Boat Poem. Spencer.
Boats. MacCaig.
Bonded. Brady.
Cargoes. Masefield.
Drunken Boat, The. Rimbaud.
Flower-Boat, The. Frost.
Paper Boats, *sel.* Tagore.
Queen of Connemara, The. Fahy.
Steamboat Bill. *Unknown.*
Unlucky Boat. Brown.
Where Go the Boats? Stevenson.
Yachts, The. Williams.
*See also* **Ships**.

**Bobwhites**
Bob White. Cooper.

**Bodies**
Bath, The. Synder.
Body, The. Herrick.
Body and Soul: A Meditation. Kumin.
Body Poems, *sels.* Barks.
First Prayer. Atwood.
Head Itself. Riding.
Her True Body. Metz.
His Body. McPherson.
Human Geography. Fuertes.
I Like My Body When It Is with Your Body. Cummings.
"It's a Whole World, the Body. A Whole World!"—Swami Satchidandanda. Young.
Old Nudists, The. Colby.
Origin of the Praise of God, The. Bly.
Praise. Matthews.
Question. Swenson.
Seven-Year Body Cycle, The. Steingass.
Soul's Garment, The. Duchess of Newcastle.
This Earthen Body. *Unknown.*
To My Body. Sullivan.
Vases of Wombs, The. Gioseffi.

Waiting. Cooper.
What Do You Say When a Man Tells You, You Have the
  Softest Skin. Mackey.
What Is Man's Body? *Unknown.*
Where I'm Staying Now. Meredith.
**Bogart, Humphrey**
Bogart. Flocos.
Bogey. Berkson.
Nobody Dies Like Humphrey Bogart. Rosten.
**Bogs**
Gullion, The. Glen.
**Boleyn, Anne**
Anne Boleyn's Song. E. Sitwell.
**Boll Weevils**
Ballit of de Boll Weevil, De. *Unknown.*
**Bones**
After X-Ray. Pastan.
Bones, The. Merwin.
Bones. Smith.
Epitaph on William Jones. *Unknown.*
Hollow Flute, The. Strauss.
Raccoon Skeleton at Long Plain Creek. Minton.
Steakbones. Wild.
Three Lectures on the Skeleton. Young.
What the Bones Do. Bissonette.
**Bonhomme Richard (ship)**
Ballad of Benjamin Bones, The. Ward.
Battle of the *Bonhomme Richard* and the *Serapis.* Whitman.
**Bonnie Prince Charlie.** *See* **Stuart, Charles Edward.**
**Bononcini, Giovanni Battista**
Epigram on Handel and Bononcini. Byron.
**Books**
Against the Evidence. Ignatow.
Book of Verses, A. Marcus.
Bookshop Idyll, A. Amis.
Book-Worms, The. Burns.
Fiction and the Reading Public. Larkin.
Fire at Alexandria, The. Weiss.
House Was Quiet and the World Was Calm, The. Stevens.
Insect Shuffle Method, The. Tapp.
On His Books. Belloc.
Over 2000 Illustrations and a Complete Concordance. Bishop.
Precious, mouldering pleasure 'tis, A. Dickinson.
Study of Reading Habits, A. Larkin.
Style. Nemerov.
There is no frigate like a book. Dickinson.
**Boomerangs**
Boomerang. Perreault.
**Boone, Daniel**
Daniel Boone. Benét.
Daniel Boone. Guiterman.
Slow Boone. Flanner.
**Booth, John Wilkes**
Booth Killed Lincoln. *Unknown.*
**Booth, William**
General William Booth Enters into Heaven. Lindsay.
**Borden, Lizzie**
Crimes of Lizzie Borden, The. *Unknown.*
**Boredom**
Dolor. Roethke.
Life, friends, is boring. We must not say so. Berryman.
Pooh! De la Mare.
Testimony Concerning a Sickness. Blazek.
Things to Do in Providence. Berrigan.
**Borges, Jorge Luis**
Borges. Barnstone.
For Borges. Berryhill.
**Borgia, Lucrezia**
On Seeing a Hair of Lucretia Borgia. Landor.
**Bosch, Hieronymus**
Homage to Hieronymus Bosch. MacGreevy.
**Boston, Massachusetts**

As a Plane Tree by the Water. Lowell.
Beasts of Boston, The. Lowry.
Boston. Bossidy.
For the Union Dead. Lowell.
South End. Aiken.
Thanksgiving in Boston Harbor, The. Butterworth.
**Boston Evening Transcript (newspaper)**
*Boston Evening Transcript,* The. Eliot.
**Boswell, James**
Poetical and Congratulatory Epistle to James Boswell Esq., A.
  "Pindar."
**Botany Bay, Australia**
Botany Bay. *Unknown.*
**Bourgeoisie**
How Beastly the Bourgeois Is. Lawrence.
Interior. Taggard.
Red-Herring. Lawrence.
Salesman is an it that stinks excuse, A. Cummings.
Unknown Citizen, The. Auden.
**Bowery, The (New York City)**
Bowery. Ignatow.
**Bowles, William Lisle**
To the Rev. W. L. Bowles. Coleridge.
**Boxer Rebellion**
Old Photo in an Old Life, An. Hoffman.
**Boxing and Boxers**
Advice to a Prizefighter. Lucilius.
Ballad of Billy Rose, The. Norris.
Black Lady in an Afro Hairdo Cheers for Cassius. Holmes.
Blues for Benny Kid Paret. Smith.
Boxer. Clancy.
Boxer Loses Face and Fortune. Lucilius.
Clay Comes Out to Meet Terrell. Ali.
Elegy for Lyn James. Norris.
Kid's Last Fight, The. *Unknown.*
Loser, The. Bukowski.
Mastering the Craft. Scannell.
Monument to a Boxer. Lucilius.
On Hurricane Jackson. Dugan.
Retired Boxer, The. Lucilius.
TKO. Peck.
Throw Him Down M'Closkey. Kelly.
To a Fighter Killed in the Ring. Lipsitz.
X of the Unknown, The. Clark.
**Boyne, Battle of the**
Battle of the Boyne, The. Blacker.
Boyne Water, The. *Unknown.*
Dialogue between King William and the Late King James on the
  Banks of the Boyne, A. Blount.
**Boys.** *See* **Childhood and Children; Youth.**
**Brahma**
Brahma. Emerson.
**Bread**
Baking Day. Joseph.
Bread. Burnshaw.
Bread. Pillin.
Bread. Urdang.
Bread Is Born. Hebert.
Evening Bread. Glatstein.
**Breakfast**
At Breakfast. Swenson.
**Brendan, Saint**
Fish at Mass, The. *Unknown.*
Lives of the Saints. Muldoon.
**Brides**
Bride, The. Akhmadulina.
Brides, The. Hope.
**Bridgeport, Connecticut**
Last Job I Held in Bridgeport, The. Donzella.
**Bridges, Robert**
To R. B. Hopkins.
**Bridges**

Address to the New Tay Bridge, An. McGonagall.
Bridge, The. Crane.
Building the Bridge. Dromgoole.
Burned Bridge, The. Stone.
London Bridge. *Unknown.*
Railway Bridge of the Silvery Tay, The. McGonagall.
Simile for Her Smile, A. Wilbur.
Tay Bridge Disaster, The. McGonagall.
**Bridget, Saint**
Giveaway, The. McGinley.
**Bristol, England**
In the Dim City. Salmon.
**Bristol, Rhode Island**
Bombardment of Bristol, R.I., The. *Unknown.*
**British Empire**
English Flag, The. Kipling.
Fuzzy-Wuzzy. Kipling.
Recessional. Kipling.
**Broadway, New York City**
Broadway. Whitman.
Broadway Pageant, A. Whitman.
Give My Regards to Broadway. Cohan.
**Brontë, Anne**
On the Death of Anne Brontë. C. Brontë.
**Brontë, Charlotte**
Sampler from Haworth. Howard.
**Brontë, Emily**
Haworth in May. Childe.
**Bronx, New York City**
Bronxomania. Cruz.
East Bronx. Ignatow.
**Brooklyn, New York City**
Brooklyn Heights. Wain.
Clickety-Clack. Blackburn.
Crossing Brooklyn Ferry. Whitman.
It's 8:54 a.m. Brooklyn it's the 28th of July and. Berrigan.
**Brooklyn Bridge**
Brooklyn Bridge. Mayakovsky.
Granite and Steel. Moore.
To Brooklyn Bridge. *Fr.* The Bridge. Crane.
**Brooklyn Dodgers**
Hometown Piece for Messrs. Alston and Reese. Moore.
**Brooks, Gwendolyn**
Afterword, An: for Gwen Brooks. Lee.
Gwendolyn Brooks. Lee.
Madimba: Gwendolyn Brooks. Harper.
**Brooks and Streams**
Bendemeer's Stream. Moore.
Brook, The. Tennyson.
Inversnaid. Hopkins.
Resolve, The. Levertov.
Runoff. Ammons.
There is a stream which rises. Bruchac.
West-running Brook. Frost.
**Brotherhood**
As It Should Be. Meschery.
Blest Be the Tie That Binds. Fawcett.
Brotherhood. Vega.
Comrade—Mister. Schneider.
Dark Testament. Murray.
Divine Image, The ("To mercy, pity, peace, and love"). *Fr.* Songs of Innocence. Blake.
Dual Site, The. Hamburger.
Fraternitas. Pound.
Hymn for Nations. *Unknown.*
I Dream a World. Hughes.
In the Mourning Time. Hayden.
In Two Fields. Williams.
Man's a Man for A' That, A. Burns.
O Blest Estate, Blest from Above. Sandys.
Poem of Distant Childhood. Sousa.
Round Table, The. Kenner.

Same Side of the Canoe, The. Espirito Santo.
Sonnet of Brotherhood. Mason.
To Some Millions Who Survive Joseph E. Mander, Sr. Wright.
Tuft of Flowers, The. Frost.
We Talked. Casiano.
**Brothers**
Atlantis. Ferguson.
Beyond the Window. Darcy.
Hidden Falls. Minczeski.
In My Brother's House. Fedullo.
In the Tree House at Night. Dickey.
My Brother's Braces. Hutchinson.
Opposite Field, The. Stuart.
Poem for My Brother. Logan.
Prodigal Son, The. Robinson.
River Kleeg, The. Kuzma.
Talk to Me, Baby. Browne.
To My Brothers. Keats.
Twa Brothers, The. *Unknown.*
Unwritten Letters. Orlen.
You Can Have It. Levine.
*Brother Songs: A Male Anthology of Poetry* (BrS). Jim Perlman, ed.
**Brown, James**
Hearing James Brown at the Café des Nattes. Long.
**Brown, John**
John Brown's Body. *Unknown.*
O Metaphysical Head. Gregory.
October 16: The Raid. Hughes.
Portent, The. Melville.
**Browning, Elizabeth Barrett**
Her—"last poems." Dickinson.
Sisters, The. A. Lowell.
To Edward Fitzgerald. R. Browning.
To the Authoress of "Aurora Leigh." Dobell.
**Browning, Robert**
After Robert Browning. Chesterton.
Last Ride Together, The. Stephen.
Sincere Flattery of R.B. Stephen.
To Robert Browning. Landor.
**Bruce, Robert**
Bruce Meets Three Men with a Wether. Barbour.
Robert Bruce's March to Bannockburn. Burns.
**Bruckner, Anton**
Bruckner. Camp.
**Bruegel, Pieter**
Brueghel's Winter. De la Mare.
Children's Games. Williams.
Dance, The. Williams.
Die Bauernhochzeit. Smithyman.
Hunters in the Snow: Brueghel. Langland.
Landscape with the Fall of Icarus. Williams.
Lines on Brueghel's *Icarus.* Hamburger.
Musée des Beaux Arts. Auden.
Two Views of a Cadaver Room. Plath.
Winter Landscape. Berryman.
**Brunanburh, Battle of**
Battle of Brunanburh. *Unknown.*
**Bryan, William Jennings**
Bryan, Bryan, Bryan, Bryan. Lindsay.
Bryan's Last Battle. *Unknown.*
Free Silver. *Unknown.*
**Bryant, William Cullen**
Bryant. *Fr.* A Fable for Critics. Lowell.
**Buckingham, George Villiers, 2d Duke of**
Death of the Duke of Buckingham. *Fr.* Moral Essays. Pope.
**Buddha**
Buddha. Melville.
Buddha took some autumn leaves. *Fr.* The City of the Moon. Rexroth.
Buddha's Birthday: April 8, 1819. *Fr.* Oraga Haru. Issa.

Buddha's Death Day: February 15, 1815. *Fr.* Oraga Haru.
  Issa.
Further Advantages of Learning. Rexroth.
Gautama in the Deer Park at Benares. Patchen.
So they rode. *Fr.* The Light of Asia. Arnold.

**Buffalo Bill (William Frederick Cody)**
Buffalo Bill's. Cummings.
To William (Whom We Have Missed). Wodehouse.

**Buffaloes**
Bison, The. Belloc.
Bison Track, The. Taylor.
Bone Yard. Barnes.
Buffalo, The. Moore.
Buffalo Dusk. Sandburg.
Buffalo, Our Sacred Beast, The. McKeown.
Buffalo Skinners, The. *Unknown.*
Caller of the Buffalo. Austin.
Crossing the Plains. Miller.
Death Chant. Blue Cloud.
Flower-fed Buffaloes, The. Lindsay.
Ghost of the Buffaloes, The. Lindsay.
I rise, I rise/ I who makes the earth to tremble. *Unknown.*
Passing of the Buffalo, The. Garland.
Rising of the Buffalo Men, The. *Unknown.*
Trail beside the River Platte, The. Heyen.

**Bull Run, Battles of**
Battle of Bull Run, The. *Unknown.*
March into Virginia, The. Melville.

**Bullfights and Bullfighters**
Bull Fight, The. *Fr.* Childe Harold's Pilgrimage. Byron.
Death Invited. Swenson.
Lament for Ignacio Sánchez Mejías. García Lorca.
Laneliest Place in the Warld, The. Campbell.
Matadors, The. Jacobsen.
Picador Bit, The. Noll.
Priest and the Matador, The. Bukowski.

**Bulls**
Black Tomintoul. Finlay.
Bull, A. Deutsch.
Bull, The. Sackville-West.
Bull, The. Williams.
Bull, The. Wright.
Hoosen Johnny. *Unknown.*
No Man's Good Bull. Seay.
Outlaw, The. Heaney.
Seventh Georgic. Economou.

**Bums.** *See* **Vagabonds.**

**Bunker Hill, Battle of**
Ballad of Bunker Hill, The. *Unknown.*
Death of Warren, The. Sargent.
Sword of Bunker Hill, The. Wallace.
Warren's Address. Pierpont.

**Bunyan, John**
For Tinkers Who Travel on Foot. Avison.

**Bureaucracy**
Bureaucrat, The. Bull.
Committee, The. Day Lewis.
Frigate Jones, the Pussyfooter. Burke.
Just Ask for a Demonstration. Weismiller.
Sharks in Shallow Water. Levinson.
Take off your hat. *Unknown.*

**Burke, Edmund**
Burke. *Fr.* Sonnets on Eminent Characters. Coleridge.
Here lies our good Edmund, whose genius was such. *Fr.*
  Retaliation. Goldsmith.

**Burlesque**
Stripper, The. Probst.

**Burne-Jones, Edward**
For "The Wind of Circe" by Burne-Jones. Rossetti.

**Burns, Robert**
At the Grave of Burns, 1803. Wordsworth.
Cemetery near Burns' Cottage, The. Smith.

Had we two met, blythe-hearted Burns. Landor.
Mute Is Thy Wild Harp, Now, O Bard Sublime. Smith.
On Visiting the Tomb of Burns. Keats.
Sonnet Written in the Cottage Where Burns Was Born. Keats.

**Burr, Aaron**
Aaron Burr's Wooing. Stedman.

**Burroughs, William**
On Burroughs' Work. Ginsberg.

**Burton, Sir Richard (1821-1890)**
Dedication: "Some nine years gone, as we dwelt together."
  Swinburne.

**Buses**
Boarding, The. Johnson.
Bus, The. Cohen.
Bus Ride. Kandel.
Motor Bus. Godley.
My Busconductor. McGough.

**Businessmen**
Executive. Betjeman.

**Butchers and Butchering**
Age of the Butcher, The. Friebert.
Blood. Murray.
Butcher, A. Hood.
Butcher Shop. Simic.
Butcherboy. Schmidt.
Cock Crowing in a Poulterer's Shop, A. Ferguson.
Fifth Hell, The. *Fr.* The Seven Hells of Jigoku Zoshi.
  Rothenberg.
Friday Lunchbreak. Orr.
Kicking from Centre Field. McFadden.
Meat Works, The. Gray.
Reuben Bright. Robinson.
Skill in Killing, A. Abbe.
Slaughter-House, The. Hayes.
Slaughter-Room Picture, The. Steingass.
Stockyard, The. Squire.

**Butler, Samuel (1612-80)**
On Butler who can think without just rage. *Fr.* A Satire.
  Oldham.

**Butler, Samuel (1835-1902)**
English Liberal. Taylor.

**Butter**
Churning Day. Heaney.

**Buttercups**
Buttercup. Dodge.
Buttercups. Radford.

**Butterflies**
Blue-Butterfly Day. Frost.
Butterflies. Sansom.
Butterflies on an Illinois Road. Minton.
Butterfly in the Fields. Campbell.
Chalk Blue Butterfly, The. Spender.
City Butterfly. Siebert.
Envoi: "Fly, white butterflies, out to sea." Swinburne.
Fauna: March. Lake.
Flying Crooked. Graves.
I was round and small like a pearl. *Unknown.*
Menashtash. Cardona-Hine.
Of the Boy and Butterfly. Bunyan.
Roots and Branches. Duncan.
September Butterfly. Boring.
To a Butterfly. Schuck.
To a Butterfly ("I've watched you now a full half hour").
  Wordsworth.
To a Butterfly ("Stay near me—do not take thy flight!").
  Wordsworth.
Was Worm. Swenson.

**Buzzards**
Buzzard. Norris.

**Byron, George Gordon Noel Byron, 6th Baron**
Byron. Coogler.
Byron vs. DiMaggio. Meinke.

Fragment: To Byron. Shelley.
Letter to Lord Byron. Auden.
Memorial Verses. Arnold.
Sketch of Lord Byron's Life. Moore.
Sonnet to Byron. Shelley.
To Lord Byron. Keats.
Very Like a Whale. Nash.
With a Wreath of Laurel. Coolbrith.

**Byzantium**
Byzantium. Yeats.
Sailing to Byzantium. Yeats.

# C

**Cactus**
Cactus Stem. Larson.
Cactuses, The. Witheford.
Night-Blooming Cereus, The. Hayden.
Organ Cactus, The. Scarborough.

**Caedmon**
Caedmon. Nicholson.

**Caesar, Julius**
Julius Caesar. *Unknown.*
Voice of Caesar, The. *Fr.* For the Time Being. Auden.

**Cain and Abel**
Abel. Lasker-Schuler.
Abel's Blood. Vaughan.
Autobiography. Pagis.
Brothers. Pagis.

**Caliban**
Caliban upon Setebos; or, Natural Theology in the Island.
 Browning.

**California**
Before the Stuff Comes Down. Snyder.
California #2. Cruz.
California Oaks, The. Winters.
California Phrasebook, The. Schmitz.
California, This Is Minnesota Speaking. Dunn.
California Winter. Shapiro.
Frankenstein Stagger, The. Lane.
How Was Your Trip to L.A.? Whalen.
In California. Simpson.
Just California. McGroarty.
Late Spring, Sur Coast. Clark.
Marin-An. Synder.
Our Beautiful West Coast Thing. Brautigan.
Vitamins and Roughage. Rexroth.

**Calliope (goddess)**
To Calliope. Graves.

**Calvary.** *See* **Crucifixion, The.**

**Calves**
Bull Calf, The. Layton.
Hey Animal—Eat This Popcorn. Kornblum.
I Would Like You for a Comrade. Parry.
New Calf, The. Hearst.
New Calf, The. Vaughan.

**Calvinism**
After the Surprising Conversions. Lowell.
Calvin in the Casino. Cassity.
McAndrew's Hymn. Kipling.
Mr. Edwards and the Spider. Lowell.
To a Calvinist in Bali. Millay.
Words. Glen.

**Calypso (mythology)**
Callypso Speaks. Doolittle ("H.D.").
Calypso's Island. MacLeish.
Forever Ambrosia. Morley.

**Cambridge, England**

Devourers, The. Macaulay.
In the Backs. Cornford.
Old Vicarage, Grantchester, The. Brooke.

**Cambridge, Massachusetts**
Professor Kelleher and the Charles River. O'Grady.

**Cambridge University**
Answer to an Invitation to Cambridge, An. Cowley.
Satire Upon the Heads. Gray.

**Cambridgeshire, England**
Cambridgeshire. Cornford.
Travelling Home. Cornford.

**Camels**
Camel. Laila Akhyaliyya.
Camel. Stallworthy.
Camels. Nordhaus.
Camel's Complaint, The. Carryl.
Camels, the Kings' Camels, The. Norris.
Dromedary. Dodat.

**Camões, Luis de**
Camões and the Debt. Andresen.
Luis de Camões. Campbell.

**Camping**
Black Lake. Nibbelink.
First Camp. Kuzma.
Last Grizzly Bear in the State. Lee.
Night in the Forest. Kinnell.
Oh, Lovely Rock. Jeffers.
Outward Bound. Simmons.
Sleeping Out in Vermont. Hilberry.
Staying Alive. Wagoner.
To Myself, Late, in a Myrtle Grove. Peterson.

**Canada**
Can. Lit. Cohen.
Canada-I-O. *Unknown.*
From Colony to Nation. Layton.
Let me put it this way. Jonas.
O Canada! Routhier.
Only Tourist in Havana Turns His Thoughts Homeward, The.
 Cohen.
Saskatchewan Dusk. Buckaway.
Un Canadien Errant (An Exiled Canadian). *Unknown.*
*New American and Canadian Poetry* (NeAC). John Gill, ed.

**Canals**
Aged Pilot Man, The. "Twain."
Lines Written on a Seat on the Grand Canal. Kavanagh.

**Canaries**
Boy, Cat, Canary. Spender.
Canary, The. Turner.

**Cancer (disease)**
Bess. Stafford.
Cancer Cells, The. Eberhart.
Cancer Match, The. Dickey.
Cancer's a Funny Thing. Haldane.
Death from Cancer. *Fr.* In Memory of Arthur Winslow.
 Lowell.
Defiant One, The. Bailey.
In the Radiotherapy Unit. Wrench.
Miss Gee. Auden.
My Family's Under Contract to Cancer. Simison.

**Candles**
Even as a dragon's eye that feels the stress. Wordsworth.
First Fig. Millay.

**Candy**
Candy Man Blues. *Unknown.*
Girtonian Funeral, A. *Unknown.*
Pennycandystore Beyond the El, The. *Fr.* A Coney Island of
 the Mind. Ferlinghetti.
Sweet Song. Scannell.
Toffee-Slab. Lee.

**Cannibals and Cannibalism**
Constant Cannibal Maiden, The. Irwin.
Yarn of the *Nancy Bell,* The. Gilbert.

**Canoes**
Canoe-Hauling Chant. Ngata.
**Cape Elizabeth, Maine**
Cape Elizabeth: A Photograph. Logan.
**Capital Punishment**
Sonnets upon the Punishment of Death. Wordsworth.
**Caravaggio, Michelangelo Merisa de**
In Santa Maria del Popolo. Gunn.
**Cardinals (birds)**
As a Child Seeing a Cardinal. Gill.
**Caribbean Islands**
O Carib Isle! Crane.
**Carmel, California**
At Carmel. Austin.
Carmel Point. Jeffers.
**Carnegie Hall, New York City**
Carnegie Hall: Rescued.
**Carnivals**
Living with the Fat Man. Delp.
**Carp**
To the Carp and Those Who Hunt Her. Hazard.
**Carpe Diem**
Beauty. Guarini.
Blue Girls. Ransom.
Carpe Diem. Frost.
Come, my Celia, let us prove. *Fr.* Volpone. Jonson.
Corinna's Going a-Maying. Herrick.
Corinna in Vendome. Ronsard.
Dream within a Dream, A. Poe.
Drink Today. *Fr.* The Bloody Brother. Fletcher.
Fading Beauty. *Unknown.*
Give me women, wine and snuff. Keats.
Go, Lovely Rose. Waller.
Let Us Drink and Be Merry. Jordan.
Lines Written at a Small Distance from My House.
  Wordsworth.
Loveliest of Trees, the Cherry Now. Housman.
My Sweetest Lesbia. Campion.
Passionate Shepherd to His Love, The. Marlowe.
Persuasions to Enjoy. Carew.
Quid Sit Futurum Cras Fuge Quaerere. Prior.
Reckoning, The. Service.
Rubáiyát of Omar Khayyám of Naishápúr, The. Omar
  Khayyám.
Sing We and Chant It. Morley.
To A. L. Persuasions to Love. Carew.
To His Coy Mistress. Marvell.
To Phyllis. Waller.
To the Virgins, to Make Much of Time. Herrick.
Villanelle of the Poet's Road. Dowson.
Vive la Compagnie. *Unknown.*
Youth and Love. *Fr.* The Beggar's Opera. Gay.
**Carpenters**
Carpenter. Smith.
Four-square Gospel. Jellema.
In Memory of G.K., for 50 Years the College Carpenter.
  Martin.
**"Carroll, Lewis" (Charles Lutwidge Dodgson)**
Lewis Carroll. Farjeon.
**Cars.** *See* **Automobiles.**
**Carson, Kit**
Imperfect Sympathies. Short.
Kit Carson's Ride. Miller.
Oliver Wiggins. "Vestal."
**Cary, Sir Lucius**
To the Immortal Memory and Friendship of That Noble Pair,
  Sir Lucius Cary and Sir H. Morison. Jonson.
**Casanova, Giovanni**
Casanova. Usborne.
**Cassandra**
Cassandra. Bogan.
Cassandra. Jeffers.

Cassandra. Robinson.
**Castlereagh, Robert Stewart, 2nd Viscount**
Epigrams on Castlereagh. Byron.
Epitaph: "Posterity will ne'er survey." Byron.
Riddle, A: "Why is a pump like V-sc--nt C-stl-r--gh?" Moore.
To Sidmouth and Castlereagh. Shelley.
**Castles**
Psalm Concerning the Castle. Levertov.
**Castro, Fidel**
Ode to Fidel Castro. Field.
One Thousand Fearful Words for Fidel Castro. Ferlinghetti.
**Catbirds**
Air: Cat Bird Singing. Creeley.
**Caterpillars**
Biology Lesson. Engle.
Caterpillar. C. Rossetti.
Caterpillar, The. Williams.
Elegies for the Hot Season. McPherson.
Only My Opinion. Shannon.
**Catfish**
Feeding Cycle of the Catfish, The. Crawford.
**Catholicism**
First Confession. Kennedy.
Habit of Perfection, The. Hopkins.
Poem against Catholics. Fenton *and* Fuller.
**Cats**
Affinities. Stoutenberg.
Angora, The. Gerard.
Appeal to Cats in the Business of Love, An: A Song. Flatman.
Auld Seceder Cat, The. *Unknown.*
Belling the Cat. *Fr.* The Vision of Piers Plowman. Langland.
Bird Fancier, The. Kirkup.
Calling in the Cat. Coatsworth.
Cat, The. Church.
Cat, The. Davies.
Cat. Farjeon.
Cat, The. Kicknosway.
Cat, The. Matthews.
Cat. Miller.
Cat. Scannell.
Cat, A. Thomas.
Cat. Tolkien.
Cat and the Bird, The. Canning.
Cat and the Moon, The. Yeats.
Cat and the Weather. Swenson.
Cat as Cat, The. Levertov.
Cat at the Cream. *Unknown.*
Cat, Caged and Shrunken, The. Freeman.
Cat Came Back, The. Miller.
Cat Heard the Cat-Bird, The. Ciardi.
Cat Morgan Introduces Himself. Eliot.
Cat of Cats, The. Rands.
Cat of Many Years. Lutz.
Cat on Couch. Howes.
Cats. Farjeon.
Cats. Scarfe.
Cats. Tessimond.
Cats and the Weather. Swenson.
Cat's Funeral. Rieu.
Cat's Life, A. Struthers.
Cheerio My Deario. *Fr.* Archy and Mehitabel. Marquis.
Chops. Dixon.
Civilization. Schmidt.
Confidence. Baird.
Cosy Cat Nap. Kirkup.
Cruel, but composed and bland. *Fr.* Matthias. Arnold.
Cruel Clever Cat. Taylor.
Death of a Cat. Jones.
Death of the Cat. Serraillier.
Diamond Cut Diamond. Milne.
Epitaph for My Cat. Garrigue.
Femme et Chatte. Verlaine.

Fiddling Cat, The. *Unknown.*
Five Eyes. De la Mare.
For a Little Girl Mourning Her Favorite Cat. Whittier.
For I Will Consider My Cat Jeoffry. *Fr.* Jubilate Agno. Smart.
Gaggle of Geese, a Pride of Lions. A. Moore.
Gift, The. Ochester.
Growltiger's Last Stand. Eliot.
Gus: The Theatre Cat. Eliot.
I Wouldn't. Ciardi.
In Memory of My Cat Domino: l951-1966. Fuller.
Intruder. Feldman.
Kindness. *Unknown.*
Kitten, A. Farjeon.
Kitten and the Falling Leaves, The. Wordsworth.
Lavender Kitten, The. Lopez.
London Tom-Cat. Hamburger.
Macavity: The Mystery Cat. Eliot.
Man and Beast. Dyment.
Moon. Smith.
Mort aux Chats. Porter.
Mother Tabbyskins. Hart.
My Cat. Syrett.
My Cats. Smith.
My Old Cat. Summers.
Naming of Cats, The. Eliot.
Nansen. Snyder.
Ode on the Death of a Favourite Cat, Drowned in a Tub of Gold Fishes. Gray.
Old Colonist, The. Taylor.
Old Trouper, The. *Fr.* Archy and Mehitabel. Marquis.
On a Cat, Ageing. Gray.
On Reading Lao-tzu. Higginson.
Open Door, The. Coatsworth.
Owl and the Pussy-Cat, The. Lear.
Pangur Ban. *Unknown.*
Poem: "As the cat." Williams.
Poem: "High on a ridge of tiles." Craig.
Prize Cat, The. Pratt.
Propinquity. Reid.
Pussy. *Unknown.*
Rescue, The. Summers.
Rum Tum Tugger, The. Eliot.
Sage, The. Levertov.
Secret in the Cat, The. Swenson.
She sights a bird, she chuckles. Dickinson.
Shuffling along in her broken shoes from the slums. *Fr.* Lady Feeding the Cats. Stewart.
Singing Cat, The. Smith.
Skimbleshanks: The Railway Cat. Eliot.
Song of the Jellicles, The. Eliot.
Stable Cat, The. Norris.
This Cat. Kicknosway.
Three Cheers for the Black, White and Blue. Pitter.
Three Little Kittens, The. *Unknown.*
To Mrs. Reynolds's Cat. Keats.
Tom-Cat, The. Marquis.
Tom Cat Blues. *Unknown.*
Tortoiseshell Cat, The. Chalmers.
Two Little Kittens. *Unknown.*
Waiting for It. Swenson.
Walk with My Cat, A. Terris.
What Could It Be? Cole.
Why Did You Go? Cummings.
Yellow Cat. Harrison.
*Poetry of Cats, The* (PCat). Samuel Carr, ed.

**Cattle**
Bags of Meat. Hardy
Blackleg. Smithyman.
Deer Among Cattle. Dickey.
Drove-Road, The. Gibson.
Friday Lunchbreak. Orr.
Good-bye, Steer. Carr.
Jersey Cattle. Currey.
Last Longhorn, The. Hall.
Night-herding Song. Stephens.
Quiet-Eyed Cattle, The. Norris.
Stampede, The. Miller.
Ten Thousand Cattle. Wister.
Upasara, the heifer after first mating. *Fr.* Walking to the Cattle-Place. Murray.
Wires. Larkin.
*See also* **Bulls; Calves; Cows; Oxen.**

**Catullus**
You Also, Gaius Valerius Catullus. MacLeish.

**Cauteretz Valley, France**
In the Valley of Cauteretz. Tennyson.

**Cavalry**
Cavalry Crossing a Ford. Whitman.
Charge of the Light Brigade, The. Tennyson.

**Caves**
Ajanta. Rukeyser.
Cave, The. Dresbach.
Cave, The. Fairburn.
Cave of Staffa, I ("We saw, but surely, in the motley crowd"). Wordsworth.
Cave of Staffa, II ("Ye shadowy beings, that have rights and claims"). Wordsworth.
Cave Where Night Sleeps, The. Broughton.
Cavern, The. Tomlinson.

**Caviar**
Virgin Sturgeon, The. *Unknown.*

**Cayuga Lake**
Far above Cayuga's Waters. *Unknown.*

**Cecilia, Saint**
Alexander's Feast. Dryden.
Ode Against St. Cecilia's Day. Barker.
Song for St. Cecilia's Day. Auden.
Song for St. Cecilia's Day, 1687, A. Dryden.

**Celandine**
Celandine. Thomas.
Small Celandine, The. Wordsworth.
To the Same Flower. Wordsworth.
To the Small Celandine. Wordsworth.

**Celibacy**
Celibates. Chuilleanáin.

**Cellars**
Root Cellar. Roethke.

**Celts**
Celt in Me, The. Wilson.

**Cemeteries**
Afternoon. Scarbrough.
Anniversary. Weissbort.
Apartments on First Avenue. Macdonald.
At the Jewish Cemetery in Prague. Levertin.
Barrow, The. Thwaite.
Burying Ground by the Ties. MacLeish.
Cemetery, A/ is sideways moving. Page.
Cemetery in New Mexico, A. Alvarez.
Cemetery Near Burns' Cottage, The. Smith.
Ceremonies, The. Brock.
Children Among the Tombstones. Hervey.
Circa 1814. Staudt.
Country Cemetery. Bunner.
Cows Near the Graveyard, The. Nelson.
Crocus. Murray.
Dead at Clonmacroise, The. *Unknown.*
Elegy in a Presbyterian Burying-Ground. Wilson.
Elegy Written in a Country Churchyard. Gray.
Epitaphs. Hughes.
Farmer Among the Tombs, A. Berry.
Funeral at Ansley. Welch.
God's Acre. Longfellow.
Graves at Elkhorn. Hugo.

Grave-Yard, The. Very.
Haleiwa Churchyard. Altizer.
In a Churchyard. Wilbur.
In a Grave-Yard. Braithwaite.
In Memoriam: Gertrud Kolmar, 1943. Hope.
In the Old Jewish Cemetery, Prague, 1970. Lowbury.
Indian at the Burial-Place of His Fathers, An. Bryant.
Indian Burying Ground, The. Freneau.
Indian Graves at Jocko. Hugo.
Indian Graveyard, The. Weeks.
Island Cemetery, An. Auden.
Jewish Cemetery, The. Tiempo.
Jewish Cemetery at Newport, The. Longfellow.
Jewish Cemetery Near Leningrad, A. Brodsky.
Levelled Churchyard, The. Hardy.
Love in Magnolia Cemetery. Rankin.
Memorial Day. Ching.
Mistress, The. Barton.
Mountain Cemetery, The. Bowers.
Night-Piece on Death, A. Parnell.
Not Like That. Rich.
Old Jewish Cemetery in Worms. Kittner.
Place of Burial in the South of Scotland, A. Wordsworth.
RIP. Garner.
Roubaix Cemetery. Brainard.
Soul Longs to Return Whence It Came, The. Eberhart.
Summer Evening Churchyard, Lechdale, Gloucestershire, A.
  Shelley.
Trinity Churchyard. Rukeyser.
Trinity Place. Sandburg.
Two Women at the JFK Gravesite. Gibson.
Voices from Things Growing in a Churchyard. Hardy.
Yugoslav Cemetery. Wright.
  *See also* **Graves.**
**Censorship**
Invocation: "Senator Smoot (Republican, Ut.)." Nash.
Letter to a Librarian. Layton.
Penal Law. Clarke.
**Centaurs**
Centaurs, The. Stephens.
**Centipedes**
Centipede, A. Holder.
**Central Park, New York City**
Central Park. Nemerov.
**Ceres.** *See* **Demeter.**
**Cereus, Night-Blooming**
Night-Blooming Cereus, The. Hayden.
**Cézanne, Paul**
Cézanne's Ports. Ginsberg.
Three Cézannes. Whipple.
**Chad, Lake**
Chad. Brathwaite.
**Chagall, Marc**
Don't Let That Horse. Ferlinghetti.
Homage to Chagall. Niatum.
Homage to Chagall. Teague.
On the Farther Wall, Marc Chagall. *Fr.* Spectator's Guide to
  Contemporary Art. McGinley.
Painting. Jacobs.
**Chamberlain, Wilt**
To Wilt Chamberlain. Meschery.
**Chameleons**
Lord's Chameleon, The. Klappert.
Tail. Saleh.
**Chamonix, France**
Hymn Before Sunrise in the Vale of Chamouni. Coleridge.
**Change**
Ancient to Ancients, An. Hardy.
Beautiful Changes, The. Wilbur.
Change-Up. Lee.
For the Old Highlands. Young.
In a World of Change. Awad.

Lack of Steadfastness. Chaucer.
Mixed Feelings. Ashbery.
Modernismus: or, Prayer for Standstill. Bull.
Mutability ("Flower that smiles to-day, The"). Shelley.
Mutability ("We are as clouds that veil the midnight moon").
  Shelley.
Mutability. *Fr.* Ecclesiastical Sonnets. Wordsworth.
Mutation. Bryant.
Nothing Gold Can Stay. Frost.
Other Fabrics, Other Mores! Lenngren.
Some Slippery Afternoon. Gioseffi.
Uprooted. Lindsay.
Western Approaches, The. Nemerov.
"World, that all contains, is ever moving, The." *Fr.* Caelica.
  Greville.
**Channing, William Henry**
Ode: Inscribed to W. H. Channing. Emerson.
**Chanukah**
Kindle the Taper. Lazarus.
**Chaplin, Charlie**
Chaplinesque. Crane.
Patriotic Ode on the Fourteenth Anniversary of the Persecution
  of Charlie Chaplin. Kaufman.
**Chapman, George**
On First Looking into Chapman's Homer. Keats.
**Chapman, John.** *See* **"Appleseed, Johnny."**
**Chardin, Jean Baptiste**
From the Painting "Back from Market" by Chardin. Boland.
**Charity**
Excelente Balade of Charitie, An. Chatterton.
Faith, Hope and Charity. Guarini.
Husband and Heathen. Foss.
Karma. Robinson.
Lovers of the Poor, The. Brooks.
My House. Garneau.
Sensitive Philanthropist, The. Enright.
Though I speak with the tongues of men and of angels. *Fr.*
  First Corinthians. Bible, *N.T.*
**Charles I, King of England**
Cavalier Tunes. Browning.
Epitaph on Charles I, King of England. Graham.
**Charles II, King of England**
Ballad Called the Haymarket Hectors, A. *Unknown.*
Britannia and Raleigh. Ayloffe.
Charles II. *Unknown.*
Commons' Petition to Charles II, The. Earl of Rochester.
Dream of the Cabal, The: A Prophetical Satire. *Unknown.*
Epitaph on Charles II. Earl of Rochester.
Essay upon Satire, An. Sheffield.
History of Insipids, The. Freke.
Impromptu on Charles II. Earl of Rochester.
Methinks I see our mighty monarch stand. *Fr.* The Royal
  Angler. Earl of Rochester.
New Ballad, to an Old Tune, Called, I Am the Duke of Norfolk,
  etc., A. *Unknown.*
On the Prorogation. *Unknown.*
Parliament Dissolved at Oxford, The. *Unknown.*
Satire on Old Rowley. *Unknown.*
Song: Old Rowley the King. *Unknown.*
Tune to the Devonshire Cant, The. *Unknown.*
Upon His Majesty's Being Made Free of the City. Marvell.
**Charles XII, King of Sweden**
Charles XII of Sweden. *Fr.* The Vanity of Human Wishes.
  Johnson.
**Charles, Ray**
Bishop of Atlanta, The: Ray Charles. Bond.
Blues Note. Kaufman.
Ray Charles. Cornish.
**Charles River, Massachusetts**
Professor Kelleher and the Charles River. O'Grady.
**Charleston, South Carolina**
Charleston. Timrod.

**Charon**
Dirce. *Fr.* Pericles and Aspasia. Landor.
Epigram: "When Bibo thought fit from the world to retreat."
   Prior.
If (aged Charon), when my life shall end. *Fr. Licia.* Fletcher
   the Elder.
Lost on a fogbound spit of sand. Auden.
There Charon stands, who rules the dreary coast. *Fr.* The
   Aeneid. Virgil.
To Dives. Belloc.

**Chatterton, Thomas**
Monody on the Death of Chatterton. Coleridge.
To Chatterton. Keats.

**Chaucer, Geoffrey**
Chaucer. Longfellow.
Lament for Chaucer and Gower. *Fr.* De Regimine Principum.
   Hoccleve.

**Cheese**
O Cheese. Hall.
Queen of Cheese. McIntyre.
What a Friend We Have in Cheeses! Cole.

**Cheetahs**
Cheetah, The. Witt.

**Chemical Warfare**
Christmas 1924. Hardy.
Dulce et Decorum Est. Owen.

**Chenango Lake**
Swimming Chenango Lake. Tomlinson.

**Cherry Trees**
Cherry Robbers. Lawrence.
Loveliest of Trees, the Cherry Now. Housman.
Oh, Fair to See. C. Rossetti.
Orchard, The. Spence.
Winter Scene. Ammons.

**Chesapeake Bay**
Middle River. Althaus.

**Chess**
Young Chess Player, The. Sinclair.

**Chesterton, Gilbert Keith**
Lines to a Don. Belloc.

**Chestnuts**
Horse Chestnut Tree, The. Eberhart.

**Chevy Chase, Battle of.** *See* **Otterburn, Battle of.**

**Chicago, Illinois**
Canal Street, Chicago. Fixmer.
Chicago. Ridge.
Chicago. Sandburg.
Chicago/ 3 Hours. Cruz.
Civic Autobiography, A. Hoover.
Foreigners at the Fair. Brooks.
Grant Park, Chicago. Pillin.
LaSalle Street. Albright.
New Day, A. Levine.
Sold. Cuscaden.
Stockyard, The. Squire.
Translation to a Chinese Tribute to Jade. Notley.

**Chicanos**
Drum. Sanchez.

**Chickadees**
Titmouse, The. Emerson.

**Chickens**
Casa de Pollos. Fraser.
Chickens, The. *Unknown.*
Fable for When There's No Way Out. Swenson.
Orphan Born. Burdette.
Poultries, The. Nash.
Prophylactic, The. Edson.
*See also* **Hens; Roosters.**

**Child Abuse**
Child Beater. Ai.
Inquest, The. Davies.
Lilith's Child. Francisco.

**Child Labor**
Chimney Sweeper, The. *Fr.* Songs of Innocence. Blake.
Golf Links Lie So Near the Mill, The. Cleghorn.

**Childhood and Children**
Aaron Nicholas, Almost Ten. Hale.
About Children. McGinley.
Afternoon with a Baby, An. Snively.
Anecdote for Fathers. Wordsworth.
Assignment. Butcher.
Autobiographical Note. Scannell.
Ballad of Chocolate Mabbie, The. Brooks.
Ballad of the Light-Eyed Little Girl, The. Brooks.
Barefoot Boy, The. Whittier.
Before You're a Stranger. Fraser.
Bells for John Whiteside's Daughter. Ransom.
Bold, Unbiddable Child, The. Letts.
Boy. Ciardi.
Boy, The. Field.
Boy, A. Graves.
Boy. Mbembe.
Boy at the Window. Wilbur.
Boy Thirteen, A. Irish.
Boy with His Hair Cut Short. Rukeyser.
Boy's Song, A. Hogg.
Centaur, The. Swenson.
Characteristics of a Child Three Years Old. Wordsworth.
Child, A. Cole.
Child, The. Hall.
Child Half-Asleep, A. Connor.
Child in the Rug, The. Haines.
Child on Top of a Greenhouse. Roethke.
Childhood. Vaughan.
Children, The. MacDonald.
Children, The. Vinz.
Children, The. Williams.
Children of Auschwitz. Korzhavin.
Children's Games. Williams.
Children's Hour, The. Johnson.
Children's Hour, The. Longfellow.
Child's Drawing. Block.
Child's Sight, The. Sobiloff.
Common Carrier. Armour.
Conversation. McCord.
Croquet in Childhood. Minton.
Cry of the Children, The. Browning.
Dead Boy. Ransom.
Dead Man Creek. Brock.
Deborah Lee. Yvonne.
Declaration of Independence. Gibbs.
Dinoland. Reiter.
Divide, The. Hanson.
Dogs Are Shakespearean, Children Are Strangers. Schwartz.
Don't Forget. Berg.
Drawing by Ronnie C., Grade One. Lechlitner.
Early Supper. Howes.
Ecce Puer. Joyce.
Efficiency Apartment. Barrax.
Elementary Scene, The. Jarrell.
Eleven. MacLeish.
Evening. Wright.
Ex Ore Infantium. Thompson.
Exigencies. Gilbert.
Eyes of the Child Do Not See Me, The. Russell.
False Security. Betjeman.
Farm Boy after Summer. Francis.
Father and Child. Harwood.
Fern Hill. Thomas.
First Song. Kinnell.
For a Junior School Poetry Book. Middleton.
For My Son Noah, Ten Years Old. Bly.
For the Crèche. *Fr.* Songs of Education. Chesterton.
Fortune/has its cookies to give out. Ferlinghetti.

Four Spacious Skies. Astor.
Game. Lucy.
Game after Supper. Atwood.
Germinal. "AE."
Getting Experience. Williams.
Going Back. Petersen.
Good and Bad Children. Stevenson.
Goodbat Nightman. McGough.
Growing Up. Perkins.
Ha Ha This-a-Way. Leadbelly.
Hard Cheese. St. John.
Heart's Needle. Snodgrass.
How We Must Teach the Children. Thomas.
Humiliation Revisited. Ashley.
I Don't Like Beetles. Fyleman.
I Don't Want to Play in Your Yard. Wingate.
I Remember, I Remember. Hood.
I Remember, I Remember. Larkin.
I Would Like You for a Comrade. Parry.
If I Could Only Live at the Pitch That Is Near Madness.
  Eberhart.
In Reference to Her Children, 23 June, 1656. Bradstreet.
In Woods Where Many Rivers Run. *Fr.* A Coney Island of the
  Mind. Ferlinghetti.
Incendiary. Scannell.
Incident in the Early Life of Ebenezer Jones, Poet, 1828, An.
  Betjeman.
Invisible Playmate, The. Widdemer.
It Is Impossible. Falconer.
It Out-Herods Herod. Pray You, Avoid It. Hecht.
Janet Waking. Ransom.
Jim, Who Ran Away from His Nurse, and Was Eaten by a Lion.
  Belloc.
Judeebug's Country. Johnson.
Key of the Kingdom, The. Reed.
Kindergarten. Rogers.
Knock on Wood. Dumas.
Land of Counterpane, The. Stevenson.
Land of Story-Books, The. Stevenson.
Little Boy, A. Bennett.
Little Boy Blue. Field.
Little Boy Lost, A. Rothenberg.
Little Brother, The. Reeves.
Little Dancers, The. Binyon.
Little Girl with Bands on Her Teeth, The. Taggard.
Lost Children, The. Jarrell.
Love. Lane.
Mama! Horne.
Memories. Moreno.
Mighty Lak' a Rose. Stanton.
Milky Way, The. Anderson.
My child, we were two children. Heine.
My Childhood's Bedroom. Tisdale.
My Father in the Night Commanding No. Simpson.
My Father's House. Orlen.
My Lost Youth. Longfellow.
My Parents Kept Me. Spender.
Nikki-Rosa. Giovanni.
Noisy Boys. Castiglione.
Nurse's Song. *Fr.* Songs of Innocence. Blake.
O God, Great Father, Lord, and King. Hoss.
Ode: Intimations of Immortality from Recollections of Early
  Childhood. Wordsworth.
Old Oaken Bucket, The. Woodworth.
On a Catholic Childhood. Hale.
On a Dead Child. Bridges.
On Children. *Fr.* The Prophet. Gibran.
On His Marks. Armour.
On My First Son. Jonson.
On The Edge. Birch.
Original Sin on the Sussex Coast. Betjeman.
Outburst from a Little Face. Woods.

Paean to Place. Niedecker.
Party, The. Whittemore.
Pastoral of the City Streets. Klein.
Pastoral with Visitor. Packer.
Pennycandystore Beyond the El, The. *Fr.* A Coney Island of
  the Mind. Ferlinghetti.
Physical Fitness. Birch.
Piano. Lawrence.
Picnic, The. Logan.
Playground, The. Bedard.
Poem of Distant Childhood. Sousa.
Praise of a Child. *Unknown.*
Rebecca, Who Slammed Doors for Fun and Perished Miserably.
  Belloc.
Remember when you couldn't. *Fr.* The Fury of Overshoes.
  Sexton.
Retreat, The. Vaughan.
Romping. Ciardi.
Rough. Spender.
Roundhouse Voices, The. Smith.
Sacred Children, The. Hays.
Self-Portrait. Romero.
September, the First Day of School. Nemerov.
Settlers, The. Hemschemeyer.
Shock. Collins.
Sick Child, A. Jarrell.
Sleeper, The. Field.
Song about Myself. Keats.
Spitting on Ira Rosenblatt. Hershon.
Stolen Child, The. Yeats.
Testing-Tree, The. Kunitz.
There Was a Child Went Forth. Whitman.
There Was a Little Girl. Longfellow.
To a Child Dancing in the Wind. Yeats.
To a Child Five Years Old. Cotton.
To a Child Trapped in a Barber Shop. Levine.
To H. C. Wordsworth.
To My Former Student on the Occasion of Birth. Bass.
Toyland. MacDonough.
Tumbling. *Unknown.*
Two Years Later. Yeats.
Underneath the House. McMaster.
Verigin, Moving in Alone. Newlove.
Walnut-Leaf Scent. Binyon.
Warning to Children. Graves.
Water. Norris.
What I Did Last Summer. Ikan
When I Learned to Whistle. Lea.
Where Knock Is Open Wide. Roethke.
Whole Duty of Children. Stevenson.
Why Did the Chidren Put Beans in Their Ears? Sandburg.
Windy Boy in a Windswept Tree. Summerfield.
Won't Go to School. Rankin.
World and the Child, The. Merrill.
Worms, The. Kizer.
Yet Another Poem About a Dying Child. Frame.
Zimmer in Grade School. Zimmer.
*See also* **Babies; Youth.**
**Children's Verse**
*Batsford Book of Light Verse for Children, The* (BBL). Gavin
  Ewart, ed.
*Callooh! Callay!: Holiday Poems for Young Readers* (CC). Myra
  Cohn Livingston, ed.
*Child's Treasury of Verse, A* (CTV). Eleanor Doan, ed.
*Ducks and Dragons: Poems for Children* (DuDr). Gene Kemp,
  ed.
*Every Child's Book of Verse* (ECBV). Sarah Chokla Gross,
  comp.
*First Poetry Book, A* (FPB). John Fodter, ed.
*In the Witch's Kitchen: Poems for Halloween* (IWK). John E.
  Brewton, Lorraine A. Blackburn *and* George M. Blackburn,
  comps.

*Listen, Children, Listen* (LCL). Myra Cohn Livingston, ed.
*Mother Goose Nursery Rhymes* (MG). Arthur Rackham, illus.
*Oxford Book of Children's Verse, The* (OxBChV). Iona *and* Peter Opie, eds.
*Poems for Children and Other People* (PCOP). George Hornby, ed.

**Chillon Castle, Switzerland**
Prisoner of Chillon, The. Byron.

**Chimney Sweepers**
Chimney Sweeper, The. *Fr.* Songs of Experience. Blake.
Chimney Sweeper, The. *Fr.* Songs of Innocence. Blake.
Wm. Brazier. Graves.

**China**
Digging for China. Wilbur.
Not-So-Good Earth, The. Dawe.
Old Photo in an Old Life, An. Hoffman.
Photographs of China. Hall.
What Is It Makes the Stranger. Hyde.

**Chinaware**
Dorchester Plate. Haste.

**Chinese, The**
Cultural Exchange. Masarik.
Hymnus ad Patrem Sinensis. Whalen.

**Chipmunks**
Chipmunk's Day, The. Jarrell.

**Chisholm Trail**
Old Chisholm Trail, The. *Unknown.*

**Christ.** *See* **Jesus Christ.**

**Christenings**
Kyran's Christening. Nowlan.
Perambulator Poem. McCord.

**Christmas**
Advent 1966. Levertov.
Almighty Spake, and Gabriel Sped, The. Richards.
Alphabet of Christmas Cheer. Weston.
Angels' Song, The. Sears.
Angels We Have Heard on High. *Unknown.*
Animals' Christmas, The. Dacey.
As I Went Down to David's Town. Stewart.
Away in a Manger. *Unknown.*
Ballad of Befana, The. McGinley.
Before the Paling of the Stars. Rossetti.
Bow Down, Mountain. Farber.
Burning Babe, The. Southwell.
Burning the Christmas Greens. Williams.
Carol: "There was a boy bedded in bracken." Short.
Ceremonies for Candlemas Day, The. Herrick.
Cherry Tree Carol, The. *Unknown.*
Christ Climbed Down. Ferlinghetti.
Christmas. Betjeman.
Christmas. Cavalieri.
Christmas ("Christmas is coming"). *Unknown.*
Christmas at Sea. Stevenson.
Christmas Carol Sung to the King at Whitehall, A. Herrick.
Christmas Comes to Moccasin Flat. Welch.
Christmas Day. Falkner.
Christmas Eve. Ammons.
Christmas Eve. Beer.
Christmas Eve. McCord.
Christmas Eve under Hooker's Statue. Lowell.
Christmas Everywhere. Brooks.
Christmas Hymn, A. Wilbur.
Christmas Morning. Behn.
Christmas Morning. Roberts.
Christmas 1959 Et Cetera. Barrax.
Christmas Tree, A. Burford.
Computer's First Christmas Card, The. Morgan.
Cultivation of Christmas Trees, The. Eliot.
December. Schuyler.
December Fragments. Lattimore.
Deck the Halls. *Unknown.*
Farewell Advent! Ryman.

First Nowell, The. *Unknown.*
For the Time Being; A Christmas Oratorio, *sels.* Auden.
For Us No Night Can Be Happier. Zinzendorf.
God Rest You Merry, Gentlemen. *Unknown.*
Hark! Hark! with Harps of Gold. Chapin.
Hark, the Herald Angels Sing. Wesley.
Holly and the Ivy, The. *Unknown.*
Hymn for Christmas Day, A. Byrom.
I Am Christmas. *Unknown.*
I am interested and amazed. Berryman.
I Heard the Bells on Christmas Day. Longfellow.
I Saw Three Ships Come Sailing In. *Unknown.*
In All the Magic of Christmas Tide. Niles.
In the Bleak Midwinter. Rossetti.
In the Week When Christmas Comes. Farjeon.
It Came upon a Midnight Clear. Sears.
It Seems That God Bestowed Somehow. Hall.
It was a night in winter. *Fr.* The Witnesses. Sansom.
It's Almost Day. Leadbelly.
Jew at Christmas Eve, The. Shapiro.
Jolly Shepherd Wat, The. *Unknown.*
Joy to the World. Watts.
Karma. Robinson.
Kid Stuff. Horne.
Landscape of the Star. Rich.
Let Christian Hearts Rejoice Today. *Unknown.*
Let me tell to you the story. Agnew.
Lines for a Christmas Card. Belloc.
Little tree. Chansons Innocentes, II. Cummings.
Nativity, The. Drummond of Hawthornden.
Nativity of Christ, The. Southwell.
Nativity of Our Lord and Saviour, The. *Fr.* Hymns and Spiritual Songs. Smart.
New Heaven, New War. Southwell.
New Prince, New Pomp. Southwell.
1913 Massacre, The. Guthrie.
No Room at the Inn. *Unknown.*
Now Is Yule Come. *Unknown.*
O Christmas Night. Selyns.
O Come, All Ye Faithful. *Unknown.*
Oh, Day of Days. Brant.
O Little Town of Bethlehem. Brooks.
Oh Tannenbaum (Oh Christmas Tree). *Unknown.*
On the Morning of Christ's Nativity. Milton.
Oxen, The. Hardy.
Precious Child, So Sweetly Sleeping. Hoppe.
Reminder, The. Hardy.
Rise Up, Shepherd, and Follow. *Unknown.*
Santa Claus. Nemerov.
Silent Night! Holy Night! Mohr.
Song Bewailing the Time of Christmas, A. *Unknown.*
Sonnets at Christmas. Tate.
Sunny Bank. *Unknown.*
Through the Dark the Dreamers Came. Marlatt.
To a Young Wretch. Frost.
Twelve Days of Christmas, The. *Unknown.*
Unto Us a Child Is Born. Dunbar.
Upon a Christmas Morning. *Unknown.*
Upon Christ's Nativity, or Christmas. Watkyns.
Visit from Saint Nicholas, A. Moore.
We Wish You a Merry Christmas. *Unknown.*
What Child Is This? Dix.
What Means This Glory Round Our Feet? Lowell.
What Tidings? Audelay.
When Jordan Hushed His Waters Still. Campbell.
White Christmas. Rodgers.
Yule Days, The. *Unknown.*
*Poems of Christmas* (PChr). Myra Cohn Livingston, ed.

**Christmas Cards**
Means Test. Enright.

**Christmas Carols**

*American Hymns, Old and New* (AH). Albert Christ-Janer, Charles W. Hughes, *and* Carleton Sprague Smith, eds.

**Chrysanthemums**
Last Chrysanthemum, The. Hardy.

**Churches**
Archaeology. Church.
At Dunwich. Thwaite.
Base Chapel, Lejeune 4/79. Hobson.
Church Going. Larkin.
Church on Comiaken Hill, The. Hugo.
Concert at Long Melford Church. Beer.
Diary of a Church Mouse. Betjeman.
Eighteen-Forty-Three. *Unknown.*
For the Lord's Day Evening. Watts.
Hymn. Walker.
Little Brown Church in the Vale, The. Pitts.
Loftiest spirit that ever flamed in flesh, The. Clause.
Manners. Shiffert.
New Coventry Cathedral, The. Bull.
Placid Pew, The. Suderman.
St. Isaac's Church, Petrograd. McKay.
Study in Punctuation. Bull.
Washington Cathedral. Shapiro.
We Love the Venerable House. Emerson.
Wednesday Night Prayer Meeting. Wright.

**Churchill, John, Duke of Marlborough.** *See* **Marlborough, John Churchill, 1st Duke of.**

**Cibber, Colley**
Cibber! write all thy verses upon glasses. Pope.
On Colley Cibber. Jonson.
Quoth Cibber to Pope, tho' in verse you foreclose. Pope.

**Cicadas**
Cicada. Stoutenberg.
Cigales. Wilbur.
Invocation: "Unwinding the spool of the morning." Miller.

**Cigars**
My First Cigar. Burdette.
To a Segar. Low.

**Cinderella**
Cinderella. Sexton.

**Circe**
Circe. Gibson.
Circe. Hope.
Circe. Tabley.
Moly. Gunn.
Strayed Reveller, The. Arnold.
To a Lady. Morton.

**Circus**
Catch me! *Fr.* Circus. Kandel.
Circus, The. Roberts.
Flying Trapeze, The. Leybourne.
Freak Show, The. Willard.
High Wire Dancers. Hoskins.
Tightrope Walker. Scannell.
What Happens. Jordan.
When I Went to the Circus. Lawrence.

**Cities**
America, America! Schwartz.
American City. Oates.
Apartment House. Raftery.
Change of Venue. Clockadale.
City. Biasotti.
City. Fisher.
City. Hughes.
City. Stembridge.
City Afternoon. Howes.
City Corruption. *Fr.* The Task. Cowper.
City Life. Lawrence.
City of Dreadful Night, The. Thomson ("B.V.").
City Psalm. Levertov.
City Rises, The. Cunningham.
City Without Smoke. Denby.

Cold Water Flat. Booth.
Commitment in a City. Tsuda.
Composed upon Westminster Bridge. Wordsworth.
Constructions: Upper East Side. Hochman.
Countryman's Return, The. Thomas.
Death in the City. Macleod.
Description of a City Shower, A. Swift.
Drat my hateful birthday. Sulpicia.
Driving at Night. Rezmerski.
Get the Gasworks. Ignatow.
Glasgow. Smith.
Going and Coming: Two Poems. Benedikt.
Green, Alas, The. Emmons.
Honored Dead, The. Doulis.
Hymn of the City. Bryant.
In the inner city. Clifton.
Lines: "Lines which are the imitation of imagined veins." Waldman.
Lost. Ignacio.
Manchester by Night. Blind.
Megalopolis. Cruz.
Metropole. Anderson.
New York. Field.
Nature of Jungles, The. Moses.
New Block. P. Dickinson.
Ode to an Urban Day. Ward.
Pastoral of the City Streets. Klein.
Pictures of a City. Fripp.
Poem: "The greater cities are." Cruz.
Poem for Democrats, A. Jones.
Preludes. Eliot.
Romanies in Town, The. Beresford.
Roof Garden, The. Moss.
Silence of a city, how awful at midnight, The! Coleridge.
Snowbound City, The. Haines.
Thaw in the City. Lipsitz.
These Lacustrine Cities. Ashbery.
Thirteen Preludes for Pioneer Square. Logan.
To Nowhere. Ignatow.
To Sextus. Martial.
Up at a Villa—Down in the City. Browning.
Upon Westminster Bridge. Wordsworth.
Urban Convalescence, An. Merrill.
Vita-Sheet. Weiss.
What It Means, Living in the City. Dickey.
What Train Will Come? Smith.
White City, The. McKay.
World Outside, The. Levertov.

**Civil Rights.** *See* **Protest, Social.**

**Civil Defense**
Civil Defense. Burke.

**Civil War, American**
Ascent of T. J. Jackson: A Soldier's Tale. "A. N."
Barbara Frietchie. Whittier.
Battle-Cry of Freedom, The. Root.
Battle-Hymn of the Republic. Howe.
Battle of Shiloh, The. *Unknown.*
Black Soldier's Civil War Chant. *Unknown.*
Blue and the Gray, The. Finch.
Bonnie Blue Flag, The. Macarthy.
Break the News to Mother. Harris.
Brother Green. *Unknown.*
Cavalry Crossing a Ford. Whitman.
Charleston. Timrod.
Cripple for Life, The. *Unknown.*
*Cumberland* and the *Merrimac*, The. *Unknown.*
*Cumberland's* Crew, The. *Unknown.*
Dan Ellis's Boys. *Unknown.*
Dixie. Emmett
Dixie (Battle Hymn). Pike.
Fabrication of Ancestors. Dugan.
Fare You Well, My Darling. *Unknown.*

For the Union Dead. Lowell.
From Trollope's Journal. Bishop.
Goin' 'Cross the Mountain. *Unknown.*
Goober Peas. *Unknown.*
Good Old Rebel, The. *Unknown.*
Grandfather. Louchheim.
History Among the Rocks. Warren.
How Do You Do, *Alabama*! Wilson.
Hunting Civil War Relics at Nimblewill Creek. Dickey.
John Brown's Body. *Unknown.*
Just Before the Battle, Mother. Root.
Kearney at Seven Pines. Stedman.
Last Fierce Charge, The. *Unknown.*
Little Giffen. Ticknor.
Lyon. Melville.
Malvern Hill. Melville.
March into Virginia, The. Melville.
Marching through Georgia. Work.
Maryland, My Maryland! Randall.
Meditation, A. Melville.
Memorial Wreath. Randall.
Negro Soldier's Civil War Chant. *Unknown.*
Ode: "Sleep sweetly in your humble graves." Timrod.
Ode Recited at the Harvard Commemoration. Lowell.
Ode to the Confederate Dead. Tate.
Portent, The. Melville.
Red, White and Red, The. *Unknown.*
Roll, *Alabama*, Roll. *Unknown.*
Sheridan's Ride. Read.
Shiloh; a Requiem. Melville.
Sight in Camp in the Daybreak Gray and Dim, A. Whitman.
Stonewall Jackson's Way. Palmer.
Tenting on the Old Camp Ground. Kittredge.
Three Hundred Thousand More. Gibbons.
Unsung Heroes, The. Dunbar.
Vigil Strange I Kept on the Field One Night. Whitman.
When Dey 'Listed Colored Soldiers. Dunbar.
When Johnny Comes Marching Home. Gilmore.
When This Cruel War Is Over. *Unknown.*
Wound-Dresser, The. Whitman.
**Civil War, Nigerian**
Nigerian Unity; or, Little Niggers Killing Little Niggers. Lee.
**Civil War, Spanish**
After the Bombing of Barcelona. Macleod.
Before Battle: [The Lincolns at Villanueva de la Canada].
    Neugass.
City of Anguish. Rolfe.
Convoy. Neugass.
Defenses, The. Maddow.
Entry. Rolfe.
Freiheit (Freedom). Ernst *and* Daniel.
Give Us This Day. Neugass.
Hans Beimler. Busch.
Jarama Valley. *Unknown.*
Los Cuatro Generales (The Four Insurgent Generals).
    *Unknown.*
Mediterranean. Rukeyser.
Near Catalonia. Davidman.
Say That We Saw Spain Die. Millay.
Si Me Quieres Escribir (If You Want to Write Me). *Unknown.*
Silence in Mallorca. Taggard.
Snow in Madrid. Davidman.
Spanish War, The. "MacDiarmid."
To the Dead of the International Brigade. Funaroff.
**Civil Wars, English**
Battle of Naseby, The. Macaulay.
Bonne Dundee. *Fr.* The Doom of Devergoil. Scott.
Cavalier Tunes. Browning.
Do not lift him from the bracken. *Fr.* The Widow of Glencoe.
    Aytoun.
Execution of Montrose, The. Aytoun.
It Was A' for Our Rightfu' King. Burns.

O What's the Rhyme to Porringer. *Unknown.*
Parliament Soldiers, The. *Unknown.*
Sally from Coventry, The. Thornbury.
Song of the Western Men, The. Hawker.
Three Troopers, The. Thornbury.
Vicar of Bray, The. *Unknown.*
**Civilization**
C Stands for Civilization. Fearing.
Long-legged Fly. Yeats.
Marx the Sign Painter. *Fr.* The New Spoon River. Masters.
Meru. Yeats.
Moral Artistry. McKain.
Waste Land, The. Eliot.
**Clams and Clamming**
Acres of Clams. *Unknown.*
Clamdigger, The. Riggs.
Clamming. Whittemore.
Clams. Moss.
Clams. Rin.
Sonnet to a Clam. Saxe.
**Clare, John**
John Clare. Anderson.
**Clark, Alfred Corning**
Alfred Corning Clark. Lowell.
**Clarke, Austin**
Visit to Bridge House, A. Weber.
**Clarke, Charles Cowden**
To Charles Cowden Clarke. Keats.
**Clay, Cassius.** *See* **Ali, Muhammed.**
**Cleopatra**
Antony to Cleopatra. Lytle.
Cleopatra to the Asp. Hughes.
Dead Cleopatra lies in a crystal casket. *Fr.* Discordants.
    Aiken.
**Clergy**
Auld Seceder Cat, The. *Unknown.*
Buddhist Priest, A. Ho Xuan Huong.
Church of England's Glory, The. *Unknown.*
Colin Clout. Skelton.
Collar, The. Herbert.
Country Clergy, The. Thomas.
Excellent New Ballad, Called the Brawny Bishop's Complaint,
    An. Mainwaring.
Father Mat. Kavanagh.
Father O'Flynn. Graves.
Fra Lippo Lippi. Browning.
Gentle Alice Brown. Gilbert.
Habit of Perfection, The. Hopkins.
Irish-American Dignitary. Clarke.
Jackdaw of Rheims, The. "Ingoldsby."
Madam and the Minister. Hughes.
Ol' Tim Legion. Moxley.
On a Clergyman's Horse Biting Him. *Unknown.*
On the Forcers of Conscience. Milton.
Paradox, The. *Unknown.*
Parson, The. *Fr.* The Deserted Village. Goldsmith.
Poor Parson, A. *Fr.* Canterbury Tales: Prologue. Chaucer.
Prayer of Holy Willie, The. Burns.
Preacher Considers His Sermon, The. Suderman.
Rival Curates, The. Gilbert.
Sentiments, The. *Unknown.*
Soliloquy of the Spanish Cloister. Browning.
Vicar, The. *Fr.* The Borough. Crabbe.
Vicar of Bray, The. *Unknown.*
You Shall. *Unknown.*
**Clerks**
Sir Joseph's Song. *Fr.* H.M.S. Pinafore. Gilbert.
Song of the GPO, A. Hamill.
Thirty Bob a Week. Davidson.
What Was Her Name? Ciardi.
**Cleveland, Ohio**
Ordinary Evening in Cleveland, An. Turco.

**Clichés**
 Clash with Cliches, A.   Miller.
 On a Lover of Books.   Grigson.
**Cliff Dwellers**
 Testament of Perpetual Change, The.   Williams.
**Clocks and Watches**
 Alarm Clock, The.   Hoover.
 Clock, The.   Beer.
 Clock in the Square, A.   Rich.
 Clocks.   Locker.
 Gold Watch, The.   Blight.
 Grandfather's Clock.   Work.
 North Infinity Street.   Aiken.
 Watch, The.   Cornford.
 Watch, The.   Swenson.
**Clonmacnoise, Ireland**
 Dead at Clonmacnoise, The.   *Unknown.*
**Clothing**
 Baby's Dress, A.   Hall.
 Because of Clothes.   Riding.
 Blue Paisley Shirt, The.   Shapcott.
 Box for Tom, A.   Tate.
 Clothes.   Jennings.
 Clothes, The.   Zychlinska.
 Clothes Do But Cheat and Cozen Us.   Herrick.
 Clothes Maketh the Man.   Weiss.
 Delight in Disorder.   Herrick.
 Divorce Dress, The.   Finley.
 Dresses.   Fraser.
 Evening Gown, The.   Swenson.
 Goodwill, Inc.   Schmitz.
 Grave Clothes.   Swenson.
 Jeans.   Brummels.
 Julia's Petticoat.   Herrick.
 Lingerie.   Hall.
 My Clothes.   Spacks.
 Nature and Art.   Herford.
 Nothing to Wear.   Butler.
 On a Girdle.   Waller.
 Overalls.   Sjoberg.
 Shirt, The.   Silkin.
 Sri Rama's Raiment.   *Unknown.*
 Stiff Shirts.   Bowman.
 This Shirt.   Trias
 Underwear.   Ferlinghetti.
 Upon Julia's Clothes.   Herrick.
 Upon Julia's Ribband.   Herrick.
**Clouds**
 Cloud, The.   Shelley.
 Cloud Factory, The.   Haines.
 Cloud-Mobile, The.   Swenson.
 Clouds.   Brooke.
 Clouds.   Fisher.
 Clouds.   Levine.
 Clouds, The.   Williams.
 Clouds That Are So Light, The.   Thomas.
 Corn-Grinding Song.   *Unknown.*
 Final Painting, The.   Harwood.
 For the Girls 'Cause They Know.   Littlebird.
 Job Hunting.   Hennen.
 O cloud that wants to be the sky's arrow.   Castellanos.
 Sea Surface Full of Clouds.   Stevens.
 Song in White.   Dressay.
 Song of the Blue-Corn Dance.   *Unknown.*
 Whispering Clouds.   Platov.
 Yellow cloud rising up from that fighting.   *Unknown.*
**Clough, Arthur Hugh**
 On Arthur Hugh Clough.   Swinburne.
 Thyrsis.   Arnold.
 To a Republican Friend, 1848.   Arnold.
 To a Republican Friend: Continued.   Arnold.
**Coal Mining and Miners**

 Avondale Mine Disaster, The.   *Unknown.*
 Blue Monday.   *Unknown.*
 Cleator Moor.   Nicholson.
 Coal Diggin' Blues.   *Unknown.*
 Coal Miner's Goodbye, A.   *Unknown.*
 Coal Miner's Grace.   Divine.
 Coal Mining Disaster's Last Trapped Man Contemplates
    Salvation, The.   Meissner.
 Collier, The.   Watkins.
 Collier's Wife, The.   Lawrence.
 Down in a Coal Mine.   Geoghegan.
 Dying Mine Brakeman, The.   Jenks.
 Gresford Disaster, The.   *Unknown.*
 Hoot Owl Shift.   Stricklin.
 John J. Curtis.   Gallagher.
 Meditation on Rhode Island Coal, A.   Bryant.
 Mine.   Hudgins.
 Miner's Doom, The.   *Unknown.*
 Miner's Helmet, The.   MacBeth.
 Mourning Letter, March 29, 1963.   Dorn.
 Old Miner's Refrain, The.   *Unknown.*
 Payday at Coal Creek.   *Unknown.*
 That Little Lump of Coal.   *Unknown.*
 Two-Cent Coal.   *Unknown.*
 Working in the Mines.   *Unknown.*
**Cobb, Tyrus Raymond (Ty)**
 Ty Cobb Story, The.   Clark.
**Cockaigne, Land of**
 Land of Cockaigne, The.   *Unknown.*
**Cockroaches**
 Aubade: N.Y.C.   Wallace.
 Roach, The.   Raven.
 Whose Scene?   Stone.
**Cocks.**   *See* **Roosters.**
**Cody, William Frederick.**   *See* **Buffalo Bill.**
**Coins**
 Cleaning a Coin.   Thwaite.
**Cold**
 Cold.   Francis.
 Cold.   Hughes.
 Cold and Heat.   *Unknown.*
 November Night, Edinburgh.   MacCaig.
 Poem of the Frost and Snow.   Morris.
 Pray to What Earth Does This Sweet Cold Belong.   Thoreau.
 Prayer for Fish.   Wallace.
 Rooftop Winter.   Thorpe.
 Snow-Girl.   Moritz.
 There Are Roughly Zones.   Frost.
 'Twas warm—at first—like us.   Dickinson.
 Young Charlotte.   *Unknown.*
**Colds (illness)**
 To Bary Jade.   Adams.
 Winter Scene, A.   Whittemore.
**Cole, Thomas**
 To Cole, the Painter, Departing for Europe.   Bryant.
**Coleridge, Samuel Taylor**
 Dedicatory Sonnet to S. T. Coleridge.   H. Coleridge.
 Deeper Into Coleridge.   Clark.
 Thoughts about the Person from Porlock.   Smith.
 To S. T. C. on his 179th Birthday, October 12th, 1951.
    Carpenter.
**Colette (Sidonie Gabrielle Colette)**
 Dear Colette.   Jong.
**Coliseum.**   *See* **Colosseum.**
**Colleges and Universities**
 Campus on the Hill, The.   Snodgrass.
 Educational Administration Professor's Prayer, The.   Bobango.
 Fisk is.   Scott.
 For a College Yearbook.   Cunningham.
 Humble Petition to the President of Harvard, A.   Beecher.
 Ode on the Despoilers of Learning in an American University,
    An.   Winters.

To a Visiting Poet in a College Dormitory. Kizer.
Town Against Gown at Oxford. Robert of Gloucester.
University Curriculum. Turner.
You Understand the Requirements. Lifshin.
**Collies**
Collies, The. Anthony.
Wonder. Raymund.
**Cologne, Germany**
Cologne. Coleridge.
**Colonna, Vittoria**
Vittoria Colonna. Marz.
**Colonus, Greece**
Colonus' Praise. *Fr.* Oedipus at Colonus. Sophocles.
**Colorado**
Anthropology in Fort Morgan, Colorado. Hamod.
**Colorado River**
Crossing the Colorado River into Yuma. Ortiz.
**Colors**
Answer to a Sonnet Ending Thus. Keats.
Blindman, The. Swenson.
Colours. Evans.
Distinctions. Tomlinson.
Green. Lawrence.
Green Eye, The. Merrill.
Making of Color, The. Seidman.
No Meaning. Brame.
Primary. Evans.
Uncle Edward's Affliction. Scannell.
What Is Pink? C. Rossetti.
**Colosseum**
Coliseum, The. Poe.
**Coltrane, John**
After the Rain. Crouch.
Blues for John Coltrane, Dead at 41. Matthews.
Dear John, Dear Coltrane. Harper.
Here Where Coltrane Is. Harper.
John Coltrane: An Impartial Review. Spellman.
JuJu. Touré.
Ode: Infinity. Storey.
Sopranosound, Memory of John. Bourke.
**Colts**
Broncho That Would Not Be Broken, The. Lindsay.
Newborn Colt, The. Kennedy.
Unclaimed. Smyth.
**Columbia University**
Columbia College, 1796. Shippey.
Poem of Solitude at Columbia University. García Lorca.
**Columbines**
Columbine, The. Very.
**Columbus, Christopher**
And of Columbus. Gregory.
Ave Maria. *Fr.* The Bridge. Crane.
Columbus. Miller.
Columbus. Nash.
Columbus. Simpson.
Columbus. Schiller.
Columbus and the Mermaids. Coatsworth.
Discovery, The. Squire.
In fourteen hundred and ninety-two. *Unknown.*
May 1506 (Christopher Columbus Speaking). Scott.
Mysterious Biography. Sandburg.
Space. Hart-Smith.
12 October. Livingston.
You, Genoese Mariner. Merwin.
**Columbus, Ohio**
Cold Feet in Columbus. Heath.
**Comets**
Comet, The. Makai.
Comet at Yell'ham, The. Hardy.
Comets and Princes. Johnson.
I am like a slip of comet. Hopkins.
**Comic Books**

Shazam. Dickey.
**Comic Strips**
Peanuts. Locklin.
**Comic Verse.** *See* **Humorous Verse.**
**Commencement Day**
Commencement. Carrier.
**Communes**
Bad Dream in the Commune, A. Hahn.
Six-forty-two Farm Communes Struggle Poem. Leifer.
**Communication**
How She Resolved to Act. Moore.
Ritual to Read to Each Other, A. Stafford.
**Communion.** *See* **Eucharist.**
**Communism**
Ballad of Tampa. Freeman.
Communism. Wilcox.
Definition. Rolfe.
Dusk of the Gods. Funaroff.
Examples of Worker Correspondence. Gold.
For the Cultural Campaign. Jigmed.
Garland for a Propagandist. Pauker.
Hymn for October. Gessner.
I Am A Red Slogan. Wright.
Just for Propaganda. Lewis.
Kral Majales. Ginsberg.
Man from Moscow, The. Lewis.
Nothing to Lose. Kalar.
Red Dawn in the East, A. Macleod.
Reichstag Trial, The. Schneider.
Reveille. Ridge.
Spring Rain. Rella.
Star Ride. Lewis.
Sweeter Our Fruits, The. Lewis.
To Otto Bauer. Hayes.
What the Thunder Said: A Fire Sermon. Funaroff.
Wreath for our Murdered Comrade Kobayashi, A. Gold.
**Commuters**
Among Commuters. Swan.
Commuters. White.
**Computers**
All Watched Over by Machines of Loving Grace. Brautigan.
Computer's First Christmas Card, The. Morgan.
Epitaph: "Here he lies moulding." Mellichamp.
Man of Letters. Knox.
Neuteronomy. Merriam.
No Holes Marred. Douglass.
No Need for, the Computer Concern Error Letter, The.
    Lifshin.
Perforated Spirit, The. Bishop.
Reason of Numbers, A. Jacobsen.
Think Tank. Merriam.
Univac to Univac. Salomon.
**Concentration Camps**
After the Fact. Cavalieri.
Camp in the Prussian Forest, A. Jarrell.
Crazed Man in Concentration Camp. Gergely.
Dachau. Brinnin.
Dachau, Now: "Roses Grow There, Fat with Blood." Ritchie.
Desnos Reading the Palms of Men on Their Way to the Gas
    Chambers. Berg.
Gift, The. Ciardi.
Golda. Wolfert.
Heart Mountain Japanese Relocation Camp, The: 30 Years
    Later. Levendosky.
June 1967 at Buchenwald. Bold.
Peat Bog Soldiers. *Unknown.*
Riddle: "From Belsen a crate of gold teeth." Heyen.
Treblinka Gas Chamber. Webb.
**Concord, Massachusetts**
Concord Hymn. Emerson.
**Concrete Poetry.** *See* **Shaped Poetry.**
**Confederacy**

Bonnie Blue Flag. Macarthy.
Dixie. Emmett.
Dixie (Battle-Hymn). Pike.
Maryland, My Maryland! Randall.
Ode: "Sleep sweetly in your humble graves." Timrod.
**Confidence**
It Couldn't Be Done. Guest.
**Conformity**
Among Friends. Kuzma.
At the Chairman's Housewarming. Stafford.
Disillusionment of Ten O'Clock. Stevens.
Let us now praise famous men. Day Lewis.
Little Boxes. Reynolds.
Love Poem Investigation for A.T. Frate.
Man in the Bowler Hat, The. Black.
Much madness is divinest sense. Dickinson.
Poetry of Departures. Larkin.
Radical in the Aligator Shirt, The. Lipsitz.
Story of My Life, The. Summers.
"Think as I Think." Black Riders, XLVII. Crane.
Traveller, The. Berryman.
Unknown Citizen, The. Auden.
**Congreve, William**
To My Dear Friend Mr. Congreve on His Comedy Called "The Double-Dealer." Dryden.
**Connecticut River**
River of Rivers in Connecticut, The. Stevens.
**Conquistadors**
El Dorado. Ryan.
**Conrad, Joseph**
Conrad. Slonimski.
**Conscience**
Conscience. Ravitch.
Conscience, The. Wickham.
Conscience Is Instinct Bred in the House. *Fr.* A Week on the Concord and Merrimack Rivers. Thoreau.
**Conscientious Objectors.** *See* **Pacifism and Pacifists.**
**Conservation.** *See* **Ecology.**
**Constellations**
Cup of the Bear, The, *abr.* Fox.
Escape at Bedtime. Stevenson.
Great Bear, The. Hollander.
**Constitution (ship)**
*Constitution* and the *Guerrière,* The. *Unknown.*
*Constitution's* Last Fight, The. Roche.
Old Ironsides. Holmes.
Resurrection. Blackmur.
**Consumerism**
Cheer for the Consumer. Waterman.
In Answer to Your Query. Lazard.
**Contentment**
Approaching Absolute Zero. Peseroff.
Art Thou Poor, Yet Hast Thou Golden Slumbers? *Fr.* The Pleasant Comedy of Patient Grissell. Dekker.
Character of a Happy Life, The. Wotton.
Contentment. Cotton.
Contentment. Estes.
Happy Life, The. Martial.
Integer Vitae. Campion.
Lake Isle of Innisfree, The. Yeats.
Maesia's Song. *Fr.* Farewell to Folly. Greene.
Mind Content, A. *Fr.* Farewell to Folly. Greene.
My Mind to Me a Kingdom Is. Dyer.
Winter deepening, the hay all in, The. Wilbur.
**Contraception**
Pill Versus the the Springhill Mine Disaster, The. Brautigan.
Poem on Inter-Uterine Device, A. Ghazi.
**Convents**
Convent, The. O'Sullivan.
**Conversion**
Mr. Davis's Experience. *Unknown.*
Mrs. Saunder's Experience. *Unknown.*

**Cooking and Cooks**
Clove as Ego. Halpern.
Grandmother's Apple Pies. Munro.
On a Gentleman Marrying His Cook. Ellis.
Savarin. Williams.
Woman Who Loved to Cook, The. Jong.
**Cooper, James Fenimore**
Cooper. *Fr.* A Fable for Critics. Lowell.
**Coral**
Coral Grove, The. Percival.
**Corinth, Greece**
To Corinth. Landor.
**Cormorants**
Green Shag. Gibson.
**Corn**
Corn-Grinding Song. Corbin.
Corn-Grinding Song. *Unknown.*
Garden Report. Kuzma.
Indian Hymn of Thanks to Mother Corn, An. *Unknown.*
Popcorn-Popper, The. Baruch.
**Corncrakes**
Corncrake, The. Cousins.
**Cornell University**
Far above Cayuga's Waters. *Unknown.*
**Cornwall, England**
April Landscape. Rowse.
Autumn in Cornwall. Swinburne.
Cape Cornwall. Mills.
Cornish Cliffs. Betjeman.
Song of the Western Man, The. Hawker.
Where deep cliffs loom enormous, where cascade. *Fr.* Sunday Afternoon in St. Enodoc Church, Cornwall. Betjeman.
**Cornwallis, Charles Cornwallis, 1st Marquis**
Cornwallis' Country Dance. *Unknown.*
**Coronado, Francisco Vasquez de**
Quivira. Guiterman.
**Cortés, Hernán**
Cortés. Rios.
**Coruña, La, Spain**
Burial of Sir John Moore at Corunna, The. Wolfe.
**Cosmetics**
Empress in the Mirror. Inez.
Maquillage. Symons.
My Mother's Moustache. Moore.
Progress of Beauty, The. Swift.
Rachel and the Truth (c. l945). Yvonne.
Valentine for a Lady, A. Lucillius.
**Cosmology**
Creation Myths. Raffel.
**Cotton**
Cotton Song. Toomer.
Design in Cotton Fabric. Macleod.
November Cotton Flower. Toomer.
Pick a Bale of Cotton. *Unknown.*
Poor Little Johnny. *Unknown.*
Roll the Cotton Down. *Unknown.*
Snapshots of the Cotton South. Davis.
**Country Life**
Above Penmaenmawr. Connor.
At Rushy Lagoon. McAuley.
Before the Thaw. Gill.
Bull, The. Sackville-West.
Cotter's Saturday Night, The. Burns.
Country Life, A: To His Brother, Master Thomas Herrick. Herrick.
Cranberry Song, The. Reynolds.
Deserted Village, The. Goldsmith.
Digging. Thomas.
Epistle to Miss Teresa Blount, on Her Leaving the Town after the Coronation. Pope.
Farm Picture, A. Whitman.
Farm, The. Miller.

Farrell O'Reilly. Gogarty.
For E. C. J. Jarrett.
Goin' Back T'morrer. Garland.
Going to Sleep in the Country. Moss.
Hardweed Path Going. Ammons.
He May Be Envied Who with Tranquil Breast. Smith.
His Content in the Country. Herrick.
Knoxville, Tennessee. Giovanni.
Lake Isle of Innisfree, The. Yeats.
Morning Chores. Heynen.
Mountain Born. Bost.
Mountain Greenery. Hart.
My Own Brand. Cuelho.
Need of Being Versed in Country Things, The. Frost.
O Country People. Hewitt.
Ode to Master Anthony Stafford to Hasten Him into the
    Country, An. Randolph.
Old Man of Verona, The. Claudian.
Ox Cart Man. Hall.
Pass of Kirkstone, The. Wordsworth.
Pasture, The. Frost.
Raleigh Was Right. Williams.
Rural Simplicity. H. Byron.
Short Pastoral. Nathan.
Silent Poem. Francis.
Solitary Reaper, The. Wordsworth.
Spraying the Potatoes. Kavanagh.
To Miss Laetitia Van Lewen (Afterwards Mrs. Pilkington), at a
    Country Assize. Grierson.
To One Who Has Been Long in City Pent. Keats.
Up at a Villa—Down in the City. Browning.
Village, The. Crabbe.
Walking through the Country. Provisor.
Wish, A. Rogers.

**Courage**
Any Complaints? Scannell.
Feigned Courage. Lamb.
Husband with No Courage in Him, The. *Unknown.*
If We Must Die. McKay.
Invictus. Henley.
Strong Men, Riding Horses. Brooks.

**Courtship**
Courtin', The. *Fr.* The Biglow Papers. Lowell.
One Perfect Rose. Parker.

**Coventry, England**
Sally from Coventry, The. Thornbury.

**Cowboys**
At a Cowboy Dance. Adams.
Breakers of Broncos. Sarett.
Bronco Busting, Event #1. Swenson.
Bucking Bronco. *Unknown.*
Buffalo Skinners, The. *Unknown.*
Clancy of the Overflow. *Unknown.*
Closing of the Rodeo, The. Smith.
Cowboy Song. Causley.
Cowboy's Dream, The. Finger.
Cowboy's Dream, The. *Unknown.*
Cowboy's Lament, The. *Unknown.*
Cowboy's Life, The. *At. to* Adams.
Cowboy's Life Is a Very Dreary Life, The. *Unknown.*
Cowboy's Love Song. O'Neill.
Cowboys: One ("Brave/ they straddle the animals"). McKuen.
Cowboys: Two ("Huddled in the pits"). McKuen.
Cowboys: Three ("They wade through beer cans"). McKuen.
Doney Gal. *Unknown.*
Dying Cowboy, The ("As I rode out by Tom Sherman's bar-
    room"). *Unknown.*
For an Indian Bronc Rider Killed in a Highway Crash Near
    Ethete, Wyoming. Roripaugh.
Git Along Little Dogies. *Unknown.*
Goodbye, Old Paint, I'm Leaving Cheyenne. Garrett.
Gunfighter. Locklin.

High-Loping Cowboy, The. Fletcher.
Hired Man on Horseback, The. Rhodes.
Hoppy. Godsey.
I Am a Cowboy in the Boat of Ra. Reed.
I Ride an Old Paint. *Unknown.*
I Want to Be a Cowboy. *Unknown.*
I'm an Old Cowhand. Mercer.
I've Got No Use for the Women. *Unknown.*
Lavender Cowboy, The. *Unknown.*
Little Joe the Wrangler. Thorp.
Love and an Old Western at the Starlite Drive-in Theater.
    Legler.
Man From Snowy River, The. Paterson.
Mocker, The. Haste.
My Own Brand. Cuelho.
New-Chum's First Trip, The. *Unknown.*
O Bury Me Not on the Lone Prairie. *Unknown.*
Old Chisholm Trail, The. *Unknown.*
Old Cowboy's Lament, The. Carr.
Old Dolores. *Unknown.*
Peeler's Lament, The. *Unknown.*
Rag Time Cowboy Joe. Clarke, Muir *and* Abrahms.
Railroad Corral, The. *Unknown.*
Red Whiskey. *Unknown.*
Ride 'Im Cowboy. Freebairn.
Ride the High Country. Slavitt.
Road outside the window was "our" The. *Fr.* Letter to an
    Imaginary Friend. McGrath.
Rodeo. Lueders.
Sandy Maranoa, The. Davis.
Silver Screen. Clark.
Tenderfoot, The. *Unknown.*
Texas Cowboy, The. *Unknown.*
Trail to Mexico. *Unknown.*
Utah Carroll. *Unknown.*
Vaquero. Dorn.
Wake Up, Jacob. *Unknown.*
Watching Jim Shoulders. Connellan.
When the Work's All Done This Fall. *Unknown.*
Whoopee-Ti-Yi-Yo! *Unknown.*
Wild Rippling Water, The. *Unknown.*
Zebra Dun, The. *Unknown.*

**Cows**
Blessing on the Cows, A. O'Sullivan.
Concert Champêtre. O'Hara.
Cow, The. Skinner.
Cow, The. Stephens.
Cow, The. Stevenson.
Cow, The. Taylor.
Cow in Apple Time, The. Frost.
Cows Are Coming Home in Maine. Coffin.
Cows Near the Graveyard, The. Nelson.
Cushy Cow, Bonny. *Unknown.*
Death on the Farm. Waterman.
Drinking Time. O'Sullivan.
Existence. Moon.
Fetching Cows. MacCaig.
Going Home. Lux.
Harmonious Heedlessness of Little Boy Blue, The. Carryl.
Lovely Big Cow. Morton.
Man and Cows. Young.
Milking Time. Roberts.
Moo! Hillyer.
My Cow. McCord.
New Cows, The. Waterman.
Purple Cow, The. Burgess.
*See also* **Cattle.**

**Coyotes**
Coyote, The. Dewey.
Coyote. Harte.
Coyotes Fighting. Wilson.
Father Coyote. Sterling.

Prairie Wolf. Haste.
Sweat Song. Blue Cloud.
Toe'osh: A Laguna Coyote Story. Silko.
**Crabbe, George**
George Crabbe. Robinson.
**Crabs**
Celibates. Chuilleanáin.
Crab, The. Aiken.
Dead Crab, The. Young.
Crustaceans. Fuller.
Ghost Crabs. Hughes.
**Cradle Songs.** *See* **Cradle Song** *and* **Lullaby** *in* **Title and First Line Index.**
**Craftmanship**
Correct Compassion, A. Kirkup.
Craftsmen. Sackville-West.
**Crane, Hart**
Hart Crane. Symons.
Orpheus. Winters.
Words for Hart Crane. Lowell.
**Cranes (birds)**
Crane Is My Neighbour, The. Neilson.
Cranes, The. Po Chü-i.
Sandhill Crane, The. Austin.
**Cranes (machines)**
Landscape with One Figure. Dunn.
**Cranmer, Thomas**
Admire Cranmer! Smith.
Cranmer. Sisson.
**Crazy Horse (Indian Chief)**
Crazy Horse Returns to South Dakota. Elliott.
Death of Crazy Horse, The. Neihardt.
Report to Crazy Horse. Stafford.
Sound from the Earth, A. Stafford.
**Creation**
Assignment. Butcher.
Beginning and an End, A. Roditi.
Chant to Io. Paraone.
Creation, The. Johnson.
Creation, The. *Unknown.*
Creation, The: According to Coyote. Ortiz.
Creation Morning. Kennedy.
Creation Myths. Raffel.
In the beginning God created the heaven and the earth. *Fr.* Genesis. Bible, *O.T.*
Kumulipo, The: A Creation Chant. Keaulumoku.
Old Creation Chant. *Unknown.*
Six Days of Creation, The. McAuley.
Six Periods of Creation, The. *Unknown.*
Song of Creation, The. *Fr.* Vedic Hymns. *Unknown.*
Spacious Firmament on High, The. Addison.
Stately Structure of This Earth, The. Brewster.
**Crécy, Battle of**
Eve of Crecy, The. Morris.
**Creede, Colorado**
Creede. Warman.
Rise and Fall of Creede, The. Warman.
**Crew Racing**
Eight Oars and a Coxswain. Guiterman.
This Shell. Van Doren.
Quarrel, A. Peck.
**Cricket (game)**
At Lord's. Thompson.
**Crickets**
Animal That Drank Up Sound, The. Stafford.
Cricket. No Ch'ŏ-myŏng.
Cricket, The. Tuckerman.
Cricket March. Sandburg.
Crickets. Saroyan.
Halloween Concert. Fisher.
On the Grasshopper and the Cricket. Keats.
Splinter. Sandburg.

To the Grasshopper and the Cricket. Hunt.
**Crime and Criminals**
Act, An. Rosen.
Ballad of Billy the Kid, The. Knibbs.
Betty and Dupree. McGhee.
Black Bart. *Unknown.*
"Black Bart, PO8." Bierce.
Bold Jack Donahue. *Unknown.*
Boston Burglar, The. *Unknown.*
Bowery, The. Hoyt.
Burglar, The. Dorman.
Captain Hall. *Unknown.*
Claude Allen. *Unknown.*
Cole Younger. *Unknown.*
Convict of Clonmel, The. Callanan.
Convicted. Mills.
Crafty Farmer, The. *Unknown.*
Crimes of Passion: The Slasher. Stokes.
Effort at Speech. Meredith.
Frank James, the Roving Gambler. *Unknown.*
Frankie Silvers. Silvers.
Full and True Account of a Horrid and Barbarous Robbery, A. Byrom.
Gentle Alice Brown. Gilbert.
He Fell Among Thieves. Newbolt.
Jesse James ("Among our country's outlaws"). Benét.
Jesse James ("Jesse James was a two-gun man") Benét.
Jim Jones at Botany Bay. *Unknown.*
Johnson-Jinkson. *Unknown.*
Last Gangster, The. Corso.
Macavity: The Mystery Cat. Eliot.
Musgrove. *Unknown.*
Newgate's Garland. Gay.
Peddler and His Wife, The. *Unknown.*
President is Not Funny, The. Heldenbrand.
Robbing and Stealing Blues. *Unknown.*
Sam Bass. *Unknown.*
Sam Hall. *Unknown.*
Somebody Call. Rogers.
Since Then. Enright.
Thief, The. Jacobsen.
Thief, The. Kunitz.
To a Fugitive. Wright.
Twenty-One Years. *Unknown.*
Wild Colonial Boy, The. *Unknown.*
**Crimean War**
Charge of the Heavy Brigade, The. Tennyson.
Charge of the Light Brigade, The. Tennyson.
**Cripples**
Crippled Child at the Window. Cannon.
Cripples. Cassian.
Cripples. Spivak.
Disabled. Owen.
Faithless Nelly Gray. Hood.
Figurehead, The. Shapiro.
Mrs. McGrath. *Unknown.*
Stumpfoot on 42nd Street. Simpson.
**Criticism and Critics**
Apology Addressed to the Critical Reviewer, The. Churchill.
Black Poet, White Critic. Randall.
Choice of Weapons, A. Kunitz.
Critic, A. Landor.
English Bards and Scotch Reviewers. Byron.
Epigram: Pipling. Roethke.
Essay on Criticism, An. Pope.
Hendecasyllabics. Tennyson.
Lines to a Critic. Shelley.
Modern Critics. Coleridge.
On Critics. Prior.
On Dennis. Pope.
Owl-Critic, The. Fields.
Popular. Tennyson.

To a Captious Critic. Dunbar.
To a Reviewer Who Admired My Book. Ciardi.
To an Author. Freneau.
To Certain Critics. Cullen.
To Christopher North. Tennyson.
To Critics. Herrick.
What is a modern poet's fate? Hood.

**Crocodiles**
Amphibious Crocodile. Ransom.
Be Careful! *Unknown.*
Crocodile, The. Belloc.
Crocodile. Chukovsky.
How Doth the Little Crocodile. *Fr.* Alice's Adventures in
  Wonderland. "Carroll."
If you should meet a crocodile. *Unknown.*
Purist, The. Nash.

**Crocuses**
Crocus. Murray.
Crocus, The. Patmore.
For the Spring Being. Carter.
Voice of the Crocus. Hoyer.

**Cromwell, Oliver**
Cromwell. Francis.
Horatian Ode upon Cromwell's Return from Ireland, An.
  Marvell.
More Power. O'Rahilly.
On the Late Metamorphosis of an Old Picture of Oliver
  Cromwell's. *Unknown.*
To the Lord General Cromwell. Milton.

**Cross, The**
Dream of the Rood, The. *Unknown.*
Ebony: Contemporary. Brand.
Making of the Cross, The. Everson.
Old Rugged Cross, The. Bennard.
Standards of the king go forth, The. Venantius Fortunatus.

**Crowds**
At the Ball Game. Williams.
Center of Attention, The. Hoffman.
I Am the People, the Mob. Sandburg.

**Crows**
Billy Magee Magaw. *Unknown.*
Biograph. Kamenetz.
Craw's Killed the Poussie, O, The! *Unknown.*
Crow. Blue Cloud.
Crow, The. Reaney.
Crow Resting. Hughes.
Crow Sat on the Willow, The. Clare.
Crows, The. Ghose.
Crows. McCord.
Crows. Witherup.
Crow's First Lesson. Hughes.
Crow's Theology. Hughes.
Fox and the Crow, The. La Fontaine.
Frog and the Crow, The. *Unknown.*
My Sister Jane. Hughes.
Night Crow. Roethke.
Note on Master Crow, A. Garrigue.
Preparations. Silko.
To Be or Not to Be. *Unknown.*
Two Old Crows. Lindsay.

**Crucifixion, The**
At the Crucifixion. *Unknown.*
Calvary. Robinson.
Christ's Passion. Cowley.
Crucifixion. *Unknown.*
Crucifixion, The. Whittier.
Early Lynching. Sandburg.
Ebony: Contemporary. Brand.
Ecce Homo. Gascoyne.
I Sigh When I Sing. *Unknown.*
Legend of the Crossbill, The. Mosen.
On Our Crucified Lord, Naked and Bloody. Crashaw.

On the Passion. *Unknown.*
Palm Sunday: Good Friday. Fletcher.
Passion, The. Vaughan.
Signature, A. Warren.
This crosse-tree here. Herrick.
To Christ on the Cross. Herrick.
To the Good Thief. Lewis.
Were You There When They Crucified My Lord? *Unknown.*
When I Survey the Wondrous Cross. Watts.
Zone of Death. Everson.

**Cruelty to Animals**
Barn Owl. *Fr.* Father and Child. Harwood.
Beasts Are Very Wise, The. Kipling.
Bells of Heaven, The. Hodgson.
Blinded Bird, The. Hardy.
Coyote, The. Dewey.
Elephant, The. Hochman.
Epigram: "Thy nags (the leanest things alive)." Prior.
Formal Application. Baker.
Gallows, The. Thomas.
Seven Mexican Children. Schmidt.
Thoughts on Capital Punishment. McKuen.
Traverse City Zoo. Harrison.
Village Tale, A. Sarton.

**Cuba**
Central Park *Some People* (3 P.M.). Morejón.
Cuba Libre. Miller.
Maceo. Lloréns Torres.

**Cuchulain (Irish legendary hero)**
Cuchulain Comforted. Yeats.

**Cuckoos**
Cuckoo, The. Chalmers.
Cuckoo. Lister.
Cuckoo, The ("The cuckoo comes in April"). *Unknown.*
Cuckoo, The ("The cuckoo is a bonny bird"). *Unknown.*
Koocoo, The. *Unknown.*
Lament for the Cuckoo. Alcuin.
Of Use. Heywood.
Oocuck, The. Richardson.
Spring. *Fr.* Love's Labour's Lost. Shakespeare.
Sumer Is Icumen In. *Unknown.*
To the Cuckoo. Wordsworth.

**Cummings, Edward Estlin**
To Chuck. Sanchez.

**Cupid**
Cheat of Cupid, The: or, The Ungentle Guest. Herrick.
Cupid Far Gone. Lovelace.
Cupid's Call. Shirley.
Duel, The. Lovelace.
Ladies Prayer to Cupid, A. Guarini.
Love Arm'd. Behn.
Love Sleeping. Plato.
Metamorphosis, The. Suckling.
Ode to Love, An. Behn.
To the God of Love. Knox.
Wounded Cupid, The. Herrick.

**Curie, Marie**
Power. Rich.

**Curlews**
Curlew. Norris.
Curlew, The. Hay.

**Curses**
Bruadar and Smith and Glinn. *Unknown.*
Curse, The. Donne.
Curse, The. Synge.
Curse for a Nation, A. E. Browning.
Curse of a Fisherman's Wife. Chalpin.
Curse on a Closed Gate, A. *Unknown.*
Curses. Duemer.
Glass of Beer, A. Stephens.
Goblin Market. C. Rossetti.
Goody Blake, and Harry Gill. Wordsworth.

I curse my bearing, childhood, youth.　Synge.
Irish Curse on the Occupying English.　*Unknown.*
Skin the Goat's Curse on Carey.　*Unknown.*
Some curse that traitor Judas life and limb.　Quarles.
Traveller's Curse after Misdirection.　Graves.
When Klopstock England defied.　Blake.
**Custer, George Armstrong**
Custer.　Stedman.
Custer's Last Charge.　Whittaker.
Tale of Last Stands, A.　Red Cloud.
**Cybele**
Mother, The.　Deutsch.
**Cyclops**
And so an easier life our Cyclops drew.　*Fr.* Idylls.　Theocritus.
Cave we found, but vacant all within, The.　*Fr.* The Odyssey.
　Homer.
**Cynicism**
Cynic, The.　Tucker.


# D


**Da Vinci, Leonardo.**　*See* **Leonardo da Vinci.**
**Dachau, Germany**
Dachau.　Brinnin.
**Daedalus**
Be Daedalus.　Alba.
Now in this while gan Daedalus a wearinesse to take.　*Fr.*
　Metamorphoses.　Ovid.
**Daffodils**
Daffodils.　Heffernan.
I Wandered Lonely as a Cloud.　Wordsworth.
Lent Lily, The.　Housman.
To Daffodils.　Herrick.
**Dahlias**
Autumn.　A. Lowell.
Giant Decorative Dahlia.　Holden.
**Daisies**
Daisies.　Nowlan.
Daisies.　Rossetti.
Diasies.　Wade.
Daisies.　Young.
Daisy, The.　Zaturenska.
Daysies.　Chaucer.　*Fr.* Legend of Good Women.
Loss.　Ammons.
To Daisies, Not To Shut So Soon.　Herrick.
**Dali, Salvador**
Salvador Dali.　Gascoyne.
**Dancing and Dancers**
Artist, The.　Williams.
At the Dancing School of the Sisters Schwarz.　Jerome.
Ballad of the Ten Casino Dancers.　Meireles.
Band Played On, The.　Palmer.
Bottled: New York.　Johnson.
Dance, The.　Williams.
Dance for Rain, A.　Bynner.
Dance Marathon, The.　Lally.
Dance Steps.　*Unknown.*
Dancer.　Page.
Dancer, The.　Waller.
Dancer: Four Poems.　Engle.
Disco Fever.　Schechter.
Harlem Dancer, The.　McKay.
Javanese Dancers.　Symons.
Lost Dancer, The.　Toomer.
Morris Dance, The.　*Unknown.*
On Her Dancing.　Shirley.
Orchestra: or, a Poem on Dancing.　Davies.
Pounding It Out.　Kroll.

Quick-Step.　Creeley.
South of the Border.　Nicholas.
Swansong.　Muske.
Waltz, The.　Byron.
Waltz Me Around Again Willie; or, Round, Round, Round.
　Cobb.
Wardance.　George.
Watching the Dance.　Merrill.
We Dance like Ella Riffs.　Rodgers.
**Dandelions**
American XVII: A Reminder of William Carlos Williams.
　Rakosi.
First Dandelion, The.　Whitman.
Sun hangs, The/ medals.　*Fr.* First Dandelions.　Wallace.
To the Dandelion.　Lowell.
**Dante Alighieri**
At Dante's Grave.　Zussman.
On the "Vita Nuova" of Dante.　Rossetti.
Study in Aesthetics, The.　Pound.
**Daphne**
Apollo and Daphne.　Winters.
**Daredevils**
On the Edge at Santorini.　Blumenthal.
**Darkness**
Dark.　Healy.
His Necessary Darkness.　Sullivan.
Phases of Darkness, The.　Petrie.
Room, The.　Aiken.
To Know the Dark.　Berry.
**Daughters**
Again.　Jones.
At a Summer Hotel.　Gardner.
Elegy for His Daughter Ellen.　Owen.
First Lesson.　Booth.
For Katherine, 1952-1961.　Hilberry.
For My Daughter.　Koertge.
Goodnight, The.　Simpson.
I Have Three Daughters.　Stone.
I see her in my sleep, my red, terrible girl.　*Fr.* Three Women.
　Plath.
Little Girl, My String Bean, My Lovely Woman.　Sexton.
Little Red Riding Hood.　NorthSun.
Madonna and Daughter.　Bergé.
Mama and Daughter.　Hughes.
Mornings.　Berger.
Mothers, Daughters.　Kaufman.
Mutant, The.　Barrows.
Name, The.　Creeley.
On My First Daughter.　Jonson.
Prayer for My Daughter, A.　Yeats.
Quicksilver Thing.　Legler.
Sara in Her Father's Arms.　Oppen.
Sleep Darling.　Sappho.
Song to Be Sung by the Father of Infant Female Children.
　Nash.
To My Infant Daughter: "Alas, that I Should Be."　Winters.
*Roses Race Around Her Name, The* (RRA).　Jonathan Cott, ed.
*Tangled Vines: A Collection of Mother and Daughter Poems* (TV).
　Lyn Lifshin, ed.
**David (Bible)**
After Goliath.　Amis.
David.　Miles.
David and Goliath.　Crouch.
David and Solomon.　Naylor.
Like David.　Preil.
Little David.　*Unknown.*
Saul.　Browning.
Song to David, A.　Smart.
That Harp You Play So Well.　Moore.
Translating.　Whitman.
**David (statue)**
Bronze David of Donatello, The.　Jarrell.

David Homindae. Rosenfeld.

**Davies, Sir John**
Four for Sir John Davies. Roethke.

**Davy, Sir Humphry**
Sir Humphry Davy. *Fr.* Clerihews. Bentley.

**Dawn**
But Venus first. *Fr.* First Dream. Juana Ines de la Cruz.
Cock-Crow. Thomas.
Dawn. Dunbar.
Dawn. Stevens.
Dawn. *Unknown.*
Dawn, The. Yeats.
Daybreak. Meyers.
Dew. Maiden.
Eagle Feather IV. George.
First Light. Kinsella.
Harbor Dawn, The. *Fr.* The Bridge. Crane.
I dreamed I saw the crescent moon. *Unknown.*
In gold sandals. Sappho.
L'Aurore Grelottante. Levi.
Miraculous Dawn. Parry.
Morning Prayer. Aua.
Now from the east. Masahongva.
Square at Dawn, The. Tate.
Starting at Dawn. Sun Yün-feng.
Sun-Rising, The. Donne.
Window to the East. Evans.
*See also* **Morning; Sunrise.**

**Day**
Curiously Young Like a Freshly-Dug Grave. Brautigan.
Days. Emerson.
Days. Larkin.
Wee Davie Daylicht. Tennant.

**Daydreams**
Instruction Manual, The. Ashbery.
Mixed Feelings. Ashbery.
*See also* **Dreams and Dreaming.**

**Deafness**
Deafness. Ryan.
Monologue of a Deaf Man. Wright.
Mutterings over the Crib of a Deaf Child. Wright.
On a Portrait of a Deaf Man. Betjeman.
On His Own Deafness. Swift.
Speechless: Upon the Marriage of Two Deaf and Dumb Persons. Marston.
To a Deaf and Dumb Little Girl. Coleridge.

**Dean, James**
For James Dean. O'Hara.

**Death and the Dead**
Adieu, Farewell Earth's Bliss. *Fr.* Summer's Last Will and Testament. Nashe.
Admiral Death. Newbolt.
After Death. Beer.
After Death. C. Rossetti.
After death nothing is, and nothing death. *Fr.* Troades. Seneca.
After Grave Deliberation. Flynn.
After Lorca. Creeley.
After My Death. Bialik.
After Tonight. Soto.
Afterwards. Hardy.
Against the Fear of Death. *Fr.* De Rerum Natura. Lucretius.
Age. Landor.
Ah, Are You Digging on My Grave? Hardy.
All Being Well. Gibson.
All the Dead Dears. Plath.
All Things Decay and Die. Herrick.
Alone in the House. Bogin.
Among Those Killed in the Dawn Raid Was a Man Aged a Hundred. Thomas.
And Death Shall Have No Dominion. Thomas.
And When I Die. Nyro.

Angel of Death, The. *Unknown.*
Angina Pectoris. Moses.
Annabel Lee. Poe.
Anthem for Doomed Youth. Owen.
Arundel Tomb, An. Larkin.
As from the darkening gloom a silver dove. Keats.
As I Ebb'd with the Ocean of Life. Whitman.
Autumn. De la Mare.
Ballad of Dead Yankees, The. Petersen.
Beautiful Youth. Benn.
Because I could not stop for Death. Dickinson.
Bed by the Window, The. Jeffers.
Before the Birth of One of Her Children. Bradstreet.
Bells for John Whiteside's Daughter. Ransom.
Bereft Child's First Night. Bellerby.
Beside the Bed. Mew.
Big Rocks, The. Kryss.
Black Death, The. Dacey.
Blind Date. Aiken.
Blue Stones. Levis.
Blue Tattoo, The. Thayne.
Book of the Dead, Prayer 14. Berssenbrugge.
Breathers, The. Reiss.
Bridal Couch. Lloyd.
Bride, The. Lawrence.
Broken Gull, A. Moore.
Broken Year, The. Talney.
Burial. Francis.
Burial. Sarton.
Burial. Tuwhare.
Burial. Walker.
Can the Circle Be Unbroken? *Unknown.*
Channel Firing. Hardy.
Charge, The. Hollo.
Child Dying, The. Muir.
City Dead-House, The. Whitman.
Clock, The. Beer.
Clorox Kid, The. Robertson.
Coming and Going. Goodman.
Conception. Miles.
Conqueror Worm, The. Poe.
Consolatio Nova: for Alan Swallow. Cunningham.
Come away, come away, death. *Fr.* Twelfth Night. Shakespeare.
Come Softly to My Wake. Brown.
Cool Tombs. Sandburg.
Creek Mother Poem. Harjo.
Crossing the Bar. Tennyson.
Darest Thou Now O Soul. Whitman.
Dark Girl. Bontemps.
David's Poem. Hiatt.
Dead, The. Blind.
Dead, The. Very.
Dead Boy. Ransom.
Dead Ponies. Chamberlain.
Death. Harjo.
Death. Herbert.
Death. Jeffrey.
Death. Jones.
Death. Knott.
Death. *Unknown.*
Death. Williams.
Death. Wright.
Death and the Arkansas River. Stanford.
Death and the Pineapple. Gerber.
Death and the Plowman. Keyes.
Death, Be Not Proud. *Fr.* Holy Sonnets. Donne.
Death Bed. Kinsella.
Death Bells. *Unknown.*
Death Came Too Late. Birch.
Death in Duke Street. Morgan.
Death in the Family. Birch.

Death Is a Door. Allcock.
Death Is Awful. *Unknown.*
Death is the supple suitor. Dickinson.
Death of a Dog. Bland.
Death of a Fair Girl. Butler.
Death of a Poet. Causley.
Death of a Son. Silkin.
Death of a Symbol, The. Storey.
Death of an Average Man. Birch.
Death of Lester Brown, House Painter, The. Taylor.
Death of the Ball Turret Gunner, The. Jarrell.
Death of the Craneman, The. Hayes.
Death of the Hired Man, The. Frost.
Death Piece. Roethke.
Death Rode A Pinto Pony. Montgomery.
Death: She Was Always Here. Wallach.
Death Snips Proud Men. Sandburg.
Death Sonnet I. Mistral.
Death Takes Only a Minute. Pratt.
Death Valley Blues. *Unknown.*
Death Watchers, The. Ryerson.
Death-Bed, The. Hood.
Death-Bed Song. *Unknown.*
Death's the Classic Look. Ciardi.
Deathwatch. Harper.
Deer Lay Down Their Bones, The. Jeffers.
Dirge, A: "Why were you born when the snow was falling." C. Rossetti.
Dirge without Music. Millay.
Do Not Go Gentle into That Good Night. Thomas.
Do the Dead Know What Time It Is? Patchen.
Dream, A. Allingham.
Dream Songs of Haka Ancestors. Lau.
Drowning is not so pitiful. Dickinson.
During Wind and Rain. Hardy.
Dwellings of Our Dead, The. Adams.
Dying. Alvarez.
Dying. Kessler.
Dying Californian, The. *Unknown.*
Dying Father's Farewell, The. *Unknown.*
Dying Gaul, The. O'Grady.
Dying Is Fine but Death. Cummings.
Dying Man, The. Roethke.
Early Purges, The. Heaney.
Earth Changes. Shire.
Edge. Plath.
Edmonton, thy cemetery. Smith.
Egyptian Book of the Dead. Henderson.
Elegy: "Death be not proud, thy hand gave not this blow." Harington.
Elegy: "My prime of youth is but a frost of cares." Tichborne.
Elegy for a School-Friend. Young.
Elegy for Alfred Hubbard. Connor.
Elegy for Jack Bowman. Bruchac.
Elegy for Jane. Roethke.
Elegy for My Father. Moss.
Elegy for My Father. Strand.
Elegy over a Tomb. Herbert of Cherbury.
Elegy Written in a Country Churchyard. Gray.
Elephants May Parade before Your House. *Unknown.*
End. Brown.
Entry. Thwaite.
Epigram: "Golden one is gone from the banquets, The." Doolittle ("H.D.").
Epilogue: "That death might not be casual." Singer.
Epitaph: "My brother is skull and skeleton now." Montgomerie.
Epitaph: "Sir, you should notice me: I am the Man." Abercrombie.
Epitaph on an Infant. Coleridge.
Epitaph on Salomon Pavy. Jonson.
Epitaph on the Lady Mary Villiers. Carew.

Epitaph upon——, An. Marvell.
Erotion's Death. Whigham.
Escape. Graves.
Evelyn Hope. Browning.
Exequy, The. King.
Exequy, An. Porter.
Exit Molloy. Mahon.
Extreme Unction. Dowson.
Fall Comes in Back-Country Vermont. Warren.
Farewell, A. Fairburn.
Fear No More the Heat o' the Sun. *Fr.* Cymbeline. Shakespeare.
Feel Me. Swenson.
Felix Randal. Hopkins.
First Death. Justice.
First Death in Nova Scotia. Bishop.
First Story. Orlen.
Five Ways to Kill a Man. Brock.
Fixing to Die. *Unknown.*
Flat One, A. Snodgrass.
For a Dead Lady. Robinson.
For Andrew. Adcock.
For My Friend Michele. Gregg.
For One Who Died Young. Hays.
For the Moment. Weber.
Force That through the Green Fuse Drives the Flower, The. Thomas.
Forsaken Garden, A. Swinburne.
Four Years After. Beer.
Fox, The. Patchen.
Friends Beyond. Hardy.
Fugue of Death. Celan.
Full fathom five thy father lies. *Fr.* The Tempest. Shakespeare.
Fun and Funerals. Glen.
Funeral at Ansley. Welch.
Funeral Oration for a Mouse. Dugan.
Funeral Poem. Jones.
Futility. Owen.
Game Called. Rice.
Game of Chance, A. Moss.
Gee I Like to Think of Dead. Cummings.
German Legion, The. Dobell.
Glories of Our Blood and State, The. *Fr.* The Contention of Ajax and Ulysses. Shirley.
Glory of the Day Was in Her Face, The. Johnson.
Go Down Death. Johnson.
Good-bye. Emerson.
Gooseberries. Wild.
Gravely. Welch.
Graves of a Household, The. Hemans.
Groundhog, The. Eberhart.
Hagen. Gregory.
Hay Derrick. Harris.
He Came to Visit Me. Seymour-Smith.
He Smelt the Smell of Death Within the Marrow. Johnson.
Hearse Song, The. *Unknown.*
Heart Burial. Grigson.
Heaven and Hell. *Unknown.*
Heaven for Railroad Men. Wojahn.
Here's Death. McMaster.
His Winding-Sheet. Herrick.
Home Burial. Frost.
How Annandale Went Out. Robinson.
How Did You Die? Cooke.
Hungry Grass. MacDonagh.
Hut Near Desolated Pines. Campbell.
Hymn to Death. Bryant.
Hymn to God My God, in My Sickness. Donne.
I heard a fly buzz when I died. Dickinson.
I Kissed Pa Twice After His Death. Peterson.
I Know Moonrise. *Unknown.*

I Shall Not Care. Teasdale.
I Thank God I'm Free at Las'. *Unknown.*
I Was Afraid of Dying. Wright.
I Went too Death. *Unknown.*
If You Should Die. Stevens.
Ignorance of Death. Empson.
In a Grave-Yard. Braithwaite.
In Memoriam (Easter 1915). Thomas.
In Memory of a Child. Lindsay.
In Memory of a Friend. Barker.
In Memory of G. K., for 50 Years the College Carpenter. Martin.
In Memory of My Cat Domino: 1951-1966. Fuller.
In Memory of My Dear Grandchild Anne Bradstreet. Bradstreet.
In Memory of My Dear Grandchild Elizabeth Bradstreet. Bradstreet.
In Tenebris. Hardy.
In the Convalescent Hospital. Pumphrey.
In the Desert. Melville.
In the House of the Dying. Cooper.
In the thirtieth year of life. Cunningham.
Incident in a Rose Garden. Justice.
Indian Burying Grounds, The. Freneau.
Inseperable. Marston.
Interlude. Shapiro.
Intimations of Immortality, Cuttingsville, Vermont, 1880. Carrier.
Invocations of Death, The. Raine.
Is It Far to Go? Day Lewis.
Is My Team Ploughing? Housman.
Is There Life Across the Street? Watson.
Isaac Leybush Peretz. Halpern.
I've seen a dying eye. Dickinson.
Ivory, Coral, Gold, The. Drummond.
Janet Waking. Ransom.
Killing of Sparrows, The. Beer.
Kind of Good-bye, A. Spencer.
Lads in their hundreds to Ludlow come in for the fair, The. Housman.
Lady Lazarus. Plath.
Lament: "I lie in darkness . . ." Hauroa.
Lament: "Listen, children:/ Your father is dead." Millay.
Lament for Taramoana. Makere.
Lamenting Tauba. Laila Akhyaliyya.
Last Journey. Martinez.
Last Lines—1916. Pearse.
Last Night that She lived, The. Dickinson.
Last Quatrain of the Ballad of Emmett Till, The. Brooks.
Last Superstition, The. Funaroff.
Last Word, A. Rodgers.
Last Words. Plath.
Layer-Out, The. Smith.
Lesson, The. Lucie-Smith.
Let Me Die a Youngman's Death. McGough.
Letter from a Death Bed. Ciardi.
Letter to a Dead Father. Shelton.
Life and Death. Turner.
Life flows to death as rivers to the sea. Cunningham.
Lights Out. Thomas.
Little Boy Blue. Field.
Little Elegy. Kennedy.
Little Libbie. Moore.
Living/Dying. Steele.
Lonesome Valley. *Unknown.*
Losses. Jarrell.
Luke Havergal. Robinson.
Lycidas. Milton.
Madam Life's a Piece in Bloom. Henley.
Madrigal. Thomas.
Malfunction. Albert.
Margaritae Sorori. Henley.

Maria Wentworth. Carew.
Matter of Urgency. Johnson.
Meditation, The. Norris.
Memorial Service. Williams.
Merlin. Hill.
Midnight Lamentation. Monro.
Mid-Term Break. Heaney.
Mill Town. Taggard.
Minor Elegy. Lisboa.
Missing. Pudney.
Morgue, The. Baxter.
Mother, they say you looked Irish. Brenner.
Mourn for Yourself. Keating.
Mourn Not the Dead. Chaplin.
Mourning-Song for Rangiaho, A. Herea.
Much Obliged. Morice.
My life closed twice before its close. Dickinson.
My Son and I. Levine.
My Son, My Executioner. Hall.
Nature. Longfellow.
Nature's Cook. Duchess of Newcastle.
Nearer, My God to Thee. Adams.
Necrological. Ransom.
Necropolis. Shapiro.
Neighbours. King.
Never Again, The. Dobzynski.
New England Protestant. *Fr.* Attitudes. Eberhart.
Newly Discovered "Homeric" Hymn, A. Olson.
News. Pomeroy.
Night-Piece on Death, A. Parnell.
Nirvana. Törel.
Nothing but Death. Neruda.
O All down within the pretty meadow. Patchen.
O Bury Me Not on the Lone Prairie. *Unknown.*
Oh! Death. *Unknown.*
O Death, Rock Me Asleep. Boleyn.
O Russian faced, woman on the grass. *Fr.* Kaddish. Ginsberg.
Oath, The. Tate.
Obit Page. Blackburn.
Ocean Burial, The. Chapin.
Ocean Said to Me Once, The. *Fr.* The Black Riders. Crane.
Of De Witt Williams on His Way to Lincoln Cemetery. Brooks.
Old King, The. De la Mare.
Old People Speak of Death, The. Troupe.
On a Dead Child. Bridges.
On a Dead Child. Middleton.
On a Death in an Old People's Home. Ivimy.
On a Dying Boy. Bell.
On Death. Killigrew.
On Death. Landor.
On My Dear Grandchild Simon Bradstreet. Bradstreet.
On My First Daughter. Jonson.
On My First Son. Jonson.
On the Acequia Madre. Corbin.
On the Countess Dowager of Pembroke. Browne.
On the Death of a Young Lady, Cousin to the Author. Byron.
On the Death of Friends in Childhood. Justice.
On the Death of His Wife. O'Dalaigh.
On the Death of Parents. Barson.
One dignity delays for all. Dickinson.
One Morning in May; or, The Young Girl Cut Down in Her Prime. *Unknown.*
Others, I am not the first. Housman.
Our journey had advanced. Dickinson.
Out of the Cradle Endlessly Rocking. Whitman.
Pale Blue Casket, The. Pitcher.
Papa's Letter. *Unknown.*
Pardon, The. Wilbur.
Pardoner's Tale Blues. Beer.
Paul. Wright.
Peace. Hughes.

Peter's Little Daughter Dies. Patchen.
Piazza Piece. Ransom.
Poem: "Old man in the crystal morning after snow." Schwartz.
Poem to Delight My Friends Who Laugh at Science-Fiction, A. Rolfe.
Poem to My Death. Burgos.
Poor Ghost, The. C. Rossetti.
Poor soul, the center of my sinful earth. *Fr.* Sonnets. Shakespeare.
Porch, The. Pain.
Portrait of a Negative. Kuo.
Post Mortem. Brain.
Post-Mortem. Smith.
Practicing My Death. Schechter.
Prayer: "Give me a death like Buddha's, let me fall." Moss.
Primary Ground, A. Rich.
Prosopopoeia Corporis Animae Valedicturi: Adios: Arrivederci. Lathum.
Prospice. Browning.
Quaker Graveyard in Nantucket, The. Lowell.
Rain. Thomas.
Raisin, The. Hall.
Raising of Lazarus, The. Clifton.
Reconciliation. Lewis.
Refusal to Mourn the Death, by Fire, of a Child in London, A. Thomas.
Remember. C. Rossetti.
Remembrance. E. Brontë.
Reminiscence, A. A. Brontë.
Requiem: "Under the wide and starry sky." Stevenson.
Requiescat. Arnold.
Responsory, 1948, A. Merton.
Resurgence. Stevenson.
Resurrection, The. Taylor.
Rumination. Eberhart.
Safe in their alabaster chambers. Dickinson.
Sailing Home from Rapallo. Lowell.
St. James Infirmary. *Unknown.*
Saunders Point. Combellick.
Sea Ritual, The. Darley.
Sea Shanty. Dyment.
Sept. 16, 1961, Poem. Kerouac.
Shape of Death, The. Swenson.
Ship of Death, The. Lawrence.
Simplify Me When I'm Dead. Douglas.
Singleman. Hayes.
Sister Lou. Brown.
Slumber Did My Spirit Seal, A. Wordsworth.
Smell of death is so powerful, The. Marguerite de Navarre.
Smile, Death. Mew.
Somebody and Somebody Else and You. Rolfe.
Song of a Man about to Die in a Strange Land. *Unknown.*
Song of a Woman Abandoned by the Tribe. *Unknown.*
Sonnet on the Death of a Friend. Keats.
Sonnet 21. Goodman.
Spark's Farewell to Its Clay, The. Mason.
Sparrow-Hawk's Complaint, The. *Unknown.*
Speculation. Nemerov.
Springfield Mountain. *Unknown.*
Staircase, The. Allen.
Stanzas: "I'll not weep that thou art going to leave me." E. Brontë.
Stanzas to——: "Well, some may hate, and some may scorn." E. Brontë.
Statue, The. Belloc.
Stone Words for Robert Lowell. Eberhart.
Stoneyard, The. Trias.
Stony Lonesome. Hughes.
Streets of Laredo, The. *Unknown.*
Summer Evening Churchyard, Lechdale, Gloucestershire, A. Shelley.
Sylvester's Dying Bed. Hughes.

Tag, I.D. Harris.
Tenancy, The. Gilmore.
Thanatopsis. Bryant.
That Dark Other Mountain. Francis.
That time of year thou mayst in me behold. *Fr.* Sonnets. Shakespeare.
That's Life? Bold.
There, on the Darkened Deathbed. Masefield.
There's been a death in the opposite house. Dickinson.
Thesis. De Bolt.
They are all gone into the world of light! Vaughan.
This Business of Dying. Skoyles.
This Houre Her Vigill. Iremonger.
Thoughts of Phena. Hardy.
Three. Corso.
Threnody: "The south-wind brings." Emerson.
Through a Glass, Darkly. Dowling.
Through the Eye of the Needle. Gioseffi.
Timor Mortis Conturbat Me. Dunbar.
Tir'd nature's sweet restorer, balmy sleep! *Fr.* Night Thoughts. Young.
To——: "The cold earth slept below." Shelley.
To a Dying Girl. Larson.
To a Troubled Friend. Wright.
To an Athlete Dying Young. Housman.
To Death. Gogarty.
To Death. Shelley.
To die—takes just a little while. Dickinson.
To His Dying Brother, Master William Herrick. Herrick.
To L. H. B. Mansfield.
To My Friend Whose Parachute Did Not Open. Wagoner.
To My Ninth Decade. Landor.
To Night. White.
To the Holy Spirit. Winters.
To the Reverend Shade of His Religious Father. Herrick.
To the Thoughtful Reader. Meredith.
Tobacconist of Eighth Street, The. Eberhart.
Tombstone with Cherubim. Gregory.
Tomorrow, and Tomorrow, and Tomorrow. *Fr.* Macbeth. Shakespeare.
Transfiguration, The. Herrick.
Transformations. Hardy.
Trifles. Everson.
Truth the Dead Know, The. Sexton.
Turning Point. Gillies.
Two Deaths. Jennings.
Two Views of a Cadaver Room. Plath.
Two White Horses in a Line. *Unknown.*
Two Women at the JFK Gravesite. Gibson.
Uncle Death. Clark.
Unhappy Diary Days. Vizenor.
Unwelcome. Dovey.
Uphill. C. Rossetti.
Upon a Child That Died. Herrick.
Upon a Dying Lady. Yeats.
Upon His Sister-in-Law, Mistress Elizabeth Herrick. Herrick.
Upon the Death of a Gentleman. Crashaw.
Upon the Image of Death. Southwell.
Upon Wedlock, and Death of Children. Taylor.
*Vale* from Carthage. Viereck.
Valediction, A: Forbidding Mourning. Donne.
Vegetable, I Will Not Be, A. Whitewing.
Villagers and Death, The. Graves.
Visit to My Father-in-Law on Memorial Day, A. Ruse.
Voice of Heroes. Gregory.
Wake. Spires.
Wake All the Dead. Davenant.
Wake Not for the World-Heard Thunder. Housman.
Waking to Snowfall. Jellema.
Warning and Reply. E. Brontë.
Watch, The. Cornford.
Water Island. Moss.

We Are Seven. Wordsworth.
We Assume: On the Death of Our Son, Reuben Masai Harper. Harper.
We slowly drove, he knew no haste. Dickinson.
Welcome, Sweet Rest. Wigglesworth.
What says my brother?/ Death is a fearful thing. *Fr.* Measure for Measure. Shakespeare.
When I Am Dead, My Dearest. C. Rossetti.
When I Have Fears That I May Cease to Be. Keats.
When I Was Home Last Christmas. Jarrell.
When the Ripe Fruit Falls. Lawrence.
Who's Most Afraid of Death? Cummings.
Wild Mustard River, The. *Unknown.*
Witness to Death. Lattimore.
Woman Mourned by Daughters, A. Rich.
Woman Shopping, A. Glover.
Written in Disgust of Vulgar Superstition. Keats.
Yahrzeit. Jaffe.
Yet Another Poem about a Dying Child. Frame.
*Death in Literature* (DL). Robert F. Weir, ed.

**Death of God**
On Listening to a Death-of-God Theologian Lecture in Chapel. Suderman.
On the Death of God. Jellema.

**Debauchery**
Disabled Debauchee, The. Earl of Rochester.

**Debussy, Claude**
1907: A Proposal from Paris. Howard.

**Decay**
Empty Glen, The. Saunders.
Hammers, The. Hodgson.
Lion's Skeleton, The. Turner.
Ozymandias. Shelley.
Since brass, nor stone, nor earth, nor boundless sea. *Fr.* Sonnets. Shakespeare.
When I have seen by Time's fell hand defaced. *Fr.* Sonnets. Shakespeare.
Wood-Pile, The. Frost.

**December**
December Stillness. Sassoon.

**Decoration Day.** *See* **Memorial Day.**

**Deer**
Buck in the Snow, The. Millay.
Crystal Moment. Coffin.
Deer. No Ch'ŏn-myŏng.
Deer. *Fr.* A Bestiary. Rexroth.
Deer, The. Sheck.
Deer among Cattle. Dickey.
Deer in the Prison, The. Bruchac.
Deer Isle. Booth.
Deer Lay Down Their Bones, The. Jeffers.
Deer Stolen. Stafford.
Fallow Deer at the Lonely House, The. Hardy.
Landscape, Deer Season. Howes.
Long Hair. Snyder.
Lost Deer, The. Bruchac.
Moment. Flanner.
Moschus Moschiferus. Hope.
Nymph Complaining for the Death of Her Fawn, The. Marvell.
Out in the Dark. Thomas.
Pet Deer, The. Tate.
Poacher, The. *Unknown.*
Psalm. Oppen.
Runnable Stag, A. Davidson.
This Poem Is for Deer. *Fr.* Myths and Texts: Hunting. Snyder.
Traveling through the Dark. Stafford.
Two Look at Two. Frost.

**Defeat**
First in the Pentathlon. Lucilius.
Mighty Runner, A (Variation of a Greek Theme). Robinson.

Snapshot for Miss Bricka Who Lost in the Semifinal Round of the Pennsylvania Lawn Tennis Tournament. Wallace.
To a Friend Whose Work Has Come to Nothing. Yeats.
Victory in Defeat. Markham.

**Defoe, Daniel**
To That Most Senseless Scoundrel, the Author of Legion's Humble Address to the Lords. Brown.
Upon the Anonymous Author of Legion's Humble Address to the Lords. Brown.

**Degas, Edgar**
Degas. Monette.
Museum Piece. Wilbur.

**Deirdre**
Deirdre. Stephens.

**Dejection.** *See* **Melancholy.**

**De Kooning, Willem**
Ode to Willem de Kooning. O'Hara.

**Delphi, Oracle of**
Last Utterance of the Delphic Oracle. Rexroth.
News for the Delphic Oracle. Yeats.

**Demeter**
Appeasement of Demeter, The. Meredith.
Demeter and Persephone. Tennyson.
Song of Ceres. Doak.

**Democracy**
As a kid I believed in democracy: I. Berryman.
Councils. Piercy.
On a General Election. Belloc.

**Dempsey, Jack**
Dempsey, Dempsey. Gregory.

**Dentists**
After the Dentist. Swenson.
Anxiety about Dying. Ostriker.
Hands folded like napkins in my lap. Peterson.
Making an Impression. Jackson.

**Denver, Colorado**
Waltz Against the Mountains. Ferril.

**Depression (economic).** *See* **Great Depression.**

**Depression (psychological).** *See* **Melancholy; Mental Illness.**

**Descartes, René**
Whoroscope. Beckett.

**Deserts**
Death in the Desert, A. Tomlinson.
Death Valley. Lee.
Desert, The. Knibbs.
Desert Bloom. Arnold.
Desert Song ("There's no hiding here in the glare of the desert"). Dresbach.
Desert Song ("When I came on from Santa Fe"). Galsworthy.
How to Write a Poem About the Desert. Carter.
I Am Drawn Still to the Desert. Bull.
New Mexican Desert. Bynner.
Rain in the Desert. *Fr.* Arizona Poems. Fletcher.
Requiem for Sonora. Shelton.
Song of the Desert. Snow.
Spring in the Desert. Hall.
Spring in the Desert. Merrill.
To the Colorado Desert. Morris.
Toll of the Desert, The. Monroe.
Tour of the Southwest, A. Lueders.
Water Tank at Dusk, The. Hall.

**Desire**
Abstinence sows sand all over. Blake.
Arrow of Desire, The. *Unknown.*
Desire is a witch. Day Lewis.
Desire Is Dead. Lawrence.
I turn you out of doors. Chartier.
Of the Birth and Bringing Up of Desire. Vere, Earl of Oxford.
Re-forming the Crystal. Rich.
Thou Blind Man's Mark. *Fr.* Astrophel and Stella. Sidney.
Two Songs. Rich.

**De Soto, Hernando**

Distant Runners, The.   Van Doren.

**Despair**
Carrion Comfort.   Hopkins.
City of Dreadful Night, The.   Thomson ("B. V.").
Delirium in Vera Cruz.   Lowry.
Defeated, The.   Gregg.
Despair.   Eberhart.
Divorce of a Lover, The.   Gascoigne.
I cannot live with you.   Dickinson.
I Wake and Feel the Fell of Dark.   Hopkins.
No Worst, There Is None.   Hopkins.
Old-World Thicket, An.   C. Rossetti.
She May Have Seen Better Days.   Thornton.
Song of Despair.   Rangiaho.
There's a certain slant of light.   Dickinson.
These.   Williams.
Thou Art Indeed Just, Lord.   Hopkins.
Warren Pryor.   Nowlan.

**Destiny.**   *See* **Fate.**

**Detroit, Michigan**
Black Day in July.   Lightfoot.
Coming Home, Detroit, 1968.   Levine.
Detroit.   Hall.
In Detroit, I walk out Woodward Avenue.   Cuscaden.

**Devil.**   *See* **Satan.**

**Dew**
Dew Sat on Julia's Hair.   Herrick.
On a Drop of Dew.   Marvell.

**Diabetes**
Day of the Pancreas, The.   McFadden.

**Diamonds**
Hope Diamonds.   DeFrees.

**Diana**
Dianae Sumus in Fide.   Catullus.
Hymn to Diana.   *Fr.* Cynthia's Revels.   Jonson.

**Dickens, Charles**
Dickens Characters.   Morgan.
Dickens in Camp.   Harte.

**Dickinson, Emily**
Altitudes.   Wilbur.
At the Birth of a Poet: Amherst, 1830.   Rubin.
Emily Dickinson—in Appreciation.   Batt.
Emily Dickinson Postage Stamp.   Strongin.
"I Am in Danger—Sir."   Rich.
Occupation: Spinster.   Cabral.
Sisters, The.   A. Lowell.
To Emily Dickinson.   Crane.
To Emily Dickinson.   Winters.
When I Consider.   Griffith.

**Dictators**
Epitaph on a Tyrant.   Auden.

**Dido**
I am that Dido which thou here do'st see.   Ausonius.

**Dieting**
Breakfast Song in Time of Diet.   King.

**Dietrich, Marlene**
Welthistoriche Perspektiven.   Watson.

**DiMaggio, Joe**
Byron vs. DiMaggio.   Meinke.

**Dinosaurs**
Deinosaurs.   Bull.
Dinosaur Bones, The.   Sandburg.
Dinosaur Tracks in Beit Zayit.   Kaufman.

**Dionysus**
Dionysus.   Andresen.
Hail, Dionysos.   Randall.

**Dirigibles**
Elegy for the U. S. N. Dirigible, Macon, The.   Winters.
Hangar at Sunnyvale, The: 1937.   Lewis.
Zeppelin.   Glaze.

**Disasters**
Albion Battleship Calamity, The.   McGonagall.
Flood Disaster in Gallup, New Mexico.   Parker.
Tay Bridge Disaster, The.   McGonagall.

**Discotheques**
Disco Fever.   Schechter.

**Disraeli, Benjamin**
To Disraeli.   Brooks.

**Diving and Divers**
Diver.   Francis.
Diver, The.   Hayden.
Divers, The.   Quennell.
Divers.   Schauffler.
Diving.   Murano.
Diving into the Wreck.   Rich.
Elegy for a Diver.   Booth.
Skin Song.   Lieberman.
Underwater.   Schmidt.

**Divorce**
Daily Courage Doesn't Count.   Alta.
Dividing the House.   Richardson.
Divorce.   Jennings.
Divorce.   Jong.
Divorce, The.   Marcus.
Divorce.   Noll.
Divorce.   Widerberg.
Mementos, 1.   Snodgrass.

**Dnieper River**
Heard at Dnieperstroi.   Gessner.

**Doctors.**   *See* **Physicians.**

**Dodoes**
Dodo.   Carlile.
Dodo, The.   Kessler.
Dodo, The.   Lucie-Smith.

**Dogs**
Addition to the Family, An.   Morgan.
Ah, Are You Digging on My Grave?   Hardy.
Argus and Ulysses.   Farjeon.
At Thieves I bark; at lovers wag my tail.   *Unknown.*
Ballad of Master McGrath, A.   *Unknown.*
Bath, The.   Lehmann.
Big Dog.   Booth.
Bingo.   *Unknown.*
Bones.   Lee.
Bony.   Ortiz.
Contentment.   Johnson.
Dame.   Astor.
Der Deitcher's Dog.   Winner.
Dog.   Ferlinghetti.
Dog, The.   Iremonger.
Dog.   Ransom.
Dog Alive.   Witt.
Dog at Night.   Untermeyer.
Dog Dream.   Welburn.
Dog Hospital.   Wild.
Dog in the Quarry, A, *sel.*   Holub.
Dog Parade, The.   Guiterman.
Dog Talk.   De Pietro.
Dogs Are Shakespearean, Children Are Strangers.   Schwartz.
Dog's Best Friend Is His Illiteracy, A.   Nash.
Dog's Cold Nose, The.   Guiterman.
Dogs of Santiago.   McCarthy.
Dogskin Rug.   Stoutenburg.
Elegy on the Death of a Mad Dog, An.   *Fr.* The Vicar of Wakefield.   Goldsmith.
Epigram Engraved on the Collar of a Dog Given to His Royal Highness.   Pope.
Epitaph on a Dog.   *Unknown.*
Epitaph to a Dog.   Byron.
Fashions in Dogs.   White.
German Shepherd.   Livingston.
Greedy Dog.   Hurley.
Hairy Dog, The.   Asquith.
Hope.   Dickey.

Integration. Kell.
Lone Dog. McLeod.
Mad Dog. Siegel.
Maltese Dog, The. Tymnes.
Montgomery. Evans.
Nemo Canem Impune Lacessit. Garioch.
Night Hunt, The. MacDonagh.
Night Song. Cornford.
Nino, the Wonder Dog. Fuller.
Ode to a Young Dog. Viidikas.
Old Blue. *Unknown.*
Old Dog, The. MacLean.
Old Dog. Souster.
Old Dog. Stafford.
Old Dog Blue. *Unknown.*
Old Dog in the Ruins of the Graves at Arles, The. Wright.
Old Dog Tray. Foster.
Old Rattler. *Unknown.*
On one of my long walks. Zukofsky.
Overland to the Islands. Levertov.
P. C. Plod Versus the Dale St. Dog Strangler. McGough.
Pardon, The. Wilbur.
Power of the Dog, The. Kipling.
Puppy. Lape.
Rake. Ratcliffe.
Rescue, The. Serraillier.
Roger the Dog. Hughes.
Scroppo's Dog. Swenson.
Seeing Eye, The. Pound.
Sheepdog Trials in Hyde Park. Day Lewis.
Silver. Ammons.
Simon and the Tarantula. Wright.
Small Poem About the Hounds and the Hares. Mueller.
Span of Life, The. Frost.
Stray Dog, Near Ecully. Avison.
Sudden Assertion. Leslie.
Sunning. Tippett.
To Our House-Dog Captain. Landor.
To robbers furious, and to lovers tame. Johnson.
Towser Shall Not Be Tied Tonight. *Unknown.*
Two Dogs Have I. Nash.
Unloved, The. Canzoneri.
Village Tale, A. Sarton.
Watchdog. Armour.
Wolf and the Dog, The. La Fontaine.
"Word" of a Watch-Dog, The. Sandag.
*Good Dog Poems* (GDP). William Cole, comp.
*See also* **individual breeds of dogs (e.g., Basset Hounds).**
**Dolls**
Barbie-Doll Goes to College. Gross.
Dialogue—2 Dollmakers. Corso.
Doll, The. Friend.
Dolls, The. Yeats.
Lost Doll, The. *Fr.* The Water Babies. Kingsley.
**Dolphins**
Dolphin Seen Alone. Lattimore.
**Don Juan**
Aubade: Donna Anna to Juan, Still Asleep. Howard.
Don Juan. Lawrence.
**Don Quixote**
Bridge of Heraclitus, The. Reavey.
**Donatello**
Bronze David of Donatello, The. Jarrell.
**Donkeys**
Dance of Burros. Laing.
Donkey, The. Chesterton.
Donkey, The. Hinde.
Donkey, The. Roethke.
Donkey and the Lapdog, The. La Fontaine.
Donkey Riding. *Unknown.*
Donkeys. Field.
Faith. Dunkels.

Little Donkey, The. Alexander.
Prayer of the Donkey, The. De Gasztold.
Time Out. Montague.
To a Young Ass. Coleridge.
**Donne, John**
Elegy upon the Death of the Dean of St. Paul's, Dr. John Donne. Carew.
John Donne Speaks from His Grave. Brain.
On Donne's Poetry. Coleridge.
**Doors**
Delights of the Door, The. Ponge.
Door, The. Tomlinson.
Doors. Sandburg.
Plate-glass doors form a dangerous duo. Fuller.
**Dorsetshire, England**
Dorset. Betjeman.
"Dorset Nose," The. Sansom.
**Dostoyevsky, Feodor**
Buzzing Doubt, The. Hill.
For Fyodor. Webb.
Now It's Happened. Lawrence.
Respectable Burgher, The. Hardy.
Will You, Won't You? Van Doren.
**Douglass, Frederick**
Frederick Douglass. Cornish.
Frederick Douglass. Dunbar.
Frederick Douglass. Hayden.
Frederick Douglass and the Slave Breaker. Randall.
Frederick Douglass: 1817-1895. Hughes.
**Doves**
Dove. Farber.
High in the afternoon the dove. *Fr.* Considerations. Smithyman.
Mourning Dove, The. Livingston.
My Doves. Browning.
Parrot and Dove. Landor.
Peace. Bukowski.
Stockdoves, The. Young.
**Dragonflies**
Dragonfly, The. Bogan.
Dragonfly, A. Farjeon.
Dragonfly, The. Nemerov.
**Dragons**
By this the dreadful beast drew nigh to hand. *Fr.* The Faerie Queene. Spenser.
Dragon Lesson. Hearst.
Dragon of Wantley, The. *Unknown.*
Dragons. Ciardi.
O to Be a Dragon. Moore.
Small Dragon, A. Patten.
**Drake, Sir Francis**
Drake's Drum. Newbolt.
Sir Francis Drake; or Eighty-Eight. *Unknown.*
To the Noble Sir Francis Drake. Beedome.
**Dreams and Dreaming**
African Dream. Kaufman.
Back Behind the Eyes. Stokesbury.
Beale Street. Hughes.
Big Dream, Little Dream. Simpson.
Calamity Jane Greets Her Dreams. Lignell.
Day-Dream from an Emigrant to His Absent Wife, The. Coleridge.
Do Not Dream. Zach.
Dream. Miles.
Dream, The. *Unknown.*
Dream Deferred. Hughes.
Dream Farmer. Boyer.
Dream of Dying. Beddoes.
Dream of Fair Women, A. Amis.
Dream Record: June 8, 1955. Ginsberg.
Dream Was of Rabbits, The. Leffler.
Dreamer, The. Childress.

Dream-Pedlary. Beddoes.
Dreams. Giovanni.
Dreams. Herrick.
Dreams. Peskett.
Dreams. Traherne.
Dreamscape. Booth.
Fidelity. Kass.
First of All My Dreams Was Of, The. Cummings.
Five Dreams, The. Woods.
Havana Dreams. Hughes.
House We Leave, The. Matteson.
It's Comforting. Simmons.
Le Rêve. Bowers.
Lenox Avenue Mural. Hughes.
Lime-Tree, The. Lucie-Smith.
Loom of Dreams, The. Symons.
Mad Scene, The. Merrill.
Mouth of the Amazon. Gira.
My Dream. Blockcolski.
My Dream. Rossetti.
Night a Sailor Came to Me in a Dream, The. Wakoski.
Nightmare, A. *Fr.* Iolanthe. Gilbert.
Ode: "We are the music makers." O'Shaughnessy.
Old Trip by Dream Train, The. Galvin.
On Dreams. Swift.
On His Deceased Wife. Milton.
Prowling the Ridge. Minty.
Rain. Murray.
Salome. Garrett.
Seven Dreams. Bayliss.
Sleep-Learning. Fainlight.
Suppose We Sleep. Ellis.
This was my dream! I saw a forest. *Fr.* Bad Dreams.
  Browning.
To the Hand. Merwin.
Tonight Everyone in the World Is Dreaming the Same Dream.
  Litwack.
Vine, The. Herrick.
Vision, The ["Methought I saw (as I did dream in bed)"].
  Herrick.
Vision, The ["Sitting alone (as one forsook)"]. Herrick.
Walter Mitty. Bird.
What Did I Dream? Graves.

**Dreiser, Theodore**
Homage to Theodore Dreiser on the Centennial of His Birth,
  *sel.* Warren.

**Dress.** *See* **Clothing.**

**Driftwood**
Driftwood. Smythe.
Driftwood Dybbuk. Lefcowitz.

**Drinking**
Anacreontic ("Born I was to be old"). Herrick.
Anacreontic to Flip. Tyler.
At the Tavern. *Unknown.*
Auld Lang Syne. Burns.
Bacchus's Opinion of Wine, and Other Beverages. *Fr.* Bacchus
  in Tuscany. Redi.
Back and Side Go Bare. *At. to* Stevenson.
Ballade of Liquid Refreshment. Bentley.
Chevaliers de la Table Ronde (Let Us Drink Knights of the
  Round Table). *Unknown.*
Drink with Something in It, A. Nash.
Drinking. Cowley.
Drinking Song. Brome.
Drinking Song. Marryat.
Drinking Song. Stephen.
Drinking Song. *Unknown.*
Drinking Song, A. Yeats.
Drinking While Driving. Brush.
Fill the Bowl, Butler. *Unknown.*
Finnegan's Wake. *Unknown.*
Five Reasons, The. Aldrich.

Friend Advises Me to Stop Drinking, A. Mei Yao Ch'en.
Frolic, A. Herrick.
Glass of Beer, A. Stephens.
Had we two met, blythe-hearted Burns. Landor.
His Farewell to Sack. Herrick.
I drink to forget, but whenever I think. Bold.
Ignacio, Colorado, for You That Time. Harjo.
In the Bar. Vander Molen.
In the 2 A.M. Club, a working man's bar. Peterson.
Interview with Doctor Drink. Cunningham.
Io Baccho! Williams.
Jacobean Merrymaking. *Fr.* The Spanish Curate. Beaumont
  *and* Fletcher.
Johnson's Ale. *Unknown.*
Jug of Punch, The. McPeake.
Landlord Fill the Flowing Bowl. *Unknown.*
Last Drink, A. *Unknown.*
Lilliputian's Beer Song. Winner.
Little Brown Jug, The. Winner.
Luck. Carver.
Mariners' Compass, The. *Unknown.*
Midget, The. Levine.
Moonshine. *Unknown.*
Morning After. Hughes.
Nothing Like Grog. Dibdin.
Ode for a Social Meeting. Holmes.
Old Filthy Beer Pail, The. Hall.
Old Wife in High Spirits. "MacDiarmid."
Pledge at Spunky Point, The. Hay.
Reflections on Ice-Breaking. Nash.
Revenue Man Blues. *Unknown.*
Rubáyát of Omar Khayyám of Naishápúr, The. Omar
  Khayyám.
Sam Swipes. Marryat.
Sir John Barleycorn. *Unknown.*
Song: "Let school-masters puzzle their brain." *Fr.* She Stoops
  to Conquer. Goldsmith.
Song: "There's a barrel of porter at Tammany Hall." Halleck.
Spoilt. Enright.
Stony Brook Tavern. Reed.
Take a Drink on Me. *Unknown.*
Tale of Lord Lovell, The. *Unknown.*
There is drink fermented. *Fr.* A Satirical Poem about Drink.
  Jigmed.
To Julius. Martial.
To Laura Phelan: 1880-1906. Stokesbury.
Tom Brown. *Unknown.*
Two shots down and I'm exalted. Dugan.
Vive la Compagnie (Vive l'Amour). *Unknown.*
Wassail Song. *Unknown.*
We Be Soldiers Three. *Unknown.*
Welcome to Sack, The. Herrick.
What Matter? *Unknown.*
Whenever you drink all night you make. Martial.
Why I Drink. Aldrich.
Willie Brew'd a Peck o' Maut. Burns.
Yellow Bittern, The. Gunna.
*See also* **Drunkards.**

**Drought**
Drought. Oumar Ba.
I Am Crying from Thirst. Lopez.
That Summer. Ragan.

**Drowning**
Along the River. Enright.
At the Discharge of Cannon Rise the Drowned. Witheford.
D'Avalos' Prayer. Masefield.
Dead Man Dragged from the Sea, The. Gardner.
Death of a Young Son by Drowning. Atwood.
Drowning Girl. Bentley.
Drowning is not so pitiful. Dickinson.
Dying off Egg Island Bar. Smith.
Elegy: "Morning after death on the bar was calm." Henderson.

Emily Drowned.  Duncan.
Emmeline Grangerford's "Ode to Stephen Dowling Bots,
  Dec'd."  *Fr.* The Adventures of Huckleberry Finn.  "Twain."
Floating Bridge.  *Unknown.*
Fourth of July Drowning, The.  Minty.
Half-Moon Lake, The.  Carson.
Jimmy Judge.  *Unknown.*
Judas Touch, The.  Malouf.
Lord, lord! methought what pain it was to drown.  *Fr.* King
  Richard III.  Shakespeare.
Not Waving but Drowning.  Smith.
On a Friend's Escape from Drowning off the Norfolk Coast.
  Barker.
Samuel Allen.  *Unknown.*
Sir Patrick Spens.  *Unknown.*
To Some Millions Who Survive Joseph E. Mander, Sr.  Wright.
Under the Moon.  Bruce.
Walking Out.  Adcock.

**Drug Addiction**
Addict, The.  Sexton.
Answer to Yo/ Question of Am I Not Yo/ Woman.  Sanchez.
Blues for Sister Sally.  Kandel.
Cocaine Blues.  *Unknown.*
Cocaine Lil and Morphine Sue.  *Unknown.*
Discovery of LSD a True Story, The.  Hollo.
Documentary on Airplane Glue, A.  Henderson.
Ho.  Young.
Idea of Ancestry, The.  Knight.
Junior Addict.  Hughes.
Junkies Is.  Coleman.
Loaded Hearts.  Viidikas.
Mainline.  Ditsky.
Not Her, She Aint No Gypsy.  Young.
"O.D."  Gilbert.
Speeding.  Durham.
Street Song.  Gunn.
Stuff.  Johnson.
Summer Words of a Sistuh Addict.  Sanchez.
Take a Whiff on Me.  *Unknown.*
To My Daughter the Junkie on a Train.  Lorde.
Uncovering.  MacDonald.
Willy the Weeper.  *Unknown.*

**Drugstores**
Drug Store.  Shapiro.

**Druids**
Hymn to the Sun.  Doughty.

**Drums**
Beat! Beat! Drums!  Whitman.
Percussions.  Welburn.
Portrait of Rudy, A.  Cunningham.

**Drunkards**
A he as o.  Cummings.
Absinthe-Drinker, The.  Symons.
Beautiful Brown Eyes.  *Unknown.*
Bowery.  Ignatow.
Calton Weaver, The.  *Unknown.*
Canned Heat Blues.  *Unknown.*
Cliff, The.  Rowbotham.
Dead Drunk Blues.  *Unknown.*
Drunk in the Furnace, The.  Merwin.
Drunk Last Night.  *Unknown.*
Drunkard, A.  *Unknown.*
Drunkard and the Pig, The.  *Unknown.*
Drunkard's Doom, The.  *Unknown.*
Drunken Man, The.  Orlen.
Eclipse.  Probst.
Epigram: "When Bibo thought fit from the world to retreat."
  Prior.
Epitaph: "Stavro's dead. A truant vine."  Durrell.
Four Nights' Drunk, The.  *Unknown.*
Good Friday.  Morgan.
Grace of God and the Meth-Drinker, The.  Smith.

Helves Surling Out of Eakspeasies Per (Reel) Hapsingly.
  Cummings.
Intoxicated Rat, The.  *Unknown.*
John Adkins' Farewell.  *Unknown.*
Little Brown Jug, The.  Winner.
Lost After All.  Tillman.
Love ("There's the wonderful love of a beautiful maid").
  *Unknown.*
Lying in a Yuma Saloon.  Barnes.
Manchild.  Bohanon.
Miniver Cheevy.  Robinson.
Mr. Flood's Party.  Robinson.
My Papa's Waltz.  Roethke.
Old Witherington.  Randall.
Original Epitaph on a Drunkard.  Tyler.
Pig, The.  *Unknown.*
Point of No Return.  Graves.
Porson's Visit to the Continent.  Porson.
Railroad to Hell.  *Unknown.*
Red Whiskey.  *Unknown.*
Reformed Drunkard.  Scannell.
Rolling English Road, The.  Chesterton.
There is drink fermented.  *Fr.* A Satirical Poem about Drink.
  Jigmed.
Two Hangovers.  Wright.
Waiting for the Bus.  Ziegler.
What Shall We Do with a Drunken Sailor.  *Unknown.*
Whisky Johnny.  *Unknown.*
Wino.  Hughes.
Zimmer Drunk and Alone, Dreaming of Old Football Games.
  Zimmer.

**Dryden, John**
How long shall I endure without reply.  *Fr.* The Medal of John
  Bays: A Satire against Folly and Knavery.  Shadwell.
Panegyric on the Author of "Absalom and Achitophel," A.
  *Unknown.*
Shadwell and Settle are both fools to Bays.  *Fr.* The Tory
  Poets: A Satire.  *At. to* Shadwell.
To Mr. Bayes.  Sackville.

**Dublin, Ireland**
Dublin.  MacNeice.
Dublin Made Me.  MacDonagh.
For James Joyce.  Ford.
No Place So Grand.  *Unknown.*
Rocky Road to Dublin, The.  *Unknown.*

**Du Bois, William Edward Burghardt**
Booker T. and W. E. B.  Randall.
For William Edward Burghardt Du Bois on His Eightieth
  Birthday.  Latimer.
Legacy for a Beboppin Gentle Giant: DuBois.  Mberi.
On the Death of William Edward Burghardt Du Bois by African
  Moonlight and Forgotten Shores.  Rivers.

**Duchamp, Marcel**
Nude Descending a Staircase.  Kennedy.

**Ducks**
Duck.  Donaghy.
Duck, The.  Nash.
Duck and the Kangaroo, The.  Lear.
Duck-Chasing.  Kinnell.
Ducks.  Hesketh.
Ducks' Ditty.  Grahame.
Notorious Glutton, The.  Taylor.
Three Moves.  Logan.
Trueblue Gentleman, A.  Patchen.

**Duddon River, England**
River Duddon, The, *sels.*  Wordsworth.

**Dumont, Margaret**
To the Lady Portrayed by Margaret Dumont.  Hollander.

**Dundee, John Graham of Claverhouse, 1st Viscount (Bonnie
Dundee)**
Bonnie Dundee.  *Fr.* The Doom of Devergoil.  Scott.

**Dunes**

Sand Dunes. Frost.
**Dunwich, England**
At Dunwich. Thwaite.
**Dürer, Albrecht**
Nuremberg. Slessor.
Steeple-Jack, The. Moore.
**Dusk.** *See* **Twilight.**
**Duty**
Duty. Clough.
Kind of an Ode to Duty. Nash.
Ode to Duty. Wordsworth.
Stopping by Woods on a Snowy Evening. Frost.


# E


**Eagles**
American Eagle, The. Lawrence.
Dalliance of Eagles, The. Whitman.
Eagle, The. Tennyson.
Eagle and the Beetle, The. La Fontaine.
Eagle and the Mole, The. Wylie.
Fire on the Hills. Jeffers.
Folding Fan, The. Cohoe.
Inability to Depict an Eagle. Eberhart.
**Earhart, Amelia**
Flight. Alexander.
**Earth**
Anatomy of Monotony. Stevens.
Aspects of the World Like Coral Reefs. Bronk.
Bonnie Broukit Bairn, The. "MacDiarmid."
Earth. Herford.
Earth's Answer. *Fr.* Songs of Experience. Blake.
Epitaph on the World. Thoreau.
Evening without Angels. Stevens.
First Psalm, The. Brecht.
God's World. Millay.
Hamatreya. Emerson.
Lute Music. Rexroth.
O Sweet Spontaneous Earth. Cummings.
On a Wednesday. Aliesan.
On Inhabiting an Orange. Miles.
Our Mother's Body Is the Earth. McAnnally.
Planet, The. Jacobsen.
Spinning Earth, The. Fisher.
Under the Hill. Eberhart.
Views of Our Sphere. Sandeen.
When Last Seen. Flexner.
World, The. Raine.
World, The. Rands.
**Earthquakes**
Crack in the Wall Holds Flowers. Emanuel.
Earthquake, The. *Unknown.*
Ruaumoko—the Earthquake God. Turei.
San Francisco Falling. Markham.
Santa Barbara Earthquake, The. *Unknown.*
**Easter**
Alleluia! Christ Is Risen Today. Hopkins.
Drizzling Easter Morning, A. Hardy.
Easter. Conkling.
Easter. Herbert.
Easter. *Fr.* Amoretti. Spenser.
Easter Communion. Hopkins.
Easter Day. Crashaw.
Easter Hymn. Housman.
Easter Morning. McCord.
Easter Sunday. Sedulius Scottus.
Easter Wings. Herbert.
Easter Zunday. Barnes.

Lift Your Glad Voices in Triumph on High. Ware.
Lord Is Risen, The. Dunbar.
O Day of Light and Gladness. Hosmer.
On Easter Day. Thaxter.
Rejoice, Let Alleluias Ring. Schaefer.
**Eatherly, Claude R.**
Song about Major Eatherly, A. Wain.
**Echoes**
Echo. Asheron.
Echo. De la Mare.
Echo to a Rock. Herbert.
Echoing Cliff, The. Young.
Gentle Echo on Woman, A. Swift.
What Makes Echo. Duchess of Newcastle.
**Eclipses**
About That of Which One Cannot Speak, One Must Be Silent.
Abele.
Baltimore Eclipse. Plymell.
**Ecology**
Above the Moving River. Kherdian.
Ain't It a Sad Thing. Taylor.
Air. Rado *and* Ragni.
Al Capone in Alaska. Reed.
As Yet. Rodríguez Nietzche.
Bedtime Story. Macbeth.
Binsey Poplars. Hopkins.
Buffalo. Brodsky.
Bungaloid Growth. Ellis.
Communion Portrait in Oil. Weirather.
Cwm Above Penrhiwceiber, The. Morgan.
Don't Look Now. Fogerty.
Earth, The. Jones.
Easier. Harrison.
Ecologue. Ginsberg.
Get the Gasworks. Ignatow.
Hamatreya. Emerson.
Hard Questions. Tsuda.
Highway Construction. Chapin.
Hymn to Moloch. Hodgson.
I Telephoned a Friend. Miles.
Inadequate Aqua Extremis. Walsh.
Inexpensive Progress. Betjeman.
Instructions for a Park. Walker.
Inversnaid. Hopkins.
Kilbarrack 1969. Crowley.
Lesson, The. Wagoner.
Looking at Power. Woessner.
Malediction. Spacks.
Martyred Earth, The. Milne.
Memo to the 21st Century. Appleman.
Moorhen Pond, The. Earley.
Moss-Gathering. Roethke.
Mower against Gardens, The. Marvell.
On the Projected Kendal and Windermere Railway.
Wordsworth.
Poem for the Year Twenty Twenty. Lee.
Pollution. Lehrer.
Poplar-Field, The. Cowper.
Pylons, The. Spender.
Rabbit, The. Brownjohn.
Requiem for a River. Williams.
Requiem for Sonora. Shelton.
Revolutionary Letter #16. Di Prima.
Rip Tide. Piercy.
Seven Preludes to Silence. Shelton.
Small War, A. Norris.
Smokey the Bear Sutra. *Unknown.*
Song of Cove Creek Dam, The. *Unknown.*
Statement on Our Higher Education. Ransom.
There Was a Lady of Rome. Nash.
To a Young Wretch. Frost.
Transcontinent. Hall.

Unless We Guard Them Well.  Merchant.
Vantage.  Ghiselin.
What Have They Done to the Rain.  Reynolds.
Why the Soup Tastes Like the Daily News.  Piercy.
Wilderness.  Mecklenburger.
Woodman, Spare that Tree.  Morris.
Working against Time.  Wagoner.
*News of the Universe: Poems of Twofold Consciousness* (NU).
    Robert Bly, ed.

**Ecuador**
Equator at Quito, The; or, The Will to Die.  Schulte.

**Eden, William**
Rondeau: "Of Eden lost, in ancient days."  Ellis.

**Eden**
Garden, The.  Very.
In the Orchard.  Friend.
Marriage in Eden, The.  Williams.
Never AgainWould Birds' Song Be the Same.  Frost.
Old Story, An.  Lee.
One Foot in Eden.  Muir.

**Edinburgh, Scotland**
Edinburgh.  Adamson.

**Editors**
Editor.  Luschei.
Editor Whedon.  *Fr.* Spoon River Anthology.  Masters.

**Education**
Educational Administration Professor's Prayer, The.  Bobango.
Elementary School Classroom in a Slum, An.  Spender.
History of Education.  McCord.
Homework for Annabelle.  McGinley.
Lines to a Don.  Belloc.
Pains of Education, The.  *Fr.* The Author.  Churchill.
Student, The.  Moore.
Tirocinium: or, A Review of Schools.  Cowper.
To David, about His Education.  Nemerov.
University Examinations in Egypt.  Enright.
Women.  Walker.
*See also* **Scholars and Scholarship; Teaching and Teachers.**

**Edward I, King of England**
Bard, The.  Gray.
Scots in Berwick, The.  *Unknown.*

**Edward II, King of England**
Four Wise Men on Edward II's Reign.  *Unknown.*

**Edward III, King of England**
On the Death of Edward III.  *Unknown.*

**Edward IV, King of England**
King Edward the Fourth and a Tanner of Tamworth.
    *Unknown.*

**Edward VII, King of England**
New Song on the Birth of the Prince of Wales, A.  *Unknown.*

**Edwards, Jonathan**
After the Surprising Conversions.  Lowell.
Mr. Edwards and the Spider.  Lowell.

**Eels**
Eel, The.  Montale.
Song of Hate for Eels.  Guiterman.
Strange the formation of the eely race.  *Fr.* Halieutica.  Diaper.

**Eggs**
At Breakfast.  Swenson.
Easter Egg.  Kieffaber.
Easter Eggs.  Behn.
Egg, The.  Bowering.
Egg Boiler, The.  Brooks.
Eggs.  Gioseffi.
In marble halls as white as milk.  *Unknown.*
Long white barn, A.  *Unknown.*
Written on an Egg.  Mörike.

**Egotism**
Ego.  Siegel.
Egotist, The.  Evans.
Immoral Proposition, The.  Creeley.

Megaceph, chosen to serve the State.  *Fr.* The Devil's
    Dictionary.  Bierce.
Talker, The.  Van Duyn.

**Egrets**
Egrets.  Wright.

**Egypt**
I Am a Cowboy in the Boat of Ra.  Reed.
Nile, The.  Hunt.
Order of Service.  Jones.
Ozymandias.  Shelley.
This Is the Life.  MacNeice.
Witch Going Down To Egypt, A.  Chalfi.

**Eichmann, Adolf**
For Adolf Eichmann.  Levi.
Peachtree, The.  Levertov.

**Einstein, Albert**
$E = mc^2$.  D. Rowbotham.
Gift to Be Simple, The.  Moss.
It did not last; the Devil howling Ho.  Squire.
Relative Sadness.  C. Rowbotham.

**Eisenhower, Dwight D.**
Eisenhower's Visit to Franco, 1959.  Wright.
On the Eisenhower Stamp.  Pereira.

**El Dorado**
Eldorado.  Poe.

**Electric Appliances**
Man About the Kitchen, A.  Hobson.
Now I Set Me.  Herman.

**Electricity**
Electric Orchard, The.  Muldoon.
High Tension Wires.  Block.
Ohms.  Layton.
Pylons, The.  Spender.

**Elephants**
America: The Elephant.  Tipton.
Blind Men and the Elephant, The.  Saxe.
Circus Elephants.  Worth.
Cool Morning Shower in Early Spring.  Levis.
Death of an Elephant, The.  Pagnucci.
Elephant, The.  *Fr.* The Progresse of the Soule.  Donne.
Elephant, The.  Hochman.
Elephant, The.  Phillips.
Elephant Is Slow to Mate, The.  Lawrence.
Elephant, or the Force of Habit, The.  Housman.
Elephants in the Circus.  Lawrence.
Eletelephony.  Richards.
Ivory Paper Weight.  Stoutenburg.
Pete at the Zoo.  Brooks.
Rat and the Elephant, The.  La Fontaine.
Retirement of the Elephant, The.  Edson.
Salute to the Elephant.  Apolebieji.
Tit for Tat: A Tale.  Aikin.
Zimmer Envying Elephants.  Zimmer.

**Elevators**
Ode to a Vanished Operator in an Automated Elevator.
    Rosenfield.

**Elgin Marbles**
On Seeing the Elgin Marbles.  Keats.

**Eliot, Thomas Stearns**
Chard Whitlow.  Reed.
I Haven't Forgotten T. S. Eliot.  Kirby.
Lines for Cuscuscaraway and Mirza Murad Ali Beg.  Eliot.
Mr. Tubbe's Morning Service.  Burnshaw.
T. S. Eliot.  Auden.
T. S. Eliot.  Lowell.
To T. S. Eliot.  Litvinoff.
Vice.  Hecht.

**Elizabeth I, Queen of England**
In Honour of That High and Mighty Princess Queen Elizabeth
    of Happy Memory.  Bradstreet.
Of Astraea.  *Fr.* Hymns of Astraea.  Davies.

**Ellington, Edward Kennedy (Duke)**

Elegy for Duke Ellington.  Mulac.
Half Note for the Duke, A.  Carter.
Morning Duke Ellington Praised the Lord, The.  Dodson.
**Elm Trees**
Elegy: "Here where the elm trees were."  Carrier.
Elm Buds.  Sandburg.
**Elves**
How to Treat Elves.  Bishop.
Little Elf, The.  Bangs.
**Embryos**
Embryos.  Piercy.
**Emerson, Ralph Waldo**
Art in America.  Weiss.
Emerson.  *Fr.* A Fable for Critics.  Lowell.
In the Garden.  Schmidt.
**Empedocles**
Death and Empedocles 444 B.C.  Gregory.
Empedocles.  Meredith.
Empedocles on Etna.  Arnold.
Empedocles on Etna.  Mallalieu.
**Empire State Building**
Looking at the Empire State Building.  Pomeroy.
New York.  Wheelock.
**Emus**
Emus.  Fullerton.
**Endymion**
Endymion, *sels.*  Keats.
Oh, sleep forever in the Latmian cave.  Millay.
**Energy Crisis**
Elegy Written in a Country Coal-Bin.  Morley.
**England**
Anglicized Utopia.  Gilbert.
Composed by the Sea-Side, near Calais, August, 1802.
  Wordsworth.
Composed in the Valley near Dover, on the Day of Landing.
  Wordsworth.
England.  De la Mare.
England.  *Fr.* King Richard II.  Shakespeare.
England in 1819.  Shelley.
"England! with all thy faults I love thee still."  *Fr.* Beppo: a
  Venetian Story.  Byron.
English Counties.  *Unknown.*
English Succession, The.  *Unknown.*
English Train, Summer.  Pomeroy.
Farewell to England.  *Unknown.*
Happy is England! I could be content.  Keats.
Hoddesdon.  Wilson.
Home-Thoughts, from Abroad.  Browning.
Homes of England, The.  Hemans.
It is not to be thought of that the flood.  Wordsworth.
Italy versus England.  *Fr.* Beppo: A Venetian Story.  Byron.
Land of Hope and Glory.  Benson.
Last of England, The.  Porter.
Lines Written in the Album at Elbingerode.  Coleridge.
On a Parisian Boulevard.  Stephen.
Properties of the Shires of England, The.  *Unknown.*
Recessional.  Kipling.
Remembering England.  Bland.
Rhyming Prophecy for a New Year.  Cooper.
Rolling English Road, The.  Chesterton.
Rule, Britannia.  *Fr.* Alfred, a Masque.  Thomson.
Soldier, The.  Brooke.
South Country, The.  Belloc.
Summer in England, 1914.  Meynell.
This Landscape, These People.  Ghose.
True-born Englishman, The.  Defoe.
We Must Be Free or Die.  Wordsworth.
When I have borne in memory what has tamed.  Wordsworth.
You Ask Me, Why, though Ill at Ease.  Tennyson.
*Poets and the English Scene* (PES).  Elinor Parker, ed.
**England, Church of**

Battle Royal between Dr. Sherlock, Dr. South, and Dr. Burnet.
  Pittis.
Church of England's Glory, The.  *Unknown.*
New Catch in Praise of the Reverend Bishops, A.  *Unknown.*
Paradox, The.  *Unknown.*
Poem upon the Imprisonment of Mr. Calamy in Newgate, A.
  Wild.
Pulpit to Be Let, A.  *Unknown.*
Sentiments, The.  *Unknown.*
Vox Clero.  *Unknown.*
**English, The**
English, The.  *Unknown.*
Englishman, The.  Gilbert.
Mad Dogs and Englishmen.  Coward.
Neutral British Gentleman, The.  "Kerr."
Observations in a Cornish Teashop.  Rexroth.
Old England Forever and Do It No More.  *Unknown.*
Secret People, The.  Chesterton.
True-born Englishman, The.  Defoe.
**Envy**
Frog Who Would Be an Ox, The.  La Fontaine.
**Epictetus**
To a Friend.  Arnold.
**Epigrams**
Epigram, An: "Epigram should be, An—if right."  Walsh.
Epigrams must be curt, nor seem.  Landor.
Her Whole Life Is an Epigram.  Blake.
Three things must epigrams, like bees, have all.  *Unknown.*
What is an epigram? a dwarfish whole.  Coleridge.
**Epstein, Sir Jacob**
Jacob Epstein.  *Unknown.*
**Erie Canal**
Erie.  *Unknown.*
Erie Canal, The.  *Unknown.*
**Ernst, Max**
Train.  Smith.
**Erotic Love**
After Love.  Kumin.
Anybody Could Write This Poem. All You Have to Say Is Yes.
  Alta.
Before the Fall.  Daniell.
Candy Man Blues.  *Unknown.*
December 18th.  *Fr.* Eighteen Days Without You.  Sexton.
Desire.  Coleridge.
Dirty Colours of Her Kiss Have Just, The.  Cummings.
Doing, a Filthy Pleasure Is, and Short.  Petronius Arbiter.
Drunk as drunk on turpentine.  Neruda.
Equilibrists, The.  Ransom.
Firebird.  Alta.
From pent-up, aching rivers.  Whitman.
Geranium, The.  Sheridan.
Goodbye, Sally.  Simmons.
I gently touched her hand: she gave.  *Unknown.*
I like my body when it is with your body.  Cummings.
Imperfect Enjoyment, The.  Earl of Rochester.
Love and Sleep.  Swinburne.
Love Poem on Theme by Walt Whitman.  Ginsberg.
Lugete O Veneres.  Mason.
Man and Woman.  Lee.
May I Feel Said He.  Cummings.
Meditation in My Favorite Position.  *Fr.* Walking into Love.
  Piercy.
Net, The.  Rodgers.
New Year's Eve.  Lawrence.
Nice.  Lifshin.
Now Ain't That Love?  Rodgers.
O It's Nice to Get Up in, the Slipshod Mucous Kiss.
  Cummings.
Oh! the time that is past.  *Unknown.*
On the Happy Corydon and Phyllis.  Sedley.
Our Bodies.  Levertov.
Over the hill and over the dale.  Keats.

Paradise Is Not a Place. Gioseffi.
Poemlove (Fragment). *Fr.* Erotic Suite. Vega.
Power of Love He Wants Shih, The. Owens.
Proverbial Man. Galvin.
Radiant Heat. Owens.
Rapping Along with Ronda Davis. Cunningham.
Seen through the Trees behind Which You're Walking. Patten.
Sex and the Over Forties. Porter.
Shelley and jazz and lieder and love and hymn-tunes. *Fr.*
	Autumn Journal. MacNeice.
Song: "O blush not so!" Keats.
Stones. Blumenthal.
Terraplane Blues. *Unknown.*
That Day. Sexton.
Thieves, The. Graves.
To His Mistress Going to Bed. Donne.
To the Fair Clarinda, Who Made Love to Me, Imagin'd More
	than Woman. Behn.
To the Tune "Soaring Clouds." Huang O.
Tubes. Mollin.
Two Songs. Rich.
Us. Sexton.
Where be ye going, you Devon maid? Keats.
Woman Waits for Me, A. Whitman.
*See also* **Sex.**
**Esau**
Esau. Kwitko.
**Eschatology**
Conclusion. Nims.
End of the World. Hoddis.
End of the World, The. MacLeish.
Eschatology. Hall.
Fire and Ice. Frost.
**Eskimos**
Bear Hunting. Aua.
Hunger. *Unknown.*
Hymn to the Air Spirit. *Unknown.*
Song of the Trout Fisher, The. Ikinilik.
Walrus Hunting. Aua.
When the Iceworms Nest Again. Service.
**Essex, England**
Map of the Western Part of the County of Essex in England, A.
	Levertov.
Out into Essex. Betjeman.
**Eternity**
Eternity. Blake.
It Was the Worm. Broughton.
World, The. Vaughan.
**Ethics**
Ethics. Pastan.
**Etiquette**
Boy Serving at the Table, The. Lydgate.
Etiquette. Gilbert.
How to Get on in Society. Betjeman.
Manners at Table When away from Home. *Unknown.*
Story of Fidgity Philip, The. Hoffman.
Table Manners. Flagg.
Table Rules for Little Folks. *Unknown.*
**Eton College**
Ode on a Distant Prospect of Eton College. Gray.
**Eucharist**
Bugler's First Communion, The. Hopkins.
Let Us Break the Bread Together. *Unknown.*
**Euclid**
Euclid Alone Has Looked On Beauty Bare. Millay.
**Euripides**
For the Hippolytus of Euripides. Church.
**Europe**
Beyond the Alps. Lowell.
Farewell to Europe. Pillen.
**Eurydice**
Dreams of Eurydice. Ryan.

Euridice. Alta.
Eurydice. Doolittle ("H.D.").
Eurydice. Thompson.
Orpheus to Beast. Lovelace.
**Eutaw Springs, South Carolina**
To the Memory of the Brave Americans. Freneau.
**Euthanasia**
To the Mercy Killers. Randall.
**Evangelism**
Faith Healer Come to Rabun County. Bottoms.
Jesus Song. Greasybear.
Revival. Garrett.
**Eve**
Adam and Eve. Sisson.
Ballad of Eve, A. Randall.
Banishment, The. *Fr.* Paradise Lost. Milton
Eve. Bull.
Eve. Fichman.
Eve. Herford.
Eve. Hodgson.
Eve. Rossetti.
Eve. *Unknown.*
Eve to Her Daughters. Wright.
Eves Apologie. Lanier.
Eve's Birth. Chernin.
Eve's Lament. *Unknown.*
Eve's Song in the Garden. Gottlieb.
First Wedding in the World, The. Rosenberg.
Fortunate Fall, The. Alvarez.
Fresco. Pastan.
Garden, The. Silverman.
Imperial Adam. Hope.
Letter to Eve. Dugan.
Marriage in Eden, The. Williams.
Never Again Would Birds' Song Be the Same. Frost.
Occasional Poem. Housman.
Reveille. Hughes.
She. Wilbur.
Waiting for Lilith. Kessler.
Way It Really Happened, The. Shpunt.
**Evening**
Evening. Aldington.
Evening. Clare.
Evening. Cotton.
Evening. Doolittle ("H. D.").
Evening. Manger.
Evening. Miller.
Evening. Taylor.
Evening in Paradise. *Fr.* Paradise Lost. Milton.
Evening: Ponte a Mare, Pisa. Shelley.
Evening Quatrains. Cotton.
Evening without Angels. Stevens.
Georgia Dusk. Toomer.
Island in the Evening, The. Porter.
It Is a Beauteous Evening. Wordsworth.
Night. Teasdale.
Ode to Evening. Collins.
Sad. . .and Glad. Lee.
Sheep-bell tolleth curfew time, The. Patmore.
Six O'Clock. Stickney.
Surprised by Evening. Bly.
Windmill of Evening, The. Reich.
*See also* **Sunset; Twilight.**
**Evening Star**
Hesperus. Clare.
To the Evening Star. Blake.
**Evers, Medgar**
Medgar Evers. Brooks.
**Evil**
Hymn to Evil. Ginsberg.
**Evolution**
Easier. Harrison.

Evolution. Brock.
Evolution. Swenson.
Evolution. Tabb.
Evolution from the Fish. Bly.
Evolutionary Hymn. Lewis.
Inheritors, The. Peskett.
Lamarck Elaborated. Wilbur.
Nature ("Subtle chain of countless rings, A"). Emerson.
On Evolution. Ciardi.
Progression of the Species. Aldiss.
Verse for Vestigials. Allen.
Wearing Breasts. Gioseffi.

**Executions**
Croppy Boy, The. *Unknown.*
Culprit, The. Housman.
Danny Deever. Kipling.
Death of Damiens or l'Apres-Midi des Lumieres. Brissenden.
Droit de Seigneur. Murphy.
Dunlavin Green. *Unknown.*
Electrocution. Ridge.
Elegy: "My prime of youth is but a frost of cares." Tichborne.
Epitaph: "They hanged him on a clement morning, swung." Scott.
Execution of Cornelius Vane, The. Read.
Execution of Montrose, The. Aytoun.
Franz Jagesttater's Epistemology. Halperin.
Mary Hamilton. *Unknown.*
More Light! More Light! Hecht.
Night Before Larry Was Stretched, The. *Unknown.*
No Speech from the Scaffold. Gunn.
Poem for Rupert Weber, 85 Years Too Late. Lipman.
Romans Angry about the Inner World. Bly.
*See also* **Hanging.**

**Exile**
By Babel's Streams. Freneau.
Castaway. Nerber.
Embracing Exile. Mabuza.
Exiles, The. Gessner.
Girl I Left Behind Me, The. *Unknown.*
House and Land. Curnow.
Thoughts in Exile. Su Tung-Po.
Un Canadien Errant (An Exiled Canadian). *Unknown.*
Where Is the Sea? Hemans.

**Exodus**
Exodus. Shapiro.

**Explorers and Exploring**
Arabia. Falkner.
Everlasting Astronauts, The. Buchan.
Into the Dark. Monette.
North Pole Story, A. Smedley.
O Pioneers! Bishop.
Pacific, The. Grant.
Sea-King, The. Tooker.
Terra Australis. Stewart.
To the Virginian Voyage. Drayton.
To the Western World. Simpson.
Voyage West. MacLeish.

**Eyes**
Astigmatic, The. Hobsbaum.
Dark Eyes. *Unknown.*
Eye, The. Benedikt.
Eye. Burr.
Eye, The. Herrick.
Eyes. Nicoidski.
Eyes. Shore.
Eyes of Night-Time. Rukeyser.
Eyesight II. Duncan.
For Sore Eyes. *Unknown.*
Her Eyes. Ransom.
Illuminating lamps, ye orbs christallite. *Fr.* Zepheria. *Unknown.*
My Father's Eye. Vakalo.

Squint. Lowbury.
Through a Glass Eye, Lightly. Kizer.
Your Eyes Have Their Silence. Barrax.

# F

**Faces**
Face. Shelton.
Faces Seen Once. Dickey.
I Have Had to Learn to Live with My Face. Wakoski.
Keep Your Face. Tsongas.
Phizzog. Sandburg.
Poem about Your Face. Alterman.
Self-Portrait. Cassian.
Two Faces. Thwaite.

**Factories**
Factory Girl, The. *Unknown.*
On the Closing of the Millom Ironworks. Nicholson.

**Failure**
Nobody Loses All the Time. Cummings.
Ordinance on Failure. Lazard.
To a Friend Whose Work Has Come to Nothing. Yeats.

**Fairies**
Beggar to Mab, the Fairy Queen, The. Herrick.
Fairies, The. Allingham.
Fairies' Farewell, The. Corbet.
Fairies Never Have a Penny to Spend, The. Fyleman.
Fairy in Armor, A. *Fr.* The Culprit Fay. Drake.
Fairy Queen, The ("Come follow follow me"). *Unknown.*
Fairy Song. *Fr.* A Midsummer Night's Dream. Shakespeare.
Fairy Thorn, The. Ferguson.
Fairy Went a-Marketing, A. Fyleman.
Goblin Market. Rossetti.
Hosting of the Sidhe, The. Yeats.
Little Orphant Annie. Riley.
Tam Lin. *Unknown.*
Thomas the Rhymer. *Unknown.*
O, then I see Queen Mab hath been with you. *Fr.* Romeo and Juliet. Shakespeare.
Oberon's Feast. Herrick.
Oberon's Palace. Herrick.
Stolen Child, The. Yeats.
Wee Wee Man, The. *Unknown.*

**Fairs**
Ballad-Singer, The. *Fr.* At Casterbridge Fair. Hardy.
Fair at Windgap, The. Clarke.
First of May, The. Housman.
Hallow-Fair. Fergusson.

**Fairy Tales**
Frog Prince, The. Smith.
Märchen, The. Jarrell.
True Story of Snow White, The. Bennett.

**Faith**
Act of Faith. Trías.
After the Burial. Lowell.
Amazing Grace. Newton.
Ballad Which Anne Askew Made and Sang When She Was in Newgate, The. Askew.
Carrion Comfort. Hopkins.
Discipline. Herbert.
Doubts. Jennings.
Dover Beach. Arnold.
Faith Healer Come to Rabun County. Bottoms.
Faith, Hope and Charity. Guarini.
"Faith" is a fine invention. Dickinson.
Faith of Our Fathers. Faber.
God and Yet a Man, A? *Unknown.*
Great God! I Ask Thee for No Meaner Pelf. Thoreau.

How brittle are the piers. Dickinson.
I never saw a moor. Dickinson.
In Faith of Rising. Kennedy.
My Faith Looks Up to Thee. Palmer.
No Coward Soul Is Mine. E. Brontë.
O, Yet We Trust. *Fr.* In Memoriam A. H. H. Tennyson.
Pagan Isms, The. McKay.
Prayer for Faith, A. Michelangelo.
Sunday Morning. Stevens.
Thou Art Indeed Just, Lord, if I Contend. Hopkins.
To Trust. Pozzi.
Trust and Obey. Sammis.

**Falcons**
Falcon, The. Lovelace.
Sparrow-Hawk's Complaint, The. *Unknown.*
Windhover, The: To Christ Our Lord. Hopkins.

**Fall.** *See* **Autumn.**

**Fame**
After Publication of Under the Volcano. Lowry.
Contemporary. Flexner.
Cool Tombs. Sandburg.
Fame. Rutsala.
Fame Makes Us Forward. Herrick.
Fan-mail from foreign countries, is that fame? *Fr.* Dream Songs. Berryman.
He that hath set his headlong heart. *Fr.* The Consolation of Philosophy. Boethius.
Hometown Elegy. Fraser.
I'm nobody! Who are you? Dickinson.
In an Album. Lowell.
Love of Fame, The Universal Passion. Young.
Ode [To Popularity]. Praed.
On Fame ("Fame, like a wayward girl, will still be coy"). Keats.
On Fame ("How fever'd is the man, who cannot look"). Keats.
Ozymandias. Shelley.
Pillar of Fame, The. Herrick.
Resolve, The. Chudleigh.
Settling Some Old Football Scores. Bishop.
Soup. Sandburg.
To an Athlete Dying Young. Housman.
There is a tall long-sided dame. *Fr.* Hudibras. Butler.
Transparent Closet, The. M. Shelley.
Wish, A. Kemble.

**Family Life**
Because. McAuley.
Chronicle. Bersssenbrugge.
Church Poem. Thomas.
Eyes, the Blood, The. Meltzer.
Family. MacCaig.
Family Reunion. Nelson.
Generations. Jones.
Good Times. Clifton.
Heaven for Railroad Men. Wojahn.
House on Buder Street, The. Gildner.
Jewish Family, The. Orlen.
Life Style, The. Brock.
Long Island Springs. Moss.
My Father in the Night Commanding No. Simpson.
Nails. Gildner.
Nikki-Rosa. Giovanni.
Remember. Soto.
To My Sister. Kherdian.

**Famine**
Famine Song. *Unknown.*
Famine Year, The. Wilde.
Hunger. Binyon.
Not-So-Good Earth, The. Dawe.

**Fans**
Eagle-Feather Fan, The. Momaday.
Fan for His Daughter, A. Mallarmé.
Folding Fan, The. Cohoe.

Present from the Emperor's New Concubine, A. Pan.

**Farming and Farmers**
Abandoned Farmhouse. Kooser.
After Winter. Brown.
American Farm, 1934. Taggard.
Black Man Talks of Reaping, A. Bontemps.
Blown Door, The. Cowley.
Code, The. Frost.
Cooney Potter. *Fr.* Spoon River Anthology. Masters.
Dakota Land. *Unknown.*
Deserted Homestead, The. Eiseley.
Drumdelgie. *Unknown.*
Enriching the Earth. Berry.
Ex M. Antonio Flaminio, Ad Agellum Suum. Ashmore.
Farm Picture, A. Whitman.
Farm Wife. Voigt.
Farmer, The. Stokes.
Farmer Is the Man, The. *Unknown.*
Farmer's Life, A. *Unknown.*
Field and Forest. Jarrell.
Floodtide. Touré.
Follower. Heaney.
For A Young South Dakota Man. Manfred.
For the Record. Thomas.
God Save the Plough. Sigourney.
Hard Way to Learn. Hearst.
Hay Derrick. Harris.
Hay for the Horses. Snyder.
Hill Farmer Speaks, The. Thomas.
Hoeing. Updike.
Huw's Farm. Morgan.
I Will Go with My Father a-Ploughing. Campbell.
Illinois Farmer. Sandburg.
Improved Farm Land. Sandburg.
Laying By. Williams.
Mad Farmer Stands Up In Kentucky For What He Thinks Is Right, The. Hall.
Marginal Field, The. Spender.
Memory of Kuhre. McNair.
Mirror Farming. Morgan.
Mowing. Frost.
My Own Brand. Cuelho.
New Farm Tractor. Sandburg.
Northern Farmer: New Style. Tennyson.
Northern Farmer: Old Style. Tennyson.
Old Field Mowed for Appearances' Sake, An. Meredith.
Old MacDonald Had a Farm. *Unknown.*
On the Debt My Mother Owed to Sears Roebuck. Dorn.
On The Land. Lindquist.
Ploughman, The. Miller.
Ploughman, The. *Unknown.*
Pretty Ploughboy, The. *Unknown.*
Prodigal, The. Bishop.
Quickview #2. Mberi.
Reapers. Blind.
Reapers. Toomer.
Robert's Farm. *Unknown.*
Rogation Sunday. Williams.
Said Hanrahan. Hartigan.
Satisfactions of the Mad Farmer, The. Berry.
Song of the Farmworker. Jahns.
Sower, The. Blind.
Spraying the Potatoes. Kavanagh.
Stump Farming. Tipton.
Thank You Poem for the Andersons, A. Hey.
Through Old Farmhouse Windows. Block.
Tom Ball's Barn. Kooser.
Vermont Conversation. Hubbell.
Warren Pryor. Nowlan.
Wife's Tale, The. Heaney.
Winter deepening, the hay all in, The. Wilbur.
*See also* **Fields and Pastures.**

**Fascism**
Autumn Song for Anti-Fascists.  Taggard.
In Praise of Fascists.  Davidman.
**Fashions**
Fashions in the 70's.  Swenson.
**Fate**
Day's Ration, The.  Emerson.
Definition of Love, The.  Marvell.
Draft Horse, The.  Frost.
Eros Turannos.  Robinson.
Eshu, the God of Fate.  *Unknown.*
Fate in Incognito.  Benedikt.
Flux.  Eberhart.
Hand of Ms. Fate, The.  Terrell.
Hap.  Hardy.
Invictus.  Henley.
Karma.  Robinson.
Lost, Dancing, The.  Field.
New Year's Eve.  Hardy.
Subalterns, The.  Hardy.
*See also*  **Fortune.**
**'athers**
All My Pretty Ones.  Sexton.
Am I Not Your Son?  Abele.
American Primitive.  Smith.
And This Is My Father.  Grapes.
Any Man's Advice to His Son.  Fearing.
Au Tombeau de Mon Père.  McCuaig.
Beryl.  Lifshin.
Bill to My Father, A.  Field.
Boy.  Ciardi.
Boy Driving His Father to Confession.  Heaney.
Cage, The.  Montague.
Carpenter.  Smith.
Christmas Eve.  Kooser.
Cleaning Up, Clearing Out.  Bronson.
Colossus, The.  Plath.
Commander Lowell.  Lowell.
Cutting Wood: After a Family Photograph.  Krapf.
Dad.  Feinstein.
Daddy.  Plath.
Day the Old Man Joined the Church (Xmas '66), The.
    Thomas.
Dream of Southern Roads.  Claire.
Efficiency Apartment.  Barrax.
Elegy for My Father.  Moss.
Elegy for My Father.  Strand.
Equality, Father!  Bruck.
Europe and America.  Ignatow.
Everybody Works but Father.  McClintock.
Eyes of Flesh, The.  Hochman.
Family Photograph.  Vizenor.
Father.  Carroll.
Father.  Gershgoren.
Father.  Kaffka.
Father.  Livingston.
Father and Son.  Higgins.
Father and Son.  Kunitz.
Father and Son.  Stafford.
Father Is Home.  *Unknown.*
Father of My Country, The.  Wakoski.
Father Son and Holy Ghost.  Lorde.
Fathers, The.  Morris.
Father's Story.  Roberts.
Father's Whiskers.  *Unknown.*
Feliks Skrzynecki.  Skrzynecki.
Finding the Father.  Bly.
Fire. 10/78.  Plantenga.
Fisherman, The.  Wells.
Follower.  Heaney.
For My Father: Two Poems.  Kherdian.

For the Poet's Father, on His Taking Up Gardening Late in
    Life.  Dacey.
Furniture Factory, The.  Rutsala.
Game, The.  Silverman.
Geese, The.  Peck.
Hallelujah: A Sestina.  Francis.
Heaven for Railroad Men.  Wojahn.
Hospital Window, The.  Dickey.
House You Looked For, The.  Root.
How My Father Died.  Ezekiel.
Hudson Hornet.  Cook.
I Put My Hand on His Head.  Kooser.
In Honor of David Anderson Brooks, My Father.  Brooks.
Irish Cliffs of Moher, The.  Stevens.
Jarashow.  Sklar.
Jim.  Howes.
Journal Entry: April 5, 1974.  Gerber.
Leaves.  Hamod.
Letter from My Son.  Hogan.
Letter to a Dead Father.  Shelton.
Letter to a Young Father in Exile.  Logan.
Life's Work.  Kumin.
Lines to His Son on Reaching Adolescence.  Logan.
Lines to My Father.  Hamod.
Listening.  Stafford.
Lost Pilot, The.  Tate.
Love from My Father.  Clemmons.
Making Money.  Woods.
My Faither.  Glen.
My Father.  Chalfi.
My Father.  Collins.
My Father.  Kherdian.
My Father.  Koertge.
My Father.  Logan.
My Father After Work.  Gildner.
My Father and the Figtree.  Shihab.
My Father Dreams of Baseball.  Lieberman.
My father gave me the freedom of love.  *Fr.* Longjaunes His
    Periplus.  McCord.
My father is a fist.  *Fr.* Hero's Father's Tombs.  Hemphill.
My Father Moved through Dooms of Love.  Cummings.
My Father Toured the South.  Nichols.
My Father, Who's Still Alive.  Kozer.
My Father's Eye.  Vakalo.
My Papa's Waltz.  Roethke.
My Son and I.  Levine.
On My First Son.  Jonson.
Parentage.  Stafford.
Paean to Place.  Niedecker.
Passing It On.  Saner.
Pawnbroker, The.  Kumin.
Phoning My Son Long Distance.  Kooser.
Placing a $2 Bet for a Man Who Will Never Go to the Horse
    Races Any More.  Wakoski.
Poem for My Father.  Delp.
Poem for My Father, A.  Sanchez.
Prayer: "Sign that I might, A."  King.
Portrait, The.  Kunitz.
Portrait of the Father.  Hough.
Reformer to His Father, A.  Simmons.
Relationships.  Van Duyn.
Requiem of a War-Baby.  Watton.
Rhythm.  Stone.
Runaway, The.  Rubin.
Safely.  Ignatow.
Sixth Day, The.  Adcock.
Stranger, The.  Gelman.
Terminal Days at Beverly Farms.  Lowell.
That Dark Other Mountain.  Francis.
Those Winter Sundays.  Hayden.
To My Father.  Fried.
To the Reverend Shade of His Religious Father.  Herrick.

Toys, The.  Patmore.
Tradition.  James.
Two Postures Beside a Fire.  Wright.
Utility.  Jahns.
Vigil.  Feela.
Waking.  Maxton.
When Father Slept.  Anderson.
Word to a Father, Dead, A.  Allen.
Worker, The.  Thomas.
Zealot without a Face.  Dobzynski.
*Brother Songs: A Male Anthology of Poetry* (BrS).  Jim Perlman,
    ed.

**Faust**
Doctor Faustus, *sels.*  Marlowe.
Faust, *sels.*  Goethe.
Progress of Faust, The.  Shapiro.
Royalties.  Enright.

**Fawns.**  *See* **Deer.**

**Fear**
Animal, The.  Block.
Cold Feet.  Lee.
Fear.  Camerino.
Fear.  Dobyns.
Fear.  Peacock.
Fear.  Pizarnik.
Fear, The.  Reynolds.
Garden, The.  Glück.
House Fear.  Frost.
Man Under the Bed, The.  Jong.
Ode to Fear.  Collins.
Ode to Fear.  Tate.
Storm Fear.  Frost.
Waste Places.  Stephens.
Witch in the Wintry Wood, The.  Fisher.
With the sun fear leaves me.  Parker.

**February**
February.  *Fr.* The Shepherd's Calendar.  Clare.
February.  Updike.
February Thaw.  Bull.
Lent Tending.  Shepherd.
When.  Aldis.

**Feet**
Baby's feet, like sea-shells pink, A.  *Fr.* Étude Réaliste.
    Swinburne.
Five Toes.  *Unknown.*
Going Barefoot.  Thurman.
My Feet.  Jenkins.
These Feet for Rosa Parks.  Bohanon.

**Fences**
Fence, A.  Sandburg.
Fence Wire.  Dickey.
Gates.  Kooser.
Mending Wall.  Frost.
Wires.  Larkin.

**Fencing**
For E. McC.  Pound.

**Ferlinghetti, Lawrence**
Clickety-Clack.  Blackburn.

**Ferns**
Japanese Fold-Song from Hyogo.  *Unknown.*

**Ferry Boats**
Crossing Brooklyn Ferry.  Whitman.
Ferry Me Across the Water.  Rossetti.
Recuerdo.  Millay.
Trip on the Staten Island Ferry, A.  Lorde.

**Feuds**
Massacre of the MacPhersons, The.  Aytoun.
Rowan County Crew, The.  Day.

**Fidelity**
Lover Beseecheth His Mistress Not to Forget His Steadfast
    Faith and True Intent, The.  Wyatt.

**Fiddlers and Fiddles**

Elegiac Lines on the Death of a Fiddler, Called Blind Jacob.
    Freneau.
Fiddler of Dooney, The.  Yeats.
My Fiddle.  Kwitko.

**Fields and Pastures**
Kilbarrack 1969.  Crowley.
Like a Field Waiting.  Chalfi.
Low Fields and Light.  Merwin.
Pasture, The.  Frost.
To Meadows.  Herrick.
*See also*  **Farming and Farmers.**

**Figs**
Figs.  Lawrence.
My Father and the Figtree.  Shihab.
Where the Slow Fig's Purple Sloth.  Warren.

**Filipinos**
Rapping with One Million Carabaos in the Dark.  Robles.

**Films.**  *See* **Motion Pictures.**

**Finches**
Birdsong.  Singer.
Finches, The.  Shapcott.
On the Lamented Death of Mrs. Throckmorton's Bullfinch.
    Cowper.
Song: "Where I walk out."  Winters.

**Fingal's Cave**
Cave of Staffa, I ("We saw, but surely, in the motley crowd").
    Wordsworth.
Cave of Staffa, II ("Ye shadowy beings, that have rights and
    claims").  Wordsworth.

**Finland**
Helsinki, 1940.  Hollo.
Washrags.  Rutsala.

**Finn, Huckleberry**
Huck Finn at Ninety, Dying in a Chicago Boarding House
    Room.  Schevill.

**Fir Trees**
Epitaph on a Fir-tree.  Murphy.

**Fire**
Aftermath.  Plath.
Armadillo, The.  Bishop.
Brooklyn Theater Fire, The.  *Unknown.*
Brother Fire.  MacNeice.
Burning Love Letters.  Moss.
Burning the Christmas Greens.  Williams.
Burning the Letters.  Grew.
Burning the Small Dead.  Snyder.
Coal Fire in Winter, A.  McGrath.
Feeding the Fire.  Finkel.
Fire.  Barrows.
Fire!  *Unknown.*
Fire and Ice.  Frost.
Fire at Alexandria, The.  Weiss.
Fire Down Below.  *Unknown.*
Fire in Enfield.  McNair.
Fire of Drift-wood, The.  Longfellow.
Fire on the Hills.  Jeffers.
Forest Fire, The.  Monroe.
Lumberyard, The.  Herschberger.
Milwaukee Fire, The.  *Unknown.*
Miramichi Fire, The.  *Unknown.*
Mister Charlie.  *Unknown.*
Psychoanalysis of Fire, The.  Morgan.
Scare-Fire, The.  Herrick.
Some Verses upon the Burning of Our House July 10th, 1666.
    Bradstreet.
Street Fire.  Halpern.
Streets of Laredo, The.  MacNeice.
Summer Oracle.  Lorde.
Within Us, Too.  Grenville.

**Fire Engines**
Fire-Truck, A.  Wilbur.
Great Figure, The.  Williams.

**Fireflies**
  Fireflies. McKain.
  Fireflies. Minton.
  Firefly. Hajime.
  Firefly. Roberts.
  Flattered Lightning Bug, The. Marquis.
  Glowworm. McCord.
  Glow-Worm, The. Mercer.
  Glow-Worm, The. Wordsworth.
  Mower to the Glowworms, The. Marvell.
  Nightingale and the Glowworm, The. Cowper.

**Fireworks**
  5th of July, The. Holman.
  Fireworks. Deutsch.
  Fireworks. Worth.
  Fourth of July Night. Aldis.
  Fourth of July Night. Sandburg.
  July 4th. Swenson.
  Pinwheel's Song, The. Ciardi.

**Fish**
  Alas, Alack! De la Mare.
  Although it's cold no clothes I wear. *Unknown.*
  And God said, let the waters generate. *Fr.* Paradise Lost.
    Milton.
  Aquarium, San Francisco, The. Sackville-West.
  Beginning of an Undergraduate Poem. *Unknown.*
  Birds and Fishes. Jeffers.
  Blow Ye Winds Westerly. *Unknown.*
  Carp, The. Malouf.
  Crawdad. *Unknown.*
  Cuttlefish. Kroll.
  Egyptian Pulled Glass Bottle in the Shape of a Fish, An.
    Moore.
  Fish, The. Bishop.
  Fish, The. Moore.
  Fish. Williams.
  Fish. Witt.
  Fish Story. Armour.
  Fish, the Man, and the Spirit, The. Hunt.
  Fishes, The. *Unknown.*
  Fishy Square Dance, A. Merriam.
  Flattered Flying Fish, The. Rieu.
  Great fish's eyes never shut, The. Castellanos.
  Grunion. Livingston.
  Halieuticks, *sel.* Oppian.
  Heaven. Brooke.
  How they Brought the Good News by Sea. Farber.
  Little Fish. Lawrence.
  Mrs. Busk. Sitwell.
  Movement of Fish, The. Dickey.
  Over the Green Sands. Bennett.
  Pesci Misti. Aaronson.
  Pike. Hughes.
  Pike, The. Roethke.
  Robbers came to our house, The. *Unknown.*
  Some Scribbles for a Lumpfish. Johnson.
  Three Movements. Yeats.
  To the Carp and Those Who Hunt Her. Hazard.

**Fishing and Fishermen**
  Angler's Song, The ("As inward love breeds outward talk").
    Walton.
  At the Fishhouses. Bishop.
  Bait, The. Donne.
  Blackfriars. Farjeon.
  Blow Ye Winds Westerly. *Unknown.*
  Careful Angler, The. Stevenson.
  Casting at Night. Hoey.
  Caulker, The. Lewis.
  Curse of a Fisherman's Wife. Chalpin.
  Don's Holiday. Hamilton.
  Dragging in Winter. McElroy.
  Drunken Fisherman, The. Lowell.

  Fish, The. Bishop.
  Fish. Williams.
  Fisherman. Booth.
  Fisherman, The. Brown.
  Fisherman. Root.
  Fisherman, The. Stuart.
  Fisherman, The. Yeats.
  Fisherman Casts His Line into the Sea, The. Holland.
  Fisherman's Wife, The. Wagoner.
  Fishermen. Bunting.
  Fishermen, The. *Fr.* Idylls. Theocritus.
  Fisher's Life, The. *Unknown.*
  Fishing at Sunrise. Curry.
  Fishing Blues. *Unknown.*
  Fishing Harbour towards Evening. Kell.
  Fishing Song. *Unknown.*
  Fishing with My Daughter in Miller's Meadow. Stryk.
  Friend with Spinning Rod. St. Cyr.
  Going Fishing. Griffiths.
  Grabbling in Yokna Bottom. Seay.
  Haddock Fishermen. Brown.
  Hard Times, But Carrying On. Smith.
  Hint for the Incomplete Angler. Smithyman.
  How to Catch Tiddlers. Jones.
  Ice-Fishing House, The: Long Lake, Minnesota. Harper.
  Impromptu Immersion in Tom's Run. Ruark.
  In a Curious Way. Smith.
  It is Hard to Catch Trout. Piuvkaq.
  Late Morning: Oahu. *Fr.* Rice and Mats. Kendrick.
  Marlin. Ghiselin.
  Master and Man. Newbolt.
  Neither Hook nor Line. Bunyan.
  Night Fishing. Stein.
  Night Fishing for Blues. Smith.
  Northern Pike. Wright.
  Not Being Wise. Elson.
  Old Fisherman, The. Hay.
  Old Man Let's Go Fishing in the Yellow Reeds of the Bay.
    Berssenbrugge.
  Once There Were Three Fishermen. *Unknown.*
  Out Fishing. Howes.
  Out from Lobster Cove. Reed.
  Paean to Place. Niedecker.
  Pike, The. Bruce.
  Poke-Pole Fishing. Schmitz.
  Prayer for Fish. Wallace.
  Purse-Seine, The. Jeffers.
  Reflections of a Trout Fisherman. Demon.
  Shark's Parlor, The. Dickey.
  Song of the Trout Fisher, The. Ikinilik.
  Talk to Me, Baby. Browne.
  Three Fishers, The. Kingsley.
  To My Father. Haines.
  Trip to the Grand Banks, A. Hanson.
  Trout, The. Montague.
  Trout Fisher. Brown.
  Uncle Roderick. MacCaig.

**Fitzgerald, Edward**
  To Edward Fitzgerald. Browning.

**Fitzgerald, Ella**
  Early Ella. Sukenick.

**Fitzgerald, F. Scott**
  Effervescence and Evanescence. Preston.

**Fitzgeralds, The**
  Geraldines, The. Davis.

**Flags**
  Battle-Flag, The. Davis.
  Foreboding. Rilke.
  Que Bonita Bandera (How Beautiful Is the Flag). *Unknown.*
  Red Flag, The. Connell.

**Flags, Confederacy**
  Bonnie Blue Flag, The. Macarthy.

**Flags, Great Britain**
English Flag, The. Kipling.
**Flags, United States**
American Flag, The. Drake.
Flag Goes By, The. Bennett.
Leaving the Flag Out All Night. St. Cyr.
Lowering, The. Swenson.
Star-spangled Banner, The. Key.
You're a Grand Old Flag. Cohan.
**Flamingos**
Boy in the Roman Zoo. MacLeish.
**Flattery**
Fox and the Crow, The. La Fontaine.
**Fleas**
Cannibal Flea, The. Hood.
Flea, The. Donne.
Fleas, The. De Morgan.
Harlots' Catch. Nichols.
**Flies**
Amber Bead, The. Herrick.
Blue-Fly, The. Graves.
Blue-tail Fly, The. *Unknown.*
Flesh-Fly and the Bea, The. Patmore.
Fly, The. Ayres.
Fly, The. *Fr.* Songs of Experience. Blake.
Fly, The. De la Mare.
Fly, The. Oldys.
Fly, The. Shapiro.
Fly That Flew into My Mistress's Eye, A. Carew.
I heard a fly buzz—when I died. Dickinson.
Lake Flies of Winnebago, The. Flaherty.
Mosca. Blackburn.
Spider and the Fly, The. Howitt.
Truth. Nemerov.
Upon a Spider Catching a Fly. Taylor.
**Flirtation**
Song in the Same Play by the Wavering Nymph. Behn.
Teasing; or, I Was Only, Only Teasing You. Mack.
**Flodden Field, England**
Flowers of the Forest, The: or, Battle of Flodden, The. Elliot.
**Floods**
Back Water Blues. *Unknown.*
Cabin Creek Flood, The. *Unknown.*
Flood. McGough.
Flood Disaster in Gallup, New Mexico. Parker.
High Water Everywhere ("The back water done rose around Sumner, now"). *Unknown.*
Rising High Water Blues. *Unknown.*
River, A. Ramanujan.
River Swelleth More and More, The. Thoreau.
**Florence, Italy**
E, the Feasting Florentines. Hoffman.
Elements of Geometry, The. Malouf.
Old Pictures in Florence. Browning.
**Florida**
Cages. Kenyon.
Causeway. Block.
Cuban Refugees on Key Biscayne. Winder.
Florida. Rakosi.
I Must Come to Terms with Florida. Taylor.
Morning in Gainesville. Whitehill.
**Florists**
Old Florist. Roethke.
**Flowers**
Because I Never Learned the Names of Flowers. Jellema.
Blossom, The. *Fr.* Songs of Innocence. Blake.
Bouquets. Francis.
Buttercups and Daisies. Howitt.
Buying Lilies. Stepanchev.
Church Calendar of English Flowers. *Unknown.*
Contemplation upon Flowers, A. King.
Cut Flower, A. Shapiro.

Cuttings ("Sticks-in-a-drowse over sugary loam"). Roethke.
Cuttings ("This urge, wrestle, resurrection of dry sticks"). Roethke.
Death of the Flowers, The. Bryant.
Divination by a Daffodil. Herrick.
Fair Flower Delice, The. *Fr.* The Shephearde's Calender. Spenser.
Fear of Flowers, The. Clare.
Flower. Schjeldahl.
Flower Dump. Roethke.
Flower in the Crannied Wall. Tennyson.
Flowers. Davies.
Flowers and Men. Lawrence.
Flowers by the Sea. Williams.
Flowers for a Funeral. *Fr.* Lycidas. Milton.
Flowers in Winter. *Fr.* The Task. Cowper.
Flowers of January. Wordsworth.
Fury of Flowers and Worms, The. Sexton.
Garden Blooms. Flocos.
Gardener to His God, The. Van Duyn.
Gift of Trilliums, A. McPherson.
Golden Glories. Rossetti.
Green-house, The. *Fr.* The Task. Cowper.
Hill-side Flowers. *Fr.* Thyrsis. Arnold.
In Back of the Real. Ginsberg.
It will be Summer eventually. Dickinson.
Lament of the Flowers, The. Very.
Leaves Compared with Flowers. Frost.
Little think'st thou, poore flower. *Fr.* The Blossome. Donne.
Love of Flowers, The. Beddoes.
Mirrorment. Ammons.
Morning Compliments. Dayre.
Odours of Flowers, The. *Fr.* Milton. Blake.
Painted Cup, The. Bryant.
Picture of Little T.C. in a Prospect of Flowers, The. Marvell.
Pot of Flowers, The. Williams.
Rhodora, The. Emerson.
Spring Flowers. *Fr.* The Seasons. Thomson.
Spring Garland. *Fr.* A Winter's Tale. Shakespeare.
Swans, The. Sitwell.
Thrice happy flowers. *Fr.* The Masque of Flowers. *Unknown.*
To Daffodils. Herrick.
To Flowers from Italy in Winter. Hardy.
Troll's Nosegay, The. Graves.
Why Flowers Change Color. Herrick.
Wild Flowers. *Fr.* A Midsummer Night's Dream. Shakespeare.
Yellow Flower, The. Williams.
*Poetry of Flowers, The* (PF). Samuel Carr, ed.
*See also* **names of flowers (e.g. Lilies).**
**Flutes**
Flute Player. *Unknown.*
Longing. *Unknown.*
Musical Instrument, A. E. Browning.
Old Orange Flute, The. *Unknown.*
Tree to Flute. Hajnal.
**Flying Dutchman (ship)**
Flying Dutchman, The. Robinson.
**Flying Saucers.** *See* **UFOs.**
**Foals**
Birth of the Foal. Juhász.
Foal. Miller.
**Fog**
Beats in a Fog. Jeffers.
Breathing, The. Levertov.
Fog. Sandburg.
Fog-Horn. Merwin.
Fog 9/76. Dey.
Ground-Mist, The. Levertov.
Haze. Thoreau.
Plaint Against the Fog. *Unknown.*
Quiet Fog, The. Piercy.

**Folk Songs.** *See* **Ballads and Folk Songs.**
**Food**
  At Breakfast. Swenson.
  Any Part of Piggy. Coward.
  Author Loving These Homely Meats, Specially, viz: Cream, Pancakes, Buttered Pippin-pies, The. Davies.
  Bagel, The. Ignatow.
  Beans, Bacon and Gravy. *Unknown.*
  Beautiful Soup. "Carroll."
  Breaded Meat, Breaded Hands. Harper.
  Broccoli. Schmidt.
  Cheerios. Meinke.
  Chips. Cook.
  Deliver Me, O Lord, from My Daily Bread. Walker.
  Dunderbeck. *Unknown.*
  Epicurean Reminiscences of a Sentimentalist. Hood.
  Epigram on Fasting. Swift.
  Expect no strange or puzzling meat, no pie. *Fr.* A Bill of Fare. Cartwright.
  Famous Hot Pepper Eating Contest, The. Hamod.
  Food of the North. Lawrence.
  Go Back. Keefe.
  Goober Peas. *Unknown.*
  Gourmet's Love-Song, The. Wodehouse.
  Grace to Be Said at the Supermarket. Nemerov.
  Green Corn. *Unknown.*
  Hasty-Pudding, The. Barlow.
  High on the Hog. Fields.
  If We Didn't Have to Eat. Waterman.
  Invention of Cuisine, The. Muske.
  Invitation to Lubberland, An. *Unknown.*
  Inviting a Friend to Supper. Jonson.
  Joy of Cooking, The, *sel.* Mus.
  Lemon Pie. Guest.
  Long Song, A. Tyler.
  Methuselah. *Unknown.*
  Miss T. De la Mare.
  No Mixed Green Salad For Me, Thanks. Galbraith.
  Oberon's Feast. Herrick.
  Observations in a Cornish Teashop. Rexroth.
  Ode to a Lebanese Crock of Olives. Wakoski.
  One Fish Ball. *Unknown.*
  Peas and Honey. *Unknown.*
  Pesci Misti. Aaronson.
  Poem to My New Jacket. Winant.
  Pumpkin Pie. Hall.
  Punkin Pie. Mills.
  Quartermaster Store, The. *Unknown.*
  Rice. Muske.
  Sausage. Guest.
  Shopping for Meat in Winter. Williams.
  Shredded Wheat. Dudek.
  Soup of Venus, The. Tate.
  Spectator Ab Extra. Clough.
  Stomach. Norris.
  Survey of Literature. Ransom.
  Tamales. "O. Henry."
  This Is Just to Say. Williams.
  Those Flapjacks of Brown's. Taylor.
  Vision of MacConglinne, The. MacConglinne.
  When De Co'n Pone's Hot. Dunbar.
  When in Rome. Evans.
**Fools**
  Epigram: "Sir, I admit your gen'ral rule." Pope.
  Epigram: "Yes, every poet is a fool." Prior.
  Fool much bit by fleas put out the light, A. Lovelace.
  To Fool, or Knave. Jonson.
  Upon a Fool. Hoskyns.
**Football**
  Autumn Begins in Martins Ferry, Ohio. Wright.
  Ballad of the Pigskin. Fiske.
  Bee, The. Dickey.

  Bubba Smith. Nash.
  Caught in the Pocket. Barney.
  Charge of the Grid Brigade. Applegarth.
  Dick Szymanski. Nash.
  Fall Practice. Stuart.
  First Practice. Gildner.
  Football. Fitzgerald.
  Football. Mason.
  For the Death of Vince Lombardi. Dickey.
  In the beginning was the. Morrison.
  In the Pocket. Dickey.
  Nearly Everybody Loves Harvey Martin. Barney.
  Out-and-Down Pattern. Kloefkorn.
  Passer, The. Abbe.
  Running Back. Smith.
  Saturday Afternoon. Rubin.
  Say Goodbye to Big Daddy. Jarrell.
  Sleeper, The. Field.
  To the Men Who Hold the Line. Barron.
  Tom Matte. Nash.
  Watching the Jets Lose to Buffalo at Shea. Swenson.
**Ford, Ford Madox**
  To Ford Madox Ford in Heaven. Williams.
**Forest Rangers**
  Jolly Forester, The. *Unknown.*
**Forests**
  Avenue in Savernake Forest. Bowles.
  Black-Forest. Watson.
  Breathing, The. Levertov.
  Darkness Comes to the Woods. Krapf.
  Departure, The. Whittemore.
  Elegy for a Forest Clear-Cut by the Weyerhaeuser Company. Wagoner.
  Forest. Garrigue.
  Forest, The. Wright.
  Forest Hymn, A. Bryant.
  Forest of Dean, The. Flower.
  Glyn Cynon Wood. *Unknown.*
  Hollow Wood, The. Thomas.
  Inscription for the Entrance to a Wood. Bryant.
  Lost. Wagoner.
  Magic Wood, The. Treece.
  On Wenlock Edge the wood's in trouble. Housman.
  Path, The. Thomas.
  Report from a Forest Logged by the Weyerhaeuser Company. Wagoner.
  Sitting in the Woods: A Contemplation. Moses.
  Solitude Late at Night in the Woods. Bly.
  Smith Brothers' Lumber Shed. Flanner.
  Stopping by Woods on a Snowy Evening. Frost.
  Talking to the Forest. Wagoner.
  Waldeinsamkeit. Emerson.
  Way through the Woods, The. Kipling.
  Wood. Ferril.
  Woodnotes I ("When the pine tosses its cones"). Emerson.
  Woodnotes II ("As sunbeams stream through liberal space"). Emerson.
**Forgiveness**
  Forgive? Montoya.
  Hymn to God the Father, A. Donne.
  'Tis true—they shut me in the cold. Dickinson.
**Forsythia**
  Forsythia Is the Color I Remember. Cherwinski.
**Fortune**
  Author, of His Own Fortune, The. Harington.
  Good Luck. Herrick.
  Hap. Hardy.
  Hughie at the Inn. Wylie.
  Lady Fortune, The. *Unknown.*
  My Stars. Ibn Ezra.
  To Fortune on Buying a Ticket in the Irish Lottery. Coleridge.
  *See also* **Fate; Luck.**

**Fountains**
Baroque Wall-Fountain in the Villa Sciarra. Wilbur.
Fountain, The. Davie.
Fountain, The. Liasides.
Fountains, The. Rodgers.
From Rome. For More Public Fountains in New York City.
Dugan.
Great Fountains, The. Hebert.
Inscription for a Fountain on a Heath. Coleridge.
Roman Fountain. Bogan.
**Fourth of July**
Chippewa Lake Park. Woessner.
Concord Hymn. Emerson.
Fourth, The. Silverstein.
Fourth of July. Field.
Fourth of July Night. Aldis.
Independence Day. Berry.
**Fox, Charles James**
On the Death of Mr. Fox. Byron.
**Foxes**
Abnegation. Rich.
Arctic Vixen. Baldwin.
Ballad of Red Fox, The. La Follette.
Cross Fox. Bruchac.
Emblem of Two Foxes, An. Spacks.
False Fox, The. *Unknown.*
Four Little Foxes. Sarett.
Fox, The. Clare.
Fox, The. Day Lewis.
Fox, The. Patchen.
Fox. *Fr.* A Bestiary. Rexroth.
Fox and the Crow, The. La Fontaine.
Fox and the Geese, The. *Unknown.*
Fox and the Goose, The. *Unknown.*
Fox and the Wolf, The. *Unknown.*
Fox's Counsel, The. Llwyd.
Gone. Thompson.
Hunt, The. De la Mare.
Hunting Song. Finkel.
Kilruddery Hunt, The. Mozeen.
Listening to Foxhounds. Dickey
Plea for a Captive. Merwin.
Thought-Fox, The. Hughes.
Trap, The. Beyer.
Vixen, The. Clare.
Wily Fox, The. Davies.
Year of the Foxes, The. Malouf.
Young Reynard. Meredith.
**France**
Four Sheets to the Wind and a One-Way Ticket to France.
Rivers.
France: An Ode. Coleridge.
September, 1802, Near Dover. Wordsworth.
**Francis of Assisi, Saint**
Assisi. MacCaig.
Mental Hospital Garden, The. Williams.
St. Francis of Assisi and the Miserable Jews. Wittlin.
Tears of Saint Francis. Duncan.
**Franco, Francisco**
Eisenhower's Visit to Franco, 1959. Wright.
Franco. Smallshaw.
**Frankenstein**
Bride of Frankenstein, The. Field.
Frankenstein. Field.
Help Is on the Way. Scott.
**Franklin, Aretha**
Poem for Aretha. Giovanni.
**Frederick Augustus, Duke of York**
On Prince Frederick. *Unknown.*
**Frederick Louis, Prince of Wales**
On Prince Frederick. *Unknown.*
**Free Will**

Free Will. Clark.
**Freedom**
Ante-Bellum Sermon, An. Dunbar.
Antiquity of Freedom, The. Bryant.
Brave New World. MacLeish.
Deer in the Prison, The. Bruchac.
Dreaming About Freedom. Baca.
France: an Ode. Coleridge.
Freedom Is a Constant Struggle. *Unknown.*
Frederick Douglass. Hayden.
Freedom. Hughes.
Freedom. Lowell.
Freedom. Stafford.
I Thank God I'm Free at Las'. *Unknown.*
If We Must Die. McKay.
In Exile. Lazarus.
Liberty. MacLeish.
Liberty. Shelley.
Liberty Tree. Paine.
No More Beneath the Oppressive Hand. *Unknown.*
Ode: "God save the Rights of Man!" Freneau.
Ode to Freedom. Zeitlin.
Ode to Liberty. Shelley.
Of Old Sat Freedom on the Heights. Tennyson.
Of the Child with the Bird on the Bush. Bunyan.
Prayers to Liberty. Shaul.
Prison Bi-Centennial Address, A. Aguila.
Prison Break. Hogan.
Shine, Perishing Republic. Jeffers.
Slave, The. Oppenheim.
So the Seeds Are Growing. South.
Sonnet on Chillon. *Fr.* The Prisoner of Chillon. Byron.
Spirit of Freedom, Thou Dost Love the Sea. Dodge.
Sympathy. Dunbar.
They shut me up in prose. Dickinson.
To Althea, from Prison. Lovelace.
To the Republicans of North America. Shelley.
Twilight of Freedom. Glaze.
We Must Be Free or Die. Wordsworth.
Wires. Larkin.
Woke up this Morning with My Mind on Freedom. *Unknown.*
Words Like Freedom. Hughes.
You Ask Me, Why, though Ill at Ease. Tennyson.
**French, The**
French, 1870-1871, The. *Unknown.*
To Henrietta, on Her Departure for Calais. Hood
**French Revolution**
Character, A. Coleridge.
Destruction of the Bastille. Coleridge.
French Revolution, The, *sel.* Blake.
Let the brothels of Paris be opened. Blake.
Poetical and Philosophical Essay on the French Revolution, A.
Courtenay.
**Freud, Sigmund**
Doctor Freud. Lazar.
Freud: Dying in London, He Recalls the Smoke of His Cigar
Beginning to Sing. Schevill.
In Memory of Sigmund Freud. Auden.
Ladders. Whittemore.
Psychology. Glen.
Sigmund Freud. Nemerov.
Song for Sigmund Freud, A. Cherry.
**Friars**
Against the Friars. *Unknown.*
Friar's Retort, The. *Unknown.*
Wanton Merry Friar, A. *Fr.* The Canterbury Tales. Chaucer.
**Friends, Society of**
At a Friends' Meeting. M. Coleridge.
First-Day Thoughts. Whittier.
Quaker Widow, The. Taylor.
**Friendship**
After He Said. Dunn.

As through the wild green hills of Wyre. Housman.
Auld Lang Syne. Burns.
Ballad: "I want to know the unity in all things." Ammons.
But. Cummings.
Commitment, A. Anderson.
Comrades. McGlennon.
Dark brother touches me, The. *Fr.* 108 Tales of a Po' Buckra. Inman.
Father, His Friend, and Another. Stafford.
Female Friend, The. Whur.
Fire of Drift Wood, The. Longfellow.
Friend. Brooks.
Friend, The. Piercy.
Friend, A. Power.
Friends. Durem.
Friends. Jennings.
Friendship's Mystery, to My Dearest Lucasia. Philips.
Friendship. Stryk.
George. Randall.
Good Friends and First Impressions. Drake.
Grasshopper, The: To My Noble Friend, Mr. Charles Cotton. Lovelace.
He Was a Friend of Mine. *Unknown.*
Hungarian, The. Stern.
Interlude. Smith.
I've Gone and Stained with the Color of Love. Acorn.
La Belle Confidante. Stanley.
My Gal Sal. Dresser.
My Ramblin' Boy. Paxton.
O! Wherefore. Peter.
Of Money. Googe.
Old Familiar Faces, The. Lamb.
One, Annie and Me. Ostriker.
Poem for Russell Nowak, A. Torgerson.
Public House Cinematics. Smith.
Song: "Circumstance has estranged my friend." Rakosi.
Song for Meeting a Friend. González.
Story, A. Torgerson.
Time to Talk, A. Frost.
To a Troubled Friend. Wright.
To Alpha Dryden Eberhart. Eberhart.
To Edward Williams. Shelley.
To My Excellent Lucasia and Our Friendship. Philips.
To My Friend. Thompson.
To Phylocles, Inviting Him to Friendship. "Ephelia."
To William Hayley. Blake.
Unbridling Our Horses. Bush.
When to the sessions of sweet silent thought. *Fr.* Sonnets. Shakespeare.

**Frietchie, Barbara**
Barbara Frietchie. Whittier.

**Frogs**
Aesop's Fable of the Frogs. La Fontaine.
As Near to Eden. Francis.
Ascend my shoulders, firmly keep thy seat. *Fr.* The Battle of the Frogs and Mice. *Unknown.*
Bullfrog. Hughes.
Bullfrog in a Pond Not Far from an Abandoned Farm, A. Locke.
Cheers. Merriam.
Death of a Naturalist. Heaney.
Early Frogs, The. Mills.
Frog, The. Belloc.
Frog, The. *Unknown.*
Frog and the Crow, The. *Unknown.*
Frog and the Toad, The. C. Rossetti.
Frog Plague, The. Dawe.
Frog Prince, The. Smith.
Frog Went a-Courting. *Unknown.*
Frogs. MacCaig.
Frogs. Simpson.
Frog's Fate, A. C. Rossetti.

Frog's Lament, The. Fisher.
Green Frog at Roadstead, Wisconsin. Schevill.
His mansion in the pool. Dickinson.
Hopping Frog. Rossetti.
Kato's Poem. Kherdian.
Marriage of the Frog and the Mouse, The. *Unknown.*
Padda Song, The. *Unknown.*
Peepers in our Meadow, The. MacLeish.
Princess Addresses the Frog Prince, The. Brewster.
Rebels from Fairy Tales. Hill.
Small Frogs Killed on the Highway. Wright.
Toad and the Frog, The. *Unknown.*
Who-Tapped-the-Frogs-In. Makidemewabe.
Wooing Frog, The. Reeves.

**Frontiersmen**
John Day, Frontiersman. Winters.

**Frost, Robert**
For Robert Frost. Kinnell.
Mending Sump. Koch.
Of Robert Frost. Brooks.
Robert Frost. Lowell.
Thanks, Robert Frost. Ray.
"Yes, But. . . ." Weiss.

**Frost**
Apparently with no surprise. Dickinson.
Cold Snap. Mangan.
Early Frost. Norris.
Frost at Midnight. Coleridge.

**Fruit**
Fruit and Vegetables. Jong.
Fruits. C. Rossetti.
Nevertheless. Moore.
This Is Just to Say. Williams.
Three from the Market. McPherson.
Tropics in New York, The. McKay.

**Fulton, Robert**
Robert Fulton. Stanford.

**Funerals**
After the Funeral. Thomas.
Agony Column. Hope.
Brown Girl Dead, A. Cullen.
Burial. Grigson.
Burial in the Country, A. Clause.
Burial of a fisherman in Hydra. Schulman.
Come Not, When I Am Dead. Tennyson.
Country Burial. Lewis.
Dirge without Music. Millay.
Do Nothing Till You Hear from Me. Henderson.
Elegy for a Polish Grandaunt. Bonk.
Finnegan's Wake. *Unknown.*
First Death. Justice.
Funeral, The. Donne.
Funeral at Ansley. Welch.
Funeral Home. Bohanon.
Funeral of Paddy Haugh. Kiely.
Grief. George.
Italian Extravaganza. Corso.
Lowering, The. Swenson.
My Grandfather's Funeral. Applewhite.
Night Funeral in Harlem. Hughes.
Question, A. Synge.
Rebel, The. Evans.
Report on a Memorial Service: A Letter to Mark Van Doren. Claire.
Returning from the Funeral. Henley.
She: At His Funeral. Hardy.
Shetland Funeral. Rankin.
Strange Funeral in Braddock, A. Gold.
Tract. Williams.
Traveler, The. Bottoms.

**Furniture**
Heirloom. Flanigan.

Inventory of the Furniture of a Collegian's Chamber, An. Winstanley.

# G

**Gadflies**
Gadfly, The. Keats.
**Galuppi, Baldassaro**
Toccata of Galuppi's, A. Browning.
**Galveston, Texas**
Sailor's Song, A. Harris.
**Gambling and Gamblers**
Camptown Races, De. Foster.
Casino. Auden.
Crapshooters. Sandburg.
Early Evening Quarrel. Hughes.
Gambler, The. *Unknown.*
Gambling. Tyler.
Heathen Chinee, The. Harte.
John Hardy. *Unknown.*
Man Who Broke the Bank at Monte Carlo, The. Gilbert.
Man Who Invented Las Vegas, The. Costanzo.
Midweek. Miles.
On a Distant Prospect of an Absconding Bookmaker. Hamilton
One Time Henry Dreamed the Number. Long.
Placing a $2 Bet for a Man Who Will Never Go to the Horse Races Any More. Wakoski.
Rambling, Gambling Man. Houston.
Root Hog or Die. *Unknown.*
Roving Gambler Blues. *Unknown.*
To Fortune on Buying a Ticket in the Irish Lottery. Coleridge.
Wednesday Cocking. *Unknown.*
**Gandhi, Mohandas Karamchand**
Vaticide. O'Higgins.
**Gangs**
Black Jackets. Gunn.
Blackstone Rangers, The. Brooks.
**Gangsters**
Last Gangster, The. Corso.
**Gannets**
Blue Booby, The. Tate.
**Garbage**
Bears in the Land-Fill, The. Turco.
Dustbin Men, The. Harrison.
Feeding Time. Beeler.
Man on the Dump, The. Stevens.
Town Dump, The. Nemerov.
**García Lorca, Federico**
Cante Jondo for Soul Brother Jack Spicer. Jonas.
Lines to Garcia Lorca. Baraka.
We Bumped Off Your Friend the Poet. Norse.
**Garda, Lake, Italy**
"Frater Ave Atque Vale." Tennyson.
**Gardens**
Alter Ego. Slade.
Center of the Garden, The. Stanford.
Chinese Garden, The. Gregory.
Elegy While Pruning Roses. Wagoner.
Erica. Bethell.
For Jim, Easter Eve. Spencer.
For the Poet's Father, on His Taking Up Gardening Late in Life. Dacey.
Forsaken Garden, A. Swinburne.
Garden, The. Grimald.
Garden, The. Marvell.
Garden, A. Shelley.
Garden, The. Very.

Garden, The. Warren.
Garden by Moonlight, The. A. Lowell.
Garden Fancies. Browning.
Garden in September, The. Bridges.
Garden Lore. Ewing.
Garden of Appleton House, The. *Fr.* Upon Appleton House. Marvell.
Gardener to His God, The. Van Duyn.
Glasgow Botanic Gardens. Rankin.
How Jack Found that Beans May Go Back on a Chap. Carryl.
Man in Overalls, The. Lueders.
Mr. Bidery's Spidery Garden. McCord.
My Garden. Brown.
My Garden. Lindon.
My Garden. Succorsa.
Old Florist. Roethke.
Public Garden, The. Lowell.
Roof Garden, The. Moss.
Summer Garden. Akhmatova.
Trance. Bethell.
Transplanting. Roethke.
Two Gardens. De Bevoise.
Weed Puller. Roethke.
Within my garden, rides a bird. Dickinson.
Winter Garden. Lewis.
**Garfield, James Abram**
Charles Guiteau. *Unknown.*
**Garfield, John**
John Garfield. Christopher.
**Gargoyles**
527 Cathedral Parkway. Lesser.
**Garlic**
To Maecenas. Horace.
**Gaslight**
Ode on Gas, An. *Unknown.*
**Gasoline Stations**
At Every Gas Station There Are Mechanics. Dunn.
Hottest Brand Goin'. *Unknown.*
**Gauguin, Paul**
Gauguin's Menhir, Tahiti. Hope.
Two Women with Mangoes. Cramer.
**Gawain, Sir**
Sir Gawaine and the Green Knight. Winters.
**Gazelles**
Gazelle Calf, The. Lawrence.
**Geese**
Aunt Rhody. *Unknown.*
Boy and the Geese, The. Fiacc.
Fox and the Goose, The. *Unknown.*
Gabble-Gabble. Reeves.
Gaggle of Geese, a Pride of Lions, A. Moore.
Geese, The. Peck.
Geese, The. Plutzik.
Goose. Braun.
Gray Goose, The. *Unknown.*
Late at Night. Stafford.
Wild Geese. Hart-Smith.
Wild Geese, The. Masefield.
**Gems**
Diamond Cutters, The. Rich.
**Genetic Engineering**
Progression of the Species. Aldiss
**Gentians**
Bavarian Gentians. Lawrence.
To the Fringed Gentian. Bryant.
**Geography**
About Scotland, & C. Todd.
Chapter from Geography, A. Pillin.
Geography. *Fr.* Songs of Education. Chesterton.
Geography Lesson. Ghose.
**Geology**
Goodnight. Ciardi.

Lyell's Hypothesis Again.  Rexroth.

**Geometry**
Plane Geometry.  Rounds.

**George I, King of England**
Epigram: "King George, observing with judicious eyes."  Trapp.
Epigram: "King to Oxford sent a troop of horse, The."  Browne.
Pasquin to the Queen's Statue at St. Paul's.  Shippen.

**George II, King of England**
George II and the Chinese Emperor.  Graves.

**George III, King of England**
England in 1819.  Shelley.
George the Third.  *Fr.* Clerihews.  Bentley.
George the Third's Soliloquy.  Freneau.
Monarch's Funeral, The.  Shelley.
Saint Peter sat by the celestial gate.  *Fr.* The Vision of Judgment.  Byron.

**Georgetown, Washington, D.C.**
Pride of Place.  Louchheim.

**Georgia**
Georgia Dusk.  Toomer.
Writing on Napkins at the Sunshine Club, Macon, Georgia 1971.  Bottoms.

**Geraniums**
Geranium, The.  Roethke.

**Germany**
No Offence.  Enright.
Song of the Cape of Good Hope.  Schubart.

**Ghettos**
Butterfly, The.  Friedmann.
For Real Ghetto, The.  Landrum.
Ghetto Twilight.  Brody.
In the Ghetto.  Sonnenschein.
Jewish Main Street.  Layton.
Summertime and the Living.  Hayden.

**Ghost Towns**
Two Views of Two Ghost Towns.  Tomlinson.

**Ghosts**
All Souls' Night.  Cornford.
Apparition, The.  Donne.
Aunt, The.  Galvin.
Autumn Ghost Sounds.  *Unknown.*
Colonel Fazackerley.  Causley.
Company.  Oakes.
Cuchulain Comforted.  Yeats.
Fall of J. W. Beane, The.  Herford.
False Dawn.  De la Mare.
Ghost, The.  De la Mare.
Ghost, The.  Lowell.
Ghost Boy.  Van Doren.
Ghosts' Stories.  Reid.
Haunted House, The.  Hood.
Haunted House.  Worth.
Highwayman's Ghost, The.  Garnett.
Listeners, The.  De la Mare.
Lost Weekend Bar, The.  Harjo.
Low Barometer.  Bridges.
Mary's Ghost.  Hood.
Mini Spooks, The.  Anderson.
Miss Bailey's Ghost.  Colman the Younger.
Molly Means.  Walker.
My Aunt's Spectre.  Collins.
Old Toby.  Wilson.
Old Wife and the Ghost, The.  Reeves.
Phantom Horsewoman, The.  Hardy.
Phantom Ship, The.  Longfellow.
Phantom Wooer, The.  Beddoes.
Shadwell Stair.  Owen.
Song of Shadows, The.  De la Mare.
Souls of the Slain, The.  Hardy.
Southern Mansion.  Bontemps.

Superstitious Ghost, The.  Guiterman.
Sweet William's Ghost.  *Unknown.*
Thirteen O'Clock.  Fearing.
Unfortunate Miss Bailey.  *Unknown.*
Wife of Usher's Well, The.  *Unknown.*

**Giacometti, Alberto**
Tall Figures of Giacometti, The.  Swenson.

**Gibbon, Edward**
Distribution of Honours for Literature.  Landor.
Lausanne.  Hardy.

**Ginkgo Trees**
Ginkgoes in Fall.  Nemerov.

**Ginsberg, Allen**
Allen Ginsberg Blesses a Bride and Groom: A Wedding Night Poem.  Peters.
For Allen Ginsberg Who Cut Off His Beard.  Pinsker.
Reprise of one of A. G.'s Best Poems!  Baraka.
Squeal.  Simpson.

**Giorgione**
For "A Venetian Pastoral" by Giorgione.  Rossetti.

**Giotto de Bondone**
Perfect Symbol, The.  Johnson.

**Gipsies.**  *See* **Gypsies.**

**Giraffes**
Baby Giraffe.  Ball.
Conversation with a Giraffe at Dusk in the Zoo.  Livingstone.
Giraffe, The.  Fuller.
Giraffe.  Plumly.
Giraffes: The American Version.  Dunn.
On the Death of the Giraffe.  Hood.

**Girdles**
On a Girdle.  Waller.
Woman with Girdle.  Sexton.

**Girls.**  *See* **Childhood and Children; Youth.**

**Gloucester, Massachusetts**
Gloucester Moors.  Moody.

**Glowworms.**  *See* **Fireflies.**

**Gluttony and Gluttons**
Glutton, The.  Oakman.
Greedy Jane.  *Unknown.*
Mouse and the Cake, The.  Cook.
Notorious Glutton, The.  Taylor.
On Gut.  Jonson.

**Gnats**
Gnat, The.  Beaumont.
Gnat-Psalm.  Hughes.

**Gnus**
Gnu, The.  Belloc.
Gnu, The.  Roethke.

**Goats**
All Goats.  Coatsworth.
April.  Winters.
Bill Groggin's Goat.  *Unknown.*
Goat.  Johnson.
Goat, The.  Young.
Goat Paths, The.  Stephens.
Hunger.  Hilberry.
Mating the Goats.  Barnstone.

**Goblins.**  *See* **Fairies.**

**God**
Accepting.  Miller.
Advice.  Gregory.
All the Way My Saviour Leads Me.  Crosby.
Bermudas.  Marvell.
Black Cliffs, Ballybunion, The.  Kennelly.
Canticle to the Waterbirds, A.  Everson.
Collector's Note.  Bull.
Counsels of O'Riordan, The Rann Maker, The.  O'Bolger.
Creation, The.  Johnson.
Crow's Theology.  Hughes.
Day After Sunday, The.  McGinley.
Design.  Frost.

Divine Image, The. *Fr.* Songs of Innocence. Blake.
Edom. Watts.
Egocentric. Smith.
Ellora. Nathan.
Eternal Dice, The. Vallejo.
Flower in the Crannied Wall. Tennyson.
For Eleanor Boylan Talking with God. Sexton.
Forgive, O Lord. Frost.
From the Batter's Box. Harford.
Furniture. Bloch.
Fury of Aerial Bombardment, The. Eberhart.
Genesis. Witt.
Give to Our God Immortal Praise. Watts.
God. Ruggles.
God. Slutsky.
God and Man. Hazo.
God Don't Never Change. *Unknown.*
God Has Pity on Kindergarten Children. Amichai.
God in Wrath, A. *Fr.* The Black Riders. Crane.
God is a distant, stately lover. Dickinson.
God Is Here Again. Angoff.
God is indeed a jealous God. Dickinson.
God Lay Dead in Heaven. *Fr.* The Black Riders. Crane.
God of Judgment, The. Swinburne.
God Opens His Mail. Rubin.
God Poem. Moss.
God, That Madest All Things. *Unknown.*
God Walks Among the Dust. Chambers.
God's Grandeur. Hopkins.
Great Sad One, The. Greenberg.
Hand and Foot, The. Very.
He Leadeth Me. Gilmore.
He Puts Me to Rest. Ignatow.
He's Got the Whole World in His Hands. *Unknown.*
Higher Pantheism, The. Tennyson.
His Necessary Darkness. Sullivan.
His Theology. Bull.
Hound of Heaven, The. Thompson.
How, Then? Crane.
Hunchback, The. Bishop.
Hymn of the City. Bryant.
Hypnopompic Poem. Cole.
I Am the Great Sun. Causley.
I know that He exists. Dickinson.
I Thank You God for Most This Amazing. Cummings.
If God Exists. Lipska.
Image of God, The. Aldana.
Immediate Kindness. Kornblum.
In Absentia. Mackie.
Incomprehensible, The. Watts.
Indian upon God, The. Yeats.
Invocation, or the Eternal Father and Mother. Snow.
Johannes Milton, Senex. Bridges.
Lauds. Berryman.
Law I Love Is Major Mover, The. Duncan.
Less and Less Human, O Savage Spirit. Stevens.
Light Shining Out of Darkness. Cowper.
Mama's God. Rodgers.
Mighty Fortress, A. Luther.
My Garden. Brown.
Nature's Hymn to the Deity. Clare.
Noah's Ark. Young.
Old Repair Man, The. Johnson.
On a Squirrel Crossing the Road in Autumn, in New England. Eberhart.
On First Knowing God. *Fr.* The Seven Days. Whittemore.
On the Universality and Other Attributes of the God of Nature. Freneau.
151st Psalm, The. Shapiro.
Pied Beauty. Hopkins.
Preacher, The: Ruminates behind the Sermon. Brooks.
Quatrain: "Strictly mathematic God, A." Bull.

Quite Apart from the Holy Ghost. Mitchell.
Search. Ritchie.
Severity. Bull.
So It Happens. Feldman.
Song: "My straying thoughts, reduced stay." Collins.
South Coast, The. Everson.
Speak. Wright.
Star Quality. Wallace-Crabbe.
Study in Punctuation. Bull.
Stupendous God! how shrinks our bounded sense. *Fr.* The Omnipresence of the Deity. Montgomery.
Testimony. Rodgers.
There is no God, as I was taught in youth. Masefield.
To a God Unknown. Eller.
To a Waterfowl. Bryant.
Twelve Lines about the Burning Bush. Ravitch.
Tyger, The. *Fr.* Songs of Experience. Blake.
Ultimate Problems. Stafford.
Universal Prayer, The. Pope.
Upon the Burning of Our House, July 10, 1666. Bradstreet.
What the Devil Said. Stephens.
What Tomas Said in a Pub. Stephens.
When God First Said. Zach.
When I Was Growing Up. Vogel.
When the God Returns. Edson.
Where Were You? Landrum.
Why God Permits Evil: For Answers to This Question of Interest to Many Write Bible Answers Dept. E-7. Williams.
Written in Exile. Raine.
Yet Do I Marvel. Cullen.
*In Love with Love* (ILwL). Anne *and* Christopher Fremantle, eds.

**Gods and Goddesses**
Dead Pan, The. Browning.
For the Unknown Goddess. Brewster.
God in Wrath, A. *Fr.* The Black Riders. Crane.
Hertha. Swinburne.
Oshun, the River Goddess. *Unknown.*
Song: "Sabrina fair." *Fr.* Comus. Milton.
Sonnet for All Greeks Living Now. Gray.
Visit of the Gods, The. Schiller.
Water of Kane, The. *Unknown.*
Weather of Olympus, The. Graves.

**Goethe, Johann Wolfgang von**
Memorial Versus. Arnold.
Sorrows of Werther, The. Thackeray.

**Gogarty, Oliver St. John**
Lay of Oliver Gogarty, The. Dawson.

**Gold Mining and Miners**
Californian, The. *Unknown.*
Clementine. *Unknown.*
Days of Forty-Nine, The. *Unknown.*
Dead Prospector, The. Chapman.
Dreary Black Hills, The. *Unknown.*
In the Mines. Swett.
Joe Bowers. *Unknown.*
Lousy Miner. *Unknown.*
Miner's Lament, The. *Unknown.*
Miner's Progress, The. *At. to* Delano.
National Miner, The. *Unknown.*
Prospecting Dream. *Unknown.*
San Francisco Company, The. *Unknown.*
Seeing the Elephant. *Unknown.*
Sweet Jane. *Unknown.*
When I Went Off to Prospect. *Unknown.*

**Golden Gate Bridge**
Geometry of Motion, The—Crossing the Golden Gate Bridge. McDonough.

**Goldfinches**
Crimson lute that comest in the dawn. Asbaje.
Mechanism. Ammons.
Song: "Where I walk out." Winters.

Yellow Flutterings. Keats.
**Goldfish**
Address to Certain Gold Fishes. Coleridge.
Goldfish. Nemerov.
**Golem**
Bella and the Golem. Ombres.
Golem, The. Reich.
**Golf**
Any Golf Championship. Rice.
Golfers. Layton.
Public Nuisance, A. Arkell.
Seaside Golf. Betjeman.
Who Taught Caddies to Count? or A Burnt Golfer Fears the
Child. Nash.
**Goliath**
David and Goliath. Crouch.
Epitaph for Goliath. Slavitt.
**Gonne, Maud**
No Second Troy. Yeats.
**Good Friday**
Good Friday, 1613. Riding Westward. Donne.
Tenebrae. Clarke.
*See also* **Crucifixion, The.**
**Gore-Booth, Eva**
In Memory of Eva Gore-Booth and Con Markiewicz. Yeats.
**Gorillas**
Au Jardin des Plantes. Wain.
Gorilla Gorilla. Dawe.
**Gossip**
Journal of Society, The. Turner.
Old Women, The. Brown.
People do gossip. Sappho.
Tattle. Turner.
**Govan, Saint**
St. Govan. Prys-Jones.
**Government**
Government! Nihoniho.
Ill Government. Herrick.
What shall we think! Can people give away. *Fr.* Absalom and
Achitophel. Dryden.
**Goya y Lucientes, Francisco José de**
In Goya's greatest scenes we seem to see. *Fr.* A Coney Island
of the Mind. Ferlinghetti.
La Pesadilla. Penfold.
**Graffiti**
From a Lavatory Wall. *Unknown.*
Graffiti. Field.
Graffiti for Lovers. Hall.
Kilroy. Viereck.
Men's Room in the College Chapel, The. Snodgrass.
Poet Finds an Ephemeral Home in Truck Stop on the New
Jersey Turnpike, ca. 1970, The. Hall.
SM. Moss.
Sunny Prestatyn. Larkin.
To Desi as Joe as Smoky the Lover of 115th Street. Lorde.
**Grammar**
How a Girl Was Too Reckless of Grammar. Carryl.
**Granada, Spain**
Moorish King Who Lost Granada, The. *Unknown.*
**Grand Canyon**
At Grand Canyon's Edge. Ray.
**Grand Rapids, Michigan**
Grand Rapids. Moore.
**Grandfathers**
Christmas Gift, A. Mura.
Dunbarton. Lowell.
Grandfather. Coleman.
Grandfather. Harper.
Grandfather. Leax.
Grandfather. Mahon.
Grandfather in the Old Men's Home. Merwin.
Grandfather never went to school. Quintana.

Grandfathers. Castro.
Grandfather's Clock. Work.
Grandpa. Rankin.
Grandpa Dropped His Glasses. Jackson.
Grandparents. Lowell.
I Want to Write a Jewish Poem. Pacernick.
Legacy II. Quintana.
Much Obliged. Morice.
On the Photograph of a Man I Never Saw. Plutzik.
Other Side, The. Reiter.
Poem for My Grandfather. Jacobs.
Two Clocks. Daniel.
When We Go Over To My Grandad's. Rosen.
With My Grandfather. Zelda.
"Write a letter to Grandpa," my mother said, but he smelled
old. *Fr.* Recovery. Van Duyn.
**Grandmothers**
Anishinabe Grandmothers. Vizenor.
Black Sheba. Braxton.
Death of My Grandmother, The. Fraser.
First Generation, The. Mirikitani.
For Great Grandmother and Her Settlement House. Darr.
For My Mother's Mother. McDaniel.
Foxfire. Willard.
From My Mother's Home. Goldberg.
Grammer's Shoes. Barnes.
Grandmother, The. Berry.
Grandmother. Carlile.
Grandmother and Child. Dallas.
Grandmother Sleeps. Bahe.
Grandmothers, The. Oliver.
Grandparents. Lowell.
History. Soto.
Legacies. Giovanni.
Lineage. Walker.
Love Necessitates. Redmond.
My Grandmother. Jennings.
My Grandmother. Shapiro.
My Grandmother Sifting. Marion.
My Grandmother Washes Her Feet. Chappell.
My Grandmother's Love Letters. Crane.
Thoughts for My Grandmothers. Firestone.
To Jesus Villanueva, with Love. Villanueva.
Touchstone. Worley.
Way and the Way Things Are, The. NorthSun.
Woman of the House, The. Murphy.
Words to Remind Me of My Grandmother. Castro Rios.
Yentel. Leider.
**Grantchester, England**
Old Vicarage, Grantchester, The. Brooke.
**Grapes**
Father and His Children, The. *Unknown.*
Grapes Making. Adams.
Harvester, The. Lawrence.
**Grasmere, England**
Grasmere Sonnets. Wright.
Recluse, The. Wordsworth.
**Grass**
Blade of Grass, The. *Fr.* The Black Riders. Crane.
Grass. Sandburg.
Grassroots. Sandburg.
Green Grass Grew All Around, The. *Unknown.*
Heavenly Grass. Williams.
Mower's Song, The. Marvell.
Rustling of Grass, The. Noyes.
What Is There. Bell.
**Grasshoppers**
Explanation of the Grasshopper, An. Lindsay.
Grasshopper, The. Cowley.
Grasshopper, The. Lovelace.
Grasshopper. McDonald.
Grasshopper, The. Stanley.

Grasshopper, A. Wilbur.
Grasshopper and the Ant, The. La Fontaine.
On the Grasshopper and the Cricket. Keats.
Ondt and the Gracehoper, The. Joyce.
R-p-o-p-h-e-s-s-a-g-r. Cummings.
To the Grasshopper and the Cricket. Hunt.

**Graves**
"Ah, Are You Digging on My Grave?" Hardy.
Arundel Tomb, An. Larkin.
At White River. Haines.
Barrow, The. Thwaite.
Burial. Walker.
Bury Me in a Free Land. Harper.
Claribel. Tennyson.
Cool Tombs. Sandburg.
Cover me over, clover. Eberhart.
Despair. Levertov.
Dig My Grave. *Unknown.*
Father Son and Holy Ghost. Lorde.
Grave, The. Winters.
Graves in Queens. Hugo.
Inscriptions. Thwaite.
Lord Cozens Hardy. Betjeman.
On the Tombs in Westminster Abbey. Beaumont.
Relique, The. Donne.
Sonnet Written in the Church-Yard at Middleton, in Sussex. Smith.
Stranger, The. De la Mare.
Temporary Problems. Rubin.
They're Moving Father's Grave. *Unknown.*
To——: "The cold earth slept below." Shelley.
To Laura Phelan: 1880-1906. Stokesbury.
Tribal Cemetery. Hale.
Unknown Grave, The. Landon.
Unquiet Grave, The. *Unknown.*
Wanderer's Grave, The. Sage.
Way of Keeping, A. Willard.
You Can Dig My Grave. *Unknown.*
Yugoslav Cemetery. Wright.

**Graveyards.** *See* **Cemeteries.**

**Gray, Thomas**
Sketch of His Own Character. Gray.

**Great Depression**
Acts of God. Maddow.
Arizona. *Unknown.*
Beans, Bacon and Gravy. *Unknown.*
Brother, Can You Spare a Dime? Harburg.
Depression: My Father Speaks to My Mother. Allen.
Great Depression, The. Goedicke.
Hellbabies. Gregory.
In a Home Relief Bureau. Hayes.
New Youngfellow. Burnshaw.
Road to Utterly. Lewis.
34 Blues. *Unknown.*
Unemployed: 2 A.M. Funaroff.
Upsurge. Gessner.
Variations on a Baedecker. Burnshaw.
Working Man Blues. *Unknown.*

**Greco, El**
El Greco: *Espolio.* Birney.
High Renaissance. Starbuck.

**Greece**
At Lindos. Sarton.
At midnight, in his guarded tent. *Fr.* Marco Bozzaris. Halleck.
Bousouki. Hanson.
First of All. Hanson.
Isles of Greece, The. *Fr.* Don Juan. Byron.
World's great age begins anew, The. *Fr.* Hellas. Shelley.

**Greed**
Bird on Nellie's Hat, The. Lamb.
Covetousness. Idley.

Greed Song, The. Goldbarth.
Greedy Richard. Taylor
Greedy the People, The. Cummings.
Mother Pin a Rose on Me. *Unknown.*
On a Favourite Cat Drowned in a Tub of Goldfishes. Gray.
To a Covetous Churl. May.

**Greeks**
Three Greeks. Packer.

**Green (color)**
Green. Lawrence.
Green Eye, The. Merrill.
Green Prose. Lux.
Variables of Green. Graves.

**Greene, Graham**
Muted Screen of Graham Greene, The. McGinley.

**Greenhouses**
Big Wind. Roethke.
Forcing House. Roethke.
New England Greenhouse. McQuilkin.

**Greenland**
Greenland Fisheries. *Unknown.*

**Greenwich Village, New York City**
Lüchow's and After. Sissman.

**Gregory, Lady Augusta**
Municipal Gallery Revisited, The. Yeats.

**Grenville, Sir Richard**
*Revenge,* The. Tennyson.

**Greyhounds**
Ballad of Master McGrath, A. *Unknown.*
Greyhounds. Gray.
How a Good Greyhound Is Shaped. *Unknown.*

**Grief**
After great pain, a formal feeling comes. Dickinson.
After the Burial. Lowell.
Aunt Laura Moves toward the Open Grave of Her Father. De Roche.
Bereavement. E. Browning.
Bereft. Hardy.
Carousel, The. Oden.
Complaint. Wright.
Cross of Snow, The. Longfellow.
David's Lament for Jonathan. Abélard.
Death of Lester Brown, House Painter, The. Taylor.
Despair. Levertov.
Dirge: "I make this dirge for you Miss Mary Binning I miss you." *Unknown.*
Do not lift him from the bracken. *Fr.* The Widow of Glencoe. Aytoun.
Elegy for Jane. Roethke.
Elegy on a Lady Whom Grief for the Death of Her Betrothed Killed. Bridges.
Elegy on the Death of Her Husband. Howard.
Exequy, The. King.
Flowers in Cellars. Ellis.
Ghost. Beer.
Glory of the Day Was in Her Face, The. Johnson.
Great grief came over me. Aleqaajik.
Grief. E. Browning.
If Ever Hapless Woman Had a Cause. Pembroke.
Kaddish for Naomi Ginsberg. Ginsberg.
Lament for Art O'Leary. O'Connell.
Lament of the Border Widow, The. *Unknown.*
Lamentation, A: "Grief, have I denied thee?" Levertov.
Lycidas. Milton.
Mad Song. Blake.
Mourning Women. Blind.
My Buried Friends. *Unknown.*
My grief on the sea. Cussrooee.
"My True Love Hath My Heart and I Have His." M. Coleridge.
Nurse No Long Grief. Gilmore.
Office for the Dead. Kinsella.

Old Familiar Faces, The.  Lamb.
Poet Is Dead, The.  Everson.
Poet's Lament on the Death of His Wife.  Ugaas.
Sestina: "September rain falls on the house."  Bishop.
Sonnet on the Death of Mr. Richard West.  Gray.
Spell Against Sorrow.  Raine.
Spring and Fall: To a Young Child.  Hopkins.
Story about Chicken Soup, A.  Simpson.
Surprised by Joy—Impatient As the Wind.  Wordsworth.
To Margaret.  Hopkins.
Valediction, A: Forbidding Mourning.  Donne.
When to the sessions of sweet silent thought.  *Fr.* Sonnets,
    XXX.  Shakespeare.
Widow's Lament in Springtime, The.  Williams.
With Rue My Heart Is Laden.  Housman.

**Griffins**
Griffin.  Matthews.

**Grocers**
"Mrs. Evans fach, you want butter again."  Davies.
Song Against Grocers, The.  Chesterton.

**Grongar Hill, Wales**
Grongar Hill.  Dyer.

**Groundhogs**
Drumlin Woodchuck, A.  Frost.
Groundhog, The.  Eberhart.
Groundhog.  *Unknown.*
Groundhog Day.  Hogan.
Woodchuck Who Lives on Top of Mt. Ritter, The.  Simon.
Woodchucks.  Kumin.

**Grünewald, Mathias**
Green at Colmar.  Aldan.

**Guernsey**
In Guernsey.  Swinburne.

**Guerrière (ship)**
*Constitution* and the *Guerrière*, The.    *Unknown.*

**Guest, Edgar A**
Edgar A. Guest Considers "The Old Woman Who Lived in a
    Shoe."  Untermeyer.
Lines to a World-Famous Poet Who Failed to Complete a
    World-Famous Poem; or, Come Clean, Mr. Guest!  Nash.

**Guevara, Ernesto ("Che")**
Guevara with Minutes to Go.  Corrington.

**Guggenheim, John Simon**
No Foundation.  Hollander.

**Guilt**
Christina.  MacNeice.
First Frost.  Clarkson.
Oedipus.  Muir.
Song about Major Eatherly, A.  Wain.
To Alpha Dryden Eberhart.  Eberhart.
Why Would I Have Survived?  Bruck.

**Guinea Pigs**
Guinea-Pig Song, A.  *Unknown.*

**Guitars**
Guitar.  García Lorca.
Guitarist Tunes Up, The.  Cornford.

**Gulf Stream**
Gulf Stream, The.  Bellamann.
Song of the Gulf Stream.  Ford.

**Gulls**
Andrew Talks to Gulls.  Roberts.
Desert Gulls.  Gillespie.
Echoing Cliff, The.  Young.
Gull, it is said, The.  Nakasuk.
Gulls.  Howes.
Gulls.  Kendrick.
Gulls.  Muir.
Gulls Land and Cease To Be.  Ciardi.
Herring-Gull.  Wheelock.
Maine Sea Gulls.  Hoban.
On the Beach.  Cornford.
Predictor of Famine, The.  Williams.

Sea-Birds.  Allen.
Seagull, The.  Dafydd ap Gwilym.
Seagull, The.  Howitt.
Sea-Gull, The.  Nash.
Sea-Gull, The.  *Unknown.*
Seagulls.  Francis.
Sea-Mew, The.  Browning.
Storm's End.  Speyer.
Tarred Gull.  Ritchie.
To a Seamew.  Swinburne.
What a View.  Montague.

**Gunpowder Plot**
Now they are met: this armèd with a spade.  *Fr.* The Locusts,
    or Appolyonists.  Fletcher.

**Guns**
A. E. F.  Sandburg.
Grandpa's .45.  Ransom.
Gun, White Castle.  Klappert.
Guns.  Woods.
Invention of the Gun, The.  Batki.
Naming of Parts.  *Fr.* Lessons of the War.  Reed.
Son of a Gun.  Fiacc.
Technique on the Firing Line.  Cassity.

**Gwyn, Nell**
Ballad Called the Haymarket Hectors, A.  *Unknown.*
Panegyric, A: "Of a great heroine I mean to tell."  *Unknown.*

**Gymnastics**
Watching Gymnasts.  Francis.

**Gypsies**
Gipsies.  Clare.
Gypsies.  Nibbelink.
Gypsies.  Nowlan.
Gypsy.  Miles.
Gypsy, The.  Thomas.
Gypsy Davy, The.  *Unknown.*
Gypsy Laddie, The.  *Unknown.*
Gypsy Rover, The.  *Unknown.*
Meg Merrilies.  Keats.
Romanies in Town, The.  Beresford.
Scholar-Gypsy, The.  Arnold.
Wraggle-Taggle Gypsies, The.  *Unknown.*

# H

**Hair**
Boy with His Hair Cut Short.  Rukeyser.
For Anne Gregory.  Yeats.
For Muh' Dear.  Rodgers.
Girl's Hair, A.  Dafydd ab Edmwnd.
Hair.  Corso.
Hair.  Silverman.
Hair Poem.  Knott.
Her Hair.  Baudelaire.
Keeping Hair.  Wilson.
Lavender Cowboy, The.  Hersey.
Oh Who Is That Young Sinner.  Housman.
On Getting a Natural.  Randall.
Poem: "After your death."  Knott.
Sam's World.  Cornish.
To Amarantha, That She Would Dishevel Her Hair.  Lovelace.
W. W.  Baraka.

**Haiti**
Coming of Dusk upon a Village in Haiti, The.  Rago.

**Hale, Nathan**
Nathan Hale.  Finch.
Nathan Hale.  *Unknown.*

**Haley, Alex**
For Kinte.  La Grone.

**Halloween**
Hallowe'en. Behn.
Halloween. Livingston.
Halloween Witches. Holman.
Hist whist. Cummings.
Litany for Halloween. *Unknown.*
Shivers. Fisher.
This Is Halloween. Thompson.
We Three. Moore.
What Night Would It Be? Ciardi.
Witch? Reavin.
*In the Witch's Kitchen* (IWK). John E. Brewton, Lorraine A. Blackburn, George M. Blackburn III, comps.

**Hamlet**
Elegy of Fortinbras. Herbert.
Midrash on Hamlet. Landy.
They All Want to Play Hamlet. Sandburg.

**Handball**
Day and Night Handball. Dunn.
Game Resumed. Lattimore.
Handball Players. Goodman.
Handball Players at Brighton Beach, The. Feldman.

**Handel, George Frideric**
Epigram on Handel and Bononcini. Byrom.

**Hands**
Bestiary for the Fingers of My Right Hand. Simic.
Case History. Drake.
Hand. Marcus.
Hand, The. Moss.
Hands. Fox.
Hands, The. Harrison.
Hands. Young.
Hold a glass of pure water to the eye of the sun! *Fr.* The Glass of Pure Water. "MacDiarmid."
In the Small Boats of Their Hands. Kircher.
Look to the Back of the Hand. Minty.
Palm of the Hand. Rilke.
Poem for My Hands. Oles.
This Hand. Wylie.
This Is the Hand. Rosen.
This Living Hand. Keats.
Your Hands. Grimké.

**Hanging**
Ballade: "Brother humans who live on after us." Villon.
Captain Hall. *Unknown.*
Carpenter's Son, The. Housman.
Clever Tom Clinch Going to Be Hanged. Swift.
Danny Deever. Kipling.
Dream of Hanging, A. Beer.
Eight O'Clock. Housman.
Epitaph: "They hanged him on a clement morning, swung." Scott.
Four Maries, The. *Unknown.*
Geordie. *Unknown.*
Hang Me, O Hang Me, and I'll Be Dead and Gone. *Unknown.*
Hanging Johnny. *Unknown.*
Hanging of Sam Archer, The. *Unknown.*
Hangman at Home, The. Sandburg.
Jeff Buckner. Beddo.
Kevin Barry: Died for Ireland, 1st November, 1920. *Unknown.*
Life of the Mannings. *Unknown.*
London Fete, A. Patmore.
MacPhersons Farewell. *Unknown.*
Maid Freed from the Gallows, The. *Unknown.*
Night before Larry Was Stretched, The. *Unknown.*
On moonlit heath and lonesome bank. Housman.
Poor Boy. *Unknown.*
River Song. Kees.
Sam Hall. *Unknown.*
Song of the Death of Mr. Thewlis, The. *Unknown.*
To His Son. Ralegh.
Two Poems (after A. E. Housman). Kingsmill.

*See also* **Executions; Lynching.**

**Hanks, Nancy**
Nancy Hanks. R. *and* S. V. Benét.
Nancy Hanks, Mother of Abraham Lincoln. Lindsay.

**Hanukkah**
Chanuke, O Chanuke. *Unknown.*
Mi Y'Malel (Who Can Retell?). *Unknown.*

**Happiness**
Anatomy of Happiness, The. Nash.
Art of Happiness, The. Young.
Breathing, The. Levertov.
Character of a Happy Life, The. Wotton.
Choice, The. Pomfret.
Christmas Poem. Hilton.
Cliff Klingenhagen. Robinson.
Elephant. Brownjohn.
Four Things Make Us Happy Here. Herrick.
Happiness. Sandburg.
Happy Life, The. Martial.
Happy the Man. Horace.
If You Happy Would Be. Fernández.
Laugh and Be Merry. Masefield.
Let Us Be Merry. Curran.
Life Is All Right. Wangberg.
Our Beautiful West Coast Thing. Brautigan.
Quiet Fog, The. Piercy.
Running. Wilbur.
Sonnet-Ballad, The. Brooks.
Wish, A. Rogers.
Wishes. Harjo.

**Harbors and Ports**
Cinque Port, A. Davidson.
Gateway to the Sea, A (I). Bruce.
Harbor Dawn, The. *Fr.* The Bridge. Crane.
Harbors. Minty.
In Felmouth Harbour. Johnson.
Long Harbour, The. Bethell.
Ode to Swansea. Watkins.
Winter Ship, A. Plath.

**Harding, Warren Gamaliel**
Two Poems About President Harding. Wright.

**Hardy, Thomas**
At Max Gate. Sassoon.
At Thomas Hardy's Birthplace, 1953. Wright.
Luncheon, A. Beerbohm.
Thomas Hardy. De la Mare.

**Hares**
Dance, The. Davies.
Epitaph on a Hare. Cowper.
Hare, A ("Eyes that glass fear, though fear on furtive foot"). De la Mare.
Hare, The. *Unknown.*
Hare and the Tortoise, The. Serraillier.
Hare in the Snow, The. Rawlinson.
Hare in Winter. Piercy.
Trapped Hare, The. Dowling.
Two Songs of a Fool. Yeats.
White Hare, The. Bowes-Lyon.
*See also* **Rabbits.**

**Harfleur, France, Battle of**
King Henry the Fifth before Harfleur. *Fr.* King Henry V. Shakespeare.

**Harlem, New York City**
De Mayor of Harlem. Henderson.
Esthete in Harlem. Hughes.
Good Morning. Hughes.
Harlem. Hughes.
Harlem Freeze Frame. Bethune.
Harlem Gallery: From the Inside. Neal.
Harlem in January. Fields.
Harlem Night Song. Hughes.
Harlem River. Spector.

Harlem Sounds: Hallelujah Corner.  Browne.
Jitterbugging in the Streets.  Hernton.
Juke Box Love Song.  Hughes.
Keep on Pushing.  Henderson.
King of Harlem, The.  García Lorca.
Lenox Avenue Mural.  Hughes.
Night Funeral in Harlem.  Hughes.
Prime.  Hughes.
Promised Land.  Engel.
Puzzled.  Hughes.
Sketches of Harlem.  Henderson.
Still Voice of Harlem, The.  Rivers.
Train Runs Late to Harlem, The.  Rivers.
Walk with de Mayor of Harlem.  Henderson.
Young Negro Poet.  Hernton.

**Harper's Ferry, West Virginia**
Narrative.  Atkins.

**Harps**
Harp of the North.  *Fr.* The Lady of the Lake.  Scott.
Harp That Once thro' Tara's Halls, The.  Moore.
Harper, The.  *Unknown.*
Military Harpist, The.  Pitter.

**Harpur, Charles**
Extinct Birds.  Wright.

**Harrison, Benjamin**
Historical Reflections.  Hollander.

**Harvard University.**
Experiential Religion.  Du Priest.
I Went to See Irving Babbitt.  Eberhart.

**Harvest**
Bringing in the Sheaves.  Shaw.
Evening in Harvest Time, An.  Turner.
Harvest Song.  Campbell.
Harvesting Wheat for the Public Share.  Li Chü.
Hock-Cart, or Harvest Home, The.  Herrick.
Hurrahing in Harvest.  Hopkins.
In the Huon Valley.  McAuley.
Reaper, The.  Allen.
Reapers.  Blind.
Reapers.  Toomer.
Solitary Reaper, The.  Wordsworth.
Threshing-Machine, The.  Meynell.

**Harvey, William**
On the Death of Mr. William Harvey.  Cowley.
Portrait of William Harvey.  Brain.

**Hastings, Warren**
Fifth Day.  Fitzgerald.

**Hate**
Consequence, The.  McDonald.
Enslaved.  McKay.
Fury's Field.  Bodker.
Hatred.  Bennett.
Immortal Hate.  *Fr.* Paradise Lost.  Milton.
Poison Tree, A.  *Fr.* Songs of Experience.  Blake.
Soliloquy of the Spanish Cloister.  Browning.
Tree of Hatred, The.  Moreh.

**Hats**
Hats.  Dillard.
My Infundibuliform Hat.  Adams.
Quangle Wangle's Hat, The.  Lear.
Where Did You Get That Hat?  Sullivan.

**Hawaii**
Born was the island.  *Unknown.*
Late Morning: Oahu.  *Fr.* Rice and Mats.  Kendrick.
Leper, The.  Ka-'ehu.
Luau, The.  Taggard.
Twenty-Third Flight.  Birney.
*Poetry Hawaii: A Contemporary Anthology* (PHC).  Frank
    Stewart *and* John Unterecker, eds.

**Hawks**
Afternoon.  Sund.
Balances.  Stuart.

Birds.  Jeffers.
Buteo Regalis.  Momaday.
Fieldmouse crouches low, A.  Sund.
Goshawk, The.  Haines.
Hawk, The.  Bloom.
Hawk Is a Woman.  Flanner.
Hawk Nailed to a Barn Door.  Blue Cloud.
Hawk Roosting.  Hughes.
Hawk's Way.  Olson.
Hurt Hawks.  Jeffers.
Over Sir John's Hill.  Thomas.
Rock and Hawk,  Jeffers.
Sea-Hawk.  Eberhart.
Shiva.  Jeffers.
Tamer and Hawk.  Gunn.
To a Marsh Hawk in Spring.  Thoreau.
Windhover, The.  Hopkins.
Windy Gap.  Campbell.
Wounded Hawk, The.  Palmer.

**Hawthorne, Nathaniel**
Hawthorne.  *Fr.* A Fable for Critics.  Lowell.
Hawthorne Garland, A.  Fogle.
On Visiting the Graves of Hawthorne and Throreau.  Very.

**Haydon, Benjamin Robert**
Addressed to Haydon ("Great spirits are now on earth
    sojourning").  Keats.
Addressed to Haydon ("Highmindedness, a jealousy for good").
    Keats.
To B. R. Haydon with the Foregoing Sonnet on the Elgin
    Marbles.  Keats.

**Haydn, Franz Joseph**
Allegro: "After a black day, I play Haydn."  Tranströmer.

**Haze.**  *See* **Fog.**

**Heads**
Thoughts on One's Head.  Meredith.

**Hearst, Patty**
Dear Patty Dear Tania.  Mathews.

**Hearst, William Randolph**
Doxology.  Taylor.

**Heat**
Cold and Heat.  *Unknown.*
Heat.  *Fr.* The Garden.  Doolittle ("H. D.").
Shade-seller, The.  Jacobsen.

**Heaven**
About the Heavenly Life.  Leon.
Celestial City, The.  *Fr.* Christ's Victory and Triumph.
    Fletcher.
Description of Elizium, The.  *Fr.* The Muses' Elizium.
    Drayton.
Evening in Paradise.  *Fr.* Paradise Lost.  Milton.
For a Lady I Know.  *Fr.* Four Epitaphs.  Cullen.
Future Life, The.  Bryant.
General William Booth Enters into Heaven.  Lindsay.
Greater Country, The.  Watkins.
He Would Have His Lady Sing.  Dolben.
Heaven.  Brooke.
Heaven.  Hughes.
Heaven, Heaven, Heaven Is the Place.  Hughes.
Heaven is so far of the mind.  Dickinson.
Heaven of Animals, The.  Dickey.
Heavenly Canaan, The.  Watts.
Heavenly City, The.  Smith.
Hierusalem, My Happy Home.  *Unknown.*
Hunchback Girl: She Thinks of Heaven.  Brooks.
I never saw a moor.  Dickinson.
Ice Cream in Paradise.  Hollander.
If There Are Any Heavens.  Cummings.
In the Sweet Bye-and-Bye.  Bennett.
Life of the Blessed, The.  León.
Nothing in Heaven Functions as It Ought.  Kennedy.
Peace.  Vaughan.

Saint Peter sat by the celestial gate. *Fr.* The Vision of Judgment. Byron.
Streets of Glory. *Unknown.*
To Ford Madox Ford in Heaven. Williams.
What is—"Paradise." Dickinson.
White Island: Or the Place of the Blest, The. Herrick.

**Hebrides**
Stormy Hebrides, The. *Fr.* An Ode on the Popular Superstitions. ˙ Collins.

**Hector**
Ballad of Hector in Hades. Muir.

**Hedgehogs**
Happy Hedgehog, The. Rieu.
Hedgehog. Muldoon.
To a Hedgehog. Thompson.

**Heine, Heinrich**
Century Piece for Poor Heine, A (1800-1856). Logan.
Translator to Translated. Pound.

**Helen of Troy**
Helen. Doolittle ("H. D.").
Helen ("I am the blue! I come from the lower world"). Valéry.
Helen like the Rose. Lloyd.
Helen of Troy. *Fr.* Doctor Faustus. Marlowe.
Helen, the Sad Queen. Valéry.
Judgment of Paris, The. Merwin.
Mythmaking. Spivack.
To Helen. Poe.
Ultimate Antientropy, The. Weiss.
White Isle of Leuce, The. Read.

**Helicopters**
Helicopter, The. Serraillier.
Street Scene. Suffolk.

**Hell**
Arrival in Hell. Huch.
Ascent into Hell. Hope.
Ballad of Hell, A. Davidson.
Hell. *Unknown.*
Hell Gate. Housman.
Hell is a city much like London. *Fr.* Peter Bell the Third. Shelley.
Ixion. Banning.
Jews in Hell, The. Goldemberg.
Lament of an Idle Demon. Lister.
Nothing in Heaven Functions as It Ought. Kennedy.
Place of the Damned, The. Swift.
Simon Legree—A Negro Sermon. Lindsay.
Slim in Hell. Brown.
Strange Meeting. Owen.
Supremacy. Robinson.
To Dives. Belloc.
Underworld. Garrett.

**Hell's Angels**
Black Jackets. Gunn.

**Hemingway, Ernest.**
Answer to Allegory, An. Payne.

**Henry I, King of England**
White Ship, The. Rossetti.

**Henry VIII, King of England**
Henry VIII. E. *and* H. Farjeon.

**Henry IV, King of France**
Ivry. MacCaulay.

**Henry the Navigator**
Portrait of Prince Henry, The. Clouts.

**Hens**
Hen Dying. Maclean.
Hen Flower, The. Kinnell.
Hen Under Bay-Tree. Pitter.
Hens. Nowlan.
Hens, The. Roberts.
Hens in Winter. Coffin.
Hen's Nest. Clare.
Janet Waking. Ransom.

Near and Far. Behn.
Song of the Battery Hen. Brock.

**Heraclitus**
From Heraclitus. Dugan.
Variation on Heraclitus. MacNeice.

**Herbs**
Lines with a Gift of Herbs. Lewis.

**Hermits**
Hermit, The. Hsü Pên.
Hermit's Song, A. *Unknown.*
Marban, a Hermit Speaks. *Unknown.*
St. Govan. Prys-Jones.
Three Hermits, The. Yeats.

**Hero and Leander**
On a Leander Gem. Keats.
On Leander's Swimming over the Hellespont to Hero. Warton, the Younger.
Written after swimming from Sestos to Abydos. Byron.

**Herod the Great**
Innocent's Song. Causley.

**Heroes and Heroines**
Abdul, the Bulbul Amir. *Unknown.*
Babe Ruth. Runyon.
Casabianca. Hemans.
Casey at the Bat. Thayer.
Casey's Daughter at the Bat. Graham.
Charlton Heston. Fried.
Commemorative of a Naval Victory. Melville.
Critics say that epics have died out, The. *Fr.* Aurora Leigh. Browning.
Hero, The. Moore.
Heroes. Creeley.
Icarus. Field.
Poem for Heros, A. Fields.
Settling Some Old Football Scores. Bishop.
Tom Matte. Nash.
Where Are You Now Superman? Patten.
Where, O Where? Bracker.

**Heroin.** *See* **Drug Addiction.**

**Herons**
Blue Heron. Welch.
Great Blue Heron, The. Kizer.
Heron, The. Murray.
Heron. Plumly.
Heron, The. Roethke.
Heron, The. Watkins.
Herons. *Unknown.*
Night Herons. Wright.

**Herrick, Robert**
Mr. Robert Herrick, His Farewell unto Poetry. Herrick.

**Herring**
Herring. *Fr.* A Bestiary. Rexroth.
Herring Is King. Graves.
Red Herring, The. MacBeth.
With the Herring Fishers. "MacDiarmid."

**Heston, Charlton**
Charlton Heston. Fried.

**Heydrich, Reinhard**
Polemical Elegy for Reinhardt Heydrich. Buchan.

**Hiawatha**
Hiawatha's Photographing. "Carroll."
Modern Hiawatha, The. Strong.

**Hicks, Edward**
Edward Hicks: The Peaceable Kingdom. Stanford.
Peaceable Kingdom, The. Piercy.

**Highwaymen**
Bold Jack Donahue. *Unknown.*
Brennan of the Moor. *Unknown.*
Death of Morgan, The. *Unknown.*
Dick Turpin and Black Bess. *Unknown.*
Mulberry Mountain. *Unknown.*
To Walk on Hills. Graves.

Walk, A. Snyder.
Wild Colonial Boy, The. *Unknown.*

**Hill, Joe**
Joe Hill Listens to the Praying. Patchen.

**Hills and Mountains**
Alaskan Mountain Poem #1. Silko.
Alpine. Thomas.
Ask the Mountains. George.
Cheyenne Mountain. Jackson.
Close-Up. Ammons.
Driving Down from the Big Horns. Curry.
Fable: "The mountain and the squirrel." Emerson.
Golgotha Is a Mountain. Bontemps.
Grongar Hill. Dyer.
Here in Katmandu. Justice.
Hills, The. Cornford.
Hills, The. Field.
In the Canadian Rockies. Hopper.
Like to these to these unmeasurable mountains. Sannazaro.
Long Hill, The. Teasdale.
Mont Blanc. Shelley.
Monument Mountain. Bryant.
Mountain Born. Bost.
Mountain Stream, The. Hughes.
Muckish Mountain (The Pig's Back). Leslie.
Myth and the Mountain, The. Robinson.
Nocturne of the Self-Evident Presence. MacGreevy.
Object Lesson. Henderson.
Paps of Dana, The. Stephens.
Pennines in April. Hughes.
Pilgrimage Song. *Unknown.*
Ridge in Wind. Curry.
Rocky Acres. Graves.
Schreckhorn, The. Hardy.
Shancoduff. Kavanagh.
Sitting Bear Mountain. Lovell.
Sleeping Giant, The. Hall.
Snow on Saddle Mountain, The. Miyazawa.
To Walk on Hills. Graves.

**Hinduism**
Mahabalipuram. MacNeice.

**Hippopotamuses**
Habits of the Hippopotamus. Guiterman.
Hippo, The. Roethke.
Hippopotamus, The. Belloc.
Hippopotamus, The. Durston.
Hippopotamus, The. Eliot.
Hippopotamuses. Spilka.
Native African Revolutionaries. Jones.

**Hiroshima, Japan**
Hiroshima. Brain.
I Come and Stand at Every Door. Hikmet.
Monuments of Hiroshima, The. Enright.
There were many of us at that time. *Fr.* Hiroshima. Bantock.

**History and Historians**
Beginnings. Fitzgerald.
Concise History of the World, A. Sadoff.
Fall of Rome, The. Auden.
History. Birch.
History. Gregor.
History. Skelton.
How many bards gild the lapses of time! Keats.
Lessons in History. Warren.
Living Truth, The. Plumpp.
Looking Backward. Bly.
Meredith Phyfe. *Fr.* The New Spoon River. Masters.
Moral Artistry. McKain.
On Sir Nathaniel Wraxall the Historian. Colman, the Younger.
Readings of History. Rich.
Speech for an Abdication. Stessel.
Written in the Beginning of Mezeray's History of France.
  Prior.

**Hitchhiking**
Faces. Ciardi.
Fort Wayne, Indiana 1964. Lewis.
Wendover. Cuelho.

**Hitler, Adolf**
Hitler, frothy-mouth, wooden-head. *Unknown.*
Round and Round Hitler's Grave. *Unknown.*

**Ho Chi Minh**
Ballad of Ho Chi Minh. MacColl.

**Hobbes, Thomas**
Hobbes, 1651. Hollander.

**Hobos.** *See* **Vagabonds.**

**Hogarth, William**
Epitaph on William Hogarth. Johnson.

**Hogg, James**
Extempore Effusion upon the Death of James Hogg.
  Wordsworth.

**Hohenlinden, Battle of**
Battle of Hohenlinden, The. Campbell.

**Hokusai, Katsushika**
Great Wave: Hokusai, The. Finkel.
Hokusai. Farrar.

**Holiday, Billie (Eleanora Fagan McKay)**
Blues and Bitterness. Bennett.
Day Lady Died, The. O'Hara.
For Our Lady. Sanchez.

**Holidays**
Adrian Henri's Talking After Christmas Blues. Henri.
Conversation with Washington. Livingston.
Rebolushinary X-mas. Rodgers.
*Callooh! Callay! Holiday Poems For Young Readers* (CC). Myra
  Cohn Livingston, ed.
*O Frabjous Day!* (OFD). Myra Cohn Livingston, ed.
*See also* **specific holidays.**

**Holland.** *See* **Netherlands.**

**Holly**
Green Grow'th the Holly. *At. to* Henry VIII, King of England.
Holly, The. De la Mare.
Holly and Mistletoe. Farjeon.
Holly and the Ivy, The. *Unknown.*
Itum Paradisun all clothed in green. *Unknown.*

**Hollywood, California**
After the Locust. Gascou.
Trying to Forget. Wieners.

**Holmes, Oliver Wendell (1809-94)**
Filling an Order. Trowbridge.
Holmes. *Fr.* A Fable for Critics. Lowell.

**Holy Family**
Cherry-Tree Carol, The. *Unknown.*

**Home**
Disturbances. Thwaite.
Family Prime. Van Doren.
Getting Home. Rodriguez.
Hearth and Home. King.
Home ("Home's home, although it reached be"). Beaumont.
Home. Guest.
Home on the Range. *Unknown.*
Home! Sweet Home! Payne.
"Home, Sweet Home," with Variations. Bunner.
Homecoming. Thompson.
Hometown Elegy. Fraser.
I've Got a Home in That Rock. Patterson.
Just Passing Through. Roberts.
Oh, Joyous House. Janzen.
On the Wide Heath. Millay.
One Home. Stafford.

**Homer**
Cure for Poetry, A. *Unknown.*
Development. Browning.
On First Looking into Chapman's Homer. Keats.
To a Friend. Arnold.
To Homer. Keats.

**Homesickness**
Home, Boys, Home.  *Unknown.*
Homesick.  Lasker-Schüler.
I Wonder How My Home Is.  *Unknown.*
*John B.* Sails.  *Unknown.*
Lament of the Banana Man.  Jones.
Les Vaches.  Clough.
Morning Chores.  Heynen.
Outcast.  McKay.
Sailor's Song, A.  Harris.
Tropics in New York, The.  McKay.
Un Canadien Errant (An Exiled Canadian).  *Unknown.*
Unreturning Native, The.  Dowling.

**Homesteaders**
Little Old Sod Shanty.  *Unknown.*
Starving to Death on a Government Claim.  *Unknown.*

**Homosexuality and Homosexuals**
Art of Enforced Deprivation, The.  Alta.
Christopher St. Liberation Day, June 28, 1970.  Winant.
Coming Out.  Lapidus.
First Time, The.  White.
For Freckle-faced Gerald.  Knight.
Homosexual Sonnets.  Pitchford.
Homosexuality.  O'Hara.
Island of Giglio.  Norse.
Lesbian Poem.  Morgan.
Note to a New Lesbian.  M. Shelley.
Pair of muscular calves, A.  *Fr.* You Must Have Been a Sensational Baby.  Norse.
Playboy of the Demi-World: 1938, The.  Plomer.
Poem to My New Jacket.  Winant.
Song: "Love a woman? You're an ass!"  Earl of Rochester.
This Form of Life Needs Sex.  Ginsberg.
Torso, The: Passages 18.  Duncan.
Wholesome.  Meredith.
Words for Hart Crane.  Lowell.

**Honey**
Sing a Song of Honey.  Todd.
Socratic.  Doolittle ("H.D.").
Wild Honey.  Schneider.

**Honey Eaters**
Nesting Time.  Stewart.

**Honeysuckle**
Wild Honey Suckle, The.  Freneau.

**Honor**
Honour ("Ambitious sir, take heed!").  Beaumont.
To Lucasta, Going to the Wars.  Lovelace.
Trail All Your Pikes.  Winchilsea.

**Hood, Thomas**
Elegy on Thomas Hood.  Fagg.

**Hope**
Dark Testament.  Murray.
Eagle Feather IV.  George.
Faith, Hope and Charity.  Guarini.
Hope.  Anderson.
Hope.  Herbert.
Hope is a strange invention.  Dickinson.
Hope is a subtle glutton.  Dickinson.
Hope is the thing with feathers.  Dickinson.
Hopes, The.  Fringell.
On Himself, upon Hearing What Was His Sentence.  Graham.
On Hope, by Way of Question and Answer between Abraham Cowley and Richard Crashaw.  Crashaw.
Plan.  McKuen.
Say Not the Struggle Naught Availeth.  Clough.
To Hope.  Keats.
Visionary Hope, The.  Coleridge.
Work Without Hope.  Coleridge.

**Hopi Indians**
Butterfly Maidens.  Lahpu.
Death in the Desert, A.  Tomlinson.
Flute Song: "Hail, fathers hail."  *Unknown.*

Hopi Lament.  Beghtol.
Hopi Prayer.  Beghtol.
Hopi Woman.  Spencer.

**Hopkins, Gerard Manley**
Breakfast with Gerard Manley Hopkins.  Brode.

**Horace**
To Horace.  Lake.

**Horatius**
Horatius.  *Fr.* Lays of Ancient Rome.  Macaulay.

**Hornsby, Rogers**
Obit Page.  Blackburn.

**Horse Racing**
At Galway Races.  Yeats.
Day Alvero Pineda Was Killed, The.  Koertge.
Day at the Races, A.  Phillips.
Grog-An'-Grumble Steeplechase.  Lawson.
Gwine to Run All Night; or, De Camptown Races.  Foster.
Hot Day at the Races.  Raworth.
Morning Workout.  Deutsch.
Old Stomping Grounds: The Half-Mile Track.  *Fr.* Desperado.  Taylor.
Placing a $2 Bet for a Man Who Will Never Go to the Horse Races Any More.  Wakoski.
To a Race Horse at Ascot.  Palen.

**Horse Shows**
Pliny Jane.  Luton.

**Horseback Riding**
Billy Could Ride.  Riley.
Flying Changes.  Wood.
Galloping.  Chitty.
Gentled Beast, The.  Laing.
Haiku, for Cinnamon.  Chaffin.
Horse.  Harrison.
Indecision Means Flexibility.  Abhau.
New Skills.  Nye.
Once Upon a Nag.  McMahon.
Riding.  Grossman.
Riding Lesson.  Taylor.
Tallyho-Hum.  Nash.

**Horseradish**
Consumer's Report.  Kennedy.

**Horses**
All through the Rains.  Snyder.
At Grass.  Larkin.
Birth of the Foal.  Juhász.
Black Horse Rider, The.  Loving.
Blessing, The.  Wright.
Blood Horse, The.  "Cornwall."
Broncho That Would Not Be Broken, The.  Lindsay.
Cariboo Horses, The.  Purdy.
Colt, The.  Knister.
Cow-ponies.  Lesemann.
Daniel Webster's Horses.  Coatsworth.
Dead Ponies.  Chamberlain.
Distant Runners, The.  Van Doren.
Draft Horse, The.  Frost.
Fly-Away Horse, The.  Field.
Foal.  Watkins.
Focus.  Norris.
Ghostly Story.  Acorn.
Glory Trail, The.  Clark.
Going Away.  Stanford.
Golden Stallion, The.  Thompson.
Gun Teams.  Frankau.
Horse.  Blasing.
Horse, The.  Coppard.
Horse.  Harrison.
Horse, The.  Merwin.
Horse, The.  Ponge.
Horse.  *Fr.* A Bestiary.  Rexroth.
Horse, The.  Smith.
Horses, The.  Hughes.

Horses. Kipling.
Horses, The ("Barely a twelvemonth after"). Muir.
Horses ("Those lumbering horses in the steady plough"). Muir.
Horses. Thomas.
Horses. Wellesley.
Horses Aboard. Hardy.
Horses Chawin' Hay. Garland.
Horses Graze. Brooks.
Horses on the Camargue. Campbell.
How We Drove the Trotter. Goodge.
Imperiously he leaps, he neighs, he bounds. *Fr.* Venus and
    Adonis. Shakespeare.
Incognito. Manifold.
Jack and His Pony, Tom. Belloc.
Kentucky Belle. Woolson.
Lovers, The. Comfort.
Lyarde Is an Old Horse. *Unknown.*
Mare. Thurman.
Mare, The. Watkins.
Mountain Corral. Sorrells.
My Fairy Steed. Benét.
My Horse, Amanda: The Summer of the Watergate Hearings.
    Kumin.
Names of Horses. Hall.
Old Gray Mare. *Unknown.*
Old Poulter's Mare. *Unknown.*
Old Timbrook Blues. *Unknown.*
Orchard. Stone.
Paiute Ponies. Barnes.
Palomino Stallion, The. Nowlan.
Pinto, The. Wister.
Pony Blues, The. *Unknown.*
Racing-Man, The. Herbert.
Rain-In-the-Face. Grow.
Riding in the Rain. Kumin.
Runaway, The. Frost.
Say This of Horses. Moody.
Slade's Anatomy of the Horse. Slade.
Stallion, The. *Fr.* Song of Myself. Whitman.
Stewball. *Unknown.*
Strawberry Roan, The. Fletcher.
Strawberry Roan, The. *Unknown.*
Tam Pierce. *Unknown.*
Tête-à-Tête. Honig.
Thracian Filly, The. Anacreon.
Three Colts Exercising in a Six-Acre. Campbell.
Three Ponies. Guiterman.
Timothy. James.
Title of a Swift Horse. *Unknown.*
To the Four Courts, Please. Stephens.
Todd. Conn.
War Horse, The. Boland.
White Horse, The. Lawrence.
White Stallion, The. Owen.
White Steed of the Prairies, The. Barber.
Zebra Dun, The. *Unknown.*
*Poetry of Horses, The* (PH). William Cole, ed.
**Hospitals**
And This Is My Father. Grapes.
And We Are Strangers to Each Other. Schechter.
Building, The. Larkin.
C44. Kent.
Corwin Psychiatric Ward, 1972. Dilsaver.
Cottage Hospital, The. Betjeman.
Death of the Sailor's Wife, The. Barton.
Dedication for a Building. Dugan.
Far Cry After a Close Call, A. Howard.
Flight. Whitman.
Ford Hospital. Reed.
Girl Clings to Coma. Mulac.
Hospital, The. Kavanagh.
Hospital. Shapiro.

Hospital Care Authorization. Gross.
Hospital Window, The. Dickey.
In Hospital. Flecker.
In Hospital. Henley.
In the Convalescent Hospital. Pumphrey.
Katrina. Dawe.
Lullaby. Sexton.
Malice of Innocence, The. Levertov.
Microcosmos. Miles.
Operation, The. Snodgrass.
Polar Bear. Guthrie.
Recovery Room, The: Lying-In. Chasin.
St. Vincent's. Merwin.
Saratoga Ending. Kees.
Semi-Private Room. Nowlan.
Slipping out of Intensive Care. Trefethen.
Stones, The. Plath.
Surgical Ward. Auden.
Them, Crying. Dickey.
Transfusion. Moore.
Tulips. Plath.
Visiting Hour. MacCaig.
**Hotels**
At the End of the Affair. Kumin.
Cairo Hotel. Rowland.
Chelsea, The. Walcott.
Delirium in Vera Cruz. Lowry.
Dolgelley Hotel, The. Hughes.
Gramercy Park Hotel. Smith.
Noises in the Dark. Lochhead.
Stirling's Hotel. *Unknown.*
Up-Hill. Rossetti.
**Houdini, Harry**
Harry Houdini, the Hippodrome, New York, January 7, 1918.
    Hilberry.
**Houses**
Buildings and Grounds. Taylor.
Deserted House, The. M. Coleridge.
Haunted House, The. Hood.
House. Clark.
House, The. Williams.
House on the Hill, The. Robinson.
Invocation: "Silent, about-to-be-parted-from house." Levertov.
Living There. Dickey.
Music in an Empty House. Davies.
My Father's House. Orlen.
My House. Stevenson.
New House, The. Thomas.
Poem for Valerie. Breit.
Selling the House. McPherson.
Song for a Little House. Morley.
Thanksgiving to God, for His House, A. Herrick.
To My Friend G. N., from Wrest. Carew.
To Saxham. Carew.
*See also* **Home.**
**Housman, Alfred Edward**
Mr. Housman's Message. Pound.
Two Poems (after A. E. Housman). Kingsmill.
**Hudson, Henry**
Weepers Tower in Amsterdam, The. Goodman.
**Hudson River**
Egyptian Passage, An. Weiss.
Lordly Hudson, The. Goodman.
Mouth of the Hudson, The. Lowell.
Scene on the Banks of the Hudson, A. Bryant.
**Hughes, Langston**
Do Nothing Till You Hear from Me. Henderson.
For All Things Black and Beautiful. Rivers.
Langston. Evans.
Langston Blues. Randall.
Langston Hughes. Blockcolski.
Reading Walt Whitman. Forbes.

Rhetoric of Langston Hughes, The. Danner.

**Hume, David**

On the Author of the *Treatise of Human Nature*. Beattie.

**Humility**

Nudus Redibo. Flatman.

Nulla Fides. Carey.

On the Vanity of Earthly Greatness. Guiterman.

Resolve, The. Chudleigh.

To Show How Humble. *Unknown.*

**Hummingbirds**

Container, The. Corman.

Hummingbird. Clarkson.

Humming Bird, The. Kemp.

Hummingbird. Lawrence.

Hummingbird. Littlebird.

Ritual, The. Gwillim.

Route of evanescence, A. Dickinson.

**Humorous Verse**

*Faber Book of Comic Verse, The* (FaBoCo). Michael Roberts and Janet Adam Smith, eds.

*Faber Book of Nonsense Verse, The* (FaBoNo). Geoffrey Grigson, ed.

*New Oxford Book of English Light Verse, The* (NOBL). Kingsley Amis, ed.

*Oh, Such Foolishness!* (OSF). William Cole, ed.

*Oxford Book of American Light Verse, The* (OBAL). William Harmon, ed.

*Poems One Line and Longer* (POL). William Cole, ed.

*Speak Roughly to Your Little Boy* (SpRo). Myra Cohn Livingston, ed.

**Hundred Years War**

Ballad of Agincourt, The. Drayton.

King Henry the Fifth before Agincourt. *Fr.* Henry V. Shakespeare.

**Hunger**

Hunger. Binyon.

Hunger. *Unknown.*

Hunger and Thirst. Bishop.

Nothing to Lose. Kalar.

Poem: "Moving thru the drifting mist." Pillin.

To an American Workman Dying of Starvation. Taggard.

**Hunt, Leigh**

Addressed to Haydon ("Great spirits are now on earth sojourning"). Keats.

Written on the Day That Mr. Leigh Left Prison. Keats.

**Hunting and Hunters**

After the Night Hunt. Dickey.

Ageing Hunter, The. Avane.

All in Green Went My Love Riding. Cummings.

Ballad of Red Fox, The. LaFollette.

Beagles. Rodgers.

Bear, The. Kinnell.

Bear Hunting. Aua.

Blackwater Mountain. Wright.

Buffalo Skinners, The. *Unknown.*

Chase, The. Cunningham.

Coon Song. Ammons.

Day of the Wolf. Wilson.

Decoys, The. Auden.

Deer Hunt. Jerome.

Deer Lay Down Their Bones, The. Jeffers.

Dream 2: Brian the Still-Hunter. Atwood.

Duck. Donaghy.

First Blood. Stallworthy.

For the Opening of the Hunting Season. Bishop.

Gallows, The. Thomas.

Hunt. Childers.

Hunt, The. De la Mare.

Hunt, The. Halpern.

Hunt, The. Kent.

Hunt, The. *Fr.* Windsor Forest. Pope.

Hunter, The. Nash.

Hunter of the Prairies, The. Bryant.

Hunter Trials. Betjeman.

Hunting Fragment. Lawless.

Hunting Song. Finkel.

Hunting Song. Fowler.

Hunting with My Father. Absher.

Huntsmen, The. De la Mare.

Hymn to the Air Spirit. *Unknown.*

I Saw a Jolly Hunter. Causley.

In Autumn. Howes.

January: Cover Shooting. *Fr.* An Idler's Calender. Blunt.

Killing, The. Smith.

Kilruddery Hunt, The. Mozeen.

Lion Hunts. Beer.

Listening to Foxhounds. Dickey.

Long Hunter, The. *Fr.* Inland Passages. Berry.

Lord Epsom. Belloc.

Lost Deer, The. Bruchac.

Magic Words for Hunting Seal. *Unknown.*

Man, The. McCombs.

March Hares. De la Mare.

Moschus Moschiferus. Hope.

Old Squire, The. Blunt.

On Dressing to Go Hunting. *Unknown.*

Opening Day. Severy.

Partridges. Masefield.

Peace. Bukowski.

Petty Murder. MacLean.

Poacher, The. *Unknown.*

Rabbit, The. Davies.

Rabbit Hunter, The. Frost.

Raid, The. Everson.

Rainbow. Huff.

Revenge of the Hunted. Ford.

Runnable Stag, A. Davidson.

Shoot, The. *Fr.* Windsor Forest. Pope.

Sportsman, The. McCord.

Springer Mountain. Dickey.

Stag-Hunt. *Unknown.*

Summons, The. Dickey.

This Poem Is for Deer. *Fr.* Myths and Texts: Hunting. Snyder.

To Christ Our Lord. Kinnell.

Tracking Rabbits: Night. Barnes.

Trapped Hare, The. Dowling.

Ulivfak's Song of the Caribou. *Unknown.*

Walrus Hunting. Aua.

Winter: East Anglia. Blunden.

**Hurdy-Gurdies**

Lines on Hearing the Organ. Calverley.

**Huron, Lake**

Huron, The. Herschberger.

**Hurricanes**

Hurricane, The. Bryant.

Hurricane, The. Crane.

Hurricane, The. Freneau.

Hurricane. MacLeish.

Wasn't That a Mighty Storm? *Unknown.*

**Husbands**

Female of the Species Is Hardier Than the Male, The. McGinley.

Henpecked Husband, A. *Unknown.*

Husband with No Courage in Him, The. *Unknown.*

Husbands. Terris.

Prowling the Ridge. Minty.

Slice of Wedding Cake, A. Graves.

To My Dear and Loving Husband. Bradstreet.

What I Want in a Husband Besides a Mustache. Wakoski.

*See also* **Marriage.**

**Hussey, Margaret**

To Mistress Margaret Hussey. Skelton.

**Hyde, Douglas**

Burial of an Irish President. Clarke.

**Hyenas**
Happy Hyena, The. Wells.
Hyaenas, The. Kipling.
Hyena. Muske.

**Hymns**
*American Hymns, Old and New* (AH). Albert Christ-Janer,
Charles W. Hughes, *and* Carleton Sprague Smith, eds.
*Best Loved Songs and Hymns* (BLSH). James Morehead *and*
Albert Morehead, eds.

**Hypochondria**
How Jack Found that Beans May Go Back on a Chap. Carryl.

**Hypocrisy**
Address to the Unco Guid, or the Rigidly Righteous. Burns.
American Heartbreak. Hughes.
Cambridge Ladies Who Live in Furnished Souls, The.
Cummings.
Domestic Asides; or, Truth in Parentheses. Hood.
Ethics for Everyman. Woddis.
Holy Willie's Prayer. Burns.
Hypocrisy will serve as well. Butler.
Hypocrite Women. Levertov.
In Westminster Abbey. Betjeman.
Johnson's Cabinet Watched by Ants. Bly.
Karma. Robinson.
Miss America. Sadowski.
On Flunking a Nice Boy Out of School. Ciardi.
She Proves the Inconsistency of the Desires and Criticism of
Men Who Accuse Women of What They Themselves Cause.
Juana Ines de la Cruz.
Terrible People, The. Nash.
Two-Faced Too. *Unknown.*
Vicar of Bray, The. *Unknown.*
We Wear the Mask. Dunbar.

**Hysteria**
Miracle Cure. Lowbury.


# I


**Ibises**
Ibis, The. Welch.

**Icarus**
I, Icarus. Nowlan.
Icarus. Field.
Icarus. Iremonger.
Icarus. Layton.
Icarus. Spender.
Landscape with the Fall of Icarus. Williams.
Lines on Brueghel's *Icarus.* Hamburger.
Now in this while gan Daedalus a wearinesse to take. *Fr.*
Metamorphoses. Ovid.
To a Friend Whose Work Has Come to Triumph. Sexton.
Waiting for Icarus. Rukeyser.

**Ice**
Fire and Ice. Frost.
Ice. Driscoll.
Ice Castle, The. Harris.
Icehouse in Summer, The. Nemerov.

**Ice-Skating.** *See* **Skating and Skaters.**

**Icebergs**
Berg, The. Melville.
Convergence of the Twain, The. Hardy.
Icebergs. *Fr.* The Rime of the Ancient Mariner. Coleridge.
*Titanic* Blues. *Unknown.*

**Iceland**
Iceland First Seen. Morris.
Journey to Iceland. Auden.

**Idaho**

Chronicle. Dorn.
Idaho. French.
Way Out in Idaho. *Unknown.*

**Identity Crisis**
After Love. Kumin.
Agony, An. As Now. Baraka.
Being Somebody. Honig.
Crazy Soliloquy. Kudaka.
Dark Reflections. Bohanon.
Give Me Five. Harris.
Had I but gone some forty days or more. Mitchell.
Heartblow: Messages. Harper.
High. Mbembe.
January of 75, The. Lau.
Main Problem in Portraiture, The. Ritchie.
My Son. Stone.
Name Giveaway. George.
Roots. Sutton.
Self-Dependence. Arnold.
To a Family Man in His Family Room. Daniell.
Vacancy. Gioseffi.
Woman at the Washington Zoo, The. Jarrell.

**Iguanas**
Royal Iguanas, The. Dehn.

**Illinois**
Elanoy. *Unknown.*
First Song. Kinnell.
Illinois Farmer. Sandburg.
Winter 1970, Fox River, Illinois. Salisbury.

**Illness**
As I lie alone. *Unknown.*
Bout with Burning. Miller.
Fever 103°. Plath.
Flat One, A. Snodgrass.
For Kenneth and Miriam Patchen. Young.
Gastric. C. T.
Hymn to God, My God, in My Sickness. Donne.
Judgment, The. Spivack.
Katrina. Dawe.
Land of Counterpane, The. Stevenson.
Litany in Time of Plague, A. Nashe.
Memphis Minnie-Jitis Blues. *Unknown.*
My Daughter Very Ill. Goodman.
Prayer in Sickness, A. "Cornwall."
Song of Sickness, A. Tangikuku.
To Mary. Cowper.
Visionary Hope, The. Coleridge.
Watch, The. Cornford.

**Imagination**
Bedpost, The. Graves.
Block City. Stevenson.
Centaur, The. Swenson.
Closet. Thurman.
Digging for China. Wilbur.
Fancy. Keats.
I saw in a poet's song. Drinkwater.
Little Exercise. Bishop.
Lucy in the Sky With Diamonds. Lennon *and* McCartney.
Mental Traveller, The. Blake.
Ode to Fancy. Freneau.
Ode to Fancy. Warton.
Poem: "O who can ever praise enough." Auden.
Sand Hill Road. Grosser.
Settlers, The. Hemschemeyer.
Sick Child, A. Jarrell.
This Last Pain. Empson.
Warning to Children. Graves.
Weary with toil, I haste me to my bed. *Fr.* Sonnets.
Shakespeare.
When Mother Reads Aloud. *Unknown.*
When the Mississippi Flowed in Indiana. Lindsay.
Woman with Finger. McKeown.

Yachting in Arkansas. Weeden.
**Immigrants**
  Canadian Boat-Song. *Unknown.*
  Elegy for Bella, Sarah, Rosie and All The Others. Dorman.
  Europe and America. Ignatow.
  Exile. Bloch.
  Feliks Skrzynecki. Skrzynecki.
  Immigrants. Frost.
  In Exile. Lazarus.
  In the Gazebo. Flocos.
  Lament of the Banana Man. Jones.
  Migrant Hostel. Skrzynecki.
  My Polish Grandma. Field.
  New Colossus, The. Lazarus.
  No Irish Need Apply. *Unknown.*
  Prospective Immigrants Please Note. Rich.
  Schwiegermutterlieder. Harrison.
  Speech for the Repeal of the McCarran Act. Wilbur.
  Stanzas on the Emigration to America, and Peopling the
    Western Country. Freneau.
**Immortality**
  Arjuna said:/ How shall I in battle against Bhisma. *Fr.* The
    Bhagavad-Gita. *Unknown.*
  Because I could not stop for death. Dickinson.
  Death Be Not Proud. *Fr.* Holy Sonnets. Donne.
  Exceptional. Lewis.
  His Immortality. Hardy.
  Mohini Chatterjee. Yeats.
  Not marble, nor the gilded monuments. *Fr.* Sonnets.
    Shakespeare.
  O May I Join the Choir Invisible. "Eliot."
  Ode: "Bards of passion and of mirth." Keats.
  Ode: Intimations of Immortality from Recollections of Early
    Childhood. Wordsworth.
  On the Beach, at Night. Whitman.
  One day I wrote her name upon the strand. *Fr.* Amoretti.
    Spenser.
  Poem in Three Parts. Bly.
  Ponce de León: A Morning Walk. Young.
  Sailing to Byzantium. Yeats.
  This Monument Will Outlast. *Fr.* Odes. Horace.
  To Inez Milholland. Millay.
  To the Stone-cutters. Jeffers.
  Whilst thus my pen strives to eternize thee. *Fr.* Idea.
    Drayton.
  Whispers of Immortality. Eliot.
  Wish, A. Kemble.
**Imperialism**
  Imperial. *Fr.* Album Leaves. Fairburn.
  Recessional. Kipling.
  Remember Suez? Mitchell.
  Training. Enright.
  White Man's Burden, The. Kipling.
**Impotence**
  Against an Old Lecher. Harington.
  Carnation, The. Hannigan.
  Disappointment, The. Behn.
  Imperfect Enjoyment, The. Earl of Rochester.
  Impotence. Bell.
  Maimed Debauchee, The. Earl of Rochester.
  To the Tune "Red Embroidered Shoes." Huang O.
**Independence**
  Declaration of Independence. Gibbs.
  Solitary, The. Teasdale.
**Independence Day.** *See* **Fourth of July.**
**India**
  Patna-Benares Express. Ginsberg.
  Phrases for Everyday Use by the British in India. Daniel.
  Relief of Lucknow, The. R. T. S. Lowell.
  This Landscape, These People. Ghose.
**Indian Ocean**
  Nights on the Indian Ocean. Rice.

**Indian Pipe (flower)**
  In Shining Groups. Higginson.
**Indian Summer**
  Indian Summer. Burr.
  Indian Summer Day on the Prairie, An. Lindsay.
  Indian Summer: Vermont. Stevenson.
  Pyre of My Indian Summer, The. Leib.
**Indiana**
  Anderson, Indiana. White.
  Fort Wayne, Indiana 1964. Lewis.
  July In Indiana. Fitzgerald.
  Memo to the 21st Century. Appleman.
  Midwest. Nims.
**Indianapolis, Indiana**
  Home in Indianapolis. Pflum.
**Indians, American**
  Alice Corbin Is Gone. Sandburg.
  American Indian, The. *Unknown.*
  America's Wounded Knee. George.
  Arrowy Dreams. Bynner.
  Ask the Mountains. George.
  At Grand Canyon's Edge. Ray.
  Ballad of Ira Hayes. La Farge.
  Bar's Fight, August 28, 1746. Terry.
  Bear Paw. Hugo.
  Blackfeet, Blood and Piegan Hunters. Welch.
  Boast not proud English, of thy birth and blood. Williams.
  Broken Arrowheads at Chilmark, Martha's Vineyard. Todd.
  Centenary Ode, A: Inscribed to Little Crow, Leader of the Sioux
    Rebellion in Minnesota, 1862. Wright.
  Choctaw Chief Helps Plan a Festival. Barnes.
  Christmas Comes to Moccasin Flat. Welch.
  Citizens' Complaint, The. Evans.
  Concealment, The: Ishi, the Last Wild Indian. Stafford.
  Crazy Horse Returns to South Dakota. Elliott.
  Custer Lives in Humbolt County. Hale.
  Dakota: October, 1822, Hunkpapa Warrior. Taylor.
  Dead in Bloody Snow. Le Sueur.
  Driving Through the Pima Indian Reservation. Cook.
  End of the Indian Poems, The. Plumly.
  From his wanderings far to eastward. *Fr.* The Song of
    Hiawatha. Longfellow.
  Grass on the Mountain, The. *Unknown.*
  Harlem, Montana: Just Off the Reservation. Welch.
  Ignacio, Colorado, for You That Time. Harjo.
  In My First Hard Springtime. Welch.
  In the Oregon Country. Stafford.
  Indian at the Burial-Place of His Fathers, An. Bryant.
  Indian Burying Ground, The. Freneau.
  Indian Convert, The. Freneau.
  Indian Graves at Jocko. Hugo.
  Indian Graveyard, The. Weeks.
  Indian Guys at the Bar. Ortiz.
  Indian Painting, Probably Paiute, in a Cave Near Madras,
    Oregon. Ramsey.
  Indian School. Russell.
  Indian Woman's Death-Song. Hemans.
  Indians, The. Fowler.
  Inscription: "Eagle, stooping from yon snow-blown peaks, The."
    Whittier.
  Kansa, The. Contoski.
  Lament of the Cherokee Reservation Indian, The. Loudermilk.
  Landscape, The. Ray.
  Memorial Ode. Buck.
  Monument in Bone. George.
  Moon of Huckleberries. George.
  My Country 'Tis of Thy People You're Dying. Sainte-Marie.
  Navajo Poem. Woessner.
  New Mexican Mountain. Jeffers.
  Night at the Napi in Browning, A. Hugo.
  Now Everyone is Writing Poems About Indians. Tipton.
  Now That the Buffalo's Gone. Sainte-Marie.

Now What Good That Do? Lewis.
Powwow. Snodgrass.
Prairies, The. Bryant.
Prophecy of King Tammany, The. Freneau.
Red Man of the South, The. Snow.
Red Man of the West, The. Snow.
Report to Crazy Horse. Stafford.
Returned to Say. Stafford.
Road outside the window was "our," The. *Fr.* Letter to an Imaginary Friend. McGrath.
Rosebud. Anderson.
Santo Domingo Corn Dance. R. P. Dickey.
Self-Portrait. Romero.
Self-Portrait: Microcosm, or, Song of Mixed-Blood. Conley.
Shaman Songs 12. Fowler.
Sioux, The. *Unknown.*
Sioux Indians, The. *Unknown.*
Sisseton Indian Reservation, The. Lyons.
Sky House for Crazy Horse, Chaka and Geronimo. Storey.
Spontaneous Requiem for the American Indian. Corso.
Spruce. George.
Vanishing Point: Urban Indian. Rose.
Variation. Wild.
Way and the Way Things Are, The. NorthSun.
We Are a People. Henson.
White Bear. Griffin.
Yaqui Women: Three Generations. Casillas.
*Carriers of the Dream Wheel* (CDW). Duane Niatum, ed.
*Voices from Wah'Kon-Tah* (VW). Robert K. Dodge *and* Joseph B. McCullough, eds.
*Voices of the Rainbow: Contemporary Poetry by American Indians* (VoR). Kenneth Rosen, ed.

**Individualism**
Big I, The. Wheelock.
Cross Fox. Bruchac.
Dual Site, The. Hamburger.
For My Son. Brownjohn.
I Don't Care. Lenox.
Letter to a Young Friend. Nowlan.
Ode: Inscribed to W. H. Channing. Emerson.
On Myselfe. Countess of Winchilsea.
Self-Dependence. Arnold.
Silence. Moore.
Solitary, The. Teasdale.

**Industrial Revolution**
Factory Girl's Come-All-Ye, The. *Unknown.*
Art on the Swing-Shift, Truck Assembly. Johnson.

**Infants.** *See* **Babies.**

**Infidelity**
Adultery. Dickey.
Adultery. Dugan.
Adultery at the Plaza. Thompson.
Ballade Against Woman Inconstant, A. Chaucer.
Bird on Nellie's Hat, The. Lamb.
Black Snake. *Unknown.*
Bold Trooper, The. *Unknown.*
Chandler's Wife, The. *Unknown.*
Clever Skipper, The. *Unknown.*
Constant Lover, The. Suckling.
Don't Fish in My Sea. *Unknown.*
Early in the Spring. *Unknown.*
Faithless Sally Brown. Hood.
Faithless Wife, The. García Lorca.
First Lawcase, The. *Unknown.*
Good Bye, My Lady Love. Howard.
Grey Cock, The. *Unknown.*
Gypsy Davy. *Unknown.*
Gypsy Laddie, The. *Unknown.*
I'm Gonna Move to the Outskirts of Town. *Unknown.*
Little Cheat, A. *Unknown.*
Little Musgrave and Lady Barnard. *Unknown.*
Little Sparrow. *Unknown.*

Lyricism of the Weak, The. Viereck.
Matty Groves. *Unknown.*
Message, The. Donne.
Mind Reader Blues. *Unknown.*
Modern Love. Cunningham.
Newcomer's Wife, The. Hardy.
Nighthawk, The. Gaughan.
Of a Heroical Answer of a Great Romantic Lady to Her Husband. Harington.
Old Devil. *Unknown.*
Old Farmer and His Young Wife, The. *Unknown.*
Only Jealousy of Emer, The. *Unknown.*
Our Goodman. *Unknown.*
Peach Orchard Mama. *Unknown.*
Pneumonia Blues. *Unknown.*
Poem: "When he came home." Sanchez.
Reaping. Lowell.
Song: "Go and catch a falling star." Donne.
Song of Longing. *Unknown.*
Take Back Your Gold. Pritzkow.
Temperaments, The. Pound.
They Flee from Me. Wyatt.
Thursday. Millay.
To His Mistress. Ovid.
Trail to Mexico, The. *Unknown.*
Two or Three a Recipe to Make a Cuckold. Pope.
Unfaithful Married Woman, The. García Lorca.
When Daisies Pied and Violets Blue. *Fr.* Love's Labour's Lost. Shakespeare.
Whoopee Blues. *Unknown.*
Why So Pale and Wan. Suckling.
You All Know the Story of the Other Woman. Sexton.

**Inflation**
Cost-of-Living Mother Goose, The. Richardson.

**Ingres, Jean Auguste Dominique**
For "Ruggiero and Angelica" by Ingres. Rossetti.

**Injustice**
Juanito's Blues. Mberi.
Patchwork. Mabuza.
Spokane Falls 1874. George.
Tired with all these, for restful death I cry. Sonnets, LXVI. Shakespeare.

**Innisfree, Ireland**
Lake Isle of Innisfree, The. Yeats.

**Inns.** *See* **Hotels.**

**Insanity.** *See* **Madness; Mental Illness.**

**Insects**
Brown Bug, The. Brown.
Considerable Speck, A. Frost.
Creatures. Kumin.
Depressed by a Book of Bad Poetry, I Walk Toward an Unused Pasture and Invite the Insects to Join Me. Wright.
Minimal, The. Roethke.
Nameless One, A. Avison.
Take thy hat, my little Laura. *Fr.* The Insect Hunters. Newman.
There Ain't No Bugs on Me. *Unknown.*

**Insomnia**
For the Sleepless. Dunn.
Insomnia. Zelvin.
Verses Written During a Sleepless Night. Pushkin.
Winter Insomnia. Carver.

**Insurance**
Injury to Insured. Daniel.
To My Daughter, 1936. Taggard.

**Intellect**
Alma; or, The Progress of the Mind. Prior.
Blue Swallows, The. Nemerov.
Explorer, The. Ignatow.
Hymn to Intellectual Beauty. Shelley.
In a Hard Intellectual Light. Eberhart.

Mind. Wilbur.
Mind, Intractable Thing, The. Moore.
Mind Is an Ancient and Famous Capital, The. Schwartz.
Mind Is an Enchanting Thing, The. Moore.
My Brain. Laurance.
My Mind to Me a Kingdom Is. Dyer.
On the Birth of His Son. Su Tung-Po.
Two Minds. Teasdale.

**Inventors**
Darius Green and His Flying-Machine. Trowbridge.
Invention of the Telephone, The. Klappert.

**Iowa**
Iowa. Browne.
Stopping Near Highway 80. Ray.
Touring the Hawkeye State. Gildner.

**Iphigenia**
Victim of Aulis, The. Abse.

**Ireland**
Antrim. Jeffers.
Bard of Armagh, The. *Unknown.*
Battle of the Boyne, The. Blacker.
Bogland. Heaney.
Bold Fenian Men, The. *Unknown.*
Carrickfergus. MacNeice.
Change, The. O'Bruadair.
Clay is the word and clay is the flesh. *Fr.* The Great Hunger. Kavanagh.
Dublin Made Me. MacDonagh.
Dunlavin Green. *Unknown.*
Easter 1916. Yeats.
Eire. O'Bruadair.
Erin Go Braugh! *Unknown.*
Famine Song. *Unknown.*
First Invasion of Ireland, The. Montague.
Go to Old Ireland. *Unknown.*
Grafted Tongue, A. Montague.
Harp That Once through Tara's Halls, The. Moore.
Hibernia. Howard-Jones.
I Am of Ireland. *Unknown.*
"I Am of Ireland." Yeats.
In Ruin Reconciled. De Vere.
Inis Fal. O'Rahilly.
Ireland, Ireland. Newbolt.
Ireland Never Was Contented. Landor.
Ireland with Emily. Betjeman.
Irish Airman Foresees His Death, An. Yeats.
Irish Cliffs of Moher, The. Stevens.
Irish Dancer, The. *Unknown.*
Irish Language, The. Mangan.
Johnson's Motor Car. *Unknown.*
Kathaleen Ny-Houlahan. Mangan.
Kennedy. Heffernan.
Kevin Barry: Died for Ireland, 1st November, 1920. *Unknown.*
Kilcash. *Unknown.*
Lament for the Death of Thomas Davis. Ferguson.
Lilli Burlero. *Unknown.*
Municipal Gallery Revisited, The. Yeats.
My Son, Forsake Your Art. O'Hefferman.
New Style, The. O'Bruadair.
Old Orange Flute. *Unknown.*
On some island I long to be. Saint Columcille.
On the Irish Club. Swift.
Orange Lily, The. *Unknown.*
Our Stars come from Ireland. Stevens.
Parnell. Yeats.
Passage at Night—The Blaskets. Flower.
Pastoral Ballad by John Bull, A. Moore.
Patriot Game, The. Behan.
Requiem for the Croppies. Heaney.
Rising of the Moon, The. *Unknown.*

Rose Tree, The. Yeats.
September 1913. Yeats.
Shan Van Vocht, The. *Unknown.*
Shancoduff. Kavanagh.
Spenser's Ireland. Moore.
This Night Sees Ireland Desolate. MacMarcius.
Time of Change, A. O'Rahilly.
To Colman Returning. Colman.
To Ireland in the Coming Times. Yeats.
Wearing of the Green, The. *Unknown.*
Where the River Shannon Flows. Russell.
Young Fenians, The. Fallon.
*Contemporary Irish Poetry* (CIP). Anthony Bradley, ed.
*Irish Poets, 1924-1974* (IPM). David Marcus, ed.
*Poems from Ireland* (PFIr). William Cole, comp.

**Iris (flower)**
Iris. Williams.

**Irish**
Ballad of Ballymote, The. Gallagher.
Barney McGee. Hovey.
Cult of the Celtic, The. Deane.
Finnegan's Wake. *Unknown.*
Gaeltacht. Hutchinson.
Insular Celts, The. Carson.
Irish Antiquities. Moore.
Irishman in Coventry, An. Hewitt.
No Irish Need Apply. *Unknown.*
Spenser's Ireland. Moore.

**Iron**
Red Iron Ore. *Unknown.*

**Ironsides (ship).** *See* **Constitution.**

**Isaac**
Akedah, The. Megged.
Isaac. Guri.
Isaac. Holtz.
Isaac. Jacobs.
Parable of the Old Man and the Young, The. Owen.
Sacrifice, The. Bloch.
Story of Isaac, The. Cohen.

**Ishtar**
Song for Ishtar. Levertov.

**Islands**
By Ferry to the Island. Smith.
Island, The. Thomson.
Islands. Rukeyser.
Lake Isle of Innisfree, The. Yeats.
Letter from an Island. Brinnin.
On This Island. Auden.

**Israel**
At Masada. Neufeld
Hear, O Israel! Spire.
Israel. Shapiro.
Reclaimed Area. Silkin.
Temple, The. Kahn.
Those Zionists. Del Monte.

**Italian-Ethiopian War**
Pacelli and the Ethiop. Cassity.

**Italy**
Four Postcards from Italy. Andrews.
Good-Bye to the Mezzogiorno. Auden.
Italia, Io Ti Saluto. C. Rossetti.
Italy Versus England. *Fr.* Beppo. Byron.
Poem: "So many pigeons at Columbus." Gregor.
Super Flumina Babylonis. Swinburne.

**Ivry-La-Bataille, France**
Ivry. Macauley.

**Ivy**
Holly and Ivy. *Unknown.*
Ivy, Chief of Trees. *Unknown.*
Ivy-Wife, The. Hardy.

# J

**Jack and the Beanstalk**
Jack Hope.  McDonald.
**Jackdaws**
Jackdaw.  Earley.
**Jackrabbits**
Jackrabbits.  Barker.
Jack Rabbit.  Stoutenberg.
To a Jack Rabbit.  Barker.
**Jackson, Mahalia**
When Mahalia Sings.  Prettyman.
**Jackson, Thomas Jonathan (Stonewall)**
Ascent of T. J. Jackson: A Soldier's Tale.  "A. N."
Stonewall Jackson's Way.  Palmer.
**Jacob**
Jacob.  Lasker-Schuler.
Jacob.  Reznikoff.
Jacob.  Schwartz.
**Jacobites**
It Was A' For Our Righfu' King.  Burns.
**Jagger, Mick**
Going Home.  Reynolds.
**Jaguars**
Jaguar, The.  Hughes.
Second Glance at a Jaguar.  Hughes.
**James, Henry**
Henry James at Newport.  Kees.
Old Mansion.  Ransom.
**James, Jesse**
Jesse James ("Among our country's outlaws").  Benét.
Jesse James ("It was on a Wednesday night, the moon was
  shining bright").  Unknown.
Jesse James ("Jesse James was a lad that killed many a man").
  Unknown.
**James II, King of England**
Clerical Cabal, The.  Unknown.
Dialogue between King William and the Late King James on the
  Banks of the Boyne, A.  Blount.
Hounslow Heath.  Unknown.
Humble Address, The.  Unknown.
Trick for Tyburn, or a Prison Rant, A.  Unknown.
Upon the King's Voyage to Chatham to Make Bulwarks against
  the Dutch.  Unknown.
**Jamestown, Virginia**
Enough.  Moore.
Jamestown.  Jarrell.
**Japan**
In the Second-Best Hotel in Tokyo.  Shapiro.
Japan.  Hecht.
**Japanese**
Asian Brother, Asian Sister.  Inada.
Caption, Circa 1972.  Inada.
Heart Mountain Japanese Relocation Camp, The: 30 Years
  Later.  Levendosky.
Japanese Children.  Kirkup.
Jasmine.  Fr. Lalla Rookh, The Light of the Haram.  Moore.
**Jason**
Golden Fleece, The.  Williams.
**Jazz**
Battle Report.  Kaufman.
"Bird Lives": Charles Parker in St. Louis.  Harper.
Elegy for Duke Ellington.  Mulac.
Half Note for the Duke, A.  Carter.
Hot Poem.  Viidikas.
In a Mist.  Young.
Jazz.  Rogers.
Jazz Fantasia.  Sandburg.
Jazzman, The.  Fields.
Jazzonia.  Hughes.

Lester Young.  Joans.
Mingus.  Kaufman.
Satchmo.  Tolson.
Something Else They Say.  Mbembe.
Song thumbed down a cruiser for a ride, A.  Cunningham.
There were blood spots on the skirt.  Cunningham.
Two Jazz Poems.  Hines.
Voodoo on the Un-Assing of Janis Joplin.  Rogers.
Walking Parker Home.  Kaufman.
Zimmer's Last Gig.  Zimmer.
**Jealousy**
Hell Hath No Fury.  Bukowski.
Jealousy.  Brooke.
Jealousy.  Elegies, I.  Donne.
Jealousy.  Unknown.
Lily of the West, The.  Unknown.
Sheffield 'Prentice, The.  Unknown.
Those Wedding Bells Shall Not Ring Out!  Rosenfeld.
What if jealousy is just a bad dream.  Palmer.
Widow's Old Broom, The.  Unknown.
Wild Bill Jones.  Unknown.
**Jeffers, Robinson.**
Poet Is Dead, The.  Everson.
Return of Robinson Jeffers, The.  Hass.
**Jefferson, Thomas**
Brave New World.  MacLeish.
Lines Addressed to Mr. Jefferson.  Freneau.
Memorial for Mr. Jefferson, A.  Rosenberger.
Monticello.  Sarton.
Twilight's Last Gleaming.  Monks.
**Jellyfish**
Jellyfish, A.  Moore.
Jellyfish, The.  Root.
Medusa, The.  Davenport.
Now is it pleasant in the summer-eve.  Fr. The Borough.
  Crabbe.
**Jenner, Edward**
What Jenner Said on Hearing in Elysium That Complaints Had
  Been Made of His Having a Statue.  Brooks.
**Jerome, Saint**
Jerome.  Jarrell.
**Jerusalem**
At the Western Wall.  Lefcowitz.
Guide to Jerusalem.  Silk.
Heavenly Jerusalem, Jerusalem of the Earth.  Goldberg.
Hierusalem, My Happy Home.  Unknown.
In Jerusalem.  Ritchie.
Jerusalem.  Ausländer.
Jerusalem.  Kanalenstein.
Jerusalem.  Slonimski.
Jerusalem.  Vinner.
Jerusalem, Port City.  Amichai.
Mirrors of Jerusalem, The.  Lefcowitz.
Shadow of the Old City.  Amichai.
Sodom's Sister City.  Amichai.
Walk in Jerusalem, Just Like John.  Unknown.
**Jesus Christ**
Adam and Eve.  Sisson.
Advent 1966.  Levertov.
All Hail the Power of Jesus' Name.  Perronet.
Away in a Manger.  Unknown.
Ballad of the Bread Man.  Causley.
Ballad of the Goodly Fere.  Pound.
Ballad of Trees and the Master, A.  Lanier.
Bambino.  Bird.
Before the Paling of the Stars.  Rossetti.
Bitter Withy, The.  Unknown.
Blessed Assurance.  Crosby.
Burning Babe, The.  Southwell.
Calvary.  Robinson.
Carpenter's Son, The.  Housman.
Cherry-Tree Carol, The.  Unknown.

Child's Nativity, A. Morris.
Child's Present, A. Herrick.
Christ Climbed Down. Ferlinghetti.
Christ in the Universe. Meynell.
Christ Walking on the Water. Rodgers.
Christmas Hymn, A. Wilbur.
Christ's Descent into Hell. Rilke.
Christ's Love Song. *Unknown.*
Church's One Foundation, The. Stone.
Corpus Christi Carol, The: "Heron flew east, the heron flew west, The." *Unknown.*
Corpus Christi Carol, The: "Lully, lulley, lully, lulley." *Unknown.*
Corpus Christi Carol, The: "Over yonder's a park, which is newly begun." *Unknown.*
Coventry Carol. *Unknown.*
Cradle Hymn. Watts.
Crucifixus pro Nobis. Carey.
Deep Spring. *Unknown.*
Easter Hymn. Housman.
Easter Song, An. *Unknown.*
Ecce Homunculus. Mason.
El Greco: Espolio. Birney.
Ex Ore Infantium. Thompson.
Fairest Lord Jesus. *Unknown.*
For God While Sleeping. Sexton.
Friday Morning. Carter.
Friendly Beasts, The. *Unknown.*
From Heaven High I Come to You. *At. to* Luther.
Gentle Jesus, Meek and Mild. Wesley.
Gift, The. Williams.
Give Me Jesus. *Unknown.*
God, That Madest All Things. *Unknown.*
Good Friday. Bastian.
Good Friday. C. Rossetti.
Good Shepherd, The. Lope de Vega.
He Was Made Man. Fletcher.
He Was One of Us. Rice.
Holly and the Ivy, The. *Unknown.*
Holy Well, The. *Unknown.*
I Have Labored Sore. *Unknown.*
I Heard Christ Sing. "MacDiarmid."
I Told Jesus. Plumpp.
I Will Sing the Wondrous Story. Rowley.
If Christ/ Had lept from the cross. Duguid.
If I Could Grasp a Wave from the Great Sea. Moreland.
Into the Woods My Master Went. Lanier.
Jehovah-Jesus. Cowper.
Jesu Christ, My Leman Swete. *Unknown.*
Jesus and His Mother. Gunn.
Jesus Borned in Bethlea. *Unknown.*
Jesus Christ ("Jesus Christ was a man that traveled through the land.") Guthrie.
Jesus, Lover of My Soul. Wesley.
Jesus Make Up My Dying Bed. *Unknown.*
Jolly Shepherd Wat, The. *Unknown.*
Joys of Mary. *Unknown.*
Just as I Am. Elliot.
Last Supper, The. Rilke.
Little Cradle Rocks Tonight in Glory, The. *Unknown.*
Little Jesus. Thompson.
Long, Long Ago. *Unknown.*
Lord of the Dance. Carter.
Mary and Her Son Alone. Ryman.
Moby Christ. Barrax.
My Heart Is Woe. *Unknown.*
My Song Is Love Unknown. Crossman.
Nails and a Cross. Mason.
Name of Jesus, The. Newton.
Nativity of Our Lord, The. Smart.
Never Said a Mumbalin' Word. *Unknown.*
New Approach Needed. Amis.

New Heaven, New War. Southwell.
O Jesu Parvule. "MacDiarmid."
On the Infancy of Our Saviour. Quarles.
On the Morning of Christ's Nativity. Milton.
On the Swag. Mason.
Once in Royal David's City. Alexander.
Paradox. Miller.
Pieta, The, Rhenish, 14th C., the Cloisters. Van Duyn.
Plastic Jesus. *Unknown.*
Poor Little Jesus. *Unknown.*
Pun for Al Gelpi, A. Kerouac.
"Receive Thy Sight." Bryant.
Redemption. Herbert.
Revive Us Again. MacKay.
Royalty. Shaw.
Second Coming, The. Clark.
Seven Virgins, The. *Unknown.*
Shepherds Had an Angel, The. Rossetti.
Softly and Tenderly Jesus Is Calling. Thompson.
Sometime During Eternity. *Fr.* A Coney Island of the Mind. Ferlinghetti.
Strong Son of God, Immortal Love. *Fr.* In Memoriam A. H. H. Tennyson.
Sweet Jesu. *Unknown.*
Take the Name of Jesus with You. Baxter.
There Is a Green Hill. Alexander.
To Jesus on His Birthday. Millay.
Under Sorrow's Sign. O'Dalaigh.
Was He Married? Smith.
Weeping Saviour, The. E. B. Browning.
When I Survey the Wondrous Cross. Watts.
White Was His Naked Breast. *Unknown.*
Words from an Old Spanish Carol. Sawyer.
Young Poet. O'Higgins.
**Jewelry**
With a Gift of Rings. Graves.
**Jews**
Alphabet, The. Shapiro.
At the Jewish Cemetery in Prague. Levertin.
Diaspora Jews. Boimwall.
Dubrovinik Poem (Emilio Tolentino). Rudolf.
Farewell to Europe. Pillen.
Hasidič Jew from Sadagora. Ausländer.
Hebrew of Your Poets, Zion, The. Reznikoff.
I Am a Jew. Martin.
I Want to Write a Jewish Poem. Pacernick.
Identity. Friend.
Jew. Morhange.
Jew. Randall.
Jew. Shapiro.
Jewish Cemetery, The. Tiempo.
Jewish Cemetery at Newport, The. Longfellow.
Jewish Cemetery Near Leningrad, A. Brodsky.
Jewish Main Street. Layton.
Jewish Woman, The. Kolmar.
Jews in Hell, The. Goldemberg.
Let Other People Come As Streams. Reznikoff.
Messias. Shapiro.
Midrash, A, *sel.* Meltzer.
On the Jewish Day of Judgment in the Year 1942 (5703). Wittlin.
One Thing to Take, Another to Keep. Del Monte.
Out of the Strong, Sweetness. Reznikoff.
Poem on the Jews, The. Yeshurun.
Portrait of a Jew Old Country Style. Rothenberg.
Roman Roman, A. Del Monte.
St. Francis of Assisi and the Miserable Jews. Wittlin.
Story About Chicken Soup, A. Simpson.
Survivors. Feinstein.
Test, The. Friend.
That Was Then. Gardner.
To the Jews in Poland. Wittlin.

View of the Organ Mountains North of Las Cruces, New
   Mexico, A.  Frumkin.
Wandering Jew, The.  Mezey.
Wandering Jews.  Keesing.
What Is a Jewish Poem?  Sklarew.
*Voices Within the Ark* (VWA).  Howard Schwartz *and* Anthony
   Rudolf, eds.

**Jezebel**
Jezebel.  Forbes.

**Jogging.**  *See* **Runners and Running.**

**John Bull**
Epigram on John Bull.  Byron.

**John Henry (folk hero)**
Birth of John Henry, The.  Tolson.
John Henry ("John Henry was a li'l baby, uh-huh").  *Unknown.*
Spike Driver Blues.  *Unknown.*

**John the Baptist, Saint**
Prophet.  Chambers.
Saint John Baptist.  Drummond of Hawthornden.

**Johnson, Lyndon Baines**
Miltonic Sonnet for Mr. Johnson on His Refusal of Peter Hurd's
   Official Portrait, A.  Wilbur.

**Johnson, Samuel**
Doctor Johnson.  Jenyns.
Epitaph: "Here Johnson lies—a sage by all allow'd."  Cowper.
Oceans of Dr. Johnson, The.  Bevington.

**Jonah**
For Lo! My Jonah How He Slumped.  Wilson.
I to the Lord from My Distress.  *Unknown.*
Jonah Is Cast into the Sea.  *Unknown.*
Ribs and Terrors, The.  *Fr.* Moby Dick.  Melville.
Who Did Swallow Jonah?  *Unknown.*

**Jones, Casey (John Luther Jones)**
Casey Jones (Union).  Hill.
Casey Jones.  Seibert.
Kassie Jones.  *Unknown.*

**Jones, John Paul**
Ballad of Benjamin Bones, The.  Ward.
Paul Jones's Victory.  *Unknown.*
*Stately Southerner,* The.  *Unknown.*
Yankee Man-of-War, The.  *Unknown.*

**Jonson, Ben**
His Prayer to Ben Jonson.  Herrick.
Ode to Himself ("Come leave the loathed stage").  Jonson.
Ode to Himself, An ("Where dost thou careless lie").  Jonson.
Ode for Him, An.  Herrick.
Upon Ben Jonson.  Herrick.
Upon Mr. Ben Jonson: Epigram.  Herrick.

**Joplin, Janis**
Burying Blues for Janis.  Piercy.
Janis Joplin and the Folding Company.  Winters.
Voodoo on the Un-Assing of Janis Joplin.  Rodgers.

**Joseph**
Pharaoh and Joseph.  Lasker-Schuler.

**Joseph, Saint**
Cherry Tree Carol.  *Unknown.*

**Joshua**
Joshua Fit de Battle ob Jerico.  *Unknown.*
Joshua's Face.  Gilboa.
Moses and Joshua.  Lasker-Schuler.

**Jowett, Benjamin**
First come I; my name is Jowett.  *Fr.* Balliol Rhymes.
   Beeching.

**Joy**
After the Second Operation.  Goedicke.
Answer, The.  Teasdale.
59th Street Bridge Song, The.  Simon.
First or Last.  Hardy.
Joy.  Creeley.
Joy.  Jeffers.
L'Allegro.  Milton.
Song of Joy.  Uvavnuk.

What Are Years?  Moore.

**Joyce, James**
D. H. Lawrence and James Joyce.  Wolfe.
For James Joyce.  Ford.
Ulysses' Library.  Daiches.

**Judas Iscariot**
Judas.  Miller.
Judas.  *Unknown.*
Judas Before.  Travis.
Judas Iscariot.  Mason.
Judas Iscariot.  Spender.
Judas, Joyous Little Son.  Farber.
Saint Judas.  Wright.

**Judges**
Circuit Judge, The.  *Fr.* Spoon River Anthology.  Masters.
Judge Somers.  *Fr.* Spoon River Anthology.  Masters
Judge with the Sore Rump, The.  Tucker.
On Rÿneveld, an Unpopular Dutch Judge.  *Unknown.*

**Judgment Day**
Blow Gabriel.  *Unknown.*
Crowdieknowe.  "MacDiarmid."
Day of Judgment, The.  Swift.
Day of Judgment, The.  Watts.
Great Round-up, The.  *Unknown.*
How long, dear Saviour, O how long.  Watts.
Jesus Is Coming Soon.  *Unknown.*
Judgement Day.  *Unknown.*
O Children, Would You Cherish?  Dock.
Rapture.  Carlson.
Revelation.  Meinke.
Second Coming, The.  Yeats.
Ten thousand times ten thousand.  Alford.
That Day of Wrath, that Direful Day.  Thomas of Celano.
When the Roll Is Called Up Yonder.  Black.

**Judith (Apocrypha)**
Deed.  Murawski.
Judith of Bethulia.  Ransom.
Judith Recalls Holofernes.  Stanton.

**Jugglers**
Juggler.  Wilbur.
Juggler and the Baron's Daughter, The.  *Unknown.*

**Jukeboxes**
Jukebox has a big square face, The.  *Fr.* King Juke.  Fearing.

**July**
July in Indiana.  Fitzgerald.
Loud is the summer's busy song.  *Fr.* The Shepherd's Calender:
   July.  Clare.

**June**
And what is so rare as a day in June?  *Fr.* The Vision of Sir
   Launfal.  Lowell.
June.  Ledwidge.
June.  *Fr.* The Earthly Paradise.  Morris.
June Is Bustin' Out All Over.  Hammerstein.

**Jungles**
In the frightened forest the tree sleeps, the leaves are dead.  *Fr.*
   Song for the Elephant Hunt.  *Unknown.*
Jungle Husband, The.  Smith.
Men in Green.  Campbell.

**Juniper**
Juniper.  Francis.
Juniper.  *Unknown.*
Sing a Song of Juniper.  Francis.

**Junk**
Junk.  Wilbur.

**Justice**
Born with a gentle heart, and born to please.  *Fr.* The Country
   Justice.  Langhorne.
Carl Hamblin.  *Fr.* Spoon River Anthology.  Masters.
Death of Justice, The.  Hawkins.
Justice.  Hughes.
Poem: "In the old days either the plaintiff or the defendant won
   or lost."  Dugan.

They Can't Do That.  *Unknown.*
Youth.  Hope.
**Juvenile Delinquency**
We Real Cool.  Brooks.

# K

**Kabul, Afghanistan**
Ford o' Kabul River.  Kipling.
**Kafka, Franz**
Letter to Kafka.  Stanton.
Tribute to Kafka for Someone Taken.  Dugan.
**Kalakaua (Hawaiian King)**
Praise Song for King Kalakaua.  *Unknown.*
**Kalamazoo, Michigan**
Sins of Kalamazoo, The.  Sandburg.
**Kali**
Invocation to Kali, The, *sels.*  Sarton.
**Kane (Hawaiian God)**
O Kane, O Lono of the blue sea.  *Unknown.*
Water of Kane, The.  *Unknown.*
**Kangaroos**
Duck and the Kangaroo, The.  Lear.
Kangaroo.  Lawrence.
Kangaroo, The.  *Unknown.*
**Kansas**
Crossing Kansas by Train.  Justice.
In Kansas.  *Unknown.*
Kansas Boy.  Lechlitner.
Moonlit Night in Kansas.  Contoski.
Outside Abilene.  Elliott.
Place in Kansas, A.  Kooser.
Trail into Kansas, The.  Merwin.
Wichita Vortex Sutra.  Ginsberg.
**Kansas City, Kansas**
Kansas City West Bottoms.  Dahlberg.
**Kansas City, Missouri**
Kansas City.  Hammerstein.
**Katmandu, Nepal**
Here in Katmandu.  Justice.
**Katydids**
To a Caty-Did.  Freneau.
**Katzenjammer Kids**
Katzenjammer Kids, The.  Reaney.
**Kavanagh, Patrick**
In Memory of Patrick Kavanagh.  McNeice.
**Kearney, Phillip**
Kearney at Seven Pines.  Stedman.
**Kearsarge (ship)**
How Do You Do, *Alabama*!  Wilson.
**Keats, John**
Adonais: An Elegy on the Death of John Keats.  Shelley.
John Keats.  Byron.
Keats.  Longfellow.
Keats to Fanny Brawne.  Masters.
Ode on a Grecian Urn Summarized.  Skirrow.
On First Looking in on Blodgett's *Keat's "Chapman's Homer."*
    Starbuck.
On Keats.  Shelley.
On the Death of Keats.  Logan.
**Kells, Book of**
Book of Kells, The.  Colum.
Library, The.  Logan.
**Kennedy, John Fitzgerald**
Assassination Raga.  Ferlinghetti.
Belief.  Ammons.
Down in Dallas.  Kennedy.
Hero.  Stafford.

History.  Skelton.
Kennedy.  Heffernan.
Kennedy.  Kazan.
Lines for a President.  Watson.
Thanksgiving 1963.  Booth.
To J.F.K. 14 Years After.  Weaver.
**Kennedy, Robert Francis**
Assassination, The.  Justice.
Assassination Raga.  Ferlinghetti.
Beyond the Presidency.  Gibson.
Lowering, The.  Swenson.
**Kent, England**
Beechwoods at Knole.  Sackville-West.
In Romney Marsh.  Davidson.
To the Men of Kent. October, 1803.  Wordsworth.
**Kent State University, Ohio**
Kent State Massacre, The.  Warshaw *and* Dane.
Kent State, May 4, 1970.  Goodman.
**Kentucky**
East Kentucky, 1967.  Berry.
Hunters of Kentucky, The.  Woodworth.
In the Corn Land.  Howard.
My Old Kentucky Home.  Foster.
Old Athens of the West is now a Blue Grass Tour, The.  Hall.
Tourism.  Chaffin.
**Kesey, Ken**
First Party at Ken Keseys with Hell's Angels.  Ginsberg.
**Kevin, Saint**
St. Kevin.  *Unknown.*
**Kew Gardens, London**
Barrel-Organ, The.  Noyes.
**Keys**
Found with Chain.  Johnson.
Liberator, The.  Coleman.
Skeleton Key.  Hollander.
**Kidd, William**
Captain Kidd.  *Unknown.*
**Kilcash, Ireland**
Kilcash.  *Unknown.*
**Killigrew, Anne**
To the Pious Memory of the Accomplished Young Lady.
    Dryden.
**King, Edward**
Lycidas.  Milton.
**King, Martin Luther, Jr.**
Alabama Bus.  *Unknown.*
Assassination.  Lee.
Death of Dr. King.  Cornish.
Funeral of Martin Luther King, Jr., The.  Giovanni.
In Memoriam: Martin Luther King, Jr.  Jordan.
King Lives.  Boyer.
Martin Luther King, Jr.  Brooks.
Martin's Blues.  Harper.
Shot with a Hot Rot Gun.  Goode.
Stopped in Memphis.  Bauer.
War War.  Goode.
**King Kong**
Fay Wray to the King.  Rechter.
**Kingfishers**
Kingfisher, The.  Davies.
Kingfisher, The.  *Fr.* Upon Appleton House.  Marvell.
Kingfishers, The.  Olson.
One Kingfisher and One Yellow Rose.  Brennan.
**Kings**
Bastard King of England, The.  *Unknown.*
English Succession, The.  *Unknown.*
Georges, The (I–IV).  Thackeray.
Ill Government.  Herrick.
Kings and Tyrants.  Herrick.
Model for the Laureate, A.  Yeats.
On King Richard the Third, Who Lies Buried under Leicester
    Bridge.  Suckling.

On the Four Georges. Landor.
**Kipling, Rudyard**
To R. K. Stephen.
**Kisses**
Did Not. Moore.
Kiss, A. Herrick.
Kiss, The. Patmore.
Kisses Loathesome. Herrick.
Love's Philosophy. Shelley.
Mark, The. Graves.
Moth's kiss, first, The! *Fr.* In a Gondola. Browning.
Not alwayes give a melting kiss. *Fr. Basia.* Johannes
    Secundus.
Some Kisses from *The Kama Sutra.* Williams.
To Anthea. Herrick.
**Kites**
Kite, The. Behn.
Kite. Dillard.
Kite, The. O'Keeffe.
Kite, A. Sherman.
Kite Day at the Washington Monument. Orfalea.
Kite is a Victim, A. Cohen.
**Klee, Paul**
Paul Klee. Todd.
**Knife-Grinders**
Sparkles from the Wheel. Whitman.
**Knight, Etheridge**
Hospital/Poem. Sanchez.
**Knighthood and Knights**
Brave Knight, A. Dodge.
Fast rode the knight. *Fr.* War Is Kind. Crane.
Knight, The. Rich.
Knight, Death, and the Devil, The. Jarrell
La Belle Dame sans Merci. Keats.
Song of Finis, The. De la Mare.
**Knoxville, Tennessee**
Knoxville, Tennessee. Giovanni.
**Koalas**
Koala. Ross.
**Kollwitz, Kathë**
Kathë Kollwitz. Rukeyser.
**Koran**
Page from the Koran. Merrill.
**Korea**
Ode for the American Dead in Korea. McGrath.
**Kosciusko, Thaddeus**
To Kosciusko. Keats.
**Kraken**
Kraken, The. Tennyson.
**Ku Klux Klan**
Ku Klux. Hughes.
Night, Death, Mississippi. Hayden.
Special Bulletin. Hughes.
**Kubla Khan**
Kubla Khan. Coleridge.

# L

**Labor and Laborers**
Apprentice Painter, The. Myers.
Black Sweeper. Bruchac.
Burying Ground by the Ties. MacLeish.
Captain Captain. *Unknown.*
Commonwealth of Toil, The. Chaplin.
Cynddylan on a Tractor. Thomas.
Docker. Heaney.
Drill, Ye Tarriers, Drill! *Unknown.*
Drover, A. Colum.

Factory Girl's Come-All-Ye, The. *Unknown.*
Florida Road Workers. Hughes.
Foundations of American Industry, The. Hall.
Freighting from Wilcox to Globe. *Unknown.*
Furniture Factory, The. Rutsala.
George. Randall.
Go Down, Old Hannah. *Unknown.*
Going Up the River. *Unknown.*
Golden Lot, A. Skipsey.
Grinders, The; or, The Saddle on the Right Horse. *Unknown.*
Hay for the Horses. Snyder.
Hoeing. Soto.
I've Been Workin' on the Railroad. *Unknown.*
John Henry *Unknown*
Labourer's Noon-Day Hymn, The. Wordsworth.
Life and Death Among the Xerox People. Cabral.
Liftman, The. Evans.
Lining Track. *Unknown.*
Lone Striker. Frost.
Man with the Hoe, The. Markham.
May I Ask You a Question, Mr. Youngtown Sheet & Tube?
    Patchen.
Muckers. Sandburg.
Night-Shift. Kalar.
Night Shift at the Plating Division of Keeler Brass. Allen.
Old Men Working Concrete. Hey.
Paper Cutter, The. Ignatow.
Paso Por Aqui. Hall.
Pastures of Plenty. Guthrie.
Pat Works on the Railway. *Unknown.*
Picture of Workers Resting. Beer.
Preacher and the Slave, The. Hill.
Proletarian Visit. Macleod.
Public-House Confidence. Cameron.
Roadmenders' Song, The. *Unknown.*
Shovelling Iron Ore. *Unknown.*
Sisyphus. Garioch.
So Handy, Me Boys, So Handy. *Unknown.*
Song of the Banana Man. Jones.
Song of the Shirt, The. Hood.
Stevedore. Collins.
Tamping Ties. *Unknown.*
Thatcher. Heaney.
This Sun Is Hot. *Unknown.*
Timeclock. Spector.
Tired Worker, The. McKay.
To the Museums. Schneider.
Toads. Larkin.
Track-Lining Song. *Unknown.*
Train Runs Late to Harlem, The. Rivers
United Front. Brecht *and* Eisler.
Unloading Rails. *Unknown.*
Verses: "Poor fellow, what is it to you." Williams.
Way Out in Idaho. *Unknown.*
Worker, The. Thomas.
Worker Uprooted. Kalar.
Youth. Wright.
**Labor Day**
Labor Day. Pacernick.
**Labor Unions**
Blackleg Miners, The. *Unknown.*
Casey Jones (Union). Hill.
Great Day ("One of these mornings bright and fair").
    *Unknown.*
Hold the Fort. *Unknown.*
Its a Good Thing to Join a Union. *Unknown.*
Joe Hill. Hayes.
Ludlow Massacre, The. Guthrie.
Picket Line Song, The. *Unknown.*
Popular Wobbly, The. Slim.
Roll the Union On. Williams *and* Hays.
Solidarity Forever. Chaplin.

Talking Union. Hays, Lampell *and* Seeger.
There Is Power. *Unknown.*
Union Maid. Guthrie.
Union Man. Morgan.
Union Train. Hays, Lampell *and* Seeger.
We Are Building a Strong Union. *Unknown.*
Which Side Are You On? Reese.
You Gotta Go Down (And Join the Union). *Unknown.*

**Labrador**
North Labrador. Crane.

**Labyrinths**
Labyrinth, The. Muir.

**Ladybirds**
Clock-a-clay (The Ladybird). Clare.
Ladybird, The, *sel.* Clare.
Ladybirds, The. Lucie-Smith.
Ladybug. Dodat.
Ladybug's Christmas. Farber.
To the Lady-Bird. Bowles.

**La Fayette, Marie Joseph, Marquis de**
La Fayette. *Fr.* Sonnets on Eminent Characters. Coleridge.
Let the brothels of Paris be opened. Blake.

**Lakes and Ponds**
By Loe Pool. Symons.
Goose Pond. Kunitz.
Imitation of Spenser. Keats.
Lake, The. Hughes.
Lake. Simpson.
Lake Above Santos, The. Wilson.
Lake Chelan. Stafford.
Overturned Lake, The. Ford.
Pond, The Thwaite.
Reason and Nature. Cunningham.
Spring Pools. Frost.
Water and Light, Light and Water. Perlberg.

**Lamb, Charles**
This Lime-Tree Bower My Prison. Coleridge.
Written after the Death of Charles Lamb. Wordsworth.

**Lambs**
Composed on a May Morning, 1838. Wordsworth.
Delivering Lambs. Campbell.
For a Lamb. Eberhart.
Lamb, The. *Fr.* Songs of Innocence. Blake.
Lamb. Browne.
Lamb. Rankin.
Lambs Frolicking Home. Lape.
Mary's Lamb. Hale.
Pet Lamb, The. Wordsworth.
Winter Lambing. Tipton.
Wolf and the Lamb, The. La Fontaine.

**Lamplighters**
Lamplighter, The. O'Sullivan.
Lamplighter, The. Stevenson.

**Lampreys**
Lamprey, glowing with uncommon fires, The. *Fr.* Halieutica. Diaper.

**Lancashire, England**
Lancashire Winter. Connor.

**Lancelot du Lac**
Lanzarote. *Unknown.*

**Landlords and Landladies**
Homely Accomodation, Suit Gent. Turner.
Landlady, The. Atwood.
Landladies. Locklin.
Leaving the Country House to the Landlord, Five Years Later. McNair.
Madam and the Rent Man. Hughes.
Pity the Down-Trodden Landlord. Woolf *and* Clayton.
Scenery. Joans.
Telephone Conversation. Soyinka.
Tragedy of the Leaves, The. Bukowski.

**Landor, Walter Savage**

Fable, A. Frere.
W. S. Landor. Moore.

**Language**
Americana IX: "Your correspondent must be kidding when he says." Rakosi.
And the whole earth was of one language and of one speech. *Fr.* Genesis. Bible, *O.T.*
Anthology of Nouns. Tyler.
Antiques. De la Mare.
As Planned. O'Hara.
Change, The. O'Bruadair.
Coal. Lorde.
Cool Web, The. Graves.
Crow's First Lesson. Hughes.
Cryptology. Kroll.
Education in Tongues, An. Swann.
Genesis. Higgins.
Goose, Moose, & Spruce. McCord.
Grafted Tongue, A. Montague.
Habla Usted Español? Reiss.
Hebrew Lesson. Brod.
History of the Word. Graves.
How a Girl Was Too Reckless of Grammar. Carryl.
How One Thing Leads to Another. Smith.
Irish Language, The. Mangan.
Just Because... McCord.
Language, The. Creeley.
Language has not the power to speak what love indites. Clare.
Language, Talk to Me. Jones.
Lapsus Linguae. Howard.
Latin for Today. *Unknown.*
Logical English *Unknown.*
Loving and Liking. D. Wordsworth.
Modern Kabbalist. Falk.
New Style, The. O'Bruadair.
Nigger. Sanchez.
Nine Parts of Speech, The. *Unknown.*
Nothingness. Amir.
Of the Manner of Addressing Clouds. Stevens.
On Reading Mr. Ytche Bashes' Stories in Yiddish. Ehrlichman.
On the Use of Jayshus. Gogarty.
One day the Nouns were clustered in the street. *Fr.* Permanently. Koch.
Scat! Scitten! McCord.
Sentence. Collins.
Spanish Is the Loving Tongue. *Unknown.*
Test. Price.
Tilth. Graves.
Traditions. Heaney.
Upon Dr. Davies's British Grammar. Howell.
Very Like a Whale. Nash.
What's in a Word? Shine.
When the Wine Was Gone. Aubert.
Why English Is So Hard! *Unknown.*
Word made flesh is seldom, A. Dickinson.
Words. Finch.
Words. Rutsala.
Yet. Hoffman.

**Laodamia**
Laodamia. Wordsworth.

**Lapwings**
Landscape with Lapwings. Aitchison.

**Larkin, James**
Inscription for a Headstone. Clarke.

**Larks**
Caged Skylark, The. Hopkins.
Shelley's Skylark. Hardy.
Skylarks. Hughes.
To a Skylark. Shelley.
To a Skylark. Wordsworth.

**Las Vegas, Nevada**
Man Who Invented Las Vegas, The. Costanzo.

**Laughter**
Laugh and Be Merry. Masefield.
Laughing Song. *Fr.* Songs of Innocence. Blake.
Mirth. *Fr.* The Knight of the Burning Pestle. Beaumont.
Not a Clown. Schechter.
Why did I laugh to-night? No voice will tell. Keats.

**Laundry and Laundering**
Bendix. Updike.
Clothesline, The. Wade.
Dolls' Wash, The. Ewing.
Goldfish Wife, The. Hochman.
Hanging Clothes. Kent.
Laundrette. Lochhead.
Laundromat. McCord.
Love Calls Us to the Things of This World  Wilbur.
Mad Scene, The. Merrill.
Mennonite Farm Wife. Kauffman.
One for the Ladies at the Troy Laundry Who Cooled
   Themselves for Zimmer. Zimmer.
Shepherd's Hut, The. Young.
Stocking and Shirt. Reeves.
Storm. Nagy.
Thinking Twice in the Laundromat. Elliott.
Wash. Updike.
Wash Day. Mollin.
Wash-Day Wonder. Faubion.

**Lavender**
I planned to have a border of lavender. Goodman.

**Lawes, Henry**
To Master Henry Lawes, the Excellent Composer of Lyrics.
   Herrick.
To Mr. Henry Lawes. Philips.

**Lawrence, David Herbert**
An Elegy for D. H. Lawrence. Williams.
D. H. Lawrence and James Joyce. Wolfe.

**Lawyers and Law**
Case at Sessions, A. Landor.
Case to the Civilians, A. *Unknown.*
Conversation in Craven Street, Strand. Smith *and* Rose
Damages, Two Hundred Pounds. Thackeray.
Judge Somers. *Fr.* Spoon River Anthology. Masters.
Law I Love Is Major Mover, The. Duncan
Law Like Love. Auden.
Laws of God, the laws of man, The. Housman.
Lawyer Clark Blues. *Unknown.*
Lawyers Know Too Much, The. Sandburg.
Legal Fiction. Empson.
To the Lawyer from His Only Lately Neglected Tort. Stager.
Who doubts? The laws fell down from heaven's height. *Fr.*
   Virgidemiarum. Hall.

**Lazarus**
Act of Faith. Trías
Come Out, Lazarus! *Unknown.*
Dives and Lazarus. *Unknown.*

**Laziness**
Lazy Man's Song. Po Chü-i.
Personal Song. Arnatkoak.
Sluggard, The. Watts.

**Lear, Edward**
How Pleasant to Know Mr. Lear. Lear.

**Lear, King**
Lear. Williams.
On Sitting Down to Read "King Lear" Once Again. Keats.

**Learning**
Arithmetic on the Frontier. Kipling.
He That Never Read a Line. *Unknown.*
Little Learning, A. *Fr.* An Essay on Criticism. Pope.
More Wisdom. Richards.
Ode on the Despoilers of Learning in an American University,
   An. Winters.
Oyfn Pripetshuk (On the Hearth). Warshawsky.
To David, About His Education. Nemerov.

Vain Learning. *Fr.* Caelica. Greville.

**Leaves**
Autumn Leaves. Webb.
Dock-Leaves. Barnes.
Gathering Leaves. Frost.
Invitation Standing. Blackburn.
Leaf Treader, A. Frost.
Leaves. Hughes.
Leaves. Shideler.
Leaves Compared with Flowers. Frost.
Les Etiquettes Jaunes. O'Hara.
My Own House. Ignatow.
One Leaf, The. Norris.
Watch long enough, and you will see the leaf. *Fr.* Preludes for
   Memnon. Aiken.

**Leda**
Leda. Rilke.
Leda. Van Duyn.
Leda and the Swan. Gogarty.
Leda and the Swan. Yeats.
Leda Reconsidered. Van Duyn.
New Leda, The. Howes.
People do gossip. Sappho.

**Leeuwenhoek, Anton**
Microscope, The. Kumin.

**Legree, Simon**
Simon Legree—A Negro Sermon. Lindsay.

**Legs**
Her Leg. Herrick.
Lament for a Leg. Abse.
Leg, The. Shapiro.
Legs, The. Graves.
Legs. Scannell.
Poem in Which My Legs Are Accepted. Fraser.
Vet's Rehabilitation. Durem.

**Leisure**
Leisure. Davies.

**Lemmings**
Lemmings, The. Masefield.

**Lemons**
Lemon. Satz.
Lemons. Hubbell.
Lemons, Lemons. Young.

**Lenin, Vladimir Ilyich**
Second Hymn to Lenin. "MacDiarmid."
To Comrade Lenin. Schneider.

**Lent**
Children's Lenten Wisdom. Houck.
To Keep a True Lent. Herrick.

**Leonardo da Vinci**
For "Our Lady of the Rocks." D. G. Rossetti.
Leonardo's Secret. Bly.

**Leopards**
Leopard. *Unknown.*

**Leopold III, King of the Belgians**
Moon and the Night and the Men, The. Berryman.

**Lepanto, Battle of**
Lepanto. Chesterton.

**Leprosy**
Leper, The. Ka-'ehu.
Pennacesse Leper Colony For Women, The. Cape Cod. 1922.
   Dubie.

**Lesbianism.** *See* Homosexuality.

**Letters**
Burning Love Letters. Moss.
Burning the Letters. Grew.
Destruction of Letters. Deutsch.
Form Rejection Letter. Dacey.
Harry. Webb.
How to Write a Letter. Turner.
Letter to a Conceivable Great-Grandson. Birney.
Way I read a letter's—this, The. Dickinson.

**Levett, Robert**
  On the Death of Mr. Robert Levet, a Practiser in Physic.
    Johnson.

**Liberalism and Liberals**
  Apology for Liberals. Davidman.
  Child of the Dead and Forgotten Gods. Wright.
  Respectabilities. Silkin.

**Liberia**
  On the Founding of Liberia. *Fr.* Libretto for the Republic of
    Liberia. Tolson.

**Liberty, Statue of**
  New Colossus, The. Lazarus.
  Statue of Liberty, The. Field.
  To the Statue. Swenson.

**Libraries**
  Fire at Alexandria, The. Weiss.
  Girl in a Library, A. Jarrell.
  Library. Armour.
  Library. Collins.
  Library, The. Gillies.
  Library, The. Shore.
  Precious, mouldering pleasure 'tis, A. Dickinson.
  Reading Room, The New York Public Library. Eberhart.
  Rhoda Pitkin. *Fr.* The New Spoon River. Masters.

**Lice**
  Louse Hunting. Rosenberg.
  To a Louse. Burns.

**Lichen**
  In Praise of Lichen. Perlberg.

**Lies and Lying**
  Ancient Custom, An. Steiger.
  Beware, Oh, Take Care. *Unknown.*
  Book of Lies, The. Tate.
  Lie, The. Kipling.
  Lying. Moore.
  Matilda, Who Told Lies, and Was Burned to Death. Belloc.
  She Said I Said He Lied. Rosen.
  Song: "Lying is an occupation." Pilkington.
  Unfortunate Coincidence. Parker.
  When my love swears that she is made of truth. Sonnets,
    CXXXVIII. Shakespeare.

**Life**
  All the World's A Stage. *Fr.* As You Like It. Shakespeare.
  Anyone Lived in a Pretty How Town. Cummings.
  April Inventory. Snodgrass.
  Arena, The. Witheford.
  Barter. Teasdale.
  Beach in August, The. Kees.
  Cold Spring, The. Levertov.
  Consumer's Report, A. Porter.
  Contra Mortem. Carruth.
  Curiosity. Reid.
  Discovery. Belloc.
  Elegy: "My prime of youth is but a frost of cares." Tichborne.
  Esthete in Harlem. Hughes.
  Flux. Eberhart.
  Fly, The. *Fr.* Songs of Experience. Blake.
  For Life I Had Never Cared Greatly. Hardy.
  Force That through the Green Fuse Drives the Flower, The.
    Thomas.
  Hating Your Life. J. Morris.
  He Never Expected Much. Hardy.
  Here and Human. Scannell.
  Horse Show, The. Williams.
  Hound, The. Francis.
  Hughie at the Inn. Wylie.
  Human Life: On the Denial of Immortality. Coleridge.
  I never cared for Life: Life cared for me. Hardy.
  I never saw any point. Dugan.
  Immortal Part, The. Housman.
  Into My Heart an Air That Kills. Housman.
  Is Life Worth Living? Austin.

Leaf Treader, A. Frost.
Lies. Yevtushenko.
Life, A. Nemerov.
Life. Steele.
Life. Treasone.
Life flows to death as rivers to the sea. Cunningham.
Life, friends, is boring. We must not say so. Berryman.
Lucinda Matlock. *Fr.* Spoon River Anthology. Masters.
Lying in a Hammock at William Duffy's Farm in Pine Island,
  Minnesota. Wright.
Mean Old Twister. *Unknown.*
Men Made Out of Words. Stevens.
Mother to Son. Hughes.
Nature's Questioning. Hardy.
Necessities of Life. Rich.
Nothing. Burgos.
Old Adam, The. Levertov.
On the Life of Man. Ralegh.
On Wenlock Edge the wood's in trouble. Housman.
Our lives are Swiss. Dickinson.
Pale Blue Casket, The. Pitcher.
Picture-Show. Sassoon.
Postscript. Hochman.
Psalm of Life, A. Longfellow.
Quickness. Vaughan.
Responding Voice. Icaza.
Sea Boy on the Giddy Mast, A. Clare.
Secret, The. Levertov.
Sestina of the Tramp-Royal. Kipling.
Shut Out That Moon. Hardy.
Sic Vita. King.
Sic Vita. Thoreau.
Sower, The. Blind.
Still Here. Hughes.
These chairs they have no words to utter. Wordsworth.
This life which seems so fair. Drummond of Hawthornden.
Tomorrow, and Tomorrow, and Tomorrow. *Fr.* Macbeth.
  Shakespeare.
Triumph of Life, The. Shelley.
Under Sorrow's Sign. O'Dalaigh.
Up-Hill. C. Rossetti.
We Are Transmitters. Lawrence.
What Is Life? Coleridge.
What Is Lived? Valle.
What Shall He Tell That Son? Sandburg.
Woman Poem. Giovanni.
World, The. Bacon.

**Lifeguards**
  Lifeguard, The. Dickey.
  Seasonal Phenomenon. Armour.

**Light**
  Holy Light. *Fr.* Paradise Lost. Milton.
  Light exists in Spring, A. Dickinson.
  Man Who Spilled Light, The. Wagoner.
  My Invention. Silverstein.
  There's a certain slant of light. Dickinson.

**Lighthouses**
  Cuvier Light. Wilson.
  Eddystone Light, The. *Unknown.*
  Inland Lighthouse, The. McMichael.
  Lighthouse, The. Anson.
  Lighthouse. Meeter.
  Lighthouse in the Night. Storni.
  Lighthouse Keeper. Sange.
  Lighthouses. Wellesley.

**Lightning**
  Lightning is a yellow fork, The. Dickinson.

**Lilacs**
  Lilacs. Lowell.

**Lilies**
  Bulb, A. Munkittrick.
  How Lilies Came White. Herrick.

Lily, The. *Fr.* Songs of Experience. Blake.
Lily of a Day, A. Jonson.
**Lilies of the Valley**
Lilies of the Valley. Silkin.
Lily of the Valley. Coleridge.
**Lilith**
Body's Beauty. *Fr.* The House of Life. Rossetti.
Lilith. Fainlight.
Lilith. Feldman.
Lilith. Grossman.
Lilith. Levi.
Waiting for Lilith. Kessler.
**Limbo**
Limbo. Coleridge.
**Limericks**
*They Discovered a Head in the Box for the Bread* (TDH). John
   E. Brewton *and* Lorraine A. Blackburn, comps.
**Limestone**
In Praise of Limestone. Auden.
**Lincoln, Abraham**
Abraham Lincoln. Benét.
Abraham Lincoln Walks at Midnight. Lindsay.
Booth Killed Lincoln. *Unknown.*
Death of Lincoln, The. Bryant.
Honest Abe Lincoln. Shulman.
In Hardin County, 1909. Thompson.
Lincoln, *sel.* Fletcher.
Lincoln and Liberty. Hutchinson.
Lincoln Monument: Washington. Hughes.
Lincoln, the Man of the People, *sel.* Markham.
Martyr, The. Melville.
O Captain! My Captain! Whitman.
Old Abe Lincoln Came out of the Wilderness. *Unknown.*
To Meet Mr. Lincoln. Merriam.
When Lilacs Last in the Dooryard Bloom'd. Whitman.
**Lindbergh, Charles**
Lindbergh. *Unknown.*
**Lindsay, Vachel**
To Lindsay. Ginsberg.
**Lions**
Circus Lions. Day Lewis.
Glory Trail, The. Clark.
Jim, Who Ran Away from His Nurse, and Was Eaten by a Lion.
   Belloc.
King, The. Livingstone.
Lion, The. Douglas.
Lion. *Fr.* A Bestiary. Rexroth.
Lion Hunts. Beer.
Lions. McPherson.
Lion's Skeleton, The. Turner.
Lucky Lion! *Unknown.*
One Lion, Once. Canzoneri.
Riverdale Lion. Colombo.
Song of the Lioness for Her Cub. *Unknown.*
Sunt Leones. Smith.
Supper for a Lion. Aldis.
**Li Po**
Li Po. Moore.
**Lippi, Fra Filippo**
Fra Lippo Lippi. Browning.
**Little Big Horn, Battle of**
Comanche. Gildner.
Tale of Last Stands, A. Red Cloud.
**Little Red Riding Hood**
Coup de Grâce. Hope.
**Little Rock, Arkansas**
Chicago *Defender* Sends a Man to Little Rock, The. Brooks.
**Livingstone, David**
Into the Dark. Monette.
**Lizards**
Gecko. Lloyd
Lizard. Lawrence.

Lizard. McLean.
Lizard, The. Markham.
Lizard. Mills.
Lizard and the Yellow Dandelion, The. Wangberg.
Lizards and Snakes. Hecht.
Lizards of La Brea, The. De Baca.
Note on Lizards' Feet, A. Van Rensselaer.
Old Man to the Lizard, The. MacLeish.
Recognition. Perry.
Tiny Baby Lizard, The. Brigham.
Witches' Menu. Nikolay.
**Lloyd George, David, 1st Earl Lloyd-George of Dwyfor**
Lloyd George. *Unknown.*
**Lobsters**
In the Case of Lobsters. Morstein.
Lobsters. Nemerov.
Lobsters in the Window. Snodgrass.
**Locusts**
Serenade: "The tin-type tune the locusts make." Donnelly.
**Lombardi, Vince**
For the Death of Vince Lombardi. Dickey.
**London, England**
Composed upon Westminster Bridge, September 3, 1802.
   Wordsworth.
Countryman's Return, The. Thomas.
Description of the Morning, A. Swift.
Empresse of townes, exalt in honour. *Fr.* In Honour of the
   City of London. Dunbar.
Farewell to Kurdistan. Tonks.
Hell is a city much like London. *Fr.* Peter Bell the Third.
   Shelley.
High Majesty of Paul's, The. *Fr.* London Voluntaries. Henley.
His Return to London. Herrick.
Latter-Day Geography Lesson. Mason.
Let due civilities be strickly paid. *Fr.* Trivia, or, The Art of
   Walking the Streets of London. *Fr.* Gay.
London. *Fr.* Songs of Experience. Blake.
London. Davidson.
London: A Poem in Imitation of the Third Satire of Juvenal.
   Johnson.
London after the Great Fire, 1666. *Fr.* Annus Mirabilis.
   Dryden.
London Beautiful. Le Gallienne.
London Lickpenny. *Unknown.*
London Rain. MacNeice.
London Snow. Bridges.
Mighty mass of brick, and smoke, and shipping, A. *Fr.* Don
   Juan. Byron.
Mountains of Mourne, The. French.
November Blue. Meynell.
Old-Fashioned Air. Berrigan.
Old Song, The. Chesterton.
To the City of London. Dunbar.
Upon His Majesty's Being Made Free of the City. Marvell.
**Lone Ranger, The**
Tonto. Koertge.
**Loneliness**
Acquainted with the Night. Frost.
Alone. Chu Shu-chen.
Alone. Manger.
Alone. Poe.
B Negative. Kennedy.
Bachelor. Meredith.
Bad Thing, The. Wain.
Bereft. Hardy.
Cognac and Farewell to My Sanity. Menebroker.
Cold Feet in Columbus. Heath.
Crowsfeet Splaying Round His Eyes. Lloyd-Evans.
Desert Places Frost.
Eleanor Rigby. Lennon *and* McCartney.
Five Sense. Wyche.
For Anne. Cohen.

Fruit of Loneliness.  Sarton.
Gone Away.  Levertov.
House by the Tracks, A.  Etter.
I Saw in Louisiana a Live-Oak Growing.  Whitman.
Interior.  Parker.
Little Ecologue.  Wylie.
Loneliness.  Carruth.
Loneliness.  Jenkins.
Loneliness.  Shegonee.
Lonely Boy.  Kitching.
Lonely Man, The.  Jarrell.
Lyricism of the Weak, The.  Viereck.
Mariana.  Tennyson.
Missing My Daughter.  Spender.
Mr. Flood's Party.  Robinson.
On the Wide Heath.  Millay.
One.  Rodgers.
Poem: "I've been a woman."  Sanchez.
Sheep-Herder's Lament, The.  Chapman.
Since You've Been Away.  Jozsef.
Sleeping Alone.  Fickert.
So lonely am I.  Ono no Komachi.
Song: "You're wondering if I'm lonely."  Rich.
Sorrow.  Chu Shu-chen.
Suite: Judy Blue Eyes.  Stills.
Summary.  Sanchez.
Talking after Christmas Blues.  Henri.
These.  Williams.
Third Day in a Strange City.  Berge.
Three Weeks in the State of Loneliness.  Piercy.
To Marguerite—Continued.  *Fr.* Switzerland.  Arnold.
Today.  Lochhead.
Tonight I've watched.  Sappho.
Wanderer's Grave, The.  Sage.
What Color Is Lonely.  Rodgers.
When I Am Not With You.  Teasdale.
"When I'm alone"—the words tripped off his tongue.  Sassoon.
Where Have You Gone?  Evans.
Wife A-Lost, The.  Barnes.
Wind blows out of the gates of the day, The.  *Fr.* The Land of
     Heart's Desire.  Yeats.

**Long Island, New York**
Bonac.  Wheelock.
In the Hamptons.  Morris.
Long Island Springs.  Moss.

**Longfellow, Henry Wadsworth**
Longfellow's Visit to Venice.  Betjeman.
Poe and Longfellow.  *Fr.* A Fable for Critics.  Lowell.

**Lorelei**
Lorelei, The.  Heine.

**Los Angeles, California**
Cold Rain Obscures L.A. Tonight, A.  Quagliano.

**Lot (Bible)**
Lot Later.  Nemerov.

**Lotus**
Lotos-Eaters, The.  Tennyson.

**Louis XIV, King of France**
Satire upon the French King, A.  Brown.

**Louisburg, Nova Scotia**
Louisburg.  *Unknown.*

**Louisiana**
Pine Barrens: Letter Home.  Mathis.
Southern Season.  Claudel.
View of Louisiana.  Mathis.

**Love**
*Book of Love Poetry, A* (BoLoP).  Jon Stallworthy, ed.
*Elizabethan Sonnets* (ESo).  Maurice Evans, ed.
*Gambit Book of Love Poems* (GBL).  Geoffrey Grigson, ed.
*Love's Aspects* (LoAs).  Jean Garrigue, comp.
*One Little Room, an Everywhere* (OLR).  Myra Cohn
     Livingston, ed.
*Scottish Love Poems* (SLP).  Antonia Fraser, ed.

**Lowell, Amy**
For Amy Lowell.  Cullen.
**Lowell, James Russell**
Lowell.  *Fr.* A Fable for Critics.  Lowell.
**Lowell, Robert**
Stone Words for Robert Lowell.  Eberhart.
**Lucifer.**  *See* Satan.
**Luck**
Good and Bad Luck.  Hay.
Good Luck.  Herrick.
Libation.  Levertov.
Luck.  Gibson.
Pain.  Södergran.
**Lucknow, India**
Relief of Lucknow, The.  R.T.S. Lowell.
**Lucretius**
Lucretius.  Tennyson.
**Luddites**
Song for the Luddites.  Byron.
**Luke, Saint**
Saint Luke the Painter.  *Fr.* The House of Life.  Rossetti.
**Lullabies.**  *See* **Cradle Song** *and* **Lullaby** *in* **Title and First Line**
***Index.***
**Lumbering and Lumbermen**
Bushfeller, The.  Duggan.
Canada-I-O.  *Unknown.*
Clearing, The.  Conn.
Colley's Run-I-O.  *Unknown.*
Farmer and the Shanty Boy, The.  *Unknown.*
Frozen Logger, The.  *Unknown.*
In Winter in the Woods Alone.  Frost.
Jam on Gerry's Rocks, The.  *Unknown.*
Johnny Carroll's Camp.  *Unknown.*
Lake of the Caogama, The.  *Unknown.*
Late Snow and Lumber Strike of the Summer of Fifty-Four,
     The.  Snyder.
Little Brown Bulls, The.  *Unknown.*
Lumberman's Alphabet, The.  *Unknown.*
Michigan I-O.  *Unknown.*
Once More A-Lumbering Go.  *Unknown.*
Peter Amberley.  *Unknown.*
Raftsmen, The.  *Unknown.*
Roving Shanty Boy, The.  *Unknown.*
Shanty Boys and the Pine, The.  *Unknown.*
Shanty Man's Life, A.  *Unknown.*
Timber (Jerry the Mule).  *Unknown.*
Turner's Camp on the Chippewa.  *Unknown.*
Wild Lumberjack, The.  *Unknown.*
Wild Mustard River, The.  *Unknown.*
Woodman Spare That Tree.  Morris.
**Lumumba, Patrice**
Lumumba's Grave.  Hughes.
**Lust**
At Times.  Wiegner.
Becoming a Nun.  Jong.
But for Lust.  Pitter.
Classroom.  Aitchison.
Conversion.  Hewitt.
Desire.  Coleridge.
Don 1958.  Alta.
Down, Wanton, Down!  Graves.
Expense of spirit in a waste of shame, Th'.  *Fr.* Sonnets.
     Shakespeare.
Filling her compact and delicious body.  Berryman.
Gentle Breeze, A.  Durfey.
In the Orchard.  Stuart.
Indomitable, The.  Rokosi.
It's Just the Same to Me.  Hesse.
Organ Solo.  Skinner.
Late-Flowering Lust.  Betjeman.
Mutes, The.  Levertov.
On Sir Voluptuous Beast.  Jonson.

Playboy.  Wilbur.
Power of Women.  Sobol.
Sic et Non.  Read.
To Barba.  May.
Twenty-Third Flight.  Birney.
Two Songs.  Rich.
Vine, The.  Herrick.
**Lutes**
Blame not my lute, for he must sound.  Wyatt.
Cat and the Lute, The.  Master.
Music's Duel.  Crashaw.
My lute, awake! Perform the last.  Wyatt.
Of My Lady Isabella Playing on the Lute.  Waller.
When to her lute Corinna sings.  Campion.
**Lynching**
Alabama.  Bohanon.
Between the World and Me.  Wright.
Haunted Oak, The.  Dunbar.
I Saw Them Lynching.  Freeman.
Lynching, The.  McKay.
Lynching and Burning.  St. John.
Plaint.  Ford.
So Quietly.  Hill.
Swimmers, The.  Tate.
**Lyonesse**
When I Set Out for Lyonesse.  Hardy.
**Lyrebirds**
Lyrebirds.  Wright.

**M**

**"MacDiarmid, Hugh" (Christopher Murray Grieve)**
To Hugh MacDiarmid.  Fraser.
To Hugh MacDiarmid.  Morgan.
**Machado, Antonio**
Street, The.  Smith.
**McHenry, Fort**
Star-Spangled Banner, The.  Key.
**Machines**
Deus Ex Machina.  Armour.
Egg and the Machine, The.  Frost.
Garbage Disposal Truck, The.  Kinnell.
La Marche des Machines.  Tessimond.
Love to My Electric Handmixer.  Wakoski.
Now I Set Me.  Herman.
Portrait of a Machine.  Untermeyer.
Portrait of an Engine Driver.  Jones.
Steam Shovel.  Malam.
Steam Threshing Machine, The.  Turner.
Steamboats, Viaducts, and Railways.  Wordsworth.
**McKinley, William**
White House Blues.  *Unknown.*
Zolgotz.  *Unknown.*
**MacLeish, Archibald**
Fresco for A. MacLeish, A.  Hayes.
On a Flimmering Floom You Shall Ride.  Sandburg.
**MacNeice, Louis**
Last Word, A.  Rodgers.
**McSorley's Bar (New York City)**
I was sitting in McSorley's.  Cummings.
**Macy's (department store)**
Macy's Poem, The.  Reiss.
**Madness**
Birdwatchers of America.  Hecht.
Counting the Mad.  Justice.
Cry.  Scott.
Curriculum Vitae: Incomplete.  Ritchie.
Evening in the Sanitarium.  Bogan.

First day's night had come, The.  Dickinson.
First Lecture.  Whitehead.
Going Home.  Roper
Heard in a Violent Ward.  Roethke.
Howl.  Ginsberg.
I Am.  Clare.
In a Dark Time.  Roethke.
Kaddish, *sels.*  Ginsberg.
Lines Written During a Period of Insanity.  Cowper.
Locked in a Home for Les Enfants Dérangés en Dieu.  Nolan.
Mad Maid's Song, The.  Herrick.
Mad Mother, The.  Wordsworth.
Mad Song.  Blake.
Mad Song.  Levertov.
Mad Tom of Bedlam.  *Unknown.*
Madhouse.  Hernton.
Madness.  Yoshihara.
Madness One Monday Evening.  Fields.
Mad-Woman, The.  Strong.
Much madness is divinest sense.  Dickinson.
Ringing the Bells.  Sexton.
Song of the Mad Prince, The.  De la Mare.
There is one, never seen, behind that window.  Smith.
Three anti-depressants and one diuretic a day.  *Fr.* Letters to
    Live Poets.  Beaver.
Time Out.  Henley.
To a Student Poet, Hospitalized, Having "Broken with Reality."
    Jellema.
To One in Bedlam.  Dowson.
Tom o' Bedlam's Song.  *Unknown.*
Tyger! Tyger!  Nolan.
Visits to St. Elizabeths.  Bishop.
Waking in the Blue.  Lowell.
Whats My Name If Not Everyone Elses.  Salinas.
Why Should Not Old Men Be Mad?  Yeats.
You, Doctor Martin.  Sexton.
*See also* **Mental Illness.**
**Madrid, Spain**
City of Anguish.  Rolfe.
**Magi**
Ballad of Befana, The.  McGinley.
Carol of the Brown King.  Hughes.
Carol of the Three Kings.  Merwin.
Gift, The.  Williams.
Heine in Scots.  Gray.
Journey of the Magi, The.  Eliot.
Magi, The.  Yeats.
Perfect Gift, The.  Cooke.
Three Holy Kings from Morgenland.  Heine.
Three Kings, The.  Dario.
Three Kings, The.  Longfellow.
Through the Dark the Dreamers Came.  Marlatt.
Twelfth Night.  Bishop.
We Three Kings of Orient Are.  Hopkins.
Wise Men and Shepherds.  Godolphin
**Magic**
For the El Paso Weather Bureau.  Wild.
Harry Houdini, the Hippodrome, New York, January 7, 1918.
    Hilberry.
Magic.  Johnson.
Sermonette.  Reed.
Testing Tree, The.  Kunitz.
Two Magicians, The.  *Unknown.*
**Magnolia Trees**
Planting a Magnolia.  Snodgrass.
**Magpies**
Magpies, The.  Piece.
Trend Spotter.  Turner.
**Maia**
Ode to May, Fragment.  Keats.
**Mail and Mailmen**
Dead Letter Office, The.  Chernoff.

Epitaph for a Postal Clerk. Browne.
Getting the Mail. Kinnell.
Henry's Mail. *Fr.* Dream Songs. Berryman.
Letter Edged in Black, The. *Unknown.*
Mailman, The. Brush.
Mailman, The. Contoski.
Mrs. G. Watters. Ormsby.
Night Mail. Auden.
Postman, The. Challis.
Postman, The. Rossetti.
Resignation Day. Friedman.
Six-Horse Limited Mail, The. Fuller.

**Maine (ship)**
Battleship of *Maine*. *Unknown.*

**Maine (state)**
District, The: Both Sides of Chandler River. Enslin.
Miss Ada. Fahy.
York Harbor Morning. Garrett.

**Majorca**
Andraitx-Pomegranate Flowers. Lawrence.

**Malachy, Saint**
St. Malachy. Merton.

**Malaga, Spain**
Malaga. Hutchinson.

**Malcolm X (Malcolm Little)**
Aardvark. Fields.
At That Moment. Patterson.
El-Hajj Malik El-Shabazz. Hayden.
For Malcolm, a Year After. Knight.
For Malcolm: After Mecca. Barrax.
For Malcolm Who Walks in the Eyes of Our Children. Troupe.
For Malcolm X. Alba.
For Malcolm X. Walker.
I Remember. Jackson.
Malcolm. Clifton.
Malcolm, a Thousandth Poem. Rivers.
Malcolm X. Brooks.
Malcolm X—An Autobiography. Neal.
Poem for Black Hearts, A. Baraka.
Portrait of Malcolm X. Knight.
Sun Came, The. Knight.
They Are Killing All the Young Men. Henderson.

**Mallarmé, Stéphane**
Mallarme on July 14, 1889. Batki.

**Manassas, Battles of.** *See* **Bull Run, Battles of.**

**Manchester, England**
Murphy in Manchester. Montague.

**Mandalay, Burma**
Mandalay. Kipling.

**Mandelstam, Osip**
Mandelstam. Young.
Osip Mandelshtam. Layton.

**Manhattan.** *See* **New York City.**

**Mankind**
Apostrophe to Man. Millay.
As Concerning Man. Radcliffe.
Awake, my St. John! leave all meaner things. *Fr.* An Essay on Man. Pope.
Away, Melancholy. Smith.
Birds and Man. Mabuza.
Brief Essay on Man. Guiterman.
Chorus Sacerdotum. Greville.
Common Dust. Johnson.
Consider the Auk. Nash.
Corruption. Vaughan.
Dead, The. Very.
Discrimination. Rexroth.
Divine Image, The. *Fr.* Songs of Innocence. Blake.
Explorations. MacNeice.
For A' That and A' That. Burns.
Four seasons fill the measure of the year. Keats.
Great Way of the Man, The. Russell.

Here. Thomas.
Hollow Men, The. Eliot.
Horror Comic. Conquest.
Human Abstract, The. *Fr.* Songs of Experience. Blake.
Human Form Divine, The. Raine.
Human Life: On the Denial of Immortality. Coleridge.
Hymn of Man. Swinburne.
If. Kipling.
In Shame and Humiliation. Wright.
Inscription on the Monument of a Newfoundland Dog. Byron.
Know then thyself, presume not God to scan. *Fr.* An Essay on Man. Pope.
Life Cycle of Common Man. Nemerov.
Lines Written in Early Spring. Wordsworth.
Man. Herbert.
Man. Vaughan.
Man Is a Snow. Birney.
Meditatio. Pound.
Mostly People. Nichols.
Nature of Man, The. Sisson.
Original Sin. Jeffers.
Pity This Busy Monster, Manunkind. Cummings.
Prayer before Birth. MacNeice.
Progress. Meinke.
Psyche. Coleridge.
Pulley, The. Herbert.
Satire against Mankind, A. Earl of Rochester.
Self-Knowledge. Coleridge.
Sic Vita. King.
That Nature Is a Heraclitean Fire. Hopkins.
To My Son Parker, Asleep in the Next Room. Kaufman.
Truant, The. Pratt.
Unnatural Powers. Jeffers.
What Is He? Lawrence.
When Serpents Bargain for the Right to Squirm. Cummings.
Windows, The. Herbert.
Worstest Beast, The. Jackson.

**Mannequins**
Window Dressing. Peskett.

**Man-of-War Birds**
To the Man-of-War Bird. Whitman.

**Mansfield, Jayne**
Of Jayne Mansfield, Flannery O'Connor, My Mother and Me. Danniell.

**Mantegna, Andrea**
For "An Allegorical Dance of Women" by Andrea Mantegna. Rossetti.

**Mao Tse-tung**
Thoughts of Chairman Mao. Young.

**Maps**
Map, The. Oden.
Map of Places, The. Riding.
Private Letter to Brazil, A. Oden.

**Marathon, Battle of**
Persian Version, The. Graves.

**Marc Antony**
Antony to Cleopatra. Lytle.
Tact. Pascal.
To Mark Anthony in Heaven. Williams.

**March**
Confrontations of March. Dillow.
Dear March, come in! Dickinson.
March. Hopper.
March. *Unknown.*
March. Williams.
March. Wright
Not to March. Hackleman.
Twenty-seventh of March, The. Bryant.
Twilight in Middle March, A. Ledwidge.
Written in March. Wordsworth.

**Mardi Gras**
Mardi Gras. Keithley.

**Marigolds**
Marigold, The. Carew.
Marigold. Haines.
Marigold, The. Wither.
Marigolds. Carman.

**Marijuana**
Marijuana Patch on the State Hospital's Former Grounds.
    Whiting.
Marijuana Notation. Ginsberg.
Smoking Drugs with Strangers. Bowering.

**Marines.** *See* **United States Marine Corps.**

**Marion, Francis**
Song of Marion's Men. Bryant.

**Mark Antony.** *See* **Marc Antony.**

**Markiewicz, Constance Georgine, Countess**
In Memory of Eva Gore-Booth and Con Markiewicz. Yeats.

**Marlborough, John Churchill, 1st Duke of**
False Favorite's Downfall, The. *Unknown.*
New Song Made in Honour of His Grace the Duke of
    Marlborough, A. Durfey.
Satirical Elegy on the Death of a Late Famous General, A.
    Swift.

**Marlin**
Marlin. Ghiselin.

**Marriage**
About a Year After He Got Married He Would Sit Alone in an
    Abandoned Shack. Whitehead.
About Marriage. Levertov.
Ache of Marriage, The. Levertov.
After Selecting the Wedding Invitations. Levenberg.
Anniversary, The. Ai.
Anniversary. Dacey.
Any Wife to Any Husband. Browning.
Applicant, The. Plath.
Bachelor Bold and Young. *Unknown.*
Ballad of Calvary Street. Baxter.
Ballad of the Despairing Husband. Creeley.
Because. McAuley.
Bed, The. Saleh.
Birthday, The. Dacey.
Bon Mot, A. *Unknown.*
Brewer's Man, The. Strong.
By Vows of Love Together Bound. Fitch.
Call It a Good Marriage. Graves.
Conspirators, The. Burke.
Crisis, The. Creeley.
Daisy Bell; or, A Bicycle Built for Two. Dacre.
Daughters Will You Marry? *Unknown.*
De Se. Weever.
Dedication to My Wife, A. Eliot.
Domesticity. Hall.
Early Thoughts of Marriage. Cotton.
Enticer. Armour.
Epigram: "As Thomas was cudgeled one day by his wife."
    Swift.
Epigram: "In the neat parlor of their honeymoon." Halpern.
Epitaph upon Husband and Wife Who Died and Were Buried
    Together, An. Crashaw.
Epithalamion: "The kingfisher falls through the dry air."
    Wright.
Epithalamion: "Ye learned sisters which have oftentimes."
    Spenser.
Epithalamion Made at Lincoln's Inn. Donne.
Essay on Marriage, *sel.* Finch.
Exequy upon His Wife. King.
Farmer's Bride, The. Mew.
Farmer's Wife, The. Sexton.
First Snow of the Year, The. Van Doren.
For a Marriage. Jong.
For Three Days. Payne.
40—Love. McGough.
From a Slave Marriage Ceremony. *Unknown.*

Gerda, My Husband's Wife. Triem.
Getting the License. Koertge.
Griesly Wife, The. Manifold.
Grim Fairy Tale. Wiggam.
Groom's Lament, The. Peterson.
Habitation. Atwood.
Happy Marriage. Blacklock.
Here Comes. Jong.
Holy Matrimony. Keble.
Home Burial. Frost.
Hymeneal Song on the Nuptials of the Lady Anne Wentworth
    and the Lord Lovelace, An. Carew.
I Am of These. Curry.
I gave myself to him. Dickinson.
I Wish I Was Single Again. *Unknown.*
In the Last Few Moments Came the Old German Cleaning
    Woman. Cooper.
In the Room of the Bride-Elect. Hardy.
Late Abed. MacLeish.
Les Sylphides. MacNeice.
Letter to an Absent Son. DeFrees.
Letter to Dafnis, A. Countess of Winchilsea.
Lines for Those to Whom Tragedy Is Denied. Oates.
Live Man's Epitaph. Hope.
Love ("She stood in her snood and arasaid"). *Unknown.*
Love's Matrimony. Duke of Newcastle.
Mad Answer to a Madman, A. Hayman.
Major Macroo. Smith.
Man and Wife. Goodman.
Man and Wife. Sexton.
Man Who Married Magdalene, The. Simpson.
Marital Journey, The. Araaya.
Marriage. Berry.
Marriage, The. Bertolino.
Marriage. Clarke.
Marriage. Corso.
Marriage. Lopes.
Marriage. Moore.
Marriage, The. Strand.
Marriage. *Unknown.*
Marriage. Williams.
Marriage and Money. *Fr.* The Happy Pair. Sedley.
Married and Single Life. *Unknown.*
Married Man Blues. *Unknown.*
Maternity Gown. Holbrook.
Meditation at Kew. Wickham.
Modern Love. Meredith.
Modern Romance. Harris.
Most Like an Arch This Marriage. Ciardi.
My Three Wives. *Unknown.*
Nesting. Saleh.
Nice Old Couple, The. Aldis.
Night Fight. Piercy.
Occasional Poem. Housman.
Old Flame, The. Lowell.
Old-Marrieds, The. Brooks.
On Giles and Joan. Jonson.
On Marriage. Flatman.
Packin' Trunk Blues. *Unknown.*
Personals, The. Feldman.
Plea for Trigamy, A. Seaman.
Portrait of a Marriage. Abse.
Proposal of Marriage, The. *Unknown.*
Prothalamium. MacDonagh.
Retired Boxer, The. Lucilius.
River-Merchant's Wife, The: A Letter. Li Po.
Robertin Tush. *Unknown.*
Rosy Apple, Lemon or Pear. *Unknown.*
Sensibility. Simpson.
She Vowed Him This. Box.
Shoes are made to fit the feet. *Unknown.*
Silver Wedding. Hodgson.

Slave Marriage Ceremony Supplement. *Unknown.*
Slice of Wedding Cake, A. Graves.
Some twenty years of marital agreement. Cunningham.
Song Ballet. *Unknown.*
Song for a Marriage. Miller.
Sonnet Reversed. Brooke.
Staying Married. Allen.
Stolen Peonies, The. Williams.
Stumbling. Lourie.
Suite for Marriage, A. Ignatow.
Then Almitra spoke again and said, "And what of Marriage,
   Master?" *Fr.* The Prophet. Gibran.
This Cold Nothing Else. Wier.
To a Friend, Who Recommended a Wife to Him. *Unknown.*
To a Lady on Her Marriage. Bell.
To My Dear and Loving Husband. Bradstreet.
"To Speak of Woe That Is in Marriage." Lowell.
To the Ladies. Chudleigh.
Twenty Year Marriage. Ai.
Upon Wedlock, and Death of Children. Taylor.
Wait for Me. Creeley.
Waiting at the Church; or, My Wife Won't Let Me. Leigh.
Way Sun Keeps Falling Away from Every Window, The.
   Lifshin.
Wedding. Brown.
Wedding Poem. Waters.
Wedding-Wind. Larkin.
Westminster Drollery, 1671. Behn.
When Charlie Bowdre married Manuela, we carried them.
   Ondaatje.
When I Was Single. *Unknown.*
Whitsun Weddings, The. Larkin.
Who Drags the Fiery Artist Down? Day.
Why Should a Foolish Marriage Vow. *Fr.* Marriage à la Mode.
   Dryden.
Wife Killer. Scannell.
Wife to Husband. Adcock.
Wife Who Would a Wanton Be, The. *Unknown.*
Wife Wrapt in Wether's Skin, The. *Unknown.*
Word to Husbands, A. Nash.
World Is Really a Sugarplum House in the Forest, The.
   Boyajian.
You were young—but that was scarcely to your credit. *Fr.*
   Monogamy. Gould.
**Marshes**
Dingman's Marsh. Moore.
In the Marsh. Higginson.
Marsh, The. Snodgrass.
Marsh, New Year's Day, The. Everwine.
Marsh Song—At Sunset. Lanier.
Marshes of Glynn, The. Lanier.
Paean to Place. Niedecker.
Sunrise. Lanier.
Winter Pond. Logue.
**Martyrs**
Admire Cranmer! Smith.
Gift of Fire, The. Mueller.
Norman Morrison. Ferguson.
Norman Morrison. Mitchell.
Of Late. Starbuck.
On the Late Massacre in Piedmont. Milton.
Sunt Leones. Smith.
Wallabout Martyrs, The. Whitman.
**Marvell, Andrew**
Marvell's Ghost. Ayloffe.
You, Andrew Marvell. MacLeish.
**Mary, the Virgin**
Annunciation. Maura.
Annunciation, The. *Unknown.*
Assumption. Fallon.
Assumption, The. *Unknown.*
At Dawn the Virgin Is Born. Lope de Vega.

Blessed Virgin Compared to the Air We Breathe, The.
   Hopkins.
Cherry-Tree Carol, The. *Unknown.*
Empryce of prys, imperatrice. *Fr.* Ane Ballat of Our Lady.
   Dunbar.
God, Woman, Egg. Minton.
"He came all so still." *Unknown.*
Hymn to the Virgin. William of Shoreham.
I Sing of a Maiden. *Unknown.*
In Praise of Mary. *Unknown.*
In the Town. *Unknown.*
Little Carol of the Virgin, A. Lope de Vega.
M and A, R and I. *Unknown.*
Mary and Her Son Alone. Ryman.
Mary Had a Baby. *Unknown.*
Mary, Mother of Christ. Cullen.
Mary's Dream. *Unknown.*
May Magnificat, The. Hopkins.
Mother of God, The. Yeats.
O, My Heart Is Woe! *Unknown.*
O Simplicitas. *Fr.* Three Songs of Mary. L'Engle.
Of One That Is So Fair and Bright. *Unknown.*
On the Blessèd Virgin's Bashfulness. Crashaw.
Orison to the Blessed Virgin, An. Herebert.
Our Lady. M. Coleridge.
Penitent Considers Another Coming of Mary, A. Brooks.
Seven Blessings of Mary, The. *Unknown.*
Song about Mary. Mitchell.
Star Song, The: A Carol to the King. Herrick.
Virgin Jewess, Rising with a Cry, The. Baker.
Virgin Mary, The. Bowers.
Virgin Mary, The. *Unknown.*
Virgin Mary Had One Son. *Unknown.*
Virgin Mary to Christ on the Cross, The. Southwell.
Virgin's Song, The. *Unknown.*
Welcome O Great Mary. O'Gallagher.
**Mary Magdalene**
Magdalene, Afterward. Whitehill.
Mary Magdalene. Kassia.
Mary Magdalene. Lewis.
Mary to Her Savior's Tomb. Newton.
On Mary Magdalen. Drummond.
Saint Mary Magdalene; or, The Weeper. Crashaw.
**Maryland**
Maryland, My Maryland! Randall.
**Maryland Yellow-throat**
Maryland Yellow-throat, The. Van Dyke.
**Marx, Groucho**
To the Lady Portrayed by Margaret Dumont. Hollander.
**Marx, Karl**
Karl Marx is a comic novelist, almost. *Fr.* The Alphabet
   Murders. Tranter.
Workers Rose on May Day or Postscript to Karl Marx. Lorde.
**Masochism**
In Francum. Davies.
**Massachusetts**
To the Governor and Legislature of Massachusetts. Nemerov.
**Massada**
At Masada. Neufeld.
Never Again, The. Dobzynski.
On an autumn night, lying restless, far from her broken
   homeland. *Fr.* Massada. Lamdan.
**Masters, Edgar Lee**
Figure. M. L. Masters.
House in Chicago, The. M. L. Masters.
Man, My Father, The. M. L. Masters.
**Matadors.** *See* **Bullfights and Bullfighters.**
**Mathematics**
Euclid. Lindsay.
Invention of Zero, The. Urdang.
Tortoise Shell. Lawrence.
**Matisse, Henri**

Matisse: "The Red Studio." Snodgrass.
Matisse's Jazz Cut-Outs at the National Gallery. Lefcowitz.

**May**
Composed on a May Morning, 1838. Wordsworth.
Corinna's Going a-Maying. Herrick.
Fountain in the Park, The. Haley.
May. Neilson.
May. C. Rossetti.
May. Wade.
May Day Carol, A. *Unknown.*
May Day Dancing, The. Nemerov.
May Magnificat, The. Hopkins.
May Poem. *Unknown.*
Mayers' Song, The. *Unknown.*
Padstow Night Song, The. *Unknown.*
Pray in May. Metcalfe.
Same Lady, The. Nichols.
Song on May Morning. Milton.
Spring in These Hills. MacLeish.
To the Lady May. Townsend.
You that in love finde lucke and habundance. Wyatt.

**Mayo, Ireland**
County Mayo, The. Raftery.

**Mechanics**
Detroit Grease Shop Poem. Levine.
Misery of Mechanics, The. Booth.

**Medals**
On a Nomination to the Legion of Honour. *Unknown.*

**Medea**
Medea. Euripides.

**Medicine**
*Poems from the Medical World* (PMW). Howard Sergeant, ed.

**Mediterranean Sea**
Mediterranean, The. Tate.
Middle of the World. Lawrence.

**Medusa**
Medusa. Bogan.
Medusa. O'Sullivan.

**Meiklejohn, Alexander**
To Alexander Meiklejohn, *sel.* Beecher.

**Melampus**
Melampus. Meredith.

**Melancholy**
Away, Melancholy. Smith.
City of Dreadful Night, The. Thomson ("B. V.").
Charles Carville's Eyes. Robinson.
Dejection; An Ode. Coleridge.
Here I sit in my infested cubicle. Greenwood.
Il Penseroso. Milton.
Like Fire Spreadin/The Joylessness. Nkabinde.
Lines Written in Dejection. Yeats.
Melancholia. Bridges.
Melancholy ("Hence, all you vain delights"). Fletcher.
Mirth and Melancholy. Duchess of Newcastle.
My Sad Self. Ginsberg.
Ode on Melancholy. Keats.
Pleasures of Melancholy, The. Warton.
Sad Child's Song, The. Van Doren.
Sadness. Cartwright.
Stanzas, Written in Dejection, near Naples. Shelley.
To Melancholy. Countess of Winchelsea.

**Melville, Herman**
At Melville's Tomb. Crane.
Herman Melville. Aiken.

**Memorial Day**
Decoration Day. Sinclair.
Rememberance Day. Scannell.

**Memory**
Brooding Grief. Lawrence.
Celandine. Thomas.
Crossing. MacLeish.
Crystals Like Blood. "MacDiarmid."

Dear Men and Women. Wheelock.
Deja Vu. Mulligan.
Embroidery. Jacobs.
Forgiven Past, The. Riding.
Grandmother, Rocking. Merriam.
He Wakes Again in Early Light. Kistler.
Heart! We will forget him! Dickinson.
Home. Blight.
Homecoming Celebration. Catacalos.
House of Hospitalities, The. Hardy.
Legende. Crane.
Letter from the Caribbean, A. Howes.
Lines Written a Few Miles above Tintern Abbey. Wordsworth.
Looking at Pictures to Be Put Away. Snyder.
Mementos, 1. Snodgrass.
Memory. Aldrich.
Memory, A. Allingham.
Memory. Deutsch.
Memory. Landor.
Mnemosyne. Stickney.
Ode to Memory. Tennyson.
Oft, in the Stilly Night. Moore.
Old Memories of Earth. Mason.
Old Upright I Did Not Learn to Play, The. Flocos.
People, The. Creeley.
Piano. Lawrence.
Proust's Madeleine. Rexroth.
Remember. C. Rossetti.
Remembering. Tóth.
Reminiscence. Irwin.
Resurrection. Fearing.
Return. Spencer.
Rhapsody on a Windy Night. Eliot.
Romantics. Lindsay.
Rustling of Grass, The. Noyes.
Scrapbooks. Giovanni.
Since. Auden.
Song: "Memory, hither come." Blake.
Stanzas: "In a drear-nighted December." Keats.
Stephen's Green Revisited. Weber.
Ten Days Leave. Snodgrass.
Thinking of the Lost World. Jarrell.
Time does not bring relief; you all have lied. Millay.
Time Reminded Me. Uceda.
Two Memories. Mathis.
Two Old Ladies. Sassoon.
Uncovering. MacDonald.
Wedded Memories. Marston.
When to the sessions of sweet silent thought. Sonnets, XXX. Shakespeare.
Within the Circuit of This Plodding Life. Thoreau.
Your Birthday in the California Mountains. Rexroth.

**Men**
Blind Spot. Birch.
Fall In. Kirstein.
Hooked on the Magic Muscle. King.
Man, Man, Man Is for the Woman Made. *Unknown.*
Man-Sized Job. Hall.
Never love unless you can. Campion.
Olaf and Sigurd. Sargent.
Ordinary Man, The. Service.
Psalm Praising the Hair of Man's Body, A. Levertov.
Resting Figure. Levertov.
Some Chicks Just Can't Tell a Cézanne from a Sears. Yates.
Stew Meat Blues. *Unknown.*
Three Men. *Unknown.*
Tired As I Can Be. *Unknown.*
Two Old Men. Niedecker.
Woman and Men. Mumin.
Word in Edgeways, A. Tomlinson.

**Menageries.** *See* **Zoos.**
**Mennonites**

Mennonite Farm Wife. Kauffman.

**Mental Illness**
Asylum for War Victims. Morgan.
But Her Eyes Spoke Another Language. Duncan.
Death of a Son. Silkin.
Dementia Praecox. Bishop.
Dropping Toward Stillness. Barba.
Evening in the Sanitarium. Bogan.
Frank Drummer. *Fr.* Spoon River Anthology. Masters.
Grandeurs of the crazy man alone, The. Roethke.
Hard Rock Returns to Prison from the Hospital for the Criminal Insane. Knight.
Hour of Feeling, The. Simpson.
In a Mental Hospital Sitting Room. Jennings.
Invisible Woman, The. Morgan.
Lines Written During a Period of Insanity. Cowper.
Local Man Remembering Betty Fuller, A. Whitehead.
Man Upstairs, The. Hilton.
Manic Depressant. Dammers.
Mental Cases. Owen.
Mental Health. Fried.
Mental Hospital Garden, The. Williams.
Patient, The: Rockland County Sanitarium. Hernton.
Repression of War Experience. Sassoon.
Ringing the Bells. Sexton.
Schizophrenia. Bartlett.
Servant to Servants, A. Frost.
Simplicity. Simpson.
Third Avenue in Sunlight. Hecht.
Visit to the Asylum, A. Millay.
Waking in the Blue. Lowell.
What Is There? Schechter.
*See also* **Madness.**

**Mental Retardation**
Art Lesson, The. Morgan.
Class, The. Jacobsen.
Dickens Characters. Morgan.
Halfwit. Dowling.
Hospital for Defectives. Blackburn.

**Mercy**
Mercy. *Unknown.*
Ode to Mercy. Collins.
Quality of Mercy, The. *Fr.* The Merchant of Venice. Shakespeare.

**Merlin**
Merlin. Emerson.
Merlin and the Gleam. Tennyson.
Merlin Enthralled. Wilbur.
Merlin, They Say. Greville.

**Mermaid Tavern**
Lines on the Mermaid Tavern. Keats.

**Mermaids and Mermen**
Ballad by Hans Breitmann. Leland.
Catch. Hughes.
Clerk Colvill. *Unknown.*
Fable of the Mermaid and the Drunks. Neruda.
Forsaken Merman, The. Arnold.
I Did Not See a Mermaid? Johnson.
Keeper of the Eddystone Light, The. *Unknown.*
Kennack Sands. Binyon.
Little Fan. Reeves.
Madness One Monday Evening. Fields.
Mermaid, The. King.
Mermaid, The. Mueller.
Mermaid, The, *sel.* Tennyson.
Mermaid, The. *Unknown.*
Mermaid, The. Yeats.
Mermaiden, A. Hennell.
Mermaidens' Vesper-Hymn, The. *Fr.* Syren Songs. Darley.
Mermaids. De la Mare.
Mermaids six or seven. *Fr.* The Vision of the Mermaids. Hopkins.

My gentle Puck, come hither. *Fr.* A Midsummer Night's Dream. Shakespeare.
Sailor Boy, The. Tennyson.
Sea-Fairies, The. Tennyson.
Song by Lady Happy, As a Sea-Goddess. *Fr.* The Convent of Pleasure. Duchess of Newcastle.

**Merrimac (ship)**
*Cumberland* and the *Merrimac*, The. *Unknown.*

**Merry-go-rounds**
Carousel, The. Oden.
Merry-go-round. Field.
Merry-go-round. McAuley.
Merry-go-round. Rawlinson.
Merry-go-round, The. Rilke.
Merry-go-round. Van Doren.
On the Merry, merry-go-round. Martin.

**Messiah**
Encounter in Safed. Yungman.
Instructions for the Messiah. Sklarew.
Messiah, The. Yungman.
When the Days Grow Long. Bialik.

**Methodism**
World, the Devil, and Tom Paine, The. *Unknown.*

**Metric System**
Elegy for Yards, Pounds, and Gallons. Wagoner.

**Metropolitan Opera**
Another Poem on the Tearing Down of the Metropolitan Opera House. Stevens.

**Mets, New York (baseball team)**
Ode to the New York Mets. Lindsay.
September Valentine. Sullivan.

**Mexican War**
Defence of the Alamo, The. Miller.
Maid of Monterey, The. *Unknown.*
Santy Anno. *Unknown.*

**Mexico**
Baja—Outside Mexicali. McClure.
In Puerto Vallarta. Ostroff.
Irapuato. Birney.
Leaving Mexico One More Time. Urdang.
Lines for a Young Wanderer in Mexico. Logan.
Mexican Village. Schulte.
Mexico. Hughes.
On the Beach. Ostroff.
Requiem for Sonora. Shelton.
Sinalóa. Birney.
Sunday, Guadalajara. Ostroff.

**Meynell, Alice**
On Looking at a Copy of Alice Meynell's Poems. A. Lowell.

**Mice**
Anne and the Field-Mouse. Serraillier.
Ascend my shoulders, frimly keep thy seat. *Fr.* The Battle of the Frogs and Mice. *Unknown.*
Church Mouse, The. Bullett.
City Mouse and the Garden Mouse, The. Rossetti.
Country Mouse and the City Mouse, The. Sharpe.
Diary of a Church Mouse. Betjeman.
Fearful Finale of the Irascible Mouse, The. Carryl.
Field Mouse, The. Sharp.
Fieldmouse crouches low, A. Sund.
Frog Went A-Courting. *Unknown.*
Funeral Oration for a Mouse. Dugan.
Leaving School. Fuller.
Madame Mouse Trots. Sitwell.
Magical Mouse, The. Patchen.
Marriage of the Frog and the Mouse, The. *Unknown.*
Meadow Mouse, The. Roethke.
Mice in the Hay. Norris.
Monstrous Mouse, A. Kennedy.
Mouse That Gnawed the Oak-Tree Down, The. Lindsay.
Mouse and the Cake, The. Cook.
Mouse Night: One of Our Games. Stafford.

Mouse's Nest. Clare.
Mouse's Petition, The. Barbauld.
Mus Ridiculus Non. Welch.
My mother's maids, when they did sew and spin. *Fr.* Satires. Wyatt.
Poor Mouse. Berssenbrugge.
Ritual Mouse, A. Meredith.
Three Blind Mice. *Unknown.*
To a Mouse. Burns.
To the Field Mice. Eberhart.
Two Mice, The. Henryson.
*Mice Are Rather Nice* (MN). Vardine Moore, comp.

**Michelangelo Buonarroti**
David Homindae. Rosenfeld.

**Michigan**
*The Third Coast: Contemporary Michigan Poetry* (TC). Conrad Hilberry, Herbert Scott, *and* James Tipton, eds.

**Michigan, Lake**
Lake Michigan. Kherdian.
November on Lake Michigan. McKeown.

**Midas**
King Midas. Moss.
King's Speech, The, *sel.* Moss.

**Middle Age**
Aging. Jong.
Ambulando. Brasch.
Birthday Card for a Psychiatrist. Van Duyn.
"Dover Beach"—a Note to That Poem. MacLeish.
Face in the Mirror, The. Graves.
For My Daughter's 20th Birthday. Lowenfels.
From a Correct Address in a Suburb of a Major City. Sorrells.
Hunger Artist, The. Kaufman.
In the Smoking Car. Whitman.
Libertine, The. MacNeice.
Love Song of J. Alfred Prufrock, The. Eliot.
Men at Forty. Justice.
Menstruation at Forty. Sexton.
Mezzo Cammin. Longfellow.
Middle-aged Conversation. Tessimond.
Middleaged Man, The. Simpson.
Next Day. Jarrell.
Ode on Celestial Music. Patten.
Professor Waking, The. Tate.
Some Slippery Afternoon. Gioseffi.
Tea Shop, The. Pound.
There Is Grey in My Eyebrows. Shapiro.
Thirty-Eight. Smith.
Thirty eighth year, The. Clifton.
To His Love in Middle-Age. Brock.

**Middlesex, England**
Middlesex. Betjeman.

**Midnight**
Midnight. Mistral.
No Time for Poetry. Fields.

**Midwifery and Midwives**
Country Midwife, The: A Day. Ai.

**Migrant Workers**
Pastures of Plenty. Guthrie.
Plane Wreck at Los Gatos. Guthrie.

**Milk**
Milkmaid. Lee.
Spilled Milk. Haines.

**Mill, John Stuart**
John Stuart Mill. *Fr.* Clerihews. Bentley.

**Millennium**
It Is Almost the Year Two Thousand. Frost.
Second Coming, The. Yeats.

**Miller, Glenn**
Glenn Miller's music is a trunk. Valle.

**Miller, Henry**
Henry Miller: A Writer. Lem.
Warrant is Out for the Arrest of Henry Miller, A. Hollo.

**Mills and Millers**
Dishonest Miller, The. *Unknown.*
Mill, The. Robinson.
Mill at Romesdal. Hugo.
Miller, The. *Unknown.*
Miller of Dee, The. *Unknown.*
Unfortunate Miller, The. Coppard.

**Milton, John**
Johannes Milton, Senex. Bridges.
Lines on Seeing a Lock of Milton's Hair. Keats.
Lines Printed under the Engraved Portrait of Milton. Dryden.
London, 1802 ("Milton! Thou shouldst be living at this hour"). Wordsworth.
Milton. Blake.
Milton. Longfellow.
Milton. Tennyson.
Milton by Firelight. Snyder.
Milton's Wife on Her Twenty-third Birthday. Conant-Bissell.
On His Blindness. Milton.
On Mr. Milton's Paradise lost. Marvell.

**Milwaukee, Wisconsin**
Walking Milwaukee. Witt.

**Mind.** *See* **Intellect.**

**Minerals**
Crystals like Blood. "MacDiarmid."
*See also* **Mining and Miners.**

**Minerva**
To Minerva. Hood.

**Mining and Miners**
Ballad of Springhill (The Springhill Mine Disaster). MacColl *and* Seeger.
Blackleg Miners, The. *Unknown.*
Blood Donor. Morgan.
Book of Stones. Morgan.
Caliban in the Coal Mines. Untermeyer.
Casey Jones ("Come all you muckers and gather here"). *Unknown.*
Childhood. Walker.
Cousin Jack Song. *At. to* Tregonning.
Derelict Valley. Morgan.
Donibristle Moss Moran Disaster, The. *Unknown.*
Dreary Black Hills, The. *Unknown.*
Drill Man Blues. Sizemore.
Dynamite Song. *Unknown.*
For Laurence Jones. Kizer.
Free Coal. Morgan.
Hard-Working Miner, The. *Unknown.*
I'll Have a Collier for My Sweetheart. Oliver.
I'm Only a Broken-Down Miner. *Unknown.*
Lament While Descending a Shaft. *Unknown.*
Ludlow Massacre, The. Guthrie.
Men in Black. Morgan.
Miner Boy, The. *Unknown.*
Miners. Wright.
Miner's Lifeguard. *Unknown.*
Mining Places. Boden.
1913 Massacre, The. Guthrie.
Oh, Give Me the Hills. *Unknown.*
Only a Miner. *Unknown.*
Prospecting. Ammons.
Prospecting Dream. *Unknown.*
Robens' Promised Land. Purdom.
78 Miners in Mannington, West Virginia. Phillips.
Strip Mining Pit. Gillespie.
Tramp Miner's Song. *Unknown.*
We Don't Know What to Plan or Say or Do. Lally.
Working in the Mines. *Unknown.*
Ye Ancient Yuba Miner of the Days of '49. Upham.

**Ministers.** *See* **Clergy.**

**Minneapolis, Minnesota**
Minneapolis. Hennen.
Minneapolis Poem, The. Wright.

**Minnesota**
Driving toward the Lac Qui Parle River.  Bly.
Ice-Fishing House, The: Long Lake, Minnesota.  Harper.
Late Lights in Minnesota.  Kooser.
**Miracles**
Distance from the Sea, A.  Kees.
Epistle Containing the Strange Medical Experience of Karshish, the Arab Physician, An.  Browning.
Miracles.  Whitman.
Why I am Offended by Miracles.  Bergman.
**Miranda, Carmen**
Carmen Miranda.  Polite.
**Miró, Joan**
Joan Miró ("After that war, when death had gone away").  Todd.
Joan Miró ("Once there were peasant pots and a dry brown hare").  Todd.
**Mirrors**
Face in the Mirror, The.  Graves.
Lady Who Offers Her Looking-Glass to Venus, The.  Prior.
Lais now old, that erst attempting lass.  Plato.
Lais to Aphrodite.  Robinson.
Looking-Glass, A.  Carew.
Looking Glass, The.  Kipling.
Man and His Image, The.  La Fontaine.
Mirror.  Chimako.
Mirror, The.  Glück.
Mirror.  Plath.
Mirror Images.  Speer.
Mirror in the Woods, The.  Rexroth.
Mirrors, The.  Andresen.
Moments of Vision.  Hardy.
On His Mistress Looking in a Glass.  Carew.
Results of a Scientific Survey.  Cutler.
To Cynthia, on Her Looking-Glass.  Kynaston.
With the Face.  Riding.
Written on a Looking-Glass.  *Unknown.*
**Mirth**
Hock-Cart, or Harvest Home, The.  Herrick.
L'Allegro.  Milton.
Lyric to Mirth, A.  Herrick.
To Live Merrily, and To Trust to Good Verses.  Herrick.
**Misanthropy**
Wishes of an Elderly Man, The.  Ralegh.
**Misers**
Aaron Stark.  Robinson.
**Mishima, Yukio**
Mysterious East.  Cole.
Poet's Prayer Para Yukio Mishima.  Aguila.
**Misogyny**
Gentle Echo on Woman, A.  Swift.
Misogynist, The.  Morgan.
**Mission Bay, California**
Mission Bay.  Koethe.
**Missionaries**
Foreign Missions in Battle Array.  Lindsay.
From Greenland's Icy Mountains.  Heber.
Memorial to a Missionary.  Sinclair.
Wake, Isles of the South.  Tappan.
**Mississippi**
Birthday Poem.  Young.
Delta Farmer in a Wet Summer.  Whitehead.
Pachuta, Mississippi/A Memoir.  Young.
Troubador.  Simmons.
**Mississippi River**
Brown River, Smile.  Toomer.
Steamboat Bill.  *Unknown.*
**Missouri**
Early June.  Dickey.
Last Look at La Plata, Missouri.  Barnes.
**Missouri River**
Foreclosure.  Brown.

**Mistletoe**
Mistletoe.  De la Mare.
Under the Mistletoe.  Cullen.
**Mithra**
Song to Mithras, A.  Kipling.
**Mithridates the Great**
Mithridates.  Emerson.
**Moccasins**
Moccasins of an Old Man, The.  Carden.
**Mockingbirds**
Bird-witted.  Moore.
Fable of the Talented Mockingbird.  Bates.
Listen to the Mockingbird.  Winner.
Mockingbird, The.  Jarrell.
Mocking-Bird, The.  *Fr.* Out of the Cradle Endlessly Rocking.  Whitman.
Mockingbird in Winter.  Kroll.
To the Mocking Bird.  Wilde.
**Models**
Looking at Models in Sears Catalogue.  Dacey.
Ode to a Model.  Nabokov.
**Moles**
Anarchist.  Dugdale.
Blue Moles.  Plath.
Eagle and the Mole, The.  Wylie.
Mole, The.  Haines.
Mole, The.  Marcus.
Moles.  Stafford.
Star-Nosed Mole, The.  Wallace.
**Monasteries**
December.  Snyder.
Stanzas from the Grande Chartreuse.  Arnold.
**Monet, Claude**
Monet: "Les Nymphéas."  Snodgrass.
**Money**
America.  Dumas.
American Primitive.  Smith.
Complaint of Chaucer to His Purse, The.  Chaucer.
Dollars.  Schneider.
Fatigue.  Belloc.
Hardship of Accounting, The.  Frost.
How Pleasant It Is to Have Money.  *Fr.* Dipsychus.  Clough.
I love sixpence, jolly little sixpence.  Mother Goose.
Impact of a dollar upon the heart, The.  *Fr.* War Is Kind.  Crane.
Inheritance, An.  Replansky.
Marriage and Money.  *Fr.* The Happy Pair.  Sedley.
Money.  Contoski.
Money.  Nemerov.
Money.  Sisson.
Money Gets the Mastery.  Herrick.
Money Is King.  *Unknown.*
Money Isn't Everything!  Hammerstein.
Money Makes the Mirth.  Herrick.
Money! Money!  *Unknown.*
My God, How the Money Rolls In.  *Unknown.*
My Purse.  *Unknown.*
Of Money.  Googe.
Poem to My Creditors.  Lux.
Sensitive Philanthropist, The.  Enright.
Splendid Shilling, The.  Philips.
Terrible People, The.  Nash.
Words, the Words, the Words, The.  Williams.
Worry About Money.  Raine.
**Mongolia**
For the Cultural Campaign.  Jigmed.
**Monitor (ship)**
Utilitarian View of the *Monitor's* Fight, A.  Melville.
**Monkeys**
At Woodward's Gardens.  Frost.
Monkey.  Read.
Monkeys.  Colum.

Monkeys and the Crocodile, The. Richards.
Monkeys on Mt. Hiei. Shiffert.
Ship of Rio, The. De la Mare.

**Monks**
Carthusians. Dowson.
For a Young Cistercian Monk. Kiely.
Soliloquy of the Spanish Cloister. Browning.
Weak Monk, The. Smith.

**Monmouth, James Scott, Duke of**
Advice to the Painter. Prior.
Ballad Called Perkin's Figary, A. *Unknown.*
Dutchess of Monmouth's Lamentation for the Loss of Her
    Duke, The. *Unknown.*
Hue and Cry after Blood and Murder, A. *Unknown.*
On the University of Cambridge's Burning the Duke of
    Monmouth's Picture. Stepney.
Western Rebel, The. *Unknown.*

**Monroe, Marilyn**
I have come to claim. Grahn.
Marilyn Monroe. Ramsey.

**Monsters**
Chimera, The. Mombert.
Kraken, The. Tennyson.
Troll, The. Prelutsky.

**Mont Blanc**
Hymn before Sun-Rise, in the Vale of Chamouni. Coleridge.
Mont Blanc. Shelley.

**Montana**
Driving Montana. Hugo.
Montana. Hanson.
Montana Pastoral. Cunningham.
Montana Ranch Abandoned. Hugo.
Night at the Napi in Browning, A. Hugo.

**Months**
Months, The. S. Coleridge.
Months, The. *Unknown.*

**Montreal, Canada**
O God! O Montreal. Butler.

**Montrose, James Graham, 5th Earl of**
Execution of Montrose, The. Aytoun.

**Monuments**
Ancient Monuments. Ormond.
City of Monuments. Rukeyser.
For the Union Dead. Lowell.
Inscription for Marye's Heights, Fredericksburg. Melville.

**Moon**
Ablow the Mune. Campbell.
All Other Love Is Like the Moon. *Unknown.*
Autumnal Moon, The. *Fr.* The Seasons. Thomson.
Ballad of the Moon, Moon. García Lorca.
Cat and the Moon, The. Yeats.
Charming the Moon. Den Boer.
Death of the Moon, The. Wagoner.
Elegy: "Tonight the moon is high, to summon all." Bell.
Epiphany on a Plot of Moonlight. Mitchell.
Flying. Westrup.
Full Moon. De la Mare.
Full Moon. Hayden.
Full Moonlight in Spring. Merwin.
Glow and beauty of the stars, The. Sappho.
Golden Moonrise. Braithwaite.
Half Moon. García Lorca.
How to Reach the Moon. Pomerantz.
Hunger Moon. Cooper.
Lady Moon. Milnes.
Lamp in the West, The. Higginson.
Landing on the Moon. Swenson.
Learn'd society of late, A. *Fr.* The Elephant in the Moon: A
    Satire. Butler.
Lunar Baedeker. Loy.
Man in the Moon, The ("Man in the moone stand and strit").
    *Unknown.*

Match with the Moon, A. Rossetti.
Moon, The. Creeley.
Moon, The. *Fr.* Passages. Duncan.
Moon, The. Upton.
Moon and the Yew Tree, The. Plath.
Moon Compasses. Frost.
Moon Is the Number 18, The. Olson.
Moon Poem. Sharp.
Moon Rock. Mally.
Moonrise. Lawrence.
Moonrise in the Rockies. Higginson.
Moon's the North Wind's Cooky, The. Lindsay.
New Moon. *Fr.* The Moon-Bone Cycle. *Unknown.*
Night Song. Cornford.
On the Telescopic Moon. Drennan.
Once Only. Snyder.
Only a Little Litter. Livingston.
Partial Eclipse. Snodgrass.
Pan and Luna. Browning.
Silver. De la Mare.
Song for Ishtar. Levertov.
Sonnet of the Moon, A. Best.
Target. Lister.
To a Solitary Disciple. Williams.
To the Moon ("Art thou pale for weariness"). Shelley.
To the Moon. Winters.
Voyage to the Moon. MacLeish.
Waning Moon, The. Shelley.
Where the Mind Meets the Moon in Revolt. *Fr.* Woman
    Against the Moon. Wolfert.
Who Knows If the Moon's. Cummings.
Wind and Silver. Lowell.
Winter Moon. Hughes.
With How Sad Steps, O Moon, Thou Climb'st the Skies. *Fr.*
    Astrophel and Stella. Sidney.
"With How Sad Steps, O Moon, Thou Climb'st the Sky."
    Wordsworth.
*Moonstruck* (Moon). Robert Phillips, ed.

**Moonshiners**
Dark Corner. Morgan.
Kentucky Bootlegger. *Unknown.*
Moonshiner. *Unknown.*
Mountain Dew. *Unknown.*
Real Old Mountain Dew. *Unknown.*

**Moore, Henry**
On a Celtic Mask by Henry Moore. Gregory.

**Moore, Sir John**
Burial of Sir John Moore at Corunna, The. Wolfe.

**Moore, Marianne**
For Marianne Moore's Birthday. Boyle.
Valentine for Marianne Moore, A. Olson.

**Moore, Thomas**
On T. Moore's Poems. *Unknown.*
Recollections of "Lalla Rookh." Trowbridge.

**Moors**
Whinlands. Heaney.

**Moose**
Bull Moose, The. Nowlan.

**Moravia**
Two Summers in Moravia. McDonald.

**Morison, Sir Henry**
To the Immortal Memory and Friendship of That Noble Pair,
    Sir Lucius Cary and Sir H. Morison. Jonson.

**Mormons**
Brigham Young. *Unknown.*
Desert Gulls. Gillespie.
Marching to Utah. *Unknown.*
Nauvoo. Taylor.
On the Death of the Dearly Beloved and Much Lamented
    Father. Snow.

**Morning**
After the Stormy Night. Kent.

Aubade: "Having bitten on life like a sharp apple." MacNeice.
Aubade: "The lark now leaves his watery nest." Davenant.
Ballad of the Morning Streets. Jones.
Breakfast Time. Stephens.
Chelsea Morning. Mitchell.
Clouded Morning, The. Very.
Cocoa Morning. Kaufman.
Composed upon Westminster Bridge. Wordsworth.
Description of the Morning, A. Swift.
Early Morning, The. Belloc.
Fair Morning, The. Very.
Fairies Break Their Dances, The. Housman.
Frosty Morning, A. Davidson.
Get Up. Levine.
Good Morning Love! Blackburn.
How in the Morning. Miller.
Impression du Matin. Wilde.
In Earliest Morning. Schuyler.
In the Naked Bed, in Plato's Cave. Schwartz.
May All Earth Be Clothed in Light. Hitchcock.
Morning. Blake.
Morning. Fainlight.
Morning. George.
Morning at the Window. Eliot.
Morning Light, The. Simpson.
Morning Song. *Fr.* Senlin, a Biography. Aiken.
New Morning. Dylan.
No Time for Poetry. Fields.
October Morning. Bethell.
On the Bright Side. Revard.
Pas de Deux for Lovers. Dransfield.
Removal from Terry Street, A. Dunn.
Reveille. Housman.
Slanted World. McMaster.
Song: "Year's at the spring, The." Browning.
This morning I threw the windows. Wright.
Waking from Sleep. Bly.
Wayside Station, The. Muir.
*See also* **Dawn; Sunrise.**

**Morris, William**
1915: A Pre-Raphaelite Ending, London. Howard.

**Morrison, Norman**
Norman Morrison. Ferguson.
Norman Morrison. Mitchell.
Of Late. Starbuck.

**Mortality**
Fire in My Meditation Burned. Ainsworth.
Fragment of Bion, A. Freneau.
Lord, thou hast been our dwelling place. Psalm XC. Bible, *O.T.*
People. Yevtushenko.
So, pure and dutiful, she sought that place. *Fr.* The Mahabharata. *Unknown.*

**Moses**
Go Down, Moses. *Unknown.*
Last View, The. Spinnanger.
Little Moses. *Unknown.*
Moses' Account. Fuest.
Moses and Joshua. Lasker-Schuler.
Moses on Mount Nebo. Regelson.
Oh, Mary Don't You Weep. *Unknown.*
Pharao's Daughter. Moran.

**Mosquitoes**
Mosquito, The. Lawrence.
Mosquito. Updike.
Mosquito Knows, The. Lawrence.
To a Mosquito. Bryant.

**Motels**
Leaving the Motel. Snodgrass.
Washyuma Motor Hotel. Ortiz.

**Mothers**
Accomplishments. MacDonald.

Adversary, The. McGinley.
Affliction of Margaret, The. Wordsworth.
After Illness. Gale.
Apples. Kaufman.
Arrival of My Mother, The. Wilson.
At My Mother's Bedside. M. L. Masters.
Before My Father Before Me. Hartman.
Belief. Miles.
Big Momma. Lee.
Black Mother Woman. Lorde.
C. L. M. Masefield.
Child Bearers, The. Sexton.
Child of Mine. Goffin *and* King.
Children, The. MacDonald.
Children, The. Urdang.
Christmas Eve. Sexton.
Claiming Kin. Voight.
Clutter of Mothers, A. Brock.
Color of Honey. Waldman.
Creek Mother Poem. Harjo.
Cruel Mother, The. *Unknown.*
Disquieting Muses, The. Plath.
Doll Poem. Derricotte.
Elegy: "My mother in the witness box." Scott.
Emma. Yvonne.
External Element, The. McFadden.
Footnote to John ii. 4. Mason.
For Mama Streek. Inez.
For My Mother. Bass.
For My Mother. Glück.
Generation Gap. Wallace.
Getting Down to Get Over. Jordan.
Good Times, *sel.* Clifton.
Her Eyes Don't Shine Like Diamonds. Marion.
Here lies,/ A worthy matron of unspotted life. Bradstreet.
Homework for Annabelle. McGinley.
Horse Show, The. Williams.
Housecleaner, The. White.
Human Geography. Whitman.
I Should be Ashamed. Uvlunuaq.
In Memory of My Mother. Kavanagh.
In the Ocean. Goedicke.
Intruder, The. Kizer.
It Is Deep. Rodgers.
Jessie Mitchell's Mother. Brooks.
Jesus Was Crucified, or, It Must Be Deep. Rodgers.
Kaddish. Ignatow.
Kaddish. Ginsberg.
Keeping You Alive. Gallagher.
Kornelia Woloszczuk. Skrzynecki.
Lacking Sense, The. Hardy.
Leroy. Baraka.
Let Me Go. *Unknown.*
Let's Talk, Mother. Bruck.
Letter to My Mother. Moraes.
Loaded. Swope.
Lost Children, The. Jarrell.
Mad Mother, The. Wordsworth.
Madonna and Daughter. Bergé.
Mama and Daughter. Hughes.
Maternity. Meynell.
Matrilineal Descent. Morgan.
Metamorphoses. Fuller.
Mommie. Kennedy.
Morning Song. Plath.
Mornings. Berger.
Mother. Bland.
Mother, The. Brooks.
Mother. Dempster.
Mother. Jong.
Mother. Libera.
Mother. Nagase Kiyoko.

Mother. Vincent.
Mother and I. Yoak.
Mother and Poet. E. Browning.
Mother, they say you looked Irish. Brenner.
Mother, to Son. Hughes.
Mothers. Giovanni.
Mothers. Sexton.
Mothers, Daughters. Kaufman.
Mother's Day. Hamod.
My Mother. Campbell.
My Mother. Taylor.
My Mother and the Americans. Kherdian.
My Mother and the Bed. Lifshin.
My Mother Tries to Visit Me in the Dead of Night. Wakoski.
My Mother Was Always Dressed. Luttinger.
My Mother Would Be a Falconress. Duncan.
My Mother's Childhood. Spacks.
My Mother's Milkman. Wakoski.
My Nightingales. Ausländer.
My Young Mother. Cooper.
Nancy Hanks, Mother of Abraham Lincoln. Lindsay.
Nani. Rios.
Night Feeding. Rukeyser.
90th Year, The. Levertov.
Old Arm-Chair, The. Cook.
Old Ladies. Dromgoole.
Old Mother turns blue and from us. Niedecker.
Olga Poems. Levertov.
Paean to Place. Niedecker.
Pavane for the Passing of a Child. Chester.
Physical for My Son. Smith.
Picnic on the Lawn. Scannell.
Poem: "I meet Mother on the street." Bruce.
Poem for My Mother. Fox.
Poem for My Mother. Jaeger.
Poem of the Mother. Sklarew.
Premonition. Yvonne.
Prodigal Thinks of his Mother, The. Simmons.
Reflections. Barrows.
Retribution often is. Birch.
Reunion. Herzberg.
Snapshot. Inez.
Someday Song for Sophia, A. Ratner.
Song for My Mother. Lau.
Song of the Old Mother, The. Yeats.
Sonnet to My Mother. Barker.
Taught Me Purple. Hunt.
To My Mother. Barker.
To My Son. Griffin.
Tricks. Olds.
Unknown Girl in the Maternity Ward. Sexton.
Upon a Young Mother of Many Children. Herrick.
Vacation Trip. Stafford.
Way It Is, The. Oden.
What a Friend We Have in Mother. Roat.
Widow's Plot, The: or, She Got What Was Coming to Her.
    Plomer.
Woman Mourned by Daughters. Rich.
Your Mother. Cornish.
*Tangled Vines: A Collection of Mother and Daughter Poems* (TV).
    Lyn Lifshin, ed.
**Mothers-in-law**
Her Place. Lochhead.
Prince Robert. *Unknown.*
Unexpected Pleasure, An. *Unknown.*
**Moths**
Getting Older Here. Hauk.
Great Moth, The. Gittings.
Lying Awake. Snodgrass.
Moth, The. Baker.
Mothsong. Harmon.
Tyranny of Moths. Vizenor.

Under the Sign of Moth. Wagoner.
Warning, The. Crapsey.
Yucca Moth, The. Ammons.
**Motion Pictures**
Answer to Allegory, An. Payne.
As a Great Prince. Honig.
At the Drive-In: "John Wayne vs. God." Dewey.
Attack of the Crab Monsters. Raab.
Autobiographical Note. Scannell.
Ave Maria. O'Hara.
Bogart. Flocos.
Bride of Frankenstein, The. Field.
Curse of the Cat Woman. Field.
Day I Stopped Dreaming about Barbara Steele, The. Dillard.
Day with the Foreign Legion, A. Whittemore.
Dick Powell. Koertge.
Drive In Movie. Sange.
Feature Time. Hammond.
Forties Flick. Ashbery.
Frankenstein. Field.
Grenadine. Griffin.
Hoppy. Godsey.
Horror Film. Scannell.
Horror Movie. Moss.
If Life's a Lousy Picture, Why Not Leave Before the End.
    McGough.
Laurel and Hardy. Bricuth.
Movie House. Updike.
Movie-Going. Hollander.
Newsreel. Day Lewis.
Nobody Dies Like Humphrey Bogart. Rosten.
Old Movies. Cotton.
Physical Imperfections of Old Films, The. Ramsey.
Projectionist's Nightmare, The. Patten.
Reel One. Stoutenburg.
Ride the High Country. Slavitt.
Schloss, The. Kirby.
Skin Flick. Chappell.
Spool, The. Belitt.
This world/ is amazingly flat. Gorbanyevskaya.
To the Film Industry in Crisis. O'Hara.
To the Lady Portrayed by Margaret Dumont. Hollander.
Triple Feature. Levertov.
Two Figures from the Movies. Meredith.
Western Movies. Jensen.
Where Are You Now Superman? Patten.
While Cecil Snores: Mom Drinks Cold Milk. Cunningham.
Working for Dr. No. Nash.
**Motorcycles**
Gypsy Motorcycle Club of South Minneapolis, The.
    Gunderson.
Motorcycle Irene. Spence.
Motorcyclist's Song, The. Bell.
On the Move. Gunn.
Sketch from Loss of Memory. Dorman.
Stoplight. Root.
Unsettled Motorcyclist's Vision of His Death, The. Gunn.
**Mountain Climbing**
Alpine. Thomas.
Climbing in Glencoe. Young.
De Gustibus. Hankin.
Finding a Poem. Merriam.
Here in Katmandu. Justice.
How the Laws of Physics Love Chocolate! Saner.
John Muir on Mt. Ritter. Snyder.
Schreckhorn, The. Hardy.
Space Eater Camps at Fifth Lake, The. Saner.
Story, A. Stafford.
Summer Solstice. Garner.
Wingwalking in Oregon. Peterson.
**Mountain Lions**
Mountain Lion. Lawrence.

**Mountains.**  *See* **Hills and Mountains.**
**Movies.**  *See* **Motion Pictures.**
**Moving Day**
Drifters.  Dawe.
Getting Loaded.  Thomas.
Moving.  Matthews.
Moving In.  Engle.
October 1.  Shapiro.
Removal from Terry Street, A.  Dunn.
**Mowing and Mowers**
Damon the Mower.  Marvell.
Haymaking.  Thomas.
Mower, Against Gardens, The.  Marvell.
Mower to the Glo-Worms, The.  Marvell.
Mower's Song, The.  Marvell.
Mowing.  Frost.
Photograph of Haymaker, 1890.  Holden.
Scything.  Dowling.
Tuft of Flowers, The.  Frost.
**Mozart, Wolfgang Amadeus**
Mozart.  Glatstein.
**Muhammed Ali.**  *See* **Ali, Muhammed.**
**Mules**
Erie Canal, The.  *Unknown.*
Kicking Mule, The.  *Unknown.*
Mule, The.  Barks.
Mules.  Fox-Smith.
My Sweetie's a Mule in the Mine.  *Unknown.*
On a mule you find two feet behind.  *Unknown.*
Poem to a Mule, Dead Twenty Years.  Owen.
Timber (Jerry the Mule).  *Unknown.*
**Mummies**
Breathing, at Last, in the Wichita Art Museum.  Clinton.
Mummy of a Lady Named Jemutesonekh XXI Dynasty.
James.
Wanting a Mummy.  McPherson.
**Munch, Edvard**
God, Woman, Egg.  Minton.
**Murder and Murderers**
Abel's Blood.  Vaughan.
Ashland Tragedy, The.  Adams.
Babylon; or, The Bonnie Banks 'o Fordie.  *Unknown.*
Bad Luck Blues.  *Unknown.*
Bad Man Ballad.  *Unknown.*
Ballad of William Bloat, The.  *Unknown.*
Bermondsey Tragedy, The.  *Unknown.*
Billy Lyons and Stack O'Lee.  *Unknown.*
Blood Hound Blues.  *Unknown.*
Brother, The.  Hardy.
Check to Song.  Meredith.
Coroner's Jury.  Strong.
Cruel Mother, The.  *Unknown.*
Death of Samuel Adams, The.  *Unknown.*
Deep Water.  *Unknown.*
Delia Holmes.  *At. to.* Ruff.
Down in the Willow Garden.  *Unknown.*
Earl Richard.  *Unknown.*
Edward, Edward.  *Unknown.*
Ella Speed.  *Unknown.*
Ellen Flannery.  *Unknown.*
Farewell to barn and stack and tree.  Housman.
Fine Flowers in the Valley.  *Unknown.*
Florella.  *Unknown.*
For Andy Goodman — Michael Schwerner — and James
Chaney.  Walker.
For the One Who Would Take Man's Life in His Hands.
Schwartz.
Fragment from the Elizabethans.  Bridges-Adams.
Frankie and Johnnie.  *Unknown.*
Fuller and Warren.  *At. to* Whitecotton.
Gatton Tragedy, The.  Manifold.

Getting Through the Fifties: The Starkweather Case Revisited.
Hahn.
Go Down You Murderers.  MacColl.
Gosport Tragedy, The.  *Unknown.*
He Fell Among Thieves.  Newbolt.
Herbert White.  Bidart.
I Should Be Ashamed.  Uvlunuaq.
Incident.  Baraka.
Indictment, The, *sel.*  Ayer.
Inquest, The.  Davies.
John Adkins' Farewell.  *Unknown.*
John Hardy.  *Unknown.*
Johnson-Jinkson.  *Unknown.*
Knoxville Girl.  *Unknown.*
Lady Isabella's Tragedy, The.  *Unknown.*
Life of the Mannings.  *Unknown.*
Lily of the West.  *Unknown.*
Little Musgrave and Lady Barnard.  *Unknown.*
Local Man Remembers the Killing Ground, A.  Whitehead.
Loose Woman.  Kennedy.
Lord Randal.  *Unknown.*
Lula Vires.  *Unknown.*
Lynching, The.  Kessler.
McAfee's Confession.  *Unknown.*
Mary Wyatt and Henry Green.  *Unknown.*
Murder of Goins, The.  *Unknown.*
Naomi Wise.  *Unknown.*
Omie Wise.  *Unknown.*
One to destroy, is murder by the law.  Young.
Oxford Girl, The.  *Unknown.*
Paris Railway-Station, The.  D. G. Rossetti.
Pearl Bryan.  *Unknown.*
Peddler and His Wife, The.  *Unknown.*
Poem for Richard Speck, A.  McMahon.
Poor Ellen Smith.  *Unknown.*
Porphyria's Lover.  Browning.
Pretty Polly.  *Unknown.*
Prince Robert.  *Unknown.*
Reason, The.  Haste.
Robin and Gandelein.  *Unknown.*
Rose Connoley.  *Unknown.*
Salute!  Ferlinghetti.
Sam Hall.  *Unknown.*
Scenery.  Joans.
Seth Dismounts Thrice.  Walsh.
Silvery Tide, The.  *Unknown.*
Stagolee.  *Unknown.*
.38, The.  Joans.
Tom Dooley.  *Unknown.*
Two Sisters, The.  *Unknown.*
Upon the Double Murther of King Charles I.  Philips.
Wexford Girl, The.  *Unknown.*
Wild Bill Jones.  *Unknown.*
Willie Taylor.  *Unknown.*
Young Hunting.  *Unknown.*
**Muses**
Muse.  Wagoner.
Ode to the Muse on Behalf of a Young Poet.  Wagoner.
Saint Harmony my patroness.  Goodman.
To the Muses.  Blake.
**Museums**
At the Museum of Modern Art.  Swenson.
At the Natural History Museum.  Meredith.
Historical Museum, Manitoulin Island.  Mueller.
Homage to the British Museum.  Empson.
In the Children's Museum in Nashville.  Salisbury.
In the Local Museum.  De la Mare.
June Fugue.  Shapcott.
Museum Item 237.  Mann.
Museum Piece.  Wilbur.
Museums.  MacNeice.
Night in the Royal Ontario Museum, A.  Atwood.

Spring Vacation: The Smithsonian. Ritchie.
Visit to the Museum. Simpson.

**Mushrooms**
Disused Shed in County Wexford, A. Mahon.
Morels. Smith.
Mushrooms. Dowling.
Mushrooms. Plath.
Slicing Button Mushrooms. Bowman.
Story for a Child, A. MacDonald.
Toadstool Wood, The. Reeves.

**Music and Musicians**
Abt Vogler. Browning.
Alexander's Feast: or, The Power of Music. Dryden.
Apocalypse. Enright.
At a Concert of Music. Aiken.
At a Solemn Music. Milton.
Autobiography Part Two: Rock and Roll Dedicated to the Poet Victor Hernandez Cruz. Hagedorn.
Bard. Bantock.
Bouzouki. Hanson.
Composers of Music. MacCaig.
Dance for Ma Rainey, A. Young.
Day They Ate the Baritone, The. Hazo.
Daybreak in Alabama. Hughes.
Elegiac Lines on the Death of a Fiddler, Called Blind Jacob. Freneau.
Evening Musicale. McGinley.
Free Thoughts on Several Eminent Composers. Lamb.
Group, The. Cruz.
Guide to the Symphony. Kees.
Guitar. García Lorca.
Guitarist Tunes Up, The. Cornford.
Harlem Sounds: Hallelujah Corner. Browne.
Hearing My Son Play. Cardona-Hine.
Here he played. *Fr.* Pine Top Smith. Ewing.
Here Where Coltrane Is. Harper.
Herrick Hospital, Fifth Floor. Young.
How High the Moon. Jeffers.
Hymn. Walker.
I Was Fair Beat. Garioch.
Impossibility, An. Vas Dias.
In Commendation of Music. Strode.
In Memory of Bryan Lathrop. Masters.
Juke Box Love Song. Hughes.
Leit. Rodríguez Frese.
Lost Chord, A. Procter.
Make Music With Your Life. O'Meally.
Man bent over his guitar, The. *Fr.* The Man With the Blue Guitar. Stevens.
Music. Herrick.
Music. A. Lowell.
Music Alone Shall Live. *Unknown.*
Music and Drum. MacLeish.
Musical Instrument, A. E. Browning.
Musician, The. Thomas.
Musician Returning from a Cafe Audition, A. Minard.
Music's Duel. Crashaw.
1907: A Proposal from Paris. Howard.
Nocturne in the Corner Phonebox, The. Taylor.
Ode: "We are the music-makers." O'Shaughnessy.
On Hearing a Symphony of Beethoven. Millay.
Orchestra. Saner.
Orchestra, The. Williams.
Passions, an Ode to Music, The. Collins.
Percussions. Welburn.
Peter Quince at the Clavier. Stevens.
Piper, A. O'Sullivan.
Piper's Progress, The. Mahony.
Piping down the Valleys Wild. *Fr.* Songs of Innocence. Blake.
Portrait of Rudy, A. Cunningham.
Pro Musica Antiqua. Hardison.
Seventy Six Trombones. Willson.

Singers to Come. Meynell.
Song for St. Cecilia's Day, 1687, A. Dryden.
Song of Shadows, The. De la Mare.
Songs, The. Bell.
Sonsito. Cruz.
Soul. Graham.
Spirits Unchained. Kgositsile.
Stanzas for Music ("There be none of Beauty's daughters"). Byron.
Symphony. Dorn.
Three Musicians, The. Beardsley.
To——: "Half in the dim light from the hall." Braithwaite.
To a Child at the Piano. Reid.
To Music. Herrick.
To Music: A Song. Herrick.
To Music, To Becalm His Fever. Herrick.
Toccata of Galuppi's, A. Browning.
View of the Capitol From the Library Of Congress. Bishop.
We Dance Like Ella Riffs. Rodgers.
When de Saints Go Ma'chin' Home. Brown.

**Mysticism**
Credo. Jeffers.
Mystic, The. Tennyson.
"Mysticism Has Not the Patience to Wait for God's Revelation." Eberhart.
*In Love with Love* (ILwL). Ann *and* Christopher Fremantle, eds.

**Mythology**
In Heavenly Realms of Hellas. Cummings.
Labors of Thor, The. Wagoner.
Priapupation of Queen Pasiphaë, The. Williams.
To Juan at the Winter Solstice. Graves.

**N**

**Names**
Choosing a Name. Lamb.
Conversation with God. Hathaway.
Crow, Straight Flier, But Dark. Firestone.
Empty Dwelling Places. Patchen.
Hallelujah: A Sestina. Francis.
Indian Names. Sigourney.
John Jacob Jingleheimer Schmidt. *Unknown.*
Kariuki. Gatuira.
Mary's a Grand Old Name. Cohan.
Mutual Problem. Cole.
My Baby Has No Name Yet. Kim Nam-jo.
My Mother Takes My Wife's Side. Kherdian.
My Name. Gold.
My Name. Hopkins.
My Name and I. Graves.
My Name Is a Name. Steele.
Name, The. Rumi.
Names. Lifshin.
Naming of Cats, The. Eliot.
Poem for My Eighth Year in Prison. Hogan.
Reason of Numbers, A. Jacobsen.
There. Harmon.
There's a Man Goin' 'Round Takin' Names. *Unknown.*
United States Tony. Kherdian.
Word Can Become the Way It Sounds, A. Arana.

**Nantucket, Massachusetts**
Nantucket. Williams.
Phenomenal Survivals of Death in Nantucket. Glück.
Quaker Graveyard in Nantucket, The. Lowell.

**Naples, Italy**
Ode to Naples. Shelley.

**Napoleon I**

Advice to a Raven in Russia. Barlow.
Boney Was a Warrior. *Unknown.*
Bonny Bunch of Roses, The. *Unknown.*
Calais, August 15, 1802. Wordsworth.
Feelings of a Republican on the Fall of Bonaparte. Shelley.
Incident of the French Camp. Browning.
Lines Written on Hearing the News of the Death of Napoleon. Shelley.
March to Moscow, The. Southey.
Napoleon. Holub.
Napoleon I. De la Mare.
Ode to Napoleon Buonaparte. Byron.

**Napoleonic Wars**
Battle of the Baltic. Campbell.
Burial of Sir John Moore at Corunna, The. Wolfe.
Field of Waterloo, The. *Fr. Childe Harold's Pilgrimage.* Byron.
Incident of the French Camp. Browning.

**Narcissus (flower)**
Narcissus. Cowper.
Window Ledge in the Atom Age. White.

**Narcotics.** *See* **Drug Addiction.**

**Naseby, Battle of**
Battle of Naseby, The. Macaulay.

**Nash, Richard (Beau Nash)**
On Mr. Nash's Picture at Full Length. Brereton.

**Nasturtiums**
Lines to a Nasturtium (A Lover Muses). Spencer.

**Nation, Carry**
That Little Hatchet. Andrews.

**Nativity**
Carol: "There was a Boy bedded in a bracken." Short.
In the Holy Nativity of Our Lord God. Crashaw.
Nativity of Our Lord and Saviour Jesus Christ, The. Smart.
Ode on the Morning of Christ's Nativity. Milton.
Salus Mundi. Coleridge.
*See also* **Christmas.**

**Naturalists**
Naturalist, The. Reynolds.
Week-End Naturalist, The. Buchan.

**Nature**
Amends to Nature. Symons.
Animal, Vegetable and Mineral. Bogan.
Apology, The. Emerson.
Apparently with no surprise. Dickinson.
Attraction. Wilcox.
Birds and Fishes. Jeffers.
Blue Horses. Roberson.
Chorus Sacerdotum. Greville.
Composed by the Side of Grasmere Lake. Wordsworth.
Correspondences. Baudelaire.
Design. Frost.
Each and All. Emerson.
Elegy for a Nature Poet. Nemerov.
Enthusiast, The; or, The Lover of Nature. Warton.
Eternity of Nature, The. Clare.
Evening Walk, An. Wordsworth.
Expostulation and Reply. Wordsworth.
Fall of Rome, The. Auden.
For Nature daily through her grand design. *Fr. Sonnets.* Tuckerman.
Force That Through the Green Fuse, The. Thomas.
Gravelly Run. Ammons.
Great Way of the Man, The. Russell.
Gully, The. Stewart.
Heaven of Animals, The. Dickey.
Holding the Mirror Up to Nature. Nemerov.
Hymn before Sun-rise, in the Vale of Chamouni. Coleridge.
I stood tip-toe upon a little hill. Keats.
I taste a liquor never brewed. Dickinson.
In All These Acts. Everson.
In Harmony with Nature. Arnold.

Innocence. Layton.
Inscription for the Entrance to a Wood. Bryant.
Kindred. Stewart.
Landscape. Simpson.
Leaves. Hughes.
Lines Written a Few Miles above Tintern Abbey. Wordsworth.
Lines Written in Early Spring. Wordsworth.
Loving and Liking. D. Wordsworth.
Marban, a Hermit Speaks. *Unknown.*
Me Imperturbe. Whitman.
Miracle, The. De la Mare.
Miracles ("Why, who makes much of a miracle"). Whitman.
Nature. Bull.
Nature ("Rounded world is fair to see, The"). Emerson.
Nature ("Subtle chain of countless rings, A"). Emerson.
Nature Lover. Nims.
Nature the gentlest mother is. Dickinson.
Nature's Hymn to the Deity. Clare.
Nature's Lineaments. Graves.
Nature's Questioning. Hardy.
Nocturnal Reverie, A. Countess of Winchilsea.
Nothing Will Die. Tennyson.
Ode: Intimations of Immortality from Recollections of Early Childhood. Wordsworth.
Ode to the Spirit of Earth in Autumn. Meredith.
On the Grasshopper and the Cricket. Keats.
On the Religion of Nature. Freneau.
On the Uniformity and Perfection of Nature. Freneau.
On the Universality and Other Attributes of the God of Nature. Freneau.
On thy stupendous summit, rock sublime! *Fr. Beachy Head.* Smith.
One Fragment for God. Everson.
Oneness of the Philosopher with Nature, The. Chesterton.
Onset, The. Frost.
Pause. Bethell.
Peace of Wild Things, The. Berry.
Pied Beauty. Hopkins.
Poets Love Nature. Clare.
Poor, Poor Country, The. Neilson.
Rainy Summer, The. Meynell.
Root of Revolution in the Vegetable Kingdom, The. Urdang.
Sky is low, the clouds are mean, The. Dickinson.
Song (Prelude). Pieterse.
Song of the Sky Loom. *Unknown.*
Spring Mountain Climb. Eberhart.
Spring Pools. Frost.
Stars, I have seen them fall. Housman.
Tables Turned, The. Wordsworth.
Thanatopsis. Bryant.
There Was a Child Went Forth. Whitman.
Three Kingdoms of Nature, The. Lessing.
To Mr. Henry Lawes. Philips.
To Nature. Coleridge.
Unison, A. Williams.
Waking, The ("I strolled across/ An open field"). Roethke.
Waking, The ("I wake to sleep, and take my waking slow"). Roethke.
What mystery pervades a well! Dickinson.
Wilderness, The. Raine.
Work without Hope. Coleridge.
World Has Many Places Many Ways, The. Russell.
Writer Indulges a Hobby, The. Randall.
Written in March. Wordsworth.
*Room for Me and a Mountain Lion* (RFM). Nancy Larrick, comp.

**Nautilus (shell)**
Chambered Nautilus, The. Holmes.

**Nauvoo, Illinois**
Nauvoo. Taylor.

**Naval Battles**
Battle of the *Bonhomme Richard* and the *Serapis.* Whitman.

Constitution and Guerriere, The. *Unknown.*
Utilitarian View of the *Monitor's* Fight, A.
  Melville.

**Navy, France**
Ballad for a Boy, A. Cory.

**Navy, Great Britain**
Admirals All. Newbolt.
Ballad for a Boy, A. Cory.
Battle of Sole Bay, The. *Unknown.*
Battle of the Baltic. Campbell.
Chief Petty Officer. Causley.
Death of Admiral Benbow, The. *Unknown.*
Instructions to a Painter. Waller.
Old Navy, The. Marryat.
Second Advice to a Painter, The. Marvell.
Third Advice to a Painter, The. Marvell.
Ye Mariners of England. Campbell.

**Navy, United States**
Anchors Aweigh. Miles.
Ballad of Benjamin Bones, The. Ward.
*Constitution's* Last Fight, The. Roche.
How Do You Do, *Alabama*! Wilson.
Navy Hymn, The. Whiting.
Warship of 1812, The. *Unknown.*
Yankee Man-of-War, The. *Unknown.*

**Nazis**
Ballade of Beauties. Scott.
Children, The. Heyen.
Construction #13. Sherwin.
Cross of Flame. Gessner.
Family Goldschmitt, The. Coulette.
In Memoriam: Gertrud Kolmar, 1943. Hope.
"More Light! More Light!" Hecht.
Mother. Tuwim.
Nazi Headquarters: El Monte, California. Burns.
Peachtree, The. Levertov.
Tailor, The. Garfinkel.

**Nebraska**
Otoe County in Nebraska. Kloefkorn.
So This Is Nebraska. Kooser.
Wild Pigs. Kooser.

**Nefertiti**
Nofretete. Pollak.

**Negro Verse.** *See* **Black Verse.**

**Negroes.** *See* **Blacks.**

**Neighbors**
Body, The. Bronk.
Mending Wall. Frost.

**Nelson, Horatio Nelson, Viscount**
Admirals All. Newbolt.
1805. Graves.
England Expects? Seaman.

**Nepal**
Here in Katmandu. Justice.

**Neptune (god)**
In Praise of Neptune. Campion.
Neptune. Farjeon.
Neptune, besides the sway. *Fr.* Comus. Milton.

**Neruda, Pablo**
Black Poppies. Miller.
Death of Neruda, The. Rendleman.
General Song of Humanity, The. Ferlinghetti.
Regard to Neruda. Lowther.
Words for Neruda. Carroll.

**Nerval, Gérard de**
Gerard de Nerval. Brush.

**Netherlands**
Character of Holland, The. Marvell.
Such Is Holland! Genestet.

**Nettles**
Nettles. Scannell.
Stinging Nettle. Head.

Tall Nettles. Thomas.

**Nevada**
January 15 as a National Holiday. Revard.
Night in Nevada with a Friend from Italy, A. Mezzetta.

**New England**
God's Controversy with New-England. Wigglesworth.
New England. Robinson.
New England: Driving Back in Early April. Steward.
New England Sampler, A. Brinnin.
Uppon the First Sight of New England, June 29, 1638. Tillam.
With hearts revived in conceit, new land and trees they eye. *Fr.*
  Good News from New England. Johnson.

**New Hampshire**
New Hampshire. Eliot.
New Hampshire. Hall.
Winter, New Hampshire. Kherdian.

**New Jersey**
Invention of New Jersey, The. Anderson.

**New Mexico**
Abiquiu—Thursday in Holy Week. Church.
How To Get To New Mexico. Brandi.
Landscape, New Mexico. Robertson.
Sand Painters, The. Belitt.
View of the Organ Mountains North of Las Cruces, New
  Mexico, A. Frumkin.

**New Orleans, Louisiana**
Alcide Pavageau. Williams.

**New Orleans, Battle of**
Ballad of New Orleans. Wilson.
Hunters of Kentucky. Woodworth.

**New Year**
Auld Lang Syne. Burns.
Both my child. Teitoku.
For a fresh start. *Fr.* Oraga Haru. Issa.
Last Day of the Year, The (New Year's Eve). Droste-Hülshoff.
Last Day of the Year, The. Su Tung P'o.
New Year, The. *Unknown.*
New Year 1974. Jones.
New Year's Day. Lowell.
New Year's Sacrifice, A: To Lucinda. Carew.
New Year's Water. *Unknown.*
Ring Out, Wild Bells. *Fr.* In Memoriam A. H. H. Tennyson.
Wish, A. Farjeon.
Year's End. Wilbur.

**New York City**
Annunciation. Maura.
B Negative. Kennedy.
Birthday Memorial to Seventh Street. Lorde.
Caesar and the Blind Men. Rella.
City of Orgies. Whitman.
Crossing Brooklyn Ferry. Whitman.
Eastside Incidents. Corso.
Give Me Splendid Silent Sun. Whitman.
Give My Regards to Broadway. Cohan.
Hymn of the City. Bryant.
I Am New York City. Cortez.
I Awoke with the Room Cold. Piercy.
Ivan Silen P.R. Poet. Sutton.
Letter to N.Y. Bishop.
Madison Square. Glanz-Leyeles.
Manhattan. Hart.
Manhattan. Hays.
Mannahatta. Whitman.
Metropolitan Nightmare. Benét.
Mouth of the Hudson, The. Lowell.
My Sad Self. Ginsberg.
New York. García Lorca.
New York Skyline. Spinnanger.
Night in New York. Spector.
Ode to New York. Whittemore.
Ode to the New York Mets. Lindsay.
Pennsylvania Station. Hughes.

Port of New York, The. Hayes.
Proud New York. Reed.
Review from Staten Island. Oden.
Saturday in New York. Beresford.
Sidewalks of New York, The. Lawlor *and* Blake.
Sign, The. Blackburn.
Snow in New York. Swenson.
Sonnet: "Five A.M. on East Fourteenth I'm out to eat." Clark.
Step Away from Them, A. O'Hara.
Steps. O'Hara.
Strawberries in Mexico. Padgett.
Stumpfoot on 42nd Street. Simpson.
Summer: West Side. Updike.
Things to Do in New York (City). Berrigan.
Tropics in New York, The. McKay.
Twentieth-Century Americanism. Davidman.
Under. Bowering.
Uptown. Ginsberg.
Walking. O'Hara.
Winter Sketches. Reznikoff.
*New York: Poems* (NYP). Howard Moss, ed.

**New Zealand**
Farewell to New Zealand. Vaughan-Thomas.
*Anthology of Twentieth Century New Zealand Poetry, An* (ATNZ). Vincent O'Sullivan, ed.

**Newark, New Jersey**
Newark, for Now (68). Rodgers.
Penn Central Station at Beacon, N.Y., The. Ochester.

**Newport, Rhode Island**
Looking at Wealth in Newport. Schevill.

**News**
Newsreel. Lewis.
Ten O'Clock News. Ortiz.

**Newspapers**
After the Last Bulletin. Wilbur.
Chicago *Defender* Sends a Man to Little Rock, Fall, 1957, The. Brooks.
Country Press. Dobson.
Dear Editor. Kicknosway.
Depression. Witherup.
Editor Whedon. *Fr.* Spoon River Anthology. Masters.
Headline History. Plomer.
Newspaper Is a Collection of Half-Injustices, A. *Fr.* War Is Kind. Crane.
Reading Today's Newspaper. Abbott.
Suggestion Made by the Posters of the *Globe,* A. Thorold Rogers.
You cannot hope. Wolfe.

**Newton, Sir Isaac**
Intended for Sir Isaac Newton. Pope.

**Niagara Falls**
Niagara. Braun.
Niagara Falls. Dugan.
Niagara Falls Nocturne. Gasparini.

**Nigeria**
Aah . . . You Ikenne Women. Wangberg.

**Night**
Acquainted with the Night. Frost.
Auld Daddy Darkness. Ferguson.
Bagley Wood. Johnson.
Casting at Night. Hoey.
Children of Night. Shelton.
Cold Front. Sharpe.
Day Is Done, The. Longfellow.
Domination of Black. Stevens.
Dread of Darkness. Keithley.
Driving to Town Late to Mail a Letter. Bly.
Evening. Doolittle ("H.D.")
Four Glimpses of Night. Davis.
Hotel in Paris. Trudell.
Hymn to the Evening, An. Wheatley.
Hymn to the Night. Longfellow.

Hymns to the Night. "Novalis."
If night takes the form of a whale and. Fraire.
In the Dark. Pridmore.
In the Dark None Dainty. Herrick.
In the Half Point Time of Night. Menebroker.
Midnight. Bethell.
Midnight. Lampman.
Moonlit Apples. Drinkwater.
Night. *Fr.* Songs of Innocence. Blake.
Night. Camerino.
Night. Lovelace.
Night. Radcliffe.
Night, The ("Through that pure Virgin-shrine"). Vaughan.
Night and Sleep. Patmore.
Night Clouds. A. Lowell.
Night Is Darkening Round Me, The. E. Brontë.
Night Piece. Strand.
Night-Piece, A. Wordsworth.
Night-Piece, to Julia, The. Herrick.
Night Sounds. *Fr.* Blunt, Master Constable. Middleton.
Night Will Never Stay, The. Farjeon.
Night Words: The Ravishing. McClure.
No Difference in the Dark. Herrick.
Nocturnal Reverie, The. Countess of Winchilsea.
Nocturnal Sketch, A. Hood.
Nocturne: "Three-toed tree toad, The." Guiterman.
Now Winter Nights Enlarge. Campion.
Omalos. Warren.
On the Night in Question. Goedicke.
Pine Tree Tops. Snyder.
Puck's Night Song. *Fr.* A Midsummer Night's Dream. Shakespeare.
Rhapsody on a Windy Night. Eliot.
She is the night: all horror of her. *Fr.* Lilith. Brennan.
Short Night, The. Buson.
Silver. De la Mare.
So Beautiful Is the Tree of Night. Hanson.
Sound of Night, The. Kumin.
Spring Night. Su Tung-P'o.
Still Life. Whittemore.
Sun has long been set, The. Wordsworth.
To Night. Shelley.
To Night. *Unknown.*
To Night. White.
Trilogy of the Night. Troupe.
Vision of the Night, The. Freneau.
Winter Night, A. Barnes.
You, Andrew Marvell. MacLeish.
*Dusk to Dawn* (DuDa). Helen Hill, Agnes Perkins, Alethea Helbig, eds.

**Nightingales**
Happy Nightingale, The. *Unknown.*
Music's Duel. Crashaw.
My Nightingale. Ausländer.
Nightingale, The. Coleridge.
Nightingale and the Glowworm, The. Cowper.
Nightingales. Bridges.
Nightingales. Norris.
Ode to a Nightingale. Keats.
On the Cliffs. Swinburne.
On the Death of a Nightingale. Randolph.
Owl Against Nightingale. *Unknown.*
Philomel. Barnfield.
Philomela. Arnold.
Philomela. Ransom.
Philomela. Sidney.
Sonnet: "O nightingale, that on yon bloomy spray." Milton.
To the Nightingale. Coleridge.
To the Nightingale. Countess of Winchilsea.

**Nightmares**
Bad Dreams. Collins.
Original Sin: A Short Story. Warren.

**Nihilism**
Nothing. Burgos.
**Nijinsky, Vaslav**
Nijinsky. Tyler.
**Nile (river)**
Nile, The. Hunt.
To the Nile. Keats.
**Nixon, Richard Milhous**
Hallelujah I'm a Bum ("I read in the news, the President said").
   Dane *and* Silber.
**Noah**
Abridged Bestiary, An. Chernoff.
And Did the Animals? Van Doren.
Animals in the Ark, The. *Unknown.*
Ballad of Mrs. Noah, The. Duncan.
Didn't It Rain. *Unknown.*
Dog's Cold Nose, The. Guiterman.
Flood, The. Mak.
Hammer, Ring. *Unknown.*
History of the Flood, The. Heath-Stubbs.
In Noah's Wake. Block.
Neighbor, The. Williams.
Noah. Bloch.
Noah's Ark. Young.
Old Ark's a-Moverin', The. *Unknown.*
One More River to Cross. *Unknown.*
Parley of Beasts. "MacDiarmid."
Proust on Noah. Silberschlag.
Still, Citizen Sparrow. Wilbur.
**Noon**
Noon. Ferrill.
Noon on Alameda Street. Flanner.
**Norfolk, England**
Coast: Norfolk, The. Cornford.
**North Carolina**
Hill Hunger. West.
**North Dakota**
North Dakota Gothic. Vinz.
Sisseton Indian Reservation, The. Lyons.
Something is Dying Here. McGrath.
**North Pole**
90 North. Jarrell.
Polar Exploration. Spender.
Scientific Proof. Foley.
**Northern Ireland**
Ballymurphy. *Unknown.*
Lisnagade. *Unknown.*
**Northwest Passage**
Looking for Asia. Dillard.
**Norway**
Going to Norway. Anderson.
Hammerfest. Auden.
**Noses**
Dong with a Luminous Nose, The. Lear.
"Dorset Nose," The. Sansom.
Hairs in My Nose, The. Boyajian.
Of One That Had a Great Nose. Turberville.
Of Tyndarus. *Unknown.*
Smell! Williams.
There's a man with a nose. *Fr.* The Devil's Dictionary.
   Bierce.
**Nostalgia**
Ballad of Dead Yankees, The. Petersen.
Family Album, A. Brody.
Fifties, The. Sadoff.
First-Class Relics: Letter to Dennis Finnell. DeFrees.
I Remember, I Remember. Larkin.
Looking for the Buckhead Boys. Dickey.
Miniver Cheevy. Robinson.
Moon Behind the Hill, The. *Unknown.*
Morning Chores. Heynen.
Nostalgia. Lawrence.

Old Furniture. Hardy.
Old Movies. Cotton.
Old Ruralities. Turner.
Old-fashioned Pitcher, The. Phair.
One day when I was a child, long ago. Paley.
Piano. Lawrence.
Straus Park. Stern.
Thinking about the Past. Justice.
TKO. Peck.
Tropics in New York, The. McKay.
**Nostradamus**
Nostradamus's Prophecy. Marvell.
Some Newly-discovered Prophecies of Nostradamus. Lake.
**Notre Dame Cathedral**
Notre Dame. Mandelstam.
**Novels**
Critical Observations. MacLeish.
Who'd Be a Hero (Fictional)? Bishop.
**November**
Late November in a Field. Wright.
November. Clare.
November. *Fr.* Sonnets on the Seasons. H. Coleridge.
November. Harvey.
November. Hughes.
November. Tuckerman.
November Sun. Daryush.
November Through a Giant Copper Beech. Honig.
**Nuclear Energy**
Looking at Power. Woessner.
Plumber Arrives at Three Mile Island, The. Stewart.
Sonnet to Seabrook. Ray.
**Nuclear War**
Canticle of the Rose, The. Sitwell.
Earth. Wheelock.
Fall 1961. Lowell.
Fifteen Million Plastic Bags. Mitchell.
Four Poems from the Strontium Age, *sels.* Johnson.
Horses, The ("Barely a twelvemonth after"). Muir.
I Saw an Army. Abbe.
Mother the Wardrobe Is Full of Infantrymen. McGough.
Relative Sadness. Rowbotham.
Song about Major Eatherly, A. Wain.
What Have They Done to the Rain? Reynolds.
Your Attention Please. Porter.
*See also* **Atomic Bomb.**
**Nudity**
"Gross, Coarse, Hideous" (Police Description of My Pictures).
   Lawrence.
Landscape as a Nude. MacLeish.
Naked and the Nude, The. Graves.
Nude Descending a Staircase. Kennedy.
On an Ecdysiast. Ciardi.
**Nuns**
Ballad of a Nun, A. Davidson.
Convent, The. O'Sullivan.
Felixstowe, or The Last of Her Order. Betjeman.
Halfway. Kumin.
Heaven-Haven. Hopkins.
Holding Pattern. McPherson.
Intercessors. Clarke.
Motet: "I am a young girl." *Unknown.*
Mother Rosarine. Kumin.
Nuns at Eve. Brinnin.
Nuns in the Wind. Rukeyser.
On Christ's Birth (To Sisters). Luecke.
Portrait of a Nun. Jones.
Psalms for a New Nun. DeFrees.
Teasing the Nuns. Shapiro.
To a Nun. Ormond.
With a Bottle of Blue Nun to All My Friends. DeFrees.
Wreck of the *Deutschland*, The. Hopkins.
**Nurses**

Malice of Innocence, The.   Levertov.
Modern American Nursing.   Hricz.
Night Duty.   MacKenzie.
Nurse.   Ivimy.
Rivalry.   Nowlan.
Wound-dresser, The.   Whitman.

**Nymphs**
To the Water Nymphs, Drinking at the Fountain.   Herrick.

# O

**Oak Trees**
Bearded Oaks.   Warren.
California Oaks, The.   Winters.
I Saw in Louisiana a Live-Oak Growing.   Whitman.
Oak, The.   Tennyson.
Oak and the Reed, The.   La Fontaine.

**Oases**
Green, Green Is El Aghir.   Cameron.

**Oates, Titus**
Panegyric upon Oates, A.   Duke.
Salamanca Doctor's Farewell, The.   *Unknown.*
Tragi-Comedy of Titus Oates, The.   *Unknown.*

**Obesity**
Washing Your Feet.   Ciardi.

**Occult, The**
Die hard.   Moffett.
Séance.   King.
Voices from the Other World.   Merrill.
*See also* **Supernatural.**

**Ocean.**   *See* **Sea.**

**O'Connor, Flannery**
Flannery O'Connor.   Walters.
Of Jayne Mansfield, Flannery O'Connor, My Mother and Me.
   Daniell.

**O'Connor, Frank**
Light Dying.   Kennelly.

**October**
Double Life.   MacCaig.
Especially When the October Wind.   Thomas.
Impulse of October, The.   Moses.
October.   Higginson.
October Dawn.   Hughes.
October in the Lane.   Norris.
October 1954.   Boyle.
Poem in October.   Thomas.
Poppies in October.   Plath.
Winter Watch.   Marion.

**Octopuses**
Octopus.   Hilton.
Octopus, The.   Nash.
Octopus.   Reavin.
Underwater.   Schmidt.

**Odin**
Descent of Odin, The; an Ode from the Norse Tongue.   Gray.

**Odysseus.**   *See* **Ulysses.**

**Oedipus**
Myth.   Rukeyser.
Oedipus.   Blackburn.
Oedipus.   Muir.
Oedipus Tyrannus.   Sophocles.

**O'Hara, Frank**
Night and Day.   Batki.

**Ohio**
Blessing at Kellenberger Road.   Valian.

**Oklahoma**
Captive Stone, The.   Barnes.
Country-Western Music.   Kooser.

Last Song, The.   Harjo.

**Old Age**
Acre of Grass, An.   Yeats.
Age.   Landor.
Aged Lover Renounceth Love, The.   Vaux.
Almswomen.   Blunden.
Am I really old, as people say?   Kim Jung-Ku.
Ancient to Ancients, An.   Hardy.
Angry Old Men.   Payne.
At Eighty.   Stanhope.
Aunt Alice in April.   Matchett.
Baucis and Philemon.   Hoskins.
Bean Eaters, The.   Brooks.
Beautiful Old Age.   Lawrence.
Birthday, The.   Johnson.
Broken Dreams.   Yeats.
But I Am Growing Old and Indolent.   Jeffers.
Certain Old Women.   Kennelly.
Childhood.   Wolfe.
City Pigeons.   Chasin.
Coming of Wisdom with Time, The.   Yeats.
Complaint.   Hamilton.
Conversation.   Giovanni.
Crabbed Age and Youth.   Shakespeare.
Crows, The.   Bogan.
Crowsfeet Splaying Round His Eyes.   Lloyd-Evans.
Cry of an Aged One, The.   Fraser.
Daguerreotype Taken in Old Age.   Atwood.
Dear Men and Women.   Wheelock.
Death Came Too Late.   Birch.
Death of a Vermont Farm Woman.   Howes.
Disturb me not, O bouyant youths!   *Unknown.*
Do Not Go Gentle into That Good Night.   Thomas.
Elders.   Reed.
Envy the Old.   Van Doren.
Fair Isle Pattern.   Rankin.
Fall.   Bethell.
Father William.   *Fr.* Alice's Adventures in Wonderland.
   "Carroll."
Fountain, The.   Wordsworth.
From the Crag.   Leib.
George.   Randall.
Geriatric.   Gonzalez.
Geriatric Huts.   Smith.
Gerontion.   Eliot.
Gold Leaves.   Chesterton.
Grandfathers, The.   Justice.
Growing Old.   Arnold.
Growing Old.   *Fr.* Don Juan.   Byron.
Hay for the Horses.   Snyder.
Heavy, Heavy — What Hangs Over?   Burke.
Hebrides.   MacLeish.
His Golden Locks Time Hath to Silver Turned.   *Fr.*
   Polyhymnia.   Peele.
How to Be Old.   Swenson.
Hut Near Desolated Pines.   Campbell.
I look into my glass.   Hardy.
I Saw from the Beach.   Moore.
Ice, The.   Gibson.
Ice-Creepers (for Cid Ricketts Sumner).   Merriam.
I'm Here.   *Fr.* Meditations of an Old Woman.   Roethke.
"I'm 92," Joe said.   Weber.
Imperialists in Retirement.   Lucie-Smith.
In Respect of the Elderly.   Peacock.
In the Convalescent Hospital.   Pumphrey.
In Time of Gold.   Doolittle ("H. D.").
In (What Few) Green (Barely) Parks.   Coleman.
Invisible Man, The.   Matthews.
John Anderson, My Jo.   Burns.
Lament of the Old Woman of Beare, The.   *Unknown.*
Lamentation of the Old Pensioner, The.   Yeats.
Last Chapter, The.   De la Mare.

Last Leaf, The. Holmes.
Letter from a Girl to Her Own Old Age, A. Meynell.
Light and Dark. Howes.
Little Old Women, The. Baudelaire.
Mad Poem Addressed to My Nephews and Nieces, A. Po Chü-i.
Miss Euphemia. Ransom.
Missing Dates. Empson.
Moccasins of an Old Man, The. Carden.
Model T. Stoutenburg.
Moonlight. Teasdale.
Nice Old Couple, The. Aldis.
90th Year, The. Levertov.
Niño Leading an Old Man to Market. Nathan.
No charm can stay, no medicine assuage. Landor.
Norfolk. Betjeman.
Nursing Home. Parker-Silverman.
Of the Last Verses in the Book. Waller.
Old Adam, The. Levertov.
Old Age. Cummings.
Old Age. Dehn.
Old Age. Jacobsen.
Old Age. *Unknown.*
Old Age in His Ailing. Melville.
Old Black Men. Johnson.
Old Couple, The. Green.
Old Folk, The. Ditlevsen.
Old Folks Home. Hennen.
Old Inmate, An. Mackenzie.
Old Jockey, The. Higgins.
Old Lady's Lament For Her Youth, The. Villon.
Old Man and the Sun, The. Aleixandre.
Old Man, Phantom Dog. Eckman.
Old Man's Comforts and How He Gained Them, The. Southey.
Old Man's Song. Scannell.
Old Man's Winter Night, An. Frost.
Old Men, The. Kipling.
Old Men. Nash.
Old Men Admiring Themselves in the Water, The. Yeats.
Old Mother turns blue and from us. Niedecker.
Old Nudists, The. Colby.
Old One and the Wind, The. Short.
Old People. Livingston.
Old Soldiers Home at Marshalltown, Iowa. Barnes.
Old Wife in High Spirits. "MacDiarmid."
Old Woman, The. Campbell.
Old Woman. Jennings.
Old Woman. Smith.
Old Woman Awaiting the Greyhound Bus. Niatum.
Old woman sits, The. Davis.
Old Women, The. Cochrane.
On Growing Old. Masefield.
On His Seventy-Fifth Birthday. *Fr.* The Last Fruit off an Old Tree. Landor.
On Living Too Long. Landor.
One Flesh. Jennings.
Phone Call to Rutherford. Blackburn.
Plaudite, or End of Life, The. Herrick.
Proposal for Recycling Wastes, A. Piercy.
Provide, Provide. Frost.
Red-Tail Hawk and Pyre of Youth. Warren.
Sair Fyel'd, Hinny. *Unknown.*
Senile. Folk.
Seventy. Reynolds.
Sex and the Over Forties. Porter.
She, to Him. Hardy.
Silver Threads among the Gold. Rexford.
Simon Lee. Wordsworth.
Something Like an Apple. Reiss.
Smile, The. Aiken.
Song for September. Fitzgerald.

Song of a Woman Abandoned by the Tribe. *Unknown.*
Spur, The. Yeats.
Stroke. Rea.
Strokes. Stafford.
Survival. Greenberg.
Survivor, The. Thomas.
Tarzan, Old. Block.
Terminus. Emerson.
That time of year thou mayest in me behold. Sonnets, LXXIII. Shakespeare.
Three Old Brothers. O'Connor.
To a Poor Old Woman. Williams.
To Age. Landor.
To an Old Lady. Empson.
To His Mistresses ("Help me! Help me! now I call"). Herrick.
To My Ninth Decade. Landor.
To Perilla. Herrick.
To Waken an Old Lady. Williams.
Tracks. Berssenbrugge.
Two Old Men. Niedecker.
Very Old, The. Galloway.
Very Old Woman, A. Eshleman.
Veteran Sirens. Robinson.
Warning. Joseph.
Weeksville Women. Loftin.
When the sword of sixty comes nigh his head. Firdosi.
When You and I Were Young, Maggie. Johnson.
When You Are Old. Yeats.
When Your Parents Grow Old. Hart.
Why Should Not Old Men Be Mad? Yeats.
Young and Old. *Fr.* The Water Babies. Kingsley.
Youth and Age. Coleridge.
*Timeless Voices* (TVo). Virginia Larrain, ed.

**Old Ironsides.** *See* **Constitution (ship).**

**O'Leary, Arthur**
Lament for Arthur O'Leary. O'Connell.

**Olson, Charles**
From Gloucester Out. Dorn.

**Olympics**
First in the Pentathlon. Lucilius.

**O'Neill, Owen Roe**
Lament for the Death of Eoghan Ruadh O'Neill. Davis.

**O'Neill, Shane**
Shane O'Neill's Cairn. Jeffers.

**Onions**
Man in the Onion Bed, The. Ciardi.
Onyons. *Fr.* Market Women's Cries. Swift.
Peeling Onions. Rich.

**Opals**
Opal. Miles.

**Opera**
Another Poem on the Tearing Down of the Metropolitan Opera House. Stevens.
Il Janitoro. Ade.
Matinees. Merrill.
Rigoletto. Levy.
Tannhäuser. Levy.

**Ophelia**
Ophelia's Song. Zaturenska.

**Opium**
Opium Den, The. *Unknown.*

**Oppen, George**
For George Oppen. Gray.

**Oppression**
Determination. Clarke.
Oppression. Hughes.

**Opossums**
Possum Tree, The. Gough.

**Optimism**
Away, Melancholy. Smith.
Difference, The. *Unknown.*
Good Time Coming, The. Mackay.

Pangloss's Song.  Wilbur.
Pessimist and Optimist.  Langbridge.
Protect Me.  Adler.
Say Not the Struggle Nought Availeth.  Clough.
When the clouds' swoln bosoms echo back the shouts.  *Fr.* In
   Tenebris.  Hardy.

**Oracles**
Hebrew Sibyl, The.  Fainlight.
Oracles, The.  Housman.

**Oranges**
Orange Tree, The.  Neilson.
Orange Tree Dream.  Serin.
Smudging.  Wakoski.

**Orchards**
Autumn Orchard.  Jacobs.
Good-by and Keep Cold.  Frost.
Lost Orchard, The.  Masters.
Orchard.  Doolittle ("H. D.").
Through Ruddy Orchards.  Oliver.

**Orchids**
Orchids.  Roethke.
Orchids.  Wratislaw.

**Oregon**
Exodus for Oregon.  Miller.
Finding Sky Ranch.  Stafford.
In Oregon.  Stafford.
Indian Painting, Probably Paiute, in a cave near Madras,
   Oregon.  Ramsey.
Looking from Oregon.  Birney.

**Oregon Trail**
Oregon Trail, The.  Guiterman.
Oregon Trail, The.  *Unknown.*
Oregon Trail: 1851.  Marshall.

**Orioles**
To hear an oriole sing.  Dickinson.

**Orion (constellation)**
Orion.  Rich.

**Orion (mythology)**
There was a slumbrous silence in the air.  *Fr.* Orion.  Horne.

**Orphans**
Child's Umbrella, The.  Souster.
Little Orphant Annie.  Riley.
Motherless Children.  *Unknown.*
Orphan, The.  *Unknown.*
Orphans.  Ray.

**Orpheus**
Ballad of Orpheus, A.  Lindsay.
Orpheus.  Herrick.
Orpheus.  Winters.
Orpheus in Greenwich Village.  Gilbert.
Orpheus in the Underworld.  Gascoyne.
Orpheus to Beasts.  Lovelace.
Orpheus to Woods.  Lovelace.
Power of Music, The.  Lisle.
Thus sung Orpheus to his strings.  *Unknown.*

**Osiris**
Hurry Hurry.  Harry.

**Ospreys**
Osprey's Nest, The.  Wagoner.

**Ostriches**
He "Digesteth Harde Yron."  Moore.
Ostrich, The.  Douglas.
Ostrich Is a Silly Bird, The.  Freeman.

**Othello**
At the Theatre.  Williams.
Speaking of Poetry.  Bishop.

**Otter (river), Devon, England**
Sonnet to the River Otter.  Coleridge.

**Otterburn, Battle of**
Battle of Otterbourne, The.  *Unknown.*
Chevy Chase.  *Unknown.*

**Otters**

Lutra, the Fisher.  McMichael.
Otter, An.  Hughes.
Otters.  Hart-Smith.
River-Mates.  Colum.

**Ouija Boards**
Voices from the Other World.  Merrill.

**Outlaws.**  *See* **Crime and Criminals.**

**Ovenbirds**
Oven Bird, The.  Frost.

**Ovid (Publius Ovidius Naso)**
Near the Death of Ovid.  Conquest.
Written in an Ovid.  Prior.

**Owls**
Aziola, The.  Shelley.
Barn Owl.  *Fr.* Father and Child.  Harwood.
Barn Owl.  Norris.
Bird of Night, The.  Jarrell.
Great Brown Owl, The.  Browne.
Hail to Thee, Blithe Owl.  Lardner.
Hitchhiker.  McCord.
Horned Owl, The.  Cornwall.
If the Owl Calls Again.  Haines.
Leaves that rustled on this oak-crowned hill, The.  Wordsworth.
Nightwatchman.  Morgan.
Owl.  MacBeth.
Owl, The.  Sackville-West.
Owl, The.  Tennyson.
Owl, The.  Thomas.
Owl Against Nightingale.  *Unknown.*
Owl and the Pussy-Cat, The.  Lear.
Owl Critic, The.  Fields.
Owl in the Rabbi's Barn, The.  Jaffe.
Owl Pellet, The.  Deagon.
Owl Seen In Rearview Mirror.  Niatum.
Owls.  Norris.
Owls.  Snodgrass.
Prayer to the Snowy Owl.  Haines.
Questioning Faces.  Frost.
Sweet Suffolk owl, so trimly dight.  *Unknown.*
Tree Animals.  Lieberman.
Town Owl.  Lee.
Wring the Swan's Neck.  Martinez.

**Oxen**
Beasts Are Very Wise, The.  Kipling.
I Have Twelve Oxen.  *Unknown.*
Musk Oxen.  Igjugarjuk.
Old Ox, The.  Hamilton.
Ox Cart Man.  Hall.
Oxen, The.  Hardy.
Oxen: Ploughing at the Fiesole.  Tomlinson.
Recantation Illustrated in the Story of the Mad Ox.  Coleridge.
Song of Praise for an Ox.  Sutskever.

**Oxford, England**
City of weathered cloister and worn court.  *Fr.* Oxford.
   Johnson.
Duns Scotus's Oxford.  Hopkins.
Going Back to Oxford.  Chuilleanáin.
Oxford Canal.  Flecker.
Town Against Gown at Oxford.  Robert of Gloucester.

**Oysters**
Ossified Oyster, An.  Wells.
Oyster, The.  Ponge.
Oystering.  Howard.

**P**

**Pacific Ocean**
Eye, The.  Jeffers.

Facing West from California's Shores. Whitman.
Once by the Pacific. Frost.
Prayer to the Pacific. Silko.
Slow Pacific Swell, The. Winters.

**Pacifism and Pacifists**
Advent 1966. Levertov.
Arsenal at Springfield, The. Longfellow.
Bring 'Em Home. Dane.
Christmas Eve under Hooker's Statue. Lowell.
Conscientious Objector. Millay.
Conscientious Objector, The. Shapiro.
Dooley Is a Traitor. Michie.
For the Minority. Peterson.
For the One Who Would Take Man's Life in His Hands.
  Schwartz.
I Just Wanna Stay Home. Silber.
I Sing of Olaf Glad and Big. Cummings.
I've Got to Know. Guthrie.
Memories of West Street and Lepke. Lowell.
Put My Name Down. Silber.
Study War No More. *Unknown.*
That Crazy War. *Unknown.*

**Paganism**
Plain of Adoration, The. *Unknown.*

**Paige, Leroy ("Satchel")**
To Satch. Allen.

**Pain**
After great pain, a formal feeling comes. Dickinson.
Dolores. Swinburne.
Flower, The. Creeley.
For Kenneth Patchen. Miller.
Horrors, The. Nash.
It's Just the Same to Me. Hesse.
My Knees Go before the Firing Squad at Dawn. Wakoski.
Pain. Södergran.
Pain — has an element of blank. Dickinson.
Prayer from a Stryker Frame. Clarkson.
Thoughts on Pain. Chesham.
Two Founts, The. Coleridge.
Quality of Pain, A. Holender.
Shot. Thayne.
Surgical Ward. Auden.
There is a Languor of the Life. Dickinson.
There is a pain—so utter. Dickinson.
Thirty Childbirths. Brand.
This Pain. Wheelock.
Villanelle: "It is the pain, it is the pain, endures." Empson.
Way of Pain, The. Berry.
Who Hurt You So? Millay.

**Paine, Thomas**
Citizen Paine. Daugherty.
Epigram: "In digging up your bones, Tom Paine." Byron.
Stanzas: "Princes and kings decay and die." Freneau.

**Painting and Painters**
All Too Little on Pictures. Black.
Andrea del Sarto. Browning.
Approaching the Canvas. Spivack.
At an Exhibition of Historical Paintings, Hobart. Smith.
Backgrounds to Italian Paintings: Fifteenth Century. Ridler.
Card-Dealer, The. Rossetti.
Dance, The. Williams.
For "A Venetian Pastoral" by Giorgione. Rossetti.
For "An Allegorical Dance of Women" by Andrea Mantegna.
  Rossetti.
For "Our Lady of the Rocks" by Leonardo da Vinci. Rossetti.
For "Ruggiero and Angelica" by Ingres. Rossetti.
For "The Wine of Circe" by Edward Burne-Jones. Rossetti.
Fra Lippo Lippi. Browning.
Fresco. Pastan.
Giovanni da Fiesole on the Sublime; or, Fra Angelico's "Last
  Judgment." Howard.

In Goya's Greatest Scenes. *Fr.* A Coney Island of the Mind.
  Ferlinghetti.
In Santa Maria del Popolo. Gunn.
Landscape with Pervert. Noll.
Landscapes. Hugo.
Last Instructions to a Painter, The. Marvell.
Museum Piece. Wilbur.
Old Pictures in Florence. Browning.
On a Painting by Patient B of the Independence State Hospital
  for the Insane. Justice.
On a Picture by Michele Da Verona, of Arion As a Boy Riding
  upon a Dolphin. Ridler.
Paint Box, The. Rieu.
Painting. Chernoff.
Painting. Jacobs.
Painture. Lovelace.
Persian Miniature. Shore.
Pictor Ignotus. Browning.
Portrait of Prince Henry, The. Clouts.
Still Life. Dobson.
Something Missing on the Left. Albrecht.
Suggested by a Picture of the Bird of Paradise. Wordsworth.
To Cole, the Painter, Departing for Europe. Bryant.
Ultimate Antientropy, The. Weiss.
Why I Am Not a Painter. O'Hara.
With Francis Furini. *Fr.* Parleyings with Certain People of
  Importance in Their Day. Browning.

**Paleontology**
Imitation of Julia A. Moore. "Twain."

**Palm Trees**
Royal Palm. Crane.

**Pan (god)**
Dead Pan, The. Browning.
Hymn of Pan. Shelley.
Hymn to Pan. *Fr.* The Faithful Shepherdess. Fletcher.
Musical Instrument, A. E. Browning.
Pan. Emerson.
Pan and Luna. Browning.
Pan Piping. Plato.

**Pandas**
Panda, The. *Fr.* Animals That Stand in Dreams. Elliott.

**Pansies**
Pansy. Bradley.

**Pantheism**
Higher Pantheism, The. Tennyson.
Higher Pantheism in a Nutshell, The. *Fr.* The Heptalogia.
  Swinburne.
There is no God, as I was taught in youth. Masefield.

**Parachuting.** *See* **Sky Diving.**

**Paradise.** *See* **Heaven.**

**Paranoia**
Dossier, The. McMahon.
Girl on the Run. Kresh.
Paranoia. Browne.
Tryst. Merriam.
Tunnel, The. Strand.

**Parenthood**
Amusing Our Daughters. Kizer.
And How It Goes. Hollo.
At the Washing of My Son. Su Tung P'o.
Because. McAuley.
Bring a Child Flowers. Tarn.
Childless. MacNamee.
Children. Kizer.
Children, The. Urdang.
Expectant Father, The. Ortiz.
For a Child Expected. Ridler.
For My Son on the Highways of His Mind. Kumin.
For Sapphires. Rodgers.
For Yvonne, My Daughter. Moreno.
Goodnight, The. Simpson.
Heart's Needle. Snodgrass.

Journal for My Daughter. Kunitz.
Letter Home, A. Nicholson.
Lost Children, The. Jarrell.
Lost Parents. Ferlinghetti.
Magic Children. Drake.
Man Holding Boy in the Rain. Dixon.
Man Who Finds That His Son Has Become a Thief, The. Souster.
On Giving a Son to the Sea. Dickey.
She's Leaving Home. Lennon *and* McCartney.
Sitting Here. Creeley.
Sons, *sel.* Lubeck.
Two Parents, The. "MacDiarmid."
Way of Pain, The. Berry.
What My Child Learns of the Sea. Lorde.
Wheel Revolves, The. Rexroth.

**Paris, France**
Enigmatic Traveler, The. Vazakas.
Four Sheets to the Wind. Rivers.
Mourning Letter from Paris, A. Rivers.
Paris. Garnett.
Paris. Young.
Paris by Night. Milbauer.
Southeast Ramparts of the Seine, The. Tóth.

**Parker, Charlie**
"Bird Lives": Charles Parker in St. Louis. Harper.
Mellowness and Flight. Barlow.
Sidewalk Restoration. Ikan.
Walking Parker Home. Kaufman.
Yardbird's Skull. Dodson.

**Parks**
Battery Park, High Noon. Belitt.
Blackstone Park. Jonas.
Central Park. Nemerov.
Central Park, 1916. Stewart.
Central Park Tourney. Weston.
Definition of Nature. Redmond.
Fountain in the Park, The. Haley.
In Golden Gate Park that day. *Fr.* A Coney Island of the Mind. Ferlinghetti.
Instructions for a Park. Walker.
On St. James's Park. Waller.
On the Fine Arts Garden, Cleveland. Atkins.
Park, The. Tippett.
Public Garden, The. Lowell.
Public Gardens, The. Lewis.
St. John's Park. McAuley.
South End. Aiken.
Umbaji Park. Kherdian.

**Parnell, Charles Stewart**
Parnell. Yeats.
Richard Pigott, the Forger, *sel.* McGonagall.

**Parodies**
*Faber Book of Comic Verse, The* (FaBoCo). Michael Roberts *and* Janet Adam Smith, eds.
*Speak Roughly to Your Little Boy* (SpRo). Myra Cohn Livingston, ed.
*See also* the special parody sections in: *Poetry and Its Conventions* (PAIC). Frederick R. Lapides *and* John T. Shawcross, eds.; *Understanding Poetry* (UnPo 1976 ed.). Cleanth Brooks *and* Robert Penn Warren, eds.

**Parrots**
Gossip, The. Halpern.
Little Miss and Her Parrot. Marchant.
Obituary. Kees.
Parrot. Brownjohn.
Parrot, The. Campbell.
Parrot, The. Flecker.
Parrot, The. Lucie-Smith.
Poor Poll. Bridges.
Sailor to His Parrot, The. Davies.
Talking Back. Wagoner.

Who Killed Lawless Lean? Smith.

**Parthenon**
On Seeing the Elgin Marbles. Keats.

**Parties**
At a Pairty. Campbell.
Dancers Inherit the Party, The. Finlay.
Feckless Dinner Party, The. De la Mare.
Odd Woman, The. DeFrees.
Office Party. McGinley.
Party, The. Avison.
Party, The. Dunbar.
Party. Justice.
Saturday Night. Moxley.
Thoughts While Driving Home. Updike.

**Parting**
Against Parting. Zach.
False Cadence. Berger.
Goodbye, My Lover, Goodbye. *Unknown.*
If He Let Us Go Now. Williams.
Leave-Taking, A. Swinburne.
No Madam Butterfly. Hajek.

**Partridges**
Another Song of the Same Woman, to Some Partridges, Sent to Her Alive. Pinar.
Partridges. Masefield.

**Passover**
Seder, 1944. Torberg.

**Pasternak, Boris**
Last Year's Discussion; The Nobel Russian. McGinley.

**Pastures.** *See* **Fields and Pastures.**

**Patience**
Damn Her. Ciardi.
Owl, The. Davison.
Patience. Horne.
Patience, Hard Thing. Hopkins.

**Patrick, Saint**
Clonfeacle. Muldoon.

**Patriotic Songs, American**
America. Smith.
America the Beautiful. Bates.
Army Goes Rolling Along, The. Gruber *and* Arberg.
As Down a Lone Valley. Dwight.
Battle-Cry of Freedom, The. Root.
Battle-Hymn of the Republic. Howe.
Bunker Hill. Niles.
Chester. Billings.
God Bless America. Berlin.
Hail, Columbia. Hopkinson.
Liberty Song, The. J. Dickinson.
Marines' Hymn, The. *Unknown.*
O Beautiful My Country. Hosmer.
O Lord Our God, Thy Mighty Hand. Van Dyke.
Pledge to the Flag, The. Bellamy.
Star-Spangled Banner, The. Key.
Tenting Tonight. Kittredge.
Tramp! Tramp! Tramp! Root.
When Johnny Comes Marching Home. Gilmore.
Yankee Doodle Boy, The. Cohan.

**Patriotic Songs, Canadian**
Maple Leaf Forever, The. Muir.
O Canada! Routhier.

**Patriotic Songs, Chinese**
Chee Lai! (Arise!). *Unknown.*

**Patriotic Songs, Confederate**
Bonnie Blue Flag, The. Macarthy.
Dixie. Emmett.
Dixie (Battle-Hymn). Pike.
Maryland, My Maryland! Randall.

**Patriotic Songs, English**
Anglo-Saxon Race, The: A Rhyme for Englishmen. Tupper.
God Save the King. *At. to* Carey.
Rule Britannia. *Fr.* Alfred, a Masque. Thomson.

**Patriotic Songs, French**
　Marseillaise, La.　Rouget de Lisle.
**Patriotic Songs, Scottish**
　Campbells are Comin', The.　*Unknown.*
**Patriotism**
　Anglo-Saxon Race, The: A Rhyme for Englishmen.　Tupper.
　As One Non-Combatant to Another.　Orwell.
　Barbara Frietchie.　Whittier.
　Columbia.　*Unknown.*
　Dulce et Decorum Est.　Owen.
　1887.　Housman
　Great men have been among us; hands that penned.
　　Wordsworth.
　Hail, Columbia.　Hopkinson.
　Homes of England, The.　Hemans.
　Long Voyage, The.　Cowley.
　Minority Report.　Updike.
　Next to of Course God America I.　Cummings.
　Patriot Game, The.　Behan.
　Pat's Opinion of Flags.　Brooks.
　Sussex.　Kipling.
　These Fought in Any Case.　*Fr.* Hugh Selwyn Mauberley.
　　Pound.
　This Is My Own, My Native Land.　*Fr.* The Lay of the Last
　　Minstrel.　Scott.
　To Horace.　Lake.
　To the Men of Kent, October, 1803.　Wordsworth.
　Weeping Sad and Lonely (When This Cruel War Is Over).
　　Sawyer.
　Yankee Doodle Boy, The.　Cohan.
　*Breathes There the Man* (BTTM).　Frank S. Meyer, ed.
**Paul, Saint**
　Our Two Worthies.　Ransom.
　Saul, Afterward Riding East.　Brinnin.
**Pawnbrokers**
　Pawnbroker, The.　Kumin.
**Peace**
　"And There Was a Great Calm."　Hardy.
　April 29, 1975.　Hilton.
　At the Un-National Monument along the Canadian Border.
　　Stafford.
　Forty Years Peace.　Sivan.
　Legend of Versailles, A.　Tolson.
　Not Marching Away to Be Killed.　Fuller.
　On Peace.　Keats.
　On The Inside Strong.　Mberi.
　Peace.　De la Mare.
　Peace.　Jonas.
　Peace, So That.　Kuzma.
　Pleading Voices.　Katav.
　Shalom Chaverim.　*Unknown.*
　Vine and Fig Tree.　Altman.
　What a Grand and Glorious Feeling.　*Unknown.*
**Peaches**
　Unripe Peach, An.　Fein.
**Peacocks**
　Domination of Black.　Stevens.
　On a Peacock.　Heyrick.
　What is it more eyes doth wear.　*Unknown.*
**Pear Trees and Pears**
　Pear Tree.　Doolittle ("H. D.").
　Pears.　Pastan.
　Sickle Pears.　Dodson.
　Study of Two Pears.　Stevens.
　To a Blossoming Pear Tree.　Wright.
**Pearls**
　Precious Pearls, The.　Wilson.
**Peasants**
　Exiles.　"AE."
**Peddling and Pedlars**
　Autolycus as Peddler.　*Fr.* The Winter's Tale.　Shakespeare.
　Negro Peddler's Song, A.　Johnson.

**Peeping Toms**
　Fiend, The.　Dickey.
**Pegasus**
　Pegasus.　Kavanagh.
　Pegasus.　Lewis.
**Pelicans**
　Frigate Pelican, The.　Moore.
　King and Queen of the Pelicans we.　*Fr.* The Pelican Chorus.
　　Lear.
　Pelican, The.　Kuzma.
**Pembroke, Mary Sidney Herbert, Countess of**
　On the Death of Mary, Countess of Pembroke.　Browne.
**Penelope (mythology)**
　Ancient Gesture, An.　Millay.
　Penelope.　Gilmore.
　Penelope, for her Ulysses' sake.　*Fr.* Amoretti.　Spenser.
　World as Meditation, The.　Stevens.
**Penguins**
　Teaching the Penguins to Fly.　Spacks.
　View from Here, The.　Stafford.
**Pennsylvania**
　Pennsylvania Places.　Daly.
　Pennsylvania Winter Indian 1974.　Littlebird.
**Pennsylvania Station, New York City**
　Pennsylvania Station.　Hughes.
**Penshurst, England**
　At Penshurst.　Waller.
　To Penshurst.　Jonson.
**Peonies**
　Selling Ruined Peonies.　Yü Hsüan-chi.
**Persephone**
　Demeter and Persephone.　Tennyson.
　Garden of Proserpine, The.　Swinburne.
　Gardens of Proserpine.　Cassity.
　Hymn to Proserpine.　Swinburne.
　Kore.　Creeley.
　Persephone.　Duncan.
**Perseverence**
　Don't Give Up.　Cary.
　Quitter, The.　*Unknown.*
**Persians**
　Persian Version, The.　Graves.
**Persimmon Trees**
　Longing for the Persimmon Tree.　Brand.
**Pessimism**
　Difference, The.　*Unknown.*
　Epitaph on a Pessimist.　Hardy.
　I to My Perils.　Housman.
　Of Misery.　Howell.
　Pessimist, The.　King.
　Pessimist and Optimist.　Langbridge.
　Said Hanrahan.　Hartigan.
　There Are Bad Times Just Around the Corner.　Coward.
　World's a Bubble, The.　Bacon.
**Peter, Saint**
　And the Cock Begins to Crow.　Avery.
**Peterloo Massacre**
　Mask of Anarchy, The.　Shelley.
　Song: To the Men of England.　Shelley.
　Sonnet: England in 1819.　Shelley.
**Petrels**
　Stormy Petrel, The.　"Cornwall."
**Pets**
　Ode of Odium on Aquariums.　Guiterman.
　Pet Shop.　MacNeice.
**Pheasants**
　Pheasant, The.　Coffin.
**Phidias**
　Death of Phidias, The.　Deagon.
**Philately**
　Philatelist Royal.　Graves.
**Philippine Islands**

On a Soldier Fallen in the Philippines. Moody.
Song for My Father. Hagedorn.
White Man's Burden, The. Kipling.
**Philosophy and Philosophers**
Alexander and the Gymnosophists. *Unknown.*
All That Glitters. Kornblum.
Dissatisfaction with Metaphysics. Empson.
Epistemologist, Over a Brandy, Opining, The. Sargent.
Epistemology. Wilbur.
Ignorance of Death. Empson.
Makhno's Philosophers. Manifold.
Maya. Robinson.
Metaphysical Amorist, The. Cunningham.
Mock On, Mock On, Voltaire, Rousseau. Blake.
Moralists, The. Winters.
New Philosophy, The. *Fr.* An Anatomy of the World. Donne.
Of the Pythagorean Philosophy. *Fr.* Metamorphoses. Ovid.
On the Death of a Metaphysician. Santayana.
Philosopher, A. Foss.
Philosopher and the Lover to a Mistress Dying, The.
　Davenant.
Reading and Talking. Zukofsky.
This, That & the Other. Nemerov.
Variation on Heraclitus. MacNeice.
Words. Glen.
**Phoenix**
About the Phoenix. Merrill.
Mutations of the Phoenix, *sel.* Read.
News of the Phoenix. Smith.
Phoenix, The. Cunningham.
Phoenix, The. *Fr.* Nepenthe. Darley.
Phoenix, The. Megged.
Phoenix and Turtle, The. Shakespeare.
**Photographs**
Developing a Wife. Taylor.
Family Album, A. Brody.
Family Man, A. Kumin.
Family Portrait. Hood-Adams.
Going Through the Old Photos. Rosen.
Hiawatha's Photographing. "Carroll."
Lines on a Young Lady's Photograph Album. Larkin.
Lost Pictures, The. Summers.
Mementos, I. Snodgrass.
Old Photographs. Harsent.
Perspective and Limits of Snapshots, The. Smith.
Photo, The. Bruce.
Photograph. Prettyman.
Photographs. Wright.
Two Stories about Cameras, *sel.* Pfingston.
**Physicians**
Arthur Ridgewood, M.D. Davis.
Bed, The. Hope.
Better Way, The. Leaf.
Clinic: Examination. Conard.
Correct Compassion, A. Kirkup.
Doctor, The. Abse.
Doctor Black. Blight.
Doctor Who Sits at the Bedside of a Rat, The. Miles.
Doctors' Row. Aiken.
Epistle, An, Containing the Strange Medical Experience of
　Karshish, The Arab Physician. Browning.
Football. Mason.
He Makes a House Call. Stone.
Hessian Doctor, The. Freneau.
Le Médecin Malgré Lui. Williams.
MD Sewed Wrong Section of Colon. Scott.
My Friend, The Doctor. Abbe.
On Dr. Isaac Letsome. *Unknown.*
On the Death of Dr. Robert Levet. Johnson.
Physician, Heal Thyself. Smith.
Portrait of a Physician. *Fr.* The Dispensary. Garth.
Remedy, Worse than the Disease, The. Prior.

Resuscitation. Stone.
Scientist, The. Burroway.
See, one physician, like a sculler, plies. Jekyll.
Smells. Koertge.
To Doctor Empiric. Jonson.
*Poems from the Medical World* (PMW). Howard Sergeant, ed.
**Pianos**
Human Firewood Piano, The. Blazek.
Investment, The. Frost.
Old Upright I Did Not Learn to Play, The. Flocos.
Piano. Lawrence.
Piano at Evening. Palea.
Piano Tuner, The. Smith.
Player Piano. Updike.
To a Child at the Piano. Reid.
**Picasso, Pablo**
Art of Picasso, The. Gascoyne.
Chicago Picasso, The. *Fr.* Two Dedications. Brooks.
"Portrait de Femme." Feldman.
**Pickles**
Meditation for a Pickle Suite. Dillard.
**Picnics**
Georgia Dusk. Toomer.
Picnic, The. Logan.
Picnic: The Liberated. Holman.
**Piedmont, Italy**
On the Late Massacre in Piedmont. Milton.
**Pigeons**
Cropped, grey, too-small, bullet, Prussian head, A. Fuller.
Fly. Merwin.
On Startling Some Pigeons. Turner.
Pigeon Pie. Bode.
Pigeons. Edson.
Pigeons. Kell.
Pigeons. Meyers.
Pigeons. Moore.
Pigeons. Reid.
Pigeons. Whisler.
Pitchfork Department. Enright.
Wild Oats. MacCaig.
**Pigs**
Animals Are Passing from Our Lives. Levine.
Any Part of Piggy. Coward.
Blood. Murray.
Ego. Siegel.
February. Chappell.
Hardweed Path Going. Ammons.
Hog at the Manger. Farber.
Hog-calling. Blount.
Hog-calling Competition. Bishop.
Hogpen. Morgan.
If Pigs Could Fly. Reeves.
Lady Who Loved a Swine, The. *Unknown.*
Laughing Faces of Pigs, The. Lape.
Little Pig, The. Landau.
Little Piggy. Hood.
Little Pigs Lie in the Best of Straw. *Unknown.*
Moly. Gunn.
Ode to a Pig while His Nose Was Being Bored. Southey.
Pig, The. *Unknown.*
Pig Poem. Waterman.
Pigs. Cotton.
Pindaric on the Grunting of a Hog, A. Wesley.
Sow. Plath.
Sow Took the Measles, The. *Unknown.*
State Fair Pigs. Pfingston.
Three Little Pigs, The. Gatty.
View of a Pig. Hughes.
Wild Pigs. Kooser.
**Pike**
Pike, The. Bruce.
Pike. Hughes.

Pike, The.  Roethke.
**Pilgrim Fathers**
Landing of the Pilgrim Fathers in New England, The.  Hemans.
Pilgrim Fathers, The.  Pierpont.
Pilgrim Fish Heads.  Bly.
**Pilgrims and Pilgrimages**
Passionate Man's Pilgrimage, The.  Ralegh.
Pilgrimage, The.  Herbert.
To Be A Pilgrim.  Bunyan.
**Pinball Machines**
Pinball Queen Of South Illinois St., The.  Tietz.
**Pindar**
Praise of Pindar, The.  *Fr.* Odes.  Horace.
**Pine Trees**
At Torrey Pines State Park.  Mazzaro.
Developing Curious Survival Patterns Against Winter Saltwinds,
The.  Lifshin.
Foxtail Pine.  Snyder.
Height.  Fitzgerald.
Hill Pines Were Sighing, The.  Bridges.
Hunchback Pine.  Russell.
My Cathedral.  Longfellow.
Pine Assessor, The.  Baker.
Pine at Timber-Line, The.  Monroe.
Pine Tree.  Page.
Pines.  Banks.
Pines, The.  Mahy.
Southern Pines.  Bishop.
**Pioneers**
Boys of Sanpete County, The.  *Unknown.*
Covered Wagon, The.  Blakeney.
Handcart Song, The.  *Unknown.*
Homestead in Idaho.  Larson.
John Day, Frontiersman.  Winters.
Once I Lived in Cottonwood.  *Unknown.*
Pioneer, The.  Field.
Pioneer, The.  Ruggles.
Pioneer Woman.  Crawford.
Prayer of the Homesteader.  Haste.
St. George.  Walker.
Sioux Indians, The.  *Unknown.*
Slow Boone.  Flanner.
Stanzas on the Emigration to America, and Peopling the
Western Country.  Freneau.
Sweet Betsy from Pike.  *Unknown.*
Tittery-Irie-Aye.  *Unknown.*
Western Wagons.  Benét.
**Pirates and Piracy**
Bounty.  Miles.
Captain Kidd.  *Unknown.*
*Flying Cloud*, The.  *Unknown.*
Henry Martin.  *Unknown.*
Salcombe Seaman's Flaunt to the Proud Pirate, The.  *Unknown.*
Sir Andrew Barton.  *Unknown.*
Tarry Buccaneer, The.  Masefield.
Teach the Rover.  *Unknown.*
Wild Barbaree, The.  *Unknown.*
**Pisa, Italy**
Evening: Ponte a Mare, Pisa.  Shelley.
**Pitt, William**
Epitaph for William Pitt.  Byron.
**Pity**
Expostulation, An.  Bickerstaffe.
Ode to Pity.  Collins.
Pity.  Mills.
Pity Me Not Because the Light of Day.  Millay.
**Place Names**
American Names.  S.V. Benét.
American Traveller, The.  "Kerr."
Englishman with an Atlas, An; or, America the
Unpronounceable.  Bishop.
Pennsylvania Places.  Daly.

Yankee Cradle.  Coffin.
**Plague**
Adieu, Farewell Earth's Bliss.  *Fr.* Summer's Last Will and
Testament.  Nashe.
Black Death, The.  Dacey.
Coming of the Plague, The.  Kees.
From a Plague Year.  Malouf.
Plague, The.  Wharton.
**Plains.**  *See* **Prairies.**
**Planetariums**
View from the Planetarium.  Barker.
**Plants**
Cuttings ("Sticks-in-a-drowse droop over sugary loam").
Roethke.
Cuttings ("This urge, wrestle, resurrection of dry sticks").
Roethke.
Giant Decorative Dahlia.  Holden.
Have You Thanked a Green Plant today.  Anderson.
Jubilate Herbis.  Farber.
La Condition Botanique.  Hecht.
Loves of the Plants, *sel.*  E. Darwin.
Moss-Gathering.  Roethke.
Old Man.  Thomas.
Plant, The.  McPherson.
Plants, The.  Browne.
Readymade.  Perreault.
Root Cellar.  Roethke.
Seed Leaves.  Wilbur.
Seedlings in the Mail.  Piercy.
Sundew, The.  Swinburne.
What Ails My Fern?  Schuyler.
Woman with Flower.  Madgett.
Woodspurge, The.  Rossetti.
*See also*  **Flowers; Trees,** *etc.*
**Plath, Sylvia**
After Reading Sylvia Plath.  Alta.
Bitter Pills for the Dark Ladies.  Jong.
Closer First to Earth.  Hazlewood-Brady.
In Sylvia Plath Country.  Jong.
On the Death of Sylvia Plath.  Herzberg.
Room of Her Own, A.  Garitano.
Sylvia's Death.  Sexton.
Your face broods from my table, Suicide.  Berryman.
**Plato**
Plato.  Duguid.
Plato in London.  Johnson.
Spirit of Plato.  *Unknown.*
What Then?  Yeats.
**Platonic Love**
La Belle Confidante.  Stanley.
No Platonic Love.  Cartwright.
**Platonism**
Idea, The. Made of Alnwick, in His Expedition to Scotland with
the Army, 1639.  Herbert.
No Platonic Love.  Cartwright.
Platonic Love.  Herbert.
**Platte, River**
Trail Beside the River Platte.  Heyen.
**Platypuses**
Old Man Platypus.  Paterson.
**Play**
Centaur, The.  Swenson.
Children's Games.  Williams.
Hide and Seek.  Scannell.
Playing Catch.  Moul.
Romping.  Ciardi.
Voyage of Jimmy Poo, The.  Emanuel.
**Plowing**
Follower.  Heaney.
**Plum Trees and Plums**
Leave the Top Plums.  Chandler.
Plum, A.  Leib.

Plum Blossoms. Chu Shu-chên.
Plum Gatherer, The. Millay.
This Is Just to Say. Williams.
To a Poor Old Woman. Williams.
Word "Plum," The. Chasin.
**Plumbing and Plumbers**
Difference, The. King.
Elegy for Alfred Hubbard. Connor.
**Po Chu-i**
As I Step Over a Puddle at the End of Winter, I Think of an
Ancient Chinese Governor. Wright.
**Poaching and Poachers**
Lincolnshire Poacher, The. *Unknown.*
Poaching in Excelsis. Menzies.
Van Diemen's Land. *Unknown.*
**Poe, Edgar Allan**
Fall of the House of Usher, The. Whittemore.
Farewell to Earth, *sel.* Doten.
Poe and Longfellow. *Fr.* A Fable for Critics. Lowell.
Tomb of Edgar Poe, The. Mallarmé.
**Poetry and Poets**
About My Poems. Justice.
Acrophobe and Lapidary. Bonk.
Adam's Curse. Yeats.
Admonition to the Muse. Taylor.
After Horace. Godley.
After Reading Nelly Sachs. Pastan.
Ah. Kuzma.
Alas! 'Tis Very Sad to Hear. Landor.
All Friends Together: A Survey of Present-Day Australian
Poetry. Simpson.
All Things Can Tempt Me. Yeats.
American Poetry. Simpson.
American Saturday Afternoon. Ikan.
And Thus in Nineveh. Pound.
Answer for Voznesensky and Evtushenko. O'Hara.
Answers for Ethelbert. Zu-Bolton, II.
Apologia Pro Vita Sua. Coleridge.
Apology: "Simplicity assuages." Cunningham.
Apology for Apostasy? Knight.
Appology, The. Countess of Winchilsea.
Ars Poetica. MacLeish.
Ars Poetica. Trías.
Art of Poetry, The. Gray.
Arthur Ridgewood, M.D. Davis.
As One Non-Combatant to Another. Orwell.
At Poetry Workshop, Winter Semester. Martin.
At the "Atlantic" Dinner. Holmes.
Author to Her Book, The. Bradstreet.
Ballad Maker, A. Colum.
Ballade of Prose and Rhyme, The. Dobson.
Bard. Everson.
Bell Too Heavy to Ring. Kryss.
Betjeman, 1984. Causley.
Beware: Do Not Read This Poem. Reed.
Biographical Note. Preil.
Birth of a Poet. Morgan.
Bitter Pills for the Dark Ladies. Jong.
Black Art. Baraka.
Boarder, The. Feirstein.
Bookshop Idyll, A. Amis.
Breadth. Circle. Desert. Monarch. Month. Wisdom. Hollander.
Breakthrough. Rodgers.
British Leftish Poetry, 1930-40. "MacDiarmid."
But I Am Growing Old and Indolent. Jeffers.
Buy One Now. Enright.
By Rail Through Istria. Conquest.
Cat Poem. Graham.
Catch. Francis.
Chances of Rhyme, The. Tomlinson.
Charge to the Poets, A. Whitehead.
Choice, The. Yeats.

Choice of Weapons, A. Kunitz.
Circus Animals' Desertion, The. Yeats.
Coat, A. Yeats.
Codicil. Rexroth.
Codicil. Walcott.
Colophon for Lan-t'ing Hsiu-Hsi. Peck.
Come, Said My Soul. Whitman.
Commission. Pound.
Comparison of the Sonnet and the Epigram. Harington.
Constantly risking absurdity. *Fr.* A Coney Island of the Mind.
Ferlinghetti.
Correspondence School Instructor Says Goodbye to his Poetry
Students, The. Kinnell.
Craftsmen. Sackville-West.
Critic, The. Wharton.
Critics say that epics have died out, The. *Fr.* Aurora Leigh.
Browning.
Cycle, A. Leax.
Dance for Militant Dilettantes, A. Young.
Dedication of the Cook. Wickham.
Digging. Heaney.
Discontents in Devon. Herrick.
Distant Drum, The. Hernton.
Draft Dodger, The. Rubin.
Dump, The. Kuzma.
Eating Poetry. Strand.
Echoes. Lazarus.
Egg Boiler, The. Brooks.
Elegy for a Nature Poet. Nemerov.
Elegy in a Presbyterian Burying-Ground. Wilson.
Emerson. *Fr.* A Fable for Critics. Lowell.
Enamoured of the Miniscule. Hartnett.
Epic, The. Tennyson.
Epigram: "Sir, I admit your gen'ral rule." Pope.
Epigram: "Yes, every poet is a fool." Prior.
Epigram on Miltonicks. Wesley.
Epilogue to Lessing's Laocoön. Arnold.
Epistle from Mr. Pope to Dr. Abuthnot, An. Pope.
Epitaph: "Here lies a poet, briefly known as Hecht." Hecht.
Epitaph on a Young Poet Who Died before Having Achieved
Success. Lowell.
Esthetique du Machiavel. Starbuck.
Every critic in the town. Murray.
Exchange of Hats, An. Moss.
Exhortation, An. Shelley.
Fashionable Poet Reading. Connor.
Father, The. O'Grady.
First Steps up Parnassus. *Fr.* To My Most Dearly Loved
Henry Reynolds. Drayton.
Fish. Berry.
Fit of Rime Against Rime, A. Jonson.
Flowering Cacti, The. Fowler.
For Black Poets Who Think of Suicide. Knight.
For J. A. R. McKellar. Lehmann.
For My Contemporaries. Cunningham.
For Poets. Young.
For Saundra. Giovanni.
For Some Poets. Jackson.
Foreword to New Numbers. Logue.
Fragment: "Where's the poet? Show him! Show him!" Keats.
Fresh Air. Koch.
Gesture. Finkel.
Getting By on Honesty. Smith.
Gift, The. Lourie.
God Opens His Mail. Rubin.
Had I the Choice. Whitman.
Hands. Finkel.
Hard Night's Daze, A. Payne.
Hat in the Ring, A. Manifold.
Hebrew of Your Poets, Zion, The. Reznikoff.
Hendecasyllabics. Tennyson.
Heraclitus. Cory.

Hexameters. Coleridge.
High-Toned Old Christian Woman, A. Stevens.
Holding Pattern. McPherson.
Holy Office, The. Joyce.
How to Become a Poet. McCloskey.
How to Eat a Poem. Merriam.
Hunt of the Poem, The. Behm.
I Am Raftery. Raftery.
I Am 25. Corso.
I Come to Bury Caesar. Harris.
I don't bother with rhymes. Caeiro.
I Dream I'm the Death of Orpheus. Rich.
I Know I'm Not Sufficiently Obscure. Durem.
I Often Want to Let My Lines Go. Neidus.
I polish, cook or clean my nest. Holsapple.
I reckon when I count at all. Dickinson.
I Think of Housman Who Said the Poem Is a Morbid Secretion,
   Like the Pearl. Kroll.
I Would Like to Describe. Herbert.
I would not paint a picture. Dickinson.
I Write for Those Unknown. Miller.
If it is a poem. Duguid.
If thou indeed derive thy light from Heaven. Wordsworth.
If U Are a Poet. Yearwood.
Illustrious Ancestors. Levertov.
Immigrant, The. Hilton.
In a Spring Still Not Written Of. Wallace.
In Defense of Black Poets. Rivers.
In My Craft or Sullen Art. Thomas.
In Poets' Defence. Wheelwright.
In the Backs. Cornford.
In the great snowfall before the bomb. Niedecker.
Inspiration. Service.
Instruction from Bly. Macdonald.
Invocation: "Ten bloody years with this quill lying."
   Iremonger.
Is it true, ye gods, who treat us. Clough.
Israfel. Poe.
It is difficult now to speak of poetry. *Fr.* Of Being Numerous.
   Oppen.
Jacob's Ladder, The. Levertov.
Jordan ("Who says that fictions only and false hair"). Herbert.
Journey of a Poem Compared to All the Sad Variety of Travel,
   The. Schwartz.
July, 1964. Davie.
Just Ask for a Demonstration. Weismiller.
Kidnap Poem. Giovanni.
Kitchen Poem. Scarfe.
Ladies and gentlemen/ This is our final word. *Fr.* Manifesto.
   Parra.
Lake Isle, The. Pound.
Lamentations of an Au Pair Girl. Feldman.
Langston Hughes. Blockcolski.
Large Red Man Reading. Stevens.
Laureate, The. Graves.
Let Me Tell You. Williams.
Let Us Honor Them. Owens.
Letter to a Chinese Poet, *sel.* Dallas.
Letter to a Friend. Stallworthy.
Letter to an American Visitor. Comfort.
Letter to Paul Celan in Memory, A. Rothenberg.
Lines Written in Ridicule of Certain Poems Published in 1777.
   Johnson.
Little Grenade, The. Harry.
Living Poetry. Margenat.
Loneliness. Young.
Loss of Black Camels, The. Hamod.
Love and Poetry. Simpson.
Love the Wild Swan. Jeffers.
MacFlecknoe. Dryden.
Makers, The. Kell.
Mastering the Craft. Scannell.

Me Again. Rexroth.
Memo. Sahl.
Metre Columbian, The. *Unknown.*
Metrical Feet. Coleridge.
Milton by Firelight. Snyder.
Miss Cho Composes in the Cafeteria. Tate.
Model for the Laureate, A. Yeats.
Modern Poetry. Skeen.
Monster, The. Rago.
Moon. Walcott.
Most Days. Ritchie.
Move On, Yiddish Poet. Glatstein.
Muse, The. Spacks.
Muse of Amergin, The. *Unknown.*
Musical Ape, The. Gray.
My Olson Elegy. Feldman.
My Poem. Hewell.
My Poetry. Takamura.
My Son, Forsake Your Art. O'Heffernan.
Namby-Pamby. Carey.
Nameless One, The. Mangan.
New Poem, A. Duncan.
New Poem, The. Wright.
New Poet Arrives, A. Ewart.
New Simile in the Manner of Swift, A. Goldsmith.
Newly Pressed Suit, The. McGough.
Night Shift at the Poetry Factory, The. Magorian.
No White Bird Sings. Ciardi.
Noises. Johnson.
Not marble, nor the gilded monuments. Sonnets, LV.
   Shakespeare.
Notes for a History of Poetry. Daiches.
O Black and Unknown Bards. Johnson.
O'Bruadair. O'Bruadair.
Obstetrician, The. Shore.
Ode: "Bards of passion and of mirth." Keats.
Ode: "We are the music-makers." O'Shaughnessy.
Ode on the Poetical Character. Collins.
Ode: Salute to the French Negro Poets. O'Hara.
Ode to Apollo. Keats.
Ode to Himself, An. Jonson.
Ode to the Medieval Poets. Auden.
Of English Verse. Waller.
Of Modern Poetry. Stevens.
Of Myself. Goldberg.
Old Southern Critic Takes a Look at My Poems, An. Gray.
Old Stories, The. Frumkin.
On an Anniversary. Synge.
On Arrival. Howard.
On First Looking into Chapman's Homer. Keats.
On Learning to Play the Guitar. Fraser.
On Poetry: A Rhapsody. Swift.
On Reading Another Poet. Brewster.
On Teaching the Youth. Winters.
On the Death of Dermody, the Poet. White.
On the Death of W. H. Auden. Morice.
On the New Laureate. *Unknown.*
On the Sonnet. Keats.
Opening the Cage: 14 Variations on 14 Words. Morgan.
Owl Pellet, The. Deagon.
Pact, A. Pound.
Paradox. Bennett.
Past Ruin'd Ilion Helen Lives. Landor.
Pastoral Poesy. Clare.
Pegasus. Kavanagh.
Persistency of Poetry. Arnold.
Petit, the Poet. *Fr.* Spoon River Anthology. Masters.
Piping down the Valleys Wild. *Fr.* Songs of Innocence. Blake.
Pitcher. Francis.
Planet on the Table, The. Stevens.
Please. Creeley.
Poem: "I want to be one of those Poets." Hilton.

Poem: "On getting a card." Williams.
Poem, The: "Painter of Dante's awful ferryride, The." Deutsch.
Poem: "You said./ don't write me/ a love poem." Lomax.
Poem about a Poem about a Poem. Conquest.
Poem About Poems About Vietnam, A. Stallworthy.
Poem for Liu Ya-tzu. Mao Tse-tung.
Poem—Good or Bad—A Thing—With One Attribute—Flat, A. Ravitch.
Poem is Mightier Than the Switchblade, The. Thomas.
Poem Like a Grenade, A. Haines.
Poem moves down a page, A. Meltzer.
Poem, or Beauty Hurts Mr. Vinal. Cummings.
Poem: Rocket. Ginsberg.
Poem That Took the Place of a Mountain, The. Stevens.
Poem You Asked For, The. Levis.
Poems. Kelso.
Poems. Severy.
Poems of the Condemned Man, The. Dybek.
Poet, The. Browning.
Poet, The. Bryant.
Poet, The. Clifton.
Poet, A. Hardy.
Poet. Hilberry.
Poet, The. Keats.
Poet, The. Randolph.
Poet. Siegel.
Poet, The. Tennyson.
Poet. Viereck.
Poet and the Rose, The. *Fr.* Fables. Gay.
Poet, A!—He Hath Put His Heart to School. Wordsworth.
Poet in Need, A. Heath-Stubbs.
Poet in Washington, The. Pauker.
Poet of Bray, The. Heath-Stubbs.
Poet of One Mood, A. Meynell.
Poet Speaks from the Visitors' Gallery, A. MacLeish.
Poeta Fit, non Nascitur. "Carroll."
Poetical Economy. Graham.
Poetry. Birch.
Poetry. Kuzma.
Poetry. Masarik.
Poetry. Moore.
Poetry. Rakosi.
Poetry. Sutskever.
Poetry. Vigee.
Poetry, a Natural Thing. Duncan.
Poetry and the Poet. Bunner.
Poetry Is in the Darkness. Boyajian.
Poetry Liberation. Pumphrey.
Poetry of one the Russians call "a broad nature," The. *Fr.* The Kind of Poetry I Want. "MacDiarmid."
Poetry Paper. Codrescu.
Poetry Perpetuates the Poet. Herrick.
Poetry Reading. Scannell.
Poetry Today. Heath-Stubbs.
Poetry Workshop in a Reform School. Adcock.
Poets Agree To Be Quiet by the Swamp, The Wagoner.
Poets Hitchhiking on the Highway. Corso.
Poet's Household, A. Kizer.
Poets light but lamps, The. Dickinson.
Poets Love Nature. Clare.
Poets of My Epoch. Stark.
Poet's Prayer. Sussman.
Poet's Prayer, The. *Unknown.*
Poet's Progress, A. Hamburger.
Poets to Come. Whitman.
Poet's Wife, A. A. Lowell.
Poet's Wife Makes Him a Door So He Can Find the Way Home, The. Willard.
Populist Manifesto. Ferlinghetti.
Prelude: "Give us another poem, he said." Kavanagh.
Prestidigitator, The. Young.
Procedure is habit. I affirm it. Meltzer.

Proem: "I love the old melodious lays." Whittier.
Profile. Schechter.
Progress of Poesy, The. Gray.
Prologue, The: "To sing of wars, of captains, and of kings." Bradstreet.
Reading and Talking. Zukofsky.
Reading Walt Whitman. Forbes.
Reason for Not Writing Orthodox Nature Poetry. Wain.
Reasons for Music. MacLeish.
Relish of the Muse, The. Beaumont.
Resignation Day. Friedman.
Rhymes (?). Leigh.
Said the Poet to the Analyst. Sexton.
Sanctimonious Poets, The. Hölderlin.
Sarasvati. Stephens.
Sasha and the Poet. Valentine.
Scottsboro, Too, Is Worth Its Song. Cullen.
Secret, The. Levertov.
Seven. Parra.
Seven-League Boots, The. Voronca.
Sharon Will Be No/Where on Nobody's Best-Selling List. Scott.
Shoplifting Poetry. Steingesser.
Since Most Poets Write Nonsense. Rosenberger.
Singing Aloud. Kizer.
Sisters, The. A. Lowell.
Sitting Bard, The. Seaman.
Six Poets in Search of a Lawyer. Hall.
Sleep and Poetry. Keats.
Solution. Emerson.
Sometimes/ the poems. Scott.
Song of Allegiance. Mason.
Song to Accompany the Bearer of Bad News. Wagoner.
Song's Eternity. Clare.
Sonnet: "Oh for a poet—for a beacon bright." Robinson.
Sonnet: "Nuns fret not at their convent's narrow room." Wordsworth.
Sonnet, The: "Sonnet is a moment's monument, A." *Fr.* The House of Life. D.G. Rossetti.
Sonnet, A: "Two voices are there: one is of the deep." Stephen.
Sonnets to Be Written from Prison. Adamson.
Souster. Fraser.
Spenser! a jealous honourer of thine. Keats.
Spicer's Instant Poetry. Reeves.
Spiritualist, The. Slade.
Spur, The. Yeats.
Strike Among the Poets, A. *Unknown.*
Survey of Literature. Ransom.
Teacher of Poetry, The. Packard.
Telling It. Sullivan.
Ten Definitions of Poetry. Sandburg.
Terence, This Is Stupid Stuff. Housman.
Terminus. Emerson.
Test, The. Emerson.
That Bright Chimeric Beast. Cullen.
That Poem. Sáez Burgos.
These poems/ they are things that I do. Jordan.
Thinking of You. Lourie.
This Is to Signify. Morice.
This was a poet — it is that. Dickinson.
Thoughts from a Bottle. Clark.
Throughout the World If It Were Sought. Wyatt.
Tin Can, The. Smith.
To a Poet, Who Would Have Me Praise Certain Bad Poets, Imitators of His and Mine. Yeats.
To a Waterfowl. Hall.
To a Young Poet Who Fled. Logan.
To an Athlete Turned Poet. Meinke.
To an Author. Freneau.
To an Elder Poet. Williams.
To an Indian Poet. Harjo.

To Chuck. Sanchez.
To His Mother. Herbert.
To Hugh MacDiarmid. Morgan.
To Ireland in the Coming Times. Yeats.
To Julia de Burgos. Burgos.
To Li Po from Tu Fu. Kizer.
To Minerva. Hood.
To My Brother George. Keats.
To My Contemporaries. Rolfe.
To My Ingenious and Worthy Friend William Lowndes, Esq.
  Gay.
To Poem. Lifshin.
To Poesy. Tennyson.
To Robert Browning. Landor.
To the Mother from Scarsdale Who Asked About Publishing
  Her Daughter's Poems. Bass.
To the Moon. Winters.
To the Nightingale. Countess of Winchilsea.
To the Reader. Bowers.
To the Rt. Hon. the Lady C. Tufton. Countess of Winchilsea.
To the Stone-Cutters. Jeffers.
To the Trade. Neugass.
To the Young Poets, Except Children, Who Haven't Earned the
  Title. Humphrey.
Today Is a Day of Great Joy. Cruz.
Traditional Grammarian as Poet, The. Hipple.
Transformation. Troupe.
Ultimate Anthology. Bell.
Untitled X. Esteves.
Up, up old Benedict, the bard who would. *Fr.* Six Reveilles to
  Match My Self-Indulgence. Bentley.
Uses of Poetry. Scott.
Valentine for Marianne Moore, A. Olson.
Variations: #21. Stephens.
Verse: "What should we know." Gogarty.
Very Like a Whale. Nash.
Villanelle: "It's all a trick, quite easy when you know it."
  Skeat.
Vision of Poets, A, *sel.* Browning.
Visiting Poet. Nims.
Voice in the Crowd. Joans.
W. C. W. Ray.
War Poets. Fuller.
What Good Is a Poet? Lanners.
What Is a Jewish Poem? Sklarew.
What is a Sonnet? Watkins.
What the Chairman Told Tom. Bunting.
What You Should Know to Be a Poet. Snyder.
Whats My Name If Not Everyone Elses. Salinas.
When He Would Have His Verses Read. Herrick.
When I Began This Funny Journey. Miller.
When the Five Prominent Poets. Jacobsen.
Where Are the War Poets? Day Lewis.
Who will believe my verse in time to come. Sonnets, XVII.
  Shakespeare.
Why I Am Not a Painter. O'Hara.
Why is my verse so barren of new pride. Sonnets, LXXVI.
  Shakespeare.
Why Write Poetry? Davis.
With Mercy for the Greedy. Sexton.
Witness to Death. Lattimore.
Wits, The. Suckling.
Woman Poet, The. Kolmar.
Word Drunk. Harrison.
Words, The. Wagoner.
Words for Neruda. Carroll.
Writing in England Now. O'Connor.
Xmas for the Boys. Ewart.
"Yes, But. . . ." Weiss.
Yes; I Write Verses. Landor.
Yes the Secret Mind Whispers. Young.
Yet Do I Marvel. Cullen.

Yiddish Poet. Jacobs.
Young Poets. Parra.
Younger Poet, A. Schjeldahl.
*See also* **names of individual poets.**

**Poker**
My Poker Girl. Masson.
Newton's Third. Hubbard.
Poker Poem. Pettit.
Rambling, Gambling Man. Houston.
Root, Hog, or Die. *Unknown.*

**Poland**
Cafe in Warsaw. Ginsberg.
Poland/1931. Rothenberg.
To the Jews in Poland. Wittlin.

**Polar Bears**
Polar Bear, The. Lucie-Smith.

**Police**
Bogong Jack and the Trooper. Manifold.
Cops and Robbers. Middleton.
Corner. Pomeroy.
Definition for Blk/Children. Sanchez.
Fish. Levis.
Idiot, The. Randall.
Knock on Wood. Dumas.
Narrative Hooper and L.D.O. Sestina with a Long Line, The.
  Whitehead.
Negro Hero. Brooks.
P.C. Plod Versus the Dale St Dog Strangler. McGough.
Poem to a Nigger Cop. Hamilton.
Police Station Ditties. Beerbohm.
Policeman's Lot, The. *Fr.* The Pirates of Penzance. Gilbert.
Secret Policeman. Buckley.
Southern Cop. Brown.
Third Degree. Hughes.
When Cotton Haymes Walks down the Street. Brigham.
Who But the Lord? Hughes.

**Politics and Politicians**
As a kid I believed in democracy: I. Berryman.
As I strole the city, oft I. *Fr.* The Legion Club. Swift.
Blest statesman he, whose mind's unselfish will. Wordsworth.
Bryan, Bryan, Bryan, Bryan. Lindsay.
Campaign, The. Miles.
Campaign Promise. Taylor.
Candidate, The. Ezell.
Demagogue, The. McGinley.
Dodger, The. *Unknown.*
Election 1960. Baxter.
Epitaph on the Politician Himself. Belloc.
Excellent Roman knives slip along the ribs. *Fr.* The Teeth
  Mother Naked at Last. Bly.
Hand That Signed the Paper, The. Thomas.
Independent, The. McGinley.
Legend of Versailles, A. Tolson.
Letter from a Candidate for the Presidency. *Fr.* The Biglow
  Papers. Lowell.
Man from Washington, The. Welch.
Misconception, A. Lowell.
Modern Leader, A. Simpson.
Next to of course God America I. Cummings.
Nocturne for the U.S. Congress. Contoski.
On a General Election. Belloc.
On Watching Politicians Perform at Martin Luther King's
  Funeral. Knight.
Politician, A. Cummings.
Politicians, 1972. Clinch.
Politics. Yeats.
Similes for Two Political Characters of 1819. Shelley.
Speech. Taylor.
Statesman, The. Belloc.
This, the last ornament among the peers. Belloc.
To a Noisy Politician. Freneau.
To Antenor. Philips.

Tory Pledges.  Moore.
Washington Interregnum.  Whittemore.
What the Moon Saw.  Lindsay.
Young Politician.  Jackson.
**Pollock, Jackson**
Number 1 by Jackson Pollock (1948).  Sullivan.
Squeeze Play.  *Fr.* Spectator's Guide to Contemporary Art.
    McGinley.
**Pollution.**  *See* **Ecology.**
**Polo**
Jigsaw Puzzle.  Deagon.
Polo Match.  Ciardi.
**Pompeii, Italy**
New Excavations.  *Fr.* Pompeii.  Speyer.
Volcanoes.  Akhmadulina.
**Ponds.**  *See* **Lakes and Ponds.**
**Ponies**
For a Shetland Pony Brood Mare Who Died In Her Barren
    Year.  Kumin.
Ponies, The.  Gibson.
**Pool (game)**
Eightball.  Morice.
Kelley.  Hershon.
Poolhall, The.  Burt.
Pool-Shootin' Roy.  Runyon.
Rotation.  Bond.
Straightening the Warp.  Blazek.
**Pope, Alexander**
Johnson on Pope.  Ferry.
Mr. Pope.  Tate.
Mr. Pope's Welcome from Greece.  Gay.
**Popeye**
Farm Implements and Rutabagas in a Landscape.  Ashbery.
**Poplar Trees**
Binsey Poplars.  Hopkins.
Poplar-Field, The.  Cowper.
To a Late Poplar.  Kavanagh.
**Poppies**
Copa de Oro.  Coolbrith.
Farewell Ballad of Poppies, A.  Brudne.
Ode to the Poppy.  Oneil.
Poppies, The.  Church.
Poppies on the Wheat.  Jackson.
**Porcupines**
Kag the Porcupine (the Misanthrope).  Guiterman.
Porcupine, The.  Kinnell.
Porcupine, The.  Kuskin.
Porcupine, The.  Nash.
Porcupines.  Huff.
Pretty Murder.  MacLean.
**Pornography**
Ode to Pornography.  Anderson.
Saturday Afternoon at the Movies.  Logan.
**Port Jefferson, New York**
Port Jefferson.  Simpson.
**Porter, Cole**
Parodies of Cole Porter's "Night and Day."  Lardner.
**Portraits**
Dorothy Q.  Holmes.
"Formerly a Slave."  Melville.
Likeness, A.  Browning.
Miltonic Sonnet for Mr. Johnson on His Refusal of Peter Hurd's
    Official Portrait, A.  Wilbur.
Miss Cecily Finch.  Galvin.
My Picture.  Procter.
On the Portrait of a Woman about to Be Hanged.  Hardy.
Portrait, The ("This is her picture as she was").  Rossetti.
Recollection, A.  Bishop.
**Ports.**  *See* **Harbors and Ports.**
**Portugal**
Camoes and the Debt.  Andresen.
**Portuguese Man-of-War.**

Medusa, The.  Davenport.
**Poseidon.**  *See* **Neptune.**
**Potatoes**
Digging.  Heaney.
Famine Song.  *Unknown.*
Potato.  Wilbur.
**Pound, Ezra**
Cage, The.  Berryman.
Epistle to the Rapalloan.  MacLeish.
Ezra Pound.  Lowell.
Ezra Pound.  Price.
Ezra Pound.  Webb.
Ezry.  MacLeish.
Homage and Lament for Ezra Pound in Captivity.  Duncan.
On the Fly-Leaf of Pound's Cantos.  Bunting.
Postscript, on a Name.  Ratcliffe.
Talking of Ezra Pound and long-dead pantos.  *Fr.* Fisbo.
    Nichols.
**Poverty**
Alice Fell.  Wordsworth.
Art thou poor, yet hast thou golden slumbers?  *Fr.* The Pleasant
    Comedy of Patient Grissell.  Dekker.
Aztec Figurine.  Beecher.
Ballad of the Man Who's Gone.  Hughes.
Bargain.  Stone.
Bean Eaters, The.  Brooks.
Bon Voyage.  Steele.
Born with a gentle heart, and born to please.  *Fr.* The Country
    Justice.  Langhorne.
Boy with His Hair Cut Short.  Rukeyser.
Brian O Linn.  *Unknown.*
Champion.  Morgan.
City Life.  Lawrence.
Come, live with me and be my love.  Day Lewis.
Crucified.  Sadowski.
Dakota Land.  *Unknown.*
Debt.  *Unknown.*
Deserted Cabin.  Haines.
Down and Out.  Hughes.
Elementary School Classroom in a Slum, An.  Spender.
Eugene Delacroix Says.  Dorn.
Furnished Lives.  Silkin.
Gleaner, The.  Taylor.
Good Times.  Clifton.
Hard Time Killin' Floor Blues.  *Unknown.*
Holy Thursday ("Is this a holy thing to see").  *Fr.* Songs of
    Experience.  Blake.
Home/grown.  Storey.
I, Jim Rogers.  Burnshaw.
Images of Poverty.  Maddow.
In (What Few) Green (Barely) Parks.  Coleman.
I've Heard Them Talk: for My Main Man.  Storey.
Jone o' Grinfield.  *Unknown.*
Last Families in the Cabins, The.  Brand.
Last of The Flock, The.  Wordsworth.
Leaden-eyed, The.  Lindsay.
Lean Street.  Fraser.
Likeness, The.  Nathan.
Lovers of the Poor, The.  Brooks.
Manchild.  Bohanon.
Mean wind wanders through the backcourt trash, A.  *Fr.*
    Glasgow Sonnets.  Morgan.
Miss Rosie.  Clifton.
Moving through the Silent Crowd.  Spender.
My Song.  Bialik.
Nikki-Rosa.  Giovanni.
No New Music.  Crouch.
One Time Henry Dreamed the Number.  Long.
Orphan Girl, The.  *Unknown.*
Other Side of Town Saturday Night, The.  Steele.
Photographing the Facade—San Miguel de Allende.  Colquitt.
Poem For the Subterranean Poor.  Di Prima.

Poor, The. Williams.
Poor Girl's Meditation, The. *Unknown.*
Poor Man, The. *Unknown.*
Poor Man Blues. *Unknown.*
Poverty. Simic.
Poverty Knock. *Unknown.*
Proletarian Portrait. Williams.
Rich and Poor. Hunt.
Rich and Poor; or, Saint and Sinner. Peacock.
Saturday's Child. Cullen.
Shoofly, The. O'Hare.
Sixth Winter, The. Rolfe.
Song of Poverty. *Unknown.*
Starving to Death on a Government Claim. *Unknown.*
Street. Oppen.
Street Window. Sandburg.
Strictly for Posterity. Simic.
Summertime and the Living. Hayden.
Sure a Poor Man. *Unknown.*
There Is No Light. Mabuza.
Things About Comin' My Way. *Unknown.*
Thirty Bob a Week. Davidson.
Tin Cup Blues. *Unknown.*
Tinker's Wife. Kavanagh.
To a Fighter Killed in the Ring. Lipsitz.
To a Red-headed Do-good Waitress. Dugan.
To the Four Courts, Please. Stephens.
West London. Arnold.
What You Goin' to Do When the Rent Comes 'Round?
   Sterling.
Wildcats Walking in the Dark. Steele.
Winter. Synge.
Woman Poem. Giovanni.
Worry About Money. Raine.

**Prairie Schooners**
Covered Wagon, The. Blakeney.
Prairie Schooner, The. Dale.
Western Wagons. Benét.
*See also* **Wagon Trains.**

**Prairies**
Bury Me Not on the Lone Prairie. *Unknown.*
Bury Me Out on the Prairie. *Unknown.*
Nebraska. Swan.
Plains, The. Dixon.
Prairie, The. Pillin.
Prairie Melts, The. Ferril.
Prairie Town. Stafford.
Prairies, The. Bryant.
Stories from Kansas. Stafford.
West of Chicago. Dimoff.

**Praxiteles**
Spoken by Venus on Seeing Her Statue Done by Praxiteles.
   *Unknown.*

**Prayer**
After the Funeral of Assam Hamady. Hamod.
And yet hath prayer, the heav'n breathing foliage of faith. *Fr.*
   The Testament of Beauty. Bridges.
Conversation of Prayer, The. Thomas.
Dark Scent of Prayer, The. Drachler.
For the Woman Who Asked Me If I Believe in God and If I
   Pray. Wiegner.
Grass on the Prayer Path. *Unknown.*
Great God, let all by tuneful pow'rs. Heginbothom.
Hour of Prayer, The. Hoy.
How the Ploughman Learned His Paternoster. *Unknown.*
Letter to the Child Lady Margaret Cavendish Holles-Harley, A.
   Prior.
Man of Prayer, The. *Fr.* A Song to David. Smart.
Matins, or Morning Prayer. Herrick.
Morning Smallfire in Lukachukai Mountains. Ortiz.
Oft have I seen at some cathedral door. *Fr.* Divina Commedia.
   Longfellow.

Our Insufficiency to Praise God Suitably, for His Mercy. *Fr.*
   God's Determinations. Taylor.
Paths of Prayer, The. Roditi.
Power of Prayer, The. *Fr.* Vanity of Human Wishes. Johnson.
Pray in May. Metcalfe.
Prayer: "Prayer the Church's banquet, angels' age." Herbert.
Prayer for the Young and Lovely, A. Rice.
Prayers, The. Schwartz.
Qui Laborat, Orat. Clough.
Sweet Hour of Prayer. Walford.
Temple, The. Sisson.
Universal Prayer, The. Pope.
What a Friend We Have in Jesus. Scriven.
What Shall I Pray For Today? Morehead.
Without Ceremony. Miller.
Worship. Suderman.

**Praying Mantis**
Confrontation. Hart.
Don't Sit under the Apple Tree with Anyone Else but Me.
   Pack.
Mantis. McCord.
"Mantis." Zukofsky.

**Preachers and Preaching**
Aimee McPherson. *Unknown.*
Music of His Steps, The. Wakefield.

**Predestination**
Calvin in the Casino. Cassity.
Written over a Gate. Sheffield.

**Pregnancy**
Angel. Soto.
Birthing, The. Bentley.
Charm Against Pregnancy, A. Stessel.
D-Day Minus. Brock.
Emergency at 8. Hewitt.
Epigram: for a Woman with Child. Cunningham.
First Pregnancy. Alta.
Foetal Song. Oates.
For a Woodscolt Miscarried. Corrington.
For Arl in Her Sixth Month. Young.
For You, Who Didn't Know. Willard.
I loved/ secretly. *Fr.* Carmina Burana. *Unknown, tr. fr. Latin.*
Kind of Love, A. Nichols.
Labour of the Brain, Ballad of the Body. Forman.
Maternity Gown. Holbrook.
Meeting, The. Spivack.
Night Watch. Magid.
Now Jentil Belly Down. *Unknown.*
Now That I Am Forever with Child. Lorde.
Oblique Birth Poem. Darr.
Poem Before Birth. Scott.
Poem Wondering If I'm Pregnant. Fraser.
Portrait of a Pregnant Woman. Jones.
Pot-Bellied Anachronism, The. Darr.
Pregnancy. Fish.
Pregnancy. McPherson.
Pregnant Teenager On the Beach. Balazs.
Timepiece, A. Merrill.
To a Child Born in Time of Small War. Sorrells.
Trouble. Wright.
Unexpected, The. Ai.
Vow, The. Hecht.
Wait, The. Janowitz.
Waiting for the Doctor. Inez.
With Child. Taggard.
Woman to Child. Wright.
Woman to Man. Wright.

**Prejudice.** *See* **Racial Prejudice.**

**Presidency, The (U.S.)**
Mild-Spoken Citizen Finally Writes to the White House, A.
   Meredith.

**Presley, Elvis**
Painkillers. Gunn.

**Pride**
　Be not proud of your sweet body.　*Unknown.*
　Conceited Man, A.　*Unknown.*
　Naturally.　Lorde.
　Ozymandias.　Shelley.
　Positive, a Coxcomb.　Plomer.
　Primer Lesson.　Sandburg.
　Proper Pride.　Lawrence.
**Priestly, Joseph**
　Priestly.　*Fr.* Sonnets on Eminent Characters.　Coleridge.
**Priests.**　*See* **Clergy.**
**Primroses**
　Evening Primroses.　Clare.
　Primrose, The.　Herrick.
　Primrose, Being at Montgomery Castle, The.　Donne.
　Primula Scotica.　Senior.
**Printing and Printers**
　Midrash.　Meltzer.
　Printing Jenny.　Mitchell.
**Prior, Matthew**
　For My Own Monument.　Prior.
**Prisoners of War**
　Between Two Prisoners.　Dickey.
　Tramp! Tramp! Tramp! or, The Prisoner's Hope.　Root.
**Prisons and Prisoners**
　Attica.　Coleman.
　Attica.　Welburn.
　Baby, Please Don't Go.　*Unknown.*
　Balls and Chain.　Aubert.
　Been in the Pen So Long.　*Unknown.*
　Boston Burglar, The.　*Unknown.*
　Botany Bay.　*Unknown.*
　Cell Song.　Knight.
　Chain Gang Blues.　*Unknown.*
　Chain Gang Trouble.　*Unknown.*
　Charlie 12.　Small.
　Clonmel Jail.　*Unknown.*
　Coming of Age in the County Jail.　Revard.
　Convict, The.　Wordsworth.
　Convicts' Ball, The.　Bierce.
　Decayed Time.　Wahl.
　Deer in the Prison, The.　Bruchac.
　Diagnostic Center.　Nicholson.
　Down in the Valley.　*Unknown.*
　Fish.　Hogan.
　Folsom, August 11th: A Question of Races.　Aguila.
　Food Strike.　Hogan.
　For Freckle-faced Gerald.　Knight.
　Gaol Song, The.　*Unknown.*
　Girl Held Without Bail.　Walker.
　Hand Me Down My Walking Cane.　*Unknown.*
　Hard Rock Returns to Prison from the Hospital for the
　　Criminal Insane.　Knight.
　He Aint Risen, Baby, Cause He Aint Gone Nowhere.
　　Coleman.
　He Sees Through Stone.　Knight.
　High Sheriff Blues.　*Unknown.*
　Idea of Ancestry, The.　Knight.
　If you see my mother . . .　Maze.
　In Jail.　Corretjer.
　In the Cage.　Lowell.
　In the Prison Pen.　Melville.
　In the Tank.　Gunn.
　Inscription.　Canning *and* Frere.
　Inside the Wall of My Cell.　Green.
　Isolation Cell Poem.　Green.
　It's Almost Done (On a Monday).　*Unknown.*
　Jailbird.　Scannell.
　Jailhouse Blues, The.　*Unknown.*
　Jim Jones at Botany Bay.　*Unknown.*
　Judge Harsh Blues.　*Unknown.*
　Lean Day in a Convict's Suit, A.　Wahl.

　Leaving the Prison.　Bruchac.
　Line-up, The.　Swift.
　Memories of West Street and Lepke.　Lowell.
　Midnight Special.　Leadbelly.
　My Crime.　*Unknown.*
　Nashville Stonewall Blues.　*Unknown.*
　O Death, Rock Me Asleep.　Boleyn.
　Of that time in a Southern jail.　*Fr.* The Call Across the Valley
　　of not Knowing.　Kinnell.
　Ol' Hannah.　*Unknown.*
　On Leaving Prison.　Leon.
　Parchman Farm Blues.　*Unknown.*
　Paul.　Saleh.
　Portland County Jail.　*Unknown.*
　Prison.　Ashley.
　Prison Bi-Centennial Address, A.　Aguila.
　Prison Cell Blues.　*Unknown.*
　Prisoner, The.　Mahon.
　Prisoner of Chillon, The.　Byron.
　Quiet and Orderly Life, A.　Hogan.
　Ritual, The.　Ashley.
　Rust.　Hogan.
　San Francisco County Jail Cell B-6.　Conyus.
　Solitary Confinement.　*Fr.* The Kropotkin Poems.　Webb.
　Sonnets to Be Written from Prison.　Adamson.
　Spring.　Hogan.
　Stalemate at Attica.　Coleman.
　Stir the Wallby Stew.　*Unknown.*
　Sympathy.　Dunbar.
　"Temporary Escape."　Keller.
　To Althea, from Prison.　Lovelace.
　Tom Mooney Walks at Midnight.　Gold.
　Trees, The: a Convict Monologue.　Shapcott.
　Visiting Hour, The.　Wagoner.
　Vivisection.　Fowler.
　What is Left?　Shakur.
　When First unto This Country.　*Unknown.*
　Written in Her French Psalter.　Elizabeth I, Queen of England.
　Written on a Wall at Woodstock.　Elizabeth I, Queen of
　　England.
　Written With a Diamond on Her Window at Woodstock.
　　Elizabeth I, Queen of England.
　*Do Not Go Gentle* (DNGG).　Michael Hogan, ed.
**Procrastination**
　Getting Started.　Hale.
**Prodigal Son (Bible)**
　Zorba.　Liddy.
**Progress**
　Dismissing Progress and its Progenitors.　Reavey.
　For the Cultural Campaign.　Jigmed.
　Moon Landing.　Auden.
　Pity This Busy Monster, Manunkind.　Cummings.
　Where Do the Children Play?　Stevens.
**Prometheus**
　Prometheus.　Byron.
　Prometheus.　Mastoraki.
　Prometheus Bound.　Aeschylus.
　Prometheus Unbound.　Shelley.
**Propertius, Sextus**
　Homage to Sextus Propertius.　Pound.
　Note on Propertius I, 5.　Adcock.
**Prophets and Prophecy**
　Advice to a Prophet.　Wilbur.
　Cassandra.　Robinson.
　Prophecy, A.　Ginsberg.
　Prophet.　Chambers.
　Prophets for a New Day.　Walker.
　Some Newly-Discovered Prophecies of Nostradamus.　Lake.
　Tiresias.　Tennyson.
　Word, The.　Kahn.
**Proserpina** *or* **Proserpine.**　*See* **Persephone.**
**Prospectors.**　*See* **Gold Mining and Miners.**

**Prostitution and Prostitutes**

As You Leave Me. Knight.
Cavalier Lyric. Simmons.
Central Maryland, 1963. Jacobik.
Fille de Joie: Congo. Jackson.
For A Masseuse and a Prostitute. Rexroth.
Greasy Spoon Blues. Gasparini.
House of the Rising Sun. *Unknown.*
In Response to a Rumor That the Oldest Whorehouse in
    Wheeling, West Virginia, Has Been Condemned. Wright.
Old Lady's Lament for Her Youth, The. Villon.
On Watching Pimps. Troupe.
Place Pigalle. Wilbur.
Prostitutes at Les Halles, The. Mayhall.
Ruined Maid, The. Hardy.
Saigon Tea. Oldham.
Scarlet Woman, The. Johnson.
She Is More to Be Pitied, than Censured. Gray.
Stranger, The. Everson.
To a Courtesan a Thousand Years Dead. Eldridge.
Violent Space, The. Knight.
Whore. King.
Wicked Lady of Gough Street. Lawson.
Young Woman of Beare, The. Clarke.

**Protest, Social**

Adultery. Dugan.
Advent 1966. Levertov.
Advice to a Prophet. Wilbur.
Advice to Young Ladies. Hope.
Africa's Plea. Dempster.
After the Industrial Revolution, All Things Happen At Once.
    Bly.
Ain't Gonna Let Nobody Turn Me Round. *Unknown.*
Alabama Bus. *Unknown.*
Alabama Centennial. Madgett.
America. Ginsberg.
Americana XV: Simplicity. Rakosi.
America's Wounded Knee. George.
And you'll say a nation totters. *Fr.* Civil Riot. Cole.
Angry Man, The. McGinley.
Apolitical Intellectuals. Castillo.
Apostrophe to Man. Millay.
April 1962. Goodman.
Bad Old Days, The. Rexroth.
Ballad of the Landlord. Hughes.
Benediction. Kaufman.
Benediction. Mitchell.
Birmingham 1963. Patterson.
Blighters. Sassoon.
Body Politic, The. Hall.
Burning of Paper Instead of Children, The. Rich.
Chic Freedom's Reflection. Walker.
Chicago Centennial or: The Town Hall Meeting. Bradford.
Child of the Romans. Sandburg.
Childhood. Walker.
Christmas Prayer, A. Mitchell.
Cinque. Hale.
Comments. Kenner.
Covenant, The. Cunningham.
Custer Lives in Humbolt County. Hale.
Dance for Militant Dilettantes, A. Young.
Dear America. Peterson.
Death to Van Gogh's Ear! Ginsberg.
Distant Drum, The. Hernton.
Don Baty, the Draft Resister. Rukeyser.
Don't Want No Hungry Woman. *Unknown.*
Draft Dodger Rag. Ochs.
Ecologue. Ginsberg.
Far Cry from Africa, A. Walcott.
First Fight. Then Fiddle. Ply the Slipping String. Brooks.
Five Ways to Kill a Man. Brock.
Florida Road Workers. Hughes.

For My People. Walker.
For Saundra. Giovanni.
Foreign Policy Commitments; or, You Get Into the Catamaran
    First, Old Buddy. Blackburn.
Free Silver. *Unknown.*
From a Speech Delivered in Freedom Hall on Afrikan
    Liberation Day: Words From a Welfare Mother. Jackson.
Girl Held Without Bail. Walker.
Gloucester Moors. Moody.
Golf Links Lie So Near the Mill, The. Cleghorn.
Great Society, Mark X, The. Nemerov.
Hallelujah I'm a Bum ("I read in the news, the President said").
    Dane *and* Silber.
Harlem. Hughes.
Home on the Range, February 1962. Dorn.
Hour of Concern. Hubbell.
House Arrest. Tsongas.
How Beastly the Bourgeois Is. Lawrence.
I Am Waiting. Ferlinghetti.
I Have Seen Black Hands. Wright.
I Sing of Olaf Glad and Big. Cummings.
If We Must Die. McKay.
In Goya's greatest scenes we seem to see. *Fr.* A Coney Island
    of the Mind. Ferlinghetti.
In Mexico. Sward.
I've Got to Know. Guthrie.
Johnson's Cabinet Watched by Ants. Bly.
Just Taking Note. Scott.
Keep Your Eyes on the Prize. *Unknown.*
Keeping Informed in D.C. Nemerov.
Kent State, May 4, 1970. Goodman.
Last of the Light Brigade, The. Kipling.
Latest Decalogue, The. Clough.
Let Us All Be Unhappy on Sunday. Neaves.
London. *Fr.* Songs of Experience. Blake.
Man of Property, The. Ballard.
March, The ("Under the too white marmorial Lincoln
    Memorial"). Lowell.
March, The ("Where two or three were heaped together, or
    fifty"). Lowell.
March on Washington, A. Squires.
Masters of War. Dylan.
May Mobilization. Ginsberg.
Meaning of Protest, The. Harper.
Miss America. Sadowski.
Montgomery. Cornish.
Mourn Not the Dead. Chaplin.
Much madness is divinest sense. Dickinson.
My Horse, Amanda: The Summer of the Watergate Hearings.
    Kumin.
Necessary Bucket, A. Meinke.
No More. Clark.
Norman Morrison. Ferguson.
Norman Morrison. Mitchell.
Note to Olga (1966), A. Levertov.
Ode: Inscribed to W. H. Channing. Emerson.
Of Late. Starbuck.
Orange Bears, The. Patchen.
Outside of a Small Circle of Friends. Ochs.
Patchwork. Mabuza.
Peaceable Kingdom, The. Piercy.
Plot to Assassinate the Chase Manhattan Bank, The. Larsen.
Poem about Birth. Sadowski.
Poem for the Subterranean Poor. Di Prima.
Poem to a Nigger Cop. Hamilton.
Proposal for Recycling Wastes, A. Piercy.
Pull Off Your Old Coat. *Unknown.*
Quaker Hero, Burning. Noll.
Rebel's Progress. Earley.
Revolution in the Revolution in the Revolution. Snyder.
Revolutionary Letter #19. Di Prima.
Revolutionary Letter #36. Di Prima.

Rich and Poor; or, Saint and Sinner. Peacock.
Riot. Brooks.
Salad la Raza. Hale.
Same in Blues. Hughes.
Season 'Tis, My Lovely Lambs, The. Cummings.
Secret People, The. Chesterton.
She Was Poor, but She Was Honest. *Unknown.*
Song of the Shirt, The. Hood.
Song for the Ragged Schools of London, A. E. Browning.
Song of the Militant Romance, The. Lewis.
Song to the Men of England. Shelley.
Sonnet on the Projected Kendal and Windermere Railway.
    Wordsworth.
Sonnet to Seabrook. Ray.
Stand Up! Lawrence.
Strange Hells. Gurney.
Street Demonstration. Walker.
Suddenly there were cakes and everything. Vargas.
Superman. Updike.
"Terres des Hommes." Schechter.
Thanks to Industrial Essex. Davie.
Thirty Bob a Week. Davidson.
To Patriotic America. Middleton.
To the Governor and Legislature of Massachusetts. Nemerov.
Un-American Investigators. Hughes.
Unlawful Assembly. Enright.
Until They Have Stopped. Wright.
Vacation. Stafford.
Vapor Trail Reflected in the Frog Pond. Kinnell.
Wack Fol the Diddle. Kearney.
Warm Protest. Enright.
We Can Be Together. Kantner.
We Real Cool. Brooks.
We Shall Overcome. *Unknown.*
Welcome Home. Purcell.
We're Gonna Move When the Spirit Says Move! *Unknown.*
What a Way to Lose the War. Salinas.
What Have They Done to the Rain? Reynolds.
Where Do the Children Play? Stevens.
Workers Rose on May Day or Postscripts to Karl Marx, The.
    Lorde.
World Is a Beautiful Place, The. Ferlinghetti.
You Can Have It. Levine.
You Get Used to It. Mitchell.
*Forerunners, The: Black Poets in America* (FB). Woodie King,
    Jr., ed.
*Social Poetry of the 1930's* (SPT). Jack Salzman *and* Leo
    Zanderer, eds.
**Proust, Marcel**
Proust on Noah. Silberschlag.
**Provincetown, Massachusetts**
Provincetown, Mass. Shapiro.
**Psyche**
Ode to Psyche. Keats.
**Psychiatry**
Birthday Card for a Psychiatrist. Van Duyn.
Couch, The. Wright.
Essay on Psychiatrists *sel.* Pinsky.
Loneliness. McPherson.
Psychiatrist. DeVries.
Walking through the Upper East Side. Jong.
**Psychoanalysis**
After the Successful Psychotherapy. Ventura.
Analysands. Randall.
Ballad of the Oedipus Complex. Durrell.
Doctor Freud. Lazar.
Interrogator, The. Jennings.
Note from an Analyst's Couch. Probst.
**Puerto Ricans**
Esperanza. Scully.
Puerto Ricans in New York. Reznikoff.
Puerto Ricans in New York II. Reznikoff.

Salsa. Moreno.
You're Nothing But a Spanish Colored Kid. Luciano.
**Puerto Rico**
African Things. Cruz.
Que Bonita Bandera (How Beautiful Is the Flag). *Unknown.*
Why I Can't Write a Poem about Lares. Silén.
*Inventing a Word: An Anthology of Twentieth-Century Puerto
    Rican Poetry* (InW). Julio Marzan, ed.
**Pumpkins**
How Come? Asheron.
Mr. Macklin's Jack-o'-Lantern. McCord.
Pumpkin, The. Graves.
Pumpkin. Worth.
Pumpkin Pie. Hall.
Theme in Yellow. Sandburg.
**Puppets**
Young Master's Account of a Puppet Show. Marchant.
**Purcell, Henry**
Bounty. Miles.
Henry Purcell. Hopkins.
Ode, An: On the Death of Mr. Purcell. Dryden.
**Purgatory**
Negrun. Travis.
**Pygmalion**
Metamorphosis of Pygmalion's Image, The, *sel.* Marston.
Pygmalion. Ruby.
Pygmalion seeing these to spend their times. *Fr.*
    Metamorphoses. Ovid.
Pygmalion's Statue Comes to Life. *Fr.* Metamorphoses. Ovid.
Twixt nature and Pygmalion there might appear great strife.
    *Fr.* Tottel's Miscellany. Tottel.
**Pyramus and Thisbe**
Epitaph of Pyramus and Thisbe. Cowley.
**Pythagoras**
Pythagorans. Hardison.
**Pythons**
Python, The. Belloc.
Python. *Unknown.*

# Q

**Quaggas**
Quagga, The. Enright.
**Quail**
Quail Walk. Miller.
**Quakers.** *See* **Friends, Society of.**
**Quarrels**
Accusation. Utahania.
Early Evening Quarrel. Hughes.
Quarrel, The. Farjeon.
Wife. Andrews.
**Queen Anne's Lace**
Queen Anne's Lace. Spinnanger.
Queen-Ann's-Lace. Williams.
Quiet Faces. Holsapple.
**Queens**
Queen Mother to New Queen. Graves.
**Queens, New York City**
Roses of Queens, The. White.
**Quilts**
Spare Quilt, The. Bishop.

# R

**Ra (Egyptian sun god)**
I Am a Cowboy in the Boat of Ra. Reed.

**Rabbits**
Myxomatosis. Larkin.
Rabbit, The. Brownjohn.
Rabbit, The. Davies.
Rabbit, The. McIntyre.
Rabbit, The. *Unknown.*
Snare, The. Stephens.
*See also* **Hares.**
**Rabelais, Francois**
In Memory of Francois Rabelais. Moritz.
**Rabies**
Elegy on the Death of a Mad Dog, An. *Fr.* The Vicar of
     Wakefield. Goldsmith.
Mad Dog. Siegal.
**Raccoons**
Babies: Just Babies. Fishback.
Coon Song. Ammons.
Dance of Gray Raccoon, The. Guiterman.
Mill Valley. Livingston.
Raccoon. *Fr.* A Bestiary. Rexroth.
Raccoon on the Road. Brennan.
Raccoon Poem. Palmer.
**Racial Prejudice**
Alarm Clock, The. Evans.
America's Wounded Knee. George.
Apartheid. Bohanon.
Backlash Blues, The. Hughes.
Ballad of Birmingham. Randall.
Ballad of Rudolph Reed, The. Brooks.
Birmingham Sunday. Farina.
Black Poet, White Critic. Randall.
Broadminded. Durem.
Cameo No. 11. Jordan.
Changeless Changes. Mabuza.
Chicago *Defender* Sends a Man to Little Rock, The. Brooks.
Children's Rhymes. Hughes.
Crispus Attucks McCoy. Brown.
Hallelujah, I'm A-Travelin'. Raymond.
In Bloemfontein. Ross.
In the Neighborhood. Miles.
Incident. Cullen.
Juanito's Blues. Mberi.
Mark This. Chesham.
May 27, 1971: No Poem. Jordan.
Moment Please, A. Allen.
Montgomery. Cornish.
Namely You. Inada.
Necessary Bucket, A. Meinke.
No Irish Need Apply. *Unknown.*
Non Poem about Vietnam, A. Rodgers.
Old Lem. Brown.
On Seeing Two Brown Boys in a Catholic Church. Horne.
Para Juaco. Casiano.
Parasitosis. Davis.
Patchwork. Mabuza.
Prejudice. Johnson.
Racialism. Blight.
Runaway Slave at Pilgrim's Point, The. E. Browning.
Society's Child. Ian.
Stereo. Lee.
Telephone Conversation. Soyinka.
Terminal. Enright.
These Feet For Rosa Parks. Bohanon.
Tiger. McKay.
To Live and Die in Dixie. Beecher.
Vietnam #4. Major.
Where? When? Which? Hughes.
White City, The. McKay.
White House, The. McKay.
With All Deliberate Speed. Lee.
Yet Do I Marvel. Cullen.
**Radar**

Radar. Ross.
**Radio**
Airwaves. Woessner.
In Memory of Radio. Baraka.
Not Lost In the Stars. Bliven.
Radio Men, The. Jennings.
Radio under the Bed, The. Whittemore.
Riders. Peavy.
Speech. Taylor.
Umbilical. Merriam.
**Radishes**
What is the silly radish doing. *Fr.* Purpose for Radishes.
     Baird.
**Railroads**
Ashtabula Disaster. Moore.
Branch Line, The. Beer.
Burying Ground by the Ties. MacLeish.
Calling Trains. *Unknown.*
Casey Jones. Seibert.
Crossing. Booth.
Echo Canyon. *Unknown.*
Express, The. Spender.
From a Railway Carriage. Stevenson.
George Allen. *Unknown.*
Great Northern. Etter.
Henry K. Sawyer. *Unknown.*
House by the Tracks, A. Etter.
I like to see it lap the miles. Dickinson.
I Rode Southern, I Rode L & N. *Unknown.*
In Texas Grass. Troupe.
I've Been Working on the Railroad. *Unknown.*
Jay Gould's Daughter. *Unknown.*
Lining Track. *Unknown.*
Metropolitan Railway, The. Betjeman.
Newport Railway, The. McGonagall.
Night Journey. Roethke.
Old Section Boss, The. *Unknown.*
Other Side, The. Reiter.
Pat Works on the Railway. *Unknown.*
Penn Central Station at Beacon, N.J., The. Ochester.
Railroad Bill. *Unknown.*
Railroad Blues, The. *Unknown.*
Railroad Cars Are Coming, The. *Unknown.*
Railroad Reverie. Young.
Railroad Song, *sel.* Chivers.
Railway Junction, The. De la Mare.
Rock Island Line, The. *Unknown.*
Salvaging Spikes. Vas Dias.
Siding near Chillicothe, A. Lattimore.
Tay Bridge Disaster, The. McGonagall.
To a Locomotive in Winter. Whitman.
Unloading Rails. *Unknown.*
Utah Iron Horse, The. *Unknown.*
Way Out in Idaho. *Unknown.*
What the Engines Said. Harte.
What's the Railroad to Me. Thoreau.
Wreck of the Royal Palm, The. *Unknown.*
*See also* **Subways; Trains; Trolleys.**
**Rain**
After Rain. Thomas.
All Day It Has Rained. Lewis.
April Rain. Loveman.
April Rain Song. Hughes.
Atavism. Lake.
Autumn Rain. Rexroth.
Beloved, Let Us Once More Praise the Rain. *Fr.* Preludes for
     Memnon. Aiken.
Biography of Southern Rain. Patchen.
Cat and the Rain, The. Swift.
City Rain. Field.
Cloud Burst. Witheford.
Cold Irish Earth, The. Skinner.

Description of a City Shower, A.  Swift.
Drums.  Chosa.
Glass Falling.  MacNeice.
Have You Ever Seen the Rain?  Fogerty.
Highland Portrait.  Smith.
In the Park beside the Marina.  Harry.
Incantation for Rain.  *Unknown.*
It Is Beautiful, It Is Rain.  Wangberg.
It Rains.  Thomas.
July the Seventh.  Norris.
June Rain.  Merwin.
Legend of the Raindrop, The.  Rice.
Little Raindrops.  Browne.
London Rain.  MacNeice.
My Party the Rain.  Stafford.
November.  Bull.
Ode to the Rain, An.  Coleridge.
Prayer for Fine Weather.  Leslie.
Prayer for Rain.  Jama.
Prayer for Rain.  *Unknown.*
Rain, The.  Creeley.
Rain, The.  Davies.
Rain.  DiPasquale.
Rain.  Evans.
Rain.  Henson.
Rain.  O'Sullivan.
Rain.  Sears.
Rain.  Smith.
Rain.  Stevenson.
Rain.  Thomas.
Rain.  Tuwhare.
Rain.  *Unknown.*
Rain in Summer.  Longfellow.
Rain in the Desert.  Fletcher.
Rain Magic Song.  *Unknown.*
Rain on the Roof.  Frame.
Rain Poem.  Coatsworth.
Rain Sleets Flat.  Brigham.
Rain Straight Down.  Makidemewabe.
Rainy Morning.  Rivera-Avilés.
Rainy Summer, The.  Meynell.
Reading in Fall Rain.  Bly.
Santo Domingo Corn Dance.  R. P. Dickey.
Seven Rainy Months.  Plomer.
Smell of Rain.  Hall.
Sophistication.  Miller.
Sudden Shower.  Clare.
Summer Rain.  Coleridge.
There's a Feeling.  Bullwinkle.
Thunderstorm in South Dakota.  Boyle.
Way Through, The.  Levertov.
Wet Day.  McAuley.
Wet Time, A.  Berry.
Wet Weather.  Low.
What Have They Done to the Rain?  Reynolds.

**Rainbows**
Epigram: "Oh, God of dust and rainbows, help us see."
  Hughes.
In a Double Rainbow.  Littlebird.
Legend.  Wright.
My Heart Leaps Up When I Behold.  Wordsworth.
Rainbow, The.  De la Mare.
Rainbow.  Lochhead.
Rainbow, The.  *Unknown.*
Red and blue and delicate green.  *Unknown.*
Watergaw, The.  "MacDiarmid."

**Rainey, Gertrude (Ma)**
Dance for Ma Rainey, A.  Young.
Ma Rainey.  Brown.

**Ralegh, Sir Walter**
Britannia and Raleigh.  Ayloffe.
Sir Walter Raleigh Sailing in the Lowlands.  *Unknown.*

**Ranching, and Ranchers**
Ranch in the Coulee, The.  Haste.
Rancher, The.  Wilson.
*See also*  **Farming and Farmers.**

**Rape**
Exodus.  Probst.
Father of the Victim.  Ballard.
On Rape Unattempted.  Dugan.
Rape.  Pickard.
Rape.  Rich.

**Rats**
Advancement of Learning, An.  Heaney.
Assailant.  Raven.
City Rat and the Country Rat, The.  La Fontaine.
Experiment with a Rat, The.  Rakosi.
Freddy the Rat Perishes.  Marquis.
Intoxicated Rat, The.  *Unknown.*
Letters from an Irishman to a Rat.  Logue.
Pack Rat, The.  Pack.
Pied Piper of Hamelin, The.  Browning.
Poem against Rats, A.  Levinson.
Rat, The.  Davies.
Rat and the Elephant, The.  La Fontaine.
Rat Riddles.  Sandburg.
Rats.  De la Mare.
Reapers.  Toomer.
Song of a Rat.  Hughes.
Three Young Rats.  *Unknown.*
Two Rats, The.  *Unknown.*
What Became of Them?  *Unknown.*
With the Woodnymphs.  Smith.

**Rattlesnakes**
Rattler, Alter.  Ghiselin.
Snake Hunt.  Wagoner.

**Ravens**
Raven, The.  Poe.
Raven, The.  Robinson.
Three Ravens.  *Unknown.*
True Facts of the Case, The.  Euwer.
Twa Corbies, The.  *Unknown.*

**Reading**
Fiction and the Reading Public.  Larkin.
House of Readers, A.  Miller.
Notes Scribbled on the Last Page of a Novel.  Hedley.
Old Susan.  De la Mare.
On My 26th Birthday.  Schechter.
Proverbial Philosophy: of Reading.  Calverley.
Reading Lesson, The.  Murphy.
Study of Reading Habits, A.  Larkin.
When Mother Reads Aloud.  *Unknown.*

**Reason**
On the Triumph of Rationalism.  Ainger.
Reason.  Miles.
Sanctimonious Poets, The.  Hölderlin.
To Hell with Commonsense.  Kavanagh.

**Rebirth**
For Life I Had Never Cared Greatly.  Hardy.
New Birth, The.  Very.

**Red**
What Is Red?  O'Neill.

**Redding, Otis**
Poem for Otis Redding.  Thomas.

**Redemption**
Amazing Grace.  Newton.
Come Ye Sinners, Poor and Needy.  Hart.
Love Lifted Me.  Rowe.
O Happy Day.  Doddridge.
Praise for the Fountain Opened.  Cowper.
Redemption.  Herbert.
Since Jesus Came into My Heart.  McDaniel.

**Redwings**
Redwing, The.  P. Dickinson.

Redwings. Wright.
**Refugees**
Address to the Refugees. Brinnin.
Epilogue: "I have just joined a raggedy line." Trudell.
My Polish Grandma. Field.
Refugees. Grade.
Refugees, The. Muir.
Road to Pengya. Tu Fu.
Two Refugees. Marcus.
**Regimentation**
Dolor. Roethke.
Perforated Spirit, The. Bishop.
**Regret**
Into My Heart an Air That Kills. Housman.
**Reincarnation**
Book of the Dead, Prayer 14. Berssenbrugge.
Meeting the Reincarnation Analyst. Gildner.
Mohini Chatterjee. Yeats.
**Reindeer**
Reindeer and Engine. Jacobsen.
Rigorists. Moore.
**Religion**
After Lorca. Creeley.
And They Were Right. Garioch.
At a Bible House. Lowell.
Boom! Nemerov.
Church Going. Larkin.
Church Poem. Thomas.
Church's One Foundation, The. Stone.
Ecclesiastical Chronicle, *sel.* Heath-Stubbs.
Evangelist, The. Sinclair.
Faith Healer Come to Rabun County. Bottoms.
For his religion it was fit. *Fr.* Hudibras. Butler.
Give Me That Old Time Religion. *Unknown.*
God Is Mr. Big, Real Big. Burke
Good Folks at the Camp Meeting, The. *Fr.* Loony.
   Kloefkorn.
Hippopotamus, The. Eliot.
Holy Willie's Prayer. Burns.
I'm ceded — I've stopped being theirs. Dickinson.
I'm Gonna Run to the City of Refuge. *Unknown.*
Indian Convert, The. Freneau.
Into Your Hands. Huck.
Latest Decalogue, The. Clough.
Law, The. Schulman.
Lay Preacher Ponders, The. Davies.
Little Vagabond, The. *Fr.* Songs of Experience. Blake.
Madam and the Minister. Hughes.
New Approach Needed. Amis.
Old Orange Flute, The. *Unknown.*
On the Religion of Nature. Freneau.
"Onward Christian Soldiers!" Davis.
Pocomania. Walcott.
Poor Can Feed the Birds, The. Neilson.
Prayer: "In the beginning/ was Sunday." Schulte.
Preacher and the Slave, The. Hill.
Priests of Serrabonne, The. Leeming.
Protestant Courts Catholic. Simmons.
Religion. Vaughan.
Religion Back Home. Stafford.
Religious Musings. Coleridge.
Revival. Wagoner.
Running Away from Home. Kizer.
Signpost. Jeffers.
Snake Sermon. Smith.
Some keep the Sabbath going to church. Dickinson.
Spokane Falls 1874. George.
Sunday. Enright.
Sunday Morning. Stevens.
Temptation, The. Smith.
That Old Time Religion. *Unknown.*
They Have Turned the Church Where I Ate God. Gildner.

To Caelia. *Unknown.*
True Religion. Anderson.
Two Memories. "MacDiarmid."
Vicar of Bray, The. *Unknown.*
Wednesday Night Prayer Meeting. Wright.
When Mahalia Sings. Prettyman.
With huntis up, with huntis up. *Unknown.*
With Mercy for the Greedy. Sexton.
Woods Gets Religion. Woods.
Written in Exile. Raine.
**Religious Life**
December. Snyder.
Walking with God. Cowper.
**Religious Verse**
*Adam Among the Television Trees* (AATT). Virginia R.
   Mollenkott, ed.
*Book of Religious Verse, A.* (BoReV). Helen Gardner, ed.
*Poems of Faith and Doubt* (PFD). R. L. Brett, ed.
**Rembrandt Harmenszoon van Rijn**
Polish Rider, The. Walcott.
**Remorse**
R-e-m-o-r-s-e. Ade.
When Oats Were Reaped. Hardy.
**Reno, Nevada**
Reno, *2 a.m.* Hamill.
**Restaurants**
Coffee Den, Cedar Rapids, The. Mulac.
Geraniums, The. Taggard.
Hamburger Mary's. Lawson.
One Fish Ball. *Unknown.*
Partial Explanation, The. Simic.
**Resurrection, The**
Quem Queritis. Carter.
Resurrection, The. Brooks.
*See also* **Easter.**
**Retirement**
Band, The. Dennis.
Death. Byatt.
Lamentation of the Old Pensioner, The. Yeats.
Retired School-Teacher. McHugh.
Swineherd. Chuilleanáin.
**Reunions**
Reunion. Forché.
**Revenge (ship)**
*Revenge, The.* Tennyson.
**Revenge**
Brian Boy Magee. Carbery.
Enslaved. McKay.
Mine enemy is growing old. Dickinson.
Revenge of Rain-in-the-Face, The. Longfellow.
Tamales. "O. Henry."
**Revere, Paul**
Paul Revere's Ride. *Fr.* Tales of a Wayside Inn. Longfellow.
**Revolution**
Abu. Randall.
And When the Revolution Came. Rodgers.
Birds and Man. Mabuza.
Black People! Baraka.
Easter 1916. Yeats.
Firebrand. Crosby.
For My People. Walker.
For Saundra. Giovanni.
For the Revolution. Davidman.
France: an Ode. Coleridge.
Great Day, The. Yeats.
Greek Crazeology. Rodgers.
In a Hotel Lobby. Schneider.
Internationale, The. Potter *and* Degeyter.
Last Poem. Donnelly.
Liberty. Shelley.
Life of the Mind, 1934. Taggard.
Militant. Hughes.

My Poem. Giovanni.
O! Start a Revolution. Lawrence.
Poem about Birth. Sadowski.
Portrait of a False Revolutionist. Schneider.
Radical War Song, A. Macaulay.
Republican Genius of Europe, The. Freneau.
Revolution is the pod. Dickinson.
Revolutionaries, The. Lister.
Revolutionary Dreams. Giovanni.
Revolutionary Letters, *sels.* DiPrima.
Revolutionary Screw, The. Lee.
Room with Revolutionists. Rolfe.
Roses and Revolutions. Randall.
Sane Revolution, A. Lawrence.
Semi-Revolution, A. Frost.
So This Is Our Revolution. Sanchez.
Song in Time of Revolution 1860, A. Swinburne.
Steel Mill Reversal. Macleod.
Strength. Wright.
Sun, the Worker, The. Schneider.
Total Revolution, A. Williams.
Transcontinental. Wright.
Tryptych for Jan Bockelson, A. Simon.
Turn of October, The. Macleod.
Warning. Hughes.
When the Revolution Really. Michelson.
Whirlwinds of Danger. *Unknown.*
Workers Rose on May Day or Postscript to Karl Marx, The.
    Lorde.
Wreath for our Murdered Comrade Kobayashi, A. Gold.
Yeah, I Is Uh Shootin off at the Mouth. Rodgers.
Young Revolutionist. · Schneider.
*See also* **American Revolution; French Revolution.**
**Reynolds, Sir Joshua**
Here Reynolds is laid and, to tell you my mind. *Fr.*
    Retaliation. Goldsmith.
Sir Joshua Reynolds. Blake.
**Rhinoceroses**
Rhinoceros. Hart-Smith.
Rhinoceros, The. Nash.
Rhinoceros. Stoutenburg.
**Riddles**
Bishop of Canterbury, The. *Unknown.*
Captain Wedderburn's Courtship. *Unknown.*
Riddles Wisely Expounded. *Unknown.*
**Rifles**
A. E. F. Sandburg.
Naming of Parts. *Fr.* Lessons of the War. Reed.
On Teaching David to Shoot. McDonald.
**Rilke, Rainer Maria**
Visions. Spivack.
**Rimbaud, Arthur**
Rimbaud in Abyssinia. Griffin.
Rimbaud's Farewell to Europe. Glavin.
**Rings**
Ring, The. Wakoski.
**Riots**
After the Riot. Pillin.
Black Day in July. Lightfoot.
For What It's Worth. Stills.
Gulf, The. Levertov.
Harlem Riot, 1943. Murray.
House-Top The: A Night Piece. Melville.
In This Year of Grace. Hewitt.
Mr. Roosevelt regrets. Murray.
Old Woman Remembers, An. Brown.
Richard Hofstadter and Michael Wallace: A Documentary
    History of American Violence. Rosenberg.
Riot. Brooks.
We are the same in our despair. *Fr.* Riot Rhymes U.S.A.
    Patterson.
Willie B. Clifton.

**Rivers**
At the Stilli's Mouth. Hugo.
Crossing the Colorado River into Yuma. Ortiz.
Duwamish. Hugo.
Estuary, The. Beer.
Green River. Bryant.
Hidden Falls. Minczeski.
In Front of the Seine, Recalling the Rio de la Plata. Ocampo.
Like Ghosts of Eagles. Francis.
Meditation at Oyster River. Roethke.
Negro Speaks of Rivers, The. Hughes.
Not envying Latian shades—if yet they throw. *Fr.* The River
    Duddon. Wordsworth.
Overlooking the River Stour. Hardy.
Repose of Rivers. Crane.
Rio Grande de Loiza. Burgos.
River, The. *Fr.* The Bridge: Powhatan's Daughter. Crane.
River, The. Kell.
River, The. Thompson.
River God, The. Smith.
River of Rivers in Connecticut, The. Stevens.
River Rhyme. Williams.
River Roads. Sandburg.
River Swelleth More and More, The. Thoreau.
River That Is East, The. Kinnell.
Riverbed. Wagoner.
Rivers. Squire.
Rivers Arise; Whether Thou Be the Son. Milton.
Riversong. Anania.
Skykomish River Running. Hugo.
Sonnet to the River Otter. Coleridge.
Stanzas to the Po. Byron.
Tide River, The. *Fr.* The Water Babies. Kingsley.
To Dean Bourn, a Rude River in Devon, by Which Sometimes
    He Lived. Herrick.
To the River Duddon. Nicholson.
To the River Itchin, Near Winton. Bowles.
Virginia. *Fr.* Landscapes. Eliot.
Watershed, The. Meynell.
**Roaches**
At Last We Killed the Roaches. Clifton.
Roaches. Field.
St. Roach. Rukeyser.
**Roads**
Blessing At Kellenberger Road. Valian.
Bound No'th Blues. Hughes.
Daybreak on a Pennsylvania Highway. Daunt.
Florida Road Workers. Hughes.
Freeway. Cardinali.
Highway, The. Merwin.
Journey, The. McMaster.
King's Highway, The. McGroarty.
Middleness of the Road, The. Frost.
Road, The. Johnson.
Road Not Taken, The. Frost.
Rolling English Road, The. Chesterton.
Roman Road, The. Hardy.
So This Is Earth. Sklar.
Song of the Open Road. Whitman.
Southern Road, The. Randall.
White in the Moon the Long Road Lies. Housman.
**Roanoke, Virginia**
Downtown Roanoke. Dillard.
**Robeson, Paul**
Paul Robeson. Brooks.
**Robin Hood**
Birth of Robin Hood, The. *Unknown.*
Bold Peddlar and Robin Hood, The. *Unknown.*
Death of Robin Hood, The. Field.
How Robin Hood Rescued the Widow's Sons. *Unknown.*
Merry Jest of Robin Hood, A. Peacock.
Robin Hood. Burr.

**Robins**

Robin Hood. Keats.

Robin Hood and Allen a Dale. *Unknown.*

Robin Hood and Little John. *Unknown.*

Robin Hood and the Bishop of Hereford. *Unknown.*

Robin Hood and the Monk. *Unknown.*

Robin Hood and the Sheriff. *Unknown.*

Robin Hood's Death. *Unknown.*

**Robins**

Autumn Robin, The. Clare.

Call for the Robin Redbreast and the Wren. Webster.

Epitaph on a Robin-Redbreast, An. Rogers.

I am called by name of man. *Unknown.*

No noise is here, or none that hinders thought. *Fr.* The Robin in Winter. Cowper.

Red Robin, The. Clare.

Robin, A. De la Mare.

Robin, The. Hardy.

Robin Redbreast. Allingham.

Robin Redbreast. Davies.

Robin Redbreast. Kunitz.

Robin Redbreast's Testament. *Unknown.*

Truth, The. Davies.

**Rocks.** *See* **Stones and Rocks.**

**Rockets**

Enough. Tom Masson.

**Rocky Mountains**

Moonrise in the Rockies. Higginson.

On Recrossing the Rocky Mountains after Many Years. Frémont.

**Rodeos**

Bronco Busting, Event #1. Swenson.

Bumper Sticker on His Pickup Said, The. Fox.

Closing of the Rodeo, The. Smith.

Rodeo. Lueders.

**Rodin, Auguste**

Rodin to Rilke. Grosholz.

**Roethke, Theodore**

Dream While Wide Awake. Garfinkel.

For Theodore Roethke. Lowell.

On the Death of Theodore Roethke. Huff.

Reading, The. Triem.

Roethke Plain. Brinnin.

Strut for Roethke, A. Berryman.

**Roland**

Silent Slain, The. MacLeish.

**Roller-Coasters**

Flight of the Roller Coaster. Souster.

**Roller Skating**

Stars Shine so Faithfully. Flanders.

**Roman Catholic Church.** *See* **Catholicism.**

**Rome**

Amours de Voyage, *sels.* Clough.

Antiquitez de Rome, *sels.* Du Bellay.

Fragment. McCrae.

Piazza di Spagna, Early Morning. Wilbur.

Roman Roman, A. Del Monte.

Rome. Cunningham.

Rome. Hardy.

Rome, Conqueror, Conquered. Sylvester.

Thief, The. Kunitz.

To an Old Philosopher in Rome. Stevens.

**Romeo and Juliet**

Silver Dagger, The. *Unknown.*

**Romney Marsh, England**

In Romney Marsh. Davidson.

**Ronkonkoma, Lake**

Dog Sacrifice at Lake Ronkonkoma. Heyen.

**Roosevelt, Franklin Delano**

Franklin D. Roosevelt's Back Again. *Unknown.*

President Roosevelt. *Unknown.*

**Roosevelt, Theodore**

T. R. Hall.

**Roosters**

Bantams in Pine-Woods. Stevens.

Bonny Grey, The. *Unknown.*

Chanticleer. *Fr.* The Canterbury Tales: The Nun's Priest's Tale. Chaucer.

Cock Crowing in a Poulterer's Shop, A. Ferguson.

Gamecock. Dickey.

I Have a Gentle Cock. *Unknown.*

Old Grey. Lape.

On a Cock at Rochester. Sedley.

Roosters. Bishop.

Roosters. Coatsworth.

To Be or Not to Be. *Unknown.*

When the sun came, the rooster expanded to meet it. Miles.

**Rosemary**

Time has an end, they say. Doolittle ("H.D.").

**Roses**

Act, The. Williams.

Bouquet of Roses in Sunlight. Stevens.

Casida of the Rose. García Lorca.

Dark Roots of the Rose, The. Everson.

Elegy While Pruning Roses. Wagoner.

Gloire de Dijon. Lawrence.

Go, Lovely Rose. Waller.

How Roses Came Red. Herrick.

I Send You Roses. Henley.

Musk Rose, The. Keats.

Of a Rose, a Lovely Rose. *Unknown.*

One Perfect Rose. Parker.

Poem: "Rose fades, The." Williams.

Rose, The. Howell.

Rose, The. Roethke.

Rose, The. Rossetti.

Rose, The. Williams.

Rose Family, The. Frost.

Rose Is Dying, The. Cummings.

Roses. *Unknown.*

Roses of Queens, The. White.

Roses of Sa'adi, The. Desbordes-Valmore.

Sea Rose. Doolittle ("H.D.").

Sepal, petal, and a thorn, A. Dickinson.

Sick Rose, The. *Fr.* Songs of Experience. Blake.

To a Friend Who Sent Me Some Roses. Keats.

To Flossie. Williams.

To the Rose upon the Rood of Time. Yeats.

White Rose, A. O'Reilly.

**Rosh Hashanah**

Feast of the Ram's Horn. Shapiro.

This is the autumn and our harvest. *Fr.* New Years's. Reznikoff.

**Rotterdam, Netherlands**

Vision of Rotterdam. Corso.

**Rouen, France**

Rouen. Cannan.

**Rousseau, Jean Jacques**

Mock on, mock on, Voltaire, Rousseau. Blake.

**Royal George (ship)**

On the Loss of the *Royal George.* Cowper.

**Rugby**

Is Football Playing? *Fr.* Is My Team Plowing? Housman.

**Rugs**

Oriental. St. Cyr.

**Runaways**

She's Leaving Home. Lennon *and* McCartney.

**Runners and Running**

For the Running of the New York City Marathon. Dickey.

Jogging at Dusk. Grossbardt.

Mighty Runner, A. Robinson.

Running under Street Lights. White.

**Rushmore, Mount**

Rushmore. Witt.

**Russell, Lucy, Countess of Bedford**

On Lucy, Countess of Bedford. Jonson.
To the Countess of Bedford. Donne.

**Russia**
"Less Nonsense." Herbert.
Meadowland. *Unknown.*
Requiem 1935-1940. Akhmatova.
Russia. Williams.
Russian Poem IV, The. Gerber.
Shootin' with Rasputin. *Unknown.*

**Ruth (Bible)**
Ruth. Hood.

**Ruth, George Herman (Babe)**
And You Are There. Clark.
Babe Ruth. Runyon.

**Rutledge, Ann**
Anne Rutledge. *Fr.* Spoon River Anthology. Masters.

# S

**Sabbath**
Light a Candle. Zelda.
Sabbath. Haan.
Softly Fades the Twilight Ray. Smith.
Thrice Welcome First and Best of Days. Chanler.
Voice Out of the Tabernacle, A. Zukofsky.

**Sacco-Vanzetti Case**
After the Storm. Kalar.
Justice Denied in Massachusetts. Millay.
Sacco-Vanzetti. Halpern.

**Sacraments**
Extreme Unction. Dowson.

**Sailing and Sailors**
Alarmed Skipper, The. Fields.
Banks of Newfoundland, The. *Unknown.*
Battle Problem. Meredith.
Bay of Biscay, The. *Unknown.*
Bell-Bottomed Trousers. *Unknown.*
Blood Red Roses. *Unknown.*
Blow the Man Down. *Unknown.*
Blow, Ye Winds. *Unknown.*
Brown Robyn's Confession. *Unknown.*
Canada-I-O. *Unknown.*
Cape Horn Gospel — 1. Masefield.
Captain Bunker. *Unknown.*
Chief Petty Officer. Causley.
Christmas at Sea. Stevenson.
Cleaning Ship. Keeler.
Clipper *Dunbar* to the Clipper *Cutty Sark*, The. Anderson.
Codfish Shanty, The. *Unknown.*
Coming around the Horn. Stone.
Commemorative of a Naval Victory. Melville.
Crowd, The. Masefield.
Dark-Eyed Sailor, The. *Unknown.*
Darned Mounseer, The. *Fr.* Ruddigore. Gilbert.
Dauber, *sels.* Masefield.
Day Sailing. Slavitt.
*Dom Pedro*, The. *Unknown.*
*Dreadnought*, The. *Unknown.*
Earlye, Earlye, in the Spring. *Unknown.*
Epitaph for a Sailor Buried Ashore. Roberts.
Fifteen Ships on Georges Banks. *Unknown.*
Figurehead, The. Garstin.
For My Grandfather. Webb.
Girls around Cape Horn, The. *Unknown.*
Girl's Song, A. Norris.
*Golden Vanity*, The. *Unknown.*
Greenland Whale Fishery, The. *Unknown.*
Harbors. Minty.

Harp Song of the Dane Women. *Fr.* Puck of Pook's Hill.
    Kipling.
Haul Away, My Rosy. *Unknown.*
Haul on the Bowline. *Unknown.*
Heaving the Lead Line. *Unknown.*
Hell's Pavement. Masefield.
Home from Sea. Singer.
Jack Is Every Inch a Sailor. *Unknown.*
Jack Was Every Inch a Sailor. *Unknown.*
Johnny Todd. *Unknown.*
Jolly Soldier. *Unknown.*
Life of a Tar, The. *Unknown.*
Life on the Ocean Wave, A. Sargent.
Lightning Flash, The. *Unknown.*
Lines to Mr. Hodgson. Byron.
Little Billee. Thackeray.
Lord Arnaldos. Flecker.
Lowson. Blight.
Luck. Gibson.
McAndrew's Hymn. Kipling.
Mariners. Morton.
Merchant Marine. Miles.
Nautical Extravaganza, A. Irwin.
Navy Hymn, The. Whiting.
Ocean Burial, The. Chapin.
Paddy, Get Back. *Unknown.*
Palmistry for Blind Mariners. Minty.
Poem to Show the Trouble That Befell Him When He Was at
    Sea, A. Prys.
Powerful Eyes o' Jeremy Tait, The. Irwin.
Putting to Sea. Bogan.
Red Iron Ore. *Unknown.*
Requiem: "Under the wide and starry sky." Stevenson.
Reuben Ranzo. *Unknown.*
Rime of the Ancient Mariner, The. Coleridge.
Rolling Home. Mackay.
Sacramento. *Unknown.*
Sailing Home from Rapallo. Lowell.
Sailing, Sailing. Burr.
Sailing Sailing. Marks.
Sailing to an Island. Murphy.
Sailor. Hughes.
Sailor Boy, The. Tennyson.
Sailor Man. Bailey.
Sailors' Alphabet, The. *Unknown.*
Sailor's Consolation, The. Dibdin.
Sailor's Yarn, A. Roche.
Santy Anno. *Unknown.*
Schooner *Fred Dunbar*, The. Hanson.
Sea Change. Masefield.
Sea Dialogue, A. Holmes.
Sea Fever. Masefield.
Sea-Voyage from Tenby to Bristol, A. Philips.
Seafarer. MacLeish.
Seafarer, The. *Unknown.*
Seaman's Life, The. *Unknown.*
Sea-Song, A. Cunningham.
Seumas Beg. Stephens.
Sir Patrick Spens. *Unknown.*
Skipper Ireson's Ride. Whittier.
Song: "To all you ladies now at land." Sackville.
Stony Brook Tavern. Reed.
Tempest, The. *Unknown.*
Things to Do Around a Ship at Sea. Snyder.
To a Seaman Dead on Land. Boyle.
Uncle Roderick. MacCaig.
Valediction, A: "We're bound for blue water where the great
    winds blow." Masefield.
We'll Go to Sea No More. *Unknown.*
Wet Sheet and a Flowing Sea, A. Cunningham.
What Shall We Do with a Drunken Sailor. *Unknown.*
Where Lies the Land. Clough.

Wind Sou'west, The.  *Unknown.*
Yachts, The.  Williams.
Yarn of the *Loch Achray*, The.  Masefield.
Yarn of the *Nancy Bell*, The.  Gilbert.
Ye Mariners of England.  Campbell.
*Rhyming in the Rigging* (RhR).  Lahaina Harry, ed.
**St. Agnes Eve**
Eve of St. Agnes, The.  Keats.
St. Agnes' Eve.  Tennyson.
**St. Cecilia's Day.**  *See* **Cecilia, Saint.**
**St. Crispin's Day**
St. Crispin's Day.  *Fr.* King Henry V.  Shakespeare.
**Saint Croix, Virgin Islands**
Beauties of Santa Cruz, The.  Bryant.
**St. David's Day**
In Honour of St. David's Day.  *Unknown.*
**St. Louis, Missouri**
Letter to Belden.  Moore.
Lucas Park (St. Louis).  Bliss.
Meet Me in St. Louis, Louis.  Sterling.
Riverfront, St. Louis.  Knoepfle.
**St. Mark's Eve**
Eve of St. Mark, The.  Keats.
**Saints**
Lives of the Saints.  Muldoon.
Mrs. Malone.  Farjeon.
When the Saints Go Marching In.  *Unknown.*
**Sales Clerks**
Sale.  Miles.
**Salt**
Ode to Salt.  Neruda.
What Is Salt?  Vernon.
**Salvation Army**
Away With Rum.  *Unknown.*
General William Booth Enters into Heaven.  Lindsay.
**Samaritan, Good**
Man Who Had Fallen Among Thieves, A.  Cummings.
**Samarkand**
Journey in the Orient.  Spaziani.
**Samson (Bible)**
History of Samson, The, *sel.*  Quarles.
If I Had My Way.  *Unknown.*
Mother of Samson to Manoah, Her Husband, The.  Whittier.
My Samsons.  Guri.
Samson.  Gilboa.
Samson Rends His Clothes.  Eldan.
Warning, The.  Longfellow.
**San Francisco, California**
After the Cries of the Birds.  Ferlinghetti.
Ballad of the Hyde Street Grip.  Burgess.
Barriers Burned.  Field.
For Paddy O'Sullivan.  Winans.
Frisco's Defi.  Hooper.
From Russian Hill.  Coolbrith.
Idyll: "San Francisco, California."  Tomlinson.
In Golden Gate Park that day.  *Fr.* A Coney Island of the
  Mind.  Ferlinghetti.
Lines Written near San Francisco.  Simpson.
Noon on Alameda Street.  Flanner.
North Beach Poem.  Winans.
Nostalgia.  Millard.
Returned to Frisco, 1946.  Snodgrass.
San Francisco.  Austin.
San Francisco.  Coolbrith.
San Francisco Arising.  Markham.
San Francisco Bay.  Miller.
San Francisco Falling.  Markham.
San Francisco from the Sea.  Harte.
San Francisco Poem.  Logan.
**San Joaquin, California**
San Joaquin.  Everson.
**Sand, George**

To George Sand.  E. Browning.
**Sand**
Burning Sand of Sinai.  Sachs.
I dug and dug amongst the snow.  C. Rossetti.
Sand.  Higham.
Sand and Snow.  Lieberman.
We Lying by Seasand.  Thomas.
**Sandpipers**
Sandpiper.  Bishop.
Sandpiper, The.  Thaxter.
**Santa Claus**
Boy Who Laughed at Santa Claus, The.  Nash.
Saint Nicholas.  Moore.
Santa Claus.  De la Mare.
Santa Claus.  Moraes.
Santa Claus.  Nemerov.
Visit from St. Nicholas, A.  Moore.
**Santa Fe, New Mexico**
Spring Morning—Santa Fe.  Riggs.
**Santa Fe Trail**
Old Santa Fe Trail, The.  Burton.
Santa Fe Trail, The.  Chapman.
**Santayana, George**
For George Santayana.  Lowell.
To an Old Philosopher in Rome.  Stevens.
Upon the Death of George Santayana.  Hecht.
**Santo Domingo**
Winter Dance, San Domingo.  Anderson.
**Sappho**
Invocation to Sappho.  Gidlow.
Sapphics.  Swinburne.
Sappho.  Cabral.
Sisters, The.  A. Lowell.
**Sarto, Andrea del**
Andrea del Sarto.  Browning.
**Saskatchewan, Canada**
Saskatchewan Dusk.  Buckaway.
**Satan**
Address to the Deil.  Burns.
Citadels.  Kell.
Copy of an Intercepted Despatch from His Excellency Don
  Strepitoso Diabolo.  Moore.
Dark Angel, The.  Johnson.
Devil and the Farmer's Wife, The.  *Unknown.*
Devil's Bag, The.  Stephens.
Devil's Thoughts, The.  Coleridge *and* Southey.
False Knight upon the Road, The.  *Unknown.*
Faust, *sels.*  Goethe.
Hell in Texas.  *Unknown.*
Incarnate Devil.  Thomas.
Lucifer in Starlight.  Meredith.
Riddles Wisely Expounded.  *Unknown.*
Satan Discovers Eden.  *Fr.* Paradise Lost.  Milton.
Truly My Satan thou art but a dunce.  *Fr.* The Gates of
  Paradise, *epilogue.*  Blake.
Tyin' a Knot in the Devil's Tail.  Gardner.
Whale, The.  *Unknown.*
**Satie, Erik**
Angel.  Merrill.
Satie, at the End of Term.  Curtis.
**Satiric Verse**
Art.  Bierce.
Beautiful Young Nymph Going to Bed, A.  Swift.
Best Line Yet, The.  Allen.
Boom!  Nemerov.
Cavalier Lyric.  Simmons.
Charming Woman, The.  Sheridan.
Contemporary Muse, The.  Rickword.
Dover Bitch, The: A Criticism of Life.  Hecht.
Epistle to Dr. Arbuthnot.  Pope.
"Faith" is a fine invention.  Dickinson.
First Satire of the Second Book of Horace, The.  Pope.

Friends. Durem.
Furniture of a Woman's Mind, The. Swift.
Giles Johnson, Ph.D. Davis.
Latest Decalogue, The. Clough.
Letter from a Candidate for the Presidency in Answer to Suttin Questions Proposed by Mr. Hosea Biglow, A. *Fr.* The Biglow Papers. Lowell.
Little Vagabond, The. *Fr.* Songs of Experience. Blake.
Lovers of the Poor, The. Brooks.
MacFlecknoe. Dryden.
Namby-Pamby. Carey.
Night Shift at the Poetry Factory, The. Magorian.
Of Alphus. *Unknown.*
Old, Filthy Beer Pail, The. Hall.
On the Vanity of Earthly Greatness. Guiterman.
Outside of a Small Circle of Friends. Ochs.
Pioneers, The. Mortimer.
Pious Editor's Creed, The. *Fr.* The Biglow Papers. Lowell.
Poem, Or Beauty Hurts Mr. Vinal. Cummings.
Prayer of Holy Willie, The. Burns.
Rape of the Lock, The. Pope.
Résumé. Parker.
Santa Claus. Nemerov.
Satire against Mankind, A. Earl of Rochester.
Satirical Elegy on the Death of a Late Famous General, A. Swift.
Spade Is Just a Spade, A. Hawkins.
Teacher of Poetry, The. Packard.
To Nysus. Sedley.
Twenty-Third Psalm, The. Simpson.
Unknown Citizen, The. Auden.
*Anthology of Poems on Affairs of State: Augustan Satirical Verse* (APAS). George deF. Lord, ed.
*English Satiric Poetry: Dryden to Byron* (ESaP). James Kinsley and James T. Boulton, eds.
*Oxford Book of Satirical Verse, The* (OBSV). Geoffrey Grigson, comp.

**Satori**
All Day Satori. Lynch.

**Satyrs**
Afternoon of a Faun, The: Ecologue. Mallarmé.

**Saul (Bible)**
King Saul. Horvitz.
Saul. Browning.
Saul. Gilboa.
Saul. Lasker-Schuler.
Saul and the Witch of Endor and the Vision of Samuel. Byron.
Song of Saul Before His Last Battle. Byron.

**Sausages**
Sausage. Guest.
Sausage, The. *Unknown.*

**Scarecrows**
Lonely Scarecrow, The. Kirkup.
Scarecrow, The. De la Mare.
Scarecrow, The. Young.
Scarecrow Independence. Kirkup.
To a Scarecrow, or Malkin, Left Long after Harvest. Turner.

**Scholars and Scholarship**
Academic. Reeves.
Academic Affair. Stockwell.
Address to the Scholars of New England. Ransom.
Antiquary, The. Campbell.
April Inventory. Snodgrass.
Baccalaureate. McCord.
Binni the Meshuggener. Siegel.
Desperate Measure, A. Dennis.
Development. Browning.
For Scholars and Pupils. Wither.
Giles Johnson, Ph.D. Davis.
Grammarian's Funeral, A. Browning.
I Want to One Morning. Turner.
Lecture Hall. Kavanagh.

Of the Manner of Addressing Clouds. Stevens.
Professor Gratt. Hall.
Professor Kelleher and the Charles River. O'Grady.
Scholars. De la Mare.
Scholars, The. Yeats.
Scholar's Life, The. *Fr.* Vanity of Human Wishes. Johnson.
Snapshot of a Pedant. Garrett.
To a Friend, on Her Examination for the Doctorate in English. Cunningham.
Wordy People, The. Fitzgerald.
Young Man's Epigram on Existence, A. Hardy.
*See also* **Students; Teaching and Teachers.**

**School**
And Two Good Things. Enright.
Description of a Good Boy, A. Dixon.
Ecole St. Luc. Fraser.
Elementary School Class Room in a Slum, An. Spender.
End of Term. *Unknown.*
Ghetto Summer School. Worth.
Hickory Stick Hierarchy. Selle.
I wake up in a morning. *Unknown.*
Kindergarten. Rogers.
Our School Now Closes Out. Dumas.
P.S. 42. Corso.
Poem Beginning with a Line Memorized at School. Jellema.
School Days. Cobb.
Schoolboy's Lot, A. *Unknown.*
Schoolchildren. Auden.
Schoolyard in April. Koch.
September, the First Day of School. Nemerov.
Two Bad Things in Infant School. Enright.
Unhappy Schoolboy, The. *Unknown.*
University. Shapiro.
University Examinations in Egypt. Enright.
Zimmer in Grade School. Zimmer.
*See also* **Colleges and Universities.**

**Schubert, Franz**
Schubertiana. Tranströmer.

**Schwartz, Delmore**
Ode to Delmore Schwartz. Carroll.
This world is gradually becoming a place. Berryman.
To Delmore Schwartz. Lowell.

**Science**
And, constantly, I seek/ A poetry of facts. *Fr.* The Kind of Poetry I Want. "MacDiarmid."
Approaching Absolute Zero. Peseroff.
"Arcturus" is his other name. Dickinson.
Blight. Emerson.
Counting Sheep. Edson.
Credibility. Ciardi.
Dr. Sigmund Freud Discovers the Sea Shell. MacLeish.
Ed and Sid and Bernard. MacDuff.
Horrid Voice of Science, The. Lindsay.
Laboratory Poem. Merrill.
Last Monster, The. Montague.
Letter to Alex Comfort. Abse.
Los Alamos: Manhattan. Rowbotham.
Microscope. Thomas.
Nuclear Physicists, The. Church.
Ode to Terminus. Auden.
Poem: "The thing/ to do/ is organize." Koch.
Problems. Scott.
Progress. Lamport.
Projection, A. Whittemore.
Richard Tolman's Universe. Bacon.
Science. Jeffers.
Science as Art. Seidman.
Science For the Young. Irwin.
Science, the agile ape, may well. Patmore.
Something Passionate for Cinda. Kornblum.
Sonnet — To Science. Poe.
Space being (don't forget to remember) curved. Cummings.

V. B. Nimble, V. B. Quick.   Updike.
*Of Quarks, Quasars, and Other Quirks* (QQQ).   Sara *and* John
   E. Brewton *and* John Brewton Blackburn, eds.

**Science Fiction**
Choice, The.   Morgan.
Discovery of the New World.   Revard.
Insect Shuffle Method, The.   Tapp.
Marrog, The.   Scriven.
Missionary.   Thomas.
Modern Romance.   Harris.
Poem to Delight My Friends Who Laugh at Science-Fiction, A.
   Rolfe.
S F.   Leverett.
Science Fiction.   Whittemore.
Southbound on the Freeway.   Swenson.
12 o'Clock News.   Bishop.

**Scopes Trial**
Bryan's Last Battle.   *Unknown.*

**Scorpions**
Scorpion, The.   Belloc.

**Scotland**
About Scotland, and C.   Todd.
Ballade of the Scottyshe Kynge, A.   Skelton.
Blue Bells of Scotland, The.   McVicar *and* Jordan.
Caledonia.   Powell.
Little White Rose, The.   Mackenzie.
My Heart's in the Highlands.   Burns.
Ode on the Popular Superstitions of the Highlands of Scotland.
   Collins.
Pterodactyl and Powhatan's Daughter, The.   Macrae.
Robert Bruce's March to Bannockburn.   Burns.
Scotland.   Gray.
Scotland 1941.   Muir.
Scotland the Wee.   Buchan.
Scotland's Winter.   Muir.
Sic Transit Gloria Scotia.   "MacDiarmid."
This Is My Own, My Native Land.   *Fr.* The Lay of the Last
   Minstrel.   Scott.
Vision, The.   Defoe.
*Made in Scotland* (MIS).   Robert Garioch, ed.
*Modern Scottish Poetry (MS).*   Maurice Lindsay, ed.

**Scots, The**
Genealogical Reflection.   Nash.
Gup, Scot.   Skelton.
Rebel Scot, The.   Cleveland.

**Scott, Sir Walter**
On Scott's "The Field of Waterloo."   Erskine.
On the Departure of Sir Walter Scott from Abbotsford, for
   Naples.   Wordsworth.
Yarrow Revisited.   Wordsworth.

**Scottish Border**
Battle of Otterbourne, The.   *Unknown.*
Flowers of the Forest, The: or, The Battle of Flodden.   Elliot.

**Scottsboro Case**
Communication to Nancy Cunard, A.   Boyle.
Lynchings of Jesus, The.   Rukeyser.
Scottsboro, Too, Is Worth Its Song.   Cullen.

**Sculpture and Sculptors**
Arundel Tomb, An.   Larkin.
Convert, The.   Danner.
Hiram Powers' "Greek Slave."   E. Browning.
On a Prize Crucifix by a Student Sculptor.   Logan.
On Seeing the Elgin Marbles.   Keats.
Rodin to Rilke.   Grosholz.
Statues, The.   Yeats.

**Sea**
And God said, let the waters generate.   *Fr.* Paradise Lost.
   Milton.
And I Have Loved Thee, Ocean!   *Fr.* Childe Harold's
   Pilgrimage.   Byron.
At Dunwich.   Thwaite.
At Melville's Tomb.   Crane.

At the Seaside.   Stevenson.
At the Western Shore.   Youngblood.
Aunt Zillah Speaks.   Palmer.
Ayii, Ayii./ I walked on the ice of the sea.   *Unknown.*
Ayii, Ayii/ The great sea has set me in motion.   *Unknown.*
Beautiful Proud Sea.   Teasdale.
Beauty of the Ocean, The.   Walker.
Break, Break, Break.   Tennyson.
By the Saltings.   Walker.
By the Sea.   C. Rossetti.
Byron's Address to the Ocean.   *Fr.* Childe Harold's Pilgrimage.
   Byron.
Captain Dobbin.   Slessor.
Cardigan Bay.   Masefield.
City in the Sea, The.   Poe.
Continent's End.   Jeffers.
Coral Grove, The.   Percival.
Crossing the Atlantic.   Sexton.
Deep, The.   Brainard.
Deep Calleth unto Deep.   Dodge.
Deep Blue Sea.   *Unknown.*
Deep-Sea Cables, The.   Kipling.
Echoes.   De la Mare.
Enigmas.   Neruda.
Even Sea, The.   Swenson.
Evening Ebb.   Jeffers.
Exiled.   Millay.
Fable, The.   Winters.
Fish, The.   Moore.
Five Bells.   Slessor.
Flowers by the Sea.   Williams.
Four Homages.   Block.
Full fathom five thy father lies.   *Fr.* The Tempest.
   Shakespeare.
Garden.   Drouet.
Grave, A.   Moore.
Hall of Ocean Life.   Hollander.
How instant joy, how clang.   *Fr.* Mediterranean Beach, Day
   after Storm.   Warren.
Hurrah for the Sea.   *Unknown.*
I have heard a voice of broken seas.   *Fr.* A Fragment.   Flecker.
I started early, took my dog.   Dickinson.
I will go back to the great sweet mother.   *Fr.* The Triumph of
   Time.   Swinburne.
Idea of Order at Key West, The.   Stevens.
Kraken, The.   Tennyson.
Land's End.   Langton.
Letter from the North Atlantic.   Williams.
Looking from Oregon.   Birney.
Love Song.   Beer.
Maggie and Milly and Molly and May.   Cummings.
Main-Deep, The.   Stephens.
Meditations of a Mariner.   Irwin.
Neither Out Far nor In Deep.   Frost.
Ocean.   Jeffers.
Ocean is a strange, The/ midnight lover.   St. Martin.
Ocean is Like a Wreath, The.   Kuapakaa.
Ocean Said to Me Once, The.   *Fr.* The Black Riders.   Crane.
Of the Sea, A Song.   Fielder.
Off Cape Leeuwen.   Joseph.
Offshore Breeze.   Acorn.
On the Sea.   Keats.
On This Island.   Auden.
Open Sea, The.   Meredith.
Oread.   Doolittle ("H.D.").
Pacific Dawn.   Birch.
Pebbles.   Melville.
Plague of Dead Sharks.   Dugan.
Pool in the Rock, The.   De la Mare.
Prayer to the Pacific.   Silko.
Quaker Graveyard in Nantucket, The.   Lowell.
Rock Pool, The.   Noyes.

Rock Pool, The. Shanks.
Sea Breeze. Mallarmé.
Sea Call. Widdemer.
Sea Calm. Hughes.
Sea Fever. Masefield.
Sea-King's Burial, The. Mackay.
Sea-Limits, The. Rossetti.
Sea Longing. Teasdale.
Sea Lullaby. Wylie.
Sea, The! O the sea! *Unknown.*
Sea Song, A. Dolben.
Sea-Sonnet. Sackville-West.
Sea Surface Full of Clouds. Stevens.
Sea Variations. Simpson.
Seafarer, The. *Unknown.*
Sealess World, A. Campbell.
Seascape. Bishop.
Seascape. Young.
Secret of the Sea, The. Longfellow.
Secret of the Sea, The. Phillips.
Shakespeare on the Sea. *Fr.* Pericles. Shakespeare.
Sleeplessly circle the waves. *Fr.* Look Not Too Deep. Binyon.
Slow Pacific Swell, The. Winters.
Snow Lies Sprinkled on the Beach, The. Bridges.
Song: "Sabrina fair." *Fr.* Comus. Milton.
Song of the Sea. Burton.
Sonnet Written in the Church-Yard at Middleton, in Sussex. Smith.
Sound of the Sea, The. Longfellow.
Spindrift. Kinnell.
Storm Tide on Mejit. *Unknown.*
Thalassa. MacNeice.
They Who Possess the Sea. Adams.
Tide Rises, the Tide Falls, The. Longfellow.
Trackless Deeps, The. Shelley.
Traveling Boy. Meredith.
Unfathomable Sea! Shelley.
Waking from a Nap on the Beach. Swenson.
Water. Lowell.
When winds that move not its calm surface sweep. Moschus.
Winter Ocean. Updike.
Winter Seascape. Betjeman.
World below the Brine, The. Whitman.
*Echoes of the Sea* (EcS). Elinor Parker, ed.
**Sea Gulls.** See **Gulls.**
**Sea Serpents**
Kraken, The. Tennyson.
Leviathan. *Fr.* Job. Bible, *O.T.*
Loch Ness Monster, The. Buchan.
Sea Wolf, The. McDougal.
Water-Snakes. *Fr.* The Rime of the Ancient Mariner. Coleridge.
**Sea Shells.** See **Shells.**
**Sea Voyages.** See **Voyages.**
**Seals**
Animals. Jeffers.
Dancing Seal, The. Gibson.
Dead Seal. Purdy.
Dead Seal Near McClure's Beach, The. Bly.
Great Silkie of Sule Skerry, The. *Unknown.*
Moon-Child, The. Sharp.
Question, A. Cole.
Seal. Smith.
Sealchie Song. *Unknown.*
Seals. Slavitt.
White Seal's Lullaby, The. Kipling.
**Seashore.** See **Shores.**
**Seasons**
Ceremonies for Candlemas Eve. Herrick.
Common Poem, A. Rodgers.
End of a Season. Scannell.
Eskimo Chant. *Unknown.*

Fight of the Year, The. McGough.
Five Students, The. Hardy.
Four seasons fill the measure of the year. Keats.
Hymn on the Seasons, A. *Fr.* The Seasons. Thomson.
In Due Season. Auden.
In the Elegy Season. Wilbur.
Insight. Spinnanger.
Metamorphosis. Stevens.
On The Inside Strong. Mberi.
Origin of Hot and Cold According to the Delawares, The. Lifshin.
Seasons, The. *Unknown.*
Signs of the Seasons. *Unknown.*
Song (Prelude). Pieterse.
Sonnet XV: "When dead the winter snows in crystals shine." Eberhart.
Still. Meriluoto.
Sunflower Moccasins. George.
Winter Flowers. Hall.
Winter's Onset from an Alienated Point of View. Dugan.
*Four Seasons Five Senses* (FSFS). Elinor Parker, ed.
**Seattle, Washington**
Thirteen Preludes for Pioneer Square. Logan.
**Seaweed**
Sea-Weed. Lawrence.
Seaweed. Longfellow.
Seaweeds. McPherson.
**Sebastian, Saint**
Martyrdom of Saint Sebastian, The. Dobson.
**Second World War.** See **World War, Second.**
**Secretaries**
Secretary. Hughes.
Secretary, The. Redgrove.
**Security**
Reckoning, The. Roethke.
**Seduction**
Dark-eyed Gentleman, The. Hardy.
Disappointment, The. Behn.
Seduced Girl. Hedylos.
Seduction. Giovanni.
Volatile Kerryman, The. O'Sullivan.
Willing Mistress, The. Behn.
**Seeds**
Seed Shop, The. Stuart.
Seeds. Reeves.
**Segovia, Andrés**
Canto del Señor Segovia. Herrstrom.
**Semele**
Semele Recycled. Kizer.
**Sennacherib, King of Assyria**
Destruction of Sennacherib, The. Byron.
**Separation**
Ancient Couple on Lu Mountain, The. Van Doren.
At the San Francisco Airport. Winters.
Barbara's Poem. Bowman.
Boudoir Lament. Yü Hsüan-chi.
Breaking Up Is Hard to Do. Walthall.
Business Trips. Taylor.
Chilterns, The. Brooke.
Cognac and Farewell to My Sanity. Menebroker.
Excuse of Absence, An. Carew.
Exile. Dowson.
Exile's Letter. Li Po.
Fatima. Tennyson.
First, Goodbye. Smith.
Frisco Whistle Blues. *Unknown.*
Gal I Left behind Me, The. *Unknown.*
Goodbye. Lewis.
Good-bye My Fancy! Whitman.
He's Gone Away. *Unknown.*
How to End the Summer Alone. Shpunt.
I let the incense grow cold. Li Ch'ing-chao.

In the Vaulted Way. Hardy.
Into the Sky. Chesham.
It Is So Long Since My Heart Has Been With Yours. Cummings.
Lake Michigan Blues. *Unknown.*
Leaving of Liverpool, The. *Unknown.*
Letter to Her Husband Absent on Public Employment, A. Bradstreet.
Long Distance Moan. *Unknown.*
Love Poem. Waterman.
Message. Ginsberg.
Missing My Daughter. Spender.
My life closed twice before its close. Dickinson.
Never Let Your Left Hand Know. *Unknown.*
New Spring. Jiménez.
Notes for a Movie Script. Holman.
O! Wherefore. Peter.
On the Departure Platform. Hardy.
Parting. Herguri.
Partings. Jewsbury.
Property Settlement. Pauker.
Remember. C. Rossetti.
Reproaches. Turner.
River-Merchant's Wife, The: A Letter. Li Po.
Round Her Neck She Wore a Yellow Ribbon. *Unknown.*
Separation. Sange.
Separation on the River Kiang. Pound.
Since there's no help, come, let us kiss and part. *Fr.* Idea. Drayton.
Song of Longing. *Unknown.*
Sonnet-Ballad, The. Gwendolyn Brooks.
Spring Thoughts Sent to Tzu-an. Yü Hsüan-chi.
Starface, The. Gleason.
Terrible Door, The. Monro.
That Lonesome Train Took My Baby Away. *Unknown.*
Three Weeks in the State of Loneliness. Piercy.
To Her In Absence: A Ship. Carew.
To His Absent Diana. Diana, *introd.* Constable.
To His Lady. Henry VIII, King of England.
To Lucasta, Going Beyond the Seas. Lovelace.
To Lucasta, Going to the Wars. Lovelace.
To My Mistress in Absence. Carew.
To Tzu-an. Yü Hsüan-chi.
Translator, The. Clary.
Two Letters from Chang-Kan. Li Po.
Upon Your Leaving. Knight.
Valediction, A: Forbidding Mourning. Donne.
Voyage. Stepanchev.
When We Two Parted. Byron.
Within the Dream You Said. Larkin.
Year after year I have watched. Li Ch'ing-chao.
You Do Not Write. Jurgensen.
You Never Miss the Water. *Unknown.*
You'll Never Miss Your Jelly. *Unknown.*
Your Light. Lee.

**September**
September. M. Coleridge.

**Sequoia Trees**
Redwoods, The. Simpson.

**Servants**
Girl Help. Lewis.

**Seurat, Georges**
Islands for Seurat. Rompf.

**Severn River, England**
Danube to the Severn gave, The. *Fr.* In Memoriam A. H. H. Tennyson.

**Sewell, Samuel**
Samuel Sewell. Hecht.

**Sewing**
Instruction. Hall.
Late Sewing. Hall.
Mending. Hall.

Red Dress, The. Bertolino.
Seams. Hall.
Stitches. Hall.
What Is She Trying to Do, to Pattern Love. Brigham.

**Sex**
After Sex. Kuzma.
Against Fruition I. Suckling.
All One. Brand.
Canticles to Men. Mannes.
Claremont. Peters.
Courtship. Strand.
Earth and Fire. Berry.
Fair Ursly, in a merry mood. *Unknown.*
From Pent-up, Aching Rivers. Whitman.
Grief of Our Genitals, The. Carlile.
Holy Roller. Frances.
I Never Saw a Man in a Negligee. Alta.
I Want to Tell You. Hochman.
I Wasn't No Mary Ellen. King.
I'd Have You, Quoth He. *Unknown.*
It Fell on a Summer's Day. Campion.
Little Ball of Yarn. *Unknown.*
Manual, The. Rubin.
May I Feel Said He. Cummings.
My Father's House. Nicoletta.
97th Kentucky Derby, The. Young.
Poet Loves a Mistress, but Not To Marry, The. Herrick.
Puberty. Wallace.
Sensualists, The. Roethke.
Shallot, A. Wilbur.
She Being Brand. Cummings
Thieves, The. Graves.
To Dianeme ("Show me thy feet; show me thy legs, thy thighs"). Herrick.
To Electra ("I'll come to thee in all those shapes"). Herrick.
Tryst, The. Soutar.
Twenty-Year Marriage. Ai.
Two Songs. Rich.
Ugly Neck. Enright.
Why Can't I Leave You? Ai.
Woman. Ai.
Woman to Man. Ai.
*See also* **Erotic Love.**

**Seymour, Jane**
Death of Queen Jane, The. *Unknown.*

**Shadows**
Escape. Johnson.
Follow Thy Fair Sun, Unhappy Shadow. Campion.
I Heard a Noise and Wished for a Sight. *Unknown.*
Lecture upon the Shadow, A. Donne.
Lectures on the Biology of the Shadow. Young.
My Shadow. Stevenson.
Nocturne Varial. Alexander.
Shadow. De la Mare.
Shadow and Substance. *Unknown.*
Shadowless Man, The. Challis.
Shadows. *Fr.* Tethy's Festival. Daniel.
Shadows. *Unknown.*
Tenebris. Grimké.

**Shadwell, Thomas**
MacFlecknoe. Dryden.
Portrait of "Og." *Fr.* Absalom and Achitophel. Dryden.

**Shaftesbury, Anthony Ashley Cooper, 1st Earl of**
Hypocrite, The. Caryll.

**Shakers**
Arrival, New York Harbor. Peters.

**Shakespeare, William**
Brush Up Your Shakespeare. Porter.
Epitaph on the Admirable Dramatic Poet, W. Shakespeare, An. Milton.
Found. Shatford.
On Sitting Down to Read "King Lear" Once Again. Keats.

Quotation from Shakespeare with Slight Improvements.
   "Carroll."
Shakespeare. Arnold.
To the Memory of My Beloved, the Author, Mr. William
   Shakespeare, and What He Hath Left Us. Jonson.
Upon the Lines and Life of the Famous Scenic Poet, Master
   William Shakespeare. Holland.
When I Read Shakespeare. Lawrence.
William Shakespeare to Mrs. Anne, Regular Servant to the Rev.
   Mr. Precentor of York. Gray.

**Shamans**
Shaman. Inman.

**Shaped Poetry**
Altar, The. Herbert.
Andy-Diana DNA Letter. Weiman.
Diamond Cut Diamond. Milne.
Easter Wings. Herbert.
Forsythia. Solt.
40—Love. McGough.
400-Meter Freestyle. Kumin.
How Everything Happens (Based on a Study of the Wave).
   Swenson.
Ice Cream. Price.
Marriage. Solt.
Message Clear. Morgan.
Moonshot Sonnet. Solt.
Out of the Sea, Early. Swenson.
Parody. Paley Francescato.
Pillar of Fame, The. Herrick.
Pomander. Morgan.
Rain Down. Solt.
Seal. Smith.
Semen. Paley Francescato.
Skeleton Key. Hollander.
Swan and Shadow. Hollander.
This crosse-tree here. Herrick.
Tribute to Henry Ford. Kostelanetz.
Two Tile Beaks. Fonte Boa.
Vitality. Fonte Boa.
Wild Crab. Solt.
Women. Swenson.
You Too? Me Too—Why Not? Soda Pop. Hollander.

**Sharks**
About the Teeth of Sharks. Ciardi.
Among Sharks. Lee.
Basking Shark. MacCaig.
Chivalrous Shark, The. *Unknown.*
Love Is a Shark. *Unknown.*
Maldive Shark, The. Melville.
Nurse Sharks. Matthews.
Plague of Dead Sharks. Dugan.
Sea-Turtle and the Shark, The. *Fr.* Harlem Gallery. Tolson.
Shark, The. Ciardi.
Shark's Parlor, The. Dickey.

**Shaw, George Bernard**
Epitaph for G. B. Shaw. Beerbohm.
Last words of Shaw, The: "I'm going to die." Bold.

**Shaw, Robert Gould**
For the Union Dead. Lowell.

**Sheep**
Bah! De la Mare.
Derby Ram, The. *Unknown.*
First Sight. Larkin.
Lambs Frolicking Home. Lape.
Little Bo-Peep. *Unknown.*
No One Talks About This. Rakosi.
Sheep. Davies.
Sheep, The. Taylor.
Sheep Child, The. Dickey.
Sheep Fair, A. Hardy.
Sheep in the Rain. Wright.
Sheep in Winter. Clare.

**Sheep Shearing**
Banks of the Condamine, The. *Unknown.*
Click Go the Shears, Boys. *Unknown.*

**Shelley, Percy Bysshe**
Cor Cordium. Swinburne.
Fishes and the Poet's Hands, The. Yerby.
Lines Written in Blank Leaf of the Prometheus Unbound.
   Beddoes.
Memorabilia. Browning.
Shelley's Skylark. Hardy.

**Shells**
Bones, The. Merwin.
Delicate shells lay on the shore, The. *Fr.* Each and All.
   Emerson.
Dr. Sigmund Freud Discovers the Sea Shell. MacLeish.
Ecstasy. Turner.
I Have seen/ A curious child. *Fr.* The Excursion.
   Wordsworth.
I have sinuous shells of pearly hue. *Fr.* Gebir. Landor.
On Some Shells Found Inland. Stickney.
Poem about a Seashell. Crosby.
Scarlett Rocks. Brown.
Sea-Limits, The. D.G. Rossetti.
Sea Shell. A. Lowell.
Sea-Shell Murmurs. Lee-Hamilton.
Secret of the Sea, The. Phillips.
Shell, The. McCord.
Shell, The. Stephens.
Shell, The. Watkins.
Shell, The. Webb.
Shells. Mahony.
Striped Shell, A. Dallas.

**Shenandoah River**
Shenandoah. *Unknown.*

**Shepherds and Shepherdesses**
Faithless Shepherd, A. Clare.
Green Shepherd, The. Simpson.
Hye Nonny Nonny Noe. *Unknown.*
Jolly Shepherd Wat, The. *Unknown.*
Nod. De la Mare.
Nymph's Reply to the Shepherd, The. Ralegh.
Passionate Shepherd to His Love, The. Marlowe.
Rise Up, Shepherd, and Follow. *Unknown.*
Sheep Country. Church.
Sheep Country. Pond.
Sheep-herder, The. Clark.
Sheep-Herder's Lament, The. Chapman.
Sheep Herding. Hall.
Sheepman. Ormsby.
Shepherd, The. Baxter.
Shepherd, The. *Fr.* Songs of Innocence. Blake.
Shepherd and Shepherdess. Hennell.
Shepherd Boy Sings in the Valley of Humiliation, The. *Fr.* The
   Pilgrim's Progress. Bunyan.
Shepherd Who Stayed, The. Garrison.
Shepherdess. Cameron.
Shepherdess, The. Meynell.
Shepherd's Song at Christmas. Hughes.
Wise Men and Shepherds. Godolphin.

**Sheridan, Philip Henry**
Sheridan's Ride. Read.

**Sherman, General William Tecumseh**
Marching through Georgia. Work.

**Shiloh, Battle of**
Battle of Shiloh, The. *Unknown.*
Drummer Boy of Shiloh, The. *Unknown.*
Shiloh; A Requiem. Melville.

**Ships**
Aboard at a Ship's Helm. Whitman.
Boats in a Fog. Jeffers.
Bonnie Ship The Diamond, The. *Unknown.*
Cargoes. Masefield.

Choosing a Mast. Campbell.
Description of a Ninety Gun Ship. Falconer.
Dismantled Ship, The. Whitman.
Golden Vanity, The. *Unknown.*
H.M.S. *Hero.* Roberts.
John B. Sails. *Unknown.*
Lines to Mr. Hodgson. Byron.
Main-Sheet Song, The. Day.
Nocturne of the Wharves. Bontemps.
Old Ship Riggers. Cody.
Old Ships, The. Flecker.
Old Ships. Morton.
Old Song Re-Sung, An. Masefield.
Passer-By, A. Bridges.
Phantom Ship, The. Longfellow.
Ritual, The. Pratt.
Rivets. Olds.
Sea-Fever. Masefield.
Ship, The. Church.
Ship, The. Hendry.
Ship and Her Makers, The. Masefield.
Ship that Never Returned, The. Work.
Where lies the land to which yon ship must go? Wordsworth.
Winter Ship, A. Plath.
*See also* **Boats; Yachts.**

**Shipwrecks**
Asleep in the Deep. Lamb.
Berg, The. Melville.
Castaway, The. Cowper.
Convergence of the Twain, The. Hardy.
Etiquette. Gilbert.
Great *Titanic.* *Unknown.*
In Memory of the Circus Ship *Euzkera.* Gibson.
Inchcape Rock, The. Southey.
Isle of Man Shore, The. *Unknown.*
Last Words. Hollander.
Loss of the *Due Dispatch,* The. *Unknown.*
Loss of the *New Columbia,* The. *Unknown.*
Mermaid, The. *Unknown.*
Old Song Re-Sung, An. Masefield.
On the Loss of the Royal George. Cowper.
Pat Cloherty's Version of *The Maisie.* Murphy.
Ritual, The. Pratt.
Shipwreck, The. Palmer.
Sinking of the *Titanic.* *Unknown.*
Sir Patrick Spens. *Unknown.*
Skipper Ireson's Ride. Whittier.
*Titanic,* The. *Unknown.*
*Titanic* Blues. *Unknown.*
White Ship, The. Rossetti.
Wreck of the *Deutschland,* The. Hopkins.
Wreck of the *Hesperus,* The. Longfellow.
Wreck of the *Julie Plante,* The. Drummond.
Yarn of the *Nancy Bell,* The. Gilbert.

**Shiva**
Shiva. Jeffers.

**Shoes**
Cartload of Shoes, A. Sutskever.
My Boots. Thoreau.
My Mother's Shoes. Zychlinska.
On Hot Days. Reiss.
Record Stride, A. Frost.
Sale. Miles.
Thinker, The. Williams.

**Shopping**
Female of the Species Is Hardier Than the Male, The.
  McGinley.
Grocery Shopping. Leax.
Oil Spots in Every Parking Place. Kornblum.
Poem to My New Jacket. Winant.
Shopping. Nitzche.
Women at the Market. Aymerich.

**Shores**
"But Still in Israel's Paths They Shine." Revard.
Corsons Inlet. Ammons.
Galloway Shore, The. Tremayne.
Guide to Dungeness Spit. Wagoner.
Headland. Ghiselin.
Long Waters, The. Roethke.
Meditation at Oyster River. Roethke.
North of Berwick. Tremayne.
Rock Pool, The. Noyes.
Rock Pool, The. Shanks.
Sea Shore. Kitching.
Shore. Bold.
Shorelines. Heaney.
We Lying by Seasand. Thomas.
Winter Shore, The. Wade.

**Shrews**
Upon a Notorious Shrew. *Unknown.*

**Shrimp**
Brineshrimp, The. McMaster.

**Shropshire, England**
Adbaston. Ash.
On Wenlock Edge. Housman.

**Siberia**
Siberia. Mangan.

**Sickness.** *See* **Illness.**

**Sidmouth, Henry Addington, Viscount**
To Sidmouth and Castlereagh. Shelley.

**Sidney, Sir Philip**
Epitaph upon the Right Honorable Sir Philip Sidney, An.
  Greville.

**Siena, Italy**
Siena. Swinburne.

**Silence**
Aprons of Silence. Sandburg.
Between the Electric Rhythm and the Melodic Mind. Schevill.
Choice of Weapons, A. McGinley.
House Was Quiet and the World Was Calm, The. Stevens.
Listening Back. Coolbrith.
On The Eclipse of the Moon of October 1865. Turner.
Pastourelle. Hayes.
Precept of Silence, The. Johnson.
Sea of Silence Exhales Secrets, The. Bialik.
Second Poem the Night-Walker Wrote, The. Goethe.
Silence. Cummings.
Silence. Hood.
Silence. Lucie-Smith.
Silence. Moore.
Silence. Turner.
Silence of a city, how awful at midnight, The! Coleridge.
Silence of Bears, The. Pflum.
Sonnet—Silence. Poe.
Sound of Silence, The. Simon.
That Silence. Taylor.
Velvet Shoes. Wylie.

**Silkworms**
Silkworms, The. Stewart.

**Simon of Cyrene**
Simon the Cyrenian Speaks. Cullen.

**Simplicity**
Familiar Epistle, A. Murry.
Ode to Simplicity. Collins.
'Tis the Gift To Be Simple. *Unknown.*

**Sin**
Adam Lay Y-Bounden. *Unknown.*
Adam's Footprint. Miller.
And Forgive Us Our Trespasses. Behn.
As a Plane Tree by the Water. Lowell.
Attend, Young Friends, While I Relate. *Unknown.*
Elegy for a Puritan Conscience. Dugan.
Fire. Hughes.
Fists. Hansen.

God from His Throne with Piercing Eye. Steward.
Going to Hell. *Unknown.*
Good Lord, what a wicked world is this. *Unknown.*
Ha! Original Sin. Nash.
Hymn to God the Father, A. Donne.
If poisonous minerals, and if that tree. *Fr.* Holy Sonnets. Donne.
My Ghostly Father, I Me Confess. Orléans.
Original Sin. Jeffers.
Penitent, The. Millay.
Portrait of the Artist As a Prematurely Old Man. Nash.
Seven Sins, The. *Unknown.*
Sin. Herbert.
Sin of Omission, The. Sangster.
There Was One I Met upon the Road. *Fr.* The Black Riders. Crane.
Two Questions, The. Meynell.
Unpardonable Sin, The. Lindsay.
Vision of Sin, The. Tennyson.
Yield Not to Temptation. Palmer.
Young People Who Delight in Sin. *Unknown.*

**Singing and Singers**
Afterword: Song of Song. Boughton.
Aim Was Song, The. Frost.
Alabama. Fields.
All Which Isn't Singing Is Mere Talking. Cummings.
And the Old Women Gathered. Evans.
Another Poem on the Tearing Down of the Metropolitan Opera House. Stevens.
Buckdancer's Choice. Dickey.
Choristers Training. *Unknown.*
Cino. Pound.
Death of an Actress. MacNeice.
Everyone Sang. Sassoon.
Fair Singer, The. Marvell.
February Morning, A. Norris.
Has Been. Worsley.
I Hear America Singing. Whitman.
I Remember How She Sang. Penny.
Idea of Order at Key West, The. Stevens.
Old Women Still Sing, The. Rowell.
Piano. Lawrence.
Poem for a Singer. Acorn.
Poem for Aretha. Giovanni.
Rivals, The. Stephens.
Singers to Come. Meynell.
Singing. Shelton.
Singing Lesson, The. Wagoner.
Solitary Reaper, The. Wordsworth.
Song for the Woman Singing at the Café Trieste. Schneider.
Steam Song. Brooks.
There was a man with tongue of wood. *Fr.* War Is Kind. Crane.
Threnody: "Let happy throats be mute." Hayes.
To Constantia Singing. Shelley.
Two Girls Singing. Smith.
When Malindy Sings. Dunbar.

**Sirens (mythology)**
Nearing Again the Legendary Isle. Day Lewis.
Siren Song. Atwood.
Sirens' Song, The. *Fr.* Inner Temple Masque. Browne.
Ulysses and the Siren. Daniel.

**Sisters**
Brother-in-Law, The. Rubin.
Letter Reaching out to My Sister 1600 Miles. Barba.
My Sister. Storni.
My Sisters the Summer of 53. Hale.
Poem for My Sister. Lochhead.
Sisters. Turner.
Three Sisters. Jong.
Twa Sisters, The. *Unknown.*

**Sitting Bull**

Song of Sitting Bull. *Unknown.*

**Skating and Skaters**
Blue Boy on Skates (Twilight). Rosenthal.
Boys of These Men Full Speed. Rukeyser.
Ice-Skaters. Olson.
Midnight Skaters, The. Blunden.
74th Street. Livingston.
Skaters, The. Williams.
Skaters, The. *Fr.* The Prelude. Wordsworth.
Three Children. *Unknown.*
To Kate, Skating Better Than Her Date. Daiches.
Woman Skating. Atwood.

**Skeletons**
I'm Skeleton. Moore.
Skeleton Once in Khartoum, A. *Unknown.*

**Skiing**
Avalanche. Emig.
Hunger. Bruce.
Skier. Francis.
Skiers. *Fr.* In the Mountains. Warren.
White Pass Ski Patrol. Logan.
Winter Trees. Diekmann.

**Skulls**
All That Is Left. Hartnett.
Lines Inscribed upon a Cup Formed from a Skull. Byron.
Scientist, The. Burroway.
Song for the Skull of Black Bear. Wagoner.
Swedenborg's Skull. Watkins.
Uppon a Deedmans Hed. Skelton.
U.S. Sailor with the Japanese Skull, The. Scott.
Yardbird's Skull. Dodson.

**Skunks**
Skunk Hour. Lowell.
Skunks, *sel.* Jeffers.
Wood Weasel, The. Moore.

**Sky**
Lewis In Summer. Thomson.
On Looking Up by Chance at the Constellations. Frost.
Richness. Bull.
Sky was candy luminous, The. Cummings.
Upper skies are palest blue, The. Bridges.
We will watch the Northern lights. *Unknown.*

**Sky Diving**
Drop. MacBeth.
Parachutist, The. Anderson.
Parachutist. Hazo.
Sky Diver. Stoutenburg.
Sky Diving. Lattimore.

**Skyjackers**
On Hearing the Airlines Will Use a Psychological Profile to Catch Potential Skyjackers. Dunn.
Raffaele Minichiello. McPherson.

**Skylarks.** *See* **Larks.**

**Skyscrapers**
Skyscrapers. Field.
Skyscrapers Stand Proud. Sandburg.

**Slaughterhouses**
Friday Lunchbreak. Orr.

**Slavery**
Alcestis on the Poetry Circuit. Jong.
Breath in My Nostrils. Jeffers.
Disillusion. *Unknown.*
*Flying Cloud,* The. *Unknown.*
"Formerly a Slave." Melville.
Frederick Douglass. Hayden.
Frederick Douglass and the Slave Breaker. Randall.
From America. Whitfield.
In Bondage. McKay.
Jack and Dinah Want Freedom. *Unknown.*
Jim Crack Corn; or, The Blue Tail Fly. *Unknown.*
John Cherokee. *Unknown.*
Middle Passage. Hayden.

My Great-Grandfather's Slaves.  Berry.
No More Auction Block.  *Unknown.*
On Being Brought from Africa to America.  Wheatley.
Poem for My Family: Hazel Griffin and Victor Hernandez Cruz.
    Jordan.
Primitive, The.  Lee.
Promises of Freedom.  *Unknown.*
Runagate Runagate.  Hayden.
Runaway Slave at Pilgrim's Point, The.  E. Browning.
Safari West.  Williams.
Sevier County Runaway, The.  Brigham.
Simon Legree—A Negro Sermon.  Lindsay.
Slave Auction, The.  Harper.
Slave Singing at Midnight, The.  Longfellow.
Slavery.  Herrick.
Slavery Chain Done Broke at Last.  *Unknown.*
Slave's Dream, The.  Longfellow.
Song of the Son.  Toomer.
Song to the Runaway Slave.  *Unknown.*
Strong Men.  Brown.
Sweet Meat Has Sour Sauce, or, the Slave-Trader in the Dumps.
    Cowper.
To Sir Toby.  Freneau.
Trellie.  Jeffers.
Wake Nicodemas.  Work.
Was It Not Curious?  Smith.
When Israel Was in Egypt's Land.  *Unknown.*
Wild Negro Bill.  *Unknown.*
Witnesses, The.  Longfellow.

**Sleep**
After I come home from the meeting with friends.  Miles.
At night I spurn the coffee cup.  Birch.
Care-charmer sleep, son of the sable night.  *Fr.* To Delia.
    Daniel.
Care-Charming Sleep.  *Fr.* The Tragedy of Valentinian.
    Fletcher.
Come, Sleep.  *Fr.* The Woman-Hater.  Beaumont *and* Fletcher.
Come Sleep! O Sleep.  *Fr.* Astrophel and Stella.  Sidney.
Country of Water.  Ames.
Disillusionment of Ten O'Clock.  Stevens.
Drowsy.  Sandburg.
Evening Song.  Fearing.
Falling Asleep.  Sassoon.
Insomnia.  Bishop.
Ivory, Coral, Gold, The.  Drummond.
Land of Nod, The.  Stevenson.
Lullaby: "Beloved, may your sleep be sound."  Yeats.
Morphine.  Heine.
Night and Sleep.  Patmore.
Night Blessing.  George.
Night-Shift.  Kalar.
11/16/75.  Pearlstein.
Now i lay (with everywhere around).  Cummings.
10/17/75.  Pearlstein.
Serenade: "Stars of the summer night!"  Longfellow.
Sleep.  Doty.
Sleep.  Imbs.
Sleep.  Knott.
Sleep, Angry Beauty, Sleep.  Campion.
Sleep Watch.  Henson.
Sleeper, The.  Clouts.
Sleeping in the Woods.  Wagoner.
Slumber Did My Spirit Seal, A.  Wordsworth.
Spell.  Francis.
To My Wife Asleep.  Tick.
To Sleep.  Clare.
To Sleep.  Keats.
To Sleep.  Smith.
To Sleep.  Wordsworth.
Touch.  Gunn.
Verses Written During a Sleepless Night.  Pushkin.
Waking From Sleep.  Bly.

Wanderer's Night Song.  Goethe.
Weary with toil, I haste me to my bed.  *Fr.* Sonnets.
    Shakespeare.
What is more gentle than a wind in summer?  *Fr.* Sleep and
    Poetry.  Keats.
When Father Slept.  Anderson.
Willie Winkie.  Miller.
Wynken, Blynken, and Nod.  Field.

**Sleeping Beauty**
Tale, The.  Beer.

**Sleighs**
Jingle Bells.  Pierpont.

**Sloth**
Sluggard, The.  Watts.

**Sloths**
Sloth, The.  Gardner.
Sloth, The.  Roethke.

**Slugs**
Slug.  Roethke.
Slugs.  Kitching.

**Slums**
Amelia Street.  Ormsby.
Bon Voyage.  Steele.
Childhood.  Latimore.
"Dangerous Condition:" Sign on Inner-City House.  Atkins.
Early Lynching.  Sandburg.
East Bronx.  Ignatow.
Elementary School Class Room in a Slum, An.  Spender.
Feeding the Lions.  Jordan.
Get the Gasworks.  Ignatow.
Judeebug's Country.  Johnson.
Letter in Winter.  Patterson.
Lovers of the Poor, The.  Brooks.
"Mean wind wanders through the backcourt trash, A."  *Fr.*
    Glasgow Sonnets.  Morgan.
On Saint-Urbain Street.  Acorn.
Other Side of Town Saturday Night, The.  Steele.
Rat, The.  Davies.
Reckoning A.M. Thursday after an Encounter between a
    Sawdust Sack and a Silly.  Turner.
Reflections in a Slum.  "MacDiarmid."
Scenery.  Joans.
6th and Walnut Street.  Moxley.
Summertime and the Living.  Hayden.
To the New Annex to the Detroit County Jail.  Thomas.
Wildcats Walking in the Dark.  Steele.

**Smells**
Alien.  Hayes.
Cologne.  Coleridge.
Epitaph on the Fart in the Parliament House.  Hoskyns.
Odours of Flowers, The.  *Fr.* Milton, II.  Blake.
Old Movies.  Cotton.
Smell of Life, The.  Sklar.
Smell of Rain.  Hall.

**Smiles**
Judy-One.  Lee.
Philosophy.  Dunbar.
Simile for Her Smile, A.  Wilbur.
Smile, The.  Blake.

**Smith, Adam**
Adam Smith.  *Fr.* Clerihews.  Bentley.

**Smith, Bessie**
Bessie Smith's Funeral.  Aubert.
Homage to the Empress of the Blues.  Hayden.

**Smith, Joseph**
Nauvoo.  Taylor.
On the Death of the Dearly Beloved and Much Lamented
    Father.  Snow.

**Smoke**
Light-winged Smoke, Icarian Bird.  Thoreau.
On the Closing of Millom Ironworks.  Nicholson.
Song of the Smoke, The.  Du Bois.

**Smoking**
He Records a Little Song for a Smoking Girl. Whitehead.
Smoker, The. Huff.
**Smugglers**
Smuggler's Song, A. *Fr.* Puck of Pook's Hill. Kipling.
**Snails**
Considering the Snail. Gunn.
Elegies for the Hot Season. McPherson.
Haughty Snail-King, The. Lindsay.
My Garden. Lindon.
Snail, The. Bourne.
Snail. Drinkwater.
Snail, The. Herbert.
Snail, The. Lovelace.
Snail, The. Reeves.
Snail, The. *Unknown.*
Snails. *Unknown.*
Snail's Monologue, The. Morgenstern.
To a Snail. Moore.
Upon a Snail. Bunyan.
Widow's Yard, The. Gardner.
**Snakes**
Andante of Snakes, The. Symons.
As Near to Eden. Francis.
Boa Constrictor. Silverstein.
Boy and His Snake, The. Lamb.
Cheers. Merriam.
Cosimo. Taylor.
Fastidious Serpent, The. Johnstone.
Garden Hose, The. Janosco.
Heaved from the Earth. Brigham.
In the Snake Park. Plomer.
Lizards and Snakes. Hecht.
Medallion. Plath.
Narrow fellow in the grass, A. Dickinson.
On a Little Boy's Endeavouring to Catch a Snake. Foxton.
Pit Viper. Momaday.
Python, The. Belloc.
Python. *Unknown.*
Rattler, Alert. Ghiselin.
Rattlesnake, The. Wrigley.
Reveille. Hughes.
Serpent, The. Roethke.
Silent Snake, The. *Unknown.*
Snake. Lawrence.
Snake. McCord.
Snake. Roethke.
Snake and the Snake-Charmer, The. Rieu.
Snake-Handling Religious Service. *Fr.* Tattoos. Wright.
Snake Hill. Bruchac.
Snake Hunt. Wagoner.
Snake Poem I. Harjo.
Snake Sermon. Smith.
Snakes. Wild.
Springfield Mountain. *Unknown.*
Summer. Wakoski.
Time We Climbed Snake Mountain, The. Silko.
To a Fair Lady Playing with a Snake. Waller.
To the Snake. Levertov.
Viper, The. Belloc.
Viper, The. Pitter.
Water-Snakes. *Fr.* The Rime of the Ancient Mariner. Coleridge.
**Snipes**
To the Snipe. Clare.
**Snobbery**
Epitaph on a Tuft-Hunter. Moore.
**Snoring**
Snoring Bedmate, The. *Unknown.*
**Snow**
After Snow. Clark.
Angels in Winter. Willard.

Boy at the Window. Wilbur.
Cynthia in the Snow. Brooks.
Desert Places. Frost.
Driving to Town Late to Mail a Letter. Bly.
Drove-Road, The. Gibson.
Dust of Snow. Frost.
Feathers of Snow. *Unknown.*
First Snow. Kay.
First Snow on an Airfield. Ciardi.
First Snowfall, The. Lowell.
Going to Remake This World. Welch.
In the Snowfall. Mechain.
It sifts from leaden sieves. Dickinson.
January. Hawley.
Jerusalem in the Snow. Bental.
Last Patch of Snow. Abbe.
London Snow. Bridges.
Long Lines. Goodman.
Metaphysic of Snow. Finkel.
Now that Snow is Falling. Kalar.
Riddles of the Weather. *Unknown.*
Sand and Snow. Lieberman.
Snow. Hanson.
Snow. Thomas.
Snow. Witheford.
Snow Chant. Broughton.
Snow in New York. Swenson.
Snow in the City. Field.
Snow in the Suburbs. Hardy.
Snow Lies Sprinkled on the Beach, The. Bridges.
Snow on Saddle Mountain, The. Miyazawa.
Snow that never drifts, The. Dickinson.
Snow-bound; a Winter Idyl. Whittier.
Snowfall, A. Eberhart.
Snowfall, The. Mechain.
Snowfall in the Afternoon. Bly.
Snow-Flake, The. De la Mare.
Snow-Flakes. Longfellow.
Snow Man, The. Stevens.
Snow-Storm, The. Emerson.
Snow Storm, The. Millay.
Soft Snow. Blake.
Stopping by Woods on a Snowy Evening. Frost.
Stories Of Snow. Page.
Storm Fear. Frost.
There was a young man of Quebec. *Unknown.*
To a Snow-Flake. Thompson.
Trying to Shovel Out. Legler.
Velvet Shoes. Wylie.
Watching Snow. Ward.
Wet Snow. MacCaig.
When the snow falls softly. Esteves.
White Fields. Stephens.
White Worlds. Luecke.
Winter Poem. Giovanni.
**Snow White**
Dwarf, The. Locklin.
True Story of Snow White, The. Bennett.
**Snowdrops**
Snowdrop, The. De la Mare.
Snowdrop, The. Tennyson.
Snowdrops, The. Coleridge.
**Snowflakes**
Snow-Flake, The. De la Mare.
Snowflake on asphodel, clear ice on rose. Aiken.
Watering the Horse. Bly.
**Snowmen**
Boy at the Window. Wilbur.
Death of a Snowman. Scannell.
**Soccer**
Rythm. Smith.
Soccer. Voznesensky.

Stanley Matthews.  Ross.
Then Strip Lads, and To It.  Scott.
**Social Protest.**  *See* **Protest, Social.**
**Social Workers**
Feeding the Lions.  Jordan.
**Socialism**
Unholy Roller.  Lewis.
**Sociology**
Trend Spotter.  Turner.
**Sodom**
And there came two angels to Sodom at even.  *Fr.* Genesis.
Bible, *O.T.*
Cities of the Plain, The.  Whittier.
Lot Later.  Nemerov.
Lot's Wife.  Akhmatova.
This Place Rumord to Have Been Sodom.  Duncan.
**Softball**
Casey's Daughter at the Bat.  Graham.
**Soldiers**
American Soldier, The.  Freneau.
Another Epitaph on an Army of Mercenaries.  "MacDiarmid."
Anthem for Doomed Youth.  Owen.
Army Corps on the March, An.  Whitman.
Arthur McBride.  *Unknown.*
Ballad of the Volunteer, The.  Stuart.
Base Chapel, Lejeune 4/79.  Hobson.
Boots.  Kipling.
Box Comes Home, A.  Ciardi.
Breakfast.  Gibson.
British Grenadiers, The.  *Unknown.*
Bugler's First Communion, The.  Hopkins.
Canadians.  Gurney.
Captain Jinks.  *Unknown.*
Cavalry Crossing a Ford.  Whitman.
Champs d'Honneur.  Hemingway.
Character of the Happy Warrior.  Wordsworth.
Come, Gaze with Me upon This Dome.  Cummings.
Comrades.  McGlennon.
Coward, The.  Spender.
Danny.  Cowley.
Danny Deever.  Kipling.
Death of a Warrior, The.  Mastoraki.
Defeated Victor, The.  Bienek.
Disabled.  Owen.
Does It Matter?  Sassoon.
Draft Dodger, The.  Rubin.
Dreamers.  Sassoon.
1887.  Housman.
Eighth Air Force.  Jarrell.
Epitaph on an Army of Mercenaries.  Housman.
Fife Tune.  Manifold.
For Our Soldiers Who Fell in Russia.  Fortini.
For the Fallen.  Binyon.
Forgive Me, Sire.  Cameron.
Fuzzy-Wuzzy.  Kipling.
Gee, But I Want to Go Home.  *Unknown.*
Gentlemen-Rankers.  Kipling.
Grenadier.  Housman.
Gunga Din.  Kipling.
He Said To.  Bell.
Heroes, The.  Simpson.
How Sleep the Brave.  Collins.
How We Heard the Name.  Dugan.
In Barracks.  Sassoon.
Incident of the French Camp.  Browning.
Innocence.  Gunn.
Insensibility.  Owen.
Into Battle.  Grenfell.
Israeli Soldier's Nightmare, An.  Carb.
Jimmy's Enlisted, or, The Recruited Collier.  *Unknown.*
Kerry Recruit, The.  *Unknown.*
Kilroy.  McCarthy.

Last of the Light Brigade, The.  Kipling.
Lessons of the War.  Reed.
Letter to Her Son's Commanding Officer.  Russell.
Lines on a Paid Militia.  *Fr.* Cymon and Iphigenia.  Dryden.
Little Girl Saw Her First Troop Parade, The.  Sandburg.
Lullaby, A: "For wars his life and half a world away."  Jarrell.
Man He Killed, The.  Hardy.
Men in Green.  Campbell.
Mrs. McGrath.  *Unknown.*
Modern Major-General, The.  *Fr.* The Pirates of Penzance.
Gilbert.
My Morose Master-Sergeants.  Holt.
New Mistress, The.  Housman.
News from the V. A.  Winans.
Oh stay at home, my lad, and plough.  Housman.
O What Is That Sound.  Auden.
Old Soldiers Home at Marshalltown, Iowa.  Barnes.
Old Soldiers Never Die.  *Unknown.*
Old Timers.  Sandburg.
On a Soldier Fallen in the Philippines.  Moody.
On the idle hill of summer.  Housman.
Peasants, The.  Lewis.
Place Pigalle.  Wilbur.
Private of the Buffs, The.  Doyle.
Prolonged Sonnet: When the Troops Were Returning from
Milan.  Albizzi.
Recruit, The.  Housman.
Recruiting Drive.  Causley.
Rendezvous.  Seeger.
Satirical Elegy, A.  Swift.
Send-off, The.  Owen.
Soldier, The.  *Fr.* 1914.  Brooke.
Soldier, A.  Frost.
Soldier from the wars returning.  Housman.
Soldier Going to the Field, The.  Davenant.
Soldier, Rest!  *Fr.* The Lady of the Lake.  Scott.
Soldiers Bathing.  Prince.
Soldier's Dream, The.  Campbell.
Soldier's Dream.  Owen.
Soldiers Plundering a Village.  Thwaite.
Soldier's Song, The.  *Unknown.*
Soldiers who wish to be a hero.  *Unknown.*
Song of the Freedman.  *Unknown.*
Sonnet-Ballad, The.  Brooks.
Sonnet to Negro Soldiers.  Cotter.
Speaking: The Hero.  Pollak.
Strange Meeting.  Owen.
Street Sounds to the Soldiers' Tread, The.  Housman.
Ten Days Leave.  Snodgrass.
There Was an Old Soldier.  *Unknown.*
"They."  Sassoon.
Things That Make a Soldier Great, The.  Guest.
To a Conscript of 1940.  Read.
To the Veterans of the Abraham Lincoln Brigade.  Taggard.
Tomb of Lt. John Learmonth, A. I. F., The.  Manifold.
Tommy.  Kipling.
Troops, The.  Sassoon.
Vale from Carthage.  Viereck.
Volunteer, The.  Asquith.
When Johnny Comes Marching Home.  Gilmore.
Working Party, A.  Sassoon.
*See also* **War.**
**Solipsism**
Argent Solipsism.  Blake.
**Solitude**
Acre of Grass, An.  Yeats.
Alastor; or, The Spirit of Solitude.  Shelley.
Alone.  Sassoon.
Anticipation of Sharks.  Wakoski.
Cave, The.  Dresbach.
Compensation.  Jeffers.
Desert Places.  Frost.

Legacy: My South.  Randall.
My South.  Glaze.
Snapshots of the Cotton South.  Davis.
Southbound.  Adcock.
Southern Mansion.  Bontemps.
Southern Road, The.  Randall.
Strange Fruit.  Allan.
Tenantry.  Scarbrough.
To Live and Die in Dixie, *sels.*  Beecher.
**South Africa**
Apartheid.  Bohanon.
Attend my fable if your ears be clean.  *Fr.* The Wayzgoose.
   Campbell.
**South America**
South American Sway.  Byers.
**South Carolina**
Carolinas, The.  Ray.
**South Dakota**
Primer Lesson.  Vinz.
Tourist Guide: How You Can Tell for Sure When You're in
   South Dakota.  Heynen.
**Southey, Robert**
Dedication: "Bob Southey! You're a poet—Poet-laureate."  *Fr.*
   Don Juan.  Byron.
Epitaph on Robert Southey.  Moore.
Vision of Judgment, The.  Byron.
**Space and Space Travel**
Apollo 113.  Finne.
Asteroid Light, The.  *Unknown.*
Astronaut's Choice.  Darcy.
Beginnings.  Fitzgerald.
Capsule Philosophy.  Lamport.
Christmas 1959 Et Cetera.  Barrax.
Earth's Bondman.  Dabney.
Far Trek.  Brady.
Faster Than Light.  Buller.
Interplanetary Limericks.  Graham.
Let's Send a Rocket.  Patrickson.
Love in a Space-Suit.  Kirkup.
Mission Uncontrolled.  Peck.
Missionary.  Thomas.
Moon Walk.  Belitt.
Moonwalk.  Engels.
Not Lost In the Stars.  Bliven.
S.F.  Leverett.
Space.  Kennedy.
Space Child's Mother Goose, The, *sels.*  Winsor.
Space Wanderer's Homecoming.  Viereck.
Tea in a Space-Ship.  Kirkup.
Unknown Shores.  Thomas.
Valentine For Earth.  F. Frost.
**Spain**
Day in Salamanca, A.  Squires.
**Spanish-American War**
Battleship of *Maine.*  *Unknown.*
There Exists the Eternal Fact of Conflict.  Crane.
**Spanish Armada**
Armada, The.  Macaulay.
Armada, 1588, The.  Wilson.
Ballade of the Armada, A.  Dobson.
Sir Francis Drake; or Eighty-Eight.  *Unknown.*
**Spanish Civil War.  See Civil War, Spanish.**
**Spanish Succession, War of the**
Jack Frenchman's Defeat.  Congreve.
**Sparrows**
Bee, the Ant and the Sparrow, The.  Cotton.
City Sparrow.  Mayhall.
Dead Sparrow, The.  Cartwright.
Haiku: "Bitter morning, A."  Hackett.
Killing of Sparrows, The.  Beer.
London Sparrow's If, A.  Lindon.
Mr. and Mrs. Spikky Sparrow.  Lear.

Phyllyp Sparrowe.  Skelton.
Rocking.  Ammons.
Song of the Reed Sparrow, The.  *Unknown.*
Sparrow, The.  Williams.
Sparrow in the Zoo, The.  Nemerov.
Sparrow in Winter.  Takahashi.
**Sparta**
Spartan Wrestler, The.  Damagetus.
**Spenser, Edmund**
Spenser! a jealous honourer of thine.  Keats.
Upon Master Edmund Spenser.  Beaumont.
**Sphinx**
Myth.  Rukeyser.
Sphinx, The.  Emerson.
What Riddle Asked the Sphinx.  MacLeish.
**Spiders**
Design.  Frost.
Homes, The.  Pitkin.
Identity.  Ammons.
Mr. Edwards and the Spider.  Lowell.
Moving North.  Deagon.
Noiseless Patient Spider, A.  Whitman.
Range-Finding.  Frost.
Spider, The.  Eberhart.
Spider.  Farber.
Spider, The.  MacKenzie.
Spider and the Fly, The.  Howitt.
Spider and the Ghost of the Fly, The.  Lindsay.
Spider as an artist, The.  Dickinson.
Spider holds a silver ball, The.  Dickinson.
Spider in the Grapes.  James.
Spider sewed at night, A.  Dickinson.
Study of a Spider, The.  Tabley.
To a Magnificent Spinner, Murdered.  Taggard.
Upon a Spider Catching a Fly.  Taylor.
Wedding, The.  Aiken.
Welcome to This House.  George.
White Spider.  Garin.
**Spinsters**
Eleanor Rigby.  Lennon *and* McCartney.
Emily Hardcastle, Spinster.  Ransom.
I'll Not Marry at All.  *Unknown.*
Miss Gee.  Auden.
Miss Loo.  De la Mare.
My Mother's Sister.  Day Lewis.
Old Ladies, The.  Ellis.
Old Maid's Song.  *Unknown.*
Single Girl.  *Unknown.*
Spinster.  Plath.
Spinster's Lullaby.  Miller.
Three Sisters.  De la Mare.
Waiting, the Hallways under Her Skin Thick with
   Dreamchildren.  Lifshin.
Woman Who Loved Worms, The.  Inez.
**Sports**
Confessions of a Born Spectator.  Nash.
Football Field: Evening.  McKellar.
Games, hard press and bruise of the flesh.  Vliet.
Life-Cycle.  Dawe.
*Literature of Sports, A* (LiSp).  Tom Dodge, ed.
*Sports Poems* (SPo).  R. R. Knudson *and* P. K. Ebert, eds.
*See also* **Athletes** *and* **individual games.**
**Spring**
After dark vapours have oppress'd our plains.  Keats.
Allotments: April.  Spencer.
Among Old Houses.  Dallas.
And every sky was blue and rain.  Hodgson.
And When the Green Man Comes.  Haines.
April.  Thompson.
April 1885.  Bridges.
April 5, 1974.  Wilbur.
Aunt Alice in April.  Matchett.

Hermit, The. Halpern.
In Commendation of a Solitary Life. Lodge.
Lake Isle of Innisfree, The. Yeats.
Little Elegy. Wylie.
Most of It, The. Frost.
O solitude! if I must with thee dwell. Keats.
Ode on Solitude. Pope.
Petition for an Absolute Retreat, The. Countess of Winchilsea.
Poem of Solitude at Columbia University. García Lorca.
Remote Country. Tremayne.
Ships That Pass in the Night. Longfellow.
Solitary Reaper, The. Wordsworth.
Solitude. Fairburn.
Solitude. Milne.
Solitude Late at Night in the Woods. Bly.
Sweet Soledad. Murguia.
Tin Can, The. Smith.
To Any M.F.H. Sackville-West.
To Marguerite — Continued. *Fr.* Switzerland. Arnold.
Tokyo West. Corn.
Wants. Larkin.

**Solomon**
David and Solomon. Naylor.
On Woman. Yeats.
Solomon and the Witch. Yeats.
Solomon to Sheba. Yeats.

**Somalia**
Independence. *Unknown.*
Our Country is Divided. Nuur.

**Somerset, Robert Carr, Earl of**
Upon the Sudden Restraint of the Earl of Somerset, Then
    Falling Out of Favor. Wotton.

**Sonnets**
Nuns fret not at their convent's narrow room. Wordsworth.
On a Magazine Sonnet. Loines.
On the Sonnet. Keats.
Scorn not the sonnet. Wordsworth.
Single Sonnet. Bogan.
Sonnet, The. *Fr.* The House of Life. D. G. Rossetti.
Sonnet, The: "Sonnet, she told the crowd of bearded, The."
    Hoffman.
What Is a Sonnet? Watkins.
What the Sonnet Is. Lee-Hamilton.

**Sons**
Am I Not Your Son? Abele.
Ancient Couple on Lu Mountain, The. Van Doren.
Andrew Talks to Gulls. Roberts.
Basketball. Vincent.
Death of a Son. Silkin.
Firstborn. Wright.
For a Father. Cronin.
For Galway. McCullough.
For My Father. Potts.
For My Son Noah, Ten Years Old. Bly.
For Stephen. Brookhouse.
Gift, The. Glück.
Graham. Gershgoren.
Hearing My Son Play. Cardona-Hine.
Heart/Song for Christopher Raymond. Pauly.
Heritage. Young.
I Walk out into the Country at Night. Lu Yu.
Kiss, The. Pack.
Lament of a Man for His Son. Austin.
Lost Son, The. Roethke.
Lullaby: "O my son, born of a winter's morn."
    Nohomaiterangi.
My Son and I. Levine.
My Son, My Executioner. Hall.
On My First Son. Jonson.
On the Birth of His Son. Su Tung-P'o.
Out-and-Down Pattern. Kloefkorn.
Passing It On. Saner.

Saunders Point. Combellick.
Son, Condemned, The. Rubin.
Son of Toad. Locklin.
This Is a Poem to My Son Peter. Meinke.
To My Father. Waterman.
To My Son. Griffin.
What Shall He Tell That Son? Sandburg.
Young Man Thinks of Sons, The. Mason.
*Brother Songs: A Male Anthology of Poetry* (BrS). Jim Perlman,
    ed.

**Sophocles**
Kaire. Eberhart.
To a Friend. Arnold.

**Sorrow**
Dark Song. Ammons.
Depths of Sorrow, The. *Unknown.*
Dolor. Roethke.
Man of Constant Sorrow. *Unknown.*
O Sorrow, Sorrow, say where dost thou dwell? *Fr.* The Noble
    Soldier. Dekker.
Poem of the Intimate Agony. Burgos.
Sadness in Spring. *Unknown.*
Sorrow Is the Only Faithful One. Dodson.
Spell Against Sorrow. Raine.
Stormy Night in Autumn. Chu Shu-chen.
Tailor Called Sorrow, A. Alver.
Tears. Reese.
Troubled Woman. Hughes.
With Rue My Heart Is Laden. Housman.
*See also* **Grief.**

**Soul**
Caged Skylark, The. Hopkins.
Dialogue between the Soul and Body, A. Marvell.
Dialogue of Self and Soul, A. Yeats.
Hadrian's Address to the Soul, When Dying. Emperor
    Hadrian.
I Know My Soul. McKay.
Indian Burying Ground, The. Freneau.
Invention of Comics, The. Baraka.
Love Calls Us to the Things of This World. Wilbur.
Maya. Robinson.
My Soul Hovers over Me. Pai.
Noiseless Patient Spider, A. Whitman.
Ode: "Bards of passion and of mirth." Keats.
Pegasus. Kavanagh.
Poor soul, the center of my sinful earth. Sonnets, CXLVI.
    Shakespeare.
Rebirth. Machado.
Scorpion. Smith.
Soul and the Body, The. *Fr.* Nosce Teipsum. Davies.
Soul has bandaged moments, The. Dickinson.
Soul selects her own society, The. Dickinson.
Speculation. Nemerov.
Terrain. Ammons.
Wake. Spires.

**Sound**
Animal That Drank Up Sound, The. Stafford.
East Hampton: The Structure of Sound. Appleman.
Frost round the House. Murray.
Now I will do nothing but listen. *Fr.* Song of Myself.
    Whitman.
On A Wednesday. Aliesan.
On the Power of Sound. Wordsworth.
Sounds. Creeley.
Sounds in the Evening, The. Farjeon.

**South, The**
Alas! for the South! Coogler.
Dealer's Choice and the Dealer Shuffles. Williams.
Dixie. Emmett.
First Families Move Over! Nash.
Georgia Dusk. Toomer.
Invitation to Madison County, An. Wright.

Backward Spring, A. Hardy.
Barren Spring. *Fr.* The House of Life. Rossetti.
Bee! I'm expecting you. Dickinson.
Canzone Pastoral in Honor of Her Majesty, A. Bolton.
Coming. Larkin.
Corinna's Going a-Maying. Herrick.
Cuckoo Song. *Unknown.*
Depression Before Spring. Stevens.
Echoing Green, The. *Fr.* Songs of Innocence. Blake.
Elm Buds. Sandburg.
Enkindled Spring, The. Lawrence.
Farewell Frost, or Welcome the Spring. Herrick.
First Sight. Larkin.
First Walk in the Park. Herschberger.
Footsteps of Spring. Bialik.
For Jane Myers. Gluck.
From you have I been absent in the spring. Sonnets, XCVIII.
  Shakespeare.
Georgian Spring. Campbell.
God's Plan for Spring. Turner.
Hillside Thaw, A. Frost.
Home-Thoughts, from Abroad. Browning.
In a Spring Still Not Written Of. Wallace.
In Just-/ Spring. *Fr.* Chansons Innocentes. Cummings.
Innocent Spring, The. Sitwell.
It's Spring Returning, It's Spring and Love. *Unknown.*
June. Ledwidge.
Last Snow. Young.
Late Spring: a Heaving, a Turning. Gill.
Late Spring Day in My Life, A. Bly.
Lent Lily, The. Housman.
Light exists in spring, A. Dickinson.
Lines Written at a Small Distance from My House.
  Wordsworth.
Love Day, The. Dunn.
Loveliest of Trees, the Cherry Now. Housman.
Lyric to Spring. Stilwell.
Manor Farm, The. Thomas.
Mardi Gras. Keithley.
May. Neilson.
May 10th. Kumin.
Miss Euphemia. Ransom.
Morning in Spring. Ginsberg.
No Spring. Corbin.
Now fades the last long streak of snow. *Fr.* In Memoriam
  A.H.H. Tennyson.
Ode on the Spring. Gray.
Prayer in Spring, A. Frost.
Question, The ("I dream'd that, as I wander'd by the way").
  Shelley.
Rich Morning. Farren.
Sailing. Murray.
Saint-Henri Spring. Acorn.
Same Lady, The. Nichols.
Screw Spring. Hoffman.
Seed Leaves. Wilbur.
Slow Spring. Tynan.
Solvitur Acris Hiems. *Fr.* Odes. Horace.
Spring. *Fr.* Songs of Innocence. Blake.
Spring, The. Carew.
Spring, The. *Fr.* The Mistress. Cowley.
Spring. Hogan.
Spring. Hopkins.
Spring. Millay.
Spring. Nashe.
Spring. Ridge.
Spring. Surrey.
Spring. *Fr.* The Seasons. Thomson.
Spring ("Lenten is come with love to towne"). *Unknown.*
Spring and All. Williams.
Spring at Fort Okanogan. Wilson.
Spring at Nant Dywelan. Jones.

Spring Coming. Ammons.
Spring Flowers. *Fr.* The Seasons. Thomson.
Spring Goeth All in White. Bridges.
Spring Images. Wright.
Spring in New Hampshire. McKay.
Spring in the Desert. Hall.
Spring in Virginia. Wilson.
Spring in Washington. Den Boer.
Spring is like a perhaps hand. Cummings.
Spring Morning, A. Clare.
Spring Morning. Lawrence.
Spring Pools. Frost.
Spring Quiet. C. Rossetti.
Spring Stops Me Suddenly. Iremonger.
Spring, the Sweet Spring. *Fr.* Summer's Last Will and
  Testament. Nashe.
Spring Thunder. Van Doren.
Springtime. Hadley.
Stay, Spring. Young.
Sunflower Moccasins. George.
Sweet spring is your. Cummings.
That Sharp Knife. Wolfe.
Thaw. Lifshin.
Thaw. Thomas.
Thaw in the City. Lipsitz.
These are the days when birds come back. Dickinson.
Time, A: A Season. Ramsey.
To a Nun. Ormond.
To Spring. Blake.
To Spring. Smith.
Twilight in Middle March, A. Ledwidge.
Twist-Rime on Spring. Guiterman.
Two Springs. Li Ch'ing-chao.
Vernal Ague, The. Freneau.
Vernal Sentiment. Roethke.
When daisies pied and violets blue. *Fr.* Love's Labour's Lost.
  Shakespeare.
When Faces Called Flowers Float out of the Ground.
  Cummings.
When, loosened from the winter's bonds. Nukada.
When Spring came,/ Leaves grew with a green fresh. *Unknown.*
When the Birds Go North Again. Higginson.
Who Calls? Clarke.
Written in March. Wordsworth.
Year's Awakening, The. Hardy.
Yin and Yang. Rexroth.

**Squid**
Squid-Jiggin' Ground. *Unknown.*

**Squirrels**
Fable: "The mountain and the squirrel." Emerson.
Five Little Squirrels. *Unknown.*
Gray Squirrel, The. Wolfe.
Migration of the Grey Squirrels, The. Howitt.
Mirror for Myself. Wescott.
On a Squirrel Crossing the Road in Autumn, in New England.
  Eberhart.
Squirrel, The ("Whisky Frisky"). *Unknown.*
Squirrel in Sunshine. Cowper.
Squirrel Near Library. Taggard.
Squirrels. Young.

**Sri Lanka**
Tea. Struthers.

**Stables**
More To It Than Riding. Lindon.
Riding Stable in Winter, The. Tagliabue.
Stable, The. Hoffman.

**Stagecoaches**
Californy Stage. *Unknown.*
Oro Stage, The. Knibbs.

**Stalin, Joseph**
"Less Nonsense." Herbert.

**Stanley, Sir Henry Morton**

Into the Dark. Monette.

**Starkweather, Charles**
Getting Through the Fifties: the Starkweather Case Revisited. Hahn.

**Starlings**
Branwen's Starling. Parry.
Rooftop Winter. Thorpe.
Smoke of Birds, A. Cowley.
Starling, The. Heath-Stubbs.
Starlings. MacCaig.

**Stars**
Awake, oh Heaven, for (lo) the Heavens Conspire. Tourneur.
Bright Star! Would I Were As Steadfast As Thou Art. Keats.
Canopus. Taylor.
Counting. Johnson.
Darkness. Campbell.
Escape at Bedtime. Stevenson.
First Star. *Unknown.*
Great Bear, The. Hollander.
If the Stars Should Fall. Allen.
Impressions, Number III. Cummings.
It Is the Stars That Govern Us. Magee.
Lightly stepped a yellow star. Dickinson.
Lights in the Sky Are Stars, The. Rexroth.
Little Star, The. *Unknown.*
Lost Lane. Wellesley.
Martial Cadenza. Stevens.
More Loving One, The. Auden.
My Star. Browning.
North Star, The. Morris-Jones.
Nova. Jeffers.
Pole Star, The. Coslett.
Speculation. Nemerov.
Star, The. Taylor.
Star. Whitebird.
Star-Talk. Graves.
Starry Night, The. Sexton.
Stars. Nowlan.
Stars Over the Dordogne. Plath.
Stars Wheel in Purple. Doolittle ("H.D.").
Summer Stars. Sandburg.
Take Something Like a Star. Frost.
To the Evening Star. Blake.
Tumultuous Plenty in the Heavens. Maclean.
Twinkle, twinkle, little star. Dehn.
Universe, The. Miller.
When I Heard the Learn'd Astronomer. Whitman.
When Sun Doth Rise. Williams.

**Statistics**
Meditation on Statistical Method. Cunningham.

**Statue of Liberty.** *See* **Liberty, Statue of.**

**Statues**
After Plotinus. Stafford.
Archaic Torso of Apollo. Rilke.
By the Statue of King Charles at Charing Cross. Johnson.
Cheap Rent. Sandburg.
Christmas Eve under Hooker's Statue. Lowell.
Duke of York's Statue, The. Landor.
Figures, The. Creeley.
Instructions for the Erection of a Statue of Myself in Central Park. Inez.
Interrupted, The. Jacobsen.
Lines to the South. Corrington.
Misdemeanor. Triem.
On a Statue of Sir Arthur Sullivan. Hamilton.
Ponder, darling, these busted statues. Cummings.
Rider Victory, The. Muir.
Six Statues in a Park. Stuart.
Statue, The. Belloc.
Statue, The. Berryman.
Statue, The. Fuller.
Statues, The. Yeats.

Statues in the Public Gardens, The. Nemerov.
Tiki. Anderson.

**Steam Rollers**
To a Steam Roller. Moore.

**Steel**
Prayers of Steel. Sandburg.

**Steeples**
Steeple-Jack, The. Moore.
To a Solitary Disciple. Williams.

**Stein, Gertrude**
Gertrude Stein. Roberts.
They Don't Speak English in Paris. Nash.
Yesterday. Winant.

**Sterne, Laurence.**
Epitaph on Laurence Sterne. Garrick.

**Stevens, Wallace**
In His Poems Are El Greco's Hands. Leverant.
Rouse for Stevens, A. Roethke.
So Long? Stevens. Berryman.

**Stinkbugs**
Dusty black beetle, A. Sund.

**Stoicism**
The Old Stoic. Brontë.

**Stonehenge**
What is Stonehenge? It is the roofless past. *Fr.* The Heart's Journey. Sassoon.

**Stones and Rocks**
As Rocks Rooted. Hanson.
Crystals Like Blood. "MacDiarmid."
Forecast. Miles.
How to Amuse a Stone. Shelton.
I've Got a Home in That Rock. Patterson.
Path among the Stones, The. Kinnell.
Petoskey Stone. Vas Dias.
Rock and Hawk. Jeffers.
Rock Climbing. Cooper.
Rocks. Packer.
Runes. Jarrett.
Serenity in Stones, The. Ortiz.
Silica Carbonate Rock. Berry.
Skipping Stones. Farber.
Stone, The. Blackburn.
Stone. Simic.
Stone Poems, The. Smith.
Stones, The. Berry.
Stones. Jeffrey.
Stonetalk. Hamelin.
Three Stones. Watson.
To the Stone-Cutters. Jeffers.
Touchstone. Worley.
Waters. Hall.
What Any Lover Learns. MacLeish.

**Storms**
Ballad of the Tempest. Fields.
Beginning to Squall. Swenson.
Big Wind. Roethke.
Blizzard, The. Dewey.
Brainstorm. Nemerov.
Channel Passage, A. Swinburne.
Cloud-Flower Lullaby, The. *Unknown.*
Equinox, The. Heyward.
Equinox, The. *Fr.* Seaweed. Longfellow.
First Winter Storm. Everson.
Found in a Storm. Stafford.
Hailstorm in June 1831, The. Clare.
Hatteras Calling. Aiken.
Ice-Storm, April, 1974. Stelzer.
In Cold Storm Light. Silko.
Interlude. Roethke.
Invocation for a Storm. *Unknown.*
June Thunder. MacNeice.
Line-Storm Song, A. Frost.

Little Exercise. Bishop.
Local Storm, A. Justice.
Low Barometer. Bridges.
Misgivings. Melville.
On a Thunder Storm. Scott.
On the Fen: A Stormy Day Near Heckington. Bull.
Once by the Pacific. Frost.
Reefing Topsails. Mitchell.
Snow-bound; a Winter Idyl. Whittier.
Snow-Storm, The. Emerson.
Squall. Moore.
Storm, The. Roethke.
Storm. Wright.
Storm at Sea, A. Donne.
Storm Cone, The. Kipling.
Storm Fear. Frost.
Storm in Summer, A. Blunt.
Storm in the Desert. Squires.
Storm on the Island. Heaney.
Storm Tide on Mejit. *Unknown.*
Storm-Wind, The. Barnes.
Stormy Day, A. *Unknown.*
Stormy Night in Autumn. Chu Shu-chen.
Summer Storm. Kent.
Tempest, The. *Unknown.*
Thunderstorm in Town, A. Hardy.
West Palm Beach Storm, The. *Unknown.*
Wind begun to rock the grass, The. Dickinson.

**Story Poems**
*The Poet's Tales; A New Book of Story Poems* (PoTa). William
    Cole, ed.

**Storytelling and Storytellers**
Andrew's Bedtime Story. Serraillier.
Aunt Sue's Stories. Hughes.
Come/ With/ Me. *Fr.* Come With Me. Chase-Riboud.
Lost Anchors. Robinson.
Story-Teller, The. Van Doren.
To Juan at the Winter Solstice. Graves.

**Stowe, Harriet Beecher**
Harriet Beecher Stowe. Dunbar.

**Strangers**
To You. Whitman.
What Is It Makes the Stranger. Hyde.

**Strauss, Richard**
1907: A Proposal from Paris. Howard.

**Strawberries**
Wild Strawberries. Graves.

**Streams.** *See* **Brooks and Streams.**

**Strikes**
Coal Strike. Macleod.
Late Snow and Lumber Strike of the Summer of Fifty-Four,
    The. Snyder.
Repentant Judas. Kalar.
Thalassa, Thalassa. Neugass.
Will and Testament. Neugass.

**Stuart, Charles Edward, the Young Pretender**
Charlie Is My Darling. Nairne.
Old Scottish Cavalier, The. Aytoun.
Wae's Me for Prince Charlie. Glen.

**Students**
About My Students. Fandel.
Discontented Student, The. Tucker.
Etudes. Thomas.
Foreign Student. Robinson.
Freshmen. Spacks.
Heathen Pass-ee, The. Hilton.
On Hearing That the Students of Our New University Have
    Joined the Agitation against Immoral Literature. Yeats.
Straying Student, The. Clarke.
Student, The. Stuart.
Theme for English B. Hughes.
To the University of Cambridge in New England. Wheatley.

Two Sec. Mods. Ghose.
University Examinations in Egypt. Enright.
Vulture and the Husbandman, The. Hilton.
Ways of Loving. Weiss.
You Understand the Requirements. Lifshin.
*See also* **Education; Scholars and Scholarship; School.**

**Stuttering**
Mister Charlie. *Unknown.*
Stutterer. Dugan.

**Stuyvesant, Peter**
Epitaph for Peter Stuyvesant. Selyns.

**Suburbs**
Before the Stuff Comes Down. Snyder.
5:32, The. McGinley.
In the city you had dirt and din. Birch.
In the Suburbs. Simpson.
Long Island Springs. Moss.
Middlesex. Betjeman.
Suburb, The. Stevenson.
Suburban. Malouf.
Suburban Dream. Muir.
Suburbia: Impossibilities of Change. Marcus.
To an American Poet Just Dead. Wilbur.
We Told You So. Keesing.

**Subways**
Approaching Washington Heights. Reiss.
Boy Who Smells Like Cocoa, A. Hershon.
Cage, The. Montague.
City Afternoon. Howes.
Clickety-Clack. Blackburn.
Curse, The. Hollander.
Going Uptown ɔ Visit Miriam. Cruz.
In a Station of the Metro. Pound.
Metropolitan Railway, The. Betjeman.
One Year to Life on the Grand Central. Lorde.
Queen, The. Pitchford.
Spirit of 34th Street, The. Shriver.
Subway, The. Tate.
This Subway Station. Reznikoff.
Train to Reflection. O'Neill.
Tubes. Mollin.
Tunnel, The. *Fr.* The Bridge. Crane.
Under the Stone I Saw Them Flow. Gregory.
Underground Poetry. Pietri.
Walk About the Subway Station. Reznikoff.

**Success**
After Publication of Under the Volcano. Lowry.
Kindly Unhitch That Star, Buddy. Nash.
Names. Enright.
Robert Whitmore. Davis.
Success is counted sweetest. Dickinson.
Success Story. Hayes.
To a Friend Whose Work Has Come to Nothing. Yeats.
To a Friend Whose Work Has Come to Triumph. Sexton.
Willie Bobo Was a Baaaa/aad Dude. Mélendez.

**Suez Canal**
Suez Crisis, The. *Unknown.*

**Suffering**
Alajire, we ask you to be patient. *Unknown.*
Long Term Suffering. Eberhart.
Musée des Beaux Arts. Auden.
Old and the New Masters, The. Jarrell.

**Suicide**
After the Surprising Conversions. Lowell.
Ballad of Hell, A. Davidson.
Bridge of Sighs, The. Hood.
Butcher Boy, The. *Unknown.*
Call It a Good Marriage. Graves.
Caroline of Edinboro' Town. *Unknown.*
Dear Girl, The. Warner.
Elderly Nobody Erases Self in Central Park. Forgotson.
Elegy for a Schoolmate. O'Sullivan.

Exeat. Smith.
Faithless Nelly Gray. Hood.
Farewell to the world, and to the night farewell. *Fr.* The Love
   Suicides at Sonezaki. Chikamatsu.
Felo De Se. Blackburn.
For Black Poets Who Think of Suicide. Knight.
Harlem River. Spector.
Henry's Understanding. Berryman.
Her Story. Madgett.
I Am Going to Sleep (Suicide Poem). Storni.
If the composition of this collection lasted three years.
   Burkard.
Justice Is Reason Enough. Wakoski.
Lady Lazarus. Plath.
Middle-Aged, Middle-Class Woman at Midnight, A. Taggard.
Mill, The. Robinson.
Monument Mountain. Bryant.
Newcomer's Wife, The. Hardy.
Notes Found Near a Suicide. Horne.
Of Late. Starbuck.
Of Suicide. Berryman.
On the Suicide of a Friend. Whittemore.
One Summer in Charleston. Hogan.
Passages. Walker.
Poor Shammes of Berditchev, The. Ratner.
Portrait, The. Kunitz.
Preface to a Twenty Volume Suicide Note. Baraka.
Quaker Hero, Burning. Noll.
Resume. Parker.
Richard Cory. Robinson.
Richard Cory. Simon.
Shot? so quick, so clean an ending? Housman.
Singular Self, The. Bukowski.
Six Feet Under. Hale.
Sportsman, The. McCord.
Suicide, The. Lowbury.
Suicide. Walker.
Suicide Off Egg Rock. Plath.
To Be, or Not to Be. *Fr.* Hamlet. Shakespeare.
To D——, Dead by Her Own Hand. Nemerov.
To Helen in a Huff. Willis.
Tragedy, A. Marzials.
221-1424. Sanchez.
Wanting to Die. Sexton.
Wedding, The. Gant.
Why I Died. Jong.
**Sumac**
Sumach Leaves, The. Very.
**Summer**
As imperceptibly as grief. Dickinson.
August Fugue. Shapcott.
Beginning, The. Stevens.
Cuckoo Song. *Unknown.*
Dog-Days. A. Lowell.
Edinburgh Courtyard in July. MacCaig.
End of Summer. Kunitz.
Exeunt. Wilbur.
Fortune. Ferlinghetti.
Ghetto Summer School. Worth.
High Summer on the Mountains. Davies.
Hymn to the Sun. Roberts.
In Fields of Summer. Kinnell.
In the Good Old Summer Time. Shields.
It will be Summer eventually. Dickinson.
July the Seventh. Norris.
Knoxville, Tennessee. Giovanni.
Late August. Atwood.
Letters of Summer, The. Buckley.
Loud is the summer's busy song. *Fr.* The Shepherd's Calender:
   July. Clare.
Misericordia. Mead.
Mounting Summer, Brilliant and Ominous, The. Schwartz.

Musings. Barnes.
My Father Paints the Summer. Wilbur.
Poem on the End of Sensation. Stange.
Rainy Summer, The. Meynell.
School Boy, The. *Fr.* Songs of Experience. Blake.
Songs to Survive the Summer. Hass.
Soote Season, The. Surrey.
Summer. C. Rossetti.
Summer. Wilson.
Summer Countries, The. Rago.
Summer Is Gone. *Unknown.*
Summer Malison, The. Hardy.
Summer Music. Sarton.
Summer Song. Ciardi.
Summer Songs. Watt.
Summer: West Side. Updike.
Summertime and the Living. Hayden.
These are the days when birds come back. Dickinson.
To Summer. Blake.
To Summer. Nadet.
**Sun**
Ask of the sun. Zukofsky.
How Can I Say It Any Other Way. Nibbelink.
Indian Summer Day on the Prairie, An. Lindsay.
Metric Figure. Williams.
Morning Light. Dudek.
Noon Glare. Brennan.
Nova. Jeffers.
November. Harvey.
November Sun. Daryush.
Ol' Hannah. *Unknown.*
Prayer, A: "Sun my relative." *Unknown.*
Song: "Stay, Phoebus, stay!" Waller.
Song for Sunsets. Birney.
Sun. Dickey.
Sun, The. Drinkwater.
Sun. Moore.
Sun Rising, The. Donne.
Sun-flower, The. Greenwell.
Sunlight. Bruchac.
Thy Rising Is Beautiful. Akhnaton.
True Account of Talking to the Sun at Fire Island, A. O'Hara.
Versions of Sunlight. Applewhite.
**Sunday**
Ain't It a Shame. *Unknown.*
Aside. Dugan.
On a Sunday Afternoon. Sterling.
Sunday. Miles.
Sunday. Rungren.
Sunday in South Carolina. Parham.
Sunday Morning. MacNeice.
When You Have Forgotten Sunday: The Love Story. Brooks.
**Sundials**
Epigram: "I who by day am function of the light."
   Cunningham.
I am a sundial, and I make a botch. Belloc.
I am a sundial. Ordinary words. Belloc.
I am a sundial, turned the wrong way round. Belloc.
Motto for a Sundial. *Unknown.*
**Sunflowers**
Ah! Sun-Flower. *Fr.* Songs of Experience. Blake.
Sun-flower, The. Greenwell.
Sunflower Sutra. Ginsberg.
Sunflowers, The. Stewart.
Tom O'Bedlam among the Sunflowers. James.
**Sunrise**
Hymn to the Morning, An. Wheatley.
I'll tell you how the sun rose. Dickinson.
Kitchen Window. Ebberts.
Lever de Rideau. Bethell.
Out of the Sea, Early. Swenson.
Pennsylvania Academy of Fine Arts. Kroll.

Plainview: 3. Momaday.
Reveille. Housman.
Sunrise. Lanier.
Sunrise at Sea. Swinburne.
Sunrise Call, The. *Unknown.*
Watching the Sun Rise Over Mount Zion. Whitman.
*See also* **Dawn; Morning.**

**Sunset**
Acceptance. Frost.
Evening: to Harriet. Shelley.
Evensong. Dufault.
Hesperos, you bring home all the bright dawn disperses. Sappho.
Mediterranean. Whitman.
Mise en Scene. Fitzgerald.
On Its Way. Swenson.
On the Setting Sun. Scott.
Prairie Sunset, A. Whitman.
Song for Sunsets. Birney.
Sunset Song. *Unknown.*
We in the Fields. Everson.
*See also* **Evening; Twilight.**

**Supermarkets**
Grace to Be Said at the Supermarket. Nemerov.
Supermarket. Holman.
Supermarket in California, A. Ginsberg.
Whistling Willie. Starbird.

**Supernatural.**
Sacred Children, The. Hays.
*Catch Your Breath: A Book of Shivery Poems* (CaYB). Lilian Moore *and* Lawrence Webster, comps.
*See also* **Occult, The.**

**Superstition**
Ode on the Popular Superstitions of the Highlands of Scotland. Collins.
Written in Disgust of Vulgar Superstition. Keats.

**Surfers and Surfing**
Surfer, The. Wright.
Surfer and Others. Dorman.
Surfers at Santa Cruz. Goodman.

**Surgery**
Correct Compassion, A. Kirkup.
Heart Surgery. Mitter.
Operation, The. Smith.

**Surrealism**
Salvador Dali. Gascoyne.
*English and American Surrealist Poetry* (EAS). Edward B. Germain, ed.

**Susquehanna River**
River, The. Thompson.

**Surrey, Henry Howard, Earl of**
Verse in Praise of Lord Henry Howard, Earl of Surrey. Turberville.

**Susanna (Bible)**
Peter Quince at the Clavier. Stevens.
Susannah and the Elders. *Unknown.*

**Sussex, England**
On Holmbury Hill. Shanks.
Puck's Song. *Fr.* Puck of Pook's Hill. Kipling.
Sussex. Kipling.

**Sutter, John**
John Sutter. Winters.

**Swallows**
Blue Swallows, The. Nemerov.
Swallow, The. Aikin.
Swallow, The. Clare.
Swallow, The. Cowley.
Swallows, The. Coatsworth.
Swallows. Ferril.
Swallow's Nest, The. Arnold.
To a Swallow. Bishop.
To the Swallow. Cowper.

Upon the Swallow. Bunyan.

**Swamps**
Alligator, The. Ravenel.
Walking in a Swamp. Wagoner.
Bereaved Swan, The. Smith.

**Swans**
Black Swan, The. Jarrell.
Hard Edge of Beauty. Stuart.
Love the Wild Swan. Jeffers.
Mating Swans. McAuley.
Mirror, The. Milne.
Native Element. Jeffrey.
Silver Swan, The. *Unknown.*
Swan Bathing, The. Pitter.
Swans, The. Dyment.
Swans, The. Sitwell.
Swan's Feet, The. Scovell.
Three Sentences for a Dead Swan. Wright.
Wild Swans. Millay.
Wild Swans at Coole, The. Yeats.
Wring the Swan's Neck. Martinez.

**Sweden**
Carriage from Sweden, A. Moore.

**Swift, Jonathan**
Hypocrite Swift. Bogan.
Lamentation of Glumdalclitch, The. Pope.
Lines on Swift's Ancestors. Pope.
On Himself. Swift.
Sermon on Swift, A. Clarke.
Swift. Schwartz.
Swift's Epitaph. Yeats.
Verses on the Death of Doctor Swift, *sels.* Swift.
Written in a Copy of Swift's Poems for Wayne Burns. Wright.

**Swimming and Swimmers**
And I Have Loved Thee, Ocean! *Fr.* Childe Harold's Pilgrimage. Byron.
Dead Man Creek. Brock.
Fall In. Kirstein.
First Lesson. Booth.
400-Meter Freestyle. Kumin.
Ice-Cart, The. Gibson.
Inside the River. Dickey.
Intimations at the Lake, 1963. Minton.
Lifeguard, The. Dickey.
Lovely Swimmers, The. Lattimore.
Moon-Bathers. Freeman.
Morning Swim. Kumin.
Old Swimmer, The. Morley.
On a Friend's Escape from Drowning off the Norfolk Coast. Barker.
Swimmer. Francis.
Swimming in the Rain. Wallace.
Swimming by Night. Merrill.
Swimming Chenango Lake. Tomlinson.
Upon Boys Diverting Themselves in the River. Foxton.
Written after Swimming from Sestos to Abydos. Byron.

**Swinburne, Algernon Charles**
After Swinburne. Chesterton.

**Swings**
Here in the scuffled dust. *Fr.* Heart's Needle. Snodgrass.
Swing, The. Stevenson.
Swing Song, A. Allingham.

**Switzerland**
Switzerland. Thwaite.
Thought of a Briton on the Subjugation of Switzerland. Wordsworth.

**Sydney, Australia**
Sydney Cove, 1788. Porter.

**Synagogues**
Cry for a Disused Synagogue in Booysens. Hirsch.

**Synge, John Millington**

Memory, A. Strong.
Municipal Gallery Revisited, The. Yeats.

# T

**Tadpoles**
Porwigles. Holder.
**Tailors**
Amendis to the Telyouris and Sowtaris for the Turnament Maid
on Thame, The. Dunbar.
Tailor. Farjeon.
**Talmud, The**
Pilpul. Kamenetz.
**Tamalpais, Mount, California**
Circumambulation of Mt. Tamalpais. Hoyem.
Mount Tamalpais. Cook.
**Tammuz**
Death of Tammuz, The. Tchernichovsky.
Tammuz. Alterman.
**Tannhäuser**
Laus Veneris. Swinburne.
Tannhauser. Levy.
**Tapestry**
Tapestry, The. Nemerov.
**Tara, Ireland**
Harp That Once thro' Tara's Halls, The. Moore.
**Tarzan**
What did Tarzan know. *Fr.* Tarzan. Koertge.
**Tasman, Abel**
Landfall in Unknown Seas. Curnow.
**Tasmania**
In Northern Tasmania. McAuley.
Van Diemen's Land. *Unknown.*
**Taverns**
Glass of Beer, A. Stephens.
Hostess of the Ferry Inn, The. Gwerfyl Mechain.
In a Prominent Bar in Secaucus One Day. Kennedy.
Lady, of anonymous flesh and face. Cunningham.
Lines on the Mermaid Tavern. Keats.
Old Wife in High Spirits. "MacDiarmid."
Railroad to Hell. *Unknown.*
Will Waterproof's Lyrical Monologue. Tennyson.
**Taxes**
Caged Rats. Elliott.
New Song on the Birth of the Prince of Wales, A. *Unknown.*
New Song on the Taxes, A. *Unknown.*
On Mr. Pitt's Hair-Powder Tax. Burns.
**Taxis**
Taxis, The. MacNeice.
**Tea**
Dish of Tea, The. Freneau.
How to Get On in Society. Betjeman.
Monody on a Tea-Kettle. Coleridge.
Twinings Orange Pekoe. Moffett.
**Teaching and Teachers**
Absent-Minded Professor. Nemerov.
Ageing Schoolmaster, An. Scannell.
Always Learning. Enright.
April Inventory. Snodgrass.
Campus on the Hill, The. Snodgrass.
Correspondence School Instructor Says Goodbye to His Poetry
Students, The. Kinnell.
Dr. Fatt, Instructor. Hall.
Dustless Chalk. Rankin.
Education. Lee.
Educators, The. Black.
Emeritus, n. Coulette.
French Master, The. Abse.

Freshmen. Spacks.
Golden Gate: The Teacher. Mastrolia.
Grouchy Good Night to the Academic Year, A. Pauker.
He Don't Know the Inside Feel. Adams.
Kindergarten Teacher. Kiesel.
Letter to a Teacher of English, A. Hillyer.
Miss Ada. Fahy.
Off to Patagonia. Weiss.
On Reading Poems to a Senior Class at South High. Berry.
*One* That Got Away, The. Miranda.
Pay Is Good, The. Kell.
Pedagogy. Locklin.
Place's Fault, The. Hobsbaum.
Preliminary to Classroom Lecture. Miles.
Professor's Song, A. Berryman.
Retired School-Teacher. McHugh.
Schoolmaster Abroad with His Son, The. Calverley.
Schoolmistress. Sansom.
School-Mistress, The. Shenstone.
Short History of the Teaching Profession, A. Maura.
Student, The. Eckman.
Syllabus, The. Jurgensen.
Teacher, The. Jong.
Teacher, A. McGregor.
Teacher, A. Whittemore.
Teacher of Poetry, The. Packard.
Teaching. Young.
Teaching Swift to Young Ladies. Dickey.
Teechur. Higgins.
To My Old Schoolmaster. Whittier.
Turn on the Footlights: The Perils of Pedagogy. Carter.
What Schoolmasters Say. Seymour-Smith.
Year's End. Barnes.
**Tears**
Eyes and Tears. Marvell.
In the Sea of Tears. Replansky.
Man in the Onion Bed, The. Ciardi.
My Lady's Tears. *Unknown.*
Peeling Onions. Rich.
Rain. Lindsay.
Tears. E. Browning.
Tears. Reese.
Tears. Sitwell.
Tears. *Unknown.*
Tears, Idle Tears. *Fr.* The Princess. Tennyson.
Upon Julia Weeping. Herrick.
Valediction, A: of Weeping. Donne.
**Teeth**
My Teeth. Ochester.
Palace for Teeth, The. Luttinger.
Poet's Farewell to His Teeth, The. Dickey.
Teeth. *Fr.* Broken Treaties. Contoski.
**Telegraph**
Cable Hymn, The. Whittier.
On the Completion of the Pacific Telegraph. Very.
**Telephones**
Crimes of Passion: The Phone Caller. Stokes.
Dial Tone, The. Nemerov.
Eletelephony. Richards.
Exchange. Stuart.
Hello! My Baby. Howard.
Hot Lines. Dunann.
I Am a Victim of Telephone. Ginsberg.
Long Distance. Stafford.
Nocturne in the Corner Phonebox, The. Taylor.
Obscene Caller, The. Dacey.
On Seeing a Torn Out Coin Telephone. Robbins.
Slight Confusion, A. Reiss.
Telephone Connection. Edgcomb.
Telephone Operator, The. Francis.
Telephone Poles. Updike.
221-1424. Sanchez.

Voice on the Other End of the Line, The. Randolph.

**Television**
A.B.S. News. Lechlitner.
Addict. Montgomery.
Aunts Watching Television. Pudney.
Day the T.V. Broke, The. Jonas.
Death. Byatt.
Dick Powell. Koertge.
Electric Cop, The. Cruz.
Goodbye, Old Paint, I'm Leaving Cheyenne. Garrett.
Jabber-Whacky. Di Caprio.
Jimmy Jet and His TV Set. Silverstein.
Mousemeal. Nemerov.
Not-So-Good Earth, The. Dawe.
Speaking of Television, *sels.* McGinley.
Teevee. Merriam.
Tee-Vee Enigma. Raskin.
Watching Television. Bly.
When Daddy Died. Ackerson.
Winning of the TV West, The. Alexander.

**Tell, William**
Archery. De la Mare.

**Temperance**
Away With Rum. *Unknown.*
Have Courage, My Boy, to Say No. Hilton.
John Barley-Corn, My Foe. Adams.

**Ten Commandments**
God Is Mr. Big, Real Big. Burke.
Latest Decalogue, The. Clough.

**Teniers, David, the Younger.**
Bench of Boors, The. Melville.

**Tennessee**
Black Bottom Bootlegger, The. Leiper.
Father in Tennessee, A. Simmons.
Tenantry. Scarbrough.

**Tennis**
40—Love. McGough.
Midnight Tennis Match, The. Lux.
Old Pro's Lament, The. Petrie.
Old Tennis Player. Brooks.
Snapshot for Miss Bricka Who Lost in the Semifinal Round of the Pennsylvania Lawn Tennis Tournament. Wallace.
Subaltern's Love Song, A. Betjeman.
Tennis. Avison.
Tennis. Pinsky.

**Tennyson, Alfred Tennyson, 1st Baron**
After Lord Tennyson. Chesterton.
To Alfred Tennyson. Landor.

**Tents**
Benediction for the Tent. *Unknown.*
Thinking of Tents. Whittemore.

**Termites**
Tree Animals. Lieberman.

**Terns**
Gracious Goodness. Piercy.

**Terrorists**
Disillusionment. Alegria.
18 West 11th Street. Merrill.
Montage. Guest.

**Texas**
At the Airport in Dallas. Mooney.
Cattle. Nance.
Crossing West Texas (1966). Robertson.
Driving North from Kingsville, Texas. Shihab.
Eyes of Texas, The. *Unknown.*
From the Observation Deck, Austin. Petroski.
Hell in Texas. *Unknown.*
Jefferson, Texas. Shihab.
Texas. Lowell.
Texas Ranger, The. Boswell.
Texas Rangers. *Unknown.*
Yellow Rose of Texas, The. *Unknown.*

**Thackeray, William Makepeace**
Divisions on a Victorian Ground. Howard.

**Thames (river), England.**
Lines Written near Richmond, upon the Thames, at Evening. Wordsworth.
Voyage on the Thames, The. *Fr.* The Rape of the Lock. Pope.

**Thanksgiving**
First Thanksgiving. Livingston.
Prayer for the Great Family. Snyder.
Thanksgiving. Herrick.
Thanksgiving. Morris.
Thanksgiving to God, for His House, A. Herrick.

**Thanksgiving Day**
Minnesota Thanksgiving. Berryman.
Thanksgiving Day. Child.
Thanksgiving in Boston Harbor, The. Butterworth.

**Theater**
Play-House, The. Addison.
Prologue Spoken at the Opening of the Theatre in Drury-Lane, 1747. Johnson.
Rehearsal, The. Gregory.

**Thebes**
Tiresias. Tennyson.

**Theology**
Respectable Burgher, The. Hardy.

**Theresa, Saint, of Avila**
Flaming Heart, The, *sels.* Crashaw.
Hymn to the Name and Honor of the Admirable St. Theresa, A. Crashaw.

**Thermopylae, Battle of**
On the Spartan Dead at Thermopylae. Simonides.
Oracles, The. Housman.

**Theseus**
Theseus: A Trilogy. Winters.
Theseus and Ariadne. Graves.

**Thirst**
Hunger and Thirst. Bishop.

**Thistles**
Looking at a Dry Canadian Thistle Brought in from the Snow. Bly.
Thistledown. Monro.
Thistles. Hughes.

**Thomas, Dylan**
Cwmrhydyceirw Elegiacs. Watkins.
Elegy for Dylan Thomas. Sitwell.
True Picture Restored, A. Watkins.

**Thomas à Becket, Saint**
Becket. Gilbert.

**Thomas the Rhymer (Thomas of Erceldoune)**
Thomas Rymer. *Unknown.*

**Thomson, James (1700-1748)**
Ode Occasion'd by the Death of Mr. Thomson. Collins.

**Thor**
Labors of Thor, The. Wagoner.

**Thoreau, Henry David**
Men of Sudbury, The. Baker.
On Visiting the Graves of Hawthorne and Thoreau. Very.

**Thrushes**
Come In. Frost.
Darkling Thrush, The. Hardy.
Reminder, The. Hardy.
Thrush Before Dawn, A. Meynell.
Thrushes. Hughes.
Thrush's Nest, The. Clare.
Thrush's Nest, The. Ryan.
What the Thrush Said. Keats.

**Thunder**
Giant Thunder. Reeves.
June Thunder. MacNeice.
Spring Thunder. Van Doren.
Thunder in a Moment of Calm. Kalar.
Thunder in the Garden. Morris.

To Redound. Harmon.
Written in a Thunder Storm July 15th 1841. Clare.

**Tides**
Between the Tides. Councilman.
Low-Tide. Millay.
Tidal Pool. Hay.
Tide Rises, the Tide Falls, The. Longfellow.
Tides. Blackwell.
Tides, The. Bryant.
Tides. Prys-Jones.

**Tigers**
O have you caught the tiger? Housman.
Tyger, The. *Fr.* Songs of Experience. Blake.

**Till, Emmett**
Emmett Till. Emanuel.
Last Quatrain of the Ballad of Emmett Till, The. Brooks.

**Timbuktu**
Timbuctu. Brathwaite.

**Time**
And the Days Are Not Full Enough. Pound.
Before. Stanford.
Birthday, The. Dacey.
Birthday Verses Written in a Child's Album. Lowell.
Burnt Norton. *Fr.* Four Quartets. Eliot.
Cat's Eyes. Scarfe.
Chronology. Cassity.
Cities and Thrones and Powers. *Fr.* Puck of Pook's Hill.
  Kipling.
Clerks, The. Robinson.
Cold Fall. Eberhart.
Confession of a Young Hegelian. Griffin.
Counting the Beats. Graves.
Days. Emerson.
Days, The. Hall.
Dear Men and Women. Wheelock.
Devouring time blunt thou the lion's paws. Sonnets, XIX.
  Shakespeare.
Dialogue betwixt Time and a Pilgrim, A. Townsend.
Dream within a Dream, A. Poe.
Driving Clock. Flanner.
During Wind and Rain. Hardy.
Elegy: "The laundry-basket is still there." Hollo.
Enemies, The. Bull.
Estuary, The. Fairburn.
Even Such Is Tyme. Ralegh.
Five Bells. Slessor.
Forever is composed of nows. Dickinson.
Four Preludes on Playthings of the Wind. Sandburg.
Four seasons fill the measure of the year. Keats.
God's Education. Hardy.
Going and Staying. Hardy.
Her Reply. Ralegh.
His Poetry His Pillar. Herrick.
Hour-Glass, The. Herrick.
How Soon Hath Time the Subtle Thief of Youth. Milton.
In Italian They Call the Bird Civetta. Warren.
In the Fleeting Hand of Time. Corso.
In Time. Graves.
In tyme the strong and statelie turrets fall. *Fr.* Licia. Fletcher
  the Elder.
Lamentation of the Old Pensioner, The. Yeats.
Light Year, The. Ridland.
Like as the waves make towards the pebbled shore. Sonnets,
  LX. Shakespeare.
L'Imprévisibilité. Hippius.
Maple in November. Russell.
Mutability. *Fr.* Ecclesiastical Sonnets. Wordsworth.
Next, Please. Larkin.
New Year, The. Rexroth.
1967. Hardy.
Nothing Gold Can Stay. Frost.
Old Furniture. Hardy.

On an Hour-Glass. Hall.
On Time. Milton.
Our Bias. Auden.
Poet Laments the Coming of Old Age, The. Sitwell.
Polo Grounds. Humphries.
"Quod Tegit Omnia." Winters.
Red Earth. Corbin.
Rising Five. Nicholson.
Roll on, sad world! not Mercury or Mars. *Fr.* Sonnets.
  Tuckerman.
Rome, Conquerer, Conquered. Sylvester.
Scene on the Banks of the Hudson, A. Bryant.
Sheep Fair, A. Hardy.
Shut Out That Moon. Hardy.
Signature for Tempo. MacLeish.
Since brass, nor stone, nor earth, nor boundless sea. Sonnets,
  LXV. Shakespeare.
Slow Starter, The. MacNeice.
Song: "Who can say." Tennyson.
Sunshade, The. Hardy.
Thistledown. Glover.
Tide Rises, the Tide Falls, The. Longfellow.
Time. Curnow.
Time. Wynne.
Time Is the Mercy of Eternity. Rexroth.
Time, Real and Imaginary. Coleridge.
Time Study. Roberts.
Time's Dedication. Schwartz.
Time's Offerings. Eberhart.
To Daffodils. Herrick.
To Every Thing There Is a Season. *Fr.* Ecclesiastes. Bible,
  *O.T.*
To His Coy Mistress. Marvell.
XXth Century. Hillyer.
Wheel Revolves, The. Rexroth.
When I have seen by Time's fell hand defaced. Sonnets, LXIV.
  Shakespeare.
Where it is. Creeley.
You, Andrew Marvell. MacLeish.

**Tiresias**
Tiresias. Tennyson.

**Titanic (ship)**
Convergence of the Twain, The. Hardy.
Great *Titanic*. *Unknown.*
I Sing of Shine. Knight.
Sinking of the *Titanic*. *Unknown.*
*Titanic*, The. *Unknown.*
*Titanic* Blues. *Unknown.*

**Tithonus**
Tithonus. Tennyson.
Wedding, The. Aiken.

**Titian**
Venus and the Lute Player. Engle.

**Toads**
Death of a Toad, The. Wilbur.
Delicate the Toad. Francis.
Friend in the Garden, A. Ewing.
History Lesson for My Son. Kooser.
Song of Mr. Toad, The. *Fr.* The Wind in the Willows.
  Grahame.
Toad. Cotton.
Toad and the Frog, The. *Unknown.*
Toad School. Meeter.

**Tobacco**
Author Loving These Homely Meats, Specially, viz., The:
  Cream, Pancakes, Buttered Pippin-pies. Davies.
Ode to Tobacco. Calverley.
On Tobacco. Cotton
Says the Miner to the Mucker. *Unknown.*
Tobacco. Freneau.
Tobacco. Harris.
Tobacco, *sels.* Kauffman.

Tobacco is a filthy weed. *Unknown.*
Tobacco Men. Applewhite.
**Toledo, Ohio**
Atlas. Flanagan.
Not Men Alone. Rolfe.
**Tolstoy, Leo**
Now It's Happened. Lawrence.
**Tools**
His Request. O'Sullivan.
Needs. Ammons.
**Toothaches**
Charm against the Toothache, A. Heath-Stubbs.
**Torah, The**
Expounding the Torah. Zukofsky.
**Tories**
Suggestion Made by the Posters of the *Globe*, A. Thorold
   Rogers.
**Tornadoes**
Interview with a Tornado Victim on April 16 1974, An. Legler.
Mid-Plains Tornado. Bierds.
Sherman Cyclone, The. *Unknown.*
Tornado. Stafford.
Tornado Warning. Shapiro.
Tornado Watch. Shuttleworth.
Tupelo Destruction, The. *Unknown.*
Under the Cellar. Salisbury.
**Toronto, Ontario**
Nights Passed on Ward's Island, Toronto Harbour. Fetherling.
**Tortoises**
Baby Tortoise. Lawrence.
Elegy for the Giant Tortoises. Atwood.
Giant Tortoise, The. Lucie-Smith.
Hare and the Tortoise, The. Serraillier.
Tortoise. De Longchamps.
Tortoise Gallantry. Lawrence.
Tortoise Shell. Lawrence.
Tortoise Shout. Lawrence.
*See also* **Turtles.**
**Tourists**
Afternoons with Baedeker. Lancaster.
Body Fished from the Seine. Corso.
Importer, An. Frost.
Manners. Shiffert.
This Is the Life. MacNeice.
Tourism. Chaffin.
Trials of a Tourist. Tibble.
Twenty-third Flight. Birney.
**Toussaint L'Ouverture, François Dominique**
To Toussaint L'Ouverture. Wordsworth.
**Towns**
Anderson, Indiana. White.
Assumptions. Hugo.
At Barstow. Tomlinson.
Good Town, The. Muir.
Midwest Town. Peterson.
Our Town. Stanford.
Sunday Dreamer's Guide to Yarrow, Missouri, A. Barnes.
They're Tearing Down a Town. Strunk.
Village, The. Le Sueur.
X. Dickey.
**Toys**
Broken Toys, The. Kirkup.
Little Boy Blue. Field.
Silver Racer, The. Murphy.
Toys, The. Patmore.
Toys. Sutskever.
**Track Athletics**
Cry of the High Hurdlers, The. Fiske.
High Jump, The. *Unknown.*
Pole Vaulter. Evans.
Pole-Vaulter, The. *Unknown.*
Runner, The. Whitman.

Sports Field. Wright.
**Tractors**
Cynddylan on a Tractor. Thomas.
**Traffic**
Before Disaster. Winters.
Drivers of Boston, The. Gross.
Eclogue: "Whores are afraid to cross the street," The.
   Bergman.
Meditations on Frost's "Stopping by Woods." De Pietro.
**Traffic Accidents**
Auto Wreck. Shapiro.
Chorus: "They were singing Old MacDonald in the schoolbus."
   Ciardi.
Obituary. Fearing.
**Traherne, Thomas**
Of Thomas Traherne and the Pebble Outside. Clouts.
**Trains**
"Are Ye Right There, Michael?" (A Lay of the Wild West
   Clare). French.
Ballade of the Old-Time Engine. Vines.
Boxcar Poem, The. Young.
By Rail through Istria. Conquest.
By Rail through the Earthly Paradise, Perhaps Bedfordshire.
   Levertov.
Evening Song. Anderson.
Express, The. Spender.
Flying Crow. *Unknown.*
Freight Train. *Unknown.*
Gambler, The. *Unknown.*
I like to see it lap the miles. Dickinson.
I Never Saw the Train. Roberts.
In a Train. Bly.
In the Train. *Fr.* City Nights. Symons.
Limerick Train, The. Kennelly.
Limited. Sandburg.
Lines Written in Objection; or, the Limpopo Express. Hey.
Metroliner. DuVall.
Midnight on the Great Western. Hardy.
Newport Railway, The. McGonagall.
Night Journey. Roethke.
Night Mail. Auden.
Night-Ride, The. Slessor.
900 Miles. *Unknown.*
Number 29. *Unknown.*
Observation Car. Hope.
Panama Limited, The. *Unknown.*
Pennsylvania Station. Hughes.
Praise of a Train. *Unknown.*
Railroad Reverie. Young.
Smokestack Lightin'. *Unknown.*
South Shore Line. Schlesinger.
Starting from San Francisco. Ferlinghetti.
This Train ("This train is bound for glory, this train").
   *Unknown.*
To a Locomotive in Winter. Whitman.
Train, The. Brownjohn.
Train: Abstraction. Taggard.
Train Journey. Wright.
Train Tune. Bogan.
Train Window. Stewart.
Transandean Railway, The. Kretz.
Travel. Millay.
12 O'Clock Freight. Flanner.
Wabash Cannonball, The. *Unknown.*
Window. Sandburg.
Women don't travel in clubcars. Jonas.
Wreck of the Old 97, The. *Unknown.*
*See also* **Railroads.**
**Translations and Translators**
Lesson in Translation, A. Preil.
On Elphinston's Translation of Martial. Burns.

On First Looking in on Blodgett's *Keats's "Chapman's Homer."* Starbuck.
On First Looking into Chapman's Homer. Keats.
On the Translation of Anacreon. Walpole.
On Tom Moore's Translation of Anacreon. Erskine.
Poem in Translation, A. Gallagher.
Translator to Translated. Pound.

**Trapeze Artists**
High Wire Dancers. Hoskins.
Last Great Flight of the Great Wallenda, The. Hyett.

**Trappers and Trapping**
Hare in Winter. Piercy.
Rabbit, The. Davies.
Trapper, The. Klappert.

**Travel**
Crossing the Atlantic. Sexton.
Dover to Munich, *sels.* Calverley.
Eight Frontiers Distant. Hutchinson.
Farewell to Kurdistan. Tonks.
Four Postcards from Italy. Andrews.
4/22/75. Pearlstein.
Frontier, The. Hewitt.
Hard Traveling. Guthrie.
I Am Going to California. *Unknown.*
Interstate, *sels.* Harris.
Journey into France, The. *Unknown.*
Lines to Mr. Hodgson. Byron.
Louise. Smith.
Old Walking Song, The. Tolkien.
On the Circuit. Auden.
Over 2000 Illustrations and a Complete Concordance. Bishop.
Questions of Travel. Bishop.
Railway Junction, The. De la Mare.
Sightseeing. O'Grady.
Starting from San Francisco. Ferlinghetti.
Traveller, The. Berryman.
Traveller Has Regrets, The. Fraser.
Travellers, The. Reeves.
Traveler's Curse after Misdirection, The. Graves.
Traveling in Europe. Althaus.
Two Travellers, The. Boland.
Unexplorer, The. Millay.

**Treason**
Gunpowder Plot, The. *Unknown.*
Of Treason. Harington.

**Trees**
All That Time. Swenson.
And When the Green Man Comes. Haines.
Ballad of Trees and the Master, A. Lanier.
Bark. Welch.
Bent Tree. Serchuk.
Binsey Poplars. Hopkins.
Bound. Roethke.
Chestnut Trees at Alton House, The. Tomlinson.
Child's Song in Spring. Nesbit.
Christmas Trees (A Christmas Circular Letter). Frost.
Circle on the Grass, The. Kenyon.
Cycads, The. Wright.
Fallen Tree, The. Bly.
Felled Plane Tree, The. Hajnal.
Foresters Arms, The. Thwaite.
Fraser, I think, tells of a Roman. Reznikoff.
Green Grass Grew All Around, The. *Unknown.*
He Praises the Trees. *Unknown.*
Holes of Green. Fisher.
I Consider the Tree. Buber.
I Had a little nut-tree, nothing would it bear. Mother Goose.
In a Wood. Hardy.
Juniper. Duggan.
Knife and Sap. Leslie.
Knockmany. Ryan.
Laurel Tree, The. Simpson.

Learning by Doing. Nemerov.
Legend of Paper Plates, The. Haines.
Lines to a Tree. Teller.
Loveliest of Trees, the Cherry Now. Housman.
New Year for Trees, The. Schwartz.
Of All Plants, the Tree. White.
Old Pines, The. Corman.
On a Great Hollow Tree. Strode.
Proper Place, A. Nye.
Second Shadow. Roethke.
Snow-Gum, The. Stewart.
Some Knots. Honig.
Song: "Love and harmony combine." Blake.
Song of the Open Road. Nash.
Sound of Trees, The. Frost.
Spruce Is Standing Lonely, A. Heine.
Stump, The. Hall.
Tenebris. Grimké.
They. Finkel.
This Time a Tree Turns into a Woman. Bentley.
3 Stanzas About a Tree. Bell.
To Blossoms. Herrick.
To Sycamores. Herrick.
Tree. Hoffman.
Tree, The. Hopewell.
Tree. Mbembe.
Tree, The. Pound.
Tree. Smith.
Tree, The. Wilson.
Tree at My Window. Frost.
Tree Is Father to the Man, The. Lipsitz.
Tree Party. MacNeice.
Trees. S. Coleridge.
Trees. Kilmer.
Trees. Merwin.
Trees, The. Rich.
Trees. Singer.
Trees, The. Williams.
Trees and Evening Sky. Momaday.
Trees Are Down, The. Mew.
Trees in the Garden. Lawrence.
Trees Lose Parts of Themselves inside a Circle of Fog. Ponge.
Trembling of the Veil, The. Ginsberg.
Uprooted. Lindsay.
Walnut-Leaf Scent. Binyon.
War Against the Trees, The. Kunitz.
Willow-Man, The. Ewing.
Winter Trees. Plath.
Woodman Spare That Tree. Morris.
Wormwood. Kinsella.
*See also* **names of trees** *(e.g.,* **Poplar Trees***).*

**Trelawny, Edward John**
Dedication to "Songs of the Springtides." Swinburne.

**Trieste**
Three Streets. Saba.

**Trinity, The.**
On Trinity Sunday. Byrom.

**Trojan War**
Iliad, The. Homer.
Judgment of Paris, The. Merwin.
Palladium. Arnold.
Return, The ("Veteran Greeks came home, The"). Muir.
Scenes from the Fall of Troy. Morris.
Wonders of "The Iliad." Goodman.

**Trolleys**
Burned Bridge, The. Stone.
Dump, The. Hall.

**Trolls**
Stone Troll, The. Tolkien.
Trolls. Terrell.

**Trout**
It Is Hard to Catch Trout. Piuvkaq.

Reflections of a Trout Fisherman. Demon.
Trout, The. Montague.
Trout of the Well, The. *Unknown.*
Winter Trout. Dickey.
Work of Art. Short.
**Troy**
Troy. Muir.
**Troy, New York**
Going and Coming: Two Poems. Benedikt.
**Trucks and Truckers**
Buffalo. Brodsky.
Daybreak on a Pennsylvania Highway. Daunt.
Julio. Robertson.
Pancho Villa. Lipsitz.
Poet Finds an Ephemeral Home in a Truck Stop on the New
    Jersey Turnpike, ca. 1970, The. Hall.
Truckdriver. Sange.
Truck Drivers. Haag.
Trucker Drives Through His Lost Youth, A. Bottoms.
Water-Truck, The. Lane.
Why Log Truck Drivers Rise Earlier than Students of Zen.
    Snyder.
**Trumpets**
How High the Moon. L. Jeffers.
**Truth**
Buddha took some Autumn leaves. *Fr.* The City of the Moon.
    Rexroth.
I died for beauty—but was scarce. Dickinson.
In a World of Change. Awad.
O, how much more doth beauty beauteous seem. *Fr.* Sonnets.
    Shakespeare.
Student. Cheng Min.
Tell all the truth but tell it slant. Dickinson.
Threnody: "Truth is a golden sunset far away." Scherzo.
True Confession, A. Stallworthy.
Truth. Duggan.
Truth. Hearst.
Truth. McKay.
Wayfarer, The. *Fr.* War Is Kind. Crane.
What is Truth. Wright.
When my love swears that she is made of truth. *Fr.* Sonnets.
    Shakespeare.
**Truth, Sojourner**
Oriflamme. Fauset.
Sojourner Truth. *Fr.* Stars. Hayden.
**Tuberculosis**
T.B. Blues. *Unknown.*
**Tubman, Harriet**
I Like to Think of Harriet Tubman. Griffin.
Runagate Runagate. Hayden.
**Tucson, Arizona**
In Old Tucson ("In old Tucson, in old Tucson,/ How swift the
    happy days ran on!"). Hall.
In Old Tucson ("In old Tucson, in old Tucson,/ What cared I
    how the days ran on?"). Conrard.
In Old Tucson ("Within a 'dobe wall"). Beghtol.
**Tulips**
To a Bed of Tulips. Herrick.
Tulips. Plath.
**Tumbleweed**
Weeds. Stanford.
**Turkeys**
Black November Turkey, A. Wilbur.
Soliloquy of a Turkey. Dunbar.
**Turner, Lana**
Poem: "Lana Turner has collapsed." O'Hara.
**Turner, Nat**
Ballad of Nat Turner, The. Hayden.
Nat Turner. Allen.
Nat Turner in the Clearing. Aubert.
Remembering Nat Turner. Brown.
**Turtle Doves**

Phoenix and Turtle, The. Shakespeare.
**Turtles**
Emancipation of George-Hector (A Colored Turtle), The.
    Evans.
Little Turtle, The. Lindsay.
Living Tenderly. Swenson.
Sea Turtle. Pope.
Sea-Turtle and the Shark, The. Tolson.
Snapper, The. Heyen.
Tony the Turtle. Rieu.
Turtle, The. Nash.
Turtle, The. *Fr.* Greed. Wakoski.
Turtle's Song, The. *Unknown.*
*See also* **Tortoises.**
**Tutsan (plant)**
Tutsan. Senior.
**"Twain, Mark" (Samuel Langhorne Clemens)**
When the Mississippi Flowed in Indiana. Lindsay.
**Twilight**
Coming of Dusk upon a Village in Haiti, The. Rago.
Georgia Dusk. Toomer.
Half past Four, October. Hajnal.
If the Owl Calls Again. Haines.
Remembering Home. Petrykewycz.
Saskatchewan Dusk. Buckaway.
Suburban Dusk. Meyers.
Winter Twilight, A. Grimké.
*See also* **Evening; Sunset.**
**Twins**
Gemini. Creeley.
Portrait of a Younger Twin. Shapcott.
Twins. Graves.
Twins, The. Leigh.
**Tyranny**
Epitaph on a Tyrant. Auden.
Foreign Ruler, A. Landor.
Kings and Tyrants. Herrick.
Song to the Men of England. Shelley.

# U

**UFOs**
Midwest U.F.O. Steingass.
**Uccello, Paolo**
Uccello. Corso.
**Ulysses**
Callypso Speaks. Doolittle ("H.D.").
Canto I: "And then went down to the ship." Pound.
Lotos-Eaters, The. Tennyson.
Odysseus. Merwin.
Return, The ("Doors flapped open in Ulysses' house, The").
    Muir.
Strayed Reveller, The. Arnold.
Tales of Brave Ulysses. Clapton *and* Sharp.
Ulysses. *Fr.* Divina Commedia: Inferno. Dante.
Ulysses. Graves.
Ulysses. Tennyson.
Ulysses and the Siren. Daniel.
World as Meditation, The. Stevens.
**Umbrellas**
Outcast, The. Sanford.
Rain It Raineth, The. Bowen.
**Uncles**
All Up and Down the Lines. Cooperman.
Fall In. Kirstein.
Nobody Loses All the Time. Cummings.
Uncle. Levine.
Uncles. Norse.

**Underground Railroad**
Runagate Runagate. Hayden.

**Unemployment**
Hellbabies. Gregory.
I Don't Want Your Millions Mister. Garland.
In a Coffee Pot. Hayes.
Moving through the Silent Crowd. Spender.
Papermill. Kalar.
Poolroom Faces. Kalar.
Soup Song. Sugar.
Tom's Garland. Hopkins.
Uprooted. Funaroff.
Young fellow walks about, The. Reznikoff.

**Unicorns**
Taliessin's Song of the Unicorn. Williams.
Talisman for the New Year, A. Metzger.
Unicorn. Gray.
Unicorn. Smith.
Unicorn, The. Young.

**Unions.** *See* **Labor Unions.**

**United States**
America. Creeley.
America. Ginsberg.
America. McKay.
America. Smith.
America. Whitman.
America a Prophecy. Blake.
America Bleeds. Lewis.
America for Me. Van Dyke.
America the Beautiful. Bates.
American Age, The. Packer.
American Dreams. Simpson.
American Eagle, The. Lawrence.
American Letter: For Gerald Murphy. Millay.
American Lights, Seen from Off Abroad. Berryman.
Another Commercial. Landrum.
Benjamin Franklin Hazard. *Fr.* The New Spoon River.
    Masters.
Brooklyn Heights. Wain.
Brown River, Smile. Toomer.
Centennial Hymn. Whittier.
Columbia. *Unknown.*
Columbia, the Gem of the Ocean. Shaw.
Coming Back to America. Dickey.
Dear America. Peterson.
England. Moore.
Flag Goes By, The. Bennett.
1492. Lazarus.
Free America. Warren.
From Paumanok Starting I Fly Like a Bird. Whitman.
Gift Outright, The. Frost.
Hail, Columbia. Hopkinson.
Happy Birthday America. Aguila.
I Am Waiting. *Fr.* Oral Messages. Ferlinghetti.
I Hear America Singing. Whitman.
I, Too. Hughes.
"In 1843,/ John James Audubon." *Fr.* Founding Fathers.
    Wyatt.
In Goya's greatest scenes we seem to see. *Fr.* A Coney Island
    of the Mind. Ferlinghetti.
Inner Part, The. Simpson.
Invocation: "American muse, whose strong and diverse heart."
    *Fr.* John Brown's Body. Benét.
Jefferson and Liberty. *Unknown.*
Long, Too Long America. Whitman.
Lyric: "From now on kill America out of your mind." Agee.
Minority Report. Updike.
Mrs. Trollope in America. Bevington.
My Blackness Is the Beauty of This Land. L. Jeffers.
N.Y. to L.A. by Jet Plane. Dorman.
New Colossus, The. Lazarus.
Next to of Course God America I. Cummings.

Night Journey. Roethke.
On the Emigration to America. Freneau.
On the Prospect of Planting Arts and Learning in America.
    Berkeley.
Our Country. Thoreau.
Poem of the Forty-eight States, A. Koch.
Poem, or Beauty Hurts Mr. Vinal. Cummings.
Pterodactyl and Powhatan's Daughter, The. Macrae.
Racist Delicious. Landrum.
Republic, The. Longfellow.
Sailing from the United States. Moss.
Shine, Perishing Republic. Jeffers.
Shine, Republic. Jeffers.
Starting from San Francisco. Ferlinghetti.
To Cole, the Painter, Departing for Europe. Bryant.
To My Son Parker, Asleep in the Next Room. Kaufman.
To the Republicans of North America. Shelley.
U.S.A., The. Rice.
Watch the Lights Fade. Jeffers.
Whenever I Say "America." Turner.
Wild Dreams of a New Beginning. Ferlinghetti.
Yonder. Eberhart.
*Traveling America with Today's Poets* (TAT). David Kherdian,
    ed.
*Visions of America* (VoA). David Kherdian, ed.

**United States Air Force**
Air Force Blue, The. *Unknown.*

**United States Army**
Caissons Go Rolling Along, The. Gruber.

**United States Marine Corps**
Marine Hymn, The. *Unknown.*
Rise and Fall of the Swagger Stick, The. Smith.

**Universe**
Imagine Grass. Skinner.
Man Said to the Universe, A. Crane.
Ode on Zero. Pettingell.
Quatrain: "Strictly mathematic God, A." Bull.
3 Models of the Universe. Swenson.
Tumultuous Plenty in the Heavens. Maclean.
Universe, The. Swenson.

**Universities.** *See* **Colleges and Universities.**

**Unknown Soldier**
Elegy for an Unknown Soldier. Baxter.
Unknown Dead, The. Timrod.

**Unwin, Mary**
To Mary. Cowper.

**Uriel**
Uriel. Emerson.

**Ursa Major**
Cup of the Bear, The, *abr.* Fox.
Great Bear, The. Hollander.

**Usury**
Canto XLV: "With Usura." Pound.
Gombeen, The. Campbell.

**Utah**
Abandoned Copper Refinery. Gillespie.
Desert Gulls. Gillespie.
Marching to Utah. *Unknown.*
Utah. Stevenson.

**Utopia**
Anglicized Utopia. Gilbert.

# V

**Vacation**
I'm Going to Rocky Island. *Unknown.*
Lake Chemo. Rowe.
School's Out. Davies.

Vacation. Stafford.

**Vagabonds**
Another Academy. Bukowski.
Big Rock Candy Mountains, The. *Unknown.*
Bums, on Waking. Dickey.
Communion of Saints: The Poor Bastard under the Bridge.
     Ponsot.
Danville Girl. *Unknown.*
Dying Hobo, The. *Unknown.*
Great American Bum, The. *Unknown.*
Hallelujah, Bum Again. *Unknown.*
Hard Traveling. Guthrie.
Hobo's Lullaby. Reeves.
Jay Gould's Daughter. *Unknown.*
Me and You and a Dog Named Boo. LaVoie.
Sunflower Rock. Blackburn.
Taking Off. Rogers.
Tramp, The. Hill.
Two Hoboes. *Unknown.*
Wanderer's Grave, The. Sage.
You See Them in the Alleys. Masarik.

**Valentine's Day**
Conversation Hearts. Payne.
February Loves. Lattimore.
Hail, Bishop Valentine, whose day this is. *Fr.* An
     Epithalamion. Donne.
St. Valentine. Moore.
Secret, A. Merriam.
Thank You for the Valentine. Wakoski.
To My Valentine. *Unknown.*
To-morrow is Saint Valentine's Day. *Fr.* Hamlet.
     Shakespeare.
Valentines. Dumas.
Valentines to My Mother, 1880. C. Rossetti.

**Vampires**
Undead, The. Wilbur.
Voices Answering Back: The Vampires. Raab.
Why Don't They Go Back to Transylvania? Peters.

**Van Doren, Mark**
Ballad of Remembrance, A. Hayden.

**Van Gogh, Vincent**
Blue Church, The. Balakian.
Dear Vincent. Bartlett.
Farewell to Van Gogh. Tomlinson.
"Truly We Can Only Allow Our Paintings to Speak."
     Pumphrey.

**Vanbrugh, Sir John**
On Sir John Vanbrugh, Architect. Evans.

**Vanderbilt, Gloria**
Poor Kid. Cole.

**Vanity**
Four Preludes on Playthings of the Wind. Sandburg.
Man and His Image, The. La Fontaine.
On the Death of a Metaphysician. Santayana.
Once in a Saintly Passion. Thomson ("B. V.").
Ozymandias. Shelley.
Palinode, A. Bolton.
Vanitas Vanitatum. *Fr.* The Devil's Law Case. Webster.
Vanity of All Worldly Things, The. Bradstreet.
Vanity of Existence, The. Freneau.

**Vaughan, Henry**
At the Grave of Henry Vaughan. Sassoon.

**Vegetables**
Cauliflower, The. Haines.
For Instance. McAlmon.
Fruit and Vegetables. Jong.
Marshall. Macbeth.
Nocturn Cabbage. Sandburg.
Root-Crops. Bowman.
Roots of Revolution in the Vegetable Kingdom, The. Urdang.
Squashes. Eaton.
Three from the Market. McPherson.

**Vegetarians**
I Don't Eat Animals (and They Don't Eat Me). Safka.

**Velázquez, Diego Rodríguez de Silva y**
Juan de Pareja: Painted by Velázquez. Long.
Portrait, A. De la Mare.
Rokeby Venus, The. Conquest.

**Venereal Disease**
Cadaver. Stone.
Hygiene. Oldham.
Pangloss's Song. Wilbur.
V.D. Clinic. Stoutenburg.

**Venice, Italy**
On the Extinction of the Venetian Republic. Wordsworth.
Venice and Sunset. *Fr.* Childe Harold's Pilgrimage. Byron.

**Venus (goddess)**
Birth of Venus. Urdang.
Death of Venus, The. Creeley.
Invocation to the Goddess, An. Wright.
Lady of the Castle, The. Hollander.
Laus Veneris. Swinburne.
Spoken by Venus on Seeing Her Statue Done by Praxiteles.
     *Unknown.*
To Venus. *Fr.* Odes. Horace.
Venus, and yong Adonis sitting by her. *Fr.* Fidessa, More
     Chaste than Kind. Griffin.
Venus of the Salty Shell. Devlin.
Venus Transiens. Lowell.
*See also* **Aphrodite.**

**Venus (planet)**
Evening Star, The. *Fr.* The Moon-Bone Cycle. *Unknown.*
Occultation of Venus, The. Hall.
Perspective. *Fr.* The Angel in the House. Patmore.
*See also* **Evening Star.**

**Venus Fly Trap**
Readymade. Perreault.

**Venus of Milo (statue)**
Venus of the Louvre. Lazarus.

**Veracruz, Mexico**
Beach at Veracruz, The. Bowering.
Veracruz. Hayden.

**Vermont**
Indian Summer: Vermont. Stevenson.
Safe Places. Urdang.
Settling In. Stuart.
Windham Thaw, The. Guiterman.
Winter Fairyland in Vermont. Osgood.

**Vesalius, Andreas**
Cider and Vesalius. Peck.

**Vesta**
To Vesta. Middleton.

**Veteran's Day**
Armistice Day. Beer.

**Veterinarians**
Vet, The. Boas.

**Victoria, Queen of England**
1887. Housman.
Ode on the Installation of His Royal Highness Prince Albert.
     Wordsworth.
On the Jubilee of Queen Victoria. Tennyson.
Queen Victoria and Me. Cohen.
To the Queen ("O loyal to the royal in thyself"). Tennyson.

**Vienna, Austria**
View of Vienna from Schonbrunn. Ruse.

**Vietnam**
Advent 1966. Levertov.
Altars in the Street, The. Levertov.
Americana XV: Simplicity. Rakosi.
And All Call Him Uncle. Mberi.
Asian Peace Offers Rejected Without Publication. Bly.
At a March against the Vietnam War. Bly.
Atlas' Daughter. Mann.
Ballad of Ho Chi Minh. MacColl.

Boy From Tennessee. Killens.
Bring 'Em Home. Dane.
Bummer, A. Casey.
Butter. Schmidt.
Containing Communism. Cobb.
Dustoff: Med Evac. Coleman.
Earth Sings Mi-Fa-Mi, The. Lowther.
Epitaph: "Here lies fierce Strephon, whose poetic rage." Hecht.
Fare Thee Well. Siegel.
Foreign Policy Commitments; or, You Get Into the Catamaran First, Old Buddy. Blackburn.
Hallowe'en 1971. Browne.
Homecoming. Dawe.
In Ca Mau. Coleman.
In Southeast Asia (Viet Nam). Rowland.
In the Mourning Time. Hayden.
Junglegrave. Anderson.
Kilroy. McCarthy.
Lost, The. Dunn.
Memo. Lynch.
National Security. MacLeish.
Negro Soldier's Viet Nam Diary, A. Martin.
Night Flare Drop, Tan Son Nhut. Coleman.
Nine Years After Viet Nam. Quintana.
Non Poem about Vietnam, A. Rodgers.
Norman Morrison. Mitchell.
Of Late. Starbuck.
Paraders for the Bomb. Bernard.
Poem About Poems About Vietnam, A. Stallworthy.
Poem to My Sister, Ethel Ennis, Who Sang "The Star-spangled Banner" at the Second Inauguration of Richard Milhous Nixon. Jordan.
Problems. Scott.
Rosie Bakungan. Smith.
Saigon Tea. Oldham.
Streets. Enright.
Teeth Mother Naked at Last, The. Bly.
Third World, The. Ferlinghetti.
Thirty-nine thousand/five hundred and seventy-two. Trudell.
Two Vietnamese Women. Krohn.
Up Rising. Fr. Passages. Duncan.
Vietnam. Major.
Vietnam #4. Major.
Voice from Danang. Redshaw.
What Were They Like? Levertov.
Wichita Vortex Sutra. Ginsberg.
Women in Vietnam, The. Paley.

**Vikings**
Abbey Tomb. Beer.
Battle of Brunanburh. Unknown.
Bettystown. Smith.
Runilda's Chant. Fr. Ethelstan. Darley.
Viking Terror, The. Unknown.
Vikings, The. Unknown.

**Villages**
Our Village—by a Villager. Hood.

**Vinci, Leonardo da.** See **Leonardo da Vinci.**

**Violence**
Beating, The. Stanford
Bloody Sire, The. Jeffers.
Beating, The. Stanford.
Formal Application. Baker.
Gagaku: "Pissed on her chest." Richmond.
Gagaku: "Put my hand through TV screen." Richmond.
Mousemeal. Nemerov.
Street Fight. Monro.

**Violets**
How Violets Came Blue. Herrick.
Sonnet: "I had no thought of violets of late." Nelson.
To Violets. Herrick.
Violet, The. Taylor.
Yellow Violet, The. Bryant.

**Violins**
Country Fiddler, The. Montague.
Ode to a Violin. Salinas.
Second Violinist's Son, The. Gregor.

**Virgil**
To Virgil. Tennyson.

**Virgin Mary.** See **Mary, the Virgin.**

**Virginia**
Carry Me Back to Old Virginny. Bland.
I went to the valley. Clifton.
Untitled. Clifton.

**Virginity**
All Night by the Rose. Unknown.
Best Line Yet, The. Allen.
Broomfield Hill, The. Unknown.
Description of Maidenhead, A. Unknown.
Dialogue After Enjoyment. Cowley.
First Time, The. Newlove.
Honour. Cowley.
How Can I Keep My Maidenhead. Burns.
In Bertram's Garden. Justice.
In Praise of Virginity. Hroswitha.
Maidenhead. Philips.
My Little Love Lies on the Ground. Paraske.
To the Virgins, to Make Much of Time. Herrick.
To Virgins. Herrick.
Twa Magicians, The. Unknown.

**Vogler, Georg Joseph**
Abt Vogler. Browning.

**Volcanoes**
Lava Tubes. Unterecker.
Volcanoes. Akhmadulina.

**Voltaire, François Marie Arouet de**
Epigram on Voltaire. Young.
Mock On, Mock On, Voltaire, Rousseau. Blake.
Voltaire at Ferney. Auden.

**Voters and Voting**
Fair and Free Elections. Unknown.
Poll. Roberson.
Voting Machine. Nathan.

**Vowels**
Five, The. Swift.
Vowels. West.

**Voyages**
Aboard at a Ship's Helm. Whitman.
Crossing the Atlantic. Sexton.
To the Virginian Voyage. Drayton.
Voyages, sels. Crane.
Where Lies the Land? Clough.

**Vulcan**
To Vulcan. Herrick.

**Vulpius, Melchior**
Melchior Vulpius. Moore.

**Vultures**
Black Vulture, The. Sterling.
Ecology. Kennedy.
Still, Citizen Sparrow. Wilbur.
Vulture, The. Belloc.
Vulture. Jeffers.
Vulture. Fr. A Bestiary. Rexroth.
Vulture of the Plains, The. Garland.

# W

**Wabash River**
Autumn on the Wabash. Etter.
**Wagner, Richard**
Tannhauser. Levy.

Wagner.  Brooke.
**Wagon Trains**
  Exodus for Oregon.  Miller.
  Oregon Trail, The.  Guiterman.
  Wagon Train, The.  Simpson.
  *See also*  **Prairie Schooners.**
**Wagtails**
  Little Trotty Wagtail.  Clare.
**Waikiki, Hawaii**
  Middle Aged Midwesterner at Waikiki Again.  Logan.
**Waiters and Waitresses**
  All-Night Waitress, The.  Stanton.
  Daily I Fall in Love with Waitresses.  Fried.
  Epitaph on a Waiter.  McCord.
  Her Story.  Madgett.
  What You Waited For.  Piercy.
**Waiting Rooms**
  Waiting-Room, The.  Fulton.
  Waiting Rooms.  Nemerov.
**Wales**
  Above Penmaenmawr.  Connor.
  Caernarfon, 2 July 1969.  Davies.
  Cymru.  Jones.
  Hiraeth in N.W.3.  Vaughan-Thomas.
  On Leaving London for Wales.  Shelley.
  Seven Wonders of North Wales, The.  *Unknown.*
  Wales.  Nicholson.
  Wales Visitation.  Ginsberg.
  Walter Llywarch.  Thomas.
  Welsh History.  Thomas.
  Welsh Landscape.  Thomas.
  *Oxford Book of Welsh Verse in English, The* (OBW).  Gwyn
    Jones, ed.
**Walking**
  How to Walk in a Crowd.  Hershon.
  Trivia; or, The Art of Walking the Streets of London.  Gay.
**Wall Street**
  Working on Wall Street.  Swenson.
**Wallendas**
  Last Flight of the Great Wallenda, The.  Hyett.
**Walls**
  I had not minded—walls.  Dickinson.
  Mending Wall.  Frost.
  There's a Red Brick Wall.  Chambers.
**Walruses**
  Walrus Hunting.  Aua.
**Wanderlust**
  Drifting.  Bushby.
  Long Gone.  Brown.
  My Bounding Bark.  *Unknown.*
  Sea-Fever.  Masefield.
  Sea Gypsy, The.  Hovey.
  Travel.  Millay.
  Ulysses.  Tennyson.
  Walking Tour, The.  Auden.
  Wanderer, The.  Auden.
  Wanderer, The.  Field.
  Wanderer's Song, A.  Masefield.
  Wandering.  *Unknown.*
  Wanderlust.  Birch.
  Wild Rover.  *Unknown.*
**War**
  A Terre.  Owen.
  Abbey Tomb.  Beer.
  Advent 1966.  Levertov.
  All Day It Has Rained.  Lewis.
  Anthem for Doomed Youth.  Owen.
  Arms and the Boy.  Owen.
  As One Non-Combatant to Another.  Orwell.
  Ash and the Oak, The.  Simpson.
  Asylum for War Victims.  Morgan.
  At Asqefar.  Thwaite.

Attack.  Sassoon.
August 1914.  Rosenberg.
Base Details.  Sassoon.
Battle Picture, A.  Melville.
Battle Won Is Lost.  George.
Battlefields.  Scannell.
Beat! Beat! Drums!  Whitman.
Boots.  Kipling.
Break of Day in the Trenches.  Rosenberg.
Breakfast.  Gibson.
Broken Promise.  Taylor.
Carentan O Carentan.  Simpson.
Censorship.  Waley.
Chances, The.  Owen.
Channel Firing.  Hardy.
Charge of the Light Brigade, The.  Tennyson.
Children Killed in War.  Enright.
Christmas Letter Home.  Fraser.
Come to the Stone.  Jarrell.
Conquerors, The.  McGinley.
Conquerors.  Treece.
Counting Small-Boned Bodies.  Bly.
Cruel War Is Raging, The.  *Unknown.*
Das Schloss.  Kirstein.
Dead Shall Be Raised Incorruptible, The.  Kinnell.
Death of the Ball Turret Gunner, The.  Jarrell.
Defeated Victor, The.  Bienek.
Deserted Village, The.  Hyde.
Disabled.  Owen.
Dreams from War.  Krysl.
Drum, The.  Scott.
Dulce et Decorum Est.  Owen.
Eighth Air Force.  Jarrell.
Elegy, An: "You might have died so many kinds of death."
  Lindsay.
Every Day.  Bachmann.
Exposure.  Owen.
"Faith and Practice."  Balaban.
Farewell, Adieu, That Courtly Life.  Pickering.
Fighting South of the Ramparts.  Li Po.
Flowers of the Forest, The.  Elliot.
For the Record.  Thomas.
Foresight.  Kirstein.
Fortunes of War, The.  *Unknown.*
Fungi.  Lake.
Fury of Aerial Bombardment, The.  Eberhart.
Futility.  Owen.
General, The.  Sassoon.
Greater Love.  Owen.
Green Tanks and Other Hidden Vehicles of Destruction.  Kuo.
Gun Teams.  Frankau.
Gunpowder Plot.  Scannell.
Hand That Signed the Paper Felled a City, The.  Thomas.
Home Front, The.  Bell.
Homecoming.  Dawe.
Hope for Those Separated by War, A.  Keyes.
How to Start a War.  McGinley.
I Am Goya.  Voznesensky.
I Did Not Lose My Heart.  Housman.
I Have a Rendezvous with Death.  Seeger.
In Distrust of Merits.  Moore.
In Flanders Fields.  McCrae.
In Southeast Asia (Viet Nam).  Rowland.
In the Dordogne.  Bishop.
In Time of "The Breaking of Nations."  Hardy.
Insensibility.  Owen.
Into Battle.  Grenfell.
It Is Dangerous to Read Newspapers.  Atwood.
Italian Spring, 1945.  Miller.
Johnny, I Hardly Knew Ye.  *Unknown.*
Lament of the Frontier Guard.  Pound.
Last War, The.  Amis.

Letter to an American Visitor. Comfort.
Life at War. Levertov.
Little Girl Saw Her First Troop Parade, The. Sandburg.
Long War, The. Lee.
Mademoiselle from Armentieres. *Unknown.*
Malvern Hill. Melville.
Man He Killed, The. Hardy.
March into Virginia, The. Melville.
Maryland Battalion, The. Palmer.
Masters of War. Dylan.
Memories of a Lost War. Simpson.
Men in Green. Campbell.
Mental Cases. Owen.
Mrs. McGrath. *Unknown.*
Montcalm and Wolfe. *Unknown.*
Mother and Poet. E. Browning.
My Sweet Old Etcetera. *Fr.* Is 5. Cummings.
National Security. MacLeish.
Night Flare Drop, Tan Son Nhut. Coleman.
Nightingales Are Not Singing. Dor.
Noon Hour. Finnigan.
Oh, It's Nine Years Ago I Was Digging in the Land. *Unknown.*
O.T.'s Blues. Cuney.
Ode for the American Dead in Korea. McGrath.
Ode upon the Occasion of His Majesty's Proclamation in the
    Year 1630, An. Fanshawe.
Ode Written in the Beginning of the Year 1746. Collins.
Of Bombs and Boys. Corbin.
Old War-Dreams. Whitman.
On Being Asked for a War Poem. Yeats.
On the Lawn at the Villa. Simpson.
One-and-Twenty. *Unknown.*
One Morning We Brought Them Order. Lee.
One to destroy, is murder by the law. Young.
Peace. Brooke.
Peasants, The. Lewis.
Performance, The. Dickey.
Perplexed by the Sunlight. Lindop.
Picture of the Times, A. Freneau.
Plato told. Cummings.
Poem to My Sister, Ethel Ennis, Who Sang "The Star-spangled
    Banner" at the Second Inauguration of Richard Milhous
    Nixon. Jordan.
Portrait: The Freedom Fighter. Jonas.
Prayer after World War. Sandburg.
Preacher, Said the General. Meinke.
Quintana Lay in the Shallow Grave of Coral. Shapiro.
Recalling War. Graves.
Remembrance Day. Scannell.
Repression of War Experience. Sassoon.
Russians. Douglas.
Scalp Dance Song. *Unknown.*
Scyros. Shapiro.
Send-Off, The. Owen.
Show, The. Owen.
Smile at the Birdie. Mann.
Snow in Europe. Gascoyne.
Soldiers Bathing. Prince.
Soldiers Plundering a Village. Thwaite.
Soldier's Song, The. *Unknown.*
Song of the Camp, The. Taylor.
Song of the Freedman. *Unknown.*
Sonnet-Ballad, The. Brooks.
Sonnet to Britain. Aytoun.
Spool, The. Belitt.
Spring Before a War. Randall.
Spring 1942. Fuller.
Strange Hells. Gurney.
Strange Meeting. Owen.
Strength through Joy. Rexroth.
Summer Night, A. Maddow.
Sunset Horn. O'Higgins.

Ten Thousand Miles. *Unknown.*
Tenting Tonight. Kittredge.
Tewa Song of War. *Unknown.*
That Crazy War. *Unknown.*
There Was a Crimson Clash of War. Crane.
These. Williams.
"They." Sassoon.
This and That. Bull.
To a Conscript of 1940. Read.
To Lucasta, Going to the Wars. Lovelace.
To R — Before Leaving to Fight in Unknown Terrain.
    Serrano.
Training. Enright.
Twenty five years of the endless war. *Fr.* The New Antigone.
    Parkinson.
Two Armies. Spender.
Ultima Ratio Regum. Spender.
U.S. Sailor with the Japanese Skull, The. Scott.
Unpardonable Sin, The. Lindsay.
Unseen Fire. Currey.
Vale from Carthage. Viereck.
Vergissmeinnicht. Douglas.
Vigil Strange I Kept on the Field One Night. Whitman.
Vitai Lampada. Newbolt.
Voices of Heroes. Gregory.
Walking Wounded. Scannell.
War. Hernandez.
War. Ramsey.
War. Shapcott.
War Is Kind. Crane.
War Is the Stateman's Game. *Fr.* Queen Mab. Shelley.
War Song. *Unknown.*
War-Song of Dinas Vawr. *Fr.* The Misfortunes of Elphin.
    Peacock.
Watching Post. Day Lewis.
What Kind of War? Rottman.
What We Said. Snodgrass.
When the War Is Over. Merwin.
Where Have All the Flowers Gone? Seeger.
Why Should Vain Mortals Tremble. Niles.
Widow's Party, The. Kipling.
Winter Warfare. Rickword.
Without Benefit of Declaration. Hughes.
*See also* **Soldiers; World War, First; World War, Second.**
**War Dead**
Anthem for Doomed Youth. Owen.
Armistice. Dehn.
At Asqefar. Thwaite.
Bobby Campbell. *Unknown.*
Cenotaph, The. Mew.
Classic Encounter. Caudwell.
Come Up from the Fields, Father. Whitman.
Counting Small-Boned Bodies. Bly.
Dead Man's Dump. Rosenberg.
Dead on the War Path. *Unknown.*
Death of a Soldier, A. Stevens.
Death of the Ball Turret Gunner, The. Jarrell.
Drummer Hodge. Hardy.
Dulce et Decorum Est. Owen.
Elegy for a Dead Soldier. Shapiro.
Epithets of War—III: Casualties. Scannell.
Futility. Owen.
Grass. Sandburg.
Greater Love. Owen.
Hunting Civil War Relics at Nimblewill Creek. Dickey.
In Flanders Fields. McCrae.
Inscription for Marye's Heights, Fredericksburg. Melville.
Investiture, The. Sassoon.
John Anderson. Douglas.
Johnny, I Hardly Knew Ye. *Unknown.*
Killed at the Ford. Longfellow.
Lines for an Interment. MacLeish.

Man He Killed, The. Hardy.
Memo. Lynch.
Memorial Rain. MacLeish.
Memorial Wreath. Randall.
Miners. Owen.
My Brother. Morice.
Ode: "Sleep sweetly in your humble graves." Timrod.
Ode to the Confederate Dead. Tate.
Ode, Written in the Beginning of the Year 1746. Collins.
Olive, The. Housman.
On a Soldier Fallen in the Philippines. Moody.
Pacific Epitaphs. Randall.
Performance, The. Dickey.
Photographs: A Vision of Massacre. Harper.
Plaque in the Reading Room for my Classmates Killed in Korea, The. Reeve.
Pro Patria. Carrier.
Rendezvous. Seeger.
Show, The. Owen.
Sight in Camp in the Daybreak Gray and Dim, A. Whitman.
Silent Slain, The. MacLeish.
Soldier, The. Brooke.
Somebody's Darling. Ravenel de la Coste.
Song of a Youth Whose Father Was Killed in the War. *Unknown.*
Song of the Dying Gunner A.A.1. Causley.
Strange Meeting. Owen.
To His Dead Body. Sassoon.
Tomb of Lieutenant John Learmonth, A.I.F., The. Manifold.
Ultima Ratio Regum. Spender.
Unknown Soldiers. *Fr.* The New Spoon River. Masters.
Vacant Chair, The. Washburn *and* Root.
Vergissmeinicht. Douglas.
Volunteer, The. Asquith.
Wall, The. Askenazy.
War. Langland.
Young Dead Soldiers, The. MacLeish.

**War of 1812**
Ballad of New Orleans. Wilson.
Banks of Champlain, The. *Unknown.*
Battle of New Orleans, The. *Unknown.*
*Constitution's* Last Fight, The. Roche.
Hunters of Kentucky. Woodworth.
James Bird. *Unknown.*
Johnny Bull, My Jo, John. *Unknown.*
Warship of 1812, The. *Unknown.*
Ye Parliament of England. *Unknown.*

**Warren, Joseph**
Death of Warren, The. Sargent.

**Warren, Robert Penn**
To a Romantic. Tate.

**Wars of the Roses**
Song at the Feast of Brougham Castle. Wordsworth.
War of the Roses, The. *Unknown.*

**Warsaw, Poland**
Conversation with a Countryman. Slonimski.
Shtil di Nacht (Silent Is the Night). Glik.
Stone and the Blade of Grass in the Warsaw Ghetto, The. Scheinert.
Zog Nit Keynmol (Tell Us No More). *Unknown.*

**Warton, Thomas, the Younger**
Lines on Thomas Warton's Poems. Johnson.

**Washington, Booker T.**
Booker T. and W.E.B. Randall.

**Washington, George**
Cameo No. II. Jordan.
February 22. Updike.
Historical Note, A. Sellers.
Mount Vernon. *Unknown.*
Patriotic Poem. Wakoski.
To His Excellency, General Washington. Wheatley.
Under the Old Elm, *sels.* Lowell.

Washington. Turner.
Washington. *Unknown.*
Washington Monument by Night. Sandburg.
Washington's Monument, February 1885. Whitman.
Which Washington? Merriam.

**Washington, D.C.**
Capitol, The: Spring. LaBombard.
Dupont Circle. Berman.
It Pleases. Snyder.
July in Washington. Lowell.
Marble. Ammons.
On Flying Into Washington over the Pentagon. Austin.
Spring in Washington. Den Boer.
Washington, D.C. Kroll.
X2s and 42s (Into Northeast Washington). Forde.

**Wasps**
Upon a Wasp Chilled with Cold. Taylor.
Wasp, The. Evans.
Wasp. Nowlan.
Waspish. Frost.
Wasps' Nest, The. MacBeth.

**Watches.** *See* **Clocks and Watches.**

**Water**
All Day I Hear. Joyce.
Anahorish. Heaney.
Appoggiatura. Hayes.
At the Mouth of the Ardyne. Lindsay.
Come, Happy Children. *Unknown.*
Desire of Water, The. Jarman.
Diviners, The. Oliver.
Gift of Water, The. Garland.
Hold a glass of pure water to the eye of the sun! *Fr.* The Glass of Pure Water. "MacDiarmid."
Meditation at Oyster River. Roethke.
Personal Helicon. Heaney.
Springs, The. Berry.
Third Thing, The. Lawrence.
To Drink. Mistral.
Water. Berry.
Water. Jabès.
Water. Norris.
Water-Drinker, The. Johnson.
Well Water. Jarrell.
What Any Lover Learns. MacLeish.
Word of Water, The. Mayo.

**Water Lilies**
Monet: "Les Nympheas." Snodgrass.
Pond Lily. Clarkson.

**Water Wheels**
Force, The. Redgrove.
Wheel. Carson.
Insomnia the Gem of the Ocean. Updike.
Rift Tide. Walsh.

**Waterfalls**
By Frazier Creek Falls. Snyder.
Cascadilla Falls. Ammons.
Cataract of Lodore, The. Southey.
Falls of Falloch, The. Tremayne.
Falls of Glomach, The. Young.
Persistent Explorer. Ransom.
Waterfall. Heaney.
Waterfall, The. Vaughan.
Waterfalls. Watkins.

**Waterfowl**
Canticle to the Waterbirds, A. Everson.
Little Militant, The. Neilson.
Pair, A. Swenson.
To a Waterfowl. Bryant.
Willets, The. Swenson.

**Watergate**
My Horse, Amanda: The Summer of the Watergate Hearings. Kumin.

Poem: On Moral Leadership as a Political Dilemma. Jordan.
Watergate Elegy, The. Dana.
**Waterloo, Battle of**
Field of Waterloo, The. *Fr.* Childe Harold's Pilgrimage.
    Byron.
**Watermelons**
Ode to the Watermelon. Neruda.
Watermelon. Joans.
Watermelons. Simic.
**Watts, Los Angeles, California**
Watts. Kaufman.
Watts. Rivers.
**Waves**
"Dover Beach"—a Note to That Poem. MacLeish.
How Everything Happens. Swenson.
If I Could Grasp a Wave from the Great Sea. Moreland.
Main-Deep, The. Stephens.
Marine. Humphries.
Spray. Lawrence.
Surfer and Others. Dorman.
Thornton Beach. McClure.
Waters. Hall.
Waves. Farjeon.
**Wealth**
Art thou poor, yet hast thou golden slumbers? *Fr.* The Pleasant
    Comedy of Patient Grisell. Dekker.
Beverly Hills, Chicago. Brooks.
Bewick Finzer. Robinson.
For A' That and A' That. Brooks.
Looking at Wealth in Newport. Schevill.
On Late-Acquired Wealth. *Unknown.*
Rich and Poor; or, Saint and Sinner. Peacock.
Rich Man and the Poor Man, The. *Unknown.*
Rich Men, Trust Not. Nashe.
Short Song of Congratulation, A. Johnson.
Spectator Ab Extra. Clough.
To Richard Boyle, Earl of Burlington: Of the Use of Riches.
    Pope.
Wealth and Wisdom. *Unknown.*
Worldly Wealth. Watkyns.
**Weasels**
Weasel. Read.
**Weather**
Gray Weather. Jeffers.
Rainbow at Night. *Unknown.*
Storm Warnings. Rich.
Weather, The. Ewart.
Weather of Olympus, The. Graves.
Weathers. Hardy.
Winter's Onset from an Alienated Point of View. Dugan.
**Weathervanes**
Upon the Weathercock. Bunyan.
**Weavers**
Jone o' Grinfield. *Unknown.*
Poverty Knocks. *Unknown.*
Weave Room Blues. *Unknown.*
Weaver's Life. *Unknown.*
Work of the Weavers, The. *Unknown.*
**Webster, Daniel**
Ichabod. Whittier.
Why did all manly gifts in Webster fail? Emerson.
**Wedding Songs**
Bridal Song. *Fr.* Hero and Leander. Chapman.
Bridal Song, A. *Fr.* The Two Noble Kinsmen. Shakespeare.
Entertainment, or Porch-Verse, at the Marriage of Master Henry
    Northleigh and the Most Witty Mistress Lettice Yard, The.
    Herrick.
Epithalamion: "Ye learned sisters which have oftentimes."
    Spenser.
Epithalamium: "We have found our peace, and move with a
    turning globe." Fairburn.

Epithalamy to Sir Thomas Southwell and His Lady, An.
    Herrick.
Good-Night, or Blessing, The. Herrick.
Nuptial Song, or Epithalamy, on Sir Clipsby Crew and His
    Lady, A. Herrick.
Sergeant's Weddin', The. Kipling.
**Weddings**
Ballade upon a Wedding, A. Sir John Suckling.
Black Wedding Song, A. Brooks.
Wedding. Brown.
**Wellington, Arthur Wellesley, 1st Duke of**
Oh Wellington! (Or "Vilainton," for Fame). *Fr.* Don Juan.
    Byron.
Ode on the Death of the Duke of Wellington. Tennyson.
**Wells**
Cleaning the Well. Chappell.
Mother. Heaney.
Personal Helicon. Heaney.
Well, The. Palés Matos.
Well, The: Two Songs. *Unknown.*
What mystery pervades a well! Dickinson.
**Wenceslaus, Saint**
Good King Wenceslas. Neale.
**Wendigos**
Wendigo, The. Nash.
**Wentworth, Thomas, Earl of Strafford**
Epitaph on the Earl of Strafford. Cleveland.
**Werewolves**
Beasts. Wilbur.
**Wessex, England**
Wessex Heights. Hardy.
**West, Richard**
Sonnet on the Death of Richard West. Gray.
**West (United States)**
Arizona Nature Myth. Michie.
Away Out West. Hall.
Goin' Back T'morrer. Garland.
Gone West. Lewis.
Home on the Range. *Unknown.*
Hoppy. Godsey.
Let the Rest of the World Go By. Brennan.
Love and an Old Western at the Starlite Drive-in Theater.
    Legler.
O Bury Me Not on the Lone Prairie. *Unknown.*
Once I heard a hobo, singing by the tie-trail. Knibbs.
Out Where the West Begins. Chapman.
Out Where the West Begins: A Parody. Douglas.
Ranch, The. Spingarn.
Song Mt. Tamalpais Sings, The. Welch.
Tour of the Southwest, A. Lueders.
Western Ways. Lattimore.
Whoopee-Ti-Yi-Yo! *Unknown.*
*Best Loved Poems of the American West* (BPAW). John J. *and*
    Barbara T. Gregg, comps.
*Women Poets of the West: An Anthology, 1850-1950* (WPW). A.
    Thomas Trusky, ed.
**West Indies**
Jamaican Bus Ride. Tessimond.
O Carib Isle! Crane.
Tales of the Islands. Walcott.
**West Virginia**
78 Miners in Mannington, West Virginia. Phillips.
**Westminster Abbey**
In Westminster Abbey. Betjeman.
On the Tombs in Westminster Abbey. Beaumont.
Refusal, A. Hardy.
**Whales and Whaling**
Before the Storm. Hanson.
Blackfish Poem. Acorn.
Blow Ye Winds in the Morning. *Unknown.*
Blue Whale, The. Watson.
Boothbay Whale, The. *Unknown.*

Coast of Peru. *Unknown.*
Father Mapple's Hymn. *Fr.* Moby Dick. Melville.
For a Coming Extinction. Merwin.
Greenland Whale, The. *Unknown.*
Harpooning, The. Walker.
Huge Leviathan, The. *Fr.* Visions of the World's Vanity. Spenser.
Killing a Whale. Gill.
Leviathan. *Fr.* Job. Bible, *O.T.*
Leviathan. Merwin.
Leviathan. Quennell.
Quaker Graveyard in Nantucket, The. Lowell.
Suicides, The. Macbeth.
To the Humpback Whales. Morowitz.
Vantage. Ghiselin.
Whale. Benét.
Whale, The. *Fr.* The Progresse of the Soule. Donne.
Whale, The. *Unknown.*
Whale at Twilight. Coatsworth.
Whale Song. Maguire.
Whales. Bates.
Whales, The. Young.
Whales Weep Not! Lawrence.
Whaling, The. *Unknown.*

**Wheat**
Color in the Wheat. Garland.
Sheaves, The. Robinson.
To a Red-Wheat Field. Turner.

**Wheelbarrows**
Red Wheelbarrow, The. Williams.

**Wheelock, Eleazer**
Eleazer Wheelock. Hovey.

**Whiskey**
Calton Weaver, The. *Unknown.*
Kentucky Bootlegger. *Unknown.*
Kentucky Moonshiner. *Unknown.*
Moonshiner. *Unknown.*
Mountain Dew. *Unknown.*
Real Old Mountain Dew. *Unknown.*
Rye Whiskey. *Unknown.*
Whiskey Johnny. *Unknown.*

**Whistler, James Abbott McNeill**
There's a combative artist named Whistler. Rossetti.
To Whistler, American. Pound.
Whistler's Father. Ryan.

**Whitman, Walt**
After Walt Whitman. Chesterton.
Late Spring, Sur Coast. Clark.
Letters to Walt Whitman. Johnson.
Love Poem on Theme by Whitman. Ginsberg.
Ode to Walt Whitman. Gold.
Old Walt. Hughes.
Pact, A. Pound.
Reading Walt Whitman. Forbes.
Sincere Flattery of W. W. (Americanus). Stephen.
Supermarket in California, A. Ginsberg.
To Walt Whitman in America. Swinburne.
Walt Whitman. Carnevali.
Walt Whitman. Honig.
Walt Whitman at Bear Mountain. Simpson.

**Whittier, John Greenleaf**
Mr. Whittier. Scott.
Whittier. *Fr.* A Fable for Critics. Lowell.

**Widows and Widowers**
After His Death. Hartman.
Dear Old Girl. Buck.
I am a widow, robed in black, alone. Pisan.
Poem for My Dead Husband. Roberts.
Portrait of a Widow. Strauss.
Racer's Widow, The. Glück.
Sequence for a Young Widow Passing. Munro.
Stony Lonesome. Hughes.

To a Lady on the Death of Her Husband. Wheatley.
Upon the Death of Sir Albert Morton's Wife. Wotton.
Urgency. Sholl.
Widow, The. Davenport.
Widow in Wintertime, A. Kizer.
Widow of Drynam, The. MacDonogh.
Widower, The. Tyler.
Widow's Lament. *Fr.* Shih Ching. *Unknown.*.
Widow's Lament in Springtime, The. Williams.
Young Widow. Beer.

**Wilberforce, William**
Sonnet to William Wilberforce, Esq. Cowper.

**Wilde, Oscar**
Arrest of Oscar Wilde at the Cadogan Hotel, The. Betjeman.

**Wilderness**
Rocky Acres. Graves.

**William III, King of England (William of Orange)**
Dialogue between King William and the Late King James on the Banks of the Boyne, A. Blount.
Duchess of York's Ghost, The. *Unknown.*
Impartial Inspection, The. *Unknown.*
Mourners, The. Higgons.
On the Late Metamorphosis of an Old Picture of Oliver Cromwell's. *Unknown.*
Panegyric, A: "Hail happy William, thou art strangely great." *Unknown.*
Shash, The. *Unknown.*
Upon the King's Return from Flanders. Hall.

**Williams, William Carlos**
Couplets For WCW. Christina.
Death News. Ginsberg.
For William Carlos Williams. Page.
Letter to William Carlos Williams, A. Rexroth.
Nuances of a Theme by Williams. Stevens.
Obit Page. Blackburn.
To W. C. W. M. D. Kreymborg.
"Yes, But. . . ." Weiss.

**Willow Trees**
Hunting Pheasants in a Cornfield. Bly.
Sauchs in the Reuch Heuch Hauch, The. "MacDiarmid."
To the Willow Tree. Herrick.
Willow Poem. Williams.

**Wills**
Last Will and Testamnet, A. Winstanley.

**Wiltshire, England**
Wiltshire Downs. Young.

**Winchester, England**
In Praise of Winchester. *Unknown.*

**Wind**
Address to a Child during a Boisterous Winter Evening. D. Wordsworth.
Aim Was Song, The. Frost.
Autumn Ghost Sounds. *Unknown.*
Big Wind. Roethke.
Blow, Blow, Thou Winter Wind. *Fr.* As You Like It. Shakespeare.
Cars once steel and green, now old. Zukofsky.
Day the Winds, The. Miles.
Dirge, A: "Rough wind, that moanest loud." Shelley.
Especially When the October Wind. Thomas.
I Saw the Wind Today. Colum.
In the Middle of a Wind Tunnel. Morice.
Invocation to the Wind. Kalar.
Irish Wind, An. Dennis.
King Wind. Van Doren.
Little Wind. Greenaway.
My Lady Wind. *Unknown.*
Night-Wind, The. E. Brontë.
North Wind in October. Bridges.
Nothing. De la Mare.
O Thirsty Wind. *Unknown.*
Ode to the North-east Wind. Kingsley.

Ode to the Norther. Chittenden.
Ode to the West Wind. Shelley.
Old One and the Wind, The. Short.
Old Prison, The. Wright.
Reminiscence II. Colum.
Snow-Storm, The. Emerson.
Sonnet: "A wind has blown the rain away and blown."
   Cummings.
Storm at Sea. *Unknown.*
Strong Wind, A. Clarke.
Sudden Gale in Spring. Thomas.
Term, The. Williams.
There came a wind like a bugle. Dickinson.
Tumbleweed. Carden.
Unknown Color, The. Cullen.
Villain, The. Davies.
Weather of Olympus, The. Graves.
West Wind, The. Masefield.
Western Wind. *Unknown.*
Who Has Seen the Wind? C. Rossetti.
Wind, The. Bull.
Wind, The. Dafydd ap Gwilym.
Wind. Dobell.
Wind. Hughes.
Wind, The. Reeves.
Wind, The. Stephens.
Wind, The. Stevenson.
Wind. *Unknown.*
Wind in a Frolic, The. Howitt.
Wind Increases, The. Williams.
Wind Secrets. Wakoski.
Wind's Lament, The. Morris-Jones.
Windy Nights. Stevenson.
Words to the Wind. Di Cicco.

**Windhovers.** *See* **Falcons.**

**Windmills**
Windmill, The. Bull.
Windmill in March. Privett.

**Windows**
Climbing. Epstein.
Kitchen Window. Ebberts.
Window, The. Aiken.
Window. Cherner.
Window to the East. Evans.
Windows, The. Loewinsohn.
Windows in Providence. Barnstone.

**Windsor Forest, England**
Lines Written in Windsor Forest. Pope.

**Wine**
Bacchus's Opinion of Wine, and Other Beverages. *Fr.* Bacchus
   in Tuscany. Redi.
Epilogue: " 'The poets pour us wine.' " Browning.
Forty Pounds of Blackberries Equals Thirteen Gallons of Wine.
   Hoeft.
Gooseberry Wine. Shumway.
Havdolah Wine. Ulinover.
On a Honey Bee. Freneau.
Song: "Hence burgundy, claret, and port." Keats.
Wine Menagerie, The. Crane.

**Winston, Harry**
Winnie. Mberi.

**Winter**
About Long Days. Ostroff.
Ancient Music. Pound.
Beyond Anguish. Kessler.
Bicentennial Winter. Pastan.
Blow, Blow, Thou Winter Wind. *Fr.* As You Like It.
   Shakespeare.
Blue Horses. Roberson.
Cold Fear. Roberts.
Cold Wave Blues. *Unknown.*
Coming on to Winter. Flaherty.

Darkling Thrush, The. Hardy.
Deep in Winter. Kooser.
Dirge for the Year. Shelley.
Evening Walk in Winter. Bethell.
Exposure. Owen.
Facts of Winter. Harris.
February Thaw. Bull.
Flowers in Winter. *Fr.* The Task. Cowper.
Frost is here, The. Tennyson.
Glass World. Donnelly.
Hillside Thaw, A. Frost.
How Still, How Happy. E. Brontë.
In December. Young.
In Winter in the Woods Alone. Frost.
Induction to "A Mirror for Magistrates." Sackville.
January Thaw. Block.
Last Leaves. Norris.
London Snow. Bridges.
Midwinter. Norris.
New Year's Song. Hughes.
No Possum, No Sop, No Taters. Stevens.
Now Winter Nights Enlarge. Campion.
Old Man's Winter Night, An. Frost.
One Horse Open Sleigh, The. Pierpont.
Onset, The. Frost.
Persia. Sackville-West.
Poem on the End of Sensation. Stange.
Reach of Winter, The. Andrews.
Sayings from the Northern Ice. Stafford.
Scotland's Winter. Muir.
Settling In. Stuart.
Signs of Winter. Clare.
Sky is low, the clouds are mean, The. Dickinson.
Snow Country. Etter.
Snow Man, The. Stevens.
Snow-bound; a Winter Idyl. Whittier.
Snowy Night. Haines.
Song: "I'd much rather sit there in the sun." Krauss.
Song in the Cold Season. Morse.
Song of Winter, A. Meyer.
Star-Talk. Graves.
Stopping by Woods on a Snowy Evening. Frost.
Thaw. Thomas.
There's a certain slant of light. Dickinson.
'Tis Winter Now. Longfellow.
To the Earl of Dorset. Philips.
To Winter. Blake.
Warning of Winter. Bethell.
Weary year his race now having run, The. *Fr.* Amoretti.
   Spenser.
White Ropes. Brainard.
Why Fires Are Lit December 21st. McMahon.
Winter. Akhmadulina.
Winter. De la Mare.
Winter. Donaghy.
Winter. Donzella.
Winter. Patmore.
Winter. *Fr.* Love's Labour's Lost. Shakespeare.
Winter. Synge.
Winter. Tynan.
Winter. Williams.
Winter; a Dirge. Burns.
Winter Burn. Hill.
Winter Day. Fried.
Winter Evening. Behn.
Winter Fairyland in Vermont. Osgood.
Winter Memories. Thoreau.
Winter Morning. Nash.
Winter Morning. Smith.
Winter, New Hampshire. Kherdian.
Winter Night, A. Barnes.
Winter Night. Day Lewis.

Winter Night, A. *Fr.* The Seasons. Thomson.
Winter Nights. Campion.
Winter Nights. Dunetz.
Winter Piece, A. Bryant.
Winter Pond. Logue.
Winter Remembered. Ransom.
Winter Scene, A. Whittemore.
Winter Scene. Young.
Winter Seascape. Betjeman.
Winter Sonnet. Waldman.
Winter Soon is Coming. Coatsworth.
Winter Time. Stevenson.
Winter Wakens All My Care. *Unknown.*
Winterfall. *Unknown.*
Wintering. Plath.
Winter's Tale, A. Thomas.
Winter with the Gulf Stream. Hopkins.
Zimmer in Winter. Zimmer.

**Wisconsin**
Driving to Sauk City. Woessner.
Walking Milwaukee. Witt.

**Wisdom**
Art of Happiness, The. Young.
Coming of Wisdom with Time, The. Yeats.
More Wisdom. Richards.
On Reading Aloud My Early Poems. Williams.
Wealth and Wisdom. *Unknown.*
Wisdom. Sobiloff.
Wisdom. Teasdale.
Wisdom is the finest beauty of a person. *Unknown.*

**Wise Men.** *See* **Magi.**

**Wishes**
Reflections at Dawn. McGinley.
Richard Roe and John Doe. Graves.
Wish, The. Cowley.
Wish, A. Farjeon.
Wishing. Allingham.

**Wit**
Ode: Of Wit. Cowley.

**Witchcraft and Witches**
Against Witches. *Unknown.*
Allison Gross. *Unknown.*
Apples of Sodom and Gomorrah, The. Holland.
Ballad of the Hoppy-Toad. Walker.
Demon Lover, The. *Unknown.*
Hag, The ("Hag is astride, The"). Herrick.
Hag, The ("Staff is now greased, The"). Herrick.
Hag-ridden. Graves.
Halloween Witches. Holman.
Her Kind. Sexton.
Her Strong Enchantments Failing. Housman.
In Salem. Clifton.
It maie be, love by death doth not pretend. *Fr.* Diana. Constable.
Laily Worm and the Machrel of the Sea, The. *Unknown.*
Mixed Brews. Sansom.
Molly Means. Walker.
Old Woman on a Broom. *Unknown.*
Ride-by-Nights, The. De la Mare.
Sabbath. Harris.
Song of Wandering Aengus, The. Yeats.
Thrice Toss These Oaken Ashes in the Air. Campion.
Two Witches, The. Graves.
Wicked Witch's Kitchen, The. Kennedy.
Witch, A. Barnes.
Witch. Beer.
Witch of Atlas, The. Shelley.
Witch of Coös, The. *Fr.* Two Witches. Frost.
Witchcraft. Johnson.
Witches, The. Smith.
Witches' Charm, The. *Fr.* The Masque of Queens. Jonson.
Witch's Ballad, The. Scott.

Witch's Broom Notes. McCord.
Witch's Broomstick Spell. *Unknown.*
Witch's Cat, The. Serraillier.
Witch's Milking Charm. *Unknown.*
Witch's Work Song, The. White.
Yellow Witch of Caribou, The. Robertson.

**Wives**
Aged Wino's Counsel to a Young Man on the Brink of Marriage, The. Kennedy.
At Flock Mass. Higgins.
Breaded Meat, Breaded Hands. Harper.
Dedication of the Cook. Wickham.
Elder's Reproof to His wife, An. Muuse.
Fisherman's Wife, The. Mitchell.
Fishermen's Wives, The. Namanworth.
For Hettie. Baraka.
For My Lover, Returning to His Wife. Sexton.
Freedom of Love. Breton.
House Carpenter's Wife, The. *Unknown.*
Housewife's Lament, The. *Unknown.*
Jealous Wife, The. Scannell.
Memory, A. Bell.
Milton's Wife on Her Twenty-Third Birthday. Conant-Bissell.
New Wife, The. *Unknown.*
Old Wife, The. Kent.
On His Dead Wife. Milton.
Red Haired Man's Wife. Stephens.
Scholar's Wife, The. Mernit.
Single Girl. *Unknown.*
To the Ladies. Chudleigh.
Wife's Lament, The. *Unknown..*
Wish for a Young Wife. Roethke.
Wives in the Sere. Hardy.
Wives of Mafiosi, The. Jong.
Young Housewife, The. Williams.
*See also* **Marriage.**

**Wolsey, Thomas, Cardinal**
Last Words of Cardinal Wolsey, The. *Fr.* King Henry VIII. Shakespeare.
On Cardinal Wolsey. *Unknown.*
Such a prelate, I trow. *Fr.* Why Come Ye Not to Court. Skelton.

**Wolverines**
For the Last Wolverine. Dickey.

**Wolves**
Coup de Grace. Hope.
Day of the Wolf. Wilson.
Four Mountain Wolves. Silko.
Fox and the Wolf, The. *Unknown.*
Howling of Wolves, The. Hughes.
Life of the Wolf, The. Gildner.
Morning of the Wolf, The. Wilson.
Prairie Wolves. Carr.
Tantanoola Tiger, The. Harris.
Wolf. Blue Cloud.
Wolf. *Fr.* A Bestiary. Rexroth.
Wolf and the Dog, The. La Fontaine.
Wolf and the Lamb, The. La Fontaine.
Wolf and the Stork, The. La Fontaine.
Wolves. Haines.
Wolves, The. Tate.
"Word" of a Wolf Encircled by the Hunt, The. Sandag.

**Wombats**
Weary Will. Paterson.

**Women**
Against Blame of Women. Desmond.
Ah! who can e'er forget so fair a being? Keats.
Bad Girl Blues. *Unknown.*
Beautiful Black Women. Baraka.
Before Bed. Waldrop.
Birthday, The. Dacey.
Black Woman. Madgett.

Bookshop Idyll, A. Amis.
Bottle Up and Go. *Unknown.*
Broken Dreams. Yeats.
C. L. M. Masefield.
Charming Woman. Sheridan.
Childhood. *Fr.* The Four Ages of Man. Bradstreet.
Cinderella. Broumas.
Combing. Cardiff.
Common Woman, The. Grahn.
Dear Colette. Jong.
Dedication of the Cook. Wickham.
Dispraise of Absalom, The. *Unknown.*
Double Looking Glass, The. Hope.
Energetic Women. Lawrence.
Epigram on Woman, An. Ayres.
Evil Devil Woman. *Unknown.*
Farmer's Curst Wife, The. *Unknown.*
Father of Women, A. Meynell.
Female, Extinct. Beer.
Female Femininity. Aguila.
Female Friend, The. Whur.
Female God, The. Rosenberg.
For Mariella, in Antrona. Simpson.
Four Women. Simone.
Frau Bauman, Frau Schmidt, and Frau Schwartze. Roethke.
From an Old House in America. Rich.
Furniture of a Woman's Mind, The. Swift.
Gentle Echo on Woman, A. Swift.
Green Apples. Randall.
Her Sister. O'Neill.
Housewife. Pillin.
Housewife. Sexton.
Hypocrite Women. Levertov.
I Am a Black Women. Evans.
I Dream I'm the Death of Orpheus. Rich.
I Knew a Woman. Roethke.
I Know a Lady. Thomas.
I Know a Spot Just Over the Hill. Mills.
I Light Your Streets. Le Sueur.
Ibo Woman. Wangberg.
If Women Could Be Fair. De Vere.
In Celebration of My Uterus. Sexton.
In Her Praise. Graves.
In Librum. Davies.
In Mind. Levertov.
In the Park. Harwood.
In the Person of Woman Kind. Jonson.
It's No Good! Lawrence.
James Alley. *Unknown.*
Jewish Woman, The. Kolmar.
Katie May. *Unknown.*
Ladies in Love. Ashley.
Lay Your Arms Aside. Ferriter.
Letter to My Sister. Spencer.
Light feet, dark violet eyes, and parted hair. Keats.
Little League Women. Metzger.
Little Old Women, The. Baudelaire.
Looking Out. Chasin.
Lord Walter's Wife. Browning.
Love Poem for All the Women I Have Known, A. Bukowski.
Mabel Kelly. O'Carolan.
Man, Man, Man Is for the Woman Made. *Unknown.*
Metamorphoses. Fuller.
Modern Fine Lady, The. Jenyns.
Mutes, The. Levertov.
My Lady Carenza of the lovely body. *Unknown.*
My Mother's Sister. Day Lewis.
Nakedness of women is the work of God, The. Blake.
Negro Women. Alexander.
Nehi Blues. *Unknown.*
New York Woman, The. Sissman.
Next Day. Jarrell.

No Images. Cuney.
No Second Troy. Yeats.
Oh, oh, you will be sorry for that word! Millay.
O Woman, Shapely As the Swan. *Unknown.*
Ode to a Beautiful Woman. Clark.
Of Jayne Mansfield, Flannery O'Connor, My Mother and Me. Daniell.
Old Wife in High Spirits. "MacDiarmid."
On the Debt My Mother Owed to Sears Roebuck. Dorn.
On Woman. Yeats.
Out on Santa-Fe—Blues. *Unknown.*
Peggy Browne. O'Carolan.
Penis Envy. Jong.
Perfect One, The. Orlen.
Picnic on the Lawn. Scannell.
Pioneer Woman. Crawford.
Planetarium. Rich.
Poem: "The person who can do." Dugan.
Portrait, The. Graves.
Portraits of 2 Lonely Women. Storey.
Power of Women. Sobol.
Prayer for My Daughter, A. Yeats.
Present. Sanchez.
Pro Femina, *sels.* Kizer.
Raising the Flag. Vizenor.
Rebel Girl, The. Hill.
Red Haired Man's Wife, The. Stephens.
Robbing and Stealing Blues. *Unknown.*
Sadie and Maud. Brooks.
Saturday Blues. *Unknown.*
Saying Goodbye. Juhasz.
Serious Merriment of Women, The. Goedicke.
She. Wilbur.
She Was a Phantom of Delight. Wordsworth.
Short Haired Woman. *Unknown.*
Sisters, The. A. Lowell.
Snapshots of a Daughter-in-Law. Rich.
Someone Is Beating a Woman. Voznesensky.
Song: Go and Catch a Falling Star. Donne.
Song: "When lovely woman stoops to folly." *Fr.* The Vicar of Wakefield. Goldsmith.
Song: "With my frailty don't upbraid me." Congreve.
Streets. A. Lowell.
Streets of New York, The. Blossom.
Tame Cat. Pound.
That Women Are but Men's Shadows. Jonson.
There Has to Be a Jail for Ladies. Merton.
There is Nothin' Like a Dame. Hammerstein.
These Women All. Heath.
Thirty eighth year, The. Clifton.
This Pretty Woman. *Unknown.*
To a Young Lady. Wordsworth.
To Caelia. *Unknown.*
To Women, As Far As I'm Concerned. Lawrence.
Transit. Wilbur.
Treat the woman tenderly, tenderly. *Unknown.*
Trial and Error. McGinley.
Two Parents, The. "MacDiarmid."
Ultimate Antientropy, The. Weiss.
Upon Some Women. Herrick.
Vierge Ouvrante. Palmer.
Volcanic Venus. Lawrence.
W.W. Baraka.
Wasn't your mother a woman? Honnamma.
Way It Was, The. Clifton.
Weeksville Women. Loftin.
What Is, and What Is Not for Woman. Snow.
What You Waited For. Piercy.
Why, Some of My Best Friends Are Women. McGinley.
Wish, A. Lerner.
Woman. Jarrell.
Woman as Artist. Taylor.

Woman Gets Restless, The. Drake.
Woman in the Field, The. Miller.
Woman Is a Worthy Thing, A. *Unknown.*
Woman Poem. Giovanni.
Woman Poet, The. Kolmar.
Woman! when I behold thee flippant, vain. Keats.
Woman with Girdle. Sexton.
Women. Bogan.
Women. Swenson.
Women and Men. Mumin.
Women in Brooklyn. Zweig.
Women in Vietnam, The. Paley.
Women Who Are Hard Inside. Gotlieb.
*Book of Women Poets from Antiquity to Now, A* (BoWoP). Aliki
    Barnstone *and* Willis Barnstone, eds.
*Mountain Moving Day: Poems by Women* (MMD). Elaine Gill,
    ed.
*New Poets: Women* (NPW). Terry Wetherby, ed.
*Penguin Book of Women Poets, The* (PBWP). Carol Cosman,
    Joan Keefe, Kathleen Weaver, eds.
*Psyche: The Feminine Poetic Consciousness* (Psy). Barbara
    Segnitz *and* Carol Rainey, eds.
*Rising Tides: 20th Century American Women Poets* (RiTi).
    Laura Chester *and* Sharon Barba, eds.
*Salt and Bitter and Good: Three Centuries of English and
    American Women Poets* (SBG). Cora Kaplan, ed.
*We Become New* (WBN). Lucille Iverson *and* Kathryn Ruby,
    eds.
*Women Poets in English, The* (WPE). Ann Stanford, ed.
*Women Poets of the West: An Anthology, 1850-1950* (WPW).
    A. Thomas Trusky, ed.

**Women's Liberation**
Advice to Young Ladies. Hope.
After Drinking Water. Gioseffi.
Alcestis on the Poetry Circuit. Jong.
Answer to a Man's Question, "What Can I Do About Women's
    Liberation?" Griffin.
Back to Africa. Jong.
Beyond What. Walker.
Cactus Tree. Mitchell.
Conversation in the Eighth Street Bookshop. Moore.
Councils. Piercy.
Departure of the Women, The. Mairs.
Free woman, A. At last free! *Unknown.*
From Sappho to myself, consider the fate of women. *Fr.* Pro
    Femina. Kizer.
Hard Is the Fortune of All Womankind. *Unknown.*
Her Sister. O'Neill.
Housewife. Schaeffer.
Housewife's Lament, The. *Unknown.*
How many wise men and heroes. Ch'iu Chin.
Hypocrite Women. Levertov.
I Like to Think of Harriet Tubman. Griffin.
I take as my theme, "The Independent Woman." *Fr.* Pro
    Femina. Kizer.
In the Men's Room(s). Piercy.
Interpretation. Koster.
Justice Has Become a Woman. Brady.
Liberation. Stone.
Little Phoebe. *Unknown.*
Morning Half-Life Blues, The. Piercy.
Mountain moving day is coming, The. Akiko *and* Weisstein.
My People. Himel.
Myth. Rukeyser.
New Lost Feminist, The. Brown.
Ninth Symphony of Beethoven Understood at Last as a Sexual
    Message, The. Rich.
No More Soft Talk. Wakoski.
Oh, Oh, you will be sorry for that word! Millay.
On a Fortification at Boston Begun by Women. Tompson.
Out of the Desert. Levenberg.
Over the fence. Dickinson.

Personal Letter No. 2. Sanchez.
Poet Recognizing the Echo of the Voice, A. Wakoski.
Quarrel, The. Di Prima.
Rearranging My Body. Mathis.
Red Haired Man's Wife, The. Stephens.
Reply of the Free Woman. Hall.
Seventeen Warnings in Search of a Feminist Poem. Jong.
She Proves the Inconsistency of the Desires and Criticism of
    Men Who Accuse Women of What They Themselves Cause.
    Juana Ines de la Cruz.
Someone Is Beating a Woman. Voznesensky.
Soul-Drift. Blind.
Spring Offensive of the Snail, The. Piercy.
Three X Three. Sanchez.
Tirade. Moore.
To Kate, Skating Better Than Her Date. Daiches.
To the Ladies. Chudleigh.
Try Brillo on the Slimy Stove. Gotlieb.
Winter Mornings. Mairs.
Women Called Bossy Cowboys. Jankola.
Women's Degrees. Godley.
YWCA. McHugh.
*I Hear My Sisters Saying* (IHMS). Carol Konek *and* Dorothy
    Walters, eds.
*No More Masks!* (NMM). Florence Howe *and* Ellen Bass, eds.

**Wood**
Anniversary. Dacey.
Old Boards. Bly.
Rail Splitting. Lawless.
Woodyards in the Rain. Marriott.
Workbox, The. Hardy.

**Wood, Grant**
Grant Wood's American Landscape. Scott.

**Woodchucks.** *See* **Groundhogs.**

**Woods.** *See* **Forests.**

**Woodstock, New York**
Woodstock. Mitchell.

**Wool**
Benediction for the Felt. *Unknown.*

**Woolf, Virginia**
Virginia Woolf. Locklin.

**Words**
A B C s. Olson.
Four Walls of My Cage, The. Reavey.
Idle Words. Lander.
Lost Word. Burden.
One day the Nouns were clustered in the street. *Fr.*
    Permanently. Koch.
Primer Lesson. Sandburg.
Threes. Sandburg.
Word Man, The. Moffi.
Word "Plum," The. Chasin.
Words. Schulte.
Words That Speak of Death. Eldan.
Words Words Words. Krysl.

**Wordsworth, William**
Addressed to Haydon ("Great spirits are now on earth
    sojourning"). Keats.
Epilogue: "There's something in a stupid ass." Byron.
Fragment in Imitation of Wordsworth. Fanshawe.
I know that what our neighbours call *longueurs*. *Fr.* Don Juan.
    Byron.
In the Lake Country. Wissinger.
Lost Leader, The. Browning.
Memorial Verses. Arnold.
On a Portrait of Wordsworth by B.R. Haydon. E. Browning.
Resolution of Dependence. Barker.
Sonnet, A: "Two voices are there: one is of the deep."
    Stephen.
To the River Duddon. Nicholson.
To William Wordsworth. Coleridge.
To William Wordsworth from Virginia. Randall.

To Wordsworth. Clare.
To Wordsworth. Landor.
To Wordsworth. Shelley.
William Wordsworth. Keyes.
Wordsworth, Unvisited. Coleridge.
Wordsworth's Grave. Watson.
**Work.** *See* **Labor and Laborers.**
**Work Songs**
Corn-Song, A. Dunbar.
Drill, Ye Tarriers, Drill! *Unknown.*
I've Been Workin' on the Railroad. *Unknown.*
*American Folk Poetry* (AmFP). Duncan Emrich, ed.
*Blues Line, The* (BluL). Eric Sackheim, ed.
**World.** *See* **Earth.**
**World War, First**
"And There Was a Great Calm." Hardy.
At the Eastern Front. Trakl.
"Blighters." Sassoon.
Break of Day in the Trenches. Rosenberg.
Channel Firing. Hardy.
Dulce et Decorum Est. Owen.
Epitaphs of the War, 1914-1918. Kipling.
Epithets of War—I: August 1914. Scannell.
Exposure. Owen.
Farmer Remembers the Somme, The. Palmer.
Fathers, The. Sassoon.
For All We Have and Are. Kipling.
Gethsemane. Kipling.
Gun Teams. Frankau.
I Have a Rendezvous with Death. Seeger.
In Flanders Fields. McCrae.
In Time of "The Breaking of Nations." Hardy.
Mademoiselle from Armentières. *Unknown.*
1914, *sels.* Brooke.
Rear-Guard, The. Sassoon.
Rouen. Cannan.
Show, The. Owen.
Silver Jubilee, 1939. Griffith.
Summer in England, 1914. Meynell.
**World War, Second**
Ballad of the D-Day Dodgers. *Unknown.*
Carentan O Carentan. Simpson.
Exodus 1940. Wolfenstein.
Face, The. Stryk.
Firebombing, The. Dickey.
Hitler, frothy-mouth, wooden-head. *Unknown.*
How They Killed My Grandmother. Slutsky.
In Westminster Abbey. Betjeman.
"Less Nonsense." Herbert.
Moon and the Night and the Men, The. Berryman.
Nerves. "Sagittarius."
Night of Battle. Winters.
Nike. Wazyk.
On Seeing Films of the War. Coxe.
1 September 1939. Berryman.
Picture Postcards. Radnóti.
Stoic, The: For Laura von Courten. Bowers.
To My Father on Pearl Harbor Day. Donzella.
Watch the Lights Fade. Jeffers.
What Lies on Us. Dawe.
**Worms**
Autobiography of a Lungworm. Fuller.
Brither Worm. Garioch.
Fish, The. Mills.
Fury of Flowers and Worms, The. Sexton.
Old Shellover. De la Mare.
This Is an African Worm. Danner.
Worm, The. Bergengren.
Worm Within. Thwaite.
Worms and the Wind. Sandburg.
**Worship**
In the First Cave. Mayne.

O my Lord, if I worship you from fear of Hell. Rabi'a the
   Mystic.
Water and Worship: An Open-Air Service on the Gatineau
   River. Avison.
*See also* **Churches; Religion.**
**Wren, Sir Christopher**
Sir Christopher Wren. *Fr.* Clerihews. Bentley.
**Wrens**
Call for the Robin Redbreast and the Wren. Webster.
Looking at a Dead Wren in My Hand. Bly.
Wren, The. *Unknown.*
**Wrestling and Wrestlers**
All-In Wrestlers. Kirkup.
Funeral Games for Patroclus, The: Wrestling to a Draw.
   Homer.
Rasslers, The. Barney.
Ripper Collins' Legacy. Johnson.
Spartan Wrestler, The. Damagetus.
Two Wrestlers. Francis.
Wrestlers. Lewandowski.
**Wright, Richard**
Heartblow: Messages. Harper.
Mourning Letter from Paris, A. Rivers.
To Richard Wright. Rivers.
**Writing and Writers.** *See* **Authors and Authorship.**
**Wyatt, Sir Thomas**
Note on Wyatt, A. Amis.
Wyatt resteth here, that quick could never rest. Earl of Surrey.
**Wyoming**
Heart Mountain Japanese Relocation Camp, The: 30 Years
   Later. Levendosky.
Old Trail Town, Cody, Wyoming. Garmon.
Snow Country. Etter.
**Wyspianski, Stanislaw**
To Stanislaw Wyspianski. Mansfield.

# X

**X-Rays**
After X-Ray. Pastan.
Sitting, The. Chernoff.
X Ray. Abse.
X-Ray. Bartlett.
**Xenophanes**
Xenophanes. Emerson.

# Y

**Yachts**
Incredible Yachts, The. Booth.
Yachts, The. Williams.
**Yaks**
Mad Yak, The. Corso.
Yak, The. Belloc.
Yak, The. Roethke.
Yaks come from far-off Tibet. Hoberman.
**Yale University**
Yale Boola! Hirsh.
**Yankee Stadium**
Tao in the Yankee Stadium Bleachers. Updike.
**Yankees, New York (baseball team)**
Ballad of Dead Yankees, The. Petersen.
Baseball and Writing. Moore.
**Yarrow or Yarrow Water, Scotland**
Yarrow Revisited. Wordsworth.

Yarrow Unvisited.  Wordsworth.
Yarrow Visited.  Wordsworth.
**Yeats, William Butler**
 After W. B. Yeats.  Chesterton.
 For the Centenary.  Simmons.
 I have moved to Dublin to have it out with you.  Berryman.
 If I Ask Whether the Islands.  Griffin.
 In Memory of W.B. Yeats.  Auden.
 William Butler Yeats.  Hope.
**Yellow**
 Yell for Yellow, A.  Merriam.
 Yellow.  Gerber.
 Yellow.  Jacobsen.
 Yellow without Poetry.  Harry.
**Yesenin, Sergey**
 Death of the Epileptic Poet Yesenin, The.  Boyajian.
 Letters to Yesenin, *sels.*  Harrison.
**Yevtushenko, Yevgeny**
 Yevtushenko!  Foreman.
**Yew Trees**
 Moon and the Yew Trees, The.  Plath.
 Yew in the Churchyard, The.  *Fr.* In Memoriam A. H. H.
  Tennyson.
 Yew Trees.  Wordsworth.
**Yiddish**
 On Reading Mr. Ytche Bashes' Stories in Yiddish.  Ehrlichman.
 Yiddish.  Herzberg.
 Yiddish.  Levitan.
**Yin and Yang**
 Yin and Yang.  Rexroth.
**Yom Kippur**
 On the Day of Atonemen.  Amichai.
 Riding Westward.  Shapiro.
 Yom Kippur.  Bloch.
 Yom Kippur.  Chaet.
 Yom Kippur.  Day.
 Yom Kippur.  Pastan.
 Yom Kippur: Fasting.  R. Whitman.
**York, England**
 Coldness, The.  Silkin.
**Yorkshire, England**
 All there was of men was the smoke above their houses.  *Fr.*
  Upon an Image from Dante.  Sitwell.
 Call of the Fells, The.  Palmer.
**Young, Brigham**
 Brigham Young.  *Unknown.*
 Nauvoo.  Taylor.
**Young, Lester**
 Lester Young.  Joans.
**Young Men's Christian Association (Y.M.C.A.)**
 Soldier's Plea for the Y.M.C.A., A.  Reed.
**Young Pretender, The.**  *See* **Stuart, Charles Edward, the Young**
 **Pretender.**
**Youth**
 Barefoot Boy, The.  Whittier.
 Boy, The.  Weismiller.
 Boys, The.  Thwaite.
 Contacts with the Past.  Simpson.
 Crabbed Age and Youth.  Shakespeare.
 Daedalus.  Reid.
 Fern Hill.  Thomas.
 For My Son on the Highways of His Mind.  Kumin.
 Getting Experience.  Williams.
 Great-Aunts.  O'Críadáin.
 Green Apples.  Randall.
 How to Be Old.  Swenson.
 I See the Boys of Summer.  Thomas.
 In a Dream.  Ignatow.

 In Youth Is Pleasure.  Wever.
 Let me ask you, Mind.  *Unknown.*
 Let's away with study.  *Fr.* Carmina Burana.  *Unknown.*
 Linda.  Stone.
 Lines to Do with Youth.  Bynner.
 Little Johnny's Final Letter.  Patten.
 My Brother's Braces.  Hutchinson.
 My Lost Youth.  Longfellow.
 My Rival.  Kipling.
 Old age sticks.  Cummings.
 Old Man's Comforts and How He Gained Them, The.
  Southey.
 On My 18th Birthday.  Corrington.
 Portrait of a Girl with Comic Book.  McGinley.
 Red-Tail Hawk and Pyre of Youth.  Warren.
 Song: "When maidens are young, and in their spring."  *Fr.* The
  Emperor of the Moon.  Behn.
 Toward Light.  Lindsay.
 When I Was One-and-Twenty.  Housman.
 World Youth Song.  *Unknown.*
 Young.  Sexton.
 Young and Old.  *Fr.* The Water Babies.  Kingsley.
 Young Ones, Flip Side, The.  Emanuel.
 Youth.  Hope.
 Youth and Age.  Coleridge.
 Youth and Love.  *Fr.* The Beggar's Opera.  Gay.
**Yuma, Arizona**
 Crossing the Colorado River into Yuma.  Ortiz.

## Z

**Zebras**
 Miscegenous Zebra, The.  Young.
 Zebra.  "Dinesen."
 Zebras, The.  Campbell.
**Zen**
 December.  Snyder.
 Last Frontier, The.  Thomas.
 Those Old Zen Blues.  Broughton.
**Zeus**
 Hymn to Zeus.  Cleanthes.
 Leda and the Swan.  Yeats.
 Praise of Zeus.  Aratus of Soli.
**Zoos**
 At the City Park Zoo.  Dickey.
 At the Zoo.  Thackeray.
 Au Jardin des Plantes.  Wain.
 Elephant, The.  Hochman.
 Encounter in the Cage Country.  Dickey.
 Invitation to the Zoological Gardens, An.  *Unknown.*
 Jaguar, The.  Hughes.
 On Visiting Central Park Zoo.  Dugan.
 Our Visit to the Zoo.  Pope.
 Polar Bear at Crandon Park Zoo, Miami, The.  Winder.
 Traverse City Zoo.  Harrison.
 Twilight at the Zoo.  Rodger.
 Woman at the Washington Zoo, The.  Jarrell.
 Zoo, The.  Ostroff.
**Zulus**
 Senzangakhona.  *Unknown.*
 Those Were the Days.  *Unknown.*
 Young viper grows as it sits, The.  *Fr.* Shaka.  *Unknown.*
**Zuni Indians**
 Songs, The.  *Unknown.*